Community So
of
ZIP Code Demog

18th Edition
2004

Business
Information
Solutions

ESRI

TABLE OF CONTENTS

Residential ZIP Code Data by State

ZIP Code Maps

Alabama	**704**	Montana	**731**
Alaska	**705**	Nebraska	**732**
Arizona	**706**	Nevada	**733**
Arkansas	**707**	New Hampshire	**734**
California	**708,709**	New Jersey	**735**
Colorado	**710**	New Mexico	**736**
Connecticut	**711**	New York	**737,738**
Delaware	**712**	North Carolina	**739**
District of Columbia	**713**	North Dakota	**740**
Florida	**714**	Ohio	**741**
Georgia	**715**	Oklahoma	**742**
Hawaii	**716**	Oregon	**743**
Idaho	**717**	Pennsylvania	**744**
Illinois	**718**	Rhode Island	**745**
Indiana	**719**	South Carolina	**746**
Iowa	**720**	South Dakota	**747**
Kansas	**721**	Tennessee	**748**
Kentucky	**722**	Texas	**749**
Louisiana	**723**	Utah	**750**
Maine	**724**	Vermont	**751**
Maryland	**725**	Virginia	**752**
Massachusetts	**726**	Washington	**753**
Michigan	**727**	West Virginia	**754**
Minnesota	**728**	Wisconsin	**755**
Mississippi	**729**	Wyoming	**756**
Missouri	**730**		

Introduction

ESRI Business Information Solutions, a division of ESRI, provides customer and market intelligence solutions to help businesses, government, and nonprofit organizations with

- Customer profiling and segmentation analysis
- Site evaluation and selection
- Market evaluation and selection
- Custom target analysis
- Direct mail campaign implementation
- Media planning
- Merchandise mix analysis
- Target marketing
- Sales forecasting

By combining demographics, consumer spending pattern intelligence, and lifestyle segmentation with innovative technology, ESRI BIS empowers you to make better business decisions.

For more than thirty years, ESRI has been the leading developer of GIS software with more than 300,000 clients worldwide. ESRI also provides consulting, implementation and technical support services. In addition to its headquarters facility in Redlands, CA, ESRI has regional offices throughout the United States, international distributors in more than 90 countries and more than 1,200 business partners.

Please contact us for more information about our products, services and solutions.

East Coast
ESRI Business Information Solutions
8620 Westwood Center Drive
Vienna, VA 22182
800-292-2224
www.esribis.com

West Coast
ESRI Business Information Solutions
3252 Holiday Court, Suite 200
La Jolla, CA 92037
800-292-2224
www.esribis.com

Features of the 18th Edition

This edition of *Community Sourcebook of ZIP Code Demographics* contains the most accurate demographic information based on ESRI Business Information Solutions' release of the 2004/2009 projections of key population and income data. Updated variables for population, households, families, income, race, age and spending potential for a wide variety of products and services are included in this reference tool. *Community Sourcebook of ZIP Code Demographics* contains these sections:

Residential and Non-Residential ZIP Codes – residential ZIP Codes are profiled using over 70 demographic variables. An appendix references the non-residential ZIP Codes with their enclosing residential ZIP Codes.

Profile Sections - demographic variables are grouped by section into profiles for Population Change, Population Composition, Income and Spending Potential. Updated demographics include population, age, race, Hispanic origin, household type and household income.

Summaries - the state and local data summaries provide a quick comparison of a ZIP Code to state and national information.

Explanation of Variables - definitions of the demographic variables and key terms used in the Sourcebook are included.

Business Data - the predominant industry by ZIP Code is listed in the Business Data section. This section also contains information about the total number of businesses and the total employment in each ZIP Code.

Community™ Tapestry™ Data - For the first time, we've included our Tapestry segmentation system, the next generation of ACORN! This section includes information about the dominant Tapestry consumer group in each ZIP Code and the proportion of households represented by the group.

Demographic and ZIP Code Update Methodologies - current data methodology statements explain how the population and income data are forecast from the Census 2000 base as well as how ZIP Code data are estimated.

ZIP Code Ranges - to find specific ZIP Codes, refer to the ZIP Code ranges listed on each page..

ZIP Code Maps – individual state maps delineating three-digit ZIP Code boundaries are included as reference.

ZIP Code to State Cross-Reference

01000-02799 Massachusetts	32000-34999 Florida	68000-69399 Nebraska
02800-02999 Rhode Island	35000-36999 Alabama	70000-71499 Louisiana
03000-03899 New Hampshire	37000-38599 Tennessee	71600-72999 Arkansas
03900-04999 Maine	38600-39799 Mississippi	73000-74999 Oklahoma
05000-05999 Vermont	40000-42799 Kentucky	75000-79999 Texas
06000-06999 Connecticut	43000-45899 Ohio	80000-81699 Colorado
07000-08999 New Jersey	46000-47999 Indiana	82000-83199 Wyoming
09000-14999 New York	48000-49999 Michigan	83200-83899 Idaho
15000-19699 Pennsylvania	50000-52899 Iowa	84000-84799 Utah
19700-19999 Delaware	53000-54999 Wisconsin	85000-86599 Arizona
20000-20599 District of Columbia	55000-56799 Minnesota	87000-88499 New Mexico
20600-21999 Maryland	57000-57799 South Dakota	89000-89899 Nevada
22000-24699 Virginia	58000-58899 North Dakota	90000-96699 California
24700-26899 West Virginia	59000-59999 Montana	96700-96899 Hawaii
27000-28999 North Carolina	60000-62999 Illinois	97000-97999 Oregon
29000-29999 South Carolina	63000-65899 Missouri	98000-99499 Washington
30000-31999 Georgia	66000-67999 Kansas	99500-99999 Alaska

There are 80 exceptions to these ranges in 5 states: Georgia (39813-39897), Kentucky (45275), New York (06390), Tennessee (42223), and Virginia (20041 and 20105-20198).

There are six residential ZIP Codes that physically exist in two states. The state that contains the largest portion of the ZIP Code is listed.

ZIP CODE	LISTED IN THIS STATE	NOT LISTED IN THIS STATE
42223	Tennessee	Kentucky
57724	South Dakota	Montana
63673	Missouri	Illinois
71749	Arkansas	Louisiana
72395	Arkansas	Tennessee
73949	Oklahoma	Texas

ESRI Business Information Solutions
Update Methodology: 2004/2009

Introduction

ESRI Business Information Solutions (ESRI BIS) presents 2004/2009 forecasts. Since releasing our 2003 updates, we have re-evaluated and revised models and continued to introduce new data sources. Changes in trends are monitored, including the effects of the recent recession and economic recovery.

The last recession's impact on business has diminished. Recovery has restored real GDP growth to over 4 percent (fourth quarter 2003). Inflation is increasing slowly, up 2.3 percent in 2003. Interest rates remain at historic lows, and personal consumption expenditures are up 4.3 percent from a year ago. However, the effects of the recession linger in the labor force.

Employment growth is erratic. Job loss continues in industries like manufacturing, agriculture, and now information services, but rapid growth characterizes health care services, real estate, and administrative/support services. The net effect is a small increase in employment, less than one percent, and an increase in the number of unemployed, now over 10 million. The jobless recovery persists while businesses rely on increased worker productivity, outsourcing and cheaper labor abroad.

Household income increased by over 3 percent in the past year—a slight (0.1 percentage point) improvement over the previous year. Again, the change is inconsistent, with growth of 4.5 percent among the highest income households compared to only 3.2 percent among the lower income households.

Despite the sluggish growth in household income, the housing market remains robust. Low interest rates, innovative financing programs, and government incentive and assistance programs have pushed up median home value from $112,000 in 2000 to almost $146,000 in 2004 and boosted the homeownership rate to over 67 percent in 2004. This fast pace of growth in homeownership is unlikely to continue for the remainder of the decade. While the number of homeowners will continue to grow, the rate of homeownership will not increase like it has since 2000.

The next wave of new homeowners will be Gen Y, who is just now maturing into household formation years. This generation rivals the Baby Boom in size, but not composition. Gen Y includes not only the children of Baby Boomers, but also waves of recent immigrants to the U.S. It is more diverse than the Baby Boom—and not as predictable.

Demographically, the effects of the echo boom are evident in the age distribution of the population, too. The increase in the median age, which has followed the aging of the Baby Boom cohorts for years, has either slowed or reversed in most areas. Although some states boast a median age of over 40 years, many areas are now experiencing a distinct "younging" of the population. This trend is likely to continue. As the echo effect of the Baby Boom wanes, births are still increasing in the U.S. with younger families arriving and, soon enough, with family formation by Gen Y.

Forecasts are developed from the Census 2000 base. Postcensal trends in the population are captured from a variety of data sources and applied to provide the most accurate update for 2004. This change is then extrapolated five years, to 2009. The 2004 update represents current events; the 2009 forecast illustrates the effects of current events and the expected recovery from the recession.

ESRI BIS' 2004/2009 forecasts include population, age by sex, race by Hispanic origin, labor force and employment by industry and occupation, households and families, housing by occupancy and tenure and home value, income, including household and family income distributions, household income by age of householder, and per capita income. Updates of household income are also extended to provide after-tax (disposable) income and a measure of household wealth, net worth.[1]

Post-2000 Geography Changes

Change is inevitable with any geographic area—political or statistical. Changes in the areas for which data are tabulated and reported are critical to the analysis of trends. In the past year, there have been two county changes, the decennial overhaul of metropolitan areas by the Office of Management and Budget, and a revision of the boundaries for Designated Market Areas (DMAs) by Nielsen Media Research in addition to the usual adjustment of ZIP Codes by the U.S. Postal Service.

County changes include the addition of Broomfield County in Colorado and the merge of Clifton Forge city (a county equivalent) with Alleghany County in Virginia. Larger political areas like counties do not change often, but these revisions affect every component area within the county, from census tracts to blocks. ESRI BIS has incorporated all the component changes and calculated estimates of base data from Census 2000 for the counties and component areas.

Metropolitan changes include 45 new metropolitan statistical areas and introduce a new class of statistical area, Micropolitan Statistical Areas. Like metropolitan areas, counties or county equivalents define micropolitan areas. As the name suggests, however, these areas are smaller. Each Micropolitan Statistical Area includes a central county and an urban cluster(s) with a population of at least 10,000, but less than 50,000, the minimum for a metropolitan area. There are

---

[1] All forecasts are mid-year, for July 1 of the forecast year.

573 new Micropolitan Statistical Areas. Collectively, Metropolitan and Micropolitan Statistical Areas are referred to as Core Based Statistical Areas (CBSAs). Geocodes for CBSAs are revised, too, from four- to five-digit codes.

DMAs represent the 2003-2004 markets defined by Nielsen. Most DMAs correspond to whole counties, but there are a few exceptions where counties are split into different DMAs. Finally, ZIP Codes, which are defined solely to expedite mail delivery, can change monthly—or whenever the U.S. Postal Service decides to revise delivery routes. ZIP Codes in the 2004/2009 forecasts represent the November 2003 inventory.

DEMOGRAPHIC UPDATE METHODOLOGY

Forecasts are prepared initially for counties and block groups (BGs). From the county database, forecasts are aggregated to CBSAs, DMAs, states or higher levels. From the block group database, forecasts can be retrieved for census tracts, places, county subdivisions , ZIP Codes, or any user-defined site, circle, or polygon. ESRI BIS also includes data for Congressional Districts (108th Congress).

Total Population: Counties

The change in total population is a function of the changes in household population and the population in group quarters, which are subject to different trends. The addition of a prison, for example, produces a sudden increase in the group quarters' population that is unlikely to yield an attendant change in the household population or the projected population growth of a county. A military base closing effects an immediate decrease in the household population with the reduction not only of military personnel, but also their families and civilian personnel; however, this drop is unlikely to continue. The disparity of trends in household versus group quarters' population is accommodated by separate projections. The group quarters' population is the Census 2000 count of group quarters plus any changes in prisons since 2000.

Forecasting change in the size and distribution of the household population begins at the county level with several sources of data. ESRI BIS uses a time series of estimates from the U.S. Bureau of the Census that includes the latest estimates, 2002, and intercensal (1991-1999) estimates adjusted for error of closure.[2] The Census Bureau's time series is consistent, but testing has revealed improvement in accuracy by using a variety of different sources to track county population trends. ESRI BIS also employs a time series of building permits and housing starts plus residential deliveries. Finally, we review local data sources that tested well against Census 2000.

Selection of an appropriate trend line for a county depends upon population size, past change, and the

projection date, one, five or ten years in the future. For example, projections for smaller counties (less than 5,000 people) or counties that are experiencing a loss of population, benefit from a longer trend line, characteristic of several years of change rather than one or two years. More recent data provide more accurate forecasts for areas that are growing rapidly, at least in the short run.[3]

Choice of the best projection technique is also guided by testing. Past studies have not shown more complex methods to be more accurate; however, the measure of population change, whether total or by component, can make a difference in projection accuracy. As noted earlier, rapid rates of change, positive or negative, do not continue indefinitely. In fact, small areas like counties can experience sharp annual fluctuations in rates of change. More conservative measures, such as a linear "model", tend to be more accurate for the extremes than techniques that can exaggerate the amount of change, like exponential extrapolation. ESRI BIS applies this research and extensive testing against Census 2000 data to calculate 2004 and 2009 county forecasts.

Total Population: Block Groups

Forecasts of subcounty population trends are built from an analysis of recent (1990-2000) change at the block group level and the latest data. Current trends are measured from local estimates, a new data source, Acxiom household counts, and time series analysis of the changes in residential delivery statistics from the U.S. Postal Service.

The U.S. Postal Service publishes counts of residential deliveries for every postal carrier route. Post office delivery counts are not the same as housing units in a carrier route, especially in rural areas. Sparsely populated areas tend to have post office box ZIPs because there are few rural addressing systems and little comparability to urban, street delivery. Comparison of the residential delivery counts to Census 2000 housing unit and household counts, combined with a time series analysis of postal carrier routes and the corresponding delivery statistics, provide useful estimates of local change—from the development of a new housing subdivision to the demolition of an old housing complex.

The first step in calculating local demographic change is the derivation of correspondence files. The correspondence between 2000 census statistical areas and postal carrier routes is developed using data from Geographic Data Technology—updated quarterly. The correspondence between block groups and places is developed from Census 2000 data at the block level.

---

[2] U.S. Bureau of the Census, Population Division, Table CO-EST2002-07-01.

[3] Lynn Wombold, 1992, *The Long and Short of Population Forecasting: A Test of County Populations against the 1990 Census*, paper presented at the 1992 Annual Meeting of the Population Association of America.

The rules of thumb on projection accuracy at the block group level are similar to county and larger area patterns; population size and rate of change show similar effects. The probability of extremes in population change (loss or growth), for example, is unlikely to continue among block groups for extended time periods. Past censuses have demonstrated that rapid population change slows to a more moderate pace in three out of four subcounty areas. The small size of block groups simply cannot sustain rapid growth indefinitely. The average land area is less than 17 square miles; average population density, 1,349 persons per square mile.

The change from 1990 to 2000 is incorporated in the analysis of future change by block group, but not extrapolated indiscriminately. More recent data establish the credibility of continued growth, or decline, and quantify recent change to improve forecast accuracy at the BG level. Testing also identifies the best techniques for projecting population change for small areas. Like counties, forecasts for block groups improve when conservative measures of extreme trends are used instead of techniques that can exaggerate the amount of change, like exponential extrapolation. Specific to the block groups, however, is the stabilizing influence of controlling projections to independent totals for larger areas. Projection accuracy improves with use of a technique that relates local change to county change.

The best techniques are derived from a combination of models. An average is used for most block groups to estimate current population change. Averages reduce overall error, bias, and the occurrence of outliers, extremely high or very low projections. Discrepant trends are checked extensively against independent sources. Finally, totals for block groups are controlled to the county projections.

Population Characteristics
The population by age and sex is projected via a cohort survival model that calculates the components of population change separately, by age and sex. Applying survival rates specific to the cohort carries the 2000 population forward. Changes in the population by age/sex diverge at the household level. For example, an area that is losing population can age more rapidly with the loss of population in prime migrant ages, 20-34 years—unless there is a college nearby. An influx of college students can offset the loss of youthful outmigrants.

To capture these variations, ESRI BIS' model first separates group quarters' population from the household population and, second, keys the calculations to the size and characteristics of the population. This stratification identifies several different patterns of change by age and sex that are applied in the cohort survival model. Births are projected from area-specific, child-woman ratios. Migration is computed as a residual, the difference between the survived population and independent projections of total population.

Forecasts by race and Hispanic origin are combined in the 2004/2009 updates. The most current data by race

and Hispanic origin are 2002 data available from the Census Bureau's estimates and the American Community Survey. Survey data is employed in conjunction with ESRI BIS' estimate of change from 1990 to 2000 by race and Hispanic origin. Tracking inter-census population change by race is encumbered by the new reporting method in Census 2000. Race was reported as a multiple-choice item-not "one person-one race" as reported in past censuses or estimates. The 2000 data are not directly comparable to 1990 Census data, or to any earlier estimates or projections. Comparisons made between single-race reporters in 2000 and 1990 underestimate the change by race. Excluding the rapid growth of the multiracial population minimizes the change by race from 1990 to 2000. Alternatively, combining single-race reporters with races reported in any combination can cut down the 63 racial groups reported in Census 2000. For example, a person who reports "White and Asian" is counted as both "White" and "Asian." This combination of single-race and multiracial reporters overcounts multiracial reporters and overestimates the change by race from 1990 to 2000. To achieve a true picture of population change by race, it is important to account for the change in multiracial reporting.

ESRI BIS takes an innovative approach in analyzing this data to make effective use of the additional information from Census 2000.[4] The Census Bureau released most race-related data by six single races and one multiple-race group. Our data preserve this format and enable a comparison of 1990 and 2000 data for six single-races and one multiracial group. Assuming that the probability of reporting more than one race varies by race group and geographic area (as shown in Census 2000), ESRI BIS estimates the number of likely multiple race reporters from 1990 Census data. The same approach is adopted for the population of Hispanic origin by race. Local trends in the distribution of the population by race and Hispanic origin are incorporated with current population estimates in the model. Forecasts by BG combine local changes in the distributions by race and projected change for counties. The last step controls block group distributions to county projections. Data are reported by Hispanic origin for seven race groups that are consistent with Census 2000 tabulations.

Households and Families
The composition of the American household continues the slow change from married couple families to nontraditional families and single-person households. Between 1990 and 2000, the dominant share of households remained married couple families in most states, but decreased from 55 percent of all households to 51.7 percent in 2000. Increased shares of single parent and single person units comprised the difference. The attendant change in average household size is the decline from 2.63 in 1990 to 2.59 in 2000.

---

[4] A more detailed discussion of ESRI BIS' 1990-2000 race analysis is available from Sangita Vashi's paper, *Trends in the U.S. Multiracial Population 1990-2000*, presented at the 2001 Southern Demographic Association's Annual Meeting.

Gone are the dramatic shifts in size and distribution in the 1970s and 1980s that were created by the Baby Boom as they entered their twenties and formed households. Fertility rates declined with fewer births and delayed childbearing. Divorce rates increased. Single-person and single parent households expanded. Average household size dropped quickly. As a result, households increased more rapidly than the population, and families, especially the traditional married-couple family, decreased proportionately. Households are still increasing more rapidly than population in many areas, but the pace has slackened as the Baby Boom, and the rest of the population, age.

The gradual change in household size makes it uniquely suitable to forecasting the change in households from the change in household population. Average household size is one of the most stable, and predictable, components of the forecasts. Household forecasts are predicated upon local patterns of change, which are controlled to the more constant trends for states and counties. Nationally, household change stabilized in the 1990s.

Local change, however, is affected more by the singular composition of the population, and trends often vary from the national norm. Nationally, average household size decreased by less than 0.4 percent annually from 1990 to 2000. By county, the change varied from a low of –2.3 percent to a high of 1.2 percent. An increase in household size can result from higher rates of fertility locally—or from an increase in multigenerational households. Census 2000 has documented the increase in multigenerational households in areas where there is high immigration or areas with housing shortages and higher costs.

Few block groups represent a cross-section of U.S. households. In areas that gained population from immigration in the 1990s, the trend in average household size actually reversed and increased. To distinguish local variation, ESRI BIS' model is keyed to the characteristics of households at the block group level. This stratification identifies several different patterns of change by household type that are applied to forecast trends in the characteristics of households-- both family composition and tenure. Local change is emphasized in the 2004/2009 forecasts of households and families for counties and block groups. National trends are monitored and applied as controls.

Home Value
Home value is again updated for all owner-occupied housing units in 2004. Previously, home value was reported for *specified* owner units, select single-family homes—excluding mobile homes, houses on ten or more acres and homes with a business or medical office. The distribution of home value from the 1990 Census of Housing was limited to *specified* owner-occupied units. Census 2000 data on home value are reported for all owner units as well as specified owner units. ESRI BIS updated the distribution of home value to represent all owner-occupied housing units.

From 1990 to 2000, home value increased by over four percent annually—down from the growth of 5.3 percent annually in the 1980s. The most rapid increase in home value was evident in Western states with rapid population growth, like Utah, Colorado, Oregon and Washington, and Midwestern states with below average home values in 1990, like Michigan, Wisconsin and Iowa. Contrary to expectations, home prices are still booming on the back of historically low mortgage rates and gradual economic expansion. Since 2003, annual growth in home value has slowed very slightly to 6.5 percent, down from almost 7 percent. California, DC, Massachusetts, New Hampshire, New Jersey, and Rhode Island are still exhibiting double-digit growth in median home value.

ESRI BIS tracks the change in home value using the Office of Federal Housing Enterprise Oversight's (OFHEO) House Price Index. The HPI is designed to monitor change in the loan-to-value ratio of mortgages held or guaranteed by Fannie Mae or Freddie Mac. OFHEO affirms the "significant advantages" of the HPI over Commerce Dept. surveys. ESRI BIS has evaluated the accuracy of the HPI in estimating change in home value through the past decade.

Data are released quarterly for states and MSAs. ESRI BIS has applied time series analysis to extrapolate both short-term (2004) and long-range (2009) trends in home value through states and metropolitan areas to block groups. Local estimates of home value incorporate supply-demand characteristics, the socioeconomic traits of householders in the area, and HPI trends assessed for larger markets. Five-year forecasts do not assume that the recession will continue indefinitely.

INCOME UPDATE METHODOLOGY

Data Sources
To estimate household income and family income, ESRI BIS employs government and independent data sources, including: (i) the U.S. Bureau of the Census' Current Population Survey, (ii) National Planning Association Data Service, and (iii) the Census Bureau's 2000-02 Supplementary Surveys.

ESRI BIS' projection base is the income reported in Census 2000. Technically, 2000 income data represent income in 1999 because the Census Bureau tabulates income received in the "last year" before the Census. Similarly, ESRI BIS' 2004 income updates represent income received in 2003, expressed in 2003 dollars. Projections for 2009 are shown in 2008 dollars, assuming an annual inflation rate of about two percent.

Income Methods
First, the state income distributions are updated to reflect current change in household and family income and 2004 households (and families). The release of Census 2000 income data has enabled careful evaluation of data sources employed in past forecasts, including the recent (2000-02) Supplementary Surveys. Data for 2000 from each source varies from the income reported in Census 2000. In fact, the most extensive data source released since the 1990 Census, the 2000

Supplementary Survey with over 750,000 households, is the most discrepant source. One point in time is just not a good measure of a data series. For any given year, any estimate of income is likely to vary from the population. However, the sources that ESRI BIS has employed throughout the 1990s proved effective measures of change in income. Testing reveals the power of time series' data in tracking income. ESRI BIS postcensus updates place a strong emphasis on maintaining and implementing time series results from household surveys.

After forecasting the state income distributions, we, estimate household income for counties, then tracts and block groups. ESRI BIS has redesigned the income forecasts to distinguish both local variation and changes in income inequality. The model is keyed to the characteristics of households at the block group level. This stratification identifies several different patterns of change by household type that are applied to forecast trends in income. The annual change in income is derived from national surveys. Modeling links the current income change to all households with similar socioeconomic characteristics. Separate forecasts of the change in income by strata are aggregated to compose the county income distributions. Finally, the models are calibrated to distinguish the change in average household income, for example, from the change in median income.

Money Income
ESRI BIS uses the Census Bureau's definition of money income, which enables direct comparison of income updates and decennial census data. For each person 15 years old and over, money income received in the preceding calendar year is tallied from each of the following sources: earnings, unemployment compensation, Social Security, Supplemental Security Income, public assistance, veterans' payments, survivor benefits, disability benefits, pension or retirement income, interest, dividends, rents, royalties, estates and trusts, educational assistance, alimony, child support, financial assistance from outside of the household, and other income.

Data on consumer income collected by the Census Bureau cover money income received (exclusive of certain money receipts such as capital gains) before payments for personal income taxes, Social Security, union dues, Medicare deductions, etc. Therefore, money income does not reflect the fact that some families receive part of their income in the form of noncash benefits, such as food stamps, health benefits, rent-free housing, or goods produced and consumed on a farm. In addition, money income does not include noncash benefits, such as the use of business transportation and facilities, full or partial payments by business for retirement, medical and educational expenses, etc.

Use of Projections
Projections are necessarily derived from current events and past trends. The past and the present are known; the future must be extrapolated from this knowledge base. While projections represent the unknown, they are not uninformed. Guidelines for the development of projections also inform the use of those projections:

1. The recent past provides a reasonable clue to the course of future events, especially if that information is tempered with a historical perspective.

2. A stable rate of growth is easier to anticipate than rapid growth or decline.

3. The risk inherent in projections is inversely related to the size of an area: the smaller the area, the greater the risk.

4. The risk increases with the length of the projection interval. Any deviation of the projected trends from actual events is amplified over time.

ESRI BIS revises its projections annually to draw upon the most recent estimates and projections of local trends. However, this data can be complemented with personal knowledge of an area to provide the qualitative, anecdotal detail that is not captured in a national database. It is incumbent upon the data user and the producers to incorporate as much information as possible when assessing local trends, especially areas that are subject to "boom-bust" cycles.

ZIP CODE UPDATE METHODOLOGY
Data for residential ZIP Codes are estimated by ESRI BIS. Census 2000 geographic areas are the building blocks for ESRI BIS' ZIP Codes. Because ZIP Code boundaries change frequently, census geography provides a comparatively stable base for the development of ZIP Code data. ZIP Code data have been estimated from block groups. BGs are assigned to residential ZIP Codes by overlaying the centroids of component blocks on ZIP boundaries. Expressed as latitude/longitude coordinates, centroids approximate the geographic centers of blocks. If the centroid of a block falls within a ZIP Code, it is included in the residential inventory; otherwise, it is classified as nonresidential. Blocks are then aggregated, and the ratio of block totals to block group data is used to apportion demographic characteristics to a ZIP Code. This edition of the Sourcebook publishes data for 29,827 residential ZIP Codes. ZIP Codes with no 2004 population have been excluded.

This geodemographic method does not provide data for ZIP Codes that are assigned to a single address or business or post office box only ZIPs. If a polygon is not defined for a ZIP Code, or no blocks are assigned to a ZIP Code polygon, data cannot be retrieved. In most cases, information about post office box ZIP Codes or single address ZIPs is incorporated with the data for the enclosing, residential ZIP Code.

Source for Boundaries
Geographic Data Technology (GDT) creates boundary files for ZIP Codes. GDT ZIP Codes include point and boundary files. ZIP Code boundaries are current as of November 2003.

Comparisons over Time

ZIP Codes are not amenable to time series analysis, preventing a direct comparison with ZIP Codes from previous editions of the Sourcebook. Changes typically include new residential ZIP Codes, deleted ZIPs, and boundary revisions. The changes reflect the U.S. Postal Service's revisions of ZIP Codes in addition to any changes in GDT's techniques of defining ZIP Code perimeters.

Spending Potential Indices
Methodology Statement

Spending potential data measure the likely expenditure for a product or service in a county, ZIP Code, or other trade area. The ESRI Business Information Solutions database includes the average expenditure per household, total expenditures and a Spending Potential Index (SPI) for over 700 products and services. The Sourcebook contains the SPIs for 20 key products or services. The SPI compares the average local expenditure for a product to the average amount spent nationally. An index of 100 is average. An SPI of 120 shows that the average spent by local consumers is 20 percent above the national average. An SPI of 85 shows that the average spent is 15 percent below the national average.

Methodology

ESRI Business Information Solutions has combined the latest Consumer Expenditure Surveys (CEX), 1999, 2000 and 2001, from the Bureau of Labor Statistics' (BLS) to estimate current spending patterns. These continuing surveys include a Diary Survey for daily purchases and an Interview Survey for general purchases. The Diary Survey represents record keeping by consumer units (CU) for two consecutive one-week periods. This component of the CEX collects data on small daily purchases that could be overlooked by the quarterly Interview Survey. The Interview Survey collects expenditures from consumers in five interviews conducted every three months. Each survey includes about 7,500 consumer units. ESRI Business Information Solutions integrates data from both surveys to provide a comprehensive database on all consumer expenditures.

Over the years, both the BLS and ESRI Business Information Solutions have updated their methods of collecting and estimating consumer spending data. In 2001, BLS revised the Interview Survey to collect income by using ranges in addition to discrete totals. The goal is to improve the accuracy of income reporting, but the change also affects expenditures derived directly from income data, like Social Security deductions.

Additionally, the values reported in 1999 and later surveys might be higher for some variables due to coding changes. Items like investments are commonly topcoded to a select upper limit. Topcoding replaces data when the value of the reported item exceeds prescribed critical values. The critical values for each topcoded variable are estimated according to Census Disclosure Review Board guidelines. The topcoded value represents the mean of the subset of all outlying observations. Any average, including average expenditures, can be influenced by the presence of extreme values. Therefore, when the topcode is changed, the average also changes. BLS can include other coding changes when an item is switched from the Diary Survey to the Interview Survey, like personal services in 2000.

ESRI Business Information Solutions has extracted demographic and economic data for households from the 1999, 2000, and 2001 Diary and Interview Surveys. To compensate for the relatively small CEX survey bases and the variability of single-year data, expenditures are combined from the 1999-2001 surveys. ESRI Business Information Solutions constructs a conditional probability model that links the spending of consumer units surveyed in the CEX to all households with similar socioeconomic characteristics. Next, ESRI Business Information

Solutions integrates consumer spending with ACORN™, a market segmentation system of households with similar characteristics. ACORN, **A** **C**lassification **O**f **R**esidential **N**eighborhoods, is a multivariate profile of U.S. consumer markets. Spending patterns are developed by ACORN type and updated to 2004 by adjusting to current levels of income. Expenditures represent 2004 annual averages and totals.

Computation of a Spending Potential Index

For any trade area, the expenditure per household for a particular product or service can be computed by linking the expenditure data to the demographic characteristics of the population. The SPI is defined as the ratio of the local average to the U.S. average expenditure. This equation shows how the index is derived:

$$SPI = \left[\frac{\text{Local Average Expenditure}}{\text{U.S. Average Expenditure}} \right] \times 100$$

How High is High?

The Spending Potential Index exhibits different value ranges for different products or services. In general, products pertaining to specific lifestyles or income levels will show a wider range of SPI values than the products or services purchased by everybody.

The SPI has an average value of 100, but the distribution of SPIs among counties varies by product. The table on the next page shows the upper range of values for select SPIs by county. This is a rough guide for determining "how high is high":

Medians and Percentiles of Spending Potential Indices: All U.S. ZIP Codes

		Somewhat High	Very High	Extremely High
Percentiles				
	Median	75th	90th	95th
Financial Services:				
Auto Loan	83	98	119	141
Home Loan	70	92	130	162
Investments	56	91	142	185
Retirement Plans	66	90	131	164
The Home:				
Home Improvements				
Home Repair	74	94	128	158
Lawn & Garden	82	101	132	163
Furnishings				
Computers and Hardware- Personal	69	89	123	151
Major Appliances	76	94	123	150
TV, Radio, Sound Equipment	74	91	118	144
Furniture	69	89	124	153
Entertainment:				
Dine Out/Carry Out	90	112	148	181
Sports Equipment	89	110	143	174
Fees & Tickets	65	89	127	158
Toys & Games	89	112	151	187
Travel	70	90	124	153
Cable TV	76	91	116	142
Personal:				
Apparel & Services	85	108	146	180
Auto Repairs	76	93	121	148
Health Insurance	84	98	118	140
Pets & Supplies	96	114	140	167

Variable Definitions

Here are definitions of the 2004 Sourcebook Spending Potential Indices:

Financial Services

Auto Loan

Reduction of principal vehicle loan, automobile finance charges, truck finance charges, motorcycle finance charges, and other vehicle finance charges. Other vehicles include motorized campers, trailer-type campers, other attachable type campers, scooters, mopeds, and boats.

Home Loan

Payments of mortgage interest and principal, property taxes, homeowners insurance, and ground rent.

Investments

Purchase price of stocks, bonds, or mutual funds.

Retirement Plans

Amount of private pension funds deducted from last pay, annualized for all consumer unit members.

The Home

Home Improvements
Home Repair

Maintenance and repair services associated with painting or papering, plumbing or water heating installation or repair, heating, air conditioning or electrical work, roofing and gutters, and other repair and maintenance work (including repair and replacement of hard surface flooring, and repair of built-in appliances such as dishwashers, garbage disposals, or range hoods). Maintenance and repair products associated with paints, wallpaper and supplies; painting and wallpapering tools and equipment; plumbing supplies and equipment; electrical supplies; heating and air conditioning; materials for hard surface flooring, roofing, gutters, downspouts, materials for plaster, panel, and siding, materials for patios, walks, fences, brick or stucco work; landscaping maintenance materials, insulation materials, materials for additions, finishing basements or attics, remodeling rooms, construction materials for jobs not started, hard surface flooring material, material for landscape maintenance.

Lawn & Garden

Gardening and lawn care services, supplies, and equipment. Expenditures for indoor plants and fresh flowers, repairs/rentals of lawn and garden equipment.

Furnishings
Computers and Hardware - Personal

Computers, computer systems, and related hardware for non-business use.

Major Appliances

Purchase of dishwashers, garbage disposals, refrigerators, freezers, washing and drying machines, cooking ovens and stoves, microwave ovens, window air conditioning units, electric floor cleaning equipment, and miscellaneous household appliances such as sewing machines, etc.

TV, Radio, Sound Equipment

Community antenna or cable TV; portion of management fees for utilities in condos or co-ops. TV and video expenditures from color TVs (console, portable, table model), VCRs, video cameras/camcorders, disc players, video cassettes, tapes, and discs, video game hardware and software, satellite dishes, rental of videos (tapes, films, and discs). Expenditures for sound equipment include sound components and component systems, CD, tape, record and video mail order clubs, records, CDs, tapes, needles, tape recorders, radios, miscellaneous equipment/accessories, musical instruments and accessories, repair and rental of musical instruments, rental and repair of TV, VCR, radio and sound equipment.

Entertainment

Dine Out/Carry-Out
Breakfast, lunch, dinner, or snacks at fast food or full service establishments, place of employment, or vending machines.

Sports Equipment
Equipment and gear for exercise, game tables, bicycles, camping, hunting and fishing, sports (water, winter, etc.). Also, rental or repair of miscellaneous sports equipment.

Fees and Tickets
Fees and admissions for social, recreation, or civic club memberships, sports participation, movie, theater, opera, ballet, sporting events, or recreational lessons.

Toys & Games
Toys, games, hobbies, tricycles, playground equipment, and play on arcade pinball/video games.

Travel
Transportation expenditures for airline fares, intercity trains, ships, and intercity buses. Also includes trip expenditures such as local transport, taxis and limousines, auto and truck rentals, gasoline, motor oil, parking fees, tolls, and lodging; Expenditures on food and drink on trips (alcoholic beverages and food); Entertainment-related expenses on trips for recreation, participant sports, admission to movies, sporting events, etc.

Cable TV
Community antenna or cable TV; portion of management fees for utilities in condos or co-ops.

Personal

Apparel and Services
Men's suits, sport coats, coats and jackets, underwear, socks, nightwear, uniforms, costumes, sweaters and vests, active sportswear, shirts, pants, shorts, and accessories. Women's coats and jackets, dresses, sport coats and tailored jackets, sweaters and vests, shirts, tops, and blouses, skirts, pants, shorts, active sportswear, sleepwear, uniforms, costumes, suits, undergarments, hosiery, and accessories. Boys' and girls' coats and jackets, sweaters, shirts, underwear, sleepwear, socks and hosiery, suits, dresses and skirts, shirts and blouses, sport coats, vests, pants, shorts and shorts sets, active sportswear, uniforms, costumes, and accessories.

Auto Repairs
Expenditures for vehicle maintenance and repairs such as coolant, additives, brake and transmission fluid, tires (purchased replaced, installed), parts, equipment, and accessories, vehicle products, miscellaneous auto repair and servicing, body work and painting, clutch, transmission, rear-end, and drive shaft repairs, brake work, steering, front end, and engine cooling system repair, motor tune up, lube, oil change, oil filters, front end alignment, wheel balance and rotation, shock absorber replacement, tire repair, exhaust and electrical system repair, motor repair and replacement, and auto repair service policies.

Health Insurance
Commercial health insurance coverage from traditional service health plans and preferred provider plans, health maintenance organizations, and Medicare payments. Coverage from Blue Cross, Blue Shield, which includes traditional fee for service health plans, preferred provider plans, health maintenance organizations, commercial Medicare supplement.

Pets & Supplies
Pets, pet supplies, medicine for pets, and veterinary services.

Community™ Tapestry™
Consumer Classification System
Methodology Statement

Based on the foundation of ACORN's proven methodology introduced more than 30 years ago, the Tapestry segmentation system classifies U.S. neighborhoods into 65 market segments. Neighborhoods with the most similar characteristics are grouped together, while neighborhoods showing divergent characteristics are separated.

What Attributes Are Used?

Each neighborhood is analyzed and sorted by over 60 attributes, including income, source of income, employment, home value, housing type, occupation, education, household composition, age and other key determinants of consumer behavior. The U.S. consumer markets are diverse in many ways. The use of large number of attributes reflects the diversity and the need to capture them with the most powerful data available. The data sources include Census 2000, ESRI BIS' proprietary demographic updates, Acxiom's InfoBase consumer database, Mediamark Research Inc.'s national consumer survey, and other sources to capture the subtlety and vibrancy of the U.S. marketplace.

Why 65 Segments?

A frequently asked question about a geodemographic segmentation is why this number of segments. Tapestry's 65 segments describe the U.S. markets. Why not 60 or some other number? We employed several statistical methods to ensure the most optimal number of segments. The most intuitive measure among the batch of statistics used is the concept of *stability*. By examining how many neighborhoods would change their assignment, we could assess the stability of a solution. From an analysis of solutions with different numbers of segments, the solution with 65 segments proved to be the most stable.

How Is Tapestry Built?

Tapestry combines the traditional statistical methodology of cluster analysis with our latest data mining techniques to provide a robust and compelling segmentation of U.S. neighborhoods. ESRI BIS incorporated and developed these data mining techniques to complement and strengthen the traditional methodology to work with large amount of geodemographic data.

Geodemographic data covers a vast number of neighborhoods with many of them having very large or small values in their attributes. Robust methods are less susceptible to extreme values and are crucial in dealing with geodemographic data. The traditional methodology of cluster analysis has a long track record in developing segmentation systems. Complementary use of data mining techniques developed in the recent years enhances the effectiveness of traditional statistical methodology in developing Tapestry.

What Verification Steps Are Taken?

Verification procedures follow the creation of the segments to ensure their stability and validity. Replicating the segments with independent samples checks stability. Validity is checked through the use of characteristics not used to generate the segments. Linking the Tapestry segmentation system to the latest consumer survey data is the critical test. A market segmentation system must be able to distinguish consumer behavior—spending patterns and lifestyle choices—as expected.

Community™ Tapestry™ Segmentation
Summary Descriptions

01 Top Rung
Top Rungs are the wealthiest consumer market—representing less than one percent of all households. Median income is over $168,000 almost four times the national median, and median home value is over $721,000. Householders are in their peak earning years, 45-64, primarily in family households with no children or older children. The median age is 43.3 years.

02 Suburban Splendor
These successful suburbanites are the epitome of upward mobility, just a couple rungs below the top and situated recently in growing neighborhoods of affluent homes with a median home value over $337,000. Most are two-income families with children. The household population is younger, median age of 40 years, well educated and well employed.

03 Connoisseurs
Second in wealth among the consumer markets, but first in conspicuous consumption, *Connoisseurs* are slightly older, with a median age of 44.5 years, and closer to retirement than child rearing. Their neighborhoods tend to be older, bastions of affluence where the median home value is almost $435,000 and growth is slow.

04 Boomburbs
The newest additions to the suburbs, these communities are home to younger families with a busy, upscale lifestyle. Median home value is almost $250,000 (and growing), and most households have two workers and two vehicles. Growth is characteristic of the communities—and the families.

05 Wealthy Seaboard Suburbs
Wealthy Seaboard Suburbs remain established quarters of affluence characteristic of coastal metropolitan areas. Neighborhoods are older and slow to change, with median home value that exceeds $304,000. The labor force is professional; the households, married couples with no or older children living at home. Median age is 41.5 years.

06 Sophisticated Squires
Sophisticated Squires enjoy cultured country living in newer home developments with low density and a median value over $195,000. These urban escapees are younger families, well educated and professionally employed, that have elected to commute to maintain their semi-rural lifestyle.

07 Exurbanites
Open areas with affluence define exurban and the resident households. Median home value is currently about $224,000, with a median household income of $78,800. Homeowners are older, primarily empty nesters, professionally employed—with many who work from home.

08 Laptops and Lattes
The most eligible and unencumbered marketplace—they're affluent, single, and still renting. *Laptops and Lattes* are educated, professional, and partial to city life, favoring major metropolitan areas like New York, Boston, Chicago, Los Angeles and San Francisco. Median household income is over $83,000; median age is 38 years.

09 Urban Chic
The *Urban Chic* are professional couples with an urbane, exclusive lifestyle. They are homeowners, but city dwellers with expensive homes in high-rise buildings or townhomes (median value over $419,000). Median age is 41.2 years.

10 Pleasant-Ville
Prosperous domesticity distinguishes the settled homes of *Pleasant-Ville*. Most are single family homes built in the 1950s with a median value of $224,000 today. Located throughout the U.S., these households range the middle ages—most with children; some approaching early retirement. Median age is 38.8 years.

11 Pacific Heights
These households are found in the high-rent districts of California and Hawaii. Median home value is almost $357,000, with residents favoring single detached or townhomes. This market is small but affluent, with one in two households earning over $69,000 annually.

12 Up and Coming Families
Up and Coming Families represent the second highest growth market—and the youngest of the affluent family markets. These days, residents are more Gen X than Baby Boom. Despite the cohort turnover, the profile remains young affluent families with young children. Homes are new, with a median value of $157,000.

13 In Style

Households that are *In Style* live in affluent neighborhoods of metropolitan areas. More suburban than urban, these households nevertheless embrace an urbane lifestyle, favoring townhomes over the traditional single-family houses. Professional couples predominate, with high labor force participation, and fewer children. Median age is 37.6 years.

14 Prosperous Empty Nesters

A third of the population is aged 55 years or older, and most households are married-couples with no children living at home. Well educated and experienced, *Prosperous Empty Nesters* are enjoying the segue from child rearing to retirement. A median income over $64,000 supports a lifestyle that focuses on the present, with travel and home renovation, and the future, through investments.

15 Silver and Gold

These are the wealthiest seniors, predominantly retired from professional occupations, with a median age of 57.6 years. Their affluence has afforded relocation to sunnier climates. More than half live in the South, mainly in Florida. California and Arizona are also popular. A quarter of the homes are located in the West. Neighborhoods are exclusive, with median home value over $250,000 and a high share of seasonal housing.

16 Enterprising Professionals

This market is home to young, highly educated, working professionals. Either single or recently married, they prefer newer neighborhoods with townhomes or apartments and renting to owning, typically in cities. Household income exceeds expectations, with a median over $62,000, and their lifestyle reflects both youth and growing consumer clout.

17 Green Acres

A little bit country, the residents of *Green Acres* enjoy select homes in a pastoral setting. This upscale market represents developing fringe areas, with more in the Midwest. Most of the families are blue collar Baby Boomers, many with children aged 6-17 years. Median household income, $60,000, and median home value, $163,000, are high compared to the U.S.

18 Cozy and Comfortable

Still older, settled married couples and still working, *Cozy and Comfortable* families are closer to retirement today. Many of the couples are still living in the homes in which they raised their children—single-family homes built before 1970 with a current market value of $139,000 and located mainly in suburban areas in the Midwest and Northeast. Most of the population is older, with a median age of 40.2 years.

19 Milk and Cookies

Upscale living with a family allowance, this market represents young, affluent married couples who are starting their families. Many have young children already. Residents of milk-and-cookie land favor single-family homes, median value over $115,000, in suburban areas largely in the South and West, especially Texas. Families with 2+ workers, 1+ children and 3+ vehicles are the norm.

20 City Lights

City lights have attracted a diverse array of residents to the Northeast. This dense urban market is a mixture of housing, household types and cultures that all share the same city walks. Households include both families and singles; while housing ranges from owner-occupied townhomes to renter-occupied apartments in buildings with two to 50+ units. The population is a bit older, with a median age of 38 years. Residents earn a good living in white collar and service occupations, with median household income of $54,500.

21 Urban Villages

Urban Villages are the multicultural enclaves of young families that are unique to gateway cities, especially in California. Families dominate this market; most have children. Although education to date is lower, college enrollment is above average. Many are two-income households, earning a median income of $53,100 in manufacturing, retail and service industries. Most residents own older, single-family homes with a median value of $188,500 and, typically Californian, multiple vehicles.

22 Metropolitans

Metropolitans favor city living, in older neighborhoods populated by singles or childless couples. The neighborhoods are an eclectic mix of single- and multi-family structures, with home values ranging between $100,000 and $200,000. Residents include both Gen X and retirees, but generally prosperous with a median household income over $53,000.

23 Trendsetters

The cutting edge in urban style—*Trendsetters* are young, diverse and mobile, and primarily West Coast. Still renting, they favor the upscale, multiunit settlements in older city districts. Well educated, professional, but not always typical, they are well employed with a median income over $51,000. Over half are single, living alone or sharing with a roommate.

24 Main Street, USA

Main Street USA is a profile of the American population: families with a growing mix of single households (household size of 2.53), median age of 35.9 years, comfortable middle income with a median of $48,000, and homeowners (60 percent) in older single family homes with a market value of $148,500. They are the suburban incumbents of smaller metropolitan cities across the U.S.

25 Salt of the Earth

Blue collar, rural or small town best describe the *Salt of the Earth*. Hard working, primarily in agriculture, manufacturing or mining, the labor force is slightly older with low unemployment. Household income parallels the U.S. median, $48,300. Mostly married couples, these households own their homes. The median age is 39.5 years.

26 Midland Crowd

The largest Community market, *Midland Crowd* represents over 10 million people, almost 4 percent of the U.S. population in one market. As expected, the largest market reflects some characteristics of the U.S. population, median age (35.9 years) and median income, about $46,000. The differences distinguish the *Midland Crowd*. These neighborhoods are located in mainly rural areas, *growing* rural areas at a rate of over 3 percent annually since 2000. Almost 95 percent of the homes are single family, or mobile homes, with a third built after 1990.

27 Metro Renters

Metro Renters are young (almost one-third in their twenties), very well educated, singles who are beginning their professional careers in the largest cities like New York, Chicago, and Los Angeles. Median household income is increasing, currently $47,200. They are primarily renters living in older high-rise units, either alone or with roommates, given the average monthly rent of $900+.

28 Aspiring Young Families

Aspiring Young Families are attracted to the large, growing metropolitan areas in the South and West, with the highest shares in California, Florida and Texas. These are mainly young, start-up families, married couples or single parents, with children. Although young, with a median age under 30 years, about half have already purchased start-up homes, with a high percent of townhouses, and half are renters, living in newer multi-unit buildings.

29 Rustbelt Retirees

As the name implies, most of these households reside in the Northeast or Midwest, especially in Pennsylvania and areas around the Great Lakes.

Although many householders are still working, labor force participation is low. Over 40 percent of the households draw retirement income. The neighborhoods are typical of the older, industrial cities—owner-occupied, single-family homes in the city with a current market value of $104,600. Unlike many retirees, those in the Rustbelt are not inclined to move.

30 Retirement Communities

Congregate housing, which commonly includes meals and other services with rent, is concentrated in this market. Although retirement communities can also offer owner-occupied housing and nursing care facilities, most are characterized by congregate housing. Denizens of *Retirement Communities* include well-educated retirees, a third aged 65 years or older, scattered throughout the U.S., but mainly city dwellers. Median household income is about $45,000, but median net worth is over $178,000.

31 Rural Resort Dwellers

Rural Resort Dwellers follow the scenic route. Favoring milder climates and pastoral settings, the population resides in rural nonfarm areas throughout the U.S. Their communities are small, but growing—primarily single-family or mobile homes, including a significant inventory of seasonal housing. The population is older, with a median age of 46.2 years, and most are married with no children at home. Although retirement officially looms for many, most are employed. Many are self-employed.

32 Rustbelt Traditions

Rustbelt Traditions are the mainstay of the older, industrial cities in the states along the Great Lakes. They are the backbone of the manufacturing and transportation industries that sustain the local economy. The majority of households in this market are owner occupied in modest, single family homes with a median value of $87,500. Median age is 36.1 years, with a mix of family and household types, including not only married couples, but a high proportion of single-parent households and singles. Median household income is $41,400.

33 Midlife Junction

Somewhere between the childraising years and retirement lies the *Midlife Junction*. Few households still have children. Most of the labor force is still employed, but approaching retirement. Almost a third are already drawing retirement income. Most still own their homes, but many have moved into multi-unit apartment buildings. The housing market is a mix of single family homes and low density apartments, somewhere between urban and rural. The residents of *Midlife Junction* have a median age

of 40.1 years and a median household income of $41,800.

34 Family Foundations

The bedrock of this market is family life—married couples, single parents, grandparents, young children and adult children. This small urban market can be found in large metropolitan areas. Their neighborhoods are comprised of row houses or single-family detached, primarily owner-occupied homes built before 1960. There is a gradual decline in population through attrition, but little turnover in the neighborhoods. Unemployment is above average, although 30 percent have completed some college.

35 International Marketplace

International Marketplace represents the cutting edge of one of the major demographic trends shaping the U.S. future, immigration. This developing urban market presents a blend of cultures and household types. With a median age of only 30.6 years, the population is young. Families with children, either married couple or single-parent, represent 45 percent of the households. Most are renting apartments in multi-unit buildings, but over 30 percent have purchased a home. This market is located primarily in gateway states on the coasts.

36 Old and Newcomers

Old and Newcomers are neighborhoods in transition, populated by renters, either starting up or retiring. Householders are either in their twenties or over the age of 75. The median age, 36.2 years, simply splits the difference. Spread throughout metropolitan areas of the US, these neighborhoods have more single-person and shared households than families. Many have moved recently. Mid- or high-rise apartment buildings constructed in the 1970s dominate the housing market.

37 Prairie Living

Small farm owners in the Midwest dominate this stable market. Family-owned farms naturally favor married couples with and without children. The population is somewhat older than the U.S, with a median age of 39.9 years. Single-family homes, most built before 1940, are characteristic of the farms, although mobile homes and seasonal housing are also common. Median home value is $88,100.

38 Industrious Urban Fringe

Settled on the fringe of metropolitan cities, this market employs both its proximity to metropolitan cities and its location to earn a living. These diverse families rely on manufacturing, construction, retail—and agriculture—for their livelihood. Family is important. Many are multigenerational households; over half of all households have children. Two thirds own their homes, mostly older, single-family houses with a median value of $90,300.

39 Young and Restless

Change is the constant in this market. The population is young, with a median age under 30 years, and on the go, over 70 percent have moved in the past five years. Still not settled, nonfamily households are the standard, almost 60 percent of this growing segment. The *Young and Restless* are renters, who favor multi-unit apartment buildings and pay over $700 in rent monthly. Many are college graduates; some are still enrolled in college. Median household income is about $38,000.

40 Military Proximity

This segment depends on the military for its livelihood. Over 75 percent of the labor force is in the Armed Forces. Civilian jobs on military bases are also included. The population is young, median age of 22.2 years, and mobile. Average household size is high, 3.40, with about 75 percent of the households either married couples or single parents with children. Median household income is $37,300.

41 Crossroads

Young, mobile families in mobile homes typify **Crossroads**. Found most often in small towns throughout the South and West, these neighborhoods are home to families with children, both married couple and single-parent. Over half of these young families own mobile homes. Median home value is $57,400, and vacancies are above average for growing neighborhoods. Employment is mainly in the manufacturing, construction and retail sectors.

42 Southern Satellites

Southern Satellites are rural settlements, primarily in the South, that include a manufacturing and/or construction industry. Single-industry employment dominates this market, however residents also benefit from agriculture. Families in this market own newer, single-family or mobile homes, with a median value of $76,200. The market is a bit older, with a median age of 36.9 years.

43 The Elders

This is the oldest market, with a *median* age of 72.9 year. Representing the highest concentration of the elderly, *The Elders* favor communities designed for senior living, primarily in warm climates. Half live in Florida, and most of the rest live in Arizona and California. Sources of income are apparently Social Security and retirement income. Over 80 percent of the households draw Social Security, over three times the U.S. ratio.

44 Urban Melting Pot
This small market, rich in ethnicity and household types, includes recently settled immigrants. Over half of the market was born abroad; half of them immigrated in the 1990s. Most rent homes in the urban canyons of large cities in high density, high rise, pre-1950s apartment buildings. Median age is 35 years, slightly younger than the U.S. population. Median household income is about $36,000.

45 City Strivers
City Strivers are urban denizens, the resident population of the most densely settled neighborhoods in major metropolitan areas, primarily New York and Chicago. The population is younger, with a median age of 31.9 years. Unemployment is above average, but labor force participation is average. Employment is also concentrated in the city, in services including local government, protective services and health care. Housing is older, rented apartments in small multi-unit buildings.

46 Rooted Rural
This older, predominantly family, market is grounded in farming, but diversified in other industries like manufacturing, construction, retail and healthcare. The population is older, with a median age of 40.4 years. About a third of the households are already drawing Social Security. Neighborhoods are rural, predominantly single family homes, with a mix of mobile homes and some seasonal housing. Median home value is $79,500.

47 Las Casas
Las Casas are the latest wave of western pioneers. Settled primarily in California, almost half were born outside the U.S. Residents are young, Hispanic and family-oriented—62 percent have children. Most households are renting, although about 40 percent own their homes, with a median value of $164,400. Housing is a real mix of single-family homes and older apartment buildings. Median age is 25.2 years; median household income is almost $34,000.

48 Great Expectations
Young singles and married couple families dominate this large urban market. The median age of the population is 33 years, but there is a high ratio of householders in the twenties. Labor force participation is high, and they are pursuing a variety of careers, primarily in manufacturing, retail and service jobs. Home ownership is increasing. Almost half now own single-family homes with a median home value of $89,500. The rest still rent in small multi-unit buildings. Their neighborhoods are older suburbs, with most homes built before 1960.

49 Senior Sun Seekers
Senior Sun Seekers are émigrés from colder winter climes. Many have relocated permanently to warmer regions; others are snowbirds, migrating only for the winter. Most are retired. The median age of the population in this market is 51.8 years, but over 60 percent of the householders are 55 years or older. The areas favored by the seniors are growth markets, especially in Florida, with available seasonal housing. Most of the housing is either single family or mobile homes, with a median home value of $90,600.

50 Heartland Communities
Heartland Communities are preferred by 6.5 million people. The towns are small, located throughout the Midwest and the South. Over 75 percent of the homes are single-family dwellings with median home value of $65,700. The population and the homes are older, most built before 1960. The median age of the population is 40.9 years; the median age of the homes, 45 years.

51 Metro City Edge
Metro City Edge incorporates older, suburban neighborhoods of metropolitan cities. Home to singles and single-parent families, this market is young, with a median age of 28.4 years. Half are homeowners—single-family homes with a median value of $69,500. The labor force is varied, with jobs primarily in the service sector. Median household income is about $30,000.

52 Inner City Tenants
Inner City Tenants are a multistoried microcosm of urban diversity. This multicultural market consists of renters in mid- or high-rise apartments. The population is young, with a median age of 27.9 years. And the household composition reflects their youth. Single persons and shared households make up a large segment of this market—45 percent of all households.

53 Home Town
Home townies stay close to home base. They may move from one house to another, but they rarely cross the county line. Single-family homes predominate in these suburban neighborhoods with low population density, mainly in the Midwest and South. Median home value is $55,300, and over half of the householders are homeowners. The local job market offers employment primarily in manufacturing, retail trade and support services.

54 Urban Rows
Row houses are characteristic of the large cities in the mid-Atlantic region. Built decades ago, few of these homes have undergone gentrification. Median home value is $51,200, and vacancies

are above average. However, most of the homes are owner-occupied. Residents are young, median age of 32.5 years.

55 College Towns
Neighborhoods in *College Towns* represent on- and off-campus living. This market has a strong presence of college students with nearly 40 percent enrolled in college and a third of these students still on-campus. The median age of the population is 24.3 years, with the high concentration of 18-24 year olds. Housing is a mix of low-income, multi-unit rentals and single family detached homes with married couples. Median home value is $116,400.

56 Rural Bypasses
Small towns and country back-roads, primarily in the South, are home to these families. Most own their homes, either single-family homes, which make up two thirds of the housing stock or mobile homes. Median home value is $52,200, and vacancies are higher. The local economy is dominated by the manufacturing and service sectors.

57 Simple Living
The median age for this market is 39.5 years, although a high percent of the population is 75 or older. Residents are primarily retired seniors living alone or in congregate housing. The majority are renters, living in multi-unit apartment buildings. There is some retirement income, but dependence on Social Security is high.

58 NeWest Residents
Among the newest residents in the West, young families, living in mid or high-rise apartments, comprise this market. Over half of the population is foreign born. The median age of the population is younger, 25.5 years. With many small children in the families, average household size is 3.56. Most of the neighborhoods are located in large cities in California and Texas.

59 Southwestern Families
These families are the bedrock of the Hispanic culture in the Southwest. Two thirds of them own their homes, mainly in suburban neighborhoods, with a median home value of $47,400. The population is young, with a median age of 27.7 years, and most have children. Median household income is $24,700.

60 City Dimensions
This market, found in large urban cities, has high diversity in multiple dimensions: housing structure, household type, and ethnic background. The age of the population is young, 28.8 years, with both younger householders and children. Two-thirds of the households are renters.

61 High Rise Renters
Nine out of ten households in this market reside in high-rise apartment buildings in densely populated centers. Residents represent a diverse mix of cultures, and many speak a language other than English. The population is younger, with a median age of only 29 years. Most of the work force is employed in the service industry.

62 Modest Income Homes
Most households in this market have a modest income, but half own their homes, mainly single-family homes in older suburbs of metropolitan cities. Median home value is $48,200. Households are family-oriented and multigenerational. The population is somewhat younger, with a median age of 34.2 years.

63 Dorms to Diplomas
Over 80 percent of this market attends college, living in dormitories or off-campus housing. The majority of off-campus housing is in multi-unit apartment buildings. Many work part-time in low paying, service jobs.

64 City Commons
Single persons or single parents head these very young households. With a median age of 23.9 years, this is one of the youngest markets. Many have young children. These homes are commonly located in cities of large metropolitan areas where mid-rise buildings predominate. Labor force participation is below average; employment in part-time jobs is common.

65 Social Security Set
Elderly and living alone characterize this market. More than four out of ten householders are over 65 years old. This market has one of the lowest household incomes. Most live in low-rent, high-rise apartment buildings in large cities across the U.S.

66 Unclassified
Unclassified neighborhoods include areas that are unpopulated (parks, golf courses, undeveloped land, etc.), predominantly institutional group quarters (prisons, juvenile detention homes, and mental hospitals) and/or have insufficient data for classification.

Business Data Note

ESRI Business Information Solutions' business data are extracted from a comprehensive list of businesses licensed from *info*USA. The *info*USA business list contains data for over ten million U.S. businesses including the business name, location, franchise code, North American Industry Classification System (NAICS) code, number of employees and sales volume. These statistics are current as of February 2004.

Data Sources

*info*USA collects and maintains its business database by referencing several sources, including directory listings (yellow pages and business white pages), annual reports, 10K's and SEC information, federal, state, and municipal government data, business magazines, newsletters and newspapers, and U.S. Postal Service information. *info*USA conducts annual telephone verifications with each business to ensure accurate and complete information.

ESRI Business Information Solutions provides reports and file extracts from the *info*USA database that include the number of businesses by NAICS code and employment size or sales volume, total employment, and total sales, where available. Industry classifications include the standard NAICS code hierarchy, plus *info*USA's proprietary detailed eight-digit industry code. Also, a special industry code for select industries is available that provides more detailed information, such as the number of rooms in hotels/motels or the number of beds in hospitals and nursing homes. Sales data are reported for business locations.

The Business Data section shows the total number of companies and employees by ZIP Code for all industries. Also shown is the top industry as determined by total employment for each ZIP Code. Industries are represented by three-digit NAICS industry. A complete list of NAICS definitions is included in Appendix II.

Business Locations

*info*USA compiles an address list of businesses from its sources and telephone verification. The addresses are geocoded to assign latitude and longitude coordinates to the business site and to append a census geographic code. Most businesses are coded at the address level and assigned to a census block group. Of course, the quality of the local address system varies: address matching is better in an urban area with street-level address systems than in rural areas. Overall, 84 percent of the businesses are coded at the address level; 86 percent are assigned to a census block group. Businesses that cannot be assigned to a block group are assigned to a census tract or county.

ESRI Business Information Solution uses the geographic codes to report business data for summary areas--states, counties, census tracts and block groups. Aggregations by ZIP Codes are created from the business database. *info*USA's ZIP Codes may differ from the residential ZIP Codes in ESRI Business Information Solutions' demographic databases due to the inclusion of business-only ZIP Codes, which are unique to a particular establishment and include no residential area.

Explanation of Variables*

Tapestry Type
Tapestry is ESRI BIS' market segmentation system. There are 65 distinct residential Tapestry segments and one unclassified segment.

Top Tapestry Type
The top Tapestry type is determined by the household distribution of the ZIP Code among the 66 Tapestry segments. The top Tapestry type has the largest share of households in a ZIP Code, usually the majority of households. However, in a large diverse ZIP Code, the top Tapestry type may not represent most of the households, but a smaller share.

Age
Age is reported for five-year age groups and select summary groups such as 18 years and over. These data are ESRI Business Information Solutions' 2004 projections.

Median Age
Median age is calculated from the distribution of age by five-year groups. ESRI Business Information Solutions' 2004 projections. See Median.

Average Household Size
See Household.

Census Tract
Tracts are small statistical subdivisions of a county. The boundaries are delineated by local committees to represent relatively homogeneous neighborhoods and to maintain stable boundaries. Census tracts generally have 1,500 to 8,000 residents.

Centile
Same as Percentile.

County
Counties are the primary legal subdivisions of a state and are identified by a two-digit state FIPS code and a three-digit county FIPS code. Because ZIP Code boundaries do not follow county lines, the dominant county reported for each ZIP Code represents the county with the largest proportion of land area in a ZIP Code. See FIPS Code.

Families
Households in which one or more persons in the household are related to the householder (formerly, the head of the household) by birth, marriage or adoption. The Census tabulates only one family per household. These data are Census 2000 and ESRI Business Information Solutions 2004 projections.

FIPS Code
Federal Information Processing Standards for numeric codes used to identify states and counties.

Hispanic Origin
Defined by self-identification, Hispanic origin refers to ethnicity, not race. Persons of Hispanic origin may be of any race. These data are Census 2000 and ESRI Business Information Solutions' 2004 projections.

Home Value
The estimate of value is presented for total owner-occupied units. For a discussion of home value projections, see the Update Methodology. These data are ESRI Business Information Solutions' 2004 projections.

Median Home Value
This estimate divides the distribution of home value into two equal parts. Linear interpolation is used if the median home value falls below $1,000,000. If the median falls in the upper home value interval of $1,000,000+, it is represented by $1,000,001.

Home Value Base
This is the sum of the home value distribution.

Household
A household is an occupied housing unit. Household type is identified by the presence of relatives and the number of persons living in the household. Family households, with or without children, include married couples and other families--a male or female householder with no spouse present. Non-family households may be a group of unrelated persons or a single person living alone. These data are Census 2000 and ESRI Business Information Solutions' 2004 and 2009 projections.

Average Household Size
The average size is calculated by dividing the number of persons in households by the number of households.

Household Income
See Income.

Household Income Base
The sum of the household income distribution.

Income
2004 Income is a forecast of Income for the calendar year 2003. Income amounts are expressed in current dollars, including an adjustment for inflation or cost-of-living increases. For a discussion of income projections, see the Update Methodology. These data are ESRI Business Information Solutions' 2004 and 2009 projections.

---

* Note: For more information about Census 2000 data, please see the 2000 Census of Population and Housing, Summary Files 1 and 3 Technical Documentation prepared by the U.S. Bureau of the Census.

Median

Median is a value that divides a distribution into two equal parts. A median is a positional measure that is unaffected by extremely high or low values in a distribution that can affect an average.

Median Household Income

This is the value that divides the distribution of household income into two equal parts. Pareto interpolation is used if the median falls in an income interval other than the first or last. For the lowest interval, <$10,000, linear interpolation is used. If the median falls in the upper income interval of $500,000+, it is represented by the value of $500,001.

Per Capita Income

This is the average income for all persons calculated from the aggregate income of persons 15 years and older.

Percentile

This is another measure that can be used to locate the position of a value for a select area relative to that value for other areas. Percentiles show the proportion of areas that have a lower value. For example, ZIP Codes are ranked on 2004 median household income by percentile, 0 to 100, in each state and nationwide. A ZIP Code with a rank of 95 on median household income has a higher median value than 95 percent of the ZIP Codes in a state or the U.S.

Population

This is the total number of residents in an area. Residence refers to the "usual place" where a person lives, not necessarily the legal residence. For example, college students are counted where they attend school. These data are Census 2000 and ESRI Business Information Solutions' 2004 and 2009 projections.

Post Office Name

Typically, the post office name is the name that appears on the city/state address line. If multiple post office names are assigned to a ZIP Code, the city name is used.

Race

Defined by self-identification, race detail from Census 2000 was expanded to include a multiracial component. For the first time, each individual could report up to six race categories, resulting in 63 possible race combinations. The six basic race categories are White, Black or African American, American Indian or Alaskan Native, Asian, Native Hawaiian or Other Pacific Islander, and "some other" race for persons who do not identify with one of the specified groups. ESRI Business Information Solutions forecasts race for all single and multiracial populations that are consistent with 2000 Census tabulations. Data are Census 2000 and ESRI Business Information Solutions' 2004 projections of White, Black and Asian/Native Hawaiian or Other Pacific Islander.

Rate, Annual Percent

Calculated as an annual compound rate of change from 2000 to 2004 for population, households, and families. For example:

$$Rate = \left[\left(\frac{P_{04}}{P_{00}} \right)^{\frac{1}{4.25}} - 1 \right] \times 100$$

The rate of population change is ranked by percentile within each state. See Percentile.

Spending Potential Index

See the Spending Potential Indices Methodology.

State

States are identified by a two-digit FIPS code. The District of Columbia is included as a state-equivalent area in the ESRI Business Information Solutions database. See FIPS Code.

ZIP Code

Created by the U.S. Postal Service to deliver the mail, ZIP Codes do not represent standard census geographic areas for data reporting. Because the ZIP Code boundaries are not contiguous with census geographic areas or stable over time, data estimated for ZIP Codes are also subject to change. The ZIP Codes in this Sourcebook are current as of November 2003. See the ZIP Code Update Methodology for a description of data estimation for ZIP Codes.

Residential ZIP Code Data
by State

The Community
Sourcebook
2004
18th EDITION
of ZIP Code
Demographics

ZIP CODE		COUNTY FIPS CODE	POPULATION			2000-2004 ANNUAL RATE		HOUSEHOLDS					FAMILIES		
#	POST OFFICE NAME		2000	2004	2009	% Rate	State Centile	2000	2004	2009	% Annual Rate 2000-2004	2004 Average HH Size	2000	2004	% Annual Rate 2000-2004
35004	MOODY	115	6664	7383	8066	2.4	94	2605	2958	3299	3.0	2.48	1951	2215	3.0
35005	ADAMSVILLE	073	9154	8465	8098	-1.8	1	3534	3339	3251	-1.3	2.53	2658	2505	-1.4
35006	ADGER	073	3194	3135	3085	-0.4	19	1218	1228	1234	0.2	2.55	931	935	0.1
35007	ALABASTER	117	19679	22316	26009	3.0	96	7213	8379	9980	3.6	2.62	5709	6621	3.6
35010	ALEXANDER CITY	123	21013	20974	21003	0.0	34	8318	8482	8642	0.5	2.40	5784	5884	0.4
35014	ALPINE	121	4378	4428	4457	0.3	48	1654	1727	1788	1.0	2.34	1236	1289	1.0
35016	ARAB	095	15655	15592	15782	-0.1	32	6350	6414	6570	0.2	2.41	4602	4641	0.2
35019	BAILEYTON	043	2255	2304	2324	0.5	61	873	910	931	1.0	2.53	651	677	0.9
35020	BESSEMER	073	31391	29754	28796	-1.3	4	12097	11658	11459	-0.9	2.51	8133	7821	-0.9
35022	BESSEMER	073	15121	15796	16032	1.0	75	5905	6272	6460	1.4	2.48	4547	4826	1.4
35023	BESSEMER	073	25160	24854	24503	-0.3	22	9359	9437	9466	0.2	2.46	7049	7101	0.2
35031	BLOUNTSVILLE	009	7898	8256	8591	1.1	75	3094	3279	3448	1.4	2.52	2328	2464	1.3
35033	BREMEN	043	3585	3559	3528	-0.2	27	1361	1379	1387	0.3	2.58	1083	1095	0.3
35034	BRENT	007	5339	5722	6146	1.6	84	1538	1720	1921	2.7	2.76	1118	1247	2.6
35035	BRIERFIELD	007	1517	1451	1506	-1.0	6	554	543	577	-0.5	2.67	444	436	-0.4
35036	BROOKSIDE	073	142	141	139	-0.2	27	61	62	62	0.4	2.23	46	47	0.5
35040	CALERA	117	7202	8223	9524	3.2	98	2731	3186	3759	3.7	2.57	2083	2423	3.6
35041	CARDIFF	073	21	21	21	0.0	37	9	9	9	0.0	2.22	7	7	0.0
35042	CENTREVILLE	007	5154	5376	5716	1.0	73	2060	2206	2409	1.6	2.32	1487	1591	1.6
35043	CHELSEA	117	4424	5346	6423	4.6	100	1571	1936	2370	5.0	2.74	1280	1575	5.0
35044	CHILDERSBURG	121	7814	8104	8274	0.9	70	2927	3106	3249	1.4	2.57	2116	2243	1.4
35045	CLANTON	021	12980	13431	14025	0.8	69	5106	5365	5685	1.2	2.45	3622	3804	1.2
35046	CLANTON	021	4747	4825	4960	0.4	55	1945	2013	2102	0.8	2.39	1458	1507	0.8
35049	CLEVELAND	009	4289	4520	4738	1.2	78	1566	1675	1774	1.6	2.69	1222	1304	1.5
35051	COLUMBIANA	117	7320	7909	8974	1.8	87	2761	3052	3537	2.4	2.55	2055	2264	2.3
35053	CRANE HILL	043	2449	2556	2602	1.0	73	1001	1067	1104	1.5	2.40	782	832	1.5
35054	CROPWELL	115	3419	3644	3882	1.5	81	1377	1491	1613	1.9	2.44	1025	1107	1.8
35055	CULLMAN	043	18568	17954	17763	-0.8	10	7863	7721	7731	-0.4	2.25	5123	5019	-0.5
35057	CULLMAN	043	11616	11987	12136	0.7	67	4482	4718	4844	1.2	2.54	3496	3671	1.2
35058	CULLMAN	043	9736	9902	9995	0.4	56	3734	3868	3957	0.8	2.55	2895	2990	0.8
35061	DOLOMITE	073	1635	1505	1437	-1.9	1	579	543	527	-1.5	2.70	438	410	-1.5
35062	DORA	073	8570	8694	8682	0.3	53	3295	3413	3474	0.8	2.54	2579	2663	0.8
35063	EMPIRE	127	5075	5184	5211	0.5	60	1916	1997	2046	1.0	2.59	1451	1511	1.0
35064	FAIRFIELD	073	12647	12117	11768	-1.0	6	4698	4561	4492	-0.7	2.52	3214	3109	-0.8
35068	FULTONDALE	073	5888	5991	5986	0.4	56	2423	2532	2584	1.0	2.36	1708	1778	1.0
35071	GARDENDALE	073	13281	13655	13691	0.7	65	5347	5643	5775	1.3	2.39	3981	4177	1.1
35072	GOODWATER	027	4657	4538	4451	-0.6	14	1770	1769	1779	-0.0	2.54	1303	1300	-0.1
35073	GRAYSVILLE	073	2884	2787	2715	-0.8	10	1144	1125	1114	-0.4	2.46	840	823	-0.5
35077	HANCEVILLE	043	12961	12956	12955	0.0	35	5058	5168	5245	0.5	2.43	3656	3718	0.4
35078	HARPERSVILLE	117	2501	2685	3041	1.7	85	949	1046	1212	2.3	2.54	715	785	2.2
35079	HAYDEN	009	6854	7380	7775	1.8	86	2553	2789	2970	2.1	2.62	2010	2195	2.1
35080	HELENA	117	11449	14148	17168	5.1	100	4265	5392	6673	5.7	2.62	3373	4252	5.6
35083	HOLLY POND	043	2945	3129	3223	1.4	80	1130	1224	1277	1.9	2.56	855	924	1.8
35085	JEMISON	021	7976	8373	8810	1.2	76	2978	3180	3396	1.6	2.62	2265	2415	1.5
35087	JOPPA	043	1891	1930	1948	0.5	59	755	785	803	0.9	2.46	567	587	0.8
35089	KELLYTON	037	2677	2683	2643	0.1	38	1039	1063	1070	0.5	2.33	768	785	0.5
35091	KIMBERLY	073	748	767	767	0.6	63	288	300	305	1.0	2.56	223	232	0.9
35094	LEEDS	073	11690	12843	13616	2.2	92	4802	5375	5793	2.7	2.39	3361	3767	2.7
35096	LINCOLN	121	6564	6762	6841	0.7	66	2561	2708	2809	1.3	2.46	1885	1989	1.3
35098	LOGAN	043	1339	1480	1552	2.4	93	514	578	615	2.8	2.56	400	449	2.8
35111	MC CALLA	073	10278	10927	11263	1.5	80	3609	3914	4109	1.9	2.73	3012	3260	1.9
35114	MAYLENE	117	3971	4518	5274	3.1	97	1412	1650	1969	3.7	2.74	1110	1294	3.7
35115	MONTEVALLO	117	14730	15629	17467	1.4	80	5340	5812	6667	2.0	2.53	3801	4138	2.0
35116	MORRIS	073	4489	4496	4442	0.0	38	1671	1698	1702	0.4	2.65	1317	1336	0.3
35117	MOUNT OLIVE	073	4916	4988	4972	0.3	53	1880	1949	1977	0.9	2.53	1473	1523	0.8
35118	MULGA	073	3473	3323	3227	-1.0	6	1344	1311	1296	-0.6	2.53	1023	993	-0.7
35120	ODENVILLE	115	8291	8915	9534	1.7	86	3018	3320	3621	2.3	2.56	2416	2656	2.3
35121	ONEONTA	009	14185	15216	16006	1.7	85	5370	5830	6196	2.0	2.53	3913	4249	2.0
35124	PELHAM	117	17120	20200	23990	4.0	99	6591	7951	9630	4.5	2.54	4836	5806	4.4
35125	PELL CITY	115	9279	9530	9971	0.6	64	3521	3681	3920	1.1	2.53	2584	2697	1.0
35126	PINSON	073	19627	21020	21550	1.6	84	6846	7452	7758	2.0	2.82	5660	6165	2.0
35127	PLEASANT GROVE	073	9969	10258	10291	0.7	65	3566	3749	3830	1.2	2.68	2885	3028	1.1
35128	PELL CITY	115	9205	9838	10508	1.6	83	3487	3799	4130	2.0	2.56	2654	2888	2.0
35130	QUINTON	127	3843	4091	4180	1.5	81	1550	1689	1762	2.0	2.42	1163	1264	2.0
35131	RAGLAND	115	3998	4232	4511	1.4	79	1519	1635	1772	1.8	2.56	1178	1267	1.7
35133	REMLAP	009	3980	4111	4269	0.8	68	1493	1568	1650	1.2	2.62	1192	1252	1.2
35135	RIVERSIDE	115	1499	1554	1631	0.9	70	644	683	730	1.4	2.28	459	487	1.4
35136	ROCKFORD	037	1841	1922	1919	1.0	74	770	826	847	1.7	2.30	538	575	1.6
35143	SHELBY	117	3357	3700	4244	2.3	92	1364	1541	1804	2.9	2.40	1002	1127	2.8
35146	SPRINGVILLE	115	9076	9623	10172	1.4	79	2949	3205	3463	2.0	2.73	2334	2533	1.9
35147	STERRETT	117	3045	3437	4000	2.9	96	1147	1323	1571	3.4	2.59	894	1026	3.3
35148	SUMITON	127	2628	2694	2704	0.6	63	1080	1134	1164	1.2	2.34	768	805	1.1
35150	SYLACAUGA	121	19088	18814	18708	-0.3	22	7766	7834	7977	0.2	2.37	5256	5289	0.2
35151	SYLACAUGA	037	8463	8307	8176	-0.4	19	3301	3315	3344	0.1	2.50	2492	2499	0.1
35160	TALLADEGA	121	28292	27816	27892	-0.4	20	10384	10554	10875	0.4	2.38	7271	7374	0.3
35171	THORSBY	021	3334	3611	3878	1.9	89	1275	1400	1523	2.2	2.56	991	1086	2.2
35172	TRAFFORD	009	3104	3093	3145	-0.1	32	1229	1247	1284	0.3	2.48	967	980	0.3
35173	TRUSSVILLE	073	19612	20441	20737	1.0	72	6939	7361	7589	1.4	2.75	5588	5926	1.4
35175	UNION GROVE	095	4920	5035	5139	0.6	62	1932	2012	2082	1.0	2.50	1480	1538	0.9
35176	VANDIVER	117	936	1082	1273	3.5	98	361	425	509	3.9	2.54	286	335	3.8
35178	VINCENT	117	3549	3670	4068	0.8	69	1410	1494	1690	1.4	2.45	1056	1114	1.3
35179	VINEMONT	043	8775	9085	9239	0.8	69	3370	3564	3679	1.3	2.54	2576	2717	1.3
35180	WARRIOR	073	12590	12735	12805	0.3	48	4698	4821	4909	0.6	2.64	3693	3784	0.6
35183	WEOGUFKA	037	156	150	144	-0.9	7	69	68	67	-0.3	2.21	52	51	-0.5
35184	WEST BLOCTON	007	5469	5870	6313	1.7	85	2073	2278	2506	2.2	2.57	1608	1765	2.2
35186	WILSONVILLE	117	4104	4349	4884	1.4	79	1575	1704	1953	1.9	2.52	1235	1332	1.8
35188	WOODSTOCK	007	2818	3052	3323	1.9	88	993	1101	1228	2.5	2.77	772	856	2.5
35203	BIRMINGHAM	073	3708	3518	3427	-1.2	4	1190	1115	1085	-1.5	1.80	440	409	-1.7
35204	BIRMINGHAM	073	13575	12643	12155	-1.7	2	5762	5448	5315	-1.3	2.21	3316	3129	-1.4
35205	BIRMINGHAM	073	21419	21099	20808	-0.4	21	11368	11342	11338	-0.1	1.67	3539	3517	-0.2
35206	BIRMINGHAM	073	21701	20678	20032	-1.1	5	8250	7855	7658	-1.2	2.54	5502	5221	-1.2
35207	BIRMINGHAM	073	11278	10559	10165	-1.5	3	4314	4143	4070	-1.0	2.54	2905	2779	-1.0
35208	BIRMINGHAM	073	19316	18688	18225	-0.8	11	6889	6710	6611	-0.6	2.63	4852	4711	-0.7
35209	BIRMINGHAM	073	25589	25438	25181	-0.1	29	12390	12387	12382	-0.0	2.00	6115	6087	-0.1
35210	BIRMINGHAM	073	14326	13997	13718	-0.6	16	5702	5673	5652	-0.1	2.35	3782	3757	-0.2
	ALABAMA					0.5					0.9	2.45			0.9
	UNITED STATES					1.2					1.3	2.58			1.1

1-A

ZIP CODE #	POST OFFICE NAME	RACE (%) White 2000	White 2004	Black 2000	Black 2004	Asian/Pacific 2000	Asian/Pacific 2004	% Hispanic Origin 2000	% Hispanic Origin 2004	2004 AGE DISTRIBUTION (%) 0-4	5-9	10-14	15-19	20-24	25-44	45-64	65-84	85+	18+	MEDIAN AGE 2004	% 2004 Males	% 2004 Females
35004	MOODY	94.4	94.1	3.4	3.4	0.3	0.3	1.2	1.5	6.9	6.7	7.0	6.9	6.1	30.1	25.1	10.1	1.1	75.2	36.5	49.0	51.0
35005	ADAMSVILLE	76.4	72.6	22.1	25.8	0.2	0.2	0.5	0.7	5.6	5.9	6.9	6.3	5.7	27.3	26.7	14.0	1.7	77.8	39.9	47.9	52.1
35006	ADGER	92.4	91.2	6.4	7.3	0.1	0.1	0.4	0.5	5.4	5.6	6.7	6.5	6.3	28.2	29.2	11.2	1.0	78.4	39.9	50.9	49.1
35007	ALABASTER	86.9	86.2	10.3	10.3	0.7	0.8	2.1	2.7	9.0	8.6	6.9	5.3	5.4	34.7	21.8	7.1	1.3	72.2	34.3	48.4	51.7
35010	ALEXANDER CITY	71.9	70.4	26.9	28.2	0.2	0.3	0.6	0.8	6.5	6.5	6.8	6.0	6.2	26.4	24.8	14.3	2.6	76.5	39.1	47.5	52.5
35014	ALPINE	45.4	44.0	53.4	54.6	0.2	0.3	0.7	0.7	6.8	6.7	6.5	6.6	7.2	30.4	25.1	9.7	1.0	76.3	35.9	53.2	46.8
35016	ARAB	98.2	97.9	0.1	0.1	0.3	0.3	0.9	1.2	6.3	6.4	6.8	6.4	5.6	28.4	25.1	13.4	1.7	76.6	39.1	49.1	50.9
35019	BAILEYTON	97.2	96.7	0.0	0.0	0.1	0.2	2.4	3.0	7.5	7.3	7.1	6.5	6.3	29.0	23.3	11.7	1.4	74.1	36.1	50.4	49.7
35020	BESSEMER	24.1	21.5	74.3	76.8	0.2	0.2	1.4	1.5	7.3	7.2	7.3	7.2	7.1	25.5	23.1	13.0	2.3	73.7	36.3	46.2	53.8
35022	BESSEMER	68.0	65.3	30.5	32.9	0.3	0.4	0.8	1.0	8.0	7.2	6.6	5.9	5.9	27.1	25.2	12.3	1.9	74.7	37.8	46.8	53.3
35023	BESSEMER	82.8	80.8	16.3	18.1	0.2	0.2	0.5	0.6	5.3	5.6	6.0	5.8	6.2	29.7	26.6	13.0	1.9	79.7	39.7	51.4	48.6
35031	BLOUNTSVILLE	95.5	94.6	0.1	0.1	0.2	0.3	6.7	8.5	6.6	6.6	6.8	6.2	6.0	29.0	24.8	12.5	1.5	76.2	37.3	50.7	49.3
35033	BREMEN	98.4	98.3	0.5	0.5	0.1	0.1	0.6	0.8	6.6	6.5	6.6	6.2	6.6	27.5	27.5	11.7	1.1	76.7	38.6	49.9	50.1
35034	BRENT	53.3	52.2	45.5	46.3	0.2	0.2	1.1	1.3	6.1	6.3	7.2	6.8	7.8	33.4	22.3	8.8	1.3	76.5	34.4	57.6	42.4
35035	BRIERFIELD	85.0	84.3	13.7	14.1	0.1	0.2	0.9	1.2	6.1	6.5	7.0	6.1	5.9	28.7	26.8	11.6	1.3	76.7	38.6	49.0	51.0
35036	BROOKSIDE	94.4	92.9	3.5	5.0	0.0	0.0	0.7	0.7	6.4	6.4	6.4	6.4	6.4	29.8	25.5	11.4	1.4	76.6	38.4	50.4	49.7
35040	CALERA	84.9	83.4	12.3	13.3	0.3	0.3	2.5	3.2	7.5	7.4	6.9	6.3	6.1	30.7	24.2	9.8	1.0	74.3	35.7	49.5	50.5
35041	CARDIFF	95.2	95.2	4.8	4.8	0.0	0.0	0.0	0.0	9.5	9.5	9.5	9.5	9.5	38.1	14.3	0.0	0.0	71.4	26.3	47.6	52.4
35042	CENTREVILLE	74.2	72.9	25.0	26.0	0.1	0.1	1.2	1.5	6.4	6.2	6.7	6.1	6.5	27.8	25.4	12.7	2.2	77.2	38.2	50.0	50.0
35043	CHELSEA	96.3	95.9	1.4	1.5	0.3	0.3	1.2	1.6	7.6	7.5	7.2	7.0	6.7	30.0	25.4	7.9	0.7	73.0	35.6	49.0	51.0
35044	CHILDERSBURG	70.8	68.7	27.9	30.0	0.2	0.2	0.6	0.7	7.5	6.9	7.1	6.5	6.8	27.3	24.5	12.1	1.2	74.5	36.3	47.6	52.4
35045	CLANTON	82.1	81.3	14.9	15.1	0.3	0.3	3.1	3.9	7.0	6.7	6.9	6.1	6.4	27.6	23.6	13.6	2.1	75.6	37.7	48.8	51.2
35046	CLANTON	97.1	96.8	1.1	1.1	0.2	0.3	2.2	2.7	6.4	6.5	6.6	5.6	5.6	30.0	26.0	12.3	1.1	77.1	38.2	50.6	49.4
35049	CLEVELAND	95.1	94.0	0.7	0.7	0.1	0.2	6.7	8.8	7.1	6.9	7.0	6.8	6.2	28.6	25.0	11.2	1.2	74.8	36.8	51.2	48.8
35051	COLUMBIANA	88.0	87.0	9.9	10.6	0.2	0.2	1.7	2.2	6.7	6.8	7.1	6.6	6.3	30.4	25.3	9.8	1.1	75.3	36.3	50.7	49.3
35053	CRANE HILL	98.7	98.6	0.0	0.0	0.2	0.2	0.5	0.7	5.7	5.4	6.2	6.1	4.9	25.2	31.0	14.0	1.5	79.1	42.7	50.4	49.7
35054	CROPWELL	86.5	85.5	12.2	12.9	0.2	0.3	0.7	0.9	5.4	5.7	5.9	5.5	4.4	24.9	31.7	15.6	1.1	79.8	44.0	49.9	50.1
35055	CULLMAN	96.9	96.4	0.3	0.3	0.4	0.4	4.1	5.1	6.4	6.1	5.9	5.9	6.2	26.3	23.6	16.7	3.0	78.0	40.1	47.7	52.3
35057	CULLMAN	97.9	97.6	0.3	0.4	0.1	0.2	1.3	1.8	6.8	6.8	7.2	6.5	6.2	28.8	25.5	11.4	1.1	75.4	37.3	50.4	49.7
35058	CULLMAN	97.1	96.6	0.1	0.1	0.3	0.3	2.7	3.5	6.9	7.0	7.1	6.3	5.9	28.0	25.3	12.3	1.2	75.1	37.3	50.2	49.8
35061	DOLOMITE	33.7	29.1	66.0	70.6	0.1	0.1	0.5	0.5	5.3	5.8	6.3	6.4	6.8	25.0	27.2	14.9	2.4	78.7	41.3	46.0	54.0
35062	DORA	93.5	92.8	4.2	4.6	0.1	0.1	0.3	0.5	6.5	6.7	6.9	6.0	5.6	28.6	26.5	12.0	1.2	76.3	38.4	49.4	50.6
35063	EMPIRE	92.0	91.6	6.6	6.9	0.1	0.1	0.8	1.0	7.1	7.2	7.2	6.5	6.1	29.2	25.0	10.6	1.0	74.5	36.1	50.0	50.0
35064	FAIRFIELD	10.6	8.6	88.4	90.4	0.2	0.3	0.6	0.6	5.5	6.2	8.1	8.9	8.6	23.8	25.1	11.3	2.5	75.4	36.1	44.4	55.6
35068	FULTONDALE	92.8	91.0	4.6	5.8	0.6	0.7	1.1	1.5	6.2	6.0	5.6	5.6	6.3	29.2	25.7	14.0	1.5	78.9	38.6	47.4	52.6
35071	GARDENDALE	96.4	95.4	2.0	2.6	0.4	0.6	0.8	1.1	5.5	5.7	6.1	5.7	5.4	25.6	27.4	16.2	2.3	79.1	42.4	47.3	52.7
35072	GOODWATER	60.3	60.5	38.5	38.1	0.0	0.0	0.4	0.4	6.6	6.5	6.6	6.6	6.7	27.2	26.1	11.7	1.9	76.4	38.0	49.7	50.3
35073	GRAYSVILLE	78.2	74.8	19.9	23.0	0.3	0.4	0.8	1.0	5.7	5.8	6.3	6.1	6.0	25.9	26.1	15.7	2.4	78.3	41.0	47.1	52.9
35077	HANCEVILLE	93.3	92.8	4.7	4.9	0.2	0.2	1.6	2.1	6.3	6.1	6.1	5.9	7.3	28.4	24.9	13.1	2.0	78.4	38.1	49.7	50.3
35078	HARPERSVILLE	72.5	70.6	25.5	27.1	0.4	0.5	0.6	0.8	6.4	6.9	7.5	6.7	6.2	28.8	24.8	11.5	1.3	74.8	37.4	49.3	50.7
35079	HAYDEN	96.2	95.6	1.1	1.1	0.2	0.2	1.8	2.4	7.4	7.3	7.2	5.9	5.9	29.3	25.4	10.5	1.2	74.5	36.4	50.8	49.2
35080	HELENA	93.4	92.4	3.9	4.3	0.9	1.1	1.8	2.3	9.7	8.3	7.1	5.3	5.4	38.3	20.1	5.3	0.5	71.6	32.4	48.3	51.7
35083	HOLLY POND	98.2	97.9	0.0	0.0	0.1	0.1	1.4	1.9	7.1	7.0	6.7	6.0	6.2	29.0	24.4	12.5	1.2	75.6	37.3	50.0	50.0
35085	JEMISON	88.6	87.3	8.1	8.7	0.1	0.1	3.9	4.9	7.2	7.2	7.0	6.5	6.3	30.3	24.5	10.0	1.0	74.6	35.4	50.4	49.6
35087	JOPPA	98.0	97.7	0.1	0.1	0.1	0.2	2.5	3.3	7.2	7.1	6.8	6.6	6.2	29.5	24.8	10.7	1.2	75.0	36.7	50.7	49.3
35089	KELLYTON	50.5	49.5	48.2	48.9	0.0	0.0	1.6	1.9	5.6	6.0	7.5	6.1	7.1	30.5	24.6	11.0	1.6	77.5	37.1	52.6	47.4
35091	KIMBERLY	97.3	96.6	1.2	1.4	0.1	0.3	0.5	0.7	6.8	7.0	7.8	6.0	5.5	29.6	24.9	11.3	1.0	74.6	37.3	49.4	50.6
35094	LEEDS	83.3	81.6	14.7	15.9	0.6	0.7	1.3	1.7	6.4	6.5	7.0	6.3	5.5	28.4	26.0	12.6	1.3	76.2	39.0	48.1	51.9
35096	LINCOLN	75.1	73.8	23.6	24.6	0.1	0.1	0.8	1.0	6.0	6.5	6.9	6.1	5.7	27.7	29.0	11.1	1.0	76.9	38.9	49.9	50.1
35098	LOGAN	98.1	97.8	0.0	0.0	0.1	0.1	1.3	1.7	6.6	6.6	7.6	6.6	6.6	28.5	25.2	11.0	1.4	75.3	37.0	50.2	49.8
35111	MC CALLA	93.0	91.7	5.4	6.4	0.1	0.2	0.9	1.2	6.9	7.0	6.6	5.8	5.4	28.3	27.6	10.7	1.7	76.0	38.6	48.9	51.1
35114	MAYLENE	92.5	91.7	5.3	5.6	0.7	0.8	1.6	2.2	9.3	8.5	7.1	5.7	5.9	36.8	21.0	5.3	0.5	71.7	32.9	49.4	50.6
35115	MONTEVALLO	83.3	82.5	14.6	15.1	0.2	0.3	2.4	3.1	6.8	6.5	6.2	8.8	11.5	29.2	21.4	8.6	0.9	76.7	31.5	48.3	51.7
35116	MORRIS	96.6	95.9	1.9	2.3	0.2	0.2	0.8	1.1	6.8	7.0	8.2	6.4	5.9	29.9	24.5	10.4	0.9	74.0	36.7	49.3	50.7
35117	MOUNT OLIVE	95.9	95.1	2.5	2.9	0.1	0.2	0.8	1.0	6.2	6.4	6.3	5.9	5.5	28.2	27.7	12.4	1.3	77.3	39.8	49.1	50.9
35118	MULGA	81.3	77.9	17.5	20.7	0.1	0.1	0.5	0.6	5.6	5.8	5.9	6.1	6.3	26.5	27.4	14.5	1.9	79.0	40.6	49.0	51.0
35120	ODENVILLE	89.2	88.9	9.1	9.1	0.2	0.2	0.9	1.2	6.7	6.8	7.2	6.7	6.1	30.9	25.0	9.5	1.1	75.1	36.5	51.3	48.7
35121	ONEONTA	91.9	90.9	2.9	2.9	0.1	0.2	9.4	11.7	6.9	6.8	6.6	6.2	6.1	27.6	24.4	13.3	2.2	75.9	38.1	49.6	50.4
35124	PELHAM	91.5	90.2	4.2	4.7	1.6	1.9	4.3	5.3	7.6	7.8	7.1	5.7	5.2	31.9	26.0	7.9	0.8	73.9	36.3	48.7	51.3
35125	PELL CITY	91.7	90.9	6.2	6.8	0.2	0.2	1.2	1.6	7.1	7.0	7.4	6.8	6.6	28.7	23.7	11.0	1.9	74.4	35.8	48.9	51.1
35126	PINSON	94.4	93.3	4.2	5.0	0.4	0.5	0.7	0.9	6.5	6.9	7.8	7.6	6.2	29.4	25.9	9.0	0.9	74.1	36.8	49.1	50.9
35127	PLEASANT GROVE	82.3	80.0	16.8	18.9	0.2	0.2	0.3	0.4	5.5	6.0	6.7	6.3	5.7	25.4	27.8	14.4	2.3	77.9	41.6	47.2	52.8
35128	PELL CITY	89.4	88.6	9.4	10.0	0.2	0.2	0.8	1.1	6.4	6.8	6.9	6.3	5.3	27.5	27.2	12.4	1.3	75.9	39.0	49.6	50.4
35130	QUINTON	90.5	89.8	6.8	7.2	0.1	0.1	0.4	0.6	5.4	5.7	7.0	5.9	5.0	28.5	27.5	13.6	1.4	78.2	40.3	49.8	50.2
35131	RAGLAND	91.4	91.0	7.8	8.0	0.1	0.1	0.5	0.6	7.2	7.1	7.1	6.5	6.4	29.0	24.5	11.2	0.9	74.6	36.5	50.1	49.9
35133	REMLAP	98.2	98.0	0.2	0.2	0.1	0.1	0.9	1.2	7.2	7.3	7.6	5.6	5.2	29.7	25.6	10.8	0.9	74.4	37.2	50.3	49.7
35135	RIVERSIDE	84.4	83.4	13.3	14.0	0.1	0.1	1.0	1.3	6.0	6.4	7.4	5.7	5.0	30.4	26.8	11.3	0.9	76.6	38.8	48.6	51.4
35136	ROCKFORD	72.0	70.1	25.3	26.9	0.1	0.1	1.7	2.1	5.9	5.9	6.8	5.9	5.3	25.6	27.0	15.7	1.9	77.7	41.6	51.4	48.6
35143	SHELBY	92.8	92.3	5.8	6.1	0.1	0.1	1.9	2.5	5.8	6.2	6.4	5.3	5.2	26.9	30.8	12.7	0.8	78.4	41.1	51.6	48.4
35146	SPRINGVILLE	88.0	87.3	10.2	10.5	0.2	0.2	1.6	2.0	6.6	6.7	6.5	5.7	6.1	33.2	25.7	8.6	0.9	76.6	36.9	54.9	45.1
35147	STERRETT	93.7	93.3	4.1	4.2	0.3	0.3	1.1	1.5	6.7	7.0	7.0	6.0	5.4	28.1	27.8	10.9	1.1	75.5	38.7	49.7	50.3
35148	SUMITON	94.2	93.5	3.2	3.5	0.2	0.2	0.8	1.0	6.3	6.3	6.6	5.9	6.4	27.4	27.2	12.7	1.2	77.6	38.5	48.3	51.7
35150	SYLACAUGA	69.7	68.5	28.7	29.7	0.3	0.3	0.9	1.1	6.8	6.7	6.8	6.7	6.6	26.0	24.6	13.7	2.2	75.7	38.3	46.2	53.8
35151	SYLACAUGA	86.5	85.7	12.3	12.9	0.0	0.0	0.7	0.9	6.8	6.8	6.9	6.1	5.5	28.7	26.2	12.0	1.2	75.8	38.4	50.1	49.9
35160	TALLADEGA	59.1	58.0	39.4	40.4	0.2	0.3	1.5	1.8	5.7	6.1	6.6	6.9	7.2	28.1	25.6	12.0	1.7	77.5	37.6	50.5	49.5
35171	THORSBY	89.9	88.4	5.9	6.4	0.2	0.3	4.9	6.2	7.1	7.0	6.8	6.3	6.5	30.3	23.9	10.7	1.4	75.2	36.3	51.0	49.0
35172	TRAFFORD	98.2	97.8	0.3	0.4	0.1	0.1	0.5	0.6	6.9	7.0	7.4	6.2	5.9	29.8	25.3	10.6	1.0	74.9	36.6	50.2	49.8
35173	TRUSSVILLE	96.0	95.1	2.4	3.0	0.4	0.5	0.8	1.1	6.2	6.8	7.6	7.1	5.4	27.3	28.0	10.2	1.5	75.0	39.3	48.9	51.1
35175	UNION GROVE	97.2	96.7	0.2	0.2	0.2	0.3	1.0	1.3	6.4	6.6	6.8	5.9	5.9	28.6	28.2	10.6	1.1	76.7	38.8	49.9	50.2
35176	VANDIVER	95.3	94.6	2.4	2.7	0.8	0.9	0.9	1.2	7.3	7.8	6.7	4.6	4.1	29.5	28.9	10.4	0.7	75.3	39.1	49.7	50.3
35178	VINCENT	81.8	80.1	16.7	18.2	0.2	0.2	0.8	1.0	6.1	6.3	6.2	5.8	4.9	27.6	28.8	13.0	1.3	77.8	40.6	49.1	50.9
35179	VINEMONT	97.7	97.3	0.1	0.1	0.2	0.2	1.0	1.4	6.3	6.5	7.1	6.4	6.3	28.9	25.9	11.5	1.2	76.2	37.9	50.3	49.7
35180	WARRIOR	93.7	92.7	4.7	5.4	0.2	0.2	0.5	0.6	6.7	6.7	6.9	6.2	6.2	28.8	25.6	11.6	1.3	75.9	37.6	49.5	50.6
35183	WEOGUFKA	94.9	94.0	2.6	2.7	0.0	0.0	1.3	1.3	4.0	4.7	6.0	4.7	4.7	25.3	32.7	16.0	2.0	82.7	45.4	51.3	48.7
35184	WEST BLOCTON	91.3	90.7	7.8	8.3	0.1	0.1	0.8	1.0	8.3	7.9	7.3	6.2	6.2	30.1	23.5	9.5	1.0	72.7	34.6	50.3	49.7
35186	WILSONVILLE	93.4	92.7	5.1	5.6	0.4	0.5	0.5	0.6	6.6	6.7	6.7	6.3	5.0	27.3	27.8	12.5	1.1	76.3	39.9	49.6	50.4
35188	WOODSTOCK	91.3	90.4	7.1	7.9	0.0	0.0	0.7	0.9	8.0	7.8	7.2	5.8	6.3	31.5	23.3	9.2	1.0	73.5	34.2	50.7	49.3
35203	BIRMINGHAM	19.4	16.4	79.1	82.0	0.4	0.4	0.8	0.8	7.0	4.7	2.6	4.0	10.7	37.1	23.5	8.2	2.1	84.1	36.4	60.1	39.9
35204	BIRMINGHAM	3.3	2.9	95.2	95.5	0.1	0.1	1.8	2.0	5.9	6.1	6.6	6.7	6.3	23.6	25.5	16.1	3.3	77.2	41.4	45.6	54.4
35205	BIRMINGHAM	51.1	47.6	40.8	43.3	4.8	5.5	2.7	3.3	4.5	3.6	3.3	6.0	11.9	41.6	18.4	8.6	2.1	86.9	32.6	49.8	50.2
35206	BIRMINGHAM	29.7	25.9	68.3	72.0	0.4	0.4	1.1	1.3	6.7	7.2	8.2	8.1	6.2	27.5	22.3	11.5	2.3	72.8	35.8	46.2	53.8
35207	BIRMINGHAM	6.1	4.9	93.1	94.3	0.0	0.1	0.7	0.7	6.9	7.0	8.2	7.7	6.4	23.5	25.7	13.1	1.7	73.4	37.4	46.4	53.6
35208	BIRMINGHAM	12.3	10.6	86.2	87.9	0.2	0.3	0.9	0.9	6.5	7.2	8.3	10.0	9.7	26.5	22.9	7.8	1.2	73.1	31.9	45.4	54.6
35209	BIRMINGHAM	68.9	65.2	25.4	28.1	2.8	3.2	4.0	4.8	6.8	5.7	5.2	7.0	11.6	37.0	17.7	7.3	1.8	78.9	31.1	47.8	52.2
35210	BIRMINGHAM	76.1	73.2	21.1	23.5	1.0	1.2	2.0	2.6	5.6	5.7	6.0	6.0	5.5	26.6	26.6	13.7	4.4	78.7	41.6	46.1	53.9
	ALABAMA	71.1	70.3	26.0	26.4	0.7	0.9	1.7	2.1	6.7	6.7	7.0	6.8	7.2	28.0	24.5	11.6	1.6	75.8	36.6	48.5	51.5
	UNITED STATES	75.1	73.6	12.3	12.5	3.8	4.2	12.5	14.1	6.9	6.7	7.2	7.0	7.3	28.6	23.8	10.8	1.7	75.1	36.0	49.1	50.9

INCOME

ZIP CODE				2004 HOUSEHOLD INCOME DISTRIBUTION (%)					MEDIAN HOUSEHOLD INCOME					2004 HOME VALUE DISTRIBUTION (%)					
#	POST OFFICE NAME	2004 Per Capita Income	2004 HH Income Base	Less than $25,000	$25,000 to $49,999	$50,000 to $99,999	$100,000 to $149,999	$150,000 or More	2004	2009	2004 National Centile	2004 State Centile	2004 Home Value Base	Less than $50,000	$50,000 to $89,999	$90,000 to $174,999	$175,000 to $399,999	$400,000 or More	2004 Median Home Value
35004	MOODY	21146	2958	25.7	31.5	32.9	7.9	2.0	44615	49472	60	86	2278	21.0	18.8	46.3	12.5	1.5	105374
35005	ADAMSVILLE	20797	3339	26.4	30.9	32.0	9.0	1.7	44055	50781	59	85	2840	23.2	33.0	39.8	3.7	0.3	82948
35006	ADGER	19423	1228	28.8	34.0	30.7	5.0	1.6	40530	46260	48	76	1033	34.0	35.7	23.4	5.5	1.4	66379
35007	ALABASTER	28062	8379	13.5	22.3	42.3	16.4	5.5	63388	74683	87	97	7330	7.4	5.5	58.7	25.5	2.9	144117
35010	ALEXANDER CITY	19662	8482	38.5	29.1	23.7	5.5	3.2	33627	37745	23	48	6128	24.7	33.3	28.4	10.4	3.3	79982
35014	ALPINE	16537	1727	38.4	31.8	24.0	5.3	0.5	34144	38152	24	50	1491	38.6	25.2	21.7	13.0	1.5	65541
35016	ARAB	21402	6414	29.5	33.6	25.9	8.1	2.9	39680	44015	45	73	5111	15.8	25.0	41.3	16.5	1.5	99358
35019	BAILEYTON	17086	910	33.1	37.5	24.0	4.1	1.4	35612	40156	30	57	764	26.6	27.8	34.4	9.3	2.0	82143
35020	BESSEMER	12757	11658	53.0	27.9	15.8	2.7	0.6	23198	26570	3	11	6977	39.9	43.6	14.2	2.2	0.1	56336
35022	BESSEMER	22432	6272	28.5	28.7	28.3	11.6	3.0	43658	49967	58	84	4832	10.4	22.7	42.3	23.4	1.2	118620
35023	BESSEMER	23087	9437	22.8	30.9	34.0	9.8	2.5	46482	52909	65	89	7972	9.9	34.9	46.0	8.6	0.7	94777
35031	BLOUNTSVILLE	16650	3279	36.5	31.9	26.4	4.2	1.0	33900	37537	24	49	2624	25.2	29.5	32.4	11.4	1.5	83800
35033	BREMEN	18793	1379	29.9	37.9	25.2	4.3	2.8	36246	40620	33	60	1222	30.5	27.6	25.0	13.8	3.1	75769
35034	BRENT	12885	1720	48.4	24.5	21.9	4.3	1.0	26107	29049	6	17	1310	41.1	22.0	27.7	8.9	0.4	60588
35035	BRIERFIELD	18872	543	25.1	30.6	37.4	5.9	1.1	46075	50746	64	88	473	36.8	18.8	25.0	19.2	0.2	74231
35036	BROOKSIDE	20677	62	32.3	29.0	32.3	4.8	1.6	37822	43633	39	66	52	23.1	25.0	34.6	17.3	0.0	92500
35040	CALERA	22374	3186	24.8	28.8	33.6	9.6	3.1	46164	53387	64	88	2660	17.6	23.3	40.5	14.9	3.8	108765
35041	CARDIFF	13447	9	44.4	33.3	22.2	0.0	0.0	27247	42288	7	21	8	0.0	25.0	50.0	25.0	0.0	125000
35042	CENTREVILLE	16770	2206	41.5	28.0	25.3	4.8	0.5	31771	35360	17	38	1661	33.4	24.6	32.0	9.6	0.4	75921
35043	CHELSEA	25607	1936	16.7	25.4	35.3	17.8	4.8	58423	68122	83	96	1683	16.0	10.1	21.4	45.3	7.2	180732
35044	CHILDERSBURG	17026	3106	43.6	27.0	22.9	4.9	1.6	29802	32802	12	28	2396	31.1	34.2	26.5	6.9	1.2	71314
35045	CLANTON	16847	5365	38.3	30.4	25.4	5.0	1.0	32966	35980	21	45	4015	22.1	27.2	37.1	12.3	1.3	91000
35046	CLANTON	19231	2013	33.1	28.6	31.7	5.1	1.4	40910	44656	49	77	1726	25.3	27.4	31.8	14.5	1.0	85354
35049	CLEVELAND	18315	1675	27.5	32.0	32.8	6.1	1.6	42165	46392	53	80	1408	25.8	25.1	31.6	14.8	2.7	88713
35051	COLUMBIANA	21622	3052	28.5	26.9	32.4	8.7	3.5	44845	51144	61	86	2454	23.4	18.5	33.7	20.5	3.9	104711
35053	CRANE HILL	22733	1067	29.8	30.1	26.8	7.7	5.6	41002	44688	50	77	968	19.2	15.2	34.1	27.9	3.6	121652
35054	CROPWELL	26826	1491	26.0	29.4	28.6	9.1	7.0	43755	48348	58	85	1317	21.2	14.8	29.4	28.5	6.2	130321
35055	CULLMAN	19782	7721	39.0	31.6	21.6	5.3	2.5	32669	35716	20	44	5151	9.9	25.0	46.2	17.1	1.8	106333
35057	CULLMAN	19517	4718	33.4	34.6	24.1	4.9	3.0	36576	40578	34	62	3957	24.8	22.4	35.0	14.7	3.1	93571
35058	CULLMAN	19977	3868	28.8	33.2	29.8	5.7	2.5	38747	42740	42	70	3207	19.2	23.5	39.9	14.7	2.7	99573
35061	DOLOMITE	17659	543	32.8	33.9	28.6	3.9	0.9	37697	43109	38	65	436	17.9	48.6	31.4	2.1	0.0	71765
35062	DORA	20691	3413	34.8	27.7	28.5	7.1	1.9	36514	41637	34	61	2890	25.5	27.3	36.2	10.8	0.1	86256
35063	EMPIRE	15183	1997	43.3	29.7	22.2	4.2	0.7	30013	33095	12	29	1659	42.7	30.2	21.9	5.1	0.1	55678
35064	FAIRFIELD	16441	4561	43.0	26.0	23.4	6.7	0.8	30146	34105	13	30	2946	18.3	42.8	36.6	2.2	0.0	77456
35068	FULTONDALE	21547	2532	27.7	32.2	30.9	8.0	1.3	41690	47053	52	79	1830	6.8	35.9	49.7	7.2	0.4	95885
35071	GARDENDALE	25950	5643	21.5	29.5	34.7	10.1	4.2	48842	55685	70	91	4796	10.3	17.8	49.4	21.3	1.2	117235
35072	GOODWATER	15571	1769	43.3	31.2	21.2	2.9	1.4	29976	32723	12	29	1492	42.1	28.2	23.5	5.8	0.5	57516
35073	GRAYSVILLE	18944	1125	35.7	30.5	26.4	5.9	1.5	37075	42010	36	63	917	24.0	42.1	27.2	6.5	0.2	75660
35077	HANCEVILLE	17264	5168	35.7	34.1	24.2	4.2	1.9	35068	38503	28	54	4037	24.7	30.0	34.3	9.5	1.6	83522
35078	HARPERSVILLE	18568	1046	35.0	29.4	27.0	6.8	1.9	37196	42864	36	63	860	39.5	18.1	28.4	6.5	7.4	66389
35079	HAYDEN	18903	2789	28.8	32.2	31.1	6.0	1.9	40038	44353	46	75	2468	25.5	23.0	35.8	14.7	1.1	92317
35080	HELENA	32121	5392	9.7	22.3	43.6	18.3	6.1	67831	79550	90	99	5010	6.9	3.5	59.7	27.2	2.7	150796
35083	HOLLY POND	18867	1224	32.6	33.2	27.1	4.8	2.3	37578	41463	38	65	1027	21.8	23.5	38.3	13.3	3.1	95640
35085	JEMISON	17619	3180	30.2	33.9	29.2	5.4	1.4	37846	41937	39	66	2698	27.5	26.7	29.8	14.8	1.2	83430
35087	JOPPA	23185	785	34.4	31.2	25.2	5.2	4.0	38094	42593	40	67	661	28.9	27.5	31.9	9.2	2.4	77927
35089	KELLYTON	17802	1063	39.4	35.3	19.3	3.3	2.7	32036	35900	18	40	868	45.6	27.9	22.6	3.5	0.5	56230
35091	KIMBERLY	19993	300	30.0	27.7	33.0	7.3	2.0	42351	49804	54	81	255	22.0	25.5	38.4	12.6	1.6	94333
35094	LEEDS	24542	5375	30.1	26.6	29.1	9.2	4.9	42749	49432	55	83	4053	15.9	24.0	37.9	16.9	5.3	104345
35096	LINCOLN	20856	2708	32.5	30.7	26.0	8.6	2.2	37333	42053	37	64	2311	32.1	26.5	23.2	13.2	5.0	74848
35098	LOGAN	16144	578	39.3	32.9	22.0	4.3	1.6	32926	35953	21	45	490	25.9	26.9	32.0	13.1	2.0	85333
35111	MC CALLA	21526	3914	18.7	29.8	38.0	11.6	2.0	51048	58919	74	93	3565	13.7	16.9	41.2	26.1	2.2	128938
35114	MAYLENE	26013	1650	15.0	23.6	40.9	16.1	4.4	60594	70352	85	96	1472	13.6	5.8	47.0	31.3	2.3	144180
35115	MONTEVALLO	20572	5812	30.0	29.0	27.9	10.3	2.8	41708	47798	52	79	4388	20.8	20.2	38.0	18.9	2.2	107363
35116	MORRIS	21326	1698	22.7	29.5	35.8	10.3	1.8	47962	55521	68	90	1466	21.8	21.1	40.9	14.1	2.2	101818
35117	MOUNT OLIVE	22999	1949	25.9	24.8	36.7	10.2	2.5	49146	57420	70	91	1717	11.3	19.7	46.4	22.3	0.4	114052
35118	MULGA	20133	1311	28.5	32.0	31.5	6.4	1.7	41592	46829	52	79	1097	25.4	32.5	35.8	5.4	0.9	79826
35120	ODENVILLE	20240	3320	28.2	31.8	29.6	7.9	2.5	42006	46584	53	80	2844	26.6	25.1	27.2	18.6	2.6	86596
35121	ONEONTA	18560	5830	35.5	31.4	25.0	5.9	2.2	35345	38690	29	55	4537	25.2	26.7	30.0	14.8	3.4	87198
35124	PELHAM	31433	7951	11.7	24.6	38.9	17.3	7.5	63538	73158	87	98	6878	13.9	4.4	45.6	29.7	6.4	153125
35125	PELL CITY	19587	3681	32.7	32.9	26.9	5.1	2.5	35009	38931	28	53	2784	24.4	27.5	34.8	12.6	0.8	87824
35126	PINSON	23874	7452	16.3	25.8	41.4	12.3	4.2	56997	64905	82	95	6782	9.4	14.9	50.4	23.6	1.7	120135
35127	PLEASANT GROVE	24451	3749	18.4	23.8	41.1	14.0	2.7	57719	66471	82	95	3407	2.4	18.2	60.6	18.5	0.4	124140
35128	PELL CITY	21833	3799	26.1	31.1	28.5	10.2	4.1	42719	47596	55	82	3300	14.8	23.1	32.0	27.2	2.9	119728
35130	QUINTON	17948	1689	35.6	32.0	27.9	3.6	1.0	34584	38998	26	52	1436	35.5	37.7	20.4	5.9	0.6	64625
35131	RAGLAND	16936	1635	32.8	33.2	29.1	3.7	1.2	36383	40440	33	61	1390	33.8	20.8	32.6	10.7	2.2	81899
35133	REMLAP	20655	1568	21.4	34.7	35.0	7.1	1.9	44475	49500	60	86	1364	19.8	25.7	36.7	16.6	1.3	96889
35135	RIVERSIDE	21626	683	30.9	32.9	26.2	6.7	3.2	35762	39803	31	57	497	24.4	17.9	33.4	22.1	2.2	105523
35136	ROCKFORD	17617	826	38.0	30.5	27.2	3.8	0.5	34647	36966	26	52	673	36.7	27.9	27.8	7.6	0.0	67239
35143	SHELBY	22519	1541	25.4	29.5	33.9	8.4	2.8	43740	50451	58	84	1314	33.4	14.1	26.5	25.0	1.0	95323
35146	SPRINGVILLE	19590	3205	25.3	29.3	33.7	8.6	3.2	45865	50785	64	88	2802	21.7	18.8	32.0	23.7	3.8	109332
35147	STERRETT	30006	1323	26.5	26.1	30.3	10.1	7.0	46581	52195	65	89	1122	24.5	20.5	20.8	22.9	11.3	101344
35148	SUMITON	17204	1134	43.6	26.4	23.0	5.6	1.4	30505	33644	14	32	904	34.4	28.3	28.9	7.6	0.8	70000
35150	SYLACAUGA	17630	7834	42.5	27.7	22.8	4.9	2.1	31366	35005	16	36	5477	33.4	29.2	27.8	8.8	0.8	73563
35151	SYLACAUGA	18416	3315	34.5	32.3	25.6	5.6	2.1	36016	39861	32	59	2824	33.4	23.2	31.1	10.8	1.6	79157
35160	TALLADEGA	17709	10554	40.4	30.0	22.3	5.1	2.2	33161	36860	21	46	7758	31.1	31.3	25.9	10.7	0.9	73569
35171	THORSBY	18212	1400	29.7	35.1	28.1	5.6	1.4	39607	43787	45	72	1183	25.4	27.7	31.9	13.4	1.6	85380
35172	TRAFFORD	18794	1247	30.5	30.6	32.4	5.2	1.3	39867	44077	45	74	1040	31.0	24.0	31.5	11.8	1.6	79630
35173	TRUSSVILLE	27325	7361	15.2	21.9	38.9	16.1	7.9	63090	72617	87	97	6633	9.5	9.3	37.3	40.2	3.8	158382
35175	UNION GROVE	21069	2012	29.4	29.7	30.5	7.2	3.2	40292	44917	47	76	1726	23.4	21.9	35.3	14.7	4.8	95857
35176	VANDIVER	49691	425	19.3	15.5	29.9	16.0	19.3	70238	79370	91	99	374	13.4	15.2	8.3	38.0	25.1	231731
35178	VINCENT	21639	1494	31.7	28.3	29.7	6.6	3.9	39494	44884	44	72	1266	32.6	23.9	25.9	14.2	3.3	77037
35179	VINEMONT	19175	3564	34.5	31.7	25.1	6.0	2.7	36201	40268	32	59	2998	29.3	20.3	32.5	15.4	2.5	90531
35180	WARRIOR	19410	4821	26.8	30.1	33.4	8.4	1.3	42808	48710	55	83	4111	16.9	23.5	42.2	16.4	1.1	102250
35183	WEOGUFKA	20267	68	32.4	32.4	27.9	7.4	0.0	40000	40763	46	74	60	21.7	35.0	33.3	10.0	0.0	80000
35184	WEST BLOCTON	17697	2278	34.4	35.6	23.1	5.8	1.2	36296	40360	33	60	1891	37.3	29.0	25.6	6.6	1.4	65483
35186	WILSONVILLE	27211	1704	23.3	28.1	33.2	9.7	5.7	48606	56024	69	91	1462	18.8	18.4	30.1	27.4	5.3	117899
35188	WOODSTOCK	18068	1101	29.0	31.5	32.2	5.8	1.5	41087	45192	50	77	921	29.2	28.7	30.9	10.0	1.2	75776
35203	BIRMINGHAM	10296	1115	82.5	7.8	8.0	1.1	0.6	9124	10116	0	0	66	22.7	9.1	68.2	0.0	0.0	113043
35204	BIRMINGHAM	13465	5448	59.8	25.0	12.0	2.2	1.1	19113	21883	2	3	2617	36.6	48.0	14.1	0.7	0.6	59199
35205	BIRMINGHAM	24127	11342	46.3	30.3	16.1	4.0	3.3	27152	31005	7	20	2964	17.2	27.2	31.2	17.2	7.1	97205
35206	BIRMINGHAM	15312	7855	43.1	32.6	19.7	2.9	1.7	29037	32450	10	25	5310	21.4	54.7	20.7	3.0	0.2	67534
35207	BIRMINGHAM	14276	4143	60.6	22.9	12.9	2.0	1.6	19234	21818	2	3	2413	47.3	39.3	12.7	0.4	0.3	51979
35208	BIRMINGHAM	15832	6710	39.5	32.3	23.1	3.4	1.6	32249	36171	18	41	4397	27.3	56.8	15.2	0.7	0.1	64400
35209	BIRMINGHAM	29700	12387	26.9	30.1	28.0	9.2	5.8	42347	47872	54	81	5363	2.6	5.2	38.8	48.4	5.1	180372
35210	BIRMINGHAM	28680	5673	22.7	27.2	31.3	12.1	6.7	50088	56815	72	92	4358	10.3	18.4	46.5	17.9	6.9	113469
	ALABAMA	20998		34.3	28.7	26.3	7.2	3.5	37534	42371				22.7	26.7	33.4	14.6	2.7	90917
	UNITED STATES	25866		24.7	27.1	30.8	10.9	6.5	48124	56710				10.9	15.0	33.7	30.1	10.4	145905

#	POST OFFICE NAME	FINANCIAL SERVICES: Auto Loan	FINANCIAL SERVICES: Home Loan	FINANCIAL SERVICES: Investments	FINANCIAL SERVICES: Retirement Plans	THE HOME: Home Improvements: Home Repair	THE HOME: Home Improvements: Lawn & Garden	THE HOME: Furnishings: Computers & Hardware	THE HOME: Furnishings: Major Appliances	THE HOME: Furnishings: TV, Radio, Sound Equipment	THE HOME: Furnishings: Furniture	ENTERTAINMENT: Dine out/ Carry out	ENTERTAINMENT: Sports Equipment	ENTERTAINMENT: Fees & Tickets	ENTERTAINMENT: Toys & Games	ENTERTAINMENT: Travel	ENTERTAINMENT: Cable TV	PERSONAL: Apparel & Services	PERSONAL: Auto Repairs	PERSONAL: Health Insurance	PERSONAL: Pets & Supplies
35004	MOODY	80	78	67	76	77	80	74	77	73	75	91	90	72	88	73	71	88	77	74	90
35005	ADAMSVILLE	72	76	78	73	77	82	73	74	73	72	91	85	75	94	74	75	89	73	75	85
35006	ADGER	88	65	38	58	73	82	62	75	71	62	85	89	55	82	64	76	78	74	89	103
35007	ALABASTER	109	118	110	121	114	112	107	108	100	110	126	127	109	127	105	95	124	105	96	122
35010	ALEXANDER CITY	81	61	40	56	67	76	62	71	70	61	83	83	56	80	62	74	77	70	83	92
35014	ALPINE	75	50	23	43	57	66	49	61	58	49	69	72	41	65	49	63	62	60	75	86
35016	ARAB	83	71	55	67	76	83	68	76	74	68	89	89	65	89	70	76	84	75	84	97
35019	BAILEYTON	79	55	28	49	62	71	54	65	63	54	75	77	47	71	54	68	68	65	79	90
35020	BESSEMER	45	40	44	37	40	47	43	44	48	44	58	48	43	56	43	50	56	45	48	50
35022	BESSEMER	79	79	81	78	79	85	78	79	79	78	98	90	79	99	78	80	96	78	80	90
35023	BESSEMER	78	79	76	76	81	88	76	79	78	75	96	90	78	100	78	80	93	77	83	92
35031	BLOUNTSVILLE	77	54	28	47	60	68	52	63	61	53	72	75	45	69	53	65	66	63	76	88
35033	BREMEN	85	65	39	59	71	79	61	72	70	62	83	86	56	81	63	73	77	71	84	99
35034	BRENT	66	46	27	40	50	59	46	55	55	47	65	64	40	60	46	59	59	55	67	74
35035	BRIERFIELD	84	70	49	65	75	82	65	74	71	66	86	89	62	86	67	74	81	73	83	98
35036	BROOKSIDE	88	59	27	51	66	76	57	71	68	58	80	85	48	76	58	74	73	70	87	100
35040	CALERA	90	82	66	80	84	90	79	85	81	80	99	98	76	98	79	81	95	83	87	102
35041	CARDIFF	58	39	18	34	44	51	37	47	45	38	53	56	32	50	38	49	48	46	58	67
35042	CENTREVILLE	70	50	28	45	56	64	50	59	58	50	69	70	44	65	50	62	63	59	72	80
35043	CHELSEA	105	109	98	110	107	108	100	103	96	102	120	120	101	121	99	93	117	100	95	119
35044	CHILDERSBURG	78	56	32	50	62	71	56	66	65	56	77	78	49	73	56	69	70	65	79	89
35045	CLANTON	71	53	34	49	58	67	54	62	61	53	73	71	49	70	54	65	67	61	73	80
35046	CLANTON	77	63	45	59	69	76	59	68	65	59	78	81	56	78	62	68	73	67	78	91
35049	CLEVELAND	79	68	51	65	71	78	66	72	70	66	85	84	63	84	66	72	81	71	78	90
35051	COLUMBIANA	91	77	55	73	81	88	74	82	79	74	96	96	69	94	74	81	90	81	89	104
35053	CRANE HILL	93	72	47	65	81	91	68	82	78	68	92	97	61	90	72	83	85	81	98	113
35054	CROPWELL	110	88	62	80	98	109	83	98	93	83	111	115	76	109	87	99	104	97	115	132
35055	CULLMAN	68	60	54	59	63	70	61	65	65	60	79	75	59	78	62	67	75	65	71	78
35057	CULLMAN	84	67	45	63	72	80	65	74	71	65	86	87	60	84	65	74	80	73	82	95
35058	CULLMAN	87	69	46	63	75	83	65	76	73	66	88	90	61	86	67	77	82	75	87	101
35061	DOLOMITE	66	68	73	65	66	74	66	66	68	68	85	72	69	83	67	69	83	66	68	75
35062	DORA	94	69	39	62	77	86	66	79	76	67	90	95	59	88	67	81	83	78	94	109
35063	EMPIRE	70	51	30	46	56	64	50	59	57	50	68	70	44	65	50	60	63	59	70	80
35064	FAIRFIELD	59	55	60	52	54	62	57	58	61	58	76	64	58	73	57	64	74	59	62	66
35068	FULTONDALE	70	70	73	68	71	77	71	72	72	70	89	83	71	91	72	73	87	72	74	81
35071	GARDENDALE	81	94	102	91	93	98	88	88	86	87	107	100	93	112	91	87	106	86	87	97
35072	GOODWATER	74	51	24	44	57	65	49	60	58	49	68	72	42	65	50	62	62	60	74	85
35073	GRAYSVILLE	75	61	45	57	66	75	61	68	68	60	82	78	58	81	62	72	76	67	79	86
35077	HANCEVILLE	74	55	33	50	61	69	54	64	62	54	74	75	49	71	55	65	68	63	75	85
35078	HARPERSVILLE	84	63	37	57	68	76	60	71	68	62	82	84	54	77	61	71	76	71	82	95
35079	HAYDEN	83	69	49	65	72	79	66	74	70	67	86	87	61	82	66	72	81	73	80	94
35080	HELENA	120	137	133	143	130	126	123	122	112	128	143	142	127	144	120	105	142	118	104	133
35083	HOLLY POND	80	65	45	61	70	78	63	71	69	63	83	84	59	82	64	72	78	70	80	92
35085	JEMISON	84	61	33	54	67	75	58	70	67	59	80	83	51	76	59	71	74	69	82	96
35087	JOPPA	97	74	47	70	81	92	74	85	83	74	99	99	67	96	74	87	92	84	98	110
35089	KELLYTON	79	55	28	49	62	70	53	65	63	54	74	77	46	71	54	67	68	64	78	91
35091	KIMBERLY	90	68	41	62	75	83	65	76	73	65	88	91	59	86	66	77	81	75	89	104
35094	LEEDS	88	81	71	79	83	91	80	85	84	80	102	97	79	101	80	85	98	83	89	100
35096	LINCOLN	89	70	45	64	76	84	67	78	74	67	89	92	60	85	68	77	83	77	88	103
35098	LOGAN	76	53	28	47	60	68	51	63	60	52	71	74	45	68	52	64	65	62	75	87
35111	MC CALLA	89	87	78	86	89	93	82	87	82	83	102	102	81	102	83	82	98	85	87	103
35114	MAYLENE	105	114	106	117	109	107	103	104	96	107	121	121	105	121	100	90	119	101	91	116
35115	MONTEVALLO	82	73	66	72	74	80	75	77	77	75	94	91	72	92	73	76	90	78	78	91
35116	MORRIS	90	81	62	77	84	90	75	83	79	76	97	98	73	97	77	80	92	81	88	104
35117	MOUNT OLIVE	90	84	71	79	87	93	78	86	82	79	100	101	77	101	80	84	96	84	91	106
35118	MULGA	69	74	76	70	74	81	70	72	71	70	89	81	73	92	73	74	86	70	75	81
35120	ODENVILLE	85	77	60	74	77	81	73	79	74	75	92	91	69	87	72	73	88	78	78	94
35121	ONEONTA	83	61	37	56	67	76	61	71	70	61	83	83	54	80	61	74	76	70	84	94
35124	PELHAM	113	123	122	126	119	120	115	115	108	117	137	135	117	137	113	104	135	114	103	128
35125	PELL CITY	86	65	40	60	70	80	65	75	73	65	87	87	58	82	65	77	81	75	87	97
35126	PINSON	96	102	97	102	102	104	95	98	92	95	115	115	96	117	96	90	112	96	93	113
35127	PLEASANT GROVE	85	102	111	100	101	104	94	94	90	93	113	107	100	119	97	90	112	91	89	103
35128	PELL CITY	95	77	53	71	82	91	73	84	80	74	96	99	67	93	74	83	90	83	94	110
35130	QUINTON	82	55	25	47	62	71	53	66	64	54	75	79	45	71	54	69	68	65	82	94
35131	RAGLAND	78	58	34	52	63	70	56	66	63	57	75	78	49	71	56	66	70	65	75	88
35133	REMLAP	84	77	66	75	79	84	74	79	76	75	93	93	72	92	74	76	89	78	81	96
35135	RIVERSIDE	82	69	49	65	71	77	66	73	70	68	85	86	61	80	66	70	81	73	77	91
35136	ROCKFORD	74	52	29	46	59	67	50	62	59	50	69	73	43	67	52	63	64	61	75	86
35143	SHELBY	93	71	46	64	80	90	68	82	77	67	92	96	60	90	71	82	85	80	97	112
35146	SPRINGVILLE	91	79	58	75	83	89	74	82	79	75	96	97	71	95	75	80	91	81	88	105
35147	STERRETT	127	110	82	104	115	123	104	115	110	106	134	135	99	131	105	111	127	114	122	145
35148	SUMITON	76	51	24	45	58	67	50	62	59	50	70	74	42	66	51	63	63	61	76	87
35150	SYLACAUGA	68	54	41	50	58	66	55	61	61	55	74	71	51	72	55	64	69	61	70	77
35151	SYLACAUGA	84	59	32	52	66	76	57	70	67	58	79	83	50	76	58	72	73	69	84	97
35160	TALLADEGA	66	53	42	48	56	64	54	60	61	54	73	69	51	70	54	64	69	60	69	75
35171	THORSBY	82	63	38	57	68	76	59	70	67	60	80	83	54	79	61	71	75	69	81	95
35172	TRAFFORD	77	65	48	61	67	73	63	69	66	64	81	81	58	76	62	67	76	69	73	86
35173	TRUSSVILLE	102	118	122	117	117	117	107	109	102	107	128	128	112	134	109	100	126	106	101	123
35175	UNION GROVE	90	72	48	67	77	85	68	78	75	69	90	93	63	89	69	78	85	77	88	104
35176	VANDIVER	189	191	170	187	194	204	173	182	173	174	214	215	178	220	177	174	208	177	184	223
35178	VINCENT	97	68	36	60	77	87	66	81	77	66	91	96	57	87	67	83	83	80	98	113
35179	VINEMONT	87	64	37	58	71	80	61	73	71	62	84	87	55	81	63	75	77	72	86	100
35180	WARRIOR	83	70	50	66	74	82	68	75	73	67	88	88	64	87	69	76	83	74	84	96
35183	WEOGUFKA	76	59	41	54	67	75	56	68	63	56	75	79	50	74	60	68	70	67	80	92
35184	WEST BLOCTON	82	60	34	54	66	74	58	69	66	59	78	81	51	75	58	69	73	68	80	93
35186	WILSONVILLE	111	99	75	94	104	111	91	101	97	92	118	120	89	119	94	99	112	99	109	130
35188	WOODSTOCK	89	66	39	60	73	82	63	75	72	64	86	89	57	84	64	76	79	74	88	103
35203	BIRMINGHAM	22	18	26	17	17	21	22	21	24	22	30	24	22	29	21	25	30	22	22	24
35204	BIRMINGHAM	43	36	40	33	35	43	40	41	45	41	55	44	39	50	39	48	53	42	47	47
35205	BIRMINGHAM	59	47	63	52	47	53	63	57	64	60	80	71	59	75	58	61	78	63	55	63
35206	BIRMINGHAM	54	51	57	48	50	58	53	54	57	54	71	59	54	69	54	60	69	54	58	61
35207	BIRMINGHAM	52	43	49	39	43	52	48	49	55	50	67	53	47	61	47	58	64	51	56	57
35208	BIRMINGHAM	58	55	64	53	53	61	58	57	61	59	77	63	60	75	58	63	75	58	59	65
35209	BIRMINGHAM	80	79	98	84	77	82	89	83	86	86	109	101	87	106	85	82	106	88	76	91
35210	BIRMINGHAM	94	103	111	103	102	107	99	98	96	99	120	113	102	121	100	94	118	98	94	109
	ALABAMA	81	70	61	67	72	80	70	75	75	70	91	87	67	89	70	76	86	75	81	92
	UNITED STATES	100	100	100	100	100	100	100	100	100	100	100	100	100	100	100	100	100	100	100	100

ALABAMA

POPULATION CHANGE

A 35211-35614

# POST OFFICE NAME	COUNTY FIPS CODE	POPULATION 2000	2004	2009	2000-2004 ANNUAL RATE % Rate	State Centile	HOUSEHOLDS 2000	2004	2009	% Annual Rate 2000-2004	2004 Average HH Size	FAMILIES 2000	2004	% Annual Rate 2000-2004
35211 BIRMINGHAM	073	31251	29749	28839	-1.2	5	12199	11896	11756	-0.6	2.47	8207	7960	-0.7
35212 BIRMINGHAM	073	15394	14266	13673	-1.8	1	5827	5488	5339	-1.4	2.56	3725	3486	-1.6
35213 BIRMINGHAM	073	13952	13905	13762	-0.1	32	6219	6291	6320	0.3	2.19	3766	3793	0.2
35214 BIRMINGHAM	073	21846	21433	21081	-0.5	18	8578	8589	8596	0.0	2.47	6195	6186	0.0
35215 BIRMINGHAM	073	46328	46886	46707	0.3	49	18010	18462	18647	0.6	2.52	12951	13248	0.5
35216 BIRMINGHAM	073	31648	31740	31478	0.1	39	14279	14512	14591	0.4	2.17	8231	8321	0.3
35217 BIRMINGHAM	073	15739	15207	14829	-0.8	9	6115	5995	5929	-0.5	2.51	4153	4054	-0.6
35218 BIRMINGHAM	073	9622	9070	8759	-1.4	3	3660	3492	3414	-1.1	2.56	2434	2322	-1.1
35221 BIRMINGHAM	073	6293	5853	5617	-1.7	2	2385	2274	2225	-1.1	2.54	1707	1624	-1.2
35222 BIRMINGHAM	073	8555	8728	8745	0.5	59	4002	4146	4218	0.8	2.08	1998	2049	0.6
35223 BIRMINGHAM	073	11636	11195	10879	-0.9	8	4659	4546	4483	-0.6	2.46	3402	3314	-0.6
35224 BIRMINGHAM	073	7215	6943	6751	-0.9	8	2720	2651	2613	-0.6	2.62	1945	1891	-0.7
35226 BIRMINGHAM	073	27797	28124	27996	0.3	49	10833	11208	11364	0.8	2.48	7692	7927	0.7
35228 BIRMINGHAM	073	11265	10890	10611	-0.8	10	4243	4149	4096	-0.5	2.58	2977	2901	-0.6
35229 BIRMINGHAM	073	2017	2058	2069	0.5	59	96	102	105	1.4	2.56	40	42	1.2
35233 BIRMINGHAM	073	259	261	261	0.2	44	101	108	111	1.6	1.50	20	21	1.2
35234 BIRMINGHAM	073	7995	7343	7016	-2.0	1	2768	2579	2499	-1.7	2.55	1817	1692	-1.7
35235 BIRMINGHAM	073	18367	18568	18510	0.3	47	7576	7834	7954	0.8	2.36	5513	5685	0.7
35242 BIRMINGHAM	117	31883	37683	44488	4.0	99	12753	15160	18100	4.2	2.48	8810	10509	4.2
35243 BIRMINGHAM	073	17033	17246	17180	0.3	50	7239	7548	7687	1.0	2.28	4567	4712	0.7
35244 BIRMINGHAM	117	26966	29538	32068	2.2	91	10634	11857	13089	2.6	2.49	7604	8469	2.6
35401 TUSCALOOSA	125	37735	37159	37555	-0.4	21	14241	14250	14714	0.0	2.08	6304	6279	-0.1
35404 TUSCALOOSA	125	18891	18890	19224	0.0	37	7744	7923	8234	0.5	2.34	4771	4829	0.3
35405 TUSCALOOSA	125	30275	31996	33550	1.3	78	12198	13179	14099	1.8	2.41	8388	8991	1.7
35406 TUSCALOOSA	125	10833	11636	12283	1.7	86	4554	4957	5315	2.0	2.34	3073	3339	2.0
35441 AKRON	065	1432	1556	1653	2.0	90	589	653	707	2.5	2.38	409	453	2.4
35442 ALICEVILLE	107	5635	6203	6773	2.3	92	2050	2301	2562	2.8	2.64	1443	1617	2.7
35443 BOLIGEE	063	1091	1096	1093	0.1	41	406	417	428	0.6	2.63	276	283	0.6
35444 BROOKWOOD	125	3242	3280	3344	0.3	48	1204	1251	1303	0.9	2.60	936	968	0.8
35446 BUHL	125	1560	1611	1649	0.8	68	595	631	659	1.4	2.54	467	493	1.3
35447 CARROLLTON	107	4387	4519	4784	0.7	66	1645	1731	1868	1.2	2.60	1182	1242	1.2
35452 COKER	125	3613	3895	4096	1.8	86	1346	1484	1592	2.3	2.58	1052	1155	2.2
35453 COTTONDALE	125	9015	9275	9508	0.7	65	3473	3666	3840	1.3	2.53	2627	2759	1.2
35456 DUNCANVILLE	125	4012	4190	4331	1.0	75	1436	1536	1620	1.6	2.73	1126	1198	1.5
35457 ECHOLA	125	38	38	38	0.0	37	13	13	13	0.0	2.92	10	10	0.0
35458 ELROD	125	484	482	485	-0.1	31	188	190	194	0.3	2.54	142	142	0.0
35459 EMELLE	119	770	746	728	-0.7	12	298	298	299	0.0	2.50	209	209	0.0
35460 EPES	119	1176	1148	1125	-0.6	15	447	449	452	0.1	2.53	295	296	0.1
35461 ETHELSVILLE	107	1837	1847	1932	0.1	41	764	786	840	0.7	2.35	540	555	0.7
35462 EUTAW	063	6303	6261	6222	-0.2	28	2517	2594	2672	0.7	2.38	1698	1746	0.7
35463 FOSTERS	125	1471	1465	1475	-0.1	31	560	574	591	0.6	2.55	438	446	0.4
35464 GAINESVILLE	119	287	278	272	-0.8	11	105	105	105	0.0	2.65	69	69	0.0
35466 GORDO	107	5413	5643	6037	1.0	72	2156	2298	2511	1.5	2.46	1576	1677	1.5
35469 KNOXVILLE	063	536	552	558	0.7	66	215	228	239	1.4	2.42	140	148	1.3
35470 LIVINGSTON	119	5421	5379	5304	-0.2	27	2195	2243	2274	0.5	2.34	1307	1333	0.5
35473 NORTHPORT	125	13591	13535	13671	-0.1	31	5472	5580	5754	0.5	2.43	3932	3984	0.3
35474 MOUNDVILLE	065	5351	5713	5982	1.6	82	2009	2183	2332	2.0	2.58	1496	1627	2.0
35475 NORTHPORT	125	10044	10603	10974	1.3	78	3681	3966	4184	1.8	2.67	2981	3194	1.6
35476 NORTHPORT	125	7077	6811	6832	-0.9	8	2908	2868	2941	-0.3	2.22	1705	1663	-0.6
35480 RALPH	125	1029	1026	1034	-0.1	33	380	390	402	0.6	2.63	296	303	0.6
35481 REFORM	107	4176	4339	4607	0.9	71	1648	1750	1896	1.4	2.44	1172	1242	1.4
35487 TUSCALOOSA	125	613	677	717	2.4	93	394	448	486	3.1	1.45	80	88	2.3
35490 VANCE	125	2702	2841	2937	1.2	77	981	1053	1110	1.7	2.70	793	849	1.6
35501 JASPER	127	11066	10764	10584	-0.7	13	4578	4536	4546	-0.2	2.27	3037	3005	-0.3
35503 JASPER	127	9144	9075	8972	-0.2	27	3598	3648	3682	0.3	2.46	2667	2699	0.3
35504 JASPER	127	12813	12381	12103	-0.8	10	5067	5003	4994	-0.3	2.43	3730	3677	-0.3
35540 ADDISON	133	2606	2593	2632	-0.1	30	1061	1076	1112	0.3	2.41	777	787	0.3
35541 ARLEY	133	3198	3433	3593	1.7	85	1282	1408	1503	2.2	2.43	974	1066	2.2
35542 BANKSTON	057	1193	1218	1221	0.5	60	454	475	487	1.1	2.56	349	363	0.9
35543 BEAR CREEK	093	1110	1085	1074	-0.5	16	447	446	445	-0.1	2.43	338	337	-0.1
35544 BEAVERTON	075	959	974	982	0.4	54	391	406	418	0.9	2.40	279	290	0.9
35546 BERRY	057	3912	3972	3995	0.4	53	1541	1593	1632	0.8	2.49	1145	1182	0.8
35548 BRILLIANT	093	1812	1778	1761	-0.4	19	744	746	746	0.1	2.35	528	530	0.1
35549 CARBON HILL	127	4596	4582	4562	-0.1	33	1935	1972	2005	0.5	2.29	1358	1385	0.5
35550 CORDOVA	127	6439	6238	6113	-0.7	12	2614	2586	2587	-0.3	2.37	1826	1803	-0.3
35552 DETROIT	093	1190	1288	1342	1.9	88	498	552	585	2.5	2.33	371	411	2.4
35553 DOUBLE SPRINGS	133	4860	4953	5064	0.5	58	1928	2010	2100	1.0	2.37	1390	1448	1.0
35554 ELDRIDGE	057	1264	1255	1239	-0.2	27	496	504	509	0.4	2.47	382	388	0.4
35555 FAYETTE	057	10989	10842	10715	-0.3	22	4551	4589	4627	0.2	2.29	3139	3162	0.2
35563 GUIN	093	4222	4299	4347	0.4	57	1787	1863	1912	1.0	2.26	1222	1273	1.0
35564 HACKLEBURG	093	2552	2508	2484	-0.4	19	1081	1086	1090	0.1	2.31	747	751	0.1
35565 HALEYVILLE	133	14156	14145	14281	0.0	35	5752	5848	5999	0.4	2.40	4089	4151	0.4
35570 HAMILTON	093	11127	11127	11159	0.1	41	4430	4545	4612	0.6	2.30	3119	3196	0.6
35571 HODGES	059	1057	1079	1078	0.5	60	432	449	455	0.9	2.40	325	338	0.9
35572 HOUSTON	133	1314	1260	1261	-1.0	7	543	533	545	-0.4	2.36	402	394	-0.5
35574 KENNEDY	075	1588	1555	1551	-0.5	18	655	655	666	0.0	2.37	488	487	-0.1
35575 LYNN	133	1423	1418	1431	-0.1	32	587	597	614	0.4	2.38	441	449	0.4
35576 MILLPORT	075	3410	3382	3399	-0.2	26	1375	1393	1431	0.3	2.42	1002	1015	0.3
35578 NAUVOO	127	5421	5434	5417	0.1	39	2165	2225	2270	0.7	2.44	1627	1669	0.6
35579 OAKMAN	127	3274	3413	3464	1.0	72	1284	1367	1416	1.5	2.50	955	1015	1.4
35580 PARRISH	127	4586	4643	4641	0.3	50	1830	1891	1930	0.8	2.45	1378	1422	0.7
35581 PHIL CAMPBELL	059	5607	5692	5684	0.4	53	2210	2274	2297	0.7	2.50	1663	1709	0.6
35582 RED BAY	059	4617	4288	4101	-1.7	2	1916	1811	1755	-1.3	2.32	1366	1288	-1.4
35585 SPRUCE PINE	059	1465	1547	1571	1.3	78	588	631	650	1.7	2.45	441	474	1.7
35586 SULLIGENT	075	4701	4796	4862	0.5	59	1920	1996	2064	0.9	2.36	1398	1452	0.9
35587 TOWNLEY	127	1019	1086	1111	1.5	81	407	443	463	2.0	2.45	305	332	2.0
35592 VERNON	075	5146	5119	5163	-0.1	30	2069	2109	2176	0.5	2.37	1499	1526	0.5
35593 VINA	059	1881	1810	1760	-0.9	8	755	740	730	-0.5	2.44	582	570	-0.5
35594 WINFIELD	093	7791	7519	7371	-0.8	9	3138	3088	3068	-0.4	2.39	2277	2238	-0.4
35601 DECATUR	103	34887	33675	33427	-0.8	9	14033	13691	13740	-0.6	2.38	9158	8912	-0.6
35603 DECATUR	103	25713	26670	27167	0.9	70	10209	10825	11208	1.4	2.45	7462	7873	1.3
35610 ANDERSON	077	2079	2150	2181	0.8	69	849	893	922	1.2	2.41	650	681	1.1
35611 ATHENS	083	22720	22993	23390	0.3	49	9243	9539	9857	0.7	2.35	6255	6452	0.7
35613 ATHENS	083	12447	13488	14221	1.9	89	4613	5072	5410	2.3	2.66	3637	3996	2.3
35614 ATHENS	083	6797	6774	6854	-0.1	32	2621	2669	2745	0.4	2.54	1983	2013	0.4
ALABAMA					0.5					0.9	2.45			0.9
UNITED STATES					1.2					1.3	2.58			1.1

2-A

#	POST OFFICE NAME	White 2000	White 2004	Black 2000	Black 2004	Asian/Pacific 2000	Asian/Pacific 2004	% Hispanic Origin 2000	% Hispanic Origin 2004	0-4	5-9	10-14	15-19	20-24	25-44	45-64	65-84	85+	18+	MEDIAN AGE 2004	% 2004 Males	% 2004 Females
35211	BIRMINGHAM	4.3	4.0	94.6	94.8	0.2	0.2	0.8	0.8	7.6	7.4	8.0	7.6	7.2	24.4	23.9	12.3	1.7	72.5	35.1	44.0	56.0
35212	BIRMINGHAM	17.7	15.7	78.2	79.8	0.3	0.3	4.6	5.0	8.8	8.7	8.2	7.4	7.1	28.8	21.4	8.4	1.3	69.8	31.7	46.5	53.6
35213	BIRMINGHAM	90.8	88.5	7.3	9.1	1.1	1.4	0.9	1.2	7.0	6.8	5.9	5.0	4.6	29.1	23.5	15.0	3.0	76.7	39.3	45.8	54.2
35214	BIRMINGHAM	34.2	31.6	64.5	67.0	0.2	0.2	0.7	0.8	6.1	6.5	7.0	6.4	6.2	25.3	27.0	13.5	2.0	76.4	39.4	45.9	54.1
35215	BIRMINGHAM	57.6	53.2	40.0	44.0	0.5	0.6	1.8	2.3	8.1	7.5	7.4	6.7	7.2	29.7	21.7	10.6	1.2	72.9	34.0	46.8	53.2
35216	BIRMINGHAM	86.1	83.0	7.0	8.4	3.3	4.1	5.5	7.1	5.7	5.4	6.1	6.6	8.1	30.7	22.7	12.2	2.6	79.0	36.2	47.7	52.3
35217	BIRMINGHAM	51.6	48.8	46.4	48.9	0.1	0.1	1.8	2.3	6.3	6.6	7.3	7.4	6.9	25.9	24.5	12.9	2.3	75.2	38.0	46.5	53.5
35218	BIRMINGHAM	5.8	4.8	93.2	94.1	0.1	0.1	1.0	1.0	7.3	7.6	9.1	8.5	7.8	26.9	23.0	8.5	1.4	70.8	32.5	45.2	54.8
35221	BIRMINGHAM	2.6	2.2	96.7	97.1	0.1	0.1	0.2	0.2	7.0	7.0	7.9	6.9	7.2	22.6	25.5	13.8	2.1	74.0	37.8	43.9	56.1
35222	BIRMINGHAM	55.4	53.4	41.4	43.1	1.2	1.3	2.7	2.9	6.2	6.5	5.8	5.4	6.7	31.3	23.8	12.4	2.0	78.3	37.6	47.7	52.3
35223	BIRMINGHAM	97.3	96.6	1.3	1.7	0.8	1.0	0.6	0.8	5.9	7.1	7.8	6.8	4.4	22.0	30.2	13.9	1.9	74.6	42.6	48.2	51.8
35224	BIRMINGHAM	43.3	39.0	54.9	59.1	0.4	0.5	0.5	0.5	6.6	6.7	8.3	7.8	6.4	25.5	23.9	12.9	2.0	73.6	36.7	46.7	53.3
35226	BIRMINGHAM	89.5	86.9	5.7	7.0	3.1	3.9	1.8	2.4	6.0	6.0	6.2	6.1	6.0	29.4	26.1	12.2	2.0	78.1	38.4	47.7	52.3
35228	BIRMINGHAM	20.5	17.3	78.5	81.7	0.2	0.2	0.3	0.3	6.6	7.0	8.2	8.0	6.9	26.3	23.5	11.5	2.0	73.3	36.2	45.2	54.8
35229	BIRMINGHAM	92.7	90.9	4.4	5.5	1.9	2.4	0.8	1.1	1.6	1.8	1.4	27.7	38.6	11.7	8.2	7.4	1.7	94.5	22.3	39.5	60.5
35233	BIRMINGHAM	37.5	36.0	49.0	49.8	10.8	11.1	1.9	2.3	2.7	2.3	1.5	12.6	19.5	29.5	16.5	12.3	3.1	92.3	31.4	48.3	51.7
35234	BIRMINGHAM	4.8	3.9	94.7	95.5	0.1	0.1	0.4	0.4	6.1	6.4	6.8	6.7	6.8	27.3	25.1	12.5	2.3	76.7	38.3	46.4	53.6
35235	BIRMINGHAM	78.9	75.4	18.7	21.8	0.9	1.0	1.3	1.6	6.4	6.4	6.1	5.8	5.5	29.6	25.5	13.2	1.7	77.5	38.9	47.4	52.6
35242	BIRMINGHAM	92.8	91.7	4.0	4.4	2.1	2.6	1.7	2.2	6.9	7.3	7.5	6.1	5.3	33.0	27.0	6.5	0.4	74.5	35.8	49.4	50.6
35243	BIRMINGHAM	96.1	95.1	1.6	2.0	1.3	1.7	1.0	1.4	5.1	5.8	6.7	6.5	7.3	29.6	27.4	10.6	1.0	78.4	37.3	48.6	51.4
35244	BIRMINGHAM	90.3	88.5	5.7	6.7	2.3	2.8	2.2	2.8	6.8	7.2	7.5	6.4	5.9	31.0	26.4	7.8	0.9	74.5	36.4	49.4	50.6
35401	TUSCALOOSA	40.7	38.7	56.0	57.5	1.8	2.1	1.2	1.3	4.8	4.2	4.6	14.6	23.7	21.8	15.8	8.8	1.7	83.8	24.6	47.5	52.5
35404	TUSCALOOSA	61.4	59.3	36.1	37.9	0.6	0.7	1.7	2.0	6.5	6.2	6.3	6.7	9.3	29.2	22.2	12.1	1.6	77.8	33.9	49.0	51.0
35405	TUSCALOOSA	61.1	59.0	36.3	37.9	1.0	1.2	1.5	1.9	7.4	7.1	7.3	6.6	8.2	31.3	22.5	8.7	0.9	74.4	32.7	48.0	52.0
35406	TUSCALOOSA	89.3	88.0	7.6	8.1	2.1	2.8	0.7	0.8	6.0	6.7	7.4	6.1	8.5	24.0	28.4	11.4	1.6	76.3	39.1	48.0	52.0
35441	AKRON	47.1	44.8	52.4	54.6	0.0	0.0	0.7	0.8	8.4	8.0	6.8	6.4	5.5	24.6	26.4	12.4	1.7	73.1	36.9	47.9	52.1
35442	ALICEVILLE	30.1	28.7	68.9	70.1	0.1	0.2	0.8	0.9	7.5	7.3	8.5	8.2	7.3	23.4	22.6	12.8	2.4	71.3	35.7	46.2	53.8
35443	BOLIGEE	11.6	11.1	87.9	88.3	0.0	0.0	1.2	1.2	10.5	10.1	8.5	7.5	8.4	20.6	23.4	9.2	1.8	66.4	29.4	44.7	55.3
35444	BROOKWOOD	96.8	96.5	1.5	1.7	0.1	0.1	0.5	0.6	7.0	7.0	7.8	6.7	6.6	30.2	24.7	8.9	1.0	74.0	35.6	49.4	50.6
35446	BUHL	93.2	92.4	4.8	5.2	0.1	0.1	2.1	2.7	6.3	6.5	7.1	6.9	5.5	26.8	27.3	12.5	1.1	75.9	38.7	49.5	50.5
35447	CARROLLTON	44.5	43.4	54.3	55.1	0.1	0.1	0.8	0.9	8.1	7.4	7.8	6.9	7.4	25.0	23.5	11.8	2.1	72.4	35.2	47.1	52.9
35452	COKER	92.4	91.9	5.2	5.3	0.2	0.2	1.7	2.1	7.5	7.2	6.9	6.2	6.4	29.0	24.7	11.1	1.0	74.6	36.7	50.1	49.9
35453	COTTONDALE	89.9	88.8	8.2	9.1	0.3	0.3	0.9	1.1	6.8	6.9	6.9	6.0	6.3	30.4	26.1	9.8	0.8	75.8	36.3	49.6	50.5
35456	DUNCANVILLE	84.3	82.2	13.6	15.4	0.5	0.6	0.7	0.9	7.0	7.2	8.1	7.7	7.2	29.0	25.3	7.9	0.6	73.1	34.5	49.5	50.5
35457	ECHOLA	94.7	97.4	2.6	2.6	0.0	0.0	0.0	0.0	5.3	5.3	5.3	5.3	5.3	26.3	31.6	15.8	0.0	84.2	42.5	50.0	50.0
35458	ELROD	95.3	94.8	2.7	2.9	0.0	0.0	1.2	1.7	6.4	6.9	7.1	5.4	4.6	28.0	28.8	11.8	1.0	75.9	39.5	49.2	50.8
35459	EMELLE	25.6	24.5	73.9	74.9	0.0	0.0	0.8	0.9	6.6	6.7	9.4	8.2	7.5	24.3	22.7	12.5	2.3	72.7	35.6	48.1	51.9
35460	EPES	21.0	20.2	78.2	78.7	0.1	0.2	1.3	1.3	8.2	7.9	9.0	7.8	7.7	26.1	21.2	10.3	1.8	70.6	31.5	47.5	52.5
35461	ETHELSVILLE	62.1	61.3	36.9	37.4	0.1	0.1	0.4	0.4	6.0	6.3	6.4	6.1	6.0	27.2	25.3	15.2	1.4	77.5	39.6	49.2	50.8
35462	EUTAW	19.6	19.4	79.7	79.9	0.1	0.1	0.5	0.5	7.3	7.2	8.1	6.9	7.6	23.1	24.6	12.7	2.5	73.2	37.0	47.0	53.0
35463	FOSTERS	65.9	62.9	33.5	36.4	0.0	0.0	0.5	0.8	6.7	6.6	6.3	6.1	5.7	27.7	26.8	12.5	1.6	76.7	39.0	48.9	51.1
35464	GAINESVILLE	13.6	13.0	84.3	84.9	0.0	0.0	0.7	0.7	6.8	6.8	9.0	10.4	6.8	23.4	21.2	12.6	2.9	70.5	34.7	45.7	54.3
35466	GORDO	82.0	81.1	16.9	17.8	0.2	0.2	0.8	0.9	6.1	6.3	6.7	6.2	5.8	26.6	26.2	14.4	1.8	77.2	39.9	48.8	51.2
35469	KNOXVILLE	26.9	26.1	72.8	73.6	0.0	0.0	1.3	1.3	5.4	5.6	6.5	6.3	8.0	25.9	26.3	14.0	2.0	78.6	40.2	51.6	48.4
35470	LIVINGSTON	32.0	30.9	67.0	67.9	0.2	0.2	1.0	1.0	7.2	6.7	7.4	7.9	12.1	25.8	21.4	9.5	2.1	75.1	30.7	47.3	52.7
35473	NORTHPORT	83.4	81.6	13.3	14.5	1.2	1.5	1.9	2.4	6.6	6.6	7.1	6.5	7.5	29.1	25.1	10.3	1.1	75.9	35.8	48.6	51.4
35474	MOUNDVILLE	64.4	62.0	33.4	35.5	0.5	0.6	1.2	1.4	7.3	7.2	7.4	7.0	6.6	29.0	23.7	10.0	1.7	73.7	35.7	48.4	51.6
35475	NORTHPORT	93.9	93.1	4.8	5.3	0.2	0.2	0.8	1.1	6.5	6.8	7.0	6.5	5.8	29.7	27.6	9.3	0.8	75.8	37.9	50.6	49.4
35476	NORTHPORT	57.0	55.8	41.2	42.1	0.4	0.5	1.4	1.6	7.2	6.5	5.8	5.5	8.0	28.2	19.4	15.4	4.1	77.4	35.7	42.9	57.1
35480	RALPH	65.8	62.8	33.5	36.4	0.0	0.0	0.6	0.9	6.6	6.5	6.3	6.2	5.9	27.5	26.9	12.5	1.6	76.7	38.9	49.1	50.9
35481	REFORM	65.2	65.3	33.6	33.3	0.1	0.1	0.6	0.7	7.0	6.8	7.2	6.5	6.0	24.8	25.0	14.5	2.4	75.0	39.0	46.6	53.5
35487	TUSCALOOSA	59.4	55.4	38.5	42.3	1.0	1.2	1.1	1.3	3.7	3.3	2.4	9.5	29.1	15.2	12.9	17.4	6.7	88.9	26.9	46.1	53.9
35490	VANCE	93.6	92.7	3.9	4.3	0.1	0.1	1.9	2.5	8.6	8.2	7.2	6.2	6.3	30.8	23.9	8.0	0.7	72.2	33.4	50.3	49.7
35501	JASPER	80.8	80.0	16.9	17.2	0.3	0.4	1.7	2.1	6.3	6.0	6.0	6.0	6.8	26.3	25.3	14.9	2.4	78.3	39.9	47.9	52.1
35503	JASPER	97.7	97.3	0.6	0.7	0.4	0.5	1.0	1.2	6.5	6.6	6.6	5.8	5.6	27.6	26.6	12.9	1.7	76.8	39.1	49.4	50.6
35504	JASPER	97.6	97.2	1.1	1.3	0.4	0.5	0.9	1.1	6.4	6.3	6.1	5.9	5.8	27.4	26.2	14.3	1.7	77.8	39.8	48.4	51.6
35540	ADDISON	98.2	97.9	0.2	0.3	0.1	0.1	0.4	0.5	6.0	6.3	7.3	6.3	6.1	29.4	25.4	12.0	1.3	76.6	38.5	50.1	49.9
35541	ARLEY	99.1	98.9	0.0	0.0	0.0	0.0	0.8	1.1	6.8	6.7	6.1	5.9	5.8	27.4	27.2	12.9	1.3	76.8	39.3	49.4	50.6
35542	BANKSTON	97.5	97.4	1.8	1.9	0.0	0.0	0.5	0.6	6.2	6.3	6.7	6.2	6.4	27.3	26.6	13.0	1.3	77.2	38.6	50.3	49.7
35543	BEAR CREEK	98.4	98.1	0.1	0.1	0.2	0.3	0.9	1.2	6.5	7.0	6.6	7.0	5.9	30.4	25.9	9.9	0.7	75.5	36.4	52.1	47.9
35544	BEAVERTON	93.5	93.3	5.4	5.5	0.2	0.2	0.2	0.3	5.4	5.4	6.6	5.8	7.1	27.3	23.7	17.0	1.6	79.3	40.2	49.7	50.3
35546	BERRY	95.3	95.0	3.1	3.3	0.1	0.1	1.0	1.2	6.9	6.9	7.0	6.1	6.4	27.8	25.4	11.9	1.4	75.4	37.4	49.7	50.3
35548	BRILLIANT	98.5	98.4	0.7	0.7	0.1	0.1	1.0	1.3	6.2	6.3	6.1	5.8	5.8	26.9	27.7	13.4	1.7	77.8	40.0	50.6	49.4
35549	CARBON HILL	94.9	94.6	4.1	4.3	0.0	0.1	0.7	0.9	6.3	6.3	6.0	5.4	5.6	26.2	27.9	14.3	2.2	78.3	41.0	47.5	52.5
35550	CORDOVA	91.5	90.9	7.3	7.8	0.1	0.1	0.7	0.9	6.3	6.6	6.8	5.8	6.0	26.5	25.1	14.6	2.4	76.8	39.3	47.1	52.9
35552	DETROIT	92.4	92.3	5.9	5.8	0.2	0.2	0.8	1.0	6.3	6.4	6.5	5.8	5.7	28.7	24.5	14.1	1.9	77.0	38.2	50.2	49.8
35553	DOUBLE SPRINGS	98.4	98.1	0.1	0.1	0.1	0.1	0.7	1.0	5.9	6.0	6.7	5.6	6.0	28.8	25.6	13.1	2.2	78.1	39.1	49.7	50.3
35554	ELDRIDGE	96.1	95.8	2.9	3.1	0.1	0.1	1.0	1.4	6.2	6.4	6.4	6.0	6.3	28.1	25.9	13.2	1.7	77.5	38.9	49.1	50.9
35555	FAYETTE	81.7	80.7	17.2	17.9	0.2	0.2	0.9	1.2	5.8	5.8	6.5	6.3	6.4	25.4	26.2	14.8	2.8	78.2	40.7	48.0	52.0
35563	GUIN	91.0	90.4	7.4	7.7	0.1	0.1	0.9	1.2	6.5	6.2	5.7	6.0	5.8	26.5	24.7	16.0	2.7	77.9	40.3	48.7	51.3
35564	HACKLEBURG	98.9	98.8	0.1	0.1	0.0	0.0	0.4	0.6	5.9	5.9	6.9	5.9	5.7	27.5	25.9	14.1	2.1	77.6	39.8	48.7	51.3
35565	HALEYVILLE	96.4	95.6	0.6	0.6	0.2	0.3	2.4	3.2	6.5	6.5	6.7	6.3	6.1	28.0	25.7	12.9	1.5	76.6	38.5	49.3	50.7
35570	HAMILTON	92.4	92.0	5.6	5.8	0.4	0.5	1.4	1.7	6.0	5.9	5.7	5.5	5.9	28.5	26.3	14.0	2.1	79.1	40.0	51.4	48.6
35571	HODGES	98.4	98.4	0.1	0.1	0.1	0.1	0.2	0.3	6.9	6.6	6.1	5.4	6.8	27.6	24.7	14.4	1.7	77.1	38.6	50.0	50.1
35572	HOUSTON	96.5	96.0	0.1	0.2	0.2	0.2	1.1	1.4	5.7	5.8	6.0	5.6	6.0	27.8	27.6	14.4	1.1	79.0	40.9	51.1	48.9
35574	KENNEDY	86.2	85.9	13.1	13.3	0.1	0.1	0.8	0.8	6.2	6.2	6.2	6.0	6.2	27.8	25.9	13.8	1.7	77.8	39.6	48.8	51.2
35575	LYNN	98.8	98.6	0.1	0.1	0.1	0.1	0.4	0.4	6.1	6.4	6.9	6.3	5.4	28.9	26.6	12.5	1.1	76.7	38.7	48.1	51.9
35576	MILLPORT	84.2	83.8	15.1	15.4	0.1	0.1	0.9	1.0	6.1	6.2	6.5	5.9	5.7	27.4	26.4	13.9	2.0	77.7	40.0	50.1	49.9
35578	NAUVOO	99.0	98.8	0.2	0.2	0.1	0.1	0.6	0.8	6.7	6.8	6.4	5.7	5.8	28.9	27.0	11.5	1.3	76.7	37.9	49.7	50.4
35579	OAKMAN	92.8	92.4	6.3	6.5	0.1	0.1	0.5	0.6	6.5	6.4	6.6	6.4	6.0	27.9	26.6	12.5	1.2	76.7	39.3	50.2	49.8
35580	PARRISH	90.1	89.5	8.4	8.8	0.1	0.1	0.5	0.7	6.3	6.4	6.6	5.8	5.9	26.8	27.4	13.6	1.2	77.2	39.5	49.4	50.6
35581	PHIL CAMPBELL	96.3	95.6	0.4	0.4	0.1	0.1	3.3	4.2	6.1	6.1	6.6	6.8	6.6	28.0	24.9	13.5	1.4	77.1	38.1	50.3	49.7
35582	RED BAY	97.1	96.7	1.4	1.4	0.0	0.1	0.8	1.1	5.7	5.8	6.2	6.1	6.0	26.6	25.6	15.3	2.7	78.6	40.4	46.9	53.1
35585	SPRUCE PINE	96.3	95.7	1.0	1.0	0.1	0.1	2.3	2.8	6.1	6.3	7.0	6.4	6.4	28.3	25.9	12.4	1.3	76.9	38.0	49.6	50.4
35586	SULLIGENT	82.3	82.0	16.3	16.6	0.0	0.0	1.7	1.7	6.0	5.9	6.4	6.3	7.0	27.5	25.0	13.6	2.4	78.0	39.0	48.0	52.0
35587	TOWNLEY	98.9	98.7	0.4	0.5	0.2	0.3	0.5	0.6	6.7	6.8	6.7	6.2	5.1	27.4	27.0	12.3	1.8	75.9	38.3	50.8	49.2
35592	VERNON	89.4	89.2	9.2	9.4	0.1	0.1	1.6	1.6	6.1	6.0	6.3	6.3	6.1	27.4	25.5	14.0	2.5	78.1	39.5	48.0	52.0
35593	VINA	98.5	98.2	0.3	0.3	0.0	0.0	1.0	1.3	6.4	6.4	6.7	6.4	5.7	28.9	24.6	13.4	1.6	76.4	38.1	49.6	50.4
35594	WINFIELD	94.9	94.6	3.8	3.9	0.2	0.2	1.0	1.3	6.1	6.0	6.3	6.2	6.1	26.4	25.5	14.8	2.7	77.8	40.3	48.8	51.2
35601	DECATUR	69.5	67.6	24.9	25.7	0.6	0.7	7.8	10.0	6.6	6.5	7.0	6.3	6.5	28.3	23.5	13.3	2.1	76.2	37.5	49.1	51.0
35603	DECATUR	87.5	85.7	9.1	10.3	1.0	1.3	1.6	2.3	6.8	6.9	7.0	6.5	6.7	29.3	26.6	9.3	0.9	75.3	37.2	48.1	52.0
35610	ANDERSON	98.2	98.1	0.6	0.7	0.1	0.1	0.3	0.3	6.6	6.6	6.5	6.3	6.2	28.9	25.1	12.5	1.3	76.4	38.2	50.4	49.6
35611	ATHENS	78.9	77.5	17.5	18.1	0.5	0.6	4.3	5.4	6.6	6.5	6.7	6.1	6.2	28.8	24.4	12.6	2.1	76.5	37.7	47.9	52.1
35613	ATHENS	88.4	87.6	9.1	9.5	0.4	0.5	1.8	2.3	6.9	7.3	7.4	6.1	5.5	30.4	25.9	9.7	0.7	74.6	37.3	49.8	50.2
35614	ATHENS	92.2	91.4	5.1	5.4	0.3	0.3	2.7	3.6	7.2	7.2	6.9	6.0	6.1	29.9	26.3	9.7	0.8	75.1	36.7	50.9	49.1
	ALABAMA	71.1	70.3	26.0	26.4	0.7	0.9	1.7	2.1	6.7	6.7	7.0	6.8	7.2	28.0	24.5	11.6	1.6	75.8	36.6	48.5	51.5
	UNITED STATES	75.1	73.6	12.3	12.5	3.8	4.2	12.5	14.1	6.9	6.7	7.2	7.0	7.3	28.6	23.8	10.8	1.7	75.1	36.0	49.1	50.9

C 35211-35614

ZIP CODE #	POST OFFICE NAME	2004 Per Capita Income	2004 HH Income Base	2004 HOUSEHOLD INCOME DISTRIBUTION (%) Less than $25,000	$25,000 to $49,999	$50,000 to $99,999	$100,000 to $149,999	$150,000 or More	MEDIAN HOUSEHOLD INCOME 2004	2009	2004 National Centile	2004 State Centile	2004 Home Value Base	2004 HOME VALUE DISTRIBUTION (%) Less than $50,000	$50,000 to $89,999	$90,000 to $174,999	$175,000 to $399,999	$400,000 or More	2004 Median Home Value
35211	BIRMINGHAM	13287	11896	51.3	28.1	16.9	2.8	0.9	24149	27756	4	12	6576	32.1	50.4	14.3	2.8	0.4	61077
35212	BIRMINGHAM	13463	5488	53.5	25.2	15.7	4.1	1.6	22583	25588	3	9	2579	33.2	36.1	27.1	3.2	0.4	64859
35213	BIRMINGHAM	55332	6291	14.3	24.4	27.6	12.1	21.7	64563	76408	88	98	4547	0.8	2.8	31.9	33.7	30.8	252197
35214	BIRMINGHAM	20434	8589	32.8	29.4	27.1	8.6	2.1	38160	43490	40	68	6522	17.1	32.1	44.8	5.9	0.2	90903
35215	BIRMINGHAM	20094	18462	26.5	32.1	32.7	7.3	1.5	42764	47622	55	83	12890	4.1	37.9	52.8	5.1	0.1	95496
35216	BIRMINGHAM	35077	14512	19.8	28.6	30.3	11.5	9.9	51594	58877	75	93	7779	0.9	9.2	31.6	50.1	8.2	188088
35217	BIRMINGHAM	15508	5995	43.4	31.1	20.4	4.0	1.1	29317	32861	11	26	4008	30.0	46.8	20.0	2.8	0.4	62904
35218	BIRMINGHAM	12252	3492	56.3	29.0	11.8	2.3	0.7	21469	24330	2	7	1818	39.2	52.0	8.1	0.4	0.3	54912
35221	BIRMINGHAM	13652	2274	47.8	30.3	18.1	3.6	0.3	26356	30743	6	18	1597	31.9	56.8	10.6	0.4	0.3	61547
35222	BIRMINGHAM	31155	4146	34.4	27.3	23.3	8.0	7.1	38344	44308	41	69	2211	10.5	11.0	50.3	18.5	9.9	133722
35223	BIRMINGHAM	71887	4546	9.1	14.8	23.2	19.0	33.9	104965	124175	99	100	3903	1.0	1.1	11.3	47.0	39.6	346301
35224	BIRMINGHAM	15034	2651	43.7	28.4	23.3	2.7	1.9	28800	32614	10	24	1914	38.7	46.5	13.9	0.9	0.0	57826
35226	BIRMINGHAM	35871	11208	12.1	22.2	33.9	17.7	14.0	69014	81404	91	99	8439	0.6	2.4	37.4	54.2	5.6	186911
35228	BIRMINGHAM	15903	4149	39.1	34.0	21.8	4.1	1.0	31734	35995	17	38	3001	24.7	60.5	14.2	0.7	0.0	65313
35229	BIRMINGHAM	9986	102	22.6	38.2	23.5	9.8	5.9	37319	43604	37	64	38	0.0	13.2	26.3	55.3	5.3	189286
35233	BIRMINGHAM	15117	108	57.4	28.7	11.1	2.8	0.0	20464	23236	2	4	11	27.3	27.3	36.4	9.1	0.0	85000
35234	BIRMINGHAM	11962	2579	56.8	28.9	11.9	1.6	0.9	21162	24129	2	6	1283	44.8	45.7	9.5	0.0	0.0	52737
35235	BIRMINGHAM	26808	7834	16.4	29.0	39.1	11.6	4.0	53361	61442	77	94	6620	2.8	20.1	62.7	13.2	1.2	114418
35242	BIRMINGHAM	43070	15160	10.9	20.3	30.3	19.6	18.9	77542	87201	94	100	11111	3.2	1.8	9.9	61.3	23.9	264241
35243	BIRMINGHAM	47472	7548	13.9	21.2	31.7	14.9	18.3	69304	80762	91	99	4976	0.9	3.7	25.7	46.4	23.2	235226
35244	BIRMINGHAM	40234	11857	10.2	20.5	32.6	20.9	15.8	74633	86386	93	100	8717	2.2	2.2	19.3	65.7	10.7	224870
35401	TUSCALOOSA	15327	14250	58.8	24.4	12.6	2.3	1.9	19929	22424	2	4	5364	18.5	38.4	35.7	6.1	1.3	83006
35404	TUSCALOOSA	19739	7923	38.2	27.8	26.3	5.6	2.1	33529	37692	22	47	4876	13.7	32.3	44.2	8.6	1.3	94654
35405	TUSCALOOSA	23697	13179	27.9	27.3	31.4	9.4	3.9	44695	49965	60	86	8407	10.5	11.9	52.2	23.7	1.7	130401
35406	TUSCALOOSA	38210	4957	21.4	23.7	25.4	14.1	15.4	58075	65424	83	96	4001	9.5	7.5	27.9	39.0	16.2	187322
35441	AKRON	14823	653	45.8	31.4	19.0	2.9	0.9	28366	31424	9	23	529	53.5	16.5	22.7	5.9	1.5	47319
35442	ALICEVILLE	14543	2301	49.2	26.9	19.3	2.6	2.1	25535	28768	5	16	1803	39.8	28.1	23.5	7.3	1.4	61767
35443	BOLIGEE	10709	417	57.8	29.3	12.0	1.0	0.0	21491	24110	2	7	305	58.4	23.3	16.7	1.6	0.0	45189
35444	BROOKWOOD	18708	1251	30.2	30.3	33.3	5.1	1.1	43163	49499	56	84	1069	35.7	24.0	29.5	10.8	0.1	73309
35446	BUHL	18719	631	35.8	22.7	33.4	5.9	2.2	41460	48516	51	78	556	29.1	22.7	34.4	9.4	4.5	86429
35447	CARROLLTON	14614	1731	48.4	26.6	20.0	3.0	2.0	26120	29148	6	18	1403	39.1	28.6	24.7	6.6	1.1	63850
35452	COKER	20737	1484	27.2	25.4	36.1	8.2	3.0	46885	53696	66	89	1236	21.1	19.3	40.4	17.7	1.5	105674
35453	COTTONDALE	21504	3666	24.5	29.8	37.0	6.8	2.0	45775	52495	63	87	3062	26.8	18.2	38.6	15.9	0.6	98564
35456	DUNCANVILLE	18006	1536	28.5	30.7	33.0	7.1	0.8	42477	48440	55	82	1324	34.3	18.3	30.1	15.6	1.7	82917
35457	ECHOLA	17566	13	23.1	38.5	23.1	15.4	0.0	42330	47338	54	81	11	18.2	36.4	36.4	9.1	0.0	75000
35458	ELROD	28767	190	24.2	41.1	22.6	9.5	2.6	38187	44003	40	68	164	19.5	29.9	36.6	11.6	2.4	93333
35459	EMELLE	14791	298	49.0	29.2	19.5	0.7	1.7	25778	29286	6	16	244	54.5	22.1	15.6	7.4	0.4	46207
35460	EPES	14284	449	55.9	26.3	15.1	1.3	1.3	21391	23844	2	7	339	54.6	18.6	21.5	4.4	0.9	45441
35461	ETHELSVILLE	16596	786	38.9	32.2	24.7	3.3	0.9	30875	35426	15	34	723	40.3	26.1	31.4	2.2	0.0	65000
35462	EUTAW	17323	2594	56.6	22.5	15.8	2.9	2.2	20854	23337	2	5	1896	44.7	29.0	20.4	4.8	1.2	58347
35463	FOSTERS	18925	574	31.9	30.7	29.1	6.3	2.1	36967	42331	35	63	522	28.2	32.6	24.0	12.1	3.3	76444
35464	GAINESVILLE	11695	105	64.8	16.2	15.2	1.9	1.9	18084	20183	1	3	87	77.0	13.8	8.1	1.2	0.0	27250
35466	GORDO	19019	2298	38.7	27.2	26.9	4.6	2.6	35506	39763	30	56	1841	21.3	32.5	36.3	9.0	0.9	85140
35469	KNOXVILLE	15090	228	45.6	28.5	19.3	4.8	1.8	27041	30762	7	20	204	60.8	20.6	16.7	2.0	0.0	39444
35470	LIVINGSTON	12713	2243	59.9	21.6	15.6	1.7	1.2	18434	20363	1	3	1465	47.2	23.8	22.0	5.2	1.9	53347
35473	NORTHPORT	24961	5580	24.1	25.6	34.7	12.4	3.3	50325	57504	73	92	3979	7.9	8.2	63.8	19.5	0.6	137057
35474	MOUNDVILLE	17143	2183	33.9	27.7	32.6	5.1	0.6	40439	45569	48	76	1776	33.6	24.5	30.6	10.3	1.1	77462
35475	NORTHPORT	25203	3966	19.1	24.3	41.3	10.7	4.5	55054	63147	80	94	3507	16.3	12.3	38.4	30.5	2.5	137599
35476	NORTHPORT	17509	2868	45.6	28.7	21.4	2.8	1.4	27807	31767	8	21	1629	15.8	23.6	57.6	2.4	0.7	98223
35480	RALPH	18347	390	32.1	30.5	29.2	6.2	2.1	37017	42168	35	63	354	28.8	32.2	24.3	11.6	3.1	76000
35481	REFORM	15125	1750	47.0	27.7	19.4	4.3	1.7	26841	30257	7	19	1397	37.2	30.8	24.9	6.1	1.1	65211
35487	TUSCALOOSA	20090	448	74.1	10.9	7.4	4.2	3.4	13286	15365	1	1	52	9.6	15.4	44.2	26.9	3.9	144444
35490	VANCE	20099	1053	22.3	31.6	35.9	9.2	1.0	46581	53434	65	89	924	27.7	22.3	39.4	10.0	0.7	90000
35501	JASPER	19648	4536	43.8	26.5	21.1	5.6	3.0	29725	33011	12	27	3222	31.9	32.1	27.1	8.0	1.0	69286
35503	JASPER	19222	3648	34.7	32.4	25.7	4.4	2.9	36073	40660	32	59	3068	26.6	30.3	32.9	9.3	1.0	81538
35504	JASPER	21707	5003	30.7	30.4	28.6	6.6	3.7	39859	45368	45	74	4063	27.0	24.1	31.5	15.7	1.7	88309
35540	ADDISON	16264	1076	41.2	30.0	23.4	4.1	1.3	30068	32597	12	29	908	36.6	25.3	23.1	10.4	4.6	74306
35541	ARLEY	17967	1408	36.5	36.1	19.7	5.0	2.7	32843	36154	20	44	1193	35.1	23.9	20.5	16.3	4.2	75368
35542	BANKSTON	14786	475	37.5	34.3	25.5	2.3	0.4	32820	36366	20	44	406	41.6	26.9	26.4	4.4	0.7	61892
35543	BEAR CREEK	15816	446	39.9	33.0	23.5	2.5	1.1	31655	35191	17	38	380	41.8	33.7	18.7	5.8	0.0	60313
35544	BEAVERTON	14729	406	44.6	33.7	18.2	2.5	1.0	29127	31893	11	25	340	46.2	37.4	15.0	1.5	0.0	53514
35546	BERRY	15473	1593	42.7	30.7	22.2	3.5	0.9	30887	34337	15	34	1306	42.0	23.4	25.3	8.1	1.2	61268
35548	BRILLIANT	15560	746	46.0	28.2	22.7	2.4	0.8	28085	30725	9	22	614	48.4	25.6	18.4	6.0	1.6	51515
35549	CARBON HILL	15585	1972	47.2	29.5	19.2	3.4	0.8	26745	30108	7	19	1601	41.3	35.4	19.4	3.7	0.3	58064
35550	CORDOVA	14399	2586	50.2	28.0	17.4	3.5	0.9	24909	28060	5	15	1937	49.8	30.6	16.4	3.1	0.1	50222
35552	DETROIT	15368	552	40.2	36.4	19.9	3.1	0.4	31457	34930	16	37	463	45.6	22.5	25.5	5.6	0.9	56613
35553	DOUBLE SPRINGS	16876	2010	39.8	36.9	17.0	4.3	2.0	30616	33232	14	32	1659	42.9	25.5	21.0	9.5	1.2	58650
35554	ELDRIDGE	17295	504	34.5	32.3	27.2	5.0	1.0	34712	38543	26	52	433	40.4	29.1	26.1	3.9	0.5	57981
35555	FAYETTE	17521	4589	40.8	31.7	22.4	3.7	1.4	30799	33475	14	33	3490	29.2	33.0	29.1	8.3	0.5	73333
35563	GUIN	18254	1863	44.0	27.7	20.9	5.1	2.3	30149	32589	13	30	1400	35.8	29.6	27.2	6.6	0.7	68529
35564	HACKLEBURG	18442	1086	42.3	35.7	17.7	2.3	2.0	29171	32637	11	25	878	43.1	31.3	18.6	6.4	0.7	57531
35565	HALEYVILLE	17812	5848	44.1	31.4	18.8	3.3	2.4	29250	31546	11	26	4629	38.0	34.4	20.1	5.9	1.7	62856
35570	HAMILTON	18652	4545	41.4	33.8	18.5	3.4	2.9	31079	34404	15	34	3543	31.2	30.0	30.7	7.3	0.8	72238
35571	HODGES	20822	449	40.8	32.3	20.9	2.7	3.3	30288	33566	13	30	378	41.8	33.3	19.6	5.3	0.0	57561
35572	HOUSTON	14115	533	48.4	30.8	17.6	2.1	1.1	25740	28409	5	16	450	50.7	17.3	20.7	10.4	0.9	48571
35574	KENNEDY	15919	655	39.1	35.7	22.8	2.0	0.5	31963	35411	18	40	543	42.9	32.4	21.4	3.1	0.2	56311
35575	LYNN	17520	597	39.2	34.5	20.4	5.0	0.8	31562	33980	17	37	497	52.9	23.1	20.7	2.8	0.4	46705
35576	MILLPORT	16335	1393	41.0	30.2	24.1	4.0	0.8	31535	34706	16	37	1143	38.9	27.2	26.8	6.4	0.7	64425
35578	NAUVOO	16216	2225	43.9	28.0	22.6	4.3	1.2	29550	32464	11	26	1884	39.1	33.2	22.7	5.0	0.0	61813
35579	OAKMAN	16811	1367	41.9	29.9	22.5	3.8	1.8	30301	33977	13	31	1121	43.5	31.9	19.7	3.2	1.6	61307
35580	PARRISH	16268	1891	41.9	30.1	21.7	5.3	0.9	30957	34384	15	34	1596	44.6	34.1	17.5	3.6	0.2	55850
35581	PHIL CAMPBELL	16632	2274	42.4	32.9	19.9	3.3	1.5	30759	34301	14	33	1831	34.1	32.8	26.5	5.9	0.7	67065
35582	RED BAY	16911	1811	42.1	32.1	20.0	4.5	1.3	29860	33228	12	28	1366	31.2	38.4	25.3	5.1	0.0	67619
35585	SPRUCE PINE	16525	631	44.1	28.1	23.0	4.0	1.0	29924	32915	12	28	520	31.7	30.6	31.9	5.6	0.2	77115
35586	SULLIGENT	16667	1996	42.2	33.5	19.6	3.5	1.2	30054	32898	12	29	1582	41.1	31.4	22.1	4.0	1.5	56438
35587	TOWNLEY	14647	443	44.5	34.8	16.9	2.3	1.6	29118	32396	11	25	369	42.3	26.0	23.6	5.4	2.7	63947
35592	VERNON	16898	2109	43.3	28.2	24.1	3.0	1.4	29633	32109	11	27	1613	35.3	29.8	26.4	6.9	1.6	68097
35593	VINA	15678	740	43.8	30.3	21.6	2.7	1.6	29436	32622	11	26	627	41.2	32.2	20.1	6.4	0.2	59250
35594	WINFIELD	17564	3088	38.7	32.3	22.3	5.0	1.7	33214	36392	22	46	2477	31.7	30.9	27.0	10.1	0.4	74109
35601	DECATUR	20160	13691	37.1	29.3	24.3	6.5	2.8	35027	39646	28	53	8867	12.9	44.9	32.6	8.3	1.4	82908
35603	DECATUR	26488	10825	24.0	25.4	33.6	12.2	4.9	50571	55774	73	93	7737	8.3	21.7	45.7	22.3	2.0	121957
35610	ANDERSON	18807	893	31.8	33.8	27.8	5.0	1.6	35987	40281	31	58	759	27.9	26.8	39.7	5.3	0.4	82283
35611	ATHENS	20235	9539	38.3	26.6	25.5	7.0	2.7	35065	39085	28	54	6716	16.4	36.4	35.6	10.0	1.5	86837
35613	ATHENS	23148	5072	22.5	27.8	34.0	12.0	3.7	49673	56199	71	92	4321	12.9	21.8	44.8	18.2	2.3	113400
35614	ATHENS	18564	2669	31.6	31.3	29.0	6.4	1.8	38422	43463	41	70	2155	27.4	34.7	30.4	7.1	0.5	76034
	ALABAMA	20998		34.3	28.7	26.3	7.2	3.5	37534	42371				22.7	26.7	33.4	14.6	2.7	90917
	UNITED STATES	25866		24.7	27.1	30.8	10.9	6.5	48124	56710				10.9	15.0	33.7	30.1	10.4	145905

ZIP CODE #	POST OFFICE NAME	FINANCIAL SERVICES: Auto Loan	Home Loan	Investments	Retirement Plans	THE HOME: Home Improvements: Home Repair	Lawn & Garden	Furnishings: Computers & Hardware	Major Appliances	TV, Radio, Sound Equipment	Furniture	ENTERTAINMENT: Dine out/ Carry out	Sports Equipment	Fees & Tickets	Toys & Games	Travel	Cable TV	PERSONAL: Apparel & Services	Auto Repairs	Health Insurance	Pets & Supplies
35211	BIRMINGHAM	45	42	48	39	41	47	45	44	48	46	60	48	45	57	45	50	58	45	48	50
35212	BIRMINGHAM	48	43	49	41	42	49	47	47	51	48	63	53	47	60	46	53	61	49	51	53
35213	BIRMINGHAM	154	181	234	184	178	189	174	170	167	175	211	197	185	217	179	166	210	169	160	185
35214	BIRMINGHAM	71	70	71	66	70	77	69	71	73	69	90	80	70	90	70	75	87	71	75	82
35215	BIRMINGHAM	70	72	76	73	71	75	73	72	71	72	89	84	73	90	72	70	87	72	69	80
35216	BIRMINGHAM	102	108	127	112	107	113	110	107	106	110	134	126	111	132	109	103	131	109	101	118
35217	BIRMINGHAM	55	51	53	49	52	59	53	54	57	53	70	60	54	70	54	59	67	54	59	62
35218	BIRMINGHAM	44	38	45	36	37	44	42	42	47	44	58	46	42	55	42	49	56	43	46	48
35221	BIRMINGHAM	49	45	50	42	44	52	47	47	50	48	63	50	48	59	47	53	61	48	52	54
35222	BIRMINGHAM	86	86	107	86	85	94	92	89	94	92	117	103	93	116	92	94	115	92	89	98
35223	BIRMINGHAM	220	271	380	277	262	281	253	243	240	257	304	281	279	319	262	239	306	240	224	267
35224	BIRMINGHAM	54	53	57	49	52	59	53	54	57	54	70	60	55	70	54	59	68	54	58	62
35226	BIRMINGHAM	117	137	157	140	136	139	129	127	121	129	153	148	135	156	131	119	152	125	118	140
35228	BIRMINGHAM	56	55	63	54	54	61	57	56	59	58	74	63	59	73	57	60	72	57	58	63
35229	BIRMINGHAM	92	74	96	83	73	81	102	89	100	95	126	114	93	118	91	92	122	101	82	99
35233	BIRMINGHAM	37	27	35	29	27	31	42	34	42	37	52	44	37	48	36	39	49	40	34	39
35234	BIRMINGHAM	42	36	39	32	35	42	39	40	44	40	54	43	39	49	39	47	51	41	46	46
35235	BIRMINGHAM	83	96	105	96	94	97	91	90	87	90	109	104	95	113	92	85	108	88	84	98
35242	BIRMINGHAM	145	163	181	171	158	161	155	150	145	157	184	177	163	185	154	138	183	150	134	166
35243	BIRMINGHAM	137	161	211	165	158	166	156	151	148	156	187	177	165	194	159	146	187	151	139	165
35244	BIRMINGHAM	135	153	177	160	148	151	145	140	136	147	173	165	153	176	144	131	172	139	126	155
35401	TUSCALOOSA	48	38	45	39	38	44	50	45	52	48	65	55	47	60	46	51	62	50	47	52
35404	TUSCALOOSA	64	61	68	61	60	67	66	64	67	65	84	74	65	83	65	67	81	66	64	72
35405	TUSCALOOSA	80	79	83	81	78	82	82	80	81	82	101	96	81	100	80	78	99	82	76	91
35406	TUSCALOOSA	123	132	144	134	131	138	128	127	123	128	155	148	131	153	129	121	152	127	121	143
35441	AKRON	67	45	20	38	50	58	43	54	52	44	61	64	37	58	44	56	55	53	66	76
35442	ALICEVILLE	67	47	31	41	52	61	48	57	58	49	68	66	43	63	48	62	63	57	69	76
35443	BOLIGEE	42	33	34	29	33	41	37	39	43	38	52	41	36	46	36	46	49	40	46	45
35444	BROOKWOOD	83	67	44	62	70	77	64	73	70	66	84	86	58	80	64	71	79	73	80	94
35446	BUHL	89	61	29	53	68	78	58	72	70	59	82	86	50	78	59	75	75	72	88	102
35447	CARROLLTON	69	47	26	41	53	61	47	57	56	48	66	67	41	62	47	61	61	57	70	78
35452	COKER	92	74	49	68	79	87	70	80	77	71	93	95	65	91	71	80	87	79	90	106
35453	COTTONDALE	86	77	61	74	79	85	74	80	77	75	94	93	71	91	74	77	90	79	83	97
35456	DUNCANVILLE	77	72	57	69	72	75	68	73	69	70	85	84	65	80	67	68	82	72	72	86
35457	ECHOLA	97	65	29	56	73	84	62	78	75	64	89	93	53	84	64	81	80	77	96	111
35458	ELROD	137	92	42	79	104	120	89	111	107	90	126	133	76	119	90	115	114	110	137	158
35459	EMELLE	68	46	23	40	52	60	45	56	55	46	64	66	39	60	46	59	59	55	69	78
35460	EPES	63	44	30	39	48	57	46	53	54	47	64	61	41	59	46	58	59	53	65	71
35461	ETHELSVILLE	73	49	22	42	56	64	47	59	57	48	67	71	40	64	48	62	61	59	73	84
35462	EUTAW	68	50	39	45	53	63	53	60	62	54	74	68	49	69	53	66	69	60	71	76
35463	FOSTERS	77	70	55	67	70	74	67	72	68	69	84	83	63	79	66	67	80	71	71	85
35464	GAINESVILLE	49	37	32	33	39	47	40	44	47	41	56	49	37	50	39	50	52	45	53	55
35466	GORDO	88	59	27	51	67	77	57	71	69	58	81	85	48	76	58	74	73	70	88	101
35469	KNOXVILLE	67	46	23	40	52	59	45	55	54	46	63	65	39	60	45	58	58	55	67	77
35470	LIVINGSTON	47	35	33	33	37	43	40	42	45	40	54	49	37	50	39	46	51	44	48	52
35473	NORTHPORT	86	88	89	89	87	91	86	86	84	86	105	101	86	105	85	82	103	86	82	98
35474	MOUNDVILLE	78	60	37	55	64	71	58	67	64	59	77	79	52	73	58	66	72	66	75	88
35475	NORTHPORT	100	101	90	97	103	107	92	98	93	93	114	115	93	117	94	93	111	96	99	118
35476	NORTHPORT	59	49	49	47	50	58	55	56	59	54	72	64	52	67	53	61	68	58	61	65
35480	RALPH	77	70	54	67	70	74	66	72	68	68	83	83	63	79	66	67	80	71	72	86
35481	REFORM	70	47	21	40	53	61	45	56	54	46	64	67	38	60	46	59	58	56	70	80
35487	TUSCALOOSA	39	33	46	35	33	38	43	38	44	40	55	47	41	53	41	43	53	43	40	43
35490	VANCE	87	78	60	75	79	83	75	81	76	77	94	93	70	88	74	75	90	80	81	96
35501	JASPER	72	58	46	53	62	72	60	66	67	59	80	75	56	76	60	71	75	66	77	82
35503	JASPER	80	63	43	60	67	75	63	71	69	63	83	82	57	78	63	71	77	70	79	89
35504	JASPER	87	71	51	66	76	86	69	79	77	69	92	91	65	91	71	81	86	77	90	100
35540	ADDISON	74	49	22	43	56	64	48	60	58	49	68	71	41	64	49	62	61	59	74	85
35541	ARLEY	77	57	35	51	65	73	54	66	63	54	74	78	48	72	57	67	68	65	79	92
35542	BANKSTON	71	48	22	41	54	62	46	58	56	47	65	69	39	62	47	60	59	57	71	82
35543	BEAR CREEK	72	49	22	42	55	63	47	59	57	48	66	70	40	63	48	61	60	58	72	83
35544	BEAVERTON	67	45	20	38	50	58	43	54	52	44	61	64	37	58	44	56	55	53	66	76
35546	BERRY	70	50	27	45	56	63	48	58	56	49	66	69	43	63	49	59	61	58	69	80
35548	BRILLIANT	69	46	21	40	52	60	45	56	54	46	63	67	38	60	45	58	58	55	69	79
35549	CARBON HILL	67	45	20	39	51	59	44	55	53	44	62	65	37	58	44	57	56	54	67	77
35550	CORDOVA	59	42	25	38	47	55	44	51	51	43	60	59	38	56	44	55	55	51	62	67
35552	DETROIT	68	45	20	39	51	59	44	55	53	44	62	65	37	58	44	57	56	54	67	77
35553	DOUBLE SPRINGS	76	51	23	44	58	67	49	62	60	50	70	74	42	66	50	64	64	61	76	88
35554	ELDRIDGE	81	54	24	47	61	70	52	65	63	53	74	78	44	70	53	68	67	65	80	93
35555	FAYETTE	70	51	34	46	56	65	52	60	59	52	71	71	46	68	52	63	65	60	71	80
35563	GUIN	71	54	34	51	59	67	54	62	61	54	73	72	49	70	54	63	67	61	72	80
35564	HACKLEBURG	80	54	24	46	61	70	52	65	63	53	73	77	44	69	53	67	67	64	80	92
35565	HALEYVILLE	77	55	30	49	62	70	54	65	62	54	74	77	47	71	54	67	68	64	77	89
35570	HAMILTON	79	54	28	47	60	69	53	65	63	54	75	77	46	71	54	68	68	64	79	90
35571	HODGES	94	63	29	54	71	82	61	76	73	62	86	91	52	82	62	79	78	75	94	108
35572	HOUSTON	63	42	19	36	48	55	41	51	49	41	58	61	35	54	41	53	52	50	63	72
35574	KENNEDY	71	48	22	41	54	62	46	58	56	47	65	69	39	62	47	60	59	57	71	82
35575	LYNN	78	52	24	45	59	68	51	63	61	52	72	76	43	68	51	66	65	63	78	90
35576	MILLPORT	75	50	23	43	57	65	48	60	58	49	68	72	41	65	49	63	62	60	74	86
35578	NAUVOO	74	50	23	43	57	65	48	60	58	49	68	72	41	64	49	63	62	60	74	85
35579	OAKMAN	79	53	24	46	60	69	51	64	62	52	72	76	43	68	52	66	66	63	79	91
35580	PARRISH	75	50	23	43	57	66	49	61	59	50	69	73	41	65	49	63	63	60	75	86
35581	PHIL CAMPBELL	78	53	25	46	59	68	51	63	61	52	72	75	44	68	52	66	65	63	77	89
35582	RED BAY	74	50	23	43	56	65	48	60	58	49	68	72	41	64	49	63	62	60	74	85
35585	SPRUCE PINE	74	52	26	46	58	66	50	61	59	51	70	73	44	67	51	63	64	61	74	85
35586	SULLIGENT	75	50	23	43	57	65	48	60	58	49	68	72	41	65	49	63	62	60	74	86
35587	TOWNLEY	68	45	20	39	51	59	44	55	53	44	62	65	37	58	44	57	56	54	67	77
35592	VERNON	74	51	24	44	57	66	50	61	60	50	70	72	43	66	51	64	64	61	75	85
35593	VINA	72	48	22	42	55	63	47	58	56	47	66	70	40	62	47	61	60	58	72	83
35594	WINFIELD	74	54	32	49	60	69	54	63	62	54	74	74	48	71	54	66	68	63	75	84
35601	DECATUR	68	65	68	64	66	73	68	68	70	67	86	78	68	86	68	71	83	69	71	77
35603	DECATUR	97	94	84	94	95	101	91	94	91	91	112	110	90	113	91	90	108	93	94	110
35610	ANDERSON	84	58	29	51	65	74	56	69	66	57	78	82	48	74	57	71	71	68	83	96
35611	ATHENS	76	63	49	60	66	75	64	70	70	63	85	81	61	83	64	72	79	70	78	86
35613	ATHENS	97	88	70	84	92	99	82	90	86	82	105	106	80	106	84	88	100	88	97	114
35614	ATHENS	82	63	39	57	68	76	60	70	68	61	81	83	55	78	61	71	76	69	80	93
	ALABAMA	81	70	61	67	72	80	70	75	75	70	91	87	67	89	70	76	86	75	81	92
	UNITED STATES	100	100	100	100	100	100	100	100	100	100	100	100	100	100	100	100	100	100	100	100

#	POST OFFICE NAME	COUNTY FIPS CODE	POPULATION 2000	2004	2009	2000-2004 ANNUAL RATE % Rate	State Centile	HOUSEHOLDS 2000	2004	2009	% Annual Rate 2000-2004	2004 Average HH Size	FAMILIES 2000	2004	% Annual Rate 2000-2004
35616	CHEROKEE	033	4819	4819	4794	0.0	37	1960	2001	2030	0.5	2.41	1467	1493	0.4
35618	COURTLAND	079	2266	2107	2061	-1.7	2	932	891	889	-1.1	2.36	635	606	-1.1
35619	DANVILLE	079	5459	5680	5797	0.9	72	2055	2177	2252	1.4	2.61	1599	1690	1.3
35620	ELKMONT	083	7794	8001	8161	0.6	64	2886	3021	3129	1.1	2.65	2295	2394	1.0
35621	EVA	103	2608	2653	2677	0.4	56	988	1026	1050	0.9	2.59	771	797	0.8
35622	FALKVILLE	103	7371	7834	8097	1.4	80	2667	2893	3036	1.9	2.60	2061	2231	1.9
35630	FLORENCE	077	30640	29966	29689	-0.5	17	13703	13700	13852	0.0	2.08	7769	7739	-0.1
35633	FLORENCE	077	19648	19799	19778	0.2	44	7664	7900	8059	0.7	2.50	5962	6115	0.6
35634	FLORENCE	077	11515	11577	11547	0.1	41	4404	4522	4599	0.6	2.54	3538	3625	0.6
35640	HARTSELLE	103	21144	21408	21619	0.3	50	8305	8568	8775	0.7	2.49	6297	6480	0.7
35643	HILLSBORO	079	3629	3628	3643	0.0	35	1386	1424	1457	0.6	2.55	1047	1076	0.6
35645	KILLEN	077	10956	11183	11228	0.5	59	4148	4325	4431	1.0	2.57	3295	3427	0.9
35646	LEIGHTON	033	4991	4881	4799	-0.5	17	1964	1970	1981	0.1	2.48	1469	1470	0.0
35647	LESTER	083	1092	1103	1114	0.2	46	414	426	437	0.7	2.59	329	337	0.6
35648	LEXINGTON	077	3823	3827	3811	0.0	37	1517	1551	1575	0.5	2.47	1121	1143	0.5
35650	MOULTON	079	14000	14344	14488	0.6	63	5472	5733	5885	1.1	2.46	4076	4262	1.1
35651	MOUNT HOPE	079	1280	1292	1292	0.2	45	490	505	512	0.7	2.56	390	401	0.7
35652	ROGERSVILLE	077	7862	8043	8098	0.5	62	3214	3342	3423	0.9	2.40	2381	2469	0.9
35653	RUSSELLVILLE	059	10686	10724	10637	0.1	39	4120	4170	4175	0.3	2.50	2916	2952	0.3
35654	RUSSELLVILLE	059	8386	8348	8249	-0.1	31	3201	3214	3208	0.1	2.60	2394	2401	0.1
35660	SHEFFIELD	033	9624	9218	9006	-1.0	6	4233	4136	4122	-0.5	2.22	2708	2646	-0.5
35661	MUSCLE SHOALS	033	16179	16144	16023	-0.1	34	6408	6528	6605	0.4	2.44	4796	4871	0.4
35670	SOMERVILLE	103	7299	7604	7755	1.0	72	2789	2965	3068	1.5	2.56	2171	2299	1.4
35671	TANNER	083	2207	2365	2473	1.6	84	858	942	1003	2.2	2.48	639	699	2.1
35672	TOWN CREEK	079	6780	6793	6817	0.1	38	2688	2762	2823	0.6	2.46	2027	2082	0.6
35673	TRINITY	079	6676	6729	6754	0.2	44	2505	2585	2638	0.7	2.59	2013	2074	0.7
35674	TUSCUMBIA	033	17585	17781	17805	0.3	47	7214	7439	7591	0.7	2.35	5069	5218	0.7
35677	WATERLOO	077	1839	1831	1820	-0.1	31	744	757	768	0.4	2.42	571	579	0.3
35739	ARDMORE	083	3799	3845	3889	0.3	49	1506	1556	1598	0.8	2.47	1101	1132	0.7
35740	BRIDGEPORT	071	3851	3871	3909	0.1	41	1602	1655	1706	0.8	2.34	1115	1149	0.7
35741	BROWNSBORO	089	2795	2964	3068	1.4	79	1043	1131	1188	1.9	2.61	857	927	1.9
35744	DUTTON	071	2723	3007	3177	2.4	93	1056	1188	1275	2.8	2.53	801	900	2.8
35745	ESTILLFORK	071	314	311	312	-0.2	24	131	133	136	0.4	2.34	100	101	0.2
35746	FACKLER	071	591	673	723	3.1	97	223	260	285	3.7	2.59	170	198	3.7
35747	GRANT	095	4728	4829	4935	0.5	60	1910	1994	2070	1.0	2.41	1415	1474	1.0
35748	GURLEY	089	4971	5431	5683	2.1	90	1858	2082	2216	2.7	2.61	1424	1583	2.5
35749	HARVEST	089	12799	14214	15023	2.5	94	4339	4927	5292	3.0	2.78	3543	4004	2.9
35750	HAZEL GREEN	089	11808	12597	13078	1.5	81	4229	4603	4850	2.0	2.73	3407	3689	1.9
35751	HOLLYTREE	071	399	396	397	-0.2	27	110	110	112	0.0	3.36	81	81	0.0
35752	HOLLYWOOD	071	2334	2432	2497	1.0	72	928	991	1037	1.6	2.45	694	739	1.5
35754	LACEYS SPRING	103	5031	5088	5136	0.3	48	1981	2041	2090	0.7	2.49	1467	1507	0.6
35755	LANGSTON	095	505	512	519	0.3	51	237	245	252	0.8	2.09	173	179	0.8
35756	MADISON	083	4095	4299	4434	1.2	76	1564	1680	1761	1.7	2.56	1158	1238	1.6
35757	MADISON	089	7798	8918	9563	3.2	98	2759	3236	3529	3.8	2.65	2237	2603	3.6
35758	MADISON	089	30307	33825	35912	2.6	95	11593	13058	13989	2.8	2.58	8304	9320	2.8
35759	MERIDIANVILLE	089	4293	4426	4536	0.7	67	1565	1659	1731	1.4	2.67	1298	1368	1.2
35760	NEW HOPE	089	5254	5121	5109	-0.6	14	2112	2107	2136	-0.1	2.43	1560	1546	-0.2
35761	NEW MARKET	089	7636	7737	7783	0.3	51	2853	2960	3027	0.9	2.61	2207	2275	0.7
35763	OWENS CROSS ROADS	089	7141	8044	8603	2.8	96	2492	2810	3020	2.9	2.85	2067	2333	2.9
35764	PAINT ROCK	071	597	596	597	0.0	34	249	254	259	0.5	2.35	192	195	0.4
35765	PISGAH	071	4424	4488	4538	0.3	53	1760	1824	1878	0.8	2.46	1343	1389	0.8
35766	PRINCETON	071	244	240	240	-0.4	20	95	95	97	0.0	2.43	70	70	0.0
35768	SCOTTSBORO	071	11614	11511	11569	-0.2	25	4739	4790	4900	0.3	2.32	3241	3275	0.3
35769	SCOTTSBORO	071	9828	9896	10054	0.2	42	4128	4271	4424	0.8	2.31	2998	3085	0.7
35771	SECTION	071	3675	3691	3735	0.1	40	1432	1467	1509	0.6	2.49	1088	1112	0.5
35772	STEVENSON	071	5270	5379	5475	0.5	59	2106	2201	2283	1.0	2.40	1522	1586	1.0
35773	TONEY	089	11854	12656	13134	1.6	82	3590	3965	4201	2.4	2.72	2821	3096	2.2
35774	TRENTON	071	268	264	265	-0.4	21	109	110	112	0.2	2.28	81	81	0.0
35775	VALHERMOSO SPRINGS	103	588	606	614	0.7	67	230	242	249	1.2	2.50	165	173	1.1
35776	WOODVILLE	071	3568	3959	4207	2.5	94	1393	1577	1702	3.0	2.50	1099	1244	3.0
35801	HUNTSVILLE	089	22900	22252	22230	-0.7	13	10521	10471	10645	-0.1	2.02	6047	5980	-0.3
35802	HUNTSVILLE	089	19429	19295	19629	-0.2	28	8875	9097	9460	0.6	2.11	5657	5761	0.4
35803	HUNTSVILLE	089	25291	25486	25951	0.2	44	9743	10079	10449	0.8	2.53	7442	7647	0.6
35805	HUNTSVILLE	089	22657	21794	21939	-0.9	7	10342	10131	10362	-0.5	2.06	5388	5240	-0.7
35806	HUNTSVILLE	089	11153	12191	12802	2.1	91	4836	5325	5635	2.3	2.27	3086	3403	2.3
35808	HUNTSVILLE	089	2365	2411	2429	0.5	58	487	510	522	1.1	3.41	444	464	1.0
35810	HUNTSVILLE	089	28634	27950	28050	-0.6	15	10840	10901	11158	0.1	2.55	7877	7858	-0.1
35811	HUNTSVILLE	089	23803	25111	25980	1.3	78	8711	9436	9953	1.9	2.48	6449	6960	1.8
35816	HUNTSVILLE	089	15365	15238	15488	-0.2	25	6632	6752	7002	0.4	2.03	3222	3202	-0.2
35824	HUNTSVILLE	089	3114	3137	3137	0.2	43	1496	1542	1567	0.7	2.03	813	828	0.4
35898	HUNTSVILLE	089	12	13	13	1.9	89	5	5	6	0.0	2.40	4	4	0.0
35901	GADSDEN	055	20601	20524	20567	-0.1	32	8339	8418	8567	0.2	2.31	5417	5482	0.3
35903	GADSDEN	055	18123	17967	17898	-0.2	25	7547	7610	7710	0.2	2.35	4994	5029	0.2
35904	GADSDEN	055	15443	14988	14891	-0.7	13	6354	6268	6333	-0.3	2.34	4428	4360	-0.4
35905	GADSDEN	055	6455	6415	6365	-0.2	29	2476	2519	2550	0.4	2.45	1903	1929	0.3
35906	RAINBOW CITY	055	8944	9233	9336	0.8	68	3773	3989	4116	1.3	2.30	2667	2805	1.2
35907	GADSDEN	055	6934	7181	7262	0.8	70	2637	2805	2898	1.5	2.55	2166	2296	1.4
35950	ALBERTVILLE	095	17211	17686	18200	0.6	65	6623	6831	7075	0.7	2.57	4719	4863	0.7
35951	ALBERTVILLE	095	10535	10665	10863	0.3	50	3856	3929	4033	0.4	2.68	2905	2955	0.4
35952	ALTOONA	055	7502	7722	7856	0.7	66	2876	3005	3100	1.0	2.55	2203	2296	1.0
35953	ASHVILLE	115	6764	7196	7656	1.5	81	2496	2713	2941	2.0	2.59	1913	2077	2.0
35954	ATTALLA	055	13011	12907	12863	-0.2	26	5110	5169	5241	0.3	2.46	3705	3732	0.2
35956	BOAZ	055	8220	8350	8379	0.4	54	3200	3314	3383	0.8	2.52	2502	2581	0.7
35957	BOAZ	095	13995	14291	14613	0.5	60	5578	5758	5947	0.8	2.45	3947	4071	0.7
35958	BRYANT	071	3549	3631	3681	0.5	62	1348	1412	1458	1.1	2.57	1061	1108	1.0
35959	CEDAR BLUFF	019	4387	4589	4860	1.1	75	1850	1987	2155	1.7	2.29	1373	1472	1.7
35960	CENTRE	019	9479	9902	10473	1.0	75	3891	4169	4518	1.6	2.32	2821	3020	1.6
35961	COLLINSVILLE	049	5224	5269	5391	0.2	44	1907	1946	2013	0.5	2.62	1365	1392	0.5
35962	CROSSVILLE	049	7173	7660	8010	1.6	82	2661	2871	3030	1.8	2.62	2024	2181	1.8
35963	DAWSON	049	1548	1567	1598	0.3	50	603	619	638	0.6	2.53	457	468	0.6
35966	FLAT ROCK	071	3842	3915	3974	0.4	57	1473	1536	1586	1.0	2.55	1141	1188	1.0
35967	FORT PAYNE	049	16495	16962	17458	0.7	65	6457	6705	6967	0.9	2.48	4554	4724	0.9
35968	FORT PAYNE	049	3668	3722	3799	0.3	53	1436	1479	1527	0.7	2.50	1089	1120	0.7
35971	FYFFE	049	4468	4474	4530	0.0	38	1737	1770	1816	0.4	2.47	1293	1315	0.4
35972	GALLANT	055	730	772	796	1.3	79	283	305	319	1.8	2.53	225	242	1.7
	ALABAMA					0.5					0.9	2.45			0.9
	UNITED STATES					1.2					1.3	2.58			1.1

POPULATION COMPOSITION

ZIP CODE #	POST OFFICE NAME	RACE (%) White 2000	White 2004	Black 2000	Black 2004	Asian/Pacific 2000	Asian/Pacific 2004	% Hispanic Origin 2000	% Hispanic Origin 2004	2004 AGE DISTRIBUTION (%) 0-4	5-9	10-14	15-19	20-24	25-44	45-64	65-84	85+	18+	MEDIAN AGE 2004	% 2004 Males	% 2004 Females
35616	CHEROKEE	86.8	85.6	11.5	12.4	0.0	0.0	1.0	1.4	6.1	6.2	6.3	5.6	5.3	25.5	28.2	15.3	1.6	78.0	41.6	50.2	49.8
35618	COURTLAND	47.8	45.8	48.6	50.4	0.1	0.1	1.0	1.0	6.6	6.8	7.6	6.7	6.4	27.2	25.6	11.4	1.7	74.9	37.1	46.7	53.3
35619	DANVILLE	89.0	88.2	4.7	5.2	0.1	0.1	0.8	1.1	7.1	7.0	7.2	7.0	6.3	31.1	24.1	9.3	0.8	74.4	35.6	51.0	49.0
35620	ELKMONT	94.4	93.8	3.9	4.3	0.1	0.1	0.9	1.2	6.6	6.9	7.8	6.8	6.0	31.1	25.1	8.9	0.7	74.5	36.3	51.0	49.0
35621	EVA	97.6	97.1	0.4	0.4	0.1	0.1	1.2	1.7	6.9	7.0	6.9	6.1	6.6	30.1	25.0	10.1	1.2	75.7	36.7	51.6	48.4
35622	FALKVILLE	96.6	96.2	1.3	1.4	0.2	0.2	1.0	1.3	6.5	6.6	6.9	6.6	5.9	28.6	24.3	12.4	2.3	76.0	38.3	49.4	50.6
35630	FLORENCE	75.6	75.1	21.7	22.2	0.6	0.7	1.5	1.5	5.8	5.3	5.7	6.9	9.8	26.0	21.5	15.9	3.2	80.0	37.0	45.4	54.6
35633	FLORENCE	92.7	92.3	5.9	6.4	0.3	0.3	0.9	1.0	5.8	6.1	6.7	6.4	6.0	28.4	27.3	12.2	1.1	77.5	39.2	49.1	50.9
35634	FLORENCE	97.1	97.0	1.5	1.6	0.3	0.3	0.8	0.9	5.7	6.2	6.8	6.2	5.5	26.8	29.2	12.5	1.3	77.7	40.5	49.8	50.3
35640	HARTSELLE	94.0	93.1	3.6	4.0	0.3	0.3	1.1	1.6	6.1	6.4	7.0	6.4	5.8	28.4	26.7	11.9	1.4	76.6	38.8	49.2	50.8
35643	HILLSBORO	64.1	63.3	29.0	29.1	0.1	0.1	1.2	1.5	6.3	6.5	7.6	6.6	6.7	29.2	26.6	9.5	1.1	75.5	37.3	49.5	50.6
35645	KILLEN	96.1	95.9	2.3	2.5	0.3	0.3	0.9	0.9	6.8	7.0	7.1	6.2	5.4	29.0	26.5	11.1	1.1	75.4	38.2	49.2	50.8
35646	LEIGHTON	74.9	73.2	22.8	24.2	0.3	0.4	1.1	1.4	6.2	6.4	7.0	6.3	5.6	26.6	27.5	13.0	1.6	76.5	39.7	48.7	51.3
35647	LESTER	97.0	96.7	1.9	2.1	0.1	0.1	0.8	1.1	7.3	7.2	7.6	7.3	6.1	28.4	24.8	10.5	0.9	73.4	36.4	50.8	49.2
35648	LEXINGTON	98.9	98.8	0.1	0.2	0.1	0.1	0.6	0.5	6.7	6.7	6.4	5.6	5.4	28.2	25.9	13.4	1.8	76.8	39.2	49.3	50.7
35650	MOULTON	85.1	83.5	5.3	6.1	0.2	0.2	0.9	1.2	6.3	6.4	7.0	6.2	6.2	29.7	24.4	12.1	1.7	76.5	37.8	49.0	51.0
35651	MOUNT HOPE	86.5	85.1	4.7	5.4	0.0	0.0	0.5	0.5	7.1	7.0	7.0	7.0	6.0	29.6	22.9	12.2	1.2	74.6	36.7	49.4	50.6
35652	ROGERSVILLE	94.0	93.7	4.8	5.1	0.2	0.2	0.3	0.4	6.0	6.1	6.4	5.6	5.2	27.0	27.4	14.8	1.5	78.0	40.9	49.3	50.8
35653	RUSSELLVILLE	82.2	80.0	9.4	9.7	0.4	0.4	11.1	13.8	6.5	6.5	6.8	6.4	6.8	27.4	23.5	13.7	2.5	76.4	37.7	48.6	51.5
35654	RUSSELLVILLE	88.6	87.0	2.9	2.8	0.2	0.2	10.3	12.7	7.0	6.9	7.1	6.1	6.8	29.7	24.1	11.3	0.9	75.4	35.5	51.3	48.8
35660	SHEFFIELD	71.2	70.5	26.3	26.6	0.3	0.4	1.5	1.8	6.5	6.3	6.5	6.0	6.0	25.7	24.4	15.8	2.9	77.1	40.0	46.4	53.6
35661	MUSCLE SHOALS	82.9	81.4	15.4	16.6	0.4	0.5	1.1	1.3	6.0	6.5	7.1	5.9	5.9	27.2	27.2	12.8	1.4	76.9	39.3	47.8	52.2
35670	SOMERVILLE	94.7	94.0	2.7	3.1	0.3	0.3	0.6	0.8	6.7	6.9	7.1	6.6	6.5	29.4	26.8	9.3	0.8	75.5	37.0	50.7	49.3
35671	TANNER	67.4	65.5	27.4	28.3	0.2	0.3	4.5	5.8	6.7	6.8	7.4	7.0	7.2	29.0	25.5	9.6	0.8	75.1	36.2	50.5	49.5
35672	TOWN CREEK	68.8	67.3	21.8	22.3	0.1	0.1	1.5	1.7	6.2	6.5	7.7	6.7	6.2	28.6	25.9	10.9	1.3	75.5	37.5	49.7	50.3
35673	TRINITY	89.0	87.9	4.6	5.1	0.2	0.2	0.9	1.2	6.7	6.9	7.4	6.5	5.9	30.3	26.0	9.7	0.8	75.0	37.2	49.8	50.3
35674	TUSCUMBIA	85.4	84.7	13.1	13.6	0.2	0.2	1.0	1.3	6.1	6.1	6.3	6.0	6.1	27.1	25.8	14.2	2.2	77.7	40.0	48.4	51.6
35677	WATERLOO	98.0	98.0	0.9	1.0	0.0	0.0	0.7	0.7	4.9	5.2	6.8	6.3	6.2	29.3	27.6	12.1	1.6	79.2	40.1	50.6	49.4
35739	ARDMORE	92.9	91.8	4.3	4.9	0.4	0.6	1.4	1.8	6.8	6.8	7.2	6.7	6.0	30.4	24.7	10.5	0.9	75.1	36.7	49.0	51.1
35740	BRIDGEPORT	88.5	87.7	6.6	6.9	0.2	0.3	1.0	1.3	6.6	6.4	6.4	6.2	6.6	27.3	25.6	13.4	1.6	77.0	38.6	48.6	51.4
35741	BROWNSBORO	90.5	89.6	6.7	7.2	0.5	0.7	1.0	1.3	8.3	8.9	8.7	5.9	4.3	28.2	26.1	8.9	0.7	70.3	37.8	49.3	50.7
35744	DUTTON	94.0	93.5	0.1	0.1	0.1	0.1	1.3	1.7	7.1	7.1	6.5	5.9	5.7	29.1	26.2	11.2	1.3	76.2	37.1	49.6	50.5
35745	ESTILLFORK	97.5	97.1	0.0	0.0	0.0	0.0	0.6	0.6	5.5	6.4	8.4	6.1	5.5	30.2	26.7	10.0	1.3	75.6	36.6	50.8	49.2
35746	FACKLER	87.0	86.0	7.6	8.2	0.5	0.5	0.9	1.0	5.7	5.9	6.8	6.1	6.2	29.9	26.3	12.0	1.0	77.9	37.9	51.7	48.3
35747	GRANT	97.8	97.4	0.3	0.3	0.3	0.4	0.6	0.8	5.8	6.1	6.7	6.0	5.5	27.9	27.7	13.3	1.2	77.6	40.4	49.8	50.2
35748	GURLEY	86.8	85.0	10.2	11.6	0.2	0.2	1.2	1.5	6.6	7.0	7.7	6.7	5.5	28.3	26.7	10.2	1.2	74.4	38.3	49.8	50.2
35749	HARVEST	75.9	73.9	20.1	21.4	1.1	1.3	1.5	1.9	8.5	8.5	7.8	7.4	5.9	32.8	22.7	5.9	0.5	71.5	34.7	48.9	51.1
35750	HAZEL GREEN	93.3	92.3	3.0	3.4	0.5	0.6	1.1	1.4	7.7	7.6	7.9	7.4	6.4	31.5	23.2	7.6	0.7	72.2	34.9	49.7	50.3
35751	HOLLYTREE	95.7	95.2	0.3	0.3	0.3	0.3	1.5	1.8	5.3	5.6	6.6	11.4	6.8	26.3	25.3	11.4	1.5	74.2	36.8	51.8	48.2
35752	HOLLYWOOD	86.4	85.2	8.8	9.5	0.2	0.3	1.4	1.7	6.3	6.6	7.2	6.2	6.4	29.2	26.2	11.1	0.9	76.2	37.1	49.8	50.3
35754	LACEYS SPRING	95.3	94.6	1.1	1.2	0.3	0.4	1.3	1.7	6.8	6.8	7.1	6.1	6.0	28.6	27.9	10.0	0.7	75.6	38.2	50.9	49.1
35755	LANGSTON	95.8	95.3	0.6	0.6	0.2	0.2	1.0	1.2	4.9	5.1	5.7	4.7	4.5	23.2	33.0	17.8	1.2	81.5	46.2	50.8	49.2
35756	MADISON	58.7	57.6	38.0	38.5	0.8	1.0	2.3	2.9	7.6	7.5	6.9	6.2	5.9	33.5	23.6	7.7	1.0	74.1	35.1	49.5	50.5
35757	MADISON	76.4	74.0	19.5	21.2	1.2	1.5	1.6	2.1	8.4	8.4	7.7	7.3	5.8	32.7	22.4	6.6	0.7	71.6	34.5	48.4	51.7
35758	MADISON	79.6	77.5	13.5	14.3	3.6	4.4	2.4	3.0	7.7	7.9	8.5	7.2	6.1	32.3	24.5	5.3	0.5	71.4	34.7	49.1	50.9
35759	MERIDIANVILLE	82.7	80.7	13.6	15.1	0.7	0.9	0.9	1.2	6.9	7.3	7.6	6.8	5.2	28.5	27.7	9.5	0.6	74.0	38.4	49.7	50.3
35760	NEW HOPE	95.6	95.0	0.7	0.8	0.2	0.2	0.8	1.1	6.4	6.5	6.8	6.0	6.2	29.8	25.5	11.5	1.2	76.7	38.1	48.8	51.2
35761	NEW MARKET	86.9	85.3	7.6	8.4	0.3	0.3	1.8	2.3	7.0	7.1	7.5	6.8	6.2	30.6	24.7	9.2	1.0	74.0	36.2	50.2	49.8
35763	OWENS CROSS ROADS	94.4	93.5	2.4	2.7	0.8	1.1	0.9	1.2	8.4	9.3	9.0	6.0	4.1	27.0	26.5	8.9	0.8	69.5	38.3	49.4	50.6
35764	PAINT ROCK	93.6	93.1	0.8	0.8	0.2	0.2	0.8	1.0	7.4	7.2	6.2	5.7	6.0	28.4	25.5	12.3	1.3	76.0	37.8	51.2	48.8
35765	PISGAH	95.3	94.8	0.1	0.0	0.1	0.1	0.9	1.2	7.0	6.9	6.5	5.7	6.1	29.1	25.1	12.4	1.3	76.1	37.2	50.6	49.4
35766	PRINCETON	95.9	95.8	0.0	0.0	0.0	0.0	1.2	1.3	5.0	5.4	6.3	7.9	6.7	27.5	26.7	12.5	2.1	78.3	39.2	51.7	48.3
35768	SCOTTSBORO	89.5	88.8	6.6	6.8	0.5	0.6	1.4	1.7	5.7	6.0	6.7	6.3	5.7	27.7	25.3	14.6	2.2	77.6	39.6	47.9	52.1
35769	SCOTTSBORO	95.3	94.5	1.8	2.1	0.4	0.5	1.2	1.6	5.9	6.1	6.7	5.8	5.7	27.0	28.8	12.8	1.2	77.9	40.3	48.6	51.4
35771	SECTION	94.8	94.2	0.7	0.7	0.1	0.1	1.0	1.4	6.1	6.4	6.9	6.1	6.0	28.6	27.0	11.9	1.0	77.1	37.7	49.3	50.7
35772	STEVENSON	85.8	84.8	9.9	10.4	0.2	0.2	1.1	1.4	6.4	6.6	6.4	6.0	5.7	28.5	26.7	12.2	1.7	76.7	38.4	49.0	51.0
35773	TONEY	77.9	76.9	18.9	19.4	0.2	0.3	1.1	1.3	6.7	6.7	6.6	6.1	7.2	36.3	23.0	7.1	0.5	76.4	35.2	57.1	42.9
35774	TRENTON	95.9	95.8	0.0	0.0	0.0	0.0	1.1	1.5	4.9	5.3	6.4	9.9	6.4	26.9	25.8	12.5	1.9	76.5	38.4	51.1	48.9
35775	VALHERMOSO SPRINGS	89.5	88.0	8.5	9.6	0.2	0.3	0.5	0.8	5.9	6.3	6.4	6.8	6.1	28.2	28.7	10.9	0.7	77.1	39.1	51.5	48.5
35776	WOODVILLE	95.0	94.5	0.5	0.6	0.1	0.1	0.8	1.1	6.5	6.6	6.7	6.1	6.3	28.6	26.6	11.6	1.0	76.4	37.9	49.5	50.5
35801	HUNTSVILLE	87.1	85.8	9.5	10.1	1.2	1.6	1.3	1.7	5.4	5.2	5.2	5.4	5.4	26.4	26.3	17.9	3.0	81.0	43.1	47.7	52.3
35802	HUNTSVILLE	89.1	87.7	5.4	5.7	3.3	4.1	1.5	1.9	4.2	4.6	5.9	5.3	5.4	23.7	28.2	20.6	2.2	82.0	45.7	47.5	52.5
35803	HUNTSVILLE	90.4	88.6	2.4	2.6	4.2	5.3	2.1	2.7	5.6	6.7	8.7	7.5	4.6	27.3	29.3	9.9	0.6	74.2	39.9	49.4	50.6
35805	HUNTSVILLE	58.4	55.9	34.2	35.5	2.5	3.1	3.9	4.8	8.1	6.7	5.9	5.8	8.9	32.7	20.3	10.3	1.4	76.2	33.0	48.9	51.2
35806	HUNTSVILLE	71.6	69.4	22.2	23.4	2.9	3.4	1.6	2.0	7.2	7.2	6.8	5.7	6.3	34.6	23.6	8.1	0.5	75.5	35.7	50.3	49.7
35808	HUNTSVILLE	56.9	53.8	31.7	33.3	2.8	3.2	9.3	11.1	8.3	11.0	9.5	12.0	11.2	42.8	5.0	0.1	0.1	67.7	24.1	60.3	39.7
35810	HUNTSVILLE	27.1	25.3	69.2	70.8	0.7	0.8	1.4	1.5	6.2	6.4	7.8	7.5	6.5	26.2	26.1	11.9	1.5	75.0	37.9	46.4	53.7
35811	HUNTSVILLE	71.6	69.7	25.3	26.8	0.5	0.7	1.0	1.2	6.4	6.4	6.5	9.5	7.7	27.3	24.4	10.9	0.9	77.0	36.3	50.0	50.0
35816	HUNTSVILLE	32.1	29.8	62.0	63.5	2.2	2.5	3.3	3.8	6.9	5.8	5.5	10.1	14.8	29.5	16.7	9.5	1.3	78.7	28.3	47.1	52.9
35824	HUNTSVILLE	68.6	65.3	22.4	24.0	5.3	6.5	2.4	3.0	7.4	6.4	6.2	5.7	6.4	40.6	21.6	5.3	0.4	76.6	32.6	49.4	50.6
35898	HUNTSVILLE	50.0	53.9	41.7	38.5	0.0	7.7	0.0	0.0	15.4	15.4	7.7	7.7	15.4	38.5	0.0	0.0	0.0	61.5	21.3	61.5	38.5
35901	GADSDEN	64.0	63.6	33.1	33.5	0.7	0.7	2.2	2.3	6.3	6.1	6.0	6.8	7.0	24.6	24.8	15.8	2.7	77.5	39.9	46.9	53.1
35903	GADSDEN	66.6	66.0	30.2	30.9	0.6	0.6	2.5	2.4	6.6	6.5	6.6	6.0	6.6	27.6	24.4	13.9	1.9	76.8	37.8	47.6	52.4
35904	GADSDEN	89.4	89.0	8.6	8.9	0.2	0.2	1.3	1.3	6.6	6.4	6.1	6.0	5.8	24.8	24.9	17.1	2.5	77.3	40.5	47.3	52.7
35905	GADSDEN	97.0	96.8	1.6	1.8	0.2	0.3	0.4	0.4	5.2	5.5	6.2	6.3	5.8	26.8	27.6	14.3	2.3	79.3	41.4	48.8	51.2
35906	RAINBOW CITY	93.3	92.7	3.4	3.8	1.4	1.5	1.4	1.5	6.4	6.3	6.2	6.0	6.1	27.4	26.6	13.5	1.5	77.5	39.4	47.6	52.4
35907	GADSDEN	98.1	98.0	0.6	0.6	0.3	0.3	0.7	0.8	6.1	6.3	6.3	6.1	5.3	28.6	29.3	11.0	1.1	77.6	39.5	49.3	50.8
35950	ALBERTVILLE	88.5	86.3	1.8	1.8	0.2	0.3	13.4	16.7	8.0	7.5	7.1	6.0	6.8	29.8	21.7	11.5	1.5	73.7	34.4	48.7	51.3
35951	ALBERTVILLE	92.0	90.3	0.9	0.9	0.4	0.5	8.5	11.1	7.7	7.5	7.4	6.0	6.5	30.0	23.0	10.5	1.5	73.8	34.7	50.2	49.8
35952	ALTOONA	96.1	95.5	0.6	0.7	0.1	0.2	3.1	3.8	7.1	7.1	6.8	6.2	6.3	28.4	25.3	11.4	1.5	75.1	36.9	49.1	50.9
35953	ASHVILLE	85.6	84.6	11.9	12.5	0.2	0.3	1.6	2.0	6.6	6.8	7.2	6.7	6.2	29.0	25.3	11.4	1.0	75.4	37.0	51.2	48.8
35954	ATTALLA	89.2	88.8	8.4	8.8	0.1	0.1	2.2	2.3	6.7	6.6	6.6	6.1	6.3	27.7	25.2	13.2	1.7	76.5	38.0	49.2	50.8
35956	BOAZ	98.1	98.0	0.2	0.3	0.2	0.2	1.5	1.6	6.7	6.9	6.9	5.7	5.8	28.8	26.3	11.8	1.2	76.1	38.0	50.4	49.6
35957	BOAZ	93.3	92.0	0.9	0.9	0.3	0.4	6.9	8.9	7.1	6.9	6.8	5.7	6.5	27.8	23.6	13.7	2.0	75.8	37.3	48.2	51.8
35958	BRYANT	95.8	95.3	0.0	0.0	0.1	0.1	0.9	1.1	7.0	6.9	6.9	6.1	6.1	30.0	25.6	10.4	1.0	75.5	37.1	49.7	50.3
35959	CEDAR BLUFF	92.5	91.9	6.0	6.4	0.1	0.2	0.7	0.9	6.0	6.2	6.6	5.4	5.2	26.5	27.3	15.4	1.5	77.8	40.8	49.4	50.6
35960	CENTRE	91.2	90.6	7.3	7.6	0.2	0.2	0.6	0.9	5.7	5.8	5.9	5.0	4.9	26.7	27.6	16.2	2.2	79.6	42.3	48.9	51.1
35961	COLLINSVILLE	83.3	81.2	6.1	6.1	0.3	0.3	14.2	17.1	6.9	7.1	7.1	6.0	6.7	28.2	22.9	12.5	2.5	75.0	36.0	49.8	50.2
35962	CROSSVILLE	96.9	96.1	0.1	0.1	0.1	0.2	4.1	5.5	7.3	7.2	7.4	6.4	6.7	29.0	23.5	10.5	2.1	74.4	35.9	49.7	50.3
35963	DAWSON	96.5	95.7	0.0	0.0	0.2	0.2	3.2	4.2	6.4	6.6	6.9	5.9	6.1	28.3	25.4	12.4	2.0	76.7	38.4	49.5	50.5
35966	FLAT ROCK	95.5	95.0	0.1	0.1	0.1	0.1	0.7	0.9	7.2	7.1	7.3	5.9	6.4	28.8	25.3	10.9	1.1	74.9	36.4	49.7	50.3
35967	FORT PAYNE	85.3	82.7	4.0	4.3	0.6	0.7	10.4	13.0	6.9	6.5	6.7	5.9	6.8	29.3	23.6	12.4	1.9	76.6	36.8	48.9	51.1
35968	FORT PAYNE	95.5	94.7	0.6	0.6	0.2	0.2	2.8	3.7	6.2	6.3	6.9	6.0	6.3	29.4	25.9	11.5	1.4	77.0	37.9	50.6	49.4
35971	FYFFE	96.6	96.1	0.7	0.7	0.1	0.1	1.3	1.7	6.9	6.7	6.5	5.5	6.0	29.2	24.7	13.1	1.4	76.8	37.8	48.8	51.2
35972	GALLANT	97.5	97.2	0.7	0.8	0.1	0.1	1.4	1.7	5.8	6.2	6.9	6.1	6.1	27.3	26.9	13.5	1.2	77.3	39.4	50.3	49.7
	ALABAMA	71.1	70.3	26.0	26.4	0.7	0.9	1.7	2.1	6.7	6.7	7.0	6.8	7.2	28.0	24.5	11.6	1.6	75.8	36.6	48.5	51.5
	UNITED STATES	75.1	73.6	12.3	12.5	3.8	4.2	12.5	14.1	6.9	6.7	7.2	7.0	7.3	28.6	23.8	10.8	1.7	75.1	36.0	49.1	50.9

ZIP CODE #	POST OFFICE NAME	2004 Per Capita Income	2004 HH Income Base	2004 HOUSEHOLD INCOME DISTRIBUTION (%) Less than $25,000	$25,000 to $49,999	$50,000 to $99,999	$100,000 to $149,999	$150,000 or More	MEDIAN HOUSEHOLD INCOME 2004	2009	2004 National Centile	2004 State Centile	2004 Home Value Base	2004 HOME VALUE DISTRIBUTION (%) Less than $50,000	$50,000 to $89,999	$90,000 to $174,999	$175,000 to $399,999	$400,000 or More	2004 Median Home Value
35616	CHEROKEE	19524	2001	37.0	32.0	22.8	4.6	3.6	32647	37072	20	44	1680	31.4	40.3	22.5	5.4	0.4	67401
35618	COURTLAND	16367	891	48.5	26.6	19.1	3.8	2.0	25907	28761	6	17	703	43.2	33.4	18.4	4.1	0.9	57090
35619	DANVILLE	18204	2177	34.0	28.8	28.9	6.4	1.9	38839	44190	42	71	1834	31.1	28.1	28.4	11.2	1.3	77959
35620	ELKMONT	18743	3021	28.8	30.0	32.4	7.0	1.8	40437	46117	48	76	2583	22.2	30.6	37.4	9.5	0.4	84630
35621	EVA	19201	1026	27.6	32.2	32.1	6.1	2.1	41410	47450	51	78	868	29.4	30.9	29.6	9.2	0.9	74833
35622	FALKVILLE	17214	2893	34.8	32.8	24.5	6.0	1.9	34849	40171	27	53	2415	34.9	29.7	25.4	8.2	1.9	71146
35630	FLORENCE	19627	13700	48.4	25.3	18.9	4.8	2.7	26088	29326	6	17	7427	17.5	36.1	36.5	9.1	0.9	86188
35633	FLORENCE	22080	7900	29.3	28.5	30.7	8.4	3.0	42698	47900	55	82	6719	15.8	29.9	40.7	12.1	1.5	96408
35634	FLORENCE	24812	4522	20.9	33.7	30.6	10.2	4.7	45987	52338	64	88	3976	14.4	21.9	38.4	20.4	4.9	110048
35640	HARTSELLE	23487	8568	26.1	28.6	32.9	8.8	3.6	45626	51554	63	87	6977	14.8	30.0	38.0	15.7	1.5	95969
35643	HILLSBORO	20799	1424	33.4	30.6	28.6	5.8	1.5	37562	41947	38	65	1191	39.0	30.6	25.4	4.5	0.5	64947
35645	KILLEN	24263	4325	23.3	28.9	33.4	10.0	4.4	47915	54440	68	90	3764	13.4	26.5	37.7	18.1	4.4	106330
35646	LEIGHTON	16001	1970	40.7	30.8	23.4	4.0	1.1	30660	34057	14	33	1648	33.5	35.5	21.9	7.9	1.2	68625
35647	LESTER	18901	426	29.8	28.6	33.1	6.8	1.6	40204	46371	47	75	358	24.6	32.1	34.1	9.2	0.0	80000
35648	LEXINGTON	18116	1551	34.6	34.0	24.5	5.7	1.1	34166	38886	25	50	1318	23.2	33.8	34.8	7.1	1.2	81238
35650	MOULTON	18678	5733	35.3	30.4	25.7	6.5	2.2	35213	39256	28	55	4639	29.8	30.4	28.3	10.8	0.7	75822
35651	MOUNT HOPE	19820	505	35.8	29.7	25.4	6.3	2.8	36894	40974	35	62	428	32.9	30.6	27.1	7.9	1.4	76923
35652	ROGERSVILLE	19899	3342	31.3	33.1	27.6	6.4	1.7	38650	43928	42	70	2778	21.7	24.8	37.9	14.3	1.4	94623
35653	RUSSELLVILLE	16021	4170	44.3	26.4	23.0	5.1	1.3	28666	31659	10	24	3025	26.5	34.8	28.0	10.4	0.2	76176
35654	RUSSELLVILLE	16923	3214	40.5	29.1	23.9	5.0	1.5	31829	35927	17	39	2553	28.5	30.4	31.7	8.3	1.1	78797
35660	SHEFFIELD	18299	4136	43.0	29.8	20.7	5.2	1.4	29732	33123	12	27	2744	19.1	48.2	26.3	5.4	1.0	73930
35661	MUSCLE SHOALS	23000	6528	28.0	31.4	30.2	7.9	2.5	43102	47969	56	84	5261	14.2	30.2	36.7	15.5	3.4	96937
35670	SOMERVILLE	19748	2965	26.4	32.5	31.4	8.3	1.6	42480	48358	55	82	2520	26.6	31.0	29.9	10.8	1.6	79917
35671	TANNER	24537	942	32.6	24.7	26.4	10.1	6.2	42138	47567	53	80	787	27.5	18.3	25.9	25.2	3.2	97128
35672	TOWN CREEK	18053	2762	36.3	30.2	26.0	6.0	1.6	35266	39227	29	55	2295	38.2	28.4	25.8	7.0	0.7	67980
35673	TRINITY	22981	2585	28.2	28.6	30.9	9.0	3.3	43918	49016	58	85	2275	23.7	27.0	38.8	9.9	0.7	89148
35674	TUSCUMBIA	20190	7439	38.5	28.2	24.7	6.1	2.6	33103	37055	21	46	5620	24.2	35.7	28.9	10.2	1.1	78545
35677	WATERLOO	17302	757	41.0	36.9	17.0	3.6	1.6	30608	34698	14	32	645	33.3	41.9	19.8	4.2	0.8	68253
35739	ARDMORE	19925	1556	32.5	29.6	30.1	6.5	1.4	39885	45387	46	74	1227	21.0	32.4	38.6	7.7	0.3	86295
35740	BRIDGEPORT	18644	1655	36.7	35.5	21.8	4.2	1.8	32479	36250	19	43	1300	38.5	23.2	29.4	8.5	0.5	68219
35741	BROWNSBORO	32861	1131	12.4	23.4	35.1	17.8	11.3	65403	76504	89	98	1048	7.7	15.5	30.9	36.8	9.1	154717
35744	DUTTON	16996	1188	37.0	32.3	24.5	5.0	1.2	34785	38743	27	52	968	30.5	29.7	29.6	9.3	1.0	72857
35745	ESTILLFORK	17409	133	34.6	36.8	25.6	3.0	0.0	35575	40434	30	56	114	42.1	29.8	22.8	5.3	0.0	56923
35746	FACKLER	19915	260	30.4	39.2	24.2	3.1	3.1	38243	43380	40	68	220	35.9	31.8	24.6	6.4	1.4	60556
35747	GRANT	21398	1994	32.6	32.3	25.2	7.6	2.5	38968	43600	43	71	1690	26.2	23.1	33.0	15.4	2.3	91053
35748	GURLEY	20897	2082	30.2	29.3	29.6	8.7	2.1	40778	46591	49	76	1740	21.3	26.0	35.9	15.0	1.8	93730
35749	HARVEST	25286	4927	13.3	26.3	39.0	17.5	3.9	61518	70202	86	97	4548	7.9	13.8	57.8	18.8	1.7	126178
35750	HAZEL GREEN	19029	4603	23.2	34.7	33.7	6.7	1.7	43972	50952	59	85	3926	19.0	29.6	44.0	6.4	1.0	91340
35751	HOLLYTREE	12774	110	31.8	37.3	25.5	2.7	2.7	37857	42475	39	66	93	34.4	34.4	25.8	4.3	1.1	65357
35752	HOLLYWOOD	18130	991	34.0	35.0	24.6	4.8	1.5	35386	39406	29	56	828	35.6	31.2	26.5	5.6	1.2	65000
35754	LACEYS SPRING	19929	2041	32.1	30.4	27.4	6.2	3.9	38233	44055	40	68	1692	38.4	22.2	25.4	10.6	3.5	69072
35755	LANGSTON	23178	245	29.8	31.8	29.4	7.4	1.6	42891	47907	56	83	213	25.4	24.4	27.7	19.3	3.3	90417
35756	MADISON	22415	1680	29.5	24.1	33.2	9.3	3.9	46902	53606	66	90	1406	12.2	30.8	49.0	5.8	2.2	93929
35757	MADISON	27693	3236	12.3	26.1	36.0	18.7	7.0	63383	73093	87	97	2956	6.8	13.3	51.2	26.3	2.4	131336
35758	MADISON	31363	13058	14.0	21.6	36.3	19.2	8.8	67435	77837	90	98	9424	2.7	9.8	47.1	36.4	4.1	149639
35759	MERIDIANVILLE	27785	1659	13.1	25.9	38.8	16.0	6.2	60198	70256	85	96	1499	9.0	9.9	59.8	20.2	1.0	117844
35760	NEW HOPE	20889	2107	30.9	31.3	30.7	5.9	1.2	38785	45000	42	70	1741	26.0	31.8	33.8	7.9	0.6	80393
35761	NEW MARKET	20223	2960	28.0	30.4	31.1	8.7	1.8	42383	49025	54	81	2539	23.8	29.2	34.5	11.0	1.6	86199
35763	OWENS CROSS ROADS	32757	2810	15.9	18.3	31.3	18.8	15.8	69195	80299	91	99	2558	8.7	12.2	23.8	41.2	14.2	190826
35764	PAINT ROCK	17685	254	30.7	44.9	21.3	1.6	1.6	36754	41552	35	62	212	25.0	34.4	28.8	11.8	0.0	80476
35765	PISGAH	16639	1824	38.8	31.0	26.1	2.9	1.3	32368	36199	19	42	1510	39.9	25.4	26.8	7.6	0.3	63814
35766	PRINCETON	17637	95	33.7	36.8	24.2	3.2	2.1	37272	42481	36	64	81	37.0	30.9	25.9	4.9	1.2	64500
35768	SCOTTSBORO	18553	4790	37.7	31.9	24.1	4.7	1.7	33550	37214	23	47	3655	26.9	33.9	32.0	6.0	1.2	76497
35769	SCOTTSBORO	22479	4271	34.9	27.6	24.6	9.4	3.5	39094	41836	43	72	3295	21.7	18.9	37.6	18.1	3.8	104386
35771	SECTION	18163	1467	37.9	28.8	26.7	5.0	1.7	35369	38822	29	55	1219	31.8	33.7	24.2	9.3	1.0	68150
35772	STEVENSON	17915	2201	35.6	32.8	26.0	4.3	1.3	34707	38253	26	52	1771	40.2	30.4	24.3	3.6	1.6	62796
35773	TONEY	19045	3965	20.3	33.6	35.8	8.4	1.9	46824	54079	66	89	3454	18.7	28.4	43.1	9.2	0.7	92861
35774	TRENTON	18499	110	31.8	39.1	24.6	2.7	1.8	37280	42475	36	64	93	36.6	32.3	25.8	4.3	1.1	64091
35775	VALHERMOSO SPRINGS	18748	242	20.3	45.9	27.3	5.0	1.7	42282	48191	54	80	205	28.8	42.9	19.0	6.3	2.9	70217
35776	WOODVILLE	18546	1577	29.8	38.0	27.0	4.1	1.1	38380	42483	41	69	1335	23.7	31.2	36.9	8.0	0.2	83762
35801	HUNTSVILLE	36304	10471	27.4	23.7	26.9	12.7	9.4	48652	55106	70	91	7184	3.6	12.6	42.0	32.2	9.6	150418
35802	HUNTSVILLE	39266	9097	15.3	23.5	35.3	16.1	9.8	61816	69553	86	97	6356	1.7	7.5	49.7	36.4	4.7	160343
35803	HUNTSVILLE	31464	10079	11.7	20.7	40.4	19.4	7.8	67969	78233	90	99	8634	4.1	10.8	61.7	22.2	1.2	133291
35805	HUNTSVILLE	16074	10131	50.4	30.3	16.0	2.8	0.5	24800	27312	4	14	3808	17.2	64.0	17.8	1.0	0.1	69849
35806	HUNTSVILLE	31225	5325	17.0	24.5	34.1	18.6	5.8	62228	72686	86	97	3566	5.1	13.7	40.8	37.7	2.8	150290
35808	HUNTSVILLE	13304	510	14.1	47.3	31.8	6.9	0.0	39649	44643	45	73	14	0.0	0.0	100.0	0.0	0.0	134091
35810	HUNTSVILLE	20288	10901	29.0	30.1	31.4	6.8	2.7	41958	48654	53	79	8273	8.1	55.0	33.5	3.2	0.2	80378
35811	HUNTSVILLE	23824	9436	20.6	28.9	36.1	10.7	3.7	50340	58153	73	92	7942	9.0	25.0	50.7	14.4	0.9	107316
35816	HUNTSVILLE	16662	6752	50.9	26.2	17.3	4.4	1.1	24331	26746	4	13	2258	17.9	41.0	39.2	1.4	0.6	81076
35824	HUNTSVILLE	35096	1542	19.4	24.6	36.5	11.4	8.1	55233	61891	80	94	626	9.7	9.9	39.3	35.5	5.6	142391
35898	HUNTSVILLE	11115	5	40.0	60.0	0.0	0.0	0.0	30833	63750	14	33	0	0.0	0.0	0.0	0.0	0.0	0
35901	GADSDEN	20298	8418	42.3	25.7	23.0	5.5	3.5	31318	34704	16	36	5601	28.7	23.4	30.8	14.5	2.6	84686
35903	GADSDEN	16831	7610	41.5	31.0	22.3	4.0	1.3	30565	33964	14	32	5264	32.1	33.1	29.3	5.2	0.4	69040
35904	GADSDEN	17403	6268	42.2	32.2	19.9	3.6	2.1	30010	33288	12	29	4814	44.0	26.9	23.8	4.6	0.7	55988
35905	GADSDEN	19707	2519	27.6	31.1	34.3	5.6	1.4	42304	47150	54	80	2129	23.6	24.7	37.3	14.2	0.2	91940
35906	RAINBOW CITY	24090	3989	26.5	30.9	30.0	8.4	4.2	42801	47486	55	83	2910	12.9	14.5	48.4	23.1	1.1	124008
35907	GADSDEN	26342	2805	17.6	25.0	37.4	14.9	5.1	60160	65964	84	96	2603	8.8	13.8	55.7	20.9	0.9	118452
35950	ALBERTVILLE	16976	6831	38.2	30.7	24.1	5.3	1.7	33866	37432	24	48	4988	16.9	38.1	33.5	10.5	1.1	84432
35951	ALBERTVILLE	17730	3929	35.7	34.3	20.9	5.8	3.3	33482	37460	22	47	3092	25.9	32.2	26.8	13.2	1.9	79246
35952	ALTOONA	15583	3005	39.7	31.8	23.5	4.0	1.0	31229	34874	16	36	2436	36.8	29.8	24.7	7.0	1.7	65568
35953	ASHVILLE	17517	2713	31.7	34.0	28.4	4.3	1.7	36604	40402	34	62	2307	32.6	26.3	29.5	9.3	2.3	75343
35954	ATTALLA	17618	5169	40.3	29.0	24.3	4.6	1.8	32135	35960	18	40	3956	34.9	33.4	25.5	5.0	1.2	65503
35956	BOAZ	16738	3314	35.4	33.9	24.9	4.9	0.9	33821	38275	24	48	2821	26.1	32.9	30.8	8.9	1.3	76947
35957	BOAZ	16622	5758	40.6	30.9	22.7	4.1	1.7	30957	34332	15	34	4254	22.5	34.6	32.8	8.5	1.7	81457
35958	BRYANT	16171	1412	34.8	32.4	28.7	3.7	0.4	36601	40685	34	62	1193	31.6	29.4	31.6	6.7	0.7	75549
35959	CEDAR BLUFF	19048	1987	36.4	31.8	26.4	4.1	1.3	35106	37906	28	54	1626	33.8	22.8	30.5	11.1	1.8	79239
35960	CENTRE	18182	4169	38.0	32.4	22.6	5.3	1.6	33288	35750	19	42	3366	26.2	28.7	26.4	16.2	2.6	82568
35961	COLLINSVILLE	15309	1946	44.1	31.9	19.0	3.7	1.3	28643	31610	10	23	1537	39.2	30.6	20.8	6.7	2.7	61503
35962	CROSSVILLE	15818	2871	39.0	32.1	23.7	3.3	1.9	31814	35205	17	38	2347	28.2	33.4	27.2	9.3	2.0	77091
35963	DAWSON	15011	619	40.1	35.5	21.2	2.3	1.0	31759	35356	17	38	517	28.8	34.8	24.4	5.8	6.2	74750
35966	FLAT ROCK	15993	1536	36.4	34.4	24.5	4.2	0.5	32203	36094	18	41	1294	39.4	30.6	23.0	6.3	0.7	65241
35967	FORT PAYNE	21045	6705	36.8	29.9	24.5	5.3	3.6	34490	37569	26	51	5028	26.0	32.0	30.0	10.1	1.9	79324
35968	FORT PAYNE	19300	1479	36.4	33.1	23.9	3.7	3.0	35545	39539	30	56	1247	26.1	33.0	31.2	6.9	2.8	77929
35971	FYFFE	17508	1770	38.3	34.4	20.9	4.7	1.7	32969	36379	21	46	1483	31.8	29.1	28.3	8.6	2.1	72670
35972	GALLANT	21972	305	32.8	31.2	29.2	4.6	2.3	36245	41079	33	60	258	29.8	26.0	36.1	6.6	1.6	81667
	ALABAMA	20998		34.3	28.7	26.3	7.2	3.5	37534	42371				22.7	26.7	33.4	14.6	2.7	90917
	UNITED STATES	25866		24.7	27.1	30.8	10.9	6.5	48124	56710				10.9	15.0	33.7	30.1	10.4	145905

# ZIP CODE	POST OFFICE NAME	FINANCIAL SERVICES: Auto Loan	Home Loan	Invest-ments	Retire-ment Plans	THE HOME: Home Improvements: Home Repair	Lawn & Garden	Furnishings: Comput-ers & Hard-ware	Major Appli-ances	TV, Radio, Sound Equip-ment	Furni-ture	ENTERTAINMENT: Dine out/ Carry out	Sports Equip-ment	Fees & Tickets	Toys & Games	Travel	Cable TV	PERSONAL: Apparel & Services	Auto Repairs	Health Insur-ance	Pets & Supplies
35616	CHEROKEE	86	60	31	53	68	78	58	71	68	58	81	85	50	77	59	74	74	71	87	100
35618	COURTLAND	66	48	32	43	52	60	50	57	57	50	68	67	45	65	50	60	63	57	66	75
35619	DANVILLE	83	64	39	58	69	77	60	71	68	61	82	84	55	79	61	72	76	70	82	96
35620	ELKMONT	81	69	51	66	72	79	66	73	70	67	86	86	63	84	67	72	81	72	79	92
35621	EVA	88	66	38	59	72	81	63	74	72	63	85	89	56	83	64	76	79	73	87	101
35622	FALKVILLE	82	60	32	53	65	74	57	69	66	58	78	82	50	74	58	70	72	68	81	94
35630	FLORENCE	57	53	61	53	53	60	59	57	61	57	75	66	58	74	58	61	73	59	60	64
35633	FLORENCE	90	76	58	71	81	89	72	82	78	73	95	96	69	94	74	81	90	80	90	105
35634	FLORENCE	100	90	72	85	95	103	84	93	89	84	108	109	82	108	86	91	103	91	100	118
35640	HARTSELLE	95	81	60	77	86	94	77	86	83	77	100	102	74	101	79	86	95	84	95	110
35643	HILLSBORO	97	68	35	60	76	86	66	80	77	67	91	95	57	86	67	82	84	80	96	111
35645	KILLEN	103	88	64	83	94	101	82	92	88	82	107	110	79	108	84	91	101	90	101	120
35646	LEIGHTON	75	50	23	43	57	65	48	60	58	49	68	72	41	65	49	63	62	60	74	86
35647	LESTER	78	70	53	66	74	79	64	72	69	65	83	85	63	85	66	70	79	70	77	92
35648	LEXINGTON	82	58	29	50	64	73	55	68	65	56	77	81	48	74	56	70	70	67	82	95
35650	MOULTON	82	60	34	54	66	75	59	69	68	59	80	82	52	77	59	72	74	69	82	93
35651	MOUNT HOPE	95	64	29	55	72	83	62	77	74	63	87	92	53	83	63	80	80	76	95	109
35652	ROGERSVILLE	86	61	33	55	68	78	60	72	70	60	83	85	53	79	61	75	76	71	87	99
35653	RUSSELLVILLE	67	52	37	48	56	63	53	59	59	52	71	70	49	69	53	61	66	59	68	76
35654	RUSSELLVILLE	81	56	28	49	63	72	54	66	64	55	76	79	47	72	55	69	69	66	80	92
35660	SHEFFIELD	56	54	57	52	55	62	56	57	59	55	72	63	56	71	56	61	69	57	61	64
35661	MUSCLE SHOALS	90	79	62	74	83	91	75	83	80	75	97	97	72	97	76	82	92	81	90	105
35670	SOMERVILLE	84	70	49	66	75	81	66	75	72	67	87	89	62	86	67	74	82	74	83	97
35671	TANNER	104	84	56	78	91	100	79	91	87	79	105	108	74	104	81	91	98	89	103	121
35672	TOWN CREEK	84	56	26	48	63	73	54	68	65	55	77	81	46	72	55	70	70	67	83	96
35673	TRINITY	100	83	58	77	88	96	78	88	85	79	102	105	74	101	79	87	96	87	98	115
35674	TUSCUMBIA	78	62	46	58	67	76	62	70	69	62	83	81	58	81	63	73	78	70	80	89
35677	WATERLOO	79	53	24	46	60	69	51	64	61	52	72	76	43	68	52	66	66	63	78	90
35739	ARDMORE	83	68	45	63	72	79	64	73	70	64	84	87	60	83	65	73	79	72	82	96
35740	BRIDGEPORT	82	55	25	47	62	72	53	66	64	54	75	79	45	71	54	69	68	66	82	94
35741	BROWNSBORO	118	135	137	136	134	135	122	123	116	123	145	145	128	151	124	113	144	120	114	140
35744	DUTTON	81	54	25	47	61	71	52	65	63	53	74	78	44	70	53	68	67	65	81	93
35745	ESTILLFORK	77	51	23	44	58	67	50	62	60	50	70	74	42	66	50	64	64	61	76	88
35746	FACKLER	97	65	29	56	74	85	63	78	76	64	89	94	53	84	64	82	81	78	97	111
35747	GRANT	91	69	42	63	76	84	65	77	74	66	89	92	60	87	67	78	82	76	90	105
35748	GURLEY	87	76	57	72	80	88	72	80	77	71	93	94	70	94	74	80	88	78	88	102
35749	HARVEST	102	111	106	113	108	108	102	103	96	104	121	121	104	123	101	92	119	101	93	116
35750	HAZEL GREEN	81	77	63	75	78	81	72	76	72	73	89	89	70	88	71	71	86	75	76	92
35751	HOLLYTREE	82	55	25	47	62	72	53	66	64	54	75	79	45	71	54	69	68	66	82	94
35752	HOLLYWOOD	82	57	29	50	64	73	55	67	65	56	77	80	48	73	56	69	70	66	81	94
35754	LACEYS SPRING	86	67	43	62	72	80	64	74	71	65	85	88	58	83	65	74	80	73	84	98
35755	LANGSTON	82	66	45	60	72	80	62	72	69	61	82	85	57	82	65	72	77	71	84	98
35756	MADISON	90	84	70	82	84	89	78	84	80	81	99	97	77	96	78	80	95	82	85	101
35757	MADISON	104	116	119	119	113	113	109	108	102	110	128	127	111	129	108	97	126	106	98	119
35758	MADISON	115	123	128	130	118	119	118	115	110	121	140	136	121	139	115	104	139	115	101	127
35759	MERIDIANVILLE	102	118	118	119	116	115	106	107	100	107	125	126	111	130	107	96	124	103	97	121
35760	NEW HOPE	88	67	42	62	73	82	65	76	73	65	87	89	59	86	66	77	81	74	87	101
35761	NEW MARKET	92	71	44	65	78	86	67	79	76	68	90	94	62	89	69	79	84	77	91	106
35763	OWENS CROSS ROADS	131	145	144	146	144	149	132	134	127	133	159	156	139	164	134	125	156	130	128	153
35764	PAINT ROCK	78	52	24	45	59	68	50	63	61	51	72	75	43	68	51	66	65	63	78	90
35765	PISGAH	77	52	23	45	58	67	50	62	60	51	71	74	42	67	51	65	64	62	77	88
35766	PRINCETON	82	55	25	47	62	72	53	66	64	54	75	79	45	71	54	69	68	66	82	94
35768	SCOTTSBORO	76	55	33	50	61	70	56	65	65	55	76	76	50	72	56	69	70	65	78	86
35769	SCOTTSBORO	82	69	58	66	73	80	70	75	75	69	91	89	66	89	70	76	86	75	82	93
35771	SECTION	83	59	31	52	66	74	56	69	66	57	78	82	49	75	57	70	72	68	82	96
35772	STEVENSON	82	55	25	47	62	71	53	66	64	54	75	79	45	71	54	69	68	65	81	94
35773	TONEY	86	79	62	76	82	87	73	80	76	74	93	95	72	94	75	77	89	78	84	100
35774	TRENTON	81	54	25	47	62	71	52	66	63	53	74	78	45	70	53	68	68	65	81	93
35775	VALHERMOSO SPRINGS	88	59	27	51	67	77	57	71	69	58	81	85	49	77	58	74	74	71	88	101
35776	WOODVILLE	80	63	40	58	68	76	59	69	66	60	80	82	55	79	61	70	74	68	79	93
35801	HUNTSVILLE	95	106	128	105	104	112	104	102	103	104	129	117	109	131	106	102	127	103	100	112
35802	HUNTSVILLE	111	119	137	121	118	127	119	117	115	119	145	135	121	142	119	114	142	118	113	129
35803	HUNTSVILLE	108	124	131	127	121	122	115	114	107	116	135	133	120	138	115	103	134	111	103	126
35805	HUNTSVILLE	45	41	48	42	41	45	48	45	49	47	61	54	47	61	46	48	60	48	45	50
35806	HUNTSVILLE	99	102	114	108	98	101	104	99	99	105	126	119	105	123	100	94	124	102	89	110
35808	HUNTSVILLE	79	50	48	57	46	54	75	64	76	69	95	86	64	85	61	69	91	76	59	73
35810	HUNTSVILLE	69	74	81	72	73	79	72	72	73	73	91	81	75	92	73	73	89	72	72	81
35811	HUNTSVILLE	85	91	93	90	90	94	87	87	85	87	106	101	89	107	87	84	104	86	85	99
35816	HUNTSVILLE	48	40	52	43	40	45	51	47	52	49	65	57	48	62	48	50	63	51	46	52
35824	HUNTSVILLE	105	90	106	101	87	93	104	98	102	106	130	120	99	120	96	95	127	105	88	110
35898	HUNTSVILLE	40	29	30	31	28	32	39	35	40	37	50	44	35	47	34	38	48	40	34	40
35901	GADSDEN	68	65	66	62	65	73	66	68	69	66	85	77	66	84	66	71	82	68	72	78
35903	GADSDEN	58	52	48	50	53	60	54	56	57	53	70	65	52	70	54	59	67	56	61	66
35904	GADSDEN	62	53	46	50	56	65	55	59	60	54	72	67	53	71	56	63	68	59	67	71
35905	GADSDEN	81	67	47	63	72	79	64	73	71	64	85	85	61	84	66	73	79	71	82	94
35906	RAINBOW CITY	83	79	70	76	81	87	76	80	78	75	96	95	75	97	77	78	92	79	83	97
35907	GADSDEN	98	102	94	100	104	107	93	98	92	93	114	115	95	119	95	92	111	95	97	117
35950	ALBERTVILLE	71	56	42	53	60	68	58	64	64	57	77	75	53	75	58	66	72	64	72	80
35951	ALBERTVILLE	82	62	40	58	67	76	62	71	69	62	83	84	56	80	62	72	77	71	81	93
35952	ALTOONA	75	50	23	43	57	65	48	61	59	49	69	72	41	65	49	63	62	60	75	86
35953	ASHVILLE	84	59	31	52	66	74	57	69	67	58	79	82	50	75	58	71	72	69	83	96
35954	ATTALLA	75	56	35	51	61	70	56	65	64	56	76	76	50	73	56	68	70	64	76	85
35956	BOAZ	76	55	31	50	61	69	53	63	61	53	72	76	47	70	54	65	67	62	75	87
35957	BOAZ	69	52	36	49	57	65	53	60	60	53	72	71	48	69	54	63	66	60	70	78
35958	BRYANT	78	52	24	45	59	68	51	63	61	52	72	76	43	68	51	66	65	63	78	90
35959	CEDAR BLUFF	80	56	29	49	63	72	54	66	64	54	75	79	46	72	55	69	69	66	81	94
35960	CENTRE	73	54	33	50	60	69	55	64	62	54	74	74	49	71	55	66	68	63	76	83
35961	COLLINSVILLE	76	51	23	44	58	67	49	62	59	50	70	74	42	66	50	64	63	61	76	87
35962	CROSSVILLE	77	53	26	47	60	68	52	63	61	53	72	75	44	68	52	65	66	63	77	88
35963	DAWSON	71	48	22	41	54	62	46	58	56	47	65	69	39	62	47	60	59	57	71	82
35966	FLAT ROCK	77	51	23	44	58	67	50	62	60	51	70	74	42	66	50	64	64	61	76	88
35967	FORT PAYNE	86	71	52	67	75	83	70	77	76	70	91	90	66	89	70	78	86	77	86	98
35968	FORT PAYNE	87	63	35	57	70	79	61	73	70	61	83	87	54	81	62	74	77	72	86	100
35971	FYFFE	80	56	29	49	63	71	54	66	64	55	75	79	47	72	55	68	69	65	80	92
35972	GALLANT	105	70	32	60	79	91	68	85	82	69	96	101	58	91	69	88	87	84	104	120
	ALABAMA	81	70	61	67	72	80	70	75	75	70	91	87	67	89	70	76	86	75	81	92
	UNITED STATES	100	100	100	100	100	100	100	100	100	100	100	100	100	100	100	100	100	100	100	100

ALABAMA

A 35973-36263

POPULATION CHANGE

# POST OFFICE NAME	COUNTY FIPS CODE	POPULATION 2000	2004	2009	2000-2004 ANNUAL RATE % Rate	State Centile	HOUSEHOLDS 2000	2004	2009	% Annual Rate 2000-2004	2004 Average HH Size	FAMILIES 2000	2004	% Annual Rate 2000-2004
35973 GAYLESVILLE	019	3117	3430	3728	2.3	92	1194	1346	1497	2.9	2.51	895	1007	2.8
35974 GERALDINE	049	1392	1466	1520	1.2	77	591	633	663	1.6	2.31	421	450	1.6
35975 GROVEOAK	049	1135	1150	1167	0.3	51	453	467	480	0.7	2.46	339	349	0.7
35976 GUNTERSVILLE	095	15758	16017	16343	0.4	55	6443	6660	6888	0.8	2.34	4502	4652	0.8
35978 HENAGAR	049	4528	4485	4566	-0.2	25	1764	1773	1827	0.1	2.53	1338	1345	0.1
35979 HIGDON	049	1141	1162	1181	0.4	57	434	453	468	1.0	2.57	338	353	1.0
35980 HORTON	095	4045	4364	4604	1.8	87	1517	1653	1759	2.0	2.64	1199	1304	2.0
35981 IDER	049	2466	2680	2830	2.0	90	995	1104	1182	2.5	2.43	748	828	2.4
35983 LEESBURG	019	3109	3175	3318	0.5	60	1272	1329	1421	1.0	2.38	958	1000	1.0
35984 MENTONE	049	1792	1943	2052	1.9	89	757	838	898	2.4	2.32	531	587	2.4
35986 RAINSVILLE	049	6595	7122	7489	1.8	87	2704	2972	3165	2.3	2.38	1972	2164	2.2
35987 STEELE	115	2567	2600	2719	0.3	50	990	1021	1087	0.7	2.52	765	789	0.7
35988 SYLVANIA	049	1942	2083	2190	1.7	85	765	837	891	2.1	2.49	591	646	2.1
35989 VALLEY HEAD	049	3046	3149	3234	0.8	69	1176	1233	1280	1.1	2.55	878	921	1.1
36003 AUTAUGAVILLE	001	2006	2298	2535	3.3	98	750	886	1002	4.0	2.58	532	627	3.9
36005 BANKS	109	1353	1321	1317	-0.6	16	535	529	535	-0.3	2.50	395	391	-0.2
36006 BILLINGSLEY	001	1368	1535	1678	2.8	95	520	595	662	3.2	2.58	396	452	3.2
36009 BRANTLEY	041	2643	2603	2596	-0.4	21	1120	1126	1143	0.1	2.31	774	776	0.1
36010 BRUNDIDGE	109	4582	4536	4593	-0.2	24	1955	1983	2052	0.3	2.28	1303	1322	0.3
36013 CECIL	101	248	242	237	-0.6	15	98	97	97	-0.2	2.49	74	73	-0.3
36016 CLAYTON	005	5345	5433	5474	0.4	55	1576	1651	1699	1.1	2.59	1106	1154	1.0
36017 CLIO	005	2958	3012	3030	0.4	57	731	772	795	1.3	2.66	510	537	1.2
36020 COOSADA	051	1397	1491	1582	1.5	82	476	518	558	2.0	2.88	382	414	1.9
36022 DEATSVILLE	051	9526	10323	11096	1.9	89	3352	3696	4041	2.3	2.70	2682	2955	2.3
36024 ECLECTIC	051	5514	5595	5867	0.3	53	2126	2194	2335	0.7	2.55	1626	1671	0.6
36025 ELMORE	051	4656	5046	5364	1.9	89	857	980	1086	3.2	3.50	708	806	3.1
36026 EQUALITY	037	1202	1203	1196	0.0	37	495	506	514	0.5	2.38	374	383	0.6
36027 EUFAULA	005	17385	17301	17295	-0.1	31	6789	6892	7000	0.4	2.48	4836	4908	0.4
36028 DOZIER	041	907	913	916	0.2	42	386	395	402	0.5	2.31	262	267	0.5
36029 FITZPATRICK	011	1010	975	969	-0.8	9	396	392	398	-0.2	2.49	288	285	-0.3
36030 FOREST HOME	013	869	860	844	-0.2	24	308	311	311	0.2	2.77	233	235	0.2
36031 FORT DAVIS	011	106	104	105	-0.5	18	41	41	43	0.0	2.54	26	26	0.0
36032 FORT DEPOSIT	085	2891	2857	2879	-0.3	22	1051	1068	1109	0.4	2.66	749	760	0.3
36033 GEORGIANA	013	4372	4513	4571	0.8	68	1792	1905	1982	1.5	2.33	1230	1307	1.4
36034 GLENWOOD	109	612	613	618	0.0	38	260	265	272	0.5	2.31	191	195	0.5
36035 GOSHEN	109	1695	1637	1628	-0.8	9	714	703	712	-0.4	2.33	486	478	-0.4
36036 GRADY	101	1935	1883	1847	-0.6	14	771	769	770	-0.1	2.45	565	560	-0.2
36037 GREENVILLE	013	14429	14128	13834	-0.5	18	5605	5612	5624	0.0	2.49	3933	3932	0.0
36038 GANTT	039	3657	3728	3764	0.5	58	1492	1544	1585	0.8	2.41	1055	1092	0.8
36039 HARDAWAY	087	394	397	404	0.2	44	146	151	158	0.8	2.62	98	101	0.7
36040 HAYNEVILLE	085	4899	5007	5132	0.5	61	1697	1796	1907	1.3	2.77	1265	1340	1.4
36041 HIGHLAND HOME	041	1362	1381	1390	0.3	51	527	545	559	0.8	2.53	382	395	0.8
36042 HONORAVILLE	041	1254	1256	1256	0.0	38	489	500	509	0.5	2.51	364	371	0.5
36043 HOPE HULL	101	3838	3784	3766	-0.3	22	1436	1453	1480	0.3	2.59	1055	1060	0.1
36046 LAPINE	041	1612	1610	1605	0.0	35	626	637	646	0.4	2.53	467	473	0.3
36047 LETOHATCHEE	085	1944	1938	1956	-0.1	33	718	738	768	0.7	2.62	520	533	0.6
36048 LOUISVILLE	005	1859	1857	1870	0.0	35	701	718	737	0.6	2.59	515	527	0.5
36049 LUVERNE	041	4862	4885	4899	0.1	41	1985	2038	2085	0.6	2.32	1353	1387	0.6
36051 MARBURY	001	1998	2158	2305	1.8	87	689	759	826	2.3	2.79	527	580	2.3
36052 MATHEWS	101	663	672	674	0.3	51	259	268	274	0.8	2.51	182	189	0.9
36053 MIDWAY	011	2382	2369	2396	-0.1	29	940	959	992	0.5	2.29	642	654	0.4
36054 MILLBROOK	051	10810	12008	13067	2.5	94	3798	4300	4753	3.0	2.79	3016	3405	2.9
36061 PEROTE	011	251	236	233	-1.4	3	107	103	104	-0.9	2.29	74	71	-1.0
36064 PIKE ROAD	101	4356	5198	5633	4.3	99	1551	1894	2091	4.8	2.74	1255	1519	4.6
36066 PRATTVILLE	001	13173	14294	15566	1.9	89	4880	5406	6001	2.4	2.64	3873	4284	2.4
36067 PRATTVILLE	001	22915	24334	26053	1.4	80	8341	9039	9865	1.9	2.67	6364	6899	1.9
36069 RAMER	101	2606	2524	2466	-0.8	11	1080	1076	1073	-0.1	2.35	756	750	-0.2
36071 RUTLEDGE	041	1058	1052	1051	-0.1	29	437	446	455	0.5	2.36	305	311	0.5
36075 SHORTER	087	2119	2195	2257	0.8	70	775	821	865	1.4	2.67	554	586	1.3
36078 TALLASSEE	051	12567	12186	12361	-0.7	12	4949	4892	5042	-0.3	2.47	3542	3487	-0.4
36079 TROY	109	9265	9372	9497	0.3	48	3772	3893	4019	0.8	2.41	2496	2574	0.7
36080 TITUS	051	2154	2324	2506	1.8	87	912	1013	1116	2.5	2.29	656	726	2.4
36081 TROY	109	13321	13769	14111	0.8	68	5331	5615	5865	1.2	2.29	3239	3413	1.2
36082 TROY	109	325	323	322	-0.2	29	0	0	0	0.0	0.00	0	0	0.0
36083 TUSKEGEE	087	11146	11308	11532	0.3	53	4476	4676	4903	1.0	2.35	2721	2839	1.0
36088 TUSKEGEE INSTITUTE	087	5573	5677	5774	0.4	57	1601	1680	1764	1.1	2.23	868	907	1.0
36089 UNION SPRINGS	011	9776	10037	10287	0.6	64	3197	3371	3547	1.3	2.52	2169	2284	1.2
36091 VERBENA	021	2975	3179	3363	1.6	82	1163	1268	1363	2.1	2.51	866	942	2.0
36092 WETUMPKA	051	18591	19187	20076	0.8	68	6130	6525	7019	1.5	2.44	4549	4828	1.4
36093 WETUMPKA	051	6607	7669	8546	3.6	98	2437	2887	3272	4.1	2.66	2055	2423	4.0
36104 MONTGOMERY	101	12686	11250	10624	-2.8	0	4993	4477	4278	-2.5	2.20	2673	2367	-2.8
36105 MONTGOMERY	101	14393	13289	12724	-1.9	1	5253	4960	4834	-1.3	2.68	3751	3523	-1.5
36106 MONTGOMERY	101	15546	14972	14640	-0.9	8	5911	5793	5749	-0.5	2.21	3550	3466	-0.6
36107 MONTGOMERY	101	9576	8960	8630	-1.6	2	4202	3988	3894	-1.2	2.19	2280	2142	-1.5
36108 MONTGOMERY	101	25377	23369	22381	-1.9	1	9333	8828	8625	-1.3	2.61	6453	6074	-1.4
36109 MONTGOMERY	101	25079	23798	23037	-1.2	4	10553	10248	10098	-0.7	2.27	7191	6939	-0.8
36110 MONTGOMERY	101	13134	12864	12645	-0.5	18	4892	4904	4906	0.1	2.54	3425	3409	-0.1
36111 MONTGOMERY	101	12296	11906	11630	-0.8	11	5340	5208	5135	-0.6	2.27	3310	3208	-0.7
36112 MONTGOMERY	101	5786	5768	5721	-0.1	33	542	534	529	-0.4	2.96	461	453	-0.4
36115 MONTGOMERY	101	845	946	991	2.7	95	193	229	248	4.1	3.33	187	222	4.1
36116 MONTGOMERY	101	38578	39531	39932	0.6	63	14798	15372	15740	0.9	2.54	10070	10405	0.8
36117 MONTGOMERY	101	37632	42267	44509	2.8	95	15243	17621	18936	3.5	2.28	9845	11491	3.7
36201 ANNISTON	015	21514	20422	19727	-1.2	4	8695	8442	8325	-0.7	2.36	5750	5580	-0.7
36203 OXFORD	015	17039	17190	17103	0.2	45	6700	6902	7010	0.7	2.47	4915	5062	0.7
36205 ANNISTON	015	19	19	19	0.0	37	9	9	9	0.0	2.00	3	3	0.0
36206 ANNISTON	015	11955	11217	10758	-1.5	3	4872	4677	4583	-1.0	2.39	3448	3301	-1.0
36207 ANNISTON	015	18050	17864	17576	-0.2	24	7786	7823	7833	0.1	2.24	5122	5154	0.2
36250 ALEXANDRIA	015	3955	4073	4077	0.7	66	1483	1569	1608	1.3	2.59	1157	1220	1.3
36251 ASHLAND	027	5507	5576	5652	0.3	50	2209	2286	2371	0.8	2.34	1557	1611	0.8
36255 CRAGFORD	027	1145	1131	1131	-0.3	22	440	442	451	0.1	2.56	331	331	0.0
36256 DAVISTON	123	1581	1702	1759	1.8	86	626	687	721	2.2	2.48	457	501	2.2
36258 DELTA	027	1668	1712	1753	0.6	64	671	706	739	1.2	2.42	500	526	1.2
36260 EASTABOGA	121	4226	4396	4428	0.9	71	1670	1784	1840	1.6	2.46	1253	1335	1.5
36262 FRUITHURST	029	1269	1239	1253	-0.6	16	490	488	504	-0.1	2.53	366	364	-0.1
36263 GRAHAM	111	733	784	820	1.6	83	263	285	301	1.8	2.75	197	213	1.9
ALABAMA					0.5					0.9	2.45			0.9
UNITED STATES					1.2					1.3	2.58			1.1

ZIP CODE #	POST OFFICE NAME	RACE (%) White 2000	White 2004	Black 2000	Black 2004	Asian/Pacific 2000	Asian/Pacific 2004	% Hispanic Origin 2000	% Hispanic Origin 2004	2004 AGE DISTRIBUTION (%) 0-4	5-9	10-14	15-19	20-24	25-44	45-64	65-84	85+	18+	MEDIAN AGE 2004	% 2004 Males	% 2004 Females
35973	GAYLESVILLE	96.3	96.0	2.1	2.2	0.1	0.2	0.3	0.3	6.2	6.2	6.8	6.1	5.5	27.4	26.6	13.6	1.6	77.1	39.2	49.2	50.9
35974	GERALDINE	98.3	98.0	0.0	0.0	0.1	0.1	0.8	1.1	7.0	7.1	7.2	6.0	5.9	26.5	23.6	14.2	2.5	75.3	38.4	48.0	52.0
35975	GROVEOAK	97.5	97.2	0.0	0.0	0.0	0.0	0.6	0.8	6.7	6.6	6.5	5.7	6.0	26.5	27.0	13.7	1.2	77.0	39.5	49.8	50.2
35976	GUNTERSVILLE	93.1	92.5	4.1	4.3	0.3	0.4	2.3	3.0	5.7	5.9	6.7	6.0	5.4	26.6	27.2	14.7	1.9	78.0	41.1	49.0	51.0
35978	HENAGAR	96.8	96.4	0.1	0.1	0.0	0.1	0.8	1.0	7.3	7.3	6.5	5.7	5.8	28.7	25.3	12.2	1.3	75.5	37.0	49.3	50.7
35979	HIGDON	98.0	97.6	0.1	0.1	0.1	0.1	0.6	0.9	6.5	6.6	7.5	6.3	6.0	29.2	24.9	12.0	1.1	75.7	37.0	49.7	50.3
35980	HORTON	94.2	92.6	0.1	0.1	0.1	0.1	5.7	7.5	7.6	7.6	7.2	6.4	6.8	30.4	23.5	9.6	1.0	73.7	34.8	50.7	49.3
35981	IDER	97.5	97.1	0.0	0.0	0.0	0.1	0.5	0.6	6.6	6.8	7.1	6.1	5.6	27.8	25.5	13.1	1.3	75.8	38.1	49.0	51.0
35983	LEESBURG	94.4	93.7	3.1	3.2	0.2	0.2	2.0	2.6	6.1	6.3	6.1	5.5	5.9	26.6	28.0	14.1	1.3	77.9	40.4	50.6	49.5
35984	MENTONE	94.6	93.9	1.1	1.2	0.1	0.1	1.2	1.5	5.5	5.7	6.3	6.1	6.2	24.2	30.9	13.3	1.8	78.7	41.8	49.7	50.3
35986	RAINSVILLE	96.7	95.9	0.2	0.2	0.2	0.2	2.2	3.1	6.6	6.8	7.0	5.6	5.9	28.9	25.3	12.5	1.5	76.2	38.0	48.5	51.5
35987	STEELE	95.2	94.4	1.6	1.8	0.1	0.1	3.3	4.2	6.3	6.3	6.4	5.8	6.0	29.1	25.9	13.0	1.2	77.2	38.6	49.3	50.7
35988	SYLVANIA	96.2	95.6	0.2	0.1	0.2	0.2	1.6	2.1	7.3	7.0	6.4	6.0	6.3	29.0	26.1	10.7	1.3	75.7	36.9	49.4	50.6
35989	VALLEY HEAD	94.0	92.8	0.8	0.9	0.1	0.2	4.0	5.4	6.9	7.0	7.0	5.7	6.5	27.5	26.4	11.9	1.2	75.7	37.4	49.2	50.8
36003	AUTAUGAVILLE	40.7	39.9	58.2	59.1	0.1	0.0	0.7	0.7	7.4	7.3	7.7	7.2	6.6	26.8	25.1	10.8	1.3	73.2	35.9	48.8	51.2
36005	BANKS	77.5	76.3	19.4	20.2	0.0	0.0	0.7	1.0	5.5	6.2	8.3	6.5	5.4	26.3	26.8	13.3	1.8	75.9	39.3	48.9	51.1
36006	BILLINGSLEY	75.3	74.7	22.7	23.1	0.2	0.2	1.2	1.4	7.7	7.6	7.7	6.8	7.0	27.8	23.4	10.7	1.2	72.8	35.0	49.6	50.4
36009	BRANTLEY	75.1	74.9	23.7	23.9	0.0	0.0	0.5	0.5	5.7	5.7	7.4	5.7	4.9	25.7	27.1	15.8	2.0	77.4	41.4	46.4	53.6
36010	BRUNDIDGE	55.5	55.6	42.0	41.8	0.2	0.2	0.9	1.0	5.7	5.8	6.5	6.5	6.2	23.9	27.4	15.9	2.2	78.1	41.7	47.0	53.0
36013	CECIL	52.8	48.8	46.0	50.0	0.0	0.0	0.8	1.2	5.8	6.2	7.0	8.7	5.8	25.2	29.3	10.3	1.7	76.0	40.4	47.5	52.5
36016	CLAYTON	40.7	39.2	57.3	58.4	0.1	0.1	1.6	2.0	6.0	6.0	6.3	5.9	9.4	34.4	21.5	9.1	1.6	78.3	34.5	59.5	40.6
36017	CLIO	48.8	47.4	46.8	47.5	0.3	0.3	3.3	3.9	3.8	4.1	4.7	5.3	9.2	37.9	23.9	9.5	1.6	84.6	36.7	65.3	34.7
36020	COOSADA	52.0	50.4	46.2	47.7	0.3	0.3	0.7	0.7	8.1	7.8	9.1	7.4	6.7	27.9	21.7	10.5	0.9	70.6	33.6	49.8	50.2
36022	DEATSVILLE	90.0	88.9	7.8	8.5	0.3	0.3	1.3	1.7	7.4	7.3	7.7	7.1	6.8	31.5	23.4	8.0	1.0	73.3	34.7	51.1	48.9
36024	ECLECTIC	85.5	84.7	12.9	13.5	0.1	0.1	1.1	1.3	6.3	6.4	7.0	6.7	5.9	26.3	27.4	12.3	1.5	76.1	39.6	49.3	50.7
36025	ELMORE	64.8	63.8	32.7	33.3	0.3	0.4	1.5	1.8	5.5	5.5	5.7	7.0	11.0	38.4	19.5	6.3	1.2	79.9	32.7	64.8	35.2
36026	EQUALITY	81.7	81.0	16.6	17.2	0.1	0.1	0.8	0.8	6.0	5.7	5.4	4.1	4.2	23.7	32.0	17.6	1.3	80.3	45.6	50.9	49.1
36027	EUFAULA	56.3	55.1	41.5	42.4	0.4	0.5	1.3	1.5	7.0	7.1	7.8	7.5	6.5	26.0	24.5	11.9	1.8	73.4	36.8	47.3	52.7
36028	DOZIER	77.5	77.1	21.3	21.6	0.1	0.1	0.3	0.3	5.9	6.0	7.3	6.8	5.7	25.0	25.9	15.2	2.2	76.3	40.3	46.9	53.1
36029	FITZPATRICK	37.2	35.8	61.9	63.2	0.2	0.2	1.6	1.6	6.3	6.5	6.9	6.7	6.6	25.6	27.5	12.1	2.0	76.5	39.6	48.9	51.1
36030	FOREST HOME	53.2	51.7	46.4	47.9	0.0	0.0	0.5	0.6	7.2	6.5	7.0	7.3	8.3	24.4	24.8	12.3	2.2	74.8	37.4	50.0	50.0
36031	FORT DAVIS	12.3	11.5	86.8	87.5	0.0	0.0	0.9	1.0	7.7	7.7	6.7	8.7	6.7	20.2	28.9	12.5	1.0	72.1	38.0	41.4	58.7
36032	FORT DEPOSIT	34.8	33.6	64.7	65.9	0.2	0.2	0.6	0.6	8.2	7.9	8.5	7.8	6.5	25.4	22.4	11.4	1.9	70.6	34.9	46.0	54.0
36033	GEORGIANA	57.8	57.7	41.6	41.6	0.0	0.0	0.6	0.6	6.3	6.2	6.5	6.6	6.3	22.6	26.5	15.9	3.1	76.8	41.6	46.8	53.2
36034	GLENWOOD	85.0	84.5	12.1	12.4	0.0	0.0	0.8	1.1	5.4	6.0	7.5	7.0	4.6	27.2	27.4	13.1	1.8	76.5	39.8	49.6	50.4
36035	GOSHEN	75.9	75.1	22.4	23.2	0.0	0.0	1.4	1.7	6.1	6.2	6.5	5.6	5.3	25.2	28.2	14.7	2.3	77.8	41.6	49.2	50.8
36036	GRADY	64.0	60.8	35.0	38.1	0.1	0.1	0.8	1.0	6.1	6.2	6.7	6.1	6.2	26.1	27.8	13.1	1.8	77.3	40.4	49.3	50.7
36037	GREENVILLE	56.8	55.3	42.4	43.7	0.2	0.3	0.7	0.8	6.7	6.4	7.7	7.3	7.6	24.6	24.7	12.6	2.3	74.6	37.5	47.2	52.8
36038	GANTT	95.2	94.8	3.5	3.7	0.1	0.1	0.3	0.4	5.6	5.9	6.4	7.0	5.7	26.3	25.9	15.2	2.0	77.8	40.8	50.8	49.2
36039	HARDAWAY	10.4	9.8	88.8	89.4	0.0	0.0	0.5	0.5	7.1	7.3	8.3	9.1	6.6	24.9	24.2	10.8	1.8	71.8	35.3	44.6	55.4
36040	HAYNEVILLE	10.0	9.2	89.5	90.1	0.1	0.1	0.5	0.5	7.6	7.7	8.9	9.1	8.6	26.0	21.3	9.5	1.4	70.3	31.7	46.4	53.6
36041	HIGHLAND HOME	71.4	71.0	27.2	27.6	0.1	0.1	0.9	0.9	6.4	6.7	7.4	6.3	7.0	26.9	25.3	12.5	1.6	75.7	37.6	49.3	50.7
36042	HONORAVILLE	78.0	77.5	20.6	21.0	0.2	0.2	0.9	1.0	6.5	6.5	7.4	6.6	6.9	27.2	25.1	12.3	1.6	75.5	37.4	49.6	50.4
36043	HOPE HULL	58.6	55.4	40.3	43.3	0.1	0.1	0.8	0.9	6.3	6.5	6.7	6.2	5.7	25.9	28.4	13.1	1.2	76.6	40.4	49.1	50.9
36046	LAPINE	75.4	74.0	23.1	24.6	0.1	0.1	0.8	0.9	6.3	6.5	7.1	6.2	6.7	26.2	27.1	12.6	1.3	76.3	38.9	50.2	49.8
36047	LETOHATCHEE	33.9	32.3	65.4	67.0	0.1	0.1	0.7	0.8	8.5	8.2	8.5	7.6	6.4	25.8	23.7	10.1	1.3	70.1	34.5	47.3	52.7
36048	LOUISVILLE	41.3	40.6	56.6	56.7	0.0	0.0	2.2	2.9	5.9	6.0	7.5	7.4	7.0	24.8	25.4	14.0	2.0	76.1	37.4	46.2	53.8
36049	LUVERNE	72.5	72.1	26.2	26.6	0.1	0.1	0.5	0.5	5.8	6.0	7.1	6.2	6.4	24.1	25.3	15.8	3.4	77.2	40.9	47.0	53.0
36051	MARBURY	82.4	81.2	15.3	16.2	0.3	0.3	1.9	2.3	6.5	6.8	7.7	7.5	6.9	27.7	24.5	11.0	1.5	74.3	36.6	49.5	50.5
36052	MATHEWS	58.8	56.4	40.3	42.7	0.3	0.3	0.9	0.9	5.7	6.3	7.3	7.6	5.2	26.9	29.2	10.7	1.2	75.7	39.4	50.7	49.3
36053	MIDWAY	19.6	19.7	79.4	79.3	0.1	0.1	0.6	0.7	5.6	5.8	7.8	7.2	7.6	27.0	24.0	12.3	2.8	76.5	37.6	49.9	50.1
36054	MILLBROOK	78.7	77.6	18.8	19.4	0.5	0.6	1.3	1.6	8.5	8.2	8.5	7.5	7.1	31.6	21.2	6.8	0.5	70.2	31.6	48.1	51.9
36061	PEROTE	37.5	36.4	61.4	62.3	0.0	0.0	1.2	0.9	6.8	7.2	8.5	6.8	5.9	23.7	25.9	12.7	2.5	72.5	38.0	47.0	53.0
36064	PIKE ROAD	57.7	54.8	40.8	43.6	0.7	0.8	0.6	0.7	7.4	7.8	8.0	7.8	5.4	27.4	27.5	7.9	0.8	71.9	36.7	48.6	51.4
36066	PRATTVILLE	89.6	88.3	7.7	8.5	0.9	1.1	1.9	2.4	7.0	7.1	8.5	7.1	5.8	29.9	23.9	9.9	0.8	73.0	36.3	48.2	51.8
36067	PRATTVILLE	77.7	76.9	20.2	20.7	0.4	0.5	1.2	1.5	7.1	7.1	8.0	7.3	6.9	28.8	24.2	9.6	1.1	73.4	35.3	48.3	51.7
36069	RAMER	59.1	54.9	40.2	44.3	0.1	0.1	0.4	0.5	5.1	5.3	6.1	6.6	5.9	25.0	29.4	15.1	1.6	79.6	42.4	49.2	50.8
36071	RUTLEDGE	73.9	73.6	24.3	24.7	0.5	0.5	0.8	0.8	6.2	6.1	6.7	6.5	6.2	27.3	25.6	13.5	2.1	77.2	38.7	48.3	51.7
36075	SHORTER	19.0	18.1	80.1	81.0	0.1	0.1	0.2	0.2	6.7	7.0	8.8	7.9	6.9	26.6	24.2	10.3	1.7	72.7	36.5	46.2	53.8
36078	TALLASSEE	77.6	76.4	20.9	22.0	0.2	0.2	1.0	1.2	6.9	6.8	7.6	6.7	6.2	26.4	24.0	13.2	2.2	74.6	37.5	48.1	51.9
36079	TROY	71.6	70.4	25.6	26.4	0.2	0.3	1.5	1.8	7.1	6.7	6.7	7.1	8.1	31.0	22.8	9.4	1.1	75.3	33.0	49.2	50.8
36080	TITUS	88.0	87.5	10.5	11.0	0.1	0.1	0.7	0.8	5.2	5.5	6.4	4.4	4.4	24.7	32.3	15.6	1.5	80.2	44.6	50.9	49.1
36081	TROY	53.3	51.9	44.0	45.1	0.6	0.7	1.1	1.4	7.0	6.6	6.6	9.2	13.1	25.3	20.6	9.8	1.9	76.1	30.2	46.4	53.6
36082	TROY	67.1	65.3	29.5	30.7	1.2	1.6	1.5	2.2	0.3	0.3	0.0	37.8	53.9	3.4	0.3	1.6	2.5	99.4	21.1	44.9	55.1
36083	TUSKEGEE	7.5	7.2	91.4	91.6	0.2	0.2	0.8	0.8	7.1	7.5	8.0	7.5	7.2	22.6	24.8	12.8	2.6	72.9	36.0	45.4	54.6
36088	TUSKEGEE INSTITUTE	2.7	2.5	94.8	94.5	1.3	1.6	0.6	0.6	4.7	4.7	4.7	18.7	23.5	17.9	14.1	10.0	1.8	83.2	23.7	46.1	53.9
36089	UNION SPRINGS	25.4	24.8	72.8	73.2	0.2	0.3	3.1	3.7	6.8	6.5	7.6	6.9	8.1	30.0	22.3	9.8	2.2	74.9	34.3	53.7	46.3
36091	VERBENA	84.0	82.8	14.3	15.3	0.2	0.2	1.2	1.5	7.1	7.3	7.6	6.8	6.2	27.2	26.1	10.6	1.2	73.8	36.1	50.7	49.3
36092	WETUMPKA	68.7	67.2	28.5	29.5	0.5	0.6	1.4	1.7	6.1	6.1	6.4	6.2	7.5	34.1	23.1	8.9	1.6	77.6	35.6	50.4	49.6
36093	WETUMPKA	90.2	89.0	7.7	8.5	0.7	0.9	1.0	1.2	6.2	6.9	7.1	6.0	4.6	26.4	31.1	10.9	0.9	76.0	40.9	49.3	50.7
36104	MONTGOMERY	13.9	12.4	85.0	86.4	0.2	0.2	0.7	0.7	8.1	8.0	7.8	8.8	8.9	26.3	19.3	10.5	2.3	72.2	31.1	47.6	52.4
36105	MONTGOMERY	9.2	8.3	89.7	90.5	0.2	0.2	0.7	0.8	7.0	7.0	8.5	8.2	7.7	25.7	23.9	10.7	1.3	72.5	34.1	45.4	54.6
36106	MONTGOMERY	67.2	64.8	30.7	32.8	0.8	1.0	1.0	1.2	5.2	5.1	5.3	11.6	11.0	24.7	23.3	11.6	2.2	81.2	34.5	46.0	54.0
36107	MONTGOMERY	65.7	62.1	31.7	35.0	0.7	0.8	1.1	1.3	6.9	6.6	7.0	6.4	6.9	31.6	20.8	11.0	2.9	75.7	35.1	46.0	54.0
36108	MONTGOMERY	15.7	14.3	82.8	84.1	0.3	0.3	0.9	0.9	7.9	8.0	8.7	8.3	7.4	24.3	23.0	11.0	1.4	70.3	32.9	45.4	54.6
36109	MONTGOMERY	89.5	87.8	8.0	9.3	1.1	1.4	1.1	1.3	5.4	5.5	6.1	6.5	6.2	24.8	26.6	16.7	2.3	79.2	42.1	46.3	53.7
36110	MONTGOMERY	45.1	42.0	51.8	54.5	1.4	1.6	1.0	1.1	6.9	7.0	8.0	7.3	6.9	29.1	22.2	11.3	1.2	73.7	35.0	47.7	52.3
36111	MONTGOMERY	62.6	59.1	35.3	38.5	0.7	0.8	1.4	1.6	6.1	6.1	6.5	6.4	7.3	24.1	23.2	17.0	3.5	77.6	40.2	45.6	54.4
36112	MONTGOMERY	62.7	58.6	31.2	34.6	1.3	1.6	3.4	4.1	4.1	4.0	2.4	9.2	36.3	36.8	7.1	0.2	0.1	88.8	24.2	73.6	26.4
36115	MONTGOMERY	63.6	59.4	29.1	32.4	3.9	4.2	3.3	3.9	9.9	9.8	9.3	8.4	15.1	43.9	3.4	0.2	0.0	66.9	24.2	54.2	45.8
36116	MONTGOMERY	29.3	29.0	68.0	68.1	1.0	1.2	1.3	1.5	8.4	8.1	8.4	7.6	8.0	32.2	20.1	6.0	1.2	70.5	30.6	45.8	54.2
36117	MONTGOMERY	69.2	66.4	26.4	28.5	2.4	2.8	1.8	2.1	6.7	6.5	6.0	6.3	7.4	33.7	24.3	8.2	0.9	77.1	35.1	49.7	50.3
36201	ANNISTON	53.0	52.5	45.1	45.4	0.2	0.3	1.2	1.5	6.7	6.9	7.2	6.5	6.3	26.4	24.5	13.7	1.9	75.4	38.1	47.1	52.9
36203	OXFORD	82.6	80.7	14.3	15.6	0.6	0.8	2.8	3.5	6.3	6.5	7.1	6.0	6.2	29.1	25.7	11.6	1.4	76.4	37.8	48.1	51.9
36205	ANNISTON	84.2	84.2	0.0	0.0	15.8	15.8	0.0	0.0	10.5	10.5	0.0	10.5	0.0	42.1	21.1	5.3	0.0	73.7	31.9	57.9	42.1
36206	ANNISTON	79.8	77.6	16.9	18.5	1.0	1.3	1.9	2.3	6.5	6.1	6.3	6.6	7.0	27.6	25.9	13.0	1.0	77.1	37.7	47.5	52.5
36207	ANNISTON	79.9	78.7	17.8	18.6	0.9	1.1	1.5	2.0	5.6	5.9	6.1	5.3	5.1	25.8	27.3	16.1	2.9	79.2	42.5	47.3	52.7
36250	ALEXANDRIA	91.3	90.1	7.0	7.8	0.5	0.7	0.6	0.8	6.7	6.9	7.2	6.5	6.5	29.9	26.4	9.2	0.6	75.3	36.3	48.6	51.4
36251	ASHLAND	85.5	84.7	13.0	13.7	0.1	0.1	2.1	2.7	6.1	6.2	6.5	6.2	5.8	27.1	24.6	14.5	3.1	77.5	39.8	48.6	51.4
36255	CRAGFORD	96.7	96.4	1.5	1.5	0.2	0.2	1.1	1.2	6.5	6.9	6.9	6.4	6.5	27.9	24.8	12.4	1.9	75.9	37.2	51.2	48.8
36256	DAVISTON	82.7	80.9	16.3	18.0	0.1	0.1	0.8	0.9	5.8	6.0	7.2	6.6	6.5	28.3	26.4	11.3	1.9	77.1	39.0	47.5	52.5
36258	DELTA	93.4	92.8	4.2	4.4	0.1	0.2	2.1	2.8	5.7	5.9	6.5	6.1	5.8	27.8	26.7	13.8	1.6	78.0	39.7	49.9	50.1
36260	EASTABOGA	85.3	84.1	12.5	13.4	0.1	0.2	1.0	1.2	6.2	6.5	6.6	6.0	6.2	29.2	27.7	10.6	1.0	77.1	38.1	49.5	50.5
36262	FRUITHURST	97.5	97.1	1.1	1.3	0.1	0.2	0.2	0.4	6.5	6.7	7.1	6.1	6.1	30.0	26.2	10.3	1.1	76.0	37.7	50.4	49.6
36263	GRAHAM	86.8	85.5	11.2	12.1	0.3	0.3	2.1	2.4	6.0	6.4	7.7	7.0	5.9	28.4	25.6	11.9	1.2	75.5	38.5	48.5	51.5
	ALABAMA	71.1	70.3	26.0	26.4	0.7	0.9	1.7	2.1	6.7	6.7	7.0	6.8	7.2	28.0	24.5	11.6	1.6	75.8	36.6	48.5	51.5
	UNITED STATES	75.1	73.6	12.3	12.5	3.8	4.2	12.5	14.1	6.9	6.7	7.2	7.0	7.3	28.6	23.8	10.8	1.7	75.1	36.0	49.1	50.9

#	POST OFFICE NAME	2004 Per Capita Income	2004 HH Income Base	2004 Household Income Distribution (%): Less than $25,000	$25,000 to $49,999	$50,000 to $99,999	$100,000 to $149,999	$150,000 or More	Median Household Income: 2004	2009	2004 National Centile	2004 State Centile	2004 Home Value Base	2004 Home Value Distribution (%): Less than $50,000	$50,000 to $89,999	$90,000 to $174,999	$175,000 to $399,999	$400,000 or More	2004 Median Home Value
35973	GAYLESVILLE	14103	1346	43.1	36.6	18.4	1.5	0.5	29938	32566	12	29	1149	34.6	31.9	26.6	6.1	0.8	68271
35974	GERALDINE	17616	633	42.7	34.6	17.4	4.3	1.1	30140	32990	13	30	520	29.2	30.2	30.8	8.1	1.7	80200
35975	GROVEOAK	18037	467	32.6	33.0	28.3	4.3	1.9	37880	42058	39	66	400	31.0	15.0	39.3	11.8	3.0	94000
35976	GUNTERSVILLE	22430	6660	33.5	31.5	24.1	7.2	3.7	35665	39632	30	57	5168	19.6	20.3	35.7	17.6	7.0	103448
35978	HENAGAR	16790	1773	35.9	33.4	25.3	4.0	1.4	34285	37883	25	50	1485	33.3	30.3	29.2	7.1	0.1	73269
35979	HIGDON	18499	453	37.5	30.5	26.5	3.5	2.0	33205	36228	22	46	383	42.8	32.9	16.2	8.1	0.0	61912
35980	HORTON	15177	1653	38.1	34.2	22.9	3.7	1.0	31834	35544	17	39	1353	34.3	23.7	30.7	9.4	2.0	74167
35981	IDER	17323	1104	38.7	30.6	25.8	3.4	1.5	32190	35525	18	41	914	39.8	29.9	24.7	5.3	0.3	66076
35983	LEESBURG	19292	1329	33.9	37.4	22.9	3.2	2.6	36179	40092	32	59	1129	33.0	29.8	26.2	9.7	1.4	72423
35984	MENTONE	16943	838	40.2	32.2	21.8	5.4	0.4	31452	34705	16	37	704	32.4	29.0	23.9	12.5	2.3	73000
35986	RAINSVILLE	18004	2972	39.9	28.9	25.5	4.2	1.6	32545	35531	19	43	2426	26.3	31.6	30.6	8.9	2.6	80495
35987	STEELE	18484	1021	31.5	34.8	26.5	4.8	2.4	37337	41431	37	65	857	28.8	32.8	29.5	6.2	2.7	75379
35988	SYLVANIA	17057	837	38.5	32.4	25.0	2.6	1.6	32895	36281	21	45	705	32.6	32.5	26.5	7.5	0.9	71349
35989	VALLEY HEAD	17740	1233	36.1	34.7	22.3	4.1	2.8	33622	37396	23	48	1024	35.4	27.0	25.7	10.3	1.8	70921
36003	AUTAUGAVILLE	15848	886	44.8	29.7	22.0	2.0	1.5	28991	32783	10	24	733	48.7	29.6	14.3	5.3	2.1	51319
36005	BANKS	19086	529	41.2	37.2	18.9	1.1	1.5	32406	36711	19	42	446	41.9	26.7	22.4	8.7	0.2	59730
36006	BILLINGSLEY	16701	595	36.8	29.2	29.2	2.9	1.9	35054	38968	28	54	505	40.4	23.0	26.5	8.1	2.0	66500
36009	BRANTLEY	16345	1126	49.3	32.2	13.3	2.6	2.6	25272	27828	5	15	897	45.2	30.6	19.2	4.8	0.3	53686
36010	BRUNDIDGE	14238	1983	53.9	28.3	14.0	2.7	1.1	22638	25734	3	9	1486	43.1	35.0	16.6	4.0	1.2	55050
36013	CECIL	22000	97	35.1	25.8	19.6	15.5	4.1	38055	43284	39	67	84	25.0	13.1	13.1	35.7	13.1	162500
36016	CLAYTON	12981	1651	50.4	27.6	17.8	2.6	1.6	24696	27583	4	14	1341	45.6	33.8	16.9	3.1	0.7	53839
36017	CLIO	12068	772	58.2	22.3	15.0	2.9	1.7	20187	22692	2	4	636	56.3	23.6	15.1	3.5	1.6	43548
36020	COOSADA	16341	518	34.2	29.0	30.1	4.3	2.5	40231	43380	47	75	432	33.6	27.6	32.4	5.1	1.4	74286
36022	DEATSVILLE	21002	3696	18.6	30.8	38.6	9.5	2.4	50378	55948	73	92	3180	18.1	21.9	43.1	15.9	1.0	99969
36024	ECLECTIC	21371	2194	28.6	31.6	28.6	8.1	3.1	40845	45395	49	77	1853	22.4	27.0	29.4	16.0	5.1	90528
36025	ELMORE	15511	980	15.8	29.3	40.7	10.4	3.8	53826	60298	78	94	871	13.0	25.4	51.0	10.2	0.5	100968
36026	EQUALITY	28412	506	28.7	23.9	29.5	8.9	9.1	45331	50000	62	87	451	14.2	18.4	31.5	26.2	9.8	133654
36027	EUFAULA	18113	6892	43.0	26.5	22.0	5.8	2.7	30369	34853	13	31	5004	26.8	31.5	27.3	12.6	1.8	77910
36028	DOZIER	15284	395	51.9	30.9	12.9	2.3	2.0	23843	26703	4	12	309	46.0	31.4	20.4	1.9	0.3	53205
36029	FITZPATRICK	16054	392	38.8	31.1	25.8	2.3	2.0	35981	40684	31	58	339	35.7	24.5	25.4	12.4	2.1	71667
36030	FOREST HOME	13474	311	47.6	27.7	19.0	3.9	1.9	26120	30246	6	18	263	42.6	28.5	20.5	7.2	1.1	59750
36031	FORT DAVIS	18732	41	46.3	26.8	17.1	7.3	2.4	31134	37388	15	35	34	50.0	17.7	26.5	5.9	0.0	50000
36032	FORT DEPOSIT	15124	1068	50.2	22.0	20.5	3.6	3.8	24862	28394	4	15	810	46.2	25.8	20.6	5.6	1.9	55439
36033	GEORGIANA	17882	1905	48.8	28.9	16.9	2.6	2.7	25824	29180	6	16	1535	53.4	25.2	14.9	5.6	0.9	46379
36034	GLENWOOD	21612	265	37.4	30.2	27.2	3.0	2.3	35819	40246	31	58	225	46.2	22.2	19.1	8.4	4.0	53269
36035	GOSHEN	17988	703	37.8	32.3	23.6	4.8	1.4	33525	37163	22	47	596	38.4	28.4	23.0	8.6	1.7	66071
36036	GRADY	18388	769	41.9	24.5	28.4	2.5	2.9	32908	36316	21	45	646	30.5	24.8	32.2	9.9	2.6	79355
36037	GREENVILLE	18573	5612	46.7	28.4	17.6	3.9	3.4	27346	30987	8	21	4192	37.5	28.6	25.6	7.1	1.2	65348
36038	GANTT	17556	1544	40.9	26.8	26.2	3.8	2.3	29797	33170	12	28	1300	34.6	25.9	27.0	9.9	2.6	70000
36039	HARDAWAY	13560	151	57.6	23.8	13.9	3.3	1.3	20480	23669	2	4	118	41.5	22.0	25.4	9.3	1.7	60000
36040	HAYNEVILLE	11196	1796	56.0	26.3	14.7	2.0	1.0	21260	24134	2	6	1421	49.9	27.5	14.4	6.3	2.0	50108
36041	HIGHLAND HOME	15907	545	41.5	35.6	17.8	3.3	1.8	30490	33052	13	32	461	45.1	31.9	18.7	3.5	0.9	55000
36042	HONORAVILLE	15151	500	38.4	37.0	20.4	3.8	0.4	32388	35855	19	42	417	41.5	28.8	24.7	3.1	1.9	58875
36043	HOPE HULL	23430	1453	29.9	30.4	28.1	7.6	4.1	40289	45643	47	75	1260	32.2	20.2	26.7	19.0	1.9	85811
36046	LAPINE	16995	637	36.9	33.4	24.7	3.3	1.7	34080	37823	24	49	544	37.3	27.0	28.1	5.0	2.6	65581
36047	LETOHATCHEE	16063	738	48.0	25.6	20.7	3.5	2.2	26366	29654	6	18	587	45.7	23.9	18.6	10.1	1.9	56375
36048	LOUISVILLE	13033	718	54.2	25.2	15.3	3.6	1.7	22927	25982	3	10	604	47.5	30.3	16.4	3.5	2.3	52381
36049	LUVERNE	16994	2038	46.0	28.8	19.1	5.0	1.2	27151	29470	7	20	1475	33.4	33.2	25.1	7.3	1.0	65945
36051	MARBURY	16941	759	32.2	28.9	32.9	4.0	2.1	38258	42491	40	69	654	38.5	23.2	24.8	12.2	1.2	70465
36052	MATHEWS	25586	268	28.0	29.5	27.6	7.1	7.8	37976	42363	39	67	224	29.0	18.8	11.6	31.3	9.4	100000
36053	MIDWAY	14798	959	56.6	23.4	13.6	4.3	2.2	21332	23906	2	6	771	49.8	24.8	18.0	4.4	3.0	50195
36054	MILLBROOK	19370	4300	21.7	33.0	36.0	7.4	1.9	46308	50907	65	88	3386	13.3	28.7	46.1	11.3	0.6	96618
36061	PEROTE	12090	103	56.3	28.2	13.6	1.9	0.0	22370	25767	3	9	82	37.8	13.4	34.2	12.2	2.4	86667
36064	PIKE ROAD	26525	1894	21.1	27.3	29.8	13.7	8.1	51626	60845	75	93	1751	14.8	14.8	27.9	33.5	9.0	145636
36066	PRATTVILLE	25368	5406	16.4	26.7	39.3	14.4	3.2	56268	62207	81	95	4436	4.7	21.2	58.7	14.5	0.9	118659
36067	PRATTVILLE	19724	9039	29.2	28.3	32.8	6.8	2.9	42916	47236	56	83	7306	28.5	28.3	29.1	12.7	1.4	81043
36069	RAMER	21620	1076	34.2	24.9	31.2	5.8	3.9	37499	42084	37	65	908	24.2	28.7	22.9	19.3	4.9	85781
36071	RUTLEDGE	15955	446	45.7	32.3	16.8	4.5	0.7	27981	30623	9	22	354	38.1	34.5	19.5	5.4	2.5	58235
36075	SHORTER	13204	821	53.5	23.9	19.2	2.8	0.6	22666	26376	3	10	680	35.6	27.2	25.6	9.7	1.9	73077
36078	TALLASSEE	17545	4892	40.3	28.1	24.4	4.8	2.4	32278	35875	19	42	3718	32.6	27.8	29.9	8.5	1.2	73682
36079	TROY	18455	3893	40.1	30.4	22.8	3.9	2.9	31331	35467	16	36	2960	39.1	20.0	27.8	10.9	2.1	71231
36080	TITUS	23834	1013	21.2	30.0	40.8	6.1	1.9	47301	51634	67	90	869	11.2	21.9	35.6	28.5	2.9	124059
36081	TROY	16907	5615	48.7	25.6	18.2	5.1	2.4	25890	29134	6	17	3424	32.2	25.0	28.0	13.3	1.5	78151
36082	TROY	9773	0	0.0	0.0	0.0	0.0	0.0	0	0	0	0	0	0.0	0.0	0.0	0.0	0.0	0
36083	TUSKEGEE	16798	4676	51.7	26.5	16.3	3.9	1.6	23462	27067	4	11	3083	24.4	38.3	31.4	5.6	0.4	76683
36088	TUSKEGEE INSTITUTE	15735	1680	53.7	23.5	15.9	4.1	2.9	21840	24937	3	8	827	22.0	40.2	31.6	6.3	0.0	78512
36089	UNION SPRINGS	12966	3371	55.4	26.8	14.2	3.0	0.7	21745	24383	2	8	2567	38.5	31.8	20.5	6.2	3.1	64587
36091	VERBENA	15813	1268	36.4	36.6	22.6	3.6	0.8	32913	36579	21	45	1067	33.9	22.1	27.5	14.3	2.2	79267
36092	WETUMPKA	18512	6525	28.7	34.9	27.7	6.5	2.2	39967	44250	46	74	5225	25.4	27.3	34.6	11.7	1.0	85823
36093	WETUMPKA	30642	2887	12.6	22.0	40.5	15.3	9.6	65993	72457	89	98	2634	7.2	10.1	46.7	32.7	3.2	148736
36104	MONTGOMERY	11881	4477	67.3	20.6	9.2	1.8	1.2	15638	17796	1	2	1451	44.1	27.9	15.6	10.3	2.1	57066
36105	MONTGOMERY	13161	4960	47.8	30.3	17.3	3.6	1.0	26474	29836	6	19	3107	35.5	44.6	15.8	3.3	0.8	58767
36106	MONTGOMERY	31434	5793	18.1	26.4	30.9	14.7	9.9	56110	64194	81	94	4132	4.2	12.0	54.6	24.0	5.1	135538
36107	MONTGOMERY	17088	3988	39.9	36.9	19.3	2.7	1.1	31198	34553	15	35	2207	19.1	69.2	10.3	0.8	0.6	63548
36108	MONTGOMERY	12681	8828	53.3	27.2	15.5	3.1	1.0	22999	26271	3	11	5432	41.3	46.2	11.1	1.0	0.4	55880
36109	MONTGOMERY	25559	10248	22.3	29.7	33.9	11.7	2.5	48195	54164	69	90	8111	4.8	30.0	57.8	6.8	0.6	99704
36110	MONTGOMERY	13863	4904	41.0	37.0	19.1	2.4	0.5	29646	32980	12	27	3524	36.5	50.9	12.1	0.3	0.3	56757
36111	MONTGOMERY	30699	5208	26.3	26.5	27.9	11.3	8.1	47241	52940	67	90	3539	2.3	25.2	43.5	22.4	6.6	126389
36112	MONTGOMERY	11821	534	31.3	38.6	23.8	5.6	0.8	36501	40626	34	61	3	0.0	100.0	0.0	0.0	0.0	72500
36115	MONTGOMERY	15674	229	9.2	20.1	68.6	2.2	0.0	57165	64335	82	95	0	0.0	0.0	0.0	0.0	0.0	0
36116	MONTGOMERY	20334	15372	31.0	32.0	27.0	7.3	2.7	38293	42741	40	69	9448	13.0	37.9	38.4	9.6	1.1	89283
36117	MONTGOMERY	32789	17621	16.1	26.4	34.0	14.6	8.9	57601	66414	82	95	12086	2.1	12.4	46.6	32.2	6.7	147596
36201	ANNISTON	14238	8442	53.6	27.4	15.2	2.7	1.2	22821	25795	3	10	5634	44.9	37.7	14.8	2.1	0.5	53997
36203	OXFORD	21041	6902	30.1	29.1	31.4	7.1	2.4	41157	45506	50	78	5275	16.3	31.0	39.5	12.1	1.1	92894
36205	ANNISTON	17004	9	0.0	100.0	0.0	0.0	0.0	34225	34225	25	50	5	0.0	100.0	0.0	0.0	0.0	68333
36206	ANNISTON	20966	4677	29.0	35.6	27.2	5.5	2.8	39649	43453	45	73	3472	22.5	37.4	31.9	7.7	0.5	80201
36207	ANNISTON	27527	7823	30.3	30.4	25.5	8.0	5.7	39584	44058	45	72	5819	16.5	21.5	40.0	17.9	4.1	109730
36250	ALEXANDRIA	21096	1569	23.5	32.7	32.8	8.0	3.0	46447	51965	65	88	1344	15.9	26.2	45.0	12.0	0.9	97361
36251	ASHLAND	15204	2286	42.8	33.3	20.3	3.0	0.6	29184	31334	11	25	1796	36.4	28.5	28.6	5.7	0.8	66000
36255	CRAGFORD	14812	442	38.0	37.8	21.0	2.3	0.9	31892	35205	18	39	373	33.0	39.7	20.4	7.0	0.0	62167
36256	DAVISTON	16328	687	33.3	39.3	23.4	3.2	0.7	35228	40129	28	55	569	34.5	39.9	19.5	6.0	0.2	63482
36258	DELTA	16815	706	32.2	39.0	25.1	2.8	1.0	34144	37233	24	50	609	32.0	33.0	26.6	5.9	2.5	74083
36260	EASTABOGA	20144	1784	30.0	33.2	29.4	5.3	2.0	37881	42457	39	66	1521	34.4	35.6	26.3	3.4	0.3	72562
36262	FRUITHURST	16755	488	34.0	38.1	24.0	2.9	1.0	35577	39155	30	57	406	36.5	29.3	22.4	11.8	0.0	67097
36263	GRAHAM	13932	285	40.7	32.6	21.8	3.5	1.4	31566	35259	17	37	240	37.1	28.8	21.7	9.2	3.3	70000
	ALABAMA	20998		34.3	28.7	26.3	7.2	3.5	37534	42371				22.7	26.7	33.4	14.6	2.7	90917
	UNITED STATES	25866		24.7	27.1	30.8	10.9	6.5	48124	56710				10.9	15.0	33.7	30.1	10.4	145905

ZIP CODE #	POST OFFICE NAME	FINANCIAL SERVICES: Auto Loan	FINANCIAL SERVICES: Home Loan	FINANCIAL SERVICES: Investments	FINANCIAL SERVICES: Retirement Plans	THE HOME: Home Improvements: Home Repair	THE HOME: Home Improvements: Lawn & Garden	THE HOME: Furnishings: Computers & Hardware	THE HOME: Furnishings: Major Appliances	THE HOME: Furnishings: TV, Radio, Sound Equipment	THE HOME: Furnishings: Furniture	ENTERTAINMENT: Dine out/ Carry out	ENTERTAINMENT: Sports Equipment	ENTERTAINMENT: Fees & Tickets	ENTERTAINMENT: Toys & Games	ENTERTAINMENT: Travel	ENTERTAINMENT: Cable TV	PERSONAL: Apparel & Services	PERSONAL: Auto Repairs	PERSONAL: Health Insurance	PERSONAL: Pets & Supplies
35973	GAYLESVILLE	66	45	21	39	51	59	43	54	52	44	61	65	37	58	44	56	56	54	66	77
35974	GERALDINE	77	51	23	44	58	67	50	62	60	50	70	74	42	66	50	64	64	61	76	88
35975	GROVEOAK	74	61	42	57	66	72	57	66	63	57	76	78	54	76	59	66	71	64	74	87
35976	GUNTERSVILLE	90	69	46	64	75	86	69	79	77	69	92	91	63	88	70	81	85	79	93	102
35978	HENAGAR	80	54	24	46	61	70	52	65	62	53	73	77	44	69	53	67	67	64	80	92
35979	HIGDON	89	60	27	52	68	78	58	72	70	59	82	86	49	77	59	75	74	71	89	103
35980	HORTON	75	51	23	44	57	66	49	61	59	50	69	73	41	65	50	63	63	60	75	87
35981	IDER	79	53	24	46	60	69	51	64	62	52	73	76	44	69	52	67	66	63	79	91
35983	LEESBURG	84	59	30	51	67	76	56	70	67	57	79	83	49	75	58	72	72	69	85	98
35984	MENTONE	70	51	29	45	58	65	49	60	57	49	67	70	42	65	51	61	61	59	72	83
35986	RAINSVILLE	76	56	32	51	61	70	55	64	63	55	75	76	49	72	55	66	69	64	76	86
35987	STEELE	83	60	34	55	66	76	59	70	68	60	81	83	53	78	60	72	75	69	83	94
35988	SYLVANIA	80	54	24	46	61	70	52	65	62	53	73	77	44	69	53	67	67	64	80	92
35989	VALLEY HEAD	85	57	27	50	65	74	55	69	66	56	78	82	47	74	56	71	71	68	85	98
36003	AUTAUGAVILLE	77	52	23	45	59	67	50	62	60	51	71	75	42	67	51	65	64	62	77	89
36005	BANKS	90	60	27	52	68	78	58	73	70	59	82	87	49	78	59	75	75	72	89	103
36006	BILLINGSLEY	81	54	25	47	62	71	52	66	63	53	74	78	45	70	53	68	67	65	81	93
36009	BRANTLEY	71	48	22	41	54	62	46	57	56	47	65	68	39	62	47	60	59	57	71	81
36010	BRUNDIDGE	58	40	24	35	44	52	40	48	48	41	57	57	35	53	41	52	52	48	59	66
36013	CECIL	74	83	88	81	82	84	77	78	76	78	94	89	81	96	78	76	93	76	75	87
36016	CLAYTON	59	40	19	35	45	52	39	48	46	40	54	57	33	51	39	49	50	48	58	67
36017	CLIO	41	27	12	24	31	36	26	33	32	27	38	40	23	35	27	34	34	33	41	47
36020	COOSADA	83	63	37	57	68	75	60	71	68	61	81	84	54	77	60	71	75	70	81	95
36022	DEATSVILLE	89	85	72	84	86	89	80	84	80	82	99	99	78	97	79	78	96	83	82	100
36024	ECLECTIC	91	74	51	69	79	87	72	81	78	72	94	95	66	91	72	80	88	80	90	104
36025	ELMORE	88	87	76	87	87	89	80	84	79	82	98	99	80	98	80	77	95	82	81	99
36026	EQUALITY	116	89	58	80	100	113	85	102	96	84	114	120	75	112	89	103	106	101	121	140
36027	EUFAULA	75	58	41	54	63	71	59	66	66	59	79	77	54	75	59	69	74	66	77	85
36028	DOZIER	67	45	20	38	50	58	43	54	52	44	61	64	37	58	44	56	55	53	66	76
36029	FITZPATRICK	74	50	25	43	56	65	49	60	59	50	69	72	42	65	50	63	63	60	74	85
36030	FOREST HOME	70	47	21	41	53	61	45	57	55	46	64	68	39	61	46	59	58	56	70	81
36031	FORT DAVIS	70	56	58	49	56	69	63	65	73	64	87	70	60	77	61	78	83	67	77	76
36032	FORT DEPOSIT	69	50	34	44	54	63	51	59	60	52	71	68	46	66	51	64	66	59	71	78
36033	GEORGIANA	71	51	34	45	56	66	53	61	63	54	74	70	48	69	53	67	68	62	74	80
36034	GLENWOOD	94	63	29	54	71	82	61	76	73	62	86	91	52	81	62	79	78	75	94	108
36035	GOSHEN	79	53	24	46	60	69	51	64	62	52	72	76	44	68	52	66	66	63	78	90
36036	GRADY	80	56	30	50	63	73	57	68	67	56	78	79	49	74	57	71	71	67	83	91
36037	GREENVILLE	80	59	39	52	64	74	59	68	68	60	81	79	53	77	59	73	75	68	82	91
36038	GANTT	79	53	25	47	61	70	52	65	62	53	73	77	44	69	53	67	66	64	79	92
36039	HARDAWAY	53	42	43	37	42	51	47	49	54	48	65	52	45	58	46	58	62	50	58	57
36040	HAYNEVILLE	46	36	37	32	37	45	41	43	47	42	57	46	39	51	40	51	54	44	51	51
36041	HIGHLAND HOME	76	51	23	44	58	66	49	61	59	50	70	73	42	66	50	64	63	61	76	87
36042	HONORAVILLE	71	48	23	42	55	62	47	58	56	47	66	69	40	62	47	60	60	57	71	82
36043	HOPE HULL	103	83	56	77	88	96	80	91	87	81	105	107	73	101	80	90	99	90	100	117
36046	LAPINE	77	56	32	49	62	70	54	65	62	55	74	77	48	71	55	66	68	64	77	88
36047	LETOHATCHEE	71	53	38	48	57	66	54	62	62	55	74	71	49	69	54	66	69	62	72	80
36048	LOUISVILLE	63	43	19	37	48	55	41	51	50	42	58	61	35	55	42	53	53	51	63	73
36049	LUVERNE	67	49	30	46	54	64	52	60	59	50	70	68	46	66	52	63	64	59	72	76
36051	MARBURY	82	65	41	59	69	76	62	71	68	63	82	84	56	78	62	70	77	71	80	93
36052	MATHEWS	108	89	63	82	95	104	83	96	91	84	110	114	78	108	85	95	103	94	107	126
36053	MIDWAY	59	39	18	34	45	51	38	48	46	39	54	57	33	51	39	50	49	47	59	67
36054	MILLBROOK	81	78	72	79	77	80	77	78	76	78	95	92	75	92	75	73	91	78	74	89
36061	PEROTE	52	35	16	30	40	46	34	42	41	34	48	50	29	45	34	44	43	42	52	60
36064	PIKE ROAD	100	111	115	111	109	113	103	103	99	105	125	117	108	125	104	98	123	101	98	116
36066	PRATTVILLE	93	104	104	105	101	102	96	96	91	97	115	112	99	117	96	88	113	94	88	106
36067	PRATTVILLE	82	76	63	73	77	82	72	77	74	73	91	90	70	89	72	75	87	77	80	93
36069	RAMER	82	70	54	64	74	82	66	75	72	67	87	87	63	87	68	75	82	73	83	96
36071	RUTLEDGE	68	47	24	42	53	61	47	57	56	47	65	67	41	62	48	60	59	56	69	77
36075	SHORTER	61	43	29	38	47	55	44	52	53	45	62	60	39	58	44	57	58	52	63	69
36078	TALLASSEE	71	57	41	53	61	69	57	64	63	57	76	74	53	74	57	66	71	63	73	81
36079	TROY	74	62	43	58	64	70	59	66	63	61	77	77	55	73	59	64	73	66	71	83
36080	TITUS	95	71	44	65	81	91	68	83	78	68	92	98	60	91	72	83	85	82	99	115
36081	TROY	59	49	48	47	50	57	55	55	59	54	72	64	52	68	53	60	69	57	60	65
36082	TROY	0	0	0	0	0	0	0	0	0	0	0	0	0	0	0	0	0	0	0	0
36083	TUSKEGEE	60	47	46	42	48	58	52	55	61	54	73	60	50	65	51	65	69	57	65	66
36088	TUSKEGEE INSTITUTE	58	49	56	46	48	57	56	55	61	57	76	62	55	71	54	63	73	57	60	63
36089	UNION SPRINGS	52	41	37	37	42	50	45	47	51	45	61	53	42	56	44	54	58	48	55	57
36091	VERBENA	73	51	26	44	57	66	49	60	58	49	68	72	42	65	50	62	62	60	73	85
36092	WETUMPKA	75	63	45	59	65	72	61	68	65	61	79	78	57	76	61	67	74	67	74	84
36093	WETUMPKA	106	129	138	129	128	128	117	117	109	116	137	136	124	144	120	107	136	113	107	129
36104	MONTGOMERY	36	30	36	28	29	35	35	34	38	35	47	39	34	44	34	39	45	36	37	39
36105	MONTGOMERY	50	45	49	42	44	51	47	48	52	49	64	52	48	60	47	54	62	49	52	55
36106	MONTGOMERY	102	113	131	115	112	117	111	108	107	111	134	126	115	136	111	105	132	108	102	119
36107	MONTGOMERY	50	51	57	51	50	54	54	52	54	53	67	61	54	68	53	53	66	53	51	57
36108	MONTGOMERY	49	42	43	39	42	49	44	46	49	45	60	51	44	56	44	51	57	47	51	54
36109	MONTGOMERY	78	87	92	84	87	94	82	84	81	82	101	94	86	103	85	82	99	82	84	92
36110	MONTGOMERY	50	47	48	46	48	53	49	50	51	48	63	56	49	62	49	52	61	50	53	57
36111	MONTGOMERY	91	100	120	99	98	107	99	97	98	99	123	110	103	124	101	98	121	97	95	107
36112	MONTGOMERY	72	46	44	52	42	49	68	59	69	63	86	78	58	77	56	63	83	69	54	67
36115	MONTGOMERY	91	57	55	66	53	62	86	74	87	80	109	98	73	97	71	79	104	87	68	84
36116	MONTGOMERY	72	71	79	72	69	74	73	72	73	75	93	84	74	91	72	72	91	73	69	81
36117	MONTGOMERY	105	114	125	118	111	113	112	108	105	112	133	128	114	134	110	101	132	109	97	119
36201	ANNISTON	56	42	32	37	44	52	43	49	50	44	60	56	40	56	43	54	56	49	58	63
36203	OXFORD	82	72	57	70	75	82	70	76	74	70	90	89	67	90	71	76	85	75	82	94
36205	ANNISTON	59	46	31	42	52	58	44	52	49	43	58	62	39	58	46	53	54	52	62	72
36206	ANNISTON	68	72	73	70	72	77	70	71	70	69	87	81	72	91	71	71	85	70	71	79
36207	ANNISTON	92	85	79	83	87	97	86	90	89	85	109	103	83	107	86	91	104	90	96	105
36250	ALEXANDRIA	88	78	59	74	82	88	72	80	77	72	93	95	71	95	74	79	89	78	87	103
36251	ASHLAND	65	47	26	41	52	59	45	54	53	46	62	64	40	60	46	56	57	54	65	74
36255	CRAGFORD	65	49	31	46	53	61	49	56	55	49	66	66	44	64	49	58	61	56	65	75
36256	DAVISTON	76	51	23	44	58	67	49	62	59	50	70	74	42	66	50	64	63	61	76	87
36258	DELTA	77	51	23	44	58	67	50	62	60	51	70	74	42	66	50	65	64	61	76	88
36260	EASTABOGA	83	66	45	63	70	79	65	74	72	66	86	86	60	83	65	74	81	73	82	93
36262	FRUITHURST	80	53	24	46	61	70	52	65	62	53	73	77	44	69	52	67	66	64	80	92
36263	GRAHAM	72	48	22	42	55	63	47	58	56	48	66	70	40	62	47	61	60	58	72	83
	ALABAMA	81	70	61	67	72	80	70	75	75	70	91	87	67	89	70	76	86	75	81	92
	UNITED STATES	100	100	100	100	100	100	100	100	100	100	100	100	100	100	100	100	100	100	100	100

ALABAMA

A 36264-36538

POPULATION CHANGE

# POST OFFICE NAME	COUNTY FIPS CODE	POPULATION 2000	2004	2009	2000-2004 ANNUAL RATE % Rate	State Centile	HOUSEHOLDS 2000	2004	2009	% Annual Rate 2000-2004	2004 Average HH Size	FAMILIES 2000	2004	% Annual Rate 2000-2004
36264 HEFLIN	029	8874	9325	9726	1.2	76	3502	3752	3986	1.6	2.46	2559	2740	1.6
36265 JACKSONVILLE	015	16558	16560	16361	0.0	37	6447	6606	6666	0.6	2.30	4092	4168	0.4
36266 LINEVILLE	027	5026	5222	5371	0.9	71	2091	2228	2346	1.5	2.32	1444	1539	1.5
36267 MILLERVILLE	027	56	53	53	-1.3	3	25	24	25	-1.0	2.21	19	18	-1.3
36268 MUNFORD	121	4958	5030	5054	0.3	53	1882	1955	2013	0.9	2.57	1439	1493	0.9
36269 MUSCADINE	029	1264	1298	1338	0.6	64	492	515	541	1.1	2.51	365	382	1.1
36271 OHATCHEE	015	5516	5820	5885	1.3	78	2143	2320	2399	1.9	2.50	1613	1741	1.8
36272 PIEDMONT	019	13748	13849	13915	0.2	43	5543	5688	5824	0.6	2.43	4041	4143	0.6
36273 RANBURNE	029	2692	2817	2928	1.1	75	1073	1145	1213	1.5	2.46	815	870	1.6
36274 ROANOKE	111	11484	11377	11499	-0.2	25	4380	4407	4520	0.1	2.49	3068	3076	0.1
36276 WADLEY	111	2343	2319	2334	-0.2	24	896	904	925	0.2	2.44	639	643	0.2
36277 WEAVER	015	5155	5055	4937	-0.5	18	2017	2026	2024	0.1	2.50	1535	1539	0.1
36278 WEDOWEE	111	3656	3890	4056	1.5	81	1462	1587	1681	2.0	2.41	1068	1158	1.9
36279 WELLINGTON	015	2433	2365	2300	-0.7	13	966	962	957	-0.1	2.45	719	714	-0.2
36280 WOODLAND	111	3678	4022	4258	2.1	91	1463	1621	1737	2.4	2.48	1103	1219	2.4
36301 DOTHAN	069	32485	32481	33095	0.0	37	13462	13760	14316	0.5	2.34	9200	9388	0.5
36303 DOTHAN	069	28682	29561	30593	0.7	67	11466	12073	12757	1.2	2.40	7867	8281	1.2
36305 DOTHAN	069	9617	10048	10397	1.0	75	3871	4158	4406	1.7	2.35	2780	2976	1.6
36310 ABBEVILLE	067	7016	7072	7202	0.2	44	2800	2886	3006	0.7	2.39	2005	2066	0.7
36311 ARITON	045	2821	2913	2963	0.8	68	1157	1226	1276	1.4	2.21	839	887	1.3
36312 ASHFORD	069	5237	5436	5635	0.9	71	2087	2216	2345	1.4	2.45	1520	1608	1.3
36314 BLACK	061	495	529	562	1.6	83	196	213	230	2.0	2.47	144	156	1.9
36316 CHANCELLOR	061	2037	2109	2192	0.8	69	832	879	931	1.3	2.40	606	639	1.3
36317 CLOPTON	067	625	639	652	0.5	61	247	259	270	1.1	2.47	186	194	1.0
36318 COFFEE SPRINGS	061	1255	1279	1320	0.5	58	507	529	557	1.0	2.42	373	388	0.9
36319 COLUMBIA	067	2597	2732	2831	1.2	77	1069	1151	1219	1.8	2.37	1038	1070	0.7
36320 COTTONWOOD	069	3494	3531	3598	0.3	47	1380	1428	1488	0.8	2.47	1038	1070	0.7
36321 COWARTS	069	1226	1399	1515	3.2	97	488	571	632	3.8	2.45	381	443	3.6
36322 DALEVILLE	045	7604	7394	7346	-0.7	13	3179	3163	3212	-0.1	2.34	2111	2095	-0.2
36323 ELBA	031	8308	8259	8399	-0.1	29	3210	3254	3379	0.3	2.43	2332	2358	0.3
36330 ENTERPRISE	031	28726	29536	30493	0.7	65	11533	12122	12783	1.2	2.41	8127	8536	1.2
36340 GENEVA	061	5680	5829	6126	0.6	64	2348	2453	2626	1.0	2.31	1597	1666	1.0
36343 GORDON	069	1372	1484	1565	1.9	88	525	584	631	2.5	2.54	393	436	2.5
36344 HARTFORD	061	5393	5560	5805	0.7	67	2155	2259	2398	1.1	2.41	1546	1618	1.1
36345 HEADLAND	067	5426	5664	5872	1.0	74	2156	2299	2434	1.5	2.46	1590	1693	1.5
36346 JACK	031	1516	1540	1571	0.4	54	616	638	664	0.8	2.41	466	481	0.8
36349 MALVERN	061	310	332	352	1.6	84	122	134	145	2.2	2.48	92	101	2.4
36350 MIDLAND CITY	045	7098	8084	8836	3.1	97	2869	3328	3708	3.6	2.43	2060	2401	3.7
36351 NEW BROCKTON	031	3227	3488	3704	1.9	88	1258	1390	1507	2.4	2.44	947	1043	2.3
36352 NEWTON	069	4625	4952	5240	1.6	83	1816	1981	2139	2.1	2.50	1375	1488	1.9
36353 NEWVILLE	067	1998	2018	2043	0.2	46	799	826	854	0.8	2.44	591	610	0.8
36360 OZARK	045	19370	19151	19217	-0.3	23	7854	7937	8146	0.3	2.36	5487	5545	0.3
36362 FORT RUCKER	045	6091	5936	5897	-0.6	14	1412	1398	1414	-0.2	3.39	1358	1343	-0.3
36370 PANSEY	069	867	977	1052	2.9	96	336	389	430	3.5	2.51	251	290	3.5
36373 SHORTERVILLE	067	1072	1067	1074	-0.1	31	432	441	454	0.5	2.42	306	312	0.5
36374 SKIPPERVILLE	045	1092	1118	1128	0.6	62	414	433	447	1.1	2.58	320	335	1.1
36375 SLOCOMB	061	6495	6782	7103	1.0	74	2576	2739	2918	1.5	2.48	1900	2017	1.4
36376 WEBB	069	2381	2814	3104	4.0	99	925	1120	1261	4.6	2.51	690	833	4.5
36401 EVERGREEN	035	8119	7995	7892	-0.4	21	3339	3372	3409	0.2	2.35	2243	2262	0.2
36420 ANDALUSIA	039	16828	17106	17388	0.4	55	6962	7221	7487	0.9	2.33	4764	4936	0.8
36425 BEATRICE	099	1369	1397	1438	0.5	59	538	564	597	1.1	2.48	360	376	1.0
36426 BREWTON	053	15875	16141	16319	0.4	55	6422	6676	6896	0.9	2.36	4481	4650	0.9
36432 CASTLEBERRY	035	3444	3434	3410	-0.1	33	1392	1427	1454	0.6	2.41	970	995	0.6
36435 COY	131	876	868	877	-0.2	25	328	339	356	0.8	2.56	213	220	0.8
36436 DICKINSON	025	793	758	749	-1.1	5	274	271	276	-0.3	2.80	200	198	-0.2
36441 FLOMATON	053	3768	3858	3905	0.6	62	1497	1570	1626	1.1	2.46	1102	1155	1.1
36442 FLORALA	039	3541	3557	3570	0.1	41	1565	1601	1636	0.5	2.22	991	1013	0.5
36444 FRANKLIN	099	924	924	944	0.0	37	366	380	400	0.9	2.43	269	279	0.9
36445 FRISCO CITY	099	5671	5886	6121	0.9	71	2217	2359	2520	1.5	2.48	1635	1737	1.4
36446 FULTON	025	227	217	215	-1.1	6	85	84	86	-0.3	2.58	63	63	0.0
36451 GROVE HILL	025	5312	5408	5447	0.4	56	2071	2168	2241	1.1	2.46	1488	1556	1.1
36453 KINSTON	031	2174	2267	2363	1.0	73	904	963	1023	1.5	2.35	658	698	1.2
36454 LENOX	035	554	567	569	0.6	62	237	249	256	1.2	2.28	172	180	1.1
36456 MC KENZIE	013	1286	1244	1211	-0.8	11	545	546	549	0.0	2.28	366	366	0.0
36460 MONROEVILLE	099	12016	12252	12659	0.5	58	4601	4821	5124	1.1	2.50	3311	3465	1.1
36467 OPP	039	10056	9907	9900	-0.4	21	4190	4216	4298	0.2	2.30	2948	2965	0.1
36471 PETERMAN	099	1321	1329	1355	0.1	42	533	555	584	1.0	2.39	345	358	0.9
36473 RANGE	035	307	314	315	0.5	61	117	123	126	1.2	2.55	85	89	1.1
36474 RED LEVEL	039	2105	2089	2088	-0.2	27	858	868	884	0.3	2.39	616	622	0.2
36475 REPTON	035	1800	1791	1777	-0.1	30	721	739	753	0.6	2.42	496	509	0.6
36477 SAMSON	061	4584	4663	4826	0.4	56	1913	1988	2098	0.9	2.35	1341	1391	0.9
36480 URIAH	099	1655	1865	2022	2.9	96	650	756	845	3.6	2.47	487	566	3.6
36481 VREDENBURGH	099	963	972	995	0.2	45	322	336	355	1.0	2.89	246	257	1.0
36482 WHATLEY	025	845	831	828	-0.4	20	318	322	330	0.3	2.57	227	230	0.3
36483 WING	039	1965	1961	1967	-0.1	34	791	808	827	0.5	2.42	575	586	0.5
36502 ATMORE	053	18515	18462	18632	-0.1	33	6289	6408	6620	0.4	2.47	4434	4516	0.4
36505 AXIS	097	1710	1718	1700	0.1	41	598	612	615	0.6	2.81	504	514	0.4
36507 BAY MINETTE	003	19081	19930	21730	1.0	75	6886	7359	8204	1.6	2.60	5185	5545	1.6
36509 BAYOU LA BATRE	097	2531	2531	2504	0.0	37	835	851	857	0.5	2.97	662	673	0.4
36511 BON SECOUR	003	482	520	575	1.8	87	187	205	231	2.2	2.54	140	153	2.1
36515 CARLTON	025	29	28	28	-0.8	9	11	11	11	0.0	2.55	9	9	0.0
36518 CHATOM	129	3316	3342	3356	0.2	44	1252	1295	1333	0.8	2.52	930	962	0.8
36521 CHUNCHULA	097	5325	5373	5334	0.2	45	1860	1912	1930	0.7	2.80	1516	1554	0.6
36522 CITRONELLE	097	5897	5867	5793	-0.1	30	2076	2101	2109	0.3	2.74	1626	1641	0.2
36523 CODEN	097	3268	3489	3576	1.6	82	1203	1321	1384	2.2	2.64	909	992	2.1
36524 COFFEEVILLE	025	1344	1293	1280	-0.9	7	585	579	588	-0.2	2.23	375	372	-0.2
36525 CREOLA	097	1540	1525	1500	-0.2	24	552	556	556	0.2	2.74	423	425	0.1
36526 DAPHNE	003	20157	22064	24612	2.2	91	7808	8651	9789	2.4	2.52	5672	6302	2.5
36527 SPANISH FORT	003	7333	8321	9447	3.0	97	2740	3133	3601	3.2	2.62	2098	2396	3.2
36528 DAUPHIN ISLAND	097	1369	1609	1721	3.9	99	600	722	787	4.5	2.23	433	521	4.5
36529 DEER PARK	129	997	1011	1019	0.3	51	338	350	361	0.8	2.89	262	271	0.8
36530 ELBERTA	003	6302	7046	7946	2.7	95	2519	2863	3281	3.1	2.46	1837	2085	3.0
36532 FAIRHOPE	003	22047	24220	27183	2.2	92	9071	10138	11578	2.7	2.36	6371	7148	2.7
36535 FOLEY	003	17330	19393	21874	2.7	95	6989	8007	9219	3.3	2.39	4993	5710	3.2
36538 FRANKVILLE	129	499	502	504	0.1	42	196	203	209	0.8	2.47	145	150	0.8
ALABAMA					0.5					0.9	2.45			0.9
UNITED STATES					1.2					1.3	2.58			1.1

ZIP CODE #	POST OFFICE NAME	RACE (%) White 2000	White 2004	Black 2000	Black 2004	Asian/Pacific 2000	Asian/Pacific 2004	% Hispanic Origin 2000	% Hispanic Origin 2004	2004 AGE DISTRIBUTION (%) 0-4	5-9	10-14	15-19	20-24	25-44	45-64	65-84	85+	18+	MEDIAN AGE 2004	% 2004 Males	% 2004 Females
36264	HEFLIN	92.1	91.5	6.1	6.4	0.2	0.2	1.9	2.4	6.2	6.3	6.9	6.2	6.0	27.6	25.8	13.2	1.7	76.8	38.8	50.4	49.6
36265	JACKSONVILLE	84.2	82.4	12.6	13.9	1.0	1.2	1.5	1.9	5.5	5.4	5.6	9.2	13.4	26.1	22.8	10.7	1.3	80.4	32.5	48.6	51.4
36266	LINEVILLE	74.7	74.0	23.4	23.8	0.2	0.2	2.2	2.7	6.2	6.2	6.6	6.0	6.2	25.9	25.0	15.9	2.2	77.5	40.2	48.8	51.2
36267	MILLERVILLE	62.5	60.4	35.7	37.7	0.0	0.0	0.0	0.0	5.7	5.7	5.7	7.6	7.6	28.3	28.3	11.3	0.0	83.0	38.1	50.9	49.1
36268	MUNFORD	79.4	78.4	19.3	20.1	0.2	0.2	0.6	0.7	6.5	6.8	7.8	6.6	6.0	28.8	26.0	10.7	0.9	74.9	36.5	48.9	51.1
36269	MUSCADINE	98.8	98.7	0.1	0.1	0.2	0.2	0.2	0.3	7.5	7.3	7.0	6.1	6.6	29.6	25.0	10.0	1.0	74.4	35.9	50.5	49.5
36271	OHATCHEE	93.4	92.6	4.8	5.4	0.2	0.2	0.6	0.8	6.6	6.5	6.3	6.6	6.6	28.3	28.2	10.3	0.8	76.8	38.1	50.4	49.6
36272	PIEDMONT	92.5	91.7	6.1	6.6	0.1	0.1	0.9	1.2	6.5	6.5	6.7	5.9	6.0	28.0	26.3	12.7	1.4	76.8	38.6	49.6	50.4
36273	RANBURNE	99.1	98.9	0.0	0.0	0.1	0.1	0.8	1.1	6.2	6.4	7.1	5.9	6.2	27.9	26.4	12.5	1.6	77.0	38.5	50.7	49.3
36274	ROANOKE	69.5	67.8	29.3	30.8	0.3	0.4	1.0	1.2	7.2	7.1	7.3	5.9	6.2	26.1	23.6	13.8	2.7	74.9	37.7	47.9	52.1
36276	WADLEY	76.0	74.3	22.2	23.7	0.1	0.1	1.5	1.8	6.6	6.4	7.3	6.9	8.9	25.4	23.9	12.9	1.8	76.6	36.1	48.3	51.7
36277	WEAVER	87.7	85.9	8.0	9.0	1.7	2.1	1.6	1.9	6.2	6.2	6.5	6.6	6.6	27.3	27.0	12.5	1.0	77.1	38.7	48.3	51.7
36278	WEDOWEE	78.4	77.2	20.2	21.2	0.2	0.3	1.1	1.4	6.0	6.1	6.3	6.1	6.0	25.8	27.2	14.8	1.7	78.0	40.6	50.3	49.7
36279	WELLINGTON	95.6	95.0	2.5	2.8	0.3	0.4	0.8	1.0	5.9	6.2	6.9	6.6	6.2	28.8	27.7	10.7	1.1	77.3	38.1	49.6	50.4
36280	WOODLAND	88.2	87.5	10.5	11.0	0.1	0.2	1.4	1.7	6.3	6.5	7.5	6.5	5.8	27.1	25.6	13.3	1.4	75.7	38.7	49.0	51.0
36301	DOTHAN	75.8	74.2	21.6	22.8	0.7	0.8	1.4	1.7	6.9	6.7	6.8	6.5	6.7	28.2	24.1	12.5	1.7	75.6	37.1	47.3	52.7
36303	DOTHAN	58.0	57.4	39.8	40.0	0.7	0.9	1.2	1.4	6.8	7.1	7.4	7.2	6.4	26.2	25.5	11.5	2.0	74.2	37.3	47.3	52.7
36305	DOTHAN	90.3	88.9	6.5	7.2	1.3	1.7	1.8	2.2	7.3	7.1	6.7	5.8	5.8	30.8	24.4	9.8	2.4	75.3	36.9	47.8	52.2
36310	ABBEVILLE	59.7	58.4	37.6	38.3	0.1	0.1	2.6	3.3	6.1	6.1	6.4	5.8	6.1	24.1	27.2	15.5	2.8	78.0	41.3	48.0	52.0
36311	ARITON	74.3	72.9	23.2	24.1	0.3	0.3	1.4	1.7	5.9	6.1	6.0	5.7	6.4	28.5	26.0	13.3	2.3	78.6	39.5	53.1	46.9
36312	ASHFORD	84.0	83.2	14.7	15.3	0.0	0.1	0.9	1.0	6.3	6.5	6.9	6.4	5.7	27.7	26.1	12.8	1.8	76.5	39.1	48.4	51.6
36314	BLACK	95.0	94.5	3.8	4.0	0.2	0.2	0.2	0.6	5.5	5.5	6.6	7.4	6.6	27.6	27.8	11.5	1.5	78.1	39.7	50.1	49.9
36316	CHANCELLOR	84.8	83.8	13.4	14.0	0.7	0.9	0.8	1.1	5.6	5.9	6.7	6.6	5.4	27.5	26.9	13.5	1.9	77.7	40.0	48.7	51.3
36317	CLOPTON	58.1	56.7	41.1	42.4	0.0	0.0	0.3	0.5	5.5	6.0	6.9	6.4	6.0	26.3	27.5	13.6	1.9	77.6	39.8	50.1	49.9
36318	COFFEE SPRINGS	94.2	93.6	4.0	4.3	0.2	0.3	0.4	0.6	5.6	5.7	5.8	5.4	5.2	26.1	28.9	15.6	1.7	79.6	42.5	48.2	51.8
36319	COLUMBIA	81.1	79.4	17.3	18.7	0.0	0.0	0.8	1.1	6.2	6.2	5.8	5.8	6.2	24.3	28.8	15.1	1.7	78.4	42.1	48.5	51.5
36320	COTTONWOOD	85.8	84.6	12.2	13.2	0.2	0.3	1.3	1.5	6.7	6.8	6.8	6.5	5.9	28.1	25.4	12.4	1.3	75.6	37.9	48.9	51.2
36321	COWARTS	86.8	85.3	11.2	12.4	0.0	0.0	0.9	1.1	6.2	6.4	6.9	6.2	6.1	28.9	26.2	12.1	1.2	76.8	38.6	48.4	51.6
36322	DALEVILLE	70.6	67.8	21.2	22.4	2.8	3.6	3.3	4.1	6.8	6.6	6.6	7.0	7.2	28.2	25.9	11.2	0.6	75.9	36.3	49.6	50.4
36323	ELBA	73.6	72.0	24.1	25.3	0.1	0.1	1.0	1.2	6.1	6.1	6.7	6.7	6.3	26.9	24.9	14.1	2.3	77.1	39.3	50.0	50.0
36330	ENTERPRISE	73.9	72.4	20.4	20.9	1.7	2.1	4.2	5.2	6.6	6.4	6.7	6.7	7.3	27.8	24.7	12.2	1.6	76.3	36.7	48.7	51.3
36340	GENEVA	85.9	85.1	12.6	13.2	0.1	0.1	1.0	1.3	5.6	5.7	6.4	6.9	6.3	25.2	26.2	15.2	2.7	78.1	41.1	48.2	51.8
36343	GORDON	64.8	62.3	33.7	36.2	0.0	0.0	1.0	0.9	6.0	7.4	7.8	7.1	5.2	26.0	27.5	11.5	1.6	74.2	38.2	50.1	49.9
36344	HARTFORD	88.2	87.7	10.2	10.5	0.1	0.1	1.5	1.9	5.5	5.8	6.9	6.4	5.4	25.2	26.0	16.1	2.8	77.8	41.6	48.8	51.2
36345	HEADLAND	73.3	72.5	25.4	26.0	0.1	0.1	0.5	0.6	6.4	7.0	7.0	6.4	5.9	26.7	27.1	11.4	2.0	75.6	38.4	47.8	52.2
36346	JACK	91.4	90.9	4.4	4.7	0.0	0.0	1.1	1.2	5.7	6.0	7.3	6.4	5.2	27.3	26.9	13.3	1.9	77.0	40.0	49.2	50.8
36349	MALVERN	94.5	93.4	2.6	2.7	0.0	0.3	1.9	2.4	6.3	6.3	6.3	6.3	6.0	31.3	25.3	11.1	0.9	77.4	36.9	49.1	50.9
36350	MIDLAND CITY	82.9	82.6	14.2	14.2	0.3	0.4	1.1	1.3	6.5	6.5	7.2	6.6	6.4	26.9	26.6	12.0	1.2	75.7	38.4	49.0	51.0
36351	NEW BROCKTON	84.3	83.3	10.9	11.5	0.3	0.4	1.3	1.7	5.4	5.9	6.3	6.8	5.5	25.5	29.2	13.9	1.4	78.2	41.5	50.5	49.5
36352	NEWTON	89.7	89.0	8.1	8.5	0.2	0.3	1.5	1.8	6.2	6.4	7.0	6.9	6.3	26.3	27.8	11.7	1.4	76.0	39.2	50.4	49.6
36353	NEWVILLE	67.6	65.7	30.8	32.5	0.1	0.1	1.1	1.2	6.6	6.7	6.6	6.1	5.6	26.7	26.2	13.6	1.9	76.4	39.2	48.9	51.1
36360	OZARK	71.4	70.2	25.6	26.3	0.7	0.8	1.9	2.4	6.5	6.2	6.5	6.8	6.6	25.4	26.4	13.5	2.2	76.7	39.5	47.5	52.5
36362	FORT RUCKER	68.6	65.2	18.1	18.9	2.8	3.4	11.6	14.7	15.3	11.1	6.3	5.9	12.6	46.0	2.6	0.2	0.0	65.1	24.5	56.7	43.3
36370	PANSEY	66.9	64.2	31.1	33.7	0.1	0.1	0.7	0.8	5.6	7.8	8.5	7.3	4.8	26.0	27.3	11.2	1.5	73.4	38.0	49.9	50.2
36373	SHORTERVILLE	66.7	64.2	31.1	33.2	0.3	0.4	1.4	1.9	5.9	5.9	6.7	6.4	6.1	26.5	27.5	13.1	2.0	77.9	39.6	48.3	51.7
36374	SKIPPERVILLE	83.9	82.5	14.2	15.4	0.1	0.1	0.7	1.0	5.2	5.6	7.8	7.4	6.2	26.0	27.6	12.6	1.5	76.8	40.3	50.8	49.2
36375	SLOCOMB	87.1	86.2	10.1	10.5	0.1	0.2	3.1	3.8	6.0	6.2	6.9	6.6	5.9	27.6	26.4	12.6	1.9	77.0	39.0	49.8	50.2
36376	WEBB	82.3	80.4	16.3	18.1	0.0	0.0	0.7	0.8	7.3	7.1	6.9	6.5	6.3	28.9	25.4	10.5	1.1	74.3	37.1	48.1	52.0
36401	EVERGREEN	51.5	50.1	47.6	48.9	0.2	0.3	0.7	0.9	6.2	6.8	8.0	6.5	6.0	24.5	25.6	13.8	2.6	75.0	39.2	46.9	53.1
36420	ANDALUSIA	82.1	81.3	16.4	17.0	0.2	0.3	0.8	1.0	6.2	6.3	6.7	6.3	6.2	25.2	25.5	15.1	2.6	77.1	40.2	47.9	52.1
36425	BEATRICE	21.3	19.7	77.8	79.2	0.4	0.4	0.7	0.6	5.1	5.7	8.9	8.1	7.7	21.9	26.1	13.7	2.8	75.3	38.9	49.2	50.8
36426	BREWTON	72.1	70.4	25.4	26.7	0.3	0.4	1.1	1.4	6.0	5.9	7.0	6.4	6.5	25.4	26.6	14.0	2.1	77.3	40.0	47.8	52.2
36432	CASTLEBERRY	62.5	61.4	36.3	37.2	0.2	0.2	0.6	0.7	6.0	6.3	7.3	6.4	6.0	26.6	26.5	13.3	1.6	76.6	39.3	48.2	51.8
36435	COY	18.7	18.1	81.2	81.8	0.0	0.0	0.3	0.2	7.3	7.0	7.4	6.8	7.5	25.4	24.4	12.3	2.0	73.9	35.9	46.1	53.9
36436	DICKINSON	42.8	41.7	56.5	57.4	0.0	0.0	0.9	0.9	7.9	7.8	8.4	7.3	7.0	28.1	21.9	10.4	1.2	71.2	34.6	48.2	51.9
36441	FLOMATON	87.6	86.3	9.2	10.1	0.0	0.1	1.2	1.5	6.2	6.3	7.2	6.7	6.6	27.0	26.3	12.5	1.2	76.1	38.2	48.6	51.4
36442	FLORALA	83.5	82.4	13.8	14.5	0.4	0.5	2.1	2.6	5.7	5.6	6.1	5.6	6.3	23.6	26.8	17.9	2.5	79.4	43.0	48.3	51.7
36444	FRANKLIN	42.8	40.6	56.4	58.7	0.0	0.0	0.5	0.5	7.3	7.1	7.1	6.7	6.9	24.4	25.8	13.0	1.7	74.6	36.9	49.5	50.5
36445	FRISCO CITY	68.7	66.8	28.7	30.5	0.3	0.4	0.8	0.9	7.8	7.7	7.5	7.0	6.5	27.5	24.0	10.5	1.7	72.9	35.5	48.9	51.1
36446	FULTON	51.1	49.8	48.0	49.3	0.0	0.0	0.9	0.9	8.3	7.8	8.3	7.8	7.4	28.1	23.0	8.8	0.5	70.1	33.8	47.5	52.5
36451	GROVE HILL	60.7	59.6	38.5	39.5	0.0	0.0	0.6	0.7	7.1	7.0	7.5	6.8	6.7	26.2	24.5	12.5	1.7	74.4	37.1	48.0	52.0
36453	KINSTON	94.1	93.5	1.7	1.8	0.1	0.1	0.6	0.7	6.1	6.2	5.8	5.7	6.0	26.2	28.1	14.2	1.8	78.6	41.2	49.9	50.1
36454	LENOX	86.8	85.9	10.5	11.1	0.0	0.0	1.3	1.6	6.7	7.1	6.5	5.5	6.7	26.5	27.0	12.9	1.2	76.7	38.3	51.0	49.0
36456	MC KENZIE	75.9	74.7	23.1	24.3	0.1	0.1	0.7	0.7	5.4	5.1	6.1	7.1	6.9	23.6	28.1	14.8	2.9	79.1	42.4	47.9	52.1
36460	MONROEVILLE	59.5	58.2	38.7	39.7	0.4	0.5	0.8	1.0	8.0	7.4	7.6	6.7	7.1	25.4	23.9	11.8	2.0	72.9	35.8	47.1	53.0
36467	OPP	87.6	87.2	11.2	11.4	0.2	0.2	0.6	0.7	6.3	6.2	6.4	5.7	5.8	25.2	26.1	15.5	2.9	77.7	41.0	46.8	53.2
36471	PETERMAN	30.4	28.5	69.3	71.0	0.1	0.2	0.6	0.6	5.7	6.2	8.8	7.2	6.7	24.7	26.0	12.6	2.2	75.0	38.1	47.6	52.5
36473	RANGE	86.6	85.7	10.4	11.2	0.0	0.0	1.3	1.6	6.7	7.0	6.4	5.4	6.7	26.1	27.4	13.1	1.3	76.4	38.8	51.0	49.0
36474	RED LEVEL	93.0	92.6	5.9	6.3	0.0	0.0	0.4	0.4	5.6	5.6	6.0	6.8	6.5	25.9	27.1	14.7	2.0	78.5	40.9	50.8	49.2
36475	REPTON	56.7	55.8	42.2	43.1	0.0	0.0	0.6	0.7	6.4	6.5	6.9	6.8	6.9	26.9	25.8	12.5	1.4	76.4	38.2	49.6	50.4
36477	SAMSON	85.8	84.9	11.0	11.5	0.2	0.2	1.9	2.3	5.9	6.2	6.8	6.1	5.7	25.8	27.0	14.5	2.0	77.3	40.2	49.5	50.5
36480	URIAH	77.0	75.8	16.5	17.4	0.3	0.3	1.2	1.3	6.7	7.1	7.8	5.5	5.7	27.9	24.7	13.4	1.3	75.2	38.2	49.5	50.5
36481	VREDENBURGH	28.0	26.3	71.0	72.7	0.0	0.0	0.4	0.3	7.6	7.6	9.4	7.9	6.8	24.5	22.4	12.0	1.8	70.6	34.0	47.9	52.1
36482	WHATLEY	40.7	40.3	58.8	59.2	0.0	0.0	0.8	0.8	7.0	7.2	8.3	6.9	6.5	27.1	22.5	12.6	1.9	73.3	36.8	47.5	52.5
36483	WING	95.2	94.7	3.8	4.2	0.1	0.1	0.8	1.0	5.6	5.7	6.2	6.6	6.2	26.6	26.2	14.8	2.0	78.6	40.9	50.2	49.8
36502	ATMORE	52.3	51.0	40.5	41.2	0.3	0.3	0.8	1.0	6.6	6.4	6.5	6.2	8.2	30.6	23.2	10.7	1.7	77.1	35.5	54.1	45.9
36505	AXIS	88.0	86.0	9.4	11.1	0.2	0.3	0.6	0.9	7.3	7.5	8.0	7.2	6.2	28.8	26.3	8.3	0.5	72.9	35.5	49.2	50.8
36507	BAY MINETTE	76.4	75.1	21.5	22.5	0.3	0.4	1.1	1.3	7.5	7.2	7.1	6.9	7.7	28.0	23.5	10.7	1.4	74.3	34.8	49.9	50.2
36509	BAYOU LA BATRE	62.9	57.7	10.2	11.1	23.9	28.0	1.3	1.5	7.1	7.1	8.5	7.5	7.4	27.1	23.9	10.6	0.8	72.8	34.2	51.3	48.7
36511	BON SECOUR	96.3	95.8	0.6	0.6	0.4	0.4	3.5	4.4	6.5	6.7	6.4	6.2	5.0	29.0	25.8	13.5	1.0	76.4	39.1	48.1	51.9
36515	CARLTON	31.0	32.1	65.5	67.9	0.0	0.0	0.0	0.0	7.1	7.1	7.1	7.1	7.1	28.6	28.6	7.1	0.0	78.6	35.0	46.4	53.6
36518	CHATOM	77.9	77.3	21.5	22.1	0.1	0.1	0.7	0.8	7.2	7.0	7.5	7.5	6.7	25.5	23.4	12.8	2.5	73.7	36.6	49.0	51.0
36521	CHUNCHULA	84.1	81.7	12.1	14.1	0.1	0.1	0.6	0.7	7.5	7.6	8.6	7.3	6.9	29.0	24.4	8.0	0.7	71.8	33.7	50.1	49.9
36522	CITRONELLE	79.4	76.7	15.6	17.9	0.1	0.2	0.8	0.9	7.8	7.5	7.6	7.2	7.4	27.3	23.4	10.4	1.4	72.6	34.5	48.7	51.3
36523	CODEN	83.1	81.7	3.7	4.0	10.1	11.0	1.2	1.4	6.0	6.1	6.6	5.9	5.7	25.4	30.6	13.0	0.8	77.6	41.1	52.0	48.0
36524	COFFEEVILLE	57.4	56.3	41.8	42.9	0.3	0.3	1.0	0.9	8.4	6.8	5.9	5.5	5.3	23.1	26.0	16.6	2.5	75.7	40.7	47.3	52.7
36525	CREOLA	70.5	67.2	27.1	30.1	0.1	0.1	0.9	1.1	7.2	7.2	7.5	6.5	5.8	27.7	26.2	10.7	1.3	74.2	37.2	48.9	51.2
36526	DAPHNE	84.4	82.9	13.3	14.5	0.6	0.8	1.6	2.0	6.4	6.5	7.3	7.0	6.4	27.8	27.3	10.3	1.1	75.3	38.2	48.6	51.5
36527	SPANISH FORT	92.1	91.2	6.0	6.4	0.7	0.9	0.9	1.1	6.1	7.0	7.9	6.7	4.1	24.5	28.6	11.9	3.2	74.3	41.6	48.5	51.5
36528	DAUPHIN ISLAND	95.2	94.4	1.2	1.4	0.6	0.8	1.0	1.3	4.9	5.1	5.3	4.9	4.8	23.9	35.6	14.7	0.9	81.6	45.6	52.3	47.7
36529	DEER PARK	76.1	75.9	21.4	21.6	0.1	0.1	0.6	0.5	7.5	7.4	7.8	7.0	6.7	26.5	24.2	11.4	1.4	73.2	36.1	49.3	50.7
36530	ELBERTA	96.1	95.5	0.9	1.0	0.3	0.4	1.9	2.4	6.5	6.6	6.9	5.8	5.5	26.3	26.4	14.9	1.2	76.5	40.1	50.2	49.8
36532	FAIRHOPE	88.7	88.0	9.4	9.7	0.5	0.6	1.2	1.6	5.6	6.0	6.7	6.2	5.0	24.3	27.7	15.8	2.8	77.7	42.6	47.2	52.8
36535	FOLEY	85.0	83.6	11.9	12.7	0.5	0.6	3.7	4.6	6.4	6.4	6.3	5.8	5.7	26.4	24.7	16.2	2.2	77.3	40.2	48.0	52.0
36538	FRANKVILLE	73.6	72.9	26.1	26.7	0.0	0.0	0.4	0.4	8.0	7.2	7.2	7.2	7.0	27.1	24.7	10.4	1.4	72.9	35.2	50.2	49.8
	ALABAMA	71.1	70.3	26.0	26.4	0.7	0.9	1.7	2.1	6.7	6.7	7.0	6.8	7.2	28.0	24.5	11.6	1.6	75.8	36.6	48.5	51.5
	UNITED STATES	75.1	73.6	12.3	12.5	3.8	4.2	12.5	14.1	6.9	6.7	7.2	7.0	7.3	28.6	23.8	10.8	1.7	75.1	36.0	49.1	50.9

#	ZIP CODE POST OFFICE NAME	2004 Per Capita Income	2004 HH Income Base	2004 HOUSEHOLD INCOME DISTRIBUTION (%) Less than $25,000	$25,000 to $49,999	$50,000 to $99,999	$100,000 to $149,999	$150,000 or More	MEDIAN HOUSEHOLD INCOME 2004	2009	2004 National Centile	2004 State Centile	2004 Home Value Base	2004 HOME VALUE DISTRIBUTION (%) Less than $50,000	$50,000 to $89,999	$90,000 to $174,999	$175,000 to $399,999	$400,000 or More	2004 Median Home Value
36264	HEFLIN	16360	3752	38.7	33.2	22.7	4.0	1.4	32150	35287	18	41	3054	33.4	26.2	28.3	11.1	1.0	75419
36265	JACKSONVILLE	18881	6606	41.2	25.8	24.1	6.0	2.9	32125	35530	18	40	4324	22.2	25.4	38.4	13.4	0.6	93355
36266	LINEVILLE	16170	2228	44.1	31.2	20.5	3.1	1.1	28236	30711	9	23	1715	31.2	33.2	25.8	7.5	2.3	74178
36267	MILLERVILLE	14292	24	54.2	20.8	25.0	0.0	0.0	22257	21076	3	8	20	25.0	50.0	25.0	0.0	0.0	76667
36268	MUNFORD	18955	1955	30.7	33.4	30.4	3.3	2.2	38829	43530	42	71	1644	38.1	29.2	23.7	7.9	1.0	63784
36269	MUSCADINE	16951	515	36.7	38.1	20.2	2.9	2.1	34035	37004	24	49	428	35.3	32.7	18.7	11.5	1.9	66857
36271	OHATCHEE	19305	2320	33.0	31.6	28.8	3.8	2.9	37926	42350	39	67	1986	25.9	31.3	27.7	12.4	2.7	80138
36272	PIEDMONT	16479	5688	39.4	32.7	22.4	4.1	1.5	31931	35544	18	39	4577	33.3	33.8	26.0	6.1	0.9	69684
36273	RANBURNE	16204	1145	40.8	32.1	22.5	3.7	1.0	32530	35273	19	43	957	32.5	25.3	29.3	10.6	2.4	78015
36274	ROANOKE	16117	4407	39.8	33.0	22.3	2.9	2.0	31708	34585	17	38	3449	34.6	30.9	27.3	6.2	1.1	70828
36276	WADLEY	16625	904	39.9	35.8	17.8	4.3	2.1	30206	33233	13	30	725	32.8	32.6	28.8	5.7	0.1	70938
36277	WEAVER	20891	2026	29.6	33.8	28.0	5.7	3.0	40110	44264	46	75	1660	24.0	35.8	34.9	4.9	0.3	80682
36278	WEDOWEE	16404	1587	45.4	26.8	22.7	3.5	1.6	28522	30977	10	23	1307	32.1	26.9	27.0	11.6	2.5	78119
36279	WELLINGTON	18129	962	30.9	37.7	25.1	4.7	1.7	36249	40768	33	60	810	27.7	27.8	34.1	10.4	0.1	82143
36280	WOODLAND	16893	1621	36.9	33.6	24.1	4.3	1.1	34243	37363	25	50	1374	36.1	22.9	26.4	13.0	1.6	74146
36301	DOTHAN	19987	13760	34.8	30.2	26.8	6.1	2.1	35699	40349	30	57	9518	22.4	42.5	28.8	5.7	0.7	76057
36303	DOTHAN	22275	12073	37.0	26.3	23.3	8.3	5.1	36243	41041	33	60	8394	18.6	25.9	37.8	15.7	2.0	97067
36305	DOTHAN	32900	4158	19.8	26.0	33.5	12.8	8.0	54093	61854	78	94	3189	6.6	17.8	52.6	17.0	6.0	122624
36310	ABBEVILLE	17403	2886	46.4	26.2	20.7	4.4	2.3	28027	31636	9	22	2338	35.4	31.2	24.4	8.6	0.5	64558
36311	ARITON	16294	1226	47.1	26.2	23.1	2.3	1.4	27116	30168	7	20	1009	44.0	30.1	16.4	8.1	1.4	57756
36312	ASHFORD	18225	2216	35.2	31.5	26.3	5.3	1.7	36490	41513	34	61	1808	31.6	35.0	26.0	7.2	0.2	69180
36314	BLACK	17067	213	30.1	39.0	26.3	4.7	0.0	36034	39337	32	59	180	40.0	29.4	24.4	6.1	0.0	64375
36316	CHANCELLOR	19316	879	42.0	28.0	24.0	3.9	2.2	30765	34098	14	33	745	35.8	28.1	22.6	9.7	3.9	72016
36317	CLOPTON	14771	259	46.0	27.0	23.6	3.5	0.0	27901	31891	8	22	217	50.7	27.2	18.0	4.2	0.0	49483
36318	COFFEE SPRINGS	18184	529	38.2	35.0	21.4	3.2	2.3	32245	36090	18	41	459	32.9	30.3	26.1	9.8	0.9	73472
36319	COLUMBIA	17280	1151	40.5	33.2	18.9	4.4	3.0	30710	34903	14	33	939	43.0	31.1	20.6	4.6	0.8	60813
36320	COTTONWOOD	16554	1428	37.8	29.7	27.5	4.6	0.4	34027	38970	24	49	1188	33.2	32.2	27.5	7.0	0.1	67143
36321	COWARTS	20173	571	32.4	30.8	31.0	3.5	2.3	38456	44060	41	70	483	31.9	43.9	20.5	3.3	0.4	65259
36322	DALEVILLE	18966	3163	35.5	30.0	28.8	4.9	0.8	36935	40424	35	63	2209	33.5	40.7	20.5	4.9	0.5	70020
36323	ELBA	17281	3254	41.3	33.3	18.8	3.7	2.9	31082	34698	15	35	2528	38.7	26.0	23.8	10.2	1.2	65839
36330	ENTERPRISE	22236	12122	31.6	29.5	27.6	7.9	3.4	39643	43817	45	73	8145	16.2	30.2	41.0	11.5	1.1	93362
36340	GENEVA	16733	2453	49.7	24.5	20.6	3.3	1.8	25189	27864	5	15	1932	38.0	32.7	22.4	5.1	1.8	59023
36343	GORDON	16467	584	40.6	29.8	24.8	3.4	1.4	34516	39412	26	51	487	40.9	25.3	29.2	3.5	1.2	63281
36344	HARTFORD	16129	2259	42.0	30.8	22.4	4.1	0.7	30352	33632	13	31	1866	34.9	33.2	27.1	3.8	1.0	62320
36345	HEADLAND	19703	2299	32.3	29.5	28.8	7.1	2.3	39719	44718	45	73	1839	17.4	28.5	38.9	13.3	2.0	95350
36346	JACK	16122	638	37.2	35.1	23.7	2.5	1.6	32608	36308	20	43	547	42.4	26.5	24.1	5.9	1.1	55321
36349	MALVERN	17754	134	32.8	34.3	26.1	4.5	2.2	38158	42791	40	68	114	29.0	45.6	19.3	5.3	0.9	72105
36350	MIDLAND CITY	17906	3328	37.5	30.8	24.6	5.7	1.4	34375	38105	25	51	2579	33.6	35.3	19.9	8.5	2.8	67370
36351	NEW BROCKTON	19522	1390	35.3	31.4	25.3	5.2	2.9	34845	39034	27	52	1182	28.7	35.1	20.3	14.0	1.9	70707
36352	NEWTON	18593	1981	30.4	34.3	28.2	5.7	1.4	38964	43573	43	71	1655	31.0	32.0	26.3	9.7	1.0	73743
36353	NEWVILLE	15828	826	42.3	28.0	25.4	4.1	0.2	31112	35000	15	35	701	41.7	32.8	23.4	1.7	0.4	56964
36360	OZARK	18946	7937	40.5	29.0	24.6	3.9	1.9	32680	35713	20	44	5735	25.2	38.4	28.7	7.0	0.7	75771
36362	FORT RUCKER	12442	1398	21.8	50.1	24.6	2.9	0.5	37810	41559	39	66	28	50.0	14.3	35.7	0.0	0.0	50000
36370	PANSEY	16920	389	40.1	35.0	19.0	3.3	2.6	32559	36574	19	43	321	44.9	29.6	23.4	1.6	0.6	55893
36373	SHORTERVILLE	15124	441	42.4	32.7	22.0	1.6	1.4	32620	37051	20	44	370	49.2	29.7	16.5	3.5	1.1	50833
36374	SKIPPERVILLE	16042	433	37.6	33.3	23.8	4.2	1.2	35164	39107	28	55	373	38.9	30.3	26.5	3.5	0.8	66875
36375	SLOCOMB	16948	2739	42.6	26.8	24.0	4.4	2.2	30164	33645	13	30	2253	31.7	34.8	27.7	4.8	1.1	70124
36376	WEBB	17871	1120	31.6	33.7	29.5	3.6	1.7	36035	41033	32	59	928	36.5	37.1	19.5	6.5	0.4	61573
36401	EVERGREEN	15566	3372	50.0	27.1	17.0	3.7	2.3	25000	28222	5	15	2514	43.6	27.3	23.9	4.5	0.8	58750
36420	ANDALUSIA	18595	7221	43.2	28.4	21.2	4.5	2.7	29715	32710	12	27	5492	36.1	29.5	24.6	7.8	2.0	68200
36425	BEATRICE	11734	564	53.2	30.5	13.7	2.1	0.5	22892	26115	3	10	451	65.6	16.2	11.8	5.8	0.7	34500
36426	BREWTON	18732	6676	41.5	27.5	22.6	5.5	3.0	32138	35982	18	40	5174	33.2	30.5	27.9	7.4	1.0	71088
36432	CASTLEBERRY	14043	1427	53.3	26.4	16.2	2.8	1.3	22816	25994	3	10	1203	42.6	30.7	22.1	4.3	0.3	57902
36435	COY	9727	339	59.6	25.7	14.8	0.0	0.0	16880	19376	1	2	296	57.8	28.4	8.1	3.7	2.0	28158
36436	DICKINSON	12340	271	53.5	21.0	19.6	5.9	0.0	22603	25481	3	9	237	52.3	28.7	17.7	0.8	0.4	46944
36441	FLOMATON	17831	1570	39.6	29.4	26.2	3.1	1.8	34217	38395	25	50	1286	37.4	34.1	24.6	3.7	0.2	63021
36442	FLORALA	13314	1601	60.5	25.7	10.9	1.8	1.1	20854	23325	2	5	1218	49.9	30.1	12.8	6.7	0.5	50094
36444	FRANKLIN	13510	380	44.2	30.8	24.0	1.1	0.0	29522	31722	11	26	328	50.3	23.5	24.7	1.5	0.0	49722
36445	FRISCO CITY	15611	2359	40.7	30.7	24.0	3.2	1.4	31432	34932	16	36	1942	47.6	26.9	22.1	3.3	0.0	53108
36446	FULTON	14563	84	48.8	19.1	27.4	4.8	0.0	26528	30000	6	19	75	48.0	32.0	18.7	1.3	0.0	55000
36451	GROVE HILL	16212	2168	45.6	24.2	23.0	6.6	0.7	28880	32903	10	24	1783	40.3	28.0	24.3	6.5	1.0	58146
36453	KINSTON	18015	963	36.5	36.8	20.9	3.0	2.9	33864	38244	24	48	804	37.4	31.1	24.1	7.0	0.4	64571
36454	LENOX	18368	249	39.4	30.9	22.9	6.0	0.8	33246	38074	22	46	226	42.9	22.6	27.0	4.4	3.1	60000
36456	MC KENZIE	16155	546	48.7	28.6	18.9	2.2	1.7	25907	28951	6	17	439	57.0	21.0	14.8	7.3	0.0	45448
36460	MONROEVILLE	19742	4821	38.7	27.8	24.1	6.3	3.1	33526	37088	22	47	3674	31.7	25.2	32.1	10.9	0.2	79011
36467	OPP	17647	4216	42.1	31.6	20.4	3.8	2.1	29320	32347	11	26	3225	37.9	31.5	23.1	5.6	1.8	63872
36471	PETERMAN	13833	555	51.2	28.8	17.1	2.3	0.5	24154	27236	4	12	464	57.3	20.5	17.7	3.2	1.3	41282
36473	RANGE	16374	123	40.7	30.1	22.8	5.7	0.8	32333	36306	19	42	112	41.1	22.3	29.5	4.5	2.7	62500
36474	RED LEVEL	15123	868	41.8	33.8	21.4	2.2	0.8	28634	32198	10	23	760	54.1	23.8	17.9	3.8	0.4	46630
36475	REPTON	14335	739	48.6	28.4	18.8	3.4	0.8	26208	29545	6	18	648	40.4	29.2	25.2	4.8	0.5	59841
36477	SAMSON	16076	1988	47.9	33.1	14.8	2.3	1.9	26377	29463	6	19	1569	38.8	35.8	16.9	7.1	1.3	60195
36480	URIAH	17445	756	36.4	32.8	24.5	5.0	1.3	35152	38898	28	54	691	46.6	31.1	18.1	4.2	0.0	54608
36481	VREDENBURGH	10791	336	45.5	37.2	15.5	1.2	0.6	27800	30799	8	21	271	63.5	17.7	17.7	0.7	0.4	36912
36482	WHATLEY	13226	322	56.8	23.0	12.7	7.1	0.3	21604	25000	2	7	267	51.3	24.3	21.0	3.0	0.4	48750
36483	WING	15328	808	44.2	33.3	17.0	5.1	0.5	28211	30900	9	23	689	32.1	30.8	28.5	8.4	0.3	68214
36502	ATMORE	15509	6408	45.1	29.8	19.5	4.2	1.5	29101	32712	11	25	4852	37.1	28.4	27.0	7.2	0.4	66721
36505	AXIS	20511	612	23.5	24.0	39.9	10.5	2.1	51805	58268	75	93	531	14.9	17.1	47.7	17.9	2.5	111995
36507	BAY MINETTE	18528	7359	32.2	32.7	26.7	6.2	2.2	37895	42305	39	67	5767	26.7	28.9	30.1	13.0	1.3	82110
36509	BAYOU LA BATRE	14094	851	45.4	28.4	22.3	2.6	1.3	27940	31522	9	22	666	49.3	27.2	15.0	7.8	0.8	51042
36511	BON SECOUR	19495	205	24.9	37.1	31.2	5.4	1.5	42575	47331	55	82	174	23.6	16.1	39.1	21.3	0.0	106818
36515	CARLTON	13750	11	45.5	27.3	27.3	0.0	0.0	27273	27273	8	21	10	40.0	40.0	20.0	0.0	0.0	60000
36518	CHATOM	18463	1295	37.5	26.6	29.8	3.5	2.7	36321	40483	33	61	1037	38.4	28.3	29.4	3.9	0.1	65643
36521	CHUNCHULA	15820	1912	30.7	32.1	31.1	5.7	0.4	39075	44432	43	71	1670	32.6	26.6	30.8	8.6	1.4	76815
36522	CITRONELLE	16827	2101	36.0	29.9	28.4	4.3	1.4	35952	40369	31	58	1691	29.8	32.2	31.3	6.0	0.8	73715
36523	CODEN	18688	1321	33.7	31.1	26.2	6.6	2.4	37017	41381	35	63	1087	31.2	20.3	25.5	17.7	5.3	87339
36524	COFFEEVILLE	15660	579	48.0	33.0	15.2	3.3	0.5	25878	29143	6	16	476	45.4	32.1	14.5	8.0	0.0	56111
36525	CREOLA	16270	556	40.8	23.0	26.8	7.7	1.6	33409	37184	22	47	443	28.9	22.4	36.3	10.8	1.6	87800
36526	DAPHNE	28575	8651	18.2	23.3	37.7	12.9	7.9	57772	64308	82	95	6667	4.1	7.3	50.4	30.2	8.0	152027
36527	SPANISH FORT	31413	3133	15.2	21.1	36.0	14.8	13.0	63558	72972	87	98	2774	7.2	6.9	34.1	46.7	5.2	180652
36528	DAUPHIN ISLAND	25557	722	27.0	31.0	29.6	9.1	3.2	42985	48084	56	84	607	20.1	16.0	29.0	25.9	9.1	119886
36529	DEER PARK	13047	350	46.9	22.6	26.3	2.0	2.3	26762	29888	7	19	317	39.4	24.6	25.6	6.6	3.8	67813
36530	ELBERTA	21141	2863	29.6	35.0	25.4	7.1	2.8	38376	43119	41	69	2366	17.1	16.3	34.2	23.5	9.0	123689
36532	FAIRHOPE	26885	10138	24.2	28.1	30.9	11.4	5.5	46895	52101	66	89	8181	9.9	8.2	35.8	35.8	10.3	165108
36535	FOLEY	21864	8007	29.7	34.7	25.9	6.5	3.2	38264	42634	40	69	6343	16.5	17.2	40.7	21.2	4.4	117847
36538	FRANKVILLE	16567	203	43.4	23.7	28.1	3.9	1.0	29793	32797	12	28	180	53.9	29.4	16.1	0.6	0.0	46316
	ALABAMA	20998		34.3	28.7	26.3	7.2	3.5	37534	42371				22.7	26.7	33.4	14.6	2.7	90917
	UNITED STATES	25866		24.7	27.1	30.8	10.9	6.5	48124	56710				10.9	15.0	33.7	30.1	10.4	145905

ZIP CODE #	POST OFFICE NAME	FINANCIAL SERVICES: Auto Loan	FINANCIAL SERVICES: Home Loan	FINANCIAL SERVICES: Invest-ments	FINANCIAL SERVICES: Retire-ment Plans	THE HOME: Home Improvements: Home Repair	THE HOME: Home Improvements: Lawn & Garden	THE HOME: Furnishings: Comput-ers & Hard-ware	THE HOME: Furnishings: Major Appli-ances	THE HOME: Furnishings: TV, Radio, Sound Equip-ment	THE HOME: Furnishings: Furni-ture	ENTERTAINMENT: Dine out/ Carry out	ENTERTAINMENT: Sports Equip-ment	ENTERTAINMENT: Fees & Tickets	ENTERTAINMENT: Toys & Games	ENTERTAINMENT: Travel	ENTERTAINMENT: Cable TV	PERSONAL: Apparel & Services	PERSONAL: Auto Repairs	PERSONAL: Health Insur-ance	PERSONAL: Pets & Supplies
36264	HEFLIN	75	51	24	44	57	66	50	61	59	50	70	73	43	66	50	64	64	61	75	85
36265	JACKSONVILLE	70	56	50	55	58	66	63	64	66	61	81	77	58	78	61	66	77	66	68	78
36266	LINEVILLE	70	48	23	41	54	62	46	57	55	47	65	68	39	62	47	59	59	57	70	81
36267	MILLERVILLE	59	40	18	34	45	52	38	48	46	39	54	57	33	51	39	50	49	48	59	68
36268	MUNFORD	86	65	39	59	70	78	62	73	70	64	84	87	56	80	63	73	78	73	84	98
36269	MUSCADINE	80	54	24	46	61	70	52	65	63	53	73	77	44	69	53	67	67	64	80	92
36271	OHATCHEE	83	65	42	60	70	78	62	72	69	63	83	85	57	81	63	72	78	71	82	96
36272	PIEDMONT	74	51	24	44	57	66	49	61	59	50	69	72	42	66	50	63	63	60	74	85
36273	RANBURNE	75	50	23	43	57	66	49	61	59	49	69	72	41	65	49	63	62	60	75	86
36274	ROANOKE	74	51	27	45	58	66	51	61	60	51	71	72	44	67	51	64	64	61	75	84
36276	WADLEY	78	52	24	45	59	68	50	63	61	51	71	75	43	67	51	65	65	62	77	89
36277	WEAVER	79	75	65	71	77	82	71	76	73	71	89	89	70	90	72	74	86	74	79	92
36278	WEDOWEE	72	51	27	45	58	66	49	60	58	49	68	72	42	65	50	62	62	60	73	85
36279	WELLINGTON	74	60	43	55	64	71	58	65	64	58	77	77	54	76	59	67	72	64	74	84
36280	WOODLAND	79	53	24	46	60	69	51	64	62	52	72	76	43	68	52	66	66	63	79	91
36301	DOTHAN	69	64	58	62	65	71	65	67	67	64	82	77	63	81	64	68	79	67	70	78
36303	DOTHAN	76	75	78	73	74	81	75	76	76	76	95	86	75	93	75	77	92	76	77	86
36305	DOTHAN	111	124	122	126	121	120	113	114	107	115	134	134	116	137	113	102	132	111	102	127
36310	ABBEVILLE	73	53	33	48	59	68	53	63	62	53	73	73	47	69	54	66	67	62	76	84
36311	ARITON	60	41	19	36	46	53	39	49	47	40	55	58	34	53	40	50	50	48	60	69
36312	ASHFORD	80	58	33	53	65	73	56	68	65	57	77	81	50	74	57	68	71	67	80	93
36314	BLACK	79	53	24	46	60	69	51	64	62	52	73	77	44	69	52	67	66	64	79	91
36316	CHANCELLOR	85	59	30	53	67	76	57	71	67	58	79	84	49	76	59	72	72	70	85	99
36317	CLOPTON	69	46	21	40	52	60	44	55	54	45	63	66	38	59	45	58	57	55	68	79
36318	COFFEE SPRINGS	81	56	28	50	63	72	55	67	64	55	76	80	47	72	55	68	69	66	80	93
36319	COLUMBIA	73	51	27	46	57	67	52	62	61	52	71	72	45	67	52	65	65	61	75	83
36320	COTTONWOOD	73	54	30	48	59	66	52	62	59	53	71	73	46	67	52	62	65	61	72	83
36321	COWARTS	93	62	28	54	71	81	60	75	73	61	85	90	51	81	61	78	77	74	93	107
36322	DALEVILLE	70	59	48	57	60	67	61	64	64	60	78	75	57	75	59	64	74	65	68	77
36323	ELBA	75	53	31	48	59	68	54	64	63	54	75	74	48	70	54	67	69	63	76	85
36330	ENTERPRISE	79	73	69	72	73	79	76	76	77	75	95	90	74	94	74	77	92	78	77	87
36340	GENEVA	69	48	26	44	54	63	50	59	58	49	68	68	43	64	50	62	62	58	71	78
36343	GORDON	79	53	24	46	60	69	51	64	61	52	72	76	43	68	52	66	66	63	78	90
36344	HARTFORD	72	49	24	43	55	64	49	59	58	49	68	70	42	64	49	62	62	59	73	82
36345	HEADLAND	77	66	50	63	70	77	65	71	70	64	84	83	61	82	65	72	79	70	79	89
36346	JACK	73	49	22	42	56	64	47	59	57	48	67	71	40	63	48	62	61	59	73	84
36349	MALVERN	70	62	49	60	63	68	61	65	62	62	76	75	58	73	60	62	73	64	66	77
36350	MIDLAND CITY	67	58	50	57	61	67	59	63	62	59	76	74	56	74	59	63	72	63	67	76
36351	NEW BROCKTON	83	66	42	60	71	78	62	72	69	62	83	85	57	81	63	72	77	71	82	96
36352	NEWTON	78	63	45	60	67	74	61	69	66	62	80	82	56	77	62	68	75	69	76	89
36353	NEWVILLE	73	49	22	42	55	64	47	59	57	48	67	70	40	63	48	61	60	58	72	84
36360	OZARK	67	61	55	59	62	69	62	65	65	61	79	74	60	78	62	66	76	65	69	76
36362	FORT RUCKER	70	45	43	51	41	48	67	57	68	62	84	76	57	76	55	62	81	68	53	65
36370	PANSEY	80	54	25	46	61	70	52	65	62	53	73	77	44	69	53	67	67	64	80	92
36373	SHORTERVILLE	68	46	22	40	52	60	45	56	54	45	63	66	38	60	46	58	57	55	68	79
36374	SKIPPERVILLE	78	52	24	45	59	68	50	63	61	51	71	75	43	68	51	66	65	62	78	90
36375	SLOCOMB	72	54	34	50	59	67	55	63	61	54	73	73	49	69	55	64	68	62	73	80
36376	WEBB	74	63	45	60	65	70	60	67	63	62	77	78	56	73	60	64	73	66	70	83
36401	EVERGREEN	65	45	27	40	50	59	46	55	54	46	64	64	40	60	46	58	59	54	67	74
36420	ANDALUSIA	74	55	35	51	60	70	56	65	64	55	76	75	50	73	57	68	70	65	77	84
36425	BEATRICE	45	35	32	30	35	43	38	41	44	39	53	45	35	47	37	47	50	42	49	50
36426	BREWTON	77	57	35	52	62	72	58	67	66	57	78	78	51	74	58	70	72	66	79	87
36432	CASTLEBERRY	64	43	19	37	48	56	41	51	50	42	58	61	35	55	42	53	53	51	63	73
36435	COY	37	29	30	26	29	36	33	34	38	34	46	37	31	41	32	41	43	35	41	40
36436	DICKINSON	65	44	20	38	49	57	42	53	51	43	60	63	36	56	43	55	54	52	65	75
36441	FLOMATON	81	55	27	48	62	72	54	66	65	55	76	78	47	72	55	69	69	66	81	92
36442	FLORALA	51	37	21	33	41	48	38	44	44	37	52	51	33	49	38	47	47	44	54	58
36444	FRANKLIN	62	41	19	36	47	54	40	50	48	41	57	60	34	54	41	52	51	49	62	71
36445	FRISCO CITY	73	49	22	42	55	64	47	59	57	48	67	71	40	63	48	61	61	58	73	84
36446	FULTON	71	47	21	41	54	62	46	57	55	47	65	68	39	61	47	60	59	57	71	81
36451	GROVE HILL	74	51	25	44	57	66	49	61	59	50	69	72	42	66	50	63	63	60	74	85
36453	KINSTON	76	55	33	49	60	68	53	64	62	54	73	76	47	70	54	65	67	63	75	87
36454	LENOX	79	53	24	46	60	69	51	64	61	52	72	76	43	68	52	66	66	63	78	90
36456	MC KENZIE	69	46	21	40	52	60	45	56	54	46	64	67	38	60	46	58	58	55	69	79
36460	MONROEVILLE	85	65	43	58	70	80	63	73	72	64	86	86	58	84	64	76	80	73	86	98
36467	OPP	71	52	33	47	57	66	52	61	60	52	71	71	47	68	53	64	66	61	73	81
36471	PETERMAN	61	42	21	36	47	54	41	50	49	41	57	59	35	54	41	53	52	50	61	70
36473	RANGE	79	53	24	45	60	69	51	64	61	52	72	76	43	68	52	66	66	63	78	90
36474	RED LEVEL	68	46	21	39	52	60	44	55	53	45	63	66	38	59	45	57	57	55	68	78
36475	REPTON	65	44	20	38	50	57	42	53	51	43	60	63	36	57	43	55	54	52	65	75
36477	SAMSON	69	47	24	42	53	62	47	57	56	47	65	67	40	62	47	59	60	57	70	79
36480	URIAH	81	54	25	47	61	71	52	65	63	53	74	78	45	70	53	68	67	65	81	93
36481	VREDENBURGH	59	39	18	34	45	51	38	48	46	39	54	57	32	51	39	49	49	47	59	67
36482	WHATLEY	63	43	21	37	48	56	42	52	50	43	59	61	36	56	42	54	54	51	63	72
36483	WING	66	46	24	41	52	60	47	56	55	46	65	65	40	61	47	59	59	56	68	75
36502	ATMORE	68	50	34	45	55	63	51	59	59	51	70	69	46	67	51	62	65	59	70	77
36505	AXIS	92	82	63	78	87	93	76	84	81	76	98	100	74	100	78	83	93	82	91	109
36507	BAY MINETTE	80	66	48	62	69	77	65	72	71	65	85	84	61	82	65	73	80	72	80	90
36509	BAYOU LA BATRE	79	53	24	46	60	69	51	64	62	52	72	76	43	68	52	66	66	63	79	91
36511	BON SECOUR	79	72	56	69	72	76	68	73	69	70	86	85	65	81	67	68	82	73	73	87
36515	CARLTON	66	44	20	38	50	58	43	53	51	43	60	64	36	57	43	55	55	53	66	76
36518	CHATOM	86	59	29	52	66	77	58	71	69	59	81	84	50	77	59	74	74	70	87	98
36521	CHUNCHULA	75	61	41	57	65	71	58	66	63	59	76	78	54	73	59	65	72	66	73	86
36522	CITRONELLE	78	62	42	58	65	74	61	69	67	61	81	80	56	78	61	69	75	68	77	87
36523	CODEN	88	64	37	57	72	82	61	75	71	61	84	88	53	81	64	76	77	74	90	104
36524	COFFEEVILLE	66	44	20	38	50	58	43	53	51	43	60	64	36	57	43	55	55	53	66	76
36525	CREOLA	69	58	52	53	59	68	59	63	65	60	79	71	57	75	59	69	75	63	72	77
36526	DAPHNE	100	111	113	113	109	111	104	104	99	105	124	122	107	127	104	96	122	103	96	116
36527	SPANISH FORT	113	118	134	123	118	123	120	119	115	119	144	140	120	141	119	111	140	120	112	130
36528	DAUPHIN ISLAND	97	76	52	68	85	96	71	86	81	71	96	101	64	95	76	86	89	85	102	118
36529	DEER PARK	71	48	22	41	54	62	46	57	55	47	65	69	39	61	47	60	59	57	71	81
36530	ELBERTA	84	73	56	70	75	82	70	77	73	71	90	89	66	86	71	74	85	77	81	94
36532	FAIRHOPE	97	88	77	85	92	103	86	93	91	86	111	105	85	109	88	94	105	91	101	111
36535	FOLEY	84	71	55	70	75	83	71	78	75	71	91	91	67	89	71	76	86	77	84	95
36538	FRANKVILLE	77	52	23	45	59	67	50	62	60	51	71	75	42	67	51	65	64	62	77	89
	ALABAMA	81	70	61	67	72	80	70	75	75	70	91	87	67	89	70	76	86	75	81	92
	UNITED STATES	100	100	100	100	100	100	100	100	100	100	100	100	100	100	100	100	100	100	100	100

POPULATION CHANGE

ZIP CODE		COUNTY FIPS CODE	POPULATION			2000-2004 ANNUAL RATE		HOUSEHOLDS					FAMILIES		
#	POST OFFICE NAME		2000	2004	2009	% Rate	State Centile	2000	2004	2009	% Annual Rate 2000-2004	2004 Average HH Size	2000	2004	% Annual Rate 2000-2004
36539	FRUITDALE	129	977	988	995	0.3	47	356	367	377	0.7	2.69	276	284	0.7
36540	GAINESTOWN	025	858	836	829	-0.6	14	278	279	285	0.1	3.00	211	212	0.1
36541	GRAND BAY	097	13299	13992	14200	1.2	77	4549	4880	5039	1.7	2.85	3679	3941	1.6
36542	GULF SHORES	003	7580	9403	11209	5.2	100	3540	4494	5465	5.8	2.09	2341	2944	5.5
36544	IRVINGTON	097	11012	11280	11291	0.6	63	3684	3852	3926	1.1	2.92	2990	3120	1.0
36545	JACKSON	025	10426	11176	11852	1.7	85	3882	4266	4645	2.2	2.60	2915	3189	2.1
36548	LEROY	129	1121	1115	1116	-0.1	29	423	432	443	0.5	2.58	315	322	0.5
36549	LILLIAN	003	4370	4912	5554	2.8	96	2061	2359	2712	3.2	2.08	1526	1744	3.2
36550	LITTLE RIVER	003	430	439	472	0.5	60	166	173	190	1.0	2.54	117	122	1.0
36551	LOXLEY	003	6023	6923	7892	3.3	98	2036	2415	2831	4.1	2.64	1547	1834	4.1
36553	MC INTOSH	129	4710	4763	4813	0.3	47	1631	1687	1746	0.8	2.82	1247	1289	0.8
36555	MAGNOLIA SPRINGS	003	589	612	665	0.9	71	269	284	314	1.3	2.15	177	187	1.3
36558	MILLRY	129	3279	3244	3240	-0.3	23	1295	1318	1351	0.4	2.46	945	961	0.4
36560	MOUNT VERNON	097	4616	4508	4414	-0.6	16	1497	1493	1489	-0.1	2.77	1146	1140	-0.1
36561	ORANGE BEACH	003	4413	5573	6714	5.6	100	2045	2615	3198	6.0	2.13	1297	1672	6.2
36562	PERDIDO	003	1551	1619	1758	1.0	73	569	607	671	1.5	2.67	446	475	1.5
36567	ROBERTSDALE	003	10381	11842	13495	3.2	97	3820	4435	5141	3.6	2.66	2939	3407	3.5
36569	SAINT STEPHENS	129	809	815	819	0.2	43	290	300	309	0.8	2.72	221	228	0.7
36571	SARALAND	097	13302	13317	13184	0.0	38	5142	5272	5324	0.6	2.50	3864	3946	0.5
36572	SATSUMA	097	6048	5982	5881	-0.3	23	2154	2179	2183	0.3	2.74	1769	1784	0.2
36574	SEMINOLE	003	1183	1305	1461	2.3	93	454	511	583	2.8	2.55	362	408	2.9
36575	SEMMES	097	15103	16393	16906	2.0	90	5298	5860	6155	2.4	2.79	4335	4772	2.3
36576	SILVERHILL	003	3692	4299	4951	3.7	99	1372	1626	1904	4.1	2.64	1054	1249	4.1
36578	STAPLETON	003	1026	1126	1257	2.2	91	375	420	477	2.7	2.66	306	342	2.7
36579	STOCKTON	003	1894	1977	2151	1.0	73	737	786	871	1.5	2.52	547	583	1.5
36580	SUMMERDALE	003	4466	4932	5527	2.4	93	1654	1859	2117	2.8	2.65	1276	1433	2.8
36582	THEODORE	097	20901	21354	21369	0.5	61	7680	8010	8162	1.0	2.66	5904	6141	0.9
36583	TIBBIE	129	299	304	308	0.4	55	116	121	125	1.0	2.51	88	91	0.8
36584	VINEGAR BEND	129	418	417	417	-0.1	34	168	172	176	0.6	2.42	132	135	0.5
36585	WAGARVILLE	129	1675	1656	1654	-0.3	23	642	652	669	0.4	2.54	483	491	0.4
36587	WILMER	097	8125	9052	9445	2.6	94	2817	3202	3403	3.1	2.82	2275	2579	3.0
36602	MOBILE	097	922	901	885	-0.5	16	552	541	536	-0.5	1.36	124	120	-0.8
36603	MOBILE	097	12369	12040	11835	-0.6	14	4143	4070	4051	-0.4	2.74	2628	2569	-0.5
36604	MOBILE	097	11682	11354	11126	-0.7	13	4739	4686	4665	-0.3	2.29	2617	2562	-0.5
36605	MOBILE	097	32617	31647	30978	-0.7	12	12085	11883	11797	-0.4	2.65	8597	8427	-0.5
36606	MOBILE	097	18559	17755	17238	-1.0	6	8034	7770	7642	-0.8	2.28	4767	4582	-0.9
36607	MOBILE	097	8483	8341	8215	-0.4	20	3557	3527	3513	-0.2	2.23	1963	1939	-0.3
36608	MOBILE	097	35164	35308	35116	0.1	40	14140	14466	14632	0.5	2.37	9248	9389	0.4
36609	MOBILE	097	24535	23972	23501	-0.5	16	10737	10605	10537	-0.3	2.26	6370	6288	-0.3
36610	MOBILE	097	19433	17702	16871	-2.2	0	6647	6189	6005	-1.7	2.74	4815	4462	-1.8
36611	MOBILE	097	6249	5950	5762	-1.2	5	2711	2624	2583	-0.8	2.26	1738	1673	-0.9
36612	MOBILE	097	5221	5043	4921	-0.8	9	1898	1886	1881	-0.2	2.67	1367	1352	-0.3
36613	EIGHT MILE	097	12370	12139	11923	-0.4	19	4276	4277	4272	0.0	2.80	3421	3412	-0.1
36615	MOBILE	097	528	566	579	1.7	85	155	168	175	1.9	3.22	118	128	1.9
36617	MOBILE	097	16431	15705	15259	-1.1	5	5988	5839	5771	-0.6	2.62	4342	4215	-0.7
36618	MOBILE	097	15475	15173	14883	-0.5	18	5784	5775	5760	0.0	2.62	4409	4389	-0.1
36619	MOBILE	097	14372	14224	14012	-0.2	24	5360	5419	5437	0.3	2.61	4172	4211	0.2
36688	MOBILE	097	1555	1555	1555	0.0	37	4	4	4	0.0	2.25	3	3	0.0
36693	MOBILE	097	18520	18319	18041	-0.3	23	7383	7433	7443	0.2	2.42	5234	5244	0.0
36695	MOBILE	097	31292	32767	33152	1.1	76	11434	12238	12613	1.6	2.65	8771	9378	1.6
36701	SELMA	047	24458	24298	23961	-0.2	29	9544	9700	9772	0.4	2.48	6752	6855	0.4
36703	SELMA	047	14210	13747	13398	-0.8	11	5314	5265	5246	-0.2	2.56	3681	3639	-0.3
36720	ALBERTA	131	1179	1301	1386	2.3	93	399	458	505	3.3	2.84	298	340	3.2
36722	ARLINGTON	131	642	654	667	0.4	57	220	231	242	1.2	2.83	167	175	1.1
36726	CAMDEN	131	5267	5397	5536	0.6	63	1926	2034	2152	1.3	2.51	1337	1411	1.3
36727	CAMPBELL	025	180	169	167	-1.5	3	67	65	67	-0.7	2.60	49	48	-0.5
36728	CATHERINE	131	662	674	688	0.4	56	221	231	243	1.1	2.92	162	170	1.1
36732	DEMOPOLIS	091	9047	9077	9181	0.1	39	3586	3698	3842	0.7	2.43	2500	2572	0.7
36736	DIXONS MILLS	091	1199	1191	1195	-0.2	28	437	451	468	0.7	2.64	327	338	0.8
36738	FAUNSDALE	091	838	887	917	1.4	79	315	343	364	2.0	2.59	217	237	2.1
36740	FORKLAND	063	2032	2016	1999	-0.2	26	790	809	830	0.6	2.49	536	548	0.5
36742	GALLION	091	2306	2341	2373	0.4	53	880	917	955	1.0	2.55	638	665	1.0
36744	GREENSBORO	065	7646	7743	7937	0.3	50	2828	2934	3080	0.9	2.57	2011	2085	0.9
36748	LINDEN	091	4395	4408	4448	0.1	39	1734	1784	1851	0.7	2.41	1233	1266	0.6
36749	JONES	001	1064	1081	1104	0.4	54	402	419	438	1.0	2.58	293	304	0.9
36750	MAPLESVILLE	021	2990	3202	3402	1.6	83	1109	1209	1303	2.1	2.65	848	923	2.0
36751	LOWER PEACH TREE	131	419	425	432	0.3	53	136	143	150	1.2	2.97	101	106	1.1
36752	LOWNDESBORO	085	1883	2051	2171	2.0	90	773	873	957	2.9	2.35	538	607	2.9
36754	MAGNOLIA	091	365	362	364	-0.2	26	146	150	155	0.6	2.41	106	109	0.7
36756	MARION	105	7702	7525	7319	-0.6	16	2815	2824	2817	0.1	2.50	1973	1978	0.1
36758	PLANTERSVILLE	047	1648	1664	1680	0.2	46	622	643	661	0.8	2.59	449	464	0.8
36759	MARION JUNCTION	047	1773	1717	1667	-0.8	11	680	675	669	-0.2	2.54	483	478	-0.2
36761	MINTER	047	1424	1393	1380	-0.5	17	525	528	537	0.1	2.64	380	383	0.2
36762	MORVIN	025	50	48	47	-1.0	7	16	16	16	0.0	3.00	13	12	-1.9
36765	NEWBERN	065	1348	1338	1358	-0.2	27	482	492	512	0.5	2.69	349	356	0.5
36767	ORRVILLE	047	2218	2150	2093	-0.7	12	828	820	815	-0.2	2.62	569	557	-0.3
36768	PINE APPLE	131	1215	1222	1242	0.1	42	475	492	515	0.8	2.47	319	330	0.8
36769	PINE HILL	131	3279	3231	3267	-0.4	21	1188	1209	1263	0.4	2.67	869	884	0.4
36773	SAFFORD	047	536	509	491	-1.2	4	205	200	198	-0.6	2.54	136	133	-0.5
36775	SARDIS	047	1052	1001	965	-1.2	5	426	419	414	-0.4	2.39	285	280	-0.4
36776	SAWYERVILLE	065	1900	1925	1957	0.3	51	667	691	718	0.8	2.79	485	501	0.8
36782	SWEET WATER	091	2318	2331	2347	0.1	41	874	904	937	0.8	2.58	675	698	0.8
36783	THOMASTON	091	1226	1240	1260	0.3	48	484	502	522	0.9	2.47	349	362	0.9
36784	THOMASVILLE	025	8878	8663	8608	-0.6	15	3402	3412	3483	0.1	2.48	2455	2461	0.1
36785	TYLER	085	745	723	719	-0.7	13	298	300	308	0.2	2.41	217	218	0.1
36786	UNIONTOWN	105	3893	3808	3699	-0.5	17	1408	1414	1412	0.1	2.69	996	998	0.1
36790	STANTON	021	309	328	346	1.4	80	130	141	150	1.9	2.33	96	104	1.9
36792	RANDOLPH	007	1043	1067	1111	0.5	62	391	408	434	1.0	2.62	301	314	1.0
36793	LAWLEY	007	663	694	733	1.1	76	245	262	284	1.6	2.65	184	198	1.7
36801	OPELIKA	081	20396	20722	22050	0.4	54	8103	8420	9139	0.9	2.38	5409	5566	0.7
36804	OPELIKA	081	14859	15625	16903	1.2	77	5405	5788	6362	1.6	2.70	4227	4514	1.6
36830	AUBURN	081	27367	29627	33272	1.9	88	12163	13329	14756	2.2	2.17	5724	6340	2.4
36832	AUBURN	081	18937	20884	22976	2.3	92	8688	9768	10935	2.8	2.05	2845	3233	3.1
36849	AUBURN UNIVERSITY	081	2209	2209	2209	0.0	37	7	7	7	0.0	3.29	4	4	0.0
36850	CAMP HILL	123	2909	2757	2720	-1.3	4	1172	1139	1145	-0.7	2.41	810	786	-0.7
	ALABAMA					0.5					0.9	2.45			0.9
	UNITED STATES					1.2					1.3	2.58			1.1

ZIP CODE #	POST OFFICE NAME	RACE (%) White 2000	White 2004	Black 2000	Black 2004	Asian/Pacific 2000	Asian/Pacific 2004	% Hispanic Origin 2000	% Hispanic Origin 2004	2004 AGE DISTRIBUTION (%) 0-4	5-9	10-14	15-19	20-24	25-44	45-64	65-84	85+	18+	MEDIAN AGE 2004	% 2004 Males	% 2004 Females
36539	FRUITDALE	85.8	85.6	12.0	12.2	0.0	0.0	1.1	1.1	9.0	8.6	8.0	6.8	7.9	27.1	22.4	9.2	1.0	70.2	32.3	50.7	49.3
36540	GAINESTOWN	20.5	19.9	78.6	79.3	0.0	0.0	0.8	1.0	8.6	9.5	9.2	7.8	6.9	27.8	20.8	8.0	1.4	68.2	30.5	47.6	52.4
36541	GRAND BAY	86.9	85.0	10.2	11.6	1.2	1.5	1.0	1.3	7.5	7.6	8.4	7.3	6.7	28.4	24.1	9.1	0.9	72.1	34.3	50.3	49.7
36542	GULF SHORES	96.8	96.4	0.3	0.3	0.3	0.4	1.5	1.9	3.5	3.7	4.8	4.8	5.3	23.1	32.7	20.7	1.5	84.9	48.0	50.0	50.0
36544	IRVINGTON	79.8	76.3	12.6	14.4	5.7	7.2	0.9	1.1	8.0	8.1	8.9	8.0	7.4	28.1	23.0	7.9	0.5	70.0	32.1	49.2	50.8
36545	JACKSON	54.9	53.2	44.0	45.5	0.2	0.3	0.6	0.6	8.3	8.1	7.4	6.6	6.3	26.6	23.9	11.2	1.8	72.2	35.6	47.5	52.5
36548	LEROY	64.9	64.2	33.2	33.8	0.2	0.2	0.4	0.4	5.9	6.4	8.3	7.0	7.0	25.6	27.4	10.9	1.6	75.0	37.4	50.0	50.0
36549	LILLIAN	95.1	94.4	2.8	3.1	0.3	0.4	1.0	1.2	2.6	2.8	3.3	2.9	2.6	11.9	31.1	40.5	2.4	89.6	61.6	48.5	51.5
36550	LITTLE RIVER	57.7	55.4	37.7	39.6	0.2	0.2	0.9	1.4	5.5	5.5	6.4	7.1	6.6	23.5	28.0	15.0	2.5	78.8	42.1	50.8	49.2
36551	LOXLEY	79.8	78.7	16.3	16.9	0.2	0.3	2.9	3.7	6.5	6.6	7.5	7.0	7.0	31.4	24.0	9.0	1.0	75.2	35.6	53.6	46.5
36553	MC INTOSH	33.7	33.8	38.7	38.8	0.1	0.1	1.2	1.1	8.8	8.6	8.9	7.5	7.1	27.1	23.1	8.4	0.6	69.2	32.3	49.2	50.8
36555	MAGNOLIA SPRINGS	95.9	95.3	0.5	0.7	1.4	1.6	1.7	2.5	4.4	4.9	5.7	4.7	4.3	22.7	34.5	16.7	2.1	82.0	46.8	48.0	52.0
36558	MILLRY	76.7	76.2	22.6	23.1	0.1	0.1	1.2	1.2	6.0	6.4	7.7	6.7	6.2	26.8	26.5	12.2	1.5	75.8	38.5	49.2	50.8
36560	MOUNT VERNON	36.5	33.5	43.9	46.0	0.2	0.2	0.2	0.2	6.8	6.9	7.7	7.1	7.0	25.9	25.4	11.7	1.4	73.9	36.8	48.8	51.2
36561	ORANGE BEACH	95.9	95.4	0.3	0.3	0.2	0.2	2.0	2.4	4.0	3.6	4.7	4.6	5.7	23.8	34.7	17.8	1.1	84.8	47.0	51.8	48.2
36562	PERDIDO	91.0	90.2	6.6	7.1	0.1	0.2	1.2	1.4	7.5	7.4	7.2	6.6	6.6	28.8	24.6	10.6	0.8	73.9	35.6	49.4	50.6
36567	ROBERTSDALE	94.7	94.1	2.8	3.1	0.2	0.3	1.4	1.7	7.3	7.2	7.5	7.5	7.0	27.7	24.0	10.7	1.1	73.3	35.3	49.4	50.6
36569	SAINT STEPHENS	78.7	78.2	20.5	21.1	0.1	0.1	0.7	0.7	6.8	6.6	7.7	7.0	6.9	28.2	25.5	10.1	1.2	74.5	36.6	50.8	49.2
36571	SARALAND	85.6	83.2	11.8	13.7	0.4	0.6	1.1	1.4	6.4	6.2	6.6	6.3	7.0	28.7	25.0	12.4	1.4	77.3	37.4	48.6	51.5
36572	SATSUMA	90.7	89.2	7.6	8.8	0.2	0.3	0.7	0.9	6.7	7.0	7.3	6.2	6.4	26.6	27.4	11.3	1.2	75.4	38.3	49.1	50.9
36574	SEMINOLE	96.4	95.9	0.4	0.5	0.3	0.3	1.6	2.1	7.0	6.8	6.7	6.7	6.4	26.6	28.1	11.1	0.7	75.4	38.9	51.4	48.6
36575	SEMMES	94.4	93.7	3.5	3.9	0.3	0.3	1.3	1.7	7.7	7.7	7.9	6.9	6.4	30.8	24.0	8.1	0.6	72.3	34.4	49.7	50.3
36576	SILVERHILL	92.2	91.2	5.1	5.7	0.4	0.5	2.0	2.6	7.3	7.3	7.4	6.8	6.1	28.9	24.5	10.6	1.2	73.5	36.5	48.7	51.3
36578	STAPLETON	88.7	87.7	9.3	10.0	0.1	0.2	1.3	1.6	7.2	7.3	8.2	7.1	6.8	28.9	24.8	9.0	0.8	72.8	34.6	51.9	48.1
36579	STOCKTON	63.6	61.4	34.3	36.4	0.1	0.1	1.0	1.0	6.4	6.6	7.2	6.9	6.3	24.9	27.7	12.2	1.8	75.6	38.9	49.6	50.4
36580	SUMMERDALE	87.5	86.4	9.1	9.8	0.3	0.3	2.7	3.4	7.9	7.9	7.7	6.5	5.8	28.4	23.5	11.5	0.8	72.6	35.6	49.6	50.4
36582	THEODORE	84.1	82.1	12.9	14.3	0.9	1.2	1.1	1.4	7.6	7.4	7.3	6.6	6.4	28.6	25.2	10.0	0.9	73.7	35.8	49.4	50.6
36583	TIBBIE	93.7	93.8	3.3	3.3	0.0	0.0	0.7	0.7	8.2	7.9	8.2	6.9	6.9	26.3	22.7	11.5	1.3	71.7	34.3	50.3	49.7
36584	VINEGAR BEND	68.2	67.4	30.1	30.9	0.0	0.0	0.5	0.5	7.0	7.0	8.2	7.0	7.0	27.1	24.5	11.3	1.2	73.6	36.9	48.7	51.3
36585	WAGARVILLE	70.6	70.1	27.2	27.7	0.1	0.1	0.5	0.6	6.8	6.7	8.4	6.3	6.5	26.5	24.3	12.7	1.8	74.2	37.6	49.4	50.6
36587	WILMER	92.4	91.3	5.3	6.0	0.1	0.1	1.2	1.5	8.3	8.2	8.1	7.0	6.4	30.4	23.1	7.8	0.7	71.0	33.4	50.5	49.6
36602	MOBILE	52.1	47.3	44.5	48.6	1.4	1.7	1.4	1.4	2.4	2.2	3.1	3.3	4.2	22.8	28.5	28.2	5.2	90.7	52.3	49.2	50.8
36603	MOBILE	4.7	4.1	94.1	94.6	0.2	0.2	0.8	0.9	10.1	9.0	8.9	7.7	8.5	23.5	20.1	9.9	2.3	67.6	29.7	46.5	53.5
36604	MOBILE	44.3	41.5	53.4	56.0	0.9	1.0	1.1	1.2	7.5	7.0	6.9	8.3	6.7	29.8	23.3	8.5	2.0	73.1	34.4	48.0	52.0
36605	MOBILE	37.4	34.8	60.0	62.3	0.7	0.8	1.3	1.5	8.1	8.3	8.8	7.9	6.7	25.4	23.1	10.3	1.4	69.9	33.6	46.7	53.3
36606	MOBILE	56.3	53.1	40.7	43.5	0.8	1.0	1.7	2.0	7.4	6.9	7.2	6.7	6.4	30.6	21.6	11.2	2.1	74.4	35.1	46.3	53.7
36607	MOBILE	39.1	36.3	59.5	62.2	0.3	0.4	1.0	1.1	6.6	6.5	6.6	7.0	7.2	25.0	21.5	14.9	4.6	75.9	38.1	43.5	56.5
36608	MOBILE	76.5	74.4	19.3	20.6	2.3	2.9	1.5	1.8	6.6	6.5	6.8	7.1	8.6	28.6	21.9	11.9	1.9	76.2	34.4	47.8	52.2
36609	MOBILE	64.0	60.3	29.0	31.5	4.3	5.2	2.2	2.6	8.3	7.1	6.3	6.1	8.5	33.0	20.0	9.4	1.2	74.6	31.8	47.2	52.8
36610	MOBILE	5.5	5.0	93.5	94.0	0.1	0.1	0.7	0.7	8.6	8.3	9.4	8.7	8.2	23.8	21.5	10.0	1.6	68.6	30.7	46.5	53.5
36611	MOBILE	87.5	85.5	9.7	11.3	0.2	0.3	1.1	1.4	7.5	7.1	6.5	5.6	5.7	25.8	21.9	16.8	3.2	75.6	38.8	47.0	53.0
36612	MOBILE	11.2	9.4	87.2	89.0	0.1	0.1	0.5	0.4	6.7	7.8	8.8	8.5	6.9	24.3	24.6	11.1	1.3	71.3	35.0	45.3	54.7
36613	EIGHT MILE	66.4	63.5	31.5	34.2	0.2	0.3	0.6	0.8	7.1	7.1	7.3	7.4	7.3	26.9	26.2	10.0	0.8	74.2	35.9	48.4	51.6
36615	MOBILE	7.2	6.0	90.2	91.0	1.5	1.8	0.6	0.7	8.7	9.2	12.4	10.4	9.2	27.6	18.2	4.1	0.4	64.0	25.1	47.7	52.3
36617	MOBILE	1.2	1.0	98.1	98.3	0.0	0.0	0.7	0.6	7.1	7.2	8.2	7.8	6.6	22.0	22.5	16.5	2.1	72.6	37.7	45.0	55.0
36618	MOBILE	60.8	56.7	37.0	40.9	0.5	0.6	1.0	1.2	6.6	6.8	7.3	7.4	6.8	26.6	25.4	12.0	1.2	74.8	37.3	47.5	52.5
36619	MOBILE	93.9	92.7	3.2	3.8	0.8	1.1	1.1	1.5	6.8	6.9	7.1	6.1	5.9	28.1	27.6	10.6	0.9	75.5	38.1	49.4	50.6
36688	MOBILE	70.6	66.4	22.1	25.0	4.3	5.3	3.0	3.7	0.1	0.0	0.0	35.2	60.2	4.4	0.1	0.0	0.0	99.7	21.2	40.3	59.7
36693	MOBILE	81.7	78.6	15.4	17.9	1.4	1.7	1.4	1.8	6.0	6.1	6.5	6.0	5.8	24.0	26.4	16.3	2.9	77.6	41.9	47.6	52.4
36695	MOBILE	86.6	84.3	9.2	10.6	2.1	2.6	1.9	2.4	7.7	7.4	7.3	6.7	6.9	30.9	25.5	6.8	0.7	73.4	35.0	49.0	51.0
36701	SELMA	43.1	42.2	55.5	56.2	0.6	0.7	0.7	0.7	7.3	7.1	7.6	7.2	6.9	25.1	24.7	12.2	1.9	73.6	36.7	45.9	54.1
36703	SELMA	24.3	22.9	74.8	76.1	0.2	0.2	0.5	0.6	8.5	8.0	8.2	8.3	7.9	24.7	21.9	11.0	1.6	70.6	32.6	44.9	55.2
36720	ALBERTA	3.9	3.8	94.6	94.6	0.0	0.0	1.8	1.9	7.2	7.7	8.8	9.5	7.5	24.8	21.6	10.7	2.2	70.4	32.1	45.9	54.1
36722	ARLINGTON	36.6	35.6	63.1	64.2	0.0	0.0	0.3	0.3	9.6	8.9	6.7	7.5	7.7	24.2	23.1	11.6	0.8	70.3	33.0	47.3	52.8
36726	CAMDEN	34.2	33.6	65.2	65.7	0.3	0.3	0.9	1.0	8.0	7.7	7.7	7.6	7.0	25.0	22.6	12.0	2.5	71.9	35.8	47.3	52.7
36727	CAMPBELL	30.6	30.2	68.3	68.6	0.0	0.0	0.0	0.6	5.3	8.3	7.7	6.5	5.3	29.6	22.5	13.6	1.2	72.8	38.3	49.7	50.3
36728	CATHERINE	22.4	21.5	77.2	78.0	0.0	0.0	0.3	0.5	6.7	7.3	10.5	8.3	7.6	23.9	24.3	9.4	2.1	70.6	34.4	45.3	54.8
36732	DEMOPOLIS	47.1	45.7	51.6	52.8	0.2	0.2	1.0	1.2	7.2	7.4	8.3	7.4	6.6	25.3	23.6	12.3	2.0	72.4	36.4	46.0	54.0
36736	DIXONS MILLS	23.3	22.3	76.3	77.1	0.2	0.3	0.3	0.4	6.6	7.4	9.0	7.1	7.0	24.6	25.4	10.9	2.1	72.4	35.0	48.0	52.0
36738	FAUNSDALE	31.5	30.6	67.5	68.4	0.2	0.2	2.0	2.3	7.2	7.3	9.7	8.1	5.9	24.7	22.9	12.7	1.5	70.7	35.7	48.8	51.2
36740	FORKLAND	19.9	19.4	79.8	80.3	0.0	0.0	0.4	0.4	8.2	8.1	8.4	6.8	6.0	23.9	25.3	11.6	1.7	71.0	36.5	48.5	51.5
36742	GALLION	62.6	61.4	36.6	37.6	0.4	0.4	1.0	1.3	6.8	7.1	8.6	8.2	6.4	25.7	25.3	10.7	1.3	72.2	36.2	49.2	50.8
36744	GREENSBORO	32.6	31.6	66.5	67.3	0.1	0.1	0.9	1.1	8.4	8.1	8.0	7.4	7.0	24.8	22.6	11.4	2.4	71.1	34.8	47.2	52.8
36748	LINDEN	52.3	51.1	46.8	47.7	0.2	0.3	1.0	1.2	7.0	7.0	7.9	6.8	6.2	23.7	24.2	14.4	2.9	73.8	38.8	46.9	53.2
36749	JONES	53.3	50.8	46.0	48.5	0.0	0.0	0.7	0.7	6.7	7.2	7.6	8.3	6.5	25.0	26.5	10.8	1.5	73.5	37.5	48.8	51.3
36750	MAPLESVILLE	76.0	75.4	22.5	22.7	0.1	0.1	1.5	1.9	7.2	7.4	7.9	7.5	6.4	27.6	23.6	11.1	1.4	73.1	35.5	51.0	49.0
36751	LOWER PEACH TREE	6.7	6.4	93.1	93.2	0.0	0.0	0.5	0.5	9.7	9.7	10.8	8.2	8.5	24.5	18.8	8.9	0.9	64.5	27.5	46.6	53.4
36752	LOWNDESBORO	55.3	53.5	42.8	44.4	0.4	0.4	0.7	0.8	6.0	6.2	7.1	6.3	5.2	23.6	29.4	14.8	1.6	76.8	42.0	48.1	51.9
36754	MAGNOLIA	43.3	42.3	55.9	57.2	0.0	0.0	0.6	0.6	7.2	7.2	8.6	6.9	6.9	25.1	22.9	13.3	1.9	72.7	35.7	47.8	52.2
36756	MARION	41.3	40.0	57.8	59.0	0.1	0.1	0.8	0.9	6.8	6.8	7.4	9.7	7.3	22.9	22.8	13.5	2.8	74.1	35.9	46.6	53.4
36758	PLANTERSVILLE	65.6	63.7	32.8	34.5	0.1	0.1	0.6	0.7	7.1	6.9	6.9	7.5	7.2	29.3	24.9	8.9	1.3	74.6	36.2	49.1	50.9
36759	MARION JUNCTION	35.5	33.8	64.0	65.6	0.0	0.0	0.9	0.9	6.2	6.6	8.2	7.2	6.6	24.6	25.6	13.2	1.9	74.6	38.6	47.1	52.9
36761	MINTER	20.8	18.9	79.0	80.9	0.0	0.0	0.4	0.4	7.1	6.3	7.2	9.1	7.4	22.3	22.5	15.5	2.6	73.6	37.9	47.6	52.4
36762	MORVIN	74.0	75.0	24.0	25.0	0.0	0.0	0.0	0.0	4.2	8.3	8.3	6.3	6.3	29.2	25.0	12.5	0.0	79.2	38.8	47.9	52.1
36765	NEWBERN	24.6	23.7	73.9	74.7	0.2	0.2	0.5	0.7	8.0	7.6	7.9	8.4	7.5	24.7	23.1	11.2	1.6	71.5	34.2	48.7	51.3
36767	ORRVILLE	15.4	13.7	84.0	85.5	0.0	0.0	1.0	1.2	7.1	7.2	8.4	7.0	7.7	25.2	23.5	11.9	2.1	73.2	35.1	45.3	54.7
36768	PINE APPLE	24.4	23.8	75.1	75.7	0.3	0.3	0.3	0.3	7.6	7.0	6.6	7.0	7.8	22.9	24.9	13.0	3.2	74.2	37.8	47.8	52.2
36769	PINE HILL	31.9	30.5	67.6	68.9	0.1	0.1	0.6	0.6	8.9	8.6	9.0	7.5	7.2	25.0	21.9	10.9	1.1	69.0	31.8	47.7	52.3
36773	SAFFORD	27.2	25.0	72.6	74.9	0.0	0.0	0.8	0.6	6.3	5.9	5.7	8.1	6.5	21.2	25.2	18.7	2.6	77.2	42.4	48.5	51.5
36775	SARDIS	25.1	23.0	74.1	76.0	0.4	0.5	0.2	0.2	4.5	5.8	7.1	6.9	6.8	24.1	25.2	16.5	3.2	78.0	41.5	47.3	52.8
36776	SAWYERVILLE	15.2	14.3	84.3	85.2	0.0	0.0	0.8	0.8	9.7	9.3	8.8	8.3	7.1	27.1	19.6	9.1	1.0	67.2	30.9	45.8	54.2
36782	SWEET WATER	52.5	51.4	46.9	48.0	0.0	0.0	0.9	0.9	7.0	7.0	6.5	6.8	6.4	25.3	26.1	13.3	1.7	75.4	38.7	49.6	50.5
36783	THOMASTON	32.9	31.7	66.1	67.1	0.2	0.2	1.1	1.3	6.1	6.2	7.9	8.5	6.9	23.7	25.0	13.4	2.3	74.3	38.4	46.6	53.4
36784	THOMASVILLE	59.2	58.1	39.7	40.7	0.2	0.2	0.7	0.9	7.2	7.2	8.0	7.2	6.5	26.3	24.1	11.5	2.0	73.2	36.3	47.6	52.4
36785	TYLER	25.1	22.8	74.6	76.9	0.0	0.0	0.5	0.7	6.2	7.5	7.9	7.8	7.2	25.2	25.6	11.5	1.2	73.7	36.1	45.9	54.1
36786	UNIONTOWN	9.5	9.0	90.1	90.5	0.0	0.0	1.0	0.9	10.0	9.2	9.8	8.1	8.0	23.5	18.9	10.7	1.9	65.9	28.9	44.0	56.0
36790	STANTON	79.9	78.7	19.4	20.4	0.0	0.0	0.7	0.9	6.4	6.7	8.2	7.9	7.0	27.1	24.4	10.7	1.5	73.5	36.0	51.5	48.5
36792	RANDOLPH	88.1	87.4	9.4	9.8	0.1	0.1	2.2	2.6	7.6	7.5	7.5	5.9	5.8	28.4	24.7	11.4	1.1	73.8	36.0	48.5	51.6
36793	LAWLEY	83.1	82.3	15.7	16.4	0.0	0.0	1.5	1.9	6.9	6.9	6.9	6.2	6.3	27.4	25.7	12.4	1.3	75.4	37.5	49.6	50.4
36801	OPELIKA	55.7	54.6	42.3	43.0	0.8	1.1	1.2	1.5	7.2	7.0	7.4	7.0	6.8	28.0	22.8	11.5	2.3	74.0	35.3	45.9	54.1
36804	OPELIKA	71.5	70.2	26.1	26.9	1.3	1.5	0.8	0.9	7.6	7.6	8.0	7.2	6.6	29.9	24.7	7.8	0.7	72.4	34.4	49.6	50.4
36830	AUBURN	77.3	75.4	17.5	18.5	3.2	3.9	1.8	2.2	5.4	5.3	5.3	8.7	21.9	27.6	17.5	7.3	1.1	81.2	26.8	50.4	49.6
36832	AUBURN	70.8	68.8	24.9	26.2	2.8	3.3	1.2	1.5	3.6	3.5	3.6	15.3	40.3	19.5	10.2	3.7	0.4	87.1	23.0	53.9	46.1
36849	AUBURN UNIVERSITY	90.1	89.0	7.6	8.2	0.9	1.2	1.0	1.3	0.1	0.1	0.1	65.1	32.9	1.3	0.4	0.0	0.0	99.4	18.8	21.4	78.6
36850	CAMP HILL	35.3	34.2	63.5	64.5	0.0	0.0	1.0	1.1	6.8	7.0	7.5	6.2	5.9	24.6	27.9	12.6	1.6	74.8	39.0	47.7	52.3
	ALABAMA	71.1	70.3	26.0	26.4	0.7	0.9	1.7	2.1	6.7	6.7	7.0	6.8	7.2	28.0	24.5	11.6	1.6	75.8	36.6	48.5	51.5
	UNITED STATES	75.1	73.6	12.3	12.5	3.8	4.2	12.5	14.1	6.9	6.7	7.2	7.0	7.3	28.6	23.8	10.8	1.7	75.1	36.0	49.1	50.9

ZIP CODE #	POST OFFICE NAME	2004 Per Capita Income	2004 HH Income Base	2004 Household Income Distribution (%): Less than $25,000	$25,000 to $49,999	$50,000 to $99,999	$100,000 to $149,999	$150,000 or More	Median Household Income: 2004	2009	2004 National Centile	2004 State Centile	2004 Home Value Base	2004 Home Value Distribution (%): Less than $50,000	$50,000 to $89,999	$90,000 to $174,999	$175,000 to $399,999	$400,000 or More	2004 Median Home Value
36539	FRUITDALE	16364	367	28.3	37.9	28.9	3.3	1.6	40072	43638	46	75	335	40.9	27.5	24.2	5.1	2.4	69792
36540	GAINESTOWN	10655	279	54.1	26.2	16.9	1.8	1.1	22882	26378	3	10	248	53.6	31.1	10.1	4.4	0.8	47500
36541	GRAND BAY	17946	4880	27.3	31.7	33.0	5.9	2.2	42372	48147	54	81	4245	25.0	28.2	33.8	10.2	2.8	85896
36542	GULF SHORES	28304	4494	26.0	29.4	31.3	7.9	5.3	44826	50693	61	86	3469	3.9	5.5	38.8	39.6	12.3	179562
36544	IRVINGTON	16488	3852	33.1	32.5	27.9	4.3	2.3	35519	39824	30	56	3201	33.4	32.1	26.2	6.8	1.5	72191
36545	JACKSON	18168	4266	40.0	24.7	26.2	6.0	3.1	34581	39849	26	51	3514	35.4	27.0	25.8	10.6	1.2	69153
36548	LEROY	17970	432	35.4	19.9	38.7	5.8	0.2	40000	42495	46	74	378	33.9	25.1	33.1	7.7	0.3	72778
36549	LILLIAN	24656	2359	26.2	37.0	30.3	4.2	2.4	41143	47576	50	78	2169	14.6	24.0	36.7	19.3	5.4	106961
36550	LITTLE RIVER	23585	173	42.8	34.1	13.3	4.1	5.8	31931	35630	18	39	155	34.8	27.1	30.3	7.7	0.0	69500
36551	LOXLEY	17881	2415	31.2	31.0	30.1	5.8	1.9	38786	43154	42	71	1983	23.5	21.8	34.5	18.2	2.0	98147
36553	MC INTOSH	13003	1687	39.5	35.6	22.1	2.5	0.4	32143	36436	18	40	1423	46.9	28.5	20.9	3.0	0.7	58241
36555	MAGNOLIA SPRINGS	28768	284	30.3	32.4	23.9	6.3	7.0	42011	47371	53	80	241	6.2	10.8	34.9	28.2	19.9	171121
36558	MILLRY	17085	1318	39.6	30.4	25.5	2.9	1.7	32848	37093	20	45	1131	43.5	27.6	25.8	2.0	1.1	56391
36560	MOUNT VERNON	12858	1493	46.6	29.1	20.2	3.5	0.6	27010	30363	7	20	1228	44.5	32.9	19.7	2.1	0.7	55877
36561	ORANGE BEACH	36019	2615	25.7	28.7	27.5	8.5	9.6	44552	50442	60	86	2010	3.2	4.2	24.4	38.9	29.4	260131
36562	PERDIDO	15824	607	28.3	40.2	27.8	3.6	0.0	36310	40975	33	61	528	40.3	30.5	24.8	4.2	0.2	58793
36567	ROBERTSDALE	19674	4435	29.5	29.8	31.9	5.7	3.1	41884	46595	53	79	3656	17.0	23.1	41.3	15.7	2.9	102321
36569	SAINT STEPHENS	16993	300	33.7	23.0	37.3	5.3	0.7	38551	41899	41	70	266	40.6	29.7	27.1	1.9	0.8	60000
36571	SARALAND	20806	5272	28.0	32.9	30.7	6.1	2.4	41261	46129	51	78	4017	14.6	31.6	45.5	7.3	1.0	92918
36572	SATSUMA	26540	2179	18.9	30.6	36.6	10.6	3.4	50514	56769	73	92	1855	9.3	21.2	56.5	12.0	1.0	109022
36574	SEMINOLE	22105	511	21.1	30.9	38.9	6.1	2.9	48281	54734	69	91	439	17.3	19.8	39.0	20.1	3.9	112269
36575	SEMMES	18406	5860	24.1	31.1	36.8	6.6	1.4	45378	50940	62	87	5075	18.2	30.1	42.1	9.2	0.5	91460
36576	SILVERHILL	20599	1626	24.1	35.9	30.7	6.7	2.6	42380	47969	54	81	1377	21.1	19.1	39.1	18.3	2.3	110539
36578	STAPLETON	19237	420	25.2	33.3	32.1	7.4	1.9	43854	49054	58	85	358	26.0	26.3	27.4	18.4	2.0	83333
36579	STOCKTON	16916	786	37.7	32.8	23.0	5.1	1.4	35969	39697	31	58	672	41.8	24.0	20.7	12.5	1.0	58462
36580	SUMMERDALE	18223	1859	31.2	32.2	27.5	7.4	1.7	38178	42548	40	68	1585	20.9	21.8	40.3	14.2	2.9	99790
36582	THEODORE	18496	8010	31.7	31.5	28.6	5.9	2.4	39347	44650	44	72	6521	19.7	28.9	37.2	11.5	2.8	91348
36583	TIBBIE	18457	121	32.2	24.8	38.8	4.1	0.0	41430	45322	51	78	107	29.9	30.8	26.2	8.4	4.7	77727
36584	VINEGAR BEND	14908	172	51.2	23.8	20.4	1.7	2.9	23956	27722	4	12	154	48.1	21.4	22.7	5.8	2.0	52143
36585	WAGARVILLE	18152	652	34.7	27.5	31.9	4.1	1.8	37893	41973	39	67	547	32.9	36.2	25.4	5.3	0.2	66172
36587	WILMER	18591	3202	31.0	31.5	30.7	4.2	2.7	39636	45011	45	72	2773	27.0	24.5	33.7	12.9	2.1	87768
36602	MOBILE	22113	541	65.4	14.8	13.9	3.1	2.8	15329	17105	1	1	139	15.1	5.8	33.1	41.7	4.3	163542
36603	MOBILE	9561	4070	70.5	16.7	10.1	1.5	1.3	13132	15270	1	1	1516	37.9	35.2	20.0	5.2	1.7	61301
36604	MOBILE	17484	4686	45.4	28.2	18.8	5.1	2.5	27871	31750	8	22	2615	14.5	26.1	39.1	19.2	1.2	101748
36605	MOBILE	13949	11883	46.4	29.1	19.9	3.3	1.3	27604	30906	8	21	7783	24.8	50.9	17.6	3.8	2.9	67207
36606	MOBILE	19159	7770	38.4	33.5	21.7	4.3	2.1	32477	36489	19	43	4693	12.2	44.2	37.6	5.4	0.7	83635
36607	MOBILE	18336	3527	51.6	26.4	14.3	4.7	3.1	23759	27055	4	12	1803	24.5	33.9	25.9	11.8	4.0	78611
36608	MOBILE	28172	14466	29.2	28.4	25.9	8.1	8.3	41618	46268	52	79	9305	6.9	19.1	41.5	23.5	9.0	122370
36609	MOBILE	22270	10605	33.5	28.3	28.4	6.4	3.4	37413	41337	37	65	5191	2.3	26.8	55.1	15.1	0.8	112394
36610	MOBILE	9961	6189	66.4	21.2	9.5	1.9	1.1	16305	18673	1	2	3049	52.5	37.3	8.4	1.6	0.1	48053
36611	MOBILE	16173	2624	42.2	33.3	20.7	3.5	0.4	30291	33816	13	31	1745	21.2	52.9	24.2	1.7	0.1	69932
36612	MOBILE	11884	1886	50.7	31.0	15.1	3.1	0.2	24573	27902	4	14	1163	36.9	47.3	14.7	1.1	0.0	58764
36613	EIGHT MILE	19687	4277	29.1	31.5	30.0	7.3	2.0	40559	46328	48	76	3635	22.0	35.5	36.6	4.8	1.0	81682
36615	MOBILE	8537	168	57.7	29.2	12.5	0.6	0.0	20296	23150	2	4	27	33.3	66.7	0.0	0.0	0.0	54500
36617	MOBILE	13402	5839	54.3	26.3	15.4	2.9	1.0	22386	25682	3	9	3807	28.5	44.8	25.1	1.7	0.0	66912
36618	MOBILE	19982	5775	26.2	30.9	33.6	7.2	2.2	43393	48762	57	84	4661	7.9	44.6	41.9	5.1	0.5	87890
36619	MOBILE	24433	5419	26.2	30.2	30.5	9.2	3.9	45384	50610	62	87	4482	10.7	32.3	39.5	15.8	1.8	96632
36688	MOBILE	10604	4	0.0	100.0	0.0	0.0	0.0	35000	40000	28	53	0	0.0	0.0	0.0	0.0	0.0	0
36693	MOBILE	28144	7433	21.8	27.0	34.5	11.4	5.4	51025	56515	74	93	5628	2.8	12.1	64.1	18.9	2.1	121815
36695	MOBILE	27735	12238	16.6	24.5	38.9	13.4	6.7	58196	64873	83	96	9634	5.2	8.9	53.0	29.7	3.2	141118
36701	SELMA	17777	9700	43.1	26.9	22.4	5.2	2.4	30654	35253	14	32	6771	28.5	32.8	28.3	8.9	1.5	76851
36703	SELMA	13056	5265	56.6	21.3	17.7	3.4	1.0	20358	23324	2	4	2963	48.5	24.0	20.0	7.0	0.5	51883
36720	ALBERTA	7499	458	67.9	22.7	7.0	2.4	0.0	13919	15860	1	1	423	55.3	24.4	8.8	11.6	0.0	43182
36722	ARLINGTON	12297	231	55.4	28.1	11.3	2.2	3.0	21331	25000	2	6	217	60.4	23.0	8.8	4.6	3.2	39643
36726	CAMDEN	13674	2034	53.5	26.2	14.4	4.5	1.4	21726	25072	2	8	1570	45.0	28.2	18.6	6.5	1.7	57290
36727	CAMPBELL	11760	65	46.2	38.5	13.9	1.5	0.0	26163	28208	6	18	58	69.0	22.4	3.5	3.5	1.7	35000
36728	CATHERINE	10095	231	59.3	25.5	11.7	2.2	1.3	20959	24064	2	5	211	56.4	25.1	11.9	2.4	4.3	44375
36732	DEMOPOLIS	19374	3698	44.9	24.6	19.6	7.7	3.3	30318	35590	13	31	2554	28.4	25.2	32.5	13.4	0.5	84945
36736	DIXONS MILLS	11909	451	57.4	20.0	17.5	4.4	0.7	19102	23259	2	3	411	52.6	27.0	14.4	1.2	4.9	45435
36738	FAUNSDALE	12322	343	55.7	24.5	14.3	5.3	0.3	21528	25497	2	7	272	57.4	21.7	10.7	9.6	0.7	42593
36740	FORKLAND	16547	809	51.9	29.2	13.8	2.4	2.7	23480	26763	4	11	704	53.3	22.4	19.7	4.6	0.0	47356
36742	GALLION	17469	917	35.3	27.0	29.8	6.5	1.3	35043	40360	28	54	777	41.6	26.0	21.0	9.4	2.1	65526
36744	GREENSBORO	14196	2934	49.4	26.8	18.2	4.1	1.5	25390	28527	5	16	2164	43.4	27.6	21.6	5.5	2.0	56792
36748	LINDEN	18125	1784	43.1	23.5	26.6	5.8	1.0	30399	35813	13	31	1401	38.3	34.8	22.5	4.0	0.5	63253
36749	JONES	15252	419	51.1	21.0	23.2	2.4	2.4	24262	27807	4	13	351	42.2	23.9	22.8	10.8	0.3	70227
36750	MAPLESVILLE	16204	1209	36.2	30.3	27.9	5.1	0.5	35025	38597	28	53	1027	29.4	28.2	34.3	7.6	0.5	80977
36751	LOWER PEACH TREE	12393	143	67.8	18.9	8.4	2.8	2.1	12230	13358	1	1	122	57.4	24.6	13.1	1.6	3.3	39444
36752	LOWNDESBORO	23875	873	34.6	23.4	29.8	7.5	4.8	40796	46243	49	77	739	36.4	20.8	28.4	13.5	0.8	81230
36754	MAGNOLIA	15777	150	50.7	21.3	20.7	6.0	1.3	24356	29681	4	14	123	49.6	26.8	17.9	5.7	0.0	50556
36756	MARION	14224	2824	48.4	27.1	19.0	3.8	1.7	26129	29422	6	18	2066	48.5	26.9	17.7	6.2	0.7	52370
36758	PLANTERSVILLE	13923	643	51.2	25.5	17.3	5.9	0.2	24300	27632	4	13	547	55.4	18.5	19.0	7.1	0.0	40484
36759	MARION JUNCTION	17165	675	50.8	17.8	25.3	3.1	3.0	24330	28328	4	13	547	44.4	26.9	15.4	8.2	5.1	60147
36761	MINTER	11965	528	55.7	30.1	9.5	2.5	2.3	21384	24777	2	6	439	48.8	18.2	20.3	8.4	4.3	52292
36762	MORVIN	12665	16	37.5	31.3	25.0	6.3	0.0	35000	45000	28	53	15	60.0	13.3	13.3	6.7	6.7	45000
36765	NEWBERN	10972	492	55.5	24.6	18.1	1.8	0.0	21932	25195	3	8	399	40.1	39.1	14.0	6.3	0.5	61103
36767	ORRVILLE	10315	820	61.1	23.2	12.8	2.9	0.0	17330	20041	1	2	648	44.6	27.9	24.1	2.8	0.6	54070
36768	PINE APPLE	13923	492	63.6	19.5	13.2	1.8	1.8	15898	18055	1	2	425	63.5	16.0	15.3	5.2	0.0	27396
36769	PINE HILL	14444	1209	54.8	24.7	15.2	3.7	1.5	20909	24116	2	5	1063	51.4	27.9	15.1	3.8	2.0	48067
36773	SAFFORD	13155	200	59.5	25.5	8.0	3.0	4.0	18797	20607	1	3	161	45.3	24.8	18.6	8.1	3.1	57500
36775	SARDIS	19272	419	50.4	24.3	21.5	1.0	2.9	24546	29257	4	14	339	32.7	20.1	30.4	16.5	0.3	85000
36776	SAWYERVILLE	12424	691	54.1	29.2	12.3	2.3	2.0	22415	25476	3	9	615	62.4	22.0	14.6	1.0	0.0	36250
36782	SWEET WATER	17686	904	39.9	24.2	26.1	8.1	1.7	34380	39825	25	51	821	51.9	26.7	13.8	4.6	3.1	47500
36783	THOMASTON	15626	502	51.0	21.1	22.1	2.6	3.2	24212	28437	4	13	429	53.4	23.1	16.8	6.8	0.0	46463
36784	THOMASVILLE	16552	3412	40.9	27.1	25.4	5.6	1.1	31612	36342	17	37	2669	39.2	28.1	24.2	6.9	1.7	65161
36785	TYLER	13816	300	51.0	23.3	24.0	1.3	0.3	24170	27171	4	13	252	42.1	26.6	21.8	9.1	0.4	58333
36786	UNIONTOWN	9557	1414	64.6	24.5	8.9	1.1	0.9	16998	19118	1	2	923	61.1	25.7	10.4	2.2	0.7	40049
36790	STANTON	19067	141	37.6	29.8	27.0	5.0	0.7	35599	40000	30	57	119	37.8	29.4	26.9	5.9	0.0	68333
36792	RANDOLPH	16546	408	31.1	36.3	27.7	4.2	0.7	37236	41941	36	64	347	38.3	24.2	24.2	11.5	1.7	67000
36793	LAWLEY	16235	262	32.1	37.0	26.3	3.8	0.8	36807	41606	35	62	223	38.1	26.5	25.6	9.4	0.5	67941
36801	OPELIKA	19700	8420	37.9	26.5	26.4	6.6	2.7	35497	40894	29	56	4936	19.9	21.5	43.1	13.8	1.7	102822
36804	OPELIKA	20105	5788	26.7	30.3	32.3	8.5	2.3	42662	49064	55	82	4808	31.2	24.6	27.0	13.6	3.7	80580
36830	AUBURN	23949	13329	44.5	19.6	23.4	8.5	4.0	31149	36271	15	35	6001	15.0	9.3	37.3	33.1	5.3	147189
36832	AUBURN	13607	9768	68.2	17.3	9.5	3.5	1.4	13381	15960	1	1	4265	53.6	12.0	14.8	17.7	2.0	39419
36849	AUBURN UNIVERSITY	10957	7	14.3	14.3	28.6	0.0	42.9	85714	91685	96	100	3	0.0	0.0	0.0	100.0	0.0	193750
36850	CAMP HILL	16715	1139	46.8	30.9	17.2	3.3	1.8	26946	30203	7	20	897	44.9	32.0	16.2	5.4	1.6	55000
	ALABAMA	20998		34.3	28.7	26.3	7.2	3.5	37534	42371				22.7	26.7	33.4	14.6	2.7	90917
	UNITED STATES	25866		24.7	27.1	30.8	10.9	6.5	48124	56710				10.9	15.0	33.7	30.1	10.4	145905

#	POST OFFICE NAME	Auto Loan	Home Loan	Invest-ments	Retire-ment Plans	Home Repair	Lawn & Garden	Comput-ers & Hard-ware	Major Appli-ances	TV, Radio, Sound Equip-ment	Furni-ture	Dine out/ Carry out	Sports Equip-ment	Fees & Tickets	Toys & Games	Travel	Cable TV	Apparel & Services	Auto Repairs	Health Insur-ance	Pets & Supplies
ZIP CODE		FINANCIAL SERVICES				THE HOME: Home Improvements		THE HOME: Furnishings				ENTERTAINMENT						PERSONAL			
36539	FRUITDALE	83	56	25	48	63	72	54	67	65	55	76	80	46	72	55	70	69	66	83	95
36540	GAINESTOWN	55	39	26	34	42	50	40	47	48	41	56	54	36	52	40	51	52	47	57	62
36541	GRAND BAY	89	69	43	63	74	82	66	77	74	67	88	91	60	84	66	77	82	76	87	102
36542	GULF SHORES	95	80	66	76	88	100	77	89	83	78	101	98	73	94	81	88	95	87	102	111
36544	IRVINGTON	85	64	38	58	69	77	62	73	69	63	83	86	55	79	62	72	77	72	83	96
36545	JACKSON	84	63	37	57	69	77	60	71	68	60	81	85	54	79	61	72	75	70	83	97
36548	LEROY	82	61	36	55	68	76	58	70	67	59	80	83	53	77	59	71	74	68	82	95
36549	LILLIAN	77	72	70	67	76	88	68	77	72	72	89	77	67	78	72	76	83	75	88	87
36550	LITTLE RIVER	106	78	46	69	88	100	74	91	86	74	102	107	65	99	78	92	94	90	109	126
36551	LOXLEY	81	69	49	64	72	77	65	72	69	66	84	85	61	81	65	70	79	72	78	92
36553	MC INTOSH	69	46	21	40	52	60	45	56	54	46	63	67	38	60	45	58	58	55	69	79
36555	MAGNOLIA SPRINGS	83	91	94	87	91	98	86	88	86	86	107	99	89	109	89	88	105	86	89	98
36558	MILLRY	79	53	24	46	60	69	51	64	62	52	73	76	44	69	52	67	66	63	79	91
36560	MOUNT VERNON	65	46	26	40	51	58	45	54	53	46	63	64	39	59	45	57	58	54	66	74
36561	ORANGE BEACH	123	103	81	96	112	124	100	114	109	98	131	134	92	130	104	113	123	113	128	149
36562	PERDIDO	79	53	24	46	60	69	51	64	62	52	73	77	44	69	52	67	66	64	79	91
36567	ROBERTSDALE	85	73	54	70	76	82	71	78	75	71	91	90	66	88	70	76	86	77	83	96
36569	SAINT STEPHENS	78	64	43	59	68	75	59	68	66	60	79	81	56	79	61	68	74	67	77	91
36571	SARALAND	79	72	60	69	75	83	71	76	75	70	91	87	69	91	72	77	86	74	82	91
36572	SATSUMA	113	105	87	101	109	116	98	107	102	98	124	126	96	126	100	104	119	104	112	132
36574	SEMINOLE	90	82	64	79	82	87	78	84	79	80	98	97	74	92	77	78	94	83	83	99
36575	SEMMES	81	75	60	72	76	80	71	76	72	72	88	89	68	86	70	71	85	75	76	92
36576	SILVERHILL	87	77	59	74	78	84	75	81	77	76	95	93	70	90	74	77	90	80	83	97
36578	STAPLETON	82	74	58	71	75	79	71	76	72	72	89	88	67	85	70	71	85	76	76	91
36579	STOCKTON	78	54	28	48	62	70	52	65	62	53	73	77	45	70	54	67	67	64	79	91
36580	SUMMERDALE	82	67	45	62	70	76	64	72	69	65	84	85	58	79	64	70	79	72	78	92
36582	THEODORE	84	65	42	61	71	79	64	73	71	64	85	86	58	83	64	74	79	72	84	96
36583	TIBBIE	87	58	26	50	66	76	56	71	68	57	80	84	48	76	57	73	73	70	87	100
36584	VINEGAR BEND	68	46	21	39	52	59	44	55	53	45	62	66	37	59	45	57	57	54	68	78
36585	WAGARVILLE	85	59	30	52	66	76	57	70	67	58	79	83	50	76	58	72	73	69	84	98
36587	WILMER	84	76	59	73	77	81	72	78	73	74	91	90	69	86	72	73	87	77	78	93
36602	MOBILE	42	38	55	39	38	45	47	43	50	45	62	51	46	61	46	51	60	47	47	48
36603	MOBILE	37	31	36	28	30	36	35	35	39	36	48	38	34	44	34	41	46	36	39	40
36604	MOBILE	55	53	63	53	52	58	58	56	59	57	74	65	58	72	57	59	72	58	56	62
36605	MOBILE	53	48	50	45	48	54	50	51	54	50	67	57	50	66	50	56	64	51	55	59
36606	MOBILE	59	58	66	58	58	64	62	60	63	61	78	70	62	78	61	63	76	62	61	67
36607	MOBILE	56	53	64	52	53	60	58	57	61	58	76	64	58	74	58	63	74	59	60	64
36608	MOBILE	91	93	109	95	92	98	98	94	96	97	120	111	98	120	96	94	118	97	90	105
36609	MOBILE	67	66	80	68	65	70	73	69	72	71	90	83	72	89	71	70	88	72	66	76
36610	MOBILE	39	32	35	28	31	38	36	37	41	37	50	40	35	46	35	44	48	38	43	43
36611	MOBILE	54	47	40	45	50	58	50	52	54	48	65	58	48	65	50	57	61	52	60	61
36612	MOBILE	45	39	44	36	38	46	42	43	47	44	58	47	42	55	42	50	56	44	48	50
36613	EIGHT MILE	85	77	66	72	79	88	74	79	79	74	97	91	73	96	75	82	92	78	87	98
36615	MOBILE	37	34	41	32	33	38	37	36	40	38	50	40	38	50	37	41	49	37	38	41
36617	MOBILE	50	44	49	41	44	52	47	48	52	49	64	51	48	60	47	55	62	49	53	55
36618	MOBILE	71	75	79	72	74	81	72	73	73	72	91	84	75	94	74	75	89	72	74	84
36619	MOBILE	99	91	75	88	95	102	87	94	90	86	110	109	85	111	88	92	105	91	99	114
36688	MOBILE	49	30	38	34	30	36	59	43	57	49	71	60	48	64	47	50	67	52	40	49
36693	MOBILE	93	101	104	100	101	108	97	98	96	96	119	112	99	121	99	96	116	97	98	110
36695	MOBILE	106	111	112	116	108	108	107	105	101	110	128	125	108	126	104	96	126	105	94	118
36701	SELMA	67	58	53	54	59	67	59	63	65	60	79	71	57	75	59	67	75	63	69	75
36703	SELMA	53	41	35	36	42	50	43	47	50	44	60	54	41	56	43	53	57	48	56	59
36720	ALBERTA	31	25	26	22	25	31	28	29	33	29	39	31	27	35	27	35	37	30	35	34
36722	ARLINGTON	63	43	24	38	48	56	43	52	51	44	61	61	37	57	43	55	56	52	64	72
36726	CAMDEN	53	42	39	39	43	52	46	49	52	47	63	53	44	58	45	56	59	50	57	57
36727	CAMPBELL	58	39	17	33	44	50	37	47	45	38	53	56	32	50	38	48	48	46	57	66
36728	CATHERINE	46	35	32	31	36	44	38	42	45	39	53	46	36	48	37	48	50	42	50	51
36732	DEMOPOLIS	72	60	54	57	62	72	63	67	69	63	84	76	61	80	63	72	80	68	75	81
36736	DIXONS MILLS	59	40	18	34	45	52	38	48	46	39	54	57	33	51	39	50	49	47	59	68
36738	FAUNSDALE	60	40	18	35	46	52	39	48	47	40	55	58	33	52	39	50	50	48	60	69
36740	FORKLAND	72	51	32	44	55	65	52	61	61	53	73	70	46	67	52	66	67	61	74	82
36742	GALLION	78	60	37	55	64	71	58	67	64	59	77	79	52	73	58	66	72	67	75	88
36744	GREENSBORO	62	45	30	40	49	58	47	54	55	47	65	61	42	60	47	59	60	54	65	70
36748	LINDEN	82	55	27	49	62	72	55	67	65	55	77	79	47	72	55	70	70	66	82	93
36749	JONES	74	50	22	43	56	65	48	60	58	49	68	72	41	64	49	62	62	59	74	85
36750	MAPLESVILLE	80	54	25	47	61	71	52	65	63	53	74	78	45	70	53	68	67	65	80	92
36751	LOWER PEACH TREE	54	43	45	38	43	53	49	51	56	50	68	54	47	60	47	60	64	52	60	59
36752	LOWNDESBORO	106	71	32	61	80	92	68	85	82	70	97	102	58	91	69	89	88	85	105	121
36754	MAGNOLIA	72	48	22	41	54	63	46	58	56	47	66	69	39	62	47	60	60	57	71	82
36756	MARION	62	44	29	39	48	57	46	53	54	46	64	61	41	59	46	58	59	53	65	70
36758	PLANTERSVILLE	67	46	21	40	52	59	44	55	53	45	62	65	38	59	45	57	57	54	67	77
36759	MARION JUNCTION	79	55	31	48	61	70	54	65	64	55	76	77	48	71	55	69	70	65	79	90
36761	MINTER	51	38	32	33	40	48	41	45	48	42	57	50	38	51	40	51	53	46	54	56
36762	MORVIN	72	48	22	41	54	62	46	58	56	47	66	69	39	62	47	60	60	57	71	82
36765	NEWBERN	54	37	19	32	41	48	36	44	44	37	51	52	31	48	37	47	47	44	54	62
36767	ORRVILLE	40	32	33	28	32	39	36	37	41	37	50	40	34	44	35	44	47	38	44	43
36768	PINE APPLE	51	40	42	36	40	50	45	47	53	47	63	51	44	56	44	56	60	49	56	55
36769	PINE HILL	65	47	34	41	50	60	49	56	58	50	69	64	44	63	49	62	64	56	68	73
36773	SAFFORD	50	39	39	35	40	49	44	46	51	45	61	50	42	54	43	55	58	48	55	55
36775	SARDIS	84	57	31	50	64	74	57	69	68	58	80	81	49	75	57	73	73	69	85	96
36776	SAWYERVILLE	65	44	20	38	49	57	42	53	51	43	60	63	36	56	43	55	54	52	65	75
36782	SWEET WATER	86	58	26	50	65	75	55	69	67	57	79	83	47	74	56	72	71	69	86	99
36783	THOMASTON	73	49	22	42	55	63	47	59	57	48	67	70	40	63	48	61	60	58	72	83
36784	THOMASVILLE	73	52	30	46	57	66	52	62	61	52	72	73	46	69	52	65	66	62	74	83
36785	TYLER	53	40	34	35	42	50	43	47	50	44	60	53	40	54	42	54	56	48	57	59
36786	UNIONTOWN	38	30	32	27	30	36	34	35	39	35	47	39	32	43	33	42	45	36	41	42
36790	STANTON	84	56	25	48	63	73	54	68	65	55	76	81	46	72	55	70	70	67	83	96
36792	RANDOLPH	80	55	27	49	62	71	53	66	63	55	75	78	46	71	54	67	68	65	79	92
36793	LAWLEY	81	54	25	47	61	71	52	65	63	53	74	78	45	70	53	68	67	65	81	93
36801	OPELIKA	68	62	66	61	62	69	66	66	69	66	85	77	65	83	65	69	82	68	68	76
36804	OPELIKA	87	78	61	75	79	84	74	80	76	76	93	94	70	90	74	76	89	80	82	98
36830	AUBURN	74	60	69	64	59	66	81	69	79	74	99	89	73	93	72	73	95	77	65	79
36832	AUBURN	40	28	33	31	28	32	45	36	44	40	55	48	38	50	38	40	52	42	34	41
36849	AUBURN UNIVERSITY	219	134	169	152	131	159	259	190	251	219	314	265	211	282	207	221	295	232	176	217
36850	CAMP HILL	69	50	35	44	54	63	51	59	60	52	71	68	46	66	51	64	66	59	71	78
	ALABAMA	81	70	61	67	72	80	70	75	75	70	91	87	67	89	70	76	86	75	81	92
	UNITED STATES	100	100	100	100	100	100	100	100	100	100	100	100	100	100	100	100	100	100	100	100

POPULATION CHANGE

ZIP CODE		COUNTY FIPS CODE	POPULATION			2000-2004 ANNUAL RATE		HOUSEHOLDS					FAMILIES		
#	POST OFFICE NAME		2000	2004	2009	% Rate	State Centile	2000	2004	2009	% Annual Rate 2000-2004	2004 Average HH Size	2000	2004	% Annual Rate 2000-2004
36852	CUSSETA	017	2041	2217	2375	2.0	90	771	852	927	2.4	2.60	578	636	2.3
36853	DADEVILLE	123	8204	8536	8710	0.9	72	3287	3515	3655	1.6	2.33	2390	2550	1.5
36854	VALLEY	017	14146	14291	14283	0.2	46	5687	5847	5955	0.7	2.42	4037	4149	0.7
36855	FIVE POINTS	017	1718	1724	1691	0.1	39	712	734	739	0.7	2.35	506	521	0.7
36856	FORT MITCHELL	113	1584	1658	1706	1.1	76	562	597	626	1.4	2.78	423	448	1.4
36858	HATCHECHUBBEE	113	762	749	751	-0.4	20	298	300	308	0.2	2.50	201	202	0.1
36860	HURTSBORO	113	1872	1835	1838	-0.5	18	796	801	821	0.2	2.29	500	501	0.1
36861	JACKSONS GAP	123	3411	3740	3908	2.2	91	1376	1536	1628	2.6	2.43	1032	1149	2.6
36862	LAFAYETTE	017	7102	7055	6893	-0.2	28	2660	2710	2711	0.4	2.49	1866	1898	0.4
36863	LANETT	017	13513	12812	12271	-1.3	4	5383	5207	5096	-0.8	2.45	3761	3635	-0.8
36866	NOTASULGA	087	3322	3350	3440	0.2	44	1367	1415	1488	0.8	2.37	923	954	0.8
36867	PHENIX CITY	113	18332	19139	19884	1.0	74	7730	8213	8680	1.4	2.30	5059	5398	1.5
36869	PHENIX CITY	113	19445	19652	19982	0.3	47	7351	7600	7894	0.8	2.53	5167	5336	0.8
36870	PHENIX CITY	081	12815	13737	14777	1.7	85	4603	4996	5441	2.0	2.75	3611	3915	1.9
36871	PITTSVIEW	113	1484	1589	1654	1.6	83	583	640	681	2.2	2.47	416	455	2.1
36874	SALEM	081	6698	7202	7776	1.7	86	2436	2674	2939	2.2	2.69	1932	2113	2.1
36875	SEALE	113	4920	5178	5344	1.2	77	1804	1936	2038	1.7	2.67	1342	1438	1.6
36877	SMITHS STATION	081	9796	10860	11946	2.5	94	3635	4092	4568	2.8	2.65	2866	3217	2.8
36879	WAVERLY	017	1094	1098	1120	0.1	40	449	461	479	0.6	2.38	309	316	0.5
36904	BUTLER	023	4863	5010	5133	0.7	66	2006	2128	2248	1.4	2.29	1399	1482	1.4
36907	CUBA	119	2010	2103	2130	1.1	75	768	820	849	1.6	2.56	533	569	1.6
36908	GILBERTOWN	023	2061	2083	2111	0.3	47	846	880	919	0.9	2.37	626	650	0.9
36910	JACHIN	023	356	342	343	-0.9	7	149	148	153	-0.2	2.31	102	101	-0.2
36912	LISMAN	023	2145	2106	2120	-0.4	19	841	851	884	0.3	2.47	580	587	0.3
36915	NEEDHAM	023	204	203	205	-0.1	30	88	90	94	0.5	2.26	67	68	0.4
36916	PENNINGTON	023	596	605	615	0.4	53	251	264	277	1.2	2.29	171	180	1.2
36919	SILAS	023	2609	2633	2671	0.2	45	983	1025	1072	1.0	2.57	746	777	1.0
36921	TOXEY	023	2353	2376	2410	0.2	46	915	951	994	0.9	2.49	683	709	0.9
36922	WARD	023	862	867	873	0.1	42	337	350	363	0.9	2.48	234	243	0.9
36925	YORK	119	4607	4454	4345	-0.8	10	1698	1677	1675	-0.3	2.58	1124	1110	-0.3
	ALABAMA					0.5					0.9	2.45			0.9
	UNITED STATES					1.2					1.3	2.58			1.1

ZIP CODE		RACE (%)						% Hispanic Origin		2004 AGE DISTRIBUTION (%)										MEDIAN AGE	% 2004 Males	% 2004 Females
		White		Black		Asian/Pacific																
#	POST OFFICE NAME	2000	2004	2000	2004	2000	2004	2000	2004	0-4	5-9	10-14	15-19	20-24	25-44	45-64	65-84	85+	18+	2004	2004	2004
36852	CUSSETA	77.7	76.5	20.7	21.7	0.3	0.3	0.8	1.0	7.6	7.3	7.7	6.6	7.0	31.1	23.5	8.3	1.0	73.3	33.8	49.2	50.8
36853	DADEVILLE	73.6	72.5	24.9	25.8	0.2	0.3	0.7	0.8	5.5	5.7	6.1	5.5	4.8	24.1	29.6	16.5	2.2	79.2	43.8	48.9	51.1
36854	VALLEY	76.9	76.2	21.9	22.4	0.3	0.3	0.9	1.0	7.0	6.9	7.0	6.0	6.0	28.0	24.1	12.9	2.1	75.5	37.3	47.6	52.4
36855	FIVE POINTS	64.5	63.3	34.8	35.9	0.0	0.0	0.4	0.5	6.0	6.4	6.8	5.5	5.2	26.2	27.7	14.6	1.8	77.4	40.7	48.6	51.4
36856	FORT MITCHELL	61.9	59.8	33.1	34.6	1.1	1.2	3.1	3.8	8.6	8.1	8.4	6.9	7.2	29.1	23.0	8.0	0.7	70.8	33.2	49.2	50.8
36858	HATCHECHUBBEE	28.4	27.1	70.6	71.7	0.1	0.1	1.2	1.2	6.8	7.5	7.9	6.5	5.7	24.7	26.4	12.6	1.9	73.8	39.1	49.3	50.7
36860	HURTSBORO	18.9	17.9	80.5	81.5	0.1	0.1	0.5	0.5	6.7	7.6	7.7	6.8	5.4	24.3	25.1	14.2	2.3	74.0	39.4	47.6	52.4
36861	JACKSONS GAP	90.2	88.6	8.8	10.3	0.2	0.2	0.7	0.9	5.3	5.5	5.8	5.4	4.8	24.6	33.1	15.0	0.8	80.2	44.1	50.7	49.3
36862	LAFAYETTE	43.1	41.6	56.0	57.4	0.1	0.2	0.9	1.0	5.9	6.0	6.6	6.2	6.7	26.3	25.6	13.7	3.1	77.8	39.7	48.1	51.9
36863	LANETT	58.4	57.2	40.5	41.5	0.2	0.2	0.8	0.9	7.1	7.0	7.2	6.3	6.4	25.9	25.0	13.0	2.1	74.9	37.5	47.7	52.3
36866	NOTASULGA	57.2	55.2	41.5	43.3	0.1	0.1	0.9	1.0	6.5	6.8	6.8	6.4	5.4	26.8	27.7	12.0	1.5	75.9	38.5	48.3	51.7
36867	PHENIX CITY	70.5	70.0	27.1	27.3	0.6	0.8	1.6	2.0	7.3	6.7	6.9	6.5	7.3	27.5	22.9	13.2	1.7	75.2	36.2	46.3	53.7
36869	PHENIX CITY	46.6	45.1	51.1	52.2	0.3	0.4	1.4	1.6	7.3	7.1	7.6	7.0	7.2	28.5	23.4	10.6	1.3	73.8	35.0	48.3	51.7
36870	PHENIX CITY	83.9	82.6	13.4	14.1	0.5	0.6	2.3	2.8	8.7	8.2	8.3	6.7	6.7	34.3	19.7	6.8	0.5	70.7	31.8	49.4	50.6
36871	PITTSVIEW	55.5	53.8	41.6	43.0	0.2	0.2	1.4	1.6	6.8	6.9	7.3	7.1	5.9	26.0	26.6	12.3	1.1	74.8	38.4	50.3	49.7
36874	SALEM	78.1	76.7	20.2	21.4	0.3	0.3	0.9	1.1	6.8	6.8	7.3	6.8	6.3	27.7	27.6	10.0	0.7	75.0	37.6	49.7	50.3
36875	SEALE	60.4	58.7	36.0	37.1	0.4	0.5	2.2	2.7	7.1	7.2	7.7	7.1	6.7	27.4	25.7	10.1	1.0	73.6	36.2	50.2	49.8
36877	SMITHS STATION	85.1	84.0	12.7	13.4	0.4	0.5	1.6	2.0	7.6	7.5	8.1	6.7	6.1	31.8	23.4	8.2	0.6	72.7	34.6	49.5	50.6
36879	WAVERLY	51.7	50.1	47.1	48.6	0.2	0.3	0.8	0.9	6.3	6.3	6.9	6.8	6.6	29.1	27.6	9.0	1.4	76.5	37.7	49.0	51.0
36904	BUTLER	60.2	58.4	39.1	40.8	0.0	0.0	0.6	0.8	6.2	5.8	6.5	6.7	6.1	24.6	27.0	14.7	2.6	77.3	41.0	46.8	53.2
36907	CUBA	30.0	28.3	69.3	70.7	0.1	0.1	1.7	1.8	7.7	6.5	7.4	8.8	6.7	23.8	25.8	11.2	2.2	72.9	36.2	47.7	52.3
36908	GILBERTOWN	81.3	80.4	17.9	18.7	0.1	0.1	1.0	1.2	7.4	7.1	5.3	5.5	5.6	25.6	27.1	14.3	2.2	77.0	40.4	49.5	50.5
36910	JACHIN	21.4	19.9	77.3	78.7	0.0	0.0	2.0	2.1	6.7	6.7	6.7	7.3	7.3	23.7	26.9	12.0	2.6	74.9	38.4	43.6	56.4
36912	LISMAN	16.2	15.2	82.8	83.7	0.0	0.0	0.7	0.7	6.3	6.3	7.2	7.7	7.3	23.8	26.9	12.6	1.9	75.5	38.3	45.4	54.7
36915	NEEDHAM	79.4	77.8	20.1	21.7	0.0	0.0	0.0	0.5	6.9	6.9	6.9	5.9	6.4	26.1	25.6	14.3	1.0	75.4	38.7	49.3	50.7
36916	PENNINGTON	41.1	39.3	58.7	60.5	0.0	0.0	0.5	0.3	6.6	9.1	8.9	5.6	4.0	28.9	24.1	11.7	1.0	71.2	38.1	49.9	50.1
36919	SILAS	48.5	46.5	50.7	52.5	0.0	0.1	0.6	0.7	8.5	7.9	7.3	6.1	6.2	26.7	25.9	10.1	1.4	72.7	35.5	48.0	52.0
36921	TOXEY	82.1	80.9	17.3	18.4	0.1	0.2	0.3	0.4	7.1	7.3	6.8	5.9	5.6	26.9	25.7	13.3	1.4	75.1	38.3	48.4	51.6
36922	WARD	20.3	19.2	79.2	80.4	0.0	0.0	1.0	1.0	7.3	8.1	8.9	6.9	5.7	26.2	23.1	12.3	1.6	70.9	36.4	44.6	55.4
36925	YORK	20.8	20.0	78.6	79.3	0.1	0.1	1.1	1.0	7.3	7.3	8.9	8.2	7.0	24.5	21.9	12.0	2.8	71.4	34.4	44.5	55.5
	ALABAMA	71.1	70.3	26.0	26.4	0.7	0.9	1.7	2.1	6.7	6.7	7.0	6.8	7.2	28.0	24.5	11.6	1.6	75.8	36.6	48.5	51.5
	UNITED STATES	75.1	73.6	12.3	12.5	3.8	4.2	12.5	14.1	6.9	6.7	7.2	7.0	7.3	28.6	23.8	10.8	1.7	75.1	36.0	49.1	50.9

ALABAMA

INCOME

C 36852-36925

#	POST OFFICE NAME	2004 Per Capita Income	2004 HH Income Base	2004 HOUSEHOLD INCOME DISTRIBUTION (%)					MEDIAN HOUSEHOLD INCOME				2004 Home Value Base	2004 HOME VALUE DISTRIBUTION (%)					2004 Median Home Value
				Less than $25,000	$25,000 to $49,999	$50,000 to $99,999	$100,000 to $149,999	$150,000 or More	2004	2009	2004 National Centile	2004 State Centile		Less than $50,000	$50,000 to $89,999	$90,000 to $174,999	$175,000 to $399,999	$400,000 or More	
36852	CUSSETA	17912	852	25.8	42.5	25.4	4.3	2.0	39803	45629	45	73	686	39.1	28.1	23.6	7.7	1.5	70667
36853	DADEVILLE	21342	3515	34.4	29.0	25.4	7.6	3.6	37317	41983	37	64	3003	24.9	24.9	21.5	21.4	7.4	90472
36854	VALLEY	18399	5847	34.9	33.0	26.4	4.1	1.7	36294	40668	33	60	4500	32.8	35.4	22.7	8.1	1.0	69055
36855	FIVE POINTS	16794	734	38.2	34.1	24.4	2.3	1.1	31226	35183	16	35	630	32.2	30.0	26.5	11.1	0.2	73878
36856	FORT MITCHELL	15904	597	30.5	37.5	27.1	3.9	1.0	36009	40438	32	58	454	28.9	30.4	35.2	4.9	0.7	81923
36858	HATCHECHUBBEE	13658	300	50.7	28.3	19.7	1.3	0.0	24525	26795	4	14	246	48.8	27.2	10.6	8.1	5.3	51667
36860	HURTSBORO	14417	801	56.6	24.6	16.7	1.6	0.5	20817	23151	2	5	635	54.0	25.7	12.8	4.4	3.2	46077
36861	JACKSONS GAP	21853	1536	29.9	31.5	27.3	7.4	4.0	40922	45554	49	77	1297	23.5	23.2	19.2	29.5	4.6	98673
36862	LAFAYETTE	14798	2710	44.9	30.1	21.0	2.7	1.3	28886	32000	10	24	2125	32.9	28.3	30.5	6.6	1.7	72926
36863	LANETT	17615	5207	41.2	31.6	21.6	3.4	2.2	31906	35305	18	39	3801	31.3	38.6	21.6	7.2	1.3	67407
36866	NOTASULGA	18074	1415	42.5	32.0	19.6	3.0	2.9	29566	33039	11	27	1138	38.3	33.7	20.7	5.5	1.8	66867
36867	PHENIX CITY	19385	8213	38.3	27.9	26.6	5.2	2.0	34024	38809	24	49	4836	17.0	27.3	41.2	13.6	1.0	97005
36869	PHENIX CITY	14544	7600	44.1	30.5	21.5	3.0	0.8	28783	31388	10	24	4881	25.6	38.7	30.7	4.0	1.0	77385
36870	PHENIX CITY	18589	4996	26.1	30.1	35.2	7.2	1.5	45680	51969	63	87	3946	18.0	20.7	53.5	7.4	0.5	102008
36871	PITTSVIEW	15309	640	42.3	27.7	26.3	3.8	0.0	31273	35057	16	36	528	34.3	29.0	27.3	8.1	1.3	68438
36874	SALEM	19554	2674	27.0	29.8	33.3	7.4	2.4	44242	50596	59	85	2243	20.5	23.0	36.5	18.1	2.0	100283
36875	SEALE	15881	1936	35.9	30.6	29.0	3.8	0.7	33668	37906	23	48	1595	34.6	28.3	26.1	10.0	1.1	72079
36877	SMITHS STATION	21952	4092	22.5	29.3	35.0	9.7	3.6	48334	54892	69	91	3469	20.8	19.6	40.2	17.2	2.2	104470
36879	WAVERLY	17797	461	39.7	26.7	25.6	6.5	1.5	32154	36799	18	41	370	27.3	21.1	30.5	15.7	5.4	92500
36904	BUTLER	19251	2128	43.1	29.0	19.4	6.3	2.3	29883	34323	12	28	1681	35.5	31.1	25.3	6.7	1.3	67069
36907	CUBA	13560	820	50.0	24.6	22.0	2.4	1.0	25000	27761	5	15	677	52.6	24.1	18.6	4.3	0.4	45513
36908	GILBERTOWN	20781	880	41.7	19.6	27.8	7.5	3.4	34384	39384	25	51	739	40.5	21.4	29.2	8.4	0.5	72556
36910	JACHIN	15210	148	58.8	25.7	8.1	4.1	3.4	21161	23275	2	6	127	46.5	33.9	13.4	6.3	0.0	53750
36912	LISMAN	14038	851	55.6	24.2	14.1	3.8	2.4	21566	24015	2	7	717	49.4	29.7	11.7	8.0	1.3	50833
36915	NEEDHAM	18425	90	51.1	26.7	17.8	2.2	2.2	24165	27825	4	12	79	59.5	24.1	15.2	1.3	0.0	41667
36916	PENNINGTON	13771	264	55.7	22.7	17.1	4.2	0.4	21756	24229	3	8	216	51.4	30.6	13.4	4.6	0.0	47273
36919	SILAS	14406	1025	52.5	26.2	17.1	2.9	1.3	23494	27099	4	11	868	53.1	25.4	16.7	4.8	0.0	46197
36921	TOXEY	17072	951	43.0	25.5	25.2	4.7	1.6	30835	35618	14	34	835	48.1	20.8	21.1	8.1	1.8	52672
36922	WARD	13254	350	52.3	28.9	15.4	3.1	0.3	23630	26852	4	11	290	54.8	28.3	13.8	3.1	0.0	45882
36925	YORK	12922	1677	57.1	25.4	13.3	2.4	1.8	21063	23266	2	5	1207	46.6	33.0	17.3	2.7	0.5	54368
	ALABAMA	20998		34.3	28.7	26.3	7.2	3.5	37534	42371				22.7	26.7	33.4	14.6	2.7	90917
	UNITED STATES	25866		24.7	27.1	30.8	10.9	6.5	48124	56710				10.9	15.0	33.7	30.1	10.4	145905

# POST OFFICE NAME	FINANCIAL SERVICES				THE HOME						ENTERTAINMENT						PERSONAL			
					Home Improvements		Furnishings													
	Auto Loan	Home Loan	Invest-ments	Retire-ment Plans	Home Repair	Lawn & Garden	Comput-ers & Hard-ware	Major Appli-ances	TV, Radio, Sound Equip-ment	Furni-ture	Dine out/ Carry out	Sports Equip-ment	Fees & Tickets	Toys & Games	Travel	Cable TV	Apparel & Services	Auto Repairs	Health Insur-ance	Pets & Supplies
36852 CUSSETA	78	65	46	61	67	73	62	70	66	64	80	81	58	76	62	67	76	69	74	87
36853 DADEVILLE	89	66	40	59	74	84	64	77	73	64	87	90	56	84	66	78	80	76	92	105
36854 VALLEY	71	60	46	56	64	71	59	65	64	59	78	76	56	78	60	67	73	64	73	82
36855 FIVE POINTS	74	50	23	43	56	65	48	60	58	49	68	72	41	64	49	62	62	59	74	85
36856 FORT MITCHELL	72	63	47	60	64	68	60	66	62	62	76	76	56	72	60	62	73	65	67	80
36858 HATCHECHUBBEE	64	43	19	37	49	56	41	52	50	42	59	62	35	56	42	54	53	51	64	74
36860 HURTSBORO	55	40	30	35	43	51	42	48	49	43	59	54	38	54	42	53	55	48	58	62
36861 JACKSONS GAP	87	71	56	67	77	85	69	79	76	69	91	93	64	89	71	79	85	79	89	102
36862 LAFAYETTE	68	47	25	40	52	60	46	56	55	47	65	66	40	61	46	59	60	56	68	77
36863 LANETT	69	56	43	51	60	68	56	62	63	56	76	72	53	75	57	67	71	62	72	79
36866 NOTASULGA	80	54	26	47	61	70	53	65	63	54	74	78	45	70	53	67	67	64	79	91
36867 PHENIX CITY	63	60	62	59	61	67	62	63	65	62	80	72	62	79	62	66	77	63	66	72
36869 PHENIX CITY	60	47	38	43	49	56	48	53	54	49	66	62	45	62	48	57	62	54	60	67
36870 PHENIX CITY	77	75	66	74	74	77	72	75	71	73	88	88	70	87	71	70	85	74	72	87
36871 PITTSVIEW	71	48	22	41	54	62	46	58	56	47	65	69	39	62	47	60	59	57	71	82
36874 SALEM	86	75	55	71	77	82	71	78	74	73	91	91	66	86	71	75	86	78	82	97
36875 SEALE	75	57	33	51	61	68	54	64	61	55	73	76	48	70	55	64	68	63	73	86
36877 SMITHS STATION	90	86	71	83	86	89	81	86	81	82	100	100	78	97	80	80	97	85	84	101
36879 WAVERLY	73	57	38	53	61	67	55	63	61	56	73	75	50	70	55	63	68	63	71	83
36904 BUTLER	83	56	27	49	63	73	55	68	66	56	77	80	47	73	56	71	70	67	83	94
36907 CUBA	59	42	30	37	46	54	44	51	52	45	62	58	40	57	44	56	57	51	61	66
36908 GILBERTOWN	93	62	28	54	70	81	60	75	72	61	85	89	51	80	61	78	77	74	92	106
36910 JACHIN	60	43	29	38	47	55	44	51	52	45	62	59	40	57	44	56	58	52	62	68
36912 LISMAN	60	43	28	37	46	55	44	51	52	45	61	59	39	57	44	56	57	51	62	68
36915 NEEDHAM	78	52	24	45	59	68	51	63	61	52	72	76	43	68	51	66	65	63	78	90
36916 PENNINGTON	59	40	18	34	45	52	38	48	46	39	54	57	33	51	39	50	49	48	59	68
36919 SILAS	70	47	21	40	53	61	45	56	54	46	64	67	38	60	46	59	58	56	69	80
36921 TOXEY	80	54	24	46	61	70	52	65	63	53	73	77	44	69	53	67	67	64	80	92
36922 WARD	60	41	22	35	46	53	40	49	49	41	57	58	35	53	41	52	52	49	60	68
36925 YORK	53	40	35	36	41	50	44	48	51	44	61	52	41	55	43	54	57	48	57	58
ALABAMA	81	70	61	67	72	80	70	75	75	70	91	87	67	89	70	76	86	75	81	92
UNITED STATES	100	100	100	100	100	100	100	100	100	100	100	100	100	100	100	100	100	100	100	100

#	POST OFFICE NAME	COUNTY FIPS CODE	POPULATION			2000-2004 ANNUAL RATE		HOUSEHOLDS					FAMILIES		
			2000	2004	2009	% Rate	State Centile	2000	2004	2009	% Annual Rate 2000-2004	2004 Average HH Size	2000	2004	% Annual Rate 2000-2004
99501	ANCHORAGE	020	16545	16414	17322	-0.2	38	7360	7312	7781	-0.2	1.98	3097	3072	-0.2
99502	ANCHORAGE	020	21730	23365	25581	1.7	88	7845	8455	9270	1.8	2.75	5673	6121	1.8
99503	ANCHORAGE	020	13847	14745	16066	1.5	84	6067	6437	7012	1.4	2.22	2903	3086	1.5
99504	ANCHORAGE	020	36961	40562	45013	2.2	92	13370	14718	16362	2.3	2.73	9391	10363	2.3
99505	FORT RICHARDSON	020	5322	5171	5406	-0.7	26	1231	1194	1266	-0.7	3.39	1137	1103	-0.7
99506	ELMENDORF AFB	020	6621	7104	7700	1.7	88	1584	1728	1893	2.1	3.63	1559	1701	2.1
99507	ANCHORAGE	020	31546	35046	38916	2.5	93	11513	12789	14201	2.5	2.73	8044	8982	2.6
99508	ANCHORAGE	020	34098	36408	39772	1.6	86	12480	13403	14724	1.7	2.60	7752	8271	1.5
99515	ANCHORAGE	020	18342	20617	23101	2.8	94	6302	7135	8024	3.0	2.88	4845	5462	2.9
99516	ANCHORAGE	020	17313	18943	20887	2.1	91	5730	6305	6976	2.3	3.00	4825	5307	2.3
99517	ANCHORAGE	020	16557	17321	18617	1.1	74	6660	6976	7504	1.1	2.47	4016	4210	1.1
99518	ANCHORAGE	020	9245	9660	10382	1.0	74	3794	3999	4318	1.3	2.41	2306	2423	1.2
99540	INDIAN	020	103	104	109	0.2	52	46	46	48	0.0	2.26	25	25	0.0
99546	ADAK	016	316	313	361	-0.2	35	159	165	199	0.9	1.78	95	99	1.0
99547	ATKA	016	96	95	110	-0.3	35	34	35	43	0.7	2.54	20	21	1.2
99549	PORT HEIDEN	164	119	108	100	-2.3	6	41	37	35	-2.4	2.92	27	25	-1.8
99551	AKIACHAK	050	426	437	459	0.6	62	97	98	102	0.2	4.46	83	84	0.3
99553	AKUTAN	013	713	852	1016	4.3	97	34	61	94	14.7	5.26	18	33	15.3
99554	ALAKANUK	270	1420	1494	1594	1.2	78	329	344	364	1.1	4.34	272	285	1.1
99555	ALEKNAGIK	070	221	225	227	0.4	58	70	71	72	0.3	3.17	54	56	0.9
99556	ANCHOR POINT	122	2412	2448	2570	0.4	55	899	925	983	0.7	2.65	603	623	0.8
99557	ANIAK	050	435	429	449	-0.3	32	137	134	139	-0.5	3.20	96	95	-0.3
99558	ANVIK	290	298	289	280	-0.7	21	90	88	85	-0.5	3.28	66	65	-0.4
99559	BETHEL	050	10695	11609	12602	2.0	90	2919	3174	3448	2.0	3.58	2143	2335	2.0
99561	CHEFORNAK	050	394	408	431	0.8	69	75	77	81	0.6	5.30	65	66	0.4
99563	CHEVAK	270	3	3	3	0.0	47	1	1	1	0.0	3.00	1	1	0.0
99564	CHIGNIK	164	79	71	67	-2.5	1	29	26	25	-2.5	2.73	19	18	-1.3
99565	CHIGNIK LAGOON	164	103	93	87	-2.4	2	33	30	28	-2.2	3.10	22	20	-2.2
99567	CHUGIAK	020	7606	7805	8303	0.6	63	2599	2682	2863	0.7	2.89	2051	2119	0.8
99568	CLAM GULCH	122	358	389	420	2.0	90	132	145	159	2.2	2.68	87	96	2.3
99569	CLARKS POINT	070	112	114	115	0.4	58	31	32	32	0.8	3.56	24	25	1.0
99571	COLD BAY	013	175	236	308	7.3	99	70	126	193	14.8	1.12	43	36	-4.1
99572	COOPER LANDING	122	357	366	382	0.6	61	155	161	171	0.9	2.20	93	97	1.0
99573	COPPER CENTER	261	1785	1800	1821	0.2	51	691	703	719	0.4	2.56	443	452	0.5
99574	CORDOVA	261	2580	2595	2624	0.1	48	964	982	1002	0.4	2.54	601	615	0.5
99575	CROOKED CREEK	050	4	4	4	0.0	47	2	2	2	0.0	2.00	1	1	0.0
99576	DILLINGHAM	070	3327	3379	3418	0.4	56	1101	1126	1145	0.5	2.97	774	794	0.6
99577	EAGLE RIVER	020	22231	24305	26803	2.1	91	7254	7978	8831	2.3	3.00	6009	6613	2.3
99578	EEK	050	555	550	576	-0.2	36	137	135	140	-0.4	4.07	105	104	-0.2
99579	EGEGIK	164	110	100	93	-2.2	7	41	37	35	-2.4	2.70	27	25	-1.8
99580	EKWOK	070	130	132	134	0.4	55	42	43	43	0.6	3.07	33	33	0.0
99583	FALSE PASS	013	64	77	91	4.5	98	22	39	61	14.4	1.97	12	4	-22.8
99584	FLAT	290	4	4	4	0.0	47	1	1	1	0.0	4.00	1	1	0.0
99585	MARSHALL	270	557	586	626	1.2	78	139	145	153	1.0	4.04	117	122	1.0
99586	GAKONA	261	328	331	334	0.2	51	149	152	155	0.5	2.16	88	90	0.5
99587	GIRDWOOD	020	1216	1337	1476	2.3	92	534	590	653	2.4	2.27	252	278	2.3
99588	GLENNALLEN	261	1118	1127	1141	0.2	50	408	414	424	0.3	2.68	274	279	0.4
99589	GOODNEWS BAY	050	230	228	239	-0.2	36	71	70	73	-0.3	3.26	54	54	0.0
99591	SAINT GEORGE ISLAND	016	152	151	173	-0.2	38	51	53	64	0.9	2.66	30	32	1.5
99602	HOLY CROSS	290	227	220	214	-0.7	20	64	62	61	-0.7	3.55	47	46	-0.5
99603	HOMER	122	8912	9473	10105	1.5	83	3529	3803	4112	1.8	2.45	2276	2463	1.9
99604	HOOPER BAY	270	1779	1872	1996	1.2	80	394	410	432	0.9	4.57	322	336	1.0
99606	ILIAMNA	164	343	311	290	-2.3	5	102	93	88	-2.2	3.34	76	70	-1.9
99607	KALSKAG	050	230	230	241	0.0	47	62	61	64	-0.4	3.77	48	48	0.0
99610	KASILOF	122	1773	1892	2019	1.5	85	691	746	807	1.8	2.53	471	510	1.9
99611	KENAI	122	14793	15484	16423	1.1	75	5283	5580	5987	1.3	2.70	3788	4012	1.4
99612	KING COVE	013	792	1191	1661	10.1	100	170	306	470	14.8	3.01	115	208	15.0
99613	KING SALMON	060	351	318	293	-2.3	4	156	143	134	-2.0	2.22	87	80	-2.0
99614	KIPNUK	050	117	121	128	0.8	68	29	30	31	0.8	4.03	25	26	0.9
99615	KODIAK	150	13889	14251	14704	0.6	63	4413	4513	4641	0.5	3.08	3249	3333	0.6
99620	KOTLIK	270	591	622	663	1.2	80	117	122	130	1.0	5.10	97	101	1.0
99622	KWIGILLINGOK	050	116	120	127	0.8	69	30	31	32	0.8	3.87	26	27	0.9
99625	LEVELOCK	164	254	230	215	-2.3	3	83	76	71	-2.1	3.03	62	57	-2.0
99626	LOWER KALSKAG	050	267	267	279	0.0	47	66	65	68	-0.4	4.11	51	51	0.0
99627	MC GRATH	290	486	472	457	-0.7	25	177	174	170	-0.4	2.71	113	112	-0.2
99628	MANOKOTAK	070	399	405	410	0.4	55	93	95	96	0.5	4.26	72	74	0.7
99630	MEKORYUK	050	210	217	229	0.8	68	73	75	79	0.6	2.89	57	59	0.8
99631	MOOSE PASS	122	531	544	568	0.6	60	229	238	253	0.9	2.22	138	144	1.0
99632	MOUNTAIN VILLAGE	270	927	975	1040	1.2	77	220	230	243	1.1	4.22	172	180	1.1
99636	NEW STUYAHOK	070	471	479	485	0.4	57	105	107	108	0.4	4.48	82	84	0.6
99638	NIKOLSKI	016	39	39	45	0.0	47	15	16	19	1.5	2.25	9	9	0.0
99639	NINILCHIK	122	996	1048	1110	1.2	78	405	431	462	1.5	2.43	279	297	1.5
99640	NONDALTON	164	221	200	187	-2.3	3	68	62	58	-2.2	3.23	51	46	-2.4
99645	PALMER	170	17924	20253	23724	2.9	95	5942	6780	8033	3.2	2.87	4435	5079	3.2
99647	PEDRO BAY	164	49	44	41	-2.5	1	16	15	14	-1.5	2.93	12	11	-2.0
99648	PERRYVILLE	164	107	97	90	-2.3	5	33	30	28	-2.2	3.23	22	20	-2.2
99649	PILOT POINT	164	108	98	91	-2.3	6	34	31	29	-2.2	3.16	23	21	-2.1
99654	WASILLA	170	33912	39094	46426	3.4	96	11565	13409	16017	3.5	2.91	8682	10084	3.6
99655	QUINHAGAK	050	284	287	299	0.3	54	78	78	80	0.0	3.68	62	62	0.0
99656	RED DEVIL	050	51	50	53	-0.5	31	18	18	18	0.0	2.78	13	12	-1.9
99658	SAINT MARYS	270	625	658	701	1.2	81	167	175	185	1.1	3.74	129	135	1.1
99659	SAINT MICHAEL	180	368	393	417	1.6	86	90	97	104	1.8	4.05	72	77	1.6
99660	SAINT PAUL ISLAND	016	495	491	565	-0.2	38	163	169	204	0.9	2.72	97	102	1.2
99661	SAND POINT	013	953	1422	1974	9.9	99	230	413	632	14.8	2.62	156	281	14.9
99662	SCAMMON BAY	270	467	491	524	1.2	77	97	101	106	1.0	4.86	79	83	1.2
99664	SEWARD	122	4630	4826	5069	1.0	72	1622	1710	1825	1.3	2.45	996	1054	1.3
99667	SKWENTNA	170	20	20	22	0.0	47	5	5	6	0.0	4.00	3	3	0.0
99668	SLEETMUTE	050	13	13	13	0.0	47	6	6	6	0.0	2.17	4	4	0.0
99669	SOLDOTNA	122	11337	11902	12607	1.2	75	4238	4506	4833	1.5	2.62	3026	3227	1.5
99670	SOUTH NAKNEK	060	907	822	757	-2.3	4	334	308	289	-1.9	2.67	214	198	-1.8
99671	STEBBINS	180	547	583	620	1.5	84	123	132	142	1.7	4.42	98	105	1.6
99672	STERLING	122	2804	2990	3190	1.5	85	1022	1102	1190	1.8	2.70	796	861	1.9
99676	TALKEETNA	170	1784	2061	2448	3.5	97	795	924	1104	3.6	2.23	449	527	3.8
99679	TULUKSAK	050	428	439	461	0.6	62	86	87	91	0.3	5.05	73	74	0.3
99681	TUNUNAK	050	1065	1100	1160	0.8	67	235	241	253	0.6	4.56	184	189	0.6
	ALASKA					1.5					1.6	2.73			1.7
	UNITED STATES					1.2					1.3	2.58			1.1

POPULATION COMPOSITION ALASKA

99501-99681 B

#	POST OFFICE NAME	RACE (%) White 2000	White 2004	Black 2000	Black 2004	Asian/Pacific 2000	Asian/Pacific 2004	% Hispanic Origin 2000	% Hispanic Origin 2004	2004 AGE DISTRIBUTION (%) 0-4	5-9	10-14	15-19	20-24	25-44	45-64	65-84	85+	18+	MEDIAN AGE 2004	% 2004 Males	% 2004 Females
99501	ANCHORAGE	60.6	59.2	8.8	8.3	7.6	7.5	8.2	9.2	5.7	5.0	5.1	5.5	8.3	32.4	25.5	10.6	1.9	81.0	37.9	51.9	48.1
99502	ANCHORAGE	75.4	73.7	3.2	3.1	8.6	8.9	4.3	4.9	7.4	7.3	8.2	7.3	7.2	31.2	25.9	5.1	0.3	72.4	33.8	49.5	50.5
99503	ANCHORAGE	59.8	57.8	4.7	4.4	12.3	12.6	9.1	10.2	7.1	6.2	6.4	6.6	8.8	33.2	23.7	7.5	0.6	76.6	34.1	52.0	48.0
99504	ANCHORAGE	67.2	65.7	9.9	9.4	5.2	5.3	5.4	6.0	8.0	7.6	8.3	7.5	7.4	30.9	23.3	6.4	0.5	71.2	32.6	49.0	51.0
99505	FORT RICHARDSON	68.3	67.4	20.2	19.5	2.1	2.2	9.2	10.7	14.7	8.8	6.4	7.5	23.7	36.1	2.7	0.2	0.0	67.9	22.7	58.5	41.5
99506	ELMENDORF AFB	77.2	76.2	12.3	11.9	3.1	3.2	7.2	8.3	14.9	11.4	9.0	6.6	20.1	36.1	1.7	0.1	0.0	61.8	22.0	54.5	45.5
99507	ANCHORAGE	73.3	71.8	5.0	4.7	6.7	6.8	6.1	6.9	7.9	7.7	8.6	8.0	8.3	31.8	23.7	3.9	0.2	70.8	31.7	50.0	50.0
99508	ANCHORAGE	58.5	56.6	9.0	8.7	9.2	9.2	7.5	8.4	8.2	7.3	7.8	8.8	9.5	29.1	22.0	6.9	0.5	71.7	30.6	49.3	50.7
99515	ANCHORAGE	77.5	75.4	2.5	2.4	6.1	6.3	5.6	6.5	7.9	8.0	8.7	7.7	6.7	30.2	25.8	4.7	0.3	70.4	33.5	49.4	50.6
99516	ANCHORAGE	89.7	88.8	1.0	0.9	2.8	2.9	2.3	2.7	5.4	7.4	9.8	8.8	4.0	24.3	35.6	4.5	0.2	71.4	40.3	50.6	49.4
99517	ANCHORAGE	71.5	69.7	3.0	2.8	10.6	10.8	5.0	5.6	6.6	6.6	6.9	6.8	7.3	30.6	27.1	7.5	0.5	75.8	36.1	50.0	50.0
99518	ANCHORAGE	74.1	72.3	5.9	5.7	6.2	6.4	5.6	6.4	7.8	7.3	6.8	5.8	7.3	34.5	24.7	5.6	0.2	74.7	33.7	49.7	50.3
99540	INDIAN	91.3	89.4	0.0	0.0	0.0	0.0	1.9	2.9	1.0	6.7	10.6	5.8	1.0	26.9	41.4	6.7	0.0	77.9	44.3	58.7	41.4
99546	ADAK	25.0	20.5	0.6	0.6	3.8	2.9	1.9	1.9	5.8	5.8	6.7	7.7	7.7	33.6	27.5	5.1	0.3	76.0	35.3	57.5	42.5
99547	ATKA	25.0	20.0	1.0	0.0	4.2	3.2	2.1	1.1	6.3	6.3	6.3	7.4	7.4	34.7	28.4	3.2	0.0	74.7	34.7	59.0	41.1
99549	PORT HEIDEN	14.3	13.9	0.0	0.0	0.8	0.9	1.7	2.8	8.3	8.3	11.1	9.3	8.3	25.9	25.0	3.7	0.0	66.7	28.1	51.9	48.2
99551	AKIACHAK	4.5	4.1	0.0	0.0	0.2	0.2	0.5	0.2	11.7	10.5	12.6	11.4	8.5	24.5	15.6	4.8	0.5	57.9	22.2	54.5	45.5
99553	AKUTAN	28.6	27.6	2.1	1.9	32.7	32.0	17.5	20.2	2.0	2.2	3.4	5.3	8.8	41.7	35.2	1.4	0.0	90.3	39.5	71.7	28.3
99554	ALAKANUK	4.1	3.9	0.1	0.1	0.1	0.1	0.5	0.5	11.9	10.8	13.1	11.7	9.4	23.8	14.2	4.9	0.2	57.0	21.4	53.7	46.3
99555	ALEKNAGIK	9.1	8.4	0.0	0.0	0.0	0.0	0.5	0.0	9.3	8.9	11.1	12.9	9.8	25.8	16.0	6.2	0.0	62.7	24.0	53.8	46.2
99556	ANCHOR POINT	89.7	88.3	0.1	0.1	0.5	0.5	1.5	1.7	6.5	6.2	9.2	8.6	6.9	21.7	33.0	7.5	0.4	72.3	39.1	52.9	47.1
99557	ANIAK	14.9	13.5	0.0	0.0	0.0	0.0	1.6	1.6	7.5	8.2	11.4	11.2	6.5	24.5	21.7	8.6	0.5	66.2	30.3	52.9	47.1
99558	ANVIK	6.0	5.5	0.0	0.0	0.0	0.0	0.3	0.4	8.7	8.7	12.5	10.7	6.2	24.6	20.4	8.3	0.0	63.0	27.4	53.3	46.7
99559	BETHEL	16.0	15.0	0.5	0.5	1.6	1.6	1.1	1.1	10.5	9.7	10.5	10.0	8.3	27.7	18.7	4.2	0.4	62.8	25.7	52.7	47.3
99561	CHEFORNAK	2.0	1.7	0.0	0.0	0.0	0.0	0.5	0.3	11.3	10.8	12.5	10.8	8.1	25.5	16.2	4.4	0.5	58.8	22.9	54.9	45.1
99563	CHEVAK	0.0	0.0	0.0	0.0	0.0	0.0	0.0	0.0	0.0	0.0	0.0	0.0	66.7	33.3	0.0	0.0	0.0	100.0	23.8	66.7	33.3
99564	CHIGNIK	15.2	14.1	0.0	0.0	0.0	0.0	2.5	0.0	8.5	8.5	14.1	8.5	8.5	23.9	23.9	4.2	0.0	60.6	26.9	52.1	47.9
99565	CHIGNIK LAGOON	14.6	14.0	0.0	0.0	1.0	1.1	1.9	3.2	7.5	7.5	11.8	8.6	8.6	25.8	25.8	4.3	0.0	66.7	29.6	50.5	49.5
99567	CHUGIAK	87.3	85.7	1.0	0.9	1.2	1.2	2.9	3.4	6.2	7.3	8.7	8.2	5.6	27.7	31.1	4.9	0.4	72.3	37.8	51.0	49.0
99568	CLAM GULCH	89.7	88.4	0.3	0.3	0.8	1.0	1.7	1.8	5.4	6.9	8.7	8.5	4.6	23.9	32.1	9.3	0.5	72.5	40.9	53.5	46.5
99569	CLARKS POINT	8.9	8.8	0.0	0.0	0.0	0.0	0.0	0.0	8.8	8.8	11.4	11.4	10.5	27.2	15.8	6.1	0.0	63.2	24.6	52.6	47.4
99571	COLD BAY	21.7	20.3	1.7	1.7	29.1	28.4	12.0	12.7	3.8	3.4	4.7	6.8	9.8	38.1	31.4	2.1	0.0	84.8	37.5	64.8	35.2
99572	COOPER LANDING	90.5	89.3	0.6	0.6	1.1	1.1	1.1	1.4	4.4	4.6	6.6	6.6	5.5	22.1	36.1	13.4	0.8	79.8	45.1	53.6	46.5
99573	COPPER CENTER	71.8	71.1	0.2	0.2	0.5	0.5	1.9	1.8	6.2	6.9	8.7	8.6	5.3	21.8	32.4	9.3	0.8	72.4	40.3	53.6	46.4
99574	CORDOVA	70.0	69.6	0.4	0.4	9.6	9.6	2.9	2.9	5.8	7.0	7.7	7.6	6.4	28.5	29.1	7.2	0.7	74.3	38.5	54.2	45.8
99575	CROOKED CREEK	25.0	25.0	0.0	0.0	0.0	0.0	0.0	0.0	0.0	0.0	0.0	0.0	50.0	50.0	0.0	0.0	0.0	100.0	25.0	50.0	50.0
99576	DILLINGHAM	28.2	27.4	0.5	0.5	0.9	0.9	2.9	2.9	9.7	9.0	10.0	8.4	6.7	25.9	23.7	6.0	0.5	65.2	31.0	50.8	49.2
99577	EAGLE RIVER	87.5	86.3	2.0	2.0	2.2	2.2	3.5	4.1	6.7	7.8	9.4	8.9	6.3	30.2	27.1	3.4	0.3	70.3	34.8	50.4	49.6
99578	EEK	4.1	3.6	0.0	0.0	0.0	0.0	0.5	0.6	8.6	8.4	10.4	10.9	6.7	29.5	18.4	6.9	0.4	65.6	28.9	52.2	47.8
99579	EGEGIK	14.6	14.0	0.0	0.0	0.9	1.0	1.8	3.0	9.0	9.0	11.0	8.0	9.0	25.0	25.0	4.0	0.0	65.0	28.3	52.0	48.0
99580	EKWOK	6.2	6.1	0.0	0.0	0.0	0.0	1.5	1.5	9.1	10.6	15.9	8.3	7.6	25.0	17.4	5.3	0.8	58.3	24.0	53.8	46.2
99583	FALSE PASS	28.1	27.3	1.6	1.3	32.8	33.8	17.2	19.5	1.3	2.6	3.9	5.2	9.1	40.3	36.4	1.3	0.0	90.9	39.8	70.1	29.9
99584	FLAT	0.0	0.0	0.0	0.0	0.0	0.0	0.0	0.0	0.0	0.0	0.0	0.0	50.0	50.0	0.0	0.0	0.0	100.0	25.0	50.0	50.0
99585	MARSHALL	5.6	5.3	0.0	0.0	0.0	0.0	0.2	0.2	11.1	10.4	12.0	13.1	10.9	22.0	16.0	4.3	0.2	56.8	21.6	50.9	49.2
99586	GAKONA	60.4	60.1	0.0	0.0	0.0	0.0	0.6	0.6	5.1	6.3	8.2	5.4	5.4	22.4	36.0	10.3	0.9	76.1	43.3	55.6	44.4
99587	GIRDWOOD	94.5	93.6	0.0	0.0	0.8	0.9	1.6	1.9	5.9	5.2	5.8	5.3	7.0	40.1	27.5	3.1	0.2	80.0	34.8	55.8	44.2
99588	GLENNALLEN	78.1	77.6	0.1	0.1	0.9	0.9	0.6	0.6	6.7	8.0	7.9	10.6	6.3	23.0	30.4	6.5	0.6	70.5	36.2	53.4	46.6
99589	GOODNEWS BAY	3.9	3.5	0.0	0.0	0.0	0.0	0.4	0.4	8.3	8.8	10.5	11.4	6.6	29.4	18.0	6.6	0.4	64.9	28.3	51.3	48.7
99591	SAINT GEORGE ISLAND	25.0	20.5	0.7	0.7	3.3	2.7	2.0	1.3	6.0	6.0	6.6	8.0	7.3	33.8	26.5	5.3	0.7	75.5	35.2	56.3	43.7
99602	HOLY CROSS	5.7	5.5	0.0	0.0	0.0	0.0	0.4	0.5	8.6	8.6	12.3	10.9	6.4	24.6	20.5	8.2	0.0	62.7	27.3	52.7	47.3
99603	HOMER	87.8	86.9	0.2	0.3	0.8	0.8	2.2	2.5	6.6	7.0	7.8	7.7	6.8	23.0	32.1	8.2	0.8	73.5	39.3	50.2	49.8
99604	HOOPER BAY	3.7	3.4	0.1	0.1	0.1	0.1	0.3	0.3	11.5	11.5	14.8	13.5	7.9	23.1	13.1	4.3	0.3	52.7	19.5	50.5	49.5
99606	ILIAMNA	22.2	20.6	0.0	0.0	0.0	0.0	0.9	0.6	8.4	8.7	12.5	10.6	8.0	24.1	21.5	5.8	0.3	64.0	26.8	52.7	47.3
99607	KALSKAG	16.5	14.8	0.4	0.4	0.4	0.4	0.4	0.4	9.1	8.7	11.7	12.2	10.4	23.0	20.4	3.9	0.4	62.6	24.0	50.9	49.1
99610	KASILOF	90.9	89.8	0.3	0.3	0.8	0.8	1.1	1.3	4.4	6.7	8.8	8.3	4.7	24.1	33.5	9.2	0.3	73.7	41.5	53.1	46.9
99611	KENAI	84.2	82.8	0.5	0.5	1.4	1.5	2.8	3.2	7.3	7.5	8.5	8.2	7.2	27.8	26.7	6.5	0.3	71.5	34.5	51.1	48.9
99612	KING COVE	15.2	14.9	1.5	1.4	24.6	24.9	6.7	7.8	5.3	4.4	5.6	7.9	10.4	36.0	27.0	3.4	0.0	79.8	35.3	58.8	41.2
99613	KING SALMON	53.6	51.3	1.1	1.3	0.9	0.9	0.6	0.3	6.6	6.6	8.2	8.2	6.9	26.7	31.1	5.4	0.3	73.3	37.9	54.7	45.3
99614	KIPNUK	1.7	1.7	0.0	0.0	0.0	0.0	0.0	0.0	11.6	10.7	14.1	10.7	7.4	24.0	16.5	5.0	0.0	56.2	21.9	55.4	44.6
99615	KODIAK	59.8	57.9	1.0	0.9	16.9	17.0	6.1	6.9	9.0	8.1	8.8	7.5	7.9	30.1	23.1	5.1	0.4	69.3	31.7	52.7	47.3
99620	KOTLIK	4.1	3.9	0.2	0.2	0.2	0.2	0.3	0.5	11.9	10.8	13.0	11.7	9.5	23.8	14.0	5.0	0.3	56.9	21.4	53.5	46.5
99622	KWIGILLINGOK	1.7	1.7	0.0	0.0	0.0	0.0	0.0	0.0	10.8	10.8	16.7	10.8	7.5	24.2	15.0	4.2	0.0	54.2	20.6	55.8	44.2
99625	LEVELOCK	22.1	20.9	0.0	0.0	0.0	0.0	0.8	0.9	8.7	8.7	10.9	8.7	8.3	25.2	22.6	6.5	0.4	65.7	29.6	51.3	48.7
99626	LOWER KALSKAG	16.5	15.0	0.4	0.4	0.4	0.4	0.4	0.4	9.4	8.6	11.6	12.7	10.5	22.5	19.9	4.5	0.4	63.3	23.7	50.6	49.4
99627	MC GRATH	42.4	40.0	0.0	0.0	0.4	0.4	1.0	1.1	6.6	7.0	10.4	10.2	7.4	22.9	27.1	8.1	0.4	69.5	35.4	53.0	47.0
99628	MANOKOTAK	9.0	8.6	0.3	0.3	0.5	0.5	0.5	0.7	9.1	8.9	11.1	12.6	9.9	25.9	16.1	6.2	0.3	63.5	24.2	53.3	46.7
99630	MEKORYUK	3.3	2.8	0.0	0.0	0.0	0.0	0.0	0.0	9.2	10.1	11.1	12.0	8.3	25.8	16.6	6.0	0.9	61.3	24.6	53.5	46.5
99631	MOOSE PASS	90.4	89.2	0.6	0.6	1.3	1.3	0.9	1.3	4.4	4.6	6.6	6.6	5.2	22.2	36.2	13.4	0.7	79.8	45.2	53.9	46.1
99632	MOUNTAIN VILLAGE	6.0	5.6	0.0	0.0	0.2	0.3	0.3	0.3	11.4	10.5	11.9	11.8	8.2	26.2	14.9	4.9	0.3	58.4	22.7	52.6	47.4
99636	NEW STUYAHOK	6.2	5.9	0.0	0.0	0.0	0.0	1.3	1.5	9.8	10.7	12.9	8.1	7.5	26.3	18.4	5.6	0.6	61.0	25.9	53.9	46.1
99638	NIKOLSKI	25.6	20.5	0.0	0.0	2.6	2.6	0.0	0.0	5.1	5.1	5.1	7.7	7.7	30.8	35.9	2.6	0.0	84.6	37.5	64.1	35.9
99639	NINILCHIK	84.6	83.0	0.0	0.0	0.7	0.7	1.5	1.7	4.6	5.0	6.3	7.4	6.0	21.7	34.2	13.9	1.1	79.4	44.6	53.3	46.7
99640	NONDALTON	22.2	20.5	0.0	0.0	0.0	0.0	0.5	0.5	8.5	8.5	12.5	10.5	8.0	24.5	21.0	6.0	0.5	64.5	27.0	52.5	47.5
99645	PALMER	86.7	85.5	1.1	1.1	0.9	0.9	2.2	2.5	6.8	7.1	8.6	9.0	7.7	26.5	26.9	6.7	0.7	71.5	34.8	51.6	48.4
99647	PEDRO BAY	22.5	20.5	0.0	0.0	0.0	0.0	0.0	0.0	9.1	9.1	15.9	9.1	9.1	22.7	22.7	2.3	0.0	61.4	23.8	54.6	45.5
99648	PERRYVILLE	15.0	13.4	0.0	0.0	0.9	1.0	1.9	3.1	8.3	9.3	9.3	8.3	9.3	25.8	25.8	4.1	0.0	67.0	29.6	52.6	47.4
99649	PILOT POINT	14.8	13.3	0.0	0.0	0.9	1.0	1.9	3.1	8.2	9.2	10.2	8.2	9.2	25.5	25.5	4.1	0.0	66.3	29.2	52.0	48.0
99654	WASILLA	87.8	86.5	0.6	0.5	0.9	0.9	2.9	3.3	7.7	7.7	9.1	8.6	7.3	28.1	25.8	5.4	0.2	69.9	33.0	51.2	48.8
99655	QUINHAGAK	1.8	1.7	0.7	0.4	0.0	0.0	0.4	0.4	9.8	9.8	13.2	10.8	7.0	27.2	15.3	6.3	0.7	60.3	24.6	54.7	45.3
99656	RED DEVIL	15.7	14.0	0.0	0.0	0.0	0.0	2.0	2.0	6.0	8.0	18.0	14.0	6.0	22.0	20.0	6.0	0.0	58.0	23.3	54.0	46.0
99658	SAINT MARYS	6.4	6.1	0.0	0.0	0.3	0.3	0.2	0.2	11.4	10.3	11.6	11.9	7.9	26.8	15.1	4.9	0.3	58.5	23.1	52.7	47.3
99659	SAINT MICHAEL	5.7	5.6	0.0	0.0	0.0	0.0	0.0	0.0	11.2	11.2	14.3	10.4	11.2	22.9	15.0	3.3	0.5	56.7	21.3	52.4	47.6
99660	SAINT PAUL ISLAND	25.1	20.4	0.6	0.6	3.4	2.9	1.8	1.6	5.9	5.9	6.5	7.5	7.9	33.6	26.9	5.3	0.4	76.4	35.2	57.0	43.0
99661	SAND POINT	27.8	28.3	1.5	1.3	23.5	23.6	13.5	14.7	6.4	6.1	6.0	6.8	7.9	36.0	27.1	3.8	0.0	77.1	35.9	59.3	40.7
99662	SCAMMON BAY	3.6	3.5	0.0	0.0	0.0	0.0	0.2	0.2	11.4	11.4	14.5	13.7	7.9	23.4	13.2	4.1	0.4	53.0	19.7	50.1	49.9
99664	SEWARD	75.6	73.6	1.6	1.5	1.7	1.7	2.2	2.5	5.6	5.6	6.6	7.8	7.9	30.3	29.5	6.3	0.4	77.1	37.4	57.9	42.1
99667	SKWENTNA	90.0	90.0	0.0	0.0	0.0	0.0	0.0	0.0	0.0	5.0	10.0	10.0	0.0	15.0	55.0	5.0	0.0	85.0	50.0	45.0	55.0
99668	SLEETMUTE	15.4	15.4	0.0	0.0	0.0	0.0	0.0	0.0	15.4	15.4	23.1	7.7	7.7	15.4	15.4	0.0	0.0	46.2	14.2	53.9	46.2
99669	SOLDOTNA	90.0	88.8	0.3	0.3	1.2	1.3	2.2	2.6	6.3	6.9	8.3	8.2	6.3	25.5	30.0	8.1	0.5	73.2	37.7	50.2	49.8
99670	SOUTH NAKNEK	52.2	50.4	0.3	0.4	0.7	0.7	0.6	0.7	7.2	7.2	8.6	9.0	7.1	27.0	29.0	4.9	0.1	71.5	36.0	53.8	46.2
99671	STEBBINS	5.9	5.5	0.2	0.2	0.0	0.0	0.2	0.2	11.0	11.2	13.0	10.6	11.3	23.2	15.4	3.6	0.7	57.8	21.9	52.7	47.3
99672	STERLING	92.5	91.6	0.4	0.4	0.6	0.6	1.3	1.5	6.4	6.9	8.6	8.4	6.6	25.4	29.4	7.9	0.3	72.7	37.6	52.1	47.9
99676	TALKEETNA	87.4	85.9	0.3	0.3	0.4	0.4	1.7	1.9	4.5	5.0	6.7	7.7	4.0	26.9	37.1	7.7	0.5	78.8	42.7	53.8	46.2
99679	TULUKSAK	4.4	4.1	0.0	0.0	0.2	0.2	0.5	0.2	11.6	10.5	12.8	11.4	8.4	24.6	15.5	4.8	0.5	57.9	22.2	54.4	45.6
99681	TUNUNAK	3.2	2.8	0.0	0.0	0.0	0.0	0.2	0.2	10.3	10.0	11.3	12.1	8.6	25.3	16.8	5.1	0.6	60.0	23.7	54.5	45.6
	ALASKA	69.3	68.2	3.5	3.3	4.5	4.6	4.1	4.7	7.6	7.3	8.3	8.1	8.1	29.3	25.1	5.8	0.5	71.7	32.9	51.4	48.6
	UNITED STATES	75.1	73.6	12.3	12.5	3.8	4.2	12.5	14.1	6.9	6.7	7.2	7.0	7.3	28.6	23.8	10.8	1.7	75.1	36.0	49.1	50.9

ZIP CODE #	POST OFFICE NAME	2004 Per Capita Income	2004 HH Income Base	2004 Household Income Distribution (%) Less than $25,000	$25,000 to $49,999	$50,000 to $99,999	$100,000 to $149,999	$150,000 or More	Median Household Income 2004	2009	2004 National Centile	2004 State Centile	2004 Home Value Base	2004 Home Value Distribution (%) Less than $50,000	$50,000 to $89,999	$90,000 to $174,999	$175,000 to $399,999	$400,000 or More	2004 Median Home Value
99501	ANCHORAGE	30587	7312	30.9	26.7	25.9	10.0	6.5	42569	51479	55	53	2341	2.6	8.1	36.4	44.6	8.2	181494
99502	ANCHORAGE	33863	8455	9.0	18.4	42.1	19.2	11.3	72592	88660	92	95	6074	0.8	4.7	32.3	56.3	6.0	190400
99503	ANCHORAGE	24035	6437	27.3	31.4	29.4	9.0	2.9	41593	49489	52	50	2359	21.2	5.0	37.6	34.1	2.1	149424
99504	ANCHORAGE	29070	14718	14.2	23.0	38.0	16.1	8.6	63254	78030	87	88	10024	12.5	3.9	35.3	47.8	0.5	171940
99505	FORT RICHARDSON	16184	1194	13.0	49.4	30.7	5.1	1.8	42155	50468	53	51	63	0.0	33.3	38.1	22.2	6.4	112500
99506	ELMENDORF AFB	16190	1728	11.5	40.8	38.8	6.6	2.3	47826	58388	68	62	17	0.0	35.3	35.3	29.4	0.0	107500
99507	ANCHORAGE	30818	12789	12.1	22.6	37.9	17.1	10.3	67322	81557	90	94	8635	8.6	4.2	27.8	52.3	7.2	190199
99508	ANCHORAGE	24727	13403	21.3	30.5	33.0	10.2	5.1	48355	56980	69	64	6615	14.5	7.8	36.9	39.2	1.7	158180
99515	ANCHORAGE	33415	7135	8.5	16.3	40.7	21.5	12.9	77235	93564	94	98	5651	7.2	4.1	27.6	54.8	6.3	197386
99516	ANCHORAGE	43514	6305	4.7	8.4	31.9	29.3	25.8	106078	128695	99	100	5826	0.6	0.8	7.3	76.0	15.2	275119
99517	ANCHORAGE	33568	6976	13.3	24.2	37.9	14.7	9.9	63323	77117	87	88	4301	3.9	4.8	39.1	47.6	4.6	178349
99518	ANCHORAGE	31662	3999	12.2	27.3	37.7	16.6	6.3	60422	75277	85	84	2386	0.8	9.5	49.3	39.1	1.2	164404
99540	INDIAN	20764	46	45.7	17.4	21.7	15.2	0.0	31099	42374	15	19	36	0.0	0.0	52.8	47.2	0.0	150000
99546	ADAK	33483	165	14.6	30.3	39.4	13.3	2.4	53735	60196	78	74	69	4.4	31.9	56.5	7.3	0.0	103125
99547	ATKA	23975	35	14.3	25.7	45.7	11.4	2.9	58518	58807	83	83	15	6.7	26.7	60.0	6.7	0.0	103125
99549	PORT HEIDEN	24269	37	16.2	35.1	27.0	13.5	8.1	49072	62105	70	67	29	10.3	17.2	51.7	20.7	0.0	112500
99551	AKIACHAK	8755	98	36.7	36.7	21.4	5.1	0.0	33143	38159	21	26	79	43.0	24.1	20.3	10.1	2.5	59167
99553	AKUTAN	16573	61	27.9	29.5	31.2	6.6	4.9	42978	51458	56	54	29	10.3	13.8	62.1	3.5	10.3	134167
99554	ALAKANUK	9253	344	36.3	32.9	27.3	2.3	1.2	33643	36235	23	30	258	50.4	12.8	19.8	16.7	0.4	49412
99555	ALEKNAGIK	14399	71	40.9	28.2	19.7	8.5	2.8	31101	38633	15	19	57	17.5	15.8	38.6	28.1	0.0	130357
99556	ANCHOR POINT	19506	925	27.4	30.4	32.0	8.3	2.0	42129	46083	53	51	778	18.6	22.4	37.3	20.4	1.3	104839
99557	ANIAK	8618	134	53.0	34.3	11.2	1.5	0.0	23106	26236	3	7	107	20.6	24.3	34.6	20.6	0.0	96875
99558	ANVIK	9864	88	47.7	33.0	15.9	3.4	0.0	26083	30940	6	11	66	56.1	18.2	16.7	7.6	1.5	44286
99559	BETHEL	16955	3174	24.8	27.3	29.7	14.5	3.7	47522	58325	67	62	1861	27.0	16.3	26.5	26.5	3.6	111566
99561	CHEFORNAK	8603	77	32.5	33.8	27.3	6.5	0.0	36364	40567	33	38	60	45.0	20.0	18.3	8.3	8.3	60000
99563	CHEVAK	0	0	0.0	0.0	0.0	0.0	0.0	0	0	0	0	0	0.0	0.0	0.0	0.0	0.0	0
99564	CHIGNIK	26111	26	19.2	34.6	26.9	7.7	11.5	47338	57172	67	59	20	10.0	20.0	45.0	25.0	0.0	112500
99565	CHIGNIK LAGOON	22684	30	20.0	30.0	23.3	16.7	10.0	50000	60000	72	69	24	8.3	16.7	54.2	20.8	0.0	113889
99567	CHUGIAK	33569	2682	7.5	19.1	34.1	23.9	15.4	83408	103616	96	99	2304	1.3	7.3	25.4	64.3	1.8	200823
99568	CLAM GULCH	20734	145	29.0	31.7	27.6	8.3	3.5	41132	47925	50	50	124	24.2	14.5	37.1	21.0	3.2	112500
99569	CLARKS POINT	12586	32	46.9	25.0	18.8	9.4	0.0	27308	37339	8	14	26	15.4	11.5	46.2	26.9	0.0	137500
99571	COLD BAY	40824	126	24.6	27.8	31.8	7.9	7.9	47375	56639	67	60	70	4.3	10.0	57.1	20.0	8.6	143000
99572	COOPER LANDING	28041	161	22.4	23.6	34.8	15.5	3.7	53884	61515	78	75	128	3.1	11.7	40.6	40.6	3.9	157500
99573	COPPER CENTER	18725	703	33.9	27.7	29.9	6.3	2.3	39650	46621	45	46	563	23.1	18.1	32.3	20.3	6.2	109423
99574	CORDOVA	29337	982	20.6	24.3	31.1	17.6	6.4	56805	68194	81	79	545	20.4	2.8	27.2	46.2	3.5	174364
99575	CROOKED CREEK	2500	2	100.0	0.0	0.0	0.0	0.0	5000	5000	0	3	0	0.0	0.0	0.0	0.0	0.0	0
99576	DILLINGHAM	22301	1126	24.4	21.6	32.6	15.0	6.4	54250	64952	79	76	693	13.0	13.1	37.8	32.3	3.8	144146
99577	EAGLE RIVER	32691	7978	5.5	16.1	40.0	25.9	12.4	82902	101915	96	99	6620	1.9	1.3	22.6	71.0	3.3	209167
99578	EEK	7843	135	45.9	37.0	14.1	3.0	0.0	26888	31251	7	12	89	60.7	20.2	10.1	7.9	1.1	39375
99579	EGEGIK	26210	37	16.2	35.1	27.0	13.5	8.1	49072	62105	70	67	29	10.3	17.2	51.7	20.7	0.0	112500
99580	EKWOK	14960	43	39.5	27.9	23.3	9.3	0.0	32317	47405	19	23	30	23.3	16.7	46.7	10.0	3.3	110000
99583	FALSE PASS	28202	39	28.2	28.2	33.3	5.1	5.1	43645	51085	58	55	19	10.5	10.5	68.4	5.3	5.3	134375
99584	FLAT	0	0	0.0	0.0	0.0	0.0	0.0	0	0	0	0	0	0.0	0.0	0.0	0.0	0.0	0
99585	MARSHALL	9880	145	36.6	39.3	20.0	2.8	1.4	34714	39688	26	33	80	33.8	11.3	30.0	22.5	2.5	94444
99586	GAKONA	19394	152	44.1	25.7	23.0	6.6	0.7	30000	36659	12	16	120	24.2	20.0	30.0	14.2	11.7	102778
99587	GIRDWOOD	42775	590	8.3	22.4	33.4	17.8	18.1	74734	101091	93	96	365	1.6	3.0	24.9	60.6	9.9	222183
99588	GLENNALLEN	20024	414	26.1	33.1	28.7	9.7	2.4	44256	50816	59	57	260	16.2	16.5	35.8	23.9	7.7	125926
99589	GOODNEWS BAY	9805	70	45.7	38.6	12.9	2.9	0.0	26911	30302	7	13	46	56.5	21.7	10.9	8.7	2.2	44000
99591	SAINT GEORGE ISLAND	22693	53	15.1	30.2	39.6	13.2	1.9	53674	58506	78	74	22	4.6	36.4	54.6	4.6	0.0	100000
99602	HOLY CROSS	9215	62	48.4	32.3	14.5	4.8	0.0	25866	30431	6	11	46	54.4	17.4	15.2	10.9	2.2	47143
99603	HOMER	25566	3803	24.2	26.0	32.7	11.8	5.3	49813	58533	72	68	2849	8.5	9.6	40.1	37.6	4.3	158393
99604	HOOPER BAY	8603	410	40.0	36.3	16.8	5.1	1.7	30134	34245	13	17	275	57.8	14.2	17.1	9.1	1.8	40227
99606	ILIAMNA	13223	93	41.9	28.0	21.5	7.5	1.1	32744	37360	20	24	56	21.4	16.1	30.4	19.6	12.5	116667
99607	KALSKAG	13805	61	32.8	31.2	24.6	9.8	1.6	36346	41138	33	37	46	6.5	13.0	52.2	26.1	2.2	138636
99610	KASILOF	23610	746	28.6	27.8	27.8	11.1	4.8	44085	50726	59	57	636	18.6	8.3	45.4	21.5	6.1	127397
99611	KENAI	24859	5580	21.6	22.9	34.1	15.7	5.7	57629	68620	82	79	4155	9.0	8.6	50.7	29.1	2.7	142077
99612	KING COVE	22019	306	21.9	26.8	32.0	9.5	9.8	51165	62385	74	70	196	0.0	7.1	54.1	30.6	8.2	158824
99613	KING SALMON	28461	143	14.7	29.4	41.3	10.5	4.2	54806	63119	79	78	66	6.1	7.6	37.9	45.5	3.0	171875
99614	KIPNUK	11216	30	33.3	33.3	30.0	3.3	0.0	37333	47394	37	41	23	43.5	17.4	21.7	8.7	8.7	65000
99615	KODIAK	26524	4513	15.2	22.4	35.2	17.8	9.4	63507	79132	87	89	2595	7.1	7.8	31.2	46.8	7.1	185844
99620	KOTLIK	7904	122	36.9	32.8	27.1	2.5	0.8	33331	36351	22	28	91	50.6	12.1	20.9	16.5	0.0	49167
99622	KWIGILLINGOK	11699	31	32.3	32.3	32.3	3.2	0.0	38625	47356	42	44	24	41.7	20.8	20.8	8.3	8.3	70000
99625	LEVELOCK	14549	76	40.8	29.0	21.1	7.9	1.3	32827	40563	20	25	46	26.1	13.0	28.3	23.9	8.7	115000
99626	LOWER KALSKAG	12659	65	32.3	33.9	23.1	9.2	1.5	36103	41141	32	36	49	6.1	14.3	51.0	26.5	2.0	136250
99627	MC GRATH	19781	174	37.9	25.9	20.7	10.3	5.2	37359	41563	37	42	103	16.5	19.4	55.3	7.8	1.0	104911
99628	MANOKOTAK	10628	95	41.1	28.4	20.0	8.4	2.1	30947	38188	15	18	77	16.9	15.6	42.9	24.7	0.0	131731
99630	MEKORYUK	15392	75	32.0	38.7	22.7	4.0	2.7	34632	38932	26	32	50	40.0	20.0	24.0	14.0	2.0	70000
99631	MOOSE PASS	27877	238	22.3	24.0	34.9	15.6	3.4	53651	60998	78	73	189	2.7	12.2	40.2	41.3	3.7	158036
99632	MOUNTAIN VILLAGE	12259	230	33.0	30.9	29.1	4.4	2.6	36606	40989	34	38	123	43.9	14.6	32.5	8.9	0.0	63000
99636	NEW STUYAHOK	10307	107	37.4	27.1	25.2	9.4	0.9	34594	46167	26	31	74	24.3	17.6	43.2	12.2	2.7	108333
99638	NIKOLSKI	25654	16	12.5	31.3	43.8	12.5	0.0	54460	66491	79	77	7	0.0	28.6	71.4	0.0	0.0	104167
99639	NINILCHIK	21189	431	33.0	29.2	25.8	9.5	2.6	38744	43865	42	45	363	16.5	22.0	33.6	27.3	0.6	106855
99640	NONDALTON	13708	62	40.3	29.0	22.6	8.1	0.0	33615	36537	23	29	37	18.9	13.5	29.7	27.0	10.8	129167
99645	PALMER	25228	6780	17.5	25.0	37.6	13.4	6.5	58423	68380	83	82	5496	7.2	8.7	43.3	36.8	4.0	158355
99647	PEDRO BAY	14661	15	33.3	33.3	26.7	6.7	0.0	37333	35000	37	41	9	22.2	0.0	44.4	33.3	0.0	131250
99648	PERRYVILLE	21748	30	20.0	30.0	23.3	16.7	10.0	50000	60000	72	69	24	8.3	16.7	54.2	20.8	0.0	113889
99649	PILOT POINT	22179	31	19.4	32.3	29.0	9.7	9.7	48639	57193	70	65	25	12.0	16.0	52.0	20.0	0.0	112500
99654	WASILLA	25069	13409	17.2	22.5	38.1	15.5	6.7	61483	72774	86	85	10748	7.2	6.7	43.0	40.5	2.6	164628
99655	QUINHAGAK	9724	78	39.7	41.0	14.1	5.1	0.0	31287	35469	16	20	64	68.8	4.7	12.5	14.1	0.0	32500
99656	RED DEVIL	9520	18	50.0	33.3	16.7	0.0	0.0	25000	25000	5	10	14	7.1	28.6	42.9	21.4	0.0	108333
99658	SAINT MARYS	14389	175	32.0	30.9	29.1	5.1	2.9	37496	42139	37	43	86	41.9	14.0	38.4	5.8	0.0	67500
99659	SAINT MICHAEL	11054	97	36.1	29.9	22.7	9.3	2.1	33264	40000	22	27	71	38.0	22.5	23.9	15.5	0.0	67500
99660	SAINT PAUL ISLAND	22330	169	15.4	29.6	39.6	13.0	2.4	53742	60381	78	75	71	4.2	32.4	56.3	7.0	0.0	102976
99661	SAND POINT	28768	413	14.3	26.2	30.8	16.5	12.4	63919	81740	88	90	255	9.0	10.2	61.6	19.2	0.0	132218
99662	SCAMMON BAY	8076	101	39.6	37.6	16.8	5.0	1.0	30268	35000	13	18	68	58.8	13.2	16.2	8.8	2.9	38333
99664	SEWARD	25824	1710	22.1	22.5	38.8	12.1	4.6	54763	64140	79	77	1129	10.1	7.4	38.5	39.7	4.3	164773
99667	SKWENTNA	12107	5	40.0	0.0	60.0	0.0	0.0	66333	65822	89	91	4	100.0	0.0	0.0	0.0	0.0	45000
99668	SLEETMUTE	8269	6	66.7	33.3	0.0	0.0	0.0	15000	7500	1	4	5	0.0	0.0	100.0	0.0	0.0	112500
99669	SOLDOTNA	26446	4506	19.4	24.2	36.3	14.0	6.2	56153	66418	81	78	3434	8.1	8.0	48.7	32.0	3.2	147228
99670	SOUTH NAKNEK	24547	308	16.2	25.0	42.5	12.0	4.2	57879	66681	83	81	163	6.8	10.4	38.7	41.7	2.5	163125
99671	STEBBINS	10184	132	36.4	31.8	22.0	8.3	1.5	32994	39484	21	26	97	36.1	22.7	27.8	13.4	0.0	69444
99672	STERLING	24100	1102	20.8	26.0	35.8	13.0	4.5	52983	62489	77	72	940	8.6	15.6	39.9	34.2	1.7	145076
99676	TALKEETNA	21645	924	37.3	27.5	26.1	5.7	3.4	36631	40985	34	39	763	23.9	18.4	42.6	8.1	7.1	103433
99679	TULUKSAK	7727	87	36.8	36.8	21.8	4.6	0.0	32840	38269	20	25	70	40.0	25.7	22.9	10.0	1.4	64000
99681	TUNUNAK	9775	241	33.2	39.4	21.6	2.9	2.9	33999	38975	24	30	161	41.0	19.3	24.8	12.4	2.5	71500
	ALASKA	27197		17.6	24.1	35.4	15.1	7.8	59655	71504				9.9	7.9	33.8	43.8	4.6	171678
	UNITED STATES	25866		24.7	27.1	30.8	10.9	6.5	48124	56710				10.9	15.0	33.7	30.1	10.4	145905

ZIP CODE	FINANCIAL SERVICES				THE HOME						ENTERTAINMENT						PERSONAL			
					Home Improvements		Furnishings													
# POST OFFICE NAME	Auto Loan	Home Loan	Investments	Retirement Plans	Home Repair	Lawn & Garden	Computers & Hardware	Major Appliances	TV, Radio, Sound Equipment	Furniture	Dine out/ Carry out	Sports Equipment	Fees & Tickets	Toys & Games	Travel	Cable TV	Apparel & Services	Auto Repairs	Health Insurance	Pets & Supplies
99501 ANCHORAGE	84	78	102	84	77	84	93	85	92	89	115	104	90	113	88	88	112	91	81	94
99502 ANCHORAGE	130	141	149	147	136	137	136	133	127	138	162	157	138	161	133	120	159	133	117	146
99503 ANCHORAGE	74	67	83	73	66	71	78	73	77	77	98	89	75	94	74	73	95	78	67	81
99504 ANCHORAGE	113	119	120	121	115	117	115	114	110	116	138	134	115	137	112	105	136	114	103	127
99505 FORT RICHARDSON	82	52	50	60	48	56	78	67	79	72	99	89	66	88	64	72	94	79	62	76
99506 ELMENDORF AFB	91	58	56	67	53	63	86	75	88	81	110	99	74	98	71	80	105	88	69	85
99507 ANCHORAGE	121	124	129	131	119	121	122	119	116	125	147	142	123	144	118	109	145	121	106	133
99508 ANCHORAGE	91	89	97	92	87	91	94	91	91	94	115	108	92	112	90	88	112	94	84	101
99515 ANCHORAGE	136	148	149	152	143	142	140	138	131	142	166	163	142	166	137	124	164	137	122	153
99516 ANCHORAGE	174	213	227	219	206	206	189	185	173	192	219	215	205	228	191	166	220	179	164	205
99517 ANCHORAGE	111	122	139	125	118	121	121	117	115	121	145	139	123	146	119	110	143	118	105	128
99518 ANCHORAGE	108	104	118	112	101	105	111	106	107	113	136	128	109	131	106	100	133	111	95	118
99540 INDIAN	66	72	72	73	69	69	68	68	64	69	81	80	69	81	67	60	80	67	59	74
99546 ADAK	90	76	90	86	73	79	89	84	87	91	112	102	85	103	82	81	108	90	75	94
99547 ATKA	91	77	90	86	74	79	90	84	88	92	113	103	85	104	83	82	109	91	76	95
99549 PORT HEIDEN	120	94	64	85	106	119	89	107	101	88	119	125	79	118	95	107	111	105	127	146
99551 AKIACHAK	60	53	44	49	51	53	54	58	56	58	70	61	49	62	51	54	69	59	54	60
99553 AKUTAN	72	79	93	76	76	80	77	76	77	80	98	85	79	101	77	77	98	77	71	82
99554 ALAKANUK	62	54	45	50	52	55	55	60	57	60	72	63	51	64	53	55	71	61	56	62
99555 ALEKNAGIK	77	61	41	55	68	77	57	69	65	57	77	81	51	76	61	69	71	68	82	94
99556 ANCHOR POINT	78	76	67	75	77	80	72	75	71	72	88	89	71	89	72	70	85	74	74	90
99557 ANIAK	38	34	37	33	33	38	39	37	41	38	50	44	38	50	38	41	49	39	39	41
99558 ANVIK	44	39	43	39	39	44	46	44	48	44	59	51	44	58	44	48	57	46	46	48
99559 BETHEL	86	89	86	88	86	87	86	88	84	89	106	101	85	102	84	80	104	88	79	95
99561 CHEFORNAK	70	61	51	57	59	62	63	68	65	68	82	72	57	72	60	63	81	69	63	71
99563 CHEVAK	0	0	0	0	0	0	0	0	0	0	0	0	0	0	0	0	0	0	0	0
99564 CHIGNIK	121	95	65	86	107	120	89	108	101	89	120	126	80	118	95	108	111	106	127	147
99565 CHIGNIK LAGOON	119	94	64	84	105	118	88	106	100	87	118	124	79	117	94	107	110	105	126	145
99567 CHUGIAK	136	156	155	161	150	146	142	141	131	145	165	165	146	168	140	123	164	137	121	154
99568 CLAM GULCH	100	70	38	66	82	92	69	85	80	68	93	103	59	92	72	84	85	84	102	119
99569 CLARKS POINT	76	60	41	54	67	75	56	68	64	56	75	79	50	74	60	68	70	67	80	93
99571 COLD BAY	88	85	84	83	85	93	85	87	87	85	108	98	84	109	84	88	105	87	88	98
99572 COOPER LANDING	106	83	57	75	93	105	78	94	88	77	105	110	70	103	83	95	97	93	111	129
99573 COPPER CENTER	80	65	46	62	71	77	63	72	68	62	81	86	57	80	64	69	76	71	80	95
99574 CORDOVA	106	116	116	118	112	111	110	109	103	111	130	129	110	131	108	97	128	109	96	120
99575 CROOKED CREEK	7	6	7	6	6	7	7	7	8	7	9	8	7	9	7	7	9	7	7	7
99576 DILLINGHAM	94	99	97	101	95	95	96	96	91	98	115	111	95	114	93	86	114	95	85	103
99577 EAGLE RIVER	137	155	160	161	149	148	144	141	133	147	169	166	149	171	141	126	167	139	123	155
99578 EEK	49	43	36	40	41	43	44	47	46	48	57	50	40	51	42	44	57	48	44	49
99579 EGEGIK	120	94	64	85	106	119	89	107	101	88	119	125	79	118	95	107	111	105	127	146
99580 EKWOK	62	56	61	55	55	63	65	62	68	62	84	72	63	83	63	69	81	65	65	68
99583 FALSE PASS	73	80	94	77	76	81	78	77	78	81	99	86	80	102	78	78	99	78	72	83
99584 FLAT	0	0	0	0	0	0	0	0	0	0	0	0	0	0	0	0	0	0	0	0
99585 MARSHALL	54	50	60	48	48	56	54	53	58	56	73	59	56	73	54	60	72	54	55	60
99586 GAKONA	71	56	38	50	63	70	52	63	59	52	70	74	47	69	56	63	65	62	75	86
99587 GIRDWOOD	136	143	148	144	142	146	138	139	133	138	167	165	137	168	138	130	163	139	131	159
99588 GLENNALLEN	76	81	79	82	79	80	77	78	73	78	92	92	77	93	76	70	90	77	70	87
99589 GOODNEWS BAY	49	43	36	40	41	43	44	47	46	48	57	50	40	51	42	44	57	48	44	49
99591 SAINT GEORGE ISLAND	90	76	90	85	73	79	89	84	87	91	112	102	85	103	82	81	108	90	75	94
99602 HOLY CROSS	44	40	43	39	39	45	46	44	49	44	60	52	45	59	45	49	58	46	46	49
99603 HOMER	91	95	90	96	93	94	90	91	86	91	108	108	89	108	89	83	106	91	84	104
99604 HOOPER BAY	54	49	59	47	47	55	53	52	58	55	72	58	55	71	53	59	71	53	54	59
99606 ILIAMNA	75	59	40	53	66	74	55	67	63	55	74	78	50	73	59	67	69	66	79	91
99607 KALSKAG	73	80	80	81	77	76	76	75	71	77	90	89	76	90	74	67	88	75	66	83
99610 KASILOF	103	80	50	75	89	98	76	90	85	76	101	108	69	101	79	88	94	88	103	122
99611 KENAI	95	102	101	103	100	101	97	97	92	97	116	115	97	118	96	89	114	97	89	109
99612 KING COVE	106	90	70	90	94	107	93	99	98	91	119	113	89	118	92	100	112	97	107	117
99613 KING SALMON	104	87	64	79	96	106	81	95	89	80	106	111	74	106	86	94	100	93	109	127
99614 KIPNUK	69	61	51	57	59	62	62	67	65	68	81	71	57	72	59	62	80	68	63	70
99615 KODIAK	114	120	131	125	117	118	120	117	113	120	143	140	119	142	116	107	141	119	104	128
99620 KOTLIK	62	54	45	50	52	55	55	60	57	60	72	63	51	64	53	55	72	61	56	62
99622 KWIGILLINGOK	69	61	51	57	59	62	62	67	65	68	81	71	57	72	59	62	80	68	63	70
99625 LEVELOCK	75	59	40	53	66	74	55	67	62	55	74	78	49	73	59	67	69	66	79	91
99626 LOWER KALSKAG	73	80	80	81	77	76	76	75	71	76	90	89	76	90	74	67	88	75	66	82
99627 MC GRATH	91	71	49	64	80	90	67	81	76	67	90	95	60	89	72	81	84	80	96	111
99628 MANOKOTAK	77	60	41	54	68	76	57	68	64	56	76	80	51	75	61	69	71	67	81	94
99630 MEKORYUK	68	60	50	56	58	61	61	66	64	67	80	70	56	70	58	61	79	67	62	69
99631 MOOSE PASS	106	83	56	75	93	105	78	94	88	77	105	110	70	103	83	94	97	93	111	129
99632 MOUNTAIN VILLAGE	72	66	75	62	63	72	70	69	75	73	95	77	71	92	69	77	92	71	72	78
99636 NEW STUYAHOK	63	56	61	55	55	63	65	62	69	63	85	73	63	83	63	69	82	65	65	69
99638 NIKOLSKI	87	74	87	83	71	77	87	81	85	88	109	99	82	100	80	79	105	88	73	91
99639 NINILCHIK	87	69	47	62	77	87	65	78	73	64	87	91	58	86	69	78	81	77	92	106
99640 NONDALTON	75	59	40	53	66	74	55	67	63	55	74	78	50	73	59	67	69	66	79	91
99645 PALMER	105	111	106	113	109	110	104	106	100	106	125	124	105	125	103	96	122	104	98	120
99647 PEDRO BAY	73	57	39	52	64	72	54	65	61	53	72	76	48	71	58	65	67	64	77	89
99648 PERRYVILLE	119	94	64	84	105	118	88	106	100	87	118	124	79	117	94	107	110	105	126	145
99649 PILOT POINT	119	93	64	84	105	118	88	106	100	87	118	124	79	116	94	106	110	104	125	145
99654 WASILLA	105	112	109	115	109	108	105	105	99	107	125	124	106	125	103	94	123	104	94	118
99655 QUINHAGAK	55	48	40	45	46	49	49	53	51	53	64	56	45	57	47	49	64	54	50	55
99656 RED DEVIL	36	32	35	31	32	36	38	36	39	36	48	42	36	48	36	40	47	37	37	39
99658 SAINT MARYS	73	68	81	64	65	75	73	71	79	75	99	80	75	98	72	81	96	73	74	81
99659 SAINT MICHAEL	61	56	68	53	54	62	61	59	66	63	82	66	62	81	60	68	80	61	62	68
99660 SAINT PAUL ISLAND	90	76	90	86	73	79	89	84	87	91	112	102	85	103	82	81	108	90	75	94
99661 SAND POINT	115	126	126	128	122	121	120	119	112	121	142	141	121	143	117	106	140	118	104	131
99662 SCAMMON BAY	54	49	59	47	47	55	53	52	57	55	72	58	55	71	53	59	70	53	54	59
99664 SEWARD	87	97	110	100	95	96	95	93	89	95	113	110	96	115	94	86	111	93	83	102
99667 SKWENTNA	82	64	44	58	73	82	61	73	69	60	81	86	54	80	65	73	76	72	87	100
99668 SLEETMUTE	24	22	24	21	22	25	25	24	27	24	33	28	24	32	24	27	32	25	25	27
99669 SOLDOTNA	102	102	94	102	103	106	98	101	96	98	119	119	96	120	97	94	116	100	98	117
99670 SOUTH NAKNEK	111	87	59	79	98	110	82	99	93	81	110	116	73	109	88	99	102	98	117	135
99671 STEBBINS	61	57	68	54	54	63	61	59	66	63	83	67	63	82	60	68	81	61	62	68
99672 STERLING	105	90	70	84	97	106	85	97	92	85	110	114	79	109	89	95	104	96	108	126
99676 TALKEETNA	82	64	44	58	72	81	61	73	69	60	81	85	54	80	65	73	75	72	86	100
99679 TULUKSAK	60	53	44	49	50	53	54	58	56	58	70	61	49	62	51	54	69	59	54	60
99681 TUNUNAK	68	60	50	56	58	61	61	66	64	67	80	70	56	71	58	61	79	67	62	69
ALASKA	106	108	111	111	106	109	107	106	104	108	130	126	107	129	105	100	128	107	98	120
UNITED STATES	100	100	100	100	100	100	100	100	100	100	100	100	100	100	100	100	100	100	100	100

POPULATION CHANGE

# ZIP CODE POST OFFICE NAME	COUNTY FIPS CODE	POPULATION 2000	2004	2009	2000-2004 ANNUAL RATE % Rate	State Centile	HOUSEHOLDS 2000	2004	2009	% Annual Rate 2000-2004	2004 Average HH Size	FAMILIES 2000	2004	% Annual Rate 2000-2004
99682 TYONEK	122	169	169	174	0.0	47	60	60	63	0.0	2.82	40	40	0.0
99683 TRAPPER CREEK	170	32	36	42	2.8	94	13	15	17	3.4	2.33	8	9	2.8
99684 UNALAKLEET	180	749	770	803	0.7	65	225	233	244	0.8	3.30	175	181	0.8
99685 UNALASKA	016	4207	5341	6491	5.8	98	796	1272	1782	11.7	2.49	452	729	11.9
99686 VALDEZ	261	4422	4457	4509	0.2	50	1632	1664	1706	0.5	2.63	1127	1154	0.6
99687 WASILLA	170	2631	2982	3500	3.0	95	1008	1153	1365	3.2	2.52	672	772	3.3
99688 WILLOW	170	1867	2121	2498	3.1	96	744	849	1006	3.2	2.50	491	564	3.3
99689 YAKUTAT	282	466	448	448	-0.9	17	184	178	178	-0.8	2.12	110	108	-0.4
99691 NIKOLAI	290	100	97	94	-0.7	23	40	39	38	-0.6	2.49	26	25	-0.9
99701 FAIRBANKS	090	17557	17728	18644	0.2	52	7165	7266	7687	0.3	2.36	4089	4161	0.4
99702 EIELSON AFB	090	5388	5659	6008	1.2	76	1445	1534	1643	1.4	3.49	1411	1498	1.4
99703 FORT WAINWRIGHT	090	5815	5978	6248	0.7	65	1437	1495	1582	0.9	3.35	1371	1427	1.0
99704 CLEAR	290	509	493	478	-0.8	19	213	207	200	-0.7	2.38	124	121	-0.6
99705 NORTH POLE	090	16380	17700	19125	1.8	89	5630	6114	6640	2.0	2.89	4249	4621	2.0
99709 FAIRBANKS	090	25545	27104	29124	1.4	83	9862	10561	11445	1.6	2.48	6220	6678	1.7
99712 FAIRBANKS	090	11083	11885	12777	1.7	87	3822	4131	4473	1.9	2.81	2870	3103	1.9
99714 SALCHA	090	1072	1158	1249	1.8	89	416	452	491	2.0	2.56	292	318	2.0
99722 ARCTIC VILLAGE	290	152	148	143	-0.6	28	52	51	50	-0.5	2.90	34	33	-0.7
99723 BARROW	185	662	652	643	-0.4	31	166	166	165	0.0	3.92	129	130	0.2
99724 BEAVER	290	84	82	79	-0.6	30	31	30	30	-0.8	2.73	20	20	0.0
99726 BETTLES FIELD	290	118	115	111	-0.6	29	46	45	44	-0.5	2.56	27	27	0.0
99727 BUCKLAND	188	406	417	428	0.6	64	84	86	88	0.6	4.85	69	71	0.7
99729 CANTWELL	068	276	279	284	0.3	54	130	136	143	1.1	2.05	72	75	1.0
99730 CENTRAL	290	176	171	166	-0.7	26	76	74	73	-0.6	2.30	45	44	-0.5
99733 CIRCLE	290	25	24	24	-1.0	16	11	11	11	0.0	2.18	6	6	0.0
99734 PRUDHOE BAY	185	5	5	5	0.0	47	1	1	1	0.0	5.00	1	1	0.0
99736 DEERING	188	105	108	111	0.7	66	29	30	30	0.8	3.60	24	25	1.0
99737 DELTA JUNCTION	240	3906	3853	3864	-0.3	33	1240	1234	1243	-0.1	2.88	924	923	0.0
99739 ELIM	180	48	50	53	1.0	72	12	13	13	1.9	3.85	9	9	0.0
99740 FORT YUKON	290	622	604	585	-0.7	25	235	230	225	-0.5	2.61	138	136	-0.3
99741 GALENA	290	17	16	16	-1.4	15	11	11	10	-1.9	1.45	7	6	-3.6
99742 GAMBELL	180	649	684	722	1.2	81	159	169	179	1.5	4.05	123	131	1.5
99743 HEALY	068	1574	1584	1602	0.2	49	675	701	733	0.9	2.17	390	406	1.0
99744 ANDERSON	068	149	150	152	0.2	49	20	21	22	1.2	5.52	13	14	1.8
99745 HUGHES	290	67	65	63	-0.7	23	18	18	17	0.0	3.61	12	11	-2.0
99746 HUSLIA	290	293	284	275	-0.7	20	88	86	83	-0.5	3.30	57	56	-0.4
99747 KAKTOVIK	185	262	259	256	-0.3	34	81	81	81	0.0	3.20	62	63	0.4
99748 KALTAG	290	223	216	209	-0.8	19	67	66	64	-0.4	3.27	51	49	-0.9
99749 KIANA	188	723	740	757	0.6	59	188	193	198	0.6	3.83	156	161	0.8
99750 KIVALINA	188	1069	1102	1129	0.7	66	182	190	196	1.0	4.45	156	163	1.0
99751 KOBUK	188	367	376	385	0.6	60	83	85	87	0.6	4.42	71	73	0.7
99752 KOTZEBUE	188	2634	2710	2779	0.7	66	703	728	750	0.8	3.64	530	551	0.9
99753 KOYUK	180	297	310	325	1.0	73	80	84	88	1.2	3.69	59	62	1.2
99755 DENALI NATIONAL PARK	068	49	49	50	0.0	47	19	20	20	1.2	2.35	11	12	2.1
99756 MANLEY HOT SPRINGS	290	136	132	128	-0.7	24	60	58	56	-0.8	2.28	35	34	-0.7
99757 LAKE MINCHUMINA	290	23	22	22	-1.0	16	11	11	11	0.0	2.00	7	7	0.0
99758 MINTO	290	265	257	249	-0.7	21	77	75	73	-0.6	3.43	45	45	0.0
99760 NENANA	290	37	36	35	-0.6	28	13	13	12	0.0	2.77	8	7	-3.1
99762 NOME	180	3847	3911	4048	0.4	56	1286	1317	1372	0.6	2.81	824	846	0.6
99763 NOORVIK	188	772	803	828	0.9	70	172	179	185	0.9	4.49	147	153	1.0
99765 NULATO	290	1121	1090	1057	-0.7	27	349	341	334	-0.5	3.01	249	245	-0.4
99766 POINT HOPE	185	574	577	574	0.1	48	145	148	148	0.5	3.87	116	119	0.6
99767 RAMPART	290	18	17	17	-1.3	15	9	9	9	0.0	1.89	5	5	0.0
99768 RUBY	290	191	185	179	-0.8	19	70	68	66	-0.7	2.72	46	44	-1.0
99769 SAVOONGA	180	294	310	327	1.3	82	62	66	70	1.5	4.70	48	51	1.4
99771 SHAKTOOLIK	180	11	11	12	0.0	47	5	5	5	0.0	2.20	4	4	0.0
99772 SHISHMAREF	180	562	576	599	0.6	61	142	146	153	0.7	3.95	102	105	0.7
99773 SHUNGNAK	188	4	4	4	0.0	47	1	1	1	0.0	4.00	1	1	0.0
99777 TANANA	290	308	299	290	-0.7	24	121	118	115	-0.6	2.53	71	70	-0.3
99778 TELLER	180	57	60	64	1.2	80	17	18	19	1.4	3.22	14	14	0.0
99780 TOK	240	2265	2233	2240	-0.3	32	857	852	857	-0.1	2.62	582	581	0.0
99781 VENETIE	290	202	196	190	-0.7	23	63	62	61	-0.4	3.16	41	40	-0.6
99782 WAINWRIGHT	185	484	472	464	-0.6	30	131	130	128	-0.2	3.63	105	105	0.0
99783 WALES	180	298	305	317	0.6	59	93	96	100	0.8	3.18	67	69	0.7
99784 WHITE MOUNTAIN	180	269	280	295	1.0	71	89	93	98	1.0	3.01	66	69	1.1
99785 BREVIG MISSION	180	276	292	308	1.3	82	68	72	77	1.4	3.90	54	58	1.7
99786 AMBLER	188	10	10	10	0.0	47	2	2	2	0.0	5.00	2	2	0.0
99788 CHALKYITSIK	290	39	38	37	-0.6	29	14	14	13	0.0	2.71	9	9	0.0
99789 NUIQSUT	185	3	3	3	0.0	47	1	1	1	0.0	3.00	1	1	0.0
99801 JUNEAU	110	28384	29463	30770	0.9	70	10521	10965	11504	1.0	2.63	7081	7406	1.1
99820 ANGOON	232	614	577	534	-1.5	14	200	194	186	-0.7	2.97	142	138	-0.7
99824 DOUGLAS	110	2064	2047	2092	-0.2	38	915	914	939	0.0	2.24	495	495	0.0
99825 ELFIN COVE	232	32	30	28	-1.5	12	15	15	14	0.0	2.00	9	8	-2.7
99826 GUSTAVUS	232	429	403	373	-1.5	12	199	193	185	-0.7	2.08	116	113	-0.6
99827 HAINES	100	2531	2501	2458	-0.3	34	1035	1037	1034	0.1	2.41	686	688	0.1
99829 HOONAH	232	1286	1210	1121	-1.4	15	485	470	451	-0.7	2.54	336	327	-0.6
99833 PETERSBURG	280	3713	3605	3453	-0.7	25	1413	1390	1351	-0.4	2.57	954	940	-0.4
99835 SITKA	220	8701	9060	9594	1.0	71	3227	3407	3662	1.3	2.58	2184	2313	1.4
99840 SKAGWAY	232	862	810	749	-1.5	14	401	387	369	-0.8	2.09	215	208	-0.8
99901 KETCHIKAN	130	13648	13570	13497	-0.1	39	5235	5251	5268	0.1	2.54	3509	3531	0.2
99903 MEYERS CHUCK	201	21	19	18	-2.3	2	9	8	8	-2.7	2.38	5	5	0.0
99919 THORNE BAY	201	409	378	346	-1.8	10	153	144	135	-1.4	2.63	109	103	-1.3
99921 CRAIG	201	1609	1487	1367	-1.8	10	579	542	505	-1.5	2.68	394	371	-1.4
99922 HYDABURG	201	69	64	58	-1.8	11	28	26	25	-1.7	2.46	19	18	-1.3
99923 HYDER	201	99	91	84	-2.0	8	49	46	42	-1.5	1.98	26	25	-0.9
99925 KLAWOCK	201	947	874	801	-1.9	8	346	324	303	-1.5	2.70	238	224	-1.4
99926 METLAKATLA	201	1452	1341	1231	-1.9	9	497	463	430	-1.7	2.90	361	337	-1.6
99927 POINT BAKER	201	114	106	98	-1.7	11	47	44	41	-1.5	2.25	29	27	-1.7
99929 WRANGELL	280	2378	2294	2193	-0.8	17	948	922	894	-0.7	2.46	644	629	-0.6
99950 KETCHIKAN	201	727	673	620	-1.8	10	286	269	252	-1.4	2.41	186	176	-1.3
ALASKA					1.5					1.6	2.73			1.7
UNITED STATES					1.2					1.3	2.58			1.1

ZIP CODE #	POST OFFICE NAME	RACE (%) White 2000	White 2004	Black 2000	Black 2004	Asian/Pacific 2000	Asian/Pacific 2004	% Hispanic Origin 2000	% Hispanic Origin 2004	2004 AGE DISTRIBUTION (%) 0-4	5-9	10-14	15-19	20-24	25-44	45-64	65-84	85+	18+	MEDIAN AGE 2004	% 2004 Males	% 2004 Females
99682	TYONEK	18.3	17.2	0.0	0.0	0.0	0.0	1.8	2.4	9.5	9.5	8.9	7.1	5.9	27.8	24.9	6.5	0.0	66.9	31.4	56.8	43.2
99683	TRAPPER CREEK	87.5	88.9	0.0	0.0	0.0	0.0	0.0	2.8	5.6	5.6	11.1	8.3	5.6	27.8	33.3	2.8	0.0	72.2	37.5	52.8	47.2
99684	UNALAKLEET	10.7	10.1	0.3	0.3	0.0	0.0	0.3	0.3	9.0	8.6	9.7	9.7	8.1	25.7	21.4	7.3	0.5	66.8	29.0	53.6	46.4
99685	UNALASKA	44.1	42.5	3.7	3.3	31.4	30.1	12.9	13.7	5.0	4.0	4.6	5.0	6.7	45.9	26.6	2.1	0.1	83.4	36.5	64.0	36.0
99686	VALDEZ	80.8	80.4	0.4	0.4	2.7	2.7	3.7	3.7	7.0	7.3	7.7	7.5	6.2	29.7	30.4	4.0	0.3	72.8	36.1	51.9	48.1
99687	WASILLA	86.6	85.3	0.4	0.4	0.5	0.5	2.2	2.5	5.6	6.2	8.0	7.9	6.7	27.6	30.2	7.6	0.3	75.1	38.4	53.8	46.2
99688	WILLOW	91.0	90.0	0.1	0.1	0.4	0.4	1.3	1.6	4.7	6.5	8.0	7.8	5.6	24.0	34.0	9.4	0.1	75.1	41.4	53.4	46.6
99689	YAKUTAT	50.4	48.9	0.2	0.2	1.9	2.0	0.9	0.9	4.9	6.3	9.2	6.9	5.8	28.6	32.8	5.6	0.0	74.3	39.3	58.9	41.1
99691	NIKOLAI	42.0	40.2	0.0	0.0	0.0	0.0	1.0	1.0	6.2	6.2	10.3	11.3	7.2	23.7	28.9	6.2	0.0	70.1	35.4	54.6	45.4
99701	FAIRBANKS	66.8	64.8	7.8	7.5	3.0	3.1	4.4	5.1	7.6	6.7	7.2	8.1	8.8	29.0	23.2	8.3	1.1	73.5	32.9	49.8	50.2
99702	EIELSON AFB	81.7	80.5	9.4	9.2	2.3	2.5	5.8	6.8	14.6	11.6	9.8	5.6	18.7	38.2	1.3	0.2	0.0	61.0	22.3	52.3	47.8
99703	FORT WAINWRIGHT	63.6	62.3	20.8	20.2	2.9	3.0	11.6	13.2	15.8	9.2	5.5	6.9	26.8	34.2	1.6	0.1	0.0	67.5	22.4	56.5	43.5
99704	CLEAR	60.9	58.4	0.4	0.4	1.4	1.4	1.6	2.2	5.3	5.3	8.1	8.1	6.5	22.5	34.1	9.3	0.8	75.3	41.8	54.0	46.0
99705	NORTH POLE	84.4	82.9	2.9	2.8	1.7	1.7	2.9	3.4	7.5	7.3	8.2	8.6	8.5	31.6	24.4	3.8	0.1	71.6	31.4	52.3	47.7
99709	FAIRBANKS	79.9	78.4	3.5	3.3	2.7	2.8	3.1	3.6	6.1	6.1	7.5	8.9	9.8	29.4	26.7	5.4	0.2	75.3	33.0	51.3	48.7
99712	FAIRBANKS	85.1	83.8	3.3	3.1	1.5	1.5	3.4	3.8	7.2	7.2	8.3	8.0	8.4	28.7	27.8	4.1	0.2	72.4	33.2	53.1	46.9
99714	SALCHA	89.4	88.1	1.2	1.2	0.9	0.9	2.2	2.5	5.4	6.1	8.3	7.6	5.9	25.2	33.4	7.4	0.7	75.6	40.1	52.1	47.9
99722	ARCTIC VILLAGE	5.3	4.7	0.0	0.0	0.0	0.0	1.3	0.7	8.1	8.1	8.8	11.5	10.1	27.0	19.6	5.4	1.4	67.6	27.8	54.7	45.3
99723	BARROW	9.7	9.4	0.3	0.3	0.3	0.3	0.2	0.2	10.0	9.1	10.6	10.1	8.9	27.6	17.6	6.0	0.2	63.7	26.0	54.9	45.1
99724	BEAVER	4.8	4.9	0.0	0.0	0.0	0.0	0.0	0.0	7.3	8.5	8.5	11.0	15.9	25.6	19.5	3.7	0.0	69.5	24.6	57.3	42.7
99726	BETTLES FIELD	21.2	20.0	0.0	0.0	0.0	0.0	0.9	0.9	6.1	7.8	7.8	14.8	5.2	26.1	24.4	7.0	0.9	68.7	32.5	57.4	42.6
99727	BUCKLAND	3.9	3.6	0.0	0.0	0.0	0.0	0.7	1.0	9.1	11.3	17.5	13.2	7.9	23.3	13.2	4.6	0.0	52.8	19.6	53.5	46.5
99729	CANTWELL	86.6	86.0	0.7	0.7	2.2	2.2	1.8	1.8	5.4	5.4	6.1	7.5	6.5	28.3	36.2	4.3	0.4	78.9	40.6	55.6	44.4
99730	CENTRAL	25.6	24.0	0.0	0.0	0.0	0.0	1.7	1.8	6.4	7.6	9.4	8.2	6.4	25.2	29.2	6.4	1.2	71.9	35.3	52.1	48.0
99733	CIRCLE	24.0	25.0	0.0	0.0	0.0	0.0	0.0	0.0	8.3	8.3	8.3	8.3	8.3	33.3	25.0	0.0	0.0	75.0	30.0	54.2	45.8
99734	PRUDHOE BAY	60.0	40.0	0.0	0.0	0.0	0.0	0.0	0.0	0.0	20.0	20.0	20.0	0.0	40.0	0.0	0.0	0.0	60.0	17.5	60.0	40.0
99736	DEERING	3.8	3.7	0.0	0.0	0.0	0.0	1.0	0.9	9.3	11.1	16.7	13.9	8.3	23.2	13.9	3.7	0.0	52.8	19.7	53.7	46.3
99737	DELTA JUNCTION	86.5	86.2	3.1	3.1	1.1	1.1	3.1	3.1	7.3	7.1	9.1	9.7	9.1	23.4	27.0	7.0	0.4	70.2	32.3	51.9	48.1
99739	ELIM	8.3	8.0	0.0	0.0	0.0	0.0	0.0	0.0	10.0	8.0	16.0	12.0	8.0	24.0	20.0	2.0	0.0	60.0	22.5	56.0	44.0
99740	FORT YUKON	24.4	23.0	0.2	0.2	0.2	0.2	1.6	1.7	6.8	7.5	9.4	8.1	6.5	24.3	30.3	6.5	0.7	71.2	35.3	53.2	46.9
99741	GALENA	5.9	6.3	0.0	0.0	0.0	0.0	0.0	0.0	6.3	12.5	12.5	12.5	12.5	25.0	18.8	0.0	0.0	68.8	22.5	56.3	43.8
99742	GAMBELL	4.0	3.7	0.0	0.0	0.3	0.4	0.3	0.2	8.2	9.2	11.1	10.1	10.4	26.0	19.2	5.1	0.7	65.1	25.8	53.2	46.8
99743	HEALY	83.4	83.0	1.1	1.1	1.9	1.9	2.3	2.3	5.1	5.3	6.3	7.5	6.8	29.5	34.9	4.4	0.4	78.7	39.8	57.0	43.0
99744	ANDERSON	83.2	82.7	4.0	4.0	1.3	1.3	4.0	4.0	4.7	4.0	5.3	7.3	8.7	40.0	27.3	2.7	0.0	81.3	34.1	62.7	37.3
99745	HUGHES	7.5	7.7	0.0	0.0	0.0	0.0	1.5	1.5	9.2	7.7	10.8	12.3	9.2	21.5	21.5	7.7	0.0	63.1	25.8	55.4	44.6
99746	HUSLIA	7.9	7.4	0.0	0.0	0.0	0.0	1.7	1.8	9.9	7.8	10.6	9.5	9.2	22.5	23.6	6.7	0.4	65.9	27.8	52.8	47.2
99747	KAKTOVIK	11.5	11.2	0.4	0.4	0.4	0.4	0.4	0.4	9.3	8.5	10.4	10.0	8.5	28.6	18.9	5.8	0.0	64.9	27.4	55.6	44.4
99748	KALTAG	8.1	7.9	0.0	0.0	0.0	0.0	0.0	0.5	6.9	8.3	13.0	11.1	10.7	24.5	18.1	7.4	0.0	64.4	25.0	50.9	49.1
99749	KIANA	7.9	7.3	0.0	0.0	0.1	0.1	0.4	0.4	13.5	10.0	12.4	10.4	9.2	22.2	15.8	6.1	0.4	57.4	22.0	54.9	45.1
99750	KIVALINA	10.0	9.4	0.3	0.3	0.0	0.0	0.7	0.7	7.8	7.2	9.1	9.8	10.6	33.2	17.9	4.3	0.2	69.4	28.0	59.5	40.5
99751	KOBUK	10.1	9.6	0.3	0.3	0.3	0.3	0.8	0.8	14.4	9.0	13.3	10.1	9.0	20.2	17.3	6.1	0.5	56.1	21.8	50.5	49.5
99752	KOTZEBUE	17.7	16.8	0.2	0.2	1.3	1.3	1.1	1.1	11.3	9.8	11.5	9.6	8.4	26.9	17.8	4.3	0.4	61.5	24.7	51.6	48.4
99753	KOYUK	7.4	7.1	0.0	0.0	0.3	0.3	0.7	0.3	10.0	9.4	11.3	11.0	8.1	24.8	19.0	5.8	0.7	62.6	25.3	54.2	45.8
99755	DENALI NATIONAL PARK	77.6	77.6	2.0	2.0	2.0	2.0	2.0	2.0	4.1	4.1	6.1	8.2	8.2	28.6	38.8	2.0	0.0	85.7	40.5	63.3	36.7
99756	MANLEY HOT SPRINGS	60.3	58.3	0.0	0.0	1.5	1.5	1.5	1.5	5.3	5.3	8.3	8.3	6.8	23.5	31.8	9.9	0.8	73.5	40.8	52.3	47.7
99757	LAKE MINCHUMINA	43.5	40.9	0.0	0.0	0.0	0.0	0.0	0.0	9.1	9.1	9.1	9.1	9.1	22.7	31.8	0.0	0.0	72.7	32.5	54.6	45.5
99758	MINTO	22.6	21.4	0.0	0.0	0.0	0.0	0.8	0.8	6.2	7.0	8.6	14.4	5.5	24.9	24.9	7.4	1.2	68.1	32.7	58.0	42.0
99760	NENANA	62.2	61.1	0.0	0.0	0.0	0.0	0.0	0.0	5.6	5.6	8.3	8.3	5.6	27.8	33.3	5.6	0.0	75.0	40.0	52.8	47.2
99762	NOME	36.6	35.0	0.8	0.8	1.5	1.5	2.0	2.2	8.3	7.7	8.8	8.6	7.4	28.8	24.0	5.7	0.7	69.3	32.0	53.4	46.6
99763	NOORVIK	3.2	3.0	0.1	0.1	0.9	0.9	0.1	0.1	12.6	10.1	14.0	13.8	10.5	20.8	12.0	5.7	0.6	54.3	19.8	51.6	48.4
99765	NULATO	21.5	20.2	0.2	0.2	0.8	0.8	1.3	1.3	7.6	7.9	10.3	12.4	8.9	26.9	20.2	5.6	0.3	65.4	28.0	53.1	46.9
99766	POINT HOPE	9.4	9.2	0.2	0.2	0.2	0.2	1.9	1.7	9.4	11.3	11.3	12.0	9.9	24.1	17.2	4.9	0.2	60.5	23.1	55.8	44.2
99767	RAMPART	22.2	23.5	0.0	0.0	0.0	0.0	0.0	0.0	11.8	11.8	11.8	11.8	5.9	29.4	17.7	0.0	0.0	64.7	22.5	64.7	35.3
99768	RUBY	7.9	7.6	0.0	0.0	0.0	0.0	1.6	1.6	9.7	7.6	10.3	10.3	9.2	22.7	23.8	6.5	0.0	66.0	27.8	52.4	47.6
99769	SAVOONGA	4.1	3.6	0.0	0.0	0.3	0.3	0.0	0.0	8.1	9.0	11.3	10.0	10.7	26.1	19.4	4.8	0.7	64.8	25.7	53.2	46.8
99771	SHAKTOOLIK	9.1	9.1	0.0	0.0	0.0	0.0	0.0	0.0	9.1	18.2	27.3	18.2	27.3	0.0	0.0	0.0	0.0	45.5	14.2	63.6	36.4
99772	SHISHMAREF	6.1	5.7	0.2	0.2	0.0	0.0	0.5	0.5	8.7	8.7	12.3	10.8	9.4	27.3	17.5	5.0	0.4	63.5	25.1	54.3	45.7
99773	SHUNGNAK	0.0	0.0	0.0	0.0	0.0	0.0	0.0	0.0	0.0	0.0	0.0	0.0	50.0	50.0	0.0	0.0	0.0	100.0	25.0	50.0	50.0
99777	TANANA	21.4	20.1	0.0	0.0	0.0	0.0	1.0	1.0	6.4	7.0	8.7	14.1	5.4	25.1	25.4	7.0	1.0	67.6	33.0	57.5	42.5
99778	TELLER	10.5	10.0	0.0	0.0	0.0	0.0	0.0	0.0	13.3	8.3	13.3	10.0	10.0	28.3	10.0	6.7	0.0	61.7	22.5	55.0	45.0
99780	TOK	66.0	65.0	0.1	0.1	0.3	0.3	2.1	2.2	6.7	6.6	8.8	8.8	6.6	24.7	30.1	7.3	0.4	72.3	36.7	51.5	48.5
99781	VENETIE	5.0	4.6	0.0	0.0	0.0	0.0	1.0	0.5	8.2	7.7	8.7	11.2	12.2	26.0	19.4	5.6	1.0	67.9	26.7	56.6	43.4
99782	WAINWRIGHT	6.2	5.9	0.2	0.2	0.2	0.2	0.0	0.0	10.2	9.5	10.4	10.4	9.5	27.3	16.1	6.4	0.2	63.6	25.0	54.0	46.0
99783	WALES	6.0	5.9	0.0	0.0	0.0	0.0	0.3	0.7	8.5	8.5	12.8	10.8	9.5	26.9	18.4	4.6	0.0	63.3	24.9	55.1	44.9
99784	WHITE MOUNTAIN	7.4	7.1	0.0	0.0	0.4	0.4	0.7	0.4	10.0	9.6	11.1	11.4	8.2	24.6	19.3	5.4	0.4	61.8	24.8	53.9	46.1
99785	BREVIG MISSION	10.9	10.3	0.0	0.0	0.0	0.0	0.7	0.7	13.7	8.6	12.0	10.3	9.9	26.7	13.7	5.1	0.0	60.3	22.8	55.1	44.9
99786	AMBLER	10.0	10.0	0.0	0.0	0.0	0.0	0.0	0.0	10.0	20.0	30.0	20.0	20.0	0.0	0.0	0.0	0.0	40.0	13.3	20.0	80.0
99788	CHALKYITSIK	5.1	5.3	0.0	0.0	0.0	0.0	0.0	0.0	10.5	7.9	10.5	10.5	7.9	26.3	21.1	5.3	0.0	63.2	26.7	55.3	44.7
99789	NUIQSUT	66.7	66.7	0.0	0.0	0.0	0.0	0.0	0.0	0.0	0.0	0.0	0.0	0.0	0.0	100.0	0.0	0.0	100.0	52.5	0.0	100.0
99801	JUNEAU	74.5	72.6	0.8	0.7	5.3	5.4	3.4	3.8	6.4	6.5	7.5	7.6	7.4	29.4	28.5	6.1	0.7	74.8	36.2	50.2	49.8
99820	ANGOON	31.6	28.9	0.3	0.4	0.5	0.5	4.7	5.2	6.2	6.9	9.4	8.2	6.6	25.7	27.4	9.0	0.7	72.4	36.3	52.9	47.1
99824	DOUGLAS	78.1	75.6	1.5	1.5	1.7	1.7	3.6	4.1	6.2	6.3	6.0	6.3	9.1	30.6	27.9	7.0	0.5	77.0	35.9	47.4	52.6
99825	ELFIN COVE	84.4	83.3	0.0	0.0	0.0	0.0	0.0	0.0	3.3	6.7	6.7	6.7	0.0	26.7	46.7	3.3	0.0	83.3	45.0	56.7	43.3
99826	GUSTAVUS	85.6	83.9	0.0	0.0	0.7	0.7	1.2	1.2	3.7	6.2	8.2	6.0	2.2	25.6	40.9	6.7	0.5	77.2	44.1	56.3	43.7
99827	HAINES	78.6	78.2	0.1	0.1	0.8	0.8	1.5	1.5	5.4	5.5	6.9	7.3	6.1	23.7	34.5	9.6	1.0	77.1	42.2	50.3	49.7
99829	HOONAH	44.5	41.6	0.2	0.2	0.3	0.3	2.9	3.1	5.6	6.1	7.9	8.2	7.8	26.6	29.6	7.5	0.7	75.0	37.7	54.3	45.7
99833	PETERSBURG	72.0	70.1	0.2	0.3	2.4	2.5	2.6	2.9	6.9	7.3	8.0	7.9	5.9	26.9	29.1	7.1	0.9	72.1	36.7	52.5	47.5
99835	SITKA	68.0	66.0	0.3	0.3	4.2	4.2	3.3	3.7	6.4	6.3	7.0	7.7	8.4	27.9	26.4	8.9	1.0	75.6	36.0	50.7	49.3
99840	SKAGWAY	92.3	91.1	0.0	0.0	0.8	0.9	2.1	2.5	4.3	4.6	7.4	5.8	5.6	29.8	33.2	8.6	0.7	80.1	40.5	51.6	48.4
99901	KETCHIKAN	74.0	73.4	0.5	0.5	4.5	4.5	2.7	2.7	6.9	6.8	7.9	7.6	7.1	27.6	27.6	7.9	0.9	73.7	36.7	50.8	49.2
99903	MEYERS CHUCK	95.2	94.7	0.0	0.0	0.0	0.0	0.0	0.0	0.0	0.0	0.0	0.0	5.3	15.8	73.7	5.3	0.0	100.0	54.2	47.4	52.6
99919	THORNE BAY	90.0	88.4	0.0	0.0	0.2	0.3	1.5	1.3	7.9	7.7	6.1	6.4	7.7	22.8	36.5	5.0	0.0	74.1	40.0	52.9	47.1
99921	CRAIG	68.7	65.6	0.1	0.1	0.4	0.4	2.8	3.0	7.6	7.3	9.0	9.1	7.5	27.6	27.4	4.2	0.2	69.2	33.7	54.9	45.1
99922	HYDABURG	39.1	35.9	0.0	0.0	0.0	0.0	0.0	0.0	4.7	7.8	9.4	7.8	7.8	21.9	32.8	7.8	0.0	71.9	37.5	54.7	45.3
99923	HYDER	95.0	94.5	0.0	0.0	0.0	0.0	1.0	1.1	4.4	4.4	4.4	4.4	5.5	19.8	47.3	9.9	0.0	84.6	49.1	52.8	47.3
99925	KLAWOCK	47.0	43.9	0.0	0.0	0.5	0.6	1.5	1.5	7.7	7.0	8.6	8.4	8.1	26.2	27.4	6.4	0.3	71.7	34.7	54.7	45.3
99926	METLAKATLA	11.1	10.1	0.3	0.3	0.1	0.2	1.7	1.6	8.7	7.7	9.0	8.1	8.4	27.8	23.3	6.6	0.5	69.7	30.9	51.2	48.8
99927	POINT BAKER	88.6	87.7	0.0	0.0	0.9	0.9	1.8	1.9	5.7	3.8	8.5	6.6	4.7	26.4	36.8	7.6	0.0	76.4	42.0	61.3	38.7
99929	WRANGELL	74.1	71.1	0.1	0.1	0.8	0.8	1.1	1.2	6.0	6.3	8.0	8.1	5.0	22.9	31.5	10.7	1.5	73.5	40.8	51.6	48.4
99950	KETCHIKAN	79.2	77.6	0.3	0.3	0.7	0.7	1.2	1.6	6.1	5.8	7.7	7.3	5.9	24.8	34.9	7.3	0.2	75.0	40.7	57.5	42.5
	ALASKA	69.3	68.2	3.5	3.3	4.5	4.6	4.1	4.7	7.6	7.3	8.3	8.1	8.1	29.3	25.1	5.8	0.5	71.7	32.9	51.4	48.6
	UNITED STATES	75.1	73.6	12.3	12.5	3.8	4.2	12.5	14.1	6.9	6.7	7.2	7.0	7.3	28.6	23.8	10.8	1.7	75.1	36.0	49.1	50.9

#	POST OFFICE NAME	2004 Per Capita Income	2004 HH Income Base	2004 HOUSEHOLD INCOME DISTRIBUTION (%) Less than $25,000	$25,000 to $49,999	$50,000 to $99,999	$100,000 to $149,999	$150,000 or More	MEDIAN HOUSEHOLD INCOME 2004	2009	2004 National Centile	2004 State Centile	2004 Home Value Base	2004 HOME VALUE DISTRIBUTION (%) Less than $50,000	$50,000 to $89,999	$90,000 to $174,999	$175,000 to $399,999	$400,000 or More	2004 Median Home Value
99682	TYONEK	11424	60	40.0	40.0	18.3	1.7	0.0	31907	36888	18	21	47	61.7	23.4	10.6	4.3	0.0	35625
99683	TRAPPER CREEK	20831	15	26.7	33.3	33.3	6.7	0.0	42343	47361	54	52	13	15.4	30.8	30.8	23.1	0.0	95000
99684	UNALAKLEET	17392	233	25.3	28.8	30.0	11.6	4.3	45957	55581	64	58	142	20.4	21.8	42.3	14.1	1.4	103125
99685	UNALASKA	29651	1272	8.0	17.1	41.4	26.3	7.3	77135	88928	94	97	297	7.7	16.2	27.3	42.1	6.7	171023
99686	VALDEZ	31819	1664	13.8	18.3	36.8	18.5	12.7	73134	88015	92	96	1199	24.8	8.4	24.1	39.9	2.8	152904
99687	WASILLA	22646	1153	24.5	29.3	33.1	9.8	3.3	46534	53766	65	59	973	14.7	17.5	40.3	23.7	3.8	121983
99688	WILLOW	26172	849	32.5	22.1	31.5	9.0	5.0	43835	52522	58	56	723	18.8	12.7	37.6	29.1	1.8	130208
99689	YAKUTAT	29849	178	20.2	27.5	42.7	5.6	3.9	51898	58692	75	71	107	15.9	18.7	43.0	19.6	2.8	124167
99691	NIKOLAI	21752	39	35.9	25.6	20.5	12.8	5.1	38637	40000	42	44	23	13.0	26.1	52.2	8.7	0.0	102500
99701	FAIRBANKS	25477	7266	28.8	27.2	28.7	10.9	4.4	43660	50614	58	56	3329	7.2	8.3	50.9	32.2	1.4	148187
99702	EIELSON AFB	13742	1534	15.9	52.6	27.4	3.0	1.0	40654	47592	48	49	10	0.0	0.0	50.0	20.0	30.0	175000
99703	FORT WAINWRIGHT	14836	1495	17.3	51.2	27.3	3.2	1.0	39263	45929	44	46	20	0.0	0.0	50.0	50.0	0.0	175000
99704	CLEAR	21098	207	35.3	25.1	29.5	6.3	3.9	38023	39446	39	43	145	25.5	25.5	38.6	10.3	0.0	89063
99705	NORTH POLE	25870	6114	13.7	21.1	42.2	16.6	6.6	65210	78061	89	91	4662	6.6	8.1	49.1	35.4	0.8	156869
99709	FAIRBANKS	30210	10561	16.9	22.3	35.1	16.7	9.0	61947	75376	86	86	6712	6.1	10.3	36.4	44.5	2.7	170048
99712	FAIRBANKS	27500	4131	11.9	21.8	40.9	17.8	7.7	66562	79117	89	93	3191	13.5	9.7	27.6	47.8	1.5	173112
99714	SALCHA	25266	452	14.2	29.7	41.2	12.6	2.4	57986	68806	83	81	377	9.0	24.1	42.2	24.7	0.0	122011
99722	ARCTIC VILLAGE	10622	51	51.0	35.3	7.8	3.9	2.0	24401	26501	4	8	35	37.1	22.9	31.4	8.6	0.0	68333
99723	BARROW	17841	166	13.9	22.9	42.8	16.3	4.2	63788	77647	88	89	111	9.9	17.1	52.3	20.7	0.0	122396
99724	BEAVER	9573	30	56.7	33.3	10.0	0.0	0.0	21436	23094	2	6	21	28.6	23.8	42.9	4.8	0.0	85000
99726	BETTLES FIELD	14196	45	48.9	22.2	24.4	4.4	0.0	26126	32347	6	12	29	44.8	37.9	13.8	3.5	0.0	57500
99727	BUCKLAND	10791	86	19.8	41.9	30.2	5.8	2.3	42685	52082	55	54	41	31.7	22.0	36.6	9.8	0.0	85000
99729	CANTWELL	34049	136	16.9	23.5	37.5	16.2	5.9	62149	70902	86	87	92	10.9	19.6	33.7	28.3	7.6	140000
99730	CENTRAL	18417	74	40.5	27.0	25.7	4.1	2.7	33625	40765	23	29	51	35.3	25.5	29.4	9.8	0.0	76250
99733	CIRCLE	15313	11	36.4	45.5	18.2	0.0	0.0	32290	47321	19	22	8	12.5	37.5	50.0	0.0	0.0	95000
99734	PRUDHOE BAY	9500	1	0.0	100.0	0.0	0.0	0.0	47500	47500	67	61	1	0.0	0.0	100.0	0.0	0.0	137500
99736	DEERING	14385	30	20.0	46.7	23.3	6.7	3.3	40000	50000	46	48	14	21.4	21.4	50.0	7.1	0.0	100000
99737	DELTA JUNCTION	21051	1234	25.1	24.2	34.8	12.0	4.0	50773	60631	73	70	866	12.5	16.1	46.3	15.7	9.5	120833
99739	ELIM	12750	13	30.8	30.8	23.1	15.4	0.0	37321	37321	37	40	8	0.0	25.0	50.0	25.0	0.0	100000
99740	FORT YUKON	15952	230	42.2	26.1	24.8	4.4	2.6	32328	38282	19	24	158	36.7	25.3	28.5	8.9	0.6	74167
99741	GALENA	24729	11	36.4	36.4	27.3	0.0	0.0	32290	30000	19	22	8	0.0	12.5	87.5	0.0	0.0	125000
99742	GAMBELL	9958	169	34.9	35.5	24.9	4.1	0.6	34687	40462	26	32	133	40.6	30.1	19.6	9.0	0.8	65417
99743	HEALY	31219	701	19.0	22.8	36.8	15.3	6.1	60710	71003	85	85	483	14.5	20.1	33.3	26.9	5.2	129167
99744	ANDERSON	14790	21	19.1	19.1	38.1	14.3	9.5	66548	75000	89	92	15	20.0	26.7	40.0	13.3	0.0	106250
99745	HUGHES	9961	18	50.0	27.8	16.7	5.6	0.0	25000	32330	5	10	13	15.4	30.8	46.2	7.7	0.0	95000
99746	HUSLIA	11145	86	46.5	29.1	19.8	4.7	0.0	27299	32329	8	14	62	24.2	22.6	37.1	9.7	6.5	94000
99747	KAKTOVIK	21616	81	12.4	27.2	40.7	16.1	3.7	60590	75636	85	84	53	3.8	17.0	54.7	24.5	0.0	131250
99748	KALTAG	10919	66	42.4	31.8	22.7	3.0	0.0	28367	33141	9	16	37	62.2	10.8	21.6	5.4	0.0	33750
99749	KIANA	15258	193	23.8	27.5	31.6	13.0	4.2	48862	58821	70	66	129	12.4	24.8	40.3	19.4	3.1	108152
99750	KIVALINA	12533	190	36.3	26.3	29.5	6.3	1.6	34044	39004	24	31	142	25.4	38.0	24.7	12.0	0.0	76842
99751	KOBUK	12539	85	22.4	30.6	30.6	11.8	4.7	48058	54457	68	63	55	12.7	21.8	38.2	23.6	3.6	117500
99752	KOTZEBUE	19944	728	17.3	19.2	39.2	18.0	6.3	64664	76505	88	90	356	7.6	15.7	39.3	35.1	2.3	141667
99753	KOYUK	11647	84	36.9	29.8	26.2	7.1	0.0	35538	43191	30	35	48	18.8	27.1	43.8	10.4	0.0	94000
99755	DENALI NATIONAL PARK	27452	20	25.0	25.0	30.0	15.0	5.0	50000	60000	72	69	13	7.7	23.1	46.2	23.1	0.0	112500
99756	MANLEY HOT SPRINGS	21994	58	34.5	24.1	32.8	6.9	1.7	40000	40000	46	48	40	25.0	25.0	37.5	12.5	0.0	90000
99757	LAKE MINCHUMINA	16705	11	36.4	45.5	18.2	0.0	0.0	32290	54545	19	22	7	0.0	14.3	71.4	14.3	0.0	118750
99758	MINTO	10789	75	46.7	24.0	25.3	4.0	0.0	27954	32969	9	15	49	46.9	30.6	16.3	6.1	0.0	55000
99760	NENANA	15556	13	38.5	23.1	30.8	7.7	0.0	32308	35000	19	23	9	11.1	22.2	66.7	0.0	0.0	118750
99762	NOME	27620	1317	17.9	17.5	38.0	18.2	8.4	66505	79685	89	92	688	12.7	21.8	33.0	30.7	1.9	126266
99763	NOORVIK	9309	179	43.6	26.3	21.2	7.8	1.1	30166	36456	13	17	112	8.9	25.0	26.8	39.3	0.0	125000
99765	NULATO	19721	341	24.6	24.1	35.5	12.9	2.9	51279	61043	74	71	205	37.1	17.6	31.2	12.7	1.5	84063
99766	POINT HOPE	20667	148	15.5	16.9	34.5	25.7	7.4	76921	89576	94	97	101	5.9	14.9	62.4	16.8	0.0	116797
99767	RAMPART	13382	9	66.7	11.1	22.2	0.0	0.0	17182	17182	1	5	6	16.7	83.3	0.0	0.0	0.0	75000
99768	RUBY	13610	68	45.6	29.4	20.6	4.4	0.0	27801	35000	8	15	49	24.5	24.5	32.7	10.2	8.2	91250
99769	SAVOONGA	8567	66	34.9	36.4	24.2	4.6	0.0	35000	45000	28	34	52	46.2	26.9	17.3	9.6	0.0	60000
99771	SHAKTOOLIK	25746	5	40.0	0.0	60.0	0.0	0.0	79167	93234	95	98	3	0.0	0.0	100.0	0.0	0.0	112500
99772	SHISHMAREF	12341	146	37.0	30.1	19.9	9.6	3.4	35000	43976	28	34	100	20.0	17.0	34.0	28.0	1.0	114063
99773	SHUNGNAK	0	0	0.0	0.0	0.0	0.0	0.0	0	0	0	0	0	0.0	0.0	0.0	0.0	0.0	0
99777	TANANA	14362	118	49.2	22.9	23.7	4.2	0.0	25738	31131	5	10	77	46.8	33.8	13.0	5.2	1.3	55000
99778	TELLER	9133	18	55.6	27.8	16.7	0.0	0.0	20000	27320	2	6	14	57.1	35.7	0.0	7.1	0.0	48333
99780	TOK	19336	852	36.9	23.5	28.1	7.6	4.0	37417	45371	37	42	662	24.2	18.3	40.3	10.9	6.3	101535
99781	VENETIE	9717	62	50.0	33.9	11.3	3.2	1.6	25000	26694	5	10	43	30.2	23.3	37.2	9.3	0.0	82500
99782	WAINWRIGHT	19939	130	17.7	13.9	48.5	15.4	4.6	67838	79866	90	94	91	16.5	13.2	56.0	14.3	0.0	112500
99783	WALES	15264	96	34.4	31.3	20.8	10.4	3.1	36288	42869	33	37	66	18.2	19.7	36.4	25.8	0.0	111364
99784	WHITE MOUNTAIN	14346	93	37.6	30.1	25.8	6.5	0.0	35236	42697	28	35	53	20.8	30.2	37.7	11.3	0.0	89286
99785	BREVIG MISSION	8932	72	50.0	33.3	15.3	0.0	1.4	25000	30557	5	10	58	55.2	32.8	5.2	6.9	0.0	48333
99786	AMBLER	0	0	0.0	0.0	0.0	0.0	0.0	0	0	0	0	0	0.0	0.0	0.0	0.0	0.0	0
99788	CHALKYITSIK	7763	14	64.3	28.6	7.1	0.0	0.0	17143	17225	1	5	10	20.0	20.0	60.0	0.0	0.0	108333
99789	NUIQSUT	15833	1	0.0	100.0	0.0	0.0	0.0	47500	47500	67	61	1	0.0	0.0	100.0	0.0	0.0	137500
99801	JUNEAU	31650	10965	12.5	20.4	38.3	19.3	9.5	71896	83442	92	95	7380	9.1	5.3	16.3	57.7	11.6	221455
99820	ANGOON	15139	194	33.0	34.0	26.8	3.6	2.6	36037	41383	32	36	107	11.2	21.5	39.3	20.6	7.5	123958
99824	DOUGLAS	34372	914	14.7	22.4	41.9	14.3	6.7	61934	77385	86	86	426	1.6	9.4	23.0	50.0	16.0	232500
99825	ELFIN COVE	26102	15	26.7	33.3	20.0	13.3	6.7	42343	40000	54	52	11	0.0	0.0	36.4	45.5	18.2	225000
99826	GUSTAVUS	25845	193	28.0	30.1	30.1	7.3	4.7	40681	47070	49	49	142	3.5	9.2	42.3	35.2	9.9	165278
99827	HAINES	26059	1037	27.0	27.7	31.3	8.0	6.0	45222	53464	62	58	768	14.6	13.9	31.4	34.1	6.0	145703
99829	HOONAH	21133	470	27.5	28.7	32.6	8.1	3.2	43540	50607	57	55	301	12.6	16.3	41.2	25.9	4.0	122794
99833	PETERSBURG	28553	1390	19.5	26.0	34.7	11.7	8.2	54095	65491	78	76	999	17.4	6.6	26.2	45.8	4.0	174247
99835	SITKA	28453	3407	15.7	25.5	36.7	13.6	8.5	58343	71825	83	82	2149	14.7	6.1	18.3	46.1	14.9	215000
99840	SKAGWAY	33513	387	14.2	28.2	37.5	15.5	4.7	57663	68793	82	80	238	3.4	9.2	34.9	47.1	5.5	179286
99901	KETCHIKAN	28229	5251	15.8	26.0	38.0	13.5	6.7	58551	68364	83	83	3412	6.2	8.5	25.6	52.6	7.1	193652
99903	MEYERS CHUCK	11579	8	75.0	0.0	25.0	0.0	0.0	12677	15000	1	3	6	16.7	33.3	50.0	0.0	0.0	85000
99919	THORNE BAY	22584	144	18.8	33.3	35.4	8.3	4.2	48507	53099	69	64	103	24.3	14.6	29.1	31.1	1.0	118750
99921	CRAIG	24666	542	17.7	28.8	37.1	11.1	5.4	53156	60442	77	72	406	44.3	4.9	20.9	27.6	2.2	93000
99922	HYDABURG	18586	26	30.8	34.6	30.8	3.9	0.0	37321	51381	37	40	20	10.0	20.0	40.0	30.0	0.0	125000
99923	HYDER	16410	46	58.7	8.7	30.4	2.2	0.0	15000	17681	1	4	37	13.5	27.0	24.3	5.4	29.7	104167
99925	KLAWOCK	18233	324	29.6	31.5	29.9	7.7	1.2	40424	45713	48	48	241	45.6	13.3	24.5	13.7	2.9	57000
99926	METLAKATLA	18899	463	22.5	29.2	38.4	9.1	0.9	48548	54280	69	65	351	21.4	8.8	42.2	25.9	1.7	119375
99927	POINT BAKER	17309	44	34.1	38.6	25.0	0.0	2.3	33590	32919	23	28	38	29.0	15.8	29.0	23.7	2.6	100000
99929	WRANGELL	25475	922	25.1	27.4	30.6	10.2	6.7	48033	56127	68	63	635	20.3	8.0	34.0	32.6	5.0	140399
99950	KETCHIKAN	21815	269	29.4	34.6	29.4	3.4	3.4	38804	41313	42	45	214	23.4	15.9	31.8	26.6	2.3	117105
	ALASKA	27197		17.6	24.1	35.4	15.1	7.8	59655	71504				9.9	7.9	33.8	43.8	4.6	171678
	UNITED STATES	25866		24.7	27.1	30.8	10.9	6.5	48124	56710				10.9	15.0	33.7	30.1	10.4	145905

ZIP CODE #	POST OFFICE NAME	FINANCIAL SERVICES: Auto Loan	FINANCIAL SERVICES: Home Loan	FINANCIAL SERVICES: Investments	FINANCIAL SERVICES: Retirement Plans	THE HOME: Home Improvements: Home Repair	THE HOME: Home Improvements: Lawn & Garden	THE HOME: Furnishings: Computers & Hardware	THE HOME: Furnishings: Major Appliances	THE HOME: Furnishings: TV, Radio, Sound Equipment	THE HOME: Furnishings: Furniture	ENTERTAINMENT: Dine out/ Carry out	ENTERTAINMENT: Sports Equipment	ENTERTAINMENT: Fees & Tickets	ENTERTAINMENT: Toys & Games	ENTERTAINMENT: Travel	ENTERTAINMENT: Cable TV	PERSONAL: Apparel & Services	PERSONAL: Auto Repairs	PERSONAL: Health Insurance	PERSONAL: Pets & Supplies
99682	TYONEK	55	43	29	39	48	54	40	49	46	40	54	57	36	53	43	49	50	48	57	67
99683	TRAPPER CREEK	79	69	52	65	71	77	65	73	68	66	83	84	61	80	66	69	79	72	77	91
99684	UNALAKLEET	80	88	88	90	85	84	84	83	78	85	99	98	84	100	82	74	98	83	73	91
99685	UNALASKA	131	130	136	140	124	125	131	127	124	135	159	152	130	153	125	116	155	130	110	140
99686	VALDEZ	111	117	109	118	113	113	109	111	104	112	131	130	109	129	107	99	128	110	100	124
99687	WASILLA	96	77	54	70	85	95	73	86	81	72	96	101	65	95	77	86	90	85	100	116
99688	WILLOW	111	87	59	78	98	110	82	99	93	81	110	116	73	109	87	99	102	97	117	135
99689	YAKUTAT	114	89	61	81	101	113	84	101	95	83	113	119	75	111	90	102	105	100	120	139
99691	NIKOLAI	92	72	49	65	81	91	68	82	77	67	91	96	61	90	72	82	85	81	97	112
99701	FAIRBANKS	84	81	91	84	79	84	88	84	86	87	108	100	86	106	84	83	105	87	79	93
99702	EIELSON AFB	75	48	46	55	44	52	71	61	72	66	90	81	61	81	58	66	86	72	57	70
99703	FORT WAINWRIGHT	74	47	45	54	43	51	70	61	71	65	89	81	60	80	58	65	85	71	56	69
99704	CLEAR	85	67	46	60	75	85	63	76	71	62	85	89	56	83	67	76	79	75	90	104
99705	NORTH POLE	106	116	115	120	111	110	109	108	102	111	129	128	111	129	106	95	127	107	94	118
99709	FAIRBANKS	104	112	121	116	109	110	110	107	104	111	132	128	112	132	108	99	130	108	96	118
99712	FAIRBANKS	108	116	121	120	113	114	113	111	107	113	135	132	114	135	111	102	132	111	100	122
99714	SALCHA	95	96	90	95	96	98	91	94	89	92	111	112	89	111	91	87	108	94	90	110
99722	ARCTIC VILLAGE	42	37	41	37	37	42	44	42	46	42	56	49	42	55	42	46	55	44	44	46
99723	BARROW	98	107	107	109	104	103	102	101	95	103	121	120	102	121	100	90	119	101	89	111
99724	BEAVER	36	32	35	31	31	36	37	35	39	36	48	41	36	47	36	39	46	37	37	39
99726	BETTLES FIELD	49	51	59	53	51	54	52	52	50	52	63	61	52	61	52	49	61	52	50	57
99727	BUCKLAND	89	70	47	63	78	88	66	79	74	65	88	93	59	87	70	79	82	78	93	108
99729	CANTWELL	97	107	107	109	103	102	102	101	95	103	120	120	102	121	100	90	119	100	89	111
99730	CENTRAL	72	56	38	51	63	71	53	64	60	53	71	75	47	70	57	64	66	63	76	87
99733	CIRCLE	57	44	30	40	50	56	42	50	47	42	56	59	37	55	45	51	52	50	60	69
99734	PRUDHOE BAY	62	77	81	77	75	74	68	67	64	68	80	80	73	85	70	62	80	66	61	75
99736	DEERING	88	69	47	62	78	87	65	78	74	64	87	92	58	86	69	79	81	77	93	107
99737	DELTA JUNCTION	87	90	87	90	90	92	86	88	84	85	104	104	86	106	86	82	102	87	83	102
99739	ELIM	67	62	74	59	59	68	66	65	72	68	90	73	68	89	66	74	88	67	68	74
99740	FORT YUKON	70	55	38	50	62	69	52	63	59	52	70	73	47	69	56	63	65	62	74	85
99741	GALENA	49	44	48	43	43	49	51	49	54	49	66	57	49	65	49	54	64	51	51	54
99742	GAMBELL	62	54	45	50	52	55	55	60	57	60	72	63	51	64	53	55	72	61	56	62
99743	HEALY	100	99	96	101	96	98	100	98	96	99	120	118	97	119	96	91	117	100	90	111
99744	ANDERSON	114	79	76	89	73	84	109	96	110	103	137	126	96	125	92	100	132	111	88	109
99745	HUGHES	49	44	48	43	43	49	51	49	54	49	66	57	49	65	49	54	64	51	51	54
99746	HUSLIA	50	45	49	44	44	50	52	50	55	50	67	58	50	66	50	55	65	52	52	55
99747	KAKTOVIK	96	106	106	108	102	101	101	100	94	102	119	118	101	120	98	89	117	99	88	110
99748	KALTAG	49	45	54	43	43	50	48	47	52	50	66	53	50	65	48	54	64	49	49	54
99749	KIANA	91	76	68	70	80	91	76	84	84	76	102	96	72	101	78	89	97	84	95	107
99750	KIVALINA	77	60	41	54	68	76	57	68	64	56	76	80	51	75	61	69	71	67	81	94
99751	KOBUK	76	70	84	66	67	77	75	73	81	77	102	82	77	101	75	84	100	75	77	84
99752	KOTZEBUE	106	109	103	110	108	110	103	106	99	104	124	125	102	124	102	96	121	105	99	122
99753	KOYUK	59	54	65	51	52	60	58	57	63	60	79	64	60	78	58	65	77	58	60	65
99755	DENALI NATIONAL PARK	97	91	84	91	91	95	92	93	91	91	113	112	88	111	89	88	109	95	90	110
99756	MANLEY HOT SPRINGS	84	67	47	61	75	84	63	76	71	63	84	88	57	83	67	76	78	74	89	103
99757	LAKE MINCHUMINA	57	44	30	40	50	56	42	50	47	42	56	59	37	55	45	51	52	50	60	69
99758	MINTO	51	52	59	54	52	55	53	53	51	53	64	62	53	63	53	50	62	53	51	58
99760	NENANA	73	57	39	52	65	72	54	65	61	54	72	76	48	72	58	65	67	64	77	89
99762	NOME	107	118	130	121	115	115	114	112	108	115	136	132	116	138	113	103	135	112	100	123
99763	NOORVIK	57	46	64	43	44	53	56	54	64	58	79	62	55	75	54	66	77	58	58	62
99765	NULATO	82	85	90	84	82	85	84	83	83	86	105	96	85	105	83	81	103	83	78	92
99766	POINT HOPE	112	122	123	125	118	117	117	115	109	118	138	137	117	139	114	103	136	115	101	127
99767	RAMPART	34	36	41	37	36	38	36	36	35	36	44	42	36	43	36	34	43	36	35	39
99768	RUBY	50	45	49	44	44	51	53	50	55	50	68	58	51	67	51	55	66	52	52	55
99769	SAVOONGA	62	54	45	50	52	55	55	60	57	60	72	63	51	64	53	55	71	61	56	62
99771	SHAKTOOLIK	79	84	87	84	81	82	81	80	78	82	99	94	82	99	80	75	97	80	73	89
99772	SHISHMAREF	66	61	74	58	59	68	66	64	71	68	90	72	68	89	65	74	87	66	67	74
99773	SHUNGNAK	0	0	0	0	0	0	0	0	0	0	0	0	0	0	0	0	0	0	0	0
99777	TANANA	49	51	59	53	52	54	52	52	50	52	63	61	52	62	52	49	61	52	50	57
99778	TELLER	39	31	43	29	30	36	38	36	43	39	53	41	37	50	36	44	52	39	39	42
99780	TOK	77	74	66	72	75	78	70	74	70	70	87	88	68	86	71	70	83	74	74	90
99781	VENETIE	42	37	41	37	37	42	44	42	46	42	56	48	42	55	42	46	54	43	43	46
99782	WAINWRIGHT	101	111	111	113	107	106	106	104	99	106	125	124	106	125	103	93	123	104	92	115
99783	WALES	66	61	73	58	58	68	66	64	71	68	89	72	68	88	65	73	87	66	67	73
99784	WHITE MOUNTAIN	59	54	65	52	52	60	58	57	63	60	79	64	60	79	58	65	78	59	60	65
99785	BREVIG MISSION	46	37	51	34	35	43	45	43	51	46	63	49	44	60	43	53	61	46	47	49
99786	AMBLER	0	0	0	0	0	0	0	0	0	0	0	0	0	0	0	0	0	0	0	0
99788	CHALKYITSIK	29	26	28	25	25	29	30	28	31	29	39	33	29	38	29	31	37	30	30	31
99789	NUIQSUT	62	77	81	77	75	74	68	67	64	68	80	80	73	85	70	62	80	66	61	75
99801	JUNEAU	113	129	138	131	125	126	121	120	114	122	144	141	125	146	121	109	142	118	108	132
99820	ANGOON	76	60	41	54	67	76	56	68	64	56	76	80	50	75	60	68	70	67	80	93
99824	DOUGLAS	98	113	139	117	111	114	111	108	106	111	133	129	115	137	112	102	132	109	98	118
99825	ELFIN COVE	89	69	47	63	78	88	65	79	74	65	88	92	59	87	70	79	82	78	93	108
99826	GUSTAVUS	91	72	49	65	81	91	68	81	76	67	91	95	60	89	72	82	84	80	96	111
99827	HAINES	105	82	56	79	91	102	82	94	90	80	108	110	74	106	84	94	100	93	107	122
99829	HOONAH	86	71	54	69	76	86	72	79	77	70	93	91	67	92	72	80	87	78	88	98
99833	PETERSBURG	103	108	108	108	109	112	104	106	101	103	126	125	104	129	105	99	123	105	102	122
99835	SITKA	104	112	112	112	110	112	106	107	102	107	127	125	107	129	106	99	125	105	99	120
99840	SKAGWAY	90	103	127	106	101	104	102	98	96	101	122	117	104	125	102	93	120	99	89	107
99901	KETCHIKAN	97	107	115	109	104	105	105	102	99	104	125	122	106	127	103	94	123	103	92	112
99903	MEYERS CHUCK	47	37	25	33	41	46	34	42	39	34	46	49	31	46	37	42	43	41	49	57
99919	THORNE BAY	94	86	67	83	86	91	82	88	83	84	103	102	78	97	81	82	98	88	87	104
99921	CRAIG	103	97	80	94	96	101	93	98	92	95	115	114	88	109	91	90	110	97	95	115
99922	HYDABURG	71	61	47	61	64	72	63	67	66	61	81	76	60	80	62	67	75	66	72	79
99923	HYDER	55	43	29	39	49	55	41	49	46	40	55	57	36	54	43	49	51	48	58	67
99925	KLAWOCK	78	71	56	69	71	75	68	73	69	70	85	84	64	80	67	68	82	73	72	87
99926	METLAKATLA	76	82	82	82	80	83	78	79	75	79	95	91	79	95	78	73	93	78	73	87
99927	POINT BAKER	70	49	25	46	57	64	48	60	55	48	65	72	41	64	50	58	59	59	71	83
99929	WRANGELL	101	87	66	82	93	102	83	94	89	82	107	110	77	106	85	91	101	92	103	121
99950	KETCHIKAN	90	70	46	67	77	84	69	80	75	69	90	94	62	88	70	77	84	79	89	103
	ALASKA	106	108	111	111	106	109	107	106	104	108	130	126	107	129	105	100	128	107	98	120
	UNITED STATES	100	100	100	100	100	100	100	100	100	100	100	100	100	100	100	100	100	100	100	100

#	POST OFFICE NAME	COUNTY FIPS CODE	POPULATION			2000-2004 ANNUAL RATE		HOUSEHOLDS					FAMILIES		
			2000	2004	2009	% Rate	State Centile	2000	2004	2009	% Annual Rate 2000-2004	2004 Average HH Size	2000	2004	% Annual Rate 2000-2004
85003	PHOENIX	013	9823	10275	11386	1.1	28	3606	3896	4451	1.8	2.12	1473	1531	0.9
85004	PHOENIX	013	4600	4813	5342	1.1	28	1972	2094	2354	1.4	2.09	788	823	1.0
85006	PHOENIX	013	33402	35355	39638	1.4	33	9643	10040	11156	1.0	3.44	6417	6682	1.0
85007	PHOENIX	013	15831	16064	17667	0.3	14	4838	4901	5409	0.3	3.01	2956	2971	0.1
85008	PHOENIX	013	57698	65356	75935	3.0	71	18867	21267	24659	2.9	2.99	11475	12801	2.6
85009	PHOENIX	013	56314	60182	67332	1.6	37	12923	13641	15256	1.3	3.92	9998	10542	1.3
85012	PHOENIX	013	6713	7277	8214	1.9	50	3014	3290	3732	2.1	2.07	1339	1458	2.0
85013	PHOENIX	013	21985	23827	27106	1.9	49	10149	11006	12487	1.9	2.15	4781	5162	1.8
85014	PHOENIX	013	27347	29547	33632	1.8	47	12510	13345	15072	1.5	2.18	5731	6118	1.6
85015	PHOENIX	013	42729	46977	54101	2.3	56	15534	16708	18985	1.7	2.80	9507	10210	1.7
85016	PHOENIX	013	36340	39033	44418	1.7	42	16590	17668	19966	1.5	2.19	8093	8560	1.3
85017	PHOENIX	013	37899	40064	45009	1.3	32	12141	12624	14043	0.9	3.12	8146	8422	0.8
85018	PHOENIX	013	35124	36871	41316	1.2	29	16019	16826	18800	1.2	2.17	8650	9018	1.0
85019	PHOENIX	013	28072	30024	33893	1.6	39	8571	8986	10005	1.1	3.34	6288	6574	1.1
85020	PHOENIX	013	34711	36673	41093	1.3	32	15255	16116	18010	1.3	2.25	8147	8552	1.2
85021	PHOENIX	013	38580	42160	48132	2.1	53	15460	16863	19194	2.1	2.46	8772	9458	1.8
85022	PHOENIX	013	45779	49756	56535	2.0	52	19561	21198	23974	1.9	2.35	11931	12873	1.8
85023	PHOENIX	013	34259	36484	41108	1.5	35	13765	14705	16526	1.6	2.48	8643	9185	1.4
85024	PHOENIX	013	16874	19472	22863	3.4	74	6209	7135	8333	3.3	2.73	4590	5259	3.3
85027	PHOENIX	013	36566	40131	46028	2.2	54	14030	15497	17787	2.4	2.54	9169	10059	2.2
85028	PHOENIX	013	21093	21374	23514	0.3	14	8677	8807	9677	0.4	2.41	5816	5892	0.3
85029	PHOENIX	013	45858	49276	55907	1.7	42	17437	18640	21036	1.6	2.63	11101	11820	1.5
85031	PHOENIX	013	27778	29703	33363	1.6	39	7496	7835	8668	1.1	3.79	5861	6115	1.0
85032	PHOENIX	013	66461	72222	82077	2.0	52	24946	27045	30619	1.9	2.64	16136	17509	1.9
85033	PHOENIX	013	51305	54108	60320	1.2	31	14119	14705	16271	1.0	3.67	11663	12114	0.9
85034	PHOENIX	013	9675	9745	10725	0.2	12	2838	2872	3170	0.3	3.25	1844	1858	0.2
85035	PHOENIX	013	42192	46625	53320	2.4	58	11133	12111	13695	2.0	3.85	8914	9672	1.9
85037	PHOENIX	013	33797	37295	42823	2.3	58	10053	11062	12632	2.3	3.37	8237	9055	2.3
85040	PHOENIX	013	28367	30495	34433	1.7	44	7467	7931	8874	1.4	3.80	5601	5934	1.4
85041	PHOENIX	013	33061	39815	45811	3.8	76	8418	9805	11537	3.7	3.91	6992	8162	3.7
85042	PHOENIX	013	33491	39106	46111	3.7	75	10036	11724	13804	3.7	3.29	7265	8418	3.5
85043	PHOENIX	013	15976	20658	26049	6.2	92	4785	6084	7582	5.8	3.39	3622	4551	5.5
85044	PHOENIX	013	39152	44023	51038	2.8	67	16647	18732	21666	2.8	2.35	10023	11165	2.6
85045	PHOENIX	013	5903	8186	10424	8.0	96	1966	2717	3442	7.9	3.01	1669	2304	7.9
85048	PHOENIX	013	31854	38853	46698	4.8	86	11125	13564	16245	4.8	2.86	8575	10429	4.7
85050	PHOENIX	013	21279	24707	28986	3.6	75	8277	9573	11171	3.5	2.58	5910	6852	3.5
85051	PHOENIX	013	41455	43010	47754	0.9	25	15597	16225	17981	0.9	2.64	10154	10510	0.8
85053	PHOENIX	013	28439	29316	32548	0.7	23	10677	11058	12263	0.8	2.65	7367	7604	0.8
85054	PHOENIX	013	2541	2987	3518	3.9	77	1140	1319	1535	3.5	2.26	724	835	3.4
85085	PHOENIX	013	1899	2891	3861	10.4	98	676	1038	1388	10.6	2.78	554	835	10.1
85086	PHOENIX	013	8786	10543	12420	4.4	84	2839	3483	4174	4.9	2.67	2210	2707	4.9
85087	NEW RIVER	013	3854	4528	5326	3.9	77	1480	1751	2062	4.0	2.54	1119	1324	4.0
85201	MESA	013	47624	52430	60191	2.3	56	18158	19958	22839	2.3	2.59	10669	11702	2.2
85202	MESA	013	44134	50818	59764	3.4	73	17973	20498	23882	3.1	2.47	10276	11682	3.1
85203	MESA	013	36938	39515	44710	1.6	39	12675	13547	15277	1.6	2.90	9000	9620	1.6
85204	MESA	013	65809	69669	78020	1.4	33	21862	23100	25776	1.3	3.00	15567	16402	1.2
85205	MESA	013	40125	44867	51569	2.7	64	16306	18239	20908	2.7	2.44	10999	12309	2.7
85206	MESA	013	31773	37325	44122	3.9	77	13468	15671	18422	3.6	2.29	8675	10101	3.7
85207	MESA	013	25836	33850	42595	6.6	93	9225	12325	15623	7.1	2.74	7199	9546	6.9
85208	MESA	013	45756	54377	64734	4.2	82	18915	22092	25978	3.7	2.46	13577	15976	3.9
85210	MESA	013	36496	39064	44187	1.6	40	12939	13735	15437	1.4	2.80	8140	8630	1.4
85212	MESA	013	9040	11515	14240	5.9	90	2953	3776	4664	6.0	3.03	2396	3079	6.1
85213	MESA	013	30002	33342	38386	2.5	61	10057	11127	12765	2.4	2.98	7766	8634	2.5
85215	MESA	013	15327	18238	21628	4.2	83	6387	7578	8943	4.1	2.40	4724	5620	4.2
85218	APACHE JUNCTION	021	6113	8538	11289	8.2	96	2831	4030	5420	8.7	2.12	2216	3168	8.8
85219	APACHE JUNCTION	021	16089	19372	23973	4.5	84	6807	8246	10311	4.6	2.35	4727	5773	4.8
85220	APACHE JUNCTION	021	32473	38201	46342	3.9	78	13869	16332	19925	3.9	2.33	9353	11077	4.1
85222	CASA GRANDE	021	37883	43839	53023	3.5	74	13194	15423	18906	3.7	2.81	9815	11482	3.8
85224	CHANDLER	013	43417	49857	58328	3.3	72	15648	17891	20816	3.2	2.76	10856	12391	3.2
85225	CHANDLER	013	66444	76462	89626	3.4	73	22158	25513	29839	3.4	2.99	16278	18680	3.3
85226	CHANDLER	013	39472	44712	51871	3.0	71	14434	16340	18879	3.0	2.73	10301	11617	2.9
85228	COOLIDGE	021	10612	11504	13444	1.9	50	3378	3696	4382	2.1	3.04	2532	2772	2.2
85231	ELOY	021	16777	18783	22176	2.7	66	4858	5574	6771	3.3	3.06	3801	4361	3.3
85232	FLORENCE	021	19935	21263	23319	1.5	36	3283	3857	4749	3.9	2.46	2300	2714	4.0
85233	GILBERT	013	38412	46469	55758	4.6	85	13123	15754	18768	4.4	2.95	10237	12283	4.4
85234	GILBERT	013	36532	43178	51230	4.0	81	11595	13635	16076	3.9	3.17	9492	11201	4.0
85236	HIGLEY	013	6059	7815	9644	6.2	92	1751	2226	2714	5.8	3.51	1544	1960	5.8
85237	KEARNY	021	2762	2969	3477	1.7	44	1031	1112	1313	1.8	2.67	765	826	1.8
85239	MARICOPA	021	7983	9707	12019	4.7	86	2511	3089	3877	5.0	3.11	1906	2348	5.0
85242	QUEEN CREEK	021	14096	22333	30907	11.4	98	4436	7082	9879	11.6	3.15	3658	5809	11.5
85247	SACATON	021	9479	10302	11996	2.0	52	2339	2562	3023	2.2	3.85	1948	2134	2.2
85248	CHANDLER	013	34710	45195	56529	6.4	92	14644	18788	23225	6.0	2.41	11256	14438	6.0
85249	CHANDLER	013	9227	17310	25349	16.0	99	3582	6396	9149	14.6	2.70	2692	4884	15.1
85250	SCOTTSDALE	013	16407	17543	19869	1.6	39	8023	8627	9770	1.7	2.03	4299	4586	1.5
85251	SCOTTSDALE	013	35671	39345	45413	2.3	58	17741	19552	22463	2.3	2.00	7907	8577	1.9
85253	PARADISE VALLEY	013	18261	19327	21596	1.3	33	7138	7553	8414	1.3	2.55	5344	5680	1.5
85254	SCOTTSDALE	013	49649	53642	60721	1.8	47	18440	20118	22819	2.1	2.65	13564	14676	1.9
85255	SCOTTSDALE	013	27721	39198	50477	8.5	97	11081	15647	20045	8.5	2.50	8630	12062	8.2
85256	SCOTTSDALE	013	5076	5674	6343	2.2	55	1347	1479	1678	2.2	3.74	932	1021	2.2
85257	SCOTTSDALE	013	30536	31274	34436	0.6	18	13525	13884	15300	0.6	2.21	7269	7435	0.5
85258	SCOTTSDALE	013	24476	26159	29457	1.6	37	11905	12779	14375	1.7	2.04	7318	7831	1.6
85259	SCOTTSDALE	013	18705	22988	27801	5.0	88	7260	8915	10742	5.0	2.58	5068	6280	5.2
85260	SCOTTSDALE	013	35478	39574	45430	2.6	63	15036	16947	19509	2.9	2.30	9685	10849	2.7
85262	SCOTTSDALE	013	12068	16282	20522	7.3	95	5253	7109	8942	7.4	2.29	4198	5670	7.3
85263	RIO VERDE	013	1543	2199	2834	8.7	97	806	1153	1484	8.8	1.91	656	937	8.8
85264	FORT MCDOWELL	013	947	1176	1423	5.2	89	284	352	423	5.2	3.34	226	281	5.3
85268	FOUNTAIN HILLS	013	20187	23808	28105	4.0	80	8634	10224	12052	4.1	2.33	6501	7697	4.1
85272	STANFIELD	021	772	847	998	2.2	54	227	250	297	2.3	3.39	175	193	2.3
85273	SUPERIOR	021	3391	3546	4080	1.1	28	1299	1375	1603	1.4	2.58	881	933	1.4
85281	TEMPE	013	54095	56175	62638	0.9	25	21981	22931	25723	1.0	2.26	8385	8671	0.8
85282	TEMPE	013	49683	53132	60333	1.6	39	20685	22134	25084	1.6	2.39	11458	12193	1.5
85283	TEMPE	013	42011	44327	49801	1.3	31	16108	17028	19103	1.3	2.58	9820	10311	1.2
85284	TEMPE	013	17282	18640	21049	1.8	46	5867	6338	7139	1.8	2.94	4885	5277	1.2
85287	TEMPE	013	550	546	573	-0.2	6	9	9	10	0.0	2.56	3	3	0.0
85292	WINKELMAN	021	2678	2697	2887	0.2	12	922	939	1016	0.4	2.87	696	710	0.5
	ARIZONA					2.7					2.7	2.64			2.9
	UNITED STATES					1.2					1.3	2.58			1.1

10-A

ZIP CODE #	POST OFFICE NAME	RACE (%) White 2000	White 2004	Black 2000	Black 2004	Asian/Pacific 2000	Asian/Pacific 2004	% Hispanic Origin 2000	% Hispanic Origin 2004	2004 AGE DISTRIBUTION (%) 0-4	5-9	10-14	15-19	20-24	25-44	45-64	65-84	85+	18+	MEDIAN AGE 2004	% 2004 Males	% 2004 Females
85003	PHOENIX	62.1	60.7	10.9	10.6	1.8	1.8	42.5	45.1	6.1	4.9	5.1	6.6	8.1	36.5	21.3	9.8	1.6	80.0	35.6	61.3	38.7
85004	PHOENIX	65.9	63.8	7.2	7.4	0.9	0.9	46.3	50.4	6.8	5.5	5.5	7.9	9.2	32.9	21.7	9.3	1.4	78.1	33.9	57.1	42.9
85006	PHOENIX	62.7	61.1	4.2	4.0	0.8	0.8	73.1	76.9	11.7	9.9	9.2	8.1	9.7	32.4	14.1	4.3	0.7	64.7	25.8	53.4	46.6
85007	PHOENIX	59.9	59.3	11.2	10.3	0.7	0.8	59.3	62.9	10.0	9.0	8.1	7.1	8.0	30.9	19.7	6.3	0.9	68.8	30.0	54.5	45.5
85008	PHOENIX	58.3	56.0	5.7	5.7	1.4	1.5	57.6	60.9	10.8	8.7	7.9	7.3	10.7	33.9	14.6	5.4	0.8	68.7	27.2	52.3	47.7
85009	PHOENIX	46.7	44.9	4.0	3.8	0.6	0.5	76.5	79.9	10.9	9.4	8.8	9.0	10.2	32.2	13.8	5.2	0.6	65.7	25.9	55.7	44.3
85012	PHOENIX	80.6	78.4	3.9	4.2	1.9	2.0	20.0	23.4	5.1	4.4	4.9	6.4	8.1	29.6	24.1	14.5	2.8	82.5	39.2	55.0	45.0
85013	PHOENIX	76.2	74.4	5.1	5.2	2.1	2.2	24.7	28.2	6.4	5.7	5.6	5.5	7.8	32.4	24.2	10.1	2.2	79.2	36.6	50.2	49.8
85014	PHOENIX	69.7	66.7	4.4	4.5	1.5	1.5	30.1	34.9	7.4	6.4	6.4	6.5	8.4	33.4	22.6	7.8	1.3	76.4	34.1	52.0	48.0
85015	PHOENIX	59.8	56.8	6.7	6.9	3.2	3.2	40.8	45.6	10.4	8.9	7.6	6.9	9.2	32.6	16.4	6.6	1.5	69.2	28.6	50.8	49.2
85016	PHOENIX	74.2	71.3	3.5	3.6	1.9	2.0	27.2	31.6	6.6	5.8	5.6	5.7	8.0	31.7	22.8	11.3	2.5	78.8	36.1	50.1	49.9
85017	PHOENIX	55.6	52.7	5.6	5.5	3.8	3.8	49.0	54.1	11.1	9.3	8.5	7.7	10.4	31.4	15.0	5.9	0.8	66.9	26.6	51.6	48.4
85018	PHOENIX	85.3	83.2	2.5	2.6	1.9	2.1	14.3	17.4	6.0	5.8	6.1	5.7	5.9	29.1	25.3	13.8	2.4	78.7	39.9	49.3	50.7
85019	PHOENIX	56.7	53.9	5.5	5.5	3.6	3.6	52.4	57.3	10.6	9.2	8.9	7.8	9.0	31.0	16.1	6.9	0.6	66.8	27.6	51.6	48.4
85020	PHOENIX	82.7	80.7	2.5	2.6	1.6	1.7	23.2	26.9	6.7	6.0	5.8	5.4	7.1	30.5	24.9	11.4	2.2	78.4	37.3	49.9	50.1
85021	PHOENIX	74.2	71.5	3.7	4.1	3.9	4.1	25.0	28.6	7.7	6.7	6.4	6.5	10.6	30.9	19.7	9.3	2.2	75.6	31.8	51.3	48.7
85022	PHOENIX	87.9	86.2	2.1	2.2	2.8	3.1	11.0	13.4	6.7	6.2	6.2	5.9	7.2	30.9	26.1	9.9	1.1	77.6	36.9	49.0	51.0
85023	PHOENIX	84.6	82.3	2.7	2.9	2.8	3.1	13.4	16.4	7.8	6.9	6.9	6.4	9.0	32.7	21.9	7.7	0.7	74.8	32.6	49.3	50.7
85024	PHOENIX	90.4	89.1	1.9	2.1	2.4	2.7	8.4	10.2	8.2	8.0	7.7	6.0	5.4	36.1	21.8	6.3	0.6	72.4	34.3	49.3	50.7
85027	PHOENIX	88.1	86.5	2.4	2.6	1.4	1.6	11.4	13.5	8.4	7.5	7.2	7.5	7.5	34.9	20.0	6.4	0.6	71.8	31.4	50.6	49.4
85028	PHOENIX	93.2	92.2	1.1	1.2	1.7	1.9	6.3	7.8	4.7	5.3	6.2	6.1	5.0	24.6	32.5	13.5	2.1	80.1	43.8	48.5	51.5
85029	PHOENIX	81.9	79.7	3.2	3.4	2.6	2.9	19.0	22.4	7.5	6.5	7.0	7.1	9.9	30.8	21.4	8.5	1.4	75.0	32.1	50.1	49.9
85031	PHOENIX	56.3	53.9	4.8	4.6	1.4	1.4	62.5	67.3	10.5	9.6	9.9	8.7	8.9	28.5	15.8	7.6	0.6	64.9	26.6	50.3	49.7
85032	PHOENIX	84.3	82.4	1.7	1.8	1.8	2.0	19.1	22.1	7.5	7.0	7.3	6.6	7.8	32.9	22.2	7.5	1.3	74.4	33.5	50.2	49.8
85033	PHOENIX	55.7	52.9	8.1	7.9	1.6	1.6	55.9	61.2	11.4	10.3	10.0	8.5	8.9	30.1	15.5	5.0	0.3	63.1	25.5	49.9	50.1
85034	PHOENIX	46.8	46.0	7.5	7.2	0.7	0.7	76.3	78.7	10.9	8.9	9.3	8.1	9.3	30.0	16.5	6.3	0.8	66.3	27.0	54.1	45.9
85035	PHOENIX	40.6	38.4	7.1	6.6	1.6	1.5	70.8	74.8	11.6	10.4	10.4	8.7	9.6	30.6	14.7	3.9	0.3	62.4	24.7	51.2	48.8
85037	PHOENIX	59.6	55.9	8.2	8.2	2.3	2.4	41.8	47.2	11.0	9.9	9.1	7.4	7.5	34.4	17.2	3.3	0.2	65.5	27.7	49.5	50.5
85040	PHOENIX	38.3	37.8	23.7	22.4	0.7	0.7	65.0	68.2	11.4	9.9	9.8	8.7	9.5	29.8	14.3	5.9	0.7	63.9	25.4	52.0	48.0
85041	PHOENIX	52.4	50.7	9.5	10.1	0.7	0.6	73.6	76.5	10.4	9.9	9.9	8.8	8.6	27.9	17.7	6.2	0.6	64.4	26.4	50.8	49.2
85042	PHOENIX	41.1	39.0	21.4	20.5	1.3	1.3	52.0	56.5	9.5	8.7	8.7	8.2	9.3	30.6	18.2	6.2	0.7	68.1	28.1	49.9	50.1
85043	PHOENIX	51.5	49.4	6.6	5.8	0.9	0.9	66.5	70.6	12.2	10.4	9.0	7.5	9.1	33.3	13.9	4.3	0.3	64.0	25.8	51.5	48.5
85044	PHOENIX	85.7	83.6	3.8	4.2	4.0	4.5	9.6	11.9	6.4	6.2	6.3	5.8	7.3	36.0	22.8	8.3	0.8	77.7	35.0	49.8	50.2
85045	PHOENIX	87.0	85.5	3.5	3.8	5.2	5.9	6.3	7.7	9.7	10.0	9.1	6.5	4.1	36.4	21.7	2.5	0.1	67.1	34.5	50.5	49.5
85048	PHOENIX	86.2	84.4	3.2	3.5	5.2	5.9	8.0	9.8	7.9	8.4	9.2	7.4	5.8	33.5	24.3	3.4	0.2	69.9	34.2	49.8	50.2
85050	PHOENIX	92.0	91.0	1.1	1.2	1.9	2.2	6.9	8.4	8.8	8.4	7.0	5.3	4.5	35.0	21.2	8.9	0.9	72.4	35.6	48.2	51.8
85051	PHOENIX	76.4	73.5	4.7	5.0	3.2	3.4	21.9	26.0	8.1	7.2	7.4	7.3	8.8	29.7	21.0	9.6	0.9	73.3	32.6	50.1	49.9
85053	PHOENIX	86.9	85.0	2.6	2.8	2.2	2.5	12.1	14.8	7.2	6.8	7.1	7.0	8.6	30.4	24.3	7.9	0.8	74.9	33.6	50.1	49.9
85054	PHOENIX	93.1	92.0	1.2	1.3	2.6	3.0	4.1	5.1	5.8	5.4	5.1	5.6	6.5	39.5	26.9	5.2	0.1	80.5	36.5	50.7	49.3
85085	PHOENIX	91.3	90.4	1.2	1.2	2.4	2.5	7.3	8.8	8.9	8.6	7.3	5.1	4.0	36.4	24.0	5.3	0.4	72.0	34.7	50.2	49.8
85086	PHOENIX	91.9	91.4	3.7	3.5	0.8	0.9	8.4	9.9	5.4	6.0	6.2	5.1	4.3	32.6	29.8	10.1	0.6	79.1	40.4	54.2	45.8
85087	NEW RIVER	95.7	95.1	0.7	0.7	0.5	0.6	4.9	6.1	5.3	6.1	6.7	6.1	4.0	27.1	32.8	11.3	0.6	78.0	42.3	51.9	48.1
85201	MESA	73.1	69.4	3.8	4.0	1.5	1.6	29.5	34.6	9.4	7.7	7.1	7.1	9.9	32.1	17.0	7.9	1.9	71.9	29.4	49.9	50.1
85202	MESA	74.3	70.9	4.5	4.8	3.5	3.8	20.1	25.1	7.9	6.3	6.1	6.9	13.0	33.7	19.6	5.8	0.8	76.0	29.1	50.0	50.0
85203	MESA	83.4	81.2	2.2	2.4	1.3	1.4	18.2	21.5	8.7	7.8	7.8	7.8	8.6	29.0	21.2	7.8	1.2	71.0	30.7	49.8	50.3
85204	MESA	76.0	73.3	2.4	2.4	1.6	1.7	30.3	34.4	9.7	8.4	8.0	7.7	9.3	30.3	17.2	8.2	1.2	69.3	28.7	50.4	49.6
85205	MESA	91.6	90.1	1.5	1.7	1.2	1.4	8.2	10.3	6.3	6.3	6.9	6.3	5.4	21.5	22.8	21.0	3.6	76.6	43.0	47.2	52.8
85206	MESA	92.0	90.4	1.5	1.7	1.3	1.5	8.0	10.1	6.4	5.7	5.4	4.6	4.8	22.5	16.8	26.8	7.1	79.6	45.8	46.4	53.7
85207	MESA	90.8	89.6	1.4	1.5	0.8	1.0	10.8	13.1	8.0	7.5	7.2	6.5	6.0	27.1	23.3	13.5	1.0	73.2	37.1	48.9	51.1
85208	MESA	90.0	88.1	1.3	1.5	1.0	1.3	12.5	15.2	7.5	6.8	6.1	4.7	4.6	24.1	19.0	24.5	2.8	76.6	41.9	48.1	51.9
85210	MESA	68.1	64.9	3.4	3.4	2.3	2.4	36.5	41.3	8.8	7.6	7.3	7.2	10.4	34.7	18.6	4.9	0.5	72.4	29.1	52.1	47.9
85212	MESA	85.6	84.1	2.3	2.3	2.0	2.2	12.9	15.6	12.7	10.6	7.2	4.8	5.4	38.3	13.0	7.6	0.5	66.6	29.7	49.2	50.8
85213	MESA	89.3	87.5	1.4	1.5	1.7	2.0	10.0	12.1	7.5	7.4	8.1	8.1	7.7	25.1	24.2	10.6	1.5	72.0	34.2	49.4	50.6
85215	MESA	94.5	93.6	1.1	1.2	0.9	1.0	5.6	7.0	5.4	5.9	6.3	5.2	3.7	21.3	26.8	22.7	2.8	79.2	46.6	48.4	51.6
85218	APACHE JUNCTION	95.4	94.4	0.3	0.4	0.6	0.7	5.1	6.3	3.9	4.3	5.3	4.2	3.2	19.9	36.1	22.1	1.1	83.8	50.6	49.2	50.8
85219	APACHE JUNCTION	93.7	92.4	0.6	0.7	0.5	0.6	6.5	8.2	4.7	5.1	5.2	4.8	4.1	20.8	29.4	24.4	1.7	82.1	49.0	48.5	51.5
85220	APACHE JUNCTION	92.5	90.6	0.8	0.9	0.6	0.8	9.1	11.7	6.9	6.3	5.6	4.6	4.8	24.8	22.5	21.9	2.7	78.3	42.6	49.5	50.6
85222	CASA GRANDE	65.1	61.3	3.6	3.8	1.0	1.0	38.0	43.1	8.5	8.1	8.2	7.7	7.4	25.6	21.2	12.2	1.1	70.5	33.1	49.6	50.4
85224	CHANDLER	80.2	77.3	3.6	3.9	4.6	5.3	15.0	18.1	7.7	7.4	7.7	6.9	7.3	34.8	21.6	5.4	1.4	73.1	32.8	49.6	50.4
85225	CHANDLER	69.2	66.5	3.7	3.8	2.8	3.0	34.5	38.0	10.2	9.1	8.0	6.8	7.6	35.4	17.4	5.0	0.6	68.6	29.8	50.3	49.7
85226	CHANDLER	81.3	78.8	3.7	4.0	6.8	7.8	11.6	13.9	8.3	8.2	8.4	7.2	6.5	36.8	20.9	3.4	0.2	70.5	32.3	49.5	50.5
85228	COOLIDGE	60.0	55.4	7.7	8.1	0.7	0.7	37.5	42.7	8.7	8.2	8.7	8.0	7.8	23.8	20.7	12.7	1.5	69.7	32.6	49.2	50.8
85231	ELOY	62.4	60.9	4.0	3.9	1.0	1.0	55.4	57.9	8.2	7.9	8.3	7.5	7.6	29.2	19.1	11.4	0.9	71.0	31.9	55.2	44.8
85232	FLORENCE	59.8	55.2	8.0	8.3	0.8	0.8	34.2	39.2	3.0	2.9	3.0	5.0	11.6	45.0	19.9	8.9	0.8	88.9	35.5	77.1	22.9
85233	GILBERT	82.8	80.7	2.7	2.9	5.4	6.0	13.3	15.8	9.8	9.0	8.2	6.6	6.6	35.6	20.0	3.9	0.3	68.9	31.5	49.7	50.4
85234	GILBERT	88.3	86.6	1.9	2.1	2.3	2.6	10.9	13.1	9.2	9.4	9.8	8.1	6.2	31.7	20.9	4.4	0.4	66.4	30.9	49.2	50.8
85236	HIGLEY	89.8	88.2	1.5	1.7	2.4	2.7	8.9	11.0	10.1	10.5	10.9	8.2	5.0	33.8	18.3	3.1	0.2	63.1	29.8	49.8	50.2
85237	KEARNY	79.3	75.5	0.4	0.5	0.2	0.2	35.7	42.1	8.1	7.3	7.8	6.9	5.9	21.0	27.3	14.7	1.2	72.2	38.8	49.4	50.6
85239	MARICOPA	59.7	56.2	1.4	1.5	0.4	0.4	39.8	45.0	8.8	8.0	9.2	8.4	7.2	26.7	23.2	8.1	0.6	68.9	32.1	52.3	47.7
85242	QUEEN CREEK	82.4	78.8	0.6	0.6	0.7	0.8	26.5	32.0	9.0	8.8	9.1	7.5	5.7	28.9	21.6	9.1	0.5	68.4	33.0	51.6	48.4
85247	SACATON	10.6	10.5	0.5	0.6	0.5	0.6	8.7	8.6	10.3	10.2	11.9	10.6	8.1	25.8	16.4	5.6	1.1	60.9	24.3	47.2	52.8
85248	CHANDLER	88.7	86.6	2.1	2.3	3.5	4.1	7.5	9.9	7.2	6.7	5.4	3.6	2.9	26.4	22.4	23.8	1.7	78.5	43.5	48.2	51.8
85249	CHANDLER	89.2	86.4	1.2	1.2	1.1	1.2	16.0	21.5	8.6	7.1	6.8	5.3	3.9	26.8	22.5	18.1	1.0	74.1	38.7	49.8	50.2
85250	SCOTTSDALE	95.0	94.3	0.9	1.0	1.2	1.4	5.1	6.4	3.7	3.6	4.5	5.0	5.1	25.9	28.3	21.3	2.7	85.3	46.6	46.5	53.5
85251	SCOTTSDALE	88.9	87.0	1.5	1.7	1.6	1.8	13.8	17.1	4.8	4.3	4.5	4.6	8.5	32.5	21.0	16.4	3.4	83.8	38.6	48.7	51.3
85253	PARADISE VALLEY	94.9	94.2	0.9	1.0	2.3	2.6	3.0	3.8	4.4	5.6	7.5	7.1	4.4	18.3	34.3	16.4	2.0	77.8	46.5	49.4	50.6
85254	SCOTTSDALE	93.6	92.5	1.1	1.2	2.5	3.0	4.3	5.5	5.4	6.4	7.9	7.2	5.8	28.0	30.1	8.1	1.1	75.6	39.2	48.9	51.1
85255	SCOTTSDALE	94.3	93.4	1.2	1.3	2.3	2.7	3.2	4.1	7.0	7.7	6.5	4.4	2.6	27.9	31.0	12.0	1.0	75.9	41.9	49.2	50.8
85256	SCOTTSDALE	23.5	22.1	0.5	0.5	0.2	0.3	16.3	17.9	9.4	9.1	10.1	8.8	6.8	23.8	18.6	11.6	1.7	66.2	29.8	46.8	53.2
85257	SCOTTSDALE	84.6	82.6	1.8	2.0	1.6	1.7	14.0	16.8	5.5	5.2	5.4	5.5	6.3	31.3	21.9	16.0	2.9	80.6	39.0	48.5	51.5
85258	SCOTTSDALE	95.1	94.4	0.7	0.8	2.2	2.5	3.2	3.9	3.4	3.8	4.6	4.4	3.9	21.7	33.6	22.5	2.1	85.5	50.4	47.0	53.0
85259	SCOTTSDALE	93.5	92.6	1.4	1.6	2.4	2.7	3.9	4.9	6.1	6.9	7.5	6.4	5.2	28.9	28.5	9.8	0.7	75.4	39.2	48.6	51.4
85260	SCOTTSDALE	93.9	93.0	1.1	1.2	2.7	3.1	3.8	4.8	5.7	6.2	6.7	5.9	5.2	30.2	27.7	10.9	1.6	77.7	39.4	47.8	52.2
85262	SCOTTSDALE	96.5	95.9	0.6	0.6	1.1	1.3	2.9	3.6	3.2	4.1	4.3	3.8	2.4	17.8	41.7	21.6	1.1	86.0	53.0	49.8	50.2
85263	RIO VERDE	98.2	97.9	0.1	0.1	0.4	0.5	1.7	2.1	2.2	2.4	2.1	1.9	1.2	11.1	29.9	46.1	3.1	92.1	64.7	48.2	51.8
85264	FORT MCDOWELL	15.4	14.1	0.4	0.4	0.1	0.1	10.0	10.5	10.7	10.5	10.5	9.8	8.6	27.5	18.3	4.0	0.2	62.2	25.0	51.0	49.0
85268	FOUNTAIN HILLS	96.3	95.7	0.6	0.7	1.0	1.1	3.1	3.8	4.4	5.0	5.4	4.8	3.3	22.2	34.2	19.2	1.6	82.1	48.0	48.2	51.8
85272	STANFIELD	52.5	48.5	2.1	2.1	0.9	0.9	61.8	67.3	10.6	9.8	9.2	8.6	7.6	27.5	18.8	7.4	0.5	65.1	28.5	52.9	47.1
85273	SUPERIOR	73.5	71.4	0.5	0.5	0.4	0.4	67.4	72.7	6.5	6.4	7.9	6.8	6.4	21.2	24.4	18.4	2.0	75.2	40.8	49.7	50.3
85281	TEMPE	70.8	67.6	3.1	3.3	6.6	7.0	25.1	29.3	5.8	4.3	4.1	12.1	23.2	35.0	11.5	3.8	0.5	83.7	25.2	54.0	46.0
85282	TEMPE	79.2	76.6	4.2	4.4	3.6	4.0	16.7	19.9	6.0	5.2	5.4	5.8	11.3	34.5	20.3	9.9	1.7	80.5	32.5	50.4	49.6
85283	TEMPE	72.1	69.8	4.3	4.6	3.7	4.1	21.8	24.8	6.2	5.9	6.3	6.4	9.8	35.1	22.6	6.7	0.9	78.0	32.1	50.4	49.6
85284	TEMPE	88.3	86.7	1.8	2.0	6.2	7.1	6.9	8.6	6.0	7.6	9.2	8.0	4.7	26.4	32.8	5.0	0.5	72.0	39.2	49.7	50.3
85287	TEMPE	86.2	84.3	1.5	1.5	3.5	3.9	8.0	9.7	0.9	1.3	0.6	46.5	19.2	21.8	7.3	1.8	0.6	96.7	20.2	53.9	46.2
85292	WINKELMAN	64.5	61.7	0.3	0.4	0.3	0.4	64.0	68.6	7.5	7.4	8.6	8.0	6.8	21.1	27.7	12.1	0.9	71.4	36.9	50.4	49.6
	ARIZONA	75.5	74.0	3.1	3.2	1.9	2.1	25.3	27.9	7.6	7.1	7.3	6.9	7.5	28.1	22.1	11.9	1.5	74.0	34.8	49.9	50.2
	UNITED STATES	75.1	73.6	12.3	12.5	3.8	4.2	12.5	14.1	6.9	6.7	7.2	7.0	7.3	28.6	23.8	10.8	1.7	75.1	36.0	49.1	50.9

ZIP CODE #	POST OFFICE NAME	2004 Per Capita Income	2004 HH Income Base	2004 Household Income Distribution (%): Less than $25,000	$25,000 to $49,999	$50,000 to $99,999	$100,000 to $149,999	$150,000 or More	Median Household Income: 2004	2009	2004 National Centile	2004 State Centile	2004 Home Value Base	2004 Home Value Distribution (%): Less than $50,000	$50,000 to $89,999	$90,000 to $174,999	$175,000 to $399,999	$400,000 or More	2004 Median Home Value
85003	PHOENIX	20486	3896	49.3	23.0	15.5	6.1	6.1	25490	32651	5	10	1244	7.2	12.5	22.4	53.5	4.3	200600
85004	PHOENIX	21329	2094	41.0	21.5	28.1	6.7	2.7	34682	45267	26	28	631	10.3	21.1	47.9	18.1	2.7	116300
85006	PHOENIX	11083	10040	44.7	31.2	18.7	3.9	1.5	28296	34510	9	14	3906	9.2	31.8	51.0	7.5	0.4	98270
85007	PHOENIX	17548	4901	45.6	24.0	18.3	7.6	4.5	28692	36328	10	16	2141	12.2	24.7	27.1	30.1	5.9	130653
85008	PHOENIX	15154	21267	33.9	35.2	23.5	5.4	2.0	35037	43319	28	30	7500	14.1	23.0	54.1	8.6	0.3	102273
85009	PHOENIX	11115	13641	41.6	33.7	19.4	3.5	1.7	30365	37539	13	18	7262	23.6	46.5	28.3	1.4	0.2	75797
85012	PHOENIX	35080	3290	26.6	27.6	23.8	11.0	11.0	45426	60377	62	59	1482	2.3	5.3	22.6	50.6	19.2	250294
85013	PHOENIX	31751	11006	25.2	28.8	29.2	9.1	7.7	44816	59373	61	58	5153	3.2	9.2	53.3	25.5	8.8	147134
85014	PHOENIX	25703	13345	28.9	34.4	24.4	8.0	4.3	39223	49282	43	43	5132	5.3	17.2	48.8	23.2	5.5	128170
85015	PHOENIX	16426	16708	33.2	35.1	24.5	5.2	2.1	34819	43694	27	29	6401	8.0	24.4	60.6	6.5	0.6	105889
85016	PHOENIX	37785	17668	24.0	29.8	26.2	9.7	10.4	46215	59527	64	61	8530	2.5	9.6	44.3	26.7	16.9	158584
85017	PHOENIX	13634	12624	35.6	35.1	24.0	4.1	1.3	33690	41076	23	26	6033	12.3	34.4	51.6	1.3	0.5	92363
85018	PHOENIX	43947	16826	19.8	27.9	26.8	11.1	14.4	52736	68845	77	73	9615	1.4	5.9	31.2	37.3	24.2	213462
85019	PHOENIX	14791	8986	28.8	35.5	28.4	5.5	1.8	38210	47034	40	41	4732	2.4	24.2	71.5	1.5	0.4	105056
85020	PHOENIX	34250	16116	22.4	27.4	28.5	11.1	10.6	50233	64869	72	69	9072	3.7	13.8	41.5	31.6	9.4	145265
85021	PHOENIX	28793	16863	24.2	31.2	27.7	8.7	8.3	44446	56555	60	56	7510	5.9	9.1	46.2	29.2	9.7	144523
85022	PHOENIX	35179	21198	17.9	28.9	30.7	13.1	9.4	53235	67999	77	73	13470	9.8	9.8	38.2	37.4	4.7	157260
85023	PHOENIX	28149	14705	19.1	29.2	34.0	11.2	6.6	51610	64722	75	71	8269	9.1	5.8	55.2	25.9	4.1	141345
85024	PHOENIX	31908	7135	8.4	21.0	41.7	20.8	8.1	71819	88649	92	88	6518	4.2	6.7	43.0	45.1	1.1	169385
85027	PHOENIX	25206	15497	15.3	30.3	39.7	11.6	3.0	53561	66057	78	74	10522	12.0	9.8	67.3	10.4	0.4	121886
85028	PHOENIX	43405	8807	10.7	20.9	34.1	18.8	15.5	73740	95224	93	89	7165	0.3	1.1	32.4	57.2	9.0	202908
85029	PHOENIX	22151	18640	20.7	31.9	33.8	10.5	3.1	47318	59348	67	63	10320	1.7	11.2	77.4	9.0	0.7	122809
85031	PHOENIX	12600	7835	26.2	37.3	29.0	6.3	1.2	39466	47538	44	44	5451	5.9	30.7	62.0	1.5	0.0	96363
85032	PHOENIX	25551	27045	16.7	29.1	36.6	12.3	5.3	53527	66418	78	74	17420	4.9	8.3	53.8	31.5	1.6	146765
85033	PHOENIX	13569	14705	24.0	34.6	33.6	6.7	1.0	42102	50759	53	51	9743	3.8	28.0	66.3	1.9	0.1	100686
85034	PHOENIX	11694	2872	45.3	30.5	18.9	4.5	0.9	28514	36167	10	15	887	31.2	40.3	23.1	5.4	0.0	66618
85035	PHOENIX	11951	12111	30.1	34.9	28.4	5.3	1.3	38119	45845	40	40	7059	3.2	35.0	61.3	0.4	0.1	95565
85037	PHOENIX	18915	11062	11.0	28.6	47.7	10.2	2.5	56625	68063	81	77	9012	1.6	11.5	81.4	5.2	0.4	118477
85040	PHOENIX	10245	7931	42.4	33.0	20.0	3.4	1.2	29559	36164	11	17	3760	14.9	42.2	39.8	2.2	0.8	84119
85041	PHOENIX	12027	9805	31.6	33.9	26.2	6.8	1.5	37561	45822	38	39	6842	17.0	44.4	33.3	3.8	1.5	82498
85042	PHOENIX	17630	11724	21.7	30.3	35.2	9.3	3.5	48055	60324	68	65	7931	8.3	22.1	53.9	13.9	1.8	108743
85043	PHOENIX	13246	6084	28.6	40.0	26.4	3.5	1.6	36109	43509	32	32	2496	27.6	20.2	42.0	9.5	0.7	92204
85044	PHOENIX	39591	18732	8.8	20.6	41.3	18.1	11.2	70982	88992	92	87	11585	0.6	0.9	37.0	54.0	7.5	192039
85045	PHOENIX	50992	2717	1.3	3.8	26.8	34.4	33.7	125517	155823	100	100	2631	0.6	0.2	2.6	67.6	29.0	327872
85048	PHOENIX	44294	13564	4.1	10.9	34.3	27.7	23.0	100832	128698	98	98	11135	0.3	0.5	12.4	69.3	17.5	251862
85050	PHOENIX	35753	9573	10.5	19.6	38.6	20.7	10.6	74610	93167	93	89	8377	10.3	11.3	25.6	49.8	3.0	180586
85051	PHOENIX	21045	16225	23.9	32.3	33.1	8.0	2.7	44664	55529	60	57	9428	2.4	15.4	76.1	5.9	0.3	116565
85053	PHOENIX	24556	11058	15.4	28.0	40.9	12.7	3.0	54670	66674	79	75	7429	1.3	4.9	76.2	16.8	0.9	133930
85054	PHOENIX	50166	1319	6.7	12.8	33.8	22.7	24.0	94325	125159	98	97	814	0.0	0.0	3.6	63.3	33.2	348689
85085	PHOENIX	34062	1038	10.3	12.9	40.3	24.4	12.1	80640	102775	95	93	973	3.9	1.3	25.5	62.8	6.5	205058
85086	PHOENIX	29803	3483	11.0	17.0	44.3	20.0	7.6	72129	87357	92	88	3238	7.9	2.8	16.0	63.0	10.3	233333
85087	NEW RIVER	31667	1751	11.8	21.3	41.3	18.3	7.4	66077	82612	89	84	1597	6.3	6.3	23.2	55.1	9.1	204310
85201	MESA	19876	19958	24.7	34.4	31.2	7.6	2.2	42682	53429	55	52	9396	11.4	17.2	60.0	10.8	0.7	113331
85202	MESA	23835	20498	20.9	31.5	34.3	9.8	3.5	47766	59068	68	65	9618	7.1	11.5	56.8	23.8	0.7	135519
85203	MESA	25042	13547	17.8	26.2	34.7	14.5	6.8	55841	70232	81	76	8633	4.8	7.6	52.1	32.0	3.5	152181
85204	MESA	19066	23100	20.2	32.9	35.6	8.5	2.8	47161	57732	66	63	14003	14.6	6.6	67.7	10.1	1.0	121947
85205	MESA	26283	18239	24.0	26.6	31.6	12.4	5.4	49266	61412	71	67	14025	12.4	8.1	55.3	20.4	3.8	130485
85206	MESA	27638	15671	19.4	29.0	36.0	11.7	4.0	51432	64643	75	71	12638	7.1	9.6	56.0	25.7	1.7	145614
85207	MESA	28085	12325	17.1	23.2	37.1	14.3	8.4	59995	73549	84	80	10942	10.5	10.2	42.3	29.0	7.9	145726
85208	MESA	23251	22092	21.5	31.7	34.0	10.2	2.6	46892	59289	66	62	19634	13.3	16.7	42.2	27.5	0.3	130052
85210	MESA	19979	13735	21.8	33.4	32.8	9.5	2.5	45693	55737	63	60	6660	11.6	12.5	56.2	19.5	0.2	125994
85212	MESA	24911	3776	9.9	20.9	47.8	17.4	4.1	68339	82577	90	86	3369	4.2	3.3	31.8	60.2	0.5	186559
85213	MESA	29657	11127	12.9	20.8	37.1	17.5	11.6	66130	83047	89	84	8831	11.6	5.4	32.6	42.5	8.0	176050
85215	MESA	35434	7578	15.2	24.3	34.8	14.6	11.0	61798	77889	86	81	6957	3.9	8.1	37.7	43.6	6.7	175534
85218	APACHE JUNCTION	41947	4030	10.6	22.0	40.9	17.3	9.2	67197	84168	90	86	3600	4.7	4.2	28.6	55.0	7.6	193886
85219	APACHE JUNCTION	25748	8246	24.4	33.5	29.5	8.7	3.9	44005	52514	59	54	6949	18.0	20.6	35.9	22.8	2.8	112881
85220	APACHE JUNCTION	20452	16332	28.1	34.8	30.6	5.2	1.3	40174	47750	47	47	13867	29.9	17.0	44.5	8.2	0.5	94501
85222	CASA GRANDE	18185	15423	29.2	32.6	27.8	7.6	2.8	39627	47161	45	44	10693	22.8	27.0	38.5	11.3	0.4	90187
85224	CHANDLER	28573	17891	10.8	22.0	41.9	18.2	7.1	66513	82555	89	85	12448	0.3	1.1	59.3	36.2	3.2	162598
85225	CHANDLER	23833	25513	14.4	25.0	41.7	14.3	4.6	59870	73926	84	80	18157	6.5	7.4	54.1	31.3	0.7	149916
85226	CHANDLER	34901	16340	6.6	18.1	42.1	21.5	11.8	77358	97823	94	91	11915	0.5	1.3	41.5	52.4	4.3	185417
85228	COOLIDGE	16751	3696	35.9	31.6	22.8	6.7	3.1	35226	42005	28	30	2631	31.2	37.1	26.7	4.8	0.2	73464
85231	ELOY	14864	5574	32.7	34.2	25.5	5.6	2.0	37269	44080	36	38	4026	22.3	36.5	33.2	7.4	0.6	79880
85232	FLORENCE	17858	3857	25.8	31.0	34.2	7.4	1.7	44590	51775	60	57	2928	21.8	26.1	42.3	7.9	1.9	92274
85233	GILBERT	32003	15754	7.0	16.1	41.7	25.9	9.4	79972	100799	95	92	12721	0.4	0.9	32.6	63.0	3.2	196898
85234	GILBERT	30705	13635	6.8	17.3	43.8	21.0	11.1	76737	95345	94	91	11690	0.7	1.7	34.6	56.2	6.8	196284
85236	HIGLEY	26046	2226	2.6	13.3	46.9	30.7	6.5	84389	105531	96	94	2082	0.1	0.8	36.4	57.8	5.0	192925
85237	KEARNY	19746	1112	26.8	31.0	33.2	6.7	2.3	44588	51845	60	57	920	28.0	48.6	21.3	2.0	0.1	69558
85239	MARICOPA	15020	3089	29.2	33.0	30.0	6.9	0.9	39760	47953	45	45	2298	21.8	23.4	47.6	6.5	0.8	96022
85242	QUEEN CREEK	22831	7082	15.3	26.6	38.0	14.0	6.2	57212	68022	82	77	6228	13.1	9.5	34.9	38.1	4.5	159125
85247	SACATON	10363	2562	49.0	26.5	15.7	6.1	2.8	25567	30703	5	11	1648	41.9	29.8	10.3	17.4	0.6	60427
85248	CHANDLER	39762	18788	10.3	19.3	37.2	21.1	12.2	75565	96589	93	90	17156	3.8	2.1	27.2	61.2	5.7	213765
85249	CHANDLER	29218	6396	12.9	23.4	40.2	14.4	9.1	63830	80192	88	82	5838	2.6	5.3	38.3	43.7	10.1	182915
85250	SCOTTSDALE	40120	8627	14.8	24.2	37.8	14.2	9.1	60692	76845	85	81	6360	0.3	1.9	41.5	49.9	6.5	186315
85251	SCOTTSDALE	37975	19552	20.9	30.1	31.6	9.8	7.6	48842	62141	70	66	9997	1.2	5.6	51.1	35.8	6.3	163580
85253	PARADISE VALLEY	97945	7553	5.9	10.8	18.2	16.3	48.8	145658	198396	100	100	6467	0.0	0.4	3.1	13.8	82.7	832230
85254	SCOTTSDALE	44202	20118	6.7	15.9	34.5	24.1	18.8	86971	113211	97	96	15344	0.5	0.8	12.6	70.8	15.3	261903
85255	SCOTTSDALE	69559	15647	6.9	9.7	23.9	22.9	36.7	118909	152755	99	99	13627	0.3	0.1	1.4	39.7	58.6	447280
85256	SCOTTSDALE	11791	1479	40.6	28.3	23.9	5.1	2.2	31606	40129	17	22	1153	46.1	26.7	14.4	8.9	4.0	55291
85257	SCOTTSDALE	26447	13884	22.5	28.6	34.1	11.1	3.7	48859	60832	70	66	9040	10.3	9.2	54.2	25.7	0.6	144687
85258	SCOTTSDALE	62272	12779	9.7	17.0	30.8	18.6	23.9	84683	113294	96	95	9451	0.5	0.2	11.3	58.8	29.3	314176
85259	SCOTTSDALE	57104	8915	10.3	13.7	28.1	19.2	28.7	94596	128980	98	98	6668	0.2	0.3	4.7	44.0	50.9	405403
85260	SCOTTSDALE	50559	16947	10.2	17.8	32.0	19.8	20.2	80540	106424	95	93	12183	0.3	0.1	10.2	61.7	27.7	291563
85262	SCOTTSDALE	80454	7109	6.5	9.6	25.6	20.7	37.5	117059	156432	99	99	6663	0.7	0.8	3.3	30.6	64.6	477960
85263	RIO VERDE	71325	1153	7.7	12.3	29.7	19.2	31.1	100529	140993	98	98	1099	0.0	0.6	5.3	38.9	55.2	431250
85264	FORT MCDOWELL	25776	352	20.5	21.6	36.7	9.4	11.9	56021	68474	81	77	305	17.4	29.5	31.5	15.1	6.6	95278
85268	FOUNTAIN HILLS	41714	10224	9.6	20.0	37.1	18.7	14.7	75500	97536	93	89	8663	0.2	1.5	17.5	58.4	22.5	257896
85272	STANFIELD	12810	250	38.0	32.0	22.0	6.0	2.0	32039	38046	18	24	156	36.5	27.6	28.9	4.5	2.6	75000
85273	SUPERIOR	14670	1375	43.0	31.4	22.0	2.2	1.4	30615	36442	14	20	999	40.5	40.1	17.0	1.8	0.5	58514
85281	TEMPE	19255	22931	36.1	32.6	23.8	5.4	2.1	34794	43836	27	28	5999	14.2	13.5	55.7	15.6	1.1	116939
85282	TEMPE	28054	22134	17.2	28.7	36.4	13.1	4.6	53467	67185	78	74	12563	9.3	5.8	56.6	27.7	0.6	145093
85283	TEMPE	30743	17028	14.3	24.2	37.2	16.2	8.1	62236	78160	86	82	10036	2.0	6.6	50.0	39.5	1.8	163273
85284	TEMPE	46103	6338	3.7	9.4	31.7	25.8	29.4	107484	138521	99	99	6020	0.2	0.7	11.0	66.6	21.5	276373
85287	TEMPE	9715	9	22.2	0.0	33.3	44.4	0.0	85912	110555	96	96	5	0.0	0.0	40.0	60.0	0.0	208333
85292	WINKELMAN	15747	939	34.4	34.1	24.9	3.7	2.9	36740	44551	34	35	759	52.3	27.4	14.9	3.4	2.0	47177
	ARIZONA	25625		22.8	27.9	31.5	11.3	6.4	49168	61784				9.8	13.0	42.4	28.8	6.1	140071
	UNITED STATES	25866		24.7	27.1	30.8	10.9	6.5	48124	56710				10.9	15.0	33.7	30.1	10.4	145905

#	POST OFFICE NAME	FINANCIAL SERVICES: Auto Loan	Home Loan	Invest-ments	Retire-ment Plans	THE HOME: Home Improvements: Home Repair	Lawn & Garden	Furnishings: Comput-ers & Hard-ware	Major Appli-ances	TV, Radio, Sound Equip-ment	Furni-ture	ENTERTAINMENT: Dine out/ Carry out	Sports Equip-ment	Fees & Tickets	Toys & Games	Travel	Cable TV	PERSONAL: Apparel & Services	Auto Repairs	Health Insur-ance	Pets & Supplies
85003	PHOENIX	59	55	68	56	54	59	62	59	63	62	79	69	60	77	60	62	77	62	58	65
85004	PHOENIX	59	54	66	56	53	58	63	59	63	62	80	70	61	77	60	61	78	63	57	65
85006	PHOENIX	54	48	48	47	47	49	53	53	54	55	69	60	50	66	50	52	69	55	49	56
85007	PHOENIX	74	69	76	70	68	71	75	74	76	78	96	86	73	95	72	73	96	77	69	80
85008	PHOENIX	65	57	60	59	56	59	64	63	65	66	82	74	61	79	60	61	81	67	58	68
85009	PHOENIX	59	51	50	50	50	52	56	57	59	60	74	64	54	71	53	55	74	60	53	61
85012	PHOENIX	97	96	126	99	95	104	110	102	109	106	136	122	108	135	107	106	134	108	98	112
85013	PHOENIX	91	90	114	95	88	94	100	93	98	98	123	113	99	122	96	94	121	98	87	103
85014	PHOENIX	78	72	85	76	71	76	81	77	81	81	102	92	79	99	78	77	100	82	73	85
85015	PHOENIX	64	59	65	60	58	61	66	63	66	66	83	75	64	81	63	63	82	67	59	69
85016	PHOENIX	112	110	133	114	108	117	120	115	118	119	149	135	119	145	116	114	146	120	109	126
85017	PHOENIX	60	54	57	54	53	56	59	59	60	61	76	67	56	72	56	57	75	61	55	63
85018	PHOENIX	124	134	173	138	131	141	137	132	134	137	170	155	142	172	138	132	167	135	125	145
85019	PHOENIX	69	66	67	64	65	68	69	69	70	71	88	79	68	87	67	68	88	71	66	74
85020	PHOENIX	103	107	131	110	106	112	111	108	109	112	137	126	112	137	110	106	135	110	101	118
85021	PHOENIX	97	93	110	97	92	98	104	98	102	102	128	118	101	125	99	97	126	103	92	108
85022	PHOENIX	117	118	127	123	116	121	118	117	114	120	145	136	119	140	116	110	142	118	108	130
85023	PHOENIX	98	96	108	101	93	98	101	97	98	102	124	116	100	120	97	93	121	101	89	108
85024	PHOENIX	125	140	136	146	134	129	127	126	117	132	148	148	131	149	124	109	147	123	107	138
85027	PHOENIX	92	94	97	97	91	93	93	92	89	95	113	108	93	110	90	85	111	93	83	102
85028	PHOENIX	137	159	183	159	157	165	149	149	143	150	180	170	157	183	153	142	178	147	141	164
85029	PHOENIX	80	80	90	83	79	82	84	81	82	84	104	96	84	103	82	78	102	84	75	89
85031	PHOENIX	72	64	58	61	62	65	66	69	68	71	86	75	62	78	63	66	85	71	66	73
85032	PHOENIX	95	98	104	101	95	98	98	96	94	99	119	113	98	117	95	89	117	97	87	105
85033	PHOENIX	72	68	64	66	66	68	70	72	71	73	89	80	67	85	67	67	89	73	66	76
85034	PHOENIX	54	47	49	46	45	49	52	52	55	55	69	59	49	64	50	53	68	55	50	56
85035	PHOENIX	68	59	55	57	57	60	64	65	66	68	83	73	60	79	60	62	84	68	60	69
85037	PHOENIX	91	100	97	102	96	94	93	92	86	95	110	108	94	109	90	81	108	91	80	101
85040	PHOENIX	57	49	47	48	48	51	54	55	56	57	70	61	51	66	51	54	70	57	52	59
85041	PHOENIX	71	63	55	59	61	64	65	69	67	69	84	74	60	76	62	65	83	70	65	73
85042	PHOENIX	85	79	79	79	76	80	82	83	82	86	104	94	79	98	78	79	103	85	76	90
85043	PHOENIX	66	57	58	58	56	59	63	63	64	66	81	72	60	78	59	61	81	66	58	68
85044	PHOENIX	132	133	148	140	129	135	134	131	129	137	164	152	135	157	130	124	160	133	121	145
85045	PHOENIX	211	251	257	260	240	238	223	219	204	230	259	255	238	265	222	194	259	213	191	242
85048	PHOENIX	176	199	211	209	191	191	184	180	171	189	217	211	193	219	182	162	216	177	157	199
85050	PHOENIX	135	146	136	150	141	138	133	134	125	139	158	157	135	156	130	117	155	131	118	149
85051	PHOENIX	74	76	87	78	75	79	80	77	78	79	99	91	81	99	79	76	97	79	72	84
85053	PHOENIX	88	94	103	97	92	94	94	92	90	94	114	108	95	114	92	86	112	93	83	101
85054	PHOENIX	163	184	177	192	175	169	166	165	152	173	193	193	171	194	162	141	191	160	139	180
85085	PHOENIX	132	154	152	158	147	143	138	137	127	142	161	160	143	164	136	119	159	133	118	150
85086	PHOENIX	106	123	122	127	118	115	111	110	102	113	129	128	115	132	109	96	128	106	95	120
85087	NEW RIVER	105	126	131	126	124	124	113	114	106	114	133	131	119	138	115	103	132	110	104	126
85201	MESA	73	69	75	72	68	72	74	72	73	74	92	86	72	88	71	70	90	75	68	80
85202	MESA	83	77	88	82	75	80	86	82	84	86	106	98	83	101	81	79	104	86	75	91
85203	MESA	100	107	112	109	105	107	105	103	100	105	127	121	106	128	103	96	125	103	94	113
85204	MESA	82	82	83	83	80	83	82	82	80	84	101	94	81	97	80	76	99	83	76	89
85205	MESA	91	96	100	95	95	102	90	93	89	93	111	102	92	106	92	88	108	92	93	102
85206	MESA	94	95	94	92	95	105	89	95	89	93	112	101	90	102	91	90	107	93	98	105
85207	MESA	112	116	112	114	117	124	107	113	106	109	132	127	108	128	109	105	127	110	113	130
85208	MESA	86	83	78	80	85	95	77	85	79	81	99	90	77	91	80	81	93	83	91	96
85210	MESA	82	76	81	80	73	76	81	79	79	83	101	93	78	96	76	74	99	82	71	87
85212	MESA	109	120	118	126	115	112	111	109	102	115	130	128	113	129	107	95	128	107	93	120
85213	MESA	122	139	145	141	136	138	127	128	120	130	151	145	133	151	128	116	149	124	117	140
85215	MESA	121	128	133	125	129	142	117	125	116	123	146	132	121	135	123	118	140	121	129	138
85218	APACHE JUNCTION	129	130	129	124	135	153	119	132	122	125	152	134	122	135	128	128	145	127	146	148
85219	APACHE JUNCTION	93	84	75	79	89	102	80	90	85	83	105	95	78	95	84	89	98	88	102	106
85220	APACHE JUNCTION	72	67	62	63	70	79	63	71	67	66	82	76	62	76	66	69	77	69	79	83
85222	CASA GRANDE	77	71	63	69	72	77	71	75	72	72	90	84	68	84	70	72	86	75	76	85
85224	CHANDLER	111	119	122	125	115	115	114	113	107	117	136	133	115	134	111	101	133	112	99	124
85225	CHANDLER	102	104	104	107	100	101	103	101	99	106	125	119	102	123	99	93	124	102	90	111
85226	CHANDLER	137	147	149	155	141	139	139	136	129	144	165	161	142	163	135	121	163	136	118	150
85228	COOLIDGE	77	69	61	65	69	76	69	74	73	71	90	83	66	85	69	74	87	75	77	85
85231	ELOY	70	59	46	56	60	66	61	66	65	62	79	73	56	73	59	65	76	66	69	75
85232	FLORENCE	50	49	52	47	50	57	48	52	49	50	62	54	48	57	50	50	59	51	55	56
85233	GILBERT	135	149	147	155	142	139	138	136	127	143	162	159	141	161	134	119	160	134	117	149
85234	GILBERT	138	157	153	163	150	145	142	140	130	147	165	165	146	167	139	122	164	137	120	154
85236	HIGLEY	130	148	144	155	141	137	134	132	122	139	156	155	138	156	130	114	154	129	113	145
85237	KEARNY	84	69	51	65	74	85	70	78	77	68	91	89	65	89	71	80	85	77	90	97
85239	MARICOPA	73	66	54	63	66	70	65	69	66	67	82	79	61	77	63	65	79	69	68	80
85242	QUEEN CREEK	109	109	96	109	107	111	101	106	99	105	123	121	100	118	100	96	120	104	100	121
85247	SACATON	55	48	58	46	46	53	54	52	58	55	72	60	53	69	52	59	70	55	54	60
85248	CHANDLER	140	145	142	143	144	155	132	141	131	140	164	150	135	152	136	131	158	137	142	156
85249	CHANDLER	115	122	120	122	120	127	111	116	108	117	136	126	114	127	113	106	131	113	113	127
85250	SCOTTSDALE	111	115	131	114	116	128	113	115	114	115	143	128	116	137	116	115	138	116	118	128
85251	SCOTTSDALE	101	103	125	106	102	111	109	106	108	108	135	123	110	132	108	105	132	109	102	116
85253	PARADISE VALLEY	313	399	521	396	392	420	356	354	334	362	421	400	395	436	374	334	424	342	332	387
85254	SCOTTSDALE	156	186	204	190	180	182	170	167	158	172	200	195	180	205	171	152	199	163	149	183
85255	SCOTTSDALE	228	284	329	289	275	281	251	247	231	257	293	284	275	303	257	225	295	239	221	271
85256	SCOTTSDALE	80	56	30	49	63	72	55	66	64	55	76	79	48	72	55	69	70	66	80	92
85257	SCOTTSDALE	80	82	91	82	81	88	83	83	83	83	104	95	84	103	83	82	101	84	82	92
85258	SCOTTSDALE	173	192	213	189	192	210	177	183	174	182	218	198	187	210	185	177	213	178	186	203
85259	SCOTTSDALE	199	222	260	232	214	223	213	206	200	217	255	241	224	254	211	192	253	206	185	228
85260	SCOTTSDALE	162	174	194	183	169	174	170	166	161	173	204	195	175	202	167	153	202	167	149	183
85262	SCOTTSDALE	237	291	358	286	288	311	259	263	246	266	311	291	284	313	274	249	310	254	254	289
85263	RIO VERDE	207	192	182	182	204	240	178	203	189	190	234	200	180	196	193	202	219	197	238	233
85264	FORT MCDOWELL	140	122	91	117	125	134	117	129	121	120	148	150	109	141	116	121	141	128	132	157
85268	FOUNTAIN HILLS	137	140	149	136	143	162	132	141	134	137	168	148	136	154	140	139	161	138	152	157
85272	STANFIELD	66	58	49	54	56	59	60	64	62	65	78	68	55	69	57	60	77	66	60	67
85273	SUPERIOR	58	51	42	47	50	55	51	56	54	55	67	59	48	60	50	54	65	57	57	60
85281	TEMPE	62	50	61	54	49	54	68	59	66	63	83	75	61	78	60	61	80	66	55	66
85282	TEMPE	91	92	107	95	90	95	97	93	95	97	119	111	97	117	95	91	117	97	87	103
85283	TEMPE	109	113	131	118	109	113	115	111	111	116	140	132	116	139	112	106	138	114	101	123
85284	TEMPE	182	222	235	230	214	214	197	192	179	201	228	223	213	235	198	172	229	186	169	212
85287	TEMPE	112	87	113	98	86	96	124	107	122	115	154	138	112	143	110	112	149	122	99	119
85292	WINKELMAN	72	62	48	58	62	66	61	67	64	65	79	75	57	73	60	63	77	68	67	77
	ARIZONA	97	96	98	96	95	101	96	97	95	98	119	111	95	114	95	93	116	98	95	108
	UNITED STATES	100	100	100	100	100	100	100	100	100	100	100	100	100	100	100	100	100	100	100	100

POPULATION CHANGE

#	POST OFFICE NAME	COUNTY FIPS CODE	POPULATION			2000-2004 ANNUAL RATE		HOUSEHOLDS					FAMILIES		
			2000	2004	2009	% Rate	State Centile	2000	2004	2009	% Annual Rate 2000-2004	2004 Average HH Size	2000	2004	% Annual Rate 2000-2004
85296	GILBERT	013	32694	42148	52220	6.2	91	10055	12943	15962	6.1	3.25	8628	11094	6.1
85297	GILBERT	013	2728	5909	9224	19.9	100	802	1749	2729	20.1	3.38	697	1519	20.1
85301	GLENDALE	013	57519	64965	75362	2.9	70	19753	22224	25654	2.8	2.91	12943	14521	2.7
85302	GLENDALE	013	37042	40036	45466	1.9	47	14461	15703	17829	2.0	2.51	9293	10034	1.8
85303	GLENDALE	013	25117	29558	34938	3.9	79	7613	8935	10511	3.8	3.30	6039	7083	3.8
85304	GLENDALE	013	29375	30781	34255	1.1	29	9876	10356	11497	1.1	2.94	7742	8084	1.0
85305	GLENDALE	013	5673	7055	8543	5.3	89	1716	2118	2546	5.1	3.32	1477	1822	5.1
85306	GLENDALE	013	25932	27808	31350	1.7	41	9329	10158	11517	2.0	2.69	6584	7128	1.9
85307	GLENDALE	013	10424	12691	15488	4.7	86	3348	4145	5091	5.2	2.93	2736	3281	4.4
85308	GLENDALE	013	64729	77362	92717	4.3	83	22652	27149	32477	4.4	2.83	17655	21177	4.4
85309	LUKE AFB	013	682	679	742	-0.1	7	0	0	0	0.0	0.00	0	0	0.0
85310	GLENDALE	013	21602	27727	34139	6.1	91	6929	8919	10959	6.1	3.10	5915	7599	6.1
85321	AJO	019	3824	3705	3901	-0.7	1	1719	1686	1792	-0.5	2.19	1125	1101	-0.5
85322	ARLINGTON	013	527	646	776	4.9	87	169	208	249	5.0	3.11	127	156	5.0
85323	AVONDALE	013	35842	47008	58812	6.6	93	10633	13982	17450	6.7	3.35	8717	11487	6.7
85324	BLACK CANYON CITY	025	2747	3061	3484	2.6	63	1263	1416	1621	2.7	2.14	794	892	2.8
85326	BUCKEYE	013	18456	21742	25563	3.9	80	5235	6282	7468	4.4	3.15	4123	4945	4.4
85328	CIBOLA	012	1363	1322	1317	-0.7	1	548	536	541	-0.5	2.47	350	346	-0.3
85331	CAVE CREEK	013	22917	28308	34210	5.1	88	8942	11038	13289	5.1	2.56	7022	8680	5.1
85332	CONGRESS	025	3362	3772	4312	2.7	67	1635	1846	2121	2.9	2.04	1073	1216	3.0
85333	DATELAND	027	477	474	503	-0.2	6	134	134	144	0.0	3.31	102	102	0.0
85335	EL MIRAGE	013	7640	13989	20116	15.3	99	2127	3983	5768	15.9	3.51	1754	3281	15.9
85337	GILA BEND	013	2183	2250	2478	0.7	22	704	728	802	0.8	3.09	524	537	0.6
85338	GOODYEAR	013	19975	31516	42872	11.3	98	6506	10782	14928	12.6	2.70	5262	8719	12.6
85339	LAVEEN	013	6150	6335	7136	0.7	22	1812	1889	2131	1.0	3.33	1431	1482	0.8
85340	LITCHFIELD PARK	013	7114	9682	12459	7.5	95	2552	3438	4387	7.3	2.81	1986	2667	7.2
85342	MORRISTOWN	013	1192	1404	1654	3.9	80	497	587	691	4.0	2.39	369	434	3.9
85343	PALO VERDE	013	104	127	153	4.8	87	37	46	55	5.3	2.76	28	34	4.7
85344	PARKER	012	15812	16128	16453	0.5	17	6699	6988	7266	1.0	2.27	4527	4741	1.1
85345	PEORIA	013	53568	59494	68736	2.5	60	18909	20918	24067	2.4	2.82	13646	15083	2.4
85347	ROLL	027	1092	1089	1151	-0.1	7	309	311	331	0.2	3.36	239	240	0.1
85348	SALOME	012	2372	2582	2712	2.0	52	1051	1162	1244	2.4	2.22	701	782	2.6
85350	SOMERTON	027	27811	32017	36115	3.4	73	6201	7218	8227	3.6	4.11	5724	6680	3.7
85351	SUN CITY	013	29975	31202	34807	1.0	26	18226	19018	21205	1.0	1.60	9559	9919	0.9
85353	TOLLESON	013	7211	9552	12285	6.8	93	2097	2791	3583	7.0	3.42	1682	2241	7.0
85354	TONOPAH	013	2721	3625	4539	7.0	94	922	1233	1542	7.1	2.93	685	914	7.0
85355	WADDELL	013	2957	3764	4606	5.8	90	886	1132	1382	5.9	3.32	767	971	5.7
85356	WELLTON	027	5466	5665	6062	0.8	24	1979	2069	2227	1.1	2.73	1530	1598	1.0
85361	WITTMANN	013	2765	3267	3858	4.0	81	912	1081	1274	4.1	3.02	697	825	4.1
85362	YARNELL	025	16	17	19	1.4	35	7	8	8	3.2	2.13	4	5	5.4
85363	YOUNGTOWN	013	2775	2851	3136	0.6	21	1563	1609	1766	0.7	1.77	742	760	0.6
85364	YUMA	027	71754	76451	83959	1.5	36	24042	25677	28316	1.6	2.92	17834	19127	1.7
85365	YUMA	027	36597	41301	46432	2.9	69	13057	14872	16836	3.1	2.65	10045	11445	3.1
85367	YUMA	027	17006	20203	23133	4.1	82	8194	9751	11186	4.2	2.07	6232	7423	4.2
85373	SUN CITY	013	13188	15517	18573	3.9	78	7240	8316	9824	3.3	1.84	4442	5194	3.8
85374	SURPRISE	013	28821	41213	53626	8.8	97	11847	16659	21451	8.4	2.47	9159	12914	8.4
85375	SUN CITY WEST	013	26009	29119	33898	2.7	66	14802	16587	19271	2.7	1.74	10239	11520	2.8
85379	SURPRISE	013	1515	3712	6039	23.5	100	518	1313	2152	24.5	2.83	396	1005	24.5
85381	PEORIA	013	21615	25283	29871	3.8	75	7159	8438	9972	3.9	2.96	5693	6648	3.7
85382	PEORIA	013	29426	39749	50171	7.3	95	11832	15834	19852	7.1	2.48	8668	11706	7.3
85383	PEORIA	013	7246	11645	16285	11.8	99	2230	3585	4986	11.8	3.24	1967	3139	11.6
85387	SURPRISE	013	1869	2214	2617	4.1	82	573	681	804	4.2	3.25	449	533	4.1
85390	WICKENBURG	013	9486	10419	11883	2.2	55	4116	4519	5137	2.2	2.30	2688	2953	2.2
85501	GLOBE	007	13239	13034	13110	-0.4	4	5030	4976	5035	-0.3	2.50	3451	3435	-0.1
85530	BYLAS	009	1846	1934	1970	1.1	28	443	470	482	1.4	4.11	366	390	1.5
85533	CLIFTON	011	414	410	409	-0.2	5	149	149	149	0.0	2.70	120	120	0.0
85534	DUNCAN	011	2988	3034	3061	0.4	15	1138	1163	1177	0.5	2.60	810	832	0.6
85535	EDEN	009	77	80	81	0.9	25	23	24	24	1.0	3.33	18	19	1.3
85539	MIAMI	007	6181	5936	6016	-1.0	1	2484	2409	2460	-0.7	2.46	1691	1647	-0.6
85540	MORENCI	011	5147	5047	5012	-0.5	3	1830	1816	1815	-0.2	2.77	1337	1333	-0.1
85541	PAYSON	007	21252	22728	23673	1.6	39	9184	9865	10329	1.7	2.28	6305	6807	1.8
85542	PERIDOT	007	6331	6614	6818	1.0	27	1581	1659	1717	1.1	3.92	1313	1381	1.2
85543	PIMA	009	3669	3801	3850	0.8	24	1194	1245	1264	1.0	3.05	954	997	1.0
85544	PINE	007	3073	3336	3501	2.0	50	1419	1558	1649	2.2	2.14	992	1094	2.3
85545	ROOSEVELT	007	59	62	64	1.2	30	40	42	44	1.2	1.48	23	21	-2.1
85546	SAFFORD	009	18110	18090	18067	0.0	8	5857	5912	5933	0.2	2.69	4236	4293	0.3
85550	SAN CARLOS	009	2587	2583	2565	0.0	8	553	558	557	0.2	4.63	505	511	0.3
85552	THATCHER	009	5903	5982	5997	0.3	14	1855	1901	1916	0.6	3.00	1395	1436	0.7
85601	ARIVACA	019	79	81	86	0.6	19	55	57	61	0.8	1.42	32	29	-2.3
85602	BENSON	003	8969	9838	10712	2.2	54	3781	4207	4640	2.5	2.32	2597	2902	2.7
85603	BISBEE	003	8420	8415	8768	0.0	8	3652	3696	3902	0.3	2.21	2071	2106	0.4
85606	COCHISE	003	1389	1468	1565	1.3	32	629	673	726	1.6	2.18	421	451	1.6
85607	DOUGLAS	003	21258	21862	22992	0.7	22	6089	6322	6739	0.9	3.15	4639	4831	1.0
85610	ELFRIDA	003	1478	1541	1629	1.0	26	530	558	595	1.2	2.71	377	398	1.3
85611	ELGIN	023	818	884	982	1.8	47	341	375	422	2.3	2.35	242	265	2.2
85613	FORT HUACHUCA	003	5107	5118	5254	0.1	11	868	884	929	0.4	4.25	824	839	0.4
85614	GREEN VALLEY	019	19696	21247	23319	1.8	46	10882	11823	13058	2.0	1.78	7081	7707	2.0
85615	HEREFORD	003	6754	7863	8825	3.6	75	2567	3014	3420	3.9	2.60	1932	2276	3.9
85616	HUACHUCA CITY	003	4777	5485	6114	3.3	72	1876	2176	2451	3.6	2.51	1287	1497	3.6
85617	MC NEAL	003	1206	1247	1293	0.8	24	514	561	612	2.1	1.15	344	158	-16.7
85618	MAMMOTH	021	1779	1908	2224	1.7	41	570	619	732	2.0	3.08	447	487	2.0
85619	MOUNT LEMMON	019	132	157	179	4.2	83	59	71	82	4.5	2.17	45	55	4.8
85621	NOGALES	023	22923	24662	27602	1.7	45	6650	7272	8255	2.1	3.36	5492	6015	2.2
85623	ORACLE	021	4349	4836	5737	2.5	62	1724	1971	2394	3.2	2.41	1297	1494	3.4
85624	PATAGONIA	023	1252	1285	1388	0.6	21	585	614	675	1.1	2.09	353	369	1.1
85625	PEARCE	003	2004	2126	2270	1.4	34	934	1003	1084	1.7	2.11	619	666	1.7
85629	SAHUARITA	019	6178	8191	10091	6.9	94	2058	2732	3374	6.9	2.95	1585	2107	6.9
85630	SAINT DAVID	003	2716	2920	3140	1.7	44	1050	1146	1249	2.1	2.54	731	799	2.1
85631	SAN MANUEL	021	5766	5776	6689	0.0	10	1932	1966	2313	0.4	2.94	1557	1584	0.4
85632	SAN SIMON	003	1479	1533	1617	0.9	25	625	656	700	1.2	2.32	426	449	1.2
85634	SELLS	019	7492	7332	7721	-0.5	2	1997	1978	2099	-0.2	3.68	1524	1505	-0.3
85635	SIERRA VISTA	003	29002	30599	32903	1.3	31	12118	12918	14047	1.5	2.34	7871	8452	1.7
85637	SONOITA	023	830	899	998	1.9	48	369	405	455	2.2	2.19	271	297	2.2
85638	TOMBSTONE	003	2032	2159	2308	1.4	35	932	998	1077	1.6	2.16	570	613	1.7
85640	TUMACACORI	023	724	742	804	0.6	19	343	359	396	1.1	2.07	218	229	1.2
	ARIZONA					2.7					2.7	2.64			2.9
	UNITED STATES					1.2					1.3	2.58			1.1

ZIP CODE #	POST OFFICE NAME	RACE (%) White 2000	White 2004	Black 2000	Black 2004	Asian/Pacific 2000	Asian/Pacific 2004	% Hispanic Origin 2000	% Hispanic Origin 2004	2004 AGE DISTRIBUTION (%) 0-4	5-9	10-14	15-19	20-24	25-44	45-64	65-84	85+	18+	MEDIAN AGE 2004	% 2004 Males	% 2004 Females
85296	GILBERT	86.3	84.0	2.5	2.7	3.2	3.5	11.7	14.6	12.1	11.0	8.9	6.0	5.0	38.0	15.8	2.9	0.2	64.1	30.2	49.9	50.1
85297	GILBERT	87.0	83.5	1.4	1.9	0.8	1.0	16.6	20.9	11.3	10.1	9.5	7.3	4.9	34.2	18.2	4.3	0.3	64.3	30.2	51.0	49.0
85301	GLENDALE	60.5	57.2	7.0	6.9	1.4	1.5	46.1	51.1	10.6	9.1	8.1	7.4	9.5	29.8	16.6	7.9	1.0	67.9	28.0	50.1	49.9
85302	GLENDALE	80.9	78.2	3.9	4.2	3.2	3.4	17.3	21.0	7.1	6.5	7.0	6.9	9.1	28.9	23.4	9.3	1.7	75.6	33.6	49.0	51.0
85303	GLENDALE	62.9	59.6	7.2	7.3	2.4	2.5	42.0	47.0	11.0	9.8	9.2	8.0	8.4	32.1	17.5	3.7	0.2	65.1	27.1	50.4	49.7
85304	GLENDALE	85.1	82.9	3.1	3.4	3.2	3.7	12.1	14.8	6.3	6.7	8.4	8.0	8.0	27.8	26.6	7.1	1.2	73.8	34.7	49.4	50.6
85305	GLENDALE	75.2	72.2	6.1	6.4	1.8	2.0	26.0	30.8	9.1	9.3	9.9	8.1	5.8	34.4	19.3	3.9	0.3	66.2	31.1	49.9	50.1
85306	GLENDALE	85.9	83.9	2.0	2.2	4.3	4.9	10.9	13.4	6.4	6.5	7.5	7.1	8.0	31.6	24.0	7.4	1.5	75.4	34.0	49.3	50.7
85307	GLENDALE	74.0	71.5	7.7	7.3	2.9	3.1	22.5	27.6	11.2	9.4	8.2	7.5	10.8	34.4	14.7	3.6	0.2	67.3	26.6	52.0	48.1
85308	GLENDALE	89.1	87.5	2.1	2.3	3.4	4.0	8.7	10.6	7.6	7.7	7.8	6.8	6.3	32.6	25.3	5.5	0.5	72.7	34.7	49.8	50.3
85309	LUKE AFB	72.6	70.3	14.2	15.2	3.2	3.4	13.2	15.9	15.6	11.9	8.4	8.4	19.2	35.2	1.2	0.2	0.0	61.6	21.5	55.5	44.5
85310	GLENDALE	91.5	90.1	1.3	1.5	2.0	2.3	7.3	9.2	8.5	9.0	9.7	7.1	5.3	32.8	23.3	4.0	0.3	68.2	33.7	49.4	50.6
85321	AJO	78.5	76.2	0.2	0.3	0.4	0.4	37.1	42.1	5.4	5.2	6.1	5.5	4.4	15.7	25.8	29.5	2.6	79.9	51.9	47.7	52.3
85322	ARLINGTON	77.6	74.3	0.8	0.8	0.2	0.2	33.0	38.5	8.1	7.6	9.6	9.3	8.1	25.4	22.1	9.4	0.5	68.7	31.3	52.3	47.7
85323	AVONDALE	63.6	62.2	5.2	5.4	2.1	2.3	45.9	47.7	9.8	9.2	9.1	7.9	7.3	32.2	19.1	4.9	0.5	67.1	29.6	50.4	49.6
85324	BLACK CANYON CITY	96.1	95.8	0.3	0.3	0.3	0.4	3.7	4.4	4.0	4.1	4.7	5.9	4.0	18.4	34.4	22.4	2.1	83.0	50.3	51.2	48.8
85326	BUCKEYE	74.7	72.1	3.4	3.3	0.4	0.5	32.1	36.5	7.7	7.8	8.5	8.3	7.0	30.6	22.3	7.3	0.6	70.5	32.7	55.2	44.9
85328	CIBOLA	82.8	79.0	1.1	1.1	0.2	0.2	30.0	35.9	6.8	6.1	7.5	8.5	8.5	24.9	24.6	12.6	0.6	74.4	36.4	51.8	48.2
85331	CAVE CREEK	95.3	94.4	0.7	0.7	1.1	1.3	4.9	6.1	6.9	7.4	6.5	5.0	3.3	28.6	30.4	11.2	0.7	76.0	41.0	49.6	50.4
85332	CONGRESS	94.9	94.4	0.2	0.2	0.2	0.2	7.6	8.9	3.0	3.3	4.4	4.2	3.4	13.6	33.0	33.1	2.0	86.7	57.8	50.6	49.4
85333	DATELAND	77.2	75.7	0.4	0.4	0.2	0.2	72.8	77.0	9.1	9.1	10.6	9.9	7.6	27.4	17.7	8.7	0.0	65.4	27.9	56.5	43.5
85335	EL MIRAGE	66.1	65.1	3.4	3.1	0.5	0.6	66.6	68.9	12.5	11.0	9.5	8.0	7.9	30.7	14.7	5.4	0.3	62.3	25.6	51.4	48.7
85337	GILA BEND	48.2	44.8	1.1	1.2	0.3	0.3	44.2	49.2	8.6	8.2	9.0	7.2	8.3	27.0	21.9	9.0	0.8	69.8	31.1	50.7	49.3
85338	GOODYEAR	78.6	77.2	5.0	4.8	1.7	1.9	21.5	24.4	6.9	6.6	6.2	5.3	6.3	31.1	25.1	11.9	0.5	77.1	37.1	50.7	49.3
85339	LAVEEN	51.0	50.4	1.9	2.0	0.6	0.7	26.6	30.9	8.2	8.3	9.4	8.2	6.8	25.3	25.4	7.8	0.7	69.1	32.9	49.5	50.5
85340	LITCHFIELD PARK	86.7	84.3	1.8	1.9	2.6	2.7	14.9	19.3	6.0	6.7	7.9	7.0	5.6	23.9	28.0	13.9	1.0	74.8	40.7	49.9	50.1
85342	MORRISTOWN	84.7	82.1	0.8	1.0	0.3	0.4	21.3	25.3	6.4	6.5	7.0	6.1	5.4	20.6	27.8	18.7	1.5	76.3	43.5	50.4	49.6
85343	PALO VERDE	77.9	74.0	1.0	0.8	0.0	0.0	32.7	39.4	8.7	7.9	7.9	8.7	8.7	25.2	22.8	10.2	0.0	70.1	32.5	53.5	46.5
85344	PARKER	71.1	70.0	0.8	0.8	0.6	0.6	21.7	23.4	4.9	4.8	5.4	5.5	5.2	18.4	27.4	26.3	2.1	81.4	49.6	51.3	48.7
85345	PEORIA	78.4	75.7	3.7	3.9	1.8	1.9	23.4	27.4	8.2	7.9	8.4	7.3	6.8	30.8	19.7	9.2	1.7	71.0	32.7	48.6	51.4
85347	ROLL	75.2	73.1	0.9	1.0	0.2	0.2	60.5	65.4	8.5	8.5	10.0	9.0	7.5	26.2	20.6	9.4	0.5	67.6	30.3	55.3	44.7
85348	SALOME	89.7	87.4	0.2	0.2	0.4	0.5	22.0	26.9	3.7	3.8	5.9	5.3	4.2	15.1	27.7	32.8	1.4	83.3	55.6	50.9	49.1
85350	SOMERTON	53.8	53.0	1.8	1.6	0.3	0.3	87.6	90.0	9.6	9.0	10.3	10.2	10.2	29.1	16.2	5.1	0.3	65.0	25.5	52.5	47.5
85351	SUN CITY	98.1	97.8	0.6	0.7	0.4	0.5	1.2	1.6	0.4	0.3	0.3	0.3	0.3	2.3	16.8	62.7	16.7	98.8	74.8	41.2	58.8
85353	TOLLESON	57.6	56.6	1.2	1.0	0.6	0.5	67.1	66.9	9.5	8.1	9.6	8.2	7.3	27.9	20.7	8.2	0.7	67.8	30.2	50.9	49.1
85354	TONOPAH	76.8	73.0	1.7	1.9	0.1	0.1	30.8	36.5	8.3	8.6	9.1	7.1	6.5	25.2	24.3	10.7	0.4	69.7	34.8	52.1	47.9
85355	WADDELL	86.3	83.9	1.0	1.1	0.7	0.7	19.8	24.0	6.8	7.4	8.6	8.0	6.2	27.5	27.9	7.0	0.5	72.0	36.5	51.1	48.9
85356	WELLTON	70.9	67.0	2.3	2.4	0.5	0.5	35.4	40.9	7.3	7.2	7.4	7.3	7.2	21.7	22.4	18.5	0.9	73.7	37.8	52.1	47.9
85361	WITTMANN	78.8	75.4	1.3	1.5	0.3	0.3	30.3	35.8	8.2	8.3	8.6	6.9	6.1	24.3	25.2	11.5	1.0	70.7	35.8	50.7	49.3
85362	YARNELL	93.8	100.0	0.0	0.0	0.0	0.0	12.5	5.9	0.0	0.0	0.0	0.0	0.0	11.8	64.7	23.5	0.0	100.0	57.5	41.2	58.8
85363	YOUNGTOWN	88.0	85.7	1.5	1.6	0.9	1.0	13.7	16.9	3.3	3.2	3.4	3.1	2.8	13.8	23.9	39.1	7.4	88.2	63.0	43.3	56.8
85364	YUMA	63.5	61.2	2.7	2.8	1.4	1.5	55.1	59.4	9.2	8.4	8.6	8.1	8.0	26.7	19.0	10.7	1.4	68.8	30.7	49.1	50.9
85365	YUMA	77.2	74.9	2.4	2.4	1.3	1.4	33.3	37.5	7.3	6.6	7.0	6.4	8.8	22.4	20.5	19.6	1.5	75.7	37.9	51.3	48.7
85367	YUMA	91.4	89.7	0.4	0.5	0.6	0.7	10.8	13.3	3.0	2.9	2.8	2.5	2.0	10.9	25.2	47.9	2.9	89.9	65.3	49.0	51.0
85373	SUN CITY	96.8	95.8	0.9	1.1	0.5	0.6	3.1	4.5	3.3	2.9	2.4	1.8	1.5	11.1	17.6	46.8	12.6	90.2	69.3	44.3	55.7
85374	SURPRISE	86.9	85.5	2.6	2.8	1.1	1.2	22.4	24.5	7.2	6.0	5.0	3.8	3.9	22.5	21.2	28.6	1.8	79.5	47.5	48.8	51.2
85375	SUN CITY WEST	98.4	98.0	0.5	0.6	0.4	0.5	1.0	1.4	0.2	0.2	0.3	0.2	0.2	1.4	13.3	74.7	9.4	99.2	74.7	44.5	55.5
85379	SURPRISE	77.9	77.4	2.2	2.6	1.2	1.4	28.1	28.4	13.0	6.8	4.9	4.7	13.9	37.8	15.0	3.7	0.1	72.8	27.4	51.1	48.9
85381	PEORIA	88.2	86.5	2.5	2.7	3.2	3.5	10.4	12.8	6.5	7.4	9.1	8.4	6.2	27.0	25.5	6.1	3.9	71.7	36.8	47.7	52.3
85382	PEORIA	91.9	90.6	1.9	2.2	1.7	2.0	7.1	8.9	7.3	6.8	6.1	5.0	4.4	25.6	21.6	19.8	3.5	76.7	41.4	47.3	52.7
85383	PEORIA	93.2	91.0	1.1	1.5	1.3	2.1	7.0	8.8	9.1	9.3	8.5	6.7	4.7	32.0	23.5	5.7	0.5	68.8	34.6	50.1	49.9
85387	SURPRISE	87.5	85.6	1.0	1.1	0.5	0.6	16.7	19.7	4.5	4.5	4.8	3.9	3.4	14.1	23.5	39.6	1.7	83.7	60.2	48.8	51.2
85390	WICKENBURG	88.5	86.5	0.4	0.4	0.4	0.4	15.7	19.1	4.9	4.9	5.9	6.0	5.3	18.3	28.9	23.0	2.8	80.6	48.6	48.8	51.2
85501	GLOBE	81.7	79.0	0.7	0.7	0.8	0.9	29.0	34.6	6.5	6.7	7.1	6.8	6.0	23.5	27.0	14.2	2.3	75.3	40.1	49.9	50.1
85530	BYLAS	1.0	1.1	0.0	0.0	0.1	0.1	2.4	2.5	10.4	12.2	13.3	11.8	7.2	25.2	15.4	4.1	0.3	56.6	21.5	49.4	50.6
85533	CLIFTON	76.1	76.1	0.2	0.2	0.0	0.0	51.0	51.5	7.1	7.1	7.8	7.3	5.9	23.4	28.1	12.7	0.7	72.7	38.3	51.7	48.3
85534	DUNCAN	83.3	83.1	0.2	0.2	0.1	0.1	28.8	29.2	8.4	7.4	7.9	7.3	7.0	23.3	25.0	12.4	1.5	71.4	36.1	51.8	48.2
85535	EDEN	83.1	82.5	0.0	0.0	0.0	0.0	15.6	16.3	8.8	8.8	8.8	8.8	6.3	23.8	21.3	12.5	1.3	66.3	32.0	53.8	46.3
85539	MIAMI	80.0	77.7	0.8	0.9	0.2	0.2	37.1	41.9	6.9	6.7	6.6	6.4	6.0	21.2	27.2	17.0	2.0	75.6	42.0	49.0	51.0
85540	MORENCI	68.7	68.4	0.7	0.7	0.3	0.3	50.7	51.0	8.7	8.3	8.9	7.8	7.4	26.9	24.5	6.9	0.8	69.4	32.8	52.2	47.8
85541	PAYSON	95.1	94.5	0.2	0.2	0.5	0.5	5.1	6.5	4.8	4.8	5.5	5.4	4.6	17.5	29.9	24.7	2.8	81.5	50.3	48.9	51.1
85542	PERIDOT	4.1	3.9	0.1	0.1	0.2	0.3	2.5	2.7	10.1	10.5	12.1	10.8	7.7	25.2	18.0	5.4	0.3	60.1	24.3	49.5	50.5
85543	PIMA	85.4	84.0	0.3	0.4	0.3	0.2	19.3	21.9	10.2	9.4	8.9	7.7	7.2	24.2	20.0	11.2	1.2	66.8	30.1	50.3	49.7
85544	PINE	96.8	96.4	0.1	0.1	0.3	0.3	2.3	3.0	2.9	3.4	4.2	4.5	2.6	13.3	41.2	26.3	1.5	86.6	55.8	49.9	50.2
85545	ROOSEVELT	96.6	95.2	0.0	0.0	0.0	0.0	3.4	3.2	3.2	3.2	1.6	3.2	3.2	9.7	37.1	35.5	3.2	91.9	60.6	53.2	46.8
85546	SAFFORD	75.0	73.3	2.4	2.5	0.8	0.9	37.0	40.7	7.3	6.9	7.1	7.3	7.9	28.5	20.8	12.4	1.7	74.5	34.1	54.7	45.3
85550	SAN CARLOS	1.1	1.2	0.0	0.1	0.0	0.1	3.2	3.2	11.5	12.4	14.1	12.4	7.7	24.2	14.6	3.1	0.2	53.8	19.9	48.9	51.1
85552	THATCHER	84.1	82.4	0.8	0.8	0.6	0.7	20.5	23.3	7.9	7.5	8.7	13.4	11.1	20.2	19.3	10.2	1.7	70.7	26.3	46.7	53.3
85601	ARIVACA	87.3	86.4	0.0	0.0	0.0	0.0	25.3	29.6	3.7	3.7	4.9	4.9	6.2	18.5	33.3	22.2	2.5	82.7	50.3	51.9	48.2
85602	BENSON	90.7	89.3	0.5	0.5	0.5	0.5	15.2	18.5	5.4	5.4	6.1	6.1	5.2	18.5	29.1	22.0	2.3	79.4	47.4	49.7	50.3
85603	BISBEE	79.6	77.3	0.7	0.7	0.5	0.5	39.7	45.5	6.0	6.0	6.5	6.0	5.7	23.6	27.8	16.0	2.4	77.7	42.4	49.1	50.9
85606	COCHISE	91.7	90.1	0.2	0.2	0.8	0.9	12.5	15.7	3.8	4.0	5.0	5.5	4.5	15.3	32.0	26.9	3.1	83.8	53.2	49.5	50.5
85607	DOUGLAS	62.5	61.1	1.5	1.4	0.5	0.5	78.3	81.2	8.4	8.1	8.8	8.8	8.0	26.2	19.7	10.5	1.4	69.6	31.0	52.0	48.0
85610	ELFRIDA	81.6	79.0	0.9	0.9	0.7	0.7	32.5	38.0	5.2	5.9	8.3	8.9	5.6	18.3	27.3	19.0	1.6	74.6	43.2	51.4	48.6
85611	ELGIN	91.2	89.9	0.2	0.3	0.4	0.3	16.0	18.9	4.0	4.0	6.5	4.8	2.8	17.4	40.8	17.9	1.9	82.4	50.7	50.1	49.9
85613	FORT HUACHUCA	61.7	59.1	20.4	20.9	3.2	3.5	14.7	17.9	13.4	9.3	6.2	11.6	22.7	33.8	2.5	0.5	0.0	69.0	22.1	57.2	42.8
85614	GREEN VALLEY	96.6	96.1	0.2	0.3	0.4	0.5	6.6	8.0	1.3	1.3	1.6	1.4	1.1	5.4	21.2	58.1	8.6	94.9	70.8	45.0	55.0
85615	HEREFORD	86.3	84.7	1.4	1.5	1.2	1.3	15.2	18.3	5.8	6.0	7.4	7.4	4.6	23.0	32.0	12.9	0.8	75.6	42.4	49.8	50.2
85616	HUACHUCA CITY	80.6	78.9	4.3	4.2	1.1	1.2	14.7	17.8	5.8	6.6	8.1	7.8	5.5	23.0	28.4	13.8	1.0	74.6	40.8	49.1	50.9
85617	MC NEAL	70.7	67.7	8.0	7.9	0.3	0.2	25.1	30.0	2.3	2.5	3.6	5.3	10.2	39.6	24.9	10.7	0.9	88.5	37.9	74.7	25.3
85618	MAMMOTH	62.1	59.9	0.1	0.1	0.5	0.5	71.6	76.3	8.3	8.1	9.1	8.9	7.2	25.1	21.4	11.1	1.0	69.2	32.5	50.2	49.8
85619	MOUNT LEMMON	92.4	91.7	0.8	0.6	2.3	2.6	6.8	8.3	3.2	4.5	6.4	6.4	4.5	19.1	38.9	15.9	1.3	81.5	48.2	50.3	49.7
85621	NOGALES	77.5	77.7	0.4	0.4	0.4	0.4	92.5	93.7	8.9	8.7	9.7	9.2	7.7	24.6	20.7	9.4	1.1	66.9	29.8	47.3	52.7
85623	ORACLE	79.1	76.5	0.2	0.2	0.6	0.6	34.0	38.6	5.2	5.6	6.1	5.8	6.3	19.4	30.2	20.2	1.2	79.7	46.1	48.7	51.3
85624	PATAGONIA	87.6	86.4	0.2	0.2	0.4	0.4	33.7	38.5	3.9	4.5	5.8	5.8	4.4	17.9	35.6	19.7	2.4	82.3	50.6	47.9	52.1
85625	PEARCE	91.1	89.5	0.4	0.4	0.6	0.7	13.1	16.2	4.0	4.2	5.2	5.7	4.5	15.0	33.1	25.5	2.8	82.9	52.5	49.6	50.4
85629	SAHUARITA	86.0	82.1	0.7	0.7	0.6	0.6	25.4	32.2	6.4	6.5	7.0	6.7	6.3	25.5	27.1	12.8	1.8	75.9	39.7	49.8	50.2
85630	SAINT DAVID	92.9	91.7	0.6	0.7	0.5	0.5	9.9	12.4	5.6	5.5	7.1	7.5	5.9	15.8	29.7	20.9	2.1	76.8	46.9	49.7	50.3
85631	SAN MANUEL	68.1	63.9	0.3	0.4	0.4	0.4	48.4	55.0	8.3	8.2	8.7	8.4	6.8	25.5	22.4	10.9	0.7	69.4	32.7	50.9	49.1
85632	SAN SIMON	79.7	76.5	0.3	0.3	0.8	0.8	32.8	38.6	6.8	6.8	6.2	7.4	5.1	19.3	27.2	19.9	1.3	75.5	43.6	52.3	47.7
85634	SELLS	2.2	2.0	0.1	0.1	0.3	0.3	3.1	3.0	10.3	10.2	10.5	10.0	8.5	25.3	18.4	6.4	0.5	62.4	25.4	48.1	51.9
85635	SIERRA VISTA	75.9	74.1	8.1	8.2	4.1	4.4	18.1	21.6	6.6	6.0	6.7	7.0	7.4	25.6	25.5	13.8	1.6	76.4	38.4	47.9	52.1
85637	SONOITA	91.2	90.0	0.5	0.6	0.4	0.3	16.0	18.8	4.5	4.1	5.8	3.9	2.6	19.4	39.5	18.8	1.6	82.8	50.8	49.4	50.6
85638	TOMBSTONE	88.9	87.3	0.5	0.6	0.8	0.8	20.1	24.4	3.5	3.6	4.0	6.1	5.1	17.0	36.8	22.1	2.0	85.3	51.8	49.6	50.4
85640	TUMACACORI	79.4	78.2	0.1	0.1	1.0	0.9	43.0	46.5	4.9	5.4	5.3	4.5	4.5	18.9	33.6	20.6	2.6	81.7	49.3	48.9	51.1
	ARIZONA	75.5	74.0	3.1	3.2	1.9	2.1	25.3	27.9	7.6	7.1	7.3	6.9	7.5	28.1	22.1	11.9	1.5	74.0	34.8	49.9	50.2
	UNITED STATES	75.1	73.6	12.3	12.5	3.8	4.2	12.5	14.1	6.9	6.7	7.2	7.0	7.3	28.6	23.8	10.8	1.7	75.1	36.0	49.1	50.9

ZIP CODE #	POST OFFICE NAME	2004 Per Capita Income	2004 HH Income Base	2004 HOUSEHOLD INCOME DISTRIBUTION (%) Less than $25,000	$25,000 to $49,999	$50,000 to $99,999	$100,000 to $149,999	$150,000 or More	MEDIAN HOUSEHOLD INCOME 2004	2009	2004 National Centile	2004 State Centile	2004 Home Value Base	2004 HOME VALUE DISTRIBUTION (%) Less than $50,000	$50,000 to $89,999	$90,000 to $174,999	$175,000 to $399,999	$400,000 or More	2004 Median Home Value
85296	GILBERT	30196	12943	3.4	12.0	46.9	27.3	10.4	84575	105464	96	95	12173	0.4	0.4	27.6	66.9	4.7	204985
85297	GILBERT	25174	1749	5.8	16.9	47.1	22.8	7.4	75906	92327	94	90	1589	1.3	0.6	14.4	71.4	12.4	247911
85301	GLENDALE	14584	22224	34.7	33.9	26.3	4.2	0.9	34989	43290	27	29	10378	24.1	27.2	44.1	4.3	0.4	88446
85302	GLENDALE	23691	15703	20.3	28.8	36.1	11.9	3.0	50751	62760	73	69	9606	3.3	11.6	70.6	14.1	0.3	133021
85303	GLENDALE	17678	8935	21.3	29.3	37.2	10.1	2.1	49332	60829	71	67	5862	3.0	11.1	71.9	13.4	0.6	126168
85304	GLENDALE	26355	10356	12.4	23.5	38.9	18.1	7.0	63895	79438	88	83	7711	0.0	2.5	69.3	27.2	1.0	148530
85305	GLENDALE	23687	2118	3.2	20.9	54.4	16.9	4.6	68387	82475	91	86	1956	6.8	2.9	72.2	17.3	0.8	145142
85306	GLENDALE	25504	10158	16.1	24.4	40.2	14.0	5.4	58396	72022	83	78	6652	1.1	8.5	67.4	21.9	1.2	140510
85307	GLENDALE	21807	4145	11.7	35.7	37.7	13.0	1.9	52505	64968	76	72	2305	8.3	11.0	53.2	25.0	2.6	143080
85308	GLENDALE	32814	27149	7.3	16.7	42.6	22.7	10.8	77809	98043	94	92	22653	0.8	2.2	41.2	52.3	3.6	187003
85309	LUKE AFB	2689	0	0.0	0.0	0.0	0.0	0.0	0	0	0	0	0	0.0	0.0	0.0	0.0	0.0	0
85310	GLENDALE	35216	8919	3.2	10.6	43.5	29.1	13.5	89654	112309	97	96	8555	0.7	1.2	31.9	60.4	5.8	199654
85321	AJO	17803	1686	42.1	35.7	16.1	4.1	2.1	29789	36042	12	17	1326	19.2	43.3	32.2	4.7	0.7	79613
85322	ARLINGTON	17961	208	29.3	31.3	28.9	6.3	4.3	40967	54112	50	49	152	19.7	15.1	44.7	17.8	2.6	108333
85323	AVONDALE	20900	13982	16.0	23.6	41.4	13.7	5.2	59577	72297	84	79	11051	9.9	10.9	41.5	37.2	0.5	157118
85324	BLACK CANYON CITY	23863	1416	35.2	31.2	23.2	6.1	4.2	36777	44442	35	36	1190	16.8	27.7	40.9	12.8	1.8	98228
85326	BUCKEYE	19426	6282	23.2	28.7	34.2	10.2	3.7	47638	60345	67	64	4686	17.0	17.2	40.3	23.5	2.0	118347
85328	CIBOLA	17492	536	34.5	26.1	35.6	3.7	0.0	40309	50479	47	47	373	55.0	7.0	30.6	3.2	4.3	38021
85331	CAVE CREEK	48450	11038	6.7	12.9	34.0	25.7	20.7	93601	121973	98	97	10185	1.1	0.4	7.3	63.2	27.9	298927
85332	CONGRESS	22707	1846	39.0	33.3	19.8	5.4	2.6	32472	38604	19	24	1582	14.7	24.6	39.7	16.1	5.0	104259
85333	DATELAND	11999	134	42.5	34.3	17.2	4.5	1.5	28675	33597	10	15	62	64.5	14.5	19.4	1.6	0.0	31000
85335	EL MIRAGE	14024	3983	22.7	39.1	29.8	6.7	1.8	40449	49576	48	48	2831	12.3	27.3	48.9	9.4	2.2	98695
85337	GILA BEND	13124	728	37.8	36.1	21.7	2.6	1.8	32734	40060	20	25	475	48.8	27.2	16.6	5.3	2.1	51196
85338	GOODYEAR	29714	10782	9.6	23.6	41.8	17.1	7.8	66539	82395	89	85	9309	3.0	3.2	38.6	51.4	3.9	185497
85339	LAVEEN	20070	1889	27.6	21.2	30.6	12.9	7.8	51238	64690	74	70	1478	16.6	14.8	22.4	42.3	3.9	162500
85340	LITCHFIELD PARK	35343	3438	11.4	22.3	33.9	18.7	13.7	71672	89859	92	88	2751	6.6	7.3	31.2	43.6	11.5	187277
85342	MORRISTOWN	21557	587	28.1	33.9	27.9	6.8	3.2	39663	49044	45	45	470	24.3	19.8	31.7	21.3	3.0	99333
85343	PALO VERDE	20002	46	28.3	30.4	30.4	6.5	4.4	41530	56611	51	50	34	23.5	14.7	41.2	17.7	2.9	105000
85344	PARKER	18756	6988	40.3	33.7	18.8	5.0	2.2	31078	37060	15	21	5574	36.7	26.2	27.1	7.7	2.3	70722
85345	PEORIA	22867	20918	17.0	28.0	41.0	11.3	2.7	53623	65794	78	75	16193	12.5	12.7	65.4	9.1	0.3	119349
85347	ROLL	13638	311	37.9	33.1	20.6	5.5	2.9	31622	38476	17	23	172	44.8	17.4	30.8	5.8	1.2	63750
85348	SALOME	14982	1162	51.2	32.2	12.5	1.8	2.3	24326	27929	4	8	977	46.2	30.8	17.9	3.6	1.5	55515
85350	SOMERTON	9278	7218	43.6	35.2	17.5	2.9	0.9	28552	33554	10	15	5094	17.6	40.3	37.4	4.0	0.9	83801
85351	SUN CITY	31111	19018	30.4	35.2	24.6	6.7	3.1	37390	46480	37	38	17029	2.1	20.5	67.4	9.6	0.4	111326
85353	TOLLESON	16594	2791	22.9	29.2	36.8	8.9	2.2	47496	59155	67	64	1958	11.3	31.4	37.6	18.0	1.7	102245
85354	TONOPAH	17127	1233	31.2	32.4	26.4	7.8	2.1	37386	49542	37	38	920	23.6	16.9	43.7	12.8	3.0	104938
85355	WADDELL	23913	1132	10.8	19.5	39.6	25.9	4.2	76266	91448	94	91	979	2.4	4.8	27.5	55.6	9.8	216035
85356	WELLTON	17131	2069	32.2	33.7	26.9	5.4	1.8	36263	44147	33	33	1507	34.4	23.2	34.4	6.7	1.2	78311
85361	WITTMANN	14944	1081	30.8	35.1	27.3	5.7	1.1	36462	45159	33	34	852	22.1	30.9	38.9	7.9	0.4	85455
85362	YARNELL	17941	8	50.0	12.5	37.5	0.0	0.0	30000	40000	12	18	7	0.0	0.0	100.0	0.0	0.0	112500
85363	YOUNGTOWN	20209	1609	45.5	35.2	13.5	4.5	1.2	26946	33371	7	13	947	8.8	56.8	33.9	0.5	0.0	83203
85364	YUMA	17805	25677	32.9	30.9	25.1	7.6	3.6	37183	45567	36	37	15892	19.8	28.9	41.9	8.8	0.7	91258
85365	YUMA	23317	14872	23.7	31.5	31.3	8.8	4.8	44734	55943	60	58	11849	23.5	21.2	37.6	15.8	1.8	98276
85367	YUMA	25188	9751	27.7	35.7	28.1	5.2	3.3	39763	48578	45	46	8979	14.3	29.6	42.4	13.3	0.5	96800
85373	SUN CITY	31464	8316	20.5	32.0	35.0	9.8	2.7	47644	60223	68	64	7335	5.0	7.4	63.0	24.4	0.3	140467
85374	SURPRISE	27132	16659	15.5	30.9	39.1	10.1	4.4	52645	65328	76	72	14658	5.4	8.2	48.6	34.3	3.6	155853
85375	SUN CITY WEST	40174	16587	14.7	33.2	34.7	11.3	6.2	51502	64076	75	71	15788	0.3	1.5	47.8	47.3	3.1	175728
85379	SURPRISE	23368	1313	7.2	32.2	47.3	11.1	2.2	58737	71076	83	79	1233	1.1	1.7	74.8	21.9	0.6	145150
85381	PEORIA	31328	8438	8.8	16.5	41.6	22.9	10.2	78026	96650	94	92	7317	0.6	3.5	42.6	50.5	2.9	180056
85382	PEORIA	31983	15834	10.5	23.6	41.2	18.1	6.5	64762	80605	88	83	13764	1.2	3.6	40.3	53.6	1.3	181437
85383	PEORIA	29862	3585	6.7	12.7	41.8	29.3	9.5	85240	106589	96	95	3492	1.7	0.1	15.6	65.5	17.3	264286
85387	SURPRISE	19517	681	19.1	33.3	33.2	9.5	4.9	47298	59532	67	63	604	8.4	12.6	32.8	43.4	2.8	166016
85390	WICKENBURG	23503	4519	30.7	31.1	27.1	7.6	3.5	39774	49883	45	46	3160	24.9	9.7	28.6	31.6	5.3	129833
85501	GLOBE	19815	4976	30.7	30.2	30.7	6.4	2.0	40478	48271	48	48	3871	22.6	29.1	38.7	8.9	0.7	87629
85530	BYLAS	5902	470	62.3	26.8	10.4	0.4	0.0	18612	21630	1	4	244	63.9	29.9	6.2	0.0	0.0	37727
85533	CLIFTON	19412	149	17.5	39.6	34.9	6.7	1.3	45200	50296	62	59	128	22.7	33.6	39.8	3.1	0.8	83846
85534	DUNCAN	16022	1163	34.7	33.9	27.8	2.8	1.0	35568	41001	30	31	936	34.5	34.4	26.5	3.7	0.9	72959
85535	EDEN	13292	24	33.3	29.2	29.2	8.3	0.0	35000	50000	28	30	19	15.8	21.1	52.6	10.5	0.0	104167
85539	MIAMI	19829	2409	34.7	30.4	26.8	5.3	2.8	36465	44132	33	34	1879	32.6	29.4	30.3	6.9	0.8	71568
85540	MORENCI	19646	1816	17.6	36.5	38.9	5.3	1.8	47852	54584	68	65	562	32.7	33.5	29.0	4.5	0.4	71250
85541	PAYSON	23989	9865	31.5	31.6	25.9	6.5	4.5	38186	47637	40	40	7938	11.6	9.7	44.2	29.0	5.4	141153
85542	PERIDOT	6966	1659	61.9	23.8	12.9	0.6	0.8	19202	21834	2	5	1197	71.6	20.6	6.0	1.3	0.6	26080
85543	PIMA	14780	1245	35.0	29.9	29.1	4.3	1.7	36352	43173	33	33	1025	21.0	25.7	43.9	8.8	0.7	93920
85544	PINE	30331	1558	24.3	29.4	29.7	9.5	7.1	46706	59121	66	61	1349	4.4	6.5	38.3	45.5	5.3	177319
85545	ROOSEVELT	25069	42	47.6	31.0	19.1	2.4	0.0	26489	30000	6	12	36	27.8	25.0	22.2	19.4	5.6	85000
85546	SAFFORD	16474	5912	35.6	29.5	28.3	4.9	1.7	36434	44842	33	33	4492	21.6	28.3	40.3	8.9	0.9	90100
85550	SAN CARLOS	6761	558	52.5	26.0	19.5	1.3	0.7	23447	27991	3	7	392	54.1	36.2	8.2	0.0	1.5	46190
85552	THATCHER	17188	1901	29.8	31.7	28.7	6.9	2.9	39335	48027	44	43	1433	12.6	24.4	49.6	13.2	0.3	104712
85601	ARIVACA	23333	57	50.9	21.1	26.3	1.8	0.0	24497	31710	4	9	43	23.3	27.9	32.6	11.6	4.7	89000
85602	BENSON	21541	4207	32.7	32.3	27.2	5.7	2.2	36454	45161	33	34	3312	26.8	26.5	33.1	11.1	2.5	84416
85603	BISBEE	19511	3696	37.0	35.0	22.9	3.5	1.7	34132	41379	24	27	2658	15.1	41.9	33.2	8.2	1.7	83428
85606	COCHISE	20314	673	42.2	26.3	25.9	4.0	1.6	31952	39290	18	23	563	19.5	26.8	40.0	11.7	2.0	93727
85607	DOUGLAS	11880	6322	51.7	25.6	18.1	2.5	2.0	23849	28310	4	8	4228	31.6	33.1	30.9	4.4	0.1	72609
85610	ELFRIDA	16338	558	44.8	29.6	19.9	3.8	2.0	27741	33511	8	13	447	32.2	26.9	28.0	9.0	4.0	79000
85611	ELGIN	33910	375	16.5	19.5	37.1	17.1	9.9	65807	90562	89	84	324	2.8	6.8	19.8	48.8	21.9	241489
85613	FORT HUACHUCA	11483	884	22.2	47.5	26.2	4.1	0.0	38208	45918	40	40	31	16.1	41.9	25.8	16.1	0.0	86875
85614	GREEN VALLEY	37802	11823	20.4	30.8	31.6	10.4	6.9	48905	61793	70	66	10544	3.7	12.0	47.2	34.0	3.2	145325
85615	HEREFORD	24411	3014	18.6	29.3	36.0	11.6	4.5	51383	62617	75	70	2582	10.5	16.6	43.8	26.5	2.6	120366
85616	HUACHUCA CITY	18459	2176	33.6	36.1	22.8	5.7	1.8	35836	42868	31	32	1677	19.1	33.7	41.4	5.5	0.4	87527
85617	MC NEAL	25339	561	42.3	25.0	28.0	3.9	0.9	31160	38356	15	21	461	19.7	33.2	34.3	10.0	2.8	86538
85618	MAMMOTH	12664	619	37.5	35.1	23.8	3.4	0.3	34921	40461	27	29	465	40.9	41.5	14.4	1.7	1.5	58854
85619	MOUNT LEMMON	61361	71	12.7	15.5	31.0	19.7	21.1	82170	111043	96	94	61	0.0	4.9	9.8	65.6	19.7	253125
85621	NOGALES	13834	7272	45.0	25.3	21.1	4.8	3.8	27930	35583	9	14	4652	17.3	19.9	45.4	13.0	4.5	106973
85623	ORACLE	27312	1971	22.4	25.6	33.0	12.7	6.2	51863	63281	75	72	1647	12.7	12.8	40.7	29.4	4.5	124632
85624	PATAGONIA	22554	614	36.5	28.5	25.2	7.5	2.3	34574	48410	26	27	470	25.3	15.1	23.8	29.8	6.0	118269
85625	PEARCE	20348	1003	42.7	27.7	24.4	3.9	1.3	30247	36947	13	18	839	20.4	27.3	37.9	11.9	2.5	92468
85629	SAHUARITA	24473	2732	18.3	25.6	36.8	13.3	5.9	55218	70082	80	76	2277	12.8	14.8	43.0	26.8	2.6	131799
85630	SAINT DAVID	18054	1146	30.5	36.7	26.5	3.3	3.0	37018	44768	35	37	927	29.5	18.0	37.5	13.3	1.7	93983
85631	SAN MANUEL	18927	1966	24.0	34.3	32.0	6.0	3.7	43078	50049	56	53	1541	26.9	40.6	29.9	1.4	1.1	74220
85632	SAN SIMON	14881	656	50.9	28.5	15.1	4.6	0.9	24482	28679	4	9	532	43.4	29.3	18.1	6.8	2.4	57143
85634	SELLS	7949	1978	56.8	25.1	15.3	2.3	0.5	20344	25364	2	5	1268	54.6	27.4	16.2	1.5	0.4	41471
85635	SIERRA VISTA	23377	12918	25.2	32.4	30.6	8.7	3.1	42988	52649	56	53	7870	8.4	18.3	59.7	13.1	0.5	111729
85637	SONOITA	36881	405	17.0	19.3	35.8	16.8	11.1	66507	93133	89	85	356	2.3	5.1	17.1	51.7	23.9	253659
85638	TOMBSTONE	19041	998	40.8	29.4	23.9	4.2	1.8	32207	39684	18	24	784	15.3	27.8	45.0	9.6	2.3	97200
85640	TUMACACORI	36836	359	30.9	23.7	21.5	16.2	7.8	45133	64438	62	59	290	13.8	19.0	25.9	29.0	12.4	145455
	ARIZONA	25625		22.8	27.9	31.5	11.3	6.4	49168	61784				9.8	13.0	42.4	28.8	6.1	140071
	UNITED STATES	25866		24.7	27.1	30.8	10.9	6.5	48124	56710				10.9	15.0	33.7	30.1	10.4	145905

ZIP CODE #	POST OFFICE NAME	FINANCIAL SERVICES: Auto Loan	FINANCIAL SERVICES: Home Loan	FINANCIAL SERVICES: Investments	FINANCIAL SERVICES: Retirement Plans	THE HOME: Home Improvements: Home Repair	THE HOME: Home Improvements: Lawn & Garden	THE HOME: Furnishings: Computers & Hardware	THE HOME: Furnishings: Major Appliances	THE HOME: Furnishings: TV, Radio, Sound Equipment	THE HOME: Furnishings: Furniture	ENTERTAINMENT: Dine out/Carry out	ENTERTAINMENT: Sports Equipment	ENTERTAINMENT: Fees & Tickets	ENTERTAINMENT: Toys & Games	ENTERTAINMENT: Travel	ENTERTAINMENT: Cable TV	PERSONAL: Apparel & Services	PERSONAL: Auto Repairs	PERSONAL: Health Insurance	PERSONAL: Pets & Supplies
85296	GILBERT	140	159	154	166	152	147	144	142	131	149	167	167	148	168	140	123	165	138	121	156
85297	GILBERT	120	138	135	142	132	128	124	123	114	128	144	144	128	146	122	107	143	119	105	135
85301	GLENDALE	61	55	57	56	54	57	60	59	61	61	76	69	58	73	57	58	75	62	56	65
85302	GLENDALE	82	84	93	87	82	85	87	84	83	86	105	100	86	104	84	80	103	86	77	93
85303	GLENDALE	84	85	85	88	82	83	84	83	81	86	102	98	83	100	81	76	101	84	74	92
85304	GLENDALE	107	116	125	120	113	114	113	110	107	114	135	130	116	136	111	101	133	110	98	121
85305	GLENDALE	113	127	123	133	121	117	115	114	105	120	134	133	118	134	112	98	133	111	97	125
85306	GLENDALE	95	102	109	105	99	100	100	98	95	101	120	116	101	120	98	90	118	99	88	108
85307	GLENDALE	97	89	88	95	85	89	94	91	91	95	115	110	90	110	88	86	112	95	82	103
85308	GLENDALE	131	147	147	152	141	139	136	134	126	139	160	157	139	161	133	119	158	132	117	148
85309	LUKE AFB	0	0	0	0	0	0	0	0	0	0	0	0	0	0	0	0	0	0	0	0
85310	GLENDALE	155	177	173	184	169	164	160	158	146	165	186	185	165	187	156	137	184	154	135	173
85321	AJO	57	55	58	50	58	70	51	59	55	55	68	55	52	57	56	59	63	57	69	64
85322	ARLINGTON	89	81	63	78	81	86	77	83	78	79	96	96	73	91	76	77	93	82	82	98
85323	AVONDALE	102	104	99	106	100	100	100	101	97	105	122	116	100	119	97	91	121	101	90	109
85324	BLACK CANYON CITY	75	72	76	66	76	92	67	77	72	72	89	72	68	75	73	77	83	75	91	84
85326	BUCKEYE	93	86	72	83	86	90	84	89	85	86	106	102	80	101	82	84	103	89	88	103
85328	CIBOLA	69	63	49	60	63	66	60	64	60	61	75	74	56	70	59	60	72	64	64	76
85331	CAVE CREEK	171	197	204	201	192	195	178	179	167	183	211	205	187	211	180	161	208	174	163	197
85332	CONGRESS	69	65	67	60	69	83	60	70	65	65	80	66	62	68	66	70	75	67	82	77
85333	DATELAND	60	52	44	49	50	53	53	58	56	58	70	61	49	62	51	54	69	59	54	60
85335	EL MIRAGE	74	61	57	60	62	65	67	69	71	71	89	80	64	87	64	68	89	73	66	77
85337	GILA BEND	62	55	45	51	53	55	56	60	58	61	73	64	51	64	53	56	72	61	56	63
85338	GOODYEAR	113	120	119	122	118	122	112	114	108	116	136	129	114	130	112	105	132	112	108	126
85339	LAVEEN	92	96	102	93	94	97	94	94	94	96	117	108	95	117	93	92	116	95	90	105
85340	LITCHFIELD PARK	140	146	147	143	148	156	138	143	137	138	170	166	140	172	141	137	166	141	142	166
85342	MORRISTOWN	82	70	53	67	73	81	70	76	74	70	90	86	65	84	70	76	85	76	83	91
85343	PALO VERDE	88	80	63	77	80	85	76	82	77	79	95	95	72	90	75	76	92	82	81	97
85344	PARKER	64	59	56	55	62	70	57	64	60	59	74	67	56	67	59	62	70	63	70	72
85345	PEORIA	93	97	95	98	95	98	92	94	89	95	112	107	92	109	91	86	109	93	88	104
85347	ROLL	70	61	51	57	58	62	63	67	65	68	82	72	58	72	60	63	81	69	63	70
85348	SALOME	49	47	49	43	49	60	43	50	47	47	58	47	44	49	47	50	54	48	59	54
85350	SOMERTON	53	46	43	45	45	46	50	51	52	53	66	57	47	63	47	49	66	54	47	54
85351	SUN CITY	74	71	75	65	74	90	66	76	71	71	88	71	67	74	72	76	82	73	89	82
85353	TOLLESON	88	79	63	74	78	82	78	84	80	82	100	93	72	92	75	79	98	85	82	94
85354	TONOPAH	80	73	57	70	73	77	70	75	70	71	87	86	66	82	69	69	83	74	74	88
85355	WADDELL	103	128	136	128	126	124	114	114	106	114	133	134	122	142	117	103	133	110	102	126
85356	WELLTON	70	63	62	59	64	75	63	69	66	67	83	70	61	71	64	68	78	69	76	75
85361	WITTMANN	72	65	51	63	65	69	62	67	63	64	78	77	59	74	62	63	75	67	67	80
85362	YARNELL	65	50	36	45	55	65	48	58	55	50	66	63	44	60	50	59	60	57	70	74
85363	YOUNGTOWN	52	50	53	46	53	64	47	54	50	50	62	50	48	52	51	54	58	52	64	58
85364	YUMA	76	71	70	71	70	74	73	75	74	76	93	84	70	87	71	71	91	77	72	82
85365	YUMA	93	88	85	84	90	101	85	92	88	88	109	98	84	100	88	90	104	91	99	105
85367	YUMA	76	73	77	67	77	93	68	79	73	73	90	74	69	76	74	78	84	76	93	85
85373	SUN CITY	83	82	88	78	85	99	78	86	81	82	101	87	79	89	83	85	95	84	96	94
85374	SURPRISE	99	97	96	95	99	110	91	99	93	96	116	103	92	103	95	94	111	97	104	110
85375	SUN CITY WEST	103	99	102	91	104	126	91	106	98	99	122	100	94	102	100	105	114	102	125	116
85379	SURPRISE	94	105	103	109	101	98	96	95	89	100	113	112	99	113	94	83	112	93	82	104
85381	PEORIA	130	146	151	150	142	145	134	134	126	137	159	154	140	158	134	121	157	131	123	148
85382	PEORIA	114	118	121	119	118	125	112	116	110	116	138	129	113	130	113	108	133	115	114	128
85383	PEORIA	134	153	158	159	148	147	141	139	130	144	165	163	146	167	139	123	163	136	122	153
85387	SURPRISE	98	91	80	87	94	106	85	94	88	90	110	99	84	96	89	91	104	93	103	110
85390	WICKENBURG	84	69	57	65	75	90	72	80	79	72	95	84	67	86	74	84	87	79	96	93
85501	GLOBE	81	65	46	62	69	80	67	74	73	66	88	85	62	84	67	76	81	74	84	90
85530	BYLAS	33	27	37	25	26	31	33	31	37	34	46	36	32	44	32	38	45	34	34	36
85533	CLIFTON	84	76	60	73	76	80	73	78	74	75	91	90	69	86	72	73	87	78	77	92
85534	DUNCAN	64	58	49	56	58	62	58	61	59	59	73	70	55	70	57	59	70	61	61	71
85535	EDEN	80	56	29	53	65	73	55	68	64	55	75	82	47	73	57	67	68	67	81	95
85539	MIAMI	75	65	56	63	68	76	66	72	70	67	86	79	63	80	67	72	81	71	78	83
85540	MORENCI	79	80	75	80	78	79	78	79	75	80	95	91	76	92	76	72	93	80	72	87
85541	PAYSON	85	75	67	70	81	95	72	82	78	75	95	84	70	83	77	83	88	80	97	97
85542	PERIDOT	38	32	37	30	31	37	36	36	40	37	49	41	35	47	35	41	48	38	39	41
85543	PIMA	75	63	44	60	66	71	60	68	64	61	77	79	55	74	61	64	73	67	72	85
85544	PINE	110	86	59	78	97	109	81	98	92	81	109	115	73	108	87	98	102	97	116	134
85545	ROOSEVELT	54	52	55	47	55	66	48	56	52	52	64	52	49	54	53	56	60	54	66	60
85546	SAFFORD	68	59	45	56	61	67	59	64	62	59	75	73	55	72	58	63	71	63	68	76
85550	SAN CARLOS	43	35	48	32	33	40	42	41	48	44	59	46	41	56	41	49	58	44	44	46
85552	THATCHER	81	71	59	70	72	77	72	76	74	72	90	90	67	87	70	72	87	77	77	91
85601	ARIVACA	48	46	49	42	49	59	43	50	46	47	58	47	44	48	47	50	54	48	59	54
85602	BENSON	78	69	58	65	71	81	67	75	71	69	87	80	64	79	69	74	82	74	82	86
85603	BISBEE	66	56	47	53	57	65	59	63	63	59	77	70	55	72	58	65	73	63	69	72
85606	COCHISE	66	61	60	56	64	78	58	67	63	61	77	64	58	66	62	67	72	65	79	74
85607	DOUGLAS	55	49	40	45	47	49	49	53	51	54	65	57	45	57	47	50	64	54	50	56
85610	ELFRIDA	72	54	35	52	59	71	60	66	67	57	79	73	53	74	59	71	72	65	79	79
85611	ELGIN	121	113	108	107	120	141	105	119	111	112	138	117	106	115	114	118	129	116	139	136
85613	FORT HUACHUCA	70	44	42	51	41	48	66	57	67	61	84	76	56	75	54	61	80	67	53	65
85614	GREEN VALLEY	99	95	98	88	100	119	89	102	95	95	118	98	90	100	96	101	110	98	118	112
85615	HEREFORD	105	88	64	84	93	101	85	95	90	86	109	112	78	105	86	91	103	94	102	120
85616	HUACHUCA CITY	74	65	49	63	66	72	64	69	66	65	81	79	60	76	63	66	77	69	71	82
85617	MC NEAL	13	10	7	10	11	13	11	12	12	10	14	14	10	14	11	13	13	12	14	15
85618	MAMMOTH	60	53	43	49	51	54	53	58	56	58	70	62	49	62	51	54	69	59	55	61
85619	MOUNT LEMMON	220	184	143	169	203	230	172	203	190	174	229	228	161	217	185	202	214	199	237	263
85621	NOGALES	71	62	53	58	60	63	64	68	66	69	83	73	59	75	61	64	83	70	64	71
85623	ORACLE	103	90	73	89	94	106	90	97	95	90	116	108	87	111	91	97	109	96	106	114
85624	PATAGONIA	76	58	41	56	63	76	63	70	70	61	83	77	57	78	63	74	76	70	83	84
85625	PEARCE	65	57	52	53	61	74	57	64	62	58	75	65	55	66	60	66	69	63	76	73
85629	SAHUARITA	112	102	83	99	105	111	97	105	100	99	123	123	93	119	97	100	117	104	107	128
85630	SAINT DAVID	74	56	37	53	61	73	62	68	69	58	81	76	55	77	61	73	74	68	81	82
85631	SAN MANUEL	88	78	62	74	81	86	75	82	78	76	96	96	71	93	75	79	91	82	86	101
85632	SAN SIMON	56	42	28	40	46	55	46	51	52	44	61	57	41	58	46	55	56	51	61	61
85634	SELLS	42	33	39	30	33	40	39	39	44	40	54	43	38	50	38	47	52	41	44	45
85635	SIERRA VISTA	74	76	85	77	75	81	78	77	77	78	97	89	79	96	78	76	95	78	75	85
85637	SONOITA	126	114	105	108	122	143	106	122	113	113	140	122	106	119	115	121	131	119	143	142
85638	TOMBSTONE	66	50	33	48	55	65	55	61	62	52	73	68	49	69	55	65	66	61	73	73
85640	TUMACACORI	121	97	74	93	105	125	102	113	112	100	134	121	94	122	103	118	123	112	134	134
	ARIZONA	97	96	98	96	95	101	96	97	95	98	119	111	95	114	95	93	116	98	95	108
	UNITED STATES	100	100	100	100	100	100	100	100	100	100	100	100	100	100	100	100	100	100	100	100

POPULATION CHANGE

#	POST OFFICE NAME	COUNTY FIPS CODE	POPULATION			2000-2004 ANNUAL RATE		HOUSEHOLDS					FAMILIES		
			2000	2004	2009	% Rate	State Centile	2000	2004	2009	% Annual Rate 2000-2004	2004 Average HH Size	2000	2004	% Annual Rate 2000-2004
85641	VAIL	019	6569	8425	10027	6.0	91	2447	3139	3744	6.0	2.68	1920	2454	5.9
85643	WILLCOX	009	9030	9470	10019	1.1	29	3053	3244	3483	1.4	2.67	2169	2312	1.5
85645	AMADO	023	2768	2965	3276	1.6	40	1071	1170	1311	2.1	2.51	753	817	1.9
85648	RIO RICO	023	10751	12974	15240	4.5	85	3044	3693	4371	4.7	3.51	2617	3175	4.7
85650	SIERRA VISTA	003	13914	15421	16834	2.5	60	5098	5758	6396	2.9	2.52	4222	4760	2.9
85653	MARANA	019	11034	12985	14865	3.9	79	3790	4573	5324	4.5	2.75	2881	3481	4.6
85701	TUCSON	019	4388	4408	4677	0.1	11	2283	2312	2475	0.3	1.82	827	840	0.4
85704	TUCSON	019	27314	29343	32122	1.7	42	12378	13501	14937	2.1	2.11	7275	7907	2.0
85705	TUCSON	019	57191	58065	61916	0.4	15	25128	25649	27487	0.5	2.24	12675	12902	0.4
85706	TUCSON	019	70348	75622	82336	1.7	44	20039	21699	23831	1.9	3.25	15624	16840	1.8
85707	TUCSON	019	6058	6030	6341	-0.1	6	1452	1462	1561	0.2	3.64	1395	1405	0.2
85709	TUCSON	019	31	31	32	0.0	10	14	14	15	0.0	2.14	8	8	0.0
85710	TUCSON	019	53504	57183	62382	1.6	37	24121	26113	28730	1.9	2.18	14069	15121	1.7
85711	TUCSON	019	43482	44823	48117	0.7	23	18160	18910	20439	1.0	2.34	10475	10842	0.8
85712	TUCSON	019	30609	31118	33046	0.4	16	14998	15434	16547	0.7	1.94	6807	6979	0.6
85713	TUCSON	019	45161	46273	49335	0.6	18	14893	15409	16578	0.8	2.87	10219	10522	0.7
85714	TUCSON	019	13703	14517	15704	1.4	34	4137	4427	4822	1.6	3.25	3218	3434	1.5
85715	TUCSON	019	19433	20668	22601	1.5	35	8701	9346	10302	1.7	2.20	5385	5770	1.6
85716	TUCSON	019	33834	34559	36980	0.5	17	16728	17230	18557	0.7	2.00	7451	7631	0.6
85718	TUCSON	019	26442	27786	29949	1.2	30	12119	12908	14042	1.5	2.11	7273	7757	1.5
85719	TUCSON	019	36277	37181	39763	0.6	19	17237	17818	19214	0.8	2.02	6355	6552	0.7
85721	TUCSON	019	6058	6062	6068	0.0	10	6	6	7	0.0	2.50	1	1	0.0
85730	TUCSON	019	37503	41687	46510	2.5	62	14124	15882	17862	2.8	2.62	10125	11337	2.7
85735	TUCSON	019	8314	9248	10207	2.5	63	3012	3377	3750	2.7	2.74	2246	2514	2.7
85736	TUCSON	019	6195	6664	7227	1.7	44	2184	2352	2555	1.8	2.83	1559	1679	1.8
85737	TUCSON	019	29751	36405	42413	4.9	87	12196	14898	17369	4.8	2.43	9434	11620	5.0
85739	TUCSON	019	11324	14028	16912	5.2	88	4753	6104	7577	6.1	2.27	3708	4807	6.3
85741	TUCSON	019	31134	33603	36923	1.8	46	11538	12681	14080	2.3	2.63	8254	8992	2.0
85742	TUCSON	019	23097	26279	29377	3.1	71	8296	9549	10752	3.4	2.75	6532	7498	3.3
85743	TUCSON	019	18708	23740	28134	5.8	90	6781	8645	10277	5.9	2.74	5291	6774	6.0
85745	TUCSON	019	30907	33508	36844	1.9	50	11968	13133	14558	2.2	2.50	7892	8633	2.1
85746	TUCSON	019	47323	52400	57809	2.4	59	14998	16625	18386	2.5	3.14	11680	12939	2.4
85747	TUCSON	019	13714	18453	22360	7.2	94	4676	6256	7576	7.1	2.95	3927	5249	7.1
85748	TUCSON	019	15434	17426	19378	2.9	70	6019	6876	7709	3.2	2.53	4575	5230	3.2
85749	TUCSON	019	18613	20988	23398	2.9	69	6842	7845	8836	3.3	2.67	5543	6316	3.1
85750	TUCSON	019	24906	27166	29853	2.1	53	10898	11909	13145	2.1	2.27	7289	7995	2.2
85901	SHOW LOW	017	24588	27043	29607	2.3	56	7766	8752	9798	2.9	3.07	6023	6803	2.9
85920	ALPINE	001	271	282	287	0.9	26	138	147	153	1.5	1.92	100	107	1.6
85922	BLUE	011	2	2	2	0.0	10	2	2	2	0.0	1.00	2	0	-100.0
85924	CONCHO	001	2111	2328	2446	2.3	58	862	969	1040	2.8	2.40	606	689	3.1
85925	EAGAR	001	3963	3893	3871	-0.4	3	1391	1405	1434	0.2	2.76	1068	1083	0.3
85928	HEBER	017	3449	3889	4311	2.9	69	1450	1649	1853	3.1	2.36	1044	1193	3.2
85929	LAKESIDE	017	7024	7806	8589	2.5	61	2683	3007	3354	2.7	2.57	1985	2236	2.8
85935	PINETOP	017	3697	4282	4813	3.5	74	1517	1782	2037	3.9	2.40	1138	1342	4.0
85936	SAINT JOHNS	001	4090	3980	3944	-0.6	2	1155	1146	1160	-0.2	3.21	918	915	-0.1
85937	SNOWFLAKE	017	8978	9869	10808	2.3	55	2800	3146	3519	2.8	3.13	2214	2499	2.9
85938	SPRINGERVILLE	001	3388	3344	3329	-0.3	5	1243	1257	1282	0.3	2.49	914	930	0.4
86001	FLAGSTAFF	005	35256	39044	42924	2.4	59	13229	14907	16704	2.9	2.44	7218	8268	3.3
86004	FLAGSTAFF	005	34014	36572	39805	1.7	44	11966	13037	14393	2.0	2.80	8627	9470	2.2
86021	COLORADO CITY	005	4637	5114	5736	2.3	58	740	817	919	2.4	6.26	661	736	2.6
86022	FREDONIA	005	1318	1344	1437	0.5	16	479	506	556	1.3	2.66	352	370	1.2
86025	HOLBROOK	017	5860	6117	6513	1.0	27	1962	2068	2237	1.3	2.87	1434	1519	1.4
86030	HOTEVILLA	017	252	252	265	0.0	10	72	72	77	0.0	3.50	48	49	0.5
86033	KAYENTA	017	8465	8676	9182	0.6	19	2181	2261	2431	0.9	3.83	1773	1845	0.9
86034	KEAMS CANYON	017	3400	3430	3631	0.2	13	938	955	1027	0.4	3.53	719	737	0.6
86035	LEUPP	005	2727	2787	2928	0.5	17	691	713	759	0.7	3.91	553	574	0.9
86036	MARBLE CANYON	005	556	571	601	0.6	21	264	276	295	1.1	2.07	147	160	2.0
86038	MORMON LAKE	005	97	102	109	1.2	30	46	49	53	1.5	2.08	30	33	2.3
86039	KYKOTSMOVI VILLAGE	017	117	120	126	0.6	20	35	36	39	0.7	3.33	27	28	0.9
86040	PAGE	005	8912	9060	9482	0.4	16	2818	2895	3069	0.6	3.12	2202	2277	0.8
86042	POLACCA	017	1597	1565	1643	-0.5	3	412	411	441	-0.1	3.81	335	336	0.1
86043	SECOND MESA	017	1587	1566	1636	-0.3	5	516	518	551	0.1	3.02	375	380	0.3
86044	TONALEA	005	131	125	127	-1.1	0	40	38	38	-1.2	3.29	28	26	-1.7
86045	TUBA CITY	005	11717	11909	12517	0.4	15	2998	3078	3278	0.6	3.84	2431	2509	0.8
86046	WILLIAMS	005	8130	8816	9564	1.9	50	3260	3554	3897	2.1	2.46	2131	2343	2.3
86047	WINSLOW	017	18999	19491	20576	0.6	20	5301	5508	5928	0.9	3.23	4057	4240	1.0
86053	KAIBITO	005	7563	7808	8227	0.8	23	1811	1882	2005	0.9	4.12	1488	1553	1.0
86054	SHONTO	017	2005	2005	2097	0.0	10	549	555	590	0.3	3.61	428	435	0.4
86301	PRESCOTT	025	16753	18750	21448	2.7	66	7271	8264	9584	3.1	2.14	4405	5097	3.5
86303	PRESCOTT	025	16433	17712	19889	1.8	45	7796	8483	9604	2.0	2.04	4575	5001	2.1
86305	PRESCOTT	025	14559	15818	17853	2.0	51	6089	6699	7652	2.3	2.25	4064	4480	2.3
86314	PRESCOTT VALLEY	025	26789	32362	38516	4.6	85	10071	12217	14601	4.7	2.63	7434	9066	4.8
86320	ASH FORK	025	862	957	1088	2.5	60	306	341	390	2.6	2.81	225	252	2.7
86321	BAGDAD	025	1487	1443	1582	-0.7	2	540	529	584	-0.5	2.73	409	401	-0.5
86322	CAMP VERDE	025	10008	10928	12292	2.1	53	3839	4238	4812	2.4	2.49	2668	2955	2.4
86323	CHINO VALLEY	025	12751	15022	17590	3.9	80	4849	5734	6739	4.0	2.62	3646	4324	4.1
86324	CLARKDALE	025	4305	4744	5376	2.3	57	1896	2109	2406	2.5	2.23	1272	1382	2.0
86325	CORNVILLE	025	3660	4127	4724	2.9	69	1463	1669	1928	3.2	2.42	1020	1170	3.3
86326	COTTONWOOD	025	19923	22336	25530	2.7	66	8036	9080	10448	2.9	2.41	5339	6045	3.0
86327	DEWEY	025	6738	7469	8493	2.5	60	2998	3336	3807	2.6	2.24	2184	2436	2.6
86332	KIRKLAND	025	1113	1195	1334	1.7	41	478	517	581	1.9	2.28	303	328	1.9
86333	MAYER	025	4872	5560	6407	3.2	71	2038	2342	2715	3.3	2.34	1341	1546	3.4
86334	PAULDEN	025	2503	2994	3532	4.3	84	833	997	1178	4.3	3.00	640	768	4.4
86335	RIMROCK	025	3296	3680	4194	2.6	64	1445	1627	1866	2.8	2.26	941	1064	2.9
86336	SEDONA	005	13870	15621	17644	2.8	68	6709	7602	8645	3.0	2.05	3973	4536	3.2
86337	SELIGMAN	025	940	1023	1151	2.0	52	433	476	538	2.3	2.15	268	295	2.3
86343	CROWN KING	025	154	165	183	1.6	40	84	91	102	1.9	1.90	47	52	2.4
86351	SEDONA	025	5472	6460	7566	4.0	80	2659	3169	3738	4.2	2.01	1664	1993	4.3
86401	KINGMAN	015	42889	46467	51877	1.9	48	17345	18899	21214	2.0	2.42	11824	12939	2.1
86403	LAKE HAVASU CITY	015	13355	14924	16866	2.7	64	5869	6589	7479	2.8	2.26	3812	4297	2.9
86404	LAKE HAVASU CITY	015	12965	15323	17811	4.0	81	5685	6759	7892	4.2	2.27	4069	4846	4.1
86406	LAKE HAVASU CITY	015	18848	22073	25522	3.8	76	7846	9274	10796	4.0	2.35	5820	6895	4.1
86413	GOLDEN VALLEY	015	7706	8670	9843	2.8	67	3221	3641	4152	2.9	2.38	2189	2479	3.0
86426	FORT MOHAVE	015	8918	11065	13167	5.2	89	3403	4259	5097	5.4	2.60	2618	3280	5.5
86429	BULLHEAD CITY	015	4560	5233	5993	2.9	72	2013	2320	2667	3.4	2.25	1294	1494	3.4
	ARIZONA					2.7					2.7	2.64			2.9
	UNITED STATES					1.2					1.3	2.58			1.1

ZIP CODE #	POST OFFICE NAME	RACE (%) White 2000	White 2004	Black 2000	Black 2004	Asian/Pacific 2000	Asian/Pacific 2004	% Hispanic Origin 2000	% Hispanic Origin 2004	2004 AGE DISTRIBUTION (%) 0-4	5-9	10-14	15-19	20-24	25-44	45-64	65-84	85+	18+	MEDIAN AGE 2004	% 2004 Males	% 2004 Females
85641	VAIL	88.0	85.8	0.7	0.7	0.6	0.6	17.0	20.4	6.6	6.8	8.3	7.0	4.3	27.0	29.2	10.2	0.7	73.7	39.5	50.4	49.6
85643	WILLCOX	76.6	74.2	1.9	1.8	0.5	0.5	35.0	40.6	6.4	6.3	6.7	7.1	7.5	26.4	24.8	13.2	1.7	76.1	37.5	54.0	46.0
85645	AMADO	84.4	83.0	0.3	0.3	0.5	0.5	34.9	38.3	5.6	6.1	7.2	5.7	4.5	18.7	29.0	19.2	4.1	77.4	46.7	47.9	52.1
85648	RIO RICO	68.0	67.3	0.5	0.5	1.1	1.1	79.2	82.4	10.5	10.1	10.7	8.8	6.1	29.8	18.0	5.7	0.3	62.8	27.9	49.4	50.6
85650	SIERRA VISTA	79.0	77.7	7.5	7.3	3.3	3.6	13.5	16.6	6.8	6.4	6.7	7.7	8.6	23.7	25.9	13.4	0.8	76.2	37.6	50.5	49.5
85653	MARANA	80.5	79.1	2.3	2.2	0.7	0.8	22.5	25.5	6.4	6.2	8.3	7.7	6.9	27.9	26.0	10.0	0.6	74.3	36.5	51.5	48.5
85701	TUCSON	67.6	65.4	3.8	3.8	1.6	1.6	49.5	54.1	5.2	4.4	5.0	6.0	10.1	34.4	23.3	10.1	1.6	82.1	34.7	50.3	49.7
85704	TUCSON	90.5	88.8	1.3	1.4	2.2	2.5	11.2	14.0	3.8	4.0	5.2	5.7	6.6	22.2	28.9	18.8	4.8	83.5	46.7	46.3	53.7
85705	TUCSON	70.1	67.1	3.6	3.5	2.8	2.9	32.2	36.8	7.4	6.3	6.5	6.8	10.3	29.9	20.1	11.1	1.6	76.2	32.4	50.1	49.9
85706	TUCSON	54.0	52.4	3.2	3.1	0.7	0.7	71.4	74.4	9.5	8.5	8.6	8.3	9.0	30.3	17.9	7.4	0.5	68.4	28.5	51.6	48.4
85707	TUCSON	67.3	64.1	13.9	14.6	4.2	4.5	15.0	18.0	16.7	11.8	8.8	7.0	15.5	37.6	2.4	0.3	0.0	59.6	21.9	54.0	46.0
85709	TUCSON	74.2	71.0	3.2	3.2	3.2	3.2	45.2	48.4	6.5	6.5	6.5	6.5	6.5	25.8	25.8	16.1	0.0	80.7	38.8	48.4	51.6
85710	TUCSON	84.2	82.1	4.0	4.3	2.2	2.4	15.4	18.6	5.6	5.3	6.0	6.2	6.9	25.6	23.3	18.0	3.2	79.6	41.2	46.8	53.2
85711	TUCSON	72.9	70.2	4.6	4.6	2.8	3.0	29.7	34.0	7.4	6.4	6.8	7.1	8.7	29.1	21.7	10.9	1.9	75.5	34.4	48.5	51.5
85712	TUCSON	81.0	78.5	3.8	4.1	2.9	3.1	18.8	22.5	6.0	5.3	5.2	5.3	7.6	30.2	22.9	13.5	4.0	80.5	38.1	47.4	52.6
85713	TUCSON	51.6	49.9	6.3	5.8	1.0	1.0	62.7	66.0	8.1	7.7	8.1	7.3	7.3	26.7	20.8	12.5	1.6	71.8	33.4	48.4	51.6
85714	TUCSON	43.6	42.4	1.6	1.5	0.5	0.5	86.5	88.2	8.9	8.5	9.4	8.4	7.9	27.3	18.9	9.5	1.1	68.0	29.6	49.3	50.7
85715	TUCSON	87.6	86.0	2.4	2.5	2.7	3.1	12.1	14.5	5.0	5.2	5.8	5.7	6.1	24.9	27.5	17.4	2.4	80.4	43.1	47.4	52.6
85716	TUCSON	79.1	76.4	3.5	3.7	2.9	3.1	21.0	24.9	6.3	5.4	5.3	5.9	9.8	33.9	22.8	8.8	1.8	79.9	33.9	49.1	50.9
85718	TUCSON	91.8	90.6	1.1	1.2	3.1	3.6	7.5	9.2	3.2	4.0	5.5	5.9	6.1	18.9	33.3	18.9	4.3	83.6	48.7	47.4	52.6
85719	TUCSON	77.0	74.4	3.1	3.2	5.4	5.8	20.0	23.4	4.8	3.9	3.9	9.3	21.5	31.2	16.7	7.1	1.7	84.9	27.7	50.8	49.2
85721	TUCSON	81.6	79.1	3.3	3.6	8.1	9.1	10.2	12.3	0.0	0.0	0.0	71.9	26.3	1.3	0.4	0.1	0.0	99.4	18.5	41.8	58.2
85730	TUCSON	76.5	73.8	6.7	6.9	3.3	3.5	20.3	24.0	7.5	7.4	7.8	7.0	6.9	30.1	22.8	9.6	0.9	73.0	34.5	48.8	51.2
85735	TUCSON	77.0	73.4	0.9	1.0	0.4	0.4	34.0	39.6	6.8	6.8	7.8	7.3	5.9	25.6	26.8	12.2	0.9	74.2	38.6	49.6	50.4
85736	TUCSON	73.7	69.9	0.6	0.6	0.5	0.5	36.7	42.3	6.6	6.6	8.5	8.9	7.6	24.6	27.0	9.4	0.8	72.6	35.7	51.4	48.6
85737	TUCSON	92.8	91.7	1.1	1.2	2.0	2.4	7.8	9.6	5.0	5.5	6.6	6.1	3.9	20.5	30.1	21.1	1.4	79.0	46.5	48.6	51.4
85739	TUCSON	90.7	89.7	0.5	0.5	0.6	0.7	14.5	16.2	3.3	3.5	3.9	4.3	3.7	14.7	29.8	35.0	1.8	86.5	58.8	48.8	51.2
85741	TUCSON	85.4	83.0	1.8	1.9	2.3	2.6	19.1	23.1	7.1	7.0	7.8	7.4	7.9	31.0	23.5	7.2	1.2	73.6	33.6	49.1	50.9
85742	TUCSON	89.1	87.4	1.6	1.8	1.8	2.0	13.6	16.5	7.1	7.3	7.9	7.0	5.9	27.8	26.5	9.4	1.0	73.1	37.2	48.4	51.6
85743	TUCSON	87.3	84.8	1.5	1.8	1.8	2.3	15.3	18.8	8.0	8.0	7.9	6.3	5.2	30.3	25.4	8.5	0.5	71.8	36.2	49.6	50.4
85745	TUCSON	66.8	65.5	3.0	2.9	2.0	2.1	48.1	51.1	6.5	6.2	6.3	6.5	7.7	28.8	26.8	10.0	1.2	77.4	36.6	48.0	52.0
85746	TUCSON	53.1	50.2	2.6	2.5	0.9	0.9	56.9	61.7	9.3	8.8	9.3	8.3	7.9	28.0	20.2	7.5	0.8	67.6	29.3	48.8	51.2
85747	TUCSON	81.9	79.5	4.8	5.1	2.4	2.6	16.5	19.8	9.8	9.2	8.5	6.7	5.2	34.5	20.5	5.4	0.3	68.0	32.7	49.9	50.1
85748	TUCSON	88.4	86.8	2.7	2.9	2.9	3.3	10.8	13.2	5.5	6.0	6.4	6.3	5.5	25.9	31.8	11.7	1.0	78.1	41.8	48.9	51.1
85749	TUCSON	93.2	91.8	1.1	1.2	2.0	2.3	7.8	9.7	4.2	5.8	8.3	7.6	4.0	21.8	36.1	11.3	0.9	76.6	44.2	50.2	49.8
85750	TUCSON	90.7	89.4	1.4	1.5	3.8	4.3	7.3	8.9	4.2	4.8	6.2	6.0	5.1	21.9	33.3	16.9	1.5	80.8	45.9	48.3	51.7
85901	SHOW LOW	52.0	52.5	0.3	0.3	0.3	0.4	5.9	7.0	9.0	8.6	9.6	9.0	7.2	24.3	22.1	9.6	0.7	66.9	31.1	48.7	51.3
85920	ALPINE	93.0	91.8	0.4	0.4	0.7	0.7	8.1	9.6	5.0	4.3	5.3	7.1	3.6	18.4	39.7	15.6	1.1	80.5	48.8	50.7	49.3
85922	BLUE	100.0	100.0	0.0	0.0	0.0	0.0	50.0	50.0	0.0	0.0	0.0	0.0	100.0	0.0	0.0	0.0	0.0	100.0	22.5	50.0	50.0
85924	CONCHO	85.6	84.1	1.2	1.3	0.6	0.6	11.5	13.2	5.7	6.1	6.7	6.7	4.0	17.9	36.2	16.2	0.5	76.8	46.6	51.5	48.5
85925	EAGAR	87.6	86.3	0.4	0.4	0.6	0.6	13.6	15.5	7.2	6.8	8.9	9.6	6.7	21.1	28.1	10.7	1.0	70.6	37.9	49.2	50.8
85928	HEBER	95.1	93.6	0.1	0.1	0.2	0.3	5.7	7.0	4.1	4.7	6.2	5.7	4.5	16.6	33.6	23.9	0.9	81.5	50.3	50.9	49.1
85929	LAKESIDE	88.7	85.8	0.7	0.8	0.5	0.5	11.9	14.4	6.6	6.5	7.3	7.1	5.7	22.3	29.9	13.5	1.0	74.8	41.2	50.1	49.9
85935	PINETOP	91.3	89.1	0.9	1.1	0.4	0.5	8.1	9.7	4.9	5.5	6.6	6.1	3.2	19.3	34.6	18.7	1.2	79.1	47.9	49.7	50.3
85936	SAINT JOHNS	79.3	77.4	1.0	1.0	0.4	0.4	23.8	26.6	8.4	7.5	8.7	8.8	7.6	24.7	23.8	9.4	1.1	69.3	33.0	52.4	47.6
85937	SNOWFLAKE	89.1	85.8	0.5	0.6	0.4	0.5	8.0	9.5	9.7	9.1	9.7	9.0	6.9	22.0	23.0	9.6	1.1	65.6	30.1	50.1	49.9
85938	SPRINGERVILLE	83.2	81.6	0.9	0.9	0.5	0.5	18.5	20.8	7.4	7.3	7.8	7.7	6.7	24.4	26.4	11.0	1.4	72.1	37.1	51.7	48.3
86001	FLAGSTAFF	82.5	80.3	1.7	1.7	1.4	1.5	12.1	13.7	5.9	5.0	5.6	8.9	20.3	30.0	18.9	4.7	0.6	79.9	27.0	49.8	50.2
86004	FLAGSTAFF	75.7	73.2	1.3	1.3	1.0	1.1	16.9	18.5	7.7	7.5	8.0	8.0	8.6	29.5	24.7	5.8	0.4	72.0	32.1	49.5	50.5
86021	COLORADO CITY	94.1	93.9	0.1	0.1	0.2	0.3	2.6	3.0	21.6	17.1	13.3	9.4	7.9	21.9	7.3	1.3	0.3	42.1	14.3	50.2	49.8
86022	FREDONIA	86.7	84.7	0.9	1.0	0.2	0.2	1.6	2.1	7.4	7.3	8.8	7.7	5.4	27.5	25.5	9.7	0.7	71.8	36.7	51.6	48.4
86025	HOLBROOK	61.2	54.0	2.2	2.3	1.0	1.1	21.8	23.4	8.8	8.9	8.7	10.1	7.1	24.2	22.2	9.1	1.0	66.9	30.7	47.9	52.2
86030	HOTEVILLA	1.6	1.2	0.0	0.0	0.0	0.0	2.8	2.4	9.1	9.5	11.5	10.7	6.4	24.2	18.3	8.7	1.6	63.1	27.3	48.4	51.6
86033	KAYENTA	4.3	2.9	0.1	0.1	0.1	0.1	0.9	0.8	10.4	10.1	12.1	11.4	8.7	24.4	17.4	5.3	0.4	60.0	23.6	48.5	51.5
86034	KEAMS CANYON	5.7	4.0	0.1	0.1	0.1	0.1	2.5	2.3	10.1	9.7	10.4	9.6	7.8	24.6	19.7	7.6	0.8	63.6	27.1	49.1	50.9
86035	LEUPP	0.8	0.7	0.0	0.0	0.0	0.0	1.4	1.3	8.5	8.8	11.5	10.8	7.6	25.1	18.1	8.6	1.0	64.5	27.3	50.8	49.2
86036	MARBLE CANYON	82.9	80.0	0.2	0.2	0.7	0.7	2.0	2.3	5.6	6.1	4.9	4.4	2.6	27.5	37.8	10.5	0.5	80.7	44.3	55.2	44.8
86038	MORMON LAKE	69.1	64.7	0.0	0.0	1.0	1.0	6.2	5.9	8.8	8.8	8.8	5.9	3.9	28.4	29.4	5.9	0.0	68.6	37.1	51.0	49.0
86039	KYKOTSMOVI VILLAGE	3.4	2.5	1.7	1.7	0.0	0.0	5.1	4.2	8.3	12.5	12.5	9.2	7.5	22.5	19.2	5.8	2.5	60.0	25.0	46.7	53.3
86040	PAGE	51.7	48.6	0.3	0.3	0.7	0.7	3.8	4.2	8.2	8.9	10.4	9.6	7.5	25.6	23.3	6.0	0.6	66.2	30.0	49.9	50.1
86042	POLACCA	1.3	1.0	0.1	0.1	0.1	0.1	0.7	0.6	11.1	10.9	10.8	10.0	7.4	22.9	17.6	8.4	1.0	60.9	24.9	48.1	51.9
86043	SECOND MESA	3.8	2.6	0.5	0.5	0.1	0.1	1.4	1.3	7.3	7.9	9.6	8.1	6.6	24.8	24.3	10.0	1.5	70.2	33.8	48.9	51.1
86044	TONALEA	0.0	0.0	0.0	0.0	0.0	0.0	3.1	2.4	9.6	12.8	8.8	7.2	5.6	23.2	15.2	17.6	0.0	63.2	29.7	56.0	44.0
86045	TUBA CITY	4.4	3.5	0.1	0.1	0.2	0.2	2.4	2.3	9.8	9.8	12.6	11.5	7.6	25.7	16.9	5.5	0.8	60.5	24.3	49.0	51.0
86046	WILLIAMS	79.5	77.3	1.6	1.6	1.0	1.0	20.4	22.6	6.5	6.5	7.0	7.4	6.6	27.8	28.9	8.7	0.6	75.4	38.2	51.9	48.1
86047	WINSLOW	35.8	31.5	2.8	2.8	0.6	0.6	15.8	16.4	8.7	8.5	9.6	9.6	9.1	26.2	18.6	8.6	1.2	67.1	28.5	52.1	47.9
86053	KAIBITO	1.3	1.0	0.1	0.1	0.0	0.0	0.5	0.5	10.8	11.0	13.2	11.2	8.0	23.6	14.4	7.1	0.7	57.8	22.4	49.2	50.8
86054	SHONTO	1.5	0.9	0.1	0.1	0.1	0.1	0.9	0.8	9.6	9.6	11.7	10.7	8.6	22.7	18.5	7.9	0.8	62.0	24.9	50.9	49.1
86301	PRESCOTT	91.2	90.8	0.5	0.6	0.8	0.9	9.4	10.2	3.8	3.9	4.8	6.2	6.9	19.7	27.2	23.7	3.8	84.2	48.5	49.6	50.4
86303	PRESCOTT	94.7	94.2	0.4	0.4	0.6	0.7	6.0	6.9	3.4	3.6	3.9	4.0	4.6	18.1	33.9	25.5	3.0	86.9	53.1	48.6	51.4
86305	PRESCOTT	94.9	94.4	0.4	0.4	0.9	1.0	6.0	6.8	3.6	3.9	4.8	6.8	7.4	16.6	33.4	20.6	2.9	84.5	49.4	50.1	49.9
86314	PRESCOTT VALLEY	90.4	89.3	0.5	0.5	0.6	0.7	12.1	13.6	7.7	7.3	7.4	6.8	6.2	25.9	22.9	14.3	1.5	73.0	36.9	49.2	50.8
86320	ASH FORK	94.6	94.5	0.9	0.9	0.1	0.1	28.2	31.6	6.0	5.6	6.4	8.5	9.1	22.9	28.3	12.5	0.7	77.0	39.2	56.0	44.0
86321	BAGDAD	93.2	92.5	0.9	0.9	0.5	0.6	17.5	20.0	7.4	6.9	8.5	8.3	8.4	25.9	27.1	7.0	0.6	72.4	34.1	50.7	49.3
86322	CAMP VERDE	86.0	84.8	0.4	0.4	0.5	0.6	10.7	12.2	6.0	5.8	6.4	6.4	5.7	21.4	28.2	18.2	1.9	77.9	43.7	50.4	49.6
86323	CHINO VALLEY	93.8	93.1	0.3	0.3	0.3	0.4	9.9	11.5	6.4	6.5	7.3	7.5	6.2	22.7	28.6	13.7	1.1	75.0	40.5	49.6	50.4
86324	CLARKDALE	85.7	84.5	0.4	0.4	0.4	0.4	10.7	12.1	5.5	5.5	5.3	6.3	5.0	19.0	28.1	22.6	2.7	79.5	47.4	48.2	51.9
86325	CORNVILLE	92.7	91.9	0.4	0.4	0.6	0.7	8.9	10.2	4.7	5.1	6.9	7.1	4.2	22.3	34.3	14.0	1.4	78.8	44.8	50.2	49.8
86326	COTTONWOOD	88.5	87.3	0.4	0.4	0.5	0.6	15.5	17.6	6.4	6.2	6.6	6.4	6.0	22.0	24.6	18.8	3.1	76.7	42.4	47.4	52.6
86327	DEWEY	96.2	95.7	0.2	0.3	0.5	0.5	5.1	6.1	3.5	4.0	5.0	5.1	3.7	15.4	32.3	28.8	2.3	84.4	54.4	49.2	50.8
86332	KIRKLAND	93.5	92.7	0.2	0.2	0.2	0.2	8.4	9.6	4.0	4.4	4.7	4.2	3.9	16.8	34.8	25.1	2.2	84.3	52.9	50.6	49.4
86333	MAYER	95.6	95.2	0.2	0.2	0.3	0.3	6.6	7.7	4.7	4.7	5.6	6.2	5.1	19.0	32.5	20.3	1.9	80.7	48.1	50.9	49.1
86334	PAULDEN	93.6	92.9	0.4	0.4	0.4	0.4	11.3	13.0	5.9	6.5	7.7	7.7	5.9	23.5	29.6	12.5	0.9	75.2	40.7	50.7	49.3
86335	RIMROCK	90.9	90.0	0.1	0.1	0.2	0.3	7.5	8.6	5.5	5.4	5.4	4.9	4.7	21.7	31.1	19.4	1.9	80.7	46.7	48.3	51.7
86336	SEDONA	93.0	92.1	0.4	0.5	0.9	1.0	8.2	9.5	3.0	3.3	3.5	3.8	3.4	17.7	38.8	23.9	2.6	87.8	53.3	47.7	52.3
86337	SELIGMAN	85.6	84.1	1.4	1.5	1.2	1.3	14.8	16.8	4.5	5.1	6.2	6.4	3.9	21.2	35.2	17.1	0.5	79.5	47.0	51.2	48.8
86343	CROWN KING	98.1	97.6	0.0	0.0	0.7	0.6	5.8	6.1	1.8	3.6	5.5	3.6	4.2	20.0	47.9	10.9	2.4	87.3	50.4	58.2	41.8
86351	SEDONA	95.2	94.6	0.4	0.4	0.8	0.9	6.7	7.8	2.5	2.9	3.7	3.1	2.7	14.6	37.1	28.9	4.5	88.9	57.3	46.1	54.0
86401	KINGMAN	90.0	89.0	0.5	0.6	1.0	1.2	8.5	9.8	6.1	5.9	6.5	6.5	5.9	21.9	27.3	18.1	1.8	77.5	43.0	49.6	50.4
86403	LAKE HAVASU CITY	92.2	91.2	0.4	0.4	0.7	0.8	10.4	12.1	5.1	5.1	5.6	5.3	5.7	20.8	27.0	22.8	2.6	81.0	46.7	49.2	50.8
86404	LAKE HAVASU CITY	94.4	93.6	0.3	0.3	0.5	0.5	8.3	9.7	4.6	4.7	5.1	4.6	3.9	19.6	30.1	25.4	1.8	82.7	50.5	49.9	50.2
86406	LAKE HAVASU CITY	95.5	94.9	0.3	0.3	0.7	0.9	6.1	7.1	4.4	4.6	5.6	5.2	4.4	19.1	29.2	25.1	2.4	82.1	49.8	49.1	50.9
86413	GOLDEN VALLEY	94.1	93.5	0.5	0.5	0.8	0.8	7.1	8.2	4.3	5.1	6.4	5.7	3.8	18.8	35.3	19.5	1.1	80.2	48.5	51.1	49.0
86426	FORT MOHAVE	90.7	89.7	0.6	0.7	1.2	1.4	11.9	13.7	6.3	6.4	7.6	6.7	5.3	23.2	26.1	17.5	1.0	75.6	41.3	49.7	50.3
86429	BULLHEAD CITY	90.6	89.6	1.1	1.2	1.2	1.4	13.6	15.6	5.2	5.0	4.8	4.5	5.3	22.2	30.3	21.4	1.3	82.3	47.2	50.3	49.7
	ARIZONA	75.5	74.0	3.1	3.2	1.9	2.1	25.3	27.9	7.6	7.1	7.3	6.9	7.5	28.1	22.1	11.9	1.5	74.0	34.8	49.9	50.2
	UNITED STATES	75.1	73.6	12.3	12.5	3.8	4.2	12.5	14.1	6.9	6.7	7.2	7.0	7.3	28.6	23.8	10.8	1.7	75.1	36.0	49.1	50.9

ZIP CODE #	POST OFFICE NAME	2004 Per Capita Income	2004 HH Income Base	2004 HOUSEHOLD INCOME DISTRIBUTION (%) Less than $25,000	$25,000 to $49,999	$50,000 to $99,999	$100,000 to $149,999	$150,000 or More	MEDIAN HOUSEHOLD INCOME 2004	2009	2004 National Centile	2004 State Centile	2004 Home Value Base	2004 HOME VALUE DISTRIBUTION (%) Less than $50,000	$50,000 to $89,999	$90,000 to $174,999	$175,000 to $399,999	$400,000 or More	2004 Median Home Value
85641	VAIL	26559	3139	13.2	28.0	40.6	12.3	5.9	58344	71927	83	78	2898	7.2	13.3	44.7	30.2	4.7	143532
85643	WILLCOX	16061	3244	39.2	28.0	24.9	6.5	1.4	35330	43057	29	31	2458	28.4	29.3	33.4	8.3	0.6	78869
85645	AMADO	31807	1170	28.2	21.8	27.1	13.2	9.7	50000	66731	72	68	927	12.0	16.5	28.1	29.3	14.1	148520
85648	RIO RICO	15487	3693	21.2	38.1	30.0	7.6	3.1	41967	52440	53	51	2919	2.6	13.7	68.2	14.7	0.9	118830
85650	SIERRA VISTA	27465	5758	13.5	26.4	39.7	14.8	5.6	60549	74071	85	80	4261	4.8	12.1	41.7	38.6	2.8	159678
85653	MARANA	20448	4573	23.8	32.3	32.1	7.5	4.3	44333	56156	60	56	3886	14.3	22.7	42.3	17.4	3.3	109020
85701	TUCSON	19209	2312	53.2	28.1	14.3	3.1	1.3	22718	27856	3	6	691	2.0	19.0	53.1	22.3	3.6	121591
85704	TUCSON	33028	13501	17.8	27.7	34.7	13.0	6.8	53860	68252	78	75	8578	6.2	4.0	34.6	52.8	2.4	186276
85705	TUCSON	16297	25649	45.9	33.0	17.0	2.9	1.2	27274	33875	8	13	11864	40.9	26.5	28.9	3.2	0.6	69116
85706	TUCSON	12604	21699	40.3	34.0	20.9	3.6	1.2	30693	37015	14	20	14366	29.4	36.3	32.5	1.5	0.3	76910
85707	TUCSON	13026	1462	13.3	50.6	33.1	2.7	0.3	40923	48053	49	48	135	66.7	17.8	15.6	0.0	0.0	40217
85709	TUCSON	24180	14	21.4	28.6	42.9	7.1	0.0	50000	52087	72	68	13	0.0	15.4	76.9	7.7	0.0	128125
85710	TUCSON	24448	26113	26.4	33.9	30.1	7.3	2.3	41070	50848	50	49	16047	6.4	9.9	71.9	11.2	0.6	126016
85711	TUCSON	21261	18910	33.8	31.0	26.1	6.5	2.6	36684	46774	34	35	9698	1.1	17.6	64.9	15.9	0.6	116524
85712	TUCSON	23334	15434	36.3	33.8	22.9	4.8	2.2	33444	41550	22	25	6501	7.3	16.3	64.8	10.0	1.6	115618
85713	TUCSON	14980	15409	40.0	34.4	19.8	3.8	2.0	30781	36925	14	21	10215	23.1	43.3	29.8	3.3	0.5	74514
85714	TUCSON	12353	4427	41.5	35.4	19.5	2.6	1.0	30406	36257	13	19	2932	17.7	53.8	27.3	1.2	0.0	77922
85715	TUCSON	34250	9346	15.7	26.2	36.3	14.2	7.7	57339	72203	82	78	6721	3.7	6.7	39.4	46.2	3.9	175220
85716	TUCSON	24400	17230	37.9	32.1	20.3	5.9	3.8	32936	41528	21	25	7032	4.6	12.8	55.2	23.3	4.1	128932
85718	TUCSON	58812	12908	13.3	17.5	28.7	17.5	23.0	80225	109998	95	93	8791	1.0	1.5	10.8	50.6	36.2	336480
85719	TUCSON	20693	17818	45.5	28.5	17.7	5.4	3.0	27917	35282	9	14	6042	9.0	12.8	52.9	22.8	2.5	125700
85721	TUCSON	14867	6	66.7	33.3	0.0	0.0	0.0	16902	20878	1	3	1	0.0	0.0	100.0	0.0	0.0	112500
85730	TUCSON	21241	15882	19.2	35.2	34.9	8.2	2.5	45911	56128	64	60	11339	7.3	14.9	69.6	7.4	0.9	116434
85735	TUCSON	19390	3377	17.3	39.9	33.9	7.5	1.5	44950	54896	61	58	2894	14.7	22.7	52.4	9.9	0.4	100809
85736	TUCSON	16847	2352	34.9	29.3	26.8	7.1	1.9	35990	47904	32	32	1901	23.8	27.3	39.6	8.6	0.7	88633
85737	TUCSON	39253	14898	8.6	17.7	41.3	20.7	11.7	76032	99278	94	90	12977	0.7	2.4	21.7	66.9	8.3	222144
85739	TUCSON	35893	6104	13.8	25.7	36.0	15.0	9.5	59833	78239	84	79	5440	5.5	6.9	25.4	49.2	13.1	225198
85741	TUCSON	23950	12681	15.0	31.0	39.3	11.9	2.9	53104	64679	77	73	8740	3.7	4.5	75.7	15.8	0.3	135751
85742	TUCSON	30339	9549	8.0	21.2	44.4	18.8	7.6	68915	84985	91	87	8279	1.9	1.0	59.3	35.5	2.3	160766
85743	TUCSON	27202	8645	10.9	25.6	42.1	16.6	4.8	62607	78500	87	82	7697	3.9	9.2	51.6	32.6	2.8	149319
85745	TUCSON	26863	13133	23.5	25.7	32.5	12.5	5.8	50835	64273	74	69	9000	5.3	12.1	45.4	33.2	4.0	148553
85746	TUCSON	16325	16625	26.4	32.1	33.3	6.4	1.8	42641	52477	55	52	12398	16.6	19.1	58.7	5.3	0.4	105200
85747	TUCSON	26831	6256	5.1	24.3	49.7	16.6	4.3	65408	79938	89	83	5886	3.1	3.6	61.3	30.8	1.3	155106
85748	TUCSON	33808	6876	9.5	20.7	41.1	19.8	8.9	69897	87071	91	87	5986	0.1	0.8	48.6	45.0	5.6	176045
85749	TUCSON	44947	7845	8.2	13.7	33.6	25.2	19.4	90256	117376	97	97	6869	0.5	1.1	8.6	63.9	25.9	283954
85750	TUCSON	51943	11909	7.8	18.6	33.2	18.4	22.0	81569	109629	95	94	8782	0.6	0.2	11.8	56.8	30.7	309989
85901	SHOW LOW	14356	8752	36.4	31.0	26.0	5.1	1.5	34728	42164	26	28	6568	26.2	21.0	37.2	14.0	1.7	94557
85920	ALPINE	30451	147	28.6	27.9	27.9	10.9	4.8	43489	53804	57	54	126	3.2	12.7	38.1	35.7	10.3	166667
85922	BLUE	0	0	0.0	0.0	0.0	0.0	0.0	0	0	0	0	0	0.0	0.0	0.0	0.0	0.0	0
85924	CONCHO	15457	969	45.2	27.0	22.1	5.3	0.4	29215	36343	11	16	856	30.8	28.3	33.4	5.6	1.9	73676
85925	EAGAR	19944	1405	25.6	28.8	34.3	8.8	2.5	44093	54307	59	55	1173	9.9	20.6	50.4	17.1	2.1	109669
85928	HEBER	19654	1649	34.2	33.8	25.2	4.1	2.7	36559	44662	34	35	1401	11.1	18.4	40.2	27.9	2.4	121786
85929	LAKESIDE	20567	3007	27.0	31.8	31.2	7.0	3.0	42244	52103	54	51	2421	7.9	18.3	47.8	24.3	1.8	124089
85935	PINETOP	32578	1782	19.0	20.7	37.1	14.4	8.9	60779	76491	85	81	1505	4.2	11.1	29.0	50.1	5.7	191383
85936	SAINT JOHNS	15454	1146	30.1	32.3	27.2	8.6	1.8	40107	48551	46	47	896	21.3	42.1	31.7	4.8	0.1	77069
85937	SNOWFLAKE	16044	3146	27.7	34.1	28.1	7.7	2.4	39702	49563	45	45	2632	14.5	22.3	48.0	13.0	2.2	106273
85938	SPRINGERVILLE	20343	1257	29.8	30.3	29.3	8.4	2.2	40026	48750	46	46	973	10.6	28.1	47.4	11.8	2.2	100526
86001	FLAGSTAFF	23108	14907	26.9	30.0	30.3	8.7	4.1	43063	53265	56	53	7313	7.2	4.3	30.8	48.4	9.4	188936
86004	FLAGSTAFF	25552	13037	18.6	25.8	35.2	14.1	6.4	55381	68283	80	76	8867	7.8	4.8	30.3	50.1	7.1	187344
86021	COLORADO CITY	7209	817	33.8	37.3	20.9	5.4	2.6	32994	39643	21	25	538	16.2	14.9	41.5	26.6	0.9	121845
86022	FREDONIA	16136	506	32.0	44.9	17.8	4.0	1.4	33985	40550	24	26	395	25.3	28.6	39.8	5.3	1.0	86310
86025	HOLBROOK	17103	2068	33.9	28.8	28.1	6.5	2.8	37003	45721	35	37	1534	31.0	41.0	23.5	3.7	0.9	71152
86030	HOTEVILLA	9089	72	69.4	9.7	15.3	5.6	0.0	15000	18342	1	1	46	34.8	8.7	6.5	28.3	21.7	150000
86033	KAYENTA	10385	2261	45.1	24.9	23.1	6.1	0.9	30667	37944	14	20	1637	64.8	18.8	12.2	2.8	1.4	30030
86034	KEAMS CANYON	10545	955	49.7	24.0	20.1	4.8	1.4	25282	32361	5	10	626	63.4	17.9	13.7	4.2	0.8	36023
86035	LEUPP	8087	713	51.3	26.7	19.2	2.8	0.0	23980	29086	4	8	569	47.8	18.1	23.9	9.5	0.7	54630
86036	MARBLE CANYON	26268	276	16.3	38.0	36.2	8.0	1.5	46986	57311	66	62	188	36.2	12.2	31.4	17.6	2.7	96000
86038	MORMON LAKE	23388	49	49.0	24.5	18.4	4.1	4.1	25534	34289	5	11	39	20.5	18.0	10.3	41.0	10.3	187500
86039	KYKOTSMOVI VILLAGE	8089	36	55.6	41.7	2.8	0.0	0.0	16421	23593	1	2	31	54.8	45.2	0.0	0.0	0.0	17500
86040	PAGE	20395	2895	22.3	23.6	35.7	14.4	4.1	54985	68519	80	75	2365	26.6	19.4	28.3	24.8	0.9	101843
86042	POLACCA	7747	411	51.8	37.2	8.3	2.7	0.0	23572	27633	4	7	347	66.6	23.6	8.9	0.6	0.3	36161
86043	SECOND MESA	8865	518	57.9	24.5	16.8	0.8	0.0	20098	22713	2	5	385	51.2	21.8	12.5	12.5	2.1	49151
86044	TONALEA	11594	38	15.8	73.7	7.9	0.0	2.6	30585	35488	14	19	36	83.3	5.6	11.1	0.0	0.0	9474
86045	TUBA CITY	11894	3078	33.5	26.6	32.8	6.4	0.7	40925	51104	49	49	2084	60.8	16.3	18.6	3.8	0.5	36800
86046	WILLIAMS	21169	3554	26.7	30.4	33.6	6.7	2.6	44270	54091	59	55	2133	19.7	14.2	40.5	21.2	4.5	119063
86047	WINSLOW	13242	5508	41.3	27.9	23.1	6.1	1.6	31503	38359	16	22	4019	36.1	33.9	23.9	3.5	2.5	68072
86053	KAIBITO	8479	1882	50.3	25.7	19.7	2.8	1.5	24813	29900	4	9	1630	66.0	15.0	16.2	2.6	0.3	28729
86054	SHONTO	9955	555	47.8	27.9	18.4	5.4	0.5	26908	32626	7	12	467	65.7	15.4	15.0	2.8	1.1	30109
86301	PRESCOTT	29270	8264	26.9	30.7	27.3	9.5	5.7	42978	54018	56	52	5840	4.3	9.7	43.3	38.9	3.8	158716
86303	PRESCOTT	30039	8483	25.6	29.9	28.5	11.1	4.9	44584	57024	60	56	6221	5.4	3.7	30.9	47.6	12.5	199822
86305	PRESCOTT	31620	6699	26.0	26.4	29.0	11.5	7.1	46883	61467	66	62	5238	15.0	6.5	21.2	43.1	14.2	195680
86314	PRESCOTT VALLEY	19527	12217	27.3	36.7	27.2	6.4	2.5	39528	47929	44	44	9083	3.8	16.6	62.3	16.6	0.8	122006
86320	ASH FORK	12852	341	41.9	33.4	22.0	1.8	0.9	30499	37105	14	19	269	40.2	28.6	25.3	4.8	1.1	65278
86321	BAGDAD	18785	529	18.7	31.8	43.1	5.9	0.6	49679	61024	71	68	127	55.1	38.6	3.2	3.2	0.0	43500
86322	CAMP VERDE	18555	4238	30.3	35.3	28.3	5.6	0.5	37776	45160	38	39	3473	16.2	21.9	39.7	19.9	2.3	108358
86323	CHINO VALLEY	22330	5734	26.8	31.7	28.6	8.4	4.5	41606	52014	52	50	4751	9.1	16.7	41.4	27.2	5.5	132043
86324	CLARKDALE	23096	2109	30.0	33.3	25.6	7.8	3.3	38211	45795	40	41	1690	12.2	20.7	43.8	21.4	2.0	113226
86325	CORNVILLE	22460	1669	23.7	30.6	33.7	9.3	2.7	46531	56714	65	61	1434	5.1	13.2	41.1	33.3	7.3	147152
86326	COTTONWOOD	21249	9080	31.6	32.7	26.4	5.9	3.5	37403	45628	37	39	6542	4.3	17.0	53.9	22.2	2.6	130490
86327	DEWEY	27600	3336	24.5	31.2	31.1	7.3	5.9	44250	56014	59	55	2918	6.2	7.6	45.3	35.7	5.2	152843
86332	KIRKLAND	20064	517	42.0	29.8	20.1	5.6	2.5	31853	38004	17	23	426	16.7	21.1	37.8	18.5	5.9	108333
86333	MAYER	19048	2342	37.0	29.4	26.5	5.1	2.1	35836	42712	31	32	1913	19.6	31.4	35.4	11.3	2.3	88588
86334	PAULDEN	21111	997	23.8	34.4	28.6	8.1	5.1	41886	52114	53	50	843	5.1	14.7	47.5	28.0	4.7	139844
86335	RIMROCK	19514	1627	31.0	36.8	27.5	2.8	1.8	38293	45368	40	42	1314	6.5	15.1	55.9	19.8	2.8	119967
86336	SEDONA	38329	7602	21.5	27.1	28.9	12.0	10.5	51280	66777	74	70	6057	7.8	3.3	18.1	46.5	24.4	242765
86337	SELIGMAN	15218	476	49.2	30.9	16.4	3.6	0.0	25476	30228	5	10	389	41.4	33.2	23.4	0.8	1.3	55982
86343	CROWN KING	34395	91	26.4	30.8	26.4	5.5	11.0	39206	54626	43	43	67	14.9	16.4	26.9	35.8	6.0	137500
86351	SEDONA	38909	3169	21.7	29.0	28.0	10.0	11.4	49172	67299	70	67	2449	0.0	1.9	14.9	56.9	26.3	281484
86401	KINGMAN	19950	18899	36.8	31.3	23.9	5.5	2.4	33868	40504	24	26	14776	21.2	29.1	37.5	11.3	1.0	89663
86403	LAKE HAVASU CITY	23495	6589	28.9	34.5	26.1	7.3	3.3	38495	46290	41	42	4852	1.7	20.4	57.5	19.2	1.3	114749
86404	LAKE HAVASU CITY	22774	6759	27.9	35.6	26.4	8.0	2.2	38236	45670	40	41	5570	6.8	20.1	48.4	21.8	2.9	118586
86406	LAKE HAVASU CITY	27007	9274	22.0	34.0	30.4	8.6	4.9	45611	54651	63	60	7755	1.3	10.2	58.6	24.5	5.3	132726
86413	GOLDEN VALLEY	17857	3641	39.4	33.0	21.2	4.5	1.9	31400	36732	16	22	3127	19.4	42.1	33.0	5.2	0.4	79914
86426	FORT MOHAVE	21292	4259	22.6	32.3	35.5	7.3	2.3	43775	52703	58	54	3310	6.9	20.1	48.4	24.3	0.3	122292
86429	BULLHEAD CITY	22839	2320	28.5	40.1	22.8	5.3	3.2	36891	43780	35	36	1280	12.7	9.8	39.2	35.9	2.3	151108
	ARIZONA	25625		22.8	27.9	31.5	11.3	6.4	49168	61784				9.8	13.0	42.4	28.8	6.1	140071
	UNITED STATES	25866		24.7	27.1	30.8	10.9	6.5	48124	56710				10.9	15.0	33.7	30.1	10.4	145905

#	POST OFFICE NAME	FINANCIAL SERVICES: Auto Loan	FINANCIAL SERVICES: Home Loan	FINANCIAL SERVICES: Investments	FINANCIAL SERVICES: Retirement Plans	THE HOME: Home Improvements: Home Repair	THE HOME: Home Improvements: Lawn & Garden	THE HOME: Furnishings: Computers & Hardware	THE HOME: Furnishings: Major Appliances	THE HOME: Furnishings: TV, Radio, Sound Equipment	THE HOME: Furnishings: Furniture	ENTERTAINMENT: Dine out/Carry out	ENTERTAINMENT: Sports Equipment	ENTERTAINMENT: Fees & Tickets	ENTERTAINMENT: Toys & Games	ENTERTAINMENT: Travel	ENTERTAINMENT: Cable TV	PERSONAL: Apparel & Services	PERSONAL: Auto Repairs	PERSONAL: Health Insurance	PERSONAL: Pets & Supplies
85641	VAIL	107	106	93	103	106	110	100	105	99	101	122	122	97	120	99	97	118	104	102	123
85643	WILLCOX	68	58	44	55	59	65	58	63	61	60	75	71	54	69	57	62	72	64	66	73
85645	AMADO	120	109	102	106	112	127	109	118	114	112	140	126	106	127	111	116	134	117	127	132
85648	RIO RICO	81	70	63	67	68	71	75	78	78	81	99	86	70	92	71	74	99	81	72	82
85650	SIERRA VISTA	105	101	95	101	100	108	101	102	100	101	124	118	98	118	99	98	120	103	101	117
85653	MARANA	90	82	64	78	83	88	78	84	79	79	98	97	74	94	77	79	94	83	85	101
85701	TUCSON	49	42	50	44	41	45	51	48	52	50	65	57	48	61	48	49	63	52	46	52
85704	TUCSON	93	99	119	101	98	105	101	99	99	101	125	115	103	123	101	97	122	101	95	108
85705	TUCSON	53	46	48	46	47	52	52	51	53	51	66	60	49	62	50	52	63	54	52	58
85706	TUCSON	57	50	47	48	49	52	53	55	55	56	69	60	50	64	50	53	68	56	52	58
85707	TUCSON	75	47	45	54	43	51	71	61	72	66	90	81	60	80	58	66	86	72	56	69
85709	TUCSON	68	79	87	75	78	85	75	75	74	74	92	83	79	96	78	76	91	73	76	81
85710	TUCSON	70	76	88	76	75	81	75	75	74	75	93	85	78	94	77	74	91	75	74	82
85711	TUCSON	66	65	76	66	65	71	72	68	72	70	90	81	71	90	70	71	88	71	68	75
85712	TUCSON	61	58	71	61	57	63	67	63	66	65	83	75	65	80	64	64	81	67	61	69
85713	TUCSON	63	58	53	54	57	61	58	62	60	62	75	66	55	67	57	59	73	63	61	66
85714	TUCSON	59	52	43	48	50	53	53	57	55	58	69	61	49	61	51	53	69	58	54	60
85715	TUCSON	98	108	130	110	107	113	108	106	105	107	132	123	111	133	109	103	130	107	100	116
85716	TUCSON	65	60	74	64	59	64	72	66	71	69	89	81	69	86	68	67	87	71	62	73
85718	TUCSON	165	188	223	188	187	201	179	179	172	180	216	203	188	214	184	171	213	177	174	197
85719	TUCSON	58	46	58	50	45	51	65	55	63	60	80	71	58	75	57	59	77	62	52	62
85721	TUCSON	27	16	21	19	16	20	32	23	31	27	39	32	26	35	25	27	36	29	22	27
85730	TUCSON	76	81	87	83	79	81	80	79	77	81	97	93	81	97	79	74	95	80	72	87
85735	TUCSON	84	77	61	74	77	81	74	79	74	76	92	91	70	87	73	73	88	78	78	93
85736	TUCSON	74	69	57	65	69	75	65	71	67	68	83	79	63	76	66	67	79	70	73	82
85737	TUCSON	139	142	142	140	145	160	131	140	131	137	164	148	135	149	137	134	158	136	147	158
85739	TUCSON	126	117	105	112	122	138	109	122	114	116	142	127	108	123	115	119	134	120	135	141
85741	TUCSON	90	93	96	97	90	91	92	90	87	93	110	107	91	109	89	82	108	91	80	100
85742	TUCSON	120	132	128	135	128	129	119	121	112	124	142	138	123	139	119	108	139	118	111	134
85743	TUCSON	111	116	105	118	113	113	107	109	102	110	128	127	107	126	105	97	125	107	99	123
85745	TUCSON	93	95	102	96	93	97	96	95	93	97	118	110	95	115	94	90	116	97	88	104
85746	TUCSON	75	72	70	71	71	75	72	74	72	74	90	84	70	85	70	70	88	75	71	82
85747	TUCSON	114	126	121	130	122	119	114	115	106	118	134	134	117	135	113	101	132	112	101	128
85748	TUCSON	115	135	140	136	131	130	124	123	115	125	146	143	129	150	124	111	145	120	110	135
85749	TUCSON	160	190	199	190	189	191	171	173	161	171	202	201	180	211	176	159	201	167	161	195
85750	TUCSON	161	181	205	185	177	187	168	168	160	172	203	189	178	201	171	158	200	164	159	186
85901	SHOW LOW	71	58	45	54	62	69	58	65	63	58	76	75	53	74	59	65	72	65	72	82
85920	ALPINE	99	78	53	70	88	98	73	88	83	73	98	103	66	97	78	89	91	87	104	121
85922	BLUE	0	0	0	0	0	0	0	0	0	0	0	0	0	0	0	0	0	0	0	0
85924	CONCHO	64	49	32	44	55	62	47	56	53	46	62	66	41	62	49	56	58	55	67	77
85925	EAGAR	92	74	52	71	80	88	73	83	78	73	94	97	66	92	74	80	88	82	91	106
85928	HEBER	79	62	42	56	69	78	58	70	66	58	78	82	52	77	62	70	72	69	83	96
85929	LAKESIDE	90	71	48	64	79	89	67	80	75	66	89	94	59	88	71	80	83	79	95	110
85935	PINETOP	133	104	71	94	117	132	98	118	111	97	132	138	88	130	105	119	122	116	140	162
85936	SAINT JOHNS	83	64	42	62	70	79	66	74	72	65	86	86	59	82	66	75	80	74	85	94
85937	SNOWFLAKE	79	71	57	69	73	78	69	74	70	70	87	87	65	84	68	70	83	73	76	89
85938	SPRINGERVILLE	83	67	49	65	72	83	69	76	75	67	90	87	64	88	69	78	84	75	86	94
86001	FLAGSTAFF	82	73	79	76	72	77	86	79	84	82	105	98	81	101	80	79	102	84	74	90
86004	FLAGSTAFF	99	106	110	109	104	106	103	101	98	104	124	119	105	124	101	95	122	101	93	113
86021	COLORADO CITY	71	64	52	62	64	68	63	66	64	64	79	77	59	75	62	63	76	66	66	78
86022	FREDONIA	62	56	44	54	57	60	54	58	55	55	67	67	51	64	53	54	65	58	58	70
86025	HOLBROOK	75	68	58	67	69	74	69	72	70	69	86	83	65	83	68	69	82	72	73	84
86030	HOTEVILLA	47	37	39	33	37	46	42	44	49	43	58	47	40	52	41	52	55	45	52	51
86033	KAYENTA	62	56	45	53	55	58	55	59	56	58	70	66	51	64	53	55	68	59	57	66
86034	KEAMS CANYON	54	47	46	44	46	52	50	52	54	52	67	57	48	61	49	55	65	54	54	58
86035	LEUPP	50	42	33	39	42	44	43	47	45	46	56	51	39	50	41	44	55	48	46	52
86036	MARBLE CANYON	87	78	60	75	79	84	74	81	76	76	94	93	70	89	74	76	90	80	82	98
86038	MORMON LAKE	83	65	44	58	73	82	61	74	69	61	82	86	55	81	65	74	76	72	87	101
86039	KYKOTSMOVI VILLAGE	41	36	30	34	35	37	37	40	38	40	48	42	34	43	35	37	48	41	38	42
86040	PAGE	96	96	84	94	95	97	90	94	88	92	109	108	88	107	89	86	107	92	89	108
86042	POLACCA	40	36	39	35	35	40	42	40	44	40	54	46	40	53	40	44	52	42	42	44
86043	SECOND MESA	41	32	27	30	33	41	36	38	41	35	48	42	33	44	35	43	45	39	45	45
86044	TONALEA	52	58	58	57	57	57	54	55	52	55	65	63	55	66	54	50	65	54	50	60
86045	TUBA CITY	67	66	60	64	64	67	64	67	64	67	80	76	62	76	63	61	78	67	62	73
86046	WILLIAMS	83	69	58	68	72	79	71	76	75	71	91	90	66	87	70	75	86	77	80	94
86047	WINSLOW	63	56	51	54	56	60	58	61	61	59	75	69	55	71	57	60	73	62	61	68
86053	KAIBITO	53	46	39	43	45	48	48	51	50	52	62	55	44	55	45	49	62	52	49	54
86054	SHONTO	55	48	40	45	47	49	49	53	51	54	64	57	45	57	47	49	64	54	50	56
86301	PRESCOTT	93	88	93	85	91	106	87	93	91	90	113	97	87	100	91	94	107	93	104	104
86303	PRESCOTT	91	86	88	83	90	104	82	90	87	86	108	94	83	96	88	91	102	89	102	104
86305	PRESCOTT	106	102	102	98	106	123	98	107	102	101	127	110	99	114	104	107	120	105	120	121
86314	PRESCOTT VALLEY	82	70	54	68	73	81	70	76	74	70	89	87	65	85	70	75	84	76	82	92
86320	ASH FORK	61	48	33	43	54	61	45	55	51	45	61	64	40	60	48	55	56	54	64	75
86321	BAGDAD	80	68	53	68	71	81	70	75	74	69	90	85	67	89	69	76	84	74	81	88
86322	CAMP VERDE	74	65	51	62	66	73	63	69	66	64	81	77	60	75	63	67	76	68	73	81
86323	CHINO VALLEY	92	84	69	81	85	92	80	87	82	83	101	98	77	93	80	82	97	86	89	102
86324	CLARKDALE	77	72	70	68	76	90	68	77	72	72	90	76	69	78	73	77	84	75	89	87
86325	CORNVILLE	92	75	51	72	80	87	73	83	77	73	94	97	66	90	73	79	88	82	89	105
86326	COTTONWOOD	78	68	60	67	72	81	71	75	74	70	90	84	67	85	71	76	85	75	83	87
86327	DEWEY	95	88	78	84	91	104	82	92	86	87	107	96	81	93	87	90	101	90	102	106
86332	KIRKLAND	73	62	55	56	67	80	58	70	65	62	80	71	57	69	63	70	74	68	83	83
86333	MAYER	67	60	58	56	64	78	59	67	64	61	78	66	58	68	63	68	72	65	79	75
86334	PAULDEN	101	92	73	88	92	98	87	94	89	90	109	107	83	102	87	88	105	93	95	112
86335	RIMROCK	71	54	36	52	59	70	59	65	66	57	78	73	53	74	59	70	71	65	77	79
86336	SEDONA	120	111	104	106	118	136	103	117	109	108	135	121	103	119	111	116	127	114	134	138
86337	SELIGMAN	55	44	30	39	49	55	41	49	46	41	55	58	37	54	44	50	51	49	58	68
86343	CROWN KING	104	83	61	75	93	106	79	94	88	79	105	107	72	102	84	94	98	92	111	125
86351	SEDONA	114	111	115	110	116	130	107	116	109	111	136	122	108	121	112	112	129	114	126	130
86401	KINGMAN	74	67	58	64	69	78	66	71	69	67	84	79	63	79	67	71	80	71	77	83
86403	LAKE HAVASU CITY	80	72	67	68	76	89	71	78	76	72	93	81	70	83	74	80	87	77	90	89
86404	LAKE HAVASU CITY	79	71	65	67	76	90	68	77	73	71	89	78	67	77	72	78	83	75	91	89
86406	LAKE HAVASU CITY	97	89	82	84	94	111	84	95	90	88	111	95	84	95	90	95	103	92	111	109
86413	GOLDEN VALLEY	67	60	50	57	62	69	57	64	60	60	74	70	55	68	58	61	70	63	68	75
86426	FORT MOHAVE	88	80	63	77	80	85	77	82	77	79	96	95	72	90	75	76	92	82	81	97
86429	BULLHEAD CITY	84	64	42	60	70	83	68	76	76	65	90	87	61	86	68	81	83	76	91	95
	ARIZONA	97	96	98	96	95	101	96	97	95	98	119	111	95	114	95	93	116	98	95	108
	UNITED STATES	100	100	100	100	100	100	100	100	100	100	100	100	100	100	100	100	100	100	100	100

A 86432-86556

ZIP CODE		COUNTY FIPS CODE	POPULATION			2000-2004 ANNUAL RATE		HOUSEHOLDS					FAMILIES		
#	POST OFFICE NAME		2000	2004	2009	% Rate	State Centile	2000	2004	2009	% Annual Rate 2000-2004	2004 Average HH Size	2000	2004	% Annual Rate 2000-2004
86432	LITTLEFIELD	015	1584	2197	2753	8.0	96	597	822	1027	7.8	2.67	431	605	8.3
86434	PEACH SPRINGS	005	980	1106	1254	2.9	69	278	319	366	3.3	3.39	222	254	3.2
86435	SUPAI	005	503	516	542	0.6	20	140	145	154	0.8	3.56	102	106	0.9
86436	TOPOCK	015	2055	2409	2788	3.8	76	1016	1198	1391	4.0	2.01	627	743	4.1
86440	MOHAVE VALLEY	015	6513	7286	8230	2.7	65	2516	2832	3215	2.8	2.55	1792	2024	2.9
86441	DOLAN SPRINGS	015	54	60	67	2.5	61	20	22	25	2.3	2.73	12	13	1.9
86442	BULLHEAD CITY	015	29787	32222	35978	1.9	48	12182	13158	14708	1.8	2.44	7955	8631	1.9
86444	MEADVIEW	015	178	198	222	2.5	63	76	85	96	2.7	2.33	45	51	3.0
86502	CHAMBERS	001	2276	2552	2710	2.7	66	647	720	769	2.6	3.54	493	551	2.7
86503	CHINLE	001	12512	12589	12610	0.1	12	3328	3416	3494	0.6	3.59	2538	2619	0.7
86505	GANADO	001	24478	24161	24054	-0.3	5	6808	6886	7023	0.3	3.46	5232	5313	0.4
86507	LUKACHUKAI	001	1749	1743	1745	-0.1	7	482	492	505	0.5	3.54	370	379	0.6
86510	PINON	017	8032	8578	9248	1.6	36	2028	2173	2371	1.6	3.95	1601	1723	1.7
86514	TEEC NOS POS	001	5620	5640	5636	0.1	11	1579	1627	1667	0.7	3.47	1219	1261	0.8
86535	DENNEHOTSO	001	1807	1786	1774	-0.3	5	450	450	455	0.0	3.97	354	355	0.1
86538	MANY FARMS	001	4789	4860	4888	0.4	14	1283	1330	1368	0.9	3.65	982	1022	0.9
86556	TSAILE	001	1924	1947	1953	0.3	13	469	485	497	0.8	3.80	369	382	0.8
	ARIZONA					2.7					2.7	2.64			2.9
	UNITED STATES					1.2					1.3	2.58			1.1

POPULATION COMPOSITION

#	POST OFFICE NAME	White 2000	White 2004	Black 2000	Black 2004	Asian/Pacific 2000	Asian/Pacific 2004	% Hispanic Origin 2000	% Hispanic Origin 2004	0-4	5-9	10-14	15-19	20-24	25-44	45-64	65-84	85+	18+	MEDIAN AGE 2004	% 2004 Males	% 2004 Females
86432	LITTLEFIELD	83.3	81.1	0.0	0.0	0.5	0.6	23.7	27.1	8.7	7.4	6.6	5.1	7.8	24.1	26.8	13.1	0.5	74.3	36.2	52.3	47.8
86434	PEACH SPRINGS	18.2	19.2	0.1	0.2	0.1	0.2	5.0	5.1	8.9	8.6	10.5	9.9	8.1	24.6	21.7	7.7	0.2	65.6	28.5	49.3	50.7
86435	SUPAI	9.9	8.3	0.0	0.0	0.0	0.0	1.8	1.7	11.1	13.4	12.0	7.6	6.8	27.5	18.0	3.3	0.4	58.1	24.4	47.7	52.3
86436	TOPOCK	95.9	95.4	0.5	0.5	0.5	0.6	5.2	6.1	2.2	2.5	3.8	4.6	2.7	14.8	32.9	34.3	2.2	88.6	58.2	50.6	49.4
86440	MOHAVE VALLEY	85.8	84.8	0.4	0.5	0.8	0.9	13.1	14.9	6.0	6.0	6.6	6.4	5.4	22.6	28.3	17.2	1.4	77.3	43.0	50.4	49.6
86441	DOLAN SPRINGS	92.6	91.7	0.0	1.7	0.0	1.7	5.6	6.7	3.3	3.3	3.3	3.3	3.3	15.0	33.3	31.7	3.3	90.0	57.5	50.0	50.0
86442	BULLHEAD CITY	85.1	83.7	0.9	1.0	1.0	1.2	20.8	23.2	6.3	6.2	6.5	5.3	5.3	22.8	27.2	18.8	1.7	77.8	43.2	49.8	50.2
86444	MEADVIEW	93.3	92.4	1.1	1.0	1.7	1.5	6.2	7.1	3.5	3.5	4.0	4.6	3.0	13.6	32.3	32.8	2.5	85.9	57.4	52.5	47.5
86502	CHAMBERS	13.0	11.4	0.4	0.4	0.1	0.1	3.6	3.7	10.3	9.8	12.0	10.9	8.0	22.8	18.5	7.0	0.7	60.6	24.4	49.3	50.7
86503	CHINLE	3.2	2.9	0.1	0.1	0.1	0.1	1.4	1.4	10.5	10.1	11.6	11.3	8.9	23.9	16.4	6.4	0.9	60.5	23.7	49.9	50.1
86505	GANADO	3.2	2.9	0.1	0.1	0.2	0.2	1.2	1.2	9.5	9.3	11.0	10.7	8.5	24.4	19.0	6.8	0.7	63.3	25.9	49.0	51.0
86507	LUKACHUKAI	1.1	1.0	0.0	0.0	0.1	0.1	1.0	1.0	9.2	9.0	11.8	11.9	9.5	24.2	16.4	7.2	0.8	62.9	24.3	48.8	51.2
86510	PINON	2.1	1.4	0.0	0.0	0.0	0.0	0.8	0.7	11.6	10.7	11.6	11.3	8.3	24.3	14.9	6.7	0.6	59.0	22.9	49.8	50.2
86514	TEEC NOS POS	1.7	1.5	0.0	0.0	0.1	0.1	0.7	0.7	9.7	9.5	11.2	10.8	7.8	24.1	17.8	8.3	0.9	62.9	25.8	50.0	50.0
86535	DENNEHOTSO	0.8	0.7	0.0	0.0	0.0	0.0	0.8	0.8	9.2	9.9	13.7	11.3	8.5	22.1	15.6	8.8	1.0	60.3	23.5	51.1	48.9
86538	MANY FARMS	3.0	2.7	0.1	0.1	0.1	0.1	0.9	0.9	10.8	10.5	12.0	11.2	9.0	24.5	16.0	5.5	0.6	59.8	23.1	49.3	50.7
86556	TSAILE	2.3	2.1	0.1	0.1	0.1	0.1	0.9	0.9	10.6	9.6	10.5	11.4	10.2	26.0	15.7	5.4	0.6	62.8	23.9	48.2	51.8
	ARIZONA	75.5	74.0	3.1	3.2	1.9	2.1	25.3	27.9	7.6	7.1	7.3	6.9	7.5	28.1	22.1	11.9	1.5	74.0	34.8	49.9	50.2
	UNITED STATES	75.1	73.6	12.3	12.5	3.8	4.2	12.5	14.1	6.9	6.7	7.2	7.0	7.3	28.6	23.8	10.8	1.7	75.1	36.0	49.1	50.9

#	POST OFFICE NAME	2004 Per Capita Income	2004 HH Income Base	2004 HOUSEHOLD INCOME DISTRIBUTION (%)					MEDIAN HOUSEHOLD INCOME				2004 Home Value Base	2004 HOME VALUE DISTRIBUTION (%)					2004 Median Home Value
				Less than $25,000	$25,000 to $49,999	$50,000 to $99,999	$100,000 to $149,999	$150,000 or More	2004	2009	2004 National Centile	2004 State Centile		Less than $50,000	$50,000 to $89,999	$90,000 to $174,999	$175,000 to $399,999	$400,000 or More	
86432	LITTLEFIELD	17037	822	27.9	39.9	25.2	5.6	1.5	36834	45205	35	36	682	23.5	17.9	43.4	12.3	2.9	103218
86434	PEACH SPRINGS	13800	319	48.9	24.5	19.1	4.1	3.5	25659	32336	5	12	200	31.0	32.0	26.5	9.5	1.0	72778
86435	SUPAI	9961	145	51.7	27.6	12.4	4.8	3.5	23793	28588	4	7	95	66.3	19.0	7.4	7.4	0.0	27917
86436	TOPOCK	19579	1198	41.8	32.9	21.3	2.4	1.6	29558	34625	11	17	997	24.1	40.2	29.9	5.6	0.2	76189
86440	MOHAVE VALLEY	17984	2832	29.6	34.5	29.0	6.1	0.9	38853	46792	42	42	2290	18.7	21.0	43.8	15.9	0.7	102296
86441	DOLAN SPRINGS	10667	22	63.6	18.2	13.6	4.6	0.0	18015	20678	1	3	19	52.6	31.6	15.8	0.0	0.0	47500
86442	BULLHEAD CITY	19160	13158	35.5	36.2	21.6	4.2	2.5	34162	40773	25	27	8872	23.9	31.9	34.4	8.4	1.6	83294
86444	MEADVIEW	11641	85	62.4	22.4	12.9	2.4	0.0	18615	22739	1	4	73	49.3	28.8	20.6	1.4	0.0	50833
86502	CHAMBERS	10002	720	49.0	29.9	17.8	1.9	1.4	25607	30945	5	11	525	22.5	32.8	34.1	4.8	5.9	83452
86503	CHINLE	9174	3416	53.4	26.9	15.8	2.1	1.8	22179	27002	3	6	2276	68.9	19.6	5.6	2.2	3.8	26463
86505	GANADO	11146	6886	43.9	28.4	21.5	5.3	1.0	29193	35939	11	16	4771	63.3	19.0	12.0	4.1	1.7	32141
86507	LUKACHUKAI	5027	492	75.4	20.5	3.7	0.4	0.2	11427	12801	1	1	363	66.7	20.4	8.5	3.3	1.1	15938
86510	PINON	6170	2173	64.1	24.3	9.9	1.4	0.2	15088	17742	1	2	1520	57.9	21.4	9.8	9.0	1.9	35962
86514	TEEC NOS POS	7461	1627	62.2	21.1	15.7	1.0	0.0	16361	19972	1	2	1366	70.5	15.2	7.9	2.3	4.1	23986
86535	DENNEHOTSO	6824	450	55.1	26.7	16.2	2.0	0.0	18568	23528	1	4	375	60.5	21.9	11.7	2.9	2.9	30682
86538	MANY FARMS	7843	1330	53.8	27.7	16.6	1.6	0.2	21542	26039	2	6	842	59.7	24.6	11.4	2.7	1.5	28226
86556	TSAILE	7876	485	60.6	20.8	14.0	4.5	0.0	18204	21992	1	3	299	65.2	21.7	10.7	1.3	1.0	21607
	ARIZONA	25625		22.8	27.9	31.5	11.3	6.4	49168	61784				9.8	13.0	42.4	28.8	6.1	140071
	UNITED STATES	25866		24.7	27.1	30.8	10.9	6.5	48124	56710				10.9	15.0	33.7	30.1	10.4	145905

ZIP CODE		FINANCIAL SERVICES				THE HOME						ENTERTAINMENT						PERSONAL			
						Home Improvements		Furnishings													
#	POST OFFICE NAME	Auto Loan	Home Loan	Invest-ments	Retire-ment Plans	Home Repair	Lawn & Garden	Comput-ers & Hard-ware	Major Appli-ances	TV, Radio, Sound Equip-ment	Furni-ture	Dine out/ Carry out	Sports Equip-ment	Fees & Tickets	Toys & Games	Travel	Cable TV	Apparel & Services	Auto Repairs	Health Insur-ance	Pets & Supplies
86432	LITTLEFIELD	72	66	52	64	66	70	63	68	64	65	79	78	60	74	62	63	76	67	67	80
86434	PEACH SPRINGS	67	58	59	56	59	68	65	65	69	63	84	75	62	82	64	70	80	67	70	75
86435	SUPAI	54	48	40	44	46	48	49	53	51	53	63	56	45	56	46	49	63	54	49	55
86436	TOPOCK	57	55	58	50	58	70	51	59	55	55	68	55	52	57	56	59	64	57	70	64
86440	MOHAVE VALLEY	75	65	49	61	67	73	62	69	65	63	79	79	58	75	62	65	75	68	72	84
86441	DOLAN SPRINGS	42	41	43	37	43	52	38	44	41	41	51	41	39	42	41	44	47	42	52	48
86442	BULLHEAD CITY	72	65	58	61	68	77	62	70	66	65	81	74	61	74	65	69	76	69	77	81
86444	MEADVIEW	40	38	40	35	40	49	35	41	38	38	47	38	36	40	39	41	44	39	48	44
86502	CHAMBERS	55	48	40	45	48	51	49	52	50	51	63	58	45	57	43	49	61	53	51	58
86503	CHINLE	45	39	45	36	38	44	44	44	48	45	60	49	43	57	43	49	58	46	46	49
86505	GANADO	58	52	47	49	51	56	53	55	55	54	68	62	50	64	52	56	66	56	57	63
86507	LUKACHUKAI	24	20	26	19	20	23	24	23	27	25	33	27	24	32	24	28	32	25	25	26
86510	PINON	37	32	28	29	31	34	33	35	35	35	44	38	31	39	32	35	43	36	36	38
86514	TEEC NOS POS	38	32	31	29	31	36	35	36	38	36	47	39	33	43	34	39	45	37	39	40
86535	DENNEHOTSO	41	36	30	34	35	37	37	40	39	40	48	43	34	43	35	37	48	41	38	42
86538	MANY FARMS	40	35	41	33	34	39	39	38	42	40	53	43	39	51	38	43	52	40	40	43
86556	TSAILE	40	33	41	30	32	38	38	38	43	39	53	43	37	51	37	44	51	40	41	44
	ARIZONA	97	96	98	96	95	101	96	97	95	98	119	111	95	114	95	93	116	98	95	108
	UNITED STATES	100	100	100	100	100	100	100	100	100	100	100	100	100	100	100	100	100	100	100	100

#	POST OFFICE NAME	COUNTY FIPS CODE	POPULATION 2000	2004	2009	% Rate	State Centile	HOUSEHOLDS 2000	2004	2009	% Annual Rate 2000-2004	2004 Average HH Size	FAMILIES 2000	2004	% Annual Rate 2000-2004
71601	PINE BLUFF	069	20214	19435	18926	-0.9	8	7154	6916	6791	-0.8	2.66	4748	4498	-1.3
71602	WHITE HALL	069	19442	19751	19716	0.4	48	6828	7047	7131	0.8	2.58	5064	5149	0.4
71603	PINE BLUFF	069	35862	35666	35264	-0.1	30	13781	13842	13835	0.1	2.49	9691	9567	-0.3
71630	ARKANSAS CITY	041	45	45	45	0.0	35	13	13	13	0.0	3.46	9	9	0.0
71631	BANKS	011	748	741	733	-0.2	27	304	305	305	0.1	2.43	201	198	-0.4
71635	CROSSETT	003	13837	13717	13668	-0.2	27	5459	5488	5547	0.1	2.48	4028	3991	-0.2
71638	DERMOTT	043	4754	4694	4620	-0.3	24	1625	1637	1645	0.2	2.64	1123	1111	-0.3
71639	DUMAS	041	6560	6446	6404	-0.4	20	2440	2438	2466	0.0	2.62	1742	1713	-0.4
71640	EUDORA	017	4119	3971	3822	-0.9	9	1554	1517	1484	-0.6	2.62	1107	1064	-0.9
71642	FOUNTAIN HILL	003	577	587	591	0.4	50	246	253	259	0.7	2.32	184	187	0.4
71643	GOULD	079	2634	2641	2683	0.1	37	657	666	689	0.3	2.56	464	463	-0.1
71644	GRADY	079	4264	4264	4299	0.0	35	783	788	807	0.2	2.78	604	599	-0.2
71646	HAMBURG	003	6815	7003	7095	0.6	59	2564	2668	2739	0.9	2.59	1916	1965	0.6
71647	HERMITAGE	011	2398	2358	2330	-0.4	21	862	853	850	-0.3	2.46	621	604	-0.7
71651	JERSEY	011	400	392	387	-0.5	19	102	101	100	-0.2	2.97	71	68	-1.0
71652	KINGSLAND	025	1052	1079	1115	0.6	58	419	432	450	0.7	2.50	308	313	0.4
71653	LAKE VILLAGE	017	5520	5398	5235	-0.5	16	2148	2145	2122	0.0	2.36	1500	1473	-0.4
71654	MC GEHEE	041	5491	5545	5592	0.2	44	2205	2274	2341	0.7	2.41	1535	1557	0.3
71655	MONTICELLO	043	15852	16654	17620	1.2	73	6235	6666	7182	1.6	2.41	4299	4516	1.2
71656	MONTICELLO	043	160	170	179	1.4	79	7	8	9	3.2	2.50	3	3	0.0
71658	MONTROSE	003	980	965	958	-0.4	23	356	356	358	0.0	2.71	258	253	-0.5
71660	NEW EDINBURG	025	1066	1082	1113	0.4	48	420	430	446	0.6	2.52	314	317	0.2
71661	PARKDALE	003	471	444	436	-1.4	4	183	176	175	-0.9	2.52	136	129	-1.2
71662	PICKENS	041	1047	1022	1013	-0.6	15	398	395	398	-0.2	2.58	291	285	-0.5
71663	PORTLAND	003	952	908	887	-1.1	6	362	352	350	-0.7	2.58	264	252	-1.1
71665	RISON	025	6171	6374	6617	0.8	64	2332	2435	2554	1.0	2.59	1814	1869	0.7
71666	MC GEHEE	041	641	643	642	0.1	38	257	261	264	0.4	2.46	179	179	0.0
71667	STAR CITY	079	7172	7335	7522	0.5	55	2668	2769	2881	0.9	2.55	1962	2007	0.5
71670	TILLAR	043	868	935	984	1.8	83	342	374	400	2.1	2.47	244	262	1.7
71671	WARREN	011	9199	9255	9284	0.1	40	3620	3677	3722	0.4	2.41	2535	2532	0.0
71674	WATSON	041	1024	1000	991	-0.6	15	409	406	409	-0.2	2.46	299	292	-0.6
71675	WILMAR	043	1280	1307	1363	0.5	53	519	539	570	0.9	2.41	364	372	0.5
71676	WILMOT	003	974	912	895	-1.5	2	370	353	352	-1.1	2.44	242	226	-1.6
71677	WINCHESTER	043	291	302	317	0.9	67	103	109	116	1.3	2.77	77	80	0.9
71678	YORKTOWN	079	857	874	895	0.5	52	319	331	344	0.9	2.64	228	232	0.4
71701	CAMDEN	103	21651	21394	21068	-0.3	24	8763	8765	8740	0.0	2.40	6050	5945	-0.4
71720	BEARDEN	103	2593	2560	2511	-0.3	24	993	995	989	0.1	2.56	715	704	-0.4
71722	BLUFF CITY	099	497	492	498	-0.2	26	204	204	209	0.0	2.41	149	147	-0.3
71725	CARTHAGE	039	1186	1198	1196	0.2	45	473	486	492	0.6	2.36	303	306	0.2
71726	CHIDESTER	103	1308	1244	1203	-1.2	6	575	556	546	-0.8	2.23	382	362	-1.3
71730	EL DORADO	139	35872	36057	36345	0.1	40	14198	14407	14665	0.3	2.44	9930	9905	-0.1
71740	EMERSON	027	1858	1875	1877	0.2	43	720	735	744	0.5	2.55	514	515	0.1
71742	FORDYCE	039	5887	5806	5736	-0.3	23	2185	2178	2176	-0.1	2.47	1499	1469	-0.5
71743	GURDON	019	4400	4560	4714	0.8	66	1775	1859	1938	1.1	2.45	1250	1284	0.6
71744	HAMPTON	013	3607	3582	3541	-0.2	29	1457	1472	1482	0.2	2.36	1010	1003	-0.2
71745	HARRELL	013	829	818	807	-0.3	23	339	341	342	0.1	2.39	245	243	-0.2
71747	HUTTIG	139	1256	1231	1226	-0.5	19	496	492	496	-0.2	2.50	348	339	-0.6
71748	IVAN	039	340	341	339	0.1	38	145	148	150	0.5	2.30	108	109	0.2
71749	JUNCTION CITY	139	3132	3073	3045	-0.5	19	1197	1188	1192	-0.2	2.55	895	881	-0.4
71751	LOUANN	103	1056	1044	1025	-0.3	25	424	426	424	0.1	2.45	319	316	-0.2
71752	MC NEIL	027	1329	1332	1331	0.1	36	512	518	524	0.3	2.57	361	359	-0.1
71753	MAGNOLIA	027	17544	17500	17524	-0.1	32	6809	6868	6957	0.2	2.39	4505	4458	-0.3
71758	MOUNT HOLLY	139	566	677	744	4.3	99	228	276	308	4.6	2.45	161	192	4.2
71762	SMACKOVER	139	2773	2747	2747	-0.2	27	1051	1053	1064	0.0	2.55	750	741	-0.3
71763	SPARKMAN	039	1802	1808	1800	0.1	38	719	732	739	0.4	2.47	522	522	0.0
71764	STEPHENS	103	2374	2283	2221	-0.9	8	933	907	893	-0.7	2.52	657	628	-1.1
71765	STRONG	139	2518	2513	2517	-0.1	32	1012	1022	1034	0.2	2.46	703	699	-0.1
71766	THORNTON	013	1308	1315	1307	0.1	40	521	533	539	0.5	2.47	374	377	0.2
71770	WALDO	027	3270	3265	3259	0.0	32	1302	1319	1334	0.3	2.48	902	897	-0.1
71801	HOPE	057	17241	17588	18069	0.5	53	6511	6649	6839	0.5	2.60	4582	4601	0.1
71822	ASHDOWN	081	9489	9569	9708	0.2	42	3766	3876	4014	0.7	2.42	2714	2750	0.3
71825	BLEVINS	057	980	999	1019	0.5	51	364	373	381	0.6	2.68	275	278	0.3
71826	BRADLEY	073	2408	2283	2162	-1.3	5	1005	974	943	-0.7	2.34	693	661	-1.1
71827	BUCKNER	073	1159	1098	1042	-1.3	4	436	420	406	-0.9	2.59	318	302	-1.2
71828	CALE	099	355	363	371	0.5	55	124	128	132	0.8	2.84	93	95	0.5
71831	COLUMBUS	057	81	81	82	0.0	35	29	29	30	0.0	2.79	20	20	0.0
71832	DE QUEEN	133	9226	9495	9812	0.7	61	3171	3227	3307	0.4	2.89	2344	2352	0.1
71833	DIERKS	061	2457	2404	2370	-0.5	17	944	935	933	-0.2	2.53	716	700	-0.5
71834	DODDRIDGE	091	1431	1436	1486	0.1	38	609	621	652	0.5	2.31	437	438	0.1
71835	EMMET	099	1562	1631	1686	1.0	70	610	642	670	1.2	2.54	435	449	0.8
71836	FOREMAN	081	2930	3037	3116	0.9	67	1178	1242	1298	1.3	2.45	1969	2030	0.7
71837	FOUKE	091	6860	7073	7443	0.7	62	2468	2574	2742	1.0	2.74	319	310	-0.7
71838	FULTON	057	1220	1199	1209	-0.4	20	455	449	453	-0.3	2.67	319	310	-0.7
71839	GARLAND CITY	091	542	548	571	0.3	45	209	214	226	0.6	2.53	156	157	0.2
71841	GILLHAM	133	878	959	1023	2.1	88	362	395	420	2.1	2.43	273	294	1.8
71842	HORATIO	133	2862	2885	2943	0.2	42	1065	1073	1090	0.2	2.69	802	798	-0.1
71845	LEWISVILLE	073	2286	2157	2040	-1.4	4	918	881	848	-1.0	2.43	641	605	-1.4
71846	LOCKESBURG	133	2864	2902	2968	0.3	47	1141	1159	1181	0.4	2.50	831	831	0.0
71847	MC CASKILL	057	689	735	768	1.5	81	265	283	296	1.6	2.60	206	218	1.3
71851	MINERAL SPRINGS	061	2647	2568	2521	-0.7	12	1037	1016	1009	-0.5	2.53	767	740	-0.8
71852	NASHVILLE	061	9217	9419	9509	0.5	54	3488	3596	3661	0.7	2.53	2450	2491	0.4
71853	OGDEN	081	438	434	439	-0.2	27	186	188	194	0.3	2.31	126	125	-0.2
71854	TEXARKANA	091	31610	33671	36189	1.5	80	12351	13340	14546	1.8	2.44	8519	9051	1.4
71855	OZAN	057	922	933	948	0.3	46	356	362	369	0.4	2.58	252	252	0.0
71857	PRESCOTT	099	5697	5804	5938	0.4	51	2222	2292	2376	0.7	2.40	1509	1529	0.3
71858	ROSSTON	099	1414	1405	1423	-0.2	29	548	553	569	0.2	2.54	404	402	-0.1
71859	SARATOGA	061	583	554	548	-1.2	5	252	241	240	-1.0	2.30	168	158	-1.4
71860	STAMPS	073	2856	2889	2823	0.3	46	1138	1169	1163	0.6	2.39	769	775	0.2
71861	TAYLOR	027	1419	1451	1462	0.5	55	560	580	591	0.8	2.45	413	421	0.5
71862	WASHINGTON	057	783	787	797	0.1	40	329	333	337	0.3	2.36	239	238	-0.1
71864	WILLISVILLE	099	776	765	773	-0.3	23	318	319	327	0.1	2.40	230	228	-0.2
71865	WILTON	081	26	26	26	0.0	35	11	11	11	0.0	2.36	9	9	0.0
71866	WINTHROP	081	753	741	744	-0.4	22	327	328	335	0.1	2.26	237	233	-0.4
71901	HOT SPRINGS NATIONAL	051	28858	29472	30363	0.5	53	11806	12117	12566	0.6	2.31	7343	7395	0.2
71909	HOT SPRINGS VILLAGE	051	13069	13880	14712	1.4	79	6368	6849	7332	1.7	2.02	4934	5232	1.4
	ARKANSAS					0.9					1.1	2.47			0.8
	UNITED STATES					1.2					1.3	2.58			1.1

ZIP CODE #	POST OFFICE NAME	RACE (%) White 2000	White 2004	Black 2000	Black 2004	Asian/Pacific 2000	Asian/Pacific 2004	% Hispanic Origin 2000	% Hispanic Origin 2004	2004 AGE DISTRIBUTION (%) 0-4	5-9	10-14	15-19	20-24	25-44	45-64	65-84	85+	18+	MEDIAN AGE 2004	% 2004 Males	% 2004 Females
71601	PINE BLUFF	16.1	14.3	82.6	84.3	0.3	0.3	0.9	1.0	7.9	7.5	8.2	9.9	9.9	24.4	20.2	10.4	1.8	71.7	30.4	45.9	54.1
71602	WHITE HALL	75.1	73.5	22.9	24.2	0.6	0.8	1.1	1.2	6.6	6.6	6.8	6.9	7.2	30.1	25.2	9.8	1.0	76.1	36.2	52.8	47.3
71603	PINE BLUFF	49.7	47.4	48.2	50.2	1.1	1.2	0.7	0.8	7.1	7.0	7.0	6.6	6.9	25.8	25.0	12.4	2.4	75.0	37.4	46.9	53.1
71630	ARKANSAS CITY	55.6	53.3	42.2	44.4	0.0	0.0	4.4	2.2	6.7	6.7	8.9	6.7	6.7	28.9	22.2	11.1	2.2	77.8	36.9	51.1	48.9
71631	BANKS	55.8	54.0	41.6	43.2	0.1	0.1	2.4	2.4	5.8	6.1	7.4	6.6	5.9	23.1	24.7	18.0	2.4	76.8	40.6	50.5	49.5
71635	CROSSETT	71.7	70.9	26.4	27.2	0.3	0.3	1.9	1.9	7.2	7.2	7.5	6.5	6.1	26.9	25.0	11.8	1.9	74.2	37.0	48.4	51.6
71638	DERMOTT	38.7	37.1	59.4	60.9	0.3	0.3	1.6	1.7	6.4	6.7	7.4	7.1	6.6	27.6	23.7	12.1	2.4	74.8	36.5	49.8	50.2
71639	DUMAS	39.8	38.9	56.0	57.0	0.4	0.4	4.5	4.5	8.5	8.1	7.6	7.8	7.5	24.7	23.6	10.6	1.8	71.1	33.6	46.7	53.3
71640	EUDORA	30.0	28.8	66.8	67.6	0.2	0.2	4.0	4.6	7.8	7.6	7.7	7.5	8.1	23.6	22.9	13.2	1.6	72.6	35.1	47.1	52.9
71642	FOUNTAIN HILL	80.6	79.1	13.2	14.5	0.0	0.0	5.7	5.8	6.5	6.3	6.8	6.6	6.6	28.6	25.6	11.8	1.2	76.3	37.4	51.3	48.7
71643	GOULD	36.9	35.4	61.2	62.6	0.0	0.0	1.1	1.3	5.4	5.1	5.3	5.3	10.3	37.8	22.1	7.3	1.4	81.0	34.4	65.4	34.6
71644	GRADY	53.5	51.3	43.7	45.6	0.2	0.2	3.0	3.4	3.7	3.6	3.8	6.1	14.9	41.0	19.3	6.6	1.0	86.1	33.2	74.5	25.5
71646	HAMBURG	76.2	74.8	18.4	19.9	0.1	0.1	5.5	5.4	6.7	6.8	7.6	6.4	6.5	27.4	25.1	11.9	1.5	74.8	37.0	49.7	50.3
71647	HERMITAGE	61.7	60.9	17.4	18.3	0.0	0.0	22.3	22.2	6.8	6.7	6.6	6.5	7.8	30.6	22.4	11.1	1.6	76.3	35.0	55.9	44.2
71651	JERSEY	60.5	59.7	15.0	15.8	0.0	0.0	24.3	23.7	4.1	4.3	4.3	5.1	7.7	33.2	26.8	12.5	2.0	84.4	40.1	62.0	38.0
71652	KINGSLAND	78.0	76.7	20.1	21.1	0.2	0.2	1.6	2.0	6.9	7.0	7.7	5.9	6.1	26.4	24.8	13.5	1.7	74.7	37.2	48.8	51.2
71653	LAKE VILLAGE	58.7	57.0	38.2	39.5	0.7	0.8	2.7	3.1	6.9	6.7	7.1	6.5	6.3	25.6	24.7	14.0	2.2	75.2	38.2	49.4	50.6
71654	MC GEHEE	54.2	53.2	43.8	44.8	0.3	0.3	1.5	1.5	7.1	6.9	7.4	7.4	6.8	24.1	24.9	12.8	2.5	73.7	37.1	46.1	53.9
71655	MONTICELLO	71.5	70.0	26.0	27.2	0.5	0.6	1.7	2.0	7.0	6.7	7.0	8.0	8.4	27.4	22.8	10.9	1.9	75.1	34.2	48.4	51.6
71656	MONTICELLO	66.9	64.7	31.9	33.5	0.6	0.6	1.3	1.2	2.9	1.8	0.6	35.3	37.7	10.6	7.7	3.5	0.0	91.8	21.3	53.5	46.5
71658	MONTROSE	54.3	53.2	40.6	41.9	0.0	0.0	6.1	5.9	6.6	6.8	8.2	8.5	7.3	28.0	22.7	10.2	1.8	73.4	34.6	49.5	50.5
71660	NEW EDINBURG	79.6	78.5	18.2	19.0	0.0	0.0	2.2	2.5	5.5	5.8	6.8	7.0	6.8	26.7	25.6	14.1	1.7	77.8	40.0	51.4	48.6
71661	PARKDALE	57.8	55.2	39.5	41.9	0.0	0.0	3.8	3.8	7.0	6.8	8.1	6.8	7.2	25.9	24.6	11.9	1.8	74.1	36.6	49.1	50.9
71662	PICKENS	62.7	61.1	33.5	35.2	0.4	0.4	4.0	3.8	7.4	7.1	7.1	7.2	7.2	24.6	26.5	11.2	1.7	73.9	37.1	48.3	51.7
71663	PORTLAND	53.4	51.0	43.2	45.2	0.0	0.0	5.2	5.6	7.1	6.9	7.8	6.7	7.4	25.3	23.8	12.9	2.1	74.3	36.6	49.1	50.9
71665	RISON	86.3	85.4	11.7	12.4	0.2	0.2	1.5	1.8	6.9	6.9	7.3	6.5	6.2	27.4	25.1	12.1	1.7	75.0	37.7	48.8	51.2
71666	MC GEHEE	56.8	54.4	41.8	44.3	0.0	0.0	2.7	2.8	7.6	7.3	7.2	6.5	7.0	24.1	27.2	11.7	1.4	73.7	38.4	47.9	52.1
71667	STAR CITY	83.8	82.4	14.2	15.4	0.1	0.1	1.5	1.8	7.0	6.9	7.6	6.8	6.8	26.3	23.2	12.9	2.6	74.5	37.2	48.3	51.7
71670	TILLAR	69.0	66.8	28.3	30.5	0.0	0.0	2.0	2.1	5.9	6.1	6.7	7.0	6.6	26.2	25.9	13.1	2.6	76.7	38.9	49.5	50.5
71671	WARREN	65.1	64.2	30.7	31.5	0.1	0.1	4.3	4.3	5.9	5.9	6.3	6.3	6.3	26.1	24.6	15.5	3.1	78.0	40.2	47.6	52.4
71674	WATSON	73.7	72.0	22.7	24.3	0.3	0.3	3.5	3.5	7.0	6.5	5.8	6.5	5.9	23.7	28.5	14.0	2.1	76.7	41.1	50.3	49.7
71675	WILMAR	52.2	51.1	45.6	46.5	0.3	0.3	1.5	1.8	6.2	6.2	6.7	7.1	7.6	26.6	26.0	12.4	1.2	76.7	37.6	49.6	50.4
71676	WILMOT	32.2	30.2	66.7	69.0	0.0	0.0	2.0	2.0	4.8	4.9	7.0	7.2	8.1	22.3	25.6	16.6	3.5	78.4	41.7	45.3	54.7
71677	WINCHESTER	72.5	71.2	24.4	25.8	0.0	0.0	2.8	3.3	7.0	6.6	8.6	7.3	7.0	28.8	22.9	10.3	1.7	73.8	34.6	49.0	51.0
71678	YORKTOWN	49.5	46.9	47.1	49.4	0.0	0.0	2.5	2.9	8.7	8.1	7.6	6.6	7.1	26.3	23.2	11.0	1.4	71.5	34.9	49.7	50.3
71701	CAMDEN	58.8	57.4	39.6	40.9	0.3	0.4	0.7	0.8	6.4	6.4	7.2	7.0	6.6	24.4	25.1	14.3	2.6	75.7	39.4	47.1	52.9
71720	BEARDEN	62.4	60.0	35.8	38.1	0.1	0.1	1.1	1.1	6.8	7.0	7.7	6.9	7.2	25.5	26.2	11.5	1.4	74.2	37.1	50.6	49.4
71722	BLUFF CITY	53.7	51.8	45.1	47.2	0.0	0.0	0.4	0.2	6.3	6.5	6.3	6.7	6.5	25.4	26.8	14.0	1.4	76.8	40.6	51.8	48.2
71725	CARTHAGE	43.0	41.5	54.9	56.3	0.0	0.0	3.2	3.2	6.0	6.5	6.9	5.8	5.7	21.5	27.6	17.0	3.0	77.3	43.0	50.8	49.2
71726	CHIDESTER	64.8	62.4	33.6	35.7	0.4	0.5	0.7	0.8	5.6	5.6	6.3	5.4	5.8	20.3	30.9	17.5	2.7	79.0	45.8	49.7	50.3
71730	EL DORADO	65.9	64.5	32.2	33.3	0.5	0.6	1.1	1.3	6.7	6.6	7.1	6.8	6.5	25.8	24.6	13.3	2.7	75.6	38.5	47.8	52.2
71740	EMERSON	67.7	66.0	31.1	32.6	0.1	0.1	1.1	1.1	5.9	6.1	7.5	6.7	6.5	27.8	23.5	13.8	2.0	76.3	38.7	49.6	50.4
71742	FORDYCE	53.2	52.0	45.1	46.2	0.4	0.4	1.4	1.4	6.4	6.5	7.9	7.7	6.5	24.9	24.3	13.0	2.9	74.4	37.8	47.6	52.4
71743	GURDON	70.8	69.3	25.7	26.6	0.1	0.1	3.3	3.9	7.3	7.0	7.1	6.9	6.6	27.1	23.5	12.7	1.8	74.3	36.7	48.8	51.2
71744	HAMPTON	75.6	74.8	22.2	23.0	0.1	0.1	1.9	1.9	5.0	5.3	7.3	6.9	6.1	25.7	26.6	14.6	2.5	78.2	41.2	48.8	51.2
71745	HARRELL	70.5	69.4	28.2	29.1	0.0	0.0	0.5	0.5	5.8	6.0	7.0	6.2	6.4	27.1	26.8	12.8	2.0	77.5	39.5	47.9	52.1
71747	HUTTIG	54.6	51.7	42.0	44.7	0.1	0.1	2.3	2.6	5.9	6.3	7.6	6.2	5.8	27.2	27.1	12.3	1.6	76.4	39.2	50.0	50.0
71748	IVAN	90.6	90.3	8.5	9.1	0.0	0.0	0.3	0.3	5.0	5.3	5.0	5.6	5.3	21.1	37.0	14.4	1.5	82.1	46.6	53.4	46.6
71749	JUNCTION CITY	71.6	69.4	27.4	29.3	0.1	0.1	0.8	1.0	6.8	6.8	7.3	6.9	7.7	25.6	24.5	12.7	1.7	75.1	37.3	50.6	49.4
71751	LOUANN	80.5	79.1	17.8	19.3	0.3	0.3	0.8	0.7	5.1	5.2	7.4	7.3	6.8	25.4	30.6	10.9	1.4	77.9	41.1	50.4	49.6
71752	MC NEIL	53.7	51.8	44.7	46.5	0.2	0.2	1.1	1.1	7.1	7.3	7.7	6.8	6.9	26.3	24.8	11.6	1.5	73.7	36.3	49.4	50.6
71753	MAGNOLIA	62.0	61.1	35.9	36.8	0.5	0.5	1.1	1.1	6.1	6.0	6.9	9.1	8.8	25.0	22.3	13.2	2.6	76.6	35.8	47.5	52.5
71758	MOUNT HOLLY	73.9	71.3	25.3	27.5	0.0	0.0	1.2	1.6	4.4	6.5	7.4	6.4	6.2	26.6	27.0	13.6	1.9	77.0	40.6	51.0	49.0
71762	SMACKOVER	74.7	73.1	24.2	25.9	0.1	0.1	0.3	0.4	5.8	5.9	6.5	6.7	6.8	24.6	24.0	16.6	3.1	77.8	40.9	48.7	51.3
71763	SPARKMAN	72.1	70.9	24.6	25.7	0.0	0.0	3.2	3.2	6.2	6.4	6.4	6.6	6.1	23.9	28.5	13.6	2.3	77.0	41.0	48.9	51.1
71764	STEPHENS	54.2	52.0	44.7	46.9	0.1	0.1	0.6	0.6	5.3	5.5	7.2	7.7	6.8	23.8	26.8	15.0	1.9	77.3	40.0	47.7	52.3
71765	STRONG	52.7	50.3	44.5	46.5	0.4	0.6	2.7	2.9	6.1	6.3	7.3	7.1	6.8	26.3	25.5	12.6	2.1	76.0	38.4	48.2	51.8
71766	THORNTON	74.2	73.2	23.7	24.6	0.0	0.0	1.2	1.1	6.8	6.8	7.2	5.9	5.9	26.7	26.4	12.9	1.4	75.6	39.5	48.6	51.4
71770	WALDO	55.1	53.4	43.5	45.2	0.1	0.1	1.2	1.2	6.9	6.6	7.0	6.7	7.5	25.7	24.8	12.8	2.1	75.5	37.6	47.8	52.2
71801	HOPE	61.3	59.6	31.7	32.5	0.2	0.3	9.7	11.0	7.9	7.5	7.2	6.9	7.2	27.5	22.1	11.5	2.4	73.3	34.7	48.1	51.9
71822	ASHDOWN	73.5	72.2	22.9	23.8	0.2	0.3	1.4	1.7	6.8	6.6	6.8	6.1	6.3	25.6	26.3	13.4	2.1	76.1	39.2	48.9	51.1
71825	BLEVINS	78.5	76.7	15.8	16.8	0.2	0.2	6.4	7.5	6.6	6.5	7.1	6.9	6.6	27.0	26.0	11.7	1.5	75.6	38.3	50.4	49.7
71826	BRADLEY	71.8	71.1	26.5	27.2	0.6	0.7	1.2	1.4	5.7	5.8	6.5	6.6	6.0	22.5	28.0	16.6	2.3	77.8	42.7	49.2	50.8
71827	BUCKNER	71.8	70.3	26.5	27.8	0.2	0.2	0.4	0.4	7.0	7.0	6.6	6.5	6.2	25.4	27.0	12.6	1.8	75.5	38.5	49.7	50.3
71828	CALE	64.8	62.5	34.4	36.6	0.0	0.0	0.3	0.3	6.9	7.4	7.2	6.6	6.3	27.8	24.0	12.7	1.1	74.4	37.1	49.9	50.1
71831	COLUMBUS	45.7	43.2	53.1	55.6	0.0	0.0	2.5	2.5	7.4	7.4	7.4	7.4	7.4	23.5	24.7	12.4	2.5	70.4	36.9	49.4	50.6
71832	DE QUEEN	74.7	72.2	4.2	4.1	0.3	0.3	28.8	32.5	8.6	8.3	8.0	6.5	7.2	28.7	20.6	10.4	1.8	71.2	32.7	50.0	50.0
71833	DIERKS	95.1	94.8	2.2	2.3	0.1	0.1	2.9	3.0	6.2	6.4	6.7	6.6	6.6	27.2	23.9	13.6	2.8	76.7	38.8	48.9	51.1
71834	DODDRIDGE	85.7	84.1	13.1	14.6	0.2	0.2	0.4	0.5	5.9	5.9	5.9	5.3	5.5	24.9	26.7	17.4	2.6	79.3	42.6	47.6	52.4
71835	EMMET	83.7	82.3	13.3	14.4	0.1	0.2	2.2	2.5	6.1	6.4	7.7	6.4	6.1	28.9	23.6	13.1	1.6	75.7	37.2	49.4	50.6
71836	FOREMAN	77.6	75.7	17.0	18.5	0.2	0.2	2.3	2.6	7.4	7.3	6.6	6.4	5.9	25.6	25.6	13.3	1.8	74.7	37.7	49.1	50.9
71837	FOUKE	95.4	95.0	2.1	2.3	0.1	0.1	1.3	1.5	7.8	7.5	7.5	7.0	7.1	29.2	23.6	9.3	0.9	72.8	34.4	51.2	48.9
71838	FULTON	59.5	57.1	37.1	39.2	0.1	0.1	2.7	3.1	7.2	7.2	7.0	6.4	6.8	24.6	26.4	12.7	1.8	74.8	37.9	50.0	50.0
71839	GARLAND CITY	82.8	80.8	14.9	16.8	0.2	0.2	0.7	1.1	6.9	7.3	7.1	6.6	6.4	27.2	26.8	10.6	1.1	74.5	37.0	51.3	48.7
71841	GILLHAM	89.9	88.2	0.6	0.6	0.1	0.2	10.3	12.5	7.1	7.1	7.0	6.7	7.0	27.7	25.9	10.7	0.8	74.8	36.5	51.0	49.0
71842	HORATIO	87.9	86.1	1.9	2.0	0.1	0.1	10.6	12.9	7.5	7.5	8.3	6.6	6.6	28.3	21.7	12.1	1.5	72.7	35.0	49.4	50.6
71845	LEWISVILLE	57.8	56.3	40.9	42.4	0.0	0.0	1.5	1.8	5.6	5.8	7.1	7.1	6.4	24.3	26.4	14.6	2.7	76.8	41.1	48.2	51.8
71846	LOCKESBURG	84.2	82.8	11.6	12.4	0.1	0.1	2.4	3.0	6.7	6.8	7.1	6.4	6.6	26.5	25.1	13.1	1.7	75.6	37.6	50.7	49.4
71847	MC CASKILL	80.4	78.9	13.9	14.4	0.2	0.1	5.4	6.4	7.4	7.1	7.2	7.1	6.3	27.9	23.5	12.0	1.6	74.0	37.0	50.1	49.9
71851	MINERAL SPRINGS	54.9	53.2	40.4	42.0	0.1	0.1	6.1	6.0	6.5	6.8	8.2	7.1	6.4	28.5	23.5	11.3	1.7	74.2	36.3	49.0	51.1
71852	NASHVILLE	73.4	72.5	21.2	22.1	0.7	0.7	5.3	5.4	7.4	7.0	7.5	7.3	6.8	27.5	22.1	12.0	2.4	73.7	36.1	49.5	50.5
71853	OGDEN	41.3	39.6	50.2	51.2	1.1	1.4	5.9	6.7	6.2	6.5	7.8	6.2	6.0	26.3	27.2	11.8	2.1	76.0	39.2	49.5	50.5
71854	TEXARKANA	68.7	67.4	28.1	29.1	0.5	0.6	1.7	2.0	7.5	7.1	6.9	6.7	7.3	27.9	23.5	11.3	1.9	74.5	35.5	48.7	51.3
71855	OZAN	57.7	55.4	38.8	40.6	0.0	0.0	3.2	3.8	7.0	7.1	7.4	6.7	5.7	25.7	26.1	12.8	1.7	74.7	38.6	49.6	50.4
71857	PRESCOTT	64.3	62.8	33.5	34.7	0.1	0.1	2.0	2.3	6.6	6.5	6.8	6.7	6.8	25.8	24.6	13.6	2.8	76.0	38.5	48.4	51.7
71858	ROSSTON	67.5	65.6	31.1	32.8	0.0	0.0	0.9	1.1	6.5	6.5	6.3	6.0	6.8	25.6	26.6	14.0	1.9	77.2	39.8	49.3	50.8
71859	SARATOGA	53.7	51.4	43.7	45.7	0.2	0.2	1.7	2.0	6.5	6.7	6.1	5.8	6.5	23.8	27.8	14.6	2.2	77.4	41.2	50.0	50.0
71860	STAMPS	54.0	52.5	44.7	46.1	0.1	0.2	0.7	0.8	6.6	6.6	7.0	7.0	6.4	24.7	23.7	14.5	3.6	75.5	38.6	48.2	51.8
71861	TAYLOR	80.3	79.1	18.8	19.9	0.3	0.3	0.4	0.3	6.1	6.3	6.2	5.8	5.8	24.5	25.8	17.0	2.7	78.0	41.4	48.7	51.3
71862	WASHINGTON	54.8	52.5	41.5	43.5	0.0	0.0	3.6	4.2	7.4	7.4	7.4	6.7	6.5	25.9	24.9	12.2	1.7	74.0	36.8	49.4	50.6
71864	WILLISVILLE	66.4	64.4	32.0	33.6	0.0	0.0	1.3	1.4	6.5	6.4	6.1	5.9	6.9	25.1	27.1	13.6	2.4	77.3	40.1	47.7	52.3
71865	WILTON	92.3	88.5	3.9	7.7	0.0	0.0	0.0	0.0	7.7	7.7	7.7	7.7	7.7	30.8	30.8	0.0	0.0	76.9	32.5	50.0	50.0
71866	WINTHROP	94.3	93.4	1.1	1.2	0.0	0.0	1.2	1.6	6.8	6.8	5.9	6.2	5.0	25.1	29.7	13.4	1.2	76.5	40.2	49.4	50.6
71901	HOT SPRINGS NATIONAL	80.7	79.8	15.3	15.7	0.7	0.9	3.3	3.9	6.1	5.9	6.3	6.5	6.3	25.3	26.1	14.7	3.0	77.9	40.8	49.0	51.0
71909	HOT SPRINGS VILLAGE	97.8	97.5	0.7	0.8	0.3	0.4	1.0	1.2	2.5	2.5	2.7	2.8	2.4	10.9	26.7	46.0	3.5	90.5	64.8	48.0	52.0
	ARKANSAS	80.0	79.3	15.7	15.8	0.8	1.0	3.3	3.8	6.9	6.7	6.9	6.8	7.3	27.3	24.1	12.2	1.8	75.7	36.7	49.0	51.0
	UNITED STATES	75.1	73.6	12.3	12.5	3.8	4.2	12.5	14.1	6.9	6.7	7.2	7.0	7.3	28.6	23.8	10.8	1.7	75.1	36.0	49.1	50.9

ZIP CODE #	POST OFFICE NAME	2004 Per Capita Income	2004 HH Income Base	2004 HOUSEHOLD INCOME DISTRIBUTION (%) Less than $25,000	$25,000 to $49,999	$50,000 to $99,999	$100,000 to $149,999	$150,000 or More	MEDIAN HOUSEHOLD INCOME 2004	2009	2004 National Centile	2004 State Centile	2004 Home Value Base	2004 HOME VALUE DISTRIBUTION (%) Less than $50,000	$50,000 to $89,999	$90,000 to $174,999	$175,000 to $399,999	$400,000 or More	2004 Median Home Value
71601	PINE BLUFF	13763	6916	47.9	27.3	20.1	3.8	1.0	26504	33364	6	11	4048	52.7	34.4	10.7	1.9	0.2	48351
71602	WHITE HALL	19924	7047	30.5	27.9	30.0	8.8	2.8	41034	51856	50	85	5251	37.7	29.8	26.9	5.0	0.6	65906
71603	PINE BLUFF	21639	13842	32.0	28.1	28.4	8.0	3.5	41006	50632	50	85	9631	31.7	37.1	25.3	4.9	1.1	68188
71630	ARKANSAS CITY	8444	13	53.9	23.1	23.1	0.0	0.0	22265	37321	3	3	10	80.0	20.0	0.0	0.0	0.0	30000
71631	BANKS	11207	305	63.3	24.9	8.2	2.3	1.3	18613	22153	1	2	260	58.9	25.0	11.9	4.2	0.0	40800
71635	CROSSETT	20097	5488	30.3	31.7	29.1	6.2	2.8	39471	48003	44	82	4138	37.9	31.7	23.0	6.6	0.9	63634
71638	DERMOTT	12968	1637	49.8	29.9	15.6	3.1	1.6	25137	31254	5	7	1128	61.0	28.6	8.3	1.1	1.0	41143
71639	DUMAS	15618	2438	43.3	27.3	22.4	4.9	2.1	30383	38329	13	28	1575	46.5	36.4	14.3	2.7	0.0	53516
71640	EUDORA	13503	1517	53.1	26.0	16.7	2.6	1.6	22968	28781	3	4	1062	57.3	26.0	11.7	5.1	0.0	44690
71642	FOUNTAIN HILL	19502	253	35.2	34.8	23.7	4.0	2.4	35661	42867	30	66	212	53.3	20.8	19.8	5.2	0.9	47083
71643	GOULD	13230	666	46.6	30.3	18.3	2.4	2.4	26807	32369	7	12	426	63.6	25.1	8.0	3.3	0.0	34688
71644	GRADY	12061	788	38.1	37.3	17.5	4.4	2.7	32044	38725	18	43	614	54.7	26.2	15.5	3.1	0.5	46420
71646	HAMBURG	18985	2668	33.0	32.7	27.2	5.1	2.0	37157	45077	36	75	2174	41.4	28.3	23.8	5.3	1.2	62994
71647	HERMITAGE	17117	853	42.7	26.5	21.9	5.4	3.5	30479	37012	13	29	663	47.8	26.1	21.9	3.0	1.2	53625
71651	JERSEY	12539	101	46.5	26.7	18.8	5.0	3.0	27300	35000	8	14	88	48.9	25.0	20.5	3.4	2.3	51429
71652	KINGSLAND	17894	432	35.7	34.0	26.2	3.2	0.9	35784	42606	31	68	356	64.3	25.8	7.6	2.0	0.3	38788
71653	LAKE VILLAGE	20842	2145	42.3	26.1	22.1	5.2	4.3	32635	41443	20	47	1532	35.7	28.2	17.0	18.3	0.9	68676
71654	MC GEHEE	17313	2274	47.9	24.0	20.2	4.8	3.0	26422	33718	6	11	1537	41.4	34.4	22.5	1.8	0.0	58129
71655	MONTICELLO	21077	6666	37.5	28.1	24.7	6.0	3.8	34750	43749	26	60	4651	39.2	25.7	25.1	9.2	0.9	66482
71656	MONTICELLO	6255	8	50.0	0.0	50.0	0.0	0.0	35000	54495	28	63	3	0.0	66.7	33.3	0.0	0.0	85000
71658	MONTROSE	17076	356	43.3	31.7	18.3	4.8	2.0	30147	36720	13	27	275	56.7	25.5	17.5	0.4	0.0	44032
71660	NEW EDINBURG	17063	430	37.0	36.5	20.7	4.4	1.4	32156	39042	18	44	362	42.3	35.1	19.6	2.2	0.8	57368
71661	PARKDALE	17082	176	37.5	32.4	24.4	4.6	1.1	34486	42134	26	58	144	52.8	24.3	20.1	2.8	0.0	47333
71662	PICKENS	16528	395	44.3	27.3	20.3	4.8	3.3	29052	36765	10	21	265	51.3	29.8	12.8	4.5	1.5	49239
71663	PORTLAND	16985	352	41.2	32.4	20.2	4.0	2.3	30770	38016	14	31	282	60.3	19.2	16.3	4.3	0.0	41471
71665	RISON	18728	2435	31.8	30.8	29.8	5.2	2.4	39156	47112	43	82	1993	38.3	31.8	23.2	5.4	1.4	63703
71666	MC GEHEE	17689	261	48.3	26.1	16.9	5.8	3.1	26175	33437	6	10	206	62.6	22.8	11.2	1.9	1.5	36364
71667	STAR CITY	17888	2769	33.8	30.2	28.5	5.9	1.7	37633	45467	38	77	2218	39.1	32.5	21.6	5.8	1.0	62731
71670	TILLAR	19312	374	38.8	24.3	27.5	5.4	4.0	33100	43234	21	49	292	45.6	29.1	21.9	3.4	0.0	54333
71671	WARREN	17544	3677	43.4	29.1	19.0	5.2	3.3	30143	36968	13	27	2679	41.8	30.7	21.5	5.3	0.8	57268
71674	WATSON	17487	406	43.6	25.6	23.7	4.2	3.0	30638	40118	14	30	312	58.0	23.4	15.4	2.2	1.0	44444
71675	WILMAR	18750	539	45.5	27.1	18.7	4.8	3.9	29294	36793	11	22	435	53.8	19.3	17.7	8.3	0.9	47155
71676	WILMOT	11866	353	61.5	21.3	13.6	2.0	1.7	16989	21668	1	1	269	68.4	21.9	7.1	1.9	0.7	36618
71677	WINCHESTER	17354	109	36.7	27.5	28.4	4.6	2.8	36383	46886	33	71	87	57.5	21.8	18.4	2.3	0.0	42778
71678	YORKTOWN	15060	331	40.5	34.7	19.0	3.9	1.8	31204	37226	15	36	270	55.6	22.6	15.2	5.6	1.1	44643
71701	CAMDEN	18003	8765	38.7	29.5	25.2	5.0	1.6	34168	41122	25	56	6069	40.0	32.3	22.3	5.1	0.3	60412
71720	BEARDEN	15736	995	38.0	33.3	23.1	4.6	1.0	32802	39959	20	48	818	50.6	39.4	9.1	1.0	0.0	49375
71722	BLUFF CITY	19573	204	34.3	35.8	22.6	3.9	3.4	32498	41229	19	46	173	55.5	25.4	18.5	0.6	0.0	44412
71725	CARTHAGE	14389	486	49.4	30.3	17.9	1.4	1.0	25391	30282	5	8	386	64.0	23.3	9.8	1.6	1.3	37875
71726	CHIDESTER	21158	556	39.9	31.3	19.6	5.8	3.4	31091	38463	15	35	444	47.8	21.0	21.9	9.2	0.2	52857
71730	EL DORADO	20256	14407	36.3	28.5	25.7	6.0	3.5	35732	44668	30	67	10276	37.8	29.8	23.4	7.7	1.4	64462
71740	EMERSON	18534	735	35.1	29.4	27.5	5.9	2.2	39112	48699	43	81	593	50.8	25.0	18.6	5.6	0.2	49318
71742	FORDYCE	17394	2178	43.2	32.7	19.2	2.2	2.7	29500	34491	11	23	1615	54.7	26.9	12.9	4.8	0.6	45000
71743	GURDON	17707	1859	36.3	35.1	23.6	3.5	1.5	33808	41178	23	54	1389	51.0	28.6	15.3	3.5	1.7	49258
71744	HAMPTON	18592	1472	39.2	32.4	22.3	3.3	2.8	32537	38745	19	46	1188	55.6	30.1	12.0	2.0	0.3	45976
71745	HARRELL	18824	341	44.3	28.2	17.6	7.3	2.6	28590	34793	10	20	284	57.4	29.2	11.3	1.8	0.4	44615
71747	HUTTIG	16081	492	40.9	30.5	24.2	3.3	1.2	31330	38633	16	37	404	65.1	27.2	6.2	0.7	0.7	39375
71748	IVAN	45551	148	18.9	39.2	27.7	5.4	8.8	41513	50648	51	87	126	38.9	39.7	12.7	8.7	0.0	59333
71749	JUNCTION CITY	19012	1188	37.2	28.7	27.1	4.8	2.2	35569	43202	30	66	996	50.4	26.3	17.2	5.3	0.8	49588
71751	LOUANN	18542	426	27.7	33.8	33.8	4.2	0.5	41072	49615	50	86	359	39.6	32.0	26.2	2.2	0.0	71452
71752	MC NEIL	16954	518	43.1	29.0	21.0	4.3	2.7	30000	39768	12	26	406	51.5	29.8	13.1	5.2	0.5	48462
71753	MAGNOLIA	19865	6868	39.1	25.5	25.5	6.8	3.1	33725	43478	23	53	4773	37.3	26.7	25.8	9.2	1.0	66038
71758	MOUNT HOLLY	18174	276	33.7	34.4	25.4	5.1	1.5	35629	44385	30	66	233	54.1	23.2	15.9	5.6	1.3	46346
71762	SMACKOVER	16631	1053	35.6	33.6	24.5	4.5	1.8	34175	41863	25	57	804	45.2	28.7	19.8	6.3	0.0	58478
71763	SPARKMAN	21280	732	36.1	31.6	25.0	3.3	4.1	33880	40676	24	55	599	56.8	28.4	12.7	2.2	0.0	43864
71764	STEPHENS	17685	907	43.4	27.7	23.8	3.4	1.7	31627	39064	17	40	726	49.2	32.6	14.3	3.4	0.4	51333
71765	STRONG	16726	1022	43.4	29.2	22.2	3.3	2.0	29916	36735	12	25	841	57.0	25.6	15.3	1.6	0.6	46020
71766	THORNTON	19507	533	35.7	35.8	19.9	4.1	4.5	35195	41802	28	63	454	54.9	24.2	16.7	1.8	2.4	43125
71770	WALDO	16158	1319	45.9	25.0	22.8	4.7	1.5	27964	36074	9	17	1016	50.6	28.4	17.2	3.4	0.4	49464
71801	HOPE	16440	6649	38.9	31.5	23.5	4.9	1.3	32796	39572	20	47	4473	37.7	33.6	21.2	6.6	0.9	62096
71822	ASHDOWN	20035	3876	35.0	28.3	26.9	7.8	2.0	35564	45593	30	66	3009	39.8	27.4	29.2	3.6	0.1	62393
71825	BLEVINS	17806	373	31.4	34.1	28.4	4.8	1.3	38702	45814	42	80	308	40.9	27.3	22.7	5.5	3.6	61250
71826	BRADLEY	19499	974	46.9	27.4	17.2	4.6	3.9	26945	33622	7	13	767	55.7	23.2	17.0	2.9	1.3	44942
71827	BUCKNER	17179	420	38.6	27.6	27.1	4.3	2.4	32081	40000	18	44	345	57.4	16.8	20.3	4.1	1.5	44688
71828	CALE	15048	128	32.8	36.7	25.0	3.1	2.3	35436	43357	29	65	111	58.6	19.8	19.8	1.8	0.0	41364
71831	COLUMBUS	12130	29	48.3	31.0	17.2	3.5	0.0	26103	30000	6	9	23	47.8	26.1	17.4	8.7	0.0	52500
71832	DE QUEEN	15037	3227	38.3	33.0	22.6	4.9	1.3	33316	39584	22	50	2398	36.6	31.6	26.4	4.9	0.6	64034
71833	DIERKS	18525	935	35.1	35.1	22.3	4.3	3.3	33367	41791	22	51	766	51.0	25.2	16.8	5.4	1.6	49024
71834	DODDRIDGE	20106	621	40.9	29.5	23.2	4.0	2.4	31539	39053	16	39	518	50.8	25.3	17.0	5.0	1.9	49344
71835	EMMET	18576	642	37.5	31.5	24.3	3.6	3.1	34872	42875	27	60	520	49.2	25.6	20.6	4.0	0.6	51250
71836	FOREMAN	17157	1242	37.9	31.1	25.2	4.4	1.4	32665	41713	20	47	1002	42.2	27.4	26.5	3.7	0.3	59398
71837	FOUKE	17503	2574	29.5	34.1	28.4	6.6	1.4	39443	49223	44	82	2120	40.7	29.5	24.8	4.5	0.5	63969
71838	FULTON	16109	449	42.8	29.4	21.4	4.9	1.6	30771	37930	14	31	364	47.8	29.7	16.5	5.2	0.8	51860
71839	GARLAND CITY	22804	214	33.6	29.0	21.5	14.0	1.9	40000	50601	46	84	177	39.0	22.6	29.4	7.9	1.1	68636
71841	GILLHAM	22800	395	29.6	37.2	24.1	7.3	1.8	38942	46823	43	81	324	39.8	23.8	29.3	6.5	0.6	59706
71842	HORATIO	16549	1073	32.7	34.7	26.2	5.0	1.4	35078	42179	28	63	858	37.3	33.1	22.3	6.1	1.3	62135
71845	LEWISVILLE	17719	881	42.3	25.4	25.7	5.0	1.6	30758	39218	14	31	716	56.7	22.9	16.6	3.2	0.6	42615
71846	LOCKESBURG	18549	1159	34.8	31.2	26.3	5.8	1.9	35205	42866	28	64	952	39.9	30.4	20.0	7.3	2.5	61262
71847	MC CASKILL	17906	283	31.8	32.9	28.6	4.6	2.1	40481	47601	48	84	235	34.5	31.5	22.6	8.9	2.6	69737
71851	MINERAL SPRINGS	16611	1016	37.3	34.1	22.3	4.8	1.5	33774	41237	23	54	794	46.9	28.2	20.3	3.7	1.0	54098
71852	NASHVILLE	19593	3596	37.0	28.5	26.5	4.4	3.6	34029	42295	24	55	2590	31.1	28.2	28.7	9.4	2.6	76627
71853	OGDEN	16352	188	36.2	39.4	21.3	2.7	0.5	32522	38428	19	46	151	49.0	16.6	30.5	4.0	0.0	55000
71854	TEXARKANA	20566	13340	36.8	26.1	27.3	6.6	3.2	36170	45594	32	69	8638	33.8	35.8	25.1	4.8	0.5	66861
71855	OZAN	16194	362	42.5	28.7	21.0	5.3	2.5	30575	37109	14	30	297	40.1	27.6	21.2	8.4	2.7	60208
71857	PRESCOTT	16022	2292	42.8	29.2	23.0	4.3	0.8	29763	36767	12	24	1614	49.3	29.3	19.6	1.8	0.0	50692
71858	ROSSTON	18335	553	40.9	26.9	26.0	3.4	2.7	31139	39353	15	35	466	53.9	28.5	14.8	2.8	0.0	46604
71859	SARATOGA	17638	241	42.7	33.2	18.3	5.0	0.8	29838	36411	12	24	195	51.8	28.7	15.9	2.6	1.0	48056
71860	STAMPS	15830	1169	43.8	30.0	21.5	3.3	1.5	29734	36522	12	24	906	61.5	23.5	10.5	4.4	0.1	40877
71861	TAYLOR	19119	580	31.4	34.5	26.9	4.8	2.4	36761	47049	35	72	479	46.6	28.4	19.2	5.9	0.0	54231
71862	WASHINGTON	16758	333	42.3	28.5	23.4	3.9	1.8	31008	37649	15	34	274	42.7	30.3	19.3	6.9	0.7	55882
71864	WILLISVILLE	20058	319	44.2	23.2	24.8	3.8	4.1	29320	36612	11	22	266	54.5	29.3	12.8	3.4	0.0	45862
71865	WILTON	18592	11	27.3	36.4	27.3	9.1	0.0	37303	54545	36	76	10	30.0	40.0	30.0	0.0	0.0	70000
71866	WINTHROP	19251	328	38.7	29.0	23.2	7.0	2.1	31740	40190	17	41	275	43.6	24.7	24.4	5.5	1.8	62200
71901	HOT SPRINGS NATIONAL	21749	12117	41.8	28.2	19.6	6.8	3.7	31177	38404	15	36	7734	28.8	23.6	30.2	14.7	2.7	85192
71909	HOT SPRINGS VILLAGE	30386	6849	18.4	31.6	37.8	9.0	3.2	50030	61194	72	96	6058	8.7	11.1	37.6	36.8	5.7	157660
	ARKANSAS	20565		33.0	30.6	26.7	6.4	3.3	37742	46417				27.1	29.3	31.4	10.3	1.8	80466
	UNITED STATES	25866		24.7	27.1	30.8	10.9	6.5	48124	56710				10.9	15.0	33.7	30.1	10.4	145905

ZIP CODE		FINANCIAL SERVICES				THE HOME						ENTERTAINMENT						PERSONAL			
						Home Improvements		Furnishings													
#	POST OFFICE NAME	Auto Loan	Home Loan	Invest-ments	Retire-ment Plans	Home Repair	Lawn & Garden	Comput-ers & Hard-ware	Major Appli-ances	TV, Radio, Sound Equip-ment	Furni-ture	Dine out/ Carry out	Sports Equip-ment	Fees & Tickets	Toys & Games	Travel	Cable TV	Apparel & Services	Auto Repairs	Health Insur-ance	Pets & Supplies
71601	PINE BLUFF	54	46	48	43	46	54	50	51	55	51	68	57	49	64	49	58	65	52	57	60
71602	WHITE HALL	86	72	56	68	76	84	71	78	77	71	93	91	67	91	71	79	88	77	86	98
71603	PINE BLUFF	78	74	73	71	75	83	74	77	78	74	96	88	74	96	75	80	93	77	81	90
71630	ARKANSAS CITY	55	37	17	32	42	48	36	45	43	36	50	53	30	48	36	46	46	44	55	63
71631	BANKS	51	34	16	30	39	45	33	41	40	34	47	49	28	44	34	43	43	41	51	59
71635	CROSSETT	85	66	45	61	71	80	65	74	73	65	87	87	60	84	65	76	81	73	85	97
71638	DERMOTT	56	42	34	38	44	54	46	50	53	46	63	56	42	58	45	57	59	51	60	62
71639	DUMAS	67	52	40	47	55	64	53	59	61	54	73	68	50	68	53	64	68	59	69	75
71640	EUDORA	55	42	39	37	43	52	46	50	54	47	64	55	43	58	45	57	60	51	59	61
71642	FOUNTAIN HILL	85	57	26	49	65	74	55	69	66	56	78	82	47	74	56	72	71	68	85	98
71643	GOULD	60	45	35	39	47	56	47	53	55	48	66	59	43	60	47	59	61	53	63	67
71644	GRADY	54	36	17	32	41	47	35	44	42	36	50	52	30	47	36	46	45	43	54	62
71646	HAMBURG	93	62	28	54	71	81	60	75	73	61	85	90	51	81	61	78	78	75	93	107
71647	HERMITAGE	81	58	32	51	65	74	55	68	65	56	76	80	48	73	57	70	70	67	82	95
71651	JERSEY	70	54	35	49	61	69	51	62	58	51	69	73	45	68	54	62	64	61	74	85
71652	KINGSLAND	84	56	26	49	64	73	54	68	66	55	77	81	46	73	55	71	70	67	84	97
71653	LAKE VILLAGE	86	66	44	61	71	81	67	76	75	67	89	88	60	84	67	78	83	76	87	97
71654	MC GEHEE	71	52	36	46	56	65	53	61	62	54	74	71	48	69	53	66	69	62	73	80
71655	MONTICELLO	85	68	51	64	72	81	69	76	75	68	91	89	64	88	68	78	85	76	85	97
71656	MONTICELLO	48	29	37	33	29	35	57	42	55	48	69	58	46	62	45	49	65	51	39	48
71658	MONTROSE	87	58	26	50	66	76	56	70	68	57	80	84	48	75	57	73	73	70	87	100
71660	NEW EDINBURG	81	54	25	47	61	71	52	65	63	53	74	78	44	70	53	68	67	65	81	93
71661	PARKDALE	67	58	52	57	61	67	58	63	61	58	75	75	55	72	58	62	71	63	67	77
71662	PICKENS	78	53	28	46	60	69	53	64	63	54	74	76	46	70	53	68	68	64	79	89
71663	PORTLAND	66	60	57	59	62	67	60	64	62	60	76	75	58	73	60	62	72	64	67	76
71665	RISON	87	64	37	58	71	80	61	73	70	62	84	87	55	81	62	75	77	72	86	101
71666	MC GEHEE	82	55	25	47	62	72	53	66	64	54	75	79	45	71	54	69	68	66	82	94
71667	STAR CITY	85	59	29	51	66	76	58	70	69	58	81	83	50	76	58	74	73	70	86	98
71670	TILLAR	90	61	28	53	69	79	59	73	70	59	82	88	50	78	60	75	75	72	90	104
71671	WARREN	72	53	34	49	58	69	57	64	65	55	76	73	50	72	56	69	70	64	77	81
71674	WATSON	80	55	27	48	62	71	53	65	63	54	74	78	46	71	54	68	68	65	80	92
71675	WILMAR	80	61	37	55	66	73	58	68	65	59	78	81	52	75	59	68	73	68	78	91
71676	WILMOT	45	35	34	31	35	43	39	41	45	40	54	44	37	48	38	48	51	42	49	49
71677	WINCHESTER	91	61	27	52	69	79	58	73	71	60	83	87	50	78	60	76	75	72	90	104
71678	YORKTOWN	75	50	23	43	57	65	48	61	58	49	69	72	41	65	49	63	62	60	75	86
71701	CAMDEN	67	57	49	53	59	67	58	62	63	58	77	71	56	75	58	66	73	62	70	76
71720	BEARDEN	75	51	24	45	58	66	49	61	59	50	70	73	42	66	50	63	63	61	75	87
71722	BLUFF CITY	89	60	27	51	67	78	57	72	69	59	81	86	49	77	58	75	74	71	89	102
71725	CARTHAGE	65	44	20	38	49	57	42	53	51	43	60	63	36	56	43	55	54	52	65	75
71726	CHIDESTER	84	59	31	53	66	77	60	71	70	59	82	83	52	78	60	75	75	71	87	95
71730	EL DORADO	79	66	54	61	69	78	67	73	73	66	88	84	63	85	67	76	83	72	81	90
71740	EMERSON	89	60	27	51	67	78	57	72	69	59	81	86	49	77	58	75	74	71	89	102
71742	FORDYCE	79	57	32	51	63	73	57	67	66	56	78	79	50	74	57	70	71	67	81	90
71743	GURDON	75	56	34	52	62	70	56	65	63	56	75	77	50	73	56	66	69	64	76	86
71744	HAMPTON	80	55	29	50	62	73	56	67	66	56	78	79	49	73	57	71	71	67	82	91
71745	HARRELL	84	57	26	49	64	74	55	69	66	56	78	82	47	74	56	71	71	68	84	97
71747	HUTTIG	76	51	23	44	57	66	49	61	59	50	69	73	42	66	50	64	63	61	75	87
71748	IVAN	178	140	95	126	157	177	132	159	149	130	177	186	118	174	140	159	164	156	188	217
71749	JUNCTION CITY	92	62	28	53	70	80	59	74	72	61	84	89	51	80	61	77	77	74	92	106
71751	LOUANN	86	57	26	49	65	75	55	69	67	56	78	83	47	74	56	72	71	68	85	98
71752	MC NEIL	71	54	41	50	57	66	57	63	64	57	77	74	52	75	57	67	73	64	72	80
71753	MAGNOLIA	76	64	55	60	67	76	66	71	72	65	87	82	63	84	66	74	82	71	79	87
71758	MOUNT HOLLY	84	56	25	48	64	73	54	68	65	55	77	81	46	73	55	71	70	67	84	96
71762	SMACKOVER	72	52	34	48	57	68	56	63	64	55	76	72	50	71	55	68	69	63	76	80
71763	SPARKMAN	99	66	30	57	75	86	64	80	77	65	91	96	54	86	65	83	82	79	99	114
71764	STEPHENS	74	55	35	52	60	71	59	66	66	57	78	75	52	74	59	70	72	66	79	82
71765	STRONG	77	52	23	45	59	68	50	63	60	51	71	75	43	67	51	65	64	62	77	89
71766	THORNTON	91	61	27	52	69	79	59	73	71	60	83	88	50	78	60	76	75	73	90	104
71770	WALDO	71	49	30	43	54	64	50	59	59	51	70	69	44	65	50	64	65	59	72	80
71801	HOPE	68	55	43	52	58	66	58	62	63	57	76	72	54	74	57	66	72	63	70	77
71822	ASHDOWN	86	63	39	58	70	79	63	73	72	63	85	87	56	81	63	76	78	73	87	98
71825	BLEVINS	90	60	27	52	68	78	58	73	70	59	82	87	49	78	59	75	75	72	89	103
71826	BRADLEY	82	59	34	52	67	76	56	69	66	57	78	82	49	75	59	71	71	68	84	97
71827	BUCKNER	84	56	26	49	64	73	55	68	66	56	77	81	47	73	55	71	70	67	84	96
71828	CALE	80	54	24	46	61	70	52	65	63	53	74	78	44	70	53	68	67	64	80	92
71831	COLUMBUS	64	43	19	37	48	56	41	52	50	42	58	62	35	55	42	54	53	51	64	73
71832	DE QUEEN	73	56	39	53	60	67	58	65	64	59	77	75	53	74	57	65	73	65	71	80
71833	DIERKS	83	61	35	56	68	77	60	71	69	60	82	84	53	79	61	72	75	70	84	96
71834	DODDRIDGE	88	59	27	51	66	76	57	71	68	58	80	85	48	76	58	74	73	70	87	100
71835	EMMET	89	60	27	52	67	78	57	72	69	59	81	86	49	77	58	75	74	71	88	102
71836	FOREMAN	79	53	24	46	60	69	51	64	62	52	72	76	43	68	52	66	66	63	79	91
71837	FOUKE	83	65	42	60	69	76	63	72	69	64	83	85	57	79	63	71	78	72	80	94
71838	FULTON	81	54	25	47	61	71	52	65	63	53	74	78	45	70	53	68	67	65	81	93
71839	GARLAND CITY	109	73	33	63	83	96	71	88	85	72	100	106	60	95	72	92	91	88	109	126
71841	GILLHAM	103	70	34	61	79	91	68	84	81	69	96	100	58	91	69	87	87	83	103	118
71842	HORATIO	84	56	26	48	64	73	54	68	65	55	77	81	46	73	55	70	70	67	83	96
71845	LEWISVILLE	81	54	26	47	61	71	53	66	64	54	75	78	45	71	54	69	68	65	81	92
71846	LOCKESBURG	87	59	27	51	66	76	57	71	68	58	80	84	48	76	57	73	73	70	87	100
71847	MC CASKILL	88	59	27	51	66	76	57	71	68	58	80	85	48	76	58	74	73	70	87	101
71851	MINERAL SPRINGS	77	54	28	48	61	69	52	63	61	53	72	76	45	69	53	65	66	63	77	89
71852	NASHVILLE	81	67	51	64	71	80	68	74	73	67	88	86	64	87	68	75	83	73	82	91
71853	OGDEN	70	48	23	42	54	62	46	57	55	47	65	68	40	62	47	59	59	57	70	81
71854	TEXARKANA	78	67	58	64	69	78	70	73	75	68	91	85	66	89	69	77	86	74	80	88
71855	OZAN	79	53	24	45	60	69	51	64	61	52	72	76	43	68	52	66	65	63	78	90
71857	PRESCOTT	65	49	34	45	53	61	52	58	59	51	70	67	47	67	51	62	65	58	68	73
71858	ROSSTON	88	59	27	51	67	77	57	71	68	58	80	85	48	76	58	74	73	70	87	101
71859	SARATOGA	76	51	23	44	58	67	49	62	60	50	70	74	42	66	50	64	64	61	76	88
71860	STAMPS	63	47	34	42	50	60	50	56	58	50	68	63	45	63	49	62	63	56	67	71
71861	TAYLOR	79	62	42	55	67	77	60	69	69	60	82	81	56	82	62	73	77	69	82	91
71862	WASHINGTON	75	50	23	43	57	65	48	60	58	49	68	72	41	65	49	63	62	60	74	86
71864	WILLISVILLE	91	61	27	52	69	79	59	73	71	60	83	87	50	78	60	76	75	72	90	104
71865	WILTON	83	55	25	48	63	72	53	67	65	54	76	80	45	72	54	70	69	66	82	95
71866	WINTHROP	82	55	25	47	62	72	53	66	64	54	75	79	45	71	54	69	68	66	82	94
71901	HOT SPRINGS NATIONAL	77	67	66	65	69	78	71	74	75	70	92	85	68	88	71	76	87	75	80	87
71909	HOT SPRINGS VILLAGE	94	87	82	82	92	108	80	92	85	86	106	91	81	89	87	91	99	89	107	106
	ARKANSAS	81	69	57	66	72	80	69	75	74	69	90	87	65	87	69	76	85	75	82	92
	UNITED STATES	100	100	100	100	100	100	100	100	100	100	100	100	100	100	100	100	100	100	100	100

POPULATION CHANGE

ZIP CODE		POPULATION			2000-2004 ANNUAL RATE		HOUSEHOLDS					FAMILIES		
# POST OFFICE NAME	COUNTY FIPS CODE	2000	2004	2009	% Rate	State Centile	2000	2004	2009	% Annual Rate 2000-2004	2004 Average HH Size	2000	2004	% Annual Rate 2000-2004
71913 HOT SPRINGS NATIONAL	051	37631	39087	40496	0.9	68	16980	17743	18481	1.0	2.19	11030	11288	0.6
71921 AMITY	019	1830	1982	2094	1.9	85	732	797	846	2.0	2.49	537	575	1.6
71922 ANTOINE	109	533	551	590	0.8	65	205	214	232	1.0	2.57	151	156	0.8
71923 ARKADELPHIA	019	16658	16800	17141	0.2	42	6139	6236	6420	0.4	2.33	3843	3817	-0.2
71929 BISMARCK	059	3022	3037	3005	0.1	40	1162	1174	1167	0.2	2.57	880	877	-0.1
71933 BONNERDALE	059	1974	2003	2010	0.3	48	763	781	790	0.6	2.56	584	589	0.2
71935 CADDO GAP	097	2402	2487	2665	0.8	66	906	940	1011	0.9	2.65	678	696	0.6
71937 COVE	113	2133	2203	2269	0.8	64	817	848	877	0.9	2.60	590	603	0.5
71940 DELIGHT	109	1643	1686	1801	0.6	59	673	700	758	0.9	2.41	480	491	0.5
71941 DONALDSON	059	2025	1957	1903	-0.8	10	810	791	775	-0.6	2.47	627	604	-0.9
71942 FRIENDSHIP	059	267	259	252	-0.7	12	106	104	102	-0.5	2.49	83	81	-0.6
71943 GLENWOOD	109	3923	4517	5131	3.4	97	1491	1740	2003	3.7	2.53	1064	1223	3.3
71944 GRANNIS	113	898	880	885	-0.5	18	329	323	327	-0.4	2.72	253	246	-0.7
71945 HATFIELD	113	1540	1500	1509	-0.6	13	588	576	583	-0.5	2.60	434	419	-0.8
71949 JESSIEVILLE	051	1658	1678	1711	0.3	46	626	642	660	0.6	2.61	482	484	0.1
71950 KIRBY	109	1035	1049	1113	0.3	47	411	422	453	0.6	2.47	312	317	0.4
71952 LANGLEY	109	272	276	293	0.3	48	104	107	115	0.7	2.58	82	83	0.3
71953 MENA	113	14403	14819	15250	0.7	61	5873	6068	6271	0.8	2.41	4187	4260	0.4
71956 MOUNTAIN PINE	051	1780	1744	1762	-0.5	18	675	669	681	-0.2	2.61	505	491	-0.7
71957 MOUNT IDA	097	3477	3900	4374	2.7	94	1500	1701	1927	3.0	2.23	1034	1154	2.6
71958 MURFREESBORO	109	3858	3980	4262	0.7	63	1589	1660	1801	1.0	2.36	1155	1190	0.7
71959 NEWHOPE	109	648	665	696	0.6	59	255	265	282	0.9	2.50	193	199	0.7
71960 NORMAN	097	766	810	878	1.3	76	324	342	371	1.3	2.37	241	251	1.0
71961 ODEN	097	852	892	961	1.1	71	340	357	386	1.2	2.50	261	271	0.9
71962 OKOLONA	019	918	1003	1064	2.1	88	379	417	444	2.3	2.41	279	302	1.9
71964 PEARCY	051	3734	3745	3777	0.1	38	1371	1393	1416	0.4	2.69	1079	1079	0.0
71965 PENCIL BLUFF	097	326	339	363	0.9	69	140	146	157	1.0	2.32	106	109	0.7
71968 ROYAL	051	4012	4459	4761	2.5	92	1477	1662	1791	2.8	2.56	1151	1273	2.4
71969 SIMS	097	639	658	703	0.7	61	250	258	277	0.7	2.55	186	190	0.5
71970 STORY	097	394	408	437	0.8	66	184	192	206	1.0	2.13	134	138	0.7
71971 UMPIRE	061	493	522	535	1.4	77	181	194	202	1.7	2.67	139	148	1.5
71972 VANDERVOORT	113	211	230	242	2.1	87	78	85	90	2.0	2.71	57	61	1.6
71973 WICKES	113	1217	1219	1228	0.0	36	424	428	433	0.2	2.85	325	323	-0.2
71998 ARKADELPHIA	019	55	55	55	0.0	35	0	0	0	0.0	0.00	0	0	0.0
72001 ADONA	105	572	573	582	0.0	36	224	227	232	0.3	2.52	171	170	-0.1
72002 ALEXANDER	125	12850	13840	15108	1.8	83	4786	5236	5802	2.1	2.62	3706	3992	1.8
72003 ALMYRA	001	773	765	765	-0.2	26	306	308	312	0.2	2.48	227	224	-0.3
72004 ALTHEIMER	069	1602	1479	1411	-1.9	1	563	528	511	-1.5	2.80	396	365	-1.9
72005 AMAGON	067	359	386	398	1.7	83	146	159	166	2.0	2.19	106	113	1.5
72006 AUGUSTA	147	3259	3430	3559	1.2	74	1324	1417	1494	1.6	2.40	927	976	1.2
72007 AUSTIN	085	4692	5417	6219	3.4	97	1699	1985	2302	3.7	2.72	1387	1599	3.4
72010 BALD KNOB	145	6772	6939	7230	0.6	57	2639	2730	2869	0.8	2.53	1931	1966	0.4
72011 BAUXITE	125	3551	4198	4796	4.0	99	1258	1497	1728	4.2	2.80	1016	1196	3.9
72012 BEEBE	145	9032	9641	10247	1.6	81	3433	3706	3977	1.8	2.58	2609	2779	1.5
72013 BEE BRANCH	141	1643	1600	1572	-0.6	13	660	648	642	-0.4	2.47	497	483	-0.7
72014 BEEDEVILLE	067	105	114	119	2.0	86	43	47	50	2.1	2.43	31	34	2.2
72015 BENTON	125	39225	41682	45240	1.4	79	14952	16141	17822	1.8	2.51	11205	11940	1.5
72016 BIGELOW	105	2605	2855	3033	2.2	89	963	1064	1137	2.4	2.67	739	804	2.0
72017 BISCOE	117	1314	1280	1260	-0.6	14	528	524	525	-0.2	2.44	389	380	-0.6
72020 BRADFORD	067	4388	4420	4525	0.2	41	1717	1752	1811	0.5	2.52	1273	1279	0.1
72021 BRINKLEY	095	5737	5611	5503	-0.5	16	2237	2212	2193	-0.3	2.49	1494	1450	-0.7
72022 BRYANT	125	8523	9642	10741	3.0	95	3092	3573	4057	3.5	2.59	2414	2748	3.1
72023 CABOT	085	24727	28534	32586	3.4	97	8817	10299	11887	3.7	2.75	7135	8231	3.4
72024 CARLISLE	085	3560	3653	3960	0.6	59	1412	1469	1613	0.9	2.40	995	1013	0.4
72025 CASA	105	751	748	758	-0.1	31	295	296	302	0.1	2.53	228	226	-0.2
72026 CASSCOE	001	558	555	555	-0.1	30	233	236	240	0.3	2.35	169	168	-0.1
72027 CENTER RIDGE	029	1631	1717	1782	1.2	75	613	652	685	1.5	2.63	463	486	1.2
72028 CHOCTAW	141	1370	1348	1328	-0.4	22	567	563	559	-0.2	2.34	399	391	-0.5
72029 CLARENDON	095	2901	2888	2855	-0.1	31	1226	1232	1231	0.1	2.33	820	809	-0.3
72030 CLEVELAND	029	401	408	415	0.4	50	161	166	171	0.7	2.46	121	123	0.4
72031 CLINTON	141	4598	4946	5175	1.7	83	1903	2092	2220	2.3	2.32	1313	1413	1.7
72032 CONWAY	045	25991	28314	31249	2.0	87	9649	10673	11947	2.4	2.52	6895	7509	2.0
72034 CONWAY	045	31592	34833	38814	2.3	90	12375	13759	15480	2.5	2.47	7920	8643	2.1
72035 CONWAY	045	1864	1864	1864	0.0	35	4	4	4	0.0	1.50	0	0	0.0
72036 COTTON PLANT	147	1503	1446	1443	-0.9	8	627	612	620	-0.6	2.36	417	400	-1.0
72038 CROCKETTS BLUFF	001	120	120	121	0.0	35	49	50	51	0.5	2.40	36	36	0.0
72039 DAMASCUS	045	865	1105	1325	5.9	100	341	438	529	6.1	2.52	263	332	5.6
72040 DES ARC	117	3511	3559	3571	0.3	47	1440	1478	1504	0.6	2.36	1015	1025	0.2
72041 DE VALLS BLUFF	117	1907	1896	1882	-0.1	29	802	812	820	0.3	2.33	569	567	-0.1
72042 DE WITT	001	5666	5789	5875	0.5	54	2274	2353	2420	0.8	2.37	1621	1649	0.4
72044 EDGEMONT	023	936	1013	1104	1.9	85	427	467	515	2.1	2.17	321	346	1.8
72045 EL PASO	145	1009	1033	1073	0.6	56	388	401	420	0.8	2.55	303	309	0.5
72046 ENGLAND	085	4627	4606	4928	-0.1	31	1789	1801	1948	0.2	2.53	1298	1281	-0.3
72047 ENOLA	045	750	796	868	1.4	79	276	295	324	1.6	2.70	207	217	1.1
72048 ETHEL	001	60	61	62	0.4	49	24	25	26	1.0	2.44	18	18	0.0
72051 FOX	137	1106	1116	1123	0.2	43	447	457	464	0.5	2.44	332	335	0.2
72052 GARNER	145	76	85	92	2.7	93	27	30	33	2.5	2.83	19	21	2.4
72055 GILLETT	001	960	950	948	-0.3	25	414	416	422	0.1	2.28	287	284	-0.3
72057 GRAPEVINE	053	1103	1147	1210	0.9	69	402	422	449	1.2	2.72	317	328	0.8
72058 GREENBRIER	045	12236	13688	15355	2.7	93	4442	5018	5679	2.9	2.73	3506	3904	2.6
72060 GRIFFITHVILLE	145	626	623	646	-0.1	31	262	264	277	0.2	2.27	184	182	-0.3
72063 HATTIEVILLE	029	1444	1480	1514	0.6	57	564	586	606	0.9	2.53	432	443	0.6
72064 HAZEN	117	1800	1777	1757	-0.3	24	721	724	728	0.1	2.36	514	507	-0.3
72065 HENSLEY	125	3880	4072	4343	1.1	72	1484	1570	1694	1.3	2.39	1159	1212	1.1
72066 HICKORY PLAINS	117	557	548	542	-0.4	22	211	210	210	-0.1	2.61	163	160	-0.4
72067 HIGDEN	023	2529	2652	2845	1.1	72	1099	1163	1260	1.3	2.28	823	858	1.0
72068 HIGGINSON	145	367	405	437	2.4	91	148	165	179	2.6	2.45	111	122	2.3
72069 HOLLY GROVE	095	1231	1203	1179	-0.5	16	493	487	482	-0.3	2.47	316	305	-0.8
72070 HOUSTON	105	783	814	840	0.9	69	300	314	326	1.1	2.58	221	228	0.7
72072 HUMNOKE	085	625	632	676	0.3	45	243	249	270	0.6	2.54	176	177	0.1
72073 HUMPHREY	001	1300	1262	1247	-0.7	12	521	515	517	-0.3	2.45	376	365	-0.7
72076 JACKSONVILLE	119	39920	40836	41841	0.5	56	15126	15654	16231	0.9	2.60	11142	11360	0.5
72079 JEFFERSON	069	573	589	589	0.7	60	212	222	226	1.1	2.64	167	172	0.7
72080 JERUSALEM	029	194	195	197	0.1	40	73	74	76	0.3	2.64	54	54	0.0
72081 JUDSONIA	145	7204	7700	8180	1.6	81	2700	2926	3141	1.9	2.56	2044	2182	1.6
ARKANSAS					0.9					1.1	2.47			0.8
UNITED STATES					1.2					1.3	2.58			1.1

#	POST OFFICE NAME	White 2000	White 2004	Black 2000	Black 2004	Asian/Pacific 2000	Asian/Pacific 2004	% Hispanic Origin 2000	% Hispanic Origin 2004	0-4	5-9	10-14	15-19	20-24	25-44	45-64	65-84	85+	18+	Median Age 2004	% 2004 Males	% 2004 Females
71913	HOT SPRINGS NATIONAL	91.1	90.1	5.4	6.0	0.5	0.6	2.7	3.1	5.6	5.6	5.5	5.0	5.1	24.6	27.6	18.3	2.6	80.3	44.0	47.9	52.1
71921	AMITY	95.8	95.3	0.6	0.7	0.1	0.1	3.0	3.4	7.2	6.9	6.6	6.1	5.8	26.2	24.7	14.5	2.1	75.6	37.9	50.9	49.1
71922	ANTOINE	74.7	72.8	21.6	23.1	0.2	0.2	1.3	1.6	7.1	7.3	7.4	7.3	5.8	24.1	24.7	14.2	2.2	73.9	38.2	49.7	50.3
71923	ARKADELPHIA	72.9	71.2	23.3	24.5	0.9	1.1	2.2	2.5	5.6	5.2	5.3	10.5	15.4	24.0	20.1	11.7	2.2	80.8	30.2	48.0	52.0
71929	BISMARCK	97.4	97.3	0.4	0.4	0.1	0.1	2.0	1.9	6.0	6.9	7.6	6.2	5.6	27.4	25.6	13.5	1.2	75.6	39.0	50.2	49.8
71933	BONNERDALE	96.3	96.0	0.3	0.4	0.6	0.6	2.0	2.2	6.5	6.6	7.3	6.5	5.5	27.3	26.9	12.0	1.3	75.5	39.0	51.5	48.5
71935	CADDO GAP	93.5	92.4	0.3	0.4	0.3	0.4	5.7	7.0	7.5	7.4	7.3	6.8	5.7	27.0	24.3	12.8	1.3	73.7	37.8	50.7	49.3
71937	COVE	93.4	92.7	0.5	0.5	0.1	0.1	4.1	4.9	6.8	6.8	7.9	7.0	7.3	26.8	23.2	12.9	1.3	74.3	36.9	51.1	48.9
71940	DELIGHT	90.2	89.3	5.1	5.4	0.4	0.5	2.4	2.7	6.5	6.6	6.7	5.8	5.0	25.6	26.2	15.0	2.6	76.6	40.9	50.9	49.1
71941	DONALDSON	97.8	97.8	0.3	0.3	0.1	0.1	1.0	1.0	6.0	6.1	6.1	6.1	6.7	26.8	27.5	13.2	1.5	78.2	40.2	50.8	49.2
71942	FRIENDSHIP	97.4	97.3	0.0	0.0	0.0	0.0	1.9	1.5	6.6	6.2	6.6	6.2	6.2	29.0	24.3	13.5	1.5	76.8	38.2	51.0	49.0
71943	GLENWOOD	92.4	91.3	0.7	0.8	0.2	0.2	7.3	8.4	7.2	6.7	6.6	6.9	6.1	25.6	22.9	14.4	3.5	75.3	38.2	49.8	50.2
71944	GRANNIS	81.2	78.4	0.3	0.3	0.3	0.3	14.8	17.8	7.4	6.9	7.1	7.8	8.1	28.5	22.7	10.5	1.0	73.9	33.3	51.0	49.0
71945	HATFIELD	94.7	94.3	0.1	0.1	0.1	0.1	1.1	1.3	8.0	7.7	6.9	6.0	5.9	24.7	25.7	13.8	1.3	73.9	38.1	48.1	51.9
71949	JESSIEVILLE	98.3	98.0	0.2	0.2	0.3	0.4	0.6	0.8	5.9	5.7	6.4	6.3	5.4	23.8	26.0	18.7	1.9	78.3	42.6	49.6	50.4
71950	KIRBY	96.2	95.7	0.9	1.0	0.2	0.2	2.4	2.6	6.2	6.4	7.0	6.7	5.7	27.3	26.0	13.5	1.2	75.8	39.1	50.7	49.3
71952	LANGLEY	99.3	98.9	0.0	0.0	0.0	0.0	1.1	1.5	6.5	7.3	6.2	6.5	5.8	24.3	27.9	14.5	1.1	75.7	40.0	51.8	48.2
71953	MENA	96.8	96.5	0.1	0.1	0.3	0.4	1.6	2.0	6.6	6.6	6.6	6.1	5.6	23.9	26.0	16.1	2.7	76.6	41.0	49.2	50.9
71956	MOUNTAIN PINE	86.0	84.1	9.9	11.3	0.6	0.8	1.9	2.2	7.4	7.6	7.6	7.0	6.1	28.6	24.1	10.5	1.2	73.2	35.6	50.2	49.8
71957	MOUNT IDA	96.5	96.2	0.3	0.3	0.3	0.3	1.0	1.2	4.4	4.9	5.6	5.8	4.5	20.9	27.7	22.3	3.9	81.4	47.7	48.0	52.1
71958	MURFREESBORO	92.9	92.2	4.0	4.5	0.2	0.2	1.7	1.9	5.9	6.1	6.6	6.2	5.5	25.4	27.3	14.6	2.4	77.2	41.0	49.3	50.7
71959	NEWHOPE	96.9	96.7	0.8	0.9	0.3	0.3	3.4	3.5	5.9	6.0	6.5	5.7	5.4	27.7	27.1	14.1	1.7	78.1	40.8	49.6	50.4
71960	NORMAN	95.3	94.8	0.3	0.3	0.4	0.6	2.6	3.1	7.0	7.3	7.9	6.5	5.1	25.4	24.4	14.7	1.6	74.0	38.1	47.8	52.2
71961	ODEN	95.7	95.2	0.0	0.0	0.9	1.1	0.7	0.8	6.3	6.5	6.1	5.8	5.3	23.9	27.5	17.0	1.7	77.8	42.4	48.4	51.6
71962	OKOLONA	80.2	78.3	17.5	19.2	0.0	0.0	0.8	1.1	6.1	6.6	6.5	5.9	4.7	24.6	28.5	15.3	1.9	77.2	41.9	51.8	48.2
71964	PEARCY	97.3	97.0	0.2	0.2	0.3	0.4	1.7	2.0	6.2	6.6	7.5	7.1	6.1	27.0	27.7	10.8	0.9	75.3	38.6	51.5	48.5
71965	PENCIL BLUFF	96.3	96.2	0.3	0.3	0.6	0.6	0.6	0.6	6.8	7.1	5.9	5.3	4.7	22.7	28.3	17.4	1.8	76.7	43.2	48.7	51.3
71968	ROYAL	93.6	92.7	3.9	4.6	0.1	0.1	1.6	2.0	5.5	5.7	6.6	8.6	6.6	26.1	28.6	11.4	0.9	77.1	39.4	51.5	48.5
71969	SIMS	97.0	96.7	0.6	0.8	0.3	0.3	0.5	0.6	7.3	7.5	5.8	4.6	4.3	21.6	29.5	17.8	1.8	76.8	44.3	49.5	50.5
71970	STORY	97.0	96.3	0.5	0.5	0.3	0.3	0.8	1.0	6.4	6.6	6.1	4.9	4.4	21.6	27.7	20.3	2.0	77.9	45.0	50.0	50.0
71971	UMPIRE	96.8	96.7	1.0	1.2	0.0	0.0	7.9	7.7	6.5	6.5	6.1	5.4	6.1	28.9	25.5	13.0	1.9	77.2	39.0	51.3	48.7
71972	VANDERVOORT	94.3	93.9	1.0	0.9	0.0	0.0	3.8	4.4	6.1	6.5	8.3	7.0	7.8	26.1	23.5	13.5	1.3	74.8	37.2	51.3	48.7
71973	WICKES	83.0	80.4	0.0	0.0	0.2	0.2	17.9	21.3	9.0	8.5	8.6	7.2	6.7	28.1	20.9	9.9	0.9	69.3	32.0	51.1	48.9
71998	ARKADELPHIA	87.3	87.3	9.1	9.1	1.8	1.8	0.0	0.0	0.0	0.0	0.0	29.1	70.9	0.0	0.0	0.0	0.0	100.0	21.5	90.9	9.1
72001	ADONA	97.0	97.0	0.5	0.5	0.2	0.2	0.7	0.7	7.2	6.8	7.3	6.8	5.9	28.1	23.6	13.1	1.2	74.5	37.0	50.6	49.4
72002	ALEXANDER	94.3	93.6	2.9	3.3	0.6	0.7	1.3	1.6	6.7	6.9	7.5	6.8	5.9	31.2	26.1	8.3	0.6	74.7	36.3	50.4	49.6
72003	ALMYRA	93.1	92.8	6.2	6.7	0.0	0.0	0.3	0.3	7.1	6.4	4.8	5.9	6.0	27.7	28.5	12.4	1.2	78.2	39.6	51.6	48.4
72004	ALTHEIMER	38.1	34.0	59.4	63.3	0.5	0.4	2.4	2.5	7.0	7.2	7.7	7.6	6.4	23.9	25.4	12.9	1.9	73.6	37.4	47.1	52.9
72005	AMAGON	89.4	88.9	7.0	7.3	0.3	0.5	2.8	3.1	5.4	5.7	4.9	6.7	7.3	28.5	25.4	14.0	2.1	80.1	39.7	50.0	50.0
72006	AUGUSTA	58.5	56.9	40.5	42.1	0.0	0.0	0.6	0.6	7.1	7.0	7.2	7.0	6.5	24.0	26.7	12.6	2.1	74.6	38.4	48.9	51.1
72007	AUSTIN	97.2	96.8	0.2	0.3	0.4	0.4	1.8	2.1	6.5	6.6	7.9	7.8	6.9	30.8	24.5	8.2	0.7	74.1	35.9	49.5	50.5
72010	BALD KNOB	94.0	93.4	3.0	3.3	0.4	0.5	2.4	2.8	6.9	7.0	7.4	6.6	6.1	28.5	24.4	11.5	1.6	74.7	36.6	49.3	50.7
72011	BAUXITE	97.8	97.6	0.7	0.7	0.2	0.3	1.1	1.2	7.5	7.4	8.3	7.5	6.7	32.3	22.8	6.9	0.6	72.2	33.8	49.5	50.6
72012	BEEBE	93.8	93.1	3.4	3.7	0.5	0.6	1.2	1.5	6.8	6.8	7.4	6.9	6.9	28.3	25.0	10.5	1.5	75.2	36.6	48.9	51.1
72013	BEE BRANCH	97.8	97.7	0.1	0.1	0.3	0.3	1.6	1.8	6.5	6.7	6.5	6.2	5.1	26.4	26.6	14.5	1.6	76.4	39.8	51.1	48.9
72014	BEEDEVILLE	94.3	93.9	1.0	1.8	0.0	0.9	2.9	2.6	6.1	6.1	5.3	7.0	4.4	26.3	27.2	14.9	2.6	77.2	41.7	50.9	49.1
72015	BENTON	94.6	94.2	3.0	3.1	0.5	0.5	1.6	1.8	6.6	6.7	6.9	6.4	6.2	29.0	25.2	11.4	1.6	75.8	37.5	49.3	50.7
72016	BIGELOW	92.7	92.3	4.6	4.7	0.2	0.2	0.9	1.1	6.8	7.2	8.0	6.8	5.6	28.4	26.8	9.4	1.0	73.7	37.2	50.5	49.5
72017	BISCOE	76.0	75.4	22.8	23.4	0.1	0.1	0.8	0.9	5.2	5.6	6.6	7.0	6.4	26.4	28.1	13.0	2.0	78.8	40.6	52.0	48.0
72020	BRADFORD	97.9	97.6	0.2	0.3	0.1	0.2	1.3	1.6	6.2	6.3	7.0	6.4	6.1	26.9	26.3	13.2	1.7	76.7	38.8	50.0	50.0
72021	BRINKLEY	57.1	55.3	40.8	42.4	0.2	0.2	1.2	1.4	7.8	7.2	8.2	7.3	6.8	21.7	24.2	14.2	2.6	72.3	37.9	46.3	53.7
72022	BRYANT	95.2	94.4	2.2	2.6	1.0	1.2	1.0	1.3	6.9	6.9	7.3	8.5	6.2	28.7	24.5	9.4	1.8	73.1	36.3	48.4	51.7
72023	CABOT	96.8	96.3	0.3	0.4	0.7	0.9	1.7	2.0	7.5	7.4	8.0	7.7	6.8	30.2	23.7	7.9	0.8	72.2	34.6	49.3	50.7
72024	CARLISLE	87.7	86.4	10.9	12.1	0.3	0.3	0.8	0.8	5.9	6.1	6.8	6.1	5.8	25.8	25.6	14.7	3.3	77.4	40.7	48.9	51.1
72025	CASA	97.2	97.3	0.5	0.5	0.1	0.1	0.4	0.5	7.4	7.0	7.2	6.4	5.6	28.7	23.1	13.4	1.2	74.5	36.8	50.0	50.0
72026	CASSCOE	74.2	72.4	24.4	25.8	0.0	0.0	0.0	0.0	6.9	6.7	5.1	5.4	5.4	24.9	30.8	13.3	1.6	78.2	42.0	52.1	47.9
72027	CENTER RIDGE	91.7	90.9	6.0	6.5	0.3	0.2	1.8	2.2	7.1	6.8	7.1	6.2	6.6	26.0	25.5	13.3	1.6	75.3	38.7	50.7	49.3
72028	CHOCTAW	97.2	97.0	0.1	0.1	0.2	0.2	1.3	1.5	5.7	5.9	6.6	5.9	5.6	22.9	28.4	16.5	2.5	77.9	43.2	49.3	50.7
72029	CLARENDON	69.8	68.4	28.5	29.8	0.1	0.1	1.9	2.1	6.0	6.4	7.2	6.4	6.2	24.6	25.9	15.0	2.3	76.7	40.1	49.5	50.6
72030	CLEVELAND	93.5	92.9	4.7	4.9	0.0	0.0	1.8	2.2	6.4	6.4	7.1	6.1	5.9	25.0	26.7	14.5	2.0	76.0	40.2	50.0	50.0
72031	CLINTON	96.0	95.5	0.4	0.4	0.3	0.4	1.6	1.9	5.3	5.5	6.7	6.1	6.1	23.1	27.3	16.9	3.1	78.6	43.0	49.4	50.6
72032	CONWAY	86.6	85.8	10.4	10.9	0.5	0.7	1.9	2.2	7.0	6.8	6.8	7.9	8.7	30.9	22.7	8.4	0.9	75.6	33.1	49.2	50.8
72034	CONWAY	85.1	84.0	11.0	11.5	1.3	1.6	2.2	2.6	7.5	6.4	6.5	7.5	13.2	31.3	18.2	8.0	1.5	75.8	29.2	48.3	51.7
72035	CONWAY	76.9	75.1	18.5	19.7	2.6	3.2	1.0	1.2	0.0	0.0	0.0	56.2	42.1	1.6	0.1	0.0	0.1	99.8	19.5	38.8	61.2
72036	COTTON PLANT	41.9	41.5	56.6	56.9	0.2	0.2	1.3	1.3	8.0	7.7	7.9	7.4	4.8	21.9	23.7	15.4	3.3	71.7	39.6	45.0	55.0
72038	CROCKETTS BLUFF	79.2	78.3	19.2	20.8	0.0	0.0	0.0	0.0	6.7	6.7	5.0	5.0	5.0	25.8	29.2	15.0	1.7	79.2	41.9	51.7	48.3
72039	DAMASCUS	81.2	79.1	16.8	18.8	0.2	0.2	0.6	0.6	6.7	6.6	7.7	7.5	6.3	27.8	23.2	12.6	1.6	74.4	37.5	50.0	50.1
72040	DES ARC	88.5	88.0	9.7	10.3	0.2	0.2	1.0	0.9	6.2	6.2	6.5	6.5	5.3	25.3	26.4	15.1	2.4	77.0	40.9	49.5	50.5
72041	DE VALLS BLUFF	82.6	81.9	16.5	17.3	0.1	0.1	0.4	0.4	5.9	6.0	6.3	6.0	5.9	24.5	29.2	13.8	2.5	78.3	41.7	48.7	51.3
72042	DE WITT	84.6	83.5	14.2	15.1	0.2	0.2	0.6	0.8	6.5	6.5	6.4	6.4	5.6	25.8	26.1	14.2	2.6	76.6	40.0	48.2	51.8
72044	EDGEMONT	98.3	98.2	0.0	0.0	0.1	0.1	0.3	0.3	3.9	3.9	5.0	4.6	4.3	16.3	31.2	29.2	1.6	84.5	55.7	50.0	50.1
72045	EL PASO	97.1	96.8	0.1	0.1	0.4	0.5	1.4	1.7	6.6	6.8	6.9	6.5	6.0	28.5	26.4	11.1	1.3	75.9	37.8	50.7	49.3
72046	ENGLAND	70.6	67.1	28.0	31.3	0.1	0.2	1.3	1.5	7.2	7.0	6.9	6.5	6.5	25.6	25.0	13.0	2.3	75.0	38.0	47.6	52.4
72047	ENOLA	97.3	97.1	0.0	0.0	0.3	0.3	1.6	2.0	7.5	7.3	7.3	7.4	6.7	27.0	24.1	11.2	1.5	73.1	36.0	51.3	48.7
72048	ETHEL	95.0	95.1	5.0	4.9	0.0	0.0	0.0	0.0	6.6	6.6	4.9	4.9	3.3	23.0	32.8	18.0	0.0	82.0	45.6	49.2	50.8
72051	FOX	97.6	97.6	0.4	0.4	0.1	0.1	1.0	1.1	5.2	5.6	5.9	6.1	5.3	21.4	31.3	17.5	1.8	79.6	45.3	51.6	48.4
72052	GARNER	94.7	92.9	1.3	1.2	0.0	0.0	2.6	3.5	7.1	7.1	7.1	7.1	5.9	27.1	23.5	14.1	1.2	71.8	37.1	50.6	49.4
72055	GILLETT	88.0	87.2	11.3	12.0	0.0	0.0	0.9	1.2	4.4	5.1	7.3	7.0	5.8	24.4	28.3	15.8	2.0	78.8	42.5	48.7	51.3
72057	GRAPEVINE	88.1	87.2	10.2	10.9	0.1	0.1	0.4	0.4	5.5	5.8	7.5	8.2	6.6	26.8	27.2	11.3	1.1	76.1	38.5	52.0	48.0
72058	GREENBRIER	96.3	95.9	1.4	1.6	0.1	0.1	0.9	1.1	7.3	7.3	8.3	7.1	6.4	30.4	23.3	9.0	1.0	72.7	34.9	49.7	50.4
72060	GRIFFITHVILLE	96.2	95.5	1.0	1.1	0.0	0.2	2.4	3.1	7.4	7.2	7.1	5.8	5.9	26.3	24.9	14.1	1.3	74.5	38.4	53.3	46.7
72063	HATTIEVILLE	96.1	95.7	2.1	2.2	0.1	0.2	0.4	0.5	5.9	6.4	7.5	6.4	5.5	25.5	27.9	13.3	1.8	76.4	40.2	49.0	51.0
72064	HAZEN	82.0	81.4	16.9	17.5	0.0	0.0	0.7	0.7	6.2	6.4	6.3	5.9	5.1	24.6	25.5	17.0	3.2	77.0	42.1	48.8	51.2
72065	HENSLEY	84.2	83.8	12.5	12.5	1.1	1.3	0.9	1.0	6.1	6.4	6.6	6.1	6.1	34.1	25.7	8.1	0.8	77.1	36.8	53.9	46.1
72066	HICKORY PLAINS	92.6	92.5	4.1	4.2	1.1	1.1	1.6	1.6	8.4	8.2	6.8	4.9	5.7	26.8	25.7	11.9	1.6	73.7	36.9	51.3	48.7
72067	HIGDEN	97.6	97.4	0.1	0.1	0.2	0.2	1.0	1.2	4.8	4.8	5.0	4.7	3.7	19.7	31.8	23.4	2.0	82.5	50.0	50.9	49.1
72068	HIGGINSON	96.7	96.3	0.0	0.0	0.5	0.5	3.3	4.0	6.2	6.2	7.2	7.4	5.9	30.9	25.2	9.9	1.2	76.1	36.3	51.1	48.9
72069	HOLLY GROVE	38.3	36.2	61.1	63.1	0.1	0.1	0.3	0.3	6.0	6.2	8.4	6.7	7.3	22.3	23.8	16.0	3.3	75.5	40.4	44.8	55.2
72070	HOUSTON	93.2	92.9	3.8	3.8	0.1	0.1	1.3	1.5	6.6	7.1	7.5	6.1	4.7	27.6	26.9	12.4	1.0	74.7	38.7	51.4	48.7
72072	HUMNOKE	69.8	65.0	27.8	32.4	0.2	0.2	1.3	1.6	6.8	6.5	7.1	6.0	7.0	27.5	25.0	12.3	1.7	75.8	37.4	48.6	51.4
72073	HUMPHREY	60.9	58.9	36.7	38.6	0.2	0.2	1.1	1.0	6.2	6.6	7.3	7.1	6.7	25.7	27.0	11.6	1.9	75.7	38.4	48.4	51.6
72076	JACKSONVILLE	74.6	71.3	19.7	22.3	1.7	2.0	3.0	3.6	9.0	8.1	7.4	6.6	8.3	31.2	20.8	8.1	0.6	71.6	31.5	49.1	50.9
72079	JEFFERSON	87.8	86.1	9.6	11.0	0.2	0.3	2.8	3.2	7.3	7.0	7.1	7.0	6.8	31.4	24.8	7.8	0.9	74.4	35.3	51.6	48.4
72080	JERUSALEM	92.3	91.8	6.7	7.2	0.0	0.0	0.0	0.5	5.1	5.6	6.7	5.6	5.6	24.6	29.7	15.4	1.5	78.5	42.8	51.3	48.7
72081	JUDSONIA	96.0	95.6	0.9	1.0	0.1	0.2	2.5	3.0	6.8	6.9	7.0	6.4	6.3	28.5	24.3	11.6	2.2	75.4	37.3	49.9	50.1
	ARKANSAS	80.0	79.3	15.7	15.8	0.8	1.0	3.3	3.8	6.9	6.7	6.9	6.8	7.3	27.3	24.1	12.2	1.8	75.7	36.7	49.0	51.0
	UNITED STATES	75.1	73.6	12.3	12.5	3.8	4.2	12.5	14.1	6.9	6.7	7.2	7.0	7.3	28.6	23.8	10.8	1.7	75.1	36.0	49.1	50.9

ZIP CODE				2004 HOUSEHOLD INCOME DISTRIBUTION (%)					MEDIAN HOUSEHOLD INCOME					2004 HOME VALUE DISTRIBUTION (%)					
#	POST OFFICE NAME	2004 Per Capita Income	2004 HH Income Base	Less than $25,000	$25,000 to $49,999	$50,000 to $99,999	$100,000 to $149,999	$150,000 or More	2004	2009	2004 National Centile	2004 State Centile	2004 Home Value Base	Less than $50,000	$50,000 to $89,999	$90,000 to $174,999	$175,000 to $399,999	$400,000 or More	2004 Median Home Value
71913	HOT SPRINGS NATIONAL	23584	17743	32.1	32.5	25.2	7.2	3.1	37139	45283	36	74	12980	19.8	26.3	33.7	15.6	4.5	94465
71921	AMITY	17617	797	39.8	32.6	22.0	3.9	1.8	31364	38250	16	38	654	45.9	23.2	19.4	9.0	2.5	55094
71922	ANTOINE	21830	214	39.7	32.7	18.7	4.2	4.7	33993	40345	24	55	179	57.5	14.5	23.5	4.5	0.0	43250
71923	ARKADELPHIA	18166	6236	40.4	25.6	26.0	5.6	2.3	34155	42302	25	56	3890	24.9	24.8	37.0	11.7	1.7	90370
71929	BISMARCK	17322	1174	31.6	38.6	23.1	4.0	2.7	35906	42338	31	68	984	29.9	24.9	32.1	11.3	1.8	84719
71933	BONNERDALE	17500	781	32.5	34.7	25.7	5.3	1.8	34884	41273	27	61	663	32.1	29.7	28.5	8.6	1.1	71000
71935	CADDO GAP	15316	940	33.1	37.1	26.0	3.4	0.4	36835	42591	35	73	780	46.2	21.2	21.3	9.0	2.4	57692
71937	COVE	16314	848	46.3	30.0	16.9	4.5	2.4	27474	33540	8	14	682	51.9	25.2	19.2	3.5	0.2	48395
71940	DELIGHT	18491	700	40.7	32.3	22.6	2.9	1.6	30861	37059	14	32	603	45.6	20.1	23.1	8.6	2.7	59138
71941	DONALDSON	18107	791	30.5	35.8	29.0	4.3	0.5	37200	43446	36	75	668	44.9	27.3	24.3	3.4	0.2	57391
71942	FRIENDSHIP	18205	104	27.9	30.8	35.6	5.8	0.0	40000	47385	46	84	87	46.0	29.9	23.0	1.2	0.0	55833
71943	GLENWOOD	17114	1740	40.0	32.8	20.8	4.5	1.8	31527	37093	16	39	1334	40.9	24.9	24.4	7.7	2.0	64000
71944	GRANNIS	17767	323	36.5	35.3	20.7	4.0	3.4	33731	40242	23	53	254	42.1	30.3	19.3	5.5	2.8	60000
71945	HATFIELD	15002	576	45.7	31.9	17.2	2.6	2.6	27704	33451	8	16	478	36.8	29.5	22.6	8.4	2.7	61923
71949	JESSIEVILLE	21224	642	25.6	33.0	31.6	5.8	4.1	41150	51464	50	86	537	38.4	17.5	31.1	12.9	0.2	79054
71950	KIRBY	18767	422	40.5	30.6	20.1	5.7	3.1	31663	38288	17	40	364	47.0	22.3	18.1	9.6	3.0	53548
71952	LANGLEY	18533	107	39.3	32.7	19.6	4.7	3.7	31266	37060	16	36	89	43.8	27.0	16.9	9.0	3.4	57857
71953	MENA	17656	6068	42.6	30.7	21.3	3.0	2.4	29600	35765	11	23	4748	28.9	33.1	26.0	9.2	2.7	75222
71956	MOUNTAIN PINE	15679	669	36.5	38.7	19.4	4.6	0.8	33910	40871	24	55	543	62.4	17.1	14.2	5.9	0.4	38214
71957	MOUNT IDA	18472	1701	39.6	33.8	19.8	4.4	2.5	31335	36666	16	37	1380	35.4	24.4	29.3	10.1	0.8	71667
71958	MURFREESBORO	19778	1660	37.5	33.1	23.0	3.8	2.7	34081	40597	24	56	1332	41.4	33.5	19.2	4.7	1.1	57703
71959	NEWHOPE	20894	265	37.4	29.1	23.0	6.0	4.5	34255	41800	25	57	225	42.7	27.6	21.3	6.2	2.2	57500
71960	NORMAN	15210	342	43.0	32.5	20.8	3.8	0.0	29554	34387	11	23	282	55.0	19.2	19.5	6.0	0.4	44400
71961	ODEN	24866	357	32.2	37.0	19.3	5.0	6.4	36256	42696	33	71	303	34.0	32.0	25.7	6.3	2.0	68281
71962	OKOLONA	18039	417	36.5	32.4	26.4	3.1	1.7	33787	41358	23	54	355	43.4	23.9	21.7	5.6	5.4	66379
71964	PEARCY	20304	1393	29.1	34.3	25.3	8.0	3.2	39110	47541	43	81	1189	26.2	25.7	31.3	13.6	3.1	87500
71965	PENCIL BLUFF	22329	146	35.6	37.7	17.1	4.1	5.5	33345	38626	22	51	125	38.4	30.4	22.4	7.2	1.6	66250
71968	ROYAL	18099	1662	25.9	34.3	33.9	4.9	1.0	42215	51593	54	89	1411	32.1	29.9	22.7	13.3	2.0	73240
71969	SIMS	16172	258	40.7	38.4	14.7	3.5	2.7	29344	35103	11	23	221	44.8	28.5	18.6	6.8	1.4	61389
71970	STORY	18059	192	41.7	35.9	16.7	3.7	2.1	30000	35588	12	26	164	45.1	25.0	22.6	6.7	0.6	61667
71971	UMPIRE	23799	194	32.5	28.9	22.7	10.3	5.7	40000	49395	46	84	161	37.9	28.0	23.6	8.1	2.5	65417
71972	VANDERVOORT	15736	85	41.2	31.8	18.8	5.9	2.4	30231	35628	13	28	70	50.0	27.1	18.6	4.3	0.0	50000
71973	WICKES	15104	428	48.1	30.8	15.7	2.1	3.3	26224	31489	6	10	327	57.2	20.2	19.3	2.8	0.6	39457
71998	ARKADELPHIA	7904	0	0.0	0.0	0.0	0.0	0.0	0	0	0	0	0	0.0	0.0	0.0	0.0	0.0	0
72001	ADONA	17282	227	35.7	34.8	22.9	4.9	1.8	35146	43076	28	63	190	41.1	30.5	21.6	4.7	2.1	63333
72002	ALEXANDER	21251	5236	20.4	31.6	38.4	7.6	2.1	48197	56826	69	95	4453	30.4	24.1	33.0	12.0	0.6	81939
72003	ALMYRA	20738	308	27.0	33.1	32.5	4.6	2.9	43228	51080	57	91	245	42.0	29.0	22.9	4.5	1.6	59750
72004	ALTHEIMER	13485	528	44.9	30.9	20.1	2.7	1.5	28973	36339	10	21	374	63.4	27.0	2.9	6.7	0.0	34444
72005	AMAGON	15142	159	52.2	32.1	13.8	0.6	1.3	23786	28278	4	5	125	64.8	26.4	8.0	0.0	0.8	36250
72006	AUGUSTA	16091	1417	49.5	28.9	17.7	2.1	1.8	25295	30261	5	8	955	57.0	29.7	11.5	1.8	0.0	44458
72007	AUSTIN	20550	1985	18.4	33.5	38.2	7.3	2.6	48203	57125	69	96	1651	24.1	25.5	36.2	12.9	1.3	90556
72010	BALD KNOB	16372	2730	40.7	29.1	24.5	4.5	1.3	32559	39835	19	46	2088	51.1	26.4	18.2	3.5	0.8	49262
72011	BAUXITE	18919	1497	17.3	35.9	40.7	4.7	1.4	47076	55483	66	94	1256	26.5	34.7	32.7	6.0	0.1	75443
72012	BEEBE	21005	3706	26.8	32.3	30.5	7.7	2.8	42226	51065	54	89	2921	21.1	27.2	40.0	9.5	2.3	91447
72013	BEE BRANCH	19044	648	32.9	35.8	22.5	5.4	3.4	34557	42005	26	58	540	35.6	25.4	25.2	10.9	3.0	73611
72014	BEEDEVILLE	11732	47	53.2	34.0	12.8	0.0	0.0	23266	28586	3	4	37	73.0	18.9	8.1	0.0	0.0	30833
72015	BENTON	22987	16141	22.0	30.3	35.4	8.5	3.8	47990	56044	68	95	12526	16.8	30.4	41.2	10.1	1.4	92958
72016	BIGELOW	20108	1064	29.8	32.1	27.6	7.1	3.5	37229	45306	36	75	894	30.4	30.4	30.4	6.8	1.9	73659
72017	BISCOE	16490	524	41.0	30.7	23.1	3.8	1.3	31620	38437	17	39	403	50.4	27.1	16.4	5.7	0.5	49531
72020	BRADFORD	16418	1752	40.2	32.0	23.7	3.0	1.0	32909	40250	21	48	1429	59.2	25.5	12.3	2.5	0.6	43995
72021	BRINKLEY	16539	2212	49.6	30.7	15.1	1.9	2.8	25267	30191	5	7	1492	43.1	35.3	18.5	2.7	0.5	55202
72022	BRYANT	23199	3573	19.2	26.5	40.0	12.0	2.4	54156	63569	79	98	2857	16.3	18.9	48.6	15.6	0.7	107132
72023	CABOT	22859	10299	16.5	27.3	41.8	11.5	2.9	55151	65853	80	98	8161	11.1	26.7	48.6	13.1	0.6	103695
72024	CARLISLE	20683	1469	39.2	24.6	27.2	5.6	3.3	36013	44260	32	69	1131	42.2	34.5	17.8	5.4	0.2	57696
72025	CASA	20972	296	37.2	34.1	22.0	5.1	1.7	34685	42352	26	59	250	42.8	30.4	20.4	4.8	1.6	62174
72026	CASSCOE	22147	236	20.3	32.2	39.8	6.4	1.3	48092	58361	69	95	194	44.3	23.2	21.7	10.8	0.0	66667
72027	CENTER RIDGE	18204	652	38.5	26.1	26.1	6.9	2.5	33999	43457	24	55	560	34.3	33.2	25.9	4.1	2.5	68929
72028	CHOCTAW	21249	563	38.7	33.4	19.4	3.7	4.8	31282	38026	16	37	462	31.6	24.2	31.8	10.2	2.2	80000
72029	CLARENDON	17381	1232	46.0	27.2	21.2	3.2	2.4	27487	34325	8	14	883	55.6	26.7	14.8	2.5	0.3	45286
72030	CLEVELAND	18664	166	39.8	26.5	24.1	7.2	2.4	33492	42105	22	52	142	35.9	28.9	23.9	8.5	2.8	67857
72031	CLINTON	19870	2092	45.8	29.9	17.4	3.6	3.3	27297	32504	8	14	1638	36.0	30.7	25.3	6.9	1.2	65740
72032	CONWAY	22488	10673	24.7	27.2	35.5	9.1	3.5	47721	58935	68	95	7613	15.1	27.5	44.7	11.3	1.5	97411
72034	CONWAY	23787	13759	29.7	27.0	28.4	9.9	5.0	43433	53333	57	91	7868	10.7	19.7	48.4	18.8	2.5	115341
72035	CONWAY	8600	4	50.0	0.0	50.0	0.0	0.0	35000	35000	28	63	0	0.0	0.0	0.0	0.0	0.0	0
72036	COTTON PLANT	12091	612	63.4	23.2	11.3	0.7	1.5	17624	20741	1	1	399	74.2	13.8	9.5	2.3	0.3	29786
72038	CROCKETTS BLUFF	20814	50	26.0	34.0	34.0	4.0	2.0	41536	55323	51	88	41	41.5	24.4	24.4	9.8	0.0	71667
72039	DAMASCUS	20083	438	27.4	34.0	30.6	5.7	2.3	41145	50799	50	86	378	31.0	34.1	26.7	7.1	1.1	70000
72040	DES ARC	19526	1478	39.2	31.5	21.0	5.4	2.9	33084	40600	21	49	1145	42.3	27.0	26.6	3.5	0.7	61080
72041	DE VALLS BLUFF	21073	812	40.3	28.5	26.6	2.7	2.0	33620	40458	23	53	629	45.5	28.6	21.9	3.8	0.2	56196
72042	DE WITT	17302	2353	43.1	28.4	22.7	4.0	1.7	29584	36260	11	23	1697	48.4	27.6	19.2	4.1	0.7	51815
72044	EDGEMONT	18466	467	37.7	36.4	21.6	3.2	1.1	31207	36048	15	36	413	22.5	9.9	44.8	20.8	1.9	118344
72045	EL PASO	21396	401	27.7	30.2	29.7	7.2	5.2	42447	51880	54	90	337	27.9	23.4	31.2	8.6	8.9	87188
72046	ENGLAND	18499	1801	35.1	32.9	24.2	5.8	2.0	35666	42777	30	66	1254	43.2	27.0	23.3	5.6	1.0	58416
72047	ENOLA	17089	295	33.6	34.6	24.8	5.8	1.4	35283	43403	29	64	249	36.6	28.1	25.7	8.8	0.8	68864
72048	ETHEL	14795	25	40.0	36.0	24.0	0.0	0.0	33600	40000	23	52	21	47.6	28.6	19.1	4.8	0.0	55000
72051	FOX	16661	457	43.8	36.8	14.7	2.0	2.8	28941	33743	10	21	390	40.0	30.8	21.3	5.9	2.1	60789
72052	GARNER	10676	30	50.0	33.3	16.7	0.0	0.0	25000	28605	5	7	24	45.8	29.2	25.0	0.0	0.0	53333
72055	GILLETT	20791	416	33.9	35.1	23.6	5.3	2.2	36738	44128	34	72	331	44.7	33.8	17.8	3.0	0.6	56731
72057	GRAPEVINE	17277	422	31.3	32.7	27.0	7.6	1.4	38402	46330	41	80	358	42.5	34.9	16.2	5.0	1.4	64000
72058	GREENBRIER	20765	5018	24.3	29.5	36.5	7.1	2.7	46603	56675	65	94	4139	21.8	30.7	36.1	10.2	1.1	86629
72060	GRIFFITHVILLE	15772	264	39.0	36.4	21.6	3.0	0.0	31555	38130	17	39	217	47.9	24.9	26.3	0.9	0.0	53750
72063	HATTIEVILLE	18504	586	30.6	35.0	26.5	6.7	1.4	37714	46737	38	78	517	25.7	31.5	34.6	6.8	1.4	80854
72064	HAZEN	20273	724	34.3	35.5	23.2	3.9	3.2	34907	41534	27	61	548	38.3	30.3	27.7	3.7	0.0	63667
72065	HENSLEY	22257	1570	21.8	26.2	42.7	8.0	1.3	51448	60860	75	97	1376	27.8	31.8	32.5	7.4	0.4	74189
72066	HICKORY PLAINS	19435	210	35.7	26.2	28.1	4.8	5.2	43073	51849	56	90	180	31.7	27.2	38.3	0.6	2.2	80000
72067	HIGDEN	20892	1163	32.5	34.7	25.6	4.2	3.0	37007	43894	35	74	1001	25.5	21.2	34.3	14.2	4.9	97283
72068	HIGGINSON	16062	165	32.1	43.6	19.4	4.9	0.0	35401	42322	29	65	134	46.3	35.1	14.2	3.0	1.5	54167
72069	HOLLY GROVE	12512	487	56.7	24.4	14.8	3.3	0.8	20795	25243	2	2	317	66.9	19.9	12.0	1.3	0.0	40614
72070	HOUSTON	15878	314	36.9	33.8	22.9	5.1	1.3	32389	38688	19	45	254	29.1	31.1	29.9	7.1	2.8	72857
72072	HUMNOKE	15781	249	45.0	30.5	21.7	0.8	2.0	27763	32714	8	16	202	73.3	21.3	3.5	2.0	0.0	33571
72073	HUMPHREY	16125	515	44.5	25.6	23.3	5.8	0.8	30211	38587	13	27	396	51.0	32.6	12.9	3.5	0.0	48889
72076	JACKSONVILLE	19482	15654	27.3	33.0	31.6	6.5	1.7	41350	51402	51	87	9096	20.8	42.7	31.7	4.1	0.8	75736
72079	JEFFERSON	18557	222	22.5	36.0	34.7	6.3	0.5	42050	51822	53	88	170	47.1	32.4	17.7	2.9	0.0	54167
72080	JERUSALEM	17910	74	36.5	32.4	17.6	10.8	2.7	35618	44192	30	66	63	33.3	27.0	20.6	15.9	3.2	69286
72081	JUDSONIA	16105	2926	36.4	32.7	26.4	2.7	1.8	34633	41894	26	59	2374	43.6	29.5	20.9	4.7	1.3	56509
	ARKANSAS	20565		33.0	30.6	26.7	6.4	3.3	37742	46417				27.1	29.3	31.4	10.3	1.8	80466
	UNITED STATES	25866		24.7	27.1	30.8	10.9	6.5	48124	56710				10.9	15.0	33.7	30.1	10.4	145905

#	POST OFFICE NAME	FINANCIAL SERVICES				THE HOME						ENTERTAINMENT						PERSONAL			
						Home Improvements		Furnishings													
ZIP CODE		Auto Loan	Home Loan	Invest-ments	Retire-ment Plans	Home Repair	Lawn & Garden	Comput-ers & Hard-ware	Major Appli-ances	TV, Radio, Sound Equip-ment	Furni-ture	Dine out/ Carry out	Sports Equip-ment	Fees & Tickets	Toys & Games	Travel	Cable TV	Apparel & Services	Auto Repairs	Health Insur-ance	Pets & Supplies
71913	HOT SPRINGS NATIONAL	82	70	58	66	74	84	69	77	74	69	90	87	65	86	71	77	84	76	86	94
71921	AMITY	82	55	25	48	63	72	53	67	64	54	76	80	45	71	54	69	69	66	82	95
71922	ANTOINE	106	71	32	61	80	92	68	86	83	70	97	102	58	92	70	89	88	85	105	121
71923	ARKADELPHIA	71	57	50	56	60	68	63	65	67	61	82	78	58	79	61	68	77	67	71	79
71929	BISMARCK	84	56	26	49	64	73	54	68	66	55	77	81	46	73	55	71	70	67	84	97
71933	BONNERDALE	79	60	35	54	65	72	57	68	65	59	77	80	51	74	58	68	72	67	77	90
71935	CADDO GAP	70	55	35	51	58	64	53	61	58	54	70	71	48	66	53	60	65	60	67	79
71937	COVE	80	53	24	46	61	70	52	65	62	53	73	77	44	69	52	67	66	64	79	92
71940	DELIGHT	84	56	25	48	64	73	54	68	65	55	77	81	46	73	55	70	70	67	84	96
71941	DONALDSON	84	56	26	49	64	74	55	68	66	56	77	81	46	73	55	71	70	67	84	97
71942	FRIENDSHIP	85	57	26	49	65	75	55	69	67	56	78	82	47	74	56	72	71	68	85	98
71943	GLENWOOD	74	55	34	51	60	70	58	65	65	56	77	75	51	73	57	69	70	65	78	83
71944	GRANNIS	91	61	28	53	69	80	59	74	71	60	83	88	50	79	60	77	76	73	91	105
71945	HATFIELD	74	49	22	43	56	64	48	59	57	48	67	71	40	64	48	62	61	59	73	84
71949	JESSIEVILLE	92	75	55	68	83	94	70	84	78	71	94	95	64	90	75	84	87	82	99	111
71950	KIRBY	88	59	27	51	67	77	57	71	68	58	80	85	48	76	58	74	73	70	87	101
71952	LANGLEY	90	60	27	52	68	79	58	73	70	59	82	87	49	78	59	76	75	72	90	103
71953	MENA	74	54	31	50	60	69	55	64	63	54	75	74	49	71	56	67	68	64	77	84
71956	MOUNTAIN PINE	75	53	27	46	59	67	51	62	60	52	70	74	44	67	51	63	65	61	74	86
71957	MOUNT IDA	70	53	34	49	58	68	54	62	62	53	73	72	48	69	55	65	67	62	75	80
71958	MURFREESBORO	80	61	39	57	66	76	61	70	69	61	82	82	56	80	61	72	76	69	81	90
71959	NEWHOPE	97	66	32	59	76	86	64	80	76	65	90	96	55	86	66	82	82	79	98	113
71960	NORMAN	68	45	21	39	51	59	44	55	53	45	62	66	37	59	45	57	56	54	68	78
71961	ODEN	117	78	35	68	89	102	76	95	91	77	107	113	64	101	77	98	97	94	117	134
71962	OKOLONA	82	55	25	47	62	71	53	66	64	54	75	79	45	71	54	69	68	65	81	94
71964	PEARCY	90	77	56	73	79	85	74	82	77	76	94	95	68	89	73	77	89	81	85	101
71965	PENCIL BLUFF	98	65	30	56	74	85	63	79	76	64	89	94	54	84	64	82	81	78	97	112
71968	ROYAL	82	64	40	58	70	77	60	71	68	61	81	84	56	80	62	71	76	70	82	96
71969	SIMS	78	52	24	45	59	68	50	63	61	51	71	75	43	67	51	65	65	62	77	89
71970	STORY	68	48	26	43	53	62	49	58	57	48	67	67	42	63	49	61	61	57	70	77
71971	UMPIRE	116	81	42	76	94	105	80	99	92	79	108	119	68	106	83	96	98	97	117	137
71972	VANDERVOORT	80	54	24	46	61	70	52	65	63	53	73	77	44	69	53	67	67	64	80	92
71973	WICKES	81	54	25	47	61	71	52	65	63	53	74	78	45	70	53	68	67	65	81	93
71998	ARKADELPHIA	0	0	0	0	0	0	0	0	0	0	0	0	0	0	0	0	0	0	0	0
72001	ADONA	82	55	25	47	62	72	53	66	64	54	75	79	45	71	54	69	68	66	82	94
72002	ALEXANDER	88	82	67	80	82	86	78	83	78	80	97	96	75	93	77	77	93	82	81	97
72003	ALMYRA	83	72	54	69	77	83	68	75	72	68	88	89	66	89	70	74	83	74	82	97
72004	ALTHEIMER	71	48	22	41	54	62	46	57	55	47	65	69	39	62	47	60	59	57	71	82
72005	AMAGON	55	37	17	32	42	48	35	44	43	36	50	53	30	47	36	46	46	44	55	63
72006	AUGUSTA	68	48	30	43	53	61	49	57	57	49	68	68	43	65	49	60	63	58	68	77
72007	AUSTIN	86	83	70	81	83	86	78	82	78	80	96	95	76	94	78	77	93	82	81	96
72010	BALD KNOB	76	53	28	47	59	68	52	63	61	52	72	74	45	69	52	65	66	62	75	86
72011	BAUXITE	84	76	59	73	77	82	73	78	75	75	92	90	69	88	72	74	88	78	79	93
72012	BEEBE	87	74	56	72	78	86	73	80	78	73	95	92	70	94	74	80	89	79	87	98
72013	BEE BRANCH	88	59	28	51	67	77	57	72	69	58	81	85	49	77	58	74	74	71	88	101
72014	BEEDEVILLE	54	36	16	31	41	47	35	43	42	35	49	52	29	46	35	45	45	43	53	61
72015	BENTON	89	83	71	81	85	92	80	85	83	80	102	99	79	101	81	83	97	84	89	102
72016	BIGELOW	89	76	54	71	78	84	72	80	76	74	93	94	67	88	72	77	88	80	85	100
72017	BISCOE	74	51	25	46	58	66	50	62	59	50	69	74	42	66	51	62	63	61	75	87
72020	BRADFORD	78	52	24	45	59	68	50	63	61	51	71	75	43	67	51	65	65	62	78	89
72021	BRINKLEY	70	51	33	47	55	66	54	61	62	53	73	70	48	69	54	66	67	61	74	78
72022	BRYANT	91	91	81	91	90	95	87	90	86	87	107	104	86	106	86	84	103	88	87	103
72023	CABOT	93	95	87	96	94	96	89	92	87	90	108	108	90	109	89	84	105	90	87	106
72024	CARLISLE	88	64	37	60	71	82	65	77	74	66	87	90	57	84	66	78	80	76	91	101
72025	CASA	100	67	30	58	76	87	64	81	78	66	91	96	55	86	66	84	83	80	99	115
72026	CASSCOE	83	74	57	71	78	84	69	76	73	69	89	91	67	91	71	75	84	74	82	98
72027	CENTER RIDGE	90	60	27	52	68	79	58	73	70	59	83	87	50	78	59	76	75	72	90	104
72028	CHOCTAW	86	62	36	57	69	81	65	75	75	64	88	86	57	83	65	80	81	75	91	97
72029	CLARENDON	75	52	25	45	58	67	50	62	59	50	70	74	43	66	51	64	64	61	76	87
72030	CLEVELAND	86	58	26	50	66	75	56	70	67	57	79	83	47	75	57	73	72	69	86	99
72031	CLINTON	79	57	34	53	63	75	61	69	70	59	82	80	53	77	61	74	75	69	84	89
72032	CONWAY	86	83	79	83	83	87	82	84	82	83	102	100	80	100	81	80	99	85	82	98
72034	CONWAY	87	78	84	83	76	82	87	83	85	86	107	101	83	102	82	81	104	87	78	94
72035	CONWAY	58	36	45	40	35	42	69	51	67	58	83	70	56	75	55	59	78	62	47	58
72036	COTTON PLANT	43	34	32	31	35	42	38	40	43	38	52	45	36	48	37	45	49	41	46	48
72038	CROCKETTS BLUFF	83	70	50	65	75	81	65	74	71	65	85	88	62	86	67	73	80	72	82	97
72039	DAMASCUS	81	73	57	70	74	79	69	75	71	71	87	87	66	84	69	71	84	74	76	91
72040	DES ARC	87	59	28	52	67	77	57	71	68	58	80	85	49	76	59	72	73	70	87	101
72041	DE VALLS BLUFF	91	62	30	56	71	81	61	75	72	61	84	90	52	81	62	76	76	74	91	106
72042	DE WITT	70	52	35	49	57	65	54	61	62	54	73	72	49	71	54	65	68	62	72	79
72044	EDGEMONT	62	56	51	53	60	70	52	60	56	55	69	60	52	59	56	60	64	58	70	70
72045	EL PASO	101	70	35	62	79	90	68	83	80	69	95	99	59	90	69	86	86	82	101	117
72046	ENGLAND	72	61	51	58	64	73	63	68	69	62	83	78	60	81	64	71	78	68	76	82
72047	ENOLA	86	59	28	51	66	75	57	70	68	58	80	84	49	75	57	72	73	69	85	98
72048	ETHEL	68	46	21	39	52	59	44	55	53	45	62	66	37	59	45	57	57	54	68	78
72051	FOX	77	51	23	44	58	67	50	62	60	50	70	74	42	66	50	64	64	61	76	88
72052	GARNER	57	38	17	33	43	50	37	46	44	38	52	55	31	49	37	48	47	46	57	65
72055	GILLETT	76	63	47	62	67	75	64	70	69	63	83	80	61	82	64	70	78	69	77	85
72057	GRAPEVINE	88	59	27	51	67	77	57	71	69	58	81	85	49	77	58	74	74	71	88	101
72058	GREENBRIER	90	81	63	77	84	89	76	83	80	77	97	98	73	97	77	80	93	82	87	104
72060	GRIFFITHVILLE	69	46	21	40	52	60	44	56	54	45	63	66	38	59	45	58	57	55	68	79
72063	HATTIEVILLE	79	64	43	59	69	76	60	69	67	60	80	83	56	80	62	69	75	68	79	92
72064	HAZEN	90	62	30	56	71	81	60	75	71	60	83	90	51	80	62	76	76	74	91	105
72065	HENSLEY	85	83	72	81	83	86	78	82	78	79	96	97	76	95	78	77	93	81	81	97
72066	HICKORY PLAINS	95	64	29	55	72	83	62	77	74	63	87	92	52	83	63	80	79	76	95	110
72067	HIGDEN	81	63	43	57	71	80	60	72	68	59	80	84	53	79	64	72	74	71	85	98
72068	HIGGINSON	74	50	23	43	56	65	48	60	58	49	68	72	41	64	49	62	62	59	74	85
72069	HOLLY GROVE	49	37	33	33	39	47	40	44	46	41	56	48	37	50	40	50	52	44	52	54
72070	HOUSTON	76	53	26	46	59	67	51	62	60	52	71	74	44	67	51	64	65	62	75	87
72072	HUMNOKE	75	51	23	44	57	66	49	61	59	50	69	73	41	65	50	63	63	60	75	87
72073	HUMPHREY	74	50	23	43	57	65	48	60	58	49	68	72	41	64	49	62	62	60	74	85
72076	JACKSONVILLE	73	69	68	70	68	73	73	72	72	72	90	85	70	88	70	70	87	74	70	81
72079	JEFFERSON	78	70	55	68	70	74	68	72	69	70	85	84	64	80	67	68	82	73	71	86
72080	JERUSALEM	89	60	27	51	67	78	57	72	69	59	81	86	49	77	58	75	74	71	89	102
72081	JUDSONIA	74	56	33	50	60	67	53	63	60	55	72	74	47	68	54	63	67	63	72	84
	ARKANSAS	81	69	57	66	72	80	69	75	74	69	90	87	65	87	69	76	85	75	82	92
	UNITED STATES	100	100	100	100	100	100	100	100	100	100	100	100	100	100	100	100	100	100	100	100

#	POST OFFICE NAME	COUNTY FIPS CODE	POPULATION 2000	2004	2009	2000-2004 ANNUAL RATE % Rate	State Centile	HOUSEHOLDS 2000	2004	2009	% Annual Rate 2000-2004	2004 Average HH Size	FAMILIES 2000	2004	% Annual Rate 2000-2004
72082	KENSETT	145	1955	1909	1963	-0.6	15	743	732	760	-0.4	2.48	499	481	-0.9
72083	KEO	085	138	145	158	1.2	73	58	62	68	1.6	2.34	44	46	1.1
72084	LEOLA	053	808	892	972	2.4	91	301	335	369	2.6	2.66	233	256	2.2
72086	LONOKE	085	9248	9736	10689	1.2	75	3437	3661	4069	1.5	2.59	2552	2671	1.1
72087	LONSDALE	125	1512	1731	1908	3.2	96	590	685	765	3.6	2.52	469	536	3.2
72088	FAIRFIELD BAY	141	2566	2510	2477	-0.5	16	1278	1258	1247	-0.4	1.91	865	838	-0.7
72099	LITTLE ROCK AIR FORC	119	1339	1418	1471	1.4	77	111	147	172	6.8	2.35	74	96	6.3
72101	MC CRORY	147	4394	4365	4387	-0.2	29	1755	1767	1803	0.2	2.41	1223	1211	-0.2
72102	MC RAE	145	2362	2628	2849	2.5	92	903	1014	1110	2.8	2.59	686	759	2.4
72103	MABELVALE	125	11637	12000	12701	0.7	63	4419	4619	4954	1.1	2.60	3368	3469	0.7
72104	MALVERN	059	20555	20412	20210	-0.2	29	8217	8217	8188	0.0	2.44	5916	5823	-0.4
72105	JONES MILL	059	2110	2256	2301	1.6	82	767	825	846	1.7	2.73	614	652	1.4
72106	MAYFLOWER	045	4074	4397	4837	1.8	84	1662	1820	2024	2.2	2.41	1175	1261	1.7
72110	MORRILTON	029	11820	11882	12057	0.1	40	4665	4740	4863	0.4	2.44	3271	3266	0.0
72111	MOUNT VERNON	045	1255	1354	1474	1.8	84	487	529	580	2.0	2.56	365	391	1.6
72112	NEWPORT	067	12502	12309	12196	-0.4	22	4544	4525	4523	-0.1	2.37	3077	3008	-0.5
72113	MAUMELLE	119	12265	13772	14637	2.8	94	4786	5445	5861	3.1	2.52	3645	4080	2.7
72114	NORTH LITTLE ROCK	119	14554	13891	13824	-1.1	6	5812	5586	5617	-0.9	2.44	3357	3143	-1.5
72116	NORTH LITTLE ROCK	119	20816	21042	21403	0.3	45	9514	9709	9983	0.5	2.16	6023	6008	-0.1
72117	NORTH LITTLE ROCK	119	12305	12142	12239	-0.3	23	4658	4665	4764	0.0	2.60	3272	3213	-0.4
72118	NORTH LITTLE ROCK	119	22553	22686	23007	0.1	40	9333	9538	9809	0.5	2.34	6195	6179	-0.1
72120	SHERWOOD	119	26649	27262	27752	0.5	56	10656	11100	11472	1.0	2.44	7768	7930	0.5
72121	PANGBURN	145	2606	2827	3042	1.9	86	1050	1151	1250	2.2	2.46	801	867	1.9
72122	PARON	125	1103	1196	1288	1.9	86	423	468	512	2.4	2.54	337	368	2.1
72125	PERRY	105	936	949	967	0.3	48	346	357	367	0.7	2.66	256	260	0.4
72126	PERRYVILLE	105	4690	4709	4777	0.1	39	1913	1939	1984	0.3	2.36	1365	1359	-0.1
72127	PLUMERVILLE	029	2317	2368	2419	0.5	54	916	949	982	0.8	2.50	661	674	0.5
72128	POYEN	053	981	985	1022	0.1	39	386	391	410	0.3	2.52	295	294	-0.1
72129	PRATTSVILLE	053	1292	1329	1396	0.7	61	498	519	550	1.0	2.56	387	397	0.6
72130	PRIM	023	356	397	440	2.6	93	136	153	172	2.8	2.59	106	118	2.6
72131	QUITMAN	023	3773	3908	4173	0.8	66	1578	1648	1776	1.0	2.37	1165	1198	0.7
72132	REDFIELD	069	2453	2484	2478	0.3	47	919	947	959	0.7	2.62	709	719	0.3
72133	REYDELL	069	53	48	46	-2.3	0	23	21	20	-2.1	2.29	17	15	-2.9
72134	ROE	095	377	393	397	1.0	69	146	154	157	1.3	2.51	101	105	0.9
72135	ROLAND	119	2855	2862	2888	0.1	37	1094	1113	1139	0.4	2.57	833	835	0.1
72136	ROMANCE	145	1510	1763	1960	3.7	98	547	643	719	3.9	2.74	442	513	3.6
72137	ROSE BUD	145	2304	2438	2595	1.3	77	870	929	997	1.6	2.62	665	701	1.3
72140	SAINT CHARLES	001	458	469	475	0.6	57	202	210	216	0.9	2.23	151	154	0.4
72141	SCOTLAND	141	1594	1600	1605	0.1	38	634	639	644	0.2	2.44	443	443	0.0
72142	SCOTT	085	2037	2249	2444	2.4	91	803	898	985	2.7	2.50	609	669	2.2
72143	SEARCY	145	28211	29780	31571	1.3	75	10875	11596	12418	1.5	2.44	7718	8094	1.1
72149	SEARCY	145	1680	1680	1680	0.0	35	1	1	1	0.0	1.00	0	0	0.0
72150	SHERIDAN	053	11565	12217	12987	1.3	76	4365	4663	5012	1.6	2.58	3318	3500	1.3
72152	SHERRILL	069	623	584	561	-1.5	3	249	237	231	-1.2	2.38	161	150	-1.7
72153	SHIRLEY	141	3182	3145	3112	-0.3	25	1292	1289	1286	-0.1	2.44	934	919	-0.4
72156	SOLGOHACHIA	029	566	584	599	0.7	63	215	224	233	1.0	2.61	167	172	0.7
72157	SPRINGFIELD	029	1298	1375	1433	1.4	78	500	535	564	1.6	2.57	374	395	1.3
72160	STUTTGART	001	11007	11015	11059	0.0	35	4497	4553	4628	0.3	2.39	3117	3102	-0.1
72165	THIDA	063	170	164	164	-0.8	9	58	57	58	-0.4	2.88	43	41	-1.1
72166	TICHNOR	001	312	309	308	-0.2	26	131	132	134	0.2	2.34	101	100	-0.2
72167	TRASKWOOD	125	1515	1488	1555	-0.4	20	572	571	606	0.0	2.60	432	423	-0.5
72168	TUCKER	069	2260	2208	2178	-0.6	15	340	325	317	-1.1	2.39	226	210	-1.7
72170	ULM	117	431	420	414	-0.6	14	184	183	183	-0.1	2.30	139	136	-0.5
72173	VILONIA	045	6607	7118	7821	1.8	84	2338	2547	2826	2.0	2.79	1907	2048	1.7
72175	WABBASEKA	069	565	543	526	-0.9	8	225	220	217	-0.5	2.47	155	149	-0.9
72176	WARD	085	5123	5619	6286	2.2	89	1801	1993	2248	2.4	2.82	1437	1565	2.0
72179	WILBURN	023	564	601	650	1.5	80	219	236	258	1.8	2.55	167	178	1.5
72199	NORTH LITTLE ROCK	119	359	370	378	0.7	62	41	43	45	1.1	7.00	28	29	0.8
72201	LITTLE ROCK	119	466	499	517	1.6	82	167	184	195	2.3	2.05	42	42	0.0
72202	LITTLE ROCK	119	10818	10429	10452	-0.9	9	5295	5237	5344	-0.3	1.89	2250	2120	-1.4
72204	LITTLE ROCK	119	32357	32581	33101	0.2	41	11824	12090	12453	0.5	2.51	7703	7685	-0.1
72205	LITTLE ROCK	119	24125	24051	24273	-0.1	31	11462	11563	11812	0.2	1.97	5728	5596	-0.6
72206	LITTLE ROCK	119	27307	26729	26966	-0.5	18	10258	10195	10431	-0.1	2.52	6928	6769	-0.5
72207	LITTLE ROCK	119	12049	12054	12137	0.0	35	6051	6114	6223	0.2	1.97	3135	3060	-0.6
72209	LITTLE ROCK	119	31924	31689	31754	-0.2	28	11921	11910	12043	0.0	2.66	8368	8181	-0.5
72210	LITTLE ROCK	119	11151	11794	12284	1.3	76	4671	5060	5368	1.9	2.33	3245	3444	1.4
72211	LITTLE ROCK	119	17049	17855	18396	1.1	71	8103	8512	8838	1.2	2.08	4407	4523	0.6
72212	LITTLE ROCK	119	13470	13916	14239	0.8	64	5356	5598	5792	1.1	2.46	3771	3852	0.5
72223	LITTLE ROCK	119	11920	13938	15195	3.8	98	4705	5420	5897	3.4	2.55	3420	3924	3.3
72227	LITTLE ROCK	119	11551	11656	11806	0.2	43	5420	5544	5685	0.5	2.08	3221	3224	0.0
72301	WEST MEMPHIS	035	27440	28139	29136	0.6	58	9960	10343	10859	0.9	2.69	7081	7241	0.5
72310	ARMOREL	093	9	9	9	8.0	35	3	3	3	0.0	3.00	2	2	0.0
72311	AUBREY	077	47	45	44	-1.0	7	23	22	22	-1.0	2.05	16	16	0.0
72313	BASSETT	093	80	74	67	-1.8	1	26	24	22	-1.9	3.08	19	17	-2.6
72315	BLYTHEVILLE	093	27246	25449	23445	-1.6	2	10208	9616	8951	-1.4	2.62	7240	6717	-1.8
72320	BRICKEYS	077	1920	1898	1887	-0.3	25	103	102	101	-0.2	2.56	79	77	-0.6
72321	BURDETTE	093	28	26	24	-1.7	2	10	10	9	0.0	2.60	7	7	0.0
72324	CHERRY VALLEY	037	2194	2238	2277	0.5	53	849	878	907	0.8	2.55	640	653	0.5
72326	COLT	123	2480	2701	2792	2.0	87	967	1072	1125	2.5	2.50	723	788	2.1
72327	CRAWFORDSVILLE	035	1877	1814	1854	-0.8	10	699	689	715	-0.3	2.62	510	494	-0.8
72328	CRUMROD	107	366	341	323	-1.7	2	105	100	96	-1.1	3.41	84	79	-1.4
72329	DRIVER	093	3	3	3	0.0	35	1	1	1	0.0	3.00	1	1	0.0
72330	DYESS	093	921	875	809	-1.2	5	325	313	293	-0.9	2.80	260	248	-1.1
72331	EARLE	035	4024	4004	4087	-0.1	30	1428	1438	1487	0.2	2.78	994	982	-0.3
72333	ELAINE	107	1348	1282	1228	-1.2	6	500	482	468	-0.9	2.66	348	330	-1.2
72335	FORREST CITY	123	20150	19999	19782	-0.2	28	6618	6607	6608	0.0	2.61	4701	4621	-0.4
72338	FRENCHMANS BAYOU	093	17	16	14	-1.4	4	7	7	6	0.0	2.29	5	5	0.0
72339	GILMORE	035	408	399	406	-0.5	16	143	143	147	0.0	2.79	112	110	-0.4
72340	GOODWIN	123	135	127	122	-1.4	3	40	38	37	-1.2	3.34	30	29	-0.8
72341	HAYNES	077	50	47	46	-1.5	3	22	21	21	-1.1	2.24	17	16	-1.4
72342	HELENA	107	6979	6744	6513	-0.8	10	2560	2490	2424	-0.7	2.60	1732	1655	-1.1
72346	HETH	123	890	835	805	-1.5	3	323	308	301	-1.1	2.71	236	222	-1.4
72347	HICKORY RIDGE	037	920	895	898	-0.7	13	366	363	371	-0.2	2.46	274	268	-0.5
72348	HUGHES	123	3303	3205	3167	-0.7	12	1241	1225	1231	-0.3	2.59	879	852	-0.7
72350	JOINER	093	1423	1285	1165	-2.4	0	528	486	447	-1.9	2.64	373	337	-2.4
	ARKANSAS					0.9					1.1	2.47			0.8
	UNITED STATES					1.2					1.3	2.58			1.1

ZIP CODE #	POST OFFICE NAME	RACE (%) White 2000	White 2004	Black 2000	Black 2004	Asian/Pacific 2000	Asian/Pacific 2004	% Hispanic Origin 2000	% Hispanic Origin 2004	2004 AGE DISTRIBUTION (%) 0-4	5-9	10-14	15-19	20-24	25-44	45-64	65-84	85+	18+	MEDIAN AGE 2004	% 2004 Males	% 2004 Females
72082	KENSETT	76.6	74.5	17.2	18.4	0.2	0.2	5.1	6.0	8.0	7.5	6.9	6.1	6.6	24.5	22.5	14.5	3.4	74.0	37.3	45.8	54.2
72083	KEO	84.8	82.1	13.0	15.9	0.0	0.0	2.2	2.1	6.9	6.9	6.9	4.8	4.8	27.6	28.3	11.7	2.1	75.9	39.8	51.0	49.0
72084	LEOLA	87.9	86.4	1.4	1.5	0.3	0.2	9.7	11.0	8.1	8.1	7.2	6.5	6.3	27.7	24.1	10.8	1.4	72.7	34.9	49.6	50.5
72086	LONOKE	84.1	82.3	13.1	14.6	0.3	0.4	2.2	2.5	7.0	7.1	7.2	6.7	6.0	27.4	25.3	11.4	2.1	74.7	37.6	49.3	50.7
72087	LONSDALE	97.2	96.9	0.5	0.6	0.2	0.2	0.9	1.1	6.0	6.1	6.2	5.4	5.1	23.9	26.7	19.4	1.3	78.4	43.1	50.0	50.0
72088	FAIRFIELD BAY	98.0	97.9	0.4	0.4	0.2	0.3	0.7	0.8	3.0	2.8	2.9	2.8	2.8	11.6	25.2	42.8	6.3	89.6	64.5	45.3	54.7
72099	LITTLE ROCK AIR FORC	73.5	70.0	21.7	24.7	1.6	1.8	2.5	2.8	2.1	1.1	1.6	9.4	38.1	42.5	4.5	0.6	0.0	94.9	24.7	80.8	19.2
72101	MC CRORY	86.4	86.0	12.0	12.3	0.3	0.3	0.9	1.0	6.8	6.7	6.3	5.6	6.2	25.5	25.7	14.3	3.0	76.7	40.1	47.6	52.4
72102	MC RAE	96.3	95.9	0.4	0.4	0.0	0.1	1.7	2.1	7.0	6.9	7.2	6.6	7.0	28.2	24.3	11.7	1.2	75.2	36.5	50.3	49.7
72103	MABELVALE	81.6	80.9	14.7	15.0	0.9	1.1	1.8	2.1	7.2	7.4	7.8	6.5	6.1	31.0	25.2	8.2	0.7	73.6	35.2	50.0	50.0
72104	MALVERN	82.5	81.9	15.0	15.7	0.3	0.3	1.2	1.2	6.4	6.5	6.8	6.2	6.1	25.5	25.8	14.5	2.3	76.6	39.7	48.3	51.7
72105	JONES MILL	98.1	97.9	0.1	0.2	0.3	0.3	1.1	1.1	6.7	7.1	8.8	7.6	6.1	28.5	26.4	8.1	0.8	72.7	36.2	50.4	49.6
72106	MAYFLOWER	86.6	85.3	11.0	12.0	0.3	0.3	1.1	1.3	5.7	5.8	6.1	6.5	6.1	28.3	28.3	12.1	1.1	78.1	40.3	49.6	50.4
72110	MORRILTON	83.6	82.6	13.3	14.1	0.3	0.4	2.3	2.6	6.7	6.8	6.8	6.4	6.2	25.9	24.0	14.7	2.4	75.7	38.9	48.4	51.6
72111	MOUNT VERNON	97.2	96.9	0.3	0.4	0.2	0.2	1.4	1.6	7.5	7.2	7.2	6.9	6.4	28.1	24.8	10.6	1.4	73.9	36.4	51.3	48.7
72112	NEWPORT	74.1	72.6	24.0	25.3	0.2	0.3	1.2	1.4	5.9	5.8	5.6	6.6	8.9	26.1	24.5	14.1	2.6	79.4	38.7	47.3	52.7
72113	MAUMELLE	89.2	87.9	8.0	8.8	0.8	0.9	1.8	2.2	7.7	7.9	7.1	5.9	5.0	31.2	27.6	7.0	0.7	73.6	37.0	48.3	51.7
72114	NORTH LITTLE ROCK	24.1	22.0	72.6	74.5	0.4	0.4	2.1	2.3	9.7	9.0	8.7	7.7	7.4	25.0	20.1	10.1	2.4	68.0	30.9	45.5	54.5
72116	NORTH LITTLE ROCK	88.4	86.9	8.7	9.7	1.0	1.2	1.6	1.9	5.1	5.1	5.2	5.4	5.8	26.6	28.5	15.9	2.5	81.4	42.9	47.1	52.9
72117	NORTH LITTLE ROCK	44.2	41.1	52.7	55.7	0.3	0.3	1.4	1.5	6.9	6.8	7.9	7.8	7.2	26.2	24.5	11.4	1.4	73.7	35.7	48.2	51.8
72118	NORTH LITTLE ROCK	75.5	72.6	20.4	22.8	0.5	0.5	3.5	4.1	6.9	6.5	6.5	6.6	6.8	29.5	24.4	11.0	1.7	76.0	36.4	48.5	51.5
72120	SHERWOOD	86.9	84.6	9.5	11.1	1.0	1.2	2.1	2.5	6.8	6.9	6.7	6.3	6.4	29.7	26.3	9.9	1.1	75.8	36.7	48.6	51.4
72121	PANGBURN	98.1	97.9	0.2	0.1	0.0	0.1	1.0	1.1	5.8	6.2	7.5	6.2	5.8	27.2	26.7	13.0	1.6	76.7	39.5	49.6	50.4
72122	PARON	97.5	97.0	0.4	0.5	0.5	0.6	0.7	0.8	4.5	5.0	5.4	4.4	3.8	19.0	30.2	26.0	1.7	82.1	50.7	49.9	50.1
72125	PERRY	96.9	96.6	0.2	0.2	0.2	0.3	1.8	1.9	6.6	6.5	7.3	7.4	7.0	28.1	24.8	11.5	0.8	75.3	36.1	50.6	49.4
72126	PERRYVILLE	97.3	97.1	0.2	0.2	0.2	0.2	1.3	1.6	6.0	5.9	6.4	6.3	5.8	24.4	26.5	16.0	2.7	77.7	41.6	49.2	50.8
72127	PLUMERVILLE	65.7	63.9	31.9	33.4	0.3	0.3	1.0	1.1	7.1	7.2	6.8	6.4	6.0	27.0	25.9	11.7	1.9	75.0	37.9	49.1	50.9
72128	POYEN	97.7	97.4	0.6	0.7	0.0	0.0	1.5	1.8	5.4	5.7	6.8	5.9	6.7	28.5	27.3	12.3	1.4	78.5	39.2	51.8	48.2
72129	PRATTSVILLE	86.7	85.5	11.8	12.8	0.3	0.5	0.5	0.6	6.4	6.3	6.4	6.6	6.6	27.5	26.4	12.3	1.7	76.9	38.4	51.2	48.8
72130	PRIM	98.9	98.7	0.0	0.0	0.0	0.0	0.3	0.3	5.8	6.3	7.3	5.5	6.1	23.7	27.0	16.9	1.5	77.6	41.6	50.4	49.6
72131	QUITMAN	98.2	98.1	0.1	0.1	0.1	0.1	1.6	1.9	6.6	6.4	6.0	6.0	5.2	24.3	26.4	17.3	1.9	77.4	42.0	49.7	50.3
72132	REDFIELD	92.0	90.7	4.6	5.5	0.9	1.1	2.3	2.7	6.1	6.2	7.3	7.0	7.4	29.6	27.2	8.4	0.9	76.2	36.7	49.6	50.4
72133	REYDELL	58.5	54.2	37.7	41.7	1.9	0.0	3.8	2.1	6.3	6.3	8.3	8.3	4.2	20.8	31.3	14.6	0.0	79.2	41.7	43.8	56.3
72134	ROE	83.0	81.9	14.1	15.0	0.3	0.3	1.1	1.0	6.6	7.1	7.1	5.9	4.8	25.7	27.5	13.2	2.0	75.8	39.5	49.4	50.6
72135	ROLAND	91.7	90.5	6.3	7.3	0.1	0.1	0.4	0.5	5.3	6.2	7.3	6.4	5.6	25.7	32.2	10.2	1.1	77.2	41.4	50.2	49.8
72136	ROMANCE	97.6	97.3	0.6	0.6	0.2	0.2	0.9	1.0	7.0	7.1	7.2	7.0	6.1	28.3	26.0	10.4	0.9	74.5	37.3	50.9	49.1
72137	ROSE BUD	97.5	97.3	0.2	0.2	0.2	0.3	1.2	1.4	6.2	6.3	7.6	6.4	6.2	26.7	27.0	12.4	1.2	76.1	38.9	50.1	49.9
72140	SAINT CHARLES	94.1	93.8	5.0	5.3	0.0	0.0	0.4	0.4	6.4	6.0	4.3	5.3	4.5	25.4	28.8	17.9	1.5	80.0	43.5	51.0	49.0
72141	SCOTLAND	96.3	96.0	0.3	0.3	0.7	0.8	1.7	2.0	5.6	5.8	6.6	6.1	5.8	24.0	26.2	16.6	3.3	78.1	42.1	49.4	50.6
72142	SCOTT	75.7	71.7	20.9	24.4	0.1	0.1	3.0	3.5	6.1	6.3	6.6	6.3	5.3	27.8	29.8	10.7	1.4	77.3	40.1	51.8	48.2
72143	SEARCY	92.3	91.6	4.9	5.2	0.4	0.5	1.7	2.0	6.3	6.1	6.4	7.0	10.0	26.5	22.3	13.0	2.3	77.5	36.0	49.2	50.8
72149	SEARCY	92.9	92.0	3.3	3.6	0.8	0.9	3.3	3.9	0.0	0.0	0.0	49.0	50.5	0.4	0.1	0.0	0.0	99.6	20.1	33.3	66.7
72150	SHERIDAN	97.5	97.3	1.0	1.0	0.2	0.2	0.7	0.8	6.6	6.8	7.1	6.7	6.0	28.9	25.7	10.6	1.6	75.3	37.6	49.4	50.6
72152	SHERRILL	49.3	45.2	49.0	53.1	0.2	0.2	1.3	1.4	5.1	5.7	6.2	8.4	5.7	22.3	29.3	15.1	2.4	77.4	42.3	50.7	49.3
72153	SHIRLEY	97.3	97.1	0.3	0.3	0.1	0.1	1.2	1.3	5.8	5.7	5.9	6.0	5.3	22.9	27.8	18.7	1.8	78.8	43.9	50.0	50.1
72156	SOLGOHACHIA	94.9	94.5	3.0	3.3	0.4	0.3	0.7	0.7	5.8	7.2	7.9	6.2	5.3	26.2	26.5	13.2	1.7	75.2	39.2	49.1	50.9
72157	SPRINGFIELD	88.9	88.2	8.9	9.5	0.3	0.3	1.0	1.2	6.7	6.8	6.9	6.4	6.6	26.8	25.7	12.7	1.5	75.9	38.5	50.9	49.1
72160	STUTTGART	66.5	64.9	31.9	33.4	0.6	0.7	0.9	1.0	7.0	6.9	7.1	6.6	6.3	25.3	25.1	13.4	2.3	74.9	38.2	47.0	53.0
72165	THIDA	95.3	95.1	1.2	1.2	0.0	0.0	0.0	0.0	4.9	4.9	7.3	7.3	6.7	25.6	29.3	12.8	1.2	78.7	40.0	49.4	50.6
72166	TICHNOR	94.6	94.2	3.5	3.9	0.0	0.0	2.9	2.9	4.2	4.9	5.2	6.2	4.9	25.9	31.7	15.5	1.6	81.9	44.2	50.5	49.5
72167	TRASKWOOD	97.8	97.5	0.3	0.3	0.1	0.1	0.8	0.9	6.8	6.9	7.7	7.3	7.0	29.0	25.7	8.9	0.7	74.0	35.6	49.7	50.3
72168	TUCKER	51.6	46.9	47.3	51.9	0.1	0.1	0.7	0.8	2.1	2.3	2.4	3.9	10.7	52.7	19.8	5.3	0.8	91.0	35.6	81.7	18.3
72170	ULM	92.6	91.9	6.5	6.9	0.0	0.0	0.5	0.5	6.0	6.0	5.0	5.2	6.0	24.1	32.4	13.8	1.7	80.2	43.6	51.0	49.1
72173	VILONIA	97.5	97.2	0.2	0.2	0.2	0.2	1.3	1.6	7.4	7.4	8.3	7.7	6.7	30.5	23.2	8.1	0.8	72.0	34.4	50.3	49.7
72175	WABBASEKA	29.6	25.8	68.7	72.4	0.0	0.0	1.6	1.7	7.7	7.6	7.9	7.4	7.2	24.1	22.8	12.9	2.4	72.4	35.3	47.0	53.0
72176	WARD	97.6	97.3	0.2	0.2	0.3	0.3	1.5	1.9	8.1	7.9	8.7	7.5	6.9	32.1	20.6	7.6	0.7	70.8	32.6	49.9	50.1
72179	WILBURN	98.4	98.2	0.2	0.2	0.0	0.0	0.4	0.5	5.8	5.8	5.8	5.8	6.0	23.6	30.0	15.8	1.3	79.0	43.2	48.3	51.8
72199	NORTH LITTLE ROCK	94.2	93.2	3.9	4.6	0.0	0.0	1.7	1.6	4.3	4.1	8.1	15.7	4.9	25.7	20.8	11.6	4.9	70.5	36.3	50.0	50.0
72201	LITTLE ROCK	41.4	37.5	55.6	59.3	0.4	0.4	2.2	2.2	3.0	2.6	1.2	3.2	10.4	45.1	27.9	5.8	0.8	92.0	37.5	60.5	39.5
72202	LITTLE ROCK	29.7	29.1	67.7	68.0	0.6	0.7	1.5	1.7	5.7	5.7	6.0	7.0	8.4	29.1	24.2	11.9	2.1	78.9	36.4	48.8	51.2
72204	LITTLE ROCK	28.7	26.6	67.3	69.2	1.2	1.2	3.1	3.5	7.0	6.9	7.2	8.1	8.6	29.4	22.7	8.6	1.6	74.5	33.1	47.9	52.1
72205	LITTLE ROCK	70.7	68.1	25.6	27.7	1.5	1.8	1.8	2.1	5.3	5.0	5.3	5.5	7.1	32.7	23.0	12.7	3.5	81.2	37.8	46.1	53.9
72206	LITTLE ROCK	45.1	45.0	52.5	52.3	0.4	0.5	1.3	1.5	6.6	6.5	6.7	6.9	6.6	27.2	26.3	11.5	1.7	76.1	38.0	49.0	51.0
72207	LITTLE ROCK	90.1	88.7	7.0	8.0	1.3	1.6	1.1	1.3	5.7	5.6	5.3	4.8	5.6	31.2	26.3	12.9	2.7	80.5	39.6	45.8	54.2
72209	LITTLE ROCK	32.4	29.1	61.3	64.0	0.8	0.8	5.7	6.3	9.4	8.9	8.8	7.8	7.9	29.7	19.5	7.3	0.7	68.1	29.7	46.5	53.5
72210	LITTLE ROCK	84.6	82.3	12.4	14.3	0.8	1.1	1.5	1.7	6.7	6.6	6.3	5.8	6.0	30.8	28.2	9.0	0.6	76.7	37.2	48.7	51.3
72211	LITTLE ROCK	79.6	76.7	13.8	15.6	4.0	4.7	2.5	2.8	7.3	6.7	5.6	4.8	7.7	37.8	21.9	6.8	1.3	77.5	33.8	47.7	52.3
72212	LITTLE ROCK	85.5	83.4	9.2	10.4	3.6	4.4	1.3	1.6	6.0	6.5	6.7	6.0	6.1	24.1	31.0	11.5	2.2	77.1	41.4	47.5	52.5
72223	LITTLE ROCK	88.8	87.4	6.6	7.3	2.8	3.4	1.3	1.5	7.7	8.3	7.9	6.4	5.0	28.9	28.1	7.0	0.9	71.9	37.1	49.7	50.3
72227	LITTLE ROCK	82.0	80.0	13.4	14.8	2.3	2.7	2.3	2.7	4.9	5.0	5.5	5.7	6.1	27.1	28.2	15.3	2.2	81.1	41.9	45.8	54.2
72301	WEST MEMPHIS	43.0	41.8	55.1	56.1	0.6	0.7	1.0	1.2	8.6	8.4	8.6	7.9	7.2	26.8	21.7	9.5	1.3	69.5	32.0	46.3	53.7
72310	ARMOREL	88.9	88.9	11.1	11.1	0.0	0.0	0.0	0.0	0.0	0.0	0.0	0.0	22.2	77.8	0.0	0.0	0.0	100.0	31.3	55.6	44.4
72311	AUBREY	46.8	46.7	51.1	53.3	0.0	0.0	0.0	0.0	6.7	6.7	6.7	4.4	6.7	17.8	28.9	17.8	4.4	80.0	45.8	42.2	57.8
72313	BASSETT	63.8	59.5	35.0	37.8	0.0	0.0	2.5	1.4	6.8	6.8	8.1	8.1	6.8	27.0	21.6	13.5	1.4	70.3	35.0	47.3	52.7
72315	BLYTHEVILLE	58.3	56.7	38.5	39.8	0.7	0.8	1.9	2.1	8.8	8.2	8.0	7.3	7.5	27.0	21.4	10.2	1.6	70.6	32.4	47.6	52.4
72320	BRICKEYS	57.2	55.9	41.8	43.1	0.0	0.0	4.8	4.9	2.7	2.9	3.2	4.3	12.2	52.1	17.5	4.6	0.6	89.3	33.2	79.8	20.2
72321	BURDETTE	89.3	88.5	7.1	7.7	0.0	0.0	7.1	3.9	7.7	7.7	7.7	7.7	7.7	30.8	30.8	0.0	0.0	76.9	32.5	50.0	50.0
72324	CHERRY VALLEY	91.3	90.5	7.6	8.3	0.1	0.1	0.8	0.9	6.2	6.7	7.3	6.2	6.7	26.7	27.4	11.5	1.4	76.2	38.2	50.8	49.2
72326	COLT	73.0	70.2	25.8	28.5	0.2	0.3	1.3	1.6	7.6	7.4	6.6	7.2	6.3	25.9	26.3	11.4	1.4	74.0	36.8	49.1	50.9
72327	CRAWFORDSVILLE	44.9	41.0	53.4	57.1	0.1	0.1	2.2	2.3	8.7	8.2	7.8	6.8	6.9	24.6	25.6	10.4	1.1	71.1	34.8	49.9	50.1
72328	CRUMROD	36.1	34.0	56.6	57.8	0.3	0.3	10.7	12.0	9.4	8.8	10.3	8.8	9.7	22.0	20.8	10.0	0.3	66.3	27.3	49.6	50.4
72329	DRIVER	100.0	100.0	0.0	0.0	0.0	0.0	0.0	0.0	0.0	0.0	0.0	0.0	66.7	33.3	0.0	0.0	0.0	100.0	23.8	66.7	33.3
72330	DYESS	91.3	90.1	3.2	3.5	0.1	0.1	6.5	7.4	8.6	8.1	7.5	6.6	7.4	29.4	22.1	9.6	0.7	71.9	33.0	48.9	51.1
72331	EARLE	32.3	29.0	66.2	69.4	0.4	0.4	0.9	0.9	9.8	8.7	8.9	8.3	7.3	23.4	20.7	11.1	1.8	67.2	31.4	46.7	53.3
72333	ELAINE	43.0	40.5	53.4	55.6	0.2	0.2	5.9	6.5	8.3	8.0	8.7	8.0	7.5	21.8	23.3	12.7	1.7	70.1	33.2	45.9	54.1
72335	FORREST CITY	44.0	43.1	53.0	53.5	0.6	0.8	6.5	7.3	7.8	7.1	7.2	6.9	7.8	30.4	21.7	9.5	1.6	73.6	33.5	53.4	46.6
72338	FRENCHMANS BAYOU	64.7	62.5	35.3	37.5	0.0	0.0	0.0	0.0	6.3	6.3	12.5	12.5	12.5	37.5	12.5	0.0	0.0	75.0	25.0	37.5	62.5
72339	GILMORE	59.3	55.1	37.3	41.1	1.2	1.3	2.5	2.3	8.0	8.0	7.8	7.5	5.8	27.6	24.6	9.8	1.0	71.2	35.2	52.4	47.6
72340	GOODWIN	60.7	56.7	37.8	41.7	0.0	0.0	3.0	3.2	6.3	6.3	7.1	8.7	7.1	25.2	26.8	11.0	1.6	74.8	37.8	49.6	50.4
72341	HAYNES	34.0	31.9	64.0	66.0	0.0	0.0	2.0	2.1	6.4	6.4	8.5	8.5	4.3	19.2	31.9	12.8	2.1	70.2	41.3	46.8	53.2
72342	HELENA	34.1	32.5	64.4	65.8	0.6	0.7	0.9	1.0	8.8	8.2	8.9	8.0	7.3	22.1	21.7	12.9	2.2	69.1	32.8	45.9	54.1
72346	HETH	60.7	57.1	37.1	40.4	0.1	0.1	2.4	2.8	6.4	7.8	7.7	7.4	6.0	25.6	27.7	10.5	1.0	74.0	36.5	50.5	49.5
72347	HICKORY RIDGE	98.3	97.9	0.1	0.2	0.1	0.1	1.5	1.9	6.5	6.7	6.9	5.6	5.8	26.5	26.3	14.3	1.5	76.5	39.7	49.6	50.4
72348	HUGHES	45.9	43.8	51.7	53.5	1.0	1.1	1.6	1.8	7.9	7.7	8.1	7.5	6.3	24.4	24.6	12.3	1.3	71.7	36.0	48.6	51.4
72350	JOINER	65.7	62.5	33.2	36.4	0.0	0.0	0.7	0.8	6.9	6.6	6.6	8.0	7.6	26.2	23.0	13.4	1.6	74.9	36.4	45.9	54.1
	ARKANSAS	80.0	79.3	15.7	15.8	0.8	1.0	3.3	3.8	6.9	6.7	6.9	6.8	7.3	27.3	24.1	12.2	1.8	75.7	36.7	49.0	51.0
	UNITED STATES	75.1	73.6	12.3	12.5	3.8	4.2	12.5	14.1	6.9	6.7	7.2	7.0	7.3	28.6	23.8	10.8	1.7	75.1	36.0	49.1	50.9

ZIP CODE				2004 HOUSEHOLD INCOME DISTRIBUTION (%)					MEDIAN HOUSEHOLD INCOME					2004 HOME VALUE DISTRIBUTION (%)					
#	POST OFFICE NAME	2004 Per Capita Income	2004 HH Income Base	Less than $25,000	$25,000 to $49,999	$50,000 to $99,999	$100,000 to $149,999	$150,000 or More	2004	2009	2004 National Centile	2004 State Centile	2004 Home Value Base	Less than $50,000	$50,000 to $89,999	$90,000 to $174,999	$175,000 to $399,999	$400,000 or More	2004 Median Home Value
72082	KENSETT	12032	732	50.1	37.2	10.1	1.9	0.7	24897	29522	4	6	461	57.5	30.4	8.7	3.5	0.0	45274
72083	KEO	20361	62	33.9	27.4	30.7	6.5	1.6	37336	43638	37	76	48	29.2	27.1	33.3	8.3	2.1	78000
72084	LEOLA	19045	335	35.8	29.0	25.7	7.2	2.4	36220	43398	32	70	270	64.1	20.4	10.4	3.7	1.5	39500
72086	LONOKE	18855	3661	29.1	29.8	32.7	7.2	1.2	41823	50667	52	88	2845	31.3	31.7	28.4	8.0	0.6	70259
72087	LONSDALE	23372	685	21.8	34.9	31.4	7.9	4.1	44149	54204	59	92	581	25.0	21.9	26.3	21.7	5.2	95968
72088	FAIRFIELD BAY	29197	1258	31.3	34.6	24.2	4.9	4.9	38388	46098	41	80	1061	21.4	35.9	31.2	10.6	0.9	83018
72099	LITTLE ROCK AIR FORC	10507	147	38.8	36.7	21.8	2.7	0.0	34648	42575	26	59	78	69.2	5.1	19.2	0.0	6.4	33636
72101	MC CRORY	17145	1767	42.7	30.9	21.1	3.7	1.6	30487	36299	13	29	1325	56.0	26.9	12.5	3.9	0.8	45031
72102	MC RAE	19203	1014	35.4	34.7	24.4	3.4	2.2	34194	41402	25	57	838	36.0	25.8	28.4	8.8	1.0	66154
72103	MABELVALE	19808	4619	22.2	37.0	33.7	5.6	1.4	42957	51172	56	90	3653	29.7	38.3	28.4	3.4	0.1	71257
72104	MALVERN	17933	8217	34.9	33.3	26.6	3.9	1.2	35416	41272	29	65	6286	33.0	32.9	28.0	5.8	0.3	67585
72105	JONES MILL	16914	825	24.9	37.1	33.5	3.8	0.9	41850	49755	52	88	693	27.3	31.9	32.6	8.2	0.0	77841
72106	MAYFLOWER	20535	1820	27.4	33.1	32.9	4.7	2.0	40362	49809	47	84	1490	29.7	34.5	31.7	3.7	0.3	71905
72110	MORRILTON	20600	4740	35.1	27.9	27.7	6.5	2.9	37742	46765	38	78	3563	28.0	34.8	29.1	7.5	0.6	74125
72111	MOUNT VERNON	19771	529	28.7	37.2	24.8	7.6	1.7	36746	44737	34	72	453	27.4	28.9	30.2	11.3	2.2	79875
72112	NEWPORT	19211	4525	43.5	27.5	19.5	5.5	4.0	29710	37184	12	24	3134	38.8	36.3	19.3	4.9	0.8	60000
72113	MAUMELLE	34321	5445	12.9	21.1	36.5	18.2	11.2	68468	87388	91	100	4474	5.8	10.0	57.2	24.6	2.4	133571
72114	NORTH LITTLE ROCK	13492	5586	56.3	28.1	11.8	2.7	1.1	21143	26666	2	2	2077	57.9	33.8	6.6	1.7	0.0	45753
72116	NORTH LITTLE ROCK	34805	9709	15.3	25.7	37.7	13.7	7.8	58547	73680	83	99	6514	2.6	15.8	62.6	17.2	1.8	119440
72117	NORTH LITTLE ROCK	16402	4665	38.8	35.7	20.9	3.1	1.5	32407	40317	19	45	3187	46.5	41.5	8.9	2.5	0.5	52517
72118	NORTH LITTLE ROCK	22448	9538	25.7	31.4	33.3	7.4	2.3	43710	54978	58	91	6416	20.3	48.9	25.3	5.2	0.3	71355
72120	SHERWOOD	26290	11100	16.4	28.8	39.3	12.0	3.5	53768	67535	78	98	8084	7.2	33.7	51.3	7.3	0.5	96820
72121	PANGBURN	19303	1151	31.4	36.2	26.7	4.3	1.5	37702	45250	38	78	957	32.2	24.8	31.9	10.3	0.8	76121
72122	PARON	30212	468	15.4	27.8	37.2	12.0	7.7	56549	68309	81	99	413	15.7	17.2	28.6	29.1	9.4	136397
72125	PERRY	17764	357	30.5	35.6	27.5	4.8	1.7	37131	45358	36	74	288	37.2	31.9	25.0	4.9	1.0	63793
72126	PERRYVILLE	20540	1939	32.2	32.3	26.5	6.5	2.6	37630	46521	38	77	1553	30.8	33.7	27.9	5.0	2.6	70387
72127	PLUMERVILLE	18455	949	35.0	32.6	26.8	4.1	1.6	36183	44453	32	70	763	40.2	34.7	22.3	2.5	0.3	61620
72128	POYEN	19547	391	28.4	34.8	28.6	6.4	1.8	39396	47154	44	82	326	31.6	31.3	33.4	3.7	0.0	75161
72129	PRATTSVILLE	20062	519	26.8	33.3	29.5	9.1	1.4	42269	50931	54	89	431	37.4	34.8	24.1	3.3	0.5	61000
72130	PRIM	15600	153	35.3	37.3	23.5	2.0	2.0	33674	40000	23	53	129	38.0	19.4	30.2	12.4	0.0	75833
72131	QUITMAN	18603	1648	33.7	36.9	24.2	3.4	1.8	35798	42294	31	68	1369	26.4	27.3	32.7	11.7	2.0	83608
72132	REDFIELD	19842	947	21.1	33.0	38.5	6.6	0.8	45909	57489	64	93	768	38.8	38.3	19.9	3.0	0.0	61226
72133	REYDELL	18382	21	38.1	38.1	19.1	4.8	0.0	31091	40000	15	35	15	73.3	13.3	0.0	13.3	0.0	29167
72134	ROE	19524	154	36.4	30.5	25.3	4.6	3.3	33159	40381	21	49	107	43.9	39.3	14.0	2.8	0.0	57222
72135	ROLAND	30978	1113	15.6	29.6	29.6	12.9	12.4	55259	71314	80	98	951	22.6	23.7	26.0	20.7	7.1	96339
72136	ROMANCE	24320	643	21.3	32.0	33.1	9.2	4.4	45800	56274	63	93	570	20.0	27.0	33.2	15.4	4.4	95000
72137	ROSE BUD	19621	929	26.6	34.2	32.4	4.2	2.6	40663	48863	48	85	783	28.0	25.4	32.1	12.9	1.7	83977
72140	SAINT CHARLES	18543	210	36.2	34.3	26.2	1.0	2.4	35781	42709	31	67	174	46.0	26.4	22.4	5.2	0.0	62000
72141	SCOTLAND	15782	639	45.2	32.6	17.2	3.6	1.4	27607	33518	8	15	515	35.2	30.3	26.2	6.4	1.9	67222
72142	SCOTT	26516	898	24.2	29.0	34.9	7.2	4.8	47399	56862	67	95	714	27.7	26.6	28.7	12.8	4.2	80000
72143	SEARCY	21297	11596	32.3	29.9	27.9	6.4	3.6	38718	47133	42	80	8028	16.4	27.8	40.5	13.5	1.8	96705
72149	SEARCY	8533	0	0.0	0.0	0.0	0.0	0.0	0	0	0	0	0	0.0	0.0	0.0	0.0	0.0	0
72150	SHERIDAN	22128	4663	25.4	31.4	33.5	6.3	3.4	44349	53180	60	92	3795	27.6	28.9	32.3	10.4	0.8	81871
72152	SHERRILL	15091	237	48.1	27.9	18.6	3.0	2.5	26446	33752	6	11	185	67.6	20.5	11.4	0.5	0.0	34342
72153	SHIRLEY	17806	1289	37.9	35.5	21.0	4.0	1.6	32281	38391	19	45	1087	37.6	25.5	26.3	9.5	1.1	69107
72156	SOLGOHACHIA	17958	224	30.8	29.5	33.0	6.3	0.5	40375	49367	47	84	194	27.8	29.9	36.1	5.2	1.0	80625
72157	SPRINGFIELD	18715	535	34.6	31.0	26.5	6.5	1.3	36273	45736	33	71	460	32.8	36.5	26.5	3.0	1.1	68980
72160	STUTTGART	23348	4553	33.9	31.8	25.4	5.8	3.1	37427	45547	37	76	3108	27.5	38.0	27.1	7.3	0.2	71270
72165	THIDA	13542	57	31.6	40.4	26.3	1.8	0.0	33324	40000	22	51	46	39.1	37.0	19.6	4.4	0.0	60000
72166	TICHNOR	22088	132	30.3	36.4	23.5	9.1	0.8	36830	43984	35	73	102	41.2	26.5	27.5	3.9	1.0	61667
72167	TRASKWOOD	18506	571	27.0	35.2	32.8	4.0	1.1	41099	48697	50	86	467	35.1	31.5	23.6	8.6	1.3	64556
72168	TUCKER	11101	325	48.0	24.3	22.5	2.8	2.5	26639	34442	7	12	252	71.8	16.7	11.1	0.4	0.0	32308
72170	ULM	19542	183	29.5	37.7	29.0	2.7	1.1	37898	43845	39	78	153	28.8	32.7	30.1	7.8	0.7	76250
72173	VILONIA	20835	2547	21.6	29.8	38.4	8.0	2.4	48415	59327	69	96	2141	24.2	24.7	40.4	9.8	0.9	91286
72175	WABBASEKA	14162	220	52.3	22.7	20.5	3.2	1.4	23130	31272	3	4	157	66.2	27.4	4.5	1.9	0.0	35682
72176	WARD	17961	1993	23.7	35.1	32.1	8.2	1.0	42384	51273	54	89	1609	25.1	34.9	29.8	9.0	1.2	81853
72179	WILBURN	19520	236	32.2	32.6	28.0	4.7	2.5	36845	44158	35	73	203	23.7	23.2	33.5	18.7	1.0	95909
72199	NORTH LITTLE ROCK	7603	43	18.6	34.9	41.9	4.7	0.0	46158	60816	64	94	33	36.4	27.3	30.3	6.1	0.0	67500
72201	LITTLE ROCK	16103	184	35.3	49.5	10.9	0.0	4.4	28605	32758	10	20	21	52.4	47.6	0.0	0.0	0.0	48333
72202	LITTLE ROCK	23804	5237	52.2	25.1	14.8	3.9	3.9	23459	29490	4	4	1786	35.7	37.1	13.8	6.9	6.5	63347
72204	LITTLE ROCK	16920	12090	36.6	32.6	24.9	4.4	1.5	33892	41857	24	55	7119	36.5	46.9	15.7	0.7	0.2	61082
72205	LITTLE ROCK	28739	11563	26.5	31.1	28.0	9.3	5.1	42943	54595	56	90	6329	4.7	29.4	52.7	12.1	1.2	102383
72206	LITTLE ROCK	18000	10195	35.0	31.4	25.7	5.8	2.1	35682	45311	30	67	7062	40.1	34.3	21.4	4.0	0.2	60574
72207	LITTLE ROCK	49900	6114	16.0	25.3	31.4	12.5	14.8	60170	78030	85	99	3880	3.0	13.2	41.4	27.9	14.5	152778
72209	LITTLE ROCK	16136	11910	35.4	34.8	24.4	3.8	1.7	34257	41648	25	57	6707	34.0	58.6	7.2	0.2	0.0	59732
72210	LITTLE ROCK	29801	5060	19.9	25.5	35.6	13.3	5.7	54591	70161	79	98	3797	21.3	16.8	47.3	12.0	2.7	109967
72211	LITTLE ROCK	35051	8512	15.8	25.2	38.2	13.7	7.1	59787	75102	84	99	4812	2.8	11.1	65.5	18.9	1.8	126985
72212	LITTLE ROCK	43493	5598	10.2	18.1	33.6	19.8	18.3	80548	100720	95	100	4185	1.0	3.4	40.3	47.4	7.8	191962
72223	LITTLE ROCK	49411	5420	11.2	13.6	31.1	20.6	23.6	88925	117118	97	100	4010	5.2	8.7	21.8	47.2	17.1	221716
72227	LITTLE ROCK	40491	5544	19.3	25.8	29.4	13.0	12.5	56107	72590	81	99	3550	1.2	6.5	66.5	20.1	5.8	145507
72301	WEST MEMPHIS	16544	10343	39.8	27.3	24.4	5.4	3.0	32341	40351	19	45	6066	25.4	44.5	25.0	4.5	0.6	68712
72310	ARMOREL	0	0	0.0	0.0	0.0	0.0	0.0	0	87500	0	0	0	0.0	0.0	0.0	0.0	0.0	0
72311	AUBREY	14556	22	50.0	31.8	18.2	0.0	0.0	25000	27273	5	7	18	77.8	22.2	0.0	0.0	0.0	25000
72313	BASSETT	10651	24	50.0	33.3	12.5	4.2	0.0	25000	32290	5	7	18	66.7	16.7	16.7	0.0	0.0	35000
72315	BLYTHEVILLE	17969	9616	38.2	28.0	24.4	7.1	2.3	34141	43048	24	56	6207	28.0	34.0	28.7	8.7	0.6	71613
72320	BRICKEYS	7367	102	39.2	31.4	22.6	3.9	2.9	33180	40834	21	50	76	59.2	30.3	10.5	0.0	0.0	42222
72321	BURDETTE	16501	10	40.0	20.0	40.0	0.0	0.0	37500	27247	37	77	8	25.0	50.0	25.0	0.0	0.0	70000
72324	CHERRY VALLEY	19286	878	34.7	37.4	20.8	3.6	3.4	32996	39893	21	49	702	45.7	32.1	17.4	4.4	0.4	54412
72326	COLT	17223	1072	35.6	34.6	23.0	4.9	2.0	34349	41853	25	57	873	42.7	31.0	20.3	4.9	1.0	58581
72327	CRAWFORDSVILLE	14798	689	40.5	33.0	21.2	4.5	0.9	31493	39428	16	38	467	49.0	24.6	21.8	3.4	1.1	53750
72328	CRUMROD	8416	100	55.0	33.0	8.0	4.0	0.0	22788	27941	3	3	46	58.7	26.1	15.2	0.0	0.0	37500
72329	DRIVER	0	0	0.0	0.0	0.0	0.0	0.0	0	0	0	0	0	0.0	0.0	0.0	0.0	0.0	0
72330	DYESS	13513	313	40.6	33.6	21.4	4.5	0.0	30906	37207	15	33	245	68.2	24.5	5.3	0.0	2.0	34659
72331	EARLE	16776	1438	50.8	28.2	15.2	3.4	2.3	24517	29314	4	6	889	67.5	20.6	10.8	0.7	0.5	36809
72333	ELAINE	15466	482	49.4	31.7	11.2	3.3	4.4	25434	30938	5	8	284	58.8	25.7	13.4	2.1	0.0	39333
72335	FORREST CITY	15270	6607	43.3	28.7	21.5	4.2	2.3	29815	35699	12	24	4005	29.9	40.6	22.0	6.8	0.7	68673
72338	FRENCHMANS BAYOU	7500	7	71.4	28.6	0.0	0.0	0.0	12071	53930	1	1	5	100.0	0.0	0.0	0.0	0.0	23750
72339	GILMORE	14885	143	41.3	23.8	28.7	4.9	1.4	33293	41442	22	50	108	61.1	25.0	13.9	0.0	0.0	42500
72340	GOODWIN	10451	38	39.5	42.1	15.8	2.6	0.0	33158	40535	21	49	30	53.3	23.3	20.0	3.3	0.0	48333
72341	HAYNES	15380	21	38.1	42.9	19.1	0.0	0.0	31091	31091	15	35	16	62.5	31.3	6.3	0.0	0.0	45000
72342	HELENA	16468	2490	51.6	24.3	15.5	4.1	4.5	23769	29684	4	5	1358	42.6	24.9	20.8	10.1	1.6	59709
72346	HETH	15570	308	45.5	27.3	19.8	5.2	2.3	28154	34842	9	18	240	57.9	20.4	15.8	5.8	0.0	43871
72347	HICKORY RIDGE	26211	363	36.4	27.0	23.7	5.5	7.4	37230	46432	36	75	275	47.3	25.8	16.0	6.2	4.7	52027
72348	HUGHES	15566	1225	47.3	28.1	18.1	4.7	1.8	27244	34032	7	14	792	46.7	25.0	23.9	3.5	0.9	55306
72350	JOINER	13685	486	45.9	27.2	22.8	3.3	0.8	28046	35566	9	17	368	54.1	25.5	19.6	0.8	0.0	45000
	ARKANSAS	20565		33.0	30.6	26.7	6.4	3.3	37742	46417				27.1	29.3	31.4	10.3	1.8	80466
	UNITED STATES	25866		24.7	27.1	30.8	10.9	6.5	48124	56710				10.9	15.0	33.7	30.1	10.4	145905

ZIP CODE		FINANCIAL SERVICES				THE HOME						ENTERTAINMENT						PERSONAL			
						Home Improvements		Furnishings													
#	POST OFFICE NAME	Auto Loan	Home Loan	Investments	Retirement Plans	Home Repair	Lawn & Garden	Computers & Hardware	Major Appliances	TV, Radio, Sound Equipment	Furniture	Dine out/ Carry out	Sports Equipment	Fees & Tickets	Toys & Games	Travel	Cable TV	Apparel & Services	Auto Repairs	Health Insurance	Pets & Supplies
72082	KENSETT	57	38	17	33	43	50	37	46	45	38	52	55	31	49	38	48	48	46	57	66
72083	KEO	86	60	31	57	70	78	59	73	68	59	80	89	51	79	62	72	73	72	87	102
72084	LEOLA	95	64	29	55	72	83	62	77	74	63	87	92	52	83	63	80	79	76	95	110
72086	LONOKE	80	68	52	65	70	77	67	73	71	67	86	84	63	82	67	72	81	73	78	90
72087	LONSDALE	88	84	79	82	86	94	80	86	82	82	102	97	80	96	83	83	97	85	91	101
72088	FAIRFIELD BAY	89	79	73	73	86	101	74	87	81	78	99	88	73	88	80	87	92	84	102	103
72099	LITTLE ROCK AIR FORC	63	42	39	47	39	45	59	52	60	55	74	68	51	67	49	55	71	60	49	59
72101	MC CRORY	72	52	32	47	57	66	54	62	62	53	73	73	47	70	54	65	68	62	74	82
72102	MC RAE	87	67	42	62	72	79	65	75	71	66	86	88	58	81	65	74	80	74	83	98
72103	MABELVALE	78	72	62	71	73	78	72	75	73	72	90	87	69	87	71	72	86	75	75	87
72104	MALVERN	71	58	42	55	61	70	59	65	64	58	77	75	55	76	59	67	72	64	73	80
72105	JONES MILL	73	65	50	63	66	72	64	68	66	64	81	78	60	78	63	66	77	67	70	81
72106	MAYFLOWER	84	68	46	63	72	78	65	74	71	67	86	87	60	81	65	72	81	74	81	95
72110	MORRILTON	83	66	47	63	71	81	68	75	75	66	89	86	63	87	68	78	83	74	86	93
72111	MOUNT VERNON	87	69	44	63	73	81	66	76	72	67	87	89	60	83	66	75	82	75	85	99
72112	NEWPORT	73	56	42	51	60	70	58	65	67	58	79	74	54	74	58	71	74	65	77	82
72113	MAUMELLE	119	135	142	139	131	131	125	124	117	127	148	146	130	151	125	112	147	122	111	137
72114	NORTH LITTLE ROCK	45	39	49	37	38	45	45	44	49	45	61	49	45	59	44	51	59	46	48	50
72116	NORTH LITTLE ROCK	99	110	126	112	108	113	108	106	104	108	131	125	111	132	109	101	129	107	99	116
72117	NORTH LITTLE ROCK	63	56	53	52	57	65	57	59	62	58	76	67	57	74	58	65	73	60	66	71
72118	NORTH LITTLE ROCK	73	75	78	74	75	80	75	75	74	73	93	88	76	95	75	74	90	75	74	85
72120	SHERWOOD	88	96	101	97	94	96	93	92	89	93	111	108	94	112	92	86	109	92	85	101
72121	PANGBURN	89	60	28	52	68	78	58	72	70	59	82	86	50	77	59	75	74	71	88	102
72122	PARON	115	114	105	110	118	128	104	113	106	107	131	124	106	126	109	109	126	110	121	134
72125	PERRY	87	61	31	54	68	77	58	71	69	59	81	85	51	78	59	73	74	70	86	100
72126	PERRYVILLE	87	62	34	57	69	80	63	74	72	62	85	87	55	81	63	77	78	74	89	99
72127	PLUMERVILLE	87	58	26	50	66	76	56	70	68	57	79	84	48	75	57	73	72	69	86	99
72128	POYEN	93	62	28	54	70	81	60	75	72	61	85	90	51	80	61	78	77	74	92	106
72129	PRATTSVILLE	97	65	29	56	73	84	63	78	75	64	89	93	53	84	64	81	81	77	96	111
72130	PRIM	72	53	32	47	59	68	50	61	58	52	70	70	45	64	52	63	64	60	74	83
72131	QUITMAN	80	57	30	50	64	73	54	67	64	55	75	79	47	72	56	69	69	66	81	94
72132	REDFIELD	83	76	59	73	76	80	72	77	73	74	90	89	68	85	71	72	86	77	77	92
72133	REYDELL	79	53	24	46	60	69	51	64	62	52	72	76	43	68	52	66	66	63	79	91
72134	ROE	93	62	28	54	71	81	60	75	73	61	85	90	51	81	61	78	78	75	93	107
72135	ROLAND	106	127	132	127	125	124	114	115	107	114	134	134	120	141	117	104	133	111	104	128
72136	ROMANCE	107	96	74	91	99	105	90	98	93	91	114	115	87	113	91	94	109	96	102	122
72137	ROSE BUD	83	72	54	69	75	82	69	75	73	68	89	89	66	89	70	75	84	74	82	95
72140	SAINT CHARLES	78	52	24	45	59	68	50	63	61	51	71	75	43	67	51	66	65	62	78	89
72141	SCOTLAND	70	48	26	43	54	63	49	59	58	49	68	69	43	64	50	62	62	58	72	79
72142	SCOTT	114	89	57	83	98	108	85	99	95	85	113	119	78	112	87	99	105	98	114	134
72143	SEARCY	84	70	57	69	74	83	73	78	78	71	94	91	69	92	72	79	89	78	84	95
72149	SEARCY	0	0	0	0	0	0	0	0	0	0	0	0	0	0	0	0	0	0	0	0
72150	SHERIDAN	96	79	55	74	84	93	75	85	82	76	99	101	71	98	77	85	93	84	95	110
72152	SHERRILL	69	46	21	40	52	60	44	55	54	45	63	66	38	59	45	58	57	55	68	79
72153	SHIRLEY	75	56	35	51	63	72	54	66	63	54	74	76	48	71	57	67	68	65	79	89
72156	SOLGOHACHIA	77	65	47	61	70	76	61	69	66	61	80	82	59	81	63	68	75	67	76	90
72157	SPRINGFIELD	91	61	27	52	69	79	59	73	71	60	83	87	50	78	60	76	75	72	90	104
72160	STUTTGART	84	75	66	72	78	87	76	80	81	75	99	92	74	98	76	84	94	80	88	97
72165	THIDA	73	49	22	42	56	64	47	59	57	48	67	71	40	64	48	62	61	59	73	84
72166	TICHNOR	94	65	34	62	76	85	65	80	74	64	87	96	55	85	67	78	79	79	95	111
72167	TRASKWOOD	78	69	53	66	70	75	66	72	68	67	83	83	62	79	65	68	80	71	73	87
72168	TUCKER	65	43	20	37	49	56	42	52	50	43	59	62	36	56	43	54	54	52	64	74
72170	ULM	81	57	30	54	66	74	56	69	64	55	76	83	48	74	58	68	69	68	82	96
72173	VILONIA	90	85	70	82	85	89	81	86	81	82	100	100	78	97	80	80	97	85	84	102
72175	WABBASEKA	66	44	20	38	50	57	43	53	51	43	60	64	36	57	43	55	55	53	66	76
72176	WARD	81	73	57	71	73	78	70	75	71	72	88	87	66	83	69	70	84	75	75	89
72179	WILBURN	94	63	28	54	71	82	60	76	73	62	86	90	51	81	62	79	78	75	93	107
72199	NORTH LITTLE ROCK	81	70	54	69	73	81	71	76	75	70	91	87	68	89	70	75	85	75	81	89
72201	LITTLE ROCK	53	42	54	46	41	46	57	51	57	54	71	64	52	66	51	53	69	57	48	57
72202	LITTLE ROCK	63	55	75	56	54	63	65	61	69	64	86	71	64	83	63	70	83	66	65	69
72204	LITTLE ROCK	58	57	67	57	56	62	61	59	62	61	78	68	62	77	60	62	76	61	59	66
72205	LITTLE ROCK	77	79	99	80	77	84	84	80	84	83	105	94	85	106	83	83	103	83	78	88
72206	LITTLE ROCK	71	61	55	57	63	71	62	66	67	63	82	75	59	78	62	70	78	66	73	81
72207	LITTLE ROCK	125	141	185	145	137	145	141	136	137	141	172	160	147	177	142	134	171	138	126	148
72209	LITTLE ROCK	58	57	65	56	55	61	60	58	62	60	77	67	61	78	59	62	76	59	58	65
72210	LITTLE ROCK	98	104	105	104	103	105	98	100	95	99	119	118	99	121	98	93	117	99	94	114
72211	LITTLE ROCK	104	105	114	112	102	104	107	104	102	109	129	123	106	125	103	96	126	106	93	114
72212	LITTLE ROCK	143	162	192	166	159	167	155	152	147	157	186	177	163	186	156	143	184	151	141	167
72223	LITTLE ROCK	171	199	215	206	193	195	184	180	170	186	216	210	194	220	184	164	215	177	160	199
72227	LITTLE ROCK	111	125	147	128	124	129	122	120	117	122	147	141	126	148	123	114	144	120	113	131
72301	WEST MEMPHIS	61	59	66	57	58	64	62	61	65	62	81	70	63	80	61	66	78	63	63	69
72310	ARMOREL	0	0	0	0	0	0	0	0	0	0	0	0	0	0	0	0	0	0	0	0
72311	AUBREY	56	38	17	32	43	49	36	45	44	37	51	54	31	49	37	47	47	45	56	64
72313	BASSETT	62	41	19	36	47	54	40	50	48	41	57	60	34	54	41	52	51	49	62	71
72315	BLYTHEVILLE	72	62	54	59	63	71	64	68	69	64	84	78	61	81	64	70	80	68	73	80
72320	BRICKEYS	8	5	2	5	6	7	5	7	6	5	7	8	4	7	5	7	7	6	8	9
72321	BURDETTE	81	54	25	47	61	71	52	65	63	53	74	78	44	70	53	68	67	65	80	93
72324	CHERRY VALLEY	93	62	28	53	70	81	60	75	72	61	85	89	51	80	61	78	77	74	92	106
72326	COLT	81	55	26	48	62	71	53	66	63	54	75	78	45	71	54	68	68	65	80	93
72327	CRAWFORDSVILLE	70	49	27	43	54	63	48	58	57	49	68	69	42	63	49	61	62	58	71	80
72328	CRUMROD	42	34	35	30	34	41	38	40	44	39	53	42	36	47	37	47	50	41	47	46
72329	DRIVER	0	0	0	0	0	0	0	0	0	0	0	0	0	0	0	0	0	0	0	0
72330	DYESS	71	48	22	41	54	62	46	57	55	47	65	69	39	62	47	60	59	57	71	81
72331	EARLE	72	56	48	52	59	70	62	66	70	62	84	74	57	78	61	74	79	67	78	80
72333	ELAINE	64	49	45	43	50	61	53	58	62	55	75	63	50	67	52	67	70	59	69	70
72335	FORREST CITY	62	52	48	49	54	61	55	58	60	55	73	67	52	70	54	62	69	59	64	70
72338	FRENCHMANS BAYOU	32	22	10	19	24	28	21	26	25	21	30	31	18	28	21	27	27	26	32	37
72339	GILMORE	78	52	24	45	59	68	51	63	61	51	72	76	43	68	51	66	65	63	78	90
72340	GOODWIN	66	44	20	38	50	57	42	53	51	43	60	64	36	57	43	55	55	53	66	75
72341	HAYNES	65	43	20	37	49	57	42	52	51	43	59	63	36	56	43	54	54	52	65	74
72342	HELENA	64	53	55	49	54	64	58	60	65	59	79	68	56	75	58	68	76	62	68	71
72346	HETH	79	53	24	46	60	69	51	64	62	52	73	77	44	69	52	67	66	64	79	91
72347	HICKORY RIDGE	122	81	37	70	92	106	79	98	95	80	111	117	67	105	80	102	101	97	121	140
72348	HUGHES	68	50	36	44	54	63	51	59	59	51	70	68	46	66	51	63	65	59	70	78
72350	JOINER	68	46	21	40	52	59	44	55	53	45	62	66	38	59	45	57	57	54	67	77
	ARKANSAS	81	69	57	66	72	80	69	75	74	69	90	87	65	87	69	76	85	75	82	92
	UNITED STATES	100	100	100	100	100	100	100	100	100	100	100	100	100	100	100	100	100	100	100	100

#	POST OFFICE NAME	COUNTY FIPS CODE	POPULATION			2000-2004 ANNUAL RATE		HOUSEHOLDS					FAMILIES		
			2000	2004	2009	% Rate	State Centile	2000	2004	2009	% Annual Rate 2000-2004	2004 Average HH Size	2000	2004	% Annual Rate 2000-2004
72351	KEISER	093	963	892	817	-1.8	1	366	345	320	-1.4	2.59	283	263	-1.7
72354	LEPANTO	111	2665	2648	2638	-0.2	29	1034	1038	1043	0.1	2.55	748	739	-0.3
72355	LEXA	107	3796	3839	3798	0.3	46	1370	1407	1409	0.6	2.64	1029	1042	0.3
72358	LUXORA	093	1905	1797	1666	-1.4	4	667	636	594	-1.1	2.55	491	461	-1.5
72360	MARIANNA	077	8639	8580	8550	-0.2	29	3268	3303	3329	0.3	2.45	2288	2276	-0.1
72364	MARION	035	12551	13470	14226	1.7	82	4564	4987	5360	2.1	2.63	3442	3700	1.7
72365	MARKED TREE	111	3809	3723	3700	-0.5	16	1524	1507	1512	-0.3	2.40	1045	1017	-0.6
72366	MARVELL	107	3062	2947	2835	-0.9	8	1188	1155	1123	-0.7	2.51	792	752	-1.2
72367	MELLWOOD	107	70	65	62	-1.7	2	17	16	16	-1.4	4.06	13	13	0.0
72368	MORO	077	1241	1187	1162	-1.0	6	501	489	487	-0.6	2.43	361	346	-1.0
72369	ONEIDA	107	72	69	66	-1.0	7	24	23	23	-1.0	3.00	18	17	-1.3
72370	OSCEOLA	093	9992	9394	8670	-1.4	3	3537	3365	3137	-1.2	2.69	2583	2417	-1.6
72372	PALESTINE	123	2046	1982	1936	-0.7	11	768	757	750	-0.3	2.60	574	557	-0.7
72373	PARKIN	037	1875	1838	1843	-0.5	19	712	711	725	0.0	2.59	487	478	-0.4
72374	POPLAR GROVE	107	988	994	976	0.1	40	377	384	382	0.4	2.58	272	273	0.1
72376	PROCTOR	035	2216	2348	2478	1.4	78	783	848	911	1.9	2.77	599	638	1.5
72379	SNOW LAKE	041	132	128	126	-0.7	11	53	52	52	-0.5	2.46	37	36	-0.6
72384	TURRELL	035	1391	1356	1379	-0.6	14	490	484	500	-0.3	2.80	359	348	-0.7
72386	TYRONZA	111	1972	1922	1895	-0.6	14	762	754	751	-0.3	2.55	564	549	-0.6
72390	WEST HELENA	107	10378	10084	9747	-0.5	13	3813	3741	3652	-0.5	2.69	2661	2569	-0.8
72392	WHEATLEY	123	436	408	393	-1.6	2	176	168	163	-1.1	2.43	132	124	-1.5
72394	WIDENER	123	773	737	715	-1.1	6	279	270	266	-0.8	2.73	199	189	-1.2
72395	WILSON	093	1037	952	870	-2.0	1	403	377	350	-1.6	2.53	294	271	-1.9
72396	WYNNE	037	14432	14719	14963	0.5	52	5428	5636	5833	0.9	2.56	4020	4114	0.6
72401	JONESBORO	031	47566	49055	51463	0.7	63	19087	19857	21035	0.9	2.35	12227	12466	0.5
72404	JONESBORO	031	16495	18330	19836	2.5	92	6207	7018	7692	2.9	2.57	4656	5153	2.4
72410	ALICIA	075	701	683	676	-0.6	14	264	259	257	-0.5	2.64	208	201	-0.8
72411	BAY	031	2381	2450	2542	0.7	61	908	946	992	1.0	2.59	696	713	0.6
72412	BEECH GROVE	055	495	506	525	0.5	54	197	203	212	0.7	2.49	162	165	0.4
72413	BIGGERS	121	1210	1184	1187	-0.5	17	486	479	483	-0.3	2.47	356	345	-0.7
72414	BLACK OAK	031	1114	1095	1126	-0.4	21	427	421	436	-0.3	2.59	317	307	-0.8
72415	BLACK ROCK	075	1684	1683	1679	0.0	33	665	670	672	0.2	2.51	480	475	-0.3
72416	BONO	031	5305	5631	5953	1.4	79	2015	2162	2307	1.7	2.59	1545	1633	1.3
72417	BROOKLAND	031	2591	2848	3064	2.3	90	973	1076	1165	2.4	2.65	759	826	2.0
72419	CARAWAY	031	1446	1429	1470	-0.3	24	591	590	612	0.0	2.37	421	412	-0.5
72421	CASH	031	779	773	796	-0.2	28	326	328	341	0.1	2.36	237	234	-0.3
72422	CORNING	021	5291	5112	4966	-0.8	10	2183	2119	2067	-0.7	2.38	1499	1429	-1.1
72424	DATTO	021	161	156	151	-0.7	11	65	63	62	-0.7	2.48	45	43	-1.1
72425	DELAPLAINE	055	499	467	479	-1.6	2	193	182	188	-1.4	2.57	144	133	-1.9
72426	DELL	093	348	327	301	-1.5	3	151	144	134	-1.1	2.27	108	101	-1.6
72428	ETOWAH	093	642	593	541	-1.9	1	241	226	210	-1.5	2.62	186	173	-1.7
72429	FISHER	111	565	542	536	-1.0	7	234	227	227	-0.7	2.39	161	154	-1.0
72430	GREENWAY	021	580	578	568	-0.1	31	245	245	243	0.0	2.36	174	172	-0.3
72432	HARRISBURG	111	6618	6965	7152	1.2	74	2516	2672	2761	1.4	2.53	1877	1964	1.1
72433	HOXIE	075	3391	3326	3293	-0.5	19	1338	1325	1319	-0.2	2.49	963	938	-0.6
72434	IMBODEN	121	1750	1794	1823	0.6	58	720	746	764	0.8	2.40	523	533	0.5
72435	KNOBEL	021	497	555	576	2.6	93	202	226	236	2.7	2.46	146	161	2.3
72436	LAFE	055	1175	1215	1269	0.8	65	434	455	480	1.1	2.67	342	354	0.8
72437	LAKE CITY	031	3320	3523	3772	1.4	79	1245	1336	1446	1.7	2.58	939	990	1.3
72438	LEACHVILLE	093	2545	2480	2316	-0.6	14	1000	982	928	-0.4	2.53	718	692	-0.9
72440	LYNN	075	319	373	401	3.8	98	136	160	174	3.9	2.33	103	120	3.7
72441	MC DOUGAL	021	968	949	927	-0.5	19	377	373	367	-0.3	2.54	282	276	-0.5
72442	MANILA	093	4506	4273	3950	-1.2	5	1757	1681	1567	-1.0	2.51	1253	1179	-1.4
72443	MARMADUKE	055	2773	3115	3421	2.8	94	1111	1267	1406	3.1	2.45	839	941	2.7
72444	MAYNARD	121	1954	1980	2015	0.3	47	803	821	843	0.5	2.41	586	591	0.2
72445	MINTURN	075	19	20	20	1.2	74	6	6	6	0.0	3.33	5	5	0.0
72447	MONETTE	031	1697	1638	1674	-0.8	9	723	705	727	-0.6	2.24	464	440	-1.2
72449	O KEAN	121	242	251	257	0.9	67	98	103	106	1.2	2.44	73	75	0.6
72450	PARAGOULD	055	31758	33269	35223	1.1	72	12570	13258	14139	1.3	2.47	9022	9370	0.9
72453	PEACH ORCHARD	021	319	350	363	2.2	90	138	151	158	2.1	2.32	100	108	1.8
72454	PIGGOTT	021	5144	5102	5010	-0.2	27	2216	2211	2183	-0.1	2.26	1465	1434	-0.5
72455	POCAHONTAS	121	12980	13326	13669	0.6	59	5184	5371	5557	0.8	2.42	3704	3778	0.5
72456	POLLARD	021	639	645	638	0.2	43	263	267	266	0.4	2.42	199	199	0.0
72457	PORTIA	075	144	148	149	0.7	60	60	62	63	0.8	2.35	42	43	0.6
72458	POWHATAN	075	612	618	620	0.2	44	242	246	249	0.4	2.51	178	178	0.0
72459	RAVENDEN	075	923	912	904	-0.3	24	363	362	360	-0.1	2.52	267	261	-0.5
72460	RAVENDEN SPRINGS	121	1077	1087	1101	0.2	43	428	436	446	0.4	2.49	316	318	0.2
72461	RECTOR	021	3458	3315	3212	-1.0	7	1503	1450	1415	-0.8	2.29	1004	951	-1.3
72464	SAINT FRANCIS	021	291	291	286	0.0	35	123	123	122	0.0	2.37	90	89	-0.3
72465	SEDGWICK	075	106	110	112	0.9	67	42	44	45	1.1	2.50	33	34	0.7
72466	SMITHVILLE	075	772	837	870	1.9	86	313	341	357	2.0	2.45	234	251	1.7
72467	STATE UNIVERSITY	031	28	27	28	-0.9	9	11	11	11	0.0	2.45	9	8	-2.7
72469	STRAWBERRY	135	1690	1723	1767	0.5	52	660	677	698	0.6	2.55	505	511	0.3
72470	SUCCESS	021	253	245	238	-0.8	11	103	100	98	-0.7	2.45	71	68	-1.0
72471	SWIFTON	067	1239	1235	1229	-0.1	31	485	487	487	0.1	2.53	356	352	-0.3
72472	TRUMANN	111	9076	9068	9062	0.0	32	3579	3612	3640	0.2	2.49	2566	2547	-0.2
72473	TUCKERMAN	067	2200	2159	2134	-0.4	20	940	934	934	-0.2	2.27	648	636	-0.6
72476	WALNUT RIDGE	075	6918	6772	6703	-0.5	18	2776	2733	2716	-0.4	2.28	1845	1783	-0.8
72478	WARM SPRINGS	121	127	153	171	4.5	99	48	59	66	5.0	2.51	36	44	4.8
72479	WEINER	111	1421	1397	1392	-0.4	21	569	563	565	-0.3	2.48	413	402	-0.6
72482	WILLIFORD	135	869	890	933	0.6	57	393	405	426	0.7	2.20	275	279	0.3
72501	BATESVILLE	063	23707	24260	24856	0.5	56	9337	9662	10004	0.8	2.41	6556	6680	0.4
72512	HORSESHOE BEND	065	3349	3348	3361	0.0	33	1570	1576	1590	0.1	2.09	1045	1031	-0.3
72513	ASH FLAT	135	2039	2242	2432	2.3	90	825	923	1016	2.7	2.35	552	607	2.3
72515	BEXAR	049	321	312	309	-0.7	13	131	128	128	-0.5	2.44	102	99	-0.7
72517	BROCKWELL	065	732	724	721	-0.3	25	283	283	284	0.0	2.56	213	211	-0.2
72519	CALICO ROCK	005	2825	2782	2792	-0.4	23	946	940	952	-0.2	2.61	659	644	-0.5
72520	CAMP	049	492	478	473	-0.7	12	192	188	187	-0.5	2.53	147	142	-0.8
72521	CAVE CITY	063	3432	3515	3668	0.6	57	1336	1378	1451	0.7	2.50	970	986	0.4
72522	CHARLOTTE	063	451	484	506	1.7	82	181	197	209	2.0	2.46	139	149	1.7
72523	CONCORD	023	1313	1393	1501	1.4	78	516	554	604	1.7	2.51	384	406	1.3
72524	CORD	063	320	323	329	0.2	43	136	138	143	0.3	2.34	103	103	0.0
72526	CUSHMAN	063	192	208	218	1.9	85	81	89	95	2.2	2.34	63	68	1.8
72527	DESHA	063	374	366	367	-0.5	17	149	148	150	-0.2	2.47	112	109	-0.6
72528	DOLPH	065	424	415	413	-0.5	18	174	170	170	-0.6	1.52	127	98	-5.9
	ARKANSAS					0.9					1.1	2.47			0.8
	UNITED STATES					1.2					1.3	2.58			1.1

ZIP CODE # POST OFFICE NAME	RACE (%) White 2000	White 2004	Black 2000	Black 2004	Asian/Pacific 2000	Asian/Pacific 2004	% Hispanic Origin 2000	% Hispanic Origin 2004	2004 AGE DISTRIBUTION (%) 0-4	5-9	10-14	15-19	20-24	25-44	45-64	65-84	85+	18+	MEDIAN AGE 2004	% 2004 Males	% 2004 Females
72351 KEISER	89.2	87.8	8.1	9.3	0.1	0.1	2.2	2.5	6.2	6.5	7.4	7.0	5.9	26.0	27.5	12.2	1.4	75.7	38.6	49.7	50.3
72354 LEPANTO	84.7	82.9	13.0	14.4	0.0	0.0	2.2	2.6	7.9	7.1	7.6	7.2	7.4	25.6	23.6	12.2	1.4	73.1	35.8	48.2	51.8
72355 LEXA	53.0	51.3	45.1	46.7	0.3	0.3	1.6	1.8	7.1	7.1	8.5	7.8	7.5	24.8	24.9	10.8	1.5	72.5	35.2	48.3	51.7
72358 LUXORA	53.2	50.4	44.0	46.6	0.1	0.1	2.5	2.8	7.5	7.1	8.2	7.6	6.8	28.3	23.2	9.2	2.1	72.5	34.1	52.3	47.8
72360 MARIANNA	34.2	33.2	64.3	65.3	0.4	0.4	1.6	1.6	7.7	7.2	8.1	8.0	7.7	23.9	22.7	12.3	2.5	72.2	34.7	47.2	52.8
72364 MARION	75.1	72.3	22.7	25.1	0.5	0.7	1.9	2.2	7.8	7.6	8.2	7.6	7.0	32.8	22.4	6.0	0.7	71.7	32.8	50.5	49.5
72365 MARKED TREE	72.9	71.6	24.6	25.5	0.2	0.3	2.1	2.4	6.9	6.8	7.1	7.0	6.2	24.3	24.4	14.9	2.4	75.1	38.7	48.1	52.0
72366 MARVELL	40.5	38.4	58.3	60.3	0.0	0.0	0.8	0.9	7.5	7.1	8.9	7.9	6.1	20.8	23.6	15.6	2.7	71.3	38.3	46.2	53.8
72367 MELLWOOD	38.6	36.9	54.3	55.4	0.0	0.0	10.0	12.3	9.2	7.7	15.4	9.2	9.2	21.5	20.0	7.7	0.0	58.5	24.6	50.8	49.2
72368 MORO	62.2	61.0	37.2	38.4	0.2	0.3	1.5	1.5	6.8	5.5	6.4	6.9	6.6	23.3	27.1	15.2	2.3	77.2	41.0	46.8	53.2
72369 ONEIDA	47.2	43.5	47.2	50.7	0.0	0.0	5.6	5.8	10.1	8.7	8.7	7.3	7.3	23.2	23.2	11.6	0.0	66.7	31.9	46.4	53.6
72370 OSCEOLA	51.9	49.7	46.4	48.3	0.2	0.3	1.6	1.8	9.2	8.2	8.1	7.9	8.2	26.2	21.4	9.3	1.5	69.8	31.3	48.4	51.6
72372 PALESTINE	67.6	64.3	31.4	34.5	0.2	0.3	0.2	0.2	6.9	6.6	7.1	7.4	7.2	25.3	26.2	11.7	1.7	74.8	37.7	49.1	50.9
72373 PARKIN	35.2	32.2	63.5	66.4	0.1	0.1	1.0	1.0	7.0	8.4	8.4	8.4	6.4	23.8	22.1	13.8	1.7	70.7	34.4	46.8	53.2
72374 POPLAR GROVE	50.4	48.5	48.5	50.2	0.1	0.1	1.2	1.5	6.1	6.7	9.0	8.3	6.7	22.7	25.7	12.9	1.9	72.9	37.6	48.3	51.7
72376 PROCTOR	48.6	45.5	49.0	51.9	0.2	0.2	1.9	2.1	7.9	7.7	7.7	7.0	6.7	26.8	25.0	9.9	1.3	72.5	35.6	50.4	49.6
72379 SNOW LAKE	65.2	63.3	31.1	33.6	0.0	0.0	3.0	3.1	7.8	6.3	5.5	6.3	4.7	20.3	32.0	14.8	2.3	75.8	44.4	52.3	47.7
72384 TURRELL	36.5	33.0	60.3	63.6	0.2	0.2	3.9	4.2	8.7	8.3	8.1	7.3	6.8	24.6	25.7	9.4	1.2	70.3	34.4	49.9	50.1
72386 TYRONZA	86.8	85.7	11.0	11.9	0.2	0.2	1.2	1.3	7.2	7.3	6.8	6.5	6.9	27.5	25.3	11.2	1.1	74.8	35.6	50.2	49.8
72390 WEST HELENA	36.5	35.3	62.0	63.0	0.3	0.4	1.1	1.2	9.5	9.0	9.1	7.8	7.3	23.4	21.4	11.1	1.5	67.5	31.4	45.8	54.2
72392 WHEATLEY	62.4	58.6	35.8	39.5	0.0	0.0	3.2	3.4	6.4	6.4	6.6	9.1	6.6	25.7	26.5	11.3	1.5	75.7	37.9	49.3	50.7
72394 WIDENER	47.2	43.3	50.8	54.7	0.1	0.1	2.9	3.1	7.7	7.6	9.2	7.9	7.1	25.0	21.9	12.2	1.5	70.6	34.2	50.5	49.5
72395 WILSON	75.0	72.3	23.1	25.5	0.0	0.0	2.7	3.2	6.5	6.4	7.0	8.6	8.0	24.8	27.1	10.2	1.4	74.9	37.6	46.2	53.8
72396 WYNNE	76.0	74.7	22.5	23.6	0.4	0.5	0.9	1.1	7.1	7.0	7.6	7.1	6.7	26.9	24.3	11.5	1.7	73.9	36.4	48.5	51.5
72401 JONESBORO	84.6	83.5	12.0	12.7	0.8	1.0	2.6	3.0	6.8	6.2	6.0	7.8	10.7	28.1	21.8	10.9	1.8	77.8	32.9	47.9	52.1
72404 JONESBORO	93.9	92.9	3.5	4.0	0.7	0.9	1.2	1.5	6.9	6.3	6.8	7.3	9.7	31.5	23.4	7.1	1.0	75.8	33.0	49.6	50.4
72410 ALICIA	99.3	99.3	0.0	0.0	0.0	0.0	0.1	0.2	4.0	8.1	9.2	6.9	5.0	27.2	24.5	13.8	1.5	74.4	38.7	50.7	49.3
72411 BAY	95.9	95.3	2.5	2.8	0.0	0.0	1.5	1.9	7.3	7.2	7.3	7.1	6.6	28.2	24.2	10.8	1.3	73.8	36.0	49.1	50.9
72412 BEECH GROVE	98.0	97.8	0.0	0.0	0.0	0.0	0.2	0.4	6.7	6.7	6.3	6.9	6.1	29.8	25.3	10.9	1.2	76.1	37.1	52.0	48.0
72413 BIGGERS	96.1	95.8	1.5	1.6	0.0	0.1	0.4	0.4	6.7	6.8	7.4	6.0	4.6	26.4	24.2	16.1	1.9	75.4	39.2	49.6	50.4
72414 BLACK OAK	97.3	96.8	0.1	0.1	0.3	0.4	1.4	1.8	5.7	6.1	6.2	6.3	5.9	26.6	27.5	14.0	1.7	78.3	40.8	50.1	49.9
72415 BLACK ROCK	98.6	98.6	0.1	0.1	0.0	0.0	0.5	0.5	5.9	6.2	7.0	6.7	5.9	24.8	27.3	14.1	2.0	76.5	40.3	50.7	49.3
72416 BONO	97.8	97.6	0.4	0.4	0.1	0.1	1.3	1.5	7.7	7.6	7.6	6.4	6.4	30.6	23.4	9.5	0.8	73.1	34.4	50.1	49.9
72417 BROOKLAND	97.4	97.1	0.5	0.5	0.0	0.0	1.2	1.5	8.5	8.5	7.9	5.9	5.6	31.1	22.1	9.4	1.2	71.5	34.0	50.4	49.7
72419 CARAWAY	97.5	97.0	0.0	0.0	0.1	0.1	3.1	3.9	6.8	7.1	7.0	6.2	5.6	26.2	26.6	12.4	2.1	75.6	38.3	48.6	51.4
72421 CASH	98.2	98.1	0.5	0.5	0.4	0.4	1.8	2.1	8.3	7.9	6.9	4.4	4.5	31.1	22.9	12.2	1.9	74.3	36.3	51.4	48.6
72422 CORNING	97.2	97.0	0.2	0.3	0.2	0.2	0.5	0.6	6.3	6.2	7.0	6.4	6.5	25.8	24.1	15.1	2.6	76.6	39.1	48.5	51.5
72424 DATTO	98.1	98.1	0.0	0.0	0.0	0.0	1.2	0.6	6.4	6.4	7.1	5.8	5.8	26.9	25.6	14.7	1.3	76.3	38.2	52.6	47.4
72425 DELAPLAINE	91.4	90.8	0.0	0.0	0.2	0.2	0.8	0.9	4.7	5.4	7.9	6.9	6.4	28.1	26.1	12.9	1.7	77.7	39.8	52.0	48.0
72426 DELL	89.4	87.8	6.6	7.7	0.3	0.3	4.9	5.5	6.1	6.4	7.3	6.1	5.2	26.3	28.4	12.8	1.2	76.5	40.3	50.2	49.9
72428 ETOWAH	93.0	92.1	1.3	1.5	0.2	0.2	6.4	7.4	8.9	7.9	7.4	6.6	6.6	28.5	22.1	11.0	1.0	71.7	33.8	50.3	49.8
72429 FISHER	96.6	96.1	1.1	1.3	0.0	0.0	2.5	3.0	5.4	5.7	7.2	5.9	5.5	27.5	29.9	11.4	1.5	78.0	41.3	50.4	49.6
72430 GREENWAY	99.0	99.1	0.0	0.0	0.0	0.0	0.5	0.5	4.5	5.0	7.1	6.1	5.0	26.1	29.4	15.1	1.7	79.4	42.5	51.2	48.8
72432 HARRISBURG	95.9	95.4	2.3	2.6	0.2	0.2	1.3	1.5	6.5	6.6	6.8	6.7	6.4	27.8	25.4	12.4	1.5	76.0	37.7	50.2	49.9
72433 HOXIE	98.4	98.3	0.4	0.4	0.1	0.1	1.2	1.2	7.0	7.0	7.3	6.9	6.5	27.2	23.9	12.4	2.0	74.7	36.8	48.3	51.7
72434 IMBODEN	97.0	96.9	0.5	0.5	0.0	0.0	0.9	1.0	5.9	6.4	7.3	6.0	5.2	24.5	27.5	15.0	2.2	76.8	41.0	49.7	50.3
72435 KNOBEL	97.6	97.7	0.4	0.4	0.0	0.0	2.0	2.0	6.9	6.9	7.2	6.3	4.5	25.6	24.3	16.6	1.8	75.0	39.7	49.9	50.1
72436 LAFE	93.5	92.8	0.0	0.0	0.1	0.1	1.1	1.4	5.8	6.0	7.1	7.2	6.4	28.2	27.7	10.8	0.7	76.8	38.5	50.5	49.5
72437 LAKE CITY	98.0	97.7	0.2	0.2	0.0	0.1	1.5	1.9	6.4	6.5	7.6	7.0	6.2	27.2	24.6	12.7	1.9	75.4	37.6	49.7	50.3
72438 LEACHVILLE	93.8	92.9	1.3	1.5	0.2	0.2	7.2	8.4	7.1	6.3	7.0	6.9	7.5	26.3	24.3	13.0	1.7	75.4	37.3	49.8	50.2
72440 LYNN	96.9	97.1	0.3	0.3	0.0	0.0	0.6	0.5	7.5	7.2	6.4	5.4	7.8	22.8	27.4	13.7	1.9	75.6	39.6	50.1	49.9
72441 MC DOUGAL	98.9	98.6	0.1	0.1	0.0	0.0	0.5	0.5	6.4	6.4	5.9	5.9	6.2	24.6	27.2	16.1	1.3	77.8	41.3	50.8	49.2
72442 MANILA	97.6	97.3	0.2	0.3	0.0	0.1	1.9	2.3	6.6	6.6	7.5	6.5	6.8	28.1	23.5	12.6	1.9	75.5	37.4	48.3	51.7
72443 MARMADUKE	96.9	96.5	0.0	0.0	0.1	0.1	1.2	1.4	6.6	6.6	7.3	6.6	6.0	28.4	24.6	12.4	1.6	75.5	37.7	49.1	51.0
72444 MAYNARD	96.8	96.5	1.0	1.0	0.1	0.1	0.5	0.7	5.7	6.1	7.4	6.9	5.6	25.6	26.5	14.9	1.3	76.5	40.2	50.2	49.8
72445 MINTURN	100.0	100.0	0.0	0.0	0.0	0.0	0.0	0.0	5.0	10.0	10.0	5.0	5.0	35.0	30.0	0.0	0.0	75.0	35.0	60.0	40.0
72447 MONETTE	95.8	95.0	0.1	0.1	0.0	0.0	4.0	4.8	6.7	6.3	5.6	5.4	5.6	24.9	23.9	18.0	3.9	78.2	41.7	45.8	54.2
72449 O KEAN	98.4	98.4	0.0	0.0	0.0	0.0	0.4	0.4	7.6	7.2	6.0	6.0	6.4	27.1	28.7	10.0	1.2	76.1	38.1	48.2	51.8
72450 PARAGOULD	97.7	97.5	0.2	0.2	0.2	0.3	1.2	1.4	6.9	6.8	7.0	6.3	6.5	28.7	23.8	12.3	1.7	75.5	36.7	49.0	51.0
72453 PEACH ORCHARD	96.9	97.1	0.3	0.3	0.0	0.0	1.6	2.3	6.6	6.9	7.4	6.6	4.6	26.0	24.3	16.0	1.7	75.4	39.4	49.7	50.3
72454 PIGGOTT	98.6	98.4	0.2	0.2	0.0	0.0	0.8	1.0	6.0	5.8	6.3	5.7	5.6	24.0	24.7	18.4	3.5	78.3	42.6	48.1	51.9
72455 POCAHONTAS	97.2	97.0	1.0	1.0	0.1	0.1	0.8	1.0	6.1	6.1	6.5	6.8	6.4	25.3	24.9	15.2	2.8	77.3	40.1	48.7	51.3
72456 POLLARD	99.1	99.1	0.0	0.0	0.0	0.0	0.8	0.8	5.7	5.9	6.7	6.2	7.0	25.7	27.6	14.0	1.2	78.0	40.1	50.1	49.9
72457 PORTIA	98.6	98.7	0.7	0.7	0.0	0.0	1.4	0.7	6.1	6.1	7.4	5.4	5.4	26.4	23.0	17.6	2.7	77.7	40.8	46.6	53.4
72458 POWHATAN	98.2	98.2	0.2	0.2	0.0	0.0	0.7	0.7	6.0	6.2	6.6	6.5	6.3	24.3	28.0	14.4	1.8	77.0	41.1	51.0	49.0
72459 RAVENDEN	96.9	96.9	0.0	0.0	0.0	0.0	0.9	0.9	6.1	6.1	6.3	7.4	7.4	25.6	26.2	13.9	1.1	77.3	40.0	50.0	50.0
72460 RAVENDEN SPRINGS	97.6	97.3	0.3	0.3	0.0	0.0	1.0	1.2	5.8	6.0	6.4	5.9	6.0	26.1	27.5	14.7	1.6	78.4	40.8	50.5	49.5
72461 RECTOR	98.2	98.0	0.2	0.2	0.1	0.2	1.1	1.2	5.9	5.9	6.0	5.4	5.7	24.3	25.9	17.6	3.4	78.8	42.7	47.5	52.5
72464 SAINT FRANCIS	98.3	97.9	0.0	0.0	0.0	0.0	1.4	1.7	7.2	6.5	7.2	5.5	4.5	26.8	27.5	13.1	1.7	75.3	39.7	50.9	49.1
72465 SEDGWICK	98.1	99.1	0.0	0.0	0.0	0.0	0.9	0.9	7.3	7.3	5.5	6.4	6.4	26.4	25.5	13.6	1.8	74.6	38.8	51.8	48.2
72466 SMITHVILLE	97.4	97.4	0.3	0.2	0.0	0.0	0.8	0.7	6.7	6.6	6.5	5.6	7.1	23.5	27.7	14.6	1.8	76.9	40.9	50.5	49.5
72467 STATE UNIVERSITY	96.4	100.0	0.0	0.0	0.0	0.0	0.0	0.0	7.4	7.4	7.4	7.4	7.4	29.6	29.6	3.7	0.0	77.8	33.8	51.9	48.2
72469 STRAWBERRY	98.2	98.1	0.4	0.4	0.1	0.1	0.5	0.5	7.1	7.3	7.3	5.8	6.1	25.1	26.1	13.6	1.6	74.7	38.8	50.8	49.2
72470 SUCCESS	98.0	97.6	0.0	0.0	0.0	0.0	0.8	1.2	6.1	6.5	7.4	6.1	6.1	26.1	24.5	15.1	2.0	75.5	38.5	51.4	48.6
72471 SWIFTON	98.1	97.8	0.4	0.5	0.1	0.1	1.8	2.1	5.9	6.6	9.0	6.5	5.1	27.5	24.8	13.7	0.9	74.6	36.8	48.4	51.6
72472 TRUMANN	94.9	94.2	3.5	3.9	0.2	0.2	1.0	1.2	7.2	7.1	7.5	6.5	6.4	27.4	23.8	12.6	1.5	74.2	36.5	48.4	51.6
72473 TUCKERMAN	89.8	89.0	8.6	9.4	0.0	0.0	0.9	0.9	5.1	5.2	6.5	6.8	6.8	24.6	26.9	15.7	2.4	79.1	42.0	47.5	52.5
72476 WALNUT RIDGE	97.0	96.9	0.9	0.9	0.1	0.1	0.6	0.6	6.8	6.0	5.5	7.0	7.8	25.1	22.3	15.9	3.6	78.5	38.5	47.1	52.9
72478 WARM SPRINGS	92.9	92.2	4.7	4.6	0.0	0.0	1.6	2.0	4.6	5.2	6.5	8.5	6.5	24.8	29.4	13.7	0.7	77.1	41.0	52.9	47.1
72479 WEINER	97.7	97.4	1.0	1.2	0.3	0.4	1.8	2.0	5.6	5.7	6.9	6.3	6.4	26.8	26.6	13.7	2.0	78.0	40.1	50.0	50.0
72482 WILLIFORD	98.3	98.0	0.1	0.1	0.1	0.1	0.7	0.8	5.1	4.9	5.5	5.4	5.4	20.3	30.0	21.6	1.8	81.5	47.3	50.2	49.8
72501 BATESVILLE	93.9	93.3	2.8	2.9	0.9	1.1	1.7	2.0	6.4	6.4	6.3	6.9	7.0	26.3	25.6	13.0	2.1	77.2	38.7	48.7	51.3
72512 HORSESHOE BEND	97.4	97.1	0.2	0.2	0.2	0.2	1.2	1.5	3.8	3.9	4.3	3.5	3.6	15.5	27.3	33.3	4.8	85.8	58.1	48.3	51.7
72513 ASH FLAT	97.4	97.0	0.6	0.8	0.2	0.2	1.1	1.3	5.0	5.2	6.4	6.4	5.5	22.0	26.5	19.6	3.4	78.9	44.7	47.4	52.6
72515 BEXAR	98.1	98.1	0.0	0.0	0.3	0.3	0.3	0.3	4.8	5.1	6.7	5.8	5.5	22.1	31.4	17.3	1.3	79.5	45.0	52.6	47.4
72517 BROCKWELL	97.5	97.1	0.1	0.1	0.0	0.0	1.0	1.4	5.8	6.4	6.9	6.1	4.8	26.0	28.7	14.0	1.4	77.1	41.1	49.3	50.7
72519 CALICO ROCK	94.6	94.1	3.2	3.5	0.2	0.3	1.3	1.5	4.6	4.9	6.2	6.3	5.9	28.2	26.3	15.6	2.0	80.2	41.5	54.4	45.7
72520 CAMP	97.0	96.9	0.0	0.0	0.0	0.0	0.8	1.1	4.8	5.2	5.7	6.1	5.9	21.1	30.5	18.6	2.1	80.5	45.8	50.0	50.0
72521 CAVE CITY	97.1	96.8	0.9	0.9	0.1	0.1	1.1	1.4	8.0	7.5	7.0	6.4	6.0	27.0	22.1	13.7	2.3	73.4	36.6	47.7	52.3
72522 CHARLOTTE	96.5	96.1	0.9	1.0	0.2	0.2	1.3	1.7	6.0	6.2	6.0	6.2	7.2	26.9	28.7	11.6	1.2	78.1	39.2	52.1	47.9
72523 CONCORD	98.1	97.9	0.0	0.0	0.1	0.1	1.1	1.2	5.4	5.8	7.5	6.8	6.5	26.6	25.2	14.9	1.5	77.3	39.1	49.8	50.2
72524 CORD	97.8	97.5	0.6	0.6	0.3	0.3	0.6	0.6	6.2	5.9	6.2	6.2	6.5	25.7	29.1	12.7	1.6	78.0	40.5	52.3	47.7
72526 CUSHMAN	96.4	95.7	0.5	0.5	0.0	0.0	1.0	1.0	5.8	6.3	7.2	7.2	6.7	27.4	28.9	9.6	1.0	76.0	37.1	51.0	49.0
72527 DESHA	98.1	97.8	0.5	0.6	0.3	0.3	0.5	0.6	5.7	6.0	6.0	6.6	6.8	26.2	29.0	12.3	1.4	78.1	40.5	47.3	52.7
72528 DOLPH	86.8	85.5	11.3	12.3	0.2	0.2	0.5	0.5	3.4	3.6	4.3	4.6	8.2	42.7	24.8	7.5	1.0	85.3	37.6	68.7	31.3
ARKANSAS	80.0	79.3	15.7	15.8	0.8	1.0	3.3	3.8	6.9	6.7	6.9	6.8	7.3	27.3	24.1	12.2	1.8	75.7	36.7	49.0	51.0
UNITED STATES	75.1	73.6	12.3	12.5	3.8	4.2	12.5	14.1	6.9	6.7	7.2	7.0	7.3	28.6	23.8	10.8	1.7	75.1	36.0	49.1	50.9

#	POST OFFICE NAME	2004 Per Capita Income	2004 HH Income Base	2004 HOUSEHOLD INCOME DISTRIBUTION (%) Less than $25,000	$25,000 to $49,999	$50,000 to $99,999	$100,000 to $149,999	$150,000 or More	MEDIAN HOUSEHOLD INCOME 2004	2009	2004 National Centile	2004 State Centile	2004 Home Value Base	2004 HOME VALUE DISTRIBUTION (%) Less than $50,000	$50,000 to $89,999	$90,000 to $174,999	$175,000 to $399,999	$400,000 or More	2004 Median Home Value
72351	KEISER	18205	345	29.6	32.5	31.6	5.2	1.2	41364	50836	51	87	227	43.2	39.7	17.2	0.0	0.0	54697
72354	LEPANTO	14697	1038	45.7	29.1	21.2	2.9	1.2	27761	33743	8	16	656	47.0	32.3	17.4	3.1	0.3	53509
72355	LEXA	17036	1407	43.3	30.6	20.5	3.6	2.1	29909	36140	12	25	998	48.5	31.4	16.9	3.2	0.0	51899
72358	LUXORA	12895	636	48.9	29.6	17.3	3.5	0.8	25552	30490	5	9	370	48.1	33.2	15.4	3.2	0.0	52333
72360	MARIANNA	14333	3303	53.0	26.6	15.6	2.6	2.2	22752	27898	3	3	1991	49.1	34.8	14.9	1.3	0.0	50907
72364	MARION	20532	4987	23.0	32.4	32.9	10.1	1.6	45693	56015	63	93	3454	21.6	24.9	39.9	13.0	0.7	94136
72365	MARKED TREE	15047	1507	46.1	29.5	20.0	3.7	0.7	27559	33575	8	15	965	32.4	41.1	21.2	4.9	0.3	66026
72366	MARVELL	17240	1155	49.1	28.4	15.7	3.5	3.4	25667	32020	5	9	783	58.1	31.4	8.6	1.4	0.5	41533
72367	MELLWOOD	6077	16	56.3	37.5	6.3	0.0	0.0	22205	27230	3	2	8	62.5	25.0	12.5	0.0	0.0	35000
72368	MORO	14764	489	50.3	28.0	17.8	2.3	1.6	24799	31232	4	6	391	55.8	31.0	12.8	0.5	0.0	43382
72369	ONEIDA	8877	23	56.5	30.4	13.0	0.0	0.0	21069	26087	2	2	14	64.3	28.6	7.1	0.0	0.0	35000
72370	OSCEOLA	14461	3365	45.6	26.8	22.0	3.7	2.1	28268	34095	9	19	1944	30.0	41.2	24.8	3.6	0.4	65845
72372	PALESTINE	15642	757	39.5	32.2	22.6	3.6	2.1	31865	38630	17	42	596	41.3	33.1	19.3	4.5	1.9	61692
72373	PARKIN	13303	711	54.3	25.0	15.2	3.7	1.8	22435	27594	3	3	476	66.2	24.6	5.7	2.5	1.1	37027
72374	POPLAR GROVE	15864	384	42.5	31.8	20.1	3.7	2.1	31387	39131	16	38	300	46.7	34.3	16.0	3.0	0.0	53226
72376	PROCTOR	17415	848	31.3	35.3	26.3	4.0	3.2	37497	46080	37	77	671	39.9	27.3	27.4	2.8	2.5	64836
72379	SNOW LAKE	15198	52	53.9	23.1	19.2	1.9	1.9	22265	26504	3	3	40	62.5	17.5	17.5	2.5	0.0	37500
72384	TURRELL	14301	484	40.3	32.2	21.3	4.8	1.5	31448	39806	16	38	330	60.0	17.9	17.9	3.3	0.9	40833
72386	TYRONZA	15593	754	37.8	33.8	23.9	3.9	0.7	33196	40855	21	50	517	51.1	30.6	16.4	1.9	0.0	49154
72390	WEST HELENA	13647	3741	47.7	29.5	18.2	3.1	1.5	26703	32519	7	12	2190	40.0	38.5	19.0	2.2	0.3	58866
72392	WHEATLEY	14025	168	39.9	41.7	16.1	2.4	0.0	32660	40109	20	47	133	56.4	24.8	15.8	3.0	0.0	47639
72394	WIDENER	19154	270	49.6	27.0	16.3	4.4	2.6	25212	30989	5	7	196	67.4	24.0	8.7	0.0	0.0	37353
72395	WILSON	21102	377	34.0	26.3	31.0	4.5	4.2	39860	50279	45	83	226	31.4	36.7	26.6	2.2	3.1	69524
72396	WYNNE	19032	5636	36.6	31.2	24.7	4.9	2.7	35304	42522	29	64	4208	32.4	31.4	28.9	6.6	0.7	71852
72401	JONESBORO	19594	19857	36.8	29.4	25.3	5.9	2.6	34703	43457	26	60	12080	17.9	32.8	37.1	10.8	1.4	89170
72404	JONESBORO	26908	7018	20.9	26.4	34.4	10.2	8.0	52664	64765	76	97	4784	11.3	16.2	49.8	18.0	4.8	116202
72410	ALICIA	14223	259	44.0	32.8	18.2	3.5	1.5	27521	30941	8	14	204	61.3	27.5	9.3	2.0	0.0	40000
72411	BAY	17505	946	30.4	35.1	28.7	4.4	1.4	38596	47313	41	80	720	38.6	42.2	15.6	3.5	0.1	57664
72412	BEECH GROVE	21607	203	26.1	34.0	34.0	3.0	3.0	41132	48827	50	86	173	26.0	23.1	34.1	14.5	2.3	91364
72413	BIGGERS	14411	479	44.9	33.8	18.8	1.3	1.3	28219	33716	9	19	382	65.5	29.1	5.2	0.3	0.0	39167
72414	BLACK OAK	17174	421	39.9	27.8	24.0	5.9	2.4	33870	42860	24	54	339	49.9	33.0	12.1	5.0	0.0	50114
72415	BLACK ROCK	15410	670	39.3	37.9	18.8	3.3	0.8	30490	35567	13	29	543	42.9	33.5	20.3	3.1	0.2	56754
72416	BONO	19153	2162	29.7	37.5	25.1	5.4	2.5	37482	46280	37	76	1723	33.5	36.8	22.9	5.9	0.9	65595
72417	BROOKLAND	18832	1076	29.1	31.1	31.2	6.6	2.0	41079	50659	50	86	876	31.4	37.1	27.9	3.0	0.7	70538
72419	CARAWAY	14951	590	46.4	31.0	18.1	3.7	0.7	27648	34829	8	15	451	61.6	30.6	6.2	1.6	0.0	41532
72421	CASH	15393	328	44.5	32.0	19.2	4.3	0.0	27779	33438	8	16	271	49.1	36.2	13.7	1.1	0.0	50926
72422	CORNING	16076	2119	46.8	32.0	17.3	2.3	1.5	27006	31468	7	13	1520	53.9	32.2	13.2	0.8	0.0	46758
72424	DATTO	22063	63	42.9	36.5	14.3	0.0	6.4	29420	36647	11	23	50	64.0	24.0	10.0	2.0	0.0	38750
72425	DELAPLAINE	15400	182	36.8	40.1	17.0	3.3	2.8	35000	40780	28	63	151	55.6	27.2	14.6	2.7	0.0	42917
72426	DELL	20107	144	35.4	29.2	29.2	4.2	2.1	37002	47378	35	74	111	42.3	31.5	14.4	11.7	0.0	59444
72428	ETOWAH	13640	226	44.3	36.3	15.5	3.1	0.9	28043	33519	9	17	158	57.6	21.5	17.1	3.8	0.0	35833
72429	FISHER	15646	227	44.5	32.2	19.4	1.3	2.6	28090	33777	9	18	174	48.3	27.6	19.5	2.9	1.7	51667
72430	GREENWAY	22413	245	35.5	32.7	20.4	5.7	5.7	33470	41479	22	52	202	56.9	20.3	13.9	7.9	1.0	46216
72432	HARRISBURG	16013	2672	42.6	26.7	24.4	4.9	1.5	31635	39674	17	40	2125	44.9	31.9	17.7	4.6	0.9	55394
72433	HOXIE	15278	1325	44.2	31.3	19.4	3.3	1.8	29145	33783	11	21	948	43.5	46.9	8.0	1.6	0.0	53974
72434	IMBODEN	17729	746	40.0	32.8	21.6	3.5	2.1	30148	35755	13	27	608	40.0	33.2	21.7	3.6	1.5	60000
72435	KNOBEL	12858	226	46.5	37.2	15.5	0.9	0.0	28171	32340	9	18	180	67.8	21.7	8.3	1.7	0.6	36071
72436	LAFE	15428	455	32.1	40.0	23.7	2.9	1.3	36820	43573	35	72	389	42.2	32.9	22.1	2.1	0.8	60729
72437	LAKE CITY	17736	1336	32.2	33.3	26.4	6.4	1.7	37003	45632	35	74	1022	44.6	36.7	15.7	2.8	0.2	53929
72438	LEACHVILLE	17993	982	39.0	35.2	20.3	3.4	2.1	32020	38922	18	43	707	53.0	27.9	17.1	2.0	0.0	47095
72440	LYNN	16841	160	39.4	35.6	20.0	4.4	0.6	32495	37850	19	46	133	39.9	36.1	23.3	0.8	0.0	60333
72441	MC DOUGAL	14288	373	43.2	29.0	25.2	2.4	0.3	30478	35140	13	29	311	58.2	23.8	13.2	4.2	0.6	44796
72442	MANILA	16348	1681	41.2	29.5	23.3	4.8	1.3	30706	37870	14	31	1275	47.8	31.4	17.7	3.1	0.0	53202
72443	MARMADUKE	15804	1267	39.5	36.3	19.9	2.2	2.1	31845	38493	17	42	983	36.3	38.1	20.9	2.0	2.8	62402
72444	MAYNARD	15498	821	45.1	30.2	20.8	2.7	1.2	29117	35317	11	21	658	52.6	26.9	18.2	2.3	0.0	48247
72445	MINTURN	10625	6	16.7	50.0	33.3	0.0	0.0	35000	45000	28	63	5	0.0	100.0	0.0	0.0	0.0	77500
72447	MONETTE	18139	705	38.0	32.3	23.4	5.0	1.3	34670	42514	26	59	503	46.9	38.2	12.1	2.8	0.0	52768
72449	O KEAN	16152	103	40.8	32.0	23.3	2.9	1.0	33804	40917	23	54	80	60.0	31.3	6.3	2.5	0.0	42000
72450	PARAGOULD	20726	13258	34.2	32.4	26.3	4.4	2.8	36314	43456	33	71	9696	19.9	35.5	33.4	10.5	0.7	83123
72453	PEACH ORCHARD	13941	151	46.4	37.1	15.9	0.7	0.0	28280	33628	9	19	121	66.9	22.3	8.3	1.7	0.8	36944
72454	PIGGOTT	18765	2211	41.5	32.3	19.9	2.9	3.4	30390	35913	13	28	1666	35.8	32.8	23.9	7.1	0.4	63804
72455	POCAHONTAS	17735	5371	37.7	33.4	22.3	4.2	2.3	33596	39748	23	52	3963	27.6	35.9	30.0	6.1	0.4	70655
72456	POLLARD	15183	267	41.2	36.7	18.4	2.3	1.5	30071	35217	12	26	223	51.1	26.9	16.1	5.4	0.5	48864
72457	PORTIA	16423	62	45.2	27.4	22.6	3.2	1.6	28601	32344	10	20	47	40.4	46.8	12.8	0.0	0.0	57500
72458	POWHATAN	14822	246	39.4	38.2	18.3	3.3	0.8	30901	35578	15	32	204	41.2	29.4	25.0	4.4	0.0	59000
72459	RAVENDEN	13062	362	48.3	39.5	9.4	1.4	1.4	26513	30794	6	11	293	45.1	41.0	8.5	4.8	0.7	53222
72460	RAVENDEN SPRINGS	16605	436	42.7	29.8	22.3	3.0	2.3	30531	36817	14	29	364	37.1	28.6	19.5	9.6	5.2	64667
72461	RECTOR	17971	1450	45.9	27.8	21.4	3.0	1.9	27871	33214	8	17	1100	51.8	35.0	9.3	3.9	0.0	48773
72464	SAINT FRANCIS	16733	123	31.7	45.5	20.3	1.6	0.8	34169	41354	25	56	102	44.1	33.3	15.7	6.9	0.0	58571
72465	SEDGWICK	24336	44	34.1	27.3	22.7	4.6	11.4	40000	42399	46	84	36	52.8	36.1	11.1	0.0	0.0	48000
72466	SMITHVILLE	15372	341	40.2	36.1	19.1	3.8	0.9	31462	37120	16	38	285	39.3	31.9	25.3	3.5	0.0	61552
72467	STATE UNIVERSITY	18241	11	36.4	27.3	27.3	9.1	0.0	37303	47321	36	76	9	33.3	44.4	22.2	0.0	0.0	65000
72469	STRAWBERRY	17172	677	37.5	28.4	26.4	6.1	1.6	34469	40822	26	58	572	39.7	23.3	25.7	6.5	4.9	61795
72470	SUCCESS	22262	100	41.0	39.0	13.0	1.0	6.0	30287	35867	13	28	79	65.8	22.8	10.1	1.3	0.0	37083
72471	SWIFTON	13877	487	44.8	32.9	18.5	3.5	0.4	28596	35322	10	20	372	53.0	32.0	12.9	2.2	0.0	48070
72472	TRUMANN	15161	3612	41.0	33.9	21.2	2.5	1.5	30885	37093	15	32	2488	34.3	41.6	22.4	1.4	0.3	60780
72473	TUCKERMAN	17059	934	40.8	32.6	21.7	4.2	0.8	31720	38495	17	41	708	49.4	38.3	10.5	1.1	0.7	50381
72476	WALNUT RIDGE	17145	2733	37.8	33.0	24.4	2.9	1.9	32606	38425	20	47	1867	37.1	46.7	13.5	2.8	0.0	61075
72478	WARM SPRINGS	16938	59	40.7	32.2	23.7	1.7	1.7	31333	36830	16	37	48	33.3	39.6	22.9	4.2	0.0	61250
72479	WEINER	20568	563	35.4	29.1	25.0	5.2	5.3	35700	44058	30	67	456	33.1	40.1	21.3	4.6	0.9	67966
72482	WILLIFORD	17250	405	48.4	32.4	12.6	4.4	2.2	25947	29690	6	9	345	37.7	38.3	18.0	5.5	0.6	59884
72501	BATESVILLE	20150	9662	34.1	31.3	27.2	4.0	3.4	36826	44408	35	72	7152	28.6	31.1	29.5	9.5	1.2	74815
72512	HORSESHOE BEND	19900	1576	40.2	37.4	18.5	2.7	1.3	31008	35818	15	34	1344	30.2	34.9	26.7	7.7	0.5	69556
72513	ASH FLAT	17644	923	49.4	29.1	15.3	2.7	3.5	25297	28987	5	8	706	27.2	39.8	23.4	8.2	1.4	70133
72515	BEXAR	16640	128	39.1	38.3	18.8	3.1	0.8	29253	35393	11	22	114	24.6	21.9	21.1	29.8	2.6	96667
72517	BROCKWELL	16461	283	42.1	32.9	19.1	4.2	1.8	31144	35892	15	35	249	36.1	25.7	23.7	11.7	2.8	73214
72519	CALICO ROCK	15327	940	43.4	33.0	18.1	2.5	3.1	29649	34616	12	24	716	33.9	28.8	26.1	10.8	0.4	71702
72520	CAMP	19899	188	42.0	24.5	25.5	3.7	4.3	31365	38977	16	38	162	21.6	29.0	32.1	16.7	0.6	88750
72521	CAVE CITY	15011	1378	41.4	35.1	20.2	2.7	0.6	30856	35373	14	32	1042	35.6	40.0	18.4	4.7	1.3	61825
72522	CHARLOTTE	19087	197	30.5	33.5	30.0	4.6	1.5	39745	48294	45	83	167	36.5	30.5	23.4	9.0	0.6	67727
72523	CONCORD	17154	554	37.2	34.3	23.8	3.1	1.6	33656	39535	23	53	473	46.9	29.4	17.8	5.9	0.0	52544
72524	CORD	21484	138	30.4	33.3	29.0	3.6	3.6	37978	46447	39	79	117	32.5	29.9	29.1	8.6	0.0	74091
72526	CUSHMAN	16238	89	31.5	41.6	25.8	1.1	0.0	33189	39679	21	50	73	52.1	30.1	11.0	6.9	0.0	48750
72527	DESHA	19793	148	16.9	45.3	32.4	3.4	2.0	40498	48373	48	84	125	16.0	28.8	48.0	4.8	2.4	94063
72528	DOLPH	17923	170	52.4	24.1	18.8	2.9	1.8	23466	27719	4	5	143	29.4	24.5	28.7	14.7	2.8	85417
	ARKANSAS	20565		33.0	30.6	26.7	6.4	3.3	37742	46417				27.1	29.3	31.4	10.3	1.8	80466
	UNITED STATES	25866		24.7	27.1	30.8	10.9	6.5	48124	56710				10.9	15.0	33.7	30.1	10.4	145905

#	POST OFFICE NAME	FINANCIAL SERVICES: Auto Loan	Home Loan	Invest-ments	Retire-ment Plans	THE HOME: Home Improvements: Home Repair	Lawn & Garden	Furnishings: Comput-ers & Hard-ware	Major Appli-ances	TV, Radio, Sound Equip-ment	Furni-ture	ENTERTAINMENT: Dine out/ Carry out	Sports Equip-ment	Fees & Tickets	Toys & Games	Travel	Cable TV	PERSONAL: Apparel & Services	Auto Repairs	Health Insur-ance	Pets & Supplies
72351	KEISER	75	62	47	62	66	74	64	69	68	63	82	79	60	82	63	70	77	68	76	83
72354	LEPANTO	71	47	21	41	54	62	46	57	55	46	65	68	39	61	46	59	59	56	70	81
72355	LEXA	75	54	35	47	59	68	54	64	64	55	76	74	49	72	55	68	70	64	76	85
72358	LUXORA	55	42	32	39	45	51	45	49	50	44	61	58	41	58	44	52	57	50	56	62
72360	MARIANNA	54	40	34	36	42	50	44	48	51	44	60	54	40	56	43	54	57	49	56	59
72364	MARION	81	81	76	80	79	82	78	79	76	79	95	92	77	93	76	74	93	79	75	90
72365	MARKED TREE	60	44	32	40	48	57	48	53	55	47	65	60	43	60	47	59	60	54	64	67
72366	MARVELL	74	53	36	48	58	69	56	64	65	56	77	73	50	72	56	70	71	64	77	83
72367	MELLWOOD	38	29	28	26	30	36	32	34	38	33	45	37	30	40	32	40	42	35	41	41
72368	MORO	67	45	20	39	51	59	44	55	53	44	62	65	37	58	44	57	56	54	67	77
72369	ONEIDA	46	33	21	28	36	42	33	39	40	34	47	45	30	43	33	43	43	39	48	52
72370	OSCEOLA	61	51	44	48	53	59	53	56	58	52	70	65	50	68	53	60	67	57	62	69
72372	PALESTINE	77	51	23	44	58	67	50	62	60	51	70	74	42	67	51	65	64	62	77	88
72373	PARKIN	59	42	28	37	46	54	43	50	51	44	61	58	39	56	43	55	56	51	61	67
72374	POPLAR GROVE	77	52	24	45	58	67	50	62	60	51	71	74	43	67	51	65	65	62	77	88
72376	PROCTOR	84	65	40	59	69	77	62	72	69	64	83	85	56	79	62	72	78	72	81	95
72379	SNOW LAKE	70	47	21	41	53	62	46	57	55	46	65	68	39	61	46	59	59	56	70	81
72384	TURRELL	69	49	34	43	53	63	50	59	60	52	71	67	45	65	50	64	66	59	71	77
72386	TYRONZA	75	50	23	43	57	65	48	60	58	49	69	72	41	65	49	63	62	60	75	86
72390	WEST HELENA	55	46	45	42	46	55	49	51	55	50	66	57	47	63	48	57	63	52	58	61
72392	WHEATLEY	64	43	19	37	49	56	41	52	50	42	59	62	35	56	42	54	53	51	64	74
72394	WIDENER	98	66	30	57	75	86	64	80	77	65	90	95	54	85	65	83	82	79	98	113
72395	WILSON	83	71	55	71	74	84	73	78	77	71	94	89	70	93	72	79	88	77	84	92
72396	WYNNE	78	65	53	61	68	76	66	71	71	66	87	82	62	83	66	74	82	71	79	87
72401	JONESBORO	68	64	63	63	64	70	67	67	68	65	84	79	65	83	66	68	81	68	69	77
72404	JONESBORO	104	102	97	104	101	105	98	100	97	100	121	119	98	120	97	94	118	100	96	118
72410	ALICIA	71	47	21	41	54	62	46	57	55	47	65	68	39	61	46	59	59	57	70	81
72411	BAY	76	59	40	56	64	72	60	67	66	59	79	78	55	77	60	68	73	66	76	85
72412	BEECH GROVE	86	77	58	73	81	87	71	79	75	71	92	94	70	94	73	77	87	77	85	102
72413	BIGGERS	67	45	20	39	51	59	43	54	52	44	61	65	37	58	44	56	56	54	67	77
72414	BLACK OAK	84	56	25	49	64	73	54	68	66	55	77	81	46	73	55	71	70	67	84	96
72415	BLACK ROCK	73	49	22	42	55	64	47	59	57	48	67	70	40	63	48	61	61	58	73	84
72416	BONO	82	67	48	64	71	79	66	74	71	66	86	86	62	84	66	73	81	72	81	93
72417	BROOKLAND	83	65	44	62	70	79	66	74	73	65	87	85	61	85	66	75	81	73	83	93
72419	CARAWAY	67	45	20	39	51	59	44	54	53	44	62	65	37	58	44	57	56	54	67	77
72421	CASH	68	46	21	39	52	60	44	55	53	45	63	66	38	59	45	57	57	55	68	78
72422	CORNING	71	48	24	42	54	63	48	58	57	48	67	69	41	63	48	61	61	58	71	80
72424	DATTO	103	69	31	59	78	90	66	83	80	68	94	99	57	89	68	86	86	82	102	118
72425	DELAPLAINE	74	50	24	44	57	65	48	60	58	49	68	72	42	65	49	62	62	59	73	85
72426	DELL	86	58	26	50	65	75	56	70	67	57	79	83	47	74	57	72	71	69	86	99
72428	ETOWAH	67	45	21	39	51	59	44	55	53	44	62	65	37	58	44	56	56	54	67	77
72429	FISHER	70	47	21	41	53	61	45	57	55	46	64	68	39	61	46	59	58	56	70	81
72430	GREENWAY	100	67	30	58	76	87	64	80	78	66	91	96	55	86	65	84	83	80	99	114
72432	HARRISBURG	72	53	34	48	59	66	52	62	60	53	71	73	46	68	53	63	66	61	72	83
72433	HOXIE	72	48	22	42	54	63	47	58	56	47	66	69	40	62	47	60	60	58	72	82
72434	IMBODEN	80	54	24	46	61	70	52	65	63	53	74	78	44	69	53	67	67	64	80	92
72435	KNOBEL	59	40	18	34	45	52	38	48	46	39	54	57	33	51	39	50	49	48	59	68
72436	LAFE	78	52	24	45	59	68	50	63	61	51	71	75	43	67	51	65	65	62	77	89
72437	LAKE CITY	87	58	27	50	66	76	56	70	68	57	80	84	48	76	57	73	73	70	87	100
72438	LEACHVILLE	86	57	26	49	65	75	55	69	67	56	78	83	47	74	56	72	71	68	85	98
72440	LYNN	74	50	22	43	56	65	48	60	58	49	68	71	41	64	49	62	62	59	74	85
72441	MC DOUGAL	68	46	21	40	52	60	44	55	53	45	63	66	38	59	45	58	57	55	68	79
72442	MANILA	78	52	24	45	59	68	50	63	61	51	71	75	43	67	51	65	65	62	77	89
72443	MARMADUKE	73	49	23	43	55	64	47	59	57	48	67	70	40	63	48	61	61	58	72	83
72444	MAYNARD	70	47	21	41	53	61	45	57	55	46	64	68	39	61	46	59	59	56	70	81
72445	MINTURN	67	45	20	39	51	58	43	54	52	44	61	64	37	58	44	56	56	53	66	77
72447	MONETTE	70	51	31	47	56	66	54	62	62	52	73	70	48	69	54	66	66	61	74	78
72449	O KEAN	74	50	22	43	56	65	48	60	58	49	68	72	41	64	49	62	62	59	74	85
72450	PARAGOULD	87	68	45	63	73	83	67	76	75	67	90	89	62	88	68	78	83	75	88	99
72453	PEACH ORCHARD	61	41	18	35	46	53	39	49	47	40	56	59	33	53	40	51	51	49	61	70
72454	PIGGOTT	74	54	32	50	60	69	55	64	63	54	75	74	49	71	56	67	68	63	76	84
72455	POCAHONTAS	73	56	36	52	61	70	57	65	64	56	76	75	51	73	57	67	70	64	76	83
72456	POLLARD	69	46	21	40	52	60	45	56	54	45	63	67	38	60	45	58	57	55	69	79
72457	PORTIA	73	49	22	42	56	64	47	59	57	48	67	71	40	64	48	62	61	59	73	84
72458	POWHATAN	70	47	21	41	53	61	45	57	55	46	64	68	39	61	46	59	58	56	70	80
72459	RAVENDEN	62	41	19	36	47	54	40	50	48	41	57	60	34	54	41	52	52	50	62	71
72460	RAVENDEN SPRINGS	78	52	24	45	59	68	50	63	61	51	71	75	43	67	51	65	65	62	78	89
72461	RECTOR	70	51	30	47	56	66	53	61	61	52	72	70	47	68	53	65	66	61	74	79
72464	SAINT FRANCIS	75	50	23	43	57	65	48	60	58	49	68	72	41	65	49	63	62	60	74	86
72465	SEDGWICK	115	77	35	66	87	100	74	93	89	75	105	111	63	99	75	96	95	92	114	131
72466	SMITHVILLE	71	48	22	41	54	62	46	57	55	47	65	69	39	61	47	60	59	57	71	82
72467	STATE UNIVERSITY	84	56	26	49	64	74	54	68	66	56	77	81	46	73	55	71	70	67	84	97
72469	STRAWBERRY	82	55	25	48	62	72	53	67	64	54	75	79	45	71	54	69	68	66	82	94
72470	SUCCESS	103	69	31	59	78	90	66	83	80	68	94	99	56	89	67	86	85	82	102	118
72471	SWIFTON	66	44	20	38	50	58	43	54	52	44	61	64	36	57	44	56	55	53	66	76
72472	TRUMANN	67	49	28	44	54	62	48	57	55	48	65	67	43	63	48	58	60	56	67	77
72473	TUCKERMAN	62	46	29	44	51	60	50	56	57	48	67	63	45	63	50	60	61	56	67	69
72476	WALNUT RIDGE	70	51	30	47	56	66	53	61	61	52	72	70	47	68	53	64	65	61	73	79
72478	WARM SPRINGS	81	54	25	47	62	71	52	66	63	53	74	78	45	70	53	68	68	65	81	93
72479	WEINER	88	63	37	59	71	83	66	77	75	64	89	89	58	85	67	80	81	76	92	100
72482	WILLIFORD	64	49	31	44	54	63	48	57	55	47	65	66	43	63	50	59	60	56	68	76
72501	BATESVILLE	83	65	45	61	71	80	65	73	72	64	86	86	60	84	66	75	80	73	84	95
72512	HORSESHOE BEND	66	57	52	52	61	74	54	63	59	57	73	63	53	63	58	64	67	62	76	74
72513	ASH FLAT	69	52	33	49	57	68	56	63	63	54	74	71	50	70	56	67	68	62	75	77
72515	BEXAR	76	51	23	44	58	67	49	62	60	50	70	74	42	66	50	64	64	61	76	88
72517	BROCKWELL	79	53	24	46	60	69	51	64	62	52	73	77	44	69	52	67	66	63	79	91
72519	CALICO ROCK	73	52	30	48	58	68	55	63	63	53	74	73	48	70	55	67	68	63	77	82
72520	CAMP	93	63	30	56	72	83	62	77	74	63	87	91	53	83	63	79	79	76	94	107
72521	CAVE CITY	69	47	24	42	53	62	47	57	56	47	66	67	41	62	48	60	60	57	70	78
72522	CHARLOTTE	87	60	29	52	67	77	58	71	69	59	81	85	50	77	59	73	74	70	86	100
72523	CONCORD	81	54	25	47	62	71	52	66	63	53	74	78	45	70	53	68	68	65	81	93
72524	CORD	86	69	45	63	74	82	64	75	72	65	86	89	60	85	66	75	80	73	85	100
72526	CUSHMAN	71	48	22	41	54	62	46	58	56	47	65	69	39	62	47	60	59	57	71	82
72527	DESHA	78	70	53	66	74	79	65	72	69	65	83	85	63	85	66	70	79	70	77	92
72528	DOLPH	67	45	20	39	51	59	44	55	53	44	62	65	37	58	44	57	56	54	67	77
	ARKANSAS	81	69	57	66	72	80	69	75	74	69	90	87	65	87	69	76	85	75	82	92
	UNITED STATES	100	100	100	100	100	100	100	100	100	100	100	100	100	100	100	100	100	100	100	100

ARKANSAS

POPULATION CHANGE

A 72529-72721

ZIP CODE		COUNTY FIPS CODE	POPULATION			2000-2004 ANNUAL RATE		HOUSEHOLDS					FAMILIES		
#	POST OFFICE NAME		2000	2004	2009	% Rate	State Centile	2000	2004	2009	% Annual Rate 2000-2004	2004 Average HH Size	2000	2004	% Annual Rate 2000-2004
72529	CHEROKEE VILLAGE	135	4584	4809	5122	1.1	72	2153	2266	2423	1.2	2.11	1556	1612	0.8
72530	DRASCO	023	1744	1856	2004	1.5	80	726	781	853	1.7	2.38	550	585	1.5
72531	ELIZABETH	049	790	790	800	0.0	35	352	356	365	0.3	2.22	250	249	-0.1
72532	EVENING SHADE	135	1657	1887	2095	3.1	96	679	780	872	3.3	2.41	498	563	2.9
72533	FIFTY SIX	137	349	356	361	0.5	53	149	154	158	0.8	2.31	111	113	0.4
72534	FLORAL	063	1236	1273	1305	0.7	61	476	495	513	0.9	2.57	364	373	0.6
72536	FRANKLIN	065	455	455	457	0.0	35	187	188	190	0.1	2.39	140	138	-0.3
72537	GAMALIEL	005	877	906	947	0.8	64	388	403	424	0.9	2.25	273	278	0.4
72538	GEPP	049	396	387	385	-0.5	16	160	158	158	-0.3	2.45	118	115	-0.6
72539	GLENCOE	049	654	643	639	-0.4	21	255	252	251	-0.3	2.52	198	194	-0.5
72540	GUION	065	267	268	268	0.1	38	111	113	114	0.4	2.36	76	76	0.0
72542	HARDY	135	3822	3998	4242	1.1	71	1599	1685	1798	1.2	2.37	1109	1150	0.9
72543	HEBER SPRINGS	023	10878	11799	12897	1.9	86	4679	5123	5654	2.2	2.25	3271	3525	1.8
72544	HENDERSON	005	684	707	738	0.8	65	288	300	316	1.0	2.36	202	206	0.5
72546	IDA	023	64	66	70	0.7	63	27	28	30	0.9	2.36	20	21	1.2
72550	LOCUST GROVE	063	641	643	654	0.1	38	256	261	268	0.5	2.46	197	197	0.0
72553	MAGNESS	063	311	316	320	0.4	49	131	135	139	0.7	2.34	91	92	0.3
72554	MAMMOTH SPRING	049	4088	4192	4256	0.6	58	1722	1781	1820	0.8	2.35	1267	1290	0.4
72555	MARCELLA	137	627	640	648	0.5	53	252	260	265	0.7	2.46	187	190	0.4
72556	MELBOURNE	065	2308	2492	2612	1.8	84	1007	1104	1170	2.2	2.19	663	714	1.8
72560	MOUNTAIN VIEW	137	6719	6901	7022	0.6	59	2824	2937	3017	0.9	2.30	2002	2049	0.6
72561	MOUNT PLEASANT	065	1455	1451	1452	-0.1	32	582	587	593	0.2	2.47	431	428	-0.2
72562	NEWARK	063	2198	2218	2247	0.2	43	873	895	918	0.6	2.48	638	642	0.2
72564	OIL TROUGH	063	534	530	536	-0.2	28	231	232	238	0.1	2.28	174	172	-0.3
72565	OXFORD	065	891	897	897	0.2	41	360	366	369	0.4	2.45	264	265	0.1
72566	PINEVILLE	065	430	421	419	-0.5	18	175	171	171	-0.5	1.81	125	121	-0.3
72567	PLEASANT GROVE	137	858	870	878	0.3	48	343	351	357	0.5	2.48	262	265	0.3
72568	PLEASANT PLAINS	063	1645	1705	1749	0.9	67	633	663	688	1.1	2.57	484	499	0.7
72569	POUGHKEEPSIE	135	689	703	735	0.5	53	272	280	294	0.7	2.51	208	212	0.5
72571	ROSIE	063	496	542	572	2.1	88	177	195	208	2.3	2.78	142	155	2.1
72572	SAFFELL	075	211	209	207	-0.2	27	87	87	87	0.0	2.40	64	63	-0.4
72573	SAGE	065	248	270	283	2.0	87	102	113	121	2.4	2.32	70	76	2.0
72576	SALEM	049	3144	3199	3226	0.4	50	1309	1347	1368	0.7	2.32	896	905	0.2
72577	SIDNEY	135	905	934	980	0.7	63	308	321	340	1.0	2.72	236	242	0.6
72578	STURKIE	049	159	155	154	-0.6	14	61	60	60	-0.4	2.58	46	44	-1.0
72579	SULPHUR ROCK	063	1011	1074	1116	1.4	79	388	418	440	1.8	2.57	289	307	1.4
72581	TUMBLING SHOALS	023	1049	1099	1178	1.1	72	452	479	520	1.4	2.29	338	353	1.0
72583	VIOLA	049	987	963	954	-0.6	14	401	394	393	-0.4	2.44	298	289	-0.7
72584	VIOLET HILL	065	311	309	308	-0.2	29	133	133	134	0.0	2.32	100	99	-0.2
72585	WIDEMAN	065	144	145	145	0.2	41	57	58	58	0.4	2.47	42	42	0.0
72587	WISEMAN	065	19	19	19	0.0	35	8	8	8	0.0	2.38	6	6	0.0
72601	HARRISON	009	27395	28235	29108	0.7	62	11203	11669	12145	1.0	2.37	7882	8078	0.6
72611	ALPENA	015	1483	1626	1745	2.2	89	574	634	684	2.4	2.56	438	476	2.0
72616	BERRYVILLE	015	9543	10211	10959	1.6	82	3634	3877	4158	1.5	2.60	2589	2719	1.2
72617	BIG FLAT	005	226	228	235	0.2	43	103	105	110	0.5	2.17	75	75	0.0
72619	BULL SHOALS	089	2367	2531	2699	1.6	82	1167	1255	1345	1.7	2.01	772	815	1.3
72623	CLARKRIDGE	005	702	755	806	1.7	83	282	306	330	1.9	2.47	226	242	1.6
72624	COMPTON	101	242	240	239	-0.2	27	111	113	115	0.4	2.12	82	82	0.0
72626	COTTER	005	1151	1176	1223	0.5	54	566	587	616	0.9	2.00	357	363	0.4
72628	DEER	101	1436	1411	1398	-0.4	20	590	594	603	0.2	2.37	408	404	-0.2
72629	DENNARD	141	1370	1327	1313	-0.8	11	554	543	542	-0.5	2.44	399	385	-0.8
72631	EUREKA SPRINGS	015	3220	3656	4045	3.0	95	1519	1737	1929	3.2	2.09	1103	1238	2.8
72632	EUREKA SPRINGS	015	4337	4594	4931	1.4	77	2008	2136	2298	1.5	2.11	1173	1227	1.1
72633	EVERTON	009	1242	1256	1275	0.3	45	471	484	497	0.6	2.60	375	380	0.3
72634	FLIPPIN	089	4304	4779	5201	2.5	92	1775	1982	2171	2.6	2.40	1268	1391	2.2
72635	GASSVILLE	005	3081	3254	3441	1.3	76	1224	1310	1402	1.6	2.41	893	940	1.2
72638	GREEN FOREST	015	7111	7488	7961	1.2	75	2583	2714	2884	1.2	2.76	1901	1961	0.7
72639	HARRIET	129	1012	1022	1043	0.2	44	420	431	448	0.6	2.37	321	325	0.3
72640	HASTY	101	275	284	288	0.8	64	108	114	118	1.3	2.49	82	86	1.1
72641	JASPER	101	1953	1968	1973	0.2	41	816	841	862	0.7	2.28	532	537	0.2
72642	LAKEVIEW	005	2014	2116	2232	1.2	73	1007	1065	1133	1.3	1.99	698	725	0.9
72644	LEAD HILL	009	2059	2153	2232	1.1	71	871	921	963	1.3	2.27	623	646	0.9
72645	LESLIE	129	1799	1882	1960	1.1	71	817	871	923	1.5	2.16	550	575	1.1
72648	MARBLE FALLS	101	892	894	894	0.1	36	350	358	366	0.5	2.49	258	260	0.2
72650	MARSHALL	129	2908	2923	2978	0.1	40	1248	1275	1319	0.5	2.25	857	860	0.1
72651	MIDWAY	005	1030	1082	1142	1.2	73	446	473	504	1.4	2.29	319	333	1.0
72653	MOUNTAIN HOME	005	26313	27547	29072	1.1	71	11767	12437	13256	1.3	2.17	8038	8348	0.9
72655	MOUNT JUDEA	101	912	895	886	-0.4	20	375	377	382	0.1	2.36	280	278	-0.2
72658	NORFORK	005	1530	1561	1621	0.5	53	641	663	696	0.8	2.35	470	479	0.5
72660	OAK GROVE	015	556	565	589	0.4	49	210	215	224	0.6	2.63	161	161	0.0
72661	OAKLAND	089	577	605	638	1.1	72	276	291	308	1.3	2.08	209	217	0.9
72662	OMAHA	009	2495	2717	2872	2.0	87	1010	1117	1194	2.4	2.43	753	819	2.0
72663	ONIA	137	480	485	488	0.2	45	195	199	203	0.5	2.44	149	150	0.2
72666	PARTHENON	101	563	557	554	-0.3	25	242	245	249	0.3	2.27	167	166	-0.1
72668	PEEL	089	658	700	744	1.5	80	303	323	345	1.5	2.17	217	228	1.2
72669	PINDALL	129	483	493	505	0.5	53	186	192	200	0.8	2.57	133	135	0.4
72670	PONCA	101	288	286	285	-0.2	29	114	116	118	0.4	2.47	84	84	0.0
72675	SAINT JOE	129	1624	1669	1724	0.7	60	667	691	723	0.8	2.41	477	486	0.4
72679	TILLY	115	66	70	74	1.4	78	30	32	34	1.5	2.19	23	24	1.0
72680	TIMBO	137	1318	1331	1341	0.2	44	549	561	570	0.5	2.37	413	417	0.2
72682	VALLEY SPRINGS	089	226	230	239	0.4	50	91	94	98	0.8	2.44	69	70	0.3
72683	VENDOR	101	816	801	794	-0.4	20	314	315	320	0.1	2.52	237	235	-0.2
72685	WESTERN GROVE	101	1046	1079	1094	0.7	63	416	437	453	1.2	2.47	317	329	0.9
72686	WITTS SPRINGS	129	676	677	689	0.0	36	277	282	292	0.4	2.40	199	199	0.0
72687	YELLVILLE	089	7595	7834	8209	0.7	63	2990	3100	3266	0.9	2.49	2202	2254	0.6
72701	FAYETTEVILLE	143	32357	35079	39163	1.9	86	12448	13700	15558	2.3	2.24	6705	7257	1.9
72703	FAYETTEVILLE	143	26145	29206	33457	2.6	93	11314	12805	14814	3.0	2.20	5995	6596	2.3
72704	FAYETTEVILLE	143	14269	16530	19187	3.5	98	5597	6539	7622	3.7	2.53	3791	4328	3.2
72712	BENTONVILLE	007	24819	30073	36182	4.6	99	9288	11324	13668	4.8	2.63	6700	8039	4.4
72714	BELLA VISTA	007	10042	11505	13417	3.3	97	4675	5357	6249	3.3	2.12	3482	3936	2.9
72715	BELLA VISTA	007	6227	6908	7922	2.5	91	3045	3393	3901	2.6	2.04	2466	2712	2.3
72717	CANEHILL	143	979	996	1075	0.4	50	366	376	408	0.6	2.62	281	284	0.3
72718	CAVE SPRINGS	007	803	920	1073	3.3	97	305	351	410	3.4	2.62	249	284	3.1
72719	CENTERTON	007	2327	2945	3602	5.7	100	791	1006	1232	5.8	2.92	632	792	5.5
72721	COMBS	087	669	648	637	-0.8	11	256	249	246	-0.8	2.60	195	188	-0.9
	ARKANSAS					0.9					1.1	2.47			0.8
	UNITED STATES					1.2					1.3	2.58			1.1

#	POST OFFICE NAME	RACE (%) White 2000	White 2004	Black 2000	Black 2004	Asian/Pacific 2000	Asian/Pacific 2004	% Hispanic Origin 2000	% Hispanic Origin 2004	2004 AGE DISTRIBUTION (%) 0-4	5-9	10-14	15-19	20-24	25-44	45-64	65-84	85+	18+	MEDIAN AGE 2004	% 2004 Males	% 2004 Females
72529	CHEROKEE VILLAGE	96.8	96.6	0.2	0.2	0.3	0.3	0.9	1.0	4.1	4.0	4.5	4.3	3.7	15.5	26.8	33.2	4.0	84.8	56.9	47.8	52.2
72530	DRASCO	98.6	98.5	0.0	0.0	0.1	0.1	0.6	0.7	5.6	5.9	6.2	5.0	5.1	25.4	29.6	15.8	1.5	79.3	43.0	50.0	50.1
72531	ELIZABETH	98.2	98.1	0.1	0.1	0.5	0.6	0.6	0.6	4.7	4.9	5.6	5.1	4.8	22.3	31.0	19.9	1.8	81.8	46.7	51.5	48.5
72532	EVENING SHADE	97.6	97.5	0.6	0.6	0.0	0.0	0.7	0.7	5.1	5.6	7.1	5.9	5.1	24.3	29.9	15.2	1.8	78.6	42.8	48.4	51.6
72533	FIFTY SIX	98.6	98.6	0.0	0.0	0.0	0.0	0.9	0.8	4.8	5.3	6.2	5.9	5.1	20.5	33.2	17.4	1.7	79.8	46.2	48.9	51.1
72534	FLORAL	98.5	98.4	0.1	0.1	0.1	0.1	1.1	1.2	6.2	6.2	6.6	7.0	7.0	25.8	26.3	13.4	1.5	76.7	39.4	49.7	50.4
72536	FRANKLIN	97.8	97.4	0.2	0.2	0.0	0.0	1.1	1.3	5.3	5.9	7.3	5.9	4.8	26.8	27.5	14.5	2.0	77.8	41.1	49.0	51.0
72537	GAMALIEL	98.8	98.6	0.0	0.0	0.1	0.1	0.5	0.6	4.8	5.1	6.1	4.0	4.0	21.5	31.9	21.4	1.3	81.8	48.8	51.0	49.0
72538	GEPP	98.7	99.0	0.0	0.0	0.0	0.0	0.5	0.5	6.5	6.5	6.5	6.2	5.2	25.1	27.4	14.7	2.1	76.7	40.3	48.3	51.7
72539	GLENCOE	97.6	97.5	0.2	0.2	0.2	0.2	0.6	0.6	5.3	5.6	6.7	6.1	5.3	22.2	29.7	17.4	1.7	78.5	44.2	50.4	49.6
72540	GUION	96.6	96.6	1.1	1.1	0.0	0.0	0.8	1.1	4.9	5.6	6.0	4.9	4.1	19.8	34.0	19.4	1.5	80.2	48.6	47.8	52.2
72542	HARDY	96.9	96.7	0.1	0.1	0.2	0.3	1.1	1.4	5.5	5.5	5.6	5.4	5.1	21.1	28.9	21.0	2.0	80.1	46.4	48.9	51.2
72543	HEBER SPRINGS	98.1	97.9	0.2	0.2	0.3	0.4	1.4	1.7	5.0	5.1	5.9	5.8	5.2	22.6	26.7	20.4	3.2	80.3	45.2	47.5	52.5
72544	HENDERSON	98.4	98.3	0.2	0.1	0.3	0.3	0.4	0.3	4.0	4.2	5.2	4.0	4.1	19.2	33.0	24.3	2.0	84.0	51.9	51.1	48.9
72546	IDA	98.4	98.5	0.0	0.0	0.0	0.0	0.0	0.0	6.1	6.1	6.1	4.6	6.1	24.2	27.3	18.2	1.5	81.8	42.5	51.5	48.5
72550	LOCUST GROVE	97.4	97.1	0.3	0.3	0.6	0.8	0.5	0.5	6.2	6.1	6.1	6.5	7.0	28.2	27.2	11.8	0.9	77.6	39.1	50.7	49.3
72553	MAGNESS	98.1	97.8	0.0	0.0	0.0	0.0	1.3	1.6	6.0	6.0	6.3	7.3	6.0	25.3	27.9	12.7	2.5	77.9	40.4	50.0	50.0
72554	MAMMOTH SPRING	97.1	96.8	0.3	0.4	0.2	0.2	0.4	0.4	5.2	5.4	6.3	6.0	5.2	21.4	29.1	19.4	2.2	79.5	45.4	48.9	51.1
72555	MARCELLA	96.8	96.6	0.2	0.2	0.0	0.0	1.0	1.1	5.5	5.9	6.4	6.1	5.2	23.4	29.8	16.3	1.4	78.4	43.2	50.2	49.8
72556	MELBOURNE	97.9	97.6	0.2	0.2	0.1	0.2	0.5	0.6	6.3	6.3	6.2	5.3	5.5	25.4	25.2	16.7	3.1	78.2	41.2	47.5	52.5
72560	MOUNTAIN VIEW	97.0	96.8	0.0	0.0	0.1	0.1	1.1	1.3	5.4	5.6	5.9	6.0	5.4	22.1	28.6	18.6	2.5	79.4	44.7	48.4	51.6
72561	MOUNT PLEASANT	98.5	98.3	0.3	0.3	0.2	0.2	0.9	1.1	6.6	6.7	6.3	6.4	5.7	25.6	27.2	13.9	1.6	76.6	39.9	51.1	48.9
72562	NEWARK	97.1	96.8	0.4	0.5	0.4	0.5	0.8	1.0	7.2	7.0	6.6	6.6	6.6	27.5	25.7	10.7	2.0	75.2	37.1	49.0	51.0
72564	OIL TROUGH	95.7	95.5	0.9	1.1	0.0	0.0	0.4	0.4	5.7	5.5	7.2	7.2	6.6	25.9	28.1	12.6	1.3	77.7	39.6	50.8	49.3
72565	OXFORD	97.1	96.7	0.1	0.1	0.1	0.1	1.1	1.3	6.2	6.0	5.8	6.4	6.1	23.3	29.8	14.4	2.0	78.0	42.2	50.3	49.7
72566	PINEVILLE	90.2	89.3	7.7	8.3	0.2	0.2	0.9	1.2	4.0	4.3	5.2	5.2	7.1	36.8	25.2	10.7	1.4	82.9	38.7	62.5	37.5
72567	PLEASANT GROVE	97.8	97.7	0.1	0.1	0.0	0.0	0.6	0.8	6.0	6.3	6.9	6.1	5.1	24.5	28.9	15.1	1.3	77.0	41.7	50.5	49.5
72568	PLEASANT PLAINS	97.0	96.7	0.1	0.1	0.2	0.2	2.0	2.4	6.3	6.3	7.2	6.9	6.7	27.7	24.7	13.1	1.0	75.8	38.5	51.2	48.8
72569	POUGHKEEPSIE	96.7	96.3	2.0	2.1	0.0	0.0	1.0	1.3	6.1	6.3	6.5	6.1	5.8	25.6	27.7	14.5	1.3	77.2	40.9	51.5	48.5
72571	ROSIE	98.0	97.8	0.2	0.2	0.0	0.0	0.8	0.7	8.1	7.8	6.8	7.0	6.5	26.8	24.9	11.4	0.7	73.1	37.0	51.3	48.7
72572	SAFFELL	99.5	99.5	0.0	0.0	0.0	0.0	0.0	0.0	7.2	7.7	7.2	5.7	5.3	24.9	26.3	13.9	1.9	74.6	38.4	50.7	49.3
72573	SAGE	98.4	97.8	0.0	0.0	0.0	0.4	0.8	0.7	6.7	6.7	6.3	5.6	5.9	26.3	24.8	15.2	2.6	77.0	40.2	48.5	51.5
72576	SALEM	97.9	97.6	0.2	0.2	0.2	0.3	0.7	0.8	6.5	6.2	5.9	6.1	5.9	23.1	25.7	17.4	3.3	77.4	42.2	47.9	52.1
72577	SIDNEY	97.2	97.2	0.8	0.8	0.0	0.0	0.4	0.4	7.0	7.0	6.9	5.3	5.1	28.3	22.4	13.0	5.3	75.9	38.8	48.8	51.2
72578	STURKIE	98.7	98.7	0.0	0.0	0.0	0.0	1.3	0.7	7.1	6.5	6.5	6.5	5.8	23.2	27.7	14.8	1.9	76.1	41.1	49.0	51.0
72579	SULPHUR ROCK	96.7	96.5	0.6	0.7	0.1	0.2	1.6	1.8	6.1	6.2	6.0	6.7	6.9	26.8	28.2	11.6	1.7	77.8	39.2	51.6	48.4
72581	TUMBLING SHOALS	98.8	98.7	0.0	0.0	0.0	0.0	0.5	0.6	4.7	5.0	5.2	4.6	4.0	24.2	32.0	18.9	1.4	82.4	46.5	48.9	51.1
72583	VIOLA	98.8	98.8	0.1	0.1	0.1	0.1	0.7	0.8	6.4	6.4	6.4	6.4	5.7	24.4	27.6	14.6	1.9	76.7	40.6	49.8	50.2
72584	VIOLET HILL	97.4	97.4	0.0	0.0	0.0	0.0	1.0	1.3	5.8	6.2	6.5	6.2	5.2	25.2	28.8	14.6	1.6	78.0	41.6	50.2	49.8
72585	WIDEMAN	96.5	96.6	0.7	0.7	0.0	0.0	1.4	1.4	5.5	5.5	6.2	6.2	6.2	23.5	31.0	13.8	2.1	78.6	42.8	51.0	49.0
72587	WISEMAN	94.7	100.0	0.0	0.0	0.0	0.0	0.0	0.0	10.5	10.5	5.3	10.5	10.5	31.6	21.1	0.0	0.0	73.7	26.3	47.4	52.6
72601	HARRISON	97.7	97.4	0.1	0.1	0.4	0.4	1.1	1.3	6.4	6.3	6.6	6.2	6.5	25.8	25.2	14.6	2.5	77.0	39.6	48.2	51.8
72611	ALPENA	97.6	97.3	0.1	0.1	0.4	0.6	1.4	1.7	6.3	6.7	7.2	6.6	6.2	25.8	27.4	12.6	1.2	75.7	38.8	50.6	49.4
72616	BERRYVILLE	94.0	93.1	0.0	0.0	0.4	0.5	10.5	12.4	7.5	7.2	6.8	6.5	6.4	26.9	23.8	12.9	2.0	74.6	37.3	49.6	50.4
72617	BIG FLAT	97.8	96.9	0.4	0.4	0.4	0.4	0.4	0.4	4.4	5.3	5.3	5.7	4.8	21.1	30.7	20.6	2.2	81.1	47.9	49.1	50.9
72619	BULL SHOALS	98.0	97.8	0.3	0.2	0.3	0.4	0.9	1.0	3.7	3.6	3.8	3.3	3.6	15.2	31.3	31.3	4.3	86.8	57.4	49.3	50.7
72623	CLARKRIDGE	98.2	98.0	0.0	0.0	0.4	0.5	1.0	1.1	3.3	5.2	7.3	6.6	3.3	27.3	32.9	13.1	1.1	79.9	43.4	51.7	48.3
72624	COMPTON	97.9	97.9	0.4	0.4	0.0	0.0	1.2	0.8	5.8	5.8	6.7	6.3	7.1	26.3	28.8	12.1	1.3	77.5	40.3	52.1	47.9
72626	COTTER	97.2	97.0	0.0	0.0	0.2	0.3	1.7	1.9	5.6	5.5	5.1	4.9	6.0	23.8	28.7	18.5	2.0	81.0	44.4	48.8	51.2
72628	DEER	97.1	97.0	0.1	0.1	0.1	0.1	1.0	1.0	4.8	5.4	6.6	6.2	5.7	23.6	32.0	14.0	1.7	79.2	43.6	52.2	47.8
72629	DENNARD	95.5	95.0	0.6	0.6	0.3	0.5	1.1	1.3	5.6	5.9	7.0	6.0	5.7	24.0	27.9	16.4	1.6	77.9	42.1	51.4	48.6
72631	EUREKA SPRINGS	96.7	96.3	0.2	0.2	0.4	0.5	1.7	2.2	3.3	3.8	4.5	4.4	4.0	17.9	36.8	23.3	2.0	85.5	52.1	49.5	50.5
72632	EUREKA SPRINGS	95.3	94.7	0.1	0.1	0.6	0.7	3.3	4.0	3.8	4.1	4.1	4.6	4.6	20.5	37.6	18.2	2.5	84.9	49.8	47.4	52.6
72633	EVERTON	98.5	98.3	0.1	0.1	0.3	0.4	0.7	0.8	5.8	7.6	7.3	6.8	5.7	28.0	26.3	11.3	1.3	75.1	37.5	48.7	51.4
72634	FLIPPIN	96.8	96.5	0.2	0.2	0.3	0.4	0.8	0.9	6.0	6.2	6.4	6.8	5.2	24.5	27.9	15.3	1.8	77.1	41.8	49.0	51.0
72635	GASSVILLE	98.0	97.7	0.1	0.1	0.2	0.3	1.2	1.4	6.0	6.3	7.2	6.2	5.1	25.5	25.5	15.6	2.6	76.5	40.5	47.5	52.6
72638	GREEN FOREST	90.2	88.9	0.2	0.2	0.5	0.6	17.6	20.3	8.2	7.8	7.5	6.7	7.0	29.3	22.2	10.3	1.1	72.5	34.0	50.7	49.3
72639	HARRIET	97.1	96.9	0.1	0.1	0.1	0.2	1.2	1.4	5.1	5.3	5.4	5.8	5.1	24.4	31.1	16.1	1.8	80.7	44.4	51.8	48.2
72640	HASTY	98.2	98.2	0.0	0.0	0.4	0.4	1.1	1.1	6.3	6.3	7.4	7.0	6.0	27.8	26.8	10.9	1.4	75.7	38.0	48.9	51.1
72641	JASPER	96.7	96.7	0.2	0.2	0.2	0.2	1.2	1.2	6.4	6.3	6.2	5.4	6.1	22.7	28.4	15.5	3.1	77.4	42.8	49.9	50.2
72642	LAKEVIEW	98.2	97.9	0.1	0.1	0.5	0.6	1.0	1.3	2.9	2.9	3.4	3.5	3.4	13.0	28.8	37.9	4.3	88.7	60.7	49.2	50.9
72644	LEAD HILL	96.7	96.5	0.0	0.0	0.5	0.6	1.0	1.2	5.2	5.4	6.1	5.3	3.8	22.2	29.0	20.9	2.1	79.9	46.6	50.7	49.3
72645	LESLIE	97.9	97.7	0.0	0.0	0.4	0.4	0.9	1.1	5.7	5.8	5.8	5.6	5.6	22.1	29.1	17.6	2.7	79.3	44.5	49.0	51.0
72648	MARBLE FALLS	97.8	97.8	0.2	0.2	0.2	0.2	1.1	1.1	5.9	5.9	6.7	6.3	6.7	26.4	28.6	12.2	1.2	77.7	40.1	50.5	49.6
72650	MARSHALL	97.8	97.6	0.1	0.1	0.0	0.0	0.8	0.9	5.5	5.5	5.7	6.2	5.9	23.2	25.9	18.7	3.5	79.2	43.7	47.6	52.4
72651	MIDWAY	97.7	97.3	0.0	0.0	0.2	0.3	1.3	1.5	4.4	4.4	4.8	4.5	4.4	18.3	29.7	26.8	2.6	83.6	52.0	49.6	50.4
72653	MOUNTAIN HOME	97.8	97.5	0.1	0.1	0.4	0.5	1.0	1.2	4.5	4.5	5.1	5.0	5.1	19.6	28.3	24.1	4.0	82.8	50.0	47.9	52.2
72655	MOUNT JUDEA	97.7	97.7	0.1	0.1	0.1	0.1	0.8	0.9	6.4	6.2	6.2	6.7	6.4	23.4	28.8	14.4	1.7	76.8	41.3	51.5	48.5
72658	NORFORK	97.5	97.3	0.5	0.5	0.1	0.2	0.6	0.8	4.8	5.5	6.1	5.8	4.6	21.7	30.9	18.7	1.9	80.0	46.1	49.9	50.1
72660	OAK GROVE	96.4	95.9	0.0	0.0	0.4	0.4	1.1	1.4	6.7	6.7	7.3	6.9	7.1	25.7	26.7	11.9	1.1	75.0	38.0	50.3	49.7
72661	OAKLAND	97.8	97.7	0.0	0.0	0.4	0.5	0.2	0.2	2.3	2.5	3.1	3.3	3.3	12.2	38.5	32.6	2.2	90.3	59.6	51.9	48.1
72662	OMAHA	97.2	96.9	0.1	0.1	0.2	0.2	0.8	1.0	6.7	6.8	6.4	6.0	5.7	26.1	27.8	13.3	1.1	76.4	40.1	51.0	49.0
72663	ONIA	97.7	97.5	0.0	0.0	0.0	0.0	1.5	1.7	6.4	6.6	6.6	5.4	4.3	23.7	29.1	16.5	1.4	77.1	43.0	50.1	49.9
72666	PARTHENON	97.0	97.0	0.2	0.2	0.2	0.2	1.2	1.3	5.2	5.8	7.2	6.1	5.2	23.3	30.9	14.5	1.8	77.9	43.2	51.7	48.3
72668	PEEL	97.9	97.7	0.0	0.0	0.0	0.0	0.5	0.7	3.9	3.9	3.7	5.1	4.6	19.3	35.7	22.3	1.6	85.6	51.3	52.1	47.9
72669	PINDALL	97.5	97.2	0.0	0.0	0.2	0.2	0.8	1.2	6.7	6.9	7.1	7.3	5.9	28.4	23.9	12.8	1.0	74.7	37.3	50.5	49.5
72670	PONCA	97.6	97.2	0.4	0.4	0.4	0.4	1.0	1.1	5.9	5.6	6.3	5.9	7.0	25.9	29.7	12.6	1.1	79.0	40.9	50.7	49.3
72675	SAINT JOE	96.1	95.8	0.0	0.0	0.1	0.2	1.2	1.4	6.4	6.4	6.5	6.6	5.9	24.5	27.4	14.7	1.7	76.8	40.9	51.7	48.4
72679	TILLY	98.5	98.6	0.0	0.0	0.0	0.0	0.0	1.4	4.3	5.7	8.6	8.6	5.7	24.3	27.1	14.3	1.4	77.1	40.8	51.4	48.6
72680	TIMBO	97.6	97.4	0.2	0.2	0.2	0.2	1.3	1.4	6.1	6.3	6.5	5.6	4.6	22.9	29.6	16.8	1.7	77.7	43.7	50.3	49.7
72682	VALLEY SPRINGS	97.8	97.4	0.0	0.0	0.4	0.4	1.3	1.7	5.7	6.1	6.5	7.0	6.1	22.6	29.1	15.7	1.3	77.4	42.5	51.7	48.3
72683	VENDOR	97.8	97.8	0.1	0.3	0.1	0.1	1.0	1.0	6.6	6.4	6.4	7.0	6.0	23.9	27.8	14.2	1.8	75.5	40.7	51.6	48.4
72685	WESTERN GROVE	98.2	98.2	0.1	0.1	0.4	0.4	1.2	1.2	6.2	6.5	7.5	7.2	5.8	27.4	26.8	11.3	1.2	75.4	37.9	49.3	50.7
72686	WITTS SPRINGS	96.5	96.0	0.0	0.0	0.3	0.3	2.1	2.4	4.7	5.3	5.6	5.2	5.5	21.7	31.8	17.9	2.4	81.1	46.3	50.7	49.3
72687	YELLVILLE	97.7	97.5	0.1	0.1	0.2	0.2	0.7	0.8	5.4	5.6	6.6	7.1	5.7	22.9	29.1	15.7	2.0	78.0	42.9	49.9	50.2
72701	FAYETTEVILLE	87.4	86.2	4.4	4.4	2.7	3.3	4.4	5.1	5.9	5.2	5.3	11.7	16.4	27.8	19.4	7.2	1.2	80.5	28.2	51.0	49.0
72703	FAYETTEVILLE	89.1	88.0	4.1	4.2	2.2	2.6	4.1	4.8	6.4	5.3	5.0	6.7	17.4	28.6	19.1	9.3	2.2	80.1	29.9	50.2	49.8
72704	FAYETTEVILLE	89.4	88.0	3.7	4.2	1.4	1.7	4.0	4.9	8.4	7.1	6.6	6.7	12.8	34.2	17.9	5.8	0.6	74.3	28.8	51.3	48.8
72712	BENTONVILLE	91.9	90.8	0.8	0.8	2.1	2.4	5.4	6.4	8.4	7.6	7.8	6.9	7.5	31.3	20.3	9.0	1.1	72.1	32.7	48.4	51.6
72714	BELLA VISTA	97.7	97.4	0.2	0.2	0.3	0.4	1.1	1.4	4.3	4.1	4.2	3.8	3.1	18.0	25.6	32.9	4.1	85.0	56.0	47.8	52.2
72715	BELLA VISTA	98.1	97.9	0.1	0.2	0.3	0.3	0.8	0.9	2.9	2.9	3.1	2.5	2.2	12.7	26.9	44.4	2.5	89.6	63.5	49.1	50.9
72717	CANEHILL	92.2	91.5	0.5	0.6	0.1	0.1	2.3	2.7	7.1	7.1	6.4	7.6	5.5	26.3	26.2	12.5	1.2	74.1	38.3	51.2	48.8
72718	CAVE SPRINGS	96.0	95.5	0.5	0.5	0.4	0.5	1.5	1.9	7.7	8.2	7.3	6.2	4.0	29.6	27.3	8.9	0.9	73.0	37.9	49.5	50.5
72719	CENTERTON	95.6	95.1	0.2	0.2	0.2	0.2	3.4	4.0	9.6	9.3	8.5	6.8	5.9	31.7	20.0	7.5	0.8	68.4	32.0	49.2	50.8
72721	COMBS	97.2	96.9	0.0	0.0	0.2	0.2	1.2	1.1	6.0	7.4	7.4	6.5	6.0	26.5	27.5	11.3	1.4	74.5	38.1	49.2	50.8
	ARKANSAS	80.0	79.3	15.7	15.8	0.8	1.0	3.3	3.8	6.9	6.7	6.9	6.8	7.3	27.3	24.1	12.2	1.8	75.7	36.7	49.0	51.0
	UNITED STATES	75.1	73.6	12.3	12.5	3.8	4.2	12.5	14.1	6.9	6.7	7.2	7.0	7.3	28.6	23.8	10.8	1.7	75.1	36.0	49.1	50.9

ZIP CODE				2004 HOUSEHOLD INCOME DISTRIBUTION (%)					MEDIAN HOUSEHOLD INCOME					2004 HOME VALUE DISTRIBUTION (%)					
#	POST OFFICE NAME	2004 Per Capita Income	2004 HH Income Base	Less than $25,000	$25,000 to $49,999	$50,000 to $99,999	$100,000 to $149,999	$150,000 or More	2004	2009	2004 National Centile	2004 State Centile	2004 Home Value Base	Less than $50,000	$50,000 to $89,999	$90,000 to $174,999	$175,000 to $399,999	$400,000 or More	2004 Median Home Value
72529	CHEROKEE VILLAGE	19800	2266	36.7	42.4	14.3	4.2	2.4	31065	35880	15	34	1899	21.9	46.3	25.1	6.7	0.0	70536
72530	DRASCO	17937	781	32.5	36.5	25.5	4.2	1.3	35673	42217	30	67	658	30.2	21.1	36.3	10.6	1.7	88043
72531	ELIZABETH	17250	356	42.7	34.6	18.8	3.1	0.8	29229	34614	11	22	303	36.3	20.8	30.7	10.9	1.3	74091
72532	EVENING SHADE	17227	780	40.6	36.2	18.3	2.4	2.4	30965	35577	15	33	667	36.9	32.7	22.8	6.5	1.2	63308
72533	FIFTY SIX	18599	154	41.6	29.9	20.8	5.2	2.6	31648	37986	17	40	131	25.2	36.6	29.0	8.4	0.8	76818
72534	FLORAL	17170	495	34.8	36.4	23.6	4.0	1.2	35430	41728	29	65	418	39.7	29.0	26.8	4.3	0.2	62162
72536	FRANKLIN	17101	188	41.5	30.9	20.7	4.8	2.1	31813	37338	17	42	158	30.4	26.0	26.6	14.6	2.5	81667
72537	GAMALIEL	16377	403	38.5	33.5	26.8	1.2	0.0	30415	35440	13	29	334	25.2	19.8	33.8	21.3	0.0	111667
72538	GEPP	14465	158	40.5	41.1	15.2	1.9	1.3	30304	35364	13	28	130	36.9	28.5	19.2	15.4	0.0	65385
72539	GLENCOE	29112	252	30.6	36.9	24.2	3.2	5.2	35839	42596	31	68	224	25.5	32.1	20.1	17.4	4.9	77333
72540	GUION	15630	113	51.3	24.8	16.8	6.2	0.9	24190	30000	4	5	96	38.5	25.0	28.1	8.3	0.0	68000
72542	HARDY	15444	1685	49.8	31.6	13.7	3.2	1.8	25110	28748	5	7	1356	33.0	34.7	23.9	6.9	1.5	66690
72543	HEBER SPRINGS	22707	5123	33.6	32.3	23.6	6.5	4.0	36766	44222	35	72	3911	13.3	27.3	37.4	18.1	3.9	104016
72544	HENDERSON	16314	300	39.7	33.7	24.7	1.7	0.3	30000	35232	12	26	251	27.5	20.3	32.3	19.5	0.4	101563
72546	IDA	18129	28	32.1	39.3	25.0	3.6	0.0	35000	40000	28	63	24	33.3	20.8	37.5	8.3	0.0	85000
72550	LOCUST GROVE	23025	261	28.7	36.0	26.4	5.0	3.8	37287	44184	36	75	221	30.8	29.0	28.1	10.4	1.8	73750
72553	MAGNESS	21278	135	35.6	33.3	22.2	5.9	3.0	33368	40668	22	51	109	33.0	31.2	26.6	9.2	0.0	68750
72554	MAMMOTH SPRING	19315	1781	44.9	30.2	20.2	2.8	2.0	28219	33428	9	19	1451	36.3	32.5	23.1	7.0	1.1	64412
72555	MARCELLA	13479	260	53.9	29.2	13.5	2.3	1.2	23181	27524	3	4	215	35.8	26.5	25.6	8.4	3.7	70455
72556	MELBOURNE	16608	1104	44.8	30.8	19.5	3.8	1.1	28252	33040	9	19	789	32.3	32.1	26.1	9.1	0.4	68494
72560	MOUNTAIN VIEW	18814	2937	47.9	29.2	16.3	3.9	2.7	26192	30817	6	10	2263	27.2	29.7	32.1	9.8	1.2	81595
72561	MOUNT PLEASANT	15619	587	39.0	33.9	22.8	3.9	0.3	31988	37261	18	43	487	37.4	23.6	24.4	11.7	2.9	67000
72562	NEWARK	17690	895	35.9	32.6	26.3	3.9	1.3	34960	41075	27	61	698	37.8	29.4	24.5	7.5	0.9	63846
72564	OIL TROUGH	19681	232	30.2	39.2	27.6	1.3	1.7	35000	41855	28	63	191	39.8	37.7	19.4	3.1	0.0	57222
72565	OXFORD	16141	366	45.4	36.1	13.4	3.6	1.6	27523	32135	8	15	320	42.5	30.6	23.1	3.1	0.6	62424
72566	PINEVILLE	17811	171	49.1	27.5	18.1	2.9	2.3	25835	29284	6	9	139	30.9	26.6	27.3	13.0	2.2	81250
72567	PLEASANT GROVE	11957	351	57.8	27.6	12.0	2.6	0.0	22034	26134	3	2	293	43.0	25.9	20.8	3.4	6.8	62333
72568	PLEASANT PLAINS	18143	663	34.5	35.3	25.2	2.3	2.7	36624	43298	34	71	564	41.0	29.6	24.1	4.6	0.7	62075
72569	POUGHKEEPSIE	17253	280	35.0	34.3	24.3	5.0	1.4	35218	41270	28	64	241	37.8	29.9	20.8	7.9	3.7	64167
72571	ROSIE	23521	195	28.2	34.4	30.3	2.1	5.1	41687	49154	52	88	166	45.8	27.1	21.1	5.4	0.6	54118
72572	SAFFELL	16871	87	47.1	24.1	21.8	6.9	0.0	26369	33610	6	11	74	43.2	23.0	28.4	4.1	1.4	57143
72573	SAGE	15935	113	42.5	31.9	21.2	3.5	0.9	30272	33951	13	27	81	32.1	28.4	25.9	12.4	1.2	71667
72576	SALEM	17522	1347	46.3	29.6	17.9	3.6	2.7	27194	32490	7	13	1028	26.6	32.8	25.4	12.4	2.9	76250
72577	SIDNEY	14374	321	46.7	27.4	17.8	5.6	2.5	27916	31906	9	17	273	33.0	31.9	24.5	8.4	2.2	70227
72578	STURKIE	14952	60	38.3	38.3	18.3	5.0	0.0	31118	37333	15	35	50	24.0	34.0	26.0	14.0	2.0	80000
72579	SULPHUR ROCK	18475	418	32.1	34.0	27.3	5.5	1.2	36980	44587	35	73	349	37.5	29.2	22.6	9.5	1.2	65962
72581	TUMBLING SHOALS	19624	479	31.1	32.2	28.6	7.9	0.2	37698	44741	38	77	395	17.2	22.5	43.0	15.4	1.8	101705
72583	VIOLA	16963	394	40.9	37.6	16.5	3.6	1.5	30000	35772	12	26	329	29.2	29.5	25.5	14.3	1.5	75313
72584	VIOLET HILL	17836	133	42.9	33.1	18.1	4.5	1.5	30590	35438	14	30	116	36.2	27.6	25.0	9.5	1.7	71429
72585	WIDEMAN	12938	58	46.6	36.2	13.8	3.5	0.0	26789	30000	7	12	51	41.2	31.4	23.5	3.9	0.0	63000
72587	WISEMAN	10132	8	50.0	50.0	0.0	0.0	0.0	25000	25000	5	7	7	28.6	42.9	28.6	0.0	0.0	82500
72601	HARRISON	20035	11669	35.8	33.8	23.0	4.3	3.1	34443	40726	26	58	8443	13.4	31.2	39.9	13.5	2.0	95606
72611	ALPENA	17800	634	36.6	33.6	21.9	5.2	2.7	35363	41940	29	65	527	20.3	33.6	32.5	10.1	3.6	84306
72616	BERRYVILLE	17785	3877	37.6	31.7	23.8	4.2	2.7	32562	39717	19	46	2981	19.6	28.2	36.0	11.1	5.0	92848
72617	BIG FLAT	19712	105	30.5	37.1	27.6	4.8	0.0	36100	43176	32	69	88	22.7	26.1	36.4	14.8	0.0	93333
72619	BULL SHOALS	20886	1255	40.2	33.6	18.9	5.1	2.3	30731	35829	14	31	998	13.8	27.8	42.1	13.9	2.4	98936
72623	CLARKRIDGE	17045	306	32.4	40.2	22.9	2.9	1.6	34551	40696	26	58	273	16.9	26.0	38.5	15.0	3.7	96290
72624	COMPTON	17300	113	37.2	38.9	21.2	2.7	0.0	32868	36418	21	48	92	37.0	25.0	28.3	6.5	3.3	68889
72626	COTTER	21227	587	45.3	28.6	20.3	3.1	2.7	27784	32591	8	16	427	25.5	31.2	29.0	13.8	0.5	79625
72628	DEER	18190	594	47.8	31.7	14.8	3.2	2.5	26342	30678	6	10	507	37.1	26.8	27.0	7.1	2.0	68784
72629	DENNARD	19816	543	44.0	32.0	16.9	3.5	3.5	28111	34088	9	18	452	44.9	30.5	20.6	3.1	0.9	55111
72631	EUREKA SPRINGS	30524	1737	35.9	29.9	21.5	6.6	6.1	34974	43393	27	61	1458	12.1	15.0	37.7	29.6	5.6	139309
72632	EUREKA SPRINGS	23000	2136	41.3	28.8	18.7	6.2	4.9	30679	37568	14	30	1586	8.3	19.4	37.8	28.5	6.1	135204
72633	EVERTON	16839	484	34.1	31.8	28.1	4.6	1.5	36151	42414	32	69	402	25.4	33.3	34.6	5.5	1.2	78372
72634	FLIPPIN	17663	1982	41.3	32.8	21.6	3.2	1.1	30838	35746	14	32	1556	20.1	31.9	32.6	14.7	0.6	86893
72635	GASSVILLE	17313	1310	39.5	33.7	21.3	3.6	1.9	31785	37244	17	42	1027	20.3	37.7	29.0	11.3	1.8	79955
72638	GREEN FOREST	16265	2714	38.0	34.1	20.6	4.5	3.0	32966	40320	21	48	2037	27.6	33.3	26.6	7.6	4.9	75804
72639	HARRIET	12652	431	52.2	31.8	13.7	1.6	0.7	23486	27012	4	5	368	49.7	27.2	18.5	4.6	0.0	50345
72640	HASTY	16199	114	36.8	40.4	18.4	3.5	0.9	31899	37290	18	42	95	32.6	27.4	29.5	10.5	0.0	66875
72641	JASPER	16946	841	47.9	28.2	19.0	2.5	2.4	26369	30451	6	11	638	33.7	29.9	27.4	7.2	1.7	68333
72642	LAKEVIEW	22182	1065	34.1	40.1	20.5	3.9	1.5	33420	38856	22	52	911	15.4	24.6	40.4	17.6	2.1	102250
72644	LEAD HILL	18456	921	40.0	38.0	16.6	3.7	1.7	30947	35969	15	33	767	28.3	34.2	26.9	9.8	0.9	74467
72645	LESLIE	13926	871	53.0	31.7	12.9	1.5	0.9	22735	26544	3	3	680	40.7	28.4	25.4	4.6	0.9	59844
72648	MARBLE FALLS	15059	358	37.4	38.8	21.0	2.5	0.3	32215	37321	18	44	292	35.6	26.0	28.1	8.2	2.1	68276
72650	MARSHALL	15750	1275	49.3	30.7	16.6	2.3	1.2	25443	29424	5	9	950	40.8	34.5	18.2	5.6	0.8	58131
72651	MIDWAY	22167	473	36.8	36.2	19.9	4.0	3.2	32441	38258	19	45	407	22.1	23.3	36.1	15.5	3.0	95441
72653	MOUNTAIN HOME	20748	12437	35.5	35.9	20.9	5.0	2.7	33644	39809	23	53	9874	13.6	23.6	45.4	15.6	1.9	104556
72655	MOUNT JUDEA	17714	377	45.9	35.8	13.3	2.9	2.1	27127	31718	7	13	322	43.8	25.5	23.3	6.5	0.9	59091
72658	NORFORK	16924	663	37.7	35.9	21.9	2.6	2.0	32166	37841	18	44	557	33.6	19.8	34.1	12.4	0.2	83393
72660	OAK GROVE	17862	215	39.5	32.1	20.0	5.6	2.8	30357	35637	13	28	176	30.1	19.3	30.1	14.2	6.3	90526
72661	OAKLAND	21999	291	42.3	28.2	19.2	5.2	5.2	29872	35467	12	25	262	18.3	31.3	26.0	22.9	1.5	91667
72662	OMAHA	19202	1117	37.3	32.7	22.7	3.2	4.1	33345	40000	22	51	904	26.0	23.2	35.8	11.3	3.7	91129
72663	ONIA	17868	199	43.2	31.2	17.6	4.5	3.5	28357	34113	9	20	169	31.4	40.8	20.7	6.5	0.6	65000
72666	PARTHENON	17673	245	47.8	30.2	16.3	2.9	2.9	26356	31046	6	10	209	30.6	25.4	31.6	10.5	1.9	79643
72668	PEEL	20760	323	39.9	31.9	20.7	3.7	3.7	31054	36311	15	34	284	23.6	26.4	36.6	11.3	2.1	90000
72669	PINDALL	15475	192	47.4	34.9	13.0	2.1	2.6	26737	30679	7	12	158	41.1	31.7	20.9	5.1	1.3	58750
72670	PONCA	15006	116	37.9	38.8	20.7	2.6	0.0	32032	36719	18	43	95	35.8	26.3	27.4	7.4	3.2	68500
72675	SAINT JOE	15621	691	49.4	32.3	15.6	1.5	1.3	25412	29610	5	8	566	34.1	32.2	25.3	6.9	1.6	66481
72679	TILLY	24872	32	28.1	37.5	21.9	9.4	3.1	40000	45000	46	84	27	37.0	33.3	22.2	3.7	3.7	58750
72680	TIMBO	17525	561	44.2	31.4	16.9	4.3	3.2	28114	33164	9	18	474	33.8	39.2	20.0	6.3	0.6	63636
72682	VALLEY SPRINGS	14430	94	40.4	39.4	20.2	0.0	0.0	30965	37315	15	33	78	24.4	33.3	30.8	9.0	2.6	78571
72683	VENDOR	14060	315	46.7	36.2	13.3	2.5	1.3	26541	30498	6	12	268	43.7	22.4	25.8	7.5	0.8	60526
72685	WESTERN GROVE	16380	437	37.3	39.4	18.3	3.9	1.1	31765	37014	17	41	365	31.5	26.6	31.0	10.7	0.3	68793
72686	WITTS SPRINGS	15682	282	51.4	31.9	13.5	1.4	1.8	24093	28126	4	5	235	36.6	29.4	26.8	3.8	3.4	63261
72687	YELLVILLE	15600	3100	40.0	35.4	20.2	2.8	1.6	31229	36577	16	36	2513	26.1	29.4	33.9	9.1	1.4	80638
72701	FAYETTEVILLE	21970	13700	37.2	26.0	24.3	8.0	4.6	36252	45207	33	70	6972	10.2	22.5	37.9	24.9	4.6	115751
72703	FAYETTEVILLE	24269	12805	33.8	28.3	25.3	7.9	4.7	38328	46574	40	79	5644	8.0	13.3	46.2	26.4	6.1	133895
72704	FAYETTEVILLE	21657	6539	24.9	32.9	32.3	7.3	2.8	43485	52478	57	91	4170	14.1	17.5	52.2	13.8	2.5	106369
72712	BENTONVILLE	25275	11324	20.9	32.6	30.3	9.2	7.0	46621	56904	65	94	7639	6.8	22.5	44.5	20.7	5.6	115152
72714	BELLA VISTA	30419	5357	15.7	32.4	37.5	9.8	4.6	51273	61239	74	97	4570	3.4	19.7	53.8	21.3	2.0	124104
72715	BELLA VISTA	33005	3393	13.6	34.7	35.0	11.6	5.2	51212	62879	74	97	3040	3.1	12.1	48.5	31.0	5.4	154158
72717	CANEHILL	18011	376	33.2	33.0	27.1	4.3	2.4	36192	45375	32	70	314	22.9	29.3	35.4	10.2	2.2	86111
72718	CAVE SPRINGS	34846	351	17.7	24.5	29.6	16.2	12.0	62162	77183	86	99	319	8.5	10.3	28.8	36.7	15.7	182813
72719	CENTERTON	19503	1006	20.2	33.2	38.3	6.0	2.4	46614	55318	65	94	845	9.7	21.5	50.2	13.4	5.2	104808
72721	COMBS	13858	249	40.2	40.6	16.1	2.4	0.8	30156	35343	13	27	215	29.3	30.7	27.9	10.7	1.4	71154
	ARKANSAS	20565		33.0	30.6	26.7	6.4	3.3	37742	46417				27.1	29.3	31.4	10.3	1.8	80466
	UNITED STATES	25866		24.7	27.1	30.8	10.9	6.5	48124	56710				10.9	15.0	33.7	30.1	10.4	145905

ZIP CODE #	POST OFFICE NAME	FINANCIAL SERVICES: Auto Loan	Home Loan	Investments	Retirement Plans	THE HOME: Home Improvements: Home Repair	Lawn & Garden	Furnishings: Computers & Hardware	Major Appliances	TV, Radio, Sound Equipment	Furniture	ENTERTAINMENT: Dine out/ Carry out	Sports Equipment	Fees & Tickets	Toys & Games	Travel	Cable TV	PERSONAL: Apparel & Services	Auto Repairs	Health Insurance	Pets & Supplies
72529	CHEROKEE VILLAGE	63	57	54	53	60	73	55	63	60	58	73	62	54	63	59	64	68	61	74	70
72530	DRASCO	78	55	29	48	62	71	52	65	62	53	73	77	45	70	54	67	67	64	79	91
72531	ELIZABETH	65	51	36	45	55	65	48	58	55	50	66	63	44	60	50	59	61	57	70	74
72532	EVENING SHADE	78	52	24	45	59	68	51	63	61	52	72	76	43	68	52	66	65	63	78	90
72533	FIFTY SIX	81	54	25	47	61	71	52	65	63	53	74	78	45	70	53	68	67	65	81	93
72534	FLORAL	82	56	27	49	63	73	54	67	65	55	76	80	47	72	55	69	69	66	82	94
72536	FRANKLIN	76	52	24	45	58	67	51	62	61	51	71	74	43	67	51	65	65	62	77	87
72537	GAMALIEL	62	49	33	44	55	62	46	56	52	46	62	65	41	61	49	56	58	55	66	76
72538	GEPP	66	45	21	39	51	58	43	54	52	44	61	64	37	58	44	56	56	53	66	76
72539	GLENCOE	133	93	49	86	107	121	93	113	108	92	126	135	80	122	95	114	115	112	136	155
72540	GUION	63	49	33	44	55	62	47	56	53	46	62	65	42	62	50	56	58	55	66	76
72542	HARDY	62	45	28	42	50	59	48	55	54	46	64	62	42	60	48	58	58	54	66	70
72543	HEBER SPRINGS	86	67	47	63	73	85	68	77	75	67	90	87	62	85	69	80	83	76	91	97
72544	HENDERSON	63	52	41	47	57	66	49	58	54	50	65	64	45	62	52	58	61	57	69	75
72546	IDA	79	54	27	47	62	71	52	65	62	53	73	77	45	70	54	67	67	64	79	92
72550	LOCUST GROVE	93	80	58	75	85	92	74	83	80	74	97	99	72	98	76	82	91	81	92	109
72553	MAGNESS	94	63	28	54	71	82	61	76	73	62	86	91	52	81	62	79	78	75	93	108
72554	MAMMOTH SPRING	76	58	39	54	64	75	59	68	66	58	78	77	52	74	60	70	72	67	82	88
72555	MARCELLA	62	42	19	36	47	55	40	50	49	41	57	60	34	54	41	52	52	50	62	72
72556	MELBOURNE	60	45	30	43	50	59	49	55	55	47	65	62	43	62	49	58	59	55	66	68
72560	MOUNTAIN VIEW	79	55	28	49	61	71	55	66	65	55	76	78	47	72	55	69	69	66	81	90
72561	MOUNT PLEASANT	71	49	24	42	55	63	47	59	57	48	66	70	41	63	48	61	60	58	72	82
72562	NEWARK	80	57	29	50	63	72	54	66	64	55	75	79	48	72	55	68	69	65	80	92
72564	OIL TROUGH	85	57	26	49	64	74	55	68	66	56	78	82	47	73	56	71	70	68	84	97
72565	OXFORD	74	50	23	43	57	65	48	60	58	49	68	72	41	64	49	63	62	60	74	85
72566	PINEVILLE	70	48	24	42	54	62	48	58	57	48	66	68	41	63	48	61	60	57	71	79
72567	PLEASANT GROVE	56	37	17	32	42	49	36	45	44	37	51	54	31	48	37	47	46	45	56	64
72568	PLEASANT PLAINS	88	59	27	51	67	77	57	71	69	58	80	85	48	76	58	74	73	70	88	101
72569	POUGHKEEPSIE	82	55	25	47	62	71	53	66	64	54	75	79	45	71	54	69	68	65	81	94
72571	ROSIE	123	82	37	71	93	108	80	100	96	81	113	119	68	107	81	103	102	98	123	141
72572	SAFFELL	76	51	23	44	58	67	49	62	60	50	70	74	42	66	50	64	64	61	76	88
72573	SAGE	64	46	27	43	51	60	49	56	56	47	66	64	43	62	49	59	60	56	68	72
72576	SALEM	69	50	31	48	56	66	54	61	61	52	72	70	48	68	54	65	66	61	74	77
72577	SIDNEY	76	51	23	44	57	66	49	61	59	50	69	73	42	65	50	64	63	61	75	87
72578	STURKIE	71	49	24	44	56	64	48	59	56	48	66	71	41	63	49	60	60	58	72	83
72579	SULPHUR ROCK	89	60	27	52	68	78	58	72	70	59	82	86	49	77	59	75	74	72	89	103
72581	TUMBLING SHOALS	79	59	37	53	67	75	56	68	65	56	76	80	49	74	59	69	70	67	82	94
72583	VIOLA	77	52	25	47	60	68	51	63	60	51	71	76	43	68	52	65	65	63	77	89
72584	VIOLET HILL	78	52	24	45	59	68	50	63	61	51	71	75	43	67	51	65	65	62	78	89
72585	WIDEMAN	60	40	18	35	46	53	39	49	47	40	55	58	33	52	40	51	50	48	60	69
72587	WISEMAN	45	30	14	26	34	40	29	37	35	30	42	44	25	39	30	38	38	36	45	52
72601	HARRISON	79	62	44	59	67	77	63	71	70	62	84	82	58	82	64	73	78	70	82	89
72611	ALPENA	82	58	32	53	66	74	57	69	66	57	78	82	50	76	58	70	72	68	82	95
72616	BERRYVILLE	80	60	38	56	66	76	60	69	68	60	81	80	54	77	61	72	75	69	82	90
72617	BIG FLAT	81	54	24	47	61	70	52	65	63	53	74	78	44	70	53	68	67	64	80	93
72619	BULL SHOALS	62	59	60	54	62	75	54	64	59	59	73	61	55	62	60	63	68	61	75	70
72623	CLARKRIDGE	76	53	28	50	62	69	52	65	60	52	71	78	45	70	54	63	65	64	77	90
72624	COMPTON	69	46	21	40	52	60	45	56	54	46	63	67	38	60	45	58	58	55	69	79
72626	COTTER	71	52	33	49	57	68	56	63	64	54	75	72	50	71	56	67	68	63	76	79
72628	DEER	81	54	25	47	62	71	53	66	63	54	75	79	45	70	53	68	68	65	81	93
72629	DENNARD	91	61	28	53	69	80	59	74	71	60	84	88	51	79	60	77	76	73	91	104
72631	EUREKA SPRINGS	97	91	87	86	96	113	84	96	89	90	111	94	85	92	91	95	103	93	112	109
72632	EUREKA SPRINGS	67	69	80	69	70	77	68	70	68	69	86	77	70	82	71	70	83	70	72	77
72633	EVERTON	80	55	28	51	64	72	54	67	63	54	74	81	46	72	56	67	68	66	81	94
72634	FLIPPIN	79	54	25	46	61	70	52	65	62	53	73	77	44	69	53	67	67	64	80	91
72635	GASSVILLE	70	57	40	54	61	68	56	62	61	56	73	73	53	73	56	63	69	61	70	79
72638	GREEN FOREST	81	58	31	52	65	73	56	68	65	57	77	81	49	74	57	69	71	67	81	94
72639	HARRIET	54	37	19	33	42	49	37	45	44	37	52	53	32	49	38	48	47	45	55	62
72640	HASTY	76	51	23	44	58	66	49	61	59	50	70	73	42	66	50	64	63	61	76	87
72641	JASPER	68	48	27	44	54	63	50	59	58	49	68	68	44	65	50	62	62	58	71	77
72642	LAKEVIEW	64	62	65	56	65	79	57	67	62	62	77	62	59	64	63	66	71	64	78	72
72644	LEAD HILL	73	56	39	49	62	72	53	65	61	56	74	71	49	67	56	66	67	63	78	83
72645	LESLIE	51	37	22	34	41	48	39	45	45	38	53	51	35	50	39	48	48	45	54	57
72648	MARBLE FALLS	71	47	22	41	54	62	46	57	55	47	65	68	39	61	47	59	59	57	70	81
72650	MARSHALL	61	44	26	41	49	58	46	53	53	45	63	61	41	59	46	57	57	53	65	69
72651	MIDWAY	85	67	50	61	74	87	64	77	73	66	87	84	59	79	68	78	80	75	92	98
72653	MOUNTAIN HOME	71	60	50	57	65	77	60	68	66	61	79	71	57	71	63	70	73	67	80	80
72655	MOUNT JUDEA	79	53	24	46	60	69	51	64	62	52	72	76	43	68	52	66	66	63	79	91
72658	NORFORK	74	50	24	44	57	66	49	61	58	50	69	72	42	65	50	63	63	60	75	85
72660	OAK GROVE	88	59	27	51	67	77	57	71	69	58	81	85	49	77	58	74	74	71	88	101
72661	OAKLAND	69	65	62	61	69	81	60	68	63	64	79	67	61	66	65	68	74	66	80	78
72662	OMAHA	87	59	28	52	67	77	57	71	68	58	80	85	49	76	58	73	73	71	87	101
72663	ONIA	82	55	25	47	62	72	53	66	64	54	75	79	45	71	54	69	68	66	82	94
72666	PARTHENON	76	51	23	44	57	66	49	61	59	50	69	73	42	65	50	64	63	61	75	87
72668	PEEL	72	62	52	58	67	78	58	68	63	60	77	72	56	69	62	67	72	66	79	84
72669	PINDALL	74	50	23	43	56	65	49	60	58	49	69	72	42	65	49	63	62	60	74	85
72670	PONCA	70	47	21	40	53	61	45	56	54	46	64	67	38	60	46	59	58	56	69	80
72675	SAINT JOE	67	47	25	42	52	61	48	57	56	47	66	66	42	62	48	60	60	56	69	76
72679	TILLY	102	69	31	59	78	89	66	83	80	67	94	99	56	89	67	86	85	82	102	118
72680	TIMBO	78	52	24	45	59	68	51	63	61	52	72	76	43	68	51	66	65	63	78	90
72682	VALLEY SPRINGS	66	44	20	38	50	58	43	54	52	44	61	64	36	57	44	56	55	53	66	76
72683	VENDOR	67	45	20	39	51	58	43	54	52	44	61	65	37	58	44	56	56	54	67	77
72685	WESTERN GROVE	76	51	23	44	58	67	49	62	59	50	70	74	42	66	50	64	63	61	76	87
72686	WITTS SPRINGS	71	47	22	41	54	62	46	57	55	47	65	68	39	61	47	60	59	57	71	81
72687	YELLVILLE	71	50	26	44	56	64	49	59	57	49	68	69	42	64	50	62	62	59	72	81
72701	FAYETTEVILLE	76	67	72	69	68	74	78	73	78	74	97	90	74	95	74	75	93	77	72	85
72703	FAYETTEVILLE	75	67	79	71	67	72	82	74	80	78	100	92	77	97	76	75	97	80	69	83
72704	FAYETTEVILLE	81	72	73	75	72	77	78	77	78	77	98	93	75	94	75	75	94	80	74	90
72712	BENTONVILLE	97	96	95	98	95	98	95	96	93	96	117	112	94	115	93	90	113	96	90	108
72714	BELLA VISTA	99	92	88	88	98	115	85	97	90	91	112	95	86	93	93	96	105	94	114	111
72715	BELLA VISTA	102	95	91	90	101	119	88	100	93	94	116	98	89	97	96	99	108	97	117	115
72717	CANEHILL	89	60	27	52	68	78	58	72	70	59	82	86	49	77	59	75	74	71	89	103
72718	CAVE SPRINGS	119	147	156	147	145	143	131	131	122	131	153	154	140	163	134	118	153	126	118	145
72719	CENTERTON	91	81	62	77	86	92	75	83	80	75	97	99	74	99	77	82	92	81	90	108
72721	COMBS	68	45	21	39	52	59	44	55	53	45	62	66	37	59	45	57	57	54	68	78
	ARKANSAS	81	69	57	66	72	80	69	75	74	69	90	87	65	87	69	76	85	75	82	92
	UNITED STATES	100	100	100	100	100	100	100	100	100	100	100	100	100	100	100	100	100	100	100	100

ARKANSAS
POPULATION CHANGE

A 72722-72955

# POST OFFICE NAME	COUNTY FIPS CODE	POPULATION 2000	2004	2009	2000-2004 ANNUAL RATE % Rate	State Centile	HOUSEHOLDS 2000	2004	2009	% Annual Rate 2000-2004	2004 Average HH Size	FAMILIES 2000	2004	% Annual Rate 2000-2004
72722 DECATUR	007	2805	3095	3546	2.3	91	994	1103	1265	2.5	2.81	778	852	2.2
72727 ELKINS	143	3187	3797	4445	4.2	99	1176	1416	1667	4.5	2.68	913	1083	4.1
72729 EVANSVILLE	143	270	275	297	0.4	50	105	108	117	0.7	2.52	81	82	0.3
72730 FARMINGTON	143	5947	6525	7335	2.2	90	2180	2408	2719	2.4	2.71	1612	1752	2.0
72732 GARFIELD	007	4526	5031	5778	2.5	92	1729	1930	2219	2.6	2.61	1323	1457	2.3
72734 GENTRY	007	6893	7749	8958	2.8	94	2548	2881	3336	2.9	2.69	1951	2174	2.6
72736 GRAVETTE	007	5071	5716	6626	2.9	95	1873	2115	2454	2.9	2.68	1405	1566	2.6
72738 HINDSVILLE	087	1754	1803	1882	0.7	60	658	682	717	0.9	2.64	512	523	0.5
72739 HIWASSE	007	453	574	704	5.7	100	169	216	265	5.9	2.66	136	172	5.7
72740 HUNTSVILLE	087	8696	9167	9481	1.3	75	3318	3519	3655	1.4	2.58	2447	2554	1.0
72742 KINGSTON	087	671	642	630	-1.0	6	276	266	263	-0.9	2.41	208	199	-1.0
72744 LINCOLN	143	4430	4653	5110	1.2	73	1739	1841	2030	1.4	2.52	1283	1335	0.9
72745 LOWELL	007	9067	11103	13390	4.9	99	3416	4184	5040	4.9	2.64	2630	3182	4.6
72747 MAYSVILLE	007	190	202	227	1.5	80	67	71	80	1.4	2.85	53	55	0.9
72749 MORROW	143	28	29	31	0.8	66	4	4	4	0.0	7.00	3	3	0.0
72751 PEA RIDGE	007	3953	4496	5228	3.1	96	1432	1629	1892	3.1	2.75	1142	1284	2.8
72752 PETTIGREW	087	463	439	430	-1.2	5	194	186	183	-1.0	2.36	132	125	-1.3
72753 PRAIRIE GROVE	143	6261	6753	7519	1.8	84	2315	2514	2811	2.0	2.66	1783	1909	1.6
72756 ROGERS	007	35650	40261	46747	2.9	95	13378	15051	17434	2.8	2.66	9724	10769	2.4
72758 ROGERS	007	18697	21043	24351	2.8	94	6720	7527	8688	2.7	2.76	5099	5637	2.4
72760 SAINT PAUL	087	658	630	618	-1.0	7	272	262	259	-0.9	2.40	193	184	-1.1
72761 SILOAM SPRINGS	007	15780	17097	19456	1.9	85	5647	6153	7044	2.0	2.64	4088	4397	1.7
72762 SPRINGDALE	143	26220	29213	33371	2.6	92	9316	10407	11917	2.6	2.77	7085	7792	2.3
72764 SPRINGDALE	143	32449	37385	43321	3.4	97	11551	13197	15247	3.2	2.80	8340	9370	2.8
72768 SULPHUR SPRINGS	007	1562	1666	1870	1.5	81	534	570	640	1.6	2.87	395	415	1.2
72769 SUMMERS	143	950	971	1051	0.5	54	336	347	377	0.8	2.80	271	276	0.4
72773 WESLEY	087	1668	1611	1583	-0.8	10	627	608	601	-0.7	2.65	496	477	-0.9
72774 WEST FORK	143	5540	5856	6452	1.3	76	2072	2208	2444	1.5	2.65	1620	1702	1.2
72776 WITTER	087	230	222	218	-0.8	9	83	81	80	-0.6	2.74	61	58	-1.2
72801 RUSSELLVILLE	115	16786	17579	18606	1.1	71	6594	6971	7462	1.3	2.30	4130	4276	0.8
72802 RUSSELLVILLE	115	17272	17933	18829	0.9	68	6401	6713	7110	1.1	2.66	4892	5050	0.8
72820 ALIX	047	476	494	511	0.9	67	183	191	199	1.0	2.59	131	135	0.7
72821 ALTUS	047	2802	2868	2945	0.6	56	1089	1125	1165	0.8	2.55	809	823	0.4
72823 ATKINS	115	6732	6993	7356	0.9	68	2559	2679	2842	1.1	2.57	1947	2014	0.9
72824 BELLEVILLE	149	1183	1305	1449	2.3	91	455	503	558	2.4	2.59	352	384	2.1
72826 BLUE MOUNTAIN	083	189	197	202	1.0	69	72	76	79	1.3	2.59	54	56	0.9
72827 BLUFFTON	149	163	172	187	1.3	75	70	74	80	1.3	2.32	52	54	0.9
72828 BRIGGSVILLE	149	148	156	169	1.3	75	59	62	67	1.2	2.52	44	45	0.5
72830 CLARKSVILLE	071	14349	14929	15637	0.9	69	5509	5730	6005	0.9	2.51	3837	3920	0.5
72832 COAL HILL	071	1387	1413	1463	0.4	51	548	559	579	0.5	2.53	395	397	0.1
72833 DANVILLE	149	4358	4639	5043	1.5	80	1462	1547	1676	1.3	2.86	1077	1124	1.0
72834 DARDANELLE	149	9847	10577	11572	1.7	83	3745	4026	4401	1.7	2.60	2773	2935	1.3
72835 DELAWARE	083	775	789	799	0.4	50	317	327	335	0.7	2.41	223	225	0.2
72837 DOVER	115	7351	7672	8120	1.0	70	2764	2908	3103	1.2	2.64	2160	2246	0.9
72838 GRAVELLY	149	166	173	186	1.0	69	68	71	76	1.0	2.44	51	52	0.5
72839 HAGARVILLE	071	709	716	737	0.2	44	269	273	282	0.4	2.62	205	205	0.0
72840 HARTMAN	071	995	1075	1148	1.8	84	389	422	451	1.9	2.55	291	311	1.6
72841 HARVEY	127	261	264	272	0.3	46	100	102	105	0.5	2.59	78	78	0.0
72842 HAVANA	149	1375	1446	1565	1.2	73	541	569	614	1.2	2.50	394	407	0.8
72843 HECTOR	115	2892	2986	3132	0.8	64	1082	1128	1193	1.0	2.65	844	869	0.7
72845 KNOXVILLE	071	1128	1166	1217	0.8	65	423	437	456	0.8	2.67	330	338	0.6
72846 LAMAR	071	3642	3981	4285	2.1	88	1367	1502	1617	2.2	2.64	1005	1087	1.9
72847 LONDON	115	1933	2181	2391	2.9	95	745	848	937	3.1	2.57	568	638	2.8
72851 NEW BLAINE	083	1001	1029	1049	0.7	60	416	432	445	0.9	2.38	303	309	0.5
72852 OARK	071	246	245	253	-0.1	31	102	102	106	0.0	2.40	75	74	-0.3
72853 OLA	149	2105	2225	2412	1.3	76	797	837	905	1.2	2.59	556	574	0.8
72854 OZONE	071	351	352	362	0.1	38	136	137	142	0.2	2.57	102	102	0.0
72855 PARIS	083	6830	6766	6840	-0.2	27	2775	2777	2833	0.0	2.37	1902	1869	-0.4
72856 PELSOR	115	63	62	64	-0.4	22	26	26	27	0.0	2.38	21	21	0.0
72857 PLAINVIEW	149	1405	1519	1668	1.9	85	581	629	690	1.9	2.41	412	439	1.5
72858 POTTSVILLE	115	1829	2052	2243	2.7	94	691	781	861	2.9	2.63	551	617	2.7
72860 ROVER	149	389	410	444	1.2	75	144	152	164	1.3	2.70	107	111	0.9
72863 SCRANTON	083	1520	1658	1746	2.1	88	555	610	648	2.3	2.72	444	481	1.9
72865 SUBIACO	083	1163	1216	1263	1.1	70	411	435	456	1.3	2.75	317	331	1.0
72901 FORT SMITH	131	22062	21694	22187	-0.4	21	9081	8924	9142	-0.4	2.33	5163	4925	-1.1
72903 FORT SMITH	131	25080	25934	27088	0.8	65	10564	11013	11568	1.0	2.27	6672	6791	0.4
72904 FORT SMITH	131	19649	19990	20725	0.4	50	7305	7410	7678	0.3	2.68	4931	4901	-0.1
72905 FORT SMITH	131	47	54	58	3.3	97	7	8	9	3.2	6.63	6	7	3.7
72908 FORT SMITH	131	11799	12093	12516	0.6	57	4689	4845	5039	0.8	2.48	3416	3461	0.3
72916 FORT SMITH	131	5271	5994	6537	3.1	96	2123	2452	2705	3.5	2.44	1552	1740	2.7
72921 ALMA	033	11386	11873	12390	1.0	69	4181	4398	4622	1.2	2.70	3293	3417	0.9
72923 BARLING	131	4149	4542	4849	2.2	88	1599	1767	1899	2.4	2.53	1117	1209	1.9
72924 BATES	127	196	200	207	0.5	53	80	82	85	0.6	2.44	59	60	0.4
72926 BOLES	127	783	793	818	0.3	47	317	323	335	0.4	2.46	252	254	0.2
72927 BOONEVILLE	083	8686	8728	8819	0.1	39	3255	3293	3353	0.3	2.57	2400	2392	-0.1
72928 BRANCH	047	640	617	624	-0.9	9	255	248	254	-0.7	2.49	199	192	-0.8
72930 CECIL	047	260	266	273	0.5	56	101	104	108	0.7	2.54	77	79	0.6
72932 CEDARVILLE	033	1060	1204	1308	3.0	95	380	438	481	3.4	2.75	306	348	3.1
72933 CHARLESTON	047	5077	5373	5626	1.3	77	1973	2111	2231	1.6	2.50	1425	1500	1.2
72934 CHESTER	033	865	916	964	1.4	77	318	340	361	1.6	2.69	243	257	1.3
72936 GREENWOOD	131	12099	13291	14200	2.2	90	4329	4789	5140	2.4	2.73	3490	3809	2.1
72937 HACKETT	131	3445	3544	3658	0.7	61	1333	1382	1433	0.9	2.56	1031	1050	0.4
72938 HARTFORD	131	1397	1432	1475	0.6	57	528	544	563	0.7	2.63	399	403	0.2
72940 HUNTINGTON	131	2782	2877	2977	0.8	65	1046	1089	1132	1.0	2.63	813	832	0.6
72941 LAVACA	131	4630	4951	5217	1.6	82	1719	1849	1957	1.7	2.67	1392	1476	1.4
72943 MAGAZINE	083	1955	2126	2236	2.0	87	738	811	862	2.2	2.62	554	600	1.9
72944 MANSFIELD	127	3138	3258	3399	0.9	68	1187	1239	1298	1.0	2.62	877	899	0.6
72946 MOUNTAINBURG	033	3627	3698	3804	0.5	52	1394	1435	1487	0.7	2.58	1045	1059	0.4
72947 MULBERRY	033	3883	3956	4054	0.4	51	1513	1555	1606	0.7	2.49	1135	1148	0.3
72948 NATURAL DAM	033	479	554	606	3.5	98	180	211	234	3.8	2.63	146	170	3.7
72949 OZARK	047	8468	8670	8911	0.6	57	3243	3344	3464	0.7	2.49	2300	2335	0.4
72950 PARKS	127	460	465	479	0.3	45	195	198	205	0.4	2.35	152	153	0.2
72951 RATCLIFF	083	611	600	602	-0.4	20	234	233	236	-0.1	2.58	174	171	-0.4
72952 RUDY	033	3077	3389	3626	2.3	90	1122	1250	1349	2.6	2.71	907	998	2.3
72955 UNIONTOWN	033	479	557	612	3.6	98	163	192	213	3.9	2.90	130	150	3.4
ARKANSAS					0.9					1.1	2.47			0.8
UNITED STATES					1.2					1.3	2.58			1.1

19-A

ZIP CODE #	POST OFFICE NAME	RACE (%) White 2000	White 2004	Black 2000	Black 2004	Asian/Pacific 2000	Asian/Pacific 2004	% Hispanic Origin 2000	% Hispanic Origin 2004	2004 AGE DISTRIBUTION (%) 0-4	5-9	10-14	15-19	20-24	25-44	45-64	65-84	85+	18+	MEDIAN AGE 2004	% 2004 Males	% 2004 Females
72722	DECATUR	89.0	87.7	0.0	0.0	0.4	0.4	7.6	9.0	8.1	7.7	7.4	7.8	7.0	29.2	22.8	9.1	0.8	72.1	33.8	52.2	47.8
72727	ELKINS	96.2	95.7	0.4	0.5	0.2	0.2	1.7	2.0	7.2	7.3	7.6	6.9	6.5	28.1	26.1	9.4	0.8	73.6	36.6	50.5	49.5
72729	EVANSVILLE	92.2	91.6	0.7	0.7	0.0	0.0	1.9	2.2	7.3	7.3	6.2	7.6	5.5	25.8	26.2	12.7	1.5	74.2	38.6	51.3	48.7
72730	FARMINGTON	93.6	93.0	1.0	1.1	0.5	0.6	3.1	3.6	7.9	7.6	7.5	6.3	8.2	31.5	21.2	8.9	0.8	73.3	32.5	49.8	50.2
72732	GARFIELD	95.4	94.9	0.0	0.0	0.2	0.3	3.4	4.1	6.3	6.4	7.4	6.7	5.8	25.4	28.7	12.4	0.9	75.8	40.3	51.5	48.5
72734	GENTRY	90.5	89.5	0.1	0.1	0.3	0.4	4.8	5.8	7.6	7.4	7.7	7.6	7.1	29.0	23.2	9.4	1.1	72.7	34.4	50.2	49.8
72736	GRAVETTE	92.3	91.6	0.3	0.2	0.3	0.3	3.9	4.6	7.7	7.3	7.8	7.7	6.1	26.8	24.0	11.0	1.7	72.4	36.2	49.4	50.6
72738	HINDSVILLE	96.8	96.4	0.3	0.3	0.1	0.1	2.2	2.5	6.4	6.4	6.2	5.8	5.7	26.8	27.8	13.4	1.5	77.4	40.5	50.9	49.1
72739	HIWASSE	96.5	96.0	0.0	0.2	0.0	0.0	2.0	2.6	8.2	7.8	7.1	6.1	5.1	27.7	22.1	14.6	1.2	72.8	36.6	49.5	50.5
72740	HUNTSVILLE	95.2	94.6	0.1	0.1	0.2	0.2	4.0	4.7	6.8	6.7	7.6	7.0	6.1	24.9	25.5	13.1	2.3	74.7	38.5	49.8	50.2
72742	KINGSTON	96.1	96.1	0.0	0.0	0.2	0.2	0.6	0.8	6.1	6.4	6.9	6.7	5.5	23.5	29.8	13.6	1.7	77.0	41.9	50.2	49.8
72744	LINCOLN	92.8	92.0	0.1	0.1	0.2	0.3	4.0	4.7	7.5	7.3	7.1	6.4	6.3	27.0	25.1	11.5	1.7	74.2	36.7	49.7	50.3
72745	LOWELL	92.7	91.3	0.6	0.6	2.0	2.4	4.9	6.2	9.1	8.3	6.5	5.5	5.5	34.1	22.1	8.2	0.8	72.8	33.5	50.3	49.7
72747	MAYSVILLE	92.6	92.6	0.0	0.0	0.5	0.5	1.6	1.5	9.4	8.9	7.9	7.4	5.9	27.7	23.3	8.4	1.0	68.8	33.2	51.0	49.0
72749	MORROW	92.9	93.1	0.0	0.0	0.0	0.0	0.0	0.0	6.9	6.9	6.9	6.9	6.9	27.6	27.6	10.3	0.0	79.3	36.3	51.7	48.3
72751	PEA RIDGE	96.6	96.1	0.2	0.2	0.4	0.4	2.0	2.4	7.3	7.4	8.2	7.2	5.7	27.9	23.9	11.0	1.4	72.5	36.5	49.8	50.2
72752	PETTIGREW	97.6	97.5	0.0	0.0	0.0	0.0	2.4	2.7	4.1	4.6	5.2	7.7	6.2	22.3	33.7	14.4	1.8	81.6	44.9	51.7	48.3
72753	PRAIRIE GROVE	95.0	94.4	0.3	0.3	0.4	0.4	2.2	2.7	7.4	7.2	7.5	6.8	6.6	27.1	24.7	11.3	1.5	73.7	36.7	48.9	51.1
72756	ROGERS	86.9	85.0	0.4	0.4	1.7	2.0	16.7	19.2	8.3	7.7	7.4	6.5	6.7	29.2	21.8	11.0	1.4	72.6	34.5	49.5	50.5
72758	ROGERS	89.1	87.3	0.5	0.5	1.0	1.2	13.8	16.3	8.6	8.2	7.8	6.4	6.4	29.9	21.3	9.6	1.8	71.4	33.9	49.2	50.8
72760	SAINT PAUL	97.6	97.6	0.0	0.0	0.0	0.0	1.8	1.9	5.1	5.7	6.4	7.3	6.2	23.8	30.5	13.5	1.6	78.3	42.3	51.3	48.7
72761	SILOAM SPRINGS	87.5	86.1	0.3	0.4	0.7	0.8	10.6	12.5	7.8	7.2	7.2	8.1	9.6	28.4	20.6	9.7	1.6	73.9	32.0	49.8	50.3
72762	SPRINGDALE	88.9	87.4	0.5	0.5	2.2	2.5	10.0	11.4	7.8	7.4	7.3	6.6	6.5	29.9	23.2	9.9	1.4	73.4	35.0	48.4	51.6
72764	SPRINGDALE	81.0	78.8	1.0	1.0	3.2	3.6	20.7	23.4	9.8	8.5	7.3	6.5	7.8	32.6	18.9	7.6	1.1	70.7	30.6	50.9	49.1
72768	SULPHUR SPRINGS	91.4	90.4	0.4	0.4	0.3	0.3	5.3	6.2	8.1	7.4	8.5	8.0	6.6	25.6	22.8	11.0	2.0	70.9	35.0	48.8	51.2
72769	SUMMERS	92.1	91.3	0.1	0.1	0.5	0.6	3.6	4.3	7.7	7.8	7.1	6.4	6.6	27.0	25.6	11.0	0.7	73.5	36.4	50.7	49.3
72773	WESLEY	97.1	96.8	0.1	0.1	0.1	0.2	1.5	1.7	6.5	7.2	7.3	6.9	5.7	27.4	27.2	10.6	1.3	74.6	37.8	50.0	50.0
72774	WEST FORK	95.7	95.2	0.4	0.4	0.4	0.4	1.6	1.9	6.7	6.8	7.6	7.2	6.4	27.8	27.4	9.4	0.8	74.6	37.1	50.5	49.5
72776	WITTER	98.3	97.8	0.4	0.5	0.0	0.0	1.3	0.9	4.1	5.0	6.8	7.2	6.3	23.0	30.6	15.3	1.8	78.8	43.7	51.4	48.7
72801	RUSSELLVILLE	89.0	87.9	5.9	6.2	1.0	1.3	3.1	3.7	7.0	6.1	5.8	9.8	11.6	26.4	18.7	11.9	2.8	77.7	31.1	48.0	52.0
72802	RUSSELLVILLE	94.8	94.1	1.9	2.0	0.8	1.0	2.0	2.4	6.9	6.8	7.3	6.9	7.0	28.6	25.5	10.1	1.1	75.0	36.5	49.7	50.3
72820	ALIX	97.3	96.8	0.2	0.2	0.4	0.4	1.7	2.0	7.7	7.3	6.7	5.9	6.1	26.5	25.3	13.0	1.6	74.7	38.4	49.6	50.4
72821	ALTUS	97.4	97.0	0.1	0.2	0.3	0.4	1.5	1.8	7.3	7.2	6.8	6.5	6.2	26.6	25.1	12.7	1.6	74.8	37.7	50.0	50.0
72823	ATKINS	95.9	95.6	1.7	1.8	0.2	0.3	0.9	1.1	6.6	6.7	7.2	6.7	6.5	27.7	24.7	12.3	1.7	75.5	37.7	49.2	50.8
72824	BELLEVILLE	86.6	84.6	2.7	2.9	3.3	4.0	7.1	8.5	5.9	6.1	7.0	7.1	6.4	27.7	24.8	13.6	1.6	76.8	38.3	50.0	50.0
72826	BLUE MOUNTAIN	97.9	97.0	0.0	0.0	0.0	0.0	0.5	1.0	5.6	6.1	8.1	7.6	6.1	25.4	26.9	13.2	1.0	75.1	38.8	51.8	48.2
72827	BLUFFTON	94.5	93.0	0.0	0.0	0.0	0.6	4.3	5.2	5.2	5.2	7.6	7.0	5.8	27.3	25.0	15.1	1.7	77.9	40.3	51.7	48.3
72828	BRIGGSVILLE	93.9	93.0	0.0	0.0	0.0	0.6	4.7	5.1	5.8	5.8	7.7	7.1	5.1	28.2	25.6	12.8	1.9	76.3	40.3	52.6	47.4
72830	CLARKSVILLE	92.0	91.0	2.0	2.1	0.3	0.4	9.2	10.7	6.9	6.4	6.8	6.2	7.3	27.4	23.5	13.1	2.4	76.4	37.1	49.5	50.5
72832	COAL HILL	96.0	95.6	0.1	0.1	0.0	0.0	2.7	3.3	7.9	7.2	7.1	6.7	6.9	28.1	22.4	12.4	1.4	73.8	35.7	48.9	51.1
72833	DANVILLE	79.9	77.3	1.3	1.3	1.0	1.2	23.6	26.7	7.3	6.7	6.8	6.9	7.5	29.0	21.9	11.4	2.5	75.2	34.9	51.7	48.3
72834	DARDANELLE	87.1	85.4	2.2	2.2	0.5	0.5	10.7	12.5	6.4	6.3	7.0	6.7	6.6	27.8	24.5	12.8	2.0	76.4	37.8	49.4	50.7
72835	DELAWARE	98.6	98.4	0.1	0.1	0.1	0.1	1.0	1.3	5.5	5.6	5.5	5.6	5.2	25.4	27.4	18.6	1.4	79.6	43.4	49.7	50.3
72837	DOVER	96.6	96.3	0.2	0.2	0.1	0.1	1.6	1.9	6.5	6.8	7.6	7.0	6.4	27.9	26.1	10.7	1.0	74.7	37.1	49.4	50.6
72838	GRAVELLY	93.4	91.9	0.6	0.6	0.0	0.6	4.2	5.2	4.6	4.6	7.5	6.4	5.8	26.0	27.8	15.0	2.3	79.2	42.0	51.5	48.6
72839	HAGARVILLE	97.0	96.5	0.3	0.3	0.1	0.3	1.3	1.8	5.9	6.3	7.4	5.9	5.3	25.8	28.5	13.6	1.4	76.7	40.4	51.3	48.7
72840	HARTMAN	97.2	96.8	0.4	0.4	0.0	0.0	2.4	3.0	8.3	7.5	6.9	6.0	6.2	27.3	23.2	13.3	1.4	73.7	36.2	49.4	50.6
72841	HARVEY	93.9	93.6	0.8	0.8	1.2	1.1	0.8	0.8	6.4	6.8	7.2	6.1	4.9	24.6	26.5	15.9	1.5	75.0	40.6	50.8	49.2
72842	HAVANA	89.8	87.9	0.1	0.1	1.1	1.3	11.6	14.0	6.3	6.2	6.9	6.5	6.2	27.6	22.9	14.9	2.5	76.7	38.9	49.1	50.9
72843	HECTOR	97.5	97.3	0.2	0.2	0.1	0.1	1.2	1.4	5.9	6.1	7.9	7.7	6.5	27.5	25.4	11.8	1.3	75.4	38.5	52.2	47.8
72845	KNOXVILLE	96.9	96.5	0.1	0.1	0.2	0.2	2.2	2.6	6.5	6.8	7.9	6.4	7.0	27.6	24.1	12.4	1.3	75.0	36.8	52.1	47.9
72846	LAMAR	96.4	95.8	0.5	0.6	0.3	0.3	2.9	3.5	6.6	7.0	7.9	6.1	6.3	27.6	25.6	11.6	1.4	74.8	37.0	51.6	48.4
72847	LONDON	97.4	97.1	0.3	0.3	0.6	0.8	0.7	0.9	5.9	6.3	7.3	6.4	5.6	27.2	27.7	12.4	1.2	76.7	39.8	49.8	50.3
72851	NEW BLAINE	98.5	98.2	0.2	0.2	0.1	0.1	0.9	1.2	5.9	6.1	6.0	5.7	5.3	26.2	26.2	17.0	1.5	78.0	41.8	50.1	50.0
72852	OARK	96.8	96.3	0.0	0.0	0.0	0.0	1.2	1.6	5.3	5.7	6.9	5.7	5.7	21.6	30.2	17.6	1.2	78.0	44.2	51.8	48.2
72853	OLA	88.3	86.2	0.2	0.2	0.3	0.3	11.9	14.3	8.1	7.6	7.2	6.7	6.9	25.9	22.3	13.3	2.0	73.0	36.0	50.0	50.0
72854	OZONE	96.6	96.3	0.3	0.3	0.0	0.0	1.7	2.0	6.0	6.3	7.1	6.0	5.4	24.7	28.4	14.8	1.4	77.3	41.2	49.7	50.3
72855	PARIS	95.1	94.6	2.5	2.7	0.1	0.2	1.6	2.0	6.2	6.3	6.8	6.4	6.1	25.5	24.3	15.4	3.1	76.7	40.1	49.2	50.8
72856	PELSOR	95.2	95.2	0.0	0.0	0.0	0.0	0.0	0.0	4.8	6.5	11.3	8.1	4.8	29.0	27.4	8.1	0.0	72.6	35.8	54.8	45.2
72857	PLAINVIEW	94.0	93.0	0.1	0.1	0.1	0.1	5.8	6.9	7.0	7.3	6.7	6.2	7.4	24.7	22.3	16.6	1.8	75.2	38.1	50.8	49.2
72858	POTTSVILLE	96.2	95.8	1.0	1.1	0.4	0.5	1.3	1.5	6.4	6.7	8.0	7.3	6.5	29.4	25.4	9.3	0.9	74.4	36.6	50.9	49.1
72860	ROVER	94.1	93.4	0.3	0.2	0.3	0.2	4.4	5.4	5.1	5.6	7.6	6.8	5.6	26.8	26.3	14.4	1.7	77.3	40.6	52.2	47.8
72863	SCRANTON	97.8	97.7	0.4	0.4	0.0	0.0	0.7	0.8	7.3	7.4	7.6	6.8	6.3	27.4	23.9	11.8	1.5	73.6	37.0	50.5	49.5
72865	SUBIACO	95.7	95.3	2.2	2.3	0.2	0.3	0.8	0.9	6.2	6.6	7.3	6.7	6.4	26.5	25.9	12.7	1.8	75.7	38.8	51.6	48.4
72901	FORT SMITH	76.5	73.8	8.7	9.2	3.2	3.8	11.1	13.1	7.5	6.8	6.4	6.7	8.2	30.1	21.8	10.8	1.9	75.5	34.4	50.7	49.3
72903	FORT SMITH	86.6	84.7	4.6	5.0	2.4	3.0	5.1	6.1	6.1	5.6	5.9	6.4	7.3	25.4	25.8	14.2	3.3	78.6	40.2	47.0	53.0
72904	FORT SMITH	56.9	52.8	17.7	18.4	10.0	11.6	15.6	18.0	9.2	7.9	7.3	6.9	7.9	27.4	20.9	10.9	1.7	71.4	32.7	48.1	51.9
72905	FORT SMITH	95.7	94.4	0.0	1.9	0.0	0.0	0.0	1.9	7.4	7.4	7.4	7.4	7.4	27.8	24.1	11.1	0.0	74.1	35.0	48.2	51.9
72908	FORT SMITH	90.1	88.6	2.8	3.1	3.0	3.8	1.7	2.1	7.7	7.4	7.5	6.5	6.1	27.6	25.8	10.3	1.1	73.4	37.2	47.8	52.2
72916	FORT SMITH	91.8	89.9	1.2	1.5	2.6	3.5	2.0	2.6	6.7	6.4	6.3	6.2	7.1	30.4	26.8	9.2	0.9	76.8	36.6	50.7	49.3
72921	ALMA	95.3	94.7	0.9	1.0	0.3	0.4	2.2	2.7	7.6	7.3	7.6	7.3	6.9	27.0	24.9	10.4	1.0	73.0	35.8	49.8	50.2
72923	BARLING	86.9	84.4	1.4	1.6	5.5	7.0	3.8	4.7	8.3	7.7	6.5	5.4	7.0	30.9	22.9	9.6	1.7	74.1	34.9	47.4	52.6
72924	BATES	94.9	94.5	0.0	0.0	1.0	1.0	1.0	1.5	8.0	9.0	6.5	6.0	5.5	27.0	26.0	11.0	1.0	73.0	36.2	51.0	49.0
72926	BOLES	95.5	95.2	0.1	0.1	0.9	1.1	0.6	0.8	5.0	7.6	7.3	7.1	3.7	25.5	28.8	13.8	1.4	75.8	40.8	52.8	47.2
72927	BOONEVILLE	96.7	96.3	0.3	0.4	0.3	0.4	1.2	1.4	7.0	6.8	7.3	6.8	6.5	25.8	25.0	12.7	2.0	74.5	37.6	49.3	50.7
72928	BRANCH	97.2	97.1	0.2	0.2	0.3	0.3	1.3	1.5	6.2	7.0	7.5	4.2	5.8	25.9	28.2	13.8	1.5	76.7	40.2	53.0	47.0
72930	CECIL	96.9	96.6	0.0	0.0	0.8	0.8	1.2	1.5	6.4	6.8	7.1	6.4	5.3	27.4	27.1	12.4	1.1	75.2	39.1	50.8	49.3
72932	CEDARVILLE	93.4	92.8	0.1	0.1	0.3	0.3	1.3	1.5	6.6	7.1	8.1	7.1	6.2	28.4	26.2	9.4	0.9	73.8	36.6	50.9	49.1
72933	CHARLESTON	95.8	95.2	0.2	0.3	0.4	0.6	1.9	2.3	6.9	7.0	7.2	6.2	5.8	27.0	24.3	13.1	2.5	75.0	38.5	49.9	50.1
72934	CHESTER	94.5	94.0	0.0	0.0	0.2	0.2	1.4	1.6	6.8	7.2	7.2	6.0	5.7	26.5	28.2	11.4	1.1	75.0	38.8	50.2	49.8
72936	GREENWOOD	96.0	95.4	0.3	0.4	0.5	0.6	1.6	2.0	7.7	7.6	7.7	7.2	6.3	30.0	23.2	9.1	1.4	72.4	35.0	49.8	50.2
72937	HACKETT	95.1	94.3	0.3	0.3	0.8	1.1	1.2	1.6	6.1	6.3	7.0	7.2	6.4	26.8	28.1	10.8	1.3	76.2	38.8	50.4	49.6
72938	HARTFORD	95.3	94.4	0.1	0.1	0.6	0.8	1.2	1.6	6.6	6.9	7.4	6.9	6.5	25.6	26.3	12.2	1.7	74.9	38.3	50.9	49.1
72940	HUNTINGTON	95.2	94.4	0.5	0.6	0.7	0.9	1.8	2.3	6.2	7.0	7.7	6.9	6.2	26.4	26.6	11.5	1.5	74.6	38.4	50.6	49.4
72941	LAVACA	95.8	95.1	0.4	0.4	0.1	0.2	1.8	2.3	6.4	6.9	7.6	6.5	5.8	30.5	25.2	10.3	0.8	75.0	37.2	49.6	50.4
72943	MAGAZINE	97.2	97.0	0.0	0.0	0.1	0.1	1.1	1.1	7.4	7.5	7.5	6.7	6.3	25.7	23.9	13.5	1.6	73.3	36.7	52.4	47.7
72944	MANSFIELD	95.2	94.5	0.2	0.3	0.8	1.0	2.0	2.5	7.3	7.3	7.0	6.9	6.6	26.6	25.4	11.3	1.7	74.1	37.5	50.3	49.7
72946	MOUNTAINBURG	96.0	95.7	0.1	0.1	0.2	0.2	1.0	1.2	6.7	7.1	7.6	6.8	6.2	26.5	25.9	11.9	1.3	74.5	37.8	50.5	49.5
72947	MULBERRY	95.9	95.6	0.3	0.3	0.2	0.3	0.8	1.0	6.1	6.2	6.7	6.5	6.1	25.5	28.0	13.3	1.7	77.1	40.5	51.1	48.9
72948	NATURAL DAM	92.5	92.1	0.0	0.0	0.2	0.4	1.3	1.6	7.2	7.6	7.4	6.9	5.6	27.8	27.3	9.0	1.3	73.5	37.4	50.2	49.8
72949	OZARK	95.9	95.5	1.0	1.1	0.3	0.3	1.9	2.3	6.6	6.2	6.7	7.7	7.2	25.1	24.1	13.9	2.5	75.8	37.7	49.3	50.7
72950	PARKS	93.9	93.3	0.9	0.9	1.1	1.3	0.9	0.9	6.5	6.9	7.3	6.2	4.7	24.5	26.5	15.9	1.5	75.5	40.6	50.5	49.5
72951	RATCLIFF	97.4	97.2	1.0	1.0	0.2	0.2	1.2	1.3	5.3	7.0	7.7	7.7	5.5	25.8	28.0	11.5	1.5	75.2	38.7	50.5	49.5
72952	RUDY	95.0	94.5	0.1	0.1	0.5	0.6	1.3	1.6	6.4	6.8	7.7	7.1	6.6	28.1	26.1	10.3	0.7	74.7	37.0	51.9	48.1
72955	UNIONTOWN	92.3	91.7	0.2	0.2	0.2	0.2	1.7	1.8	6.5	7.0	8.4	7.2	5.9	28.4	26.2	9.5	0.9	73.4	36.7	49.7	50.3
	ARKANSAS	80.0	79.3	15.7	15.8	0.8	1.0	3.3	3.8	6.9	6.7	6.9	6.8	7.3	27.3	24.1	12.2	1.8	75.7	36.7	49.0	51.0
	UNITED STATES	75.1	73.6	12.3	12.5	3.8	4.2	12.5	14.1	6.9	6.7	7.2	7.0	7.3	28.6	23.8	10.8	1.7	75.1	36.0	49.1	50.9

ZIP CODE #	POST OFFICE NAME	2004 Per Capita Income	2004 HH Income Base	2004 Household Income Distribution (%): Less than $25,000	$25,000 to $49,999	$50,000 to $99,999	$100,000 to $149,999	$150,000 or More	Median Household Income: 2004	2009	2004 National Centile	2004 State Centile	2004 Home Value Base	2004 Home Value Distribution (%): Less than $50,000	$50,000 to $89,999	$90,000 to $174,999	$175,000 to $399,999	$400,000 or More	2004 Median Home Value
72722	DECATUR	17549	1103	26.4	40.4	23.8	6.8	2.5	39023	46631	43	81	847	25.2	20.9	32.4	16.7	5.0	95492
72727	ELKINS	20140	1416	24.0	33.1	34.3	6.2	2.3	43735	54032	58	92	1201	18.5	26.4	35.7	17.0	2.4	96685
72729	EVANSVILLE	18866	108	34.3	32.4	26.9	4.6	1.9	35984	45321	31	69	91	23.1	28.6	36.3	11.0	1.1	87000
72730	FARMINGTON	18856	2408	26.7	29.9	34.2	8.0	1.2	44276	54216	59	92	1703	12.8	23.7	47.6	14.1	1.8	104194
72732	GARFIELD	20097	1930	26.2	32.0	32.8	5.9	3.1	43481	51921	57	91	1651	17.8	27.9	30.4	21.0	3.0	97178
72734	GENTRY	19026	2881	27.3	35.7	27.7	6.9	2.5	39818	47568	45	83	2209	20.6	26.5	34.5	14.0	4.4	93896
72736	GRAVETTE	19141	2115	29.8	33.6	27.1	6.2	3.2	39423	47361	44	82	1658	24.0	24.0	34.6	13.3	4.1	92895
72738	HINDSVILLE	22705	682	29.8	34.9	27.1	4.0	4.3	37857	44531	39	78	572	21.3	21.9	33.4	18.5	4.9	99750
72739	HIWASSE	23303	216	20.8	33.3	34.7	7.4	3.7	46150	55413	64	94	184	10.9	19.0	45.7	17.4	7.1	110000
72740	HUNTSVILLE	17064	3519	39.0	34.1	20.4	4.3	2.2	32224	38033	18	44	2761	24.6	25.5	31.5	12.5	5.9	89921
72742	KINGSTON	17027	266	40.2	30.5	24.4	4.9	0.0	31671	37470	17	40	227	24.2	31.3	31.3	7.9	5.3	79545
72744	LINCOLN	17819	1841	35.0	33.1	25.5	4.6	1.8	35180	44242	28	63	1404	20.9	29.6	35.0	10.8	3.8	89464
72745	LOWELL	25496	4184	16.4	28.0	39.1	11.3	5.3	54593	66478	79	98	3438	11.2	12.3	53.6	19.4	3.6	120910
72747	MAYSVILLE	19555	71	19.7	50.7	18.3	8.5	2.8	42233	49362	54	89	60	15.0	18.3	48.3	15.0	3.3	106667
72749	MORROW	112	0	0.0	0.0	0.0	0.0	0.0	0	87500	0	0	0	0.0	0.0	0.0	0.0	0.0	0
72751	PEA RIDGE	18741	1629	22.0	33.8	36.4	6.1	1.7	45370	53624	62	93	1336	9.0	30.7	43.6	15.2	1.6	99650
72752	PETTIGREW	16815	186	44.6	32.8	17.2	2.7	2.7	28140	32788	9	18	160	39.4	24.4	24.4	11.9	0.0	66154
72753	PRAIRIE GROVE	18126	2514	31.9	29.4	31.3	5.7	1.8	40946	51003	49	85	2049	17.5	24.0	44.9	11.1	2.5	97554
72756	ROGERS	21807	15051	26.7	30.4	30.2	8.6	4.1	43422	52085	57	91	10384	9.2	23.9	46.7	17.3	3.0	110094
72758	ROGERS	25020	7527	18.9	30.2	33.4	9.8	7.8	50723	60448	73	97	5750	7.0	17.7	50.6	21.0	3.6	118412
72760	SAINT PAUL	16040	262	43.5	34.4	17.6	2.7	1.9	28706	33451	10	21	226	35.8	27.0	23.9	12.4	0.9	67826
72761	SILOAM SPRINGS	19428	6153	26.7	33.1	31.1	5.7	3.5	41214	49659	50	87	4119	15.0	25.3	43.4	13.2	3.2	100523
72762	SPRINGDALE	21768	10407	20.6	29.8	35.8	10.5	3.3	49540	60597	71	96	8032	5.8	18.9	55.9	16.1	3.3	114091
72764	SPRINGDALE	19249	13197	26.9	34.1	29.6	5.3	4.1	40540	50714	48	85	7876	16.6	25.2	42.6	12.6	3.1	98357
72768	SULPHUR SPRINGS	15937	570	30.0	37.4	26.8	3.7	2.1	39520	47021	44	82	444	26.4	28.4	34.0	8.6	2.7	83438
72769	SUMMERS	16215	347	33.7	33.7	26.5	4.9	1.2	35301	44676	29	64	278	22.7	31.7	21.6	20.5	3.6	82000
72773	WESLEY	18584	608	37.2	40.1	18.9	2.8	1.0	33414	39470	22	51	519	27.9	27.0	32.4	10.4	2.3	80556
72774	WEST FORK	18406	2208	27.7	32.2	33.2	5.5	1.4	41484	51410	51	87	1823	21.4	28.9	34.5	13.3	1.9	89688
72776	WITTER	11600	81	49.4	33.3	14.8	2.5	0.0	25356	31834	5	8	70	21.4	37.1	35.7	5.7	0.0	70000
72801	RUSSELLVILLE	19071	6971	35.7	31.0	25.6	5.6	2.1	34642	42626	26	59	3689	13.3	41.3	36.3	8.8	0.4	85993
72802	RUSSELLVILLE	20838	6713	28.9	27.5	31.1	8.9	3.6	43092	53792	56	90	5227	15.4	28.0	39.4	15.3	1.9	97628
72820	ALIX	15511	191	39.3	35.1	20.9	2.6	2.1	31540	37161	16	39	155	38.1	31.6	25.2	4.5	0.7	65909
72821	ALTUS	19627	1125	34.7	33.9	25.0	3.7	2.8	34601	40969	26	58	927	33.0	31.1	26.5	8.9	0.5	73138
72823	ATKINS	17875	2679	36.1	30.5	25.9	5.2	2.4	35411	43754	29	65	2179	32.1	35.9	25.6	5.8	0.6	68262
72824	BELLEVILLE	20135	503	34.6	33.0	26.8	3.0	2.6	34935	43149	27	61	412	35.2	29.1	25.0	8.3	2.4	73438
72826	BLUE MOUNTAIN	14410	76	43.4	36.8	17.1	0.0	2.6	30000	35443	12	26	63	60.3	28.6	9.5	1.6	0.0	43500
72827	BLUFFTON	19084	74	40.5	29.7	23.0	4.1	2.7	31828	37844	17	42	60	45.0	35.0	16.7	1.7	1.7	56000
72828	BRIGGSVILLE	17628	62	41.9	29.0	22.6	3.2	3.2	31120	36728	15	35	50	44.0	30.0	24.0	2.0	0.0	57500
72830	CLARKSVILLE	18826	5730	39.4	32.2	22.4	4.2	1.8	32261	38658	18	45	4178	26.4	37.5	28.0	7.2	0.9	73590
72832	COAL HILL	15418	559	44.5	27.7	22.5	3.9	1.3	27970	33265	9	17	440	43.4	31.8	22.3	1.8	0.7	58056
72833	DANVILLE	16235	1547	39.5	30.6	23.5	3.7	2.7	31917	38718	18	43	1116	34.7	33.1	23.0	7.6	1.6	67126
72834	DARDANELLE	19898	4026	33.4	32.3	27.0	5.3	2.0	36982	45166	35	73	3008	24.1	36.1	27.6	10.7	1.4	79122
72835	DELAWARE	17014	327	47.1	25.7	20.2	4.3	2.8	27799	33262	8	16	278	36.3	32.4	22.3	5.4	3.6	68571
72837	DOVER	17529	2908	32.7	30.6	29.9	5.2	1.7	38028	47342	39	79	2425	28.1	32.3	31.0	7.8	0.8	75594
72838	GRAVELLY	18900	71	40.9	29.6	22.5	4.2	2.8	31348	37840	16	37	58	41.4	32.8	20.7	3.5	1.7	60000
72839	HAGARVILLE	16580	273	36.3	32.6	25.6	3.7	1.8	32947	40299	21	48	232	32.3	29.3	22.4	13.8	2.2	71875
72840	HARTMAN	17483	422	43.8	28.2	21.6	3.3	3.1	29236	35070	11	22	341	51.3	27.6	17.0	1.8	2.4	48953
72841	HARVEY	15833	102	37.3	41.2	17.7	1.0	2.9	30975	35239	15	34	87	37.9	32.2	18.4	10.3	1.2	66429
72842	HAVANA	15600	569	41.5	33.7	19.9	3.7	1.2	32007	38955	18	43	448	42.6	31.5	16.1	8.7	1.1	55593
72843	HECTOR	18375	1128	34.6	35.6	21.3	5.9	2.7	35000	43413	28	63	948	42.0	28.2	22.5	4.9	2.5	58837
72845	KNOXVILLE	18004	437	31.6	34.1	26.5	5.5	2.3	38044	46240	39	79	375	27.2	33.6	27.7	9.3	2.1	75000
72846	LAMAR	16664	1502	36.9	33.2	23.4	4.4	2.1	33082	39764	21	49	1187	30.5	34.3	24.3	8.9	2.0	69866
72847	LONDON	22537	848	27.7	31.7	28.5	7.2	4.8	41157	51827	50	87	713	21.3	34.4	30.3	12.9	1.1	83017
72851	NEW BLAINE	18829	432	43.5	27.8	21.8	3.7	3.2	30555	36504	14	30	369	36.6	31.4	22.8	5.7	3.5	68125
72852	OARK	15139	102	47.1	24.5	24.5	2.0	2.0	26949	32333	7	13	86	39.5	31.4	20.9	5.8	2.3	61250
72853	OLA	14704	837	44.6	33.6	15.9	4.5	1.4	27691	32702	8	15	596	45.5	29.4	19.3	5.9	0.0	54737
72854	OZONE	15712	137	38.7	29.9	27.0	4.4	0.0	31776	38774	17	41	116	35.3	27.6	25.9	10.3	0.9	70000
72855	PARIS	17671	2777	40.5	32.6	20.5	4.1	2.3	31624	37640	17	40	2146	30.9	37.5	24.4	6.2	1.0	66747
72856	PELSOR	14476	26	42.3	38.5	19.2	0.0	0.0	30000	36120	12	26	22	50.0	31.8	18.2	0.0	0.0	50000
72857	PLAINVIEW	19796	629	46.6	34.3	13.5	2.7	2.9	27242	33003	7	13	483	50.3	27.1	19.3	2.3	1.0	49700
72858	POTTSVILLE	18569	781	33.2	28.7	28.7	7.7	1.8	37238	46788	36	75	630	28.1	30.0	30.6	11.1	0.2	78448
72860	ROVER	15738	152	42.1	29.6	21.7	3.3	3.3	30801	36848	14	32	124	44.4	33.1	19.4	1.6	1.6	56364
72863	SCRANTON	21601	610	29.2	33.9	30.0	2.1	4.8	38371	45000	41	79	515	31.8	26.8	29.7	7.8	3.9	78548
72865	SUBIACO	17210	435	33.3	35.9	26.4	2.1	2.3	35819	42261	31	68	367	31.3	32.7	27.8	6.8	1.4	69306
72901	FORT SMITH	17946	8924	40.6	31.9	21.2	4.1	2.2	30934	38042	15	33	4566	34.6	41.2	17.5	5.8	0.9	62509
72903	FORT SMITH	30423	11013	24.7	28.9	28.2	10.1	8.1	45657	57301	63	93	6690	7.6	26.3	44.2	17.8	4.1	109276
72904	FORT SMITH	15394	7410	44.6	30.1	20.2	3.4	1.7	28646	34709	10	20	4209	46.4	38.4	13.0	1.7	0.5	52218
72905	FORT SMITH	7454	8	25.0	25.0	50.0	0.0	0.0	42500	66667	55	90	7	0.0	57.1	42.9	0.0	0.0	85000
72908	FORT SMITH	28500	4845	20.5	27.9	32.8	11.0	7.8	51557	64285	75	97	3423	8.7	32.1	42.2	15.2	1.9	98504
72916	FORT SMITH	25462	2452	22.8	29.7	32.9	9.8	4.7	47814	59015	68	95	1719	14.5	21.4	44.5	15.3	4.3	108982
72921	ALMA	18792	4398	31.2	32.7	25.4	7.4	3.2	37532	44387	38	77	3387	24.3	29.8	36.7	8.6	0.6	84163
72923	BARLING	20322	1767	25.7	32.1	32.9	7.6	1.7	44468	54147	60	92	1282	25.4	51.8	21.1	1.1	0.6	68073
72924	BATES	16142	82	37.8	39.0	17.1	3.7	2.4	31672	35366	17	41	69	52.2	29.0	8.7	8.7	1.5	47000
72926	BOLES	15996	323	42.7	35.6	19.2	0.3	2.2	31216	35764	16	36	275	44.7	26.2	21.8	6.2	1.1	60600
72927	BOONEVILLE	15980	3293	36.9	34.9	22.4	4.0	1.8	33221	39332	22	50	2437	33.5	36.3	24.6	5.0	0.6	67327
72928	BRANCH	16931	248	38.7	34.7	18.6	8.1	0.0	32706	38701	20	47	210	30.5	20.5	29.1	17.6	2.4	86667
72930	CECIL	18206	104	35.6	30.8	25.0	6.7	1.9	35000	40433	28	63	88	31.8	21.6	36.4	8.0	2.3	84000
72932	CEDARVILLE	15831	438	31.5	37.4	26.9	3.0	1.1	36241	42431	32	70	370	33.5	33.2	24.9	7.0	1.4	67500
72933	CHARLESTON	17887	2111	34.4	30.7	27.9	5.6	1.4	37359	43458	37	76	1694	24.1	35.7	32.9	6.0	1.3	77026
72934	CHESTER	15443	340	37.4	36.2	20.6	4.1	1.8	34185	40244	25	57	291	30.6	34.0	24.7	10.0	0.7	71667
72936	GREENWOOD	19808	4789	22.4	34.2	33.6	7.7	2.1	43954	54723	58	92	4003	16.8	37.5	38.4	6.4	1.0	85522
72937	HACKETT	19487	1382	27.3	33.4	31.3	6.5	1.5	41964	51384	53	88	1175	34.6	32.3	24.0	8.2	1.0	66795
72938	HARTFORD	15852	544	35.1	36.0	23.2	4.8	0.9	35268	42447	29	64	449	50.1	32.3	14.0	2.0	1.6	49884
72940	HUNTINGTON	19157	1089	27.1	34.5	30.5	6.1	1.8	39153	49195	43	81	903	37.8	35.9	19.4	6.5	0.4	63533
72941	LAVACA	21743	1849	21.1	28.5	37.8	9.8	2.9	50271	61579	72	96	1559	24.4	30.0	35.5	9.3	0.9	79882
72943	MAGAZINE	16032	811	40.0	34.9	20.8	2.7	1.6	31523	37030	16	39	658	43.5	32.8	18.5	4.9	0.3	58269
72944	MANSFIELD	18418	1239	34.4	35.0	23.7	5.0	1.9	34856	41538	27	60	976	41.7	33.2	18.9	5.2	1.0	58617
72946	MOUNTAINBURG	18099	1435	34.3	35.5	24.0	3.8	2.3	35823	41871	31	68	1180	31.2	33.6	24.2	9.5	1.4	71081
72947	MULBERRY	18313	1555	33.6	33.8	25.0	5.3	2.2	36147	42696	32	69	1256	34.3	31.0	27.2	5.6	2.0	69706
72948	NATURAL DAM	16272	211	36.0	33.2	23.7	5.7	1.4	34853	41215	27	60	186	37.1	28.5	28.0	6.5	0.0	65000
72949	OZARK	16282	3344	35.9	35.7	23.6	3.8	1.0	34870	40686	27	60	2515	29.5	34.6	28.7	5.6	1.6	71831
72950	PARKS	20112	198	37.9	40.4	17.2	1.5	3.0	30734	35931	14	31	169	38.5	31.4	17.8	10.7	1.8	65357
72951	RATCLIFF	22723	233	33.1	39.1	21.0	4.3	2.6	33779	40345	23	54	192	30.7	31.3	28.7	6.8	2.6	71538
72952	RUDY	16053	1250	31.0	38.3	25.0	5.2	0.6	36413	42638	33	71	1064	30.9	34.0	23.8	9.1	2.2	66779
72955	UNIONTOWN	16281	192	29.2	35.9	30.7	2.1	2.1	38274	45205	40	79	158	30.4	32.3	29.1	7.0	1.3	78182
	ARKANSAS	20565		33.0	30.6	26.7	6.4	3.3	37742	46417				27.1	29.3	31.4	10.3	1.8	80466
	UNITED STATES	25866		24.7	27.1	30.8	10.9	6.5	48124	56710				10.9	15.0	33.7	30.1	10.4	145905

#	POST OFFICE NAME	FINANCIAL SERVICES: Auto Loan	FINANCIAL SERVICES: Home Loan	FINANCIAL SERVICES: Invest-ments	FINANCIAL SERVICES: Retire-ment Plans	THE HOME: Home Improvements: Home Repair	THE HOME: Home Improvements: Lawn & Garden	THE HOME: Furnishings: Comput-ers & Hard-ware	THE HOME: Furnishings: Major Appli-ances	THE HOME: Furnishings: TV, Radio, Sound Equip-ment	THE HOME: Furnishings: Furni-ture	ENTERTAINMENT: Dine out/ Carry out	ENTERTAINMENT: Sports Equip-ment	ENTERTAINMENT: Fees & Tickets	ENTERTAINMENT: Toys & Games	ENTERTAINMENT: Travel	ENTERTAINMENT: Cable TV	PERSONAL: Apparel & Services	PERSONAL: Auto Repairs	PERSONAL: Health Insur-ance	PERSONAL: Pets & Supplies
72722	DECATUR	83	65	43	61	71	79	64	73	71	64	85	86	59	84	65	74	79	72	83	95
72727	ELKINS	89	76	55	71	81	88	70	79	76	71	92	95	68	93	72	79	87	77	88	104
72729	EVANSVILLE	90	60	27	52	68	79	58	73	70	59	82	87	49	78	59	76	75	72	90	103
72730	FARMINGTON	79	68	57	68	72	79	70	74	73	69	89	87	67	89	69	74	85	74	78	90
72732	GARFIELD	86	73	54	69	78	85	69	78	74	69	89	91	65	88	71	76	84	77	85	100
72734	GENTRY	83	70	51	67	74	82	68	75	73	67	88	88	65	88	69	75	83	74	83	95
72736	GRAVETTE	82	71	54	69	74	82	69	75	74	69	89	88	67	90	70	75	84	74	82	93
72738	HINDSVILLE	107	77	45	71	87	100	75	91	86	76	103	106	66	96	78	92	94	90	110	124
72739	HIWASSE	98	88	70	84	93	102	82	91	87	82	106	105	80	105	85	89	100	88	100	115
72740	HUNTSVILLE	80	56	29	51	64	72	55	67	65	55	76	80	48	73	56	68	69	66	81	93
72742	KINGSTON	74	53	28	47	58	67	52	62	60	52	71	73	45	68	52	64	65	61	74	84
72744	LINCOLN	81	58	32	52	64	73	57	68	66	57	78	80	50	75	57	70	72	67	80	92
72745	LOWELL	102	103	90	104	103	104	94	99	92	97	115	116	94	116	94	90	111	96	94	117
72747	MAYSVILLE	89	79	60	75	84	90	73	81	78	73	95	97	72	97	76	80	90	79	88	105
72749	MORROW	0	0	0	0	0	0	0	0	0	0	0	0	0	0	0	0	0	0	0	0
72751	PEA RIDGE	81	70	55	69	74	82	70	75	74	69	90	86	67	89	70	76	85	74	82	91
72752	PETTIGREW	74	50	24	44	57	65	49	60	58	49	69	72	42	65	49	63	62	60	74	85
72753	PRAIRIE GROVE	82	65	43	61	71	79	63	72	69	63	83	85	58	82	64	72	78	71	82	95
72756	ROGERS	87	81	76	81	82	88	81	84	82	82	102	97	79	99	80	81	98	84	84	97
72758	ROGERS	103	102	93	101	102	107	98	101	97	98	120	119	97	120	97	95	116	100	99	117
72760	SAINT PAUL	72	49	23	43	55	63	47	59	57	48	67	70	41	63	48	61	61	58	72	82
72761	SILOAM SPRINGS	81	70	58	69	74	83	72	77	76	71	93	89	69	92	72	78	87	76	83	92
72762	SPRINGDALE	91	88	79	88	90	94	84	89	85	85	105	104	83	105	85	83	101	87	88	104
72764	SPRINGDALE	81	74	70	74	74	79	76	77	77	77	96	91	74	94	74	75	93	78	76	89
72768	SULPHUR SPRINGS	73	63	49	62	67	73	62	67	66	61	80	78	60	80	63	67	75	66	73	83
72769	SUMMERS	85	57	26	49	65	75	55	69	67	56	78	83	47	74	56	72	71	68	85	98
72773	WESLEY	93	62	28	54	70	81	60	75	72	61	85	90	51	80	61	78	77	74	92	106
72774	WEST FORK	79	68	51	65	72	79	64	72	69	64	84	85	62	85	66	71	79	70	78	92
72776	WITTER	50	42	33	42	44	50	43	46	46	43	56	53	41	55	43	47	52	46	50	55
72801	RUSSELLVILLE	70	57	53	57	60	67	64	66	68	62	83	78	60	80	62	67	78	68	70	78
72802	RUSSELLVILLE	82	78	73	77	80	85	77	80	78	76	96	94	76	97	77	78	93	79	81	95
72820	ALIX	74	52	26	45	58	66	50	61	58	50	69	72	43	66	50	62	63	60	73	85
72821	ALTUS	86	65	40	60	71	81	65	75	73	65	87	87	59	84	65	76	80	74	86	98
72823	ATKINS	83	60	33	54	66	75	58	70	68	59	80	82	52	77	59	72	74	69	83	94
72824	BELLEVILLE	98	66	30	57	75	86	64	80	77	65	90	95	54	85	65	83	82	79	98	113
72826	BLUE MOUNTAIN	70	47	21	41	53	61	45	57	55	46	64	68	39	61	46	59	59	56	70	81
72827	BLUFFTON	84	56	25	48	63	73	54	68	65	55	77	81	46	72	55	70	70	67	83	96
72828	BRIGGSVILLE	84	56	25	48	63	73	54	68	65	55	77	81	46	72	55	70	70	67	83	96
72830	CLARKSVILLE	81	61	41	57	66	76	63	71	71	62	85	83	57	82	63	74	78	71	82	90
72832	COAL HILL	73	49	22	42	56	64	47	59	57	48	67	71	40	64	48	62	61	59	73	84
72833	DANVILLE	83	59	37	54	64	72	60	70	69	62	84	83	54	80	60	72	79	71	80	92
72834	DARDANELLE	86	67	46	63	72	82	68	77	76	67	91	90	62	88	68	79	84	76	88	98
72835	DELAWARE	77	52	23	45	59	67	50	62	60	51	71	75	42	67	51	65	64	62	77	89
72837	DOVER	78	63	42	58	68	75	59	69	66	60	79	82	55	78	61	69	74	67	78	91
72838	GRAVELLY	87	58	26	50	66	76	56	70	68	57	79	84	48	75	57	73	72	69	86	100
72839	HAGARVILLE	82	55	25	47	62	72	53	66	64	54	75	79	45	71	54	69	68	66	82	94
72840	HARTMAN	84	56	25	48	64	73	54	68	65	55	77	81	46	73	55	70	70	67	84	96
72841	HARVEY	77	52	23	45	59	67	50	62	60	51	71	75	42	67	51	65	64	62	77	89
72842	HAVANA	74	50	22	43	56	65	48	60	58	49	68	71	41	64	49	62	62	59	74	85
72843	HECTOR	86	63	40	57	69	78	62	73	71	62	84	87	55	80	62	74	78	73	86	98
72845	KNOXVILLE	79	63	44	61	67	76	64	71	70	63	84	82	60	82	64	72	78	70	80	88
72846	LAMAR	82	56	27	49	63	72	54	67	65	55	76	80	47	72	55	69	69	66	81	94
72847	LONDON	91	79	61	77	83	92	78	85	83	77	101	98	75	101	79	85	95	83	92	103
72851	NEW BLAINE	83	58	29	50	64	74	55	68	65	56	77	81	48	74	56	70	71	67	82	95
72852	OARK	68	46	21	40	52	60	44	55	53	45	63	66	38	59	45	58	57	55	68	79
72853	OLA	72	49	22	42	55	63	47	59	57	48	66	70	40	63	48	61	60	58	72	83
72854	OZONE	73	51	27	46	57	66	50	61	59	51	70	72	44	67	51	63	64	60	73	84
72855	PARIS	75	53	29	48	59	69	54	64	63	53	74	74	47	70	54	67	67	63	78	85
72856	PELSOR	65	44	20	38	49	57	42	53	51	43	60	63	36	56	43	55	54	52	65	75
72857	PLAINVIEW	89	60	28	52	68	78	58	72	70	60	83	86	50	78	59	75	75	72	89	102
72858	POTTSVILLE	88	64	35	57	70	80	61	74	71	62	84	88	54	81	62	75	77	73	87	101
72860	ROVER	80	54	24	46	61	70	52	65	62	53	73	77	44	69	53	67	67	64	80	92
72863	SCRANTON	97	82	58	77	88	95	76	86	83	77	100	103	73	101	78	86	94	84	96	114
72865	SUBIACO	84	63	37	57	70	78	60	71	69	61	82	85	54	80	61	73	76	70	84	98
72901	FORT SMITH	58	56	61	56	56	61	61	59	62	59	76	69	60	77	60	61	74	60	60	65
72903	FORT SMITH	95	101	112	101	100	107	101	100	99	100	124	115	103	125	101	98	121	100	98	110
72904	FORT SMITH	63	51	46	49	53	61	56	58	61	55	74	68	53	72	55	63	70	60	65	70
72905	FORT SMITH	80	71	54	67	75	80	66	73	70	66	85	86	64	86	67	71	80	71	79	94
72908	FORT SMITH	101	104	99	104	104	109	100	102	99	99	123	119	101	125	100	98	119	100	100	116
72916	FORT SMITH	98	81	74	84	84	91	86	89	89	86	110	108	80	105	83	87	104	92	91	110
72921	ALMA	84	68	48	64	72	81	66	74	73	66	88	88	62	87	67	76	82	73	84	96
72923	BARLING	80	68	58	69	70	79	72	75	75	71	92	87	69	90	70	75	87	75	79	88
72924	BATES	74	50	22	43	56	65	48	60	58	49	68	72	41	64	49	62	62	59	74	85
72926	BOLES	74	50	22	43	56	65	48	60	58	49	68	71	41	64	49	62	62	59	74	85
72927	BOONEVILLE	73	53	30	48	58	67	53	62	61	53	73	73	47	69	53	65	66	62	75	83
72928	BRANCH	79	53	24	46	60	69	51	64	62	52	73	76	44	69	52	67	66	63	79	91
72930	CECIL	79	60	38	58	67	75	60	70	67	60	80	82	54	79	61	69	74	69	80	91
72932	CEDARVILLE	82	55	25	47	62	72	53	66	64	54	75	79	45	71	54	69	68	66	82	94
72933	CHARLESTON	73	58	41	57	63	72	60	67	66	59	79	77	56	77	60	68	73	66	76	83
72934	CHESTER	78	52	24	45	59	68	51	63	61	52	72	76	43	68	51	66	65	63	78	90
72936	GREENWOOD	87	76	58	73	80	88	73	80	77	72	94	94	71	95	74	79	89	78	86	100
72937	HACKETT	83	69	48	65	74	81	65	74	71	65	85	88	62	86	66	73	80	72	82	97
72938	HARTFORD	78	53	24	45	60	69	51	63	61	52	72	76	43	68	52	66	65	63	78	90
72940	HUNTINGTON	86	69	46	64	75	82	65	75	72	65	86	89	61	86	66	75	81	73	85	100
72941	LAVACA	93	83	63	79	88	94	77	85	81	77	99	101	75	101	79	84	94	83	92	110
72943	MAGAZINE	79	53	24	46	60	69	51	64	62	52	72	76	44	68	52	66	66	63	79	91
72944	MANSFIELD	86	62	35	56	69	79	61	73	71	61	84	86	54	81	62	75	77	72	86	98
72946	MOUNTAINBURG	88	59	27	51	67	77	57	71	69	58	80	85	48	76	58	74	73	70	87	101
72947	MULBERRY	87	58	26	50	66	76	56	70	68	57	80	84	48	75	57	73	72	70	87	100
72948	NATURAL DAM	80	54	24	46	61	70	52	65	63	53	74	78	44	70	53	68	67	64	80	92
72949	OZARK	70	53	34	50	58	66	54	61	60	53	72	71	49	70	54	63	66	61	71	79
72950	PARKS	89	60	27	51	67	78	57	72	69	59	81	86	49	77	58	75	74	71	89	102
72951	RATCLIFF	110	74	33	64	84	96	71	89	86	73	101	106	61	95	72	93	92	88	110	126
72952	RUDY	79	57	30	50	63	71	54	66	63	55	75	78	48	72	55	67	69	65	79	91
72955	UNIONTOWN	89	60	27	51	67	78	57	72	69	59	81	86	49	77	58	75	74	71	89	102
	ARKANSAS	81	69	57	66	72	80	69	75	74	69	90	87	65	87	69	76	85	75	82	92
	UNITED STATES	100	100	100	100	100	100	100	100	100	100	100	100	100	100	100	100	100	100	100	100

ZIP CODE			POPULATION			2000-2004 ANNUAL RATE		HOUSEHOLDS					FAMILIES		
#	POST OFFICE NAME	COUNTY FIPS CODE	2000	2004	2009	% Rate	State Centile	2000	2004	2009	% Annual Rate 2000-2004	2004 Average HH Size	2000	2004	% Annual Rate 2000-2004
72956	VAN BUREN	033	29220	30538	32066	1.0	70	10760	11332	11992	1.2	2.66	8202	8531	0.9
72958	WALDRON	127	7476	7714	8040	0.7	63	2949	3059	3206	0.9	2.49	2064	2104	0.5
72959	WINSLOW	143	2795	3066	3440	2.2	89	1066	1178	1327	2.4	2.60	817	890	2.0
	ARKANSAS					0.9					1.1	2.47			0.8
	UNITED STATES					1.2					1.3	2.58			1.1

ZIP CODE		RACE (%)							2004 AGE DISTRIBUTION (%)										MEDIAN AGE			
#	POST OFFICE NAME	White		Black		Asian/Pacific		% Hispanic Origin		0-4	5-9	10-14	15-19	20-24	25-44	45-64	65-84	85+	18+	2004	% 2004 Males	% 2004 Females
		2000	2004	2000	2004	2000	2004	2000	2004													
72956	VAN BUREN	89.7	88.5	1.2	1.2	2.0	2.4	4.6	5.4	7.8	7.5	7.6	7.1	6.6	28.8	23.5	9.8	1.3	72.8	35.1	49.1	51.0
72958	WALDRON	92.9	91.9	0.2	0.2	0.9	1.1	7.9	9.3	7.9	7.4	6.7	6.6	6.1	26.3	23.8	13.0	2.2	74.3	37.1	50.9	49.1
72959	WINSLOW	95.4	95.0	0.4	0.4	0.4	0.4	1.0	1.2	6.1	6.3	7.7	7.1	5.9	26.0	29.4	10.4	1.0	75.4	38.8	50.8	49.2
	ARKANSAS	80.0	79.3	15.7	15.8	0.8	1.0	3.3	3.8	6.9	6.7	6.9	6.8	7.3	27.3	24.1	12.2	1.8	75.7	36.7	49.0	51.0
	UNITED STATES	75.1	73.6	12.3	12.5	3.8	4.2	12.5	14.1	6.9	6.7	7.2	7.0	7.3	28.6	23.8	10.8	1.7	75.1	36.0	49.1	50.9

ARKANSAS

C 72956-72959

#	POST OFFICE NAME	2004 Per Capita Income	2004 HH Income Base	2004 HOUSEHOLD INCOME DISTRIBUTION (%)					MEDIAN HOUSEHOLD INCOME				2004 Home Value Base	2004 HOME VALUE DISTRIBUTION (%)					2004 Median Home Value
				Less than $25,000	$25,000 to $49,999	$50,000 to $99,999	$100,000 to $149,999	$150,000 or More	2004	2009	2004 National Centile	2004 State Centile		Less than $50,000	$50,000 to $89,999	$90,000 to $174,999	$175,000 to $399,999	$400,000 or More	
72956	VAN BUREN	17535	11332	30.0	34.9	28.1	5.4	1.6	38419	45549	41	80	8578	23.1	37.8	31.3	6.8	1.1	77221
72958	WALDRON	15401	3059	41.4	33.6	20.4	3.2	1.3	30025	34397	12	26	2199	41.8	32.5	17.5	6.9	1.4	58167
72959	WINSLOW	16652	1178	30.7	35.3	29.4	3.9	0.8	36983	45824	35	73	994	26.4	30.9	27.9	13.4	1.5	79211
	ARKANSAS	20565		33.0	30.6	26.7	6.4	3.3	37742	46417				27.1	29.3	31.4	10.3	1.8	80466
	UNITED STATES	25866		24.7	27.1	30.8	10.9	6.5	48124	56710				10.9	15.0	33.7	30.1	10.4	145905

SPENDING POTENTIAL INDICES

ARKANSAS

72956-72959 **D**

ZIP CODE		FINANCIAL SERVICES				THE HOME						ENTERTAINMENT						PERSONAL			
						Home Improvements		Furnishings													
#	POST OFFICE NAME	Auto Loan	Home Loan	Invest-ments	Retire-ment Plans	Home Repair	Lawn & Garden	Comput-ers & Hard-ware	Major Appli-ances	TV, Radio, Sound Equip-ment	Furni-ture	Dine out/ Carry out	Sports Equip-ment	Fees & Tickets	Toys & Games	Travel	Cable TV	Apparel & Services	Auto Repairs	Health Insur-ance	Pets & Supplies
72956	VAN BUREN	75	64	49	60	67	73	63	68	67	62	82	81	59	80	63	69	77	68	75	86
72958	WALDRON	70	48	24	43	54	63	48	58	57	48	67	69	41	63	48	61	61	58	71	80
72959	WINSLOW	75	59	37	54	64	71	55	64	62	56	74	77	51	73	57	65	69	63	74	87
	ARKANSAS	81	69	57	66	72	80	69	75	74	69	90	87	65	87	69	76	85	75	82	92
	UNITED STATES	100	100	100	100	100	100	100	100	100	100	100	100	100	100	100	100	100	100	100	100

20-D Copyright © 2004 ESRI BIS. All rights reserved. Reproduction by any method is prohibited.

#	POST OFFICE NAME	COUNTY FIPS CODE	POPULATION 2000	POPULATION 2004	POPULATION 2009	2000-2004 ANNUAL RATE % Rate	2000-2004 ANNUAL RATE State Centile	HOUSEHOLDS 2000	HOUSEHOLDS 2004	HOUSEHOLDS 2009	% Annual Rate 2000-2004	2004 Average HH Size	FAMILIES 2000	FAMILIES 2004	% Annual Rate 2000-2004
90001	LOS ANGELES	037	54519	55173	56614	0.3	23	12537	12585	12810	0.1	4.38	10705	10734	0.1
90002	LOS ANGELES	037	44494	45870	47402	0.7	42	10670	10855	11094	0.4	4.21	8740	8880	0.4
90003	LOS ANGELES	037	57653	60120	62510	1.0	55	14344	14856	15335	0.8	4.03	11513	11899	0.8
90004	LOS ANGELES	037	67751	70409	73733	0.9	51	23081	23888	24864	0.8	2.92	15007	15401	0.6
90005	LOS ANGELES	037	40371	43093	45576	1.6	70	13832	14648	15367	1.4	2.93	8994	9476	1.2
90006	LOS ANGELES	037	60562	61527	63465	0.4	26	18079	18262	18704	0.2	3.33	13133	13231	0.2
90007	LOS ANGELES	037	44040	44820	46164	0.4	28	12405	12656	13036	0.5	3.07	6931	6981	0.2
90008	LOS ANGELES	037	32985	34057	35450	0.8	43	14167	14582	15091	0.7	2.33	8033	8220	0.5
90010	LOS ANGELES	037	4015	4289	4526	1.6	71	2225	2352	2455	1.3	1.82	898	952	1.4
90011	LOS ANGELES	037	101611	103745	106934	0.5	31	21780	21999	22456	0.2	4.70	18362	18537	0.2
90012	LOS ANGELES	037	31699	32830	33814	0.8	47	8500	8864	9215	1.0	2.25	4148	4326	1.0
90013	LOS ANGELES	037	8628	8796	8993	0.5	29	3028	3125	3228	0.7	1.49	368	377	0.6
90014	LOS ANGELES	037	3690	3784	3893	0.6	36	2653	2732	2813	0.7	1.12	268	274	0.5
90015	LOS ANGELES	037	17551	18412	19433	1.1	60	5616	5949	6285	1.4	2.98	3392	3516	0.9
90016	LOS ANGELES	037	44334	45837	47729	0.8	45	15540	15960	16512	0.6	2.86	10442	10674	0.5
90017	LOS ANGELES	037	20489	23577	25866	3.4	93	6350	7331	8024	3.4	3.08	4058	4658	3.3
90018	LOS ANGELES	037	48584	50797	52967	1.1	56	15602	16168	16722	0.8	3.09	10452	10795	0.8
90019	LOS ANGELES	037	68841	70775	73335	0.7	39	24246	24759	25469	0.5	2.81	15232	15507	0.4
90020	LOS ANGELES	037	42474	45204	47771	1.5	69	16970	17902	18752	1.3	2.51	9722	10206	1.2
90021	LOS ANGELES	037	3124	3152	3242	0.2	20	1330	1349	1396	0.3	1.72	352	362	0.7
90022	LOS ANGELES	037	67882	70952	74065	1.1	56	17011	17667	18305	0.9	4.01	14152	14681	0.9
90023	LOS ANGELES	037	45397	46426	48022	0.5	33	10302	10477	10763	0.4	4.40	8868	9007	0.4
90024	LOS ANGELES	037	44313	46902	49433	1.4	65	16894	17980	19025	1.5	1.99	5829	6104	1.1
90025	LOS ANGELES	037	40667	42610	44770	1.1	58	20982	21838	22790	1.0	1.92	7688	7977	0.9
90026	LOS ANGELES	037	73417	74996	77604	0.5	32	24452	24845	25538	0.4	2.98	15042	15233	0.3
90027	LOS ANGELES	037	49960	53064	56078	1.4	67	22521	23912	25161	1.4	2.17	10298	10845	1.2
90028	LOS ANGELES	037	29790	31176	33084	1.1	58	14352	14870	15673	0.8	2.04	5085	5287	0.9
90029	LOS ANGELES	037	40546	42526	44697	1.1	60	13239	13811	14419	1.0	3.02	8832	9202	1.0
90031	LOS ANGELES	037	39923	40486	41551	0.3	24	10760	10850	11056	0.2	3.69	8556	8609	0.2
90032	LOS ANGELES	037	46727	47278	48442	0.3	23	12636	12721	12946	0.2	3.67	10185	10231	0.1
90033	LOS ANGELES	037	49126	49193	50460	0.0	15	12325	12257	12496	-0.1	3.84	9627	9568	-0.1
90034	LOS ANGELES	037	58300	60526	62897	0.9	50	25849	26614	27435	0.7	2.26	12158	12462	0.6
90035	LOS ANGELES	037	27853	28833	29975	0.8	47	12920	13283	13707	0.7	2.13	6223	6363	0.5
90036	LOS ANGELES	037	32366	34390	36274	1.4	68	17045	17987	18822	1.3	1.89	6051	6328	1.1
90037	LOS ANGELES	037	55766	56426	57942	0.3	23	14695	14752	15026	0.1	3.80	11077	11095	0.0
90038	LOS ANGELES	037	32342	33485	34720	0.8	47	12127	12434	12777	0.6	2.67	6565	6742	0.6
90039	LOS ANGELES	037	29470	29671	30450	0.2	19	11456	11504	11745	0.1	2.55	6347	6327	-0.1
90040	LOS ANGELES	037	12861	13516	14172	1.2	61	3317	3458	3599	1.0	3.85	2721	2838	1.0
90041	LOS ANGELES	037	28274	28857	29768	0.5	31	9522	9671	9920	0.4	2.85	6445	6524	0.3
90042	LOS ANGELES	037	63386	65241	67623	0.7	40	19074	19477	20028	0.5	3.30	13740	14001	0.4
90043	LOS ANGELES	037	45398	47808	50159	1.2	62	16022	16731	17403	1.0	2.84	11003	11462	1.0
90044	LOS ANGELES	037	88417	90387	93038	0.5	33	24777	25157	25695	0.4	3.58	18890	19129	0.3
90045	LOS ANGELES	037	42304	43850	45802	0.9	48	17263	17843	18546	0.8	2.32	9988	10291	0.7
90046	LOS ANGELES	037	50279	52350	54656	1.0	53	28811	29922	31074	0.9	1.73	9029	9283	0.7
90047	LOS ANGELES	037	47736	48609	50056	0.4	28	15872	16048	16395	0.3	3.02	11544	11645	0.2
90048	LOS ANGELES	037	21381	21716	22452	0.4	26	11798	11929	12265	0.3	1.76	3928	3932	0.0
90049	LOS ANGELES	037	33570	35468	37351	1.3	64	16551	17442	18266	1.2	1.99	7775	8162	1.2
90056	LOS ANGELES	037	8188	8280	8474	0.3	22	3397	3417	3474	0.1	2.42	2322	2329	0.1
90057	LOS ANGELES	037	43460	46988	49899	1.9	77	14579	15598	16419	1.6	2.93	8962	9596	1.6
90058	LOS ANGELES	037	3525	3670	3819	1.0	53	952	986	1021	0.8	3.66	748	773	0.8
90059	LOS ANGELES	037	38258	39118	40310	0.5	33	9411	9526	9725	0.3	4.06	7665	7751	0.3
90061	LOS ANGELES	037	23752	24366	25132	0.6	36	5975	6067	6201	0.4	3.96	4798	4863	0.3
90062	LOS ANGELES	037	29104	29546	30485	0.4	25	8680	8722	8918	0.1	3.35	6189	6197	0.0
90063	LOS ANGELES	037	56090	56860	58552	0.3	24	13157	13261	13549	0.2	4.28	11079	11148	0.2
90064	LOS ANGELES	037	23874	24537	25407	0.7	39	10496	10755	11077	0.6	2.25	5675	5777	0.4
90065	LOS ANGELES	037	47201	48028	49399	0.4	28	14214	14385	14697	0.3	3.32	10366	10465	0.2
90066	LOS ANGELES	037	54434	56213	58416	0.8	43	23096	23680	24414	0.6	2.36	12537	12818	0.5
90067	LOS ANGELES	037	2555	2545	2599	-0.1	11	1584	1568	1590	-0.2	1.61	642	636	-0.2
90068	LOS ANGELES	037	21810	23131	24847	1.4	66	12542	13130	13950	1.1	1.75	3828	4092	1.6
90069	WEST HOLLYWOOD	037	20569	21315	22366	0.8	48	13712	14165	14780	0.8	1.50	2728	2777	0.4
90071	LOS ANGELES	037	7	7	7	0.0	15	1	1	1	0.0	7.00	0	0	0.0
90077	LOS ANGELES	037	9070	9371	9683	0.8	44	3559	3658	3755	0.7	2.52	2469	2533	0.6
90089	LOS ANGELES	037	240	207	205	-3.4	0	136	116	114	-3.7	1.78	0	0	0.0
90095	LOS ANGELES	037	66	75	81	3.1	90	1	1	1	0.0	3.00	1	1	0.0
90201	BELL	037	104594	108448	113185	0.9	49	23691	24328	25166	0.6	4.42	20837	21389	0.6
90210	BEVERLY HILLS	037	23460	23850	24557	0.4	27	9612	9702	9905	0.2	2.45	6097	6131	0.1
90211	BEVERLY HILLS	037	8221	8567	8903	1.0	54	3704	3822	3935	0.7	2.24	2022	2082	0.7
90212	BEVERLY HILLS	037	11444	11741	12160	0.6	36	5768	5874	6037	0.4	2.00	2691	2726	0.3
90220	COMPTON	037	48173	49837	51731	0.8	46	12719	13064	13456	0.6	3.79	10211	10475	0.6
90221	COMPTON	037	51086	52171	53922	0.5	32	11102	11227	11498	0.3	4.62	9640	9733	0.2
90222	COMPTON	037	29861	31282	32704	1.1	58	7136	7397	7659	0.9	4.21	5886	6102	0.9
90230	CULVER CITY	037	31693	32317	33340	0.5	29	12588	12812	13145	0.4	2.51	7571	7669	0.3
90232	CULVER CITY	037	16649	17051	17658	0.6	34	7084	7242	7465	0.5	2.33	3950	3999	0.3
90240	DOWNEY	037	23153	23956	24814	0.8	47	7354	7491	7668	0.4	3.19	5790	5887	0.4
90241	DOWNEY	037	40446	41565	42812	0.6	38	13736	13856	14078	0.2	2.97	10055	10119	0.2
90242	DOWNEY	037	43665	45201	46734	0.8	47	12889	13109	13383	0.4	3.36	10143	10293	0.4
90245	EL SEGUNDO	037	15926	16628	17411	1.0	55	7021	7303	7602	0.9	2.27	3888	4016	0.8
90247	GARDENA	037	47160	49084	51069	1.0	53	15874	16432	16985	0.8	2.95	10887	11221	0.7
90248	GARDENA	037	9430	10084	10652	1.6	71	3135	3347	3517	1.6	3.01	2346	2496	1.5
90249	GARDENA	037	26216	28027	29558	1.6	71	8825	9366	9802	1.4	2.97	6482	6861	1.4
90250	HAWTHORNE	037	93724	99400	104395	1.4	66	31534	32870	34067	1.0	3.01	22122	22993	0.9
90254	HERMOSA BEACH	037	18694	18842	19386	0.2	19	9535	9555	9758	0.1	1.96	3583	3577	0.0
90255	HUNTINGTON PARK	037	78858	83662	88225	1.4	67	18799	19784	20694	1.2	4.22	16139	16954	1.2
90260	LAWNDALE	037	33641	34336	35258	0.5	31	10174	10226	10374	0.1	3.35	7511	7535	0.1
90262	LYNWOOD	037	68930	70653	72761	0.6	35	14193	14365	14643	0.3	4.77	12762	12902	0.3
90263	MALIBU	037	1525	1662	1769	2.2	82	3	4	4	7.0	2.50	2	2	0.0
90265	MALIBU	037	18084	19146	20186	1.4	65	7267	7745	8182	1.5	2.30	4634	4940	1.5
90266	MANHATTAN BEACH	037	33857	33913	34717	0.0	16	14480	14417	14658	-0.1	2.35	8394	8335	-0.2
90270	MAYWOOD	037	28083	28877	30046	0.7	39	6469	6609	6827	0.5	4.36	5698	5819	0.5
90272	PACIFIC PALISADES	037	22709	23197	23980	0.5	32	9247	9392	9634	0.4	2.46	6428	6514	0.3
90274	PALOS VERDES PENINSU	037	24905	25980	27143	1.0	55	9256	9599	9957	0.9	2.70	7573	7839	0.8
90275	RANCHO PALOS VERDES	037	41900	43453	45446	0.9	49	15690	16165	16785	0.7	2.66	12431	12790	0.7
90277	REDONDO BEACH	037	33943	34848	36141	0.6	37	16926	17327	17873	0.6	2.01	7890	7973	0.3
90278	REDONDO BEACH	037	37410	39611	41597	1.4	65	15490	16329	17035	1.3	2.42	9431	9904	1.2
90280	SOUTH GATE	037	97841	99734	102651	0.5	29	23524	23715	24170	0.2	4.20	20340	20470	0.2
	CALIFORNIA					1.4					1.2	2.90			1.2
	UNITED STATES					1.2					1.3	2.58			1.1

# ZIP CODE	POST OFFICE NAME	RACE (%) White 2000	White 2004	Black 2000	Black 2004	Asian/Pacific 2000	Asian/Pacific 2004	% Hispanic Origin 2000	% Hispanic Origin 2004	2004 AGE DISTRIBUTION (%) 0-4	5-9	10-14	15-19	20-24	25-44	45-64	65-84	85+	18+	MEDIAN AGE 2004	% 2004 Males	% 2004 Females
90001	LOS ANGELES	24.6	24.7	14.4	12.7	0.2	0.2	84.6	86.5	11.7	10.4	11.2	9.4	9.7	29.1	13.5	4.5	0.6	61.0	23.8	50.4	49.7
90002	LOS ANGELES	16.8	17.4	35.8	32.1	0.2	0.2	63.3	67.1	11.2	10.4	12.1	10.3	9.6	26.9	14.0	4.9	0.7	60.0	23.2	48.6	51.4
90003	LOS ANGELES	19.5	20.1	31.8	28.6	0.5	0.4	66.8	70.2	11.5	10.4	11.0	9.6	9.4	28.7	14.1	4.6	0.6	61.3	24.0	49.3	50.7
90004	LOS ANGELES	34.1	32.6	3.4	3.2	23.8	23.4	55.6	58.5	8.1	7.4	7.6	6.9	8.1	35.1	19.6	6.4	0.8	72.9	31.8	50.6	49.4
90005	LOS ANGELES	27.9	27.1	4.7	4.3	26.2	25.3	61.6	64.3	8.7	7.7	7.7	6.3	8.8	37.5	17.1	5.6	0.7	72.4	30.3	52.3	47.7
90006	LOS ANGELES	26.6	26.4	4.0	3.6	14.4	13.4	78.0	80.2	9.3	8.3	8.8	7.6	9.2	33.6	16.9	5.7	0.7	69.3	28.7	51.3	48.7
90007	LOS ANGELES	31.7	30.0	13.0	11.7	10.9	11.6	58.1	60.8	6.8	6.0	6.8	15.5	21.8	25.9	12.2	4.5	0.5	76.8	23.4	50.4	49.6
90008	LOS ANGELES	6.8	7.0	77.4	75.7	3.1	3.2	15.4	17.2	7.0	7.0	7.6	6.5	6.1	27.0	23.4	13.3	2.1	74.4	37.5	43.7	56.4
90010	LOS ANGELES	32.5	29.7	8.1	7.9	44.0	45.0	21.8	25.0	5.3	4.4	4.7	3.9	5.9	36.0	22.2	15.6	2.2	83.6	38.7	50.3	49.7
90011	LOS ANGELES	28.0	28.1	13.5	11.8	0.6	0.5	85.3	87.3	12.1	10.7	10.8	9.1	9.9	31.1	12.4	3.5	0.5	61.0	23.7	51.4	48.6
90012	LOS ANGELES	20.4	18.7	16.5	15.3	38.9	40.1	30.0	32.4	3.1	3.2	3.6	5.7	10.5	41.5	19.2	11.1	2.1	88.0	36.1	61.1	38.9
90013	LOS ANGELES	27.0	25.3	37.2	35.8	14.3	14.5	27.4	31.4	2.8	2.8	2.5	2.5	4.3	36.1	34.4	12.8	1.8	90.6	44.6	66.5	33.5
90014	LOS ANGELES	27.2	24.7	33.2	32.7	20.7	20.9	23.0	26.4	2.4	2.0	1.5	1.7	2.8	26.2	36.9	23.8	2.8	93.3	50.9	65.0	35.0
90015	LOS ANGELES	29.9	29.0	4.7	4.5	10.1	10.7	80.3	80.6	9.0	7.7	7.8	8.7	11.1	33.2	15.5	6.2	0.8	70.7	27.8	52.3	47.7
90016	LOS ANGELES	18.5	19.1	47.0	44.0	3.5	3.6	45.0	48.6	8.3	7.9	8.8	7.8	7.6	29.1	20.3	9.0	1.4	70.2	31.7	47.0	53.0
90017	LOS ANGELES	30.2	29.6	4.2	3.7	5.2	5.0	86.2	88.0	10.7	8.7	7.7	7.1	11.5	34.8	13.2	5.5	0.8	69.3	26.9	55.6	44.4
90018	LOS ANGELES	16.2	16.7	43.5	39.9	3.3	3.2	49.3	53.5	8.4	8.0	9.2	8.3	7.9	29.4	18.7	8.3	1.7	69.4	30.7	47.7	52.3
90019	LOS ANGELES	23.5	23.0	31.7	29.8	12.9	13.0	44.0	47.3	7.5	6.9	7.6	7.1	8.1	32.6	20.7	8.2	1.4	73.7	32.8	48.5	51.5
90020	LOS ANGELES	25.9	25.4	7.0	6.5	43.3	42.5	37.6	40.8	7.8	6.9	6.8	5.4	7.4	39.6	19.3	6.2	0.6	75.6	32.7	50.3	49.7
90021	LOS ANGELES	29.9	28.5	25.2	24.3	7.5	7.4	51.1	54.1	4.5	4.0	4.3	4.5	6.5	39.3	31.8	4.9	0.3	85.0	39.3	66.5	33.5
90022	LOS ANGELES	41.4	40.8	0.5	0.4	0.8	0.8	96.3	97.0	9.9	9.2	10.0	8.6	8.9	30.1	15.4	6.9	0.9	65.7	27.0	50.2	49.8
90023	LOS ANGELES	39.3	38.7	0.4	0.4	0.9	0.8	96.9	97.6	10.6	9.4	10.1	8.8	9.4	30.8	14.4	5.8	0.8	64.8	26.0	50.9	49.1
90024	LOS ANGELES	64.6	60.4	2.1	2.2	24.3	26.7	7.3	9.0	2.3	1.9	1.8	15.0	27.9	26.0	13.6	9.3	2.3	93.0	25.7	47.4	52.6
90025	LOS ANGELES	66.1	61.5	3.0	3.1	17.1	18.8	16.1	19.6	3.8	3.1	3.0	3.6	9.0	46.5	19.8	9.4	1.8	88.3	34.6	50.4	49.7
90026	LOS ANGELES	35.7	34.3	2.6	2.4	18.5	17.7	63.7	67.4	7.9	7.1	7.8	7.3	8.7	34.4	18.9	7.1	0.9	72.9	31.4	51.1	48.9
90027	LOS ANGELES	61.8	57.7	3.7	3.8	12.6	13.6	25.1	29.0	4.7	4.4	5.0	5.4	7.4	37.1	23.2	11.1	1.8	82.9	37.2	50.1	50.0
90028	LOS ANGELES	54.9	50.5	7.6	7.3	7.7	8.1	39.4	45.7	5.6	4.8	5.5	6.0	9.7	41.7	17.7	8.0	1.0	80.9	32.5	54.8	45.2
90029	LOS ANGELES	38.2	35.7	2.8	2.7	15.3	14.6	61.0	65.7	8.0	7.2	8.0	7.4	8.9	33.4	18.7	7.3	1.2	72.6	31.2	51.2	48.9
90031	LOS ANGELES	29.6	29.5	1.1	1.0	24.8	23.3	68.9	71.5	9.1	8.4	9.0	8.5	8.3	29.3	18.1	8.1	1.3	68.5	29.3	49.5	50.5
90032	LOS ANGELES	35.8	35.2	2.2	1.9	12.1	11.3	80.1	82.3	8.8	8.3	8.9	8.0	8.3	30.6	17.7	8.3	1.0	69.2	29.6	49.3	50.7
90033	LOS ANGELES	33.6	33.1	1.6	1.4	3.7	3.4	92.2	93.3	10.1	9.4	10.3	9.6	9.2	28.9	15.3	6.1	1.2	64.2	25.9	51.0	49.0
90034	LOS ANGELES	46.4	43.2	15.1	14.5	16.2	17.1	28.9	33.0	6.2	5.3	5.8	6.1	9.4	41.4	18.8	6.1	1.1	79.5	32.1	49.6	50.5
90035	LOS ANGELES	71.3	67.9	12.6	13.0	5.6	6.4	9.1	11.2	5.8	5.3	5.2	4.8	6.2	35.6	22.8	11.2	3.3	80.9	37.6	47.3	52.7
90036	LOS ANGELES	69.3	65.5	7.8	8.2	16.6	18.7	6.7	8.4	4.7	3.9	4.3	4.0	7.0	45.2	18.8	9.4	2.7	84.7	34.8	48.4	51.6
90037	LOS ANGELES	20.8	21.3	29.9	26.7	0.6	0.6	67.8	71.5	10.9	9.6	10.2	9.0	9.8	29.7	14.9	5.2	0.7	63.9	25.3	49.7	50.3
90038	LOS ANGELES	42.4	39.4	4.5	4.1	8.2	8.1	62.1	67.0	7.7	6.9	7.5	7.1	9.3	37.7	17.2	5.8	0.8	73.9	30.6	53.0	47.0
90039	LOS ANGELES	49.6	46.4	2.5	2.6	19.2	19.5	45.0	49.3	6.1	5.8	6.2	5.9	6.8	33.8	24.0	9.8	1.7	78.5	36.7	50.9	49.1
90040	LOS ANGELES	44.3	43.4	1.0	0.9	1.2	1.1	93.5	94.9	9.2	8.6	9.9	9.0	8.6	28.8	16.8	8.4	0.9	66.7	28.1	49.4	50.6
90041	LOS ANGELES	48.3	45.2	2.2	2.2	25.4	25.8	39.5	44.1	6.4	6.2	6.8	7.2	8.1	29.2	23.8	10.3	2.0	76.7	35.9	48.3	51.7
90042	LOS ANGELES	40.9	39.2	3.1	2.9	12.4	12.0	69.8	73.4	9.0	8.1	8.9	8.1	8.5	31.1	18.9	6.5	0.9	69.2	29.4	49.7	50.3
90043	LOS ANGELES	8.4	8.7	72.5	69.8	0.8	0.8	22.6	25.6	7.5	7.5	8.6	7.7	6.8	26.9	22.7	11.1	1.4	71.7	34.9	45.9	54.1
90044	LOS ANGELES	17.1	17.9	45.2	41.5	0.6	0.6	52.6	56.7	10.7	9.8	11.0	9.6	8.7	27.8	15.8	6.0	0.7	62.7	25.2	47.9	52.1
90045	LOS ANGELES	62.0	59.8	16.5	15.6	9.7	10.8	16.9	20.1	6.1	5.9	5.7	7.9	8.1	31.5	23.4	9.9	1.6	79.4	36.3	47.9	52.1
90046	LOS ANGELES	85.5	82.7	3.6	3.9	4.3	5.1	8.1	10.5	2.6	2.2	2.7	3.4	6.5	43.5	23.1	13.4	2.6	90.6	39.3	52.9	47.1
90047	LOS ANGELES	8.4	9.1	73.0	70.4	0.6	0.6	24.3	27.1	7.8	8.2	9.6	8.1	6.4	26.4	21.7	10.8	1.1	69.4	33.4	45.4	54.6
90048	LOS ANGELES	85.9	83.2	2.4	2.7	5.5	6.4	6.2	8.1	3.4	2.7	2.6	2.8	4.7	43.0	21.6	13.9	5.2	89.7	39.8	47.1	52.9
90049	LOS ANGELES	87.3	84.6	1.4	1.6	6.8	8.1	4.6	6.1	4.1	4.4	4.2	3.8	5.2	35.2	25.8	14.8	2.5	85.1	40.5	46.3	53.7
90056	LOS ANGELES	18.8	16.9	71.6	72.4	3.2	3.5	3.9	4.6	5.5	6.0	6.3	5.4	4.5	23.6	29.7	16.5	2.7	79.0	44.3	45.3	54.7
90057	LOS ANGELES	28.7	28.2	5.5	4.9	18.4	17.3	69.5	72.6	9.3	8.1	7.5	6.4	9.7	36.0	15.5	6.5	1.1	71.7	29.2	53.5	46.5
90058	LOS ANGELES	29.3	29.2	12.6	11.1	6.2	5.7	77.7	80.3	10.2	11.9	13.1	10.1	7.6	27.8	15.2	3.9	0.4	58.5	23.2	49.5	50.5
90059	LOS ANGELES	13.5	14.2	45.9	42.2	0.4	0.4	52.3	56.3	11.2	10.7	12.1	10.0	8.7	26.5	14.3	5.7	0.8	59.9	23.5	47.1	52.9
90061	LOS ANGELES	14.1	14.8	45.9	42.1	0.4	0.4	52.7	56.7	9.8	9.7	11.1	9.8	8.3	27.3	15.8	7.3	0.8	63.2	25.9	48.2	51.8
90062	LOS ANGELES	14.5	15.4	51.8	47.9	1.7	1.6	44.3	48.5	8.8	8.7	9.7	8.2	7.5	28.5	19.0	8.2	1.2	67.6	30.1	46.9	53.1
90063	LOS ANGELES	36.7	36.3	0.5	0.5	1.3	1.2	96.8	97.3	10.3	9.3	10.0	8.6	9.3	30.2	15.0	6.5	0.8	65.2	26.4	50.6	49.4
90064	LOS ANGELES	71.9	68.4	2.6	2.7	14.4	15.9	15.6	18.6	5.4	5.5	5.2	4.4	4.9	33.5	25.5	12.5	3.1	81.4	39.7	48.6	51.4
90065	LOS ANGELES	41.5	39.9	2.0	1.9	15.4	15.0	66.3	69.6	8.3	7.7	8.5	7.5	7.7	30.7	20.6	8.2	1.0	71.1	31.6	50.1	49.9
90066	LOS ANGELES	61.3	57.7	4.0	3.9	13.4	14.2	32.3	37.2	6.0	5.5	5.4	5.0	7.0	36.3	23.2	10.0	1.6	80.1	36.4	49.8	50.2
90067	LOS ANGELES	85.6	82.8	2.3	2.6	8.5	10.1	4.0	5.3	2.5	2.2	1.9	2.1	3.2	22.6	26.1	31.2	8.1	92.2	57.7	44.2	55.8
90068	LOS ANGELES	81.3	78.3	4.7	5.0	5.4	6.3	9.3	11.6	3.4	2.8	2.6	2.6	5.0	45.2	26.8	10.0	1.5	89.8	39.6	55.0	45.0
90069	WEST HOLLYWOOD	87.6	85.1	3.0	3.4	3.9	4.6	7.4	9.6	1.8	1.3	1.1	1.2	4.7	49.3	26.1	12.2	2.4	95.2	40.9	58.6	41.4
90071	LOS ANGELES	28.6	28.6	14.3	14.3	57.1	57.1	14.3	14.3	0.0	0.0	0.0	0.0	0.0	0.0	0.0	71.4	28.6	100.0	81.3	28.6	71.4
90077	LOS ANGELES	86.9	84.1	1.7	1.9	6.8	8.1	4.1	5.4	5.2	6.4	6.3	4.8	2.7	23.6	31.7	17.0	2.4	79.1	45.6	48.4	51.7
90089	LOS ANGELES	47.9	43.5	4.6	4.4	28.3	30.4	14.6	16.9	0.0	0.0	0.0	81.6	16.9	0.5	1.0	0.0	0.0	97.1	18.1	44.4	55.6
90095	LOS ANGELES	62.1	57.3	1.5	1.3	21.2	24.0	18.2	20.0	0.0	0.0	2.7	2.7	16.0	28.0	10.7	14.7	25.3	96.0	45.8	38.7	61.3
90201	BELL	47.1	46.2	1.1	1.0	0.9	0.8	92.7	94.3	11.6	10.4	10.8	9.0	9.4	30.9	13.8	3.7	0.5	61.9	24.4	50.4	49.6
90210	BEVERLY HILLS	88.2	85.6	1.4	1.5	5.0	5.9	4.8	6.3	4.7	5.3	5.9	5.2	4.6	24.3	29.8	17.2	3.1	80.8	45.0	46.8	53.2
90211	BEVERLY HILLS	83.2	79.9	1.8	2.0	9.1	10.8	4.3	5.6	4.0	4.2	6.9	7.6	7.1	30.0	26.2	11.6	2.4	80.2	39.2	46.7	53.3
90212	BEVERLY HILLS	84.8	81.6	2.2	2.4	7.7	9.2	4.0	5.2	3.2	3.9	6.5	7.3	5.2	31.4	27.3	12.6	2.6	81.5	40.5	44.6	55.4
90220	COMPTON	15.7	16.1	46.7	43.7	1.9	1.9	47.2	50.7	9.5	9.5	11.1	9.6	8.0	26.7	17.2	7.9	0.6	64.0	26.8	48.2	51.8
90221	COMPTON	20.4	20.9	30.2	27.1	1.1	1.0	67.1	70.6	11.4	10.3	11.2	9.6	9.4	28.6	14.9	4.3	0.3	61.3	24.0	49.7	50.3
90222	COMPTON	18.7	19.5	37.6	34.1	0.4	0.4	61.4	65.1	10.6	9.9	11.1	9.6	8.8	27.2	15.1	6.9	0.9	62.5	25.0	49.4	50.6
90230	CULVER CITY	52.2	49.1	13.1	13.3	12.6	13.3	32.9	36.1	5.7	5.9	7.1	6.4	6.3	29.5	25.7	11.7	1.7	77.4	38.3	47.9	52.1
90232	CULVER CITY	58.6	54.5	7.7	7.7	13.8	14.7	28.4	33.2	5.6	5.5	6.5	6.2	7.0	32.4	25.8	9.6	1.5	78.7	37.7	47.6	52.4
90240	DOWNEY	59.4	56.0	1.8	1.7	10.2	10.3	52.4	58.3	6.9	6.9	8.0	7.3	6.9	28.5	22.2	11.4	2.0	73.8	35.1	48.7	51.3
90241	DOWNEY	55.8	52.5	2.8	2.6	7.2	7.2	57.6	63.5	8.1	7.4	7.9	7.2	7.7	30.2	20.0	9.7	2.0	72.3	32.7	47.7	52.3
90242	DOWNEY	48.2	45.3	5.7	5.3	7.5	7.5	61.0	66.4	8.8	8.1	8.5	9.0	8.1	30.5	18.8	7.3	1.0	68.9	29.8	49.5	50.5
90245	EL SEGUNDO	83.6	80.7	1.2	1.2	6.7	7.7	11.0	13.9	5.9	5.8	6.6	6.2	5.8	34.0	26.1	8.5	1.2	77.8	37.9	49.5	50.5
90247	GARDENA	24.4	23.6	19.2	17.7	27.5	27.6	42.0	45.2	8.2	7.5	8.0	7.0	7.2	31.0	19.6	10.3	1.2	72.1	32.8	49.3	50.7
90248	GARDENA	29.7	28.2	17.8	16.8	31.3	31.9	33.5	36.1	7.0	6.8	7.4	6.1	5.6	28.1	22.0	15.8	1.3	75.1	37.5	49.3	50.7
90249	GARDENA	27.6	25.9	35.1	34.4	16.8	16.8	29.1	32.6	7.9	7.7	8.1	6.7	6.6	29.8	23.2	9.0	1.0	72.3	34.1	49.0	51.0
90250	HAWTHORNE	32.1	30.9	30.1	28.3	8.0	8.0	44.4	49.1	9.8	8.8	9.0	7.4	8.5	32.6	17.6	5.7	0.6	68.1	28.9	48.4	51.6
90254	HERMOSA BEACH	89.5	87.1	0.8	0.9	4.7	5.5	6.8	8.9	4.1	3.1	3.3	2.9	5.9	51.6	21.9	6.3	0.9	87.4	35.0	52.9	47.1
90255	HUNTINGTON PARK	42.1	41.6	0.7	0.7	0.8	0.7	95.6	96.5	10.6	9.5	10.1	8.6	9.5	31.4	15.0	4.8	0.5	64.7	26.0	50.4	49.6
90260	LAWNDALE	43.8	41.2	11.5	10.7	11.5	11.5	50.1	55.4	9.1	8.6	9.2	7.5	7.7	33.1	18.4	5.9	0.6	68.5	30.1	50.5	49.5
90262	LYNWOOD	33.5	33.4	13.7	12.2	1.2	1.1	82.1	84.6	10.8	9.8	10.8	9.7	10.0	30.1	14.7	3.7	0.5	63.0	24.5	51.2	48.8
90263	MALIBU	84.6	81.5	3.4	3.8	5.3	6.2	7.3	9.5	2.6	2.6	2.8	28.2	29.6	13.7	16.3	4.0	0.4	90.4	22.3	44.5	55.5
90265	MALIBU	89.8	87.6	1.6	1.8	3.3	3.9	6.4	8.5	4.5	5.2	5.9	8.8	6.7	23.8	32.1	11.7	1.3	80.1	42.1	49.7	50.3
90266	MANHATTAN BEACH	89.0	86.7	0.6	0.7	6.2	7.3	5.2	6.8	6.2	6.8	6.7	5.1	3.7	33.7	27.3	9.6	1.1	77.1	38.9	50.4	49.7
90270	MAYWOOD	43.0	42.4	0.4	0.3	0.5	0.5	96.3	97.2	11.4	10.4	10.5	8.4	9.2	32.0	13.9	3.7	0.5	62.6	25.0	50.8	49.2
90272	PACIFIC PALISADES	91.3	89.3	0.8	0.9	4.7	5.7	3.6	4.8	6.0	7.3	7.7	5.5	2.8	21.5	31.9	15.0	2.4	75.2	44.6	48.2	51.8
90274	PALOS VERDES PENINSU	76.8	73.2	1.2	1.3	18.0	20.7	3.8	5.0	4.9	6.4	7.7	6.2	3.5	18.1	32.3	19.0	1.9	76.9	46.9	48.6	51.4
90275	RANCHO PALOS VERDES	66.9	62.8	2.3	2.4	25.8	28.7	6.2	7.6	4.9	5.9	7.0	6.3	4.0	20.4	31.2	18.4	1.9	77.9	45.8	48.2	51.8
90277	REDONDO BEACH	83.8	80.7	1.8	2.0	7.7	8.9	9.2	11.8	4.4	4.3	4.3	4.2	4.7	38.3	28.1	10.4	1.4	84.4	40.2	50.0	50.0
90278	REDONDO BEACH	75.1	71.3	2.9	3.0	11.1	12.4	16.0	19.8	6.3	6.2	6.0	5.5	5.5	36.5	25.5	7.7	0.8	78.2	37.7	50.0	50.0
90280	SOUTH GATE	41.7	40.6	1.0	0.9	1.0	0.9	91.9	93.5	10.2	9.4	10.2	8.8	9.2	30.8	16.1	4.6	0.7	64.9	26.2	49.7	50.3
	CALIFORNIA	59.6	57.1	6.7	6.5	11.3	11.8	32.4	35.5	7.4	7.1	7.8	7.3	7.7	29.8	22.1	9.3	1.4	73.3	33.8	49.8	50.2
	UNITED STATES	75.1	73.6	12.3	12.5	3.8	4.2	12.5	14.1	6.9	6.7	7.2	7.0	7.3	28.6	23.8	10.8	1.7	75.1	36.0	49.1	50.9

#	ZIP CODE POST OFFICE NAME	2004 Per Capita Income	2004 HH Income Base	2004 Household Income Distribution (%) Less than $25,000	$25,000 to $49,999	$50,000 to $99,999	$100,000 to $149,999	$150,000 or More	Median Household Income 2004	2009	2004 National Centile	2004 State Centile	2004 Home Value Base	2004 Home Value Distribution (%) Less than $50,000	$50,000 to $89,999	$90,000 to $174,999	$175,000 to $399,999	$400,000 or More	2004 Median Home Value
90001	LOS ANGELES	8703	12585	46.0	31.1	18.5	3.2	1.3	26943	31331	7	6	4883	1.7	1.4	18.5	77.3	1.1	220599
90002	LOS ANGELES	9832	10855	48.3	28.0	18.3	3.9	1.5	26049	30717	6	6	4550	1.8	1.5	25.7	69.4	1.6	204318
90003	LOS ANGELES	8945	14856	49.6	29.5	16.3	3.0	1.6	25175	29213	5	5	5535	2.5	1.4	21.7	72.6	1.8	212925
90004	LOS ANGELES	18739	23888	41.2	30.3	18.1	5.1	5.4	30892	35168	15	12	4576	2.1	2.0	2.8	28.2	65.0	546518
90005	LOS ANGELES	13813	14648	50.9	28.8	14.2	3.1	3.0	24482	27403	4	4	1376	6.1	0.0	4.4	30.9	58.6	486765
90006	LOS ANGELES	11472	18262	54.6	27.9	12.6	3.3	1.6	22570	25386	3	3	1913	3.8	0.8	7.1	68.0	20.3	282971
90007	LOS ANGELES	11522	12656	58.3	24.2	13.4	2.9	1.3	20212	23082	2	2	1687	3.1	0.5	7.9	72.6	15.9	272258
90008	LOS ANGELES	24070	14582	38.5	25.4	22.7	7.7	5.8	33875	40890	24	18	4871	0.6	0.6	5.3	53.0	40.6	361664
90010	LOS ANGELES	31992	2352	48.5	25.0	15.4	4.0	7.1	25938	31199	6	5	295	1.0	1.7	18.6	13.6	65.1	1000001
90011	LOS ANGELES	9047	21999	46.6	31.7	16.1	3.4	2.2	26608	30820	7	6	6887	2.3	1.6	17.5	73.1	5.5	224510
90012	LOS ANGELES	19426	8864	55.0	20.2	14.5	6.2	4.0	21517	25788	2	2	1195	8.0	0.3	16.2	59.3	16.2	244900
90013	LOS ANGELES	18018	3125	77.8	12.4	6.1	2.4	1.4	9475	10886	0	1	81	9.9	0.0	16.1	60.5	13.6	258654
90014	LOS ANGELES	19360	2732	85.9	8.1	4.3	0.6	1.1	8249	9169	0	1	36	38.9	2.8	13.9	44.4	0.0	165000
90015	LOS ANGELES	12603	5949	59.4	24.5	10.1	2.9	3.2	20089	22488	2	2	674	1.6	3.3	26.9	46.3	22.0	275000
90016	LOS ANGELES	16700	15960	36.9	29.8	23.7	6.9	2.7	34323	41426	25	19	6502	0.6	0.5	16.0	72.6	10.4	246930
90017	LOS ANGELES	10343	7331	68.8	22.4	6.3	0.8	1.7	16220	17602	1	2	93	0.0	0.0	4.3	21.5	74.2	442453
90018	LOS ANGELES	13212	16168	46.3	28.7	18.6	4.5	1.9	27537	32971	8	7	5060	0.6	0.3	7.9	78.3	13.0	258579
90019	LOS ANGELES	20324	24759	35.5	26.9	24.5	7.7	5.4	36285	44685	33	23	7140	1.0	0.4	3.8	40.9	53.8	420073
90020	LOS ANGELES	18952	17902	46.8	30.2	16.0	3.4	3.5	26676	30611	7	6	1604	5.3	3.4	13.7	29.4	48.2	365882
90021	LOS ANGELES	17042	1349	65.1	21.7	8.2	4.3	0.7	15111	17865	1	2	116	0.0	8.6	0.0	36.2	55.2	420000
90022	LOS ANGELES	11194	17667	39.4	32.6	21.9	4.1	2.1	30955	36229	15	12	6977	1.2	0.3	10.3	82.0	6.2	251628
90023	LOS ANGELES	9561	10477	40.8	33.0	20.5	3.6	2.1	29942	34766	12	10	3372	1.2	0.5	11.5	81.1	5.7	248159
90024	LOS ANGELES	57539	17980	30.2	15.4	21.5	12.0	21.0	58121	77962	83	66	5953	0.2	0.1	1.2	16.6	81.9	993928
90025	LOS ANGELES	45597	21838	20.9	22.2	30.8	14.1	12.1	57446	73900	82	64	5659	0.3	0.5	1.2	25.9	72.2	534356
90026	LOS ANGELES	17088	24845	38.4	30.5	20.6	6.7	3.8	32276	38424	19	14	6428	1.7	0.8	6.2	58.0	33.2	327893
90027	LOS ANGELES	30703	23912	34.6	26.4	22.2	8.8	8.0	38221	49130	40	27	5807	0.2	1.0	5.0	22.2	71.6	633278
90028	LOS ANGELES	18042	14870	48.4	29.1	17.0	4.2	1.3	25886	31467	6	5	616	0.7	0.5	15.4	42.4	41.1	340217
90029	LOS ANGELES	11767	13811	50.2	30.7	14.9	2.8	1.4	24881	28517	4	4	1710	1.6	0.3	5.5	54.3	38.3	353037
90031	LOS ANGELES	11960	10850	43.3	31.1	18.8	4.7	2.1	28817	33636	10	9	3732	5.5	1.2	13.8	71.0	8.6	245091
90032	LOS ANGELES	13992	12721	32.0	31.5	25.8	7.8	3.0	37979	45204	39	26	6593	3.0	0.6	12.9	79.1	4.5	237385
90033	LOS ANGELES	9347	12257	50.2	31.2	15.0	2.2	1.4	24855	28707	4	4	2629	0.7	0.8	15.7	73.6	9.3	238752
90034	LOS ANGELES	28752	26614	25.4	31.1	27.4	9.6	6.6	43773	53877	58	39	5958	1.5	1.1	4.4	32.6	60.5	474850
90035	LOS ANGELES	43401	13283	21.5	20.5	28.7	16.0	13.3	60197	78937	85	68	4697	0.0	0.2	1.0	15.9	82.9	661276
90036	LOS ANGELES	45218	17987	20.1	22.5	31.8	13.6	12.1	58164	75663	83	66	3350	0.8	0.3	1.0	9.1	88.9	722985
90037	LOS ANGELES	9632	14752	53.8	27.9	13.9	2.9	1.5	22408	25920	3	3	4267	2.3	2.4	14.0	75.2	6.1	229028
90038	LOS ANGELES	13338	12434	49.8	31.2	14.4	2.9	1.7	25099	28509	5	5	1102	0.2	0.0	6.2	62.1	31.6	342978
90039	LOS ANGELES	31809	11504	21.4	25.6	31.2	12.7	9.2	52839	65133	77	58	5415	0.7	0.3	5.4	49.0	44.6	373214
90040	LOS ANGELES	13021	3458	33.0	30.8	26.8	7.9	1.6	38564	45448	41	28	1761	1.5	0.0	12.2	82.6	3.8	244037
90041	LOS ANGELES	25544	9671	20.7	24.2	31.3	15.4	8.5	55881	68279	81	62	5349	1.9	0.4	3.4	61.7	32.5	336601
90042	LOS ANGELES	16780	19477	30.1	29.3	28.0	8.9	3.7	40612	48000	48	33	8460	1.4	1.2	14.0	74.3	9.2	242203
90043	LOS ANGELES	21730	16731	32.9	26.6	24.8	10.1	5.5	39011	47239	43	28	9080	0.9	0.8	8.4	65.9	24.0	272219
90044	LOS ANGELES	10343	25157	49.1	29.6	16.6	3.2	1.4	25554	30212	5	5	8923	1.3	1.1	18.6	75.4	3.6	223728
90045	LOS ANGELES	37211	17843	15.4	21.2	31.5	17.4	14.5	68583	86302	91	76	9703	0.5	0.8	1.5	20.6	76.6	549795
90046	LOS ANGELES	50011	29922	28.2	25.1	25.0	10.6	11.1	46530	60411	65	44	6919	0.3	0.4	4.5	19.2	75.7	710948
90047	LOS ANGELES	16954	16048	33.3	27.0	29.5	7.8	2.4	39421	47722	44	30	9635	0.7	0.4	9.2	86.6	3.1	240943
90048	LOS ANGELES	52300	11929	20.7	21.5	29.9	14.1	13.8	58288	78369	83	66	3724	0.4	0.5	1.5	10.6	87.0	710891
90049	LOS ANGELES	101129	17442	10.0	11.8	25.4	17.2	35.6	106100	143646	99	95	9583	0.3	0.2	1.1	6.1	92.4	1000001
90056	LOS ANGELES	56040	3417	8.2	16.0	30.2	18.0	27.6	90335	117897	97	91	2562	0.0	0.2	0.2	13.2	86.5	643514
90057	LOS ANGELES	10447	15598	58.1	28.0	11.0	2.2	0.7	21194	23304	2	2	772	7.0	12.7	24.6	51.8	3.9	188415
90058	LOS ANGELES	8860	986	57.3	24.7	13.7	3.0	1.3	20843	23653	2	2	155	0.0	0.0	21.9	67.7	10.3	234868
90059	LOS ANGELES	9660	9526	50.9	25.3	18.0	4.0	1.8	24360	28755	4	4	3999	1.3	1.9	25.8	68.3	2.7	206935
90061	LOS ANGELES	10495	6067	41.7	30.8	21.2	4.6	1.8	30233	35338	13	11	2984	1.6	0.8	19.5	75.5	2.6	219316
90062	LOS ANGELES	14306	8722	42.2	29.6	20.5	5.4	2.4	30859	37484	14	12	3853	2.0	1.4	11.6	81.9	3.2	233822
90063	LOS ANGELES	10917	13261	36.6	32.2	24.5	4.8	1.9	33152	38712	21	16	5421	2.9	0.9	15.2	74.9	6.1	231162
90064	LOS ANGELES	54739	10755	15.5	18.9	27.5	16.1	22.1	73217	98203	93	80	6225	0.6	0.9	1.2	9.7	87.7	707386
90065	LOS ANGELES	19391	14385	27.2	28.2	27.8	11.0	5.8	44411	52906	60	41	7434	1.5	1.0	7.5	69.2	20.8	287366
90066	LOS ANGELES	33980	23680	20.5	25.1	29.9	13.6	10.9	54814	70338	79	60	9875	0.5	0.8	1.8	21.7	75.1	547794
90067	LOS ANGELES	106978	1568	18.9	13.4	21.1	14.4	32.1	85833	131063	96	90	1075	0.0	0.0	0.5	8.2	91.4	839015
90068	LOS ANGELES	75001	13130	18.2	20.6	25.0	14.2	22.1	67808	96332	90	76	5895	0.5	0.2	2.3	12.7	84.3	783356
90069	WEST HOLLYWOOD	81409	14165	20.0	19.9	28.7	14.0	17.5	62568	81665	87	70	5050	0.1	0.0	3.9	31.7	64.3	583541
90071	LOS ANGELES	0	0	0.0	0.0	0.0	0.0	0.0	0	0	0	0	0	0.0	0.0	0.0	0.0	0.0	0
90077	LOS ANGELES	129906	3658	7.0	6.6	14.4	15.1	56.8	182633	239692	100	100	3320	0.1	0.0	0.5	1.5	97.9	1000001
90089	LOS ANGELES	5072	116	92.2	7.8	0.0	0.0	0.0	6905	7703	0	1	0	0.0	0.0	0.0	0.0	0.0	0
90095	LOS ANGELES	8498	0	0.0	0.0	0.0	0.0	0.0	0	0	0	0	0	0.0	0.0	0.0	0.0	0.0	0
90201	BELL	10214	24328	35.0	36.4	22.7	4.3	1.6	33233	38430	22	16	6598	10.9	0.8	7.4	70.3	10.6	256172
90210	BEVERLY HILLS	113679	9702	10.3	9.6	18.4	16.3	45.4	133638	178602	100	98	7077	0.1	0.0	0.3	2.9	96.8	1000001
90211	BEVERLY HILLS	54250	3822	16.4	17.4	27.9	16.1	22.3	73810	103238	93	81	1579	0.0	0.2	0.8	2.7	96.3	1000001
90212	BEVERLY HILLS	69818	5874	16.2	15.7	28.5	14.5	25.1	78314	108517	95	85	1764	0.0	0.7	1.5	4.6	93.1	1000001
90220	COMPTON	12941	13064	32.8	30.3	28.2	6.9	1.9	38382	45303	41	27	8183	4.2	7.7	19.0	67.2	2.0	207582
90221	COMPTON	10544	11227	34.2	31.0	26.0	6.1	2.8	35966	42633	31	22	6032	2.2	0.9	16.0	79.1	1.8	218907
90222	COMPTON	11902	7397	37.4	29.5	24.5	5.7	2.9	33295	39095	22	17	3966	1.8	0.5	22.8	73.2	1.7	211738
90230	CULVER CITY	32451	12812	17.9	22.5	33.7	15.2	10.7	60480	74843	85	68	7393	1.4	1.7	8.4	40.0	48.5	388617
90232	CULVER CITY	31421	7242	19.7	27.1	32.7	12.7	7.9	53273	66070	77	58	3074	0.2	0.9	2.9	32.4	63.7	468627
90240	DOWNEY	26297	7491	17.9	18.5	37.6	16.5	9.6	64874	79130	88	72	5450	1.0	0.2	1.4	57.2	40.2	368776
90241	DOWNEY	22199	13856	23.1	27.5	31.6	11.6	6.2	49470	59140	71	51	6584	0.8	0.8	3.5	61.3	33.6	346505
90242	DOWNEY	18012	13109	22.3	29.3	33.3	11.1	4.0	48666	56758	70	50	6697	2.1	0.6	4.1	80.4	12.9	289265
90245	EL SEGUNDO	42064	7303	10.0	19.7	37.6	20.4	12.2	73879	92583	93	81	3061	0.0	0.0	1.8	14.9	83.2	600132
90247	GARDENA	17000	16432	30.6	29.8	30.0	7.6	2.0	39756	47397	45	30	6418	7.6	0.8	9.2	72.4	10.1	261328
90248	GARDENA	22922	3347	20.8	28.3	31.8	15.2	3.8	50793	60946	73	54	2349	8.5	4.3	6.3	70.5	10.5	263020
90249	GARDENA	22652	9366	23.3	24.6	32.9	14.7	4.6	52283	62702	76	57	5403	2.2	0.5	5.2	87.1	4.9	277167
90250	HAWTHORNE	17786	32870	31.3	32.6	25.4	7.5	3.3	37669	44137	38	26	10933	1.1	0.4	4.4	75.4	18.7	283659
90254	HERMOSA BEACH	71267	9555	7.9	14.0	27.0	23.5	27.7	101780	135461	98	95	4284	0.4	0.5	0.9	6.5	91.6	831181
90255	HUNTINGTON PARK	10881	19784	35.2	33.6	24.5	5.1	1.6	33572	38772	23	17	6771	0.8	0.7	8.7	84.2	5.7	257249
90260	LAWNDALE	16669	10226	23.4	30.4	34.4	9.0	2.8	46364	54113	65	44	4060	1.3	0.5	7.4	80.7	10.2	282860
90262	LYNWOOD	10622	14365	28.7	34.6	28.7	6.6	1.4	39635	45607	45	30	6805	1.5	1.2	8.8	84.9	3.8	234545
90263	MALIBU	9846	4	0.0	0.0	0.0	0.0	100.0	225000	250000	100	100	3	0.0	0.0	0.0	0.0	100.0	1000001
90265	MALIBU	95144	7745	9.0	10.5	21.0	17.5	42.0	124568	163102	99	98	5967	0.2	0.2	1.7	7.8	90.1	1000001
90266	MANHATTAN BEACH	80103	14417	6.4	9.3	23.4	21.9	39.1	122115	159398	99	98	9783	0.1	0.3	0.5	2.3	96.9	1000001
90270	MAYWOOD	10126	6609	35.1	35.2	24.1	4.2	1.5	33464	38719	22	17	2210	1.6	0.0	5.5	85.5	7.4	248582
90272	PACIFIC PALISADES	104930	9392	5.6	8.9	19.1	16.7	49.7	148980	195061	100	99	8048	0.5	0.6	1.3	4.1	93.6	1000001
90274	PALOS VERDES PENINSU	83294	9599	4.4	9.2	18.9	20.6	46.9	141598	181015	100	99	8782	0.1	0.3	0.9	3.0	95.8	1000001
90275	RANCHO PALOS VERDES	58933	16165	6.4	12.4	24.6	22.7	34.0	111321	142330	99	96	13449	0.2	0.6	0.9	6.7	91.6	894155
90277	REDONDO BEACH	56132	17327	10.1	15.9	33.8	19.8	20.4	82639	109226	96	88	8262	0.4	0.8	1.2	12.0	85.5	670964
90278	REDONDO BEACH	43203	16329	11.5	15.8	33.6	21.8	17.2	82096	105246	96	87	9331	2.2	0.3	0.8	21.4	75.3	510081
90280	SOUTH GATE	12007	23715	27.5	34.7	29.5	6.4	1.9	39909	46199	46	31	11364	2.2	0.6	4.4	88.4	4.5	253366
	CALIFORNIA	27293		21.8	24.4	30.5	13.7	9.7	54267	64547				3.3	2.7	13.3	42.9	37.9	319678
	UNITED STATES	25866		24.7	27.1	30.8	10.9	6.5	48124	56710				10.9	15.0	33.7	30.1	10.4	145905

ZIP CODE #	POST OFFICE NAME	FINANCIAL SERVICES Auto Loan	Home Loan	Invest-ments	Retire-ment Plans	THE HOME: Home Improvements Home Repair	Lawn & Garden	Furnishings Comput-ers & Hard-ware	Major Appli-ances	TV, Radio, Sound Equip-ment	Furni-ture	ENTERTAINMENT Dine out/ Carry out	Sports Equip-ment	Fees & Tickets	Toys & Games	Travel	Cable TV	PERSONAL Apparel & Services	Auto Repairs	Health Insur-ance	Pets & Supplies
90001	LOS ANGELES	55	47	46	46	46	48	53	53	55	56	70	60	50	68	49	52	70	56	48	56
90002	LOS ANGELES	60	51	51	50	50	53	57	58	60	60	76	65	54	72	54	57	76	61	54	62
90003	LOS ANGELES	52	44	44	43	43	45	50	50	52	53	66	57	47	63	46	49	66	53	46	53
90004	LOS ANGELES	62	65	124	63	62	71	74	68	81	76	103	79	75	110	75	85	104	74	69	75
90005	LOS ANGELES	46	48	89	48	47	52	55	52	59	56	76	61	55	80	56	61	76	56	50	56
90006	LOS ANGELES	45	44	79	41	41	48	50	48	57	53	73	54	50	76	51	60	74	51	48	52
90007	LOS ANGELES	43	34	46	35	33	37	47	41	49	46	61	50	43	60	42	46	60	46	39	45
90008	LOS ANGELES	76	72	87	68	70	81	76	75	81	78	102	83	78	99	77	84	99	77	79	85
90010	LOS ANGELES	68	71	118	73	70	78	82	75	85	80	107	90	83	111	83	86	106	81	76	82
90011	LOS ANGELES	62	52	51	52	51	53	59	59	61	62	78	67	56	76	55	57	78	62	53	62
90012	LOS ANGELES	55	57	85	63	58	60	65	61	63	63	79	76	64	79	64	60	78	66	56	66
90013	LOS ANGELES	33	29	44	31	29	34	36	33	38	35	48	39	36	47	36	39	46	36	36	37
90014	LOS ANGELES	28	24	36	25	25	29	31	28	32	29	40	33	30	40	30	33	39	31	30	31
90015	LOS ANGELES	50	43	48	44	42	44	51	49	52	52	66	57	48	65	47	49	66	53	45	52
90016	LOS ANGELES	65	61	70	58	59	65	66	65	69	68	87	73	65	85	64	69	86	67	65	71
90017	LOS ANGELES	43	37	44	36	36	38	42	41	45	45	57	47	40	57	40	43	58	44	39	44
90018	LOS ANGELES	51	50	73	47	47	54	55	53	59	57	75	59	54	76	55	61	75	56	53	58
90019	LOS ANGELES	69	71	116	71	68	76	79	74	83	80	106	87	81	111	80	85	106	79	73	81
90020	LOS ANGELES	51	57	113	57	54	62	66	59	70	65	89	71	68	99	68	74	90	64	59	65
90021	LOS ANGELES	38	32	43	35	32	35	41	37	41	40	52	46	39	51	38	39	51	41	36	41
90022	LOS ANGELES	66	56	54	55	55	57	62	63	65	66	82	71	59	79	58	61	82	66	57	66
90023	LOS ANGELES	61	51	50	51	51	52	58	58	60	61	76	66	55	74	54	56	77	61	53	62
90024	LOS ANGELES	181	166	259	180	160	181	206	179	205	199	258	221	202	257	194	197	252	194	169	200
90025	LOS ANGELES	110	109	197	123	104	115	126	113	128	128	162	138	131	170	124	126	161	120	105	125
90026	LOS ANGELES	62	61	100	61	59	65	70	65	75	71	95	76	71	101	70	76	96	70	63	71
90027	LOS ANGELES	76	83	155	85	78	90	93	84	98	93	125	100	98	137	95	102	126	90	83	93
90028	LOS ANGELES	43	42	76	43	40	46	52	46	55	50	70	56	51	74	51	56	69	51	46	51
90029	LOS ANGELES	39	40	81	38	38	44	47	43	52	48	67	49	48	73	48	56	68	46	44	47
90031	LOS ANGELES	62	56	58	56	55	56	62	61	63	64	79	71	59	77	58	58	79	65	55	65
90032	LOS ANGELES	75	67	63	64	65	68	71	73	73	76	93	81	67	87	67	70	93	76	68	77
90033	LOS ANGELES	49	42	43	42	41	43	47	47	50	50	63	54	45	61	44	46	63	50	43	50
90034	LOS ANGELES	85	81	122	88	78	86	93	86	94	94	120	104	93	121	90	92	118	92	80	95
90035	LOS ANGELES	117	121	198	131	115	127	133	122	134	135	170	147	139	177	133	133	169	128	114	135
90036	LOS ANGELES	108	107	193	121	102	113	123	110	125	125	158	135	129	166	122	123	157	117	102	122
90037	LOS ANGELES	53	45	46	44	44	46	51	50	53	53	67	57	48	65	47	50	67	53	47	54
90038	LOS ANGELES	41	40	79	39	38	45	48	44	53	49	68	50	48	72	48	56	69	48	45	48
90039	LOS ANGELES	104	112	151	112	108	114	115	111	115	117	146	129	118	152	115	113	146	114	102	120
90040	LOS ANGELES	74	64	58	62	63	65	69	72	72	74	90	79	64	84	65	68	90	74	66	75
90041	LOS ANGELES	90	103	143	99	98	106	103	99	104	105	132	113	107	141	105	105	133	101	93	107
90042	LOS ANGELES	78	73	78	72	70	74	77	77	79	81	100	87	76	99	74	75	100	80	71	82
90043	LOS ANGELES	83	81	97	77	79	90	84	83	89	86	112	91	87	109	85	92	109	85	87	94
90044	LOS ANGELES	53	46	48	44	44	48	51	51	54	53	68	57	49	65	48	53	67	53	50	55
90045	LOS ANGELES	112	128	175	130	123	130	128	122	124	129	157	143	133	163	128	122	156	124	110	132
90046	LOS ANGELES	107	107	194	118	102	115	123	111	127	124	161	134	129	170	123	127	160	118	105	123
90047	LOS ANGELES	71	67	74	64	65	75	69	69	74	72	93	75	71	89	70	76	90	71	73	79
90048	LOS ANGELES	118	117	210	131	111	123	134	120	137	136	173	147	140	182	133	135	172	128	112	134
90049	LOS ANGELES	253	285	458	302	274	301	291	272	286	297	363	320	315	381	297	286	364	277	254	300
90056	LOS ANGELES	172	207	245	204	203	214	193	191	185	194	233	218	205	239	199	185	231	188	181	209
90057	LOS ANGELES	35	35	63	33	33	38	40	37	45	42	57	43	40	61	40	47	58	40	38	41
90058	LOS ANGELES	46	39	40	39	38	39	44	44	46	46	58	50	42	56	41	43	58	46	40	47
90059	LOS ANGELES	55	48	51	46	46	51	53	53	57	56	71	59	51	68	51	56	70	56	53	58
90061	LOS ANGELES	60	52	51	50	51	55	56	58	59	60	75	64	54	71	54	57	74	60	55	62
90062	LOS ANGELES	67	60	67	57	58	66	65	65	70	67	87	72	65	84	64	71	85	67	67	72
90063	LOS ANGELES	68	58	55	57	57	59	65	65	67	69	85	74	61	82	60	63	85	69	60	69
90064	LOS ANGELES	155	176	250	180	170	183	178	168	174	179	220	198	187	229	180	172	219	172	157	184
90065	LOS ANGELES	88	87	96	86	85	88	90	90	91	94	115	102	89	115	88	88	116	93	83	96
90066	LOS ANGELES	97	108	164	109	104	113	113	106	115	113	145	125	117	155	115	116	145	110	101	116
90067	LOS ANGELES	218	237	308	237	232	256	245	235	245	242	308	271	253	313	249	247	303	242	233	257
90068	LOS ANGELES	164	172	292	189	165	180	188	172	189	191	240	208	199	252	188	187	239	180	159	190
90069	WEST HOLLYWOOD	154	153	278	173	145	162	175	156	177	178	225	191	184	236	173	176	224	166	146	174
90071	LOS ANGELES	0	0	0	0	0	0	0	0	0	0	0	0	0	0	0	0	0	0	0	0
90077	LOS ANGELES	402	541	742	530	528	569	471	467	439	482	555	525	535	585	503	443	564	449	434	507
90089	LOS ANGELES	13	8	10	9	8	9	15	11	15	13	18	15	12	16	12	13	17	14	10	13
90095	LOS ANGELES	0	0	0	0	0	0	0	0	0	0	0	0	0	0	0	0	0	0	0	0
90201	BELL	65	55	54	55	54	56	62	62	65	66	82	71	59	80	58	60	83	66	56	66
90210	BEVERLY HILLS	342	420	617	426	408	445	397	382	381	404	482	439	439	505	414	383	485	379	358	418
90211	BEVERLY HILLS	150	161	269	175	154	168	174	159	173	176	220	191	184	232	174	172	219	165	147	175
90212	BEVERLY HILLS	175	173	313	196	165	183	199	178	202	203	257	218	209	269	197	200	255	189	166	199
90220	COMPTON	71	64	63	62	63	68	67	69	70	71	88	76	65	83	65	69	87	71	67	75
90221	COMPTON	71	61	58	60	60	62	67	68	70	71	88	77	64	84	63	66	89	72	63	72
90222	COMPTON	72	64	64	62	62	67	69	69	72	72	91	77	67	88	66	70	90	72	67	75
90230	CULVER CITY	101	112	161	112	107	116	115	109	116	117	146	126	120	154	116	116	146	112	103	119
90232	CULVER CITY	92	102	136	103	99	105	105	100	103	104	131	118	108	135	105	102	130	103	93	109
90240	DOWNEY	107	124	149	118	119	125	118	116	116	121	147	131	123	155	119	116	149	117	108	125
90241	DOWNEY	87	91	109	88	87	93	92	91	93	95	118	103	93	120	91	92	118	93	85	98
90242	DOWNEY	83	83	92	81	80	84	84	84	85	88	108	94	84	108	82	83	108	86	78	90
90245	EL SEGUNDO	124	137	168	142	134	139	138	133	133	138	168	159	141	169	137	128	165	136	122	146
90247	GARDENA	64	68	89	70	67	68	72	70	70	72	88	84	70	88	71	66	88	74	63	75
90248	GARDENA	88	96	123	103	98	97	101	100	94	100	119	122	98	115	101	88	118	104	87	106
90249	GARDENA	90	92	108	91	90	96	94	93	95	97	120	106	95	120	94	94	119	96	89	102
90250	HAWTHORNE	67	68	99	68	65	72	74	70	77	76	98	82	75	103	74	78	99	74	68	77
90254	HERMOSA BEACH	175	180	311	199	171	188	200	181	202	203	256	220	210	270	199	200	255	191	168	201
90255	HUNTINGTON PARK	67	57	55	56	56	58	64	64	66	67	84	73	60	81	59	62	84	68	58	68
90260	LAWNDALE	75	77	87	75	74	78	78	77	79	81	100	87	78	101	76	77	100	79	71	83
90262	LYNWOOD	71	61	59	60	60	62	68	68	70	72	89	77	64	86	63	66	89	72	62	72
90263	MALIBU	287	386	529	378	376	406	336	333	313	344	396	375	382	417	358	316	402	320	310	362
90265	MALIBU	281	378	503	369	368	393	330	327	308	336	389	369	372	411	350	310	394	314	302	354
90266	MANHATTAN BEACH	227	284	416	287	273	292	269	257	258	273	327	298	295	351	279	259	330	255	234	279
90270	MAYWOOD	64	54	53	54	53	55	61	61	64	65	81	70	58	79	57	59	81	65	55	65
90272	PACIFIC PALISADES	309	424	580	411	412	442	368	365	343	375	433	410	417	462	393	347	441	350	336	394
90274	PALOS VERDES PENINSU	270	366	492	355	356	380	320	318	300	326	378	359	359	403	340	302	384	306	293	342
90275	RANCHO PALOS VERDES	184	256	344	247	249	261	226	224	211	228	265	257	250	286	240	211	269	218	201	238
90277	REDONDO BEACH	141	154	234	165	149	159	162	151	159	163	201	181	169	211	162	157	200	156	139	166
90278	REDONDO BEACH	136	153	187	156	148	154	151	146	144	152	183	172	156	186	150	140	181	148	132	159
90280	SOUTH GATE	73	63	61	62	62	65	70	71	73	74	92	80	66	88	66	68	92	74	65	75
	CALIFORNIA	107	111	131	112	109	115	113	111	111	114	140	129	114	141	112	109	139	113	104	122
	UNITED STATES	100	100	100	100	100	100	100	100	100	100	100	100	100	100	100	100	100	100	100	100

ZIP CODE			POPULATION			2000-2004 ANNUAL RATE		HOUSEHOLDS					FAMILIES		
#	POST OFFICE NAME	COUNTY FIPS CODE	2000	2004	2009	% Rate	State Centile	2000	2004	2009	% Annual Rate 2000-2004	2004 Average HH Size	2000	2004	% Annual Rate 2000-2004
90290	TOPANGA	037	6240	6301	6466	0.2	21	2541	2547	2592	0.1	2.46	1661	1660	0.0
90291	VENICE	037	31689	32078	33071	0.3	23	15853	16019	16431	0.3	1.98	5643	5639	0.0
90292	MARINA DEL REY	037	17529	18174	19094	0.9	48	10620	10984	11473	0.8	1.65	3756	3878	0.8
90293	PLAYA DEL REY	037	8668	9257	9800	1.6	70	4623	4940	5190	1.6	1.86	1918	2030	1.3
90301	INGLEWOOD	037	38159	38970	40296	0.5	32	12180	12355	12695	0.3	3.08	8392	8481	0.3
90302	INGLEWOOD	037	30350	30817	31733	0.4	25	10881	10996	11249	0.3	2.78	7141	7189	0.2
90303	INGLEWOOD	037	26040	26572	27456	0.5	31	7081	7175	7356	0.3	3.70	5755	5820	0.3
90304	INGLEWOOD	037	28989	29570	30491	0.5	30	6559	6646	6800	0.3	4.43	5605	5670	0.3
90305	INGLEWOOD	037	13763	13632	13877	-0.2	9	5615	5531	5596	-0.4	2.46	3665	3598	-0.4
90401	SANTA MONICA	037	5013	5374	5689	1.7	73	3004	3274	3487	2.1	1.43	613	641	1.1
90402	SANTA MONICA	037	12428	12685	13161	0.5	31	5540	5656	5843	0.5	2.24	3220	3258	0.3
90403	SANTA MONICA	037	22538	23243	24178	0.7	42	13276	13630	14092	0.6	1.67	4460	4552	0.5
90404	SANTA MONICA	037	21051	21482	22239	0.5	31	9772	9890	10162	0.3	2.06	3986	4020	0.2
90405	SANTA MONICA	037	25135	25712	26579	0.5	33	13848	14090	14470	0.4	1.81	5068	5122	0.3
90501	TORRANCE	037	40796	41691	43000	0.5	32	13916	14116	14447	0.3	2.94	9750	9878	0.3
90502	TORRANCE	037	16915	17314	17826	0.6	34	5515	5621	5755	0.5	2.95	3896	3963	0.4
90503	TORRANCE	037	42388	43142	44547	0.4	28	16896	17047	17454	0.2	2.49	11110	11231	0.3
90504	TORRANCE	037	31823	32435	33443	0.5	29	11704	11859	12137	0.3	2.73	8373	8458	0.2
90505	TORRANCE	037	34520	35496	36767	0.7	39	13750	14056	14457	0.5	2.50	9356	9538	0.5
90601	WHITTIER	037	31365	31774	32606	0.3	23	10902	10952	11146	0.1	2.87	7899	7910	0.0
90602	WHITTIER	037	25717	26347	27116	0.6	35	8109	8186	8328	0.2	3.13	5685	5729	0.2
90603	WHITTIER	037	19068	19059	19444	0.0	12	6722	6682	6774	-0.1	2.82	5169	5127	-0.2
90604	WHITTIER	037	38656	39914	41500	0.8	43	11944	12216	12585	0.5	3.26	9474	9679	0.5
90605	WHITTIER	037	37282	37657	38474	0.2	21	9967	9960	10082	0.0	3.76	8295	8273	-0.1
90606	WHITTIER	037	32663	33444	34510	0.6	34	8682	8816	9027	0.4	3.68	7090	7187	0.3
90620	BUENA PARK	059	44780	45228	46575	0.2	21	13288	13353	13649	0.1	3.34	10742	10765	0.1
90621	BUENA PARK	059	33504	34806	36325	0.9	51	10006	10251	10570	0.6	3.37	7817	7994	0.5
90623	LA PALMA	059	15550	16232	17032	1.0	55	4999	5213	5440	1.0	3.11	4295	4472	1.0
90630	CYPRESS	059	46939	48167	50199	0.6	37	15923	16294	16878	0.5	2.94	12370	12634	0.5
90631	LA HABRA	059	66827	69182	72286	0.8	47	21544	22124	22935	0.6	3.10	16204	16607	0.6
90638	LA MIRADA	037	45377	46907	48689	0.8	45	14561	14967	15419	0.7	3.09	11539	11822	0.6
90639	LA MIRADA	037	2003	2043	2080	0.5	30	200	207	213	0.8	5.02	113	117	0.8
90640	MONTEBELLO	037	60908	62564	64685	0.6	38	18381	18733	19219	0.5	3.32	14549	14805	0.4
90650	NORWALK	037	103369	108263	113004	1.1	58	26907	27868	28800	0.8	3.84	22542	23285	0.8
90660	PICO RIVERA	037	63417	63879	65291	0.2	19	16464	16460	16695	0.0	3.86	13870	13839	-0.1
90670	SANTA FE SPRINGS	037	16558	16718	17139	0.2	21	4592	4604	4690	0.1	3.36	3569	3574	0.0
90680	STANTON	059	30329	32116	33851	1.4	65	8820	9271	9688	1.2	3.42	6359	6630	1.0
90701	ARTESIA	037	16635	16805	17213	0.2	21	4548	4567	4646	0.1	3.55	3695	3706	0.1
90703	CERRITOS	037	51221	51836	53350	0.3	23	15286	15396	15736	0.2	3.36	13565	13651	0.2
90704	AVALON	037	3696	3767	3858	0.5	29	1281	1288	1306	0.1	2.72	800	802	0.1
90706	BELLFLOWER	037	72835	76062	79140	1.0	56	23347	23909	24527	0.6	3.16	17105	17461	0.5
90710	HARBOR CITY	037	25630	26330	27183	0.6	38	8710	8876	9088	0.5	2.95	6248	6355	0.4
90712	LAKEWOOD	037	31396	32203	33276	0.6	36	11263	11476	11768	0.4	2.80	8271	8403	0.4
90713	LAKEWOOD	037	27381	27803	28603	0.4	25	9562	9640	9838	0.2	2.87	7363	7408	0.1
90715	LAKEWOOD	037	20385	21836	23079	1.6	72	6061	6434	6738	1.4	3.39	4895	5190	1.4
90716	HAWAIIAN GARDENS	037	14964	15173	15606	0.3	24	3503	3504	3567	0.0	4.33	2862	2859	0.0
90717	LOMITA	037	20955	21325	21926	0.4	28	8382	8475	8648	0.3	2.50	5302	5343	0.2
90720	LOS ALAMITOS	059	21686	21873	22549	0.2	20	7900	7965	8171	0.2	2.69	5970	6001	0.1
90723	PARAMOUNT	037	54828	57049	59445	0.9	52	13888	14280	14722	0.7	3.97	11255	11557	0.6
90731	SAN PEDRO	037	61153	62801	64999	0.6	38	22266	22700	23359	0.5	2.65	13957	14164	0.4
90732	SAN PEDRO	037	18170	18607	19289	0.6	34	7602	7745	7979	0.4	2.37	5118	5197	0.4
90740	SEAL BEACH	059	23760	23579	24204	-0.2	9	12875	12804	13097	-0.1	1.82	5854	5774	-0.3
90742	SUNSET BEACH	059	945	899	912	-1.2	2	519	494	498	-1.2	1.82	221	208	-1.4
90743	SURFSIDE	059	456	437	443	-1.0	2	200	191	192	-1.1	2.29	113	107	-1.3
90744	WILMINGTON	037	52403	54359	56419	0.9	49	13557	13928	14326	0.6	3.89	11160	11453	0.6
90745	CARSON	037	55559	57409	59429	0.8	44	14732	15128	15547	0.6	3.76	12174	12472	0.6
90746	CARSON	037	24495	25020	25866	0.5	32	7229	7307	7485	0.3	3.36	5924	5990	0.3
90747	CARSON	037	718	716	729	-0.1	11	98	97	99	-0.2	6.51	65	64	-0.4
90755	SIGNAL HILL	037	9441	10146	10706	1.7	74	3662	3909	4094	1.6	2.58	2131	2267	1.5
90802	LONG BEACH	037	39307	40933	42746	1.0	53	18977	19618	20358	0.8	2.04	6943	7106	0.6
90803	LONG BEACH	037	32434	33096	34256	0.5	31	18369	18683	19231	0.4	1.76	7095	7161	0.2
90804	LONG BEACH	037	42623	43746	45109	0.6	37	14969	15116	15398	0.2	2.84	8613	8680	0.2
90805	LONG BEACH	037	90666	93995	97399	0.9	48	25750	26112	26648	0.3	3.56	19817	20041	0.3
90806	LONG BEACH	037	43038	45026	47043	1.1	57	12010	12408	12830	0.8	3.56	8976	9230	0.7
90807	LONG BEACH	037	30249	30749	31536	0.4	27	12118	12187	12386	0.1	2.45	7300	7319	0.1
90808	LONG BEACH	037	37901	38773	40109	0.5	33	14473	14727	15134	0.4	2.62	10364	10519	0.4
90810	LONG BEACH	037	35635	36882	38295	0.8	47	9142	9362	9624	0.6	3.87	7501	7668	0.5
90813	LONG BEACH	037	61667	62556	64338	0.3	25	16093	16214	16550	0.2	3.76	12079	12136	0.1
90814	LONG BEACH	037	18270	18634	19161	0.5	30	8816	8871	9025	0.2	2.06	3611	3618	0.1
90815	LONG BEACH	037	37016	37786	39196	0.5	31	14847	15090	15565	0.4	2.43	9439	9570	0.3
90840	LONG BEACH	037	1714	1715	1716	0.0	15	11	12	13	2.1	1.08	0	0	0.0
91001	ALTADENA	037	35741	35970	36856	0.2	18	12267	12279	12499	0.0	2.87	8942	8933	0.0
91006	ARCADIA	037	30180	31616	33057	1.1	58	10466	10881	11285	0.9	2.90	8157	8454	0.9
91007	ARCADIA	037	30668	31754	33114	0.8	47	11265	11638	12084	0.8	2.66	7916	8146	0.7
91010	DUARTE	037	27388	28302	29440	0.8	45	8057	8276	8552	0.6	3.33	6000	6141	0.6
91011	LA CANADA FLINTRIDGE	037	20599	21169	21892	0.6	38	6914	7074	7268	0.5	2.96	5745	5863	0.5
91016	MONROVIA	037	41070	42053	43458	0.6	34	14792	15030	15409	0.4	2.78	10110	10250	0.3
91020	MONTROSE	037	7608	8131	8584	1.6	71	3215	3420	3587	1.5	2.32	1862	1966	1.3
91024	SIERRA MADRE	037	10599	10921	11361	0.7	41	4765	4888	5053	0.6	2.21	2750	2814	0.5
91030	SOUTH PASADENA	037	24153	24210	24775	0.1	16	10434	10402	10569	-0.1	2.31	5981	5951	-0.1
91040	SUNLAND	037	18683	19309	20034	0.8	45	6980	7173	7392	0.6	2.64	6408	6558	0.6
91042	TUJUNGA	037	26147	26953	27930	0.7	42	9548	9789	10078	0.6	2.71	6408	6558	0.6
91101	PASADENA	037	16486	17178	17916	1.0	54	8603	8947	9284	0.9	1.85	2956	3062	0.8
91103	PASADENA	037	28906	30077	31388	0.9	52	8459	8739	9052	0.8	3.32	6059	6248	0.7
91104	PASADENA	037	37939	39919	41865	1.2	61	12769	13291	13803	1.0	2.96	8781	9131	0.9
91105	PASADENA	037	10847	11201	11651	0.8	43	5011	5146	5317	0.6	2.11	2856	2924	0.6
91106	PASADENA	037	23224	25336	27144	2.1	80	10154	11025	11747	2.0	2.23	5011	5391	1.7
91107	PASADENA	037	32155	32449	33260	0.2	20	12567	12628	12862	0.1	2.54	8175	8189	0.0
91108	SAN MARINO	037	13166	13203	13516	0.1	17	4344	4337	4410	0.0	3.04	3714	3700	-0.1
91123	PASADENA	037	32	32	33	0.0	15	7	7	7	0.0	4.43	4	4	0.0
91201	GLENDALE	037	24005	25700	27221	1.6	72	8357	8887	9342	1.5	2.88	6037	6399	1.4
91202	GLENDALE	037	21789	22403	23171	0.7	39	8659	8811	9027	0.4	2.53	5835	5930	0.4
91203	GLENDALE	037	14381	15075	15768	1.1	59	5363	5572	5775	0.9	2.68	3555	3690	0.9
91204	GLENDALE	037	16889	18344	19519	2.0	79	5491	5925	6259	1.8	3.01	3975	4283	1.8
91205	GLENDALE	037	41221	41747	42962	0.3	23	14009	14092	14397	0.1	2.90	9753	9769	0.0
	CALIFORNIA					1.4					1.2	2.90			1.2
	UNITED STATES					1.2					1.3	2.58			1.1

ZIP CODE #	POST OFFICE NAME	RACE (%) White 2000	White 2004	Black 2000	Black 2004	Asian/Pacific 2000	Asian/Pacific 2004	% Hispanic Origin 2000	% Hispanic Origin 2004	2004 AGE DISTRIBUTION (%) 0-4	5-9	10-14	15-19	20-24	25-44	45-64	65-84	85+	18+	MEDIAN AGE 2004	% 2004 Males	% 2004 Females
90290	TOPANGA	90.5	88.3	1.0	1.1	3.6	4.4	5.0	6.7	5.3	6.4	6.9	5.4	3.3	25.6	37.7	8.6	0.8	77.8	43.7	50.4	49.6
90291	VENICE	71.7	68.4	6.7	6.6	3.9	4.4	24.9	29.3	4.6	3.6	4.2	3.9	7.3	46.3	23.1	6.2	0.9	85.4	35.4	52.6	47.4
90292	MARINA DEL REY	82.6	79.3	4.0	4.4	8.1	9.6	6.7	8.9	3.1	2.2	1.7	1.7	4.1	41.7	30.6	13.5	1.4	92.0	42.7	50.8	49.2
90293	PLAYA DEL REY	80.7	77.3	4.9	5.3	7.5	8.8	8.5	11.1	3.6	3.1	3.4	3.7	5.6	39.3	29.5	10.5	1.2	87.8	40.2	49.6	50.4
90301	INGLEWOOD	24.0	24.0	34.8	32.2	2.0	1.9	57.5	61.3	9.4	8.4	9.3	8.0	8.8	30.6	18.6	5.9	1.0	68.0	28.9	48.3	51.7
90302	INGLEWOOD	18.1	18.2	54.5	51.8	1.2	1.3	37.4	41.0	9.3	8.6	9.2	7.9	7.8	31.7	19.7	5.1	0.7	68.0	29.6	46.7	53.3
90303	INGLEWOOD	19.9	20.1	40.5	38.5	1.4	1.3	55.0	57.6	9.9	9.5	10.5	9.0	8.4	29.0	17.6	5.6	0.5	64.6	26.9	48.8	51.2
90304	INGLEWOOD	31.8	31.1	5.5	4.9	2.5	2.2	86.3	88.4	10.7	9.8	11.0	9.6	9.5	30.7	14.7	3.7	0.4	62.7	24.7	51.4	48.6
90305	INGLEWOOD	4.8	4.6	87.8	86.9	0.7	0.7	6.8	7.9	5.7	6.4	7.5	6.4	5.1	25.3	27.5	14.3	1.7	76.3	41.0	44.0	56.0
90401	SANTA MONICA	78.2	74.7	4.3	4.7	6.9	7.8	12.3	15.3	2.3	2.0	2.2	2.7	5.7	43.4	24.8	13.4	3.5	91.9	40.7	52.2	47.8
90402	SANTA MONICA	89.6	87.3	0.6	0.7	6.2	7.4	3.8	5.0	5.0	6.0	6.7	5.3	3.3	24.2	31.8	15.2	2.6	78.8	44.8	47.8	52.2
90403	SANTA MONICA	86.4	83.6	1.5	1.6	6.9	8.1	5.7	7.5	3.3	3.1	3.6	4.1	4.5	37.5	27.7	13.3	3.0	87.5	42.1	46.5	53.5
90404	SANTA MONICA	62.7	58.8	8.4	8.5	8.4	9.0	28.1	32.8	4.2	4.0	4.9	5.7	7.8	37.0	23.9	9.6	3.0	83.5	37.3	48.6	51.4
90405	SANTA MONICA	79.7	76.1	3.2	3.4	7.2	8.3	12.4	15.6	4.2	3.9	4.1	4.2	5.4	36.9	29.2	10.2	2.0	85.3	40.7	49.1	51.0
90501	TORRANCE	48.2	45.0	6.1	5.8	18.8	19.7	39.0	43.1	7.9	7.4	8.5	7.4	7.8	31.6	21.1	7.5	0.9	71.7	32.2	50.4	49.6
90502	TORRANCE	41.2	38.3	7.9	7.5	28.6	29.4	33.0	37.1	6.7	6.5	6.6	6.1	6.3	29.3	24.1	12.5	1.9	76.5	37.6	48.3	51.7
90503	TORRANCE	57.5	53.3	1.8	1.8	33.1	36.0	9.7	11.8	5.6	5.7	6.6	6.6	6.6	28.7	26.0	12.1	2.1	77.9	39.9	48.6	51.4
90504	TORRANCE	46.9	42.7	3.5	3.5	36.2	38.3	17.2	20.2	5.9	5.9	7.0	6.8	6.9	28.8	25.4	12.0	1.4	77.0	38.4	49.1	50.9
90505	TORRANCE	65.9	61.5	1.7	1.7	25.5	28.4	8.7	10.8	5.6	6.0	6.7	6.3	5.2	27.1	27.2	13.8	2.1	77.6	41.4	48.1	51.9
90601	WHITTIER	58.8	55.9	1.3	1.3	6.1	6.1	62.0	67.4	7.6	7.2	7.7	7.3	7.4	30.5	22.2	8.9	1.3	73.5	33.7	48.1	51.9
90602	WHITTIER	52.5	49.5	1.2	1.1	3.2	3.2	68.2	73.3	9.5	8.4	8.9	8.2	8.3	30.9	16.8	7.4	1.7	68.8	29.3	48.6	51.4
90603	WHITTIER	77.8	74.2	0.7	0.7	4.7	5.1	34.7	41.2	6.1	6.4	8.1	7.1	5.7	24.9	24.2	15.0	2.5	75.0	40.1	47.9	52.2
90604	WHITTIER	62.8	59.3	1.6	1.6	3.9	4.0	55.1	61.5	8.0	7.8	8.9	8.1	7.6	29.7	20.0	9.0	0.9	70.3	31.9	49.7	50.4
90605	WHITTIER	52.9	50.1	1.2	1.1	3.1	3.1	68.9	73.8	8.5	8.4	9.7	8.7	7.9	29.1	19.2	7.6	1.0	68.1	29.9	49.9	50.1
90606	WHITTIER	52.9	51.1	1.2	1.1	1.9	1.8	81.7	85.3	8.3	8.0	9.0	10.3	7.9	28.2	18.5	8.6	1.4	68.3	29.7	50.4	49.7
90620	BUENA PARK	57.7	53.8	3.3	3.2	21.5	22.6	27.3	31.9	7.2	7.2	8.1	7.4	7.2	29.5	22.4	10.1	1.1	73.1	34.7	49.2	50.8
90621	BUENA PARK	45.0	42.0	4.7	4.4	21.8	22.0	43.2	47.9	9.5	8.8	9.1	7.5	7.9	32.3	17.9	6.5	0.7	68.2	29.5	50.0	50.0
90623	LA PALMA	44.0	40.2	4.2	4.2	44.0	46.6	12.0	14.1	5.6	5.7	6.7	6.9	7.1	26.9	28.5	11.8	0.8	77.8	39.4	48.9	51.1
90630	CYPRESS	66.2	62.1	2.8	2.9	20.7	22.7	15.7	18.9	6.1	6.5	8.1	7.4	6.5	27.7	26.1	10.7	1.0	74.7	37.8	48.5	51.5
90631	LA HABRA	64.0	60.2	1.5	1.5	7.4	8.0	45.4	50.8	8.1	7.8	8.1	7.3	7.3	29.2	20.8	9.9	1.6	71.6	33.0	49.3	50.8
90638	LA MIRADA	63.7	59.7	1.9	1.9	15.6	16.8	34.1	39.5	6.6	6.7	8.0	7.8	7.0	26.9	23.1	12.6	1.4	74.2	36.7	48.6	51.4
90639	LA MIRADA	77.8	74.0	2.3	2.4	11.0	12.6	15.4	19.4	2.3	2.4	2.6	26.7	31.0	11.7	10.5	8.6	4.3	90.6	22.6	41.7	58.4
90640	MONTEBELLO	47.0	45.6	0.9	0.8	11.3	11.2	75.0	77.8	8.2	7.7	8.2	7.4	7.6	29.5	18.9	11.1	1.5	71.5	32.0	48.1	51.9
90650	NORWALK	44.8	42.7	4.6	4.3	11.9	11.7	63.0	67.4	8.8	8.4	9.4	8.5	8.1	29.3	18.6	8.0	0.9	68.3	29.7	49.5	50.5
90660	PICO RIVERA	49.5	48.3	0.7	0.7	2.8	2.6	88.3	90.5	8.5	8.1	9.1	8.2	8.0	28.7	18.9	9.5	1.1	69.4	30.6	49.0	51.0
90670	SANTA FE SPRINGS	51.2	48.8	4.0	3.8	4.2	4.1	70.3	74.8	7.2	6.9	8.7	8.1	7.6	28.0	20.4	12.0	1.1	72.2	33.8	50.1	49.9
90680	STANTON	49.8	46.4	2.4	2.3	16.7	16.9	47.0	51.9	8.9	8.0	8.4	7.4	8.1	31.0	18.2	8.5	1.7	70.4	30.9	50.3	49.7
90701	ARTESIA	43.9	40.8	3.6	3.5	28.5	29.6	37.8	41.2	7.4	7.1	7.7	7.3	7.8	28.4	22.2	10.3	1.8	73.4	34.0	50.3	49.7
90703	CERRITOS	27.0	24.2	6.7	6.5	58.4	60.5	10.6	12.2	4.7	5.1	7.0	7.4	7.2	25.2	31.7	10.8	0.9	78.6	40.4	48.6	51.5
90704	AVALON	70.8	66.1	0.8	0.9	1.1	1.1	44.4	51.8	7.6	7.3	8.7	8.1	7.0	29.6	23.1	7.4	1.2	71.0	33.4	50.3	49.7
90706	BELLFLOWER	46.1	42.6	13.1	12.6	10.4	10.6	43.2	48.9	9.6	8.7	8.9	7.6	8.1	30.4	18.6	7.0	1.1	68.2	29.6	48.8	51.2
90710	HARBOR CITY	46.5	44.1	14.0	13.4	14.6	15.3	41.8	45.9	8.2	7.7	8.1	6.6	7.2	30.5	20.9	9.7	1.2	72.0	33.0	48.7	51.3
90712	LAKEWOOD	64.8	60.5	8.6	8.8	11.9	13.0	20.7	25.0	6.9	7.0	8.1	7.0	6.2	28.3	23.8	10.9	1.8	73.7	37.0	47.9	52.1
90713	LAKEWOOD	77.6	73.8	3.1	3.2	7.7	8.8	17.3	21.5	6.8	7.0	7.7	7.1	5.8	27.5	25.5	11.1	1.6	74.0	38.3	48.6	51.4
90715	LAKEWOOD	39.9	37.0	11.5	11.2	25.1	25.7	33.4	37.8	7.9	7.6	9.0	8.2	8.6	30.5	20.5	7.2	0.5	70.6	30.8	49.2	50.8
90716	HAWAIIAN GARDENS	38.2	36.7	4.7	4.3	10.3	9.9	71.9	75.4	10.5	9.4	10.3	9.5	10.0	29.1	15.2	5.5	0.6	64.2	25.2	51.3	48.7
90717	LOMITA	66.2	62.0	3.8	3.8	12.2	13.2	26.8	31.9	7.5	7.4	7.7	5.9	5.8	30.6	24.0	9.6	1.5	73.8	36.2	48.2	51.8
90720	LOS ALAMITOS	82.5	79.6	2.0	2.1	8.1	9.2	11.5	14.5	5.1	5.6	7.9	7.5	6.3	24.0	26.8	14.2	2.6	76.7	41.2	47.7	52.3
90723	PARAMOUNT	34.7	33.6	13.6	12.5	4.2	4.0	72.3	75.8	11.1	10.1	10.4	8.8	9.0	30.7	14.9	4.5	0.5	63.2	25.4	49.2	50.9
90731	SAN PEDRO	58.8	56.0	7.6	7.3	5.0	5.1	46.9	51.9	7.9	7.3	7.8	7.3	7.6	31.7	21.2	8.1	1.2	72.9	33.0	50.4	49.6
90732	SAN PEDRO	80.1	77.0	3.2	3.3	5.8	6.6	21.0	25.5	5.5	5.8	6.0	5.3	4.7	26.3	27.7	16.2	2.5	79.6	42.8	47.3	52.7
90740	SEAL BEACH	89.0	87.2	1.4	1.5	5.9	6.8	6.4	8.2	3.1	3.3	4.0	3.7	3.5	19.1	23.9	29.8	9.6	87.3	56.4	44.0	56.0
90742	SUNSET BEACH	88.8	86.7	0.1	0.1	2.8	3.1	6.0	7.8	2.9	2.6	3.9	3.6	5.8	38.0	30.3	11.6	1.5	88.5	41.2	54.3	45.7
90743	SURFSIDE	96.1	95.0	0.0	0.0	1.3	1.8	7.7	9.8	4.6	4.8	5.7	5.0	4.1	30.7	35.5	9.4	0.2	81.5	42.3	53.1	46.9
90744	WILMINGTON	35.9	34.9	3.3	2.9	3.6	3.3	85.9	88.2	10.6	9.7	10.4	8.7	9.1	30.1	15.7	5.2	0.6	64.1	25.9	50.9	49.1
90745	CARSON	29.5	28.1	8.7	8.0	35.2	34.9	40.0	43.5	7.2	7.1	8.4	7.8	7.6	28.4	22.3	10.2	1.1	72.6	33.5	48.8	51.2
90746	CARSON	13.7	13.5	65.6	63.7	7.3	7.6	17.9	20.6	6.3	6.6	8.1	8.0	7.0	25.8	25.6	11.8	0.8	74.2	36.7	47.2	52.8
90747	CARSON	17.7	16.5	67.8	67.0	4.7	5.2	12.0	14.3	4.6	4.8	7.3	8.8	11.0	24.6	24.3	13.6	1.1	80.7	35.5	44.1	55.9
90755	SIGNAL HILL	45.3	41.6	13.1	12.8	18.5	19.2	29.2	33.6	8.1	6.8	7.6	6.6	6.8	33.2	23.6	6.6	0.7	73.3	34.1	49.1	50.9
90802	LONG BEACH	46.5	43.7	17.4	16.8	6.0	6.3	39.7	44.1	7.6	6.2	5.9	5.7	9.1	37.2	19.7	7.1	1.5	77.3	32.9	52.4	47.7
90803	LONG BEACH	85.5	82.7	2.3	2.5	4.8	5.6	10.0	12.9	3.6	3.1	3.0	3.1	5.8	39.0	29.1	11.6	1.8	88.6	40.9	49.1	50.9
90804	LONG BEACH	37.9	35.4	17.0	16.2	15.2	15.2	38.7	43.2	9.2	8.0	8.8	8.5	11.1	34.3	15.3	4.1	0.9	69.3	27.2	48.7	51.3
90805	LONG BEACH	29.6	28.1	23.9	22.2	13.1	13.0	46.0	50.5	10.0	9.6	10.8	9.0	8.3	29.6	16.8	5.2	0.7	64.0	26.6	48.9	51.1
90806	LONG BEACH	25.0	24.2	21.5	19.9	19.8	19.7	45.0	48.6	10.0	9.3	10.2	9.0	8.9	28.6	17.1	5.9	1.0	65.0	26.7	49.3	50.7
90807	LONG BEACH	54.9	51.0	16.2	16.3	14.7	15.9	17.7	21.2	6.2	6.1	7.0	6.6	6.2	28.9	25.3	10.3	3.5	76.7	38.5	47.0	53.0
90808	LONG BEACH	80.6	77.2	2.8	3.0	7.0	8.0	13.8	17.3	6.3	6.7	7.0	6.2	5.1	27.2	27.0	12.6	2.0	76.2	40.2	48.6	51.4
90810	LONG BEACH	23.8	23.2	16.4	15.1	26.2	25.6	45.6	49.2	8.7	8.5	10.0	9.0	8.4	26.9	18.4	8.9	1.2	67.3	28.9	48.9	51.1
90813	LONG BEACH	25.2	24.6	13.5	12.3	16.6	15.9	61.3	64.7	12.0	10.0	11.0	10.1	10.7	28.7	12.8	4.2	0.5	61.0	23.2	51.1	48.9
90814	LONG BEACH	66.7	62.8	9.1	9.2	7.5	8.2	21.1	25.5	5.7	4.8	4.8	4.5	8.2	40.3	22.4	7.6	1.7	82.1	35.4	48.6	51.4
90815	LONG BEACH	76.5	73.0	3.9	4.1	9.5	10.7	12.5	15.6	5.8	6.0	5.9	6.5	7.4	27.8	24.5	13.7	2.4	79.2	39.5	48.0	52.1
90840	LONG BEACH	56.2	51.5	11.3	11.7	17.9	19.5	16.5	19.9	0.0	0.0	0.0	68.0	30.9	0.9	0.1	0.0	0.1	99.6	18.7	35.4	64.6
91001	ALTADENA	42.4	40.1	36.6	36.2	3.9	4.2	21.8	25.0	6.8	7.3	8.1	6.9	5.5	26.2	26.9	10.5	1.8	73.2	38.5	48.0	52.0
91006	ARCADIA	48.2	44.0	0.9	0.9	42.0	44.7	13.1	15.5	5.0	5.6	7.2	7.3	6.6	24.6	29.1	12.9	1.7	77.8	41.1	47.9	52.1
91007	ARCADIA	46.4	42.2	1.3	1.4	44.6	47.4	10.6	12.6	4.5	4.8	6.1	6.4	6.7	25.9	28.0	14.2	3.5	80.7	42.3	46.5	53.5
91010	DUARTE	49.9	47.4	10.0	9.4	10.8	11.2	47.2	51.8	7.6	7.5	8.5	7.4	6.8	27.6	22.0	10.0	2.8	71.8	34.4	47.6	52.4
91011	LA CANADA FLINTRIDGE	74.4	70.3	0.8	0.8	20.1	23.1	5.1	6.5	5.1	6.7	9.4	9.1	4.7	17.6	32.5	12.9	2.0	72.9	43.4	48.2	51.8
91016	MONROVIA	63.0	59.7	8.3	8.0	7.1	7.6	35.6	41.2	7.9	7.6	8.3	7.1	6.9	30.2	22.1	8.4	1.5	71.9	34.0	48.3	51.7
91020	MONTROSE	72.1	67.7	0.6	0.7	16.9	19.1	13.0	16.2	5.1	5.0	6.4	7.3	8.0	28.9	26.6	10.1	2.6	79.0	38.9	46.3	53.7
91024	SIERRA MADRE	85.8	82.9	1.2	1.3	5.7	6.6	9.9	12.8	4.9	5.4	5.5	5.0	4.1	26.8	32.2	13.7	2.3	80.9	44.0	47.4	52.6
91030	SOUTH PASADENA	60.3	56.2	3.0	3.1	26.7	28.9	16.1	19.4	4.7	4.8	6.7	7.4	7.1	31.0	26.8	10.0	1.6	79.2	38.3	46.6	53.5
91040	SUNLAND	78.0	74.1	1.5	1.6	6.5	7.3	20.2	25.0	6.2	6.4	7.1	6.3	5.7	27.9	27.9	10.9	1.7	76.4	39.7	49.4	50.6
91042	TUJUNGA	71.8	68.0	2.4	2.4	6.3	7.0	26.5	31.3	7.1	7.0	7.4	6.9	6.4	29.5	26.0	8.5	1.3	74.4	36.6	50.6	49.4
91101	PASADENA	53.9	50.2	11.7	11.7	15.0	16.4	28.8	32.4	5.5	4.2	4.2	3.7	8.1	43.7	17.9	9.6	3.2	84.2	34.2	48.9	51.2
91103	PASADENA	34.4	33.6	27.3	25.6	4.6	4.7	50.9	54.5	8.4	8.3	9.2	8.4	7.9	28.3	19.6	8.3	1.5	69.0	30.6	49.9	50.2
91104	PASADENA	54.3	51.0	14.5	14.2	6.0	6.3	36.4	41.2	7.7	7.6	7.9	6.8	6.8	31.1	22.4	8.3	1.5	72.8	34.4	48.8	51.2
91105	PASADENA	79.4	76.5	4.4	4.5	9.0	10.3	12.3	15.0	4.5	5.0	4.7	4.0	3.3	25.2	31.0	18.6	3.8	83.4	47.1	48.2	51.8
91106	PASADENA	56.8	52.6	9.3	9.4	16.1	17.3	25.7	30.3	6.2	5.2	5.0	5.5	10.0	38.2	20.3	8.1	1.4	80.8	33.4	49.6	50.4
91107	PASADENA	63.9	60.4	5.8	5.8	15.1	16.3	23.7	27.6	6.1	6.1	6.1	5.4	5.5	30.9	25.1	12.3	2.4	78.3	38.9	48.6	51.4
91108	SAN MARINO	48.3	43.6	0.3	0.3	47.9	52.0	4.6	5.5	4.8	6.2	8.2	8.1	4.9	20.5	30.8	14.6	2.1	75.7	43.4	48.3	51.7
91123	PASADENA	84.4	84.4	3.1	3.1	9.4	9.4	6.3	6.3	6.3	6.3	3.1	3.1	6.3	25.0	25.0	21.9	3.1	84.4	45.0	50.0	50.0
91201	GLENDALE	65.6	61.0	1.5	1.5	11.2	12.3	22.1	25.6	6.1	6.1	7.2	7.1	7.5	31.4	23.2	9.8	1.6	76.5	36.0	48.7	51.3
91202	GLENDALE	68.1	63.4	1.1	1.2	18.4	20.6	10.7	13.0	4.9	5.1	5.7	6.5	6.9	29.5	25.7	13.6	2.2	80.3	40.2	47.4	52.6
91203	GLENDALE	58.2	53.3	1.8	1.7	16.2	17.2	21.1	25.0	5.6	5.4	6.3	6.8	7.9	31.6	24.0	10.7	1.8	78.7	36.8	48.4	51.6
91204	GLENDALE	44.2	40.3	1.5	1.4	19.7	20.0	40.8	45.3	7.1	6.7	7.4	6.6	7.9	33.3	20.5	8.9	1.5	75.0	33.3	49.2	50.8
91205	GLENDALE	57.8	53.0	1.4	1.4	13.5	14.4	28.5	33.1	6.2	6.0	7.5	7.2	8.1	30.5	22.0	10.6	1.9	76.0	35.2	48.1	51.9
	CALIFORNIA	59.6	57.1	6.7	6.5	11.3	11.8	32.4	35.5	7.4	7.1	7.8	7.3	7.7	29.8	22.1	9.3	1.4	73.3	33.8	49.8	50.2
	UNITED STATES	75.1	73.6	12.3	12.5	3.8	4.2	12.5	14.1	6.9	6.7	7.2	7.0	7.3	28.6	23.8	10.8	1.7	75.1	36.0	49.1	50.9

#	POST OFFICE NAME	2004 Per Capita Income	2004 HH Income Base	2004 Household Income Distribution (%): Less than $25,000	$25,000 to $49,999	$50,000 to $99,999	$100,000 to $149,999	$150,000 or More	Median Household Income: 2004	2009	2004 National Centile	2004 State Centile	2004 Home Value Base	2004 Home Value Distribution (%): Less than $50,000	$50,000 to $89,999	$90,000 to $174,999	$175,000 to $399,999	$400,000 or More	2004 Median Home Value
90290	TOPANGA	61863	2547	10.6	13.0	23.1	19.2	34.0	106982	140229	99	96	1996	2.5	1.1	1.2	6.7	88.7	832702
90291	VENICE	46844	16019	19.0	25.0	28.9	14.1	13.0	56713	75440	81	63	5109	0.3	0.6	2.4	11.0	85.7	639037
90292	MARINA DEL REY	85961	10984	12.2	14.2	30.1	19.6	24.0	86830	114588	97	90	3497	1.7	0.7	2.8	9.7	85.2	631996
90293	PLAYA DEL REY	69043	4940	9.6	17.3	32.0	18.5	22.6	83405	110197	96	88	2404	0.3	0.0	2.7	30.9	66.2	639303
90301	INGLEWOOD	15616	12355	35.7	33.1	22.7	6.7	1.9	35090	40848	28	20	3440	0.4	0.7	18.3	72.0	8.6	237902
90302	INGLEWOOD	17348	10996	32.5	33.5	26.4	5.5	2.0	36717	42627	34	24	3285	0.4	1.5	23.8	63.1	11.2	232320
90303	INGLEWOOD	14497	7175	31.5	28.2	28.7	7.9	3.6	40380	47521	47	32	3179	0.5	0.0	4.9	84.1	10.4	274147
90304	INGLEWOOD	10221	6646	37.3	33.9	21.6	4.2	3.1	32995	38372	21	16	2345	1.0	0.7	5.6	85.4	7.3	251780
90305	INGLEWOOD	27362	5531	22.7	25.0	34.0	12.4	5.8	52452	63035	76	57	3670	0.2	0.0	1.5	88.9	9.4	294357
90401	SANTA MONICA	44787	3274	33.4	24.0	24.4	9.7	8.6	42128	54279	53	36	288	0.0	0.0	0.0	16.7	83.3	728916
90402	SANTA MONICA	120544	5656	8.9	9.4	19.3	15.9	46.4	137766	186355	100	99	3837	0.0	0.0	0.9	4.1	95.0	1000001
90403	SANTA MONICA	61725	13630	18.7	18.4	28.3	15.5	19.1	68923	94786	91	77	3686	0.1	0.4	0.8	11.2	87.6	737533
90404	SANTA MONICA	30723	9890	27.3	25.2	28.2	12.9	6.4	47145	60548	66	46	2597	4.9	0.7	1.7	29.9	62.9	465205
90405	SANTA MONICA	54815	14090	19.2	19.2	29.4	15.5	16.8	65013	89176	89	72	5613	0.5	0.3	1.2	10.8	87.2	780242
90501	TORRANCE	22045	14116	23.0	28.3	30.4	12.1	6.3	48622	59131	70	49	6472	5.3	1.6	3.5	41.6	48.1	389868
90502	TORRANCE	24293	5621	18.1	24.8	35.3	15.9	5.9	56110	67932	81	63	3903	7.4	1.9	13.0	68.6	9.1	265241
90503	TORRANCE	35915	17047	14.1	21.0	34.0	19.7	11.3	68905	86356	91	77	9382	1.5	1.7	1.3	16.3	79.2	538005
90504	TORRANCE	25804	11859	18.7	24.3	34.4	16.6	6.1	57686	69692	82	65	7337	2.9	1.6	0.9	54.1	40.5	374116
90505	TORRANCE	38756	14056	13.4	19.8	33.5	19.0	14.2	71410	89624	92	79	8372	0.7	1.7	2.5	11.9	83.3	614102
90601	WHITTIER	27471	10952	15.6	23.9	35.6	14.8	10.2	61505	74190	86	69	6809	0.8	0.4	4.5	59.1	35.2	336355
90602	WHITTIER	19635	8186	27.4	29.4	27.8	9.3	6.0	44055	51560	59	40	3115	0.3	0.2	2.7	63.7	33.0	324573
90603	WHITTIER	31084	6682	13.9	19.6	34.8	21.5	10.3	68930	85355	91	77	5497	1.3	0.7	1.0	68.2	28.9	347960
90604	WHITTIER	20490	12216	17.0	25.7	37.7	15.6	3.9	56296	66423	81	63	8010	0.9	0.3	3.1	90.5	5.2	286519
90605	WHITTIER	19682	9960	15.7	27.1	37.3	13.5	6.3	56192	65588	81	63	6865	1.0	0.3	3.4	79.5	15.9	277289
90606	WHITTIER	16515	8816	19.9	30.2	36.1	10.7	3.1	49925	57904	72	52	5942	2.6	1.4	4.6	88.7	2.6	262307
90620	BUENA PARK	21977	13353	14.4	24.4	40.0	16.0	5.2	60991	71519	85	69	8776	1.8	2.1	2.6	83.4	10.2	320128
90621	BUENA PARK	18256	10251	21.3	30.8	31.7	11.3	4.9	47933	55572	68	48	4119	0.3	0.5	3.3	68.0	28.0	301998
90623	LA PALMA	30676	5213	9.6	18.6	34.7	22.1	15.0	79193	96618	95	85	3884	1.0	1.2	0.8	28.2	68.7	456357
90630	CYPRESS	30684	16294	11.9	20.0	36.2	20.8	11.2	72415	86530	92	80	11704	2.0	1.3	2.8	47.7	46.2	387136
90631	LA HABRA	24947	22124	18.6	24.0	33.9	15.1	8.4	57751	68238	82	65	13507	2.6	2.3	5.6	54.8	34.7	337674
90638	LA MIRADA	27601	14967	13.0	18.9	39.4	19.7	9.0	70014	84027	91	78	12105	0.9	0.9	3.6	73.3	21.3	326371
90639	LA MIRADA	15647	207	24.2	23.7	35.3	11.6	5.3	52874	64557	77	58	130	0.0	0.0	0.0	85.4	14.6	350000
90640	MONTEBELLO	17726	18733	28.3	28.8	28.7	9.8	4.3	43336	51178	57	39	9431	2.7	0.7	5.4	65.7	25.5	310882
90650	NORWALK	15903	27868	18.9	29.2	38.3	10.7	2.9	51447	59681	75	55	18423	2.5	0.9	6.9	87.2	2.6	251268
90660	PICO RIVERA	14707	16460	24.6	28.3	34.3	9.9	2.8	47248	54825	67	46	11379	2.2	1.2	4.3	86.8	5.5	262668
90670	SANTA FE SPRINGS	18411	4604	20.9	27.2	37.2	11.2	3.6	51362	59491	74	55	3035	4.9	0.3	5.4	87.5	1.9	260856
90680	STANTON	17097	9271	25.2	28.7	34.0	8.7	3.4	46435	53642	65	44	4582	11.7	6.2	9.1	67.0	6.0	237882
90701	ARTESIA	19075	4567	18.6	29.7	34.6	11.7	5.4	51578	61823	75	56	2763	4.7	1.5	8.3	63.5	22.2	290644
90703	CERRITOS	30217	15396	8.9	16.2	35.3	23.8	15.7	83088	103145	96	88	12593	3.3	2.0	2.0	27.1	65.6	452276
90704	AVALON	24219	1288	22.1	32.5	29.5	10.7	5.2	45602	53789	63	43	390	0.8	0.0	2.1	9.2	88.0	634868
90706	BELLFLOWER	18272	23909	25.6	30.8	30.5	9.8	3.3	44385	51926	60	41	10246	10.5	0.9	4.8	72.2	11.6	267570
90710	HARBOR CITY	22071	8876	25.0	25.8	30.4	13.1	5.8	49192	59333	70	50	4805	7.3	9.2	10.7	44.5	28.3	303116
90712	LAKEWOOD	28138	11476	17.5	18.3	38.6	19.6	6.1	65322	78909	89	73	8636	1.2	0.1	1.4	81.2	16.0	321560
90713	LAKEWOOD	28027	9640	11.8	17.0	43.0	21.8	6.5	71661	85817	92	79	8000	0.6	0.1	1.4	85.7	12.3	331717
90715	LAKEWOOD	19807	6434	18.6	26.0	35.3	15.1	5.0	55273	65833	80	61	3378	2.5	0.9	7.8	81.8	7.0	277553
90716	HAWAIIAN GARDENS	11761	3504	31.3	30.2	30.5	6.2	1.8	40324	47219	47	32	1485	12.9	2.2	22.6	59.6	2.6	196505
90717	LOMITA	26357	8475	20.7	28.6	31.2	13.8	5.8	50881	62489	74	54	4213	8.1	1.6	4.5	40.0	45.7	382872
90720	LOS ALAMITOS	38378	7965	10.4	17.5	35.8	18.8	17.6	77146	94728	94	84	5325	0.9	1.0	1.7	17.9	78.4	582230
90723	PARAMOUNT	13216	14280	28.3	32.9	30.4	6.2	2.3	40741	46826	49	33	6169	12.8	3.8	19.9	60.6	3.0	213407
90731	SAN PEDRO	21659	22700	31.6	26.3	26.7	10.7	4.7	41493	50069	51	35	8197	1.6	0.8	5.0	51.9	40.7	360058
90732	SAN PEDRO	38253	7745	13.7	17.2	34.8	21.1	13.2	75340	92392	93	82	5983	0.4	0.3	5.2	34.2	60.0	453843
90740	SEAL BEACH	43221	12804	25.5	24.4	24.1	14.3	11.7	50153	61567	72	53	9800	1.0	12.6	30.9	17.6	37.8	211503
90742	SUNSET BEACH	83640	494	14.6	8.5	34.0	17.4	25.5	83829	112688	96	89	205	0.5	4.4	1.5	11.2	82.4	1000001
90743	SURFSIDE	42614	191	12.0	16.8	34.6	14.7	22.0	80220	102937	95	86	130	0.0	0.0	4.6	0.0	95.4	1000001
90744	WILMINGTON	12658	13928	36.1	31.5	23.5	5.9	3.0	33262	38737	22	17	5742	2.9	0.8	11.1	80.4	4.8	249816
90745	CARSON	18324	15128	17.9	24.8	38.2	14.3	4.8	56893	66466	82	63	11046	5.5	4.5	8.8	73.9	7.4	265198
90746	CARSON	25153	7307	13.5	19.2	41.7	17.3	8.3	66928	79803	90	75	6319	2.4	5.2	3.6	76.3	12.5	301598
90747	CARSON	10202	97	25.8	25.8	32.0	12.4	4.1	48389	59345	69	49	80	10.0	16.3	8.8	56.3	8.8	227778
90755	SIGNAL HILL	28508	3909	16.6	26.1	36.1	14.6	6.6	56842	69554	82	63	1896	1.2	0.7	7.3	74.2	16.7	272941
90802	LONG BEACH	20983	19618	43.1	29.4	19.8	5.2	2.6	29580	35318	11	10	4127	3.2	10.8	35.7	33.8	16.6	176219
90803	LONG BEACH	63303	18683	12.5	19.6	32.5	17.1	18.4	73256	96456	93	80	8346	1.8	2.2	3.7	16.1	76.3	627757
90804	LONG BEACH	16016	15116	38.2	29.6	24.1	5.5	2.5	33044	38779	21	16	3352	2.6	0.9	18.2	64.0	14.2	257007
90805	LONG BEACH	13817	26112	33.1	31.6	26.4	6.6	2.3	36907	43105	35	24	11511	7.2	1.8	10.0	79.1	2.0	227898
90806	LONG BEACH	13919	12408	37.8	28.2	23.8	7.7	2.5	33305	39419	22	17	4685	1.5	0.6	8.8	83.7	5.5	262347
90807	LONG BEACH	35362	12187	17.1	24.0	31.3	16.2	11.4	59791	74510	84	67	6988	0.5	1.4	6.7	50.1	41.3	361313
90808	LONG BEACH	33439	14727	13.5	17.6	36.9	21.4	10.6	73163	89412	93	80	11977	0.3	0.1	1.5	61.6	36.6	370461
90810	LONG BEACH	14573	9362	29.9	28.4	30.8	8.2	2.8	41685	49110	52	35	5463	1.8	3.8	10.4	81.6	2.4	230632
90813	LONG BEACH	8602	16214	56.4	27.9	12.5	2.1	1.0	21671	24168	2	3	2310	1.2	2.1	27.1	64.9	4.7	216085
90814	LONG BEACH	34558	8871	21.5	30.8	28.7	11.7	7.4	48271	59074	69	49	2870	0.3	0.5	10.8	33.0	55.4	437470
90815	LONG BEACH	35852	15090	13.9	19.4	34.9	20.8	11.0	70646	86770	91	78	10695	0.6	0.2	2.2	52.2	44.8	385623
90840	LONG BEACH	18943	12	91.7	0.0	0.0	0.0	8.3	17321	21383	1	2	0	0.0	0.0	0.0	0.0	0.0	0
91001	ALTADENA	35014	12279	13.7	18.8	31.7	19.5	16.3	75162	93355	93	82	9583	0.2	0.2	3.5	44.8	51.3	407463
91006	ARCADIA	32820	10881	15.2	20.7	32.1	17.0	15.2	68811	85490	91	77	8098	3.5	3.3	2.1	27.2	64.0	532721
91007	ARCADIA	34086	11638	18.6	23.5	29.4	15.4	13.1	59799	74465	84	67	7029	1.7	2.5	2.6	28.8	64.4	546704
91010	DUARTE	23012	8276	19.0	23.8	34.3	15.9	7.1	57630	68755	82	65	5804	2.5	0.3	7.7	73.3	16.1	257294
91011	LA CANADA FLINTRIDGE	67079	7074	7.6	9.6	19.6	20.7	42.4	130478	167875	100	98	6355	0.3	0.9	1.2	4.4	93.1	984226
91016	MONROVIA	25709	15030	21.1	26.3	32.2	13.2	7.3	52732	63607	77	58	7660	2.0	1.0	4.0	58.5	34.5	341964
91020	MONTROSE	33498	3420	21.0	23.6	32.1	15.3	8.0	57462	73623	82	64	1502	2.2	0.3	3.5	44.9	49.2	397297
91024	SIERRA MADRE	52571	4888	9.4	18.1	34.8	16.5	21.2	79126	102355	95	85	3313	0.0	0.5	0.7	17.5	81.4	603480
91030	SOUTH PASADENA	41875	10402	14.6	21.3	32.5	15.5	16.2	67571	87820	90	75	4970	1.4	1.9	1.9	21.3	73.5	598444
91040	SUNLAND	29507	7173	17.7	22.6	33.4	17.4	8.9	60955	75443	85	68	5145	3.5	0.7	4.8	64.0	27.0	307025
91042	TUJUNGA	24576	9789	22.7	27.6	32.1	11.7	5.9	49646	60071	71	51	5880	1.0	0.4	10.6	61.3	26.7	294444
91101	PASADENA	33527	8947	28.6	26.4	28.8	11.0	5.3	45573	55548	63	43	1566	1.7	0.0	12.0	74.4	11.9	258421
91103	PASADENA	23132	8739	32.5	24.9	23.3	9.6	9.7	40120	48999	46	31	4123	0.4	0.1	10.0	51.1	38.4	318515
91104	PASADENA	25979	13291	24.7	25.5	24.9	15.1	9.8	49702	62862	71	52	7288	0.7	0.2	2.5	47.6	49.1	395890
91105	PASADENA	75667	5146	12.5	14.8	24.7	16.8	31.2	94597	125446	98	93	3774	0.2	0.2	1.3	9.5	88.9	756348
91106	PASADENA	43247	11025	20.6	25.4	27.4	13.6	13.1	55170	69795	80	61	4151	0.6	0.9	6.5	44.7	47.4	382007
91107	PASADENA	41542	12628	16.0	20.5	29.5	17.0	17.0	67268	86850	90	75	7931	0.5	1.1	2.8	27.7	67.9	498441
91108	SAN MARINO	78111	4337	6.3	7.6	19.8	19.3	47.1	141634	183752	100	99	3961	0.1	1.9	3.2	3.0	91.8	1000001
91123	PASADENA	45706	7	0.0	0.0	42.9	0.0	57.1	208785	285714	100	100	4	0.0	0.0	0.0	25.0	75.0	500000
91201	GLENDALE	22261	8887	27.7	28.6	26.6	11.1	6.1	43127	51013	56	38	3202	2.0	0.5	3.0	34.4	60.1	453477
91202	GLENDALE	32533	8811	21.3	22.3	31.7	14.3	10.5	57477	70285	82	64	4174	0.7	0.5	5.0	31.8	62.0	483223
91203	GLENDALE	19094	5572	31.0	33.1	25.6	7.4	2.9	38151	45328	40	27	1532	0.9	0.0	8.5	72.6	18.1	277817
91204	GLENDALE	16112	5925	34.7	27.6	29.9	6.4	1.4	37236	43889	36	25	1035	2.2	0.0	7.1	66.0	24.7	274457
91205	GLENDALE	16309	14092	40.0	28.8	22.5	6.1	2.6	32364	38497	19	15	3148	2.5	0.5	8.6	57.4	31.1	311045
	CALIFORNIA	27293		21.8	24.4	30.5	13.7	9.7	54267	64547				3.3	2.7	13.3	42.9	37.9	319678
	UNITED STATES	25866		24.7	27.1	30.8	10.9	6.5	48124	56710				10.9	15.0	33.7	30.1	10.4	145905

ZIP CODE #	POST OFFICE NAME	FINANCIAL SERVICES: Auto Loan	FINANCIAL SERVICES: Home Loan	FINANCIAL SERVICES: Investments	FINANCIAL SERVICES: Retirement Plans	THE HOME: Home Improvements: Home Repair	THE HOME: Home Improvements: Lawn & Garden	THE HOME: Furnishings: Computers & Hardware	THE HOME: Furnishings: Major Appliances	THE HOME: Furnishings: TV, Radio, Sound Equipment	THE HOME: Furnishings: Furniture	ENTERTAINMENT: Dine out/Carry out	ENTERTAINMENT: Sports Equipment	ENTERTAINMENT: Fees & Tickets	ENTERTAINMENT: Toys & Games	ENTERTAINMENT: Travel	ENTERTAINMENT: Cable TV	PERSONAL: Apparel & Services	PERSONAL: Auto Repairs	PERSONAL: Health Insurance	PERSONAL: Pets & Supplies
90290	TOPANGA	181	255	321	244	244	253	219	216	203	221	256	245	245	281	231	204	261	207	192	231
90291	VENICE	117	116	203	129	110	122	133	120	135	135	172	146	138	180	132	134	171	128	112	133
90292	MARINA DEL REY	175	187	319	203	178	196	203	185	203	206	257	222	215	273	204	202	257	193	171	204
90293	PLAYA DEL REY	161	166	285	184	159	174	184	167	186	187	235	203	194	248	184	184	234	176	155	185
90301	INGLEWOOD	67	59	67	59	58	62	66	65	69	69	88	74	65	86	64	68	87	69	63	71
90302	INGLEWOOD	65	61	74	60	59	66	66	64	70	68	88	74	67	88	65	70	87	67	64	72
90303	INGLEWOOD	76	68	71	67	67	72	74	74	77	77	97	83	73	95	71	75	97	77	71	80
90304	INGLEWOOD	65	56	55	56	55	57	63	63	65	66	83	72	60	81	59	61	83	66	57	66
90305	INGLEWOOD	92	90	101	86	88	102	91	91	96	94	121	97	95	116	93	100	118	92	97	104
90401	SANTA MONICA	83	78	140	88	75	85	94	84	97	94	122	102	96	126	92	96	121	90	81	93
90402	SANTA MONICA	332	395	608	410	382	417	384	365	372	393	472	425	423	496	397	373	475	366	340	401
90403	SANTA MONICA	131	131	233	147	125	139	149	134	152	151	192	163	156	202	148	151	191	142	125	149
90404	SANTA MONICA	79	78	141	85	74	83	91	81	94	91	120	99	94	127	90	95	119	87	78	90
90405	SANTA MONICA	125	129	214	141	123	135	142	130	143	144	181	157	149	190	142	142	180	136	121	144
90501	TORRANCE	85	90	107	91	88	91	92	91	91	94	115	106	92	116	91	87	115	94	82	97
90502	TORRANCE	92	103	129	105	102	103	104	103	99	105	126	121	104	127	104	95	126	106	91	109
90503	TORRANCE	111	134	177	139	132	133	133	129	122	131	154	157	135	157	134	116	154	133	111	137
90504	TORRANCE	86	99	137	105	100	99	103	100	96	101	122	123	102	123	104	91	122	105	87	106
90505	TORRANCE	119	146	188	143	143	149	139	137	133	140	168	158	145	175	143	132	169	138	125	146
90601	WHITTIER	102	115	138	112	111	116	112	110	110	114	139	126	116	144	112	108	139	111	101	118
90602	WHITTIER	84	81	92	81	79	83	87	85	88	89	111	98	86	111	84	84	111	88	79	91
90603	WHITTIER	111	133	153	129	131	138	125	123	121	124	152	140	133	160	129	121	150	121	119	134
90604	WHITTIER	89	96	106	93	93	97	94	93	93	96	118	105	96	121	94	92	118	94	87	101
90605	WHITTIER	101	104	113	100	100	106	103	104	104	107	131	116	104	131	102	101	131	105	97	111
90606	WHITTIER	86	83	83	79	79	84	84	86	86	89	108	94	81	104	81	83	108	88	80	91
90620	BUENA PARK	95	106	126	103	103	108	104	102	102	106	130	116	106	134	104	101	130	103	95	110
90621	BUENA PARK	85	82	92	82	80	83	87	86	87	90	111	99	85	110	84	83	111	89	78	92
90623	LA PALMA	112	144	198	151	145	142	142	139	127	138	160	172	143	164	145	119	161	143	116	145
90630	CYPRESS	114	138	167	134	133	139	129	127	124	130	156	145	136	165	131	123	157	126	116	137
90631	LA HABRA	103	111	126	109	108	113	110	109	108	112	136	125	111	137	110	105	135	111	102	118
90638	LA MIRADA	108	127	153	128	126	128	123	122	117	123	147	143	127	152	125	113	147	122	110	131
90639	LA MIRADA	86	89	103	93	90	94	91	90	88	90	110	106	91	107	91	85	107	91	87	99
90640	MONTEBELLO	83	79	84	78	77	80	83	84	83	86	105	95	80	101	80	79	105	87	77	89
90650	NORWALK	83	83	92	81	81	85	85	85	86	89	109	95	84	108	83	84	109	87	79	91
90660	PICO RIVERA	85	76	67	71	73	77	78	83	81	84	102	89	73	93	74	78	101	85	77	87
90670	SANTA FE SPRINGS	85	82	91	79	79	85	86	86	88	89	111	95	84	107	84	87	110	89	83	92
90680	STANTON	80	81	88	79	79	83	82	82	82	85	104	92	81	103	80	80	104	84	76	88
90701	ARTESIA	87	96	120	99	95	95	99	97	93	98	118	117	97	118	98	88	118	101	84	103
90703	CERRITOS	122	145	205	165	151	140	156	152	135	148	170	198	147	164	156	119	168	162	120	157
90704	AVALON	101	90	82	87	96	104	91	97	95	89	115	116	86	116	92	96	110	98	104	120
90706	BELLFLOWER	78	79	89	77	77	81	81	80	82	83	103	90	81	104	79	80	103	82	75	86
90710	HARBOR CITY	85	89	108	89	87	91	93	91	92	93	116	106	93	117	92	89	115	94	84	97
90712	LAKEWOOD	102	118	134	116	115	119	112	111	109	113	137	128	118	142	114	107	136	110	103	121
90713	LAKEWOOD	102	124	140	121	121	124	115	114	110	115	138	131	122	147	118	108	138	111	105	124
90715	LAKEWOOD	88	95	111	92	92	97	94	93	94	97	119	105	96	122	94	92	119	94	86	100
90716	HAWAIIAN GARDENS	72	65	66	64	63	65	71	70	73	75	93	80	69	92	67	69	93	74	64	75
90717	LOMITA	88	92	108	92	89	95	94	91	93	95	117	106	95	118	93	90	116	94	86	100
90720	LOS ALAMITOS	132	157	196	156	152	160	150	146	143	151	181	169	158	187	152	141	181	146	133	158
90723	PARAMOUNT	76	66	64	65	65	67	73	74	75	77	95	83	69	92	68	71	96	77	67	78
90731	SAN PEDRO	78	77	88	77	75	80	81	80	82	83	103	92	81	103	79	79	103	83	75	86
90732	SAN PEDRO	110	144	178	138	139	146	130	128	124	130	155	146	141	167	136	124	156	125	119	138
90740	SEAL BEACH	105	114	142	110	115	130	109	114	110	113	138	120	114	133	115	114	134	112	118	123
90742	SUNSET BEACH	184	215	334	223	206	222	217	203	214	220	270	240	233	290	222	214	271	207	187	221
90743	SURFSIDE	124	143	176	148	141	145	141	137	134	140	169	163	145	173	142	130	167	138	125	149
90744	WILMINGTON	72	62	59	61	60	63	68	69	71	72	89	78	64	86	64	67	90	73	63	73
90745	CARSON	86	98	129	106	99	96	103	101	93	100	118	126	99	115	102	85	117	106	84	106
90746	CARSON	112	123	137	119	120	130	118	117	118	120	149	131	124	150	121	119	147	117	116	130
90747	CARSON	81	80	88	76	78	90	79	80	83	82	105	85	84	101	81	87	102	80	86	91
90755	SIGNAL HILL	100	100	117	102	97	102	105	101	104	107	132	118	104	131	102	100	130	105	94	111
90802	LONG BEACH	57	50	71	54	48	53	62	56	63	61	80	69	60	79	58	60	79	62	53	62
90803	LONG BEACH	140	148	240	161	142	154	160	147	159	162	202	178	168	212	160	157	201	153	136	162
90804	LONG BEACH	62	55	70	57	53	58	65	61	66	65	84	73	62	83	61	63	83	65	56	66
90805	LONG BEACH	68	63	71	62	61	65	68	67	71	71	89	77	67	89	66	68	89	70	63	73
90806	LONG BEACH	69	63	67	63	62	64	69	68	70	72	89	79	67	88	66	66	89	72	63	73
90807	LONG BEACH	113	128	158	129	124	130	126	122	122	127	154	143	130	158	126	119	153	124	112	133
90808	LONG BEACH	107	137	168	132	133	138	125	123	120	125	150	142	135	162	130	119	151	121	113	133
90810	LONG BEACH	75	75	89	75	74	77	79	79	79	81	100	91	78	98	78	76	100	82	72	84
90813	LONG BEACH	44	38	42	38	37	39	44	43	46	46	58	49	42	57	41	43	58	46	40	46
90814	LONG BEACH	97	89	122	98	87	94	105	96	104	104	131	118	103	128	99	99	129	104	89	107
90815	LONG BEACH	108	131	169	128	127	135	126	123	122	126	153	142	133	161	130	122	153	123	114	132
90840	LONG BEACH	56	34	43	39	34	41	67	49	65	56	81	68	54	73	53	57	76	60	45	56
91001	ALTADENA	125	157	194	149	151	158	144	142	139	146	175	161	154	186	149	139	176	140	131	153
91006	ARCADIA	114	143	191	148	143	142	140	138	128	138	161	168	142	166	143	121	162	141	118	145
91007	ARCADIA	110	132	186	148	137	129	140	137	122	133	153	176	134	150	140	109	153	144	109	142
91010	DUARTE	103	111	125	105	107	113	108	109	107	112	136	121	109	135	108	106	135	110	102	116
91011	LA CANADA FLINTRIDGE	241	326	439	318	317	339	285	282	266	290	336	318	321	357	303	268	341	271	260	305
91016	MONROVIA	94	101	119	101	98	104	102	100	100	103	126	115	103	128	101	98	126	101	93	108
91020	MONTROSE	104	111	135	114	108	113	113	109	110	114	139	129	115	139	112	106	137	112	100	120
91024	SIERRA MADRE	142	180	229	178	175	181	168	164	159	168	200	192	179	213	173	157	201	163	148	177
91030	SOUTH PASADENA	119	135	202	143	132	139	140	132	136	140	171	159	146	179	142	133	171	137	120	143
91040	SUNLAND	99	118	141	116	115	118	112	110	108	112	136	127	117	143	114	106	135	109	101	119
91042	TUJUNGA	82	96	127	92	92	98	94	91	94	95	118	104	98	126	96	95	119	92	86	98
91101	PASADENA	81	76	126	84	73	81	90	81	92	90	117	98	91	120	87	91	115	87	78	90
91103	PASADENA	106	105	119	103	102	108	108	108	109	113	138	122	108	137	106	106	139	111	101	116
91104	PASADENA	102	110	128	108	107	111	109	108	108	112	136	123	111	139	108	105	136	109	99	116
91105	PASADENA	197	246	327	241	240	258	229	225	220	231	277	255	248	291	239	222	278	222	213	244
91106	PASADENA	123	124	203	133	118	131	139	127	142	141	180	153	143	187	138	141	179	135	120	141
91107	PASADENA	131	156	213	156	150	159	151	146	147	154	186	170	160	196	154	146	187	147	133	158
91108	SAN MARINO	287	373	517	381	370	385	345	340	315	345	398	400	372	409	361	307	401	337	303	364
91123	PASADENA	312	292	280	277	309	364	270	307	285	289	355	301	274	295	294	305	332	298	360	351
91201	GLENDALE	72	84	141	81	80	89	88	82	92	89	117	95	93	130	91	96	119	86	80	90
91202	GLENDALE	99	112	170	111	107	117	115	109	117	116	149	126	121	159	118	119	149	113	104	119
91203	GLENDALE	55	60	119	60	57	66	70	62	76	69	96	73	72	108	72	80	98	68	63	69
91204	GLENDALE	54	58	107	57	55	63	66	60	71	66	91	70	68	100	68	75	92	65	60	66
91205	GLENDALE	52	56	108	56	53	62	64	58	70	64	89	68	67	99	67	74	90	63	59	64
	CALIFORNIA	107	111	131	112	109	115	113	111	111	114	140	129	114	141	112	109	139	113	104	122
	UNITED STATES	100	100	100	100	100	100	100	100	100	100	100	100	100	100	100	100	100	100	100	100

ZIP CODE		COUNTY FIPS CODE	POPULATION			2000-2004 ANNUAL RATE		HOUSEHOLDS					FAMILIES		
#	POST OFFICE NAME		2000	2004	2009	% Rate	State Centile	2000	2004	2009	% Annual Rate 2000-2004	2004 Average HH Size	2000	2004	% Annual Rate 2000-2004
91206	GLENDALE	037	33010	34229	35662	0.9	49	13283	13681	14144	0.7	2.47	8704	8928	0.6
91207	GLENDALE	037	10072	10238	10596	0.4	27	4062	4097	4206	0.2	2.50	2761	2768	0.1
91208	GLENDALE	037	15495	16245	17012	1.1	59	6027	6275	6521	1.0	2.55	4144	4315	1.0
91214	LA CRESCENTA	037	29504	30110	31159	0.5	31	10473	10648	10954	0.4	2.81	8108	8201	0.3
91301	AGOURA HILLS	037	26625	28616	30328	1.7	74	9114	9731	10236	1.6	2.94	7073	7529	1.5
91302	CALABASAS	037	23076	24956	26475	1.9	77	8099	8630	9046	1.5	2.88	6414	6812	1.4
91303	CANOGA PARK	037	23799	24354	25103	0.5	33	7622	7678	7821	0.2	3.17	5048	5075	0.1
91304	CANOGA PARK	037	47584	49541	51531	1.0	53	16034	16463	16934	0.6	2.97	11594	11912	0.6
91306	WINNETKA	037	45217	46640	48237	0.7	42	14094	14317	14636	0.4	3.24	10510	10662	0.3
91307	WEST HILLS	111	23657	24768	25894	1.1	58	8081	8417	8739	1.0	2.90	6507	6774	1.0
91311	CHATSWORTH	037	35579	37205	38856	1.1	57	13300	13855	14383	1.0	2.63	9335	9693	0.9
91316	ENCINO	037	24959	24934	25482	0.0	12	11812	11678	11827	-0.3	2.13	6459	6387	-0.3
91320	NEWBURY PARK	111	36492	38479	41003	1.3	63	12458	13135	13962	1.3	2.90	9714	10197	1.2
91321	NEWHALL	037	31022	34514	37410	2.5	86	10407	11459	12327	2.3	2.94	7097	7809	2.3
91324	NORTHRIDGE	037	24185	24424	25078	0.2	21	8076	8087	8236	0.0	2.99	5652	5655	0.0
91325	NORTHRIDGE	037	30944	32808	34511	1.4	66	11619	12322	12925	1.4	2.53	7415	7832	1.3
91326	NORTHRIDGE	037	27628	29701	31415	1.7	74	9583	10208	10700	1.5	2.90	7857	8381	1.5
91330	NORTHRIDGE	037	1963	2143	2270	2.1	80	149	172	187	3.4	2.56	61	72	4.0
91331	PACOIMA	037	97873	101916	106072	1.0	53	21546	22307	23049	0.8	4.55	18604	19217	0.8
91335	RESEDA	037	68421	73060	77005	1.6	70	22019	23272	24307	1.3	3.09	15479	16315	1.3
91340	SAN FERNANDO	037	34880	35703	36845	0.6	34	8228	8347	8537	0.3	4.26	6937	7029	0.3
91342	SYLMAR	037	79818	87438	93583	2.2	82	20846	22662	24081	2.0	3.75	●16723	18137	1.9
91343	NORTH HILLS	037	57708	59754	61947	0.8	47	16574	16863	17260	0.4	3.50	13110	13321	0.4
91344	GRANADA HILLS	037	48245	49907	51958	0.8	46	16089	16580	17162	0.7	2.97	12483	12816	0.6
91345	MISSION HILLS	037	17242	17447	17846	0.3	23	5064	5064	5130	0.0	3.37	3890	3884	0.0
91350	SANTA CLARITA	037	25056	28875	32081	3.4	93	7734	8824	9704	3.2	3.25	6659	7591	3.1
91351	CANYON COUNTRY	037	27997	30569	32867	2.1	80	8991	9700	10323	1.8	3.14	6910	7433	1.7
91352	SUN VALLEY	037	47060	49982	52676	1.4	67	11999	12670	13268	1.3	3.91	9793	10317	1.2
91354	VALENCIA	037	17887	20626	22815	3.4	93	5918	6812	7500	3.4	3.03	4768	5517	3.5
91355	VALENCIA	037	27402	30340	33341	2.4	85	10518	11622	12739	2.4	2.57	7209	7864	2.1
91356	TARZANA	037	29028	31040	32720	1.6	71	11579	12371	12984	1.6	2.47	7471	7906	1.3
91360	THOUSAND OAKS	111	42528	44827	48104	1.3	63	14526	15374	16502	1.3	2.82	10764	11262	1.1
91361	WESTLAKE VILLAGE	111	19937	21600	23422	1.9	78	8055	8637	9289	1.7	2.50	5665	6051	1.6
91362	THOUSAND OAKS	111	33775	37669	41419	2.6	87	12428	13779	15069	2.5	2.73	9367	10384	2.5
91364	WOODLAND HILLS	037	23801	24611	25639	0.8	45	9659	9974	10346	0.8	2.42	6495	6665	0.6
91367	WOODLAND HILLS	037	36436	37047	38076	0.4	27	15751	15918	16233	0.3	2.32	9537	9604	0.2
91371	WOODLAND HILLS	037	4	4	4	0.0	15	1	1	1	0.0	4.00	1	0	-100.0
91377	OAK PARK	111	14215	16321	18282	3.3	92	5034	5799	6484	3.4	2.81	3851	4426	3.3
91381	STEVENSON RANCH	037	7910	9618	10783	4.7	97	2845	3407	3778	4.3	2.82	2124	2525	4.2
91384	CASTAIC	037	22234	26384	29866	4.1	96	4655	5755	6639	5.1	3.32	3810	4770	5.4
91387	CANYON COUNTRY	037	30272	34370	37602	3.0	90	10366	11653	12626	2.8	2.95	7672	8609	2.8
91390	SANTA CLARITA	037	14853	16606	18054	2.7	88	4805	5359	5792	2.6	3.05	3863	4302	2.6
91401	VAN NUYS	037	41323	43075	44871	1.0	54	14994	15354	15783	0.6	2.80	9655	9887	0.6
91402	PANORAMA CITY	037	66620	69344	71901	1.0	53	17628	17906	18262	0.4	3.85	14077	14269	0.3
91403	SHERMAN OAKS	037	20465	21322	22244	1.0	54	10329	10712	11106	0.9	1.99	4961	5099	0.7
91405	VAN NUYS	037	48410	51843	54791	1.6	72	15374	16137	16818	1.2	3.16	10580	11069	1.1
91406	VAN NUYS	037	53685	56297	58894	1.1	59	18374	18987	19641	0.8	2.95	12372	12762	0.7
91411	VAN NUYS	037	23743	24744	25784	1.0	54	8979	9229	9520	0.7	2.66	5283	5420	0.6
91423	SHERMAN OAKS	037	28040	29080	30278	0.9	49	14144	14557	15039	0.7	1.99	6480	6649	0.6
91436	ENCINO	037	15131	15474	15999	0.5	33	5921	6032	6199	0.4	2.55	4433	4503	0.4
91501	BURBANK	037	19708	20547	21431	1.0	55	8040	8359	8670	0.9	2.45	5023	5163	0.7
91502	BURBANK	037	11466	11723	12068	0.5	33	4741	4822	4930	0.4	2.43	2593	2621	0.3
91504	BURBANK	037	24238	24487	25118	0.2	21	9047	9053	9214	0.1	2.67	6174	6177	0.0
91505	BURBANK	037	29083	29464	30251	0.3	23	13031	13098	13336	0.1	2.24	6811	6834	0.1
91506	BURBANK	037	19201	19294	19730	0.1	18	8024	8011	8133	0.0	2.35	4591	4571	-0.1
91522	BURBANK	037	3	3	3	0.0	15	1	1	1	0.0	3.00	0	0	0.0
91601	NORTH HOLLYWOOD	037	38062	38812	39954	0.5	29	15208	15423	15767	0.3	2.49	7754	7806	0.2
91602	NORTH HOLLYWOOD	037	15391	15605	16097	0.3	24	8464	8540	8751	0.2	1.83	3125	3146	0.2
91604	STUDIO CITY	037	25740	26796	28059	1.0	53	13387	13921	14503	0.9	1.89	5711	5897	0.8
91605	NORTH HOLLYWOOD	037	54956	56583	58535	0.7	40	14679	14940	15309	0.4	3.74	11635	11827	0.4
91606	NORTH HOLLYWOOD	037	45128	46553	48216	0.7	42	14544	14837	15215	0.5	3.12	10038	10209	0.4
91607	VALLEY VILLAGE	037	30163	32206	34043	1.6	70	14011	14885	15634	1.4	2.13	6654	7039	1.3
91701	RANCHO CUCAMONGA	071	39431	42399	46311	1.7	74	12863	13767	14921	1.6	3.07	10315	11036	1.6
91702	AZUSA	037	57286	59639	62125	1.0	53	15219	15716	16252	0.8	3.69	11751	12096	0.7
91706	BALDWIN PARK	037	76177	78571	81363	0.7	42	17077	17450	17914	0.5	4.47	15147	15451	0.5
91709	CHINO HILLS	071	65830	80035	94150	4.7	97	19812	23865	27799	4.5	3.35	16877	20320	4.5
91710	CHINO	071	76637	82029	89593	1.6	72	19355	20773	22743	1.7	3.48	15815	16953	1.7
91711	CLAREMONT	037	34636	35640	36861	0.7	39	11428	11836	12270	0.8	2.55	7840	8052	0.6
91722	COVINA	037	35520	37258	39020	1.1	60	10711	11090	11492	0.8	3.33	8346	8632	0.8
91723	COVINA	037	16063	16784	17518	1.0	56	5755	5949	6151	0.8	2.78	3959	4092	0.8
91724	COVINA	037	25766	27139	28488	1.2	63	8647	9044	9422	1.1	2.96	6650	6930	1.0
91730	RANCHO CUCAMONGA	071	52146	57069	62988	2.2	82	16728	18374	20253	2.2	2.97	12090	13238	2.2
91731	EL MONTE	037	28548	30120	31606	1.3	63	7121	7441	7736	1.0	4.02	5859	6108	1.0
91732	EL MONTE	037	64388	67345	70249	1.1	57	14953	15485	16011	0.8	4.29	12764	13195	0.8
91733	SOUTH EL MONTE	037	45375	46594	48230	0.6	38	9793	9985	10253	0.5	4.65	8713	8878	0.4
91737	RANCHO CUCAMONGA	071	22669	24178	26253	1.5	70	7200	7654	8252	1.5	3.16	5960	6298	1.3
91739	RANCHO CUCAMONGA	071	13704	17754	21314	6.3	98	4162	5410	6476	6.4	3.09	3517	4585	6.4
91740	GLENDORA	037	24630	24852	25491	0.2	20	8214	8244	8400	0.1	2.93	6224	6230	0.0
91741	GLENDORA	037	25724	26357	27291	0.6	35	9033	9205	9467	0.4	2.80	6882	6998	0.4
91744	LA PUENTE	037	83665	87985	92091	1.2	61	18163	18938	19653	1.0	4.64	16080	16746	1.0
91745	HACIENDA HEIGHTS	037	52671	53208	54663	0.2	21	15675	15784	16125	0.2	3.35	13184	13256	0.1
91746	LA PUENTE	037	34216	34772	35736	0.4	26	7801	7874	8029	0.2	4.39	6796	6852	0.2
91748	ROWLAND HEIGHTS	037	46340	48099	50006	0.9	50	13462	13838	14259	0.7	3.47	11422	11755	0.7
91750	LA VERNE	037	33491	33857	34820	0.3	22	11502	11546	11798	0.1	2.86	8624	8658	0.1
91752	MIRA LOMA	065	19003	20414	23470	1.7	74	5795	6158	7004	1.4	3.30	4212	4411	1.1
91754	MONTEREY PARK	037	31977	33113	33485	0.8	47	10809	11133	11514	0.7	2.97	8297	8531	0.7
91755	MONTEREY PARK	037	29409	31109	32793	1.3	65	9247	9731	10187	1.2	3.17	7310	7671	1.1
91759	MT BALDY	071	573	622	681	2.0	78	228	247	269	1.9	2.34	171	184	1.7
91761	ONTARIO	071	56239	62598	69837	2.6	87	14931	16561	18347	2.5	3.76	12532	13849	2.4
91762	ONTARIO	071	54228	58473	64021	1.8	75	15796	16823	18213	1.5	3.45	12241	12991	1.4
91763	MONTCLAIR	071	33616	35305	38034	1.2	60	8988	9331	9947	0.9	3.72	7178	7427	0.8
91764	ONTARIO	071	49584	52193	56445	1.2	62	13395	13995	15006	1.0	3.70	10427	10807	0.9
91765	DIAMOND BAR	037	49353	51770	54269	1.1	60	15451	16053	16679	0.9	3.22	12936	13452	0.9
91766	POMONA	037	70447	73261	76436	0.9	52	17045	17528	18118	0.7	4.15	14264	14651	0.6
91767	POMONA	037	47178	49563	51826	1.2	61	13365	13892	14389	0.9	3.51	9868	10205	0.8
	CALIFORNIA					1.4					1.2	2.90			1.2
	UNITED STATES					1.2					1.3	2.58			1.1

ZIP CODE		RACE (%)						% Hispanic Origin		2004 AGE DISTRIBUTION (%)										MEDIAN AGE		
#	POST OFFICE NAME	White		Black		Asian/Pacific																
		2000	2004	2000	2004	2000	2004	2000	2004	0-4	5-9	10-14	15-19	20-24	25-44	45-64	65-84	85+	18+	2004	% 2004 Males	% 2004 Females
91206	GLENDALE	63.6	59.2	1.6	1.7	20.0	21.7	15.1	18.2	5.0	4.8	5.3	5.8	6.9	30.1	26.2	13.9	2.1	81.6	40.4	46.8	53.2
91207	GLENDALE	79.5	76.0	0.7	0.7	10.9	12.4	9.4	12.0	4.9	5.1	4.9	4.4	4.7	27.9	29.1	16.2	2.7	82.3	43.9	47.3	52.7
91208	GLENDALE	75.2	71.3	0.6	0.7	15.0	16.9	9.0	11.2	5.6	6.0	6.6	5.7	4.7	26.1	28.3	14.2	2.7	78.2	42.3	47.4	52.6
91214	LA CRESCENTA	72.6	68.5	0.5	0.6	20.0	22.6	9.1	11.5	5.6	6.1	7.7	8.0	6.4	24.1	29.6	10.9	1.6	75.4	40.7	48.3	51.7
91301	AGOURA HILLS	86.7	84.0	1.4	1.5	6.6	7.8	6.9	8.9	6.0	7.2	9.0	7.8	5.1	27.3	30.5	6.5	0.7	72.6	38.1	49.6	50.4
91302	CALABASAS	88.0	85.4	1.1	1.2	7.1	8.5	4.7	6.2	5.9	7.3	9.4	7.7	4.5	23.8	31.3	9.3	0.8	72.3	40.4	48.6	51.4
91303	CANOGA PARK	50.6	47.9	4.0	3.8	8.9	8.9	59.4	64.0	9.5	8.5	8.2	7.3	9.2	35.6	16.5	4.8	0.4	69.7	28.9	51.8	48.2
91304	CANOGA PARK	61.7	58.2	4.5	4.5	12.3	13.2	32.7	36.7	7.8	7.5	7.8	6.7	6.8	31.0	22.6	8.5	1.3	72.8	34.2	49.8	50.2
91306	WINNETKA	52.4	48.3	4.4	4.2	15.4	16.0	40.4	45.6	7.9	7.5	8.1	7.0	7.6	32.1	20.9	8.0	0.9	72.3	32.7	50.1	49.9
91307	WEST HILLS	79.1	75.6	2.1	2.2	11.6	13.4	10.4	12.9	6.0	6.8	7.6	6.5	4.6	25.3	28.4	13.2	1.6	75.3	41.4	49.1	50.9
91311	CHATSWORTH	73.7	69.6	3.0	3.2	14.4	16.4	13.6	16.9	5.4	5.8	6.4	6.1	5.3	27.5	29.0	12.8	1.7	78.4	41.2	48.5	51.5
91316	ENCINO	82.8	79.5	2.6	2.9	5.1	5.9	10.2	12.9	4.8	4.7	4.6	4.4	4.7	30.8	26.3	16.7	3.0	83.2	42.6	47.0	53.1
91320	NEWBURY PARK	84.5	82.0	1.2	1.3	6.0	6.7	14.2	17.0	7.4	7.8	7.7	6.2	5.3	29.4	26.3	8.6	1.4	73.3	37.5	49.7	50.4
91321	NEWHALL	72.3	69.0	1.9	2.0	4.2	4.8	35.7	40.0	8.1	7.4	7.4	7.3	8.5	31.5	19.8	8.4	1.6	73.1	32.0	50.1	49.9
91324	NORTHRIDGE	59.1	55.5	4.3	4.3	14.8	16.0	31.9	35.5	6.7	6.5	7.3	6.8	7.9	30.5	22.0	11.0	1.3	75.5	34.0	49.6	50.5
91325	NORTHRIDGE	62.8	58.6	6.1	6.2	14.3	15.7	23.1	27.2	5.6	5.3	6.1	8.6	10.7	30.1	22.0	10.4	1.3	79.4	33.2	48.5	51.5
91326	NORTHRIDGE	65.6	60.8	2.7	2.8	25.4	28.9	8.8	10.7	5.4	6.1	6.8	6.3	5.2	25.5	31.3	12.3	1.1	77.5	41.8	48.7	51.3
91330	NORTHRIDGE	48.5	44.3	16.6	16.7	19.8	21.4	18.2	21.9	2.5	1.9	1.7	27.3	31.6	23.6	8.5	2.7	0.3	92.5	22.6	45.0	55.0
91331	PACOIMA	36.9	35.9	5.5	5.0	4.7	4.5	81.8	84.2	9.3	8.7	10.0	9.1	9.5	30.1	16.9	5.9	0.6	66.6	27.0	50.6	49.4
91335	RESEDA	57.4	53.6	4.2	4.2	11.3	11.6	41.9	47.2	7.6	7.2	7.7	7.1	7.4	31.5	20.8	8.8	2.0	73.3	33.6	49.1	50.9
91340	SAN FERNANDO	41.2	40.0	2.9	2.5	1.3	1.2	87.8	90.0	9.9	9.1	9.7	8.8	9.1	30.4	16.4	5.9	0.8	66.0	27.1	50.6	49.4
91342	SYLMAR	49.1	46.8	6.6	6.2	3.9	3.9	66.1	70.7	8.6	8.4	9.4	8.8	7.7	29.7	19.6	7.0	0.9	68.1	29.9	50.2	49.8
91343	NORTH HILLS	51.3	48.8	4.9	4.7	12.5	12.8	52.7	56.9	9.3	8.4	8.8	7.9	8.2	30.0	18.6	7.9	1.0	68.7	30.0	49.9	50.1
91344	GRANADA HILLS	66.0	61.6	3.7	3.8	16.3	18.0	20.4	24.7	6.0	6.3	7.3	6.9	6.0	28.2	26.3	11.7	1.3	76.1	38.6	49.1	50.9
91345	MISSION HILLS	52.2	49.1	4.0	3.7	10.7	10.7	54.4	59.8	7.5	7.2	8.1	7.3	6.8	28.0	21.8	11.1	2.2	72.8	34.6	49.2	50.8
91350	SANTA CLARITA	83.2	79.8	1.7	1.9	5.5	6.5	14.9	18.6	7.9	8.6	9.9	8.0	5.8	29.6	25.1	4.8	0.4	68.4	34.4	49.7	50.3
91351	CANYON COUNTRY	74.8	70.7	2.6	2.8	4.9	5.5	26.6	32.2	8.0	8.1	9.1	7.7	6.4	32.3	21.5	6.3	0.6	70.0	32.8	49.4	50.6
91352	SUN VALLEY	49.8	47.8	1.6	1.5	6.4	6.3	69.9	73.3	8.7	8.4	9.4	8.2	8.5	29.8	19.3	6.8	0.9	68.6	29.3	50.8	49.2
91354	VALENCIA	82.8	79.3	1.8	2.0	8.5	10.2	11.4	14.4	10.4	10.7	9.1	5.8	4.0	34.1	21.3	4.3	0.4	66.1	33.8	49.2	50.8
91355	VALENCIA	85.3	82.1	1.5	1.8	6.6	7.9	10.2	13.0	6.4	6.9	7.7	6.5	5.3	29.1	28.1	8.6	1.6	74.9	38.5	48.6	51.4
91356	TARZANA	79.1	75.2	3.6	4.0	5.6	6.4	13.1	16.6	5.7	6.1	6.5	5.8	6.0	28.0	26.6	13.2	2.2	78.1	40.2	48.3	51.7
91360	THOUSAND OAKS	84.5	81.5	0.9	1.0	5.2	5.8	14.9	18.8	6.4	6.7	7.6	7.1	6.9	26.4	25.5	11.0	2.4	75.3	38.3	49.4	50.6
91361	WESTLAKE VILLAGE	90.2	88.4	0.9	1.0	5.1	5.8	6.0	7.9	4.4	5.2	6.6	5.9	4.6	21.8	33.1	16.5	2.1	80.2	45.9	48.7	51.3
91362	THOUSAND OAKS	85.5	83.0	1.1	1.2	6.8	7.9	11.2	13.5	6.9	7.7	8.0	6.5	4.7	27.5	29.0	8.9	1.0	73.3	39.0	48.5	51.5
91364	WOODLAND HILLS	85.0	82.1	2.5	2.6	5.3	6.3	6.9	9.0	5.8	6.0	5.7	5.0	4.5	28.9	28.8	13.2	2.2	79.3	41.9	49.3	50.7
91367	WOODLAND HILLS	82.0	78.8	3.5	3.8	7.5	8.7	7.7	9.9	5.1	5.2	5.5	5.3	5.6	29.4	26.4	15.3	2.1	80.8	41.4	48.7	51.3
91371	WOODLAND HILLS	50.0	50.0	0.0	0.0	0.0	25.0	50.0	50.0	0.0	0.0	0.0	0.0	50.0	50.0	0.0	0.0	0.0	100.0	25.0	50.0	50.0
91377	OAK PARK	88.2	85.9	1.0	1.0	7.2	8.5	4.4	5.7	7.0	8.5	10.2	7.7	4.2	27.5	29.1	5.4	0.5	69.3	37.8	48.4	51.6
91381	STEVENSON RANCH	73.2	69.2	2.7	2.9	14.5	16.3	12.9	16.1	10.4	10.1	7.9	5.3	5.0	38.1	19.5	3.4	0.3	68.2	32.8	50.6	49.4
91384	CASTAIC	68.9	66.0	11.5	12.3	5.4	5.9	32.8	39.1	6.5	6.7	7.2	7.2	9.6	42.3	17.7	2.7	0.2	76.5	31.4	64.9	35.1
91387	CANYON COUNTRY	77.8	74.0	4.2	4.4	5.4	6.1	18.7	23.3	8.5	8.4	9.1	7.3	7.3	32.7	22.0	4.4	0.4	69.5	31.6	50.0	50.0
91390	SANTA CLARITA	85.3	82.3	2.0	2.1	4.5	5.3	13.3	17.0	7.4	8.0	10.3	7.6	4.6	30.8	26.2	4.7	0.5	69.4	35.9	49.7	50.3
91401	VAN NUYS	60.0	55.8	5.0	5.0	4.7	4.9	43.5	49.3	8.2	7.3	7.6	6.9	8.1	32.7	20.3	7.7	1.3	72.9	32.4	50.0	50.0
91402	PANORAMA CITY	35.8	34.3	4.7	4.3	12.4	12.0	69.3	72.9	10.8	9.6	9.7	8.1	8.8	32.0	15.3	5.1	0.7	65.3	26.8	50.4	49.6
91403	SHERMAN OAKS	82.7	79.3	3.5	3.8	5.9	6.9	8.6	11.1	5.0	4.6	4.2	3.9	5.6	37.4	25.3	12.0	2.0	83.9	39.2	48.0	52.1
91405	VAN NUYS	49.2	46.3	6.2	5.7	8.1	7.9	58.0	63.6	9.8	8.6	8.5	7.1	8.5	33.2	16.8	6.4	1.3	69.0	29.4	50.5	49.5
91406	VAN NUYS	54.5	51.2	6.2	5.8	7.0	7.1	51.2	56.8	9.0	8.2	8.2	6.9	7.6	34.2	18.7	6.3	0.9	70.6	31.0	50.9	49.1
91411	VAN NUYS	56.9	53.7	5.1	5.0	5.5	5.7	50.5	55.1	8.1	7.3	7.4	6.5	8.0	36.5	19.3	6.0	1.0	73.6	31.9	51.1	48.9
91423	SHERMAN OAKS	82.5	79.2	4.3	4.7	5.2	6.0	9.8	12.6	5.0	4.7	4.7	4.4	5.5	36.2	25.7	11.3	2.4	82.9	39.2	47.4	52.6
91436	ENCINO	89.0	86.7	1.7	1.9	4.3	5.2	5.0	6.6	5.4	6.4	6.2	5.0	3.4	23.3	29.7	18.3	2.4	78.7	45.3	48.1	51.9
91501	BURBANK	72.2	67.7	1.9	2.0	11.6	12.9	16.0	19.9	5.5	5.4	6.5	7.0	7.3	32.1	24.7	10.0	1.5	78.5	37.1	47.7	52.3
91502	BURBANK	60.4	56.5	2.9	2.9	9.6	10.0	39.5	44.5	6.5	6.0	7.4	7.3	7.8	34.1	17.7	11.5	1.7	75.8	33.9	48.4	51.7
91504	BURBANK	68.0	64.2	2.2	2.2	10.5	11.4	28.6	33.1	6.1	6.1	7.2	6.7	7.1	30.2	24.1	10.7	1.8	76.6	36.8	48.4	51.7
91505	BURBANK	77.6	74.0	2.1	2.2	7.6	8.4	22.3	27.3	5.1	5.0	5.9	6.1	6.8	33.8	24.8	10.2	2.2	80.3	38.3	49.2	50.8
91506	BURBANK	75.6	71.9	1.8	1.8	8.3	9.1	24.9	30.0	5.7	5.8	6.2	5.7	5.9	31.4	25.6	10.9	2.8	78.8	39.3	49.1	50.9
91522	BURBANK	66.7	100.0	0.0	0.0	0.0	0.0	0.0	0.0	0.0	0.0	0.0	0.0	66.7	33.3	0.0	0.0	0.0	100.0	23.8	66.7	33.3
91601	NORTH HOLLYWOOD	52.9	49.5	8.3	8.1	5.3	5.4	49.2	54.2	7.6	6.7	7.2	6.7	8.7	38.0	18.3	5.8	0.9	74.6	31.8	50.7	49.3
91602	NORTH HOLLYWOOD	78.5	75.1	6.1	6.5	6.1	6.8	12.9	16.3	4.1	3.5	3.8	3.6	6.6	42.9	25.0	9.0	1.4	86.5	37.9	49.7	50.4
91604	STUDIO CITY	85.4	82.6	3.5	3.9	5.3	6.3	6.6	8.7	4.4	4.3	4.1	3.7	4.8	37.4	27.2	11.6	2.6	85.0	40.7	49.9	50.2
91605	NORTH HOLLYWOOD	45.2	42.7	3.0	2.8	10.4	10.2	64.2	68.6	9.2	8.5	9.4	8.1	8.4	31.4	17.7	6.4	0.8	68.0	28.9	50.6	49.4
91606	NORTH HOLLYWOOD	52.7	49.3	3.9	3.7	5.1	5.1	57.6	62.8	8.6	8.0	8.6	7.5	8.2	32.5	18.7	6.9	1.0	70.3	30.6	50.4	49.6
91607	VALLEY VILLAGE	73.9	69.9	5.7	6.0	5.3	5.9	19.9	24.5	5.5	5.0	5.3	5.4	6.8	35.6	24.3	10.0	2.2	81.0	37.3	48.3	51.7
91701	RANCHO CUCAMONGA	72.7	69.5	6.0	6.1	7.0	7.5	22.0	26.0	6.5	7.0	8.3	7.7	6.7	28.9	26.7	7.4	0.8	73.3	35.9	48.8	51.2
91702	AZUSA	51.7	49.2	3.4	3.2	6.1	6.0	66.4	70.9	9.4	8.7	9.1	9.0	9.8	30.5	16.8	6.0	0.7	68.1	27.5	49.8	50.2
91706	BALDWIN PARK	40.2	39.5	1.6	1.4	11.7	10.9	78.7	81.5	9.7	9.2	10.0	8.9	8.8	29.7	17.5	5.6	0.6	65.7	27.1	50.0	50.0
91709	CHINO HILLS	56.5	53.4	5.6	5.6	22.5	23.6	25.1	28.5	8.8	9.0	9.1	7.2	5.7	33.1	22.6	4.2	0.4	68.5	33.0	49.7	50.4
91710	CHINO	56.6	53.9	8.0	7.5	5.0	5.0	46.8	51.8	7.3	7.2	8.1	7.8	9.1	33.7	20.7	5.5	0.7	73.0	31.4	53.4	46.6
91711	CLAREMONT	72.9	69.4	5.5	5.7	11.3	12.5	16.1	19.6	4.4	4.7	6.1	12.2	11.5	21.9	23.9	12.9	2.5	80.2	36.2	47.2	52.8
91722	COVINA	56.6	53.3	4.9	4.6	9.7	9.9	49.7	55.7	7.7	7.7	9.1	8.0	7.7	29.9	20.8	8.1	1.1	70.8	32.0	48.6	51.4
91723	COVINA	62.7	58.8	4.9	4.9	7.6	7.8	43.0	49.6	8.4	7.6	8.2	7.4	8.1	31.3	19.7	8.2	1.2	71.4	31.6	47.8	52.3
91724	COVINA	66.4	62.6	3.9	3.9	11.4	12.2	33.5	39.2	6.6	6.8	8.1	7.5	6.9	27.7	24.3	10.6	1.4	73.8	36.3	48.2	51.8
91730	RANCHO CUCAMONGA	58.9	55.4	9.6	9.6	5.5	5.8	35.7	39.9	7.7	7.2	8.1	7.8	9.1	34.3	20.0	5.4	0.6	72.6	30.6	50.2	49.8
91731	EL MONTE	38.8	38.0	0.9	0.8	18.1	17.2	72.4	75.2	9.9	9.0	9.3	8.5	8.9	30.4	16.6	6.6	0.9	66.7	27.7	50.4	49.6
91732	EL MONTE	35.2	34.2	0.8	0.8	18.5	17.7	71.7	74.6	10.0	9.2	9.6	8.6	9.0	30.3	16.6	5.9	0.7	66.0	27.2	50.6	49.4
91733	SOUTH EL MONTE	36.5	36.0	0.4	0.4	14.2	13.4	80.3	82.4	10.3	9.3	9.7	8.4	9.2	31.5	15.4	5.7	0.6	65.7	26.8	50.7	49.3
91737	RANCHO CUCAMONGA	72.0	69.2	7.5	7.6	7.8	8.2	19.6	23.1	6.4	7.1	9.0	7.8	6.4	29.3	27.9	5.6	0.5	72.5	35.3	49.5	50.5
91739	RANCHO CUCAMONGA	69.3	66.4	7.3	7.0	4.9	5.0	27.6	32.0	7.7	7.9	9.4	8.8	7.6	33.1	21.8	3.5	0.3	69.7	31.4	51.9	48.1
91740	GLENDORA	74.5	70.6	2.1	2.2	7.5	8.2	28.0	33.8	6.9	7.0	8.1	7.6	6.9	28.3	23.8	9.8	1.6	73.2	35.7	48.5	51.5
91741	GLENDORA	85.8	83.1	0.9	1.0	5.2	5.9	15.4	19.6	5.6	6.2	8.4	8.7	6.6	24.1	26.6	12.1	1.6	74.6	39.0	48.0	52.0
91744	LA PUENTE	40.0	38.8	2.3	2.1	7.8	7.4	80.6	83.4	9.2	8.8	9.9	8.9	8.7	29.7	17.7	6.7	0.6	66.7	28.0	49.8	50.2
91745	HACIENDA HEIGHTS	40.9	38.5	1.6	1.5	36.3	37.0	38.1	41.5	5.7	5.9	7.3	7.4	7.5	26.8	26.3	12.0	1.0	76.7	37.5	48.8	51.2
91746	LA PUENTE	45.0	44.0	2.0	1.8	8.0	7.6	81.0	83.8	8.7	8.3	9.1	8.3	8.4	29.8	18.3	8.4	0.7	68.9	29.4	50.1	49.9
91748	ROWLAND HEIGHTS	28.6	26.8	2.5	2.4	51.2	51.7	28.7	31.2	6.7	6.6	7.3	7.1	7.7	29.9	25.3	8.6	0.8	75.2	34.9	49.3	50.7
91750	LA VERNE	77.2	73.7	3.2	3.4	7.2	8.1	23.0	28.1	5.7	6.2	7.2	7.8	6.8	25.9	27.1	11.5	1.9	76.4	38.7	48.4	51.6
91752	MIRA LOMA	65.4	60.8	2.9	3.0	1.5	1.5	44.4	50.8	7.7	7.6	9.1	8.8	7.7	25.5	22.8	9.5	1.2	70.2	33.0	50.0	50.0
91754	MONTEREY PARK	23.4	22.9	0.4	0.4	58.1	57.6	32.2	34.3	5.5	5.4	6.3	6.0	6.1	28.5	22.9	16.9	2.4	79.2	39.7	47.8	52.2
91755	MONTEREY PARK	19.6	19.0	0.5	0.4	65.0	64.3	26.0	28.1	5.9	5.6	6.1	6.1	7.2	30.3	23.6	13.5	1.8	78.8	37.8	48.4	51.6
91759	MT BALDY	78.9	76.2	3.7	3.7	4.9	5.3	16.2	19.3	4.8	6.0	7.2	7.6	6.3	28.1	31.5	8.0	0.5	77.7	40.0	52.9	47.1
91761	ONTARIO	48.2	46.0	9.1	8.8	5.3	5.3	56.9	60.7	9.5	9.0	9.6	8.4	8.3	31.7	19.0	4.2	0.4	66.9	28.1	50.1	50.0
91762	ONTARIO	49.8	47.0	5.9	5.6	4.0	3.9	59.1	63.7	9.9	9.0	9.3	7.7	8.3	30.9	17.7	6.4	0.9	67.2	28.5	49.5	50.5
91763	MONTCLAIR	44.8	42.6	6.2	5.8	8.2	7.8	60.5	65.0	9.1	8.5	9.1	8.8	8.9	29.1	18.3	7.1	1.1	67.9	28.6	50.1	49.9
91764	ONTARIO	45.2	42.9	7.1	6.7	3.4	3.3	64.3	68.2	10.3	9.2	9.5	8.4	8.9	31.3	16.4	5.2	0.8	65.9	27.1	50.7	49.3
91765	DIAMOND BAR	40.9	37.3	4.8	4.7	43.5	45.7	17.4	20.1	5.6	6.2	7.7	7.6	6.9	27.7	29.6	7.9	0.7	75.6	37.6	48.9	51.1
91766	POMONA	39.8	38.3	6.9	6.3	9.2	9.0	69.7	73.1	10.2	9.4	10.5	9.2	8.9	29.9	16.9	4.6	0.4	64.2	26.1	51.0	49.0
91767	POMONA	42.4	40.4	13.7	12.4	5.2	5.1	57.7	62.7	9.2	8.6	9.7	8.5	8.8	29.7	17.3	6.8	1.4	67.3	28.3	49.3	50.7
	CALIFORNIA	59.6	57.1	6.7	6.5	11.3	11.8	32.4	35.5	7.4	7.1	7.8	7.3	7.7	29.8	22.1	9.3	1.4	73.3	33.8	49.8	50.2
	UNITED STATES	75.1	73.6	12.3	12.5	3.8	4.2	12.5	14.1	6.9	6.7	7.2	7.0	7.3	28.6	23.8	10.8	1.7	75.1	36.0	49.1	50.9

#	POST OFFICE NAME	2004 Per Capita Income	2004 HH Income Base	2004 HOUSEHOLD INCOME DISTRIBUTION (%) Less than $25,000	$25,000 to $49,999	$50,000 to $99,999	$100,000 to $149,999	$150,000 or More	MEDIAN HOUSEHOLD INCOME 2004	2009	2004 National Centile	2004 State Centile	2004 Home Value Base	2004 HOME VALUE DISTRIBUTION (%) Less than $50,000	$50,000 to $89,999	$90,000 to $174,999	$175,000 to $399,999	$400,000 or More	2004 Median Home Value
91206	GLENDALE	30827	13681	25.7	25.2	27.7	10.8	10.6	49091	58456	70	50	5913	0.4	0.7	7.9	33.8	57.3	465221
91207	GLENDALE	45187	4097	14.7	16.6	31.1	16.7	21.0	73683	94303	93	81	2770	0.1	0.2	3.7	14.2	81.8	653082
91208	GLENDALE	44998	6275	12.5	14.9	31.0	20.3	21.4	82152	106202	96	87	4462	0.8	1.1	1.8	13.8	82.5	624337
91214	LA CRESCENTA	35719	10648	12.3	17.4	35.1	19.3	15.8	76170	94247	94	83	7947	1.2	1.1	2.0	29.1	66.6	463043
91301	AGOURA HILLS	50259	9731	7.5	11.9	30.4	21.8	28.4	100361	125559	98	94	7828	0.5	0.4	3.5	19.2	76.5	608494
91302	CALABASAS	70655	8630	6.6	10.5	22.4	18.1	42.4	125128	162502	99	98	7282	0.6	1.5	1.2	8.8	87.9	948043
91303	CANOGA PARK	16790	7678	27.2	32.6	30.4	7.4	2.5	41594	48614	52	35	2498	1.0	1.4	18.4	71.4	7.8	240886
91304	CANOGA PARK	28245	16463	19.1	24.4	30.4	15.0	11.1	57805	70151	82	65	9194	3.1	4.1	5.0	45.2	42.5	370976
91306	WINNETKA	20950	14317	21.0	25.5	33.2	15.0	5.4	54047	64975	78	59	8103	1.3	0.0	4.8	82.9	11.0	290240
91307	WEST HILLS	39382	8417	8.6	15.0	32.7	24.5	19.2	87972	109608	97	91	7467	0.2	0.0	0.3	44.5	54.9	424599
91311	CHATSWORTH	36174	13855	11.9	18.4	37.4	18.3	14.0	71841	87584	92	79	9802	3.9	2.9	2.5	42.4	48.3	391577
91316	ENCINO	45629	11678	21.2	23.8	29.7	12.4	12.9	54881	68199	80	60	6231	0.2	0.3	9.6	45.1	44.9	369793
91320	NEWBURY PARK	36662	13135	8.2	15.0	33.7	26.2	17.0	87774	106085	97	90	10698	1.9	2.5	4.2	28.6	62.8	450570
91321	NEWHALL	27084	11459	19.8	22.9	32.5	15.4	9.4	59004	71385	84	67	7205	5.5	1.7	11.3	51.7	29.7	283243
91324	NORTHRIDGE	28285	8087	20.9	21.3	29.8	15.8	12.2	59972	75279	84	67	4780	3.4	0.6	1.4	45.3	49.3	396906
91325	NORTHRIDGE	32889	12322	19.0	24.8	29.3	14.8	12.1	56675	70736	81	63	6232	0.8	0.4	2.5	43.7	52.6	419451
91326	NORTHRIDGE	46515	10208	8.7	12.4	28.8	23.1	27.1	100249	126303	98	94	8701	0.5	0.8	1.1	16.7	81.0	559774
91330	NORTHRIDGE	12105	172	32.6	28.5	26.2	5.2	7.6	40000	51392	46	31	48	4.2	0.0	2.1	56.3	37.5	340000
91331	PACOIMA	12342	22307	24.8	32.4	30.9	9.3	2.6	44128	50681	59	40	13754	4.4	1.6	12.7	80.1	1.2	227042
91335	RESEDA	19814	23272	24.5	28.4	31.8	11.0	4.3	46843	56018	66	45	12582	1.0	0.7	9.0	80.4	8.9	262667
91340	SAN FERNANDO	12674	8347	25.5	30.7	33.6	8.3	1.9	45047	51679	61	42	4608	2.2	1.7	16.5	77.2	2.5	223304
91342	SYLMAR	18393	22662	18.0	26.1	36.6	14.2	5.2	55340	64592	80	61	16391	2.3	2.8	13.8	70.6	10.5	251174
91343	NORTH HILLS	18578	16863	26.6	25.9	28.9	12.8	5.8	47455	56049	67	47	9034	1.1	0.7	9.3	69.2	19.7	314402
91344	GRANADA HILLS	31429	16580	12.5	19.1	35.3	19.1	14.0	72820	88436	92	80	12651	0.7	0.3	1.7	54.4	42.9	376422
91345	MISSION HILLS	21361	5064	16.8	23.0	39.8	14.2	6.3	61274	71993	86	69	3837	3.9	5.3	6.4	79.6	4.9	269088
91350	SANTA CLARITA	32996	8824	5.6	11.7	38.9	27.8	16.1	90147	110582	97	91	7884	0.6	1.6	3.7	54.7	39.5	371121
91351	CANYON COUNTRY	25047	9700	10.0	22.1	42.8	18.8	6.3	66935	80013	90	75	7314	6.1	5.7	9.3	67.8	11.1	269094
91352	SUN VALLEY	16041	12670	25.8	27.6	31.1	10.4	5.2	46551	54921	65	44	7464	2.5	0.8	9.5	73.1	14.0	249041
91354	VALENCIA	39933	6812	6.9	8.5	35.1	29.4	20.1	99091	121417	98	94	6052	0.3	0.2	0.5	41.7	57.4	433358
91355	VALENCIA	42965	11622	10.2	14.4	31.8	24.0	19.7	87333	110724	97	90	8420	0.2	0.3	2.1	42.1	55.3	420859
91356	TARZANA	48129	12371	19.1	22.9	24.3	13.3	20.4	62789	78900	87	70	7297	0.3	0.6	9.4	22.4	67.4	663582
91360	THOUSAND OAKS	35163	15374	10.5	16.7	33.4	23.1	16.4	81575	98482	95	87	11295	0.4	0.0	1.5	32.7	65.4	455458
91361	WESTLAKE VILLAGE	57608	8637	8.9	15.0	27.5	19.0	29.6	96664	121491	98	93	6648	0.2	0.4	1.0	14.1	84.3	671975
91362	THOUSAND OAKS	51010	13779	9.6	14.2	27.0	22.3	26.9	97992	118854	98	93	11059	1.1	0.7	2.0	20.1	76.1	607875
91364	WOODLAND HILLS	56795	9974	9.7	13.8	29.0	19.6	27.9	94259	124044	98	93	7311	1.4	0.9	1.2	15.4	81.3	605493
91367	WOODLAND HILLS	44611	15918	17.0	17.4	30.1	18.4	17.1	72763	92887	92	80	9395	0.5	0.5	3.0	29.7	66.5	491721
91371	WOODLAND HILLS	0	0	0.0	0.0	0.0	0.0	0.0	0	0	0	0	0	0.0	0.0	0.0	0.0	0.0	0
91377	OAK PARK	45974	5799	8.1	13.6	26.3	25.3	26.7	102668	124755	98	95	4821	0.0	0.3	0.7	22.3	76.7	567839
91381	STEVENSON RANCH	43500	3407	6.1	11.1	32.8	25.3	24.7	99969	125225	98	94	2667	0.1	0.2	0.2	25.2	74.4	507106
91384	CASTAIC	28345	5755	8.2	12.4	36.9	26.8	15.6	87999	109800	97	91	4884	2.7	3.8	2.6	58.0	32.9	349179
91387	CANYON COUNTRY	31477	11653	10.6	20.0	38.1	20.4	11.0	70714	84914	92	78	7402	3.4	1.3	10.0	52.2	33.2	326604
91390	SANTA CLARITA	35142	5359	8.9	12.6	37.7	26.8	14.1	85975	106021	96	90	4751	3.6	2.2	5.4	39.2	49.7	397702
91401	VAN NUYS	23265	15354	28.8	31.3	21.9	10.7	7.3	40273	49104	47	32	5547	0.4	0.6	5.0	47.0	47.0	388212
91402	PANORAMA CITY	12606	17906	31.7	34.8	24.7	6.7	2.0	36296	41049	33	23	6634	0.5	2.2	20.7	74.6	1.9	227869
91403	SHERMAN OAKS	59969	10712	17.0	19.8	28.7	15.0	19.5	67793	89040	90	76	4849	0.1	0.0	2.0	24.0	73.9	674452
91405	VAN NUYS	15221	16137	36.8	30.7	23.0	6.7	2.8	33706	39603	23	18	4523	1.9	0.4	15.9	73.9	7.9	266060
91406	VAN NUYS	18718	18987	28.8	30.0	28.2	9.1	3.8	41361	49578	51	35	8171	2.9	0.5	6.3	78.7	11.6	276824
91411	VAN NUYS	22173	9229	27.3	31.0	27.4	10.1	4.3	42214	51235	54	36	2907	0.4	0.7	9.1	61.0	28.8	318127
91423	SHERMAN OAKS	53602	14557	15.4	22.1	31.1	15.7	15.8	65134	84595	89	73	6419	0.7	0.6	1.6	21.3	75.9	597774
91436	ENCINO	76539	6032	9.8	11.6	20.4	18.0	40.3	121905	158703	99	98	5090	0.1	0.1	0.8	4.1	94.9	968664
91501	BURBANK	30555	8359	22.4	25.4	29.8	13.8	8.7	52683	65307	76	57	3270	0.6	0.7	3.2	30.3	65.1	498802
91502	BURBANK	19649	4822	39.4	28.1	23.2	6.5	2.9	33598	40509	23	17	602	0.7	2.7	6.8	76.6	13.3	291912
91504	BURBANK	31312	9053	18.1	22.0	33.4	16.2	10.3	61505	75236	86	69	5276	0.6	0.2	2.6	43.6	53.1	418192
91505	BURBANK	34686	13098	16.8	23.4	35.0	17.3	7.6	61441	76926	86	69	6630	0.8	0.2	3.1	62.6	33.3	359532
91506	BURBANK	33427	8011	17.2	24.6	33.8	14.9	9.4	59192	73912	84	67	4339	1.0	0.4	2.5	45.0	51.1	403594
91522	BURBANK	0	0	0.0	0.0	0.0	0.0	0.0	0	0	0	0	0	0.0	0.0	0.0	0.0	0.0	0
91601	NORTH HOLLYWOOD	20170	15423	32.7	32.4	25.4	6.3	3.3	36744	43623	34	24	3439	0.0	0.4	5.6	59.8	34.2	321542
91602	NORTH HOLLYWOOD	48692	8540	16.5	25.2	33.6	13.9	10.8	58486	75973	83	66	3129	0.0	0.0	5.6	27.3	67.2	541090
91604	STUDIO CITY	64451	13921	12.9	19.2	31.7	16.7	19.5	72875	96233	92	80	6670	0.0	0.3	0.7	17.8	81.2	686682
91605	NORTH HOLLYWOOD	13629	14940	33.3	29.6	25.7	8.7	2.7	36590	42907	34	23	6374	2.0	1.5	5.9	85.2	5.4	262936
91606	NORTH HOLLYWOOD	15702	14837	33.1	33.1	23.8	7.0	3.0	36194	42527	32	22	5499	0.6	0.6	8.9	81.4	8.5	262286
91607	VALLEY VILLAGE	33559	14885	22.4	29.7	29.3	10.6	8.0	48065	60912	68	48	4979	0.2	0.3	5.5	35.2	58.8	444026
91701	RANCHO CUCAMONGA	30412	13767	11.6	17.5	37.6	22.3	11.0	76551	88949	94	83	11300	2.9	3.0	3.9	67.1	23.1	308985
91702	AZUSA	16137	15716	22.5	29.6	34.2	10.6	3.1	48004	55829	68	48	9013	4.2	1.7	13.2	76.7	4.3	229403
91706	BALDWIN PARK	13274	17450	22.2	31.8	33.8	9.3	3.0	46983	54022	66	45	10614	3.5	1.5	13.4	79.5	2.1	228188
91709	CHINO HILLS	31331	23865	6.7	12.4	37.5	27.6	15.8	89293	106894	97	91	20558	1.5	1.6	5.1	46.2	45.6	382201
91710	CHINO	20659	20773	16.1	22.9	37.6	17.0	6.3	61294	70218	86	69	14665	3.4	1.5	9.5	75.6	10.1	268917
91711	CLAREMONT	36657	11836	15.2	17.7	31.4	20.2	15.5	75000	91810	93	82	7942	1.7	0.8	2.2	46.1	49.2	396236
91722	COVINA	19865	11090	18.6	25.4	38.7	13.2	4.1	55387	64579	80	62	7409	4.5	1.3	4.7	85.5	4.1	261895
91723	COVINA	22866	5949	25.0	28.0	32.1	11.8	3.1	47079	56161	66	45	2441	0.6	0.1	3.7	80.6	15.0	292352
91724	COVINA	28209	9044	14.9	21.3	35.8	18.3	9.7	66521	81291	89	74	6804	6.3	3.5	4.1	60.5	25.7	305441
91730	RANCHO CUCAMONGA	23156	18374	16.3	26.6	39.6	13.3	4.3	55514	63914	80	62	11202	4.2	1.7	13.6	78.3	2.3	232551
91731	EL MONTE	11988	7441	33.1	31.8	26.4	7.0	1.8	35850	42013	31	22	3201	7.3	1.0	5.9	79.0	6.9	246857
91732	EL MONTE	12299	15485	30.8	33.5	26.1	7.0	2.5	37454	43728	37	26	7236	10.5	1.2	9.3	73.9	5.2	235504
91733	SOUTH EL MONTE	11070	9985	31.2	34.5	25.0	7.0	2.4	36860	43071	35	24	4399	10.1	0.8	8.9	75.9	4.3	238189
91737	RANCHO CUCAMONGA	31630	7654	9.4	13.8	37.7	24.9	14.2	82780	96950	96	88	5881	1.4	1.4	2.1	51.8	43.3	369924
91739	RANCHO CUCAMONGA	31729	5410	6.8	15.4	44.1	20.5	13.2	78932	91080	95	85	4425	0.4	0.3	7.2	58.0	34.1	288695
91740	GLENDORA	25578	8244	15.0	23.5	40.0	15.6	5.9	60908	72353	85	68	6036	6.4	1.7	2.9	77.0	12.1	289134
91741	GLENDORA	36880	9205	13.3	18.9	32.7	19.0	16.2	76283	93612	94	83	7108	2.9	1.0	1.3	37.9	56.9	432173
91744	LA PUENTE	13374	18938	18.4	28.7	39.4	10.4	3.0	52159	60306	76	56	13265	4.3	1.7	7.3	85.3	1.4	232540
91745	HACIENDA HEIGHTS	26069	15784	14.7	20.1	37.1	17.3	10.7	67619	81166	90	76	12469	4.6	2.2	3.5	48.5	41.2	354479
91746	LA PUENTE	14307	7874	21.2	28.9	35.4	9.9	4.7	49963	58274	72	52	5658	4.0	1.8	6.5	81.4	6.3	241431
91748	ROWLAND HEIGHTS	23685	13838	19.3	22.6	31.2	16.5	10.4	60960	75045	85	68	8961	5.5	4.0	3.5	47.3	39.8	341186
91750	LA VERNE	32103	11546	14.2	19.5	34.3	19.8	12.2	69951	84306	91	78	9223	7.7	6.2	8.1	41.8	36.2	344394
91752	MIRA LOMA	16919	6158	27.5	31.6	27.3	10.3	3.3	40689	46261	49	33	3999	12.0	2.4	15.2	68.2	2.1	228357
91754	MONTEREY PARK	22326	11133	24.7	28.0	28.4	12.5	6.4	47248	57619	67	46	6465	5.7	1.1	3.9	53.6	35.7	340927
91755	MONTEREY PARK	19816	9731	27.3	26.0	29.2	11.7	5.8	46893	55900	66	45	4881	6.4	1.5	3.7	64.1	24.4	317556
91759	MT BALDY	40957	247	15.8	10.9	40.9	14.2	18.2	72629	85867	92	80	202	8.4	4.0	17.3	34.2	36.1	279167
91761	ONTARIO	17962	16561	16.7	26.9	38.9	12.9	4.6	55012	62694	80	61	11442	6.2	4.3	12.4	72.5	4.7	238672
91762	ONTARIO	15588	16823	25.9	31.0	33.1	7.5	2.6	44226	50250	59	41	9216	1.7	1.5	25.6	67.9	3.3	216438
91763	MONTCLAIR	14768	9331	26.7	29.6	31.9	9.6	2.2	44096	49887	59	40	5342	7.9	1.6	19.6	69.8	1.1	211008
91764	ONTARIO	14384	13995	23.5	35.1	32.0	7.2	2.2	43072	48756	56	38	7092	6.4	1.1	27.5	63.9	1.1	200644
91765	DIAMOND BAR	30516	16053	10.4	16.0	35.8	23.8	14.0	80214	100121	95	86	13148	3.4	1.3	4.8	44.2	46.3	385331
91766	POMONA	15056	17528	25.8	27.9	29.6	11.2	5.6	46319	53669	65	44	10300	4.3	1.5	20.6	64.2	9.4	216314
91767	POMONA	16277	13892	27.3	28.1	31.8	9.2	3.5	45270	52435	62	42	7863	3.4	1.6	16.2	75.2	3.7	217188
	CALIFORNIA	27293		21.8	24.4	30.5	13.7	9.7	54267	64547				3.3	2.7	13.3	42.9	37.9	319678
	UNITED STATES	25866		24.7	27.1	30.8	10.9	6.5	48124	56710				10.9	15.0	33.7	30.1	10.4	145905

ZIP CODE		FINANCIAL SERVICES				THE HOME						ENTERTAINMENT						PERSONAL			
						Home Improvements		Furnishings													
#	POST OFFICE NAME	Auto Loan	Home Loan	Invest-ments	Retire-ment Plans	Home Repair	Lawn & Garden	Comput-ers & Hard-ware	Major Appli-ances	TV, Radio, Sound Equip-ment	Furni-ture	Dine out/ Carry out	Sports Equip-ment	Fees & Tickets	Toys & Games	Travel	Cable TV	Apparel & Services	Auto Repairs	Health Insur-ance	Pets & Supplies
91206	GLENDALE	84	102	176	98	96	107	106	98	110	105	139	115	112	156	111	115	142	103	95	107
91207	GLENDALE	124	165	261	157	157	170	158	150	158	158	199	173	172	225	167	164	203	151	140	161
91208	GLENDALE	140	179	230	172	172	181	165	162	158	166	199	185	177	213	171	159	201	160	149	173
91214	LA CRESCENTA	120	158	203	149	152	158	143	141	137	145	173	160	154	188	149	138	175	139	127	150
91301	AGOURA HILLS	194	234	266	237	226	232	213	209	198	215	251	242	228	260	216	193	251	204	187	230
91302	CALABASAS	262	322	401	326	312	329	293	286	273	298	346	329	320	356	301	268	349	280	260	314
91303	CANOGA PARK	75	69	75	70	67	70	75	73	76	78	96	85	73	95	71	72	96	77	67	79
91304	CANOGA PARK	107	121	157	120	116	123	119	115	117	121	149	133	124	155	120	116	149	117	106	126
91306	WINNETKA	90	95	112	94	92	96	96	94	95	99	121	107	97	122	95	93	121	96	86	102
91307	WEST HILLS	132	190	246	177	181	189	164	162	154	165	194	183	182	216	174	156	198	156	145	172
91311	CHATSWORTH	121	145	181	141	140	148	137	134	132	139	167	154	144	175	140	131	167	134	123	145
91316	ENCINO	123	136	175	136	133	144	138	133	137	138	172	154	143	175	140	136	170	136	129	145
91320	NEWBURY PARK	140	168	187	168	162	164	154	151	144	156	182	175	163	191	155	140	183	148	135	165
91321	NEWHALL	111	113	123	113	111	117	113	113	112	116	141	129	114	139	112	109	139	115	108	124
91324	NORTHRIDGE	110	116	143	116	113	121	122	116	120	122	152	136	123	154	120	117	151	121	108	126
91325	NORTHRIDGE	113	114	139	117	110	118	124	116	121	123	153	139	123	151	119	116	151	122	107	128
91326	NORTHRIDGE	165	218	271	213	209	217	194	190	181	196	229	218	213	246	201	180	232	185	169	205
91330	NORTHRIDGE	83	51	64	57	50	60	98	72	95	83	119	100	80	107	78	84	112	88	67	82
91331	PACOIMA	81	73	72	71	71	74	78	79	80	82	101	88	74	97	74	76	102	82	73	84
91335	RESEDA	78	84	110	81	81	87	85	83	87	87	110	93	87	115	86	87	111	85	79	90
91340	SAN FERNANDO	79	69	65	67	67	70	75	76	78	80	98	85	71	93	70	73	98	80	70	81
91342	SYLMAR	96	96	101	92	92	97	96	97	97	101	123	109	95	122	94	95	123	99	90	104
91343	NORTH HILLS	85	92	108	89	89	93	91	90	91	95	115	103	94	120	91	89	117	92	83	96
91344	GRANADA HILLS	118	142	175	137	137	144	133	131	129	136	163	148	141	172	136	128	164	130	120	141
91345	MISSION HILLS	97	103	114	98	99	104	101	101	101	105	128	112	102	129	100	100	128	102	95	109
91350	SANTA CLARITA	150	173	173	178	166	163	156	155	144	161	183	181	163	185	155	136	181	151	135	170
91351	CANYON COUNTRY	112	118	119	121	115	116	113	113	108	116	137	131	114	134	111	103	134	113	102	125
91352	SUN VALLEY	87	84	89	81	81	85	87	88	89	92	113	99	86	112	84	85	113	91	80	93
91354	VALENCIA	169	193	195	200	185	182	176	174	162	181	206	203	182	209	173	154	204	170	151	190
91355	VALENCIA	148	167	192	171	161	166	160	156	153	162	193	183	167	197	160	148	191	156	142	171
91356	TARZANA	136	167	269	163	160	178	167	157	169	167	215	181	180	235	175	176	217	161	153	172
91360	THOUSAND OAKS	126	155	187	152	150	157	144	141	137	144	173	163	153	181	148	136	172	139	131	153
91361	WESTLAKE VILLAGE	178	226	280	221	221	234	205	204	194	206	245	231	222	255	214	195	245	199	191	221
91362	THOUSAND OAKS	182	219	250	223	211	216	201	197	187	204	238	229	215	246	203	181	238	193	175	215
91364	WOODLAND HILLS	163	218	300	212	210	221	199	193	189	200	238	223	218	259	208	190	241	190	175	207
91367	WOODLAND HILLS	129	153	195	151	149	159	148	144	143	148	180	166	156	187	151	142	180	144	134	156
91371	WOODLAND HILLS	0	0	0	0	0	0	0	0	0	0	0	0	0	0	0	0	0	0	0	0
91377	OAK PARK	181	211	210	219	201	197	189	186	172	195	219	217	198	222	186	162	218	181	160	204
91381	STEVENSON RANCH	176	199	192	208	189	183	180	178	164	187	209	208	185	209	175	153	207	173	151	194
91384	CASTAIC	150	168	167	173	160	157	154	153	143	160	182	178	158	183	151	135	180	150	132	167
91387	CANYON COUNTRY	133	134	143	143	129	131	135	131	128	139	163	156	135	158	129	120	160	133	115	145
91390	SANTA CLARITA	152	173	170	177	167	164	157	156	145	160	183	183	162	187	155	138	181	152	137	173
91401	VAN NUYS	81	84	122	84	81	88	91	86	94	92	119	100	92	125	91	94	119	90	82	94
91402	PANORAMA CITY	68	62	67	61	61	63	68	67	70	71	88	77	66	88	64	66	89	70	61	71
91403	SHERMAN OAKS	151	159	256	173	153	167	170	157	169	173	215	189	180	223	171	167	214	163	146	174
91405	VAN NUYS	62	58	80	57	56	61	66	63	70	68	89	73	65	92	64	69	90	68	60	68
91406	VAN NUYS	72	72	95	71	69	74	77	74	79	79	101	85	77	104	76	79	101	77	70	80
91411	VAN NUYS	79	75	101	79	72	78	83	79	85	86	108	93	83	109	81	82	107	84	73	86
91423	SHERMAN OAKS	135	145	220	155	140	151	153	143	151	154	191	171	160	198	153	149	190	147	133	157
91436	ENCINO	232	316	425	304	306	328	278	275	263	282	331	310	311	355	296	266	335	266	255	296
91501	BURBANK	89	98	158	98	93	103	105	97	108	105	137	115	109	148	106	110	138	102	93	107
91502	BURBANK	63	57	77	59	55	61	67	63	70	67	88	74	65	88	64	69	87	68	61	69
91504	BURBANK	102	122	165	118	117	125	118	115	117	120	148	132	125	159	121	118	150	116	107	123
91505	BURBANK	100	108	146	112	105	110	111	106	109	112	138	125	114	143	111	107	137	108	98	116
91506	BURBANK	102	113	144	114	110	116	113	109	111	114	140	127	117	145	114	109	139	111	102	119
91522	BURBANK	0	0	0	0	0	0	0	0	0	0	0	0	0	0	0	0	0	0	0	0
91601	NORTH HOLLYWOOD	68	62	80	65	60	65	72	67	73	72	92	81	70	91	68	70	91	72	63	74
91602	NORTH HOLLYWOOD	113	113	192	126	108	119	127	115	128	129	163	140	133	169	126	126	161	122	107	128
91604	STUDIO CITY	154	172	254	181	167	178	177	166	173	178	219	198	186	229	178	171	218	170	154	182
91605	NORTH HOLLYWOOD	71	66	70	65	64	67	71	70	72	74	92	80	69	91	67	69	92	73	65	75
91606	NORTH HOLLYWOOD	64	62	82	61	59	64	68	65	71	70	90	75	67	93	66	70	90	69	62	71
91607	VALLEY VILLAGE	93	92	134	97	89	97	102	95	103	103	131	114	103	133	101	102	130	101	90	106
91701	RANCHO CUCAMONGA	132	144	140	147	141	143	134	135	128	136	160	157	138	163	133	123	157	132	124	151
91702	AZUSA	83	79	84	77	77	80	83	83	84	86	107	93	81	105	80	81	107	86	77	89
91706	BALDWIN PARK	85	77	77	75	75	78	82	83	85	87	107	93	79	103	78	81	107	87	77	89
91709	CHINO HILLS	148	167	168	173	159	157	153	151	141	157	179	176	158	180	150	133	178	148	131	165
91710	CHINO	101	106	110	106	102	105	103	103	100	106	127	118	104	126	101	97	126	103	94	113
91711	CLAREMONT	131	149	180	149	147	157	145	142	140	145	177	162	151	179	148	140	174	142	137	155
91722	COVINA	87	95	110	92	91	97	93	92	93	95	118	104	95	121	93	92	117	93	86	99
91723	COVINA	88	86	99	88	83	88	91	88	90	93	114	103	90	113	88	86	113	92	81	96
91724	COVINA	106	126	150	121	121	128	118	117	116	120	146	133	125	153	121	115	146	116	109	127
91730	RANCHO CUCAMONGA	100	97	104	103	93	96	101	98	97	103	123	116	99	118	96	91	121	101	87	108
91731	EL MONTE	69	62	63	61	61	63	67	67	69	71	87	76	64	85	64	65	87	70	62	72
91732	EL MONTE	74	68	71	67	66	69	73	73	75	77	95	84	71	93	70	71	95	77	67	78
91733	SOUTH EL MONTE	75	64	63	64	63	65	72	72	74	76	93	82	68	90	67	69	94	76	66	76
91737	RANCHO CUCAMONGA	142	159	154	165	153	152	145	144	134	149	170	168	150	171	142	127	168	140	127	159
91739	RANCHO CUCAMONGA	124	143	148	149	138	137	130	129	120	133	152	150	137	155	130	114	151	126	113	141
91740	GLENDORA	101	111	121	110	108	112	107	106	104	108	132	123	110	135	107	102	131	106	99	117
91741	GLENDORA	131	158	189	156	155	162	149	147	143	149	180	169	158	187	153	141	179	145	137	159
91744	LA PUENTE	88	84	84	80	81	85	86	88	88	91	111	97	83	107	83	85	111	90	82	93
91745	HACIENDA HEIGHTS	108	126	167	134	128	125	129	127	118	127	149	157	127	148	130	110	149	132	108	134
91746	LA PUENTE	93	85	77	80	82	86	86	91	89	93	112	98	82	103	83	86	112	93	86	96
91748	ROWLAND HEIGHTS	101	117	160	129	120	115	123	121	110	119	139	153	119	136	123	100	139	127	99	126
91750	LA VERNE	126	140	152	137	139	148	130	133	127	133	159	148	136	158	134	127	156	131	130	146
91752	MIRA LOMA	78	75	80	74	74	79	78	78	79	79	99	89	77	96	77	78	97	80	76	86
91754	MONTEREY PARK	81	94	130	106	98	92	100	99	88	96	111	126	96	108	100	79	111	104	79	102
91755	MONTEREY PARK	76	90	126	102	93	87	96	94	83	91	105	122	91	102	96	74	105	100	75	97
91759	MT BALDY	118	147	156	147	144	142	131	130	121	130	152	152	140	162	134	118	152	126	117	144
91761	ONTARIO	97	100	97	101	96	96	97	97	93	100	118	112	96	117	93	88	117	97	86	105
91762	ONTARIO	75	72	76	72	70	73	76	75	76	78	96	86	75	96	73	73	96	77	69	81
91763	MONTCLAIR	77	75	79	72	72	76	76	77	77	80	98	86	75	97	74	75	98	79	71	83
91764	ONTARIO	75	70	72	70	68	71	75	74	76	78	96	85	72	93	71	72	95	77	68	80
91765	DIAMOND BAR	122	144	189	155	146	141	147	144	132	143	166	179	144	165	147	121	166	149	120	151
91766	POMONA	89	83	84	83	81	83	88	87	88	92	112	100	86	109	83	83	112	90	79	94
91767	POMONA	80	78	83	76	75	80	79	80	81	83	102	90	78	99	78	78	101	82	76	86
	CALIFORNIA	107	111	131	112	109	115	113	111	111	114	140	129	114	141	112	109	139	113	104	122
	UNITED STATES	100	100	100	100	100	100	100	100	100	100	100	100	100	100	100	100	100	100	100	100

#	POST OFFICE NAME	COUNTY FIPS CODE	POPULATION			2000-2004 ANNUAL RATE		HOUSEHOLDS					FAMILIES		
			2000	2004	2009	% Rate	State Centile	2000	2004	2009	% Annual Rate 2000-2004	2004 Average HH Size	2000	2004	% Annual Rate 2000-2004
91768	POMONA	037	32821	34275	35667	1.0	56	8100	8320	8552	0.6	3.87	6378	6549	0.6
91770	ROSEMEAD	037	61490	63360	65710	0.7	41	16111	16457	16928	0.5	3.80	13411	13681	0.5
91773	SAN DIMAS	037	34482	34623	35508	0.1	17	11961	11930	12152	-0.1	2.81	8964	8917	-0.1
91775	SAN GABRIEL	037	23568	24910	26152	1.3	64	8388	8791	9156	1.1	2.81	6142	6407	1.0
91776	SAN GABRIEL	037	37897	39142	40625	0.8	43	11579	11872	12228	0.6	3.25	8826	9007	0.5
91780	TEMPLE CITY	037	33170	33511	34497	0.2	21	11406	11450	11700	0.1	2.89	8644	8655	0.0
91784	UPLAND	071	23108	23914	25815	0.8	47	7909	8200	8816	0.9	2.91	6644	6866	0.8
91786	UPLAND	071	48498	52173	57536	1.7	74	17744	19022	20838	1.7	2.71	12128	12943	1.5
91789	WALNUT	037	45492	48088	50621	1.3	64	12520	13159	13764	1.2	3.52	11016	11576	1.2
91790	WEST COVINA	037	44220	45969	47923	0.9	52	12882	13263	13700	0.7	3.43	10430	10730	0.7
91791	WEST COVINA	037	30578	32380	34139	1.4	65	9769	10321	10828	1.3	3.12	7714	8127	1.2
91792	WEST COVINA	037	31244	32670	34259	1.1	57	8895	9238	9614	0.9	3.53	7375	7658	0.9
91801	ALHAMBRA	037	54872	58063	61098	1.3	65	19580	20557	21459	1.2	2.79	13375	14018	1.1
91803	ALHAMBRA	037	30147	31646	33194	1.2	60	9525	9956	10382	1.1	3.07	7284	7594	1.0
91901	ALPINE	073	16648	17374	18597	1.0	55	5775	5975	6326	0.8	2.80	4411	4544	0.7
91902	BONITA	073	17953	18985	19746	1.3	65	6026	6301	6472	1.1	3.00	4914	5128	1.0
91905	BOULEVARD	073	1441	1576	1746	2.1	81	491	538	595	2.2	2.66	344	375	2.1
91906	CAMPO	073	3094	3143	3371	0.4	26	1036	1045	1112	0.2	2.77	742	744	0.1
91910	CHULA VISTA	073	74065	77732	77601	1.1	60	26571	27449	26993	0.8	2.80	18677	19193	0.6
91911	CHULA VISTA	073	71266	80324	86829	2.9	89	22408	25129	26845	2.7	3.19	17345	19391	2.7
91913	CHULA VISTA	073	12231	23284	32980	16.4	100	3892	7152	9935	15.4	3.26	3251	6039	15.7
91914	CHULA VISTA	073	3054	5514	8047	14.9	100	939	1635	2320	13.9	3.37	831	1434	13.7
91915	CHULA VISTA	073	8747	15528	22281	14.5	100	2531	4245	5841	12.9	3.66	2290	3835	12.9
91916	DESCANSO	073	2231	2294	2389	0.7	39	840	857	880	0.5	2.63	579	588	0.4
91917	DULZURA	073	604	617	693	0.5	32	232	235	261	0.3	2.62	174	176	0.3
91932	IMPERIAL BEACH	073	26979	27495	28344	0.5	29	9267	9366	9544	0.3	2.86	6448	6479	0.1
91934	JACUMBA	073	792	808	867	0.5	30	313	316	334	0.2	2.56	195	196	0.1
91935	JAMUL	073	8443	9705	12198	3.3	92	2726	3112	3875	3.2	3.04	2256	2575	3.2
91941	LA MESA	073	43700	44440	46327	0.4	27	18150	18296	18846	0.2	2.40	11269	11285	0.0
91942	LA MESA	073	23290	23441	24250	0.2	18	10608	10625	10886	0.0	2.15	5577	5533	-0.2
91945	LEMON GROVE	073	25105	25475	26523	0.3	25	8537	8595	8847	0.2	2.90	6048	6057	0.0
91950	NATIONAL CITY	073	52928	53928	55384	0.4	29	15305	15442	15657	0.2	3.45	12065	12127	0.1
91962	PINE VALLEY	073	1963	2085	2422	1.4	67	756	797	916	1.3	2.54	554	582	1.2
91963	POTRERO	073	1031	1025	1106	-0.1	10	341	336	358	-0.4	3.03	256	251	-0.5
91977	SPRING VALLEY	073	55395	56868	59549	0.6	37	17684	18018	18641	0.4	3.13	13769	13972	0.3
91978	SPRING VALLEY	073	8002	8438	9068	1.3	63	2910	3030	3192	1.0	2.78	2158	2245	0.9
91980	TECATE	073	229	226	242	-0.3	7	67	66	69	-0.4	3.42	50	49	-0.5
92003	BONSALL	073	3954	4343	4936	2.2	82	1429	1557	1752	2.0	2.78	1058	1150	2.0
92004	BORREGO SPRINGS	073	2895	3153	3971	2.0	79	1299	1397	1735	1.7	2.25	826	882	1.6
92007	CARDIFF BY THE SEA	073	11342	11611	12342	0.6	34	4848	4948	5199	0.5	2.33	2772	2799	0.2
92008	CARLSBAD	073	35914	39116	41696	2.0	79	14493	15577	16413	1.7	2.47	9024	9683	1.7
92009	CARLSBAD	073	42332	53579	62014	5.7	98	17028	21062	23908	5.1	2.54	11870	14659	5.1
92014	DEL MAR	073	16527	17869	20497	1.9	77	6936	7362	8183	1.4	2.42	4458	4755	1.5
92019	EL CAJON	073	40969	42467	43807	0.9	48	14358	14743	14957	0.6	2.86	11006	11255	0.5
92020	EL CAJON	073	57172	58216	60214	0.4	28	20613	20783	21227	0.2	2.74	14072	14106	0.1
92021	EL CAJON	073	59905	61465	64670	0.6	37	21561	21944	22810	0.4	2.75	15001	15191	0.3
92024	ENCINITAS	073	47498	51288	57076	1.8	76	18263	19509	21433	1.6	2.60	11759	12509	1.5
92025	ESCONDIDO	073	45420	47150	49315	0.9	50	13965	14306	14784	0.6	3.23	10043	10237	0.5
92026	ESCONDIDO	073	47100	49035	53298	1.0	53	16584	17058	18378	0.7	2.84	11760	12041	0.6
92027	ESCONDIDO	073	46717	49693	53474	1.5	68	15020	15769	16744	1.2	3.13	11065	11608	1.1
92028	FALLBROOK	073	42428	45494	49706	1.7	73	14453	15379	16646	1.5	2.93	11256	11940	1.4
92029	ESCONDIDO	073	17892	18692	20300	1.0	56	6569	6809	7290	0.9	2.73	4960	5132	0.8
92036	JULIAN	073	3527	3829	4622	2.0	78	1456	1566	1870	1.7	2.42	1010	1083	1.7
92037	LA JOLLA	073	43712	45731	47983	1.1	57	18220	19057	19958	1.1	2.08	9657	9934	0.7
92040	LAKESIDE	073	42747	44039	46228	0.7	41	15006	15304	15832	0.5	2.86	11155	11334	0.4
92054	OCEANSIDE	073	74702	77855	84650	1.0	54	24426	25299	27503	0.8	2.84	16527	17001	0.7
92055	CAMP PENDLETON	073	11813	11856	12033	0.1	17	2224	2214	2244	-0.1	2.98	2163	2152	-0.1
92056	OCEANSIDE	073	51696	53554	55946	0.8	47	19021	19427	20055	0.5	2.74	13512	13751	0.4
92057	OCEANSIDE	073	47372	53802	61755	3.0	90	15820	17592	19774	2.5	3.04	11800	13129	2.5
92059	PALA	073	1488	1623	1808	2.1	80	405	437	482	1.8	3.63	318	342	1.7
92061	PAUMA VALLEY	073	2081	2049	2195	-0.4	6	667	652	690	-0.5	3.14	511	496	-0.7
92064	POWAY	073	48199	50657	52820	1.2	61	15528	16157	16619	0.9	3.11	12875	13343	0.8
92065	RAMONA	073	33102	35100	36881	1.4	66	10704	11265	11698	1.2	3.10	8739	9172	1.1
92066	RANCHITA	073	426	449	521	1.2	63	165	173	200	1.1	2.43	110	115	1.1
92067	RANCHO SANTA FE	073	3778	4126	4651	2.1	80	1375	1489	1657	1.9	2.77	1104	1192	1.8
92069	SAN MARCOS	073	54316	61745	69408	3.1	90	18406	20675	23051	2.8	2.98	13148	14730	2.7
92070	SANTA YSABEL	073	1270	1369	1622	1.8	75	522	559	654	1.6	2.42	348	370	1.5
92071	SANTEE	073	53380	54188	56675	0.4	25	18619	18768	19422	0.2	2.83	14098	14145	0.1
92075	SOLANA BEACH	073	12005	12163	12683	0.3	23	5324	5380	5566	0.3	2.26	2995	2996	0.0
92078	SAN MARCOS	073	6197	8819	13868	8.7	100	2451	3366	5195	7.8	2.62	1730	2363	7.6
92081	VISTA	073	25564	27645	31327	1.9	77	9706	10341	11589	1.5	2.57	6675	7104	1.5
92082	VALLEY CENTER	073	17079	18887	21457	2.4	84	5707	6273	7054	2.3	2.99	4550	4983	2.2
92083	VISTA	073	36553	37890	40005	0.9	48	10359	10607	11117	0.6	3.51	7843	7992	0.4
92084	VISTA	073	44262	46391	48917	1.1	59	14039	14499	15152	0.8	3.14	10422	10713	0.7
92086	WARNER SPRINGS	073	1175	1239	1438	1.3	63	467	490	566	1.1	2.37	313	326	1.0
92091	RANCHO SANTA FE	073	1061	1505	2372	8.6	99	534	755	1182	8.5	1.99	421	592	8.4
92101	SAN DIEGO	073	21814	25801	34939	4.0	95	11364	13924	20022	4.9	1.47	2219	2709	4.8
92102	SAN DIEGO	073	47313	48128	49322	0.4	27	14167	14262	14472	0.2	3.33	9460	9464	0.0
92103	SAN DIEGO	073	29994	31163	34098	0.9	51	17470	18031	19661	0.8	1.68	4986	5073	0.4
92104	SAN DIEGO	073	48430	49607	52039	0.6	35	21817	22075	22910	0.3	2.23	9520	9529	0.0
92105	SAN DIEGO	073	70815	72687	75639	0.6	37	20527	20686	21159	0.2	3.50	15371	15400	0.0
92106	SAN DIEGO	073	18936	19145	19754	0.3	22	7141	7191	7402	0.2	2.33	4231	4226	0.0
92107	SAN DIEGO	073	28176	28710	29361	0.4	29	14150	14291	14456	0.2	1.95	5905	5918	0.1
92108	SAN DIEGO	073	12161	13704	15530	2.9	89	7220	8025	8948	2.5	1.69	2112	2346	2.5
92109	SAN DIEGO	073	46181	47041	48421	0.4	29	23947	24129	24587	0.2	1.94	7470	7435	-0.1
92110	SAN DIEGO	073	22801	23341	24028	0.6	34	9909	10093	10328	0.4	2.08	4642	4681	0.2
92111	SAN DIEGO	073	46254	48066	50734	0.9	51	16975	17759	18791	1.1	2.68	10809	11132	0.7
92113	SAN DIEGO	073	47242	48552	50210	0.7	39	11881	12082	12329	0.4	3.96	9729	9865	0.3
92114	SAN DIEGO	073	65804	67158	69195	0.5	31	17157	17349	17661	0.3	3.86	14628	14749	0.2
92115	SAN DIEGO	073	60158	62676	67921	1.0	54	22258	22947	24844	0.7	2.56	11660	11892	0.5
92116	SAN DIEGO	073	33317	34084	35874	0.5	33	16660	16870	17516	0.3	2.01	6778	6789	0.0
92117	SAN DIEGO	073	50672	51496	52941	0.4	26	20450	20599	20919	0.2	2.49	12667	12676	0.0
92118	CORONADO	073	18922	18937	19815	0.0	15	7682	7655	8078	-0.1	2.28	4892	4837	-0.3
92119	SAN DIEGO	073	23443	24174	24604	0.7	42	9676	9891	9957	0.5	2.44	6580	6689	0.4
92120	SAN DIEGO	073	23946	24662	26002	0.7	41	10229	10450	10879	0.5	2.35	6788	6885	0.5
	CALIFORNIA					1.4					1.2	2.90			1.2
	UNITED STATES					1.2					1.3	2.58			1.1

ZIP CODE #	POST OFFICE NAME	RACE (%) White 2000	White 2004	Black 2000	Black 2004	Asian/Pacific 2000	Asian/Pacific 2004	% Hispanic Origin 2000	% Hispanic Origin 2004	2004 AGE DISTRIBUTION (%) 0-4	5-9	10-14	15-19	20-24	25-44	45-64	65-84	85+	18+	MEDIAN AGE 2004	% 2004 Males	% 2004 Females
91768	POMONA	45.6	43.6	8.7	7.9	4.9	4.8	66.7	71.3	9.9	9.0	9.8	9.1	9.6	29.6	16.7	5.5	0.9	66.1	26.7	51.2	48.8
91770	ROSEMEAD	27.3	26.9	0.7	0.6	47.8	46.3	42.2	45.5	7.5	7.4	8.0	7.1	7.7	30.5	20.9	9.6	1.4	72.9	33.1	49.2	50.8
91773	SAN DIMAS	74.6	70.8	3.4	3.5	9.5	10.5	23.7	28.9	5.9	6.3	7.3	7.4	7.0	27.0	26.9	10.5	1.7	75.8	37.7	48.0	52.0
91775	SAN GABRIEL	47.0	43.1	1.4	1.4	38.8	40.7	22.1	25.6	6.6	6.6	6.6	5.8	5.8	29.2	25.6	11.7	2.2	76.7	38.7	48.0	52.0
91776	SAN GABRIEL	28.9	27.9	1.2	1.2	50.5	49.8	34.3	37.4	6.8	6.5	6.9	6.6	7.4	32.7	21.6	9.8	1.9	75.9	34.7	48.6	51.4
91780	TEMPLE CITY	49.3	45.5	1.0	1.0	37.7	39.7	22.0	25.4	5.6	5.8	7.1	6.8	6.7	26.8	27.1	11.9	2.2	77.5	39.2	47.8	52.2
91784	UPLAND	78.9	76.5	3.9	4.1	9.3	10.0	13.3	16.0	4.7	5.8	7.6	7.1	5.2	22.4	33.9	12.4	1.1	77.5	43.3	48.2	51.8
91786	UPLAND	62.8	59.7	8.9	8.7	6.4	6.6	33.4	38.0	8.1	7.2	7.8	7.2	8.6	30.1	20.3	9.0	1.6	72.6	32.0	48.0	52.0
91789	WALNUT	32.6	29.9	4.5	4.3	49.6	51.2	21.9	24.3	5.0	5.6	7.8	8.9	9.0	26.3	29.0	7.6	0.9	76.8	36.1	49.5	50.5
91790	WEST COVINA	47.7	45.0	4.9	4.6	16.5	16.6	52.9	57.9	8.3	8.0	8.4	7.5	7.3	29.0	20.7	9.7	1.2	70.7	32.6	48.8	51.2
91791	WEST COVINA	50.8	48.0	5.4	5.1	20.4	20.9	40.5	45.4	6.9	6.9	8.0	7.4	7.2	27.7	23.1	11.2	1.5	73.7	35.4	48.2	51.8
91792	WEST COVINA	31.8	30.7	8.6	7.9	33.7	33.4	42.1	45.8	7.7	7.4	8.0	7.4	8.0	31.2	22.6	7.2	0.6	72.5	32.2	48.5	51.5
91801	ALHAMBRA	29.2	27.6	1.7	1.6	48.9	48.5	33.2	36.5	6.2	5.9	6.3	6.1	7.4	33.4	22.4	10.4	2.0	78.1	35.7	47.0	53.0
91803	ALHAMBRA	31.4	29.9	1.5	1.4	44.8	44.6	39.5	42.6	6.2	6.0	6.9	6.9	7.9	31.1	21.8	10.9	2.3	76.9	35.3	47.7	52.3
91901	ALPINE	89.2	87.3	1.4	1.4	2.1	2.4	11.0	13.9	6.0	6.6	7.8	7.1	5.2	27.4	28.8	9.9	1.2	75.3	39.6	51.6	48.4
91902	BONITA	69.0	65.9	3.6	3.6	11.6	12.2	31.3	36.4	5.1	5.7	7.2	7.1	6.3	24.7	30.2	12.4	1.4	77.7	41.0	48.6	51.4
91905	BOULEVARD	70.5	67.8	3.5	3.7	0.8	0.8	18.3	22.1	5.8	6.2	7.0	6.2	5.0	28.6	29.4	11.0	0.8	76.8	40.1	55.8	44.2
91906	CAMPO	72.1	68.2	2.4	2.5	1.0	1.1	28.1	33.5	5.9	6.7	7.9	12.7	5.9	22.4	27.3	10.3	1.0	69.4	36.8	54.7	45.3
91910	CHULA VISTA	57.1	54.1	4.6	4.4	11.7	11.8	45.8	51.0	7.8	7.3	7.4	6.8	7.3	30.3	21.0	10.2	1.8	73.4	34.1	48.3	51.7
91911	CHULA VISTA	52.4	49.5	4.7	4.6	7.2	8.5	60.1	63.0	7.9	7.5	8.3	7.9	8.1	29.0	19.6	10.5	1.2	71.5	32.1	48.6	51.5
91913	CHULA VISTA	58.4	49.9	4.5	5.8	18.7	22.8	35.6	38.2	10.1	9.5	8.7	6.1	5.2	36.9	18.8	4.4	0.4	67.9	32.2	47.9	52.1
91914	CHULA VISTA	57.1	55.4	5.6	5.2	18.7	18.9	35.7	38.1	12.2	11.2	8.3	5.4	4.2	41.2	15.1	2.4	0.1	64.8	31.6	49.1	50.9
91915	CHULA VISTA	49.0	45.4	5.6	5.9	29.5	28.8	29.6	38.7	9.4	9.3	9.0	7.2	5.9	32.2	21.4	5.5	0.3	67.9	32.6	50.3	49.7
91916	DESCANSO	87.4	85.1	0.5	0.6	1.2	1.3	9.6	12.1	5.1	6.0	7.0	7.8	6.1	21.5	36.1	9.4	1.0	76.7	42.7	51.2	48.8
91917	DULZURA	90.1	88.3	0.8	0.8	1.2	1.3	22.2	27.1	4.5	6.5	8.4	7.3	3.2	24.0	31.9	13.5	0.7	76.0	43.0	52.2	47.8
91932	IMPERIAL BEACH	62.2	58.8	5.2	5.1	7.2	7.3	40.2	45.5	8.4	7.4	8.3	8.5	10.3	31.5	18.2	6.7	0.7	71.2	28.8	49.8	50.2
91934	JACUMBA	69.7	65.2	4.0	4.3	0.1	0.1	32.3	38.1	6.9	6.9	6.6	6.2	6.2	19.3	30.7	14.9	2.4	75.9	43.6	47.4	52.6
91935	JAMUL	86.3	83.6	1.6	1.8	2.6	3.0	17.0	20.7	5.3	6.9	8.7	8.0	4.7	24.2	32.1	9.4	0.7	74.2	40.7	51.4	48.7
91941	LA MESA	80.3	77.2	5.4	5.7	4.1	4.5	14.0	17.2	6.0	5.8	6.2	6.0	6.8	29.0	24.9	12.8	2.5	78.4	38.7	48.2	51.8
91942	LA MESA	83.1	80.3	3.7	4.0	4.4	4.9	11.1	13.9	4.9	4.5	5.2	5.6	7.6	30.8	22.0	14.6	4.9	82.2	39.3	46.1	54.0
91945	LEMON GROVE	59.5	55.6	12.4	12.5	6.3	6.6	28.8	33.7	7.0	6.9	8.1	7.7	7.7	28.3	22.9	9.6	1.8	73.3	34.7	48.4	51.7
91950	NATIONAL CITY	34.4	33.0	4.6	4.3	19.6	18.9	61.6	65.0	8.7	8.2	9.2	8.5	8.4	27.8	17.9	10.0	1.4	68.9	29.8	48.7	51.3
91962	PINE VALLEY	92.4	90.9	0.7	0.7	0.6	0.7	8.8	11.0	4.6	5.7	7.8	8.5	5.1	19.8	35.3	12.1	1.2	76.8	44.1	50.9	49.1
91963	POTRERO	80.3	76.9	1.3	1.4	0.9	1.1	28.4	34.1	6.0	6.6	8.9	8.4	5.8	23.4	28.4	11.7	0.9	72.4	39.5	51.7	48.3
91977	SPRING VALLEY	57.0	53.3	13.4	13.5	8.7	9.1	28.1	32.6	8.0	7.8	8.7	7.8	7.7	28.9	21.8	8.2	1.2	70.6	32.1	48.7	51.3
91978	SPRING VALLEY	75.0	71.6	6.5	6.6	5.1	5.6	17.4	21.4	6.6	6.5	7.0	7.0	7.9	29.3	24.8	9.8	1.2	75.7	36.0	48.7	51.3
91980	TECATE	79.0	75.7	1.3	1.3	0.9	0.9	29.3	35.4	6.2	6.6	8.9	9.3	6.2	23.9	27.4	11.1	0.4	70.8	37.7	51.8	48.2
92003	BONSALL	84.9	82.1	1.1	1.1	2.7	3.1	19.0	23.3	5.0	5.6	6.5	5.8	4.7	22.8	28.1	19.0	2.5	79.3	44.7	49.0	51.0
92004	BORREGO SPRINGS	82.1	78.6	0.9	0.9	0.4	0.5	31.5	37.7	4.8	5.1	5.3	4.6	3.6	20.7	28.2	24.9	2.7	82.0	49.4	51.5	48.5
92007	CARDIFF BY THE SEA	86.9	84.5	0.8	0.9	2.9	3.3	13.8	16.6	4.7	4.8	5.4	5.3	6.2	34.7	28.9	8.7	1.4	81.9	38.7	50.2	49.8
92008	CARLSBAD	83.8	81.3	1.0	1.0	3.5	4.0	17.9	20.9	5.2	5.3	6.1	6.1	6.5	29.2	25.8	13.4	2.4	79.5	39.8	49.6	50.4
92009	CARLSBAD	88.8	85.9	1.0	1.3	5.2	6.2	6.6	8.9	7.4	7.8	7.1	5.3	3.7	28.7	28.0	11.0	1.2	74.2	40.1	48.0	52.0
92014	DEL MAR	91.6	90.1	0.5	0.6	4.7	5.5	4.4	5.6	4.0	5.1	6.2	5.7	3.7	23.1	35.4	15.0	1.8	81.0	46.2	49.9	50.1
92019	EL CAJON	83.3	80.3	2.9	3.1	3.4	3.9	13.4	16.5	6.4	6.7	7.8	7.4	7.3	27.3	27.0	9.2	1.0	74.5	36.9	49.0	51.0
92020	EL CAJON	73.5	70.0	5.8	6.0	3.1	3.3	22.4	26.5	8.3	7.5	7.4	6.8	9.0	28.9	19.8	10.4	2.0	72.9	32.5	48.8	51.2
92021	EL CAJON	80.0	76.8	3.7	3.9	2.4	2.6	18.1	22.0	7.7	7.2	7.7	7.3	8.1	29.2	22.1	9.5	1.4	73.1	33.7	49.1	50.9
92024	ENCINITAS	86.7	84.2	0.5	0.6	3.3	3.8	14.9	17.9	5.9	6.2	7.0	6.5	6.1	28.6	28.9	8.9	2.0	76.7	39.2	49.6	50.4
92025	ESCONDIDO	64.4	61.2	1.9	1.9	3.6	3.8	46.4	50.8	9.0	8.2	8.6	7.3	8.1	30.0	19.1	7.7	2.0	69.8	30.6	50.5	49.5
92026	ESCONDIDO	73.8	71.0	2.4	2.4	5.1	5.5	29.9	33.3	7.9	7.5	7.8	6.6	6.9	27.9	21.0	11.7	2.7	72.9	35.0	48.7	51.3
92027	ESCONDIDO	69.6	66.4	2.0	2.0	3.8	4.1	36.4	40.8	8.3	8.0	8.4	7.5	7.7	29.0	20.5	9.1	1.6	70.8	32.4	50.1	49.9
92028	FALLBROOK	76.1	73.3	1.2	1.2	2.1	2.3	30.8	34.7	7.0	6.6	7.6	7.1	7.7	24.0	24.6	13.5	2.1	74.6	37.1	50.6	49.4
92029	ESCONDIDO	82.5	79.6	1.8	1.9	6.0	6.7	14.3	17.6	6.4	6.8	6.8	6.2	5.7	25.2	28.9	12.3	1.6	76.0	40.5	49.3	50.7
92036	JULIAN	89.2	87.3	0.8	0.9	0.4	0.5	9.0	11.4	4.3	5.6	7.7	6.5	3.8	19.6	36.0	15.4	1.2	77.7	46.3	49.3	50.7
92037	LA JOLLA	82.1	79.4	0.9	0.9	11.7	13.1	7.0	8.7	3.6	3.4	3.7	12.5	7.9	27.3	23.1	15.5	3.1	87.2	38.3	48.0	52.0
92040	LAKESIDE	88.2	85.9	1.3	1.4	1.6	1.8	11.5	14.5	7.3	7.2	7.8	7.0	6.7	28.5	24.9	9.5	1.1	73.3	35.9	49.6	50.4
92054	OCEANSIDE	62.9	59.4	7.2	7.3	4.8	5.1	36.9	41.2	8.9	7.1	7.1	7.9	14.6	30.5	15.7	7.2	1.0	73.2	27.3	54.2	45.8
92055	CAMP PENDLETON	63.7	59.3	12.8	13.3	3.9	4.2	22.0	26.4	11.5	5.6	3.9	12.1	43.2	22.7	1.0	0.1	0.0	77.7	22.0	71.6	28.4
92056	OCEANSIDE	73.0	69.5	4.9	5.1	6.7	7.3	21.0	24.7	6.8	6.8	7.6	6.6	6.4	27.7	21.2	15.2	2.0	74.8	37.3	48.4	51.7
92057	OCEANSIDE	63.9	60.3	8.2	8.4	9.2	9.7	27.7	31.9	7.7	7.6	8.6	7.2	6.7	29.1	19.9	11.5	1.9	71.7	34.1	48.7	51.3
92059	PALA	61.3	59.0	1.5	1.5	3.0	3.2	35.2	40.8	8.5	8.4	9.2	7.7	6.5	29.9	22.1	7.2	0.6	68.6	32.4	50.6	49.4
92061	PAUMA VALLEY	44.5	41.6	0.6	0.6	1.3	1.3	41.1	47.0	7.2	8.2	11.2	10.0	6.9	24.8	22.1	8.6	1.0	66.5	32.2	53.0	47.1
92064	POWAY	82.8	79.9	1.7	1.8	7.8	8.9	10.5	12.9	6.1	7.3	9.7	8.4	5.5	26.0	27.9	8.0	1.2	71.4	37.8	49.2	50.8
92065	RAMONA	86.1	83.5	0.7	0.7	1.3	1.5	17.1	20.9	7.1	7.6	8.6	8.0	6.4	26.0	26.8	8.6	0.9	71.5	36.4	50.3	49.7
92066	RANCHITA	83.8	81.7	2.1	2.2	1.6	1.8	12.2	15.4	3.6	4.0	5.8	5.6	4.2	21.6	34.5	18.9	1.8	82.6	47.8	48.8	51.2
92067	RANCHO SANTA FE	93.3	91.9	0.3	0.4	2.9	3.4	5.4	7.0	4.0	6.0	9.0	8.8	3.3	13.9	35.3	16.5	3.2	75.2	47.6	48.7	51.3
92069	SAN MARCOS	68.1	65.4	1.9	1.9	4.5	5.2	36.6	39.4	8.5	7.9	7.6	6.2	6.6	29.6	19.5	11.7	2.5	72.2	34.2	49.2	50.8
92070	SANTA YSABEL	74.0	72.0	1.6	1.7	1.3	1.4	15.3	18.5	5.1	5.8	6.9	5.7	4.8	21.2	32.8	16.9	0.8	78.4	45.2	49.8	50.2
92071	SANTEE	87.0	84.4	1.5	1.6	3.0	3.4	11.2	14.1	6.7	6.8	7.7	7.3	6.6	30.4	24.9	8.5	1.1	74.2	36.2	48.2	51.9
92075	SOLANA BEACH	86.6	84.7	0.5	0.6	3.5	4.1	15.6	17.9	4.6	4.6	5.3	5.1	5.2	30.1	28.2	14.6	2.3	82.4	42.1	49.5	50.5
92078	SAN MARCOS	81.9	77.5	1.9	2.1	6.5	8.0	13.7	17.4	7.7	7.6	6.7	4.6	4.4	29.1	23.2	14.3	2.4	75.1	38.7	48.4	51.6
92081	VISTA	77.8	74.7	4.2	4.3	6.1	6.8	17.1	20.4	7.0	6.6	6.5	6.5	8.1	31.8	21.9	10.5	1.2	76.2	34.9	49.6	50.4
92082	VALLEY CENTER	78.6	75.8	0.6	0.6	1.6	1.8	21.7	26.2	6.1	7.0	8.7	7.4	5.2	23.3	28.2	12.7	1.4	73.4	40.3	50.6	49.4
92083	VISTA	57.3	53.8	4.5	4.4	4.2	4.3	49.0	53.8	9.3	8.6	9.2	8.2	9.0	32.0	16.9	5.9	0.9	67.9	28.4	50.2	49.8
92084	VISTA	67.7	64.4	3.0	3.0	2.9	3.1	38.5	42.8	8.3	7.7	8.4	7.3	7.6	28.2	20.6	9.8	2.2	71.3	32.7	49.9	50.1
92086	WARNER SPRINGS	82.8	80.6	2.0	2.2	1.5	1.8	12.2	15.3	3.7	4.3	6.0	5.6	4.4	21.7	34.0	18.6	1.8	81.8	47.4	48.8	51.3
92091	RANCHO SANTA FE	92.6	91.2	0.2	0.2	4.7	5.5	3.7	4.7	3.9	5.7	7.8	7.2	3.5	14.6	38.2	17.1	2.0	78.0	48.8	48.6	51.4
92101	SAN DIEGO	68.8	66.5	10.3	10.3	5.7	6.3	23.0	25.6	2.2	1.9	1.9	2.8	7.5	41.3	27.2	13.2	2.0	92.9	40.9	62.1	37.9
92102	SAN DIEGO	37.5	36.2	15.0	13.8	6.1	5.9	63.0	66.7	9.8	8.8	9.6	8.6	9.6	31.8	15.5	5.6	0.8	66.7	27.0	50.6	49.4
92103	SAN DIEGO	85.1	82.5	2.5	2.7	3.8	4.3	13.2	16.4	2.9	2.5	2.7	2.7	6.3	41.2	25.4	12.9	3.5	90.4	40.5	51.4	48.6
92104	SAN DIEGO	57.1	53.6	12.1	12.0	5.8	6.0	34.4	39.2	6.7	6.0	6.1	5.9	8.3	38.3	20.6	6.7	1.4	77.7	33.6	50.9	49.1
92105	SAN DIEGO	32.9	31.5	15.2	14.3	17.7	17.3	48.9	52.6	11.0	9.6	10.1	8.9	9.8	30.2	14.5	5.3	0.7	64.0	25.3	49.9	50.1
92106	SAN DIEGO	89.6	87.7	1.7	1.8	2.8	3.2	7.8	9.9	4.0	4.1	4.3	6.2	8.8	28.7	25.5	15.1	3.1	85.0	40.7	52.1	47.9
92107	SAN DIEGO	88.1	85.9	1.6	1.8	2.2	2.5	8.6	10.8	4.0	3.7	3.8	4.6	10.7	40.4	22.6	8.4	1.8	86.5	34.6	51.1	48.9
92108	SAN DIEGO	76.5	73.0	5.3	5.6	8.1	9.1	13.6	16.5	2.9	1.9	1.6	2.2	14.2	47.0	19.9	8.8	1.6	92.8	33.7	48.8	51.2
92109	SAN DIEGO	87.4	85.1	1.4	1.6	3.2	3.6	10.7	13.1	3.4	2.7	2.6	2.9	14.8	46.4	17.0	8.4	1.7	89.9	31.8	53.4	46.6
92110	SAN DIEGO	80.3	77.6	3.9	4.1	5.7	6.3	14.5	17.8	5.0	3.8	3.6	9.3	11.4	32.0	20.4	12.2	2.4	85.4	34.6	49.7	50.3
92111	SAN DIEGO	59.4	56.8	5.5	5.5	19.3	19.9	22.3	25.3	6.9	6.6	7.0	6.3	7.4	31.3	21.4	11.7	1.5	75.7	35.1	49.1	50.9
92113	SAN DIEGO	31.5	31.3	18.2	16.7	3.5	3.3	74.5	76.8	10.8	9.8	11.3	9.8	9.4	28.6	14.1	5.7	0.7	62.2	24.5	49.3	50.7
92114	SAN DIEGO	20.9	20.0	29.3	28.1	27.1	26.8	29.8	32.9	7.5	7.8	9.6	9.4	8.0	26.1	22.3	8.5	0.8	69.3	31.1	48.9	51.1
92115	SAN DIEGO	56.9	53.7	10.8	10.7	13.1	13.6	24.3	27.9	7.0	5.7	5.6	10.1	15.2	31.5	15.3	7.9	1.8	78.8	28.1	50.1	49.9
92116	SAN DIEGO	65.7	62.4	11.3	11.4	5.1	5.4	25.0	29.2	6.0	5.2	5.2	5.0	8.1	39.1	22.8	7.0	1.6	80.8	35.3	49.6	50.4
92117	SAN DIEGO	77.3	73.8	2.0	2.1	9.1	10.1	16.1	19.5	5.7	5.5	5.8	5.6	6.5	32.1	23.7	13.3	1.7	79.6	38.7	49.9	50.1
92118	CORONADO	90.2	88.6	1.9	2.0	3.2	3.6	8.6	10.9	4.9	5.1	5.8	5.7	6.7	26.1	25.6	16.8	3.4	81.0	42.0	50.0	50.0
92119	SAN DIEGO	86.6	84.3	2.5	2.7	4.4	5.0	9.1	11.3	5.1	5.4	5.8	5.3	5.5	25.7	26.4	18.5	2.3	80.5	43.3	47.6	52.4
92120	SAN DIEGO	85.7	83.2	2.8	3.0	4.6	5.2	9.1	11.3	4.8	5.1	5.3	4.5	4.5	26.1	27.2	20.2	2.5	82.1	44.9	48.6	51.4
	CALIFORNIA	59.6	57.1	6.7	6.5	11.3	11.8	32.4	35.5	7.4	7.1	7.8	7.3	7.7	29.8	22.1	9.3	1.4	73.3	33.8	49.8	50.2
	UNITED STATES	75.1	73.6	12.3	12.5	3.8	4.2	12.5	14.1	6.9	6.7	7.2	7.0	7.3	28.6	23.8	10.8	1.7	75.1	36.0	49.1	50.9

ZIP CODE #	POST OFFICE NAME	2004 Per Capita Income	2004 HH Income Base	2004 Household Income Distribution (%) Less than $25,000	$25,000 to $49,999	$50,000 to $99,999	$100,000 to $149,999	$150,000 or More	Median Household Income 2004	2009	2004 National Centile	2004 State Centile	2004 Home Value Base	2004 Home Value Distribution (%) Less than $50,000	$50,000 to $89,999	$90,000 to $174,999	$175,000 to $399,999	$400,000 or More	2004 Median Home Value
91768	POMONA	15294	8320	29.0	29.9	28.0	9.2	3.9	41608	48615	52	35	4584	4.4	1.1	24.9	61.5	8.1	201997
91770	ROSEMEAD	14507	16457	27.8	29.6	30.6	8.9	3.1	43328	50807	57	39	9000	7.2	1.2	5.6	69.4	16.7	275874
91773	SAN DIMAS	35895	11930	11.7	19.2	34.7	21.4	13.0	74320	90593	93	81	9044	5.0	2.5	3.1	51.5	37.9	348616
91775	SAN GABRIEL	29071	8791	16.6	22.7	31.5	18.7	10.5	64070	78323	88	71	5747	3.6	1.7	1.3	31.6	61.8	448601
91776	SAN GABRIEL	16515	11872	26.2	31.3	30.2	9.8	2.4	43376	51537	57	39	5068	6.7	1.2	4.7	66.6	20.8	307955
91780	TEMPLE CITY	24084	11450	19.1	25.3	34.8	14.7	6.1	55486	67268	80	62	7220	6.4	1.7	2.0	50.2	39.8	365201
91784	UPLAND	40002	8200	6.7	12.6	36.3	24.0	20.5	90529	107555	97	92	7486	0.8	0.5	2.6	37.6	58.6	430279
91786	UPLAND	21741	19022	27.9	29.3	29.3	8.8	4.7	42320	48950	54	37	9033	6.7	2.9	13.9	65.0	11.5	254368
91789	WALNUT	29389	13159	11.0	14.6	33.8	24.2	16.3	84143	103970	96	89	11336	4.4	4.7	2.1	31.8	57.0	431813
91790	WEST COVINA	19964	13263	16.3	26.1	39.0	14.8	3.8	56990	66485	82	64	9284	2.2	0.8	2.7	88.4	5.9	282569
91791	WEST COVINA	28114	10321	15.0	21.9	34.5	17.7	10.9	65917	80672	89	74	7472	1.2	1.3	3.0	60.5	34.0	344660
91792	WEST COVINA	21290	9238	13.5	25.5	39.1	15.9	6.1	61873	73104	86	70	6239	3.8	0.6	8.3	74.8	12.5	280120
91801	ALHAMBRA	20776	20557	27.3	29.2	29.0	10.2	4.4	44084	52535	59	40	7680	5.3	0.7	3.3	62.7	28.0	317681
91803	ALHAMBRA	19779	9956	26.1	25.5	32.6	11.5	4.4	47913	57365	68	48	4943	4.9	0.4	3.3	70.7	20.6	320017
91901	ALPINE	33157	5975	14.6	18.5	35.0	20.1	11.9	70823	83798	92	79	4273	5.4	3.1	1.9	23.5	66.1	465948
91902	BONITA	35494	6301	9.1	19.0	33.8	21.1	17.0	79561	96800	95	86	5041	0.0	0.3	3.1	29.7	67.0	476706
91905	BOULEVARD	18793	538	35.7	25.3	27.7	6.5	4.8	40126	46562	47	31	409	6.6	2.7	32.3	43.8	14.7	209766
91906	CAMPO	19551	1045	31.6	27.4	27.2	10.2	3.6	41805	49208	52	36	789	12.6	3.3	13.4	58.9	11.8	241098
91910	CHULA VISTA	22391	27449	23.2	28.4	31.8	11.7	4.9	48321	56030	69	49	14412	6.1	0.9	4.6	57.4	31.0	338217
91911	CHULA VISTA	17504	25129	23.3	33.8	32.0	8.5	2.5	44026	51482	59	40	13667	9.3	3.6	8.5	67.8	10.8	270948
91913	CHULA VISTA	34955	7152	4.9	15.7	43.0	22.2	14.1	82152	101723	96	87	6105	0.9	1.4	2.3	44.5	50.9	402916
91914	CHULA VISTA	26138	1635	6.1	12.5	52.2	20.9	8.3	78239	90148	95	85	1530	0.0	0.0	1.2	53.0	45.8	385388
91915	CHULA VISTA	26393	4245	6.5	16.5	41.4	22.5	13.1	81886	89316	96	87	3818	0.5	1.5	1.1	44.6	52.4	406808
91916	DESCANSO	23645	857	21.4	32.7	30.1	12.0	3.9	46074	53092	64	43	685	12.3	3.7	5.0	53.9	25.3	278538
91917	DULZURA	25024	235	20.9	28.1	28.9	17.9	4.3	51702	62915	75	56	188	9.6	5.3	5.3	40.4	39.4	364286
91932	IMPERIAL BEACH	18222	9366	27.6	35.6	28.2	6.4	2.2	39358	45229	44	29	2910	6.3	2.7	4.9	75.0	11.2	281091
91934	JACUMBA	15427	316	37.0	34.2	22.8	6.0	0.0	33549	38178	23	17	235	10.6	0.0	46.4	29.8	13.2	165625
91935	JAMUL	39441	3112	10.7	13.3	30.4	23.2	22.4	90240	110855	97	91	2765	2.1	2.2	1.5	26.3	68.0	498904
91941	LA MESA	29783	18296	21.3	27.3	32.1	12.0	7.4	51430	61311	75	55	10705	1.1	0.4	4.0	48.5	46.0	383885
91942	LA MESA	27045	10625	20.9	31.3	34.6	9.8	3.4	48029	56195	68	48	5111	1.3	0.5	5.0	71.9	21.4	321179
91945	LEMON GROVE	19322	8595	23.3	31.2	34.9	8.3	2.3	45362	52316	62	42	5032	1.5	0.2	4.2	87.5	6.7	274451
91950	NATIONAL CITY	12730	15442	36.9	33.4	23.6	4.4	1.7	32932	37386	21	16	5796	3.9	1.3	13.3	76.5	5.0	235369
91962	PINE VALLEY	28045	797	14.6	23.1	37.6	20.0	4.8	63678	77057	88	71	678	0.0	0.3	6.5	52.8	40.4	366146
91963	POTRERO	18370	336	32.1	27.1	25.6	11.6	3.6	43114	50474	56	38	263	14.5	3.8	14.1	54.4	13.3	226500
91977	SPRING VALLEY	20040	18018	19.3	28.5	37.1	11.2	4.0	51793	60249	75	56	11500	4.5	1.3	5.3	73.2	15.8	277289
91978	SPRING VALLEY	24800	3030	18.3	27.3	34.4	15.0	5.1	53689	64095	78	59	2157	18.4	5.2	9.0	45.8	21.7	277904
91980	TECATE	15532	66	33.3	27.3	24.2	10.6	4.6	42351	49313	54	37	52	15.4	1.9	17.3	57.7	7.7	211538
92003	BONSALL	40950	1557	14.3	20.7	33.8	16.0	15.3	65578	79032	89	73	1296	1.1	0.0	4.2	37.5	57.2	458491
92004	BORREGO SPRINGS	24212	1397	29.5	33.8	24.9	8.5	3.3	40764	47339	49	33	1102	16.5	9.3	21.6	38.3	14.3	187946
92007	CARDIFF BY THE SEA	44722	4948	11.2	17.4	34.8	18.5	18.1	76441	97736	94	83	2885	0.3	0.1	0.4	19.6	79.6	677115
92008	CARLSBAD	34136	15577	15.9	22.7	34.2	16.5	10.7	63509	76934	87	71	9283	0.5	0.6	2.0	33.4	63.6	461915
92009	CARLSBAD	46880	21062	9.9	16.8	29.7	22.1	21.6	87102	107290	97	90	16329	0.2	1.5	2.4	21.8	74.1	578481
92014	DEL MAR	79535	7362	8.7	11.8	19.9	21.7	37.9	118860	151070	99	97	5636	0.1	0.0	0.4	5.1	94.4	1000001
92019	EL CAJON	29659	14743	15.1	23.5	33.9	17.6	10.0	64181	77011	88	71	10794	4.9	1.3	4.0	43.9	46.0	379625
92020	EL CAJON	20238	20783	28.2	32.5	26.4	8.9	4.1	40259	46392	47	32	8890	4.3	1.8	4.5	49.5	39.9	351590
92021	EL CAJON	20790	21944	24.8	31.3	30.9	9.4	3.6	44758	51473	61	41	11742	15.3	4.9	9.1	46.6	24.2	283451
92024	ENCINITAS	42235	19509	13.3	18.9	30.8	18.4	18.6	75135	92678	93	82	12949	1.7	1.0	2.7	18.3	76.3	598807
92025	ESCONDIDO	19739	14306	25.4	29.7	27.9	10.7	6.3	44655	52101	60	41	7043	3.3	0.3	7.4	47.1	41.8	348394
92026	ESCONDIDO	22795	17058	19.9	27.9	34.8	12.5	4.9	51803	60463	75	56	10403	1.9	1.0	7.6	58.1	31.4	331509
92027	ESCONDIDO	21874	15769	20.4	28.5	32.6	12.7	5.9	51022	61035	74	55	9980	7.7	3.5	6.2	59.3	23.3	288172
92028	FALLBROOK	25975	15379	20.2	25.3	31.4	14.2	8.9	54870	65880	80	60	10792	4.5	0.9	3.8	38.2	52.6	415069
92029	ESCONDIDO	36585	6809	14.4	19.0	31.6	18.2	16.7	71788	84743	92	79	5168	5.1	3.4	9.1	22.5	60.0	480438
92036	JULIAN	27641	1566	21.7	28.5	35.3	9.3	5.2	49860	56970	72	52	1242	5.0	1.7	8.6	47.3	37.4	325943
92037	LA JOLLA	62228	19057	15.2	16.9	26.4	16.0	25.6	80682	102168	95	87	11253	0.1	0.1	1.1	10.0	88.7	1000001
92040	LAKESIDE	23330	15304	18.8	26.4	36.6	13.1	5.1	54186	63156	79	59	10617	9.9	6.5	7.4	47.6	28.6	323858
92054	OCEANSIDE	19969	25299	26.5	33.3	28.3	8.1	3.8	41356	48360	51	35	10999	6.3	7.6	7.6	53.8	24.7	285896
92055	CAMP PENDLETON	16391	2214	23.7	47.8	24.8	3.3	0.4	36336	41706	33	23	110	19.1	31.8	23.6	15.5	10.0	88750
92056	OCEANSIDE	26343	19427	15.3	25.3	38.8	14.7	5.9	58672	67956	83	66	14135	2.1	1.8	6.5	54.0	35.6	348403
92057	OCEANSIDE	23160	17592	16.5	27.4	35.8	14.9	5.5	55318	64321	80	61	13031	1.0	1.8	12.7	57.0	27.6	283920
92059	PALA	17881	437	22.4	30.0	31.4	11.0	5.3	47987	56839	68	48	333	6.3	3.3	9.9	45.1	35.4	340123
92061	PAUMA VALLEY	19101	652	26.4	33.9	26.7	7.5	5.5	41866	47104	52	36	434	9.7	6.5	15.0	38.5	30.4	298529
92064	POWAY	34252	16157	9.5	18.5	33.3	21.6	17.2	80107	95975	95	86	13007	1.8	1.8	2.3	35.7	58.5	453769
92065	RAMONA	27348	11265	13.5	21.1	38.1	18.1	9.2	67525	78656	90	75	8870	1.9	1.7	2.6	42.0	51.8	406617
92066	RANCHITA	24613	173	32.4	29.5	25.4	9.3	3.5	39082	46559	43	29	141	5.0	5.0	28.4	46.8	14.9	238333
92067	RANCHO SANTA FE	128439	1489	6.7	8.9	9.4	12.3	62.7	224221	268020	100	100	1335	0.0	0.0	0.0	0.0	100.0	1000001
92069	SAN MARCOS	21762	20675	18.6	29.1	34.3	13.7	4.2	52108	61656	76	56	14124	3.3	6.0	11.6	49.6	29.6	315641
92070	SANTA YSABEL	32364	559	30.2	29.9	20.8	8.2	10.9	38419	45000	41	27	419	20.5	3.8	12.9	23.4	39.4	271875
92071	SANTEE	24858	18768	14.6	23.9	41.2	16.2	4.1	60652	70168	85	68	14285	6.4	4.1	10.4	62.3	16.9	291843
92075	SOLANA BEACH	59229	5380	14.4	17.1	26.1	17.7	24.8	82123	103256	96	87	3218	0.5	0.0	0.8	10.5	88.2	817906
92078	SAN MARCOS	30553	3366	17.7	23.0	33.8	16.7	8.7	62156	71796	86	70	2859	6.8	4.0	13.8	31.7	43.8	367555
92081	VISTA	27572	10341	13.6	28.8	36.5	14.3	6.8	56900	66430	82	64	6267	1.9	0.8	2.7	49.9	44.7	383291
92082	VALLEY CENTER	29074	6273	15.5	20.2	34.0	18.1	12.2	67642	80971	90	76	5344	5.2	2.3	6.7	27.5	58.3	439694
92083	VISTA	16936	10607	20.6	32.3	33.8	10.2	3.1	47656	54766	68	47	5673	5.5	2.0	6.7	72.0	13.8	274438
92084	VISTA	21418	14499	21.6	29.0	31.4	11.7	6.4	49435	58279	71	51	8844	5.2	2.6	4.0	48.1	40.1	356150
92086	WARNER SPRINGS	25457	490	32.0	29.6	25.3	9.2	3.9	39181	46361	43	29	401	6.2	5.5	27.7	43.9	16.7	234302
92091	RANCHO SANTA FE	137296	755	8.9	9.4	16.2	14.2	51.4	155789	193302	100	99	682	0.0	0.0	0.0	3.1	96.9	1000001
92101	SAN DIEGO	31416	13924	45.8	24.2	18.4	6.6	5.1	28278	34704	9	8	1937	3.6	0.3	3.7	31.1	61.3	481530
92102	SAN DIEGO	12047	14262	42.7	33.6	18.1	4.1	1.6	29177	33514	11	9	4409	7.0	1.7	22.4	56.4	12.5	230694
92103	SAN DIEGO	43897	18031	24.4	28.8	26.8	11.0	9.0	46908	57577	66	45	5749	0.5	0.6	4.3	29.5	65.1	540242
92104	SAN DIEGO	20963	22075	34.0	33.1	24.7	6.0	2.2	34991	40310	27	20	5920	0.4	1.7	11.2	60.1	26.6	296602
92105	SAN DIEGO	11552	20686	44.3	32.4	18.5	3.0	1.8	27959	31412	9	8	6361	3.2	2.5	21.6	70.3	2.4	218000
92106	SAN DIEGO	44424	7191	14.3	23.0	28.7	17.1	16.9	70665	86342	91	78	4821	0.8	0.3	0.9	10.4	87.5	766824
92107	SAN DIEGO	34320	14291	20.7	29.8	31.2	12.3	6.0	49525	59530	71	51	5653	0.7	0.9	3.7	25.1	69.6	542007
92108	SAN DIEGO	34337	8025	21.8	31.0	34.1	9.7	3.4	47518	56565	67	47	2477	0.9	0.8	31.5	56.8	10.0	224127
92109	SAN DIEGO	37523	24129	21.6	26.2	31.8	13.2	7.2	51952	63761	75	56	7503	2.1	2.4	4.7	19.9	70.9	577471
92110	SAN DIEGO	29766	10093	25.6	28.8	28.3	11.0	6.3	45585	54549	63	43	4368	2.0	0.3	5.4	35.9	56.3	433822
92111	SAN DIEGO	23498	17759	23.1	28.7	32.9	11.4	4.0	48355	55764	69	49	9761	4.6	3.9	5.9	61.9	23.7	325392
92113	SAN DIEGO	9473	12082	47.5	31.4	16.8	2.9	1.5	26200	29834	6	6	4168	1.9	2.6	31.9	58.8	4.8	202351
92114	SAN DIEGO	15311	17349	20.8	28.1	37.4	10.9	2.7	50908	58386	74	54	12374	1.4	0.8	8.3	86.1	3.4	254810
92115	SAN DIEGO	19599	22947	36.1	29.4	23.7	7.8	3.0	35551	41265	30	21	8547	0.9	1.9	6.9	67.1	23.3	298139
92116	SAN DIEGO	27549	16870	29.3	34.2	24.5	7.0	5.0	38586	44675	41	28	5163	0.2	0.7	8.6	47.9	42.6	353739
92117	SAN DIEGO	26893	20599	17.9	28.0	36.2	12.8	5.1	53548	63189	78	59	12461	0.9	0.3	2.2	55.5	41.1	376728
92118	CORONADO	47916	7655	11.3	19.8	31.0	18.6	19.4	77869	97798	94	84	4279	0.4	0.6	0.5	2.3	96.2	1000001
92119	SAN DIEGO	33949	9891	13.8	21.6	39.7	16.6	8.3	64803	76146	88	72	7424	0.0	0.5	7.8	50.4	41.4	372473
92120	SAN DIEGO	36331	10450	13.8	22.8	37.7	15.9	9.8	65055	76612	89	73	8007	1.3	1.6	5.3	42.3	49.5	398170
	CALIFORNIA	27293		21.8	24.4	30.5	13.7	9.7	54267	64547				3.3	2.7	13.3	42.9	37.9	319678
	UNITED STATES	25866		24.7	27.1	30.8	10.9	6.5	48124	56710				10.9	15.0	33.7	30.1	10.4	145905

ZIP CODE #	POST OFFICE NAME	FINANCIAL SERVICES: Auto Loan	Home Loan	Invest-ments	Retire-ment Plans	THE HOME: Home Improvements: Home Repair	Lawn & Garden	Furnishings: Comput-ers & Hard-ware	Major Appli-ances	TV, Radio, Sound Equip-ment	Furni-ture	ENTERTAINMENT: Dine out/ Carry out	Sports Equip-ment	Fees & Tickets	Toys & Games	Travel	Cable TV	PERSONAL: Apparel & Services	Auto Repairs	Health Insur-ance	Pets & Supplies
91768	POMONA	83	75	77	74	73	76	82	81	84	85	106	93	78	103	77	79	106	85	75	87
91770	ROSEMEAD	69	76	102	85	79	75	82	81	74	80	93	103	78	90	82	66	93	86	66	84
91773	SAN DIMAS	134	155	176	156	151	155	147	144	140	148	176	168	154	182	148	136	176	143	131	158
91775	SAN GABRIEL	98	122	165	129	123	120	122	120	110	119	138	148	122	140	124	102	138	123	100	125
91776	SAN GABRIEL	65	74	106	81	76	74	80	77	73	77	92	97	77	91	80	67	92	82	65	81
91780	TEMPLE CITY	86	100	133	108	101	98	104	102	94	101	119	126	101	118	104	87	119	106	85	107
91784	UPLAND	149	187	212	186	183	188	167	166	155	168	196	189	181	205	173	153	197	160	152	181
91786	UPLAND	80	80	92	82	78	84	85	82	84	85	105	96	84	104	83	81	104	85	77	90
91789	WALNUT	130	149	200	164	152	147	157	153	141	152	178	193	152	174	157	128	177	161	128	161
91790	WEST COVINA	90	98	114	95	94	100	96	95	96	99	122	107	98	123	96	95	121	97	89	103
91791	WEST COVINA	110	131	162	127	127	133	125	123	121	126	153	141	130	160	127	120	153	123	113	132
91792	WEST COVINA	94	106	139	107	104	107	107	105	104	108	132	124	108	135	108	101	132	108	94	112
91801	ALHAMBRA	70	83	115	93	86	81	88	86	77	84	98	111	84	95	88	69	97	91	70	90
91803	ALHAMBRA	75	87	118	95	89	85	91	89	82	88	103	113	88	101	91	74	103	94	74	93
91901	ALPINE	129	144	150	145	142	145	135	136	128	136	161	159	139	164	136	125	159	134	125	152
91902	BONITA	129	170	212	163	164	171	152	150	144	153	181	171	165	196	159	144	183	147	137	161
91905	BOULEVARD	81	61	40	58	66	79	67	74	75	64	88	83	60	83	66	79	81	74	88	89
91906	CAMPO	87	71	51	69	75	85	74	80	79	73	95	91	68	90	73	82	89	80	90	96
91910	CHULA VISTA	85	88	101	88	85	90	89	87	88	91	111	100	90	111	88	87	110	89	82	95
91911	CHULA VISTA	77	76	83	74	74	78	78	78	79	81	100	87	76	98	76	77	99	80	74	84
91913	CHULA VISTA	160	181	181	187	173	171	165	164	153	171	195	190	171	196	162	145	193	160	142	179
91914	CHULA VISTA	126	143	138	149	136	131	129	128	118	134	150	149	133	150	126	110	148	124	108	139
91915	CHULA VISTA	133	149	158	151	142	143	138	137	131	144	167	157	143	170	137	126	166	135	121	149
91916	DESCANSO	113	79	42	75	92	103	78	96	90	77	105	116	67	103	81	94	96	95	115	134
91917	DULZURA	83	97	107	92	96	105	92	92	91	91	113	102	97	118	95	93	111	90	93	100
91932	IMPERIAL BEACH	74	68	74	70	66	70	74	72	75	76	94	85	72	91	71	71	93	76	67	79
91934	JACUMBA	64	48	32	46	52	63	53	58	59	50	70	65	47	66	52	63	64	58	70	70
91935	JAMUL	158	195	212	197	191	193	175	173	162	175	205	199	189	214	179	158	205	167	157	190
91941	LA MESA	95	99	118	102	98	103	104	99	101	102	127	118	105	127	102	97	125	102	93	109
91942	LA MESA	78	79	96	82	78	84	84	81	83	83	104	96	84	103	83	80	102	84	77	89
91945	LEMON GROVE	75	80	89	81	78	81	81	79	78	80	99	92	82	100	80	76	97	79	73	86
91950	NATIONAL CITY	60	57	64	57	56	58	61	61	62	63	79	70	59	77	59	59	79	64	56	65
91962	PINE VALLEY	100	111	109	109	112	114	101	104	98	100	121	122	103	126	104	97	119	101	101	122
91963	POTRERO	86	81	67	77	81	86	77	82	78	79	96	94	74	92	77	78	93	81	82	96
91977	SPRING VALLEY	84	91	99	91	89	92	90	88	87	90	110	102	91	112	89	85	109	89	82	96
91978	SPRING VALLEY	101	101	98	103	98	101	99	99	95	101	120	117	98	117	96	91	117	100	91	112
91980	TECATE	85	77	60	74	77	82	74	79	74	76	92	91	70	87	73	73	88	79	78	94
92003	BONSALL	164	167	170	161	173	195	154	168	156	161	196	173	159	175	165	163	187	163	183	188
92004	BORREGO SPRINGS	91	73	52	66	82	92	69	82	77	69	92	95	62	90	73	83	86	81	97	111
92007	CARDIFF BY THE SEA	133	145	209	153	140	148	150	141	147	151	186	169	156	194	150	144	185	145	129	155
92008	CARLSBAD	114	123	140	126	121	126	121	120	117	123	148	139	124	148	121	114	146	121	112	131
92009	CARLSBAD	160	183	204	187	180	185	171	170	161	174	204	195	179	204	173	157	201	167	157	187
92014	DEL MAR	235	300	424	300	291	313	274	267	260	280	329	306	305	347	288	261	332	262	247	291
92019	EL CAJON	114	128	139	131	124	127	123	120	116	123	147	141	127	149	122	111	145	120	109	132
92020	EL CAJON	76	75	85	77	74	79	79	77	78	79	99	90	79	97	78	76	97	79	73	85
92021	EL CAJON	79	80	86	81	78	82	82	80	81	82	101	95	82	100	80	78	99	82	76	89
92024	ENCINITAS	143	166	200	169	162	169	159	155	151	160	191	180	167	196	160	148	190	154	142	169
92025	ESCONDIDO	88	87	94	89	86	89	91	89	90	93	113	104	90	112	88	85	113	92	82	97
92026	ESCONDIDO	88	92	101	92	90	95	92	91	91	93	114	105	93	114	91	89	112	92	87	100
92027	ESCONDIDO	94	98	104	98	97	101	97	97	95	99	120	110	98	119	96	92	118	98	92	106
92028	FALLBROOK	105	109	117	108	108	117	107	109	106	109	133	122	109	130	108	105	131	109	107	119
92029	ESCONDIDO	138	148	161	152	145	152	143	142	137	145	174	165	147	172	143	134	171	142	132	158
92036	JULIAN	108	91	69	85	99	109	87	100	95	86	114	117	81	114	91	99	107	98	113	130
92037	LA JOLLA	180	205	293	211	200	218	205	196	199	207	252	228	218	259	209	199	250	198	185	215
92040	LAKESIDE	92	98	104	99	96	99	96	95	92	96	116	111	97	116	95	89	114	95	88	105
92054	OCEANSIDE	81	74	80	77	73	78	82	79	81	82	102	94	79	99	78	78	100	83	74	88
92055	CAMP PENDLETON	69	44	42	50	40	48	65	56	67	61	83	75	56	74	54	61	80	67	52	64
92056	OCEANSIDE	101	107	113	107	105	111	102	104	100	105	126	116	104	122	103	98	122	103	100	114
92057	OCEANSIDE	97	103	112	103	101	106	99	100	97	103	123	112	101	121	100	96	121	100	95	109
92059	PALA	103	93	73	89	93	99	89	96	91	92	112	110	84	105	88	90	108	96	96	114
92061	PAUMA VALLEY	95	80	61	74	80	85	81	90	86	86	106	98	73	96	78	84	103	91	89	101
92064	POWAY	145	167	176	170	163	164	154	153	144	156	182	179	161	186	155	139	181	150	137	169
92065	RAMONA	116	130	137	134	127	127	123	121	115	124	146	142	126	147	122	110	144	120	109	134
92066	RANCHITA	103	81	55	73	91	102	76	92	86	75	102	107	68	101	81	92	95	90	108	125
92067	RANCHO SANTA FE	431	580	795	569	565	610	505	501	471	517	595	563	574	627	539	475	605	481	465	544
92069	SAN MARCOS	92	92	96	92	91	97	91	93	90	94	114	103	91	109	90	88	111	93	90	101
92070	SANTA YSABEL	130	99	66	93	110	128	103	117	116	99	137	134	92	131	105	123	126	117	140	149
92071	SANTEE	98	106	108	107	104	107	101	102	97	102	122	118	102	122	101	94	119	101	94	113
92075	SOLANA BEACH	166	198	267	199	194	206	191	185	184	192	232	215	203	242	196	183	231	185	173	201
92078	SAN MARCOS	112	121	124	118	120	129	111	116	110	116	138	125	115	132	115	110	133	113	117	127
92081	VISTA	100	104	115	109	101	104	103	101	99	105	126	119	105	123	101	95	123	102	92	112
92082	VALLEY CENTER	121	134	133	133	134	137	123	126	118	124	148	146	127	151	125	117	145	123	120	144
92083	VISTA	84	80	85	82	78	81	85	83	84	87	106	97	83	104	81	79	105	86	75	90
92084	VISTA	91	96	106	96	95	99	96	95	94	97	118	109	97	119	95	91	117	96	89	103
92086	WARNER SPRINGS	104	81	55	74	91	103	77	93	88	76	104	108	69	102	82	93	96	91	110	126
92091	RANCHO SANTA FE	331	446	611	437	435	469	389	385	362	398	458	433	441	482	414	365	465	370	358	418
92101	SAN DIEGO	67	58	88	64	57	64	74	66	75	72	95	81	72	93	70	73	92	73	64	73
92102	SAN DIEGO	57	49	51	50	48	51	56	55	57	58	73	64	53	70	52	54	72	58	51	59
92103	SAN DIEGO	96	95	149	104	92	101	108	98	108	108	137	119	110	140	106	106	135	104	93	109
92104	SAN DIEGO	64	57	70	62	56	60	69	63	68	67	86	78	65	82	64	63	84	69	58	70
92105	SAN DIEGO	58	51	52	51	49	52	57	56	58	59	74	64	54	72	53	55	74	59	52	60
92106	SAN DIEGO	141	164	206	163	161	172	159	156	155	159	195	180	167	200	164	155	193	156	149	170
92107	SAN DIEGO	90	86	112	92	84	90	100	92	98	97	123	113	97	121	95	92	121	99	84	101
92108	SAN DIEGO	69	61	79	66	59	65	74	67	73	72	93	83	71	89	69	69	90	73	63	75
92109	SAN DIEGO	97	86	125	96	84	93	107	96	107	104	135	120	104	132	101	102	132	105	90	107
92110	SAN DIEGO	86	78	99	83	77	86	95	86	94	90	118	105	91	115	89	91	115	93	83	95
92111	SAN DIEGO	83	86	108	87	84	91	89	87	89	90	113	100	90	113	89	89	111	89	83	95
92113	SAN DIEGO	54	46	45	45	45	47	51	52	54	54	68	58	49	65	48	51	68	54	48	55
92114	SAN DIEGO	78	83	98	83	81	84	84	84	82	85	104	97	84	102	84	80	103	86	77	90
92115	SAN DIEGO	68	58	75	62	57	62	75	66	75	71	94	83	70	91	69	70	91	74	62	74
92116	SAN DIEGO	75	70	92	75	68	73	81	75	80	80	101	92	79	99	77	76	99	81	68	83
92117	SAN DIEGO	86	95	116	96	93	99	96	93	93	95	118	108	99	120	96	92	116	94	87	101
92118	CORONADO	147	169	214	169	166	179	163	160	158	164	199	184	172	202	167	158	197	160	153	175
92119	SAN DIEGO	106	121	144	119	120	128	118	116	115	117	144	132	123	146	121	114	142	116	113	126
92120	SAN DIEGO	110	126	146	124	125	135	121	120	118	121	148	136	127	151	125	119	146	119	118	131
	CALIFORNIA	107	111	131	112	109	115	113	111	111	114	140	129	114	141	112	109	139	113	104	122
	UNITED STATES	100	100	100	100	100	100	100	100	100	100	100	100	100	100	100	100	100	100	100	100

POPULATION CHANGE

ZIP CODE		POPULATION			2000-2004 ANNUAL RATE		HOUSEHOLDS					FAMILIES		
# POST OFFICE NAME	COUNTY FIPS CODE	2000	2004	2009	% Rate	State Centile	2000	2004	2009	% Annual Rate 2000-2004	2004 Average HH Size	2000	2004	% Annual Rate 2000-2004
92121 SAN DIEGO	073	4188	4285	4428	0.5	33	1799	1824	1859	0.3	2.34	962	975	0.3
92122 SAN DIEGO	073	33280	35570	39366	1.6	71	15888	16994	18769	1.6	2.09	7444	7760	1.0
92123 SAN DIEGO	073	26532	28159	31056	1.4	67	9791	10277	11149	1.2	2.63	6328	6595	1.0
92124 SAN DIEGO	073	30187	31119	32224	0.7	42	10576	10910	11303	0.7	2.85	7540	7649	0.3
92126 SAN DIEGO	073	67786	69610	72289	0.6	38	22148	22647	23316	0.5	3.06	16173	16422	0.4
92127 SAN DIEGO	073	17503	19286	21285	2.3	83	6094	6718	7408	2.3	2.82	4577	5020	2.2
92128 SAN DIEGO	073	44251	47176	49572	1.5	69	19305	20152	20837	1.0	2.33	12785	13332	1.0
92129 SAN DIEGO	073	50360	55840	57688	2.5	85	15959	17329	17613	2.0	3.22	13415	14633	2.1
92130 SAN DIEGO	073	28264	39147	44851	8.0	99	10590	14381	16035	7.5	2.71	7481	10264	7.7
92131 SAN DIEGO	073	27369	31328	35044	3.2	92	9774	11144	12161	3.1	2.79	7681	8653	2.8
92133 SAN DIEGO	073	194	194	194	0.0	15	5	5	5	0.0	2.60	4	2	-15.1
92134 SAN DIEGO	073	1140	1141	1142	0.0	15	0	0	0	0.0	0.00	0	0	0.0
92135 SAN DIEGO	073	5174	5176	5180	0.0	15	51	51	52	0.0	2.84	42	42	0.0
92136 SAN DIEGO	073	9821	9821	9821	0.0	15	8	8	8	0.0	5.25	7	7	0.0
92139 SAN DIEGO	073	36491	36734	37401	0.2	19	10490	10427	10462	-0.1	3.50	8885	8809	-0.2
92140 SAN DIEGO	073	4279	4279	4279	0.0	15	5	5	5	0.0	2.80	5	5	0.0
92145 SAN DIEGO	073	6470	6489	6513	0.1	17	542	542	540	0.0	4.11	537	537	0.0
92154 SAN DIEGO	073	69050	77234	87609	2.7	88	16767	18759	21228	2.7	3.74	14428	16228	2.8
92173 SAN YSIDRO	073	27861	28891	29835	0.9	49	7183	7375	7516	0.6	3.91	6258	6413	0.6
92182 SAN DIEGO	073	589	649	810	2.3	83	1	1	2	0.0	3.00	0	0	0.0
92201 INDIO	065	56443	66213	79862	3.8	95	16611	19566	23531	3.9	3.34	12946	15061	3.6
92203 INDIO	065	2751	3604	4586	6.6	99	875	1176	1503	7.2	3.06	681	893	6.6
92210 INDIAN WELLS	065	3912	4366	5113	2.6	87	2020	2242	2603	2.5	1.95	1342	1477	2.3
92211 PALM DESERT	065	19344	23804	29309	5.0	97	9467	11697	14346	5.1	2.03	6403	7866	5.0
92220 BANNING	065	25782	28656	33397	2.5	86	9535	10716	12528	2.8	2.58	6671	7414	2.5
92223 BEAUMONT	065	17768	20595	24653	3.5	94	6452	7388	8742	3.2	2.76	4604	5212	3.0
92225 BLYTHE	065	15976	17483	20326	2.1	81	5352	5764	6616	1.8	3.00	3893	4160	1.6
92227 BRAWLEY	025	23314	24304	25966	1.0	54	7047	7335	7806	1.0	3.27	5580	5771	0.8
92230 CABAZON	065	2348	2529	2896	1.8	75	746	794	903	1.5	3.03	526	555	1.3
92231 CALEXICO	025	27756	31959	35855	3.4	93	6982	8009	8942	3.3	3.98	6121	7007	3.2
92233 CALIPATRIA	025	9316	9666	10076	0.9	49	1677	1777	1892	1.4	3.23	1246	1311	1.2
92234 CATHEDRAL CITY	065	42832	52065	63649	4.7	97	14144	16840	20261	4.2	3.08	9717	11571	4.2
92236 COACHELLA	065	23262	27394	32995	3.9	95	4949	5779	6892	3.7	4.73	4586	5344	3.7
92239 DESERT CENTER	065	9776	9910	10119	0.3	24	463	508	588	2.2	2.29	303	328	1.9
92240 DESERT HOT SPRINGS	065	23489	26236	30713	2.6	88	8340	9136	10533	2.2	2.85	5457	5923	2.0
92241 DESERT HOT SPRINGS	065	5809	6895	8330	4.1	96	2684	3115	3699	3.6	2.21	1667	1919	3.4
92242 EARP	071	1535	1678	1845	2.1	81	730	797	871	2.1	2.11	458	497	1.9
92243 EL CENTRO	025	45298	47580	50600	1.2	60	13329	13968	14796	1.1	3.30	10538	11009	1.0
92249 HEBER	025	3574	3886	4264	2.0	79	870	973	1087	2.7	3.72	803	886	2.3
92250 HOLTVILLE	025	7994	8368	8969	1.1	58	2337	2446	2616	1.1	3.36	1972	2053	1.0
92251 IMPERIAL	025	10080	11666	13033	3.5	94	3030	3498	3889	3.4	3.32	2508	2885	3.4
92252 JOSHUA TREE	071	8105	8448	9134	1.0	54	3455	3591	3861	0.9	2.30	2063	2133	0.8
92253 LA QUINTA	065	23727	30784	38792	6.3	98	8455	10911	13630	6.2	2.82	6566	8422	6.0
92254 MECCA	065	8674	10271	12357	4.1	96	1774	2074	2470	3.7	4.83	1580	1841	3.7
92256 MORONGO VALLEY	071	3541	3783	4110	1.6	71	1525	1627	1758	1.5	2.32	889	943	1.4
92257 NILAND	025	1067	1101	1158	0.7	43	565	584	612	0.8	1.86	319	326	0.5
92259 OCOTILLO	025	419	413	427	-0.3	7	207	206	214	-0.1	1.48	119	111	-1.6
92260 PALM DESERT	065	29479	33516	39640	3.1	90	13945	15721	18420	2.9	2.11	7838	8704	2.5
92262 PALM SPRINGS	065	25238	27311	31457	1.9	77	11190	11968	13650	1.6	2.23	5410	5692	1.2
92264 PALM SPRINGS	065	18112	19107	21736	1.3	63	9521	10010	11305	1.2	1.90	4179	4316	0.8
92267 PARKER DAM	071	123	110	114	-2.6	0	46	41	43	-2.7	2.68	27	24	-2.7
92270 RANCHO MIRAGE	065	13283	15473	18534	3.7	94	6831	7881	9344	3.4	1.95	4020	4599	3.2
92274 THERMAL	025	22466	24345	27405	1.9	78	4403	4785	5430	2.0	4.08	3614	3931	2.0
92276 THOUSAND PALMS	065	5859	6275	7197	1.6	72	2262	2418	2756	1.6	2.59	1478	1561	1.3
92277 TWENTYNINE PALMS	071	17977	20051	22348	2.6	87	7001	7758	8588	2.5	2.51	4638	5122	2.4
92278 TWENTYNINE PALMS	071	13300	13063	13293	-0.4	6	1220	1153	1209	-1.3	3.61	1205	1138	-1.3
92280 VIDAL	071	47	42	44	-2.6	0	20	18	18	-2.5	2.33	13	11	-3.9
92281 WESTMORLAND	025	2443	2552	2706	1.0	56	726	758	800	1.0	3.36	585	607	0.9
92282 WHITE WATER	065	808	924	1086	3.2	91	276	316	371	3.2	2.63	169	191	2.9
92283 WINTERHAVEN	025	4209	4187	4348	-0.1	11	1592	1563	1612	-0.4	2.57	1038	1010	-0.6
92284 YUCCA VALLEY	071	20839	22170	24042	1.5	68	8585	9123	9842	1.4	2.40	5535	5858	1.3
92285 LANDERS	071	2127	2179	2333	0.6	35	1008	1033	1100	0.6	2.11	608	619	0.4
92301 ADELANTO	071	18972	21036	23271	2.5	85	5015	5459	5968	2.0	3.59	4047	4397	2.0
92304 AMBOY	071	18	20	22	2.5	86	8	9	10	2.8	2.22	5	5	0.0
92305 ANGELUS OAKS	071	171	176	189	0.7	40	74	76	81	0.6	2.32	49	50	0.5
92307 APPLE VALLEY	071	30580	33392	36783	2.1	80	10699	11622	12706	2.0	2.86	8278	8981	1.9
92308 APPLE VALLEY	071	29528	31605	34477	1.6	72	10095	10869	11840	1.8	2.88	7644	8183	1.6
92309 BAKER	071	978	1139	1316	3.7	94	246	280	322	3.1	3.23	161	180	2.7
92310 FORT IRWIN	071	9464	10252	11153	1.9	78	2359	2586	2834	2.2	3.41	2202	2407	2.1
92311 BARSTOW	071	31121	31394	33496	0.2	20	11095	11196	11896	0.2	2.76	7915	7950	0.1
92313 GRAND TERRACE	071	11506	11907	12756	0.8	47	4183	4316	4598	0.7	2.71	3019	3108	0.7
92314 BIG BEAR CITY	071	15447	16069	17228	0.9	52	6163	6401	6825	0.9	2.48	4269	4410	0.8
92315 BIG BEAR LAKE	071	4653	4779	5116	0.6	38	1989	2036	2167	0.6	2.34	1271	1293	0.4
92316 BLOOMINGTON	071	26922	28425	30692	1.3	64	7014	7334	7841	1.1	3.84	5828	6073	1.0
92317 BLUE JAY	071	1013	1052	1127	0.9	50	372	386	411	0.9	2.73	304	315	0.8
92320 CALIMESA	065	7074	8136	9786	3.4	92	2958	3444	4160	3.6	2.33	2038	2349	3.4
92321 CEDAR GLEN	071	1209	1256	1344	0.9	51	451	468	498	0.9	2.68	306	315	0.7
92322 CEDARPINES PARK	071	768	799	860	0.9	52	303	315	337	0.9	2.54	208	215	0.8
92324 COLTON	071	51797	55901	61410	1.8	76	15827	16904	18388	1.6	3.28	11928	12666	1.4
92325 CRESTLINE	071	7708	7985	8537	0.8	47	3029	3133	3330	0.8	2.55	2081	2144	0.7
92327 DAGGETT	071	240	229	241	-1.1	2	97	92	97	-1.2	2.49	63	59	-1.5
92328 DEATH VALLEY	027	360	350	351	-0.7	3	208	203	204	-0.6	1.72	94	92	-0.5
92332 ESSEX	071	69	74	82	1.7	73	32	34	38	1.4	2.18	20	20	0.0
92335 FONTANA	071	81634	88389	96799	1.9	77	21136	22493	24293	1.5	3.91	17433	18500	1.4
92336 FONTANA	071	53848	61334	69136	3.1	91	13721	15539	17377	3.0	3.93	12158	13772	3.0
92337 FONTANA	071	29583	33731	38062	3.1	91	7744	8706	9704	2.8	3.87	6740	7567	2.9
92338 LUDLOW	071	68	70	74	0.7	40	25	26	27	0.9	2.69	16	16	0.0
92339 FOREST FALLS	071	1171	1228	1321	1.1	59	509	533	570	1.1	2.30	314	324	0.7
92342 HELENDALE	071	4841	5174	5640	1.6	71	1921	2055	2229	1.6	2.51	1456	1550	1.5
92345 HESPERIA	071	68470	74369	81680	2.0	79	21831	23629	25770	1.9	3.13	17349	18752	1.9
92346 HIGHLAND	071	46666	50259	55172	1.8	75	15017	16086	17543	1.6	3.02	11509	12329	1.6
92347 HINKLEY	071	1915	1884	2003	-0.4	6	670	657	695	-0.5	2.85	480	469	-0.5
92350 LOMA LINDA	071	24	24	26	0.0	15	14	14	15	0.0	1.71	7	7	0.0
92352 LAKE ARROWHEAD	071	5101	5557	6102	2.0	80	1782	1937	2113	2.0	2.87	1437	1556	1.9
92354 LOMA LINDA	071	18144	19406	21184	1.6	71	6937	7384	8010	1.5	2.55	4369	4616	1.3
CALIFORNIA					1.4					1.2	2.90			1.2
UNITED STATES					1.2					1.3	2.58			1.1

POPULATION COMPOSITION

CALIFORNIA

92121-92354 **B**

ZIP CODE #	POST OFFICE NAME	RACE (%) White 2000	White 2004	Black 2000	Black 2004	Asian/Pacific 2000	Asian/Pacific 2004	% Hispanic Origin 2000	% Hispanic Origin 2004	2004 AGE DISTRIBUTION (%) 0-4	5-9	10-14	15-19	20-24	25-44	45-64	65-84	85+	18+	MEDIAN AGE 2004	% 2004 Males	% 2004 Females
92121	SAN DIEGO	58.6	54.2	1.8	1.9	33.6	36.8	6.1	7.3	6.1	5.1	3.2	3.0	19.3	40.6	18.1	4.2	0.4	84.3	30.6	50.5	49.5
92122	SAN DIEGO	74.1	70.2	1.5	1.6	18.5	20.9	6.8	8.3	4.2	3.6	4.0	4.4	9.6	41.0	20.4	11.2	1.7	86.0	34.6	49.6	50.4
92123	SAN DIEGO	66.0	62.6	8.8	9.0	12.2	13.3	14.1	16.8	7.9	6.3	5.7	6.6	9.9	33.7	18.1	10.6	1.3	75.8	31.9	49.6	50.4
92124	SAN DIEGO	70.7	67.2	8.3	8.7	10.8	12.0	10.5	12.7	9.2	9.4	8.9	5.7	5.1	35.3	19.9	6.0	0.5	68.6	31.6	49.3	50.7
92126	SAN DIEGO	44.7	40.7	4.6	4.7	40.5	42.8	10.2	11.9	7.1	6.7	6.3	5.6	7.0	37.4	22.5	6.8	0.7	76.5	34.0	50.7	49.3
92127	SAN DIEGO	77.8	74.7	2.4	2.6	13.0	14.5	7.5	9.2	6.8	7.8	8.8	7.0	5.4	30.0	22.2	8.5	3.5	72.0	36.2	47.8	52.2
92128	SAN DIEGO	78.1	74.5	2.0	2.1	14.9	17.1	6.1	7.6	6.2	6.3	5.8	4.7	4.1	28.2	23.7	17.4	3.7	78.8	41.9	46.9	53.1
92129	SAN DIEGO	63.0	58.7	2.6	2.6	26.5	29.5	8.3	9.7	7.6	8.3	9.1	7.5	5.5	30.7	26.0	5.0	0.5	70.3	35.3	49.5	50.5
92130	SAN DIEGO	80.4	76.0	0.6	0.8	14.1	16.4	5.9	7.8	8.5	9.1	8.7	6.4	4.1	32.8	25.3	4.7	0.5	69.4	36.2	48.8	51.2
92131	SAN DIEGO	79.1	75.7	2.3	2.5	12.6	14.3	6.9	8.6	8.1	8.8	8.1	5.9	4.3	31.3	27.6	5.5	0.4	71.3	36.9	48.9	51.1
92133	SAN DIEGO	77.8	74.7	10.8	11.9	4.1	4.6	7.7	9.3	0.0	0.5	0.0	34.0	52.1	12.9	0.5	0.0	0.0	99.5	21.5	67.0	33.0
92134	SAN DIEGO	55.4	51.5	16.0	16.6	18.9	20.3	12.2	14.6	0.0	0.0	0.0	8.1	30.4	56.4	5.1	0.0	0.0	99.9	27.3	74.1	25.9
92135	SAN DIEGO	63.2	59.1	17.1	17.9	7.0	7.8	14.4	17.6	0.4	0.1	0.2	14.1	57.1	26.4	1.6	0.1	0.0	99.2	23.1	88.6	11.4
92136	SAN DIEGO	60.2	55.9	17.2	17.9	7.9	8.6	16.2	19.7	0.1	0.0	0.0	14.2	59.1	25.4	1.1	0.0	0.0	99.8	23.0	89.8	10.2
92139	SAN DIEGO	29.3	27.0	14.2	13.6	35.6	36.3	28.2	30.9	8.4	7.5	8.2	7.6	8.4	30.1	20.9	8.0	0.8	71.2	31.1	48.7	51.3
92140	SAN DIEGO	67.8	63.3	8.8	9.2	3.2	3.5	23.0	27.9	0.0	0.0	0.0	49.6	40.0	10.0	0.4	0.0	0.0	96.7	20.0	98.4	1.6
92145	SAN DIEGO	62.1	57.4	13.1	13.6	6.0	6.5	20.6	24.9	6.6	4.7	3.3	10.1	55.5	19.2	0.6	0.1	0.0	84.3	22.3	78.3	21.7
92154	SAN DIEGO	43.6	40.7	7.1	8.4	16.0	14.7	55.3	57.9	7.2	6.9	7.9	8.3	9.2	33.0	19.6	7.3	0.5	73.1	31.1	53.6	46.4
92173	SAN YSIDRO	44.5	43.6	2.2	2.0	3.5	3.2	88.9	90.5	9.4	9.2	11.0	10.2	9.0	27.4	16.5	6.7	0.6	64.1	25.8	47.4	52.6
92182	SAN DIEGO	75.9	72.3	6.1	6.5	6.5	7.1	16.0	19.9	0.2	0.0	0.0	48.4	46.4	4.2	0.6	0.3	0.0	99.7	20.2	44.8	55.2
92201	INDIO	52.0	50.8	2.7	2.5	1.7	1.8	70.0	72.1	10.1	8.8	9.2	8.1	8.9	28.4	17.4	8.2	0.9	66.9	28.2	50.3	49.7
92203	INDIO	71.1	73.0	0.7	0.6	1.0	1.1	43.9	42.0	4.2	4.0	4.4	3.7	3.4	12.8	18.6	45.9	3.1	85.3	64.3	47.3	52.8
92210	INDIAN WELLS	91.0	89.2	0.8	0.9	2.3	2.5	10.2	12.7	3.0	3.4	4.3	3.3	3.1	16.0	31.0	32.8	3.1	87.4	57.2	47.5	52.5
92211	PALM DESERT	89.9	87.9	1.1	1.1	2.0	2.2	11.9	15.0	3.3	3.4	3.6	3.1	2.6	14.5	27.9	38.3	3.3	87.6	60.6	47.3	52.8
92220	BANNING	63.2	61.2	8.3	8.0	5.3	5.4	29.7	33.3	6.6	6.3	7.3	6.9	6.4	20.3	19.7	23.7	2.8	75.6	41.5	48.4	51.7
92223	BEAUMONT	76.2	72.5	2.1	2.2	1.6	1.7	27.5	32.7	7.4	6.7	7.8	7.0	6.9	23.4	22.1	16.2	2.5	73.6	37.8	47.8	52.2
92225	BLYTHE	55.5	51.2	7.8	7.6	1.4	1.4	46.5	52.5	9.7	8.4	9.1	8.2	7.2	25.9	21.2	9.1	1.1	67.4	31.1	50.2	49.8
92227	BRAWLEY	53.9	52.2	2.4	2.3	1.5	1.5	72.4	75.1	9.0	8.5	9.4	8.9	8.1	27.2	19.5	8.4	1.0	67.5	29.6	49.6	50.4
92230	CABAZON	67.6	64.1	3.8	3.9	1.2	1.2	28.8	33.9	6.6	7.0	10.0	9.2	8.3	26.7	22.1	9.0	1.1	70.6	33.5	47.4	52.6
92231	CALEXICO	46.7	46.6	0.5	0.5	1.8	1.8	95.0	95.4	8.1	8.1	9.9	9.8	8.2	26.2	19.4	9.4	0.8	67.6	29.6	46.9	53.1
92233	CALIPATRIA	40.8	38.3	16.5	15.7	1.4	1.3	55.0	59.5	5.1	4.8	5.5	5.9	9.5	43.6	18.5	6.6	0.6	81.3	33.4	71.0	29.0
92234	CATHEDRAL CITY	65.3	61.8	2.8	2.8	3.8	3.9	49.8	55.1	9.1	8.1	8.6	7.4	7.5	28.9	18.7	10.5	1.3	69.5	31.7	50.5	49.5
92236	COACHELLA	39.4	38.5	0.5	0.4	0.4	0.3	96.3	96.9	11.5	10.3	11.0	10.1	9.9	27.6	14.2	5.1	0.4	61.0	23.6	50.0	50.0
92239	DESERT CENTER	28.9	26.0	23.2	21.6	1.9	1.9	45.4	50.3	0.7	0.7	0.6	1.9	19.2	59.2	14.1	3.4	0.2	97.7	32.6	94.4	5.6
92240	DESERT HOT SPRINGS	69.7	66.3	4.9	4.9	1.8	1.9	41.0	46.9	8.8	8.1	8.9	7.5	7.3	26.0	19.5	12.3	1.6	69.5	32.4	49.7	50.3
92241	DESERT HOT SPRINGS	83.3	80.1	0.9	0.9	0.6	0.6	27.4	33.4	5.0	4.6	5.7	5.5	4.2	17.9	27.2	26.1	4.0	81.4	50.1	49.6	50.4
92242	EARP	87.2	85.1	2.2	2.3	0.8	0.9	8.2	10.2	5.1	4.7	4.8	4.9	3.2	14.0	28.1	31.6	3.6	82.4	56.7	47.8	52.2
92243	EL CENTRO	48.5	46.8	2.9	2.8	3.4	3.4	73.0	76.0	8.6	8.3	9.2	9.1	8.3	27.5	20.1	8.1	0.9	68.3	30.0	50.0	50.0
92249	HEBER	34.2	35.1	0.9	0.9	0.4	0.4	94.9	94.9	7.9	7.6	9.3	10.0	8.6	29.2	18.5	8.3	0.6	69.3	29.9	51.3	48.7
92250	HOLTVILLE	58.9	56.6	0.6	0.6	1.2	1.2	67.9	72.0	7.9	8.0	9.5	8.5	7.3	25.0	21.9	10.2	1.8	69.1	32.6	49.3	50.7
92251	IMPERIAL	59.9	57.2	2.4	2.3	2.4	2.4	58.9	63.2	9.2	8.9	9.3	8.3	7.2	30.3	20.0	6.3	0.6	67.3	30.8	49.5	50.5
92252	JOSHUA TREE	88.2	86.3	1.7	1.7	1.4	1.6	10.5	12.8	5.4	5.7	7.0	6.6	5.6	23.0	25.9	17.9	2.9	77.5	42.7	49.4	50.6
92253	LA QUINTA	77.1	74.1	1.4	1.5	1.9	2.1	34.0	38.3	8.1	7.9	8.0	6.6	5.9	26.1	23.7	12.9	0.9	72.0	36.9	49.0	51.0
92254	MECCA	32.2	31.1	0.2	0.2	0.7	0.6	94.7	95.8	11.4	9.9	10.7	10.1	11.2	28.4	14.0	3.9	0.4	61.8	23.6	55.5	44.6
92256	MORONGO VALLEY	91.1	89.4	1.0	1.0	0.6	0.8	10.2	12.6	4.5	4.9	7.1	7.6	6.2	20.8	31.4	15.3	2.2	78.4	44.2	49.8	50.3
92257	NILAND	85.6	84.1	7.6	8.1	0.6	0.5	10.8	12.6	2.3	2.0	2.1	2.2	1.5	8.5	25.0	50.4	6.0	92.3	67.6	49.0	51.0
92259	OCOTILLO	69.0	66.6	9.1	8.7	0.5	0.5	28.2	32.0	3.9	3.9	3.9	4.8	9.2	29.5	27.1	16.7	1.0	86.2	41.5	65.9	34.1
92260	PALM DESERT	87.4	84.9	1.0	1.1	2.5	2.8	17.7	21.9	4.1	3.8	4.6	4.6	5.1	19.2	26.0	28.0	4.8	84.9	52.4	47.4	52.6
92262	PALM SPRINGS	74.3	70.7	5.5	5.7	3.5	3.7	27.8	33.1	5.9	5.5	5.7	5.5	6.0	24.2	26.5	17.6	3.2	79.6	43.1	51.6	48.4
92264	PALM SPRINGS	84.8	82.9	1.4	1.5	4.5	4.6	17.8	20.9	3.3	3.2	3.4	3.0	3.3	18.2	31.0	29.7	5.0	88.4	56.0	52.9	47.1
92267	PARKER DAM	64.2	61.8	0.8	0.9	0.0	0.0	17.9	20.0	4.6	6.4	8.2	4.6	1.8	17.3	33.6	20.0	3.6	77.3	48.6	51.8	48.2
92270	RANCHO MIRAGE	92.1	90.3	0.9	1.0	1.5	1.7	10.3	13.0	2.8	3.0	3.1	2.9	2.5	12.9	30.4	37.2	5.3	89.2	61.2	47.8	52.2
92274	THERMAL	38.8	37.2	6.6	5.9	1.0	1.0	75.8	79.0	9.2	7.5	7.8	7.9	11.6	34.5	14.7	6.4	0.5	71.0	27.9	62.6	37.5
92276	THOUSAND PALMS	77.1	74.9	0.7	0.7	1.0	1.0	40.1	44.1	6.3	6.4	7.4	6.0	5.2	22.2	21.5	22.0	3.1	76.3	42.3	50.0	50.0
92277	TWENTYNINE PALMS	72.8	69.1	8.5	9.1	4.9	5.4	14.3	17.3	9.4	7.4	7.8	8.1	11.4	27.4	18.7	8.8	1.0	71.1	28.1	51.9	48.1
92278	TWENTYNINE PALMS	70.2	66.9	10.9	11.2	3.3	3.5	19.1	22.7	6.4	2.6	2.0	13.2	47.5	27.1	1.2	0.1	0.0	88.1	22.7	81.0	19.0
92280	VIDAL	66.0	64.3	0.0	0.0	2.1	2.4	17.0	19.1	4.8	4.8	9.5	4.8	4.8	21.4	26.2	19.1	4.8	81.0	45.0	57.1	42.9
92281	WESTMORLAND	55.8	53.9	1.2	1.3	0.7	0.6	79.6	82.8	9.3	7.9	10.0	9.5	8.2	25.1	19.8	9.2	1.0	67.2	29.6	48.9	51.1
92282	WHITE WATER	71.9	68.3	7.4	7.6	1.5	1.6	32.9	38.4	8.2	6.8	8.3	16.0	6.2	22.4	18.5	12.5	1.1	63.1	28.7	57.9	42.1
92283	WINTERHAVEN	41.7	39.9	3.5	3.4	0.5	0.5	32.2	35.9	8.2	7.4	8.4	7.7	6.2	22.6	23.8	14.4	1.4	71.3	36.1	51.6	48.4
92284	YUCCA VALLEY	87.8	85.9	2.1	2.2	1.5	1.6	11.1	13.5	5.7	5.7	7.0	7.2	6.0	20.8	26.0	18.3	3.3	77.0	43.2	48.3	51.7
92285	LANDERS	91.7	90.3	1.4	1.5	0.7	0.7	9.0	11.0	2.8	3.1	5.3	5.4	4.5	16.5	35.3	24.7	2.4	85.4	52.0	51.0	49.0
92301	ADELANTO	52.0	48.5	12.3	11.9	1.8	1.8	44.5	49.8	10.7	10.0	10.3	8.1	7.4	32.8	15.2	5.3	0.4	63.9	27.2	53.4	46.6
92304	AMBOY	77.8	70.0	0.0	5.0	0.0	0.0	16.7	15.0	5.0	5.0	5.0	10.0	10.0	20.0	35.0	10.0	0.0	85.0	40.0	60.0	40.0
92305	ANGELUS OAKS	91.8	90.3	0.0	0.0	1.2	1.1	6.4	8.0	4.6	5.7	6.8	5.7	3.4	23.3	37.5	11.9	1.1	79.0	45.3	50.0	50.0
92307	APPLE VALLEY	78.4	75.7	7.1	7.4	2.4	2.6	16.6	19.8	6.9	7.0	8.6	8.5	6.5	22.7	25.4	13.3	1.3	72.1	37.6	48.8	51.2
92308	APPLE VALLEY	76.1	73.5	7.7	7.8	2.3	2.4	19.6	23.1	7.1	7.4	9.4	8.6	6.5	23.2	22.9	13.5	1.5	70.5	36.1	47.9	52.1
92309	BAKER	69.2	66.9	5.2	4.0	0.9	1.0	51.5	58.7	10.1	7.6	7.2	6.1	12.2	38.6	14.6	3.4	0.3	71.6	27.8	59.3	40.7
92310	FORT IRWIN	56.6	52.5	17.3	17.5	3.9	4.1	19.0	22.3	15.3	9.4	6.6	5.8	22.2	37.8	2.7	0.3	0.0	66.2	22.9	57.6	42.4
92311	BARSTOW	61.6	58.5	9.6	9.5	3.4	3.5	34.5	39.2	8.2	7.6	8.3	8.0	8.6	26.2	21.6	10.5	1.1	71.1	32.3	50.3	49.7
92313	GRAND TERRACE	73.6	70.9	4.6	4.6	6.2	6.6	25.4	29.3	6.6	6.5	7.4	7.2	6.9	29.3	25.2	9.5	1.6	75.3	35.8	47.0	53.0
92314	BIG BEAR CITY	89.5	87.6	0.7	0.7	0.7	0.7	11.4	13.9	5.4	6.1	7.7	7.5	5.5	23.9	30.1	13.0	0.8	75.8	41.3	50.2	49.8
92315	BIG BEAR LAKE	90.6	89.1	0.8	0.8	0.9	0.9	14.7	17.6	5.3	5.5	6.6	5.9	4.9	22.3	31.1	16.8	1.6	78.9	44.6	51.3	48.7
92316	BLOOMINGTON	51.9	49.2	6.7	6.3	2.0	1.9	61.8	66.5	9.3	9.0	10.4	9.1	8.4	28.0	18.7	6.4	0.7	65.7	27.5	50.1	49.9
92317	BLUE JAY	93.1	91.8	0.2	0.2	1.3	1.4	11.5	14.1	4.7	5.3	6.4	7.1	6.4	19.9	34.3	15.0	1.0	79.3	45.2	49.2	50.8
92320	CALIMESA	88.1	85.6	0.5	0.6	1.4	1.5	16.2	20.2	5.1	5.3	7.1	6.6	5.9	22.2	26.0	18.5	3.4	78.3	43.5	47.9	52.1
92321	CEDAR GLEN	88.1	85.9	0.9	1.0	0.6	0.6	16.9	20.4	5.9	6.2	7.4	7.6	6.3	23.7	30.0	11.9	0.9	75.7	40.4	49.5	50.5
92322	CEDARPINES PARK	89.6	87.9	0.9	0.9	0.7	0.8	10.7	12.9	6.9	6.6	7.9	7.5	4.9	24.8	32.3	8.8	0.4	74.0	40.4	50.9	49.1
92324	COLTON	44.1	42.0	10.4	10.0	5.4	5.5	59.8	63.0	9.9	8.8	9.8	8.6	8.9	30.0	17.3	6.0	0.8	66.3	27.4	49.4	50.6
92325	CRESTLINE	87.5	85.2	0.8	0.9	0.7	0.8	10.9	13.3	5.8	6.5	8.4	7.8	5.5	24.3	31.3	9.7	0.7	74.1	39.9	49.8	50.2
92327	DAGGETT	74.6	72.1	3.3	3.5	1.7	1.8	15.0	17.5	5.2	5.7	7.4	6.6	6.6	23.6	31.0	12.7	1.3	76.9	41.6	52.0	48.0
92328	DEATH VALLEY	81.7	80.3	0.3	0.3	1.9	2.0	6.7	7.7	3.1	4.3	3.7	4.0	4.3	24.0	38.9	16.0	1.7	86.0	47.6	52.6	47.4
92332	ESSEX	73.9	70.3	1.5	2.7	1.5	1.4	17.4	18.9	5.4	5.4	5.4	6.8	8.1	18.9	29.7	16.2	4.1	77.0	45.0	54.1	46.0
92335	FONTANA	47.6	45.5	6.1	5.6	1.7	1.6	68.7	72.9	10.9	9.8	10.6	9.1	9.4	29.0	15.5	5.1	0.6	63.2	25.2	50.3	49.7
92336	FONTANA	44.0	42.0	14.4	13.9	6.4	6.7	51.4	54.3	9.9	9.4	10.4	9.0	8.1	31.3	17.7	3.8	0.4	64.6	27.3	49.5	50.5
92337	FONTANA	41.6	39.2	12.6	12.0	5.7	5.7	58.7	62.8	10.3	9.7	10.7	8.9	7.6	32.5	16.7	3.4	0.3	63.8	26.9	50.0	50.0
92338	LUDLOW	85.3	82.9	1.5	1.4	0.0	1.4	16.2	18.6	5.7	5.7	5.7	5.7	5.7	18.6	31.4	18.6	2.9	80.0	47.0	52.9	47.1
92339	FOREST FALLS	79.9	76.4	0.3	0.3	0.5	0.5	9.7	11.6	4.8	5.0	7.3	8.0	8.1	24.7	33.6	8.2	0.4	78.1	40.5	49.4	50.7
92342	HELENDALE	87.9	86.1	2.2	2.3	1.2	1.4	14.5	17.2	5.1	5.8	7.4	6.5	3.5	19.1	27.8	23.4	1.3	77.5	46.8	49.7	50.3
92345	HESPERIA	75.2	72.0	3.9	4.0	1.2	1.3	28.3	32.9	7.9	7.8	9.5	8.7	7.1	25.9	22.3	9.6	1.1	69.4	32.7	49.5	50.5
92346	HIGHLAND	61.0	58.3	11.9	11.7	6.3	6.6	29.4	33.3	8.1	7.9	8.7	7.7	7.1	28.5	23.2	7.9	0.8	70.4	33.2	49.2	50.8
92347	HINKLEY	76.3	73.1	2.1	2.1	1.3	1.3	27.4	32.0	6.1	6.5	9.1	8.6	6.9	23.8	26.7	11.3	1.0	73.0	38.2	50.6	49.4
92350	LOMA LINDA	62.5	62.5	4.2	4.2	16.7	16.7	16.7	16.7	8.3	8.3	4.2	4.2	16.7	45.8	12.5	0.0	0.0	79.2	27.0	45.8	54.2
92352	LAKE ARROWHEAD	91.8	90.3	0.5	0.5	1.2	1.3	9.3	11.3	5.5	6.7	8.9	8.2	5.0	20.8	32.4	11.9	0.7	73.7	41.9	49.8	50.2
92354	LOMA LINDA	52.1	49.0	6.9	6.8	25.6	26.6	18.5	21.2	6.9	6.4	6.8	6.6	7.6	30.9	20.3	11.2	3.3	76.0	34.0	46.9	53.1
	CALIFORNIA	59.6	57.1	6.7	6.5	11.3	11.8	32.4	35.5	7.4	7.1	7.8	7.3	7.7	29.8	22.1	9.3	1.4	73.3	33.8	49.8	50.2
	UNITED STATES	75.1	73.6	12.3	12.5	3.8	4.2	12.5	14.1	6.9	6.7	7.2	7.0	7.3	28.6	23.8	10.8	1.7	75.1	36.0	49.1	50.9

ZIP CODE #	POST OFFICE NAME	2004 Per Capita Income	2004 HH Income Base	2004 HOUSEHOLD INCOME DISTRIBUTION (%) Less than $25,000	$25,000 to $49,999	$50,000 to $99,999	$100,000 to $149,999	$150,000 or More	MEDIAN HOUSEHOLD INCOME 2004	2009	2004 National Centile	2004 State Centile	2004 Home Value Base	2004 HOME VALUE DISTRIBUTION (%) Less than $50,000	$50,000 to $89,999	$90,000 to $174,999	$175,000 to $399,999	$400,000 or More	2004 Median Home Value
92121	SAN DIEGO	40524	1824	14.7	16.9	28.6	24.0	15.8	78643	99760	95	85	1079	0.6	0.1	0.2	27.3	71.9	501667
92122	SAN DIEGO	41831	16994	19.1	21.8	30.9	16.3	11.9	61369	77648	86	69	6878	0.3	0.3	2.4	26.6	70.4	530513
92123	SAN DIEGO	27239	10277	14.6	29.0	36.8	15.1	4.6	56356	66870	81	63	5195	0.8	0.0	4.2	65.5	29.5	354698
92124	SAN DIEGO	31235	10910	9.9	24.1	37.1	17.4	11.5	67124	81812	90	75	5625	1.3	1.0	0.4	37.5	59.8	444891
92126	SAN DIEGO	26074	22647	10.6	21.1	42.9	19.2	6.3	67666	78667	90	76	14658	1.4	1.4	5.5	61.7	30.1	343760
92127	SAN DIEGO	40016	6718	6.0	18.2	35.6	24.3	16.0	83813	103451	96	89	4361	0.4	0.6	1.4	35.1	62.5	453110
92128	SAN DIEGO	41952	20152	10.6	17.5	36.0	21.7	14.2	77903	95064	94	84	15042	0.5	0.3	1.7	38.8	58.7	441182
92129	SAN DIEGO	32154	17329	7.2	13.0	36.3	28.7	14.9	89091	106641	97	91	12909	0.6	0.3	2.5	22.7	74.0	480054
92130	SAN DIEGO	59078	14381	8.3	10.4	24.2	21.9	35.2	113848	143641	99	96	11050	0.0	0.9	0.5	11.5	87.1	837699
92131	SAN DIEGO	48282	11144	4.7	10.5	31.8	27.9	25.0	103680	126753	98	95	9610	0.3	0.4	0.8	23.7	74.9	582249
92133	SAN DIEGO	20946	5	0.0	0.0	60.0	40.0	0.0	93234	103773	97	92	0	0.0	0.0	0.0	0.0	0.0	0
92134	SAN DIEGO	18773	0	0.0	0.0	0.0	0.0	0.0	0	0	0	0	0	0.0	0.0	0.0	0.0	0.0	0
92135	SAN DIEGO	20050	51	0.0	0.0	0.0	52.9	47.1	146435	193405	100	99	0	0.0	0.0	0.0	0.0	0.0	0
92136	SAN DIEGO	18725	0	0.0	0.0	0.0	0.0	0.0	0	0	0	0	0	0.0	0.0	0.0	0.0	0.0	0
92139	SAN DIEGO	18472	10427	14.9	30.5	39.8	11.4	3.5	53370	61422	77	58	6692	1.5	0.5	9.3	84.9	3.8	265432
92140	SAN DIEGO	18858	5	0.0	0.0	60.0	40.0	0.0	93234	103773	97	92	0	0.0	0.0	0.0	0.0	0.0	0
92145	SAN DIEGO	16546	542	14.8	41.3	37.5	5.9	0.6	43205	50311	56	38	6	0.0	0.0	0.0	100.0	0.0	275000
92154	SAN DIEGO	17125	18759	20.4	28.4	35.9	11.2	4.1	50972	62560	74	55	12311	7.8	3.5	5.9	66.3	16.6	275244
92173	SAN YSIDRO	10085	7375	42.3	31.6	21.1	4.3	0.7	29944	33531	12	10	2674	7.1	4.6	12.2	71.5	4.7	257873
92182	SAN DIEGO	10308	0	0.0	0.0	0.0	0.0	0.0	0	5000	0	0	0	0.0	0.0	0.0	0.0	0.0	0
92201	INDIO	17804	19566	29.3	31.4	26.1	8.9	4.4	40766	46883	49	33	10755	7.4	4.7	41.4	38.3	8.2	167872
92203	INDIO	22777	1176	20.8	33.6	26.8	12.6	6.2	46724	54078	66	44	1017	2.9	3.9	20.3	40.8	32.2	321087
92210	INDIAN WELLS	76519	2242	12.3	19.5	25.5	15.8	26.9	78873	96654	95	85	1834	0.7	1.5	10.4	26.8	60.6	510638
92211	PALM DESERT	46892	11697	16.7	26.7	28.4	14.5	13.7	57205	67476	82	64	9664	1.7	2.5	12.2	46.0	37.7	333669
92220	BANNING	19029	10716	34.8	30.1	26.3	6.4	2.5	36269	41575	33	22	7980	9.2	9.2	40.1	37.8	3.7	153892
92223	BEAUMONT	18497	7388	33.0	30.5	26.0	7.6	2.9	36813	42159	35	24	4853	11.0	4.1	44.8	34.5	5.6	157554
92225	BLYTHE	15780	5764	36.1	26.5	28.1	7.3	2.0	35728	40681	30	21	3548	8.1	10.2	52.0	27.8	2.0	138644
92227	BRAWLEY	15337	7335	37.1	26.4	25.7	8.3	2.5	35553	41577	30	21	4352	8.3	5.4	46.1	35.2	5.0	159624
92230	CABAZON	12153	794	50.9	25.6	16.9	5.2	1.5	24364	27732	4	4	501	32.5	28.3	29.7	9.4	0.0	78871
92231	CALEXICO	11351	8009	40.2	30.2	21.3	5.9	2.4	31802	36497	17	13	4789	5.2	2.8	43.0	46.6	2.4	173869
92233	CALIPATRIA	14791	1777	41.1	32.6	20.0	5.7	0.5	29631	33666	11	10	1242	28.5	19.0	43.3	9.0	0.2	96739
92234	CATHEDRAL CITY	18574	16840	26.3	30.3	30.2	8.7	4.5	43734	50259	58	39	11099	8.6	7.1	30.1	51.6	2.6	183867
92236	COACHELLA	8206	5779	39.1	35.2	21.2	4.0	0.6	30748	34415	14	12	3419	8.7	6.1	72.4	12.1	0.8	133027
92239	DESERT CENTER	18719	508	37.4	30.1	27.6	4.9	0.0	30432	35000	13	11	358	13.7	8.7	62.9	14.3	0.6	126075
92240	DESERT HOT SPRINGS	13942	9136	41.4	32.1	21.4	3.8	1.3	30346	34769	13	11	5314	13.9	17.6	47.0	20.6	0.9	121746
92241	DESERT HOT SPRINGS	19261	3115	39.8	32.3	20.9	4.7	2.3	31072	35538	15	12	2563	27.7	17.8	36.2	17.5	0.9	100296
92242	EARP	15521	797	52.1	31.0	12.8	3.5	0.6	24078	27415	4	4	654	24.5	24.8	40.8	9.3	0.6	91087
92243	EL CENTRO	16377	13968	34.0	28.3	26.2	7.8	3.8	38399	44401	41	27	8022	11.1	5.9	43.2	35.4	4.4	157863
92249	HEBER	12524	973	36.2	33.9	21.5	6.3	2.2	33753	38450	23	18	701	10.1	7.7	54.1	26.3	1.9	147720
92250	HOLTVILLE	16729	2446	27.7	29.5	29.1	10.3	3.4	43868	49881	58	40	1669	12.5	8.3	41.3	34.8	3.0	156700
92251	IMPERIAL	20911	3498	18.7	22.2	41.6	13.2	4.4	57808	66413	82	65	2722	1.7	2.9	44.7	47.1	3.6	177058
92252	JOSHUA TREE	16224	3591	42.4	33.7	19.7	2.9	1.4	28996	33005	10	9	2519	10.7	25.7	46.0	17.4	0.3	107711
92253	LA QUINTA	32672	10911	16.0	24.8	33.2	13.4	12.7	58804	68903	83	66	8733	4.2	1.0	20.9	47.5	26.3	254782
92254	MECCA	8165	2074	48.1	32.0	16.6	2.2	1.1	25779	29102	6	5	885	16.2	8.3	63.6	6.1	5.9	119069
92256	MORONGO VALLEY	21482	1627	33.6	29.1	27.4	6.6	3.4	36847	43652	35	24	1165	9.9	21.6	54.3	11.6	2.7	111565
92257	NILAND	19658	584	48.0	36.3	9.6	3.4	2.7	25937	30359	6	5	521	55.3	25.0	13.4	6.3	0.0	45417
92259	OCOTILLO	23306	206	44.7	30.6	20.4	4.4	0.0	29524	34072	11	9	166	9.6	28.3	54.8	6.0	1.2	101630
92260	PALM DESERT	35018	15721	23.9	27.4	29.0	10.4	9.5	48458	56585	69	49	10423	2.9	4.3	19.6	49.1	24.1	242165
92262	PALM SPRINGS	25790	11968	33.9	29.6	22.1	8.8	5.7	36440	42765	33	23	6380	4.7	5.3	27.9	46.5	15.7	208647
92264	PALM SPRINGS	38307	10010	27.8	27.0	25.8	10.2	9.2	44578	52371	60	41	6736	14.7	5.6	19.3	37.7	22.6	211316
92267	PARKER DAM	11136	41	51.2	26.8	22.0	0.0	0.0	24034	30734	4	4	26	7.7	19.2	53.9	19.2	0.0	129167
92270	RANCHO MIRAGE	67417	7881	18.1	22.2	24.7	13.4	21.7	64925	77598	88	72	6525	7.9	5.6	11.3	29.3	45.9	369637
92274	THERMAL	12052	4785	45.4	32.1	15.8	4.3	2.4	27180	30641	7	7	2557	30.7	14.2	32.0	12.3	10.8	99457
92276	THOUSAND PALMS	19495	2418	36.0	31.8	23.8	6.0	2.4	36073	40174	32	22	1929	8.1	22.9	46.2	21.7	1.0	121190
92277	TWENTYNINE PALMS	16299	7758	37.1	34.6	22.4	5.3	0.7	32563	37169	19	15	3568	16.0	20.7	49.9	13.1	0.4	109320
92278	TWENTYNINE PALMS	16273	1153	32.0	44.3	19.7	4.0	0.0	33159	38322	21	16	23	21.7	30.4	47.8	0.0	0.0	88333
92280	VIDAL	18151	18	38.9	16.7	38.9	5.6	0.0	35000	35000	28	20	12	0.0	0.0	41.7	58.3	0.0	187500
92281	WESTMORLAND	11396	758	45.4	29.0	19.9	4.6	1.1	28258	32500	9	8	474	4.6	7.8	69.6	15.2	2.7	136728
92282	WHITE WATER	16508	316	39.2	30.7	22.8	5.1	2.2	31991	36784	18	14	219	14.2	22.8	51.6	7.8	3.7	113942
92283	WINTERHAVEN	12305	1563	56.3	27.5	12.7	2.0	1.5	21822	24472	3	3	1118	44.3	17.6	27.4	5.8	4.9	63585
92284	YUCCA VALLEY	18075	9123	38.8	32.6	21.4	5.3	1.9	32467	37344	19	15	6704	11.6	17.0	50.2	19.2	2.0	121073
92285	LANDERS	16880	1033	49.6	29.9	15.5	4.6	0.5	25280	29174	5	5	849	20.3	31.5	38.6	8.5	1.2	87583
92301	ADELANTO	11671	5459	35.1	34.8	26.7	2.8	0.6	34813	39388	27	19	3377	5.6	12.5	69.3	11.8	0.8	126247
92304	AMBOY	20875	9	11.1	44.4	44.4	0.0	0.0	42288	54272	54	36	6	16.7	0.0	50.0	33.3	0.0	137500
92305	ANGELUS OAKS	34173	76	17.1	19.7	39.5	10.5	13.2	64898	75496	88	72	58	5.2	3.5	12.1	65.5	13.8	241667
92307	APPLE VALLEY	21952	11622	24.3	28.0	32.4	11.5	3.8	47877	55755	68	48	8495	3.5	2.2	40.4	49.1	4.8	184734
92308	APPLE VALLEY	18640	10869	29.0	28.8	29.6	9.2	3.5	41213	47811	50	35	7925	6.8	4.3	52.1	34.1	2.8	149656
92309	BAKER	14293	280	35.7	32.5	25.0	6.1	0.7	32193	36711	18	14	151	54.3	0.7	19.2	16.6	9.3	14917
92310	FORT IRWIN	14427	2586	18.2	51.1	25.2	4.8	0.7	37960	43361	39	26	232	28.5	41.0	17.7	12.9	0.0	62500
92311	BARSTOW	18709	11196	30.3	30.0	29.6	7.9	2.2	41129	46942	50	34	6717	12.3	13.8	59.4	13.6	0.9	118479
92313	GRAND TERRACE	25927	4316	14.9	20.8	45.6	14.6	4.3	62267	72633	86	70	2918	4.7	1.6	16.1	73.5	4.0	223919
92314	BIG BEAR CITY	22781	6401	27.5	30.3	29.6	9.0	3.6	41992	49103	53	36	4831	0.3	4.8	42.3	43.4	9.2	183718
92315	BIG BEAR LAKE	24872	2036	33.3	26.3	26.0	9.2	5.2	38417	44974	41	27	1304	10.7	0.8	13.9	48.6	25.9	270513
92316	BLOOMINGTON	13658	7334	27.7	33.2	29.0	8.1	2.1	41754	47062	52	36	5424	12.7	3.4	43.6	38.0	2.3	161851
92317	BLUE JAY	40544	386	11.7	13.5	38.6	18.4	17.9	80631	95790	95	86	338	0.0	0.0	2.7	49.4	47.9	386000
92320	CALIMESA	23241	3444	27.5	29.8	32.8	6.8	3.1	42967	48932	56	38	2738	20.3	4.6	31.6	38.5	4.9	159462
92321	CEDAR GLEN	30949	468	17.5	21.2	32.3	18.8	10.3	66982	79218	90	75	350	0.0	0.0	20.6	55.7	23.7	252885
92322	CEDARPINES PARK	24668	315	23.2	20.3	41.3	9.8	5.4	55363	64238	80	61	256	1.2	0.8	41.8	49.2	7.0	192391
92324	COLTON	15522	16904	29.8	31.5	29.1	6.9	2.7	40183	45549	47	32	9334	4.9	5.2	47.4	39.1	3.5	162473
92325	CRESTLINE	23364	3133	23.2	30.9	29.3	12.6	4.1	46554	54300	65	44	2387	3.4	4.3	39.5	49.0	3.9	182827
92327	DAGGETT	15872	92	47.8	17.4	30.4	4.4	0.0	27332	32365	8	7	58	39.7	12.1	36.2	10.3	1.7	86667
92328	DEATH VALLEY	26764	203	37.0	22.2	30.5	10.3	0.0	39067	43638	43	28	81	49.4	19.8	8.6	12.4	9.9	50625
92332	ESSEX	25403	34	14.7	35.3	38.2	8.8	2.9	50000	51652	72	52	22	13.6	9.1	36.4	40.9	0.0	140000
92335	FONTANA	12500	22493	30.0	33.5	28.9	5.7	1.9	38171	42745	40	27	11984	4.8	3.4	48.6	41.9	1.2	166551
92336	FONTANA	18230	15539	14.5	24.1	41.6	15.5	4.4	61429	70940	86	69	12397	1.3	0.7	20.3	74.6	3.1	232079
92337	FONTANA	17773	8706	12.4	25.7	45.7	12.5	3.7	59759	67911	84	67	6884	2.0	0.5	22.4	73.2	2.0	213000
92338	LUDLOW	14679	26	38.5	26.9	30.8	3.9	0.0	37321	48630	37	25	18	0.0	0.0	61.1	33.3	5.6	145000
92339	FOREST FALLS	29690	533	23.6	22.9	30.4	13.7	9.4	53599	64757	78	59	346	0.0	1.2	22.0	64.5	12.4	233333
92342	HELENDALE	25454	2055	18.0	26.2	39.1	13.8	3.0	53562	61593	78	59	1713	1.8	1.1	36.5	54.1	6.5	197339
92345	HESPERIA	18111	23629	24.7	29.3	34.9	8.2	2.9	46384	52830	65	44	17563	3.5	4.4	56.8	33.7	1.6	151719
92346	HIGHLAND	21922	16086	22.0	25.6	34.1	12.6	5.7	52388	60235	76	57	11281	8.8	4.2	26.0	55.9	5.1	209087
92347	HINKLEY	14593	657	34.9	34.7	24.1	5.3	1.1	31479	36104	16	12	477	4.8	27.5	55.4	11.1	1.3	106078
92350	LOMA LINDA	28291	14	35.7	28.6	21.4	14.3	0.0	35000	42343	28	20	4	0.0	0.0	25.0	75.0	0.0	200000
92352	LAKE ARROWHEAD	35660	1937	12.1	14.7	35.9	21.8	15.5	80021	95476	95	86	1665	0.2	0.0	4.0	48.8	47.0	385735
92354	LOMA LINDA	22829	7384	30.2	27.8	27.0	9.6	5.3	41997	48629	53	36	3299	6.8	2.7	19.5	60.0	11.1	234973
	CALIFORNIA	27293		21.8	24.4	30.5	13.7	9.7	54267	64547				3.3	2.7	13.3	42.9	37.9	319678
	UNITED STATES	25866		24.7	27.1	30.8	10.9	6.5	48124	56710				10.9	15.0	33.7	30.1	10.4	145905

ZIP CODE #	POST OFFICE NAME	FINANCIAL SERVICES: Auto Loan	Home Loan	Invest-ments	Retire-ment Plans	THE HOME: Home Improvements: Home Repair	Lawn & Garden	Furnishings: Comput-ers & Hard-ware	Major Appli-ances	TV, Radio, Sound Equip-ment	Furni-ture	ENTERTAINMENT: Dine out/ Carry out	Sports Equip-ment	Fees & Tickets	Toys & Games	Travel	Cable TV	PERSONAL: Apparel & Services	Auto Repairs	Health Insur-ance	Pets & Supplies
92121	SAN DIEGO	135	121	128	130	116	121	148	128	140	140	176	162	137	167	132	126	170	138	113	142
92122	SAN DIEGO	111	115	181	123	111	122	125	116	125	126	158	138	130	163	125	124	157	121	109	128
92123	SAN DIEGO	98	96	123	101	93	101	104	98	104	104	131	117	105	131	101	101	128	103	93	109
92124	SAN DIEGO	123	122	149	130	116	123	130	122	126	130	159	148	130	159	124	120	157	127	110	135
92126	SAN DIEGO	101	114	149	125	115	111	120	117	108	117	136	147	115	132	118	98	135	123	96	123
92127	SAN DIEGO	158	178	187	184	171	170	166	163	154	170	195	191	171	196	163	146	193	161	142	178
92128	SAN DIEGO	135	149	160	149	147	155	138	142	134	143	168	157	143	164	141	132	164	139	136	155
92129	SAN DIEGO	139	162	178	167	156	158	150	146	139	152	177	170	158	181	149	134	177	144	129	161
92130	SAN DIEGO	216	249	293	261	238	241	232	224	217	238	276	263	247	284	232	209	276	221	198	247
92131	SAN DIEGO	181	220	236	226	211	211	196	193	180	201	229	224	210	236	197	173	229	187	168	211
92133	SAN DIEGO	157	100	95	114	91	108	148	128	151	138	188	170	127	168	122	137	180	151	118	145
92134	SAN DIEGO	0	0	0	0	0	0	0	0	0	0	0	0	0	0	0	0	0	0	0	0
92135	SAN DIEGO	289	184	175	210	168	199	273	236	278	255	347	314	234	311	225	253	332	278	218	268
92136	SAN DIEGO	0	0	0	0	0	0	0	0	0	0	0	0	0	0	0	0	0	0	0	0
92139	SAN DIEGO	86	90	109	94	89	90	94	92	90	94	113	111	92	111	92	84	112	96	81	99
92140	SAN DIEGO	157	100	95	114	91	108	148	128	151	138	188	170	127	168	122	137	180	151	118	145
92145	SAN DIEGO	81	51	49	59	47	56	76	66	78	71	97	88	65	87	63	71	93	78	61	75
92154	SAN DIEGO	77	78	85	75	75	79	78	79	79	82	100	88	78	99	77	77	100	80	73	84
92173	SAN YSIDRO	57	49	49	49	48	50	55	55	57	58	72	62	52	70	51	53	72	58	50	58
92182	SAN DIEGO	0	0	0	0	0	0	0	0	0	0	0	0	0	0	0	0	0	0	0	0
92201	INDIO	88	78	75	76	77	82	82	85	85	87	107	94	78	99	79	82	105	88	81	92
92203	INDIO	106	98	91	92	102	117	92	104	97	99	121	104	92	102	98	102	115	102	116	116
92210	INDIAN WELLS	220	209	211	201	219	256	197	219	207	209	258	220	201	222	212	219	243	215	251	249
92211	PALM DESERT	140	135	135	129	141	164	126	140	132	133	165	141	129	144	136	140	156	137	160	159
92220	BANNING	71	68	67	63	68	78	66	72	69	70	86	74	65	77	68	71	83	72	77	78
92223	BEAUMONT	73	70	70	68	71	79	70	74	72	72	90	80	70	85	71	73	86	73	77	81
92225	BLYTHE	71	65	57	63	64	67	66	69	67	69	83	77	62	78	63	65	82	70	66	76
92227	BRAWLEY	74	69	63	67	67	69	69	73	70	74	88	80	66	82	67	68	88	74	68	78
92230	CABAZON	57	44	35	41	47	53	47	51	53	47	64	60	43	62	47	55	60	52	58	64
92231	CALEXICO	69	61	50	56	58	61	62	67	64	67	81	71	57	71	59	62	80	68	63	70
92233	CALIPATRIA	51	45	37	41	43	45	46	49	47	50	59	52	42	52	43	46	59	50	46	51
92234	CATHEDRAL CITY	83	81	80	80	80	85	80	83	80	84	101	91	79	95	79	78	98	83	80	90
92236	COACHELLA	57	49	45	48	48	50	54	55	56	57	70	62	50	67	50	53	71	57	50	58
92239	DESERT CENTER	66	54	40	51	58	67	55	61	60	54	72	68	50	67	56	63	67	61	71	75
92240	DESERT HOT SPRINGS	57	52	50	50	52	57	55	57	57	56	71	62	52	66	54	57	69	58	58	62
92241	DESERT HOT SPRINGS	67	58	50	53	63	72	55	64	60	56	73	69	52	69	58	64	68	62	73	79
92242	EARP	48	46	48	42	48	58	42	49	46	46	57	46	44	48	47	49	53	48	58	53
92243	EL CENTRO	78	73	70	71	71	74	75	77	76	79	96	86	72	91	72	73	95	79	71	83
92249	HEBER	61	54	45	50	52	55	55	59	57	60	72	63	50	63	52	55	71	60	56	62
92250	HOLTVILLE	84	76	67	71	73	77	77	82	80	83	100	88	72	90	74	77	100	84	77	86
92251	IMPERIAL	99	105	101	105	101	101	99	101	95	103	120	114	99	117	96	91	119	99	90	109
92252	JOSHUA TREE	55	48	42	46	50	58	51	53	54	49	66	60	48	64	51	57	62	53	60	62
92253	LA QUINTA	133	137	134	137	136	143	129	134	126	134	159	149	130	150	130	124	154	132	131	149
92254	MECCA	55	47	46	47	46	47	53	53	55	56	70	61	51	68	49	51	71	56	48	56
92256	MORONGO VALLEY	77	63	49	61	67	78	68	73	73	65	88	83	62	85	67	76	81	73	83	88
92257	NILAND	53	51	53	46	53	65	47	55	51	51	63	51	48	53	51	54	58	53	64	59
92259	OCOTILLO	43	34	23	31	38	43	32	39	36	32	43	45	29	42	34	39	40	38	46	53
92260	PALM DESERT	106	103	112	100	107	122	100	108	104	104	129	113	102	118	106	108	123	107	118	121
92262	PALM SPRINGS	80	77	88	75	78	86	80	81	82	80	103	91	79	101	81	84	100	83	84	91
92264	PALM SPRINGS	106	102	107	96	106	124	97	107	102	102	127	108	98	112	103	108	120	105	121	120
92267	PARKER DAM	51	40	27	36	45	50	37	45	42	37	50	53	34	50	40	45	47	44	53	62
92270	RANCHO MIRAGE	195	186	187	177	194	227	175	195	184	186	229	194	178	196	188	194	216	191	223	220
92274	THERMAL	60	52	51	51	52	56	56	58	59	60	74	64	54	70	54	57	74	61	56	62
92276	THOUSAND PALMS	77	69	64	63	72	82	66	76	71	71	88	77	64	77	69	74	84	75	84	85
92277	TWENTYNINE PALMS	61	49	48	51	48	55	59	56	60	57	75	68	55	71	54	58	72	60	56	63
92278	TWENTYNINE PALMS	63	40	38	46	37	43	60	51	61	56	76	68	51	68	49	55	72	61	48	58
92280	VIDAL	71	56	41	52	62	69	54	63	60	54	72	74	49	70	57	63	67	63	73	85
92281	WESTMORLAND	58	51	43	48	49	52	52	56	54	57	68	60	48	60	50	52	68	58	53	59
92282	WHITE WATER	67	60	48	57	59	63	59	63	60	62	75	71	55	69	57	59	73	64	62	72
92283	WINTERHAVEN	44	37	30	35	38	44	38	42	41	39	50	45	35	45	38	42	48	42	46	47
92284	YUCCA VALLEY	68	55	41	52	59	69	58	64	64	56	76	71	54	73	58	67	70	63	74	76
92285	LANDERS	56	49	43	44	53	62	45	54	50	47	61	56	44	55	49	54	57	52	63	65
92301	ADELANTO	57	57	56	57	55	57	57	57	56	58	71	67	56	70	56	54	69	58	53	63
92304	AMBOY	78	61	45	57	68	76	59	69	66	59	79	82	53	77	62	69	74	69	80	93
92305	ANGELUS OAKS	125	99	68	89	111	124	93	112	105	92	124	131	83	123	99	112	116	110	132	152
92307	APPLE VALLEY	89	90	88	88	91	97	88	90	88	87	109	104	88	111	88	88	106	89	90	103
92308	APPLE VALLEY	79	74	70	73	76	83	74	78	76	74	94	89	73	92	75	77	90	77	81	90
92309	BAKER	52	44	41	43	43	45	48	49	51	51	64	56	46	62	45	47	64	52	45	53
92310	FORT IRWIN	75	48	46	55	44	52	71	61	72	66	90	82	61	81	59	66	86	72	57	70
92311	BARSTOW	73	70	68	70	70	76	73	73	74	71	91	85	71	91	72	73	88	74	74	82
92313	GRAND TERRACE	97	103	112	105	100	103	102	100	98	103	123	117	103	123	100	94	121	101	91	110
92314	BIG BEAR CITY	96	76	52	68	85	95	71	86	80	71	95	100	64	94	76	86	89	84	101	117
92315	BIG BEAR LAKE	98	77	52	69	86	97	72	87	82	72	97	102	65	96	77	88	90	86	103	119
92316	BLOOMINGTON	78	72	64	68	69	72	72	76	74	77	93	83	68	85	70	71	92	78	71	81
92317	BLUE JAY	187	147	100	133	166	186	139	167	157	137	186	195	124	183	148	168	173	164	197	228
92320	CALIMESA	78	75	73	72	77	88	74	79	77	75	95	85	74	90	76	80	90	78	86	89
92321	CEDAR GLEN	141	110	75	100	124	140	104	126	118	103	140	147	93	138	111	126	130	124	148	172
92322	CEDARPINES PARK	99	85	69	79	92	103	81	92	88	80	106	107	77	107	86	93	101	91	105	119
92324	COLTON	75	68	67	68	66	69	72	73	72	75	91	82	69	85	68	69	90	75	67	78
92325	CRESTLINE	89	84	76	82	86	91	82	87	83	81	103	102	79	103	83	83	99	86	88	104
92327	DAGGETT	66	49	31	46	54	63	52	59	59	51	69	67	46	66	52	62	64	59	70	73
92328	DEATH VALLEY	59	62	81	63	61	68	65	62	65	64	82	72	67	83	66	66	81	64	62	69
92332	ESSEX	93	73	53	67	81	91	70	83	79	70	94	97	63	92	74	83	87	82	96	112
92335	FONTANA	71	63	61	61	61	64	68	69	70	72	88	77	64	84	64	67	88	72	64	73
92336	FONTANA	103	107	102	109	103	102	102	103	98	107	124	118	102	120	99	92	123	102	91	111
92337	FONTANA	100	104	100	107	100	98	99	99	94	104	119	114	99	117	95	88	119	99	86	107
92338	LUDLOW	73	50	25	44	57	65	48	60	58	49	68	72	42	65	50	62	62	59	73	85
92339	FOREST FALLS	116	91	62	82	102	115	86	103	97	85	115	121	77	114	91	104	107	102	122	141
92342	HELENDALE	98	90	84	85	95	112	83	95	89	89	110	94	84	92	90	95	103	93	112	110
92345	HESPERIA	82	81	76	79	81	85	79	81	80	79	99	95	78	99	79	79	95	81	81	93
92346	HIGHLAND	94	97	98	96	94	98	94	95	92	97	116	108	94	112	93	90	114	95	90	104
92347	HINKLEY	77	53	26	46	59	67	51	63	61	52	72	75	44	68	52	65	66	63	76	88
92350	LOMA LINDA	66	56	71	62	56	61	73	65	71	69	89	82	67	84	66	66	87	72	61	72
92352	LAKE ARROWHEAD	174	136	93	123	153	172	128	155	145	127	172	181	115	170	137	155	160	152	183	211
92354	LOMA LINDA	78	81	97	84	81	86	85	83	82	84	103	98	84	101	84	79	100	85	78	90
	CALIFORNIA	107	111	131	112	109	115	113	111	111	114	140	129	114	141	112	109	139	113	104	122
	UNITED STATES	100	100	100	100	100	100	100	100	100	100	100	100	100	100	100	100	100	100	100	100

POPULATION CHANGE

ZIP CODE			POPULATION			2000-2004 ANNUAL RATE		HOUSEHOLDS					FAMILIES		
#	POST OFFICE NAME	COUNTY FIPS CODE	2000	2004	2009	% Rate	State Centile	2000	2004	2009	% Annual Rate 2000-2004	2004 Average HH Size	2000	2004	% Annual Rate 2000-2004
92356	LUCERNE VALLEY	071	5309	5391	5730	0.4	25	2050	2080	2198	0.3	2.58	1352	1366	0.2
92358	LYTLE CREEK	071	742	728	774	-0.5	5	311	304	321	-0.5	2.39	208	202	-0.7
92359	MENTONE	071	7594	8015	8672	1.3	64	2646	2794	3012	1.3	2.78	1813	1904	1.2
92363	NEEDLES	071	5469	5585	5966	0.5	32	2240	2281	2422	0.4	2.44	1442	1462	0.3
92364	NIPTON	071	203	207	223	0.5	29	92	92	99	0.0	2.09	46	44	-1.0
92365	NEWBERRY SPRINGS	071	4523	4495	4774	-0.2	10	1777	1761	1857	-0.2	2.54	1232	1208	-0.5
92368	ORO GRANDE	071	987	965	1024	-0.5	5	341	333	352	-0.6	2.88	231	224	-0.7
92371	PHELAN	071	12461	13569	14898	2.0	79	4080	4430	4832	2.0	3.04	3246	3513	1.9
92372	PINON HILLS	071	3863	4179	4580	1.9	77	1359	1465	1595	1.8	2.85	1044	1121	1.7
92373	REDLANDS	071	30123	35011	40019	3.6	94	12855	14863	16849	3.5	2.32	7933	9102	3.3
92374	REDLANDS	071	37846	41848	46487	2.4	84	12532	13857	15335	2.4	2.92	9155	10091	2.3
92376	RIALTO	071	76138	79966	86268	1.2	60	20291	21018	22411	0.8	3.78	16688	17247	0.8
92377	RIALTO	071	18548	20897	23416	2.9	89	5085	5664	6275	2.6	3.64	4448	4947	2.5
92382	RUNNING SPRINGS	071	567	583	621	0.7	39	213	220	233	0.8	2.55	160	164	0.6
92384	SHOSHONE	027	196	190	191	-0.7	3	105	102	103	-0.7	1.86	48	46	-1.0
92385	SKYFOREST	071	2175	2248	2401	0.8	45	809	835	887	0.8	2.69	605	623	0.7
92389	TECOPA	027	82	80	80	-0.6	4	37	36	36	-0.6	2.22	17	16	-1.4
92392	VICTORVILLE	071	62237	69154	76846	2.5	86	20660	22785	25088	2.3	3.01	15806	17440	2.3
92394	VICTORVILLE	071	13572	15889	17542	3.8	95	4339	4777	5254	2.3	3.12	3334	3653	2.2
92397	WRIGHTWOOD	071	4618	4773	5096	0.8	45	1781	1836	1948	0.7	2.60	1273	1306	0.6
92399	YUCAIPA	071	41731	45191	49629	1.9	77	15395	16486	17915	1.6	2.71	10839	11571	1.6
92401	SAN BERNARDINO	071	1614	1774	1963	2.3	83	542	587	641	1.9	2.97	362	385	1.5
92404	SAN BERNARDINO	071	54875	58300	63430	1.4	67	17702	18514	19911	1.1	3.06	12664	13203	1.0
92405	SAN BERNARDINO	071	27792	29713	32364	1.6	71	9117	9637	10386	1.3	3.05	6371	6699	1.2
92407	SAN BERNARDINO	071	53400	58442	64566	2.2	82	15935	17355	19067	2.0	3.26	12002	13041	2.0
92408	SAN BERNARDINO	071	13854	15135	16641	2.1	81	3935	4262	4657	1.9	3.32	2821	3045	1.8
92410	SAN BERNARDINO	071	43276	46176	50701	1.5	70	11894	12482	13527	1.1	3.64	9084	9496	1.1
92411	SAN BERNARDINO	071	23152	25714	28767	2.5	86	6083	6746	7510	2.5	3.74	4899	5417	2.4
92501	RIVERSIDE	065	18919	20561	23647	2.0	79	6161	6663	7650	1.9	2.86	3834	4117	1.7
92503	RIVERSIDE	065	69737	77234	90106	2.4	85	20758	22806	26379	2.2	3.34	16012	17459	2.1
92504	RIVERSIDE	065	47992	52774	61514	2.3	83	15795	17224	19916	2.1	3.00	11334	12288	1.9
92505	RIVERSIDE	065	38863	43325	50683	2.6	87	11399	12554	14539	2.3	3.37	8789	9640	2.2
92506	RIVERSIDE	065	41744	45600	52873	2.1	81	14759	15991	18387	1.9	2.79	11112	12011	1.9
92507	RIVERSIDE	065	47835	52688	61410	2.3	83	16616	18364	21381	2.4	2.79	9773	10684	2.1
92508	RIVERSIDE	065	18069	24829	32309	7.8	99	5380	7332	9446	7.6	3.37	4656	6329	7.5
92509	RIVERSIDE	065	63571	71708	84771	2.9	89	17187	19233	22530	2.7	3.69	14121	15707	2.5
92518	MARCH AIR FORCE BASE	065	990	964	1095	-0.6	4	523	506	570	-0.8	1.90	310	296	-1.1
92521	RIVERSIDE	065	885	885	885	0.0	15	9	9	9	0.0	2.11	2	2	0.0
92530	LAKE ELSINORE	065	38723	43812	51722	3.0	90	12161	13613	15891	2.7	3.21	9246	10319	2.6
92532	LAKE ELSINORE	065	4285	5206	6366	4.7	97	1330	1609	1951	4.6	3.23	1075	1298	4.5
92536	AGUANGA	065	2347	2687	3190	3.2	92	863	982	1154	3.1	2.73	622	701	2.9
92539	ANZA	065	3769	4067	4680	1.8	76	1475	1582	1804	1.7	2.57	998	1059	1.4
92543	HEMET	065	29460	31968	36929	1.9	78	12318	13185	15061	1.6	2.39	7306	7733	1.4
92544	HEMET	065	38831	43130	50340	2.5	86	14205	15677	18161	2.4	2.70	10184	11141	2.1
92545	HEMET	065	25006	28779	34256	3.4	93	11345	12818	15070	2.9	2.18	6988	7820	2.7
92548	HOMELAND	065	4904	5671	6762	3.5	94	2005	2313	2738	3.4	2.45	1309	1492	3.1
92549	IDYLLWILD	065	3708	3954	4515	1.5	69	1679	1782	2023	1.4	2.16	1003	1051	1.1
92551	MORENO VALLEY	065	22707	26254	31440	3.5	93	5863	6715	7957	3.2	3.90	5187	5921	3.2
92553	MORENO VALLEY	065	61030	67093	78008	2.3	83	16217	17647	20302	2.0	3.79	13686	14825	1.9
92555	MORENO VALLEY	065	13349	16349	20124	4.9	97	3883	4754	5816	4.9	3.42	3395	4133	4.7
92557	MORENO VALLEY	065	46051	51283	60199	2.6	87	13520	14932	17356	2.4	3.42	11233	12340	2.2
92561	MOUNTAIN CENTER	065	1499	1619	1863	1.8	76	664	715	818	1.8	2.23	406	431	1.4
92562	MURRIETA	065	36461	48240	61606	6.8	99	12019	15705	19805	6.5	3.06	9674	12583	6.4
92563	MURRIETA	065	18037	25126	33336	8.1	99	5760	7873	10276	7.6	3.11	4557	6197	7.5
92567	NUEVO	065	7355	8429	10001	3.3	92	2323	2652	3123	3.2	3.17	1829	2076	3.0
92570	PERRIS	065	36831	41036	47990	2.6	87	10376	11458	13268	2.4	3.55	8321	9132	2.2
92571	PERRIS	065	26188	29936	35502	3.2	91	6819	7631	8909	2.7	3.90	5881	6554	2.6
92582	SAN JACINTO	065	4507	5212	6202	3.5	94	1603	1866	2223	3.6	2.65	1105	1273	3.4
92583	SAN JACINTO	065	21541	23673	27570	2.3	83	7488	8185	9459	2.1	2.84	5137	5560	1.9
92584	MENIFEE	065	14348	19623	25435	7.7	99	4764	6511	8380	7.6	3.01	3881	5255	7.4
92585	SUN CITY	065	9244	11054	13383	4.3	96	3312	3953	4757	4.3	2.77	2321	2726	3.9
92586	SUN CITY	065	17839	20083	23601	2.8	89	8740	9830	11500	2.8	2.00	5159	5698	2.4
92587	SUN CITY	065	13310	15939	19336	4.3	96	4650	5509	6607	4.1	2.89	3762	4429	3.9
92590	TEMECULA	065	3044	3532	4217	3.6	94	1004	1153	1361	3.3	3.06	767	875	3.2
92591	TEMECULA	065	25955	33738	43287	6.4	98	8307	10689	13564	6.1	3.14	6791	8729	6.1
92592	TEMECULA	065	46480	60689	76747	6.5	98	14480	18545	23092	6.0	3.27	12371	15800	5.9
92595	WILDOMAR	065	18828	22504	27330	4.3	96	6092	7190	8628	4.0	3.12	4926	5797	3.9
92596	WINCHESTER	065	3754	6077	8629	12.0	100	1202	1965	2782	12.3	3.04	1004	1656	12.5
92602	IRVINE	059	4066	5486	6491	7.3	99	1422	1913	2250	7.2	2.87	1148	1549	7.3
92603	IRVINE	059	2815	3216	3524	3.2	91	1056	1195	1298	3.0	2.68	808	908	2.8
92604	IRVINE	059	29708	29840	30838	0.1	17	10688	10699	10980	0.0	2.78	7827	7802	-0.1
92606	IRVINE	059	17480	20088	22148	3.3	92	6616	7580	8314	3.3	2.65	4497	5100	3.0
92610	FOOTHILL RANCH	059	10953	13936	16148	5.8	98	3830	4847	5578	5.7	2.87	2989	3798	5.8
92612	IRVINE	059	26393	31007	34779	3.9	95	10428	12091	13405	3.5	2.51	5910	6845	3.5
92614	IRVINE	059	21909	23268	24733	1.4	67	8306	8816	9346	1.4	2.64	5681	6018	1.4
92618	IRVINE	059	6015	6475	6860	1.8	75	2383	2564	2712	1.7	2.16	1245	1334	1.4
92620	IRVINE	059	26428	29265	31741	2.4	85	9037	9951	10716	2.3	2.94	6981	7687	2.3
92624	CAPISTRANO BEACH	059	7560	7475	7635	-0.3	8	2818	2782	2826	-0.3	2.65	1905	1872	-0.4
92625	CORONA DEL MAR	059	12482	12855	13418	0.7	41	6066	6265	6518	0.8	2.01	3289	3384	0.7
92626	COSTA MESA	059	47538	48445	50187	0.5	29	17649	17962	18530	0.4	2.59	10581	10695	0.3
92627	COSTA MESA	059	62946	66683	70301	1.4	66	22270	23220	24195	1.0	2.81	12599	13089	0.9
92629	DANA POINT	059	27834	28241	29265	0.3	25	11765	11952	12327	0.4	2.36	7353	7448	0.3
92630	LAKE FOREST	059	60811	64255	68322	1.3	64	20783	21778	22945	1.1	2.91	15268	15964	1.1
92646	HUNTINGTON BEACH	059	57113	57246	59138	0.1	16	21868	21813	22370	-0.1	2.62	15233	15133	-0.2
92647	HUNTINGTON BEACH	059	58750	58876	60634	0.1	16	20214	20189	20658	0.0	2.90	14144	14072	-0.1
92648	HUNTINGTON BEACH	059	42292	42932	44354	0.4	25	18096	18291	18763	0.3	2.32	10121	10184	0.2
92649	HUNTINGTON BEACH	059	32099	32661	34120	0.4	29	13811	14029	14548	0.4	2.33	8432	8513	0.2
92651	LAGUNA BEACH	059	24798	24926	25778	0.1	18	11931	11978	12318	0.1	2.07	6095	6094	0.1
92653	LAGUNA HILLS	059	46802	49213	52431	1.2	61	21892	22521	23604	0.7	2.16	11853	12245	0.8
92655	MIDWAY CITY	059	7472	7782	8126	1.0	53	2150	2205	2274	0.6	3.50	1627	1665	0.5
92656	ALISO VIEJO	059	41578	51906	59511	5.4	98	16795	20773	23591	5.1	2.50	10829	13413	5.2
92657	NEWPORT COAST	059	5119	6875	8186	7.2	99	2194	2860	3340	6.4	2.40	1410	1900	7.3
92660	NEWPORT BEACH	059	29848	31787	33820	1.5	69	13345	14179	14991	1.4	2.24	7984	8434	1.2
92661	NEWPORT BEACH	059	4076	3966	4041	-0.6	4	2025	1969	1996	-0.7	2.01	902	870	-0.9
92662	NEWPORT BEACH	059	3210	3065	3133	-1.1	2	1785	1702	1732	-1.1	1.80	783	741	-1.3
	CALIFORNIA					1.4					1.2	2.90			1.2
	UNITED STATES					1.2					1.3	2.58			1.1

ZIP CODE #	POST OFFICE NAME	RACE (%) White 2000	White 2004	Black 2000	Black 2004	Asian/Pacific 2000	Asian/Pacific 2004	% Hispanic Origin 2000	% Hispanic Origin 2004	2004 AGE DISTRIBUTION (%) 0-4	5-9	10-14	15-19	20-24	25-44	45-64	65-84	85+	18+	MEDIAN AGE 2004	% 2004 Males	% 2004 Females
92356	LUCERNE VALLEY	84.4	82.0	2.2	2.4	1.3	1.4	14.5	17.5	5.7	5.9	7.3	7.6	5.8	22.3	28.7	15.4	1.4	75.9	42.2	50.5	49.5
92358	LYTLE CREEK	88.3	86.4	0.8	0.8	2.8	3.0	9.2	11.1	4.3	5.6	7.1	5.8	5.6	22.0	36.3	12.2	1.1	79.0	44.8	50.7	49.3
92359	MENTONE	76.4	73.4	4.0	4.0	2.8	2.9	23.4	27.5	7.3	7.1	8.5	8.9	7.8	28.1	23.3	7.8	1.5	71.4	33.0	49.2	50.9
92363	NEEDLES	76.2	73.6	1.5	1.6	1.5	1.6	18.4	21.7	6.7	6.4	7.7	7.6	5.8	20.9	28.5	14.5	2.0	74.1	41.2	49.7	50.4
92364	NIPTON	80.8	77.8	2.5	2.4	0.5	0.5	19.2	22.7	5.3	4.8	5.3	5.8	8.2	21.7	33.3	13.0	2.4	80.7	44.0	59.4	40.6
92365	NEWBERRY SPRINGS	81.3	78.7	2.6	2.7	2.1	2.2	16.0	19.2	5.4	6.3	7.3	7.3	5.8	23.0	30.0	13.7	1.3	76.4	41.8	51.8	48.2
92368	ORO GRANDE	74.0	71.0	2.5	2.5	0.2	0.2	43.3	48.9	8.0	7.4	10.5	8.1	4.7	22.9	24.6	13.2	0.8	68.5	36.5	54.1	45.9
92371	PHELAN	80.1	77.1	2.2	2.3	1.5	1.6	20.3	24.2	6.1	6.6	9.0	9.2	7.3	24.2	27.4	9.7	0.6	72.6	37.2	51.3	48.7
92372	PINON HILLS	88.8	86.8	0.7	0.7	0.8	0.9	13.8	16.8	5.6	6.1	7.8	8.2	7.3	21.7	30.1	12.4	0.9	75.6	41.0	50.1	49.9
92373	REDLANDS	81.4	79.3	3.1	3.2	6.6	7.3	13.2	15.5	5.2	5.2	6.3	6.5	7.0	26.4	27.2	13.1	3.1	79.2	40.3	47.0	53.0
92374	REDLANDS	66.4	64.2	5.6	5.3	5.1	5.3	32.6	35.9	7.1	7.0	8.4	9.3	9.3	27.1	22.4	8.3	1.2	72.6	31.6	47.8	52.2
92376	RIALTO	37.5	35.8	21.9	20.6	2.7	2.6	54.5	58.8	10.1	9.5	10.7	9.8	8.8	27.2	17.4	5.9	0.6	63.6	25.8	48.8	51.3
92377	RIALTO	45.1	43.0	24.8	23.8	3.6	3.6	37.8	42.4	8.6	8.8	10.0	8.5	6.7	30.8	20.4	5.7	0.4	67.1	30.5	50.0	50.0
92382	RUNNING SPRINGS	90.3	88.9	0.4	0.3	0.5	0.5	10.6	12.9	4.8	5.2	9.3	9.3	6.2	22.8	34.3	7.2	1.0	73.8	41.3	52.3	47.7
92384	SHOSHONE	81.6	79.5	0.5	0.5	1.5	2.1	6.6	7.9	3.2	4.7	3.7	3.7	4.2	23.7	39.0	16.3	1.6	85.8	47.6	51.6	48.4
92385	SKYFOREST	89.8	87.8	0.2	0.2	1.2	1.3	8.4	10.3	6.0	6.5	8.5	7.8	6.3	23.9	30.5	9.8	0.7	74.2	38.9	49.6	50.4
92389	TECOPA	81.7	80.0	0.0	0.0	2.4	2.5	6.1	8.8	2.5	5.0	3.8	3.8	5.0	23.8	37.5	17.5	1.3	85.0	47.3	55.0	45.0
92392	VICTORVILLE	64.9	61.8	9.7	9.7	3.7	3.8	30.5	35.0	8.2	8.0	9.4	8.2	6.9	25.9	21.1	11.1	1.3	69.1	32.9	48.6	51.4
92394	VICTORVILLE	57.9	54.5	15.6	16.1	3.3	3.7	33.6	37.3	9.0	8.8	9.7	8.4	7.2	29.3	19.1	8.0	0.6	67.3	30.0	51.0	49.0
92397	WRIGHTWOOD	90.8	89.1	0.4	0.4	1.1	1.2	8.8	10.9	5.9	6.5	7.8	7.7	6.6	22.6	31.2	10.9	0.8	75.1	41.0	50.9	49.2
92399	YUCAIPA	85.3	82.9	0.9	0.9	1.3	1.4	18.3	21.8	6.6	6.8	8.3	7.8	6.3	24.9	24.5	12.1	2.7	73.2	37.9	48.5	51.5
92401	SAN BERNARDINO	33.3	32.0	17.8	16.2	2.0	1.9	62.3	66.9	13.3	11.2	9.9	7.5	9.9	29.8	14.0	4.0	0.5	61.2	24.1	50.1	49.9
92404	SAN BERNARDINO	53.2	50.3	16.0	15.3	2.9	3.0	38.2	43.1	9.8	8.9	9.2	8.8	7.9	26.6	18.4	9.0	1.5	66.5	28.8	48.4	51.6
92405	SAN BERNARDINO	50.0	47.5	13.6	13.0	2.3	2.3	48.2	52.6	10.5	9.1	9.2	8.2	8.9	29.1	17.2	6.6	1.3	66.4	27.6	48.6	51.4
92407	SAN BERNARDINO	57.7	54.7	12.0	11.7	3.8	3.9	36.0	40.5	8.8	8.4	9.5	9.0	9.1	30.2	19.1	5.4	0.4	68.0	28.2	50.0	50.0
92408	SAN BERNARDINO	37.8	36.4	14.5	13.3	15.2	15.4	44.9	48.4	9.9	8.7	8.9	8.3	9.4	31.9	16.0	6.0	0.8	67.6	27.7	51.5	48.5
92410	SAN BERNARDINO	37.9	36.1	14.5	13.4	4.0	3.9	61.8	66.0	11.8	10.6	10.7	9.1	8.8	27.5	15.2	5.6	0.7	61.4	24.5	49.4	50.6
92411	SAN BERNARDINO	28.4	28.3	24.7	22.9	2.4	2.2	66.8	69.6	10.4	10.1	11.4	9.6	7.6	25.3	16.4	8.3	1.0	62.2	25.8	49.0	51.0
92501	RIVERSIDE	56.9	52.6	9.0	8.9	2.8	2.8	42.8	48.5	8.4	7.7	8.4	7.7	8.9	31.8	18.8	6.6	1.7	71.2	30.2	51.3	48.7
92503	RIVERSIDE	59.8	56.0	5.4	5.4	5.3	5.5	43.5	48.7	9.2	8.4	9.2	8.6	8.6	29.1	19.3	6.7	1.0	67.9	29.0	49.4	50.6
92504	RIVERSIDE	64.6	61.5	6.7	6.6	3.8	3.9	35.2	40.0	7.6	7.1	8.3	8.1	8.8	27.5	21.3	9.6	1.7	72.2	32.2	48.7	51.3
92505	RIVERSIDE	57.2	53.2	5.8	5.6	5.5	5.6	45.2	50.9	8.6	8.0	9.2	8.7	9.4	29.6	19.1	6.6	0.9	69.3	28.8	49.9	50.1
92506	RIVERSIDE	76.0	72.7	5.7	6.0	5.5	6.3	19.1	22.7	5.8	6.3	7.8	7.5	6.7	25.5	27.7	10.9	1.7	75.4	38.9	48.3	51.7
92507	RIVERSIDE	43.9	41.7	11.9	11.4	10.9	11.3	43.0	45.8	8.6	7.0	7.0	10.0	15.3	29.4	16.1	6.0	0.7	73.7	26.1	49.7	50.3
92508	RIVERSIDE	69.8	66.4	8.5	8.7	6.6	7.3	21.9	25.7	8.3	8.6	9.5	7.9	5.8	31.7	22.3	5.5	0.4	68.3	32.8	49.1	50.9
92509	RIVERSIDE	56.8	53.0	5.2	5.0	2.7	2.7	50.1	55.6	8.7	8.6	9.8	8.9	8.3	27.8	20.8	6.2	0.7	67.4	29.1	50.5	49.5
92518	MARCH AIR FORCE BASE	86.4	84.2	7.0	7.7	1.9	2.2	3.9	5.0	2.9	2.9	4.5	2.6	2.6	11.4	6.4	54.7	12.0	87.9	77.2	48.2	51.8
92521	RIVERSIDE	33.5	30.9	11.5	11.2	40.0	40.8	19.4	22.2	0.0	0.2	0.0	86.6	11.4	1.5	0.2	0.1	0.0	98.3	17.9	47.5	52.5
92530	LAKE ELSINORE	69.3	65.5	4.1	4.2	2.0	2.1	36.2	41.6	9.3	9.0	9.9	8.3	7.5	29.3	19.2	6.8	0.7	66.5	29.6	49.8	50.2
92532	LAKE ELSINORE	80.1	76.7	3.3	3.7	2.7	3.0	21.4	25.8	7.9	8.4	9.1	7.0	5.6	26.9	25.1	9.3	0.6	70.0	36.0	49.7	50.3
92536	AGUANGA	85.6	82.8	1.1	1.2	1.4	1.6	18.5	22.8	6.4	7.2	8.6	6.3	3.6	22.6	30.0	14.4	0.9	73.8	42.3	51.5	48.5
92539	ANZA	85.1	82.6	0.6	0.6	0.8	0.9	17.8	21.8	5.4	5.9	8.2	7.3	4.5	20.2	29.8	17.4	1.3	75.3	44.0	50.5	49.5
92543	HEMET	76.8	73.3	2.8	2.9	1.5	1.6	29.6	34.8	7.8	6.7	6.6	6.2	7.3	21.3	18.0	20.7	5.5	75.3	39.5	46.4	53.6
92544	HEMET	82.3	79.2	1.6	1.7	1.6	1.8	20.0	24.2	6.6	6.6	8.2	7.6	6.4	22.4	22.9	15.9	3.4	73.8	39.2	48.1	51.9
92545	HEMET	85.9	82.9	2.2	2.5	1.4	1.6	15.1	18.8	5.1	4.6	5.0	4.5	4.5	16.7	19.1	32.2	8.4	82.4	55.9	45.5	54.5
92548	HOMELAND	80.0	76.0	0.7	0.8	0.7	0.8	28.8	34.6	5.4	5.9	7.0	6.4	5.5	20.2	22.1	24.2	3.4	77.9	44.7	48.4	51.6
92549	IDYLLWILD	90.1	87.9	0.9	0.9	0.7	0.8	9.6	12.1	3.2	4.0	5.7	6.8	4.4	20.3	37.3	16.9	1.4	82.4	48.0	51.0	49.0
92551	MORENO VALLEY	40.7	38.2	23.2	22.6	7.2	7.2	41.6	46.1	9.8	9.1	10.5	9.5	8.7	28.9	18.3	4.9	0.3	64.6	26.6	48.9	51.1
92553	MORENO VALLEY	42.0	39.4	20.5	19.6	6.1	6.0	45.3	50.1	10.1	9.5	10.9	10.1	9.2	27.6	17.6	4.7	0.4	63.3	25.2	48.7	51.3
92555	MORENO VALLEY	60.7	57.2	15.3	15.2	5.5	5.9	27.5	32.1	6.9	7.2	9.1	9.3	7.8	26.5	25.3	7.3	0.5	70.5	32.9	49.7	50.4
92557	MORENO VALLEY	53.1	49.6	18.5	18.4	6.6	6.9	30.6	35.3	8.0	7.9	9.4	8.7	8.2	28.3	23.0	6.1	0.5	69.2	30.2	48.7	51.3
92561	MOUNTAIN CENTER	85.5	83.8	1.1	1.3	1.1	1.2	14.3	16.9	4.6	4.0	6.4	5.9	3.6	21.3	38.1	15.3	0.8	80.8	46.8	52.8	47.3
92562	MURRIETA	82.5	79.8	3.2	3.5	4.1	4.5	17.2	21.0	7.7	8.6	10.0	8.1	5.0	27.7	20.7	11.2	1.1	68.4	35.5	49.1	51.0
92563	MURRIETA	79.3	75.0	3.6	4.1	4.7	5.3	18.1	22.5	8.1	8.0	9.1	8.3	7.5	27.8	19.2	11.0	1.1	70.1	32.8	48.8	51.2
92567	NUEVO	73.9	69.6	2.6	2.7	1.1	1.1	32.9	39.0	7.0	7.1	8.9	8.2	6.6	24.5	25.5	11.2	1.0	71.7	36.5	50.3	49.7
92570	PERRIS	50.1	47.4	13.3	12.6	1.5	1.5	49.1	54.0	8.7	8.8	9.9	8.8	7.4	25.6	21.0	8.8	1.0	67.1	30.1	50.5	49.5
92571	PERRIS	42.4	39.8	16.1	15.2	3.8	3.7	54.7	59.7	11.2	10.5	11.4	9.3	7.8	29.6	15.1	4.7	0.6	61.2	25.0	49.1	50.9
92582	SAN JACINTO	79.8	77.1	2.2	2.3	1.2	1.3	26.4	31.1	6.7	6.9	7.7	6.3	5.1	24.4	21.0	18.8	3.3	74.8	40.2	48.5	51.5
92583	SAN JACINTO	68.8	65.7	2.6	2.6	1.3	1.4	40.7	45.4	8.3	8.2	8.8	7.5	6.7	24.6	19.2	14.6	2.1	70.0	34.2	48.4	51.6
92584	MENIFEE	84.8	82.1	1.5	1.6	2.6	2.9	18.6	22.7	7.2	7.7	9.5	7.8	5.4	27.1	22.2	12.2	0.9	70.6	36.6	50.0	50.0
92585	SUN CITY	73.5	69.5	2.7	2.8	1.8	1.9	32.4	38.0	6.9	7.0	8.3	7.2	6.2	23.1	21.7	17.5	2.3	73.3	38.6	48.1	51.9
92586	SUN CITY	89.6	87.7	2.2	2.4	1.4	1.5	12.6	15.4	3.4	3.7	4.6	3.6	2.2	12.4	18.1	42.8	9.2	85.8	66.1	43.9	56.1
92587	SUN CITY	86.6	83.6	1.3	1.5	2.0	2.2	17.2	21.6	6.8	7.5	8.7	7.5	4.9	26.3	24.8	12.5	1.0	72.2	38.4	49.8	50.2
92590	TEMECULA	70.7	66.7	2.0	2.0	3.1	3.3	39.4	45.6	9.3	8.7	8.1	7.7	8.7	26.6	21.8	8.4	0.8	69.7	30.9	51.1	48.9
92591	TEMECULA	78.9	74.6	3.1	3.5	4.7	5.2	19.8	24.6	8.5	8.3	9.4	8.6	8.1	29.4	20.3	6.8	0.7	68.5	30.7	49.8	50.2
92592	TEMECULA	79.1	75.9	3.8	4.1	5.3	6.0	16.8	20.2	9.2	9.5	10.0	7.7	5.5	30.9	20.2	6.6	0.5	66.3	32.7	49.1	50.9
92595	WILDOMAR	81.4	78.3	1.9	2.1	2.3	2.5	22.5	27.0	7.0	7.6	9.4	7.9	6.0	26.3	23.8	10.6	1.3	70.8	36.4	49.7	50.3
92596	WINCHESTER	78.4	73.9	3.2	4.1	2.9	3.7	24.1	26.9	8.0	8.1	9.5	8.4	7.0	30.1	20.5	7.9	0.6	69.2	32.5	51.0	49.0
92602	IRVINE	53.4	48.9	1.1	1.1	38.6	41.8	7.3	8.8	11.9	10.9	6.3	3.2	2.6	44.9	17.2	2.9	0.1	68.8	34.1	49.3	50.7
92603	IRVINE	78.9	75.6	0.3	0.3	17.2	19.7	3.2	4.0	5.5	6.8	7.5	5.5	3.1	21.8	33.0	14.6	2.2	76.4	44.9	48.8	51.2
92604	IRVINE	68.4	64.5	1.1	1.1	23.6	26.2	8.0	9.8	5.3	6.2	7.9	7.5	6.3	27.0	29.3	9.3	1.3	76.0	38.8	48.1	51.9
92606	IRVINE	49.2	44.6	2.2	2.3	40.0	43.1	7.8	9.3	7.9	7.1	6.8	6.1	7.6	38.4	21.1	4.8	0.3	74.7	33.4	48.7	51.3
92610	FOOTHILL RANCH	74.2	70.5	1.9	1.9	15.2	16.9	11.2	14.0	12.2	11.3	8.0	4.0	3.4	41.5	17.2	2.3	0.2	65.8	33.1	49.8	50.2
92612	IRVINE	63.5	58.8	1.3	1.3	28.0	31.3	6.1	7.3	3.6	4.4	6.0	10.5	15.7	24.4	24.9	8.7	1.8	82.3	33.2	48.1	51.9
92614	IRVINE	61.3	57.0	1.4	1.4	28.9	31.8	7.6	9.1	5.8	6.4	7.9	7.2	7.3	33.2	26.1	5.8	0.4	75.5	35.4	48.6	51.4
92618	IRVINE	62.0	57.2	2.3	2.3	22.0	24.9	15.0	16.9	5.6	4.9	4.4	5.5	8.4	46.7	19.6	4.4	0.3	82.6	33.6	55.4	44.6
92620	IRVINE	65.0	60.3	1.2	1.2	27.6	31.1	6.8	8.3	6.7	7.5	8.3	6.9	5.7	29.9	27.2	6.9	0.9	73.1	36.9	48.4	51.6
92624	CAPISTRANO BEACH	90.1	88.0	0.5	0.6	2.0	2.3	13.5	17.3	5.2	5.4	6.3	5.9	5.5	26.0	28.8	14.5	2.4	79.3	42.5	50.2	49.8
92625	CORONA DEL MAR	93.3	91.9	0.3	0.3	4.0	4.7	3.8	5.0	3.6	4.1	4.4	3.7	3.4	30.8	29.3	17.8	2.9	85.5	45.1	47.4	52.7
92626	COSTA MESA	71.7	67.9	1.8	1.9	12.5	13.5	19.1	23.1	5.8	5.4	5.8	6.7	9.5	34.6	21.7	9.4	1.1	79.6	34.3	50.4	49.6
92627	COSTA MESA	68.3	64.7	1.1	1.1	3.6	3.8	40.7	45.8	8.0	7.1	7.3	6.4	7.9	37.9	18.5	6.0	1.1	74.0	32.1	51.9	48.1
92629	DANA POINT	86.9	84.8	0.9	0.9	2.7	3.2	15.5	18.3	5.4	5.3	5.4	5.3	6.0	28.6	29.8	13.0	1.3	80.8	41.4	49.5	50.5
92630	LAKE FOREST	75.8	71.8	1.8	1.9	9.8	10.8	19.1	23.7	7.1	7.4	7.8	6.4	6.1	31.2	24.7	7.4	1.9	73.8	35.9	49.2	50.8
92646	HUNTINGTON BEACH	83.1	80.2	0.7	0.7	9.5	10.8	9.4	12.1	5.6	6.0	6.6	5.7	5.4	29.5	27.8	12.0	1.5	78.2	40.0	49.5	50.5
92647	HUNTINGTON BEACH	69.9	66.4	1.2	1.2	12.0	13.1	24.3	28.0	7.5	7.1	7.4	6.5	7.5	33.6	21.3	8.2	0.8	74.1	33.5	50.4	49.6
92648	HUNTINGTON BEACH	82.2	78.9	0.6	0.6	8.2	9.4	12.3	15.5	5.7	5.3	5.2	5.0	7.1	36.9	24.4	8.7	1.7	80.9	36.6	50.1	49.9
92649	HUNTINGTON BEACH	84.9	82.0	0.6	0.6	7.5	8.6	9.8	12.7	5.2	5.4	5.8	5.1	5.3	31.3	28.1	12.6	1.3	80.5	40.5	50.1	50.0
92651	LAGUNA BEACH	92.3	90.7	0.7	0.8	2.1	2.4	6.6	8.6	3.9	4.5	4.8	4.3	3.8	27.9	34.6	13.9	2.3	84.0	45.4	50.6	49.4
92653	LAGUNA HILLS	83.0	80.1	1.1	1.1	7.7	8.8	11.9	14.7	4.3	4.7	5.4	4.7	3.8	19.2	22.4	25.2	10.2	82.5	51.5	43.8	56.2
92655	MIDWAY CITY	41.5	38.1	1.1	1.1	42.0	43.2	22.4	25.8	7.3	6.9	7.2	6.9	7.6	31.7	22.4	9.0	1.1	74.5	34.2	50.1	49.9
92656	ALISO VIEJO	78.0	74.7	2.1	2.1	11.1	12.6	12.7	15.3	9.7	8.4	6.5	4.3	4.7	43.2	18.2	4.0	0.8	72.6	33.8	48.0	52.0
92657	NEWPORT COAST	82.2	78.3	0.5	0.4	13.8	16.9	3.8	5.0	8.0	8.4	5.9	4.2	3.3	31.6	30.3	7.9	0.4	75.0	39.7	48.8	51.2
92660	NEWPORT BEACH	91.2	89.3	0.5	0.6	5.4	6.4	4.1	5.4	5.1	5.9	6.3	5.1	3.8	25.3	29.9	16.6	2.1	79.5	44.2	48.5	51.5
92661	NEWPORT BEACH	94.1	92.7	0.6	0.6	1.5	1.8	5.2	6.8	3.1	2.8	3.8	4.0	5.6	38.8	25.8	14.4	1.8	87.9	40.0	52.7	47.3
92662	NEWPORT BEACH	94.9	93.7	0.4	0.5	2.2	2.6	3.2	4.2	2.6	2.4	2.7	3.8	5.6	28.6	31.6	19.2	3.5	90.3	48.4	44.5	55.5
	CALIFORNIA	59.6	57.1	6.7	6.5	11.3	11.8	32.4	35.5	7.4	7.1	7.8	7.3	7.7	29.8	22.1	9.3	1.4	73.3	33.8	49.8	50.2
	UNITED STATES	75.1	73.6	12.3	12.5	3.8	4.2	12.5	14.1	6.9	6.7	7.2	7.0	7.3	28.6	23.8	10.8	1.7	75.1	36.0	49.1	50.9

#	POST OFFICE NAME	2004 Per Capita Income	2004 HH Income Base	2004 HOUSEHOLD INCOME DISTRIBUTION (%) Less than $25,000	$25,000 to $49,999	$50,000 to $99,999	$100,000 to $149,999	$150,000 or More	MEDIAN HOUSEHOLD INCOME 2004	2009	2004 National Centile	2004 State Centile	2004 Home Value Base	2004 HOME VALUE DISTRIBUTION (%) Less than $50,000	$50,000 to $89,999	$90,000 to $174,999	$175,000 to $399,999	$400,000 or More	2004 Median Home Value
92356	LUCERNE VALLEY	16092	2080	42.8	24.0	26.5	5.8	0.9	32486	37952	19	15	1513	11.8	16.9	51.6	17.8	2.0	119886
92358	LYTLE CREEK	22194	304	30.9	26.6	28.0	12.8	1.6	42027	48006	53	36	246	6.9	7.3	49.6	33.3	2.9	155233
92359	MENTONE	21999	2794	24.1	28.7	31.5	11.2	4.5	47165	54590	66	46	1938	9.4	3.2	27.7	52.9	6.9	204253
92363	NEEDLES	17079	2281	45.4	25.6	23.0	4.2	1.8	28713	33608	10	8	1359	19.1	18.0	47.5	13.0	2.4	109862
92364	NIPTON	19437	92	32.6	43.5	18.5	4.4	1.1	35773	40650	31	22	56	42.9	3.6	25.0	14.3	14.3	106250
92365	NEWBERRY SPRINGS	16416	1761	40.2	27.1	26.3	5.3	1.1	34362	38978	25	19	1268	16.6	18.0	46.6	14.7	4.1	108438
92368	ORO GRANDE	13005	333	47.8	32.1	13.8	4.2	2.1	26272	29554	6	6	193	7.8	21.8	52.3	14.0	4.2	116827
92371	PHELAN	18755	4430	24.0	26.4	36.6	10.0	3.0	49505	55696	71	51	3635	3.4	7.0	49.8	36.5	3.2	155217
92372	PINON HILLS	18146	1465	28.3	26.1	35.8	7.7	2.1	43957	51205	59	40	1221	3.2	7.1	37.3	49.6	2.9	181527
92373	REDLANDS	35408	14863	19.1	25.9	29.4	13.6	12.1	55235	64257	80	61	8388	1.5	1.3	13.1	55.3	28.9	293056
92374	REDLANDS	22047	13857	22.0	27.3	33.6	12.5	4.6	50598	58520	73	53	9089	6.0	4.9	24.6	61.3	3.2	208816
92376	RIALTO	13483	21018	27.9	32.7	29.9	7.7	1.8	40967	46528	50	34	12888	8.5	2.4	49.3	39.4	0.4	163078
92377	RIALTO	20805	5664	11.0	23.0	44.2	17.0	4.9	64425	74579	88	72	5099	2.3	1.4	12.9	82.6	0.8	228619
92382	RUNNING SPRINGS	32184	220	6.4	28.2	40.5	10.5	14.6	67073	78692	90	75	188	0.0	0.0	16.5	44.2	39.4	297222
92384	SHOSHONE	24888	102	35.3	23.5	30.4	10.8	0.0	39294	43639	44	29	41	46.3	19.5	9.8	12.2	12.2	53750
92385	SKYFOREST	25824	835	13.2	27.0	38.2	15.3	6.4	61019	70831	85	69	667	0.0	1.8	29.1	68.2	0.9	215070
92389	TECOPA	20829	36	36.1	25.0	30.6	8.3	0.0	38165	45000	40	27	14	57.1	14.3	7.1	7.1	14.3	35000
92392	VICTORVILLE	17981	22785	27.6	28.7	32.6	8.1	3.0	43947	50650	58	40	15869	3.5	4.5	48.6	40.9	2.6	164738
92394	VICTORVILLE	14860	4777	36.7	27.7	29.0	5.1	1.6	35619	40943	30	21	2794	8.1	7.4	62.6	21.1	0.8	139558
92397	WRIGHTWOOD	25490	1836	21.4	23.3	36.4	11.6	7.3	55183	64385	80	61	1357	0.8	0.9	15.5	72.4	10.4	243214
92399	YUCAIPA	22150	16486	27.7	27.6	28.2	11.7	4.8	44349	51818	60	41	12365	25.9	2.6	19.6	43.7	8.2	181928
92401	SAN BERNARDINO	8142	587	64.9	23.9	9.5	1.4	0.3	17438	19245	1	2	107	3.7	3.7	88.8	1.9	1.9	123355
92404	SAN BERNARDINO	15698	18514	37.2	29.4	24.7	6.6	2.2	34251	38969	25	18	9660	2.5	1.9	60.3	32.9	2.5	153286
92405	SAN BERNARDINO	14599	9637	37.8	30.8	23.8	5.9	1.7	33232	38152	22	16	4855	1.0	2.9	68.0	26.0	2.2	145214
92407	SAN BERNARDINO	18091	17355	24.1	28.3	33.9	10.3	3.5	47752	54308	68	47	10960	2.1	2.3	42.0	48.7	4.9	182063
92408	SAN BERNARDINO	11597	4262	47.0	28.2	20.1	3.8	0.9	26986	30890	7	6	1854	12.7	8.5	43.6	34.7	0.5	148571
92410	SAN BERNARDINO	9975	12482	48.9	30.6	16.7	2.8	1.0	25567	28361	5	5	5668	25.5	8.9	51.2	13.3	1.2	118192
92411	SAN BERNARDINO	10361	6746	48.4	28.2	18.1	3.6	1.7	25968	29854	6	5	3833	5.0	10.8	74.3	9.6	0.4	127258
92501	RIVERSIDE	17451	6663	35.4	30.5	24.7	6.5	2.8	35109	40176	28	20	3074	1.4	3.0	47.3	45.5	2.8	172500
92503	RIVERSIDE	18769	22806	22.5	29.7	32.5	10.8	4.6	47824	54409	68	48	14560	7.0	3.4	22.5	58.8	8.4	206714
92504	RIVERSIDE	20884	17224	24.6	30.2	30.5	10.0	4.7	45969	52674	64	43	10560	2.1	1.9	30.7	55.0	10.4	200511
92505	RIVERSIDE	17818	12554	20.4	33.3	31.4	10.4	4.5	46832	53194	66	45	7258	3.8	1.1	20.3	71.6	3.2	216950
92506	RIVERSIDE	34570	15991	14.6	20.5	32.3	19.3	13.3	70245	82673	91	78	12287	0.5	0.4	10.5	64.5	24.2	289068
92507	RIVERSIDE	18145	18364	38.4	25.9	23.3	9.1	3.3	34808	40700	27	19	6802	4.6	3.0	30.9	55.6	5.9	199809
92508	RIVERSIDE	27178	7332	8.0	14.3	41.8	27.4	8.6	80529	94626	95	86	6738	1.0	1.0	6.1	80.3	11.6	286232
92509	RIVERSIDE	16907	19233	23.1	26.3	36.0	10.8	3.8	50499	57270	73	53	14006	7.1	2.8	29.3	57.8	2.9	202896
92518	MARCH AIR FORCE BASE	44145	506	13.4	12.3	48.0	15.8	10.5	73146	82527	93	80	83	9.6	7.2	3.6	53.0	26.5	283000
92521	RIVERSIDE	18402	0	0.0	0.0	0.0	0.0	0.0	0	0	0	0	0	0.0	0.0	0.0	0.0	0.0	0
92530	LAKE ELSINORE	17534	13613	28.2	27.5	30.7	10.4	3.3	44547	51205	60	41	8951	4.4	5.0	30.2	55.9	4.6	203662
92532	LAKE ELSINORE	24711	1609	16.2	18.9	37.1	18.3	9.5	64904	76656	88	72	1325	2.8	2.6	17.7	48.5	28.4	306066
92536	AGUANGA	21869	982	28.1	27.6	29.6	10.7	4.0	44409	51104	60	41	802	4.2	4.4	29.4	49.0	13.0	203535
92539	ANZA	17065	1582	36.0	33.3	23.8	5.1	2.0	32748	37916	20	15	1219	9.2	6.6	37.9	42.3	4.0	168456
92543	HEMET	16181	13185	46.4	31.6	17.3	3.3	1.5	26878	30952	7	6	7912	26.1	19.8	40.2	11.7	2.3	97247
92544	HEMET	20092	15677	31.5	27.5	28.3	9.1	3.7	40865	47268	49	34	11448	11.1	5.7	41.9	34.8	6.6	152983
92545	HEMET	21253	12818	35.8	34.7	23.4	4.5	1.8	33850	38432	24	18	9530	22.7	16.1	31.8	27.5	1.8	126398
92548	HOMELAND	14531	2313	47.6	32.3	15.7	3.4	1.0	25937	29137	6	5	1840	15.6	36.3	31.7	13.9	2.6	88440
92549	IDYLLWILD	26546	1782	30.2	27.7	28.5	7.7	6.0	40796	48155	49	34	1202	3.9	2.1	11.7	67.0	15.3	254726
92551	MORENO VALLEY	15797	6715	17.9	27.4	41.1	10.8	2.8	54235	62197	79	59	5328	3.3	1.1	42.4	52.4	0.8	179509
92553	MORENO VALLEY	13621	17647	27.8	31.3	30.2	9.0	1.7	42731	48333	55	37	10705	2.2	2.5	56.7	38.0	0.7	159934
92555	MORENO VALLEY	22423	4754	13.6	21.7	39.6	19.3	5.8	65576	75783	89	73	4136	3.1	0.6	21.4	68.0	7.0	228128
92557	MORENO VALLEY	20507	14932	13.7	25.6	41.0	15.3	4.4	60273	68034	85	68	11257	1.7	1.1	24.3	69.7	3.2	217234
92561	MOUNTAIN CENTER	26705	715	26.0	27.1	30.4	9.5	7.0	47301	54165	67	46	559	5.4	8.1	24.3	33.1	29.2	225633
92562	MURRIETA	28843	15705	13.1	20.2	37.8	19.3	9.7	67608	79416	90	76	12596	0.8	0.6	2.9	72.4	23.4	313121
92563	MURRIETA	22976	7873	16.4	24.7	36.9	16.3	5.8	58568	67786	83	66	6329	0.4	1.5	16.2	73.6	8.3	269110
92567	NUEVO	18440	2652	22.5	26.4	38.2	9.5	3.4	50632	57815	73	53	2057	1.5	3.9	39.6	47.7	7.2	189500
92570	PERRIS	13803	11458	34.6	29.5	25.4	7.8	2.7	36582	41712	34	23	8025	5.7	14.0	39.8	30.9	9.7	148882
92571	PERRIS	12900	7631	24.2	35.5	31.4	7.8	1.1	43221	48791	57	38	5413	2.4	5.5	61.3	29.0	1.8	145750
92582	SAN JACINTO	15917	1866	33.9	36.2	25.4	3.5	1.0	35339	39918	29	21	1456	12.6	20.1	47.5	18.3	1.6	124725
92583	SAN JACINTO	14777	8185	40.4	29.3	23.8	5.3	1.2	31742	36657	17	13	5460	25.2	12.1	36.7	24.7	1.2	120094
92584	MENIFEE	22218	6511	14.8	26.6	40.7	13.4	4.5	57538	66047	82	64	5579	1.5	2.2	15.2	73.6	7.7	242554
92585	SUN CITY	16615	3953	31.9	32.4	28.0	6.6	1.2	36916	42798	35	24	2953	8.4	6.0	36.3	47.3	2.0	173897
92586	SUN CITY	21699	9830	37.6	34.5	21.4	4.8	1.6	32548	37509	19	15	8261	6.0	6.6	48.8	38.6	0.0	150379
92587	SUN CITY	29471	5509	14.8	20.3	35.9	19.2	9.9	65852	77511	89	73	4676	0.4	2.3	13.9	53.4	30.0	310536
92590	TEMECULA	26776	1153	37.9	21.9	15.0	10.7	14.6	35791	42381	31	22	543	0.0	0.2	4.2	21.6	74.0	744213
92591	TEMECULA	25042	10689	12.1	21.1	41.3	18.4	7.2	65536	77658	89	73	7631	2.8	1.0	3.0	71.9	21.4	303296
92592	TEMECULA	27677	18545	8.7	16.0	43.8	22.4	9.1	76035	88420	94	83	15774	0.4	0.4	3.1	70.9	25.3	313682
92595	WILDOMAR	22745	7190	18.7	24.9	37.6	13.2	5.7	55938	64569	81	62	6136	1.7	3.4	22.1	66.2	6.6	224493
92596	WINCHESTER	25506	1965	10.5	22.7	43.1	17.2	6.6	65328	77611	89	73	1674	0.6	1.7	12.3	68.9	16.6	280248
92602	IRVINE	53266	1913	3.2	2.6	26.8	38.5	29.0	119066	140146	99	97	1847	0.1	3.5	1.1	14.9	80.5	577510
92603	IRVINE	60230	1195	6.6	11.7	22.9	22.1	36.7	116678	143288	99	97	1090	0.8	1.1	1.6	12.0	84.5	697329
92604	IRVINE	35323	10699	11.2	15.0	35.2	22.3	16.4	81383	99940	95	87	7640	2.3	2.8	1.4	34.8	58.8	436201
92606	IRVINE	37503	7580	11.5	13.9	33.7	23.4	17.6	83820	104584	96	89	4204	2.2	1.6	0.9	28.5	66.8	486220
92610	FOOTHILL RANCH	44538	4847	3.1	8.2	36.2	31.0	21.5	102658	124603	98	95	4005	0.4	0.4	0.1	23.8	75.4	494470
92612	IRVINE	45430	12091	18.2	16.6	27.4	17.3	20.6	73501	91893	93	81	6017	0.9	0.7	0.7	20.7	77.0	575513
92614	IRVINE	41688	8816	9.2	14.3	35.0	22.2	19.3	85727	105547	96	90	5301	0.8	1.4	0.8	37.0	60.0	451110
92618	IRVINE	39342	2564	10.7	15.9	41.9	18.9	12.6	69857	87037	91	78	1283	0.2	2.7	7.6	61.5	28.1	310064
92620	IRVINE	43671	9951	7.9	12.3	29.9	24.2	25.8	99832	119709	98	94	7886	0.6	1.2	3.0	22.4	72.8	528356
92624	CAPISTRANO BEACH	38474	2782	13.7	19.6	36.3	15.4	15.0	67677	83562	90	76	1912	2.4	4.8	5.1	25.3	62.5	478289
92625	CORONA DEL MAR	99736	6265	7.9	13.0	20.5	18.9	39.7	121468	155703	99	98	4208	0.0	0.0	0.4	1.2	98.4	1000001
92626	COSTA MESA	32275	17962	13.5	21.5	38.3	16.2	10.5	65863	79477	89	74	8550	0.2	0.1	0.5	35.0	64.2	440152
92627	COSTA MESA	25472	23220	19.4	26.9	34.0	12.4	7.4	53312	64545	77	58	8590	7.8	2.8	1.3	38.6	49.5	397693
92629	DANA POINT	48719	11952	11.5	17.4	33.4	18.9	19.0	77343	98175	94	84	7462	0.4	0.3	2.6	16.7	80.1	601927
92630	LAKE FOREST	33169	21778	9.5	19.4	36.2	21.2	13.8	76731	91123	94	83	15950	2.0	3.9	5.8	36.0	52.4	409554
92646	HUNTINGTON BEACH	37115	21813	10.1	17.5	35.2	23.0	14.3	79142	97190	95	85	16920	1.5	2.6	4.2	27.4	64.3	459037
92647	HUNTINGTON BEACH	27645	20189	13.4	22.7	37.7	17.7	8.5	64779	77397	88	72	10663	2.0	2.0	2.1	29.4	64.4	441108
92648	HUNTINGTON BEACH	47157	18291	13.8	18.4	30.7	17.9	19.2	76606	96031	94	83	9483	1.9	2.9	3.4	17.6	74.1	595353
92649	HUNTINGTON BEACH	49763	14029	9.7	15.8	35.4	21.3	17.8	81272	100359	95	87	9262	2.1	3.7	4.2	26.5	63.5	467844
92651	LAGUNA BEACH	78199	11978	10.4	14.7	27.8	19.3	27.9	93396	121653	97	92	7621	0.6	0.8	1.4	5.9	91.3	1000001
92653	LAGUNA HILLS	41356	22521	22.6	23.6	28.4	12.9	12.6	54614	65591	79	60	18405	1.1	3.7	29.7	33.9	31.6	246681
92655	MIDWAY CITY	19225	2205	24.0	18.6	35.1	17.6	4.6	56899	68542	82	64	1222	4.6	3.2	3.5	59.4	29.3	325369
92656	ALISO VIEJO	40985	20773	6.3	13.2	39.7	25.3	15.4	85297	105481	96	89	13746	0.4	0.4	1.3	47.0	51.0	403848
92657	NEWPORT COAST	110847	2860	4.3	5.4	20.7	21.1	48.5	145542	187783	100	99	2180	0.0	0.0	0.1	0.9	99.0	1000001
92660	NEWPORT BEACH	87190	14179	8.2	12.0	22.1	19.7	38.1	116086	145948	99	97	9128	0.7	1.2	1.5	5.2	91.4	1000001
92661	NEWPORT BEACH	66341	1969	9.9	16.5	29.9	16.9	26.8	84115	113702	96	89	959	0.9	0.0	0.0	0.8	98.2	1000001
92662	NEWPORT BEACH	92977	1702	10.6	15.2	26.3	19.5	28.6	94045	126407	98	93	783	0.0	0.0	3.3	0.6	96.0	1000001
	CALIFORNIA	27293		21.8	24.4	30.5	13.7	9.7	54267	64547				3.3	2.7	13.3	42.9	37.9	319678
	UNITED STATES	25866		24.7	27.1	30.8	10.9	6.5	48124	56710				10.9	15.0	33.7	30.1	10.4	145905

#	POST OFFICE NAME	FINANCIAL SERVICES: Auto Loan	Home Loan	Invest-ments	Retire-ment Plans	THE HOME: Home Improvements: Home Repair	Lawn & Garden	Furnishings: Comput-ers & Hard-ware	Major Appli-ances	TV, Radio, Sound Equip-ment	Furni-ture	ENTERTAINMENT: Dine out/Carry out	Sports Equip-ment	Fees & Tickets	Toys & Games	Travel	Cable TV	PERSONAL: Apparel & Services	Auto Repairs	Health Insur-ance	Pets & Supplies
92356	LUCERNE VALLEY	70	51	31	48	57	67	54	62	62	52	73	71	48	69	54	66	66	62	75	79
92358	LYTLE CREEK	95	68	38	65	79	87	67	82	76	66	90	98	58	88	69	80	82	80	96	113
92359	MENTONE	89	85	82	85	86	92	87	88	87	86	108	102	85	108	86	86	104	88	87	100
92363	NEEDLES	62	52	50	50	55	64	57	59	61	56	75	66	54	70	57	64	70	60	67	69
92364	NIPTON	59	51	38	48	53	58	48	54	51	49	62	63	45	60	49	52	59	54	58	68
92365	NEWBERRY SPRINGS	70	53	34	50	57	66	55	62	62	54	73	71	49	69	55	64	67	62	72	78
92368	ORO GRANDE	57	50	42	47	48	51	51	55	53	56	67	59	47	59	49	51	66	56	52	58
92371	PHELAN	90	83	67	80	83	88	79	84	80	81	98	98	75	94	78	79	95	84	83	100
92372	PINON HILLS	88	70	46	67	76	82	68	78	73	68	88	93	61	85	69	75	83	78	86	102
92373	REDLANDS	109	118	139	120	116	123	119	116	115	118	145	136	121	144	119	112	142	118	109	127
92374	REDLANDS	91	93	96	93	90	94	92	92	90	94	114	106	92	110	90	87	112	93	85	100
92376	RIALTO	74	69	66	66	67	70	71	73	72	75	91	81	68	86	68	69	90	74	68	78
92377	RIALTO	104	115	112	117	111	110	106	106	99	109	126	124	108	126	104	94	124	104	94	117
92382	RUNNING SPRINGS	141	111	76	100	125	140	104	126	118	104	140	147	93	138	111	126	130	124	149	172
92384	SHOSHONE	59	62	81	63	61	68	65	63	66	65	83	72	67	83	66	66	81	65	63	69
92385	SKYFOREST	109	99	82	93	106	114	92	103	97	91	117	121	88	118	96	100	111	101	113	132
92389	TECOPA	59	62	81	63	61	68	65	63	66	65	83	72	67	83	66	66	81	65	63	69
92392	VICTORVILLE	78	78	74	78	77	81	76	78	76	78	95	89	76	92	75	74	92	78	75	86
92394	VICTORVILLE	63	63	66	64	62	65	65	64	64	65	81	75	64	80	64	62	79	65	60	70
92397	WRIGHTWOOD	112	88	61	80	99	111	84	100	94	83	111	118	75	110	89	100	104	99	117	136
92399	YUCAIPA	85	86	84	84	86	92	84	86	84	84	104	99	84	103	85	84	101	86	87	98
92401	SAN BERNARDINO	33	27	34	26	26	30	32	31	35	34	44	36	31	42	31	35	44	34	32	35
92404	SAN BERNARDINO	65	63	69	62	62	67	67	66	69	68	86	76	67	85	66	68	84	68	65	72
92405	SAN BERNARDINO	63	58	62	58	56	60	63	62	64	64	80	72	61	77	60	61	79	64	59	67
92407	SAN BERNARDINO	85	82	79	82	81	84	82	84	82	84	103	97	80	99	80	79	100	85	79	94
92408	SAN BERNARDINO	53	47	50	47	46	49	52	51	53	54	67	59	50	64	49	51	66	54	48	56
92410	SAN BERNARDINO	52	45	45	44	44	47	49	51	52	52	65	56	47	61	47	50	65	53	48	54
92411	SAN BERNARDINO	57	50	45	46	48	51	52	55	55	56	69	60	49	62	50	54	68	57	53	59
92501	RIVERSIDE	67	65	70	65	64	68	69	68	69	70	86	79	67	84	67	67	85	70	65	74
92503	RIVERSIDE	88	88	90	88	86	90	89	89	88	91	111	102	88	108	87	84	109	90	83	97
92504	RIVERSIDE	84	89	97	89	87	92	90	88	88	89	110	103	90	111	89	86	109	89	83	96
92505	RIVERSIDE	84	84	90	83	81	85	85	85	84	88	107	96	84	105	83	82	106	86	79	92
92506	RIVERSIDE	127	147	164	148	145	149	140	138	133	140	167	159	146	171	141	130	166	136	128	150
92507	RIVERSIDE	70	62	70	65	61	65	74	69	74	73	93	84	70	89	69	69	91	74	64	75
92508	RIVERSIDE	129	147	145	152	141	138	134	133	123	138	156	155	138	158	131	116	155	129	114	145
92509	RIVERSIDE	90	89	85	87	86	88	88	90	87	92	110	101	86	106	85	83	109	91	83	97
92518	MARCH AIR FORCE BASE	114	118	137	123	119	125	121	120	117	120	146	141	121	142	120	113	142	121	115	131
92521	RIVERSIDE	0	0	0	0	0	0	0	0	0	0	0	0	0	0	0	0	0	0	0	0
92530	LAKE ELSINORE	80	79	79	80	77	80	81	80	79	82	99	93	79	97	78	76	98	81	74	88
92532	LAKE ELSINORE	119	125	113	127	121	120	115	117	109	119	137	136	115	134	112	103	134	115	105	131
92536	AGUANGA	96	84	65	79	89	97	79	89	84	79	101	104	74	100	81	86	96	88	97	114
92539	ANZA	68	62	55	57	64	73	58	66	61	61	75	70	56	68	61	64	71	64	73	77
92543	HEMET	55	50	51	48	52	60	52	55	56	53	69	59	51	64	53	58	65	55	62	62
92544	HEMET	77	75	75	73	77	86	75	78	77	75	95	86	75	92	77	79	91	77	83	88
92545	HEMET	69	64	63	61	67	78	62	69	66	65	81	71	62	72	65	69	76	68	78	77
92548	HOMELAND	57	49	42	45	52	60	46	54	50	49	62	56	45	55	49	53	58	52	61	64
92549	IDYLLWILD	98	77	52	69	87	97	73	87	82	72	97	102	65	96	77	88	90	86	103	120
92551	MORENO VALLEY	88	93	91	95	89	89	89	89	84	92	107	103	89	106	86	79	106	88	78	96
92553	MORENO VALLEY	74	73	71	74	71	72	74	74	72	76	91	85	72	88	71	68	89	75	67	80
92555	MORENO VALLEY	105	122	123	124	119	117	111	111	103	112	130	130	115	134	111	99	129	108	99	123
92557	MORENO VALLEY	99	108	108	112	104	103	102	101	95	104	121	118	103	121	99	90	119	100	88	111
92561	MOUNTAIN CENTER	87	84	85	82	87	93	82	87	84	82	103	101	80	103	84	84	99	87	89	104
92562	MURRIETA	127	139	136	141	136	139	126	129	119	131	151	144	130	145	126	116	147	125	121	142
92563	MURRIETA	103	113	111	115	110	112	102	105	97	107	123	117	105	119	102	94	120	102	98	115
92567	NUEVO	91	86	71	83	85	89	82	86	81	84	101	100	78	97	80	80	97	86	84	101
92570	PERRIS	75	67	56	64	66	69	67	72	69	71	87	80	63	80	65	67	85	73	69	79
92571	PERRIS	74	66	62	65	64	66	70	71	72	74	90	81	67	87	66	67	90	74	65	76
92582	SAN JACINTO	64	54	47	51	57	69	56	62	61	56	74	65	53	67	57	64	68	61	72	71
92583	SAN JACINTO	63	55	49	53	57	65	57	62	60	58	74	66	54	68	57	62	70	62	67	69
92584	MENIFEE	96	103	98	103	101	103	95	97	92	97	115	112	97	115	95	89	112	95	90	109
92585	SUN CITY	77	61	41	57	65	73	61	69	67	61	80	79	55	76	61	69	75	68	77	86
92586	SUN CITY	64	62	63	58	64	76	58	65	61	62	76	64	59	66	62	64	71	63	74	71
92587	SUN CITY	116	134	137	135	130	131	123	123	115	124	145	143	127	148	123	111	143	120	111	135
92590	TEMECULA	124	113	97	106	109	113	113	121	116	122	146	130	106	131	109	112	145	123	113	127
92591	TEMECULA	114	121	121	128	115	114	115	113	107	119	136	133	116	134	111	100	134	112	97	124
92592	TEMECULA	127	144	144	150	138	135	132	130	121	136	154	153	136	155	129	114	153	127	113	143
92595	WILDOMAR	109	107	92	106	105	108	100	104	98	103	122	121	98	118	99	95	118	103	99	120
92596	WINCHESTER	112	123	117	125	119	118	112	113	105	116	133	131	114	133	111	100	131	110	101	126
92602	IRVINE	219	248	238	258	236	227	223	221	204	233	260	259	230	261	217	190	257	215	188	242
92603	IRVINE	196	265	334	255	256	270	230	229	216	234	272	257	256	292	243	218	275	220	211	246
92604	IRVINE	123	152	188	149	146	154	140	138	134	142	169	158	150	177	144	133	170	136	126	149
92606	IRVINE	132	136	186	148	131	138	144	135	139	146	177	164	147	178	141	133	175	141	121	149
92610	FOOTHILL RANCH	184	208	200	217	197	191	187	185	171	195	218	217	193	218	182	159	215	181	157	203
92612	IRVINE	146	162	219	165	157	169	170	157	163	166	205	188	175	210	167	158	204	162	144	171
92614	IRVINE	148	165	194	174	159	163	160	154	150	162	191	182	167	192	158	143	190	154	136	169
92618	IRVINE	125	114	175	129	109	119	133	121	133	135	169	148	133	168	127	128	166	130	111	136
92620	IRVINE	174	200	221	207	193	197	185	181	173	189	220	210	196	222	185	167	219	179	163	200
92624	CAPISTRANO BEACH	134	155	179	153	154	164	145	147	140	147	176	165	152	176	150	141	173	145	143	161
92625	CORONA DEL MAR	255	296	444	305	288	316	288	277	281	295	356	318	314	368	298	283	356	277	263	305
92626	COSTA MESA	110	121	157	124	117	124	122	117	118	123	150	138	126	153	122	115	149	120	107	128
92627	COSTA MESA	99	96	113	100	94	99	103	100	102	105	129	118	102	127	99	97	128	104	91	109
92629	DANA POINT	150	171	203	174	168	175	165	162	157	166	199	188	171	201	167	154	197	162	150	178
92630	LAKE FOREST	133	146	160	149	141	144	140	137	133	143	169	159	144	168	138	128	167	137	124	151
92646	HUNTINGTON BEACH	121	152	186	147	147	154	139	138	132	140	166	157	148	175	144	132	166	135	127	149
92647	HUNTINGTON BEACH	107	116	138	118	112	117	116	112	111	117	141	132	118	143	114	108	140	114	101	123
92648	HUNTINGTON BEACH	145	153	204	161	148	159	158	151	154	160	196	178	163	196	157	151	193	155	140	166
92649	HUNTINGTON BEACH	150	171	215	173	167	176	166	162	160	168	202	188	174	206	168	157	200	163	150	177
92651	LAGUNA BEACH	198	247	336	245	240	256	231	225	222	234	280	259	251	296	241	222	281	223	209	244
92653	LAGUNA HILLS	124	132	147	127	134	150	123	131	124	129	155	137	128	145	129	127	150	128	137	143
92655	MIDWAY CITY	84	96	127	103	97	95	99	98	91	97	115	120	97	114	100	85	115	102	83	103
92656	ALISO VIEJO	148	155	157	164	148	148	149	146	140	154	178	172	150	174	144	131	175	146	128	161
92657	NEWPORT COAST	330	404	581	414	391	421	380	365	362	388	459	421	420	482	394	361	463	361	337	400
92660	NEWPORT BEACH	245	295	407	296	289	314	276	271	266	282	336	307	302	346	289	268	336	268	259	297
92661	NEWPORT BEACH	166	176	302	193	168	186	190	174	190	194	242	209	203	254	191	189	241	181	162	193
92662	NEWPORT BEACH	219	239	312	246	237	256	237	233	232	240	292	267	247	292	242	231	287	234	226	258
	CALIFORNIA	107	111	131	112	109	115	113	111	111	114	140	129	114	141	112	109	139	113	104	122
	UNITED STATES	100	100	100	100	100	100	100	100	100	100	100	100	100	100	100	100	100	100	100	100

POPULATION CHANGE

#	POST OFFICE NAME	COUNTY FIPS CODE	POPULATION 2000	2004	2009	2000-2004 ANNUAL RATE % Rate	State Centile	HOUSEHOLDS 2000	2004	2009	% Annual Rate 2000-2004	2004 Average HH Size	FAMILIES 2000	2004	% Annual Rate 2000-2004
92663	NEWPORT BEACH	059	21747	22380	23746	0.7	40	10409	10630	11174	0.5	2.05	4360	4519	0.9
92672	SAN CLEMENTE	073	45432	46966	48765	0.8	45	14667	15152	15692	0.8	2.73	9496	9775	0.7
92673	SAN CLEMENTE	059	15592	17957	19818	3.4	93	5513	6243	6790	3.0	2.87	4385	4973	3.0
92675	SAN JUAN CAPISTRANO	059	35193	40151	44480	3.2	91	11354	12900	14219	3.1	3.08	8598	9860	3.3
92676	SILVERADO	059	2553	2790	3010	2.1	81	963	1020	1077	1.4	2.69	663	709	1.6
92677	LAGUNA NIGUEL	059	64000	67907	71718	1.4	67	24067	25322	26511	1.2	2.67	17301	18179	1.2
92679	TRABUCO CANYON	059	32652	39722	44976	4.7	97	10055	12152	13641	4.6	3.26	8763	10590	4.6
92683	WESTMINSTER	059	88312	89202	91934	0.2	21	26425	26417	26954	0.0	3.35	20308	20240	-0.1
92688	RANCHO SANTA MARGARI	059	43666	54074	61911	5.2	97	15807	19312	21876	4.8	2.80	11603	14211	4.9
92691	MISSION VIEJO	059	46208	46869	48639	0.3	24	15493	15708	16240	0.3	2.92	12211	12321	0.2
92692	MISSION VIEJO	059	41284	46692	51374	2.9	90	14924	16897	18547	3.0	2.76	11475	12883	2.8
92694	LADERA RANCH	059	356	676	931	16.3	100	122	231	315	16.2	2.93	102	192	16.1
92697	IRVINE	059	11539	11652	11877	0.2	21	2192	2199	2260	0.1	2.42	1036	1032	-0.1
92701	SANTA ANA	059	58671	60245	62612	0.6	37	12449	12624	12983	0.3	4.71	10234	10353	0.3
92703	SANTA ANA	059	70381	72747	75802	0.8	45	12652	12956	13393	0.6	5.39	11126	11365	0.5
92704	SANTA ANA	059	90649	94197	98592	0.9	51	19768	20263	20951	0.6	4.63	15964	16320	0.5
92705	SANTA ANA	059	44447	45519	47592	0.6	34	14315	14283	14658	-0.1	3.16	11231	11212	0.0
92706	SANTA ANA	059	35820	38079	40277	1.5	68	9231	9649	10076	1.1	3.89	7391	7708	1.0
92707	SANTA ANA	059	62965	63568	65563	0.2	20	13307	13357	13680	0.1	4.70	10864	10806	-0.1
92708	FOUNTAIN VALLEY	059	54526	55400	57661	0.4	26	17945	18165	18785	0.3	3.02	14167	14296	0.2
92780	TUSTIN	059	54622	58241	62221	1.5	69	18133	18868	19801	0.9	3.07	12554	12938	0.7
92782	TUSTIN	059	16174	20097	22991	5.2	97	6816	8565	9805	5.5	2.35	4260	5278	5.2
92801	ANAHEIM	059	56728	59110	63062	1.3	64	16334	17024	17714	1.0	3.47	12313	12803	0.9
92802	ANAHEIM	059	44476	48639	52338	2.1	81	12000	12839	13603	1.6	3.75	9305	9925	1.5
92804	ANAHEIM	059	85558	88558	92098	0.8	47	25658	26062	26730	0.4	3.32	19291	19548	0.3
92805	ANAHEIM	059	68833	71626	74609	0.9	52	16909	17223	17663	0.4	4.13	13302	13511	0.4
92806	ANAHEIM	059	34350	35504	36946	0.8	45	10734	10932	11242	0.4	3.24	7862	7978	0.4
92807	ANAHEIM	059	35074	35504	36813	0.3	23	12187	12307	12681	0.2	2.86	9605	9675	0.2
92808	ANAHEIM	059	19936	23463	26244	3.9	95	7140	8447	9414	4.0	2.77	5478	6341	3.5
92821	BREA	059	33176	33652	35013	0.3	25	12228	12451	12913	0.4	2.69	8653	8778	0.3
92823	BREA	059	1411	1440	1498	0.5	31	523	532	550	0.4	2.71	389	393	0.2
92831	FULLERTON	059	33900	34917	36297	0.7	41	12800	13153	13608	0.6	2.57	7558	7688	0.4
92832	FULLERTON	059	23957	24431	25449	0.5	29	7512	7554	7777	0.1	3.14	4798	4804	0.0
92833	FULLERTON	059	45814	46940	48832	0.6	35	14580	14833	15304	0.4	3.13	11301	11450	0.3
92835	FULLERTON	059	22001	22539	23423	0.6	35	8471	8654	8936	0.5	2.56	5988	6095	0.4
92840	GARDEN GROVE	059	51471	53853	56368	1.1	57	14818	15262	15779	0.7	3.48	11161	11457	0.6
92841	GARDEN GROVE	059	30850	31828	33139	0.7	43	8860	9035	9308	0.5	3.46	6927	7015	0.3
92843	GARDEN GROVE	059	44553	46586	48598	1.1	57	10602	10940	11283	0.7	4.21	8873	9129	0.7
92844	GARDEN GROVE	059	24052	26459	28594	2.3	83	6560	7112	7592	1.9	3.67	5371	5813	1.9
92845	GARDEN GROVE	059	16351	16269	16662	-0.1	11	5697	5653	5757	-0.2	2.86	4488	4445	-0.2
92860	NORCO	065	24165	26539	30462	2.2	82	6138	6825	7968	2.5	3.18	4982	5529	2.5
92861	VILLA PARK	059	5923	5856	5990	-0.3	8	1934	1906	1938	-0.3	3.06	1742	1714	-0.4
92862	ORANGE	059	18	22	25	4.8	97	6	7	8	3.7	3.14	5	6	4.4
92865	ORANGE	059	18007	18430	19179	0.6	34	5907	5993	6182	0.3	3.06	4509	4560	0.3
92866	ORANGE	059	15312	15839	16502	0.8	46	5869	6039	6250	0.7	2.58	3571	3668	0.6
92867	ORANGE	059	41476	42722	44502	0.7	41	12631	12918	13359	0.5	3.22	9992	10216	0.5
92868	ORANGE	059	23213	24051	24966	0.8	48	6553	6754	6984	0.7	3.02	4211	4318	0.6
92869	ORANGE	059	37859	39422	41401	1.0	53	11742	12221	12775	1.0	3.20	9358	9716	0.9
92870	PLACENTIA	059	48211	50007	52309	0.9	49	15784	16331	16990	0.8	3.04	12077	12448	0.7
92879	CORONA	065	44444	51645	61824	3.6	94	13414	15588	18563	3.6	3.29	10284	11849	3.4
92880	CORONA	065	16146	22335	29747	7.9	99	4669	6363	8345	7.6	3.49	3981	5393	7.4
92881	CORONA	065	22153	28977	36845	6.5	98	6659	8576	10766	6.1	3.37	5660	7335	6.3
92882	CORONA	065	60261	69315	82798	3.4	92	17876	20383	24105	3.1	3.39	14492	16467	3.1
92883	CORONA	065	12695	16711	21200	6.7	99	3943	5161	6491	6.5	3.23	3318	4322	6.4
92886	YORBA LINDA	059	38383	41094	43687	1.6	72	12881	13799	14605	1.6	2.97	10552	11268	1.6
92887	YORBA LINDA	059	23592	26061	28256	2.4	84	7478	8265	8928	2.4	3.15	6417	7106	2.4
93001	VENTURA	111	32620	33284	34811	0.5	31	12772	12955	13493	0.3	2.51	7432	7504	0.2
93003	VENTURA	111	47009	49850	53412	1.4	66	18235	19350	20707	1.4	2.50	12051	12673	1.2
93004	VENTURA	111	27205	29110	31256	1.6	72	9589	10170	10839	1.4	2.85	7230	7676	1.4
93010	CAMARILLO	111	42744	45675	49224	1.6	71	15040	16102	17336	1.6	2.76	11166	11938	1.6
93012	CAMARILLO	111	24961	28136	31355	2.9	89	9772	10852	12002	2.5	2.57	6936	7800	2.8
93013	CARPINTERIA	083	16965	17079	17421	0.2	19	6071	6104	6217	0.1	2.78	4049	4068	0.1
93015	FILLMORE	111	17448	18590	19838	1.5	69	4826	5119	5436	1.4	3.57	3900	4128	1.4
93021	MOORPARK	111	32958	37034	40937	2.8	88	9461	10598	11669	2.7	3.49	8085	9024	2.6
93022	OAK VIEW	111	6018	6182	6517	0.6	38	2023	2073	2179	0.6	2.92	1482	1514	0.5
93023	OJAI	111	22278	22739	23786	0.5	31	8351	8495	8857	0.4	2.60	5775	5852	0.3
93030	OXNARD	111	46401	52790	59224	3.1	90	11563	12824	14170	2.5	4.04	9252	10322	2.6
93033	OXNARD	111	77705	80262	84445	0.8	43	16693	16976	17682	0.4	4.65	14404	14619	0.4
93035	OXNARD	111	25403	26441	27945	1.0	53	9172	9503	10002	0.8	2.77	6201	6370	0.6
93036	OXNARD	111	33151	36074	39045	2.0	79	9684	10452	11235	1.8	3.41	7714	8269	1.7
93041	PORT HUENEME	111	19682	20299	21374	0.7	42	6833	7006	7336	0.6	2.85	4556	4657	0.5
93042	POINT MUGU NAWC	111	3060	3536	3924	3.5	93	658	769	859	3.7	3.87	642	750	3.7
93043	PORT HUENEME CBC BAS	111	3026	3032	3103	0.1	16	628	629	647	0.0	3.40	607	608	0.0
93060	SANTA PAULA	111	32391	33358	35179	0.7	40	9051	9229	9665	0.5	3.52	7147	7273	0.4
93063	SIMI VALLEY	111	49096	52063	55834	1.4	66	16419	17377	18571	1.3	2.97	12991	13729	1.3
93065	SIMI VALLEY	111	64703	68018	72804	1.2	61	20857	21899	23360	1.2	3.09	16596	17358	1.1
93066	SOMIS	111	3121	3207	3376	0.6	38	1007	1032	1082	0.6	3.02	818	837	0.5
93067	SUMMERLAND	083	611	606	611	-0.2	9	295	295	298	0.0	2.05	164	163	-0.1
93101	SANTA BARBARA	083	31513	32020	32816	0.4	26	12163	12264	12515	0.2	2.56	5798	5848	0.2
93103	SANTA BARBARA	083	20811	22309	23596	1.7	73	7440	7835	8218	1.2	2.80	4403	4641	1.3
93105	SANTA BARBARA	083	26629	27309	28078	0.6	36	11492	11877	12446	0.8	2.22	6491	6676	0.7
93106	SANTA BARBARA	083	403	438	460	2.0	79	77	84	88	2.1	5.21	3	3	0.0
93108	SANTA BARBARA	083	12496	12359	12518	-0.3	8	4806	4779	4855	-0.1	2.37	3089	3066	-0.2
93109	SANTA BARBARA	083	11165	11323	11594	0.3	24	4555	4655	4783	0.5	2.42	2602	2637	0.3
93110	SANTA BARBARA	083	14668	14648	14855	0.0	12	5727	5724	5801	0.0	2.48	3418	3404	-0.1
93111	SANTA BARBARA	083	16906	16809	17019	-0.1	10	5922	5935	6026	0.1	2.78	4359	4351	0.0
93117	GOLETA	083	49578	53720	57534	1.9	78	15428	16923	18257	2.2	2.82	7971	8853	2.5
93202	ARMONA	031	1745	1784	1909	0.5	33	468	474	503	0.3	3.73	400	405	0.3
93203	ARVIN	029	14477	16359	18257	2.9	90	3403	3793	4182	2.6	4.29	2965	3295	2.5
93204	AVENAL	031	14699	15263	16008	0.9	50	1937	2020	2157	1.0	4.24	1649	1716	0.9
93205	BODFISH	029	1935	1954	2054	0.2	21	886	891	931	0.1	2.19	573	571	-0.1
93206	BUTTONWILLOW	029	1904	1957	2076	0.7	39	516	527	555	0.5	3.69	426	434	0.4
93207	CALIFORNIA HOT SPRIN	107	786	828	888	1.2	63	233	244	261	1.1	3.39	184	193	1.1
93210	COALINGA	019	17811	18162	19106	0.5	29	3957	4021	4253	0.4	3.37	2972	3009	0.3
93212	CORCORAN	107	23607	24195	25226	0.6	35	3548	3686	3945	0.9	3.50	2874	2978	0.8
	CALIFORNIA					1.4					1.2	2.90			1.2
	UNITED STATES					1.2					1.3	2.58			1.1

ZIP CODE #	POST OFFICE NAME	RACE (%) White 2000	White 2004	Black 2000	Black 2004	Asian/Pacific 2000	Asian/Pacific 2004	% Hispanic Origin 2000	% Hispanic Origin 2004	2004 AGE DISTRIBUTION (%) 0-4	5-9	10-14	15-19	20-24	25-44	45-64	65-84	85+	18+	MEDIAN AGE 2004	% 2004 Males	% 2004 Females
92663	NEWPORT BEACH	91.9	90.3	0.7	0.7	3.2	3.7	6.6	8.5	3.4	3.5	4.1	4.6	7.9	38.0	23.9	11.9	2.7	86.4	38.0	51.8	48.3
92672	SAN CLEMENTE	81.0	78.2	4.0	4.0	2.8	3.2	19.1	23.1	7.4	6.0	5.9	7.3	15.5	28.2	19.2	9.1	1.4	77.8	30.2	56.0	44.0
92673	SAN CLEMENTE	90.1	88.4	0.7	0.7	3.4	3.9	10.4	13.0	7.1	8.2	9.0	6.7	4.4	26.5	27.6	9.6	1.0	71.2	39.0	50.4	49.6
92675	SAN JUAN CAPISTRANO	78.1	76.7	0.8	0.8	2.4	2.8	33.2	34.9	7.3	7.7	8.5	6.9	5.3	26.6	25.5	10.4	1.8	72.0	37.0	49.4	50.6
92676	SILVERADO	89.4	86.5	0.9	1.0	3.2	4.2	6.0	8.1	6.6	7.7	8.4	5.3	4.0	31.4	32.6	3.8	0.3	74.3	39.6	51.0	49.0
92677	LAGUNA NIGUEL	83.4	80.4	1.3	1.4	7.8	9.0	10.6	13.4	6.8	7.5	8.0	6.1	4.9	28.9	28.4	8.5	1.0	73.8	38.7	48.7	51.3
92679	TRABUCO CANYON	87.4	84.9	1.0	1.1	5.9	6.8	7.8	10.2	9.7	10.7	10.6	7.0	3.7	30.5	24.5	3.2	0.2	64.3	34.4	49.8	50.2
92683	WESTMINSTER	46.4	43.0	1.0	1.0	37.8	38.9	22.2	25.6	7.4	7.2	7.5	6.5	6.7	31.0	22.2	10.3	1.2	73.9	34.8	49.9	50.1
92688	RANCHO SANTA MARGARI	80.0	76.6	2.0	2.0	8.3	9.6	13.9	17.2	10.3	9.7	8.5	5.7	4.8	38.0	18.0	4.7	0.3	67.8	32.6	49.0	51.0
92691	MISSION VIEJO	83.9	81.0	1.1	1.2	7.0	7.9	13.1	16.6	6.6	7.1	7.7	6.4	5.5	28.2	27.7	9.2	1.7	74.5	38.7	49.1	50.9
92692	MISSION VIEJO	82.9	80.1	1.1	1.2	8.9	10.2	10.4	12.8	6.9	7.7	8.0	6.2	4.8	27.1	26.4	11.3	1.7	73.3	39.5	48.5	51.5
92694	LADERA RANCH	92.7	91.1	0.3	0.3	3.9	4.4	7.0	9.0	4.7	6.2	8.0	7.0	4.3	20.3	35.5	12.9	1.2	76.2	44.7	48.1	51.9
92697	IRVINE	44.4	40.7	2.3	2.3	43.0	45.2	10.4	12.3	2.6	1.9	2.0	28.9	28.6	28.8	6.0	1.3	0.1	92.2	22.6	47.6	52.4
92701	SANTA ANA	42.5	41.4	1.3	1.3	3.4	3.1	88.3	90.2	12.2	10.6	10.2	8.5	9.9	33.1	11.5	3.6	0.5	62.1	24.4	52.5	47.5
92703	SANTA ANA	39.6	38.5	2.0	1.8	11.0	10.6	79.9	82.1	10.5	9.5	9.7	8.3	9.5	33.2	14.2	4.7	0.5	65.6	26.4	53.0	47.1
92704	SANTA ANA	38.8	37.3	1.8	1.6	15.6	14.9	68.1	71.3	9.6	8.7	9.4	8.1	9.2	32.9	16.5	5.2	0.5	67.6	27.9	51.1	48.9
92705	SANTA ANA	71.6	67.6	1.5	1.5	6.4	7.0	33.2	38.7	8.2	8.1	7.9	6.5	6.2	28.2	22.2	11.2	1.5	71.8	35.1	49.5	50.5
92706	SANTA ANA	48.8	46.3	1.7	1.6	6.9	6.6	67.8	72.2	10.4	9.4	9.0	7.6	8.3	31.8	15.7	6.6	1.3	66.7	28.3	50.8	49.2
92707	SANTA ANA	45.6	44.0	1.4	1.4	6.8	6.7	78.9	81.3	10.2	9.0	9.5	8.2	9.9	33.2	15.2	4.2	0.5	66.5	26.7	51.6	48.4
92708	FOUNTAIN VALLEY	63.9	59.6	1.1	1.1	26.1	28.7	11.2	13.6	6.0	6.1	6.8	6.1	6.1	28.4	27.2	11.8	1.5	77.3	39.3	48.8	51.3
92780	TUSTIN	57.9	54.1	3.2	3.0	11.5	11.7	41.4	47.1	8.5	7.9	7.9	6.8	7.9	33.2	19.2	7.6	1.0	71.5	31.6	49.2	50.8
92782	TUSTIN	68.2	64.3	1.8	1.8	22.4	24.7	8.9	11.2	7.7	6.8	5.4	3.9	5.6	42.0	23.0	5.3	0.4	77.8	35.2	49.1	50.9
92801	ANAHEIM	47.8	44.4	4.1	3.9	13.3	13.3	51.7	56.9	9.9	8.9	8.7	7.3	8.2	31.6	16.9	7.1	1.4	68.3	29.3	49.5	50.5
92802	ANAHEIM	48.2	45.5	2.3	2.1	11.3	11.3	58.1	62.7	10.2	9.1	8.9	7.4	8.8	31.8	16.3	6.5	1.1	67.5	28.3	50.5	49.5
92804	ANAHEIM	52.1	48.2	3.1	2.9	18.0	18.3	39.2	44.7	8.8	8.1	8.4	7.2	7.8	31.1	18.8	8.6	1.2	70.5	31.3	49.6	50.4
92805	ANAHEIM	48.8	46.4	1.7	1.6	5.1	4.9	74.1	78.2	10.8	9.7	9.9	8.0	8.5	32.7	14.9	4.8	0.7	64.9	26.8	51.6	48.4
92806	ANAHEIM	59.2	55.5	2.5	2.4	10.8	11.0	44.5	50.2	8.5	7.7	7.7	6.7	7.8	33.4	19.0	8.3	0.8	72.1	31.5	50.0	50.0
92807	ANAHEIM	76.2	72.7	1.8	1.8	12.9	14.4	14.4	17.8	5.6	6.1	7.1	6.4	5.8	27.0	30.3	10.2	1.5	77.1	40.2	48.8	51.2
92808	ANAHEIM	68.9	64.6	2.1	2.2	21.2	23.7	11.0	13.7	9.0	8.7	7.3	5.0	4.4	37.5	23.4	4.5	0.2	71.9	35.1	49.1	50.9
92821	BREA	76.7	73.0	1.3	1.3	9.5	10.5	20.9	25.4	6.0	6.1	7.3	7.3	7.3	28.3	25.5	10.7	1.6	76.2	37.2	48.7	51.3
92823	BREA	88.1	85.8	1.1	1.2	5.2	6.0	11.8	15.1	5.8	6.2	6.9	6.8	5.8	23.2	30.4	13.8	1.3	76.9	41.9	48.5	51.5
92831	FULLERTON	65.6	61.9	2.6	2.6	12.0	12.9	29.5	33.8	6.5	5.7	5.9	7.6	12.2	33.4	18.8	8.6	1.2	78.4	31.1	50.0	50.0
92832	FULLERTON	58.2	54.7	2.5	2.4	7.5	7.6	49.8	55.4	8.6	7.8	8.1	7.1	8.6	33.5	17.3	7.8	1.2	71.3	30.4	50.0	50.0
92833	FULLERTON	53.6	50.0	2.4	2.4	25.7	26.2	28.7	33.8	7.4	7.3	8.1	7.4	7.0	29.4	23.4	9.0	1.1	72.6	34.4	49.5	50.6
92835	FULLERTON	78.8	75.2	1.3	1.3	12.3	13.9	12.0	15.0	5.6	5.8	6.3	5.7	5.6	25.4	26.1	15.9	3.6	78.8	42.0	47.7	52.3
92840	GARDEN GROVE	51.1	47.7	1.6	1.5	24.1	24.6	37.9	42.8	8.0	7.5	8.1	7.1	7.8	31.5	20.2	8.6	1.2	72.1	32.4	49.6	50.4
92841	GARDEN GROVE	48.2	44.4	1.4	1.4	32.1	33.1	26.7	31.0	7.8	7.4	7.9	6.6	7.0	30.8	21.7	9.5	1.3	72.9	34.1	49.8	50.2
92843	GARDEN GROVE	37.1	35.4	1.1	1.0	35.0	34.1	45.0	49.3	9.1	8.7	8.8	7.8	7.8	31.9	18.3	6.8	0.8	68.6	30.0	50.5	49.5
92844	GARDEN GROVE	30.9	28.4	1.4	1.4	52.6	53.4	21.9	24.5	7.9	7.6	8.0	6.8	7.0	33.1	21.0	8.0	0.6	72.3	33.3	50.8	49.2
92845	GARDEN GROVE	81.1	78.0	0.9	1.0	11.0	12.5	10.9	13.7	6.1	6.4	7.5	6.5	5.5	27.1	26.0	13.3	1.6	75.9	40.3	48.6	51.4
92860	NORCO	82.1	79.6	6.3	6.2	1.4	1.6	23.1	27.5	5.4	5.7	6.9	6.5	6.9	36.0	25.4	6.7	0.5	78.0	36.6	55.7	44.3
92861	VILLA PARK	82.8	80.1	0.6	0.7	12.7	14.6	6.3	8.1	4.1	5.4	8.1	7.3	4.7	20.2	32.0	17.1	1.1	77.7	45.2	50.4	49.6
92862	ORANGE	66.7	63.6	0.0	0.0	27.8	27.3	11.1	13.6	9.1	9.1	9.1	4.6	0.0	36.4	31.8	0.0	0.0	72.7	37.5	45.5	54.6
92865	ORANGE	72.0	67.9	1.6	1.7	6.4	7.0	30.2	35.4	7.4	7.3	8.2	7.1	6.7	30.7	21.8	9.9	1.0	72.7	34.6	49.3	50.7
92866	ORANGE	73.3	69.7	2.0	1.9	5.2	5.7	33.3	38.8	7.8	7.3	7.5	6.1	6.9	35.2	19.6	7.8	2.0	73.9	33.5	48.8	51.2
92867	ORANGE	72.6	69.0	1.1	1.1	9.5	10.6	30.2	34.7	7.6	7.6	8.5	7.8	7.4	29.3	22.2	8.8	0.9	72.1	33.5	49.8	50.2
92868	ORANGE	61.4	57.9	2.7	2.6	11.9	12.1	44.5	50.2	7.2	6.5	6.8	8.6	9.0	34.1	17.4	8.4	2.0	74.3	31.6	53.5	46.5
92869	ORANGE	72.0	69.0	1.3	1.3	10.7	11.6	31.0	34.8	7.2	7.2	7.7	6.4	6.2	30.4	25.3	8.7	0.9	74.0	35.9	49.6	50.4
92870	PLACENTIA	68.0	64.7	1.8	1.8	11.5	12.7	30.3	33.9	7.5	7.2	7.4	6.5	7.1	31.6	23.0	8.6	1.0	73.9	34.1	49.6	50.4
92879	CORONA	55.1	51.6	7.3	7.6	8.9	9.5	41.7	45.1	9.8	8.6	8.7	7.3	8.0	32.6	17.9	6.1	1.1	68.5	29.6	49.3	50.7
92880	CORONA	68.7	65.3	4.9	4.9	5.3	5.2	34.3	39.8	10.0	9.6	9.3	7.9	6.5	33.5	18.9	4.0	0.2	66.0	29.8	50.6	49.4
92881	CORONA	69.7	65.9	7.4	8.1	6.6	7.3	24.2	27.9	10.1	9.4	8.7	7.0	5.8	33.4	19.6	5.5	0.6	67.3	31.8	49.0	51.0
92882	CORONA	62.7	59.3	4.5	4.7	6.6	7.2	40.1	43.8	9.8	9.2	9.2	7.5	7.3	32.2	18.9	5.3	0.6	67.2	29.8	49.7	50.3
92883	CORONA	74.5	71.2	6.3	6.7	3.9	4.3	24.7	29.0	10.8	10.3	9.5	6.7	5.3	33.7	18.5	4.8	0.3	64.7	31.1	49.4	50.6
92886	YORBA LINDA	84.3	81.4	1.1	1.1	8.1	9.3	11.4	14.5	5.8	6.7	8.4	7.3	5.5	25.5	30.1	9.8	1.0	74.6	39.8	48.8	51.2
92887	YORBA LINDA	77.4	73.8	1.5	1.6	15.5	17.7	8.7	11.0	6.2	7.7	10.2	8.3	5.4	26.5	30.1	5.2	0.5	70.5	37.1	49.3	50.7
93001	VENTURA	74.8	71.2	1.4	1.4	2.1	2.2	32.4	37.4	6.8	6.6	6.9	6.3	7.1	31.4	24.6	9.1	1.2	75.8	35.9	50.7	49.3
93003	VENTURA	80.7	77.1	1.5	1.6	3.8	4.2	20.0	24.5	6.0	6.1	6.7	6.6	6.5	27.5	25.6	12.3	2.7	77.1	39.1	48.7	51.3
93004	VENTURA	79.0	75.2	1.2	1.3	3.1	3.4	24.5	29.8	7.1	7.5	8.5	7.2	5.9	27.1	25.2	10.1	1.3	72.3	36.9	48.7	51.4
93010	CAMARILLO	78.4	75.2	1.9	2.0	7.0	7.9	18.7	22.4	6.6	6.8	7.5	6.9	6.2	26.2	25.4	12.6	2.0	75.0	38.6	48.9	51.1
93012	CAMARILLO	86.4	83.7	0.9	0.9	6.8	7.9	9.2	11.9	6.0	6.7	7.3	6.3	4.4	23.3	26.8	15.0	4.3	76.1	42.7	48.0	52.0
93013	CARPINTERIA	75.7	72.8	0.6	0.6	2.6	2.7	39.2	44.1	5.8	6.3	7.4	6.9	6.5	28.6	25.7	11.0	1.8	76.2	37.8	50.3	49.7
93015	FILLMORE	54.4	50.3	0.3	0.3	1.2	1.1	65.6	71.2	8.5	8.2	9.2	8.6	8.2	27.7	19.6	8.5	1.5	68.9	30.2	50.6	49.4
93021	MOORPARK	74.5	71.2	1.5	1.7	5.7	6.2	27.9	31.9	8.0	8.6	9.7	8.2	6.3	29.4	24.6	4.8	0.5	68.6	32.7	49.8	50.2
93022	OAK VIEW	86.7	83.5	0.6	0.6	1.1	1.3	16.3	20.8	5.7	6.4	7.9	7.0	5.9	25.9	29.7	9.8	1.9	75.7	40.1	49.1	51.0
93023	OJAI	88.2	85.5	0.5	0.6	1.3	1.4	15.8	19.9	5.0	5.7	7.7	8.0	6.5	21.9	29.6	12.9	2.9	76.5	42.0	48.2	51.9
93030	OXNARD	38.9	36.3	3.8	3.3	4.7	4.5	74.1	78.6	9.4	8.7	8.8	8.4	9.5	30.2	17.2	6.9	0.9	68.2	28.0	51.8	48.3
93033	OXNARD	35.5	33.6	3.4	3.1	9.5	8.9	73.9	77.4	9.6	8.7	9.6	8.8	9.5	30.4	16.6	6.2	0.7	66.8	27.2	51.7	48.3
93035	OXNARD	67.0	64.1	3.9	3.8	6.4	6.5	33.4	37.5	6.9	6.7	6.9	6.3	6.4	29.6	26.0	10.3	0.9	75.5	37.0	50.1	49.9
93036	OXNARD	49.1	46.1	4.0	3.8	6.9	6.9	60.9	65.1	9.2	8.4	8.7	8.2	8.1	29.8	19.2	7.8	0.7	68.8	29.8	49.9	50.1
93041	PORT HUENEME	56.7	52.6	5.1	5.0	5.9	5.9	46.0	51.9	8.0	7.2	7.7	7.2	8.2	28.6	20.1	11.2	1.8	73.0	32.8	48.5	51.5
93042	POINT MUGU NAWC	64.3	60.1	10.5	11.0	12.0	13.0	15.3	18.8	14.4	11.0	8.8	6.6	14.9	41.7	2.4	0.1	0.0	62.6	23.1	58.3	41.7
93043	PORT HUENEME CBC BAS	60.9	56.5	11.3	11.8	13.1	14.2	12.7	15.6	13.2	7.7	6.2	9.2	27.1	34.1	2.3	0.3	0.0	71.0	22.6	61.4	38.7
93060	SANTA PAULA	55.9	52.2	0.5	0.5	0.9	0.9	68.8	74.2	8.7	8.3	8.8	8.0	8.1	29.4	19.0	8.3	1.4	69.6	30.3	51.7	48.3
93063	SIMI VALLEY	82.8	79.7	1.2	1.3	6.3	7.2	15.2	18.6	6.9	7.3	8.1	6.9	5.8	29.7	26.6	7.9	1.0	73.5	36.8	49.4	50.6
93065	SIMI VALLEY	80.6	77.3	1.3	1.3	6.4	7.1	17.9	21.8	7.6	7.9	8.2	6.8	6.2	30.8	24.5	7.4	0.7	72.0	35.2	49.6	50.5
93066	SOMIS	72.3	67.7	1.4	1.3	2.8	3.0	35.0	41.4	6.3	6.9	7.6	7.8	6.0	25.5	27.2	11.6	1.1	74.7	38.2	52.1	47.9
93067	SUMMERLAND	90.7	89.1	0.5	0.5	2.1	2.3	10.2	12.4	3.1	3.6	5.1	5.5	4.8	28.9	33.2	14.0	1.8	84.7	44.4	47.9	52.2
93101	SANTA BARBARA	66.6	63.4	1.9	1.9	2.5	2.6	46.5	51.3	6.6	5.7	6.0	6.2	9.8	38.5	18.8	6.9	1.4	78.4	31.8	50.9	49.1
93103	SANTA BARBARA	66.2	63.1	2.4	2.3	2.0	2.1	49.7	55.0	6.4	6.0	6.9	6.4	8.0	32.1	22.9	9.7	1.7	77.1	34.6	50.6	49.4
93105	SANTA BARBARA	86.9	84.8	1.0	1.0	2.9	3.2	15.9	18.7	4.7	4.9	5.1	4.9	5.1	26.9	27.2	15.8	5.3	82.2	43.9	47.0	53.0
93106	SANTA BARBARA	84.1	81.3	1.0	0.9	5.7	6.4	8.9	10.7	0.0	0.0	0.0	15.8	81.7	1.8	0.5	0.2	0.0	100.0	22.1	43.8	56.2
93108	SANTA BARBARA	92.7	91.2	0.6	0.6	1.6	1.9	7.4	9.2	3.4	4.6	6.1	8.5	7.5	18.5	30.4	17.1	3.9	82.3	46.0	46.3	53.7
93109	SANTA BARBARA	82.8	80.4	1.3	1.3	3.9	4.3	19.7	22.8	4.9	4.9	5.2	5.7	8.2	30.1	26.0	12.8	2.3	82.2	39.3	49.6	50.4
93110	SANTA BARBARA	82.3	79.9	1.2	1.3	4.2	4.6	19.4	22.5	5.3	5.4	6.6	6.3	6.0	26.0	25.5	15.6	3.5	79.0	41.3	47.6	52.4
93111	SANTA BARBARA	81.5	79.2	1.0	1.0	5.6	6.0	19.6	22.6	5.3	5.7	6.9	6.5	5.7	24.6	28.3	14.8	2.2	78.0	42.0	48.9	51.1
93117	GOLETA	73.1	69.5	1.8	1.8	9.3	9.9	23.5	27.7	4.8	4.5	4.9	14.7	25.2	23.7	15.1	6.2	0.9	83.0	24.2	50.5	49.5
93202	ARMONA	54.4	50.1	4.5	4.4	1.7	1.6	50.9	56.8	8.6	9.1	11.8	9.3	7.5	27.1	20.4	5.8	0.6	64.9	28.0	48.6	51.4
93203	ARVIN	47.6	45.5	1.1	1.0	1.2	1.1	84.6	87.7	11.4	10.2	10.8	9.8	9.5	28.3	14.3	5.2	0.5	61.5	24.1	52.8	47.2
93204	AVENAL	35.9	33.1	12.6	11.8	0.4	0.4	65.8	70.2	6.6	5.9	6.2	6.3	11.1	45.2	15.8	2.7	0.4	78.1	30.9	73.7	26.3
93205	BODFISH	90.9	89.0	0.1	0.1	0.8	0.9	5.6	7.3	3.9	4.1	5.7	5.8	4.3	15.8	31.1	26.2	3.1	82.6	51.7	49.3	50.7
93206	BUTTONWILLOW	43.6	38.6	3.2	3.0	0.3	0.3	59.8	66.0	9.5	9.1	10.3	10.3	8.9	26.9	17.8	6.4	0.7	65.2	26.4	52.3	47.7
93207	CALIFORNIA HOT SPRIN	62.1	58.2	0.6	0.6	0.8	0.9	41.2	45.8	8.8	8.5	9.1	7.7	6.2	25.0	23.1	10.9	0.9	68.7	33.5	51.5	48.6
93210	COALINGA	52.3	48.7	8.3	8.0	1.4	1.5	51.1	56.6	7.7	6.7	7.6	7.6	10.7	37.3	16.3	5.3	0.8	73.9	30.0	62.2	37.8
93212	CORCORAN	32.7	29.3	17.0	16.1	0.7	0.6	56.2	61.2	5.5	5.1	5.3	5.8	11.4	46.4	16.1	4.0	0.5	81.0	31.9	73.9	26.2
	CALIFORNIA	59.6	57.1	6.7	6.5	11.3	11.8	32.4	35.5	7.4	7.1	7.8	7.3	7.7	29.8	22.1	9.3	1.4	73.3	33.8	49.8	50.2
	UNITED STATES	75.1	73.6	12.3	12.5	3.8	4.2	12.5	14.1	6.9	6.7	7.2	7.0	7.3	28.6	23.8	10.8	1.7	75.1	36.0	49.1	50.9

#	POST OFFICE NAME	2004 Per Capita Income	2004 HH Income Base	2004 Household Income Distribution (%): Less than $25,000	$25,000 to $49,999	$50,000 to $99,999	$100,000 to $149,999	$150,000 or More	Median Household Income: 2004	2009	2004 National Centile	2004 State Centile	2004 Home Value Base	2004 Home Value Distribution (%): Less than $50,000	$50,000 to $89,999	$90,000 to $174,999	$175,000 to $399,999	$400,000 or More	2004 Median Home Value
92663	NEWPORT BEACH	64218	10630	12.5	15.0	32.0	17.8	22.8	81756	106457	95	87	5132	4.2	1.1	0.6	12.1	82.0	964098
92672	SAN CLEMENTE	33211	15152	13.7	23.9	33.0	15.0	14.5	63886	78824	88	71	8084	0.1	0.6	1.0	19.0	79.2	599368
92673	SAN CLEMENTE	43235	6243	7.1	14.1	28.7	25.7	24.3	100051	120757	98	94	5237	0.0	0.4	0.7	16.7	82.3	612989
92675	SAN JUAN CAPISTRANO	38943	12900	11.3	18.4	32.1	19.1	19.2	77581	99228	94	84	10448	1.6	3.1	11.0	24.2	60.2	493146
92676	SILVERADO	42624	1020	6.8	11.3	27.4	30.9	23.7	105551	128412	99	95	834	1.1	0.0	1.6	32.7	64.6	526361
92677	LAGUNA NIGUEL	47471	25322	7.3	14.4	31.7	22.3	24.3	93014	114418	97	92	19183	0.1	0.2	1.2	22.4	76.1	579630
92679	TRABUCO CANYON	56631	12152	2.5	6.3	23.8	26.2	41.2	130650	155700	100	98	11279	0.0	0.1	0.5	16.3	83.2	671652
92683	WESTMINSTER	21060	26417	20.7	23.3	34.4	15.2	6.4	56077	66565	81	62	15876	7.5	3.2	2.6	57.3	29.5	341995
92688	RANCHO SANTA MARGARI	37874	19312	6.2	15.4	37.5	25.7	15.2	85645	104601	96	90	14624	0.3	0.1	3.4	42.2	54.1	417749
92691	MISSION VIEJO	36766	15708	6.8	15.8	36.2	24.8	16.4	85373	103770	96	89	12867	0.5	0.3	2.0	30.6	66.7	450590
92692	MISSION VIEJO	44059	16897	7.4	14.1	31.3	24.3	23.0	94323	113074	98	93	13895	0.9	0.4	0.6	32.8	65.4	478826
92694	LADERA RANCH	71088	231	8.2	7.4	17.3	21.7	45.5	137857	171191	100	99	222	0.9	0.0	10.8	3.6	84.7	1000001
92697	IRVINE	22629	2199	39.8	18.0	21.7	9.9	10.5	39314	50595	44	29	555	15.9	1.1	2.2	39.5	41.4	324603
92701	SANTA ANA	10516	12624	30.6	36.0	25.4	5.7	2.4	36783	41642	35	24	3439	0.7	3.4	18.3	73.4	4.2	258624
92703	SANTA ANA	10999	12956	23.8	31.0	34.3	8.5	2.4	45505	51893	63	42	6895	10.4	4.3	10.6	71.8	3.0	250673
92704	SANTA ANA	14408	20263	16.3	27.4	39.3	13.2	3.8	55364	63562	80	62	11343	10.1	3.6	9.3	67.4	9.6	270980
92705	SANTA ANA	37338	14283	12.2	21.8	28.5	17.1	20.5	73392	88550	93	81	10006	1.3	1.1	3.6	19.6	74.5	564179
92706	SANTA ANA	18109	9649	18.9	29.2	31.6	13.3	7.0	51880	60814	75	56	5115	0.3	0.0	5.0	57.0	37.7	358651
92707	SANTA ANA	14412	13357	15.7	29.7	38.4	11.8	4.4	53549	61397	78	59	7030	0.9	0.7	8.4	79.4	10.7	273126
92708	FOUNTAIN VALLEY	31345	18165	9.2	17.4	36.3	23.9	13.3	79553	96459	95	86	13768	2.1	1.6	1.6	24.0	70.9	462036
92780	TUSTIN	22232	18868	16.8	29.5	34.9	12.9	6.0	53114	61708	77	58	8415	3.9	3.5	6.7	42.8	43.1	362156
92782	TUSTIN	55775	8565	5.1	11.0	34.5	24.1	25.2	98690	122490	98	93	5556	0.5	0.9	2.4	32.1	64.1	492335
92801	ANAHEIM	16347	17024	21.3	33.6	33.9	8.7	2.5	46246	52872	64	44	7177	8.1	3.6	6.4	73.8	8.1	278802
92802	ANAHEIM	16061	12839	21.8	30.9	33.3	10.5	3.5	47415	54643	67	47	5709	8.4	2.6	3.7	72.7	12.7	295145
92804	ANAHEIM	18401	26062	22.1	30.9	32.5	10.7	3.8	47118	55506	66	46	12050	3.9	2.1	4.9	79.0	10.2	302676
92805	ANAHEIM	14119	17223	22.8	33.8	31.3	9.1	3.2	44161	50664	59	40	7543	4.8	1.0	3.2	81.7	9.2	287609
92806	ANAHEIM	21097	10932	14.7	28.1	37.8	14.7	4.7	56676	65995	81	63	5603	4.9	2.9	4.9	66.3	21.0	334522
92807	ANAHEIM	40401	12307	9.0	15.4	32.8	23.2	19.7	87102	105812	97	90	9878	2.0	1.1	2.6	34.8	59.5	441782
92808	ANAHEIM	44798	8447	4.1	9.6	35.3	28.6	22.5	101162	122080	98	94	6958	0.2	0.7	0.6	35.1	63.5	481321
92821	BREA	30566	12451	14.1	21.2	35.7	18.8	10.3	66644	80301	90	74	8224	2.0	3.8	5.5	39.6	49.2	396859
92823	BREA	31991	532	7.9	25.2	38.4	17.7	10.9	68708	82583	91	76	469	17.3	11.3	4.7	20.3	46.5	362500
92831	FULLERTON	28449	13153	19.4	29.0	30.9	12.6	8.1	51561	60615	75	56	5596	0.7	0.4	4.0	48.6	46.2	385724
92832	FULLERTON	19999	7554	23.4	28.0	34.6	9.8	4.3	48871	56483	70	50	3213	2.9	2.4	3.8	70.0	21.0	301113
92833	FULLERTON	24035	14833	18.3	25.3	34.0	14.6	7.8	57274	67366	82	64	9465	3.6	2.4	2.4	59.5	32.1	329243
92835	FULLERTON	43145	8654	11.5	18.9	33.4	19.3	17.0	75977	91552	94	82	6328	0.1	0.7	3.1	29.3	66.9	475852
92840	GARDEN GROVE	19306	15262	19.0	28.0	36.0	12.3	4.7	52436	61327	76	57	8823	5.6	2.9	5.6	75.8	10.1	295136
92841	GARDEN GROVE	19833	9035	19.9	26.8	34.9	12.0	6.4	53060	62291	77	58	5307	4.2	1.2	3.4	74.6	16.7	324217
92843	GARDEN GROVE	13667	10940	22.7	30.8	34.2	10.0	2.4	46567	52955	65	44	5968	7.6	2.7	4.8	79.8	5.1	281277
92844	GARDEN GROVE	15778	7112	23.8	28.8	34.8	9.8	2.9	47816	55937	68	47	3475	7.2	0.8	6.4	77.4	8.4	271769
92845	GARDEN GROVE	31347	5653	9.2	17.7	37.5	25.8	9.8	78794	95089	95	85	4741	0.6	0.0	0.2	55.2	43.9	385732
92860	NORCO	26168	6825	11.5	18.6	38.3	21.5	10.2	72253	85248	92	79	5862	0.9	0.1	4.3	66.3	28.4	327476
92861	VILLA PARK	65517	1906	4.0	9.5	22.0	21.9	42.5	132114	163607	100	98	1847	0.0	0.2	1.6	2.0	96.3	995427
92862	ORANGE	43603	7	0.0	0.0	28.6	42.9	28.6	129468	150000	100	98	6	0.0	0.0	0.0	0.0	100.0	625000
92865	ORANGE	24489	5993	15.3	25.1	35.8	16.2	7.6	60830	72857	85	68	4078	3.3	2.1	4.4	56.3	33.9	357162
92866	ORANGE	26345	6039	21.0	26.0	35.4	12.8	4.9	52708	63245	76	57	2700	3.3	2.2	7.0	42.7	44.8	381555
92867	ORANGE	31426	12918	12.5	18.9	34.0	19.4	15.2	75027	88815	93	82	9050	3.0	1.9	1.4	36.6	57.1	432870
92868	ORANGE	20474	6754	21.5	27.8	34.9	11.4	4.3	50615	60178	73	53	2786	4.4	1.5	6.7	76.9	10.5	278003
92869	ORANGE	35128	12221	8.5	15.9	33.8	23.0	18.8	85326	104190	96	89	9759	0.8	0.5	2.4	34.7	61.7	457646
92870	PLACENTIA	28360	16331	11.2	21.2	36.6	20.5	10.5	70496	84553	91	78	11169	2.7	1.2	3.1	36.9	56.1	417884
92879	CORONA	21817	15588	16.2	23.4	38.3	17.2	4.9	59450	69938	84	67	9544	3.8	2.1	9.7	71.7	12.7	269557
92880	CORONA	22618	6363	11.8	20.4	40.2	21.6	6.1	71065	78916	92	79	4705	2.7	2.1	3.1	76.3	15.8	314894
92881	CORONA	29391	8576	7.9	13.2	40.1	26.3	12.6	83480	101188	96	88	7330	1.0	0.9	3.3	63.2	31.7	347721
92882	CORONA	23153	20383	14.9	23.1	37.7	17.6	6.8	63220	73911	87	70	14044	3.1	1.0	9.8	62.4	23.8	298238
92883	CORONA	25956	5161	7.8	15.8	47.6	21.8	7.0	76148	87185	94	83	4738	4.3	3.3	7.4	72.1	12.9	279762
92886	YORBA LINDA	39491	13799	6.8	14.2	32.4	26.5	20.2	93503	113087	98	92	11873	0.4	1.3	2.0	25.2	71.2	481522
92887	YORBA LINDA	51655	8265	4.1	7.8	26.8	27.2	34.0	118496	142493	99	97	7110	0.4	0.3	0.8	14.2	84.4	648462
93001	VENTURA	27124	12955	23.2	26.6	31.3	11.2	7.7	50164	60325	72	53	6025	4.7	1.9	7.4	45.8	40.3	345400
93003	VENTURA	31224	19350	15.5	22.5	38.8	15.6	7.7	62043	73682	86	70	12236	2.0	2.3	8.4	49.4	37.9	361151
93004	VENTURA	29691	10170	13.7	20.7	36.2	20.0	9.5	69199	82783	91	77	7470	2.1	3.4	1.8	50.7	42.1	379699
93010	CAMARILLO	34616	16102	12.3	19.6	35.1	19.1	13.9	73019	87503	92	80	11480	1.2	1.1	1.2	41.5	54.9	420977
93012	CAMARILLO	40957	10852	12.6	16.8	31.1	20.5	19.0	80490	99892	95	86	9392	0.8	1.5	2.5	41.6	53.7	419161
93013	CARPINTERIA	31407	6104	16.0	25.1	32.3	16.2	10.4	59660	73267	84	67	3849	2.8	0.9	7.6	20.7	67.9	604937
93015	FILLMORE	18123	5119	22.4	26.5	33.4	13.2	4.4	50914	60073	74	54	3133	6.3	3.9	8.6	67.9	13.3	268310
93021	MOORPARK	29538	10598	8.0	16.3	35.0	25.8	14.9	85382	101338	96	89	8875	0.4	0.8	3.5	37.2	58.1	435493
93022	OAK VIEW	29599	2073	14.7	21.5	35.0	17.8	11.0	64329	77864	88	71	1652	4.4	2.7	2.5	53.2	37.2	359924
93023	OJAI	31974	8495	17.9	24.1	32.2	15.8	10.0	60155	74194	84	67	6087	5.8	4.9	2.5	36.6	50.3	401630
93030	OXNARD	15982	12824	23.3	26.6	33.3	11.8	5.1	50156	59628	72	53	6901	4.4	0.7	4.0	69.8	21.2	298447
93033	OXNARD	13380	16976	19.3	29.6	36.7	10.9	3.4	50841	58353	74	54	10071	8.7	3.7	6.3	78.8	2.5	263210
93035	OXNARD	31009	9503	9.7	23.0	41.6	16.2	9.5	66733	79036	90	75	5943	0.1	1.1	5.5	52.0	41.3	371636
93036	OXNARD	20441	10452	18.1	26.7	33.7	15.1	6.4	55337	65145	80	61	6133	5.8	3.1	6.4	54.1	30.6	318278
93041	PORT HUENEME	20928	7006	22.5	28.4	37.1	9.1	3.0	49277	56975	71	51	3598	0.7	0.5	11.4	80.8	6.6	257799
93042	POINT MUGU NAWC	13761	769	15.3	43.8	35.5	3.8	1.6	43345	50914	57	39	0	0.0	0.0	0.0	0.0	0.0	0
93043	PORT HUENEME CBC BAS	13491	629	25.3	53.4	18.8	2.5	0.0	33312	38450	22	17	22	13.6	18.2	18.2	50.0	0.0	162500
93060	SANTA PAULA	18058	9229	23.7	27.6	32.7	10.6	5.4	48335	56065	69	49	5387	7.6	3.9	11.9	59.1	17.6	265963
93063	SIMI VALLEY	29834	17377	10.7	17.4	37.4	23.5	11.0	77815	91831	94	84	13796	1.7	1.3	3.4	53.8	39.8	370839
93065	SIMI VALLEY	33225	21899	8.2	15.8	37.8	23.4	14.8	82251	99233	96	88	17019	0.8	0.4	1.2	53.6	44.0	383293
93066	SOMIS	40617	1032	9.7	19.6	32.3	14.0	24.5	74058	92452	93	81	694	1.6	1.2	1.6	21.5	74.2	951299
93067	SUMMERLAND	58762	295	13.9	20.7	34.6	13.6	17.3	66454	84851	89	74	199	0.0	0.0	1.0	17.1	81.9	1000001
93101	SANTA BARBARA	25419	12264	26.8	26.1	30.8	10.2	6.1	46903	56882	66	45	3523	1.7	1.1	1.5	9.0	86.7	673496
93103	SANTA BARBARA	34901	7835	17.2	25.8	28.4	14.1	14.6	57082	70891	82	64	3945	2.2	2.5	0.7	6.9	87.8	991055
93105	SANTA BARBARA	46564	11877	14.7	20.2	30.8	17.9	16.3	69902	87836	91	78	7028	1.3	0.3	1.0	5.3	92.2	932600
93106	SANTA BARBARA	5114	84	54.8	34.5	9.5	1.2	0.0	21467	26258	2	2	0	0.0	0.0	0.0	0.0	0.0	0
93108	SANTA BARBARA	84392	4779	8.9	12.2	21.6	19.4	38.0	116167	150559	99	97	3698	0.1	0.9	0.7	3.4	95.1	1000001
93109	SANTA BARBARA	38066	4655	17.6	19.5	30.6	17.3	15.0	66178	84715	89	74	2795	0.3	0.0	1.3	4.0	94.4	937767
93110	SANTA BARBARA	37133	5724	16.8	26.2	30.1	14.9	12.0	57808	71357	82	65	3623	0.3	1.6	10.6	14.8	72.9	725323
93111	SANTA BARBARA	38418	5935	7.9	17.7	37.0	23.0	14.4	80056	99066	95	86	4687	0.1	0.2	0.3	6.6	92.8	748759
93117	GOLETA	23460	16923	28.7	23.6	28.6	12.0	7.1	47453	56606	67	47	7282	0.6	1.3	4.6	12.6	80.9	640596
93202	ARMONA	11965	474	32.5	39.9	23.0	2.3	2.3	35701	38994	30	21	353	1.4	3.4	84.4	10.5	0.3	132685
93203	ARVIN	8192	3793	47.7	32.5	16.4	2.1	1.3	25974	29135	6	6	1969	8.9	14.3	70.2	6.1	0.5	110547
93204	AVENAL	14432	2020	37.5	37.0	20.8	2.5	2.1	31895	35167	18	14	1032	7.6	17.7	69.8	4.9	0.0	115296
93205	BODFISH	15001	891	53.5	31.0	12.8	1.2	1.5	23254	26210	3	3	738	15.7	38.9	34.6	10.7	0.1	84603
93206	BUTTONWILLOW	12348	527	36.1	37.0	20.3	4.0	2.7	31690	35159	17	13	308	10.7	18.8	58.1	11.4	1.0	112195
93207	CALIFORNIA HOT SPRIN	15762	244	33.6	33.6	21.7	5.7	5.3	34697	38919	26	19	180	11.7	11.1	38.9	28.3	10.0	142105
93210	COALINGA	16026	4021	28.7	31.6	29.4	8.2	2.2	41390	47559	51	35	2320	10.1	11.2	57.1	19.1	2.5	129538
93212	CORCORAN	14712	3686	40.2	34.2	20.8	3.7	1.2	31081	34381	15	12	2266	4.6	12.5	62.0	18.8	2.1	125333
	CALIFORNIA	27293		21.8	24.4	30.5	13.7	9.7	54267	64547				3.3	2.7	13.3	42.9	37.9	319678
	UNITED STATES	25866		24.7	27.1	30.8	10.9	6.5	48124	56710				10.9	15.0	33.7	30.1	10.4	145905

ZIP CODE		FINANCIAL SERVICES				THE HOME						ENTERTAINMENT						PERSONAL			
						Home Improvements		Furnishings													
#	POST OFFICE NAME	Auto Loan	Home Loan	Invest-ments	Retire-ment Plans	Home Repair	Lawn & Garden	Comput-ers & Hard-ware	Major Appli-ances	TV, Radio, Sound Equip-ment	Furni-ture	Dine out/ Carry out	Sports Equip-ment	Fees & Tickets	Toys & Games	Travel	Cable TV	Apparel & Services	Auto Repairs	Health Insur-ance	Pets & Supplies
92663	NEWPORT BEACH	171	183	275	195	178	193	191	180	189	194	239	214	201	246	193	187	237	185	170	199
92672	SAN CLEMENTE	130	136	160	140	133	142	138	134	134	139	169	156	140	167	136	130	166	137	126	147
92673	SAN CLEMENTE	171	192	205	198	187	193	178	176	167	182	213	202	188	210	179	162	210	174	162	196
92675	SAN JUAN CAPISTRANO	162	180	202	179	178	187	170	172	165	174	208	194	177	208	173	163	206	170	163	188
92676	SILVERADO	155	188	195	192	182	179	167	166	154	170	195	193	178	203	169	147	194	160	146	183
92677	LAGUNA NIGUEL	170	198	221	204	191	196	183	180	171	187	217	208	194	220	184	165	217	177	161	198
92679	TRABUCO CANYON	250	302	321	312	291	290	268	263	245	275	312	305	289	320	269	235	312	255	231	290
92683	WESTMINSTER	90	101	128	106	101	101	103	102	96	102	122	124	102	122	103	91	121	105	88	108
92688	RANCHO SANTA MARGARI	152	164	165	172	157	156	154	152	144	160	183	178	157	180	150	135	180	151	132	167
92691	MISSION VIEJO	138	169	203	167	163	168	156	154	147	158	186	178	165	195	159	144	186	152	138	166
92692	MISSION VIEJO	166	188	204	192	184	191	174	174	164	178	208	196	183	206	175	160	205	170	162	191
92694	LADERA RANCH	252	339	465	332	331	357	295	293	275	302	348	329	335	366	315	278	353	281	272	318
92697	IRVINE	89	66	104	75	64	74	103	81	102	94	128	108	93	123	90	94	123	95	76	92
92701	SANTA ANA	71	61	62	61	60	62	69	68	71	72	90	78	66	88	64	66	90	72	62	72
92703	SANTA ANA	80	71	73	71	70	72	78	78	80	82	101	90	75	99	74	75	102	82	71	83
92704	SANTA ANA	92	88	100	89	86	89	94	93	95	98	120	107	92	119	91	90	120	97	84	99
92705	SANTA ANA	151	178	215	174	173	181	168	166	163	171	205	189	178	213	171	160	206	165	153	179
92706	SANTA ANA	95	97	109	94	94	98	98	98	99	102	126	111	99	127	96	96	126	100	90	105
92707	SANTA ANA	96	86	91	87	84	88	95	93	97	99	123	108	92	120	89	91	123	98	85	101
92708	FOUNTAIN VALLEY	114	149	192	144	144	149	137	135	129	137	162	156	146	173	142	127	163	133	120	143
92780	TUSTIN	90	95	114	94	92	96	97	94	96	99	121	109	98	124	95	93	122	97	86	102
92782	TUSTIN	176	190	245	204	182	187	189	179	181	194	230	213	197	235	186	174	229	181	160	198
92801	ANAHEIM	77	77	87	76	75	79	79	79	80	82	102	89	79	102	78	78	101	81	74	85
92802	ANAHEIM	82	82	90	79	79	83	84	83	85	87	108	94	84	109	82	83	108	86	77	90
92804	ANAHEIM	82	83	97	82	80	85	86	84	86	89	110	96	86	111	84	84	110	87	78	91
92805	ANAHEIM	83	75	77	74	73	76	81	81	84	85	106	92	79	103	77	79	106	85	75	87
92806	ANAHEIM	93	95	110	96	92	98	97	95	96	100	122	109	97	121	95	93	120	98	88	104
92807	ANAHEIM	149	182	212	180	176	182	166	165	157	168	198	190	177	207	170	154	198	161	150	180
92808	ANAHEIM	174	199	205	207	190	188	181	179	167	187	212	208	189	214	178	157	211	174	154	195
92821	BREA	110	120	139	123	118	123	118	116	114	119	144	135	121	144	118	111	142	117	108	127
92823	BREA	108	138	157	134	134	136	124	123	117	123	147	142	133	158	128	115	147	119	112	133
92831	FULLERTON	98	98	123	101	95	102	107	101	105	107	133	120	107	132	103	101	131	106	92	110
92832	FULLERTON	88	82	94	85	80	85	90	87	90	92	114	101	87	110	86	86	112	91	81	95
92833	FULLERTON	97	106	131	108	105	107	108	107	104	109	132	126	108	133	108	100	132	110	95	114
92835	FULLERTON	146	166	194	166	164	173	159	158	153	160	192	180	165	194	162	151	190	157	150	172
92840	GARDEN GROVE	89	95	111	94	92	96	95	94	94	97	119	108	96	121	94	91	119	96	86	101
92841	GARDEN GROVE	87	100	124	100	98	100	98	97	94	99	119	114	100	122	99	91	120	99	86	103
92843	GARDEN GROVE	76	78	92	80	78	78	82	82	80	84	101	96	80	100	80	75	101	85	72	86
92844	GARDEN GROVE	70	82	114	92	85	80	88	86	77	84	97	110	84	94	88	69	97	91	69	89
92845	GARDEN GROVE	113	140	161	137	137	142	128	127	122	128	153	146	136	160	133	121	152	125	119	138
92860	NORCO	111	135	145	133	131	132	123	122	116	123	146	142	130	154	125	113	146	119	111	133
92861	VILLA PARK	245	325	419	316	317	338	286	285	268	290	338	321	318	356	303	270	341	274	265	308
92862	ORANGE	194	223	218	232	212	206	200	198	183	208	233	231	208	234	196	171	231	192	169	217
92865	ORANGE	99	111	123	110	108	111	107	106	103	109	130	122	110	134	107	100	130	106	97	115
92866	ORANGE	93	95	107	98	93	97	98	96	96	99	121	113	98	120	95	91	119	98	88	104
92867	ORANGE	132	154	177	151	150	155	145	143	140	148	177	164	153	185	147	137	178	142	131	155
92868	ORANGE	78	83	99	83	81	85	84	83	82	86	104	96	84	105	83	80	104	85	76	89
92869	ORANGE	148	172	195	171	166	170	161	159	154	165	195	182	169	201	162	150	196	158	143	172
92870	PLACENTIA	114	129	149	129	125	129	124	122	119	126	150	141	128	154	124	115	150	122	110	132
92879	CORONA	105	105	100	108	103	104	103	103	100	106	125	120	102	124	99	95	123	103	94	115
92880	CORONA	112	122	119	126	118	116	114	114	107	118	135	133	116	135	111	100	134	112	99	125
92881	CORONA	141	159	155	164	152	148	144	143	133	149	169	167	148	170	141	125	167	140	123	157
92882	CORONA	111	116	117	119	112	112	113	112	108	117	137	130	114	137	109	102	136	112	99	122
92883	CORONA	122	135	128	140	129	125	122	122	113	127	143	142	125	143	119	106	141	119	105	134
92886	YORBA LINDA	148	189	218	187	184	187	169	167	157	169	198	193	182	211	174	154	199	162	150	182
92887	YORBA LINDA	217	266	284	273	256	257	236	231	216	240	274	268	255	284	238	208	275	223	204	255
93001	VENTURA	94	95	104	97	94	98	98	96	96	98	121	113	97	120	96	92	119	99	90	106
93003	VENTURA	103	115	135	116	112	118	113	110	109	113	138	129	117	140	114	107	136	111	103	121
93004	VENTURA	114	132	138	133	129	131	122	122	115	123	145	141	127	148	123	111	143	119	111	134
93010	CAMARILLO	124	147	172	145	144	149	138	136	132	139	166	157	146	173	141	130	166	135	126	148
93012	CAMARILLO	145	165	175	164	162	172	149	153	143	154	180	168	158	177	153	142	177	148	148	168
93013	CARPINTERIA	117	128	145	123	125	132	123	123	122	125	153	140	126	155	124	121	152	123	118	135
93015	FILLMORE	93	89	89	85	89	95	89	93	91	93	114	102	87	109	88	90	112	94	91	101
93021	MOORPARK	142	163	168	167	157	156	149	147	139	153	176	171	157	179	148	132	176	144	129	161
93022	OAK VIEW	115	134	145	134	132	135	125	125	118	125	149	144	131	153	127	115	147	122	115	136
93023	OJAI	110	126	138	125	124	130	120	119	115	119	145	137	124	148	122	114	143	118	114	131
93030	OXNARD	92	85	85	84	83	86	90	91	92	94	116	103	87	113	86	87	116	94	83	97
93033	OXNARD	87	83	87	81	81	85	86	87	88	90	111	98	84	109	83	84	111	90	81	93
93035	OXNARD	116	126	142	127	124	129	123	122	119	124	150	140	125	150	123	116	148	122	114	134
93036	OXNARD	94	99	106	95	95	99	97	98	96	101	121	110	97	122	95	93	121	99	89	105
93041	PORT HUENEME	82	85	94	82	84	91	83	85	83	86	105	93	84	102	84	83	103	85	84	92
93042	POINT MUGU NAWC	80	51	48	58	46	55	75	65	77	70	96	87	64	86	62	70	92	77	60	74
93043	PORT HUENEME CBC BAS	62	39	37	45	36	43	58	50	59	54	74	67	50	66	48	54	71	59	47	57
93060	SANTA PAULA	91	86	85	83	84	88	88	91	90	93	113	100	86	109	86	87	113	93	85	97
93063	SIMI VALLEY	122	138	142	140	134	135	128	127	121	129	152	149	132	155	128	116	151	125	115	141
93065	SIMI VALLEY	139	158	171	161	152	154	149	146	140	151	177	171	154	180	148	134	176	145	130	160
93066	SOMIS	148	192	238	181	186	197	172	172	165	175	208	192	186	221	180	167	209	168	160	184
93067	SUMMERLAND	155	176	216	182	174	179	174	169	166	173	209	201	179	214	175	161	207	171	155	185
93101	SANTA BARBARA	88	84	109	88	81	87	94	88	94	95	119	105	93	118	90	90	118	94	82	97
93103	SANTA BARBARA	130	139	162	137	135	142	139	138	138	143	174	158	141	176	138	134	174	141	127	148
93105	SANTA BARBARA	133	155	197	155	152	161	151	147	146	151	183	171	158	189	154	144	182	148	137	160
93106	SANTA BARBARA	38	23	29	26	23	28	45	33	43	38	54	46	36	49	36	38	51	40	30	37
93108	SANTA BARBARA	272	334	422	331	329	353	303	304	288	309	363	342	330	370	318	289	362	296	289	332
93109	SANTA BARBARA	116	132	169	131	128	137	133	127	129	132	162	149	138	167	134	127	162	130	118	138
93110	SANTA BARBARA	123	134	163	134	134	145	132	133	130	133	163	149	136	159	135	129	159	133	130	144
93111	SANTA BARBARA	130	170	216	164	165	173	154	152	146	155	184	173	167	196	161	146	185	149	139	163
93117	GOLETA	91	85	104	88	83	90	103	91	99	97	125	112	98	121	95	93	121	98	84	101
93202	ARMONA	68	60	50	55	57	60	61	66	63	66	79	70	56	70	58	61	79	67	62	69
93203	ARVIN	51	43	41	43	43	44	48	49	50	51	64	56	46	61	45	47	64	52	45	52
93204	AVENAL	53	45	44	45	44	45	51	51	53	54	67	58	48	65	47	49	67	54	46	54
93205	BODFISH	48	46	48	42	49	59	43	50	46	46	57	47	43	48	47	49	53	48	59	54
93206	BUTTONWILLOW	70	63	51	59	61	64	62	67	64	67	80	73	58	72	60	62	79	68	64	73
93207	CALIFORNIA HOT SPRIN	90	69	46	65	75	82	69	81	76	71	92	93	61	87	70	78	87	81	88	102
93210	COALINGA	72	69	64	66	67	69	69	72	70	73	88	79	66	82	67	67	87	73	67	76
93212	CORCORAN	53	46	40	44	45	47	48	51	50	52	63	55	44	56	46	48	62	53	48	54
	CALIFORNIA	107	111	131	112	109	115	113	111	111	114	140	129	114	141	112	109	139	113	104	122
	UNITED STATES	100	100	100	100	100	100	100	100	100	100	100	100	100	100	100	100	100	100	100	100

POPULATION CHANGE

ZIP CODE			POPULATION			2000-2004 ANNUAL RATE		HOUSEHOLDS					FAMILIES		
#	POST OFFICE NAME	COUNTY FIPS CODE	2000	2004	2009	% Rate	State Centile	2000	2004	2009	% Annual Rate 2000-2004	2004 Average HH Size	2000	2004	% Annual Rate 2000-2004
93215	DELANO	029	45059	48369	52292	1.7	73	9661	10377	11220	1.7	4.12	8374	8965	1.6
93219	EARLIMART	107	10236	10610	11283	0.9	48	2415	2492	2635	0.7	4.26	2077	2138	0.7
93221	EXETER	107	13514	14269	15367	1.3	64	4458	4676	5004	1.1	3.03	3513	3677	1.1
93223	FARMERSVILLE	107	8935	9357	10023	1.1	58	2191	2284	2436	1.0	4.03	1899	1975	0.9
93224	FELLOWS	029	614	615	635	0.0	16	211	213	223	0.2	1.62	167	131	-5.6
93225	FRAZIER PARK	029	6854	6859	7237	0.0	15	2680	2675	2807	-0.2	2.56	1873	1854	-0.2
93226	GLENNVILLE	029	242	240	254	-0.2	9	101	100	105	-0.2	2.40	72	70	-0.7
93230	HANFORD	031	54413	59163	65045	2.0	79	18055	19459	21216	1.8	2.99	13644	14697	1.8
93234	HURON	019	8889	9375	10021	1.3	63	1874	1986	2131	1.4	3.97	1635	1727	1.3
93235	IVANHOE	107	4524	4758	5086	1.2	61	1156	1204	1277	1.0	3.95	979	1020	1.0
93238	KERNVILLE	029	1063	1059	1112	-0.1	11	480	477	500	-0.2	1.97	282	277	-0.4
93239	KETTLEMAN CITY	031	1810	1808	1901	0.0	12	383	379	395	-0.3	4.61	340	335	-0.4
93240	LAKE ISABELLA	029	5571	5912	6381	1.4	67	2537	2685	2880	1.3	2.18	1555	1629	1.1
93241	LAMONT	029	15903	16315	17365	0.6	36	3723	3795	4005	0.5	4.30	3221	3270	0.4
93242	LATON	019	2939	3044	3246	0.8	47	872	899	951	0.7	3.38	718	738	0.7
93243	LEBEC	037	543	552	579	0.4	27	182	185	192	0.4	2.98	134	135	0.2
93244	LEMON COVE	107	134	131	138	-0.5	5	54	53	56	-0.4	2.47	40	39	-0.6
93245	LEMOORE	031	30550	32938	35922	1.8	75	9322	10000	10843	1.7	3.18	7489	8018	1.6
93247	LINDSAY	107	15282	16093	17258	1.2	62	4166	4341	4617	1.0	3.67	3397	3530	0.9
93249	LOST HILLS	029	2684	2792	2980	0.9	52	519	536	568	0.8	5.18	465	479	0.7
93250	MC FARLAND	029	10974	12002	13105	2.1	81	2300	2531	2770	2.3	4.21	2071	2273	2.2
93251	MC KITTRICK	029	444	448	460	0.2	20	147	150	158	0.5	1.33	118	55	-16.4
93252	MARICOPA	111	4228	4239	4393	0.1	16	627	620	649	-0.3	4.62	463	456	-0.4
93254	NEW CUYAMA	083	647	642	648	-0.2	9	232	231	234	-0.1	2.78	165	164	-0.1
93255	ONYX	029	371	361	380	-0.6	4	170	165	173	-0.7	2.15	108	104	-0.9
93256	PIXLEY	107	4039	4210	4477	1.0	54	1049	1073	1127	0.5	3.91	886	906	0.5
93257	PORTERVILLE	107	64699	69331	75013	1.6	72	19250	20483	22030	1.5	3.30	15000	15955	1.5
93260	POSEY	107	245	230	240	-1.5	1	103	97	101	-1.4	2.37	71	67	-1.4
93262	SEQUOIA NATIONAL PAR	107	1	1	1	0.0	15	1	1	1	0.0	1.00	1	0	-100.0
93263	SHAFTER	029	15190	16154	17417	1.5	68	3982	4208	4512	1.3	3.62	3333	3508	1.2
93265	SPRINGVILLE	107	3773	3872	4119	0.6	37	1612	1656	1759	0.6	2.27	1098	1126	0.6
93266	STRATFORD	031	1653	1790	1964	1.9	77	392	412	443	1.2	4.34	341	358	1.2
93267	STRATHMORE	107	5700	5898	6287	0.8	47	1494	1535	1623	0.6	3.83	1236	1267	0.6
93268	TAFT	029	14943	15521	16573	0.9	51	5211	5402	5744	0.9	2.73	3743	3851	0.7
93270	TERRA BELLA	107	6076	6401	6849	1.2	63	1591	1676	1788	1.2	3.81	1353	1423	1.2
93271	THREE RIVERS	107	2276	2344	2506	0.7	41	1001	1031	1098	0.7	2.27	672	688	0.6
93272	TIPTON	107	2744	2910	3129	1.4	66	744	782	833	1.2	3.72	625	657	1.2
93274	TULARE	107	56103	60628	65889	1.8	76	17096	18395	19882	1.7	3.27	13720	14729	1.7
93276	TUPMAN	029	92	93	96	0.3	22	30	31	32	0.8	1.65	24	20	-4.2
93277	VISALIA	107	44932	47799	51647	1.5	68	16530	17553	18901	1.4	2.68	11866	12581	1.4
93280	WASCO	029	22519	24055	25925	1.6	70	4328	4695	5140	1.9	3.79	3704	4003	1.8
93283	WELDON	029	2116	2094	2209	-0.3	8	925	914	958	-0.3	2.29	604	592	-0.5
93285	WOFFORD HEIGHTS	029	3320	3319	3512	0.0	12	1647	1642	1727	-0.1	2.00	990	977	-0.3
93286	WOODLAKE	107	9235	9752	10485	1.3	64	2662	2814	3018	1.3	3.46	2187	2306	1.3
93287	WOODY	029	132	131	139	-0.2	9	55	54	57	-0.4	2.43	39	38	-0.6
93291	VISALIA	107	36738	40481	44635	2.3	83	10356	11473	12666	2.4	3.39	8110	8981	2.4
93292	VISALIA	107	29940	32891	36086	2.2	83	9862	10837	11850	2.2	3.00	7687	8419	2.2
93301	BAKERSFIELD	029	12842	13467	14511	1.1	59	5020	5253	5655	1.1	2.37	2852	2947	0.8
93304	BAKERSFIELD	029	45762	47505	50967	0.9	50	14995	15431	16412	0.7	3.05	10799	11054	0.6
93305	BAKERSFIELD	029	35663	37292	40081	1.1	57	10446	10798	11493	0.8	3.35	7780	7998	0.7
93306	BAKERSFIELD	029	53424	56319	60742	1.3	63	17620	18415	19696	1.0	3.03	13298	13823	0.9
93307	BAKERSFIELD	029	59205	63282	68725	1.6	71	16139	17124	18429	1.4	3.68	13090	13829	1.3
93308	BAKERSFIELD	029	44853	48500	53007	1.9	77	16131	17430	18982	1.8	2.65	11208	12068	1.8
93309	BAKERSFIELD	029	58086	60802	65566	1.1	58	22241	23178	24834	1.0	2.60	14899	15423	0.8
93311	BAKERSFIELD	029	20267	23645	26925	3.7	95	7307	8266	9191	2.9	2.82	5340	6072	3.1
93312	BAKERSFIELD	029	27698	35137	41666	5.8	98	9043	11345	13303	5.5	3.09	7472	9371	5.5
93313	BAKERSFIELD	029	25760	29739	33639	3.4	93	7719	8806	9855	3.2	3.31	6500	7398	3.1
93314	BAKERSFIELD	029	13166	15539	17768	4.0	95	3992	4711	5361	4.0	3.27	3543	4168	3.9
93401	SAN LUIS OBISPO	079	27041	28277	30365	1.1	57	11739	12276	13214	1.1	2.24	5579	5858	1.2
93402	LOS OSOS	079	14786	14908	15730	0.2	19	6063	6160	6528	0.4	2.41	3998	4022	0.1
93405	SAN LUIS OBISPO	079	31461	32259	33798	0.6	36	9144	9580	10301	1.1	2.30	3642	3713	0.5
93407	SAN LUIS OBISPO	079	1395	1409	1428	0.2	21	12	12	13	0.0	2.58	1	1	0.0
93420	ARROYO GRANDE	079	25144	27170	29564	1.8	76	9965	10799	11779	1.9	2.50	6982	7536	1.8
93422	ATASCADERO	079	29528	31224	33603	1.3	65	10643	11328	12264	1.5	2.62	7657	8077	1.3
93426	BRADLEY	053	1427	1465	1544	0.6	37	581	602	634	0.8	2.43	417	427	0.6
93427	BUELLTON	083	5501	5952	6252	1.9	77	2004	2184	2300	2.0	2.72	1423	1547	2.0
93428	CAMBRIA	079	6462	7001	7601	1.9	78	2911	3167	3448	2.0	2.21	1944	2097	1.8
93429	CASMALIA	083	1	1	1	0.0	15	0	1	1	0.0	1.00	0	0	0.0
93430	CAYUCOS	079	3261	3264	3429	0.0	15	1529	1537	1621	0.1	2.11	888	883	-0.1
93432	CRESTON	079	1274	1423	1568	2.6	88	484	544	603	2.8	2.58	369	413	2.7
93433	GROVER BEACH	079	13002	13301	14049	0.5	33	4984	5121	5425	0.6	2.57	3285	3348	0.5
93434	GUADALUPE	083	5701	6050	6290	1.4	67	1424	1525	1591	1.6	3.97	1224	1309	1.6
93436	LOMPOC	083	52095	52028	52621	0.0	12	17149	17050	17276	-0.1	2.82	12479	12383	-0.2
93437	LOMPOC	083	6168	5347	5260	-3.3	0	1714	1478	1455	-3.4	3.30	1608	1385	-3.5
93441	LOS OLIVOS	083	1132	1166	1193	0.7	41	419	435	446	0.9	2.67	323	334	0.8
93442	MORRO BAY	079	11060	11346	11968	0.6	36	5259	5417	5733	0.7	2.05	2782	2833	0.4
93444	NIPOMO	079	14927	16760	18576	2.8	88	4912	5523	6130	2.8	3.03	3983	4461	2.7
93445	OCEANO	079	7295	7587	8056	0.9	52	2453	2569	2741	1.1	2.94	1721	1788	0.9
93446	PASO ROBLES	079	37012	41383	45648	2.7	88	13284	14891	16471	2.7	2.71	9674	10788	2.6
93449	PISMO BEACH	079	8551	9019	9674	1.3	63	4230	4470	4814	1.3	2.01	2320	2421	1.0
93450	SAN ARDO	053	874	854	874	-0.5	5	286	281	287	-0.4	3.04	209	204	-0.6
93451	SAN MIGUEL	053	1825	2001	2189	2.2	82	628	692	759	2.3	2.87	473	521	2.3
93452	SAN SIMEON	079	528	554	591	1.1	60	242	252	267	1.0	2.19	137	141	0.7
93453	SANTA MARGARITA	079	2255	2544	2821	2.9	89	885	1008	1123	3.1	2.50	597	677	3.0
93454	SANTA MARIA	083	30167	31644	33065	1.1	60	10247	10736	11209	1.1	2.78	7123	7475	1.1
93455	SANTA MARIA	083	37724	38308	39334	0.4	25	13319	13607	13997	0.5	2.78	10313	10510	0.5
93458	SANTA MARIA	083	44028	47108	49643	1.6	72	10665	11316	11858	1.4	4.13	8603	9074	1.3
93460	SANTA YNEZ	083	5529	5719	5883	0.8	46	2024	2108	2175	1.0	2.69	1580	1639	0.9
93461	SHANDON	079	1309	1408	1523	1.7	74	385	417	453	1.9	3.35	322	346	1.7
93463	SOLVANG	083	8085	8122	8244	0.1	18	3193	3225	3278	0.2	2.46	2185	2201	0.2
93465	TEMPLETON	079	8148	9161	10144	2.8	89	2806	3158	3503	2.8	2.88	2177	2438	2.7
93501	MOJAVE	029	4790	5121	5600	1.6	71	1784	1902	2069	1.5	2.68	1191	1262	1.4
93505	CALIFORNIA CITY	029	8269	8540	9084	0.8	43	3020	3112	3290	0.7	2.73	2221	2273	0.6
93510	ACTON	037	7146	7910	8475	2.4	84	2313	2550	2717	2.3	3.02	1816	2001	2.3
93512	BENTON	051	190	204	225	1.7	73	75	81	89	1.8	2.52	54	59	2.1
	CALIFORNIA					1.4					1.2	2.90			1.2
	UNITED STATES					1.2					1.3	2.58			1.1

ZIP CODE #	POST OFFICE NAME	RACE (%) White 2000	White 2004	Black 2000	Black 2004	Asian/Pacific 2000	Asian/Pacific 2004	% Hispanic Origin 2000	% Hispanic Origin 2004	2004 AGE DISTRIBUTION (%) 0-4	5-9	10-14	15-19	20-24	25-44	45-64	65-84	85+	18+	MEDIAN AGE 2004	% 2004 Males	% 2004 Females
93215	DELANO	26.7	25.2	5.1	4.6	14.3	13.6	70.1	73.4	9.7	8.5	9.2	8.7	9.9	31.5	15.6	6.2	0.8	67.5	27.3	56.3	43.7
93219	EARLIMART	25.7	24.3	1.4	1.3	6.4	6.0	80.9	83.0	12.0	10.9	11.1	10.1	9.5	25.9	14.7	5.5	0.5	60.0	23.2	51.9	48.1
93221	EXETER	72.1	68.1	0.6	0.6	1.2	1.4	34.7	39.9	8.4	8.1	9.1	8.1	7.5	25.2	22.5	9.6	1.6	69.4	32.5	48.8	51.3
93223	FARMERSVILLE	41.8	38.5	0.3	0.3	1.0	1.0	72.8	77.2	10.6	9.9	11.0	9.5	9.1	27.4	16.3	5.6	0.6	62.7	25.0	50.5	49.5
93224	FELLOWS	76.6	72.5	9.1	9.8	2.3	2.4	13.4	17.1	4.1	4.1	4.6	5.5	8.0	42.3	23.6	6.8	1.1	84.1	35.9	71.5	28.5
93225	FRAZIER PARK	86.6	83.7	0.5	0.6	1.2	1.3	12.5	15.9	6.3	6.9	8.4	7.3	4.9	23.5	30.9	11.1	0.8	73.8	40.9	50.2	49.8
93226	GLENNVILLE	83.5	80.0	0.8	1.3	1.2	1.7	7.4	9.6	5.0	5.4	6.7	5.8	5.4	21.3	32.9	15.4	2.1	78.8	45.2	54.6	45.4
93230	HANFORD	64.4	61.4	4.7	4.6	2.9	3.0	38.1	42.3	8.6	8.1	8.7	7.9	7.7	28.2	20.5	8.9	1.4	69.8	31.5	49.5	50.5
93234	HURON	24.1	23.0	3.2	3.0	0.7	0.6	90.7	92.3	9.9	8.4	9.2	9.4	11.8	32.8	14.8	3.4	0.2	66.8	25.7	61.0	39.0
93235	IVANHOE	49.2	46.2	0.4	0.4	0.8	0.8	73.6	78.1	10.5	9.7	9.9	9.4	9.2	28.5	16.8	5.3	0.7	64.2	25.8	52.9	47.1
93238	KERNVILLE	86.7	84.9	1.8	2.0	0.9	0.9	9.3	11.9	2.9	3.0	4.3	13.4	2.6	14.0	32.6	24.6	2.6	77.8	52.3	55.1	45.0
93239	KETTLEMAN CITY	31.7	30.0	0.4	0.3	0.3	0.2	91.9	93.5	9.8	8.1	10.1	9.9	13.1	28.4	16.9	3.5	0.2	66.0	24.6	56.2	43.8
93240	LAKE ISABELLA	91.3	89.6	0.4	0.4	0.7	0.7	5.9	7.6	4.6	4.6	5.5	6.1	5.2	16.5	29.1	24.3	4.2	81.3	50.4	48.2	51.8
93241	LAMONT	45.2	43.5	2.5	2.6	1.0	0.9	88.9	91.2	11.3	9.9	10.9	9.9	10.3	27.9	14.5	4.8	0.6	61.9	23.9	52.2	47.8
93242	LATON	57.5	53.3	0.5	0.5	0.8	0.8	54.2	59.5	9.5	8.7	9.4	8.6	8.0	27.9	19.3	8.0	0.8	67.0	29.1	51.1	48.9
93243	LEBEC	79.6	75.2	0.9	1.1	1.3	1.5	19.2	23.9	7.1	7.3	7.8	7.3	6.3	23.9	27.0	12.5	0.9	73.6	38.8	50.0	50.0
93244	LEMON COVE	90.3	89.3	0.0	0.0	0.8	0.8	9.7	11.5	3.8	5.3	6.9	6.1	3.8	19.9	35.1	17.6	1.5	79.4	47.0	50.4	49.6
93245	LEMOORE	60.6	56.9	7.3	7.5	7.7	8.0	28.7	32.7	11.1	8.9	8.3	8.3	11.4	30.6	15.5	5.5	0.5	67.3	26.1	51.5	48.5
93247	LINDSAY	48.2	45.3	0.5	0.4	1.6	1.6	70.6	74.7	10.6	9.3	9.9	8.8	8.2	26.6	17.1	8.2	1.4	64.9	27.3	50.9	49.1
93249	LOST HILLS	25.2	23.2	2.8	2.9	0.5	0.4	89.6	91.9	13.0	11.2	11.3	8.5	10.7	29.5	13.3	2.4	0.2	60.0	22.9	56.1	44.0
93250	MC FARLAND	30.4	27.9	3.4	3.1	1.0	1.0	82.1	85.6	9.7	8.9	9.4	9.3	10.2	32.8	15.1	4.3	0.5	66.5	26.4	57.1	42.9
93251	MC KITTRICK	71.0	66.3	12.2	13.0	2.5	2.9	15.3	19.4	3.6	3.4	3.8	4.9	8.3	50.7	21.2	4.0	0.2	86.6	34.9	79.0	21.0
93252	MARICOPA	76.8	72.7	7.1	7.6	1.8	2.0	17.0	21.0	4.7	4.8	5.8	6.3	7.2	39.8	24.0	7.0	0.5	81.0	35.8	68.0	32.0
93254	NEW CUYAMA	78.2	75.6	0.8	0.8	0.6	0.6	42.4	47.7	6.7	7.3	9.0	7.5	5.1	26.0	27.9	9.7	0.8	72.3	37.6	53.6	46.4
93255	ONYX	87.9	85.6	0.5	0.8	0.3	0.3	5.9	7.5	3.9	3.6	5.3	11.6	4.2	12.5	34.1	21.9	3.1	78.4	50.6	52.1	47.9
93256	PIXLEY	36.8	33.0	4.4	3.9	0.7	0.7	65.4	70.4	12.0	10.9	10.5	9.3	8.7	25.9	16.0	6.2	0.6	61.0	24.2	52.8	47.2
93257	PORTERVILLE	55.0	50.6	1.0	0.9	4.3	4.5	49.8	55.1	9.5	8.6	9.3	8.7	8.6	26.8	19.0	8.2	1.4	67.3	28.8	49.7	50.3
93260	POSEY	92.2	90.4	0.8	0.9	0.4	0.4	6.5	8.7	5.7	5.7	6.5	4.4	1.7	17.8	33.0	24.4	0.9	79.6	51.0	50.4	49.6
93262	SEQUOIA NATIONAL PAR	100.0	100.0	0.0	0.0	0.0	0.0	0.0	0.0	0.0	0.0	0.0	0.0	100.0	0.0	0.0	0.0	0.0	100.0	22.5	100.0	0.0
93263	SHAFTER	45.7	41.2	1.8	1.8	0.6	0.6	66.4	72.0	10.5	9.4	9.9	9.0	9.3	28.0	16.3	6.5	1.1	64.7	26.2	52.0	48.0
93265	SPRINGVILLE	81.1	79.0	1.2	1.3	1.1	1.3	10.7	13.3	4.9	5.5	6.9	6.1	5.3	21.8	31.8	16.1	1.7	78.7	44.8	50.8	49.2
93266	STRATFORD	37.7	34.3	1.2	1.2	1.8	1.6	71.3	75.6	10.5	9.9	11.2	9.5	9.3	27.2	16.8	5.0	0.6	62.6	24.8	50.7	49.3
93267	STRATHMORE	51.6	47.4	0.3	0.3	1.3	1.4	58.6	63.9	9.6	9.1	9.9	9.2	8.4	25.4	19.7	7.9	0.9	65.8	27.8	50.7	49.3
93268	TAFT	83.5	80.1	1.4	1.5	1.8	1.9	16.9	21.2	8.1	7.1	7.9	7.6	8.6	27.7	21.5	10.1	1.4	72.6	32.6	51.7	48.3
93270	TERRA BELLA	42.2	39.5	0.5	0.6	2.6	2.5	67.6	70.9	10.4	9.0	9.3	9.0	9.5	26.1	19.0	7.0	0.7	65.8	26.9	53.0	47.0
93271	THREE RIVERS	89.9	87.9	0.2	0.2	0.8	0.9	7.4	9.0	3.8	4.7	6.1	5.7	4.1	18.9	36.4	18.1	2.4	81.7	48.7	49.4	50.6
93272	TIPTON	38.9	34.6	0.2	0.2	0.8	0.8	61.3	65.9	11.6	10.5	10.3	8.5	9.2	29.2	15.1	5.3	0.6	62.5	25.0	52.6	47.4
93274	TULARE	57.5	53.8	4.1	3.9	1.9	2.0	45.6	50.5	9.7	9.3	9.5	8.2	8.0	27.8	18.6	7.9	1.1	66.5	28.7	49.2	50.8
93276	TUPMAN	69.6	64.5	9.8	10.8	2.2	2.2	20.7	24.7	4.3	4.3	5.4	5.4	8.6	46.2	22.6	3.2	0.0	81.7	34.4	74.2	25.8
93277	VISALIA	80.4	77.4	1.9	2.0	2.8	3.1	25.6	30.2	7.2	7.0	7.6	7.3	7.7	26.7	23.2	11.2	2.2	73.7	35.3	47.7	52.3
93280	WASCO	35.2	31.3	9.8	9.1	0.8	0.8	66.5	72.2	8.2	7.4	7.9	7.8	12.2	36.4	14.9	4.7	0.5	72.2	28.1	63.4	36.6
93283	WELDON	89.5	88.1	0.3	0.4	0.4	0.5	6.4	8.2	4.0	4.3	6.0	7.1	4.4	15.0	31.0	25.8	2.6	81.4	51.9	49.4	50.6
93285	WOFFORD HEIGHTS	93.4	92.0	0.1	0.1	0.8	0.8	5.7	7.3	2.9	3.4	4.3	4.3	3.5	14.1	31.3	31.8	4.4	86.7	57.5	50.0	50.1
93286	WOODLAKE	56.4	54.3	0.4	0.4	0.9	1.0	69.0	72.6	9.3	8.9	9.7	8.7	8.2	26.4	20.1	7.7	0.9	66.7	28.7	51.2	48.8
93287	WOODY	83.3	80.2	0.8	1.5	1.5	1.5	7.6	9.9	5.3	5.3	6.9	5.3	5.3	20.6	32.8	16.0	2.3	77.9	45.6	55.7	44.3
93291	VISALIA	54.6	52.8	2.1	2.0	7.4	7.4	53.7	56.7	9.2	8.6	9.8	9.1	8.6	28.1	18.4	7.3	1.0	66.8	28.2	50.3	49.7
93292	VISALIA	73.3	70.0	1.5	1.4	3.6	3.9	33.2	38.0	8.2	7.9	8.5	7.9	7.4	28.0	22.6	8.5	1.2	70.5	32.5	49.2	50.8
93301	BAKERSFIELD	62.9	59.1	11.2	11.2	2.4	2.5	31.3	36.5	9.4	7.6	7.2	6.6	9.3	29.5	17.8	9.9	2.6	72.0	30.6	49.5	50.5
93304	BAKERSFIELD	48.7	44.6	13.3	12.9	4.6	4.7	42.3	48.1	10.0	8.9	9.3	8.3	8.7	27.0	18.4	8.1	1.2	66.7	28.3	48.5	51.5
93305	BAKERSFIELD	45.7	42.5	5.7	5.4	1.2	1.2	65.8	70.8	11.5	9.9	10.0	9.2	9.3	26.4	15.9	6.7	1.2	62.9	25.1	49.9	50.1
93306	BAKERSFIELD	64.5	60.4	3.6	3.7	2.5	2.6	42.2	48.0	8.6	7.7	9.0	8.5	8.7	25.0	21.4	9.7	1.4	69.5	30.8	48.9	51.1
93307	BAKERSFIELD	40.1	37.2	11.7	10.9	2.4	2.4	60.4	64.9	10.1	9.8	10.8	9.4	8.4	26.8	17.6	6.6	0.6	63.5	26.1	50.5	49.5
93308	BAKERSFIELD	87.2	85.0	1.1	1.1	1.4	1.5	12.2	15.0	7.4	6.9	7.9	7.5	8.0	27.9	23.6	9.7	1.2	73.4	34.3	49.9	50.1
93309	BAKERSFIELD	70.6	66.7	8.6	8.9	3.9	4.3	22.8	27.4	7.9	7.0	7.6	7.9	9.2	27.4	22.1	9.7	1.4	72.9	31.9	47.6	52.4
93311	BAKERSFIELD	74.2	70.2	4.1	4.3	9.6	11.0	16.2	19.6	7.1	7.1	8.2	8.1	7.9	29.6	24.9	6.2	0.8	72.2	33.5	48.2	51.8
93312	BAKERSFIELD	86.1	83.1	1.9	2.1	2.5	3.0	13.0	16.8	8.9	8.7	9.2	7.7	6.5	31.6	21.4	5.3	0.6	68.1	31.8	49.2	50.8
93313	BAKERSFIELD	64.5	59.6	7.8	8.0	6.1	6.7	27.5	33.0	9.4	9.0	9.5	7.9	7.2	31.8	19.4	5.3	0.6	67.0	29.9	49.3	50.7
93314	BAKERSFIELD	84.8	82.0	1.7	1.9	2.2	2.5	14.4	17.7	6.4	8.0	10.5	9.1	5.9	26.7	27.2	5.6	0.6	69.1	35.7	50.2	49.8
93401	SAN LUIS OBISPO	86.5	84.5	1.3	1.5	3.7	4.2	11.4	13.4	4.1	4.1	5.2	6.7	17.2	26.8	22.5	11.0	2.5	83.2	33.6	49.6	50.4
93402	LOS OSOS	88.3	86.6	0.6	0.7	4.6	5.2	9.0	10.6	4.2	4.6	6.2	6.2	6.3	22.4	31.8	15.7	2.6	81.1	45.1	47.9	52.1
93405	SAN LUIS OBISPO	80.5	78.6	7.2	7.2	5.6	6.3	16.8	18.9	1.8	1.8	2.4	14.7	26.2	27.2	16.8	7.7	1.5	92.3	27.0	63.8	36.2
93407	SAN LUIS OBISPO	81.9	79.1	1.0	1.2	9.8	11.0	10.5	12.6	0.2	0.1	0.1	58.0	37.0	3.8	0.5	0.2	0.0	99.1	19.3	59.4	40.6
93420	ARROYO GRANDE	88.8	87.0	0.5	0.6	2.8	3.1	11.2	13.2	5.3	5.8	6.6	6.4	5.3	21.6	29.9	16.6	2.6	78.3	44.4	48.1	51.9
93422	ATASCADERO	89.1	87.3	2.2	2.3	1.3	1.5	10.3	12.3	5.4	5.9	7.7	7.7	6.5	26.6	28.4	10.2	1.6	76.1	39.4	51.3	48.7
93426	BRADLEY	82.4	79.9	1.1	1.1	1.0	1.1	20.0	23.6	5.9	6.6	7.4	6.0	4.8	22.5	31.2	14.5	1.2	76.3	42.8	52.4	47.6
93427	BUELLTON	81.8	79.2	0.5	0.5	1.3	1.3	26.5	30.7	7.0	7.3	8.2	6.7	5.2	27.2	26.1	10.6	1.7	73.2	38.3	50.1	49.9
93428	CAMBRIA	91.1	89.5	0.4	0.4	1.3	1.5	14.0	17.0	3.6	4.1	4.8	4.2	3.9	16.5	36.3	24.0	2.6	84.8	52.5	48.1	52.0
93429	CASMALIA	100.0	100.0	0.0	0.0	0.0	0.0	0.0	0.0	0.0	0.0	0.0	0.0	100.0	0.0	0.0	0.0	0.0	100.0	22.5	100.0	0.0
93430	CAYUCOS	93.6	92.5	0.3	0.3	1.3	1.5	7.6	9.2	3.5	4.0	4.8	4.8	4.4	23.2	34.6	17.8	2.9	84.9	47.8	48.7	51.4
93432	CRESTON	89.5	87.7	0.4	0.4	1.0	1.2	13.0	15.6	5.8	6.3	7.7	7.1	4.8	24.5	32.5	10.6	0.8	75.4	41.6	51.3	48.7
93433	GROVER BEACH	79.8	77.1	1.0	1.1	4.1	4.5	22.4	26.0	6.9	6.5	7.0	6.8	7.6	29.7	23.7	10.3	1.5	75.4	35.8	48.4	51.6
93434	GUADALUPE	45.9	45.2	0.7	0.7	6.0	5.6	84.2	86.0	9.7	9.1	9.9	9.3	9.4	27.8	16.5	7.3	0.9	65.6	26.6	51.2	48.8
93436	LOMPOC	69.5	67.1	6.7	6.9	4.0	4.2	32.4	36.1	7.4	7.2	8.2	7.2	7.0	29.1	21.9	10.7	1.2	72.7	34.8	52.5	47.5
93437	LOMPOC	72.3	69.3	11.7	12.1	4.5	5.0	11.1	13.2	15.1	10.7	9.1	5.5	14.5	42.8	2.1	0.2	0.0	62.1	23.3	52.1	47.9
93441	LOS OLIVOS	90.9	89.4	0.5	0.5	0.4	0.4	14.3	17.1	5.2	7.0	9.3	6.0	2.8	23.5	34.4	10.6	1.2	73.7	42.8	49.9	50.1
93442	MORRO BAY	89.5	87.9	0.7	0.7	1.9	2.1	11.3	13.5	3.6	3.7	4.6	4.7	5.7	23.9	29.9	20.3	3.8	85.6	47.5	47.8	52.2
93444	NIPOMO	77.1	74.2	0.6	0.7	1.6	1.8	32.1	36.6	7.1	7.8	8.7	7.5	5.6	25.6	24.9	11.7	1.2	71.7	37.1	49.6	50.4
93445	OCEANO	69.0	66.6	1.1	1.2	1.9	2.0	44.5	48.3	8.4	7.8	8.1	6.9	7.8	28.1	22.5	9.4	1.1	71.7	32.9	49.3	50.7
93446	PASO ROBLES	80.5	78.4	2.5	2.6	1.6	1.7	22.0	24.9	6.6	6.8	8.0	9.3	6.6	25.0	24.5	11.5	1.7	73.0	36.6	50.4	49.6
93449	PISMO BEACH	91.3	89.8	0.6	0.7	3.0	3.5	6.9	8.4	3.9	3.7	4.5	4.9	5.1	23.4	29.4	22.0	3.2	84.9	47.9	48.0	52.0
93450	SAN ARDO	75.2	70.8	1.4	1.5	1.0	1.2	27.6	33.3	7.7	7.9	8.6	7.0	6.0	24.6	27.8	9.6	0.9	71.2	36.9	52.6	47.4
93451	SAN MIGUEL	75.6	73.4	1.3	1.4	0.7	0.9	24.2	27.1	6.8	7.0	8.5	8.0	7.4	27.8	26.3	7.7	0.7	72.6	35.3	51.3	48.7
93452	SAN SIMEON	79.9	77.6	0.2	0.4	1.0	1.1	37.1	41.9	4.7	5.6	5.8	4.2	4.7	28.0	28.3	16.6	2.2	81.2	43.2	51.1	48.9
93453	SANTA MARGARITA	90.3	88.7	0.3	0.4	0.8	0.8	12.6	15.0	5.0	6.3	8.0	6.8	5.0	25.0	32.4	10.7	0.9	76.6	41.7	51.3	48.7
93454	SANTA MARIA	74.8	72.2	2.2	2.2	4.3	4.5	40.5	45.6	7.2	6.9	7.6	7.3	7.3	28.0	21.3	12.2	2.3	74.1	35.1	49.9	50.1
93455	SANTA MARIA	83.5	80.9	1.4	1.5	3.7	4.2	19.4	23.0	5.9	6.4	8.1	7.9	6.0	22.4	25.8	15.7	2.0	74.5	40.9	48.6	51.4
93458	SANTA MARIA	45.2	44.3	1.7	1.6	5.0	4.9	75.8	77.8	11.1	9.6	9.7	8.4	9.7	29.9	13.5	7.0	1.1	64.7	25.8	51.5	48.5
93460	SANTA YNEZ	86.9	85.3	0.2	0.2	1.4	1.6	15.6	18.4	4.9	6.2	7.9	6.9	4.0	24.0	31.2	13.3	1.6	76.3	42.9	48.3	51.7
93461	SHANDON	75.6	73.2	0.5	0.5	0.6	0.7	38.9	42.8	8.3	8.2	9.3	10.5	8.6	27.3	20.5	6.6	0.7	68.1	29.5	52.8	47.2
93463	SOLVANG	88.3	86.6	0.4	0.5	1.0	1.1	18.0	20.6	4.9	5.3	7.2	7.0	5.3	21.8	28.3	16.4	3.7	78.2	43.9	48.3	51.7
93465	TEMPLETON	90.6	89.1	0.9	1.0	0.9	1.1	10.5	12.5	5.6	6.6	8.9	8.3	5.2	23.7	28.8	11.2	1.6	73.4	40.6	48.9	51.1
93501	MOJAVE	70.3	66.2	4.7	4.7	2.0	2.1	25.8	30.7	8.2	7.1	8.5	7.7	7.6	24.1	25.2	10.8	1.0	71.6	35.4	50.6	49.4
93505	CALIFORNIA CITY	68.1	64.1	12.9	13.7	4.0	4.4	16.9	20.6	6.9	7.0	8.4	8.5	7.2	24.9	25.9	10.4	0.9	72.5	36.1	49.5	50.5
93510	ACTON	88.2	85.5	1.6	1.8	1.2	1.4	11.7	15.3	5.6	6.9	10.2	8.1	4.4	27.0	30.3	6.8	0.6	72.0	39.4	51.6	48.4
93512	BENTON	84.2	81.9	0.0	0.0	0.0	0.0	11.6	13.2	4.9	5.4	7.4	8.8	1.5	21.6	35.3	13.7	1.5	76.0	45.2	49.0	51.0
	CALIFORNIA	59.6	57.1	6.7	6.5	11.3	11.8	32.4	35.5	7.4	7.1	7.8	7.3	7.7	29.8	22.1	9.3	1.4	73.3	33.8	49.8	50.2
	UNITED STATES	75.1	73.6	12.3	12.5	3.8	4.2	12.5	14.1	6.9	6.7	7.2	7.0	7.3	28.6	23.8	10.8	1.7	75.1	36.0	49.1	50.9

ZIP CODE #	POST OFFICE NAME	2004 Per Capita Income	2004 HH Income Base	2004 Household Income Distribution (%): Less than $25,000	$25,000 to $49,999	$50,000 to $99,999	$100,000 to $149,999	$150,000 or More	Median Household Income: 2004	2009	2004 National Centile	2004 State Centile	2004 Home Value Base	2004 Home Value Distribution (%): Less than $50,000	$50,000 to $89,999	$90,000 to $174,999	$175,000 to $399,999	$400,000 or More	2004 Median Home Value
93215	DELANO	11435	10377	41.8	33.4	18.5	3.9	2.4	29702	33312	12	10	5752	5.7	11.9	73.5	8.0	0.9	118734
93219	EARLIMART	8280	2492	50.8	33.5	12.2	2.1	1.4	24517	26725	4	4	1340	15.5	32.5	46.9	4.0	1.1	91286
93221	EXETER	18509	4676	29.1	31.4	26.4	9.0	4.1	40672	47075	48	33	3294	5.1	14.7	49.2	22.7	8.3	135664
93223	FARMERSVILLE	9903	2284	42.1	33.4	20.2	2.9	1.3	29841	32972	12	10	1443	3.0	30.7	57.2	7.5	1.6	101349
93224	FELLOWS	30214	213	26.3	27.2	31.9	11.7	2.8	46977	52152	66	45	140	20.0	23.6	41.4	12.1	2.9	96000
93225	FRAZIER PARK	22978	2675	23.7	31.4	29.1	10.8	4.9	44836	51909	61	41	2113	3.8	7.3	49.8	34.8	4.3	155400
93226	GLENNVILLE	25026	100	34.0	22.0	21.0	16.0	7.0	40914	48394	49	34	80	10.0	13.8	33.8	36.3	6.3	156250
93230	HANFORD	20253	19459	29.1	29.7	29.2	7.4	4.7	41100	47315	50	34	12384	4.3	5.7	45.3	40.0	4.6	165247
93234	HURON	12441	1986	41.0	40.5	14.5	2.0	2.1	29330	32105	11	9	602	10.3	13.6	68.9	5.7	1.5	115183
93235	IVANHOE	10104	1204	40.2	39.5	14.5	3.1	2.7	29108	32694	11	9	808	5.8	31.3	51.1	11.8	0.0	99043
93238	KERNVILLE	25347	477	43.2	23.9	20.8	8.0	4.2	31492	36257	16	13	358	20.1	10.9	33.8	26.0	9.2	133571
93239	KETTLEMAN CITY	7917	379	45.4	33.5	17.9	3.2	0.0	27199	29925	7	7	175	28.0	9.7	52.0	10.3	0.0	103618
93240	LAKE ISABELLA	16547	2685	51.0	29.0	15.1	2.7	2.3	24470	27593	4	4	2035	22.5	26.3	38.7	11.9	0.6	91346
93241	LAMONT	8451	3795	45.2	35.4	15.2	2.9	1.3	26880	30398	7	6	1787	10.4	25.2	58.7	5.6	0.1	102171
93242	LATON	14768	899	31.9	38.0	20.5	5.7	3.9	35924	40433	31	22	578	4.7	13.3	39.8	35.1	7.1	146429
93243	LEBEC	16523	185	24.9	36.8	30.8	6.5	1.1	42874	48821	56	37	142	10.6	12.0	32.4	35.2	9.9	164063
93244	LEMON COVE	30504	53	22.6	20.8	32.1	17.0	7.6	58561	77383	83	66	46	6.5	2.2	15.2	65.2	10.9	237500
93245	LEMOORE	17986	10000	24.9	33.7	28.7	9.2	3.5	42454	48739	54	37	5237	4.5	2.0	40.1	48.2	5.3	181603
93247	LINDSAY	12253	4341	40.7	31.8	20.0	5.5	2.1	30061	33842	12	11	2701	9.7	18.3	55.8	14.9	1.3	111093
93249	LOST HILLS	10336	536	33.0	38.3	21.8	4.3	2.6	33559	37581	23	17	202	33.2	17.3	34.7	12.4	2.5	89231
93250	MC FARLAND	10249	2531	45.5	32.3	17.1	3.5	1.7	27104	30246	7	7	1431	3.9	15.8	72.8	4.9	2.6	110644
93251	MC KITTRICK	29599	150	25.3	29.3	31.3	10.7	3.3	47135	53482	66	46	90	16.7	24.4	41.1	15.6	2.2	98000
93252	MARICOPA	14372	620	35.7	33.2	22.6	4.4	4.2	35651	40825	30	21	442	27.6	30.5	25.1	8.6	8.1	77083
93254	NEW CUYAMA	24163	231	28.1	32.9	26.4	6.5	6.1	42334	47039	54	37	137	2.9	9.5	39.4	16.8	31.4	169318
93255	ONYX	14328	165	60.0	21.2	15.8	3.0	0.0	20118	22094	2	2	131	32.1	25.2	26.7	14.5	1.5	65833
93256	PIXLEY	9847	1073	48.3	28.4	17.9	2.6	2.8	25985	28621	6	6	640	10.3	26.4	49.8	8.6	4.8	102062
93257	PORTERVILLE	14343	20483	36.7	30.7	24.9	5.5	2.3	34438	38516	26	19	12396	7.5	15.8	59.2	15.9	1.6	116403
93260	POSEY	17679	97	40.2	34.0	18.6	5.2	2.1	30718	34593	14	11	83	16.9	20.5	41.0	15.7	6.0	117708
93262	SEQUOIA NATIONAL PAR	0	0	0.0	0.0	0.0	0.0	0.0	0	0	0	0	0	0.0	0.0	0.0	0.0	0.0	0
93263	SHAFTER	12577	4208	38.1	35.3	20.8	3.9	1.9	31855	35872	17	14	2607	11.3	14.1	63.4	10.0	1.3	112529
93265	SPRINGVILLE	25656	1656	31.8	26.3	27.4	8.6	5.9	41542	48978	51	35	1261	8.6	5.2	33.4	44.4	8.4	186993
93266	STRATFORD	12427	412	38.6	33.7	24.0	2.2	1.5	31032	34428	15	12	312	2.2	22.1	64.7	9.3	1.6	114943
93267	STRATHMORE	11135	1535	37.5	36.9	19.5	4.4	1.6	31723	35612	17	13	1039	13.2	24.8	36.5	21.9	3.7	107245
93268	TAFT	16372	5402	36.3	31.3	24.6	6.1	1.7	34873	39055	27	19	3319	14.9	31.4	44.9	8.4	0.4	94023
93270	TERRA BELLA	11273	1676	36.9	35.3	21.6	3.7	2.5	31766	35762	17	13	1027	11.1	17.9	50.1	18.6	2.3	115134
93271	THREE RIVERS	30424	1031	26.4	22.9	31.0	11.2	8.5	50677	60217	73	54	823	6.6	4.0	18.6	58.0	12.9	230866
93272	TIPTON	12208	782	40.3	34.7	17.7	4.6	2.8	30546	34351	14	11	444	5.0	21.6	55.2	9.0	9.2	108409
93274	TULARE	15461	18395	32.1	32.6	26.1	6.5	2.7	37206	41847	36	25	11541	5.9	13.9	62.2	15.1	2.9	120648
93276	TUPMAN	29468	31	25.8	25.8	35.5	9.7	3.2	48639	52103	70	50	19	15.8	26.3	47.4	10.5	0.0	97500
93277	VISALIA	24487	17553	23.4	27.3	32.1	11.4	5.8	49328	57193	71	51	11552	6.6	2.5	58.2	30.4	2.4	148027
93280	WASCO	14495	4695	37.8	35.1	21.0	4.0	2.2	31561	35538	17	13	2647	6.0	14.7	70.5	7.9	0.9	114826
93283	WELDON	16258	914	54.9	27.2	12.6	1.6	3.6	22128	25264	3	3	769	18.5	39.7	32.4	6.8	2.7	80530
93285	WOFFORD HEIGHTS	20631	1642	45.3	31.1	17.2	3.7	2.9	27302	30994	8	7	1365	13.8	29.9	39.1	13.2	4.1	99105
93286	WOODLAKE	13386	2814	42.0	30.3	20.7	3.5	3.6	29823	33483	12	10	1685	3.7	16.5	55.1	20.8	3.9	117408
93287	WOODY	24968	54	33.3	20.4	22.2	16.7	7.4	43205	49092	56	38	43	11.6	14.0	32.6	34.9	7.0	153125
93291	VISALIA	18131	11473	31.1	31.2	23.6	8.1	6.0	38217	44317	40	27	7094	5.0	13.9	48.1	25.4	7.6	123794
93292	VISALIA	21195	10837	23.6	28.0	32.9	10.5	5.2	48458	55480	69	49	7695	3.2	8.1	51.4	33.0	4.3	149622
93301	BAKERSFIELD	19592	5253	44.3	27.6	18.7	5.6	3.9	28479	32796	10	8	2027	21.1	11.2	39.8	24.8	3.2	131940
93304	BAKERSFIELD	12933	15431	40.3	33.1	21.8	3.7	1.1	31527	35882	16	13	8669	5.1	16.2	73.4	4.9	0.4	111952
93305	BAKERSFIELD	10952	10798	48.1	31.4	15.9	3.3	1.4	25979	28685	6	6	5011	3.3	24.3	64.2	7.1	1.1	110277
93306	BAKERSFIELD	19415	18415	27.8	29.6	27.3	10.7	4.7	43040	49842	56	38	12404	6.0	10.9	59.7	20.1	3.2	130169
93307	BAKERSFIELD	10493	17124	42.8	32.0	20.4	3.8	1.1	29283	33029	11	9	10359	7.7	26.0	57.9	7.8	0.7	106469
93308	BAKERSFIELD	20531	17430	34.2	28.1	24.4	9.8	3.5	37171	42985	36	25	10797	10.4	12.5	44.8	29.9	2.4	132468
93309	BAKERSFIELD	23541	23178	27.3	29.0	28.4	10.1	5.1	44669	51145	60	41	12209	2.2	5.4	60.2	28.4	3.8	147459
93311	BAKERSFIELD	34390	8266	11.6	18.3	40.7	17.8	11.7	69665	82144	91	77	6068	0.3	1.4	38.5	46.0	13.8	199793
93312	BAKERSFIELD	27106	11345	10.3	20.6	44.4	18.9	5.9	66586	77682	90	74	9961	2.0	0.5	42.8	50.5	4.3	183145
93313	BAKERSFIELD	19184	8806	17.7	25.4	41.4	12.7	2.8	55496	64350	80	62	7393	2.7	6.1	62.2	28.3	0.7	150088
93314	BAKERSFIELD	27335	4711	10.4	16.8	37.4	24.1	11.3	78041	91214	94	84	4216	2.6	2.2	19.2	64.0	12.1	242002
93401	SAN LUIS OBISPO	29596	12276	29.1	26.7	25.8	11.4	7.0	42917	50556	56	37	6059	3.1	4.2	8.0	21.2	63.5	476833
93402	LOS OSOS	29960	6160	20.5	26.3	32.3	13.9	6.9	53395	62774	78	58	4529	0.5	1.7	8.7	50.0	39.0	361089
93405	SAN LUIS OBISPO	22455	9580	40.1	23.4	20.6	9.8	6.1	34490	40090	26	19	3642	1.5	2.0	4.2	26.1	66.3	471411
93407	SAN LUIS OBISPO	14810	12	83.3	16.7	0.0	0.0	0.0	12041	13400	1	1	0	0.0	0.0	0.0	0.0	0.0	0
93420	ARROYO GRANDE	30949	10799	18.4	24.3	34.2	13.9	9.1	56756	66596	81	63	8115	2.7	2.7	3.3	32.5	58.8	449413
93422	ATASCADERO	24594	11328	19.2	26.3	37.1	12.8	4.7	54441	63090	79	60	7814	2.6	1.8	4.5	51.8	39.2	353455
93426	BRADLEY	28390	602	24.4	27.2	31.1	8.8	8.5	48802	56878	70	50	428	4.0	2.8	11.0	49.3	32.9	338136
93427	BUELLTON	26667	2184	19.5	23.4	35.4	15.3	6.5	57224	69299	82	64	1637	8.7	7.5	11.4	14.7	57.6	434777
93428	CAMBRIA	36354	3167	18.6	29.5	31.1	11.5	9.3	51528	61012	75	56	2514	0.7	1.0	1.6	21.2	75.5	541386
93429	CASMALIA	0	0	0.0	0.0	0.0	0.0	0.0	0	0	0	0	0	0.0	0.0	0.0	0.0	0.0	0
93430	CAYUCOS	32111	1537	20.3	32.0	30.3	10.5	7.0	47992	54662	68	48	954	3.1	0.6	1.8	21.0	73.5	516376
93432	CRESTON	27717	544	18.6	25.9	37.7	10.7	7.2	54328	62711	79	60	413	1.5	0.5	5.6	37.8	54.7	431967
93433	GROVER BEACH	21910	5121	24.6	34.0	29.5	8.4	3.5	43042	49619	56	38	2843	4.0	1.0	3.1	66.3	25.6	308267
93434	GUADALUPE	13082	1525	33.5	31.0	26.6	4.8	4.1	34923	41216	27	19	889	0.2	0.5	27.9	68.8	2.6	204381
93436	LOMPOC	21590	17050	23.0	29.7	32.6	10.6	4.1	47446	54765	67	47	10345	3.7	1.7	8.2	69.5	16.9	264013
93437	LOMPOC	16276	1478	15.4	44.0	31.1	8.8	0.7	44641	51278	60	41	123	65.9	17.9	4.9	10.6	0.8	32679
93441	LOS OLIVOS	50572	435	13.1	17.5	30.6	19.1	19.8	78475	102668	95	85	311	2.3	0.0	0.6	5.1	92.0	814583
93442	MORRO BAY	25088	5417	30.9	30.5	27.8	7.8	3.1	39662	46163	45	30	3344	6.0	2.4	5.9	34.1	51.6	407835
93444	NIPOMO	22801	5523	16.2	28.0	36.2	13.3	6.4	54950	62520	80	61	4322	1.0	1.0	7.5	47.0	43.5	361264
93445	OCEANO	18967	2569	29.1	32.1	27.5	8.5	2.9	41722	46910	52	36	1473	8.3	8.0	18.1	51.8	13.9	237447
93446	PASO ROBLES	23587	14891	22.8	30.1	32.0	9.9	5.2	47509	54979	67	47	10054	1.5	1.5	5.7	62.2	29.2	297768
93449	PISMO BEACH	37686	4470	23.3	22.9	28.5	15.5	9.8	54323	65838	79	60	2830	6.4	4.7	6.5	23.9	58.5	451282
93450	SAN ARDO	17307	281	29.5	29.5	29.2	8.9	2.9	40160	47196	47	32	168	8.3	4.8	19.1	36.3	31.6	247500
93451	SAN MIGUEL	22246	692	21.2	34.3	29.3	10.3	4.9	46087	53713	64	43	480	1.5	1.7	10.2	62.9	23.8	283553
93452	SAN SIMEON	36703	252	11.9	39.7	34.1	7.5	6.8	49417	57410	71	51	136	16.2	5.9	5.9	29.4	42.7	289286
93453	SANTA MARGARITA	24065	1008	21.8	28.1	36.4	10.1	3.6	50075	57324	72	52	761	8.2	7.0	11.6	41.0	32.3	307877
93454	SANTA MARIA	21228	10736	25.4	30.1	31.1	9.5	3.9	45118	52337	61	42	6550	2.2	1.3	9.9	72.0	14.8	260636
93455	SANTA MARIA	26813	13607	15.0	26.2	36.0	16.7	6.2	60098	71062	84	67	11291	4.6	2.4	7.7	55.8	29.4	308761
93458	SANTA MARIA	11243	11316	31.6	36.1	26.0	4.7	1.6	35927	40671	31	22	5826	7.1	7.0	11.0	71.2	3.7	222033
93460	SANTA YNEZ	47259	2108	12.7	16.7	28.7	22.7	19.3	83657	106838	96	88	1654	0.1	0.8	2.2	6.2	90.8	828076
93461	SHANDON	17981	417	22.1	31.9	34.3	7.4	4.3	45986	52095	64	43	305	1.0	0.0	25.3	55.4	18.4	240865
93463	SOLVANG	35638	3225	17.8	24.9	26.6	18.0	12.7	59024	73567	84	67	2163	0.4	1.1	9.3	10.2	79.0	699797
93465	TEMPLETON	25566	3158	18.4	22.3	37.8	15.4	6.2	58911	67209	83	66	2564	3.4	3.5	6.9	34.3	52.0	411591
93501	MOJAVE	15513	1902	39.8	28.8	24.8	6.1	0.6	32263	37368	18	14	1098	21.4	41.4	31.7	5.0	0.5	80000
93505	CALIFORNIA CITY	22806	3112	26.2	22.7	36.0	11.8	3.3	51014	58499	74	55	2283	8.6	20.5	62.3	8.2	0.3	113786
93510	ACTON	36157	2550	11.6	19.9	32.1	19.0	17.4	74609	95302	93	81	2307	5.6	1.7	3.7	39.5	49.5	397289
93512	BENTON	19289	81	22.2	34.6	37.0	6.2	0.0	42380	45774	54	37	69	0.0	2.9	43.5	40.6	13.0	187500
	CALIFORNIA	27293		21.8	24.4	30.5	13.7	9.7	54267	64547				3.3	2.7	13.3	42.9	37.9	319678
	UNITED STATES	25866		24.7	27.1	30.8	10.9	6.5	48124	56710				10.9	15.0	33.7	30.1	10.4	145905

ZIP CODE #	POST OFFICE NAME	FINANCIAL SERVICES: Auto Loan	FINANCIAL SERVICES: Home Loan	FINANCIAL SERVICES: Investments	FINANCIAL SERVICES: Retirement Plans	THE HOME: Home Improvements: Home Repair	THE HOME: Home Improvements: Lawn & Garden	THE HOME: Furnishings: Computers & Hardware	THE HOME: Furnishings: Major Appliances	THE HOME: Furnishings: TV, Radio, Sound Equipment	THE HOME: Furnishings: Furniture	ENTERTAINMENT: Dine out/Carry out	ENTERTAINMENT: Sports Equipment	ENTERTAINMENT: Fees & Tickets	ENTERTAINMENT: Toys & Games	ENTERTAINMENT: Travel	ENTERTAINMENT: Cable TV	PERSONAL: Apparel & Services	PERSONAL: Auto Repairs	PERSONAL: Health Insurance	PERSONAL: Pets & Supplies
93215	DELANO	57	49	45	48	48	50	53	55	56	57	70	61	50	66	50	52	70	57	51	58
93219	EARLIMART	52	44	42	43	43	44	49	49	51	52	64	56	46	62	46	48	65	52	45	52
93221	EXETER	84	77	68	77	79	84	78	81	80	78	98	94	75	97	77	79	95	81	82	93
93223	FARMERSVILLE	59	50	46	49	49	51	54	56	56	58	71	62	51	66	51	53	71	59	52	59
93224	FELLOWS	31	22	11	21	25	28	22	27	25	21	29	32	18	29	22	26	27	26	32	37
93225	FRAZIER PARK	96	80	59	76	85	95	78	88	84	77	101	101	72	99	79	87	95	86	97	111
93226	GLENNVILLE	109	76	40	72	88	99	75	93	86	74	101	112	64	99	78	91	92	91	110	129
93230	HANFORD	89	85	80	83	84	89	85	88	86	87	106	100	82	103	83	84	104	88	85	98
93234	HURON	57	48	47	48	47	48	54	54	56	57	71	62	52	70	50	52	72	57	49	57
93235	IVANHOE	60	52	46	50	51	53	55	58	57	59	72	63	51	66	52	55	72	60	54	61
93238	KERNVILLE	83	70	58	63	77	89	66	78	73	67	88	84	62	82	71	78	82	76	92	98
93239	KETTLEMAN CITY	50	42	41	42	42	43	47	48	49	50	62	54	45	60	44	46	63	50	43	50
93240	LAKE ISABELLA	53	47	47	44	49	59	48	53	52	49	63	54	47	57	50	55	59	52	62	59
93241	LAMONT	53	45	43	45	44	45	51	51	53	53	66	58	48	64	47	49	67	54	46	54
93242	LATON	78	67	53	62	66	70	68	74	71	73	89	80	62	79	65	69	87	75	72	81
93243	LEBEC	82	68	48	65	72	77	66	74	70	67	84	87	60	81	66	70	80	74	79	93
93244	LEMON COVE	105	117	115	115	118	120	105	110	102	105	127	128	109	133	109	101	124	106	105	128
93245	LEMOORE	83	79	79	81	76	79	82	81	81	83	102	96	79	98	78	76	99	84	74	90
93247	LINDSAY	66	60	54	57	58	60	62	64	64	66	80	71	59	75	59	61	80	66	60	68
93249	LOST HILLS	77	65	64	65	64	66	74	74	77	78	98	85	71	95	69	72	98	78	67	78
93250	MC FARLAND	56	48	44	47	47	49	53	54	55	56	69	60	49	65	49	52	69	57	50	57
93251	MC KITTRICK	0	0	0	0	0	0	0	0	0	0	0	0	0	0	0	0	0	0	0	0
93252	MARICOPA	100	72	40	64	79	89	70	84	81	72	97	99	61	90	70	85	90	84	98	113
93254	NEW CUYAMA	103	90	75	84	87	91	92	100	96	100	120	106	85	106	88	92	119	101	93	104
93255	ONYX	45	41	40	38	44	53	39	45	42	41	52	45	38	45	42	45	48	44	53	52
93256	PIXLEY	58	50	44	48	49	51	53	56	55	57	69	61	49	63	50	52	69	58	52	59
93257	PORTERVILLE	68	64	62	62	62	66	65	67	67	68	84	75	63	80	63	65	82	68	64	72
93260	POSEY	72	56	37	50	63	70	53	63	60	52	71	74	47	70	56	64	65	63	75	87
93262	SEQUOIA NATIONAL PAR	0	0	0	0	0	0	0	0	0	0	0	0	0	0	0	0	0	0	0	0
93263	SHAFTER	63	58	53	55	56	59	59	62	61	63	77	68	56	71	57	59	76	64	58	66
93265	SPRINGVILLE	90	79	65	76	84	93	79	86	84	77	102	98	75	100	80	87	96	85	95	104
93266	STRATFORD	77	65	60	64	64	67	72	73	75	76	95	83	67	91	67	71	95	77	68	79
93267	STRATHMORE	65	58	49	54	57	60	58	63	61	62	76	68	54	69	57	59	74	64	61	68
93268	TAFT	58	56	57	55	56	62	60	59	61	58	75	69	58	75	59	62	73	60	61	66
93270	TERRA BELLA	66	55	46	53	55	58	58	62	62	62	77	70	54	72	56	59	76	64	61	70
93271	THREE RIVERS	96	101	100	96	103	111	94	99	96	93	118	113	96	122	99	99	115	97	103	116
93272	TIPTON	67	57	53	56	56	58	63	64	65	67	83	72	59	78	59	62	83	67	59	68
93274	TULARE	74	69	65	67	68	72	70	73	71	73	89	82	68	86	68	70	88	74	70	79
93276	TUPMAN	23	21	16	20	21	22	20	21	20	20	25	24	19	23	19	20	24	21	21	25
93277	VISALIA	89	96	100	96	95	98	94	93	91	94	114	109	96	116	94	89	112	93	88	103
93280	WASCO	74	64	56	61	62	65	68	71	70	73	89	78	63	81	64	67	88	73	66	75
93283	WELDON	54	52	55	48	55	67	48	56	52	52	65	52	50	54	53	56	60	54	66	61
93285	WOFFORD HEIGHTS	61	58	60	53	61	74	54	62	58	58	72	59	55	61	59	62	67	60	74	68
93286	WOODLAKE	72	58	49	57	60	64	63	67	67	65	83	77	58	80	60	65	81	69	67	77
93287	WOODY	110	77	40	72	89	100	76	93	87	75	102	113	65	100	78	91	93	92	111	130
93291	VISALIA	86	83	82	82	81	84	85	86	85	88	106	98	83	103	82	81	106	87	79	93
93292	VISALIA	91	93	90	92	92	94	90	92	89	91	111	107	90	111	89	86	108	92	87	103
93301	BAKERSFIELD	61	59	74	58	58	65	65	63	68	65	84	73	65	84	65	68	82	65	64	69
93304	BAKERSFIELD	55	52	52	50	50	54	55	55	57	56	71	63	53	68	53	55	69	57	54	59
93305	BAKERSFIELD	51	47	47	46	46	48	50	50	51	52	65	57	49	63	48	49	65	52	47	54
93306	BAKERSFIELD	83	83	83	82	81	85	83	84	82	85	103	96	82	100	81	80	102	85	79	91
93307	BAKERSFIELD	58	51	44	48	49	52	53	56	55	57	69	61	49	62	50	53	68	58	53	59
93308	BAKERSFIELD	75	74	78	74	74	80	77	76	78	75	97	88	77	97	76	78	94	77	76	85
93309	BAKERSFIELD	84	86	95	88	85	89	88	86	86	88	108	101	88	107	87	83	105	88	82	95
93311	BAKERSFIELD	138	153	153	161	146	144	142	139	131	146	166	164	146	166	138	123	165	137	120	153
93312	BAKERSFIELD	117	131	132	135	127	126	121	121	113	124	143	141	125	145	120	108	141	118	107	133
93313	BAKERSFIELD	91	99	95	102	95	94	91	91	85	94	108	107	93	108	89	80	106	90	80	101
93314	BAKERSFIELD	127	143	137	148	137	133	129	129	119	134	151	151	133	152	126	112	149	125	111	142
93401	SAN LUIS OBISPO	92	87	100	91	86	92	100	92	96	96	121	112	96	117	94	91	117	97	86	102
93402	LOS OSOS	98	106	116	105	106	113	102	104	100	103	125	116	105	123	104	99	122	103	102	114
93405	SAN LUIS OBISPO	75	67	82	70	66	74	84	74	82	79	103	92	79	98	78	78	99	81	71	82
93407	SAN LUIS OBISPO	20	12	15	14	12	14	23	17	23	20	28	24	19	25	19	20	27	21	16	20
93420	ARROYO GRANDE	103	116	125	114	116	123	109	111	106	109	133	124	114	134	112	107	130	109	110	122
93422	ATASCADERO	86	96	103	97	95	97	93	92	89	92	111	107	95	114	93	86	110	91	85	101
93426	BRADLEY	113	97	72	91	102	110	92	103	97	93	118	120	85	114	93	99	112	102	110	130
93427	BUELLTON	107	109	99	108	107	110	103	106	100	105	125	124	102	123	102	97	122	105	99	121
93428	CAMBRIA	122	114	108	108	121	142	105	120	111	113	138	118	107	116	114	119	130	116	140	137
93429	CASMALIA	0	0	0	0	0	0	0	0	0	0	0	0	0	0	0	0	0	0	0	0
93430	CAYUCOS	115	91	63	82	102	114	86	102	96	85	114	120	77	113	91	103	107	101	120	139
93432	CRESTON	108	107	93	104	109	114	98	105	99	99	122	123	98	124	100	99	118	102	105	127
93433	GROVER BEACH	74	80	89	82	79	81	82	79	79	80	99	94	83	102	81	75	97	80	73	86
93434	GUADALUPE	78	67	60	64	65	68	72	75	75	77	94	82	67	87	67	71	94	78	69	79
93436	LOMPOC	84	86	90	86	85	89	87	86	86	87	108	100	87	107	86	83	106	87	82	95
93437	LOMPOC	85	54	52	62	50	59	80	69	82	75	102	92	69	91	66	75	98	82	64	79
93441	LOS OLIVOS	178	215	229	214	212	214	194	195	182	194	228	225	205	238	199	178	227	188	179	215
93442	MORRO BAY	72	70	78	70	71	80	72	73	73	72	91	81	72	86	73	74	88	74	77	82
93444	NIPOMO	94	105	108	104	104	107	98	100	94	99	118	114	101	120	99	93	117	98	94	110
93445	OCEANO	87	71	57	68	73	81	75	81	81	77	99	91	69	94	73	81	96	83	85	93
93446	PASO ROBLES	93	90	86	89	92	98	89	93	90	89	111	108	88	112	90	90	107	92	94	108
93449	PISMO BEACH	107	106	116	105	108	122	105	110	106	108	133	118	105	121	108	108	127	110	116	122
93450	SAN ARDO	84	76	60	73	76	81	73	78	74	75	91	90	69	86	72	73	87	78	77	93
93451	SAN MIGUEL	87	96	99	96	95	96	92	91	88	91	110	108	93	113	92	85	108	91	85	102
93452	SAN SIMEON	135	109	76	100	121	134	102	121	114	102	136	142	94	135	108	121	127	119	140	163
93453	SANTA MARGARITA	92	86	72	84	88	94	83	88	84	83	104	103	81	103	83	85	99	87	90	106
93454	SANTA MARIA	80	84	91	84	83	88	85	84	83	84	104	96	86	104	84	82	102	84	81	92
93455	SANTA MARIA	99	113	121	110	111	117	106	107	103	107	129	120	111	131	108	102	127	105	103	116
93458	SANTA MARIA	68	60	56	58	59	62	64	66	66	68	83	73	61	78	61	63	83	68	62	70
93460	SANTA YNEZ	166	201	219	200	199	204	183	183	172	183	216	210	193	223	188	170	214	178	171	201
93461	SHANDON	88	86	79	82	84	86	84	89	84	89	106	97	81	99	82	81	105	89	82	94
93463	SOLVANG	115	131	149	131	130	137	126	125	122	126	153	143	131	155	129	121	151	124	121	137
93465	TEMPLETON	112	108	94	106	112	116	101	108	102	101	125	129	99	127	103	102	120	106	110	132
93501	MOJAVE	60	53	52	52	53	60	58	58	61	57	75	67	55	72	57	61	72	60	61	66
93505	CALIFORNIA CITY	90	91	84	91	92	96	88	90	87	87	107	105	87	108	87	86	104	89	88	103
93510	ACTON	144	179	190	179	175	173	159	159	148	159	186	186	170	198	163	143	185	153	142	176
93512	BENTON	77	71	55	68	71	74	67	72	68	69	84	83	64	79	66	67	81	72	72	85
	CALIFORNIA	107	111	131	112	109	115	113	111	111	114	140	129	114	141	112	109	139	113	104	122
	UNITED STATES	100	100	100	100	100	100	100	100	100	100	100	100	100	100	100	100	100	100	100	100

CALIFORNIA

POPULATION CHANGE

# POST OFFICE NAME	COUNTY FIPS CODE	POPULATION 2000	2004	2009	2000-2004 ANNUAL RATE % Rate	State Centile	HOUSEHOLDS 2000	2004	2009	% Annual Rate 2000-2004	2004 Average HH Size	FAMILIES 2000	2004	% Annual Rate 2000-2004
93513 BIG PINE	027	1743	1756	1773	0.2	19	693	701	711	0.3	2.45	494	498	0.2
93514 BISHOP	051	14504	14994	15567	0.8	45	6115	6326	6576	0.8	2.36	4041	4170	0.7
93516 BORON	029	2025	1867	1952	-1.9	1	801	737	767	-1.9	2.53	536	489	-2.1
93517 BRIDGEPORT	051	391	415	455	1.4	67	158	169	186	1.6	2.34	106	114	1.7
93518 CALIENTE	029	982	1048	1136	1.5	70	414	441	474	1.5	2.36	288	305	1.4
93519 CANTIL	029	143	129	134	-2.4	1	81	73	76	-2.4	1.77	44	39	-2.8
93523 EDWARDS	029	7872	8327	8977	1.3	65	2351	2484	2673	1.3	3.13	2045	2158	1.3
93524 EDWARDS	029	25	26	28	0.9	52	14	14	15	0.0	1.79	10	10	0.0
93526 INDEPENDENCE	027	779	760	763	-0.6	4	368	361	364	-0.5	2.11	216	211	-0.6
93527 INYOKERN	029	2148	2151	2258	0.0	15	899	897	936	-0.1	2.40	603	596	-0.3
93528 JOHANNESBURG	029	189	170	177	-2.5	0	92	83	86	-2.4	2.05	49	44	-2.5
93529 JUNE LAKE	051	611	653	719	1.6	71	263	281	309	1.6	2.32	169	181	1.6
93531 KEENE	029	226	255	283	2.9	89	85	96	106	2.9	2.65	67	75	2.7
93532 LAKE HUGHES	037	2817	2925	3026	0.9	50	989	1024	1054	0.8	2.64	694	716	0.7
93534 LANCASTER	037	34734	37393	39787	1.8	75	12758	13580	14324	1.5	2.64	7950	8460	1.5
93535 LANCASTER	037	57531	61487	65298	1.6	71	18026	18987	19939	1.2	3.21	13798	14527	1.2
93536 LANCASTER	037	49930	54577	58331	2.1	81	15500	16786	17807	1.9	2.95	11776	12711	1.8
93541 LEE VINING	051	496	531	586	1.6	72	191	203	223	1.4	2.61	130	138	1.4
93543 LITTLEROCK	037	11607	12187	12704	1.2	60	3445	3600	3727	1.0	3.36	2687	2803	1.0
93544 LLANO	037	1244	1267	1299	0.4	28	520	526	535	0.3	2.24	351	354	0.2
93545 LONE PINE	027	2247	2219	2231	-0.3	7	960	951	957	-0.2	2.30	601	592	-0.4
93546 MAMMOTH LAKES	051	7129	7950	8937	2.6	87	2831	3170	3583	2.7	2.44	1527	1713	2.7
93550 PALMDALE	037	65931	73921	80516	2.7	88	19390	21430	23062	2.4	3.44	15506	17135	2.4
93551 PALMDALE	037	34983	41594	46277	4.2	96	11021	12972	14297	3.9	3.21	9132	10745	3.9
93552 PALMDALE	037	26530	30309	33122	3.2	91	7390	8236	8852	2.6	3.67	6238	6958	2.6
93553 PEARBLOSSOM	037	1280	1278	1306	0.0	12	499	496	504	-0.1	2.57	337	334	-0.2
93554 RANDSBURG	029	42	38	39	-2.3	1	27	24	25	-2.7	1.58	15	13	-3.3
93555 RIDGECREST	071	30101	30907	33140	0.6	37	11919	12174	12962	0.5	2.51	8185	8298	0.3
93560 ROSAMOND	029	14945	17113	19236	3.2	92	5216	5946	6632	3.1	2.88	3771	4268	3.0
93561 TEHACHAPI	029	27145	29014	31257	1.6	71	8374	9040	9800	1.8	2.72	6394	6874	1.7
93562 TRONA	071	1988	1823	1913	-2.0	1	785	718	749	-2.1	2.54	524	478	-2.1
93563 VALYERMO	037	861	776	773	-2.4	0	250	211	208	-3.9	2.96	152	130	-3.6
93591 PALMDALE	037	6616	6844	7173	0.8	46	1877	1933	2014	0.7	3.53	1520	1564	0.7
93601 AHWAHNEE	039	1620	1997	2340	5.1	97	598	732	849	4.9	2.71	462	563	4.8
93602 AUBERRY	019	3400	3528	3756	0.9	49	1237	1279	1354	0.8	2.66	939	965	0.6
93604 BASS LAKE	039	493	534	587	1.9	78	242	260	283	1.7	2.05	167	180	1.8
93608 CANTUA CREEK	019	1927	1925	2016	0.0	12	413	411	429	-0.1	4.39	359	356	-0.2
93609 CARUTHERS	019	5278	5449	5792	0.8	43	1406	1432	1505	0.4	3.77	1189	1207	0.4
93610 CHOWCHILLA	039	19472	20628	22055	1.4	66	4079	4381	4768	1.7	3.13	3121	3350	1.7
93611 CLOVIS	019	47037	55380	63299	3.9	95	15184	17663	19952	3.6	3.11	12778	14859	3.6
93612 CLOVIS	019	33969	35877	38650	1.3	64	13400	14063	15023	1.1	2.54	8457	8815	1.0
93614 COARSEGOLD	039	9720	11202	12712	3.4	93	3744	4264	4781	3.1	2.62	2949	3355	3.1
93615 CUTLER	107	5373	5387	5661	0.1	16	1157	1153	1206	-0.1	4.66	1034	1031	-0.1
93616 DEL REY	019	1780	1825	1928	0.6	36	477	488	513	0.5	3.68	405	413	0.5
93618 DINUBA	107	24395	25696	27557	1.2	63	6529	6819	7254	1.0	3.73	5426	5659	1.0
93620 DOS PALOS	047	9666	10117	10883	1.1	58	2900	3027	3241	1.0	3.33	2320	2414	0.9
93621 DUNLAP	019	309	311	329	0.2	18	108	108	114	0.0	2.87	81	81	0.0
93622 FIREBAUGH	019	9663	10771	11897	2.6	87	2406	2655	2902	2.3	4.02	2073	2285	2.3
93623 FISH CAMP	043	64	66	68	0.7	42	33	34	36	0.7	1.09	18	8	-17.4
93625 FOWLER	019	5693	6068	6535	1.5	69	1736	1839	1964	1.4	3.24	1357	1432	1.3
93626 FRIANT	039	1211	1338	1486	2.4	84	500	546	599	2.1	2.44	357	389	2.0
93627 HELM	019	63	63	66	0.0	15	14	14	14	0.0	4.21	12	12	0.0
93630 KERMAN	019	14450	15947	17542	2.4	84	4039	4397	4779	2.0	3.61	3323	3608	2.0
93631 KINGSBURG	107	14469	15634	16997	1.8	76	4848	5216	5629	1.7	2.97	3802	4071	1.6
93633 KINGS CANYON NATIONA	019	171	181	194	1.4	65	60	63	67	1.2	2.83	39	41	1.2
93635 LOS BANOS	047	29081	33204	37358	3.2	91	8704	9773	10860	2.8	3.37	7002	7860	2.8
93637 MADERA	039	28228	30861	34111	2.1	81	8856	9573	10464	1.9	3.20	6909	7455	1.8
93638 MADERA	039	49238	52834	57838	1.7	73	12840	13551	14640	1.3	3.84	10798	11389	1.3
93640 MENDOTA	019	9106	9625	10311	1.3	64	2076	2165	2290	1.0	4.39	1751	1824	1.0
93641 MIRAMONTE	019	594	632	679	1.5	68	232	247	265	1.5	2.48	150	159	1.4
93643 NORTH FORK	039	2728	2939	3221	1.8	75	1067	1139	1234	1.6	2.58	799	852	1.5
93644 OAKHURST	039	8919	9755	10803	2.1	81	3740	4046	4432	1.9	2.38	2647	2857	1.8
93645 O NEALS	039	140	172	202	5.0	97	49	60	69	4.9	2.87	36	44	4.8
93646 ORANGE COVE	107	8490	9427	10367	2.5	85	1918	2109	2295	2.3	4.47	1682	1846	2.2
93647 OROSI	107	9732	10492	11402	1.8	75	2301	2463	2655	1.6	4.26	1998	2136	1.6
93648 PARLIER	019	12167	13302	14527	2.1	81	2732	2957	3197	1.9	4.43	2395	2589	1.9
93650 FRESNO	019	3968	4493	4992	3.0	90	1135	1273	1398	2.7	3.53	760	850	2.7
93651 PRATHER	019	1293	1472	1648	3.1	91	454	514	570	3.0	2.86	376	424	2.9
93652 RAISIN	019	242	249	264	0.7	39	66	67	71	0.4	3.70	57	58	0.4
93653 RAYMOND	039	1159	1320	1484	3.1	91	449	508	566	3.0	2.60	344	387	2.8
93654 REEDLEY	019	26434	27410	29122	0.9	49	7493	7702	8109	0.7	3.50	6080	6236	0.6
93656 RIVERDALE	019	5632	6222	6835	2.4	84	1585	1736	1889	2.2	3.57	1322	1443	2.1
93657 SANGER	019	29022	30526	32780	1.2	61	8560	8975	9572	1.1	3.37	6940	7247	1.0
93660 SAN JOAQUIN	019	4213	4478	4826	1.5	68	912	959	1022	1.2	4.67	832	873	1.1
93662 SELMA	019	26447	28152	30313	1.5	69	7566	7959	8476	1.2	3.50	6193	6500	1.1
93664 SHAVER LAKE	019	958	963	1026	0.1	18	382	382	404	0.0	2.48	289	288	-0.1
93667 TOLLHOUSE	019	2538	2904	3242	3.2	91	843	960	1064	3.1	2.98	695	789	3.0
93668 TRANQUILLITY	019	1453	1472	1541	0.3	23	423	426	443	0.2	3.46	350	353	0.2
93669 WISHON	039	575	631	699	2.2	82	247	269	295	2.0	2.35	184	200	2.0
93675 SQUAW VALLEY	019	3205	3294	3490	0.7	39	1225	1254	1321	0.6	2.57	914	933	0.5
93701 FRESNO	019	13750	14315	15346	1.0	53	3396	3514	3738	0.8	4.04	2546	2619	0.7
93702 FRESNO	019	46619	47235	49678	0.3	23	10928	10898	11311	-0.1	4.27	9134	9081	-0.1
93703 FRESNO	019	32522	33223	35041	0.5	32	10000	10028	10421	0.1	3.26	7279	7269	0.0
93704 FRESNO	019	26280	27177	28945	0.8	45	11030	11282	11889	0.5	2.41	6580	6685	0.4
93705 FRESNO	019	37492	39469	42434	1.2	62	12803	13296	14123	0.9	2.95	8960	9243	0.7
93706 FRESNO	019	35668	36917	39203	0.8	47	9560	9781	10281	0.5	3.70	7431	7577	0.5
93710 FRESNO	019	27894	29783	32270	1.6	70	10695	11379	12246	1.5	2.58	6786	7152	1.2
93711 FRESNO	019	35311	36951	39658	1.1	57	14659	15233	16205	0.9	2.42	10074	10396	0.7
93720 FRESNO	019	44623	51131	57275	3.3	92	16710	18998	21078	3.1	2.68	12021	13655	3.0
93721 FRESNO	019	6813	6889	7113	0.3	22	1618	1618	1687	0.0	2.41	792	787	-0.2
93722 FRESNO	019	59560	67354	74924	2.9	90	19335	21649	23836	2.7	3.10	14992	16738	2.6
93725 FRESNO	019	21369	22392	24092	1.1	59	5648	5863	6249	0.9	3.76	4644	4803	0.8
93726 FRESNO	019	38540	39597	41969	0.6	38	14069	14270	14948	0.3	2.77	9062	9143	0.2
93727 FRESNO	019	55865	60150	65340	1.8	75	18025	19028	20378	1.3	3.10	13034	13727	1.2
93728 FRESNO	019	16643	17104	18095	0.6	38	5929	6035	6324	0.4	2.80	3438	3471	0.2
CALIFORNIA					1.4					1.2	2.90			1.2
UNITED STATES					1.2					1.3	2.58			1.1

#	ZIP CODE POST OFFICE NAME	RACE (%) White 2000	White 2004	Black 2000	Black 2004	Asian/Pacific 2000	Asian/Pacific 2004	% Hispanic Origin 2000	% Hispanic Origin 2004	2004 AGE DISTRIBUTION (%) 0-4	5-9	10-14	15-19	20-24	25-44	45-64	65-84	85+	18+	MEDIAN AGE 2004	% 2004 Males	% 2004 Females
93513	BIG PINE	71.6	69.3	0.3	0.5	0.5	0.5	7.8	9.1	4.8	5.1	6.6	6.8	5.8	19.9	28.0	19.4	3.8	78.8	45.7	47.3	52.7
93514	BISHOP	82.3	80.7	0.1	0.1	1.0	1.1	11.3	13.2	5.3	5.9	7.2	7.3	4.9	21.2	31.1	15.0	2.2	76.8	43.9	49.2	50.8
93516	BORON	85.0	82.3	2.2	2.4	1.7	1.9	9.0	11.5	7.5	6.4	7.2	7.6	6.8	21.8	28.5	13.3	1.0	74.3	39.9	49.9	50.1
93517	BRIDGEPORT	86.2	85.3	0.8	0.7	1.5	1.7	14.8	17.4	4.3	5.1	6.0	5.3	3.4	26.0	33.5	15.7	0.7	81.5	44.9	55.2	44.8
93518	CALIENTE	85.5	82.4	1.4	1.6	1.2	1.3	8.9	11.6	3.3	4.2	6.3	5.9	4.1	14.0	38.2	22.1	1.8	82.1	51.4	52.0	48.0
93519	CANTIL	84.6	81.4	0.7	0.8	0.7	0.8	7.7	10.9	3.1	3.1	4.7	3.9	3.9	14.7	36.4	27.9	2.3	85.3	56.0	53.5	46.5
93523	EDWARDS	74.2	70.3	9.5	10.4	4.7	5.2	11.2	14.0	13.4	8.9	8.6	6.1	17.6	36.8	6.2	2.3	0.1	65.9	23.7	54.3	45.8
93524	EDWARDS	76.0	73.1	4.0	3.9	4.0	3.9	24.0	19.2	7.7	7.7	7.7	7.7	7.7	30.8	30.8	0.0	0.0	76.9	32.5	50.0	50.0
93526	INDEPENDENCE	82.0	80.0	0.0	0.0	1.2	1.2	9.4	11.2	4.5	4.7	5.3	7.4	6.5	15.8	34.0	19.2	2.8	81.1	48.0	47.6	52.4
93527	INYOKERN	90.4	88.6	0.4	0.4	1.5	1.8	6.2	7.9	4.5	4.7	7.4	6.8	4.5	20.6	37.0	12.7	1.7	78.8	45.7	50.7	49.3
93528	JOHANNESBURG	84.1	81.2	1.1	1.2	0.5	0.6	8.5	10.6	2.9	3.5	4.1	4.1	3.5	15.3	35.9	27.7	2.9	85.9	55.3	54.1	45.9
93529	JUNE LAKE	89.0	87.3	0.0	0.0	0.7	0.8	15.6	18.2	3.8	5.4	7.0	5.8	3.8	26.2	39.1	8.9	0.0	80.7	43.9	53.1	46.9
93531	KEENE	86.7	83.9	1.8	2.0	0.4	0.8	9.3	11.0	4.7	6.3	7.5	6.7	3.5	17.7	32.9	19.6	1.2	76.9	47.4	51.0	49.0
93532	LAKE HUGHES	83.1	79.7	4.0	4.3	1.6	1.8	15.9	20.2	6.3	7.3	8.0	12.3	5.8	26.1	26.8	6.8	0.7	69.2	36.1	53.7	46.3
93534	LANCASTER	64.1	60.2	15.7	15.9	3.5	3.9	24.2	29.3	8.9	8.0	8.4	9.3	8.1	26.8	18.2	10.3	2.0	68.7	30.4	48.7	51.3
93535	LANCASTER	60.7	56.4	16.2	16.6	3.0	3.3	28.2	33.7	8.9	8.7	10.6	9.0	7.5	27.8	19.9	6.8	0.7	66.0	29.4	48.6	51.4
93536	LANCASTER	70.3	66.8	11.6	11.8	4.6	5.2	18.0	22.2	6.3	6.7	8.4	7.9	7.3	29.7	24.8	7.9	1.0	73.5	35.6	53.6	46.5
93541	LEE VINING	73.6	71.0	0.6	0.6	1.0	1.1	24.2	27.5	7.2	7.7	5.8	4.9	4.9	28.8	31.8	8.3	0.6	76.3	39.5	55.0	45.0
93543	LITTLEROCK	64.3	60.3	9.6	9.3	0.9	1.0	37.1	43.7	7.3	8.0	10.5	9.1	6.2	24.7	24.6	8.7	1.0	68.3	34.6	51.4	48.6
93544	LLANO	84.4	81.7	5.6	6.0	0.4	0.5	16.6	21.2	4.3	5.0	6.3	5.8	4.6	23.8	34.3	14.9	1.2	80.7	45.2	54.2	45.8
93545	LONE PINE	79.0	77.1	0.1	0.1	0.9	1.0	23.9	27.5	6.2	6.3	6.7	5.9	6.1	20.4	29.3	16.6	2.6	77.0	43.7	48.6	51.4
93546	MAMMOTH LAKES	83.2	81.0	0.4	0.5	1.4	1.5	22.1	25.4	5.6	5.2	6.1	7.3	9.6	36.3	24.4	5.4	0.2	79.2	33.4	56.4	43.6
93550	PALMDALE	50.9	47.1	14.8	14.4	2.9	3.1	43.7	49.5	10.4	10.0	11.5	9.4	7.7	28.6	17.0	5.0	0.5	62.3	25.9	49.2	50.8
93551	PALMDALE	71.1	67.0	8.7	9.2	5.8	6.5	19.4	23.8	6.9	7.9	10.6	9.0	5.7	25.8	26.6	7.1	0.6	68.8	36.2	49.3	50.7
93552	PALMDALE	51.5	48.0	17.1	16.4	4.0	4.1	41.3	47.4	9.2	10.0	12.0	8.8	6.0	30.1	18.2	5.3	0.5	63.2	28.6	49.2	50.8
93553	PEARBLOSSOM	87.0	84.2	1.1	1.3	0.8	0.9	18.8	23.9	5.3	6.3	8.3	6.3	5.2	22.6	31.6	12.6	1.7	75.9	42.4	49.8	50.2
93554	RANDSBURG	83.3	84.2	0.0	0.0	0.0	0.0	7.1	10.5	5.3	5.3	5.3	5.3	5.3	21.1	29.0	21.1	2.6	84.2	46.7	55.3	44.7
93555	RIDGECREST	83.1	80.2	3.1	3.4	4.0	4.5	11.5	14.3	6.9	7.1	8.1	7.6	6.6	24.9	26.1	11.7	1.2	73.3	37.7	49.9	50.1
93560	ROSAMOND	72.3	68.3	6.4	6.6	3.1	3.3	25.6	31.0	7.6	7.6	9.4	8.6	7.7	27.6	23.0	7.9	0.7	70.2	33.2	50.6	49.4
93561	TEHACHAPI	74.3	71.8	6.3	5.9	1.1	1.2	21.3	25.1	5.5	6.0	7.7	7.2	7.8	29.2	24.1	11.7	1.0	76.3	36.9	57.5	42.6
93562	TRONA	86.6	84.4	1.5	1.6	1.1	1.2	15.5	18.7	7.2	6.6	8.5	8.5	8.2	22.5	26.2	11.1	1.2	72.5	36.4	51.0	49.0
93563	VALYERMO	75.8	72.8	10.0	10.4	3.5	3.6	16.4	20.8	4.5	4.8	5.7	5.2	6.8	31.4	30.9	9.9	0.8	81.7	40.8	59.5	40.5
93591	PALMDALE	61.6	57.0	11.2	11.3	1.5	1.6	32.9	39.3	7.6	9.5	12.6	10.6	6.1	24.9	22.1	6.3	0.3	63.1	29.1	51.2	48.8
93601	AHWAHNEE	88.3	85.9	0.1	0.2	0.7	0.8	9.0	11.7	5.5	5.8	6.5	6.6	4.8	21.1	31.5	16.7	1.6	78.0	44.8	48.9	51.1
93602	AUBERRY	84.1	81.7	0.4	0.4	0.7	0.8	7.2	9.2	5.1	6.3	7.4	7.1	5.2	20.0	32.6	14.4	2.0	76.5	44.3	49.7	50.3
93604	BASS LAKE	89.7	87.1	0.0	0.0	0.4	0.4	7.3	9.6	4.5	4.7	4.5	3.0	3.4	18.0	28.1	30.5	3.4	84.3	55.2	49.1	50.9
93608	CANTUA CREEK	41.3	39.6	0.6	0.6	1.0	0.9	89.4	91.5	9.6	8.8	9.2	10.1	10.8	30.4	17.7	3.1	0.3	66.3	25.8	59.1	40.9
93609	CARUTHERS	52.4	48.0	0.7	0.7	6.8	6.9	54.3	60.2	7.9	7.8	9.8	9.9	8.6	27.2	19.4	8.3	1.1	68.3	29.5	52.0	48.1
93610	CHOWCHILLA	58.7	54.1	12.3	12.3	1.8	1.8	32.5	38.8	5.8	5.6	6.3	5.4	8.1	42.6	18.4	6.9	1.0	79.1	34.0	33.6	66.4
93611	CLOVIS	82.5	79.5	1.2	1.3	6.0	6.9	14.1	17.1	6.9	7.4	9.3	8.4	5.8	26.2	27.2	7.8	1.2	71.1	36.8	48.9	51.2
93612	CLOVIS	70.6	66.3	2.4	2.5	6.6	7.2	25.2	30.0	8.1	7.2	7.9	7.5	8.5	29.9	19.9	9.5	1.5	72.2	31.7	47.6	52.4
93614	COARSEGOLD	92.1	90.4	0.4	0.4	0.9	1.0	7.1	9.4	4.6	5.6	7.6	6.2	3.9	21.0	32.5	17.3	1.3	77.9	45.6	49.4	50.6
93615	CUTLER	38.2	37.3	0.3	0.3	1.3	1.2	91.3	92.8	10.3	9.2	10.8	9.2	10.8	29.3	14.4	5.5	0.4	64.1	24.9	55.0	45.0
93616	DEL REY	45.8	43.6	0.4	0.4	4.8	4.8	78.6	81.7	9.2	8.3	8.8	8.3	8.1	25.3	20.7	10.3	1.2	68.8	30.3	50.6	49.4
93618	DINUBA	54.1	51.4	0.3	0.3	2.6	2.6	71.9	75.8	10.1	9.2	9.6	8.7	9.3	27.9	16.9	7.3	1.1	65.9	26.9	51.4	48.6
93620	DOS PALOS	63.1	60.4	5.1	4.7	0.6	0.6	53.6	58.7	9.1	8.9	9.9	8.8	7.6	26.8	19.6	8.4	1.1	66.4	29.2	50.8	49.2
93621	DUNLAP	90.0	88.1	1.9	2.3	0.3	0.6	7.4	9.3	4.8	5.1	6.4	6.8	5.5	22.2	33.1	14.8	1.3	78.8	44.5	49.5	50.5
93622	FIREBAUGH	44.3	42.2	1.3	1.2	0.9	0.9	84.6	87.7	10.2	9.1	11.0	10.6	10.1	27.1	16.2	5.3	0.5	63.3	24.6	53.1	46.9
93623	FISH CAMP	82.8	80.3	1.6	1.5	1.6	1.5	15.6	18.2	4.6	3.0	3.0	4.6	10.6	45.5	25.8	3.0	0.0	89.4	34.2	62.1	37.9
93625	FOWLER	50.7	47.2	1.7	1.6	6.6	6.6	62.2	67.5	7.7	7.5	9.0	8.9	8.2	25.6	21.2	10.1	1.9	70.5	32.0	50.2	49.8
93626	FRIANT	87.2	85.1	0.7	0.8	2.0	2.2	7.5	9.5	3.7	4.3	7.3	6.5	4.0	21.5	33.6	17.3	1.9	80.3	46.5	50.6	49.4
93627	HELM	41.3	39.7	1.6	1.6	1.6	1.6	88.9	88.9	9.5	7.9	9.5	9.5	14.3	31.8	17.5	0.0	0.0	65.1	24.7	60.3	39.7
93630	KERMAN	45.5	41.3	0.3	0.3	6.6	6.6	62.6	68.2	9.1	8.5	9.6	9.2	9.1	28.1	18.0	7.6	0.8	67.3	28.0	51.2	48.8
93631	KINGSBURG	69.1	64.6	0.5	0.5	3.2	3.5	38.3	44.0	7.8	8.0	8.8	7.6	6.8	27.6	21.4	10.3	1.7	70.5	33.4	49.6	50.5
93633	KINGS CANYON NATIONA	90.1	88.4	0.0	0.0	0.6	0.6	9.4	11.6	5.0	5.0	6.1	5.5	5.5	24.9	33.2	13.8	1.1	80.7	44.0	50.3	49.7
93635	LOS BANOS	59.0	55.7	3.8	3.7	2.5	2.6	50.4	55.0	9.7	9.0	9.2	8.2	7.8	28.4	18.9	7.7	1.2	66.8	29.5	50.1	49.9
93637	MADERA	58.7	55.0	2.8	2.8	2.2	2.3	53.0	58.5	9.5	8.6	8.9	7.7	8.0	27.7	19.6	8.8	1.2	68.2	29.8	50.1	49.9
93638	MADERA	51.9	49.1	3.7	3.5	1.2	1.2	62.7	67.2	9.5	8.6	9.8	9.0	9.3	26.8	19.3	6.9	0.7	66.6	27.5	51.7	48.3
93640	MENDOTA	29.2	28.4	0.6	0.5	0.9	0.8	94.3	95.5	9.6	8.2	8.6	9.6	11.8	31.1	16.2	4.8	0.3	68.1	26.2	57.2	42.8
93641	MIRAMONTE	87.0	84.7	1.5	1.6	0.7	0.8	10.6	13.5	4.1	4.9	7.3	6.0	5.4	24.8	32.6	14.1	0.8	79.8	43.7	51.0	49.1
93643	NORTH FORK	79.5	76.5	0.2	0.2	1.1	1.3	9.3	12.0	5.0	5.4	6.6	6.3	5.0	19.4	33.3	17.2	1.9	78.7	46.5	49.8	50.2
93644	OAKHURST	89.3	87.1	0.3	0.3	1.0	1.1	7.2	9.6	4.2	4.6	5.8	5.7	5.1	19.4	30.6	21.3	3.3	81.8	48.3	48.3	51.7
93645	O NEALS	84.3	82.0	1.4	1.2	1.4	1.2	6.4	8.7	4.7	5.2	9.3	7.6	3.5	22.7	30.8	14.5	1.7	75.0	43.2	50.0	50.0
93646	ORANGE COVE	37.3	35.6	0.3	0.3	1.7	1.7	86.4	88.9	11.0	10.2	11.1	9.7	10.0	27.8	14.3	5.4	0.5	61.9	24.0	51.7	48.3
93647	OROSI	34.9	33.5	0.4	0.4	9.6	9.3	79.6	81.7	10.2	9.3	10.0	8.8	9.8	28.1	15.7	7.3	0.9	65.3	26.2	52.6	47.4
93648	PARLIER	35.5	34.4	0.8	0.8	1.9	1.7	92.3	93.8	10.7	9.6	10.1	9.4	10.3	29.6	15.0	5.0	0.6	64.3	25.0	52.3	47.7
93650	FRESNO	47.3	43.2	4.6	4.5	13.4	13.6	43.1	48.4	9.3	8.2	9.7	9.3	10.4	29.8	16.4	6.3	0.6	67.2	26.7	47.8	52.2
93651	PRATHER	89.4	87.2	0.6	0.8	0.7	0.9	7.3	9.5	5.8	6.9	9.2	8.6	4.1	25.1	30.0	9.7	0.8	72.3	40.2	49.5	50.5
93652	RAISIN	53.3	49.4	0.4	0.4	5.4	5.6	58.7	64.7	8.8	7.6	9.6	10.0	8.8	26.5	20.5	6.8	1.2	67.9	28.3	53.8	46.2
93653	RAYMOND	90.5	88.7	0.5	0.6	0.6	0.6	9.9	13.0	5.1	5.7	6.4	6.3	5.5	19.3	34.8	15.4	1.7	78.9	46.0	48.7	51.3
93654	REEDLEY	54.7	51.7	0.4	0.4	4.4	4.5	62.9	67.2	9.2	8.2	8.9	8.0	8.7	27.9	18.2	9.0	1.9	68.9	29.6	51.4	48.6
93656	RIVERDALE	51.5	47.5	3.0	2.6	1.4	1.4	56.1	61.4	9.1	8.9	10.7	8.9	8.1	26.9	18.3	8.0	1.1	66.2	28.2	52.0	48.0
93657	SANGER	58.2	56.0	0.5	0.6	3.3	3.6	62.7	65.2	8.1	7.8	8.8	8.5	7.7	25.7	22.0	10.1	1.4	70.2	32.1	50.3	49.7
93660	SAN JOAQUIN	35.9	34.7	0.3	0.3	2.8	2.6	90.0	91.8	12.0	10.3	11.4	10.7	11.2	27.4	13.2	3.5	0.3	59.9	22.5	53.4	46.7
93662	SELMA	45.0	41.7	0.8	0.8	4.3	4.4	68.5	73.0	9.3	8.6	9.0	8.6	8.5	28.1	17.8	8.8	1.3	67.8	28.8	50.9	49.2
93664	SHAVER LAKE	94.7	93.7	0.0	0.0	0.2	0.3	9.2	11.0	4.2	5.8	8.5	5.2	3.6	21.4	37.4	13.3	0.6	78.0	45.6	52.5	47.5
93667	TOLLHOUSE	87.4	85.2	0.6	0.6	0.8	0.9	7.8	10.0	5.5	6.7	8.7	8.2	4.4	23.5	31.9	10.0	1.0	73.4	41.2	49.8	50.2
93668	TRANQUILLITY	49.3	45.2	0.6	0.5	2.3	2.3	68.6	74.3	9.7	8.6	9.0	8.9	9.0	26.2	20.3	7.5	0.8	66.9	28.5	52.7	47.4
93669	WISHON	77.0	72.1	0.0	0.0	0.7	0.8	5.9	7.8	2.9	3.8	5.2	5.2	4.6	19.3	36.6	20.6	1.7	84.6	50.4	52.5	47.5
93675	SQUAW VALLEY	86.7	84.3	2.2	2.4	0.7	0.8	11.8	15.1	4.5	5.2	7.0	7.1	5.0	22.9	32.8	14.5	1.0	78.1	44.0	50.7	49.3
93701	FRESNO	28.2	27.1	7.0	6.3	16.8	16.0	64.2	67.6	13.0	10.5	11.9	10.6	11.1	25.5	12.8	4.2	0.5	58.2	21.8	52.1	47.9
93702	FRESNO	27.3	25.9	4.6	4.2	17.1	16.4	66.0	69.4	11.4	10.4	11.9	11.2	9.5	25.2	14.5	5.1	0.7	59.2	22.6	50.9	49.1
93703	FRESNO	44.1	40.8	5.2	5.0	14.4	14.3	50.0	55.1	10.6	9.3	10.1	8.7	8.8	26.5	15.8	8.3	1.7	64.6	26.6	49.0	51.0
93704	FRESNO	70.3	66.3	3.9	4.1	5.7	6.2	27.5	32.2	6.6	6.2	7.0	6.8	7.0	25.9	24.5	13.4	2.6	76.0	37.9	47.2	52.8
93705	FRESNO	51.8	47.6	9.5	9.2	7.0	7.3	42.1	47.5	10.4	8.8	8.9	7.9	9.0	26.8	17.3	9.2	1.7	67.1	28.4	47.9	52.1
93706	FRESNO	28.9	27.4	25.3	23.7	9.4	9.6	50.3	54.2	9.5	9.1	10.5	10.1	8.8	24.4	17.7	8.7	1.3	64.7	26.6	51.1	48.9
93710	FRESNO	64.5	60.0	6.2	6.3	10.0	10.9	24.4	29.0	7.1	5.7	6.3	7.7	13.0	27.0	20.4	10.8	1.9	77.1	30.2	48.0	52.0
93711	FRESNO	78.4	74.7	3.6	3.9	7.3	8.3	14.8	18.3	5.2	5.4	6.6	6.4	6.7	24.6	29.6	13.8	1.8	78.8	41.3	48.3	51.7
93720	FRESNO	78.2	74.4	2.5	2.7	9.9	11.4	13.4	16.6	7.8	7.6	7.7	6.9	6.8	30.8	24.2	7.1	1.2	72.8	34.4	48.0	52.0
93721	FRESNO	39.2	36.7	14.4	13.3	2.9	2.9	61.1	66.1	7.4	5.4	4.6	6.7	13.5	37.0	15.4	7.1	2.9	80.2	30.5	64.7	35.3
93722	FRESNO	57.4	53.6	7.7	7.5	9.8	10.4	34.9	39.7	9.5	8.8	8.7	7.4	7.5	31.6	19.6	6.4	0.6	68.5	30.7	49.3	50.7
93725	FRESNO	36.6	34.0	6.6	6.2	8.6	8.9	63.2	67.1	9.0	8.6	10.2	9.6	8.2	26.8	18.7	7.9	1.0	66.1	28.3	50.9	49.1
93726	FRESNO	53.7	49.4	7.6	7.5	11.2	11.8	35.4	40.6	8.6	7.2	7.8	8.1	12.7	27.2	17.5	9.7	1.2	71.9	28.3	48.1	51.9
93727	FRESNO	48.9	45.1	8.0	7.8	13.3	13.7	38.1	43.0	9.6	8.3	9.2	8.6	9.4	25.6	18.2	9.3	1.7	67.9	28.3	48.4	51.6
93728	FRESNO	50.0	45.9	4.6	4.4	7.4	7.6	48.7	54.2	8.3	7.7	8.5	8.4	8.9	30.0	19.3	7.7	1.2	70.4	30.0	50.6	49.4
	CALIFORNIA	59.6	57.1	6.7	6.5	11.3	11.8	32.4	35.5	7.4	7.1	7.8	7.3	7.7	29.8	22.1	9.3	1.4	73.3	33.8	49.8	50.2
	UNITED STATES	75.1	73.6	12.3	12.5	3.8	4.2	12.5	14.1	6.9	6.7	7.2	7.0	7.3	28.6	23.8	10.8	1.7	75.1	36.0	49.1	50.9

INCOME

ZIP CODE #	POST OFFICE NAME	2004 Per Capita Income	2004 HH Income Base	2004 HOUSEHOLD INCOME DISTRIBUTION (%) Less than $25,000	$25,000 to $49,999	$50,000 to $99,999	$100,000 to $149,999	$150,000 or More	MEDIAN HOUSEHOLD INCOME 2004	2009	2004 National Centile	2004 State Centile	2004 Home Value Base	2004 HOME VALUE DISTRIBUTION (%) Less than $50,000	$50,000 to $89,999	$90,000 to $174,999	$175,000 to $399,999	$400,000 or More	2004 Median Home Value
93513	BIG PINE	21699	701	30.5	29.5	29.4	8.0	2.6	39101	45984	43	29	510	12.9	1.8	17.8	61.4	6.1	208421
93514	BISHOP	24178	6326	27.5	28.1	30.3	10.5	3.7	44169	50967	59	40	4644	17.1	4.4	13.1	44.4	21.0	251852
93516	BORON	19094	737	36.1	23.1	32.4	6.2	2.2	44891	50396	61	41	483	20.1	42.0	35.6	2.3	0.0	81397
93517	BRIDGEPORT	19101	169	23.1	42.0	31.4	3.6	0.0	40682	45483	49	33	119	10.1	4.2	15.1	67.2	3.4	215179
93518	CALIENTE	21261	441	40.4	22.5	28.8	4.3	4.1	33872	39179	24	18	373	7.2	9.9	44.0	33.0	5.9	145719
93519	CANTIL	42731	73	38.4	20.6	31.5	4.1	5.5	31722	36550	17	13	57	45.6	28.1	26.3	0.0	0.0	56250
93523	EDWARDS	16035	2484	19.3	42.9	30.8	6.4	0.7	41746	48076	52	36	501	41.9	30.5	25.8	1.8	0.0	59878
93524	EDWARDS	26939	14	28.6	35.7	28.6	7.1	0.0	40000	37333	46	31	8	0.0	25.0	25.0	50.0	0.0	175000
93526	INDEPENDENCE	24229	361	25.8	33.0	31.6	7.8	1.9	43155	50323	56	38	249	11.7	10.0	42.2	32.5	3.6	147348
93527	INYOKERN	23796	897	29.0	26.4	29.4	11.2	4.0	42809	52143	55	37	739	16.1	42.4	36.0	5.6	0.0	85079
93528	JOHANNESBURG	36698	83	38.6	21.7	31.3	3.6	4.8	30440	35000	13	11	65	44.6	29.2	26.2	0.0	0.0	57000
93529	JUNE LAKE	28780	281	33.1	12.5	39.9	4.6	10.0	52054	56420	76	56	186	3.2	0.0	8.1	38.7	50.0	400000
93531	KEENE	29934	96	18.8	17.7	42.7	12.5	8.3	63233	72392	87	71	84	3.6	2.4	26.2	51.2	16.7	228571
93532	LAKE HUGHES	26565	1024	15.9	22.6	41.1	15.6	4.8	60299	70265	85	68	820	2.2	1.7	21.3	68.4	6.3	217870
93534	LANCASTER	18876	13580	35.4	29.8	25.3	6.6	2.9	35792	42339	31	22	5833	2.7	5.2	63.6	26.3	2.1	140713
93535	LANCASTER	17828	18987	26.0	29.5	32.7	8.8	3.0	45360	53058	62	42	13507	13.6	5.2	54.2	26.2	0.8	139259
93536	LANCASTER	24818	16786	18.9	20.9	35.7	17.3	7.2	61793	75474	86	70	12660	3.9	2.2	23.7	64.8	5.4	215194
93541	LEE VINING	40639	203	16.3	36.5	32.0	2.5	12.8	48962	55411	70	50	139	4.3	5.0	20.1	56.1	14.4	208654
93543	LITTLEROCK	17988	3600	26.3	23.7	34.3	11.6	4.1	49934	60616	72	52	2892	3.0	3.3	50.7	38.9	4.2	163368
93544	LLANO	29042	526	24.5	20.9	32.1	15.8	6.7	54438	65818	79	60	445	10.3	6.7	23.4	45.8	13.7	213406
93545	LONE PINE	17043	951	43.9	29.9	19.2	5.9	1.2	29589	33399	11	10	601	19.0	11.5	27.6	31.3	10.7	143351
93546	MAMMOTH LAKES	29979	3170	20.4	28.9	31.0	10.6	9.2	50620	58586	73	53	1672	7.6	3.3	3.2	30.5	55.4	432042
93550	PALMDALE	15280	21430	29.3	28.4	31.1	9.0	2.1	43016	50496	56	38	12893	4.1	4.5	54.9	34.7	1.8	150839
93551	PALMDALE	29526	12972	9.5	16.6	40.9	22.9	10.1	76756	91772	94	83	11255	2.7	1.5	11.4	68.5	15.9	253185
93552	PALMDALE	17710	8236	15.0	28.3	40.4	13.7	2.6	56197	65431	81	63	6968	3.6	1.1	44.5	49.6	1.2	176121
93553	PEARBLOSSOM	20618	496	35.1	19.6	32.7	9.5	3.2	42828	54280	56	37	401	5.7	7.0	39.2	41.4	6.7	168534
93554	RANDSBURG	34737	24	37.5	20.8	33.3	4.2	4.2	30000	37367	12	11	19	52.6	26.3	21.1	0.0	0.0	49375
93555	RIDGECREST	25136	12174	24.4	24.8	32.4	13.3	5.0	50781	60153	73	54	8415	18.7	27.0	40.5	13.0	0.8	95972
93560	ROSAMOND	20014	5946	23.9	27.8	36.6	10.0	1.8	48172	54819	69	48	4299	14.9	11.7	59.6	12.7	1.0	119347
93561	TEHACHAPI	22834	9040	25.7	21.7	36.0	12.4	4.3	52392	60945	76	57	6816	2.8	4.6	44.3	40.3	8.0	171892
93562	TRONA	17860	718	33.0	29.4	31.2	5.4	1.0	39144	42184	43	29	453	66.0	23.2	9.9	0.9	0.0	43640
93563	VALYERMO	23907	211	23.7	20.4	33.7	14.7	7.6	55490	65751	80	62	174	15.5	7.5	27.0	25.3	24.7	175000
93591	PALMDALE	14618	1933	23.6	33.4	32.6	8.4	2.0	43236	50305	57	38	1441	2.1	10.7	73.1	10.8	3.4	124852
93601	AHWAHNEE	22605	732	23.9	37.2	23.0	10.3	5.7	41958	47905	53	36	586	0.9	2.9	14.9	64.7	16.7	245608
93602	AUBERRY	21305	1279	26.4	25.7	33.9	11.0	3.1	46950	54196	66	45	1088	9.8	3.1	28.5	51.7	6.9	196729
93604	BASS LAKE	26784	260	30.0	35.4	19.2	10.0	5.4	33364	38273	22	17	210	3.3	15.2	15.7	32.9	32.9	238710
93608	CANTUA CREEK	11982	411	34.3	52.8	9.7	0.7	2.4	30931	34264	15	12	107	38.3	30.8	18.7	8.4	3.7	68333
93609	CARUTHERS	14568	1432	32.2	29.2	27.2	7.2	4.2	39929	44751	46	31	905	4.3	4.4	52.6	30.9	7.7	148604
93610	CHOWCHILLA	16801	4381	36.7	32.3	23.2	5.0	2.9	34930	38937	27	19	2513	3.6	10.2	54.5	25.2	6.5	136879
93611	CLOVIS	28115	17663	10.5	18.1	41.1	20.4	9.8	73029	86443	92	80	15376	0.9	0.5	18.8	65.4	14.3	240079
93612	CLOVIS	16758	14063	35.8	36.6	21.5	4.9	1.3	33161	37382	21	16	6062	12.3	3.7	59.3	23.3	1.3	138049
93614	COARSEGOLD	24328	4264	22.9	27.5	31.8	13.0	4.9	49695	56905	71	52	3557	3.3	2.8	18.3	64.8	10.8	228999
93615	CUTLER	7682	1153	44.4	36.0	16.1	2.4	1.0	27951	31464	9	8	656	1.4	13.7	71.3	10.8	2.7	114326
93616	DEL REY	11832	488	36.9	32.8	21.7	7.4	1.2	32368	36544	19	15	327	2.1	4.3	63.9	19.9	9.8	123452
93618	DINUBA	13165	6819	34.2	34.8	23.6	4.6	2.8	35985	40110	31	22	4315	8.2	9.8	60.4	18.4	3.2	124280
93620	DOS PALOS	13932	3027	42.3	28.5	21.8	4.4	3.0	29330	33191	11	9	1837	3.8	3.2	53.2	28.9	10.9	157244
93621	DUNLAP	21688	108	23.2	31.5	25.0	13.9	6.5	45759	52962	63	43	87	5.8	3.5	35.6	47.1	8.1	186250
93622	FIREBAUGH	10231	2655	38.0	38.0	19.6	3.0	1.4	31707	35344	17	13	1231	7.0	8.1	65.7	18.1	1.1	125723
93623	FISH CAMP	35995	34	17.7	38.2	35.3	5.9	2.9	45000	52952	61	42	15	13.3	6.7	26.7	33.3	20.0	187500
93625	FOWLER	15930	1839	31.4	31.8	26.4	6.8	3.7	38369	43242	41	27	1136	3.8	7.9	46.2	32.3	9.8	152041
93626	FRIANT	21081	546	28.4	35.4	23.3	10.6	2.4	39305	46149	44	29	444	11.3	4.3	38.7	18.5	27.3	151250
93627	HELM	7513	14	35.7	64.3	0.0	0.0	0.0	30000	30000	12	11	4	50.0	50.0	0.0	0.0	0.0	65000
93630	KERMAN	13186	4397	38.2	33.3	20.4	5.2	3.0	32115	36351	18	14	2537	7.9	7.0	46.8	28.3	10.0	153013
93631	KINGSBURG	18862	5216	27.2	31.3	29.1	9.6	2.8	43647	50565	58	39	3627	4.3	6.6	37.1	43.4	8.5	179951
93633	KINGS CANYON NATIONA	19245	63	36.5	30.2	23.8	4.8	4.8	35436	43358	29	21	46	0.0	13.0	34.8	34.8	17.4	180000
93635	LOS BANOS	17567	9773	22.4	29.9	34.7	9.2	3.8	47799	54467	68	47	6738	2.9	1.7	20.6	64.8	10.0	233668
93637	MADERA	17835	9573	29.7	31.4	27.3	7.2	4.4	40856	46427	49	34	5763	2.9	4.0	47.9	38.6	6.6	165970
93638	MADERA	14261	13551	31.5	30.6	27.4	7.2	3.3	38349	42981	41	27	8872	2.5	5.2	50.3	38.3	3.7	157020
93640	MENDOTA	8371	2165	47.9	33.7	15.9	1.7	0.8	25862	28972	6	5	930	5.8	14.6	73.1	4.8	1.6	121716
93641	MIRAMONTE	19225	247	33.2	34.0	26.3	3.2	3.2	36837	41914	35	24	183	1.6	14.8	43.7	21.9	18.0	145833
93643	NORTH FORK	22489	1139	30.6	32.6	21.7	9.1	6.1	39689	45432	45	30	903	7.3	4.7	22.5	53.5	12.1	211232
93644	OAKHURST	23455	4046	30.5	29.8	26.7	8.4	4.6	40039	46475	46	31	3011	5.9	4.5	14.3	59.1	16.1	236360
93645	O NEALS	17701	60	36.7	30.0	21.7	8.3	3.3	41547	50349	51	35	48	12.5	0.0	18.8	41.7	27.1	250000
93646	ORANGE COVE	8947	2109	47.2	30.9	16.2	3.8	1.9	26383	30080	6	6	1053	8.1	11.1	64.5	11.6	4.8	128761
93647	OROSI	9546	2463	37.0	34.4	24.1	3.3	1.2	33088	36707	21	16	1496	6.6	12.9	67.3	12.7	0.5	114685
93648	PARLIER	8635	2957	45.5	34.7	15.2	3.2	1.5	27418	31078	8	7	1671	4.0	6.9	76.1	9.1	4.0	129392
93650	FRESNO	13586	1273	38.7	33.3	21.3	4.3	2.4	30827	34701	14	12	448	2.0	18.8	52.9	21.7	4.7	123454
93651	PRATHER	23382	514	16.9	32.1	30.7	14.6	5.6	50896	59821	74	54	440	3.2	3.0	25.9	45.0	23.0	234375
93652	RAISIN	21351	67	31.3	25.4	26.9	9.0	7.5	42985	52178	56	38	35	5.7	2.9	25.7	42.9	22.9	217857
93653	RAYMOND	22532	508	31.7	26.4	28.0	7.1	6.9	42268	48466	54	36	410	1.7	2.4	22.0	54.4	19.5	245205
93654	REEDLEY	14543	7702	31.7	30.2	27.2	7.8	3.1	38561	44328	41	28	4876	4.8	3.7	48.1	38.6	4.9	162401
93656	RIVERDALE	13879	1736	36.8	31.9	22.9	4.6	3.9	33269	37472	22	17	1035	7.7	12.4	49.9	23.1	7.0	133890
93657	SANGER	17772	8975	29.2	31.3	26.6	8.5	4.5	40526	46743	48	33	6098	4.2	6.2	44.6	33.5	11.5	160365
93660	SAN JOAQUIN	8944	959	47.9	32.6	14.9	2.5	2.1	25945	29428	6	5	424	4.5	13.2	71.0	9.2	2.1	129042
93662	SELMA	14558	7959	30.6	34.3	26.3	6.0	2.8	38135	43337	40	27	5038	6.5	7.6	53.8	25.6	6.5	144664
93664	SHAVER LAKE	26865	382	17.3	28.8	34.3	14.1	5.5	53605	62716	78	59	274	2.9	4.0	12.0	47.8	33.2	324590
93667	TOLLHOUSE	22808	960	17.3	27.1	34.6	14.9	6.2	55153	65003	80	61	820	3.2	2.4	20.2	53.2	21.0	241503
93668	TRANQUILLITY	15752	426	31.7	30.1	29.1	5.6	3.5	35688	40601	30	21	230	0.9	16.1	53.0	27.0	3.0	137264
93669	WISHON	22047	269	24.9	30.9	36.8	6.7	0.7	46729	52811	66	45	219	0.0	0.0	22.4	66.2	11.4	229435
93675	SQUAW VALLEY	21418	1254	29.5	29.9	27.0	10.3	3.3	40673	46939	48	33	1059	4.3	7.7	43.8	39.4	4.8	158104
93701	FRESNO	6671	3514	68.8	22.5	6.6	1.0	1.2	15226	16452	1	2	632	4.6	45.6	37.3	6.0	6.5	89904
93702	FRESNO	8297	10898	52.3	30.1	13.8	2.5	1.3	23829	26320	4	3	5059	3.5	31.8	61.2	3.4	0.1	98936
93703	FRESNO	10966	10028	44.6	35.7	16.1	2.6	1.1	27748	31079	8	7	4542	0.8	11.6	85.8	1.7	0.0	114056
93704	FRESNO	24959	11282	29.7	29.9	25.5	9.6	5.4	40813	47617	49	34	6833	4.7	6.6	41.3	43.0	4.4	167761
93705	FRESNO	14711	13296	38.4	33.1	22.1	4.8	1.6	32763	36793	20	15	6906	6.3	6.0	76.8	10.0	0.9	124892
93706	FRESNO	9987	9781	51.5	28.9	14.6	3.2	1.8	24039	26620	4	4	4856	6.6	27.3	43.1	18.2	4.8	111496
93710	FRESNO	19929	11379	32.6	27.9	27.0	9.3	3.1	37672	43396	38	26	5695	2.0	2.6	52.1	43.2	0.1	168560
93711	FRESNO	42130	15233	15.1	22.2	32.2	17.1	13.4	64784	77719	88	72	10424	0.6	1.0	16.1	61.9	20.5	264335
93720	FRESNO	34253	18998	11.8	21.0	36.2	19.1	11.9	70509	84291	91	78	13798	3.1	0.8	11.9	70.0	14.1	241538
93721	FRESNO	15837	1618	70.5	20.8	6.4	0.6	1.9	14573	16007	1	2	217	2.8	30.4	50.2	14.3	2.3	114722
93722	FRESNO	19413	21649	21.0	28.9	37.6	9.5	3.0	50086	57794	72	53	15335	4.2	2.1	52.1	37.5	4.2	162625
93725	FRESNO	12843	5863	38.3	31.5	22.0	5.6	2.7	32633	37132	20	15	3769	9.6	11.9	51.2	21.2	6.1	129246
93726	FRESNO	14705	14270	39.2	34.7	21.2	3.6	1.4	31618	36004	17	13	6902	1.5	5.5	84.7	8.3	0.1	130647
93727	FRESNO	16838	19028	35.3	29.7	25.0	6.6	3.4	36216	41388	32	22	9808	2.9	5.6	53.9	33.0	4.6	149428
93728	FRESNO	13350	6035	44.7	35.2	16.2	2.7	1.1	28006	31744	9	8	3023	15.9	13.2	61.0	7.5	2.4	109484
	CALIFORNIA	27293		21.8	24.4	30.5	13.7	9.7	54267	64547				3.3	2.7	13.3	42.9	37.9	319678
	UNITED STATES	25866		24.7	27.1	30.8	10.9	6.5	48124	56710				10.9	15.0	33.7	30.1	10.4	145905

#	POST OFFICE NAME	FINANCIAL SERVICES: Auto Loan	FINANCIAL SERVICES: Home Loan	FINANCIAL SERVICES: Invest-ments	FINANCIAL SERVICES: Retire-ment Plans	THE HOME: Home Improvements: Home Repair	THE HOME: Home Improvements: Lawn & Garden	THE HOME: Furnishings: Comput-ers & Hard-ware	THE HOME: Furnishings: Major Appli-ances	THE HOME: Furnishings: TV, Radio, Sound Equip-ment	THE HOME: Furnishings: Furni-ture	ENTERTAINMENT: Dine out/Carry out	ENTERTAINMENT: Sports Equip-ment	ENTERTAINMENT: Fees & Tickets	ENTERTAINMENT: Toys & Games	ENTERTAINMENT: Travel	ENTERTAINMENT: Cable TV	PERSONAL: Apparel & Services	PERSONAL: Auto Repairs	PERSONAL: Health Insur-ance	PERSONAL: Pets & Supplies
93513	BIG PINE	86	65	43	62	71	85	72	79	80	68	94	88	64	89	71	85	86	79	94	95
93514	BISHOP	79	84	89	83	84	88	81	82	79	81	98	94	82	97	82	78	96	81	80	91
93516	BORON	70	64	58	62	66	74	67	69	70	65	85	79	65	84	67	72	81	69	75	80
93517	BRIDGEPORT	76	60	41	54	67	75	56	68	64	56	75	79	50	74	60	68	70	67	80	92
93518	CALIENTE	89	65	39	58	74	84	62	76	72	63	85	90	55	83	65	78	79	75	92	106
93519	CANTIL	110	106	112	97	112	135	98	114	106	106	131	107	101	111	108	113	122	110	133	123
93523	EDWARDS	79	54	49	60	51	59	74	66	76	70	94	86	65	86	63	70	90	76	64	76
93524	EDWARDS	75	63	58	62	63	72	67	70	70	70	87	76	63	75	65	69	84	72	73	78
93526	INDEPENDENCE	82	62	41	59	68	81	69	75	77	65	90	84	61	85	68	81	82	75	90	91
93527	INYOKERN	84	85	79	82	85	91	79	84	79	81	98	94	79	94	81	79	95	82	84	96
93528	JOHANNESBURG	110	105	111	96	111	135	98	114	105	106	131	106	100	110	107	113	121	109	134	123
93529	JUNE LAKE	113	89	61	80	100	113	84	101	95	83	113	118	75	111	89	101	105	100	119	138
93531	KEENE	129	108	88	100	117	137	102	119	112	107	137	125	98	119	108	120	127	116	142	146
93532	LAKE HUGHES	103	107	103	109	106	106	103	104	98	103	123	124	102	124	101	94	120	104	96	118
93534	LANCASTER	68	66	75	67	65	70	71	69	71	71	89	81	70	88	69	70	87	71	67	76
93535	LANCASTER	83	83	80	83	81	84	82	82	80	83	100	95	80	98	80	78	98	82	78	92
93536	LANCASTER	104	115	117	116	112	114	108	108	102	109	129	125	110	130	107	99	127	106	99	119
93541	LEE VINING	180	141	96	127	159	179	133	161	151	132	179	188	119	176	142	161	166	158	190	220
93543	LITTLEROCK	85	90	88	90	88	88	87	87	83	88	105	101	86	103	85	79	103	87	79	96
93544	LLANO	105	93	76	87	100	111	87	99	93	87	113	115	82	112	92	98	107	98	111	128
93545	LONE PINE	63	47	31	46	52	62	53	58	59	50	69	65	47	65	52	62	63	58	69	70
93546	MAMMOTH LAKES	114	100	94	101	103	110	102	107	104	103	129	127	96	125	101	103	123	109	108	130
93550	PALMDALE	76	75	75	75	72	74	75	75	74	77	93	86	74	90	72	71	91	76	68	82
93551	PALMDALE	132	152	152	157	146	143	138	137	127	141	161	159	143	163	136	120	159	133	119	150
93552	PALMDALE	92	103	101	107	99	96	95	94	88	98	111	110	97	112	93	82	110	92	81	103
93553	PEARBLOSSOM	82	68	52	66	73	85	72	78	78	69	93	87	67	89	72	81	86	77	89	92
93554	RANDSBURG	80	77	81	70	81	98	71	83	77	77	96	77	73	80	78	83	89	80	98	90
93555	RIDGECREST	87	92	96	92	91	94	91	90	88	90	110	105	91	111	90	86	108	90	85	100
93560	ROSAMOND	87	85	74	84	84	87	81	84	80	83	100	98	79	97	80	78	96	84	81	97
93561	TEHACHAPI	92	91	88	89	93	101	89	92	90	89	111	104	88	108	90	91	107	92	96	106
93562	TRONA	71	60	47	60	63	71	62	66	66	61	80	76	59	79	61	67	75	65	72	78
93563	VALYERMO	130	96	58	89	110	124	93	114	106	92	125	135	81	123	98	113	115	112	135	157
93591	PALMDALE	72	78	79	79	76	76	75	74	71	76	89	88	75	90	73	67	88	74	66	82
93601	AHWAHNEE	83	86	87	82	88	98	85	87	87	83	107	97	86	108	87	90	103	86	93	97
93602	AUBERRY	91	76	56	72	82	92	76	84	82	74	98	97	70	96	77	86	92	83	96	106
93604	BASS LAKE	92	74	53	67	82	93	69	83	78	69	93	95	63	90	74	83	86	82	98	111
93608	CANTUA CREEK	74	62	61	62	61	63	70	70	73	75	93	81	67	90	66	68	93	75	64	75
93609	CARUTHERS	84	73	61	68	71	74	75	81	78	82	98	86	69	87	71	75	97	83	76	84
93610	CHOWCHILLA	65	56	48	55	57	63	59	62	62	60	76	70	55	72	57	61	73	63	64	71
93611	CLOVIS	120	139	141	141	135	134	127	126	118	129	149	148	132	153	127	113	148	123	112	140
93612	CLOVIS	59	57	63	58	56	60	61	59	61	60	76	70	60	74	59	59	74	61	57	66
93614	COARSEGOLD	95	93	85	91	97	105	86	94	88	88	108	105	86	105	90	90	104	92	100	112
93615	CUTLER	53	46	41	44	45	47	49	51	51	53	65	56	46	60	46	49	65	53	48	54
93616	DEL REY	66	58	49	54	56	59	59	64	61	64	77	68	55	69	56	59	77	65	60	67
93618	DINUBA	74	64	56	61	63	66	67	71	70	72	88	77	62	80	64	67	87	73	67	75
93620	DOS PALOS	71	61	51	58	60	64	64	68	66	68	83	74	59	76	61	64	81	69	65	73
93621	DUNLAP	112	79	43	74	92	103	78	96	89	77	105	115	67	103	81	94	96	94	114	133
93622	FIREBAUGH	60	51	48	50	50	52	57	58	59	60	74	65	53	71	53	55	75	60	53	61
93623	FISH CAMP	91	72	51	65	81	91	68	81	76	68	91	94	61	88	73	82	85	80	96	110
93625	FOWLER	75	71	68	67	69	72	71	75	73	76	92	81	68	86	69	71	91	76	70	79
93626	FRIANT	86	67	44	62	73	83	67	77	75	66	89	89	61	86	68	79	83	76	89	99
93627	HELM	42	36	35	36	35	36	41	40	42	43	53	46	39	52	38	39	54	43	37	43
93630	KERMAN	73	63	53	59	62	65	65	70	68	70	85	76	60	78	62	66	84	71	67	76
93631	KINGSBURG	84	76	68	76	79	85	77	82	79	77	97	95	74	95	77	79	93	82	84	96
93633	KINGS CANYON NATIONA	96	71	43	65	81	91	68	83	78	68	92	99	60	91	72	83	85	82	99	115
93635	LOS BANOS	86	87	82	86	84	85	84	86	82	88	104	97	83	100	82	78	103	86	78	92
93637	MADERA	80	80	79	78	78	81	80	81	80	83	101	92	79	98	78	78	100	82	76	87
93638	MADERA	78	75	72	74	74	76	76	78	77	79	96	89	74	94	74	73	96	79	72	85
93640	MENDOTA	53	44	44	44	44	45	50	50	53	53	66	58	48	65	47	49	67	53	46	53
93641	MIRAMONTE	85	62	36	55	70	79	59	72	69	59	81	85	51	78	61	74	75	71	87	101
93643	NORTH FORK	94	71	48	68	78	93	77	86	86	74	102	96	69	96	77	92	93	86	103	105
93644	OAKHURST	87	75	64	71	81	95	73	83	80	75	97	87	71	87	77	85	90	82	98	99
93645	O NEALS	85	62	39	59	69	82	67	76	75	64	89	87	59	84	67	80	81	76	91	95
93646	ORANGE COVE	59	49	47	49	49	50	55	56	58	58	73	64	52	71	52	54	73	59	52	60
93647	OROSI	61	52	46	50	51	53	56	59	58	60	73	64	52	68	53	55	73	61	55	62
93648	PARLIER	55	47	45	46	46	47	52	53	54	55	68	59	49	66	49	51	69	55	48	56
93650	FRESNO	71	63	65	66	61	64	69	68	68	71	86	79	65	79	64	64	85	71	62	74
93651	PRATHER	107	95	73	91	101	108	88	98	94	88	114	117	87	116	91	96	108	95	106	126
93652	RAISIN	121	106	88	98	102	107	108	117	112	118	141	124	99	125	103	108	140	119	110	122
93653	RAYMOND	97	72	47	69	80	94	77	87	87	74	102	99	69	97	78	92	94	87	104	109
93654	REEDLEY	73	70	67	68	69	72	71	73	71	73	89	82	69	86	69	69	88	74	69	79
93656	RIVERDALE	76	66	55	62	64	67	68	73	71	73	89	78	62	79	65	68	88	75	69	77
93657	SANGER	87	83	77	80	82	87	83	86	84	86	105	97	80	102	82	83	103	87	84	95
93660	SAN JOAQUIN	61	51	50	51	50	52	58	58	61	61	77	66	55	75	54	56	77	61	53	61
93662	SELMA	75	68	64	65	66	70	70	73	72	75	91	80	67	86	68	70	90	75	69	78
93664	SHAVER LAKE	112	90	64	82	101	112	85	101	95	84	113	118	77	112	90	101	105	99	118	137
93667	TOLLHOUSE	99	104	96	101	106	109	94	99	93	94	115	117	96	120	97	93	112	96	98	119
93668	TRANQUILLITY	83	73	61	68	70	74	75	80	78	81	98	86	69	87	71	75	97	82	75	84
93669	WISHON	88	69	47	62	77	87	65	78	73	64	87	91	58	86	69	78	81	77	92	107
93675	SQUAW VALLEY	102	70	34	62	80	91	68	84	80	68	94	101	58	90	70	85	86	83	102	119
93701	FRESNO	39	33	32	33	32	34	37	37	39	39	49	42	35	47	35	36	49	39	34	39
93702	FRESNO	52	45	40	43	43	45	48	50	50	52	63	55	45	59	45	47	63	52	46	52
93703	FRESNO	51	46	44	44	45	47	49	50	51	51	64	56	47	61	47	49	63	52	48	53
93704	FRESNO	78	83	98	82	82	89	85	84	85	85	106	95	86	106	86	84	104	85	82	91
93705	FRESNO	60	56	61	55	55	60	61	60	63	62	78	68	59	76	59	62	77	62	59	65
93706	FRESNO	54	46	43	43	45	49	50	52	53	53	66	56	46	60	47	52	65	54	51	56
93710	FRESNO	68	69	83	71	68	72	75	71	73	73	91	85	74	91	73	70	90	74	67	78
93711	FRESNO	140	148	167	152	146	154	146	144	140	148	178	167	149	173	146	137	174	145	136	159
93720	FRESNO	130	142	145	149	137	136	134	132	125	137	158	155	137	157	131	118	156	130	116	145
93721	FRESNO	35	30	31	30	30	33	35	34	36	35	45	39	33	44	33	35	45	36	33	37
93722	FRESNO	86	90	89	91	86	87	86	86	83	89	105	100	86	103	84	79	103	86	78	95
93725	FRESNO	72	64	56	60	62	65	66	70	69	71	86	76	62	79	63	66	86	72	65	74
93726	FRESNO	55	51	58	52	51	55	58	56	59	57	74	65	56	72	56	57	72	59	54	61
93727	FRESNO	73	70	73	69	69	74	73	73	74	74	93	83	72	90	71	73	91	75	71	80
93728	FRESNO	54	49	49	48	48	51	52	53	53	54	67	60	50	63	50	52	66	55	51	57
	CALIFORNIA	107	111	131	112	109	115	113	111	111	114	140	129	114	141	112	109	139	113	104	122
	UNITED STATES	100	100	100	100	100	100	100	100	100	100	100	100	100	100	100	100	100	100	100	100

POPULATION CHANGE

ZIP CODE #	POST OFFICE NAME	COUNTY FIPS CODE	POPULATION 2000	POPULATION 2004	POPULATION 2009	2000-2004 ANNUAL RATE % Rate	State Centile	HOUSEHOLDS 2000	HOUSEHOLDS 2004	HOUSEHOLDS 2009	% Annual Rate 2000-2004	2004 Average HH Size	FAMILIES 2000	FAMILIES 2004	% Annual Rate 2000-2004
93740	FRESNO	019	861	861	861	0.0	15	0	0	0	0.0	0.00	0	0	0.0
93741	FRESNO	019	23	23	24	0.0	15	16	16	16	0.0	1.44	8	7	-3.1
93901	SALINAS	053	35675	35500	36236	-0.1	11	10126	10107	10360	0.0	2.60	6622	6544	-0.3
93905	SALINAS	053	58712	63544	67837	1.9	77	11645	12541	13292	1.8	4.98	10473	11241	1.7
93906	SALINAS	053	53856	58701	63074	2.1	80	15558	16789	17860	1.8	3.47	12305	13264	1.8
93907	SALINAS	053	21814	22819	24049	1.1	57	7089	7461	7840	1.2	3.05	5448	5706	1.1
93908	SALINAS	053	14707	16447	17825	2.7	88	4918	5538	5992	2.8	2.96	4080	4569	2.7
93920	BIG SUR	053	998	964	991	-0.8	3	420	402	411	-1.0	2.27	225	215	-1.1
93923	CARMEL	053	16593	17297	18305	1.0	54	8158	8502	8944	1.0	2.02	4723	4873	0.7
93924	CARMEL VALLEY	053	6596	6873	7185	1.0	54	2701	2833	2955	1.1	2.41	1802	1869	0.9
93925	CHUALAR	053	95	105	113	2.4	84	30	33	36	2.3	3.18	28	31	2.4
93926	GONZALES	053	8453	9231	9861	2.1	80	1922	2112	2252	2.2	4.35	1691	1851	2.2
93927	GREENFIELD	053	13959	14888	15711	1.5	70	3055	3239	3388	1.4	4.59	2688	2838	1.3
93930	KING CITY	053	14621	15224	15873	1.0	53	3801	3948	4089	0.9	3.84	3121	3227	0.8
93932	LOCKWOOD	053	966	987	1029	0.5	32	332	342	357	0.7	2.75	245	250	0.5
93933	MARINA	053	27926	28633	29747	0.6	36	7863	8191	8586	1.0	2.73	5445	5607	0.7
93940	MONTEREY	053	32399	32660	33669	0.2	19	13794	13987	14415	0.3	2.14	7313	7322	0.0
93943	MONTEREY	053	385	378	382	-0.4	6	79	77	78	-0.6	2.71	50	48	-1.0
93950	PACIFIC GROVE	053	15492	15335	15793	-0.2	8	7301	7269	7470	-0.1	2.09	3967	3904	-0.4
93953	PEBBLE BEACH	053	4530	4390	4484	-0.7	3	2091	2040	2080	-0.6	2.15	1453	1404	-0.8
93955	SEASIDE	053	31957	31393	32137	-0.4	6	9913	9702	9869	-0.5	3.22	7427	7198	-0.7
93960	SOLEDAD	053	13197	14902	16206	2.9	90	3026	3432	3719	3.0	4.33	2686	3036	2.9
94002	BELMONT	081	25372	25491	25663	0.1	18	10547	10662	10762	0.3	2.33	6663	6701	0.1
94005	BRISBANE	081	3597	3804	3948	1.3	65	1620	1730	1800	1.6	2.18	859	913	1.4
94010	BURLINGAME	081	40090	40347	40674	0.2	18	16564	16770	16914	0.3	2.37	10422	10450	0.1
94014	DALY CITY	081	46645	48395	49483	0.9	49	12780	13259	13530	0.9	3.63	9913	10265	0.8
94015	DALY CITY	081	63452	64347	65085	0.3	24	20065	20318	20492	0.3	3.14	14691	14879	0.3
94019	HALF MOON BAY	081	17919	18115	18169	0.3	22	6122	6215	6236	0.4	2.77	4356	4410	0.3
94020	LA HONDA	081	1169	1139	1130	-0.6	4	443	434	431	-0.5	2.44	288	282	-0.5
94021	LOMA MAR	081	450	445	443	-0.3	8	199	198	197	-0.1	2.08	128	127	-0.2
94022	LOS ALTOS	085	18508	18596	18918	0.1	18	6983	7021	7130	0.1	2.59	5273	5299	0.1
94024	LOS ALTOS	085	21980	22010	22372	0.0	15	8032	8058	8175	0.1	2.70	6441	6447	0.0
94025	MENLO PARK	081	41574	42853	43734	0.7	42	16212	16642	16906	0.6	2.51	9655	9903	0.6
94027	ATHERTON	081	7528	7598	7667	0.2	20	2528	2558	2581	0.3	2.84	2050	2069	0.2
94028	PORTOLA VALLEY	081	6631	6699	6727	0.2	21	2503	2532	2538	0.3	2.61	1920	1938	0.2
94030	MILLBRAE	081	21052	21117	21362	0.1	17	8050	8091	8176	0.1	2.57	5581	5590	0.1
94035	MOUNTAIN VIEW	085	313	309	310	-0.3	7	10	10	10	0.0	2.60	10	10	0.0
94038	MOSS BEACH	081	5730	5533	5522	-0.8	3	1971	1910	1904	-0.7	2.83	1455	1406	-0.8
94040	MOUNTAIN VIEW	085	30161	29942	30402	-0.2	10	12929	12815	12967	-0.2	2.31	7061	6980	-0.3
94041	MOUNTAIN VIEW	085	13470	14017	14497	0.9	52	6132	6396	6600	1.0	2.19	2900	3007	0.9
94043	MOUNTAIN VIEW	085	27360	27905	28972	0.5	30	12041	12234	12629	0.4	2.26	6072	6097	0.1
94044	PACIFICA	081	38451	38249	38469	-0.1	11	14022	14005	14087	0.0	2.72	9666	9647	-0.1
94060	PESCADERO	081	1689	1675	1670	-0.2	9	457	455	453	-0.1	3.13	316	313	-0.2
94061	REDWOOD CITY	081	36478	36230	36253	-0.2	10	13929	13795	13759	-0.2	2.59	8989	8873	-0.3
94062	REDWOOD CITY	081	25953	25235	25186	-0.7	3	10196	9982	9984	-0.5	2.48	7056	6862	-0.7
94063	REDWOOD CITY	081	30612	31463	32016	0.7	39	8437	8698	8852	0.7	3.48	5797	5905	0.4
94065	REDWOOD CITY	081	10648	12182	13215	3.2	91	4649	5224	5603	2.8	2.33	2909	3277	2.8
94066	SAN BRUNO	081	39812	39609	39677	-0.1	11	14574	14454	14422	-0.2	2.73	9840	9727	-0.3
94070	SAN CARLOS	081	27533	27517	27681	0.0	12	11357	11389	11459	0.1	2.39	7489	7480	0.0
94074	SAN GREGORIO	081	94	91	90	-0.8	3	28	27	26	-0.9	3.11	18	17	-1.3
94080	SOUTH SAN FRANCISCO	081	60590	61894	62718	0.5	32	19683	20051	20238	0.4	3.06	14639	14875	0.4
94085	SUNNYVALE	085	21741	22182	22945	0.5	30	8062	8283	8564	0.6	2.66	4828	4900	0.4
94086	SUNNYVALE	085	44872	46420	47945	0.8	46	19324	19826	20320	0.6	2.33	10871	11142	0.6
94087	SUNNYVALE	085	50211	51362	52699	0.5	33	19548	20026	20501	0.6	2.54	13383	13637	0.4
94089	SUNNYVALE	085	16144	16184	16467	0.1	16	6249	6211	6276	-0.1	2.61	3801	3751	-0.3
94102	SAN FRANCISCO	075	29577	30575	31204	0.8	45	16384	16836	17128	0.6	1.69	3949	4062	0.7
94103	SAN FRANCISCO	075	23099	24685	25656	1.6	71	9584	10320	10752	1.8	2.05	2907	3125	1.7
94104	SAN FRANCISCO	075	246	227	222	-1.9	1	105	95	93	-2.3	2.29	43	39	-2.3
94105	SAN FRANCISCO	075	2094	2563	2856	4.9	97	1289	1629	1841	5.7	1.41	293	362	5.1
94107	SAN FRANCISCO	075	17117	18720	19690	2.1	81	8988	9904	10440	2.3	1.81	3050	3321	2.0
94108	SAN FRANCISCO	075	13381	13761	14091	0.7	39	7475	7721	7922	0.8	1.77	2660	2697	0.3
94109	SAN FRANCISCO	075	53849	55666	56707	0.8	45	32074	33156	33735	0.8	1.64	8096	8332	0.7
94110	SAN FRANCISCO	075	73837	74170	74602	0.1	18	25802	25852	25945	0.1	2.82	12192	12198	0.0
94111	SAN FRANCISCO	075	2997	2973	3015	-0.2	9	2060	2033	2056	-0.3	1.46	573	558	-0.6
94112	SAN FRANCISCO	075	75635	76533	76909	0.3	23	20954	20990	20970	0.0	3.60	15430	15440	0.0
94114	SAN FRANCISCO	075	32373	31601	31390	-0.6	4	17644	17231	17094	-0.6	1.82	4362	4235	-0.7
94115	SAN FRANCISCO	075	32046	32998	33646	0.7	40	16887	17365	17677	0.7	1.86	5479	5640	0.7
94116	SAN FRANCISCO	075	42869	42530	42419	-0.2	9	15075	14901	14814	-0.3	2.83	10247	10117	-0.3
94117	SAN FRANCISCO	075	39148	38285	38040	-0.5	5	18186	17755	17606	-0.6	2.01	4770	4653	-0.6
94118	SAN FRANCISCO	075	38933	38333	38234	-0.4	6	17269	17039	16995	-0.3	2.21	8066	7935	-0.4
94121	SAN FRANCISCO	075	42386	41926	41790	-0.3	8	17287	17088	17000	-0.3	2.43	9546	9421	-0.3
94122	SAN FRANCISCO	075	55498	56075	56429	0.2	21	21539	21698	21773	0.2	2.56	11816	11878	0.1
94123	SAN FRANCISCO	075	25240	25638	25947	0.4	26	15638	15889	16060	0.4	1.61	4238	4310	0.4
94124	SAN FRANCISCO	075	33355	33644	33797	0.2	20	9346	9294	9265	-0.1	3.57	7153	7117	-0.1
94127	SAN FRANCISCO	075	18403	18027	17918	-0.5	5	7157	7007	6958	-0.5	2.56	4745	4640	-0.5
94129	SAN FRANCISCO	075	2299	2727	2976	4.1	96	829	984	1073	4.1	2.76	388	458	4.0
94130	SAN FRANCISCO	075	1453	1170	1118	-5.0	0	460	356	337	-5.9	2.71	159	123	-5.9
94131	SAN FRANCISCO	075	28619	28318	28253	-0.3	8	13593	13459	13417	-0.2	2.00	5583	5503	-0.3
94132	SAN FRANCISCO	075	26340	28262	29453	1.7	73	9869	10470	10838	1.4	2.56	5818	6164	1.4
94133	SAN FRANCISCO	075	27334	27476	27604	0.1	18	13898	13999	14055	0.2	1.96	5443	5462	0.1
94134	SAN FRANCISCO	075	38570	40403	41335	1.1	58	10310	10665	10834	0.8	3.77	8194	8485	0.8
94158	SAN FRANCISCO	075	101	134	155	6.9	99	21	31	37	9.6	3.19	6	8	7.0
94301	PALO ALTO	085	16186	15693	15749	-0.7	3	7655	7432	7443	-0.7	2.06	3669	3546	-0.8
94303	PALO ALTO	085	44019	45774	47199	0.9	52	12523	12737	12976	0.4	3.58	9318	9488	0.4
94304	PALO ALTO	085	2253	2506	2684	2.5	86	1124	1291	1400	3.3	1.87	503	545	1.9
94305	STANFORD	085	13311	13609	14086	0.5	33	3206	3477	3840	1.9	2.14	1322	1305	-0.3
94306	PALO ALTO	085	24514	24128	24337	-0.4	6	10546	10367	10418	-0.4	2.31	6602	6659	-0.2
94401	SAN MATEO	081	31155	31693	32075	0.4	27	11932	12010	12058	0.2	2.59	6491	6376	-0.4
94402	SAN MATEO	081	24735	24291	24185	-0.4	6	10025	9864	9806	-0.4	2.43	6491	6376	-0.4
94403	SAN MATEO	081	38162	38047	38103	-0.1	11	15364	15302	15284	-0.1	2.45	9817	9747	-0.2
94404	SAN MATEO	081	31816	32937	33550	0.8	47	13306	13879	14177	1.0	2.37	8635	8978	0.9
94501	ALAMEDA	001	58561	57692	58234	-0.4	7	25060	24502	24479	-0.5	2.31	14039	13641	-0.7
94502	ALAMEDA	001	13698	14387	14975	1.2	60	5166	5351	5500	0.8	2.67	3819	3941	0.8
94503	AMERICAN CANYON	055	9984	12543	14645	5.5	98	3283	4108	4768	5.4	3.02	2516	3144	5.4
94506	DANVILLE	013	23351	25492	27592	2.1	80	7606	8246	8849	1.9	3.06	6706	7249	1.9
	CALIFORNIA					1.4					1.2	2.90			1.2
	UNITED STATES					1.2					1.3	2.58			1.1

#	POST OFFICE NAME	White 2000	White 2004	Black 2000	Black 2004	Asian/Pacific 2000	Asian/Pacific 2004	% Hispanic Origin 2000	% Hispanic Origin 2004	0-4	5-9	10-14	15-19	20-24	25-44	45-64	65-84	85+	18+	Median Age 2004	% 2004 Males	% 2004 Females
93740	FRESNO	55.9	51.0	12.4	12.7	16.8	18.6	16.8	20.2	0.0	0.0	0.0	56.8	37.4	5.8	0.0	0.0	0.0	100.0	19.4	48.4	51.6
93741	FRESNO	78.3	73.9	4.4	4.4	4.4	4.4	26.1	30.4	8.7	8.7	8.7	8.7	8.7	34.8	21.7	0.0	0.0	73.9	28.8	47.8	52.2
93901	SALINAS	55.8	51.9	6.8	6.6	5.4	5.6	40.4	45.5	6.0	5.5	5.9	6.0	7.9	36.6	21.6	8.7	1.9	79.2	35.7	59.5	40.5
93905	SALINAS	37.2	36.0	1.2	1.2	3.2	3.2	88.1	89.5	11.6	10.1	10.3	9.3	10.4	31.8	12.5	3.6	0.4	62.6	24.2	53.0	47.0
93906	SALINAS	47.3	43.9	2.8	2.7	10.0	10.2	54.8	59.7	9.5	8.8	9.0	7.8	8.1	31.2	18.0	6.7	0.8	67.9	29.3	49.7	50.3
93907	SALINAS	67.4	64.4	2.2	2.1	6.7	6.8	30.8	34.9	6.3	6.8	8.2	7.8	6.8	27.3	27.9	8.1	0.8	73.8	36.9	50.1	49.9
93908	SALINAS	73.2	71.1	0.8	0.8	5.6	6.2	26.1	28.1	6.9	7.7	8.9	7.2	5.1	23.7	29.3	10.3	1.0	72.0	39.1	50.1	49.9
93920	BIG SUR	89.4	86.7	1.5	1.9	1.7	2.2	8.8	11.3	4.9	5.3	6.4	6.1	4.7	24.3	37.3	10.1	0.9	79.3	44.0	53.8	46.2
93923	CARMEL	93.4	92.1	0.4	0.5	3.1	3.5	3.7	4.9	2.4	2.8	4.3	4.4	3.3	14.2	37.9	25.5	5.3	87.7	55.5	45.6	54.5
93924	CARMEL VALLEY	91.9	90.2	0.3	0.4	2.1	2.3	7.4	9.4	3.3	4.2	6.5	6.4	4.6	18.4	38.9	15.8	2.0	82.0	48.4	48.7	51.4
93925	CHUALAR	37.9	35.2	1.1	1.0	3.2	2.9	74.7	79.1	10.5	9.5	12.4	9.5	8.6	30.5	15.2	3.8	0.0	61.9	24.7	52.4	47.6
93926	GONZALES	36.1	33.9	0.7	0.6	2.4	2.3	82.1	85.3	10.4	9.5	10.1	9.3	9.8	29.4	15.8	5.2	0.6	64.5	25.5	52.1	47.9
93927	GREENFIELD	41.1	39.4	1.0	0.9	1.0	0.9	85.2	87.9	10.6	9.6	10.3	9.7	10.1	30.0	14.5	4.8	0.4	63.6	24.9	52.2	47.8
93930	KING CITY	47.2	44.3	0.6	0.6	2.0	2.0	72.9	77.2	9.8	8.7	9.4	9.0	10.2	30.0	16.6	5.7	0.6	66.6	26.7	53.0	47.1
93932	LOCKWOOD	75.8	71.8	2.3	2.5	2.8	3.3	23.3	27.7	8.2	7.8	8.2	7.0	6.6	26.4	27.2	7.9	0.7	70.9	35.3	52.9	47.1
93933	MARINA	44.9	41.3	14.3	14.3	17.7	18.4	22.7	25.9	5.9	5.4	6.3	7.3	12.2	35.9	19.4	7.2	0.5	78.9	31.4	55.9	44.1
93940	MONTEREY	81.5	78.6	2.4	2.5	7.5	8.5	10.3	12.6	5.0	4.5	4.6	6.4	8.7	31.2	24.3	12.6	2.7	83.3	38.0	48.8	51.2
93943	MONTEREY	77.1	74.3	3.6	3.7	9.6	10.6	13.8	16.4	2.7	3.2	5.8	5.3	11.6	48.2	19.8	2.9	0.5	85.7	33.1	70.1	29.9
93950	PACIFIC GROVE	88.1	85.9	1.1	1.2	4.8	5.4	7.1	9.0	3.5	3.7	5.2	6.2	5.7	23.8	32.3	16.3	3.4	83.9	46.1	46.2	53.8
93953	PEBBLE BEACH	91.3	89.8	0.4	0.4	5.5	6.4	2.3	3.0	2.2	3.0	3.7	3.6	2.7	11.3	36.3	31.8	5.5	88.9	58.9	46.3	53.7
93955	SEASIDE	49.4	46.1	12.5	12.3	11.3	11.7	34.4	38.7	9.6	7.9	8.0	7.1	8.9	32.7	17.4	7.6	0.8	70.4	29.7	50.9	49.1
93960	SOLEDAD	34.3	32.5	1.1	1.0	2.2	2.1	83.9	86.6	10.9	9.5	10.0	8.7	9.7	30.6	14.6	5.3	0.7	64.4	25.7	52.1	47.9
94002	BELMONT	75.4	71.8	1.7	1.8	15.8	17.9	8.3	9.9	5.9	5.8	5.4	5.0	5.3	32.2	26.9	11.9	1.6	79.8	39.9	49.1	50.9
94005	BRISBANE	72.3	68.1	1.0	1.1	14.6	16.7	17.1	19.9	4.4	4.5	5.4	5.0	4.7	33.0	33.7	8.6	0.7	82.4	41.7	50.5	49.5
94010	BURLINGAME	75.7	72.4	0.9	0.9	16.9	18.9	8.4	10.0	5.3	5.8	6.3	5.8	4.9	28.8	27.1	13.6	2.6	79.0	41.2	48.0	52.0
94014	DALY CITY	24.7	23.4	4.7	4.3	46.5	46.5	32.9	35.0	6.4	6.2	6.8	6.4	7.2	31.7	23.4	10.6	1.2	76.9	35.8	49.4	50.6
94015	DALY CITY	28.7	26.2	4.2	4.0	53.8	55.5	14.8	15.9	5.8	5.5	6.0	5.9	7.4	31.6	24.3	11.8	1.7	79.2	36.9	49.0	51.0
94019	HALF MOON BAY	79.6	76.6	2.7	2.8	3.4	3.8	21.3	25.1	6.0	6.4	6.8	6.2	6.2	28.5	30.5	8.5	0.9	76.9	39.5	52.3	47.8
94020	LA HONDA	89.4	87.4	0.8	0.8	2.1	2.4	12.3	14.9	4.3	4.8	6.0	7.5	6.3	27.0	37.1	6.2	0.8	79.5	41.9	53.9	46.1
94021	LOMA MAR	87.6	85.6	0.4	0.5	1.8	2.0	18.2	22.0	4.5	4.5	5.8	6.5	7.0	26.5	37.5	6.5	1.1	80.7	42.2	51.7	48.3
94022	LOS ALTOS	80.3	77.4	0.6	0.6	15.8	18.1	2.9	3.6	4.8	6.0	7.1	6.2	3.5	19.2	32.2	17.5	3.3	77.8	46.8	48.3	51.7
94024	LOS ALTOS	78.5	75.3	0.4	0.4	17.2	19.6	3.2	3.8	5.9	7.3	7.8	6.0	3.0	21.0	31.4	15.1	2.5	75.0	44.5	48.9	51.1
94025	MENLO PARK	71.8	69.8	6.0	5.7	8.0	8.8	19.5	21.5	6.8	6.7	6.8	5.4	5.3	31.8	23.5	11.2	2.5	76.2	37.8	49.5	50.6
94027	ATHERTON	85.2	82.7	0.7	0.8	9.9	11.5	3.4	4.2	5.3	6.7	7.7	7.1	4.8	18.4	30.3	16.8	2.9	76.6	45.1	48.5	51.6
94028	PORTOLA VALLEY	92.6	91.2	0.4	0.4	4.2	4.9	3.8	4.6	5.1	6.6	7.3	6.3	3.1	17.9	33.7	17.0	3.1	76.5	47.2	50.0	50.1
94030	MILLBRAE	63.1	59.1	0.8	0.8	28.2	31.0	11.7	13.4	4.6	4.8	5.8	6.2	5.8	25.2	26.3	17.0	4.2	80.7	43.5	47.2	52.8
94035	MOUNTAIN VIEW	60.7	57.0	10.9	11.0	13.7	14.6	16.3	19.1	9.4	8.1	4.9	2.6	16.2	54.1	4.9	0.0	0.0	75.7	28.3	65.7	34.3
94038	MOSS BEACH	85.1	83.3	0.8	0.9	3.1	3.5	15.3	17.0	6.0	7.1	7.6	6.2	5.0	26.2	34.4	6.5	1.2	75.2	40.9	49.7	50.3
94040	MOUNTAIN VIEW	65.6	62.2	2.0	2.0	20.4	22.2	16.8	18.9	5.9	5.5	5.5	5.6	7.3	36.2	21.8	10.5	1.7	79.7	36.1	51.4	48.6
94041	MOUNTAIN VIEW	65.7	62.4	2.1	2.1	19.1	20.9	20.8	23.1	6.3	5.0	4.3	4.3	7.6	44.1	20.7	6.6	1.2	82.1	34.7	52.4	47.6
94043	MOUNTAIN VIEW	60.7	56.5	3.9	3.9	21.9	24.2	18.7	21.2	5.9	4.9	4.9	4.7	6.6	41.6	22.2	8.1	1.1	81.6	35.7	51.8	48.2
94044	PACIFICA	69.5	66.2	3.3	3.3	16.0	17.4	14.6	17.0	5.5	5.8	6.6	6.4	6.2	30.0	28.8	9.8	1.0	78.1	39.1	49.2	50.8
94060	PESCADERO	76.7	74.3	0.5	0.5	1.2	1.3	46.7	51.5	6.3	5.4	6.3	7.2	8.4	32.7	26.5	6.3	1.0	78.5	34.4	56.0	44.0
94061	REDWOOD CITY	75.8	72.9	2.2	2.2	6.1	6.7	28.8	32.8	7.2	6.6	6.3	5.7	6.9	32.7	22.6	9.7	2.3	76.4	36.2	49.1	51.0
94062	REDWOOD CITY	87.3	84.8	0.8	0.8	5.4	6.3	8.7	10.8	5.7	6.4	6.2	5.4	3.9	27.1	31.3	12.0	1.9	78.2	42.6	49.8	50.2
94063	REDWOOD CITY	50.6	48.4	3.4	3.5	6.4	6.5	64.5	67.5	8.6	7.6	8.1	7.8	9.4	35.3	17.2	5.3	0.7	71.3	29.5	54.1	46.0
94065	REDWOOD CITY	62.7	57.8	1.8	1.8	29.6	33.5	5.9	6.9	8.1	7.6	5.4	3.8	3.9	37.7	26.4	6.5	0.6	76.4	37.9	48.5	51.5
94066	SAN BRUNO	57.5	53.9	2.0	2.0	21.7	23.0	24.1	27.1	6.0	5.9	6.6	6.4	6.8	31.8	25.1	10.1	1.4	77.6	37.3	49.4	50.7
94070	SAN CARLOS	84.6	81.9	0.8	0.8	8.2	9.4	7.7	9.2	6.6	7.0	6.3	4.9	3.6	29.1	28.3	11.8	2.4	76.9	41.4	48.5	51.5
94074	SAN GREGORIO	87.2	85.7	0.0	0.0	1.1	1.1	21.3	24.2	4.4	4.4	6.6	6.6	6.6	28.6	36.3	6.6	0.0	79.1	40.9	56.0	44.0
94080	SOUTH SAN FRANCISCO	44.3	41.4	2.8	2.7	30.3	31.2	31.8	34.8	6.5	6.3	7.1	6.4	7.1	30.1	23.6	11.6	1.4	76.3	36.6	49.6	50.4
94085	SUNNYVALE	45.9	43.0	2.2	2.2	31.0	32.4	30.5	32.7	7.5	6.0	5.6	5.1	7.9	42.8	18.3	6.1	0.7	77.9	32.4	54.1	45.9
94086	SUNNYVALE	48.3	44.7	2.8	2.7	36.9	38.8	15.5	17.8	7.2	5.5	4.3	4.0	7.0	44.6	18.9	7.5	1.1	80.8	33.7	52.5	47.5
94087	SUNNYVALE	61.0	57.0	1.6	1.6	30.8	33.7	7.2	8.3	6.8	6.6	6.3	5.1	4.9	32.9	23.8	12.0	1.6	77.0	38.5	49.8	50.2
94089	SUNNYVALE	50.5	47.4	2.6	2.5	31.7	33.1	19.3	21.4	6.3	5.6	5.3	4.8	5.7	33.7	24.4	12.5	1.8	80.0	38.0	49.6	50.4
94102	SAN FRANCISCO	47.1	43.9	15.3	14.9	25.9	27.9	13.4	15.3	3.0	2.7	2.9	3.8	7.3	40.6	26.3	12.3	1.1	89.4	39.6	60.5	39.5
94103	SAN FRANCISCO	44.9	42.0	11.7	11.3	24.1	25.8	25.6	27.6	3.1	2.8	3.2	4.1	8.1	43.6	23.8	9.7	1.5	88.7	37.6	60.4	39.6
94104	SAN FRANCISCO	32.1	28.6	0.4	0.4	61.8	64.8	6.1	7.1	1.8	1.8	4.0	2.2	5.7	31.3	31.7	20.7	0.9	91.2	47.2	50.7	49.3
94105	SAN FRANCISCO	70.3	67.2	7.4	7.3	16.0	18.1	6.3	7.6	1.0	0.6	0.1	0.8	5.4	60.3	27.9	3.5	0.5	98.0	37.9	61.9	38.1
94107	SAN FRANCISCO	61.9	58.5	13.3	13.2	16.1	18.2	9.6	11.2	3.7	2.8	3.1	3.1	5.3	48.0	22.7	9.7	1.7	88.7	37.8	54.2	45.8
94108	SAN FRANCISCO	36.2	34.2	1.6	1.6	58.2	59.6	4.2	4.8	2.5	2.2	2.9	3.4	6.5	34.6	24.8	20.0	3.1	90.7	43.5	49.3	50.7
94109	SAN FRANCISCO	60.4	56.6	3.3	3.3	28.9	31.7	7.9	9.1	2.3	1.9	1.9	2.8	6.7	45.0	22.9	13.6	3.0	92.6	38.8	52.0	48.0
94110	SAN FRANCISCO	52.6	49.9	4.2	4.0	12.6	13.0	45.9	49.7	5.3	4.6	4.9	5.0	7.9	43.1	20.9	7.5	1.0	82.4	34.4	52.4	47.7
94111	SAN FRANCISCO	63.6	59.1	2.2	2.2	30.9	35.1	3.3	3.7	1.6	1.6	1.3	1.2	1.9	25.5	37.1	26.2	3.6	94.8	54.2	54.0	46.0
94112	SAN FRANCISCO	29.1	27.3	6.3	5.8	45.4	46.3	27.6	29.6	5.6	5.5	6.0	5.6	6.3	32.0	24.4	12.6	2.1	79.6	38.1	49.3	50.7
94114	SAN FRANCISCO	82.6	80.0	2.3	2.4	7.6	8.7	8.9	10.6	2.6	1.9	1.9	1.7	3.5	53.0	27.0	7.3	1.2	92.6	39.2	60.1	39.9
94115	SAN FRANCISCO	60.2	57.5	17.6	17.5	16.1	17.8	5.5	6.4	3.4	2.6	3.1	3.8	6.4	44.8	22.0	11.6	2.3	88.7	36.9	48.3	51.7
94116	SAN FRANCISCO	42.8	38.9	1.1	1.1	51.3	54.6	4.8	5.4	4.1	4.3	5.0	5.1	5.6	31.0	26.8	15.3	2.8	83.5	41.8	48.2	51.8
94117	SAN FRANCISCO	71.4	68.6	11.9	12.1	9.0	10.1	7.4	8.8	2.6	1.9	2.1	4.3	8.4	53.9	19.4	6.2	1.3	92.1	34.3	53.4	46.6
94118	SAN FRANCISCO	56.0	52.2	1.9	1.8	36.9	40.0	4.5	5.2	3.8	3.4	3.8	5.0	6.7	40.3	23.0	11.9	2.1	86.3	37.5	46.8	53.2
94121	SAN FRANCISCO	49.0	44.8	1.5	1.5	44.2	47.7	4.4	5.0	3.8	3.6	4.0	4.6	6.3	35.6	25.6	14.2	2.4	85.8	40.1	47.8	52.2
94122	SAN FRANCISCO	47.3	43.3	1.5	1.4	45.8	49.2	5.0	5.6	3.9	3.7	4.0	4.4	6.2	38.9	24.4	12.4	2.1	85.7	38.4	48.5	51.5
94123	SAN FRANCISCO	86.3	84.1	0.6	0.6	9.8	11.3	3.9	4.7	2.9	1.5	1.4	1.3	3.7	54.6	21.1	11.1	2.4	93.3	37.0	46.7	53.3
94124	SAN FRANCISCO	9.7	9.4	47.7	45.4	28.1	29.1	16.7	18.6	7.2	7.6	9.1	8.4	7.4	28.9	20.9	9.1	1.3	70.9	32.5	47.9	52.1
94127	SAN FRANCISCO	63.8	60.0	3.9	3.8	25.8	28.5	7.5	8.7	4.8	5.2	5.1	4.8	4.0	26.4	31.5	15.4	2.9	81.8	44.8	49.2	50.8
94129	SAN FRANCISCO	76.4	73.5	4.5	4.6	9.4	10.5	9.3	11.0	6.8	4.8	3.9	3.8	16.2	52.8	10.5	1.2	0.1	83.2	29.0	53.3	46.7
94130	SAN FRANCISCO	65.3	62.0	12.2	12.2	12.0	13.4	10.2	12.1	3.1	2.4	2.1	10.9	29.4	42.3	9.2	0.6	0.0	89.5	25.6	58.9	41.1
94131	SAN FRANCISCO	67.5	64.3	5.8	5.7	17.1	18.9	12.1	14.2	3.7	3.5	3.3	3.7	3.8	38.2	28.4	12.9	2.5	87.1	41.9	52.0	48.1
94132	SAN FRANCISCO	42.0	38.1	11.7	11.4	38.3	41.3	7.8	9.0	4.2	4.0	4.5	7.9	10.2	30.9	22.7	12.8	2.9	84.6	36.9	47.1	52.9
94133	SAN FRANCISCO	40.1	37.1	1.4	1.4	54.9	57.4	3.4	3.8	2.8	2.6	3.3	3.8	5.1	35.3	25.6	18.6	3.0	89.1	43.1	49.6	50.4
94134	SAN FRANCISCO	18.6	17.1	13.1	12.5	53.0	54.0	19.4	20.8	6.2	6.3	6.8	6.3	6.8	30.6	23.0	12.5	1.5	76.9	36.6	48.9	51.1
94158	SAN FRANCISCO	76.2	73.1	5.9	6.7	5.9	6.7	10.9	14.2	0.8	0.8	0.8	3.7	9.0	63.4	18.7	3.0	0.0	97.0	34.5	76.1	23.9
94301	PALO ALTO	84.3	81.8	1.9	2.0	9.6	11.0	3.4	4.2	4.4	5.1	5.5	4.4	3.5	31.5	27.9	13.5	4.3	82.2	42.5	48.5	51.5
94303	PALO ALTO	42.8	40.7	15.6	15.0	14.2	14.6	38.8	42.0	8.6	8.4	9.2	7.9	7.6	29.9	19.8	7.9	0.9	69.1	30.8	50.6	49.5
94304	PALO ALTO	76.7	73.1	1.8	1.9	19.2	22.2	3.3	4.0	4.0	4.0	4.2	4.2	4.2	34.3	25.5	15.8	3.8	84.6	42.0	53.9	46.1
94305	STANFORD	60.5	57.4	4.9	4.8	25.7	27.7	9.0	10.5	2.9	1.7	1.5	21.2	38.6	23.4	6.1	4.1	0.6	92.9	23.0	53.6	46.4
94306	PALO ALTO	72.1	68.6	2.3	2.4	19.6	21.9	6.7	7.9	4.9	5.2	6.3	6.5	6.2	29.7	26.9	12.2	2.2	79.6	40.0	49.0	51.0
94401	SAN MATEO	57.3	53.9	4.4	4.4	15.8	16.4	34.4	38.6	6.3	5.8	6.2	5.8	7.1	35.1	21.0	9.8	3.0	78.2	35.7	50.0	50.0
94402	SAN MATEO	74.2	70.8	1.3	1.3	15.6	17.4	11.4	13.2	5.8	6.3	6.0	5.7	4.3	27.8	27.5	14.1	2.5	78.2	41.7	48.6	51.4
94403	SAN MATEO	68.4	64.8	1.8	1.8	18.5	20.3	14.6	16.9	6.0	5.8	5.6	5.2	5.8	32.1	24.4	12.4	2.6	79.4	39.1	49.1	50.9
94404	SAN MATEO	60.7	56.5	2.2	2.2	31.7	34.8	5.4	6.3	5.6	5.6	5.6	5.1	5.1	33.2	28.2	10.6	1.0	80.0	39.5	48.8	51.2
94501	ALAMEDA	57.7	53.9	7.0	7.0	24.3	26.6	10.3	11.8	5.3	5.1	5.9	6.3	7.3	31.2	25.8	11.1	2.0	80.0	38.5	48.2	51.8
94502	ALAMEDA	53.6	48.5	2.8	2.8	37.1	41.0	5.1	5.8	6.0	7.2	7.7	5.9	3.7	23.7	32.2	11.7	2.0	75.4	42.9	47.5	52.5
94503	AMERICAN CANYON	59.9	57.5	7.3	6.8	17.1	17.4	17.3	20.3	6.3	6.8	8.4	7.3	5.9	26.3	25.5	12.0	1.5	73.9	38.2	49.3	50.7
94506	DANVILLE	77.9	74.8	2.0	2.2	16.0	18.2	4.4	5.2	7.0	8.7	9.4	7.3	3.9	24.1	32.8	6.2	0.6	69.9	40.2	49.4	50.6
	CALIFORNIA	59.6	57.1	6.7	6.5	11.3	11.8	32.4	35.5	7.4	7.1	7.8	7.3	7.7	29.8	22.1	9.3	1.4	73.3	33.8	49.8	50.2
	UNITED STATES	75.1	73.6	12.3	12.5	3.8	4.2	12.5	14.1	6.9	6.7	7.2	7.0	7.3	28.6	23.8	10.8	1.7	75.1	36.0	49.1	50.9

ZIP CODE				2004 HOUSEHOLD INCOME DISTRIBUTION (%)					MEDIAN HOUSEHOLD INCOME					2004 HOME VALUE DISTRIBUTION (%)					
#	POST OFFICE NAME	2004 Per Capita Income	2004 HH Income Base	Less than $25,000	$25,000 to $49,999	$50,000 to $99,999	$100,000 to $149,999	$150,000 or More	2004	2009	2004 National Centile	2004 State Centile	2004 Home Value Base	Less than $50,000	$50,000 to $89,999	$90,000 to $174,999	$175,000 to $399,999	$400,000 or More	2004 Median Home Value
93740	FRESNO	18806	0	0.0	0.0	0.0	0.0	0.0	0	0	0	0	0	0.0	0.0	0.0	0.0	0.0	0
93741	FRESNO	37950	16	18.8	25.0	50.0	6.3	0.0	64018	60000	88	71	10	0.0	0.0	50.0	50.0	0.0	175000
93901	SALINAS	23556	10107	22.4	28.1	32.4	11.7	5.4	49428	57297	71	51	5089	1.5	0.6	1.2	45.1	51.6	405467
93905	SALINAS	10800	12541	26.7	33.7	29.5	7.4	2.7	40449	46211	48	32	6005	5.0	1.6	10.2	68.9	14.3	265903
93906	SALINAS	19587	16789	17.0	27.6	37.9	13.7	3.8	54949	63510	80	61	9815	3.4	1.0	2.3	61.6	31.7	340637
93907	SALINAS	27278	7461	12.7	22.0	37.6	18.8	8.9	66558	78745	89	74	5557	3.4	1.3	5.5	32.2	57.6	437611
93908	SALINAS	43530	5538	9.2	15.5	30.1	23.0	22.3	90688	109931	97	92	4617	0.4	0.7	0.7	13.7	84.6	698570
93920	BIG SUR	31659	402	22.1	29.1	26.4	9.5	12.9	48946	60651	70	50	187	2.1	0.0	0.0	9.6	88.2	1000001
93923	CARMEL	58958	8502	14.9	18.6	28.8	17.1	20.6	75682	92366	93	82	6221	0.1	0.3	0.8	6.2	92.7	1000001
93924	CARMEL VALLEY	54826	2833	12.7	17.5	29.4	16.1	24.3	79584	100883	95	86	2148	2.1	0.9	0.6	7.4	89.1	919799
93925	CHUALAR	22989	33	9.1	27.3	42.4	18.2	3.0	64819	68090	88	72	25	0.0	4.0	4.0	68.0	24.0	296875
93926	GONZALES	13985	2112	19.5	37.1	30.7	9.4	3.3	45350	50071	62	42	1218	1.2	1.3	7.6	71.5	18.5	279605
93927	GREENFIELD	10898	3239	23.7	36.7	31.9	6.3	1.5	41711	46634	52	36	1886	4.7	1.1	14.6	71.2	8.4	217208
93930	KING CITY	15034	3948	28.8	27.8	29.2	10.6	3.5	43218	49595	57	38	2125	4.5	4.8	15.3	63.3	12.1	232328
93932	LOCKWOOD	18940	342	26.9	31.3	31.6	7.9	2.3	41080	47375	50	34	178	6.2	3.9	15.7	36.5	37.6	308333
93933	MARINA	21128	8191	23.6	30.1	31.8	10.8	3.7	47058	54047	66	45	3394	6.4	2.4	5.5	37.2	48.5	393946
93940	MONTEREY	34998	13987	17.3	24.4	35.7	14.1	8.5	58008	70380	83	66	6356	0.2	0.3	1.4	13.5	84.6	678119
93943	MONTEREY	25098	77	23.4	16.9	36.4	11.7	11.7	56304	69102	81	63	25	0.0	0.0	0.0	28.0	72.0	534091
93950	PACIFIC GROVE	38787	7269	15.8	25.3	34.6	14.8	9.4	58229	71748	83	66	3635	0.3	0.3	2.4	7.0	90.0	721856
93953	PEBBLE BEACH	90155	2040	5.5	8.5	26.4	25.5	34.0	115428	140386	99	97	1814	0.0	0.3	1.4	1.2	97.1	1000001
93955	SEASIDE	17532	9702	21.8	32.3	33.6	9.5	2.8	46296	52970	65	44	4409	4.0	1.2	2.1	44.6	48.1	392240
93960	SOLEDAD	13425	3432	22.8	30.4	35.4	8.0	3.5	47377	52750	67	47	2048	0.8	1.5	8.7	78.7	10.3	260000
94002	BELMONT	55230	10662	7.9	14.2	29.1	22.4	26.4	97378	124388	98	93	6603	0.2	0.3	0.4	4.4	94.7	884246
94005	BRISBANE	44124	1730	14.5	14.9	32.2	24.8	13.6	77518	99282	94	84	1142	4.6	2.2	0.9	19.4	73.0	546723
94010	BURLINGAME	75536	16770	9.5	13.7	26.4	18.5	31.9	100872	127679	98	94	10230	0.1	0.2	1.3	2.9	95.5	1000001
94014	DALY CITY	23409	13259	12.7	19.8	37.9	19.8	9.8	68978	82954	91	77	8321	3.0	2.6	3.5	31.1	59.9	434620
94015	DALY CITY	27905	20318	13.5	17.8	36.4	20.9	11.3	74945	88883	93	81	11670	0.9	1.6	1.1	19.7	76.7	500532
94019	HALF MOON BAY	49058	6215	10.1	13.1	27.0	22.5	27.3	99555	124791	98	94	4629	1.6	2.4	4.1	6.5	85.5	741939
94020	LA HONDA	53396	434	7.4	15.9	25.8	23.5	27.4	101405	127425	98	94	306	2.6	0.7	0.0	7.5	89.2	738636
94021	LOMA MAR	56341	198	9.1	14.1	31.3	22.2	23.2	88649	113341	97	91	135	2.2	0.0	0.0	7.4	90.4	700581
94022	LOS ALTOS	106125	7021	4.3	8.5	16.7	15.2	55.3	167024	203494	100	100	5963	0.0	0.2	0.7	1.0	98.0	1000001
94024	LOS ALTOS	87543	8058	4.3	8.0	16.8	19.8	51.1	152795	183626	100	99	7245	0.0	0.4	0.7	1.6	97.3	1000001
94025	MENLO PARK	66481	16642	10.2	13.3	24.6	18.3	33.7	104255	134866	98	95	9999	0.5	0.4	0.3	5.9	93.0	1000001
94027	ATHERTON	137138	2558	2.2	4.5	13.6	12.9	67.0	235347	291050	100	100	2385	0.0	0.0	0.0	0.3	99.7	1000001
94028	PORTOLA VALLEY	131719	2532	3.4	6.4	13.0	14.1	63.1	202057	248842	100	100	2185	0.4	0.0	0.6	1.6	97.4	1000001
94030	MILLBRAE	40804	8091	13.4	15.8	32.2	22.4	16.2	79508	98790	95	85	5212	0.4	1.5	1.5	3.7	92.9	837466
94035	MOUNTAIN VIEW	11494	10	0.0	20.0	70.0	0.0	10.0	63627	75000	88	71	0	0.0	0.0	0.0	0.0	0.0	0
94038	MOSS BEACH	49474	1910	4.3	12.0	30.1	26.4	27.2	104537	127220	98	95	1674	4.5	3.3	3.5	4.4	84.4	694338
94040	MOUNTAIN VIEW	51822	12815	12.4	15.6	29.5	19.1	23.5	83668	107059	96	88	5739	2.4	1.6	0.9	12.0	83.1	834065
94041	MOUNTAIN VIEW	50879	6396	9.6	14.2	35.2	20.5	20.5	83992	107622	96	89	2327	2.2	2.4	4.9	12.6	78.0	714319
94043	MOUNTAIN VIEW	46419	12234	11.3	15.9	32.1	22.5	18.2	83140	105963	96	88	5183	1.4	2.7	3.7	20.9	71.4	535149
94044	PACIFICA	36837	14005	8.3	16.1	36.9	24.2	14.5	82707	101522	96	88	9934	0.7	1.0	0.4	13.6	84.2	553200
94060	PESCADERO	29732	455	11.4	22.9	30.3	17.1	18.2	72357	93304	92	80	246	0.8	0.0	3.7	6.9	88.6	734375
94061	REDWOOD CITY	40387	13795	11.8	19.4	33.5	19.2	16.1	75614	93789	93	82	6942	0.4	0.5	0.7	4.6	93.8	742545
94062	REDWOOD CITY	79726	9982	6.8	12.5	22.8	19.2	38.7	117785	148251	99	97	7663	0.1	0.3	0.4	4.3	94.9	1000001
94063	REDWOOD CITY	20040	8698	17.5	27.5	35.2	13.9	5.9	55493	65135	80	62	3124	13.0	5.4	6.6	21.1	53.8	419833
94065	REDWOOD CITY	74681	5224	4.8	8.5	21.8	25.2	39.7	126322	157519	100	98	3835	0.2	1.0	0.0	2.3	96.5	896944
94066	SAN BRUNO	31693	14454	11.4	21.9	35.9	20.4	10.5	71871	85992	92	79	9247	0.5	0.9	2.3	21.8	74.5	536629
94070	SAN CARLOS	60256	11389	8.7	12.3	26.3	22.8	29.9	104357	130539	98	95	8216	0.3	0.2	0.3	4.0	95.2	918835
94074	SAN GREGORIO	50482	27	3.7	14.8	22.2	14.8	44.4	130494	136451	100	98	19	0.0	0.0	0.0	5.3	94.7	1000001
94080	SOUTH SAN FRANCISCO	27827	20051	12.8	20.3	37.1	20.3	9.6	70059	83417	91	78	12479	3.6	1.3	0.5	18.8	75.8	503754
94085	SUNNYVALE	37650	8283	9.8	14.1	37.4	24.3	14.5	81384	102242	95	87	3340	4.2	3.5	6.2	21.4	64.6	453217
94086	SUNNYVALE	46305	19826	10.0	15.4	32.9	22.2	19.6	85519	107947	96	90	6775	3.7	3.1	2.1	14.8	76.3	605075
94087	SUNNYVALE	50988	20026	8.3	12.1	28.0	23.7	27.9	102229	127878	98	95	12073	0.5	1.3	0.9	2.9	94.4	822379
94089	SUNNYVALE	35601	6211	12.7	16.9	36.6	21.1	12.8	76572	92755	94	83	4206	4.2	11.9	29.2	22.4	32.3	204251
94102	SAN FRANCISCO	24566	16836	47.0	26.5	18.3	5.9	2.3	27009	34188	7	7	873	0.0	0.0	2.6	22.5	74.9	584839
94103	SAN FRANCISCO	27779	10320	39.5	20.4	24.5	8.7	7.0	37685	48807	38	26	1514	2.5	0.0	1.3	24.8	71.4	602594
94104	SAN FRANCISCO	20085	95	48.4	20.0	19.0	9.5	3.2	26352	38666	6	6	0	0.0	0.0	0.0	0.0	0.0	0
94105	SAN FRANCISCO	119901	1629	6.8	10.7	26.5	25.1	30.9	108357	139624	99	96	882	0.0	0.0	0.0	22.8	77.2	577795
94107	SAN FRANCISCO	71699	9904	22.1	14.1	24.0	16.0	23.9	75153	101201	93	82	3194	0.0	0.3	2.4	12.8	84.6	715988
94108	SAN FRANCISCO	41709	7721	36.0	25.0	19.5	9.8	9.8	38181	48311	40	27	910	1.8	0.7	2.9	13.1	81.7	889908
94109	SAN FRANCISCO	56295	33156	24.7	23.4	25.9	12.9	13.1	52189	66597	76	57	5886	0.6	0.8	3.8	18.4	76.4	717901
94110	SAN FRANCISCO	30906	25852	16.6	20.9	34.7	16.3	11.5	64169	81138	88	71	8754	1.1	1.1	0.8	19.2	77.9	581617
94111	SAN FRANCISCO	87695	2033	29.8	15.6	19.9	12.8	21.8	57653	74109	82	65	427	0.0	0.0	1.4	1.4	97.2	877747
94112	SAN FRANCISCO	23042	20990	12.9	22.1	36.1	19.1	9.8	66133	80638	89	74	15075	4.1	2.2	0.8	26.6	66.3	461763
94114	SAN FRANCISCO	75661	17231	9.8	13.4	30.2	21.0	25.6	92989	124121	97	92	6959	0.3	0.1	0.5	5.0	94.2	960504
94115	SAN FRANCISCO	71467	17365	20.0	16.5	26.9	14.8	21.8	71869	94293	92	79	4756	2.3	1.1	1.4	8.7	86.5	985021
94116	SAN FRANCISCO	35074	14901	12.7	17.5	33.2	20.9	15.7	78168	95750	94	84	10804	1.9	5.0	0.4	7.5	85.1	605587
94117	SAN FRANCISCO	52989	17755	14.3	17.4	30.4	19.3	18.6	77715	102735	94	84	4849	0.2	0.4	1.4	8.4	89.7	893313
94118	SAN FRANCISCO	58852	17039	13.8	17.1	29.1	17.2	22.7	78120	103992	94	84	6733	0.4	1.4	3.7	3.7	90.8	982220
94121	SAN FRANCISCO	41535	17088	13.9	19.3	33.2	19.0	14.6	73297	91068	93	80	7925	0.9	2.4	1.2	7.7	87.9	757212
94122	SAN FRANCISCO	36266	21698	14.6	18.0	33.9	18.9	14.6	72650	90984	92	80	11088	2.3	4.6	1.5	7.4	84.2	625220
94123	SAN FRANCISCO	109485	15889	8.3	12.5	25.3	19.6	34.3	108775	142399	99	96	4566	0.2	0.0	1.0	3.0	95.8	1000001
94124	SAN FRANCISCO	16650	9294	31.6	24.2	26.8	11.7	5.7	43636	53331	58	39	4936	5.3	1.3	2.2	50.8	40.4	366737
94127	SAN FRANCISCO	60963	7007	7.8	12.4	23.0	22.0	34.8	114420	141927	99	97	6119	0.3	0.5	0.8	4.2	94.1	835231
94129	SAN FRANCISCO	48376	984	6.7	16.4	32.8	21.4	22.7	89083	118277	97	91	49	0.0	0.0	2.0	0.0	98.0	1000001
94130	SAN FRANCISCO	33586	356	8.7	16.9	30.6	26.7	17.1	88361	104745	97	91	0	0.0	0.0	0.0	0.0	0.0	0
94131	SAN FRANCISCO	64365	13459	9.4	14.3	31.2	21.7	23.5	90776	118185	97	92	7565	0.2	0.9	0.5	11.3	87.1	703984
94132	SAN FRANCISCO	33094	10470	16.6	21.2	33.3	17.1	11.8	64566	79643	88	72	4442	3.5	1.1	0.9	12.3	82.2	602227
94133	SAN FRANCISCO	48475	13999	30.8	18.2	24.4	13.1	13.6	51433	67821	75	55	3119	1.1	0.8	2.4	7.2	88.5	901286
94134	SAN FRANCISCO	19416	10665	19.3	21.0	34.7	17.4	7.7	60633	74275	85	68	7297	8.2	2.8	1.0	33.0	55.0	420547
94158	SAN FRANCISCO	29717	31	6.5	19.4	41.9	12.9	19.4	61145	73763	85	69	6	0.0	0.0	100.0	0.0	0.0	140000
94301	PALO ALTO	96324	7432	11.9	10.8	19.4	18.5	39.5	119035	153208	99	97	4055	0.2	0.2	0.8	2.8	95.9	1000001
94303	PALO ALTO	32517	12737	14.8	18.5	28.3	16.8	21.6	76340	90997	94	83	7837	1.3	0.8	1.5	15.1	81.3	757210
94304	PALO ALTO	72426	1291	11.7	15.8	26.1	20.6	25.8	91626	114132	97	92	315	0.0	0.0	0.0	1.0	99.1	1000001
94305	STANFORD	37144	3477	25.2	25.5	20.9	9.1	19.4	49193	58838	70	51	853	0.0	0.0	0.5	7.3	92.3	1000001
94306	PALO ALTO	65725	10367	12.6	13.0	23.8	19.6	31.0	101158	129608	98	94	5713	2.6	0.4	2.0	3.2	91.9	953695
94401	SAN MATEO	35033	12010	15.8	21.2	34.6	17.8	10.6	64284	78364	88	71	5509	0.5	0.7	1.1	22.9	74.8	538384
94402	SAN MATEO	59912	9864	8.0	14.6	29.5	19.4	28.5	95259	121039	98	93	6477	0.1	0.6	0.8	4.2	94.3	930127
94403	SAN MATEO	43714	15302	10.4	17.6	32.6	20.6	18.9	80507	102178	95	86	9059	0.5	0.5	0.3	9.6	89.1	707756
94404	SAN MATEO	59255	13879	6.0	10.1	27.6	27.2	29.0	109292	136909	99	96	8551	0.2	0.5	0.8	6.2	92.3	773747
94501	ALAMEDA	34647	24502	16.6	23.1	34.2	16.6	9.5	61373	75667	86	69	10314	1.6	1.3	3.2	28.1	65.7	495409
94502	ALAMEDA	49654	5351	7.0	11.1	29.6	25.8	26.6	103278	124104	98	95	4639	0.5	1.4	0.1	13.0	85.0	588129
94503	AMERICAN CANYON	21983	4108	18.4	22.5	40.2	15.0	3.9	60992	71141	85	69	3577	11.7	6.8	8.4	57.3	15.8	275455
94506	DANVILLE	76841	8246	2.1	4.5	13.7	22.1	57.5	167610	204384	100	100	7731	0.2	0.5	0.8	1.0	97.5	1000001
	CALIFORNIA	27293		21.8	24.4	30.5	13.7	9.7	54267	64547				3.3	2.7	13.3	42.9	37.9	319678
	UNITED STATES	25866		24.7	27.1	30.8	10.9	6.5	48124	56710				10.9	15.0	33.7	30.1	10.4	145905

ZIP CODE #	POST OFFICE NAME	FINANCIAL SERVICES: Auto Loan	FINANCIAL SERVICES: Home Loan	FINANCIAL SERVICES: Invest-ments	FINANCIAL SERVICES: Retire-ment Plans	THE HOME: Home Improvements: Home Repair	THE HOME: Home Improvements: Lawn & Garden	THE HOME: Furnishings: Comput-ers & Hard-ware	THE HOME: Furnishings: Major Appli-ances	THE HOME: Furnishings: TV, Radio, Sound Equip-ment	THE HOME: Furnishings: Furni-ture	ENTERTAINMENT: Dine out/ Carry out	ENTERTAINMENT: Sports Equip-ment	ENTERTAINMENT: Fees & Tickets	ENTERTAINMENT: Toys & Games	ENTERTAINMENT: Travel	ENTERTAINMENT: Cable TV	PERSONAL: Apparel & Services	PERSONAL: Auto Repairs	PERSONAL: Health Insur-ance	PERSONAL: Pets & Supplies
93740	FRESNO	0	0	0	0	0	0	0	0	0	0	0	0	0	0	0	0	0	0	0	0
93741	FRESNO	70	80	98	83	79	81	79	76	75	78	95	91	81	97	79	73	94	77	69	83
93901	SALINAS	83	88	101	88	86	91	89	88	88	90	111	101	90	112	89	86	110	89	83	95
93905	SALINAS	77	67	65	67	66	67	74	74	76	78	97	85	71	94	69	71	97	78	67	78
93906	SALINAS	92	97	108	94	93	97	95	95	95	99	121	107	97	123	94	93	121	96	87	102
93907	SALINAS	109	127	139	125	124	127	118	118	114	119	143	135	123	150	120	112	143	116	109	129
93908	SALINAS	169	200	229	200	195	202	184	183	174	188	220	208	197	226	188	171	221	179	167	199
93920	BIG SUR	121	100	74	92	110	121	94	110	104	94	124	129	86	123	99	109	116	109	125	146
93923	CARMEL	169	176	188	170	181	204	162	175	164	169	205	183	168	188	173	171	197	170	188	197
93924	CARMEL VALLEY	169	205	240	205	204	214	189	189	179	190	226	215	202	230	196	178	224	185	178	206
93925	CHUALAR	112	99	82	91	95	100	100	109	104	109	131	115	92	116	96	101	130	111	102	113
93926	GONZALES	91	79	70	75	76	79	84	88	87	90	110	96	78	102	79	83	110	91	81	92
93927	GREENFIELD	73	63	60	62	62	64	69	70	72	74	91	79	66	87	65	67	91	74	64	74
93930	KING CITY	84	76	72	75	74	76	81	82	82	85	104	93	77	100	76	77	104	85	74	87
93932	LOCKWOOD	79	77	66	76	76	79	73	77	72	75	90	89	71	87	72	70	87	76	73	89
93933	MARINA	79	81	98	81	78	83	85	81	84	86	107	95	85	107	83	82	106	85	75	89
93940	MONTEREY	103	107	133	110	105	113	113	108	110	112	139	127	113	137	111	108	136	112	102	118
93943	MONTEREY	112	112	128	110	106	114	116	112	117	118	148	129	116	149	112	114	147	117	105	122
93950	PACIFIC GROVE	106	116	141	118	115	122	116	114	113	116	142	132	119	143	117	111	139	115	109	125
93953	PEBBLE BEACH	294	275	263	261	291	343	254	289	269	272	334	283	258	278	276	287	313	281	339	330
93955	SEASIDE	78	75	82	74	72	77	80	77	81	81	102	90	79	102	77	78	101	81	72	84
93960	SOLEDAD	86	75	69	72	73	76	80	83	83	86	105	92	76	99	76	79	105	86	76	87
94002	BELMONT	163	200	255	198	194	203	188	184	179	189	225	214	199	237	192	177	225	183	168	198
94005	BRISBANE	128	146	167	151	142	143	140	137	132	141	167	162	144	170	139	126	165	137	122	149
94010	BURLINGAME	221	267	394	273	258	277	258	247	250	262	315	288	281	335	266	249	317	247	227	269
94014	DALY CITY	104	121	167	135	126	119	128	127	113	123	143	161	123	138	129	102	142	133	103	132
94015	DALY CITY	105	123	179	138	127	121	133	129	118	127	149	165	127	146	133	107	148	137	105	134
94019	HALF MOON BAY	167	228	287	219	219	227	200	197	188	202	237	225	220	259	210	188	241	191	176	211
94020	LA HONDA	173	224	253	223	217	219	197	194	182	198	229	225	214	245	203	178	231	187	173	213
94021	LOMA MAR	160	200	212	200	196	193	178	177	165	177	207	207	190	221	182	160	207	171	158	196
94022	LOS ALTOS	336	458	626	446	445	479	398	394	371	406	469	443	451	497	424	375	476	379	364	427
94024	LOS ALTOS	289	385	530	378	375	404	339	334	317	346	401	377	383	423	360	320	407	323	310	363
94025	MENLO PARK	210	252	355	251	242	261	241	233	234	246	296	268	260	311	248	234	298	233	215	252
94027	ATHERTON	488	659	905	645	642	692	575	569	536	588	678	641	652	716	613	541	689	547	528	618
94028	PORTOLA VALLEY	429	554	743	548	543	584	495	491	464	504	586	556	551	609	522	465	590	475	458	534
94030	MILLBRAE	128	163	209	157	158	165	151	149	144	152	181	170	160	194	156	144	183	147	135	159
94035	MOUNTAIN VIEW	127	81	77	93	74	87	120	104	122	112	153	138	103	137	99	111	146	122	96	118
94038	MOSS BEACH	186	232	256	233	224	228	204	201	189	207	239	232	222	250	209	185	240	195	181	223
94040	MOUNTAIN VIEW	150	161	264	173	154	168	172	159	172	175	217	190	182	229	173	170	217	164	147	174
94041	MOUNTAIN VIEW	141	138	246	156	132	146	159	143	162	162	205	175	166	215	157	160	204	152	133	159
94043	MOUNTAIN VIEW	135	139	215	149	133	144	151	140	151	153	191	168	156	197	149	148	189	146	130	155
94044	PACIFICA	125	154	187	152	150	154	144	142	137	144	172	165	152	181	147	134	172	141	128	153
94060	PESCADERO	128	149	171	144	143	148	140	138	136	143	173	157	146	180	141	135	173	138	128	151
94061	REDWOOD CITY	133	158	197	155	152	160	150	147	145	152	183	170	158	191	153	143	183	148	134	159
94062	REDWOOD CITY	241	315	432	310	304	325	286	279	271	290	342	319	316	366	300	272	346	273	256	301
94063	REDWOOD CITY	95	93	109	92	90	96	97	96	100	101	126	110	97	127	95	98	126	99	90	105
94065	REDWOOD CITY	215	236	387	253	226	246	248	229	247	252	313	274	265	330	251	245	312	237	212	252
94066	SAN BRUNO	107	130	167	128	126	131	124	121	119	125	150	141	130	158	127	117	150	122	109	130
94070	SAN CARLOS	172	231	312	224	223	235	207	203	196	210	247	233	228	267	218	197	250	198	184	218
94074	SAN GREGORIO	194	275	344	260	265	271	237	235	222	238	277	269	262	309	251	222	283	226	209	251
94080	SOUTH SAN FRANCISCO	106	123	160	125	122	125	123	121	117	123	148	143	125	152	125	114	148	124	108	129
94085	SUNNYVALE	126	136	200	147	134	138	146	138	140	146	178	168	146	181	145	135	177	145	123	149
94086	SUNNYVALE	134	144	231	158	140	148	156	145	153	157	194	177	161	201	156	149	193	152	130	158
94087	SUNNYVALE	152	199	285	196	192	201	187	180	178	187	224	211	202	244	195	178	227	180	162	192
94089	SUNNYVALE	130	130	151	135	131	134	133	134	129	133	161	162	129	157	132	123	158	138	123	150
94102	SAN FRANCISCO	49	49	96	52	47	54	59	52	62	58	79	63	60	86	59	64	79	57	52	58
94103	SAN FRANCISCO	70	69	132	76	65	75	82	72	86	82	109	88	85	116	82	87	108	78	71	81
94104	SAN FRANCISCO	55	66	93	75	69	64	71	69	61	67	77	90	67	75	71	54	77	73	55	72
94105	SAN FRANCISCO	84	81	152	93	76	86	96	85	98	97	125	104	100	131	94	97	124	91	79	95
94107	SAN FRANCISCO	170	162	272	182	155	172	190	171	192	191	244	209	193	249	185	189	240	183	161	190
94108	SAN FRANCISCO	91	96	161	109	95	98	109	100	104	107	132	126	109	135	108	100	132	107	88	108
94109	SAN FRANCISCO	115	113	211	127	108	121	133	119	137	134	174	145	138	184	132	137	173	128	112	132
94110	SAN FRANCISCO	102	108	197	113	102	115	122	110	128	123	163	132	127	177	124	132	164	118	107	122
94111	SAN FRANCISCO	159	163	281	187	159	168	187	171	182	186	231	214	189	237	184	175	229	182	151	186
94112	SAN FRANCISCO	100	119	167	134	124	116	127	124	110	121	139	160	121	135	127	98	139	131	99	129
94114	SAN FRANCISCO	174	168	314	192	158	178	198	175	202	201	257	215	206	270	194	201	255	188	163	196
94115	SAN FRANCISCO	171	164	291	185	157	176	193	173	197	195	249	212	199	258	190	194	247	185	163	192
94116	SAN FRANCISCO	119	145	204	161	150	141	151	148	132	145	166	190	146	163	153	119	166	156	119	154
94117	SAN FRANCISCO	140	134	250	154	127	142	159	141	163	162	207	173	165	217	156	162	205	151	132	157
94118	SAN FRANCISCO	163	170	284	194	168	175	193	178	186	191	235	224	194	239	191	177	233	190	156	193
94121	SAN FRANCISCO	123	143	209	162	148	140	154	149	136	148	172	191	148	168	154	123	171	157	121	156
94122	SAN FRANCISCO	114	126	196	144	128	126	140	133	128	136	162	170	136	160	139	117	160	141	110	140
94123	SAN FRANCISCO	222	217	400	247	205	230	252	224	257	256	326	275	264	342	249	255	324	239	209	250
94124	SAN FRANCISCO	76	77	104	79	77	82	84	81	84	84	106	96	83	105	83	83	105	85	78	89
94127	SAN FRANCISCO	177	258	350	244	249	259	225	222	209	226	262	254	249	291	240	210	268	215	196	234
94129	SAN FRANCISCO	168	163	304	187	154	173	191	169	195	194	248	208	200	260	188	194	246	181	158	189
94130	SAN FRANCISCO	137	108	141	122	107	119	150	132	148	141	187	169	137	174	135	136	181	149	122	147
94131	SAN FRANCISCO	162	180	299	192	171	186	191	175	190	193	240	211	202	256	193	189	240	182	161	192
94132	SAN FRANCISCO	104	115	177	126	116	116	130	121	121	124	152	154	126	154	128	113	151	130	103	128
94133	SAN FRANCISCO	117	126	202	144	127	127	141	132	132	138	167	169	139	167	140	123	165	141	112	141
94134	SAN FRANCISCO	89	103	145	116	107	101	111	109	98	106	123	140	105	119	111	88	122	115	88	113
94158	SAN FRANCISCO	173	110	105	126	100	119	164	141	166	153	208	188	140	186	135	152	199	167	131	161
94301	PALO ALTO	254	296	427	305	289	312	289	278	279	293	352	323	311	365	296	277	352	278	260	304
94303	PALO ALTO	147	174	214	166	168	176	164	162	161	169	203	184	173	214	167	159	206	162	149	174
94304	PALO ALTO	173	184	314	201	176	194	198	181	198	202	252	217	212	264	199	197	251	188	169	201
94305	STANFORD	152	120	156	128	117	136	180	143	173	159	216	187	160	202	155	157	207	163	133	161
94306	PALO ALTO	180	228	340	227	218	232	218	207	211	220	266	242	237	290	226	212	269	207	188	223
94401	SAN MATEO	120	128	156	127	124	134	129	126	128	131	163	144	132	164	129	127	161	129	120	138
94402	SAN MATEO	178	224	309	220	216	229	209	203	201	212	254	233	227	272	217	201	256	201	186	219
94403	SAN MATEO	131	159	220	157	153	162	154	148	150	155	189	172	163	201	158	150	190	149	136	160
94404	SAN MATEO	166	212	312	211	202	215	201	191	194	203	244	222	219	267	208	195	247	190	173	206
94501	ALAMEDA	100	111	159	115	108	114	116	110	113	116	143	132	119	148	117	111	143	114	101	119
94502	ALAMEDA	164	215	262	218	210	210	194	190	176	194	223	224	209	235	200	170	225	187	165	204
94503	AMERICAN CANYON	96	99	95	98	97	99	95	96	92	96	115	112	94	114	93	89	113	96	89	108
94506	DANVILLE	306	388	449	396	376	386	341	334	312	347	397	383	378	414	351	305	401	321	300	368
	CALIFORNIA	107	111	131	112	109	115	113	111	111	114	140	129	114	141	112	109	139	113	104	122
	UNITED STATES	100	100	100	100	100	100	100	100	100	100	100	100	100	100	100	100	100	100	100	100

CALIFORNIA

POPULATION CHANGE

A 94507-94709

# ZIP CODE / POST OFFICE NAME	COUNTY FIPS CODE	POPULATION 2000	2004	2009	2000-2004 ANNUAL RATE % Rate	State Centile	HOUSEHOLDS 2000	2004	2009	% Annual Rate 2000-2004	2004 Average HH Size	FAMILIES 2000	2004	% Annual Rate 2000-2004
94507 ALAMO	013	14684	15483	16514	1.3	63	5071	5288	5580	1.0	2.89	4237	4426	1.0
94508 ANGWIN	055	3912	3999	4170	0.5	33	1111	1140	1196	0.6	2.65	791	808	0.5
94509 ANTIOCH	013	61978	65241	69536	1.2	62	21067	21950	23152	1.0	2.96	15878	16506	0.9
94510 BENICIA	095	26926	29332	32138	2.0	79	10351	11195	12186	1.9	2.62	7261	7828	1.8
94512 BIRDS LANDING	095	115	114	119	-0.2	9	43	43	44	0.0	2.63	34	34	0.0
94513 BRENTWOOD	013	28402	37223	44285	6.6	99	9127	11865	13976	6.4	3.12	7407	9606	6.3
94514 BYRON	013	9135	9748	10460	1.5	70	3457	3656	3884	1.3	2.63	2688	2834	1.3
94515 CALISTOGA	055	6800	7109	7563	1.1	56	2682	2773	2923	0.8	2.51	1660	1703	0.6
94517 CLAYTON	013	12446	13486	14592	1.9	78	4490	4820	5163	1.7	2.79	3602	3854	1.6
94518 CONCORD	013	27452	28864	31032	1.2	61	10329	10776	11487	1.0	2.63	7205	7491	0.9
94519 CONCORD	013	18695	18898	20015	0.3	22	6767	6778	7112	0.0	2.75	4767	4748	-0.1
94520 CONCORD	013	36360	39933	43718	2.2	82	12685	13806	14983	2.0	2.87	7829	8315	1.4
94521 CONCORD	013	41599	43456	46529	1.0	56	15000	15578	16542	0.9	2.76	11146	11486	0.7
94523 PLEASANT HILL	013	32652	33772	35717	0.8	46	13669	14080	14781	0.7	2.37	8401	8565	0.5
94525 CROCKETT	013	3184	3263	3413	0.6	35	1488	1510	1561	0.4	2.16	844	851	0.2
94526 DANVILLE	013	28924	30222	32112	1.0	56	10710	11115	11712	0.9	2.69	8320	8590	0.8
94528 DIABLO	013	936	994	1059	1.4	67	322	339	358	1.2	2.92	278	292	1.2
94530 EL CERRITO	013	22871	23568	24865	0.7	41	10089	10298	10755	0.5	2.27	5890	5971	0.3
94531 ANTIOCH	013	27787	33506	38188	4.5	96	8060	9642	10881	4.3	3.46	7033	8386	4.2
94533 FAIRFIELD	095	68583	71738	76242	1.1	57	20916	21772	23131	1.0	3.01	15433	16025	0.9
94534 FAIRFIELD	095	27833	32312	36406	3.6	94	9296	10784	12136	3.6	2.97	7634	8819	3.5
94535 TRAVIS AFB	095	9966	9779	10093	-0.4	5	2383	2316	2409	-0.7	3.35	2295	2229	-0.7
94536 FREMONT	001	65880	67515	69338	0.6	35	23341	23700	24080	0.4	2.81	16958	17099	0.2
94538 FREMONT	001	56960	59955	62448	1.2	62	19496	20209	20737	0.9	2.94	14029	14512	0.8
94539 FREMONT	001	47018	48851	50452	0.9	51	14729	15133	15452	0.6	3.21	12591	12938	0.6
94541 HAYWARD	001	59057	62273	64505	1.3	63	20117	20834	21257	0.8	2.91	13247	13710	0.8
94542 HAYWARD	001	12331	12511	12710	0.3	25	4342	4359	4380	0.1	2.72	2891	2887	0.0
94544 HAYWARD	001	71592	74642	76874	1.0	55	21824	22448	22816	0.7	3.30	16402	16768	0.5
94545 HAYWARD	001	27571	27863	28380	0.3	22	8697	8697	8761	0.0	3.18	6554	6537	-0.1
94546 CASTRO VALLEY	001	41967	42916	43866	0.5	33	16521	16749	16940	0.3	2.51	10989	11117	0.3
94547 HERCULES	013	18999	21269	23418	2.7	88	6259	6964	7601	2.5	3.05	4860	5384	2.4
94548 KNIGHTSEN	013	161	161	166	0.0	15	56	56	57	0.0	2.86	41	41	0.0
94549 LAFAYETTE	013	27709	29095	30947	1.2	60	10516	10942	11525	0.9	2.64	7824	8142	0.9
94550 LIVERMORE	001	41183	44261	46596	1.7	74	14902	15845	16484	1.5	2.78	11147	11854	1.5
94551 LIVERMORE	001	34323	36529	38236	1.5	69	12016	12680	13141	1.3	2.88	8972	9452	1.2
94552 CASTRO VALLEY	001	14168	15018	15790	1.4	66	4835	5092	5305	1.2	2.95	3959	4155	1.1
94553 MARTINEZ	013	47177	49404	52491	1.1	58	18672	19386	20416	0.9	2.47	12057	12484	0.8
94555 FREMONT	001	33863	35093	36451	0.8	48	10759	11088	11422	0.7	3.16	8726	8955	0.6
94556 MORAGA	013	16403	16847	17728	0.6	38	5698	5824	6103	0.5	2.63	4367	4444	0.4
94558 NAPA	055	63549	66900	71518	1.2	62	23352	24474	26019	1.1	2.68	16485	17194	1.0
94559 NAPA	055	27144	28116	29771	0.8	47	9975	10281	10835	0.7	2.58	6122	6273	0.6
94560 NEWARK	001	42471	43580	44588	0.6	37	12992	13190	13337	0.4	3.30	10345	10487	0.3
94561 OAKLEY	013	30373	33364	36227	2.2	82	9795	10612	11379	1.9	3.14	7720	8374	1.9
94563 ORINDA	013	17714	18134	19083	0.6	34	6644	6739	7025	0.3	2.68	5160	5213	0.2
94564 PINOLE	013	18752	19220	20216	0.6	35	6590	6699	6979	0.4	2.85	5002	5070	0.3
94565 PITTSBURG	013	77902	82549	88267	1.4	66	24224	25404	26879	1.1	3.22	18305	19128	1.0
94566 PLEASANTON	001	36158	38192	40112	1.3	64	13370	14001	14531	1.1	2.71	9888	10291	0.9
94567 POPE VALLEY	055	706	767	834	2.0	79	258	280	303	1.9	2.72	175	188	1.7
94568 DUBLIN	001	29118	32640	35239	2.7	88	9005	10298	11179	3.2	2.66	6238	7059	3.0
94569 PORT COSTA	013	232	242	256	1.0	55	108	112	117	0.9	2.16	74	76	0.6
94571 RIO VISTA	095	5415	6637	7695	4.9	97	2168	2689	3130	5.2	2.44	1470	1817	5.1
94572 RODEO	013	8403	8417	8772	0.0	16	2839	2818	2905	-0.2	2.97	2130	2102	-0.3
94574 SAINT HELENA	055	9269	9840	10585	1.4	67	3683	3878	4138	1.2	2.52	2387	2495	1.1
94576 DEER PARK	055	249	252	264	0.3	23	105	106	110	0.2	2.32	71	72	0.3
94577 SAN LEANDRO	001	43246	44572	45719	0.7	41	16708	17001	17221	0.4	2.59	10628	10726	0.2
94578 SAN LEANDRO	001	37140	38430	39513	0.8	47	14176	14418	14612	0.4	2.59	8850	8985	0.4
94579 SAN LEANDRO	001	19727	20128	20556	0.5	30	6872	6904	6951	0.1	2.91	5100	5117	0.1
94580 SAN LORENZO	001	25953	26749	27477	0.7	41	8866	9037	9174	0.5	2.96	6650	6750	0.4
94583 SAN RAMON	013	44487	49477	54326	2.5	86	16868	18616	20236	2.4	2.65	12123	13324	2.3
94585 SUISUN CITY	095	25940	26733	28230	0.7	41	7954	8178	8619	0.7	3.26	6417	6575	0.6
94586 SUNOL	001	895	976	1029	2.1	80	338	364	379	1.8	2.68	257	278	1.9
94587 UNION CITY	001	66818	70073	72550	1.1	60	18627	19259	19663	0.8	3.62	15685	16182	0.7
94588 PLEASANTON	001	28948	30463	31738	1.2	62	10491	10966	11311	1.1	2.77	7917	8257	1.0
94589 VALLEJO	095	32500	33866	36055	1.0	54	9711	10087	10711	0.9	3.27	7550	7841	0.9
94590 VALLEJO	095	37026	37888	39717	0.5	33	14114	14357	14985	0.4	2.62	8763	8860	0.3
94591 VALLEJO	095	50298	54717	59655	2.0	79	16765	18101	19600	1.8	2.99	12635	13625	1.8
94592 VALLEJO	095	149	156	162	1.1	58	36	39	42	1.9	2.28	10	11	2.3
94595 WALNUT CREEK	013	16289	17089	18195	1.1	60	9327	9744	10314	1.0	1.71	4028	4163	0.8
94596 WALNUT CREEK	013	19245	20133	21508	1.1	57	8752	9085	9611	0.9	2.19	4794	4975	0.9
94597 WALNUT CREEK	013	21128	21758	22939	0.7	40	10446	10710	11206	0.6	2.03	5195	5257	0.3
94598 WALNUT CREEK	013	25286	26308	27918	0.9	52	9929	10294	10844	0.9	2.52	7124	7323	0.7
94599 YOUNTVILLE	055	3114	3168	3288	0.4	28	1126	1148	1201	0.5	1.99	606	613	0.3
94601 OAKLAND	001	54070	55611	56755	0.7	39	14771	15002	15127	0.4	3.63	10982	11119	0.3
94602 OAKLAND	001	30137	30117	30420	0.0	12	11889	11782	11779	-0.2	2.52	7207	7100	-0.4
94603 OAKLAND	001	30822	32275	33340	1.1	58	8583	8836	8991	0.7	3.62	6816	7000	0.6
94605 OAKLAND	001	41287	41900	42681	0.4	25	14854	14870	14950	0.0	2.79	10309	10295	0.0
94606 OAKLAND	001	41898	43287	44620	0.8	44	14930	15244	15532	0.5	2.81	8506	8653	0.4
94607 OAKLAND	001	21626	22592	23334	1.0	56	7765	8087	8292	1.0	2.62	4488	4653	0.9
94608 EMERYVILLE	001	24541	25502	26174	0.9	51	10911	11193	11342	0.6	2.25	4852	4972	0.6
94609 OAKLAND	001	21244	21840	22390	0.7	39	9555	9729	9871	0.4	2.19	4030	4077	0.3
94610 OAKLAND	001	28747	29808	30872	0.9	49	15007	15375	15748	0.6	1.93	5901	6048	0.6
94611 OAKLAND	001	34934	35409	36129	0.3	24	16295	16351	16489	0.1	2.16	8275	8304	0.1
94612 OAKLAND	001	12744	13176	13580	0.8	45	7478	7574	7683	0.3	1.65	2056	2087	0.4
94613 OAKLAND	001	144	143	143	-0.2	10	50	48	48	-1.0	1.13	32	11	-22.2
94618 OAKLAND	001	15633	15953	16315	0.5	31	7314	7394	7480	0.3	2.14	3810	3841	0.2
94619 OAKLAND	001	24830	25209	25652	0.4	25	8968	9025	9092	0.2	2.71	5867	5882	0.1
94621 OAKLAND	001	30939	31383	31857	0.3	25	8777	8743	8740	-0.1	3.57	6566	6522	-0.2
94702 BERKELEY	001	15271	15359	15568	0.1	18	6948	6914	6927	-0.1	2.21	3254	3219	-0.3
94703 BERKELEY	001	20526	20247	20396	-0.3	7	9085	8890	8864	-0.5	2.25	3995	3880	-0.7
94704 BERKELEY	001	19687	21647	22983	2.3	83	8245	9218	9846	2.7	1.96	1428	1576	2.4
94705 BERKELEY	001	12230	12261	12427	0.1	16	5531	5495	5509	-0.2	2.21	2555	2514	-0.4
94706 ALBANY	001	16149	16229	16515	0.1	16	7050	7029	7082	-0.1	2.30	4070	4027	-0.3
94707 BERKELEY	001	11676	11909	12241	0.5	30	4883	4942	5030	0.3	2.41	3242	3266	0.2
94708 BERKELEY	013	11150	11179	11397	0.1	16	4867	4838	4881	-0.1	2.30	3027	2997	-0.2
94709 BERKELEY	001	10344	10530	10817	0.4	28	5116	5185	5292	0.3	1.84	1414	1401	-0.2
CALIFORNIA					1.4					1.2	2.90			1.2
UNITED STATES					1.2					1.3	2.58			1.1

ZIP CODE #	POST OFFICE NAME	RACE (%) White 2000	White 2004	Black 2000	Black 2004	Asian/Pacific 2000	Asian/Pacific 2004	% Hispanic Origin 2000	% Hispanic Origin 2004	2004 AGE DISTRIBUTION (%) 0-4	5-9	10-14	15-19	20-24	25-44	45-64	65-84	85+	18+	MEDIAN AGE 2004	% 2004 Males	% 2004 Females
94507	ALAMO	90.3	88.5	0.5	0.6	6.2	7.2	4.1	5.0	5.9	7.5	8.3	7.0	3.8	18.5	34.7	12.6	1.8	73.3	44.5	49.2	50.8
94508	ANGWIN	78.9	77.0	2.8	2.7	9.0	9.2	11.9	14.3	5.4	4.4	4.1	10.2	18.1	26.6	21.5	8.3	1.5	83.8	28.6	49.1	50.9
94509	ANTIOCH	69.2	66.1	7.4	7.6	5.2	5.7	24.7	28.0	8.2	7.9	8.5	7.5	7.6	28.7	22.5	8.0	1.1	70.7	32.5	49.0	51.0
94510	BENICIA	78.1	75.2	5.0	5.3	8.4	9.4	9.1	10.7	5.6	6.5	8.2	7.4	5.7	25.7	30.7	9.1	1.1	74.9	40.0	48.5	51.5
94512	BIRDS LANDING	86.1	83.3	0.0	0.0	1.7	2.6	14.8	15.8	7.9	7.9	7.0	7.9	7.0	24.6	25.4	10.5	1.8	71.1	37.1	52.6	47.4
94513	BRENTWOOD	71.1	67.7	3.7	4.0	3.8	4.2	28.6	32.1	9.9	9.5	9.0	6.9	6.0	31.4	18.8	7.8	0.8	67.1	32.2	49.5	50.5
94514	BYRON	88.2	86.3	1.8	2.0	2.0	2.2	10.5	12.6	6.2	7.0	6.8	6.1	3.6	27.7	30.8	11.2	0.6	75.9	41.3	51.3	48.7
94515	CALISTOGA	79.7	77.1	0.4	0.4	1.1	1.1	33.2	37.9	6.1	6.1	5.7	5.7	6.7	25.7	25.8	14.9	3.2	78.6	40.3	51.0	49.1
94517	CLAYTON	86.1	83.5	1.6	1.8	6.4	7.5	6.9	8.3	6.6	7.7	7.3	5.9	4.2	25.9	32.4	9.3	0.8	74.6	41.2	49.1	50.9
94518	CONCORD	74.7	71.4	2.4	2.4	10.8	12.0	14.5	16.8	6.2	6.3	6.5	5.9	6.1	28.9	26.7	11.6	1.8	77.4	39.3	48.4	51.6
94519	CONCORD	76.2	72.8	2.5	2.7	8.0	8.9	17.3	20.3	7.0	6.9	7.1	6.1	6.4	30.2	24.8	9.9	1.6	75.1	37.1	49.6	50.4
94520	CONCORD	59.3	56.0	4.5	4.5	9.1	9.5	39.6	43.8	8.6	7.5	7.3	6.5	8.8	35.0	17.9	7.3	1.3	72.9	31.1	51.5	48.5
94521	CONCORD	75.4	72.1	2.5	2.7	11.5	12.7	12.4	14.6	6.3	6.5	7.3	6.9	6.3	28.2	27.1	10.1	1.3	75.6	38.4	48.1	51.9
94523	PLEASANT HILL	82.1	79.3	1.5	1.7	9.5	10.8	8.2	9.8	5.7	5.8	5.9	5.8	6.0	29.2	27.7	11.6	2.2	79.0	40.1	48.4	51.6
94525	CROCKETT	82.1	79.6	5.2	5.5	2.6	2.9	12.8	15.3	4.9	4.9	5.5	6.0	6.1	26.3	31.9	12.1	2.5	81.2	43.1	48.9	51.1
94526	DANVILLE	88.8	86.9	0.8	0.9	6.9	7.9	4.8	5.9	6.1	7.2	7.8	6.5	4.1	23.0	32.3	11.5	1.5	74.4	42.5	48.6	51.4
94528	DIABLO	93.8	92.5	0.3	0.4	3.3	3.8	4.8	6.0	6.5	8.0	8.2	6.8	4.1	19.7	32.6	12.8	1.3	72.6	43.2	50.1	49.9
94530	EL CERRITO	58.2	54.4	8.6	8.8	24.2	26.5	7.9	9.0	4.5	4.5	4.5	4.4	5.1	29.4	27.6	16.4	3.6	83.9	43.5	47.2	52.8
94531	ANTIOCH	62.0	58.3	12.5	13.0	11.8	12.8	15.9	18.4	9.6	9.8	9.5	7.3	5.6	32.0	21.6	4.3	0.4	66.2	32.7	49.3	50.7
94533	FAIRFIELD	51.8	48.8	18.4	18.3	10.7	11.4	22.8	25.6	7.6	7.0	7.4	7.3	8.5	30.9	21.0	9.2	1.1	73.5	32.9	51.8	48.2
94534	FAIRFIELD	67.8	64.0	9.0	9.4	12.4	13.9	11.7	13.7	7.4	7.8	7.9	6.8	5.3	27.4	27.6	8.6	1.1	72.4	37.8	49.0	51.0
94535	TRAVIS AFB	65.0	61.4	11.4	11.8	10.0	11.0	11.1	13.1	13.0	8.7	6.7	7.2	27.3	35.0	1.8	0.3	0.0	69.5	22.6	56.7	43.3
94536	FREMONT	56.0	51.8	3.6	3.6	27.2	29.6	16.2	18.3	7.1	6.6	6.4	5.8	6.8	34.3	22.9	8.8	1.3	76.3	35.5	50.2	49.8
94538	FREMONT	52.1	48.3	3.6	3.6	28.5	29.9	19.4	22.2	7.7	6.9	6.8	6.2	7.1	36.6	20.1	7.7	0.9	74.8	33.5	51.0	49.0
94539	FREMONT	41.9	37.9	1.6	1.6	50.2	53.5	6.0	6.7	6.5	7.4	8.7	7.1	5.0	27.1	29.2	8.2	0.8	72.7	39.2	49.6	50.4
94541	HAYWARD	50.4	47.5	13.0	12.8	11.3	11.8	35.8	39.3	8.1	7.4	7.5	6.6	7.3	31.9	20.6	8.5	2.1	73.0	33.2	50.1	49.9
94542	HAYWARD	54.9	51.4	12.6	12.7	20.2	21.9	15.1	17.1	5.2	5.1	5.3	7.6	10.0	33.4	25.2	7.6	0.7	81.4	34.5	48.9	51.1
94544	HAYWARD	41.3	39.0	10.4	10.0	20.5	21.1	39.0	41.9	8.5	7.8	8.3	7.2	7.8	32.7	18.7	8.1	1.0	71.2	31.2	50.0	50.0
94545	HAYWARD	37.2	34.5	9.4	9.1	31.5	32.4	25.1	27.5	6.8	6.5	7.2	7.0	7.5	29.4	23.3	11.0	1.3	75.2	35.6	48.7	51.3
94546	CASTRO VALLEY	75.8	72.8	3.9	4.0	10.3	11.5	12.7	14.8	5.6	5.7	6.5	6.4	5.9	27.2	26.5	13.0	3.2	78.2	40.8	48.1	51.9
94547	HERCULES	29.4	26.6	18.5	18.5	42.2	43.8	10.7	11.8	5.8	6.1	7.5	7.5	7.1	27.3	30.2	7.9	0.7	76.1	38.3	47.5	52.5
94548	KNIGHTSEN	74.5	71.4	0.6	0.6	0.6	0.6	31.1	35.4	6.2	6.2	8.7	6.2	5.6	28.6	26.1	11.2	1.2	76.4	37.3	50.9	49.1
94549	LAFAYETTE	86.7	84.6	0.7	0.7	8.3	9.4	4.3	5.1	5.2	6.4	7.8	7.1	4.5	21.2	32.8	13.1	1.8	75.7	43.6	48.9	51.1
94550	LIVERMORE	84.7	82.3	1.5	1.6	5.0	5.7	12.1	14.4	6.9	7.4	8.0	6.5	5.5	29.4	26.3	8.8	1.2	73.5	37.6	49.7	50.3
94551	LIVERMORE	79.0	76.2	1.7	1.8	7.2	8.1	16.7	19.1	8.4	8.4	8.2	6.2	5.4	34.6	22.8	5.5	0.6	71.2	34.7	50.2	49.8
94552	CASTRO VALLEY	58.6	54.1	3.6	3.7	30.5	33.5	7.2	8.4	7.1	7.8	7.0	5.7	4.0	30.2	30.0	7.6	0.6	74.5	39.2	48.9	51.1
94553	MARTINEZ	79.7	77.0	3.5	3.7	7.2	8.1	11.5	13.6	5.6	5.8	6.4	6.4	6.3	29.3	29.2	9.7	1.3	78.1	39.5	49.5	50.5
94555	FREMONT	32.0	28.9	3.5	3.5	54.2	56.1	8.7	9.7	8.5	8.3	7.4	5.5	5.0	35.1	23.2	6.4	0.6	72.3	35.2	49.7	50.3
94556	MORAGA	81.6	78.9	1.0	1.0	12.1	13.6	4.8	5.7	4.0	5.5	7.3	10.6	8.1	16.8	30.9	15.0	1.9	78.7	43.4	47.3	52.7
94558	NAPA	82.9	80.8	0.5	0.5	2.0	2.1	21.6	24.7	6.0	6.3	7.1	6.8	6.0	24.5	27.3	13.5	2.6	76.3	40.5	49.1	50.9
94559	NAPA	78.0	75.6	1.4	1.3	1.5	1.5	31.5	35.6	6.6	6.3	6.8	6.5	7.7	31.7	23.3	9.0	2.1	76.3	35.3	52.1	47.9
94560	NEWARK	52.2	48.5	4.0	4.0	22.3	23.5	28.6	32.0	7.3	6.9	7.7	7.3	7.5	32.0	22.6	8.0	0.7	73.7	34.1	50.3	49.7
94561	OAKLEY	74.8	71.3	4.2	4.5	3.8	4.3	23.2	27.0	8.3	8.5	9.4	7.9	6.4	30.3	22.2	6.5	0.6	68.8	33.1	50.0	50.0
94563	ORINDA	86.5	84.3	0.5	0.5	9.2	10.5	3.2	3.9	5.0	6.6	8.0	6.9	3.4	17.6	33.3	17.0	2.2	75.9	46.4	48.1	51.9
94564	PINOLE	53.7	50.0	11.6	11.9	22.3	23.9	13.7	15.7	5.7	5.9	7.1	7.4	6.6	26.1	28.5	11.3	1.5	76.6	39.9	48.2	51.8
94565	PITTSBURG	44.6	41.9	17.2	17.0	12.6	13.2	34.1	37.3	8.8	8.3	8.6	7.9	8.3	29.9	20.2	7.1	0.9	69.5	30.4	49.2	50.8
94566	PLEASANTON	84.0	81.5	1.0	1.1	8.8	10.0	7.8	9.2	6.2	7.3	8.8	7.1	4.6	26.9	29.2	8.5	1.4	73.0	39.7	48.8	51.3
94567	POPE VALLEY	86.1	84.2	0.3	0.3	1.3	1.3	14.6	17.7	4.8	5.6	6.7	6.4	5.5	23.3	33.5	12.9	1.3	78.4	43.7	52.0	48.0
94568	DUBLIN	69.3	65.7	10.3	10.9	10.5	11.8	13.7	16.1	6.0	5.8	5.9	5.7	7.4	41.4	22.8	4.8	0.4	79.3	35.0	52.6	47.4
94569	PORT COSTA	87.1	84.7	2.2	2.5	2.6	2.9	9.1	11.2	2.9	3.7	4.6	6.2	3.7	21.9	38.0	16.5	2.5	84.7	48.5	50.4	49.6
94571	RIO VISTA	83.8	80.1	1.6	1.9	1.8	1.9	16.4	20.7	6.6	6.6	6.8	6.5	5.5	24.7	25.5	15.8	2.0	75.9	40.3	50.7	49.3
94572	RODEO	53.5	50.4	15.2	15.5	16.4	17.2	16.7	19.0	7.4	7.3	7.7	7.4	6.8	27.0	25.5	9.3	1.5	72.9	35.5	48.5	51.5
94574	SAINT HELENA	83.7	81.5	0.5	0.5	1.2	1.2	25.2	29.3	5.6	6.1	6.7	6.3	5.3	24.7	28.3	13.5	3.4	77.4	41.9	47.5	52.5
94576	DEER PARK	90.4	88.9	0.4	0.4	2.8	2.8	10.0	12.3	5.2	5.6	6.0	5.2	6.8	25.8	31.8	10.7	3.2	79.8	41.9	47.2	52.8
94577	SAN LEANDRO	51.4	48.4	12.8	12.7	19.2	20.1	22.2	24.8	6.3	6.3	6.7	5.7	6.0	29.8	24.6	11.8	2.8	77.2	38.7	48.3	51.7
94578	SAN LEANDRO	44.9	41.9	17.9	17.7	18.5	19.5	24.2	27.2	7.3	6.9	6.9	6.9	7.2	31.7	21.6	9.7	1.8	74.6	34.4	49.4	50.6
94579	SAN LEANDRO	51.3	47.2	4.7	4.7	32.1	34.9	16.4	18.2	6.5	6.4	6.6	6.1	5.8	28.6	23.4	14.6	2.1	76.8	38.8	47.9	52.1
94580	SAN LORENZO	58.8	55.1	4.9	4.9	17.8	18.9	24.8	28.3	6.5	6.6	7.7	6.9	6.6	28.7	23.5	11.8	1.6	75.0	36.9	48.6	51.4
94583	SAN RAMON	77.7	74.4	1.9	2.0	14.4	16.4	7.1	8.5	7.2	7.7	7.4	5.9	4.7	31.4	28.8	6.1	0.9	74.0	38.0	49.1	50.9
94585	SUISUN CITY	44.5	41.0	19.2	19.2	18.8	20.0	17.9	20.0	7.8	7.8	9.1	8.1	7.4	30.3	23.2	5.7	0.6	70.1	32.2	49.3	50.7
94586	SUNOL	86.0	83.4	0.6	0.6	7.9	9.3	5.1	6.3	5.4	6.9	8.4	6.5	4.0	25.1	34.8	8.0	0.9	75.2	41.7	50.6	49.4
94587	UNION CITY	30.4	27.9	6.7	6.4	44.2	45.7	24.0	25.3	7.4	7.3	7.8	6.9	7.2	31.7	23.0	7.8	0.9	73.4	33.9	49.7	50.3
94588	PLEASANTON	76.2	72.7	1.8	1.9	15.3	17.4	8.0	9.5	7.1	7.8	8.2	6.3	4.6	32.7	26.9	6.1	0.5	72.9	37.0	49.7	50.3
94589	VALLEJO	24.5	22.7	29.8	29.2	30.7	31.4	15.3	17.0	6.9	7.0	8.2	7.5	7.2	26.9	24.0	10.7	1.7	73.2	35.2	48.1	51.9
94590	VALLEJO	42.7	40.2	25.3	24.9	12.4	13.1	22.1	24.7	8.3	7.5	7.9	7.1	7.3	29.2	22.1	9.1	1.6	72.1	33.4	48.6	51.4
94591	VALLEJO	39.2	35.5	18.3	18.0	29.9	32.5	12.6	13.8	6.7	6.8	7.5	7.1	6.9	28.2	26.3	9.1	1.4	74.6	36.2	48.6	51.4
94592	VALLEJO	42.3	38.5	20.1	19.9	20.1	21.8	7.4	8.3	1.9	0.6	0.0	19.2	41.7	32.1	3.2	1.3	0.0	97.4	23.4	57.7	42.3
94595	WALNUT CREEK	92.8	91.6	0.5	0.5	4.4	5.1	2.1	2.6	2.6	3.1	3.2	2.7	1.8	11.6	19.2	38.9	17.0	89.4	69.8	39.9	60.1
94596	WALNUT CREEK	83.3	80.8	1.2	1.3	8.7	9.9	8.2	9.8	5.0	5.1	5.8	5.9	6.8	30.6	27.4	11.2	2.3	80.4	39.4	49.0	51.0
94597	WALNUT CREEK	80.9	77.9	1.6	1.7	10.7	12.1	7.4	8.9	4.8	4.6	4.8	4.8	6.1	34.7	27.0	11.1	2.1	82.9	39.3	48.8	51.2
94598	WALNUT CREEK	82.3	79.6	1.0	1.1	11.8	13.4	4.8	5.8	4.7	5.6	6.9	6.2	4.3	22.3	31.5	16.2	2.3	78.4	45.0	48.1	51.9
94599	YOUNTVILLE	91.6	90.5	1.1	1.1	1.4	1.5	10.7	12.8	2.6	3.0	3.4	3.3	2.6	16.2	26.1	35.2	7.7	88.5	59.2	56.1	43.9
94601	OAKLAND	25.6	25.3	23.6	22.1	16.8	16.7	49.9	52.6	9.2	8.4	9.1	8.2	9.4	32.1	16.6	6.0	1.0	68.5	28.2	50.9	49.1
94602	OAKLAND	44.5	42.0	21.0	20.6	23.5	25.0	12.5	14.0	6.4	6.4	6.5	6.1	6.0	30.3	27.0	9.3	2.1	77.0	38.2	46.5	53.6
94603	OAKLAND	17.0	17.7	53.6	50.6	3.9	4.0	38.3	41.6	9.5	9.4	9.9	8.6	8.3	29.1	17.5	6.8	0.8	65.9	27.7	48.5	51.5
94605	OAKLAND	20.3	19.3	60.3	59.3	5.3	5.6	16.8	18.9	7.4	7.6	8.2	6.8	6.4	27.9	25.0	9.5	1.2	72.6	35.2	46.7	53.3
94606	OAKLAND	19.3	17.9	24.4	23.0	38.9	40.1	20.7	22.5	7.1	6.5	7.3	7.2	9.3	34.5	19.6	7.5	1.1	74.9	31.6	49.7	50.3
94607	OAKLAND	11.1	10.6	51.5	49.7	26.0	27.4	12.8	13.8	7.1	6.7	7.8	7.0	7.4	29.9	21.8	10.7	1.7	74.4	34.4	48.9	51.1
94608	EMERYVILLE	25.3	23.3	52.4	52.4	11.7	12.4	9.9	11.1	5.6	5.5	6.6	6.2	7.3	34.3	23.9	9.0	1.6	78.6	35.3	47.8	52.2
94609	OAKLAND	37.1	34.6	42.9	43.0	8.6	9.3	9.5	10.9	5.2	4.8	5.3	5.6	7.9	40.0	21.7	7.8	1.8	81.5	34.5	46.9	53.1
94610	OAKLAND	53.5	50.4	23.4	24.0	14.8	15.9	6.9	7.9	4.2	4.1	4.6	4.9	5.7	37.3	28.5	9.0	2.0	84.3	39.3	47.2	52.9
94611	OAKLAND	71.9	69.2	9.8	9.8	11.7	13.2	5.1	6.0	4.7	5.1	5.3	4.9	4.4	30.7	31.5	11.0	2.5	82.0	42.2	47.5	52.5
94612	OAKLAND	25.3	23.0	37.3	37.4	25.9	26.5	10.9	12.7	4.3	3.9	3.8	4.1	7.2	33.4	23.6	16.0	3.7	85.8	40.6	52.0	48.0
94613	OAKLAND	56.3	53.2	20.8	21.0	13.2	14.0	8.3	9.1	2.8	3.5	2.8	25.9	33.6	18.9	10.5	2.1	0.0	88.8	22.2	18.9	81.1
94618	OAKLAND	78.5	75.9	6.6	6.8	8.8	10.1	4.9	5.8	5.6	5.3	4.2	3.9	4.7	34.8	29.3	10.2	2.0	82.7	40.5	48.2	51.8
94619	OAKLAND	34.1	31.7	32.4	32.0	20.4	21.6	14.7	16.3	6.3	6.3	7.1	7.0	7.2	29.1	26.2	9.1	1.8	76.5	36.7	46.3	53.7
94621	OAKLAND	15.8	16.3	48.4	45.7	5.9	5.9	41.5	44.6	9.7	9.5	10.3	8.8	8.4	29.1	16.3	6.9	0.9	65.1	27.0	49.0	51.0
94702	BERKELEY	44.0	41.1	31.9	31.9	11.0	11.9	13.3	15.4	5.2	4.9	5.5	5.3	7.1	34.7	25.6	9.7	2.0	81.3	37.6	47.2	52.8
94703	BERKELEY	51.4	48.4	24.4	24.4	12.8	14.2	10.7	12.2	5.2	4.6	5.0	5.6	9.2	38.4	23.1	7.5	1.5	82.1	33.8	49.0	51.0
94704	BERKELEY	50.1	46.1	4.0	4.0	33.9	36.4	10.3	11.7	1.3	1.0	1.1	16.3	41.4	24.1	10.3	3.6	1.0	95.9	23.7	51.9	48.1
94705	BERKELEY	76.3	73.2	6.1	6.3	10.3	11.7	5.6	6.7	3.8	3.8	4.2	4.9	8.3	33.1	29.1	11.0	1.8	85.5	39.8	48.2	51.8
94706	ALBANY	64.6	60.7	4.4	4.5	22.4	24.6	7.5	8.8	4.9	4.9	6.0	7.0	7.1	29.8	29.0	9.5	2.0	80.0	39.3	46.6	53.4
94707	BERKELEY	83.2	80.4	2.1	2.3	9.3	10.8	4.1	4.9	4.8	5.7	5.6	4.7	3.0	23.5	34.4	15.7	2.7	80.8	46.7	47.2	52.8
94708	BERKELEY	83.1	80.5	2.2	2.3	9.4	10.7	3.7	4.5	4.4	5.0	4.5	3.8	3.3	24.0	35.2	17.2	2.6	83.6	48.0	48.3	51.7
94709	BERKELEY	67.7	63.5	3.1	3.2	21.7	24.5	5.7	6.7	2.4	1.8	1.9	6.2	16.8	43.9	19.7	6.4	1.0	93.0	31.0	51.0	49.0
	CALIFORNIA	59.6	57.1	6.7	6.5	11.3	11.8	32.4	35.5	7.4	7.1	7.8	7.3	7.7	29.8	22.1	9.3	1.4	73.3	33.8	49.8	50.2
	UNITED STATES	75.1	73.6	12.3	12.5	3.8	4.2	12.5	14.1	6.9	6.7	7.2	7.0	7.3	28.6	23.8	10.8	1.7	75.1	36.0	49.1	50.9

ZIP CODE #	POST OFFICE NAME	2004 Per Capita Income	2004 HH Income Base	2004 Household Income Distribution (%): Less than $25,000	$25,000 to $49,999	$50,000 to $99,999	$100,000 to $149,999	$150,000 or More	Median Household Income: 2004	2009	2004 National Centile	2004 State Centile	2004 Home Value Base	2004 Home Value Distribution (%): Less than $50,000	$50,000 to $89,999	$90,000 to $174,999	$175,000 to $399,999	$400,000 or More	2004 Median Home Value
94507	ALAMO	87003	5288	5.8	6.0	14.7	18.6	54.9	163076	204915	100	100	4883	0.4	0.1	0.3	1.8	97.5	1000001
94508	ANGWIN	35170	1140	10.7	22.3	33.9	15.6	17.5	70839	88951	92	79	734	1.5	2.0	2.9	25.8	67.9	594444
94509	ANTIOCH	23682	21950	19.0	23.7	36.2	15.1	6.0	58041	68692	83	66	14241	0.7	1.2	9.0	76.8	12.3	271576
94510	BENICIA	36250	11195	11.9	18.4	34.4	22.1	13.1	76603	86679	94	83	8238	0.8	1.3	3.6	35.2	59.1	438386
94512	BIRDS LANDING	27858	43	14.0	27.9	37.2	14.0	7.0	60974	65200	85	68	32	0.0	0.0	3.1	87.5	9.4	241176
94513	BRENTWOOD	28761	11865	9.8	17.6	38.3	23.1	11.2	77176	92090	94	84	9568	1.9	2.1	2.2	44.7	49.1	396457
94514	BYRON	53015	3656	6.5	11.7	30.0	25.5	26.3	102435	126818	98	95	3243	1.5	0.6	0.9	17.4	79.7	584722
94515	CALISTOGA	32723	2773	20.8	30.8	27.2	11.2	10.0	48275	57010	69	49	1738	9.7	10.6	6.2	16.1	57.4	444912
94517	CLAYTON	49279	4820	5.2	9.7	27.8	26.5	30.9	110939	135999	99	96	4395	0.7	0.2	2.6	15.8	80.8	579488
94518	CONCORD	35316	10776	12.1	18.9	35.0	21.1	13.0	75175	90432	93	82	7617	5.6	3.0	8.1	27.7	55.6	425341
94519	CONCORD	27449	6778	11.9	21.1	42.5	18.9	5.7	66666	79694	90	74	4895	1.4	0.4	4.5	67.5	26.1	334076
94520	CONCORD	20342	13806	24.1	30.7	34.2	8.0	3.0	45803	52733	63	43	5362	2.8	6.1	16.5	68.6	6.0	249902
94521	CONCORD	34040	15578	9.6	17.6	38.6	21.1	13.0	76065	91514	94	83	11350	0.3	0.3	3.8	44.5	51.1	404005
94523	PLEASANT HILL	41432	14080	11.2	16.4	35.9	21.5	15.0	78941	97823	95	85	9087	0.5	0.1	2.0	31.7	65.7	469883
94525	CROCKETT	32375	1510	21.0	25.9	28.9	17.9	6.4	53450	66138	78	58	885	1.5	0.0	7.0	64.6	26.9	305760
94526	DANVILLE	65811	11115	5.0	9.0	22.5	24.7	38.9	124457	153990	99	98	9502	0.3	0.2	0.2	4.1	95.2	866797
94528	DIABLO	88028	339	4.4	10.0	14.8	23.0	47.8	144240	177994	100	99	316	0.0	0.0	0.0	6.3	93.7	947115
94530	EL CERRITO	40311	10298	13.9	21.3	34.1	17.9	12.9	67295	83661	90	75	6491	1.7	1.5	1.4	25.0	70.4	472910
94531	ANTIOCH	32178	9642	4.3	8.4	41.6	31.4	14.3	93493	112592	97	92	8965	0.8	0.1	1.0	56.4	41.7	380073
94533	FAIRFIELD	20165	21772	20.0	28.9	36.0	11.8	3.4	50969	58236	74	55	12668	2.5	2.1	11.3	73.5	10.6	243732
94534	FAIRFIELD	36112	10784	6.7	14.2	38.3	25.3	15.5	86541	100645	97	90	9435	0.8	0.5	1.5	46.4	50.9	404169
94535	TRAVIS AFB	15087	2316	21.2	42.4	31.5	4.5	0.6	40979	47242	50	34	49	22.5	0.0	49.0	28.6	0.0	157500
94536	FREMONT	34773	23700	9.3	16.3	38.1	22.8	13.5	79490	97345	95	85	14268	1.0	1.7	1.0	21.2	75.1	545319
94538	FREMONT	31640	20209	10.0	14.8	41.3	22.1	11.8	78227	94354	94	85	10629	1.4	1.7	2.5	23.3	71.2	469064
94539	FREMONT	50509	15133	6.3	9.3	24.5	25.5	34.4	117430	141394	99	97	12727	0.6	1.8	2.0	7.2	88.5	875524
94541	HAYWARD	22662	20834	18.4	26.7	37.0	12.8	5.1	54324	64166	79	60	9494	1.2	0.1	2.8	62.2	33.7	350449
94542	HAYWARD	37139	4359	12.5	14.3	32.4	21.6	19.2	82590	102982	96	88	2744	0.0	0.3	1.1	21.2	77.3	557489
94544	HAYWARD	20716	22448	16.5	26.8	36.9	14.7	5.2	56316	66350	81	63	11805	2.0	3.0	8.5	55.8	30.6	343337
94545	HAYWARD	23521	8697	13.7	20.3	42.2	17.3	6.6	64720	76449	88	72	6092	2.1	4.2	5.0	50.0	38.7	361889
94546	CASTRO VALLEY	35100	16749	13.0	20.4	37.5	18.5	10.6	67613	81486	90	76	11294	3.0	0.4	2.1	33.5	61.0	441042
94547	HERCULES	32818	6964	5.0	16.3	40.0	25.3	13.4	84084	102016	96	89	5651	1.1	0.5	2.8	51.0	44.6	376318
94548	KNIGHTSEN	28164	56	14.3	30.4	37.5	12.5	5.4	57188	64564	82	64	37	0.0	0.0	5.4	37.8	56.8	441667
94549	LAFAYETTE	67397	10942	5.8	10.4	24.6	20.5	38.7	120692	152330	99	98	8724	0.1	0.2	0.4	3.1	96.2	908766
94550	LIVERMORE	38065	15845	8.7	15.7	34.6	22.9	18.2	84770	104049	96	89	11909	0.1	0.2	1.2	17.7	80.8	554370
94551	LIVERMORE	35498	12680	7.7	13.8	38.1	26.0	14.5	85414	103858	96	89	9757	0.6	1.6	1.8	32.4	63.6	460268
94552	CASTRO VALLEY	46781	5092	4.4	7.8	24.7	31.4	31.8	119080	141331	99	97	4739	0.5	1.4	0.7	7.2	90.1	673764
94553	MARTINEZ	34769	19386	13.2	19.6	36.2	20.1	10.9	70570	85736	91	78	13718	2.5	1.8	3.6	46.8	45.4	379508
94555	FREMONT	37030	11088	6.7	10.5	34.2	28.3	20.3	97352	116610	98	93	8261	1.6	3.7	1.8	12.4	80.5	559774
94556	MORAGA	60009	5824	5.9	10.5	25.4	19.7	38.6	118700	149543	99	97	5020	0.4	0.7	0.5	5.8	92.6	882092
94558	NAPA	34174	24474	15.0	23.5	32.1	17.2	12.3	64409	77400	88	72	17819	2.8	1.9	3.1	33.0	59.3	451313
94559	NAPA	26149	10281	20.5	30.8	31.4	11.5	5.8	48724	57566	70	50	5189	2.2	1.7	2.0	52.5	41.6	371349
94560	NEWARK	27762	13190	9.5	16.7	39.1	23.7	11.0	77421	91630	94	84	8890	0.7	0.9	1.0	26.9	70.5	475134
94561	OAKLEY	26227	10612	11.9	16.4	45.6	20.4	5.8	71417	83337	92	79	9001	6.0	1.9	4.2	72.6	15.3	294059
94563	ORINDA	85247	6739	6.4	8.7	19.2	19.3	46.5	139646	175888	100	99	6039	0.0	0.4	0.5	2.9	96.2	1000001
94564	PINOLE	30099	6699	11.0	17.1	40.5	22.0	9.3	73471	87927	93	81	5117	0.9	0.4	3.3	57.5	38.0	363017
94565	PITTSBURG	20458	25404	19.5	25.9	37.0	13.7	3.9	54653	64085	79	60	15704	4.5	3.5	13.2	70.9	7.9	245893
94566	PLEASANTON	52624	14001	8.1	11.0	28.9	23.2	28.8	103106	125822	98	95	10365	0.6	0.4	2.9	7.2	89.0	728247
94567	POPE VALLEY	41391	280	13.2	21.8	33.2	14.3	17.5	65027	79472	89	72	206	8.7	2.4	4.4	33.0	51.5	433333
94568	DUBLIN	36452	10298	5.8	13.6	38.0	26.1	16.5	88439	108763	97	91	6759	0.1	0.2	1.0	17.5	81.1	518586
94569	PORT COSTA	40320	112	7.1	25.0	34.8	25.0	8.0	75889	87759	94	82	97	0.0	0.0	2.1	59.8	38.1	354000
94571	RIO VISTA	26872	2689	24.0	26.9	32.0	11.8	5.4	49075	55389	70	50	1975	7.1	0.7	6.1	66.8	19.3	265352
94572	RODEO	25228	2818	14.1	22.9	37.5	20.5	5.2	66870	79807	90	75	1877	1.3	0.0	3.6	71.6	23.4	318679
94574	SAINT HELENA	45991	3878	15.0	18.1	31.5	17.3	18.2	71822	90601	92	79	2408	1.4	1.0	2.0	11.9	83.7	887270
94576	DEER PARK	43211	106	9.4	17.0	42.5	15.1	16.0	73821	91104	93	81	64	4.7	0.0	0.0	12.5	82.8	964286
94577	SAN LEANDRO	27942	17001	16.5	25.3	37.0	14.6	6.6	57981	68321	83	65	10085	2.1	0.5	2.7	57.2	37.5	361640
94578	SAN LEANDRO	24515	14418	19.6	28.9	35.2	11.5	4.7	51323	61321	74	55	6615	4.8	0.6	2.1	62.3	30.3	342420
94579	SAN LEANDRO	27120	6904	14.5	21.5	36.2	19.0	8.8	66117	79832	89	74	5504	2.9	4.3	5.5	48.0	39.4	369344
94580	SAN LORENZO	24889	9037	15.9	22.0	39.6	16.1	6.4	61556	72677	86	69	6481	1.7	0.3	1.4	69.2	27.4	350672
94583	SAN RAMON	52086	18616	4.4	9.5	28.2	27.1	30.9	111298	136817	99	96	13524	0.3	0.3	0.4	8.6	90.5	685971
94585	SUISUN CITY	23305	8178	11.5	19.7	46.3	18.1	4.4	67329	76342	90	75	6209	0.6	0.2	3.7	87.2	8.3	269439
94586	SUNOL	62737	364	3.9	7.1	32.1	28.6	28.3	108403	132601	99	96	311	0.0	0.0	0.3	19.0	80.7	738333
94587	UNION CITY	26802	19259	10.7	14.3	37.6	23.3	14.1	81124	98169	95	87	13710	2.0	4.0	2.8	26.3	64.9	473753
94588	PLEASANTON	49127	10966	4.5	9.4	31.4	28.0	26.8	106118	128325	99	96	8404	0.1	0.4	0.2	9.3	90.0	653212
94589	VALLEJO	20748	10087	16.1	25.6	39.1	14.8	4.4	60175	67231	85	68	7552	5.2	1.1	9.9	78.5	5.3	250906
94590	VALLEJO	19118	14357	30.7	30.1	29.0	8.4	1.8	39983	46360	46	31	6886	5.8	3.0	16.1	64.5	10.6	236565
94591	VALLEJO	27986	18101	11.5	20.9	38.5	20.3	8.8	69368	79694	91	77	13468	0.8	0.5	6.7	62.3	29.7	322544
94592	VALLEJO	17195	39	48.7	33.3	10.3	7.7	0.0	25523	28150	5	5	1	0.0	0.0	0.0	0.0	100.0	450000
94595	WALNUT CREEK	49828	9744	18.6	25.4	28.9	14.5	12.5	58044	70610	83	66	8569	0.1	1.5	17.6	31.3	49.5	393127
94596	WALNUT CREEK	51179	9085	10.2	17.7	35.3	18.5	18.3	77976	98406	94	84	4434	0.6	0.4	2.4	12.7	84.1	690867
94597	WALNUT CREEK	48207	10710	12.3	17.8	36.4	20.1	13.5	75598	93868	93	82	5504	0.7	0.0	3.8	29.5	66.0	495856
94598	WALNUT CREEK	52208	10294	7.3	14.0	28.8	22.3	27.6	99646	124101	98	94	8324	0.4	0.6	1.9	11.2	85.9	681707
94599	YOUNTVILLE	39557	1148	21.0	26.1	27.8	11.9	13.2	53901	65434	78	59	840	11.3	10.4	13.3	16.2	48.8	387342
94601	OAKLAND	13784	15002	32.4	30.8	26.4	8.0	2.4	37626	44696	38	26	5252	1.7	0.9	16.1	73.5	7.9	244735
94602	OAKLAND	35358	11782	18.1	21.2	31.5	16.1	13.1	64449	78609	88	72	6559	2.3	0.4	2.0	33.2	62.2	471422
94603	OAKLAND	14362	8836	33.3	29.9	27.1	7.6	2.2	38239	45155	40	27	4563	1.9	0.8	27.7	67.0	2.7	208122
94605	OAKLAND	26108	14870	23.3	22.5	31.4	13.9	9.0	54843	65698	79	60	9230	1.1	0.6	6.2	52.7	39.5	346431
94606	OAKLAND	18905	15244	31.9	31.7	24.9	7.8	3.7	37839	45669	39	26	3513	7.5	1.7	8.9	62.0	19.9	270021
94607	OAKLAND	16152	8087	50.5	23.5	19.0	4.8	2.2	24508	30405	4	4	1840	5.1	2.8	18.4	60.4	13.4	254808
94608	EMERYVILLE	24807	11193	32.7	28.1	25.0	9.9	4.3	39288	49159	44	29	3692	1.3	0.7	13.2	67.2	17.6	269397
94609	OAKLAND	27860	9729	30.6	25.2	27.4	11.6	5.3	43388	55140	57	39	2750	1.6	0.5	4.3	40.8	52.7	412821
94610	OAKLAND	48210	15375	16.2	25.0	32.3	13.4	13.1	59682	73849	84	67	5658	0.8	0.5	6.6	22.7	69.4	595970
94611	OAKLAND	63370	16351	13.1	16.8	26.9	17.3	25.9	84044	106570	96	89	9576	0.4	0.4	2.6	8.8	87.9	759810
94612	OAKLAND	21518	7574	51.2	28.2	14.4	4.6	1.6	23997	30022	4	3	531	4.3	0.9	12.1	57.3	25.4	306115
94613	OAKLAND	30481	48	4.2	56.3	35.4	4.2	0.0	39572	55000	45	30	12	0.0	0.0	0.0	33.3	66.7	466667
94618	OAKLAND	65553	7394	9.9	13.3	28.7	19.5	28.6	95661	122900	98	93	4717	0.1	0.2	0.4	7.2	92.2	836072
94619	OAKLAND	30461	9025	17.2	22.4	32.3	17.1	11.0	62878	76808	87	70	5564	1.9	0.6	3.3	48.1	46.2	384972
94621	OAKLAND	12289	8743	38.5	32.3	22.7	4.4	2.1	33140	39097	21	16	3834	1.6	1.9	26.0	66.2	4.3	211984
94702	BERKELEY	28627	6914	26.8	24.9	30.0	12.5	5.8	48016	61253	68	48	3179	0.6	0.3	3.6	43.8	51.8	407376
94703	BERKELEY	30872	8890	24.7	23.4	29.8	13.5	8.6	51887	66332	75	56	3239	0.5	0.0	2.3	27.3	69.9	478216
94704	BERKELEY	22167	9218	53.0	20.6	16.5	5.7	4.2	22272	29170	3	3	1030	0.0	1.6	3.2	18.3	77.0	625000
94705	BERKELEY	65119	5495	16.5	15.3	25.0	15.3	27.8	83617	109794	96	88	2915	0.1	0.0	0.5	7.9	91.4	902465
94706	ALBANY	37134	7029	13.8	20.3	36.2	18.9	10.8	69214	85866	91	77	3872	1.1	0.3	1.6	29.2	67.8	481346
94707	BERKELEY	74179	4942	5.9	10.8	24.0	21.8	37.5	119725	148555	99	98	4265	0.2	0.7	0.4	3.9	94.8	779634
94708	BERKELEY	69299	4838	7.1	9.8	23.5	22.7	36.8	118093	145479	99	97	4079	0.0	0.1	0.3	4.5	95.1	802385
94709	BERKELEY	37848	5185	29.4	20.1	27.4	13.6	9.5	50675	67141	73	54	1390	1.2	0.0	1.1	16.8	80.9	641198
	CALIFORNIA	27293		21.8	24.4	30.5	13.7	9.7	54267	64547				3.3	2.7	13.3	42.9	37.9	319678
	UNITED STATES	25866		24.7	27.1	30.8	10.9	6.5	48124	56710				10.9	15.0	33.7	30.1	10.4	145905

Copyright © 2004 ESRI BIS. All rights reserved. Reproduction by any method is prohibited.

ZIP CODE		FINANCIAL SERVICES				THE HOME						ENTERTAINMENT						PERSONAL			
						Home Improvements		Furnishings													
#	POST OFFICE NAME	Auto Loan	Home Loan	Invest-ments	Retire-ment Plans	Home Repair	Lawn & Garden	Comput-ers & Hard-ware	Major Appli-ances	TV, Radio, Sound Equip-ment	Furni-ture	Dine out/ Carry out	Sports Equip-ment	Fees & Tickets	Toys & Games	Travel	Cable TV	Apparel & Services	Auto Repairs	Health Insur-ance	Pets & Supplies
94507	ALAMO	307	415	559	406	404	433	361	358	336	369	425	403	409	450	384	339	432	344	330	388
94508	ANGWIN	134	162	200	163	159	163	155	151	147	154	185	177	162	192	157	143	184	151	137	164
94509	ANTIOCH	94	102	110	104	100	102	101	99	97	101	122	116	103	124	100	94	120	99	91	108
94510	BENICIA	125	146	164	148	143	147	136	135	129	137	162	156	143	166	138	125	161	133	124	148
94512	BIRDS LANDING	93	114	125	111	111	114	105	104	100	104	126	120	112	134	108	99	126	101	97	113
94513	BRENTWOOD	129	141	136	143	135	134	130	131	122	135	155	149	132	152	127	116	153	128	115	142
94514	BYRON	188	227	240	233	221	223	203	200	187	205	237	231	219	246	205	181	237	193	180	222
94515	CALISTOGA	110	122	134	117	121	132	115	118	115	118	144	129	120	143	119	116	141	116	119	128
94517	CLAYTON	178	224	250	227	218	221	198	195	182	201	231	224	217	242	203	178	233	188	175	214
94518	CONCORD	119	143	173	139	138	146	133	132	128	135	162	150	141	169	136	128	162	130	122	143
94519	CONCORD	97	114	131	112	111	115	108	106	104	108	131	123	114	138	110	102	131	105	99	116
94520	CONCORD	75	76	102	77	74	80	82	78	84	83	106	91	83	109	81	83	105	82	75	86
94521	CONCORD	123	144	167	145	140	144	136	133	129	137	163	154	143	169	137	125	162	132	120	145
94523	PLEASANT HILL	129	143	177	147	139	146	142	137	137	143	173	162	147	175	142	133	171	139	126	150
94525	CROCKETT	90	99	114	99	98	103	100	97	98	98	123	114	102	126	100	96	120	98	93	106
94526	DANVILLE	218	286	368	278	278	295	254	252	239	258	301	285	280	318	267	240	304	244	233	273
94528	DIABLO	312	420	576	412	410	442	366	363	341	375	431	408	416	454	390	344	438	348	337	394
94530	EL CERRITO	110	138	192	138	134	140	132	127	126	132	159	149	141	170	136	125	160	127	115	137
94531	ANTIOCH	160	181	174	189	172	166	163	162	149	170	190	189	168	190	159	139	188	157	137	177
94533	FAIRFIELD	83	87	93	87	85	88	87	86	85	87	107	100	88	108	86	83	105	86	80	94
94534	FAIRFIELD	147	171	177	175	166	166	156	154	145	159	183	179	163	186	156	139	181	150	138	169
94535	TRAVIS AFB	76	48	46	55	44	52	72	62	73	67	91	83	62	82	59	67	87	73	57	71
94536	FREMONT	122	147	188	149	144	147	142	140	134	143	169	165	147	175	145	129	170	141	123	149
94538	FREMONT	120	132	171	132	127	134	133	128	130	135	166	150	135	170	133	128	165	132	118	140
94539	FREMONT	202	255	316	267	252	249	240	234	215	237	273	282	250	280	244	204	274	234	200	251
94541	HAYWARD	88	94	109	94	92	96	94	92	92	95	117	107	96	119	93	90	116	94	86	100
94542	HAYWARD	136	151	183	154	147	153	150	145	143	151	182	171	153	184	149	139	180	147	132	158
94544	HAYWARD	93	94	109	96	92	95	98	96	96	100	122	113	96	120	95	92	121	100	87	105
94545	HAYWARD	96	106	134	111	105	106	109	107	103	109	130	129	108	129	108	97	129	111	93	114
94546	CASTRO VALLEY	112	133	165	132	129	135	128	124	122	128	154	144	134	161	129	121	154	124	114	135
94547	HERCULES	131	154	180	163	152	146	148	146	134	149	170	178	149	169	147	123	169	148	122	156
94548	KNIGHTSEN	105	116	137	111	111	117	112	111	112	116	143	124	115	148	113	112	143	112	104	120
94549	LAFAYETTE	214	287	389	281	278	294	255	250	240	259	302	285	284	325	269	241	307	243	228	270
94550	LIVERMORE	138	167	187	168	162	164	153	150	143	154	181	174	162	188	155	139	180	147	136	164
94551	LIVERMORE	141	160	166	164	154	153	148	146	138	152	175	170	153	178	146	132	174	144	128	160
94552	CASTRO VALLEY	186	224	237	232	216	215	200	196	183	204	233	227	215	239	201	175	233	190	172	216
94553	MARTINEZ	114	133	151	134	129	131	126	123	119	126	150	144	131	155	126	115	149	122	111	134
94555	FREMONT	142	169	233	189	175	166	177	174	155	170	196	223	171	190	178	139	194	183	141	181
94556	MORAGA	199	273	361	263	265	279	240	238	226	243	284	270	267	307	255	227	288	230	216	255
94558	NAPA	124	136	151	134	135	143	130	132	127	132	160	149	134	159	132	126	157	130	128	145
94559	NAPA	91	95	106	96	94	99	98	96	97	97	121	112	98	122	97	94	119	97	92	105
94560	NEWARK	116	135	168	132	131	138	130	129	126	132	160	147	134	165	132	124	160	130	118	138
94561	OAKLEY	119	129	122	132	125	124	118	119	112	122	141	139	120	141	116	106	138	117	107	133
94563	ORINDA	277	369	494	360	359	384	326	323	306	331	385	366	364	407	345	307	390	312	299	349
94564	PINOLE	108	130	156	125	126	132	122	120	118	123	149	137	128	157	125	117	149	120	112	130
94565	PITTSBURG	92	92	97	93	90	94	94	93	93	96	117	107	93	115	91	90	115	94	86	102
94566	PLEASANTON	184	224	265	226	217	225	206	201	193	208	245	233	221	253	210	189	245	198	183	220
94567	POPE VALLEY	176	159	134	154	170	185	151	168	157	150	191	197	145	190	156	161	181	165	182	211
94568	DUBLIN	125	135	145	140	131	132	132	128	124	133	158	152	134	158	129	118	156	129	114	142
94569	PORT COSTA	110	129	142	122	127	139	122	122	121	120	151	136	129	157	127	124	148	119	124	133
94571	RIO VISTA	94	91	89	90	94	103	91	95	93	91	115	106	91	111	93	94	110	94	99	107
94572	RODEO	97	110	122	110	108	111	108	105	104	106	130	124	111	135	108	101	129	105	99	115
94574	SAINT HELENA	148	173	207	172	171	181	165	164	160	165	200	189	173	206	170	159	198	163	156	179
94576	DEER PARK	130	152	182	155	150	155	146	143	139	146	175	168	152	179	149	136	173	143	132	156
94577	SAN LEANDRO	93	105	127	104	102	107	103	101	101	104	127	117	106	130	104	99	126	103	94	110
94578	SAN LEANDRO	85	87	107	89	84	90	91	88	90	92	114	103	91	114	90	88	113	91	82	96
94579	SAN LEANDRO	99	116	144	115	115	120	113	112	108	113	136	130	116	139	116	106	136	113	104	120
94580	SAN LORENZO	95	108	125	104	104	110	104	102	102	105	129	116	108	134	105	102	129	102	97	111
94583	SAN RAMON	182	216	247	222	209	214	200	194	186	202	236	226	214	242	201	180	236	191	174	214
94585	SUISUN CITY	108	117	115	120	113	112	110	109	103	113	131	128	111	131	108	98	129	108	97	120
94586	SUNOL	215	273	312	273	267	270	242	240	223	243	282	277	262	299	249	219	283	231	216	264
94587	UNION CITY	121	137	181	149	140	135	144	142	130	141	164	178	138	160	144	119	164	149	118	149
94588	PLEASANTON	184	210	232	218	203	206	197	192	184	201	234	226	207	237	196	176	233	191	170	212
94589	VALLEJO	90	97	113	98	96	100	98	97	94	97	118	114	97	118	98	91	117	99	90	105
94590	VALLEJO	67	67	76	68	66	71	72	69	71	70	89	82	71	89	70	70	87	71	67	76
94591	VALLEJO	110	123	143	128	122	122	122	120	115	122	145	143	123	146	122	109	143	121	107	129
94592	VALLEJO	50	40	52	45	39	44	55	48	54	52	68	62	50	64	49	50	66	55	45	54
94595	WALNUT CREEK	120	125	141	118	129	148	117	128	120	123	150	129	121	136	125	125	143	124	139	138
94596	WALNUT CREEK	143	160	229	166	153	164	162	153	158	164	200	182	170	208	163	156	199	157	140	168
94597	WALNUT CREEK	122	137	199	144	133	141	140	133	137	141	173	158	147	181	141	135	172	135	122	145
94598	WALNUT CREEK	162	208	269	205	203	213	190	187	179	191	226	216	206	239	198	178	227	184	171	202
94599	YOUNTVILLE	130	136	155	132	139	156	130	138	131	135	164	145	134	153	136	135	158	136	145	150
94601	OAKLAND	69	64	71	62	62	66	69	68	71	72	90	77	67	89	66	69	90	71	64	73
94602	OAKLAND	109	131	177	131	128	133	128	124	124	128	156	147	134	165	131	122	156	126	113	134
94603	OAKLAND	74	67	70	64	65	71	71	72	75	75	94	80	69	90	69	74	93	74	71	79
94605	OAKLAND	96	102	122	98	99	109	101	100	103	103	130	112	106	132	103	105	128	100	99	111
94606	OAKLAND	64	67	110	72	66	70	76	71	76	75	96	88	76	99	76	74	96	76	65	77
94607	OAKLAND	51	50	66	51	50	54	55	54	56	55	70	64	55	68	55	56	69	57	52	59
94608	EMERYVILLE	75	70	95	71	67	77	78	74	82	79	103	85	79	102	76	83	101	77	75	84
94609	OAKLAND	82	74	106	80	72	81	88	81	90	87	113	98	88	112	85	88	111	87	79	91
94610	OAKLAND	116	123	206	135	118	128	134	122	133	135	168	149	140	176	134	131	168	128	112	135
94611	OAKLAND	167	199	297	203	192	207	196	186	190	198	240	217	211	255	201	190	241	187	171	202
94612	OAKLAND	47	41	56	45	41	46	52	48	53	50	66	59	50	63	50	51	64	52	47	53
94613	OAKLAND	76	65	83	72	64	70	84	75	82	79	103	95	78	98	77	76	100	83	69	83
94618	OAKLAND	170	205	310	210	196	210	201	190	196	204	248	223	218	267	206	196	250	192	173	206
94619	OAKLAND	101	124	166	121	120	126	119	115	115	119	145	134	125	155	122	115	146	116	106	124
94621	OAKLAND	63	56	56	53	54	58	60	61	63	63	79	68	58	75	57	62	79	63	59	66
94702	BERKELEY	82	86	109	88	84	91	90	86	90	90	113	101	92	113	90	89	111	89	83	95
94703	BERKELEY	92	86	121	93	84	92	102	93	101	100	128	115	100	126	97	97	125	100	87	103
94704	BERKELEY	63	41	55	46	40	48	74	55	72	63	90	76	62	82	60	64	85	67	51	63
94705	BERKELEY	182	191	319	208	182	202	207	189	207	210	262	228	219	274	207	205	261	198	176	210
94706	ALBANY	106	121	176	126	116	123	123	116	120	124	152	138	129	160	124	118	151	118	106	126
94707	BERKELEY	204	297	402	280	286	302	254	252	238	258	299	284	287	331	273	242	306	242	227	268
94708	BERKELEY	183	261	354	247	251	263	228	224	215	230	270	255	254	300	243	218	276	217	202	238
94709	BERKELEY	95	83	145	95	79	90	109	92	110	106	139	117	107	140	102	105	136	102	86	103
	CALIFORNIA	107	111	131	112	109	115	113	111	111	114	140	129	114	141	112	109	139	113	104	122
	UNITED STATES	100	100	100	100	100	100	100	100	100	100	100	100	100	100	100	100	100	100	100	100

ZIP CODE		COUNTY FIPS CODE	POPULATION			2000-2004 ANNUAL RATE		HOUSEHOLDS					FAMILIES		
#	POST OFFICE NAME		2000	2004	2009	% Rate	State Centile	2000	2004	2009	% Annual Rate 2000-2004	2004 Average HH Size	2000	2004	% Annual Rate 2000-2004
94710	BERKELEY	001	8290	8240	8303	-0.1	10	3294	3250	3241	-0.3	2.50	1892	1850	-0.5
94720	BERKELEY	001	1000	1047	1077	1.1	58	112	127	137	3.0	2.76	7	8	3.2
94801	RICHMOND	013	28627	29745	31527	0.9	51	8644	8805	9199	0.4	3.34	5989	6067	0.3
94803	EL SOBRANTE	013	24927	26312	28140	1.3	64	9033	9479	10051	1.1	2.75	6490	6766	1.0
94804	RICHMOND	013	39659	41588	44316	1.1	59	14546	15120	15959	0.9	2.73	9273	9560	0.7
94805	RICHMOND	013	13640	14161	15008	0.9	50	5226	5354	5607	0.6	2.64	3455	3518	0.4
94806	SAN PABLO	013	56336	60727	65639	1.8	75	17830	18920	20195	1.4	3.14	12608	13342	1.3
94901	SAN RAFAEL	041	40132	41164	41877	0.6	36	15501	15672	15814	0.3	2.57	8945	9033	0.2
94903	SAN RAFAEL	041	28615	29562	30278	0.8	44	11687	12150	12471	0.9	2.31	7219	7407	0.6
94904	GREENBRAE	041	12311	12718	12958	0.8	44	5570	5757	5855	0.8	2.17	3252	3338	0.6
94920	BELVEDERE TIBURON	041	12118	12344	12522	0.4	29	5325	5375	5417	0.2	2.28	3377	3404	0.2
94922	BODEGA	097	168	172	176	0.6	34	58	60	61	0.8	2.83	38	39	0.6
94923	BODEGA BAY	097	1753	1764	1798	0.2	18	821	831	848	0.3	2.11	507	511	0.2
94924	BOLINAS	041	1519	1482	1469	-0.6	4	593	576	569	-0.7	2.30	318	308	-0.8
94925	CORTE MADERA	041	9349	9500	9560	0.4	26	3867	3903	3907	0.2	2.43	2499	2533	0.3
94928	ROHNERT PARK	097	41449	41898	43106	0.3	22	15005	15110	15496	0.2	2.68	9507	9528	0.1
94929	DILLON BEACH	041	322	336	342	1.0	55	157	163	166	0.9	2.06	99	102	0.7
94930	FAIRFAX	041	8553	8518	8563	-0.1	11	3782	3757	3767	-0.2	2.26	2142	2125	-0.2
94931	COTATI	097	8547	8936	9317	1.1	56	3405	3564	3711	1.1	2.49	2149	2242	1.0
94933	FOREST KNOLLS	041	913	917	913	0.1	17	381	380	376	-0.1	2.41	240	239	-0.1
94937	INVERNESS	041	1554	1518	1510	-0.6	4	637	624	620	-0.5	2.18	341	334	-0.5
94938	LAGUNITAS	041	378	384	385	0.4	26	160	161	161	0.2	2.32	103	104	0.2
94939	LARKSPUR	041	6930	7097	7218	0.6	34	3428	3519	3578	0.6	2.01	1734	1777	0.6
94940	MARSHALL	041	122	121	121	-0.2	9	58	58	57	0.0	2.00	38	38	0.0
94941	MILL VALLEY	041	29540	29667	29793	0.1	17	13052	13093	13122	0.1	2.23	7450	7458	0.0
94945	NOVATO	041	16508	16624	16714	0.2	19	6369	6403	6420	0.1	2.58	4476	4496	0.1
94946	NICASIO	041	1061	1046	1041	-0.3	7	334	329	327	-0.4	2.92	218	214	-0.4
94947	NOVATO	041	24637	24632	24702	0.0	15	9288	9283	9292	0.0	2.57	6388	6347	-0.2
94949	NOVATO	041	13402	13333	13305	-0.1	11	5525	5486	5458	-0.2	2.40	3532	3498	-0.2
94951	PENNGROVE	097	3981	4266	4495	1.6	72	1550	1665	1752	1.7	2.55	1032	1101	1.5
94952	PETALUMA	041	31955	32753	33861	0.6	35	12218	12597	13039	0.7	2.53	8057	8264	0.6
94954	PETALUMA	097	35465	38490	40795	1.9	78	12334	13331	14068	1.9	2.86	9199	9900	1.7
94956	POINT REYES STATION	041	1136	1121	1120	-0.3	7	508	499	497	-0.4	2.15	297	291	-0.5
94960	SAN ANSELMO	041	16362	16125	16083	-0.3	7	6613	6493	6457	-0.4	2.43	4287	4208	-0.4
94963	SAN GERONIMO	041	752	755	755	0.1	17	291	290	288	-0.1	2.46	191	190	-0.1
94964	SAN QUENTIN	041	6437	6432	6435	0.0	12	93	92	94	-0.3	2.39	58	56	-0.8
94965	SAUSALITO	041	10854	10630	10557	-0.4	6	5880	5765	5711	-0.5	1.83	2497	2443	-0.5
94970	STINSON BEACH	041	753	718	708	-1.1	2	367	350	344	-1.1	2.02	177	168	-1.2
94971	TOMALES	041	287	277	274	-0.8	3	107	103	102	-0.9	2.54	70	67	-1.0
94972	VALLEY FORD	097	128	126	128	-0.4	6	47	46	47	-0.5	2.67	33	33	0.0
94973	WOODACRE	041	1635	1596	1582	-0.6	4	644	623	615	-0.8	2.45	447	433	-0.8
95002	ALVISO	085	2068	1980	1982	-1.0	2	489	467	466	-1.1	4.14	388	370	-1.1
95003	APTOS	087	25075	25154	25337	0.1	17	10425	10466	10513	0.1	2.39	6688	6693	0.0
95004	AROMAS	053	4083	4288	4518	1.2	60	1311	1376	1439	1.2	3.12	1057	1106	1.1
95005	BEN LOMOND	087	7216	7336	7435	0.4	27	2707	2747	2766	0.4	2.65	1846	1865	0.2
95006	BOULDER CREEK	087	9505	9545	9659	0.1	17	3803	3820	3853	0.1	2.48	2414	2417	0.0
95008	CAMPBELL	085	44962	46720	48478	0.9	51	18563	19387	20120	1.0	2.39	10952	11334	0.8
95010	CAPITOLA	087	9398	9335	9324	-0.2	10	4478	4440	4419	-0.2	2.07	2150	2115	-0.4
95012	CASTROVILLE	053	9168	9996	10775	2.1	80	2228	2447	2636	2.2	4.08	1889	2052	2.0
95013	COYOTE	085	239	240	242	0.1	17	64	65	66	0.4	3.11	50	51	0.5
95014	CUPERTINO	085	54328	56447	58366	0.9	51	19576	20343	20974	0.9	2.76	14799	15348	0.9
95017	DAVENPORT	087	444	491	516	2.4	84	146	162	171	2.5	2.85	99	110	2.5
95018	FELTON	087	10013	9989	10008	-0.1	11	3413	3407	3407	0.0	2.54	2219	2206	-0.1
95019	FREEDOM	087	6523	7049	7329	1.8	76	1688	1794	1844	1.4	3.91	1240	1313	1.5
95020	GILROY	085	49712	52776	55223	1.4	67	14212	15095	15751	1.4	3.43	11494	12201	1.4
95023	HOLLISTER	069	47247	52197	57072	2.4	84	13855	15133	16345	2.1	3.42	11392	12413	2.0
95030	LOS GATOS	085	12620	12333	12444	-0.5	5	5202	5084	5120	-0.5	2.39	3314	3251	-0.5
95032	LOS GATOS	085	24654	24207	24430	-0.4	6	9866	9669	9726	-0.5	2.45	6466	6340	-0.5
95033	LOS GATOS	087	9231	9073	9078	-0.4	6	3531	3474	3467	-0.4	2.59	2430	2383	-0.5
95035	MILPITAS	085	62955	65381	67516	0.9	50	17222	17832	18335	0.8	3.49	14075	14549	0.8
95037	MORGAN HILL	085	41268	43558	45238	1.3	64	13265	13952	14421	1.2	3.08	10606	11149	1.2
95039	MOSS LANDING	053	1615	1662	1720	0.7	40	483	498	513	0.7	3.32	365	373	0.5
95043	PAICINES	069	762	777	812	0.5	29	289	293	303	0.3	2.47	202	203	0.1
95045	SAN JUAN BAUTISTA	069	3827	3830	4004	0.0	15	1262	1253	1298	-0.2	3.03	934	924	-0.3
95046	SAN MARTIN	085	5979	6082	6175	0.4	27	1720	1750	1772	0.4	3.43	1415	1438	0.4
95050	SANTA CLARA	085	35672	36117	36926	0.3	23	13973	14117	14394	0.2	2.43	7877	7948	0.2
95051	SANTA CLARA	085	51985	53395	55131	0.6	38	19871	20368	20948	0.6	2.61	13201	13498	0.5
95053	SANTA CLARA	085	776	759	759	-0.5	5	0	0	0	0.0	0.00	0	0	0.0
95054	SANTA CLARA	085	13013	14895	16166	3.2	92	4274	4960	5406	3.6	2.93	2792	3215	3.4
95060	SANTA CRUZ	087	44425	45311	45958	0.5	30	17233	17599	17807	0.5	2.49	9033	9160	0.3
95062	SANTA CRUZ	087	35982	36284	36532	0.2	20	14660	14751	14796	0.2	2.40	7704	7727	0.1
95064	SANTA CRUZ	087	4179	4155	4148	-0.1	10	420	411	408	-0.5	2.47	257	250	-0.7
95065	SANTA CRUZ	087	7948	7855	7861	-0.3	8	3065	3010	2994	-0.4	2.58	2006	1960	-0.5
95066	SCOTTS VALLEY	087	15013	15511	15741	0.6	37	5693	5827	5887	0.6	2.58	3988	4081	0.5
95070	SARATOGA	085	31721	31875	32579	0.1	18	11082	11134	11350	0.1	2.84	9069	9083	0.0
95073	SOQUEL	087	9400	9256	9257	-0.4	6	3698	3642	3633	-0.4	2.53	2369	2316	-0.5
95076	WATSONVILLE	087	78597	81467	83418	0.9	48	20890	21397	21703	0.6	3.76	16401	16764	0.5
95110	SAN JOSE	085	18253	18851	19363	0.8	43	4655	4797	4918	0.7	3.53	2983	3059	0.6
95111	SAN JOSE	085	57670	60632	63023	1.2	61	14073	14486	14850	0.7	4.18	11631	11972	0.7
95112	SAN JOSE	085	51800	53544	55212	0.8	45	16617	17148	17645	0.7	2.93	9295	9565	0.7
95113	SAN JOSE	085	430	429	439	-0.1	11	266	258	261	-0.7	1.59	64	62	-0.7
95116	SAN JOSE	085	54212	54204	54820	0.0	15	12744	12601	12641	-0.3	4.26	10217	10094	-0.3
95117	SAN JOSE	085	30847	31681	32511	0.6	38	11728	11967	12205	0.5	2.63	7113	7223	0.4
95118	SAN JOSE	085	33366	33813	34705	0.3	23	11860	12032	12314	0.3	2.80	8559	8685	0.3
95119	SAN JOSE	085	10169	9953	10026	-0.5	5	3174	3116	3135	-0.4	3.19	2588	2539	-0.5
95120	SAN JOSE	085	36964	37413	38237	0.3	23	12274	12442	12692	0.3	3.00	10532	10668	0.3
95121	SAN JOSE	085	37049	38501	39758	0.9	51	8911	9246	9517	0.9	4.14	7747	8018	0.7
95122	SAN JOSE	085	60275	61787	63324	0.6	35	12072	12269	12478	0.4	5.02	10557	10717	0.4
95123	SAN JOSE	085	58847	58503	59309	-0.1	10	20099	19993	20210	-0.1	2.92	15030	14922	-0.2
95124	SAN JOSE	085	44946	45016	45690	0.0	16	16149	16208	16424	0.1	2.75	11835	11865	0.1
95125	SAN JOSE	085	46427	48785	51087	1.2	61	19069	19900	20697	1.0	2.43	11868	12393	1.0
95126	SAN JOSE	085	27771	28621	29532	0.7	41	11185	11538	11888	0.7	2.43	5838	5974	0.5
95127	SAN JOSE	085	58165	60514	62937	0.9	52	14760	15282	15804	0.8	3.92	12275	12671	0.8
95128	SAN JOSE	085	31429	32109	32876	0.5	32	11947	12112	12324	0.3	2.58	7295	7371	0.2
95129	SAN JOSE	085	36521	37380	38283	0.6	34	13303	13599	13871	0.5	2.72	9660	9830	0.4
	CALIFORNIA					1.4					1.2	2.90			1.2
	UNITED STATES					1.2					1.3	2.58			1.1

ZIP CODE #	POST OFFICE NAME	RACE (%) White 2000	White 2004	Black 2000	Black 2004	Asian/Pacific 2000	Asian/Pacific 2004	% Hispanic Origin 2000	% Hispanic Origin 2004	2004 AGE DISTRIBUTION (%) 0-4	5-9	10-14	15-19	20-24	25-44	45-64	65-84	85+	18+	MEDIAN AGE 2004	% 2004 Males	% 2004 Females
94710	BERKELEY	37.2	34.6	25.4	25.1	16.0	16.5	22.7	25.4	7.9	6.3	5.6	6.3	8.4	38.1	20.3	6.2	0.9	76.5	32.2	49.0	51.0
94720	BERKELEY	50.6	46.4	2.3	2.3	36.6	39.3	9.0	10.2	0.1	0.1	0.2	41.2	40.2	15.7	2.5	0.1	0.0	99.0	21.1	61.8	38.2
94801	RICHMOND	30.7	30.4	33.6	32.0	6.1	6.1	45.1	47.8	10.1	9.4	9.5	8.1	8.4	29.5	17.9	6.3	0.9	66.2	27.8	49.9	50.1
94803	EL SOBRANTE	53.2	49.7	15.1	15.5	18.9	20.0	12.9	15.0	5.7	6.0	6.9	6.7	6.0	26.6	29.1	11.4	1.6	77.1	40.2	48.2	51.8
94804	RICHMOND	26.7	25.7	44.3	43.1	11.7	12.3	22.5	24.6	7.8	7.6	8.1	7.1	7.0	30.2	21.9	8.9	1.4	72.2	33.4	47.5	52.5
94805	RICHMOND	48.0	45.0	18.9	19.0	15.6	16.4	20.6	23.1	6.4	6.5	6.6	6.0	6.0	28.7	27.8	10.2	1.9	76.9	38.8	47.9	52.2
94806	SAN PABLO	33.7	31.6	23.2	22.6	16.4	16.8	35.2	38.1	7.9	7.4	8.3	8.0	8.1	30.6	20.1	8.4	1.2	71.6	31.7	49.3	50.7
94901	SAN RAFAEL	72.8	70.2	2.3	2.3	5.3	5.6	29.2	32.3	6.3	6.0	5.7	5.1	6.9	33.2	25.9	9.4	1.6	79.3	37.2	50.8	49.2
94903	SAN RAFAEL	84.6	82.2	2.0	2.1	6.5	7.3	7.8	9.4	4.4	5.2	6.0	5.5	4.5	23.8	29.6	16.5	4.4	80.6	45.3	47.6	52.4
94904	GREENBRAE	92.9	91.6	0.6	0.6	3.4	3.9	2.9	3.6	4.6	5.8	6.3	5.7	3.3	19.9	32.5	18.1	4.1	79.4	47.7	46.0	54.0
94920	BELVEDERE TIBURON	91.7	90.1	0.8	0.9	4.2	5.0	3.5	4.3	5.2	6.4	6.4	5.4	3.1	19.7	34.3	17.3	2.3	78.3	47.2	47.3	52.7
94922	BODEGA	89.9	88.4	0.6	0.6	1.8	1.7	10.1	12.8	2.3	3.5	3.5	2.9	2.9	18.6	39.5	25.6	1.2	88.4	55.0	51.7	48.3
94923	BODEGA BAY	88.0	86.2	0.4	0.4	1.4	1.6	12.5	14.7	3.3	3.7	4.1	3.1	3.2	20.7	38.7	21.7	1.5	86.9	52.5	51.6	48.4
94924	BOLINAS	91.3	89.7	1.8	1.9	2.0	2.4	6.3	7.7	2.6	3.9	5.8	8.4	5.8	23.6	40.4	8.6	0.9	81.2	45.0	53.3	46.7
94925	CORTE MADERA	87.4	85.4	0.9	1.0	6.3	7.1	5.0	6.0	6.5	7.0	6.7	5.2	4.0	26.6	30.7	11.8	1.5	76.4	42.0	47.0	53.0
94928	ROHNERT PARK	80.6	78.1	2.0	2.0	5.9	6.5	13.2	15.4	6.2	6.0	6.8	8.9	10.5	31.4	21.9	7.0	1.2	76.8	32.0	48.4	51.6
94929	DILLON BEACH	92.9	91.7	0.3	0.3	2.8	3.3	5.3	6.6	2.7	3.6	4.8	4.5	2.7	17.9	42.9	19.6	1.5	85.7	52.5	50.3	49.7
94930	FAIRFAX	91.5	90.0	1.1	1.2	2.3	2.6	5.4	6.6	4.7	5.1	5.5	5.7	4.9	26.8	36.4	9.6	1.2	80.9	43.6	47.8	52.2
94931	COTATI	82.6	80.3	2.0	2.1	3.9	4.3	13.7	15.9	6.3	6.2	7.3	6.9	7.2	33.5	24.8	7.0	0.9	76.0	34.9	49.1	50.9
94933	FOREST KNOLLS	88.9	87.2	1.2	1.3	1.5	1.7	5.5	6.7	5.9	6.3	6.7	7.1	5.9	24.4	38.7	4.7	0.3	76.6	41.9	49.7	50.3
94937	INVERNESS	85.7	84.1	0.6	0.7	1.3	1.5	16.7	18.8	4.5	4.7	5.6	4.7	4.4	21.0	37.5	15.2	2.6	82.2	48.3	48.0	52.0
94938	LAGUNITAS	88.4	86.2	1.6	1.8	1.3	1.6	5.8	6.8	3.7	4.2	7.0	8.3	6.3	23.2	39.8	7.0	0.5	78.9	43.7	47.7	52.3
94939	LARKSPUR	92.3	90.7	0.6	0.7	3.3	3.8	4.3	5.4	5.0	5.4	5.1	5.1	4.1	25.1	35.4	13.1	1.7	81.3	45.1	46.7	53.4
94940	MARSHALL	83.6	81.8	0.0	0.0	0.0	0.0	25.4	30.6	6.6	6.6	5.8	5.8	5.0	28.1	30.6	9.9	1.7	77.7	39.7	56.2	43.8
94941	MILL VALLEY	89.7	88.2	1.1	1.2	5.4	6.1	3.8	4.7	5.2	6.0	6.2	5.3	3.5	26.1	34.7	11.2	1.9	79.1	43.8	47.3	52.7
94945	NOVATO	84.7	82.3	1.8	1.9	5.3	5.9	10.9	13.1	5.3	5.8	7.0	6.7	5.7	24.7	32.3	11.1	1.3	77.5	41.9	49.2	50.8
94946	NICASIO	81.6	78.9	0.8	0.8	2.1	2.3	18.6	21.5	5.5	6.5	7.2	5.9	4.4	25.2	36.0	8.3	1.1	77.2	42.3	52.0	48.0
94947	NOVATO	83.6	80.8	1.8	1.9	5.3	5.9	11.7	14.1	5.6	5.9	6.6	6.6	5.8	25.8	29.7	11.6	2.4	77.5	41.3	47.8	52.2
94949	NOVATO	83.4	80.9	1.8	2.0	4.7	5.2	14.4	17.3	6.0	6.0	6.0	5.3	5.1	29.1	27.2	13.6	1.7	78.5	40.7	48.8	51.2
94951	PENNGROVE	90.1	88.6	0.5	0.5	3.4	3.8	7.1	8.5	4.7	5.1	6.1	5.6	5.6	26.8	32.0	12.8	1.4	80.5	42.7	48.9	51.2
94952	PETALUMA	87.7	85.8	0.8	0.8	1.8	2.0	12.6	14.7	5.7	6.0	6.7	6.8	6.8	27.3	29.1	10.0	1.7	77.4	39.4	49.8	50.3
94954	PETALUMA	82.2	80.0	1.3	1.3	5.2	5.8	15.7	18.0	6.8	7.4	8.1	7.0	5.8	28.4	25.9	9.0	1.6	73.3	37.4	48.9	51.1
94956	POINT REYES STATION	89.6	88.1	0.6	0.6	1.0	1.1	12.0	14.2	3.9	4.3	4.9	6.5	6.2	20.6	37.7	13.7	2.1	82.4	47.2	46.6	53.4
94960	SAN ANSELMO	92.3	91.0	0.9	0.9	2.8	3.2	3.7	4.6	5.4	6.3	6.9	6.3	4.3	23.8	34.6	10.7	1.8	76.8	43.5	47.5	52.5
94963	SAN GERONIMO	88.4	86.6	1.3	1.3	1.6	1.7	6.7	8.1	3.3	3.8	6.6	7.7	6.1	23.2	40.8	7.6	0.9	80.7	44.6	48.2	51.8
94964	SAN QUENTIN	51.2	50.2	39.3	39.4	2.1	2.2	20.7	23.5	0.2	0.2	0.3	1.7	13.9	64.7	17.9	1.0	0.3	99.3	36.2	97.5	2.5
94965	SAUSALITO	78.8	77.1	11.2	11.5	5.0	5.6	4.5	5.5	3.9	3.3	3.1	3.5	4.7	32.7	35.7	11.9	1.2	87.5	44.4	48.2	51.9
94970	STINSON BEACH	95.4	94.3	0.7	0.7	0.8	1.0	3.5	4.2	3.8	4.2	5.7	5.0	3.8	21.6	39.6	14.8	1.7	82.9	48.4	49.3	50.7
94971	TOMALES	89.6	87.7	0.4	0.4	1.1	1.1	11.5	13.4	3.6	4.3	5.8	6.1	6.9	22.0	37.9	11.9	1.4	82.0	45.7	49.5	50.5
94972	VALLEY FORD	86.7	85.7	1.6	1.6	2.3	2.4	8.6	10.3	3.2	4.8	7.1	6.4	4.8	22.2	39.7	10.3	1.6	80.2	45.9	50.8	49.2
94973	WOODACRE	92.6	91.4	0.6	0.6	1.3	1.4	6.1	7.5	3.8	4.5	6.8	6.8	5.7	21.2	41.5	8.3	1.3	80.7	45.6	47.9	52.1
95002	ALVISO	41.7	39.2	0.6	0.6	3.7	3.6	75.3	78.9	8.7	8.5	9.7	7.7	9.2	31.1	18.3	6.4	0.4	68.8	28.6	52.3	47.7
95003	APTOS	89.8	87.9	0.6	0.6	2.6	3.0	8.2	10.2	4.7	5.2	5.9	6.0	5.2	25.5	33.2	12.5	1.8	80.5	43.5	48.4	51.6
95004	AROMAS	77.5	73.5	0.3	0.4	2.7	2.9	24.4	29.2	5.1	6.0	7.9	7.7	5.5	26.2	31.7	9.0	0.8	76.2	40.1	50.7	49.3
95005	BEN LOMOND	91.2	89.4	0.6	0.6	1.6	1.8	5.9	7.4	4.9	5.4	6.5	7.5	6.8	28.5	33.4	6.2	0.8	78.6	39.8	50.7	49.3
95006	BOULDER CREEK	90.4	88.6	0.7	0.7	1.7	1.9	6.1	7.8	5.1	5.4	6.7	7.1	6.6	28.3	34.6	5.6	0.7	78.4	40.4	51.1	49.0
95008	CAMPBELL	73.1	69.7	2.5	2.6	14.4	15.9	12.8	15.3	6.3	6.0	6.1	5.7	6.5	35.9	23.6	8.6	1.3	78.1	36.5	49.9	50.1
95010	CAPITOLA	85.0	82.3	1.1	1.1	3.6	4.1	11.9	14.8	4.5	4.2	5.1	5.9	8.4	29.7	27.7	12.0	2.5	82.7	39.8	47.6	52.4
95012	CASTROVILLE	46.0	45.0	1.1	1.1	3.9	4.0	70.3	71.6	9.1	8.5	9.4	9.1	8.6	28.7	19.1	6.9	0.7	67.5	28.5	51.0	49.0
95013	COYOTE	70.3	68.3	0.8	0.8	13.0	13.8	29.7	33.8	4.6	6.3	9.2	21.3	4.6	23.3	23.8	6.3	0.8	62.1	31.0	60.0	40.0
95014	CUPERTINO	50.2	46.2	0.8	0.8	44.2	47.6	4.3	4.9	6.0	7.1	8.3	6.8	4.5	29.7	26.7	9.6	1.3	74.2	39.0	50.2	49.8
95017	DAVENPORT	84.2	81.3	1.6	1.6	2.3	2.7	14.2	17.5	4.7	5.1	5.5	6.9	8.2	27.1	33.8	7.7	1.0	81.1	40.7	53.2	46.8
95018	FELTON	87.4	84.9	0.8	0.8	4.0	4.6	6.5	8.3	5.0	4.8	5.9	10.7	11.8	27.2	28.2	5.8	0.9	80.5	35.1	50.2	49.8
95019	FREEDOM	41.4	38.2	0.7	0.6	3.3	3.2	74.1	78.4	9.3	8.5	8.9	8.7	8.9	29.3	16.6	8.2	1.6	67.9	28.5	50.5	49.5
95020	GILROY	60.3	57.3	1.7	1.7	4.6	4.9	51.1	54.9	9.0	8.8	8.8	7.5	7.2	30.8	20.8	6.4	0.9	68.9	31.2	49.9	50.1
95023	HOLLISTER	64.2	61.5	1.1	1.1	2.6	2.7	49.4	53.6	9.4	8.9	8.8	7.6	7.3	30.4	20.1	6.8	0.9	68.3	30.9	50.5	49.5
95030	LOS GATOS	88.1	86.0	0.3	0.4	7.7	9.0	3.8	4.7	4.8	5.7	6.8	6.2	4.3	25.2	32.8	12.9	2.2	78.5	43.4	48.5	51.5
95032	LOS GATOS	85.8	83.5	0.9	0.9	8.3	9.4	6.0	7.3	5.4	6.0	7.0	6.0	4.1	26.9	28.4	13.7	2.5	77.3	42.2	48.3	51.7
95033	LOS GATOS	92.1	90.6	0.4	0.4	2.2	2.5	5.2	6.6	5.5	6.5	6.8	6.0	3.8	27.2	35.6	8.0	0.7	77.1	42.3	51.9	48.1
95035	MILPITAS	31.1	28.4	3.7	3.5	52.2	53.7	16.6	18.3	7.1	6.8	6.6	6.4	7.3	35.5	22.6	7.2	0.6	75.8	34.5	52.5	47.5
95037	MORGAN HILL	72.2	68.8	1.6	1.6	6.7	7.2	27.2	31.2	7.6	8.1	8.4	7.3	5.9	28.8	25.8	7.3	0.9	71.2	35.6	50.0	50.0
95039	MOSS LANDING	53.0	50.0	1.3	1.3	4.2	4.3	59.8	63.4	8.2	7.6	8.2	8.8	8.9	29.6	20.2	7.8	0.7	70.7	30.1	52.4	47.7
95043	PAICINES	76.0	72.6	0.3	0.3	1.4	1.5	32.0	37.1	6.4	6.7	7.9	5.8	5.3	29.5	28.2	9.0	1.3	75.4	37.6	54.3	45.7
95045	SAN JUAN BAUTISTA	67.9	64.7	0.8	0.7	2.5	2.6	43.1	47.9	7.1	7.3	7.8	7.4	6.8	27.1	26.0	9.3	1.2	73.0	35.8	50.9	49.1
95046	SAN MARTIN	69.1	65.4	0.8	0.8	6.6	7.1	35.1	39.9	6.1	6.7	7.9	7.6	6.3	27.1	28.6	8.7	1.0	74.6	37.4	50.5	49.5
95050	SANTA CLARA	61.8	58.5	2.5	2.4	21.2	22.6	19.6	22.3	6.4	5.5	4.9	6.7	10.8	35.6	19.0	9.1	2.1	80.6	33.5	50.4	49.6
95051	SANTA CLARA	55.9	52.1	2.0	2.0	30.9	33.1	14.3	16.4	6.6	5.9	5.7	5.1	6.2	37.0	22.4	10.2	1.0	78.7	36.1	50.5	49.5
95053	SANTA CLARA	71.3	67.6	2.2	2.2	12.0	13.2	18.7	22.0	2.1	1.2	1.2	37.7	29.4	14.4	10.0	3.6	0.5	94.6	21.3	48.8	51.3
95054	SANTA CLARA	38.2	34.6	2.5	2.4	47.1	49.5	14.1	15.5	6.8	5.6	5.3	5.3	8.4	40.6	20.1	7.0	0.9	79.2	33.0	53.2	46.8
95060	SANTA CRUZ	80.2	77.2	1.6	1.7	3.9	4.3	17.5	20.9	5.1	4.6	4.9	5.8	10.5	34.5	25.4	7.9	1.4	82.4	34.9	50.8	49.2
95062	SANTA CRUZ	80.6	77.2	1.3	1.3	3.5	3.9	17.6	21.4	5.3	5.0	5.5	6.2	8.3	34.3	25.1	8.1	2.2	80.7	36.2	49.3	50.7
95064	SANTA CRUZ	63.5	59.0	2.6	2.6	16.9	18.3	16.0	19.2	2.5	2.0	1.2	49.0	31.5	11.2	2.4	0.2	0.0	93.6	19.5	45.5	54.5
95065	SANTA CRUZ	84.6	81.7	0.8	0.8	3.2	3.5	14.6	17.9	5.3	5.8	6.5	6.6	5.7	26.8	30.9	9.8	2.5	78.0	41.1	49.1	50.9
95066	SCOTTS VALLEY	89.4	87.3	0.5	0.6	4.3	4.9	5.9	7.5	6.1	6.6	7.8	6.7	5.4	25.7	28.7	10.2	2.9	75.5	40.6	49.0	51.0
95070	SARATOGA	67.3	63.6	0.5	0.5	28.8	31.9	3.5	4.2	5.2	6.7	8.3	7.1	3.9	20.1	31.8	15.1	1.9	75.1	44.3	49.1	50.9
95073	SOQUEL	86.9	84.3	1.0	1.1	3.1	3.5	11.1	14.0	4.9	5.4	6.9	7.1	6.4	26.2	31.9	9.7	1.5	78.5	41.0	48.1	51.9
95076	WATSONVILLE	52.4	49.4	0.7	0.7	3.5	3.4	63.3	67.7	8.6	8.1	9.1	8.5	8.5	28.9	19.8	7.4	1.2	69.1	29.9	50.9	49.1
95110	SAN JOSE	40.4	38.4	3.5	3.2	6.2	6.3	69.9	73.1	8.1	7.1	7.9	8.2	9.5	38.1	15.4	5.0	0.7	71.9	29.5	56.8	43.2
95111	SAN JOSE	31.8	30.0	4.1	3.7	30.6	30.7	46.7	49.6	8.9	8.2	8.7	7.6	8.3	33.0	18.9	5.8	0.5	69.6	30.1	50.9	49.1
95112	SAN JOSE	43.6	41.2	4.1	3.9	18.6	18.8	50.1	53.7	7.2	6.2	6.3	8.0	12.2	35.9	17.0	6.2	1.0	77.2	29.8	53.5	46.5
95113	SAN JOSE	46.1	43.1	4.2	4.2	32.3	33.3	25.1	27.7	3.0	2.1	2.3	2.3	5.4	33.8	11.0	34.5	5.6	91.4	46.5	45.0	55.0
95116	SAN JOSE	30.5	29.5	3.1	2.8	21.8	21.2	64.4	66.9	9.6	8.6	8.8	7.8	9.3	33.0	15.7	6.4	0.9	68.4	28.2	51.9	48.1
95117	SAN JOSE	56.8	53.0	4.7	4.7	20.8	22.3	24.3	27.4	7.5	6.5	6.3	5.8	7.8	39.1	18.4	7.4	1.3	76.4	32.8	51.5	48.5
95118	SAN JOSE	72.8	69.4	2.3	2.3	10.5	11.5	19.0	22.0	7.4	7.2	7.0	6.1	5.9	32.8	23.2	9.3	1.2	74.7	36.2	49.1	50.9
95119	SAN JOSE	66.6	63.0	3.4	3.4	15.2	16.6	19.9	23.1	7.4	7.6	7.6	7.0	6.3	31.4	25.2	6.8	0.6	73.0	35.3	51.1	48.9
95120	SAN JOSE	70.6	66.9	1.0	1.0	22.8	25.4	5.4	6.4	6.2	7.5	8.2	6.6	4.0	25.2	31.4	10.1	0.7	73.8	41.1	49.4	50.6
95121	SAN JOSE	27.6	26.2	4.8	4.5	45.8	45.7	29.5	31.9	7.7	7.4	7.9	7.1	7.7	32.4	22.4	6.8	0.7	72.6	32.7	50.5	49.5
95122	SAN JOSE	23.9	23.4	3.0	2.7	31.5	30.6	57.8	60.0	8.9	8.2	8.8	8.3	9.5	33.1	17.1	5.7	0.4	69.2	28.3	52.3	47.7
95123	SAN JOSE	65.3	61.7	4.0	4.1	15.3	16.6	20.4	23.6	7.4	7.2	7.3	6.5	6.6	33.6	23.6	6.9	1.0	74.3	34.9	49.5	50.5
95124	SAN JOSE	80.0	76.9	1.6	1.7	9.0	10.1	12.3	14.7	7.0	7.2	7.1	6.2	5.2	30.4	24.6	11.0	1.4	74.6	38.4	49.8	50.2
95125	SAN JOSE	74.1	70.2	2.5	2.6	8.0	9.2	22.5	25.9	7.1	6.7	5.9	5.1	5.7	32.2	24.1	10.9	2.5	77.4	38.3	48.4	51.6
95126	SAN JOSE	61.0	57.7	4.7	4.6	9.4	10.0	36.1	40.2	6.9	6.0	5.9	5.8	8.3	38.0	20.4	7.0	1.7	77.9	33.7	51.1	49.0
95127	SAN JOSE	43.0	41.2	3.5	3.2	18.6	18.5	52.8	56.0	8.1	7.7	8.2	7.4	7.9	31.5	20.4	7.9	0.9	71.7	31.7	51.0	49.0
95128	SAN JOSE	62.1	58.6	4.0	4.0	13.5	14.4	29.0	32.9	7.4	6.5	6.1	5.5	7.2	36.5	19.9	8.7	2.3	76.9	34.4	50.3	49.7
95129	SAN JOSE	49.8	46.0	1.4	1.4	42.1	44.9	6.7	7.7	6.3	6.5	7.0	6.4	5.7	31.2	24.7	10.8	1.4	76.1	38.2	50.0	50.0
	CALIFORNIA	59.6	57.1	6.7	6.5	11.3	11.8	32.4	35.5	7.4	7.1	7.8	7.3	7.7	29.8	22.1	9.3	1.4	73.3	33.8	49.8	50.2
	UNITED STATES	75.1	73.6	12.3	12.5	3.8	4.2	12.5	14.1	6.9	6.7	7.2	7.0	7.3	28.6	23.8	10.8	1.7	75.1	36.0	49.1	50.9

ZIP CODE				2004 HOUSEHOLD INCOME DISTRIBUTION (%)					MEDIAN HOUSEHOLD INCOME					2004 HOME VALUE DISTRIBUTION (%)					
#	POST OFFICE NAME	2004 Per Capita Income	2004 HH Income Base	Less than $25,000	$25,000 to $49,999	$50,000 to $99,999	$100,000 to $149,999	$150,000 or More	2004	2009	2004 National Centile	2004 State Centile	2004 Home Value Base	Less than $50,000	$50,000 to $89,999	$90,000 to $174,999	$175,000 to $399,999	$400,000 or More	2004 Median Home Value
94710	BERKELEY	21875	3250	29.9	26.9	29.9	9.9	3.3	41631	53777	52	35	1007	0.7	1.0	1.8	48.2	48.4	393452
94720	BERKELEY	15616	127	59.8	29.1	5.5	3.9	1.6	11027	15535	1	1	3	0.0	0.0	0.0	33.3	66.7	1000001
94801	RICHMOND	16337	8805	35.0	27.5	26.4	7.5	3.6	38819	45921	42	28	3525	4.3	7.0	26.8	42.6	19.4	212883
94803	EL SOBRANTE	31443	9479	13.6	22.5	34.2	19.4	10.3	68411	82412	91	76	6978	1.5	0.4	4.8	56.3	37.0	354898
94804	RICHMOND	23431	15120	25.4	26.3	33.0	10.6	4.8	48182	58173	69	48	7439	1.1	0.9	12.7	71.2	14.1	259144
94805	RICHMOND	26608	5354	15.7	27.4	35.6	15.1	6.2	57378	68658	82	64	3698	0.4	0.6	5.7	68.4	24.9	294935
94806	SAN PABLO	19400	18920	23.2	27.1	34.6	11.7	3.4	49755	58649	71	52	10440	5.7	1.7	12.7	73.6	6.3	243425
94901	SAN RAFAEL	46903	15672	16.1	19.9	27.7	15.1	21.3	71214	90835	92	79	8088	0.7	0.3	0.5	9.1	89.4	792686
94903	SAN RAFAEL	45948	12150	11.1	16.8	31.6	21.8	18.8	82176	105416	96	88	8353	0.2	1.4	2.5	15.2	80.6	613794
94904	GREENBRAE	88432	5757	9.7	14.3	25.9	16.1	34.0	100326	130042	98	94	3901	1.0	0.5	0.6	6.1	91.9	1000001
94920	BELVEDERE TIBURON	123325	5375	8.2	8.1	21.1	16.4	46.3	136032	185018	100	99	3597	0.0	0.3	0.5	2.2	97.1	1000001
94922	BODEGA	38842	60	8.3	13.3	43.3	15.0	20.0	72707	90674	92	80	47	0.0	0.0	0.0	2.1	97.9	703947
94923	BODEGA BAY	44308	831	14.4	16.9	39.2	14.7	14.8	65793	76767	89	73	621	0.8	0.8	2.3	9.2	87.0	664749
94924	BOLINAS	39379	576	17.4	20.5	33.5	10.9	17.7	63070	81748	87	70	371	1.6	0.8	2.4	13.2	81.9	692045
94925	CORTE MADERA	62271	3903	7.8	13.3	30.9	19.5	28.5	95619	125790	98	93	2799	0.6	0.3	1.2	4.4	93.5	854730
94928	ROHNERT PARK	26791	15110	16.5	25.1	37.1	15.6	5.8	59253	68021	84	67	9180	3.5	4.2	6.6	50.1	35.6	351309
94929	DILLON BEACH	39705	163	7.4	39.3	25.2	13.5	14.7	51977	61446	75	56	136	15.4	2.2	0.0	18.4	64.0	521277
94930	FAIRFAX	46375	3757	12.0	18.2	36.7	16.9	16.2	73506	92922	93	81	2463	0.5	0.2	0.5	11.5	87.3	626156
94931	COTATI	29099	3564	14.4	28.8	36.9	14.0	6.0	57267	65343	82	64	2321	3.4	2.6	7.6	53.3	33.1	346752
94933	FOREST KNOLLS	35154	380	17.6	20.3	27.4	20.3	14.5	65725	87353	89	73	245	0.0	0.0	0.0	25.3	74.7	505859
94937	INVERNESS	36647	624	19.1	26.1	25.3	17.6	11.9	59632	77167	84	67	372	1.6	0.8	0.0	12.6	85.0	709746
94938	LAGUNITAS	44028	161	19.3	16.2	28.0	20.5	16.2	75423	97109	93	82	106	0.9	2.8	0.0	7.6	88.7	695946
94939	LARKSPUR	77601	3519	10.8	13.8	30.0	16.9	28.5	89935	122233	97	91	2057	2.9	1.3	1.0	4.1	90.8	942780
94940	MARSHALL	47692	58	27.6	17.2	25.9	13.8	15.5	57193	66754	82	64	27	3.7	0.0	0.0	3.7	92.6	1000001
94941	MILL VALLEY	78965	13093	9.7	11.3	23.5	19.6	35.9	111889	147990	99	96	8823	0.1	0.1	0.3	3.4	96.1	1000001
94945	NOVATO	43208	6403	12.0	16.7	32.5	18.2	20.7	79635	102035	95	86	4581	1.8	0.6	0.7	13.3	83.7	592930
94946	NICASIO	57081	329	10.6	14.3	28.6	14.9	31.6	89603	124354	97	91	210	1.0	2.4	0.0	3.3	93.3	1000001
94947	NOVATO	40726	9283	10.2	17.7	35.6	20.5	16.0	77699	98292	94	84	6654	0.4	0.3	0.1	22.3	76.8	554074
94949	NOVATO	46067	5486	10.1	19.1	30.9	17.6	22.2	79709	101853	95	86	3798	0.5	5.0	7.5	12.4	74.7	596799
94951	PENNGROVE	34802	1665	12.4	26.1	33.0	15.9	12.6	64362	76337	88	72	1279	4.4	2.1	3.3	11.6	78.7	646256
94952	PETALUMA	35892	12597	14.6	21.0	34.1	17.6	12.7	66370	80279	89	74	7995	0.8	0.2	1.1	20.9	77.2	575646
94954	PETALUMA	31372	13331	11.4	17.7	36.7	22.7	11.5	76145	88801	94	83	10454	3.4	2.6	1.8	33.8	58.5	436608
94956	POINT REYES STATION	44717	499	14.6	23.7	29.1	16.0	16.6	62525	80802	87	70	319	0.3	0.3	2.5	10.7	86.2	738782
94960	SAN ANSELMO	57916	6493	9.9	15.7	28.0	19.6	26.9	92589	121279	97	92	4731	0.0	0.0	0.4	3.8	95.8	885309
94963	SAN GERONIMO	38790	290	17.2	17.6	30.7	20.7	13.8	73323	93573	93	80	202	1.0	2.0	1.0	7.4	88.6	673333
94964	SAN QUENTIN	19601	92	6.5	26.1	30.4	17.4	19.6	78824	100000	95	85	17	17.7	11.8	0.0	0.0	70.6	604167
94965	SAUSALITO	91615	5765	12.3	13.7	24.1	18.0	31.9	99752	135303	98	94	2526	3.3	0.9	1.4	10.0	84.5	820388
94970	STINSON BEACH	96029	350	12.9	10.6	22.6	21.1	32.9	106695	137840	99	96	222	0.0	0.0	1.4	5.0	93.7	1000001
94971	TOMALES	31300	103	20.4	23.3	31.1	9.7	15.5	59176	73024	84	67	61	9.8	0.0	8.2	18.0	63.9	494444
94972	VALLEY FORD	54516	46	8.7	10.9	34.8	23.9	21.7	93501	110875	98	92	37	0.0	0.0	0.0	10.8	89.2	721154
94973	WOODACRE	43628	623	13.0	19.3	31.8	20.1	15.9	74287	96315	93	81	467	0.0	0.0	1.1	10.3	88.7	629248
95002	ALVISO	18363	467	10.5	24.2	39.0	17.3	9.0	65105	75265	89	73	249	2.0	7.2	20.5	49.0	21.3	300694
95003	APTOS	44131	10466	11.4	16.9	32.6	21.1	18.1	81183	101049	95	87	7714	1.3	1.2	3.1	11.3	83.3	639625
95004	AROMAS	29390	1376	13.2	15.5	39.0	20.0	12.4	78620	90210	95	85	1168	0.9	0.9	0.6	16.9	80.7	575368
95005	BEN LOMOND	37604	2747	9.6	17.4	38.3	22.7	12.1	77526	95069	94	84	1991	0.3	0.3	2.1	27.2	70.2	492529
95006	BOULDER CREEK	45021	3820	13.3	18.4	28.6	22.2	17.7	80753	102136	95	87	2650	0.8	1.0	1.7	32.1	64.5	476954
95008	CAMPBELL	43015	19387	10.6	15.1	35.2	21.7	17.5	81524	102290	95	87	9966	0.4	1.1	2.2	13.0	83.3	607217
95010	CAPITOLA	34157	4440	19.5	26.5	31.7	16.0	6.2	53472	66032	78	58	2091	2.1	3.9	8.7	21.8	63.6	495455
95012	CASTROVILLE	15303	2447	20.2	33.1	32.2	9.6	4.9	47886	55037	68	48	1429	3.6	2.4	11.1	43.9	39.1	342463
95013	COYOTE	44556	65	12.3	16.9	23.1	27.7	20.0	93541	117630	98	92	41	7.3	4.9	0.0	9.8	78.1	875000
95014	CUPERTINO	56636	20343	7.9	8.8	24.0	25.3	34.1	115757	143576	99	97	13266	0.3	1.7	3.4	2.2	92.4	914331
95017	DAVENPORT	40869	162	10.5	14.8	28.4	24.7	21.6	92056	116593	97	92	106	0.9	0.9	5.7	10.4	82.1	681818
95018	FELTON	35195	3407	10.7	16.9	37.1	23.7	11.7	76574	93555	94	83	2518	0.4	1.0	1.8	31.4	65.4	462927
95019	FREEDOM	13064	1794	29.2	32.3	29.2	7.8	1.6	40351	46608	47	32	930	3.0	9.5	18.5	43.9	25.2	286434
95020	GILROY	27396	15095	12.2	19.7	34.4	21.2	12.7	74041	87372	93	81	10105	1.5	1.5	1.9	21.7	73.3	490659
95023	HOLLISTER	23770	15133	14.3	21.8	36.1	19.5	8.5	66605	77820	90	74	10951	1.3	1.8	1.5	28.6	66.9	465374
95030	LOS GATOS	92209	5084	6.2	10.2	19.2	18.2	46.2	138376	171211	100	99	3731	0.1	0.2	0.8	1.4	97.6	1000001
95032	LOS GATOS	67975	9669	7.6	11.0	24.5	21.1	35.8	113906	142926	99	96	6986	0.5	0.7	1.3	4.5	93.0	946824
95033	LOS GATOS	64512	3474	6.3	11.5	22.9	23.7	35.6	117787	142759	99	97	2868	1.1	0.4	0.7	9.1	88.6	822736
95035	MILPITAS	33509	17832	7.5	12.7	31.6	25.1	23.1	96308	114030	98	93	12377	1.9	3.0	1.8	18.8	74.6	499656
95037	MORGAN HILL	41035	13952	9.3	13.7	28.6	22.6	25.8	96465	115558	98	93	10750	1.6	2.2	3.3	13.2	79.8	637894
95039	MOSS LANDING	21329	498	17.9	30.3	34.1	11.7	6.0	51676	60285	75	56	277	7.9	8.3	10.5	36.5	36.8	344697
95043	PAICINES	25453	293	25.6	26.6	29.4	10.6	7.9	47553	56556	67	47	178	0.0	3.4	9.0	21.9	65.7	602941
95045	SAN JUAN BAUTISTA	24816	1253	20.0	24.3	33.2	14.2	8.3	57671	68149	82	65	822	3.8	1.7	0.9	23.2	70.4	514124
95046	SAN MARTIN	33594	1750	9.3	15.4	31.0	24.5	19.9	87027	107259	97	90	1382	0.4	1.1	1.5	9.6	87.6	775956
95050	SANTA CLARA	36844	14117	16.0	18.5	32.8	19.7	13.1	70787	89008	92	78	5657	0.5	0.2	0.6	15.7	83.1	550140
95051	SANTA CLARA	41376	20368	9.2	15.1	33.5	25.0	17.3	86415	107213	97	90	11158	1.0	1.2	1.2	17.8	78.8	548332
95053	SANTA CLARA	10093	0	0.0	0.0	0.0	0.0	0.0	0	0	0	0	0	0.0	0.0	0.0	0.0	0.0	0
95054	SANTA CLARA	40088	4960	6.9	11.8	29.3	27.3	24.8	102404	124713	98	95	2239	0.0	0.6	0.0	19.1	80.4	520087
95060	SANTA CRUZ	35199	17599	20.4	19.9	28.9	17.7	13.2	64232	80454	88	71	9171	0.8	0.9	1.4	13.8	83.1	633611
95062	SANTA CRUZ	31009	14751	19.8	25.8	31.8	14.5	8.1	54595	67926	79	60	7378	3.7	4.5	7.2	16.5	68.1	505899
95064	SANTA CRUZ	19563	411	37.0	19.7	27.5	10.0	5.8	39158	49512	43	29	107	20.6	0.0	16.8	39.3	23.4	217188
95065	SANTA CRUZ	38291	3010	16.1	19.6	31.5	19.7	13.1	67530	82186	90	75	1976	0.5	1.5	0.7	10.2	87.2	643194
95066	SCOTTS VALLEY	43597	5827	10.3	17.0	28.7	21.6	22.5	86021	106615	96	90	4326	0.7	1.2	4.7	17.7	75.7	617248
95070	SARATOGA	85061	11134	6.3	6.5	14.9	18.0	54.3	161044	193505	100	99	9869	0.1	0.4	1.0	1.3	97.2	1000001
95073	SOQUEL	41873	3642	15.8	20.2	29.4	17.4	17.2	69091	85533	91	77	2542	2.6	7.0	8.0	13.5	68.9	603519
95076	WATSONVILLE	18950	21397	21.1	27.8	32.1	12.0	7.0	51102	59789	74	55	12875	1.5	2.3	6.3	41.0	48.8	394037
95110	SAN JOSE	20219	4797	22.5	22.4	33.2	14.6	7.4	55499	67800	80	62	1620	0.7	0.5	2.2	46.3	50.3	401087
95111	SAN JOSE	19782	14486	13.9	21.9	36.8	17.6	9.9	65598	77576	89	73	9356	9.6	4.2	6.7	34.3	45.2	377147
95112	SAN JOSE	22876	17148	26.8	23.7	29.8	12.8	6.9	49351	61350	71	51	5857	4.8	4.8	4.5	31.6	54.3	417645
95113	SAN JOSE	26475	258	64.0	10.1	11.6	4.7	9.7	11466	15414	1	1	16	0.0	0.0	0.0	12.5	87.5	500000
95116	SAN JOSE	15793	12601	20.3	24.7	34.4	15.1	5.5	54874	64988	80	60	5479	6.2	1.6	3.0	53.2	36.0	355430
95117	SAN JOSE	32293	11967	14.1	19.9	36.6	19.0	10.5	68091	84176	90	76	4172	0.4	1.3	2.5	16.6	79.2	555970
95118	SAN JOSE	35387	12032	10.7	14.6	33.5	25.9	15.5	84826	104212	96	89	8095	0.6	0.7	0.4	15.0	83.3	553453
95119	SAN JOSE	33723	3116	7.8	10.3	31.6	31.5	18.8	100267	116245	98	94	2456	0.9	0.8	0.0	12.2	86.1	536187
95120	SAN JOSE	58253	12442	3.4	5.9	20.2	27.3	43.2	136050	161870	100	99	11344	0.2	0.8	1.1	2.8	95.2	877378
95121	SAN JOSE	28100	9246	7.4	13.3	36.2	24.5	18.6	87906	105501	97	91	6818	1.2	2.0	2.2	25.6	69.0	471287
95122	SAN JOSE	16273	12269	15.0	19.0	39.4	18.5	8.2	66898	78179	90	75	7031	0.9	2.4	4.8	47.2	44.8	383679
95123	SAN JOSE	35099	19993	7.4	14.7	36.0	26.1	15.8	86253	104686	96	90	14321	1.1	2.6	3.7	22.6	70.1	482934
95124	SAN JOSE	42794	16208	9.1	14.0	29.9	23.9	23.1	93814	115102	98	92	11950	0.1	0.8	0.2	10.5	88.4	614669
95125	SAN JOSE	46317	19900	13.1	16.5	30.5	19.0	20.9	80018	101427	95	86	12525	1.8	1.2	3.2	9.3	84.5	677972
95126	SAN JOSE	35019	11538	18.4	23.2	31.3	14.5	12.6	58916	73538	83	66	3922	0.4	0.1	0.5	21.4	77.6	576583
95127	SAN JOSE	25190	15282	12.1	18.7	34.9	19.1	15.3	74777	88453	93	81	10843	0.5	0.4	1.1	31.6	66.5	459065
95128	SAN JOSE	32232	12112	13.9	22.3	34.2	18.5	11.1	66009	82490	89	74	5239	0.7	1.2	2.4	16.2	79.5	547038
95129	SAN JOSE	42227	13599	8.8	13.5	30.1	23.8	23.8	94771	117032	98	93	8783	1.1	3.1	1.6	7.0	87.2	780707
	CALIFORNIA	27293		21.8	24.4	30.5	13.7	9.7	54267	64547				3.3	2.7	13.3	42.9	37.9	319678
	UNITED STATES	25866		24.7	27.1	30.8	10.9	6.5	48124	56710				10.9	15.0	33.7	30.1	10.4	145905

ZIP CODE		FINANCIAL SERVICES				THE HOME						ENTERTAINMENT						PERSONAL			
						Home Improvements		Furnishings													
#	POST OFFICE NAME	Auto Loan	Home Loan	Invest-ments	Retire-ment Plans	Home Repair	Lawn & Garden	Comput-ers & Hard-ware	Major Appli-ances	TV, Radio, Sound Equip-ment	Furni-ture	Dine out/ Carry out	Sports Equip-ment	Fees & Tickets	Toys & Games	Travel	Cable TV	Apparel & Services	Auto Repairs	Health Insur-ance	Pets & Supplies
94710	BERKELEY	71	69	95	73	67	73	79	73	79	78	100	88	78	100	76	77	98	78	69	81
94720	BERKELEY	36	22	28	25	22	26	43	32	42	36	52	44	35	47	34	37	49	39	29	36
94801	RICHMOND	76	71	78	69	69	73	76	75	78	79	98	86	74	96	73	76	98	78	72	81
94803	EL SOBRANTE	112	127	149	126	124	129	124	122	120	124	151	141	128	155	125	118	150	122	114	132
94804	RICHMOND	85	83	107	83	80	90	89	86	92	91	116	98	91	116	88	93	114	89	85	96
94805	RICHMOND	88	104	130	100	100	106	99	97	97	101	123	110	104	130	101	97	124	97	90	105
94806	SAN PABLO	82	83	97	82	80	86	86	84	86	88	109	96	86	110	84	85	109	86	79	91
94901	SAN RAFAEL	152	174	243	176	168	181	174	166	170	175	215	194	183	225	176	169	216	169	154	181
94903	SAN RAFAEL	137	160	212	161	157	167	156	152	151	157	190	176	165	198	160	151	189	152	143	165
94904	GREENBRAE	239	293	401	291	286	311	276	269	266	279	336	306	301	349	288	268	336	266	256	293
94920	BELVEDERE TIBURON	337	457	634	445	443	475	402	396	377	410	476	448	453	509	427	381	484	382	364	428
94922	BODEGA	168	157	150	149	166	196	145	165	153	156	191	162	147	159	158	164	179	160	193	189
94923	BODEGA BAY	147	130	116	122	140	162	122	140	131	127	160	146	119	142	131	140	150	137	164	170
94924	BOLINAS	123	141	174	146	139	142	139	135	132	138	167	161	143	171	140	128	165	136	122	147
94925	CORTE MADERA	183	241	311	237	233	242	217	212	204	219	257	245	238	277	226	203	260	208	191	229
94928	ROHNERT PARK	100	107	115	110	104	106	105	103	100	106	126	121	106	126	103	96	124	103	94	113
94929	DILLON BEACH	139	109	74	98	123	138	103	124	116	102	138	145	92	136	109	124	128	122	146	169
94930	FAIRFAX	133	154	191	159	152	156	152	147	144	151	182	175	157	187	153	140	180	148	134	160
94931	COTATI	100	104	115	108	101	104	105	102	101	106	128	122	105	126	103	96	125	104	92	113
94933	FOREST KNOLLS	108	124	153	128	122	125	123	119	117	122	147	142	126	151	123	113	145	120	108	130
94937	INVERNESS	120	123	128	118	126	141	114	123	116	120	146	128	118	133	121	121	140	120	132	138
94938	LAGUNITAS	132	152	187	157	149	153	150	145	143	149	180	173	154	184	151	138	178	147	132	158
94939	LARKSPUR	193	226	327	233	218	232	224	212	217	226	275	250	239	290	228	216	275	215	196	232
94940	MARSHALL	125	143	176	148	141	144	141	137	134	140	169	163	145	173	142	130	167	138	124	149
94941	MILL VALLEY	214	284	383	277	275	292	254	250	240	257	302	285	281	323	268	241	305	244	229	270
94945	NOVATO	137	177	219	173	171	176	161	158	151	162	190	182	173	204	166	149	192	155	141	170
94946	NICASIO	218	279	371	274	272	291	250	247	237	256	300	279	277	313	263	237	303	241	230	269
94947	NOVATO	134	162	198	162	159	165	153	151	145	153	183	175	161	190	157	143	182	149	138	163
94949	NOVATO	132	177	229	171	171	177	160	157	151	160	189	181	173	206	167	150	192	154	141	167
94951	PENNGROVE	115	136	148	134	134	140	126	126	121	126	152	143	134	158	130	121	151	123	120	137
94952	PETALUMA	120	137	157	139	134	138	133	129	126	132	159	153	137	164	133	123	157	129	118	141
94954	PETALUMA	122	141	148	143	137	139	129	129	122	132	154	148	136	157	130	118	153	126	117	141
94956	POINT REYES STATION	127	148	175	149	146	151	141	139	135	142	170	162	147	173	144	132	168	139	129	152
94960	SAN ANSELMO	171	226	297	221	220	230	205	201	193	206	242	232	223	259	214	192	245	197	182	216
94963	SAN GERONIMO	125	144	177	149	142	145	142	137	135	141	170	164	146	174	143	131	168	139	125	150
94964	SAN QUENTIN	61	58	109	67	55	61	69	61	70	70	89	75	72	94	67	70	89	65	57	68
94965	SAUSALITO	216	235	349	250	227	246	242	227	236	246	299	269	256	307	243	232	298	233	210	251
94970	STINSON BEACH	333	261	179	236	294	330	247	297	279	244	330	347	221	326	263	298	307	292	350	405
94971	TOMALES	111	117	133	118	118	124	115	116	113	114	140	138	115	143	116	111	137	116	112	133
94972	VALLEY FORD	192	239	254	239	235	231	213	213	198	212	248	249	227	265	218	192	248	205	190	235
94973	WOODACRE	133	170	217	167	165	170	158	154	149	158	188	180	168	200	163	147	188	153	139	166
95002	ALVISO	116	102	85	95	98	103	104	113	108	114	136	120	96	120	99	104	135	115	106	118
95003	APTOS	136	162	189	160	160	166	150	150	144	150	180	175	158	189	155	143	179	148	140	167
95004	AROMAS	119	148	157	148	145	143	132	131	122	131	154	154	140	164	135	119	153	127	118	145
95005	BEN LOMOND	134	158	164	159	154	152	145	144	135	145	170	170	150	177	145	129	169	141	128	159
95006	BOULDER CREEK	147	177	193	177	172	172	162	160	151	162	191	189	170	200	164	146	190	157	143	176
95008	CAMPBELL	130	150	204	152	144	152	148	142	144	150	181	167	156	190	149	141	181	144	129	154
95010	CAPITOLA	91	101	127	104	99	105	102	98	99	101	125	116	105	127	103	97	123	100	93	108
95012	CASTROVILLE	88	86	86	84	84	86	87	88	88	91	111	100	86	109	85	84	111	90	81	95
95013	COYOTE	195	248	286	247	243	247	220	219	204	221	257	254	239	273	228	201	258	211	198	241
95014	CUPERTINO	189	236	322	251	239	235	233	229	209	227	263	281	236	266	238	195	263	234	193	241
95017	DAVENPORT	133	203	272	186	193	202	172	170	161	173	202	192	193	230	185	164	207	163	151	179
95018	FELTON	125	147	164	150	144	145	139	136	130	138	164	161	144	170	139	125	162	135	122	150
95019	FREEDOM	76	67	60	64	65	68	70	74	73	76	92	80	66	85	67	70	92	76	69	78
95020	GILROY	130	141	147	140	136	138	135	135	130	139	165	155	137	165	133	125	164	134	122	146
95023	HOLLISTER	116	123	120	123	119	119	116	118	112	121	141	135	117	139	114	107	140	117	105	128
95030	LOS GATOS	271	339	501	343	328	356	317	305	303	324	384	351	352	405	331	305	388	302	283	333
95032	LOS GATOS	201	267	362	260	258	274	241	236	229	243	287	270	265	310	253	230	291	231	216	254
95033	LOS GATOS	221	275	298	282	267	268	243	238	222	246	282	276	265	294	248	215	284	229	212	263
95035	MILPITAS	139	167	236	188	174	163	177	174	154	169	194	224	170	189	178	137	193	183	139	180
95037	MORGAN HILL	168	201	224	203	194	198	182	179	171	186	217	205	195	225	185	167	218	175	162	197
95039	MOSS LANDING	98	96	102	94	94	97	99	99	100	103	127	112	98	127	96	96	127	101	91	106
95043	PAICINES	116	81	42	77	94	106	80	99	92	79	108	119	68	106	83	97	99	98	118	138
95045	SAN JUAN BAUTISTA	99	113	129	110	108	113	106	105	104	109	132	119	111	137	107	103	132	105	97	114
95046	SAN MARTIN	150	179	201	177	175	178	165	164	157	167	199	188	174	208	168	155	199	161	150	180
95050	SANTA CLARA	117	125	170	130	122	130	133	126	129	132	164	150	134	166	131	126	162	131	115	137
95051	SANTA CLARA	129	161	229	164	157	161	157	152	148	157	187	181	164	198	161	144	188	154	133	161
95053	SANTA CLARA	0	0	0	0	0	0	0	0	0	0	0	0	0	0	0	0	0	0	0	0
95054	SANTA CLARA	145	164	243	186	169	163	179	172	161	173	204	220	173	201	178	147	202	183	142	181
95060	SANTA CRUZ	115	124	156	128	121	127	130	123	125	127	157	147	131	160	127	120	155	127	112	134
95062	SANTA CRUZ	99	106	126	109	104	108	109	105	105	107	132	125	109	134	107	101	130	107	97	115
95064	SANTA CRUZ	77	47	59	53	46	56	91	66	88	76	110	92	74	98	72	77	103	81	62	76
95065	SANTA CRUZ	130	149	171	149	146	151	142	141	136	143	171	164	148	175	144	132	170	140	129	153
95066	SCOTTS VALLEY	151	183	203	186	178	179	165	163	153	167	194	189	177	201	168	149	194	159	146	179
95070	SARATOGA	292	396	539	385	385	413	345	342	323	353	407	385	390	433	368	325	414	329	316	370
95073	SOQUEL	135	163	188	163	161	165	153	150	144	152	181	175	161	189	156	141	180	148	138	164
95076	WATSONVILLE	100	98	102	95	96	100	99	101	100	104	127	112	98	124	97	97	126	103	94	108
95110	SAN JOSE	101	90	107	93	87	92	101	98	104	106	132	115	99	130	96	98	131	104	90	106
95111	SAN JOSE	109	116	139	118	114	116	119	117	114	120	145	138	118	145	117	109	145	121	104	125
95112	SAN JOSE	89	87	116	89	84	91	97	91	98	97	124	108	96	125	94	95	122	96	86	100
95113	SAN JOSE	54	49	75	52	48	56	60	55	63	59	79	65	60	79	59	64	77	60	58	61
95116	SAN JOSE	94	87	94	88	86	87	95	94	95	98	121	110	91	118	90	89	121	99	84	100
95117	SAN JOSE	109	115	161	117	110	119	121	114	121	123	154	134	123	158	120	120	153	119	107	125
95118	SAN JOSE	124	153	190	149	147	153	142	139	136	144	171	161	151	182	145	134	172	138	125	150
95119	SAN JOSE	122	178	236	164	169	177	153	151	145	155	181	171	170	204	163	147	186	146	135	160
95120	SAN JOSE	213	289	365	283	279	291	251	247	232	254	293	281	281	315	263	231	298	237	222	267
95121	SAN JOSE	146	168	217	182	171	165	173	170	157	170	198	211	170	195	173	144	197	177	142	179
95122	SAN JOSE	108	113	137	116	111	114	117	115	114	119	144	136	116	143	115	108	144	120	103	123
95123	SAN JOSE	129	158	194	154	153	159	147	144	140	149	176	166	155	186	150	138	177	143	131	156
95124	SAN JOSE	136	193	253	180	184	192	169	166	159	170	200	189	186	222	178	161	204	161	149	176
95125	SAN JOSE	140	170	219	168	165	173	162	158	155	163	196	183	171	206	166	154	196	158	145	170
95126	SAN JOSE	115	115	154	121	110	118	123	117	122	125	154	138	124	155	120	118	153	122	107	128
95127	SAN JOSE	126	145	175	140	139	146	139	138	137	143	174	156	144	181	141	135	175	139	127	148
95128	SAN JOSE	113	117	142	121	113	119	121	116	118	123	150	138	122	148	118	113	148	120	105	128
95129	SAN JOSE	137	173	237	183	175	170	172	169	154	167	194	210	172	197	176	144	194	174	141	177
	CALIFORNIA	107	111	131	112	109	115	113	111	111	114	140	129	114	141	112	109	139	113	104	122
	UNITED STATES	100	100	100	100	100	100	100	100	100	100	100	100	100	100	100	100	100	100	100	100

POPULATION CHANGE

ZIP CODE		COUNTY FIPS CODE	POPULATION			2000-2004 ANNUAL RATE		HOUSEHOLDS					FAMILIES		
#	POST OFFICE NAME		2000	2004	2009	% Rate	State Centile	2000	2004	2009	% Annual Rate 2000-2004	2004 Average HH Size	2000	2004	% Annual Rate 2000-2004
95130	SAN JOSE	085	12818	13104	13456	0.5	33	4659	4764	4876	0.5	2.74	3255	3319	0.5
95131	SAN JOSE	085	26568	28280	29621	1.5	69	8187	8763	9174	1.6	3.21	6208	6611	1.5
95132	SAN JOSE	085	40375	40311	40825	0.0	12	11510	11485	11594	-0.1	3.51	9591	9562	-0.1
95133	SAN JOSE	085	25927	25892	26241	0.0	12	6993	6961	7017	-0.1	3.69	5905	5870	-0.1
95134	SAN JOSE	085	9703	10871	11779	2.7	88	4089	4548	4887	2.5	2.27	2283	2534	2.5
95135	SAN JOSE	085	16730	18692	20061	2.6	88	6084	6700	7121	2.3	2.79	4668	5182	2.5
95136	SAN JOSE	085	36993	39725	41911	1.7	73	12751	13589	14223	1.5	2.92	9119	9669	1.4
95138	SAN JOSE	085	14874	16237	17242	2.1	80	4816	5305	5645	2.3	3.06	3885	4286	2.3
95139	SAN JOSE	085	6945	6727	6750	-0.8	3	2276	2210	2214	-0.7	3.04	1775	1722	-0.7
95140	MOUNT HAMILTON	085	304	326	348	1.7	73	112	120	128	1.6	2.65	89	96	1.8
95148	SAN JOSE	085	43134	45962	48215	1.5	69	10651	11274	11753	1.4	4.07	9516	10075	1.4
95202	STOCKTON	077	6649	6869	7470	0.8	44	2886	3024	3311	1.1	2.16	1211	1247	0.7
95203	STOCKTON	077	16689	17240	18819	0.8	44	5631	5777	6265	0.6	2.91	3654	3732	0.5
95204	STOCKTON	077	28822	30290	33239	1.2	61	11506	12036	13135	1.1	2.48	7293	7539	0.8
95205	STOCKTON	077	34221	36296	40068	1.4	66	9816	10300	11269	1.1	3.50	7437	7750	1.0
95206	STOCKTON	077	50038	58169	68042	3.6	94	12927	15116	17718	3.8	3.75	10698	12515	3.8
95207	STOCKTON	077	50078	52739	58531	1.2	63	18451	19388	21422	1.2	2.68	12163	12633	0.9
95209	STOCKTON	077	30692	34032	38688	2.5	85	9419	10468	11883	2.5	3.20	7782	8598	2.4
95210	STOCKTON	077	40590	44605	50402	2.2	83	11301	12282	13762	2.0	3.59	9127	9865	1.9
95211	STOCKTON	077	1719	1713	1715	-0.1	11	24	19	20	-5.4	1.37	4	3	-6.5
95212	STOCKTON	077	6868	9037	11221	6.7	99	2559	3325	4088	6.4	2.68	1933	2497	6.2
95215	STOCKTON	077	23479	24999	27482	1.5	69	6478	6885	7583	1.4	3.23	4982	5267	1.3
95219	STOCKTON	077	18721	22534	26665	4.5	96	7831	9230	10754	3.9	2.44	5005	5882	3.9
95220	ACAMPO	077	7542	8133	9107	1.8	75	2656	2847	3171	1.7	2.83	2128	2273	1.6
95222	ANGELS CAMP	009	4648	5247	5933	2.9	89	1848	2114	2414	3.2	2.43	1259	1429	3.0
95223	ARNOLD	009	5782	6012	6501	0.9	52	2546	2669	2906	1.1	2.25	1808	1884	1.0
95228	COPPEROPOLIS	009	2694	3261	3807	4.6	96	1081	1307	1527	4.6	2.46	810	974	4.4
95230	FARMINGTON	099	843	976	1136	3.5	94	294	337	389	3.3	2.89	234	268	3.2
95231	FRENCH CAMP	077	4997	5731	6565	3.3	92	860	1065	1297	5.2	3.20	647	796	5.0
95232	GLENCOE	009	317	324	346	0.5	33	136	140	152	0.7	2.31	91	93	0.5
95236	LINDEN	077	3364	3815	4342	3.0	90	1111	1262	1436	3.0	2.87	898	1014	2.9
95237	LOCKEFORD	077	3221	3461	3836	1.7	74	1113	1194	1317	1.7	2.87	870	927	1.5
95240	LODI	077	45660	48860	54048	1.6	72	15682	16677	18350	1.5	2.85	10889	11493	1.3
95242	LODI	077	23135	26148	29803	2.9	90	8945	10060	11398	2.8	2.58	6441	7198	2.7
95245	MOKELUMNE HILL	009	3195	3285	3530	0.7	39	1375	1427	1544	0.9	2.28	931	960	0.7
95246	MOUNTAIN RANCH	009	2023	2094	2256	0.8	47	864	902	980	1.0	2.27	591	613	0.9
95247	MURPHYS	009	3946	4140	4491	1.1	60	1748	1850	2023	1.3	2.19	1200	1262	1.2
95249	SAN ANDREAS	009	3545	3681	3968	0.9	50	1481	1546	1678	1.0	2.29	922	956	0.9
95251	VALLECITO	009	197	205	221	0.9	52	81	85	93	1.1	2.25	57	60	1.2
95252	VALLEY SPRINGS	009	11608	13382	15348	3.4	93	4207	4868	5608	3.5	2.75	3348	3862	3.4
95255	WEST POINT	009	1983	2045	2202	0.7	42	826	860	933	1.0	2.37	543	562	0.8
95257	WILSEYVILLE	009	449	459	491	0.5	33	204	210	226	0.7	2.19	133	136	0.5
95258	WOODBRIDGE	077	3764	4110	4597	2.1	80	1225	1337	1489	2.1	3.06	1015	1104	2.0
95301	ATWATER	047	26884	28887	31648	1.7	74	8357	8911	9690	1.5	3.20	6605	7031	1.5
95303	BALLICO	047	978	1129	1277	3.4	93	300	346	389	3.4	3.24	233	266	3.2
95304	TRACY	077	11651	13540	15487	3.6	94	2677	3276	3893	4.9	2.93	2040	2468	4.6
95306	CATHEYS VALLEY	043	1036	1057	1101	0.5	30	398	408	427	0.6	2.58	282	288	0.5
95307	CERES	099	33602	37177	41727	2.4	84	10440	11433	12672	2.2	3.24	8286	9057	2.1
95309	CHINESE CAMP	109	24	26	28	1.9	78	11	12	13	2.1	2.17	8	8	0.0
95310	COLUMBIA	109	1368	1539	1670	2.8	89	641	723	788	2.9	2.11	407	459	2.9
95311	COULTERVILLE	043	2007	2158	2313	1.7	74	850	917	985	1.8	2.34	595	637	1.6
95313	CROWS LANDING	099	1364	1518	1695	2.6	87	436	482	531	2.4	3.15	342	376	2.3
95315	DELHI	047	9965	11590	13155	3.6	94	2643	3049	3435	3.4	3.77	2262	2603	3.4
95316	DENAIR	099	5831	6025	6572	0.8	44	1886	1925	2072	0.5	3.12	1554	1582	0.4
95317	EL NIDO	047	793	827	886	1.0	55	245	255	273	1.0	3.23	197	204	0.8
95318	EL PORTAL	043	578	591	608	0.5	33	256	265	279	0.8	1.25	138	98	-7.7
95320	ESCALON	077	11539	13007	14799	2.9	89	3837	4310	4879	2.8	3.00	3030	3380	2.6
95321	GROVELAND	109	3965	3857	3931	-0.7	4	1776	1742	1788	-0.5	2.21	1253	1224	-0.6
95322	GUSTINE	047	8102	9120	10183	2.8	89	2792	3130	3473	2.7	2.91	2061	2299	2.6
95323	HICKMAN	099	921	1031	1153	2.7	88	305	337	372	2.4	3.05	237	261	2.3
95324	HILMAR	047	7191	7642	8291	1.4	68	2345	2488	2686	1.4	3.07	1925	2035	1.3
95326	HUGHSON	099	7318	8256	9268	2.9	89	2346	2616	2895	2.6	3.15	1905	2117	2.5
95327	JAMESTOWN	109	9573	10039	10427	1.1	59	2161	2358	2527	2.1	2.48	1485	1614	2.0
95329	LA GRANGE	109	1720	1863	1992	1.9	78	674	733	786	2.0	2.54	524	568	1.9
95330	LATHROP	077	11122	13061	15170	3.9	95	3148	3681	4250	3.8	3.55	2662	3106	3.7
95333	LE GRAND	047	4274	4484	4842	1.1	60	1103	1149	1233	1.0	3.87	972	1012	1.0
95334	LIVINGSTON	047	13363	15032	16807	2.8	89	3264	3646	4049	2.6	4.11	2842	3172	2.6
95335	LONG BARN	109	625	631	643	0.2	21	201	205	211	0.5	2.62	130	132	0.4
95336	MANTECA	077	36528	41945	48192	3.3	92	12103	13853	15841	3.2	2.99	9343	10623	3.1
95337	MANTECA	077	19928	23866	28153	4.3	96	6605	7804	9109	4.0	3.04	5027	5964	4.1
95338	MARIPOSA	043	9835	10314	10971	1.1	60	4038	4241	4523	1.2	2.39	2772	2906	1.1
95340	MERCED	047	62541	66753	73178	1.6	70	18877	20077	21905	1.5	3.25	14420	15330	1.5
95345	MIDPINES	043	737	753	789	0.5	32	308	316	334	0.6	2.10	195	199	0.5
95346	MI WUK VILLAGE	109	1157	1167	1194	0.2	20	497	505	521	0.4	2.17	343	347	0.3
95348	MERCED	047	23016	25675	28143	2.6	87	8058	8729	9537	1.9	2.84	5509	5918	1.7
95350	MODESTO	099	53248	55668	60503	1.1	56	19856	20526	22049	0.8	2.65	13475	13862	0.7
95351	MODESTO	099	47915	51688	57032	1.8	75	12541	13287	14424	1.4	3.87	10245	10825	1.3
95354	MODESTO	099	26594	28212	30865	1.4	67	9154	9585	10359	1.1	2.86	6317	6581	1.0
95355	MODESTO	099	41554	46472	52624	2.7	88	15032	16604	18548	2.4	2.76	10878	12003	2.3
95356	MODESTO	099	33047	35741	39714	1.9	77	12363	13142	14367	1.5	2.70	8670	9204	1.4
95357	MODESTO	099	13135	15380	17958	3.8	95	4149	4785	5501	3.4	3.20	3326	3847	3.5
95358	MODESTO	099	32564	36248	40760	2.6	87	9088	9869	10898	2.0	3.56	7470	8128	2.0
95360	NEWMAN	099	8329	9084	10020	2.1	80	2491	2682	2917	1.8	3.36	2014	2159	1.7
95361	OAKDALE	099	25412	29570	34289	3.6	94	9124	10506	12031	3.4	2.80	6843	7811	3.2
95363	PATTERSON	099	16756	18762	21019	2.7	88	4507	4980	5508	2.4	3.67	3728	4102	2.3
95364	PINECREST	109	2	2	2	0.0	15	1	1	1	0.0	2.00	1	1	0.0
95366	RIPON	077	12474	14287	16388	3.2	92	4144	4724	5389	3.1	2.99	3288	3730	3.0
95367	RIVERBANK	099	16911	18936	21302	2.7	88	4946	5462	6059	2.4	3.44	4133	4564	2.4
95368	SALIDA	099	10233	12609	14804	5.0	97	2977	3620	4190	4.7	3.46	2579	3123	4.6
95369	SNELLING	047	1209	1339	1480	2.4	85	419	464	512	2.4	2.87	304	334	2.2
95370	SONORA	109	25897	27195	28580	1.2	60	10934	11537	12196	1.3	2.32	7178	7562	1.2
95372	SOULSBYVILLE	109	1538	1573	1620	0.5	33	588	605	627	0.7	2.60	433	445	0.7
95374	STEVINSON	047	1689	1742	1856	0.7	42	519	535	568	0.7	3.23	405	416	0.7
95376	TRACY	077	47931	54859	63080	3.2	92	15096	17131	19549	3.0	3.18	12049	13640	3.0
95377	TRACY	077	9809	14250	18296	9.2	100	2795	4021	5117	8.9	3.54	2468	3531	8.8
	CALIFORNIA					1.4					1.2	2.90			1.2
	UNITED STATES					1.2					1.3	2.58			1.1

ZIP CODE #	POST OFFICE NAME	RACE (%) White 2000	White 2004	Black 2000	Black 2004	Asian/Pacific 2000	Asian/Pacific 2004	% Hispanic Origin 2000	% Hispanic Origin 2004	2004 AGE DISTRIBUTION (%) 0-4	5-9	10-14	15-19	20-24	25-44	45-64	65-84	85+	18+	MEDIAN AGE 2004	% 2004 Males	% 2004 Females
95130	SAN JOSE	66.3	62.4	2.9	3.0	18.6	20.4	13.6	16.0	7.5	7.1	7.0	6.3	6.5	33.2	23.1	8.4	1.1	74.7	36.2	50.0	50.0
95131	SAN JOSE	22.4	20.2	3.5	3.4	64.0	65.4	12.2	13.3	8.2	7.1	6.1	5.3	6.1	39.7	20.9	6.3	0.5	75.4	34.1	50.7	49.4
95132	SAN JOSE	33.6	30.8	3.5	3.3	51.8	53.6	14.8	16.3	6.7	6.5	7.0	6.6	6.4	31.8	25.7	8.6	0.6	75.7	36.4	50.3	49.8
95133	SAN JOSE	25.5	24.0	3.3	3.1	55.2	55.8	24.7	26.2	7.5	7.0	7.1	6.9	7.9	32.7	22.7	7.6	0.7	74.2	33.5	50.9	49.1
95134	SAN JOSE	53.3	51.1	5.5	5.1	28.5	29.3	15.9	18.5	7.3	5.1	4.5	4.3	6.1	47.2	21.0	4.2	0.3	80.5	33.9	52.3	47.7
95135	SAN JOSE	51.7	47.5	2.5	2.4	37.3	40.6	11.5	12.9	7.8	7.5	6.1	4.6	3.4	27.3	22.7	18.6	2.1	75.6	41.2	48.4	51.6
95136	SAN JOSE	56.8	52.1	4.7	4.7	23.3	25.4	18.1	21.1	7.4	6.9	6.4	5.8	6.7	36.8	22.9	6.5	0.6	75.8	33.9	49.6	50.4
95138	SAN JOSE	48.7	45.1	4.3	4.1	32.4	34.4	17.8	20.0	9.5	8.8	7.1	5.3	5.6	37.4	21.9	4.1	0.3	71.4	33.4	49.6	50.4
95139	SAN JOSE	68.8	65.2	3.6	3.6	15.1	16.5	16.9	19.9	7.6	8.0	7.7	6.2	5.2	32.0	26.5	6.1	0.5	72.7	36.1	50.1	50.0
95140	MOUNT HAMILTON	65.5	60.7	2.3	2.5	19.1	21.5	16.8	20.3	5.2	6.1	8.0	5.2	3.7	26.7	33.1	11.0	0.9	76.7	42.2	50.9	49.1
95148	SAN JOSE	28.0	26.0	5.2	4.8	50.2	51.5	24.0	25.7	7.1	7.0	8.0	7.7	7.7	30.8	24.3	7.0	0.6	73.4	33.9	50.7	49.3
95202	STOCKTON	39.1	36.4	15.2	14.6	11.5	12.2	45.2	48.7	9.4	7.1	6.6	7.0	8.3	26.9	20.1	12.7	2.0	73.3	33.2	53.0	47.0
95203	STOCKTON	46.2	43.3	9.1	8.9	12.6	12.6	43.8	48.0	9.5	8.0	8.3	7.8	8.9	28.2	19.7	8.3	1.4	69.6	30.0	51.0	49.0
95204	STOCKTON	64.5	60.4	4.2	4.2	10.2	11.2	27.9	32.0	7.5	7.1	7.3	6.6	6.8	26.4	22.4	13.1	2.9	74.2	36.6	47.2	52.8
95205	STOCKTON	38.1	35.8	8.6	7.9	8.2	8.1	58.2	62.0	10.3	9.4	9.8	8.6	8.7	27.3	17.1	7.8	1.1	65.1	27.0	50.6	49.4
95206	STOCKTON	27.6	27.2	15.8	15.1	18.9	19.0	50.4	51.3	10.0	9.6	10.1	8.7	8.0	29.2	17.1	6.5	0.8	64.8	27.4	50.9	49.2
95207	STOCKTON	52.4	48.8	10.1	10.0	19.2	20.5	23.8	26.7	8.4	7.4	8.1	8.0	9.2	25.7	20.2	11.3	1.8	71.4	31.0	47.6	52.4
95209	STOCKTON	56.1	52.5	8.9	8.8	19.7	21.1	17.7	20.5	7.4	7.6	8.9	8.7	7.3	25.4	25.1	8.0	1.7	70.7	33.8	48.1	51.9
95210	STOCKTON	32.3	29.5	12.2	11.8	36.6	37.8	24.5	27.1	9.0	8.8	10.5	9.8	8.7	25.7	19.1	7.5	0.9	65.6	27.3	48.5	51.6
95211	STOCKTON	61.4	55.9	2.7	2.8	12.5	13.7	8.8	10.3	0.0	0.0	0.1	45.1	50.9	3.2	0.4	0.4	0.0	99.7	20.5	41.9	58.1
95212	STOCKTON	77.1	73.5	1.6	1.6	8.9	9.9	16.5	19.7	5.7	6.3	6.9	6.7	5.5	22.4	28.9	15.8	1.9	76.8	42.6	49.0	51.0
95215	STOCKTON	58.6	54.6	4.4	4.1	4.2	4.4	41.0	46.3	7.0	7.0	8.0	11.7	9.7	25.8	20.4	9.3	1.2	72.1	30.3	53.1	47.0
95219	STOCKTON	66.6	62.5	7.4	7.4	13.1	15.6	15.0	17.0	6.8	6.8	7.5	6.9	7.0	27.3	26.9	9.7	1.1	74.6	36.8	48.2	51.8
95220	ACAMPO	85.6	82.9	0.6	0.7	2.9	3.3	17.3	20.8	6.1	6.7	7.4	6.5	5.0	23.8	28.5	14.5	1.5	75.5	41.7	50.8	49.2
95222	ANGELS CAMP	92.6	91.6	0.6	0.6	0.6	0.7	7.1	8.3	4.8	5.1	6.7	6.4	5.4	22.4	30.3	16.3	2.5	79.3	44.5	48.9	51.1
95223	ARNOLD	95.0	94.2	0.2	0.2	0.6	0.7	3.7	4.3	3.3	4.3	5.9	5.0	3.4	16.8	39.2	21.0	1.2	83.3	51.7	50.8	49.2
95228	COPPEROPOLIS	89.2	87.8	1.2	1.2	2.2	2.4	8.3	9.5	5.0	5.6	6.5	5.8	4.3	20.8	33.4	17.6	1.0	79.4	46.3	49.9	50.1
95230	FARMINGTON	83.0	79.4	0.7	0.7	1.2	1.3	20.5	25.3	5.3	6.3	8.5	7.2	5.3	24.1	29.8	12.1	1.4	75.6	40.7	50.9	49.1
95231	FRENCH CAMP	45.5	40.9	11.6	11.5	6.6	6.8	42.5	47.6	6.1	6.5	7.7	11.0	9.4	35.6	16.8	6.3	0.7	73.2	30.1	61.3	38.7
95232	GLENCOE	92.4	91.4	0.0	0.0	1.3	1.5	7.3	8.6	3.4	3.4	7.7	7.4	3.1	20.1	36.1	17.9	0.9	80.9	47.5	49.4	50.6
95236	LINDEN	77.6	73.9	0.5	0.6	1.3	1.4	27.4	32.3	6.6	7.0	8.1	7.7	6.3	25.4	26.7	10.9	1.4	73.7	37.8	51.3	48.7
95237	LOCKEFORD	77.1	73.2	0.3	0.3	1.6	1.7	25.2	30.0	6.2	6.4	7.3	7.9	7.1	25.6	25.5	12.7	1.4	75.3	38.1	51.2	48.8
95240	LODI	70.1	66.4	0.6	0.7	4.9	5.4	33.6	37.7	8.5	7.5	7.7	7.3	8.4	27.1	20.2	10.9	2.5	72.0	32.7	49.8	50.2
95242	LODI	81.6	78.5	0.6	0.6	4.8	5.7	15.6	18.3	6.1	6.3	7.1	7.0	6.0	25.2	26.4	13.8	2.1	76.2	40.1	48.6	51.4
95245	MOKELUMNE HILL	92.8	91.8	0.6	0.6	0.8	0.9	4.8	5.6	3.8	4.6	6.0	6.5	4.3	18.2	37.3	17.5	1.7	81.1	48.7	50.4	49.6
95246	MOUNTAIN RANCH	92.0	90.9	1.0	1.1	1.0	1.1	5.4	6.2	3.1	3.7	5.4	6.1	4.4	16.6	37.3	21.2	2.3	83.4	50.8	50.2	49.8
95247	MURPHYS	93.0	92.0	1.0	1.0	0.7	0.8	4.7	5.6	3.5	4.3	6.4	6.4	4.2	19.3	34.2	19.4	2.4	81.5	48.4	49.5	50.5
95249	SAN ANDREAS	91.8	90.6	0.3	0.3	0.7	0.7	6.1	7.1	5.0	5.1	6.4	7.7	6.0	18.9	28.7	18.3	4.1	78.3	45.7	47.8	52.2
95251	VALLECITO	91.4	90.2	2.5	2.4	0.5	0.5	4.6	4.9	3.9	3.9	5.4	6.3	5.4	25.4	33.7	14.6	1.5	82.4	44.9	52.7	47.3
95252	VALLEY SPRINGS	88.3	86.7	1.1	1.2	1.2	1.4	10.0	11.6	5.0	6.0	8.0	7.1	4.9	22.8	32.1	13.3	1.0	76.6	42.9	50.1	49.9
95255	WEST POINT	87.5	86.4	0.7	0.6	0.6	0.6	5.9	6.8	4.3	4.9	6.4	5.8	4.7	18.6	32.7	20.1	2.5	80.6	48.5	49.0	51.0
95257	WILSEYVILLE	90.7	89.8	0.2	0.2	0.2	0.2	3.8	4.6	3.5	4.1	5.5	5.5	4.1	17.2	36.6	21.8	1.7	83.2	51.2	50.3	49.7
95258	WOODBRIDGE	80.9	77.4	0.1	0.1	4.7	5.3	21.4	25.7	6.3	7.1	9.5	8.2	6.3	24.6	27.7	9.6	0.8	71.8	37.2	49.8	50.2
95301	ATWATER	59.0	55.8	4.6	4.4	5.9	6.3	39.6	43.5	9.3	8.7	9.5	8.3	7.9	27.5	18.9	9.0	0.9	67.3	29.6	49.1	50.9
95303	BALLICO	58.4	54.5	0.3	0.4	7.8	8.1	44.1	49.0	8.7	8.6	8.5	7.3	6.1	29.9	21.3	9.1	0.5	69.6	32.5	53.5	46.5
95304	TRACY	64.6	62.0	12.7	11.7	2.1	2.5	24.6	29.2	4.6	4.9	5.3	5.9	8.8	37.1	24.6	7.7	1.0	81.9	36.5	65.0	35.0
95306	CATHEYS VALLEY	91.5	90.3	0.0	0.0	0.3	0.3	6.2	7.3	4.9	6.2	8.0	8.0	4.0	22.2	31.1	13.7	1.7	75.7	43.0	49.4	50.6
95307	CERES	67.0	64.1	2.0	2.0	3.9	4.0	36.9	40.9	8.8	8.4	9.3	8.5	8.1	28.0	19.9	8.2	0.9	68.3	30.0	49.6	50.4
95309	CHINESE CAMP	91.7	92.3	0.0	0.0	0.0	0.0	4.2	3.9	7.7	7.7	7.7	7.7	7.7	26.9	30.8	3.9	0.0	76.9	35.0	50.0	50.0
95310	COLUMBIA	93.4	92.3	0.5	0.6	0.8	0.9	4.3	5.1	4.0	4.5	4.7	4.8	4.9	15.9	37.0	21.4	2.9	84.0	51.8	49.1	50.9
95311	COULTERVILLE	91.0	89.8	0.4	0.4	0.8	0.8	7.1	8.4	4.5	5.0	6.2	5.4	3.9	17.2	36.6	19.7	1.8	80.7	49.8	50.9	49.1
95313	CROWS LANDING	69.7	65.7	0.4	0.5	1.0	0.9	44.1	49.6	9.6	8.8	8.5	7.5	6.5	30.2	18.8	9.1	1.0	68.7	31.0	51.8	48.2
95315	DELHI	53.7	49.8	1.5	1.5	3.4	3.6	53.1	58.1	9.9	9.3	10.4	9.1	8.3	29.9	16.6	6.0	0.6	64.9	27.2	50.8	49.2
95316	DENAIR	81.7	78.9	0.2	0.2	1.3	1.5	21.5	25.1	6.3	7.0	8.2	8.5	6.6	25.6	26.9	9.8	1.2	73.1	36.6	49.7	50.3
95317	EL NIDO	66.7	63.1	1.4	1.3	1.6	1.7	45.3	50.5	10.3	9.2	9.3	8.2	8.3	29.6	17.7	6.5	0.9	65.8	28.0	55.4	44.6
95318	EL PORTAL	83.2	80.9	1.6	1.5	1.2	1.2	16.4	19.0	3.9	3.7	4.1	5.3	11.2	41.8	25.7	4.1	0.3	86.0	35.5	59.2	40.8
95320	ESCALON	82.7	79.6	0.4	0.5	1.2	1.4	22.6	26.8	7.0	7.2	8.3	8.3	7.0	25.9	24.2	10.7	1.4	72.3	35.6	50.5	49.5
95321	GROVELAND	92.6	91.3	0.6	0.7	0.8	0.9	4.8	5.8	3.6	3.9	4.4	4.6	3.8	14.7	35.2	28.2	1.6	85.2	55.0	48.6	51.4
95322	GUSTINE	68.1	64.0	0.7	0.7	1.2	1.2	38.6	43.6	8.3	7.9	8.7	7.8	6.8	26.9	21.1	10.8	1.7	70.3	33.2	51.5	48.6
95323	HICKMAN	80.6	77.4	0.4	0.5	0.4	0.4	22.4	26.3	7.0	7.1	7.8	6.9	5.5	27.5	26.3	10.9	1.2	73.8	37.1	52.4	47.6
95324	HILMAR	77.9	74.1	0.3	0.4	2.1	2.3	16.3	19.1	7.1	7.1	8.2	7.8	6.8	29.3	21.9	10.6	1.2	72.8	34.7	50.1	49.9
95326	HUGHSON	74.7	71.5	0.5	0.5	2.4	2.6	29.4	33.5	6.9	7.3	8.9	8.6	7.5	26.5	23.5	9.8	1.0	71.4	33.8	49.4	50.6
95327	JAMESTOWN	74.3	72.4	10.0	10.1	1.2	1.3	18.2	20.4	3.9	3.9	4.0	4.6	11.0	40.1	22.2	9.0	1.2	85.9	36.3	70.1	29.9
95329	LA GRANGE	91.0	89.5	0.7	0.8	0.7	0.8	8.8	10.6	5.3	5.7	6.2	5.5	4.1	19.9	35.1	17.5	0.7	79.4	46.9	50.2	49.8
95330	LATHROP	52.0	47.7	4.3	4.4	13.6	14.6	37.8	41.8	8.9	9.1	10.1	8.6	7.3	29.9	19.8	5.9	0.5	66.5	30.0	50.4	49.6
95333	LE GRAND	40.6	37.9	0.6	0.6	0.9	0.9	77.5	80.9	9.7	9.6	11.7	10.3	8.0	26.4	17.0	6.5	0.7	61.8	25.5	51.4	48.6
95334	LIVINGSTON	41.8	39.8	0.7	0.7	13.0	12.9	65.2	68.2	9.7	9.0	10.1	9.9	9.5	27.4	17.1	6.5	0.8	65.2	26.2	50.9	49.1
95335	LONG BARN	94.1	93.2	0.5	0.5	0.5	0.5	4.6	5.7	4.0	4.0	3.8	5.1	4.8	23.9	37.1	16.2	1.3	84.6	47.2	54.2	45.8
95336	MANTECA	75.0	71.1	2.5	2.6	3.6	4.1	23.8	28.0	7.6	7.5	8.7	8.2	7.4	27.7	22.7	9.1	1.2	71.3	33.5	48.9	51.1
95337	MANTECA	73.8	70.1	3.0	3.2	3.8	4.4	26.7	30.7	7.8	8.0	9.2	8.7	7.3	28.6	22.0	7.3	1.2	69.4	32.4	49.7	50.3
95338	MARIPOSA	89.9	88.6	0.5	0.5	0.8	0.9	5.7	6.8	4.3	5.2	7.3	6.8	4.4	19.7	31.8	18.1	2.4	78.8	46.3	49.2	50.8
95340	MERCED	52.7	50.5	4.8	4.7	11.1	11.4	43.5	46.3	8.9	8.4	9.8	9.4	9.0	25.9	19.3	8.2	1.0	67.0	28.4	50.1	49.9
95345	MIDPINES	84.7	83.0	2.0	2.1	1.4	1.5	9.8	11.4	4.1	4.3	5.2	7.0	6.5	25.6	32.0	13.4	1.9	82.3	43.6	52.1	47.9
95346	MI WUK VILLAGE	93.7	92.5	0.3	0.3	0.5	0.6	4.8	5.9	3.9	4.9	6.2	6.0	4.5	21.9	35.7	15.4	1.4	80.8	46.3	52.3	47.7
95348	MERCED	56.9	54.0	6.8	6.5	9.9	10.4	35.7	39.4	9.7	8.2	8.6	8.1	9.3	26.7	19.0	8.8	1.9	68.8	29.1	47.9	52.1
95350	MODESTO	74.9	72.1	3.6	3.6	5.1	5.4	19.6	22.7	7.1	6.7	7.3	7.3	7.6	26.1	22.7	12.6	2.5	74.5	35.9	47.6	52.4
95351	MODESTO	47.8	45.2	4.7	4.4	8.3	8.3	54.5	58.4	10.4	9.5	10.5	9.4	9.0	27.8	16.7	6.1	0.6	63.8	25.8	50.6	49.4
95354	MODESTO	68.1	64.9	3.4	3.4	5.1	5.5	30.7	34.2	8.4	8.0	8.7	7.7	7.7	30.4	20.4	7.6	1.2	70.3	31.3	49.8	50.2
95355	MODESTO	78.6	75.7	3.0	3.1	5.2	6.0	15.9	18.6	6.7	6.8	7.7	7.4	7.5	26.7	25.7	9.9	1.6	74.4	36.1	48.1	51.9
95356	MODESTO	76.0	72.7	3.5	3.6	6.3	7.0	17.9	21.0	7.1	6.7	7.6	7.5	8.2	26.8	24.5	10.1	1.6	74.0	34.7	48.1	51.9
95357	MODESTO	72.3	68.6	1.9	2.1	5.6	6.9	26.9	29.6	7.8	7.8	8.7	8.0	7.3	28.0	22.6	9.0	0.9	70.6	33.5	48.9	51.1
95358	MODESTO	61.5	57.5	3.4	3.3	4.4	4.7	42.5	47.7	8.8	8.4	9.4	9.1	8.0	29.4	19.1	7.0	0.9	67.9	29.5	51.0	49.0
95360	NEWMAN	61.5	57.8	1.2	1.2	1.7	1.7	50.1	55.2	9.1	8.5	10.0	8.6	7.4	28.7	18.7	8.0	1.1	66.9	29.7	50.5	49.5
95361	OAKDALE	85.6	82.7	0.4	0.5	1.2	1.4	17.1	20.9	7.0	7.1	7.8	7.1	6.4	26.7	25.1	11.1	1.8	73.7	37.0	49.1	50.9
95363	PATTERSON	56.2	52.9	1.6	1.7	2.1	2.2	56.7	61.2	9.5	8.9	9.8	8.8	8.1	29.2	18.3	6.6	0.8	66.3	28.4	51.1	48.9
95364	PINECREST	100.0	100.0	0.0	0.0	0.0	0.0	0.0	0.0	0.0	0.0	0.0	0.0	100.0	0.0	0.0	0.0	0.0	100.0	22.5	50.0	50.0
95366	RIPON	83.7	80.4	0.3	0.4	1.7	1.9	19.1	23.1	7.1	7.5	9.0	8.2	6.6	26.4	24.4	8.9	1.9	71.3	35.2	49.0	51.1
95367	RIVERBANK	68.3	65.6	1.5	1.6	1.5	1.6	43.9	47.4	9.2	8.5	9.0	7.8	7.8	29.3	20.4	7.3	0.8	68.5	30.5	49.5	50.6
95368	SALIDA	68.3	65.1	3.3	3.3	4.9	5.4	31.8	35.5	10.9	10.3	9.7	7.0	6.2	34.2	16.7	4.4	0.6	64.6	29.2	49.8	50.2
95369	SNELLING	76.3	73.4	0.3	0.4	1.3	1.4	35.4	40.3	9.0	8.9	8.3	8.1	7.4	26.2	21.8	9.4	0.9	68.3	31.6	50.8	49.2
95370	SONORA	93.1	91.9	0.4	0.5	0.9	1.0	6.5	7.8	4.7	4.9	6.0	6.2	5.9	20.1	30.7	18.8	2.8	80.6	46.4	48.2	51.8
95372	SOULSBYVILLE	93.4	92.1	0.0	0.0	0.5	0.5	7.5	9.2	5.5	6.2	8.3	7.7	6.0	21.2	28.8	14.7	1.7	75.3	41.6	50.2	49.8
95374	STEVINSON	79.2	76.2	2.1	2.2	0.3	0.3	28.4	32.8	8.0	7.4	7.8	7.6	8.6	28.1	23.3	8.6	0.8	72.2	32.7	50.4	49.6
95376	TRACY	65.4	61.7	5.3	5.5	7.7	8.5	29.5	33.1	9.3	8.9	9.5	7.8	6.7	31.8	19.4	5.6	1.0	67.4	31.1	49.9	50.1
95377	TRACY	66.2	62.1	5.8	6.0	13.1	14.5	18.5	21.8	10.9	10.5	9.9	7.2	4.3	36.2	17.1	3.6	0.2	64.0	30.9	50.8	49.2
	CALIFORNIA	59.6	57.1	6.7	6.5	11.3	11.8	32.4	35.5	7.4	7.1	7.8	7.3	7.7	29.8	22.1	9.3	1.4	73.3	33.8	49.8	50.2
	UNITED STATES	75.1	73.6	12.3	12.5	3.8	4.2	12.5	14.1	6.9	6.7	7.2	7.0	7.3	28.6	23.8	10.8	1.7	75.1	36.0	49.1	50.9

ZIP CODE				2004 HOUSEHOLD INCOME DISTRIBUTION (%)					MEDIAN HOUSEHOLD INCOME					2004 HOME VALUE DISTRIBUTION (%)					
#	POST OFFICE NAME	2004 Per Capita Income	2004 HH Income Base	Less than $25,000	$25,000 to $49,999	$50,000 to $99,999	$100,000 to $149,999	$150,000 or More	2004	2009	2004 National Centile	2004 State Centile	2004 Home Value Base	Less than $50,000	$50,000 to $89,999	$90,000 to $174,999	$175,000 to $399,999	$400,000 or More	2004 Median Home Value
95130	SAN JOSE	37599	4764	10.4	16.6	32.8	23.9	16.4	82195	102796	96	88	2859	0.2	0.8	0.4	5.5	93.1	627453
95131	SAN JOSE	37053	8763	7.2	10.1	32.0	28.4	22.3	100766	120710	98	94	5718	3.8	4.4	2.6	20.0	69.3	489951
95132	SAN JOSE	32269	11485	6.8	11.5	34.0	27.3	20.4	95869	113125	98	93	8516	2.3	2.0	0.8	17.1	77.8	503284
95133	SAN JOSE	25665	6961	12.8	17.2	33.9	20.9	15.2	77494	93342	94	84	4295	1.8	3.5	1.8	31.6	61.4	453571
95134	SAN JOSE	52093	4548	8.3	12.9	29.1	26.0	23.8	99575	122830	98	94	2362	6.2	13.9	23.1	11.6	45.2	332335
95135	SAN JOSE	53136	6700	7.7	12.2	23.2	24.3	32.7	111404	134129	99	96	6233	0.1	0.6	0.9	12.6	85.8	676094
95136	SAN JOSE	37065	13589	7.2	14.2	35.0	26.2	17.5	88704	108293	97	91	8843	2.1	5.0	5.6	14.5	72.9	508868
95138	SAN JOSE	53427	5305	4.1	8.0	30.2	25.3	32.3	111583	134239	99	96	4618	2.3	3.2	5.1	13.3	76.1	598127
95139	SAN JOSE	35450	2210	7.1	10.2	30.3	34.4	18.0	102141	118959	98	95	1888	1.1	0.4	0.0	18.0	80.5	513564
95140	MOUNT HAMILTON	56595	120	12.5	5.8	18.3	32.5	30.8	125000	148109	99	98	104	1.9	0.0	0.0	4.8	93.3	904762
95148	SAN JOSE	29503	11274	5.7	9.7	32.1	30.9	21.7	102669	121092	98	95	9408	1.0	1.7	1.8	12.7	82.9	553169
95202	STOCKTON	10645	3024	73.9	18.4	5.1	1.2	1.4	12202	13643	1	2	256	0.0	3.5	41.8	51.2	3.5	195000
95203	STOCKTON	13973	5777	42.8	28.3	23.0	4.3	1.5	29553	34087	11	10	2729	3.7	7.4	55.8	29.9	3.2	148637
95204	STOCKTON	22764	12036	30.0	31.7	26.2	8.0	4.2	40189	46381	47	32	7402	0.6	0.8	48.5	43.9	6.3	175324
95205	STOCKTON	10923	10300	44.2	32.8	19.0	2.7	1.4	28276	31741	9	8	5702	7.1	7.9	72.0	11.3	1.7	131283
95206	STOCKTON	13738	15116	31.4	27.8	31.5	6.9	2.4	41619	48939	52	35	10132	2.3	5.0	42.4	48.6	1.8	175988
95207	STOCKTON	19340	19388	34.3	28.8	26.4	7.1	3.4	36844	42023	35	24	8813	2.0	2.6	30.4	57.8	7.3	202537
95209	STOCKTON	23805	10468	16.3	20.9	40.8	16.4	5.6	62769	73034	87	70	7839	0.4	0.6	9.3	86.4	3.3	237071
95210	STOCKTON	13724	12282	29.8	32.3	29.4	6.6	1.9	40109	45898	46	31	7212	4.9	3.6	44.3	46.3	0.8	171384
95211	STOCKTON	18585	19	100.0	0.0	0.0	0.0	0.0	5588	6667	0	1	0	0.0	0.0	0.0	0.0	0.0	0
95212	STOCKTON	32550	3325	22.5	23.9	26.1	15.4	12.1	56139	65900	81	63	2873	23.4	4.7	4.3	38.3	29.3	259980
95215	STOCKTON	15748	6885	33.0	31.6	26.1	6.4	3.0	37404	42327	37	25	4990	11.7	6.2	39.7	30.8	11.6	157015
95219	STOCKTON	34473	9230	19.1	24.7	28.9	15.0	12.3	58367	68553	83	66	5734	1.2	1.3	11.0	60.5	26.1	298831
95220	ACAMPO	27353	2847	20.5	22.4	36.3	11.8	9.0	55491	63927	80	62	2421	3.6	6.6	9.4	38.5	41.9	348005
95222	ANGELS CAMP	23851	2114	29.0	29.9	26.9	9.1	5.2	40461	46238	48	33	1604	7.2	4.4	13.3	52.9	22.2	249281
95223	ARNOLD	34577	2669	22.9	28.7	27.8	12.1	8.5	48829	56289	70	50	2240	1.3	1.0	10.5	63.3	24.0	280266
95228	COPPEROPOLIS	27940	1307	20.1	33.9	28.4	9.4	8.3	47161	53302	66	46	1072	0.8	1.4	16.6	51.6	29.7	282298
95230	FARMINGTON	23821	337	23.4	25.8	28.8	12.5	9.5	50652	58227	73	53	273	2.9	2.9	12.1	40.7	41.4	360169
95231	FRENCH CAMP	16868	1065	35.7	28.8	26.1	6.3	3.1	31814	36153	17	13	670	0.0	9.0	29.0	43.4	18.7	222152
95232	GLENCOE	19221	140	33.6	35.7	22.9	5.7	2.1	34081	40651	24	18	117	0.0	2.6	29.9	62.4	5.1	217000
95236	LINDEN	24795	1262	17.5	25.2	35.7	13.2	8.4	55254	63726	80	61	989	0.0	1.9	10.6	51.7	35.8	345753
95237	LOCKEFORD	23537	1194	27.4	22.8	29.0	14.4	6.5	49832	60500	72	52	950	12.4	5.7	7.3	57.9	16.7	238250
95240	LODI	19061	16677	31.4	30.2	27.1	7.3	4.0	38649	44239	42	28	9153	4.5	3.2	23.2	57.7	11.4	218502
95242	LODI	27598	10060	19.4	26.1	34.3	12.7	7.5	54292	63100	79	59	7042	3.8	0.8	8.7	69.3	17.4	262737
95245	MOKELUMNE HILL	22404	1427	29.1	28.9	30.7	8.9	2.4	42614	48189	55	37	1125	2.7	3.8	15.8	58.8	18.8	252638
95246	MOUNTAIN RANCH	24128	902	34.8	24.2	27.4	10.0	3.7	39194	44869	43	29	738	3.3	5.8	14.2	49.7	27.0	268110
95247	MURPHYS	29217	1850	25.6	27.3	28.5	12.6	6.0	47087	54519	66	46	1468	1.6	4.6	11.2	50.5	32.0	306028
95249	SAN ANDREAS	19771	1546	33.8	34.4	24.9	4.7	2.1	36502	41172	34	23	1056	4.5	13.5	23.7	43.7	14.8	206803
95251	VALLECITO	29270	85	25.9	22.4	31.8	14.1	5.9	53430	58598	78	58	69	0.0	5.8	13.0	50.7	30.4	297222
95252	VALLEY SPRINGS	23648	4868	17.5	27.0	39.4	12.0	4.2	53739	62098	78	59	4212	3.3	1.4	10.5	68.2	16.6	257953
95255	WEST POINT	17570	860	42.3	32.2	18.1	4.7	2.7	29514	33592	11	9	669	5.1	6.9	35.7	43.4	9.0	184226
95257	WILSEYVILLE	22604	210	40.0	27.1	23.3	4.8	4.8	35000	40000	28	20	169	4.1	6.5	29.0	50.3	10.1	207609
95258	WOODBRIDGE	26391	1337	15.1	21.7	36.7	17.5	9.1	65496	76525	89	73	1155	4.9	1.1	13.1	54.0	26.9	281338
95301	ATWATER	17171	8911	26.4	34.0	30.0	7.0	2.7	41305	46936	51	35	5842	5.0	1.7	43.5	45.3	4.5	174758
95303	BALLICO	17714	346	24.0	35.0	30.1	9.0	2.0	42022	46231	53	36	195	2.1	4.6	18.0	35.4	40.0	302500
95304	TRACY	24136	3276	22.4	23.8	29.4	15.3	9.1	55280	64018	80	61	2624	6.3	6.5	19.5	16.1	51.7	413580
95306	CATHEYS VALLEY	23444	408	39.0	17.4	25.5	9.3	8.8	39109	48678	43	29	317	1.6	3.5	32.5	43.2	19.2	268750
95307	CERES	15776	11433	30.0	30.9	30.1	7.2	1.8	40650	46109	48	33	7539	9.3	1.5	30.3	53.0	6.0	190218
95309	CHINESE CAMP	25192	12	25.0	33.3	25.0	16.7	0.0	45000	47338	61	42	10	0.0	0.0	20.0	60.0	20.0	266667
95310	COLUMBIA	27488	723	23.9	38.7	24.3	7.6	5.4	41222	46126	50	35	580	11.6	12.8	12.6	41.0	22.1	239855
95311	COULTERVILLE	18268	917	40.2	27.0	26.9	3.6	2.2	31835	36851	17	14	729	8.4	5.9	26.1	52.3	7.4	206500
95313	CROWS LANDING	17616	482	32.0	33.2	27.4	3.3	4.2	36511	41461	34	23	242	7.9	5.8	17.4	33.1	36.0	257500
95315	DELHI	14047	3049	25.3	36.1	30.9	5.4	2.3	42334	46826	54	37	2231	2.0	3.2	42.7	48.5	3.7	178331
95316	DENAIR	22077	1925	21.4	28.2	32.5	11.9	6.1	50513	59506	73	53	1555	7.5	1.0	21.0	41.7	28.8	240819
95317	EL NIDO	16834	255	27.8	37.3	27.8	3.5	3.5	36616	41207	34	23	121	9.1	3.3	23.1	34.7	29.8	241667
95318	EL PORTAL	35347	265	17.4	35.9	35.1	5.7	6.0	47203	53648	67	46	113	15.9	6.2	30.1	30.1	17.7	169792
95320	ESCALON	21222	4310	20.6	26.1	36.8	13.0	3.6	53167	61369	77	58	3104	2.0	3.2	13.4	57.9	23.5	263707
95321	GROVELAND	29432	1742	25.0	30.9	29.5	8.8	5.9	43851	50396	58	39	1437	3.6	2.2	18.2	54.3	21.7	267459
95322	GUSTINE	18693	3130	31.0	28.1	31.4	5.5	3.9	42124	47578	53	36	2046	9.7	6.3	26.3	45.3	12.3	196667
95323	HICKMAN	21322	337	29.7	23.2	33.8	8.9	4.5	43961	51396	59	40	240	3.8	1.7	27.1	25.8	41.7	289474
95324	HILMAR	17465	2488	22.1	32.3	37.1	7.1	1.5	45916	51101	64	43	1943	4.3	7.1	17.6	54.9	16.1	214587
95326	HUGHSON	19420	2616	27.9	23.6	34.8	8.9	4.8	48279	54457	69	49	1985	5.5	1.2	24.4	49.4	19.4	228018
95327	JAMESTOWN	20289	2358	35.0	30.0	24.4	6.9	3.8	37169	41956	36	25	1672	7.6	6.3	22.7	49.0	14.5	215000
95329	LA GRANGE	24815	733	21.3	29.5	36.4	6.7	6.1	48544	53694	69	49	622	1.8	1.3	15.6	68.5	12.9	242935
95330	LATHROP	18496	3681	14.8	25.0	44.5	12.9	2.8	60748	67083	85	68	2837	6.0	2.4	11.8	72.6	7.1	242080
95333	LE GRAND	12534	1149	35.5	34.8	21.1	5.7	3.0	31961	35546	18	14	836	1.7	3.6	69.3	16.8	8.7	140809
95334	LIVINGSTON	11376	3646	30.2	38.6	23.8	5.2	2.2	35951	40058	31	22	2100	2.4	2.9	57.5	30.0	7.3	159703
95335	LONG BARN	19887	205	45.9	21.0	22.4	5.4	5.4	26699	30406	7	6	168	0.0	0.0	36.9	53.6	9.5	198913
95336	MANTECA	21389	13853	18.5	28.2	38.2	11.0	4.1	52582	60553	76	57	9513	3.9	2.3	11.6	73.4	8.9	247212
95337	MANTECA	21041	7804	19.9	30.3	34.1	11.9	3.7	49770	57465	71	52	5042	2.4	2.2	12.0	67.6	15.8	276671
95338	MARIPOSA	21493	4241	33.2	29.5	26.7	7.7	2.9	38086	43768	40	26	3148	1.9	4.4	19.1	61.7	12.9	234771
95340	MERCED	16289	20077	34.4	28.4	26.2	6.8	4.2	36312	41374	33	23	11992	3.0	2.4	42.7	41.1	10.9	180786
95345	MIDPINES	23300	316	31.0	31.0	24.4	11.7	1.9	39731	45224	45	30	224	6.3	3.6	13.8	59.8	16.5	253333
95346	MI WUK VILLAGE	30267	505	27.7	27.7	32.3	6.9	5.4	43788	49324	58	39	415	1.7	0.5	25.3	61.5	11.1	223317
95348	MERCED	17804	8729	32.6	32.0	25.6	6.8	3.0	36870	41707	35	24	4100	6.0	3.8	32.8	51.5	5.8	189960
95350	MODESTO	20806	20526	29.0	28.9	29.7	8.7	3.8	42718	49104	55	37	12327	1.7	1.8	26.3	62.9	7.4	208415
95351	MODESTO	11602	13287	37.3	32.2	24.3	4.7	1.5	33365	37172	22	17	7648	5.5	3.4	53.0	36.7	1.4	158646
95354	MODESTO	17264	9585	32.6	32.0	26.8	5.9	2.8	37442	43010	37	25	5191	1.7	1.2	43.5	49.1	4.5	181562
95355	MODESTO	24555	16604	19.4	27.7	34.0	12.5	6.4	52865	61727	77	58	10879	2.5	2.3	9.6	74.3	11.3	239275
95356	MODESTO	27727	13142	22.7	27.2	30.1	11.8	8.2	50092	57749	72	53	8032	6.3	2.2	9.5	60.6	21.4	247456
95357	MODESTO	23496	4785	20.5	27.0	35.1	12.0	5.5	52352	61207	76	57	3923	9.4	1.8	15.8	57.4	15.5	243972
95358	MODESTO	16802	9869	25.6	29.2	32.3	9.3	3.6	44909	50555	61	42	7167	2.2	2.8	31.8	50.6	12.7	206574
95360	NEWMAN	17004	2682	28.2	29.3	32.4	7.2	3.0	43704	48690	58	39	1878	2.2	1.9	36.9	53.1	5.9	189877
95361	OAKDALE	24549	10506	21.6	29.5	31.3	11.8	5.8	49025	55735	70	50	7389	5.1	1.3	17.2	50.2	26.1	249333
95363	PATTERSON	16366	4980	22.3	28.2	36.8	9.0	3.8	49442	55805	71	51	3565	4.0	1.6	23.4	60.3	10.7	222034
95364	PINECREST	0	0	0.0	0.0	0.0	0.0	0.0	0	0	0	0	0	0.0	0.0	0.0	0.0	0.0	0
95366	RIPON	24039	4724	14.9	25.4	41.3	13.1	5.3	61075	68232	85	69	3621	0.4	0.4	7.8	66.8	24.6	284583
95367	RIVERBANK	18209	5462	20.4	29.2	37.3	8.9	4.2	50323	57185	73	53	4145	4.1	4.2	27.7	55.1	9.0	203456
95368	SALIDA	21149	3620	12.0	21.9	47.2	14.1	4.7	64458	75523	88	72	3112	0.3	0.4	10.6	83.8	4.9	246567
95369	SNELLING	19657	464	29.5	39.4	20.7	5.8	4.5	33996	37905	24	18	260	9.2	5.4	37.3	32.3	15.8	170536
95370	SONORA	24128	11537	28.7	31.4	27.6	8.3	3.9	40976	46160	50	34	8308	7.1	3.2	16.3	55.3	18.1	238381
95372	SOULSBYVILLE	25508	605	18.2	30.7	38.8	9.4	2.8	50517	56685	73	53	520	2.3	0.6	18.3	68.9	10.0	225956
95374	STEVINSON	14565	535	30.3	37.0	25.1	7.5	0.2	39533	44644	44	30	354	4.8	11.9	12.2	59.3	11.9	236301
95376	TRACY	24182	17131	14.4	19.6	40.5	18.7	6.8	67415	78080	90	75	12481	1.7	1.9	3.6	65.9	26.9	333460
95377	TRACY	27356	4021	6.5	12.5	40.2	30.0	10.8	87341	102726	97	90	3675	1.2	0.4	1.1	39.1	58.2	422317
	CALIFORNIA	27293		21.8	24.4	30.5	13.7	9.7	54267	64547				3.3	2.7	13.3	42.9	37.9	319678
	UNITED STATES	25866		24.7	27.1	30.8	10.9	6.5	48124	56710				10.9	15.0	33.7	30.1	10.4	145905

Copyright © 2004 ESRI BIS. All rights reserved. Reproduction by any method is prohibited.

ZIP CODE #	POST OFFICE NAME	FINANCIAL SERVICES Auto Loan	Home Loan	Investments	Retirement Plans	THE HOME Home Improvements Home Repair	Lawn & Garden	Furnishings Computers & Hardware	Major Appliances	TV, Radio, Sound Equipment	Furniture	ENTERTAINMENT Dine out/ Carry out	Sports Equipment	Fees & Tickets	Toys & Games	Travel	Cable TV	PERSONAL Apparel & Services	Auto Repairs	Health Insurance	Pets & Supplies
95130	SAN JOSE	131	154	191	149	148	156	146	144	143	149	180	164	153	189	149	142	181	144	132	155
95131	SAN JOSE	146	170	233	192	177	166	181	179	159	173	200	231	171	192	181	141	198	189	144	186
95132	SAN JOSE	135	163	230	183	170	159	172	169	150	164	189	218	165	185	173	134	188	178	135	175
95133	SAN JOSE	115	135	189	152	141	131	144	141	126	138	159	182	137	154	144	112	158	150	113	147
95134	SAN JOSE	172	156	212	170	151	164	175	165	176	178	223	200	173	219	168	170	218	174	155	188
95135	SAN JOSE	209	224	234	221	227	250	204	216	201	212	252	230	213	233	215	206	244	210	225	242
95136	SAN JOSE	137	158	206	158	152	160	154	149	150	157	190	173	162	199	156	148	190	151	136	162
95138	SAN JOSE	221	263	278	270	252	253	236	232	218	242	278	268	252	285	236	210	278	225	204	255
95139	SAN JOSE	128	177	220	169	170	174	155	153	145	155	181	176	169	200	162	144	184	148	136	164
95140	MOUNT HAMILTON	197	252	282	256	243	246	220	215	201	223	256	248	243	269	226	196	259	207	191	237
95148	SAN JOSE	147	176	235	193	180	172	180	177	160	175	202	222	177	200	181	146	202	184	145	186
95202	STOCKTON	30	25	33	25	25	28	30	29	33	31	41	33	30	40	29	33	40	31	30	32
95203	STOCKTON	55	52	57	52	51	55	57	56	58	57	72	64	55	71	55	56	71	58	54	60
95204	STOCKTON	73	77	88	76	77	84	80	78	81	78	100	89	82	103	80	81	98	79	78	85
95205	STOCKTON	58	50	43	47	49	51	52	56	54	57	68	60	48	62	50	52	68	57	52	58
95206	STOCKTON	75	71	68	70	69	71	72	73	72	76	91	82	69	86	69	69	90	74	67	78
95207	STOCKTON	69	70	82	70	69	74	74	71	74	74	93	83	74	92	73	72	91	73	69	79
95209	STOCKTON	101	116	127	118	113	114	110	109	104	111	131	128	113	135	110	100	130	108	98	119
95210	STOCKTON	66	69	77	68	67	70	70	69	69	71	87	79	69	86	69	66	86	71	64	74
95211	STOCKTON	8	5	6	6	5	6	10	7	9	8	12	10	8	11	8	8	11	9	7	8
95212	STOCKTON	124	132	131	129	132	140	123	128	120	124	150	146	125	148	126	120	146	125	125	145
95215	STOCKTON	72	66	59	62	66	71	66	71	69	70	85	76	63	78	65	68	83	71	71	77
95219	STOCKTON	115	121	134	126	118	122	122	119	116	122	147	141	122	145	119	111	144	120	109	131
95220	ACAMPO	106	118	119	115	119	123	108	112	106	108	132	130	112	137	112	106	129	109	110	128
95222	ANGELS CAMP	90	76	60	74	81	93	79	85	85	77	102	97	74	100	79	88	95	84	96	102
95223	ARNOLD	130	104	75	95	117	132	98	118	110	98	131	135	89	127	105	118	122	116	139	157
95228	COPPEROPOLIS	115	90	62	82	102	114	85	103	97	85	114	120	76	113	91	103	106	101	121	141
95230	FARMINGTON	123	88	48	82	102	114	86	106	99	85	116	127	74	114	90	104	106	104	126	147
95231	FRENCH CAMP	61	53	44	50	52	55	54	59	57	58	71	63	50	64	52	55	70	60	56	62
95232	GLENCOE	67	63	60	60	67	79	58	66	62	62	77	65	59	64	63	66	72	64	78	76
95236	LINDEN	117	99	75	96	107	114	96	107	101	95	122	128	90	123	97	103	116	106	116	137
95237	LOCKEFORD	101	98	90	94	97	103	94	98	95	96	118	113	92	116	94	94	115	98	97	114
95240	LODI	78	73	71	72	74	79	76	77	77	76	96	88	74	95	74	76	94	78	77	86
95242	LODI	100	103	104	102	103	110	100	102	100	100	124	118	101	124	101	99	120	101	102	115
95245	MOKELUMNE HILL	73	73	74	70	76	86	69	74	71	71	89	78	71	82	73	75	85	73	83	84
95246	MOUNTAIN RANCH	83	78	76	74	83	97	72	82	76	77	95	81	74	80	79	81	89	80	95	93
95247	MURPHYS	92	93	95	89	96	110	87	94	89	90	111	97	89	101	93	94	106	91	104	105
95249	SAN ANDREAS	72	58	43	55	62	74	61	67	67	59	80	73	56	74	61	71	74	67	79	80
95251	VALLECITO	85	99	110	94	98	107	94	94	94	93	117	105	100	121	98	96	115	92	96	102
95252	VALLEY SPRINGS	97	96	85	94	99	103	89	94	90	89	111	111	90	114	91	90	107	92	96	114
95255	WEST POINT	66	54	43	52	58	69	55	62	61	55	73	66	52	66	57	64	67	61	73	73
95257	WILSEYVILLE	75	70	67	66	74	87	65	74	68	69	85	72	66	71	70	73	80	72	86	84
95258	WOODBRIDGE	111	126	128	127	123	122	117	117	110	117	138	138	120	142	116	105	136	115	104	129
95301	ATWATER	79	77	73	76	76	79	77	79	77	79	96	91	75	95	75	74	95	80	74	87
95303	BALLICO	83	79	75	74	76	80	79	83	81	85	102	89	76	96	77	79	102	84	78	88
95304	TRACY	84	100	106	100	98	97	91	91	85	91	107	106	96	113	92	83	107	88	81	100
95306	CATHEYS VALLEY	108	76	41	72	88	99	77	93	88	75	103	111	66	100	79	92	94	92	111	126
95307	CERES	74	71	67	69	70	74	71	74	72	73	90	84	69	87	70	71	88	74	71	82
95309	CHINESE CAMP	99	69	36	65	80	90	68	84	78	67	92	102	58	90	71	82	84	83	100	117
95310	COLUMBIA	88	80	76	75	85	100	77	87	82	81	101	87	76	88	82	87	94	85	101	98
95311	COULTERVILLE	70	56	40	53	61	70	56	63	62	55	74	73	51	72	57	65	68	63	73	81
95313	CROWS LANDING	85	75	62	69	72	76	76	82	79	83	99	87	70	88	73	76	98	84	77	86
95315	DELHI	76	77	73	75	74	75	75	77	73	78	93	87	73	89	73	70	91	77	70	83
95316	DENAIR	102	100	90	100	102	107	96	101	96	95	118	118	95	120	96	95	114	99	100	119
95317	EL NIDO	83	73	61	68	70	74	75	81	78	81	97	86	69	86	71	75	97	82	76	84
95318	EL PORTAL	103	80	55	73	91	102	76	91	86	75	102	107	68	100	81	92	95	90	108	125
95320	ESCALON	98	88	72	86	91	98	87	94	90	87	110	108	83	109	87	90	105	93	97	111
95321	GROVELAND	100	91	83	86	97	113	85	97	91	90	112	98	84	96	92	97	105	95	114	113
95322	GUSTINE	86	73	56	71	75	82	74	80	78	75	95	91	69	91	73	78	91	80	84	94
95323	HICKMAN	118	82	43	78	96	107	81	100	93	80	110	121	69	107	84	98	100	99	119	140
95324	HILMAR	92	72	46	66	77	86	69	80	77	70	92	94	63	90	70	80	86	79	91	105
95326	HUGHSON	95	85	69	81	87	92	83	91	86	85	106	103	78	102	82	85	103	90	91	106
95327	JAMESTOWN	86	65	44	63	71	84	70	78	78	67	92	88	63	87	70	82	84	78	92	96
95329	LA GRANGE	98	89	78	85	95	107	83	93	88	86	108	100	83	99	88	92	102	91	106	113
95330	LATHROP	94	98	96	97	95	97	93	94	91	96	114	108	93	113	92	88	112	94	87	105
95333	LE GRAND	75	63	52	60	63	66	66	71	69	70	86	78	60	80	63	67	85	72	69	78
95334	LIVINGSTON	69	59	54	58	58	61	64	66	67	68	84	74	60	80	61	64	84	69	62	71
95335	LONG BARN	89	70	48	63	79	89	66	80	75	65	89	93	59	87	70	80	82	78	94	109
95336	MANTECA	89	92	94	93	91	95	91	91	89	91	111	106	92	112	90	87	109	91	87	101
95337	MANTECA	92	93	92	94	91	94	91	91	89	92	111	108	91	110	89	85	109	92	85	103
95338	MARIPOSA	79	68	56	65	73	84	69	76	74	68	90	83	65	85	71	78	84	75	87	90
95340	MERCED	74	72	73	71	71	74	75	74	75	75	94	86	73	93	73	73	92	76	71	81
95345	MIDPINES	82	63	42	59	69	81	66	75	74	64	88	85	59	84	67	79	80	74	89	94
95346	MI WUK VILLAGE	114	90	61	81	101	113	84	102	96	84	113	119	76	112	90	102	105	100	120	139
95348	MERCED	70	68	74	68	67	71	72	71	72	72	90	82	70	87	70	70	88	73	67	77
95350	MODESTO	73	77	85	76	76	82	78	77	78	77	98	89	80	99	79	78	95	78	77	85
95351	MODESTO	66	58	56	56	57	60	62	64	64	66	81	71	59	77	59	61	81	66	59	68
95354	MODESTO	67	67	72	66	66	70	70	69	70	70	88	79	70	88	69	68	86	70	66	74
95355	MODESTO	94	100	104	102	98	101	98	97	94	98	118	114	98	118	96	91	116	97	90	108
95356	MODESTO	105	106	115	108	105	112	107	106	105	107	132	123	107	129	106	103	128	108	103	119
95357	MODESTO	116	109	92	107	109	114	103	110	105	106	130	128	100	127	102	104	125	109	109	130
95358	MODESTO	89	84	74	82	83	85	83	87	84	86	105	99	79	100	81	81	103	88	83	97
95360	NEWMAN	88	77	63	72	74	79	78	85	82	85	102	90	72	91	75	79	101	86	81	89
95361	OAKDALE	97	97	94	96	98	104	97	98	97	95	120	114	96	121	96	97	116	97	98	112
95363	PATTERSON	89	86	76	83	83	84	84	88	84	89	105	98	81	98	81	80	104	88	80	94
95364	PINECREST	0	0	0	0	0	0	0	0	0	0	0	0	0	0	0	0	0	0	0	0
95366	RIPON	103	110	104	111	107	108	103	104	99	105	124	120	104	123	101	95	122	103	96	115
95367	RIVERBANK	93	90	82	88	88	90	88	91	87	93	110	102	85	104	85	84	109	92	85	99
95368	SALIDA	106	116	110	119	110	108	106	106	99	111	126	123	108	124	103	93	124	104	92	116
95369	SNELLING	92	75	55	68	76	82	75	84	81	80	100	93	68	91	73	81	96	85	87	97
95370	SONORA	81	77	76	74	80	90	77	81	80	77	98	90	76	95	79	82	94	80	88	93
95372	SOULSBYVILLE	86	97	104	93	96	106	92	93	93	91	115	104	97	119	96	95	112	91	96	103
95374	STEVINSON	75	68	53	65	68	71	65	70	66	67	81	80	61	76	64	65	78	70	69	82
95376	TRACY	108	118	117	120	113	113	111	110	105	114	133	129	113	133	109	100	131	109	98	120
95377	TRACY	138	157	152	164	150	145	142	140	130	147	165	164	146	166	138	121	163	137	119	154
	CALIFORNIA	107	111	131	112	109	115	113	111	111	114	140	129	114	141	112	109	139	113	104	122
	UNITED STATES	100	100	100	100	100	100	100	100	100	100	100	100	100	100	100	100	100	100	100	100

#	POST OFFICE NAME	COUNTY FIPS CODE	POPULATION			2000-2004 ANNUAL RATE		HOUSEHOLDS					FAMILIES		
			2000	2004	2009	% Rate	State Centile	2000	2004	2009	% Annual Rate 2000-2004	2004 Average HH Size	2000	2004	% Annual Rate 2000-2004
95379	TUOLUMNE	109	3909	3971	4094	0.4	26	1483	1518	1576	0.6	2.60	1059	1079	0.4
95380	TURLOCK	099	36851	41387	46603	2.8	88	11505	12759	14184	2.5	3.16	8546	9409	2.3
95382	TURLOCK	099	27732	30849	34607	2.5	86	9733	10729	11914	2.3	2.78	7092	7759	2.1
95383	TWAIN HARTE	109	5463	5611	5814	0.6	38	2311	2393	2498	0.8	2.34	1647	1699	0.7
95385	VERNALIS	099	194	201	217	0.8	48	64	66	70	0.7	2.95	55	56	0.4
95386	WATERFORD	099	8548	9716	10963	3.1	90	2551	2858	3177	2.7	3.39	2110	2356	2.6
95388	WINTON	047	11611	13654	14940	3.9	95	3228	3523	3858	2.1	3.57	2653	2886	2.0
95389	YOSEMITE NATL PARK	043	611	619	633	0.3	23	165	170	178	0.7	1.85	86	88	0.5
95391	TRACY	077	475	592	699	5.3	98	144	179	210	5.3	3.28	114	141	5.1
95401	SANTA ROSA	097	36289	37421	38739	0.7	42	12821	13159	13567	0.6	2.75	8095	8258	0.5
95403	SANTA ROSA	097	39171	42200	44690	1.8	75	14441	15609	16526	1.9	2.64	9556	10216	1.6
95404	SANTA ROSA	097	35830	37191	38677	0.9	50	14293	14749	15269	0.7	2.47	8631	8913	0.8
95405	SANTA ROSA	097	21923	22108	22675	0.2	20	8740	8831	9049	0.2	2.45	5677	5707	0.1
95407	SANTA ROSA	097	30862	33930	36254	2.3	83	9468	10311	10940	2.0	3.24	6599	7161	1.9
95409	SANTA ROSA	097	25781	26926	28169	1.0	56	11417	11839	12318	0.9	2.23	7104	7382	0.9
95410	ALBION	045	1024	1040	1058	0.4	26	487	497	507	0.5	2.04	254	257	0.3
95412	ANNAPOLIS	097	201	208	214	0.8	47	58	60	62	0.8	3.49	39	40	0.6
95415	BOONVILLE	045	1363	1377	1398	0.2	21	485	492	501	0.3	2.75	339	342	0.2
95417	BRANSCOMB	045	499	482	485	-0.8	3	212	205	207	-0.8	2.35	134	129	-0.9
95420	CASPAR	045	317	338	355	1.5	69	145	154	162	1.4	2.18	92	97	1.3
95421	CAZADERO	097	2130	2098	2129	-0.4	6	952	941	955	-0.3	2.19	538	530	-0.4
95422	CLEARLAKE	033	13629	14047	14774	0.7	41	5755	5911	6199	0.6	2.36	3434	3506	0.5
95423	CLEARLAKE OAKS	033	3877	3998	4215	0.7	42	1866	1925	2028	0.7	2.07	1079	1106	0.6
95425	CLOVERDALE	097	9217	9860	10362	1.6	72	3380	3625	3808	1.7	2.67	2366	2527	1.6
95427	COMPTCHE	045	441	456	470	0.8	45	191	199	205	1.0	2.25	126	131	0.9
95428	COVELO	045	2309	2287	2316	-0.2	8	856	850	862	-0.2	2.69	580	574	-0.2
95429	DOS RIOS	045	62	60	61	-0.8	3	26	25	26	-0.9	2.40	15	14	-1.6
95432	ELK	045	174	177	180	0.4	27	88	90	92	0.5	1.92	46	46	0.0
95436	FORESTVILLE	097	6086	6163	6320	0.3	23	2550	2592	2657	0.4	2.35	1491	1512	0.3
95437	FORT BRAGG	045	14289	14542	14906	0.4	28	5847	5963	6125	0.5	2.38	3637	3703	0.4
95439	FULTON	097	719	743	765	0.8	45	250	259	268	0.8	2.78	162	167	0.7
95441	GEYSERVILLE	097	2797	2887	2990	0.8	43	877	913	950	1.0	2.91	657	681	0.9
95442	GLEN ELLEN	097	4340	4578	4770	1.3	63	1416	1519	1599	1.7	2.34	873	932	1.6
95443	GLENHAVEN	033	164	173	185	1.3	63	72	76	81	1.3	2.28	47	50	1.5
95444	GRATON	097	845	823	835	-0.6	4	289	283	287	-0.5	2.80	197	192	-0.6
95445	GUALALA	045	2020	2020	2050	0.0	15	902	904	918	0.1	2.22	544	542	-0.1
95446	GUERNEVILLE	097	5369	5799	6128	1.8	76	2493	2722	2886	2.1	2.06	1157	1254	1.9
95448	HEALDSBURG	097	17195	17859	18592	0.9	51	6298	6507	6750	0.8	2.67	4345	4479	0.7
95449	HOPLAND	045	1856	1928	1989	0.9	51	583	602	619	0.8	3.09	413	425	0.7
95450	JENNER	097	303	299	303	-0.3	7	147	146	148	-0.2	2.00	84	83	-0.3
95451	KELSEYVILLE	033	11498	12534	13564	2.1	80	4552	4950	5347	2.0	2.50	3104	3362	1.9
95452	KENWOOD	097	1593	1591	1632	0.0	12	664	666	683	0.1	2.36	438	437	-0.1
95453	LAKEPORT	033	11156	11977	12844	1.7	73	4324	4659	5007	1.8	2.45	2839	3046	1.7
95454	LAYTONVILLE	045	1844	1842	1869	0.0	12	715	715	726	0.0	2.58	493	491	-0.1
95456	LITTLERIVER	045	1107	1111	1128	0.1	17	560	565	576	0.2	1.93	302	303	0.1
95457	LOWER LAKE	033	3347	3598	3864	1.7	74	1348	1449	1554	1.7	2.48	932	998	1.6
95458	LUCERNE	033	2670	2757	2899	0.8	43	1233	1271	1335	0.7	2.16	720	738	0.6
95459	MANCHESTER	045	542	565	583	1.0	54	237	248	257	1.1	2.22	141	147	1.0
95460	MENDOCINO	045	2043	2121	2192	0.9	50	982	1026	1065	1.0	2.06	564	586	0.9
95461	MIDDLETOWN	033	6895	7636	8329	2.4	85	2623	2908	3173	2.5	2.57	1882	2079	2.4
95462	MONTE RIO	097	1525	1502	1528	-0.4	6	762	756	770	-0.2	1.96	338	334	-0.3
95464	NICE	033	2337	2459	2612	1.2	61	1059	1116	1184	1.2	2.19	592	621	1.1
95465	OCCIDENTAL	097	2534	2475	2510	-0.6	4	1046	1026	1040	-0.5	2.38	621	604	-0.7
95466	PHILO	045	1312	1350	1385	0.7	39	450	466	479	0.8	2.81	292	302	0.8
95468	POINT ARENA	045	1365	1398	1431	0.6	34	543	559	573	0.7	2.49	335	343	0.6
95469	POTTER VALLEY	045	1774	1868	1943	1.2	62	643	681	710	1.4	2.65	458	483	1.3
95470	REDWOOD VALLEY	045	6014	6199	6399	0.7	42	2095	2172	2250	0.9	2.81	1613	1669	0.8
95472	SEBASTOPOL	097	31073	31268	32005	0.2	18	12148	12272	12564	0.2	2.50	7983	8021	0.1
95476	SONOMA	097	34300	34908	35997	0.4	28	14124	14322	14719	0.3	2.41	8677	8751	0.2
95480	STEWARTS POINT	097	94	97	100	0.7	43	38	40	41	1.2	2.38	25	26	0.9
95482	UKIAH	045	30716	31875	32968	0.9	50	11322	11745	12166	0.9	2.61	7551	7809	0.9
95485	UPPER LAKE	033	2466	2583	2736	1.1	58	1019	1070	1133	1.2	2.38	660	689	1.0
95488	WESTPORT	045	335	323	325	-0.9	2	156	151	152	-0.8	2.09	77	74	-0.9
95490	WILLITS	045	13738	13994	14398	0.4	29	5280	5391	5565	0.5	2.56	3586	3654	0.4
95492	WINDSOR	097	24582	27079	28945	2.3	83	8002	8811	9408	2.3	3.00	6021	6617	2.3
95493	WITTER SPRINGS	033	88	92	97	1.1	56	36	37	40	0.7	2.41	24	25	1.0
95494	YORKVILLE	045	153	156	160	0.5	29	68	70	71	0.7	2.14	45	46	0.5
95497	THE SEA RANCH	097	1080	1119	1152	0.8	48	539	561	578	1.0	1.95	358	371	0.8
95501	EUREKA	023	23255	23159	23394	-0.1	11	9733	9744	9914	0.0	2.22	5101	5083	-0.1
95503	EUREKA	023	23872	24288	24769	0.4	28	9525	9762	10027	0.6	2.44	6340	6469	0.5
95511	ALDERPOINT	023	298	283	283	-1.2	2	107	101	102	-1.4	2.25	67	63	-1.4
95514	BLOCKSBURG	023	155	147	147	-1.2	1	54	51	52	-1.3	2.31	34	32	-1.4
95519	MCKINLEYVILLE	023	15682	16349	16876	1.0	54	6095	6402	6657	1.2	2.55	4171	4362	1.1
95521	ARCATA	023	20922	21216	21690	0.3	24	8790	8996	9277	0.6	2.20	3884	3940	0.3
95524	BAYSIDE	023	1388	1463	1522	1.3	63	543	575	602	1.4	2.54	369	389	1.3
95525	BLUE LAKE	023	633	627	634	-0.2	9	257	257	261	0.0	2.44	175	173	-0.3
95526	BRIDGEVILLE	023	716	714	724	-0.1	11	298	300	307	0.2	2.37	205	205	0.0
95527	BURNT RANCH	105	339	342	350	0.2	20	160	164	169	0.6	2.09	103	105	0.5
95528	CARLOTTA	023	921	1025	1094	2.6	87	358	401	431	2.7	2.56	255	286	2.7
95531	CRESCENT CITY	015	23376	23891	24316	0.5	32	7598	7803	7977	0.6	2.60	5216	5345	0.6
95536	FERNDALE	023	2942	2922	2946	-0.2	10	1183	1182	1199	0.0	2.44	787	783	-0.1
95540	FORTUNA	023	12473	13271	13832	1.5	68	4960	5303	5561	1.6	2.46	3352	3568	1.5
95542	GARBERVILLE	023	2394	2533	2657	1.3	65	997	1063	1124	1.5	2.30	592	628	1.4
95543	GASQUET	015	851	844	840	-0.2	8	349	348	348	-0.1	2.30	234	232	-0.2
95546	HOOPA	023	3085	3173	3249	0.7	39	1004	1033	1062	0.7	3.07	716	735	0.6
95547	HYDESVILLE	023	1215	1224	1237	0.2	19	458	464	472	0.3	2.64	344	348	0.3
95548	KLAMATH	015	1203	1108	1088	-1.9	1	431	394	388	-2.1	2.37	284	258	-2.2
95549	KNEELAND	023	426	463	490	2.0	79	149	162	173	2.0	2.84	106	115	1.9
95550	KORBEL	023	184	190	195	0.8	43	70	73	75	1.0	2.56	47	48	0.5
95551	LOLETA	023	1222	1233	1248	0.2	20	494	497	504	0.1	2.48	304	305	0.1
95552	MAD RIVER	105	17	17	18	0.0	15	6	6	6	0.0	2.83	4	4	0.0
95554	MYERS FLAT	023	3014	2977	3000	-0.3	7	1301	1293	1313	-0.2	2.21	751	742	-0.1
95555	ORICK	023	242	232	232	-1.0	2	101	97	98	-1.0	2.38	58	56	-0.8
95556	ORLEANS	023	450	430	431	-1.1	2	180	174	176	-0.8	2.47	109	105	-0.9
95558	PETROLIA	023	283	283	285	0.0	15	128	128	130	0.0	2.13	83	83	0.0
	CALIFORNIA					1.4					1.2	2.90			1.2
	UNITED STATES					1.2					1.3	2.58			1.1

ZIP CODE #	POST OFFICE NAME	RACE (%) White 2000	White 2004	Black 2000	Black 2004	Asian/Pacific 2000	Asian/Pacific 2004	% Hispanic Origin 2000	% Hispanic Origin 2004	2004 AGE DISTRIBUTION (%) 0-4	5-9	10-14	15-19	20-24	25-44	45-64	65-84	85+	18+	MEDIAN AGE 2004	% 2004 Males	% 2004 Females
95379	TUOLUMNE	88.7	87.4	0.2	0.3	0.7	0.8	5.6	6.9	6.1	6.4	7.7	6.9	6.8	23.5	28.9	12.1	1.7	75.6	40.0	49.4	50.6
95380	TURLOCK	67.3	64.0	1.0	1.0	3.7	3.8	39.3	44.0	9.0	8.4	8.9	7.9	8.3	28.5	19.0	8.7	1.4	68.9	29.9	49.5	50.5
95382	TURLOCK	79.3	76.3	1.8	1.9	5.1	5.7	17.4	20.5	7.4	6.8	7.2	7.6	8.9	28.6	20.6	10.6	2.4	74.3	32.6	47.4	52.6
95383	TWAIN HARTE	93.5	92.4	0.1	0.1	1.0	1.1	5.0	6.0	3.9	4.8	6.9	6.8	4.6	18.9	35.3	17.5	1.3	79.8	47.3	50.5	49.5
95385	VERNALIS	47.4	44.3	1.0	1.0	0.5	0.5	67.0	70.2	9.5	8.5	9.0	8.5	8.5	28.9	18.4	8.0	1.0	67.2	29.5	51.7	48.3
95386	WATERFORD	74.1	70.5	0.5	0.5	1.0	1.0	32.5	37.3	8.6	8.4	10.0	8.9	7.9	28.4	19.7	7.3	0.9	67.4	29.8	50.4	49.6
95388	WINTON	50.9	47.4	2.1	2.0	5.6	6.6	54.5	57.9	9.9	9.0	10.3	9.1	9.0	26.6	18.3	7.1	0.7	65.2	26.8	50.7	49.3
95389	YOSEMITE NATL PARK	82.3	79.8	1.6	1.8	1.3	1.3	17.0	19.9	4.0	3.6	3.2	5.0	13.1	43.5	24.7	2.8	0.2	87.4	34.4	60.9	39.1
95391	TRACY	74.3	70.3	4.4	4.7	5.1	5.6	18.5	22.6	7.4	7.9	7.9	6.1	4.4	29.4	27.9	8.1	0.8	72.3	37.5	51.9	48.1
95401	SANTA ROSA	74.6	71.5	2.2	2.3	4.8	5.2	21.5	24.8	6.6	6.3	6.9	6.8	8.1	30.9	24.2	8.7	1.6	76.1	34.9	49.6	50.4
95403	SANTA ROSA	77.2	74.4	2.5	2.5	4.7	5.2	18.8	21.6	6.6	6.5	7.2	7.1	8.0	29.2	24.4	9.1	1.9	75.5	35.4	49.8	50.2
95404	SANTA ROSA	82.3	80.0	1.6	1.6	2.8	3.1	16.6	19.1	5.7	5.7	6.1	6.0	7.0	27.4	28.4	11.3	2.4	78.9	39.6	49.0	51.0
95405	SANTA ROSA	88.2	86.5	1.2	1.3	2.9	3.2	9.0	10.6	5.2	5.4	6.3	6.5	6.3	25.5	29.1	12.7	2.9	78.7	41.7	47.3	52.7
95407	SANTA ROSA	60.0	56.7	3.1	3.0	4.9	5.2	39.3	43.1	9.0	8.4	8.4	7.4	8.3	32.3	19.5	5.8	0.9	70.0	30.1	51.1	48.9
95409	SANTA ROSA	89.5	88.0	1.0	1.1	2.5	2.9	7.1	8.3	4.6	4.9	5.7	6.1	5.1	19.9	26.4	21.7	5.5	80.6	47.6	46.6	53.4
95410	ALBION	93.5	92.3	0.3	0.3	1.1	1.3	2.7	3.3	2.4	2.6	5.2	4.6	3.9	17.3	44.2	16.4	3.4	86.4	51.4	47.2	52.8
95412	ANNAPOLIS	84.1	81.7	0.5	0.5	1.0	1.4	14.9	17.8	3.4	3.9	3.4	3.4	3.4	13.9	39.4	27.4	1.9	86.5	56.4	49.5	50.5
95415	BOONVILLE	64.5	60.3	1.1	1.1	1.2	1.2	39.3	44.1	6.5	7.0	7.0	7.5	6.7	26.4	28.0	9.7	1.2	74.8	37.1	53.4	46.6
95417	BRANSCOMB	86.6	84.7	0.8	0.8	1.0	1.0	5.8	6.9	3.7	5.4	7.7	7.3	6.0	21.6	37.3	10.2	0.8	79.1	44.0	52.1	47.9
95420	CASPAR	92.1	90.8	0.6	0.6	1.0	0.9	3.8	4.4	3.6	4.1	5.6	6.2	3.9	21.9	38.8	13.9	2.1	82.3	47.4	50.3	49.7
95421	CAZADERO	87.0	85.1	0.6	0.6	1.4	1.5	8.5	10.2	3.2	4.4	6.0	5.2	3.9	22.6	40.3	13.4	1.1	82.9	47.4	50.7	49.3
95422	CLEARLAKE	82.7	80.7	5.1	5.4	1.3	1.4	10.8	12.6	6.1	6.1	7.1	6.7	5.6	20.6	26.8	18.3	2.8	76.6	43.4	48.3	51.7
95423	CLEARLAKE OAKS	88.4	87.0	3.6	3.8	0.8	0.9	6.7	7.9	4.2	4.3	4.9	5.0	3.9	17.2	32.6	25.3	2.7	83.4	52.6	50.2	49.8
95425	CLOVERDALE	79.2	76.2	0.2	0.2	1.1	1.2	25.1	29.0	6.3	6.5	7.2	6.7	6.7	26.3	26.2	12.0	2.0	75.7	38.4	51.0	49.1
95427	COMPTCHE	85.0	82.7	0.5	0.4	0.9	1.1	18.1	21.5	4.6	5.7	5.7	7.0	5.7	22.4	37.5	10.1	1.3	79.0	44.2	53.1	46.9
95428	COVELO	49.7	47.8	0.8	0.8	0.6	0.6	7.2	8.1	7.1	7.8	8.4	7.3	5.4	22.7	27.9	12.0	1.4	72.2	37.8	49.0	51.0
95429	DOS RIOS	75.8	71.7	1.6	1.7	1.6	1.7	6.5	6.7	5.0	6.7	6.7	6.7	5.0	21.7	36.7	10.0	1.7	78.3	44.0	53.3	46.7
95432	ELK	93.7	92.1	0.6	0.6	1.2	1.1	2.3	2.8	2.3	2.3	5.1	4.5	4.0	17.5	44.1	17.0	3.4	87.0	51.4	46.3	53.7
95436	FORESTVILLE	90.8	89.3	0.6	0.6	1.3	1.4	8.6	10.3	3.9	5.1	6.5	7.5	5.9	23.0	37.0	9.6	1.5	79.4	43.8	49.3	50.7
95437	FORT BRAGG	84.2	82.0	0.6	0.7	1.0	1.1	15.9	18.3	5.4	5.3	5.8	6.5	6.3	24.7	30.7	13.2	2.1	79.7	42.3	50.0	50.1
95439	FULTON	81.4	78.9	2.0	2.0	5.0	5.4	14.3	16.8	6.1	6.1	6.7	6.6	7.0	30.0	25.7	10.1	1.8	77.3	37.3	50.2	49.8
95441	GEYSERVILLE	72.6	70.0	0.3	0.4	0.4	0.4	35.2	39.2	5.0	5.9	7.0	6.6	5.6	29.3	30.1	9.2	1.3	77.8	39.8	55.5	44.5
95442	GLEN ELLEN	89.0	87.4	2.1	2.2	2.4	2.7	9.1	10.9	3.4	4.1	5.7	7.7	5.7	25.4	37.2	9.7	1.1	81.7	44.0	52.8	47.2
95443	GLENHAVEN	79.9	76.9	3.7	3.5	1.2	1.7	12.8	14.5	5.2	5.2	5.8	5.8	6.4	20.2	31.2	18.5	1.7	79.8	46.1	50.3	49.7
95444	GRATON	78.9	76.1	0.5	0.6	1.2	1.2	25.7	29.4	4.7	6.1	8.0	6.9	6.4	26.9	32.0	7.9	1.1	76.8	39.7	50.9	49.1
95445	GUALALA	89.8	87.9	0.2	0.2	1.1	1.3	11.1	13.2	4.5	4.9	5.1	4.8	4.1	19.7	38.1	16.8	2.1	82.4	49.3	49.2	50.8
95446	GUERNEVILLE	87.2	85.2	1.0	1.0	1.2	1.3	11.0	12.9	4.0	4.1	5.9	6.7	7.2	26.4	36.3	8.2	1.2	82.0	42.6	52.5	47.5
95448	HEALDSBURG	81.0	78.6	0.5	0.5	0.9	1.0	26.4	30.1	5.6	5.9	7.3	7.1	6.8	25.5	28.7	11.0	2.2	76.9	39.5	50.5	49.5
95449	HOPLAND	63.9	60.4	0.3	0.3	0.9	0.9	29.3	33.3	7.0	7.0	7.6	8.9	8.2	26.8	25.8	8.1	0.7	72.6	34.2	52.3	47.7
95450	JENNER	85.8	84.0	0.7	0.7	1.3	1.3	8.3	9.7	3.3	4.7	6.4	5.4	4.4	22.4	41.5	11.0	1.0	81.9	46.7	50.2	49.8
95451	KELSEYVILLE	86.6	84.6	0.8	0.8	1.0	1.1	14.4	16.8	4.7	5.1	7.2	6.9	5.2	22.0	31.3	15.7	1.9	78.4	44.3	50.3	49.8
95452	KENWOOD	93.4	92.1	0.3	0.3	1.4	1.6	5.8	7.0	2.5	3.4	5.4	6.0	3.5	16.8	39.4	20.1	3.1	85.0	51.3	49.0	51.0
95453	LAKEPORT	86.3	84.7	0.9	0.9	1.1	1.1	14.2	16.4	5.3	5.4	6.9	7.0	6.4	22.9	27.8	15.6	2.8	77.8	42.5	49.9	50.1
95454	LAYTONVILLE	78.5	76.4	0.3	0.3	1.3	1.4	7.5	8.7	6.0	6.3	7.2	7.0	6.5	24.2	31.2	10.6	1.2	76.4	40.3	50.8	49.2
95456	LITTLERIVER	94.0	92.9	0.4	0.4	1.2	1.4	2.1	2.6	2.7	3.0	5.3	5.0	4.3	17.0	43.7	15.8	3.2	85.3	51.0	47.3	52.8
95457	LOWER LAKE	88.4	86.6	1.2	1.3	1.0	1.1	8.5	9.8	4.6	5.3	6.9	5.9	4.9	21.9	33.6	15.4	1.5	79.4	45.3	50.3	49.7
95458	LUCERNE	87.9	86.3	1.7	1.8	0.5	0.5	8.5	10.0	4.7	4.9	5.7	5.6	4.9	18.1	32.4	21.4	2.3	81.1	48.9	49.7	50.3
95459	MANCHESTER	84.3	82.3	0.9	0.9	0.7	0.9	15.9	18.8	4.3	4.4	5.8	5.8	4.4	22.7	32.9	17.7	2.0	81.1	46.5	51.5	48.5
95460	MENDOCINO	94.6	93.7	0.2	0.2	1.2	1.3	2.4	2.9	2.3	3.3	5.8	4.8	3.5	17.1	42.1	19.2	1.9	85.1	52.3	46.3	53.8
95461	MIDDLETOWN	90.7	89.4	0.5	0.6	1.1	1.2	9.3	10.9	5.6	6.3	8.0	7.3	4.6	23.6	30.2	13.2	1.3	75.1	42.0	50.5	49.5
95462	MONTE RIO	91.1	89.5	0.7	0.7	1.5	1.7	6.3	7.4	4.1	4.1	5.4	6.1	5.5	24.3	38.4	11.2	0.9	82.5	45.2	52.3	47.7
95464	NICE	88.1	86.8	2.2	2.3	0.6	0.7	8.0	9.2	5.5	5.8	6.6	5.6	4.3	19.6	29.3	20.5	2.8	78.4	46.8	48.6	51.4
95465	OCCIDENTAL	89.9	88.3	0.8	0.9	1.3	1.4	8.0	9.5	3.4	3.9	6.3	7.4	6.4	22.9	38.6	10.1	1.1	81.7	44.8	50.1	49.9
95466	PHILO	78.7	75.9	0.6	0.6	0.9	1.0	24.1	27.6	5.1	6.1	6.4	7.0	5.6	23.9	35.1	9.6	1.2	77.6	42.4	52.7	47.3
95468	POINT ARENA	70.8	68.3	0.6	0.6	0.6	0.6	19.7	22.5	6.1	6.4	7.7	6.5	4.7	24.2	32.6	10.7	1.1	75.8	40.9	51.1	48.9
95469	POTTER VALLEY	83.1	80.5	0.2	0.2	0.5	0.5	14.9	17.6	3.9	5.3	7.4	7.3	7.3	25.1	33.0	9.7	1.1	78.2	40.7	53.8	46.3
95470	REDWOOD VALLEY	84.6	82.7	0.3	0.4	1.1	1.2	12.5	14.5	5.0	5.9	7.8	7.7	6.1	24.1	31.8	10.3	1.3	76.1	40.4	50.7	49.3
95472	SEBASTOPOL	89.4	87.7	0.7	0.7	1.6	1.8	9.1	10.8	4.0	4.7	6.7	7.4	6.5	22.4	34.9	11.3	2.1	79.8	43.9	48.2	51.9
95476	SONOMA	86.8	85.1	0.4	0.4	1.5	1.7	19.8	22.4	5.6	5.7	6.2	6.0	5.8	23.8	28.5	15.4	3.1	78.8	42.9	48.2	51.8
95480	STEWARTS POINT	84.0	81.4	1.1	1.0	1.1	1.0	14.9	18.6	4.1	4.1	4.1	4.1	3.1	14.4	36.1	27.8	2.1	85.6	55.7	52.6	47.4
95482	UKIAH	77.4	74.7	0.8	0.9	2.1	2.3	22.0	25.3	7.1	6.7	7.3	7.4	7.9	26.2	24.5	10.8	2.1	74.3	35.4	49.4	50.7
95485	UPPER LAKE	82.1	80.6	1.2	1.3	0.4	0.4	11.6	13.4	5.9	6.3	7.0	6.8	5.5	21.5	30.2	14.7	2.1	76.2	42.8	49.2	50.8
95488	WESTPORT	86.9	84.8	0.9	0.9	0.3	0.3	5.1	5.9	3.4	3.7	5.3	4.3	5.3	22.0	42.4	11.8	1.9	85.8	48.8	54.8	45.2
95490	WILLITS	86.6	85.0	0.4	0.5	0.8	0.9	11.2	13.1	6.2	6.4	7.4	7.4	6.3	23.1	29.3	12.1	1.8	75.5	40.2	48.9	51.1
95492	WINDSOR	79.2	76.7	0.9	0.9	2.3	2.6	23.5	26.6	7.5	8.0	8.6	6.9	5.5	29.2	23.6	9.3	1.4	71.5	36.2	50.3	49.8
95493	WITTER SPRINGS	87.5	87.0	1.1	1.1	0.0	0.0	6.8	7.6	3.3	4.4	6.5	7.6	5.4	18.5	40.2	13.0	1.1	79.4	47.5	48.9	51.1
95494	YORKVILLE	64.7	60.9	0.7	0.6	0.7	0.6	33.3	37.2	5.8	7.1	7.7	7.1	5.8	26.3	30.1	9.0	1.3	75.0	38.6	52.6	47.4
95497	THE SEA RANCH	84.3	81.8	0.7	0.7	1.2	1.3	14.9	17.8	3.4	3.5	3.5	3.7	3.0	14.3	39.3	27.3	2.1	87.1	56.3	50.5	49.5
95501	EUREKA	83.3	81.3	1.5	1.6	2.9	3.2	8.0	9.3	5.8	5.4	6.1	6.9	9.2	29.0	24.5	10.9	2.4	79.0	36.2	49.1	50.9
95503	EUREKA	86.8	85.0	0.9	0.9	3.0	3.4	5.4	6.3	5.3	5.6	6.7	6.9	6.6	24.9	29.5	12.5	2.1	78.4	41.0	49.0	51.0
95511	ALDERPOINT	86.9	85.9	3.0	3.2	0.7	0.7	6.0	7.4	4.6	4.6	5.0	6.4	7.4	35.3	30.4	5.7	0.7	81.6	37.7	56.2	43.8
95514	BLOCKSBURG	87.1	85.0	3.2	3.4	1.3	1.4	6.5	6.8	4.8	4.8	4.8	6.1	7.5	35.4	31.3	5.4	0.0	81.6	37.9	56.5	43.5
95519	MCKINLEYVILLE	88.0	86.3	0.3	0.4	1.1	1.3	4.3	5.0	6.6	6.5	7.0	6.7	7.0	28.5	27.1	9.6	1.1	75.9	36.8	49.0	51.0
95521	ARCATA	85.4	83.4	1.4	1.5	2.2	2.4	6.5	7.7	4.0	3.5	4.7	9.8	21.3	27.7	19.7	7.9	1.3	84.5	27.9	49.9	50.1
95524	BAYSIDE	91.1	89.8	0.4	0.5	1.2	1.4	2.9	3.4	3.7	4.7	7.4	6.7	5.9	24.4	34.7	11.3	1.3	79.5	43.3	49.7	50.3
95525	BLUE LAKE	89.1	87.9	0.2	0.2	1.1	1.3	2.2	2.4	4.5	5.4	7.5	5.9	5.9	24.1	35.9	9.4	1.4	79.0	43.1	50.7	49.3
95526	BRIDGEVILLE	87.0	85.9	0.8	0.8	0.6	0.6	1.5	1.7	3.5	5.6	10.6	7.8	3.5	23.4	33.8	11.5	0.3	74.9	42.3	49.6	50.4
95527	BURNT RANCH	87.9	86.0	0.3	0.3	0.6	0.6	1.8	2.3	4.1	5.6	6.7	5.9	3.2	24.9	35.7	14.0	0.0	79.8	44.8	50.3	49.7
95528	CARLOTTA	89.9	88.5	1.1	1.2	0.2	0.2	3.7	4.5	4.9	5.6	8.8	8.0	6.2	22.2	33.0	10.1	1.4	75.6	42.0	50.5	49.5
95531	CRESCENT CITY	80.0	78.3	4.9	5.0	2.6	2.9	13.7	15.7	5.6	5.5	6.8	7.3	7.6	31.3	24.1	10.4	1.5	77.5	36.6	55.7	44.3
95536	FERNDALE	92.0	90.7	0.3	0.3	0.5	0.6	7.4	8.8	6.0	6.3	6.7	6.4	5.2	23.9	30.6	13.3	1.6	77.1	41.8	49.0	51.0
95540	FORTUNA	88.4	86.8	0.4	0.4	1.1	1.2	9.8	11.5	6.7	6.3	7.2	7.3	6.6	24.0	25.1	13.9	2.8	75.4	39.5	48.0	52.0
95542	GARBERVILLE	92.0	91.0	1.3	1.3	0.8	1.0	4.5	5.3	5.1	4.8	6.3	7.3	6.4	24.4	34.3	10.4	0.9	78.9	42.0	51.3	48.7
95543	GASQUET	86.7	84.6	0.5	0.5	0.5	0.6	4.2	5.2	5.8	5.3	7.9	10.1	3.7	22.5	31.8	12.3	0.6	73.7	41.8	52.5	47.5
95546	HOOPA	14.7	13.9	0.1	0.1	0.4	0.5	4.5	5.0	10.1	9.6	10.2	9.8	7.2	24.5	20.0	7.5	1.1	63.5	27.4	49.2	50.8
95547	HYDESVILLE	90.1	88.8	0.1	0.1	0.3	0.3	6.3	7.6	5.3	6.3	7.4	6.6	5.7	23.3	32.8	11.3	1.2	77.0	42.2	50.7	49.4
95548	KLAMATH	63.1	61.2	2.2	2.5	0.6	0.6	9.1	10.7	5.0	5.3	5.5	6.1	7.2	26.7	28.5	14.2	1.5	80.1	41.7	55.0	45.0
95549	KNEELAND	91.6	90.1	0.5	0.7	0.5	0.7	3.3	3.7	4.3	5.2	6.7	6.9	6.3	22.5	36.1	10.6	1.5	79.7	43.9	50.8	49.2
95550	KORBEL	91.3	90.0	0.5	0.5	0.5	1.1	2.7	2.6	4.2	5.3	6.8	6.3	6.8	23.7	34.7	10.5	1.6	80.0	43.0	50.5	49.5
95551	LOLETA	81.7	80.1	0.1	0.1	0.5	0.5	16.5	19.2	8.0	7.5	6.7	5.8	5.8	27.7	27.5	9.3	1.8	74.3	36.9	50.1	49.9
95552	MAD RIVER	88.2	88.2	0.0	0.0	0.0	0.0	0.0	0.0	0.0	0.0	11.8	5.9	0.0	17.7	52.9	11.8	0.0	88.2	51.3	52.9	47.1
95554	MYERS FLAT	89.2	87.7	1.1	1.1	0.7	0.7	4.6	5.4	5.0	5.0	6.7	7.1	6.1	24.9	34.7	9.3	1.3	78.8	41.8	51.1	48.9
95555	ORICK	86.4	84.5	0.4	0.4	0.4	0.4	4.6	5.2	3.9	3.9	6.0	6.9	4.3	22.0	38.8	12.9	1.3	81.5	46.3	50.4	49.6
95556	ORLEANS	64.4	62.6	0.2	0.2	0.4	0.5	3.3	4.2	7.0	5.6	8.6	7.0	4.9	21.9	31.4	11.9	1.9	73.7	41.3	48.6	51.4
95558	PETROLIA	90.5	89.1	0.4	0.4	0.4	0.7	8.1	9.5	5.7	5.7	6.7	7.1	5.7	24.4	32.9	10.6	1.4	77.7	41.7	51.6	48.4
	CALIFORNIA	59.6	57.1	6.7	6.5	11.3	11.8	32.4	35.5	7.4	7.1	7.8	7.3	7.7	29.8	22.1	9.3	1.4	73.3	33.8	49.8	50.2
	UNITED STATES	75.1	73.6	12.3	12.5	3.8	4.2	12.5	14.1	6.9	6.7	7.2	7.0	7.3	28.6	23.8	10.8	1.7	75.1	36.0	49.1	50.9

#	POST OFFICE NAME	2004 Per Capita Income	2004 HH Income Base	2004 Household Income Distribution (%) Less than $25,000	$25,000 to $49,999	$50,000 to $99,999	$100,000 to $149,999	$150,000 or More	Median Household Income 2004	2009	2004 National Centile	2004 State Centile	2004 Home Value Base	2004 Home Value Distribution (%) Less than $50,000	$50,000 to $89,999	$90,000 to $174,999	$175,000 to $399,999	$400,000 or More	2004 Median Home Value
95379	TUOLUMNE	20343	1518	25.2	35.2	29.6	7.9	2.0	42347	48546	54	37	1082	1.2	0.3	29.2	53.7	15.6	215447
95380	TURLOCK	16416	12759	32.8	31.2	27.1	5.7	3.2	37844	42736	39	26	7329	6.0	3.8	29.0	49.6	11.6	198497
95382	TURLOCK	23102	10729	26.5	25.7	32.0	10.8	5.0	47705	54803	68	47	6623	1.3	0.9	10.8	75.7	11.3	238725
95383	TWAIN HARTE	28626	2393	16.6	30.6	39.2	9.3	4.4	52168	58606	76	57	1946	0.9	0.4	16.7	67.6	14.4	255685
95385	VERNALIS	16961	66	27.3	28.8	37.9	6.1	0.0	43216	51032	57	38	43	4.7	9.3	46.5	27.9	11.6	163750
95386	WATERFORD	17251	2858	24.9	34.4	32.8	6.1	1.9	42803	48422	55	37	2125	5.7	0.6	38.9	40.7	14.1	184063
95388	WINTON	13314	3523	32.7	37.3	23.5	3.7	2.8	34254	38084	25	18	2255	1.9	5.7	58.3	23.8	10.3	147055
95389	YOSEMITE NATL PARK	26138	170	15.9	36.5	35.3	5.9	6.5	47866	55079	68	48	68	22.1	8.8	23.5	25.0	20.6	164286
95391	TRACY	26221	179	14.0	24.0	31.8	16.8	13.4	70637	80230	91	78	140	0.0	2.1	5.7	17.1	75.0	682927
95401	SANTA ROSA	23659	13159	18.0	27.0	35.5	14.9	4.6	54524	62558	79	60	8051	1.9	2.8	6.1	61.1	28.1	330415
95403	SANTA ROSA	27775	15609	16.6	24.6	35.0	16.7	7.1	59768	68339	84	67	9698	5.6	3.0	6.1	41.2	44.2	375371
95404	SANTA ROSA	34342	14749	18.2	22.1	32.3	15.4	12.0	60415	71508	85	68	9148	2.1	0.7	1.5	34.8	60.9	466846
95405	SANTA ROSA	35768	8831	12.0	22.5	37.6	17.4	10.6	65125	76222	89	73	6005	0.0	0.0	2.0	46.8	51.2	406028
95407	SANTA ROSA	18762	10311	22.6	27.9	35.7	10.2	3.6	49552	56049	71	51	5646	9.5	3.1	4.8	56.3	26.3	308556
95409	SANTA ROSA	38718	11839	14.6	23.8	32.9	17.4	11.3	61783	72622	86	69	8863	3.7	2.4	2.0	31.8	60.1	451534
95410	ALBION	34813	497	25.4	29.2	24.1	9.5	11.9	47321	55809	67	46	382	1.3	0.0	3.1	41.1	54.5	434694
95412	ANNAPOLIS	28661	60	13.3	18.3	35.0	18.3	15.0	68504	84164	91	76	46	0.0	0.0	0.0	19.6	80.4	616667
95415	BOONVILLE	17428	492	31.3	33.5	25.4	7.9	1.8	37320	41960	37	25	276	6.2	1.5	13.4	48.2	30.8	288571
95417	BRANSCOMB	18129	205	40.5	30.7	19.5	7.3	2.0	31574	35202	17	13	150	6.7	5.3	20.0	55.3	12.7	237037
95420	CASPAR	28105	154	24.7	33.1	27.9	6.5	7.8	43620	49143	58	39	128	4.7	0.8	7.0	54.7	32.8	318519
95421	CAZADERO	33320	941	25.3	28.7	27.2	11.1	7.8	45060	51867	61	42	625	1.8	1.0	6.1	41.1	50.1	400658
95422	CLEARLAKE	13914	5911	55.0	29.0	12.8	2.3	0.9	22010	24524	3	3	4152	18.7	21.0	41.3	15.3	3.7	108115
95423	CLEARLAKE OAKS	19317	1925	41.6	34.7	16.2	5.2	2.3	29982	33448	12	10	1512	7.2	9.7	35.7	35.6	11.8	168289
95425	CLOVERDALE	24644	3625	23.8	25.3	32.8	12.4	5.7	50867	57918	74	54	2583	4.7	2.4	4.9	57.3	30.8	330505
95427	COMPTCHE	28435	199	30.2	30.7	21.1	11.1	7.0	39783	47699	45	31	139	3.6	0.0	2.9	38.9	54.7	432500
95428	COVELO	15287	850	39.5	31.1	22.8	4.5	2.1	31777	35916	17	13	559	12.3	11.3	31.5	27.7	17.2	151250
95429	DOS RIOS	13458	25	52.0	24.0	20.0	4.0	0.0	24000	30000	4	4	19	5.3	0.0	21.1	52.6	21.1	235000
95432	ELK	36992	90	25.6	30.0	22.2	10.0	12.2	46710	55871	66	44	69	1.5	0.0	2.9	40.6	55.1	438889
95436	FORESTVILLE	34574	2592	18.5	24.7	32.6	15.2	9.0	56414	67410	81	63	1844	1.6	1.4	5.5	49.1	42.4	363566
95437	FORT BRAGG	21758	5963	31.4	31.6	27.0	6.6	3.3	37222	42670	36	25	3882	6.0	0.8	8.8	56.9	27.5	290293
95439	FULTON	23945	259	17.4	25.9	35.1	17.4	4.3	57660	67874	82	65	179	8.4	2.2	7.8	36.9	44.7	376829
95441	GEYSERVILLE	29559	913	11.4	29.6	32.1	12.7	14.2	62267	72973	86	70	583	1.9	1.4	4.0	25.6	67.2	641250
95442	GLEN ELLEN	34562	1519	13.6	22.5	35.8	14.2	13.9	69129	83318	91	77	934	0.0	0.0	1.2	14.5	84.4	688953
95443	GLENHAVEN	16010	76	39.5	39.5	19.7	1.3	0.0	28817	31972	10	9	62	1.6	21.0	40.3	35.5	1.6	155000
95444	GRATON	25745	283	18.7	16.6	37.1	20.1	7.4	63756	75575	88	71	205	0.0	0.0	5.4	36.1	58.5	451471
95445	GUALALA	31288	904	20.4	28.1	34.0	9.0	8.6	50952	57238	74	55	701	3.0	5.1	6.9	36.0	49.1	395255
95446	GUERNEVILLE	27364	2722	25.3	29.5	32.6	8.6	4.0	44612	52633	60	41	1679	2.3	1.4	9.8	56.9	29.6	297707
95448	HEALDSBURG	31796	6507	16.4	25.0	33.2	14.8	10.7	58563	68263	83	66	4355	0.4	0.4	1.7	34.3	63.2	486652
95449	HOPLAND	19550	602	29.9	27.9	29.4	8.1	4.7	40506	45833	48	33	346	7.8	4.9	10.1	35.6	41.6	325641
95450	JENNER	31313	146	26.0	29.5	27.4	11.0	6.2	44219	50000	59	40	93	3.2	1.1	6.5	37.6	51.6	411538
95451	KELSEYVILLE	23018	4950	29.7	29.5	27.0	9.1	4.7	39654	45645	45	30	3895	7.4	4.2	23.2	48.3	16.9	216992
95452	KENWOOD	41103	666	8.1	19.1	40.8	18.2	13.8	73973	88834	93	81	529	0.0	0.4	2.3	22.9	74.5	605620
95453	LAKEPORT	20093	4659	30.8	33.9	25.4	7.0	3.0	37514	43014	38	26	3420	10.4	4.7	25.0	45.3	14.7	204376
95454	LAYTONVILLE	23877	715	36.8	32.5	24.2	3.8	2.8	36952	41217	35	25	456	3.1	3.3	33.6	51.1	9.0	211194
95456	LITTLERIVER	45684	565	24.8	30.1	22.3	9.7	13.1	47176	56192	67	46	434	0.9	0.7	2.3	34.3	61.8	483607
95457	LOWER LAKE	19676	1449	30.0	29.7	32.1	6.7	1.6	40219	45671	47	32	1191	1.9	11.0	27.6	50.4	9.2	199674
95458	LUCERNE	16548	1271	44.7	34.7	15.1	5.0	0.6	27441	30402	8	7	914	12.0	17.4	44.6	19.9	6.0	128024
95459	MANCHESTER	27310	248	33.9	33.9	23.4	5.2	3.6	37822	43867	39	26	146	1.4	3.4	8.2	34.9	52.1	412000
95460	MENDOCINO	41183	1026	24.1	25.9	28.8	11.6	9.7	50000	61103	72	52	793	0.0	1.9	1.8	14.8	81.6	589652
95461	MIDDLETOWN	22626	2908	25.0	26.4	36.7	8.8	3.1	48615	55676	70	49	2323	1.4	2.5	18.9	62.7	14.5	241061
95462	MONTE RIO	32112	756	29.0	28.2	30.8	6.5	5.6	43447	51317	57	39	466	0.4	0.0	9.4	74.7	15.5	274370
95464	NICE	14509	1116	50.1	32.5	13.4	3.5	0.5	24941	26937	5	4	751	10.9	19.4	42.2	20.8	6.7	129535
95465	OCCIDENTAL	32535	1026	20.6	23.8	31.4	14.4	9.8	57554	69122	82	65	729	1.2	0.8	5.1	21.8	71.1	622835
95466	PHILO	21395	466	29.2	31.6	22.3	10.7	6.2	40000	46521	46	31	315	4.1	0.0	2.2	36.2	57.5	457317
95468	POINT ARENA	19467	559	37.0	28.4	24.2	6.1	4.3	33502	38550	22	17	313	1.9	4.5	13.7	42.8	37.1	336719
95469	POTTER VALLEY	25344	681	28.2	23.9	33.2	9.8	4.9	44898	51749	61	41	490	1.4	1.6	11.6	44.3	41.0	315385
95470	REDWOOD VALLEY	25932	2172	19.6	31.1	33.8	10.4	5.1	49415	57346	71	51	1789	3.6	4.8	9.3	51.9	30.4	319381
95472	SEBASTOPOL	35278	12272	18.3	20.6	32.1	16.8	12.1	63704	77812	88	71	8667	1.3	0.4	1.3	18.0	78.9	601003
95476	SONOMA	34419	14322	17.7	25.3	32.3	14.6	10.2	57748	67727	82	65	9552	6.0	2.3	2.6	27.6	61.6	468249
95480	STEWARTS POINT	40079	40	15.0	17.5	37.5	17.5	12.5	68141	82163	90	76	31	0.0	0.0	0.0	19.4	80.7	612500
95482	UKIAH	22286	11745	29.9	29.3	27.9	8.6	4.4	40197	46180	47	32	7250	10.3	3.7	11.1	54.4	20.5	247278
95485	UPPER LAKE	16881	1070	41.7	31.7	20.2	5.1	1.4	30530	34382	14	11	786	8.5	8.3	32.7	37.9	12.6	176515
95488	WESTPORT	38665	151	31.8	27.8	26.5	9.3	4.6	40753	46543	49	33	105	0.0	0.0	21.0	23.8	55.2	461111
95490	WILLITS	20662	5391	32.8	31.3	26.4	7.1	2.4	37847	43062	39	26	3801	7.7	5.3	17.6	58.8	10.5	219942
95492	WINDSOR	28124	8811	13.0	19.6	36.6	21.5	9.4	70248	81671	91	78	7348	3.1	3.8	3.0	36.7	53.4	415054
95493	WITTER SPRINGS	23247	37	29.7	29.7	27.0	8.1	5.4	38635	47372	42	28	30	6.7	10.0	16.7	50.0	16.7	216667
95494	YORKVILLE	25754	70	28.6	31.4	28.6	8.6	2.9	40000	44311	46	31	44	4.6	2.3	2.3	25.0	65.9	557692
95497	THE SEA RANCH	49171	561	13.0	19.6	33.7	18.9	14.8	68488	80974	91	76	429	0.0	0.0	1.6	18.0	80.4	616135
95501	EUREKA	19494	9744	43.8	28.8	21.1	4.1	2.3	29189	33103	11	9	4479	2.1	2.4	36.6	52.7	6.2	191688
95503	EUREKA	21481	9762	28.5	31.9	29.3	6.6	3.7	40192	45993	47	32	7098	6.3	1.9	27.5	54.7	9.7	212992
95511	ALDERPOINT	19290	101	33.7	42.6	17.8	3.0	3.0	32532	37586	19	15	82	0.0	0.0	37.8	50.0	12.2	207143
95514	BLOCKSBURG	18783	51	31.4	43.1	19.6	3.9	2.0	33314	37321	22	17	41	0.0	0.0	34.2	53.7	12.2	225000
95519	MCKINLEYVILLE	22217	6402	28.2	30.9	30.1	7.3	3.6	43560	49811	57	39	4439	4.4	5.2	19.6	56.1	14.7	223643
95521	ARCATA	20116	8996	46.4	25.1	19.4	6.3	2.7	27824	31519	8	7	3818	10.9	4.9	14.5	54.8	14.9	225760
95524	BAYSIDE	28770	575	20.2	28.0	28.7	14.6	8.5	51735	62130	75	56	453	6.4	1.1	5.7	50.1	36.6	333516
95525	BLUE LAKE	24450	257	24.5	30.4	30.7	8.2	6.2	45486	52395	63	42	188	3.7	8.0	18.6	37.8	31.9	258333
95526	BRIDGEVILLE	16273	300	43.7	29.3	23.7	2.7	0.7	28061	31398	9	8	211	8.5	15.2	41.2	29.4	5.7	143359
95527	BURNT RANCH	19253	164	42.7	32.3	16.5	6.7	1.8	28324	31527	9	8	120	5.0	13.3	41.7	36.7	3.3	149000
95528	CARLOTTA	19116	401	29.4	33.7	28.4	5.7	2.7	38922	44606	42	28	309	2.3	5.5	30.4	54.4	7.4	210776
95531	CRESCENT CITY	17561	7803	40.0	26.5	24.3	7.5	1.8	33645	38919	23	18	5208	11.9	8.0	30.6	41.9	7.6	173663
95536	FERNDALE	24268	1182	23.4	35.5	27.8	7.0	6.3	41109	46804	50	34	822	2.4	2.8	16.6	51.7	26.5	283475
95540	FORTUNA	19274	5303	34.2	33.4	24.7	4.5	3.2	34788	38888	27	19	3628	3.7	5.5	25.7	54.9	10.3	212221
95542	GARBERVILLE	28882	1063	35.3	32.1	26.1	3.1	3.5	36719	41385	34	24	751	3.2	2.4	15.2	53.7	25.6	300811
95543	GASQUET	15156	348	49.1	24.4	22.7	3.7	0.0	25517	28906	5	5	251	21.1	13.9	14.3	46.2	4.4	176250
95546	HOOPA	11074	1033	53.5	25.9	16.6	2.9	1.1	22708	25173	3	3	759	20.8	12.9	34.8	25.3	6.2	130478
95547	HYDESVILLE	21409	464	24.1	30.6	32.3	9.9	3.0	45545	52279	63	42	402	6.0	2.7	22.1	41.8	27.4	260784
95548	KLAMATH	21029	394	36.6	27.4	23.4	3.8	8.9	35000	39533	28	20	308	21.4	10.7	46.1	13.6	8.1	119712
95549	KNEELAND	23693	162	21.0	31.5	30.9	10.5	6.2	47644	55916	68	47	133	3.0	2.3	14.3	55.6	24.8	288043
95550	KORBEL	25380	73	23.3	30.1	31.5	8.2	6.9	46750	53154	66	45	53	0.0	5.7	15.1	47.2	32.1	305000
95551	LOLETA	18081	497	36.4	33.2	20.9	6.4	3.0	32079	36183	18	14	320	10.0	0.6	28.1	43.4	17.8	204444
95552	MAD RIVER	5735	6	100.0	0.0	0.0	0.0	0.0	16902	16902	1	2	5	0.0	0.0	100.0	0.0	0.0	162500
95554	MYERS FLAT	18825	1293	42.6	33.3	17.6	3.5	3.0	29063	32783	10	9	921	4.3	7.0	27.8	44.1	16.8	218814
95555	ORICK	18409	97	43.3	26.8	20.6	6.2	3.1	30365	34068	13	11	66	15.2	10.6	21.2	22.7	30.3	200000
95556	ORLEANS	15050	174	42.0	35.1	17.2	5.8	0.0	28976	31982	10	9	110	24.6	29.1	26.4	13.6	6.4	83333
95558	PETROLIA	27730	128	24.2	40.6	20.3	7.8	7.0	38597	42549	41	28	90	5.6	2.2	23.3	33.3	35.6	275000
	CALIFORNIA	27293		21.8	24.4	30.5	13.7	9.7	54267	64547				3.3	2.7	13.3	42.9	37.9	319678
	UNITED STATES	25866		24.7	27.1	30.8	10.9	6.5	48124	56710				10.9	15.0	33.7	30.1	10.4	145905

ZIP CODE #	POST OFFICE NAME	FINANCIAL SERVICES: Auto Loan	FINANCIAL SERVICES: Home Loan	FINANCIAL SERVICES: Investments	FINANCIAL SERVICES: Retirement Plans	THE HOME: Home Improvements: Home Repair	THE HOME: Home Improvements: Lawn & Garden	THE HOME: Furnishings: Computers & Hardware	THE HOME: Furnishings: Major Appliances	THE HOME: Furnishings: TV, Radio, Sound Equipment	THE HOME: Furnishings: Furniture	ENTERTAINMENT: Dine out/ Carry out	ENTERTAINMENT: Sports Equipment	ENTERTAINMENT: Fees & Tickets	ENTERTAINMENT: Toys & Games	ENTERTAINMENT: Travel	ENTERTAINMENT: Cable TV	PERSONAL: Apparel & Services	PERSONAL: Auto Repairs	PERSONAL: Health Insurance	PERSONAL: Pets & Supplies
95379	TUOLUMNE	75	75	72	74	75	80	75	76	75	73	92	88	74	93	75	74	89	76	76	86
95380	TURLOCK	76	69	66	67	68	73	72	74	74	73	92	84	69	89	70	72	90	75	72	82
95382	TURLOCK	89	92	99	94	90	93	93	91	90	93	113	108	93	113	91	86	111	93	84	100
95383	TWAIN HARTE	113	90	62	81	101	113	85	101	95	84	113	119	76	112	90	101	105	100	119	138
95385	VERNALIS	74	67	60	64	65	67	69	73	71	74	90	79	65	83	66	68	89	74	67	77
95386	WATERFORD	90	82	69	78	81	85	81	86	83	84	103	97	76	96	78	81	100	87	84	97
95388	WINTON	69	60	53	58	59	62	63	66	66	67	82	73	59	77	60	63	82	68	63	71
95389	YOSEMITE NATL PARK	104	82	56	74	92	104	77	93	87	76	103	109	69	102	82	93	96	92	110	127
95391	TRACY	112	139	148	139	137	135	124	124	115	124	144	145	132	154	127	112	144	119	111	137
95401	SANTA ROSA	90	93	100	95	91	94	94	92	92	95	115	109	94	115	92	88	113	94	86	102
95403	SANTA ROSA	101	108	118	110	106	110	106	105	102	107	129	122	108	128	105	98	126	105	97	115
95404	SANTA ROSA	114	123	140	125	121	126	123	120	119	123	150	140	125	150	122	115	148	121	112	131
95405	SANTA ROSA	112	131	157	132	129	133	127	124	122	126	153	146	133	158	129	119	152	124	115	135
95407	SANTA ROSA	85	88	89	86	85	88	86	86	85	88	107	99	86	107	84	82	106	87	80	95
95409	SANTA ROSA	117	128	143	126	129	139	122	125	120	124	151	137	126	146	126	121	146	123	126	137
95410	ALBION	109	102	97	97	108	127	94	107	100	101	124	105	95	103	102	107	116	104	126	123
95412	ANNAPOLIS	166	130	89	117	146	165	123	148	139	121	164	173	110	162	131	148	153	145	175	202
95415	BOONVILLE	74	64	52	61	63	68	66	71	69	69	85	77	61	78	63	67	83	71	69	77
95417	BRANSCOMB	72	53	33	49	58	68	55	63	63	54	74	73	49	71	55	66	68	63	75	82
95420	CASPAR	78	90	107	90	89	94	88	86	85	87	107	100	91	110	89	84	105	86	82	94
95421	CAZADERO	125	98	67	88	110	124	92	111	104	91	124	130	82	122	98	111	115	109	131	152
95422	CLEARLAKE	51	42	33	39	45	54	43	48	48	43	57	52	40	53	44	51	53	48	57	58
95423	CLEARLAKE OAKS	63	53	44	49	58	68	52	60	57	53	69	64	49	63	55	61	64	59	71	73
95425	CLOVERDALE	92	93	93	89	92	99	91	94	93	93	116	106	91	115	92	94	114	94	94	105
95427	COMPTCHE	116	81	44	77	95	106	80	99	92	79	108	119	69	106	83	97	99	98	118	137
95428	COVELO	66	50	33	48	55	65	55	61	62	52	73	68	49	69	55	65	66	61	73	73
95429	DOS RIOS	52	39	26	38	43	51	43	48	49	41	57	53	39	54	43	51	52	48	57	58
95432	ELK	109	102	98	97	108	127	94	107	100	101	124	105	95	103	102	106	116	104	125	122
95436	FORESTVILLE	105	122	144	125	121	124	118	115	112	117	140	136	122	145	119	109	139	115	106	126
95437	FORT BRAGG	72	70	71	69	72	79	72	73	74	70	91	85	71	93	73	75	88	74	77	84
95439	FULTON	87	95	102	97	92	94	93	91	88	93	112	107	94	112	91	85	110	91	83	100
95441	GEYSERVILLE	116	130	152	125	125	132	124	123	123	128	157	138	129	161	126	123	156	124	116	134
95442	GLEN ELLEN	123	136	148	137	135	141	131	131	126	131	157	152	134	158	132	123	154	130	124	145
95443	GLENHAVEN	58	45	32	43	49	59	49	54	54	47	64	59	44	60	49	58	59	54	65	64
95444	GRATON	97	115	118	115	114	114	104	105	98	104	123	122	109	130	106	96	122	101	97	117
95445	GUALALA	118	93	64	84	104	117	88	105	99	87	117	123	79	116	93	105	109	103	124	143
95446	GUERNEVILLE	73	80	97	83	79	83	82	79	79	81	100	94	83	102	82	77	98	81	74	87
95448	HEALDSBURG	115	129	141	127	128	133	121	122	118	122	148	140	125	151	124	116	146	121	117	136
95449	HOPLAND	96	85	68	84	89	94	82	90	85	82	103	108	77	102	82	84	98	89	93	112
95450	JENNER	107	84	57	76	95	106	79	96	90	79	106	112	71	105	85	96	99	94	113	131
95451	KELSEYVILLE	93	77	60	71	83	93	75	86	82	75	99	98	69	95	78	86	93	85	97	110
95452	KENWOOD	131	147	158	143	148	158	136	140	133	138	167	154	143	165	142	135	163	137	141	155
95453	LAKEPORT	73	67	61	64	70	78	67	72	70	67	86	80	65	82	68	72	81	72	78	83
95454	LAYTONVILLE	101	80	56	77	86	98	82	91	90	81	108	105	76	105	82	93	100	90	102	113
95456	LITTLERIVER	130	129	130	124	135	154	119	132	123	126	153	134	123	134	128	129	145	128	147	149
95457	LOWER LAKE	82	64	43	61	70	78	64	73	70	63	84	85	58	81	65	73	78	72	83	94
95458	LUCERNE	54	48	46	45	51	62	47	54	51	49	62	53	46	55	50	55	58	52	64	60
95459	MANCHESTER	104	81	55	73	92	103	77	92	87	76	103	108	69	102	82	93	96	91	109	126
95460	MENDOCINO	118	120	133	118	123	139	116	122	118	120	148	130	119	137	122	122	142	121	131	136
95461	MIDDLETOWN	94	80	60	77	86	94	77	86	83	77	100	101	74	101	79	85	94	84	95	109
95462	MONTE RIO	88	90	99	90	92	97	88	91	88	88	109	108	88	111	90	87	106	91	89	106
95464	NICE	50	41	33	38	45	53	41	47	46	41	55	51	39	51	43	49	51	47	56	58
95465	OCCIDENTAL	104	113	132	115	113	117	111	110	108	110	135	131	112	137	112	105	132	111	104	124
95466	PHILO	104	78	49	75	88	99	78	92	87	77	103	107	70	100	80	90	95	90	106	121
95468	POINT ARENA	77	64	49	64	68	77	66	71	70	65	85	82	62	84	66	72	79	70	78	86
95469	POTTER VALLEY	99	98	90	94	102	108	92	99	94	91	116	116	92	119	95	95	112	97	102	120
95470	REDWOOD VALLEY	109	110	97	106	113	117	100	106	101	100	124	126	101	129	103	101	120	103	108	130
95472	SEBASTOPOL	116	134	150	134	133	138	127	126	122	126	153	146	132	157	129	120	150	125	119	139
95476	SONOMA	111	122	138	121	122	131	117	119	115	119	145	133	121	143	120	115	141	118	117	130
95480	STEWARTS POINT	163	128	87	115	144	162	120	145	136	119	162	170	108	160	128	146	150	143	172	199
95482	UKIAH	81	82	85	82	82	87	83	83	83	82	103	97	82	102	82	82	100	84	82	93
95485	UPPER LAKE	66	51	34	47	57	66	52	60	59	50	69	69	46	67	53	62	64	59	71	77
95488	WESTPORT	105	120	148	124	118	121	119	115	113	118	142	137	122	146	119	109	140	116	104	125
95490	WILLITS	81	70	59	67	73	82	72	76	76	70	93	89	68	92	72	78	88	76	84	93
95492	WINDSOR	122	132	127	134	128	128	121	123	114	125	144	141	123	143	120	110	142	120	111	136
95493	WITTER SPRINGS	96	75	51	68	85	95	71	85	80	70	95	100	63	94	76	86	88	84	101	117
95494	YORKVILLE	92	73	51	71	79	89	74	83	81	73	97	97	68	95	74	83	90	82	93	104
95497	THE SEA RANCH	165	129	88	117	146	163	122	147	138	121	163	172	109	161	130	147	152	145	174	201
95501	EUREKA	59	56	62	57	56	62	62	60	63	60	78	71	61	77	60	62	75	62	60	67
95503	EUREKA	70	75	80	74	75	81	74	74	74	73	91	85	76	94	75	74	89	73	74	82
95511	ALDERPOINT	68	58	45	58	61	68	59	63	63	58	76	72	57	76	59	64	72	62	69	75
95514	BLOCKSBURG	68	58	45	57	60	68	59	63	63	58	76	72	57	76	59	64	71	62	69	75
95519	MCKINLEYVILLE	79	81	81	81	81	86	81	81	80	79	99	95	80	100	80	78	96	81	79	91
95521	ARCATA	61	50	60	54	50	56	68	59	67	62	83	75	62	79	61	62	80	65	56	66
95524	BAYSIDE	93	109	130	111	108	111	105	103	100	105	126	121	110	129	107	98	125	103	95	112
95525	BLUE LAKE	80	91	95	91	90	91	85	85	81	84	102	100	89	106	86	79	100	84	79	95
95526	BRIDGEVILLE	64	51	35	48	55	62	50	57	56	50	67	67	46	65	51	58	62	57	66	74
95527	BURNT RANCH	74	50	25	44	57	66	50	61	59	50	70	72	43	66	50	63	63	60	74	84
95528	CARLOTTA	78	68	52	66	72	78	65	71	69	65	84	84	63	85	66	71	80	70	77	90
95531	CRESCENT CITY	61	56	53	55	58	63	58	60	60	57	74	69	57	73	58	61	71	60	62	69
95536	FERNDALE	103	74	43	71	84	97	76	90	87	74	102	106	66	99	78	91	93	89	108	120
95540	FORTUNA	69	63	57	61	64	72	66	67	69	64	84	77	64	83	65	70	80	68	72	78
95542	GARBERVILLE	99	92	85	91	96	102	92	97	95	91	116	115	90	118	93	95	112	97	100	116
95543	GASQUET	56	42	28	40	46	55	46	51	52	44	61	57	41	58	46	55	56	51	61	61
95546	HOOPA	47	41	47	40	41	47	47	46	50	47	62	52	46	60	46	52	60	47	49	52
95547	HYDESVILLE	91	81	61	76	85	91	74	83	79	74	96	98	73	98	77	81	91	80	89	106
95548	KLAMATH	82	62	41	59	67	81	68	75	76	65	90	84	61	85	68	81	82	75	90	91
95549	KNEELAND	92	99	105	98	100	104	94	96	93	94	116	113	97	120	96	92	113	95	93	110
95550	KORBEL	84	97	111	99	96	97	94	92	89	93	112	109	98	117	95	86	111	92	84	101
95551	LOLETA	70	60	47	59	62	70	61	65	65	60	79	75	59	78	61	66	74	64	71	77
95552	MAD RIVER	28	22	15	20	24	27	20	25	23	20	27	29	18	27	22	25	25	24	29	34
95554	MYERS FLAT	63	53	43	52	56	64	57	60	61	55	73	69	53	71	56	63	68	61	67	71
95555	ORICK	74	58	40	53	66	74	55	66	62	54	74	78	49	73	59	66	69	65	78	91
95556	ORLEANS	60	45	30	43	49	59	50	55	56	47	66	62	44	62	49	59	60	55	66	66
95558	PETROLIA	108	75	39	71	88	98	75	92	86	74	101	111	64	99	77	90	92	91	110	128
	CALIFORNIA	107	111	131	112	109	115	113	111	111	114	140	129	114	141	112	109	139	113	104	122
	UNITED STATES	100	100	100	100	100	100	100	100	100	100	100	100	100	100	100	100	100	100	100	100

POPULATION CHANGE

ZIP CODE		POPULATION			2000-2004 ANNUAL RATE		HOUSEHOLDS					FAMILIES		
# POST OFFICE NAME	COUNTY FIPS CODE	2000	2004	2009	% Rate	State Centile	2000	2004	2009	% Annual Rate 2000-2004	2004 Average HH Size	2000	2004	% Annual Rate 2000-2004
95560 REDWAY	023	415	412	415	-0.2	10	193	193	196	0.0	2.03	104	104	0.0
95562 RIO DELL	023	3271	3244	3269	-0.2	9	1264	1258	1274	-0.1	2.57	859	850	-0.3
95563 SALYER	105	868	875	893	0.2	19	379	388	401	0.6	2.26	229	233	0.4
95564 SAMOA	023	394	411	424	1.0	55	158	166	172	1.2	2.48	87	91	1.1
95565 SCOTIA	023	1096	1075	1083	-0.5	5	357	353	357	-0.3	3.05	281	277	-0.3
95567 SMITH RIVER	015	2019	1956	1937	-0.7	3	767	746	742	-0.7	2.62	542	525	-0.8
95568 SOMES BAR	093	340	316	310	-1.7	1	148	139	137	-1.5	2.27	95	89	-1.5
95569 REDCREST	023	698	686	690	-0.4	6	251	249	253	-0.2	2.60	169	167	-0.3
95570 TRINIDAD	023	2601	2524	2536	-0.7	3	1191	1165	1178	-0.5	2.16	673	654	-0.7
95573 WILLOW CREEK	023	1531	1552	1575	0.3	24	684	699	715	0.5	2.22	423	430	0.4
95585 LEGGETT	045	654	644	651	-0.4	6	259	254	257	-0.5	2.49	151	148	-0.5
95587 PIERCY	045	334	330	334	-0.3	8	153	151	153	-0.3	2.13	86	85	-0.3
95589 WHITETHORN	023	711	666	667	-1.5	1	339	320	323	-1.4	2.08	199	187	-1.5
95595 ZENIA	105	401	420	441	1.1	58	166	175	186	1.3	2.39	114	119	1.0
95602 AUBURN	061	17488	19333	22470	2.4	84	6448	7159	8377	2.5	2.58	4881	5385	2.3
95603 AUBURN	061	25051	28403	34386	3.0	90	10388	11813	14345	3.1	2.37	6660	7515	2.9
95605 WEST SACRAMENTO	113	12749	13054	14026	0.6	34	4127	4200	4480	0.4	3.09	2872	2905	0.3
95606 BROOKS	113	277	289	313	1.0	55	115	121	130	1.2	2.39	78	81	0.9
95607 CAPAY	113	302	309	330	0.5	33	119	122	129	0.6	2.53	80	80	0.0
95608 CARMICHAEL	067	58916	62918	69069	1.6	70	24708	26258	28630	1.4	2.34	15537	16297	1.1
95610 CITRUS HEIGHTS	067	43542	46352	50800	1.5	69	16869	17782	19289	1.3	2.58	10972	11445	1.0
95612 CLARKSBURG	113	1351	1335	1422	-0.3	8	433	425	450	-0.4	3.04	344	337	-0.5
95614 COOL	017	3531	3844	4297	2.0	79	1291	1411	1581	2.1	2.72	1058	1150	2.0
95615 COURTLAND	067	778	772	824	-0.2	9	243	239	254	-0.4	3.01	179	175	-0.5
95616 DAVIS	113	66669	73828	82800	2.4	85	24461	27028	30285	2.4	2.52	12403	13691	2.4
95618 EL MACERO	113	935	1148	1345	5.0	97	379	469	549	5.1	2.39	286	352	5.0
95619 DIAMOND SPRINGS	017	3721	3885	4249	1.0	55	1440	1514	1662	1.2	2.55	990	1028	0.9
95620 DIXON	095	18839	19627	20839	1.0	54	5794	5984	6316	0.8	3.23	4700	4841	0.7
95621 CITRUS HEIGHTS	067	42226	45169	49741	1.6	72	16973	18036	19704	1.4	2.48	10911	11452	1.2
95623 EL DORADO	017	4252	4593	5124	1.8	76	1705	1846	2061	1.9	2.48	1277	1372	1.7
95624 ELK GROVE	067	38538	47331	56169	5.0	97	12450	14982	17494	4.5	3.14	10258	12357	4.5
95626 ELVERTA	067	6006	6381	7017	1.4	68	1843	1953	2136	1.4	3.26	1511	1588	1.2
95627 ESPARTO	113	2514	3019	3506	4.4	96	853	1020	1177	4.3	2.94	632	752	4.2
95628 FAIR OAKS	067	41073	43642	47922	1.4	68	16101	16909	18361	1.2	2.55	11445	11936	1.0
95629 FIDDLETOWN	017	806	848	919	1.2	61	335	353	383	1.2	2.40	245	257	1.1
95630 FOLSOM	067	51884	61420	71065	4.1	96	17196	20512	23800	4.2	2.66	12527	14939	4.2
95631 FORESTHILL	061	5777	6416	7694	2.5	86	2201	2452	2946	2.6	2.62	1670	1846	2.4
95632 GALT	067	24409	27879	31670	3.2	91	7622	8611	9679	2.9	3.21	6217	7014	2.9
95633 GARDEN VALLEY	017	3072	3307	3701	1.8	75	1134	1226	1377	1.9	2.65	855	917	1.7
95634 GEORGETOWN	017	2307	2453	2706	1.5	68	888	948	1050	1.6	2.51	645	683	1.4
95635 GREENWOOD	017	862	936	1043	2.0	79	321	351	394	2.1	2.53	236	256	1.9
95636 GRIZZLY FLATS	017	563	619	695	2.3	83	226	249	280	2.3	2.49	168	184	2.2
95637 GUINDA	113	261	271	292	0.9	50	101	105	112	0.9	2.58	68	70	0.7
95638 HERALD	067	1682	1816	1999	1.8	76	557	596	649	1.6	3.01	463	493	1.5
95640 IONE	005	9819	10654	11439	1.9	78	2056	2361	2644	3.3	2.72	1537	1760	3.2
95641 ISLETON	067	2006	2132	2334	1.4	68	871	920	998	1.3	2.31	534	557	1.0
95642 JACKSON	005	5930	6247	6687	1.2	63	2535	2679	2875	1.3	2.23	1651	1740	1.2
95645 KNIGHTS LANDING	101	1675	1732	1860	0.8	45	563	580	618	0.7	2.98	391	400	0.5
95648 LINCOLN	061	15478	20182	26442	6.4	98	5390	7025	9202	6.4	2.85	4312	5598	6.3
95650 LOOMIS	061	10953	12744	15641	3.6	94	3915	4580	5638	3.8	2.77	3095	3600	3.6
95651 LOTUS	017	700	736	814	1.2	61	263	276	305	1.1	2.66	203	212	1.0
95652 MCCLELLAN	067	1062	1063	1126	0.0	15	285	283	301	-0.2	2.95	228	223	-0.5
95653 MADISON	113	891	904	950	0.3	25	160	163	174	0.4	4.10	127	129	0.4
95655 MATHER	067	914	670	679	-7.1	0	369	269	270	-7.2	2.49	220	158	-7.5
95658 NEWCASTLE	061	5894	6858	8427	3.6	94	2266	2661	3285	3.9	2.57	1724	2003	3.6
95659 NICOLAUS	101	730	774	835	1.4	66	270	284	303	1.2	2.73	194	204	1.2
95660 NORTH HIGHLANDS	067	30431	32520	35679	1.6	71	9995	10587	11499	1.4	3.06	7391	7760	1.2
95661 ROSEVILLE	061	25197	28995	35395	3.4	93	9694	11237	13811	3.5	2.51	6643	7625	3.3
95662 ORANGEVALE	067	32024	33128	35651	0.8	46	11691	11989	12776	0.6	2.73	8620	8770	0.4
95663 PENRYN	061	2022	2249	2700	2.5	86	738	825	993	2.7	2.72	588	655	2.6
95664 PILOT HILL	017	1169	1347	1550	3.4	93	415	480	554	3.5	2.81	334	385	3.4
95665 PINE GROVE	005	3962	4395	4845	2.5	85	1616	1801	1993	2.6	2.40	1207	1340	2.5
95666 PIONEER	005	5924	6141	6522	0.9	48	2611	2714	2888	0.9	2.26	1881	1950	0.9
95667 PLACERVILLE	017	34922	38224	43145	2.2	82	13650	15006	16994	2.3	2.51	9676	10542	2.0
95668 PLEASANT GROVE	101	1046	1066	1161	0.5	29	374	384	419	0.6	2.78	290	297	0.6
95669 PLYMOUTH	005	1943	2005	2142	0.7	43	764	785	838	0.6	2.55	555	569	0.6
95670 RANCHO CORDOVA	067	49713	53337	58774	1.7	73	18762	19968	21785	1.5	2.66	12708	13356	1.2
95672 RESCUE	017	3691	4114	4670	2.6	87	1259	1408	1601	2.7	2.92	1041	1157	2.5
95673 RIO LINDA	067	13933	15063	16756	1.9	77	4605	4950	5467	1.7	3.03	3520	3758	1.6
95674 RIO OSO	101	944	970	1029	0.6	38	330	337	354	0.5	2.88	247	252	0.5
95677 ROCKLIN	061	21327	25502	31744	4.3	96	8142	9739	12139	4.3	2.60	5863	7016	4.3
95678 ROSEVILLE	061	30633	36086	44608	3.9	95	11802	13858	17111	3.9	2.59	7959	9298	3.7
95679 RUMSEY	113	17	17	18	0.0	15	11	11	12	0.0	1.55	7	7	0.0
95681 SHERIDAN	061	1151	1278	1535	2.5	85	380	424	511	2.6	3.01	307	341	2.5
95682 SHINGLE SPRINGS	017	25228	28119	31923	2.6	87	9230	10319	11731	2.7	2.72	7230	8026	2.5
95683 SLOUGHHOUSE	067	4779	5628	6472	3.9	95	1958	2292	2615	3.8	2.41	1565	1819	3.6
95684 SOMERSET	017	3156	3513	3974	2.6	87	1206	1348	1529	2.7	2.61	940	1043	2.5
95685 SUTTER CREEK	005	5540	5874	6318	1.4	66	2340	2480	2668	1.4	2.37	1612	1698	1.2
95687 VACAVILLE	095	57587	63049	68673	2.2	82	19267	21240	23228	2.3	2.73	14051	15484	2.3
95688 VACAVILLE	095	32553	33978	36143	1.0	55	11300	11730	12424	0.9	2.88	8866	9199	0.9
95689 VOLCANO	005	1331	1383	1471	0.9	51	566	589	628	0.9	2.35	429	445	0.9
95690 WALNUT GROVE	067	2381	2615	2922	2.2	82	858	927	1023	1.8	2.74	581	625	1.7
95691 WEST SACRAMENTO	113	19050	21759	24995	3.2	91	7344	8341	9522	3.0	2.59	4772	5442	3.1
95692 WHEATLAND	115	3576	3860	4142	1.8	76	1227	1312	1399	1.6	2.94	936	997	1.5
95693 WILTON	067	5802	6073	6574	1.1	58	1910	1984	2129	0.9	3.04	1603	1657	0.8
95694 WINTERS	113	8540	9420	10476	2.3	84	2699	2981	3307	2.4	3.13	2159	2378	2.3
95695 WOODLAND	113	38185	40466	44072	1.4	66	13571	14406	15658	1.4	2.75	9671	10214	1.3
95698 ZAMORA	113	247	260	281	1.2	62	87	91	98	1.1	2.85	65	68	1.1
95701 ALTA	061	839	900	1060	1.7	73	308	331	391	1.7	2.71	220	235	1.6
95703 APPLEGATE	061	1502	1676	2014	2.6	87	565	630	758	2.6	2.64	408	453	2.5
95709 CAMINO	017	4405	5079	5854	3.4	93	1703	1970	2273	3.5	2.58	1284	1468	3.2
95713 COLFAX	061	8676	9781	11808	2.9	89	3337	3780	4580	3.0	2.56	2437	2739	2.8
95714 DUTCH FLAT	061	559	615	734	2.3	83	232	256	307	2.3	2.39	166	181	2.1
95715 EMIGRANT GAP	061	38	41	48	1.8	75	12	13	15	1.9	3.15	9	9	0.0
95717 GOLD RUN	061	171	195	237	3.1	91	72	82	100	3.1	2.37	52	59	3.0
CALIFORNIA					1.4					1.2	2.90			1.2
UNITED STATES					1.2					1.3	2.58			1.1

ZIP CODE #	POST OFFICE NAME	RACE (%) White 2000	White 2004	Black 2000	Black 2004	Asian/Pacific 2000	Asian/Pacific 2004	% Hispanic Origin 2000	% Hispanic Origin 2004	2004 AGE DISTRIBUTION (%) 0-4	5-9	10-14	15-19	20-24	25-44	45-64	65-84	85+	18+	MEDIAN AGE 2004	% 2004 Males	% 2004 Females
95560	REDWAY	90.1	88.4	1.2	1.5	0.5	0.7	4.3	5.1	4.9	4.6	6.8	6.8	5.3	25.7	36.2	8.7	1.0	79.4	42.2	51.5	48.5
95562	RIO DELL	85.7	83.6	0.2	0.2	0.4	0.4	10.8	12.7	7.0	6.8	7.5	7.2	7.5	24.9	25.1	12.6	1.4	74.4	36.7	50.4	49.6
95563	SALYER	82.8	81.1	0.0	0.0	0.0	0.1	2.2	2.9	4.0	6.4	6.9	7.1	3.4	21.7	34.2	14.9	1.5	77.3	45.3	52.1	47.9
95564	SAMOA	85.0	83.0	0.8	1.0	1.0	1.2	6.4	7.1	4.1	4.1	7.1	8.3	9.3	31.4	27.3	7.5	1.0	80.1	35.5	52.8	47.2
95565	SCOTIA	90.5	89.0	0.2	0.2	1.2	1.4	7.3	8.7	9.0	9.8	10.5	7.1	5.7	30.8	21.4	5.2	0.6	65.8	30.2	52.4	47.6
95567	SMITH RIVER	71.1	68.0	0.1	0.1	1.9	2.0	24.1	28.0	7.1	7.0	7.3	6.0	6.4	21.4	27.7	15.0	2.2	75.1	41.1	49.7	50.3
95568	SOMES BAR	79.7	77.5	0.3	0.3	0.6	0.6	4.4	5.4	2.9	4.8	10.1	7.3	3.2	20.6	38.0	12.3	1.0	76.9	45.6	52.5	47.5
95569	REDCREST	87.5	86.0	1.2	1.2	0.9	1.0	5.9	7.1	5.5	6.0	7.0	7.6	7.4	27.3	29.9	8.0	1.3	76.7	37.8	51.2	48.8
95570	TRINIDAD	87.0	85.5	0.4	0.4	0.6	0.7	4.1	4.8	4.0	4.2	5.6	6.2	5.0	23.5	38.0	11.8	1.6	82.2	45.7	50.1	49.9
95573	WILLOW CREEK	81.8	80.1	0.5	0.5	0.9	0.9	5.4	6.3	4.8	5.0	5.2	5.8	5.1	19.5	34.5	18.2	1.9	81.4	47.5	49.8	50.2
95585	LEGGETT	86.1	84.2	1.2	1.4	1.5	1.7	6.3	7.6	4.4	5.6	7.1	6.4	6.1	24.4	36.8	8.7	0.6	78.9	42.6	53.1	46.9
95587	PIERCY	85.9	83.9	1.2	1.2	1.5	1.5	6.0	7.0	4.9	5.5	7.0	5.8	6.1	24.2	37.0	8.8	0.9	79.1	42.8	54.2	45.8
95589	WHITETHORN	93.0	92.0	0.3	0.3	0.7	0.8	3.1	3.8	4.7	4.5	6.2	6.3	4.4	20.9	40.1	12.5	0.6	80.3	46.2	51.4	48.7
95595	ZENIA	88.8	87.6	0.0	0.0	0.8	0.7	3.0	3.3	3.8	5.2	11.0	6.7	1.9	23.1	37.6	9.8	1.0	75.5	44.1	52.1	47.9
95602	AUBURN	92.9	91.7	0.5	0.5	1.3	1.5	5.7	6.9	4.8	5.2	6.8	6.9	5.9	20.1	29.5	17.4	3.4	79.2	45.2	48.9	51.1
95603	AUBURN	92.7	91.5	0.5	0.5	1.6	1.8	6.5	7.9	5.1	5.6	6.8	6.5	5.7	22.8	29.4	15.1	3.0	78.2	43.3	47.6	52.4
95605	WEST SACRAMENTO	58.8	55.4	3.2	3.1	7.8	7.9	38.1	42.5	7.9	8.4	10.2	9.4	7.2	25.5	19.8	10.5	1.1	67.6	31.3	50.0	50.0
95606	BROOKS	80.9	77.9	1.8	1.7	1.1	1.4	16.6	19.4	5.5	6.2	6.2	5.2	4.5	23.2	33.2	14.5	1.4	78.6	44.4	50.9	49.1
95607	CAPAY	75.5	72.2	2.3	2.3	2.3	2.3	19.9	23.0	5.5	6.2	6.5	5.5	4.9	23.6	31.7	14.2	1.9	78.0	43.4	51.1	48.9
95608	CARMICHAEL	86.1	83.7	2.9	3.2	4.0	4.6	7.0	8.6	5.2	5.4	6.5	6.7	6.6	24.7	26.7	15.5	2.8	78.9	41.6	47.0	53.0
95610	CITRUS HEIGHTS	84.2	81.7	2.9	3.1	3.4	3.8	10.6	12.6	7.1	6.6	7.1	6.9	8.2	29.9	22.9	9.8	1.5	75.2	34.2	48.9	51.1
95612	CLARKSBURG	72.5	69.7	0.7	0.7	5.2	5.1	42.5	47.3	6.9	7.3	9.0	6.1	5.3	26.7	26.0	11.6	1.1	72.7	37.8	51.5	48.5
95614	COOL	95.1	94.0	0.2	0.2	1.0	1.2	4.8	6.1	5.1	6.6	8.2	6.6	4.1	23.1	31.9	13.6	1.0	75.5	43.2	49.4	50.7
95615	COURTLAND	58.9	54.7	0.8	0.9	6.9	7.1	44.6	49.6	5.4	5.8	7.1	5.8	6.7	25.4	29.3	12.8	1.6	77.7	40.6	55.7	44.3
95616	DAVIS	69.1	65.8	2.4	2.4	18.3	19.7	10.3	12.1	4.8	4.6	5.3	13.7	21.4	27.0	16.9	5.5	0.9	82.2	25.1	47.5	52.5
95618	EL MACERO	84.5	82.9	1.4	1.4	8.8	9.6	7.0	7.9	3.5	3.9	6.1	5.9	4.3	18.0	32.1	23.0	3.2	82.7	51.4	48.9	51.1
95619	DIAMOND SPRINGS	91.4	89.7	0.1	0.1	0.7	0.9	7.3	9.1	5.1	5.6	6.9	7.3	6.0	21.9	27.4	16.1	3.6	77.6	43.2	47.0	53.0
95620	DIXON	70.5	67.0	1.8	1.8	3.3	3.6	34.3	38.6	8.5	8.4	8.6	7.7	7.2	29.9	22.0	6.9	0.8	69.8	32.1	50.1	49.9
95621	CITRUS HEIGHTS	85.0	82.5	2.9	3.2	3.1	3.5	9.5	11.5	6.8	6.5	6.9	6.3	7.0	28.9	22.4	12.9	2.3	75.9	36.3	47.6	52.4
95623	EL DORADO	93.0	91.7	0.2	0.3	0.8	0.9	5.9	7.4	4.5	5.4	6.6	7.0	5.2	21.0	33.1	15.6	1.7	78.6	45.2	48.7	51.3
95624	ELK GROVE	71.2	67.0	5.0	5.4	10.9	12.6	12.7	14.9	7.6	7.9	8.6	7.8	6.3	28.4	25.1	7.3	1.1	70.8	34.8	48.8	51.2
95626	ELVERTA	81.3	78.6	2.3	2.3	3.5	3.9	12.2	14.6	5.7	6.7	8.9	9.1	7.2	25.7	27.1	8.8	0.8	73.1	36.6	49.6	50.5
95627	ESPARTO	66.4	61.9	0.8	0.7	1.9	2.0	37.1	42.4	7.0	7.6	9.7	8.9	5.8	25.8	22.6	11.4	1.2	70.2	35.0	50.8	49.2
95628	FAIR OAKS	88.2	86.2	1.7	1.9	4.1	4.7	6.4	7.8	5.3	5.7	6.7	6.7	5.6	25.4	29.5	13.6	1.5	78.0	41.7	48.8	51.2
95629	FIDDLETOWN	94.4	93.5	0.1	0.2	0.5	0.5	5.3	6.5	3.9	4.8	5.7	5.7	3.9	19.1	37.9	17.6	1.5	81.5	48.7	49.4	50.6
95630	FOLSOM	77.9	75.8	6.0	5.4	7.4	9.0	9.5	10.8	7.2	7.3	6.8	5.5	5.8	35.3	23.5	7.4	1.1	75.3	36.3	54.1	45.9
95631	FORESTHILL	92.9	91.9	0.5	0.5	0.7	0.7	4.9	5.9	4.0	5.2	8.3	7.2	5.6	22.7	31.8	13.9	1.3	77.8	43.3	50.5	49.5
95632	GALT	73.0	69.2	1.2	1.3	2.7	3.1	30.2	34.5	8.6	8.7	9.5	7.7	6.7	29.4	20.4	8.2	0.9	68.2	32.1	49.9	50.2
95633	GARDEN VALLEY	93.8	92.7	0.8	0.8	0.6	0.8	4.8	6.1	4.5	5.5	6.6	6.8	4.8	22.7	34.3	13.5	1.3	79.1	44.5	51.6	48.4
95634	GEORGETOWN	93.8	92.7	1.1	1.2	0.7	0.8	4.2	5.3	4.1	5.0	6.7	6.6	4.8	20.8	34.9	15.5	1.6	80.0	46.1	51.8	48.2
95635	GREENWOOD	92.5	91.2	2.1	2.2	0.7	0.9	5.2	6.4	4.6	5.3	6.7	7.5	5.5	22.4	32.6	13.9	1.5	79.2	43.8	53.4	46.6
95636	GRIZZLY FLATS	92.0	90.5	0.4	0.3	0.5	0.8	5.7	7.3	5.3	5.8	5.7	5.3	3.1	22.3	37.0	14.4	1.1	79.2	46.2	51.9	48.1
95637	GUINDA	79.3	76.0	1.9	1.9	1.5	1.5	17.6	20.7	5.5	5.9	6.3	5.2	4.4	23.3	34.0	14.0	1.5	78.6	44.6	50.2	49.8
95638	HERALD	90.1	88.3	0.6	0.6	2.1	2.5	10.4	12.7	6.3	8.1	7.8	6.6	4.0	25.4	31.8	9.2	0.9	73.4	40.5	50.4	49.6
95640	IONE	66.8	64.9	13.1	13.1	1.8	1.9	17.1	19.2	4.1	4.2	4.7	11.2	8.7	36.2	22.7	7.4	0.8	80.6	35.1	69.4	30.6
95641	ISLETON	76.7	73.7	1.4	1.4	6.2	6.8	24.1	27.5	4.6	5.0	5.1	4.6	4.6	22.6	33.9	18.1	1.6	82.6	47.3	52.9	47.1
95642	JACKSON	92.7	91.3	0.3	0.4	0.6	0.8	6.4	7.7	5.0	5.3	5.9	5.8	5.5	19.7	29.3	19.0	4.5	80.1	46.9	46.9	53.1
95645	KNIGHTS LANDING	60.3	56.8	1.1	1.0	1.7	1.7	52.4	57.6	7.5	6.8	7.4	7.9	7.8	27.7	22.3	11.4	1.2	73.8	35.1	54.2	45.8
95648	LINCOLN	81.7	78.7	0.5	0.5	1.5	1.7	21.2	25.0	8.2	8.3	8.3	7.5	7.4	28.5	21.7	8.8	1.4	70.8	33.1	49.0	51.1
95650	LOOMIS	90.2	88.8	0.4	0.4	3.1	3.4	6.3	7.6	5.3	6.2	7.8	7.8	5.4	22.8	30.2	13.0	1.5	75.5	42.1	49.6	50.4
95651	LOTUS	94.4	93.3	0.6	0.5	0.7	1.1	3.4	4.4	5.3	6.5	7.5	7.9	5.7	21.2	34.2	10.5	1.2	76.1	42.8	51.1	48.9
95652	MCCLELLAN	60.3	57.1	16.9	17.1	7.6	8.2	16.2	18.8	12.0	6.0	5.3	6.0	26.3	30.3	10.3	3.6	0.3	74.6	23.9	55.2	44.8
95653	MADISON	47.7	44.1	0.7	0.7	0.8	0.8	67.3	71.9	10.3	9.3	8.4	10.0	7.2	25.7	21.1	7.4	0.7	66.7	29.8	50.4	49.6
95655	MATHER	44.0	39.4	12.9	12.7	9.0	9.4	15.2	17.3	7.3	7.6	10.5	8.8	6.1	33.6	18.1	7.5	0.6	69.0	32.2	51.2	48.8
95658	NEWCASTLE	91.5	90.2	0.3	0.2	2.4	2.6	5.1	6.0	4.6	5.4	7.0	6.5	4.0	20.7	34.2	15.8	1.8	78.7	45.9	49.3	50.7
95659	NICOLAUS	86.0	83.7	0.1	0.1	2.1	2.2	15.2	18.5	4.3	5.2	6.6	6.9	5.7	24.0	30.9	15.3	1.3	79.6	43.5	55.2	44.8
95660	NORTH HIGHLANDS	66.2	62.6	11.8	12.1	6.0	6.6	16.6	19.3	8.7	8.2	9.3	8.2	8.1	26.8	19.5	10.4	0.9	68.9	30.8	48.8	51.2
95661	ROSEVILLE	88.5	86.7	1.3	1.3	3.9	4.5	7.9	9.4	6.1	6.5	7.3	6.9	7.3	25.7	26.3	11.0	3.1	75.8	38.6	47.1	52.9
95662	ORANGEVALE	89.4	87.5	1.2	1.3	2.9	3.4	6.9	8.3	5.7	6.2	7.9	7.7	6.6	27.2	27.4	10.1	1.3	75.3	38.0	49.5	50.5
95663	PENRYN	90.7	89.3	0.3	0.2	3.0	3.3	6.4	7.7	5.0	6.1	7.3	6.9	4.9	21.7	32.3	14.1	1.7	77.3	44.0	50.0	50.0
95664	PILOT HILL	92.9	91.5	0.2	0.2	1.9	2.1	5.9	7.4	3.9	7.0	7.9	7.7	3.9	22.5	37.2	9.5	0.5	75.9	43.7	51.2	48.8
95665	PINE GROVE	91.9	90.1	0.6	0.7	1.5	1.8	6.2	7.9	4.0	4.7	5.9	6.2	5.4	16.7	34.0	21.0	2.2	81.9	49.2	50.9	49.2
95666	PIONEER	95.1	94.2	0.2	0.2	0.5	0.6	5.1	6.2	3.7	4.3	5.5	4.9	3.4	17.2	35.2	23.9	1.7	83.3	51.5	50.1	49.9
95667	PLACERVILLE	91.6	90.0	0.4	0.4	0.9	1.0	7.7	9.6	4.9	5.6	7.1	7.1	5.4	21.9	31.3	14.3	2.5	77.9	43.8	48.7	51.3
95668	PLEASANT GROVE	84.5	82.0	1.2	1.2	1.4	1.7	12.8	15.4	6.0	6.4	7.1	6.9	6.8	23.8	28.9	12.8	1.3	76.4	39.5	52.8	47.2
95669	PLYMOUTH	91.7	90.1	0.3	0.4	1.1	1.3	6.2	7.5	4.9	5.7	6.6	6.2	4.8	22.7	32.4	14.9	1.7	78.6	44.4	48.8	51.2
95670	RANCHO CORDOVA	70.8	67.7	8.8	9.0	9.1	10.2	11.4	13.3	7.7	7.3	7.7	7.3	7.4	28.8	22.4	10.3	1.1	72.7	34.2	48.7	51.3
95672	RESCUE	92.3	90.9	0.3	0.3	1.4	1.6	5.1	6.3	5.4	6.7	8.3	7.5	4.8	21.8	33.7	10.6	1.2	74.9	42.5	51.0	49.0
95673	RIO LINDA	82.4	79.3	2.2	2.4	3.3	3.9	11.3	13.7	6.7	6.9	8.8	8.2	7.2	27.1	24.7	9.6	1.0	72.6	35.7	49.4	50.6
95674	RIO OSO	83.8	81.2	0.0	0.0	3.2	3.6	19.2	22.8	4.9	5.9	9.5	8.1	6.6	24.2	25.1	14.4	1.3	75.0	40.2	51.2	48.8
95677	ROCKLIN	89.0	87.4	0.8	0.8	3.8	4.1	7.9	9.4	7.0	7.4	7.8	6.9	6.8	28.9	24.3	9.8	1.2	73.6	36.4	48.5	51.5
95678	ROSEVILLE	82.7	80.7	1.3	1.3	4.1	4.6	17.9	20.1	7.8	7.4	7.5	6.6	6.8	32.5	21.5	8.7	1.3	73.2	34.2	48.9	51.1
95679	RUMSEY	70.6	64.7	0.0	0.0	0.0	5.9	23.5	23.5	5.9	5.9	11.8	0.0	5.9	17.7	47.1	5.9	0.0	76.5	46.3	52.9	47.1
95681	SHERIDAN	84.9	82.7	0.4	0.4	0.9	0.9	13.7	16.2	5.7	6.8	8.6	7.3	6.1	25.3	28.2	10.9	1.2	74.3	39.5	49.8	50.2
95682	SHINGLE SPRINGS	92.5	91.1	0.6	0.6	1.6	1.9	6.3	7.9	6.0	6.7	7.9	7.2	5.7	24.2	29.3	11.6	1.4	74.9	40.4	48.7	51.3
95683	SLOUGHHOUSE	88.5	86.9	2.6	2.7	3.3	3.8	6.2	7.4	5.0	5.9	6.4	6.1	2.4	19.8	33.7	19.4	1.3	78.4	47.9	49.9	50.1
95684	SOMERSET	93.5	92.2	0.3	0.3	0.5	0.6	4.9	6.2	4.6	5.2	7.0	7.2	3.4	21.0	37.1	13.9	0.7	78.3	45.8	50.3	49.7
95685	SUTTER CREEK	92.4	90.9	0.2	0.3	1.0	1.1	5.8	7.1	4.2	4.7	6.3	6.9	5.2	18.9	32.4	18.5	3.0	80.2	47.6	47.7	52.3
95687	VACAVILLE	71.1	68.2	10.8	10.9	5.2	5.8	15.7	18.1	6.8	6.7	7.6	7.0	7.8	32.9	22.3	7.9	1.1	74.6	34.0	52.7	47.3
95688	VACAVILLE	79.6	77.3	4.0	4.0	3.6	4.0	19.5	21.9	7.2	7.3	8.0	7.2	6.2	27.8	26.3	9.1	1.0	73.0	36.5	49.1	50.9
95689	VOLCANO	95.7	94.8	0.2	0.3	0.5	0.6	3.7	4.5	3.3	4.1	5.4	4.9	3.5	15.0	39.8	23.0	1.1	84.1	52.4	49.5	50.5
95690	WALNUT GROVE	64.8	61.5	1.2	1.4	8.0	8.0	39.4	43.6	6.2	6.3	7.0	6.1	5.6	26.4	25.1	15.6	1.6	76.6	39.4	52.5	47.5
95691	WEST SACRAMENTO	69.2	66.9	2.2	2.1	7.8	8.1	24.5	27.7	7.3	7.1	7.6	7.2	6.9	25.4	24.9	11.8	1.7	73.6	36.9	49.1	50.9
95692	WHEATLAND	77.2	74.1	0.8	0.8	4.4	4.9	19.0	21.9	6.7	7.3	10.5	9.1	5.7	24.6	23.4	11.6	1.1	69.6	35.6	48.9	51.1
95693	WILTON	84.1	81.5	2.0	2.1	2.6	2.9	10.9	13.1	4.8	6.4	8.0	7.4	4.5	22.9	33.0	11.9	1.0	75.9	42.8	50.6	49.4
95694	WINTERS	71.1	67.8	0.8	0.8	1.6	1.5	42.7	47.9	7.8	7.7	9.0	8.3	7.4	27.7	23.3	7.8	1.1	70.4	32.9	50.9	49.1
95695	WOODLAND	69.8	66.6	1.2	1.2	3.3	3.4	35.7	40.2	7.2	6.9	7.7	7.9	7.7	27.3	23.3	10.0	2.1	73.3	34.6	49.2	50.8
95698	ZAMORA	71.3	67.7	4.5	4.6	3.2	3.5	28.3	32.7	5.8	6.2	8.5	8.1	5.8	26.2	26.2	11.9	1.5	75.0	37.8	53.1	46.9
95701	ALTA	94.8	93.9	0.1	0.1	0.6	0.7	4.1	5.0	5.1	6.9	7.0	6.9	5.6	25.4	29.6	12.7	0.9	76.4	41.6	52.0	48.0
95703	APPLEGATE	92.3	91.2	0.2	0.2	1.0	1.1	6.2	7.5	4.4	6.0	6.4	6.4	4.5	22.7	32.3	15.5	1.9	79.5	44.8	49.8	50.2
95709	CAMINO	92.0	90.2	0.3	0.3	0.8	1.0	8.1	10.3	4.9	5.8	7.2	6.3	4.6	21.6	32.8	15.2	1.6	78.1	44.8	50.1	49.9
95713	COLFAX	93.0	91.8	0.5	0.5	1.0	1.0	5.6	6.8	5.0	6.0	7.5	6.7	5.1	23.1	32.5	12.6	1.5	77.1	43.0	49.8	50.2
95714	DUTCH FLAT	94.3	93.3	0.4	0.5	0.7	0.8	4.3	5.0	5.9	6.5	7.8	6.3	3.9	24.6	31.5	11.9	1.6	75.6	42.2	49.4	50.6
95715	EMIGRANT GAP	94.7	95.1	0.0	0.0	0.0	0.0	5.3	4.9	4.9	7.3	7.3	7.3	7.3	26.8	29.3	9.8	0.0	80.5	39.2	53.7	46.3
95717	GOLD RUN	94.7	93.9	0.0	0.0	0.6	0.5	4.7	5.1	6.2	6.7	8.2	6.7	4.1	26.7	29.2	11.3	1.0	74.4	40.7	51.8	48.2
	CALIFORNIA	59.6	57.1	6.7	6.5	11.3	11.8	32.4	35.5	7.4	7.1	7.8	7.3	7.7	29.8	22.1	9.3	1.4	73.3	33.8	49.8	50.2
	UNITED STATES	75.1	73.6	12.3	12.5	3.8	4.2	12.5	14.1	6.9	6.7	7.2	7.0	7.3	28.6	23.8	10.8	1.7	75.1	36.0	49.1	50.9

#	POST OFFICE NAME	2004 Per Capita Income	2004 HH Income Base	2004 Household Income Distribution (%): Less than $25,000	$25,000 to $49,999	$50,000 to $99,999	$100,000 to $149,999	$150,000 or More	Median Household Income: 2004	2009	2004 National Centile	2004 State Centile	2004 Home Value Base	2004 Home Value Distribution (%): Less than $50,000	$50,000 to $89,999	$90,000 to $174,999	$175,000 to $399,999	$400,000 or More	2004 Median Home Value
95560	REDWAY	21036	193	44.6	32.1	16.1	2.6	4.7	27875	31617	8	7	138	5.1	8.0	23.2	50.7	13.0	228571
95562	RIO DELL	14376	1258	38.9	38.9	20.2	1.0	1.0	31212	34412	16	12	747	2.4	4.0	53.0	35.6	5.0	161442
95563	SALYER	15589	388	47.4	35.6	11.6	4.9	0.5	25936	28952	6	5	288	14.9	2.1	29.2	43.4	10.4	183871
95564	SAMOA	17250	166	35.5	38.6	17.5	8.4	0.0	33186	37630	21	16	64	7.8	10.9	42.2	35.9	3.1	144444
95565	SCOTIA	14614	353	21.5	47.0	27.5	3.4	0.6	40340	44925	47	32	110	6.4	10.9	26.4	30.0	26.4	194444
95567	SMITH RIVER	16186	746	37.7	33.5	21.3	4.6	3.0	33172	36759	21	16	565	16.6	5.8	34.3	32.2	11.0	147877
95568	SOMES BAR	21089	139	46.8	21.6	22.3	5.0	4.3	27305	32769	8	7	98	9.2	13.3	36.7	32.7	8.2	148214
95569	REDCREST	15229	249	37.0	37.8	20.9	4.0	0.4	32939	37748	21	16	154	2.0	6.5	37.7	32.5	21.4	191667
95570	TRINIDAD	24123	1165	34.0	30.4	22.6	9.2	3.9	35510	40422	30	21	839	7.3	3.9	15.9	38.4	34.6	297222
95573	WILLOW CREEK	21283	699	38.6	26.8	24.9	6.7	3.0	32270	37059	18	14	478	9.4	9.2	36.4	37.5	7.5	162500
95585	LEGGETT	14805	254	50.4	26.4	17.7	4.7	0.8	24806	28265	4	4	169	9.5	7.7	26.0	40.2	16.6	209483
95587	PIERCY	18333	151	47.7	27.2	19.2	5.3	0.7	26767	31646	7	6	96	8.3	6.3	27.1	28.1	30.2	227778
95589	WHITETHORN	22591	320	31.9	35.6	24.4	5.9	2.2	38486	43158	41	27	268	1.9	3.4	7.5	49.6	37.7	328261
95595	ZENIA	16573	175	50.3	21.7	21.1	4.6	2.3	24822	26735	4	4	124	12.9	12.1	24.2	33.1	17.7	178571
95602	AUBURN	29875	7159	18.1	28.3	30.2	14.2	9.2	53861	63580	78	59	5639	1.5	4.7	4.9	42.8	46.2	383473
95603	AUBURN	29800	11813	19.5	26.2	34.1	12.4	7.7	54136	63971	79	59	8090	4.8	3.7	5.4	50.6	35.5	332510
95605	WEST SACRAMENTO	12859	4200	42.8	33.8	19.5	2.8	1.1	29458	33181	11	9	2002	7.2	5.6	59.2	27.1	0.9	151744
95606	BROOKS	27026	121	24.8	21.5	31.4	17.4	5.0	56082	67450	81	62	94	1.1	2.1	7.5	31.9	57.5	443750
95607	CAPAY	25342	122	26.2	22.1	33.6	13.1	4.9	52213	63429	76	57	90	3.3	1.1	5.6	27.8	62.2	473333
95608	CARMICHAEL	31895	26258	20.7	28.1	30.2	12.9	8.1	51284	59477	74	55	15631	0.4	0.3	9.3	65.7	24.3	288481
95610	CITRUS HEIGHTS	23863	17782	19.6	30.3	34.9	11.3	4.0	50114	56741	72	53	9821	2.2	1.5	10.0	82.1	4.3	241815
95612	CLARKSBURG	24601	425	26.6	25.2	26.8	12.5	8.9	48319	57983	69	49	239	3.8	0.0	14.2	35.6	46.4	381915
95614	COOL	31047	1411	7.6	26.1	36.9	20.7	8.7	69306	82857	91	77	1275	0.5	0.1	2.0	64.2	33.3	341022
95615	COURTLAND	18213	239	25.1	33.5	28.0	9.6	3.8	39873	46172	46	31	149	5.4	1.3	18.1	48.3	26.9	317857
95616	DAVIS	27905	27028	29.2	21.6	24.2	14.4	10.6	48782	60859	70	50	12160	3.2	1.1	2.2	40.9	52.7	410715
95618	EL MACERO	85675	469	10.2	8.7	14.5	23.2	43.3	136092	160695	100	99	408	0.0	0.0	0.0	4.9	95.1	761792
95619	DIAMOND SPRINGS	23644	1514	23.6	34.9	29.9	8.1	3.5	42493	48524	55	37	1201	3.1	5.8	23.1	57.1	10.9	227281
95620	DIXON	21948	5984	12.8	26.8	39.5	15.9	5.0	60827	68488	85	68	4396	1.1	1.2	3.1	76.5	18.1	288681
95621	CITRUS HEIGHTS	22913	18036	20.4	33.9	34.6	8.6	2.6	46518	52472	65	44	11356	6.1	4.1	24.2	64.6	1.1	200696
95623	EL DORADO	27089	1846	17.9	30.7	35.5	9.3	6.6	51248	59701	74	55	1549	3.7	2.5	10.9	55.4	27.6	280976
95624	ELK GROVE	27468	14982	7.9	19.5	41.3	22.6	8.7	74496	86194	93	81	12942	0.5	1.3	6.4	69.9	21.8	289742
95626	ELVERTA	20432	1953	16.5	31.4	33.5	15.0	3.5	52499	60892	76	57	1637	1.3	0.1	40.0	47.1	11.5	200102
95627	ESPARTO	17887	1020	25.6	29.3	35.9	7.2	2.1	45997	51822	64	43	753	8.5	1.5	16.7	51.7	21.7	229583
95628	FAIR OAKS	35086	16909	13.6	22.0	34.9	17.8	11.8	67379	78532	90	75	12488	0.2	0.2	6.5	59.7	33.4	326078
95629	FIDDLETOWN	26556	353	24.1	25.8	33.4	12.5	4.3	50134	57379	72	53	297	1.4	3.4	16.5	50.8	28.0	293919
95630	FOLSOM	37154	20512	10.0	16.0	34.5	24.4	15.1	83285	100585	96	88	16453	2.0	1.4	3.4	51.6	41.7	373596
95631	FORESTHILL	26072	2452	17.5	26.9	38.4	11.1	6.1	56345	64730	81	63	2070	6.6	2.3	7.4	69.9	13.7	279292
95632	GALT	19133	8611	18.3	30.3	37.0	11.7	2.8	51240	58699	74	55	6914	3.6	1.7	14.3	71.2	9.1	228040
95633	GARDEN VALLEY	24632	1226	18.9	25.8	37.6	13.0	4.7	54899	63891	80	61	1076	1.3	2.2	5.5	71.4	19.6	268203
95634	GEORGETOWN	22949	948	20.4	31.9	35.1	9.0	3.7	48447	55596	69	49	785	2.6	0.8	9.9	69.0	17.7	260971
95635	GREENWOOD	23327	351	21.9	29.9	35.0	8.6	4.6	49131	57531	70	50	294	1.0	0.0	6.1	73.8	19.1	271429
95636	GRIZZLY FLATS	25123	249	22.5	31.7	32.5	8.0	5.2	46932	52900	66	45	210	0.0	0.0	19.5	58.6	21.9	237500
95637	GUINDA	24932	105	25.7	22.9	31.4	16.2	3.8	52229	63883	76	57	80	1.3	2.5	6.3	30.0	60.0	461538
95638	HERALD	26287	596	8.6	17.8	47.7	20.3	5.7	75945	85726	94	82	528	1.7	1.0	5.5	52.5	39.4	359420
95640	IONE	21426	2361	23.6	26.4	33.6	11.4	5.0	49975	58707	72	52	1812	6.1	1.2	15.1	62.1	15.5	234227
95641	ISLETON	25425	920	28.3	28.4	29.8	7.5	6.1	40000	46253	46	31	703	23.6	8.3	22.1	31.0	15.1	161779
95642	JACKSON	29106	2679	27.7	27.0	27.6	9.6	8.1	45692	52457	63	43	1830	4.9	4.6	15.1	53.4	21.9	248462
95645	KNIGHTS LANDING	15354	580	29.1	34.1	30.5	5.2	1.0	40799	45676	49	34	341	12.3	3.8	33.4	41.6	8.8	177083
95648	LINCOLN	24667	7025	19.0	23.8	37.2	14.2	5.8	57355	65908	82	64	5076	2.4	0.6	8.7	65.6	22.7	269814
95650	LOOMIS	39976	4580	13.0	20.4	32.3	18.8	15.5	75075	87442	93	82	3884	4.6	0.8	2.3	45.5	46.8	379703
95651	LOTUS	26821	276	14.5	32.3	33.0	14.1	6.2	54097	64221	79	59	236	0.0	0.9	4.2	69.5	25.4	282857
95652	MCCLELLAN	13709	283	36.4	46.6	14.1	2.8	0.0	33402	37202	22	17	50	8.0	4.0	62.0	10.0	16.0	141071
95653	MADISON	13553	163	33.7	35.0	21.5	8.6	1.2	37451	42918	37	25	115	8.7	0.0	21.7	48.7	20.9	198438
95655	MATHER	4463	269	87.0	13.0	0.0	0.0	0.0	8567	9574	0	1	0	0.0	0.0	0.0	0.0	0.0	0
95658	NEWCASTLE	37557	2661	13.3	19.8	37.2	17.4	12.4	69394	81472	91	77	2350	6.1	2.1	3.5	31.2	57.2	442857
95659	NICOLAUS	25364	284	21.5	26.1	30.6	12.0	9.9	52823	61148	77	58	217	6.9	4.2	14.8	40.6	33.6	288393
95660	NORTH HIGHLANDS	14584	10587	31.6	36.8	26.2	4.1	1.3	36104	40326	32	22	6312	9.4	1.7	66.9	21.2	0.8	147114
95661	ROSEVILLE	35966	11237	14.6	21.8	35.0	17.2	11.4	66828	79592	90	75	7124	0.8	1.3	4.2	62.0	31.7	334521
95662	ORANGEVALE	27937	11989	13.3	24.9	39.8	15.4	6.6	61150	70307	85	69	9107	2.5	2.2	7.8	71.1	16.3	253407
95663	PENRYN	31384	825	12.4	19.4	39.6	18.6	10.1	70163	82878	91	78	724	0.8	0.8	2.8	38.8	56.8	430247
95664	PILOT HILL	35600	480	5.4	31.3	30.4	22.5	10.4	70816	83908	92	78	438	1.8	0.2	3.9	45.4	48.6	393333
95665	PINE GROVE	30078	1801	19.2	26.2	38.4	9.4	6.8	54193	62022	79	59	1527	3.1	2.1	7.4	70.0	17.4	283795
95666	PIONEER	25105	2714	23.2	33.4	31.7	8.7	3.1	44185	50891	59	40	2278	3.5	2.5	16.1	64.7	13.3	235910
95667	PLACERVILLE	26538	15006	22.7	25.4	32.4	14.2	5.3	51933	61599	75	56	11494	3.4	2.5	6.7	59.8	27.6	289377
95668	PLEASANT GROVE	23760	384	23.4	27.1	32.3	11.2	6.0	49279	58571	71	51	306	4.9	2.3	17.0	44.1	31.7	288750
95669	PLYMOUTH	27138	785	25.5	23.4	31.2	12.7	7.1	50924	58524	74	54	646	1.2	9.1	21.2	34.4	34.1	257609
95670	RANCHO CORDOVA	25644	19968	20.6	28.5	32.6	12.4	5.9	50889	58250	74	54	11203	2.7	2.3	24.2	54.1	16.8	219428
95672	RESCUE	38800	1408	8.2	12.9	39.6	18.9	20.5	83355	102331	96	88	1263	0.8	1.1	4.1	39.7	54.3	418167
95673	RIO LINDA	19553	4950	21.9	30.2	34.6	10.6	2.7	47909	55022	68	48	3785	0.6	2.5	39.0	53.4	4.5	188115
95674	RIO OSO	18253	337	25.5	30.0	35.0	8.3	1.2	44415	50606	60	41	250	0.0	4.0	12.4	53.6	30.0	263636
95677	ROCKLIN	30696	9739	15.3	22.7	36.1	16.6	9.4	63860	75406	88	71	6968	3.8	1.4	2.9	61.4	30.5	317775
95678	ROSEVILLE	26431	13858	16.4	26.9	37.0	14.5	5.2	56097	65424	81	63	9181	0.5	2.0	13.0	67.7	16.7	268114
95679	RUMSEY	32500	11	27.3	27.3	36.4	9.1	0.0	37303	47500	36	25	8	0.0	0.0	0.0	25.0	75.0	583333
95681	SHERIDAN	25421	424	15.3	29.0	35.4	12.0	8.3	54181	63314	79	59	356	2.5	0.0	16.9	34.6	46.1	358824
95682	SHINGLE SPRINGS	34231	10319	12.8	18.3	39.3	18.6	11.0	70886	82976	92	79	8091	3.1	2.5	3.9	50.5	40.1	363896
95683	SLOUGHHOUSE	49155	2292	8.4	13.7	33.9	21.5	22.5	88889	104831	97	91	2084	0.0	0.7	5.8	41.1	52.4	412626
95684	SOMERSET	29894	1348	20.8	27.9	34.6	11.6	5.2	51393	60737	75	55	1166	0.4	0.6	14.0	55.2	29.8	277338
95685	SUTTER CREEK	26369	2480	23.8	27.9	32.7	9.6	6.0	48302	55330	69	49	1795	1.6	3.7	13.3	53.3	28.0	282556
95687	VACAVILLE	26166	21240	13.8	23.6	39.9	16.6	6.0	62990	71962	87	70	14457	2.3	2.7	5.6	74.8	14.6	283364
95688	VACAVILLE	29984	11730	12.8	21.2	35.8	19.7	10.6	69798	80272	91	77	8928	2.0	0.8	4.3	52.1	40.8	359466
95689	VOLCANO	27272	589	15.8	30.9	37.5	12.9	2.9	52780	61567	77	58	516	0.6	1.0	10.5	57.6	30.4	305607
95690	WALNUT GROVE	20251	927	27.9	31.6	26.7	9.7	4.1	43854	49018	58	39	543	12.3	9.2	12.9	35.4	30.2	271923
95691	WEST SACRAMENTO	20730	8341	32.1	27.1	27.9	10.1	2.9	41017	48532	50	34	5051	15.1	1.7	23.2	51.2	8.9	203555
95692	WHEATLAND	17658	1312	33.2	27.0	29.2	7.5	3.2	40678	45795	48	33	916	2.6	4.9	33.3	51.4	7.8	194811
95693	WILTON	32704	1984	8.4	21.4	33.8	19.4	17.1	79602	94312	95	86	1778	0.7	0.6	14.2	32.8	51.7	407543
95694	WINTERS	20795	2981	17.0	27.3	37.1	14.8	3.9	55442	63825	80	62	2154	1.7	2.1	5.3	64.2	26.7	270362
95695	WOODLAND	21970	14406	22.2	29.5	33.1	11.4	3.8	48646	56343	70	50	8375	1.2	0.6	8.1	70.1	20.0	266509
95698	ZAMORA	22772	91	17.6	45.1	26.4	4.4	6.6	40644	46815	48	33	66	3.0	6.1	12.1	21.2	57.6	438462
95701	ALTA	24127	331	23.0	26.3	33.8	12.4	4.5	50937	60466	74	54	256	2.0	3.1	9.4	65.2	20.3	278261
95703	APPLEGATE	27148	630	17.0	25.2	38.7	11.8	7.3	57581	66704	82	65	544	3.1	0.9	12.1	48.4	35.5	338281
95709	CAMINO	24387	1970	19.3	29.1	34.4	12.0	5.2	50987	57968	74	55	1585	4.0	0.3	8.9	61.1	25.7	272500
95713	COLFAX	27114	3780	19.1	25.7	34.4	14.6	6.2	54734	64262	79	60	3065	1.4	1.7	7.2	56.9	32.8	323991
95714	DUTCH FLAT	27759	256	19.5	19.5	40.6	16.8	3.5	60395	72375	85	68	200	2.0	0.0	6.5	66.5	25.0	310714
95715	EMIGRANT GAP	20018	13	15.4	30.8	38.5	15.4	0.0	54580	54606	79	60	10	0.0	0.0	0.0	80.0	20.0	300000
95717	GOLD RUN	23836	82	24.4	30.5	32.9	8.5	3.7	47312	56445	67	46	68	2.9	0.0	7.4	72.1	17.7	259091
	CALIFORNIA	27293		21.8	24.4	30.5	13.7	9.7	54267	64547				3.3	2.7	13.3	42.9	37.9	319678
	UNITED STATES	25866		24.7	27.1	30.8	10.9	6.5	48124	56710				10.9	15.0	33.7	30.1	10.4	145905

ZIP CODE #	POST OFFICE NAME	FINANCIAL SERVICES: Auto Loan	FINANCIAL SERVICES: Home Loan	FINANCIAL SERVICES: Invest-ments	FINANCIAL SERVICES: Retire-ment Plans	THE HOME: Home Improvements: Home Repair	THE HOME: Home Improvements: Lawn & Garden	THE HOME: Furnishings: Comput-ers & Hard-ware	THE HOME: Furnishings: Major Appli-ances	THE HOME: Furnishings: TV, Radio, Sound Equip-ment	THE HOME: Furnishings: Furni-ture	ENTERTAINMENT: Dine out/ Carry out	ENTERTAINMENT: Sports Equip-ment	ENTERTAINMENT: Fees & Tickets	ENTERTAINMENT: Toys & Games	ENTERTAINMENT: Travel	ENTERTAINMENT: Cable TV	PERSONAL: Apparel & Services	PERSONAL: Auto Repairs	PERSONAL: Health Insur-ance	PERSONAL: Pets & Supplies
95560	REDWAY	63	55	49	55	58	65	60	62	63	57	76	72	56	74	59	63	72	62	67	71
95562	RIO DELL	55	46	40	45	48	55	51	53	55	49	66	60	48	64	50	56	62	53	58	61
95563	SALYER	59	46	32	42	52	59	44	53	50	44	59	62	40	58	47	54	55	52	63	72
95564	SAMOA	55	58	66	60	58	60	62	59	60	60	75	72	62	77	61	57	74	61	55	64
95565	SCOTIA	71	63	48	60	67	72	59	65	62	59	76	77	58	77	60	64	72	63	70	83
95567	SMITH RIVER	64	60	57	56	62	71	57	64	59	60	74	65	56	65	59	62	69	62	70	72
95568	SOMES BAR	78	59	39	56	65	77	64	71	71	61	84	81	57	80	64	75	77	71	85	88
95569	REDCREST	63	50	35	48	54	62	52	58	58	51	69	66	48	66	52	60	63	57	67	70
95570	TRINIDAD	76	73	75	72	76	82	71	75	73	71	89	89	70	90	73	73	86	75	77	91
95573	WILLOW CREEK	78	60	40	56	66	77	62	70	69	60	82	80	55	79	63	74	75	70	84	90
95585	LEGGETT	52	48	47	48	49	54	52	52	53	50	65	61	50	65	51	53	62	53	54	59
95587	PIERCY	51	54	63	56	54	56	57	54	55	55	69	66	57	70	56	53	68	56	51	59
95589	WHITETHORN	79	63	44	57	70	79	59	71	67	59	79	83	54	78	63	71	74	69	83	96
95595	ZENIA	66	51	34	47	56	65	51	59	58	50	68	68	46	66	53	61	63	59	70	77
95602	AUBURN	105	117	127	116	118	124	111	112	107	111	134	126	115	133	114	107	132	110	111	124
95603	AUBURN	95	102	112	101	102	111	100	101	99	99	123	114	102	123	102	99	120	100	101	111
95605	WEST SACRAMENTO	59	53	47	50	51	54	55	58	57	59	71	62	51	65	52	55	71	59	54	61
95606	BROOKS	82	98	109	95	97	100	92	91	88	91	111	104	97	117	94	88	110	89	86	99
95607	CAPAY	81	96	106	92	95	101	90	90	89	89	111	101	96	116	94	90	109	88	89	98
95608	CARMICHAEL	98	107	125	109	105	111	108	105	105	107	132	123	110	133	108	102	130	106	100	115
95610	CITRUS HEIGHTS	84	87	98	90	85	88	89	86	86	89	109	102	89	108	87	83	107	88	80	95
95612	CLARKSBURG	115	103	93	98	107	116	100	109	107	102	131	127	96	132	102	109	126	109	116	135
95614	COOL	110	136	145	136	134	132	122	121	113	121	142	142	129	151	124	109	142	117	109	134
95615	COURTLAND	87	73	56	68	73	78	74	82	78	79	97	89	67	87	71	77	94	83	81	92
95616	DAVIS	99	81	100	89	80	88	113	95	109	103	137	122	102	129	99	100	131	106	87	106
95618	EL MACERO	256	331	442	329	323	344	298	293	279	302	352	335	329	368	312	278	355	285	271	319
95619	DIAMOND SPRINGS	94	77	60	75	82	95	82	89	89	79	106	100	76	102	82	92	98	88	101	105
95620	DIXON	100	108	107	108	104	104	102	102	97	105	123	117	103	123	100	93	122	101	91	111
95621	CITRUS HEIGHTS	75	82	93	82	80	85	81	80	79	81	100	93	83	101	81	78	98	80	76	87
95623	EL DORADO	94	96	93	93	98	107	94	97	95	91	116	109	94	118	95	97	112	95	101	109
95624	ELK GROVE	118	138	140	141	133	131	125	124	116	128	147	145	131	151	125	111	146	121	109	136
95626	ELVERTA	88	102	108	102	100	100	96	95	91	96	114	111	99	119	96	88	113	93	86	104
95627	ESPARTO	79	72	62	69	71	77	72	77	75	75	93	85	69	88	71	74	91	77	76	84
95628	FAIR OAKS	115	137	158	137	134	139	129	127	123	129	154	147	136	161	132	120	154	125	117	138
95629	FIDDLETOWN	90	93	95	89	95	107	86	93	88	89	110	97	89	102	92	92	105	90	101	104
95630	FOLSOM	146	161	167	167	157	158	151	151	142	155	180	174	155	178	150	136	177	148	136	165
95631	FORESTHILL	95	104	103	103	104	106	96	98	93	96	116	115	99	121	98	92	114	96	94	113
95632	GALT	88	92	89	92	90	92	87	89	84	90	106	101	87	104	86	81	104	88	82	98
95633	GARDEN VALLEY	84	102	111	100	100	102	93	93	89	93	112	107	99	118	96	88	111	90	87	102
95634	GEORGETOWN	83	84	80	81	87	92	79	84	80	78	99	98	79	102	82	82	96	82	87	101
95635	GREENWOOD	75	92	101	90	90	92	85	84	81	84	102	97	91	109	87	80	102	82	78	92
95636	GRIZZLY FLATS	113	79	41	75	92	103	78	96	90	77	105	116	67	103	81	94	96	95	115	134
95637	GUINDA	81	97	108	94	96	101	91	90	88	90	111	103	97	117	94	89	110	88	88	98
95638	HERALD	103	128	136	128	126	124	114	114	106	114	133	134	122	142	117	103	133	110	102	126
95640	IONE	97	82	62	80	87	97	81	89	87	80	105	104	77	105	82	89	98	87	98	110
95641	ISLETON	94	72	49	69	78	93	79	87	88	75	104	97	71	99	78	93	95	87	103	104
95642	JACKSON	98	88	80	84	92	105	89	96	95	88	115	107	86	113	91	99	109	95	107	112
95645	KNIGHTS LANDING	70	62	51	58	60	63	63	68	65	68	82	72	58	73	60	63	81	69	64	71
95648	LINCOLN	99	108	105	109	105	107	101	101	97	102	121	119	103	123	100	93	119	100	94	113
95650	LOOMIS	151	171	176	172	170	176	158	160	151	157	189	184	165	195	161	149	186	155	151	179
95651	LOTUS	91	111	122	109	109	110	102	101	97	101	122	117	109	129	105	95	121	98	93	111
95652	MCCLELLAN	54	42	43	43	40	46	53	49	55	51	68	60	49	64	48	53	66	54	48	55
95653	MADISON	73	65	55	60	63	66	66	71	68	71	86	75	61	76	63	66	85	72	67	74
95655	MATHER	15	12	17	11	12	14	15	14	17	15	21	16	15	20	14	18	20	15	16	16
95658	NEWCASTLE	124	149	164	146	147	153	137	137	131	137	165	156	146	172	142	131	163	133	131	150
95659	NICOLAUS	125	87	46	82	102	114	86	107	99	85	117	129	74	114	89	104	106	105	127	149
95660	NORTH HIGHLANDS	59	60	66	60	60	65	63	62	64	62	79	72	64	81	63	63	77	62	61	68
95661	ROSEVILLE	125	141	148	145	138	138	132	131	124	134	156	154	136	157	132	119	154	129	118	144
95662	ORANGEVALE	101	115	125	116	113	115	110	109	105	109	132	128	114	136	111	101	130	108	100	119
95663	PENRYN	114	134	140	133	133	135	122	123	116	122	145	142	128	151	125	114	143	119	115	136
95664	PILOT HILL	130	161	171	161	158	156	144	143	133	143	168	168	153	179	147	129	167	138	128	158
95665	PINE GROVE	102	105	108	100	108	122	98	105	101	101	125	109	101	116	104	106	120	102	116	117
95666	PIONEER	89	75	62	71	81	96	75	85	82	76	99	90	71	89	78	87	91	83	100	101
95667	PLACERVILLE	92	96	98	96	97	103	94	95	93	92	115	111	95	118	95	93	112	94	95	108
95668	PLEASANT GROVE	115	86	53	82	98	107	84	101	94	83	111	121	75	110	87	98	103	99	116	136
95669	PLYMOUTH	96	99	97	97	100	110	96	99	98	95	120	112	98	122	98	99	116	97	103	112
95670	RANCHO CORDOVA	93	94	104	96	93	99	98	95	96	97	120	112	98	120	96	94	118	97	91	106
95672	RESCUE	147	183	194	183	180	177	163	163	151	163	190	191	174	203	167	147	190	157	146	180
95673	RIO LINDA	81	88	89	87	87	91	84	85	82	84	102	98	86	106	85	81	100	83	81	94
95674	RIO OSO	95	66	35	63	77	87	66	81	76	65	89	98	56	87	68	79	81	80	97	113
95677	ROCKLIN	114	119	119	123	116	118	116	115	111	117	139	134	116	138	113	106	136	114	105	127
95678	ROSEVILLE	95	103	107	106	100	101	100	98	94	100	119	115	101	120	98	90	117	97	88	107
95679	RUMSEY	64	74	82	71	74	80	70	70	70	70	87	79	75	91	73	71	85	69	71	77
95681	SHERIDAN	117	113	97	110	115	119	105	111	106	106	131	133	104	133	106	105	126	109	112	136
95682	SHINGLE SPRINGS	123	147	158	148	143	144	134	133	126	135	158	156	141	165	136	122	157	130	120	146
95683	SLOUGHHOUSE	154	185	208	183	184	194	170	171	162	171	204	193	181	207	177	162	202	167	164	186
95684	SOMERSET	108	119	118	117	120	124	109	113	106	108	132	131	112	137	112	106	129	109	110	130
95685	SUTTER CREEK	87	88	88	85	90	101	86	90	88	86	109	98	87	107	89	91	104	88	96	101
95687	VACAVILLE	101	107	109	110	104	105	102	102	97	105	123	118	103	120	100	93	120	102	93	112
95688	VACAVILLE	116	132	138	133	129	129	124	123	118	126	149	144	129	154	124	113	148	121	111	134
95689	VOLCANO	93	92	91	87	95	110	85	94	89	89	111	95	87	98	92	94	105	91	106	106
95690	WALNUT GROVE	93	73	52	69	79	88	73	84	80	75	97	94	66	90	73	82	91	83	93	104
95691	WEST SACRAMENTO	74	73	75	72	73	80	76	75	77	74	95	87	75	95	75	77	92	76	77	84
95692	WHEATLAND	78	72	62	70	74	82	72	75	74	71	91	86	70	90	72	75	86	74	79	87
95693	WILTON	129	161	171	161	158	156	143	143	133	143	167	167	153	178	147	129	167	138	129	158
95694	WINTERS	91	95	96	93	92	95	92	94	90	95	114	105	92	112	91	88	113	94	86	101
95695	WOODLAND	84	85	87	84	83	87	86	86	85	87	106	98	85	104	84	83	104	86	81	93
95698	ZAMORA	112	86	54	81	94	104	84	99	93	85	111	117	74	107	85	95	103	98	111	130
95701	ALTA	103	91	73	84	98	108	85	97	92	84	111	113	80	112	90	96	105	95	109	126
95703	APPLEGATE	91	112	122	110	110	111	103	102	97	102	122	118	109	130	105	96	122	99	94	111
95709	CAMINO	85	91	93	88	92	100	88	89	88	87	109	101	90	112	90	89	106	87	91	100
95713	COLFAX	92	106	111	105	106	108	99	100	95	98	119	115	103	125	101	94	117	97	95	111
95714	DUTCH FLAT	84	102	113	100	100	102	95	94	90	94	114	108	101	121	97	89	113	91	87	102
95715	EMIGRANT GAP	107	84	57	76	95	106	79	95	90	78	106	112	71	105	84	96	99	94	113	130
95717	GOLD RUN	72	87	96	85	85	87	81	80	77	80	97	92	86	103	83	76	97	78	74	87
	CALIFORNIA	107	111	131	112	109	115	113	111	111	114	140	129	114	141	112	109	139	113	104	122
	UNITED STATES	100	100	100	100	100	100	100	100	100	100	100	100	100	100	100	100	100	100	100	100

# POST OFFICE NAME	COUNTY FIPS CODE	POPULATION 2000	2004	2009	2000-2004 ANNUAL RATE % Rate	State Centile	HOUSEHOLDS 2000	2004	2009	% Annual Rate 2000-2004	2004 Average HH Size	FAMILIES 2000	2004	% Annual Rate 2000-2004
95720 KYBURZ	017	171	171	185	0.0	15	80	80	86	0.0	2.11	45	45	0.0
95721 ECHO LAKE	017	60	62	67	0.8	44	5	5	5	0.0	2.60	3	3	0.0
95722 MEADOW VISTA	061	3669	4080	4900	2.5	86	1346	1504	1812	2.7	2.69	1080	1200	2.5
95724 NORDEN	061	113	119	136	1.2	62	53	56	64	1.3	2.13	36	38	1.3
95726 POLLOCK PINES	017	8602	9569	10827	2.5	86	3422	3814	4320	2.6	2.51	2493	2754	2.4
95728 SODA SPRINGS	057	97	100	104	0.7	42	39	40	42	0.6	2.48	23	23	0.0
95742 RANCHO CORDOVA	067	156	158	167	0.3	23	80	79	84	-0.3	1.97	43	42	-0.6
95746 GRANITE BAY	061	20848	24964	31067	4.3	96	6865	8212	10214	4.3	3.04	5925	7065	4.2
95747 ROSEVILLE	061	25616	34673	45768	7.4	99	9970	13676	18169	7.7	2.53	7685	10425	7.4
95758 ELK GROVE	067	47517	63680	78537	7.1	99	15625	20847	25501	7.0	3.00	12407	16463	6.9
95762 EL DORADO HILLS	017	21704	27139	32636	5.4	98	7140	8957	10808	5.5	3.03	6293	7870	5.4
95765 ROCKLIN	061	15454	22311	30223	9.0	100	5232	7583	10303	9.1	2.94	4247	6115	9.0
95776 WOODLAND	113	15373	17992	20702	3.8	95	4552	5133	5758	2.9	3.44	3663	4125	2.8
95814 SACRAMENTO	067	15881	16359	17528	0.7	41	8228	8496	9177	0.8	1.53	1754	1751	0.0
95815 SACRAMENTO	067	25684	26796	29009	1.0	55	9271	9538	10203	0.7	2.80	5456	5568	0.5
95816 SACRAMENTO	067	16199	16623	17853	0.6	37	9464	9654	10299	0.5	1.67	2589	2574	-0.1
95817 SACRAMENTO	067	15297	15860	17192	0.9	48	6106	6272	6742	0.6	2.48	3145	3190	0.3
95818 SACRAMENTO	067	21645	22056	23565	0.4	29	10100	10206	10806	0.3	2.14	5043	5019	-0.1
95819 SACRAMENTO	067	15955	16372	17516	0.6	37	7554	7697	8176	0.4	2.02	3752	3768	0.1
95820 SACRAMENTO	067	37058	38485	41564	0.9	50	12674	13036	13934	0.7	2.92	8213	8356	0.4
95821 SACRAMENTO	067	34488	36675	40084	1.5	68	15251	16069	17392	1.2	2.25	8526	8885	1.0
95822 SACRAMENTO	067	46243	48917	53417	1.3	65	16508	17225	18586	1.0	2.81	11153	11549	0.8
95823 SACRAMENTO	067	72395	77728	85513	1.7	73	22462	23780	25843	1.4	3.23	16917	17825	1.2
95824 SACRAMENTO	067	30242	32287	35322	1.6	70	8749	9202	9941	1.2	3.48	6574	6876	1.1
95825 SACRAMENTO	067	29854	32345	35709	1.9	78	14976	16116	17652	1.7	1.95	5912	6245	1.3
95826 SACRAMENTO	067	38670	40813	44630	1.3	64	15921	16689	18098	1.1	2.40	9183	9481	0.8
95827 SACRAMENTO	067	19577	20758	22694	1.4	66	7105	7473	8107	1.2	2.69	4678	4869	1.0
95828 SACRAMENTO	067	54942	60973	68412	2.5	85	16684	18320	20328	2.2	3.31	13124	14369	2.2
95829 SACRAMENTO	067	11369	14623	17612	6.1	98	3664	4683	5589	5.9	3.11	3032	3854	5.8
95830 SACRAMENTO	067	553	616	687	2.5	86	185	204	226	2.3	2.99	157	173	2.3
95831 SACRAMENTO	067	41566	44780	49395	1.8	75	17413	18598	20311	1.6	2.38	11241	11830	1.2
95832 SACRAMENTO	067	8720	9575	10623	2.2	82	1986	2164	2382	2.0	4.30	1664	1805	1.9
95833 SACRAMENTO	067	31523	34582	38505	2.2	82	12205	13499	15016	2.4	2.56	7311	7861	1.7
95834 SACRAMENTO	067	8339	10652	13207	5.9	98	3187	4192	5249	6.7	2.53	1998	2592	6.3
95835 SACRAMENTO	067	874	2679	4571	30.2	100	293	886	1494	29.7	3.02	218	641	28.9
95836 SACRAMENTO	067	40	40	43	0.0	15	17	17	18	0.0	2.35	13	13	0.0
95837 SACRAMENTO	067	254	256	276	0.2	19	110	110	117	0.0	2.33	72	69	-1.0
95838 SACRAMENTO	067	34723	36432	39483	1.1	60	10145	10521	11273	0.9	3.43	7528	7756	0.7
95841 SACRAMENTO	067	20836	21626	23366	0.9	50	8638	8894	9525	0.7	2.39	5143	5235	0.4
95842 SACRAMENTO	067	31833	33132	35869	1.0	53	11704	12056	12912	0.7	2.74	8089	8256	0.5
95843 ANTELOPE	067	36675	45872	54770	5.4	98	11744	14548	17163	5.2	3.15	9410	11598	5.0
95864 SACRAMENTO	067	24117	25037	27143	0.9	50	10285	10548	11300	0.6	2.37	6719	6813	0.3
95901 MARYSVILLE	115	38142	39756	41987	1.0	54	12904	13416	14133	0.9	2.90	9028	9358	0.9
95903 BEALE AFB	115	5399	5828	6251	1.8	76	1590	1714	1843	1.8	3.14	1423	1531	1.7
95910 ALLEGHANY	091	50	50	51	0.0	15	22	22	23	0.0	2.27	12	12	0.0
95912 ARBUCKLE	011	4444	4573	4677	0.7	40	1349	1374	1387	0.4	3.32	1062	1080	0.4
95914 BANGOR	007	161	151	155	-1.5	1	76	71	73	-1.6	2.13	53	49	-1.8
95915 BELDEN	063	16	16	17	0.0	15	11	11	12	0.0	1.45	7	6	-3.6
95916 BERRY CREEK	007	1284	1308	1357	0.4	29	538	549	571	0.5	2.38	363	370	0.5
95917 BIGGS	007	3044	3041	3144	0.0	12	1017	1016	1049	0.0	2.99	789	786	-0.1
95918 BROWNS VALLEY	115	1785	1865	1965	1.0	56	702	733	771	1.0	2.54	520	541	0.9
95919 BROWNSVILLE	115	1037	1054	1093	0.4	26	469	477	494	0.4	2.18	311	314	0.2
95920 BUTTE CITY	021	307	291	290	-1.3	1	105	99	99	-1.4	2.94	78	74	-1.2
95922 CAMPTONVILLE	091	631	621	639	-0.4	6	289	285	294	-0.3	2.18	169	165	-0.6
95923 CANYONDAM	063	28	28	28	0.0	15	17	17	17	0.0	1.65	13	10	-6.0
95925 CHALLENGE	115	341	342	354	0.1	17	139	139	144	0.0	2.42	88	87	-0.3
95926 CHICO	007	35794	37455	39638	1.1	57	14503	15150	16025	1.0	2.36	7301	7612	1.0
95928 CHICO	007	32759	35555	38464	2.0	78	12557	13655	14768	2.0	2.52	6663	7300	2.2
95932 COLUSA	011	7351	7411	7530	0.2	19	2636	2633	2644	0.0	2.78	1897	1887	-0.1
95934 CRESCENT MILLS	063	185	187	191	0.3	22	82	83	86	0.3	2.25	51	52	0.5
95935 DOBBINS	115	1505	1530	1588	0.4	27	628	638	661	0.4	2.38	422	426	0.2
95936 DOWNIEVILLE	091	189	189	192	0.0	15	93	94	96	0.3	2.01	56	56	0.0
95937 DUNNIGAN	113	1206	1266	1371	1.2	60	408	427	460	1.1	2.96	315	329	1.0
95938 DURHAM	007	3536	3704	3912	1.1	58	1287	1350	1425	1.1	2.73	969	1014	1.1
95939 ELK CREEK	021	237	234	236	-0.3	7	54	53	53	-0.4	3.62	39	39	0.0
95941 FORBESTOWN	007	759	744	768	-0.5	5	344	338	349	-0.4	2.20	210	205	-0.6
95942 FOREST RANCH	007	1323	1351	1402	0.5	31	543	555	576	0.5	2.38	379	387	0.5
95943 GLENN	021	971	971	985	0.0	15	330	329	333	-0.1	2.83	238	236	-0.2
95944 GOODYEARS BAR	091	207	206	210	-0.1	11	106	107	109	0.2	1.93	61	61	0.0
95945 GRASS VALLEY	057	23662	25183	26920	1.5	69	10064	10736	11501	1.5	2.31	6300	6693	1.4
95946 PENN VALLEY	057	8540	9158	9846	1.7	73	3539	3790	4073	1.6	2.42	2733	2918	1.6
95947 GREENVILLE	063	2327	2334	2383	0.1	17	971	979	1007	0.2	2.36	651	654	0.1
95948 GRIDLEY	007	9867	10211	10727	0.8	47	3353	3466	3641	0.8	2.88	2485	2559	0.7
95949 GRASS VALLEY	057	18837	20302	21879	1.8	75	7392	7973	8596	1.8	2.55	5657	6083	1.7
95951 HAMILTON CITY	021	2153	2185	2221	0.4	25	577	583	589	0.2	3.75	483	487	0.2
95953 LIVE OAK	101	8544	9088	9795	1.5	68	2536	2667	2845	1.2	3.29	1991	2086	1.1
95954 MAGALIA	007	11460	12078	12823	1.2	63	4744	5000	5312	1.2	2.40	3458	3632	1.2
95955 MAXWELL	011	1355	1380	1403	0.4	28	454	458	459	0.2	3.01	345	347	0.1
95956 MEADOW VALLEY	063	2	2	2	0.0	15	1	1	1	0.0	2.00	1	1	0.0
95957 MERIDIAN	101	785	768	807	-0.5	5	288	280	292	-0.7	2.59	206	199	-0.8
95959 NEVADA CITY	057	18047	18700	19770	0.8	48	7217	7502	7960	0.9	2.44	4976	5164	0.9
95960 NORTH SAN JUAN	057	565	544	559	-0.9	2	252	243	251	-0.9	2.20	158	151	-1.1
95961 OLIVEHURST	115	6899	7129	7497	0.8	44	2208	2279	2389	0.8	3.10	1654	1699	0.6
95963 ORLAND	021	14317	14869	15361	0.9	50	5122	5283	5417	0.7	2.81	3767	3875	0.7
95965 OROVILLE	007	19050	19935	21021	1.1	57	6701	7031	7427	1.1	2.70	4532	4736	1.0
95966 OROVILLE	007	28630	29159	30433	0.4	28	10924	11089	11547	0.4	2.60	7536	7629	0.3
95968 PALERMO	007	1311	1417	1517	1.9	77	423	454	485	1.7	3.09	312	335	1.7
95969 PARADISE	007	27544	28060	29269	0.4	29	12069	12303	12836	0.5	2.23	7584	7694	0.3
95970 PRINCETON	011	439	432	436	-0.4	6	163	159	159	-0.6	2.72	122	119	-0.6
95971 QUINCY	063	6453	6563	6707	0.4	27	2806	2880	2971	0.6	2.24	1774	1815	0.5
95972 RACKERBY	115	242	245	254	0.3	23	106	107	111	0.2	2.28	68	69	0.3
95973 CHICO	007	26900	29435	31869	2.1	81	10609	11509	12392	1.9	2.52	6822	7374	1.9
95975 ROUGH AND READY	057	1822	1848	1923	0.3	24	737	749	781	0.4	2.47	514	520	0.3
95977 SMARTVILLE	057	1365	1519	1662	2.6	87	503	560	613	2.6	2.71	391	434	2.5
95979 STONYFORD	011	811	843	867	0.9	51	295	306	312	0.9	2.39	202	209	0.9
CALIFORNIA					1.4					1.2	2.90			1.2
UNITED STATES					1.2					1.3	2.58			1.1

#	POST OFFICE NAME	RACE (%) White 2000	White 2004	Black 2000	Black 2004	Asian/Pacific 2000	Asian/Pacific 2004	% Hispanic Origin 2000	% Hispanic Origin 2004	2004 AGE DISTRIBUTION (%) 0-4	5-9	10-14	15-19	20-24	25-44	45-64	65-84	85+	18+	MEDIAN AGE 2004	% 2004 Males	% 2004 Females
95720	KYBURZ	83.0	80.1	0.6	0.6	1.2	1.2	12.3	14.6	2.3	4.1	5.9	6.4	2.3	18.1	44.4	14.0	2.3	83.0	48.9	55.0	45.0
95721	ECHO LAKE	88.3	85.5	3.3	3.2	3.3	3.2	6.7	8.1	1.6	3.2	4.8	11.3	8.1	21.0	35.5	14.5	0.0	90.3	45.0	59.7	40.3
95722	MEADOW VISTA	95.3	94.4	0.2	0.2	0.8	0.9	4.4	5.4	4.3	6.5	7.7	7.2	4.2	21.2	32.6	14.9	1.5	77.0	44.5	49.9	50.1
95724	NORDEN	94.7	93.3	0.0	0.0	0.0	0.8	4.4	4.2	5.0	6.7	6.7	6.7	5.9	25.2	31.1	12.6	0.0	76.5	41.9	52.9	47.1
95726	POLLOCK PINES	93.2	91.9	0.2	0.2	0.9	1.1	5.6	7.0	4.8	5.4	7.0	7.1	5.2	22.5	31.1	15.5	1.5	78.4	43.8	49.6	50.4
95728	SODA SPRINGS	92.8	92.0	0.0	0.0	1.0	1.0	3.1	4.0	3.0	4.0	6.0	7.0	5.0	25.0	44.0	6.0	0.0	83.0	45.0	51.0	49.0
95742	RANCHO CORDOVA	87.2	85.4	0.0	0.6	3.2	3.2	5.1	5.7	4.4	4.4	3.8	5.1	3.8	20.9	42.4	15.2	0.0	83.5	47.5	55.7	44.3
95746	GRANITE BAY	90.7	89.4	0.7	0.8	4.3	4.8	4.8	5.8	6.4	7.8	9.5	8.3	4.8	21.7	32.1	8.6	0.8	70.7	40.7	49.8	50.2
95747	ROSEVILLE	88.1	86.8	1.4	1.4	4.9	5.3	7.6	8.8	7.5	7.4	7.0	5.2	4.5	25.1	19.8	22.2	1.5	74.7	40.8	47.4	52.6
95758	ELK GROVE	58.3	54.9	10.4	10.4	18.0	19.4	14.7	16.9	9.6	9.4	8.7	6.5	5.3	35.5	19.9	4.7	0.4	68.1	32.8	49.6	50.4
95762	EL DORADO HILLS	90.5	88.7	0.7	0.7	3.9	4.6	5.1	6.3	7.4	8.7	9.8	7.7	4.5	25.0	29.1	7.4	0.6	69.3	38.5	49.7	50.3
95765	ROCKLIN	88.0	86.5	1.1	1.1	5.0	5.3	7.5	9.0	8.9	8.9	8.4	6.8	5.3	31.9	22.4	7.0	0.4	69.4	34.8	48.8	51.2
95776	WOODLAND	60.3	57.2	1.6	1.6	5.4	5.8	45.7	49.2	9.9	9.0	8.8	7.5	7.8	32.4	18.0	5.8	0.8	67.9	29.6	50.2	49.8
95814	SACRAMENTO	61.7	59.1	13.8	13.9	9.4	10.0	19.5	22.1	2.9	2.6	2.7	3.8	9.5	40.4	24.3	10.9	3.0	90.3	38.2	57.4	42.7
95815	SACRAMENTO	53.6	50.3	9.4	9.4	11.5	11.9	30.1	33.5	9.1	7.9	8.2	7.7	9.7	29.0	19.5	7.9	1.1	70.4	29.5	50.1	50.0
95816	SACRAMENTO	78.2	75.3	5.0	5.3	4.1	4.6	14.3	16.9	3.4	2.9	2.8	3.5	9.9	42.4	23.1	8.9	3.1	89.1	36.2	48.5	51.5
95817	SACRAMENTO	45.7	43.2	23.1	22.7	9.5	10.0	24.3	27.2	8.2	7.8	8.1	6.7	8.4	29.8	20.3	9.2	1.7	72.0	32.3	47.7	52.3
95818	SACRAMENTO	60.7	57.7	8.7	8.7	17.5	18.6	14.2	16.2	6.0	5.6	5.6	5.3	6.5	32.0	26.4	10.0	2.5	79.6	38.1	47.0	53.0
95819	SACRAMENTO	87.6	85.7	1.8	1.9	3.5	4.0	8.7	10.5	4.4	4.3	4.3	6.8	6.5	29.6	26.9	13.2	4.1	84.4	41.2	45.6	54.4
95820	SACRAMENTO	47.5	44.8	12.0	11.6	11.8	12.1	36.1	39.6	8.2	8.0	9.1	8.1	7.6	27.8	20.1	9.3	1.6	69.6	31.4	48.3	51.7
95821	SACRAMENTO	76.8	73.9	6.8	7.1	4.5	5.1	12.6	14.8	6.9	6.1	6.3	6.1	7.6	27.0	23.7	14.0	2.6	77.3	38.1	47.7	52.3
95822	SACRAMENTO	38.9	36.0	19.6	19.5	21.3	21.9	23.5	26.1	7.0	7.2	8.6	8.1	7.0	24.2	21.8	13.9	2.3	72.3	35.4	47.4	52.6
95823	SACRAMENTO	31.6	29.3	25.7	25.0	21.6	22.6	23.8	26.0	9.5	8.7	9.6	8.7	8.8	28.2	18.2	7.3	1.1	66.9	28.3	48.3	51.7
95824	SACRAMENTO	35.0	32.5	10.9	10.6	27.1	27.5	33.9	36.8	10.4	9.3	10.0	8.8	8.9	26.6	17.3	7.8	1.0	64.9	26.8	49.9	50.1
95825	SACRAMENTO	67.9	64.1	9.1	9.5	7.8	8.6	16.2	18.9	5.9	4.6	4.3	5.7	13.4	32.9	19.8	10.5	2.9	82.8	32.8	47.4	52.6
95826	SACRAMENTO	67.8	64.3	9.0	9.4	10.8	11.8	13.4	15.6	6.0	5.4	5.6	7.1	10.9	32.9	21.5	9.7	1.0	79.4	32.6	49.6	50.4
95827	SACRAMENTO	62.7	59.0	13.2	13.6	11.2	12.3	12.6	14.7	7.3	6.8	6.8	7.8	7.7	30.5	22.4	9.6	1.1	73.6	33.5	48.9	51.1
95828	SACRAMENTO	41.1	38.1	16.0	15.7	25.4	26.8	18.0	20.0	8.1	8.0	9.6	8.4	7.7	27.9	21.1	8.3	0.9	69.0	31.1	48.5	51.5
95829	SACRAMENTO	66.5	62.5	6.0	6.4	16.0	17.8	12.9	15.0	8.0	8.2	9.1	7.5	6.0	31.2	22.9	6.6	0.6	69.7	35.1	49.6	50.5
95830	SACRAMENTO	76.0	72.9	3.3	3.6	10.9	11.9	13.2	15.8	5.4	6.7	10.1	7.2	4.4	24.9	28.3	12.0	1.1	73.0	40.6	52.7	47.3
95831	SACRAMENTO	49.3	45.3	11.4	11.6	29.9	32.4	10.4	11.8	5.0	5.1	6.2	6.3	6.3	26.2	29.7	13.4	1.9	79.7	41.6	46.8	53.2
95832	SACRAMENTO	20.1	18.7	23.3	22.6	34.1	34.4	22.9	24.8	8.7	9.6	12.6	13.5	9.1	22.4	16.7	6.7	0.5	60.5	23.0	48.9	51.1
95833	SACRAMENTO	52.4	49.4	14.2	14.1	9.4	10.0	29.7	32.5	7.6	7.0	7.8	7.6	9.4	33.3	21.2	5.6	0.5	73.1	30.6	48.9	51.1
95834	SACRAMENTO	44.0	44.7	19.9	17.9	12.5	13.0	28.7	29.0	8.5	7.4	7.0	6.5	8.7	35.2	19.1	7.0	0.7	73.3	31.3	48.2	51.8
95835	SACRAMENTO	69.7	65.4	4.7	5.0	8.7	9.8	18.9	22.4	8.4	7.7	7.1	5.6	6.6	35.1	22.3	7.1	0.3	73.6	33.4	50.3	49.7
95836	SACRAMENTO	82.5	80.0	0.0	0.0	2.5	2.5	15.0	17.5	5.0	5.0	5.0	7.5	7.5	22.5	30.0	17.5	0.0	85.0	43.3	52.5	47.5
95837	SACRAMENTO	82.7	80.1	1.2	1.2	3.9	4.3	12.6	15.2	5.5	4.7	3.5	6.6	5.5	24.6	35.2	14.1	0.4	82.8	44.7	52.0	48.1
95838	SACRAMENTO	41.8	39.1	22.6	22.3	17.7	18.6	19.2	21.5	9.5	9.7	11.1	9.4	7.5	26.9	18.3	6.7	0.9	63.6	27.1	48.9	51.1
95841	SACRAMENTO	77.5	74.6	6.7	7.1	5.7	6.4	10.1	12.0	7.8	7.2	6.8	6.6	8.8	29.0	21.3	11.0	1.6	74.6	33.5	47.3	52.7
95842	SACRAMENTO	70.0	66.7	11.5	12.0	5.5	6.1	13.7	15.9	9.1	8.0	8.3	7.4	8.6	30.9	20.0	7.1	0.6	70.3	30.2	48.4	51.6
95843	ANTELOPE	65.6	62.3	10.0	10.1	12.4	13.8	10.7	12.4	9.8	9.2	9.4	7.3	6.9	35.0	18.3	3.8	0.3	66.8	30.1	48.8	51.3
95864	SACRAMENTO	85.9	83.5	2.4	2.6	4.9	5.5	7.6	9.3	5.5	5.9	6.4	6.2	5.7	23.0	28.0	16.6	2.6	78.5	43.2	47.2	52.8
95901	MARYSVILLE	67.4	64.1	3.1	3.1	9.9	10.8	18.7	21.3	8.4	7.7	8.9	8.8	8.0	26.1	21.5	9.5	1.1	69.6	31.5	50.2	49.8
95903	BEALE AFB	71.6	68.8	10.6	10.9	5.8	6.4	11.1	13.0	13.4	11.1	9.0	6.2	19.4	38.7	2.1	0.1	0.1	63.4	22.7	53.2	46.8
95910	ALLEGHANY	94.0	94.0	0.0	0.0	0.0	0.0	2.0	2.0	2.0	4.0	6.0	8.0	0.0	20.0	42.0	16.0	2.0	80.0	50.0	50.0	50.0
95912	ARBUCKLE	59.1	56.2	0.2	0.2	1.4	1.4	57.8	62.2	9.2	8.8	8.6	8.8	9.4	26.1	20.0	8.2	0.9	68.2	29.1	51.6	48.4
95914	BANGOR	85.7	84.1	1.2	1.3	1.2	1.3	6.2	7.3	4.0	3.3	4.6	8.0	4.0	17.9	36.4	20.5	1.3	82.8	49.5	50.3	49.7
95915	BELDEN	93.8	87.5	0.0	0.0	0.0	0.0	6.3	6.3	0.0	0.0	0.0	6.3	0.0	18.8	75.0	0.0	0.0	100.0	50.0	50.0	50.0
95916	BERRY CREEK	83.8	81.7	0.5	0.5	0.7	0.8	5.1	6.0	3.8	4.7	6.8	6.6	3.8	17.6	36.1	19.2	1.5	80.3	48.6	51.7	48.3
95917	BIGGS	79.6	76.4	0.4	0.4	0.8	0.9	21.7	25.4	6.8	7.3	9.9	9.4	6.1	25.8	22.3	11.3	1.2	69.6	34.7	49.8	50.2
95918	BROWNS VALLEY	91.5	90.0	0.2	0.2	1.2	1.5	5.9	7.1	5.2	5.7	5.4	5.6	4.1	21.8	36.5	14.5	1.1	80.1	46.2	50.4	49.6
95919	BROWNSVILLE	88.1	86.5	1.0	1.0	1.1	1.2	4.2	4.9	4.3	4.7	5.4	5.6	4.7	18.4	34.4	19.7	2.7	82.0	49.1	49.0	51.0
95920	BUTTE CITY	72.0	68.7	0.0	0.0	0.3	0.3	42.4	47.4	9.6	9.6	10.0	7.2	6.2	26.5	22.3	7.2	1.4	65.6	29.9	53.3	46.7
95922	CAMPTONVILLE	90.7	89.4	0.0	0.0	0.5	0.5	4.1	4.8	4.5	5.0	6.0	6.1	3.4	21.6	36.7	15.1	1.6	80.8	47.2	52.0	48.0
95923	CANYONDAM	96.4	100.0	0.0	0.0	0.0	0.0	7.1	3.6	3.6	3.6	3.6	3.6	0.0	7.1	46.4	32.1	0.0	89.3	60.0	57.1	42.9
95925	CHALLENGE	88.0	86.6	0.6	0.6	0.9	0.9	4.4	4.7	4.7	5.3	5.6	5.6	4.7	20.2	33.6	18.1	2.3	81.3	47.7	49.7	50.3
95926	CHICO	85.2	83.2	2.0	2.0	3.7	4.2	9.9	11.6	5.2	4.6	5.3	10.3	20.4	24.5	19.0	8.8	1.9	81.5	27.5	49.2	50.8
95928	CHICO	81.5	79.2	1.7	1.8	4.4	4.9	13.5	15.7	6.0	5.8	6.4	8.7	18.4	26.5	19.3	7.4	1.7	78.3	27.9	50.1	49.9
95932	COLUSA	69.7	66.6	0.4	0.4	2.0	2.2	37.6	41.9	8.1	7.1	8.4	8.1	7.4	26.1	23.1	10.4	1.4	71.5	33.9	50.0	50.0
95934	CRESCENT MILLS	91.4	90.4	0.0	0.0	0.5	0.5	6.5	7.5	5.4	5.9	5.4	7.0	5.4	20.9	33.7	15.0	1.6	79.1	45.1	49.2	50.8
95935	DOBBINS	89.2	87.7	0.9	0.9	0.9	1.0	4.7	5.6	3.9	4.6	6.2	5.8	4.3	19.0	38.4	15.6	2.0	81.6	48.2	49.4	50.7
95936	DOWNIEVILLE	94.7	94.7	0.0	0.0	0.5	0.5	6.4	6.4	2.7	2.7	4.8	5.3	3.2	19.6	38.6	19.6	3.7	86.2	51.6	49.2	50.8
95937	DUNNIGAN	63.0	59.7	12.8	12.7	0.9	1.0	32.6	37.2	6.6	7.2	8.5	6.6	5.5	25.1	26.1	13.3	1.3	73.7	37.7	51.7	48.3
95938	DURHAM	91.8	90.4	0.1	0.1	0.6	0.7	9.6	11.6	6.0	6.5	8.1	7.9	6.5	24.0	28.5	10.9	1.6	74.4	39.2	50.0	50.0
95939	ELK CREEK	87.8	86.3	5.1	5.1	0.0	0.0	13.5	16.2	4.7	5.1	6.0	5.6	5.1	33.8	23.5	15.4	0.9	80.8	39.8	61.1	38.9
95941	FORBESTOWN	88.1	87.0	1.3	1.3	0.4	0.4	4.9	5.7	3.5	3.9	4.7	6.1	4.4	17.3	36.3	22.0	1.8	84.3	51.1	51.1	48.9
95942	FOREST RANCH	93.6	92.5	0.3	0.4	1.2	1.4	4.0	5.0	4.5	5.1	5.7	6.9	5.5	24.1	36.5	11.2	0.5	80.5	44.0	50.8	49.2
95943	GLENN	82.0	79.7	0.1	0.1	1.9	2.1	21.0	23.7	8.3	9.0	8.9	7.1	5.7	27.4	22.9	9.0	1.9	68.9	34.6	52.9	47.1
95944	GOODYEARS BAR	95.2	94.7	0.0	0.0	0.5	0.5	5.3	5.3	1.9	2.9	4.4	5.3	2.4	19.9	40.3	18.0	4.9	86.9	51.6	51.5	48.5
95945	GRASS VALLEY	93.4	92.3	0.2	0.2	0.9	1.0	5.5	6.7	5.5	5.6	6.9	6.6	6.2	21.6	28.3	15.4	4.0	77.9	43.4	47.4	52.6
95946	PENN VALLEY	95.1	94.1	0.3	0.4	0.8	0.9	3.7	4.6	3.7	4.4	6.5	5.5	3.3	16.7	32.1	25.6	2.2	81.7	51.6	48.6	51.4
95947	GREENVILLE	87.6	86.5	0.0	0.0	0.4	0.4	7.5	8.6	5.3	5.7	6.6	6.8	4.4	19.4	32.1	17.5	2.2	77.9	46.0	50.0	50.0
95948	GRIDLEY	69.9	66.8	0.3	0.3	3.4	3.7	33.7	37.2	7.0	6.9	8.1	8.4	7.0	24.6	22.3	13.1	2.6	72.8	35.5	49.6	50.4
95949	GRASS VALLEY	95.1	94.2	0.3	0.3	0.8	0.9	3.9	4.7	3.9	4.8	6.9	6.7	4.4	18.7	34.2	18.4	2.1	80.1	47.6	49.4	50.6
95951	HAMILTON CITY	39.4	37.1	0.4	0.4	0.3	0.3	77.5	80.8	8.3	7.7	9.1	10.0	9.1	28.4	19.9	6.7	0.9	69.1	28.7	52.0	48.0
95953	LIVE OAK	57.0	53.1	1.2	1.1	9.2	9.5	40.7	45.4	7.4	7.7	9.4	8.5	7.6	27.4	20.9	9.7	1.6	70.1	32.2	49.0	51.0
95954	MAGALIA	94.3	93.3	0.4	0.5	0.8	1.0	4.9	5.8	4.4	4.7	6.1	7.9	5.6	17.6	28.1	23.4	2.2	81.0	47.5	48.7	51.3
95955	MAXWELL	76.7	74.3	0.5	0.7	1.7	1.8	31.0	35.2	8.3	8.6	9.6	6.9	5.6	25.7	23.5	10.4	1.5	69.0	33.9	49.5	50.5
95956	MEADOW VALLEY	100.0	100.0	0.0	0.0	0.0	0.0	0.0	0.0	0.0	0.0	0.0	0.0	100.0	0.0	0.0	0.0	0.0	100.0	22.5	50.0	50.0
95957	MERIDIAN	85.5	83.3	0.0	0.0	0.3	0.3	24.7	28.5	5.7	5.5	6.8	7.7	7.7	31.0	22.9	10.9	1.8	76.6	37.5	54.2	45.8
95959	NEVADA CITY	93.9	92.9	0.4	0.4	0.9	1.0	3.7	4.5	3.6	4.6	7.0	7.6	4.7	19.9	36.6	14.1	2.0	79.9	46.3	50.4	49.6
95960	NORTH SAN JUAN	91.7	90.4	0.4	0.4	0.7	0.7	3.9	4.4	4.2	4.6	7.2	8.1	3.5	21.5	37.1	12.1	1.7	78.3	45.5	51.5	48.5
95961	OLIVEHURST	67.3	63.7	1.2	1.2	4.8	5.3	24.8	28.1	8.4	7.8	9.6	8.9	7.0	26.3	21.2	9.8	1.1	68.5	32.0	50.5	49.5
95963	ORLAND	74.8	71.6	0.4	0.5	1.3	1.4	28.7	32.9	7.9	7.4	8.0	7.7	7.2	25.5	22.8	11.9	1.6	71.6	35.3	50.2	49.8
95965	OROVILLE	79.0	76.5	2.1	2.2	6.7	7.4	8.9	10.3	7.6	7.2	8.3	9.0	7.6	23.1	24.0	11.9	1.6	72.0	35.0	49.9	50.1
95966	OROVILLE	81.2	79.0	2.3	2.3	5.3	5.9	8.1	9.6	5.7	6.2	7.9	7.6	5.7	20.4	26.6	17.5	2.5	75.4	42.4	49.1	50.9
95968	PALERMO	76.5	73.6	0.8	0.9	3.2	3.5	21.2	24.4	7.3	7.3	8.2	7.3	6.8	24.0	24.0	13.0	2.3	72.9	36.5	50.6	49.4
95969	PARADISE	93.6	92.5	0.2	0.2	1.1	1.3	4.3	5.1	4.3	4.6	5.8	6.1	5.4	19.1	28.6	21.4	4.8	81.4	48.1	46.9	53.1
95970	PRINCETON	80.4	77.8	0.5	0.5	2.1	2.1	25.7	29.9	8.6	8.6	8.6	6.3	5.6	25.7	24.5	10.9	1.4	70.4	35.0	50.2	49.8
95971	QUINCY	92.1	91.1	1.5	1.6	0.8	0.9	3.7	4.4	4.3	4.6	6.6	8.2	7.0	22.4	32.3	12.9	1.8	79.5	43.2	50.1	50.0
95972	RACKERBY	88.8	86.5	1.2	1.2	1.2	1.6	3.3	4.1	4.1	4.5	4.5	5.3	3.7	14.7	33.9	26.9	2.5	83.3	53.5	48.6	51.4
95973	CHICO	86.3	83.9	1.0	1.1	2.4	2.8	10.7	12.6	6.8	6.6	7.3	7.1	7.4	27.6	24.4	10.4	2.5	74.9	36.4	48.4	51.6
95975	ROUGH AND READY	92.8	91.5	0.2	0.3	0.6	0.6	6.2	7.2	3.9	4.7	7.9	7.6	3.7	23.1	31.8	15.5	2.0	78.3	44.6	51.2	48.8
95977	SMARTVILLE	90.8	88.9	0.3	0.3	1.3	1.5	7.7	9.5	5.1	6.1	7.5	6.5	4.3	23.0	33.3	13.0	1.3	77.1	43.5	50.0	50.0
95979	STONYFORD	85.0	83.8	4.1	4.0	0.9	1.0	14.1	16.3	3.7	4.2	5.3	15.9	6.9	17.2	27.6	17.3	1.9	75.2	42.5	56.1	43.9
	CALIFORNIA	59.6	57.1	6.7	6.5	11.3	11.8	32.4	35.5	7.4	7.1	7.8	7.3	7.7	29.8	22.1	9.3	1.4	73.3	33.8	49.8	50.2
	UNITED STATES	75.1	73.6	12.3	12.5	3.8	4.2	12.5	14.1	6.9	6.7	7.2	7.0	7.3	28.6	23.8	10.8	1.7	75.1	36.0	49.1	50.9

#	POST OFFICE NAME	2004 Per Capita Income	2004 HH Income Base	2004 HOUSEHOLD INCOME DISTRIBUTION (%) Less than $25,000	$25,000 to $49,999	$50,000 to $99,999	$100,000 to $149,999	$150,000 or More	MEDIAN HOUSEHOLD INCOME 2004	2009	2004 National Centile	2004 State Centile	2004 Home Value Base	2004 HOME VALUE DISTRIBUTION (%) Less than $50,000	$50,000 to $89,999	$90,000 to $174,999	$175,000 to $399,999	$400,000 or More	2004 Median Home Value
95720	KYBURZ	27939	80	26.3	30.0	28.8	8.8	6.3	38639	45000	42	28	60	0.0	0.0	21.7	48.3	30.0	276923
95721	ECHO LAKE	8642	5	0.0	0.0	100.0	0.0	0.0	71033	87500	92	79	4	0.0	0.0	25.0	25.0	50.0	350000
95722	MEADOW VISTA	32407	1504	7.2	21.1	44.5	17.7	9.5	68820	82281	91	77	1327	1.6	1.2	2.0	50.8	44.5	378254
95724	NORDEN	28356	56	25.0	32.1	28.6	8.9	5.4	45000	52929	61	42	41	0.0	2.4	12.2	68.3	17.1	282143
95726	POLLOCK PINES	23849	3814	21.5	27.6	37.6	9.9	3.4	50555	57639	73	53	3055	9.1	1.3	9.4	65.6	14.6	243413
95728	SODA SPRINGS	20282	40	30.0	35.0	27.5	5.0	2.5	36511	42367	34	23	26	0.0	7.7	23.1	53.9	15.4	250000
95742	RANCHO CORDOVA	26785	79	10.1	24.1	63.3	2.5	0.0	52172	57816	76	57	62	67.7	0.0	1.6	12.9	17.7	17500
95746	GRANITE BAY	56036	8212	7.3	9.5	25.0	23.0	35.3	114987	139113	99	97	7594	2.4	0.1	0.8	12.4	84.3	694520
95747	ROSEVILLE	34286	13676	10.4	19.6	43.1	18.5	8.4	69744	80107	91	77	12060	0.1	0.5	1.5	60.1	37.8	364772
95758	ELK GROVE	29615	20847	8.1	15.8	45.0	21.7	9.4	76539	87729	94	83	17922	1.2	0.4	3.2	82.5	12.7	273221
95762	EL DORADO HILLS	47364	8957	4.0	9.7	31.5	27.9	27.0	106170	126884	99	96	8249	0.4	0.1	1.1	33.3	65.1	463151
95765	ROCKLIN	35719	7583	6.2	12.8	36.9	28.8	15.4	90288	108192	97	91	6219	0.0	0.0	0.3	48.1	51.6	405218
95776	WOODLAND	17103	5133	18.9	28.5	39.8	11.5	1.4	51748	59675	75	56	3549	9.1	6.5	4.8	71.3	8.2	248644
95814	SACRAMENTO	21555	8496	53.1	25.5	15.9	3.9	1.6	22743	26562	3	3	786	1.8	2.3	36.8	52.3	6.9	197785
95815	SACRAMENTO	13496	9538	44.4	31.8	19.2	3.5	1.1	28254	31641	9	8	3817	9.1	8.0	60.4	21.0	1.6	134695
95816	SACRAMENTO	35877	9654	30.5	29.4	26.6	8.1	5.5	40261	47798	47	32	2629	0.8	0.0	8.8	55.3	35.1	328558
95817	SACRAMENTO	17759	6272	43.6	26.9	22.3	5.3	1.9	29538	34102	11	10	2438	1.4	5.0	42.9	48.0	2.8	176891
95818	SACRAMENTO	31237	10206	31.8	22.4	24.9	12.2	8.7	44004	52025	59	40	5170	1.2	0.9	9.3	56.1	32.5	311384
95819	SACRAMENTO	37163	7697	15.8	21.9	37.8	17.1	7.5	62569	74303	87	70	5310	0.2	0.2	4.6	69.1	26.0	311696
95820	SACRAMENTO	14991	13036	36.9	31.9	24.8	4.9	1.5	34659	38788	26	19	7573	1.7	5.1	64.0	28.5	0.7	147891
95821	SACRAMENTO	23801	16069	32.1	30.1	25.6	8.6	3.7	38600	44277	41	28	7527	4.0	0.4	15.9	68.4	11.3	242170
95822	SACRAMENTO	18429	17225	30.7	31.8	26.8	7.4	3.3	38555	43524	41	28	10832	1.9	1.5	45.6	44.0	7.0	178179
95823	SACRAMENTO	15170	23780	29.7	33.6	28.7	6.5	1.4	39402	44464	44	30	13301	8.4	2.0	41.2	47.8	0.7	173305
95824	SACRAMENTO	11349	9202	41.6	33.6	19.9	3.9	1.0	30214	33572	13	11	4404	4.8	4.1	77.0	14.0	0.2	138737
95825	SACRAMENTO	27513	16116	29.4	33.2	26.0	7.7	3.7	38645	43591	42	28	4279	0.0	2.4	31.0	59.1	7.6	222407
95826	SACRAMENTO	24227	16689	21.5	31.7	33.6	10.0	3.3	47163	53531	66	46	9012	2.7	2.3	17.8	75.8	1.5	215556
95827	SACRAMENTO	22009	7473	21.9	31.4	33.9	10.2	2.7	47178	53537	67	46	4283	14.2	5.2	26.2	53.0	1.5	182119
95828	SACRAMENTO	18338	18320	20.5	29.5	35.8	11.1	3.1	49994	56537	72	52	13601	7.5	3.8	31.3	56.4	0.9	186733
95829	SACRAMENTO	26626	4683	5.6	19.0	49.7	19.1	6.8	71380	81619	92	79	4150	0.2	0.0	4.6	79.6	15.6	254020
95830	SACRAMENTO	34502	204	5.4	19.1	34.3	25.5	15.7	83285	97503	96	88	169	0.6	0.0	1.8	27.8	69.8	532986
95831	SACRAMENTO	34813	18598	12.6	24.1	35.5	18.0	9.8	65242	75920	89	73	11560	1.1	0.4	4.4	69.3	24.8	308178
95832	SACRAMENTO	9827	2164	40.7	30.3	23.0	4.9	1.2	31211	35251	16	12	1344	0.8	4.6	83.6	9.2	1.7	137434
95833	SACRAMENTO	23174	13499	19.6	31.6	36.1	9.3	3.5	48676	54699	70	50	6155	2.1	2.1	35.3	57.4	3.3	193923
95834	SACRAMENTO	25658	4192	18.3	32.3	36.8	10.1	2.5	49520	56794	71	51	2331	11.1	8.8	16.9	55.2	8.1	201795
95835	SACRAMENTO	29101	886	8.1	18.5	41.7	23.0	8.7	75722	86027	93	82	752	0.0	0.0	3.1	67.2	29.8	335593
95836	SACRAMENTO	27786	17	23.5	29.4	29.4	11.8	5.9	47361	50000	67	47	13	0.0	0.0	15.4	46.2	38.5	325000
95837	SACRAMENTO	40098	110	19.1	19.1	19.1	20.0	22.7	81966	95854	96	87	73	1.4	0.0	1.4	21.9	75.3	645000
95838	SACRAMENTO	13345	10521	34.1	34.9	24.7	4.3	2.0	34711	39106	26	19	5936	5.3	4.8	55.0	33.8	1.0	153733
95841	SACRAMENTO	20222	8894	30.7	35.6	24.2	6.5	3.0	36803	41144	35	24	3523	10.4	3.4	20.2	57.5	8.5	212977
95842	SACRAMENTO	19080	12056	21.1	36.9	33.3	7.4	1.4	43889	49544	58	40	6570	5.8	4.9	33.6	55.2	0.5	183515
95843	ANTELOPE	24649	14548	8.2	24.0	45.6	17.9	4.2	66580	76894	89	74	10833	0.2	0.3	11.1	86.5	2.0	245655
95864	SACRAMENTO	42307	10548	15.1	24.0	29.9	15.4	15.6	63867	75081	88	71	7576	0.6	0.1	10.1	41.9	47.3	381835
95901	MARYSVILLE	15961	13416	38.7	32.1	22.2	4.7	2.3	31987	35496	18	14	7508	9.2	5.9	53.2	27.5	4.2	144162
95903	BEALE AFB	14758	1714	16.0	59.7	21.1	2.2	1.0	37513	42370	37	26	156	44.9	17.3	8.3	29.5	0.0	54211
95910	ALLEGHANY	23288	22	31.8	18.2	36.4	9.1	4.6	50000	42372	72	52	13	0.0	7.7	38.5	38.5	15.4	212500
95912	ARBUCKLE	17170	1374	27.8	32.5	29.1	6.4	4.2	41053	46220	50	34	917	4.9	2.4	33.5	48.4	10.8	196778
95914	BANGOR	24239	71	45.1	28.2	15.5	8.5	2.8	27263	33345	8	7	58	3.5	10.3	27.6	44.8	13.8	212500
95915	BELDEN	30125	11	54.6	9.1	27.3	9.1	0.0	22247	42500	3	3	8	0.0	12.5	37.5	50.0	0.0	175000
95916	BERRY CREEK	19510	549	37.9	37.2	16.0	4.9	4.0	31515	36005	16	13	448	5.8	6.0	38.0	38.6	11.6	175610
95917	BIGGS	16672	1016	28.6	34.7	27.2	7.4	2.1	39211	44082	43	29	751	1.5	5.2	64.3	23.6	5.5	140826
95918	BROWNS VALLEY	23503	733	24.8	30.0	30.6	8.2	6.4	46454	52191	65	44	608	0.5	2.0	27.6	52.6	17.3	248315
95919	BROWNSVILLE	19758	477	42.1	31.2	19.7	4.8	2.1	30393	33746	13	11	375	6.9	3.5	40.5	43.2	5.9	173380
95920	BUTTE CITY	14559	99	38.4	39.4	14.1	4.0	4.0	30209	33440	13	11	50	10.0	2.0	40.0	28.0	20.0	166667
95922	CAMPTONVILLE	19254	285	38.6	31.2	23.9	4.6	1.8	31844	35666	17	14	205	4.4	12.7	38.1	36.6	8.3	154808
95923	CANYONDAM	31071	17	17.7	29.4	47.1	5.9	0.0	50894	63223	74	54	15	0.0	0.0	6.7	46.7	46.7	375000
95925	CHALLENGE	14878	139	43.2	34.5	18.7	2.9	0.7	28808	33003	10	8	105	5.7	7.6	45.7	36.2	4.8	156731
95926	CHICO	20859	15150	39.2	26.3	23.6	7.4	3.5	32919	38522	21	16	7054	4.6	2.0	15.8	69.5	8.2	228717
95928	CHICO	21050	13655	36.2	28.6	23.9	7.0	4.2	35222	40988	28	20	6679	3.4	3.6	23.6	54.8	14.5	227641
95932	COLUSA	17691	2633	31.2	33.3	26.8	5.7	3.0	37996	42912	39	26	1679	3.1	4.0	35.1	53.4	4.4	198138
95934	CRESCENT MILLS	19215	83	43.4	19.3	28.9	6.0	2.4	32359	33632	19	15	62	16.1	17.7	38.7	22.6	4.8	128125
95935	DOBBINS	21269	638	35.9	25.4	24.9	9.4	4.4	39652	44695	45	30	517	6.4	2.5	32.3	48.7	10.1	203440
95936	DOWNIEVILLE	24027	94	28.7	28.7	40.4	2.1	0.0	43909	49085	58	40	65	0.0	0.0	20.0	67.7	12.3	236458
95937	DUNNIGAN	18451	427	21.1	32.1	37.5	7.0	2.3	46517	52492	65	44	323	5.0	10.5	34.4	29.4	20.7	176389
95938	DURHAM	33395	1350	19.2	21.4	35.6	13.1	10.7	61265	72523	86	69	1032	1.2	0.5	15.2	49.4	33.7	302326
95939	ELK CREEK	14644	53	30.2	34.0	26.4	5.7	3.8	39426	43338	44	30	37	5.4	16.2	32.4	32.4	13.5	156250
95941	FORBESTOWN	21374	338	39.9	30.2	21.3	5.6	3.0	33187	37221	21	16	271	13.7	9.6	36.2	31.0	9.6	151389
95942	FOREST RANCH	31322	555	18.0	20.5	40.0	16.2	5.2	62903	75495	87	70	457	5.7	1.3	14.9	49.2	28.9	272177
95943	GLENN	21606	329	29.5	33.1	27.1	5.2	5.2	38813	43469	42	28	205	5.9	4.4	23.4	39.0	27.3	262500
95944	GOODYEARS BAR	25495	107	26.2	33.6	33.6	4.7	1.9	43070	47033	56	38	74	0.0	1.4	21.6	67.6	9.5	236000
95945	GRASS VALLEY	24347	10736	30.8	31.8	25.6	7.5	4.5	38513	44379	41	28	6928	3.1	2.8	8.9	62.2	22.9	273189
95946	PENN VALLEY	32214	3790	15.0	25.5	37.9	13.8	7.8	58560	68113	83	66	3277	2.0	0.9	2.8	55.2	39.0	352991
95947	GREENVILLE	17069	979	37.8	32.3	25.5	3.6	0.8	32866	37300	20	15	720	14.6	10.4	28.1	36.4	10.6	154630
95948	GRIDLEY	17117	3466	37.8	29.8	23.6	6.6	2.2	34005	37998	24	18	2291	4.0	6.6	44.8	39.4	5.3	162801
95949	GRASS VALLEY	29349	7973	17.3	27.3	33.9	12.7	8.8	55665	64587	80	62	6986	2.8	4.0	7.2	53.1	32.9	322798
95951	HAMILTON CITY	10440	583	30.0	46.8	20.9	1.7	0.5	34955	37621	27	20	373	7.0	15.8	58.2	13.4	5.6	136405
95953	LIVE OAK	14778	2667	39.9	28.7	24.0	4.4	3.1	32907	37465	21	16	1812	5.0	3.8	59.0	21.5	10.7	147776
95954	MAGALIA	19815	5000	34.7	33.0	24.8	5.8	1.7	36397	40557	33	23	4141	2.0	12.3	40.9	40.8	4.0	161924
95955	MAXWELL	18717	458	29.5	28.8	28.6	7.6	5.5	39624	45852	45	30	326	6.1	3.7	50.0	33.1	7.1	156395
95956	MEADOW VALLEY	0	0	0.0	0.0	0.0	0.0	0.0	0	0	0	0	0	0.0	0.0	0.0	0.0	0.0	0
95957	MERIDIAN	18962	280	35.7	29.6	23.2	7.9	3.6	36594	41351	34	23	165	8.5	15.2	36.4	30.3	9.7	152083
95959	NEVADA CITY	30179	7502	20.9	28.4	29.6	12.9	8.2	50683	60271	73	54	5904	1.3	1.3	7.4	49.3	40.7	345491
95960	NORTH SAN JUAN	22335	243	35.4	26.8	25.5	7.4	4.9	35517	39361	30	21	170	4.1	7.7	28.8	44.1	15.3	215217
95961	OLIVEHURST	12274	2279	39.1	38.2	18.8	2.4	1.5	30393	32847	13	11	1464	7.5	14.1	71.2	6.7	0.5	123509
95963	ORLAND	16119	5283	34.5	34.5	23.1	5.6	2.2	34346	37939	25	19	3747	7.8	6.2	37.3	37.8	10.9	171907
95965	OROVILLE	14164	7031	45.9	30.8	18.4	3.2	1.8	27140	30403	7	7	4159	15.1	9.8	46.7	22.0	6.4	135470
95966	OROVILLE	18573	11089	36.5	31.4	24.2	5.5	2.4	35052	39602	28	20	8257	8.4	7.9	46.1	32.1	5.6	146714
95968	PALERMO	13112	454	36.8	38.1	19.6	3.7	1.8	33560	37433	23	17	345	12.8	12.2	56.5	15.7	2.9	129327
95969	PARADISE	22338	12303	35.2	31.3	24.8	5.3	3.4	35734	41004	31	21	8954	10.6	6.0	30.4	45.1	7.8	183897
95970	PRINCETON	20440	159	32.7	27.7	27.7	6.9	5.0	37589	44608	38	26	110	7.3	3.6	42.7	36.4	10.0	165909
95971	QUINCY	23411	2880	32.7	27.0	27.6	9.0	3.7	41118	47099	50	34	1997	8.7	4.1	23.8	57.3	6.1	209757
95972	RACKERBY	23853	107	41.1	35.5	19.6	1.9	1.9	29704	30726	12	10	87	14.9	9.2	21.8	50.6	3.5	189583
95973	CHICO	25354	11509	25.0	29.9	30.3	9.7	5.2	46046	52202	64	43	7403	12.6	3.7	11.2	58.7	13.7	225065
95975	ROUGH AND READY	22755	749	25.4	25.8	36.1	9.0	3.9	49028	56034	70	50	614	2.8	1.3	13.2	57.5	25.2	284470
95977	SMARTVILLE	23011	560	24.5	25.5	33.2	11.6	5.2	50000	58013	72	52	477	0.8	0.0	8.0	61.4	29.8	297566
95979	STONYFORD	17551	306	44.4	28.1	18.0	8.2	1.3	28717	32996	10	8	258	13.6	7.8	37.2	32.2	9.3	148182
	CALIFORNIA	27293		21.8	24.4	30.5	13.7	9.7	54267	64547				3.3	2.7	13.3	42.9	37.9	319678
	UNITED STATES	25866		24.7	27.1	30.8	10.9	6.5	48124	56710				10.9	15.0	33.7	30.1	10.4	145905

SPENDING POTENTIAL INDICES

CALIFORNIA

95720-95979 D

ZIP CODE #	POST OFFICE NAME	FINANCIAL SERVICES: Auto Loan	Home Loan	Invest-ments	Retire-ment Plans	THE HOME: Home Improvements: Home Repair	Lawn & Garden	Furnishings: Comput-ers & Hard-ware	Major Appli-ances	TV, Radio, Sound Equip-ment	Furni-ture	ENTERTAINMENT: Dine out/ Carry out	Sports Equip-ment	Fees & Tickets	Toys & Games	Travel	Cable TV	PERSONAL: Apparel & Services	Auto Repairs	Health Insur-ance	Pets & Supplies
95720	KYBURZ	100	79	54	71	89	100	74	89	84	74	100	105	66	98	79	90	93	88	106	122
95721	ECHO LAKE	128	100	68	91	113	127	95	114	107	94	127	133	85	125	101	115	118	112	135	156
95722	MEADOW VISTA	112	138	150	137	135	136	125	124	118	125	148	145	134	158	128	115	148	121	113	137
95724	NORDEN	102	80	55	72	90	101	76	91	86	75	101	107	68	100	81	91	94	90	108	125
95726	POLLOCK PINES	83	86	85	84	87	95	83	86	84	82	103	97	84	104	85	85	100	84	89	97
95728	SODA SPRINGS	85	67	46	60	75	85	63	76	72	63	85	89	57	84	67	76	79	75	90	104
95742	RANCHO CORDOVA	77	75	80	69	79	95	70	80	74	75	92	76	72	79	76	80	86	77	93	87
95746	GRANITE BAY	224	279	302	286	270	272	246	241	225	249	285	279	269	298	251	218	287	232	214	267
95747	ROSEVILLE	124	134	134	134	132	139	122	128	118	128	149	138	126	141	124	117	144	124	124	139
95758	ELK GROVE	126	143	138	149	136	132	129	128	118	134	150	149	133	151	126	110	148	124	109	140
95762	EL DORADO HILLS	194	234	244	242	226	224	208	205	190	213	242	238	223	249	209	182	242	198	179	225
95765	ROCKLIN	151	170	164	178	162	156	154	152	141	160	179	178	158	179	150	131	177	148	129	166
95776	WOODLAND	86	86	79	86	83	83	83	85	81	87	102	97	81	99	80	77	101	85	76	93
95814	SACRAMENTO	44	38	51	41	38	42	49	44	49	46	61	54	46	59	46	47	60	49	43	49
95815	SACRAMENTO	52	47	51	47	46	51	53	52	55	53	69	60	51	67	51	54	67	54	51	56
95816	SACRAMENTO	82	72	96	79	71	77	91	81	89	87	112	102	86	108	84	83	109	89	75	90
95817	SACRAMENTO	58	56	67	57	56	61	63	60	64	62	79	71	62	78	61	63	77	63	59	66
95818	SACRAMENTO	84	93	121	95	92	96	98	93	94	96	118	112	98	120	97	91	117	96	85	101
95819	SACRAMENTO	98	112	136	115	111	114	111	108	106	110	134	128	114	137	112	104	132	109	99	118
95820	SACRAMENTO	60	59	63	58	58	62	61	61	62	62	78	69	61	77	60	61	77	62	59	66
95821	SACRAMENTO	70	72	85	72	71	78	76	74	77	75	96	86	77	96	76	76	94	76	73	81
95822	SACRAMENTO	69	71	81	70	70	75	73	72	73	73	92	81	73	91	73	73	90	73	71	78
95823	SACRAMENTO	67	66	74	66	65	70	69	68	70	70	87	77	69	87	67	69	86	69	65	74
95824	SACRAMENTO	56	53	53	52	52	53	55	57	55	57	70	64	52	65	53	53	69	59	52	60
95825	SACRAMENTO	72	65	84	70	64	71	80	73	79	76	99	90	76	96	75	75	97	79	69	80
95826	SACRAMENTO	78	79	92	81	78	82	85	80	82	83	104	96	84	103	82	79	102	83	75	88
95827	SACRAMENTO	82	85	94	87	83	87	85	84	83	86	104	98	85	103	84	80	102	85	78	92
95828	SACRAMENTO	85	90	92	90	88	90	86	87	84	88	106	100	87	105	85	82	104	87	81	96
95829	SACRAMENTO	117	134	132	139	128	125	121	119	111	125	141	139	125	142	119	104	139	116	103	131
95830	SACRAMENTO	142	165	169	167	161	164	148	148	138	150	175	171	157	178	150	135	174	144	135	166
95831	SACRAMENTO	111	121	142	126	118	122	121	118	115	121	145	139	123	144	120	110	143	119	106	128
95832	SACRAMENTO	59	56	56	54	55	57	57	60	58	60	73	66	54	68	56	56	72	61	56	63
95833	SACRAMENTO	84	80	90	85	77	81	86	83	84	87	106	98	84	102	81	79	104	86	74	91
95834	SACRAMENTO	92	90	98	94	87	92	93	91	91	95	116	107	93	111	90	87	113	93	84	100
95835	SACRAMENTO	126	143	138	149	136	131	129	127	118	134	150	149	132	150	125	110	148	124	108	139
95836	SACRAMENTO	116	84	47	79	97	108	82	100	94	81	110	121	71	108	85	98	101	99	118	138
95837	SACRAMENTO	127	141	148	139	143	152	130	135	127	130	158	154	135	159	136	128	155	132	134	154
95838	SACRAMENTO	64	61	64	60	59	64	65	64	66	65	82	74	63	80	63	64	80	65	62	70
95841	SACRAMENTO	65	63	75	66	62	67	70	66	69	69	87	79	69	85	68	67	85	70	63	73
95842	SACRAMENTO	73	74	80	77	72	74	76	74	73	76	92	88	75	91	73	69	90	75	67	81
95843	ANTELOPE	111	125	121	130	119	115	114	112	104	118	132	132	116	133	111	97	131	110	96	123
95864	SACRAMENTO	128	148	175	146	145	154	144	141	139	142	174	163	150	179	146	137	172	140	133	153
95901	MARYSVILLE	65	60	60	59	60	66	64	64	66	63	82	74	63	81	63	66	79	66	65	72
95903	BEALE AFB	73	46	44	53	42	50	69	59	70	64	87	79	59	78	57	64	84	70	55	68
95910	ALLEGHANY	90	70	48	64	79	89	66	80	75	66	89	94	59	88	71	80	83	79	95	109
95912	ARBUCKLE	88	77	63	72	75	80	78	84	82	83	102	91	72	92	75	80	100	85	82	91
95914	BANGOR	70	72	84	76	73	77	74	74	71	74	90	86	74	87	74	69	87	74	70	80
95915	BELDEN	71	53	35	51	58	70	59	65	66	56	78	73	52	73	58	70	71	65	78	78
95916	BERRY CREEK	76	63	49	57	69	79	59	70	66	60	79	78	54	75	63	70	73	69	83	91
95917	BIGGS	82	65	46	63	70	77	66	75	72	67	87	85	60	83	66	73	82	74	81	91
95918	BROWNS VALLEY	106	77	45	73	88	98	75	92	86	75	101	110	66	99	78	89	93	90	107	125
95919	BROWNSVILLE	66	56	48	54	59	69	59	63	63	58	76	70	55	71	59	65	70	63	72	73
95920	BUTTE CITY	66	58	48	53	55	58	59	64	61	64	77	67	54	68	56	59	76	65	60	66
95922	CAMPTONVILLE	69	52	35	49	57	68	55	62	62	53	73	71	49	70	56	66	67	62	74	78
95923	CANYONDAM	87	68	46	61	77	86	64	77	73	64	86	91	57	85	68	78	80	76	91	106
95925	CHALLENGE	58	44	29	42	48	57	48	53	54	46	64	60	43	60	48	57	58	53	64	64
95926	CHICO	67	60	71	63	59	65	75	66	73	70	91	82	70	88	69	69	88	72	63	74
95928	CHICO	73	68	76	71	66	71	80	72	77	76	97	89	76	94	74	73	94	77	68	80
95932	COLUSA	75	65	54	64	67	75	68	72	71	67	87	82	64	85	67	72	82	71	76	83
95934	CRESCENT MILLS	70	52	35	50	57	69	58	64	65	55	77	72	52	72	57	69	70	64	77	77
95935	DOBBINS	72	69	71	70	71	77	72	73	72	70	89	85	70	86	71	71	85	74	75	82
95936	DOWNIEVILLE	74	68	63	64	72	85	63	72	67	67	83	72	63	71	68	72	78	70	85	85
95937	DUNNIGAN	84	80	66	76	79	84	76	80	77	78	95	93	73	91	75	76	91	80	80	94
95938	DURHAM	127	137	137	138	137	142	130	132	126	130	157	153	133	160	131	124	153	129	126	148
95939	ELK CREEK	80	60	40	58	66	79	67	73	75	63	88	82	59	83	66	79	80	73	88	89
95941	FORBESTOWN	78	62	45	57	69	79	60	71	67	60	80	80	55	77	63	72	74	70	84	92
95942	FOREST RANCH	117	108	90	101	115	123	99	112	104	99	126	131	95	128	104	108	121	109	121	143
95943	GLENN	108	79	46	74	88	98	78	94	88	79	105	111	68	101	80	91	97	93	107	124
95944	GOODYEARS BAR	79	68	56	63	74	85	63	74	69	65	84	79	60	76	68	74	78	72	87	92
95945	GRASS VALLEY	78	77	80	76	79	86	79	80	80	77	99	92	78	99	80	81	95	80	83	91
95946	PENN VALLEY	110	114	116	110	117	131	105	114	107	110	134	119	109	123	112	111	128	110	123	128
95947	GREENVILLE	64	52	40	49	56	67	53	60	59	53	71	64	50	64	55	62	65	59	71	72
95948	GRIDLEY	75	65	54	62	67	73	67	72	71	68	87	81	63	84	66	71	84	72	75	83
95949	GRASS VALLEY	103	113	117	110	114	122	104	108	102	105	127	119	108	125	108	103	124	105	110	121
95951	HAMILTON CITY	60	53	44	49	51	53	54	58	56	59	70	62	49	62	51	54	69	59	54	61
95953	LIVE OAK	76	64	49	60	64	68	65	72	69	69	85	78	59	77	63	67	83	73	71	80
95954	MAGALIA	68	63	61	59	67	79	61	69	66	63	80	70	61	73	65	70	75	67	80	78
95955	MAXWELL	102	71	37	67	83	93	70	87	81	70	95	105	60	93	73	85	87	86	104	121
95956	MEADOW VALLEY	0	0	0	0	0	0	0	0	0	0	0	0	0	0	0	0	0	0	0	0
95957	MERIDIAN	85	61	36	56	67	78	63	74	73	63	86	84	56	81	63	77	79	73	87	94
95959	NEVADA CITY	100	110	116	108	111	118	104	106	102	103	127	122	107	130	107	103	124	104	106	120
95960	NORTH SAN JUAN	81	61	41	58	68	80	65	73	73	62	86	83	58	82	66	77	79	73	87	92
95961	OLIVEHURST	55	50	47	48	50	55	52	53	55	52	68	61	50	66	51	55	65	54	55	61
95963	ORLAND	72	59	46	56	62	68	61	67	65	62	80	76	56	76	60	66	76	67	71	79
95965	OROVILLE	56	48	44	46	49	56	52	53	55	51	67	61	49	65	51	56	64	54	58	62
95966	OROVILLE	69	66	64	63	68	76	66	69	69	66	84	78	65	83	67	71	81	69	74	80
95968	PALERMO	73	53	29	47	58	65	51	61	59	52	70	72	45	66	51	62	64	60	71	83
95969	PARADISE	74	67	61	63	70	82	67	73	72	67	88	78	66	82	70	76	82	72	84	84
95970	PRINCETON	101	70	37	66	82	92	69	86	80	68	94	103	59	92	72	84	85	84	102	119
95971	QUINCY	74	75	74	74	75	80	74	75	74	73	91	88	73	92	74	74	88	75	75	86
95972	RACKERBY	79	76	81	70	80	97	71	82	76	77	95	77	72	79	78	82	88	79	97	89
95973	CHICO	88	94	100	95	93	97	92	92	89	92	111	106	93	111	92	86	109	91	87	101
95975	ROUGH AND READY	71	83	92	79	82	90	78	79	78	78	97	88	83	101	82	80	95	77	80	85
95977	SMARTVILLE	86	95	94	93	94	97	88	90	85	88	106	104	90	109	89	84	104	88	86	102
95979	STONYFORD	68	50	33	48	55	66	55	61	62	53	73	69	49	69	55	66	67	61	74	75
	CALIFORNIA	107	111	131	112	109	115	113	111	111	114	140	129	114	141	112	109	139	113	104	122
	UNITED STATES	100	100	100	100	100	100	100	100	100	100	100	100	100	100	100	100	100	100	100	100

 Copyright © 2004 ESRI BIS. All rights reserved. Reproduction by any method is prohibited.

ZIP CODE			POPULATION			2000-2004 ANNUAL RATE		HOUSEHOLDS					FAMILIES		
#	POST OFFICE NAME	COUNTY FIPS CODE	2000	2004	2009	% Rate	State Centile	2000	2004	2009	% Annual Rate 2000-2004	2004 Average HH Size	2000	2004	% Annual Rate 2000-2004
95981	STRAWBERRY VALLEY	063	155	153	157	-0.3	7	74	73	76	-0.3	2.10	45	44	-0.5
95982	SUTTER	101	3285	3549	3861	1.8	76	1054	1130	1218	1.7	3.14	877	938	1.6
95983	TAYLORSVILLE	063	300	307	315	0.5	33	126	130	134	0.7	2.36	83	85	0.6
95984	TWAIN	063	111	112	114	0.2	20	53	54	55	0.4	2.07	33	33	0.0
95987	WILLIAMS	011	4528	4946	5224	2.1	81	1244	1336	1389	1.7	3.51	981	1051	1.6
95988	WILLOWS	021	8780	8842	8995	0.2	19	3090	3079	3105	-0.1	2.79	2217	2206	-0.1
95991	YUBA CITY	101	34925	37523	40740	1.7	74	12432	13180	14149	1.4	2.80	8587	9108	1.4
95993	YUBA CITY	101	27849	29978	32574	1.8	75	9487	10143	10923	1.6	2.92	7359	7829	1.5
96001	REDDING	089	32399	35296	38609	2.0	80	13008	14163	15523	2.0	2.45	8598	9380	2.1
96002	REDDING	089	30528	32049	34381	1.2	60	11340	11939	12854	1.2	2.63	7994	8379	1.1
96003	REDDING	089	41221	43849	47161	1.5	68	16478	17624	19058	1.6	2.40	10938	11662	1.5
96006	ADIN	049	209	207	205	-0.2	8	92	92	91	0.0	2.23	64	64	0.0
96007	ANDERSON	089	21018	22732	24698	1.9	77	7923	8592	9364	1.9	2.63	5702	6157	1.8
96008	BELLA VISTA	089	1359	1448	1577	1.5	69	530	563	614	1.4	2.56	398	423	1.4
96010	BIG BAR	105	322	323	330	0.1	17	120	121	126	0.2	2.63	81	82	0.3
96013	BURNEY	089	4525	5047	5620	2.6	87	1829	2050	2295	2.7	2.42	1264	1409	2.6
96014	CALLAHAN	093	228	217	213	-1.2	2	94	90	90	-1.0	2.40	64	61	-1.1
96015	CANBY	049	370	368	366	-0.1	10	86	86	86	0.0	3.19	61	61	0.0
96016	CASSEL	089	465	461	484	-0.2	9	210	209	220	-0.1	2.21	154	153	-0.2
96019	SHASTA LAKE	089	6511	7183	7874	2.3	84	2449	2715	2989	2.5	2.64	1685	1860	2.4
96020	CHESTER	063	2665	2738	2815	0.6	38	1130	1172	1215	0.9	2.30	777	802	0.8
96021	CORNING	103	14448	14877	15518	0.7	40	5133	5244	5441	0.5	2.80	3659	3721	0.4
96022	COTTONWOOD	103	11100	11916	12804	1.7	73	3992	4285	4615	1.7	2.78	3087	3307	1.6
96023	DORRIS	093	1277	1253	1240	-0.5	5	494	487	485	-0.3	2.57	358	352	-0.4
96024	DOUGLAS CITY	105	629	648	670	0.7	41	275	287	301	1.0	2.26	183	191	1.0
96025	DUNSMUIR	093	2565	2464	2436	-0.9	2	1166	1129	1126	-0.8	2.17	686	661	-0.9
96027	ETNA	093	2221	2152	2124	-0.7	3	899	879	876	-0.5	2.44	630	614	-0.6
96028	FALL RIVER MILLS	089	2106	2075	2170	-0.4	7	765	756	797	-0.3	2.50	526	518	-0.4
96031	FORKS OF SALMON	093	268	253	249	-1.4	1	117	111	110	-1.2	2.28	77	72	-1.6
96032	FORT JONES	093	2492	2506	2507	0.1	18	1032	1043	1050	0.3	2.38	715	719	0.1
96033	FRENCH GULCH	089	369	340	352	-1.9	1	158	146	152	-1.8	2.33	110	101	-2.0
96034	GAZELLE	093	181	180	178	-0.1	10	73	73	73	0.0	2.45	51	51	0.0
96035	GERBER	103	3765	3862	4009	0.6	36	1305	1329	1371	0.4	2.91	979	993	0.3
96038	GRENADA	093	736	758	765	0.7	41	284	293	297	0.7	2.56	200	205	0.6
96039	HAPPY CAMP	093	1208	1101	1074	-2.2	1	517	475	467	-2.0	2.32	313	286	-2.1
96040	HAT CREEK	089	334	330	347	-0.3	8	129	128	135	-0.2	2.58	92	91	-0.3
96041	HAYFORK	105	1884	1866	1907	-0.2	8	790	793	824	0.1	2.35	504	504	0.0
96044	HORNBROOK	093	980	997	999	0.4	28	430	441	446	0.6	2.24	282	287	0.4
96046	HYAMPOM	105	256	257	263	0.1	17	130	132	137	0.4	1.95	70	71	0.3
96047	IGO	089	655	758	852	3.5	94	262	305	344	3.6	2.47	201	232	3.4
96048	JUNCTION CITY	105	552	568	587	0.7	39	245	256	269	1.0	2.14	165	171	0.8
96050	KLAMATH RIVER	093	576	556	551	-0.8	3	266	260	260	-0.5	2.14	177	171	-0.8
96051	LAKEHEAD	089	1478	1502	1589	0.4	26	676	690	732	0.5	2.18	459	467	0.4
96052	LEWISTON	105	2511	2602	2695	0.8	48	1027	1079	1136	1.2	2.29	712	746	1.1
96054	LOOKOUT	049	388	384	381	-0.2	8	164	164	163	0.0	2.32	114	114	0.0
96055	LOS MOLINOS	103	3729	3960	4217	1.4	67	1425	1511	1605	1.4	2.59	1012	1074	1.4
96056	MCARTHUR	035	2429	2449	2521	0.2	19	903	912	945	0.2	2.47	672	678	0.2
96057	MCCLOUD	093	1541	1467	1444	-1.2	2	675	650	645	-0.9	2.26	457	438	-1.0
96058	MACDOEL	093	693	677	670	-0.6	4	265	260	259	-0.5	2.60	190	186	-0.5
96059	MANTON	089	462	465	484	0.2	18	199	201	209	0.2	2.17	140	141	0.2
96062	MILLVILLE	089	933	1034	1136	2.5	85	338	378	417	2.7	2.74	263	292	2.5
96063	MINERAL	103	143	147	151	0.7	39	68	70	72	0.7	1.89	47	48	0.5
96064	MONTAGUE	093	4586	4711	4756	0.6	38	1817	1885	1920	0.9	2.44	1302	1345	0.8
96065	MONTGOMERY CREEK	089	843	838	881	-0.1	10	344	344	363	0.0	2.38	243	241	-0.2
96067	MOUNT SHASTA	093	7232	7487	7613	0.8	47	3176	3314	3400	1.0	2.23	1984	2060	0.9
96069	OAK RUN	089	1283	1396	1531	2.0	79	493	538	592	2.1	2.57	360	392	2.0
96071	OLD STATION	089	174	172	180	-0.3	8	86	85	90	-0.3	2.02	59	58	-0.4
96073	PALO CEDRO	089	4047	4391	4770	1.9	78	1422	1550	1690	2.1	2.82	1188	1290	2.0
96075	PAYNES CREEK	103	459	470	486	0.6	34	183	188	194	0.6	2.25	127	130	0.6
96076	PLATINA	089	116	137	154	4.0	95	47	55	62	3.8	2.47	33	40	4.6
96080	RED BLUFF	103	27976	28875	30110	0.8	43	10909	11252	11713	0.7	2.51	7510	7722	0.7
96085	SCOTT BAR	093	13	13	13	0.0	15	7	7	7	0.0	1.86	5	5	0.0
96086	SEIAD VALLEY	093	67	63	62	-1.4	1	27	26	25	-0.9	2.42	18	17	-1.3
96087	SHASTA	089	70	69	73	-0.3	7	30	30	31	0.0	2.30	21	21	0.0
96088	SHINGLETOWN	089	4231	4526	4902	1.6	72	1739	1867	2028	1.7	2.42	1324	1417	1.6
96091	TRINITY CENTER	105	559	594	626	1.4	68	265	286	305	1.8	2.08	172	186	1.9
96093	WEAVERVILLE	105	3355	3468	3588	0.8	45	1433	1503	1579	1.1	2.25	911	952	1.0
96094	WEED	093	6006	6208	6306	0.8	45	2439	2548	2614	1.0	2.38	1680	1748	0.9
96096	WHITMORE	089	767	847	930	2.4	84	312	348	384	2.6	2.43	242	268	2.4
96097	YREKA	093	9507	9596	9674	0.2	20	4050	4114	4181	0.4	2.26	2540	2584	0.4
96101	ALTURAS	049	5090	5106	5110	0.1	17	2088	2103	2115	0.2	2.32	1385	1391	0.1
96103	BLAIRSDEN-GRAEAGLE	063	1830	1902	1965	0.9	51	879	922	960	1.1	2.06	597	625	1.1
96104	CEDARVILLE	049	849	823	810	-0.7	3	376	367	363	-0.6	2.22	246	240	-0.6
96105	CHILCOOT	063	532	562	586	1.3	64	215	228	240	1.4	2.46	151	160	1.4
96106	CLIO	063	217	225	233	0.9	49	105	110	115	1.1	2.05	72	75	1.0
96107	COLEVILLE	051	1303	1323	1425	0.4	25	532	542	587	0.4	2.32	376	383	0.4
96108	DAVIS CREEK	049	426	410	402	-0.9	2	143	138	136	-0.8	2.59	101	97	-1.0
96109	DOYLE	035	1364	1442	1520	1.3	65	543	574	606	1.3	2.51	380	400	1.2
96111	FLORISTON	057	106	109	114	0.7	39	41	42	45	0.6	2.57	24	25	1.0
96112	FORT BIDWELL	049	214	209	206	-0.6	4	96	94	94	-0.5	2.15	61	60	-0.4
96113	HERLONG	035	952	1049	1137	2.3	83	390	426	460	2.1	2.45	265	291	2.2
96114	JANESVILLE	063	3158	3406	3629	1.8	75	1147	1237	1321	1.8	2.73	894	964	1.8
96115	LAKE CITY	049	238	232	229	-0.6	4	102	100	100	-0.5	2.25	65	64	-0.4
96116	LIKELY	049	290	291	289	0.1	17	128	129	130	0.2	2.23	88	89	0.3
96117	LITCHFIELD	035	170	173	179	0.4	28	70	72	74	0.7	2.35	53	54	0.4
96118	LOYALTON	091	1364	1392	1428	0.5	31	537	553	574	0.7	2.48	375	385	0.6
96119	MADELINE	035	66	66	66	0.0	15	23	24	25	1.0	2.54	16	2	-38.7
96120	MARKLEEVILLE	003	933	994	1077	1.5	69	375	398	429	1.4	2.50	231	244	1.3
96121	MILFORD	035	460	465	479	0.3	22	185	187	193	0.3	2.49	124	125	0.2
96122	PORTOLA	063	4109	4251	4382	0.8	46	1655	1718	1781	0.9	2.46	1138	1178	0.8
96123	RAVENDALE	035	5	5	5	0.0	15	2	2	2	0.0	1.00	1	0	-100.0
96124	CALPINE	091	315	319	326	0.3	23	144	147	153	0.5	2.15	93	95	0.5
96125	SIERRA CITY	091	287	286	290	-0.1	11	136	137	140	0.2	2.09	77	78	0.3
96126	SIERRAVILLE	091	402	408	418	0.4	25	159	163	169	0.6	2.52	106	108	0.4
96128	STANDISH	035	253	258	267	0.5	29	98	100	104	0.5	2.52	74	75	0.3
	CALIFORNIA					1.4					1.2	2.90			1.2
	UNITED STATES					1.2					1.3	2.58			1.1

ZIP CODE #	POST OFFICE NAME	RACE (%) White 2000	White 2004	Black 2000	Black 2004	Asian/Pacific 2000	Asian/Pacific 2004	% Hispanic Origin 2000	% Hispanic Origin 2004	2004 AGE DISTRIBUTION (%) 0-4	5-9	10-14	15-19	20-24	25-44	45-64	65-84	85+	18+	MEDIAN AGE 2004	% 2004 Males	% 2004 Females
95981	STRAWBERRY VALLEY	91.0	89.5	0.0	0.0	0.0	0.7	4.5	5.2	4.6	5.2	6.5	5.9	3.9	20.9	37.3	14.4	1.3	79.7	46.7	51.6	48.4
95982	SUTTER	85.2	82.5	0.2	0.3	1.1	1.2	11.5	14.0	7.1	8.2	9.9	9.2	5.7	26.2	23.7	9.3	0.7	69.0	35.1	50.9	49.1
95983	TAYLORSVILLE	91.0	89.6	0.0	0.0	0.7	0.7	6.3	7.5	5.5	5.9	5.5	6.5	4.2	19.5	35.5	15.6	1.6	78.8	46.4	50.8	49.2
95984	TWAIN	91.0	90.2	0.0	0.0	0.0	0.0	6.3	8.0	5.4	5.4	4.5	6.3	5.4	20.5	36.6	14.3	1.8	79.5	46.4	53.6	46.4
95987	WILLIAMS	52.5	49.6	0.4	0.4	1.2	1.3	61.6	65.7	8.9	8.5	8.9	8.6	9.2	27.6	19.0	7.5	1.7	68.6	28.6	51.4	48.6
95988	WILLOWS	73.5	70.1	0.8	0.8	8.1	8.9	20.4	23.6	7.7	7.9	8.6	8.7	7.2	25.3	21.9	10.7	1.9	70.5	33.0	50.5	49.5
95991	YUBA CITY	67.7	64.6	2.6	2.5	7.8	8.5	26.0	28.9	8.2	7.4	8.0	7.5	8.7	27.6	20.1	10.5	2.1	71.8	32.1	48.8	51.3
95993	YUBA CITY	66.6	63.2	1.8	1.8	19.5	20.9	12.8	14.8	7.0	7.0	7.8	6.9	6.2	27.4	24.8	11.9	1.1	73.8	36.9	49.8	50.2
96001	REDDING	89.8	88.6	0.9	1.0	2.1	2.4	5.3	6.2	5.7	6.1	7.4	7.5	6.5	23.3	28.2	13.4	2.0	75.9	40.7	48.7	51.3
96002	REDDING	87.0	85.2	1.1	1.1	4.0	4.6	5.7	6.7	7.1	6.5	7.6	7.8	8.4	24.0	23.5	12.6	2.4	74.0	36.3	48.3	51.7
96003	REDDING	90.6	89.2	0.9	1.0	1.8	2.1	4.8	5.6	6.0	5.9	6.7	7.2	7.8	24.9	25.7	13.7	2.1	77.3	38.9	48.6	51.4
96006	ADIN	91.4	91.3	0.0	0.0	0.0	0.0	8.1	8.7	4.8	5.3	6.8	6.8	5.3	20.3	31.9	17.4	1.5	78.7	45.4	51.7	48.3
96007	ANDERSON	88.8	87.2	0.5	0.5	1.2	1.4	6.6	7.8	6.5	6.3	7.7	7.7	7.1	23.1	26.5	13.2	2.0	74.8	39.0	48.4	51.6
96008	BELLA VISTA	91.6	90.5	0.3	0.4	0.4	0.4	3.9	4.6	3.7	5.2	8.0	7.2	4.6	22.4	34.9	12.6	1.4	78.1	44.4	50.1	49.9
96010	BIG BAR	85.7	84.5	0.0	0.0	1.2	1.2	5.3	5.9	4.0	4.6	9.3	9.3	2.8	21.7	32.2	15.2	0.9	76.2	44.1	49.9	50.2
96013	BURNEY	88.4	87.2	0.2	0.2	0.7	0.8	6.6	7.9	5.3	5.4	6.8	7.5	6.2	21.7	30.3	14.7	2.1	77.5	42.9	48.7	51.3
96014	CALLAHAN	84.7	83.0	0.0	0.0	0.4	0.5	4.8	5.5	3.2	4.2	6.9	8.3	4.2	18.9	37.3	15.7	1.4	79.7	47.2	53.5	46.5
96015	CANBY	92.4	92.1	1.1	1.1	0.5	0.5	5.7	5.7	4.4	4.9	7.3	12.0	6.0	19.6	32.1	13.0	0.8	74.2	41.7	52.7	47.3
96016	CASSEL	88.6	87.4	0.0	0.0	0.4	0.4	3.2	3.9	3.9	4.8	5.4	4.6	3.7	16.1	36.7	22.6	2.4	82.7	52.4	52.3	47.7
96019	SHASTA LAKE	87.0	85.3	0.7	0.8	0.4	0.5	6.4	7.6	6.8	6.8	7.9	7.7	7.2	26.1	24.1	11.6	1.9	73.6	37.1	49.1	50.9
96020	CHESTER	93.2	92.0	0.2	0.2	0.6	0.6	5.7	6.9	4.6	5.4	7.8	6.5	4.7	20.4	33.1	15.2	2.2	77.9	45.3	50.0	50.0
96021	CORNING	77.1	74.0	0.6	0.7	0.7	0.7	25.4	29.3	7.7	7.2	7.9	8.0	7.5	24.5	22.9	12.7	1.6	72.0	35.5	49.9	50.1
96022	COTTONWOOD	89.7	88.2	0.3	0.3	1.3	1.5	6.8	8.1	5.5	5.9	8.2	8.2	6.7	22.7	29.8	12.1	1.0	75.0	40.5	49.4	50.6
96023	DORRIS	79.4	76.1	0.1	0.2	0.8	0.8	22.7	27.0	6.8	7.2	8.6	7.1	5.9	23.5	26.7	12.5	1.8	73.0	37.5	50.7	49.3
96024	DOUGLAS CITY	90.9	89.4	0.3	0.3	0.6	0.6	2.7	3.4	5.4	5.9	6.2	6.2	3.7	20.2	34.7	17.0	0.8	78.6	46.2	49.9	50.2
96025	DUNSMUIR	90.1	88.6	2.1	2.2	0.7	0.8	9.2	11.2	4.4	4.7	6.9	7.1	4.9	21.4	30.8	17.1	2.8	79.3	45.4	50.1	49.9
96027	ETNA	87.8	86.1	0.1	0.1	0.7	0.8	4.3	5.3	4.0	4.5	7.0	7.9	5.4	18.0	34.5	16.6	2.1	79.0	46.7	50.5	49.5
96028	FALL RIVER MILLS	84.9	83.0	0.1	0.1	0.2	0.2	12.3	14.4	6.3	6.5	7.0	8.4	5.6	21.6	27.6	14.7	2.3	73.9	40.9	50.8	49.2
96031	FORKS OF SALMON	83.6	81.4	0.0	0.0	0.4	0.4	4.9	5.9	3.2	3.6	7.9	8.7	4.0	20.2	36.8	14.2	1.6	78.7	46.2	53.0	47.0
96032	FORT JONES	90.0	88.4	0.4	0.5	0.5	0.6	6.0	7.3	5.0	5.4	5.7	5.8	5.0	19.7	35.3	16.2	2.0	79.3	46.9	49.5	50.5
96033	FRENCH GULCH	94.0	93.5	0.0	0.0	0.5	0.6	1.9	2.4	2.9	4.1	8.2	5.3	2.1	21.5	42.7	12.4	0.9	80.9	47.9	50.9	49.1
96034	GAZELLE	90.1	88.3	0.0	0.0	0.6	0.6	4.4	5.6	5.6	6.1	7.8	7.2	5.0	20.6	30.6	15.0	2.2	75.6	43.5	51.1	48.9
96035	GERBER	74.1	70.5	0.5	0.4	0.6	0.6	26.8	30.9	6.7	7.0	9.5	8.2	7.0	24.7	22.9	12.8	1.3	71.6	35.6	51.2	48.8
96038	GRENADA	90.9	89.7	0.1	0.1	0.4	0.5	4.1	5.2	5.3	6.1	7.8	6.7	4.9	20.1	31.4	15.8	2.0	76.3	44.4	50.5	49.5
96039	HAPPY CAMP	70.9	68.5	0.4	0.5	0.6	0.6	4.2	5.0	4.1	5.5	7.8	6.0	4.2	20.7	34.8	15.3	1.7	78.9	45.9	52.0	48.1
96040	HAT CREEK	88.6	87.9	0.0	0.0	0.3	0.3	3.9	3.9	4.2	4.6	5.2	4.6	4.2	17.0	36.1	21.8	2.4	83.0	51.6	51.5	48.5
96041	HAYFORK	85.4	83.5	0.1	0.2	0.2	0.2	5.0	6.1	5.5	6.0	7.6	7.1	5.5	21.3	31.9	14.0	1.2	76.5	43.0	51.1	48.9
96044	HORNBROOK	88.4	86.7	0.3	0.3	0.5	0.5	5.7	6.9	4.7	4.9	4.9	6.1	4.9	18.8	33.0	20.8	1.9	81.6	48.8	49.0	51.1
96046	HYAMPOM	89.5	88.7	0.0	0.0	1.2	1.2	0.8	0.8	0.8	4.3	7.8	5.8	0.4	22.2	39.7	18.7	0.4	81.7	48.9	51.8	48.3
96047	IGO	90.7	89.2	0.3	0.3	0.9	1.1	4.4	5.0	4.1	5.2	6.3	6.6	5.0	19.9	38.1	13.9	0.9	80.1	46.5	50.3	49.7
96048	JUNCTION CITY	90.8	89.3	0.2	0.2	0.4	0.4	4.0	4.9	3.2	4.2	7.8	6.7	3.4	20.4	38.6	14.8	1.1	80.1	47.2	50.4	49.7
96050	KLAMATH RIVER	81.1	78.8	0.5	0.5	0.7	0.9	5.0	5.9	4.7	5.2	6.3	6.1	4.5	18.4	36.9	16.6	1.4	79.9	47.8	49.3	50.7
96051	LAKEHEAD	93.0	92.3	0.1	0.1	0.3	0.4	3.3	3.9	2.6	3.3	4.5	4.2	3.4	16.5	43.7	19.8	1.9	87.2	52.5	50.7	49.3
96052	LEWISTON	90.6	89.2	1.4	1.5	0.6	0.7	5.5	6.4	3.6	4.3	6.4	5.9	4.5	20.1	35.7	18.2	1.4	81.5	48.2	53.0	47.0
96054	LOOKOUT	91.0	90.6	0.3	0.3	0.3	0.3	8.3	8.3	5.0	5.5	7.0	6.5	5.2	20.3	31.3	18.0	1.3	78.1	45.3	51.6	48.4
96055	LOS MOLINOS	88.8	87.5	0.1	0.1	0.4	0.3	17.0	19.3	6.0	6.3	7.4	7.0	5.9	22.8	26.3	16.1	2.2	76.0	41.6	49.9	50.1
96056	MCARTHUR	88.0	86.8	1.5	1.6	0.3	0.3	11.7	13.9	4.9	5.3	7.2	8.5	5.3	23.9	30.1	13.2	1.6	76.5	41.7	53.9	46.1
96057	MCCLOUD	89.9	88.5	1.6	1.7	1.3	1.4	6.0	7.4	4.8	5.3	6.2	5.5	4.8	18.3	33.1	19.4	2.6	80.5	48.3	48.4	51.6
96058	MACDOEL	80.5	77.6	0.3	0.3	0.9	0.9	21.1	24.8	6.7	7.1	8.0	6.9	5.9	23.0	27.3	13.2	1.9	74.0	38.6	50.2	49.8
96059	MANTON	88.7	87.3	1.5	1.7	0.7	0.7	8.0	9.7	3.4	4.3	6.2	6.5	4.3	22.4	32.5	18.9	1.5	81.9	46.7	54.6	45.4
96062	MILLVILLE	92.9	91.8	0.3	0.4	0.5	0.6	4.2	4.9	4.0	5.3	7.5	7.3	2.9	19.9	38.4	13.2	1.6	77.5	46.7	51.0	49.0
96063	MINERAL	87.4	85.0	2.8	2.7	0.7	0.7	10.5	12.9	3.4	4.1	6.8	6.1	4.8	23.8	32.7	17.0	1.4	81.6	45.6	54.4	45.6
96064	MONTAGUE	90.2	88.7	0.5	0.5	0.7	0.8	4.8	5.8	4.4	5.0	6.8	7.1	4.9	20.4	32.4	17.3	1.6	79.2	45.8	50.0	50.0
96065	MONTGOMERY CREEK	86.8	85.1	0.6	0.7	0.6	0.6	3.6	4.2	3.9	6.6	7.9	6.8	3.9	23.0	33.8	12.8	1.3	76.6	43.8	53.6	46.4
96067	MOUNT SHASTA	92.8	91.6	0.9	1.0	1.5	1.7	4.6	5.5	4.2	4.7	6.0	7.1	6.1	19.8	35.1	14.8	2.3	80.5	46.2	48.1	51.9
96069	OAK RUN	90.1	89.0	0.2	0.3	0.6	0.7	3.4	4.0	3.9	5.9	7.2	7.1	3.2	19.9	37.8	13.5	1.4	77.4	46.4	51.7	48.4
96071	OLD STATION	89.1	87.8	0.0	0.0	0.6	0.6	5.2	5.8	4.7	5.2	5.8	5.2	4.7	18.0	33.1	20.4	2.9	80.8	49.2	50.0	50.0
96073	PALO CEDRO	93.3	92.2	0.4	0.4	0.9	1.0	3.6	4.3	3.7	5.1	8.7	8.8	3.9	19.3	35.5	13.9	1.2	76.4	45.4	49.5	50.5
96075	PAYNES CREEK	87.2	85.5	2.4	2.6	0.4	0.4	10.5	12.8	3.6	4.3	6.4	6.2	4.7	24.0	31.9	17.2	1.7	81.7	45.5	54.9	45.1
96076	PLATINA	90.5	89.8	0.0	0.0	0.9	0.7	5.2	5.8	2.9	5.1	6.6	5.8	5.1	19.0	42.3	13.1	0.0	81.0	47.5	54.7	45.3
96080	RED BLUFF	88.6	86.8	0.6	0.6	1.2	1.3	10.8	12.8	6.2	6.2	7.4	7.1	6.8	23.8	25.4	14.6	2.5	75.6	39.9	48.5	51.5
96085	SCOTT BAR	92.3	92.3	0.0	0.0	0.0	0.0	0.0	7.7	0.0	0.0	0.0	0.0	0.0	0.0	100.0	0.0	0.0	100.0	52.9	38.5	61.5
96086	SEIAD VALLEY	76.1	74.6	0.0	0.0	1.5	1.6	4.5	3.2	3.2	4.8	6.4	6.4	3.2	20.6	41.3	14.3	0.0	82.5	47.9	49.2	50.8
96087	SHASTA	90.0	89.9	0.0	0.0	1.4	1.5	2.9	4.4	2.9	2.9	5.8	10.1	5.8	20.3	34.8	15.9	1.5	79.7	46.1	49.3	50.7
96088	SHINGLETOWN	92.8	91.6	0.2	0.3	0.4	0.4	3.9	4.8	3.5	4.6	6.7	6.4	3.8	19.3	34.6	19.8	1.3	80.9	48.4	51.0	49.0
96091	TRINITY CENTER	89.3	88.1	0.2	0.2	1.4	1.5	1.4	1.9	2.0	4.4	5.7	4.0	2.7	14.8	39.1	25.9	1.4	85.7	54.3	52.5	47.5
96093	WEAVERVILLE	91.5	90.3	0.2	0.3	0.8	1.0	4.4	5.1	5.3	5.6	7.0	6.9	6.3	20.2	30.4	15.3	2.9	77.4	44.0	48.5	51.5
96094	WEED	82.7	81.1	5.2	5.1	3.1	3.3	8.8	10.3	5.7	5.4	6.8	8.0	6.8	21.0	28.8	15.4	2.2	77.9	42.6	49.2	50.9
96096	WHITMORE	92.8	91.7	0.4	0.4	0.5	0.6	4.3	5.1	4.0	5.2	7.4	7.2	3.1	19.8	37.8	13.9	1.5	77.7	46.7	50.9	49.1
96097	YREKA	87.6	86.1	0.6	0.6	1.5	1.7	5.1	6.1	5.3	5.4	6.8	7.6	6.2	21.0	28.4	16.6	2.9	77.5	43.5	48.3	51.7
96101	ALTURAS	87.7	87.6	0.7	0.7	0.9	0.9	10.2	10.3	5.8	6.2	6.9	7.2	5.7	21.8	29.2	15.2	2.0	76.1	42.5	50.0	50.0
96103	BLAIRSDEN-GRAEAGLE	96.8	96.2	0.2	0.3	0.5	0.6	2.2	2.6	2.1	2.7	3.8	4.4	2.8	13.4	41.2	27.8	1.7	88.4	56.1	49.6	50.4
96104	CEDARVILLE	86.3	86.3	0.1	0.1	0.2	0.2	7.7	7.8	4.7	5.4	6.0	5.2	4.7	20.1	32.0	19.2	2.8	80.3	47.9	49.8	50.2
96105	CHILCOOT	91.9	91.1	0.2	0.2	0.4	0.4	5.3	6.1	4.3	4.8	9.8	7.3	2.9	22.6	34.0	13.5	0.9	75.6	44.0	51.4	48.6
96106	CLIO	97.7	96.9	0.0	0.4	0.5	0.4	1.8	2.2	2.2	2.2	3.1	4.0	2.7	12.0	41.3	30.7	1.8	89.8	57.1	50.2	49.8
96107	COLEVILLE	82.7	80.9	1.2	1.3	1.4	1.6	10.7	12.6	5.9	6.0	6.4	5.4	6.4	24.3	28.5	15.7	1.5	78.6	41.8	53.1	46.9
96108	DAVIS CREEK	85.2	84.4	3.8	3.9	1.4	1.5	9.9	10.2	3.4	3.9	4.6	6.6	5.4	25.6	35.9	13.7	1.0	83.2	45.3	57.8	42.2
96109	DOYLE	88.8	87.5	1.5	1.6	0.4	0.4	7.4	9.0	5.6	6.0	6.7	6.8	5.1	21.0	31.8	15.7	1.3	77.5	44.2	49.9	50.1
96111	FLORISTON	93.4	92.7	0.0	0.0	0.9	0.9	2.8	3.7	3.7	3.7	6.4	7.3	4.6	26.6	42.2	5.5	0.0	82.6	43.9	52.3	47.7
96112	FORT BIDWELL	79.9	79.4	0.0	0.0	0.9	1.0	7.5	7.7	4.8	5.3	6.2	5.7	5.7	18.2	31.6	19.1	3.4	79.0	48.0	48.3	51.7
96113	HERLONG	78.1	74.8	6.2	7.2	0.7	0.8	10.2	12.0	7.2	6.5	6.3	6.4	5.6	23.4	32.1	11.4	1.1	75.7	41.5	53.6	46.4
96114	JANESVILLE	92.7	91.6	0.5	0.6	0.6	0.7	6.2	7.7	5.9	6.4	9.3	8.2	3.7	25.8	29.3	10.5	1.0	72.7	40.2	51.3	48.7
96115	LAKE CITY	79.8	79.3	0.0	0.0	0.8	0.9	7.6	7.8	5.2	5.6	5.6	5.6	6.0	18.1	31.5	19.0	3.5	78.9	48.0	47.8	52.2
96116	LIKELY	89.7	90.0	0.3	0.3	0.3	0.3	9.7	10.0	4.5	5.5	6.9	6.2	3.4	19.6	32.7	20.3	1.0	78.7	47.9	50.9	49.1
96117	LITCHFIELD	88.2	86.7	0.6	0.6	0.6	0.6	11.8	13.9	6.4	6.9	9.8	8.1	6.9	24.9	27.8	8.7	0.6	71.7	36.5	52.0	48.0
96118	LOYALTON	94.0	93.9	0.4	0.4	0.3	0.3	6.5	6.8	5.2	5.6	7.7	7.5	5.7	21.1	30.5	14.5	2.3	76.2	43.2	49.1	50.9
96119	MADELINE	68.2	68.2	27.3	27.3	0.0	0.0	25.8	30.3	0.0	0.0	0.0	3.0	16.7	68.2	12.1	0.0	0.0	100.0	33.0	100.0	0.0
96120	MARKLEEVILLE	72.6	72.5	0.6	0.6	0.4	0.4	7.9	8.3	5.2	5.4	5.7	7.2	6.4	28.3	31.4	9.1	1.2	78.8	40.2	52.4	47.6
96121	MILFORD	81.1	78.9	5.7	6.5	0.7	0.7	10.0	11.8	5.4	5.8	6.2	6.7	5.4	21.3	32.7	15.3	1.3	78.5	44.5	51.0	49.0
96122	PORTOLA	88.1	86.3	0.5	0.5	0.8	0.9	10.6	12.5	5.3	6.1	8.8	7.7	5.4	22.9	29.4	12.7	1.7	74.6	40.9	50.0	50.0
96123	RAVENDALE	60.0	80.0	20.0	20.0	0.0	0.0	20.0	40.0	0.0	0.0	0.0	0.0	20.0	80.0	0.0	0.0	0.0	100.0	32.5	100.0	0.0
96124	CALPINE	94.3	94.4	0.0	0.0	0.0	0.0	5.4	5.3	4.1	4.7	5.3	6.0	3.5	27.9	31.0	15.7	1.9	82.1	44.3	52.7	47.3
96125	SIERRA CITY	95.1	95.1	0.0	0.0	0.4	0.4	4.5	4.6	2.5	3.2	4.6	5.9	2.1	19.6	39.9	17.1	5.2	85.7	51.3	52.1	47.9
96126	SIERRAVILLE	92.8	92.9	0.0	0.0	0.5	0.5	6.7	6.9	4.9	5.6	7.6	7.1	4.4	21.8	31.4	15.4	1.7	76.5	44.1	50.0	50.0
96128	STANDISH	88.1	86.8	0.4	0.8	0.4	0.4	11.5	14.3	6.2	6.6	8.1	8.5	7.0	25.2	28.3	9.3	0.8	74.0	37.8	51.9	48.1
	CALIFORNIA	59.6	57.1	6.7	6.5	11.3	11.8	32.4	35.5	7.4	7.1	7.8	7.3	7.7	29.8	22.1	9.3	1.4	73.3	33.8	49.8	50.2
	UNITED STATES	75.1	73.6	12.3	12.5	3.8	4.2	12.5	14.1	6.9	6.7	7.2	7.0	7.3	28.6	23.8	10.8	1.7	75.1	36.0	49.1	50.9

#	POST OFFICE NAME	2004 Per Capita Income	2004 HH Income Base	2004 Household Income Distribution (%): Less than $25,000	$25,000 to $49,999	$50,000 to $99,999	$100,000 to $149,999	$150,000 or More	Median Household Income: 2004	2009	2004 National Centile	2004 State Centile	2004 Home Value Base	2004 Home Value Distribution (%): Less than $50,000	$50,000 to $89,999	$90,000 to $174,999	$175,000 to $399,999	$400,000 or More	2004 Median Home Value
95981	STRAWBERRY VALLEY	19464	73	37.0	34.3	23.3	5.5	0.0	32722	35000	20	15	57	3.5	10.5	33.3	47.4	5.3	184375
95982	SUTTER	18324	1130	27.6	27.1	35.0	8.5	1.8	46345	52569	65	44	909	1.5	1.5	40.3	41.8	14.9	188268
95983	TAYLORSVILLE	18723	130	38.5	23.9	30.8	5.4	1.5	37340	41553	37	25	102	13.7	11.8	31.4	35.3	7.8	153125
95984	TWAIN	20736	54	46.3	18.5	27.8	7.4	0.0	30000	32336	12	11	40	20.0	17.5	37.5	22.5	2.5	112500
95987	WILLIAMS	15088	1336	28.7	33.7	29.8	5.2	2.5	39941	44704	46	31	896	3.6	2.9	47.1	34.4	12.1	171624
95988	WILLOWS	15818	3079	34.9	34.1	24.7	5.3	1.1	35224	38998	28	20	1884	3.1	4.9	49.6	38.5	3.8	158960
95991	YUBA CITY	17802	13180	33.6	29.3	26.9	7.5	2.7	37356	43087	37	25	7164	4.9	4.8	39.2	46.3	4.8	176896
95993	YUBA CITY	24624	10143	19.5	28.0	33.6	12.7	6.3	52525	61377	76	57	7662	3.6	1.8	17.3	67.2	10.2	228851
96001	REDDING	24825	14163	32.3	26.5	26.0	9.4	5.9	39390	46517	44	30	9325	3.8	2.3	32.0	51.4	10.6	206127
96002	REDDING	19046	11939	31.6	32.9	26.5	6.2	2.9	37361	42111	37	25	7327	12.5	1.9	35.1	43.7	6.8	176187
96003	REDDING	22215	17624	30.7	30.0	28.1	7.9	3.4	40603	46521	48	33	11488	8.3	5.3	29.1	50.5	6.8	190079
96006	ADIN	18238	92	40.2	33.7	19.6	3.3	3.3	30737	35367	14	12	76	17.1	15.8	35.5	19.7	11.8	126923
96007	ANDERSON	16072	8592	37.7	33.9	22.9	3.7	1.8	32830	37068	20	15	5998	8.8	5.3	47.6	34.5	3.9	153879
96008	BELLA VISTA	23174	563	25.8	33.6	24.9	10.5	5.3	43181	49435	56	38	473	4.7	7.2	32.6	38.3	17.3	201087
96010	BIG BAR	14920	121	44.6	29.8	17.4	8.3	0.0	28939	30000	10	9	90	1.1	5.6	37.8	41.1	14.4	195833
96013	BURNEY	19573	2050	38.0	31.4	24.4	4.6	1.7	34746	38404	26	19	1447	8.7	13.3	54.5	19.8	3.7	130277
96014	CALLAHAN	21360	90	36.7	28.9	22.2	7.8	4.4	36854	42862	35	24	70	11.4	8.6	25.7	37.1	17.1	190000
96015	CANBY	16929	86	30.2	27.9	29.1	12.8	0.0	40000	47347	46	31	69	13.0	29.0	21.7	27.5	8.7	117500
96016	CASSEL	24959	209	22.5	36.4	28.7	8.1	4.3	45516	50742	63	42	170	0.0	4.1	35.9	53.5	6.5	204082
96019	SHASTA LAKE	15488	2715	42.6	32.3	21.6	2.0	1.6	29193	33036	11	9	1816	5.0	11.1	65.7	18.1	0.1	135165
96020	CHESTER	21200	1172	28.3	31.3	31.3	7.0	2.1	39869	45905	45	31	837	3.2	1.3	25.5	59.0	11.0	214950
96021	CORNING	14728	5244	42.6	31.1	20.7	3.9	1.9	30817	34180	14	12	3534	10.1	12.1	48.9	24.9	4.0	135881
96022	COTTONWOOD	17989	4285	28.8	33.9	27.9	6.5	2.9	39210	44771	43	29	3488	8.4	5.1	30.9	48.9	6.7	189640
96023	DORRIS	14133	487	46.4	32.0	17.7	2.5	1.4	27033	31140	7	7	329	11.6	33.1	32.8	16.4	6.1	96034
96024	DOUGLAS CITY	20360	287	39.7	26.8	24.4	5.9	3.1	35329	38642	29	21	230	9.6	7.8	34.4	37.4	10.9	171667
96025	DUNSMUIR	17956	1129	46.4	31.8	15.7	3.9	2.2	26732	30057	7	6	670	9.1	3.6	60.8	21.9	4.6	142358
96027	ETNA	23695	879	37.5	30.9	20.8	7.5	3.2	35419	40315	29	21	692	7.1	6.5	30.8	42.8	12.9	191250
96028	FALL RIVER MILLS	18478	756	36.0	34.0	21.3	4.8	4.0	34888	39275	27	19	554	11.7	9.0	39.4	33.6	6.3	151667
96031	FORKS OF SALMON	28881	111	36.9	27.9	21.6	8.1	5.4	36638	41542	34	23	83	10.8	9.6	26.5	37.4	15.7	187500
96032	FORT JONES	23651	1043	39.4	26.8	23.4	7.5	3.0	35646	40789	30	21	827	4.2	4.5	35.0	42.1	14.3	194022
96033	FRENCH GULCH	18797	146	34.9	30.1	28.8	4.1	2.1	35000	40928	28	20	113	8.0	11.5	38.9	29.2	12.4	162500
96034	GAZELLE	16764	73	37.0	34.3	23.3	4.1	1.4	36601	41119	34	23	53	11.3	7.6	43.4	26.4	11.3	143269
96035	GERBER	17400	1329	36.7	36.0	20.8	3.5	3.0	31398	35163	16	12	967	6.7	12.5	55.1	20.3	5.4	130309
96038	GRENADA	19495	293	35.8	34.1	23.6	4.4	2.1	36833	41277	35	24	217	13.4	8.3	38.3	29.5	10.6	145427
96039	HAPPY CAMP	15790	475	52.0	25.1	17.5	4.0	1.5	23689	26801	4	3	296	20.3	15.2	37.8	20.6	6.1	112766
96040	HAT CREEK	20476	128	24.2	35.9	28.9	7.0	3.9	44307	48976	59	41	102	2.9	6.9	38.2	45.1	6.9	182143
96041	HAYFORK	16687	793	49.9	32.8	10.3	5.8	1.1	25022	27112	5	4	568	11.3	11.3	47.4	24.8	5.3	134949
96044	HORNBROOK	18963	441	41.7	31.8	18.4	5.4	2.7	29487	33410	11	9	354	9.9	12.4	39.8	30.2	7.6	143750
96046	HYAMPOM	18351	132	59.1	13.6	16.7	8.3	2.3	17687	19760	1	2	111	5.4	27.9	24.3	29.7	12.6	121023
96047	IGO	27931	305	32.8	24.6	25.9	10.8	5.9	39770	46281	45	30	257	7.8	5.5	21.4	41.6	23.7	256731
96048	JUNCTION CITY	21242	256	31.6	33.6	26.6	7.0	1.2	36851	40523	35	24	216	0.9	8.8	30.1	46.8	13.4	217857
96050	KLAMATH RIVER	19964	260	45.0	26.9	20.0	6.2	1.9	28447	32166	9	8	187	7.5	8.6	36.9	33.7	13.4	163542
96051	LAKEHEAD	22442	690	30.0	33.8	24.9	9.0	2.3	38418	43881	41	27	554	4.3	6.0	32.5	42.6	14.6	202525
96052	LEWISTON	20590	1079	33.0	33.6	24.9	6.2	2.3	36017	40206	32	22	864	8.8	5.8	35.9	39.4	10.2	173876
96054	LOOKOUT	17950	164	40.9	33.5	20.7	3.1	1.8	30397	35670	13	11	136	15.4	16.2	35.3	20.6	12.5	127500
96055	LOS MOLINOS	17099	1511	34.8	31.0	27.9	4.8	1.5	35278	39021	29	20	1115	12.8	8.5	35.0	34.1	9.6	154972
96056	MCARTHUR	17391	912	40.1	31.1	22.6	4.1	2.1	31734	35830	17	13	721	10.3	12.9	31.1	34.7	11.1	159750
96057	MCCLOUD	19080	650	39.2	31.1	23.2	4.2	2.3	33213	37955	22	16	447	3.6	9.4	50.3	31.8	4.9	153125
96058	MACDOEL	14340	260	45.0	31.5	18.9	2.7	1.9	28056	32052	9	8	176	10.2	29.6	35.8	18.2	6.3	105556
96059	MANTON	20921	201	34.3	35.8	24.9	4.0	1.0	35145	39798	28	20	165	6.7	13.3	32.7	33.9	13.3	167969
96062	MILLVILLE	23531	378	25.4	28.3	31.2	9.5	5.6	46390	52232	65	44	313	4.8	3.5	15.7	54.0	22.0	268902
96063	MINERAL	23311	70	37.1	40.0	15.7	5.7	1.4	31488	35000	16	13	58	10.3	15.5	34.5	25.9	13.8	146429
96064	MONTAGUE	17478	1885	38.9	33.8	21.1	4.6	1.6	32620	37141	20	15	1515	4.8	12.7	45.2	29.5	7.8	145048
96065	MONTGOMERY CREEK	18913	344	35.5	33.1	23.0	6.4	2.0	35221	39366	28	20	274	10.2	8.4	32.5	32.5	16.4	171591
96067	MOUNT SHASTA	24322	3314	35.6	27.1	25.4	6.9	5.0	36952	42887	35	25	2325	7.6	4.0	19.9	54.2	14.3	236861
96069	OAK RUN	22252	538	31.0	28.4	27.5	8.9	4.1	41193	47116	50	34	442	7.7	5.0	22.2	42.8	22.4	242708
96071	OLD STATION	24102	85	29.4	37.7	23.5	5.9	3.5	38619	43907	41	28	65	4.6	7.7	40.0	38.5	9.2	168750
96073	PALO CEDRO	26154	1550	14.6	29.0	34.0	15.1	7.4	57577	67746	82	65	1371	1.1	1.8	15.3	63.8	18.0	264080
96075	PAYNES CREEK	19926	188	38.3	38.3	16.5	5.3	1.6	31183	35000	15	12	156	10.3	15.4	34.0	26.3	14.1	148684
96076	PLATINA	14940	55	45.5	20.0	30.9	3.6	0.0	29062	31529	10	9	47	4.3	10.6	51.1	27.7	6.4	123958
96080	RED BLUFF	19688	11252	33.7	31.9	25.7	5.8	2.9	36074	40509	32	22	7414	6.8	4.7	40.9	40.0	7.6	170061
96085	SCOTT BAR	23077	7	57.1	0.0	42.9	0.0	0.0	22183	22183	3	3	5	0.0	0.0	60.0	40.0	0.0	162500
96086	SEIAD VALLEY	13611	26	53.9	23.1	19.2	3.9	0.0	22265	26093	3	3	18	5.6	5.6	44.4	33.3	11.1	150000
96087	SHASTA	24220	30	23.3	30.0	33.3	10.0	3.3	47351	48639	67	46	23	0.0	4.4	43.5	47.8	4.4	181250
96088	SHINGLETOWN	22483	1867	29.7	31.0	30.9	5.3	3.2	39119	44475	43	29	1562	3.7	5.1	28.0	53.7	9.6	210510
96091	TRINITY CENTER	22741	286	33.2	30.8	28.3	4.9	2.8	35346	39186	29	21	236	3.0	5.1	34.8	42.4	14.8	193478
96093	WEAVERVILLE	21604	1503	34.6	35.3	20.6	5.7	3.8	34299	39100	25	18	997	5.3	5.0	29.5	51.2	9.0	196875
96094	WEED	19797	2548	38.8	29.1	24.5	5.7	1.9	34359	38793	25	19	1773	4.9	9.2	42.2	34.1	9.6	159879
96096	WHITMORE	26214	348	25.9	28.2	31.6	8.9	5.5	46213	51972	64	43	289	5.2	3.5	17.0	53.3	21.1	261184
96097	YREKA	22598	4114	39.0	29.2	22.9	5.1	3.7	33953	38776	24	18	2660	9.2	5.4	39.7	39.5	6.2	164507
96101	ALTURAS	21958	2103	42.4	25.8	23.7	5.5	2.6	29639	33484	11	10	1522	7.0	24.1	45.1	19.1	4.7	116604
96103	BLAIRSDEN-GRAEAGLE	29527	922	20.8	23.0	40.5	13.8	2.0	55669	63585	80	62	784	2.7	3.1	17.7	51.2	25.4	271923
96104	CEDARVILLE	23238	367	35.2	34.6	21.5	3.3	5.5	34238	40125	25	18	253	8.7	16.2	39.1	25.7	10.3	135069
96105	CHILCOOT	24693	228	31.1	23.3	31.6	9.7	4.4	46732	52210	66	45	189	5.8	4.2	24.3	34.4	31.2	240625
96106	CLIO	29532	110	20.9	23.6	40.0	13.6	1.8	54979	62471	80	61	94	2.1	3.2	16.0	52.1	26.6	276471
96107	COLEVILLE	20006	542	23.3	39.5	31.6	4.4	1.3	39660	44509	45	30	364	17.9	1.4	20.1	49.2	11.5	211905
96108	DAVIS CREEK	18291	138	35.5	18.1	40.6	5.8	0.0	47563	52844	67	47	113	17.7	8.9	31.0	32.7	9.7	133929
96109	DOYLE	16373	574	41.6	30.3	21.3	4.7	2.1	31858	35359	17	14	483	12.4	17.4	36.4	26.9	6.8	134949
96111	FLORISTON	19567	42	33.3	33.3	26.2	4.8	2.4	35000	41155	28	20	27	0.0	7.4	22.2	51.9	18.5	256250
96112	FORT BIDWELL	25919	94	37.2	34.0	18.1	5.3	5.3	32324	36857	19	14	71	15.5	15.5	36.6	23.9	8.5	123958
96113	HERLONG	19207	426	27.0	35.0	28.9	8.7	0.5	39368	44406	44	29	255	11.4	14.5	40.0	29.8	4.3	132083
96114	JANESVILLE	25011	1237	21.3	31.0	32.2	11.6	4.0	48244	53883	69	48	1046	0.9	2.6	22.4	61.4	12.8	238333
96115	LAKE CITY	24836	100	37.0	35.0	18.0	5.0	5.0	31964	35909	18	14	75	14.7	14.7	33.3	26.7	10.7	134722
96116	LIKELY	20168	129	39.5	31.0	20.9	5.4	3.1	32880	37709	21	15	103	7.8	12.6	38.8	27.2	13.6	140625
96117	LITCHFIELD	23722	72	26.4	27.8	33.3	8.3	4.2	46854	51863	66	45	55	7.3	3.6	25.5	54.6	9.1	198438
96118	LOYALTON	20369	553	31.7	33.6	25.7	5.6	3.4	36975	41490	35	25	391	6.9	4.9	40.4	34.0	13.8	168145
96119	MADELINE	30348	24	54.2	16.7	25.0	4.2	0.0	22257	23565	3	3	20	20.0	10.0	15.0	30.0	25.0	200000
96120	MARKLEEVILLE	28916	398	24.4	27.4	33.7	8.3	6.3	48291	56582	69	49	271	7.4	3.3	14.8	49.5	25.1	294767
96121	MILFORD	19860	187	26.7	34.8	26.2	11.8	0.5	40250	45226	47	32	143	11.9	14.7	38.5	30.8	4.2	134559
96122	PORTOLA	18528	1718	37.8	28.4	25.8	5.5	2.5	34228	39433	25	18	1219	6.4	8.8	40.4	36.2	8.2	163190
96123	RAVENDALE	17643	0	0.0	0.0	0.0	0.0	0.0	0	0	0	0	0	0.0	0.0	0.0	0.0	0.0	0
96124	CALPINE	23706	147	25.2	36.1	29.3	6.1	3.4	45555	50484	63	43	115	0.0	11.3	29.6	44.4	14.8	212500
96125	SIERRA CITY	23696	137	26.3	36.5	29.2	5.1	2.9	41601	45813	52	35	95	0.0	3.2	20.0	68.4	8.4	235156
96126	SIERRAVILLE	18032	163	31.3	36.2	24.5	6.1	1.8	36027	40610	32	22	120	10.8	5.0	27.5	41.7	15.0	210000
96128	STANDISH	22342	100	27.0	27.0	33.0	8.0	5.0	46993	51632	66	45	77	6.5	3.9	27.3	53.3	9.1	194792
	CALIFORNIA	27293		21.8	24.4	30.5	13.7	9.7	54267	64547				3.3	2.7	13.3	42.9	37.9	319678
	UNITED STATES	25866		24.7	27.1	30.8	10.9	6.5	48124	56710				10.9	15.0	33.7	30.1	10.4	145905

#	POST OFFICE NAME	FINANCIAL SERVICES				THE HOME						ENTERTAINMENT						PERSONAL			
						Home Improvements		Furnishings													
		Auto Loan	Home Loan	Invest-ments	Retire-ment Plans	Home Repair	Lawn & Garden	Comput-ers & Hard-ware	Major Appli-ances	TV, Radio, Sound Equip-ment	Furni-ture	Dine out/ Carry out	Sports Equip-ment	Fees & Tickets	Toys & Games	Travel	Cable TV	Apparel & Services	Auto Repairs	Health Insur-ance	Pets & Supplies
95981	STRAWBERRY VALLEY	67	51	34	48	57	66	53	61	60	51	71	69	48	68	54	64	65	60	72	77
95982	SUTTER	94	79	59	78	85	90	77	86	81	77	98	103	71	97	78	81	92	85	92	110
95983	TAYLORSVILLE	70	56	43	54	61	73	59	65	65	58	78	71	55	71	60	69	71	65	78	78
95984	TWAIN	69	52	34	50	57	68	58	64	65	55	76	71	51	72	57	68	69	63	76	77
95987	WILLIAMS	83	70	54	65	69	74	71	78	75	76	93	85	64	83	68	73	91	79	77	86
95988	WILLOWS	64	60	55	59	61	66	61	63	63	60	77	73	59	77	61	62	74	63	65	73
95991	YUBA CITY	70	67	69	67	67	72	70	70	71	70	88	81	69	87	69	70	86	71	70	78
95993	YUBA CITY	94	107	119	104	105	110	102	101	100	102	125	116	106	130	103	99	124	101	97	112
96001	REDDING	82	86	93	86	86	92	87	86	86	85	107	99	88	109	87	86	104	86	85	95
96002	REDDING	72	69	67	69	69	75	71	72	71	70	88	83	69	86	70	71	85	72	72	81
96003	REDDING	76	75	74	74	76	83	75	77	76	74	94	88	74	92	75	76	90	77	79	88
96006	ADIN	66	49	33	47	54	65	55	60	61	52	72	67	49	68	54	65	66	60	72	73
96007	ANDERSON	66	54	43	52	57	65	57	61	62	56	74	70	53	72	57	64	70	61	69	73
96008	BELLA VISTA	102	80	52	76	87	95	78	90	84	78	101	107	70	98	79	86	95	89	99	117
96010	BIG BAR	63	47	31	46	52	62	53	58	59	50	69	65	47	65	52	62	63	58	69	70
96013	BURNEY	80	58	35	54	64	76	62	70	71	60	83	80	55	79	62	75	76	70	85	89
96014	CALLAHAN	89	67	42	62	77	86	64	78	73	64	87	93	57	85	68	78	80	77	93	108
96015	CANBY	93	65	35	62	76	85	65	80	75	64	88	96	56	86	67	79	80	79	95	110
96016	CASSEL	93	73	49	66	82	92	69	83	79	69	93	97	62	91	74	84	86	82	98	112
96019	SHASTA LAKE	61	53	46	52	55	62	57	59	60	55	72	68	54	70	56	61	68	59	64	68
96020	CHESTER	80	64	45	62	70	79	65	73	71	64	85	85	60	84	65	73	79	72	82	92
96021	CORNING	65	54	43	52	56	62	56	60	60	56	72	69	52	69	55	61	69	60	64	73
96022	COTTONWOOD	75	71	62	69	73	78	69	72	70	68	86	84	68	87	69	71	83	71	75	86
96023	DORRIS	68	46	21	40	52	60	44	55	53	45	63	66	38	59	45	58	57	55	68	79
96024	DOUGLAS CITY	78	61	42	55	69	77	58	69	65	57	77	81	52	76	61	70	72	68	82	95
96025	DUNSMUIR	63	48	31	45	52	62	52	58	58	50	69	65	46	65	52	62	63	58	69	70
96027	ETNA	100	73	44	69	83	95	74	88	84	72	99	103	64	96	76	89	91	87	105	118
96028	FALL RIVER MILLS	75	56	37	54	62	74	62	68	69	59	81	77	55	77	61	73	74	68	82	83
96031	FORKS OF SALMON	112	86	57	79	97	110	83	100	94	82	111	117	74	109	88	100	103	98	118	135
96032	FORT JONES	92	70	47	67	77	90	75	84	83	72	98	96	67	94	75	88	90	83	99	104
96033	FRENCH GULCH	78	56	32	53	65	72	55	67	63	55	74	81	48	73	57	66	68	66	79	92
96034	GAZELLE	67	50	33	48	56	66	55	61	61	52	72	69	49	69	55	65	66	61	73	75
96035	GERBER	83	66	47	62	69	76	67	75	73	69	89	84	61	82	66	74	85	76	81	90
96038	GRENADA	78	63	46	60	67	80	68	73	74	64	88	82	62	84	67	78	81	73	86	87
96039	HAPPY CAMP	59	44	29	43	49	58	49	54	55	47	65	61	44	61	49	58	59	54	65	65
96040	HAT CREEK	88	69	46	63	77	88	67	79	76	66	90	92	60	88	70	81	83	78	94	105
96041	HAYFORK	64	48	32	46	53	63	52	58	59	50	69	65	47	66	52	62	63	58	69	71
96044	HORNBROOK	68	51	34	49	56	68	57	63	64	54	75	70	51	71	56	67	69	63	75	76
96046	HYAMPOM	58	43	29	42	47	57	48	53	54	45	63	59	43	60	47	57	58	53	63	64
96047	IGO	103	92	79	90	97	111	95	101	100	92	120	113	91	117	96	104	113	100	112	117
96048	JUNCTION CITY	74	56	37	53	61	73	61	67	69	58	81	76	55	76	61	73	74	67	81	82
96050	KLAMATH RIVER	69	52	35	50	57	68	57	63	64	54	76	71	51	71	57	68	69	63	75	76
96051	LAKEHEAD	83	65	44	59	73	82	61	74	69	61	82	86	55	81	65	74	76	73	87	101
96052	LEWISTON	78	63	46	58	70	79	60	71	67	60	80	82	55	79	64	72	75	70	83	94
96054	LOOKOUT	68	51	32	49	56	66	55	62	62	53	73	70	49	69	55	66	67	62	74	76
96055	LOS MOLINOS	78	55	31	52	63	72	57	67	65	55	76	79	49	73	57	69	70	67	81	90
96056	MCARTHUR	72	52	32	50	59	69	56	64	63	54	74	73	49	71	56	67	68	64	76	81
96057	MCCLOUD	70	52	34	50	57	69	58	64	65	55	76	71	51	72	57	68	70	64	76	77
96058	MACDOEL	69	47	23	41	53	61	46	57	55	47	65	67	40	61	47	59	59	56	69	78
96059	MANTON	77	61	41	55	68	77	58	69	65	57	77	81	52	76	61	70	72	68	82	94
96062	MILLVILLE	117	81	43	77	95	106	80	99	93	79	109	120	69	106	83	97	99	98	118	138
96063	MINERAL	76	60	41	54	67	76	56	68	64	56	76	80	50	75	60	68	70	67	80	93
96064	MONTAGUE	68	56	41	53	59	67	57	63	62	56	74	72	53	71	57	64	69	63	71	76
96065	MONTGOMERY CREEK	79	58	33	55	66	73	57	69	65	57	76	82	50	74	59	67	70	68	80	93
96067	MOUNT SHASTA	78	74	72	73	76	84	76	78	78	74	95	90	74	94	76	79	91	78	82	89
96069	OAK RUN	104	72	38	68	84	95	72	89	82	71	97	107	61	95	74	87	88	87	105	123
96071	OLD STATION	81	62	42	58	69	80	63	73	71	61	84	84	56	81	65	76	77	72	87	94
96073	PALO CEDRO	104	108	104	104	111	118	101	107	102	100	126	124	103	130	105	104	122	104	110	125
96075	PAYNES CREEK	76	60	41	54	68	76	57	68	64	56	76	80	51	75	60	68	71	67	81	93
96076	PLATINA	61	46	31	43	51	60	49	55	54	47	64	62	43	61	49	58	59	55	65	69
96080	RED BLUFF	74	65	58	63	68	77	67	71	71	66	87	80	65	84	68	74	82	71	79	83
96085	SCOTT BAR	69	52	34	50	57	68	58	63	64	55	76	71	51	72	57	68	69	63	76	76
96086	SEIAD VALLEY	53	40	26	38	44	52	44	49	50	42	58	55	39	55	44	52	53	49	58	59
96087	SHASTA	70	86	95	84	84	86	79	78	76	79	95	91	85	101	81	75	95	77	73	86
96088	SHINGLETOWN	89	70	51	66	77	90	71	81	79	71	95	90	65	88	73	84	87	80	97	101
96091	TRINITY CENTER	80	63	43	57	71	79	59	71	67	59	79	84	53	78	63	72	74	70	84	98
96093	WEAVERVILLE	75	62	47	59	66	78	66	71	72	63	86	80	61	83	66	76	80	71	83	84
96094	WEED	66	63	64	61	64	72	66	67	68	64	83	76	65	82	66	70	80	67	72	75
96096	WHITMORE	114	80	43	76	93	105	80	98	92	79	108	118	69	106	83	97	99	97	117	135
96097	YREKA	77	67	56	64	71	82	70	75	75	67	90	84	66	88	70	79	84	74	85	87
96101	ALTURAS	82	64	46	62	69	80	69	75	76	66	90	87	62	87	68	79	83	76	87	92
96103	BLAIRSDEN-GRAEAGLE	91	88	85	84	92	106	81	90	84	86	105	90	82	97	87	89	99	88	103	103
96104	CEDARVILLE	83	63	41	60	69	82	69	76	78	66	91	86	62	86	69	82	83	76	91	92
96105	CHILCOOT	103	81	55	73	91	102	76	92	86	76	102	108	68	101	81	92	95	91	109	126
96106	CLIO	92	86	82	81	91	107	79	90	84	85	104	88	80	87	86	89	97	87	105	103
96107	COLEVILLE	80	56	38	55	62	70	62	68	68	60	82	84	53	78	60	69	76	71	76	90
96108	DAVIS CREEK	76	57	38	55	63	75	64	70	71	60	84	78	57	79	63	75	76	70	84	84
96109	DOYLE	76	52	25	45	58	67	51	62	61	51	71	74	44	67	51	65	65	62	76	87
96111	FLORISTON	86	67	46	61	76	85	63	76	72	63	85	89	57	84	67	77	79	75	90	104
96112	FORT BIDWELL	91	68	45	66	75	90	76	83	85	72	100	93	67	94	75	89	91	83	100	100
96113	HERLONG	74	57	45	57	61	71	64	68	70	62	84	78	58	79	63	72	78	69	77	81
96114	JANESVILLE	97	106	101	104	105	106	97	100	93	98	116	116	98	118	98	91	114	97	93	113
96115	LAKE CITY	91	68	45	65	75	89	76	83	85	72	100	93	67	94	75	89	91	83	99	100
96116	LIKELY	82	57	30	54	68	74	56	70	65	56	76	84	48	75	58	68	69	69	83	97
96117	LITCHFIELD	89	81	63	78	81	86	77	83	78	79	97	96	73	91	76	77	93	83	83	98
96118	LOYALTON	81	63	44	61	68	80	68	74	75	65	89	84	62	86	68	79	82	74	87	89
96119	MADELINE	0	0	0	0	0	0	0	0	0	0	0	0	0	0	0	0	0	0	0	0
96120	MARKLEEVILLE	123	96	65	87	108	122	91	109	103	90	121	128	81	120	97	110	113	107	129	149
96121	MILFORD	80	60	39	57	66	79	66	73	74	63	87	82	59	82	66	79	80	73	87	88
96122	PORTOLA	72	62	48	60	65	72	62	67	65	62	79	77	59	78	62	66	75	66	72	81
96123	RAVENDALE	0	0	0	0	0	0	0	0	0	0	0	0	0	0	0	0	0	0	0	0
96124	CALPINE	86	68	46	61	76	86	64	77	73	63	86	90	57	85	68	77	80	76	91	105
96125	SIERRA CITY	80	67	54	62	74	85	63	74	70	65	84	81	59	78	68	74	78	73	88	95
96126	SIERRAVILLE	73	55	37	53	61	72	60	67	67	57	79	75	53	75	60	71	72	66	80	82
96128	STANDISH	90	82	64	79	82	87	78	84	79	80	98	97	74	92	77	78	94	83	83	99
	CALIFORNIA	107	111	131	112	109	115	113	111	111	114	140	129	114	141	112	109	139	113	104	122
	UNITED STATES	100	100	100	100	100	100	100	100	100	100	100	100	100	100	100	100	100	100	100	100

POPULATION CHANGE

ZIP CODE		COUNTY FIPS CODE	POPULATION			2000-2004 ANNUAL RATE		HOUSEHOLDS					FAMILIES		
#	POST OFFICE NAME		2000	2004	2009	% Rate	State Centile	2000	2004	2009	% Annual Rate 2000-2004	2004 Average HH Size	2000	2004	% Annual Rate 2000-2004
96130	SUSANVILLE	035	21536	22112	22997	0.6	37	6390	6643	7016	0.9	2.57	4389	4543	0.8
96132	TERMO	035	55	55	55	0.0	15	27	28	29	0.9	1.96	19	1	-50.0
96133	TOPAZ	051	535	536	570	0.0	16	188	188	201	0.0	2.58	139	140	0.2
96134	TULELAKE	093	2500	2384	2343	-1.1	2	898	857	846	-1.1	2.78	639	607	-1.2
96135	VINTON	063	3	3	3	0.0	15	1	1	1	0.0	3.00	1	1	0.0
96136	WENDEL	035	174	178	183	0.5	33	57	58	60	0.4	2.98	43	44	0.5
96137	WESTWOOD	063	2074	2136	2205	0.7	41	940	976	1017	0.9	2.19	696	721	0.8
96140	CARNELIAN BAY	061	666	718	849	1.8	75	299	324	385	1.9	2.22	172	183	1.5
96141	HOMEWOOD	061	267	292	348	2.1	81	135	149	177	2.4	1.96	60	64	1.5
96142	TAHOMA	061	1454	1589	1824	2.1	81	616	676	779	2.2	2.34	349	379	2.0
96143	KINGS BEACH	061	4549	5202	6331	3.2	91	1635	1850	2239	3.0	2.81	924	1034	2.7
96145	TAHOE CITY	061	5752	6343	7557	2.3	84	2422	2688	3223	2.5	2.29	1273	1392	2.1
96146	OLYMPIC VALLEY	061	502	580	709	3.5	93	216	251	307	3.6	2.31	98	112	3.2
96148	TAHOE VISTA	061	1156	1335	1633	3.5	93	446	509	619	3.2	2.62	268	302	2.9
96150	SOUTH LAKE TAHOE	017	33082	34634	37958	1.1	58	13097	13733	15070	1.1	2.51	7989	8286	0.9
96161	TRUCKEE	057	15550	17168	18884	2.4	84	5785	6402	7064	2.4	2.67	4014	4422	2.3
96162	TRUCKEE	057	123	127	135	0.8	43	61	63	67	0.8	2.00	35	36	0.7
	CALIFORNIA					1.4					1.2	2.90			1.2
	UNITED STATES					1.2					1.3	2.58			1.1

#	ZIP CODE POST OFFICE NAME	RACE (%) White 2000	White 2004	Black 2000	Black 2004	Asian/Pacific 2000	Asian/Pacific 2004	% Hispanic Origin 2000	% Hispanic Origin 2004	2004 AGE DISTRIBUTION (%) 0-4	5-9	10-14	15-19	20-24	25-44	45-64	65-84	85+	18+	MEDIAN AGE 2004	% 2004 Males	% 2004 Females
96130	SUSANVILLE	80.2	78.9	8.2	8.4	1.5	1.6	13.6	15.7	5.6	5.7	6.4	6.7	10.4	34.1	22.0	7.9	1.2	78.4	33.8	60.5	39.5
96132	TERMO	67.3	67.3	27.3	27.3	0.0	0.0	27.3	30.9	0.0	0.0	0.0	3.6	16.4	67.3	12.7	0.0	0.0	100.0	32.1	100.0	0.0
96133	TOPAZ	83.6	81.3	1.9	1.9	1.5	1.7	8.8	10.3	8.2	7.7	6.9	5.8	9.0	28.4	20.5	12.1	1.5	74.1	32.1	53.9	46.1
96134	TULELAKE	74.6	72.6	0.6	0.7	0.3	0.3	34.4	37.5	8.6	8.3	9.1	8.0	5.1	24.1	22.8	12.5	1.6	69.2	34.8	50.5	49.5
96135	VINTON	100.0	100.0	0.0	0.0	0.0	0.0	0.0	0.0	0.0	0.0	0.0	0.0	66.7	33.3	0.0	0.0	0.0	100.0	23.8	66.7	33.3
96136	WENDEL	88.5	87.1	0.6	0.6	0.6	0.6	12.1	13.5	6.2	6.7	7.9	9.0	6.7	25.8	28.7	8.4	0.6	74.2	37.5	51.1	48.9
96137	WESTWOOD	95.7	95.1	0.1	0.1	0.4	0.4	3.6	4.4	3.1	3.5	4.3	3.4	3.2	12.5	37.7	30.7	1.6	86.9	57.6	50.9	49.1
96140	CARNELIAN BAY	94.1	93.3	0.0	0.0	4.4	4.9	2.4	2.9	3.5	3.9	6.0	5.4	4.5	31.2	32.6	12.8	0.1	83.4	42.3	53.6	46.4
96141	HOMEWOOD	95.5	95.2	0.4	0.3	1.5	1.7	3.4	3.8	2.4	2.4	4.1	6.2	5.5	30.1	39.4	9.6	0.3	88.0	44.4	54.8	45.2
96142	TAHOMA	94.3	93.3	0.3	0.3	0.8	0.8	4.3	5.3	5.4	5.2	5.5	6.0	7.7	35.3	26.6	8.1	0.2	80.2	37.5	54.3	45.8
96143	KINGS BEACH	72.6	70.2	0.7	0.6	0.6	0.6	43.8	47.7	7.5	6.9	7.8	7.2	9.2	36.1	21.3	4.0	0.2	73.7	31.0	54.3	45.7
96145	TAHOE CITY	95.6	95.0	0.4	0.4	1.2	1.3	2.9	3.4	3.4	3.4	4.9	5.5	7.1	36.3	29.7	8.6	1.1	84.8	38.9	54.0	46.0
96146	OLYMPIC VALLEY	94.2	93.1	0.2	0.3	1.2	1.4	4.0	4.8	2.2	2.1	3.6	6.9	9.8	43.3	24.1	7.6	0.3	88.5	34.2	59.3	40.7
96148	TAHOE VISTA	84.2	81.5	0.1	0.1	0.9	0.9	22.6	26.7	6.1	5.8	6.5	6.3	7.3	34.3	27.8	5.4	0.5	78.0	35.3	52.1	47.9
96150	SOUTH LAKE TAHOE	80.9	78.6	0.7	0.7	4.8	5.2	20.6	23.5	6.2	6.1	7.2	7.2	8.0	30.1	26.6	8.2	0.6	76.3	35.8	51.6	48.4
96161	TRUCKEE	89.1	87.6	0.2	0.3	1.0	1.1	12.3	14.1	6.0	6.5	7.9	6.8	5.5	32.5	28.9	5.6	0.4	75.2	37.1	52.7	47.3
96162	TRUCKEE	93.5	92.1	0.0	0.0	0.8	0.8	3.3	3.9	3.9	4.7	6.3	6.3	5.5	26.0	40.2	7.1	0.0	81.1	43.7	54.3	45.7
	CALIFORNIA	59.6	57.1	6.7	6.5	11.3	11.8	32.4	35.5	7.4	7.1	7.8	7.3	7.7	29.8	22.1	9.3	1.4	73.3	33.8	49.8	50.2
	UNITED STATES	75.1	73.6	12.3	12.5	3.8	4.2	12.5	14.1	6.9	6.7	7.2	7.0	7.3	28.6	23.8	10.8	1.7	75.1	36.0	49.1	50.9

#	POST OFFICE NAME	2004 Per Capita Income	2004 HH Income Base	2004 HOUSEHOLD INCOME DISTRIBUTION (%)					MEDIAN HOUSEHOLD INCOME				2004 Home Value Base	2004 HOME VALUE DISTRIBUTION (%)					2004 Median Home Value
				Less than $25,000	$25,000 to $49,999	$50,000 to $99,999	$100,000 to $149,999	$150,000 or More	2004	2009	2004 National Centile	2004 State Centile		Less than $50,000	$50,000 to $89,999	$90,000 to $174,999	$175,000 to $399,999	$400,000 or More	
96130	SUSANVILLE	19357	6643	29.9	30.8	29.9	7.5	2.0	40389	45752	47	32	4546	9.5	4.8	39.2	41.1	5.4	168118
96132	TERMO	17897	28	42.9	25.0	28.6	3.6	0.0	30000	32361	12	11	23	26.1	13.0	17.4	30.4	13.0	137500
96133	TOPAZ	18474	188	22.9	43.1	27.1	3.7	3.2	36523	41150	34	23	113	25.7	0.0	16.8	42.5	15.0	220313
96134	TULELAKE	13509	857	44.6	29.5	20.9	4.9	0.1	29707	33031	12	10	554	21.7	27.1	30.7	13.4	7.2	93500
96135	VINTON	0	0	0.0	0.0	0.0	0.0	0.0	0	0	0	0	0	0.0	0.0	0.0	0.0	0.0	0
96136	WENDEL	18905	58	27.6	27.6	32.8	6.9	5.2	46137	53780	64	43	45	6.7	4.4	26.7	55.6	6.7	194643
96137	WESTWOOD	27750	976	22.9	30.0	31.6	9.3	6.3	47822	54359	68	47	856	3.0	1.4	14.8	45.0	35.8	310949
96140	CARNELIAN BAY	30402	324	18.2	25.0	35.5	16.1	5.3	57550	69766	82	65	225	0.0	0.0	0.0	24.4	75.6	527985
96141	HOMEWOOD	28318	149	10.1	36.9	45.6	6.7	0.7	50922	58990	74	54	94	0.0	0.0	0.0	53.2	46.8	387500
96142	TAHOMA	33781	676	11.2	18.2	45.4	15.8	9.3	67624	79774	90	76	473	1.5	0.0	1.5	49.3	47.8	388587
96143	KINGS BEACH	20363	1850	27.3	31.2	28.8	9.4	3.3	41224	47341	50	35	778	5.0	1.4	9.8	42.3	41.5	352857
96145	TAHOE CITY	42548	2688	13.4	23.4	32.2	15.4	15.5	66626	81817	90	74	1771	0.0	0.1	1.1	21.6	77.2	657051
96146	OLYMPIC VALLEY	61172	251	10.4	17.9	29.1	16.7	25.9	84682	108054	96	89	154	0.0	0.0	3.3	11.7	85.1	1000001
96148	TAHOE VISTA	29190	509	17.5	27.7	31.2	11.8	11.8	57935	68216	83	65	341	13.5	0.6	13.8	24.1	48.1	383333
96150	SOUTH LAKE TAHOE	23726	13733	22.5	34.5	30.0	8.7	4.3	45093	51204	61	42	7655	4.6	0.9	6.0	65.4	23.1	274672
96161	TRUCKEE	33095	6402	9.8	22.7	43.1	14.0	10.5	65533	77008	89	73	4954	3.6	0.9	2.8	40.8	52.0	410860
96162	TRUCKEE	24567	63	36.5	28.6	23.8	6.4	4.8	34296	39304	25	18	42	2.4	4.8	28.6	50.0	14.3	220000
	CALIFORNIA	27293		21.8	24.4	30.5	13.7	9.7	54267	64547				3.3	2.7	13.3	42.9	37.9	319678
	UNITED STATES	25866		24.7	27.1	30.8	10.9	6.5	48124	56710				10.9	15.0	33.7	30.1	10.4	145905

#	POST OFFICE NAME	FINANCIAL SERVICES				THE HOME						ENTERTAINMENT						PERSONAL			
						Home Improvements		Furnishings													
		Auto Loan	Home Loan	Invest-ments	Retire-ment Plans	Home Repair	Lawn & Garden	Comput-ers & Hard-ware	Major Appli-ances	TV, Radio, Sound Equip-ment	Furni-ture	Dine out/ Carry out	Sports Equip-ment	Fees & Tickets	Toys & Games	Travel	Cable TV	Apparel & Services	Auto Repairs	Health Insur-ance	Pets & Supplies
96130	SUSANVILLE	70	71	71	71	71	74	71	71	70	71	87	84	70	88	70	68	85	72	69	81
96132	TERMO	0	0	0	0	0	0	0	0	0	0	0	0	0	0	0	0	0	0	0	0
96133	TOPAZ	79	52	42	56	52	60	69	66	72	65	88	85	59	81	60	68	84	73	66	80
96134	TULELAKE	59	48	37	46	49	55	51	56	55	53	67	60	46	61	49	55	64	56	59	62
96135	VINTON	0	0	0	0	0	0	0	0	0	0	0	0	0	0	0	0	0	0	0	0
96136	WENDEL	90	82	64	79	82	87	78	84	79	81	98	97	74	92	77	78	94	84	83	100
96137	WESTWOOD	102	81	56	73	91	102	76	92	86	76	102	107	68	101	81	92	95	90	108	125
96140	CARNELIAN BAY	114	90	61	81	101	113	85	102	96	84	113	119	76	112	90	102	105	100	120	139
96141	HOMEWOOD	94	74	50	67	83	93	70	84	79	69	93	98	62	92	74	84	87	83	99	115
96142	TAHOMA	135	105	72	95	119	133	99	120	113	99	133	140	89	132	106	120	124	118	142	164
96143	KINGS BEACH	87	73	70	73	74	79	79	81	82	81	102	95	74	99	76	79	100	84	80	94
96145	TAHOE CITY	165	133	97	121	148	165	126	149	140	125	167	175	114	165	133	149	156	147	173	201
96146	OLYMPIC VALLEY	240	188	128	170	212	238	177	214	201	176	238	250	159	235	189	214	221	210	253	292
96148	TAHOE VISTA	122	104	87	98	114	125	100	114	108	99	130	134	93	129	105	113	123	113	127	148
96150	SOUTH LAKE TAHOE	85	81	84	81	81	85	85	84	84	84	105	101	82	104	83	82	102	87	81	97
96161	TRUCKEE	136	130	113	126	133	140	121	130	122	122	150	153	117	151	123	123	145	128	133	160
96162	TRUCKEE	82	67	48	61	74	82	63	74	70	62	83	87	57	82	67	74	78	73	86	100
	CALIFORNIA	107	111	131	112	109	115	113	111	111	114	140	129	114	141	112	109	139	113	104	122
	UNITED STATES	100	100	100	100	100	100	100	100	100	100	100	100	100	100	100	100	100	100	100	100

POPULATION CHANGE

#	POST OFFICE NAME	COUNTY FIPS CODE	POPULATION			2000-2004 ANNUAL RATE		HOUSEHOLDS					FAMILIES		
			2000	2004	2009	% Rate	State Centile	2000	2004	2009	% Annual Rate 2000-2004	2004 Average HH Size	2000	2004	% Annual Rate 2000-2004
80002	ARVADA	059	14670	14742	14901	0.1	15	6237	6337	6467	0.4	2.32	3808	3854	0.3
80003	ARVADA	059	33913	33814	34461	-0.1	10	12599	12826	13225	0.4	2.62	8810	8858	0.1
80004	ARVADA	059	37493	37071	37262	-0.3	8	14515	14616	14896	0.2	2.51	10255	10250	0.0
80005	ARVADA	059	24742	24845	25102	0.1	15	9198	9445	9684	0.6	2.62	7004	7122	0.4
80007	ARVADA	059	5896	7451	8413	5.7	90	1970	2505	2846	5.8	2.97	1735	2194	5.7
80010	AURORA	001	43381	47510	54391	2.2	53	13953	14881	16805	1.5	3.16	9417	9904	1.2
80011	AURORA	005	45764	49625	56112	1.9	48	16858	18393	20896	2.1	2.66	11278	12102	1.7
80012	AURORA	005	42858	45649	49881	1.5	41	17817	19207	21194	1.8	2.36	10812	11441	1.3
80013	AURORA	005	57464	63860	71926	2.5	62	20054	22583	25698	2.8	2.83	15226	17011	2.6
80014	AURORA	005	34141	37463	41610	2.2	54	16624	18495	20737	2.5	2.00	8590	9416	2.2
80015	AURORA	005	53784	64636	76296	4.4	82	17905	21648	25691	4.6	2.98	14453	17474	4.6
80016	AURORA	005	7616	12263	16578	11.9	98	2389	3907	5343	12.3	3.13	2148	3512	12.3
80017	AURORA	005	29312	31411	34526	1.6	43	11270	12321	13734	2.1	2.55	7419	7934	1.6
80018	AURORA	005	1402	2167	2866	10.8	98	489	754	1002	10.7	2.87	397	611	10.7
80019	AURORA	001	61	66	77	1.9	47	17	19	23	2.7	3.11	13	14	1.8
80020	BROOMFIELD	014	49433	57016	64159	3.4	74	17279	20149	22828	3.7	2.83	13333	15545	3.7
80021	BROOMFIELD	059	28359	29458	30339	0.9	31	10704	11392	11930	1.5	2.57	7325	7650	1.0
80022	COMMERCE CITY	001	28238	32395	39129	3.3	73	9003	10345	12525	3.3	3.09	6764	7704	3.1
80026	LAFAYETTE	013	24933	27767	30907	2.6	63	9467	10612	11863	2.7	2.61	6446	7141	2.4
80027	LOUISVILLE	013	28356	31654	35214	2.6	63	10738	12074	13493	2.8	2.62	7337	8092	2.3
80030	WESTMINSTER	001	16310	17620	20570	1.8	46	6256	6797	7973	2.0	2.55	3951	4228	1.6
80031	WESTMINSTER	001	34842	39842	48081	3.3	73	12947	15106	18366	3.7	2.64	9091	10496	3.4
80033	WHEAT RIDGE	059	26260	26698	27110	0.4	21	11600	11958	12277	0.7	2.17	6633	6742	0.4
80101	AGATE	039	256	320	385	5.4	87	100	126	151	5.6	2.54	71	89	5.5
80102	BENNETT	001	4233	4989	5999	3.9	77	1478	1766	2141	4.3	2.83	1152	1363	4.0
80103	BYERS	005	2265	2508	2818	2.4	60	800	896	1017	2.7	2.80	623	691	2.5
80104	CASTLE ROCK	035	15043	21922	31784	9.3	96	5518	8192	12047	9.7	2.67	4156	6101	9.5
80105	DEER TRAIL	005	1198	1361	1549	3.1	70	444	503	572	2.9	2.71	314	352	2.7
80106	ELBERT	039	3571	4581	5495	6.0	92	1233	1606	1949	6.4	2.85	1042	1349	6.3
80107	ELIZABETH	039	10555	12583	14788	4.2	80	3522	4225	4980	4.4	2.98	3013	3600	4.3
80108	CASTLE ROCK	035	9122	15212	23384	12.8	99	3251	5502	8568	13.2	2.73	2735	4650	13.3
80109	CASTLE ROCK	035	5743	10750	17354	15.9	100	1835	3405	5480	15.7	3.15	1655	3054	15.5
80110	ENGLEWOOD	005	22376	23854	26225	1.5	42	9248	10002	11123	1.9	2.36	5493	5831	1.4
80111	ENGLEWOOD	005	26170	28325	31346	1.9	47	9503	10615	12005	2.6	2.62	7020	7719	2.3
80112	ENGLEWOOD	005	21503	22992	25439	1.6	42	7764	8379	9351	1.8	2.66	5758	6132	1.5
80113	ENGLEWOOD	005	21593	22373	24327	0.8	29	9660	10209	11274	1.3	2.12	5220	5402	0.8
80116	FRANKTOWN	035	3853	5088	7163	6.8	93	1377	1888	2719	7.7	2.69	1190	1607	7.3
80117	KIOWA	039	2171	2450	2802	2.9	67	762	862	987	2.9	2.84	612	687	2.8
80118	LARKSPUR	035	4035	5092	6859	5.6	89	1463	1898	2606	6.3	2.65	1244	1598	6.1
80120	LITTLETON	005	29301	30995	33860	1.3	39	12584	13528	14975	1.7	2.25	7530	8003	1.4
80121	LITTLETON	005	18171	19178	20960	1.3	38	6711	7209	7979	1.7	2.63	5202	5530	1.5
80122	LITTLETON	005	31761	32901	35703	0.8	29	11892	12580	13859	1.3	2.60	8958	9373	1.1
80123	LITTLETON	059	39708	44643	48561	2.8	65	15926	18254	20093	3.3	2.44	10746	12151	2.9
80124	LITTLETON	035	12401	13883	18014	2.7	64	4372	5004	6597	3.2	2.77	3504	3995	3.1
80125	LITTLETON	035	5778	10453	16624	15.0	100	2112	3910	6319	15.6	2.67	1729	3176	15.4
80126	LITTLETON	035	31613	38556	51965	4.8	85	10793	13068	17617	4.6	2.95	8625	10385	4.5
80127	LITTLETON	059	39265	43450	46106	2.4	59	13371	15110	16266	2.9	2.87	11014	12352	2.7
80128	LITTLETON	059	34480	37628	39681	2.1	52	12517	13980	14966	2.6	2.68	9560	10569	2.4
80129	LITTLETON	035	20043	25693	35035	6.0	91	6822	8825	12136	6.2	2.91	5625	7227	6.1
80130	LITTLETON	035	17056	21307	28687	5.4	87	6215	7952	10881	6.0	2.68	4845	6118	5.6
80132	MONUMENT	041	13689	17121	20073	5.4	87	4590	5827	6906	5.8	2.94	3964	5014	5.7
80133	PALMER LAKE	041	2273	2470	2681	2.0	49	898	1001	1104	2.6	2.47	675	739	2.2
80134	PARKER	035	30955	46064	67438	9.8	97	10208	15408	22767	10.2	2.99	8722	13022	9.9
80135	SEDALIA	035	3683	5157	7351	8.2	95	1367	1954	2825	8.8	2.63	1090	1555	8.7
80136	STRASBURG	001	2540	3055	3698	4.4	82	873	1055	1284	4.6	2.88	686	821	4.3
80137	WATKINS	005	2164	2337	2611	1.8	46	768	845	956	2.3	2.75	603	656	2.0
80138	PARKER	035	19752	27464	38358	8.1	95	6660	9379	13248	8.4	2.92	5699	8009	8.3
80202	DENVER	031	4315	4745	5032	2.3	56	2949	3272	3481	2.5	1.38	610	655	1.7
80203	DENVER	031	18577	19095	19508	0.7	26	12819	13271	13569	0.8	1.38	1883	1891	0.1
80204	DENVER	031	32956	32600	32620	-0.3	8	11177	11045	11031	-0.3	2.91	6702	6490	-0.8
80205	DENVER	031	29604	30174	30694	0.5	23	10318	10546	10740	0.5	2.75	5987	5991	0.0
80206	DENVER	031	20706	20040	19929	-0.8	3	11737	11432	11382	-0.6	1.70	3667	3478	-1.2
80207	DENVER	031	23771	23395	23332	-0.4	7	7954	7841	7810	-0.3	2.62	5424	5276	-0.7
80208	DENVER	031	1966	1935	1930	-0.4	7	379	372	371	-0.4	2.96	77	74	-0.9
80209	DENVER	031	20553	20104	20127	-0.5	4	11648	11484	11517	-0.3	1.75	4313	4174	-0.8
80210	DENVER	031	30459	29805	29762	-0.5	4	15327	15083	15072	-0.4	1.91	6563	6326	-0.9
80211	DENVER	031	38788	38288	38872	-0.3	8	14472	14334	14358	-0.2	2.61	8351	8146	-0.6
80212	DENVER	031	18140	18407	18809	0.3	20	8326	8524	8722	0.6	2.12	4279	4299	0.1
80214	DENVER	059	25992	25461	25425	-0.5	5	11236	11074	11144	-0.3	2.20	5763	5580	-0.8
80215	DENVER	059	19053	18687	18691	-0.5	5	8256	8228	8327	-0.1	2.21	5008	4922	-0.4
80216	DENVER	031	10933	11035	11141	0.2	18	2856	2891	2934	0.3	3.69	2191	2170	-0.2
80218	DENVER	031	16485	16236	16303	-0.4	7	10253	10177	10233	-0.2	1.57	2270	2180	-1.0
80219	DENVER	031	59908	59859	59946	0.0	11	19321	19139	19035	-0.2	3.12	13805	13516	-0.5
80220	DENVER	031	33582	33437	33659	-0.1	10	15505	15394	15434	-0.2	2.16	7799	7605	-0.6
80221	DENVER	001	38306	41788	48359	2.1	51	13205	14405	16665	2.1	2.86	9221	9949	1.8
80222	DENVER	031	19446	19183	19359	-0.3	7	9244	9155	9235	-0.2	2.02	4487	4365	-0.7
80223	DENVER	031	19404	19287	19348	-0.1	10	7131	7056	7045	-0.3	2.72	4175	4082	-0.5
80224	DENVER	031	17967	18236	18513	0.4	20	8471	8590	8695	0.3	2.08	4220	4198	-0.1
80226	DENVER	059	29429	29507	29849	0.1	13	11914	12215	12551	0.6	2.35	7311	7355	0.1
80227	DENVER	059	32228	33296	34050	0.8	27	14090	14844	15368	1.2	2.24	8606	8870	0.7
80228	DENVER	059	30927	31709	32256	0.6	25	12847	13359	13746	0.9	2.36	8254	8528	0.8
80229	DENVER	001	40557	47489	58131	3.8	77	14348	16897	20777	3.9	2.80	10166	11854	3.7
80230	DENVER	031	2185	3660	4742	12.9	99	892	1477	1901	12.6	2.47	511	831	12.1
80231	DENVER	031	34663	37759	40576	2.0	50	18887	20347	21716	1.8	1.85	7686	8096	1.2
80232	DENVER	059	21294	20829	20790	-0.5	4	8576	8528	8617	-0.1	2.41	5756	5644	-0.5
80233	DENVER	001	35969	43111	53435	4.4	81	12550	15494	19527	5.1	2.77	9399	11329	4.5
80234	DENVER	001	21554	26964	33956	5.4	87	8714	10846	13626	5.3	2.48	5662	7003	5.1
80235	DENVER	059	7927	8640	9065	2.1	50	3148	3478	3682	2.4	2.19	1843	2029	2.3
80236	DENVER	031	16210	17469	18268	1.8	45	5974	6446	6732	1.8	2.58	4002	4279	1.6
80237	DENVER	031	16459	17030	17690	0.8	28	8427	8740	9039	0.9	1.94	4157	4213	0.3
80239	DENVER	031	28734	32194	34346	2.7	65	8369	9476	10161	3.0	3.40	6797	7598	2.7
80241	DENVER	001	27445	36135	46670	6.7	93	9379	12543	16329	7.1	2.86	7465	9885	6.8
80246	DENVER	031	13098	14263	15503	2.0	50	7017	7577	8203	1.8	1.88	2521	2701	1.6
80247	DENVER	005	17161	19459	21768	3.0	69	9107	10257	11431	2.8	1.90	3732	4088	2.2
80249	DENVER	031	7947	13457	17630	13.2	99	2704	4675	6184	13.8	2.88	2031	3466	13.4
	COLORADO					2.4					2.6	2.52			2.5
	UNITED STATES					1.2					1.3	2.58			1.1

#	POST OFFICE NAME	RACE (%) White 2000	White 2004	Black 2000	Black 2004	Asian/Pacific 2000	Asian/Pacific 2004	% Hispanic Origin 2000	% Hispanic Origin 2004	2004 AGE DISTRIBUTION (%) 0-4	5-9	10-14	15-19	20-24	25-44	45-64	65-84	85+	18+	MEDIAN AGE 2004	% 2004 Males	% 2004 Females
80002	ARVADA	89.2	88.3	0.9	1.0	1.6	1.8	14.1	15.7	7.8	7.3	6.7	6.3	7.4	30.3	24.7	8.6	1.0	74.6	35.4	50.5	49.5
80003	ARVADA	86.5	84.8	0.8	0.9	4.0	4.7	14.1	16.2	6.5	6.6	7.4	7.0	6.8	30.4	25.8	9.0	0.7	75.3	36.2	49.6	50.4
80004	ARVADA	92.6	91.8	0.6	0.6	1.7	1.9	7.9	9.0	6.3	6.4	7.1	7.0	6.3	26.5	25.7	12.7	2.1	75.8	39.5	48.0	52.0
80005	ARVADA	93.5	92.7	0.6	0.6	1.9	2.3	6.9	7.9	5.5	6.4	7.3	7.0	5.9	26.5	32.3	8.3	0.8	76.3	40.3	48.9	51.2
80007	ARVADA	95.8	95.2	0.4	0.4	1.2	1.5	5.0	5.9	7.6	8.6	8.9	7.3	4.4	27.5	29.6	5.8	0.2	69.8	38.0	49.5	50.5
80010	AURORA	54.3	52.5	15.5	15.6	2.8	3.0	49.7	53.2	10.9	9.0	8.0	7.0	9.2	33.7	15.6	5.8	0.8	68.1	27.9	52.9	47.1
80011	AURORA	61.9	59.6	17.8	18.5	3.7	4.1	24.8	27.4	8.8	8.0	7.8	6.9	8.4	31.0	19.9	8.6	0.7	71.5	31.4	50.1	49.9
80012	AURORA	62.8	60.7	19.3	19.8	6.0	6.5	16.9	19.0	7.4	6.8	6.6	6.6	8.2	31.9	22.9	8.8	0.8	75.4	33.6	48.7	51.4
80013	AURORA	77.7	75.7	8.5	9.0	5.2	6.0	10.8	12.2	8.0	7.9	8.3	7.6	7.1	34.1	23.4	3.3	0.2	71.1	32.4	49.8	50.2
80014	AURORA	80.8	79.3	8.3	8.8	5.1	5.7	6.9	8.0	4.3	4.3	5.1	5.9	6.5	28.4	28.5	14.0	3.0	82.7	41.9	46.5	53.5
80015	AURORA	82.2	80.3	5.7	6.0	6.0	6.9	7.3	8.4	8.4	8.7	9.5	8.0	5.7	33.6	23.1	2.6	0.4	68.2	32.6	49.3	50.7
80016	AURORA	88.7	88.0	3.0	2.9	5.1	5.8	4.3	4.9	5.9	8.7	10.6	9.4	3.8	24.3	32.9	4.2	0.2	68.2	38.9	50.9	49.1
80017	AURORA	69.4	67.3	14.8	15.5	5.0	5.6	13.0	14.8	8.6	7.9	7.5	6.7	7.8	35.9	22.0	3.5	0.2	72.1	31.4	48.9	51.1
80018	AURORA	80.6	76.8	6.6	7.8	5.1	6.3	8.8	10.8	10.0	9.0	6.4	5.0	4.0	38.7	20.8	5.7	0.4	71.4	34.0	49.8	50.2
80019	AURORA	77.1	74.2	3.3	3.0	4.9	6.1	21.3	24.2	3.0	6.1	6.1	18.2	10.6	24.2	27.3	4.6	0.0	78.8	31.3	62.1	37.9
80020	BROOMFIELD	88.1	87.1	0.9	0.9	5.0	5.5	9.1	10.2	7.9	7.9	8.2	7.1	6.2	32.4	24.2	5.8	0.5	71.6	34.7	50.0	50.0
80021	BROOMFIELD	89.6	88.2	1.1	1.1	4.0	4.9	8.7	9.9	6.8	6.9	7.4	7.0	7.9	36.2	23.1	4.3	0.5	74.7	33.1	50.1	49.9
80022	COMMERCE CITY	66.8	64.5	2.0	2.1	0.8	0.8	50.9	54.7	8.9	8.1	8.5	7.5	8.0	29.7	20.3	8.4	0.8	70.1	30.7	52.2	47.8
80026	LAFAYETTE	86.0	85.0	0.9	0.9	3.4	3.8	15.7	16.7	7.8	7.6	7.3	6.3	6.3	34.1	24.3	5.7	0.7	73.3	35.0	49.4	50.6
80027	LOUISVILLE	89.8	88.4	1.0	1.1	4.8	5.7	5.0	5.7	7.2	7.7	8.2	7.0	5.7	34.4	25.2	4.2	0.5	72.5	34.8	50.3	49.7
80030	WESTMINSTER	74.6	71.9	1.0	1.2	8.0	8.9	30.2	33.8	7.6	6.8	7.1	7.1	8.0	30.1	20.8	10.6	1.9	74.3	33.8	50.3	49.7
80031	WESTMINSTER	82.0	79.9	1.4	1.6	5.4	6.3	17.9	20.1	6.9	6.8	7.3	6.5	7.2	31.9	25.3	7.7	0.6	75.2	34.7	49.9	50.1
80033	WHEAT RIDGE	90.0	88.9	0.9	0.9	1.4	1.5	12.3	13.9	5.8	5.6	5.8	5.7	6.0	26.6	25.0	15.4	4.1	79.2	41.5	47.2	52.8
80101	AGATE	93.0	93.1	0.0	0.0	0.0	0.0	7.8	8.1	5.9	6.9	7.2	5.6	6.9	23.8	28.4	13.1	2.2	76.3	41.3	50.3	49.7
80102	BENNETT	93.6	92.8	0.8	0.9	0.6	0.8	5.5	6.6	8.3	8.4	8.5	7.6	6.2	29.5	24.7	6.0	0.7	70.0	34.2	50.9	49.1
80103	BYERS	95.7	95.3	0.4	0.4	0.2	0.2	4.0	4.7	7.2	7.5	8.8	8.5	5.6	28.5	25.8	7.2	0.8	71.0	35.8	51.1	48.9
80104	CASTLE ROCK	94.1	93.5	0.4	0.5	1.1	1.3	5.8	6.4	8.9	9.0	8.2	6.4	5.7	33.3	22.3	5.6	0.5	69.8	33.4	49.6	50.5
80105	DEER TRAIL	95.7	95.4	0.5	0.5	0.7	0.7	3.2	3.7	7.4	7.7	7.8	8.2	5.8	25.8	24.5	11.0	1.8	71.6	37.1	50.8	49.2
80106	ELBERT	94.3	93.8	1.4	1.5	0.5	0.6	4.1	4.9	6.4	7.5	8.9	7.5	5.2	27.6	31.7	4.9	0.3	72.3	38.5	50.4	49.6
80107	ELIZABETH	95.3	94.9	0.4	0.5	0.6	0.7	4.0	4.5	6.7	7.7	8.6	7.9	4.6	29.9	29.2	5.2	0.3	71.9	38.0	50.0	50.0
80108	CASTLE ROCK	94.9	94.3	0.9	1.0	1.3	1.5	4.5	5.1	7.6	8.9	8.9	6.0	4.5	25.4	32.5	5.9	0.4	70.8	39.3	50.8	49.2
80109	CASTLE ROCK	94.8	94.5	0.5	0.6	1.2	1.5	5.3	5.5	10.3	10.7	9.1	6.4	4.1	31.5	24.0	3.8	0.2	65.8	34.5	51.1	48.9
80110	ENGLEWOOD	81.9	80.3	2.0	2.1	2.3	2.5	21.5	24.2	7.0	6.4	6.3	7.0	8.3	31.4	22.6	9.8	1.3	76.4	35.2	51.0	49.1
80111	ENGLEWOOD	89.8	88.7	1.9	2.1	5.1	5.8	5.6	6.2	5.1	6.7	8.7	8.4	6.4	24.8	32.7	6.6	0.6	73.8	38.6	50.7	49.3
80112	ENGLEWOOD	92.9	92.0	1.9	2.3	2.6	2.9	4.8	5.6	5.3	6.6	8.1	8.1	5.4	25.9	32.9	7.4	0.4	74.8	39.9	50.1	49.9
80113	ENGLEWOOD	91.3	90.3	1.3	1.5	1.8	2.1	7.8	9.1	5.0	5.3	5.9	6.1	8.2	28.5	25.6	11.7	3.8	80.1	39.2	48.7	51.3
80116	FRANKTOWN	97.0	96.9	0.2	0.3	0.6	0.7	2.7	3.0	3.9	6.1	8.4	7.5	4.2	19.8	41.1	8.5	0.6	76.5	45.1	50.5	49.6
80117	KIOWA	94.6	94.2	0.8	0.9	0.6	0.7	3.7	4.2	7.4	8.5	8.3	7.8	4.6	28.5	27.3	6.8	0.8	70.2	37.3	51.1	48.9
80118	LARKSPUR	96.7	96.3	0.3	0.3	0.8	1.0	3.3	3.7	5.4	6.9	7.7	7.0	3.9	23.4	36.4	9.1	0.4	75.2	43.1	50.2	49.8
80120	LITTLETON	91.5	90.7	1.2	1.3	1.8	2.0	8.6	9.9	5.6	5.7	6.6	6.5	6.8	26.2	27.2	13.3	2.2	78.1	40.5	48.6	51.4
80121	LITTLETON	94.2	93.6	0.9	0.9	1.7	1.9	4.2	4.9	5.5	6.7	8.0	7.0	4.7	22.3	31.7	13.1	1.2	75.3	42.5	49.1	50.9
80122	LITTLETON	94.9	94.4	0.7	0.7	2.0	2.3	4.0	4.6	5.2	6.1	8.1	8.0	5.2	23.3	32.0	10.9	1.3	75.1	41.7	48.0	52.0
80123	LITTLETON	91.5	90.5	0.9	1.0	2.4	2.8	8.5	9.7	6.2	6.4	6.8	6.6	6.5	30.6	26.9	9.1	0.8	76.5	37.0	48.6	51.4
80124	LITTLETON	91.8	90.6	1.3	1.4	3.5	4.4	4.5	5.0	8.9	9.2	8.3	5.9	4.6	32.0	26.7	4.3	0.2	69.9	35.8	49.6	50.4
80125	LITTLETON	94.4	93.7	0.4	0.4	1.4	1.7	5.2	6.1	8.7	9.0	7.7	5.6	3.9	33.3	26.2	5.5	0.1	71.2	36.4	50.9	49.1
80126	LITTLETON	91.1	90.0	1.3	1.3	3.8	4.6	5.0	5.5	9.2	10.0	9.5	6.8	4.6	32.5	23.5	3.8	0.3	66.9	34.0	49.3	50.7
80127	LITTLETON	93.9	93.2	0.5	0.6	2.0	2.3	6.0	6.9	7.1	8.5	9.5	7.7	4.9	29.9	27.8	4.3	0.3	69.8	36.3	50.2	49.8
80128	LITTLETON	93.6	92.9	0.7	0.7	1.6	1.8	6.5	7.5	6.7	7.3	7.8	7.4	5.7	30.3	27.3	7.1	0.5	73.4	36.6	49.4	50.6
80129	LITTLETON	91.2	90.2	1.2	1.3	3.4	4.1	6.5	7.2	12.5	11.8	8.1	4.7	3.4	40.1	17.0	2.3	0.1	64.6	32.4	49.7	50.3
80130	LITTLETON	89.5	87.9	1.6	1.7	5.3	6.5	5.2	6.0	10.8	9.8	7.7	4.9	5.2	38.1	19.6	3.7	0.2	68.5	32.5	49.6	50.4
80132	MONUMENT	94.7	94.0	0.9	1.0	1.4	1.6	3.7	4.3	6.2	8.1	9.5	7.8	4.0	24.1	32.9	6.9	0.5	70.7	40.3	50.7	49.3
80133	PALMER LAKE	94.2	93.5	0.6	0.7	0.9	1.1	5.5	6.4	6.1	7.4	8.5	6.7	5.0	28.1	30.7	6.8	0.7	73.3	39.1	50.4	49.6
80134	PARKER	93.5	92.6	0.9	1.0	1.9	2.4	4.8	5.6	10.2	10.5	9.3	6.4	4.3	34.0	22.1	3.1	0.1	65.6	33.1	49.8	50.2
80135	SEDALIA	96.5	96.0	0.2	0.3	0.7	1.0	3.6	4.2	4.9	6.5	7.9	6.6	3.6	21.6	37.7	10.9	0.5	76.2	44.6	51.4	48.6
80136	STRASBURG	95.4	94.9	0.8	0.8	0.3	0.4	3.9	4.8	6.9	7.5	9.0	7.6	4.8	28.0	26.8	8.3	1.2	71.6	37.8	50.6	49.4
80137	WATKINS	89.5	88.3	1.8	1.9	1.0	1.2	8.7	10.1	8.5	8.5	7.6	6.5	5.9	28.4	27.7	6.4	0.6	71.5	35.4	51.1	48.9
80138	PARKER	94.5	93.9	0.8	0.9	1.0	1.2	4.7	5.4	8.4	9.1	8.6	6.4	4.3	31.9	25.6	5.2	0.6	69.8	35.7	49.4	50.6
80202	DENVER	79.9	78.5	5.7	5.9	6.4	6.8	10.9	12.7	1.2	0.7	0.5	1.0	5.9	39.2	33.5	16.3	1.9	97.4	46.0	57.9	42.1
80203	DENVER	80.5	78.5	5.4	5.7	2.9	3.3	14.6	17.3	2.0	1.3	1.3	2.5	11.7	50.9	21.9	7.1	1.3	94.6	34.3	58.1	42.0
80204	DENVER	52.0	50.6	4.2	3.9	2.9	3.0	66.4	69.7	10.0	8.6	8.4	7.5	9.6	32.0	16.4	6.6	1.0	68.6	28.0	51.3	48.7
80205	DENVER	32.1	32.3	36.6	34.2	1.0	1.1	43.9	47.5	8.5	7.7	7.9	7.8	8.3	32.1	18.7	7.9	1.2	71.2	30.8	52.0	48.0
80206	DENVER	85.0	83.9	6.7	6.9	2.1	2.5	8.1	9.6	3.7	3.0	3.1	3.6	6.9	40.9	28.0	9.1	1.8	88.3	38.3	50.4	49.6
80207	DENVER	33.3	33.1	53.3	52.2	1.0	1.1	17.6	20.0	6.8	7.0	7.2	7.2	7.1	31.3	22.8	9.6	1.0	74.9	35.5	50.7	49.3
80208	DENVER	78.1	76.0	4.4	4.4	8.3	9.5	8.5	10.1	2.4	1.5	1.3	25.3	33.9	27.2	6.8	1.5	0.2	93.9	22.9	52.6	47.4
80209	DENVER	91.3	90.2	1.3	1.4	1.7	1.9	7.3	8.6	4.0	3.4	3.0	3.0	5.4	41.1	27.2	10.8	2.1	88.0	39.2	49.9	50.2
80210	DENVER	90.6	89.7	1.4	1.5	2.6	2.9	6.4	7.6	4.4	4.2	4.2	4.4	8.2	37.5	23.4	10.2	3.4	85.0	37.3	48.8	51.2
80211	DENVER	59.0	56.7	1.8	1.8	1.3	1.4	60.4	64.5	7.8	7.0	6.9	6.5	7.9	34.3	19.2	8.3	2.2	74.6	32.7	50.7	49.3
80212	DENVER	79.1	76.8	1.0	1.0	1.5	1.7	30.0	34.1	5.6	5.4	5.6	5.6	6.4	32.4	24.7	11.3	3.0	80.2	38.5	48.2	51.8
80214	DENVER	78.2	76.5	2.1	2.2	1.6	1.8	29.2	32.2	7.6	6.3	6.0	6.1	8.8	31.6	21.8	9.4	2.5	76.9	34.4	50.0	50.0
80215	DENVER	90.7	89.7	1.4	1.5	1.7	1.9	9.5	11.0	5.9	5.7	6.0	6.0	6.6	25.1	26.6	15.5	2.7	78.9	41.6	48.1	51.9
80216	DENVER	42.1	41.0	6.1	5.6	0.6	0.5	77.9	80.3	10.0	9.3	9.3	8.5	9.0	31.0	16.2	6.1	0.8	66.4	27.3	54.1	45.9
80218	DENVER	82.4	80.8	7.0	7.1	2.1	2.4	11.3	13.6	3.4	2.6	2.6	3.3	9.3	48.0	22.4	7.4	1.2	89.8	34.7	53.9	46.1
80219	DENVER	57.3	55.2	1.4	1.4	4.1	4.2	62.3	66.2	9.2	8.6	8.3	7.4	7.9	30.6	18.4	8.6	1.0	69.4	30.4	50.8	49.2
80220	DENVER	71.6	69.6	14.6	14.9	2.7	3.1	15.1	17.7	6.7	6.1	5.9	5.8	7.2	34.1	24.8	8.0	1.4	77.8	35.8	49.6	50.4
80221	DENVER	70.6	68.4	1.1	1.2	3.4	3.8	45.8	50.1	7.8	7.0	7.2	7.6	8.8	30.6	20.2	9.9	0.9	73.9	32.2	51.1	48.9
80222	DENVER	83.4	81.9	4.9	5.0	3.7	4.2	11.9	14.0	5.5	5.2	5.2	4.7	6.4	31.6	24.0	14.0	3.6	81.4	39.7	48.8	51.2
80223	DENVER	62.9	60.9	2.6	2.5	2.6	2.8	57.6	61.9	8.4	7.9	7.3	7.1	7.8	34.0	19.3	7.5	0.8	72.3	31.5	52.9	47.1
80224	DENVER	77.9	76.1	9.3	9.5	4.5	5.4	10.5	12.2	5.3	4.9	4.7	4.7	6.2	29.0	25.1	16.8	3.3	82.5	41.6	48.2	51.8
80226	DENVER	86.1	84.5	1.1	1.2	2.9	3.4	19.2	21.5	5.9	5.5	5.9	6.7	8.5	29.7	23.2	12.3	2.3	78.9	36.5	48.7	51.3
80227	DENVER	86.3	84.8	1.2	1.3	3.7	4.2	14.9	16.9	5.9	5.4	6.0	6.1	7.7	31.4	25.6	11.2	0.7	79.2	36.8	48.4	51.6
80228	DENVER	91.2	90.2	1.1	1.2	2.9	3.4	7.1	8.2	5.8	6.1	6.6	6.4	7.5	30.6	27.4	8.9	0.7	77.7	37.1	49.7	50.3
80229	DENVER	75.5	73.0	1.6	1.7	1.8	2.0	32.4	36.3	8.9	8.0	7.9	7.1	8.8	33.6	18.9	6.3	0.6	71.1	30.1	49.8	50.3
80230	DENVER	67.2	63.0	19.0	21.2	2.0	2.2	11.8	14.4	10.4	9.3	7.1	5.9	6.6	36.8	16.5	5.2	2.3	69.8	31.0	48.1	51.9
80231	DENVER	75.7	74.3	10.4	10.5	5.7	6.4	9.7	11.1	5.4	4.5	3.8	3.8	9.1	37.6	24.0	10.1	1.8	84.2	35.7	48.3	51.7
80232	DENVER	87.3	85.9	1.0	1.0	3.6	4.1	15.3	17.3	5.8	6.0	6.6	6.4	6.3	28.1	25.7	13.2	1.9	77.7	39.3	48.5	51.5
80233	DENVER	84.3	82.3	1.2	1.3	2.7	3.1	19.0	21.6	7.7	7.5	7.5	6.8	6.6	32.9	21.6	7.5	1.8	73.2	34.0	49.4	50.6
80234	DENVER	85.1	83.1	1.7	1.9	4.7	5.5	13.4	15.6	7.7	7.0	6.4	6.0	8.1	34.6	22.9	7.0	0.4	75.5	33.6	50.0	50.0
80235	DENVER	81.5	80.5	3.8	3.8	4.0	4.4	17.4	19.2	5.4	5.1	5.1	6.5	7.9	37.5	22.4	9.4	0.6	80.2	34.6	55.0	45.0
80236	DENVER	74.7	72.3	1.9	1.9	5.0	5.4	32.0	36.1	6.4	6.2	6.6	7.0	7.6	29.9	21.8	12.8	1.7	76.4	36.0	50.3	49.7
80237	DENVER	84.8	83.4	6.6	6.8	2.9	3.4	6.6	7.8	4.5	4.4	4.2	4.4	6.8	31.5	26.4	15.6	2.1	84.3	40.8	47.5	52.5
80239	DENVER	26.0	26.3	44.8	42.4	3.1	3.3	36.0	39.2	9.9	9.5	9.9	8.2	8.0	31.9	18.3	4.2	0.2	65.6	27.7	50.1	49.9
80241	DENVER	87.9	86.1	1.2	1.4	3.0	3.7	13.2	15.4	9.3	8.8	8.1	6.6	6.3	36.2	20.9	3.4	0.6	69.8	32.1	49.8	50.2
80246	DENVER	73.9	72.5	7.4	7.5	5.2	5.5	20.6	23.1	5.5	4.1	3.9	4.9	13.4	42.0	18.1	7.1	1.0	84.3	31.4	52.9	47.1
80247	DENVER	67.6	66.7	14.1	14.0	4.3	5.0	17.4	18.5	6.4	5.0	4.8	5.1	9.4	35.7	16.8	12.9	4.0	81.1	33.9	46.0	54.0
80249	DENVER	51.2	50.3	30.8	29.9	4.6	4.9	16.5	19.2	10.6	9.3	7.7	5.7	6.5	40.7	17.6	1.8	0.1	68.9	30.1	49.5	50.5
	COLORADO	82.8	81.7	3.8	3.9	2.3	2.6	17.1	18.6	7.0	6.8	7.1	7.0	7.5	30.6	24.3	8.6	1.2	75.1	35.0	50.3	49.7
	UNITED STATES	75.1	73.6	12.3	12.5	3.8	4.2	12.5	14.1	6.9	6.7	7.2	7.0	7.3	28.6	23.8	10.8	1.7	75.1	36.0	49.1	50.9

ZIP CODE #	POST OFFICE NAME	2004 Per Capita Income	2004 HH Income Base	2004 HOUSEHOLD INCOME DISTRIBUTION (%) Less than $25,000	$25,000 to $49,999	$50,000 to $99,999	$100,000 to $149,999	$150,000 or More	MEDIAN HOUSEHOLD INCOME 2004	2009	2004 National Centile	2004 State Centile	2004 Home Value Base	2004 HOME VALUE DISTRIBUTION (%) Less than $50,000	$50,000 to $89,999	$90,000 to $174,999	$175,000 to $399,999	$400,000 or More	2004 Median Home Value
80002	ARVADA	26275	6337	19.9	31.8	34.1	9.6	4.6	48256	58281	69	58	3663	7.2	1.6	32.8	49.4	9.0	189416
80003	ARVADA	26334	12826	11.6	26.4	43.7	14.6	3.7	60945	71213	85	79	9836	0.2	0.2	29.0	69.4	1.2	200631
80004	ARVADA	28405	14616	15.9	25.2	38.1	14.5	6.2	59560	69513	84	77	10815	0.2	0.2	15.6	78.8	5.2	226607
80005	ARVADA	34960	9445	8.4	18.7	39.3	22.5	11.1	78644	89875	95	92	8311	0.2	0.4	15.3	75.4	8.7	251364
80007	ARVADA	44407	2505	5.0	6.0	35.2	28.6	25.2	105543	125900	99	100	2408	0.0	0.0	1.4	42.6	56.0	419890
80010	AURORA	14074	14881	29.5	38.6	26.2	4.6	1.2	36860	43072	35	25	6627	2.2	4.0	65.6	27.8	0.4	152177
80011	AURORA	19880	18393	22.0	35.0	34.7	6.4	1.9	44568	51691	60	51	10723	14.4	5.7	42.3	37.0	0.7	159874
80012	AURORA	24725	19207	18.4	34.2	35.4	9.1	3.0	47782	55408	68	58	10432	1.0	5.9	40.4	51.9	0.8	178783
80013	AURORA	28302	22583	6.3	21.7	48.4	17.9	5.6	70044	80376	91	87	18097	0.6	1.3	27.4	70.4	0.4	198975
80014	AURORA	33999	18495	16.8	29.8	35.5	11.8	6.1	52986	61597	77	68	12164	0.3	3.1	38.2	56.5	1.9	188848
80015	AURORA	33019	21648	5.0	17.1	42.1	23.8	12.0	81272	96819	95	93	18988	0.7	1.0	17.2	72.6	8.6	237666
80016	AURORA	60228	3907	2.9	8.2	18.9	27.9	42.0	135477	165195	100	100	3761	0.0	0.2	1.1	27.6	71.2	492608
80017	AURORA	25988	12321	10.4	30.5	45.1	11.4	2.7	57599	66607	82	75	7992	0.7	3.7	42.8	52.5	0.3	178061
80018	AURORA	28693	754	5.7	17.4	54.4	16.6	6.0	72869	83176	92	89	718	1.1	2.0	7.9	82.2	6.8	230243
80019	AURORA	24893	19	0.0	0.0	89.5	10.5	0.0	75691	86673	93	90	11	0.0	0.0	0.0	100.0	0.0	258333
80020	BROOMFIELD	31324	20149	8.1	18.0	44.2	21.0	8.7	76268	85656	94	90	16939	3.9	3.0	8.1	71.9	13.0	243242
80021	BROOMFIELD	31999	11392	6.1	18.9	48.7	19.7	6.6	71542	83907	92	88	7982	0.0	0.4	18.2	75.0	6.4	226389
80022	COMMERCE CITY	15724	10345	27.3	36.4	30.1	4.1	2.1	38938	44271	43	33	6959	10.5	4.6	59.4	23.8	1.7	141830
80026	LAFAYETTE	34535	10612	12.0	21.0	38.3	17.0	11.6	69545	85124	91	87	8254	7.9	2.0	15.1	52.3	22.7	240046
80027	LOUISVILLE	39688	12074	7.9	15.5	37.8	22.5	16.3	83040	101284	96	95	8719	2.1	0.6	4.8	63.1	29.5	320811
80030	WESTMINSTER	20593	6797	22.4	35.4	32.2	8.2	1.8	43715	50547	58	49	4010	0.6	0.9	44.9	53.5	0.2	178705
80031	WESTMINSTER	31178	15106	10.5	26.4	39.3	15.5	8.3	62274	70344	86	82	10950	2.7	1.2	25.0	65.7	5.4	210458
80033	WHEAT RIDGE	26529	11958	23.1	32.9	31.7	8.9	3.5	44414	52597	60	51	6877	0.9	1.8	26.3	64.3	6.8	213945
80101	AGATE	20137	126	15.1	42.1	35.7	6.4	0.8	46113	52340	64	54	98	12.2	12.2	32.7	32.7	10.2	153125
80102	BENNETT	24242	1766	13.5	28.3	42.9	11.4	3.9	56584	63530	81	74	1500	14.9	6.6	29.8	42.0	6.7	172460
80103	BYERS	22126	896	17.8	29.9	37.7	11.6	3.0	52161	58669	76	67	742	10.0	8.1	33.3	45.6	3.1	172093
80104	CASTLE ROCK	31804	8192	8.8	19.7	42.9	20.0	8.6	71943	83308	92	88	6144	0.5	0.1	11.3	76.1	12.0	241036
80105	DEER TRAIL	20364	503	22.3	37.4	29.0	7.6	3.8	42496	50578	55	45	403	17.9	12.2	31.8	27.1	11.2	134167
80106	ELBERT	35051	1606	7.7	16.6	39.5	25.8	10.5	82880	99315	96	94	1473	2.7	1.0	8.1	70.5	17.8	278203
80107	ELIZABETH	29652	4225	7.3	17.2	45.1	20.2	10.2	76451	86922	94	90	3931	1.3	0.6	10.0	62.7	25.3	310295
80108	CASTLE ROCK	70520	5502	2.5	13.3	22.3	23.1	38.8	124217	140173	99	100	4754	0.4	0.0	0.6	26.5	72.6	545328
80109	CASTLE ROCK	39148	3405	2.3	6.7	42.2	29.4	19.4	98284	115060	98	99	3282	1.7	1.3	1.6	67.3	28.2	317014
80110	ENGLEWOOD	21208	10002	25.6	35.1	30.9	6.6	1.8	41573	48993	52	42	5629	7.9	2.8	38.3	49.8	1.2	176220
80111	ENGLEWOOD	56182	10615	6.1	12.3	30.4	20.8	30.4	102208	124068	98	99	7770	0.1	0.7	6.0	45.7	47.6	389600
80112	ENGLEWOOD	43750	8379	6.8	14.5	33.7	22.4	22.6	90792	107836	97	97	6829	0.3	0.4	6.3	78.5	14.6	294755
80113	ENGLEWOOD	49193	10209	19.4	27.7	31.3	9.1	12.6	53301	62559	77	70	5836	0.6	0.4	29.2	41.6	28.2	219456
80116	FRANKTOWN	45379	1888	6.0	15.4	31.2	20.0	27.3	94258	105250	98	97	1752	0.0	0.0	0.2	25.2	74.7	572566
80117	KIOWA	26744	862	9.7	29.4	39.1	13.8	8.0	60226	69052	85	78	731	5.6	3.7	12.6	53.1	25.0	286149
80118	LARKSPUR	42033	1898	7.6	14.7	34.6	22.5	20.6	88870	101123	97	96	1759	1.5	1.6	7.2	36.6	53.2	417492
80120	LITTLETON	32512	13528	19.0	26.9	32.0	13.1	9.0	54705	63023	79	73	8243	3.9	2.7	14.7	68.5	10.2	230494
80121	LITTLETON	52617	7209	7.6	17.6	36.5	18.0	20.3	82243	97343	96	94	6307	0.1	0.1	9.6	65.6	24.5	249859
80122	LITTLETON	39639	12580	8.1	17.3	37.9	20.9	15.9	80440	93370	95	93	10807	0.3	0.7	13.0	75.0	11.0	254596
80123	LITTLETON	38924	18254	9.7	20.1	38.6	18.9	12.7	73652	85683	93	89	13566	0.3	0.7	16.1	65.2	17.7	242748
80124	LITTLETON	45651	5004	4.3	12.5	32.9	25.4	25.0	100489	115219	98	99	4405	0.2	0.0	1.1	52.9	45.9	382536
80125	LITTLETON	40637	3910	5.7	11.0	45.1	22.8	15.5	84578	96619	96	95	3677	0.7	0.5	1.7	65.3	31.9	292144
80126	LITTLETON	43221	13068	3.9	10.9	36.3	25.9	23.1	98239	113028	98	99	11042	0.6	0.1	2.5	66.5	30.5	336097
80127	LITTLETON	40767	15110	4.4	11.6	38.7	26.8	18.6	92755	109294	97	97	13748	0.1	0.1	6.7	73.4	19.7	278422
80128	LITTLETON	33880	13980	5.8	18.9	44.4	21.3	9.6	76803	88386	94	91	12394	0.1	1.1	16.4	76.2	6.1	235601
80129	LITTLETON	37762	8825	2.6	10.1	39.6	31.8	15.9	96736	113505	98	98	8060	0.1	0.0	0.5	79.4	20.0	325988
80130	LITTLETON	41206	7952	3.5	10.5	39.5	29.2	17.4	95205	111812	98	98	6807	0.3	0.0	0.7	76.5	22.6	324033
80132	MONUMENT	42558	5827	6.9	12.7	31.8	26.0	22.6	97333	113859	98	98	5362	3.0	0.9	7.0	58.2	30.9	339634
80133	PALMER LAKE	33027	1001	13.0	22.7	38.0	15.1	11.3	65030	73590	89	83	842	8.7	1.4	20.1	54.6	15.2	222188
80134	PARKER	38912	15408	4.1	9.6	41.0	26.6	18.7	93009	107702	97	97	14106	0.2	0.3	2.5	70.4	26.8	318489
80135	SEDALIA	43511	1954	13.9	12.4	30.3	23.3	20.1	87775	102407	97	96	1770	2.9	2.2	5.4	34.4	55.1	426149
80136	STRASBURG	22568	1055	16.6	25.7	42.3	11.8	3.7	58249	63297	83	76	907	8.7	5.6	26.2	54.0	5.4	199569
80137	WATKINS	27149	845	12.7	24.6	47.0	11.8	3.9	61771	70566	86	80	771	39.8	10.3	4.8	37.4	7.8	89773
80138	PARKER	36122	9379	5.5	11.4	40.8	26.4	16.0	89290	105064	97	97	8816	0.0	0.3	4.9	67.4	27.4	326689
80202	DENVER	65569	3272	42.2	17.4	16.6	8.6	15.3	34504	39381	26	18	1153	1.8	0.8	8.8	47.9	40.8	348301
80203	DENVER	31901	13271	36.0	33.9	22.2	5.3	2.7	34380	41921	25	18	2674	0.6	5.7	37.3	48.6	7.9	190122
80204	DENVER	15663	11045	40.4	29.7	22.1	5.2	2.6	32054	37508	18	12	4087	0.9	4.5	58.0	30.7	6.0	155285
80205	DENVER	16798	10546	41.0	27.2	22.9	6.2	2.8	32167	37339	18	12	4830	1.6	5.0	48.1	40.0	5.3	166835
80206	DENVER	53628	11432	23.8	27.5	24.4	10.5	13.9	48498	59767	69	59	4353	0.3	0.9	13.4	46.1	39.3	349511
80207	DENVER	24903	7841	24.9	27.9	29.7	9.1	8.4	47161	55192	66	56	5465	0.6	2.4	35.2	50.9	11.0	201377
80208	DENVER	13933	372	41.7	35.2	18.8	3.5	0.8	29190	32686	11	6	39	0.0	0.0	48.7	51.3	0.0	177500
80209	DENVER	63092	11484	16.6	21.1	28.6	15.3	18.3	68344	84394	90	86	6211	0.1	0.3	7.2	53.8	38.6	354682
80210	DENVER	42541	15083	18.5	25.0	31.7	13.6	11.3	58321	70610	83	77	9153	0.1	0.1	13.7	68.2	17.9	260298
80211	DENVER	20011	14334	31.8	29.4	27.8	8.3	2.9	39574	46238	45	34	7496	0.4	2.4	38.5	56.5	2.4	192350
80212	DENVER	26592	8524	22.0	33.0	32.8	9.2	3.0	45963	54734	64	54	5401	5.4	2.2	33.2	56.2	3.0	189470
80214	DENVER	23236	11074	25.7	36.6	29.4	6.0	2.4	41128	50147	50	40	4607	2.3	5.3	39.1	51.1	2.1	179950
80215	DENVER	32310	8228	16.1	30.5	34.8	11.4	7.2	53198	62026	77	69	5195	0.3	1.2	16.7	69.1	12.7	249978
80216	DENVER	12191	2891	35.2	32.2	26.3	5.1	1.3	35474	40030	29	21	1710	4.3	13.2	65.9	13.1	3.6	124180
80218	DENVER	41247	10177	30.2	31.0	22.9	8.1	7.9	39392	48778	44	34	2917	0.2	2.8	21.1	41.3	34.6	286186
80219	DENVER	16525	19139	27.3	33.1	31.4	6.2	2.1	40885	46749	49	39	12388	1.9	3.1	62.0	32.5	0.5	157699
80220	DENVER	38472	15394	22.4	25.9	27.3	12.5	12.0	52083	62857	76	66	8525	0.4	1.8	22.5	50.6	24.7	262527
80221	DENVER	18712	14405	22.8	35.5	32.4	7.6	1.8	44104	50565	59	50	9914	5.4	2.1	44.6	47.0	0.9	172455
80222	DENVER	30403	9155	19.8	31.4	33.1	11.0	4.8	48937	56987	70	60	5115	1.0	4.1	23.7	69.0	2.2	208405
80223	DENVER	18776	7056	30.6	33.0	27.5	5.9	3.0	37382	43742	37	27	3672	3.4	3.3	59.4	33.1	0.7	158645
80224	DENVER	34522	8590	20.5	28.6	31.3	11.4	8.3	50921	58246	74	64	5024	0.9	2.4	29.6	61.4	5.8	213624
80226	DENVER	26447	12215	18.2	29.8	36.8	11.8	3.4	51871	60729	75	66	7601	3.4	1.7	25.9	66.8	2.2	202133
80227	DENVER	32534	14844	12.3	29.1	38.4	13.9	6.3	57079	67312	82	75	9395	0.3	1.8	27.9	61.3	8.9	218466
80228	DENVER	36614	13359	9.4	23.5	40.8	16.5	9.8	68288	80424	90	86	8792	0.2	1.3	13.7	75.1	9.7	241733
80229	DENVER	19803	16897	17.7	33.3	40.2	7.4	1.4	49202	55577	71	61	11458	11.2	5.0	43.6	39.8	0.4	161309
80230	DENVER	38484	1477	19.1	26.6	24.9	15.4	14.0	56907	66537	82	75	598	0.0	0.0	3.9	53.5	42.6	377551
80231	DENVER	37769	20347	16.6	32.6	32.6	11.4	6.9	50778	59913	73	64	9011	0.6	4.7	34.2	53.3	7.2	206101
80232	DENVER	27742	8528	11.8	29.7	40.9	13.6	4.0	57027	67073	82	75	6216	0.5	1.5	27.4	69.0	1.6	203363
80233	DENVER	24015	15494	12.9	26.0	45.0	13.5	2.7	60569	65950	85	79	11808	0.6	0.6	28.2	70.4	0.3	198308
80234	DENVER	30171	10846	11.1	27.0	41.9	13.4	6.7	61844	68877	86	81	7105	5.6	5.4	18.4	63.6	7.0	218383
80235	DENVER	33758	3478	13.9	31.3	34.5	11.9	8.4	54799	65086	79	73	2028	0.3	10.1	29.3	42.5	17.9	209873
80236	DENVER	25264	6446	17.2	28.7	37.1	13.1	3.9	53338	62349	77	70	4320	2.3	3.5	25.4	65.2	3.6	203154
80237	DENVER	41742	8740	14.0	27.8	34.4	13.8	10.1	60430	71255	85	78	4944	0.5	3.6	28.6	54.6	12.7	245878
80239	DENVER	18188	9476	17.2	31.8	37.9	9.9	3.2	50822	58321	74	64	6865	0.8	0.4	50.1	48.3	0.3	173834
80241	DENVER	31164	12543	4.4	18.2	48.2	20.4	8.9	76986	86180	94	91	10128	0.4	0.3	10.4	82.6	6.4	244157
80246	DENVER	31867	7577	27.7	34.3	24.8	8.1	5.2	39501	46925	44	34	2021	0.0	0.5	32.5	44.4	22.7	213558
80247	DENVER	27160	10257	26.5	36.6	27.5	6.7	2.7	39804	46097	45	35	4275	1.5	15.4	54.6	27.2	1.3	129631
80249	DENVER	26484	4675	5.6	23.4	48.9	17.1	5.0	67338	79578	90	85	3747	0.0	0.4	24.7	74.0	1.0	203914
	COLORADO	28803		19.1	26.9	34.1	12.5	7.5	54077	63465				4.8	4.7	28.0	49.9	12.6	203984
	UNITED STATES	25866		24.7	27.1	30.8	10.9	6.5	48124	56710				10.9	15.0	33.7	30.1	10.4	145905

ZIP CODE # POST OFFICE NAME	FINANCIAL SERVICES: Auto Loan	FINANCIAL SERVICES: Home Loan	FINANCIAL SERVICES: Invest-ments	FINANCIAL SERVICES: Retire-ment Plans	THE HOME: Home Improvements: Home Repair	THE HOME: Home Improvements: Lawn & Garden	THE HOME: Furnishings: Comput-ers & Hard-ware	THE HOME: Furnishings: Major Appli-ances	THE HOME: Furnishings: TV, Radio, Sound Equip-ment	THE HOME: Furnishings: Furni-ture	ENTERTAINMENT: Dine out/ Carry out	ENTERTAINMENT: Sports Equip-ment	ENTERTAINMENT: Fees & Tickets	ENTERTAINMENT: Toys & Games	ENTERTAINMENT: Travel	ENTERTAINMENT: Cable TV	PERSONAL: Apparel & Services	PERSONAL: Auto Repairs	PERSONAL: Health Insur-ance	PERSONAL: Pets & Supplies
80002 ARVADA	84	86	95	90	84	87	88	85	85	88	107	102	89	107	86	81	105	87	78	95
80003 ARVADA	94	103	111	106	100	101	100	98	95	100	120	116	102	121	99	90	118	98	88	108
80004 ARVADA	95	105	116	107	104	107	103	101	99	103	124	118	105	125	103	96	122	101	95	111
80005 ARVADA	123	142	153	145	139	140	132	131	124	133	157	153	138	161	133	120	155	129	118	144
80007 ARVADA	180	216	223	223	207	205	192	188	175	197	223	219	205	228	191	167	223	182	164	207
80010 AURORA	62	57	59	57	56	59	63	62	64	64	80	71	61	79	60	60	80	65	57	66
80011 AURORA	73	74	79	75	72	76	76	74	75	76	94	87	76	93	74	73	92	76	71	82
80012 AURORA	82	79	91	84	76	81	85	81	82	86	105	97	83	101	81	78	102	85	74	90
80013 AURORA	113	124	125	129	119	117	117	115	108	120	138	135	119	138	114	102	136	114	99	126
80014 AURORA	95	95	110	99	94	100	98	96	96	99	121	112	98	117	96	93	118	99	91	106
80015 AURORA	140	153	156	161	146	145	144	141	133	148	170	166	147	168	140	125	168	139	122	155
80016 AURORA	243	304	348	309	293	300	268	263	246	274	312	303	293	323	274	239	314	254	235	289
80017 AURORA	96	92	100	99	88	91	97	93	93	99	118	112	95	113	91	86	115	96	82	103
80018 AURORA	115	132	133	136	127	126	120	119	111	123	140	138	124	141	119	105	139	116	104	130
80019 AURORA	112	123	123	125	119	118	117	116	110	118	138	138	118	139	114	103	136	115	102	127
80020 BROOMFIELD	122	138	143	142	134	134	128	127	120	131	152	148	133	153	127	114	150	125	112	140
80021 BROOMFIELD	116	125	130	132	120	120	120	118	113	123	143	139	122	141	117	106	141	118	103	129
80022 COMMERCE CITY	73	66	58	62	64	68	67	71	69	71	87	77	63	80	65	67	86	72	68	76
80026 LAFAYETTE	128	135	140	141	130	131	131	128	124	134	157	152	133	155	127	117	154	129	114	142
80027 LOUISVILLE	142	160	181	169	153	153	151	146	141	155	180	172	157	183	149	134	178	145	128	161
80030 WESTMINSTER	74	73	77	74	72	77	75	74	74	75	93	86	74	92	73	73	90	75	73	83
80031 WESTMINSTER	113	123	132	127	120	121	119	117	113	120	142	137	121	144	117	108	141	116	105	129
80033 WHEAT RIDGE	76	79	94	80	78	85	83	80	83	82	103	94	84	104	83	82	101	82	79	88
80101 AGATE	93	65	34	61	75	84	64	79	74	63	86	95	54	85	66	77	79	78	94	110
80102 BENNETT	97	105	103	106	102	102	99	99	93	100	118	117	100	118	97	89	116	98	89	110
80103 BYERS	92	93	83	91	93	95	87	91	85	88	106	106	86	105	87	84	103	90	87	106
80104 CASTLE ROCK	118	132	136	136	127	125	124	122	115	126	146	144	127	147	122	109	144	121	106	133
80105 DEER TRAIL	93	76	52	74	82	88	72	83	77	73	93	100	66	92	74	79	87	82	91	109
80106 ELBERT	141	162	159	168	155	150	146	145	134	151	170	169	151	172	143	125	168	140	124	158
80107 ELIZABETH	127	143	138	149	136	131	129	128	118	134	150	150	133	151	126	110	149	124	108	140
80108 CASTLE ROCK	256	310	356	319	300	308	281	273	259	285	329	316	305	338	284	251	331	267	245	302
80109 CASTLE ROCK	174	200	198	208	191	187	180	178	165	186	210	208	188	211	177	155	208	173	153	195
80110 ENGLEWOOD	67	68	77	70	67	71	73	70	71	71	89	83	72	89	71	69	87	72	66	76
80111 ENGLEWOOD	192	225	260	231	218	226	209	204	195	212	248	237	223	252	211	189	248	201	185	225
80112 ENGLEWOOD	155	189	210	194	184	185	171	167	158	173	201	195	185	208	174	153	201	163	150	185
80113 ENGLEWOOD	141	150	184	156	148	156	154	149	148	154	187	176	157	187	152	143	184	152	137	163
80116 FRANKTOWN	161	201	217	206	194	195	177	173	161	179	205	200	194	214	180	156	206	166	154	191
80117 KIOWA	109	122	118	127	117	113	111	110	102	115	129	129	114	130	108	95	128	107	94	120
80118 LARKSPUR	147	181	199	184	177	181	161	159	149	163	189	182	176	194	165	146	189	154	145	175
80120 LITTLETON	97	106	124	109	104	109	106	103	102	106	129	121	109	130	106	100	127	104	96	113
80121 LITTLETON	180	217	252	217	213	221	200	197	188	201	237	227	214	247	205	185	237	193	182	216
80122 LITTLETON	133	160	182	162	157	161	148	146	139	149	176	169	158	182	151	136	175	143	134	160
80123 LITTLETON	130	143	158	148	139	142	138	135	130	140	165	158	141	165	136	124	162	135	121	148
80124 LITTLETON	175	206	210	213	197	195	184	181	168	189	214	211	195	218	183	160	214	176	157	199
80125 LITTLETON	150	176	178	182	169	166	158	156	145	162	184	182	166	188	157	137	183	151	135	171
80126 LITTLETON	179	203	207	212	195	192	186	182	171	191	217	213	194	219	182	161	216	179	158	200
80127 LITTLETON	160	188	196	194	181	180	170	167	156	174	199	196	179	203	169	149	198	163	146	184
80128 LITTLETON	125	143	150	146	138	138	132	130	123	134	156	152	137	158	131	117	154	128	116	143
80129 LITTLETON	157	176	171	184	167	163	161	159	148	167	188	186	165	188	156	138	186	155	135	174
80130 LITTLETON	155	174	182	182	165	163	161	158	149	167	190	185	166	191	157	140	188	155	136	173
80132 MONUMENT	165	204	219	209	198	198	181	177	165	183	210	206	196	219	184	160	211	171	157	196
80133 PALMER LAKE	106	132	140	132	129	127	117	117	109	117	137	137	125	146	120	106	137	113	105	129
80134 PARKER	163	187	188	195	179	176	169	167	156	175	198	195	177	199	167	146	196	163	144	183
80135 SEDALIA	151	182	197	185	178	180	165	163	153	166	194	190	176	200	168	149	193	159	149	181
80136 STRASBURG	97	96	86	95	98	101	90	96	90	90	111	114	89	112	91	88	107	94	94	115
80137 WATKINS	113	112	96	109	111	115	105	110	104	107	129	128	102	125	104	102	125	109	106	128
80138 PARKER	147	169	172	176	162	159	154	151	141	158	180	177	161	181	151	133	179	148	131	166
80202 DENVER	121	113	167	120	112	127	133	123	137	130	171	146	133	171	131	137	167	132	126	136
80203 DENVER	60	51	74	58	50	56	67	59	66	64	84	75	63	81	62	62	82	66	55	66
80204 DENVER	65	56	61	55	54	59	64	63	67	66	83	72	60	78	60	64	82	67	61	68
80205 DENVER	64	58	65	58	57	63	65	63	67	65	84	73	64	81	63	66	82	66	63	69
80206 DENVER	120	114	181	126	110	122	135	122	135	134	171	150	136	173	130	131	169	131	114	135
80207 DENVER	92	94	108	92	92	101	95	94	97	96	121	106	98	120	96	98	119	95	94	105
80208 DENVER	51	31	39	35	30	37	60	44	58	51	73	61	49	65	48	51	68	54	41	50
80209 DENVER	143	144	214	155	141	154	158	147	158	158	199	175	162	201	157	156	196	154	142	164
80210 DENVER	108	115	143	120	114	119	121	115	116	119	147	138	122	147	119	112	144	118	106	126
80211 DENVER	72	70	77	69	68	72	74	73	75	76	94	84	73	92	72	72	93	76	69	79
80212 DENVER	74	80	97	82	79	83	82	79	79	81	99	94	83	101	82	77	98	80	74	87
80214 DENVER	71	69	80	73	68	72	75	72	73	75	93	86	74	90	72	70	90	75	67	79
80215 DENVER	96	104	119	106	103	109	104	102	100	103	126	119	106	126	104	98	124	103	96	111
80216 DENVER	67	58	52	55	56	59	61	64	64	66	80	70	57	74	58	61	80	66	60	68
80218 DENVER	86	78	117	87	76	84	96	86	96	94	121	107	94	119	91	91	118	94	80	96
80219 DENVER	74	70	68	67	68	72	72	74	73	75	92	81	69	88	69	71	91	75	70	79
80220 DENVER	110	111	144	118	109	116	122	114	118	120	149	138	122	149	118	113	147	119	105	125
80221 DENVER	75	75	78	74	73	77	76	76	75	77	95	87	75	93	74	73	93	77	72	83
80222 DENVER	81	85	106	88	84	90	90	86	88	89	111	102	91	111	89	86	109	89	81	94
80223 DENVER	72	66	72	66	64	68	72	72	73	75	92	81	69	88	69	71	92	75	68	77
80224 DENVER	96	102	124	104	100	108	103	101	101	104	128	117	105	127	104	100	125	103	97	111
80226 DENVER	83	88	103	89	86	92	90	87	88	89	111	102	91	111	89	86	109	89	83	96
80227 DENVER	101	101	115	106	98	103	105	102	102	106	129	120	105	126	102	98	127	105	93	112
80228 DENVER	119	125	140	132	122	126	126	122	120	127	152	144	128	150	123	114	149	124	110	135
80229 DENVER	80	78	79	80	76	80	79	78	78	80	98	93	78	96	77	75	95	80	74	88
80230 DENVER	138	134	145	144	128	131	139	133	133	142	169	160	137	162	131	124	165	138	118	148
80231 DENVER	97	92	117	99	90	96	101	96	99	102	126	115	100	122	97	95	123	101	89	106
80232 DENVER	89	98	112	99	96	100	96	94	93	96	117	110	99	119	96	90	116	95	88	103
80233 DENVER	91	100	106	102	97	98	96	94	91	97	115	111	98	117	95	88	114	94	85	104
80234 DENVER	104	108	120	114	104	107	109	105	104	111	132	125	109	130	105	98	129	107	94	116
80235 DENVER	110	106	128	113	103	110	114	109	111	115	141	130	113	136	110	106	138	114	100	121
80236 DENVER	87	95	108	94	94	99	94	93	92	94	116	107	97	118	95	91	115	93	89	101
80237 DENVER	108	113	140	117	111	119	116	112	114	117	144	131	118	142	116	112	141	115	107	124
80239 DENVER	87	90	93	92	87	88	89	88	85	91	108	102	89	107	86	81	107	88	79	96
80241 DENVER	128	138	140	146	132	130	131	128	121	135	154	151	133	153	126	113	152	127	110	141
80246 DENVER	80	72	98	79	70	77	89	80	87	86	110	100	85	107	83	82	108	88	74	89
80247 DENVER	75	68	76	72	67	73	73	73	73	76	92	83	71	85	71	70	89	75	70	80
80249 DENVER	110	117	117	124	112	110	111	109	104	115	132	129	113	130	107	96	130	109	94	120
COLORADO	103	104	110	107	103	108	105	104	102	105	128	122	104	127	103	99	125	105	98	116
UNITED STATES	100	100	100	100	100	100	100	100	100	100	100	100	100	100	100	100	100	100	100	100

ZIP CODE			POPULATION			2000-2004 ANNUAL RATE		HOUSEHOLDS					FAMILIES		
#	POST OFFICE NAME	COUNTY FIPS CODE	2000	2004	2009	% Rate	State Centile	2000	2004	2009	% Annual Rate 2000-2004	2004 Average HH Size	2000	2004	% Annual Rate 2000-2004
80260	DENVER	001	28487	32223	38614	2.9	67	11418	12970	15573	3.0	2.48	7199	8049	2.7
80262	DENVER	031	45	44	44	-0.5	3	0	0	0	0.0	0.00	0	0	0.0
80301	BOULDER	013	22616	23258	24741	0.7	26	9670	10004	10698	0.8	2.27	5252	5321	0.3
80302	BOULDER	013	26557	27027	28644	0.4	21	12022	12425	13333	0.8	2.01	4134	4153	0.1
80303	BOULDER	013	23638	24471	26371	0.8	28	10822	11299	12252	1.0	2.13	4919	5031	0.5
80304	BOULDER	013	23771	25426	27734	1.6	43	10098	10862	11901	1.7	2.33	5514	5756	1.0
80305	BOULDER	013	16477	16755	17904	0.4	21	6852	7046	7581	0.7	2.37	3577	3576	0.0
80309	BOULDER	013	5604	5735	5878	0.6	25	0	0	0	0.0	0.00	0	0	0.0
80401	GOLDEN	059	38481	38746	39174	0.2	16	15550	15900	16276	0.5	2.34	9992	10115	0.3
80403	GOLDEN	047	17764	19481	21009	2.2	54	7119	7896	8599	2.5	2.46	4895	5390	2.3
80421	BAILEY	093	8170	9663	11740	4.0	79	3152	3811	4726	4.6	2.54	2363	2841	4.4
80422	BLACK HAWK	047	582	608	662	1.0	34	290	307	338	1.4	1.98	135	142	1.2
80423	BOND	037	164	172	196	1.1	35	71	75	85	1.3	2.29	42	43	0.6
80424	BRECKENRIDGE	117	7448	9032	11401	4.6	83	2997	3678	4680	4.9	2.42	1386	1680	4.6
80428	CLARK	107	692	916	1164	6.8	94	272	365	471	7.2	2.51	199	266	7.1
80430	COALMONT	057	124	129	132	0.9	31	51	54	56	1.4	2.37	36	38	1.3
80433	CONIFER	059	7979	8250	8398	0.8	27	3029	3203	3311	1.3	2.58	2402	2518	1.1
80435	DILLON	117	9848	11516	14246	3.8	76	3874	4595	5757	4.1	2.41	2030	2381	3.8
80439	EVERGREEN	059	24312	25768	26756	1.4	41	9406	10158	10698	1.8	2.52	7109	7605	1.6
80440	FAIRPLAY	093	2695	3251	3980	4.5	82	1162	1429	1786	5.0	2.23	722	881	4.8
80446	GRANBY	049	7726	9615	12805	5.3	86	3138	4005	5470	5.9	2.33	1880	2376	5.7
80447	GRAND LAKE	049	1854	2373	3210	6.0	91	857	1123	1553	6.6	2.10	573	746	6.4
80449	HARTSEL	093	159	202	254	5.8	90	75	98	126	6.5	2.06	54	70	6.3
80452	IDAHO SPRINGS	019	5809	6114	6544	1.2	37	2567	2759	3010	1.7	2.20	1540	1639	1.5
80455	JAMESTOWN	013	351	405	459	3.4	74	164	192	219	3.8	2.11	90	103	3.2
80456	JEFFERSON	093	601	733	904	4.8	85	283	352	443	5.3	2.08	195	240	5.0
80459	KREMMLING	049	2170	2632	3467	4.7	83	825	1025	1384	5.2	2.51	583	719	5.1
80461	LEADVILLE	065	7570	7998	8595	1.3	39	2867	3041	3277	1.4	2.60	1837	1933	1.2
80463	MC COY	037	115	122	140	1.4	41	49	52	60	1.4	2.35	32	33	0.7
80465	MORRISON	059	15442	15566	15720	0.2	16	5568	5755	5911	0.8	2.66	4353	4466	0.6
80466	NEDERLAND	013	3379	3422	3634	0.3	19	1481	1518	1624	0.6	2.25	873	874	0.0
80467	OAK CREEK	107	2031	2486	3042	4.9	85	855	1069	1333	5.4	2.33	535	659	5.0
80468	PARSHALL	049	375	478	642	5.9	90	141	185	257	6.6	2.48	100	131	6.6
80470	PINE	059	3561	4073	4517	3.2	72	1359	1584	1783	3.7	2.57	1042	1205	3.5
80479	TOPONAS	107	789	897	1057	3.1	71	326	380	458	3.7	2.36	216	251	3.6
80480	WALDEN	057	1453	1481	1507	0.5	23	610	636	660	1.0	2.31	407	421	0.8
80481	WARD	013	899	1039	1171	3.5	75	380	444	503	3.7	2.33	211	241	3.7
80487	STEAMBOAT SPRINGS	107	13873	15743	18538	3.0	70	5632	6510	7805	3.5	2.38	3198	3656	3.2
80498	SILVERTHORNE	117	6569	7899	9918	4.4	82	2363	2864	3635	4.6	2.62	1432	1721	4.4
80501	LONGMONT	013	55498	59532	65191	1.7	44	20699	22268	24459	1.7	2.65	14145	14992	1.4
80503	LONGMONT	013	25380	29323	33281	3.5	75	9635	11307	12953	3.8	2.57	7097	8191	3.4
80504	LONGMONT	123	10335	15828	22759	10.6	97	3512	5439	7892	10.8	2.90	2906	4424	10.4
80510	ALLENSPARK	013	187	198	213	1.4	39	89	96	104	1.8	2.01	53	56	1.3
80512	BELLVUE	069	2207	2389	2633	1.9	47	928	1030	1156	2.5	2.32	621	677	2.1
80513	BERTHOUD	069	9889	10885	12246	2.3	56	3566	3992	4553	2.7	2.72	2819	3122	2.4
80514	DACONO	123	2992	3775	5108	5.6	89	1080	1371	1859	5.8	2.75	751	935	5.3
80515	DRAKE	069	958	1045	1156	2.1	51	443	496	559	2.7	2.07	319	351	2.3
80516	ERIE	123	8377	11898	15830	8.6	95	3000	4275	5724	8.7	2.78	2362	3334	8.5
80517	ESTES PARK	069	9557	10473	11615	2.2	54	4371	4909	5543	2.8	2.11	2814	3090	2.2
80521	FORT COLLINS	069	28943	30467	33425	1.2	37	11779	12584	14001	1.6	2.37	5093	5275	0.8
80523	FORT COLLINS	069	4408	4414	4439	0.0	13	227	236	260	0.9	1.25	45	42	-1.6
80524	FORT COLLINS	069	27219	29876	33821	2.2	55	11082	12289	14061	2.5	2.39	6777	7490	2.4
80525	FORT COLLINS	069	42859	48740	55782	3.1	71	16949	19389	22387	3.2	2.48	10896	12405	3.1
80526	FORT COLLINS	069	41357	45746	51275	2.4	59	15742	17698	20102	2.8	2.57	10248	11350	2.4
80528	FORT COLLINS	069	6116	8926	11399	9.3	96	2229	3347	4355	10.0	2.67	1687	2474	9.4
80530	FREDERICK	123	1942	3092	4681	11.6	98	648	1064	1633	12.4	2.91	509	819	11.8
80534	JOHNSTOWN	123	5092	6681	9205	6.6	93	1783	2353	3251	6.7	2.84	1413	1838	6.4
80535	LAPORTE	069	2372	2478	2685	1.0	34	928	991	1090	1.6	2.50	646	675	1.0
80536	LIVERMORE	069	1425	1559	1724	2.1	53	601	674	759	2.7	2.26	454	501	2.3
80537	LOVELAND	069	33406	36871	41331	2.4	58	12860	14453	16444	2.8	2.52	9146	10163	2.5
80538	LOVELAND	069	34879	39239	44743	2.8	66	13219	15142	17511	3.3	2.57	9947	11298	3.0
80540	LYONS	013	4297	4472	4788	0.9	31	1802	1908	2066	1.4	2.34	1270	1321	0.9
80542	MEAD	123	2151	2979	4204	8.0	95	698	977	1385	8.2	3.05	579	801	7.9
80543	MILLIKEN	123	3317	4862	7029	9.4	97	1014	1494	2167	9.6	3.25	833	1213	9.3
80545	RED FEATHER LAKES	069	827	905	1002	2.1	53	385	432	487	2.8	2.05	265	291	2.2
80549	WELLINGTON	069	4682	5088	5647	2.0	49	1673	1849	2077	2.4	2.75	1274	1387	2.0
80550	WINDSOR	123	11815	15805	21871	7.1	94	4234	5751	8029	7.5	2.72	3228	4326	7.1
80601	BRIGHTON	001	22061	28310	36187	6.0	92	7147	9260	11931	6.3	2.92	5381	6908	6.1
80602	BRIGHTON	001	6203	9960	14043	11.8	98	2069	3334	4712	11.9	2.99	1755	2801	11.6
80603	BRIGHTON	001	5738	8381	11900	9.3	97	1884	2783	3967	9.6	2.99	1547	2262	9.4
80610	AULT	123	2517	3003	3969	4.2	81	937	1128	1498	4.5	2.66	690	819	4.1
80611	BRIGGSDALE	123	453	549	729	4.6	83	170	209	279	5.0	2.60	124	149	4.4
80612	CARR	123	244	315	420	6.2	92	95	124	168	6.5	2.54	72	93	6.2
80615	EATON	123	5205	7401	10566	8.6	96	1872	2694	3871	8.9	2.73	1434	2035	8.6
80620	EVANS	123	9557	14302	20987	10.0	97	3265	4909	7214	10.1	2.91	2381	3493	9.4
80621	FORT LUPTON	123	12240	15301	20730	5.4	87	3835	4829	6570	5.6	3.15	3056	3798	5.3
80624	GILL	123	833	1060	1440	5.8	90	256	328	446	6.0	3.23	200	253	5.7
80631	GREELEY	123	43469	49954	64582	3.3	73	15375	17643	22937	3.3	2.72	9210	10470	3.1
80634	GREELEY	123	40790	52686	72549	6.2	92	15579	20273	28016	6.4	2.58	11020	14135	6.0
80639	GREELEY	123	2373	2382	2418	0.1	14	57	61	76	1.6	2.44	9	9	0.0
80640	HENDERSON	001	2078	4772	7773	21.6	100	680	1616	2662	22.6	2.93	545	1294	22.6
80642	HUDSON	123	2776	3396	4515	4.9	85	916	1126	1501	5.0	3.02	730	887	4.7
80643	KEENESBURG	123	2147	2537	3316	4.0	79	742	884	1161	4.2	2.86	582	685	3.9
80644	KERSEY	123	2963	3788	5162	6.0	91	980	1257	1717	6.0	3.01	805	1024	5.8
80645	LA SALLE	123	3776	4383	5703	3.6	75	1294	1520	1994	3.9	2.85	1011	1173	3.6
80648	NUNN	123	776	1050	1465	7.4	94	272	371	519	7.6	2.83	205	274	7.1
80649	ORCHARD	087	332	362	400	2.1	51	136	149	165	2.2	2.43	100	108	1.8
80650	PIERCE	123	1337	1606	2130	4.4	82	476	582	778	4.8	2.76	378	454	4.4
80651	PLATTEVILLE	123	5154	6528	8861	5.7	90	1677	2150	2935	6.0	3.03	1306	1649	5.6
80652	ROGGEN	123	544	661	880	4.7	84	195	239	319	4.9	2.77	156	189	4.6
80653	WELDONA	087	548	597	645	2.0	50	225	246	266	2.1	2.43	169	184	2.0
80654	WIGGINS	087	2142	2381	2607	2.5	62	708	789	863	2.6	3.02	562	623	2.5
80701	FORT MORGAN	087	15425	16182	17133	1.1	35	5433	5679	5989	1.1	2.81	3960	4111	0.9
80705	LOG LANE VILLAGE	087	1122	1163	1223	0.9	29	332	346	363	1.0	3.36	271	281	0.9
80720	AKRON	121	2748	2753	2780	0.0	13	1122	1138	1163	0.3	2.38	764	767	0.1
	COLORADO					2.4					2.6	2.52			2.5
	UNITED STATES					1.2					1.3	2.58			1.1

ZIP CODE #	POST OFFICE NAME	RACE (%) White 2000	White 2004	Black 2000	Black 2004	Asian/Pacific 2000	Asian/Pacific 2004	% Hispanic Origin 2000	% Hispanic Origin 2004	2004 AGE DISTRIBUTION (%) 0-4	5-9	10-14	15-19	20-24	25-44	45-64	65-84	85+	18+	MEDIAN AGE 2004	% 2004 Males	% 2004 Females
80260	DENVER	80.4	78.1	1.8	2.0	4.2	4.6	23.5	27.0	8.5	7.2	7.1	6.9	8.8	31.0	20.1	9.7	0.8	73.2	31.8	49.0	51.0
80262	DENVER	71.1	68.2	8.9	9.1	11.1	13.6	11.1	13.6	4.6	0.0	0.0	0.0	11.4	54.6	20.5	6.8	2.3	95.5	33.8	40.9	59.1
80301	BOULDER	88.0	86.8	1.5	1.6	3.8	4.3	8.7	9.8	5.3	5.5	6.3	6.4	7.3	33.6	27.3	7.1	1.1	79.0	36.5	50.7	49.3
80302	BOULDER	92.2	91.3	0.9	0.9	2.7	3.1	4.3	5.1	2.7	2.5	2.6	10.3	28.7	27.7	18.5	5.8	1.3	90.5	26.6	51.6	48.4
80303	BOULDER	87.4	86.2	1.4	1.5	4.9	5.5	8.7	9.9	3.8	3.6	4.4	6.3	17.8	29.6	22.2	10.0	2.3	85.3	32.5	51.7	48.3
80304	BOULDER	90.5	89.3	0.8	0.8	1.9	2.2	10.0	11.4	5.1	5.4	6.0	5.9	7.4	33.7	28.6	6.9	1.0	79.8	36.8	50.1	49.9
80305	BOULDER	91.6	90.7	0.9	0.9	3.6	4.1	4.5	5.1	3.6	3.7	4.8	5.6	13.4	33.1	25.4	9.3	1.0	84.9	34.9	52.8	47.2
80309	BOULDER	80.9	79.0	2.2	2.3	10.9	12.3	6.2	7.1	2.8	1.1	0.6	60.4	21.8	12.1	1.0	0.1	0.0	94.8	18.8	50.5	49.5
80401	GOLDEN	91.9	91.0	0.9	0.9	2.5	2.9	6.3	7.1	5.1	5.4	6.2	7.8	7.5	27.2	29.6	10.4	0.9	79.5	39.4	52.1	47.9
80403	GOLDEN	94.6	94.0	0.3	0.3	1.4	1.7	4.4	5.1	5.8	6.5	6.6	5.8	4.5	30.8	32.4	7.1	0.6	77.4	40.3	52.2	47.8
80421	BAILEY	95.4	95.0	0.4	0.4	0.5	0.6	4.3	4.9	5.9	7.4	7.9	6.3	3.5	29.7	32.9	6.1	0.3	74.7	40.3	51.2	48.9
80422	BLACK HAWK	91.1	90.6	0.9	0.8	1.7	2.0	8.3	9.1	4.4	4.1	4.3	6.3	6.3	31.7	35.0	7.6	0.3	83.7	41.7	53.5	46.6
80423	BOND	84.2	83.1	0.6	0.6	0.0	0.0	12.8	14.0	5.2	6.4	4.7	6.4	6.4	37.2	25.6	7.6	0.6	79.7	38.5	59.3	40.7
80424	BRECKENRIDGE	95.5	95.2	0.2	0.2	0.7	0.8	4.7	5.3	4.5	3.6	3.7	4.3	11.0	48.9	21.1	3.0	0.1	86.0	31.7	59.2	40.9
80428	CLARK	98.8	98.8	0.1	0.1	0.1	0.1	1.3	1.4	5.4	5.7	6.3	6.9	4.0	32.0	34.8	4.6	0.3	77.1	39.6	51.3	48.7
80430	COALMONT	96.0	96.1	0.0	0.0	0.0	0.0	7.3	6.2	6.2	6.2	7.0	6.2	3.9	24.0	32.6	12.4	1.6	76.0	43.0	51.2	48.8
80433	CONIFER	96.2	95.9	0.3	0.4	0.7	0.8	2.7	3.2	5.5	6.6	7.5	6.6	3.2	28.6	36.3	5.6	0.3	76.0	41.6	51.4	48.6
80435	DILLON	92.2	91.5	0.7	0.7	0.9	1.1	10.2	11.5	5.0	4.4	4.4	5.4	11.1	43.6	21.3	4.7	0.2	83.6	32.4	57.7	42.3
80439	EVERGREEN	97.2	96.9	0.3	0.3	0.6	0.7	2.3	2.7	5.3	6.6	7.6	6.5	3.7	24.5	36.3	8.8	0.9	76.2	43.0	50.0	50.0
80440	FAIRPLAY	94.3	94.0	0.8	0.9	0.3	0.3	4.3	4.9	5.6	6.3	5.4	4.0	3.5	38.4	31.0	5.5	0.2	80.0	39.6	53.9	46.1
80446	GRANBY	95.6	95.1	0.7	0.7	0.9	1.1	3.2	3.7	5.1	5.2	5.3	5.5	6.8	36.5	28.2	7.2	0.3	80.9	36.9	52.9	47.1
80447	GRAND LAKE	97.3	97.1	0.3	0.4	0.9	1.0	2.5	2.8	4.3	4.3	5.0	5.1	3.4	25.2	40.3	11.6	0.8	83.3	46.2	52.8	47.2
80449	HARTSEL	95.6	95.5	0.0	0.0	0.0	0.0	4.4	4.0	3.0	4.0	3.0	3.5	2.5	16.3	46.0	21.3	0.5	87.1	53.2	53.5	46.5
80452	IDAHO SPRINGS	95.7	95.3	0.3	0.3	0.5	0.5	4.8	5.4	5.2	5.6	6.0	6.5	6.1	28.8	33.4	7.8	0.7	79.2	40.7	52.5	47.5
80455	JAMESTOWN	96.0	96.1	0.3	0.3	0.9	1.0	2.0	2.2	4.9	5.2	6.2	7.7	6.2	27.7	36.3	5.7	0.3	79.3	41.3	52.4	47.7
80456	JEFFERSON	93.8	93.3	0.8	1.0	0.5	0.6	6.7	7.5	3.0	4.4	5.5	5.6	1.6	25.5	42.2	11.9	0.4	83.4	47.1	51.3	48.7
80459	KREMMLING	91.2	90.2	0.1	0.0	0.4	0.5	10.5	11.8	8.7	8.3	7.0	6.3	6.3	30.7	25.5	6.0	1.2	71.9	34.8	51.6	48.4
80461	LEADVILLE	77.7	76.0	0.2	0.2	0.4	0.4	36.2	39.3	8.0	7.1	6.9	7.3	9.7	31.9	21.9	6.5	0.8	74.0	31.0	53.5	46.5
80463	MC COY	83.5	82.0	0.0	0.0	0.0	0.0	20.0	23.0	7.4	7.4	5.7	6.6	6.6	36.9	22.1	6.6	0.8	75.4	35.6	56.6	43.4
80465	MORRISON	94.6	94.0	0.6	0.6	1.1	1.2	5.8	6.7	5.9	6.9	7.4	7.0	5.1	28.3	32.2	6.2	0.9	75.0	39.5	51.2	48.8
80466	NEDERLAND	96.4	96.1	0.3	0.3	0.8	0.9	2.0	2.3	5.2	5.2	5.7	5.6	5.2	36.6	31.0	5.1	0.5	80.5	38.3	52.1	47.9
80467	OAK CREEK	95.5	95.3	0.1	0.1	0.6	0.8	3.6	3.9	6.2	6.7	6.2	6.0	5.1	32.5	30.8	5.9	0.6	77.1	37.7	52.5	47.5
80468	PARSHALL	96.5	96.2	0.0	0.0	0.0	0.0	3.5	4.0	6.9	6.9	6.3	6.5	4.6	29.7	29.9	8.8	0.4	75.9	39.6	54.4	45.6
80470	PINE	96.1	95.8	0.3	0.3	0.7	0.8	3.2	3.7	5.2	6.4	7.5	6.5	3.1	27.2	36.8	7.0	0.4	76.5	42.5	51.9	48.1
80479	TOPONAS	96.8	96.7	0.1	0.1	0.1	0.1	3.9	4.5	5.2	6.0	7.7	6.9	3.7	27.9	32.9	8.9	0.8	76.1	40.3	52.6	47.4
80480	WALDEN	96.2	96.2	0.3	0.3	0.1	0.1	6.5	6.7	5.5	6.4	6.8	7.7	4.2	24.2	31.1	12.9	1.4	75.9	42.2	50.4	49.6
80481	WARD	96.3	96.0	0.4	0.5	0.8	0.9	1.9	2.1	4.3	4.6	5.9	6.8	5.9	27.8	37.4	6.7	0.5	81.2	42.4	52.7	47.3
80487	STEAMBOAT SPRINGS	97.1	96.9	0.1	0.2	0.5	0.6	2.8	3.2	4.8	5.0	5.8	6.2	7.8	36.4	28.8	4.6	0.4	80.8	35.5	54.5	45.5
80498	SILVERTHORNE	87.3	86.1	1.2	1.2	1.2	1.4	14.7	16.4	6.3	5.1	5.0	5.4	10.0	42.9	21.8	3.5	0.1	80.7	31.5	56.9	43.1
80501	LONGMONT	82.8	81.1	0.5	0.6	1.5	1.8	22.6	24.9	8.1	7.6	7.4	6.8	7.1	31.5	22.4	7.7	1.5	72.8	33.5	49.5	50.6
80503	LONGMONT	93.1	92.2	0.5	0.5	2.2	2.7	5.5	6.3	6.0	6.8	7.9	7.0	5.0	26.7	31.3	8.3	0.9	74.7	40.1	49.7	50.3
80504	LONGMONT	89.7	88.0	0.2	0.2	1.3	1.5	14.2	16.6	7.9	8.2	7.9	6.8	5.3	29.2	27.6	6.6	0.4	71.7	36.1	50.6	49.4
80510	ALLENSPARK	96.3	96.0	0.5	0.5	0.5	1.0	1.6	2.0	3.0	3.0	4.0	3.5	3.5	27.3	42.9	11.6	1.0	87.4	47.5	53.0	47.0
80512	BELLVUE	94.9	94.6	0.3	0.3	0.5	0.6	3.4	3.9	4.0	5.1	6.0	5.4	3.9	29.1	37.5	8.4	0.6	81.0	43.4	52.6	47.4
80513	BERTHOUD	94.5	93.9	0.2	0.2	0.6	0.7	6.4	7.2	5.7	6.8	9.1	8.9	3.9	28.5	29.8	6.7	0.7	72.5	38.7	50.7	49.4
80514	DACONO	77.2	74.8	0.3	0.4	1.0	1.2	32.2	36.2	8.1	7.7	8.2	6.5	6.9	30.9	22.3	8.6	0.9	71.8	33.5	49.8	50.2
80515	DRAKE	97.6	97.3	0.2	0.3	0.2	0.3	2.2	2.6	3.0	3.9	5.7	6.7	3.1	27.1	40.2	9.1	1.2	83.7	45.2	51.2	48.8
80516	ERIE	90.7	89.2	0.4	0.5	1.9	2.2	10.2	12.3	9.1	9.0	7.3	5.6	4.8	33.2	24.7	5.8	0.5	71.0	35.7	50.8	49.3
80517	ESTES PARK	96.2	95.8	0.3	0.3	0.7	0.8	3.9	4.4	3.6	4.2	4.8	5.0	3.7	22.8	35.4	18.7	1.8	84.5	48.3	49.0	51.0
80521	FORT COLLINS	87.8	86.4	1.1	1.2	2.8	3.3	11.5	12.9	5.1	4.3	4.3	8.8	23.9	32.2	14.7	6.0	0.8	83.5	26.4	51.4	48.6
80523	FORT COLLINS	87.6	86.3	2.7	2.9	3.5	4.0	7.1	8.0	0.3	0.3	0.2	80.6	14.9	3.4	0.4	0.1	0.0	98.9	18.1	46.2	53.8
80524	FORT COLLINS	87.5	86.1	0.5	0.6	1.0	1.1	14.4	16.4	6.1	5.9	6.2	6.4	8.4	29.8	25.3	10.5	1.5	78.1	35.8	50.4	49.6
80525	FORT COLLINS	91.6	90.8	0.8	0.9	2.4	2.8	6.7	7.5	6.5	6.6	7.0	6.8	7.4	31.3	24.6	8.4	1.5	75.8	34.6	49.5	50.5
80526	FORT COLLINS	91.4	90.6	0.9	0.9	2.3	2.5	7.1	8.0	6.6	6.6	7.4	7.6	9.9	32.9	22.6	5.5	0.9	75.2	31.2	49.8	50.2
80528	FORT COLLINS	90.5	89.2	0.6	0.7	2.9	3.5	6.5	7.5	9.3	9.0	7.7	5.8	4.5	37.1	22.4	4.1	0.3	70.4	33.3	50.4	49.6
80530	FREDERICK	83.9	82.2	0.7	1.0	0.5	0.5	27.2	30.1	9.2	8.7	8.5	7.2	6.0	33.6	20.1	6.2	0.7	69.2	31.5	49.0	51.0
80534	JOHNSTOWN	86.6	84.5	0.2	0.2	0.3	0.4	22.6	26.2	9.0	8.5	8.1	6.0	5.5	32.4	22.7	7.1	0.8	70.5	32.9	50.2	49.8
80535	LAPORTE	92.8	92.2	0.2	0.2	0.4	0.5	7.5	8.4	5.6	6.3	7.1	7.0	6.0	28.6	31.4	7.6	0.5	76.7	39.0	50.4	49.6
80536	LIVERMORE	96.8	96.6	0.1	0.1	0.4	0.5	2.1	2.4	4.0	4.8	5.2	5.0	2.7	24.3	38.7	14.6	0.7	82.4	46.9	50.0	50.0
80537	LOVELAND	92.8	92.0	0.3	0.4	0.7	0.8	8.9	10.1	6.7	6.7	7.2	7.0	6.4	28.6	26.2	9.5	1.8	75.0	37.3	49.4	50.6
80538	LOVELAND	93.9	93.3	0.3	0.4	0.9	1.0	6.9	7.7	6.8	7.1	7.5	7.1	5.5	27.2	26.4	11.0	1.5	74.1	38.1	49.2	50.8
80540	LYONS	95.4	94.8	0.3	0.3	0.7	0.9	4.6	5.3	4.2	5.0	6.3	6.3	3.6	27.7	37.8	8.5	0.7	80.5	43.5	51.0	49.0
80542	MEAD	93.4	92.5	0.1	0.1	0.6	0.7	12.0	14.1	7.9	7.9	9.1	7.3	6.1	29.7	24.9	6.6	0.7	70.6	34.6	50.8	49.2
80543	MILLIKEN	76.5	73.6	0.3	0.4	0.4	0.4	37.1	42.2	10.6	9.9	9.4	7.3	7.5	31.7	17.9	5.2	0.5	65.6	28.1	49.0	51.0
80545	RED FEATHER LAKES	96.9	96.5	0.0	0.0	0.4	0.4	1.5	1.9	2.7	2.9	3.5	4.5	1.6	17.5	44.9	21.6	1.0	88.0	53.1	48.3	51.7
80549	WELLINGTON	90.0	89.1	0.3	0.3	0.7	0.8	9.3	10.3	7.5	7.7	8.0	7.3	5.2	32.9	25.0	6.0	0.5	72.0	34.5	50.0	50.0
80550	WINDSOR	92.2	91.0	0.4	0.5	0.5	0.7	10.3	12.1	8.5	8.1	7.5	6.4	6.9	32.4	22.7	6.4	1.0	71.8	33.4	49.6	50.5
80601	BRIGHTON	77.4	75.8	1.0	1.1	1.2	1.4	37.2	40.0	8.7	7.9	7.5	6.6	7.4	31.7	20.5	8.1	1.6	71.9	32.5	51.7	48.4
80602	BRIGHTON	89.4	88.0	1.1	1.2	2.0	2.2	13.5	15.6	8.8	8.9	8.3	6.6	5.0	33.8	24.6	3.7	0.2	69.8	34.4	50.5	49.5
80603	BRIGHTON	80.5	78.3	0.8	0.8	0.8	0.9	26.7	30.5	6.9	7.0	7.8	7.2	6.7	28.8	26.6	8.5	0.5	73.9	36.2	52.6	47.4
80610	AULT	83.6	82.1	0.1	0.1	0.7	0.9	23.6	26.0	7.4	7.3	7.4	7.5	6.9	28.1	24.9	9.4	1.2	73.4	35.5	51.5	48.5
80611	BRIGGSDALE	94.3	93.4	0.2	0.4	0.4	0.4	8.2	9.8	6.2	6.7	7.7	7.7	5.1	25.5	27.5	11.8	1.8	74.3	39.8	52.3	47.7
80612	CARR	90.2	88.6	0.4	0.3	0.4	0.3	12.3	14.6	6.4	6.7	8.6	7.3	5.4	29.8	26.0	9.2	0.6	73.7	37.8	50.8	49.2
80615	EATON	90.0	88.6	0.1	0.1	0.7	0.8	15.3	17.7	7.3	7.7	8.0	7.1	5.7	25.9	26.8	10.0	1.4	72.6	37.5	49.0	51.0
80620	EVANS	70.3	68.4	0.8	0.8	0.7	0.7	41.5	45.0	10.5	9.2	8.5	7.4	8.3	32.8	16.9	5.8	0.7	67.5	28.1	50.1	49.9
80621	FORT LUPTON	73.9	72.5	0.4	0.4	0.9	1.0	40.9	43.7	8.1	8.0	8.4	8.0	7.4	29.5	22.8	7.0	0.7	70.6	32.1	52.1	47.9
80624	GILL	83.0	80.8	0.2	0.3	0.2	0.4	21.1	24.3	6.7	7.4	9.8	7.6	5.3	26.7	25.2	10.1	1.2	71.3	36.8	52.2	47.8
80631	GREELEY	73.1	70.8	0.8	0.9	1.0	1.1	42.6	46.2	8.6	7.6	7.1	8.7	13.7	29.3	16.3	7.3	1.5	72.8	27.2	50.6	49.4
80634	GREELEY	88.4	86.9	0.7	0.8	1.1	1.3	15.8	18.3	6.9	6.7	7.2	7.1	7.8	28.1	24.7	10.0	1.6	74.9	35.2	48.8	51.2
80639	GREELEY	80.3	77.9	3.2	3.6	8.5	10.0	8.0	9.4	0.1	0.1	0.1	69.6	25.9	2.0	0.5	0.8	0.9	99.5	18.6	42.3	57.7
80640	HENDERSON	82.7	81.2	0.9	0.9	1.7	1.9	24.3	27.3	8.2	8.2	6.7	6.0	5.1	32.2	25.4	7.6	0.4	73.1	35.6	52.4	47.6
80642	HUDSON	84.8	82.9	0.4	0.5	0.6	0.7	19.4	22.1	8.5	8.5	8.3	7.5	5.8	29.7	24.5	6.7	0.6	70.2	34.0	52.0	48.0
80643	KEENESBURG	88.9	87.3	0.3	0.4	0.9	1.1	11.6	13.6	7.3	8.0	8.5	7.5	4.3	29.3	24.1	9.8	1.2	71.2	36.2	51.6	48.4
80644	KERSEY	89.7	88.2	0.2	0.2	0.8	0.9	17.0	19.7	7.4	7.6	9.0	8.2	6.7	28.0	24.0	8.1	1.0	70.9	34.3	50.6	49.5
80645	LA SALLE	79.1	76.8	0.3	0.4	0.6	0.7	29.5	33.2	6.6	6.8	8.4	7.8	7.7	27.0	25.5	9.1	1.3	73.5	35.3	51.5	48.5
80648	NUNN	88.8	87.1	0.1	0.2	0.1	0.2	15.1	17.4	6.6	7.1	8.9	7.3	6.1	28.5	24.8	10.1	0.8	73.0	36.9	50.0	50.0
80649	ORCHARD	94.0	93.1	0.0	0.0	0.0	0.0	10.5	12.4	5.5	7.2	6.9	6.9	3.9	29.3	27.4	12.2	0.8	75.4	39.4	52.8	47.2
80650	PIERCE	87.9	86.6	0.0	0.0	0.6	0.8	19.2	21.7	6.6	7.1	8.5	6.7	5.7	29.4	25.9	9.3	0.8	73.5	37.1	50.3	49.8
80651	PLATTEVILLE	76.9	74.7	0.1	0.1	0.7	0.9	32.0	35.2	8.4	8.2	8.8	7.8	7.2	29.9	22.3	6.8	0.7	69.9	32.4	51.6	48.5
80652	ROGGEN	88.4	86.4	0.2	0.3	0.6	1.1	10.7	12.7	6.8	7.7	8.3	8.8	3.3	28.0	25.7	9.8	1.5	71.1	37.7	53.4	46.6
80653	WELDONA	93.4	92.5	0.4	0.3	0.0	0.2	11.1	12.6	6.4	7.4	6.9	7.0	4.4	28.0	27.3	11.9	0.8	74.4	39.2	52.1	47.9
80654	WIGGINS	87.1	85.5	0.9	1.1	0.1	0.2	18.4	20.9	8.0	8.8	9.5	7.4	5.6	27.6	24.6	7.2	1.3	69.1	34.7	51.2	48.9
80701	FORT MORGAN	77.0	75.1	0.3	0.3	0.5	0.5	34.9	38.0	9.1	8.6	8.1	7.0	7.1	27.9	20.4	10.2	1.7	69.9	32.6	50.9	49.1
80705	LOG LANE VILLAGE	79.9	78.0	0.4	0.3	0.6	0.7	36.6	40.4	9.0	8.9	8.5	7.8	7.2	27.3	21.2	9.4	0.6	68.9	31.9	51.4	48.6
80720	AKRON	95.1	95.1	0.1	0.1	0.2	0.2	8.8	9.0	6.7	6.7	7.4	6.7	5.7	22.1	25.5	16.6	2.6	74.4	41.3	50.4	49.6
	COLORADO	82.8	81.7	3.8	3.9	2.3	2.6	17.1	18.6	7.0	6.8	7.1	7.0	7.5	30.6	24.3	8.6	1.2	75.1	35.0	50.3	49.7
	UNITED STATES	75.1	73.6	12.3	12.5	3.8	4.2	12.5	14.1	6.9	6.7	7.2	7.0	7.3	28.6	23.8	10.8	1.7	75.1	36.0	49.1	50.9

ZIP CODE #	POST OFFICE NAME	2004 Per Capita Income	2004 HH Income Base	2004 HOUSEHOLD INCOME DISTRIBUTION (%) Less than $25,000	$25,000 to $49,999	$50,000 to $99,999	$100,000 to $149,999	$150,000 or More	MEDIAN HOUSEHOLD INCOME 2004	2009	2004 National Centile	2004 State Centile	2004 Home Value Base	2004 HOME VALUE DISTRIBUTION (%) Less than $50,000	$50,000 to $89,999	$90,000 to $174,999	$175,000 to $399,999	$400,000 or More	2004 Median Home Value
80260	DENVER	20276	12970	22.7	37.7	32.5	5.5	1.5	42599	49692	55	46	8510	37.8	19.9	20.4	21.9	0.1	71862
80262	DENVER	359	0	0.0	0.0	0.0	0.0	0.0	0	0	0	0	0	0.0	0.0	0.0	0.0	0.0	0
80301	BOULDER	39337	10004	13.8	24.7	31.0	17.8	12.8	65272	80631	89	83	6690	8.0	1.8	12.3	46.2	31.7	303777
80302	BOULDER	33522	12425	31.6	25.7	22.5	10.1	10.1	40732	50660	49	38	4598	0.8	0.1	4.7	33.5	60.9	461642
80303	BOULDER	35159	11299	26.0	23.1	27.1	13.4	10.5	51180	63598	74	65	5517	2.2	0.6	8.6	49.8	38.9	353457
80304	BOULDER	44725	10862	13.7	22.5	30.4	17.4	16.0	70353	87092	91	88	7052	10.6	1.6	6.6	30.0	51.3	408106
80305	BOULDER	36833	7046	13.9	18.7	35.8	19.5	12.2	74841	92039	93	90	4397	0.7	0.0	2.1	66.4	30.9	339634
80309	BOULDER	12083	0	0.0	0.0	0.0	0.0	0.0	0	0	0	0	0	0.0	0.0	0.0	0.0	0.0	0
80401	GOLDEN	41173	15900	15.8	22.3	30.2	15.5	16.3	66216	78515	89	85	11466	6.7	3.5	11.8	49.9	28.2	271008
80403	GOLDEN	38950	7896	10.5	18.0	37.6	21.2	12.9	77809	89967	94	91	6565	0.9	0.7	13.2	61.6	23.6	278923
80421	BAILEY	28795	3811	11.2	23.4	45.6	14.7	5.1	62749	70887	87	82	3427	1.7	2.8	17.5	65.7	12.3	237921
80422	BLACK HAWK	27940	307	23.8	37.1	28.0	7.2	3.9	40626	48053	48	38	177	4.5	5.1	31.6	54.2	4.5	201875
80423	BOND	25642	75	10.7	44.0	28.0	17.3	0.0	44041	50521	59	50	48	0.0	0.0	29.2	25.0	45.8	371429
80424	BRECKENRIDGE	36796	3678	11.9	27.2	33.4	16.2	11.5	61834	71414	86	80	2200	5.0	0.4	7.6	33.3	53.8	423714
80428	CLARK	32590	365	4.4	29.6	41.4	14.0	10.7	65436	75677	89	83	315	2.9	1.6	9.2	32.1	54.3	432143
80430	COALMONT	20235	54	25.9	38.9	27.8	3.7	3.7	38196	46550	40	29	35	5.7	5.7	42.9	37.1	8.6	162500
80433	CONIFER	43107	3203	5.7	13.2	39.5	26.8	14.7	87167	102135	97	96	2952	0.0	0.1	5.8	72.4	21.7	311052
80435	DILLON	33516	4595	12.0	23.1	39.2	16.1	9.6	65083	75477	89	83	2704	4.9	4.8	16.6	39.1	34.6	321321
80439	EVERGREEN	49030	10158	9.4	16.4	29.9	22.1	22.3	89062	105160	97	96	8815	0.1	0.4	6.2	52.0	41.2	360364
80440	FAIRPLAY	29080	1429	15.1	31.4	39.3	9.6	4.8	53271	59078	77	69	1186	7.9	3.7	23.8	60.3	4.3	203901
80446	GRANBY	30597	4005	15.4	28.9	36.6	11.7	7.5	54612	62510	79	72	2840	4.5	3.4	16.9	48.7	26.6	267637
80447	GRAND LAKE	37369	1123	15.1	30.4	36.9	7.9	9.8	53410	61119	78	71	860	2.4	0.6	11.6	54.5	30.8	298276
80449	HARTSEL	29770	98	18.4	44.9	23.5	6.1	7.1	40550	45000	48	37	88	2.3	12.5	26.1	52.3	6.8	200000
80452	IDAHO SPRINGS	28333	2759	19.1	30.2	36.1	10.2	4.4	50510	59301	73	63	2006	10.8	6.9	23.6	52.3	6.4	195423
80455	JAMESTOWN	39717	192	14.6	16.7	42.2	17.2	9.4	69357	90937	91	87	136	0.0	0.7	14.7	59.6	25.0	308108
80456	JEFFERSON	27453	352	23.9	27.8	36.9	6.8	4.6	47744	54894	68	57	315	7.9	11.1	29.2	47.6	4.1	178618
80459	KREMMLING	23961	1025	19.3	30.8	39.5	8.9	1.5	49877	55505	72	61	801	15.5	6.6	27.6	44.1	6.2	175694
80461	LEADVILLE	21622	3041	23.8	36.7	29.8	6.3	3.4	42409	46824	54	44	1944	13.7	14.6	43.0	26.9	1.9	133712
80463	MC COY	26299	52	9.6	40.4	34.6	13.5	1.9	50000	55719	72	62	35	17.1	14.3	20.0	20.0	28.6	170833
80465	MORRISON	39609	5755	7.3	12.5	44.9	21.2	14.2	81707	95214	95	94	5209	0.1	0.4	10.8	65.6	23.1	243720
80466	NEDERLAND	39304	1518	14.2	16.2	38.5	17.7	13.5	72129	88871	92	89	1069	0.9	1.0	8.0	55.5	34.6	334462
80467	OAK CREEK	28313	1069	18.2	30.5	35.4	11.2	4.7	50985	57905	74	65	836	8.7	7.5	42.3	19.9	21.5	156053
80468	PARSHALL	27919	185	15.1	30.8	38.4	11.4	4.3	53489	60222	78	71	155	5.8	3.9	10.3	60.0	20.0	254630
80470	PINE	37407	1584	7.3	16.7	40.3	25.2	10.5	82491	96414	96	94	1438	0.0	0.8	6.8	71.4	21.1	283214
80479	TOPONAS	28184	380	21.1	41.3	28.7	5.0	4.0	41329	46354	51	41	296	6.4	4.1	38.5	20.3	30.7	178125
80480	WALDEN	20077	636	31.8	35.7	25.9	4.1	2.5	35181	39401	28	20	442	23.5	16.1	38.7	17.2	4.5	106322
80481	WARD	32265	444	17.8	18.2	40.1	17.6	6.3	62683	81651	87	82	324	0.0	1.5	13.6	63.0	21.9	295455
80487	STEAMBOAT SPRINGS	37403	6510	14.2	20.3	40.1	15.5	10.0	65792	76958	89	84	4483	7.7	2.7	10.5	37.7	41.4	354519
80498	SILVERTHORNE	35316	2864	11.1	20.3	41.8	16.4	10.4	67966	80379	90	85	1885	1.3	0.3	13.3	50.8	34.4	332609
80501	LONGMONT	24783	22268	17.7	26.9	38.4	13.0	4.0	54935	68230	80	73	14673	5.5	1.1	20.5	68.6	4.3	204719
80503	LONGMONT	42964	11307	9.9	17.7	32.8	21.3	18.4	83433	100965	96	95	9090	0.6	0.5	4.3	59.5	35.1	334619
80504	LONGMONT	35474	5439	11.1	19.3	36.6	16.7	16.3	75457	83883	93	90	4833	6.7	5.3	11.2	42.6	34.2	287181
80510	ALLENSPARK	32295	96	24.0	25.0	31.3	16.7	3.1	50935	59072	74	64	78	0.0	2.6	10.3	57.7	29.5	300000
80512	BELLVUE	35482	1030	12.0	22.8	42.7	15.3	7.1	61940	71235	86	81	872	0.9	2.0	17.1	54.2	25.8	270000
80513	BERTHOUD	32526	3992	9.9	22.9	40.3	17.4	9.5	68246	78234	90	86	3452	4.9	2.5	11.7	60.5	20.5	272883
80514	DACONO	18370	1371	18.6	40.0	35.3	5.5	0.6	45290	53785	62	53	1096	3.2	15.2	64.9	16.2	0.6	124829
80515	DRAKE	30459	496	16.9	31.3	41.1	7.5	3.2	50921	59916	74	64	413	1.5	1.5	25.7	54.7	16.7	231322
80516	ERIE	36275	4275	8.1	15.4	39.4	23.4	13.7	82997	99276	96	95	3779	1.6	0.8	7.2	60.0	30.4	327702
80517	ESTES PARK	36481	4909	16.4	28.4	36.0	11.5	7.7	54959	62300	80	73	3392	0.3	0.4	10.0	66.3	22.9	302236
80521	FORT COLLINS	19888	12584	36.6	30.2	24.5	6.2	2.5	35665	42344	30	22	5295	4.9	1.2	38.0	51.1	4.8	181829
80523	FORT COLLINS	16521	236	73.3	18.6	6.4	1.7	0.0	15227	16480	1	1	9	0.0	0.0	44.4	55.6	0.0	181250
80524	FORT COLLINS	27077	12289	23.1	28.8	30.7	10.7	6.7	48030	56630	68	58	8543	16.2	6.6	19.3	44.6	13.3	194593
80525	FORT COLLINS	31966	19389	16.6	23.2	36.1	14.1	9.9	61287	71855	86	80	13581	5.2	2.2	16.8	66.3	9.5	229656
80526	FORT COLLINS	28547	17698	15.7	25.0	37.8	15.1	6.5	60169	68656	85	78	12358	4.5	1.2	20.3	66.3	7.7	209881
80528	FORT COLLINS	36336	3347	7.4	14.6	42.9	21.4	13.6	80426	93967	95	93	2956	0.3	2.5	20.2	56.9	20.2	274938
80530	FREDERICK	21083	1064	20.1	26.8	40.3	10.9	1.9	52711	59889	76	67	903	0.3	1.7	45.3	52.3	0.4	178460
80534	JOHNSTOWN	24455	2353	18.0	25.5	40.2	11.3	5.1	56737	62967	81	74	1950	4.0	1.4	25.1	59.3	10.3	212865
80535	LAPORTE	25012	991	14.2	28.5	45.2	11.2	0.9	56265	64119	81	74	759	3.8	5.3	26.8	53.8	10.4	200850
80536	LIVERMORE	32416	674	13.8	25.1	41.7	12.2	7.3	60000	68824	84	77	611	2.1	2.8	12.9	61.2	21.0	244149
80537	LOVELAND	26785	14453	18.1	27.9	37.3	11.1	5.5	53842	62219	78	71	10711	2.5	2.3	30.1	54.8	10.4	198336
80538	LOVELAND	27890	15142	16.4	24.6	39.0	14.4	5.7	60044	68411	84	78	11993	4.8	1.4	18.0	67.9	7.8	212861
80540	LYONS	36336	1908	12.3	24.0	35.5	17.0	11.3	65010	78918	89	82	1622	2.7	2.1	8.5	55.6	31.1	303762
80542	MEAD	35736	977	8.7	16.5	40.4	18.8	15.6	77980	89575	94	92	855	1.1	6.6	15.6	37.2	39.7	310606
80543	MILLIKEN	18766	1494	17.5	32.5	38.8	7.8	3.4	49958	56584	72	62	1221	3.0	2.2	45.0	44.3	5.6	174846
80545	RED FEATHER LAKES	28123	432	26.2	30.3	30.6	8.3	4.6	45153	51403	62	52	380	0.5	1.3	26.1	54.2	17.9	227857
80549	WELLINGTON	25144	1849	12.7	27.6	46.4	9.5	3.9	57667	65879	82	76	1570	1.1	4.7	35.4	44.1	14.7	193583
80550	WINDSOR	27962	5751	15.5	23.4	41.9	14.1	5.2	60829	68441	85	79	4781	1.0	0.7	21.9	66.8	9.5	212748
80601	BRIGHTON	20589	9260	17.9	30.4	37.6	10.5	3.7	51553	56787	75	66	6892	6.5	2.6	28.7	58.4	3.8	193283
80602	BRIGHTON	31929	3334	6.9	12.3	51.2	19.4	10.2	79731	89189	95	92	3106	0.2	0.1	8.5	66.4	24.8	261538
80603	BRIGHTON	23297	2783	13.9	27.7	41.4	12.2	4.8	57660	65473	82	76	2319	7.2	8.4	29.1	42.2	13.0	196696
80610	AULT	20630	1128	28.8	30.6	30.8	7.4	2.5	40919	46279	49	39	871	11.5	7.7	40.0	31.1	9.8	156766
80611	BRIGGSDALE	19197	209	31.6	33.0	25.8	6.7	2.9	38412	41892	41	31	166	12.7	12.7	32.5	28.3	13.9	148529
80612	CARR	24425	124	22.6	28.2	36.3	8.9	4.0	49218	54224	71	61	101	5.9	13.9	26.7	38.6	14.9	185938
80615	EATON	26010	2694	20.5	29.2	34.7	10.5	5.1	50228	56369	72	62	1992	3.4	4.7	30.2	49.6	12.2	203876
80620	EVANS	17814	4909	26.0	32.7	34.6	4.3	2.5	42591	50358	55	46	3262	12.3	5.9	54.0	27.2	0.6	150307
80621	FORT LUPTON	20050	4829	21.0	29.8	34.1	10.3	4.7	49198	56409	71	60	3668	8.6	4.0	31.6	45.3	10.4	185263
80624	GILL	18585	328	27.7	23.8	34.5	11.0	3.1	48642	54389	70	59	259	8.5	12.0	23.9	40.5	15.1	204730
80631	GREELEY	15871	17643	38.1	33.3	22.3	4.4	2.0	31892	38405	18	11	9055	16.6	8.7	46.9	24.5	3.4	139484
80634	GREELEY	28031	20273	18.7	26.6	36.1	12.2	6.5	54261	62406	79	72	14992	1.5	2.9	33.0	56.1	6.4	192573
80639	GREELEY	15942	61	59.0	34.4	6.6	0.0	0.0	18702	21226	1	2	7	0.0	14.3	57.1	28.6	0.0	137500
80640	HENDERSON	30034	1616	10.8	27.6	35.8	13.4	12.4	62728	68449	87	82	1404	6.3	1.4	10.9	62.7	18.7	247671
80642	HUDSON	22456	1126	15.0	29.5	38.2	13.4	3.9	54673	62007	79	72	948	9.5	6.0	31.3	40.6	12.6	182576
80643	KEENESBURG	21875	884	21.8	29.2	35.4	9.3	4.3	49018	54491	70	60	683	4.7	6.3	27.2	49.3	12.5	198958
80644	KERSEY	19474	1257	19.3	30.3	38.8	9.4	2.2	50240	56452	72	63	1059	9.0	5.6	35.2	40.0	10.2	175573
80645	LA SALLE	20441	1520	23.6	28.6	36.8	8.6	2.4	47702	54161	68	57	1175	4.5	2.8	49.9	35.0	7.8	165894
80648	NUNN	20626	371	24.5	30.2	32.1	8.6	4.6	46240	51934	64	55	300	9.3	14.7	30.3	35.0	10.7	160227
80649	ORCHARD	18982	149	29.5	39.6	24.2	4.0	2.7	37971	43517	39	27	116	14.7	14.7	40.5	26.7	3.5	125000
80650	PIERCE	21245	582	23.7	31.1	35.1	7.2	2.9	44466	50120	60	51	489	5.7	7.0	56.0	23.1	8.2	148864
80651	PLATTEVILLE	22351	2150	20.5	26.4	39.2	9.2	4.7	52358	59332	76	67	1721	10.1	4.0	34.4	38.6	12.9	178140
80652	ROGGEN	20188	239	24.3	29.7	36.0	7.1	2.9	45228	48447	62	53	191	4.7	6.8	17.8	48.2	22.5	257292
80653	WELDONA	20398	246	28.1	39.0	25.6	4.1	3.3	39224	43358	43	33	191	12.6	13.6	38.7	28.3	6.8	130357
80654	WIGGINS	16795	789	26.4	35.5	30.0	4.6	3.6	40340	44269	47	36	622	7.4	12.1	45.7	29.7	5.1	143125
80701	FORT MORGAN	17933	5679	27.6	36.6	28.2	5.2	2.4	38618	43417	41	31	4106	10.0	13.4	51.8	22.7	2.1	124139
80705	LOG LANE VILLAGE	17302	346	26.9	33.8	30.4	4.1	4.9	41288	45980	51	41	269	16.0	21.9	37.6	22.7	1.9	105580
80720	AKRON	19910	1138	32.3	36.1	24.0	4.6	3.1	35446	40101	29	21	859	17.2	24.5	43.8	11.3	3.3	102083
	COLORADO	28803		19.1	26.9	34.1	12.5	7.5	54077	63465				4.8	4.7	28.0	49.9	12.6	203984
	UNITED STATES	25866		24.7	27.1	30.8	10.9	6.5	48124	56710				10.9	15.0	33.7	30.1	10.4	145905

#	POST OFFICE NAME	FINANCIAL SERVICES: Auto Loan	FINANCIAL SERVICES: Home Loan	FINANCIAL SERVICES: Invest-ments	FINANCIAL SERVICES: Retire-ment Plans	THE HOME: Home Improvements: Home Repair	THE HOME: Home Improvements: Lawn & Garden	THE HOME: Furnishings: Comput-ers & Hard-ware	THE HOME: Furnishings: Major Appli-ances	THE HOME: Furnishings: TV, Radio, Sound Equip-ment	THE HOME: Furnishings: Furni-ture	ENTERTAINMENT: Dine out/ Carry out	ENTERTAINMENT: Sports Equip-ment	ENTERTAINMENT: Fees & Tickets	ENTERTAINMENT: Toys & Games	ENTERTAINMENT: Travel	ENTERTAINMENT: Cable TV	PERSONAL: Apparel & Services	PERSONAL: Auto Repairs	PERSONAL: Health Insur-ance	PERSONAL: Pets & Supplies
80260	DENVER	75	70	67	71	69	73	71	72	71	73	89	84	69	84	69	69	86	74	69	83
80262	DENVER	0	0	0	0	0	0	0	0	0	0	0	0	0	0	0	0	0	0	0	0
80301	BOULDER	123	130	153	136	127	133	130	127	125	132	158	149	133	157	129	121	156	129	116	140
80302	BOULDER	95	82	107	88	80	88	109	91	105	100	132	117	101	127	97	97	128	101	84	102
80303	BOULDER	100	96	122	102	94	101	115	101	110	108	138	126	110	136	107	103	135	108	93	112
80304	BOULDER	137	151	187	155	147	154	151	145	145	151	183	172	156	185	150	140	181	147	132	160
80305	BOULDER	113	121	150	123	119	126	129	121	124	125	155	145	129	156	126	119	153	125	111	132
80309	BOULDER	0	0	0	0	0	0	0	0	0	0	0	0	0	0	0	0	0	0	0	0
80401	GOLDEN	131	145	168	149	143	148	143	139	136	142	171	163	148	173	142	132	169	139	128	152
80403	GOLDEN	128	150	161	153	146	146	139	137	129	140	164	161	145	169	139	124	163	134	122	151
80421	BAILEY	98	115	120	117	112	111	106	105	98	106	124	123	110	128	106	94	123	103	93	116
80422	BLACK HAWK	71	81	100	84	80	82	80	77	76	80	96	92	82	98	80	74	95	78	70	85
80423	BOND	76	86	105	89	85	87	85	83	81	85	102	98	87	104	85	78	101	83	75	90
80424	BRECKENRIDGE	128	114	149	122	114	125	126	123	129	127	161	148	123	160	123	127	157	129	121	145
80428	CLARK	131	114	89	106	124	135	106	122	115	105	137	143	99	138	112	120	130	120	137	160
80430	COALMONT	82	64	44	58	72	81	60	73	68	60	81	85	54	80	64	73	75	72	86	99
80433	CONIFER	149	181	192	186	175	176	160	158	147	163	186	183	173	193	162	142	187	152	141	175
80435	DILLON	126	109	95	108	114	123	108	117	112	109	138	138	102	134	109	113	131	117	122	146
80439	EVERGREEN	162	199	221	201	195	198	178	177	166	180	209	204	192	217	183	162	209	171	161	195
80440	FAIRPLAY	108	89	66	82	98	108	84	98	92	84	110	115	77	109	88	97	104	97	111	130
80446	GRANBY	118	99	76	93	108	118	94	108	102	94	122	127	87	121	98	106	115	107	121	142
80447	GRAND LAKE	133	105	71	94	118	132	99	119	112	98	132	139	88	131	105	119	123	117	141	163
80449	HARTSEL	104	82	56	74	92	103	77	93	87	76	103	109	69	102	82	93	96	91	110	127
80452	IDAHO SPRINGS	85	94	102	95	92	94	90	89	86	90	107	106	91	110	90	83	106	89	82	100
80455	JAMESTOWN	107	125	151	129	122	125	121	117	115	121	145	140	126	149	122	111	143	118	106	128
80456	JEFFERSON	97	76	52	69	86	96	72	86	81	71	96	101	64	95	76	87	89	85	102	118
80459	KREMMLING	88	90	85	90	90	91	86	88	83	86	104	104	84	104	85	81	101	88	83	102
80461	LEADVILLE	78	79	82	80	78	80	81	80	79	80	99	95	80	100	79	76	97	81	74	88
80463	MC COY	85	90	97	91	89	92	88	88	85	88	107	104	88	107	88	83	105	89	83	99
80465	MORRISON	141	168	177	171	163	163	152	151	141	154	178	176	161	184	153	136	178	147	134	166
80466	NEDERLAND	118	133	151	136	131	135	127	125	121	127	152	148	131	156	128	118	150	125	116	140
80467	OAK CREEK	91	99	103	100	97	98	95	95	90	95	114	112	95	114	94	87	112	94	86	105
80468	PARSHALL	119	94	64	84	105	118	88	106	100	87	118	125	79	117	94	107	110	105	126	145
80470	PINE	129	156	162	159	151	150	139	138	128	141	162	161	148	168	140	123	162	133	122	152
80479	TOPONAS	120	84	44	79	98	110	83	103	96	82	112	124	71	110	86	100	102	101	122	143
80480	WALDEN	82	60	36	56	69	77	58	71	67	58	78	85	51	77	61	70	72	70	84	98
80481	WARD	105	107	116	107	110	116	105	108	105	104	130	128	104	131	107	104	126	108	107	127
80487	STEAMBOAT SPRINGS	126	130	144	135	127	131	129	127	124	130	157	151	129	157	127	120	154	128	117	143
80498	SILVERTHORNE	147	143	122	141	145	150	131	140	131	134	161	164	128	161	132	130	155	137	140	170
80501	LONGMONT	91	96	101	99	94	97	95	94	91	95	115	110	95	114	93	88	112	94	87	103
80503	LONGMONT	150	176	187	181	171	171	161	158	149	163	188	185	170	193	161	143	188	155	141	174
80504	LONGMONT	145	162	159	164	158	159	148	149	139	150	175	174	152	177	148	134	173	146	135	167
80510	ALLENSPARK	111	87	60	79	98	111	82	99	93	82	111	116	74	109	88	100	103	98	117	136
80512	BELLVUE	109	127	138	127	126	127	117	118	111	117	140	139	122	146	120	109	138	115	109	132
80513	BERTHOUD	123	140	139	141	136	135	128	128	120	129	151	150	132	154	128	115	149	125	115	143
80514	DACONO	80	72	56	70	73	78	70	75	71	71	88	86	66	84	69	71	84	74	76	89
80515	DRAKE	108	84	58	76	95	107	80	96	90	79	107	112	71	105	85	96	99	94	113	131
80516	ERIE	141	161	160	165	155	152	147	146	136	150	172	171	151	175	145	128	170	142	127	160
80517	ESTES PARK	124	107	88	99	116	133	99	116	108	102	132	125	95	120	107	116	123	114	136	146
80521	FORT COLLINS	65	52	64	57	51	56	74	62	72	67	90	81	66	84	65	65	86	70	57	69
80523	FORT COLLINS	34	21	26	24	21	25	41	30	39	34	49	41	33	44	32	35	46	36	28	34
80524	FORT COLLINS	92	92	95	93	91	96	94	92	91	93	114	109	92	112	92	89	111	94	88	104
80525	FORT COLLINS	110	117	128	122	114	117	116	112	110	117	139	133	118	138	113	104	137	113	102	124
80526	FORT COLLINS	103	106	114	112	103	105	108	103	102	108	129	124	108	127	104	96	127	105	92	115
80528	FORT COLLINS	137	157	155	164	150	146	141	140	129	147	165	163	147	166	139	121	163	136	119	153
80530	FREDERICK	86	94	94	95	91	90	89	88	84	90	106	105	90	106	87	79	104	88	78	97
80534	JOHNSTOWN	97	108	108	111	104	103	101	100	94	103	119	118	103	120	99	89	117	99	88	110
80535	LAPORTE	83	99	103	99	96	95	90	90	84	90	106	106	94	110	91	81	105	88	80	99
80536	LIVERMORE	101	116	118	115	116	117	104	107	100	104	124	126	109	131	107	98	123	104	101	123
80537	LOVELAND	91	101	105	102	99	102	97	96	93	97	117	113	100	120	97	91	115	96	90	106
80538	LOVELAND	98	110	115	112	108	110	103	103	98	104	123	119	107	126	104	95	122	101	95	113
80540	LYONS	115	132	137	131	132	133	120	123	115	120	143	144	125	150	123	113	142	119	115	140
80542	MEAD	155	177	171	184	168	163	159	158	146	165	185	185	164	187	156	136	183	153	134	173
80543	MILLIKEN	85	94	94	96	91	90	89	88	83	90	105	104	90	106	87	78	103	87	77	97
80545	RED FEATHER LAKES	95	80	61	74	88	97	75	87	82	74	98	102	69	98	79	86	92	86	99	116
80549	WELLINGTON	95	109	110	110	106	104	100	100	93	101	118	118	103	121	100	89	116	98	89	110
80550	WINDSOR	108	120	118	124	116	113	111	110	103	114	131	130	113	132	109	97	129	109	96	121
80601	BRIGHTON	84	90	91	91	88	89	87	87	84	88	105	101	88	105	86	80	103	87	80	95
80602	BRIGHTON	130	154	156	158	149	146	138	137	127	141	161	161	145	166	138	121	160	133	120	151
80603	BRIGHTON	102	106	97	104	106	109	98	102	96	99	119	119	98	120	99	94	116	100	98	118
80610	AULT	86	75	60	75	79	86	75	80	78	74	95	94	72	95	75	79	90	79	85	97
80611	BRIGGSDALE	90	63	33	60	74	82	62	77	72	62	84	93	53	83	65	75	77	76	92	107
80612	CARR	106	83	54	79	93	101	80	94	88	79	105	113	72	104	82	91	97	93	107	127
80615	EATON	97	107	108	106	107	109	101	102	98	100	122	120	103	127	102	96	120	100	98	116
80620	EVANS	75	73	70	73	72	74	74	74	73	75	91	87	72	90	72	70	89	75	69	83
80621	FORT LUPTON	95	90	79	87	89	93	88	93	89	91	110	105	84	105	86	87	108	93	89	104
80624	GILL	108	76	40	72	88	99	75	92	86	74	101	111	64	99	78	90	92	91	110	129
80631	GREELEY	62	55	56	55	55	59	62	60	62	61	78	71	58	75	59	60	75	63	58	67
80634	GREELEY	99	107	115	109	105	108	105	103	100	105	126	121	106	126	104	96	124	103	95	113
80639	GREELEY	35	22	27	24	21	26	42	31	40	35	51	43	34	45	33	36	47	37	28	35
80640	HENDERSON	115	141	150	141	139	137	127	127	118	126	149	148	135	158	130	115	148	122	114	140
80642	HUDSON	96	103	99	103	102	103	96	98	92	97	116	117	97	118	96	89	113	97	91	112
80643	KEENESBURG	97	90	76	89	93	97	86	93	87	86	107	111	82	107	86	86	102	92	93	113
80644	KERSEY	83	88	86	88	87	88	84	85	80	84	101	100	84	102	83	77	99	84	79	96
80645	LA SALLE	84	86	82	85	87	89	82	85	80	82	100	100	82	102	82	79	97	84	82	99
80648	NUNN	106	74	39	70	86	96	73	90	84	72	98	109	62	96	76	88	90	89	107	125
80649	ORCHARD	77	62	45	57	69	76	59	69	65	59	78	81	54	77	62	69	73	68	79	93
80650	PIERCE	93	80	62	79	84	92	79	86	84	79	102	100	76	101	80	85	96	85	92	105
80651	PLATTEVILLE	104	100	85	98	100	104	94	99	94	96	117	117	92	114	94	92	113	98	97	118
80652	ROGGEN	99	72	41	69	82	91	71	86	80	70	94	103	62	93	73	83	87	84	100	117
80653	WELDONA	84	66	45	61	74	82	63	75	70	62	83	88	56	82	66	74	78	74	87	101
80654	WIGGINS	87	68	44	65	74	81	66	77	72	67	86	91	59	83	67	74	81	76	85	100
80701	FORT MORGAN	74	69	62	68	70	74	70	73	72	71	89	84	68	87	69	71	86	73	73	82
80705	LOG LANE VILLAGE	93	84	66	81	84	89	81	86	81	83	101	100	76	95	79	80	97	86	86	102
80720	AKRON	80	58	36	56	65	77	63	71	71	60	83	82	55	79	63	75	76	71	85	90
	COLORADO	103	104	110	107	103	108	105	104	102	105	128	122	104	127	103	99	125	105	98	116
	UNITED STATES	100	100	100	100	100	100	100	100	100	100	100	100	100	100	100	100	100	100	100	100

POPULATION CHANGE

#	POST OFFICE NAME	COUNTY FIPS CODE	POPULATION 2000	POPULATION 2004	POPULATION 2009	2000-2004 ANNUAL RATE % Rate	State Centile	HOUSEHOLDS 2000	HOUSEHOLDS 2004	HOUSEHOLDS 2009	% Annual Rate 2000-2004	2004 Average HH Size	FAMILIES 2000	FAMILIES 2004	% Annual Rate 2000-2004
80721	AMHERST	095	190	195	201	0.6	26	68	71	73	1.0	2.75	55	57	0.8
80722	ATWOOD	075	288	303	314	1.2	37	104	113	119	2.0	2.47	80	85	1.4
80723	BRUSH	087	6825	7084	7478	0.9	30	2437	2535	2675	0.9	2.69	1704	1759	0.8
80726	CROOK	075	420	424	429	0.2	18	171	176	181	0.7	2.41	129	131	0.4
80727	ECKLEY	125	443	451	451	0.4	21	156	160	161	0.6	2.82	112	114	0.4
80728	FLEMING	075	976	997	1017	0.5	24	374	398	415	1.5	2.14	283	299	1.3
80729	GROVER	123	539	655	870	4.7	84	237	292	390	5.0	2.22	172	208	4.6
80731	HAXTUN	095	1650	1682	1728	0.5	23	668	685	709	0.6	2.40	467	476	0.5
80733	HILLROSE	121	525	583	633	2.5	61	184	206	225	2.7	2.83	146	163	2.6
80734	HOLYOKE	095	2817	2876	2959	0.5	24	1112	1142	1179	0.6	2.47	767	781	0.4
80735	IDALIA	125	418	443	451	1.4	41	165	178	184	1.8	2.49	128	137	1.6
80736	ILIFF	075	766	812	844	1.4	41	287	314	332	2.1	2.43	219	237	1.9
80737	JULESBURG	115	1800	1808	1807	0.1	15	756	767	772	0.3	2.28	513	516	0.1
80740	LINDON	121	117	116	117	-0.2	9	48	48	50	0.0	2.42	35	35	0.0
80741	MERINO	075	781	820	850	1.2	36	288	306	320	1.4	2.68	223	235	1.2
80742	NEW RAYMER	123	273	331	439	4.6	83	106	130	174	4.9	2.52	77	93	4.5
80743	OTIS	121	1085	1130	1164	1.0	32	436	461	482	1.3	2.45	323	340	1.2
80744	OVID	115	542	512	500	-1.3	0	239	229	226	-1.0	2.24	169	161	-1.1
80745	PADRONI	075	52	53	54	0.5	23	21	22	22	1.1	2.41	16	16	0.0
80747	PEETZ	075	510	515	522	0.2	18	188	194	199	0.7	2.65	142	145	0.5
80749	SEDGWICK	115	405	407	407	0.1	15	170	173	176	0.4	2.35	122	124	0.4
80750	SNYDER	087	520	590	650	3.0	70	183	207	228	2.9	2.85	136	153	2.8
80751	STERLING	075	16581	17404	18101	1.2	36	6066	6451	6777	1.5	2.42	3933	4152	1.3
80754	STONEHAM	123	131	159	211	4.7	84	56	69	92	5.0	2.28	41	49	4.3
80755	VERNON	125	162	171	175	1.3	38	58	63	65	2.0	2.71	45	48	1.5
80757	WOODROW	121	274	272	275	-0.2	10	106	107	110	0.2	2.54	78	79	0.3
80758	WRAY	125	3781	3703	3643	-0.5	5	1480	1464	1452	-0.3	2.48	1004	986	-0.4
80759	YUMA	125	4492	4453	4406	-0.2	9	1730	1726	1719	-0.1	2.54	1189	1177	-0.2
80801	ANTON	121	171	168	169	-0.4	6	70	70	71	0.0	2.40	52	51	-0.5
80802	ARAPAHOE	017	346	346	346	0.0	12	123	125	126	0.4	2.77	84	85	0.3
80804	ARRIBA	073	399	423	459	1.4	41	171	184	201	1.7	2.30	121	129	1.5
80805	BETHUNE	063	431	411	400	-1.1	1	157	152	150	-0.8	2.70	120	116	-0.8
80807	BURLINGTON	063	4837	4883	4878	0.2	18	1714	1751	1768	0.5	2.49	1173	1190	0.3
80808	CALHAN	041	5902	7006	7964	4.1	79	2020	2426	2783	4.4	2.87	1580	1872	4.1
80809	CASCADE	041	2540	2624	2785	0.8	27	1101	1166	1258	1.4	2.22	706	728	0.7
80810	CHEYENNE WELLS	017	1279	1276	1275	-0.1	11	511	519	523	0.4	2.43	354	356	0.1
80812	COPE	121	344	336	337	-0.6	3	142	140	143	-0.3	2.40	105	103	-0.5
80813	CRIPPLE CREEK	119	1614	1896	2192	3.9	77	681	819	965	4.4	2.26	435	518	4.2
80814	DIVIDE	119	3495	3958	4504	3.0	68	1323	1526	1765	3.4	2.57	1016	1165	3.3
80815	FLAGLER	063	973	963	951	-0.2	9	413	413	413	0.0	2.31	271	269	-0.2
80816	FLORISSANT	119	4343	4955	5675	3.2	72	1795	2085	2424	3.6	2.37	1266	1460	3.4
80817	FOUNTAIN	041	15708	17448	19196	2.5	61	5247	5934	6609	2.9	2.94	4224	4720	2.7
80818	GENOA	073	392	409	433	1.0	33	152	164	181	1.8	1.68	106	113	1.5
80820	GUFFEY	093	809	935	1125	3.5	75	365	432	530	4.1	2.16	250	294	3.9
80821	HUGO	073	1239	1312	1422	1.4	40	492	525	574	1.5	2.37	330	349	1.3
80822	JOES	125	274	304	317	2.5	60	108	121	127	2.7	2.51	84	94	2.7
80823	KARVAL	073	286	311	342	2.0	49	117	129	143	2.3	2.41	88	97	2.3
80824	KIRK	125	286	314	326	2.2	55	111	124	130	2.6	2.53	87	96	2.3
80825	KIT CARSON	017	606	595	591	-0.4	6	246	247	247	0.1	2.35	165	164	-0.1
80827	LAKE GEORGE	093	803	928	1109	3.5	75	363	430	524	4.1	2.16	259	305	3.9
80828	LIMON	073	3606	3812	4098	1.3	39	1049	1138	1256	1.9	2.60	685	736	1.7
80829	MANITOU SPRINGS	041	5247	5323	5606	0.3	20	2561	2660	2846	0.9	1.99	1337	1342	0.1
80830	MATHESON	039	291	330	379	3.0	69	111	128	147	3.4	2.55	82	93	3.4
80831	PEYTON	041	10507	12533	14311	4.2	81	3510	4279	4962	4.8	2.92	2910	3500	4.4
80832	RAMAH	039	742	830	925	2.7	64	274	309	347	2.9	2.66	208	232	2.6
80833	RUSH	073	676	802	917	4.1	79	255	305	352	4.3	2.63	197	234	4.1
80834	SEIBERT	063	293	287	283	-0.5	5	135	134	134	-0.2	2.14	95	93	-0.5
80835	SIMLA	039	902	970	1079	1.7	44	325	350	391	1.8	2.73	244	261	1.6
80836	STRATTON	063	1184	1163	1149	-0.4	6	455	456	457	0.1	2.54	339	338	-0.1
80840	U S A F ACADEMY	041	7536	7725	7998	0.6	25	1131	1211	1308	1.6	3.52	1115	1193	1.6
80861	VONA	063	293	296	296	0.2	18	116	120	121	0.8	2.47	82	84	0.6
80863	WOODLAND PARK	119	11286	12425	13958	2.3	57	4278	4769	5425	2.6	2.60	3259	3619	2.5
80864	YODER	041	1248	1576	1844	5.6	89	444	569	673	6.0	2.77	351	443	5.6
80903	COLORADO SPRINGS	041	15059	15027	15827	-0.1	11	6451	6591	7106	0.5	1.95	2673	2617	-0.5
80904	COLORADO SPRINGS	041	20744	21738	23373	1.1	35	9846	10611	11616	1.8	2.03	5383	5599	0.9
80905	COLORADO SPRINGS	041	3287	3337	3574	0.4	20	1391	1451	1586	1.0	2.20	718	720	0.1
80906	COLORADO SPRINGS	041	49182	50945	54388	0.8	29	19761	20827	22534	1.2	2.39	12622	13036	0.8
80907	COLORADO SPRINGS	041	26801	26910	28466	0.1	15	12063	12391	13317	0.6	2.14	6784	6764	-0.1
80908	COLORADO SPRINGS	041	9238	10464	11622	3.0	68	3179	3684	4154	3.5	2.84	2706	3101	3.3
80909	COLORADO SPRINGS	041	38282	38230	40355	0.0	11	16141	16417	17574	0.4	2.30	9696	9613	-0.2
80910	COLORADO SPRINGS	041	27783	28292	30145	0.4	22	10720	11123	12019	0.9	2.47	6763	6830	0.2
80911	COLORADO SPRINGS	041	29433	30499	33327	1.2	36	9825	10516	11469	1.6	2.94	8067	8525	1.3
80913	COLORADO SPRINGS	041	10771	11529	12253	1.6	43	1698	1947	2180	3.3	3.61	1636	1872	3.2
80914	COLORADO SPRINGS	041	366	345	358	-1.4	0	1	1	1	0.0	3.00	1	1	0.0
80915	COLORADO SPRINGS	041	19746	21544	23774	2.1	51	7270	8095	9057	2.6	2.65	5465	5986	2.2
80916	COLORADO SPRINGS	041	31669	34190	37213	1.8	45	11069	12216	13497	2.4	2.77	8183	8838	1.8
80917	COLORADO SPRINGS	041	30482	31109	33019	0.5	23	12274	12813	13812	1.0	2.40	8168	8318	0.4
80918	COLORADO SPRINGS	041	49398	56233	63363	3.1	71	18600	21612	24704	3.6	2.56	13175	15130	3.3
80919	COLORADO SPRINGS	041	27968	29841	32319	1.5	42	10271	11181	12283	2.0	2.65	7816	8359	1.6
80920	COLORADO SPRINGS	041	31666	37020	41985	3.7	76	10246	12102	13852	4.0	3.06	8505	9982	3.7
80921	COLORADO SPRINGS	041	7572	10857	13602	8.9	96	2613	3826	4862	9.4	2.84	2257	3279	9.2
80922	COLORADO SPRINGS	041	13074	21591	29060	12.5	99	4152	6961	9475	12.9	3.10	3583	5944	12.7
80925	COLORADO SPRINGS	041	3061	3726	4284	4.7	85	960	1188	1383	5.1	3.14	827	1014	4.9
80926	COLORADO SPRINGS	041	1317	1448	1584	2.3	56	535	598	662	2.7	2.41	412	453	2.3
80928	COLORADO SPRINGS	041	851	1069	1247	5.5	88	276	352	415	5.9	3.03	223	280	5.2
80929	COLORADO SPRINGS	041	574	708	820	5.1	86	212	267	313	5.6	2.65	175	217	5.2
80930	COLORADO SPRINGS	041	687	848	981	5.1	86	241	302	353	5.5	2.80	202	251	5.2
81001	PUEBLO	101	29450	30386	32124	0.7	26	11279	11884	12778	1.2	2.47	7388	7648	0.8
81003	PUEBLO	101	14515	14512	15118	0.0	12	5397	5489	5837	0.4	2.26	3044	3034	-0.1
81004	PUEBLO	101	25875	26132	27399	0.2	18	10802	11082	11781	0.6	2.32	6451	6487	0.1
81005	PUEBLO	101	27256	28770	30804	1.3	38	10738	11572	12588	1.8	2.45	7816	8319	1.5
81006	PUEBLO	101	13028	13496	14239	0.8	29	4711	4976	5333	1.3	2.69	3633	3796	1.0
81007	PUEBLO	101	17145	21992	25882	6.0	91	6085	7858	9327	6.2	2.78	4914	6304	5.9
81008	PUEBLO	101	6973	7870	8722	2.9	67	2793	3191	3577	3.2	2.46	1992	2251	2.9
81019	COLORADO CITY	101	1491	1664	1823	2.6	63	577	654	727	3.0	2.54	439	491	2.7
	COLORADO					2.4					2.6	2.52			2.5
	UNITED STATES					1.2					1.3	2.58			1.1

ZIP CODE		RACE (%)						% Hispanic Origin		2004 AGE DISTRIBUTION (%)										MEDIAN AGE		
#	POST OFFICE NAME	White		Black		Asian/Pacific																
		2000	2004	2000	2004	2000	2004	2000	2004	0-4	5-9	10-14	15-19	20-24	25-44	45-64	65-84	85+	18+	2004	% 2004 Males	% 2004 Females
80721	AMHERST	96.3	96.4	0.0	0.0	0.0	0.0	4.2	4.1	7.2	7.7	7.7	6.7	5.6	22.1	30.3	11.8	1.0	73.3	40.2	52.3	47.7
80722	ATWOOD	93.4	93.1	2.1	2.0	0.4	0.7	8.7	9.9	6.6	7.9	7.3	6.9	6.3	29.0	25.1	9.9	1.0	72.9	36.6	53.8	46.2
80723	BRUSH	79.8	77.8	0.4	0.4	0.2	0.2	31.2	34.4	8.2	7.6	7.9	6.7	6.8	24.6	21.6	13.3	3.4	72.1	36.1	48.8	51.2
80726	CROOK	96.7	96.5	0.0	0.0	0.2	0.2	6.2	7.1	6.4	6.8	6.8	7.8	5.4	24.5	26.9	13.2	2.1	75.7	40.5	51.7	48.4
80727	ECKLEY	91.0	90.7	0.2	0.2	0.2	0.2	12.9	13.3	7.8	8.4	10.0	6.0	4.4	26.2	23.1	13.3	0.9	69.8	35.9	49.7	50.3
80728	FLEMING	94.1	93.6	4.2	4.5	0.3	0.4	6.4	7.3	5.1	5.5	6.1	5.8	8.2	29.0	26.5	12.4	1.3	79.7	39.1	58.2	41.8
80729	GROVER	94.3	93.3	0.2	0.3	0.4	0.5	8.4	9.8	6.3	6.7	7.8	7.5	5.2	26.0	27.3	11.6	1.7	74.4	39.6	52.1	47.9
80731	HAXTUN	96.9	96.8	0.6	0.7	0.3	0.3	2.4	2.5	6.0	6.5	7.3	5.6	4.8	22.6	25.7	17.2	4.5	77.0	43.2	48.6	51.4
80733	HILLROSE	96.2	95.7	0.2	0.2	0.2	0.2	8.2	9.4	6.7	7.0	7.7	7.2	5.7	25.2	26.9	12.7	0.9	74.1	39.4	51.6	48.4
80734	HOLYOKE	90.9	90.7	0.0	0.0	0.5	0.5	17.2	17.5	7.7	7.6	7.8	6.3	5.0	24.5	24.3	13.9	3.1	72.7	38.9	48.3	51.7
80735	IDALIA	96.2	96.6	0.0	0.0	0.0	0.0	5.3	5.2	6.1	6.6	9.0	8.1	5.2	25.1	26.6	11.5	1.8	72.2	38.5	52.1	47.9
80736	ILIFF	94.3	93.8	1.4	1.5	0.4	0.5	6.9	7.9	6.7	6.9	7.5	6.5	6.3	26.7	27.0	11.5	1.0	74.9	38.1	55.9	44.1
80737	JULESBURG	89.8	89.7	0.3	0.3	0.7	0.7	12.6	12.9	6.1	6.3	6.9	5.5	5.7	22.7	23.8	19.0	4.0	77.1	42.5	48.9	51.1
80740	LINDON	98.3	99.1	0.0	0.0	0.0	0.0	0.9	0.9	5.2	4.3	7.8	8.6	3.5	25.9	32.8	11.2	0.9	76.7	42.0	55.2	44.8
80741	MERINO	95.5	95.0	0.1	0.1	0.5	0.6	6.2	7.1	6.8	8.3	8.3	7.2	5.0	26.2	26.0	11.2	1.0	71.0	37.9	49.8	50.2
80742	NEW RAYMER	94.1	93.1	0.4	0.3	0.4	0.6	8.1	9.4	6.3	6.7	7.9	7.6	5.1	24.8	27.8	12.1	1.8	74.0	39.9	52.0	48.0
80743	OTIS	98.3	98.2	0.0	0.0	0.1	0.1	3.2	3.4	6.5	6.6	7.0	6.5	5.6	24.3	27.2	14.3	2.3	76.0	40.5	52.0	48.1
80744	OVID	89.3	89.1	1.1	1.2	1.1	1.2	13.3	13.3	4.3	4.7	5.5	5.9	4.9	21.5	31.1	19.7	2.5	82.0	47.0	52.9	47.1
80745	PADRONI	96.2	96.2	0.0	0.0	0.0	0.0	7.7	5.7	7.6	7.6	7.6	7.6	5.7	22.6	24.5	15.1	1.9	77.4	39.2	52.8	47.2
80747	PEETZ	96.7	96.3	0.0	0.0	0.2	0.2	6.3	7.2	6.6	6.8	6.8	7.6	5.4	25.2	26.4	13.2	1.9	75.2	40.4	51.7	48.4
80749	SEDGWICK	95.1	95.3	0.7	0.7	1.5	1.5	4.0	3.7	5.7	6.1	5.7	4.9	4.9	21.4	32.4	17.0	2.0	79.6	45.8	53.6	46.4
80750	SNYDER	92.7	92.4	0.4	0.3	0.2	0.2	5.2	6.1	8.8	9.5	10.2	6.8	4.1	24.1	23.6	12.4	0.7	67.3	36.0	48.5	51.5
80751	STERLING	90.8	90.1	2.2	2.3	0.5	0.6	13.2	14.7	6.6	6.3	6.3	7.5	8.7	26.9	23.1	12.3	2.4	77.1	36.2	52.8	47.2
80754	STONEHAM	93.9	94.3	0.0	0.0	0.0	0.0	8.4	8.8	6.3	6.3	7.6	7.6	5.7	24.5	27.7	12.6	1.9	74.2	39.8	52.8	47.2
80755	VERNON	96.3	96.5	0.0	0.0	0.0	0.0	4.9	5.3	5.9	6.4	8.8	8.2	5.3	25.2	26.9	11.1	2.3	72.5	39.0	52.1	48.0
80757	WOODROW	98.2	97.8	0.0	0.0	0.0	0.0	1.8	1.8	5.2	4.4	8.5	9.9	3.7	25.7	30.2	11.4	1.1	75.0	40.5	54.0	46.0
80758	WRAY	95.8	95.7	0.1	0.1	0.1	0.1	7.9	8.1	6.5	6.6	7.4	7.1	6.1	23.4	25.7	14.3	2.9	74.6	39.8	49.1	50.9
80759	YUMA	92.3	92.2	0.1	0.1	0.1	0.1	19.2	19.5	7.1	7.1	8.0	7.0	6.2	25.9	23.1	12.9	2.8	73.4	37.0	48.7	51.3
80801	ANTON	97.7	97.0	0.0	0.0	0.0	0.0	2.9	3.6	5.4	5.4	7.1	7.1	4.8	24.4	30.4	14.3	1.2	78.0	42.3	53.0	47.0
80802	ARAPAHOE	93.4	93.4	0.3	0.3	0.0	0.0	7.8	7.8	8.1	7.8	7.8	7.5	6.9	27.5	22.5	10.7	1.2	70.5	36.3	50.6	49.4
80804	ARRIBA	95.7	94.8	0.0	0.0	1.8	2.1	3.5	4.0	5.2	6.2	7.8	5.7	5.9	24.1	28.6	14.9	1.7	77.3	42.0	53.0	47.0
80805	BETHUNE	89.6	89.3	0.2	0.2	0.2	0.2	12.8	13.4	6.8	7.1	8.0	7.1	7.5	24.1	26.0	12.2	1.2	73.5	37.9	50.9	49.2
80807	BURLINGTON	82.2	82.0	2.9	2.9	0.5	0.5	18.8	19.0	6.9	6.6	6.8	6.6	7.0	30.6	22.7	10.6	2.2	75.3	36.5	54.9	45.1
80808	CALHAN	91.1	90.0	1.5	1.7	0.6	0.7	6.2	7.3	7.7	7.9	8.9	8.1	6.4	28.8	24.7	7.0	0.6	70.0	34.2	50.7	49.3
80809	CASCADE	94.6	94.0	0.4	0.5	0.6	0.7	4.5	5.1	4.0	4.9	6.8	6.6	3.4	25.9	37.6	10.1	0.7	79.3	44.1	50.9	49.1
80810	CHEYENNE WELLS	92.7	92.6	0.6	0.6	0.2	0.2	8.4	8.7	7.1	7.1	7.5	7.3	6.3	25.5	25.8	11.8	1.7	73.6	38.4	51.3	48.7
80812	COPE	97.1	96.7	0.0	0.0	0.3	0.3	4.4	4.5	5.4	5.7	7.4	6.9	5.1	23.5	28.3	16.7	1.2	77.1	42.4	52.4	47.6
80813	CRIPPLE CREEK	92.9	92.5	0.8	0.8	0.6	0.7	5.0	5.5	4.5	5.0	6.9	6.4	5.3	26.7	34.6	10.2	0.6	80.3	42.3	51.3	48.7
80814	DIVIDE	95.1	94.8	0.6	0.7	0.5	0.7	2.9	3.2	5.3	6.6	7.4	6.5	2.8	29.3	34.4	7.3	0.5	76.2	41.6	51.0	49.0
80815	FLAGLER	97.3	97.4	0.0	0.0	0.0	0.0	2.6	2.6	4.6	5.3	7.6	7.2	6.1	21.6	27.5	16.2	4.0	77.4	43.6	49.4	50.6
80816	FLORISSANT	94.9	94.6	0.6	0.6	0.4	0.4	4.0	4.4	5.5	5.6	6.7	6.1	4.3	26.3	35.7	9.7	0.3	78.3	42.6	50.4	49.6
80817	FOUNTAIN	75.6	73.4	8.3	8.9	2.6	2.9	15.1	17.1	9.5	8.6	9.1	8.1	7.6	32.0	19.2	5.7	0.3	68.0	30.1	49.5	50.6
80818	GENOA	76.5	74.6	10.5	11.0	1.0	1.0	11.2	12.7	3.9	4.7	5.6	5.1	7.6	38.4	24.7	8.8	1.2	82.9	37.7	68.0	32.0
80820	GUFFEY	95.3	95.1	0.4	0.4	0.0	0.0	3.5	4.0	4.2	3.7	4.8	5.2	2.7	21.2	43.0	14.8	0.4	83.3	48.9	50.2	49.8
80821	HUGO	95.7	95.4	0.9	1.1	0.3	0.4	3.9	4.3	5.1	5.4	7.2	7.1	6.4	24.4	27.4	13.9	3.1	77.8	41.6	48.3	51.8
80822	JOES	98.5	98.7	0.0	0.0	0.0	0.0	4.0	4.3	5.6	6.3	7.6	6.9	4.9	25.3	29.3	12.2	2.0	76.3	41.2	51.0	49.0
80823	KARVAL	97.6	97.8	0.4	0.3	0.0	0.0	2.8	3.5	4.2	4.5	8.0	7.4	4.8	21.9	28.0	18.7	2.6	78.8	44.5	49.5	50.5
80824	KIRK	98.3	98.1	0.0	0.0	0.0	0.0	4.2	4.5	5.7	6.1	7.6	7.3	5.1	25.8	28.7	11.8	1.9	76.1	40.4	51.0	49.0
80825	KIT CARSON	92.9	92.8	0.3	0.3	0.0	0.0	7.6	7.6	5.4	5.6	6.1	7.4	5.4	21.7	26.6	16.1	5.9	77.7	44.2	48.6	51.4
80827	LAKE GEORGE	95.0	94.9	0.5	0.5	0.4	0.3	4.4	5.0	4.0	5.0	5.3	4.5	3.0	21.1	41.6	14.7	0.9	82.8	48.7	53.1	46.9
80828	LIMON	81.5	80.1	6.9	7.2	0.6	0.6	11.1	12.5	5.6	5.7	6.5	7.2	7.6	32.0	23.0	10.1	2.3	77.7	36.7	59.3	40.7
80829	MANITOU SPRINGS	93.8	93.3	0.5	0.6	1.1	1.3	3.9	4.6	4.0	4.3	5.2	6.3	6.6	28.1	34.3	9.9	1.3	82.7	42.4	49.0	51.0
80830	MATHESON	94.5	94.6	0.0	0.0	0.0	0.0	4.8	5.2	6.4	6.7	7.9	7.0	6.4	23.6	27.0	12.7	2.4	74.2	40.2	50.6	49.4
80831	PEYTON	91.9	90.9	1.1	1.2	0.7	0.8	5.4	6.5	6.9	7.6	9.0	7.9	5.2	30.4	27.5	5.3	0.3	71.1	36.5	50.9	49.1
80832	RAMAH	93.8	93.1	0.7	0.7	0.4	0.5	4.0	4.6	6.6	7.1	8.4	8.3	6.1	26.3	26.5	9.4	1.2	72.2	37.5	50.5	49.5
80833	RUSH	93.6	92.8	0.9	1.0	0.4	0.5	5.6	6.6	7.1	7.0	8.5	7.6	6.0	25.8	25.4	11.2	1.4	72.2	37.4	50.6	49.4
80834	SEIBERT	98.6	99.0	0.0	0.0	0.0	0.0	1.7	1.4	4.5	6.3	7.3	6.6	2.8	23.3	30.0	17.1	2.1	76.7	44.5	53.7	46.3
80835	SIMLA	95.3	95.2	0.2	0.2	0.1	0.1	3.4	3.8	6.3	6.7	7.7	7.7	6.2	24.0	26.2	12.7	2.5	73.6	39.4	50.8	49.2
80836	STRATTON	94.4	94.2	0.0	0.0	0.3	0.3	6.8	7.1	6.5	6.9	8.5	7.4	5.8	23.5	26.5	13.5	1.6	73.1	39.7	51.0	49.0
80840	U S A F ACADEMY	83.6	81.9	5.8	6.3	3.1	3.5	8.7	10.0	8.8	7.4	5.0	18.1	36.0	22.3	2.2	0.1	0.0	76.9	21.5	66.2	33.8
80861	VONA	93.9	93.9	0.0	0.0	0.3	0.3	6.8	7.1	5.4	6.4	8.1	7.1	4.4	23.3	28.7	14.9	1.7	75.0	42.3	52.4	47.6
80863	WOODLAND PARK	95.2	94.8	0.5	0.5	0.8	0.9	3.3	3.7	5.8	6.5	7.5	7.5	5.8	25.9	33.0	7.6	0.5	75.5	40.6	50.4	49.6
80864	YODER	90.6	89.6	1.4	1.6	0.6	0.8	7.5	8.8	8.8	8.6	9.3	7.7	6.6	28.5	23.6	6.4	0.5	67.6	32.1	51.1	48.9
80903	COLORADO SPRINGS	79.2	77.6	7.7	8.0	1.5	1.7	13.9	15.7	5.1	4.2	4.4	9.5	16.0	31.6	19.9	7.6	1.8	83.7	30.7	50.4	49.6
80904	COLORADO SPRINGS	89.3	88.1	1.7	1.8	1.3	1.4	10.5	12.1	5.2	4.9	5.6	6.0	6.8	28.5	27.7	12.9	2.3	80.6	40.7	48.1	51.9
80905	COLORADO SPRINGS	83.1	81.6	3.5	3.7	1.3	1.4	17.3	19.6	6.1	5.5	5.8	7.2	8.1	32.2	24.2	8.6	2.4	78.4	36.2	48.2	51.8
80906	COLORADO SPRINGS	79.9	78.1	6.2	6.7	3.1	3.5	13.0	14.5	7.0	6.5	6.9	6.8	7.4	29.2	24.3	10.5	1.5	75.4	35.5	49.5	50.5
80907	COLORADO SPRINGS	86.9	85.5	2.3	2.5	2.2	2.5	11.0	12.5	6.1	5.7	5.9	5.9	6.7	30.6	25.4	11.8	2.0	78.8	38.3	49.4	50.7
80908	COLORADO SPRINGS	95.2	94.7	0.8	0.9	0.8	0.9	3.2	3.8	4.9	6.9	9.4	8.5	3.3	24.4	35.2	7.1	0.4	72.9	41.9	50.4	49.6
80909	COLORADO SPRINGS	78.9	77.3	7.2	7.5	1.9	2.1	15.5	17.4	7.4	6.3	6.3	6.7	8.2	27.7	21.9	13.2	2.3	76.4	36.0	48.2	51.8
80910	COLORADO SPRINGS	58.9	56.2	17.0	17.7	3.4	3.8	25.9	28.9	9.2	7.3	7.0	7.1	9.9	30.5	17.3	10.0	1.7	72.4	30.0	49.4	50.6
80911	COLORADO SPRINGS	74.0	71.6	10.6	11.4	3.6	4.1	12.7	14.5	7.2	7.3	8.6	8.5	7.0	29.2	22.3	9.5	0.4	71.6	34.2	49.2	50.8
80913	COLORADO SPRINGS	63.0	60.4	19.8	20.9	2.9	3.2	15.3	17.3	12.2	7.9	4.5	8.9	32.4	32.4	1.5	0.1	0.0	73.9	22.5	66.7	33.3
80914	COLORADO SPRINGS	74.6	72.5	13.1	13.9	3.6	4.1	9.6	11.0	13.6	11.9	7.3	8.7	13.6	39.4	5.2	0.3	0.0	64.4	23.1	55.7	44.4
80915	COLORADO SPRINGS	81.2	79.8	7.0	7.2	2.6	2.9	11.1	12.7	8.3	7.6	7.8	7.2	7.3	30.8	21.6	8.8	0.7	72.0	33.0	49.7	50.3
80916	COLORADO SPRINGS	60.4	57.9	18.3	19.0	4.6	5.1	19.1	21.5	10.7	9.1	8.4	7.1	9.5	35.5	15.7	3.9	0.2	67.9	27.7	49.8	50.3
80917	COLORADO SPRINGS	84.8	83.2	5.3	5.7	2.8	3.2	8.7	10.1	6.9	6.5	6.8	6.6	8.0	30.2	25.1	8.9	1.0	75.8	34.9	48.8	51.3
80918	COLORADO SPRINGS	85.3	83.8	4.0	4.3	3.5	4.0	8.4	9.6	7.7	7.4	7.2	7.2	7.2	32.2	23.6	6.9	0.7	73.9	33.7	49.9	50.1
80919	COLORADO SPRINGS	90.4	89.3	1.7	1.9	3.9	4.5	4.7	5.5	6.2	7.0	8.1	7.3	5.4	28.9	30.2	6.4	0.6	73.9	38.0	49.7	50.3
80920	COLORADO SPRINGS	89.2	87.9	3.0	3.3	3.2	3.7	5.7	6.6	8.0	8.8	9.7	8.9	6.3	30.5	23.5	4.1	0.3	67.8	33.1	49.9	50.1
80921	COLORADO SPRINGS	94.5	93.6	1.1	1.3	1.7	2.0	3.6	4.2	6.3	7.8	9.0	7.0	3.9	22.8	32.5	9.4	1.4	72.2	41.6	50.0	50.1
80922	COLORADO SPRINGS	82.1	80.4	5.5	6.1	4.7	5.4	8.7	9.8	11.1	10.2	9.0	6.7	5.7	39.3	15.5	2.5	0.1	65.5	30.6	49.6	50.5
80925	COLORADO SPRINGS	78.0	75.9	8.6	9.2	2.5	2.8	12.7	14.6	9.3	8.8	9.0	7.7	7.2	34.1	20.0	3.7	0.2	68.1	30.9	50.5	49.5
80926	COLORADO SPRINGS	91.5	90.5	1.9	2.1	2.6	3.0	4.9	5.6	5.4	6.4	7.0	6.2	3.7	25.6	34.8	10.1	0.9	77.0	42.9	49.7	50.4
80928	COLORADO SPRINGS	87.8	86.6	3.1	3.3	1.1	1.1	8.7	10.1	9.0	8.8	9.1	7.6	6.6	29.9	22.5	6.0	0.5	67.8	31.9	50.9	49.1
80929	COLORADO SPRINGS	84.3	82.8	4.7	5.1	1.4	1.6	9.9	11.6	7.6	7.8	8.5	7.2	5.8	31.8	25.3	5.9	0.1	71.6	35.4	51.1	48.9
80930	COLORADO SPRINGS	83.8	82.1	5.1	5.5	1.3	1.5	10.3	12.0	9.2	8.8	9.1	7.8	6.8	33.7	20.2	4.1	0.2	67.8	31.3	51.1	48.9
81001	PUEBLO	73.4	71.8	1.7	1.8	1.3	1.4	49.7	53.2	7.3	6.9	7.5	7.6	8.2	25.9	21.5	12.6	2.5	74.1	34.1	47.9	52.1
81003	PUEBLO	75.2	73.2	3.8	3.9	0.6	0.6	42.4	46.7	6.2	6.0	6.0	7.7	8.0	30.2	21.8	12.1	2.0	77.6	35.5	52.3	47.8
81004	PUEBLO	72.1	70.0	3.1	3.1	0.3	0.3	47.0	51.2	7.3	6.6	6.6	6.6	7.2	26.5	22.5	14.0	2.8	75.6	37.0	48.4	51.6
81005	PUEBLO	84.2	82.8	1.9	2.0	0.5	0.5	35.3	39.3	5.9	6.1	7.0	6.8	6.3	23.1	26.0	16.1	2.6	76.8	41.2	47.4	52.6
81006	PUEBLO	82.2	80.4	0.5	0.5	0.4	0.4	34.2	38.1	6.0	6.7	7.6	7.8	6.2	24.6	27.3	12.5	1.4	74.7	39.1	50.0	50.0
81007	PUEBLO	88.5	87.1	0.8	0.9	1.1	1.2	18.2	21.0	8.3	8.4	8.0	6.7	5.7	29.9	23.5	9.0	0.5	70.8	35.0	49.8	50.2
81008	PUEBLO	82.5	80.3	1.5	1.7	1.3	1.5	32.0	36.2	6.8	6.7	6.7	6.4	6.5	25.6	26.1	13.7	1.7	75.8	38.6	48.4	51.6
81019	COLORADO CITY	93.3	92.3	0.7	0.9	0.3	0.4	8.5	10.0	5.5	7.0	8.2	8.1	4.2	24.6	29.9	11.8	0.6	73.7	40.2	49.3	50.7
	COLORADO	82.8	81.7	3.8	3.9	2.3	2.6	17.1	18.6	7.0	6.8	7.1	7.0	7.5	30.6	24.3	8.6	1.2	75.1	35.0	50.3	49.7
	UNITED STATES	75.1	73.6	12.3	12.5	3.8	4.2	12.5	14.1	6.9	6.7	7.2	7.0	7.3	28.6	23.8	10.8	1.7	75.1	36.0	49.1	50.9

#	POST OFFICE NAME	2004 Per Capita Income	2004 HH Income Base	2004 Household Income Distribution (%): Less than $25,000	$25,000 to $49,999	$50,000 to $99,999	$100,000 to $149,999	$150,000 or More	Median Household Income: 2004	2009	2004 National Centile	2004 State Centile	2004 Home Value Base	2004 Home Value Distribution (%): Less than $50,000	$50,000 to $89,999	$90,000 to $174,999	$175,000 to $399,999	$400,000 or More	2004 Median Home Value
80721	AMHERST	20453	71	26.8	28.2	31.0	7.0	7.0	45567	50706	63	54	57	8.8	14.0	47.4	28.1	1.8	124038
80722	ATWOOD	21413	113	18.6	40.7	28.3	8.9	3.5	43962	48085	59	49	90	12.2	21.1	44.4	20.0	2.2	122917
80723	BRUSH	17248	2535	33.0	34.5	25.6	5.5	1.5	37096	41370	36	26	1792	9.6	13.6	56.6	17.9	2.3	116736
80726	CROOK	18316	176	28.4	42.1	23.9	3.4	2.3	38031	42553	39	28	139	20.9	28.1	26.6	19.4	5.0	91875
80727	ECKLEY	15018	160	34.4	35.0	25.6	3.8	1.3	35000	38102	28	20	116	16.4	28.5	31.0	16.4	7.8	100000
80728	FLEMING	19611	398	32.2	37.9	22.9	5.0	2.0	35394	39740	29	21	322	18.0	16.8	40.7	24.5	0.0	112295
80729	GROVER	22481	292	32.2	33.2	25.0	6.5	3.1	37789	42245	38	27	232	12.5	13.8	32.8	27.2	13.8	145833
80731	HAXTUN	18755	685	31.0	38.4	25.1	3.5	2.0	36075	40049	32	23	548	13.5	25.6	45.1	15.7	0.2	105165
80733	HILLROSE	16755	206	28.2	38.4	26.7	3.4	3.4	38193	41043	40	29	164	17.7	8.5	39.6	32.3	1.8	122414
80734	HOLYOKE	19093	1142	34.3	34.1	23.5	3.9	4.3	35835	40974	31	22	895	13.1	23.6	47.7	15.0	0.7	109236
80735	IDALIA	19969	178	18.5	41.0	36.0	2.8	1.7	39719	45000	45	35	132	18.9	22.0	32.6	13.6	12.9	110938
80736	ILIFF	20830	314	27.4	36.9	27.7	5.1	2.9	39671	43294	45	35	246	16.3	20.7	35.4	24.0	3.7	116406
80737	JULESBURG	17940	767	38.2	36.8	19.8	3.4	1.8	31697	35511	17	10	567	23.8	32.6	37.0	5.5	1.1	83707
80740	LINDON	16358	48	33.3	43.8	18.8	2.1	2.1	31591	36461	17	10	33	27.3	6.1	45.5	18.2	3.0	127500
80741	MERINO	20284	306	19.6	41.2	27.1	8.5	3.6	43190	48793	56	47	244	10.3	23.8	42.2	19.7	4.1	121970
80742	NEW RAYMER	19847	130	31.5	33.9	25.4	6.2	3.1	37973	42355	39	28	103	13.6	13.6	34.0	24.3	14.6	142045
80743	OTIS	24919	461	25.8	36.9	26.7	6.7	3.9	38967	43587	43	33	384	20.8	29.7	36.7	11.2	1.6	89231
80744	OVID	18472	229	41.1	36.2	17.0	3.5	2.2	29597	32545	11	6	181	34.8	27.1	30.9	5.5	1.7	65952
80745	PADRONI	16132	22	31.8	40.9	27.3	0.0	0.0	35000	35000	28	20	17	5.9	29.4	35.3	23.5	5.9	112500
80747	PEETZ	16735	194	28.4	42.3	23.2	3.6	2.6	38189	43530	40	29	153	21.6	27.5	26.1	19.6	5.2	91667
80749	SEDGWICK	21278	173	34.7	39.3	17.9	4.1	4.1	31707	35000	17	10	136	32.4	24.3	35.3	4.4	3.7	80000
80750	SNYDER	18093	207	25.1	32.9	32.9	5.8	3.4	43332	46565	57	47	162	21.0	14.2	45.1	15.4	4.3	109868
80751	STERLING	19494	6451	35.2	29.4	28.0	4.6	2.8	36510	42067	34	25	4588	11.8	21.9	42.3	23.5	0.5	112809
80754	STONEHAM	21810	69	31.9	33.3	24.6	7.3	2.9	37978	42863	39	28	55	12.7	12.7	32.7	27.3	14.6	147917
80755	VERNON	18185	63	17.5	41.3	36.5	3.2	1.6	40560	44524	48	37	47	19.2	23.4	31.9	12.8	12.8	107500
80757	WOODROW	18846	107	33.6	38.3	21.5	3.7	2.8	32641	36200	20	14	73	23.3	6.9	45.2	19.2	5.5	131250
80758	WRAY	19603	1464	31.9	33.7	27.4	4.8	2.3	37025	41558	36	26	1119	17.3	24.5	42.5	13.1	2.7	100071
80759	YUMA	17457	1726	34.3	32.7	26.5	4.5	2.0	35000	39363	28	20	1286	11.7	26.2	48.1	12.1	1.9	105792
80801	ANTON	23427	70	32.9	41.4	15.7	4.3	5.7	33568	38606	23	16	50	24.0	24.0	36.0	14.0	2.0	100000
80802	ARAPAHOE	19102	125	23.2	37.6	30.4	6.4	2.4	43380	48893	57	48	97	25.8	25.8	40.2	8.3	0.0	88125
80804	ARRIBA	20904	184	32.6	33.2	23.4	7.1	3.8	36924	38322	35	26	147	13.6	24.5	39.5	14.3	8.2	109239
80805	BETHUNE	21293	152	32.2	25.7	26.3	8.6	7.2	42015	48229	53	43	124	15.3	21.0	31.5	24.2	8.1	125000
80807	BURLINGTON	20132	1751	31.9	27.7	31.0	6.3	3.1	39181	45580	43	33	1315	16.4	21.8	45.2	15.4	1.1	104659
80808	CALHAN	19520	2426	22.5	32.0	36.2	6.8	2.4	46232	51812	64	55	2044	11.0	10.0	39.5	34.8	4.7	156780
80809	CASCADE	33511	1166	17.8	29.2	32.9	10.8	9.4	52393	59247	76	67	954	3.3	2.1	27.8	49.6	17.3	203736
80810	CHEYENNE WELLS	21080	519	27.0	33.3	29.9	7.5	2.3	43520	48224	57	48	405	24.0	25.2	40.5	9.4	1.0	91522
80812	COPE	25406	140	31.4	42.9	14.3	4.3	7.1	35000	39232	28	20	103	26.2	28.2	32.0	11.7	1.9	85909
80813	CRIPPLE CREEK	25469	819	15.0	40.3	34.3	8.2	2.2	47246	55720	67	56	581	4.8	7.8	47.7	36.5	3.3	157500
80814	DIVIDE	29168	1526	10.8	28.7	39.6	14.0	7.0	61103	69995	85	79	1353	0.6	5.3	25.9	55.1	13.1	223399
80815	FLAGLER	19293	413	38.0	31.0	23.0	5.8	2.2	33252	39158	22	15	314	21.7	30.6	36.9	10.2	0.6	87586
80816	FLORISSANT	26230	2085	18.7	31.3	38.6	7.2	4.2	50018	58250	72	62	1744	2.4	9.9	38.9	42.7	6.1	173077
80817	FOUNTAIN	19186	5934	17.9	33.7	38.7	7.5	2.2	48819	55933	70	59	4352	6.5	4.9	65.1	22.8	0.7	142837
80818	GENOA	23583	164	29.3	37.2	26.2	5.5	1.8	36368	39781	33	24	128	18.0	25.0	38.3	14.1	4.7	99000
80820	GUFFEY	26313	432	23.6	37.0	28.7	6.5	4.2	42257	48498	54	44	378	5.8	7.4	24.1	54.2	8.5	205556
80821	HUGO	18306	525	35.1	33.9	25.7	3.8	1.5	34311	37856	25	17	381	17.1	27.8	45.1	7.6	2.4	95132
80822	JOES	24780	121	27.3	32.2	24.0	8.3	8.3	43826	51284	58	49	97	11.3	20.6	41.2	19.6	7.2	118750
80823	KARVAL	19497	129	31.8	35.7	26.4	3.9	2.3	32725	36924	20	14	102	21.6	21.6	34.3	16.7	5.9	104167
80824	KIRK	23680	124	25.8	33.9	25.8	7.3	7.3	43159	51271	56	46	98	13.3	20.4	39.8	18.4	8.2	117647
80825	KIT CARSON	19488	247	41.3	26.3	24.3	6.1	2.0	32328	37351	19	13	201	31.8	30.9	29.9	7.0	0.5	72647
80827	LAKE GEORGE	26264	430	22.8	29.3	35.8	9.1	3.0	47382	53125	67	57	372	4.6	5.4	33.6	45.2	11.3	190385
80828	LIMON	18227	1138	26.9	38.1	25.2	7.5	2.3	38092	44229	40	28	786	16.9	18.3	47.5	15.8	1.5	109574
80829	MANITOU SPRINGS	30101	2660	27.5	27.4	27.7	10.7	6.7	43928	51630	58	49	1662	0.4	3.4	33.0	54.0	9.2	200169
80830	MATHESON	19965	128	21.9	41.4	27.3	7.0	2.3	41138	48321	50	40	99	7.1	12.1	38.4	31.3	11.1	148438
80831	PEYTON	25175	4279	13.9	23.3	44.5	12.3	6.0	60698	68725	85	79	3882	3.1	2.4	31.4	58.4	4.7	197164
80832	RAMAH	21528	309	23.3	34.0	31.7	7.4	3.6	44391	50926	60	50	253	10.3	10.7	34.8	34.8	9.5	160500
80833	RUSH	18538	305	28.5	36.1	28.2	4.9	2.3	37347	42087	37	26	249	17.3	17.3	36.6	24.9	4.0	124583
80834	SEIBERT	21390	134	38.1	35.8	20.2	2.2	3.7	33338	39304	22	15	108	39.8	12.0	33.3	13.9	0.9	85000
80835	SIMLA	18785	350	28.0	39.1	22.3	6.6	4.0	38459	45257	41	31	271	4.8	11.4	41.7	29.5	12.6	143750
80836	STRATTON	19329	456	30.5	37.7	25.7	4.2	2.0	37501	43248	37	27	359	28.1	17.0	40.1	12.0	2.8	101607
80840	U S A F ACADEMY	15811	1211	7.4	50.5	35.5	5.2	1.4	47013	52142	66	56	22	0.0	27.3	9.1	63.6	0.0	193750
80861	VONA	20732	120	31.7	40.0	21.7	2.5	4.2	36344	41430	33	24	95	33.7	16.8	36.8	11.6	1.1	89167
80863	WOODLAND PARK	27504	4769	14.1	25.8	38.9	15.2	6.1	61299	69566	86	80	3968	5.1	0.5	22.0	62.0	10.4	222097
80864	YODER	17893	569	26.9	36.2	29.9	5.5	1.6	40758	46143	49	38	475	15.0	14.1	38.5	30.1	2.3	137500
80903	COLORADO SPRINGS	21423	6591	39.4	31.7	21.6	4.6	2.7	31821	37670	17	11	2869	4.4	6.6	56.0	29.4	3.7	154524
80904	COLORADO SPRINGS	26685	10611	25.6	36.3	27.8	7.1	3.3	41524	48396	51	42	6212	3.6	5.0	48.4	37.8	5.1	163591
80905	COLORADO SPRINGS	19568	1451	33.4	34.7	26.4	4.1	1.4	35283	41222	29	20	870	4.7	11.5	64.6	17.0	2.2	131030
80906	COLORADO SPRINGS	31078	20827	22.0	29.0	29.6	10.1	9.4	49096	56434	70	60	12821	5.4	4.2	30.6	42.0	17.9	200860
80907	COLORADO SPRINGS	26209	12391	26.7	31.7	29.7	7.6	4.3	43187	50003	56	47	7778	10.4	3.1	50.3	32.2	4.1	159466
80908	COLORADO SPRINGS	36039	3684	8.2	15.6	36.6	23.5	16.1	83686	95772	96	95	3410	0.8	0.4	10.9	62.1	25.9	305626
80909	COLORADO SPRINGS	21180	16417	29.8	34.7	27.5	5.6	2.5	38585	44655	41	31	8524	0.9	3.2	63.6	31.3	1.0	157787
80910	COLORADO SPRINGS	17198	11123	33.2	36.6	25.5	3.5	1.2	35156	41271	28	20	5238	4.6	10.1	77.2	8.0	0.1	125626
80911	COLORADO SPRINGS	20645	10516	15.1	30.1	42.8	9.9	2.1	53383	61188	77	70	8779	0.9	2.1	74.2	22.5	0.4	148849
80913	COLORADO SPRINGS	13585	1947	15.7	58.9	23.2	1.9	0.3	38217	42507	40	30	41	0.0	0.0	51.2	22.0	26.8	168750
80914	COLORADO SPRINGS	2721	0	0.0	0.0	0.0	0.0	0.0	0	0	0	0	0	0.0	0.0	0.0	0.0	0.0	0
80915	COLORADO SPRINGS	23294	8095	14.0	32.4	39.8	10.6	3.2	53234	60654	77	69	5737	11.5	4.5	56.6	25.5	1.9	148277
80916	COLORADO SPRINGS	18573	12216	18.8	39.0	36.3	4.8	1.2	45257	51863	62	53	7144	16.6	6.3	62.5	14.5	0.1	129139
80917	COLORADO SPRINGS	25674	12813	17.1	31.4	36.8	11.3	3.4	51386	57951	75	65	7903	0.5	3.6	49.3	45.4	1.2	171478
80918	COLORADO SPRINGS	28749	21612	12.6	25.3	42.5	14.1	5.5	62079	70889	86	81	15576	1.8	1.6	37.8	56.2	2.6	183896
80919	COLORADO SPRINGS	37491	11181	9.5	15.9	38.0	20.2	16.5	79644	90549	95	92	9021	0.0	1.2	16.7	68.4	13.7	257011
80920	COLORADO SPRINGS	28944	12102	5.2	16.9	46.8	22.8	8.3	78550	91296	95	92	10162	0.2	0.4	20.7	77.1	1.7	218256
80921	COLORADO SPRINGS	40518	3826	3.3	11.6	38.2	28.1	18.8	95536	113484	98	98	3453	0.1	0.1	2.4	76.7	20.7	307274
80922	COLORADO SPRINGS	24493	6961	3.3	19.5	59.5	13.8	3.9	68636	79250	91	87	6426	0.7	0.1	31.1	67.6	0.6	190525
80925	COLORADO SPRINGS	20783	1188	10.0	26.7	48.6	12.1	2.6	59696	66733	84	77	1019	7.4	2.2	50.5	37.7	2.3	166543
80926	COLORADO SPRINGS	50533	598	11.0	17.7	30.8	17.4	23.1	80231	89576	95	93	522	6.3	1.2	4.4	49.0	39.1	356818
80928	COLORADO SPRINGS	17392	352	23.0	33.8	34.7	7.1	1.4	45000	50246	61	52	296	13.5	11.2	40.5	32.4	2.4	150543
80929	COLORADO SPRINGS	23273	267	14.2	28.8	43.8	10.1	3.0	54426	61207	79	72	236	5.5	2.1	41.5	47.0	3.8	176351
80930	COLORADO SPRINGS	21624	302	14.6	26.5	48.7	8.3	2.0	55895	62700	81	74	262	6.5	2.7	50.0	39.3	1.5	167000
81001	PUEBLO	18423	11884	39.9	30.5	22.3	4.5	2.7	31186	35300	15	9	7543	11.8	25.5	50.5	11.4	0.8	103869
81003	PUEBLO	16295	5489	43.4	34.4	18.1	2.9	1.2	28117	32766	9	4	2908	11.0	37.4	46.0	5.3	0.3	91066
81004	PUEBLO	16894	11082	45.1	32.6	18.0	2.4	1.9	28139	32047	9	4	6883	6.7	37.3	51.7	3.5	0.7	93821
81005	PUEBLO	22629	11572	27.0	32.6	29.3	7.7	3.4	41406	46978	51	41	9129	4.3	10.2	66.1	17.9	1.5	123254
81006	PUEBLO	21500	4976	26.8	28.5	33.3	7.9	3.5	45319	51468	62	53	4215	11.2	17.2	42.5	27.5	1.6	132533
81007	PUEBLO	23646	7858	16.0	29.9	39.8	9.3	4.9	53109	60444	77	69	6539	3.2	8.0	51.8	35.3	1.6	156835
81008	PUEBLO	23866	3191	25.8	33.2	29.0	8.2	3.7	41830	47876	52	43	2551	13.5	12.6	57.6	14.9	1.5	118792
81019	COLORADO CITY	21696	654	24.2	27.8	39.9	4.3	3.8	48069	54251	68	58	547	7.9	9.1	50.8	23.8	8.4	136285
	COLORADO	28803		19.1	26.9	34.1	12.5	7.5	54077	63465				4.8	4.7	28.0	49.9	12.6	203984
	UNITED STATES	25866		24.7	27.1	30.8	10.9	6.5	48124	56710				10.9	15.0	33.7	30.1	10.4	145905

ZIP CODE		FINANCIAL SERVICES				THE HOME						ENTERTAINMENT						PERSONAL			
						Home Improvements		Furnishings													
#	POST OFFICE NAME	Auto Loan	Home Loan	Investments	Retirement Plans	Home Repair	Lawn & Garden	Computers & Hardware	Major Appliances	TV, Radio, Sound Equipment	Furniture	Dine out/ Carry out	Sports Equipment	Fees & Tickets	Toys & Games	Travel	Cable TV	Apparel & Services	Auto Repairs	Health Insurance	Pets & Supplies
80721	AMHERST	102	71	37	67	83	93	70	87	81	69	95	104	60	93	73	85	86	85	103	121
80722	ATWOOD	83	59	32	56	68	76	58	71	67	57	78	86	50	77	60	70	72	70	85	99
80723	BRUSH	72	61	50	60	65	72	63	68	67	63	81	78	59	78	63	68	76	68	73	81
80726	CROOK	80	56	29	53	65	73	55	68	63	54	74	82	47	73	57	67	68	67	81	95
80727	ECKLEY	77	53	28	51	62	70	53	65	61	52	71	79	45	70	55	64	65	64	78	91
80728	FLEMING	59	41	21	39	48	53	40	50	46	40	55	60	34	53	42	49	50	49	59	69
80729	GROVER	91	63	33	60	74	82	62	77	72	62	84	93	53	83	65	75	77	76	92	107
80731	HAXTUN	78	56	33	53	64	73	58	68	66	56	78	80	51	75	59	70	71	68	82	90
80733	HILLROSE	86	60	31	57	70	78	59	73	68	58	80	88	51	78	61	72	73	72	87	102
80734	HOLYOKE	77	59	40	58	65	76	63	70	70	61	83	80	57	80	63	73	76	70	82	87
80735	IDALIA	90	63	33	59	73	82	62	77	71	61	84	92	53	82	64	75	76	76	91	107
80736	ILIFF	82	57	30	54	67	75	56	70	65	56	76	84	48	75	59	68	70	69	83	97
80737	JULESBURG	67	50	32	48	55	66	55	61	61	52	72	69	48	68	54	65	66	61	73	75
80740	LINDON	72	50	26	47	58	65	49	61	57	49	67	74	42	65	51	60	61	60	73	85
80741	MERINO	98	69	36	65	80	90	68	84	78	67	92	101	58	90	70	82	84	83	100	117
80742	NEW RAYMER	91	63	33	60	74	83	62	77	72	62	84	93	53	83	65	76	77	76	92	108
80743	OTIS	111	77	40	73	90	101	76	94	88	75	103	114	65	101	79	92	94	93	112	131
80744	OVID	68	50	32	48	56	66	55	62	62	52	72	70	48	69	55	65	66	61	74	77
80745	PADRONI	70	49	26	46	57	64	48	60	56	48	66	72	41	64	50	59	60	59	71	84
80747	PEETZ	80	56	29	53	65	73	55	69	64	55	75	83	47	73	57	67	68	68	82	95
80749	SEDGWICK	90	63	34	60	73	82	63	77	72	62	85	92	54	83	65	76	77	76	92	106
80750	SNYDER	93	65	35	62	76	85	64	80	74	64	87	96	55	85	67	78	79	78	94	111
80751	STERLING	74	61	49	59	65	73	63	69	68	62	82	81	59	80	63	69	77	69	76	85
80754	STONEHAM	90	63	33	59	73	82	62	77	72	61	84	93	53	82	64	75	77	76	92	107
80755	VERNON	89	62	33	59	73	81	62	76	71	61	83	92	53	82	64	74	76	75	91	106
80757	WOODROW	87	61	32	57	71	79	60	74	69	59	81	89	51	79	62	72	74	73	88	103
80758	WRAY	85	61	35	58	69	79	63	74	71	61	84	87	54	81	64	75	76	73	88	98
80759	YUMA	73	56	37	54	61	71	59	66	65	57	78	76	53	75	59	68	71	66	77	82
80801	ANTON	102	71	37	67	83	93	70	87	81	69	95	105	60	93	73	85	86	86	103	121
80802	ARAPAHOE	96	67	35	63	78	87	66	82	76	65	89	98	56	87	68	80	81	80	97	114
80804	ARRIBA	87	61	32	57	71	79	60	74	69	59	81	89	51	79	62	73	74	73	88	103
80805	BETHUNE	104	73	38	69	85	95	72	89	83	71	97	107	61	95	74	87	88	87	106	124
80807	BURLINGTON	77	69	63	69	72	79	71	75	73	70	89	88	68	88	71	73	85	75	78	89
80808	CALHAN	88	83	68	80	82	86	78	83	78	81	97	96	75	93	77	76	94	82	81	97
80809	CASCADE	96	112	134	114	111	115	108	106	102	107	129	124	112	131	109	100	127	105	98	115
80810	CHEYENNE WELLS	93	65	34	61	76	85	64	79	74	63	87	96	55	85	66	78	79	78	94	110
80812	COPE	110	77	40	73	90	100	76	94	88	75	103	113	65	101	79	92	94	93	112	131
80813	CRIPPLE CREEK	98	77	53	70	87	98	73	88	82	72	98	103	65	96	78	88	91	86	104	120
80814	DIVIDE	98	122	129	122	119	118	108	108	101	108	126	127	115	135	111	98	126	104	97	119
80815	FLAGLER	75	55	34	52	61	72	59	67	66	56	78	77	52	74	59	70	71	67	80	84
80816	FLORISSANT	96	90	76	86	95	101	83	92	86	82	105	108	81	107	86	89	100	90	98	116
80817	FOUNTAIN	79	85	85	86	82	83	82	81	78	82	98	95	82	98	80	74	96	80	73	89
80818	GENOA	38	28	17	27	31	35	28	33	31	27	37	39	25	36	28	32	34	32	38	44
80820	GUFFEY	97	76	52	68	85	96	71	86	81	71	96	101	64	95	76	86	89	85	102	118
80821	HUGO	71	53	33	50	58	69	57	64	64	54	75	73	50	71	57	67	68	64	77	80
80822	JOES	113	79	41	74	92	103	78	96	89	77	105	116	66	103	81	94	96	95	114	134
80823	KARVAL	85	59	31	56	69	77	59	73	68	58	79	87	50	78	61	71	72	71	86	101
80824	KIRK	109	76	40	72	88	99	75	93	86	74	101	112	64	99	78	90	92	91	110	129
80825	KIT CARSON	76	56	35	54	62	74	61	68	68	58	81	78	54	77	61	72	73	68	82	85
80827	LAKE GEORGE	93	77	57	71	86	95	72	85	80	72	95	100	67	95	77	84	89	84	98	114
80828	LIMON	66	55	42	55	59	66	57	61	61	56	73	70	54	73	57	62	69	60	67	73
80829	MANITOU SPRINGS	77	89	108	91	88	91	87	85	82	86	104	100	90	106	88	80	103	85	78	92
80830	MATHESON	92	64	34	61	75	84	64	79	73	63	86	95	54	84	66	77	78	78	94	110
80831	PEYTON	109	113	104	115	111	112	105	107	100	107	126	126	105	127	103	97	123	105	99	123
80832	RAMAH	94	81	59	78	84	90	78	86	81	79	98	101	72	94	77	81	93	85	90	107
80833	RUSH	82	67	46	64	71	77	65	73	69	65	83	86	59	80	65	70	78	73	79	94
80834	SEIBERT	83	58	30	55	67	76	57	71	66	56	77	85	49	76	59	69	70	70	84	98
80835	SIMLA	93	65	34	61	75	84	64	79	74	63	87	95	55	85	66	77	79	78	94	110
80836	STRATTON	89	62	32	59	72	81	61	76	71	61	83	91	52	81	64	74	76	75	90	106
80840	U S A F ACADEMY	87	55	53	63	51	60	82	71	84	77	104	95	70	94	68	76	100	84	66	81
80861	VONA	93	65	34	61	75	84	64	79	74	63	86	95	54	85	66	77	79	78	94	110
80863	WOODLAND PARK	96	114	118	115	111	109	104	103	96	104	121	121	108	126	104	92	120	100	91	113
80864	YODER	79	72	56	69	72	76	69	73	69	70	86	85	65	81	68	68	82	73	73	87
80903	COLORADO SPRINGS	58	53	65	55	52	57	64	58	64	61	79	71	61	77	60	61	77	63	57	65
80904	COLORADO SPRINGS	73	76	87	78	76	80	78	76	76	77	95	89	79	95	78	74	93	77	73	84
80905	COLORADO SPRINGS	57	60	68	62	60	62	63	61	61	61	76	73	63	77	62	58	75	62	57	66
80906	COLORADO SPRINGS	103	105	115	107	103	109	108	105	105	107	132	124	108	131	106	103	129	107	100	116
80907	COLORADO SPRINGS	76	78	88	79	77	82	81	79	79	80	100	92	81	99	80	78	97	80	76	87
80908	COLORADO SPRINGS	134	167	178	170	162	162	148	146	136	149	172	169	160	180	150	131	172	140	130	161
80909	COLORADO SPRINGS	65	67	76	67	66	71	70	68	69	68	86	79	70	87	69	68	84	69	66	74
80910	COLORADO SPRINGS	57	55	63	57	54	57	60	57	59	59	75	69	59	73	58	57	73	60	54	63
80911	COLORADO SPRINGS	82	94	97	94	91	92	87	87	83	88	104	101	91	107	87	80	103	85	78	95
80913	COLORADO SPRINGS	69	44	42	50	40	48	65	56	66	61	83	75	56	74	54	60	79	66	52	64
80914	COLORADO SPRINGS	0	0	0	0	0	0	0	0	0	0	0	0	0	0	0	0	0	0	0	0
80915	COLORADO SPRINGS	87	93	92	93	91	93	89	89	85	89	107	104	89	107	88	82	105	88	82	100
80916	COLORADO SPRINGS	75	71	73	75	69	71	75	73	73	76	92	88	73	88	71	68	89	75	65	81
80917	COLORADO SPRINGS	86	89	97	92	86	88	90	87	86	90	109	104	90	107	87	82	107	89	79	96
80918	COLORADO SPRINGS	102	111	120	116	108	109	108	105	102	109	129	124	110	128	106	97	127	105	94	116
80919	COLORADO SPRINGS	135	159	170	164	154	153	145	142	133	147	169	166	153	173	145	128	169	139	125	156
80920	COLORADO SPRINGS	126	143	140	149	136	132	129	128	118	134	151	150	133	151	126	111	149	125	109	140
80921	COLORADO SPRINGS	154	176	194	183	173	177	166	163	155	167	196	191	174	197	166	150	194	161	150	180
80922	COLORADO SPRINGS	109	123	119	129	117	113	111	110	102	116	129	129	114	130	108	95	128	107	93	120
80925	COLORADO SPRINGS	93	106	102	110	101	97	95	94	87	99	111	111	98	111	93	81	110	92	80	103
80926	COLORADO SPRINGS	161	199	213	202	194	194	176	173	162	177	205	202	191	215	179	157	205	167	155	193
80928	COLORADO SPRINGS	82	79	65	77	78	80	74	78	73	76	91	90	72	87	73	71	88	77	75	91
80929	COLORADO SPRINGS	93	94	83	95	94	96	86	90	84	88	105	106	87	106	86	82	102	87	86	106
80930	COLORADO SPRINGS	86	96	94	99	92	90	89	88	82	91	104	103	90	104	86	77	103	86	76	96
81001	PUEBLO	63	60	65	59	59	64	65	64	66	65	82	73	63	80	63	65	80	66	62	69
81003	PUEBLO	48	47	52	46	47	52	51	49	52	49	64	57	50	65	50	52	62	50	51	54
81004	PUEBLO	53	51	54	49	51	58	55	54	57	53	70	62	54	71	54	58	68	55	57	60
81005	PUEBLO	75	80	84	78	80	86	78	79	78	77	97	90	80	99	80	78	94	78	79	88
81006	PUEBLO	81	85	82	82	85	90	81	83	81	80	100	95	82	103	82	81	98	82	83	95
81007	PUEBLO	94	103	98	104	100	100	95	96	89	96	112	112	96	113	94	86	111	94	87	108
81008	PUEBLO	78	85	90	83	84	88	84	83	82	83	102	95	85	105	84	81	100	82	80	90
81019	COLORADO CITY	100	70	36	66	81	91	69	85	79	68	93	103	59	91	71	83	85	84	101	119
	COLORADO	103	104	110	107	103	108	105	104	102	105	128	122	104	127	103	99	125	105	98	116
	UNITED STATES	100	100	100	100	100	100	100	100	100	100	100	100	100	100	100	100	100	100	100	100

COLORADO

POPULATION CHANGE

A 81020-81334

# POST OFFICE NAME	COUNTY FIPS CODE	POPULATION 2000	POPULATION 2004	POPULATION 2009	2000-2004 ANNUAL RATE % Rate	2000-2004 ANNUAL RATE State Centile	HOUSEHOLDS 2000	HOUSEHOLDS 2004	HOUSEHOLDS 2009	% Annual Rate 2000-2004	2004 Average HH Size	FAMILIES 2000	FAMILIES 2004	% Annual Rate 2000-2004
81020 AGUILAR	071	1008	1031	1058	0.5	25	422	439	458	0.9	2.35	285	293	0.7
81021 ARLINGTON	061	24	23	22	-1.0	2	10	10	9	0.0	2.30	7	7	0.0
81022 AVONDALE	101	1435	1584	1726	2.4	58	482	541	599	2.8	2.90	381	422	2.4
81023 BEULAH	101	1183	1313	1434	2.5	60	503	573	637	3.1	2.29	374	419	2.7
81025 BOONE	101	1275	1338	1420	1.1	35	498	533	574	1.6	2.49	370	391	1.3
81027 BRANSON	071	169	176	183	1.0	32	74	78	82	1.3	2.26	56	58	0.8
81029 CAMPO	009	483	478	464	-0.2	9	187	187	184	0.0	2.56	144	143	-0.2
81036 EADS	061	1124	1121	1106	-0.1	11	462	468	470	0.0	2.34	303	305	0.2
81039 FOWLER	101	1946	1955	1942	0.1	15	793	809	813	0.5	2.36	546	553	0.3
81040 GARDNER	055	303	333	367	2.3	56	138	156	177	2.9	2.13	89	99	2.5
81041 GRANADA	099	903	943	975	1.0	34	275	288	299	1.1	3.27	205	213	0.9
81043 HARTMAN	099	115	114	116	-0.2	9	41	41	42	0.0	2.78	31	31	0.0
81044 HASTY	011	396	435	480	2.2	55	155	172	191	2.5	2.53	113	124	2.2
81045 HASWELL	061	130	123	119	-1.3	1	51	49	49	-0.9	2.51	37	36	-0.6
81047 HOLLY	099	2004	2010	2034	0.1	14	729	735	748	0.2	2.67	529	530	0.1
81049 KIM	071	301	290	294	-0.9	2	135	131	134	-0.7	2.21	94	90	-1.0
81050 LA JUNTA	089	11424	11213	10928	-0.4	5	4437	4431	4389	0.0	2.44	3045	3020	-0.2
81052 LAMAR	099	10726	10832	11008	0.2	18	3994	4069	4163	0.4	2.60	2765	2796	0.3
81054 LAS ANIMAS	011	4971	5192	5544	1.0	34	1630	1734	1890	1.5	2.46	1116	1180	1.3
81055 LA VETA	055	1576	1720	1887	2.1	52	732	822	925	2.8	2.06	459	510	2.5
81057 MC CLAVE	011	549	603	666	2.2	55	187	207	231	2.4	2.91	136	150	2.3
81058 MANZANOLA	089	1069	1057	1042	-0.3	8	405	408	411	0.2	2.46	284	285	0.1
81059 MODEL	071	256	266	274	0.9	31	94	99	103	1.2	2.68	70	73	1.0
81062 OLNEY SPRINGS	025	1978	2185	2526	2.4	58	342	409	518	4.3	3.15	252	299	4.1
81063 ORDWAY	025	3022	3406	4056	2.9	66	817	962	1206	3.9	2.67	560	653	3.7
81064 PRITCHETT	009	158	156	153	-0.3	8	62	62	61	0.0	2.52	47	46	-0.5
81067 ROCKY FORD	089	6187	5916	5696	-1.1	1	2389	2321	2269	-0.7	2.50	1682	1623	-0.8
81069 RYE	101	1940	2099	2271	1.9	47	757	834	916	2.3	2.52	558	606	2.0
81071 SHERIDAN LAKE	061	337	319	308	-1.3	1	139	134	132	-0.9	2.38	102	98	-0.9
81073 SPRINGFIELD	009	2278	2205	2126	-0.8	3	1008	991	968	-0.4	2.16	636	618	-0.7
81076 SUGAR CITY	025	488	540	624	2.4	59	191	228	289	4.3	1.43	141	115	-4.7
81081 TRINCHERA	071	72	80	86	2.5	62	31	35	38	2.9	2.29	23	26	2.9
81082 TRINIDAD	071	12095	12517	12986	0.8	28	4895	5151	5422	1.2	2.36	3195	3334	1.0
81084 TWO BUTTES	009	99	95	91	-1.0	2	47	46	45	-0.5	2.07	34	33	-0.7
81087 VILAS	009	145	141	136	-0.7	3	57	56	55	-0.4	2.52	44	43	-0.5
81089 WALSENBURG	055	5870	6118	6515	1.0	33	2169	2326	2558	1.7	2.25	1340	1424	1.4
81090 WALSH	009	1372	1342	1298	-0.5	4	551	550	542	0.0	2.39	369	364	-0.3
81091 WESTON	071	1312	1436	1528	2.2	53	524	587	635	2.7	2.38	374	415	2.5
81092 WILEY	099	829	831	848	0.1	13	304	309	319	0.4	2.69	225	227	0.2
81101 ALAMOSA	003	13906	14419	15078	0.9	30	5117	5423	5795	1.4	2.48	3376	3549	1.2
81102 ALAMOSA	003	66	68	71	0.7	26	2	2	2	0.0	2.50	1	1	0.0
81120 ANTONITO	021	2604	2660	2714	0.5	24	997	1040	1080	1.0	2.55	712	737	0.8
81121 ARBOLES	007	134	158	199	4.0	78	42	51	66	4.7	3.10	32	39	4.8
81122 BAYFIELD	067	6064	6873	7794	3.0	68	2385	2772	3215	3.6	2.47	1745	2005	3.3
81123 BLANCA	023	798	893	970	2.7	64	291	333	371	3.2	2.68	213	242	3.1
81125 CENTER	109	3878	4308	4978	2.5	62	1297	1455	1708	2.7	2.95	998	1115	2.6
81130 CREEDE	079	833	875	875	1.2	36	378	403	403	1.5	2.17	252	267	1.4
81132 DEL NORTE	105	3247	3257	3374	0.1	14	1241	1269	1338	0.5	2.52	900	917	0.4
81133 FORT GARLAND	023	829	867	909	1.1	34	331	354	381	1.6	2.45	247	262	1.4
81136 HOOPER	003	275	287	301	1.0	33	93	98	105	1.2	2.93	75	79	1.2
81137 IGNACIO	067	5122	5593	6263	2.1	52	1880	2107	2417	2.7	2.63	1406	1559	2.5
81140 LA JARA	021	2711	2772	2826	0.5	24	924	965	1002	1.0	2.83	678	705	0.9
81143 MOFFAT	109	1438	1712	2066	4.2	80	698	866	1081	5.2	1.95	377	460	4.8
81144 MONTE VISTA	105	7616	7775	8024	0.5	24	2818	2912	3048	0.8	2.61	2055	2108	0.6
81146 MOSCA	003	643	670	704	1.0	32	226	239	256	1.3	2.80	177	186	1.2
81147 PAGOSA SPRINGS	007	9260	11388	14607	5.0	86	3729	4708	6197	5.6	2.40	2682	3364	5.5
81149 SAGUACHE	109	943	1066	1253	2.9	67	412	475	572	3.4	2.21	266	310	3.7
81151 SANFORD	023	4121	4202	4302	0.5	23	1507	1579	1656	1.1	2.66	1102	1147	1.0
81152 SAN LUIS	023	295	299	308	0.3	19	132	139	148	1.2	2.15	85	89	1.1
81153 SAN PABLO	023	650	654	672	0.1	16	282	294	313	1.0	2.22	190	196	0.7
81154 SOUTH FORK	105	1210	1521	1742	5.5	88	532	682	796	6.0	2.23	380	485	5.9
81155 VILLA GROVE	109	120	155	194	6.2	92	47	62	79	6.7	2.50	35	46	6.6
81201 SALIDA	015	8678	9558	10851	2.3	57	3844	4316	4997	2.8	2.19	2414	2686	2.5
81210 ALMONT	051	267	325	379	4.7	85	117	144	171	5.0	2.25	74	91	5.0
81211 BUENA VISTA	015	6735	7421	8341	2.3	57	2360	2719	3193	3.4	2.27	1662	1896	3.2
81212 CANON CITY	043	29046	31249	34722	1.7	45	9866	10894	12475	2.4	2.34	6527	7144	2.2
81220 CIMARRON	085	124	141	160	3.1	71	56	65	75	3.6	2.11	41	47	3.3
81223 COTOPAXI	043	1253	1736	2202	8.0	95	520	727	930	8.2	2.39	401	554	7.9
81224 CRESTED BUTTE	051	3433	3893	4381	3.0	69	1494	1718	1963	3.3	2.27	660	748	3.2
81226 FLORENCE	043	9654	10689	11843	2.4	60	2483	2861	3334	3.4	2.54	1731	1975	3.2
81228 GRANITE	065	89	101	113	3.0	70	40	46	52	3.3	2.20	29	33	3.1
81230 GUNNISON	051	9342	9684	10353	0.9	29	3653	3874	4244	1.4	2.25	1969	2064	1.1
81231 GUNNISON	051	24	25	26	1.0	32	10	11	12	2.3	1.73	6	6	0.0
81233 HOWARD	043	1529	1736	2001	3.0	70	670	774	904	3.5	2.24	508	580	3.2
81235 LAKE CITY	053	750	804	804	1.7	44	344	372	372	1.9	2.16	237	254	1.6
81236 NATHROP	015	844	997	1173	4.0	78	385	465	558	4.5	2.14	290	347	4.3
81239 PARLIN	051	112	145	174	6.3	93	47	63	77	7.1	2.29	36	47	6.5
81240 PENROSE	043	4585	5057	5748	2.3	57	1665	1871	2155	2.8	2.68	1313	1462	2.6
81241 PITKIN	051	124	165	201	7.0	94	47	64	79	7.5	2.58	36	48	7.0
81243 POWDERHORN	051	93	103	115	2.4	60	34	39	44	3.3	2.51	24	27	2.8
81251 TWIN LAKES CPU	065	170	191	212	2.8	65	78	88	98	2.9	2.17	56	62	2.4
81252 WESTCLIFFE	027	2825	3348	4143	4.1	79	1210	1467	1856	4.6	2.27	867	1045	4.5
81253 WETMORE	027	636	756	935	4.2	80	254	310	394	4.8	2.39	199	242	4.7
81301 DURANGO	067	24275	26619	29584	2.2	54	9883	11104	12652	2.8	2.25	5480	6123	2.6
81303 DURANGO	067	7131	7529	8239	1.3	38	2680	2890	3228	1.8	2.58	1889	2013	1.5
81320 CAHONE	033	530	572	636	2.6	63	233	268	307	3.4	2.13	136	154	3.0
81321 CORTEZ	083	13041	13225	13432	0.3	19	5052	5247	5447	0.9	2.47	3504	3612	0.8
81323 DOLORES	083	4013	4048	4105	0.2	17	1636	1701	1767	0.9	2.37	1177	1215	0.8
81324 DOVE CREEK	033	1331	1397	1505	1.2	36	552	595	659	1.8	2.35	406	437	1.8
81325 EGNAR	113	156	157	166	0.2	16	61	63	68	0.8	2.49	41	42	0.6
81326 HESPERUS	067	1777	2008	2265	2.9	67	694	801	923	3.4	2.51	508	580	3.2
81327 LEWIS	083	813	867	901	1.5	42	312	341	361	2.1	2.54	239	259	1.9
81328 MANCOS	083	3650	3662	3704	0.1	14	1460	1508	1561	0.8	2.34	1022	1046	0.6
81331 PLEASANT VIEW	083	286	309	323	1.8	46	109	120	129	2.3	2.58	84	92	2.3
81334 TOWAOC	083	1914	2031	2109	1.4	41	589	641	679	2.0	3.15	457	494	1.9
COLORADO					2.4					2.6	2.52			2.5
UNITED STATES					1.2					1.3	2.58			1.1

#	ZIP CODE POST OFFICE NAME	RACE (%) White 2000	White 2004	Black 2000	Black 2004	Asian/Pacific 2000	Asian/Pacific 2004	% Hispanic Origin 2000	% Hispanic Origin 2004	2004 AGE DISTRIBUTION (%) 0-4	5-9	10-14	15-19	20-24	25-44	45-64	65-84	85+	18+	MEDIAN AGE 2004	% 2004 Males	% 2004 Females
81020	AGUILAR	85.7	85.0	0.0	0.0	0.5	0.6	42.5	45.9	4.9	5.0	6.3	5.4	5.9	19.9	32.0	17.5	3.2	80.7	47.2	48.5	51.5
81021	ARLINGTON	95.8	100.0	0.0	0.0	0.0	0.0	0.0	0.0	8.7	8.7	8.7	8.7	8.7	34.8	21.7	0.0	0.0	73.9	28.8	47.8	52.2
81022	AVONDALE	88.6	87.9	0.1	0.1	0.2	0.2	37.6	41.4	6.3	6.4	7.2	7.2	6.8	26.6	25.7	12.9	1.0	75.8	37.6	51.1	48.9
81023	BEULAH	94.3	93.4	0.5	0.5	0.2	0.2	9.6	11.4	4.5	5.5	6.9	6.8	2.2	22.8	37.2	13.0	1.1	78.5	45.7	50.9	49.1
81025	BOONE	90.4	89.5	0.4	0.4	0.5	0.5	27.1	30.9	5.9	6.1	6.7	6.9	5.8	25.1	28.0	14.1	1.5	77.1	41.0	50.1	49.9
81027	BRANSON	93.5	93.2	0.6	0.6	0.0	0.0	12.4	13.6	4.6	5.1	10.2	7.4	4.0	26.1	27.8	13.1	1.7	74.4	41.2	50.0	50.0
81029	CAMPO	96.7	96.7	0.0	0.0	0.2	0.2	2.7	2.7	5.2	6.1	7.1	7.5	5.4	21.8	27.0	17.8	2.1	76.8	42.9	53.1	46.9
81036	EADS	96.1	96.1	0.5	0.5	0.0	0.0	3.2	3.1	6.2	6.2	6.9	6.5	6.5	22.8	26.1	15.3	3.6	76.5	41.6	50.0	50.0
81039	FOWLER	94.7	94.1	0.2	0.2	0.1	0.1	12.5	14.5	6.6	6.5	6.0	5.9	6.0	22.5	25.8	17.1	3.6	77.5	42.3	48.1	51.9
81040	GARDNER	75.6	73.3	0.3	0.3	0.0	0.0	32.0	36.3	3.0	4.2	7.5	9.0	5.1	18.6	42.0	9.6	0.9	79.3	46.1	50.8	49.3
81041	GRANADA	64.3	62.3	0.1	0.2	0.0	0.0	59.8	63.3	8.3	8.2	9.9	10.6	7.7	26.9	19.8	7.7	0.9	67.0	28.6	53.2	46.8
81043	HARTMAN	91.3	89.5	0.0	0.0	0.0	0.0	18.3	20.2	6.1	6.1	9.7	6.1	6.1	27.2	23.7	13.2	1.8	72.8	39.1	53.5	46.5
81044	HASTY	85.6	84.1	0.3	0.2	0.8	0.7	17.4	19.8	7.8	7.8	7.6	6.4	6.0	26.9	24.4	12.2	0.9	72.6	36.7	51.0	49.0
81045	HASWELL	96.2	95.9	0.8	0.8	0.0	0.0	3.1	2.4	6.5	6.5	6.5	5.7	7.3	24.4	28.5	13.0	1.6	75.6	40.8	52.9	47.2
81047	HOLLY	80.6	78.8	0.2	0.2	0.1	0.1	29.4	32.5	8.1	7.8	8.7	7.0	6.1	25.3	22.1	12.0	2.8	70.6	36.4	52.3	47.7
81049	KIM	97.7	97.2	0.7	0.7	0.3	0.3	6.3	7.2	3.5	4.1	7.6	5.9	3.8	22.1	30.3	20.7	2.1	81.0	47.4	52.8	47.2
81050	LA JUNTA	78.2	76.5	1.0	1.1	0.8	0.9	36.3	39.5	6.9	6.4	7.7	7.8	7.6	23.8	24.1	13.6	2.1	74.3	37.0	48.7	51.3
81052	LAMAR	78.6	76.9	0.3	0.4	0.5	0.6	32.6	35.4	8.2	7.8	7.6	7.6	8.1	26.7	21.8	10.4	1.8	72.1	32.4	50.2	49.9
81054	LAS ANIMAS	78.3	77.0	4.4	4.5	0.5	0.6	32.9	35.7	5.9	5.6	5.8	6.5	8.0	28.7	23.2	14.0	2.3	78.5	37.9	57.1	42.9
81055	LA VETA	91.4	90.5	0.3	0.4	0.6	0.8	12.7	14.8	3.7	4.5	6.8	6.9	5.3	17.1	37.4	16.3	2.1	80.7	47.6	49.8	50.2
81057	MC CLAVE	85.6	84.1	0.2	0.2	0.7	0.8	17.5	19.7	7.6	7.6	7.6	6.5	6.1	26.9	24.5	12.1	1.0	73.1	36.9	50.6	49.4
81058	MANZANOLA	81.5	79.8	1.6	1.8	0.6	0.7	30.5	33.9	6.4	6.3	7.1	6.4	6.3	25.7	26.7	13.5	1.4	76.6	39.4	52.1	47.9
81059	MODEL	91.4	90.6	0.4	0.4	0.4	0.4	16.0	17.3	4.5	5.3	9.8	7.5	4.9	25.9	27.1	13.5	1.5	74.4	40.8	49.6	50.4
81062	OLNEY SPRINGS	82.7	81.7	8.3	8.7	1.2	1.3	18.1	19.8	4.3	4.5	4.9	4.7	8.3	43.3	21.7	7.1	1.1	83.3	36.1	70.6	29.4
81063	ORDWAY	83.4	82.7	5.8	5.8	0.6	0.6	26.0	28.4	5.3	5.1	6.1	6.1	8.3	33.2	24.1	10.1	1.8	79.8	38.0	61.3	38.7
81064	PRITCHETT	96.8	97.4	0.0	0.0	0.0	0.0	3.2	3.2	5.1	5.1	7.1	7.1	5.1	21.8	28.9	18.0	1.9	77.6	44.2	52.6	47.4
81067	ROCKY FORD	75.8	74.3	0.4	0.5	1.0	1.2	48.0	51.2	6.5	6.5	8.0	7.4	6.9	23.4	24.3	14.5	2.6	74.2	38.3	50.3	49.7
81069	RYE	93.6	92.7	0.3	0.3	0.2	0.2	9.2	10.9	4.3	6.2	7.6	7.5	3.8	22.4	33.0	14.3	0.9	76.6	43.9	50.2	49.8
81071	SHERIDAN LAKE	96.1	96.6	0.3	0.3	0.0	0.0	3.0	3.1	6.6	6.6	7.2	5.6	6.9	23.8	27.6	13.8	1.9	75.9	40.5	51.1	48.9
81073	SPRINGFIELD	94.3	93.7	0.0	0.1	0.3	0.4	6.3	7.2	6.0	5.9	5.9	5.8	5.9	20.9	25.9	19.6	4.3	78.6	44.8	48.3	51.7
81076	SUGAR CITY	83.2	82.4	8.0	8.3	1.2	1.3	17.2	18.9	4.3	4.6	5.0	4.8	8.2	42.8	21.7	7.4	1.3	82.8	36.2	69.6	30.4
81081	TRINCHERA	94.4	95.0	0.0	0.0	0.0	0.0	16.7	17.5	2.5	3.8	7.5	7.5	2.5	27.5	36.3	12.5	0.0	80.0	44.4	42.5	57.5
81082	TRINIDAD	81.2	80.2	0.5	0.5	0.6	0.7	44.4	47.5	5.9	6.0	7.0	7.1	6.7	22.6	26.9	14.9	3.0	77.0	41.1	48.7	51.3
81084	TWO BUTTES	96.0	95.8	0.0	0.0	0.0	0.0	5.1	5.3	3.2	7.4	8.4	7.4	4.2	19.0	39.0	10.5	1.1	74.7	45.2	51.6	48.4
81087	VILAS	92.4	92.2	0.0	0.0	0.7	0.7	7.6	8.5	6.4	6.4	5.7	7.1	5.7	20.6	29.1	16.3	2.8	76.6	43.6	53.9	46.1
81089	WALSENBURG	78.3	77.3	3.6	3.7	0.4	0.5	41.8	45.1	4.5	4.6	5.8	6.1	6.7	26.8	27.9	15.0	2.7	80.9	42.0	55.5	44.5
81090	WALSH	91.6	90.8	0.1	0.1	0.2	0.2	10.4	11.6	6.9	7.8	6.1	6.0	4.3	22.1	28.4	15.6	2.9	74.6	42.7	51.1	48.9
81091	WESTON	86.1	85.3	0.1	0.1	0.5	0.6	32.6	35.6	4.7	5.2	6.2	5.9	4.4	23.4	35.2	13.7	1.5	80.2	45.2	51.4	48.6
81092	WILEY	88.1	86.5	0.1	0.1	0.2	0.2	16.0	18.2	7.8	7.5	8.4	7.0	6.9	31.7	21.2	8.2	1.4	71.7	33.5	50.2	49.8
81101	ALAMOSA	70.2	68.4	1.0	1.1	1.0	1.1	43.3	46.5	7.3	6.7	7.6	8.7	11.9	26.2	22.1	8.1	1.5	74.3	30.3	49.7	50.3
81102	ALAMOSA	75.8	73.5	3.0	2.9	1.5	1.5	27.3	29.4	10.3	5.9	2.9	13.2	27.9	23.5	13.2	1.5	1.5	80.9	23.2	39.7	60.3
81120	ANTONITO	68.8	68.1	0.3	0.3	0.3	0.3	78.8	81.1	7.4	7.3	7.9	7.6	6.4	22.3	24.7	15.0	1.5	72.6	37.6	51.2	48.8
81121	ARBOLES	74.6	72.8	0.0	0.0	0.0	0.0	26.9	29.8	5.1	6.3	8.9	6.3	4.4	19.6	34.8	13.3	1.3	75.3	44.6	55.1	44.9
81122	BAYFIELD	92.3	91.7	0.2	0.3	0.2	0.2	8.1	9.1	5.5	6.2	7.5	6.2	5.2	27.1	32.4	9.5	0.5	76.7	40.8	50.7	49.3
81123	BLANCA	62.8	60.0	1.0	1.0	2.6	2.8	48.8	53.2	5.8	6.7	9.0	8.3	5.8	23.9	27.4	12.2	0.9	73.2	38.0	52.0	48.0
81125	CENTER	62.1	59.5	0.2	0.3	0.2	0.2	62.2	66.5	9.0	8.6	8.7	8.4	7.9	26.5	22.0	8.2	0.7	68.6	30.6	50.7	49.4
81130	CREEDE	96.9	96.9	0.0	0.0	0.0	0.0	2.0	2.1	4.5	4.8	6.1	5.1	3.4	21.6	35.5	17.7	1.3	81.3	47.5	51.1	48.9
81132	DEL NORTE	73.5	71.8	0.3	0.3	0.3	0.3	43.6	46.6	6.6	7.5	7.9	6.7	6.4	23.5	27.5	11.8	2.1	73.8	39.0	49.6	50.4
81133	FORT GARLAND	62.4	60.3	0.5	0.6	2.2	2.1	56.3	60.2	6.3	6.7	6.5	6.6	5.5	21.3	28.3	17.9	0.9	76.4	42.8	49.4	50.6
81136	HOOPER	84.0	81.9	0.4	0.4	1.1	1.4	17.1	19.2	6.6	8.0	10.1	8.7	4.9	28.6	22.3	10.1	0.7	69.3	36.4	51.9	48.1
81137	IGNACIO	66.3	65.6	0.2	0.2	0.3	0.3	21.7	23.2	6.3	7.0	9.0	8.1	6.5	26.6	27.4	8.5	0.8	72.5	36.2	50.6	49.4
81140	LA JARA	71.2	69.5	0.1	0.1	0.3	0.3	52.8	56.2	8.3	8.0	8.6	8.2	7.0	22.1	23.0	12.5	2.3	69.7	35.1	48.4	51.6
81143	MOFFAT	90.9	89.5	0.1	0.1	0.9	1.1	8.1	10.7	3.6	5.1	5.8	4.9	3.5	20.6	44.0	11.3	1.2	82.6	48.1	51.1	48.9
81144	MONTE VISTA	70.7	67.9	0.4	0.5	0.3	0.3	46.1	50.4	7.5	7.2	7.9	7.6	6.8	24.3	24.3	12.4	2.2	72.5	36.5	48.8	51.2
81146	MOSCA	83.4	81.6	0.6	0.6	1.1	1.3	17.7	20.0	6.4	7.6	9.9	8.4	5.4	27.6	24.3	9.9	0.6	70.6	36.6	51.8	48.2
81147	PAGOSA SPRINGS	89.2	88.2	0.4	0.4	0.3	0.4	16.0	17.8	5.3	6.0	7.6	7.1	4.1	24.7	33.7	10.9	0.7	76.3	42.3	50.5	49.5
81149	SAGUACHE	83.8	81.1	0.0	0.0	0.5	0.6	26.7	32.8	4.9	5.3	6.3	6.2	5.0	22.6	34.6	13.1	2.1	79.6	44.9	51.1	48.9
81151	SANFORD	73.2	72.0	0.3	0.3	0.2	0.2	56.7	59.6	7.8	7.7	8.6	8.1	7.6	23.0	22.6	12.8	1.8	70.7	34.3	49.7	50.3
81152	SAN LUIS	64.8	62.9	1.7	1.7	0.0	0.0	50.5	54.5	5.7	6.0	5.4	6.0	4.7	18.7	37.8	14.1	1.7	78.9	47.1	52.5	47.5
81153	SAN PABLO	55.1	54.4	0.9	1.1	0.3	0.5	88.2	89.8	5.5	5.8	6.7	7.0	6.0	18.7	31.0	17.1	2.1	78.3	45.2	49.2	50.8
81154	SOUTH FORK	92.2	91.4	0.1	0.1	0.2	0.2	12.9	15.3	4.5	5.1	5.9	5.3	4.5	22.0	32.2	19.7	0.8	81.1	46.9	49.6	50.4
81155	VILLA GROVE	91.7	89.7	0.0	0.0	1.7	1.3	10.0	14.2	4.5	3.9	5.8	7.1	3.9	20.0	45.8	7.7	1.3	81.3	47.2	51.6	48.4
81201	SALIDA	93.7	93.0	0.1	0.1	0.5	0.5	8.6	9.8	5.0	5.2	6.1	6.4	4.7	24.0	29.7	16.5	2.4	79.5	44.1	49.6	50.4
81210	ALMONT	95.9	95.1	0.0	0.3	0.8	0.9	4.9	5.5	5.2	4.6	6.2	7.1	5.5	35.4	27.7	7.7	0.6	79.4	36.6	53.5	46.5
81211	BUENA VISTA	86.7	85.7	3.7	3.9	0.5	0.6	9.3	10.3	3.8	4.6	5.3	5.3	7.8	29.5	29.7	13.0	1.1	83.0	41.2	57.7	42.4
81212	CANON CITY	91.1	90.6	4.3	4.4	0.5	0.6	10.5	11.7	5.0	5.0	6.0	6.1	7.7	29.4	24.3	13.8	2.7	80.2	39.6	55.4	44.6
81220	CIMARRON	91.1	91.5	0.0	0.0	0.8	0.7	4.8	5.7	5.0	5.7	6.4	6.4	3.6	25.5	36.2	11.4	0.0	78.0	43.3	51.1	48.9
81223	COTOPAXI	94.9	94.6	0.2	0.2	0.5	0.6	4.1	4.7	3.6	5.9	7.0	6.9	2.1	22.3	38.6	13.3	0.4	78.2	46.1	50.9	49.1
81224	CRESTED BUTTE	97.3	97.0	0.2	0.2	0.4	0.5	2.7	3.1	4.6	3.6	4.0	4.8	8.0	49.8	22.4	2.8	0.0	84.8	32.9	56.4	43.6
81226	FLORENCE	80.4	79.5	12.3	13.0	0.8	0.8	13.2	14.9	4.7	4.6	5.0	5.1	6.6	39.2	24.0	9.6	1.3	82.6	37.4	64.6	35.4
81228	GRANITE	82.0	81.2	0.0	0.0	0.0	0.0	24.7	25.7	5.9	6.9	7.9	6.9	5.0	27.7	32.7	6.9	0.0	73.3	38.2	55.5	44.6
81230	GUNNISON	94.4	93.8	0.6	0.7	0.6	0.7	5.9	6.8	4.1	4.3	5.7	14.1	12.9	28.7	21.6	7.6	1.0	81.9	29.6	52.9	47.1
81231	GUNNISON	95.8	96.0	0.0	0.0	0.0	0.0	8.3	4.0	0.0	0.0	8.0	20.0	16.0	32.0	24.0	0.0	0.0	92.0	28.8	56.0	44.0
81233	HOWARD	96.9	96.5	0.2	0.2	0.1	0.2	4.3	5.1	3.3	4.3	4.9	5.0	4.0	18.6	39.9	18.6	1.5	84.2	50.1	50.2	49.8
81235	LAKE CITY	97.3	97.4	0.0	0.0	0.3	0.3	1.6	1.6	6.0	4.7	5.1	3.9	3.6	27.5	37.6	10.8	0.9	81.3	44.7	51.5	48.5
81236	NATHROP	96.2	96.0	0.1	0.2	0.7	0.8	3.1	3.5	3.5	3.8	5.0	4.7	2.6	19.6	40.8	19.2	0.8	84.6	50.9	50.5	49.6
81239	PARLIN	94.6	94.5	0.0	0.0	0.9	1.4	6.3	7.6	5.5	4.1	7.6	8.3	3.5	27.6	31.7	11.0	0.7	77.2	41.4	51.7	48.3
81240	PENROSE	95.1	94.7	0.6	0.7	0.4	0.5	7.2	8.3	6.2	6.8	7.4	7.2	6.0	25.0	30.4	10.5	0.6	75.0	39.8	51.1	48.9
81241	PITKIN	94.4	94.6	0.0	0.0	0.8	1.2	6.5	7.3	5.5	4.2	7.3	7.9	3.0	27.3	33.3	10.9	0.6	77.6	42.2	53.3	46.7
81243	POWDERHORN	90.3	90.3	0.0	0.0	0.0	1.0	2.2	2.9	4.9	5.8	6.8	6.8	2.9	28.2	35.0	9.7	0.0	78.6	40.4	54.4	45.6
81251	TWIN LAKES CPU	72.9	71.2	0.6	0.5	0.0	0.0	35.9	38.7	8.4	8.4	10.0	7.9	6.3	31.4	22.0	5.8	0.0	68.1	30.8	56.5	43.5
81252	WESTCLIFFE	95.8	95.5	0.4	0.4	0.3	0.3	2.3	2.5	5.3	5.9	5.9	5.1	4.1	19.4	37.5	16.0	0.9	79.5	47.4	51.0	49.0
81253	WETMORE	95.8	95.8	0.9	0.9	0.3	0.4	3.6	4.1	4.2	5.2	6.9	5.0	3.8	21.2	38.2	15.0	0.5	80.2	46.8	51.7	48.3
81301	DURANGO	89.2	88.4	0.4	0.4	0.7	0.8	9.4	10.6	4.3	4.5	5.6	9.6	13.0	26.8	25.9	9.0	1.4	81.8	34.2	50.8	49.2
81303	DURANGO	89.4	88.2	0.2	0.2	0.3	0.3	9.8	11.2	5.5	5.9	6.9	6.8	7.4	28.0	31.0	7.9	0.6	77.6	38.8	51.0	49.0
81320	CAHONE	93.2	93.0	0.0	0.0	1.4	1.6	3.3	3.5	4.2	3.3	4.6	5.1	5.9	31.6	32.7	11.2	1.4	85.3	42.6	54.9	45.1
81321	CORTEZ	82.9	82.1	0.2	0.2	0.3	0.4	11.5	12.8	7.3	6.9	7.0	7.4	7.3	23.9	25.7	12.7	2.0	74.2	37.7	48.7	51.3
81323	DOLORES	91.0	90.3	0.1	0.1	0.3	0.3	8.0	9.0	5.4	5.9	7.1	6.5	4.7	23.2	32.9	13.1	1.2	77.2	43.2	49.9	50.1
81324	DOVE CREEK	96.1	95.9	0.1	0.1	0.1	0.1	4.1	4.5	5.2	5.8	6.8	6.5	5.4	21.3	30.1	16.4	2.4	78.1	44.1	50.3	49.8
81325	EGNAR	97.4	97.5	0.0	0.0	0.0	0.0	3.2	4.5	4.5	5.7	7.0	7.0	6.4	23.6	35.7	9.6	0.6	78.3	42.5	53.5	46.5
81326	HESPERUS	93.3	92.5	0.3	0.3	0.1	0.1	6.9	7.9	6.2	7.1	8.3	6.3	5.5	25.4	32.0	8.5	0.9	74.6	39.6	51.7	48.3
81327	LEWIS	94.1	93.5	0.0	0.0	0.4	0.4	5.3	6.0	6.9	7.3	6.7	6.2	4.7	23.6	30.0	13.6	0.9	75.3	41.8	50.5	49.5
81328	MANCOS	91.6	90.9	0.1	0.1	0.2	0.3	7.8	8.9	5.0	5.3	6.4	7.3	6.0	21.8	32.0	13.8	2.4	78.4	43.8	49.3	50.7
81331	PLEASANT VIEW	94.1	93.9	0.0	0.0	0.0	0.0	5.6	6.5	7.8	7.8	6.2	5.8	4.2	23.6	28.8	14.9	1.0	74.4	41.8	50.8	49.2
81334	TOWAOC	27.9	27.6	0.2	0.2	0.1	0.1	4.9	5.2	10.0	10.0	10.5	9.3	7.7	28.4	17.9	5.5	0.5	63.2	26.8	49.8	50.2
	COLORADO	82.8	81.7	3.8	3.9	2.3	2.6	17.1	18.6	7.0	6.8	7.1	7.0	7.5	30.6	24.3	8.6	1.2	75.1	35.0	50.3	49.7
	UNITED STATES	75.1	73.6	12.3	12.5	3.8	4.2	12.5	14.1	6.9	6.7	7.2	7.0	7.3	28.6	23.8	10.8	1.7	75.1	36.0	49.1	50.9

ZIP CODE #	POST OFFICE NAME	2004 Per Capita Income	2004 HH Income Base	2004 HOUSEHOLD INCOME DISTRIBUTION (%) Less than $25,000	$25,000 to $49,999	$50,000 to $99,999	$100,000 to $149,999	$150,000 or More	MEDIAN HOUSEHOLD INCOME 2004	2009	2004 National Centile	2004 State Centile	2004 Home Value Base	2004 HOME VALUE DISTRIBUTION (%) Less than $50,000	$50,000 to $89,999	$90,000 to $174,999	$175,000 to $399,999	$400,000 or More	2004 Median Home Value
81020	AGUILAR	14542	439	49.2	33.7	10.9	4.3	1.8	25426	26503	5	3	361	21.3	33.2	27.2	10.3	8.0	85286
81021	ARLINGTON	15870	10	40.0	30.0	30.0	0.0	0.0	30000	32265	12	7	7	0.0	42.9	57.1	0.0	0.0	103125
81022	AVONDALE	16382	541	27.2	41.4	23.8	4.8	2.8	36192	41469	32	24	443	17.2	23.7	44.0	12.0	3.2	102083
81023	BEULAH	27695	573	16.1	28.5	41.9	8.9	4.7	53245	61730	77	69	496	6.3	2.4	46.8	40.9	3.6	164925
81025	BOONE	21410	533	32.7	37.2	20.5	5.6	4.1	33954	39042	24	17	439	22.6	28.7	32.4	11.9	4.6	88659
81027	BRANSON	19938	78	34.6	32.1	28.2	3.9	1.3	31832	35000	17	11	59	17.0	25.4	40.7	6.8	10.2	101250
81029	CAMPO	15635	187	40.6	38.0	17.1	2.1	2.1	31444	35000	16	9	155	47.7	16.8	25.2	5.8	4.5	55000
81036	EADS	19282	468	36.5	34.4	19.9	6.0	3.2	33364	37774	22	16	355	36.1	34.1	27.3	1.7	0.9	67500
81039	FOWLER	19625	809	35.7	34.1	23.5	5.4	1.2	33113	38263	21	14	604	8.6	33.3	48.5	9.6	0.0	98167
81040	GARDNER	21250	156	42.3	22.4	26.3	5.8	3.2	28846	30781	10	6	117	12.0	25.6	29.9	27.4	5.1	104808
81041	GRANADA	12098	288	42.0	33.7	19.4	2.8	2.1	28655	31334	10	5	194	38.1	28.4	28.9	4.6	0.0	65333
81043	HARTMAN	14211	41	31.7	43.9	19.5	4.9	0.0	34277	38596	25	17	34	38.2	17.7	29.4	14.7	0.0	75000
81044	HASTY	20321	172	30.2	39.0	22.7	5.2	2.9	38308	42877	40	30	126	29.4	22.2	35.7	10.3	2.4	87500
81045	HASWELL	16707	49	38.8	30.6	22.5	8.2	0.0	32276	39076	19	12	35	31.4	25.7	31.4	8.6	2.9	78333
81047	HOLLY	15778	735	41.8	35.1	17.4	2.7	3.0	30195	32314	13	7	567	38.8	30.3	21.7	9.0	0.2	65426
81049	KIM	30569	131	29.8	45.8	18.3	2.3	3.8	38473	43457	41	31	111	38.7	22.5	14.4	10.8	13.5	74375
81050	LA JUNTA	17970	4431	38.3	30.0	24.8	5.5	1.4	33712	38746	23	16	3169	17.3	30.9	41.8	9.7	0.3	92407
81052	LAMAR	16871	4069	34.7	36.3	22.8	4.7	1.6	33573	38062	23	16	2799	23.9	25.2	40.7	9.6	0.7	91183
81054	LAS ANIMAS	15932	1734	41.1	32.8	21.4	2.9	1.9	29609	33312	11	7	1251	30.1	31.1	33.0	3.9	1.9	76593
81055	LA VETA	24451	822	36.3	30.4	24.2	6.1	3.0	34666	39389	26	18	600	7.3	11.5	46.8	29.8	4.5	135616
81057	MC CLAVE	17686	207	30.0	38.2	23.7	5.8	2.4	38707	42630	42	32	152	29.0	22.4	35.5	11.2	2.0	88000
81058	MANZANOLA	16113	408	40.9	33.3	21.1	3.2	1.5	31032	34910	15	8	321	21.8	34.0	30.5	13.4	0.3	82885
81059	MODEL	16451	99	37.4	30.3	26.3	5.1	1.0	31124	35370	15	9	76	14.5	25.0	40.8	10.5	9.2	105769
81062	OLNEY SPRINGS	15622	409	40.8	31.5	23.5	1.7	2.4	30681	32444	14	8	328	18.6	25.9	34.5	15.6	5.5	97500
81063	ORDWAY	16755	962	42.3	37.3	14.9	2.7	2.8	28168	31736	9	5	703	26.2	30.9	37.6	4.8	0.6	81161
81064	PRITCHETT	17662	62	40.3	40.3	16.1	1.6	1.6	31812	35435	17	11	52	44.2	17.3	28.9	5.8	3.9	65000
81067	ROCKY FORD	16293	2321	41.0	31.1	21.8	4.3	1.8	31092	34535	15	8	1678	17.3	37.8	36.6	7.9	0.4	84785
81069	RYE	24266	834	25.1	31.7	32.1	6.0	5.2	44746	51239	61	52	716	7.3	11.3	52.8	21.7	7.0	134956
81071	SHERIDAN LAKE	20345	134	37.3	30.6	20.9	9.0	2.2	33274	36518	22	15	96	31.3	26.0	33.3	8.3	1.0	77778
81073	SPRINGFIELD	17848	991	44.4	32.8	19.0	2.5	1.3	28706	32442	10	5	751	35.4	30.2	29.2	4.5	0.7	68917
81076	SUGAR CITY	27561	228	41.2	29.0	25.0	1.8	3.1	30922	32854	15	8	182	17.6	25.8	33.5	17.6	5.5	98571
81081	TRINCHERA	20091	35	37.1	25.7	25.7	11.4	0.0	32368	33576	19	13	25	8.0	20.0	44.0	24.0	4.0	114583
81082	TRINIDAD	20483	5151	40.5	30.1	23.2	3.9	2.4	31528	35838	16	10	3586	12.7	17.7	48.9	17.6	3.1	115984
81084	TWO BUTTES	22728	46	32.6	37.0	23.9	4.4	2.2	36108	40748	32	23	34	23.5	23.5	35.3	14.7	2.9	95000
81087	VILAS	25291	56	32.1	32.1	30.4	1.8	3.6	40603	44086	48	37	45	28.9	24.4	33.3	11.1	2.2	87000
81089	WALSENBURG	17322	2326	46.3	31.2	17.6	2.8	2.1	27040	30724	7	4	1665	13.2	32.6	35.0	14.2	5.1	94862
81090	WALSH	17065	550	38.0	36.2	20.0	3.5	2.4	32295	35821	19	13	436	39.5	27.8	24.1	7.3	1.4	65135
81091	WESTON	19195	587	36.8	38.3	18.7	3.4	2.7	31737	36096	17	10	478	13.2	23.0	37.2	24.5	2.1	110135
81092	WILEY	17269	309	30.4	35.6	28.8	3.2	1.9	38981	42068	43	33	238	15.6	27.3	45.0	12.2	0.0	99444
81101	ALAMOSA	18240	5423	38.3	30.5	22.5	6.5	2.2	32704	38186	20	14	3559	14.6	19.4	46.2	17.6	2.2	111182
81102	ALAMOSA	2257	2	100.0	0.0	0.0	0.0	0.0	5000	5000	0	1	0	0.0	0.0	0.0	0.0	0.0	0
81120	ANTONITO	13856	1040	51.2	28.7	15.8	3.0	1.4	24163	26689	4	3	826	32.6	30.2	27.5	7.1	2.7	73889
81121	ARBOLES	14442	51	31.4	35.3	31.4	2.0	0.0	34507	40000	26	18	44	11.4	11.4	27.3	29.6	20.5	175000
81122	BAYFIELD	23913	2772	23.5	29.5	34.1	8.4	4.5	47222	54888	67	56	2325	7.9	3.7	27.1	49.1	12.3	207588
81123	BLANCA	12042	333	47.2	35.4	15.3	1.2	0.9	26130	29879	6	4	274	40.2	27.0	17.9	12.0	2.9	64783
81125	CENTER	13659	1455	42.5	34.2	17.8	3.3	2.3	28401	31637	9	5	1007	28.0	29.5	30.2	8.5	3.8	80563
81130	CREEDE	29348	403	28.0	37.2	26.6	5.2	3.0	38695	43633	42	32	322	13.7	9.6	32.6	34.8	9.3	152381
81132	DEL NORTE	17968	1269	38.7	31.6	22.9	4.3	2.4	32178	35581	18	12	986	20.4	26.7	29.6	18.9	4.5	94394
81133	FORT GARLAND	15931	354	49.2	29.1	16.7	2.5	2.5	25496	28490	5	3	292	23.6	21.2	34.9	19.9	0.3	103333
81136	HOOPER	17324	98	28.6	32.7	27.6	10.2	1.0	40983	46781	50	39	81	16.1	24.7	30.9	23.5	4.9	108750
81137	IGNACIO	20161	2107	28.8	30.0	32.2	6.1	2.9	42174	48006	53	43	1611	12.8	9.7	28.6	35.6	13.4	171443
81140	LA JARA	14167	965	40.8	29.4	24.4	4.3	1.1	30956	35709	15	8	787	30.9	26.9	32.9	8.8	0.5	75391
81143	MOFFAT	19036	866	48.6	27.7	18.0	4.9	0.8	25860	27857	6	3	687	18.5	15.9	40.0	18.6	7.0	116466
81144	MONTE VISTA	17176	2912	34.7	36.1	23.7	2.1	3.5	34509	39074	26	18	2084	15.2	22.8	44.4	15.4	2.2	100954
81146	MOSCA	18297	239	30.1	28.0	29.3	10.0	2.5	41477	46348	51	41	196	13.8	23.5	33.7	25.0	4.1	116667
81147	PAGOSA SPRINGS	26773	4708	25.1	33.7	29.0	6.6	5.7	43386	49730	57	48	3811	7.2	9.2	26.3	41.8	15.5	196895
81149	SAGUACHE	17480	475	42.7	33.9	19.2	3.0	1.3	28972	32870	10	6	375	24.8	26.4	33.3	6.9	8.5	87857
81151	SANFORD	12911	1579	51.7	28.5	14.8	4.2	0.8	23948	26726	4	2	1238	31.2	31.6	31.7	5.3	0.2	73220
81152	SAN LUIS	14955	139	51.1	31.7	13.0	4.3	0.0	23788	24465	4	2	116	38.8	37.1	20.7	0.9	2.6	66250
81153	SAN PABLO	10715	294	62.9	29.3	6.8	1.0	0.0	18494	20404	1	2	259	31.3	24.3	37.5	7.0	0.0	81944
81154	SOUTH FORK	27751	682	23.2	30.8	33.9	7.3	4.8	45163	51849	62	52	552	11.1	8.7	44.0	31.7	4.5	143182
81155	VILLA GROVE	20139	62	22.6	46.8	24.2	4.8	1.6	33353	39764	22	15	54	20.4	14.8	33.3	7.4	24.1	134375
81201	SALIDA	21375	4316	33.6	34.9	22.5	6.0	3.1	35889	40802	31	23	3142	9.2	7.0	34.4	40.0	9.3	173824
81210	ALMONT	36001	144	15.3	29.2	38.2	8.3	9.0	54187	63093	79	71	104	4.8	1.0	13.5	59.6	21.2	260714
81211	BUENA VISTA	22238	2719	27.7	33.8	28.9	6.3	3.4	41084	46361	50	40	2220	9.2	6.9	29.1	44.1	10.8	188789
81212	CANON CITY	19877	10894	31.3	32.0	29.0	5.9	1.8	38784	43979	42	32	7989	8.5	13.7	53.8	21.9	2.2	130689
81220	CIMARRON	23169	65	24.6	40.0	30.8	4.6	0.0	43022	50263	56	46	52	0.0	3.9	28.9	42.3	25.0	300000
81223	COTOPAXI	21074	727	31.0	32.3	28.1	5.0	3.7	38380	42937	41	30	660	3.5	10.3	51.8	29.6	4.9	148626
81224	CRESTED BUTTE	38139	1718	13.3	30.5	34.1	10.7	11.5	55070	67357	80	74	971	1.0	2.5	13.0	43.9	39.7	335987
81226	FLORENCE	16628	2861	33.9	35.2	25.3	4.5	1.0	34880	40069	27	19	2224	12.8	16.8	56.8	13.1	0.5	112278
81228	GRANITE	24560	46	26.1	28.3	39.1	4.4	2.2	46537	48210	65	55	38	18.4	18.4	13.2	39.5	10.5	175000
81230	GUNNISON	21731	3874	32.3	31.4	27.8	6.1	2.4	36791	41591	35	25	2147	8.1	6.1	24.9	51.4	9.6	193631
81231	GUNNISON	23019	11	36.4	18.2	45.5	0.0	0.0	32290	35000	19	13	6	0.0	0.0	16.7	83.3	0.0	225000
81233	HOWARD	21565	774	30.5	35.5	27.1	4.9	1.9	37981	43107	39	28	643	0.9	3.7	45.1	39.5	10.7	175694
81235	LAKE CITY	28054	372	20.7	40.1	26.3	4.0	8.9	42511	48814	55	45	247	4.5	5.7	23.1	44.1	22.7	266379
81236	NATHROP	43963	465	16.3	21.3	34.0	13.1	15.3	65596	76919	89	84	406	9.6	6.2	5.9	45.6	32.8	295238
81239	PARLIN	29054	63	14.3	30.2	41.3	4.8	9.5	52938	60524	77	68	49	2.0	0.0	14.3	71.4	12.2	239583
81240	PENROSE	18216	1871	25.4	34.3	34.2	5.1	1.0	42077	46704	53	43	1607	9.4	12.1	43.1	32.9	2.5	151450
81241	PITKIN	25879	64	14.1	29.7	42.2	4.7	9.4	53033	59616	77	68	50	2.0	0.0	14.0	72.0	12.0	241667
81243	POWDERHORN	16038	39	25.6	41.0	30.8	2.6	0.0	42266	47377	54	44	31	0.0	6.5	22.6	48.4	22.6	322727
81251	TWIN LAKES CPU	27160	88	15.9	37.5	38.6	3.4	4.6	47349	53541	67	56	68	33.8	27.9	16.2	17.7	4.4	68571
81252	WESTCLIFFE	23445	1467	31.8	30.3	26.7	7.0	4.2	38367	44889	41	30	1195	11.3	12.2	25.0	36.7	14.7	180833
81253	WETMORE	25718	310	19.7	37.7	29.0	8.4	5.2	45789	53508	63	54	268	2.2	10.8	26.1	44.4	16.4	225000
81301	DURANGO	28725	11104	26.3	28.8	28.1	9.2	7.6	44554	53661	60	51	6892	11.2	2.6	16.0	52.2	18.0	232901
81303	DURANGO	26584	2890	21.3	25.2	34.8	12.4	6.4	53321	62182	77	70	2283	10.6	4.9	18.7	44.8	21.1	226575
81320	CAHONE	24714	268	29.9	30.2	30.2	5.2	4.5	42448	48939	54	45	192	9.4	14.1	43.8	29.7	3.1	143519
81321	CORTEZ	20079	5247	33.0	34.4	25.0	4.8	2.7	35682	41379	30	22	3824	13.0	14.3	48.8	20.0	3.9	121554
81323	DOLORES	20930	1701	31.2	34.2	25.2	5.9	3.6	37133	41866	36	26	1399	10.2	8.8	33.7	39.2	8.2	168873
81324	DOVE CREEK	18656	595	38.0	32.3	25.7	2.2	1.9	33136	37121	21	15	492	19.7	32.1	36.4	11.0	0.8	87805
81325	EGNAR	22074	63	23.8	31.8	34.9	7.9	1.6	44436	50000	60	51	50	10.0	2.0	44.0	30.0	14.0	164286
81326	HESPERUS	23948	801	23.0	29.0	32.5	11.7	3.9	48441	56104	69	59	677	5.8	7.5	27.2	40.6	18.9	210238
81327	LEWIS	20549	341	20.8	34.9	35.5	6.2	2.6	43322	48333	57	47	293	3.1	12.6	38.2	39.6	6.5	165086
81328	MANCOS	23240	1508	29.8	30.4	27.3	8.5	4.0	41128	46342	50	40	1160	9.5	6.6	37.5	38.4	8.0	167553
81331	PLEASANT VIEW	20303	120	20.0	31.7	39.2	6.7	2.5	47393	51292	67	57	103	0.0	12.6	39.8	43.7	3.9	169318
81334	TOWAOC	11430	641	49.0	31.5	14.5	2.7	2.3	25626	28617	5	3	443	37.5	18.5	30.3	9.9	3.8	78167
	COLORADO	28803		19.1	26.9	34.1	12.5	7.5	54077	63465				4.8	4.7	28.0	49.9	12.6	203984
	UNITED STATES	25866		24.7	27.1	30.8	10.9	6.5	48124	56710				10.9	15.0	33.7	30.1	10.4	145905

ZIP CODE #	POST OFFICE NAME	FINANCIAL SERVICES: Auto Loan	FINANCIAL SERVICES: Home Loan	FINANCIAL SERVICES: Invest-ments	FINANCIAL SERVICES: Retire-ment Plans	THE HOME: Home Improvements: Home Repair	THE HOME: Home Improvements: Lawn & Garden	THE HOME: Furnishings: Comput-ers & Hard-ware	THE HOME: Furnishings: Major Appli-ances	THE HOME: Furnishings: TV, Radio, Sound Equip-ment	THE HOME: Furnishings: Furni-ture	ENTERTAINMENT: Dine out/ Carry out	ENTERTAINMENT: Sports Equip-ment	ENTERTAINMENT: Fees & Tickets	ENTERTAINMENT: Toys & Games	ENTERTAINMENT: Travel	ENTERTAINMENT: Cable TV	PERSONAL: Apparel & Services	PERSONAL: Auto Repairs	PERSONAL: Health Insur-ance	PERSONAL: Pets & Supplies
81020	AGUILAR	55	41	27	40	45	54	46	50	51	43	60	57	41	57	45	54	55	50	60	61
81021	ARLINGTON	66	46	24	44	54	60	46	56	52	45	62	68	39	60	47	55	56	56	67	78
81022	AVONDALE	66	67	64	64	68	74	66	67	68	64	84	75	67	87	67	69	81	66	70	76
81023	BEULAH	115	80	42	76	93	105	79	98	91	78	107	118	68	105	82	96	98	97	117	136
81025	BOONE	82	69	54	66	73	84	73	78	78	70	94	87	68	91	72	81	88	77	88	92
81027	BRANSON	81	57	30	54	66	74	56	69	65	55	76	84	48	74	58	68	69	68	83	97
81029	CAMPO	72	50	26	48	59	66	50	62	57	49	67	74	43	66	52	60	61	61	73	86
81036	EADS	75	55	35	53	61	73	60	67	68	57	80	77	53	76	60	71	73	67	81	84
81039	FOWLER	75	58	39	55	62	74	63	69	69	60	82	77	56	77	62	73	75	69	81	83
81040	GARDNER	77	60	41	54	68	76	57	69	64	56	76	80	51	75	61	69	71	68	81	94
81041	GRANADA	62	53	42	49	52	56	54	59	57	58	70	64	49	63	52	55	69	60	58	65
81043	HARTMAN	72	50	26	47	58	65	49	61	57	49	67	73	42	65	51	60	61	60	73	85
81044	HASTY	93	65	34	61	76	85	64	79	74	63	87	96	55	85	67	78	79	78	94	110
81045	HASWELL	76	53	28	50	62	69	52	65	60	52	71	78	45	69	54	63	64	64	77	90
81047	HOLLY	70	55	37	53	60	67	55	63	61	55	73	74	51	72	56	63	67	62	71	80
81049	KIM	122	85	45	81	100	112	84	104	97	83	114	126	72	112	88	102	104	103	124	145
81050	LA JUNTA	68	57	47	56	62	69	59	64	64	58	76	75	55	75	60	65	72	64	72	79
81052	LAMAR	65	58	53	58	60	65	61	63	63	60	77	73	58	76	60	63	74	64	65	73
81054	LAS ANIMAS	63	47	31	45	52	62	52	58	59	50	69	65	46	65	52	62	63	58	69	70
81055	LA VETA	83	63	42	59	70	82	66	75	75	64	88	86	59	84	67	79	81	75	90	95
81057	MC CLAVE	93	65	34	61	76	85	64	79	74	64	87	96	55	85	67	78	79	78	95	111
81058	MANZANOLA	60	45	30	43	49	59	50	55	56	47	65	61	44	62	49	59	60	55	65	66
81059	MODEL	79	55	30	52	64	72	56	68	64	55	75	81	48	73	57	67	68	67	81	92
81062	OLNEY SPRINGS	66	50	33	48	54	65	55	61	62	52	73	68	49	69	55	65	66	61	73	73
81063	ORDWAY	56	42	28	40	46	55	47	51	52	44	61	58	41	58	46	55	56	51	62	62
81064	PRITCHETT	80	56	29	53	65	73	55	69	64	55	75	83	47	73	58	67	68	68	82	95
81067	ROCKY FORD	61	53	46	51	55	60	56	59	59	56	72	67	52	69	55	59	69	60	62	68
81069	RYE	105	80	51	73	91	102	76	93	87	76	103	109	68	101	81	92	95	91	110	128
81071	SHERIDAN LAKE	88	61	32	58	71	80	60	75	70	60	82	90	52	80	63	73	74	74	89	104
81073	SPRINGFIELD	64	47	30	45	53	62	51	58	58	49	68	66	45	65	51	61	62	58	69	72
81076	SUGAR CITY	81	61	40	58	67	80	67	74	75	64	88	83	60	84	66	79	81	74	89	90
81081	TRINCHERA	72	66	54	64	70	74	62	68	64	61	77	81	59	79	63	65	74	67	72	86
81082	TRINIDAD	74	62	53	60	66	75	66	70	71	64	86	80	62	84	66	74	81	71	79	84
81084	TWO BUTTES	85	59	31	56	69	77	59	72	67	58	79	87	50	78	61	71	72	71	86	101
81087	VILAS	115	80	42	76	94	105	79	98	92	78	107	118	68	105	82	96	98	97	117	137
81089	WALSENBURG	64	49	33	46	54	64	52	58	58	50	69	66	46	66	52	62	63	58	70	73
81090	WALSH	69	50	31	48	56	66	54	61	61	52	71	70	47	68	54	64	65	61	73	78
81091	WESTON	80	59	35	55	67	76	58	70	66	57	78	83	50	76	60	70	71	69	83	95
81092	WILEY	74	61	46	61	65	73	63	68	67	62	81	78	59	80	63	69	76	67	75	83
81101	ALAMOSA	65	61	63	62	61	64	65	64	65	64	81	76	63	79	63	63	79	66	62	73
81102	ALAMOSA	7	5	7	6	5	6	8	7	7	7	9	9	7	9	7	7	9	7	6	7
81120	ANTONITO	45	41	68	37	40	47	46	46	52	48	67	51	44	68	47	56	66	48	49	53
81121	ARBOLES	81	57	30	53	66	74	56	69	64	55	75	83	48	74	58	68	69	68	82	96
81122	BAYFIELD	89	86	76	84	90	95	80	87	82	80	100	102	79	102	83	83	96	85	90	106
81123	BLANCA	51	47	37	45	47	49	45	48	45	46	56	55	42	53	44	45	54	48	48	57
81125	CENTER	66	53	39	50	55	59	54	61	58	56	71	68	48	65	53	57	68	61	63	71
81130	CREEDE	108	85	58	76	95	107	80	96	90	79	107	113	71	106	85	97	100	95	114	132
81132	DEL NORTE	76	58	38	54	62	70	60	68	66	60	79	78	53	74	59	68	74	68	77	84
81133	FORT GARLAND	66	53	37	48	58	65	50	59	55	50	66	69	45	65	52	58	62	58	68	79
81136	HOOPER	82	72	54	69	74	79	69	76	71	71	87	88	64	83	69	71	83	75	78	92
81137	IGNACIO	82	71	60	69	74	80	72	77	76	72	93	91	68	91	72	77	88	78	81	93
81140	LA JARA	73	51	26	46	58	65	50	61	58	50	68	73	43	66	51	61	63	61	73	85
81143	MOFFAT	60	48	34	46	51	59	50	55	55	49	65	63	46	62	50	57	61	55	62	66
81144	MONTE VISTA	75	58	38	55	63	70	59	67	65	59	78	78	53	75	59	66	72	67	75	85
81146	MOSCA	86	70	48	67	75	81	68	77	73	69	88	91	62	84	68	74	82	77	84	99
81147	PAGOSA SPRINGS	112	84	54	77	96	108	81	98	92	80	109	116	71	107	85	98	100	97	116	135
81149	SAGUACHE	63	49	33	46	53	62	51	57	57	49	67	65	46	64	52	60	62	57	67	72
81151	SANFORD	51	45	46	42	44	48	46	49	49	49	62	54	43	59	45	50	61	50	49	55
81152	SAN LUIS	55	43	29	39	48	54	40	49	46	40	54	57	36	53	43	49	50	48	57	66
81153	SAN PABLO	28	27	51	24	25	30	31	30	36	33	46	33	30	48	31	39	46	32	31	33
81154	SOUTH FORK	105	82	56	74	93	104	78	94	88	77	104	109	69	103	83	94	97	92	111	128
81155	VILLA GROVE	85	67	46	60	75	85	63	76	71	63	85	89	56	84	67	76	79	75	90	104
81201	SALIDA	74	61	47	58	66	75	63	69	68	61	81	79	58	79	63	70	76	69	79	85
81210	ALMONT	129	106	93	106	111	123	109	118	116	110	142	140	102	137	109	116	134	120	125	147
81211	BUENA VISTA	74	54	33	51	62	70	55	65	62	53	73	76	48	71	56	66	67	64	77	86
81212	CANON CITY	74	63	51	61	67	76	66	70	70	64	85	80	62	83	66	73	80	70	78	84
81220	CIMARRON	85	64	41	59	73	82	61	75	70	61	83	88	54	81	65	74	76	73	88	102
81223	COTOPAXI	85	67	46	60	75	85	63	76	71	63	85	89	56	84	67	76	79	75	90	104
81224	CRESTED BUTTE	135	111	107	114	114	125	119	123	123	120	153	148	110	145	116	122	146	128	126	152
81226	FLORENCE	66	55	41	54	58	65	56	61	60	56	72	69	53	70	56	61	68	60	66	73
81228	GRANITE	88	76	57	72	79	85	72	81	76	73	92	93	67	89	73	77	88	80	85	101
81230	GUNNISON	73	62	65	64	63	68	73	70	73	70	91	86	68	88	69	70	87	74	68	82
81231	GUNNISON	67	54	48	53	56	61	63	60	65	59	80	76	58	78	59	63	75	64	62	75
81233	HOWARD	77	67	56	62	73	84	62	73	68	64	82	77	60	74	67	72	77	71	85	90
81235	LAKE CITY	103	81	55	73	91	102	76	92	86	75	102	107	68	101	81	92	95	90	108	125
81236	NATHROP	150	130	111	121	141	163	121	141	132	126	161	149	118	143	131	141	150	138	166	174
81239	PARLIN	113	89	61	81	100	112	84	101	95	83	112	118	75	111	89	101	104	99	118	137
81240	PENROSE	76	69	53	66	71	75	65	71	67	66	82	83	62	81	65	67	79	69	73	87
81241	PITKIN	113	89	61	80	100	112	84	101	95	83	112	118	75	111	89	101	104	99	119	138
81243	POWDERHORN	68	54	37	48	60	68	51	61	57	50	68	71	45	67	54	61	63	60	72	83
81251	TWIN LAKES CPU	94	86	67	82	86	90	82	87	83	84	102	101	77	96	80	81	98	87	87	104
81252	WESTCLIFFE	91	71	48	64	80	90	67	81	76	66	90	94	60	89	71	81	83	79	95	110
81253	WETMORE	103	81	55	73	91	102	76	92	86	75	102	107	68	101	81	92	95	90	108	125
81301	DURANGO	94	89	95	91	89	95	96	93	94	94	118	113	92	114	92	91	114	97	90	107
81303	DURANGO	98	104	101	103	103	105	98	100	94	98	118	117	99	119	98	92	116	98	93	113
81320	CAHONE	92	69	42	63	78	88	66	80	75	65	89	95	58	87	70	80	82	79	95	111
81321	CORTEZ	79	67	52	65	70	77	68	73	71	68	86	85	63	83	67	72	82	73	78	89
81323	DOLORES	85	62	37	59	70	80	64	75	73	63	86	88	56	82	65	76	78	75	89	98
81324	DOVE CREEK	74	54	33	51	60	71	57	66	65	55	76	76	50	73	58	68	70	65	79	83
81325	EGNAR	100	69	36	66	81	91	69	85	79	68	93	102	59	91	71	83	85	84	101	118
81326	HESPERUS	92	89	75	87	89	92	84	88	83	86	103	102	81	100	83	82	100	88	86	103
81327	LEWIS	95	66	35	62	77	86	65	81	75	64	88	97	56	86	68	79	80	79	96	112
81328	MANCOS	96	72	43	68	81	90	70	84	79	69	93	100	61	91	72	82	86	83	98	114
81331	PLEASANT VIEW	95	66	35	62	77	86	65	81	75	64	88	97	56	86	68	79	80	80	96	112
81334	TOWAOC	51	46	46	45	45	51	50	50	52	49	65	58	48	63	49	52	62	51	51	56
	COLORADO	103	104	110	107	103	108	105	104	102	105	128	122	104	127	103	99	125	105	98	116
	UNITED STATES	100	100	100	100	100	100	100	100	100	100	100	100	100	100	100	100	100	100	100	100

ZIP CODE		COUNTY FIPS CODE	POPULATION			2000-2004 ANNUAL RATE		HOUSEHOLDS					FAMILIES		
#	POST OFFICE NAME		2000	2004	2009	% Rate	State Centile	2000	2004	2009	% Annual Rate 2000-2004	2004 Average HH Size	2000	2004	% Annual Rate 2000-2004
81335	YELLOW JACKET	083	227	245	257	1.8	45	86	95	102	2.4	2.58	66	73	2.4
81401	MONTROSE	085	25901	28766	32405	2.5	61	10301	11604	13242	2.8	2.44	7297	8170	2.7
81410	AUSTIN	029	1536	1669	1805	2.0	49	625	691	759	2.4	2.31	477	523	2.2
81411	BEDROCK	085	218	234	259	1.7	44	87	95	107	2.1	2.46	58	63	2.0
81413	CEDAREDGE	029	4475	4949	5440	2.4	59	1999	2234	2480	2.7	2.21	1411	1566	2.5
81415	CRAWFORD	085	1465	1664	1849	3.0	70	604	696	784	3.4	2.38	450	514	3.2
81416	DELTA	029	11970	12594	13467	1.2	37	4409	4679	5055	1.4	2.55	3183	3358	1.3
81418	ECKERT	029	1661	1986	2259	4.3	81	656	800	922	4.8	2.46	510	617	4.6
81419	HOTCHKISS	029	3469	3656	3915	1.2	38	1401	1499	1626	1.6	2.40	992	1052	1.4
81422	NATURITA	085	518	556	615	1.7	44	212	232	260	2.1	2.39	141	152	1.8
81423	NORWOOD	113	1184	1195	1257	0.2	18	504	524	566	0.9	2.28	335	347	0.8
81424	NUCLA	085	1529	1595	1736	1.0	33	653	695	767	1.5	2.29	440	463	1.2
81425	OLATHE	085	4578	5067	5679	2.4	59	1522	1704	1933	2.7	2.89	1188	1319	2.5
81426	OPHIR	113	345	394	443	3.2	72	167	195	225	3.7	2.02	86	100	3.6
81427	OURAY	091	757	859	1006	3.0	70	352	406	483	3.4	2.10	229	261	3.1
81428	PAONIA	029	3953	4027	4228	0.4	22	1626	1685	1794	0.8	2.34	1128	1158	0.6
81430	PLACERVILLE	113	730	801	881	2.2	54	330	370	416	2.7	2.16	170	188	2.4
81431	REDVALE	085	511	529	574	0.8	28	217	229	252	1.3	2.31	147	153	1.0
81432	RIDGWAY	091	2432	2795	3299	3.3	73	999	1168	1399	3.8	2.38	714	828	3.6
81433	SILVERTON	111	558	558	558	0.0	12	269	283	283	1.2	1.95	158	165	1.0
81434	SOMERSET	051	197	219	244	2.5	62	84	95	108	2.9	2.31	55	62	2.9
81435	TELLURIDE	113	4179	4869	5528	3.7	76	1953	2342	2730	4.4	2.07	793	953	4.4
81501	GRAND JUNCTION	077	20703	21035	22715	0.4	21	8927	9167	10055	0.6	2.12	4422	4442	0.1
81503	GRAND JUNCTION	077	23384	25616	28651	2.2	53	9107	10168	11526	2.6	2.51	6980	7714	2.4
81504	GRAND JUNCTION	077	22442	25281	28651	2.8	66	8683	9990	11504	3.4	2.50	6418	7295	3.1
81505	GRAND JUNCTION	077	7587	8738	10001	3.4	74	2917	3416	3967	3.8	2.47	2071	2408	3.6
81506	GRAND JUNCTION	077	8906	9692	10787	2.0	49	3890	4306	4869	2.4	2.20	2576	2806	2.0
81520	CLIFTON	077	11599	13027	14709	2.8	65	4211	4789	5471	3.1	2.70	3097	3475	2.8
81521	FRUITA	077	9038	10095	11356	2.6	64	3386	3878	4443	3.2	2.53	2474	2798	2.9
81522	GATEWAY	077	1029	1117	1239	2.0	48	394	435	488	2.4	2.55	303	331	2.1
81524	LOMA	077	1507	1887	2247	5.4	88	534	682	825	5.9	2.76	420	531	5.7
81525	MACK	077	433	544	649	5.5	88	167	214	259	6.0	2.54	131	167	5.9
81526	PALISADE	077	5331	5814	6459	2.1	51	2047	2273	2567	2.5	2.47	1481	1625	2.2
81527	WHITEWATER	077	1199	1410	1626	3.9	77	430	519	610	4.5	2.62	331	395	4.3
81601	GLENWOOD SPRINGS	045	12282	13741	16062	2.7	64	4798	5427	6400	2.9	2.48	3093	3466	2.7
81610	DINOSAUR	081	421	404	412	-1.0	2	163	157	162	-0.9	2.45	109	104	-1.1
81611	ASPEN	097	9073	9823	11153	1.9	48	4321	4750	5467	2.3	2.00	1819	1961	1.8
81621	BASALT	097	5579	6585	7944	4.0	78	2110	2509	3043	4.2	2.62	1310	1532	3.8
81623	CARBONDALE	097	13371	15575	18621	3.7	76	4674	5477	6578	3.8	2.81	3256	3773	3.5
81624	COLLBRAN	077	1389	1503	1654	1.9	47	463	511	574	2.4	2.61	346	377	2.0
81625	CRAIG	081	12180	12635	13228	0.9	30	4610	4878	5203	1.3	2.53	3312	3478	1.2
81630	DE BEQUE	045	885	974	1093	2.3	56	331	370	421	2.7	2.61	250	277	2.4
81631	EAGLE	037	7121	8373	10102	3.9	77	2210	2601	3136	3.9	3.20	1598	1860	3.6
81633	DINOSAUR	081	7	7	7	0.0	12	4	4	4	0.0	1.50	3	2	-9.1
81635	PARACHUTE	045	4980	5873	7050	4.0	78	2033	2414	2917	4.1	2.42	1420	1672	3.9
81637	GYPSUM	037	4806	6069	7581	5.6	89	1548	1967	2462	5.8	3.08	1211	1523	5.5
81638	HAMILTON	081	199	215	230	1.8	46	76	84	91	2.4	2.56	58	64	2.3
81639	HAYDEN	107	2298	2559	2983	2.6	62	865	985	1172	3.1	2.58	627	709	2.9
81640	MAYBELL	081	341	346	358	0.3	20	116	119	124	0.6	2.86	81	83	0.6
81641	MEEKER	103	3304	3509	3789	1.4	41	1345	1463	1619	2.0	2.35	927	1002	1.9
81642	MEREDITH	097	48	50	56	1.0	32	27	28	32	0.9	1.79	12	12	0.0
81643	MESA	077	923	1009	1123	2.1	52	373	415	469	2.5	2.40	287	316	2.3
81647	NEW CASTLE	045	4317	4942	5851	3.2	72	1555	1797	2142	3.5	2.75	1189	1367	3.3
81648	RANGELY	103	2543	2640	2811	0.9	30	903	961	1050	1.5	2.59	679	719	1.4
81650	RIFLE	103	10392	12055	14332	3.6	75	3647	4284	5145	3.9	2.73	2602	3032	3.7
81652	SILT	045	3313	3956	4780	4.3	81	1230	1479	1797	4.4	2.67	934	1115	4.3
81653	SLATER	081	43	46	49	1.6	43	17	19	20	2.7	2.32	15	16	1.5
81654	SNOWMASS	097	2969	3351	3894	2.9	67	1338	1531	1798	3.2	2.18	684	772	2.9
81657	VAIL	037	22115	25222	29985	3.1	72	8719	10007	11929	3.3	2.49	4388	4952	2.9
	COLORADO					2.4					2.6	2.52			2.5
	UNITED STATES					1.2					1.3	2.58			1.1

#	POST OFFICE NAME	White 2000	White 2004	Black 2000	Black 2004	Asian/Pacific 2000	Asian/Pacific 2004	% Hispanic Origin 2000	% Hispanic Origin 2004	0-4	5-9	10-14	15-19	20-24	25-44	45-64	65-84	85+	18+	MEDIAN AGE 2004	% 2004 Males	% 2004 Females
81335	YELLOW JACKET	94.3	93.5	0.0	0.0	0.0	0.0	5.7	6.5	7.8	7.8	6.5	5.7	4.5	23.3	29.0	14.7	0.8	74.3	41.6	50.2	49.8
81401	MONTROSE	90.6	89.7	0.3	0.3	0.6	0.7	14.5	16.1	6.8	6.7	7.3	6.5	6.1	23.5	27.2	13.6	2.2	74.9	40.1	48.9	51.1
81410	AUSTIN	93.6	92.9	0.1	0.1	0.7	0.8	9.2	10.5	4.7	5.5	6.8	6.5	4.3	19.2	29.4	19.2	4.4	78.7	47.0	49.1	50.9
81411	BEDROCK	93.6	93.6	0.0	0.0	0.0	0.0	5.5	6.4	6.8	6.8	9.0	7.3	6.0	25.2	23.9	13.7	1.3	72.2	37.8	49.2	50.9
81413	CEDAREDGE	96.3	96.1	0.0	0.0	0.4	0.5	4.9	5.6	4.4	4.5	4.8	5.6	4.1	16.5	33.1	24.0	3.0	82.6	51.9	49.5	50.5
81415	CRAWFORD	95.4	94.8	0.1	0.1	0.1	0.2	4.8	5.7	6.0	7.0	7.8	5.6	4.6	21.9	31.9	13.4	1.7	75.4	43.1	51.4	48.6
81416	DELTA	87.6	86.3	1.2	1.3	0.4	0.4	18.8	21.1	6.9	6.7	7.0	6.2	6.8	24.8	25.0	14.2	2.4	75.4	39.0	50.6	49.4
81418	ECKERT	94.5	93.8	0.1	0.2	0.4	0.5	7.0	8.2	3.7	4.2	5.6	6.6	4.1	17.6	30.4	24.4	3.4	82.1	50.6	48.9	51.1
81419	HOTCHKISS	94.6	94.1	0.0	0.0	0.3	0.4	8.2	9.3	5.3	5.7	6.4	6.1	5.8	21.3	32.5	14.9	2.0	78.7	44.6	50.7	49.3
81422	NATURITA	93.8	93.2	0.0	0.0	0.2	0.2	5.6	6.5	6.5	6.5	7.7	7.0	5.9	25.4	25.2	14.2	1.6	74.1	39.3	50.0	50.0
81423	NORWOOD	97.3	97.2	0.0	0.0	0.2	0.2	3.8	4.2	4.9	5.4	6.8	6.8	6.4	23.7	36.2	8.9	1.0	78.7	42.6	52.4	47.6
81424	NUCLA	95.4	95.2	0.1	0.1	0.1	0.1	2.9	3.3	5.2	5.5	6.8	7.2	6.3	22.6	30.2	14.7	1.4	77.9	42.6	50.5	49.5
81425	OLATHE	84.3	83.0	0.4	0.4	0.3	0.3	22.2	24.4	7.8	7.3	7.9	7.4	7.6	23.1	26.2	10.7	2.1	72.2	36.7	50.6	49.4
81426	OPHIR	95.4	94.7	0.0	0.3	0.6	0.8	3.2	3.6	5.3	5.1	5.1	4.3	5.1	38.1	34.0	3.1	0.0	82.2	39.2	54.8	45.2
81427	OURAY	96.4	96.3	0.1	0.1	0.4	0.6	4.6	5.4	5.1	5.9	7.0	5.9	2.8	27.4	33.0	11.4	1.5	78.2	42.7	50.5	49.5
81428	PAONIA	96.8	96.6	0.1	0.1	0.2	0.2	5.0	5.7	5.5	5.8	6.6	6.9	5.6	20.4	31.4	15.2	2.8	77.3	44.5	50.5	49.5
81430	PLACERVILLE	96.6	96.3	0.0	0.0	0.7	0.9	2.1	2.4	5.2	5.4	5.1	4.4	3.8	36.8	36.0	3.3	0.1	81.7	40.1	54.6	45.4
81431	REDVALE	95.9	95.7	0.2	0.2	0.2	0.2	2.2	2.5	4.9	5.3	6.6	7.4	6.4	22.1	30.8	15.1	1.3	78.6	43.2	49.7	50.3
81432	RIDGWAY	96.2	96.0	0.1	0.1	0.3	0.4	4.2	4.7	4.8	5.8	7.1	5.8	2.9	23.9	36.9	12.1	0.9	78.6	44.9	50.8	49.2
81433	SILVERTON	97.1	97.1	0.0	0.0	0.5	0.5	7.4	7.4	4.7	4.1	5.4	7.0	2.5	25.6	43.7	7.0	0.0	80.7	45.3	52.9	47.1
81434	SOMERSET	94.4	94.5	0.0	0.0	1.0	0.9	4.1	4.6	4.6	5.5	4.6	3.2	2.3	26.5	41.1	11.4	0.9	82.7	46.9	55.3	44.8
81435	TELLURIDE	91.7	91.1	0.5	0.5	1.1	1.2	8.7	9.6	4.1	3.6	4.4	4.6	9.1	47.4	24.1	2.5	0.1	85.4	33.5	55.2	44.8
81501	GRAND JUNCTION	89.7	88.7	0.9	1.0	1.0	1.2	13.5	15.3	6.0	5.4	5.1	8.3	10.9	27.6	20.7	12.9	3.2	80.1	34.3	49.0	51.0
81503	GRAND JUNCTION	94.5	94.1	0.3	0.3	0.6	0.7	7.1	8.0	5.2	6.0	7.2	7.0	4.9	23.2	31.0	14.1	1.4	77.1	42.8	49.1	50.9
81504	GRAND JUNCTION	92.1	91.3	0.4	0.5	0.6	0.7	10.9	12.3	7.6	7.2	7.4	6.7	6.9	27.1	23.4	12.5	1.3	73.6	36.2	48.8	51.3
81505	GRAND JUNCTION	92.1	91.6	0.3	0.3	0.6	0.7	12.6	13.6	5.1	6.0	7.2	7.2	5.8	25.7	28.9	12.5	1.5	77.4	40.5	50.4	49.6
81506	GRAND JUNCTION	95.9	95.5	0.3	0.3	0.8	0.9	4.4	5.0	4.0	4.8	5.6	6.0	4.7	17.3	29.7	22.3	5.6	81.7	49.9	46.2	53.8
81520	CLIFTON	88.5	87.4	0.6	0.7	0.4	0.5	13.6	15.3	9.5	8.1	8.0	8.0	9.2	28.1	19.6	8.4	1.0	69.8	29.6	48.4	51.6
81521	FRUITA	91.9	91.3	0.3	0.3	0.3	0.4	10.7	12.0	6.4	6.6	7.5	7.4	6.4	25.4	25.3	12.4	2.5	74.7	38.4	48.4	51.7
81522	GATEWAY	95.4	95.0	0.2	0.2	1.4	1.5	4.3	4.9	5.5	6.5	6.7	6.5	5.1	20.8	37.1	10.9	1.1	77.0	44.3	49.7	50.3
81524	LOMA	94.5	94.0	0.1	0.2	0.5	0.6	5.6	6.3	6.6	7.3	8.0	6.2	5.2	25.3	30.8	9.5	1.1	74.2	40.1	52.7	47.3
81525	MACK	94.5	93.8	0.2	0.2	0.5	0.7	5.3	6.3	6.6	7.4	7.9	6.3	5.2	25.2	30.9	9.6	1.1	74.3	40.1	52.9	47.1
81526	PALISADE	93.9	93.3	0.2	0.2	0.7	0.8	7.7	8.7	5.5	5.7	7.0	7.3	5.7	23.2	28.9	14.1	2.6	77.3	42.5	49.5	50.5
81527	WHITEWATER	95.2	94.6	0.3	0.3	0.5	0.6	10.6	12.1	6.0	6.1	7.7	7.5	5.0	24.2	32.6	9.9	1.0	75.4	41.3	51.6	48.4
81601	GLENWOOD SPRINGS	90.5	89.4	0.2	0.2	0.8	0.9	14.3	16.2	6.2	6.1	6.4	7.1	8.0	30.0	27.9	7.3	1.1	77.2	36.2	50.7	49.4
81610	DINOSAUR	93.8	93.6	0.0	0.0	0.0	0.0	13.8	15.1	5.9	5.9	6.9	7.9	5.9	29.5	27.2	9.7	1.0	76.5	39.1	55.0	45.1
81611	ASPEN	95.1	94.7	0.6	0.6	1.4	1.7	5.3	5.9	3.5	3.6	4.0	5.1	6.6	36.5	31.7	8.6	0.5	85.9	39.9	52.9	47.1
81621	BASALT	88.5	87.4	0.3	0.4	1.1	1.3	19.9	22.0	6.9	6.6	6.8	6.6	7.2	34.4	27.8	3.6	0.3	75.5	35.1	52.5	47.6
81623	CARBONDALE	87.1	85.9	0.5	0.5	0.7	0.9	25.3	28.0	7.2	6.8	6.3	6.5	7.5	32.7	26.9	5.4	0.8	75.6	34.6	52.2	47.8
81624	COLLBRAN	92.9	92.4	1.5	1.5	0.1	0.2	7.6	8.5	4.5	6.1	7.7	16.6	5.2	19.2	28.7	10.1	1.9	71.5	37.7	52.0	48.0
81625	CRAIG	93.5	92.9	0.2	0.3	0.4	0.4	9.4	10.6	7.1	6.8	7.4	8.0	7.6	27.4	26.7	7.8	1.3	73.5	35.4	51.7	48.3
81630	DE BEQUE	94.9	94.4	0.1	0.1	0.3	0.4	5.2	5.9	5.9	6.3	7.9	6.9	4.4	22.9	31.1	13.6	1.1	74.9	41.9	51.3	48.7
81631	EAGLE	84.6	83.3	0.3	0.3	0.5	0.6	22.1	24.0	8.2	8.0	7.9	6.6	6.4	36.0	23.3	3.3	0.3	71.6	33.1	52.7	47.4
81633	DINOSAUR	100.0	100.0	0.0	0.0	0.0	0.0	14.3	14.3	0.0	0.0	0.0	0.0	28.6	71.4	0.0	0.0	0.0	100.0	28.8	57.1	42.9
81635	PARACHUTE	93.4	92.9	0.5	0.5	0.4	0.4	9.3	10.4	7.3	7.2	7.5	5.4	5.1	26.6	22.0	17.7	1.3	74.5	38.7	49.7	50.4
81637	GYPSUM	82.4	80.9	0.2	0.2	0.2	0.3	30.7	33.3	8.9	8.3	8.3	7.6	7.7	34.9	21.2	3.0	0.2	69.6	30.5	51.8	48.2
81638	HAMILTON	96.0	95.4	0.0	0.0	0.5	0.5	4.0	5.1	3.7	4.7	10.7	8.8	3.7	22.3	35.8	10.2	0.0	74.4	42.8	54.4	45.6
81639	HAYDEN	96.2	95.9	0.1	0.1	0.2	0.2	5.6	6.5	6.7	7.5	8.1	7.2	6.5	30.5	26.8	5.9	0.7	73.0	35.2	51.7	48.3
81640	MAYBELL	94.1	93.9	0.0	0.0	0.0	0.0	7.3	8.1	4.6	7.2	6.1	7.8	3.5	25.4	31.2	13.9	0.3	76.6	42.7	53.8	46.2
81641	MEEKER	95.8	95.4	0.1	0.1	0.2	0.3	4.6	5.2	6.1	6.2	6.2	6.8	6.0	23.9	30.3	12.7	2.0	76.9	41.4	50.2	49.8
81642	MEREDITH	93.8	94.0	0.0	0.0	0.0	0.0	6.3	6.0	4.0	4.0	6.0	8.0	4.0	32.0	38.0	4.0	0.0	78.0	40.0	58.0	42.0
81643	MESA	95.8	95.3	0.0	0.1	0.2	0.3	3.8	4.2	5.4	5.9	7.7	7.1	4.2	21.8	32.7	14.0	1.3	75.8	43.5	51.9	48.1
81647	NEW CASTLE	93.2	92.6	0.3	0.3	0.3	0.4	11.6	12.9	8.3	8.0	7.6	6.6	6.4	32.6	24.6	5.4	0.4	72.0	33.6	50.8	49.2
81648	RANGELY	93.9	93.4	0.4	0.4	0.4	0.5	5.4	6.1	5.9	5.5	7.2	9.9	10.4	28.3	24.8	7.5	0.6	76.4	33.2	50.2	49.8
81650	RIFLE	89.7	88.8	0.7	0.8	0.3	0.4	17.0	19.0	8.7	8.0	8.0	7.5	8.0	30.4	21.4	6.8	1.3	70.3	32.0	51.7	48.3
81652	SILT	92.0	91.2	0.3	0.4	0.1	0.1	11.1	12.5	7.3	7.4	8.0	7.4	6.0	30.8	25.7	6.9	0.6	72.8	35.5	52.1	47.9
81653	SLATER	97.7	100.0	0.0	0.0	0.0	0.0	11.6	10.9	4.4	4.4	6.5	8.7	4.4	28.3	37.0	6.5	0.0	80.4	41.3	56.5	43.5
81654	SNOWMASS	95.8	95.3	0.4	0.4	0.8	0.9	5.1	5.7	3.9	4.1	5.4	6.1	5.7	33.5	34.1	7.0	0.3	82.6	40.4	54.2	45.8
81657	VAIL	85.0	83.7	0.5	0.5	1.1	1.3	22.1	24.1	6.0	4.9	4.7	4.9	9.0	46.6	20.2	3.7	0.1	81.7	31.8	56.2	43.8
	COLORADO	82.8	81.7	3.8	3.9	2.3	2.6	17.1	18.6	7.0	6.8	7.1	7.0	7.5	30.6	24.3	8.6	1.2	75.1	35.0	50.3	49.7
	UNITED STATES	75.1	73.6	12.3	12.5	3.8	4.2	12.5	14.1	6.9	6.7	7.2	7.0	7.3	28.6	23.8	10.8	1.7	75.1	36.0	49.1	50.9

#	POST OFFICE NAME	2004 Per Capita Income	2004 HH Income Base	2004 HOUSEHOLD INCOME DISTRIBUTION (%) Less than $25,000	$25,000 to $49,999	$50,000 to $99,999	$100,000 to $149,999	$150,000 or More	MEDIAN HOUSEHOLD INCOME 2004	2009	2004 National Centile	2004 State Centile	2004 Home Value Base	2004 HOME VALUE DISTRIBUTION (%) Less than $50,000	$50,000 to $89,999	$90,000 to $174,999	$175,000 to $399,999	$400,000 or More	2004 Median Home Value
81335	YELLOW JACKET	20203	95	20.0	29.5	42.1	6.3	2.1	50177	53358	72	62	82	0.0	12.2	40.2	45.1	2.4	169444
81401	MONTROSE	21494	11604	28.5	32.9	29.1	6.7	2.7	41533	46494	51	42	8863	11.5	7.3	44.0	30.0	7.2	151227
81410	AUSTIN	19752	691	29.8	35.8	30.0	3.0	1.5	40762	45238	49	38	583	9.3	6.2	46.1	34.0	4.5	150543
81411	BEDROCK	14581	95	42.1	35.8	21.1	1.1	0.0	30267	33806	13	7	78	34.6	30.8	20.5	12.8	1.3	70000
81413	CEDAREDGE	22720	2234	32.4	33.6	26.2	5.1	2.8	36842	41082	35	25	1858	5.7	9.0	40.7	36.5	8.1	161425
81415	CRAWFORD	22425	696	32.3	29.2	28.3	5.9	4.3	40345	43220	47	36	564	7.6	9.2	36.0	38.7	8.5	167453
81416	DELTA	17408	4679	33.6	35.9	23.6	5.1	1.8	34259	39284	25	17	3483	10.7	9.4	50.1	24.6	5.2	132017
81418	ECKERT	19717	800	28.4	35.8	30.3	3.1	2.5	39783	44654	45	35	683	1.6	5.0	58.4	32.4	2.6	154167
81419	HOTCHKISS	20761	1499	35.7	30.2	26.6	4.9	2.7	36297	41010	33	24	1202	9.7	10.2	35.9	33.2	11.0	155978
81422	NATURITA	15027	232	40.1	36.2	21.6	1.3	0.9	31410	34682	16	9	189	32.8	31.2	21.7	11.6	2.7	72333
81423	NORWOOD	24057	524	23.9	32.4	32.6	9.0	2.1	44410	50452	60	50	414	9.2	3.1	44.2	29.5	14.0	163934
81424	NUCLA	18827	695	31.6	36.8	27.3	2.9	1.4	35678	40897	30	22	567	18.5	22.4	33.5	20.5	5.1	107212
81425	OLATHE	15041	1704	33.5	35.8	27.2	2.5	1.1	35931	40394	31	23	1317	8.7	13.1	47.5	25.1	5.5	129115
81426	OPHIR	51315	195	9.2	25.1	36.9	16.4	12.3	67001	80976	90	85	129	4.7	0.0	9.3	42.6	43.4	367308
81427	OURAY	30625	406	22.7	36.5	28.1	5.7	7.1	43619	51503	58	48	316	14.2	2.9	9.8	53.2	19.9	271111
81428	PAONIA	20750	1685	30.3	32.3	28.3	7.0	2.1	38205	43787	40	29	1333	5.6	7.4	47.7	34.7	4.7	154670
81430	PLACERVILLE	46826	370	7.8	25.1	38.1	17.6	11.4	67604	82093	90	85	263	4.9	0.0	7.6	44.5	43.0	370161
81431	REDVALE	19516	229	30.1	36.7	28.4	3.5	1.3	36188	41870	32	23	187	14.4	19.8	37.4	22.5	5.9	116250
81432	RIDGWAY	29766	1168	22.9	28.6	32.1	8.8	7.6	48545	56621	69	59	929	8.2	2.5	11.4	43.4	34.6	316570
81433	SILVERTON	20867	283	36.8	35.0	21.9	3.9	2.5	32498	35282	19	13	196	3.6	3.6	47.5	42.9	2.6	168571
81434	SOMERSET	26935	95	27.4	35.8	23.2	7.4	6.3	39642	44301	45	34	74	2.7	28.4	13.5	39.2	16.2	200000
81435	TELLURIDE	49229	2342	19.6	23.4	30.3	12.1	14.6	57913	73039	83	76	1020	0.6	0.8	6.6	29.6	62.5	545322
81501	GRAND JUNCTION	17731	9167	43.8	32.7	19.3	3.0	1.3	28247	32561	9	5	4504	5.5	12.3	70.4	11.3	0.6	115419
81503	GRAND JUNCTION	27929	10168	17.5	30.9	35.0	10.3	6.4	51393	59017	75	65	8537	2.1	5.0	48.6	38.4	5.8	164124
81504	GRAND JUNCTION	19621	9990	24.4	36.7	31.9	5.2	1.8	41068	46731	50	39	7894	7.0	9.5	67.4	15.9	0.2	131213
81505	GRAND JUNCTION	27655	3416	27.1	31.4	24.8	8.2	8.5	42305	48772	54	44	2680	9.7	7.5	30.2	39.8	12.8	180912
81506	GRAND JUNCTION	33936	4306	21.0	28.5	30.6	10.3	9.7	50549	56463	73	63	3335	1.0	4.1	34.7	54.4	5.9	190379
81520	CLIFTON	14302	4789	35.0	38.0	24.3	2.5	0.2	35293	40160	29	21	3004	20.8	12.9	54.3	10.7	1.4	105143
81521	FRUITA	19613	3878	28.7	35.3	26.8	6.3	2.8	39827	44747	45	36	3019	4.7	10.5	50.8	30.5	3.6	143703
81522	GATEWAY	25626	435	15.6	32.9	37.5	10.3	3.7	51556	58520	75	66	382	4.2	3.4	35.9	52.6	3.9	188298
81524	LOMA	20265	682	25.8	31.8	27.4	9.8	5.1	42222	46126	54	44	576	2.8	6.4	29.9	53.3	7.6	197500
81525	MACK	21979	214	26.2	31.8	26.6	9.8	5.6	41692	45174	52	42	181	2.8	6.1	29.8	53.6	7.7	198295
81526	PALISADE	20723	2273	30.6	33.4	25.7	6.1	4.2	38924	44140	42	32	1740	10.1	6.7	39.9	39.5	3.8	156719
81527	WHITEWATER	21107	519	29.5	29.5	31.6	6.4	3.1	43657	48939	58	49	459	3.5	6.3	36.6	48.2	5.5	186149
81601	GLENWOOD SPRINGS	28827	5427	16.6	30.6	33.0	12.4	7.4	52768	59874	77	67	3601	5.2	5.4	9.9	52.1	27.3	295640
81610	DINOSAUR	15487	157	37.6	36.9	24.2	1.3	0.0	35603	38920	30	21	128	45.3	35.2	14.8	2.3	2.3	55455
81611	ASPEN	57512	4750	12.7	22.3	33.6	13.1	18.3	70080	84835	91	88	2561	0.7	2.9	16.4	18.9	61.1	762801
81621	BASALT	34145	2509	10.3	21.6	41.7	16.4	10.0	68634	79994	91	87	1779	7.7	9.8	10.2	18.7	53.6	420673
81623	CARBONDALE	28512	5477	13.1	22.3	40.4	15.4	8.9	66087	75784	89	84	3922	6.3	6.6	8.5	36.4	42.3	357762
81624	COLLBRAN	21755	511	26.0	35.4	28.2	5.7	4.7	39923	44748	46	36	416	4.1	4.8	44.5	37.5	9.1	166860
81625	CRAIG	21294	4878	21.4	33.1	38.9	5.5	1.1	46390	51318	65	55	3565	12.2	11.6	49.8	24.7	1.8	126546
81630	DE BEQUE	19304	370	28.4	32.4	29.7	6.5	3.0	40000	44709	46	36	295	10.2	6.8	42.7	31.5	8.8	154643
81631	EAGLE	31408	2601	9.7	16.2	43.3	18.7	12.2	77274	86657	94	91	1846	8.0	3.5	3.0	29.0	56.6	431105
81633	DINOSAUR	782	0	0.0	0.0	0.0	0.0	0.0	0	55000	0	0	0	0.0	0.0	0.0	0.0	0.0	
81635	PARACHUTE	21165	2414	23.5	34.2	35.3	5.3	1.6	42415	48470	54	45	1400	6.9	10.6	36.1	37.0	9.4	169048
81637	GYPSUM	25730	1967	7.0	23.2	47.9	14.1	7.7	65641	74953	89	84	1607	9.6	6.3	10.6	49.5	24.1	285222
81638	HAMILTON	17348	84	26.2	46.4	23.8	3.6	0.0	41409	46260	51	41	70	15.7	7.1	27.1	32.9	17.1	175000
81639	HAYDEN	22834	985	15.4	33.8	39.2	10.4	1.2	50735	57725	73	63	740	12.3	3.0	46.1	29.1	9.6	160211
81640	MAYBELL	16832	119	36.1	24.4	33.6	0.0	5.9	42573	46318	55	46	95	22.1	26.3	22.1	20.0	9.5	106250
81641	MEEKER	20184	1463	29.1	32.2	34.1	3.4	1.2	40717	45143	49	38	1120	7.6	9.7	50.0	28.0	4.7	142170
81642	MEREDITH	55609	28	7.1	25.0	46.4	7.1	14.3	61836	75000	86	81	16	0.0	6.3	25.0	0.0	68.8	1000001
81643	MESA	21477	415	28.9	31.6	29.6	6.3	3.6	40513	44720	48	37	349	10.6	6.6	41.3	32.7	8.9	157012
81647	NEW CASTLE	25116	1797	12.6	27.9	43.1	12.2	4.1	58570	65779	83	77	1516	10.3	5.9	18.1	54.6	11.0	215043
81648	RANGELY	20874	961	20.4	35.4	34.0	8.0	2.2	45336	50433	62	54	748	13.5	27.9	46.4	12.2	0.0	96400
81650	RIFLE	20806	4284	18.1	32.2	39.4	8.1	2.3	49813	57798	72	61	2848	14.6	10.9	28.3	38.9	7.3	166509
81652	SILT	24361	1479	17.2	29.0	41.0	8.9	3.9	53024	59522	77	68	1247	4.1	6.0	29.5	47.3	13.1	201729
81653	SLATER	23578	19	15.8	31.6	52.6	0.0	0.0	54641	62891	79	72	17	5.9	11.8	35.3	47.1	0.0	170833
81654	SNOWMASS	47654	1531	11.2	22.9	35.1	13.9	16.9	68093	81969	90	86	906	0.9	2.0	10.8	20.0	66.3	729381
81657	VAIL	47702	10007	9.2	20.9	34.9	18.6	16.4	74761	89673	93	89	5311	5.1	3.8	7.1	31.7	52.3	417425
	COLORADO	28803		19.1	26.9	34.1	12.5	7.5	54077	63465				4.8	4.7	28.0	49.9	12.6	203984
	UNITED STATES	25866		24.7	27.1	30.8	10.9	6.5	48124	56710				10.9	15.0	33.7	30.1	10.4	145905

#	POST OFFICE NAME	Auto Loan	Home Loan	Investments	Retirement Plans	Home Repair	Lawn & Garden	Computers & Hardware	Major Appliances	TV, Radio, Sound Equipment	Furniture	Dine out/ Carry out	Sports Equipment	Fees & Tickets	Toys & Games	Travel	Cable TV	Apparel & Services	Auto Repairs	Health Insurance	Pets & Supplies
81335	YELLOW JACKET	94	66	34	62	77	86	65	80	75	64	88	97	55	86	67	79	80	79	96	112
81401	MONTROSE	85	70	53	68	76	84	70	79	75	70	91	91	65	87	71	78	85	78	87	98
81410	AUSTIN	81	59	36	56	68	77	58	70	66	58	78	82	51	74	61	69	71	69	84	95
81411	BEDROCK	68	45	21	39	51	59	44	55	53	45	62	65	37	59	44	57	56	54	67	78
81413	CEDAREDGE	78	67	55	63	71	85	67	75	72	67	88	78	64	78	69	77	81	73	88	87
81415	CRAWFORD	95	69	39	65	79	87	68	82	77	67	91	98	59	88	70	80	83	81	95	112
81416	DELTA	73	57	39	54	62	70	59	66	65	58	78	76	54	75	59	68	72	66	75	83
81418	ECKERT	65	70	74	67	71	78	67	69	68	66	84	77	69	85	70	70	81	68	72	78
81419	HOTCHKISS	88	62	35	59	72	82	64	76	73	62	85	90	55	83	65	76	78	75	91	103
81422	NATURITA	68	45	21	39	51	59	44	55	53	45	62	65	37	59	44	57	56	54	67	78
81423	NORWOOD	99	69	36	66	81	90	68	85	79	68	93	102	59	91	71	83	84	83	101	118
81424	NUCLA	79	55	28	51	63	71	54	66	62	53	73	80	46	71	55	66	67	66	80	93
81425	OLATHE	72	58	40	54	61	66	57	65	62	60	75	74	51	70	57	62	72	65	69	80
81426	OPHIR	136	156	181	161	152	153	150	146	142	151	179	174	155	182	150	136	177	147	131	160
81427	OURAY	117	81	43	77	95	106	80	99	93	79	109	120	69	107	83	97	99	98	118	139
81428	PAONIA	85	61	34	58	69	79	62	74	71	61	84	87	54	81	64	75	76	73	88	99
81430	PLACERVILLE	129	148	183	154	146	150	147	142	139	146	176	169	151	180	147	135	174	143	129	155
81431	REDVALE	82	57	30	54	66	74	56	70	65	56	76	84	48	75	58	68	69	69	83	97
81432	RIDGWAY	120	96	66	92	106	116	92	108	100	91	120	129	84	119	95	104	112	106	121	143
81433	SILVERTON	69	54	37	49	61	69	51	62	58	51	69	72	46	68	55	62	64	61	73	84
81434	SOMERSET	105	83	56	75	93	104	78	94	88	77	104	110	70	103	83	94	97	92	111	128
81435	TELLURIDE	135	138	207	152	131	138	147	135	145	151	185	164	153	191	144	141	183	140	122	150
81501	GRAND JUNCTION	52	46	53	48	47	52	55	52	55	52	69	62	52	67	52	54	66	55	52	58
81503	GRAND JUNCTION	96	106	108	105	106	110	99	101	96	99	120	117	102	123	101	95	117	99	97	114
81504	GRAND JUNCTION	73	70	65	69	71	75	69	71	69	69	85	83	67	84	68	68	82	71	71	83
81505	GRAND JUNCTION	100	98	95	96	101	110	96	100	97	95	119	115	95	118	98	99	115	99	105	117
81506	GRAND JUNCTION	100	113	125	112	113	121	106	109	103	107	130	121	111	128	110	104	126	106	108	119
81520	CLIFTON	56	53	50	53	54	57	54	55	55	53	68	65	53	68	54	54	65	56	56	63
81521	FRUITA	78	70	56	68	72	78	68	73	70	68	86	86	65	85	68	71	82	72	76	90
81522	GATEWAY	85	106	112	106	104	102	94	94	87	94	110	110	100	117	97	85	110	91	84	104
81524	LOMA	101	71	38	67	83	92	70	86	80	69	95	104	60	93	73	84	86	85	102	120
81525	MACK	101	71	37	67	82	92	70	86	80	69	94	104	60	92	72	84	86	85	103	120
81526	PALISADE	80	68	55	66	73	80	70	76	74	68	89	89	65	89	70	75	84	76	83	93
81527	WHITEWATER	101	70	37	66	82	92	70	86	80	69	94	104	59	92	72	84	86	85	102	120
81601	GLENWOOD SPRINGS	96	108	120	110	105	107	104	102	99	104	125	120	107	127	104	96	123	101	93	112
81610	DINOSAUR	68	48	25	45	56	62	47	58	54	47	64	70	40	62	49	57	58	57	69	81
81611	ASPEN	153	157	235	169	153	165	168	158	167	169	211	191	173	219	168	165	209	163	149	178
81621	BASALT	128	143	139	148	137	134	130	130	120	135	153	152	133	153	127	113	151	127	112	143
81623	CARBONDALE	113	127	129	131	122	121	117	115	108	120	138	135	121	139	115	103	136	113	101	128
81624	COLLBRAN	106	74	39	70	86	96	73	90	84	72	99	109	62	97	76	88	90	89	108	126
81625	CRAIG	83	76	64	75	78	83	75	80	76	75	94	94	71	92	74	76	90	79	81	95
81630	DE BEQUE	88	64	39	61	73	82	64	77	72	63	85	93	56	84	66	75	79	76	89	104
81631	EAGLE	145	163	157	171	155	150	147	146	135	153	172	171	152	172	143	126	170	142	124	160
81633	DINOSAUR	0	0	0	0	0	0	0	0	0	0	0	0	0	0	0	0	0	0	0	0
81635	PARACHUTE	79	64	49	62	68	80	70	75	76	67	91	85	64	87	69	79	84	75	86	89
81637	GYPSUM	115	127	120	132	122	119	115	115	107	120	135	135	118	135	112	100	133	112	100	127
81638	HAMILTON	80	57	31	54	65	73	56	68	64	55	75	82	48	74	58	67	69	67	81	95
81639	HAYDEN	87	89	82	88	88	89	84	86	81	85	101	101	83	100	83	79	99	85	80	98
81640	MAYBELL	90	61	28	54	69	79	59	74	70	60	83	88	50	79	60	75	75	73	90	104
81641	MEEKER	73	66	55	65	68	74	66	70	68	65	83	81	63	81	65	68	78	69	73	83
81642	MEREDITH	168	132	90	119	149	167	125	150	141	123	167	176	111	165	133	151	155	148	177	205
81643	MESA	93	65	34	62	76	85	64	80	74	64	87	96	55	85	67	78	79	78	95	111
81647	NEW CASTLE	100	109	103	112	105	104	100	100	93	103	118	117	101	117	98	88	116	98	89	112
81648	RANGELY	81	79	72	80	79	83	78	79	76	78	95	93	76	94	76	74	92	79	76	90
81650	RIFLE	85	85	77	84	84	86	81	84	79	82	99	98	79	97	80	77	96	83	79	95
81652	SILT	90	101	101	102	98	97	94	94	88	95	111	111	96	113	93	84	110	93	83	104
81653	SLATER	88	79	60	75	83	89	73	81	77	73	94	96	71	96	75	79	89	78	87	104
81654	SNOWMASS	152	152	148	149	157	164	143	151	144	143	177	178	142	180	147	144	171	149	153	182
81657	VAIL	174	163	187	173	160	169	170	167	169	173	212	200	167	208	165	163	207	172	157	193
	COLORADO	103	104	110	107	103	108	105	104	102	105	128	122	104	127	103	99	125	105	98	116
	UNITED STATES	100	100	100	100	100	100	100	100	100	100	100	100	100	100	100	100	100	100	100	100

ZIP CODE #	POST OFFICE NAME	COUNTY FIPS CODE	POPULATION			2000-2004 ANNUAL RATE		HOUSEHOLDS					FAMILIES		
			2000	2004	2009	% Rate	State Centile	2000	2004	2009	% Annual Rate 2000-2004	2004 Average HH Size	2000	2004	% Annual Rate 2000-2004
06001 AVON		003	16011	16686	17161	1.0	73	6303	6650	6922	1.3	2.48	4539	4752	1.1
06002 BLOOMFIELD		003	19585	19781	20047	0.2	29	7901	8125	8353	0.7	2.37	5155	5233	0.4
06010 BRISTOL		003	59992	60624	61560	0.3	31	24849	25525	26290	0.6	2.34	16160	16385	0.3
06013 BURLINGTON		003	8216	8542	8722	0.9	71	2853	3020	3129	1.4	2.82	2428	2559	1.2
06016 BROAD BROOK		003	5201	5389	5500	0.8	67	2064	2183	2265	1.3	2.44	1429	1499	1.1
06018 CANAAN		005	2591	2586	2634	-0.1	16	1102	1113	1147	0.2	2.25	696	695	0.0
06019 CANTON		003	8807	9036	9263	0.6	55	3507	3652	3795	1.0	2.45	2486	2578	0.9
06021 COLEBROOK		005	277	280	287	0.3	31	115	118	122	0.6	2.37	85	87	0.6
06023 EAST BERLIN		003	1397	1514	1581	1.9	97	496	547	580	2.3	2.73	382	418	2.1
06024 EAST CANAAN		005	753	748	762	-0.2	11	237	239	247	0.2	2.79	166	166	0.0
06026 EAST GRANBY		003	4811	4930	5005	0.6	52	1872	1947	2004	0.9	2.53	1370	1415	0.8
06027 EAST HARTLAND		003	1569	1578	1581	0.1	23	549	562	572	0.6	2.79	456	464	0.4
06029 ELLINGTON		013	13046	13973	14889	1.6	91	5240	5734	6225	2.1	2.43	3499	3793	1.9
06031 FALLS VILLAGE		005	1526	1530	1560	0.1	20	649	658	680	0.3	2.28	419	420	0.1
06032 FARMINGTON		003	17741	18631	19153	1.2	79	7221	7671	7977	1.4	2.39	4738	4980	1.2
06033 GLASTONBURY		003	26282	26451	26674	0.2	24	10267	10469	10688	0.5	2.50	7417	7511	0.3
06035 GRANBY		003	7322	7475	7578	0.5	47	2755	2860	2941	0.9	2.58	2103	2165	0.7
06037 BERLIN		003	16822	17261	17540	0.6	55	6299	6552	6742	0.9	2.62	4776	4938	0.8
06039 LAKEVILLE		005	2049	2085	2142	0.4	42	894	919	954	0.7	2.20	547	554	0.3
06040 MANCHESTER		003	54668	56127	57495	0.6	56	23166	24148	25075	1.0	2.28	13987	14451	0.8
06043 BOLTON		013	5103	5167	5353	0.3	35	1944	2001	2105	0.7	2.58	1471	1502	0.5
06051 NEW BRITAIN		003	27767	28314	28928	0.5	45	11474	11762	12119	0.6	2.38	6419	6504	0.3
06052 NEW BRITAIN		003	8377	8138	8124	-0.7	2	3374	3314	3349	-0.4	2.31	2073	2011	-0.7
06053 NEW BRITAIN		003	35363	35091	35306	-0.2	10	13700	13797	14066	0.2	2.38	8443	8384	-0.2
06057 NEW HARTFORD		005	6110	6432	6727	1.2	82	710	720	745	0.3	2.40	488	490	0.1
06058 NORFOLK		005	1740	1738	1775	0.0	17	710	720	745	0.3	2.40	488	490	0.1
06060 NORTH GRANBY		003	1938	2039	2096	1.2	81	639	681	709	1.5	2.99	560	594	1.4
06062 PLAINVILLE		003	17325	16975	16986	-0.5	3	7384	7346	7452	-0.1	2.29	4645	4568	-0.4
06063 BARKHAMSTED		005	3179	3388	3565	1.5	89	1201	1302	1391	1.9	2.60	937	1008	1.7
06065 RIVERTON		003	555	566	574	0.5	45	205	213	219	0.9	2.66	162	168	0.9
06066 VERNON ROCKVILLE		013	28043	28367	29566	0.3	32	12257	12627	13388	0.7	2.22	7268	7409	0.5
06067 ROCKY HILL		003	17938	18475	18942	0.7	60	7544	7948	8304	1.2	2.22	4511	4718	1.1
06068 SALISBURY		005	1471	1458	1487	-0.2	9	636	639	661	0.1	2.17	373	370	-0.2
06069 SHARON		005	2879	2839	2881	-0.3	5	1201	1202	1239	0.0	2.24	746	737	-0.3
06070 SIMSBURY		003	14944	15377	15760	0.7	59	5461	5702	5917	1.0	2.67	4227	4390	0.9
06071 SOMERS		013	10733	11098	11532	0.8	65	2994	3177	3386	1.4	2.76	1450	1564	1.8
06073 SOUTH GLASTONBURY		003	5203	5565	5795	1.6	91	1850	2002	2108	1.9	2.77	1450	1564	1.8
06074 SOUTH WINDSOR		003	24409	25045	25516	0.6	55	8903	9227	9503	0.8	2.69	6767	6974	0.7
06076 STAFFORD SPRINGS		013	11585	11765	12265	0.4	40	4537	4699	4984	0.8	2.48	3206	3291	0.6
06078 SUFFIELD		003	10321	10437	10528	0.3	32	3473	3567	3649	0.6	2.46	2425	2468	0.4
06081 TARIFFVILLE		003	1371	1391	1401	0.3	38	618	639	654	0.8	2.18	377	383	0.4
06082 ENFIELD		003	45140	46024	46941	0.5	45	16392	17057	17696	0.9	2.48	11377	11712	0.7
06084 TOLLAND		013	13143	14253	15267	1.9	97	4587	5064	5516	2.4	2.79	3785	4155	2.2
06085 UNIONVILLE		003	5731	6248	6547	2.1	99	2167	2392	2536	2.4	2.61	1540	1686	2.2
06088 EAST WINDSOR		003	4689	4864	4984	0.9	67	2040	2155	2242	1.3	2.16	1149	1197	1.0
06089 WEATOGUE		003	3319	3307	3333	-0.1	14	1290	1297	1320	0.1	2.55	965	958	-0.2
06090 WEST GRANBY		003	1087	1143	1177	1.2	81	387	414	432	1.6	2.75	331	352	1.5
06092 WEST SIMSBURY		003	3605	3928	4144	2.0	98	1159	1276	1360	2.3	3.03	1024	1123	2.2
06093 WEST SUFFIELD		003	3165	3264	3338	0.7	63	1163	1224	1272	1.2	2.67	910	952	1.1
06095 WINDSOR		003	28336	27908	27941	-0.4	5	10612	10601	10753	0.0	2.58	7624	7566	-0.2
06096 WINDSOR LOCKS		003	12043	12002	12042	-0.1	15	4935	5005	5097	0.3	2.39	3306	3320	0.1
06098 WINSTED		005	11891	12033	12352	0.3	33	4851	4983	5187	0.6	2.40	3199	3249	0.4
06103 HARTFORD		003	738	712	708	-0.8	2	361	349	351	-0.8	1.62	68	65	-1.1
06105 HARTFORD		003	19268	20213	20967	1.1	78	9483	9994	10459	1.2	1.97	3888	4025	0.8
06106 HARTFORD		003	40224	41034	41935	0.5	47	13858	14199	14638	0.6	2.68	8600	8756	0.4
06107 WEST HARTFORD		003	18160	18011	18078	-0.2	10	7351	7385	7503	0.1	2.41	5134	5117	-0.1
06108 EAST HARTFORD		003	24111	23821	23879	-0.3	8	9585	9523	9634	-0.2	2.44	7435	7629	0.6
06109 WETHERSFIELD		003	26370	26941	27534	0.5	48	11248	11642	12044	0.8	2.29	7435	7629	0.6
06110 WEST HARTFORD		003	12234	12586	12959	0.7	59	4994	5191	5403	0.9	2.40	3232	3327	0.7
06111 NEWINGTON		003	29306	28917	28937	-0.3	7	12014	12067	12256	0.1	2.35	8254	8213	-0.1
06112 HARTFORD		003	21555	21088	21193	-0.5	2	7461	7366	7478	-0.3	2.83	5342	5241	-0.5
06114 HARTFORD		003	26186	26916	27441	0.7	57	9412	9592	9792	0.5	2.76	6279	6340	0.2
06117 WEST HARTFORD		003	17597	17706	17934	0.2	24	5362	5453	5599	0.4	2.49	3889	3925	0.2
06118 EAST HARTFORD		003	25848	25511	25583	-0.3	7	10758	10782	10959	0.1	2.35	7079	7024	-0.2
06119 WEST HARTFORD		003	15632	15733	15900	0.2	24	6883	6989	7137	0.4	2.20	3690	3717	0.2
06120 HARTFORD		003	13437	12431	12267	-1.8	1	4355	4074	4073	-1.6	2.81	2984	2764	-1.8
06226 WILLIMANTIC		015	17862	17878	18249	0.0	19	6351	6419	6645	0.3	2.45	3680	3671	-0.1
06231 AMSTON		013	3783	4018	4258	1.4	89	1356	1464	1575	1.8	2.74	1086	1167	1.7
06232 ANDOVER		013	3046	3197	3378	1.1	78	1149	1222	1309	1.5	2.61	861	908	1.3
06234 BROOKLYN		015	5006	5261	5482	1.2	80	1607	1734	1846	1.8	2.67	1254	1341	1.6
06235 CHAPLIN		015	1680	1993	2223	4.1	100	636	769	871	4.6	2.59	456	547	4.4
06237 COLUMBIA		013	4529	4764	5021	1.2	81	1703	1823	1955	1.6	2.60	1328	1411	1.4
06238 COVENTRY		013	11531	12506	13428	1.9	97	4273	4707	5133	2.3	2.65	3201	3495	2.1
06239 DANIELSON		015	13079	13289	13707	0.4	41	5125	5279	5523	0.7	2.46	3325	3394	0.5
06241 DAYVILLE		015	6153	6418	6682	1.0	74	2379	2535	2687	1.5	2.50	1690	1776	1.2
06242 EASTFORD		015	1046	1063	1090	0.4	41	398	410	425	0.7	2.59	290	296	0.5
06243 EAST KILLINGLY		015	71	71	72	0.0	18	25	26	26	0.9	2.73	18	18	0.0
06247 HAMPTON		015	2482	2593	2696	1.0	75	921	976	1029	1.4	2.66	686	721	1.2
06248 HEBRON		013	5222	5292	5486	0.3	36	1782	1835	1933	0.7	2.88	1501	1537	0.6
06249 LEBANON		011	6829	7105	7348	0.9	72	2419	2564	2697	1.4	2.72	1913	2013	1.2
06250 MANSFIELD CENTER		013	4841	5223	5610	1.8	94	1948	2148	2350	2.3	2.39	1309	1416	1.9
06254 NORTH FRANKLIN		011	1904	2059	2177	1.9	95	712	782	840	2.2	2.63	544	593	2.1
06255 NORTH GROSVENORDALE		015	4573	4792	4991	1.1	77	1802	1921	2033	1.5	2.49	1269	1340	1.3
06256 NORTH WINDHAM		015	1935	1930	1972	-0.1	16	832	845	877	0.4	2.27	582	585	0.1
06259 POMFRET CENTER		015	4238	4331	4449	0.5	48	1583	1635	1699	0.8	2.64	1168	1197	0.6
06260 PUTNAM		015	9107	9217	9459	0.3	33	3723	3831	3995	0.7	2.34	2318	2360	0.4
06262 QUINEBAUG		015	374	380	389	0.4	41	182	187	194	0.6	2.03	124	127	0.6
06264 SCOTLAND		015	158	175	188	2.4	100	60	68	74	3.0	2.57	46	52	2.9
06266 SOUTH WINDHAM		015	377	372	379	-0.3	7	138	138	143	0.0	2.70	101	101	0.0
06268 STORRS MANSFIELD		013	13861	14418	15045	0.9	72	3384	3671	4001	1.9	2.33	1844	1966	1.5
06269 STORRS MANSFIELD		013	2137	2199	2248	0.7	60	3	5	7	12.8	2.60	2	3	10.0
06277 THOMPSON		015	3437	3505	3614	0.5	45	1318	1369	1434	0.9	2.55	953	981	0.7
06278 ASHFORD		013	4177	4335	4491	0.9	68	1624	1711	1800	1.2	2.52	1119	1169	1.0
06279 WILLINGTON		013	6034	6245	6524	0.8	66	2377	2509	2669	1.3	2.48	1453	1514	1.0
06280 WINDHAM		015	3415	3371	3445	-0.3	8	1310	1321	1374	0.2	2.48	936	936	0.0
CONNECTICUT						0.5					0.7	2.51			0.5
UNITED STATES						1.2					1.3	2.58			1.1

ZIP CODE #	POST OFFICE NAME	RACE (%) White 2000	White 2004	Black 2000	Black 2004	Asian/Pacific 2000	Asian/Pacific 2004	% Hispanic Origin 2000	% Hispanic Origin 2004	2004 AGE DISTRIBUTION (%) 0-4	5-9	10-14	15-19	20-24	25-44	45-64	65-84	85+	18+	MEDIAN AGE 2004	% 2004 Males	% 2004 Females
06001	AVON	95.0	93.6	1.0	1.2	3.0	3.9	1.6	2.0	6.1	7.2	8.1	6.0	3.6	21.5	31.3	14.1	2.2	74.7	43.7	47.9	52.2
06002	BLOOMFIELD	40.0	36.5	54.1	57.0	1.3	1.5	3.7	4.1	5.0	5.4	6.3	6.1	4.7	21.9	28.5	18.1	4.1	79.5	45.5	44.8	55.2
06010	BRISTOL	91.6	89.8	2.7	3.2	1.5	1.9	5.3	6.5	6.2	6.1	6.6	6.1	5.8	29.8	25.0	12.3	2.2	77.3	38.9	48.5	51.5
06013	BURLINGTON	97.4	96.7	0.6	0.7	0.8	1.1	1.4	1.7	7.1	8.1	8.1	6.3	4.1	27.2	31.2	7.3	0.8	72.7	39.7	50.4	49.6
06016	BROAD BROOK	92.9	91.3	3.5	4.3	1.4	1.8	1.9	2.4	6.6	6.7	7.1	6.4	5.3	29.6	25.7	11.0	1.6	75.6	38.9	49.2	50.8
06018	CANAAN	96.8	96.4	1.2	1.3	0.2	0.3	2.7	3.1	5.5	5.7	6.8	6.4	6.0	25.9	25.9	14.2	3.8	78.0	41.3	48.3	51.7
06019	CANTON	97.2	96.5	0.5	0.6	0.8	1.0	1.3	1.7	6.2	7.0	7.5	5.9	4.0	26.0	30.5	10.8	2.1	75.4	41.5	48.3	51.7
06021	COLEBROOK	97.1	96.4	0.7	0.7	0.7	0.7	2.5	2.9	5.7	6.8	7.5	6.1	3.2	25.7	30.7	12.1	2.1	75.7	42.5	50.4	49.6
06023	EAST BERLIN	96.8	95.9	0.6	0.7	1.8	2.4	1.9	2.4	5.9	6.4	6.8	6.5	5.3	25.0	28.6	13.6	1.9	76.3	41.8	49.9	50.1
06024	EAST CANAAN	97.5	96.9	1.1	1.2	0.1	0.3	1.3	1.7	4.8	5.2	6.8	5.9	5.6	26.5	24.3	15.4	5.5	79.4	41.9	48.1	51.9
06026	EAST GRANBY	95.6	94.5	1.4	1.7	1.0	1.4	1.5	2.0	6.7	7.2	7.5	6.5	4.0	26.0	29.3	11.7	1.3	74.5	41.0	48.9	51.1
06027	EAST HARTLAND	98.3	98.0	0.2	0.2	0.6	0.8	0.4	0.5	5.5	6.5	8.2	7.0	5.2	24.3	33.5	8.9	1.0	75.0	41.4	50.2	49.8
06029	ELLINGTON	96.2	95.5	1.0	1.1	1.3	1.7	1.4	1.7	6.4	6.7	7.1	6.2	5.5	31.5	26.4	9.2	1.1	75.9	38.1	49.3	50.7
06031	FALLS VILLAGE	96.8	96.5	1.4	1.5	0.5	0.5	0.7	0.8	4.6	5.6	6.4	6.0	4.4	21.7	32.0	15.7	3.6	79.5	45.7	47.2	52.8
06032	FARMINGTON	92.4	90.4	1.6	2.0	4.1	5.3	2.3	2.9	5.4	5.8	7.0	6.6	4.9	25.4	28.7	13.3	2.9	77.5	42.1	46.5	53.5
06033	GLASTONBURY	92.7	90.9	1.6	1.9	3.6	4.7	2.7	3.4	6.5	7.5	7.9	5.9	3.8	25.2	29.4	11.7	2.2	74.1	41.4	47.0	53.0
06035	GRANBY	97.7	97.1	0.6	0.7	0.8	1.0	1.2	1.5	6.7	7.7	8.0	5.7	3.6	25.5	29.6	11.6	1.7	73.8	41.6	49.2	50.8
06037	BERLIN	97.1	96.2	0.3	0.4	1.7	2.2	1.4	1.8	5.5	6.1	7.3	6.8	5.0	23.9	29.0	14.2	2.3	76.7	42.3	48.5	51.5
06039	LAKEVILLE	95.6	95.0	1.7	1.9	1.2	1.5	1.6	1.9	3.7	5.3	8.4	8.5	4.3	16.9	34.6	15.2	3.1	76.6	46.7	48.1	51.9
06040	MANCHESTER	82.8	80.2	8.4	9.4	3.2	3.9	6.5	7.8	6.2	5.8	6.4	6.0	7.0	30.2	24.4	11.4	2.6	77.9	37.7	47.8	52.2
06043	BOLTON	97.7	97.3	0.7	0.8	0.5	0.7	1.7	2.0	5.8	6.6	7.4	7.0	4.4	23.7	32.4	11.2	1.4	75.7	42.4	48.4	51.6
06051	NEW BRITAIN	63.0	58.8	13.5	14.5	1.5	1.7	35.1	39.7	7.9	7.1	7.7	7.6	8.4	28.4	20.0	10.8	2.0	72.8	32.5	47.8	52.2
06052	NEW BRITAIN	81.2	77.9	7.3	8.3	1.5	1.9	15.7	18.7	5.5	5.6	6.5	6.0	5.7	28.3	24.0	14.6	3.8	78.6	40.0	47.8	52.2
06053	NEW BRITAIN	71.6	68.0	9.7	10.6	3.4	4.1	22.8	25.8	6.0	5.7	6.1	8.4	10.3	27.8	20.3	12.9	2.6	78.6	34.1	48.3	51.7
06057	NEW HARTFORD	97.7	97.2	0.6	0.7	0.8	1.1	1.3	1.6	6.3	7.4	8.1	6.4	3.7	25.9	32.1	9.2	1.0	74.1	41.0	49.8	50.2
06058	NORFOLK	97.2	96.9	0.5	0.5	0.5	0.6	1.0	1.2	5.9	6.7	7.0	5.1	3.3	25.1	32.2	13.1	1.6	77.1	43.1	49.4	50.6
06060	NORTH GRANBY	97.0	96.0	0.6	0.7	0.9	1.2	1.7	2.2	5.9	7.8	9.1	7.5	4.3	23.4	35.5	5.9	0.6	72.4	41.4	51.6	48.4
06062	PLAINVILLE	93.5	92.0	2.3	2.7	1.7	2.2	3.6	4.6	4.8	5.1	6.4	6.3	5.8	28.6	27.6	13.2	2.3	79.9	41.0	48.8	51.2
06063	BARKHAMSTED	98.5	98.3	0.1	0.1	0.4	0.5	0.9	1.0	5.3	6.2	7.5	5.9	4.4	27.4	32.0	10.2	1.0	77.1	41.4	49.9	50.1
06065	RIVERTON	98.2	97.7	0.0	0.0	0.7	0.9	1.4	1.8	5.5	6.0	6.4	8.0	4.6	25.4	33.2	10.1	0.9	77.0	42.3	50.4	49.7
06066	VERNON ROCKVILLE	90.0	88.5	4.0	4.3	2.7	3.4	3.6	4.1	6.0	5.8	6.3	5.9	6.0	29.8	25.8	12.2	2.1	78.2	39.0	47.9	52.1
06067	ROCKY HILL	90.2	87.8	3.4	4.1	4.0	5.3	3.2	4.1	4.9	5.2	5.6	5.4	5.4	28.7	28.4	14.0	2.6	81.0	42.0	49.5	50.5
06068	SALISBURY	95.8	95.3	1.7	1.9	0.6	0.8	1.5	1.7	3.1	3.8	6.3	6.0	3.2	17.6	34.2	18.9	6.8	82.3	50.6	46.0	54.0
06069	SHARON	96.8	96.3	0.9	1.0	0.6	0.8	2.0	2.3	3.9	4.5	6.6	6.0	4.1	21.0	32.0	17.6	4.3	80.5	47.1	48.6	51.4
06070	SIMSBURY	95.2	93.9	1.3	1.6	2.2	2.9	1.6	2.0	7.0	8.3	9.0	6.7	3.6	23.0	29.2	11.3	1.9	71.1	40.9	48.6	51.4
06071	SOMERS	83.4	82.5	9.5	9.8	0.7	0.9	7.9	8.6	4.3	5.2	6.6	7.0	8.6	30.9	26.9	9.3	1.2	79.7	38.2	60.0	40.0
06073	SOUTH GLASTONBURY	96.0	94.9	0.6	0.7	2.3	3.1	1.1	1.5	7.9	9.4	8.9	5.7	2.8	24.4	29.5	10.2	1.4	69.7	40.9	48.7	51.3
06074	SOUTH WINDSOR	91.5	89.4	3.0	3.5	3.7	4.9	2.3	2.9	6.1	7.3	8.3	6.7	4.3	26.0	28.9	10.9	1.4	73.8	40.6	48.2	51.8
06076	STAFFORD SPRINGS	96.9	96.4	0.6	0.7	0.9	1.2	1.6	1.9	6.4	6.6	7.0	6.5	5.9	28.6	27.3	9.7	2.0	76.1	39.2	49.1	50.9
06078	SUFFIELD	85.8	83.6	8.9	10.0	1.1	1.4	5.3	6.3	5.2	5.7	6.2	6.3	6.9	30.1	25.1	11.9	2.7	79.4	39.7	55.3	44.7
06081	TARIFFVILLE	92.4	90.9	2.7	3.2	2.0	2.7	1.0	1.2	6.6	6.5	6.0	6.0	5.2	30.3	26.8	10.9	1.7	77.3	39.3	48.7	51.3
06082	ENFIELD	89.7	88.3	5.6	6.1	1.4	1.8	3.7	4.5	5.6	5.9	6.5	6.0	6.4	31.4	24.0	12.4	1.7	78.2	38.6	52.3	47.7
06084	TOLLAND	96.8	96.1	0.8	0.9	1.2	1.6	1.2	1.4	7.3	8.0	7.9	6.6	5.2	27.3	29.1	7.8	0.9	72.7	38.7	49.7	50.3
06085	UNIONVILLE	94.2	92.8	1.3	1.6	2.8	3.6	2.2	2.7	6.1	7.1	8.2	7.4	4.0	26.7	28.5	10.5	1.5	73.7	40.1	49.9	50.1
06088	EAST WINDSOR	89.9	87.8	4.7	5.5	2.8	3.5	2.4	3.0	4.8	5.0	5.2	5.6	4.7	29.9	26.8	15.2	2.8	81.4	42.3	49.2	50.8
06089	WEATOGUE	95.2	94.0	0.9	1.1	2.7	3.5	1.9	2.4	6.8	7.8	7.7	7.6	3.6	25.6	29.6	10.3	1.0	72.8	40.3	48.4	51.7
06090	WEST GRANBY	97.8	97.3	1.0	1.2	0.6	0.7	1.3	1.7	6.5	7.4	7.9	6.3	3.9	23.4	32.9	10.8	1.0	73.7	42.1	50.3	49.7
06092	WEST SIMSBURY	97.1	96.4	0.4	0.6	1.3	1.8	1.4	1.7	6.7	8.8	10.4	7.4	3.1	19.9	31.3	10.9	1.6	68.9	41.7	49.2	50.8
06093	WEST SUFFIELD	97.9	97.4	0.8	0.9	0.6	0.8	1.0	1.2	5.2	6.4	7.7	6.8	4.8	24.9	32.2	10.6	1.4	76.4	41.8	49.5	50.5
06095	WINDSOR	64.9	60.8	27.3	30.1	3.2	3.9	5.0	5.8	5.8	6.4	7.0	6.4	5.1	25.7	28.7	12.5	2.5	76.7	41.3	47.3	52.7
06096	WINDSOR LOCKS	92.5	90.6	2.7	3.2	2.6	3.4	2.2	2.8	5.9	6.1	6.8	6.4	5.3	28.0	25.2	14.5	1.9	77.3	40.5	48.5	51.5
06098	WINSTED	94.7	93.9	1.2	1.3	0.9	1.2	3.1	3.6	5.7	5.9	6.7	6.6	5.8	26.5	27.9	12.6	2.3	77.8	40.9	48.7	51.3
06103	HARTFORD	61.5	56.9	14.8	16.3	5.4	6.6	24.7	27.1	2.0	2.1	3.2	4.5	4.9	36.2	35.1	11.0	1.0	90.2	43.3	61.7	38.3
06105	HARTFORD	34.2	30.8	43.2	44.7	2.5	2.8	27.1	29.4	7.7	6.7	6.0	6.4	9.3	33.6	20.9	8.2	1.2	76.1	32.1	47.6	52.4
06106	HARTFORD	35.3	32.5	17.1	17.0	2.6	2.9	57.8	61.1	8.2	7.6	8.4	9.8	11.1	27.4	18.0	7.5	2.1	70.7	28.3	48.5	51.5
06107	WEST HARTFORD	93.2	91.6	1.5	1.8	3.2	4.2	2.8	3.5	6.1	6.9	6.8	6.1	4.0	21.7	29.2	15.5	3.8	76.2	44.0	46.8	53.2
06108	EAST HARTFORD	55.8	51.2	23.3	24.9	5.2	6.1	19.3	22.1	7.0	6.5	7.2	7.2	7.2	29.3	22.7	10.9	1.9	74.8	35.7	48.4	51.6
06109	WETHERSFIELD	93.1	91.6	2.1	2.5	1.6	2.1	4.3	5.4	5.2	5.6	6.0	5.4	4.2	23.5	27.1	19.3	3.8	79.9	45.1	46.6	53.4
06110	WEST HARTFORD	72.9	69.6	10.0	10.5	8.1	9.9	13.2	14.8	5.8	6.1	6.9	6.7	5.4	26.8	23.7	14.5	4.2	76.9	40.3	46.5	53.5
06111	NEWINGTON	92.5	90.7	2.1	2.5	2.9	3.7	3.7	4.7	5.1	5.5	6.1	5.5	4.6	26.4	27.7	16.3	2.9	79.8	43.1	47.0	53.0
06112	HARTFORD	3.7	3.5	86.1	86.1	0.4	0.4	9.4	9.9	8.8	8.5	9.0	8.3	8.4	25.6	20.9	9.6	0.9	68.5	30.8	44.8	55.2
06114	HARTFORD	39.6	36.2	15.6	15.9	1.5	1.7	52.2	56.1	8.6	7.8	8.4	8.4	8.7	29.5	19.3	7.7	1.5	70.2	30.6	48.3	51.7
06117	WEST HARTFORD	90.7	88.5	3.6	4.3	3.6	4.6	2.7	3.3	4.4	5.2	5.8	13.8	13.0	13.5	22.4	16.0	5.9	81.4	40.0	45.4	54.6
06118	EAST HARTFORD	73.2	69.6	14.5	15.9	3.0	3.7	11.4	13.4	5.9	6.0	6.5	5.8	5.4	26.5	25.5	16.1	2.3	78.0	41.1	47.2	52.8
06119	WEST HARTFORD	82.5	79.6	5.8	6.4	5.8	7.1	8.9	10.6	5.6	5.5	5.9	6.4	6.7	30.5	23.5	12.5	3.5	78.9	38.3	46.1	53.9
06120	HARTFORD	9.6	9.4	61.2	60.1	0.5	0.5	36.2	37.7	9.6	9.4	9.4	10.0	10.0	26.6	17.9	6.4	0.8	65.8	26.1	49.2	50.8
06226	WILLIMANTIC	70.3	66.7	5.9	6.2	1.6	2.0	31.0	35.3	6.5	5.8	6.4	11.5	13.6	26.7	18.5	8.9	2.1	77.7	29.1	48.6	51.4
06231	AMSTON	97.4	97.0	0.6	0.7	0.7	0.9	1.2	1.5	7.9	8.7	7.7	6.4	3.8	28.1	30.1	6.8	0.5	71.3	38.6	49.8	50.2
06232	ANDOVER	96.7	96.1	0.9	1.1	0.5	0.6	1.5	1.9	7.2	7.9	7.8	5.8	4.1	28.6	30.1	7.6	1.0	72.7	39.2	50.9	49.1
06234	BROOKLYN	92.2	91.6	4.6	4.8	0.5	0.6	3.0	3.6	5.2	5.6	6.4	6.3	6.2	31.7	26.9	9.5	2.2	78.7	38.9	53.2	46.8
06235	CHAPLIN	97.3	96.9	0.7	0.8	0.4	0.6	1.9	2.4	6.5	6.8	6.9	5.9	5.1	31.4	28.2	8.6	0.7	76.2	38.3	50.5	49.5
06237	COLUMBIA	97.4	97.0	0.4	0.4	0.7	1.0	1.7	2.0	6.3	7.2	8.0	5.9	3.8	25.7	31.0	10.9	1.2	74.4	41.4	48.8	51.2
06238	COVENTRY	97.0	96.4	0.6	0.7	0.6	0.8	1.7	2.1	6.9	7.4	7.4	6.4	4.8	30.6	27.5	7.9	1.0	74.1	38.1	50.6	49.4
06239	DANIELSON	93.8	92.8	1.5	1.6	1.5	1.9	2.6	3.3	6.0	6.0	7.6	7.5	6.7	27.9	24.0	11.8	2.5	75.8	37.7	48.9	51.1
06241	DAYVILLE	94.3	93.2	1.2	1.3	1.4	1.8	1.4	1.8	6.4	7.0	8.4	7.2	5.8	28.2	24.8	10.3	1.8	73.6	37.2	49.3	50.7
06242	EASTFORD	97.8	97.4	0.4	0.5	0.4	0.5	1.3	1.8	6.1	6.8	7.9	5.9	4.9	26.3	29.2	11.3	1.7	75.5	40.9	51.2	48.8
06243	EAST KILLINGLY	94.4	94.4	1.4	1.4	1.4	1.4	0.0	0.0	5.6	7.0	7.0	5.6	5.6	28.2	29.6	9.9	1.4	74.7	39.6	49.3	50.7
06247	HAMPTON	97.0	96.3	0.3	0.4	0.8	1.0	1.9	2.5	6.2	6.9	7.5	6.7	4.6	26.3	31.1	9.8	1.0	75.2	40.8	50.4	49.6
06248	HEBRON	97.9	97.5	0.5	0.6	0.5	0.7	1.0	1.2	8.9	9.5	8.1	6.4	4.2	28.1	28.6	5.8	0.5	69.4	37.5	50.4	49.6
06249	LEBANON	96.9	96.4	0.8	0.9	0.3	0.4	1.7	2.1	6.4	6.9	8.1	8.0	4.5	26.5	30.0	8.5	1.2	72.9	40.0	50.6	49.4
06250	MANSFIELD CENTER	90.6	88.4	1.6	1.8	4.8	6.3	3.4	4.2	5.1	5.4	7.3	7.4	6.5	25.1	28.7	12.5	2.1	77.5	40.8	48.2	51.8
06254	NORTH FRANKLIN	97.7	97.5	0.7	0.9	0.2	0.2	1.2	1.5	5.3	5.8	6.7	6.3	5.4	26.4	30.2	12.5	1.4	77.9	41.8	51.1	48.9
06255	NORTH GROSVENORDALE	98.1	97.9	0.5	0.5	0.2	0.3	0.9	1.2	5.8	6.0	7.0	6.9	6.3	27.6	25.9	12.8	1.7	76.9	40.1	49.6	50.4
06256	NORTH WINDHAM	88.6	87.1	1.5	1.6	0.4	0.5	10.3	12.0	6.4	6.3	6.7	5.8	6.0	27.2	28.8	11.7	1.2	77.1	39.5	48.2	51.8
06259	POMFRET CENTER	97.3	96.7	0.4	0.4	0.7	1.0	1.5	2.1	5.8	6.3	7.7	7.1	5.7	26.1	30.2	9.5	1.6	75.6	40.5	49.3	50.7
06260	PUTNAM	95.4	94.7	1.3	1.4	0.4	0.5	1.8	2.3	5.9	5.9	6.5	6.6	6.8	27.2	24.5	13.1	3.5	77.4	39.2	48.0	52.1
06262	QUINEBAUG	98.4	98.2	1.1	1.3	0.3	0.3	0.0	0.0	5.5	5.8	7.1	5.8	4.7	24.5	26.6	16.8	3.2	77.6	42.8	50.3	49.7
06264	SCOTLAND	97.5	97.7	0.6	0.6	0.6	0.6	2.5	2.3	6.9	7.4	7.4	7.4	5.1	27.4	28.0	9.1	1.1	73.1	38.0	50.9	49.1
06266	SOUTH WINDHAM	95.0	93.8	0.8	0.8	0.3	0.3	5.6	7.0	5.7	6.2	5.9	5.1	5.1	29.0	31.2	10.0	1.9	79.0	41.1	50.3	49.7
06268	STORRS MANSFIELD	82.1	79.3	5.7	6.0	7.9	10.0	4.6	5.2	2.5	2.3	3.3	22.9	31.3	17.0	12.6	7.1	0.9	89.8	23.0	50.2	49.8
06269	STORRS MANSFIELD	81.2	78.1	7.0	7.7	7.8	9.7	4.4	5.0	0.3	0.2	0.2	48.0	46.8	3.9	0.4	0.3	0.0	99.0	20.2	46.6	53.4
06277	THOMPSON	97.7	97.2	0.3	0.3	0.7	0.9	0.7	0.8	6.0	6.6	7.4	6.5	5.1	29.6	27.4	10.1	1.3	75.6	39.6	50.6	49.4
06278	ASHFORD	95.8	95.0	1.0	1.1	1.0	1.3	2.0	2.5	6.0	6.3	7.1	6.7	6.1	30.5	28.3	8.0	1.1	76.4	37.7	50.2	49.8
06279	WILLINGTON	94.0	92.8	1.0	1.1	3.1	4.0	1.8	2.1	4.6	4.7	5.8	6.8	13.6	30.2	26.2	7.2	0.9	80.9	34.0	50.1	49.9
06280	WINDHAM	87.9	86.3	2.1	2.3	0.9	1.2	11.5	13.3	5.8	6.0	6.4	5.8	5.7	24.9	29.0	13.8	2.7	78.1	41.9	47.8	52.2
	CONNECTICUT	81.6	80.0	9.1	9.5	2.5	3.1	9.4	10.5	6.4	6.7	7.1	6.9	6.3	27.5	25.4	11.7	2.2	75.8	38.5	48.5	51.5
	UNITED STATES	75.1	73.6	12.3	12.5	3.8	4.2	12.5	14.1	6.9	6.7	7.2	7.0	7.3	28.6	23.8	10.8	1.7	75.1	36.0	49.1	50.9

INCOME

#	POST OFFICE NAME	2004 Per Capita Income	2004 HH Income Base	2004 Household Income Distribution (%): Less than $25,000	$25,000 to $49,999	$50,000 to $99,999	$100,000 to $149,999	$150,000 or More	Median Household Income: 2004	2009	2004 National Centile	2004 State Centile	2004 Home Value Base	2004 Home Value Distribution (%): Less than $50,000	$50,000 to $89,999	$90,000 to $174,999	$175,000 to $399,999	$400,000 or More	2004 Median Home Value
06001	AVON	64030	6650	7.5	12.7	29.0	19.3	31.6	101636	119590	98	91	5704	0.2	0.8	9.6	51.0	38.4	337782
06002	BLOOMFIELD	33778	8125	18.8	22.6	33.0	14.9	10.7	61017	71215	85	37	6244	0.7	3.1	37.3	54.0	4.9	187345
06010	BRISTOL	27369	25525	20.7	26.6	36.2	12.5	4.0	52747	61420	77	22	16749	1.4	4.7	46.3	45.9	1.8	171540
06013	BURLINGTON	44601	3020	5.0	11.7	38.3	25.2	19.9	91898	108239	97	87	2874	0.3	1.2	9.4	70.3	18.8	276947
06016	BROAD BROOK	26934	2183	13.9	26.5	42.6	13.2	3.9	58023	66816	83	31	1581	1.1	1.5	31.4	59.1	6.8	210140
06018	CANAAN	22577	1113	28.2	28.8	32.3	9.5	1.3	41353	47792	51	11	803	1.1	7.5	38.5	49.3	3.6	180649
06019	CANTON	40212	3652	10.1	19.1	35.3	21.7	13.8	75925	91311	94	69	2997	0.2	2.4	18.3	63.1	16.0	244697
06021	COLEBROOK	36668	118	13.6	19.5	42.4	15.3	9.3	66108	75805	89	49	104	0.0	1.0	20.2	58.7	20.2	255556
06023	EAST BERLIN	31364	547	6.8	16.6	44.8	23.2	8.6	79417	94795	95	76	473	2.3	1.1	12.5	79.7	4.4	225171
06024	EAST CANAAN	19725	239	16.3	33.9	37.2	11.3	1.3	49851	55969	72	19	194	0.0	2.1	41.8	49.5	6.7	186538
06026	EAST GRANBY	35949	1947	8.5	22.1	35.9	21.9	11.6	76973	91368	94	71	1634	1.0	1.9	13.0	74.5	9.5	232322
06027	EAST HARTLAND	31288	562	5.7	19.9	48.2	18.7	7.5	71523	81975	92	61	519	0.0	1.0	16.2	75.7	7.1	229559
06029	ELLINGTON	32770	5734	11.2	20.2	41.3	19.6	7.7	70174	79184	91	58	4240	0.8	4.3	22.2	67.4	5.3	218450
06031	FALLS VILLAGE	44333	658	17.5	22.2	34.4	12.9	13.1	63659	76016	88	44	543	0.7	2.6	16.4	55.6	24.7	254500
06032	FARMINGTON	50703	7671	11.9	19.2	28.8	18.6	21.6	81021	99787	95	78	5847	0.4	2.6	14.0	54.8	28.2	266755
06033	GLASTONBURY	46675	10469	9.5	15.5	32.0	21.3	21.8	87185	105042	97	84	8677	0.1	1.7	12.2	62.5	23.4	286254
06035	GRANBY	39109	2860	7.4	17.9	34.8	24.2	15.8	84115	101753	96	80	2510	0.5	0.3	16.1	74.6	8.5	233311
06037	BERLIN	33131	6552	11.0	19.6	37.0	21.8	10.6	76335	89937	94	70	5729	0.6	1.2	11.9	76.5	9.8	237529
06039	LAKEVILLE	46334	919	18.9	21.7	35.4	8.5	15.6	61039	69095	85	37	671	0.0	1.5	14.2	39.3	45.0	367157
06040	MANCHESTER	30506	24148	17.8	26.4	36.0	13.9	6.0	55624	64985	80	28	14465	1.3	2.3	49.0	44.0	3.3	171364
06043	BOLTON	34207	2001	9.7	20.3	36.8	21.6	11.6	75784	85353	94	68	1726	0.0	0.8	21.8	65.5	11.9	242342
06051	NEW BRITAIN	18030	11762	41.2	30.9	22.5	3.9	1.5	30907	34355	15	3	4017	3.7	12.0	68.9	15.3	0.2	129109
06052	NEW BRITAIN	31348	3314	21.9	24.7	33.0	14.3	6.0	53404	61765	78	24	2056	2.6	6.0	40.1	49.4	1.8	177126
06053	NEW BRITAIN	21472	13797	27.2	31.8	30.9	7.4	2.8	40914	47037	49	10	7336	1.9	8.4	68.9	20.1	0.8	136915
06057	NEW HARTFORD	36199	2380	10.3	13.9	39.1	22.2	14.5	80706	94888	95	77	2092	0.1	4.0	15.1	69.8	11.0	244670
06058	NORFOLK	39698	720	13.3	24.9	34.0	15.6	12.2	63458	73719	87	43	589	0.3	0.9	22.2	48.4	28.2	261620
06060	NORTH GRANBY	40537	681	2.6	8.2	31.3	33.6	24.2	108642	127274	99	93	657	0.0	0.0	3.4	71.7	25.0	325566
06062	PLAINVILLE	27295	7346	19.7	25.7	37.5	14.0	3.0	54092	63287	78	26	5111	1.9	4.7	45.6	47.2	0.6	171954
06063	BARKHAMSTED	33110	1302	7.5	18.1	42.2	24.2	8.0	75584	85694	93	67	1156	0.0	0.0	10.9	80.4	8.7	232486
06065	RIVERTON	31436	213	6.6	18.3	47.4	22.5	5.2	78023	87088	94	74	194	0.0	0.0	11.3	82.5	6.2	224638
06066	VERNON ROCKVILLE	29493	12627	19.5	27.4	35.5	13.5	4.1	52858	60070	77	22	7493	3.4	4.8	37.4	52.7	1.7	181907
06067	ROCKY HILL	35667	7948	11.2	21.1	41.2	18.6	7.9	67016	79236	90	52	5251	1.5	4.8	21.8	64.1	7.8	219536
06068	SALISBURY	41156	639	25.8	18.6	32.9	9.2	13.5	58472	67202	83	31	488	1.0	2.3	14.1	45.5	37.1	318182
06069	SHARON	51690	1202	15.8	23.3	35.5	12.8	12.6	61614	71539	86	39	971	0.7	0.7	13.3	51.9	33.4	280044
06070	SIMSBURY	48772	5702	7.4	12.3	32.3	22.6	25.6	95971	114189	98	89	4994	0.4	0.3	8.8	62.5	28.1	322544
06071	SOMERS	29428	3177	9.5	21.2	38.9	19.2	11.2	73545	83559	93	65	2792	0.0	0.3	10.1	74.6	15.0	273917
06073	SOUTH GLASTONBURY	62386	2002	7.1	8.2	27.0	23.9	33.7	113451	133884	99	94	1852	0.1	0.2	3.4	56.4	40.0	355072
06074	SOUTH WINDSOR	36733	9227	7.7	14.8	39.8	23.0	14.8	83049	100769	96	79	8248	1.2	3.0	17.7	69.9	8.3	228294
06076	STAFFORD SPRINGS	26273	4699	16.0	24.6	41.5	15.0	2.9	60280	67382	85	34	3646	1.4	2.5	45.1	47.6	3.4	176699
06078	SUFFIELD	33376	3567	15.2	17.0	34.9	21.3	11.8	75130	89166	93	66	2933	0.0	1.9	16.7	68.1	13.3	235095
06081	TARIFFVILLE	35776	639	12.4	24.3	39.9	14.1	9.4	67480	81206	90	53	440	0.0	2.7	23.4	73.4	0.5	196341
06082	ENFIELD	26219	17057	15.2	25.4	41.2	14.1	4.1	59258	67671	84	32	13201	0.5	1.5	51.2	45.9	0.9	171699
06084	TOLLAND	35141	5064	6.4	13.3	40.1	27.0	13.3	85653	100039	96	83	4738	0.0	0.7	17.0	71.7	10.6	235034
06085	UNIONVILLE	35281	2392	16.2	19.8	34.0	16.6	13.4	67604	80544	90	54	1873	0.0	0.4	14.7	72.5	12.5	242730
06088	EAST WINDSOR	32025	2155	16.4	25.9	42.4	11.0	4.3	56411	65059	81	29	1462	8.3	4.5	46.9	39.1	1.3	159333
06089	WEATOGUE	46158	1297	5.3	13.5	37.3	23.5	20.4	90154	107774	97	86	1090	0.0	1.7	11.5	63.8	23.0	286242
06090	WEST GRANBY	47257	414	3.4	12.6	31.2	29.0	23.9	103205	118715	98	92	393	0.0	0.5	16.3	59.8	23.4	304128
06092	WEST SIMSBURY	50832	1276	3.7	7.5	28.0	23.0	37.8	122935	145963	99	94	1215	0.5	0.0	1.7	57.9	39.9	367070
06093	WEST SUFFIELD	35885	1224	10.1	13.8	42.7	20.1	13.2	78584	93798	95	75	1109	0.0	1.4	14.7	73.9	10.0	253356
06095	WINDSOR	32924	10601	12.2	19.8	38.6	20.1	9.4	71033	82692	92	60	8676	0.6	2.3	33.2	60.5	3.5	196767
06096	WINDSOR LOCKS	27188	5005	16.3	27.9	37.7	15.1	2.9	55838	64921	81	29	3919	0.1	2.6	54.9	41.8	0.7	167452
06098	WINSTED	27217	4983	21.7	24.7	37.5	12.0	4.2	53720	61501	78	25	3469	1.1	3.7	41.7	47.3	6.3	180800
06103	HARTFORD	50538	349	26.1	19.8	20.1	14.3	19.8	61452	71997	86	39	102	0.0	1.0	45.1	42.2	11.8	187500
06105	HARTFORD	20784	9994	51.9	27.1	14.5	3.3	3.2	23593	26095	4	2	1710	6.4	9.5	22.6	46.9	14.6	203101
06106	HARTFORD	13849	14199	47.8	28.4	19.0	3.4	1.4	26455	29705	6	3	3526	3.0	15.5	66.7	14.2	0.7	128443
06107	WEST HARTFORD	48983	7385	9.0	15.8	34.1	20.0	21.2	85150	102898	96	81	6314	0.5	0.8	6.9	74.7	17.1	272222
06108	EAST HARTFORD	22317	9523	28.1	31.2	28.9	9.3	2.5	41689	47331	52	11	4531	3.0	4.3	63.5	28.6	0.6	148039
06109	WETHERSFIELD	34176	11642	17.1	23.4	35.3	15.8	8.4	61134	72186	85	38	9009	0.9	1.1	23.8	67.3	6.8	222897
06110	WEST HARTFORD	26009	5191	19.6	28.3	35.8	13.4	3.0	52023	61326	76	22	3632	0.6	1.7	52.5	45.2	0.1	169437
06111	NEWINGTON	32265	12067	14.2	21.0	40.2	18.2	6.4	64752	76704	88	46	9712	0.2	3.0	29.3	65.7	1.9	198117
06112	HARTFORD	14818	7366	39.8	30.8	22.9	4.4	2.1	31695	36279	17	4	3005	1.8	9.7	65.8	19.7	3.1	132196
06114	HARTFORD	14517	9592	40.7	31.4	23.4	3.5	1.1	31469	34841	16	4	3244	4.0	11.3	62.3	21.8	0.6	136478
06117	WEST HARTFORD	44644	5453	11.3	13.0	30.5	17.1	28.0	89136	107945	97	86	4785	0.2	0.4	4.4	67.9	27.1	297606
06118	EAST HARTFORD	27478	10782	21.4	28.3	34.6	11.8	3.9	50264	57376	72	20	7720	5.1	4.8	53.7	36.0	0.4	156829
06119	WEST HARTFORD	35204	6989	18.9	23.7	33.0	16.0	8.5	58529	68324	83	31	3739	1.8	3.3	24.6	60.6	9.7	217191
06120	HARTFORD	10545	4074	59.3	25.8	11.4	2.4	1.1	17961	20994	1	1	809	9.5	15.0	46.2	23.4	5.9	130191
06226	WILLIMANTIC	18641	6419	38.2	28.2	26.1	5.5	2.1	33820	36733	23	6	2730	4.1	6.4	69.4	19.5	0.7	136849
06231	AMSTON	37328	1464	6.4	12.5	44.3	22.1	14.6	82099	93656	96	78	1345	0.0	0.7	17.8	73.1	8.3	241498
06232	ANDOVER	34527	1222	8.4	17.8	44.8	19.8	9.2	77862	88262	94	73	1068	0.7	1.2	21.6	72.2	4.3	221344
06234	BROOKLYN	25858	1734	13.6	22.5	41.2	16.6	6.1	63901	70715	88	44	1500	1.5	2.1	41.7	49.1	5.6	185380
06235	CHAPLIN	25736	769	14.3	25.8	44.3	13.0	2.6	59622	64633	84	34	617	0.5	6.8	46.8	43.6	2.3	169504
06237	COLUMBIA	34526	1823	9.3	16.7	41.2	24.6	8.1	77564	88664	94	72	1679	0.9	0.2	20.7	69.7	8.4	228363
06238	COVENTRY	31448	4707	9.9	21.6	39.4	20.8	8.2	72404	82100	92	63	4154	0.2	1.4	30.1	64.2	4.0	204235
06239	DANIELSON	21701	5279	27.8	29.3	31.3	8.9	2.7	43352	47685	57	14	3354	3.1	3.3	63.5	28.7	1.3	151243
06241	DAYVILLE	23219	2535	23.3	35.9	28.4	8.2	4.3	43025	47793	56	13	1864	6.7	4.7	57.7	29.9	1.0	148048
06242	EASTFORD	30158	410	15.9	23.4	38.8	13.9	8.1	62307	68651	87	41	350	1.1	2.9	33.4	56.9	5.7	200581
06243	EAST KILLINGLY	23082	26	19.2	26.9	42.3	11.5	0.0	54580	60000	79	28	22	0.0	0.0	63.6	36.4	0.0	156250
06247	HAMPTON	28728	976	14.0	22.0	43.0	14.0	6.9	62615	69326	87	41	868	0.9	2.9	36.4	54.5	5.3	189655
06248	HEBRON	36310	1835	8.1	10.4	42.2	25.5	13.8	85149	100280	96	81	1673	0.7	0.6	9.8	78.9	10.0	239481
06249	LEBANON	30680	2564	7.9	23.6	46.3	16.9	5.3	66997	76208	90	51	2291	0.4	1.9	21.6	70.2	6.0	219010
06250	MANSFIELD CENTER	30573	2148	16.3	23.4	37.2	16.5	6.7	60634	68877	85	36	1635	1.1	0.9	36.6	56.3	5.1	193072
06254	NORTH FRANKLIN	29681	782	13.0	21.4	39.9	20.2	5.5	67942	76922	90	55	694	0.4	1.2	24.8	66.9	6.8	218649
06255	NORTH GROSVENORDALE	21979	1921	25.6	26.7	36.1	9.3	2.3	47908	53081	68	17	1472	2.1	2.0	54.6	38.3	3.0	162302
06256	NORTH WINDHAM	22794	845	26.3	32.7	31.7	7.6	1.8	41173	45556	50	10	648	17.8	19.4	35.7	26.9	0.3	127000
06259	POMFRET CENTER	29697	1635	15.2	18.5	43.2	14.4	8.7	64401	73188	88	45	1304	1.9	2.2	27.3	58.1	10.5	220751
06260	PUTNAM	23393	3831	25.4	28.0	34.7	9.2	2.7	46959	51598	66	15	2371	0.0	7.0	58.8	31.8	2.5	146490
06262	QUINEBAUG	24888	187	30.5	28.3	32.1	7.0	2.1	41587	46412	52	11	172	14.5	4.1	39.5	36.1	5.8	157500
06264	SCOTLAND	28245	68	10.3	17.7	54.4	11.8	5.9	64813	71226	88	47	60	0.0	1.7	33.3	61.7	3.3	192308
06266	SOUTH WINDHAM	29125	138	3.6	22.5	54.4	14.5	5.1	64619	72035	88	46	119	5.0	1.7	53.8	39.5	0.0	160119
06268	STORRS MANSFIELD	24378	3671	30.3	19.6	26.5	13.6	10.0	50096	55899	72	20	1963	7.9	4.0	18.9	63.5	5.8	209925
06269	STORRS MANSFIELD	13115	5	40.0	60.0	0.0	0.0	0.0	40833	42248	49	9	2	0.0	0.0	0.0	100.0	0.0	225000
06277	THOMPSON	27752	1369	18.8	23.7	41.1	11.5	5.0	55773	62715	80	28	1194	0.8	1.9	46.7	45.3	5.2	175773
06278	ASHFORD	31406	1711	17.6	21.3	40.4	14.4	6.4	60620	67209	85	36	1325	2.2	2.3	30.9	61.6	3.0	194273
06279	WILLINGTON	30411	2509	19.5	23.4	36.3	15.3	5.4	57193	64839	82	30	1691	1.3	1.5	29.9	62.6	4.6	201265
06280	WINDHAM	26394	1321	18.2	26.8	37.6	13.5	3.9	54090	59466	78	26	1021	1.7	2.2	42.9	49.9	3.4	179408
	CONNECTICUT	34999		18.8	22.0	32.8	15.1	11.4	61358	72202				1.5	2.7	24.6	51.4	19.8	230968
	UNITED STATES	25866		24.7	27.1	30.8	10.9	6.5	48124	56710				10.9	15.0	33.7	30.1	10.4	145905

ZIP CODE		FINANCIAL SERVICES				THE HOME						ENTERTAINMENT						PERSONAL			
						Home Improvements		Furnishings													
#	POST OFFICE NAME	Auto Loan	Home Loan	Invest-ments	Retire-ment Plans	Home Repair	Lawn & Garden	Comput-ers & Hard-ware	Major Appli-ances	TV, Radio, Sound Equip-ment	Furni-ture	Dine out/ Carry out	Sports Equip-ment	Fees & Tickets	Toys & Games	Travel	Cable TV	Apparel & Services	Auto Repairs	Health Insur-ance	Pets & Supplies
06001	AVON	212	251	283	254	247	257	228	228	215	232	272	259	245	275	235	212	270	222	214	251
06002	BLOOMFIELD	108	114	131	114	113	123	114	113	114	115	143	128	118	141	115	114	139	114	113	125
06010	BRISTOL	85	92	102	92	91	96	92	90	90	91	113	105	95	117	92	89	111	90	87	99
06013	BURLINGTON	164	204	219	205	199	198	182	179	168	182	212	209	196	224	185	163	212	173	161	198
06016	BROAD BROOK	86	95	106	96	94	97	96	93	92	94	115	110	98	119	95	89	114	93	86	101
06018	CANAAN	73	69	72	67	71	79	70	72	73	69	90	84	69	92	72	75	87	73	78	86
06019	CANTON	128	155	174	158	152	152	143	141	133	143	168	165	151	176	145	129	168	138	126	155
06021	COLEBROOK	113	140	149	141	138	136	125	125	116	125	146	146	133	156	128	113	146	120	112	138
06023	EAST BERLIN	110	134	147	131	131	133	123	122	117	122	147	141	131	157	126	115	147	119	113	133
06024	EAST CANAAN	80	78	73	74	81	90	77	80	82	74	100	91	78	106	80	85	95	79	89	95
06026	EAST GRANBY	117	141	158	141	139	142	130	129	123	130	155	150	138	162	134	121	154	126	119	141
06027	EAST HARTLAND	114	141	150	142	139	137	126	126	117	126	147	147	134	157	129	113	147	121	113	139
06029	ELLINGTON	106	119	133	123	117	118	115	113	109	116	138	133	119	141	115	105	136	113	102	124
06031	FALLS VILLAGE	178	133	82	125	152	169	129	156	146	128	173	186	114	170	135	153	159	154	183	213
06032	FARMINGTON	159	188	214	190	185	190	176	174	166	176	209	203	185	215	179	163	207	171	161	191
06033	GLASTONBURY	150	183	214	184	178	184	169	165	159	169	200	191	180	209	173	156	200	162	152	180
06035	GRANBY	131	161	173	160	159	160	146	145	137	145	172	168	155	182	150	134	171	141	134	160
06037	BERLIN	112	136	147	133	133	137	124	124	118	123	148	142	132	157	128	117	147	120	116	135
06039	LAKEVILLE	141	155	168	153	157	166	146	150	142	145	177	173	150	179	151	143	174	147	147	171
06040	MANCHESTER	94	98	112	100	96	102	101	98	99	100	124	115	102	125	100	96	122	100	93	107
06043	BOLTON	113	137	154	138	135	135	127	125	120	126	150	147	134	158	129	116	150	123	114	138
06051	NEW BRITAIN	56	53	68	52	52	59	60	57	63	59	79	66	59	80	59	64	77	60	59	63
06052	NEW BRITAIN	98	105	122	106	104	110	108	104	105	106	132	123	110	133	108	103	129	106	100	114
06053	NEW BRITAIN	65	68	95	66	66	74	72	69	75	73	95	79	74	99	73	77	94	72	70	76
06057	NEW HARTFORD	126	155	169	156	152	151	141	140	131	140	165	164	149	174	144	127	164	136	125	154
06058	NORFOLK	123	140	170	145	139	142	138	134	131	137	165	160	142	170	139	127	164	135	122	147
06060	NORTH GRANBY	160	199	216	205	193	194	175	171	160	178	203	198	192	212	179	155	205	165	152	190
06062	PLAINVILLE	80	91	104	90	90	94	89	87	87	88	109	101	93	114	91	86	108	87	84	95
06063	BARKHAMSTED	112	139	148	139	137	135	124	124	115	124	144	145	132	154	127	112	144	119	111	137
06065	RIVERTON	108	135	143	135	132	131	120	120	111	120	140	140	128	149	123	108	140	116	107	132
06066	VERNON ROCKVILLE	87	92	106	95	91	96	95	92	92	94	116	108	96	117	94	89	114	93	86	101
06067	ROCKY HILL	104	117	143	118	115	121	115	112	113	115	142	130	120	146	117	111	140	113	107	123
06068	SALISBURY	152	124	93	114	138	153	118	138	131	117	156	162	107	155	125	138	146	137	159	185
06069	SHARON	154	184	212	185	183	190	172	171	163	172	205	197	181	209	177	161	203	168	161	186
06070	SIMSBURY	170	207	234	210	202	207	189	185	176	190	222	215	203	230	192	172	222	181	169	203
06071	SOMERS	102	123	133	122	121	122	113	112	106	112	134	130	119	141	115	104	133	109	102	123
06073	SOUTH GLASTONBURY	227	282	307	289	273	278	250	244	229	253	291	281	274	303	255	223	293	236	220	270
06074	SOUTH WINDSOR	129	154	173	155	151	155	142	141	134	142	169	163	151	175	145	132	168	138	130	155
06076	STAFFORD SPRINGS	91	95	97	95	96	99	92	93	91	91	113	110	93	116	93	89	110	93	90	107
06078	SUFFIELD	117	139	156	138	138	144	130	129	124	129	156	148	137	161	134	123	154	126	123	141
06081	TARIFFVILLE	99	114	140	118	112	115	113	109	107	112	135	130	116	138	113	104	134	110	99	119
06082	ENFIELD	85	97	106	96	96	100	93	92	91	92	113	106	97	119	95	90	112	91	88	101
06084	TOLLAND	129	156	169	158	153	152	142	141	132	143	167	165	150	174	144	128	166	137	126	155
06085	UNIONVILLE	115	146	172	143	141	146	132	130	125	133	157	150	142	167	136	123	157	127	119	140
06088	EAST WINDSOR	91	103	121	103	102	107	101	99	99	100	124	115	105	129	103	98	122	99	95	108
06089	WEATOGUE	153	187	211	193	181	184	170	165	157	172	199	193	183	206	172	152	200	162	148	182
06090	WEST GRANBY	168	206	226	205	204	208	186	187	175	186	220	215	198	228	193	172	219	181	173	205
06092	WEST SIMSBURY	204	253	277	259	246	250	225	220	206	227	262	254	245	271	230	201	263	213	199	243
06093	WEST SUFFIELD	124	152	165	151	150	151	137	137	128	137	161	158	146	169	141	126	161	133	126	151
06095	WINDSOR	112	130	144	129	127	132	122	121	118	122	148	139	129	153	124	116	146	119	114	133
06096	WINDSOR LOCKS	84	97	106	95	95	99	93	91	90	91	113	105	97	118	94	89	111	90	87	100
06098	WINSTED	91	94	92	91	94	101	91	93	92	90	114	108	93	117	92	92	110	92	94	107
06103	HARTFORD	121	116	219	129	109	124	136	122	143	140	182	148	141	190	135	144	181	131	116	136
06105	HARTFORD	53	47	68	48	46	53	58	53	61	57	77	64	56	76	56	61	75	58	54	60
06106	HARTFORD	45	43	74	41	41	47	50	47	55	52	71	54	49	72	50	58	71	51	48	52
06107	WEST HARTFORD	149	183	222	180	180	190	169	168	162	170	204	191	181	212	176	162	203	165	159	182
06108	EAST HARTFORD	73	73	83	72	72	79	78	75	79	76	99	87	78	100	77	79	96	77	75	82
06109	WETHERSFIELD	99	115	135	112	113	123	111	110	109	110	137	124	117	141	115	110	135	109	108	119
06110	WEST HARTFORD	81	90	104	88	89	95	89	87	87	88	110	100	92	113	90	87	108	87	85	95
06111	NEWINGTON	98	114	129	111	113	119	108	107	106	107	133	122	114	138	112	106	131	106	105	117
06112	HARTFORD	57	52	64	49	50	59	57	55	62	59	77	61	58	75	56	64	75	58	59	64
06114	HARTFORD	47	47	84	43	44	52	53	50	59	56	77	56	52	80	53	64	77	54	52	55
06117	WEST HARTFORD	165	209	262	204	205	217	191	189	182	192	229	215	207	239	200	183	229	185	179	205
06118	EAST HARTFORD	88	90	98	88	90	98	91	90	91	90	114	104	92	116	91	92	111	91	91	102
06119	WEST HARTFORD	99	111	147	113	108	116	112	107	110	112	138	126	116	142	113	109	137	110	101	117
06120	HARTFORD	39	33	47	30	31	37	38	37	44	40	54	42	38	52	37	46	53	40	40	42
06226	WILLIMANTIC	61	59	76	60	58	65	67	63	69	65	86	74	66	87	66	68	84	66	63	69
06231	AMSTON	134	166	178	168	162	161	148	146	136	148	172	170	159	182	151	132	172	141	130	162
06232	ANDOVER	120	143	150	144	140	138	131	130	121	131	153	153	136	160	132	117	152	126	115	143
06234	BROOKLYN	84	102	109	102	100	100	93	92	87	92	109	108	98	114	94	84	108	90	84	102
06235	CHAPLIN	88	103	109	102	100	101	96	95	91	96	114	111	100	119	97	88	113	93	86	104
06237	COLUMBIA	116	142	155	141	140	142	129	129	121	129	152	149	137	160	133	119	152	125	118	141
06238	COVENTRY	111	127	138	130	125	126	120	119	113	121	143	140	124	146	121	109	141	118	108	131
06239	DANIELSON	74	75	75	74	76	81	76	76	76	74	94	89	76	96	76	76	91	76	77	86
06241	DAYVILLE	90	78	64	77	81	91	79	84	84	78	102	98	77	102	79	85	97	83	91	101
06242	EASTFORD	125	112	86	106	118	126	103	114	109	103	133	136	101	136	106	112	127	111	123	147
06243	EAST KILLINGLY	101	90	68	85	95	102	83	92	88	83	107	110	81	110	86	90	102	90	100	119
06247	HAMPTON	99	123	131	123	121	119	110	110	102	109	128	128	117	136	112	99	128	106	98	121
06248	HEBRON	140	170	178	174	165	163	152	150	139	154	176	174	162	183	153	133	176	144	132	165
06249	LEBANON	113	133	137	132	133	133	120	122	113	119	141	143	125	150	123	111	140	118	113	138
06250	MANSFIELD CENTER	94	110	131	113	109	110	107	104	101	106	127	123	111	131	107	98	126	104	94	114
06254	NORTH FRANKLIN	100	122	133	121	120	121	112	111	106	111	133	129	119	141	114	103	132	108	102	121
06255	NORTH GROSVENORDALE	73	78	80	75	79	86	76	77	77	74	96	87	79	101	78	79	93	75	79	85
06256	NORTH WINDHAM	75	75	74	73	74	77	73	75	72	74	91	86	71	89	72	71	88	75	72	85
06259	POMFRET CENTER	105	122	130	123	121	121	112	113	106	112	133	132	117	138	114	103	131	110	104	126
06260	PUTNAM	73	79	84	78	79	84	78	77	78	76	97	90	81	102	79	77	95	77	77	86
06262	QUINEBAUG	64	75	83	71	74	81	71	71	70	70	88	79	75	91	74	72	86	69	72	77
06264	SCOTLAND	94	117	125	117	115	114	105	104	97	104	122	122	111	130	107	94	122	101	93	115
06266	SOUTH WINDHAM	99	121	134	118	118	121	112	111	107	111	134	128	119	143	115	105	134	108	103	121
06268	STORRS MANSFIELD	97	89	109	94	88	95	112	97	107	103	134	122	105	130	102	100	130	105	89	107
06269	STORRS MANSFIELD	39	24	30	27	23	28	46	34	45	39	56	47	37	50	37	39	52	41	31	38
06277	THOMPSON	94	110	115	110	108	109	102	102	96	102	121	119	106	126	103	93	120	99	93	112
06278	ASHFORD	104	120	135	122	118	120	114	113	108	114	136	133	118	141	115	105	135	112	103	124
06279	WILLINGTON	100	103	122	108	102	105	111	104	106	108	134	127	110	134	107	101	132	109	95	115
06280	WINDHAM	85	98	114	97	96	100	94	93	91	94	115	108	98	119	96	90	114	92	88	102
	CONNECTICUT	116	129	153	129	127	135	127	124	124	126	156	144	132	161	128	124	154	124	119	137
	UNITED STATES	100	100	100	100	100	100	100	100	100	100	100	100	100	100	100	100	100	100	100	100

CONNECTICUT

POPULATION CHANGE

A 06281-06607

# POST OFFICE NAME	COUNTY FIPS CODE	POPULATION 2000	2004	2009	2000-2004 ANNUAL RATE % Rate	State Centile	HOUSEHOLDS 2000	2004	2009	% Annual Rate 2000-2004	2004 Average HH Size	FAMILIES 2000	2004	% Annual Rate 2000-2004
06281 WOODSTOCK	015	6572	6963	7291	1.4	86	2523	2705	2867	1.7	2.57	1854	1971	1.5
06282 WOODSTOCK VALLEY	015	1205	1275	1335	1.3	85	436	467	495	1.6	2.73	339	361	1.5
06320 NEW LONDON	011	25619	25185	25517	-0.4	4	10163	10110	10406	-0.1	2.22	5375	5259	-0.5
06330 BALTIC	011	3445	3428	3501	-0.1	12	1284	1300	1349	0.3	2.60	931	935	0.1
06331 CANTERBURY	015	4694	4790	4954	0.5	47	1718	1785	1875	0.9	2.68	1340	1383	0.8
06333 EAST LYME	011	5957	6520	6941	2.2	99	2065	2293	2477	2.5	2.83	1727	1907	2.4
06334 BOZRAH	011	2509	2627	2732	1.1	76	935	997	1054	1.5	2.60	708	748	1.3
06335 GALES FERRY	011	6742	6774	6904	0.1	21	2475	2535	2629	0.6	2.67	1906	1938	0.4
06336 GILMAN	011	39	42	44	1.8	94	16	18	19	2.8	2.28	11	12	2.1
06339 LEDYARD	011	7920	8121	8373	0.6	54	2805	2934	3076	1.1	2.77	2193	2277	0.9
06340 GROTON	011	31787	32215	33054	0.3	37	12256	12743	13356	0.9	2.33	7822	8011	0.6
06349 GROTON	011	1	1	1	0.0	18	0	0	0	0.0	0.00	0	0	0.0
06351 JEWETT CITY	011	14757	15510	16212	1.2	80	5672	6057	6429	1.6	2.54	4040	4298	1.5
06353 MONTVILLE	011	226	244	258	1.8	95	103	113	121	2.2	2.16	62	68	2.2
06354 MOOSUP	015	5555	5778	6011	0.9	72	2114	2237	2363	1.3	2.58	1470	1539	1.1
06355 MYSTIC	011	11638	11974	12371	0.7	59	4739	4951	5197	1.0	2.35	3117	3222	0.8
06357 NIANTIC	011	12161	12313	12586	0.3	35	4243	4391	4586	0.8	2.28	2807	2871	0.5
06359 NORTH STONINGTON	011	4968	5067	5195	0.5	47	1822	1896	1978	0.9	2.66	1415	1462	0.8
06360 NORWICH	011	33807	34738	35918	0.6	56	14157	14795	15548	1.0	2.30	8476	8748	0.8
06365 PRESTON	011	4721	4784	4892	0.3	36	1849	1912	1991	0.8	2.50	1368	1402	0.6
06370 OAKDALE	011	6533	6593	6767	0.2	28	2352	2414	2519	0.6	2.73	1826	1860	0.4
06371 OLD LYME	011	9422	9710	10023	0.7	61	3812	3977	4162	1.0	2.44	2765	2860	0.8
06374 PLAINFIELD	015	8597	8907	9287	0.8	67	3152	3321	3518	1.2	2.63	2314	2418	1.0
06375 QUAKER HILL	011	4191	4272	4395	0.5	43	1427	1475	1543	0.8	2.50	1044	1071	0.6
06377 STERLING	015	2728	2872	2998	1.2	82	987	1055	1117	1.6	2.72	741	786	1.4
06378 STONINGTON	011	5779	6105	6401	1.3	85	2544	2714	2880	1.5	2.24	1615	1702	1.2
06379 PAWCATUCK	011	8651	8726	8956	0.2	27	3615	3707	3865	0.6	2.35	2333	2366	0.3
06380 TAFTVILLE	011	2360	2350	2388	-0.1	14	974	988	1021	0.3	2.38	624	625	0.0
06382 UNCASVILLE	011	11536	11985	12445	0.9	69	3855	4091	4336	1.4	2.53	2708	2846	1.2
06384 VOLUNTOWN	011	2526	2546	2624	0.2	26	951	972	1016	0.5	2.62	702	712	0.3
06385 WATERFORD	011	15013	15129	15453	0.2	26	6133	6284	6523	0.6	2.34	4184	4245	0.3
06401 ANSONIA	009	18540	18330	18426	-0.3	8	7502	7475	7560	-0.1	2.44	4977	4911	-0.3
06403 BEACON FALLS	009	5284	5582	5778	1.3	85	2050	2184	2275	1.5	2.56	1463	1546	1.3
06405 BRANFORD	009	28562	28911	29454	0.3	35	12504	12771	13107	0.5	2.24	7635	7693	0.2
06409 CENTERBROOK	007	558	600	641	1.7	92	256	279	303	2.0	2.11	171	183	1.6
06410 CHESHIRE	009	28377	28725	29084	0.3	35	9290	9457	9633	0.4	2.70	7208	7291	0.3
06412 CHESTER	007	3743	3837	3989	0.6	54	1510	1582	1674	1.1	2.33	1006	1043	0.9
06413 CLINTON	007	13094	13216	13696	0.2	28	5134	5272	5547	0.6	2.51	3616	3681	0.4
06415 COLCHESTER	011	15305	16136	16879	1.3	83	5526	5879	6225	1.5	2.71	4216	4462	1.3
06416 CROMWELL	007	12871	13411	14081	1.0	73	5212	5512	5872	1.3	2.32	3265	3413	1.1
06417 DEEP RIVER	007	4610	4715	4897	0.5	49	1824	1889	1988	0.8	2.43	1262	1294	0.6
06418 DERBY	009	12371	12216	12263	-0.3	8	5243	5214	5266	-0.1	2.30	3240	3189	-0.4
06419 KILLINGWORTH	007	6014	6545	7041	2.0	98	2194	2410	2619	2.2	2.72	1763	1923	2.1
06420 SALEM	011	3798	3945	4076	0.9	69	1337	1411	1481	1.3	2.79	1059	1111	1.1
06422 DURHAM	007	6594	7054	7508	1.6	91	2267	2469	2669	2.0	2.80	1863	2018	1.9
06423 EAST HADDAM	007	4982	5373	5751	1.8	94	1861	2038	2213	2.2	2.60	1367	1484	1.8
06424 EAST HAMPTON	007	13564	14389	15201	1.4	88	4217	4591	4964	2.0	2.59	848	879	0.9
06426 ESSEX	007	3145	3267	3434	0.9	69	1492	1576	1682	1.3	2.01	6027	6182	0.6
06437 GUILFORD	009	21359	21928	22508	0.6	56	8137	8382	8644	0.7	2.58	6027	6182	0.6
06438 HADDAM	007	2351	2424	2531	0.7	62	898	942	998	1.1	2.56	680	708	1.0
06441 HIGGANUM	007	4490	4685	4922	1.0	75	1676	1779	1898	1.4	2.63	1334	1405	1.2
06442 IVORYTON	007	2802	3025	3243	1.8	95	1063	1158	1256	2.0	2.59	758	817	1.8
06443 MADISON	009	17869	18070	18324	0.3	32	6519	6620	6747	0.4	2.71	5123	5181	0.3
06447 MARLBOROUGH	003	5734	6128	6356	1.6	90	2015	2201	2318	2.1	2.73	1634	1774	2.0
06450 MERIDEN	009	34539	34748	35238	0.1	23	13700	13822	14071	0.2	2.44	8790	8783	0.0
06451 MERIDEN	009	23806	23696	23925	-0.1	13	9293	9286	9416	0.0	2.54	6205	6157	-0.2
06455 MIDDLEFIELD	007	2959	3030	3150	0.6	51	1143	1192	1258	1.0	2.54	830	857	0.8
06457 MIDDLETOWN	007	43104	44571	46879	0.8	65	18489	19420	20739	1.2	2.20	10382	10780	0.9
06459 MIDDLETOWN	007	147	136	139	-1.8	1	92	85	87	-1.8	1.56	30	27	-2.5
06460 MILFORD	009	52288	52864	53771	0.3	32	20894	21278	21782	0.4	2.46	14062	14201	0.2
06468 MONROE	001	18940	18931	19217	0.0	17	6379	6432	6563	0.2	2.93	5267	5283	0.1
06469 MOODUS	007	2628	2749	2892	1.1	76	1022	1090	1165	1.5	2.46	708	747	1.3
06470 NEWTOWN	001	14961	15715	16350	1.2	79	5015	5302	5541	1.3	2.88	4087	4298	1.2
06471 NORTH BRANFORD	009	7514	7970	8316	1.4	88	2908	3083	3226	1.4	2.57	2034	2137	1.2
06472 NORTHFORD	009	6501	6530	6590	0.1	20	2258	2284	2319	0.3	2.86	1857	1870	0.2
06473 NORTH HAVEN	009	23327	23550	23901	0.2	28	8697	8840	9026	0.4	2.64	6555	6617	0.2
06475 OLD SAYBROOK	007	10367	10561	10965	0.4	43	4184	4327	4558	0.8	2.38	2922	2992	0.6
06477 ORANGE	009	13250	13562	13838	0.6	50	4745	4887	5015	0.7	2.75	3901	3996	0.6
06478 OXFORD	009	9988	10550	10912	1.3	85	3408	3629	3777	1.5	2.91	2840	3010	1.4
06479 PLANTSVILLE	003	9812	9900	10019	0.2	27	3570	3666	3766	0.6	2.62	2702	2766	0.6
06480 PORTLAND	007	8845	9497	10150	1.7	92	3427	3735	4050	2.1	2.49	2451	2652	1.9
06481 ROCKFALL	007	1181	1217	1270	0.7	61	478	502	532	1.2	2.42	352	366	0.9
06482 SANDY HOOK	001	10376	10883	11271	1.1	78	3412	3608	3758	1.3	2.90	2771	2919	1.2
06483 SEYMOUR	009	15298	15316	15414	0.0	19	6090	6142	6222	0.2	2.47	4162	4162	0.0
06484 SHELTON	001	38121	39067	40103	0.6	52	14195	14674	15156	0.8	2.62	10545	10818	0.6
06488 SOUTHBURY	009	18582	19737	20531	1.4	89	7232	7687	8005	1.5	2.42	4838	5135	1.4
06489 SOUTHINGTON	003	29957	30081	30377	0.1	20	11531	11766	12049	0.5	2.53	8590	8731	0.4
06492 WALLINGFORD	009	43013	44102	45141	0.6	50	16692	17267	17799	0.8	2.50	11577	11870	0.6
06498 WESTBROOK	007	6292	6845	7354	2.0	98	2605	2868	3121	2.3	2.37	1694	1842	2.0
06510 NEW HAVEN	009	2799	3029	3174	1.9	96	1328	1481	1581	2.6	1.53	274	301	2.2
06511 NEW HAVEN	009	52752	53930	55050	0.5	49	20286	20855	21437	0.7	2.23	9709	9843	0.3
06512 EAST HAVEN	009	28374	28714	29235	0.3	33	11697	11923	12214	0.5	2.39	7503	7574	0.2
06513 NEW HAVEN	009	35195	36328	37464	0.8	63	13346	13657	14061	0.5	2.63	8479	8604	0.3
06514 HAMDEN	009	25189	25519	25977	0.3	36	9969	10137	10371	0.4	2.40	6416	6444	0.1
06515 NEW HAVEN	009	16619	16799	17125	0.3	31	6374	6484	6653	0.4	2.37	3845	3882	0.2
06516 WEST HAVEN	009	52307	52114	52580	-0.1	14	21067	21124	21443	0.1	2.41	13107	12996	-0.2
06517 HAMDEN	009	14322	14914	15396	1.0	72	6190	6540	6822	1.3	2.24	3685	3819	0.8
06518 HAMDEN	009	17152	18033	18641	1.2	81	6157	6580	6884	1.6	2.32	3867	4091	1.4
06519 NEW HAVEN	009	16114	16278	16628	0.2	30	5306	5391	5540	0.4	2.89	3552	3555	0.0
06524 BETHANY	009	5058	5237	5357	0.8	66	1761	1838	1891	1.0	2.85	1454	1510	0.9
06525 WOODBRIDGE	009	8965	9318	9555	0.9	70	3097	3235	3335	1.0	2.83	2548	2649	0.8
06604 BRIDGEPORT	001	27804	28898	30085	1.0	73	9581	9989	10380	1.0	2.76	5978	6189	0.8
06605 BRIDGEPORT	001	24015	24745	25586	0.7	61	8683	8942	9253	0.7	2.74	5281	5367	0.2
06606 BRIDGEPORT	001	44629	45531	46622	0.5	47	16743	17066	17496	0.5	2.60	11160	11252	0.2
06607 BRIDGEPORT	001	7600	7529	7664	-0.2	9	2673	2674	2735	0.0	2.81	1864	1849	-0.2
CONNECTICUT					0.5					0.7	2.51			0.5
UNITED STATES					1.2					1.3	2.58			1.1

ZIP CODE #	POST OFFICE NAME	RACE (%) White 2000	White 2004	Black 2000	Black 2004	Asian/Pacific 2000	Asian/Pacific 2004	% Hispanic Origin 2000	% Hispanic Origin 2004	2004 AGE DISTRIBUTION (%) 0-4	5-9	10-14	15-19	20-24	25-44	45-64	65-84	85+	18+	MEDIAN AGE 2004	% 2004 Males	% 2004 Females
06281	WOODSTOCK	97.6	97.2	0.1	0.1	0.4	0.6	0.8	1.0	5.3	6.0	7.6	6.9	5.2	25.9	29.8	11.3	2.0	76.6	41.4	49.7	50.4
06282	WOODSTOCK VALLEY	96.3	95.8	0.5	0.6	0.5	0.6	1.1	1.4	5.8	6.5	7.8	7.3	5.3	28.7	29.5	8.3	0.9	75.4	39.4	50.2	49.8
06320	NEW LONDON	63.5	60.9	18.7	19.4	2.2	2.7	19.7	21.7	6.7	5.8	6.4	9.0	13.0	28.0	19.9	9.2	2.0	77.5	31.0	49.2	50.8
06330	BALTIC	95.7	94.9	0.7	0.8	1.3	1.7	1.2	1.6	5.1	5.8	8.3	7.2	5.7	28.7	27.3	10.4	1.5	76.2	39.1	48.5	51.5
06331	CANTERBURY	97.3	96.9	0.4	0.4	0.3	0.4	1.1	1.4	5.3	6.1	7.6	7.6	5.6	28.5	29.6	8.6	1.1	76.2	39.5	50.8	49.2
06333	EAST LYME	90.7	88.7	1.1	1.3	5.9	7.7	1.8	2.2	6.0	7.8	9.5	7.6	3.3	24.2	31.6	9.1	0.9	71.4	40.6	49.6	50.4
06334	BOZRAH	96.2	95.6	0.6	0.7	0.6	0.8	1.8	2.1	5.4	5.9	7.0	6.3	4.8	27.0	30.1	11.7	1.8	77.4	41.7	50.2	49.8
06335	GALES FERRY	92.2	90.9	2.0	2.3	2.2	2.8	2.6	3.1	5.3	8.0	8.9	7.4	4.6	27.6	28.3	9.2	0.8	72.5	38.9	49.2	50.8
06336	GILMAN	97.4	97.6	0.0	0.0	0.0	0.0	0.0	0.0	4.8	4.8	4.8	4.8	4.8	28.6	31.0	14.3	2.4	85.7	43.8	47.6	52.4
06339	LEDYARD	84.9	83.1	2.9	3.2	2.3	2.9	2.9	3.4	6.8	7.4	7.5	7.3	5.6	28.4	27.6	8.9	0.6	73.8	37.8	49.4	50.6
06340	GROTON	81.3	78.9	8.2	8.9	3.8	4.8	5.8	6.8	8.8	7.3	6.2	7.0	10.2	31.4	17.6	9.7	2.0	74.5	30.9	51.7	48.4
06349	GROTON	100.0	100.0	0.0	0.0	0.0	0.0	0.0	0.0	0.0	0.0	0.0	0.0	100.0	0.0	0.0	0.0	0.0	100.0	22.5	100.0	0.0
06351	JEWETT CITY	94.9	94.3	1.1	1.2	0.8	1.0	1.6	1.9	5.9	6.3	7.5	6.7	5.7	29.4	27.4	9.8	1.3	75.9	38.9	49.6	50.4
06353	MONTVILLE	93.4	92.2	1.3	1.6	0.9	1.2	3.1	3.3	4.5	4.5	7.0	6.2	6.2	25.8	27.9	16.0	2.1	80.3	42.8	48.8	51.2
06354	MOOSUP	96.2	95.4	0.5	0.6	0.7	1.0	2.8	3.5	6.9	6.8	8.1	7.2	6.7	29.9	23.8	9.4	1.3	73.8	35.8	49.3	50.7
06355	MYSTIC	93.6	92.5	1.6	1.8	2.0	2.6	1.7	2.1	5.0	5.7	6.7	5.9	3.8	26.5	29.7	14.1	2.6	78.5	43.0	48.4	51.6
06357	NIANTIC	85.6	84.2	8.9	9.5	1.4	1.8	6.0	6.8	4.1	4.6	5.2	5.4	5.7	33.9	26.4	12.9	1.8	83.0	40.1	47.1	52.9
06359	NORTH STONINGTON	94.3	93.5	0.6	0.7	1.1	1.4	1.5	1.8	5.5	6.3	6.8	6.5	5.4	26.1	31.9	10.7	0.9	76.9	41.5	50.0	50.0
06360	NORWICH	82.8	80.7	7.1	7.7	2.3	2.8	6.1	7.1	6.4	6.1	6.6	6.8	7.1	27.9	24.1	12.8	2.4	76.9	37.8	47.6	52.4
06365	PRESTON	95.6	94.8	0.7	0.8	1.2	1.6	1.4	1.8	4.5	5.1	6.5	6.2	5.3	25.9	30.7	14.5	1.4	80.1	43.0	49.8	50.2
06370	OAKDALE	92.8	91.6	2.0	2.2	1.5	2.0	2.8	3.4	6.0	6.7	8.2	7.0	5.2	29.9	27.5	9.0	0.6	74.6	38.7	50.1	49.9
06371	OLD LYME	97.5	97.1	0.2	0.2	1.2	1.6	1.0	1.2	5.3	6.3	7.1	5.7	3.1	21.3	32.9	16.3	2.1	77.5	45.7	49.5	50.5
06374	PLAINFIELD	96.2	95.5	0.9	1.1	0.6	0.7	2.4	3.0	6.4	6.3	7.4	6.9	6.9	29.3	24.6	10.3	2.0	75.7	37.1	48.9	51.1
06375	QUAKER HILL	90.3	88.7	2.8	3.2	2.9	3.7	2.2	2.7	4.7	5.5	5.6	9.2	12.2	21.0	24.9	14.6	2.3	80.7	39.3	48.5	51.5
06377	STERLING	96.2	95.6	0.2	0.2	0.3	0.4	1.3	1.6	7.2	7.6	8.1	6.4	5.3	33.8	24.2	6.7	0.8	73.1	35.6	51.5	48.5
06378	STONINGTON	97.4	97.0	0.3	0.3	0.9	1.1	1.1	1.4	4.5	5.2	6.0	5.2	3.6	23.5	32.6	17.2	2.2	80.9	46.1	49.0	51.0
06379	PAWCATUCK	94.7	93.8	0.8	0.9	1.5	2.0	1.3	1.6	6.3	6.4	6.9	6.3	5.5	27.1	26.3	13.2	2.1	76.5	40.3	48.6	51.4
06380	TAFTVILLE	88.4	86.9	3.1	3.5	0.6	0.8	7.0	8.3	6.7	6.2	6.8	7.6	8.6	31.6	22.0	9.4	1.2	75.7	34.5	48.4	51.6
06382	UNCASVILLE	82.1	80.1	7.6	8.1	2.1	2.7	7.0	8.1	5.2	5.5	6.3	6.5	7.6	33.3	23.3	10.8	1.6	79.2	37.2	56.1	43.9
06384	VOLUNTOWN	96.6	96.1	0.6	0.6	0.3	0.4	1.2	1.4	6.4	7.0	8.0	5.9	4.5	33.3	25.9	8.3	0.9	74.9	37.9	50.9	49.1
06385	WATERFORD	92.9	91.7	2.1	2.3	2.4	3.1	2.5	3.0	4.8	5.6	6.7	6.1	4.3	23.8	28.8	17.0	3.0	78.8	44.3	48.0	52.0
06401	ANSONIA	85.5	83.3	8.4	9.5	1.1	1.5	7.4	9.0	6.9	6.6	6.8	6.2	6.4	29.4	23.0	12.3	2.4	75.9	37.5	47.8	52.2
06403	BEACON FALLS	97.0	96.3	0.7	0.9	1.1	1.4	2.1	2.7	6.5	6.5	6.8	6.6	5.6	31.0	27.2	8.7	1.2	76.1	38.2	50.5	49.5
06405	BRANFORD	94.1	92.7	1.3	1.6	2.8	3.6	2.6	3.3	5.2	5.5	5.9	5.7	4.9	26.6	29.3	14.3	2.8	79.9	42.9	46.9	53.1
06409	CENTERBROOK	97.1	96.3	0.5	0.7	0.4	0.7	2.3	2.8	7.7	8.2	6.5	4.7	3.8	26.5	28.5	12.3	1.8	74.2	41.1	47.5	52.5
06410	CHESHIRE	89.4	87.8	4.7	5.0	2.7	3.5	3.8	4.5	5.6	6.5	7.3	8.4	5.8	26.3	27.7	10.2	2.3	75.8	39.5	53.2	46.8
06412	CHESTER	96.8	96.3	0.9	0.9	0.9	1.2	1.7	2.0	6.2	6.5	6.1	5.7	4.2	25.2	30.0	11.8	4.4	77.2	42.8	47.8	52.2
06413	CLINTON	95.9	95.1	0.6	0.6	1.2	1.5	4.0	4.7	6.3	6.8	7.2	6.0	5.0	28.3	28.5	10.6	1.3	75.9	39.8	48.4	51.6
06415	COLCHESTER	95.6	94.9	1.3	1.5	0.6	0.8	1.9	2.4	8.3	8.6	8.4	6.4	4.6	30.8	23.9	7.6	1.5	70.4	36.6	48.6	51.4
06416	CROMWELL	93.1	92.1	3.1	3.4	1.2	1.6	3.2	3.7	5.2	5.6	6.0	6.0	5.0	28.0	28.1	12.8	3.4	79.3	41.8	48.3	51.7
06417	DEEP RIVER	94.6	93.8	2.4	2.6	0.9	1.1	3.0	3.4	5.1	6.1	7.2	6.9	4.5	27.8	29.1	11.7	1.7	76.8	40.6	49.5	50.5
06418	DERBY	90.1	88.3	3.6	4.1	1.8	2.3	7.7	9.2	6.1	6.0	6.3	5.5	5.3	31.3	23.4	13.5	2.7	78.1	39.0	48.6	51.4
06419	KILLINGWORTH	97.5	97.1	0.4	0.4	0.8	1.1	1.2	1.4	7.2	8.4	8.1	5.4	3.2	25.1	30.4	10.8	1.4	72.7	41.3	49.4	50.6
06420	SALEM	95.5	94.5	0.8	1.0	1.5	2.0	1.2	1.6	6.5	7.5	9.2	7.1	4.5	27.2	30.8	6.4	0.8	72.3	38.9	49.7	50.3
06422	DURHAM	96.7	96.1	1.2	1.2	0.8	1.1	1.6	1.8	6.5	7.8	8.4	7.3	4.1	25.7	30.0	8.8	1.3	71.9	39.9	50.1	49.9
06423	EAST HADDAM	97.1	96.7	1.1	1.1	0.4	0.5	1.0	1.2	7.1	7.7	7.1	5.9	3.7	29.4	29.4	8.5	1.1	73.7	39.7	49.9	50.1
06424	EAST HAMPTON	93.4	92.5	2.0	2.1	2.5	3.1	1.7	1.9	5.1	5.6	6.1	12.6	14.8	23.4	24.1	7.4	1.0	79.8	32.5	49.5	50.5
06426	ESSEX	98.5	98.3	0.3	0.3	0.5	0.6	1.0	1.1	4.1	4.6	5.1	4.1	2.5	18.8	31.3	21.8	7.7	83.0	51.9	45.9	54.1
06437	GUILFORD	96.0	95.1	0.9	1.1	1.6	2.1	2.1	2.7	5.8	6.8	7.3	6.3	4.2	22.6	33.4	11.9	1.9	76.1	43.4	48.1	51.9
06438	HADDAM	96.3	95.8	1.4	1.5	1.1	1.4	1.1	1.3	5.4	6.4	6.9	6.2	4.0	26.0	33.6	10.3	1.2	76.9	42.2	49.8	50.3
06441	HIGGANUM	97.2	96.8	0.9	1.0	0.6	0.8	1.0	1.2	5.5	6.9	7.9	5.9	3.5	26.8	32.9	9.8	0.8	75.8	41.9	50.9	49.1
06442	IVORYTON	97.0	96.5	0.8	0.8	0.8	1.0	1.7	2.0	8.3	8.8	7.4	5.1	4.1	28.4	27.0	9.4	1.4	71.9	39.2	48.5	51.5
06443	MADISON	96.6	95.8	0.4	0.5	1.7	2.3	1.3	1.7	6.4	7.8	8.8	6.5	3.7	21.4	30.7	12.9	1.9	72.7	42.6	48.4	51.6
06447	MARLBOROUGH	97.5	97.0	0.8	0.9	0.7	1.0	1.1	1.3	6.2	7.3	8.1	6.4	4.1	26.2	32.7	7.6	1.3	74.2	40.8	49.7	50.3
06450	MERIDEN	80.5	78.1	6.7	7.3	1.5	1.9	20.4	23.4	7.0	6.7	7.0	6.2	6.2	28.3	24.3	11.9	2.5	75.5	37.6	48.5	51.6
06451	MERIDEN	79.9	77.6	6.0	6.4	1.2	1.5	22.0	25.1	7.2	7.3	7.5	6.9	6.4	28.1	23.6	11.2	1.8	73.7	36.3	48.7	51.3
06455	MIDDLEFIELD	97.9	97.6	0.5	0.6	0.3	0.5	1.5	1.8	5.6	6.2	7.7	6.9	4.4	25.8	28.3	13.4	1.8	76.2	41.6	50.5	49.5
06457	MIDDLETOWN	80.1	78.0	12.2	13.1	2.7	3.4	5.3	6.0	6.4	6.1	5.9	5.8	6.9	32.1	23.6	11.0	2.3	77.8	37.4	48.4	51.6
06459	MIDDLETOWN	78.2	75.0	10.9	11.8	4.1	5.2	5.4	5.2	5.2	3.7	2.9	5.9	30.2	22.1	16.2	11.8	2.2	88.2	26.7	47.8	52.2
06460	MILFORD	93.6	92.3	1.9	2.2	2.4	3.0	3.4	4.1	5.8	6.1	6.2	5.8	5.0	28.5	27.5	13.0	2.1	78.2	40.7	48.4	51.6
06468	MONROE	95.9	94.9	1.2	1.4	1.5	2.0	2.5	3.1	7.3	8.1	8.6	6.8	4.2	25.8	27.9	10.3	1.2	71.6	39.7	49.2	50.9
06469	MOODUS	97.7	97.3	0.5	0.6	0.4	0.6	0.9	1.1	6.3	6.8	7.4	5.8	4.8	28.2	27.5	10.4	2.9	75.7	40.2	49.6	50.5
06470	NEWTOWN	95.4	94.3	1.7	2.0	1.3	1.7	2.4	3.0	7.3	8.4	8.3	6.5	3.8	26.7	28.9	8.9	1.2	71.7	39.8	51.2	48.8
06471	NORTH BRANFORD	95.8	95.0	1.3	1.6	0.9	1.1	2.2	2.8	6.5	6.8	7.5	6.4	4.8	26.4	25.4	12.9	3.2	75.2	40.3	48.0	52.0
06472	NORTHFORD	97.1	96.5	1.1	1.2	1.1	1.4	1.3	1.7	6.2	6.9	7.6	6.3	5.0	25.7	30.8	10.5	1.1	75.3	40.7	49.3	50.7
06473	NORTH HAVEN	93.0	91.5	2.2	2.6	3.4	4.3	1.9	2.3	5.4	5.9	6.7	6.1	4.7	24.3	28.1	16.3	2.7	78.2	43.2	48.4	51.6
06475	OLD SAYBROOK	95.8	94.9	1.0	1.1	1.8	2.4	1.9	2.2	5.5	6.2	6.6	4.9	3.4	21.8	29.6	18.5	3.6	78.6	46.0	47.3	52.7
06477	ORANGE	94.1	92.6	0.8	0.9	3.8	5.0	1.4	1.8	5.4	6.2	7.5	6.6	4.3	20.8	29.2	17.2	2.9	76.5	44.6	48.7	51.3
06478	OXFORD	97.6	97.0	0.5	0.6	0.8	1.0	1.9	2.3	6.4	7.2	7.8	6.4	4.7	27.7	30.6	8.1	1.2	74.6	40.2	50.2	49.8
06479	PLANTSVILLE	96.9	96.1	0.8	0.9	0.7	1.0	1.8	2.3	6.5	6.6	6.7	6.1	5.4	28.7	25.8	11.9	2.2	76.2	39.5	48.6	51.4
06480	PORTLAND	95.1	94.7	2.4	2.5	0.6	0.7	1.9	2.3	6.7	7.5	7.6	5.8	4.1	27.3	26.6	12.2	2.3	74.3	40.2	48.7	51.3
06481	ROCKFALL	97.5	97.0	1.2	1.3	0.5	0.7	0.9	1.1	5.0	5.8	7.5	7.2	4.0	23.0	30.7	14.8	2.0	77.1	43.5	49.6	50.5
06482	SANDY HOOK	94.8	93.7	1.8	2.1	1.6	2.1	2.3	2.9	8.4	9.1	8.5	6.2	4.1	30.1	25.3	6.8	1.5	69.6	37.2	51.4	48.6
06483	SEYMOUR	94.8	93.5	1.4	1.6	1.8	2.3	3.1	3.8	5.9	6.0	6.8	6.2	5.6	29.0	26.5	11.9	2.1	77.3	39.8	48.5	51.5
06484	SHELTON	94.4	93.2	1.1	1.3	2.1	2.7	3.5	4.3	6.1	6.4	6.7	6.1	4.9	26.8	27.7	13.0	2.6	77.0	41.2	48.4	51.6
06488	SOUTHBURY	97.3	96.7	0.5	0.5	1.2	1.6	1.6	2.0	5.0	6.1	7.0	5.7	3.1	19.5	27.8	19.7	6.1	77.9	47.2	46.5	53.5
06489	SOUTHINGTON	96.2	95.3	0.9	1.1	1.2	1.5	2.1	2.7	5.8	6.2	6.7	6.2	5.0	26.0	28.7	13.7	1.9	77.6	41.7	48.6	51.4
06492	WALLINGFORD	94.8	93.7	1.0	1.2	1.8	2.3	4.5	5.5	5.9	6.4	7.0	6.1	5.1	27.6	26.9	12.1	3.1	76.9	40.5	48.2	51.8
06498	WESTBROOK	95.8	95.0	0.7	0.8	1.7	2.1	2.5	3.0	5.2	5.7	6.3	5.4	4.4	26.1	29.5	15.2	2.2	79.2	43.2	48.9	51.1
06510	NEW HAVEN	56.0	51.1	21.7	23.1	13.0	15.5	11.6	13.1	3.2	1.7	1.7	11.3	29.0	36.6	11.2	4.7	0.6	92.8	25.9	52.0	48.0
06511	NEW HAVEN	38.0	35.2	46.0	46.8	6.4	7.7	11.4	12.4	6.0	5.5	6.1	10.2	15.5	32.0	16.9	6.7	1.2	78.4	28.3	49.3	50.8
06512	EAST HAVEN	91.9	90.5	2.3	2.5	1.7	2.2	6.4	7.6	5.7	5.6	5.9	5.9	5.2	28.9	25.2	14.8	2.8	79.2	40.7	47.9	52.1
06513	NEW HAVEN	56.5	54.3	21.8	22.3	2.2	2.6	30.7	32.8	8.3	7.7	8.3	7.7	7.7	28.9	19.4	10.1	2.0	71.1	32.1	46.8	53.2
06514	HAMDEN	70.5	67.1	21.2	23.1	3.9	4.8	5.2	6.0	5.7	5.9	6.3	6.1	7.9	28.4	22.9	13.5	3.4	78.4	38.5	46.3	53.7
06515	NEW HAVEN	49.9	47.1	41.8	43.5	2.0	2.4	8.6	9.6	7.1	6.8	6.8	11.1	10.1	26.1	21.0	9.2	1.8	75.2	31.4	45.6	54.4
06516	WEST HAVEN	74.2	71.7	16.3	17.3	3.0	3.6	9.1	10.5	6.2	6.0	6.5	6.9	7.6	28.8	24.0	12.0	2.1	77.5	37.4	47.7	52.3
06517	HAMDEN	76.2	74.0	17.3	18.3	2.8	3.5	4.6	5.4	5.6	6.1	6.7	6.6	4.8	24.3	25.7	15.8	4.4	77.2	42.4	46.0	54.0
06518	HAMDEN	88.9	86.6	5.1	5.9	3.7	4.9	2.6	3.2	4.3	4.4	4.9	12.8	10.6	25.2	22.3	12.7	2.7	83.5	35.6	45.1	54.9
06519	NEW HAVEN	25.9	24.9	41.0	40.2	0.5	0.6	45.4	48.2	9.0	8.6	9.7	9.6	9.3	26.7	16.9	7.7	2.6	67.0	27.6	47.9	52.1
06524	BETHANY	95.0	94.0	1.8	2.1	1.6	2.1	2.0	2.6	5.9	7.1	8.3	6.8	4.2	22.7	32.2	11.7	1.2	74.4	42.3	50.1	49.9
06525	WOODBRIDGE	91.3	89.4	1.5	1.7	5.1	6.6	1.5	1.9	5.3	6.8	8.6	7.4	3.8	18.4	32.3	14.6	2.9	74.4	44.8	48.7	51.3
06604	BRIDGEPORT	41.1	38.7	27.9	28.1	6.1	6.8	34.6	37.2	8.8	7.6	7.7	8.2	10.3	30.0	17.7	8.2	1.4	71.4	29.2	49.3	50.7
06605	BRIDGEPORT	44.8	42.7	29.2	29.3	4.8	5.4	33.8	36.1	9.7	8.3	7.8	7.9	8.8	30.5	18.2	7.6	1.3	69.7	29.7	49.3	50.7
06606	BRIDGEPORT	54.9	52.3	27.6	28.5	2.6	3.1	21.0	23.4	6.8	6.5	7.1	7.1	7.5	29.5	21.6	11.5	2.3	75.4	35.4	47.6	52.4
06607	BRIDGEPORT	14.2	14.1	69.2	68.6	0.5	0.5	24.8	26.1	9.2	9.0	9.2	9.1	8.4	27.0	20.1	7.5	0.7	67.3	28.9	45.3	54.7
	CONNECTICUT	81.6	80.0	9.1	9.5	2.5	3.1	9.4	10.5	6.4	6.7	7.1	6.9	6.3	27.5	25.4	11.7	2.2	75.8	38.5	48.5	51.5
	UNITED STATES	75.1	73.6	12.3	12.5	3.8	4.2	12.5	14.1	6.9	6.7	7.2	7.0	7.3	28.6	23.8	10.8	1.7	75.1	36.0	49.1	50.9

#	POST OFFICE NAME (ZIP CODE)	2004 Per Capita Income	2004 HH Income Base	2004 Household Income Distribution (%): Less than $25,000	$25,000 to $49,999	$50,000 to $99,999	$100,000 to $149,999	$150,000 or More	Median Household Income: 2004	2009	2004 National Centile	2004 State Centile	2004 Home Value Base	2004 Home Value Distribution (%): Less than $50,000	$50,000 to $89,999	$90,000 to $174,999	$175,000 to $399,999	$400,000 or More	2004 Median Home Value
06281	WOODSTOCK	28968	2705	16.6	24.4	38.0	12.5	8.5	59785	66311	84	34	2290	1.0	1.9	37.5	53.3	6.3	197166
06282	WOODSTOCK VALLEY	27252	467	12.9	18.4	47.3	13.9	7.5	65616	75568	89	48	428	0.0	0.5	38.1	52.3	9.1	201376
06320	NEW LONDON	21149	10110	33.6	33.4	25.0	5.5	2.4	36506	40114	34	8	3991	1.8	3.3	55.9	35.4	3.6	155434
06330	BALTIC	24161	1300	21.3	26.5	33.2	15.7	3.4	53026	60742	77	23	979	0.7	3.1	32.5	58.2	5.5	197720
06331	CANTERBURY	25960	1785	17.4	21.1	43.0	14.7	3.9	62145	68015	86	40	1574	1.3	1.4	42.0	53.2	2.1	180929
06333	EAST LYME	41394	2293	7.0	10.7	35.3	28.0	19.1	95178	110052	98	89	2099	0.0	0.0	8.7	62.2	29.1	298209
06334	BOZRAH	30417	997	9.1	24.5	42.2	17.8	6.4	63204	71974	87	43	867	0.0	2.0	23.4	65.7	8.9	218192
06335	GALES FERRY	30359	2535	10.1	17.3	46.4	18.4	7.8	70679	81253	92	59	2193	3.1	2.4	16.6	73.5	4.3	221333
06336	GILMAN	28551	18	16.7	27.8	33.3	16.7	5.6	54495	63158	79	27	15	0.0	0.0	20.0	66.7	13.3	225000
06339	LEDYARD	29387	2934	10.5	20.3	44.5	15.2	9.5	67325	78023	90	53	2460	0.5	1.0	29.6	59.1	9.8	217439
06340	GROTON	25312	12743	19.2	34.7	32.7	10.0	3.3	46695	52291	65	14	5915	7.8	4.4	32.8	43.8	11.2	184807
06349	GROTON	12598	0	0.0	0.0	0.0	0.0	0.0	0	0	0	0	0	0.0	0.0	0.0	0.0	0.0	0
06351	JEWETT CITY	24922	6057	16.1	26.0	42.8	12.5	2.6	56956	63789	82	30	4719	3.5	3.7	36.6	53.5	2.7	184711
06353	MONTVILLE	27135	113	23.9	26.6	34.5	13.3	1.8	49687	57104	71	19	78	7.7	1.3	30.8	59.0	1.3	191667
06354	MOOSUP	20454	2237	24.0	29.3	37.3	7.4	1.9	47178	51725	67	15	1518	0.9	3.3	65.0	29.2	1.7	150339
06355	MYSTIC	38769	4951	10.7	19.5	38.1	19.8	11.9	71979	82977	92	62	3972	3.9	0.4	14.7	57.0	24.0	247651
06357	NIANTIC	31212	4391	16.1	18.0	41.5	17.5	7.0	66105	76999	89	49	3545	0.2	1.0	19.0	68.9	10.8	227865
06359	NORTH STONINGTON	29958	1896	11.3	22.6	42.0	15.9	8.2	64768	73608	88	47	1695	2.2	0.5	16.9	64.4	16.0	240891
06360	NORWICH	23483	14795	28.9	28.1	31.1	9.0	2.9	42831	48030	56	12	8414	5.0	5.4	49.0	38.4	2.4	160617
06365	PRESTON	28771	1912	14.2	21.3	42.9	17.1	4.5	61278	68950	86	38	1641	0.3	1.2	24.7	64.8	9.0	219410
06370	OAKDALE	27041	2414	11.4	23.0	42.8	17.5	5.4	65743	75165	89	48	2099	4.3	1.1	32.4	57.6	4.5	191004
06371	OLD LYME	48384	3977	11.2	19.0	33.9	16.7	19.3	77359	89459	94	72	3492	0.0	0.2	4.1	49.0	46.7	384820
06374	PLAINFIELD	22073	3321	21.3	31.1	34.9	9.5	3.3	47867	52891	68	17	2453	4.6	4.1	63.4	26.6	1.4	145701
06375	QUAKER HILL	28290	1475	12.7	20.3	44.3	15.3	7.4	66172	76338	89	50	1315	0.5	0.6	18.9	69.1	10.8	227472
06377	STERLING	22065	1055	16.5	27.3	43.5	10.2	2.5	54159	60547	79	27	904	3.5	3.8	53.9	37.6	1.2	162623
06378	STONINGTON	42566	2714	14.3	20.5	34.1	19.1	12.2	67711	79212	90	55	2199	6.2	0.6	7.3	49.4	36.5	315483
06379	PAWCATUCK	26842	3707	22.7	26.4	35.7	10.8	4.4	50679	56621	73	20	2630	0.5	1.9	22.6	65.1	9.9	217994
06380	TAFTVILLE	23044	988	28.2	35.0	23.9	8.2	4.7	41894	46925	53	12	519	2.1	5.6	51.8	37.4	3.1	163542
06382	UNCASVILLE	25468	4091	17.4	24.3	41.2	12.2	4.9	58695	65083	83	32	3162	3.9	2.9	33.3	57.1	2.9	187908
06384	VOLUNTOWN	27944	972	13.0	23.5	41.9	17.8	3.9	63806	72149	88	44	839	0.7	1.0	36.4	57.3	4.7	191210
06385	WATERFORD	33253	6284	15.4	24.5	35.7	15.0	9.3	60474	67883	85	35	5375	1.0	1.2	24.4	59.9	13.5	226136
06401	ANSONIA	23868	7475	24.8	26.6	34.6	11.3	2.7	48471	55807	69	18	4649	0.6	1.5	23.5	73.9	0.5	207737
06403	BEACON FALLS	29193	2184	11.6	26.3	39.4	14.7	8.0	63039	72436	87	42	1774	6.3	0.6	24.3	64.8	4.0	215735
06405	BRANFORD	38048	12771	15.1	22.5	35.9	16.2	10.2	64480	76664	88	45	9054	1.9	1.8	20.0	55.9	20.4	249506
06409	CENTERBROOK	42738	279	10.4	25.5	37.6	11.5	15.1	68083	77555	90	56	232	1.3	1.3	10.3	67.7	19.4	275806
06410	CHESHIRE	40579	9457	10.1	14.5	31.6	23.7	20.1	88600	105860	97	85	8378	0.3	0.7	9.7	63.0	26.3	310271
06412	CHESTER	39478	1582	12.5	22.1	31.5	19.2	14.8	73506	84744	93	64	1252	0.0	0.2	15.3	65.2	19.3	263090
06413	CLINTON	31126	5272	14.0	19.7	39.7	19.8	6.9	68178	78945	90	56	4269	2.5	3.2	17.3	70.5	6.5	228210
06415	COLCHESTER	32235	5879	11.9	18.6	39.8	21.5	8.2	73095	83300	92	64	4798	1.8	2.5	15.0	72.5	8.2	241008
06416	CROMWELL	34872	5512	11.3	21.5	41.2	16.7	9.4	67297	78126	90	52	4316	1.0	5.7	35.3	51.3	6.8	190547
06417	DEEP RIVER	37518	1889	17.5	23.6	36.1	13.0	9.8	59560	68068	84	33	1487	0.5	1.1	13.9	71.1	13.5	229475
06418	DERBY	26503	5214	22.5	26.2	35.0	12.5	3.8	51260	59407	74	21	3328	0.5	0.2	36.8	60.6	1.9	194962
06419	KILLINGWORTH	36234	2410	8.6	16.4	32.1	29.8	13.2	87737	102536	97	85	2310	3.5	6.2	5.7	54.3	30.3	323012
06420	SALEM	32907	1411	9.3	17.6	39.6	23.5	10.0	75412	87075	93	67	1268	2.8	1.7	6.9	74.2	14.4	268571
06422	DURHAM	34463	2469	7.4	13.8	39.3	27.0	12.5	85224	100602	96	82	2260	0.3	1.6	7.6	74.0	16.6	276524
06423	EAST HADDAM	34378	2038	7.9	19.7	43.4	19.1	9.9	73445	84262	93	64	1810	0.6	0.2	12.9	68.6	17.8	262313
06424	EAST HAMPTON	28408	4591	10.2	19.3	40.7	23.1	6.7	75206	85915	93	67	3721	1.0	2.7	24.9	65.0	6.4	212199
06426	ESSEX	59525	1576	14.3	18.9	27.3	17.3	22.3	79110	90952	95	75	1210	0.0	1.1	4.6	44.0	50.4	403378
06437	GUILFORD	44662	8382	8.5	13.9	34.9	22.5	20.3	87654	105216	97	84	7381	0.0	0.6	6.1	57.1	36.2	347524
06438	HADDAM	35564	942	7.9	14.9	38.4	30.3	8.6	85161	100822	96	81	805	0.0	0.3	7.7	79.0	13.0	263654
06441	HIGGANUM	35211	1779	10.9	12.4	39.0	25.5	12.3	82752	97240	96	79	1607	0.8	0.6	11.8	75.4	11.5	246286
06442	IVORYTON	41817	1158	8.2	17.4	43.2	17.1	14.2	76401	88050	94	70	986	0.5	0.6	7.9	72.0	19.0	284713
06443	MADISON	48809	6620	8.4	11.2	29.2	24.1	27.1	101999	120173	98	91	5918	0.1	0.5	1.5	51.6	46.3	385459
06447	MARLBOROUGH	42695	2201	8.0	13.2	37.1	21.4	20.5	87647	105044	97	84	2004	1.3	0.0	9.7	78.5	10.5	248547
06450	MERIDEN	24057	13822	24.3	26.7	34.4	11.5	3.2	48985	55666	70	19	8670	2.7	4.5	45.6	45.9	1.4	171213
06451	MERIDEN	23121	9286	26.1	27.0	31.8	11.4	3.7	46539	53225	65	14	5649	0.8	2.6	50.9	44.3	1.4	169246
06455	MIDDLEFIELD	30040	1192	14.5	18.6	43.7	14.9	8.3	65984	76923	89	48	989	0.8	0.3	21.3	67.0	10.5	228654
06457	MIDDLETOWN	30471	19420	20.8	25.6	33.0	13.9	6.6	53431	61344	78	24	10609	1.5	4.0	37.9	53.7	2.9	187324
06459	MIDDLETOWN	29913	85	40.0	27.1	21.2	7.1	4.7	32837	34589	20	5	22	0.0	0.0	45.5	50.0	4.6	180000
06460	MILFORD	34293	21278	13.3	19.5	39.6	18.7	8.9	68835	80794	91	57	16850	0.8	1.2	14.1	72.5	11.4	243326
06468	MONROE	43227	6432	7.3	11.8	30.6	26.8	23.6	100425	122992	98	90	6037	0.2	0.0	4.3	53.7	41.8	372440
06469	MOODUS	32734	1090	14.4	19.9	40.8	18.8	6.1	67363	78582	90	53	834	0.0	0.5	17.0	76.1	6.4	222673
06470	NEWTOWN	51195	5302	6.5	9.2	29.0	25.1	30.2	107493	133942	99	92	4908	0.9	0.8	1.3	48.2	48.8	395773
06471	NORTH BRANFORD	33417	3083	11.2	22.1	40.2	17.3	9.3	67012	79391	90	52	2495	1.2	1.0	15.2	72.4	10.3	253342
06472	NORTHFORD	33008	2284	8.5	18.6	40.5	24.3	8.1	75754	89116	94	68	2045	0.0	0.7	9.7	78.1	11.5	265349
06473	NORTH HAVEN	35589	8840	10.5	19.7	38.7	18.6	12.5	74177	86781	93	66	7814	0.3	0.7	5.8	78.5	14.8	264901
06475	OLD SAYBROOK	36367	4327	13.1	17.4	39.9	18.2	11.4	71010	81694	92	59	3743	0.2	0.7	10.5	69.7	19.0	276615
06477	ORANGE	43695	4887	9.3	14.9	31.4	22.6	21.7	89038	106097	97	86	4518	0.8	0.1	3.0	54.3	41.9	379890
06478	OXFORD	33864	3629	8.1	13.1	40.2	26.1	12.5	84287	101612	96	80	3321	0.0	0.8	5.7	68.6	24.9	313281
06479	PLANTSVILLE	30112	3666	8.7	19.9	43.2	21.3	6.9	70146	81586	91	58	2886	0.0	0.4	21.4	73.0	5.2	217986
06480	PORTLAND	33542	3735	14.4	19.0	37.1	20.9	8.7	72503	82796	92	63	3018	0.3	0.7	25.6	67.1	6.4	215900
06481	ROCKFALL	31360	502	13.0	21.1	40.6	16.7	8.6	65390	76967	89	47	434	0.0	1.2	13.8	74.2	10.8	228662
06482	SANDY HOOK	41155	3608	7.7	8.5	32.8	26.6	24.5	101251	123799	98	90	3330	0.8	0.7	3.1	54.2	41.2	365114
06483	SEYMOUR	27721	6142	16.1	25.0	38.1	16.3	4.5	59403	69319	84	33	4627	0.0	2.3	15.3	75.0	7.4	228135
06484	SHELTON	36611	14674	11.4	16.4	36.9	21.5	13.8	77700	97884	94	73	11992	1.0	1.3	7.2	67.5	23.1	305136
06488	SOUTHBURY	38045	7687	11.9	22.4	32.0	18.2	15.4	71219	82681	92	61	6843	0.4	0.8	18.8	50.4	29.7	295233
06489	SOUTHINGTON	31686	11766	14.2	20.0	37.4	19.4	9.0	67909	80747	90	55	9805	2.9	2.5	19.8	66.1	8.8	225352
06492	WALLINGFORD	31012	17267	15.3	22.1	37.6	17.3	7.7	64488	75758	88	45	12979	2.0	1.8	16.6	71.1	8.6	231857
06498	WESTBROOK	33244	2868	19.8	19.9	33.8	17.7	8.8	62624	72267	87	42	2214	6.9	3.9	9.1	64.4	15.7	264865
06510	NEW HAVEN	28093	1481	51.1	23.2	14.3	4.3	7.1	23741	27825	4	2	95	0.0	0.0	0.0	35.8	64.2	454000
06511	NEW HAVEN	20105	20855	40.3	28.6	22.2	5.4	3.5	32274	36969	19	5	5489	1.9	9.6	41.7	35.2	11.6	166531
06512	EAST HAVEN	25775	11923	22.7	26.4	35.2	12.4	3.3	50739	58368	73	21	8379	1.3	3.1	40.5	53.6	1.6	181874
06513	NEW HAVEN	17628	13657	39.1	24.8	26.2	8.1	1.8	34925	39807	27	8	5860	2.3	10.7	51.3	34.7	1.0	146179
06514	HAMDEN	27015	10137	18.9	27.9	35.8	11.9	5.6	53273	61781	77	23	6739	0.5	1.9	44.2	50.6	2.7	180093
06515	NEW HAVEN	25617	6484	30.4	25.1	27.6	9.9	6.9	43148	50883	56	13	3114	0.9	4.2	39.1	50.2	5.7	186466
06516	WEST HAVEN	24348	21124	23.7	28.7	33.2	10.8	3.5	47392	54423	67	16	12519	2.0	4.0	45.1	47.2	1.8	173465
06517	HAMDEN	38402	6540	22.5	18.4	33.0	14.3	11.7	60568	70947	85	36	4509	1.1	2.9	29.0	57.8	9.3	205407
06518	HAMDEN	32294	6580	18.0	19.6	34.4	18.4	9.6	67481	79736	90	54	4799	0.5	0.1	20.4	70.4	8.6	226871
06519	NEW HAVEN	12499	5391	51.1	25.1	18.9	3.7	1.3	24132	26796	4	2	1509	6.8	17.9	55.9	18.8	0.5	116863
06524	BETHANY	37289	1838	6.5	16.9	36.4	21.7	18.4	85705	103460	96	83	1700	2.2	1.0	4.1	64.0	28.7	338225
06525	WOODBRIDGE	57120	3235	6.0	12.0	23.6	22.0	36.5	116529	139360	99	94	2961	0.3	0.5	1.6	32.0	65.7	479366
06604	BRIDGEPORT	17266	9989	39.2	27.5	22.9	6.5	3.8	33013	38506	21	6	3219	12.7	12.5	32.3	40.8	1.8	158506
06605	BRIDGEPORT	18996	8942	35.2	28.5	23.5	8.7	4.0	36459	42358	33	8	2897	4.8	10.3	40.0	39.8	5.1	161830
06606	BRIDGEPORT	23010	17066	23.9	27.1	34.3	11.2	3.5	48897	58554	70	18	10227	4.0	7.3	39.1	48.8	0.8	174311
06607	BRIDGEPORT	15438	2674	38.6	31.2	23.7	5.0	1.5	32590	37789	20	5	1010	22.1	22.0	43.9	10.6	1.5	104533
	CONNECTICUT	34999		18.8	22.0	32.8	15.1	11.4	61358	72202				1.5	2.7	24.6	51.4	19.8	230968
	UNITED STATES	25866		24.7	27.1	30.8	10.9	6.5	48124	56710				10.9	15.0	33.7	30.1	10.4	145905

ZIP CODE #	POST OFFICE NAME	FINANCIAL SERVICES: Auto Loan	FINANCIAL SERVICES: Home Loan	FINANCIAL SERVICES: Invest-ments	FINANCIAL SERVICES: Retire-ment Plans	THE HOME: Home Improvements: Home Repair	THE HOME: Home Improvements: Lawn & Garden	THE HOME: Furnishings: Comput-ers & Hard-ware	THE HOME: Furnishings: Major Appli-ances	THE HOME: Furnishings: TV, Radio, Sound Equip-ment	THE HOME: Furnishings: Furni-ture	ENTERTAINMENT: Dine out/ Carry out	ENTERTAINMENT: Sports Equip-ment	ENTERTAINMENT: Fees & Tickets	ENTERTAINMENT: Toys & Games	ENTERTAINMENT: Travel	ENTERTAINMENT: Cable TV	PERSONAL: Apparel & Services	PERSONAL: Auto Repairs	PERSONAL: Health Insur-ance	PERSONAL: Pets & Supplies
06281	WOODSTOCK	105	109	105	107	112	118	103	108	103	102	127	124	105	131	106	104	123	105	109	125
06282	WOODSTOCK VALLEY	98	119	125	119	118	117	107	107	100	106	125	125	113	133	109	97	124	103	97	119
06320	NEW LONDON	65	63	75	63	62	68	70	66	71	68	89	79	69	88	68	70	86	69	66	73
06330	BALTIC	81	93	104	93	92	94	91	89	87	89	109	104	94	115	91	85	108	88	82	96
06331	CANTERBURY	92	109	115	108	106	106	100	99	94	100	119	116	105	124	101	91	118	97	90	109
06333	EAST LYME	153	190	204	193	185	185	169	166	155	169	196	194	182	207	172	151	197	161	149	184
06334	BOZRAH	103	119	133	119	118	121	114	113	109	113	137	131	119	141	116	107	135	111	106	123
06335	GALES FERRY	104	129	139	128	126	126	116	116	109	116	137	135	124	146	119	106	137	112	105	127
06336	GILMAN	84	102	112	99	100	102	94	93	90	93	113	108	100	120	97	89	113	91	87	102
06339	LEDYARD	108	128	134	128	125	124	117	117	110	117	138	137	122	144	118	106	137	114	104	128
06340	GROTON	85	78	90	81	76	84	88	84	89	86	111	100	86	108	84	86	108	88	81	93
06349	GROTON	0	0	0	0	0	0	0	0	0	0	0	0	0	0	0	0	0	0	0	0
06351	JEWETT CITY	83	96	103	96	94	96	91	90	87	90	109	105	95	114	92	85	108	89	83	99
06353	MONTVILLE	75	82	86	77	83	92	81	80	84	78	104	89	85	112	84	87	100	78	86	88
06354	MOOSUP	70	74	79	72	74	79	74	73	75	73	93	85	76	97	75	75	91	73	73	81
06355	MYSTIC	120	142	159	141	140	144	132	132	126	132	159	152	139	164	136	124	157	129	123	144
06357	NIANTIC	100	117	137	118	116	120	113	111	108	112	136	129	118	141	115	106	134	110	103	120
06359	NORTH STONINGTON	102	125	136	124	123	124	114	113	108	114	136	132	122	144	117	106	135	110	104	124
06360	NORWICH	72	73	83	73	72	78	78	75	78	76	97	88	78	97	77	77	94	77	74	83
06365	PRESTON	91	109	121	106	107	112	102	101	99	101	124	116	108	131	105	99	123	99	97	110
06370	OAKDALE	96	116	125	115	114	114	106	105	100	106	125	123	112	133	108	97	125	102	96	115
06371	OLD LYME	158	182	193	180	183	190	166	170	160	166	199	195	174	205	173	159	196	165	164	192
06374	PLAINFIELD	82	83	82	83	84	89	83	84	82	81	102	97	83	103	83	81	99	83	83	94
06375	QUAKER HILL	97	115	127	110	114	122	107	108	105	107	132	121	114	136	112	107	130	105	107	117
06377	STERLING	84	92	92	94	89	88	88	87	82	88	104	103	88	104	86	77	102	86	76	95
06378	STONINGTON	126	144	161	142	143	152	135	136	131	136	164	153	141	164	140	131	161	134	134	150
06379	PAWCATUCK	86	89	94	89	90	96	89	89	89	87	110	103	91	113	90	89	107	88	89	100
06380	TAFTVILLE	71	75	85	77	74	77	80	76	77	77	97	92	80	99	78	74	95	78	71	82
06382	UNCASVILLE	89	103	111	101	102	106	98	97	95	96	119	111	103	127	100	95	118	95	93	106
06384	VOLUNTOWN	102	112	112	114	108	107	107	106	100	108	126	125	107	127	104	94	124	105	93	116
06385	WATERFORD	102	118	131	114	117	126	111	111	109	110	137	126	117	141	115	111	134	109	111	122
06401	ANSONIA	76	80	91	80	79	85	83	80	83	81	103	94	85	106	83	82	101	82	79	88
06403	BEACON FALLS	104	112	114	112	111	114	106	107	102	106	128	127	108	131	106	100	125	106	101	122
06405	BRANFORD	110	127	153	128	125	132	123	121	118	122	148	140	128	151	125	116	146	120	114	132
06409	CENTERBROOK	142	133	108	127	139	147	122	133	127	122	155	158	122	160	126	129	149	130	140	168
06410	CHESHIRE	146	182	207	182	178	183	164	162	153	165	193	186	177	203	169	151	193	157	148	177
06412	CHESTER	123	142	162	146	141	143	136	134	129	135	162	158	141	166	137	125	160	133	123	147
06413	CLINTON	104	118	125	116	117	121	110	111	107	109	133	130	114	139	113	106	131	109	106	125
06415	COLCHESTER	124	136	133	138	133	133	126	127	120	128	150	149	129	152	126	115	147	125	116	142
06416	CROMWELL	108	125	143	127	124	126	120	118	114	119	143	138	124	147	121	111	141	117	109	129
06417	DEEP RIVER	120	139	152	138	137	141	133	131	127	131	160	153	139	167	135	125	158	129	123	143
06418	DERBY	80	85	97	86	84	89	88	85	87	86	108	101	90	111	88	85	107	87	81	93
06419	KILLINGWORTH	131	156	168	156	154	159	140	141	132	142	166	159	149	169	144	130	164	137	134	156
06420	SALEM	119	148	158	149	146	144	132	132	123	132	154	155	141	164	135	119	154	127	118	146
06422	DURHAM	127	157	169	157	154	154	140	140	130	140	164	162	150	172	144	127	164	135	127	154
06423	EAST HADDAM	118	144	153	144	142	141	129	129	121	129	152	152	137	161	132	118	151	125	117	144
06424	EAST HAMPTON	108	127	137	129	124	123	118	116	110	118	139	137	122	144	118	106	138	114	104	128
06426	ESSEX	158	184	222	187	183	192	176	174	167	176	210	201	184	213	179	164	207	172	163	190
06437	GUILFORD	151	183	204	185	180	183	167	165	156	167	197	192	178	205	171	152	196	161	151	182
06438	HADDAM	118	147	156	146	144	142	131	131	122	131	154	153	140	164	134	119	153	126	118	144
06441	HIGGANUM	119	148	159	147	145	144	133	132	124	132	156	154	142	167	136	121	156	128	120	146
06442	IVORYTON	162	167	150	166	167	170	152	158	149	154	185	187	154	189	153	146	180	154	153	188
06443	MADISON	176	211	233	214	208	215	190	189	177	192	224	216	205	229	195	175	224	183	176	210
06447	MARLBOROUGH	154	191	204	193	187	186	170	169	157	170	198	198	182	210	174	153	198	163	151	187
06450	MERIDEN	78	83	95	82	81	87	84	82	84	83	105	95	86	108	84	84	104	83	80	90
06451	MERIDEN	75	81	95	80	80	86	83	81	83	82	104	94	85	107	84	83	102	82	80	88
06455	MIDDLEFIELD	98	117	131	116	115	118	109	108	104	108	131	125	115	137	112	103	130	106	101	118
06457	MIDDLETOWN	91	95	110	97	93	99	99	95	96	97	121	112	100	121	97	94	119	97	90	104
06459	MIDDLETOWN	65	52	67	58	51	57	72	63	71	67	89	80	65	83	64	65	86	71	58	70
06460	MILFORD	109	128	146	127	125	130	121	119	116	121	146	138	127	152	124	115	145	118	112	130
06468	MONROE	166	206	224	209	201	203	183	181	169	184	213	209	198	223	187	164	214	174	163	199
06469	MOODUS	105	122	146	125	120	122	118	115	112	117	141	137	122	145	119	108	139	115	104	126
06470	NEWTOWN	195	246	272	250	239	241	217	213	199	219	252	246	238	265	222	194	254	205	190	234
06471	NORTH BRANFORD	112	130	144	130	129	133	123	122	118	122	148	141	129	153	125	116	146	120	115	134
06472	NORTHFORD	122	150	163	151	147	146	136	135	127	135	159	158	144	169	139	123	159	131	121	149
06473	NORTH HAVEN	120	144	163	140	142	149	134	133	129	133	162	152	142	169	139	129	160	130	128	145
06475	OLD SAYBROOK	120	131	135	125	132	143	121	126	121	121	150	141	126	152	127	124	146	123	130	143
06477	ORANGE	148	193	234	187	188	197	173	172	163	173	204	195	187	216	181	162	205	167	159	185
06478	OXFORD	128	159	169	159	156	154	142	141	131	141	165	165	151	176	145	128	165	136	127	156
06479	PLANTSVILLE	102	124	135	122	122	123	114	113	108	113	136	132	121	145	117	106	136	110	104	124
06480	PORTLAND	111	130	140	129	127	130	121	120	115	121	145	138	127	150	123	113	143	117	112	131
06481	ROCKFALL	97	114	126	109	113	121	107	107	105	106	131	120	113	137	111	106	129	104	106	116
06482	SANDY HOOK	162	199	213	203	193	194	177	174	162	179	206	202	191	214	180	157	206	168	156	192
06483	SEYMOUR	88	104	116	102	102	106	98	97	95	97	119	112	103	126	100	94	117	95	91	106
06484	SHELTON	127	148	165	148	147	153	138	138	132	139	166	158	145	168	142	130	163	136	131	152
06488	SOUTHBURY	131	146	157	145	145	155	134	138	130	138	163	151	141	158	138	130	159	134	137	152
06489	SOUTHINGTON	105	124	134	122	122	126	115	114	110	114	138	132	121	144	118	108	136	112	108	126
06492	WALLINGFORD	103	117	130	117	115	119	112	111	108	111	135	129	117	140	113	106	134	110	104	122
06498	WESTBROOK	122	112	93	106	119	129	105	117	111	104	134	136	101	135	109	115	127	115	127	147
06510	NEW HAVEN	68	56	82	64	55	61	75	66	75	72	94	84	71	90	69	70	92	74	61	73
06511	NEW HAVEN	62	55	77	57	53	61	66	60	69	65	86	72	65	85	63	68	84	65	60	68
06512	EAST HAVEN	79	88	101	86	87	94	87	85	87	86	108	98	91	113	89	87	106	85	85	94
06513	NEW HAVEN	61	59	76	59	58	64	65	63	67	65	85	73	64	85	64	68	83	65	63	69
06514	HAMDEN	85	94	110	94	92	98	95	92	93	93	117	107	97	119	95	92	115	93	89	100
06515	NEW HAVEN	83	82	107	84	80	88	91	85	91	90	115	101	91	114	89	89	113	89	82	94
06516	WEST HAVEN	77	82	94	82	81	87	84	82	84	83	105	95	86	107	84	83	103	83	80	89
06517	HAMDEN	111	124	152	124	122	130	124	121	121	123	152	140	128	155	125	120	150	122	116	132
06518	HAMDEN	105	119	153	121	117	124	117	114	115	118	145	132	123	150	120	115	143	114	109	125
06519	NEW HAVEN	46	42	63	40	41	47	49	47	53	50	67	53	48	67	48	56	66	50	49	52
06524	BETHANY	138	170	183	170	168	167	153	152	142	152	179	177	162	189	157	139	178	147	138	168
06525	WOODBRIDGE	204	261	335	259	255	270	234	231	219	237	276	264	258	289	244	218	278	225	214	251
06604	BRIDGEPORT	60	58	90	56	56	64	66	62	71	67	90	71	66	92	66	73	89	66	63	69
06605	BRIDGEPORT	67	64	93	64	61	69	72	68	76	74	97	79	71	97	71	77	96	73	68	75
06606	BRIDGEPORT	76	81	107	79	79	87	84	81	86	84	109	92	87	113	85	88	108	83	81	89
06607	BRIDGEPORT	58	54	67	51	52	60	59	57	64	60	80	64	60	79	58	66	78	59	60	65
	CONNECTICUT	116	129	153	129	127	135	127	124	124	126	156	144	132	161	128	124	154	124	119	137
	UNITED STATES	100	100	100	100	100	100	100	100	100	100	100	100	100	100	100	100	100	100	100	100

POPULATION CHANGE

#	POST OFFICE NAME	COUNTY FIPS CODE	POPULATION 2000	2004	2009	2000-2004 ANNUAL RATE % Rate	State Centile	HOUSEHOLDS 2000	2004	2009	% Annual Rate 2000-2004	2004 Average HH Size	FAMILIES 2000	2004	% Annual Rate 2000-2004
06608	BRIDGEPORT	001	13407	13218	13623	-0.3	5	4127	4097	4232	-0.2	3.19	3141	3088	-0.4
06610	BRIDGEPORT	001	22026	22896	23706	0.9	71	8482	8817	9138	0.9	2.52	5294	5457	0.7
06611	TRUMBULL	001	34354	35176	36117	0.6	51	11954	12323	12711	0.7	2.80	9736	9994	0.6
06612	EASTON	001	7170	7376	7558	0.7	59	2429	2513	2585	0.8	2.94	2047	2109	0.7
06614	STRATFORD	001	31976	32028	32614	0.0	19	12794	12882	13172	0.2	2.46	9027	9019	0.0
06615	STRATFORD	001	17979	18107	18509	0.2	25	7097	7158	7333	0.2	2.53	4604	4604	0.0
06702	WATERBURY	009	4074	4002	4022	-0.4	3	1885	1842	1850	-0.5	1.94	662	632	-1.1
06704	WATERBURY	009	24560	24460	24708	-0.1	14	9423	9428	9571	0.0	2.57	6268	6202	-0.3
06705	WATERBURY	009	26179	26613	27244	0.4	41	10964	11133	11414	0.4	2.35	6713	6763	0.2
06706	WATERBURY	009	13801	13785	13928	0.0	17	5172	5188	5265	0.1	2.65	3624	3608	-0.1
06708	WATERBURY	009	28442	28270	28482	-0.1	11	11532	11505	11650	-0.1	2.39	7295	7211	-0.3
06710	WATERBURY	009	10000	9646	9663	-0.8	2	3579	3459	3476	-0.8	2.72	2297	2184	-1.2
06712	PROSPECT	009	8710	9220	9547	1.4	86	3020	3224	3362	1.6	2.81	2456	2608	1.4
06716	WOLCOTT	009	15199	15460	15675	0.4	42	5406	5540	5653	0.6	2.77	4242	4323	0.5
06750	BANTAM	005	1388	1401	1432	0.2	28	582	599	622	0.7	2.34	372	378	0.4
06751	BETHLEHEM	005	3422	3558	3693	0.9	71	1246	1315	1383	1.3	2.65	936	980	1.1
06752	BRIDGEWATER	005	1824	1861	1911	0.5	47	703	723	751	0.7	2.53	526	536	0.4
06754	CORNWALL BRIDGE	005	1277	1339	1397	1.1	77	529	561	592	1.4	2.39	353	371	1.2
06755	GAYLORDSVILLE	005	1613	1709	1804	1.4	86	562	602	643	1.6	2.83	433	459	1.4
06756	GOSHEN	005	2592	2809	2981	1.9	97	1024	1130	1217	2.3	2.48	782	856	2.2
06757	KENT	005	2313	2389	2469	0.8	64	933	974	1019	1.0	2.39	606	624	0.7
06758	LAKESIDE	005	311	335	354	1.8	94	113	123	132	2.0	2.72	78	84	1.8
06759	LITCHFIELD	005	5826	5868	5989	0.2	25	2335	2390	2473	0.6	2.37	1611	1632	0.3
06762	MIDDLEBURY	009	6698	6661	6707	-0.1	12	2472	2477	2510	0.1	2.66	1892	1892	-0.1
06763	MORRIS	005	1961	2067	2162	1.3	83	786	840	890	1.6	2.46	553	585	1.3
06770	NAUGATUCK	009	30981	31545	32247	0.4	42	11830	12114	12455	0.6	2.59	8299	8419	0.3
06776	NEW MILFORD	005	25069	26287	27683	1.1	77	9288	9910	10590	1.5	2.63	6714	7088	1.3
06777	NEW PRSTN MRBL DALE	005	1852	1879	1937	0.3	38	727	752	787	0.8	2.48	509	521	0.6
06778	NORTHFIELD	005	1362	1372	1408	0.2	25	487	500	520	0.6	2.72	394	402	0.5
06779	OAKVILLE	005	8373	8262	8408	-0.3	7	3199	3208	3312	0.1	2.57	2319	2304	-0.2
06782	PLYMOUTH	005	2082	2161	2240	0.9	68	735	776	817	1.3	2.74	552	578	1.1
06783	ROXBURY	005	2118	2260	2379	1.5	90	839	908	968	1.9	2.49	615	659	1.6
06784	SHERMAN	001	4161	4410	4595	1.4	87	1561	1655	1728	1.4	2.66	1189	1252	1.2
06785	SOUTH KENT	005	468	486	504	0.9	68	182	191	201	1.1	2.43	121	126	1.0
06786	TERRYVILLE	005	9458	9685	9970	0.6	51	3688	3837	4007	0.9	2.51	2653	2736	0.7
06787	THOMASTON	005	7449	7926	8345	1.5	89	2898	3123	3328	1.8	2.53	2048	2192	1.6
06790	TORRINGTON	005	35339	36429	38061	0.7	62	14787	15359	16209	0.9	2.32	9170	9477	0.8
06791	HARWINTON	005	5330	5509	5707	0.8	64	1978	2082	2191	1.2	2.65	1561	1632	1.1
06793	WASHINGTON	005	1320	1340	1383	0.4	38	506	524	552	0.8	2.27	325	333	0.6
06794	WASHINGTON DEPOT	005	1005	1049	1096	1.0	75	425	449	475	1.3	2.32	291	304	1.0
06795	WATERTOWN	005	13345	13707	14216	0.6	56	4871	5093	5360	1.1	2.66	3691	3826	0.9
06796	WEST CORNWALL	005	969	982	1005	0.3	36	404	412	426	0.5	2.37	262	264	0.2
06798	WOODBURY	005	9186	9877	10444	1.7	92	3711	4042	4326	2.0	2.44	2570	2768	1.8
06801	BETHEL	001	18060	18313	18710	0.3	37	6502	6628	6800	0.5	2.75	4843	4913	0.3
06804	BROOKFIELD	001	16104	16479	16862	0.5	50	5724	5907	6078	0.7	2.78	4463	4578	0.6
06807	COS COB	001	7079	7395	7703	1.0	75	2716	2853	2981	1.2	2.59	2018	2108	1.0
06810	DANBURY	001	44545	47241	49395	1.4	87	16262	17233	18050	1.4	2.67	10063	10538	1.1
06811	DANBURY	001	29843	30715	31556	0.7	60	10761	11215	11608	1.0	2.58	7717	7977	0.8
06812	NEW FAIRFIELD	001	14111	14515	14965	0.7	59	4695	4849	5013	0.8	2.99	3949	4055	0.6
06820	DARIEN	001	19522	19440	19670	-0.1	14	6564	6526	6605	-0.1	2.95	5359	5302	-0.3
06824	FAIRFIELD	001	32784	32934	33532	0.1	21	11401	11455	11685	0.1	2.65	8356	8355	0.0
06825	FAIRFIELD	001	20195	19845	20020	-0.4	4	7349	7257	7357	-0.3	2.53	5274	5173	-0.5
06830	GREENWICH	001	24966	25099	25604	0.1	23	10135	10232	10469	0.2	2.74	3897	4091	1.2
06831	GREENWICH	001	14298	15060	15734	1.2	83	5098	5383	5635	1.3	2.83	5283	5337	0.2
06840	NEW CANAAN	001	19400	19698	20113	0.4	40	6826	6931	7085	0.4	2.44	4622	4597	-0.1
06850	NORWALK	001	17952	17942	18214	0.0	17	7220	7257	7391	0.1	2.44	6616	6711	0.3
06851	NORWALK	001	25586	25983	26608	0.4	40	10312	10539	10838	0.5	2.44	947	930	-0.4
06853	NORWALK	001	3344	3286	3319	-0.4	4	1417	1402	1423	-0.3	2.34	6774	6782	0.0
06854	NORWALK	001	27829	27966	28515	0.1	22	10446	10491	10552	0.2	2.63	1917	1902	-0.2
06855	NORWALK	001	7938	7915	8016	-0.1	15	3212	3215	3265	0.0	2.41	1972	2025	0.6
06870	OLD GREENWICH	001	6929	7159	7389	0.8	64	2576	2664	2755	0.8	2.68	2097	2065	-0.4
06877	RIDGEFIELD	001	23652	24313	25075	0.7	57	8438	8686	8974	0.7	2.78	6612	6772	0.6
06878	RIVERSIDE	001	7867	7790	7875	-0.2	9	2720	2699	2733	-0.2	2.88	7249	7375	0.4
06880	WESTPORT	001	26040	26596	27315	0.5	48	9682	9899	10185	0.5	2.66	2856	2909	0.4
06883	WESTON	001	10166	10422	10686	0.6	54	3366	3443	3529	0.5	3.03	1152	1164	0.3
06890	SOUTHPORT	001	4306	4372	4463	0.4	40	1623	1645	1680	0.3	2.60	2418	2555	1.3
06896	REDDING	001	8293	8759	9111	1.3	84	2922	3100	3235	1.4	2.82	4860	4887	0.1
06897	WILTON	001	17597	17770	18075	0.2	29	5908	5975	6091	0.3	2.91	1274	1351	1.4
06901	STAMFORD	001	6543	7037	7404	1.7	93	3225	3475	3662	1.8	1.95	14714	15052	0.5
06902	STAMFORD	001	62535	64555	66630	0.8	63	23695	24465	25278	0.8	2.60	4239	4277	0.2
06903	STAMFORD	001	14453	14535	14790	0.1	23	4961	5028	5146	0.3	2.84	4466	4556	0.5
06905	STAMFORD	001	17019	17436	17912	0.6	52	6809	7000	7211	0.7	2.48	1942	1966	0.3
06906	STAMFORD	001	8050	8210	8398	0.5	45	3277	3359	3449	0.6	2.42	2315	2298	-0.2
06907	STAMFORD	001	8483	8427	8545	-0.2	11	3429	3424	3486	0.0	2.45			
	CONNECTICUT					0.5					0.7	2.51			0.5
	UNITED STATES					1.2					1.3	2.58			1.1

46-A

#	POST OFFICE NAME	RACE (%) White 2000	White 2004	Black 2000	Black 2004	Asian/Pacific 2000	Asian/Pacific 2004	% Hispanic Origin 2000	% Hispanic Origin 2004	2004 AGE DISTRIBUTION (%) 0-4	5-9	10-14	15-19	20-24	25-44	45-64	65-84	85+	18+	MEDIAN AGE 2004	% 2004 Males	% 2004 Females
06608	BRIDGEPORT	34.0	33.7	26.0	25.6	2.0	2.1	65.1	66.2	9.6	9.2	10.5	10.3	9.8	26.7	17.6	5.6	0.6	64.4	25.4	47.6	52.4
06610	BRIDGEPORT	47.7	45.0	32.1	33.1	1.7	2.0	30.8	33.4	7.4	6.9	7.6	7.2	7.4	28.4	20.9	11.6	2.6	73.8	34.8	46.7	53.3
06611	TRUMBULL	94.0	92.6	1.9	2.2	2.4	3.2	2.7	3.4	6.8	7.5	7.7	6.2	4.0	24.5	26.2	14.4	2.8	74.0	41.4	48.3	51.7
06612	EASTON	96.8	95.9	0.2	0.3	2.0	2.6	1.8	2.2	7.3	8.6	8.6	6.3	3.1	22.4	30.1	12.3	1.4	71.4	42.0	48.5	51.5
06614	STRATFORD	92.9	91.6	3.2	3.7	1.3	1.7	4.9	6.1	5.7	6.0	6.3	5.5	4.4	25.2	25.8	17.6	3.5	78.5	43.1	46.9	53.1
06615	STRATFORD	70.3	68.1	21.5	22.6	1.6	2.0	10.2	11.7	6.3	6.3	7.6	7.3	6.2	27.4	24.7	12.1	2.2	75.4	38.3	47.6	52.4
06702	WATERBURY	47.8	44.9	21.2	21.4	0.6	0.7	44.8	48.7	7.2	5.8	6.5	7.1	6.6	20.7	19.2	21.0	5.9	75.9	41.7	47.2	52.8
06704	WATERBURY	50.6	48.1	29.8	30.5	1.2	1.5	26.1	28.5	8.6	8.0	8.3	8.1	7.5	27.1	20.1	10.5	2.0	70.2	32.6	47.6	52.4
06705	WATERBURY	75.7	72.5	12.5	13.7	1.9	2.3	14.0	16.6	6.9	6.5	6.7	6.3	6.9	29.1	22.2	12.6	2.8	76.1	36.7	46.8	53.2
06706	WATERBURY	65.6	63.1	9.2	9.5	1.7	2.0	34.8	37.7	8.0	7.9	8.1	7.7	7.7	27.3	21.7	9.7	1.8	71.5	33.1	48.8	51.2
06708	WATERBURY	83.0	80.7	7.5	8.2	1.7	2.2	11.8	13.8	6.8	6.4	6.5	5.8	6.3	28.8	23.5	13.2	2.7	76.8	38.0	47.2	52.8
06710	WATERBURY	49.9	47.0	26.2	26.9	1.3	1.5	32.9	36.0	8.6	7.7	8.8	8.6	8.0	27.2	20.4	8.8	1.8	69.5	31.5	48.5	51.5
06712	PROSPECT	96.3	95.5	1.4	1.7	0.7	1.0	1.9	2.4	6.4	6.9	6.9	6.1	4.3	27.0	28.3	12.2	1.9	75.8	40.9	48.7	51.3
06716	WOLCOTT	96.2	95.5	1.2	1.5	0.8	1.0	1.8	2.3	6.3	6.9	7.8	6.6	4.6	27.8	26.8	11.7	1.6	74.9	39.9	48.8	51.2
06750	BANTAM	97.1	96.7	0.4	0.4	0.4	0.6	1.4	1.7	4.3	5.2	8.9	8.1	4.7	22.6	29.7	14.1	2.4	76.5	43.1	46.8	53.3
06751	BETHLEHEM	97.5	97.1	0.3	0.3	0.8	1.0	0.6	0.8	4.8	6.0	7.7	6.4	4.0	22.8	34.9	11.4	2.0	77.0	44.1	49.1	50.9
06752	BRIDGEWATER	97.5	97.2	0.9	1.0	0.7	0.9	0.5	0.6	3.9	5.0	6.4	6.3	4.0	20.8	37.8	14.2	1.6	80.1	46.9	49.2	50.8
06754	CORNWALL BRIDGE	97.7	97.4	0.2	0.2	0.8	1.1	0.8	0.8	5.0	6.6	7.5	5.2	3.4	25.1	30.8	14.0	2.4	77.2	43.6	50.5	49.5
06755	GAYLORDSVILLE	94.9	94.1	1.4	1.5	1.7	2.2	2.3	2.6	7.6	8.3	8.3	6.2	4.0	29.1	27.7	7.9	0.8	71.7	38.3	48.8	51.2
06756	GOSHEN	98.3	97.9	0.5	0.5	0.7	1.0	1.2	1.5	4.9	5.8	6.5	5.8	4.1	21.9	34.0	15.0	2.0	78.8	45.5	49.1	50.9
06757	KENT	95.9	95.3	0.6	0.6	1.0	1.2	2.6	3.0	5.7	6.7	7.1	5.5	3.6	23.9	29.1	14.9	3.4	76.9	43.5	48.1	52.0
06758	LAKESIDE	97.4	97.3	0.3	0.6	0.6	0.9	1.0	1.2	4.8	5.7	6.6	6.0	4.8	23.0	34.9	12.5	1.8	79.4	44.6	49.3	50.8
06759	LITCHFIELD	96.8	96.4	0.8	0.9	0.5	0.7	1.8	2.0	4.7	5.9	7.6	7.4	3.5	20.7	31.5	15.6	3.1	76.0	45.1	48.0	52.0
06762	MIDDLEBURY	96.9	96.2	0.5	0.6	1.3	1.7	1.3	1.7	5.3	6.2	7.3	6.2	4.1	22.5	31.4	14.4	2.7	77.1	44.1	48.5	51.5
06763	MORRIS	97.5	97.2	0.7	0.8	0.9	1.1	0.8	1.0	5.8	6.3	6.8	6.4	4.5	24.8	30.8	12.9	1.7	77.1	42.3	50.1	49.9
06770	NAUGATUCK	91.8	90.1	2.8	3.3	1.7	2.2	4.5	5.5	7.0	6.8	7.4	7.0	6.6	29.9	23.8	9.6	1.9	74.4	36.3	48.7	51.3
06776	NEW MILFORD	94.3	93.3	1.4	1.6	2.0	2.5	2.8	3.3	6.9	7.4	7.9	6.4	4.6	29.6	27.1	8.7	1.5	73.7	38.5	49.3	50.7
06777	NEW PRSTN MRBL DALE	97.5	97.1	0.3	0.3	0.5	0.6	1.1	1.3	4.7	6.3	7.7	6.0	3.6	24.8	31.0	14.4	1.6	77.3	43.2	50.6	49.4
06778	NORTHFIELD	97.7	97.5	0.8	0.9	0.4	0.6	0.9	1.0	5.4	6.9	8.0	6.6	3.6	24.8	32.6	10.9	1.4	74.6	42.4	50.3	49.7
06779	OAKVILLE	95.5	94.8	1.3	1.4	1.2	1.5	2.9	3.4	6.0	6.0	7.2	6.8	6.0	28.6	25.8	11.6	1.9	76.5	39.0	47.5	52.5
06782	PLYMOUTH	97.3	96.9	0.6	0.7	0.4	0.5	0.9	1.0	5.4	6.0	7.5	6.9	5.2	27.1	28.6	11.6	1.9	76.7	41.0	49.5	50.5
06783	ROXBURY	97.3	96.8	0.2	0.2	0.9	1.2	1.3	1.6	4.7	5.8	6.2	6.3	3.5	21.8	36.3	14.3	1.2	79.4	45.9	51.3	48.7
06784	SHERMAN	97.0	96.4	0.7	0.8	0.9	1.1	1.7	2.1	6.3	7.5	8.2	6.3	3.3	22.1	32.5	12.3	1.6	74.0	43.1	48.9	51.1
06785	SOUTH KENT	95.3	94.7	0.6	0.6	1.3	1.7	2.1	2.5	5.8	7.0	6.8	4.7	3.3	25.1	29.0	14.0	4.3	77.2	43.5	48.8	51.2
06786	TERRYVILLE	97.4	97.0	0.8	0.9	0.4	0.6	1.3	1.6	6.2	6.4	7.6	7.0	5.7	29.1	25.8	10.5	1.8	75.3	38.3	50.1	49.9
06787	THOMASTON	97.8	97.5	0.6	0.7	0.5	0.6	1.5	1.7	5.8	6.3	7.6	6.8	5.4	29.2	26.8	10.5	1.5	75.9	39.1	49.4	50.6
06790	TORRINGTON	93.1	92.2	2.1	2.2	1.8	2.4	3.3	3.7	6.0	6.0	6.6	6.4	5.8	27.6	25.2	13.3	3.2	77.4	40.2	48.6	51.4
06791	HARWINTON	98.7	98.5	0.1	0.1	0.6	0.7	0.9	1.1	5.7	6.6	7.3	6.5	4.1	23.8	32.2	12.3	1.6	76.3	42.7	50.1	49.9
06793	WASHINGTON	93.9	92.8	1.3	1.3	3.3	4.0	2.6	3.0	3.2	5.5	9.6	8.7	5.6	18.9	33.0	13.7	1.9	75.5	44.0	49.9	50.1
06794	WASHINGTON DEPOT	95.9	95.5	0.3	0.3	0.9	1.1	2.4	2.8	4.5	5.8	7.6	6.1	3.2	22.7	32.7	15.5	1.8	78.2	45.0	50.4	49.6
06795	WATERTOWN	97.0	96.3	0.5	0.5	1.4	1.8	1.3	1.5	5.7	6.2	7.3	6.7	5.2	25.6	29.0	12.2	2.2	76.5	41.2	48.1	51.9
06796	WEST CORNWALL	97.4	97.2	0.3	0.3	0.5	0.7	1.7	1.8	4.3	5.7	7.2	7.1	4.0	20.8	32.6	15.8	2.6	78.0	45.5	48.3	51.7
06798	WOODBURY	97.3	96.8	0.5	0.6	1.2	1.5	1.7	1.9	5.6	6.3	7.4	6.2	3.8	25.4	31.8	11.9	1.7	76.7	42.5	48.7	51.3
06801	BETHEL	92.4	90.7	1.3	1.4	3.6	4.7	3.7	4.6	6.8	7.4	7.9	6.7	5.2	28.6	27.0	9.2	1.3	73.7	38.3	48.8	51.2
06804	BROOKFIELD	95.1	93.9	0.8	0.9	2.5	3.3	2.4	3.0	6.3	7.3	8.4	6.3	4.1	25.8	29.9	10.6	1.4	73.8	40.9	48.3	51.7
06807	COS COB	90.5	88.1	0.4	0.5	7.2	9.3	4.3	5.2	7.1	8.1	8.0	5.7	3.2	26.1	27.8	12.6	1.5	73.1	40.8	48.2	51.9
06810	DANBURY	71.1	67.8	7.1	7.6	5.9	7.1	21.2	24.0	6.6	6.0	5.8	6.5	8.1	35.2	21.0	9.0	1.9	78.3	34.6	50.5	49.5
06811	DANBURY	83.0	80.5	6.3	6.8	5.0	6.3	7.8	9.0	6.3	6.5	6.2	5.5	6.4	30.6	26.9	10.3	1.4	77.7	38.7	47.0	53.0
06812	NEW FAIRFIELD	96.8	96.0	0.4	0.5	1.3	1.7	2.8	3.5	7.5	8.4	9.1	6.6	4.0	26.8	28.1	8.3	1.1	70.6	38.7	50.0	50.0
06820	DARIEN	96.0	95.0	0.5	0.5	2.4	3.2	2.2	2.7	9.6	11.2	9.8	6.0	2.6	23.3	25.7	10.1	1.7	65.3	38.5	49.4	50.6
06824	FAIRFIELD	95.8	94.9	1.0	1.2	1.8	2.4	2.1	2.5	7.0	7.7	7.1	9.0	6.7	24.4	24.6	11.3	2.2	74.5	37.9	48.2	51.8
06825	FAIRFIELD	94.1	92.9	1.3	1.5	2.5	3.3	3.0	3.6	6.3	6.7	6.5	8.7	5.3	24.2	24.1	14.0	4.4	77.1	40.5	47.0	53.0
06830	GREENWICH	87.4	85.3	3.1	3.4	4.7	6.0	9.7	11.4	5.8	6.4	7.1	5.9	4.4	27.6	26.3	13.5	3.0	76.9	40.9	46.9	53.1
06831	GREENWICH	93.6	91.9	0.7	0.8	3.8	5.0	3.8	4.8	6.6	7.8	7.9	5.7	3.2	23.0	28.2	14.7	2.8	73.7	42.6	47.9	52.1
06840	NEW CANAAN	95.3	94.1	1.0	1.2	2.3	3.1	1.7	2.2	7.5	9.4	10.1	6.9	3.4	20.4	28.9	11.7	1.9	68.2	40.9	47.8	52.2
06850	NORWALK	79.4	76.8	10.7	11.5	4.6	5.8	11.3	13.1	6.6	6.5	6.0	5.0	4.9	32.3	24.4	12.4	1.9	77.8	38.9	49.2	50.8
06851	NORWALK	83.3	80.9	7.9	8.7	3.7	4.7	10.1	11.8	6.4	6.3	5.9	5.1	4.6	31.4	25.6	12.7	2.1	78.2	39.9	48.6	51.4
06853	NORWALK	95.1	94.2	1.2	1.4	1.1	1.4	3.2	3.9	8.5	7.5	5.4	3.4	2.5	26.5	31.3	13.3	1.6	76.2	42.9	48.2	51.8
06854	NORWALK	56.7	54.5	28.7	29.4	2.6	3.2	25.3	27.7	7.0	6.6	7.1	6.4	7.2	33.9	22.2	8.5	1.0	75.3	34.4	48.9	51.1
06855	NORWALK	82.2	79.9	8.7	9.5	2.4	3.0	15.1	17.5	6.2	6.0	5.7	5.1	5.7	33.2	23.7	11.9	2.5	78.9	38.3	49.4	50.6
06870	OLD GREENWICH	90.9	88.7	1.0	1.1	6.1	7.9	3.5	4.3	8.5	10.3	9.8	5.5	2.6	24.3	25.7	11.7	1.6	67.6	39.9	47.7	52.3
06877	RIDGEFIELD	96.1	95.1	0.6	0.7	2.1	2.8	2.0	2.5	7.5	9.0	9.4	6.9	3.4	22.1	30.2	10.2	1.4	69.6	40.8	48.4	51.6
06878	RIVERSIDE	90.5	88.3	0.7	0.8	6.6	8.5	4.3	5.2	8.1	9.8	9.6	6.0	3.0	22.8	26.6	12.3	1.8	68.4	40.4	48.7	51.3
06880	WESTPORT	95.2	94.0	1.2	1.3	2.4	3.2	2.3	2.9	7.0	8.6	9.1	6.0	2.8	21.6	29.8	13.3	1.8	71.1	42.5	47.7	52.3
06883	WESTON	95.7	94.8	0.9	1.1	2.1	2.7	2.1	2.6	7.3	9.7	11.2	7.3	2.9	20.0	31.5	9.4	0.8	67.0	40.9	49.1	50.9
06890	SOUTHPORT	96.8	95.9	0.5	0.6	1.8	2.3	1.4	1.8	7.6	8.6	7.6	5.6	2.8	21.7	27.7	15.4	3.0	72.1	42.8	47.9	52.1
06896	REDDING	96.2	95.3	0.8	0.9	1.8	2.4	1.5	1.9	6.6	8.1	8.7	6.9	3.2	21.5	33.9	10.0	1.2	72.0	42.5	49.7	50.3
06897	WILTON	95.6	94.4	0.6	0.7	2.7	3.5	1.5	1.9	7.3	9.2	9.9	7.1	3.1	20.4	30.3	10.4	2.3	68.7	41.4	48.6	51.4
06901	STAMFORD	55.0	52.2	24.5	24.9	7.7	9.2	23.3	25.5	4.4	3.8	4.8	5.4	7.8	37.4	21.9	12.7	1.7	83.8	36.7	50.4	49.6
06902	STAMFORD	59.3	56.6	22.4	23.0	4.4	5.4	23.8	26.1	6.9	6.5	6.4	6.2	6.8	33.5	21.3	10.4	2.1	76.5	35.5	48.4	51.6
06903	STAMFORD	91.8	90.0	3.0	3.5	3.5	4.5	2.7	3.3	7.4	8.8	7.7	5.0	2.6	23.8	29.8	13.4	1.6	72.7	42.3	49.2	50.8
06905	STAMFORD	82.2	79.2	5.6	6.3	7.6	9.3	7.8	9.2	7.0	6.9	6.0	4.9	4.5	31.2	23.5	13.3	2.6	76.9	39.2	48.4	51.6
06906	STAMFORD	79.1	75.7	8.4	9.3	5.6	7.0	11.6	13.7	6.2	5.5	5.0	5.3	6.1	35.6	22.3	12.1	2.0	80.2	37.5	47.5	52.5
06907	STAMFORD	87.5	85.1	3.9	4.3	4.5	5.8	7.2	8.6	6.6	6.7	6.2	5.1	4.3	31.9	25.4	11.8	2.0	77.4	39.4	48.1	51.9
	CONNECTICUT	81.6	80.0	9.1	9.5	2.5	3.1	9.4	10.5	6.4	6.7	7.1	6.9	6.3	27.5	25.4	11.7	2.2	75.8	38.5	48.5	51.5
	UNITED STATES	75.1	73.6	12.3	12.5	3.8	4.2	12.5	14.1	6.9	6.7	7.2	7.0	7.3	28.6	23.8	10.8	1.7	75.1	36.0	49.1	50.9

C 06608-06907

#	POST OFFICE NAME	2004 Per Capita Income	2004 HH Income Base	2004 HOUSEHOLD INCOME DISTRIBUTION (%)					MEDIAN HOUSEHOLD INCOME				2004 Home Value Base	2004 HOME VALUE DISTRIBUTION (%)					2004 Median Home Value
				Less than $25,000	$25,000 to $49,999	$50,000 to $99,999	$100,000 to $149,999	$150,000 or More	2004	2009	2004 National Centile	2004 State Centile		Less than $50,000	$50,000 to $89,999	$90,000 to $174,999	$175,000 to $399,999	$400,000 or More	
06608	BRIDGEPORT	12128	4097	50.5	26.6	18.2	3.5	1.2	24677	28253	4	3	1066	6.9	15.9	51.1	24.3	1.9	131081
06610	BRIDGEPORT	19488	8817	32.2	30.7	28.3	6.5	2.2	38675	45628	42	9	4272	12.6	15.7	40.7	30.3	0.7	136977
06611	TRUMBULL	43258	12323	8.7	12.9	32.5	22.8	23.1	91912	115233	97	88	11284	0.3	0.0	1.0	54.5	44.2	382377
06612	EASTON	68199	2513	5.0	9.4	16.0	20.1	49.5	148395	191130	100	97	2379	0.0	0.1	0.3	7.7	91.9	672949
06614	STRATFORD	34479	12882	14.3	20.4	37.6	18.0	9.8	66476	82029	89	50	11318	1.5	4.0	9.7	76.1	8.8	241406
06615	STRATFORD	27056	7158	20.0	25.5	35.4	13.2	6.0	53935	65405	78	25	4742	0.0	3.9	26.2	63.4	6.5	207600
06702	WATERBURY	9973	1842	77.5	15.7	5.7	1.0	0.1	12282	14315	1	1	105	9.5	3.8	62.9	23.8	0.0	121591
06704	WATERBURY	17951	9428	37.8	29.5	23.7	6.4	2.6	33363	37230	22	6	4448	5.7	12.1	61.1	20.8	0.3	134791
06705	WATERBURY	21396	11133	29.3	31.6	30.9	6.0	2.2	40505	46164	48	9	5569	3.2	7.5	62.4	26.4	0.7	143034
06706	WATERBURY	18356	5188	36.0	29.4	25.2	7.5	1.9	34593	39214	26	7	2748	2.3	7.6	61.5	28.5	0.1	143324
06708	WATERBURY	24795	11505	26.2	26.0	32.4	11.1	4.4	47453	54218	67	16	6994	2.7	4.1	53.2	38.9	1.1	161231
06710	WATERBURY	16693	3459	38.6	28.4	23.2	6.7	3.2	34819	37472	27	7	1416	2.1	9.5	61.2	27.2	0.0	141536
06712	PROSPECT	31523	3224	7.9	18.5	40.5	22.6	10.6	76311	88875	94	70	3008	2.1	1.5	11.4	72.9	12.1	260738
06716	WOLCOTT	29436	5540	10.9	18.9	43.4	19.5	7.4	69052	80610	91	58	4959	0.0	0.7	22.0	72.0	5.3	215775
06750	BANTAM	29296	599	27.1	25.4	31.2	7.7	8.7	47455	54556	67	16	433	0.0	0.9	29.6	56.8	12.7	212028
06751	BETHLEHEM	34620	1315	11.5	13.1	39.3	22.0	14.1	79239	92904	95	75	1171	1.2	0.3	8.1	64.4	26.1	306801
06752	BRIDGEWATER	52444	723	7.8	12.2	33.9	21.0	25.2	92316	109511	97	88	655	0.5	0.2	2.6	43.8	53.0	421667
06754	CORNWALL BRIDGE	45621	561	15.0	20.7	36.7	15.0	12.7	66649	77946	90	51	478	0.0	1.1	8.4	58.0	32.6	300000
06755	GAYLORDSVILLE	35686	602	9.0	16.9	39.4	20.8	14.0	79829	93183	95	77	538	3.9	3.0	9.1	64.7	19.3	282258
06756	GOSHEN	40455	1130	11.9	18.5	40.1	17.6	12.0	72501	83522	92	63	1014	0.5	1.2	8.8	61.9	27.6	299301
06757	KENT	42789	974	17.0	21.5	35.9	12.4	13.1	61063	70846	85	38	747	0.9	0.0	7.1	63.2	28.8	271565
06758	LAKESIDE	41688	123	12.2	19.5	43.9	13.8	10.6	68401	77056	91	56	107	0.0	1.9	10.3	65.4	22.4	275000
06759	LITCHFIELD	38246	2390	14.7	19.4	35.9	17.0	13.1	69046	79951	91	57	1953	0.6	0.6	14.9	58.1	25.8	267674
06762	MIDDLEBURY	38221	2477	13.0	13.7	36.4	21.6	15.3	78028	93044	94	74	2244	0.9	0.6	7.4	62.8	28.3	291412
06763	MORRIS	37536	840	18.0	18.7	39.6	16.0	7.7	61952	70879	86	40	704	0.0	0.7	14.6	63.5	21.2	255155
06770	NAUGATUCK	26844	12114	17.5	24.5	39.9	13.7	4.5	57321	65823	82	30	8471	2.9	6.6	29.5	59.1	1.9	189820
06776	NEW MILFORD	34906	9910	11.3	17.8	38.7	20.6	11.6	73991	84316	93	66	7858	0.8	3.1	12.0	70.6	13.5	247519
06777	NEW PRSTN MRBL DALE	40428	752	18.2	18.1	36.8	17.6	9.3	66313	77417	89	50	649	0.3	1.1	5.6	60.7	32.4	315185
06778	NORTHFIELD	32601	500	9.0	16.8	44.6	19.6	10.0	72378	84305	92	62	467	0.2	0.9	9.4	69.2	20.3	259375
06779	OAKVILLE	24577	3208	17.3	28.6	38.2	13.1	2.9	53754	61179	78	25	2358	0.8	1.3	45.9	51.2	0.8	177463
06782	PLYMOUTH	26091	776	15.1	24.4	40.0	15.6	5.0	61632	69249	86	39	683	1.6	4.3	45.0	46.3	2.9	173942
06783	ROXBURY	69461	908	8.9	13.4	25.0	23.4	29.3	104446	125428	98	92	820	0.0	0.0	1.1	28.3	70.6	547210
06784	SHERMAN	48219	1655	6.6	13.8	35.2	24.1	20.3	90667	112517	97	87	1517	0.5	0.3	2.8	52.2	44.2	377154
06785	SOUTH KENT	40503	191	12.6	19.4	41.4	11.0	15.7	70383	80673	91	59	153	0.0	0.0	5.2	61.4	33.3	305556
06786	TERRYVILLE	27187	3837	15.3	23.7	41.7	15.0	4.3	60374	68085	85	35	2972	1.1	3.2	50.4	44.2	1.1	169290
06787	THOMASTON	29315	3123	17.6	23.4	39.7	13.1	6.2	59613	66682	84	33	2293	0.6	5.1	40.2	51.6	2.5	181750
06790	TORRINGTON	24878	15359	24.5	27.4	34.0	11.3	2.9	47858	54417	68	17	10371	1.5	4.6	56.7	35.9	1.3	156598
06791	HARWINTON	40537	2082	11.0	17.2	38.0	20.9	13.0	75911	86691	94	69	1944	0.5	0.8	20.3	64.5	13.9	229032
06793	WASHINGTON	48839	524	11.1	13.7	32.8	23.1	19.3	85794	103116	96	83	449	0.5	0.0	5.8	38.8	55.0	439474
06794	WASHINGTON DEPOT	51571	449	13.6	15.1	28.3	23.4	19.6	85354	101709	96	82	376	1.3	0.0	4.3	47.3	47.1	378000
06795	WATERTOWN	34295	5093	10.6	19.0	38.4	21.4	10.6	75812	86574	94	69	4331	0.5	1.7	18.9	68.1	10.9	231459
06796	WEST CORNWALL	54380	412	14.1	26.0	30.3	11.4	18.2	62852	75000	87	42	329	0.0	1.2	12.5	46.2	40.1	340909
06798	WOODBURY	45617	4042	10.8	19.5	35.3	18.5	15.9	77216	88811	94	71	3173	0.4	1.5	16.3	48.3	33.5	325464
06801	BETHEL	34788	6628	8.8	17.1	37.7	22.3	14.2	80444	101154	95	77	5282	0.2	0.1	7.4	68.0	24.4	314665
06804	BROOKFIELD	46050	5907	7.2	12.7	34.0	23.8	22.4	92984	115860	97	88	5298	0.3	0.2	6.3	55.6	37.7	351014
06807	COS COB	81126	2853	7.6	11.2	21.7	17.4	42.1	124613	165249	99	95	7862	0.0	0.0	0.5	3.5	96.0	906170
06810	DANBURY	24326	17233	19.9	27.1	34.4	12.9	5.7	52958	64086	77	23	8760	2.2	2.8	20.6	65.6	8.9	226238
06811	DANBURY	37230	11215	11.3	15.3	35.3	20.5	15.4	77981	98644	94	73	8760	1.2	2.0	10.5	67.8	18.5	283418
06812	NEW FAIRFIELD	43255	4849	6.4	11.8	31.7	25.4	24.6	100064	121945	98	89	4548	0.6	0.6	4.8	60.4	33.6	334099
06820	DARIEN	103145	6526	5.0	7.3	16.4	14.3	57.1	180417	232438	100	100	5844	0.2	0.2	0.4	4.8	94.3	1000001
06824	FAIRFIELD	63068	11455	8.9	12.0	24.8	19.8	34.5	108158	138646	99	93	9641	0.2	0.1	1.6	31.1	67.1	521862
06825	FAIRFIELD	40717	7257	11.0	16.6	30.3	22.3	19.8	84302	108202	96	80	5838	0.5	0.0	2.4	52.0	45.1	382802
06830	GREENWICH	92883	10232	13.2	14.0	22.1	15.4	35.3	101443	132489	98	91	5978	0.0	0.0	0.4	13.3	86.1	923977
06831	GREENWICH	122746	5383	6.0	9.1	20.7	14.4	49.9	149431	198569	100	98	4431	0.0	0.2	0.2	4.9	94.7	1000001
06840	NEW CANAAN	111546	6931	5.6	7.9	17.8	12.9	55.8	175473	227183	100	100	5989	0.2	0.2	0.3	3.5	95.9	1000001
06850	NORWALK	39843	7257	12.6	19.7	34.0	18.3	15.4	71808	91227	92	61	4832	0.1	1.2	6.8	48.9	43.0	368606
06851	NORWALK	41665	10539	12.2	16.5	34.8	20.7	15.8	77259	98270	94	72	7546	1.2	0.9	4.4	54.3	39.2	365329
06853	NORWALK	99819	1402	7.4	9.2	18.4	18.8	46.2	137082	180807	100	96	1198	0.0	0.0	1.0	9.6	89.4	730667
06854	NORWALK	29326	10552	18.6	28.0	30.0	13.9	9.6	54390	67705	79	27	5082	0.6	0.8	12.5	60.1	26.0	298721
06855	NORWALK	39487	3215	14.2	18.8	31.3	19.2	16.6	73833	95729	93	65	1885	0.3	0.2	7.1	44.4	48.1	392843
06870	OLD GREENWICH	96092	2664	5.6	6.8	20.2	17.0	50.5	151319	192498	100	98	2351	0.1	0.0	0.5	5.6	93.8	886456
06877	RIDGEFIELD	68174	8686	7.4	9.2	21.5	19.3	42.7	128522	165999	100	95	7542	0.2	0.1	2.3	14.4	83.0	645619
06878	RIVERSIDE	84788	2699	8.3	8.4	17.6	17.8	47.9	143324	185188	100	97	2290	0.3	0.0	0.5	5.6	93.7	994444
06880	WESTPORT	103655	9899	6.1	9.6	17.4	17.4	49.6	148603	194140	100	98	8748	0.5	0.1	0.6	5.8	93.0	881799
06883	WESTON	105952	3443	2.7	6.5	17.5	14.1	59.2	179569	228413	100	100	3225	0.0	0.3	0.3	3.2	96.2	913639
06890	SOUTHPORT	90106	1645	7.8	10.8	19.0	16.7	45.7	135392	174917	100	96	1382	0.0	0.0	0.5	22.1	77.4	676809
06896	REDDING	62206	3100	5.4	9.4	21.7	25.7	37.8	125105	158690	99	94	2841	0.0	0.0	0.4	15.0	84.7	600292
06897	WILTON	92990	5975	4.2	7.9	15.7	16.6	55.7	168462	213788	100	99	5451	0.0	0.0	0.4	7.1	92.5	800665
06901	STAMFORD	32991	3475	33.2	22.6	23.7	14.3	6.2	43322	53764	57	13	452	0.0	5.5	33.0	44.9	16.6	227941
06902	STAMFORD	37602	24465	18.3	21.8	30.9	14.7	14.3	62387	78201	87	41	11888	0.6	1.3	14.1	42.5	41.5	352501
06903	STAMFORD	81057	5028	6.9	9.9	16.6	18.3	48.4	144672	189004	100	97	4820	0.0	0.0	0.4	2.9	96.7	814462
06905	STAMFORD	46986	7000	13.9	14.4	30.6	17.8	23.3	82505	107231	96	78	5073	0.2	0.0	3.6	31.7	64.5	456447
06906	STAMFORD	36215	3359	14.6	18.3	34.8	19.4	13.0	71192	90466	92	60	2029	1.0	0.3	5.2	49.4	44.0	377032
06907	STAMFORD	44293	3424	14.8	14.5	31.8	19.4	19.5	79698	103442	95	76	2498	0.0	0.6	1.6	43.2	54.6	420751
	CONNECTICUT	34999		18.8	22.0	32.8	15.1	11.4	61358	72202				1.5	2.7	24.6	51.4	19.8	230968
	UNITED STATES	25866		24.7	27.1	30.8	10.9	6.5	48124	56710				10.9	15.0	33.7	30.1	10.4	145905

ZIP CODE		FINANCIAL SERVICES				THE HOME							ENTERTAINMENT						PERSONAL			
						Home Improvements		Furnishings														
#	POST OFFICE NAME	Auto Loan	Home Loan	Invest-ments	Retire-ment Plans	Home Repair	Lawn & Garden	Comput-ers & Hard-ware	Major Appli-ances	TV, Radio, Sound Equip-ment	Furni-ture	Dine out/ Carry out	Sports Equip-ment	Fees & Tickets	Toys & Games	Travel	Cable TV	Apparel & Services	Auto Repairs	Health Insur-ance	Pets & Supplies
06608	BRIDGEPORT	45	44	82	40	41	49	51	48	58	54	75	53	50	77	51	62	75	52	50	52
06610	BRIDGEPORT	64	63	78	62	62	69	70	67	72	69	90	77	69	91	69	73	88	69	67	73
06611	TRUMBULL	150	196	238	189	191	199	175	174	165	176	208	197	190	221	183	166	209	169	161	187
06612	EASTON	242	326	447	320	318	343	284	282	265	291	335	317	323	352	303	267	340	271	262	306
06614	STRATFORD	110	126	141	122	125	136	119	120	118	119	148	134	126	152	124	120	145	118	121	131
06615	STRATFORD	88	96	110	95	95	102	97	94	96	95	120	109	100	125	98	96	118	95	93	104
06702	WATERBURY	23	21	32	21	21	24	26	24	27	25	34	27	25	34	25	28	33	26	26	26
06704	WATERBURY	61	59	70	58	59	66	65	63	67	64	84	72	65	84	64	68	82	64	64	69
06705	WATERBURY	67	69	80	69	68	74	72	70	72	71	90	81	73	91	72	71	88	71	69	76
06706	WATERBURY	62	63	81	60	62	70	67	65	71	66	89	73	68	92	68	74	87	66	68	71
06708	WATERBURY	78	84	96	83	83	89	85	83	85	83	106	95	87	109	86	85	104	83	82	91
06710	WATERBURY	59	58	73	56	57	63	64	61	67	63	83	70	63	84	63	68	82	63	62	67
06712	PROSPECT	116	142	152	141	140	140	128	128	120	128	151	149	136	161	132	118	151	124	117	141
06716	WOLCOTT	105	128	140	127	125	126	117	116	111	117	139	136	124	147	120	108	138	113	106	127
06750	BANTAM	114	84	53	80	93	110	91	102	102	87	120	117	80	114	90	108	109	102	122	128
06751	BETHLEHEM	121	150	159	150	147	145	134	133	124	133	156	156	142	166	137	120	156	129	119	147
06752	BRIDGEWATER	173	209	235	207	208	218	191	192	181	192	228	217	203	231	199	180	225	187	183	209
06754	CORNWALL BRIDGE	162	156	145	153	165	177	147	160	151	147	184	186	146	184	153	153	177	157	168	195
06755	GAYLORDSVILLE	131	163	173	163	160	158	146	145	135	145	170	170	155	181	149	131	170	140	130	160
06756	GOSHEN	158	143	117	134	153	165	132	150	140	131	169	175	126	171	139	145	161	146	164	193
06757	KENT	133	156	185	159	155	160	150	147	142	149	179	172	156	182	152	139	177	146	137	160
06758	LAKESIDE	147	183	195	184	180	177	163	163	151	163	190	191	174	203	167	147	190	157	146	180
06759	LITCHFIELD	123	140	148	137	140	149	130	133	127	129	158	151	136	162	135	128	155	130	131	148
06762	MIDDLEBURY	132	159	175	157	158	164	146	146	138	145	174	166	155	180	151	138	172	142	138	160
06763	MORRIS	131	137	129	137	138	145	130	134	128	128	159	155	132	163	131	127	154	130	132	152
06770	NAUGATUCK	96	100	102	101	99	103	100	99	97	99	122	116	100	123	98	95	119	99	94	110
06776	NEW MILFORD	122	144	155	145	141	141	133	132	125	133	157	154	139	164	134	120	156	129	118	145
06777	NEW PRSTN MRBL DALE	159	140	115	136	152	165	133	150	141	133	170	177	127	169	139	145	161	147	164	190
06778	NORTHFIELD	116	144	153	144	141	139	128	128	119	128	149	150	136	159	131	115	149	123	114	141
06779	OAKVILLE	85	91	93	89	91	98	89	89	89	87	110	102	91	115	90	89	107	88	90	100
06782	PLYMOUTH	116	103	78	98	109	117	95	105	101	95	123	126	93	125	98	104	117	103	114	136
06783	ROXBURY	220	283	340	286	275	285	248	243	228	253	289	278	277	302	257	225	293	234	220	268
06784	SHERMAN	159	208	241	202	203	207	184	183	172	184	216	211	199	231	192	170	217	177	167	199
06785	SOUTH KENT	130	156	178	156	155	163	145	145	137	145	173	165	153	175	150	136	171	142	137	158
06786	TERRYVILLE	99	99	92	97	100	106	95	98	96	94	119	114	96	122	96	96	114	96	99	114
06787	THOMASTON	98	110	116	108	109	114	106	105	103	104	128	122	109	133	107	102	126	104	102	117
06790	TORRINGTON	82	81	79	80	82	89	81	82	83	79	102	95	81	104	82	83	98	82	85	94
06791	HARWINTON	138	170	186	169	166	169	154	152	144	154	182	175	165	190	158	141	181	148	140	167
06793	WASHINGTON	155	188	213	187	187	196	172	173	163	173	205	195	183	208	179	162	203	168	165	188
06794	WASHINGTON DEPOT	156	187	208	185	186	195	171	172	162	171	204	195	181	207	178	161	202	168	165	189
06795	WATERTOWN	120	142	153	142	140	143	131	131	125	130	156	152	138	164	134	123	155	128	122	145
06796	WEST CORNWALL	218	173	121	160	194	216	165	196	183	163	218	230	149	216	174	193	203	192	227	263
06798	WOODBURY	144	171	198	175	168	171	161	157	151	161	190	185	169	197	163	147	189	156	143	173
06801	BETHEL	126	149	164	152	146	146	139	136	129	139	163	161	145	169	140	125	162	134	122	150
06804	BROOKFIELD	165	205	229	207	201	202	185	182	171	185	216	212	198	228	189	167	217	177	164	200
06807	COS COB	252	334	471	329	323	348	299	292	282	305	356	332	335	380	316	284	362	284	269	317
06810	DANBURY	81	90	124	88	86	94	92	88	93	92	118	101	95	125	93	94	118	90	84	96
06811	DANBURY	130	150	174	153	147	150	144	140	136	144	171	165	150	176	144	132	170	140	127	154
06812	NEW FAIRFIELD	170	209	223	209	205	206	185	185	173	186	217	216	198	230	190	169	217	179	168	207
06820	DARIEN	372	496	665	486	484	517	437	433	408	445	515	489	490	544	463	410	522	417	400	468
06824	FAIRFIELD	215	282	365	276	274	287	255	251	240	257	302	289	278	323	266	239	305	246	229	270
06825	FAIRFIELD	129	171	218	165	165	172	155	152	147	155	185	175	168	199	162	147	186	149	139	163
06830	GREENWICH	283	331	463	334	322	352	322	312	314	326	397	357	346	410	332	316	396	313	298	340
06831	GREENWICH	408	556	747	537	540	576	487	482	457	494	576	544	546	617	518	461	584	465	444	519
06840	NEW CANAAN	384	507	680	499	494	527	452	445	423	459	534	507	503	563	476	423	540	432	410	483
06850	NORWALK	129	142	171	144	138	146	141	137	136	141	171	160	145	173	141	132	169	138	127	150
06851	NORWALK	128	155	192	154	151	157	147	144	140	147	177	167	155	185	150	138	176	143	131	155
06853	NORWALK	277	384	521	370	372	398	333	330	310	339	391	371	376	420	355	314	399	316	303	355
06854	NORWALK	97	105	145	104	101	110	108	104	110	109	139	120	112	146	110	111	139	107	100	114
06855	NORWALK	124	142	173	143	139	146	138	136	133	139	168	158	143	171	140	130	166	136	125	147
06870	OLD GREENWICH	302	426	579	407	412	439	367	364	343	373	432	410	415	469	393	347	441	349	332	390
06877	RIDGEFIELD	240	304	382	306	297	311	273	268	254	277	321	308	301	334	283	251	324	261	245	293
06878	RIVERSIDE	288	403	548	387	390	416	348	345	325	354	409	388	394	442	372	329	417	331	316	370
06880	WESTPORT	337	451	608	441	440	472	395	392	369	403	466	442	445	492	420	372	473	377	363	425
06883	WESTON	388	523	716	512	510	550	455	451	424	466	537	507	517	565	485	428	545	433	419	490
06890	SOUTHPORT	284	391	534	379	380	407	339	336	316	346	399	378	384	427	362	320	407	323	309	363
06896	REDDING	223	288	349	290	279	290	252	247	232	257	294	283	281	308	262	229	298	238	224	272
06897	WILTON	336	444	602	438	433	465	392	388	366	400	463	439	440	486	415	368	469	375	359	421
06901	STAMFORD	80	79	139	85	76	87	92	83	96	92	122	100	95	128	92	98	121	90	83	93
06902	STAMFORD	119	132	201	132	127	140	138	130	141	139	178	152	144	189	141	143	178	135	126	143
06903	STAMFORD	283	382	512	374	371	397	332	329	309	339	391	371	376	414	353	311	397	316	303	357
06905	STAMFORD	141	181	238	176	175	184	167	164	160	168	200	188	180	215	174	160	202	161	150	175
06906	STAMFORD	111	124	172	130	121	127	127	120	123	127	156	143	132	161	127	121	154	123	111	132
06907	STAMFORD	134	167	208	165	163	170	156	152	148	156	187	176	166	197	161	147	187	151	141	165
	CONNECTICUT	116	129	153	129	127	135	127	124	124	126	156	144	132	161	128	124	154	124	119	137
	UNITED STATES	100	100	100	100	100	100	100	100	100	100	100	100	100	100	100	100	100	100	100	100

# ZIP CODE	POST OFFICE NAME	COUNTY FIPS CODE	POPULATION 2000	2004	2009	2000-2004 ANNUAL RATE % Rate	State Centile	HOUSEHOLDS 2000	2004	2009	% Annual Rate 2000-2004	2004 Average HH Size	FAMILIES 2000	2004	% Annual Rate 2000-2004
19701	BEAR	003	32112	35695	38294	2.5	68	11422	12765	13761	2.7	2.78	8539	9410	2.3
19702	NEWARK	003	44558	49058	52638	2.3	61	16170	18009	19488	2.6	2.71	11541	12637	2.2
19703	CLAYMONT	003	15325	14948	15192	-0.6	4	6437	6358	6518	-0.3	2.35	3970	3812	-1.0
19707	HOCKESSIN	003	13859	14816	15623	1.6	46	4735	5130	5462	1.9	2.84	4012	4293	1.6
19709	MIDDLETOWN	003	20267	24458	27377	4.5	93	6758	8171	9176	4.6	2.99	5579	6693	4.4
19711	NEWARK	003	56116	58385	60712	0.9	32	19262	20274	21315	1.2	2.55	12195	12640	0.9
19713	NEWARK	003	31276	32577	34036	1.0	33	12076	12711	13391	1.2	2.53	7918	8156	0.7
19716	NEWARK	003	680	701	715	0.7	28	30	34	36	3.0	5.03	6	6	0.0
19720	NEW CASTLE	003	57778	59296	61587	0.6	25	21317	22052	23069	0.8	2.64	14850	15035	0.3
19734	TOWNSEND	003	5523	6159	6684	2.6	70	1985	2187	2363	2.3	2.82	1607	1749	2.0
19736	YORKLYN	003	52	60	65	3.4	86	16	19	21	4.1	3.00	12	14	3.7
19801	WILMINGTON	003	14809	14984	15412	0.3	19	5666	5854	6104	0.8	2.39	3206	3208	0.0
19802	WILMINGTON	003	27759	27537	28058	-0.2	9	9951	9943	10215	0.0	2.54	6265	6095	-0.7
19803	WILMINGTON	003	21260	20794	21093	-0.5	5	8466	8379	8580	-0.2	2.45	6266	6094	-0.7
19804	WILMINGTON	003	17914	17829	18260	-0.1	14	7418	7447	7681	0.1	2.39	4830	4746	-0.4
19805	WILMINGTON	003	40106	39833	40601	-0.2	11	15288	15245	15640	-0.1	2.56	9614	9355	-0.6
19806	WILMINGTON	003	9590	9700	10018	0.3	18	5517	5719	5995	0.9	1.64	1879	1823	-0.7
19807	WILMINGTON	003	8073	8294	8597	0.6	26	3411	3513	3665	0.7	2.30	2292	2324	0.3
19808	WILMINGTON	003	39411	40107	41411	0.4	23	15793	16210	16863	0.6	2.43	10685	10765	0.2
19809	WILMINGTON	003	14565	14267	14454	-0.5	7	6330	6281	6421	-0.2	2.25	3933	3801	-0.8
19810	WILMINGTON	003	25296	25177	25685	-0.1	14	10065	10126	10418	0.1	2.44	7256	7173	-0.3
19901	DOVER	001	31538	33093	35835	1.1	37	12355	13200	14527	1.6	2.45	8452	8847	1.1
19902	DOVER AFB	001	455	417	434	-2.0	2	23	21	23	-2.1	2.57	23	21	-2.1
19904	DOVER	001	27944	30303	33270	1.9	53	9933	10988	12322	2.4	2.53	6692	7294	2.1
19930	BETHANY BEACH	005	2577	2884	3310	2.7	74	1303	1476	1718	3.0	1.95	868	967	2.6
19931	BETHEL	005	223	234	259	1.1	37	95	101	114	1.5	2.32	68	71	1.0
19933	BRIDGEVILLE	005	6546	6897	7682	1.2	39	2389	2543	2868	1.5	2.70	1770	1861	1.2
19934	CAMDEN WYOMING	001	8978	9744	10686	2.0	54	3285	3608	4008	2.2	2.70	2495	2717	2.0
19938	CLAYTON	001	5838	6220	6725	1.5	42	2078	2242	2455	1.8	2.77	1627	1735	1.5
19939	DAGSBORO	005	4530	5097	5877	2.8	75	1856	2127	2493	3.3	2.39	1353	1531	3.0
19940	DELMAR	005	4868	4946	5487	0.4	21	1865	1925	2171	0.8	2.52	1330	1354	0.4
19941	ELLENDALE	005	2404	2946	3539	4.9	96	845	1049	1277	5.2	2.80	629	771	4.9
19943	FELTON	001	9182	10158	11288	2.4	65	3417	3828	4310	2.7	2.65	2611	2892	2.4
19944	FENWICK ISLAND	005	633	708	813	2.7	72	332	376	438	3.0	1.88	221	246	2.6
19945	FRANKFORD	005	7778	8822	10247	3.0	82	3004	3487	4125	3.6	2.53	2183	2490	3.1
19946	FREDERICA	001	3418	3791	4203	2.5	67	1379	1551	1744	2.8	2.44	954	1055	2.4
19947	GEORGETOWN	005	15153	16433	18415	1.9	53	4711	5177	5931	2.2	2.80	3418	3703	1.9
19950	GREENWOOD	005	5984	6459	7234	1.8	47	2183	2381	2700	2.1	2.69	1653	1785	1.8
19951	HARBESON	005	1076	1315	1578	4.8	95	427	528	641	5.1	2.49	315	385	4.8
19952	HARRINGTON	001	8409	8973	9789	1.5	44	3168	3420	3778	1.8	2.62	2322	2471	1.5
19953	HARTLY	001	4196	4359	4667	0.9	30	1488	1573	1711	1.3	2.77	1143	1193	1.0
19954	HOUSTON	001	1597	1694	1834	1.4	40	583	629	691	1.8	2.69	457	487	1.5
19956	LAUREL	005	13754	15054	17116	2.2	60	5226	5777	6646	2.4	2.60	3871	4229	2.1
19958	LEWES	005	14585	16998	19949	3.7	88	6541	7750	9240	4.1	2.16	4310	5055	3.8
19960	LINCOLN	005	4788	5218	5916	2.0	58	1720	1899	2182	2.4	2.74	1291	1408	2.1
19962	MAGNOLIA	001	5761	6490	7250	2.8	81	1970	2242	2535	3.1	2.89	1551	1743	2.8
19963	MILFORD	001	14891	16766	19042	2.8	79	5925	6785	7829	3.2	2.43	4157	4700	2.9
19964	MARYDEL	001	1102	1216	1343	2.3	63	412	463	521	2.8	2.63	312	346	2.5
19966	MILLSBORO	005	16932	19053	21967	2.8	77	7305	8315	9712	3.1	2.27	5077	5685	2.7
19967	MILLVILLE	005	307	436	560	8.6	100	130	187	245	8.9	2.33	89	126	8.5
19968	MILTON	005	6819	7997	9405	3.8	89	2737	3252	3878	4.1	2.45	1916	2243	3.8
19970	OCEAN VIEW	005	3935	5102	6305	6.3	98	1844	2419	3028	6.6	2.11	1298	1679	6.2
19971	REHOBOTH BEACH	005	9318	11062	13083	4.1	91	4594	5519	6612	4.4	2.00	2587	3046	3.9
19973	SEAFORD	005	21259	23168	26277	2.0	58	8043	8901	10261	2.4	2.54	5743	6277	2.1
19975	SELBYVILLE	005	5786	6588	7633	3.1	84	2544	2928	3433	3.4	2.25	1807	2051	3.0
19977	SMYRNA	001	14074	15226	16493	1.9	49	4678	5167	5721	2.4	2.57	3376	3675	2.0
19979	VIOLA	001	624	628	660	0.2	16	235	241	258	0.6	2.61	170	172	0.3

						2000-2004 ANNUAL RATE					% Annual Rate	2004 Average HH Size			% Annual Rate
DELAWARE						1.4					1.7	2.52			1.3
UNITED STATES						1.2					1.3	2.58			1.1

# ZIP CODE POST OFFICE NAME	RACE (%) White 2000	White 2004	Black 2000	Black 2004	Asian/Pacific 2000	Asian/Pacific 2004	% Hispanic Origin 2000	% Hispanic Origin 2004	0-4	5-9	10-14	15-19	20-24	25-44	45-64	65-84	85+	18+	MEDIAN AGE 2004	% 2004 Males	% 2004 Females
19701 BEAR	76.0	73.4	18.3	19.9	2.5	3.2	3.6	4.1	8.4	8.2	8.1	6.8	6.3	34.5	22.2	5.1	0.4	71.0	33.0	49.0	51.0
19702 NEWARK	70.3	67.2	21.7	23.3	3.9	5.0	4.5	5.1	9.0	8.3	8.1	6.8	7.5	36.7	19.6	3.7	0.4	70.4	30.8	49.3	50.7
19703 CLAYMONT	69.1	66.1	24.8	26.8	2.1	2.7	3.8	4.5	7.1	6.7	7.3	6.7	6.5	30.4	21.6	11.9	1.8	74.5	36.1	47.1	52.9
19707 HOCKESSIN	89.0	86.3	2.6	2.8	7.1	9.3	2.0	2.5	6.2	7.5	8.2	6.6	4.5	22.6	31.7	10.3	2.4	73.6	41.9	49.0	51.0
19709 MIDDLETOWN	86.7	85.4	10.3	11.1	0.8	1.0	2.7	3.3	8.2	8.7	9.1	7.1	5.5	31.3	23.4	6.2	0.6	69.3	34.7	49.8	50.3
19711 NEWARK	86.2	83.9	5.7	6.2	4.6	6.0	4.5	5.2	5.3	5.3	5.6	12.8	15.7	24.9	21.6	8.0	1.0	80.9	29.3	48.1	51.9
19713 NEWARK	78.0	75.3	14.3	15.5	3.4	4.3	4.7	5.5	6.8	6.5	6.7	6.4	8.6	31.6	22.6	9.7	1.1	76.4	34.5	48.6	51.4
19716 NEWARK	92.1	90.4	2.9	3.3	2.4	3.1	2.9	3.4	0.3	0.0	0.1	46.8	46.9	3.0	1.6	1.1	0.1	99.6	20.3	41.9	58.1
19720 NEW CASTLE	63.9	61.1	29.5	31.4	1.7	2.1	7.1	8.0	6.8	6.7	7.4	6.7	6.7	31.0	23.6	10.1	1.0	75.0	35.6	48.1	51.9
19734 TOWNSEND	91.2	90.2	6.9	7.6	0.3	0.4	1.7	1.9	5.9	6.6	7.9	6.8	4.4	29.5	28.3	9.7	1.0	75.2	39.2	50.6	49.4
19736 YORKLYN	92.3	90.0	1.9	1.7	5.8	6.7	0.0	1.7	3.3	6.7	6.7	6.7	3.3	16.7	31.7	18.3	6.7	80.0	49.0	46.7	53.3
19801 WILMINGTON	12.6	11.8	81.7	82.1	0.6	0.7	6.8	7.2	8.1	8.0	8.6	7.7	8.0	28.1	20.4	9.5	1.6	70.7	32.1	45.7	54.3
19802 WILMINGTON	20.9	19.4	75.1	76.3	0.6	0.7	3.2	3.5	7.0	6.8	7.7	7.7	8.4	29.6	23.2	8.8	0.9	74.1	34.0	49.6	50.5
19803 WILMINGTON	92.4	91.0	3.7	4.1	2.9	3.8	1.5	1.8	5.2	5.9	6.3	5.3	3.8	21.9	29.2	19.1	3.4	79.1	46.0	47.7	52.3
19804 WILMINGTON	88.6	87.2	6.4	6.9	0.9	1.2	5.6	6.8	6.0	6.0	6.6	6.0	5.9	28.3	23.9	15.3	2.1	77.8	39.7	48.3	51.7
19805 WILMINGTON	59.9	57.4	26.7	27.6	0.9	1.1	18.5	20.9	7.5	7.1	7.6	7.1	7.4	29.8	21.0	10.4	2.0	73.4	34.3	48.3	51.7
19806 WILMINGTON	84.0	82.5	12.5	13.3	1.3	1.8	2.9	3.3	3.1	2.8	2.9	3.9	6.3	35.0	23.5	17.8	4.8	88.6	45.1	54.9
19807 WILMINGTON	89.9	87.9	4.8	5.5	3.7	4.7	2.3	2.8	5.0	5.6	5.4	5.3	3.7	20.4	30.0	18.7	5.9	80.2	48.0	47.0	53.0
19808 WILMINGTON	88.5	86.6	5.4	5.9	3.3	4.3	4.3	5.1	6.0	6.1	6.3	6.0	5.9	27.8	26.1	14.2	1.7	78.1	40.2	48.2	51.8
19809 WILMINGTON	80.5	78.2	14.7	15.9	2.6	3.4	2.3	2.8	5.9	6.2	6.6	6.2	5.1	30.0	25.6	12.1	2.2	77.3	39.2	47.6	52.4
19810 WILMINGTON	87.8	85.7	6.9	7.7	3.9	5.1	1.3	1.6	5.2	5.7	6.3	5.7	4.5	25.1	29.3	15.7	2.5	78.9	43.4	48.2	51.8
19901 DOVER	64.7	62.0	27.4	28.9	2.4	3.1	4.4	4.9	8.0	7.3	7.4	6.8	8.6	29.2	21.0	10.5	1.2	73.4	32.9	48.4	51.6
19902 DOVER AFB	72.8	70.5	16.5	17.5	2.2	2.9	7.3	8.4	15.4	10.3	7.2	7.4	21.1	36.7	1.9	0.0	0.0	64.3	22.3	54.7	45.3
19904 DOVER	63.4	61.8	29.8	30.3	2.7	3.5	3.2	3.6	6.7	6.4	7.0	9.3	8.8	26.4	22.5	11.0	2.0	75.7	34.8	47.4	52.6
19930 BETHANY BEACH	98.1	97.7	0.7	0.8	0.5	0.7	1.1	1.4	1.8	2.2	3.1	2.5	1.8	12.6	37.7	36.2	2.1	91.3	60.5	48.7	51.3
19931 BETHEL	83.9	82.5	13.0	13.7	0.9	1.3	2.2	2.1	8.1	8.1	6.8	6.0	6.0	30.3	22.7	10.7	1.3	73.1	35.9	47.0	53.0
19933 BRIDGEVILLE	66.6	63.8	27.0	28.9	0.6	0.7	6.5	7.7	8.0	7.7	8.3	7.3	6.7	27.6	22.8	10.4	1.3	71.5	35.0	48.5	51.5
19934 CAMDEN WYOMING	80.2	78.1	14.8	16.0	2.0	2.6	2.5	2.8	6.4	6.9	8.2	7.8	6.2	27.4	25.9	10.3	1.0	73.5	37.4	49.2	50.8
19938 CLAYTON	91.3	90.5	6.0	6.6	0.3	0.3	1.8	2.2	6.6	6.9	8.1	7.3	6.3	29.0	26.1	9.0	0.9	74.1	36.7	50.4	49.6
19939 DAGSBORO	86.7	86.0	10.6	11.0	0.7	0.9	2.1	2.5	5.0	5.1	5.5	4.9	4.3	22.5	29.7	21.6	1.4	81.4	47.0	47.8	52.2
19940 DELMAR	83.8	82.1	13.3	14.6	0.7	1.0	1.4	1.6	7.0	6.9	7.0	6.3	6.1	26.4	26.0	12.3	2.1	75.2	38.8	48.2	51.8
19941 ELLENDALE	62.5	59.2	33.0	35.7	0.1	0.2	4.4	5.0	6.8	7.1	8.1	7.5	6.6	29.0	23.7	10.4	0.8	73.1	36.3	48.5	51.5
19943 FELTON	84.0	82.6	12.2	13.0	0.9	1.1	2.1	2.4	6.8	6.9	7.5	7.4	6.0	29.5	25.8	9.3	0.7	74.1	36.6	48.8	51.2
19944 FENWICK ISLAND	98.1	97.9	0.6	0.7	0.5	0.7	1.1	1.4	1.8	2.1	3.1	2.5	1.8	12.4	37.9	36.2	2.1	91.2	60.5	48.7	51.3
19945 FRANKFORD	82.5	81.3	13.1	13.7	0.6	0.8	4.9	5.7	5.4	5.7	6.2	5.6	5.3	25.4	28.9	16.2	1.2	79.3	42.8	49.8	50.3
19946 FREDERICA	81.4	79.7	13.9	14.8	0.9	1.2	2.8	3.4	7.3	7.1	7.5	7.2	6.0	27.9	24.7	11.3	1.1	73.8	37.2	48.8	51.2
19947 GEORGETOWN	69.0	66.8	20.5	21.6	0.5	0.6	14.4	16.1	6.4	6.0	6.1	6.6	9.0	32.1	22.3	10.3	1.3	77.9	34.9	55.1	44.9
19950 GREENWOOD	84.8	83.4	12.3	13.1	0.7	1.0	2.0	2.4	7.2	7.3	7.5	6.4	5.3	27.8	24.6	12.2	1.7	73.9	37.6	49.4	50.6
19951 HARBESON	81.0	78.7	15.4	17.2	0.4	0.4	2.4	2.8	4.6	5.2	6.5	5.9	4.4	22.8	29.8	19.5	1.3	80.0	45.4	48.7	51.3
19952 HARRINGTON	83.1	81.8	13.7	14.6	0.5	0.7	2.1	2.4	7.7	7.4	7.8	6.9	6.3	27.2	24.3	11.5	1.1	72.8	36.3	47.5	52.5
19953 HARTLY	91.3	90.4	5.3	5.8	0.5	0.7	1.4	1.7	7.9	7.9	8.1	7.1	5.9	28.4	24.7	9.4	0.8	71.9	35.7	49.3	50.7
19954 HOUSTON	81.5	79.8	15.6	16.9	0.6	0.8	2.1	2.5	7.0	7.1	7.9	6.5	5.7	28.5	26.2	10.2	1.0	73.1	37.3	48.7	51.3
19956 LAUREL	81.6	79.9	14.9	16.0	1.0	1.4	1.7	2.1	7.5	7.3	7.3	6.5	6.2	27.5	24.3	12.1	1.3	73.9	37.0	48.3	51.7
19958 LEWES	90.0	88.7	6.9	7.6	0.9	1.1	1.5	1.8	4.5	4.7	4.6	4.2	3.8	20.3	30.8	24.6	2.6	83.6	50.3	47.4	52.6
19960 LINCOLN	68.3	66.3	27.1	28.4	0.5	0.7	4.9	5.7	6.2	6.7	8.6	7.4	6.2	26.2	25.9	11.7	1.2	73.9	38.2	48.7	51.3
19962 MAGNOLIA	74.6	72.1	18.8	20.3	1.8	2.3	3.8	4.3	9.1	8.5	8.9	8.4	7.5	30.3	19.8	7.1	0.6	68.5	31.2	48.8	51.2
19963 MILFORD	80.3	78.8	14.0	14.7	0.9	1.2	5.4	6.2	6.2	6.2	7.0	7.0	6.0	25.4	25.5	14.5	2.3	76.1	40.0	48.2	51.8
19964 MARYDEL	93.3	92.6	3.2	3.5	0.4	0.5	1.4	1.5	7.1	7.2	7.9	7.0	5.5	28.5	26.0	9.9	1.0	73.4	37.5	50.1	49.9
19966 MILLSBORO	82.1	80.7	12.6	13.4	0.7	0.9	2.8	3.4	4.8	4.8	5.6	5.0	4.6	21.5	28.2	23.5	1.9	81.6	47.6	47.8	52.3
19967 MILLVILLE	97.1	97.0	1.0	1.2	0.3	0.5	0.7	0.9	4.6	4.8	4.6	3.7	3.4	21.8	31.0	24.8	1.4	83.5	50.2	49.3	50.7
19968 MILTON	78.9	76.5	15.8	17.3	0.5	0.7	5.3	6.2	6.2	6.4	6.5	5.5	4.8	25.6	27.9	15.7	1.5	77.6	41.8	48.0	52.0
19970 OCEAN VIEW	97.8	97.4	0.8	0.9	0.4	0.5	0.9	1.1	3.7	3.9	4.0	3.3	2.7	17.3	33.7	29.7	1.6	86.3	55.7	48.7	51.3
19971 REHOBOTH BEACH	90.8	89.4	6.2	7.1	1.1	1.4	2.2	2.7	4.1	4.1	4.0	3.5	3.2	20.2	34.4	23.9	2.6	85.5	52.2	49.2	50.8
19973 SEAFORD	71.0	69.1	24.2	25.4	1.2	1.5	3.6	4.2	6.8	6.7	7.5	7.0	6.4	25.7	24.7	12.7	2.6	74.8	38.3	47.7	52.3
19975 SELBYVILLE	83.3	81.4	11.0	11.8	1.3	1.7	9.1	10.6	4.4	4.6	5.2	4.5	3.7	20.8	28.8	26.2	1.8	83.0	50.3	49.9	50.2
19977 SMYRNA	77.7	76.0	18.9	20.0	0.8	1.0	2.3	2.7	6.3	6.2	6.5	6.3	7.2	32.0	23.1	10.7	1.7	77.2	36.9	53.5	46.6
19979 VIOLA	81.7	79.9	14.3	15.3	1.0	1.3	2.9	3.2	5.7	6.1	7.5	7.2	7.0	26.1	27.2	12.1	1.1	76.4	39.1	48.6	51.4
DELAWARE	74.6	72.8	19.2	20.0	2.1	2.7	4.8	5.4	6.6	6.6	7.0	7.0	7.1	28.2	24.3	11.8	1.5	76.0	37.0	48.6	51.4
UNITED STATES	75.1	73.6	12.3	12.5	3.8	4.2	12.5	14.1	6.9	6.7	7.2	7.0	7.3	28.6	23.8	10.8	1.7	75.1	36.0	49.1	50.9

C   19701-19979

#	POST OFFICE NAME	2004 Per Capita Income	2004 HH Income Base	2004 HOUSEHOLD INCOME DISTRIBUTION (%)					MEDIAN HOUSEHOLD INCOME				2004 Home Value Base	2004 HOME VALUE DISTRIBUTION (%)					2004 Median Home Value
				Less than $25,000	$25,000 to $49,999	$50,000 to $99,999	$100,000 to $149,999	$150,000 or More	2004	2009	2004 National Centile	2004 State Centile		Less than $50,000	$50,000 to $89,999	$90,000 to $174,999	$175,000 to $399,999	$400,000 or More	
19701	BEAR	29660	12765	9.0	21.5	41.9	19.8	7.8	70798	84758	92	88	10140	9.6	3.5	25.8	59.5	1.7	194828
19702	NEWARK	29217	18009	10.8	22.8	42.1	18.4	5.9	65532	79786	89	81	12713	8.0	2.7	37.5	51.0	0.8	177618
19703	CLAYMONT	24705	6358	21.6	30.2	35.2	10.3	2.6	48194	57337	69	51	3439	1.7	4.5	53.7	39.5	0.5	164288
19707	HOCKESSIN	50779	5130	5.0	7.1	28.3	28.6	31.0	113493	136272	99	96	4771	0.6	0.4	2.3	71.3	25.4	330871
19709	MIDDLETOWN	29252	8171	11.5	16.9	38.1	24.8	8.8	77870	97764	94	91	7160	6.1	2.3	17.8	67.8	6.1	243506
19711	NEWARK	32546	20274	15.6	18.1	32.5	19.8	14.1	73376	89483	93	89	13989	0.8	2.1	22.7	66.4	8.0	218374
19713	NEWARK	27340	12711	15.9	26.3	39.0	13.7	5.1	57092	68614	82	75	8546	3.7	3.0	68.0	24.8	0.5	154195
19716	NEWARK	11158	34	52.9	26.5	11.8	8.8	0.0	23107	25000	3	2	6	0.0	0.0	33.3	66.7	0.0	183333
19720	NEW CASTLE	24014	22052	18.7	26.7	38.1	12.8	3.8	54497	66168	79	72	15852	1.9	6.3	63.0	27.9	0.9	144348
19734	TOWNSEND	27917	2187	13.2	20.6	44.3	16.1	5.9	64084	77716	88	79	1977	2.4	2.8	28.9	60.2	5.8	203916
19736	YORKLYN	55399	19	0.0	0.0	21.1	21.1	57.9	158242	165652	100	100	15	0.0	0.0	0.0	40.0	60.0	450000
19801	WILMINGTON	16288	5854	46.8	26.9	19.3	5.2	1.9	27147	32611	7	4	2064	9.1	31.9	49.5	9.5	0.1	100189
19802	WILMINGTON	20660	9943	31.5	27.6	27.5	9.3	4.2	40761	49734	49	12	5709	3.5	16.5	62.5	15.8	1.7	120181
19803	WILMINGTON	51889	8379	7.0	13.0	36.8	22.0	21.2	87607	107871	97	95	7568	0.3	0.3	9.7	72.3	17.5	251390
19804	WILMINGTON	25260	7447	16.9	29.0	40.9	11.6	1.6	53414	65009	78	68	5738	1.3	2.4	73.0	23.0	0.3	149292
19805	WILMINGTON	22686	15245	28.2	28.8	30.3	8.7	4.0	42322	51721	54	19	9501	2.3	14.8	67.0	13.3	2.6	124853
19806	WILMINGTON	57312	5719	17.7	29.0	25.5	12.9	14.8	53580	69845	78	70	2850	1.7	8.5	34.0	44.3	11.6	188088
19807	WILMINGTON	91269	3513	6.6	13.6	23.1	16.5	40.3	118443	149946	99	98	2688	0.0	0.2	4.9	29.2	65.7	542024
19808	WILMINGTON	34558	16210	12.0	20.4	38.8	18.3	10.4	68506	83952	91	86	13268	3.8	2.7	30.0	61.5	2.0	191163
19809	WILMINGTON	32887	6281	16.3	25.4	35.4	14.9	8.1	58023	70371	83	77	4495	1.6	7.7	34.6	53.5	2.7	184505
19810	WILMINGTON	40043	10126	9.5	18.5	35.2	20.7	16.1	79009	99230	95	93	8347	2.8	1.4	10.7	81.4	3.7	237518
19901	DOVER	23142	13200	27.0	30.9	29.2	9.1	3.9	42572	49716	55	23	8151	15.8	10.0	46.4	26.2	1.6	127187
19902	DOVER AFB	3730	21	19.1	42.9	33.3	4.8	0.0	38596	43612	41	7	0	0.0	0.0	0.0	0.0	0.0	0
19904	DOVER	23702	10988	22.6	27.6	33.8	11.4	4.7	49887	57906	72	60	7539	6.1	7.7	54.3	29.9	2.0	145243
19930	BETHANY BEACH	58502	1476	15.9	19.9	31.0	16.9	16.4	68191	99628	90	84	1309	2.2	0.1	10.4	53.9	33.4	310124
19931	BETHEL	22610	101	33.7	25.7	27.7	8.9	4.0	42340	48215	54	21	81	27.2	12.4	32.1	23.5	4.9	118056
19933	BRIDGEVILLE	16748	2543	33.5	33.9	25.2	5.4	2.0	34553	39153	26	5	1988	17.8	14.3	46.3	19.5	2.1	116754
19934	CAMDEN WYOMING	24448	3608	18.7	28.3	35.5	11.6	5.9	52159	61024	76	65	2997	9.4	7.5	45.9	30.4	6.7	144338
19938	CLAYTON	20523	2242	18.4	31.3	39.0	9.6	1.7	50214	58252	72	61	1982	11.2	9.9	50.1	27.3	1.5	136515
19939	DAGSBORO	26004	2127	23.3	28.7	34.2	9.2	4.6	47732	57947	68	49	1841	4.4	6.4	39.8	42.8	6.7	173474
19940	DELMAR	23309	1925	27.0	33.5	29.0	6.2	4.4	41893	46804	53	16	1514	13.1	12.4	48.6	23.4	2.4	122988
19941	ELLENDALE	19474	1049	26.8	33.1	32.8	5.4	1.9	42748	48648	55	28	870	24.3	15.6	38.7	20.1	1.3	108526
19943	FELTON	21286	3828	17.6	31.8	40.3	8.6	1.7	50342	58289	73	63	3315	14.4	9.4	48.4	26.6	1.2	131014
19944	FENWICK ISLAND	60719	376	16.0	20.0	30.9	16.8	16.5	67815	100000	90	82	334	2.4	0.0	10.5	53.6	33.5	309836
19945	FRANKFORD	22143	3487	24.1	33.0	32.5	7.4	3.0	42885	49878	56	30	2923	6.8	10.1	45.9	32.5	4.7	142787
19946	FREDERICA	23125	1551	25.7	29.2	35.1	8.3	1.7	45030	52697	61	39	1314	23.1	19.4	33.7	22.2	1.7	108639
19947	GEORGETOWN	19436	5177	25.8	30.2	32.7	7.5	3.8	44065	50628	59	37	4013	12.0	12.6	46.1	26.7	2.6	130241
19950	GREENWOOD	21544	2381	19.5	31.3	38.4	7.9	2.9	49388	56513	71	54	1957	7.7	9.2	48.5	30.4	4.3	137365
19951	HARBESON	20374	528	24.8	34.7	32.0	7.0	1.5	43555	50139	57	33	474	15.4	14.8	34.6	31.9	3.4	139844
19952	HARRINGTON	19628	3420	27.3	32.9	31.4	6.4	2.0	41769	48448	52	14	2677	11.0	18.5	47.6	21.1	1.9	118161
19953	HARTLY	21077	1573	20.2	32.8	34.4	8.2	4.5	46822	54951	66	46	1369	15.2	9.8	49.6	24.0	1.5	126095
19954	HOUSTON	20816	629	20.2	30.7	38.5	9.4	1.3	49445	57324	71	56	544	9.4	13.8	45.6	28.5	2.8	131048
19956	LAUREL	20092	5777	28.9	30.7	30.6	6.7	3.2	42737	49112	55	26	4620	17.1	13.9	42.0	24.1	2.9	125214
19958	LEWES	30842	7750	21.5	28.7	32.8	10.7	6.4	49839	59918	72	58	6702	13.0	8.3	18.7	48.7	11.3	201942
19960	LINCOLN	18361	1899	24.9	34.1	34.2	5.1	1.7	42204	48654	54	18	1626	15.3	7.5	56.3	19.7	1.2	130496
19962	MAGNOLIA	19532	2242	23.9	29.5	34.8	9.9	1.9	47023	54428	66	47	1801	22.8	8.1	31.2	36.8	1.2	148635
19963	MILFORD	22969	6785	27.0	29.7	31.8	8.1	3.4	42716	49730	55	25	4977	5.6	9.8	46.1	35.6	2.9	151339
19964	MARYDEL	20723	463	21.4	31.5	38.2	6.1	2.8	46521	53596	65	42	404	11.1	9.4	55.0	22.8	1.7	128358
19966	MILLSBORO	22593	8315	28.2	34.9	27.6	6.3	2.9	38912	45426	42	9	7084	23.7	16.5	38.0	19.1	2.7	108525
19967	MILLVILLE	27392	187	21.9	29.4	36.4	8.6	3.7	48509	57460	69	53	162	5.6	4.9	34.0	51.9	3.7	184783
19968	MILTON	23797	3252	25.1	31.1	30.9	9.0	4.1	45109	51321	61	40	2698	9.7	7.8	39.3	38.1	5.2	156972
19970	OCEAN VIEW	36843	2419	18.8	26.5	34.9	12.1	7.7	54677	68720	79	74	2172	3.3	3.5	25.2	56.5	11.5	217805
19971	REHOBOTH BEACH	42667	5519	19.8	27.9	29.2	10.9	12.3	52464	66854	76	67	4730	11.3	9.3	16.5	37.6	25.3	236504
19973	SEAFORD	20754	8901	30.2	29.9	28.9	7.8	3.2	40085	46515	46	11	6741	14.3	10.3	45.5	26.7	3.2	132773
19975	SELBYVILLE	26075	2928	23.2	33.7	31.7	8.3	3.1	43201	52160	56	32	2439	8.5	8.8	30.6	45.6	6.7	180701
19977	SMYRNA	21423	5167	23.6	29.6	34.1	9.3	3.4	46759	54197	66	44	3984	16.6	8.2	39.8	32.1	3.4	138663
19979	VIOLA	18735	241	24.5	34.4	34.4	6.2	0.4	43750	49236	58	35	206	28.2	12.6	40.8	18.0	0.5	114423
	DELAWARE	28477		19.6	25.7	34.1	13.2	7.3	54581	65195				7.3	7.1	39.1	41.1	5.4	167398
	UNITED STATES	25866		24.7	27.1	30.8	10.9	6.5	48124	56710				10.9	15.0	33.7	30.1	10.4	145905

# ZIP CODE POST OFFICE NAME	Auto Loan	Home Loan	Invest-ments	Retire-ment Plans	Home Repair	Lawn & Garden	Comput-ers & Hard-ware	Major Appli-ances	TV, Radio, Sound Equip-ment	Furni-ture	Dine out/ Carry out	Sports Equip-ment	Fees & Tickets	Toys & Games	Travel	Cable TV	Apparel & Services	Auto Repairs	Health Insur-ance	Pets & Supplies
19701 BEAR	119	128	126	133	122	121	120	119	112	124	143	140	122	141	117	105	140	118	104	131
19702 NEWARK	114	115	120	121	111	113	115	113	110	118	140	134	114	135	110	103	137	114	100	125
19703 CLAYMONT	76	80	92	80	79	85	83	80	82	81	102	94	84	104	83	81	100	82	78	88
19707 HOCKESSIN	190	234	267	239	229	234	210	207	194	212	246	239	229	255	215	190	247	200	187	228
19709 MIDDLETOWN	127	132	124	135	129	131	125	126	121	127	151	147	126	151	123	116	147	124	117	141
19711 NEWARK	118	123	142	127	120	127	131	122	125	127	158	147	131	156	127	119	155	126	113	135
19713 NEWARK	94	98	111	101	97	101	100	97	97	100	122	116	101	123	99	94	120	99	91	107
19716 NEWARK	48	29	37	33	29	35	57	42	55	48	69	58	46	62	45	48	65	51	39	47
19720 NEW CASTLE	86	91	97	91	89	94	90	89	88	90	111	103	92	112	90	87	109	89	85	99
19734 TOWNSEND	121	116	97	113	119	125	107	114	109	107	134	135	106	137	108	109	129	111	117	141
19736 YORKLYN	209	282	386	276	275	297	246	243	229	251	289	274	279	305	262	231	294	234	226	264
19801 WILMINGTON	53	48	61	47	46	54	55	52	58	55	73	59	55	71	54	60	71	55	55	59
19802 WILMINGTON	73	69	81	67	67	77	73	72	77	75	97	80	75	93	73	79	94	74	75	82
19803 WILMINGTON	162	198	233	194	195	206	182	182	174	183	219	207	195	226	190	174	217	178	173	197
19804 WILMINGTON	78	87	97	85	86	93	86	84	84	84	106	96	89	109	87	85	104	84	83	92
19805 WILMINGTON	77	80	94	79	78	85	83	80	83	82	104	93	84	106	83	83	102	82	79	88
19806 WILMINGTON	122	129	190	136	125	137	137	129	137	138	173	152	143	178	138	136	171	133	123	142
19807 WILMINGTON	268	337	443	335	331	355	306	303	288	310	363	344	336	375	320	288	364	295	284	330
19808 WILMINGTON	113	126	138	126	124	130	121	120	117	121	147	138	126	150	122	115	145	119	114	132
19809 WILMINGTON	95	109	128	110	108	112	107	104	103	106	129	122	111	133	108	100	127	104	98	114
19810 WILMINGTON	131	146	167	148	144	152	142	140	136	142	171	162	146	170	143	133	168	140	132	154
19901 DOVER	82	79	79	79	78	83	82	81	81	81	101	96	80	100	80	79	98	83	79	92
19902 DOVER AFB	76	48	46	55	44	52	72	62	73	67	91	82	61	81	59	66	87	73	57	70
19904 DOVER	87	89	94	89	88	92	89	89	87	89	109	104	89	108	88	85	107	89	85	99
19930 BETHANY BEACH	194	152	104	137	171	192	143	173	162	142	192	202	128	190	153	173	179	170	204	236
19931 BETHEL	92	70	41	63	77	86	66	78	75	67	90	94	60	88	68	80	83	77	92	107
19933 BRIDGEVILLE	72	60	47	57	62	69	61	66	66	61	80	77	57	77	60	67	75	66	71	81
19934 CAMDEN WYOMING	95	98	92	95	98	102	92	95	91	92	113	111	93	116	93	91	110	94	94	111
19938 CLAYTON	90	80	62	78	83	90	77	84	80	78	98	98	74	97	77	81	93	82	88	103
19939 DAGSBORO	93	86	79	82	90	105	83	92	88	85	108	95	83	98	87	93	102	90	105	105
19940 DELMAR	98	80	56	76	84	94	79	88	85	79	103	102	73	100	79	87	97	87	96	110
19941 ELLENDALE	88	79	61	76	79	84	75	81	77	77	94	94	71	90	74	76	90	81	82	97
19943 FELTON	87	83	70	81	84	88	78	83	78	79	97	97	76	95	78	78	93	82	82	99
19944 FENWICK ISLAND	194	152	104	137	171	192	143	173	162	142	192	202	128	190	153	173	179	170	204	236
19945 FRANKFORD	94	74	51	69	82	91	72	84	80	72	96	98	66	94	75	84	89	83	96	110
19946 FREDERICA	89	78	61	77	80	88	78	83	81	78	99	96	74	95	77	81	93	82	87	99
19947 GEORGETOWN	87	78	65	75	80	87	78	83	81	79	100	95	74	96	77	82	96	83	86	97
19950 GREENWOOD	91	81	64	78	85	93	78	85	82	78	100	99	76	101	79	84	95	83	91	105
19951 HARBESON	91	66	37	58	74	84	63	77	73	63	87	91	54	83	65	79	79	76	93	108
19952 HARRINGTON	81	70	56	68	73	79	70	75	74	70	90	88	66	88	70	75	85	75	80	91
19953 HARTLY	93	85	66	81	85	90	81	87	82	83	101	100	76	95	80	81	97	86	86	103
19954 HOUSTON	90	80	62	77	83	89	75	82	79	76	96	97	73	95	76	79	92	81	86	103
19956 LAUREL	84	72	55	68	76	83	70	76	75	70	91	89	67	90	71	77	86	75	84	96
19958 LEWES	107	93	79	86	101	116	86	101	94	90	115	107	83	103	93	101	107	99	119	125
19960 LINCOLN	84	67	47	64	71	80	67	75	73	67	88	87	62	85	67	75	82	74	83	94
19962 MAGNOLIA	84	84	75	83	83	85	80	83	78	82	98	97	78	95	79	75	95	82	77	95
19963 MILFORD	87	76	63	74	79	87	77	82	81	76	98	95	73	97	77	82	93	81	88	98
19964 MARYDEL	91	76	54	71	79	85	73	81	77	75	94	95	67	89	72	78	89	81	86	102
19966 MILLSBORO	85	68	50	63	75	86	66	78	74	67	88	87	61	83	69	78	82	76	91	99
19967 MILLVILLE	108	85	59	77	96	108	80	96	91	80	108	112	72	106	86	97	100	95	114	131
19968 MILTON	98	76	51	72	84	95	76	87	84	75	101	101	69	97	77	88	93	86	101	113
19970 OCEAN VIEW	127	106	83	97	116	133	99	117	109	101	132	129	93	123	106	117	123	114	138	150
19971 REHOBOTH BEACH	140	116	88	106	128	146	108	129	120	110	145	144	101	136	116	129	135	126	152	168
19973 SEAFORD	82	71	59	69	74	82	72	77	77	71	94	89	69	93	72	78	89	76	83	92
19975 SELBYVILLE	94	78	65	73	84	98	76	87	84	79	102	93	73	91	80	89	95	86	102	107
19977 SMYRNA	90	80	66	79	83	90	80	85	83	79	102	99	77	101	80	84	97	84	89	101
19979 VIOLA	78	71	55	68	71	75	67	72	68	69	84	84	64	80	67	68	81	72	73	87
DELAWARE	104	103	104	102	103	110	102	103	102	102	127	120	102	126	102	102	123	104	103	119
UNITED STATES	100	100	100	100	100	100	100	100	100	100	100	100	100	100	100	100	100	100	100	100

ZIP CODE		COUNTY FIPS CODE	POPULATION			2000-2004 ANNUAL RATE		HOUSEHOLDS					FAMILIES		
#	POST OFFICE NAME		2000	2004	2009	% Rate	State Centile	2000	2004	2009	% Annual Rate 2000-2004	2004 Average HH Size	2000	2004	% Annual Rate 2000-2004
20001	WASHINGTON	001	33660	35037	35500	1.0	92	12018	12753	13086	1.4	2.35	5769	6098	1.3
20002	WASHINGTON	001	49657	48885	48325	-0.4	46	21179	20960	20852	-0.2	2.24	10187	10154	-0.1
20003	WASHINGTON	001	23122	22504	22041	-0.6	29	10195	9990	9848	-0.5	1.96	4031	3961	-0.4
20004	WASHINGTON	001	901	976	1005	1.9	100	694	764	795	2.3	1.21	199	214	1.7
20005	WASHINGTON	001	10638	11054	11168	0.9	88	6290	6522	6609	0.9	1.67	1393	1459	1.1
20006	WASHINGTON	001	2501	2575	2606	0.7	83	784	845	873	1.8	1.29	50	55	2.3
20007	WASHINGTON	001	24047	23641	23265	-0.4	42	12383	12231	12112	-0.3	1.86	4130	4104	-0.2
20008	WASHINGTON	001	26181	26068	25814	-0.1	63	15979	15963	15901	0.0	1.61	4587	4628	0.2
20009	WASHINGTON	001	46501	47179	47223	0.3	75	24961	25522	25754	0.5	1.80	6768	7005	0.8
20010	WASHINGTON	001	30294	30030	29638	-0.2	50	11363	11272	11174	-0.2	2.62	5753	5733	-0.1
20011	WASHINGTON	001	56363	55222	54235	-0.5	38	22394	22066	21823	-0.4	2.48	13033	12878	-0.3
20012	WASHINGTON	001	13459	13011	12719	-0.8	21	5498	5343	5258	-0.7	2.29	3269	3180	-0.7
20015	WASHINGTON	001	15824	15427	15115	-0.6	33	6177	6031	5932	-0.6	2.31	3678	3600	-0.5
20016	WASHINGTON	001	31134	30874	30520	-0.2	54	13837	13855	13812	0.0	1.95	6136	6134	0.0
20017	WASHINGTON	001	17260	16653	16247	-0.8	13	7005	6788	6662	-0.7	2.27	3818	3722	-0.6
20018	WASHINGTON	001	16552	16002	15631	-0.8	21	6898	6730	6630	-0.6	2.28	3769	3693	-0.5
20019	WASHINGTON	001	53260	50995	49617	-1.0	4	21453	20645	20220	-0.9	2.44	13122	12691	-0.8
20020	WASHINGTON	001	49432	50255	50395	0.4	79	19242	19519	19634	0.3	2.55	12063	12369	0.6
20024	WASHINGTON	001	11856	12797	13318	1.8	96	6896	7287	7521	1.3	1.72	2272	2534	2.6
20032	WASHINGTON	001	36922	35507	34653	-0.9	8	12917	12460	12224	-0.8	2.68	8760	8467	-0.8
20036	WASHINGTON	001	4169	4037	3941	-0.8	25	3182	3104	3053	-0.6	1.25	371	366	-0.3
20037	WASHINGTON	001	12267	12170	12041	-0.2	58	7002	6966	6918	-0.1	1.38	1026	1034	0.2
20057	WASHINGTON	001	4467	4472	4474	0.0	71	28	30	31	1.6	2.77	8	9	2.8
20064	WASHINGTON	001	1753	1751	1749	0.0	67	38	37	35	-0.6	1.46	1	1	0.0
DISTRICT OF COLUMBIA						-0.2					-0.1	2.15			0.0
UNITED STATES						1.2					1.3	2.58			1.1

#	POST OFFICE NAME	White 2000	White 2004	Black 2000	Black 2004	Asian/Pacific 2000	Asian/Pacific 2004	% Hispanic Origin 2000	% Hispanic Origin 2004	0-4	5-9	10-14	15-19	20-24	25-44	45-64	65-84	85+	18+	MEDIAN AGE 2004	% 2004 Males	% 2004 Females
20001	WASHINGTON	8.9	10.8	81.9	77.1	3.1	4.0	7.4	10.7	5.5	5.6	6.6	9.7	11.5	29.3	21.3	9.2	1.3	78.9	32.3	47.8	52.2
20002	WASHINGTON	18.1	19.1	78.1	76.1	0.9	1.2	2.2	3.2	5.8	5.7	6.5	6.0	6.8	32.1	24.6	10.8	1.8	78.6	37.0	47.5	52.5
20003	WASHINGTON	40.5	41.9	54.7	52.1	1.8	2.2	3.1	4.4	4.5	3.9	4.2	5.5	7.7	40.0	24.9	8.4	0.9	84.8	36.4	54.2	45.8
20004	WASHINGTON	50.4	48.4	13.8	10.9	33.5	38.3	4.2	5.5	1.6	1.5	2.5	3.8	6.9	35.0	31.1	14.7	3.0	92.9	44.3	52.1	48.0
20005	WASHINGTON	44.7	45.8	30.1	24.2	7.3	8.5	25.2	32.4	3.6	2.7	3.4	4.0	11.4	46.4	19.2	7.5	1.8	88.4	33.7	59.0	41.0
20006	WASHINGTON	73.4	71.6	7.5	6.1	15.5	18.2	4.8	6.4	0.2	0.0	0.0	43.1	37.2	12.8	3.3	2.8	0.6	99.5	20.9	44.6	55.4
20007	WASHINGTON	86.5	85.8	3.8	3.1	5.9	6.9	6.1	8.2	3.7	2.6	2.3	4.6	11.1	41.1	23.4	9.6	1.7	89.9	34.7	46.4	53.6
20008	WASHINGTON	84.5	83.9	5.4	4.3	6.0	7.0	6.6	9.0	2.7	2.3	2.6	3.1	6.7	41.5	27.2	11.6	2.4	90.4	39.4	44.3	55.7
20009	WASHINGTON	49.2	50.4	31.1	25.7	4.5	5.2	20.3	26.4	4.4	3.5	3.8	3.9	8.6	48.9	20.5	5.6	0.9	86.2	33.6	52.5	47.5
20010	WASHINGTON	23.2	25.1	47.5	39.2	3.7	4.1	32.8	41.5	6.9	6.2	6.3	5.8	7.9	37.4	20.9	7.5	1.3	77.3	33.4	50.9	49.1
20011	WASHINGTON	7.7	9.9	81.0	74.8	0.7	1.0	12.6	17.8	5.6	5.9	6.2	5.8	5.8	27.7	26.2	14.6	2.3	78.9	40.6	46.1	53.9
20012	WASHINGTON	16.8	19.1	74.0	68.7	1.5	1.9	8.0	11.4	4.2	4.7	5.2	5.2	6.3	26.7	29.5	16.1	2.1	82.8	43.5	46.5	53.5
20015	WASHINGTON	82.5	82.7	9.5	8.0	4.1	5.0	4.8	6.6	5.3	5.8	5.3	4.8	3.3	24.0	29.3	17.5	4.8	80.3	46.0	48.8	51.3
20016	WASHINGTON	83.9	83.6	5.9	4.9	5.1	6.0	6.9	9.3	4.0	4.0	3.7	9.1	8.8	29.2	25.2	12.9	3.1	86.0	38.6	43.5	56.5
20017	WASHINGTON	13.4	15.1	81.8	78.6	1.2	1.6	3.1	4.4	4.6	4.7	5.8	6.0	6.5	26.4	26.8	16.3	2.9	81.6	42.3	45.7	54.3
20018	WASHINGTON	3.0	3.6	93.8	92.1	0.6	0.8	2.2	3.1	5.2	5.5	6.7	6.2	5.2	23.3	26.5	18.2	3.3	78.7	43.6	44.3	55.7
20019	WASHINGTON	0.7	0.9	97.7	97.0	0.2	0.3	0.9	1.2	7.5	8.0	8.9	7.2	6.1	25.5	23.2	11.9	1.7	71.0	35.4	43.6	56.4
20020	WASHINGTON	1.8	2.0	96.6	95.9	0.2	0.3	0.9	1.2	8.9	9.6	10.0	7.5	6.4	27.0	21.1	8.8	0.8	66.9	30.8	43.6	56.4
20024	WASHINGTON	26.3	26.8	64.8	62.4	2.7	3.4	4.4	6.1	4.5	5.0	5.2	4.7	5.4	30.7	29.8	13.2	1.5	82.2	41.4	47.5	52.5
20032	WASHINGTON	9.3	9.4	87.5	86.9	0.8	1.0	1.9	2.4	10.0	9.6	10.1	8.0	8.0	28.8	18.8	6.3	0.5	65.7	28.1	45.8	54.2
20036	WASHINGTON	80.3	79.5	6.7	5.4	8.3	9.8	6.9	9.2	1.1	0.4	0.2	1.2	13.2	53.9	21.4	7.1	1.4	98.0	34.0	51.9	48.1
20037	WASHINGTON	79.0	78.0	6.6	5.3	10.7	12.5	5.8	7.9	0.8	0.4	0.3	14.4	23.4	28.9	18.4	11.3	2.1	98.2	29.5	45.6	54.4
20057	WASHINGTON	87.9	87.6	5.4	4.5	6.7	7.8	1.7	2.4	0.1	0.0	0.0	59.3	38.1	1.1	0.7	0.5	0.3	99.2	19.2	45.5	54.5
20064	WASHINGTON	89.1	88.8	4.6	3.8	3.8	4.6	4.6	6.1	0.0	0.1	0.0	52.5	28.2	9.2	3.8	3.6	2.7	99.5	19.8	50.7	49.3
	DISTRICT OF COLUMBIA	30.8	31.6	60.0	57.0	2.7	3.3	7.9	10.6	5.6	5.5	6.0	7.1	8.2	32.1	23.2	10.6	1.7	79.8	35.4	47.1	52.9
	UNITED STATES	75.1	73.6	12.3	12.5	3.8	4.2	12.5	14.1	6.9	6.7	7.2	7.0	7.3	28.6	23.8	10.8	1.7	75.1	36.0	49.1	50.9

#	POST OFFICE NAME	2004 Per Capita Income	2004 HH Income Base	2004 HOUSEHOLD INCOME DISTRIBUTION (%)					MEDIAN HOUSEHOLD INCOME				2004 Home Value Base	2004 HOME VALUE DISTRIBUTION (%)					2004 Median Home Value
				Less than $25,000	$25,000 to $49,999	$50,000 to $99,999	$100,000 to $149,999	$150,000 or More	2004	2009	2004 National Centile	2004 State Centile		Less than $50,000	$50,000 to $89,999	$90,000 to $174,999	$175,000 to $399,999	$400,000 or More	
20001	WASHINGTON	18330	12753	43.5	25.7	20.5	7.0	3.3	30271	36307	13	21	4034	1.2	0.6	22.7	61.6	14.0	231430
20002	WASHINGTON	26780	20960	30.4	29.3	24.5	10.3	5.6	40382	47393	47	38	10021	0.4	1.6	32.7	49.5	15.9	209961
20003	WASHINGTON	39898	9990	24.3	21.0	26.4	15.3	13.1	58446	69563	83	71	4577	0.7	0.4	11.7	47.7	39.5	337678
20004	WASHINGTON	73289	764	41.2	10.7	21.2	10.6	16.2	47736	59196	68	54	193	0.0	0.0	0.0	54.4	45.6	315000
20005	WASHINGTON	33687	6522	33.9	28.0	23.3	9.7	5.1	37447	46198	37	29	1404	2.0	7.7	14.3	43.7	32.3	293447
20006	WASHINGTON	14558	845	67.8	24.9	4.1	1.7	1.5	11328	14109	1	8	54	0.0	38.9	40.7	11.1	9.3	92727
20007	WASHINGTON	79767	12231	14.3	17.1	24.5	16.4	27.8	84459	106802	96	88	5969	0.2	1.0	7.9	16.0	74.9	678704
20008	WASHINGTON	83441	15963	11.1	18.9	30.1	17.4	22.5	80021	98494	95	83	6309	0.0	1.5	7.8	28.0	62.6	580984
20009	WASHINGTON	41908	25522	24.7	26.9	27.6	10.5	10.3	48479	58390	69	58	7318	0.3	1.8	12.7	39.2	46.0	370518
20010	WASHINGTON	21611	11272	32.6	29.2	23.0	10.0	5.2	38137	46054	40	33	3726	1.1	1.2	18.1	53.2	26.4	262082
20011	WASHINGTON	25792	22066	25.8	30.0	27.2	11.3	5.7	44657	51755	60	50	12676	0.8	1.0	12.7	72.9	12.8	234730
20012	WASHINGTON	38673	5343	18.1	21.9	27.2	19.0	13.8	66155	77260	89	79	3705	0.3	0.4	7.3	47.8	44.2	372558
20015	WASHINGTON	63841	6031	9.5	11.7	20.7	21.9	36.2	114570	144380	99	100	4570	0.2	0.3	3.5	5.4	90.7	663330
20016	WASHINGTON	75183	13855	12.2	15.2	25.3	17.7	29.7	93106	114022	97	92	8421	0.1	0.5	7.9	18.4	73.2	625312
20017	WASHINGTON	26897	6788	23.2	28.0	32.8	11.4	4.6	48987	56313	70	63	4301	0.3	1.3	16.7	77.8	3.9	226066
20018	WASHINGTON	24393	6730	31.0	25.1	28.7	11.0	4.2	42570	51402	55	46	4102	0.6	0.6	22.8	71.6	4.4	230277
20019	WASHINGTON	17044	20645	41.6	30.6	21.0	5.2	1.6	31164	35608	15	25	8712	0.7	2.3	56.0	39.1	1.9	165266
20020	WASHINGTON	16700	19519	43.0	30.3	19.7	5.5	1.6	29645	32890	12	17	6715	1.6	4.3	39.5	49.7	4.9	184750
20024	WASHINGTON	30473	7287	31.4	27.9	29.2	7.4	4.1	41444	46888	51	42	2570	2.5	8.3	35.0	45.3	9.0	188568
20032	WASHINGTON	16153	12460	42.8	30.4	19.4	5.0	2.4	29214	32490	11	13	3468	1.8	3.3	56.4	37.8	0.7	165060
20036	WASHINGTON	73679	3104	16.8	24.7	30.1	15.0	13.4	61233	74838	86	75	933	0.0	8.4	23.4	36.6	31.7	244423
20037	WASHINGTON	57550	6966	28.5	20.4	24.4	13.1	13.5	51381	63457	75	67	2100	0.0	2.5	25.0	33.9	38.6	300000
20057	WASHINGTON	12886	30	0.0	0.0	50.0	13.3	36.7	100000	117288	98	96	17	0.0	0.0	0.0	52.9	47.1	246875
20064	WASHINGTON	12215	37	83.8	0.0	16.2	0.0	0.0	6607	7292	0	4	0	0.0	0.0	0.0	0.0	0.0	0
	DISTRICT OF COLUMBIA	34983		28.5	25.6	24.7	11.1	10.1	45445	53484				0.6	1.8	21.7	44.7	31.2	256143
	UNITED STATES	25866		24.7	27.1	30.8	10.9	6.5	48124	56710				10.9	15.0	33.7	30.1	10.4	145905

# POST OFFICE NAME	FINANCIAL SERVICES				THE HOME						ENTERTAINMENT						PERSONAL			
					Home Improvements		Furnishings													
	Auto Loan	Home Loan	Invest-ments	Retire-ment Plans	Home Repair	Lawn & Garden	Comput-ers & Hard-ware	Major Appli-ances	TV, Radio, Sound Equip-ment	Furni-ture	Dine out/ Carry out	Sports Equip-ment	Fees & Tickets	Toys & Games	Travel	Cable TV	Apparel & Services	Auto Repairs	Health Insur-ance	Pets & Supplies
20001 WASHINGTON	62	55	71	54	53	62	63	60	67	63	84	69	63	81	61	69	82	63	63	68
20002 WASHINGTON	83	76	102	76	73	86	84	81	90	86	113	92	86	109	83	93	110	85	85	92
20003 WASHINGTON	113	104	158	110	100	114	119	110	124	121	156	130	121	156	116	125	153	117	110	125
20004 WASHINGTON	117	112	211	129	106	119	132	117	136	135	172	144	138	181	130	134	171	126	109	131
20005 WASHINGTON	68	67	127	73	63	72	80	71	84	80	106	86	82	114	79	85	106	77	68	79
20006 WASHINGTON	32	20	25	22	19	23	38	28	37	32	46	39	31	41	30	32	43	34	26	32
20007 WASHINGTON	192	196	338	217	188	208	219	199	220	222	280	240	230	292	218	219	278	209	186	220
20008 WASHINGTON	171	167	308	190	159	177	194	173	198	197	251	211	203	264	192	196	250	184	161	193
20009 WASHINGTON	93	91	175	101	86	98	108	96	113	109	144	117	112	153	108	114	143	103	92	107
20010 WASHINGTON	66	68	126	69	64	75	78	71	84	79	107	83	81	116	80	88	107	76	71	79
20011 WASHINGTON	84	84	109	81	82	94	88	85	92	89	116	94	91	116	89	96	114	88	89	96
20012 WASHINGTON	120	131	156	126	128	143	128	126	129	130	163	139	135	163	132	133	160	127	129	141
20015 WASHINGTON	194	238	354	242	230	248	228	218	220	232	278	253	250	296	236	221	280	218	201	237
20016 WASHINGTON	204	228	354	240	220	242	233	219	230	237	291	258	250	303	238	230	291	224	206	241
20017 WASHINGTON	87	83	96	81	82	94	88	86	92	89	115	95	90	110	88	94	111	88	91	98
20018 WASHINGTON	78	73	84	70	72	84	77	77	82	78	103	83	79	98	78	86	99	79	84	87
20019 WASHINGTON	58	52	61	48	50	59	56	56	62	58	77	61	57	73	56	64	74	57	61	64
20020 WASHINGTON	58	52	65	49	50	59	58	56	63	60	79	63	59	76	57	65	77	59	60	64
20024 WASHINGTON	68	65	100	68	62	71	73	68	76	74	96	80	75	97	72	77	94	72	68	76
20032 WASHINGTON	61	53	64	51	50	59	60	58	65	61	82	66	60	79	58	67	79	61	60	66
20036 WASHINGTON	120	115	216	132	108	122	136	120	139	138	177	148	142	186	133	138	176	129	112	134
20037 WASHINGTON	122	114	211	131	108	121	138	121	141	139	179	150	142	186	134	139	177	131	113	135
20057 WASHINGTON	175	107	135	121	105	127	207	152	201	175	251	212	169	225	165	177	235	186	141	173
20064 WASHINGTON	21	13	16	14	12	15	25	18	24	21	30	25	20	27	20	21	28	22	17	21
DISTRICT OF COLUMBIA	102	98	146	100	94	108	109	102	114	110	144	118	112	145	108	116	141	107	103	115
UNITED STATES	100	100	100	100	100	100	100	100	100	100	100	100	100	100	100	100	100	100	100	100

ZIP CODE		COUNTY FIPS CODE	POPULATION			2000-2004 ANNUAL RATE		HOUSEHOLDS					FAMILIES		
#	POST OFFICE NAME		2000	2004	2009	% Rate	State Centile	2000	2004	2009	% Annual Rate 2000-2004	2004 Average HH Size	2000	2004	% Annual Rate 2000-2004
32003	ORANGE PARK	019	13097	16236	19907	5.2	91	4275	5339	6600	5.4	3.03	3701	4597	5.2
32008	BRANFORD	067	3543	3908	4244	2.3	62	1427	1584	1733	2.5	2.45	1016	1117	2.3
32009	BRYCEVILLE	089	3095	3406	3829	2.3	61	1069	1181	1337	2.4	2.88	898	985	2.2
32011	CALLAHAN	089	11276	12013	13325	1.5	42	4084	4370	4880	1.6	2.75	3233	3441	1.5
32013	DAY	067	2181	2249	2306	0.7	20	380	409	433	1.8	2.59	282	301	1.6
32024	LAKE CITY	023	17332	19031	20818	2.2	60	6406	7117	7870	2.5	2.67	4987	5496	2.3
32025	LAKE CITY	023	17681	18593	20112	1.2	33	6271	6668	7339	1.5	2.48	4199	4435	1.3
32033	ELKTON	109	2090	2282	2706	2.1	57	822	908	1084	2.4	2.51	628	682	2.0
32034	FERNANDINA BEACH	089	24786	28519	32893	3.4	78	10230	11889	13850	3.6	2.38	7257	8404	3.5
32038	FORT WHITE	023	5040	5554	6089	2.3	61	1979	2210	2456	2.6	2.51	1426	1577	2.4
32040	GLEN SAINT MARY	003	6507	6882	7488	1.3	37	2208	2366	2614	1.6	2.78	1787	1906	1.5
32043	GREEN COVE SPRINGS	019	19694	22890	27191	3.6	80	7283	8575	10317	3.9	2.61	5561	6507	3.8
32044	HAMPTON	007	2165	2313	2462	1.6	44	805	869	935	1.8	2.63	599	643	1.7
32046	HILLIARD	089	7756	8340	9286	1.7	48	2722	2942	3303	1.9	2.77	2149	2308	1.7
32052	JASPER	047	8113	8616	9147	1.4	41	2187	2422	2676	2.4	2.54	1552	1706	2.3
32053	JENNINGS	047	3485	3742	4022	1.7	47	1271	1388	1516	2.1	2.68	949	1029	1.9
32054	LAKE BUTLER	125	10718	11138	11694	0.9	26	3035	3228	3479	1.5	2.71	2339	2473	1.3
32055	LAKE CITY	023	15720	16550	17814	1.3	35	5972	6416	7014	1.7	2.45	4098	4357	1.5
32058	LAWTEY	007	5184	5207	5322	0.1	5	1081	1102	1157	0.5	2.78	814	825	0.3
32059	LEE	079	1549	1653	1790	1.5	43	620	674	743	2.0	2.45	448	483	1.8
32060	LIVE OAK	121	17435	18508	19726	1.4	40	6803	7290	7840	1.6	2.48	4880	5188	1.5
32061	LULU	023	354	429	496	4.6	89	137	170	200	5.2	2.52	101	124	5.0
32062	MC ALPIN	121	2306	2486	2670	1.8	50	867	943	1021	2.0	2.63	661	715	1.9
32063	MACCLENNY	003	10893	12013	13369	2.3	62	3614	4065	4610	2.8	2.78	2822	3158	2.7
32064	LIVE OAK	121	6152	6345	6666	0.7	20	2263	2358	2501	1.0	2.61	1568	1619	0.8
32065	ORANGE PARK	019	16973	18226	20822	1.7	47	5928	6466	7478	2.1	2.82	4738	5125	1.9
32066	MAYO	067	4167	4416	4627	1.4	39	1486	1591	1681	1.6	2.69	1102	1172	1.5
32068	MIDDLEBURG	019	36108	43149	52056	4.3	86	12330	14892	18142	4.5	2.89	10200	12248	4.4
32071	O BRIEN	121	3007	3057	3228	0.4	12	1206	1236	1316	0.6	2.47	884	899	0.4
32073	ORANGE PARK	019	41282	45795	53279	2.5	66	15259	17138	20188	2.8	2.61	11330	12614	2.6
32080	SAINT AUGUSTINE	109	16832	19611	24108	3.7	81	8012	9495	11791	4.1	2.06	4925	5718	3.6
32082	PONTE VEDRA BEACH	109	28287	33469	41273	4.0	84	12101	14431	17887	4.2	2.31	8241	9636	3.8
32083	RAIFORD	125	2707	2824	2930	1.0	27	325	372	416	3.2	2.85	261	297	3.1
32084	SAINT AUGUSTINE	109	22828	25759	31066	2.9	71	9103	10447	12788	3.3	2.34	5483	6189	2.9
32086	SAINT AUGUSTINE	109	19512	21641	25837	2.5	66	7883	8862	10691	2.8	2.39	5477	6065	2.4
32087	SANDERSON	003	4692	4963	5348	1.3	37	1161	1260	1401	1.9	3.05	942	1018	1.8
32091	STARKE	007	15413	16173	17086	1.1	32	5220	5557	5966	1.5	2.60	3782	3996	1.3
32092	SAINT AUGUSTINE	109	6528	8279	10626	5.8	93	2463	3174	4112	6.2	2.60	1848	2357	5.9
32094	WELLBORN	121	2153	2558	2887	4.1	85	843	1012	1151	4.4	2.53	633	754	4.2
32095	SAINT AUGUSTINE	109	5284	5804	6873	2.2	60	1922	2152	2589	2.7	2.57	1350	1487	2.3
32096	WHITE SPRINGS	047	2501	2708	2936	1.9	53	994	1097	1210	2.4	2.44	709	778	2.2
32097	YULEE	089	10638	11749	13229	2.4	63	3837	4285	4879	2.6	2.69	2963	3291	2.5
32102	ASTOR	069	2385	2557	2956	1.7	46	1113	1192	1375	1.6	2.13	764	807	1.3
32110	BUNNELL	035	6232	8030	11101	6.2	94	2344	3089	4347	6.7	2.55	1772	2318	6.5
32112	CRESCENT CITY	107	9091	9618	10178	1.3	37	3605	3817	4058	1.4	2.49	2446	2566	1.1
32113	CITRA	083	5596	6121	6943	2.1	58	2122	2381	2766	2.8	2.34	1545	1716	2.5
32114	DAYTONA BEACH	127	35264	36642	39561	0.9	26	14480	15219	16619	1.2	2.11	6813	6932	0.4
32117	DAYTONA BEACH	127	23605	24071	25781	0.5	13	9919	10125	10841	0.5	2.32	5772	5772	0.0
32118	DAYTONA BEACH	127	18860	20110	21965	1.5	43	10098	10770	11756	1.5	1.86	4756	4994	1.2
32119	DAYTONA BEACH	127	21864	22484	24115	0.7	18	10218	10513	11272	0.7	2.12	6152	6230	0.3
32124	DAYTONA BEACH	127	4167	4271	4421	0.6	17	439	468	509	1.5	3.64	322	338	1.2
32127	PORT ORANGE	127	29034	31411	34689	1.9	53	12494	13472	14849	1.8	2.30	8409	9000	1.6
32128	PORT ORANGE	127	8682	11981	14826	7.9	98	3716	5015	6218	8.0	2.39	2858	3915	7.7
32129	PORT ORANGE	127	18391	20275	22537	2.3	61	8349	9246	10295	2.4	2.18	5234	5679	1.9
32130	DE LEON SPRINGS	127	4835	5794	6697	4.4	87	1648	1950	2239	4.0	2.95	1227	1436	3.8
32131	EAST PALATKA	107	5164	5108	5227	-0.3	2	1879	1878	1947	0.0	2.50	1352	1342	-0.2
32132	EDGEWATER	127	7145	7448	8068	1.0	27	3038	3159	3418	0.9	2.35	2042	2093	0.6
32134	FORT MC COY	083	9353	10166	11554	2.0	55	4027	4419	5072	2.2	2.28	2718	2954	2.0
32136	FLAGLER BEACH	035	7006	9072	12534	6.3	95	3519	4588	6400	6.4	1.98	2225	2876	6.2
32137	PALM COAST	035	21632	28059	38965	6.3	95	9362	12310	17311	6.7	2.26	6931	9036	6.4
32139	GEORGETOWN	107	794	828	867	1.0	27	382	399	420	1.0	2.08	259	268	0.8
32140	FLORAHOME	107	1638	1733	1828	1.3	38	619	658	699	1.5	2.63	473	499	1.3
32141	EDGEWATER	127	15659	17306	19189	2.4	63	6495	7199	7988	2.5	2.40	4818	5274	2.2
32145	HASTINGS	109	3962	4666	5744	3.9	83	1399	1656	2048	4.1	2.79	1017	1192	3.8
32148	INTERLACHEN	107	12437	13669	14721	2.2	60	4843	5342	5794	2.3	2.56	3448	3775	2.2
32159	LADY LAKE	069	26199	33307	43288	5.8	93	13110	17033	22513	6.4	1.95	9711	12542	6.2
32162	LADY LAKE	119	3166	4480	6052	8.5	99	1661	2391	3287	9.0	1.87	1279	1820	8.7
32164	PALM COAST	035	14156	18875	26571	7.0	96	5703	7666	10895	7.2	2.45	4473	5982	7.1
32168	NEW SMYRNA BEACH	127	20507	21592	23431	1.2	34	9063	9497	10272	1.1	2.27	5855	6061	0.8
32169	NEW SMYRNA BEACH	127	10648	11167	12043	1.1	31	5319	5590	6032	1.2	1.97	3231	3339	0.8
32174	ORMOND BEACH	127	40311	44714	50258	2.5	66	17006	18924	21321	2.6	2.29	11687	12912	2.4
32176	ORMOND BEACH	127	16030	16466	17700	0.6	18	7899	8120	8720	0.7	2.02	4801	4855	0.3
32177	PALATKA	107	24467	24656	25543	0.2	7	9366	9566	10025	0.5	2.50	6544	6638	0.3
32179	OCKLAWAHA	083	8855	9648	11039	2.0	56	3690	4042	4660	2.2	2.38	2549	2762	1.9
32180	PIERSON	127	4892	5370	5885	2.2	60	1259	1413	1577	2.8	3.07	914	1015	2.5
32181	POMONA PARK	107	1409	1459	1519	0.8	23	603	628	658	1.0	2.31	411	425	0.8
32187	SAN MATEO	107	1537	1553	1603	0.2	8	635	649	677	0.5	2.39	444	450	0.3
32189	SATSUMA	107	5775	6149	6508	1.5	42	2581	2765	2948	1.6	2.22	1767	1877	1.4
32190	SEVILLE	127	1182	1250	1353	1.3	37	398	419	453	1.2	2.92	286	298	1.0
32195	WEIRSDALE	083	2928	3282	3808	2.7	69	1120	1270	1488	3.0	2.56	845	950	2.8
32202	JACKSONVILLE	031	5122	5166	5363	0.2	8	1413	1505	1653	1.5	1.66	315	317	0.2
32204	JACKSONVILLE	031	6978	7301	7890	1.1	30	3044	3291	3649	1.9	1.97	1231	1292	1.1
32205	JACKSONVILLE	031	29896	30226	32008	0.3	9	13254	13564	14520	0.6	2.22	7331	7368	0.1
32206	JACKSONVILLE	031	21240	21168	22342	-0.1	4	8309	8394	8970	0.2	2.44	4730	4684	-0.2
32207	JACKSONVILLE	031	35195	35882	38141	0.5	13	15783	16292	17507	0.8	2.18	8882	9005	0.3
32208	JACKSONVILLE	031	34657	35377	37582	0.5	14	12922	13391	14401	0.8	2.62	8926	9127	0.5
32209	JACKSONVILLE	031	38556	38466	40697	-0.1	4	14885	15051	16110	0.3	2.54	9777	9732	-0.1
32210	JACKSONVILLE	031	56797	59819	64591	1.2	34	22090	23528	25662	1.5	2.53	15230	16031	1.2
32211	JACKSONVILLE	031	32158	32426	34350	0.2	8	12689	12961	13890	0.5	2.47	8184	8250	0.2
32212	JACKSONVILLE	031	2485	2474	2562	-0.1	4	346	347	370	0.1	4.42	311	310	-0.1
32215	JACKSONVILLE	031	24	29	34	4.6	88	11	14	16	5.8	2.07	10	13	6.4
32216	JACKSONVILLE	031	30737	31399	33344	0.5	15	12544	13036	14040	0.9	2.37	8125	8317	0.6
32217	JACKSONVILLE	031	20212	21678	23591	1.7	46	8494	9243	10183	2.0	2.32	5409	5807	1.7
32218	JACKSONVILLE	031	37946	41700	46033	2.2	60	13825	15361	17146	2.5	2.64	10275	11298	2.3
32219	JACKSONVILLE	031	9516	9708	10329	0.5	14	3523	3651	3934	0.8	2.65	2556	2615	0.5
	FLORIDA					2.1					2.2	2.45			2.0
	UNITED STATES					1.2					1.3	2.58			1.1

ZIP CODE #	POST OFFICE NAME	RACE (%) White 2000	White 2004	Black 2000	Black 2004	Asian/Pacific 2000	Asian/Pacific 2004	% Hispanic Origin 2000	% Hispanic Origin 2004	2004 AGE DISTRIBUTION (%) 0-4	5-9	10-14	15-19	20-24	25-44	45-64	65-84	85+	18+	MEDIAN AGE 2004	% 2004 Males	% 2004 Females
32003	ORANGE PARK	89.5	88.0	4.5	5.0	2.9	3.5	4.3	5.3	7.3	8.1	9.4	7.3	4.7	29.0	26.3	7.2	0.5	70.0	37.1	49.7	50.3
32008	BRANFORD	94.6	93.6	1.7	2.1	0.3	0.4	5.2	6.6	5.6	5.9	6.7	6.3	6.1	24.7	27.5	16.1	1.2	77.9	41.2	50.4	49.6
32009	BRYCEVILLE	97.2	96.7	0.9	1.1	0.4	0.5	0.7	0.9	7.3	7.4	8.3	7.0	6.2	30.0	24.7	8.5	0.7	72.7	35.9	50.0	50.0
32011	CALLAHAN	92.1	91.0	6.0	6.8	0.3	0.3	0.8	1.1	6.7	6.7	7.7	7.3	6.4	27.9	26.1	10.3	0.8	74.1	37.1	49.0	51.0
32013	DAY	62.6	59.9	31.2	33.2	0.4	0.4	8.7	10.0	2.9	3.2	3.4	3.0	13.2	50.7	16.4	6.6	0.6	88.9	33.5	76.9	23.1
32024	LAKE CITY	89.9	88.1	6.5	7.7	0.7	0.9	3.3	4.2	6.8	6.7	7.6	7.6	6.9	24.8	26.4	12.3	1.0	74.3	38.2	49.2	50.8
32025	LAKE CITY	79.5	77.1	17.2	19.2	0.7	0.8	3.1	3.7	6.1	5.8	6.5	6.5	8.1	26.7	23.0	15.1	2.1	77.8	38.0	52.4	47.6
32033	ELKTON	83.7	80.1	13.4	16.7	0.7	0.8	2.3	2.8	5.7	6.0	6.3	6.1	5.4	23.0	27.1	19.2	1.4	77.9	43.4	50.0	50.0
32034	FERNANDINA BEACH	88.1	87.1	9.6	10.2	0.7	0.8	2.1	2.6	5.2	5.5	5.7	5.7	4.8	24.1	31.1	16.5	1.6	80.1	44.4	48.4	51.6
32038	FORT WHITE	87.5	85.4	9.2	10.9	0.2	0.3	2.5	3.2	6.0	6.3	6.6	6.4	5.5	24.2	30.5	13.6	1.1	77.3	41.9	49.8	50.2
32040	GLEN SAINT MARY	87.7	86.0	10.6	12.1	0.2	0.2	1.5	1.9	8.1	7.4	7.6	8.0	8.0	28.8	23.3	8.1	0.6	71.9	33.0	51.1	48.9
32043	GREEN COVE SPRINGS	86.2	84.9	9.7	10.4	0.8	0.9	3.7	4.6	6.5	6.6	7.1	6.6	6.1	26.9	26.3	12.4	1.6	75.7	39.1	49.8	50.2
32044	HAMPTON	92.1	90.8	4.9	5.5	0.3	0.4	2.7	3.4	7.7	7.2	6.8	6.8	7.9	26.7	24.1	11.8	1.0	74.1	35.6	50.5	49.6
32046	HILLIARD	91.6	90.4	6.7	7.8	0.3	0.3	0.8	1.0	7.3	7.3	7.7	7.3	6.5	28.2	24.6	10.1	1.2	73.1	36.0	49.2	50.9
32052	JASPER	55.3	52.5	41.7	44.2	0.2	0.2	5.9	7.1	5.9	5.8	5.2	6.1	9.5	34.3	22.7	9.0	1.4	79.4	35.3	61.5	38.5
32053	JENNINGS	69.1	66.7	25.1	26.7	0.4	0.5	10.3	12.1	7.2	7.4	8.0	6.7	5.7	26.8	25.7	11.5	1.1	73.2	36.5	51.0	49.0
32054	LAKE BUTLER	75.3	72.9	21.4	23.3	0.3	0.3	3.3	4.1	6.5	6.0	6.6	7.5	8.1	34.6	22.3	7.6	0.7	76.3	34.6	59.6	40.4
32055	LAKE CITY	67.1	64.9	30.0	32.0	0.9	1.0	2.1	2.5	7.0	6.8	7.0	7.1	7.6	27.1	25.0	11.1	1.4	75.0	36.0	50.8	49.2
32058	LAWTEY	64.1	60.8	31.8	34.4	0.6	0.7	4.6	5.6	3.9	3.9	4.5	5.0	9.5	42.1	23.9	6.5	0.7	84.8	35.8	70.8	29.2
32059	LEE	93.3	92.4	4.2	4.9	0.1	0.1	2.7	3.4	5.8	6.1	7.1	7.0	5.6	25.1	27.7	14.4	1.3	76.7	41.1	50.7	49.3
32060	LIVE OAK	86.7	84.7	10.0	11.4	0.5	0.6	4.4	5.5	6.2	6.2	6.3	5.7	6.0	24.3	26.2	16.5	2.7	77.8	41.7	48.6	51.5
32061	LULU	92.9	91.6	5.1	5.8	0.0	0.2	1.7	2.1	6.1	6.1	8.2	8.2	6.8	27.3	25.6	11.2	0.7	74.6	36.4	50.6	49.4
32062	MC ALPIN	90.5	88.8	6.5	7.7	0.9	1.0	4.3	5.5	6.1	6.2	6.4	5.4	5.5	24.5	28.6	16.0	1.4	78.0	42.3	49.4	50.6
32063	MACCLENNY	87.4	85.8	10.7	11.9	0.7	0.8	1.6	2.1	7.2	6.9	6.9	7.9	8.4	27.1	24.1	10.2	1.3	74.3	35.0	49.6	50.4
32064	LIVE OAK	64.6	61.9	31.8	34.1	0.7	0.8	6.9	8.0	6.7	6.8	7.3	7.1	7.9	25.7	22.9	13.8	1.9	75.2	36.7	49.7	50.3
32065	ORANGE PARK	84.6	82.6	7.7	8.6	2.9	3.5	5.6	6.9	6.9	6.9	7.7	7.4	7.2	29.5	26.6	7.3	0.6	74.0	34.9	48.8	51.2
32066	MAYO	85.3	82.7	7.9	9.2	0.0	0.0	10.4	12.9	7.2	7.5	7.5	6.4	5.9	27.7	22.7	13.4	1.7	74.0	36.1	52.5	47.5
32068	MIDDLEBURG	91.4	89.9	4.0	4.7	1.4	1.7	3.5	4.4	7.6	7.7	8.4	7.5	6.7	30.4	24.5	6.9	0.5	71.7	34.5	49.7	50.3
32071	O BRIEN	92.0	90.7	5.0	5.8	0.5	0.6	4.3	5.5	6.0	6.1	6.2	6.0	6.1	24.8	27.3	16.4	1.3	78.2	41.3	49.8	50.3
32073	ORANGE PARK	81.4	78.8	10.3	11.4	3.4	4.0	5.8	7.1	6.1	6.0	6.8	7.2	8.4	27.4	26.3	10.6	1.5	76.9	36.8	48.5	51.6
32080	SAINT AUGUSTINE	96.9	96.3	0.6	0.7	1.1	1.3	2.4	3.0	3.2	3.4	4.1	4.5	5.7	20.9	33.2	23.0	2.0	86.7	50.3	48.7	51.3
32082	PONTE VEDRA BEACH	96.3	95.5	1.0	1.4	1.2	1.4	2.5	3.2	4.7	5.3	6.8	6.2	4.9	23.9	32.0	14.6	1.6	79.2	44.0	48.1	51.9
32083	RAIFORD	67.1	64.2	28.3	30.8	0.5	0.6	4.4	5.4	2.7	2.7	2.7	3.8	4.4	51.5	28.1	3.8	0.3	89.2	39.0	81.6	18.5
32084	SAINT AUGUSTINE	76.3	73.9	20.4	22.5	0.5	0.6	2.9	3.6	5.5	5.4	6.1	8.2	8.7	25.0	26.2	12.9	2.2	79.2	38.6	47.3	52.7
32086	SAINT AUGUSTINE	94.7	93.6	2.5	3.3	1.1	1.2	3.2	4.0	4.9	5.2	6.2	6.1	5.5	22.7	27.9	18.5	2.9	79.8	44.6	47.1	52.9
32087	SANDERSON	70.9	68.3	26.4	28.8	0.2	0.2	3.1	3.7	6.3	5.8	6.5	7.6	9.6	34.4	22.8	6.5	0.5	76.9	33.4	60.5	39.5
32091	STARKE	75.9	73.4	21.6	23.7	0.8	0.9	1.8	2.2	6.2	6.1	6.5	6.4	7.0	29.7	24.5	11.7	1.8	77.3	37.3	52.5	47.5
32092	SAINT AUGUSTINE	94.1	92.1	3.9	5.6	0.4	0.5	1.6	2.0	6.1	6.5	6.7	6.3	5.1	28.3	29.4	10.6	0.9	76.5	40.0	50.9	49.1
32094	WELLBORN	91.0	89.6	6.0	6.9	0.4	0.5	3.4	4.3	6.2	6.6	7.2	5.8	5.6	24.8	28.7	13.9	1.4	76.5	40.6	48.7	51.3
32095	SAINT AUGUSTINE	94.7	93.6	2.9	3.7	0.5	0.6	2.7	3.4	6.0	6.2	6.8	6.7	6.5	31.1	27.3	8.8	0.6	77.0	38.0	52.9	47.1
32096	WHITE SPRINGS	60.7	58.2	37.6	40.1	0.1	0.2	0.7	0.9	6.4	6.4	7.3	8.1	7.5	25.1	26.7	11.5	1.2	75.1	37.6	50.1	49.9
32097	YULEE	89.1	87.4	8.1	9.5	0.5	0.6	1.6	1.9	6.8	7.0	7.4	7.0	6.0	30.1	26.2	9.1	0.4	74.6	36.4	51.4	48.6
32102	ASTOR	92.2	91.0	1.2	1.4	0.1	0.1	14.4	17.2	6.1	5.9	5.4	4.9	4.6	20.3	31.0	20.4	1.5	79.5	47.2	50.9	49.1
32110	BUNNELL	80.3	78.2	15.5	17.0	1.2	1.5	4.7	5.8	6.3	6.1	6.5	6.6	5.4	24.2	26.1	17.2	1.8	76.9	41.8	48.2	51.8
32112	CRESCENT CITY	68.9	65.0	16.2	18.2	1.0	1.1	18.3	21.0	6.7	6.4	6.8	5.9	5.7	19.8	24.2	22.1	2.5	76.5	43.9	49.8	50.2
32113	CITRA	75.9	73.1	20.8	23.3	0.4	0.4	3.7	4.4	5.3	5.7	6.3	6.6	6.8	26.9	27.9	13.1	1.3	78.7	40.5	50.1	49.9
32114	DAYTONA BEACH	48.8	45.9	45.9	48.2	1.8	2.1	3.6	4.3	5.6	4.9	5.3	11.0	15.0	24.9	18.4	12.3	2.7	81.0	30.2	50.4	49.6
32117	DAYTONA BEACH	72.3	69.0	23.8	26.6	1.1	1.3	3.6	4.4	5.6	5.5	6.3	6.0	6.2	26.2	25.0	15.6	3.4	78.9	41.2	47.7	52.3
32118	DAYTONA BEACH	94.4	93.3	1.7	2.1	1.7	2.0	2.8	3.6	2.9	2.8	3.0	3.2	4.4	22.5	29.6	27.4	4.2	89.5	52.9	50.3	49.8
32119	DAYTONA BEACH	89.2	86.8	6.7	8.4	1.8	2.1	3.2	4.1	4.8	4.6	4.7	4.6	6.6	25.5	24.6	21.5	3.1	83.3	44.4	48.2	51.8
32124	DAYTONA BEACH	70.9	65.3	24.7	30.0	0.3	0.3	5.0	5.9	2.2	2.7	2.9	11.0	7.9	47.1	21.3	4.1	0.9	84.5	35.4	74.0	26.0
32127	PORT ORANGE	96.7	95.8	1.1	1.4	0.9	1.1	2.3	3.0	4.2	4.6	5.4	5.2	4.4	20.8	30.1	22.1	3.3	82.5	48.6	47.9	52.1
32128	PORT ORANGE	95.7	94.6	1.3	1.7	1.6	1.9	2.1	2.7	4.1	4.5	5.3	4.2	3.7	18.8	34.4	23.7	1.5	83.6	51.1	48.8	51.3
32129	PORT ORANGE	95.0	93.8	2.0	2.6	1.2	1.4	2.4	3.1	3.8	3.8	5.0	5.3	5.6	23.2	25.9	24.3	3.2	84.1	47.4	47.9	52.2
32130	DE LEON SPRINGS	81.0	77.1	3.9	4.8	0.6	0.6	23.1	28.1	7.0	7.0	7.4	6.8	6.4	25.9	23.8	14.3	1.5	74.5	37.8	50.0	50.0
32131	EAST PALATKA	71.1	67.4	26.7	30.2	0.6	0.7	1.8	2.2	5.1	5.4	6.1	5.9	5.6	26.6	27.9	16.0	1.4	80.1	42.1	54.0	46.0
32132	EDGEWATER	96.5	95.7	1.3	1.8	0.4	0.5	2.1	2.7	5.3	5.4	6.0	6.0	5.7	23.0	27.2	18.7	2.8	79.7	44.1	46.8	53.2
32134	FORT MC COY	95.4	94.7	1.7	2.1	0.3	0.4	1.9	2.3	4.5	4.8	5.9	5.7	4.5	20.2	31.0	21.5	1.9	81.2	47.9	50.7	49.3
32136	FLAGLER BEACH	97.5	97.1	0.8	0.9	0.5	0.6	1.8	2.4	2.3	2.6	3.0	3.2	3.3	15.8	36.8	30.5	2.5	90.1	56.5	48.6	51.4
32137	PALM COAST	88.8	87.5	7.2	7.9	1.2	1.4	5.4	6.6	3.6	3.8	4.5	4.5	3.8	16.4	29.8	30.9	2.9	85.1	55.2	47.8	52.2
32139	GEORGETOWN	79.6	76.5	7.9	9.1	1.3	1.7	13.5	16.1	5.1	5.2	5.4	4.4	3.7	17.6	29.0	27.7	1.9	81.8	52.1	50.5	49.5
32140	FLORAHOME	94.3	93.5	1.9	2.4	0.2	0.2	2.8	3.4	6.8	6.8	6.9	7.0	6.1	25.1	27.4	13.0	0.8	75.1	39.1	50.0	50.0
32141	EDGEWATER	96.7	95.9	1.3	1.7	0.5	0.6	1.7	2.2	4.4	4.7	5.9	6.0	4.7	21.0	27.3	24.1	2.0	81.2	47.3	48.8	51.2
32145	HASTINGS	67.2	66.6	30.0	30.2	0.3	0.4	3.2	3.9	7.2	7.2	8.7	8.3	6.0	28.0	23.6	10.1	0.8	71.5	35.5	49.9	50.2
32148	INTERLACHEN	89.7	87.6	3.9	4.8	0.4	0.5	8.5	10.6	6.3	6.4	7.2	6.8	6.0	23.2	26.7	15.9	1.4	75.9	40.8	50.2	49.9
32159	LADY LAKE	96.3	95.8	2.2	2.5	0.5	0.6	1.7	2.1	1.8	1.8	2.0	1.7	1.7	7.8	23.2	56.6	3.4	93.3	67.7	47.2	52.8
32162	LADY LAKE	94.6	93.7	3.8	4.3	0.4	0.5	2.4	3.0	2.3	2.3	2.8	2.8	2.5	10.6	27.0	47.6	2.1	90.9	64.9	48.3	51.7
32164	PALM COAST	82.7	80.8	12.6	13.7	1.7	2.0	6.6	8.2	4.9	5.0	5.6	5.4	4.9	19.9	27.3	25.2	1.8	81.1	48.3	47.6	52.4
32168	NEW SMYRNA BEACH	89.6	88.4	7.9	8.9	0.6	0.8	1.5	1.9	4.2	4.3	5.1	5.1	4.5	20.9	29.0	24.0	3.0	83.3	48.9	48.1	51.9
32169	NEW SMYRNA BEACH	97.5	97.0	0.6	0.8	0.5	0.6	1.6	2.1	2.3	2.6	3.1	2.9	3.3	16.1	33.2	32.2	4.5	90.3	57.5	47.7	52.3
32174	ORMOND BEACH	93.8	92.7	3.4	4.1	1.2	1.5	2.2	2.8	4.3	4.8	5.9	5.6	4.3	21.4	29.7	20.8	3.4	81.4	47.4	48.1	52.0
32176	ORMOND BEACH	97.0	96.5	0.4	0.5	0.9	1.1	2.6	3.3	3.0	3.3	3.9	3.8	3.3	17.7	30.5	30.2	4.3	87.5	55.2	46.8	53.2
32177	PALATKA	70.2	67.8	27.4	29.4	0.4	0.5	2.7	3.3	7.2	6.7	7.2	7.2	7.0	24.6	24.5	13.7	1.9	74.7	37.7	47.9	52.1
32179	OCKLAWAHA	93.3	92.4	3.4	3.9	0.2	0.3	3.1	3.8	5.3	5.6	6.0	5.4	4.5	21.8	28.9	20.7	1.9	79.6	46.1	49.7	50.3
32180	PIERSON	84.0	81.8	2.6	3.1	0.4	0.4	44.9	51.2	6.2	6.0	5.7	6.2	9.1	34.3	21.2	10.1	1.2	78.6	33.2	55.5	44.5
32181	POMONA PARK	88.1	85.8	7.0	8.3	0.3	0.3	5.9	7.3	4.9	4.8	5.6	5.1	4.4	18.7	28.2	26.1	2.2	81.5	50.7	49.5	50.5
32187	SAN MATEO	88.2	86.5	10.2	11.7	0.3	0.3	1.8	2.1	4.9	5.6	5.7	5.0	4.9	21.4	30.2	21.3	1.0	80.9	46.7	51.1	48.9
32189	SATSUMA	92.3	90.9	4.8	5.7	0.4	0.4	2.8	3.6	5.1	5.2	5.4	4.9	4.5	18.3	29.7	25.1	1.8	81.4	50.2	49.8	50.2
32190	SEVILLE	65.9	61.5	17.0	18.9	0.3	0.2	30.0	34.6	7.1	7.1	8.4	6.4	6.5	24.1	25.4	13.6	1.4	73.4	37.1	51.8	48.2
32195	WEIRSDALE	90.0	88.1	8.0	9.5	0.5	0.6	3.6	4.4	4.7	4.9	6.2	5.6	4.9	21.3	27.9	22.7	1.8	80.8	46.8	49.7	50.3
32202	JACKSONVILLE	30.4	25.9	67.0	71.5	0.5	0.5	2.2	2.4	2.4	2.5	2.4	6.1	9.5	36.7	20.5	15.5	4.4	90.3	40.2	64.7	35.3
32204	JACKSONVILLE	51.0	49.8	45.0	45.9	1.3	1.4	2.5	2.9	4.7	4.7	4.9	5.6	7.9	32.1	19.8	14.2	6.2	82.6	38.8	47.5	52.5
32205	JACKSONVILLE	73.6	69.6	20.7	24.1	2.3	2.6	3.0	3.6	7.0	6.2	6.5	6.2	6.8	31.8	23.0	10.5	1.9	76.6	35.9	47.7	52.3
32206	JACKSONVILLE	15.1	12.5	82.4	85.1	0.5	0.5	1.8	1.9	7.9	7.4	8.3	8.6	7.4	24.8	24.3	9.9	1.5	71.2	34.8	48.2	51.8
32207	JACKSONVILLE	72.7	69.0	21.1	24.3	2.1	2.3	4.8	5.6	7.0	6.4	6.4	6.2	6.5	29.3	24.4	11.7	2.3	76.6	37.8	47.5	52.5
32208	JACKSONVILLE	22.4	19.5	76.1	79.0	0.3	0.3	1.0	1.0	6.9	7.1	8.2	7.9	6.9	24.1	25.9	11.6	1.5	72.9	36.7	45.8	54.2
32209	JACKSONVILLE	1.3	1.1	97.7	98.0	0.1	0.1	0.7	0.8	7.1	7.1	8.9	8.2	6.6	23.0	22.0	14.9	2.2	71.9	36.4	44.7	55.3
32210	JACKSONVILLE	68.1	63.8	24.4	28.0	3.2	3.5	4.2	5.0	7.5	7.0	7.6	7.4	7.6	28.5	22.6	10.4	1.3	73.4	34.4	47.8	52.2
32211	JACKSONVILLE	65.1	59.8	28.8	33.7	1.7	1.9	5.0	5.8	7.8	7.3	7.3	7.0	7.9	29.9	21.4	10.3	1.2	73.6	33.6	48.1	51.9
32212	JACKSONVILLE	63.7	58.3	25.3	29.5	2.9	3.2	11.2	13.1	10.9	8.8	6.3	10.6	26.3	30.6	4.7	1.7	0.1	71.8	22.5	62.4	37.6
32215	JACKSONVILLE	54.2	48.3	33.3	37.9	4.2	3.5	8.3	6.9	20.7	13.8	13.8	6.9	6.9	37.9	0.0	0.0	0.0	51.7	16.3	48.3	51.7
32216	JACKSONVILLE	72.5	68.4	20.7	24.1	2.8	3.1	5.6	6.6	6.9	6.4	6.8	7.0	7.6	29.4	23.2	11.1	1.5	75.6	35.7	48.2	51.8
32217	JACKSONVILLE	77.6	74.9	13.7	15.8	3.4	3.7	6.1	7.2	6.1	5.9	6.5	6.4	7.1	27.0	25.3	13.2	2.5	77.8	39.0	47.1	52.9
32218	JACKSONVILLE	57.7	53.5	39.8	43.9	0.5	0.5	1.7	1.9	7.4	7.3	7.7	7.3	7.2	29.8	23.9	8.6	1.0	73.2	34.5	48.3	51.7
32219	JACKSONVILLE	57.0	56.4	41.5	41.9	0.2	0.2	1.0	1.2	6.3	6.4	7.3	7.4	6.6	26.6	27.2	11.3	0.9	75.5	38.0	49.1	50.9
	FLORIDA	78.0	76.5	14.6	15.2	1.7	2.0	16.8	19.0	6.0	5.9	6.4	6.4	6.5	26.6	24.5	15.5	2.4	78.1	40.0	48.8	51.2
	UNITED STATES	75.1	73.6	12.3	12.5	3.8	4.2	12.5	14.1	6.9	6.7	7.2	7.0	7.3	28.6	23.8	10.8	1.7	75.1	36.0	49.1	50.9

#	POST OFFICE NAME	2004 Per Capita Income	2004 HH Income Base	2004 Household Income Distribution (%): Less than $25,000	$25,000 to $49,999	$50,000 to $99,999	$100,000 to $149,999	$150,000 or More	Median Household Income: 2004	2009	2004 National Centile	2004 State Centile	2004 Home Value Base	2004 Home Value Distribution (%): Less than $50,000	$50,000 to $89,999	$90,000 to $174,999	$175,000 to $399,999	$400,000 or More	2004 Median Home Value
32003	ORANGE PARK	30507	5339	6.8	17.9	43.9	20.8	10.5	76942	84718	94	95	4865	0.7	0.7	31.9	56.6	10.1	208565
32008	BRANFORD	16352	1584	39.6	35.0	20.6	3.1	1.7	31452	35884	16	14	1349	28.0	26.8	31.2	12.1	1.9	82229
32009	BRYCEVILLE	21649	1181	17.3	27.4	42.5	10.2	2.6	52775	60130	77	78	1079	6.1	27.5	40.1	25.9	0.4	114089
32011	CALLAHAN	20922	4370	23.1	28.5	36.7	8.8	2.9	48844	55534	70	71	3721	15.4	19.4	41.3	23.2	0.8	112056
32013	DAY	15815	409	35.7	34.5	22.3	5.6	2.0	35049	39604	28	26	345	26.4	29.0	29.3	15.4	0.0	77632
32024	LAKE CITY	17390	7117	31.1	33.7	28.3	5.0	2.0	37461	43026	37	35	6133	15.1	24.9	42.7	15.6	1.8	104616
32025	LAKE CITY	18157	6668	32.8	34.7	24.7	6.1	1.7	35747	40511	31	28	4733	14.4	27.7	43.4	12.0	2.5	100332
32033	ELKTON	23206	908	22.5	36.5	31.3	7.3	2.5	45716	52786	63	62	789	6.0	14.3	47.8	29.4	2.5	138047
32034	FERNANDINA BEACH	34205	11889	19.3	23.9	35.3	12.0	9.6	56818	64793	82	83	9496	4.6	7.8	29.8	40.6	17.2	198246
32038	FORT WHITE	17968	2210	32.7	31.5	29.6	4.4	1.8	35735	40577	31	28	1883	17.3	29.9	33.4	18.3	1.1	94688
32040	GLEN SAINT MARY	18745	2366	24.6	30.0	36.5	7.2	1.7	46145	50992	64	64	1952	21.4	22.0	36.6	16.6	3.4	101384
32043	GREEN COVE SPRINGS	23143	8575	23.4	28.5	34.1	10.3	3.7	48547	55210	69	70	6864	9.4	18.4	40.3	27.6	4.4	131685
32044	HAMPTON	23544	869	28.8	35.9	29.7	2.8	2.9	38246	43930	40	38	716	21.5	31.6	34.4	10.9	1.7	85417
32046	HILLIARD	18801	2942	24.8	31.0	35.2	6.7	2.3	45201	51475	62	60	2417	25.4	20.3	34.0	19.5	0.8	96926
32052	JASPER	14702	2422	44.2	31.8	20.0	2.7	1.3	28718	32721	10	8	1819	33.4	31.7	27.7	6.3	0.9	72556
32053	JENNINGS	13948	1388	44.2	28.6	23.0	3.4	0.8	28538	32481	10	7	1150	35.0	26.6	30.0	6.3	2.2	70000
32054	LAKE BUTLER	16676	3228	30.8	34.4	28.9	3.5	2.4	37393	42106	37	34	2533	26.1	27.9	34.0	11.0	1.0	85915
32055	LAKE CITY	16451	6416	42.2	31.0	20.7	4.6	1.5	29699	33799	12	10	4573	27.3	30.0	27.3	11.9	3.6	79176
32058	LAWTEY	17291	1102	30.3	30.0	34.0	4.1	1.6	40000	45038	46	43	909	24.2	26.4	37.4	11.9	0.1	89154
32059	LEE	19314	674	37.4	27.0	28.5	4.2	3.0	34506	39593	26	24	569	39.7	27.6	18.8	11.6	2.3	61000
32060	LIVE OAK	17542	7290	36.9	31.4	25.1	4.6	2.1	33805	38199	23	22	6015	21.1	29.5	30.6	15.2	3.7	89170
32061	LULU	17997	170	30.6	32.9	28.8	5.9	1.8	37110	43200	36	32	145	27.6	26.2	29.7	11.0	5.5	84500
32062	MC ALPIN	16396	943	33.1	34.5	27.6	3.1	1.8	35572	40476	30	28	850	19.2	28.6	33.3	14.6	4.4	93393
32063	MACCLENNY	18678	4065	27.2	31.4	33.2	5.4	2.9	43594	48494	58	56	3247	16.2	22.8	41.2	17.2	2.6	103495
32064	LIVE OAK	15173	2358	40.6	32.2	22.4	3.8	1.0	30609	34705	14	12	1801	23.5	35.7	31.4	7.6	1.9	78691
32065	ORANGE PARK	22406	6466	15.5	30.7	38.9	12.1	2.8	53098	60177	77	78	5045	2.4	10.5	60.3	25.6	1.2	135888
32066	MAYO	18205	1591	36.3	31.3	26.6	2.3	3.5	34211	38362	25	23	1298	22.9	23.7	35.7	14.6	3.1	94583
32068	MIDDLEBURG	22302	14892	14.9	28.9	41.8	10.7	3.7	54865	62136	79	80	13138	7.6	14.8	50.1	24.7	2.8	129772
32071	O BRIEN	17470	1236	35.7	34.0	23.8	5.0	1.5	33275	37924	22	20	1058	19.9	34.3	29.0	14.1	2.7	83077
32073	ORANGE PARK	25928	17138	15.7	28.9	37.3	12.9	5.2	54501	61688	79	80	11756	1.5	9.6	54.6	31.0	3.3	149506
32080	SAINT AUGUSTINE	34989	9495	21.8	28.1	31.6	9.8	8.8	50091	59567	72	74	7329	1.0	5.1	29.7	52.0	12.3	209760
32082	PONTE VEDRA BEACH	56970	14431	10.7	17.3	30.0	18.5	23.5	83036	100457	96	97	11116	0.3	0.6	14.1	41.3	43.7	361593
32083	RAIFORD	16211	372	19.9	34.7	37.1	7.5	0.8	44676	49154	60	58	267	29.6	34.8	31.1	4.1	0.4	72794
32084	SAINT AUGUSTINE	21712	10447	33.3	31.0	25.0	6.4	4.3	36094	43351	32	29	6916	14.9	17.6	37.3	21.0	9.3	117569
32086	SAINT AUGUSTINE	23363	8862	23.5	28.3	36.5	9.0	2.7	48017	56069	68	68	7086	3.1	7.3	57.3	30.1	2.2	145969
32087	SANDERSON	15342	1260	29.8	30.2	33.3	5.5	1.3	41472	46741	51	49	1033	29.2	25.1	35.6	9.7	0.4	81275
32091	STARKE	16909	5557	35.0	31.7	27.9	4.0	1.4	35174	39286	28	26	4374	19.3	29.5	38.7	10.6	1.9	92113
32092	SAINT AUGUSTINE	24832	3174	18.7	25.7	39.5	13.1	3.1	56113	65219	81	82	2763	11.4	12.1	38.1	27.4	11.0	145271
32094	WELLBORN	17840	1012	35.7	30.0	28.0	4.2	2.2	34669	39459	26	25	853	20.6	27.3	29.1	15.5	7.5	93365
32095	SAINT AUGUSTINE	22262	2152	20.6	32.4	35.0	7.5	4.5	47610	55428	67	67	1768	8.5	26.0	42.6	15.5	7.5	114547
32096	WHITE SPRINGS	16406	1097	44.0	24.3	28.2	2.8	0.7	28651	32569	10	8	923	33.8	31.7	23.7	8.7	2.1	69933
32097	YULEE	21911	4285	20.6	32.2	35.5	8.4	3.4	47436	54008	67	66	3622	10.0	21.0	48.5	16.8	3.8	114522
32102	ASTOR	19519	1192	33.3	36.2	25.6	4.0	0.8	33792	38164	23	22	990	17.6	34.7	35.2	9.8	2.8	87215
32110	BUNNELL	20132	3089	27.1	31.1	32.8	7.0	2.1	42848	48746	56	54	2534	6.5	14.8	47.6	29.6	1.5	138422
32112	CRESCENT CITY	17657	3817	43.7	34.4	16.3	2.8	2.8	27854	31727	8	6	3085	27.3	31.0	28.0	11.7	2.0	78617
32113	CITRA	18882	2381	40.2	32.1	18.5	6.3	3.0	32801	36733	20	18	1996	44.2	25.1	17.6	9.1	4.0	56150
32114	DAYTONA BEACH	17120	15219	49.3	31.4	15.1	2.4	1.8	25320	27877	5	3	5712	10.6	36.6	42.6	9.2	1.0	92908
32117	DAYTONA BEACH	16449	10125	41.7	34.7	19.4	3.0	1.3	29144	32689	11	8	6582	12.6	41.1	41.7	4.3	0.4	86639
32118	DAYTONA BEACH	29594	10770	35.2	31.2	21.4	7.3	5.0	34776	39338	27	25	6720	0.7	12.6	53.7	27.5	5.6	139198
32119	DAYTONA BEACH	24197	10513	31.4	34.8	25.3	5.2	3.4	36678	42109	34	31	7323	17.6	11.6	54.7	14.5	1.7	116164
32124	DAYTONA BEACH	16532	468	15.6	30.1	36.1	16.2	1.9	54833	59029	79	80	409	2.9	11.5	46.0	35.2	4.4	147083
32127	PORT ORANGE	27057	13472	24.2	29.6	32.6	8.6	4.9	46132	52659	64	64	11225	13.6	9.5	48.1	24.7	4.2	135339
32128	PORT ORANGE	36631	5015	12.1	23.2	38.7	15.8	10.3	64608	76902	88	91	4712	1.6	4.0	31.8	50.4	12.3	207846
32129	PORT ORANGE	21141	9246	30.7	37.3	26.0	3.8	2.2	36245	40985	33	30	6859	18.2	24.5	51.1	6.1	0.1	102201
32130	DE LEON SPRINGS	16506	1950	30.8	31.7	30.9	4.1	2.5	36689	40239	34	31	1648	10.9	24.5	45.7	17.1	1.8	106574
32131	EAST PALATKA	21120	1878	33.4	28.4	27.1	6.9	4.2	37835	44252	39	36	1557	12.7	25.5	42.3	14.3	5.2	105030
32132	EDGEWATER	18875	3159	31.9	38.6	22.4	5.2	1.8	35709	40598	30	28	2562	13.0	23.4	51.3	10.6	1.8	103296
32134	FORT MC COY	18215	4419	37.7	32.8	24.2	4.1	1.1	32248	36363	18	17	3784	35.6	29.9	24.6	8.6	1.4	68000
32136	FLAGLER BEACH	30673	4588	27.4	32.5	25.9	8.7	5.5	41214	47158	50	48	3733	6.1	9.2	36.7	37.2	10.9	170218
32137	PALM COAST	27984	12310	21.9	32.3	30.9	9.0	6.0	46173	52897	64	64	10670	2.5	7.5	42.7	40.7	6.5	168866
32139	GEORGETOWN	34418	399	36.3	35.6	15.0	3.8	9.3	33184	38060	21	20	358	22.4	40.2	23.5	13.1	0.8	76389
32140	FLORAHOME	20197	658	24.6	40.9	26.8	4.0	3.8	38794	45787	42	39	583	16.1	38.4	32.4	11.8	1.2	85093
32141	EDGEWATER	20305	7199	25.1	37.9	31.0	4.0	2.1	40173	45586	47	44	6148	4.3	18.4	67.4	9.3	0.7	113311
32145	HASTINGS	15745	1656	31.7	32.4	30.6	4.7	0.7	37978	47454	39	37	1360	15.7	38.3	42.4	2.9	0.7	86099
32148	INTERLACHEN	15595	5342	43.6	32.5	19.2	3.3	1.3	28376	32567	9	7	4488	35.7	32.5	25.2	5.5	1.2	62669
32159	LADY LAKE	26816	17033	24.5	40.0	27.2	5.2	3.1	40457	45514	48	46	16008	5.2	17.3	42.1	33.6	1.8	140704
32162	LADY LAKE	28599	2391	25.2	39.5	28.2	4.6	2.6	40158	44961	47	44	2241	9.8	9.2	51.8	27.0	2.2	133149
32164	PALM COAST	22673	7666	22.0	31.2	37.2	7.4	2.2	47299	53626	67	66	6526	2.4	3.5	51.6	41.7	0.9	162500
32168	NEW SMYRNA BEACH	23799	9497	32.2	31.2	26.2	6.3	4.2	37254	42371	36	34	7452	9.5	20.0	43.7	23.4	3.5	121411
32169	NEW SMYRNA BEACH	33375	5590	22.9	31.0	30.1	9.8	6.2	46955	54294	66	65	4553	0.6	4.7	44.0	40.9	9.8	176501
32174	ORMOND BEACH	27951	18924	23.2	31.0	30.3	9.5	6.0	46223	52703	64	64	15819	8.2	13.2	45.1	29.5	4.1	136747
32176	ORMOND BEACH	31120	8120	24.5	32.1	29.1	8.3	6.0	43589	50416	58	56	6596	0.5	10.1	56.2	27.1	6.1	142483
32177	PALATKA	18461	9566	40.7	26.8	24.5	5.3	2.8	31705	36555	17	15	6794	19.2	33.9	35.1	10.0	1.7	86703
32179	OCKLAWAHA	16284	4042	39.1	35.3	21.2	3.0	1.5	30394	34089	13	11	3417	32.5	32.4	25.3	8.5	1.3	69325
32180	PIERSON	14535	1413	29.5	41.3	23.7	3.8	1.7	35436	40697	29	27	1145	12.8	27.5	39.6	17.4	2.8	105869
32181	POMONA PARK	16434	628	42.8	33.8	19.0	2.9	1.6	28311	32209	9	7	538	26.8	29.4	29.4	13.2	1.3	80833
32187	SAN MATEO	16871	649	35.8	36.2	24.2	3.2	0.6	32772	37475	20	18	559	18.6	32.6	36.7	8.8	3.4	88700
32189	SATSUMA	18828	2765	40.7	32.7	21.2	3.9	1.6	30189	34471	13	10	2388	25.5	34.9	31.5	7.4	0.8	77273
32190	SEVILLE	14783	419	33.2	40.1	20.5	5.0	1.2	35975	41037	31	29	341	17.6	29.0	33.4	12.3	7.6	98846
32195	WEIRSDALE	24912	1270	25.2	26.8	35.5	8.7	3.9	48486	54550	69	70	1098	11.7	17.5	40.4	21.9	8.7	125620
32202	JACKSONVILLE	15266	1505	76.4	18.1	4.1	0.0	1.5	10363	12035	1	0	163	30.7	27.0	37.4	3.1	1.8	79583
32204	JACKSONVILLE	19717	3291	43.0	34.0	17.4	4.2	1.4	29383	35407	11	9	1297	15.8	26.5	30.8	20.4	6.6	104605
32205	JACKSONVILLE	24347	13564	29.8	34.3	26.0	6.0	4.0	38621	45064	41	39	7980	5.1	37.5	40.7	13.1	3.7	96524
32206	JACKSONVILLE	11981	8394	57.1	27.0	13.3	2.1	0.6	20508	24061	2	1	3698	36.8	40.1	19.6	2.7	1.0	60914
32207	JACKSONVILLE	25622	16292	31.7	29.4	26.7	7.8	4.4	39598	45835	45	42	9283	5.5	24.5	44.3	19.6	6.1	114245
32208	JACKSONVILLE	17324	13391	37.6	31.1	25.0	4.9	1.5	34136	38936	24	23	9526	12.6	50.1	34.0	3.2	0.1	80344
32209	JACKSONVILLE	13895	15051	49.5	30.3	16.2	2.9	1.3	25296	29084	5	3	8912	26.6	51.8	20.1	1.4	0.2	69153
32210	JACKSONVILLE	22824	23528	23.4	33.9	31.4	7.2	4.1	44037	50277	59	57	15359	6.3	30.7	44.7	13.6	4.8	100426
32211	JACKSONVILLE	19965	12961	27.9	35.9	28.4	5.8	2.0	39328	45137	44	41	7355	6.1	27.3	57.6	7.8	1.3	103425
32212	JACKSONVILLE	11501	347	24.2	46.7	25.4	2.6	1.2	36246	41086	33	30	47	17.0	40.4	23.4	19.2	0.0	84167
32215	JACKSONVILLE	22279	14	14.3	42.9	42.9	0.0	0.0	45000	45000	61	59	2	0.0	0.0	100.0	0.0	0.0	137500
32216	JACKSONVILLE	22979	13036	24.8	32.5	30.9	9.1	2.7	45041	50882	61	59	7951	4.4	21.4	60.5	13.0	0.8	112095
32217	JACKSONVILLE	29835	9243	22.5	32.6	28.3	9.9	6.7	44806	51668	61	58	5579	1.3	9.1	53.3	30.1	6.2	145730
32218	JACKSONVILLE	20445	15361	23.5	33.4	33.1	7.9	2.2	45286	51346	62	60	11133	9.5	27.4	48.3	14.3	0.5	104066
32219	JACKSONVILLE	19525	3651	29.3	28.3	33.0	6.7	2.7	42630	49105	55	53	2929	14.2	31.5	42.4	11.4	0.5	94094
	FLORIDA	25506		26.4	29.9	29.1	9.1	5.6	44138	51288				8.8	15.8	40.2	28.3	7.0	137042
	UNITED STATES	25866		24.7	27.1	30.8	10.9	6.5	48124	56710				10.9	15.0	33.7	30.1	10.4	145905

ZIP CODE #	POST OFFICE NAME	FINANCIAL SERVICES: Auto Loan	FINANCIAL SERVICES: Home Loan	FINANCIAL SERVICES: Invest-ments	FINANCIAL SERVICES: Retire-ment Plans	THE HOME: Home Improvements: Home Repair	THE HOME: Home Improvements: Lawn & Garden	THE HOME: Furnishings: Comput-ers & Hard-ware	THE HOME: Furnishings: Major Appli-ances	THE HOME: Furnishings: TV, Radio, Sound Equip-ment	THE HOME: Furnishings: Furni-ture	ENTERTAINMENT: Dine out/ Carry out	ENTERTAINMENT: Sports Equip-ment	ENTERTAINMENT: Fees & Tickets	ENTERTAINMENT: Toys & Games	ENTERTAINMENT: Travel	ENTERTAINMENT: Cable TV	PERSONAL: Apparel & Services	PERSONAL: Auto Repairs	PERSONAL: Health Insur-ance	PERSONAL: Pets & Supplies
32003	ORANGE PARK	133	150	145	157	143	138	136	134	124	141	158	157	139	158	132	115	156	131	114	147
32008	BRANFORD	72	51	27	45	56	65	50	60	59	51	70	71	44	66	51	63	64	60	73	82
32009	BRYCEVILLE	99	91	71	87	91	96	86	93	87	89	108	107	82	102	85	86	104	92	92	110
32011	CALLAHAN	89	85	70	82	85	89	80	85	80	81	99	98	77	96	79	79	95	84	84	100
32013	DAY	62	42	19	36	47	54	40	50	48	41	57	60	34	54	41	52	52	50	62	71
32024	LAKE CITY	74	67	52	65	68	72	64	69	65	66	80	80	61	76	63	64	77	68	69	82
32025	LAKE CITY	72	60	46	58	63	72	62	67	66	61	80	76	58	76	62	68	75	67	74	80
32033	ELKTON	94	76	54	73	81	93	78	86	85	76	102	98	72	98	78	88	95	85	98	105
32034	FERNANDINA BEACH	115	118	120	116	120	130	113	118	114	115	141	131	115	137	116	115	137	116	121	133
32038	FORT WHITE	72	66	51	63	66	69	63	67	63	64	78	77	59	74	62	62	75	67	66	79
32040	GLEN SAINT MARY	81	74	58	71	74	78	70	75	71	72	88	87	66	83	69	70	84	75	75	89
32043	GREEN COVE SPRINGS	89	87	81	85	87	94	85	88	86	85	106	100	84	105	85	86	102	87	89	101
32044	HAMPTON	99	90	71	87	90	95	86	92	87	89	108	107	81	102	85	86	103	92	92	109
32046	HILLIARD	85	75	56	71	76	81	72	78	74	73	91	90	67	85	71	73	86	78	79	94
32052	JASPER	54	37	22	32	41	48	38	45	45	38	53	52	33	49	38	48	49	45	55	61
32053	JENNINGS	70	47	21	41	53	62	46	57	55	46	65	68	39	61	46	59	59	56	70	81
32054	LAKE BUTLER	74	67	52	65	67	72	64	69	66	66	81	80	61	77	64	65	77	69	69	82
32055	LAKE CITY	62	52	42	48	54	60	52	57	56	53	68	65	49	64	52	58	65	57	62	70
32058	LAWTEY	48	37	23	34	40	44	36	41	39	37	47	48	32	45	36	41	44	41	46	54
32059	LEE	78	67	49	63	69	74	64	71	67	66	82	82	59	77	63	67	78	70	73	87
32060	LIVE OAK	72	61	45	57	63	69	58	65	62	60	75	75	54	70	58	63	71	65	70	81
32061	LULU	72	66	52	63	66	70	63	67	64	65	79	78	59	74	62	63	75	67	67	80
32062	MC ALPIN	69	63	49	60	63	66	60	64	60	61	75	74	56	70	59	60	72	64	64	76
32063	MACCLENNY	82	75	61	72	76	81	73	78	74	74	91	89	69	87	72	74	87	77	79	91
32064	LIVE OAK	65	51	37	47	54	61	52	58	58	52	70	67	48	66	52	60	65	58	66	73
32065	ORANGE PARK	88	100	99	102	97	95	91	91	85	93	108	107	94	109	91	81	106	89	81	101
32066	MAYO	82	66	46	63	70	78	65	73	71	66	86	85	60	83	65	73	80	72	81	92
32068	MIDDLEBURG	97	99	88	100	97	97	92	95	88	95	111	110	91	108	90	85	108	93	87	107
32071	O BRIEN	69	62	47	59	62	66	60	64	61	61	75	74	56	71	59	61	71	64	65	76
32073	ORANGE PARK	96	100	106	103	98	101	98	97	94	99	119	114	99	118	97	91	117	97	89	108
32080	SAINT AUGUSTINE	104	102	106	100	106	116	99	105	100	100	124	118	99	119	102	102	119	104	110	122
32082	PONTE VEDRA BEACH	179	194	222	197	195	208	186	189	181	189	227	213	193	221	191	180	222	187	186	209
32083	RAIFORD	18	16	13	16	16	17	15	17	16	16	19	19	15	18	15	15	19	17	16	20
32084	SAINT AUGUSTINE	75	69	69	68	70	77	72	73	74	72	92	84	70	88	71	75	88	74	76	84
32086	SAINT AUGUSTINE	88	79	66	76	83	92	75	84	79	76	96	94	73	92	78	81	91	82	91	101
32087	SANDERSON	64	58	46	56	58	62	56	60	56	57	70	69	53	66	55	56	67	59	59	71
32091	STARKE	72	56	38	52	60	68	56	64	62	56	74	73	51	70	56	64	69	63	72	81
32092	SAINT AUGUSTINE	96	98	87	96	97	100	91	95	89	92	111	110	90	110	91	87	108	93	91	110
32094	WELLBORN	72	65	51	63	65	69	62	67	63	64	78	77	59	74	62	62	75	67	66	79
32095	SAINT AUGUSTINE	91	85	70	83	85	89	81	86	81	83	100	99	78	96	80	80	97	85	84	101
32096	WHITE SPRINGS	70	52	30	47	56	63	50	59	57	51	68	70	44	64	50	60	63	59	68	80
32097	YULEE	92	87	71	84	87	92	82	88	83	84	102	102	79	98	82	82	98	87	87	104
32102	ASTOR	72	56	36	50	61	68	53	63	59	53	71	74	47	69	55	63	66	62	73	85
32110	BUNNELL	83	70	52	67	75	84	68	76	74	68	89	88	65	88	70	76	83	75	85	96
32112	CRESCENT CITY	71	58	47	53	62	74	57	66	64	58	77	70	54	70	59	68	71	65	78	80
32113	CITRA	72	52	27	46	57	64	50	60	58	51	69	71	43	65	50	61	63	60	71	83
32114	DAYTONA BEACH	50	43	54	44	43	49	53	49	55	51	68	58	51	65	50	54	66	53	50	55
32117	DAYTONA BEACH	53	50	51	48	51	58	53	53	56	52	68	60	52	67	53	57	65	54	58	60
32118	DAYTONA BEACH	79	74	81	72	76	88	75	79	78	77	97	85	75	89	78	80	93	80	86	89
32119	DAYTONA BEACH	71	70	78	69	72	82	71	73	73	72	91	79	72	85	73	75	87	73	79	81
32124	DAYTONA BEACH	7	6	5	6	6	7	5	6	6	5	7	7	5	7	6	6	7	6	7	8
32127	PORT ORANGE	87	92	96	89	93	103	86	91	86	88	108	97	88	102	90	89	104	89	96	101
32128	PORT ORANGE	133	124	116	118	131	153	115	130	121	122	151	130	116	128	124	129	141	126	151	150
32129	PORT ORANGE	65	64	68	61	65	75	63	67	65	64	81	70	63	75	65	67	77	66	73	74
32130	DE LEON SPRINGS	75	68	57	63	69	75	65	72	69	69	85	79	63	79	66	69	82	71	74	83
32131	EAST PALATKA	88	70	50	66	75	87	72	80	79	71	95	91	66	90	72	83	88	80	92	99
32132	EDGEWATER	68	58	50	56	62	74	59	66	64	60	78	69	57	71	61	68	72	65	76	76
32134	FORT MC COY	68	57	46	52	61	70	54	63	59	56	72	67	51	65	56	62	67	61	72	76
32136	FLAGLER BEACH	92	86	82	82	91	107	79	90	84	85	105	89	81	87	86	90	98	88	106	103
32137	PALM COAST	97	90	83	85	95	110	83	94	88	88	109	97	84	96	89	94	103	92	109	110
32139	GEORGETOWN	110	98	92	89	105	126	92	108	101	98	124	107	91	107	99	109	115	105	128	124
32140	FLORAHOME	93	72	44	65	77	85	69	80	76	70	92	94	62	87	69	79	86	79	90	105
32141	EDGEWATER	72	69	67	66	72	81	65	72	68	68	84	76	66	79	69	71	80	70	79	82
32145	HASTINGS	69	59	49	56	60	67	60	64	64	61	78	72	56	72	59	65	74	64	68	76
32148	INTERLACHEN	71	52	31	46	57	65	50	60	58	51	69	70	45	64	51	62	63	60	72	80
32159	LADY LAKE	78	74	73	69	78	92	68	78	73	73	90	77	69	77	74	78	85	76	91	88
32162	LADY LAKE	80	76	75	71	80	95	70	80	75	75	93	77	71	77	76	80	86	78	94	90
32164	PALM COAST	85	77	71	74	82	96	74	83	78	77	96	84	73	84	78	83	90	80	95	95
32168	NEW SMYRNA BEACH	80	73	70	69	76	88	72	79	77	74	95	84	71	87	75	81	89	78	89	91
32169	NEW SMYRNA BEACH	100	94	90	89	99	117	87	99	92	93	114	97	88	95	94	98	107	96	116	113
32174	ORMOND BEACH	89	92	96	90	94	103	88	92	89	89	110	102	90	107	91	90	106	91	96	104
32176	ORMOND BEACH	95	87	84	82	92	109	83	94	89	87	110	94	83	94	89	95	102	91	109	106
32177	PALATKA	73	60	49	56	63	71	62	67	68	62	82	77	58	79	62	70	77	67	75	82
32179	OCKLAWAHA	63	52	42	47	56	66	50	58	55	52	67	62	47	60	52	59	62	57	69	72
32180	PIERSON	76	58	37	52	61	67	57	67	64	60	78	76	50	71	56	66	74	67	73	83
32181	POMONA PARK	59	52	49	47	56	67	49	57	54	52	66	57	48	57	53	58	61	56	68	66
32187	SAN MATEO	67	55	42	50	59	67	52	61	58	54	70	66	49	63	54	61	65	60	70	75
32189	SATSUMA	65	57	53	52	61	73	53	63	59	57	72	63	53	63	58	64	67	61	75	73
32190	SEVILLE	81	54	25	47	62	71	53	66	63	54	74	78	45	70	53	68	68	65	81	93
32195	WEIRSDALE	99	92	81	86	94	105	86	96	90	90	111	103	84	101	89	92	105	94	103	111
32202	JACKSONVILLE	30	26	36	26	26	31	32	30	35	31	43	35	31	41	32	36	41	33	34	34
32204	JACKSONVILLE	53	45	57	46	45	51	55	52	58	54	72	61	53	68	53	57	69	56	53	58
32205	JACKSONVILLE	70	73	88	74	72	77	77	74	77	76	96	88	78	98	77	75	94	76	71	81
32206	JACKSONVILLE	41	34	39	31	34	41	39	39	44	40	54	43	38	49	38	46	51	41	44	45
32207	JACKSONVILLE	74	76	89	77	76	81	80	78	80	78	99	92	81	100	80	78	97	79	76	85
32208	JACKSONVILLE	62	59	66	57	59	68	62	61	66	63	82	67	64	80	62	68	79	62	66	70
32209	JACKSONVILLE	51	43	47	39	43	51	47	48	53	48	64	52	46	59	46	56	62	49	55	56
32210	JACKSONVILLE	78	82	89	82	81	85	82	81	81	82	102	94	84	103	82	80	100	82	78	90
32211	JACKSONVILLE	65	68	76	68	67	72	71	68	70	69	88	80	71	89	70	69	86	69	67	75
32212	JACKSONVILLE	67	43	41	49	39	46	64	55	65	59	81	73	54	72	52	59	77	65	51	62
32215	JACKSONVILLE	74	50	46	56	47	54	69	62	70	66	88	80	60	79	59	65	84	71	58	71
32216	JACKSONVILLE	74	75	86	78	74	79	79	76	77	78	97	90	79	96	77	74	95	78	72	84
32217	JACKSONVILLE	93	100	116	103	98	103	100	98	96	100	122	115	102	121	99	93	120	99	91	107
32218	JACKSONVILLE	81	78	71	76	78	82	76	79	76	76	94	92	74	94	75	75	91	78	78	92
32219	JACKSONVILLE	82	71	58	67	73	81	69	75	74	71	90	85	66	86	69	76	86	75	81	92
	FLORIDA	89	87	95	86	87	96	87	89	89	89	111	100	87	107	88	90	108	90	91	101
	UNITED STATES	100	100	100	100	100	100	100	100	100	100	100	100	100	100	100	100	100	100	100	100

#	POST OFFICE NAME	COUNTY FIPS CODE	POPULATION 2000	2004	2009	2000-2004 ANNUAL RATE % Rate	State Centile	HOUSEHOLDS 2000	2004	2009	% Annual Rate 2000-2004	2004 Average HH Size	FAMILIES 2000	2004	% Annual Rate 2000-2004
32220	JACKSONVILLE	031	10954	11437	12234	1.0	28	3993	4251	4613	1.5	2.69	3046	3209	1.2
32221	JACKSONVILLE	031	17990	20303	22656	2.9	72	6263	7194	8143	3.3	2.78	4929	5615	3.1
32222	JACKSONVILLE	031	5312	5924	6737	2.6	68	1924	2158	2470	2.7	2.75	1477	1642	2.5
32223	JACKSONVILLE	031	25399	26860	29165	1.3	37	9597	10322	11343	1.7	2.60	7400	7845	1.4
32224	JACKSONVILLE	031	30943	37513	43293	4.6	89	11925	14834	17437	5.3	2.43	7771	9499	4.8
32225	JACKSONVILLE	031	45778	54837	63207	4.3	87	16614	19803	22856	4.2	2.76	12655	15135	4.3
32226	JACKSONVILLE	031	8017	9659	11147	4.5	88	2960	3607	4204	4.8	2.66	2315	2801	4.6
32227	JACKSONVILLE	031	5250	5111	5213	-0.6	1	586	558	591	-1.2	3.85	577	549	-1.2
32233	ATLANTIC BEACH	031	25398	27322	29677	1.7	49	9846	10784	11871	2.2	2.52	6614	7143	1.8
32234	JACKSONVILLE	031	6134	6635	7364	1.9	53	2200	2419	2717	2.3	2.74	1681	1830	2.0
32244	JACKSONVILLE	031	47763	53443	59509	2.7	69	17650	20026	22556	3.0	2.66	12708	14263	2.8
32246	JACKSONVILLE	031	35532	39454	43565	2.5	66	13083	14633	16281	2.7	2.69	9437	10466	2.5
32250	JACKSONVILLE BEACH	031	25540	26952	29099	1.3	35	11595	12450	13625	1.7	2.14	6518	6916	1.4
32254	JACKSONVILLE	031	15708	15546	16395	-0.2	2	5548	5554	5919	0.0	2.79	3944	3897	-0.3
32256	JACKSONVILLE	031	29136	33017	37228	3.0	73	14032	15737	17725	2.7	2.09	7053	7983	3.0
32257	JACKSONVILLE	031	36389	40459	44802	2.5	67	14869	16683	18638	2.8	2.41	9722	10767	2.4
32258	JACKSONVILLE	031	12637	14998	17161	4.1	85	4332	5223	6050	4.5	2.84	3500	4186	4.3
32259	JACKSONVILLE	109	17955	25728	34660	8.8	99	5952	8532	11519	8.8	3.01	5164	7346	8.7
32266	NEPTUNE BEACH	031	7270	7285	7646	0.1	5	3282	3332	3536	0.4	2.19	1857	1850	-0.1
32277	JACKSONVILLE	031	27754	30702	33828	2.4	64	10816	12159	13575	2.8	2.47	7586	8420	2.5
32301	TALLAHASSEE	073	26763	29816	33159	2.6	68	12029	13702	15580	3.1	1.94	4654	5160	2.5
32303	TALLAHASSEE	073	43232	45362	49193	1.1	32	18730	19988	21831	1.4	2.27	10483	10991	1.1
32304	TALLAHASSEE	073	40229	41934	44753	1.0	27	15878	16757	18226	1.3	2.09	4256	4364	0.6
32305	TALLAHASSEE	073	18444	19136	20502	0.9	24	7074	7427	8044	1.2	2.56	4889	5075	0.9
32306	TALLAHASSEE	073	64	64	64	0.0	5	0	0	0	0.0	0.00	0	0	0.0
32307	TALLAHASSEE	073	890	902	917	0.3	10	0	0	0	0.0	0.00	0	0	0.0
32308	TALLAHASSEE	073	19961	21182	23004	1.4	40	8626	9347	10331	1.9	2.14	4974	5280	1.4
32309	TALLAHASSEE	073	28613	30193	32503	1.3	35	11027	11800	12851	1.6	2.55	8314	8784	1.3
32310	TALLAHASSEE	073	16798	17135	18346	0.5	14	6918	7134	7731	0.7	2.28	4002	4057	0.3
32311	TALLAHASSEE	073	9807	11640	13355	4.1	85	3922	4746	5541	4.6	2.37	2622	3126	4.2
32312	TALLAHASSEE	073	24451	27561	30684	2.9	71	8685	9856	11066	3.0	2.79	7131	8066	2.9
32317	TALLAHASSEE	073	10703	12499	14121	3.7	82	3817	4516	5161	4.0	2.76	3114	3648	3.8
32320	APALACHICOLA	037	3834	4261	4932	2.5	67	1493	1701	2019	3.1	2.31	975	1101	2.9
32321	BRISTOL	077	5339	5481	5579	0.6	18	1515	1592	1650	1.2	2.54	1088	1133	1.0
32322	CARRABELLE	037	3870	3893	4224	0.1	6	1234	1263	1443	0.6	2.08	776	788	0.4
32324	CHATTAHOOCHEE	039	5098	4991	5043	-0.5	1	1741	1723	1776	-0.2	2.34	1189	1166	-0.5
32327	CRAWFORDVILLE	129	18669	21625	25261	3.5	79	6661	7882	9390	4.0	2.61	4988	5861	3.9
32328	EASTPOINT	037	3002	3161	3571	1.2	34	1188	1281	1480	1.8	2.38	861	918	1.5
32331	GREENVILLE	079	4679	4845	5177	0.8	23	1777	1877	2048	1.3	2.49	1269	1330	1.1
32332	GRETNA	039	1758	1696	1715	-0.8	1	525	517	533	-0.4	3.28	403	394	-0.5
32333	HAVANA	039	11499	12397	13122	1.8	51	4493	4945	5335	2.3	2.50	3242	3538	2.1
32334	HOSFORD	077	1719	1751	1780	0.4	12	723	752	777	0.9	2.31	478	493	0.7
32336	LAMONT	065	1316	1366	1508	0.9	24	503	536	606	1.5	2.55	364	385	1.3
32340	MADISON	079	12688	13546	14616	1.6	44	4313	4711	5209	2.1	2.55	3036	3290	1.9
32343	MIDWAY	039	1361	1404	1445	0.7	20	455	477	500	1.1	2.94	353	368	1.0
32344	MONTICELLO	065	10386	11201	12404	1.8	51	3725	4134	4725	2.5	2.46	2609	2874	2.3
32346	PANACEA	037	1839	1934	2189	1.2	33	859	914	1047	1.5	2.12	576	608	1.3
32347	PERRY	123	9218	9353	9605	0.3	10	3217	3316	3463	0.7	2.66	2338	2393	0.6
32348	PERRY	123	8239	8741	9157	1.4	39	3149	3400	3623	1.8	2.37	2234	2391	1.6
32350	PINETTA	079	967	1013	1085	1.1	31	377	402	439	1.5	2.49	266	282	1.4
32351	QUINCY	039	18670	19139	19773	0.6	17	6334	6594	6938	1.0	2.69	4518	4669	0.8
32352	QUINCY	039	6707	6803	7001	0.3	10	2322	2395	2510	0.7	2.83	1727	1769	0.6
32355	SAINT MARKS	129	225	240	260	1.5	43	114	131	153	3.3	1.83	76	19	-27.8
32356	SALEM	123	198	180	179	-2.2	0	82	76	78	-1.8	2.37	59	55	-1.6
32358	SOPCHOPPY	129	2481	2747	3148	2.4	65	997	1119	1298	2.8	2.45	712	792	2.5
32359	STEINHATCHEE	029	1447	1397	1422	-0.8	1	658	646	668	-0.4	2.14	437	426	-0.6
32401	PANAMA CITY	005	24269	24813	26403	0.5	15	10246	10587	11412	0.8	2.26	6136	6288	0.6
32403	PANAMA CITY	005	3116	2950	3071	-1.3	0	846	807	854	-1.1	3.17	765	724	-1.3
32404	PANAMA CITY	005	34811	36596	39396	1.2	33	13166	13987	15248	1.4	2.53	9464	10001	1.3
32405	PANAMA CITY	005	26120	27386	29586	1.1	31	10559	11214	12277	1.4	2.39	7070	7430	1.2
32407	PANAMA CITY BEACH	005	5532	7086	8504	6.0	94	2399	3159	3865	6.7	2.22	1537	1986	6.2
32408	PANAMA CITY	005	13146	14301	15668	2.0	56	6030	6625	7337	2.2	2.15	3612	3926	2.0
32409	PANAMA CITY	005	7371	7977	8708	1.9	53	2749	3000	3307	2.1	2.66	2122	2301	1.9
32413	PANAMA CITY BEACH	005	9329	10578	11903	3.0	73	4220	4812	5460	3.1	2.20	2679	3035	3.0
32420	ALFORD	063	1955	2284	2548	3.7	82	806	953	1078	4.0	2.40	583	684	3.8
32421	ALTHA	013	4311	4465	4585	0.8	23	1643	1718	1782	1.1	2.59	1200	1245	0.9
32423	BASCOM	063	1345	1332	1383	-0.2	3	545	547	575	0.1	2.40	383	381	-0.1
32424	BLOUNTSTOWN	013	7919	8023	8141	0.3	10	2502	2577	2651	0.7	2.45	1700	1737	0.5
32425	BONIFAY	059	13570	13695	13995	0.2	8	4874	4981	5167	0.5	2.41	3425	3472	0.3
32426	CAMPBELLTON	063	868	921	978	1.4	39	340	364	391	1.6	2.52	244	259	1.4
32427	CARYVILLE	133	1222	1186	1225	-0.7	1	478	469	489	-0.5	2.49	336	327	-0.6
32428	CHIPLEY	133	14239	15131	16067	1.4	41	5267	5671	6103	1.8	2.49	3726	3984	1.6
32430	CLARKSVILLE	013	257	272	283	1.3	38	113	121	127	1.6	2.25	80	84	1.2
32431	COTTONDALE	063	4704	5074	5463	1.8	52	1869	2038	2207	2.1	2.49	1335	1443	1.9
32433	DEFUNIAK SPRINGS	131	12806	14703	17743	3.3	77	4610	5388	6661	3.7	2.46	3231	3763	3.7
32435	DEFUNIAK SPRINGS	131	6272	6761	8033	1.8	50	2583	2792	3349	1.9	2.36	1738	1873	1.8
32437	EBRO	133	556	593	636	1.5	43	226	243	262	1.7	2.41	164	175	1.5
32438	FOUNTAIN	005	3035	3592	4102	4.0	84	1145	1368	1578	4.3	2.61	824	977	4.1
32439	FREEPORT	131	6289	7230	8811	3.3	77	2596	2992	3669	3.4	2.42	1772	2031	3.3
32440	GRACEVILLE	063	5487	5446	5599	-0.2	3	2148	2156	2246	0.1	2.43	1496	1488	-0.1
32442	GRAND RIDGE	063	3623	3841	4074	1.4	39	1402	1506	1617	1.7	2.53	1032	1098	1.5
32443	GREENWOOD	063	2644	2773	2906	1.1	31	1070	1166	1262	2.0	1.89	757	818	1.8
32444	LYNN HAVEN	005	15878	17266	18897	2.0	55	6181	6809	7546	2.3	2.53	4706	5148	2.1
32445	MALONE	063	2699	2742	2812	0.4	11	472	492	523	1.0	2.83	321	331	0.7
32446	MARIANNA	063	11189	11442	11903	0.5	16	3785	3907	4130	0.8	2.45	2598	2656	0.5
32448	MARIANNA	063	8980	9463	10041	1.2	35	3446	3693	3985	1.6	2.40	2339	2492	1.5
32449	WEWAHITCHKA	013	505	523	537	0.8	23	200	209	216	1.0	2.50	142	147	0.8
32455	PONCE DE LEON	131	3700	4096	4699	2.4	65	1521	1694	1957	2.6	2.42	1070	1185	2.4
32456	PORT SAINT JOE	045	7939	8883	9757	2.7	69	3242	3693	4117	3.1	2.32	2281	2584	3.0
32459	SANTA ROSA BEACH	131	6148	7453	9320	4.6	89	2784	3399	4289	4.8	2.18	1745	2124	4.7
32460	SNEADS	063	4897	5103	5326	1.0	27	1381	1488	1602	1.8	2.40	999	1067	1.6
32462	VERNON	133	3502	3584	3752	0.6	16	1393	1452	1547	1.0	2.20	1005	1039	0.8
32464	WESTVILLE	059	3762	4111	4432	2.1	58	1535	1702	1861	2.5	2.40	1106	1218	2.3
32465	WEWAHITCHKA	045	6051	6885	7599	3.1	74	2032	2397	2717	4.0	2.43	1464	1715	3.8
32466	YOUNGSTOWN	005	5428	6061	6726	2.6	68	1934	2182	2448	2.9	2.75	1484	1664	2.7
	FLORIDA					2.1					2.2	2.45			2.0
	UNITED STATES					1.2					1.3	2.58			1.1

ZIP CODE #	POST OFFICE NAME	RACE (%) White 2000	White 2004	Black 2000	Black 2004	Asian/Pacific 2000	Asian/Pacific 2004	% Hispanic Origin 2000	% Hispanic Origin 2004	2004 AGE DISTRIBUTION (%) 0-4	5-9	10-14	15-19	20-24	25-44	45-64	65-84	85+	18+	MEDIAN AGE 2004	% 2004 Males	% 2004 Females
32220	JACKSONVILLE	92.3	90.6	4.9	6.2	0.8	0.9	1.8	2.3	7.0	6.8	7.5	7.4	7.2	28.8	26.1	8.6	0.6	74.2	36.0	50.8	49.2
32221	JACKSONVILLE	82.3	78.7	11.9	14.6	2.7	3.2	3.1	3.9	7.5	7.3	7.7	7.2	6.9	29.4	24.4	8.9	0.9	73.2	34.7	48.6	51.4
32222	JACKSONVILLE	78.8	74.7	13.8	17.1	3.1	3.6	4.5	5.4	8.3	8.1	8.4	6.9	7.0	31.8	23.1	5.9	0.5	71.0	33.5	50.0	50.0
32223	JACKSONVILLE	91.8	89.8	4.2	5.4	1.8	2.2	3.5	4.6	6.0	6.6	7.3	6.8	5.6	27.6	30.7	8.5	0.9	75.9	39.6	48.4	51.6
32224	JACKSONVILLE	83.3	80.1	8.0	10.0	4.4	5.1	5.7	6.9	8.8	6.7	6.0	6.3	12.5	35.8	17.4	5.5	1.1	75.9	29.4	48.8	51.2
32225	JACKSONVILLE	74.6	69.9	15.7	18.9	5.4	6.3	5.5	6.8	7.6	7.4	7.9	7.0	6.8	32.7	23.3	6.6	0.7	72.8	34.3	48.7	51.3
32226	JACKSONVILLE	97.1	96.5	1.1	1.4	0.4	0.5	1.7	2.2	5.7	6.1	6.7	6.1	5.4	28.4	30.5	10.2	0.7	77.6	40.5	50.3	49.7
32227	JACKSONVILLE	61.0	55.6	25.5	29.6	3.3	3.5	11.9	13.8	8.1	7.1	3.9	12.7	38.0	28.7	1.3	0.1	0.0	79.4	22.4	70.9	29.1
32233	ATLANTIC BEACH	74.8	70.6	16.9	20.1	2.6	2.9	6.0	7.2	8.1	7.2	7.3	7.1	8.2	31.6	20.9	8.2	1.4	73.2	32.7	49.7	50.3
32234	JACKSONVILLE	89.9	88.1	8.1	9.7	0.5	0.5	1.5	1.8	7.2	7.2	7.8	7.5	7.0	28.0	26.0	8.5	0.8	73.3	35.9	49.2	50.8
32244	JACKSONVILLE	68.1	63.5	22.5	26.1	4.4	4.9	5.4	6.4	8.1	7.7	8.1	7.3	7.3	32.3	21.5	7.0	0.7	71.6	32.5	48.5	51.5
32246	JACKSONVILLE	71.6	67.4	16.1	18.9	6.6	7.5	6.5	7.7	8.5	7.7	7.5	7.1	7.7	33.9	21.0	6.3	0.4	72.1	32.3	48.9	51.1
32250	JACKSONVILLE BEACH	90.9	89.1	4.7	5.7	1.9	2.3	3.0	3.8	5.3	5.1	5.0	5.0	6.3	33.2	27.2	11.3	1.7	81.6	39.5	49.9	50.1
32254	JACKSONVILLE	41.4	37.2	55.8	60.0	0.6	0.6	1.6	1.8	8.1	8.2	9.8	8.7	6.9	27.1	21.8	8.5	0.9	68.4	31.8	47.5	52.5
32256	JACKSONVILLE	75.5	72.3	12.5	14.4	7.3	8.2	6.2	7.2	6.6	5.4	5.1	5.3	10.5	38.3	20.2	7.4	1.2	80.0	32.2	49.2	50.8
32257	JACKSONVILLE	84.2	81.1	8.6	10.6	3.7	4.4	5.1	6.3	6.7	6.7	7.0	6.7	6.8	31.1	25.8	7.9	1.4	75.5	36.1	47.9	52.1
32258	JACKSONVILLE	86.2	82.9	6.8	8.6	3.9	4.7	4.0	5.0	8.6	8.5	7.1	6.1	5.5	32.8	25.0	5.0	1.3	71.8	35.5	49.1	50.9
32259	JACKSONVILLE	94.8	93.4	2.1	2.9	1.7	2.0	2.4	3.1	7.4	8.3	9.3	7.6	4.6	27.6	28.0	6.1	1.2	70.0	37.7	50.2	49.8
32266	NEPTUNE BEACH	96.1	95.3	0.7	0.9	1.1	1.3	2.1	2.7	4.2	4.3	5.4	5.9	7.3	30.3	29.8	11.5	1.4	82.8	40.5	50.8	49.2
32277	JACKSONVILLE	63.0	57.3	30.8	35.9	2.4	2.7	4.6	5.4	7.5	6.7	7.4	8.1	9.4	29.5	22.2	8.6	0.7	74.0	32.6	47.8	52.2
32301	TALLAHASSEE	50.3	47.9	44.8	46.7	1.9	2.2	4.5	5.3	5.0	4.1	4.0	10.4	15.9	34.5	18.1	6.8	1.2	84.6	29.0	45.6	54.4
32303	TALLAHASSEE	71.8	68.7	23.5	25.9	1.9	2.3	3.5	4.2	6.4	5.7	5.7	7.0	11.1	33.6	21.3	8.0	1.2	78.8	31.7	47.8	52.3
32304	TALLAHASSEE	58.0	54.3	36.3	39.2	2.2	2.5	6.0	7.2	3.4	2.6	2.4	24.1	33.2	21.6	8.4	3.6	0.6	89.9	22.6	49.5	50.5
32305	TALLAHASSEE	46.8	43.9	50.5	53.1	0.4	0.4	1.9	2.2	6.9	7.0	7.7	7.9	7.4	28.6	25.4	8.4	0.7	73.6	34.4	47.2	52.8
32306	TALLAHASSEE	75.0	73.4	15.6	17.2	4.7	4.7	7.8	9.4	0.0	0.0	0.0	79.7	14.1	6.3	0.0	0.0	0.0	100.0	18.1	45.3	54.7
32307	TALLAHASSEE	4.3	3.7	94.9	95.6	0.1	0.1	2.3	2.6	1.3	1.1	0.6	76.3	13.0	4.4	2.0	0.9	0.4	95.9	18.1	44.7	55.3
32308	TALLAHASSEE	75.0	71.3	20.0	22.9	2.6	3.1	3.0	3.7	4.9	4.7	5.7	6.4	7.9	28.3	25.7	12.3	4.1	80.9	39.0	44.9	55.1
32309	TALLAHASSEE	83.3	80.5	12.5	14.6	2.3	2.7	2.7	3.4	5.6	6.4	7.3	6.5	5.5	25.8	31.8	10.1	1.1	76.6	40.8	48.1	51.9
32310	TALLAHASSEE	45.3	43.4	48.9	50.5	2.9	2.9	2.3	2.7	7.6	7.0	7.3	10.3	9.3	31.1	19.2	7.4	0.8	73.9	29.7	49.7	50.3
32311	TALLAHASSEE	66.9	61.7	30.1	35.0	0.8	0.9	3.3	3.9	7.1	7.1	6.9	5.6	6.3	34.5	25.5	6.4	0.6	75.4	35.7	45.7	54.3
32312	TALLAHASSEE	86.6	84.9	10.2	11.3	1.8	2.3	2.2	2.9	6.5	7.6	8.8	7.6	4.5	26.2	30.1	8.1	0.8	72.3	38.5	48.7	51.3
32317	TALLAHASSEE	79.9	76.7	15.9	18.3	2.3	2.8	2.8	3.5	6.6	7.9	8.6	7.1	4.0	27.7	29.9	7.7	0.7	72.3	39.0	48.4	51.6
32320	APALACHICOLA	72.6	70.2	25.4	27.6	0.3	0.3	1.5	1.9	5.6	5.7	6.0	5.7	5.6	27.5	28.6	13.0	2.3	79.3	41.5	52.5	47.5
32321	BRISTOL	69.5	66.6	24.2	26.3	0.2	0.2	5.7	6.9	5.3	5.3	5.8	5.9	7.4	39.4	21.3	8.7	0.9	79.8	35.1	62.1	37.9
32322	CARRABELLE	77.1	75.0	19.8	21.5	0.3	0.3	4.5	5.6	3.9	3.8	3.3	3.8	6.6	37.5	25.8	13.6	1.7	86.9	40.1	65.1	34.9
32324	CHATTAHOOCHEE	49.2	45.9	48.0	51.0	0.7	0.8	3.1	3.9	5.6	5.6	5.2	5.4	6.6	28.0	27.0	14.7	1.9	80.6	41.1	51.4	48.6
32327	CRAWFORDVILLE	85.3	83.8	12.2	13.5	0.3	0.3	1.9	2.4	6.3	6.4	7.2	7.0	6.7	30.0	26.5	9.1	0.8	75.8	37.2	51.5	48.5
32328	EASTPOINT	95.9	95.2	2.0	2.3	0.1	0.2	1.2	1.6	4.8	5.1	5.2	5.6	4.7	25.6	31.0	16.2	1.8	81.3	44.4	50.7	49.3
32331	GREENVILLE	59.6	56.4	38.6	41.7	0.5	0.5	1.2	1.5	5.7	6.1	7.5	8.7	5.8	23.6	27.2	13.8	1.5	74.6	39.2	49.9	50.1
32332	GRETNA	18.8	17.2	74.6	75.5	0.1	0.1	10.4	11.9	7.3	8.7	9.9	8.6	8.3	27.7	20.5	8.0	1.1	68.6	29.8	49.1	50.9
32333	HAVANA	53.2	49.9	45.2	48.4	0.2	0.2	1.1	1.3	6.2	6.2	6.8	6.4	6.2	26.1	29.6	11.2	1.4	77.0	40.2	47.8	52.2
32334	HOSFORD	98.0	97.7	0.5	0.6	0.1	0.1	0.8	0.9	6.9	6.3	5.9	6.1	6.6	28.4	26.8	12.2	0.8	77.0	38.3	50.5	49.5
32336	LAMONT	53.8	50.7	43.8	46.8	0.4	0.4	2.2	2.6	5.2	5.3	6.1	6.3	7.1	25.9	30.4	12.2	1.5	79.7	40.7	48.3	51.7
32340	MADISON	52.5	49.6	45.1	47.8	0.3	0.4	4.0	4.7	5.9	5.8	6.6	6.9	7.7	29.8	23.2	11.8	2.3	77.6	36.3	53.0	47.0
32343	MIDWAY	15.2	15.0	83.8	83.9	0.2	0.2	0.8	1.0	8.3	8.7	8.3	8.5	7.7	25.8	24.2	7.6	0.9	69.7	31.7	46.1	53.9
32344	MONTICELLO	59.2	56.2	38.5	41.1	0.4	0.4	2.3	2.8	5.3	5.6	6.3	6.2	6.1	28.1	27.9	12.7	1.9	79.1	40.4	51.5	48.5
32346	PANACEA	93.8	92.9	4.1	4.7	0.1	0.2	1.1	1.4	4.2	4.6	5.4	5.9	5.0	22.4	33.8	17.6	1.1	82.0	46.6	51.0	49.0
32347	PERRY	83.8	81.8	12.7	14.2	0.4	0.5	1.8	2.2	6.0	6.2	6.9	6.8	6.4	28.3	26.6	11.8	1.2	76.8	38.1	51.7	48.3
32348	PERRY	67.2	65.2	30.0	31.8	0.5	0.6	1.5	1.8	6.5	6.4	7.1	6.7	6.8	28.1	25.0	11.6	1.8	76.0	37.1	51.2	48.8
32350	PINETTA	79.0	76.3	19.3	21.9	0.2	0.2	1.3	1.7	6.2	6.2	6.2	6.2	6.4	24.4	25.6	16.3	2.5	77.5	41.2	49.3	50.7
32351	QUINCY	36.1	33.6	57.5	59.1	0.3	0.3	10.6	12.5	7.1	7.0	7.5	7.1	8.0	29.4	21.8	10.4	1.7	74.2	34.0	46.9	53.1
32352	QUINCY	23.0	20.4	73.5	75.8	0.3	0.3	4.8	5.5	7.2	7.1	7.7	7.9	8.5	27.5	23.8	9.1	1.1	73.1	33.3	48.0	52.0
32355	SAINT MARKS	68.4	65.8	27.6	30.0	0.0	0.0	5.3	6.7	2.9	3.3	3.3	3.3	9.2	45.4	25.0	7.5	0.0	87.9	37.4	74.2	25.8
32356	SALEM	96.0	95.0	0.0	0.0	1.5	1.7	0.0	0.0	4.4	5.0	5.6	7.8	3.9	24.4	30.6	16.1	2.2	80.6	44.3	50.6	49.4
32358	SOPCHOPPY	89.4	88.1	8.5	9.5	0.4	0.5	2.0	2.5	5.6	5.6	5.8	6.4	5.8	23.2	31.1	15.0	1.7	79.2	43.4	50.4	49.6
32359	STEINHATCHEE	97.2	96.8	1.0	1.2	0.3	0.4	0.7	0.9	2.9	3.2	4.5	5.4	4.7	16.0	34.5	26.6	2.3	86.2	54.4	49.3	50.8
32401	PANAMA CITY	67.6	64.6	26.8	29.1	2.2	2.5	2.3	2.8	6.5	6.2	6.6	6.4	6.8	26.3	23.5	14.9	2.9	76.9	38.8	46.9	53.1
32403	PANAMA CITY	77.2	73.5	12.7	14.9	2.9	3.4	7.5	9.2	11.7	10.2	9.0	8.4	12.3	38.1	6.3	3.8	0.3	65.9	24.4	54.2	45.8
32404	PANAMA CITY	80.3	77.2	12.9	15.1	2.6	3.0	3.0	3.7	6.3	6.3	7.0	6.6	6.9	30.8	24.8	10.5	0.8	76.4	36.4	51.0	49.0
32405	PANAMA CITY	84.7	82.5	10.4	11.8	1.9	2.4	2.5	3.2	6.5	6.4	6.8	6.5	6.8	28.1	24.4	12.8	1.8	76.4	37.7	48.2	51.8
32407	PANAMA CITY BEACH	94.7	93.9	1.5	1.7	1.1	1.4	2.6	3.4	4.6	4.8	5.0	4.8	4.9	29.2	28.0	17.6	1.1	82.8	43.0	51.1	48.9
32408	PANAMA CITY	94.5	93.4	1.2	1.5	1.5	1.8	2.6	3.3	4.7	4.9	6.0	5.6	5.6	29.2	28.3	14.7	1.0	81.1	41.7	50.7	49.4
32409	PANAMA CITY	96.2	95.6	0.5	0.6	0.5	0.6	0.9	1.1	6.5	6.6	7.6	6.7	6.2	29.8	26.5	9.5	0.7	75.3	37.1	49.9	50.1
32413	PANAMA CITY BEACH	95.9	95.2	0.8	1.0	0.8	1.1	1.5	2.0	4.4	4.5	4.9	4.3	4.4	26.4	31.6	18.4	1.1	83.5	45.6	50.3	49.7
32420	ALFORD	93.0	92.0	5.0	5.9	0.2	0.2	1.1	1.4	5.8	6.0	6.1	6.0	5.3	25.4	28.5	15.9	1.1	78.5	42.2	49.5	50.5
32421	ALTHA	93.8	92.7	2.5	3.0	0.3	0.3	2.7	3.5	6.5	6.5	7.1	6.9	5.7	26.9	26.5	12.3	1.6	75.4	38.5	49.7	50.3
32423	BASCOM	66.4	62.5	32.2	36.1	0.2	0.2	1.6	2.0	5.8	6.2	6.5	6.1	5.6	24.0	28.2	15.1	2.6	77.8	41.9	50.8	49.3
32424	BLOUNTSTOWN	70.8	67.8	24.5	26.9	0.8	1.0	4.7	5.7	5.9	5.5	5.5	5.7	8.1	33.3	21.7	12.1	2.3	79.8	36.2	56.8	43.2
32425	BONIFAY	87.0	85.3	9.1	10.2	0.4	0.6	2.1	2.7	5.7	5.7	6.3	6.4	7.2	29.9	23.6	13.1	2.2	78.6	37.6	54.3	45.8
32426	CAMPBELLTON	25.9	22.7	72.9	76.1	0.1	0.1	0.9	1.0	5.7	6.2	7.1	6.8	7.5	23.5	28.3	13.1	1.9	77.2	40.2	46.5	53.5
32427	CARYVILLE	82.1	80.6	13.3	14.2	0.1	0.2	2.5	2.8	5.8	6.2	7.0	6.2	5.5	25.4	26.9	15.3	1.8	76.9	40.9	49.1	50.9
32428	CHIPLEY	83.1	81.3	12.7	14.0	0.5	0.6	2.3	2.9	6.3	6.2	6.4	5.7	6.1	27.5	25.9	13.6	2.4	77.6	39.6	51.6	48.4
32430	CLARKSVILLE	96.1	95.2	0.4	0.7	0.0	0.4	0.8	1.1	6.3	6.3	7.0	6.3	5.2	26.5	26.5	14.3	1.8	76.5	39.5	50.7	49.3
32431	COTTONDALE	74.3	71.6	22.0	24.3	0.4	0.5	1.8	2.2	6.7	6.8	7.1	6.7	6.3	26.1	26.1	12.7	1.5	75.3	38.2	47.8	52.2
32433	DEFUNIAK SPRINGS	82.2	80.3	13.4	14.9	0.4	0.4	2.5	3.1	5.9	5.9	6.6	6.2	6.2	29.4	25.9	12.6	1.3	77.8	38.5	54.1	45.9
32435	DEFUNIAK SPRINGS	84.9	82.1	10.8	13.0	0.4	0.5	2.7	3.4	5.4	5.6	6.6	6.5	5.8	24.1	26.2	17.0	2.8	78.3	42.3	48.1	51.9
32437	EBRO	68.0	67.0	25.7	26.8	0.2	0.2	1.8	2.2	6.6	6.6	6.4	6.2	6.2	26.8	28.2	12.3	0.7	76.6	39.9	49.8	50.3
32438	FOUNTAIN	95.3	94.5	0.6	0.8	0.5	0.6	2.5	3.2	5.7	5.9	8.2	8.2	6.7	27.0	27.4	10.2	0.7	75.2	38.7	51.6	48.4
32439	FREEPORT	92.5	91.2	1.1	1.5	0.6	0.7	2.1	2.7	5.9	6.4	7.1	5.7	5.0	26.2	28.8	14.0	0.9	77.1	41.4	51.3	48.7
32440	GRACEVILLE	82.2	80.3	15.8	17.5	0.1	0.1	1.1	1.4	6.4	6.3	6.7	6.4	7.1	26.2	23.4	15.0	2.6	77.1	38.1	48.6	51.4
32442	GRAND RIDGE	86.5	84.6	10.9	12.3	0.2	0.2	1.8	2.3	6.7	6.8	6.4	5.5	5.8	27.4	26.2	13.4	1.8	76.8	39.0	49.3	50.7
32443	GREENWOOD	51.5	47.3	45.7	49.5	0.2	0.3	3.9	4.6	4.5	4.6	5.8	6.1	6.9	33.3	27.3	10.2	1.3	81.3	38.9	54.3	45.7
32444	LYNN HAVEN	88.1	85.9	7.6	9.1	1.7	2.1	1.6	2.1	6.0	6.2	6.9	7.1	6.3	26.2	28.0	12.1	1.1	76.5	39.9	48.5	51.5
32445	MALONE	55.0	50.8	40.1	43.7	0.1	0.1	5.6	6.7	3.0	3.2	3.9	3.9	7.8	45.2	25.8	6.4	1.1	87.5	37.1	74.1	25.9
32446	MARIANNA	70.7	67.2	25.5	28.4	0.9	1.0	4.3	5.3	5.3	5.1	5.7	5.8	7.0	28.9	25.4	14.1	2.8	80.6	40.2	50.3	49.7
32448	MARIANNA	66.6	65.0	30.5	31.8	0.4	0.4	1.8	2.3	6.6	6.5	7.0	8.7	7.4	25.9	24.5	11.7	1.7	74.3	35.9	49.6	50.4
32449	WEWAHITCHKA	95.1	94.3	1.2	1.5	0.2	0.2	1.0	1.0	4.6	5.2	7.7	6.7	5.0	25.8	28.7	14.9	1.5	78.6	41.6	51.4	48.6
32455	PONCE DE LEON	89.1	86.4	6.1	8.4	0.3	0.3	1.2	1.5	5.6	6.2	7.4	6.7	5.6	25.3	28.7	12.6	1.8	76.5	40.6	50.7	49.3
32456	PORT SAINT JOE	80.9	79.5	16.7	17.9	0.5	0.6	0.8	1.0	4.8	4.9	5.4	5.6	5.4	22.9	29.6	19.4	2.1	81.5	45.7	49.4	50.6
32459	SANTA ROSA BEACH	94.7	93.8	0.5	0.6	0.7	0.9	2.6	3.4	4.5	4.6	4.9	4.3	4.2	27.1	33.3	15.5	1.0	83.3	45.2	49.9	50.1
32460	SNEADS	71.7	69.0	23.8	25.9	0.3	0.3	4.6	5.5	4.4	4.5	4.7	5.1	10.2	36.5	23.6	9.7	1.4	83.7	36.5	63.4	36.6
32462	VERNON	75.8	73.3	17.9	20.0	0.4	0.4	2.6	3.2	6.0	5.9	5.7	6.0	6.2	28.5	27.3	13.3	1.2	78.4	40.1	53.7	46.3
32464	WESTVILLE	96.7	96.2	0.4	0.5	0.4	0.4	1.3	1.6	5.7	5.9	6.9	6.6	5.5	25.9	27.6	14.1	1.8	76.9	40.6	49.8	50.2
32465	WEWAHITCHKA	80.3	77.4	15.5	17.9	0.5	0.5	3.7	4.5	5.4	5.5	6.8	5.9	6.4	31.2	26.0	11.6	1.2	78.4	38.4	57.3	42.7
32466	YOUNGSTOWN	94.3	93.3	1.5	1.9	0.5	0.6	1.4	1.8	6.1	6.3	7.9	7.4	7.1	29.7	26.3	8.6	0.5	75.3	36.9	51.1	48.9
	FLORIDA	78.0	76.5	14.6	15.2	1.7	2.0	16.8	19.0	6.0	5.9	6.4	6.4	6.5	26.6	24.5	15.5	2.4	78.1	40.0	48.8	51.2
	UNITED STATES	75.1	73.6	12.3	12.5	3.8	4.2	12.5	14.1	6.9	6.7	7.2	7.0	7.3	28.6	23.8	10.8	1.7	75.1	36.0	49.1	50.9

ZIP CODE #	POST OFFICE NAME	2004 Per Capita Income	2004 HH Income Base	2004 HOUSEHOLD INCOME DISTRIBUTION (%) Less than $25,000	$25,000 to $49,999	$50,000 to $99,999	$100,000 to $149,999	$150,000 or More	MEDIAN HOUSEHOLD INCOME 2004	2009	2004 National Centile	2004 State Centile	2004 Home Value Base	2004 HOME VALUE DISTRIBUTION (%) Less than $50,000	$50,000 to $89,999	$90,000 to $174,999	$175,000 to $399,999	$400,000 or More	2004 Median Home Value
32220	JACKSONVILLE	20161	4251	23.6	31.3	37.1	6.2	1.8	46108	52772	64	63	3504	18.3	26.6	42.7	12.1	0.4	98072
32221	JACKSONVILLE	20795	7194	17.9	34.3	35.4	9.7	2.8	48032	54823	68	68	5996	13.2	16.7	55.1	14.7	0.3	113041
32222	JACKSONVILLE	21312	2158	17.7	34.0	36.9	8.9	2.6	48378	56287	69	69	1711	14.7	10.3	53.4	20.8	0.8	127072
32223	JACKSONVILLE	36516	10322	8.9	20.6	39.9	19.1	11.6	73026	81671	92	94	8354	0.3	4.1	41.1	46.3	8.2	184150
32224	JACKSONVILLE	33245	14834	13.9	26.1	37.1	13.3	9.6	60766	69118	85	87	8254	10.6	5.8	25.1	49.3	9.2	191131
32225	JACKSONVILLE	28270	19803	11.0	24.9	42.3	15.0	6.7	63357	74305	87	90	15570	1.6	4.9	58.0	29.1	6.4	154970
32226	JACKSONVILLE	26957	3607	18.1	26.0	36.4	14.4	5.1	58257	65565	83	85	3191	8.6	16.8	40.5	29.7	4.4	137856
32227	JACKSONVILLE	13645	558	17.6	47.1	32.4	2.9	0.0	41823	47144	52	51	49	63.3	36.7	0.0	0.0	0.0	47292
32233	ATLANTIC BEACH	25000	10784	21.4	35.1	27.6	10.4	5.6	45038	50838	61	59	6320	7.7	15.7	36.5	24.9	15.2	131010
32234	JACKSONVILLE	18441	2419	25.2	35.5	30.8	6.4	2.2	41188	47587	50	48	1977	21.7	31.5	35.6	10.9	0.4	86295
32244	JACKSONVILLE	20638	20026	21.3	33.9	35.2	7.7	1.9	46075	52357	64	63	14086	11.2	20.1	62.0	6.6	0.2	109718
32246	JACKSONVILLE	21333	14633	20.6	30.4	37.2	9.4	2.4	49098	56246	70	71	10293	6.0	22.1	54.1	17.6	0.3	116634
32250	JACKSONVILLE BEACH	33989	12450	18.3	25.0	35.8	13.6	7.3	56018	65179	81	82	7924	3.5	2.9	37.5	46.4	9.7	188080
32254	JACKSONVILLE	12727	5554	45.1	33.0	18.2	2.7	1.1	27522	30970	8	6	3455	23.8	53.0	20.4	2.5	0.3	66763
32256	JACKSONVILLE	40277	15737	16.2	31.2	31.1	10.8	10.7	52206	60688	76	77	5561	5.1	6.0	26.1	39.6	23.2	249937
32257	JACKSONVILLE	28157	16683	16.7	29.4	35.8	13.0	5.2	53574	60730	78	79	11149	0.5	5.2	63.7	28.2	2.4	150886
32258	JACKSONVILLE	31603	5223	6.9	17.7	43.3	22.8	9.2	78107	90816	94	96	4672	1.5	3.6	46.2	46.9	1.8	173392
32259	JACKSONVILLE	36968	8532	5.0	13.0	38.4	27.1	16.4	90438	109581	97	98	7958	1.1	2.1	10.8	71.7	14.3	246161
32266	NEPTUNE BEACH	41465	3332	12.0	28.8	35.4	15.8	8.0	61603	72041	86	88	2048	0.9	1.7	29.9	57.5	10.0	209259
32277	JACKSONVILLE	24895	12159	18.7	31.1	36.2	10.1	3.9	50144	56903	72	74	7488	0.5	10.1	61.7	26.1	1.7	133726
32301	TALLAHASSEE	21651	13702	38.2	30.1	24.8	5.2	1.6	33937	41059	24	23	5012	4.3	26.3	58.5	10.7	0.3	109249
32303	TALLAHASSEE	25075	19898	25.9	30.7	31.6	8.5	3.3	44307	52351	59	58	11812	5.6	15.1	59.9	17.7	1.7	118909
32304	TALLAHASSEE	12447	16757	66.0	23.5	8.6	1.4	0.6	16460	19050	1	1	3394	27.1	40.3	27.3	4.4	1.0	74566
32305	TALLAHASSEE	18682	7427	31.9	34.2	25.2	6.3	2.4	35829	43554	31	29	5489	24.9	40.4	29.5	4.9	0.3	75548
32306	TALLAHASSEE	14788	0	0.0	0.0	0.0	0.0	0.0	0	0	0	0	0	0.0	0.0	0.0	0.0	0.0	0
32307	TALLAHASSEE	11492	0	0.0	0.0	0.0	0.0	0.0	0	0	0	0	0	0.0	0.0	0.0	0.0	0.0	0
32308	TALLAHASSEE	33432	9347	18.8	26.6	34.3	12.3	7.9	55054	64710	80	81	5339	1.6	8.9	50.5	34.3	4.7	155876
32309	TALLAHASSEE	35725	11800	10.3	19.0	39.5	20.4	10.8	73013	84527	92	94	9849	2.8	4.1	40.9	46.6	5.6	179085
32310	TALLAHASSEE	15962	7134	46.8	30.1	19.1	3.0	1.1	27612	33535	8	6	3961	28.6	33.5	30.2	7.5	0.2	76268
32311	TALLAHASSEE	27216	4746	15.3	36.2	36.7	9.4	2.5	48826	56777	70	70	3654	8.7	17.9	56.4	16.3	0.7	113723
32312	TALLAHASSEE	40229	9856	7.3	13.1	39.9	23.0	16.7	84493	102243	96	97	8936	2.3	3.0	32.3	50.9	11.5	200259
32317	TALLAHASSEE	33093	4516	7.6	17.5	44.9	19.9	10.2	75688	85834	93	95	4227	4.0	7.0	32.0	55.6	1.4	185417
32320	APALACHICOLA	15704	1701	45.5	28.7	20.7	4.2	0.9	27308	31029	8	5	1350	21.9	23.3	27.8	23.6	3.6	103333
32321	BRISTOL	17402	1592	39.1	32.7	20.6	4.2	3.5	31293	36494	16	14	1314	32.9	25.3	29.6	9.4	2.9	75526
32322	CARRABELLE	16236	1263	48.2	30.7	16.6	3.8	0.7	25864	29165	6	4	1049	23.1	23.8	32.0	16.6	4.5	94392
32324	CHATTAHOOCHEE	18627	1723	35.2	33.8	24.7	4.6	1.6	33687	37860	23	21	1206	33.3	36.7	23.2	5.2	1.7	66633
32327	CRAWFORDVILLE	20375	7882	23.9	33.8	31.7	8.4	2.2	43442	49502	57	55	6746	12.6	19.9	41.5	23.3	2.7	121274
32328	EASTPOINT	22040	1281	28.6	30.2	31.2	4.6	5.4	40956	48288	50	48	1083	17.7	16.4	16.2	28.2	21.5	172917
32331	GREENVILLE	15676	1877	39.0	34.8	22.1	3.4	0.6	31500	36532	16	14	1590	36.4	22.8	27.6	12.0	1.3	74419
32332	GRETNA	11515	517	41.6	33.5	19.0	5.2	0.8	28870	33328	10	8	412	42.7	29.9	19.2	6.1	2.2	59375
32333	HAVANA	19380	4945	31.4	28.9	31.4	5.9	2.4	40498	46309	48	46	4107	20.9	22.6	36.4	18.6	1.5	99692
32334	HOSFORD	25823	752	35.0	27.1	29.9	5.6	2.4	37188	42863	36	33	619	38.5	13.6	33.6	13.3	1.1	81667
32336	LAMONT	20208	536	35.6	26.3	29.1	6.2	2.8	39452	45792	44	41	445	13.9	25.8	38.0	17.1	5.2	109844
32340	MADISON	15455	4711	45.2	28.2	20.9	3.7	2.1	28466	32423	9	7	3550	26.4	29.9	30.6	10.8	2.3	82100
32343	MIDWAY	14310	477	38.8	37.5	19.1	2.9	1.7	30948	34844	15	13	397	32.2	29.7	21.4	16.1	0.5	78906
32344	MONTICELLO	21029	4134	34.1	29.8	25.7	7.4	3.1	36961	42998	35	32	3374	19.2	20.2	36.0	19.2	5.4	105888
32346	PANACEA	20762	914	39.5	34.5	17.3	6.6	2.2	30384	34962	13	11	725	19.6	15.7	27.5	29.4	7.9	136089
32347	PERRY	17204	3316	30.3	33.2	28.8	6.6	1.1	38557	45012	41	39	2744	30.5	23.8	36.8	7.8	1.1	82171
32348	PERRY	17280	3400	42.8	30.4	19.9	5.0	1.9	29426	33365	11	9	2581	30.0	24.1	34.3	9.3	2.3	81808
32350	PINETTA	22170	402	27.4	38.8	25.1	3.0	5.7	37458	43054	37	35	344	23.8	22.1	37.5	14.8	1.7	96364
32351	QUINCY	16099	6594	37.7	32.5	23.5	4.8	1.5	33693	38086	23	22	4825	28.4	35.2	27.5	8.4	0.5	74158
32352	QUINCY	14641	2395	36.0	33.0	26.3	2.8	1.9	34610	39884	26	24	1933	36.0	28.2	21.3	12.5	2.1	71738
32355	SAINT MARKS	22701	131	38.9	28.2	26.7	5.3	0.8	33816	38308	23	22	105	17.1	16.2	52.4	12.4	1.9	107738
32356	SALEM	16985	76	39.5	34.2	23.7	1.3	1.3	28817	34274	10	8	68	27.9	29.4	26.5	11.8	4.4	74000
32358	SOPCHOPPY	22311	1119	27.7	32.2	29.7	7.2	3.3	40716	46131	49	47	963	15.6	18.2	35.3	28.7	2.3	120871
32359	STEINHATCHEE	20454	646	45.5	27.7	15.8	6.5	4.5	28469	31968	9	7	571	31.7	23.6	26.3	15.6	2.8	83068
32401	PANAMA CITY	18345	10587	44.0	29.6	20.7	3.6	2.1	28906	32813	10	8	6339	22.2	32.8	34.4	7.2	3.5	84758
32403	PANAMA CITY	14904	807	19.7	49.3	24.8	4.3	1.9	36970	41703	35	32	158	8.9	18.4	34.2	27.2	11.4	143333
32404	PANAMA CITY	19562	13987	27.9	32.3	31.7	6.2	1.8	41543	47349	51	50	10333	13.7	20.9	48.7	15.8	1.0	109913
32405	PANAMA CITY	24001	11214	25.5	31.9	30.5	8.3	3.8	43868	50048	58	56	7557	9.7	19.8	43.1	24.1	3.3	119878
32407	PANAMA CITY BEACH	29708	3159	21.3	34.2	31.7	7.8	5.1	46509	52327	65	65	2312	8.9	11.9	43.1	31.0	5.2	141869
32408	PANAMA CITY	28522	6625	27.7	30.3	27.0	9.1	5.9	42296	47803	54	52	4282	3.5	15.3	39.0	31.9	10.3	150793
32409	PANAMA CITY	17542	3000	27.8	36.1	30.1	4.9	1.1	40407	46115	48	45	2628	20.8	32.9	34.9	9.8	1.6	86340
32413	PANAMA CITY BEACH	25929	4812	26.7	33.2	29.4	7.2	3.5	42003	47418	53	51	3900	8.4	12.7	45.8	28.6	4.5	131028
32420	ALFORD	19563	953	33.1	32.5	27.0	4.2	3.3	35937	41181	31	29	817	21.3	22.5	39.3	14.0	2.9	96733
32421	ALTHA	17353	1718	36.4	32.5	26.0	3.7	1.5	33222	37743	22	20	1456	33.5	28.1	31.1	6.9	0.4	72000
32423	BASCOM	17340	547	36.4	37.3	22.7	2.6	1.1	33714	38432	23	22	465	28.6	30.3	25.8	15.1	0.2	80568
32424	BLOUNTSTOWN	15035	2577	45.4	30.1	19.4	4.2	1.1	28041	31285	9	6	1976	27.7	28.6	33.8	8.9	1.0	81830
32425	BONIFAY	17347	4981	42.9	30.5	20.4	4.0	2.2	30665	35100	14	12	3955	26.4	27.4	31.8	12.4	2.1	85372
32426	CAMPBELLTON	14967	364	48.1	30.8	14.8	3.9	2.5	26429	29355	6	4	302	27.8	29.1	32.8	10.3	0.0	82759
32427	CARYVILLE	15451	469	43.1	30.5	21.5	3.2	1.7	29298	34132	11	9	399	30.6	26.3	31.8	11.3	0.0	78542
32428	CHIPLEY	18463	5671	39.6	30.0	22.4	5.8	2.3	31817	36831	17	16	4606	18.2	23.5	39.3	16.5	2.5	103280
32430	CLARKSVILLE	17931	121	39.7	31.4	22.3	5.0	1.7	31411	36145	16	14	108	37.0	20.4	34.3	7.4	0.9	73333
32431	COTTONDALE	15214	2038	41.4	33.3	21.3	3.3	0.8	29482	33884	11	10	1665	26.4	27.9	35.0	8.8	1.9	84624
32433	DEFUNIAK SPRINGS	16184	5388	39.0	33.4	22.7	4.0	1.0	31877	36334	17	16	4357	28.4	24.0	35.6	9.3	2.7	86362
32435	DEFUNIAK SPRINGS	16735	2792	38.0	36.3	20.7	4.3	0.8	31992	36539	18	16	2121	20.9	23.4	33.7	16.9	5.2	101277
32437	EBRO	19475	243	41.6	30.0	20.2	5.4	2.9	31805	35695	17	16	206	27.2	28.6	25.2	12.6	6.3	84286
32438	FOUNTAIN	15217	1368	43.0	36.6	16.3	2.5	1.6	30290	34871	13	11	1261	48.4	29.5	18.8	2.9	0.4	51752
32439	FREEPORT	19640	2992	34.8	34.9	22.7	5.4	2.2	36074	40748	32	29	2478	21.5	20.3	33.6	19.4	5.3	107358
32440	GRACEVILLE	17357	2156	41.8	27.2	25.0	4.2	1.9	30213	34298	13	11	1604	24.8	26.4	37.3	11.1	0.3	88230
32442	GRAND RIDGE	17881	1506	33.9	32.0	28.0	5.2	0.9	36315	41318	33	30	1267	24.9	31.4	30.7	10.9	2.1	81719
32443	GREENWOOD	24484	1166	32.1	37.9	23.8	4.0	2.3	35389	40150	29	27	987	28.4	22.2	36.8	11.8	0.9	89236
32444	LYNN HAVEN	26311	6809	18.7	28.5	35.9	12.2	4.7	52375	59640	76	77	5418	4.2	12.8	45.1	34.8	3.1	143358
32445	MALONE	14094	492	47.4	23.6	24.6	3.5	1.0	27534	31141	8	6	403	27.1	20.4	40.7	11.9	0.0	95833
32446	MARIANNA	20892	3907	30.7	30.9	26.5	8.0	4.0	39927	45196	46	43	2964	16.0	18.8	44.1	19.1	2.1	111159
32448	MARIANNA	14845	3693	44.1	35.8	15.6	3.5	1.0	28096	31909	9	6	2708	22.8	35.2	31.7	8.5	1.9	80227
32449	WEWAHITCHKA	12228	209	56.0	25.4	16.3	2.4	0.0	22010	25234	3	2	187	53.5	22.5	10.2	12.3	1.6	46176
32455	PONCE DE LEON	16311	1694	40.6	30.4	25.9	2.1	1.0	32039	36252	18	17	1452	33.6	29.6	25.3	9.5	2.1	72473
32456	PORT SAINT JOE	19928	3693	33.8	34.0	25.7	4.2	2.4	36211	41255	32	30	2930	10.9	18.6	39.9	24.4	6.3	122395
32459	SANTA ROSA BEACH	32256	3399	24.0	28.0	31.8	8.6	7.6	47925	54041	68	68	2739	7.2	13.9	23.4	35.7	19.9	202832
32460	SNEADS	17881	1488	33.3	32.1	27.8	5.0	1.9	36708	41844	34	31	1240	26.3	32.2	32.2	8.2	1.2	77500
32462	VERNON	17019	1452	43.3	31.3	20.5	3.8	1.1	29028	33246	10	8	1231	28.7	22.0	35.1	12.4	1.9	89066
32464	WESTVILLE	17412	1702	38.8	34.4	22.1	3.1	1.6	31743	35996	17	15	1486	31.8	33.0	23.0	7.3	4.8	70467
32465	WEWAHITCHKA	16780	2397	39.4	31.3	23.6	4.5	1.3	30857	35308	14	13	1997	28.5	29.5	28.7	11.3	1.9	81175
32466	YOUNGSTOWN	17569	2182	26.8	36.6	29.7	4.5	2.5	40223	46058	47	45	1908	24.8	30.4	34.3	9.3	1.3	85147
	FLORIDA	25506		26.4	29.9	29.1	9.1	5.6	44138	51288				8.8	15.8	40.2	28.3	7.0	137042
	UNITED STATES	25866		24.7	27.1	30.8	10.9	6.5	48124	56710				10.9	15.0	33.7	30.1	10.4	145905

Copyright © 2004 ESRI BIS. All rights reserved. Reproduction by any method is prohibited.

ZIP CODE #	POST OFFICE NAME	FINANCIAL SERVICES: Auto Loan	FINANCIAL SERVICES: Home Loan	FINANCIAL SERVICES: Investments	FINANCIAL SERVICES: Retirement Plans	THE HOME: Home Improvements: Home Repair	THE HOME: Home Improvements: Lawn & Garden	THE HOME: Furnishings: Computers & Hardware	THE HOME: Furnishings: Major Appliances	THE HOME: Furnishings: TV, Radio, Sound Equipment	THE HOME: Furnishings: Furniture	ENTERTAINMENT: Dine out/ Carry out	ENTERTAINMENT: Sports Equipment	ENTERTAINMENT: Fees & Tickets	ENTERTAINMENT: Toys & Games	ENTERTAINMENT: Travel	ENTERTAINMENT: Cable TV	PERSONAL: Apparel & Services	PERSONAL: Auto Repairs	PERSONAL: Health Insurance	PERSONAL: Pets & Supplies
32220	JACKSONVILLE	86	78	61	74	78	84	74	80	76	76	94	92	71	90	74	76	90	80	81	96
32221	JACKSONVILLE	85	85	79	84	84	88	82	84	81	83	101	98	81	99	81	79	98	84	81	95
32222	JACKSONVILLE	89	88	77	88	87	89	83	86	81	85	101	99	81	97	81	78	98	85	81	99
32223	JACKSONVILLE	130	142	158	150	138	142	138	133	129	140	165	157	144	164	135	123	163	133	119	148
32224	JACKSONVILLE	116	120	130	127	117	120	120	118	114	122	144	139	120	140	117	108	141	119	107	129
32225	JACKSONVILLE	109	123	125	127	119	117	114	113	105	116	134	132	117	134	112	100	132	110	99	123
32226	JACKSONVILLE	105	109	101	107	110	113	100	105	98	101	122	122	101	124	102	97	119	102	102	122
32227	JACKSONVILLE	74	47	45	54	43	51	70	61	71	65	89	81	60	80	58	65	85	71	56	69
32233	ATLANTIC BEACH	89	82	94	88	81	86	92	87	90	91	114	107	89	109	87	85	110	92	81	97
32234	JACKSONVILLE	87	69	46	64	73	80	67	76	72	68	87	89	60	82	66	74	82	75	83	97
32244	JACKSONVILLE	80	80	80	83	78	80	79	79	76	81	96	93	78	94	77	73	94	79	72	88
32246	JACKSONVILLE	82	86	84	88	84	84	83	82	79	84	100	97	83	99	81	75	97	82	75	92
32250	JACKSONVILLE BEACH	96	104	124	107	103	107	106	102	102	105	128	121	108	129	105	99	126	104	95	112
32254	JACKSONVILLE	52	44	46	41	44	51	47	49	52	48	64	55	47	62	47	55	62	50	54	58
32256	JACKSONVILLE	122	108	129	120	104	112	123	116	120	125	153	141	119	143	114	112	149	124	104	130
32257	JACKSONVILLE	96	97	107	104	94	97	99	96	94	101	120	114	99	116	95	89	117	98	86	106
32258	JACKSONVILLE	126	135	142	142	132	133	131	129	123	133	156	152	132	154	128	117	153	129	116	142
32259	JACKSONVILLE	156	170	177	178	166	166	162	160	151	165	191	188	164	189	159	143	188	158	143	175
32266	NEPTUNE BEACH	115	129	170	135	126	131	131	125	126	131	159	150	135	164	131	122	157	127	114	137
32277	JACKSONVILLE	85	88	99	91	86	89	90	87	86	90	109	103	90	109	88	83	107	89	80	96
32301	TALLAHASSEE	60	51	64	55	50	55	65	58	65	62	81	73	61	77	60	61	79	64	55	65
32303	TALLAHASSEE	79	76	86	81	74	78	84	79	81	83	102	96	82	100	80	76	100	83	72	88
32304	TALLAHASSEE	36	24	28	26	23	28	40	32	40	35	49	42	34	45	33	36	47	37	30	36
32305	TALLAHASSEE	73	68	59	65	67	72	66	69	68	68	84	79	64	80	65	67	81	70	70	81
32306	TALLAHASSEE	0	0	0	0	0	0	0	0	0	0	0	0	0	0	0	0	0	0	0	0
32307	TALLAHASSEE	0	0	0	0	0	0	0	0	0	0	0	0	0	0	0	0	0	0	0	0
32308	TALLAHASSEE	101	102	120	108	100	105	107	103	103	107	131	123	107	127	104	99	128	107	95	114
32309	TALLAHASSEE	126	141	147	144	138	140	131	131	123	134	156	152	136	156	131	119	154	129	119	145
32310	TALLAHASSEE	54	47	47	46	47	51	52	51	53	52	66	60	49	62	49	52	64	53	51	59
32311	TALLAHASSEE	91	97	102	100	94	95	95	93	90	96	114	111	96	114	93	85	112	94	83	103
32312	TALLAHASSEE	153	178	186	182	173	174	162	161	151	165	191	186	171	194	163	145	190	157	144	177
32317	TALLAHASSEE	122	147	155	149	144	144	132	131	122	133	154	152	140	160	134	118	154	127	118	145
32320	APALACHICOLA	62	46	30	43	51	60	47	55	54	47	64	61	42	59	48	57	58	54	66	70
32321	BRISTOL	83	61	35	54	68	76	58	70	67	59	80	83	51	76	60	71	74	70	83	97
32322	CARRABELLE	43	31	19	29	34	40	33	37	38	32	44	43	29	42	33	40	40	37	45	48
32324	CHATTAHOOCHEE	65	53	47	51	55	64	57	60	63	57	77	68	55	74	57	66	72	61	68	72
32327	CRAWFORDVILLE	86	78	61	75	79	83	74	80	76	76	93	93	70	89	74	75	89	79	81	96
32328	EASTPOINT	94	69	43	62	77	89	66	80	77	68	91	91	60	83	69	82	84	79	97	107
32331	GREENVILLE	67	50	33	44	54	62	50	58	57	51	68	67	45	64	50	61	63	58	68	77
32332	GRETNA	57	48	45	44	48	56	51	53	56	52	68	59	48	62	50	59	65	54	59	63
32333	HAVANA	76	69	54	66	70	76	66	72	68	67	84	83	63	81	66	69	80	71	74	86
32334	HOSFORD	112	76	35	66	86	98	73	91	88	75	103	109	62	98	74	94	94	90	112	129
32336	LAMONT	88	70	46	65	74	81	68	77	74	69	89	91	61	84	67	76	83	77	85	100
32340	MADISON	70	50	31	44	54	63	50	59	58	51	69	69	44	65	50	62	64	59	70	79
32343	MIDWAY	65	62	52	60	62	65	59	62	59	60	72	72	57	70	58	58	70	62	61	73
32344	MONTICELLO	86	71	53	67	74	83	72	79	77	72	93	90	66	87	71	79	88	79	86	96
32346	PANACEA	81	56	28	49	63	73	54	67	64	54	75	80	46	72	55	69	69	66	82	94
32347	PERRY	79	62	40	57	66	74	60	69	67	61	80	81	55	77	60	69	74	68	78	89
32348	PERRY	71	51	34	46	56	65	53	61	61	53	73	71	47	69	53	65	67	61	73	81
32350	PINETTA	104	70	32	60	79	91	68	84	82	69	96	101	57	90	69	88	87	84	104	120
32351	QUINCY	66	57	51	53	57	66	59	62	64	60	78	69	56	72	58	66	74	62	68	73
32352	QUINCY	66	59	46	56	59	63	57	61	59	58	72	70	53	68	56	59	69	61	63	73
32355	SAINT MARKS	66	60	47	58	60	64	58	62	58	59	72	71	54	68	57	57	69	61	61	73
32356	SALEM	68	54	36	48	60	68	50	61	57	50	68	71	45	67	54	61	63	60	72	83
32358	SOPCHOPPY	97	72	43	67	80	88	70	83	79	71	94	99	62	90	71	82	87	82	95	111
32359	STEINHATCHEE	75	58	40	53	66	74	55	66	62	55	74	78	49	73	59	67	69	65	79	91
32401	PANAMA CITY	60	52	52	50	53	61	58	58	62	56	75	66	55	72	56	63	71	60	64	67
32403	PANAMA CITY	75	53	50	57	50	60	70	64	71	67	89	79	62	79	61	67	85	72	63	73
32404	PANAMA CITY	76	71	60	70	72	77	70	73	70	70	87	85	67	85	69	70	83	72	73	85
32405	PANAMA CITY	81	82	84	81	82	88	82	82	81	81	101	95	82	101	82	81	98	82	82	93
32407	PANAMA CITY BEACH	103	91	78	85	97	107	88	97	94	87	113	114	83	113	91	97	108	97	107	123
32408	PANAMA CITY	83	87	100	88	87	92	87	87	86	86	107	102	87	108	88	85	104	88	85	99
32409	PANAMA CITY	74	68	53	65	68	71	65	69	65	66	81	80	61	76	64	64	77	69	69	82
32413	PANAMA CITY BEACH	96	76	53	69	85	95	72	86	81	72	96	101	65	95	76	86	90	85	100	116
32420	ALFORD	85	60	33	53	68	78	58	71	68	58	80	84	50	77	60	73	73	70	86	100
32421	ALTHA	73	64	47	61	65	70	61	67	63	62	77	78	57	74	61	63	74	67	69	83
32423	BASCOM	74	53	30	48	59	67	53	63	61	53	72	73	47	68	53	65	66	62	74	83
32424	BLOUNTSTOWN	53	43	31	41	45	51	44	48	47	43	57	56	40	54	43	49	53	48	54	60
32425	BONIFAY	76	54	31	48	59	69	54	64	63	54	74	75	47	70	54	67	68	64	77	86
32426	CAMPBELLTON	71	48	22	41	54	62	46	57	56	47	65	68	39	62	47	60	59	57	71	81
32427	CARYVILLE	68	51	31	47	55	62	49	58	55	51	66	68	44	63	50	58	62	57	66	77
32428	CHIPLEY	82	59	34	54	66	75	59	70	68	59	81	82	52	77	60	72	74	70	83	93
32430	CLARKSVILLE	69	56	37	52	58	63	53	60	57	55	70	71	49	66	53	59	66	60	65	77
32431	COTTONDALE	68	50	28	45	54	61	48	57	55	49	65	68	42	62	48	58	60	57	66	77
32433	DEFUNIAK SPRINGS	65	54	41	51	56	62	54	59	58	54	70	68	50	66	54	59	66	59	64	73
32435	DEFUNIAK SPRINGS	66	49	31	46	53	63	52	59	59	51	70	67	47	66	52	63	64	59	70	73
32437	EBRO	84	62	35	56	68	76	60	71	68	61	81	84	53	77	60	72	75	70	83	96
32438	FOUNTAIN	67	55	38	52	57	62	53	59	56	54	69	69	49	65	53	57	65	59	63	75
32439	FREEPORT	78	66	48	62	70	76	63	71	67	63	81	83	58	78	64	69	76	70	77	91
32440	GRACEVILLE	69	53	39	50	57	66	56	62	63	55	75	71	51	71	56	66	69	63	72	77
32442	GRAND RIDGE	75	63	44	59	65	71	61	68	64	62	78	79	56	74	60	65	74	67	72	84
32443	GREENWOOD	51	47	36	45	47	49	44	48	45	46	55	55	42	52	44	44	53	47	47	56
32444	LYNN HAVEN	87	101	110	101	99	101	96	95	91	95	114	111	100	119	97	88	113	93	87	103
32445	MALONE	32	24	16	23	26	31	26	29	29	25	35	32	23	33	26	31	32	29	35	35
32446	MARIANNA	79	69	54	66	73	81	68	75	73	67	88	86	65	86	69	76	83	74	83	91
32448	MARIANNA	57	46	37	43	48	54	47	52	52	48	63	59	44	59	47	54	59	52	58	64
32449	WEWAHITCHKA	58	39	17	33	44	50	37	47	45	38	53	56	32	50	38	48	48	46	57	66
32455	PONCE DE LEON	70	52	31	47	57	64	50	59	57	51	68	70	45	65	51	60	63	59	69	80
32456	PORT SAINT JOE	73	62	52	58	67	76	61	68	67	61	81	77	58	78	63	71	76	68	78	85
32459	SANTA ROSA BEACH	117	97	71	89	105	117	91	106	100	92	120	122	84	115	95	105	112	105	121	138
32460	SNEADS	57	48	35	45	49	54	47	51	49	47	60	59	43	56	46	50	57	51	54	63
32462	VERNON	71	48	22	42	54	63	46	58	56	47	66	69	40	62	47	60	60	57	71	82
32464	WESTVILLE	78	53	25	46	60	69	51	63	61	52	72	76	44	68	52	66	66	63	78	90
32465	WEWAHITCHKA	70	54	35	50	59	67	54	62	60	54	72	72	49	69	55	63	67	62	72	80
32466	YOUNGSTOWN	78	70	53	67	70	75	66	72	68	68	84	83	62	79	66	68	80	72	73	87
	FLORIDA	89	87	95	86	87	96	87	89	89	89	111	100	87	107	88	90	108	90	91	101
	UNITED STATES	100	100	100	100	100	100	100	100	100	100	100	100	100	100	100	100	100	100	100	100

A 32501-32759

# POST OFFICE NAME	COUNTY FIPS CODE	POPULATION 2000	2004	2009	2000-2004 ANNUAL RATE % Rate	State Centile	HOUSEHOLDS 2000	2004	2009	% Annual Rate 2000-2004	2004 Average HH Size	FAMILIES 2000	2004	% Annual Rate 2000-2004
32501 PENSACOLA	033	14937	14748	15165	-0.3	2	5791	5779	6038	-0.1	2.25	3130	3069	-0.5
32502 PENSACOLA	033	1303	1232	1258	-1.3	0	537	510	533	-1.2	1.87	253	234	-1.8
32503 PENSACOLA	033	34219	33932	35030	-0.2	3	13317	13417	14115	0.2	2.24	7987	7929	-0.2
32504 PENSACOLA	033	23705	24315	25416	0.6	18	10451	10879	11527	1.0	2.22	6616	6813	0.7
32505 PENSACOLA	033	29055	29275	30544	0.2	7	10666	10874	11493	0.5	2.66	7290	7357	0.2
32506 PENSACOLA	033	33555	36689	39766	2.1	58	13321	14633	15995	2.2	2.43	9208	10094	2.2
32507 PENSACOLA	033	28636	30679	32889	1.6	46	11264	12158	13179	1.8	2.45	7263	7780	1.6
32508 PENSACOLA	033	10389	10345	10383	-0.1	4	383	376	390	-0.4	3.81	379	372	-0.4
32514 PENSACOLA	033	33429	35687	37833	1.6	44	13795	15046	16247	2.1	2.24	8384	8989	1.7
32526 PENSACOLA	033	31971	33701	35801	1.3	35	12008	12892	13894	1.7	2.57	8993	9570	1.5
32531 BAKER	091	3826	4162	4576	2.0	56	1462	1604	1781	2.2	2.59	1147	1251	2.1
32533 CANTONMENT	033	23894	25773	27607	1.8	52	8560	9382	10197	2.2	2.73	6844	7442	2.0
32534 PENSACOLA	033	12125	12662	13403	1.0	28	4808	5099	5477	1.4	2.46	3370	3527	1.1
32535 CENTURY	033	6640	6863	7133	0.8	21	1971	2088	2222	1.4	2.55	1443	1514	1.1
32536 CRESTVIEW	091	13552	15029	16712	2.5	65	5051	5651	6352	2.7	2.61	3861	4301	2.6
32539 CRESTVIEW	091	20150	22296	24753	2.4	64	6897	7754	8754	2.8	2.68	5290	5910	2.6
32541 DESTIN	091	12488	14278	16115	3.2	76	5505	6433	7387	3.7	2.20	3531	4069	3.4
32542 EGLIN AFB	091	10763	10835	11511	0.2	7	2606	2675	2908	0.6	3.34	2442	2494	0.5
32544 HURLBURT FIELD	091	1867	2152	2426	3.4	78	378	450	520	4.2	4.30	312	369	4.0
32547 FORT WALTON BEACH	091	29695	31719	34768	1.6	44	12577	13594	15094	1.9	2.28	7685	8223	1.6
32548 FORT WALTON BEACH	091	21996	23044	25021	1.1	31	9570	10153	11158	1.4	2.25	5862	6146	1.1
32550 MIRAMAR BEACH	131	3024	5053	7338	12.8	100	1480	2539	3746	13.5	1.94	911	1549	13.3
32561 GULF BREEZE	033	8095	8300	9010	0.6	17	3590	3708	4054	0.8	2.23	2350	2405	0.6
32563 GULF BREEZE	113	17428	20707	24638	4.1	85	6823	8195	9839	4.4	2.51	5155	6148	4.2
32564 HOLT	113	2527	3001	3460	4.1	85	939	1129	1319	4.4	2.61	718	857	4.3
32565 JAY	113	5284	5553	6263	1.2	33	2046	2166	2464	1.4	2.51	1537	1614	1.2
32566 NAVARRE	113	21505	25703	30664	4.3	86	7961	9563	11471	4.4	2.69	6179	7366	4.2
32567 LAUREL HILL	091	3598	4111	4786	3.2	75	1447	1666	1958	3.4	2.47	1048	1197	3.2
32568 MC DAVID	033	3385	3434	3568	0.3	10	1254	1293	1363	0.7	2.64	980	1003	0.6
32569 MARY ESTHER	091	11380	12185	13295	1.6	45	4463	4833	5333	1.9	2.52	3122	3348	1.7
32570 MILTON	113	24767	26967	30633	2.0	56	9210	10130	11624	2.3	2.60	6873	7502	2.1
32571 MILTON	113	23417	26659	31066	3.1	75	8418	9617	11260	3.2	2.77	6700	7624	3.1
32577 MOLINO	033	4396	4537	4755	0.8	21	1589	1663	1766	1.1	2.73	1270	1318	0.9
32578 NICEVILLE	091	27909	30709	34138	2.3	61	10733	11966	13476	2.6	2.53	8193	9094	2.5
32579 SHALIMAR	091	10110	10636	11604	1.2	34	4283	4560	5034	1.5	2.33	3083	3252	1.3
32580 VALPARAISO	091	3921	4056	4373	0.8	22	1671	1746	1906	1.0	2.30	1125	1163	0.8
32583 MILTON	113	19662	21688	24738	2.3	62	6950	7801	9050	2.8	2.59	5185	5771	2.6
32601 GAINESVILLE	001	19364	19929	21358	0.7	19	8693	8981	9712	0.8	2.08	2489	2523	0.3
32603 GAINESVILLE	001	7372	7256	7492	-0.4	2	2219	2174	2313	-0.5	1.89	712	661	-1.7
32605 GAINESVILLE	001	22507	23308	25074	0.8	23	9260	9713	10564	1.1	2.37	5890	6126	0.9
32606 GAINESVILLE	001	18229	20525	22983	2.8	71	7551	8542	9630	2.9	2.36	5006	5658	2.9
32607 GAINESVILLE	001	26350	29866	33657	3.0	73	11961	13743	15649	3.3	2.15	5174	5780	2.6
32608 GAINESVILLE	001	34243	39490	44915	3.4	79	15270	17673	20212	3.5	2.21	6214	7126	3.3
32609 GAINESVILLE	001	19044	20456	22320	1.7	48	6799	7375	8171	1.9	2.41	3954	4282	1.9
32611 GAINESVILLE	001	4708	4624	4640	-0.4	2	205	169	176	-4.4	2.69	113	93	-4.5
32615 ALACHUA	001	12719	13249	14307	1.0	27	4880	5145	5608	1.3	2.57	3635	3816	1.2
32617 ANTHONY	083	3277	3748	4379	3.2	76	1220	1414	1670	3.5	2.64	905	1036	3.2
32618 ARCHER	001	6288	7136	8088	3.0	73	2404	2748	3138	3.2	2.60	1708	1940	3.0
32619 BELL	041	3849	4167	4520	1.9	53	1447	1582	1730	2.1	2.55	1087	1181	2.0
32621 BRONSON	075	3625	4367	5096	4.5	88	1269	1548	1828	4.8	2.72	925	1118	4.6
32622 BROOKER	007	1982	2069	2181	1.0	28	740	785	840	1.4	2.26	554	583	1.1
32625 CEDAR KEY	075	1606	1657	1782	0.7	20	740	775	845	1.1	2.14	471	485	0.7
32626 CHIEFLAND	075	8538	8986	9775	1.2	34	3506	3742	4120	1.5	2.38	2453	2595	1.3
32628 CROSS CITY	029	5073	5236	5510	0.8	21	1535	1613	1738	1.2	2.61	1095	1142	1.0
32631 EARLETON	001	781	800	861	0.6	16	321	331	359	0.7	2.42	215	221	0.7
32640 HAWTHORNE	001	10131	10572	11252	1.0	28	4039	4259	4575	1.3	2.48	2856	2988	1.1
32641 GAINESVILLE	001	12897	13135	14034	0.4	12	4560	4687	5051	0.7	2.79	3294	3367	0.5
32643 HIGH SPRINGS	001	8800	9573	10499	2.0	56	3385	3729	4131	2.3	2.55	2454	2684	2.1
32648 HORSESHOE BEACH	029	416	400	418	-0.9	0	172	167	177	-0.7	2.36	123	119	-0.8
32653 GAINESVILLE	001	12201	13104	14343	1.7	47	4943	5339	5881	1.8	2.45	3428	3683	1.7
32656 KEYSTONE HEIGHTS	019	11669	12965	15008	2.5	67	4533	5081	5933	2.7	2.54	3359	3728	2.5
32666 MELROSE	107	5808	5940	6322	0.5	16	2469	2550	2738	0.8	2.33	1722	1765	0.6
32667 MICANOPY	001	4145	4132	4505	-0.1	4	1791	1804	1986	0.2	2.28	1193	1193	0.0
32668 MORRISTON	075	4279	4798	5421	2.7	70	1658	1880	2146	3.0	2.53	1187	1333	2.8
32669 NEWBERRY	001	8220	9123	10140	2.5	66	3126	3500	3921	2.7	2.60	2311	2577	2.6
32680 OLD TOWN	029	7975	8618	9337	1.8	52	3361	3674	4028	2.1	2.33	2343	2544	2.0
32686 REDDICK	083	6231	6654	7501	1.6	44	2391	2584	2946	1.8	2.55	1697	1817	1.6
32693 TRENTON	041	9869	10773	11757	2.1	57	3376	3755	4169	2.5	2.56	2436	2686	2.3
32694 WALDO	001	1430	1521	1657	1.5	41	608	652	716	1.7	2.33	403	429	1.5
32696 WILLISTON	075	8869	9526	10504	1.7	48	3480	3790	4231	2.0	2.47	2459	2657	1.8
32701 ALTAMONTE SPRINGS	117	22563	24447	27408	1.9	53	10016	10977	12411	2.2	2.20	5520	5915	1.6
32702 ALTOONA	069	2727	3065	3669	2.8	70	1096	1235	1486	2.9	2.44	779	868	2.6
32703 APOPKA	095	43532	46958	52332	1.8	50	15613	16885	18849	1.9	2.76	11154	11922	1.6
32707 CASSELBERRY	117	31664	34120	37931	1.8	50	13029	14183	15897	2.0	2.40	8688	9346	1.7
32708 WINTER SPRINGS	117	40612	44529	49894	2.2	59	14850	16473	18625	2.5	2.69	11174	12251	2.2
32709 CHRISTMAS	095	2295	2635	3013	3.3	77	829	960	1101	3.5	2.74	639	734	3.4
32712 APOPKA	095	28878	33044	37749	3.2	76	10202	11717	13394	3.3	2.82	8116	9229	3.1
32713 DEBARY	127	15666	17519	19544	2.7	69	6606	7365	8199	2.6	2.35	4750	5229	2.3
32714 ALTAMONTE SPRINGS	117	34414	35721	39279	0.9	24	14516	15201	16858	1.1	2.34	8652	8939	0.8
32720 DELAND	127	25264	27416	30532	1.9	54	10124	11049	12357	2.1	2.36	6631	7183	1.9
32724 DELAND	127	26751	28407	30938	1.4	40	10640	11308	12343	1.4	2.37	6860	7196	1.1
32725 DELTONA	127	37742	41433	45807	2.2	60	14257	15578	17164	2.1	2.65	10750	11629	1.9
32726 EUSTIS	069	17619	19862	23948	2.9	71	7340	8323	10107	3.0	2.33	4800	5390	2.8
32730 CASSELBERRY	117	5332	5586	6148	1.1	31	2343	2480	2758	1.4	2.20	1442	1500	0.9
32732 GENEVA	117	4632	5046	5631	2.0	56	1643	1812	2041	2.3	2.76	1297	1418	2.1
32735 GRAND ISLAND	069	2444	2848	3488	3.7	81	1051	1227	1506	3.7	2.32	794	909	3.2
32736 EUSTIS	069	7848	9433	11725	4.4	87	2897	3520	4408	4.7	2.67	2215	2662	4.4
32738 DELTONA	127	34255	38884	43801	3.0	73	11580	13114	14741	3.0	2.96	9436	10599	2.8
32744 LAKE HELEN	127	3383	3602	3919	1.5	42	1359	1443	1566	1.4	2.50	979	1026	1.1
32746 LAKE MARY	117	32314	38224	44606	4.0	84	12162	14543	17132	4.3	2.58	8925	10602	4.1
32750 LONGWOOD	117	24194	25425	28096	1.2	32	8766	9287	10355	1.4	2.67	6674	7012	1.2
32751 MAITLAND	095	20384	21117	23210	0.9	23	8122	8507	9404	1.1	2.45	5332	5501	0.7
32754 MIMS	009	9932	10671	11610	1.7	48	3912	4253	4672	2.0	2.51	2881	3099	1.7
32757 MOUNT DORA	095	18905	21659	26158	3.3	76	7999	9327	11407	3.7	2.28	5261	6061	3.4
32759 OAK HILL	127	2385	2518	2745	1.3	36	1026	1088	1188	1.4	2.31	735	770	1.1
FLORIDA					2.1					2.2	2.45			2.0
UNITED STATES					1.2					1.3	2.58			1.1

ZIP CODE #	POST OFFICE NAME	RACE (%) White 2000	White 2004	Black 2000	Black 2004	Asian/Pacific 2000	Asian/Pacific 2004	% Hispanic Origin 2000	% Hispanic Origin 2004	2004 AGE DISTRIBUTION (%) 0-4	5-9	10-14	15-19	20-24	25-44	45-64	65-84	85+	18+	MEDIAN AGE 2004	% 2004 Males	% 2004 Females
32501	PENSACOLA	36.6	33.1	59.9	63.3	1.1	1.2	1.6	1.8	5.7	5.7	6.4	6.6	7.4	28.6	23.0	13.7	3.0	78.4	38.3	50.3	49.7
32502	PENSACOLA	53.2	49.8	42.7	45.9	1.3	1.5	2.5	3.0	3.8	3.5	3.8	4.5	6.4	24.9	27.4	20.5	5.2	86.4	46.7	50.2	49.8
32503	PENSACOLA	65.5	63.2	30.0	31.8	2.0	2.3	1.8	2.2	5.1	4.8	5.5	10.7	12.0	22.7	23.0	14.1	2.2	81.1	35.7	46.1	53.9
32504	PENSACOLA	82.5	79.9	12.1	13.9	2.2	2.6	2.6	3.2	5.5	5.4	6.0	6.6	7.4	26.4	26.6	14.5	1.7	79.2	40.2	47.3	52.7
32505	PENSACOLA	46.2	42.1	47.5	51.2	2.8	3.1	2.1	2.4	8.1	7.7	8.4	7.7	7.4	25.7	22.1	11.6	1.3	71.2	34.1	47.0	53.0
32506	PENSACOLA	76.3	72.5	13.1	15.3	4.9	5.7	3.7	4.7	7.5	6.9	6.9	6.9	7.9	30.0	21.3	11.4	1.2	74.8	33.9	48.8	51.2
32507	PENSACOLA	77.0	75.0	15.8	17.0	2.8	3.2	3.1	3.7	6.7	6.6	6.7	6.8	7.1	28.0	24.5	12.3	1.3	76.7	36.7	49.8	50.2
32508	PENSACOLA	75.3	71.5	13.1	15.2	2.7	3.2	9.8	11.8	2.6	2.0	1.6	23.5	27.2	40.5	2.5	0.0	0.0	93.2	23.7	83.7	16.3
32514	PENSACOLA	82.2	79.0	12.3	14.7	2.0	2.4	2.7	3.3	5.9	5.3	5.6	6.0	8.5	30.2	22.5	13.2	2.9	80.1	36.7	47.1	52.9
32526	PENSACOLA	81.5	78.9	11.8	13.5	2.7	3.1	2.7	3.3	6.1	6.3	6.9	6.7	6.5	28.1	27.2	11.2	1.0	76.5	38.2	49.0	51.0
32531	BAKER	93.1	92.1	3.1	3.6	0.4	0.5	1.0	1.3	5.9	6.3	7.5	6.9	6.1	26.2	26.8	12.6	1.5	76.0	39.1	50.0	50.0
32533	CANTONMENT	84.7	82.7	11.4	12.8	1.0	1.3	1.5	1.8	6.4	6.8	7.6	7.4	5.8	27.5	27.4	10.4	0.8	74.5	38.0	49.3	50.7
32534	PENSACOLA	72.2	68.9	23.3	26.1	1.3	1.5	1.8	2.2	6.4	6.5	6.9	6.4	6.2	26.7	26.3	12.9	1.8	76.2	39.3	47.8	52.2
32535	CENTURY	63.3	60.1	31.7	34.6	0.4	0.5	3.8	4.6	5.9	5.9	6.3	6.2	7.6	34.3	21.8	10.1	1.9	78.1	35.4	58.0	42.0
32536	CRESTVIEW	78.5	76.3	15.6	16.7	2.0	2.5	3.0	3.8	7.9	7.3	7.8	7.3	6.9	29.0	22.5	10.4	0.9	72.6	34.9	48.9	51.1
32539	CRESTVIEW	85.2	83.4	9.3	10.3	1.7	2.1	2.8	3.6	6.4	6.3	7.1	7.0	7.1	30.7	24.6	9.9	1.1	75.9	36.5	51.4	48.6
32541	DESTIN	96.2	95.6	0.4	0.5	1.1	1.3	2.6	3.3	4.0	4.4	5.5	5.6	4.5	26.5	30.8	17.3	1.4	82.6	44.7	50.3	49.7
32542	EGLIN AFB	72.3	69.3	15.3	16.6	3.1	3.6	11.8	14.2	14.3	9.6	6.7	6.5	19.4	37.1	5.4	1.0	0.1	67.0	23.4	57.5	42.5
32544	HURLBURT FIELD	74.3	71.3	13.6	14.9	2.7	3.2	8.3	10.2	11.2	9.8	9.3	8.5	13.3	33.0	7.5	6.9	0.6	65.9	24.2	51.7	48.3
32547	FORT WALTON BEACH	79.6	76.7	11.2	12.6	3.3	4.0	5.0	6.3	6.1	5.6	6.0	7.0	8.7	31.5	22.0	11.8	1.3	78.2	35.3	49.9	50.1
32548	FORT WALTON BEACH	78.1	75.6	13.8	15.2	3.0	3.6	3.9	4.9	5.5	5.2	6.0	6.2	7.2	28.8	24.8	15.0	1.3	79.7	39.8	49.5	50.5
32550	MIRAMAR BEACH	96.8	96.1	0.6	0.8	0.7	0.9	1.3	1.6	3.3	3.2	2.6	2.5	2.4	23.1	35.4	25.3	2.1	89.2	53.1	50.0	50.1
32561	GULF BREEZE	97.2	96.9	0.4	0.4	0.7	0.9	1.4	1.7	3.4	4.3	6.2	6.5	4.1	21.5	34.2	17.8	1.9	81.9	46.9	48.7	51.3
32563	GULF BREEZE	95.7	94.9	0.8	0.9	1.1	1.4	2.4	3.0	5.5	6.3	7.2	6.6	4.7	26.2	29.5	13.0	1.2	76.8	41.6	49.0	51.0
32564	HOLT	94.7	94.2	2.1	2.1	0.3	0.3	1.4	1.8	5.1	5.4	6.8	7.2	6.1	28.4	28.7	11.0	1.2	77.7	39.7	50.8	49.2
32565	JAY	96.1	95.6	0.9	1.1	0.2	0.2	0.9	1.1	6.1	6.4	6.6	6.7	5.7	27.3	27.6	12.1	1.5	76.6	39.6	50.4	49.6
32566	NAVARRE	89.1	87.7	3.7	4.2	2.4	2.8	4.1	5.1	7.2	7.3	7.7	6.9	5.5	31.9	23.6	9.4	0.5	73.5	37.1	50.3	49.7
32567	LAUREL HILL	89.0	87.2	7.7	9.2	0.3	0.4	0.8	1.1	6.0	6.2	6.8	6.4	5.5	24.4	29.1	14.3	1.4	77.3	41.7	49.7	50.3
32568	MC DAVID	84.7	82.7	9.3	10.9	0.1	0.2	0.7	0.9	6.1	6.5	7.3	6.5	5.5	25.4	28.5	12.8	1.4	76.4	40.0	51.1	48.9
32569	MARY ESTHER	81.0	78.4	8.5	9.4	4.4	5.3	4.9	6.1	6.5	6.4	6.6	6.3	7.0	32.9	24.8	9.1	0.5	76.7	35.8	51.2	48.8
32570	MILTON	85.6	83.7	8.6	9.8	1.8	2.1	2.3	2.9	7.6	7.0	6.8	6.8	6.8	28.0	23.8	11.8	1.5	74.4	36.1	48.7	51.4
32571	MILTON	94.2	93.4	1.3	1.5	1.2	1.5	2.0	2.6	6.8	6.9	7.9	7.5	6.7	28.2	26.5	8.9	0.6	73.7	36.7	49.3	50.7
32577	MOLINO	86.0	83.4	10.2	12.4	0.3	0.4	1.0	1.3	6.8	7.1	8.1	7.0	5.8	26.3	26.1	12.1	0.8	73.7	38.2	50.1	49.9
32578	NICEVILLE	89.8	88.4	3.8	4.2	2.6	3.1	3.5	4.4	5.5	5.9	7.2	7.0	5.9	25.0	28.8	13.7	1.1	77.0	41.3	49.5	50.5
32579	SHALIMAR	84.9	82.5	7.2	8.2	3.1	3.7	4.6	5.8	5.0	5.3	6.6	6.6	6.6	25.7	28.2	14.9	1.1	79.2	41.5	48.8	51.2
32580	VALPARAISO	87.8	86.1	4.1	4.5	3.2	3.8	4.1	5.2	5.4	5.1	6.3	7.4	5.7	25.5	25.8	17.3	1.6	78.6	42.0	49.0	51.0
32583	MILTON	87.2	85.8	7.9	8.7	0.8	1.0	2.5	3.1	6.5	6.3	6.4	6.7	6.8	30.6	26.7	9.6	0.6	76.9	37.3	53.4	46.6
32601	GAINESVILLE	67.2	63.6	21.8	24.0	6.4	7.4	7.4	8.8	3.1	2.6	3.5	17.9	25.8	28.6	12.1	5.3	1.3	88.2	24.5	49.4	50.6
32603	GAINESVILLE	77.4	74.6	7.1	7.9	10.1	11.4	10.3	12.3	2.0	1.3	1.3	41.1	25.1	20.3	6.0	2.2	0.6	94.6	20.9	51.2	48.8
32605	GAINESVILLE	86.4	84.2	7.2	8.3	3.3	4.0	5.6	6.9	4.7	4.9	5.9	6.8	7.3	27.7	27.8	13.0	2.0	80.6	39.9	47.7	52.3
32606	GAINESVILLE	86.1	83.7	6.1	7.0	4.8	5.7	6.2	7.7	5.7	5.8	6.9	7.7	5.6	28.3	25.7	11.6	2.8	76.9	38.4	47.2	52.8
32607	GAINESVILLE	76.5	73.4	14.5	16.2	4.0	4.8	7.6	9.2	4.9	4.0	4.9	11.3	21.0	29.7	16.5	6.4	1.3	83.0	26.5	49.5	50.5
32608	GAINESVILLE	79.4	76.8	10.7	11.7	5.2	6.2	7.4	9.0	4.4	3.7	4.1	13.6	22.9	29.3	15.0	5.9	1.0	85.2	25.5	48.9	51.1
32609	GAINESVILLE	53.9	50.3	41.4	44.7	0.8	0.9	4.1	4.7	5.7	5.6	7.1	9.3	8.2	32.1	22.8	8.3	1.0	76.4	33.7	52.2	47.8
32611	GAINESVILLE	70.7	66.9	12.3	13.8	10.8	12.3	11.3	13.4	1.1	0.6	0.4	73.0	16.2	7.9	0.4	0.6	0.0	97.5	18.3	45.1	54.9
32615	ALACHUA	77.6	75.2	19.4	21.4	0.8	0.9	4.0	4.8	6.3	6.8	7.7	7.2	6.1	25.3	29.4	10.2	1.0	74.7	39.1	48.2	51.8
32617	ANTHONY	82.0	78.8	13.5	15.9	0.3	0.4	4.7	5.8	6.8	6.9	7.3	7.4	6.4	27.0	26.9	10.5	1.1	74.7	37.6	50.6	49.4
32618	ARCHER	77.2	74.2	19.4	22.0	0.7	0.8	3.4	4.2	6.7	6.8	7.7	7.0	6.9	25.4	28.4	10.1	1.0	74.5	38.0	49.0	51.0
32619	BELL	95.3	94.7	2.6	2.9	0.1	0.1	2.3	2.9	5.8	6.4	6.8	6.9	7.4	24.9	26.7	14.0	1.1	76.5	39.6	51.1	48.9
32621	BRONSON	83.9	80.9	11.1	13.5	0.2	0.2	7.0	8.4	5.8	5.8	7.4	6.8	7.0	26.5	26.8	12.8	1.2	76.7	38.5	48.3	51.7
32622	BROOKER	82.8	80.2	15.3	17.6	0.2	0.2	1.8	2.2	5.0	5.0	5.5	6.3	6.5	32.1	26.9	11.5	1.2	80.8	39.2	56.7	43.3
32625	CEDAR KEY	97.8	97.4	0.6	0.7	0.3	0.3	1.3	1.6	5.3	5.1	4.8	4.4	4.5	19.9	34.2	19.8	2.0	82.1	49.1	48.2	51.8
32626	CHIEFLAND	86.7	85.3	10.5	11.6	0.6	0.8	2.5	3.0	6.2	5.8	6.6	6.3	5.9	21.7	26.8	18.9	1.9	77.5	43.0	48.5	51.5
32628	CROSS CITY	76.5	73.8	21.1	23.6	0.4	0.5	1.9	2.2	6.3	5.9	5.8	5.9	7.6	32.8	23.3	11.2	1.3	78.4	36.7	58.1	41.9
32631	EARLETON	90.7	89.1	6.8	8.0	0.3	0.3	1.8	2.1	4.0	4.5	5.3	5.6	5.5	24.3	35.4	14.1	1.4	82.6	45.5	50.9	49.1
32640	HAWTHORNE	79.2	76.1	18.2	20.9	0.1	0.2	2.5	3.1	5.4	5.6	6.7	6.4	5.7	22.9	30.2	15.7	1.5	78.4	43.3	49.5	50.5
32641	GAINESVILLE	22.8	20.7	75.0	77.1	0.2	0.2	1.3	1.4	8.4	8.4	10.1	9.9	7.2	23.4	22.4	9.3	1.0	67.1	30.1	45.3	54.7
32643	HIGH SPRINGS	84.1	81.6	13.2	15.4	0.3	0.3	3.6	4.4	5.8	6.1	7.1	7.0	6.1	25.5	28.7	12.0	1.7	76.6	40.3	48.3	51.7
32648	HORSESHOE BEACH	98.1	97.8	1.0	1.3	0.0	0.0	0.2	0.3	4.5	5.0	7.0	6.0	6.0	21.8	28.3	20.3	1.3	79.5	44.8	49.3	50.8
32653	GAINESVILLE	80.5	77.8	13.4	15.1	3.6	4.2	5.2	6.2	6.5	6.7	6.7	6.4	5.4	27.1	27.3	12.3	1.7	76.0	39.8	46.8	53.2
32656	KEYSTONE HEIGHTS	96.4	95.9	1.3	1.5	0.3	0.4	1.8	2.2	5.6	5.9	7.4	7.1	6.0	24.0	27.5	14.6	1.9	76.7	41.3	48.9	51.2
32666	MELROSE	86.4	84.4	10.4	12.0	0.6	0.7	2.3	2.8	5.0	5.6	6.6	5.8	4.7	22.9	30.9	16.9	1.8	79.2	44.7	50.1	49.9
32667	MICANOPY	79.4	76.1	18.2	21.2	0.3	0.3	3.5	4.2	4.0	4.8	5.8	6.0	4.7	22.7	35.5	14.4	2.0	81.6	46.0	49.6	50.4
32668	MORRISTON	91.6	90.1	5.3	6.3	0.4	0.5	5.7	6.9	5.6	5.8	5.8	5.8	5.2	24.1	30.4	15.7	1.5	79.2	43.4	49.7	50.3
32669	NEWBERRY	85.0	82.8	12.4	14.3	0.7	0.9	2.9	3.6	6.2	6.6	7.2	6.8	6.2	27.4	28.4	10.2	1.1	75.9	38.9	49.4	50.6
32680	OLD TOWN	95.8	95.0	2.0	2.4	0.2	0.3	1.9	2.4	5.5	5.5	5.8	5.4	5.4	21.7	29.2	20.1	1.4	79.7	45.5	50.6	49.4
32686	REDDICK	64.8	61.1	32.0	35.4	0.3	0.4	5.0	5.9	5.9	6.2	7.1	7.0	5.2	24.0	30.6	12.6	1.6	76.4	41.6	48.8	51.2
32693	TRENTON	87.7	86.2	9.7	10.7	0.2	0.3	3.2	3.9	5.8	5.8	6.5	7.1	11.3	24.4	23.4	13.9	1.7	78.2	36.1	52.8	47.2
32694	WALDO	81.5	78.3	14.7	17.4	0.4	0.4	2.1	2.6	5.7	6.3	7.7	6.7	4.5	25.4	30.4	11.8	1.4	76.2	40.7	49.2	50.8
32696	WILLISTON	74.1	72.6	22.5	23.6	0.5	0.6	5.0	6.1	6.4	6.5	6.8	6.3	6.1	24.6	26.1	15.3	2.0	76.5	40.4	48.2	51.8
32701	ALTAMONTE SPRINGS	77.2	75.2	13.5	14.1	2.1	2.4	14.0	17.1	5.9	5.3	5.6	5.9	7.9	30.8	24.0	12.6	2.2	79.9	37.7	48.1	51.9
32702	ALTOONA	94.8	94.0	2.5	3.0	0.2	0.2	2.6	3.2	5.9	6.1	6.5	6.5	5.7	24.9	25.9	16.4	2.1	77.5	41.4	49.7	50.3
32703	APOPKA	71.4	68.9	18.5	19.5	2.0	2.3	16.3	19.4	8.0	7.5	7.8	7.2	7.3	30.9	21.7	8.5	1.2	72.4	33.6	49.2	50.8
32707	CASSELBERRY	85.9	83.8	6.1	6.8	2.3	2.7	13.0	15.8	5.6	5.7	6.5	6.3	6.6	30.0	26.6	11.5	1.3	78.4	38.5	48.9	51.1
32708	WINTER SPRINGS	88.0	86.0	4.5	5.2	2.4	2.9	11.4	14.1	5.9	6.4	7.7	7.3	6.4	27.8	27.7	9.9	1.1	75.4	38.5	48.7	51.4
32709	CHRISTMAS	95.8	95.0	0.5	0.6	0.9	1.1	3.4	4.3	5.1	5.7	7.7	6.8	5.5	26.3	30.7	11.4	0.8	77.2	41.2	51.4	48.6
32712	APOPKA	83.7	81.1	9.0	10.4	1.8	2.1	12.2	14.9	7.2	7.4	7.8	6.6	5.7	28.1	25.9	10.3	1.0	73.4	37.6	49.3	50.8
32713	DEBARY	94.8	93.6	1.9	2.5	1.1	1.4	4.6	5.9	4.7	5.1	6.1	5.3	4.2	22.2	29.3	20.3	2.8	80.6	46.5	47.7	52.3
32714	ALTAMONTE SPRINGS	79.2	76.5	9.2	10.1	3.0	3.5	17.9	21.4	6.2	5.6	6.2	6.6	8.8	35.1	22.3	8.2	1.0	78.1	34.0	48.8	51.2
32720	DELAND	81.2	79.9	14.1	14.7	0.7	0.8	6.6	7.9	5.4	5.5	6.1	6.5	6.2	24.2	27.1	15.5	3.6	79.4	42.3	48.4	51.6
32724	DELAND	87.4	85.5	7.8	8.8	0.9	1.1	7.2	8.5	5.4	5.3	5.8	7.2	7.8	22.0	24.0	18.7	3.8	80.2	42.3	46.7	53.3
32725	DELTONA	85.2	82.4	6.1	7.5	1.1	1.3	18.5	22.2	5.8	5.9	6.8	6.7	5.9	25.1	25.0	16.5	2.3	77.3	41.0	47.9	52.1
32726	EUSTIS	78.9	76.6	17.1	18.9	0.8	0.9	6.0	7.2	6.0	5.8	6.2	5.7	6.1	21.0	23.5	21.6	4.2	78.6	44.5	46.4	53.6
32730	CASSELBERRY	83.5	80.9	8.6	9.7	1.7	2.0	14.6	18.1	6.3	5.7	5.4	5.8	7.0	29.2	23.9	14.5	2.2	79.5	38.5	48.0	52.0
32732	GENEVA	93.6	92.5	3.7	4.4	0.7	0.8	2.8	3.6	5.3	5.8	7.4	7.3	5.7	25.8	31.5	10.0	1.4	76.7	41.5	51.5	48.5
32735	GRAND ISLAND	96.0	95.0	1.7	2.1	0.5	0.5	4.7	5.9	5.2	5.0	5.7	5.3	4.3	20.9	24.6	26.4	2.7	80.9	47.8	48.9	51.1
32736	EUSTIS	95.5	94.6	1.2	1.5	0.5	0.6	4.3	5.3	5.5	6.1	7.6	6.4	4.8	24.7	29.6	14.2	1.2	76.9	42.1	51.1	49.0
32738	DELTONA	84.0	80.7	7.7	9.6	0.8	0.9	17.0	20.7	6.8	7.0	8.4	7.9	6.8	28.6	23.5	10.0	1.0	72.9	35.5	48.9	51.1
32744	LAKE HELEN	88.9	86.2	8.1	10.2	0.4	0.5	5.1	6.6	5.4	5.5	6.4	6.9	6.3	24.2	27.3	16.2	1.8	78.5	42.3	48.1	51.9
32746	LAKE MARY	84.7	82.6	6.0	6.8	4.6	5.3	9.4	11.3	6.6	6.8	7.5	6.8	5.8	30.5	27.0	8.2	0.8	74.8	37.1	49.4	50.6
32750	LONGWOOD	88.2	86.2	3.7	4.3	2.9	3.5	9.3	11.5	5.7	6.3	7.5	6.9	5.4	27.5	27.9	10.7	2.1	76.1	39.8	49.3	50.8
32751	MAITLAND	82.5	80.7	12.1	13.1	1.5	1.8	7.8	9.5	5.9	6.1	7.2	6.8	5.8	24.9	26.4	14.6	2.5	76.7	41.0	47.1	52.9
32754	MIMS	88.2	86.7	9.5	10.8	0.4	0.4	1.2	1.5	4.7	5.4	6.5	6.6	5.1	22.2	29.5	18.6	1.5	79.3	44.8	49.7	50.3
32757	MOUNT DORA	81.9	79.7	14.1	15.7	0.9	1.0	7.7	8.8	5.7	5.7	6.0	5.4	5.0	22.1	26.4	19.7	4.0	79.2	45.1	47.5	52.6
32759	OAK HILL	87.0	85.4	10.7	12.2	0.5	0.5	1.1	1.3	4.2	4.3	4.3	4.0	4.4	18.6	29.5	28.9	2.0	85.0	52.6	49.7	50.3
	FLORIDA	78.0	76.5	14.6	15.2	1.7	2.0	16.8	19.0	6.0	5.9	6.4	6.4	6.5	26.6	24.5	15.5	2.4	78.1	40.0	48.8	51.2
	UNITED STATES	75.1	73.6	12.3	12.5	3.8	4.2	12.5	14.1	6.9	6.7	7.2	7.0	7.3	28.6	23.8	10.8	1.7	75.1	36.0	49.1	50.9

ZIP CODE #	POST OFFICE NAME	2004 Per Capita Income	2004 HH Income Base	2004 Household Income Distribution (%) Less than $25,000	$25,000 to $49,999	$50,000 to $99,999	$100,000 to $149,999	$150,000 or More	Median Household Income 2004	2009	2004 National Centile	2004 State Centile	2004 Home Value Base	2004 Home Value Distribution (%) Less than $50,000	$50,000 to $89,999	$90,000 to $174,999	$175,000 to $399,999	$400,000 or More	2004 Median Home Value
32501	PENSACOLA	16715	5779	51.0	28.7	14.7	2.6	3.0	24300	27394	4	3	3062	27.6	32.8	25.6	12.3	1.7	74587
32502	PENSACOLA	22383	510	41.8	31.0	16.3	6.7	4.3	28484	32949	10	7	302	11.9	38.4	22.5	20.2	7.0	89231
32503	PENSACOLA	23806	13417	32.2	31.1	25.5	6.7	4.6	38503	44105	41	38	8844	10.1	26.2	42.9	17.2	3.7	108164
32504	PENSACOLA	28273	10879	23.5	33.5	29.8	8.5	4.7	44230	51149	59	57	7217	3.2	21.9	53.1	18.4	3.5	117861
32505	PENSACOLA	13882	10874	45.1	32.5	18.0	3.1	1.3	27634	31087	8	6	6834	33.2	45.3	16.7	4.4	0.4	63514
32506	PENSACOLA	20398	14633	28.9	34.3	28.5	6.3	2.0	39480	45367	44	42	9473	12.0	27.6	47.1	12.3	1.0	100399
32507	PENSACOLA	21803	12158	30.3	31.1	27.3	7.9	3.5	39255	45292	44	41	8623	14.1	26.5	32.2	21.1	6.1	108512
32508	PENSACOLA	14533	376	13.0	51.1	30.1	5.9	0.0	39525	44484	44	42	22	100.0	0.0	0.0	0.0	0.0	45000
32514	PENSACOLA	25177	15046	24.3	32.3	31.1	8.8	3.6	44299	50318	59	58	8983	5.5	20.5	56.5	16.0	1.6	116205
32526	PENSACOLA	22308	12892	21.8	33.1	34.7	7.3	3.1	45822	52085	63	62	10474	13.6	26.4	46.9	12.0	1.1	99020
32531	BAKER	18705	1604	28.2	31.6	31.9	6.5	1.9	38893	44652	42	39	1375	16.3	31.6	32.4	17.5	2.2	95278
32533	CANTONMENT	23180	9382	23.1	28.6	34.8	9.5	4.1	48241	54876	69	69	8120	10.8	20.1	46.3	21.5	1.3	119716
32534	PENSACOLA	20379	5099	31.9	31.7	27.6	5.7	3.1	37244	42551	36	33	3955	17.5	26.5	39.9	15.3	0.9	99316
32535	CENTURY	15087	2088	43.7	31.4	20.8	3.2	1.0	28748	32736	10	8	1640	42.7	31.2	19.8	6.2	0.1	60000
32536	CRESTVIEW	20064	5651	27.7	33.4	29.9	6.7	2.4	40464	46737	48	46	4328	10.8	26.1	52.5	10.2	0.4	102789
32539	CRESTVIEW	18600	7754	26.9	33.4	31.6	6.4	1.7	41710	47589	52	50	6278	13.0	28.2	46.0	12.3	0.4	98691
32541	DESTIN	38171	6433	15.9	24.9	37.7	12.6	9.0	60518	67727	85	87	5054	2.3	5.6	31.7	41.6	18.8	199347
32542	EGLIN AFB	12830	2675	18.3	56.7	22.2	2.3	0.5	35412	39942	29	27	305	61.6	3.0	15.4	16.4	3.6	33106
32544	HURLBURT FIELD	12239	450	20.7	40.0	30.7	6.9	1.8	39827	45255	45	43	119	6.7	2.5	6.7	80.7	3.4	224457
32547	FORT WALTON BEACH	23559	13594	22.4	37.1	30.6	7.3	2.6	42678	48656	55	53	7733	9.4	19.1	51.4	17.2	2.9	116371
32548	FORT WALTON BEACH	24551	10153	23.5	34.3	31.5	8.1	2.6	43672	49991	58	56	6400	4.5	23.4	54.8	14.4	3.0	112458
32550	MIRAMAR BEACH	36541	2539	22.0	25.2	32.3	10.4	10.2	52823	61474	77	78	2188	0.0	4.1	18.4	50.1	27.5	257789
32561	GULF BREEZE	42845	3708	17.0	21.8	32.8	13.8	14.6	63585	73566	88	90	2998	1.8	2.6	32.9	40.6	22.1	210592
32563	GULF BREEZE	33490	8195	16.7	24.5	35.7	13.6	9.5	58929	67488	83	85	6808	3.3	5.5	41.9	38.9	10.4	173633
32564	HOLT	17294	1129	31.9	31.3	31.1	3.6	2.1	39634	45266	45	42	967	33.7	31.4	22.7	11.4	0.8	71908
32565	JAY	18273	2166	34.7	32.0	25.7	5.7	1.9	35084	40776	28	26	1835	30.4	27.0	34.4	7.6	0.5	75000
32566	NAVARRE	23176	9563	17.5	31.7	37.6	9.5	3.8	50674	57487	73	75	8101	9.5	10.1	49.5	27.1	3.8	135176
32567	LAUREL HILL	15862	1666	42.3	32.2	20.4	3.5	1.7	30451	34263	13	11	1428	29.2	24.5	29.2	16.7	0.4	84700
32568	MC DAVID	18096	1293	27.4	36.9	28.5	5.2	2.0	40812	46621	49	47	1127	31.3	28.7	31.1	6.9	2.0	73542
32569	MARY ESTHER	23710	4833	16.1	36.0	35.8	8.5	3.7	48718	54881	70	70	3603	5.3	12.9	62.9	15.4	3.5	121602
32570	MILTON	19091	10130	30.1	32.2	30.1	5.7	2.0	40083	45916	46	43	7677	14.7	27.8	45.6	10.8	1.1	97807
32571	MILTON	22818	9617	21.0	29.5	35.1	10.0	4.5	49586	56083	71	72	8232	11.4	18.5	45.6	22.3	2.2	118959
32577	MOLINO	21251	1663	21.1	32.4	35.1	8.9	2.5	45523	52441	63	61	1464	18.6	20.3	40.0	19.3	1.8	109195
32578	NICEVILLE	29547	11966	16.1	24.4	36.9	15.7	6.9	60623	69572	85	87	9450	4.1	7.5	43.7	39.5	5.1	162195
32579	SHALIMAR	29430	4560	17.8	25.2	37.2	14.5	5.4	57933	64338	83	84	3323	2.5	7.8	38.7	42.0	9.0	177233
32580	VALPARAISO	24731	1746	25.3	28.6	35.9	8.6	1.6	46482	52368	65	64	1182	3.5	25.0	48.1	20.3	3.1	112500
32583	MILTON	19461	7801	26.4	34.3	30.2	6.3	2.8	40483	46880	48	46	6514	19.2	28.7	36.1	14.7	1.3	92731
32601	GAINESVILLE	14494	8981	58.4	25.2	12.7	2.4	1.3	20229	23397	2	1	2177	15.9	38.9	32.4	12.0	0.8	85379
32603	GAINESVILLE	15148	2174	64.6	20.4	8.6	5.1	1.4	16587	19375	1	1	349	3.2	6.9	47.0	43.0	0.0	165577
32605	GAINESVILLE	32210	9713	19.7	22.5	35.0	13.5	9.3	57760	68378	82	84	7235	1.1	12.2	56.5	27.7	2.6	139141
32606	GAINESVILLE	32886	8542	15.4	24.8	34.9	15.5	9.4	60251	72349	85	86	5654	0.3	6.6	51.0	37.3	4.8	163434
32607	GAINESVILLE	21726	13743	43.8	25.2	20.3	7.2	3.6	29653	34562	12	10	4889	10.8	12.4	44.8	27.8	4.3	134896
32608	GAINESVILLE	21744	17673	46.5	24.4	17.6	6.5	5.0	27772	32897	8	6	6542	16.2	15.8	32.9	28.4	6.8	133784
32609	GAINESVILLE	16440	7375	38.4	34.4	22.3	3.8	1.1	31275	37256	16	13	4250	19.5	46.6	29.2	4.8	0.1	78287
32611	GAINESVILLE	13934	169	89.4	6.5	4.1	0.0	0.0	11551	12995	1	0	0	0.0	0.0	0.0	0.0	0.0	0
32615	ALACHUA	24278	5145	26.5	24.5	34.6	9.2	5.2	48342	59169	69	69	4235	11.5	25.4	36.2	22.6	4.5	113519
32617	ANTHONY	17455	1414	28.4	36.9	26.8	6.2	1.8	38020	43830	39	37	1109	16.5	24.9	34.8	18.4	5.4	102627
32618	ARCHER	21230	2748	30.1	27.9	32.1	7.0	3.0	41791	50090	52	51	2337	19.9	27.7	34.2	16.4	1.8	93897
32619	BELL	17441	1582	37.6	32.7	23.8	4.0	1.9	33393	37490	22	21	1343	21.0	30.1	31.1	16.9	0.9	88117
32621	BRONSON	14747	1548	40.4	36.0	18.2	3.6	1.9	29806	34017	12	10	1272	28.5	35.0	28.9	6.8	0.9	72128
32622	BROOKER	19905	785	25.9	37.2	31.6	4.3	1.0	38547	44151	41	39	674	19.9	25.2	39.2	15.0	0.7	97500
32625	CEDAR KEY	22007	775	34.3	32.0	25.2	5.7	2.8	35263	40125	28	27	643	12.3	15.1	34.5	31.9	6.2	140441
32626	CHIEFLAND	15734	3742	42.6	31.9	21.0	3.7	0.9	29222	32335	11	9	3092	23.1	34.6	29.0	12.2	1.2	79843
32628	CROSS CITY	14136	1613	47.4	30.8	17.5	2.9	1.4	26438	29909	6	4	1244	39.1	29.2	25.6	6.1	0.0	64783
32631	EARLETON	23426	331	23.0	32.0	31.1	10.6	3.3	47157	56434	66	66	280	10.7	22.1	38.6	24.3	4.3	122222
32640	HAWTHORNE	18647	4259	32.3	32.5	28.3	5.4	1.5	37545	44328	38	35	3573	23.3	27.7	32.1	13.9	3.0	88668
32641	GAINESVILLE	12512	4687	47.9	29.4	18.8	2.8	1.1	26241	30837	6	4	2794	26.0	47.3	22.9	2.8	0.9	67872
32643	HIGH SPRINGS	19174	3729	31.5	30.0	31.7	4.9	1.9	39228	46936	44	40	3124	16.6	29.4	40.4	13.0	0.7	95526
32648	HORSESHOE BEACH	22401	167	28.1	29.9	28.7	9.6	3.6	42603	48646	55	53	148	33.8	25.7	30.4	7.4	2.7	75000
32653	GAINESVILLE	27868	5339	16.9	27.3	37.0	13.4	5.4	54942	65991	80	81	4301	5.6	13.9	54.0	24.2	2.3	129587
32656	KEYSTONE HEIGHTS	21710	5081	22.9	32.7	35.3	7.1	2.1	45662	52117	63	62	4322	16.2	23.6	43.3	14.7	2.2	103417
32666	MELROSE	23697	2550	27.3	33.5	29.4	6.5	3.4	41366	48586	51	49	2145	15.4	19.2	39.3	24.0	2.2	116931
32667	MICANOPY	26974	1804	28.8	24.2	29.8	12.3	4.9	45462	54006	62	61	1474	16.2	21.4	30.9	24.4	7.1	114442
32668	MORRISTON	18766	1880	36.3	33.0	23.5	3.9	3.4	33074	37739	21	19	1634	16.9	26.8	33.0	17.3	6.0	99115
32669	NEWBERRY	21691	3500	24.9	30.1	33.5	8.2	3.3	45824	54343	63	62	3017	13.0	23.1	37.2	24.8	2.0	113846
32680	OLD TOWN	17319	3674	44.1	31.5	18.9	3.3	2.2	28650	32508	10	8	3244	33.2	27.3	26.8	10.3	2.4	70905
32686	REDDICK	23022	2584	34.8	27.1	23.2	8.1	6.8	37199	42729	36	33	2142	23.6	23.2	24.7	16.3	12.2	96389
32693	TRENTON	16697	3755	37.1	35.4	21.4	4.4	1.7	31575	35521	17	15	3124	22.3	27.6	37.5	10.5	2.1	90149
32694	WALDO	24911	652	31.3	30.1	24.7	7.8	6.1	40309	48610	47	45	545	24.6	29.2	32.8	10.1	3.3	85816
32696	WILLISTON	17653	3790	39.2	33.0	20.8	5.0	2.0	31360	35416	16	14	3083	21.3	29.0	35.0	12.2	2.4	89460
32701	ALTAMONTE SPRINGS	26651	10977	22.5	32.8	31.1	9.9	3.7	44837	51364	61	59	5645	3.6	15.9	55.5	23.5	1.5	132578
32702	ALTOONA	17544	1235	32.3	34.2	29.4	3.6	0.6	37301	42836	36	34	987	23.0	27.7	25.7	22.6	1.0	89167
32703	APOPKA	20845	16885	22.5	33.6	31.5	8.9	3.6	45234	52194	62	60	11774	9.6	14.6	56.9	16.6	2.4	124391
32707	CASSELBERRY	25741	14183	20.0	29.4	35.6	10.8	4.3	50447	58305	73	74	10167	6.4	9.4	65.3	18.3	0.6	131139
32708	WINTER SPRINGS	29547	16473	12.7	27.8	34.1	16.6	8.8	59989	69007	84	86	13254	4.3	8.6	41.8	39.8	5.4	164396
32709	CHRISTMAS	22404	960	17.0	39.0	30.0	8.1	5.9	45293	52473	62	61	826	15.4	23.2	32.8	19.7	8.8	115407
32712	APOPKA	26197	11717	16.5	27.3	34.8	12.8	8.7	56028	63999	81	82	10172	9.5	11.5	38.6	37.9	2.6	148948
32713	DEBARY	27476	7365	22.6	29.4	33.8	8.9	5.3	47987	55103	68	68	6384	5.5	20.5	40.9	31.5	1.7	121466
32714	ALTAMONTE SPRINGS	26466	15201	16.4	34.0	34.8	11.0	3.8	49621	57438	71	72	7541	2.2	13.2	53.7	27.6	3.3	143002
32720	DELAND	20917	11049	32.0	31.6	27.1	6.3	3.0	37507	42823	37	35	7887	8.7	21.6	46.9	20.4	2.4	114538
32724	DELAND	22261	11308	29.8	34.1	26.0	6.7	3.6	37836	42895	39	36	8231	12.0	26.3	42.1	17.5	2.1	103874
32725	DELTONA	19840	15578	23.2	35.2	32.4	7.0	2.2	42816	49492	55	53	13111	2.2	19.1	66.6	11.5	0.6	117731
32726	EUSTIS	22575	8323	33.3	30.9	25.6	7.1	3.1	37194	42384	36	33	5755	13.3	22.4	38.5	20.3	5.5	109889
32730	CASSELBERRY	27303	2480	22.0	30.7	32.8	10.7	4.0	47762	54639	68	67	1484	1.5	5.5	65.6	26.6	0.9	147910
32732	GENEVA	25764	1812	15.2	31.7	31.8	13.4	7.9	52313	60500	76	77	1591	4.7	9.2	39.7	35.1	11.3	162920
32735	GRAND ISLAND	22625	1227	28.4	33.4	28.7	7.0	2.4	39274	43458	44	41	1125	25.4	19.1	33.3	20.2	2.0	99762
32736	EUSTIS	25811	3520	24.6	29.0	31.1	9.4	5.8	47295	53653	67	66	3104	12.7	20.3	31.6	29.6	5.8	129569
32738	DELTONA	18651	13114	17.8	37.5	36.1	6.7	2.0	46498	52665	65	64	11392	0.8	14.7	73.6	10.4	0.4	117519
32744	LAKE HELEN	19539	1443	26.1	37.6	30.5	4.7	1.1	40158	45605	47	44	1232	14.5	22.3	47.5	15.3	0.3	105583
32746	LAKE MARY	40847	14543	12.5	19.4	35.2	16.9	16.1	72242	85333	92	94	10438	0.4	4.7	32.5	44.6	17.7	208703
32750	LONGWOOD	27830	9287	13.0	23.2	40.9	16.0	7.0	63729	75141	88	90	7719	1.2	6.6	49.2	41.0	2.0	162067
32751	MAITLAND	36461	8507	20.3	25.0	29.1	13.2	12.5	56086	65178	81	82	5910	0.7	9.2	33.6	41.0	15.5	192409
32754	MIMS	20770	4253	31.6	28.7	30.5	7.0	2.2	40799	46698	49	47	3635	18.5	28.7	31.1	19.7	1.9	93699
32757	MOUNT DORA	24870	9327	29.0	29.7	29.1	7.2	4.9	42339	48332	54	52	7064	9.6	16.4	43.9	23.2	6.9	124309
32759	OAK HILL	19105	1088	35.9	35.7	21.3	5.3	1.8	32999	37002	21	19	904	14.4	27.4	42.6	14.5	1.1	101618
	FLORIDA	25506		26.4	29.9	29.1	9.1	5.6	44138	51288				8.8	15.8	40.2	28.3	7.0	137042
	UNITED STATES	25866		24.7	27.1	30.8	10.9	6.5	48124	56710				10.9	15.0	33.7	30.1	10.4	145905

ZIP CODE #	POST OFFICE NAME	FINANCIAL SERVICES: Auto Loan	FINANCIAL SERVICES: Home Loan	FINANCIAL SERVICES: Invest-ments	FINANCIAL SERVICES: Retire-ment Plans	THE HOME: Home Improvements: Home Repair	THE HOME: Home Improvements: Lawn & Garden	THE HOME: Furnishings: Comput-ers & Hard-ware	THE HOME: Furnishings: Major Appli-ances	THE HOME: Furnishings: TV, Radio, Sound Equip-ment	THE HOME: Furnishings: Furni-ture	ENTERTAINMENT: Dine out/ Carry out	ENTERTAINMENT: Sports Equip-ment	ENTERTAINMENT: Fees & Tickets	ENTERTAINMENT: Toys & Games	ENTERTAINMENT: Travel	ENTERTAINMENT: Cable TV	PERSONAL: Apparel & Services	PERSONAL: Auto Repairs	PERSONAL: Health Insur-ance	PERSONAL: Pets & Supplies
32501	PENSACOLA	53	46	51	44	46	54	51	51	56	52	68	57	50	64	50	58	66	53	56	59
32502	PENSACOLA	65	57	65	55	56	65	64	63	68	64	84	72	62	78	62	69	81	66	67	72
32503	PENSACOLA	76	74	83	73	73	82	79	77	81	78	100	89	78	97	78	81	97	79	80	87
32504	PENSACOLA	82	88	103	90	88	93	91	88	88	89	111	103	92	111	90	86	109	89	84	96
32505	PENSACOLA	52	46	49	45	46	54	50	50	54	50	67	57	50	65	50	56	64	51	54	58
32506	PENSACOLA	73	69	65	69	69	75	70	71	71	69	88	82	69	87	69	71	84	71	72	81
32507	PENSACOLA	77	75	73	73	76	82	75	77	76	74	94	88	74	94	75	77	91	77	79	89
32508	PENSACOLA	77	49	47	56	45	53	73	63	74	68	93	84	63	83	60	68	89	75	58	72
32514	PENSACOLA	79	80	90	83	79	84	83	81	81	83	102	95	83	100	81	78	99	83	77	90
32526	PENSACOLA	85	83	76	81	85	90	79	83	81	79	99	97	79	101	81	81	96	82	85	98
32531	BAKER	85	65	40	61	71	78	63	74	69	63	83	87	56	80	63	72	77	73	83	97
32533	CANTONMENT	96	92	80	89	95	100	86	92	88	86	108	108	86	110	88	89	104	90	95	113
32534	PENSACOLA	76	71	62	69	73	78	69	73	71	69	87	85	67	85	69	71	83	73	76	87
32535	CENTURY	50	35	24	31	38	45	36	42	43	37	51	48	33	47	36	46	48	43	51	56
32536	CRESTVIEW	81	75	63	74	76	81	72	77	74	73	91	90	70	89	72	74	87	76	79	92
32539	CRESTVIEW	77	73	63	72	73	77	70	74	71	71	88	86	68	85	69	70	84	73	73	87
32541	DESTIN	111	122	143	124	122	128	120	119	117	120	147	138	123	146	122	115	144	120	114	131
32542	EGLIN AFB	67	42	40	48	39	46	63	54	64	59	80	72	54	71	52	58	76	64	50	62
32544	HURLBURT FIELD	83	52	50	60	48	57	78	67	79	73	99	90	67	89	64	72	95	80	62	77
32547	FORT WALTON BEACH	75	77	82	79	76	79	78	77	76	78	95	91	78	94	77	73	93	78	72	85
32548	FORT WALTON BEACH	72	79	89	78	78	83	79	77	77	78	97	89	81	99	79	77	95	78	75	84
32550	MIRAMAR BEACH	121	96	69	88	108	122	91	109	102	91	121	125	83	118	97	109	113	107	128	146
32561	GULF BREEZE	138	140	139	137	145	157	131	140	132	133	163	155	132	156	137	134	157	137	147	162
32563	GULF BREEZE	116	130	132	129	130	132	119	121	115	118	143	143	123	149	121	113	141	118	115	140
32564	HOLT	70	64	50	61	64	67	61	65	61	62	76	75	57	72	60	61	73	65	65	77
32565	JAY	77	60	42	56	65	74	60	68	67	60	80	80	55	77	61	70	74	68	79	88
32566	NAVARRE	90	97	92	98	94	94	89	90	85	91	106	106	91	108	88	81	104	88	81	102
32567	LAUREL HILL	71	49	25	44	55	64	49	59	58	49	68	70	42	64	50	61	62	59	72	81
32568	MC DAVID	90	60	27	52	68	79	58	73	70	59	82	87	49	78	59	76	75	72	90	103
32569	MARY ESTHER	81	92	95	92	89	89	86	86	81	87	103	101	89	105	86	78	102	85	77	94
32570	MILTON	74	67	61	65	69	76	68	71	71	67	87	83	66	87	68	72	84	71	75	85
32571	MILTON	97	95	80	94	94	97	88	93	87	90	108	108	87	107	87	86	105	91	90	109
32577	MOLINO	99	79	52	73	86	94	74	86	83	75	99	103	69	98	76	86	93	84	98	115
32578	NICEVILLE	101	113	119	112	111	116	108	107	104	107	130	124	111	131	109	102	128	106	102	118
32579	SHALIMAR	95	102	106	102	101	106	98	98	94	98	118	113	99	116	98	92	116	98	94	109
32580	VALPARAISO	73	83	93	80	83	89	80	80	80	79	99	90	84	103	83	81	97	79	80	87
32583	MILTON	74	69	56	67	70	74	66	70	67	67	82	81	63	79	65	66	79	70	71	83
32601	GAINESVILLE	42	31	40	34	30	35	47	38	47	42	58	50	42	54	41	43	56	44	37	43
32603	GAINESVILLE	41	26	32	29	25	30	49	36	47	41	59	50	40	53	39	41	55	44	33	41
32605	GAINESVILLE	100	109	130	112	108	114	111	107	107	109	134	127	113	135	111	104	132	109	101	117
32606	GAINESVILLE	103	112	136	117	110	114	113	110	108	113	137	131	115	137	112	104	135	112	100	120
32607	GAINESVILLE	65	50	61	55	49	55	74	61	72	67	90	79	66	83	64	65	86	69	56	68
32608	GAINESVILLE	68	54	62	59	53	58	76	63	73	69	92	82	68	86	66	66	88	71	58	71
32609	GAINESVILLE	53	48	53	48	47	52	53	51	54	53	68	61	51	66	51	53	66	54	51	59
32611	GAINESVILLE	22	13	17	15	13	16	26	19	25	22	31	26	21	28	20	22	29	23	17	21
32615	ALACHUA	95	91	79	89	91	96	87	91	87	88	108	106	85	106	86	86	104	90	90	107
32617	ANTHONY	73	67	52	64	67	70	63	68	64	65	79	79	60	75	63	63	76	68	67	81
32618	ARCHER	85	80	66	78	80	85	77	81	77	78	95	94	74	92	76	77	91	80	81	95
32619	BELL	79	60	36	54	64	71	58	67	64	59	77	79	51	73	58	67	72	67	76	89
32621	BRONSON	66	57	41	54	58	62	54	60	57	56	69	69	50	65	54	57	66	59	62	73
32622	BROOKER	57	52	41	50	52	55	50	54	51	51	62	62	47	59	49	50	60	53	53	64
32625	CEDAR KEY	71	67	64	63	71	83	62	70	65	66	81	69	62	67	67	70	76	68	82	80
32626	CHIEFLAND	58	51	43	49	53	60	51	55	53	52	65	61	48	61	51	55	62	55	60	65
32628	CROSS CITY	57	38	18	33	43	50	37	46	45	38	52	55	31	50	38	48	48	46	57	66
32631	EARLETON	78	83	83	79	83	89	79	81	79	79	98	91	80	99	81	80	96	80	82	91
32640	HAWTHORNE	80	61	37	55	66	75	59	69	67	60	80	81	53	76	60	71	74	69	81	92
32641	GAINESVILLE	48	43	50	41	42	49	47	47	51	48	64	52	47	61	46	53	62	48	50	54
32643	HIGH SPRINGS	76	69	56	66	70	76	67	72	70	68	85	82	64	82	67	70	81	71	75	85
32648	HORSESHOE BEACH	90	71	48	64	80	89	67	80	75	66	89	94	60	88	71	81	83	79	95	110
32653	GAINESVILLE	91	102	115	104	101	102	98	97	93	98	117	115	101	120	99	90	116	97	89	107
32656	KEYSTONE HEIGHTS	88	78	62	75	81	89	75	82	78	76	95	92	72	90	76	79	90	81	87	99
32666	MELROSE	88	75	59	71	79	89	74	82	79	75	96	91	69	89	75	82	90	81	92	99
32667	MICANOPY	85	89	92	86	89	96	86	88	86	86	107	101	87	108	87	87	104	87	88	100
32668	MORRISTON	75	69	54	66	69	74	66	71	67	67	82	81	62	77	65	66	79	70	72	84
32669	NEWBERRY	84	84	76	83	84	87	79	83	78	80	97	96	79	96	79	77	94	81	80	96
32680	OLD TOWN	72	52	32	46	58	68	50	61	59	52	70	70	45	64	52	63	64	60	75	82
32686	REDDICK	95	81	59	77	84	91	78	86	82	79	99	101	72	95	78	82	94	86	91	108
32693	TRENTON	69	63	50	60	63	67	60	64	61	62	75	74	57	70	59	60	72	64	64	76
32694	WALDO	94	82	62	77	84	91	78	86	82	80	100	100	74	96	78	83	96	86	90	106
32696	WILLISTON	70	58	45	55	60	67	59	64	63	60	77	73	55	72	58	65	73	64	70	77
32701	ALTAMONTE SPRINGS	80	78	94	81	76	83	84	81	84	84	106	95	84	103	82	82	103	84	77	89
32702	ALTOONA	68	60	50	57	62	68	58	64	60	59	74	73	55	70	59	62	70	63	68	78
32703	APOPKA	83	81	83	83	80	83	82	82	81	83	101	96	81	99	80	78	99	83	77	92
32707	CASSELBERRY	85	89	94	91	88	91	89	88	86	88	108	103	89	108	88	84	105	88	83	97
32708	WINTER SPRINGS	109	121	130	124	118	121	115	113	109	116	137	132	119	138	114	105	136	112	103	125
32709	CHRISTMAS	97	89	71	86	89	94	85	91	86	88	106	105	81	101	84	85	102	91	90	108
32712	APOPKA	102	112	113	112	110	113	105	106	101	106	127	122	108	129	106	99	125	104	99	118
32713	DEBARY	93	94	93	91	95	105	90	94	90	91	112	104	91	108	92	92	108	92	98	106
32714	ALTAMONTE SPRINGS	89	81	94	89	79	84	90	86	88	92	112	104	88	105	85	83	109	91	78	96
32720	DELAND	69	69	72	68	69	76	71	71	71	69	88	81	70	88	71	71	85	71	72	80
32724	DELAND	75	74	77	72	75	84	75	76	77	74	94	86	75	93	76	78	91	76	81	86
32725	DELTONA	72	76	76	73	77	83	73	75	74	72	91	85	74	93	75	75	88	74	78	85
32726	EUSTIS	77	71	70	68	74	85	72	76	76	72	93	83	71	87	74	79	88	76	85	88
32730	CASSELBERRY	78	85	105	87	84	88	87	84	85	86	107	99	89	109	87	83	105	86	79	92
32732	GENEVA	106	108	96	105	107	110	100	105	98	102	122	121	99	121	100	96	119	103	100	121
32735	GRAND ISLAND	78	74	74	69	78	93	68	79	73	74	91	75	70	76	75	78	85	76	92	88
32736	EUSTIS	108	101	84	97	101	109	95	102	96	98	119	116	92	112	95	96	114	101	103	121
32738	DELTONA	79	83	79	83	82	83	79	80	76	79	95	94	79	96	78	74	93	79	75	90
32744	LAKE HELEN	73	68	63	67	70	78	67	72	69	68	85	78	66	81	68	70	81	70	76	81
32746	LAKE MARY	145	173	181	177	167	165	155	153	142	158	180	178	164	186	155	136	180	148	134	168
32750	LONGWOOD	101	118	124	119	115	114	109	108	102	109	128	126	113	132	109	98	127	105	97	118
32751	MAITLAND	116	128	159	129	126	136	128	125	125	128	158	144	133	159	130	124	156	126	120	137
32754	MIMS	84	71	58	66	75	85	68	78	74	71	90	85	65	82	70	78	85	77	88	94
32757	MOUNT DORA	85	78	72	76	81	92	78	83	81	78	99	93	76	94	79	84	94	83	91	97
32759	OAK HILL	74	59	45	52	64	76	56	67	63	58	77	72	52	68	59	68	70	66	81	84
	FLORIDA	89	87	95	86	87	96	87	89	89	89	111	100	87	107	88	90	108	90	91	101
	UNITED STATES	100	100	100	100	100	100	100	100	100	100	100	100	100	100	100	100	100	100	100	100

#	POST OFFICE NAME	COUNTY FIPS CODE	POPULATION 2000	2004	2009	% Rate	State Centile	HOUSEHOLDS 2000	2004	2009	% Annual Rate 2000-2004	2004 Average HH Size	FAMILIES 2000	2004	% Annual Rate 2000-2004
32763	ORANGE CITY	127	15990	17286	18965	1.9	52	6989	7540	8260	1.8	2.27	4426	4705	1.5
32764	OSTEEN	127	2562	2995	3416	3.7	82	1028	1209	1381	3.9	2.47	776	902	3.6
32765	OVIEDO	117	43687	51854	60512	4.1	85	14822	17661	20709	4.2	2.93	11888	14027	4.0
32766	OVIEDO	117	7192	9467	11606	6.7	96	2410	3180	3914	6.7	2.97	2006	2628	6.6
32767	PAISLEY	069	2355	2699	3281	3.3	76	966	1114	1361	3.4	2.42	693	790	3.1
32771	SANFORD	117	30611	35712	41846	3.7	81	11555	13646	16145	4.0	2.59	7850	9228	3.9
32773	SANFORD	117	23801	26670	30216	2.7	69	8600	9763	11180	3.0	2.67	5861	6573	2.7
32776	SORRENTO	069	6567	7935	9895	4.6	88	2404	2930	3675	4.8	2.71	1871	2258	4.5
32778	TAVARES	069	14329	16709	20382	3.7	81	6545	7787	9660	4.2	2.04	4277	5009	3.8
32779	LONGWOOD	117	25935	27932	31105	1.8	50	9679	10604	11942	2.2	2.63	7528	8134	1.8
32780	TITUSVILLE	009	31005	32354	34896	1.0	28	13606	14364	15662	1.3	2.23	8849	9239	1.0
32784	UMATILLA	069	9587	11133	13439	3.6	80	3707	4331	5256	3.7	2.55	2687	3103	3.4
32789	WINTER PARK	095	24107	24634	26812	0.5	15	10617	10937	11987	0.7	2.14	5808	5853	0.2
32792	WINTER PARK	117	47064	49974	55609	1.4	40	20348	21778	24392	1.6	2.25	11216	11779	1.2
32796	TITUSVILLE	009	20130	20557	21828	0.5	15	7850	8117	8728	0.8	2.46	5489	5621	0.6
32798	ZELLWOOD	095	1850	1920	2084	0.9	24	998	1044	1137	1.1	1.83	624	636	0.5
32801	ORLANDO	095	8212	8609	9494	1.1	31	4734	5038	5629	1.5	1.56	1183	1199	0.3
32803	ORLANDO	095	19961	20606	22642	0.8	21	9470	9919	11013	1.1	1.96	4221	4311	0.5
32804	ORLANDO	095	17922	17759	19228	-0.2	3	8593	8579	9316	0.0	2.06	4511	4407	-0.6
32805	ORLANDO	095	25625	25787	27970	0.2	6	9203	9331	10177	0.3	2.66	5647	5635	-0.1
32806	ORLANDO	095	28538	28569	30977	0.0	5	12237	12347	13462	0.2	2.22	7171	7093	-0.3
32807	ORLANDO	095	33776	34555	37743	0.5	16	12755	13125	14371	0.7	2.61	8116	8201	0.3
32808	ORLANDO	095	50312	52239	57377	0.9	25	17072	17653	19322	0.8	2.93	12053	12295	0.5
32809	ORLANDO	095	22260	24991	28339	2.8	70	8049	9023	10215	2.7	2.77	5841	6463	2.4
32810	ORLANDO	095	30729	32903	36377	1.6	45	11135	11985	13276	1.8	2.72	7649	8115	1.4
32811	ORLANDO	095	32612	36537	41444	2.7	69	12644	14247	16180	2.9	2.56	7290	8062	2.4
32812	ORLANDO	095	30537	33125	36989	1.9	54	12390	13489	15071	2.0	2.45	7832	8399	1.7
32817	ORLANDO	095	35533	39327	44239	2.4	65	13536	15004	16861	2.5	2.61	7535	8115	1.8
32818	ORLANDO	095	36061	39933	45183	2.4	65	12072	13387	15141	2.5	2.96	9262	10219	2.3
32819	ORLANDO	095	25064	26799	29854	1.6	45	8926	9589	10684	1.7	2.79	6867	7311	1.5
32820	ORLANDO	095	2919	3663	4377	5.5	92	1030	1303	1560	5.7	2.81	746	931	5.4
32821	ORLANDO	095	11988	13626	15530	3.1	74	5724	6522	7434	3.1	2.06	2934	3284	2.7
32822	ORLANDO	095	46524	50117	56125	1.8	50	19134	20680	23186	1.9	2.42	11808	12524	1.4
32824	ORLANDO	095	19453	26433	32838	7.5	97	5994	8148	10114	7.5	3.24	4939	6666	7.3
32825	ORLANDO	095	39527	45318	51829	3.3	76	13719	15918	18304	3.6	2.79	10200	11680	3.2
32826	ORLANDO	095	18976	21484	24362	3.0	72	6388	7230	8253	3.0	2.64	3872	4352	2.8
32827	ORLANDO	095	2060	2595	3145	5.6	92	724	929	1136	6.0	2.79	551	696	5.7
32828	ORLANDO	095	22105	31928	40703	9.0	99	7629	10808	13623	8.5	2.95	5847	8189	8.3
32829	ORLANDO	095	13433	15163	17129	2.9	72	3695	4251	4870	3.4	3.20	2948	3355	3.1
32830	ORLANDO	095	27	33	38	4.8	90	11	13	16	4.0	2.54	6	8	7.0
32831	ORLANDO	095	57	67	77	3.9	83	22	27	33	4.9	2.00	17	22	6.3
32832	ORLANDO	095	1860	2530	3138	7.5	97	695	953	1185	7.7	2.65	539	730	7.4
32833	ORLANDO	095	5096	6031	7003	4.0	84	1832	2180	2535	4.2	2.77	1410	1659	3.9
32835	ORLANDO	095	31686	38299	44981	4.6	88	12699	15588	18432	4.9	2.44	7534	9021	4.3
32836	ORLANDO	095	10931	13840	16663	5.7	93	3834	4863	5855	5.8	2.84	2918	3658	5.5
32837	ORLANDO	095	36797	44161	52107	4.4	87	12357	14974	17740	4.6	2.93	9527	11412	4.3
32839	ORLANDO	095	41627	46307	52223	2.5	67	13988	15748	17920	2.8	2.69	8952	9856	2.3
32901	MELBOURNE	009	22939	25320	28001	2.4	63	9842	11097	12528	2.9	2.04	5239	5852	2.6
32903	INDIALANTIC	009	12396	13232	14338	1.6	44	5496	5930	6488	1.8	2.23	3550	3776	1.5
32904	MELBOURNE	009	17851	20122	22508	2.9	71	7826	8962	10161	3.2	2.18	5091	5724	2.8
32905	PALM BAY	009	22129	23045	24850	1.0	26	9945	10498	11450	1.3	2.17	5732	5938	0.8
32907	PALM BAY	009	33688	36207	39331	1.7	48	12088	13112	14379	1.9	2.76	9553	10292	1.8
32908	PALM BAY	009	5913	6574	7270	2.5	67	2042	2298	2568	2.8	2.85	1588	1771	2.6
32909	PALM BAY	009	18076	20336	22635	2.8	70	6394	7291	8207	3.1	2.79	4982	5627	2.9
32920	CAPE CANAVERAL	009	8888	9447	10200	1.5	41	6331	6456	6931	0.5	2.31	3706	3725	0.1
32922	COCOA	009	14827	15060	16034	0.4	11	6331	6456	6931	0.5	2.31	3706	3725	0.1
32925	PATRICK AFB	009	2232	2221	2342	-0.1	3	581	573	608	-0.3	3.50	560	551	-0.4
32926	COCOA	009	20389	21184	22842	0.9	25	7955	8335	9070	1.1	2.51	5762	5989	0.9
32927	COCOA	009	26938	29210	31768	1.9	54	8747	9624	10627	2.3	2.77	6681	7290	2.1
32931	COCOA BEACH	009	14851	16020	17591	1.8	52	7748	8498	9449	2.2	1.88	4086	4393	1.7
32934	MELBOURNE	009	16691	19240	21954	3.4	78	6559	7510	8584	3.2	2.54	4828	5599	3.6
32935	MELBOURNE	009	39187	41018	44415	1.1	30	17276	18296	20002	1.4	2.24	10465	10919	1.0
32937	SATELLITE BEACH	009	26984	27261	28921	0.2	8	11513	11795	12646	0.6	2.31	8063	8141	0.2
32940	MELBOURNE	009	19127	25335	30526	6.4	96	8096	10795	13111	7.0	2.32	6101	8043	6.7
32948	FELLSMERE	061	4928	5742	6668	3.7	81	1267	1486	1747	3.8	3.59	1034	1205	3.7
32949	GRANT	009	1855	1987	2155	1.6	46	840	911	998	1.9	2.18	532	571	1.7
32950	MALABAR	009	4106	4433	4830	1.8	52	1615	1765	1943	2.1	2.51	1213	1313	1.9
32951	MELBOURNE BEACH	009	10822	11964	13317	2.4	64	4984	5557	6238	2.6	2.15	3472	3830	2.3
32952	MERRITT ISLAND	009	20695	21674	23369	1.1	30	8372	8840	9624	1.3	2.41	5902	6192	1.1
32953	MERRITT ISLAND	009	21695	22694	24554	1.1	29	9041	9518	10393	1.2	2.34	6035	6308	1.1
32955	ROCKLEDGE	009	24507	28271	32086	3.4	79	9755	11414	13122	3.8	2.44	7055	8197	3.6
32958	SEBASTIAN	061	20462	23271	26804	3.1	74	8995	10376	12091	3.4	2.24	6288	7177	3.2
32960	VERO BEACH	061	20191	21521	24046	1.5	42	9444	10197	11553	1.8	2.04	5061	5367	1.4
32962	VERO BEACH	061	20181	22098	25082	2.2	59	8683	9630	11051	2.5	2.29	5945	6517	2.2
32963	VERO BEACH	061	14077	16123	18741	3.2	76	7011	8117	9535	3.5	1.98	4924	5669	3.4
32966	VERO BEACH	061	13120	14475	16396	2.3	62	6374	7133	8193	2.7	1.96	4002	4407	2.3
32967	VERO BEACH	061	11824	13480	15588	3.1	75	4499	5211	6114	3.5	2.50	3149	3605	3.2
32968	VERO BEACH	061	8160	9525	11139	3.7	82	2862	3404	4041	4.2	2.76	2303	2716	4.0
32976	SEBASTIAN	009	8557	8846	9405	0.8	21	4735	4963	5337	1.1	1.78	2942	3037	0.8
33004	DANIA	011	14782	15495	16596	1.1	31	6722	7085	7577	1.3	2.14	3560	3653	0.6
33009	HALLANDALE	011	36234	37236	39458	0.6	18	19157	19623	20665	0.6	1.88	9208	9204	0.0
33010	HIALEAH	086	46778	47927	50217	0.6	16	15169	15600	16350	0.7	2.97	11419	11620	0.4
33012	HIALEAH	086	73132	75459	80021	0.7	20	23595	24470	25991	0.9	3.04	18903	19425	0.6
33013	HIALEAH	086	33595	33833	35214	0.2	7	10056	10151	10552	0.2	3.30	8267	8281	0.0
33014	HIALEAH	086	38538	40891	43875	1.4	39	13401	14264	15281	1.5	2.86	10078	10623	1.3
33015	HIALEAH	086	48740	54048	59105	2.5	65	16497	18153	19716	2.3	2.97	12567	13693	2.0
33016	HIALEAH	086	44038	50107	55720	3.1	74	13324	15146	16794	3.1	3.26	11555	13122	3.0
33018	HIALEAH	086	35486	42027	47438	4.1	84	9833	11437	12759	3.6	3.67	8959	10372	3.5
33019	HOLLYWOOD	011	15965	18389	20578	3.4	78	8788	10165	11341	3.5	1.80	4029	4515	2.7
33020	HOLLYWOOD	011	40452	41840	44649	0.8	22	17986	18632	19836	0.8	2.20	9037	9128	0.2
33021	HOLLYWOOD	011	45783	49738	54551	2.0	55	20188	22111	24225	2.2	2.22	12017	12773	1.5
33023	HOLLYWOOD	011	60916	63632	67902	1.0	28	19719	20483	21710	0.9	3.10	15213	15607	0.6
33024	HOLLYWOOD	011	58915	63218	68833	1.7	46	20990	22473	24338	1.6	2.81	15384	16270	1.3
33025	HOLLYWOOD	011	46414	52930	59574	3.1	75	16840	19090	21366	3.0	2.74	12046	13513	2.7
33026	HOLLYWOOD	011	29582	31275	33610	1.3	37	11495	12157	13012	1.3	2.57	8253	8585	0.9
	FLORIDA					2.1					2.2	2.45			2.0
	UNITED STATES					1.2					1.3	2.58			1.1

# ZIP CODE	POST OFFICE NAME	RACE (%) White 2000	White 2004	Black 2000	Black 2004	Asian/Pacific 2000	Asian/Pacific 2004	% Hispanic Origin 2000	% Hispanic Origin 2004	2004 AGE DISTRIBUTION (%) 0-4	5-9	10-14	15-19	20-24	25-44	45-64	65-84	85+	18+	MEDIAN AGE 2004	% 2004 Males	% 2004 Females
32763	ORANGE CITY	94.2	92.8	2.4	3.1	0.6	0.8	5.5	7.1	5.2	5.2	5.6	5.2	4.7	21.4	24.7	22.9	5.1	80.7	47.0	46.9	53.1
32764	OSTEEN	92.4	90.7	5.0	6.4	0.3	0.4	4.5	5.5	4.7	5.3	6.6	6.3	4.7	23.8	31.3	15.8	1.5	79.3	44.1	50.5	49.5
32765	OVIEDO	84.9	82.8	7.5	8.2	2.9	3.4	11.1	13.8	7.6	7.8	8.0	6.8	6.8	32.0	22.9	7.3	0.9	72.6	34.4	49.0	51.0
32766	OVIEDO	91.5	89.8	3.2	3.8	1.4	1.7	8.1	10.4	7.8	8.1	8.8	7.1	5.3	31.7	24.1	6.7	0.5	70.7	35.4	49.4	50.6
32767	PAISLEY	97.1	96.7	0.5	0.6	0.4	0.5	2.8	3.4	4.9	5.3	7.5	6.8	5.2	24.8	28.4	15.8	1.3	78.1	42.5	51.6	48.4
32771	SANFORD	56.1	56.1	38.9	38.3	0.8	1.0	5.7	6.7	7.2	7.2	7.3	6.5	6.5	27.2	25.2	11.5	1.5	74.4	37.2	48.2	51.8
32773	SANFORD	77.1	74.0	13.7	15.3	1.7	2.0	11.9	14.5	7.4	6.9	7.5	7.4	8.2	31.7	22.3	7.9	0.9	74.0	33.3	50.4	49.6
32776	SORRENTO	91.1	89.5	3.9	4.7	1.0	1.2	6.1	7.6	6.4	6.6	7.1	6.9	5.6	27.2	27.9	11.4	0.9	75.7	39.6	49.8	50.2
32778	TAVARES	90.4	88.8	6.7	7.8	0.7	0.8	3.4	4.1	3.4	3.5	4.3	4.2	4.2	18.5	25.5	31.6	4.8	86.2	55.1	47.7	52.4
32779	LONGWOOD	93.3	92.1	2.0	2.3	2.7	3.3	5.2	6.5	4.7	5.8	7.5	7.3	5.0	22.4	34.9	10.9	1.6	77.2	43.5	48.6	51.4
32780	TITUSVILLE	86.1	84.2	10.1	11.5	1.1	1.3	3.7	4.5	5.4	5.3	6.2	5.9	5.6	22.9	25.9	20.1	2.7	79.5	44.2	47.8	52.2
32784	UMATILLA	90.9	89.2	5.0	5.9	0.4	0.5	4.5	5.6	6.6	6.7	6.9	6.2	5.5	24.9	26.0	15.2	2.2	76.0	40.8	49.5	50.5
32789	WINTER PARK	84.3	82.6	11.6	12.7	1.6	1.9	4.6	5.7	5.2	5.4	5.4	7.2	6.7	25.5	26.2	14.9	3.6	80.8	41.6	47.0	53.0
32792	WINTER PARK	83.3	80.4	5.8	6.7	3.1	3.6	15.6	19.2	5.1	4.8	5.6	6.5	9.9	32.3	21.6	11.7	2.6	81.0	35.1	49.1	50.9
32796	TITUSVILLE	85.6	84.0	11.0	12.2	0.9	1.1	2.9	3.6	5.7	5.7	7.0	7.0	5.7	23.4	26.2	17.1	2.3	77.3	42.2	48.1	51.9
32798	ZELLWOOD	94.9	93.9	2.3	2.7	0.1	0.1	5.6	7.1	1.5	1.4	1.6	1.4	1.3	7.3	20.2	56.3	9.0	94.6	70.8	44.4	55.6
32801	ORLANDO	80.0	78.4	13.4	14.2	1.7	1.9	11.6	13.9	3.3	2.3	2.6	2.5	5.7	35.2	17.4	22.3	8.8	90.5	43.9	46.6	53.4
32803	ORLANDO	87.6	85.8	5.5	6.2	2.7	3.2	8.7	10.6	4.3	3.8	3.8	4.0	6.1	37.1	23.0	14.7	3.2	85.8	39.6	49.9	50.1
32804	ORLANDO	92.3	90.9	2.9	3.4	1.9	2.3	4.7	5.9	5.1	4.9	5.4	5.3	5.0	33.6	26.2	12.3	2.3	81.4	40.1	48.7	51.3
32805	ORLANDO	15.8	13.8	78.0	80.0	0.5	0.5	5.0	5.4	8.0	7.9	8.5	7.3	6.7	26.1	23.5	10.4	1.6	71.0	34.5	48.7	51.3
32806	ORLANDO	88.6	86.6	5.0	5.8	1.4	1.7	9.7	12.0	5.5	5.4	5.6	5.3	5.2	31.0	25.8	14.2	2.1	80.2	40.6	49.5	50.5
32807	ORLANDO	72.5	69.5	7.7	8.3	3.1	3.4	37.7	43.0	6.7	6.2	6.8	6.9	9.3	33.4	19.9	9.7	1.1	76.4	32.5	50.2	49.8
32808	ORLANDO	33.7	30.2	53.0	55.7	2.6	2.7	12.4	13.9	8.8	8.4	9.2	8.5	8.2	29.7	19.4	7.0	0.9	68.4	29.6	47.6	52.5
32809	ORLANDO	70.0	66.9	12.1	13.4	3.2	3.5	32.4	37.1	7.3	7.0	7.1	6.7	7.4	29.8	23.4	10.4	0.9	74.7	35.5	50.2	49.8
32810	ORLANDO	63.3	59.2	25.7	28.5	2.9	3.2	14.0	16.5	7.8	7.4	8.0	7.5	7.4	31.7	21.8	7.6	0.9	72.2	32.9	49.3	50.7
32811	ORLANDO	34.5	32.0	53.0	54.6	3.2	3.5	13.2	15.1	7.4	6.2	7.3	8.0	12.2	35.3	17.1	6.0	0.6	74.8	29.0	48.6	51.4
32812	ORLANDO	80.6	77.6	7.1	8.0	2.3	2.6	22.3	26.7	6.4	6.2	7.1	6.9	7.8	32.3	22.8	9.5	1.0	76.1	35.0	48.3	51.7
32817	ORLANDO	78.6	75.3	6.2	7.2	6.1	7.0	19.5	23.4	5.4	5.0	5.2	10.9	20.1	29.7	17.9	5.3	0.5	81.2	26.7	51.1	48.9
32818	ORLANDO	44.5	40.8	42.1	44.9	3.7	4.0	13.7	15.6	7.9	7.5	8.1	7.5	7.2	30.1	22.8	8.0	0.8	71.8	33.1	48.0	52.0
32819	ORLANDO	74.6	71.9	12.4	13.2	7.2	8.4	9.3	11.3	5.5	6.2	7.7	7.6	6.7	27.7	29.7	8.4	0.7	75.8	38.4	49.3	50.7
32820	ORLANDO	93.8	92.5	0.9	1.2	0.4	0.4	8.8	11.4	5.9	5.8	8.4	8.2	8.7	27.2	26.2	9.2	0.4	75.1	35.8	51.7	48.4
32821	ORLANDO	84.1	81.4	4.4	5.2	5.5	6.4	12.4	15.4	3.8	3.0	3.4	5.2	9.6	35.1	20.3	17.8	1.7	86.7	38.3	49.8	50.2
32822	ORLANDO	73.1	70.0	8.3	9.2	2.7	3.0	35.4	40.5	6.7	6.2	6.8	6.4	8.1	34.3	21.0	9.8	0.9	76.5	33.8	49.0	51.0
32824	ORLANDO	67.3	64.8	11.7	12.6	4.3	4.4	43.8	48.9	7.5	7.4	8.2	7.6	7.0	31.6	22.7	7.5	0.5	72.3	33.4	48.8	51.2
32825	ORLANDO	73.1	70.0	7.5	8.4	3.4	3.8	32.6	37.1	7.4	6.9	7.3	6.7	7.8	35.2	20.7	7.2	0.8	74.5	32.3	50.0	50.0
32826	ORLANDO	80.1	76.5	7.0	8.3	3.2	3.7	17.5	21.5	6.0	5.1	5.1	16.6	18.2	26.3	14.1	7.7	0.9	80.7	24.7	49.9	50.1
32827	ORLANDO	73.7	73.0	6.8	7.0	1.0	1.0	50.7	53.6	8.8	7.8	7.5	7.6	7.6	33.6	20.2	6.7	0.3	71.4	32.3	49.0	51.0
32828	ORLANDO	78.8	75.5	7.0	8.0	4.7	5.3	20.5	24.6	8.8	8.0	7.6	6.2	6.8	38.5	19.3	4.5	0.3	71.9	31.4	49.4	50.6
32829	ORLANDO	71.4	67.9	11.7	13.3	2.7	3.0	32.0	36.3	7.0	6.8	7.2	6.6	7.1	37.5	21.5	5.9	0.4	75.0	33.9	53.9	46.1
32830	ORLANDO	66.7	66.7	7.4	6.1	3.7	3.0	37.0	39.4	6.1	6.1	9.1	9.1	15.2	36.4	18.2	0.0	0.0	78.8	26.5	48.5	51.5
32831	ORLANDO	70.2	65.7	17.5	19.4	3.5	3.0	24.6	29.9	6.0	6.0	6.0	6.0	7.5	47.8	19.4	1.5	0.0	79.1	34.1	58.2	41.8
32832	ORLANDO	95.8	95.0	0.8	1.0	0.7	0.8	4.4	5.7	5.7	6.8	6.6	4.9	3.6	32.1	31.9	8.1	0.4	77.8	40.9	52.2	47.8
32833	ORLANDO	87.0	84.7	4.0	4.8	4.4	5.1	8.8	11.0	6.8	6.8	6.8	6.5	6.4	30.4	26.4	9.4	0.6	75.7	37.2	51.2	48.8
32835	ORLANDO	72.9	69.9	11.9	13.2	6.7	7.6	12.8	15.3	6.6	6.2	6.5	6.7	9.3	38.8	20.5	4.9	0.7	76.9	32.3	49.8	50.2
32836	ORLANDO	79.9	76.9	3.2	3.7	8.6	9.9	12.8	15.5	6.4	6.8	8.4	7.7	6.5	28.5	26.8	8.1	0.8	73.5	36.7	49.4	50.6
32837	ORLANDO	70.2	67.5	8.0	8.8	8.4	9.3	27.8	31.3	7.5	6.9	7.6	7.5	8.5	33.1	22.1	6.1	0.7	73.3	33.0	48.8	51.2
32839	ORLANDO	44.7	42.3	35.1	36.7	4.2	4.2	28.2	30.7	7.8	6.6	6.5	7.1	10.9	37.5	17.5	5.6	0.5	75.2	30.1	53.4	46.6
32901	MELBOURNE	73.9	71.9	20.1	21.1	1.9	2.3	5.5	6.9	5.3	4.6	4.9	6.6	8.3	22.6	21.4	21.0	5.3	81.9	43.2	48.5	51.5
32903	INDIALANTIC	96.2	95.5	0.7	0.9	1.3	1.6	3.0	3.8	4.3	4.8	5.7	5.0	3.8	22.4	30.5	21.0	2.4	82.0	47.2	49.5	50.5
32904	MELBOURNE	94.7	93.6	1.4	1.6	1.8	2.1	3.5	4.4	4.3	4.4	5.0	5.1	4.4	20.8	26.4	25.1	4.7	83.2	49.1	46.9	53.1
32905	PALM BAY	79.1	76.1	12.5	14.3	2.2	2.5	9.3	11.4	5.8	5.3	5.8	6.0	7.3	26.3	22.4	18.5	2.6	79.6	40.4	48.0	52.0
32907	PALM BAY	82.6	79.8	10.9	12.7	1.7	2.0	8.5	10.4	5.9	6.4	8.1	7.9	5.9	25.7	25.4	13.5	1.1	74.5	39.3	48.8	51.2
32908	PALM BAY	82.8	80.3	9.8	11.3	1.0	1.2	7.9	9.7	7.9	7.7	9.1	8.0	7.4	30.9	20.4	8.3	0.4	70.0	32.3	48.3	51.7
32909	PALM BAY	82.7	79.9	10.8	12.6	1.5	1.8	8.1	9.9	6.9	6.9	8.0	7.6	6.6	28.6	24.7	10.1	0.7	73.4	36.5	49.2	50.8
32920	CAPE CANAVERAL	94.6	93.7	1.4	1.7	1.7	2.1	3.5	4.4	3.0	3.0	3.3	3.8	5.1	26.8	30.9	21.7	2.4	88.4	47.8	52.2	47.8
32922	COCOA	57.3	54.1	37.5	40.3	0.9	1.0	4.9	5.8	7.3	6.8	7.4	7.4	7.6	26.2	22.6	13.0	1.7	74.0	36.2	47.6	52.4
32925	PATRICK AFB	67.7	63.7	18.9	21.1	3.0	3.4	11.8	14.1	12.0	12.3	8.8	6.5	15.8	39.4	3.6	1.6	0.1	63.4	23.3	53.8	46.2
32926	COCOA	81.7	80.8	14.4	14.7	0.8	1.0	3.4	4.2	5.8	6.1	7.5	6.9	5.9	26.0	27.2	13.5	1.0	76.3	40.4	49.8	50.2
32927	COCOA	87.8	86.2	7.6	8.6	1.0	1.2	3.7	4.6	5.7	6.4	8.2	8.2	7.7	30.5	23.4	9.2	0.7	75.0	36.4	52.5	47.5
32931	COCOA BEACH	96.6	96.1	0.6	0.7	1.1	1.3	2.5	3.1	2.3	2.5	3.3	3.5	3.6	18.4	30.7	31.6	4.1	89.7	55.6	49.8	50.2
32934	MELBOURNE	91.3	89.9	3.3	3.9	2.6	3.1	5.2	6.5	6.2	6.5	7.4	6.5	5.6	24.6	27.4	14.4	1.5	76.0	41.2	48.4	51.6
32935	MELBOURNE	89.7	87.9	4.3	5.2	2.3	2.8	5.4	6.7	5.3	5.2	5.9	5.9	6.6	28.5	25.5	15.3	1.8	80.1	40.7	48.6	51.4
32937	SATELLITE BEACH	93.6	92.7	1.9	2.1	1.8	2.2	3.7	4.6	4.3	4.5	6.1	6.2	5.2	21.8	28.4	21.1	2.3	81.0	46.1	48.3	51.7
32940	MELBOURNE	92.7	91.5	2.7	3.1	2.4	2.9	4.3	5.3	4.9	5.3	5.6	4.7	3.1	20.7	27.2	25.7	2.8	80.9	49.0	47.4	52.6
32948	FELLSMERE	68.2	65.0	4.8	5.0	0.2	0.2	57.8	64.1	9.2	8.2	8.0	7.6	9.2	33.3	17.4	6.5	0.6	70.4	29.1	56.7	43.3
32949	GRANT	97.8	97.3	0.9	1.1	0.4	0.6	1.6	2.0	1.8	1.7	2.1	2.5	1.9	9.3	28.1	46.4	6.4	92.9	66.3	46.6	53.5
32950	MALABAR	93.9	92.8	2.6	3.1	1.2	1.5	2.4	3.1	4.4	5.1	6.3	6.5	4.4	21.7	36.7	13.7	1.3	80.0	45.7	51.1	48.9
32951	MELBOURNE BEACH	97.9	97.6	0.2	0.2	0.9	1.1	2.1	2.7	3.1	3.5	4.7	3.8	2.4	16.9	35.9	27.2	2.5	86.1	53.8	49.9	50.1
32952	MERRITT ISLAND	95.0	94.1	0.9	1.0	1.7	2.1	3.6	4.5	4.4	5.3	6.6	6.4	4.1	22.2	29.6	17.9	3.5	79.8	45.6	49.2	50.8
32953	MERRITT ISLAND	86.6	84.9	8.5	9.4	1.8	2.2	4.2	5.2	5.8	5.8	6.3	6.0	5.6	24.3	26.9	16.8	2.5	78.6	42.9	48.5	51.5
32955	ROCKLEDGE	83.0	81.1	12.9	14.2	1.7	2.0	3.2	4.0	5.4	5.7	6.3	6.0	5.0	24.4	28.2	17.0	1.9	78.7	43.4	48.0	52.1
32958	SEBASTIAN	92.8	91.2	4.0	4.8	0.8	1.0	3.7	4.9	4.1	4.4	5.4	5.3	4.5	18.5	28.2	26.9	2.7	82.9	50.1	48.0	52.1
32960	VERO BEACH	90.8	89.2	4.6	5.3	1.4	1.7	5.8	7.6	4.7	4.4	4.7	4.8	6.5	23.5	24.4	22.0	5.0	83.3	46.1	47.2	52.8
32962	VERO BEACH	87.6	85.5	9.3	10.8	0.7	0.8	3.7	4.8	5.3	5.4	6.1	5.8	5.0	22.7	23.5	23.0	3.3	79.7	44.9	47.3	52.7
32963	VERO BEACH	98.4	98.0	0.3	0.4	0.7	0.9	1.7	2.2	2.0	2.5	3.4	2.9	1.8	9.3	31.3	42.6	4.3	90.1	63.4	47.3	52.7
32966	VERO BEACH	95.6	94.6	2.1	2.6	0.5	0.7	3.2	4.2	3.0	3.3	3.6	4.6	2.8	14.2	22.1	36.6	9.9	87.7	62.2	47.3	52.7
32967	VERO BEACH	53.2	51.4	41.9	42.9	0.3	0.4	7.4	8.8	6.9	6.7	7.2	6.8	6.3	24.7	24.9	14.4	2.2	75.1	39.0	49.2	50.8
32968	VERO BEACH	94.7	93.9	1.8	2.1	0.7	0.8	4.1	5.3	6.2	6.7	7.5	7.8	4.8	26.1	27.1	12.7	1.1	75.0	39.6	50.2	49.8
32976	SEBASTIAN	98.6	98.3	0.4	0.5	0.3	0.3	1.5	1.9	1.5	1.6	1.9	2.0	2.1	8.7	28.0	48.0	6.2	93.8	66.7	47.2	52.8
33004	DANIA	65.8	64.2	29.1	30.0	1.0	1.2	10.6	12.8	5.3	4.9	5.4	5.0	6.2	27.4	27.8	15.4	2.7	81.2	42.3	49.2	50.8
33009	HALLANDALE	77.7	75.3	15.5	17.1	1.0	1.1	18.8	21.7	3.9	3.8	3.7	3.4	3.8	20.8	24.3	28.8	7.6	86.6	54.2	46.2	53.8
33010	HIALEAH	87.7	87.8	3.8	3.5	0.2	0.2	91.6	93.4	5.6	5.4	6.1	6.4	6.6	27.7	22.7	17.2	2.4	79.0	40.0	50.0	50.1
33012	HIALEAH	90.1	90.1	1.6	1.6	0.5	0.5	89.9	92.0	5.2	5.2	6.0	6.4	6.2	26.7	23.5	18.2	2.6	79.5	41.2	47.1	52.9
33013	HIALEAH	91.4	91.3	1.4	1.3	0.3	0.3	90.4	92.6	5.0	5.0	5.5	5.7	5.6	27.7	24.1	19.2	2.2	81.0	41.9	49.2	50.8
33014	HIALEAH	86.7	86.6	3.4	3.3	1.0	1.0	78.2	81.9	6.1	6.2	7.3	7.3	6.8	31.1	22.5	11.6	1.2	75.9	36.3	48.2	51.8
33015	HIALEAH	68.4	69.1	18.1	16.8	2.4	2.4	62.1	67.1	8.3	7.6	7.6	7.0	8.0	34.7	19.5	6.6	0.6	72.2	31.8	47.7	52.3
33016	HIALEAH	84.4	84.8	3.0	2.8	0.8	0.8	88.5	90.6	7.5	7.4	7.9	7.4	7.0	31.3	21.3	9.1	1.1	72.5	33.7	47.7	52.3
33018	HIALEAH	86.8	86.9	2.4	2.3	1.2	1.2	87.3	89.6	7.6	7.7	8.4	7.2	6.7	32.1	22.0	7.6	0.7	71.7	33.8	48.5	51.6
33019	HOLLYWOOD	95.1	94.1	1.5	1.8	1.0	1.2	13.5	16.8	3.8	3.8	2.8	2.4	2.6	26.9	28.9	22.3	6.5	88.2	50.1	48.4	51.6
33020	HOLLYWOOD	65.9	63.4	23.5	24.8	1.5	1.7	21.5	24.9	6.2	5.8	6.2	6.3	7.0	30.6	24.7	10.9	2.3	78.0	38.0	49.9	50.1
33021	HOLLYWOOD	85.7	83.4	6.9	8.0	2.1	2.4	17.6	21.0	5.1	5.1	5.4	4.9	5.0	25.7	25.6	18.1	5.3	81.4	44.4	47.0	53.0
33023	HOLLYWOOD	42.8	39.5	45.0	47.8	1.8	1.8	24.2	26.2	7.8	7.7	8.8	7.9	7.5	29.4	21.7	8.2	1.1	70.9	32.6	47.7	52.3
33024	HOLLYWOOD	76.8	74.3	9.8	10.9	3.3	3.5	30.9	35.3	6.9	7.0	7.7	7.0	7.0	30.1	23.2	9.7	1.4	74.0	35.6	48.2	51.8
33025	HOLLYWOOD	46.3	44.5	40.1	41.3	4.3	4.6	24.1	27.5	8.2	7.3	7.4	6.7	7.7	34.3	19.6	7.5	1.3	73.1	32.4	46.7	53.3
33026	HOLLYWOOD	84.6	82.1	7.0	8.2	3.0	3.5	19.6	23.3	5.4	5.9	7.5	7.1	6.0	26.3	27.6	12.2	2.1	76.8	40.6	46.0	54.0
	FLORIDA	78.0	76.5	14.6	15.2	1.7	2.0	16.8	19.0	6.0	5.9	6.4	6.4	6.5	26.6	24.5	15.5	2.4	78.1	40.0	48.8	51.2
	UNITED STATES	75.1	73.6	12.3	12.5	3.8	4.2	12.5	14.1	6.9	6.7	7.2	7.0	7.3	28.6	23.8	10.8	1.7	75.1	36.0	49.1	50.9

INCOME

#	POST OFFICE NAME	2004 Per Capita Income	2004 HH Income Base	2004 Household Income Distribution (%): Less than $25,000	$25,000 to $49,999	$50,000 to $99,999	$100,000 to $149,999	$150,000 or More	Median Household Income: 2004	2009	2004 National Centile	2004 State Centile	2004 Home Value Base	2004 Home Value Distribution (%): Less than $50,000	$50,000 to $89,999	$90,000 to $174,999	$175,000 to $399,999	$400,000 or More	2004 Median Home Value
32763	ORANGE CITY	19878	7540	35.0	31.8	25.3	6.0	1.9	34176	38658	25	23	5878	16.3	27.9	42.0	12.7	1.2	96287
32764	OSTEEN	28426	1209	21.9	36.7	24.9	9.4	7.1	45561	50854	63	62	1111	5.0	19.7	38.9	30.6	5.9	141250
32765	OVIEDO	30252	17661	10.2	20.4	40.1	19.0	10.4	71515	82707	92	93	15514	2.3	4.7	35.0	53.6	4.4	190973
32766	OVIEDO	25652	3180	9.0	23.3	44.3	17.9	5.6	64506	75929	88	91	2953	0.0	6.5	45.0	44.8	3.7	172274
32767	PAISLEY	17768	1114	35.1	36.3	22.5	4.9	1.3	34431	39202	25	24	947	24.7	25.0	37.0	11.2	2.1	90417
32771	SANFORD	22270	13646	30.3	29.4	26.8	9.0	4.6	40095	47840	46	44	9276	8.9	23.4	38.1	24.0	5.7	115687
32773	SANFORD	19934	9763	25.0	34.8	29.3	8.1	2.8	42585	48858	55	52	6493	9.1	22.0	55.3	12.0	1.6	107887
32776	SORRENTO	23469	2930	20.6	29.6	37.0	8.5	4.4	49917	56716	72	74	2531	13.6	17.1	39.0	24.6	5.8	121479
32778	TAVARES	24125	7787	31.7	35.3	23.7	5.7	3.5	37151	41887	36	33	6515	17.8	30.4	34.5	14.4	2.9	92560
32779	LONGWOOD	42824	10604	7.1	17.9	34.9	21.3	18.9	82627	96288	96	97	8620	0.9	0.7	22.3	64.0	12.1	228340
32780	TITUSVILLE	24923	14364	27.1	29.7	30.1	9.7	3.4	43225	49473	57	54	10019	5.7	26.4	47.8	18.2	1.9	110862
32784	UMATILLA	17963	4331	35.0	33.0	25.5	4.1	2.5	35570	40506	30	27	3509	25.8	24.4	31.2	15.6	3.1	89632
32789	WINTER PARK	44736	10937	22.8	25.7	24.0	12.7	14.9	52382	61197	76	77	7133	0.9	9.4	25.6	35.4	28.7	233281
32792	WINTER PARK	25357	21778	23.6	32.4	31.3	9.3	3.4	45644	52150	63	62	10979	1.2	7.4	61.7	28.0	1.8	145120
32796	TITUSVILLE	20769	8117	28.0	30.8	31.0	8.2	2.1	41808	48527	52	51	6184	5.9	28.7	51.9	12.3	1.3	106144
32798	ZELLWOOD	25384	1044	34.5	42.9	16.9	3.6	2.1	33852	38496	24	22	981	8.7	46.2	43.5	1.6	0.0	86289
32801	ORLANDO	37704	5038	42.2	27.2	17.8	6.7	6.2	30757	36677	14	12	1355	1.1	9.6	27.1	51.1	11.1	203919
32803	ORLANDO	34398	9919	20.9	29.8	32.1	10.4	6.8	49267	58895	71	71	5996	1.3	5.4	43.8	41.1	8.4	174036
32804	ORLANDO	37543	8579	19.6	29.3	30.5	12.5	8.2	51118	60757	74	75	5739	5.5	6.0	39.2	37.9	11.4	173010
32805	ORLANDO	13007	9331	50.6	30.2	15.2	3.0	0.9	24583	28201	4	3	3730	7.9	32.9	51.4	7.6	0.3	98289
32806	ORLANDO	30923	12347	22.4	28.2	32.1	9.9	7.5	49417	57784	71	71	8239	1.1	7.6	52.4	31.8	7.1	153865
32807	ORLANDO	17283	13125	29.6	37.9	27.1	4.3	1.1	37032	42651	36	32	7007	3.3	24.3	66.0	6.0	0.4	107577
32808	ORLANDO	14581	17653	34.6	36.1	23.9	4.1	1.3	33889	38155	24	22	9513	1.9	23.5	70.0	4.4	0.2	108295
32809	ORLANDO	20787	9023	25.9	34.9	28.1	7.6	3.7	40944	46207	49	48	5742	7.2	11.5	60.1	16.1	5.2	117027
32810	ORLANDO	20355	11985	22.5	33.0	33.1	8.6	2.8	45353	51921	62	61	7724	5.5	14.3	68.6	11.0	0.6	119326
32811	ORLANDO	17183	14247	28.6	41.0	25.6	3.5	1.2	36644	41283	34	31	4611	5.8	35.4	57.2	1.3	0.4	95145
32812	ORLANDO	24943	13489	20.1	32.4	33.1	10.4	4.1	47944	55250	68	68	7920	4.8	10.8	50.4	32.1	1.9	144001
32817	ORLANDO	21471	15004	25.1	32.2	29.6	9.6	3.6	43733	49380	58	56	7819	2.1	9.1	56.1	29.8	2.9	149048
32818	ORLANDO	19628	13387	21.8	30.0	35.4	10.3	2.4	48232	55283	69	69	10300	8.8	7.2	66.1	17.2	0.7	130586
32819	ORLANDO	35689	9589	12.6	19.1	31.9	20.0	16.4	76521	87165	94	95	7732	0.7	6.7	19.7	58.4	14.6	223407
32820	ORLANDO	18015	1303	23.3	42.1	27.3	3.7	3.7	41683	49024	52	50	1045	31.8	31.4	27.4	7.9	1.6	79595
32821	ORLANDO	31475	6522	15.0	32.4	39.6	9.6	3.5	51854	62541	75	76	3680	0.0	2.0	58.9	36.9	2.3	157609
32822	ORLANDO	21077	20680	24.3	36.9	30.9	5.8	2.1	40920	47120	49	47	11061	16.0	21.4	51.6	10.7	0.3	105922
32824	ORLANDO	19017	8148	15.9	32.1	39.5	9.8	2.7	51761	59394	75	76	6763	3.3	7.9	59.2	28.2	1.4	145033
32825	ORLANDO	22439	15918	16.7	30.4	38.5	11.4	3.0	52361	60486	76	77	11999	3.4	7.9	64.9	22.6	1.3	138350
32826	ORLANDO	20120	7230	24.4	33.2	32.5	6.9	3.0	42648	49303	55	53	4736	20.7	17.8	43.1	17.5	0.9	113117
32827	ORLANDO	22296	929	16.4	41.3	32.6	4.6	5.1	45259	51884	62	60	888	1.5	2.5	83.1	2.9	10.0	119850
32828	ORLANDO	27086	10808	11.8	21.1	43.2	17.5	6.5	66049	77124	89	91	8930	3.1	7.2	32.6	55.4	1.7	187510
32829	ORLANDO	19294	4251	11.8	30.6	43.3	12.6	1.7	56512	64678	81	83	3785	4.1	6.9	65.4	23.6	0.0	143644
32830	ORLANDO	17197	13	30.8	38.5	23.1	7.7	0.0	37321	35000	37	34	0	0.0	0.0	0.0	0.0	0.0	0
32831	ORLANDO	32285	27	3.7	25.9	55.6	14.8	0.0	68452	78263	91	92	24	0.0	0.0	58.3	41.7	0.0	167857
32832	ORLANDO	46441	953	8.1	17.6	38.8	19.5	16.0	77700	91976	94	96	853	3.9	6.1	25.7	46.7	17.7	207839
32833	ORLANDO	23000	2180	23.1	29.8	29.6	13.7	3.9	47493	55356	67	67	1731	13.6	17.2	38.5	30.6	0.0	140869
32835	ORLANDO	31754	15588	15.7	28.0	34.4	13.1	8.8	56073	64528	81	82	7289	0.4	6.4	37.8	45.5	10.0	193459
32836	ORLANDO	46348	4863	17.0	17.5	22.4	17.0	26.1	83101	98654	96	97	3655	7.7	4.4	2.9	48.2	36.8	346321
32837	ORLANDO	26689	14974	11.4	24.0	41.5	15.1	8.1	63823	75424	88	90	10344	0.7	1.6	43.7	51.7	2.3	180966
32839	ORLANDO	16082	15748	34.4	38.0	22.5	3.8	1.3	33375	37466	22	21	5667	12.8	19.7	57.5	8.3	1.8	108767
32901	MELBOURNE	19170	11097	42.9	31.7	19.5	3.9	2.0	29152	33565	11	9	6338	15.9	27.9	47.7	8.5	0.1	98128
32903	INDIALANTIC	40882	5930	16.5	23.2	31.7	15.8	12.8	63847	73235	88	90	4777	1.1	2.7	34.9	49.2	12.2	204910
32904	MELBOURNE	27759	8962	22.3	34.1	30.1	8.6	4.8	43352	49224	57	55	7129	8.6	28.9	37.7	22.9	1.9	111715
32905	PALM BAY	19028	10498	38.7	34.5	21.4	4.4	1.1	31516	36351	16	15	6068	9.8	41.9	37.8	10.2	0.3	88500
32907	PALM BAY	20541	13112	19.8	33.9	36.1	8.2	2.0	47149	54234	66	66	11164	2.2	17.2	70.4	10.0	0.2	116650
32908	PALM BAY	19177	2298	18.0	39.3	36.4	4.3	2.0	45316	51695	62	61	1808	0.4	34.9	61.2	2.9	0.7	99366
32909	PALM BAY	18181	7291	21.1	36.4	35.4	5.8	1.3	43524	50128	57	55	5917	1.2	27.6	64.7	6.4	0.1	108413
32920	CAPE CANAVERAL	27663	5483	33.9	31.0	27.3	5.6	2.3	35324	40662	29	27	2981	15.4	17.3	45.6	20.4	1.3	117515
32922	COCOA	16955	6456	47.4	28.8	18.0	3.8	2.0	26551	30206	6	4	3306	17.1	44.2	27.3	9.4	2.1	78797
32925	PATRICK AFB	13907	573	12.2	48.3	36.8	1.9	0.7	45231	50841	62	60	32	50.0	0.0	28.1	21.9	0.0	70000
32926	COCOA	21698	8335	25.3	31.1	31.7	9.7	2.2	45226	51879	62	60	6955	11.6	24.0	43.6	19.9	0.9	109442
32927	COCOA	19668	9624	18.9	31.4	39.6	8.9	1.2	49678	56595	71	73	8220	5.8	19.6	66.4	8.0	0.2	111172
32931	COCOA BEACH	35290	8498	22.7	30.0	30.7	10.6	6.0	47773	54611	68	67	6000	1.9	6.8	45.0	39.6	6.7	168397
32934	MELBOURNE	27878	7510	20.2	26.1	32.6	12.9	8.3	54137	63925	79	80	6255	15.2	5.1	25.5	50.0	4.2	184766
32935	MELBOURNE	22595	18296	25.2	36.2	30.1	6.7	1.8	41351	47837	51	49	12205	7.0	26.2	55.1	10.8	0.8	107150
32937	SATELLITE BEACH	31310	11795	17.2	27.5	36.2	12.2	6.9	54584	62565	79	80	8908	0.6	4.4	51.9	37.2	6.0	163735
32940	MELBOURNE	35625	10795	10.5	21.7	41.6	17.9	8.3	68327	79396	90	92	9621	1.3	1.9	33.8	58.5	4.5	196515
32948	FELLSMERE	14175	1486	31.0	33.0	27.7	6.5	1.8	39133	46181	43	40	1149	10.9	27.0	40.0	21.5	0.6	104092
32949	GRANT	21310	911	35.6	32.7	25.1	4.1	2.5	32434	37221	19	17	850	10.4	51.3	25.3	11.9	1.2	79730
32950	MALABAR	26899	1765	18.2	25.5	37.7	14.4	4.3	57555	65807	82	84	1626	8.9	8.8	28.2	47.5	6.6	182727
32951	MELBOURNE BEACH	39997	5557	14.8	25.5	35.2	14.0	10.4	61433	71722	86	88	4790	5.1	6.2	24.7	48.8	15.2	211964
32952	MERRITT ISLAND	30468	8840	18.1	27.1	32.5	14.6	7.6	55871	64441	81	81	7291	4.1	9.2	37.4	38.8	10.5	172977
32953	MERRITT ISLAND	27185	9518	23.4	29.3	29.4	11.8	6.1	47693	54565	68	67	7025	6.1	12.8	38.3	37.2	5.6	154620
32955	ROCKLEDGE	25292	11414	17.2	30.6	36.8	12.2	3.2	51768	60379	75	76	9396	4.5	15.4	53.4	23.9	2.8	126488
32958	SEBASTIAN	23207	10376	26.4	33.1	31.9	6.4	2.2	42291	49651	54	52	8964	6.1	10.7	56.3	24.9	2.0	136264
32960	VERO BEACH	23091	10197	34.0	32.7	24.9	5.8	2.6	34768	40847	27	25	6188	7.3	21.6	45.5	20.2	5.4	119240
32962	VERO BEACH	24250	9630	25.2	34.5	30.5	6.5	3.3	42091	48841	53	51	7985	6.6	22.3	51.9	18.2	1.0	116968
32963	VERO BEACH	96232	8117	9.3	14.7	22.8	18.7	34.5	107155	138767	99	99	7453	0.5	0.2	7.4	37.9	54.0	438516
32966	VERO BEACH	29102	7133	25.5	36.3	27.4	6.5	4.2	40290	46696	47	45	6220	27.0	17.6	32.6	20.3	2.5	100235
32967	VERO BEACH	24437	5211	34.1	26.3	25.6	8.4	5.5	40287	47741	47	45	3648	13.4	16.8	30.4	27.5	12.0	134576
32968	VERO BEACH	26297	3404	16.6	27.7	37.2	11.6	6.9	55271	65175	80	81	3020	3.3	10.6	41.5	39.6	5.1	150154
32976	SEBASTIAN	25624	4963	36.0	35.9	22.4	3.4	2.3	32038	36307	18	17	4521	13.2	50.6	26.4	8.1	1.7	78666
33004	DANIA	24439	7085	32.8	30.0	24.3	8.4	4.4	38178	45329	40	37	3633	8.5	12.7	44.7	31.2	3.0	132563
33009	HALLANDALE	25021	19623	40.8	28.7	21.9	5.5	3.1	30979	36333	15	13	13217	12.3	24.2	42.8	17.3	3.5	111991
33010	HIALEAH	12458	15600	49.5	27.4	18.5	3.5	1.2	25306	29299	5	3	5703	5.7	4.5	40.8	48.5	0.6	173637
33012	HIALEAH	14691	24470	39.5	31.6	22.6	4.5	1.8	31660	36500	17	15	13217	3.6	10.2	43.4	42.2	0.6	157397
33013	HIALEAH	13830	10151	35.5	31.7	24.8	6.5	1.6	34891	39572	27	25	6671	0.9	3.6	39.6	55.3	0.6	182662
33014	HIALEAH	20937	14264	28.8	27.7	29.8	8.9	4.9	43463	50379	57	55	8025	0.5	3.8	44.3	47.0	4.4	178317
33015	HIALEAH	21756	18153	19.5	30.9	35.3	9.8	4.4	49572	57841	71	72	10552	0.5	1.2	42.8	53.4	2.2	182973
33016	HIALEAH	17293	15146	28.8	33.1	27.7	6.9	3.6	40537	46959	48	46	9611	1.6	11.1	53.2	28.1	5.9	140240
33018	HIALEAH	17454	11437	16.7	32.4	36.8	10.2	3.9	50622	58312	73	75	9601	4.6	1.3	43.8	47.8	2.5	175332
33019	HOLLYWOOD	46686	10165	21.6	24.7	29.5	12.4	11.8	53972	63764	78	79	6543	0.7	4.8	23.5	49.8	21.2	241130
33020	HOLLYWOOD	18724	18632	39.0	33.0	21.4	5.1	1.5	31849	37595	17	16	7965	7.7	16.9	47.8	25.4	2.2	132861
33021	HOLLYWOOD	29053	22111	24.6	29.1	29.5	10.6	6.4	46011	54069	64	63	15370	10.0	17.0	26.8	41.6	4.7	164000
33023	HOLLYWOOD	16664	20483	26.8	33.5	30.9	6.8	2.0	41479	47777	51	49	14583	1.8	5.3	69.7	23.0	0.3	143716
33024	HOLLYWOOD	20723	22473	22.0	29.9	36.4	9.1	2.7	48183	55335	69	69	15928	1.8	6.1	58.4	32.8	0.9	153918
33025	HOLLYWOOD	23223	19090	16.3	29.1	38.7	12.6	3.3	53882	63614	78	79	12074	3.4	11.6	32.4	51.7	1.1	179752
33026	HOLLYWOOD	30493	12157	14.9	22.9	37.5	16.8	8.0	63487	73425	87	90	10388	0.5	8.2	40.0	46.4	4.9	178436
	FLORIDA	25506		26.4	29.9	29.1	9.1	5.6	44138	51288				8.8	15.8	40.2	28.3	7.0	137042
	UNITED STATES	25866		24.7	27.1	30.8	10.9	6.5	48124	56710				10.9	15.0	33.7	30.1	10.4	145905

#	ZIP CODE POST OFFICE NAME	FINANCIAL SERVICES: Auto Loan	FINANCIAL SERVICES: Home Loan	FINANCIAL SERVICES: Invest-ments	FINANCIAL SERVICES: Retire-ment Plans	THE HOME: Home Improvements: Home Repair	THE HOME: Home Improvements: Lawn & Garden	THE HOME: Furnishings: Comput-ers & Hard-ware	THE HOME: Furnishings: Major Appli-ances	THE HOME: Furnishings: TV, Radio, Sound Equip-ment	THE HOME: Furnishings: Furni-ture	ENTERTAINMENT: Dine out/ Carry out	ENTERTAINMENT: Sports Equip-ment	ENTERTAINMENT: Fees & Tickets	ENTERTAINMENT: Toys & Games	ENTERTAINMENT: Travel	ENTERTAINMENT: Cable TV	PERSONAL: Apparel & Services	PERSONAL: Auto Repairs	PERSONAL: Health Insur-ance	PERSONAL: Pets & Supplies
32763	ORANGE CITY	66	63	61	61	65	75	61	66	64	62	79	70	61	74	64	66	74	65	73	75
32764	OSTEEN	114	98	75	93	105	117	92	105	99	93	120	119	88	115	96	103	112	102	118	133
32765	OVIEDO	125	143	142	148	137	133	129	128	119	133	151	150	134	153	127	112	150	125	110	140
32766	OVIEDO	105	123	124	126	119	116	111	110	102	113	129	129	116	133	110	97	128	107	96	121
32767	PAISLEY	67	62	53	59	63	69	59	64	60	61	75	70	57	68	59	61	71	63	67	74
32771	SANFORD	78	80	90	80	79	85	81	80	82	82	102	91	83	101	81	82	100	81	79	89
32773	SANFORD	76	77	78	79	76	78	77	76	74	77	94	90	76	93	75	71	91	77	71	85
32776	SORRENTO	101	92	71	88	94	99	86	94	89	88	109	110	83	106	87	89	105	93	96	115
32778	TAVARES	72	71	75	68	74	85	67	74	70	71	87	75	69	77	72	73	82	72	83	81
32779	LONGWOOD	146	177	201	181	173	175	163	159	151	163	191	186	174	199	165	147	191	156	143	175
32780	TITUSVILLE	79	79	80	76	80	90	76	80	78	77	97	87	77	92	79	81	93	79	86	91
32784	UMATILLA	78	60	39	55	65	74	59	68	67	59	80	80	54	77	60	70	74	68	79	89
32789	WINTER PARK	128	142	179	143	139	150	141	137	138	141	173	159	146	174	143	137	171	139	132	151
32792	WINTER PARK	77	77	93	81	76	81	83	79	81	83	103	95	83	101	81	78	100	83	74	88
32796	TITUSVILLE	70	72	74	70	72	78	71	72	71	70	88	82	72	89	72	72	86	72	73	81
32798	ZELLWOOD	70	65	65	59	68	83	60	70	65	65	81	67	61	69	66	70	75	68	83	78
32801	ORLANDO	79	74	116	80	73	83	88	80	91	87	114	96	89	116	87	91	112	86	82	89
32803	ORLANDO	89	92	123	97	90	96	99	93	97	98	123	112	101	125	98	95	121	97	87	102
32804	ORLANDO	101	112	135	116	111	114	112	109	107	111	135	129	114	136	112	104	133	110	100	119
32805	ORLANDO	48	42	48	39	41	48	46	46	51	47	63	51	46	59	45	54	61	48	51	53
32806	ORLANDO	90	100	120	101	98	104	100	97	98	99	123	113	103	126	101	96	121	98	93	106
32807	ORLANDO	61	59	71	61	57	62	65	61	65	65	82	73	64	81	62	63	80	64	58	68
32808	ORLANDO	60	55	63	56	54	59	60	59	62	61	77	69	60	75	58	61	75	61	57	66
32809	ORLANDO	73	79	105	77	77	83	80	78	81	82	104	88	82	106	81	83	103	79	76	85
32810	ORLANDO	79	76	82	79	75	78	80	78	78	80	99	92	79	96	77	75	96	80	72	87
32811	ORLANDO	63	55	64	59	53	59	62	60	63	64	80	70	61	75	59	61	78	63	57	68
32812	ORLANDO	87	84	93	89	82	85	89	86	86	90	109	102	87	105	85	81	106	89	77	95
32817	ORLANDO	80	69	80	76	67	72	85	76	82	82	104	95	79	97	77	75	100	82	68	85
32818	ORLANDO	80	87	90	89	85	86	84	83	80	85	101	97	85	101	83	77	99	82	75	91
32819	ORLANDO	132	152	177	157	148	154	143	139	135	145	171	161	153	173	144	131	171	138	127	154
32820	ORLANDO	81	74	58	71	74	78	70	75	71	72	88	87	66	83	69	70	84	75	75	89
32821	ORLANDO	90	90	106	92	90	98	93	93	92	94	115	105	93	109	92	90	112	94	91	102
32822	ORLANDO	74	69	73	71	68	72	73	72	72	74	91	85	70	87	70	69	88	74	68	81
32824	ORLANDO	89	98	94	102	94	92	90	89	83	93	105	105	92	105	88	78	104	87	78	99
32825	ORLANDO	88	95	98	98	92	92	92	90	86	93	109	106	92	109	89	82	108	90	79	99
32826	ORLANDO	79	73	79	77	71	77	80	77	78	81	99	90	77	92	76	74	95	80	72	85
32827	ORLANDO	80	92	112	88	88	94	87	86	86	90	110	96	91	113	88	86	110	86	81	93
32828	ORLANDO	115	130	125	135	123	119	117	116	107	122	136	136	120	136	114	100	135	113	98	127
32829	ORLANDO	91	99	96	100	95	94	91	91	86	95	109	106	92	109	89	82	108	90	81	101
32830	ORLANDO	65	55	62	61	53	58	63	60	62	64	79	73	60	74	59	59	77	65	56	69
32831	ORLANDO	104	118	113	123	112	108	106	105	97	111	124	123	109	124	103	90	122	102	89	115
32832	ORLANDO	160	199	211	199	195	193	178	177	164	177	207	207	189	220	182	160	207	171	158	196
32833	ORLANDO	88	100	98	99	98	99	91	92	86	91	108	108	93	111	92	84	106	90	85	104
32835	ORLANDO	111	111	119	119	107	109	113	109	108	116	137	130	113	133	108	101	134	112	96	121
32836	ORLANDO	173	211	242	217	204	210	190	185	175	193	223	214	208	229	193	170	224	181	166	205
32837	ORLANDO	110	122	125	126	117	116	114	112	107	117	135	131	116	135	111	101	134	111	99	123
32839	ORLANDO	52	50	62	51	48	52	55	52	55	56	70	62	54	69	53	54	69	55	49	58
32901	MELBOURNE	55	52	60	52	52	59	56	56	58	56	72	63	56	69	56	58	69	57	58	62
32903	INDIALANTIC	120	137	153	135	138	147	128	130	124	129	156	145	135	155	134	125	153	128	129	143
32904	MELBOURNE	83	89	98	88	90	98	86	88	85	87	106	97	88	103	88	86	103	87	90	97
32905	PALM BAY	58	54	59	54	55	62	58	58	59	57	74	66	57	71	58	60	71	59	61	66
32907	PALM BAY	79	86	85	85	85	87	80	82	78	81	97	95	82	99	81	76	95	80	77	92
32908	PALM BAY	76	84	84	85	81	80	80	79	75	81	94	94	80	95	78	70	93	79	69	87
32909	PALM BAY	74	75	70	75	75	77	71	73	70	72	87	87	71	88	71	68	85	73	70	86
32920	CAPE CANAVERAL	62	65	81	64	64	72	67	66	67	67	85	73	68	84	68	68	83	67	67	72
32922	COCOA	53	50	59	49	49	56	55	53	57	54	71	61	55	70	54	58	69	55	56	59
32925	PATRICK AFB	78	50	48	57	46	55	73	64	74	69	93	84	63	83	61	68	89	75	60	73
32926	COCOA	75	79	78	78	78	82	75	77	74	76	93	87	76	91	76	73	90	76	75	86
32927	COCOA	81	83	76	85	81	83	79	80	76	80	94	93	78	93	77	73	92	79	74	90
32931	COCOA BEACH	93	94	101	90	96	110	90	96	93	93	116	99	92	106	95	97	111	94	106	107
32934	MELBOURNE	96	110	116	110	108	111	101	102	96	103	121	116	106	123	103	95	120	99	95	112
32935	MELBOURNE	66	71	80	71	70	75	72	70	71	71	89	82	73	91	72	71	87	71	69	77
32937	SATELLITE BEACH	97	105	115	103	105	115	101	103	100	102	125	114	105	123	104	102	122	102	105	113
32940	MELBOURNE	126	119	113	113	125	145	110	124	115	117	143	123	111	121	118	122	135	120	143	141
32948	FELLSMERE	76	64	58	64	65	69	70	72	73	72	91	82	67	90	67	71	90	74	70	79
32949	GRANT	67	66	70	62	69	82	61	70	65	66	80	67	63	70	67	69	75	67	80	76
32950	MALABAR	88	109	116	109	107	105	97	97	90	97	113	113	103	121	99	87	113	93	87	107
32951	MELBOURNE BEACH	127	124	123	119	130	150	114	128	119	121	148	128	117	128	124	125	140	124	145	145
32952	MERRITT ISLAND	95	111	127	110	110	116	105	104	102	105	128	119	111	131	108	101	126	103	100	114
32953	MERRITT ISLAND	88	91	97	90	92	100	89	91	90	90	112	103	91	110	91	91	108	90	93	102
32955	ROCKLEDGE	84	93	97	90	93	99	86	89	85	87	107	99	90	107	89	86	104	87	89	99
32958	SEBASTIAN	77	74	74	69	77	92	68	78	72	73	90	75	70	76	74	77	84	75	90	86
32960	VERO BEACH	65	65	73	63	66	75	66	68	68	66	84	73	67	80	68	69	81	68	72	74
32962	VERO BEACH	77	82	85	79	82	89	77	81	77	79	96	87	79	92	80	77	93	79	82	89
32963	VERO BEACH	274	282	304	270	291	335	256	281	261	271	327	285	268	291	277	276	313	272	311	317
32966	VERO BEACH	82	82	87	79	85	97	79	85	81	82	101	89	81	93	83	84	96	83	92	94
32967	VERO BEACH	89	84	86	80	85	96	84	88	89	87	109	96	84	102	85	91	105	88	94	100
32968	VERO BEACH	96	116	123	116	114	114	105	105	98	105	123	122	111	129	107	95	122	102	96	116
32976	SEBASTIAN	67	64	68	59	67	82	59	69	64	64	79	64	61	67	65	69	74	66	81	75
33004	DANIA	69	69	86	68	68	77	74	71	76	73	95	81	75	94	74	77	93	74	74	79
33009	HALLANDALE	66	63	72	59	65	77	63	68	67	66	84	68	64	75	66	71	79	68	77	74
33010	HIALEAH	43	41	81	37	39	46	48	45	55	51	72	50	47	74	48	60	72	49	47	49
33012	HIALEAH	52	50	98	45	47	56	58	55	67	62	87	61	57	90	59	72	88	59	57	60
33013	HIALEAH	53	51	100	46	48	57	59	56	68	64	89	62	58	92	60	74	89	61	59	61
33014	HIALEAH	75	74	116	71	70	79	81	78	87	85	113	88	80	114	81	90	113	82	77	85
33015	HIALEAH	83	85	121	82	80	88	89	86	93	93	119	97	89	121	88	94	119	89	82	94
33016	HIALEAH	67	67	120	62	63	73	74	71	83	79	108	79	74	112	75	89	109	76	73	77
33018	HIALEAH	77	78	132	72	73	83	85	82	94	91	122	91	85	125	86	99	122	86	82	89
33019	HOLLYWOOD	106	121	156	119	119	130	119	116	117	118	147	133	125	152	122	118	146	117	113	128
33020	HOLLYWOOD	53	53	70	54	52	57	59	55	59	58	75	65	59	75	58	59	73	58	54	61
33021	HOLLYWOOD	87	92	108	92	92	100	91	92	90	93	114	103	93	110	93	90	111	92	91	101
33023	HOLLYWOOD	69	73	84	71	71	75	73	72	73	74	92	81	74	93	72	72	91	72	68	79
33024	HOLLYWOOD	78	82	95	81	80	85	82	81	82	83	103	92	83	105	82	81	102	82	77	89
33025	HOLLYWOOD	92	91	98	96	88	92	92	91	89	95	113	105	92	107	89	84	110	92	83	100
33026	HOLLYWOOD	106	115	130	118	114	121	111	111	108	113	136	126	115	134	112	106	133	111	106	122
	FLORIDA	89	87	95	86	87	96	87	89	89	89	111	100	87	107	88	90	108	90	91	101
	UNITED STATES	100	100	100	100	100	100	100	100	100	100	100	100	100	100	100	100	100	100	100	100

ZIP CODE		COUNTY FIPS CODE	POPULATION			2000-2004 ANNUAL RATE		HOUSEHOLDS					FAMILIES		
#	POST OFFICE NAME		2000	2004	2009	% Rate	State Centile	2000	2004	2009	% Annual Rate 2000-2004	2004 Average HH Size	2000	2004	% Annual Rate 2000-2004
33027	HOLLYWOOD	011	25470	32916	39125	6.2	94	11810	14839	17322	5.5	2.22	6937	8767	5.7
33028	HOLLYWOOD	011	22367	28905	34208	6.2	94	7104	9169	10799	6.2	3.15	5922	7573	6.0
33029	HOLLYWOOD	011	35971	46009	54193	6.0	94	10731	13489	15684	5.5	3.36	9540	11930	5.4
33030	HOMESTEAD	086	27464	29067	31004	1.3	38	8188	8566	9063	1.1	3.34	6145	6359	0.8
33031	HOMESTEAD	086	5661	5955	6320	1.2	34	1881	1977	2093	1.2	2.97	1543	1610	1.0
33032	HOMESTEAD	086	19632	21653	23594	2.3	62	5525	6038	6534	2.1	3.54	4522	4902	1.9
33033	HOMESTEAD	086	32189	35503	38648	2.3	62	9474	10369	11213	2.2	3.42	7517	8151	1.9
33034	HOMESTEAD	086	15371	16320	17325	1.4	40	3899	4152	4422	1.5	3.34	2972	3150	1.4
33035	HOMESTEAD	086	2773	3104	3412	2.7	69	1097	1273	1425	3.6	2.36	675	767	3.1
33036	ISLAMORADA	087	3499	3778	4001	1.8	52	1764	1900	2015	1.8	1.97	973	1044	1.7
33037	KEY LARGO	087	12894	13398	13837	0.9	26	5790	6009	6213	0.9	2.23	3641	3740	0.6
33039	KEY LARGO	086	446	453	459	0.4	11	13	14	15	1.8	5.00	12	13	1.9
33040	KEY WEST	087	34228	34750	35514	0.4	10	14526	14849	15249	0.5	2.28	7716	7812	0.3
33042	SUMMERLAND KEY	087	6088	6535	6818	1.7	47	2737	2949	3089	1.8	2.22	1793	1913	1.5
33043	BIG PINE KEY	087	5140	5180	5247	0.2	7	2309	2321	2353	0.1	2.21	1443	1433	-0.2
33050	MARATHON	087	12029	11757	11741	-0.5	1	5505	5410	5427	-0.4	2.14	3288	3186	-0.7
33054	OPA LOCKA	086	29272	29143	30300	-0.1	4	8915	8896	9253	-0.1	3.13	6627	6552	-0.3
33055	OPA LOCKA	086	45068	46749	49344	0.9	24	12358	12809	13478	0.9	3.61	10678	11009	0.7
33056	OPA LOCKA	086	33185	35476	38204	1.6	44	9376	10083	10863	1.7	3.49	7874	8388	1.5
33060	POMPANO BEACH	011	34082	35065	37297	0.7	19	13172	13488	14274	0.6	2.55	7843	7882	0.1
33062	POMPANO BEACH	011	23984	24510	25861	0.5	15	13634	13941	14663	0.5	1.73	6372	6346	-0.1
33063	POMPANO BEACH	011	49146	51655	55474	1.2	33	21907	22919	24467	1.1	2.24	13268	13597	0.6
33064	POMPANO BEACH	011	53174	53988	56980	0.4	10	21124	21282	22300	0.2	2.50	12976	12824	-0.3
33065	POMPANO BEACH	011	51610	52445	55154	0.4	11	17934	18175	19022	0.3	2.86	13083	13115	0.1
33066	POMPANO BEACH	011	16959	17893	19403	1.3	35	9270	9707	10463	1.1	1.83	4861	5010	0.7
33067	POMPANO BEACH	011	23999	29521	34556	5.0	91	7930	9759	11365	5.0	3.02	6510	7965	4.9
33068	POMPANO BEACH	011	48137	50300	53473	1.0	29	15913	16614	17583	1.0	3.02	11760	12099	0.7
33069	POMPANO BEACH	011	23338	24953	27121	1.6	45	10574	11304	12263	1.6	2.02	5462	5772	1.3
33070	TAVERNIER	087	5565	5453	5440	-0.5	1	2371	2325	2325	-0.5	2.27	1497	1444	-0.8
33071	POMPANO BEACH	011	38618	40935	44240	1.4	39	13076	13849	14903	1.4	2.95	10752	11320	1.2
33073	POMPANO BEACH	011	20091	24467	28131	4.8	90	7820	9456	10786	4.6	2.58	5397	6422	4.2
33076	POMPANO BEACH	011	18759	25548	31096	7.5	97	5816	7942	9641	7.6	3.22	5181	7035	7.5
33109	MIAMI BEACH	086	467	673	834	9.0	99	218	330	417	10.3	1.83	76	107	8.4
33125	MIAMI	086	49773	51043	53521	0.6	17	17519	17971	18799	0.6	2.81	11828	11988	0.3
33126	MIAMI	086	45760	49666	53865	2.0	54	16106	17534	18996	2.0	2.80	11838	12727	1.7
33127	MIAMI	086	27894	28045	29388	0.1	6	8785	8861	9283	0.2	3.07	6144	6124	-0.1
33128	MIAMI	086	6300	6567	6934	1.0	27	2554	2705	2876	1.4	2.35	1225	1268	0.8
33129	MIAMI	086	11074	12037	13144	2.0	55	5520	5944	6429	1.8	2.01	2642	2828	1.6
33130	MIAMI	086	20429	21159	22366	0.8	23	8449	8785	9280	0.9	2.39	4702	4797	0.5
33131	MIAMI	086	4723	5511	6169	3.7	82	2841	3389	3831	4.2	1.59	1070	1239	3.5
33132	MIAMI	086	5265	6481	7683	5.0	91	1941	2541	3094	6.5	1.82	639	845	6.8
33133	MIAMI	086	29895	30920	32640	0.8	22	13062	13607	14376	1.0	2.25	7224	7397	0.6
33134	MIAMI	086	33809	34158	35820	0.2	8	14510	14681	15369	0.3	2.32	8700	8697	0.0
33135	MIAMI	086	35861	36545	38265	0.5	13	13935	14232	14880	0.5	2.55	8898	8966	0.2
33136	MIAMI	086	13367	14430	15615	1.8	52	4936	5386	5854	2.1	2.51	2648	2822	1.5
33137	MIAMI	086	18112	18220	19173	0.1	6	6797	6954	7370	0.5	2.45	3538	3498	-0.3
33138	MIAMI	086	29204	29445	30868	0.2	7	11672	11798	12355	0.3	2.47	6532	6506	-0.1
33139	MIAMI BEACH	086	38238	38069	40186	-0.1	4	23211	23157	24444	-0.1	1.60	6500	6329	-0.6
33140	MIAMI BEACH	086	20136	21270	22863	1.3	36	9854	10499	11311	1.5	2.01	4760	4919	0.8
33141	MIAMI BEACH	086	37023	39109	41718	1.3	36	16668	17569	18669	1.3	2.21	8845	9170	0.9
33142	MIAMI	086	53124	54175	57011	0.5	13	16428	16807	17747	0.5	2.97	11280	11390	0.2
33143	MIAMI	086	30607	31490	33201	0.7	19	12686	13017	13667	0.6	2.41	7487	7566	0.3
33144	MIAMI	086	23899	24394	25572	0.5	14	7903	8086	8462	0.5	2.98	6090	6175	0.3
33145	MIAMI	086	28161	29161	30889	0.8	23	9911	10279	10870	0.9	2.82	7121	7314	0.6
33146	MIAMI	086	13398	13586	14086	0.3	10	4004	4092	4284	0.5	2.48	2729	2756	0.2
33147	MIAMI	086	48569	48093	50142	-0.2	3	14269	14111	14665	-0.3	3.38	10925	10714	-0.5
33149	KEY BISCAYNE	086	10513	10853	11397	0.8	21	4262	4346	4518	0.5	2.50	2902	2941	0.3
33150	MIAMI	086	26537	27237	28882	0.6	18	8709	8953	9479	0.7	3.02	5989	6090	0.4
33154	MIAMI BEACH	086	13293	13636	14281	0.6	18	6735	6842	7111	0.4	1.99	3417	3406	-0.1
33155	MIAMI	086	44067	45065	47440	0.5	16	14951	15329	16117	0.6	2.91	11334	11525	0.4
33156	MIAMI	086	30790	31678	33395	0.7	19	10516	10766	11288	0.6	2.93	8146	8274	0.4
33157	MIAMI	086	61037	63865	67819	1.1	30	19881	20793	22020	1.1	3.05	15482	16074	0.9
33158	MIAMI	086	6855	7061	7448	0.7	19	2246	2322	2448	0.8	3.04	1945	2001	0.7
33160	NORTH MIAMI BEACH	086	31711	34757	38216	2.2	59	16536	17846	19392	1.8	1.93	8163	8635	1.3
33161	MIAMI	086	53766	55871	58866	0.9	26	17518	17942	18727	0.6	3.01	12030	12166	0.3
33162	MIAMI	086	44435	46671	49589	1.2	32	13591	14014	14713	0.7	3.30	10131	10340	0.5
33165	MIAMI	086	56819	57775	60488	0.4	12	17875	18263	19120	0.5	3.13	14515	14713	0.3
33166	MIAMI	086	22493	22768	23756	0.3	9	8118	8195	8536	0.2	2.61	5463	5444	-0.1
33167	MIAMI	086	19339	19884	20918	0.7	18	5598	5747	6024	0.6	3.46	4429	4512	0.4
33168	MIAMI	086	24869	26417	28259	1.4	41	6470	6794	7199	1.2	3.89	5416	5654	1.0
33169	MIAMI	086	36081	38131	40751	1.3	37	11485	12072	12825	1.2	3.11	8459	8810	1.0
33170	MIAMI	086	7169	7572	8081	1.3	36	2083	2210	2360	1.4	3.37	1673	1759	1.2
33172	MIAMI	086	39952	44576	49282	2.6	68	14347	15888	17454	2.4	2.81	10367	11408	2.3
33173	MIAMI	086	37739	38467	40317	0.5	13	13412	13671	14297	0.5	2.76	9727	9831	0.3
33174	MIAMI	086	27852	28445	29955	0.5	15	9130	9389	9890	0.7	3.02	7417	7559	0.5
33175	MIAMI	086	51439	53854	57313	1.1	30	15210	16030	17082	1.2	3.27	13380	14018	1.1
33176	MIAMI	086	48124	49719	52615	0.8	21	17338	18020	19073	0.9	2.75	12739	13040	0.6
33177	MIAMI	086	45585	52063	57648	3.2	75	12279	13821	15186	2.8	3.65	10865	12195	2.8
33178	MIAMI	086	20332	28387	35145	8.2	98	6304	9156	11524	9.2	2.74	4800	6922	9.0
33179	MIAMI	086	38255	40382	43080	1.3	36	15646	16455	17463	1.2	2.43	9742	10081	0.8
33180	MIAMI	086	22417	24497	26664	2.1	58	11212	12304	13377	2.2	1.97	6068	6518	1.7
33181	MIAMI	086	17934	18552	19500	0.8	22	7797	7983	8331	0.6	2.25	4222	4246	0.1
33182	MIAMI	086	13942	15634	17137	2.7	70	3857	4340	4752	2.8	3.59	3559	3992	2.7
33183	MIAMI	086	37994	40114	42962	1.3	36	12512	13180	14050	1.2	3.03	10000	10451	1.0
33184	MIAMI	086	19368	20643	22118	1.5	42	5869	6274	6719	1.6	3.21	5071	5404	1.5
33185	MIAMI	086	13046	15586	17671	4.3	86	3308	3962	4492	4.3	3.74	2961	3532	4.2
33186	MIAMI	086	57553	62257	67355	1.9	53	19553	21070	22694	1.8	2.94	15153	16227	1.6
33187	MIAMI	086	14107	16496	18509	3.8	82	4162	4823	5372	3.5	3.40	3632	4192	3.4
33189	MIAMI	086	21829	23614	25512	1.9	53	7308	7925	8547	1.9	2.96	5462	5829	1.5
33190	MIAMI	086	4251	4968	5580	3.7	82	1458	1678	1864	3.4	2.96	1121	1285	3.3
33193	MIAMI	086	38501	46188	52615	4.4	87	11745	13930	15734	4.1	3.31	9865	11690	4.1
33196	MIAMI	086	35529	41594	46870	3.8	83	11095	12702	14123	3.2	3.26	9076	10398	3.3
33199	MIAMI	086	1464	1566	1657	1.6	45	293	327	357	2.6	2.82	20	22	2.3
33301	FORT LAUDERDALE	011	11951	11824	12384	-0.3	2	5615	5496	5750	-0.5	1.83	2044	1952	-1.1
33304	FORT LAUDERDALE	011	18948	19293	20490	0.4	12	9799	10016	10637	0.5	1.85	3345	3309	-0.3
	FLORIDA					2.1					2.2	2.45			2.0
	UNITED STATES					1.2					1.3	2.58			1.1

ZIP CODE #	POST OFFICE NAME	RACE (%) White 2000	White 2004	Black 2000	Black 2004	Asian/Pacific 2000	Asian/Pacific 2004	% Hispanic Origin 2000	% Hispanic Origin 2004	2004 AGE DISTRIBUTION (%) 0-4	5-9	10-14	15-19	20-24	25-44	45-64	65-84	85+	18+	MEDIAN AGE 2004	% 2004 Males	% 2004 Females
33027	HOLLYWOOD	79.9	77.1	11.0	12.7	2.9	3.2	31.3	35.3	6.1	5.8	4.8	3.7	3.4	24.2	17.5	28.6	5.9	81.0	47.0	43.9	56.1
33028	HOLLYWOOD	73.3	70.8	12.6	13.8	5.9	6.3	36.2	40.4	9.0	8.9	8.2	6.3	5.1	36.4	20.9	4.9	0.3	70.0	33.8	48.2	51.8
33029	HOLLYWOOD	74.3	71.9	13.9	15.2	4.1	4.4	36.7	40.8	10.0	9.9	8.6	6.4	5.0	35.4	20.0	4.4	0.3	67.2	33.4	48.0	52.0
33030	HOMESTEAD	63.5	63.2	21.2	20.5	0.8	0.8	49.1	54.2	10.2	9.1	9.1	8.1	9.6	29.9	17.2	6.1	0.9	67.0	27.4	53.1	46.9
33031	HOMESTEAD	91.3	90.4	2.4	2.5	1.6	1.8	32.1	38.4	5.7	6.5	7.3	6.2	5.1	27.3	31.2	10.0	1.0	76.7	40.8	52.0	48.0
33032	HOMESTEAD	53.1	54.0	34.1	32.5	1.7	1.7	42.3	47.5	9.2	9.2	10.4	9.4	7.7	28.2	19.7	5.6	0.6	65.3	28.1	49.7	50.3
33033	HOMESTEAD	64.6	65.0	19.3	18.1	0.9	0.9	59.6	64.6	10.4	9.4	9.6	8.6	9.0	28.7	16.8	7.1	0.6	65.5	27.1	49.7	50.3
33034	HOMESTEAD	49.2	49.6	37.7	36.4	0.7	0.7	39.4	44.0	9.3	8.9	8.8	7.9	8.4	32.0	17.8	6.3	0.6	68.4	29.1	51.8	48.2
33035	HOMESTEAD	79.9	79.3	11.3	11.3	2.4	2.5	26.6	31.6	7.1	6.5	6.2	4.8	5.6	31.5	21.9	14.0	2.4	77.4	37.0	45.9	54.1
33036	ISLAMORADA	97.4	97.0	0.3	0.3	0.4	0.4	6.9	9.1	2.2	3.0	3.2	3.4	3.3	23.5	42.6	17.2	1.5	89.5	50.3	55.0	45.0
33037	KEY LARGO	94.7	94.0	2.0	2.1	0.4	0.5	15.4	19.2	4.5	4.9	5.2	5.1	4.3	24.7	33.2	16.4	1.8	82.3	45.7	51.6	48.4
33039	HOMESTEAD	48.7	49.9	39.5	37.1	0.9	0.9	46.2	51.7	11.9	11.0	8.8	5.3	7.1	34.2	17.4	3.5	0.7	66.5	29.0	50.8	49.2
33040	KEY WEST	85.4	84.0	8.4	9.1	1.3	1.5	19.8	23.7	4.8	4.5	4.7	4.7	6.3	32.5	30.0	11.2	1.3	83.4	40.9	54.4	45.6
33042	SUMMERLAND KEY	95.7	95.0	1.1	1.3	0.7	0.9	6.2	7.9	3.3	4.0	4.3	3.9	3.1	23.7	42.2	14.6	1.0	85.9	48.5	52.3	47.7
33043	BIG PINE KEY	94.8	94.2	1.1	1.2	0.6	0.7	6.7	8.7	3.5	3.8	5.4	4.7	3.1	28.0	36.7	13.6	1.2	84.0	45.6	52.5	47.5
33050	MARATHON	92.2	91.0	4.0	4.6	0.5	0.6	17.9	21.7	3.7	3.9	4.9	4.4	4.2	24.5	35.4	17.3	1.7	84.9	47.4	52.4	47.6
33054	OPA LOCKA	17.9	18.9	76.6	75.4	0.2	0.3	21.0	23.1	8.1	8.0	9.2	10.1	9.4	25.2	19.5	9.4	1.1	69.0	29.1	46.4	53.7
33055	OPA LOCKA	48.3	49.9	40.4	38.3	0.6	0.6	52.6	56.6	7.0	7.2	8.5	8.2	7.6	27.9	23.5	9.4	0.7	72.1	33.5	48.5	51.6
33056	OPA LOCKA	6.8	7.4	88.5	87.6	0.4	0.4	9.3	10.9	7.8	8.2	9.8	10.0	8.4	26.3	22.4	6.8	0.4	67.9	29.6	46.6	53.4
33060	POMPANO BEACH	54.4	51.8	35.5	37.2	0.9	1.0	12.0	14.0	7.3	6.6	6.9	6.3	7.0	28.0	23.2	11.3	3.5	75.5	37.5	49.7	50.3
33062	POMPANO BEACH	96.9	96.3	0.7	0.9	0.5	0.7	5.1	6.4	2.4	2.4	2.2	1.9	2.1	19.4	32.2	30.9	6.6	91.9	57.7	48.0	52.0
33063	POMPANO BEACH	82.6	79.7	8.7	10.3	2.7	3.1	13.9	16.6	5.8	5.5	5.3	4.9	5.2	27.2	23.7	17.2	5.2	80.4	42.5	46.6	53.4
33064	POMPANO BEACH	68.5	65.1	19.8	22.0	1.4	1.6	14.0	16.2	6.6	6.4	6.6	5.9	6.0	29.4	23.9	12.5	2.6	76.9	38.6	50.0	50.0
33065	POMPANO BEACH	75.1	71.8	13.3	15.2	3.6	4.1	19.2	22.4	7.4	7.0	8.2	8.3	8.6	29.6	22.2	6.8	1.9	72.0	32.8	48.3	51.7
33066	POMPANO BEACH	93.4	91.7	3.2	4.1	1.1	1.4	5.7	7.4	3.0	2.9	3.0	2.6	2.7	16.3	19.4	36.7	13.5	89.7	65.2	41.7	58.3
33067	POMPANO BEACH	88.6	86.9	4.4	5.1	3.9	4.4	9.9	12.0	7.4	8.1	9.6	7.8	5.5	29.5	27.7	4.1	0.4	69.8	35.7	49.0	51.0
33068	POMPANO BEACH	54.6	50.6	30.5	33.4	3.3	3.5	22.8	25.4	7.9	7.5	8.2	7.6	8.2	32.4	20.8	6.4	1.2	71.9	31.7	49.0	51.0
33069	POMPANO BEACH	64.3	61.9	30.8	32.7	0.9	1.0	10.6	12.5	4.5	4.1	4.2	4.6	6.3	27.5	20.7	22.0	6.3	84.9	44.2	48.9	51.1
33070	TAVERNIER	96.5	96.0	0.7	0.8	0.8	1.0	11.8	14.5	4.8	5.0	5.4	5.4	3.5	26.4	34.6	13.2	1.8	81.2	44.8	51.1	49.0
33071	POMPANO BEACH	87.0	84.9	5.9	6.9	3.1	3.6	13.4	16.1	5.8	6.5	8.4	8.6	6.9	27.6	30.6	5.1	0.6	73.7	36.5	49.0	51.0
33073	POMPANO BEACH	82.3	79.3	7.5	8.7	3.3	3.8	15.7	18.9	8.3	7.8	6.7	4.9	4.6	37.5	21.2	8.1	0.9	74.1	35.3	49.9	50.1
33076	POMPANO BEACH	86.6	84.5	5.7	6.6	3.9	4.5	11.9	14.2	8.3	9.0	9.8	7.9	5.2	30.8	25.7	3.1	0.3	67.8	34.2	49.3	50.7
33109	MIAMI BEACH	91.2	90.8	3.2	3.1	1.7	1.8	38.8	45.9	1.6	1.8	2.1	2.8	1.3	18.0	27.2	34.6	10.6	92.6	62.6	44.9	55.1
33125	MIAMI	82.5	82.5	4.7	4.5	0.8	0.7	89.3	91.5	6.2	5.6	6.0	6.0	6.8	28.1	21.7	17.0	2.6	78.5	39.0	49.5	50.5
33126	MIAMI	87.3	87.2	2.0	2.0	0.7	0.6	91.2	93.1	5.8	5.6	6.0	6.0	6.4	29.7	22.4	15.4	2.7	79.0	39.0	47.0	53.0
33127	MIAMI	23.5	24.6	65.7	64.4	0.3	0.3	31.8	34.2	7.8	7.6	8.7	8.7	7.8	26.5	21.5	10.5	1.0	70.5	32.7	49.3	50.7
33128	MIAMI	78.2	78.3	6.4	6.3	0.4	0.3	91.0	92.6	5.9	5.5	5.9	5.9	6.7	28.4	21.3	17.7	2.7	79.6	39.7	55.5	44.5
33129	MIAMI	92.7	92.2	1.4	1.4	1.3	1.3	62.9	69.6	4.2	3.8	4.0	3.9	5.5	35.0	24.9	15.6	2.9	85.7	41.1	46.9	53.1
33130	MIAMI	78.9	79.0	4.9	4.7	0.4	0.4	90.6	92.3	6.1	5.4	5.7	6.2	6.7	28.5	22.2	16.7	2.6	79.3	39.6	50.8	49.3
33131	MIAMI	90.3	89.9	2.3	2.3	2.3	2.3	55.2	62.1	3.2	2.4	2.5	3.8	8.6	43.8	23.9	10.0	1.7	90.1	37.1	51.8	48.2
33132	MIAMI	72.7	71.1	19.4	19.5	1.6	1.5	54.0	61.8	2.7	2.4	2.4	3.5	8.4	43.0	25.9	10.1	1.7	90.8	39.4	64.6	35.4
33133	MIAMI	77.8	78.0	16.2	15.7	0.9	1.0	44.9	49.4	4.9	4.8	4.9	5.4	5.9	32.0	25.8	13.8	2.4	82.2	40.1	48.7	51.3
33134	MIAMI	93.3	93.1	0.9	0.9	0.9	0.9	68.7	73.9	4.6	4.6	4.7	4.3	5.2	31.1	24.8	17.5	3.3	83.5	42.3	46.1	53.9
33135	MIAMI	86.6	86.6	2.3	2.2	0.5	0.5	92.7	94.3	5.3	4.9	5.6	6.0	6.4	27.1	22.8	18.5	3.5	80.6	41.6	48.8	51.2
33136	MIAMI	29.6	29.9	61.9	61.1	1.2	1.3	30.3	32.5	8.2	7.7	8.2	8.1	8.2	30.5	19.6	8.2	1.3	71.2	31.4	49.6	50.4
33137	MIAMI	46.5	47.4	38.1	36.3	1.3	1.4	37.3	42.5	6.4	5.7	6.0	6.6	8.8	30.9	23.9	8.5	3.2	78.1	36.0	51.8	48.2
33138	MIAMI	46.4	46.8	40.1	39.4	1.7	1.8	22.2	26.0	6.7	6.2	6.6	6.7	7.0	28.7	26.3	10.5	1.4	76.6	38.1	51.0	49.1
33139	MIAMI BEACH	87.3	86.7	3.9	3.9	1.8	1.9	49.8	56.3	2.5	2.0	2.2	3.2	7.6	41.6	20.7	16.2	4.1	91.7	39.7	54.2	45.8
33140	MIAMI BEACH	93.5	93.0	1.6	1.6	1.1	1.2	41.0	47.6	4.5	4.4	4.4	3.8	4.3	29.6	25.1	19.5	4.4	84.3	44.4	48.6	51.4
33141	MIAMI BEACH	81.7	81.2	5.7	5.6	1.5	1.5	62.6	68.8	5.0	4.5	5.1	5.9	7.4	32.5	24.5	12.8	2.4	82.1	39.0	49.2	50.8
33142	MIAMI	33.6	34.1	54.5	53.8	0.2	0.2	45.3	47.0	7.0	7.1	8.0	8.1	8.2	28.2	20.4	11.6	1.4	73.2	33.6	51.6	48.4
33143	MIAMI	80.3	80.1	11.9	11.5	2.7	2.9	43.0	49.3	5.6	5.8	6.4	6.2	6.9	30.4	25.2	11.7	1.7	78.4	38.1	47.4	52.6
33144	MIAMI	92.9	92.9	1.0	1.0	0.4	0.4	88.3	90.9	4.2	4.3	5.1	4.9	5.1	26.3	23.9	22.5	3.7	83.3	45.1	46.5	53.5
33145	MIAMI	90.7	90.6	1.5	1.5	1.0	0.9	85.2	88.4	4.7	4.6	5.3	5.7	6.0	28.1	23.4	19.1	3.2	81.9	42.3	47.6	52.4
33146	MIAMI	88.7	87.9	5.5	5.7	3.0	3.2	36.9	43.1	4.7	5.0	4.7	14.4	15.6	22.3	20.9	10.4	2.1	83.4	30.2	47.6	52.4
33147	MIAMI	25.9	27.4	66.1	64.1	0.2	0.2	31.6	34.4	7.6	8.4	9.2	8.9	7.6	26.1	20.9	10.5	1.0	69.4	31.6	47.7	52.3
33149	KEY BISCAYNE	95.5	95.2	0.5	0.5	0.9	1.0	49.8	57.1	7.2	7.8	7.6	5.3	3.5	26.3	26.4	14.1	1.8	74.0	41.0	46.6	53.4
33150	MIAMI	16.2	17.7	71.9	70.3	0.5	0.5	18.3	21.2	8.1	7.8	8.9	8.9	8.0	25.8	22.5	9.0	1.0	69.9	31.7	47.8	52.2
33154	MIAMI BEACH	92.9	92.3	1.6	1.6	1.1	1.3	35.1	41.5	4.3	4.4	5.1	4.1	3.3	26.0	24.8	21.9	6.2	83.7	47.1	44.6	55.4
33155	MIAMI	93.0	92.9	1.1	1.1	0.7	0.7	75.8	80.4	5.4	5.4	5.8	5.4	5.1	28.2	24.3	17.8	2.7	80.2	41.8	47.2	52.8
33156	MIAMI	90.7	90.0	2.0	2.0	3.7	4.1	34.8	41.1	5.9	7.0	8.7	7.7	5.2	24.4	29.0	10.9	1.2	73.4	40.0	48.0	52.0
33157	MIAMI	57.9	58.4	31.9	30.7	2.2	2.4	30.7	35.6	7.5	7.8	8.3	7.5	6.5	27.5	24.2	9.3	1.4	71.5	35.2	47.9	52.2
33158	MIAMI	89.7	88.8	3.1	3.2	3.5	3.9	27.0	32.9	6.5	7.6	8.8	7.5	5.1	22.6	30.6	10.5	1.0	72.2	40.4	48.9	51.1
33160	NORTH MIAMI BEACH	87.9	87.3	5.4	5.2	1.6	1.7	31.6	38.1	4.0	3.7	3.9	3.4	4.2	25.8	25.1	23.1	6.8	86.3	49.0	45.7	54.3
33161	MIAMI	31.9	31.9	56.3	55.7	2.0	2.2	21.5	24.8	8.5	7.6	7.7	8.1	8.5	29.1	20.7	8.0	1.7	71.7	31.9	47.7	52.4
33162	MIAMI	37.6	37.9	47.9	46.7	4.0	4.3	25.6	29.7	7.5	7.4	8.5	8.2	8.0	27.9	22.4	8.6	1.6	71.7	32.9	47.8	52.2
33165	MIAMI	92.6	92.5	1.1	1.1	1.0	0.9	82.7	86.3	4.8	4.8	5.5	5.9	6.3	26.9	24.5	18.5	2.8	81.4	42.2	46.9	53.1
33166	MIAMI	84.7	84.6	5.4	5.3	2.1	2.1	62.1	67.7	5.6	5.6	6.4	7.9	7.5	31.8	23.0	10.4	1.8	77.7	36.9	50.0	50.0
33167	MIAMI	18.2	19.2	72.5	71.0	0.5	0.5	20.8	23.4	7.8	7.9	9.2	9.5	8.7	26.1	22.3	7.9	0.7	69.3	29.9	47.3	52.7
33168	MIAMI	22.5	23.6	66.7	65.2	1.3	1.5	21.3	24.4	7.0	7.5	9.4	9.5	8.9	25.7	23.7	7.5	0.8	70.3	31.2	48.5	51.5
33169	MIAMI	13.4	13.7	79.6	79.0	1.1	1.2	11.0	12.9	8.0	7.7	8.7	8.3	8.3	28.8	20.9	8.2	1.1	70.5	31.1	46.5	53.5
33170	MIAMI	34.7	35.4	59.1	57.8	0.6	0.7	19.7	23.2	8.7	8.3	9.4	8.7	7.0	25.6	22.0	9.3	0.9	68.2	31.8	47.4	52.6
33172	MIAMI	85.3	85.3	2.1	2.0	2.2	2.1	85.5	88.1	6.4	6.0	6.1	6.3	7.5	34.2	21.6	10.7	1.2	77.8	35.2	47.2	52.9
33173	MIAMI	88.8	88.6	2.6	2.4	2.3	2.3	65.2	71.1	5.9	5.8	6.2	6.1	6.9	31.0	24.0	12.2	2.1	78.6	37.9	46.9	53.1
33174	MIAMI	89.4	89.4	0.9	0.9	0.5	0.5	90.3	92.5	4.7	5.0	6.1	6.7	6.7	27.9	24.3	16.3	2.4	80.3	40.4	46.8	53.2
33175	MIAMI	89.8	89.8	1.9	1.8	1.1	1.1	83.2	86.7	5.4	5.7	6.9	6.7	6.5	29.5	25.2	12.3	1.8	77.9	38.5	48.5	51.5
33176	MIAMI	73.4	73.3	18.9	18.4	2.7	2.9	37.5	43.7	5.8	6.2	7.3	7.0	6.8	27.8	27.3	10.5	1.4	76.2	38.2	47.2	52.8
33177	MIAMI	67.3	68.7	19.2	17.3	1.9	1.9	63.7	68.9	8.4	8.0	8.6	7.6	7.5	33.2	19.6	6.5	0.7	70.3	31.4	50.2	49.8
33178	MIAMI	78.6	81.0	10.8	8.2	3.8	3.8	62.9	69.8	8.9	7.8	5.7	5.2	6.8	42.2	18.3	4.9	0.3	75.0	33.1	54.3	45.7
33179	MIAMI	57.1	56.3	31.7	31.6	3.2	3.4	25.4	30.2	6.5	6.1	6.6	6.5	6.4	27.8	23.7	13.3	3.2	76.9	38.5	45.3	54.7
33180	MIAMI	92.7	92.1	2.3	2.4	1.5	1.6	21.7	27.0	3.8	3.8	3.7	3.6	3.8	25.3	26.1	24.7	5.3	86.4	49.7	45.8	54.2
33181	MIAMI	57.8	56.9	33.2	33.5	2.3	2.5	26.0	30.6	7.3	6.0	5.5	6.0	8.5	32.6	21.9	10.2	1.9	78.0	35.1	48.9	51.1
33182	MIAMI	88.0	87.9	1.1	1.0	1.0	1.0	87.0	89.8	7.8	7.3	7.4	6.5	7.1	34.4	21.1	7.6	0.8	73.3	33.5	47.9	52.1
33183	MIAMI	86.3	86.3	2.8	2.6	2.0	1.9	74.1	78.7	6.5	6.6	7.2	6.6	6.6	31.6	23.5	10.1	1.3	75.6	35.7	47.0	53.0
33184	MIAMI	89.6	89.7	2.2	2.2	0.5	0.5	87.2	89.8	5.3	5.7	6.9	6.9	6.6	30.0	25.5	11.9	1.4	77.9	38.3	48.6	51.4
33185	MIAMI	87.5	87.9	4.8	4.3	1.4	1.3	76.9	81.3	6.7	7.0	7.8	6.9	6.0	33.9	22.9	7.9	0.8	74.2	35.2	50.0	50.0
33186	MIAMI	81.1	80.8	7.1	7.0	3.4	3.5	58.1	63.8	7.0	7.0	7.3	6.8	7.1	33.5	23.5	7.1	0.8	74.5	34.2	47.1	52.9
33187	MIAMI	81.3	81.3	7.3	6.8	2.3	2.3	59.4	65.9	8.8	8.6	8.2	6.4	5.6	33.5	21.3	6.9	0.5	70.2	33.6	49.7	50.3
33189	MIAMI	61.8	62.3	26.3	25.0	2.1	2.2	41.0	46.7	8.9	8.3	8.5	7.5	7.5	30.3	19.8	8.4	0.8	69.8	31.5	47.8	52.2
33190	MIAMI	66.3	67.0	21.4	20.1	1.7	1.9	46.8	52.2	9.9	8.9	8.2	6.5	7.5	34.5	18.4	5.8	0.4	69.1	30.6	48.4	51.6
33193	MIAMI	81.8	82.0	4.6	4.3	1.9	1.9	79.3	83.1	8.2	7.6	8.2	7.4	8.4	34.2	19.1	6.4	0.6	71.5	31.2	47.4	52.6
33196	MIAMI	78.5	78.8	7.5	7.0	3.1	3.0	64.3	70.1	8.4	7.7	7.7	7.5	8.2	35.4	19.3	5.5	0.4	71.7	31.4	47.6	52.4
33199	MIAMI	47.7	46.2	33.8	33.8	7.9	8.4	26.0	30.2	0.1	0.3	0.1	26.4	63.5	7.1	2.1	0.3	0.1	98.8	21.8	41.3	58.8
33301	FORT LAUDERDALE	83.9	81.7	12.5	14.3	0.7	0.9	6.9	8.2	3.0	3.0	2.9	4.7	7.6	36.6	28.8	11.4	2.0	88.7	40.9	59.6	40.4
33304	FORT LAUDERDALE	72.7	70.7	17.7	19.0	1.5	1.7	9.0	10.5	4.4	3.7	3.7	4.9	7.7	34.3	26.7	12.1	2.5	85.8	40.4	55.1	44.9
	FLORIDA	78.0	76.5	14.6	15.2	1.7	2.0	16.8	19.0	6.0	5.9	6.4	6.4	6.5	26.6	24.5	15.5	2.4	78.1	40.0	48.8	51.2
	UNITED STATES	75.1	73.6	12.3	12.5	3.8	4.2	12.5	14.1	6.9	6.7	7.2	7.0	7.3	28.6	23.8	10.8	1.7	75.1	36.0	49.1	50.9

ZIP CODE #	POST OFFICE NAME	2004 Per Capita Income	2004 HH Income Base	2004 Household Income Distribution (%) Less than $25,000	$25,000 to $49,999	$50,000 to $99,999	$100,000 to $149,999	$150,000 or More	Median Household Income 2004	2009	2004 National Centile	2004 State Centile	2004 Home Value Base	2004 Home Value Distribution (%) Less than $50,000	$50,000 to $89,999	$90,000 to $174,999	$175,000 to $399,999	$400,000 or More	2004 Median Home Value
33027	HOLLYWOOD	28571	14839	32.0	23.8	25.9	12.5	5.8	41355	51268	51	49	13499	3.0	15.3	39.8	36.7	5.2	143127
33028	HOLLYWOOD	32732	9169	5.1	12.2	42.6	26.5	13.7	86224	105063	96	98	7588	0.1	0.1	4.5	81.0	14.4	277442
33029	HOLLYWOOD	31457	13489	5.8	10.7	40.8	29.3	13.6	89735	108159	97	98	12973	0.5	1.8	7.6	78.2	12.0	264200
33030	HOMESTEAD	13047	8566	39.1	29.9	22.3	7.0	1.6	32167	37681	18	17	3766	5.1	8.1	50.8	31.6	4.3	141759
33031	HOMESTEAD	26108	1977	14.8	21.2	37.6	18.6	7.8	63954	78272	88	90	1793	1.8	2.2	10.1	64.5	21.4	270981
33032	HOMESTEAD	14453	6038	28.8	30.0	31.1	8.2	2.0	41629	49024	52	50	4175	5.6	4.8	64.4	22.6	2.6	141787
33033	HOMESTEAD	12409	10369	38.4	31.8	23.4	4.6	1.8	31902	36575	18	16	5384	5.9	9.5	67.1	16.4	1.2	127159
33034	HOMESTEAD	11730	4152	47.4	29.0	18.3	3.1	2.3	26746	31771	7	5	2192	8.7	25.7	49.5	13.4	2.7	105645
33035	HOMESTEAD	21135	1273	29.5	30.2	31.8	4.5	4.0	41723	48906	52	50	897	0.0	28.0	57.0	14.2	0.9	107297
33036	ISLAMORADA	38124	1900	23.8	33.3	21.8	11.6	9.6	44649	52676	60	58	1385	13.4	1.7	5.0	34.4	45.6	372120
33037	KEY LARGO	35543	6009	20.9	28.3	30.6	11.7	8.5	50725	58456	73	75	4795	6.0	5.0	20.6	43.5	24.9	230413
33039	HOMESTEAD	13073	14	100.0	0.0	0.0	0.0	0.0	16399	23514	1	1	0	0.0	0.0	0.0	0.0	0.0	0
33040	KEY WEST	30586	14849	22.6	27.5	33.0	9.7	7.1	49898	58856	72	74	8167	7.2	4.9	9.1	39.0	39.8	337937
33042	SUMMERLAND KEY	32835	2949	17.8	23.2	38.7	12.4	7.8	60608	69470	85	87	2471	0.7	2.7	13.1	42.9	40.7	354084
33043	BIG PINE KEY	26028	2321	25.4	24.8	38.0	8.9	3.0	49779	56034	71	73	1899	6.2	4.5	17.3	55.6	16.4	244756
33050	MARATHON	28056	5410	29.7	28.7	28.1	6.8	6.7	40650	47735	48	47	3853	17.4	2.4	15.1	37.5	27.6	241218
33054	OPA LOCKA	11827	8896	47.5	28.5	18.7	4.3	0.9	26512	31458	6	4	5136	3.5	23.7	67.5	5.0	0.3	108260
33055	OPA LOCKA	14720	12809	25.4	31.9	33.6	6.4	2.7	43455	49932	57	55	10878	8.1	10.0	64.5	17.4	0.0	134145
33056	OPA LOCKA	15003	10083	27.0	30.9	32.2	8.0	2.0	43501	50216	57	55	7528	0.5	6.6	79.0	13.0	0.9	132412
33060	POMPANO BEACH	21164	13488	32.3	29.9	25.7	7.7	4.4	37690	44373	38	36	7052	6.6	12.3	41.4	33.3	6.4	147076
33062	POMPANO BEACH	45163	13941	22.8	27.5	26.5	12.1	11.0	49668	59356	71	72	10205	0.5	3.7	29.0	49.6	17.3	222232
33063	POMPANO BEACH	25291	22919	26.1	30.3	30.9	9.9	2.8	44323	52437	59	58	17559	12.5	21.5	36.3	29.4	0.4	126735
33064	POMPANO BEACH	23264	21282	28.0	32.3	27.5	7.5	4.7	40072	47161	46	43	14557	10.0	15.2	49.9	15.3	9.7	126502
33065	POMPANO BEACH	21872	18175	21.7	30.2	32.0	11.3	4.7	47990	56310	68	68	10269	2.7	20.9	20.8	51.2	4.5	198550
33066	POMPANO BEACH	31150	9707	25.7	34.0	28.3	8.9	3.2	42964	50344	56	54	8463	0.5	10.3	72.3	16.2	0.7	123611
33067	POMPANO BEACH	41499	9759	6.6	15.1	31.2	24.9	22.2	93992	111229	98	99	7581	0.1	0.3	2.2	58.3	39.0	361323
33068	POMPANO BEACH	17520	16614	23.4	33.6	33.8	7.8	1.4	44511	51558	60	58	10983	6.2	10.4	63.4	20.1	0.0	136707
33069	POMPANO BEACH	25158	11304	28.2	32.9	28.3	7.5	3.1	39614	46184	45	42	7177	4.5	17.6	65.9	11.7	0.4	119338
33070	TAVERNIER	29537	2325	19.3	30.6	33.4	9.5	7.3	50145	57010	72	74	1777	3.6	3.3	13.8	48.6	30.7	284245
33071	POMPANO BEACH	33938	13849	9.1	19.9	36.2	19.6	15.1	75499	88371	93	95	9978	0.2	3.4	9.8	70.8	15.8	273746
33073	POMPANO BEACH	29263	9456	14.4	23.8	39.1	17.2	5.6	62746	74424	87	89	6389	17.8	3.9	9.0	67.3	1.9	227540
33076	POMPANO BEACH	44021	7942	4.1	9.3	29.5	28.7	28.4	109969	130134	99	99	7197	0.3	0.3	3.6	48.5	47.4	387999
33109	MIAMI BEACH	68267	330	56.4	8.2	10.3	8.5	16.7	20679	26066	2	2	150	0.0	0.0	11.3	20.7	68.0	637931
33125	MIAMI	11997	17971	53.1	27.5	15.4	2.8	1.2	23153	26369	3	2	6046	3.2	5.8	44.8	45.4	0.9	168616
33126	MIAMI	14499	17534	39.6	34.2	20.9	3.9	1.4	31568	36709	17	15	7599	1.0	12.1	52.7	33.7	0.5	145585
33127	MIAMI	10256	8861	54.0	28.4	15.5	1.3	0.8	22394	25900	3	2	3595	6.4	27.4	59.7	6.4	0.2	103044
33128	MIAMI	10701	2705	68.4	23.2	6.8	0.8	0.8	13649	15803	1	1	170	4.7	10.6	70.0	14.7	0.0	112791
33129	MIAMI	48602	5944	21.9	19.7	26.6	16.2	15.7	63094	81005	87	89	3552	0.6	1.0	13.9	63.9	20.5	276291
33130	MIAMI	9930	8785	67.2	23.0	7.9	1.4	0.4	15503	17791	1	1	1115	4.8	30.8	47.7	13.9	2.9	107500
33131	MIAMI	63835	3389	22.8	13.9	27.9	15.0	20.3	72030	96771	92	94	1576	0.8	0.0	18.5	54.0	26.7	266258
33132	MIAMI	24342	2541	47.3	22.6	14.7	8.6	6.9	27282	32244	8	5	678	8.3	11.5	15.2	46.2	18.9	216026
33133	MIAMI	47054	13607	25.4	21.6	24.9	10.7	17.4	53685	68485	78	79	7255	0.2	2.4	16.4	38.9	42.0	337796
33134	MIAMI	37406	14681	22.8	23.6	28.3	14.0	11.3	54285	67861	79	80	8903	1.1	1.1	14.7	53.2	30.0	297321
33135	MIAMI	12855	14232	56.3	25.8	14.3	2.9	0.7	21273	24195	2	2	3824	3.5	9.5	38.4	47.7	1.0	171636
33136	MIAMI	10953	5386	63.4	21.8	11.0	3.4	0.4	16702	19939	1	1	659	19.3	13.8	38.2	25.2	3.5	113663
33137	MIAMI	22625	6954	40.4	25.4	22.6	5.3	6.4	32965	41654	21	19	1934	4.2	11.2	39.4	25.9	19.3	153302
33138	MIAMI	23776	11798	37.2	23.3	23.4	9.5	6.6	37298	45542	36	34	6117	6.3	6.0	29.2	42.2	16.4	199789
33139	MIAMI BEACH	38463	23157	39.1	27.1	19.8	7.3	6.7	33006	43792	21	19	7101	1.2	7.7	40.5	27.9	22.8	176985
33140	MIAMI BEACH	52937	10499	27.0	20.6	23.3	11.6	17.5	53931	66257	78	79	6085	1.4	3.2	15.6	42.5	37.3	299957
33141	MIAMI BEACH	20996	17569	45.2	27.0	19.3	4.9	3.6	28101	33934	9	6	5736	2.2	13.9	39.6	29.9	14.4	153364
33142	MIAMI	11207	16807	57.5	25.4	13.8	2.4	0.9	20607	23726	2	2	6465	11.6	23.9	54.1	10.3	0.1	105890
33143	MIAMI	42025	13017	24.3	24.1	25.0	11.3	15.2	51593	64133	75	76	7767	0.7	7.5	23.2	34.7	33.9	289462
33144	MIAMI	17225	8086	33.4	28.0	27.8	8.4	2.4	37846	45590	39	36	5585	3.4	3.4	31.0	61.2	1.0	194195
33145	MIAMI	18142	10279	34.0	28.8	25.5	8.2	3.6	36996	45239	35	32	5556	1.5	1.1	26.9	68.2	2.4	212387
33146	MIAMI	53891	4092	10.9	11.1	22.2	20.4	35.4	112425	140596	99	100	3387	0.0	0.5	3.3	24.1	72.0	540805
33147	MIAMI	11813	14111	50.2	25.9	18.4	3.7	1.8	24845	28683	4	3	7958	12.3	19.2	60.9	7.2	0.4	111197
33149	KEY BISCAYNE	70733	4346	12.7	11.2	23.5	18.2	34.5	106068	136635	99	99	3214	0.0	0.0	1.3	23.1	75.6	630784
33150	MIAMI	12555	8953	49.2	27.5	17.8	4.0	1.5	25422	29945	5	3	4190	15.4	13.7	56.7	14.3	0.0	116927
33154	MIAMI BEACH	49148	6842	25.1	23.3	26.8	10.8	14.0	52038	64042	76	76	3971	0.3	3.3	26.8	41.8	27.8	256384
33155	MIAMI	22484	15329	22.8	25.9	32.9	12.6	5.8	51405	62072	75	76	11464	0.2	0.6	21.6	72.4	5.2	220272
33156	MIAMI	62145	10766	10.9	14.3	21.5	15.9	37.5	108296	136276	99	99	8678	0.1	1.3	9.2	24.5	64.9	544736
33157	MIAMI	26016	20793	25.8	20.6	28.7	14.3	10.6	54245	64888	79	80	14951	1.1	3.5	37.6	44.4	13.5	189453
33158	MIAMI	56590	2322	9.1	6.7	17.7	26.5	40.1	132281	161074	100	100	2115	1.0	1.7	0.2	42.4	54.7	421490
33160	NORTH MIAMI BEACH	37085	17846	34.5	27.3	23.3	7.2	7.8	38223	46046	40	38	11334	2.9	17.0	41.9	24.0	14.3	141240
33161	MIAMI	14970	17942	39.2	32.4	21.6	4.7	2.1	31880	37334	17	16	8255	8.8	10.3	54.2	25.5	1.3	138732
33162	MIAMI	13815	14014	34.6	31.0	27.4	5.0	2.0	36101	41889	32	29	8807	8.8	8.6	58.9	22.9	0.8	138706
33165	MIAMI	19572	18263	25.4	26.7	31.9	11.7	4.4	47863	56709	68	68	13398	0.1	1.3	24.7	70.0	3.9	212319
33166	MIAMI	25524	8195	21.2	27.8	34.4	10.3	6.4	50897	61939	74	75	4260	2.2	3.1	19.2	69.7	5.9	221754
33167	MIAMI	12226	5747	37.6	32.8	23.6	4.7	1.4	32840	38123	20	18	3718	3.6	11.3	75.4	8.3	1.3	121340
33168	MIAMI	12073	6794	31.0	34.0	26.9	6.5	1.6	36436	42876	33	30	5258	1.5	8.0	74.2	15.8	0.6	133001
33169	MIAMI	16614	12072	30.1	30.3	29.6	7.6	2.4	40094	47346	46	44	6776	4.7	8.0	66.7	20.1	0.4	139093
33170	MIAMI	14200	2210	41.9	26.3	20.2	7.9	3.7	31808	38695	17	16	1411	2.9	12.5	45.0	29.1	10.5	141273
33172	MIAMI	16954	15888	29.9	35.2	27.6	5.1	2.2	38829	45083	42	39	8132	9.2	9.3	66.0	15.0	0.5	124277
33173	MIAMI	26406	13671	18.4	24.1	36.2	14.3	7.1	56926	68663	82	83	9417	0.5	2.7	32.5	57.2	7.2	205978
33174	MIAMI	18257	9389	29.5	30.9	27.2	8.9	3.6	40414	47917	48	46	5891	0.9	5.4	38.2	53.6	2.0	184864
33175	MIAMI	20760	16030	18.2	26.5	36.7	13.4	5.2	54653	63869	79	80	13336	1.4	2.5	36.5	52.6	7.0	195240
33176	MIAMI	35174	18020	18.7	20.5	29.7	15.5	15.7	62854	76843	87	89	12949	0.7	4.5	29.2	45.3	20.3	250536
33177	MIAMI	17151	13821	16.3	29.1	41.9	9.9	2.8	53081	62210	77	78	11626	0.6	2.2	55.0	41.1	1.1	164839
33178	MIAMI	30718	9156	14.6	20.8	33.2	16.0	15.5	68963	85621	91	92	6861	1.8	0.5	13.6	63.0	21.0	252949
33179	MIAMI	23712	16455	30.1	30.8	27.0	7.5	4.7	40460	48008	48	46	12676	13.1	23.8	40.0	19.5	3.6	111511
33180	MIAMI	48513	12304	20.4	23.1	27.3	14.3	14.9	58421	73215	83	85	9319	2.6	7.1	29.6	40.8	20.0	213864
33181	MIAMI	29242	7983	32.6	28.5	22.3	8.4	8.2	38652	46635	42	39	3857	9.1	12.9	34.2	24.3	19.5	151345
33182	MIAMI	21333	4340	11.5	23.0	39.7	20.7	5.2	66277	80399	89	91	4066	0.3	0.3	17.8	76.1	5.5	225067
33183	MIAMI	21388	13180	19.3	31.9	33.3	10.3	5.2	49135	57744	70	71	10272	0.0	4.7	55.1	37.4	2.8	150559
33184	MIAMI	19253	6274	21.3	30.1	33.9	10.5	4.3	48703	56505	70	70	5067	13.6	4.0	31.7	46.0	4.8	176740
33185	MIAMI	21761	3962	12.0	19.6	40.9	17.6	9.9	67825	80255	90	92	3678	0.0	0.1	18.5	77.0	4.4	231152
33186	MIAMI	25584	21070	12.8	25.7	38.3	15.2	8.1	61428	73460	86	88	15726	0.3	0.8	38.0	57.9	3.1	193610
33187	MIAMI	23571	4823	12.7	19.2	41.8	19.5	6.7	69419	82709	91	92	4464	1.0	4.6	16.2	68.9	9.4	224864
33189	MIAMI	18452	7925	28.0	27.2	32.3	9.5	3.1	45005	52846	61	59	4491	0.5	3.4	55.1	40.8	0.2	163003
33190	MIAMI	22285	1678	22.2	23.4	37.5	11.4	5.5	53106	64236	77	78	1030	0.0	3.3	52.9	43.8	0.0	167040
33193	MIAMI	16597	13930	22.9	32.4	33.6	8.9	2.2	45456	53306	62	61	8796	0.3	4.7	43.7	51.0	0.2	177186
33196	MIAMI	22125	12702	13.4	24.9	41.0	14.9	5.7	60464	72649	85	86	9143	0.3	1.2	28.3	67.9	2.4	207114
33199	MIAMI	11372	327	66.7	16.8	14.7	1.8	0.0	11973	14385	1	1	55	14.6	0.0	25.5	40.0	20.0	213889
33301	FORT LAUDERDALE	54591	5496	19.1	22.6	27.1	12.1	19.1	62108	77195	86	89	2668	0.4	1.5	12.4	25.5	60.2	503138
33304	FORT LAUDERDALE	31822	10016	32.0	29.6	24.0	7.7	6.7	39276	48296	44	41	4068	1.0	6.2	30.9	39.1	22.9	219261
	FLORIDA	25506		26.4	29.9	29.1	9.1	5.6	44138	51288				8.8	15.8	40.2	28.3	7.0	137042
	UNITED STATES	25866		24.7	27.1	30.8	10.9	6.5	48124	56710				10.9	15.0	33.7	30.1	10.4	145905

SPENDING POTENTIAL INDICES FLORIDA
33027-33304 D

ZIP CODE #	POST OFFICE NAME	FINANCIAL SERVICES: Auto Loan	FINANCIAL SERVICES: Home Loan	FINANCIAL SERVICES: Investments	FINANCIAL SERVICES: Retirement Plans	THE HOME: Home Improvements: Home Repair	THE HOME: Home Improvements: Lawn & Garden	THE HOME: Furnishings: Computers & Hardware	THE HOME: Furnishings: Major Appliances	THE HOME: Furnishings: TV, Radio, Sound Equipment	THE HOME: Furnishings: Furniture	ENTERTAINMENT: Dine out/Carry out	ENTERTAINMENT: Sports Equipment	ENTERTAINMENT: Fees & Tickets	ENTERTAINMENT: Toys & Games	ENTERTAINMENT: Travel	ENTERTAINMENT: Cable TV	PERSONAL: Apparel & Services	PERSONAL: Auto Repairs	PERSONAL: Health Insurance	PERSONAL: Pets & Supplies
33027	HOLLYWOOD	91	95	96	92	95	105	87	94	87	92	109	97	89	100	90	88	105	91	97	102
33028	HOLLYWOOD	148	167	161	175	159	154	151	149	138	157	176	175	155	176	147	129	174	145	127	163
33029	HOLLYWOOD	153	173	166	180	164	159	156	154	143	162	181	181	160	182	152	133	179	150	131	169
33030	HOMESTEAD	59	57	67	56	56	59	60	60	62	62	79	68	60	79	59	61	78	62	56	64
33031	HOMESTEAD	101	123	134	122	120	121	112	111	105	112	132	129	118	140	114	103	132	108	101	122
33032	HOMESTEAD	70	71	78	69	69	73	71	71	72	73	91	80	72	91	70	72	90	72	68	78
33033	HOMESTEAD	59	55	63	53	54	57	58	59	61	61	77	65	57	75	57	60	77	61	56	63
33034	HOMESTEAD	55	47	49	45	46	51	51	53	55	54	68	58	49	62	49	54	67	55	52	58
33035	HOMESTEAD	70	65	79	70	63	68	72	69	72	73	91	82	71	87	69	69	89	73	64	76
33036	ISLAMORADA	125	102	77	93	113	129	96	114	106	97	128	128	89	121	103	114	119	112	134	149
33037	KEY LARGO	123	112	97	106	118	129	105	117	111	107	135	134	101	131	110	114	128	116	127	145
33039	HOMESTEAD	24	21	22	21	21	23	24	23	25	24	31	27	23	31	23	25	31	25	23	25
33040	KEY WEST	96	98	117	100	96	103	101	98	99	101	125	116	101	124	100	97	122	101	94	110
33042	SUMMERLAND KEY	113	103	88	97	110	119	96	108	101	96	123	125	92	123	101	105	117	106	118	137
33043	BIG PINE KEY	89	84	72	80	88	94	77	85	80	78	98	98	75	96	80	82	94	84	91	105
33050	MARATHON	94	82	74	79	88	97	80	89	85	80	104	103	76	101	83	88	98	89	97	112
33054	OPA LOCKA	50	45	57	42	44	51	49	49	54	51	67	53	49	65	49	56	66	50	52	55
33055	OPA LOCKA	66	66	103	61	62	72	71	69	78	75	100	75	71	102	72	82	100	72	70	75
33056	OPA LOCKA	72	69	79	66	67	77	71	70	75	73	95	77	74	92	72	78	92	71	74	80
33060	POMPANO BEACH	72	75	87	74	73	79	77	75	77	77	96	87	78	95	76	76	94	77	73	83
33062	POMPANO BEACH	111	112	122	108	115	132	107	115	110	111	137	119	110	124	113	114	131	113	125	128
33063	POMPANO BEACH	79	79	88	78	79	87	79	81	80	81	100	89	80	95	80	80	97	81	82	89
33064	POMPANO BEACH	77	80	96	79	79	86	82	81	83	82	104	93	83	105	83	83	102	82	80	89
33065	POMPANO BEACH	85	91	103	93	89	92	90	88	87	91	110	104	91	109	89	84	108	89	82	97
33066	POMPANO BEACH	83	80	85	75	83	99	76	85	80	81	100	83	77	86	81	84	94	83	97	93
33067	POMPANO BEACH	170	199	215	207	191	194	182	177	168	185	214	206	194	217	182	160	214	174	156	196
33068	POMPANO BEACH	72	74	86	74	71	75	75	73	74	77	95	85	76	94	74	73	94	75	68	80
33069	POMPANO BEACH	72	71	83	71	72	79	74	74	75	74	93	84	74	89	74	75	90	75	76	82
33070	TAVERNIER	114	92	65	84	102	114	87	103	96	87	115	119	79	112	92	102	108	101	119	137
33071	POMPANO BEACH	137	154	166	161	149	150	146	142	136	148	172	167	151	173	144	129	171	141	126	157
33073	POMPANO BEACH	112	116	108	117	113	114	108	110	103	111	130	128	108	127	106	99	127	109	101	125
33076	POMPANO BEACH	198	231	230	240	220	216	206	203	189	213	240	237	217	243	204	178	239	197	175	223
33109	MIAMI BEACH	206	193	185	183	204	241	178	203	189	191	235	199	181	195	194	202	220	197	238	232
33125	MIAMI	39	38	72	35	36	42	44	42	50	47	65	46	44	67	45	54	66	45	44	46
33126	MIAMI	47	46	89	41	43	51	53	50	61	57	79	55	52	82	53	66	80	54	52	55
33127	MIAMI	40	37	54	33	35	42	41	40	46	43	58	44	41	57	41	49	57	42	43	45
33128	MIAMI	29	28	51	26	27	31	33	31	37	34	48	35	32	49	33	40	48	34	33	34
33129	MIAMI	120	117	218	123	110	126	136	124	145	140	185	146	139	193	135	148	184	133	121	137
33130	MIAMI	27	27	52	24	25	29	31	29	35	33	46	32	30	48	31	38	46	31	30	32
33131	MIAMI	123	118	222	135	111	125	139	123	143	142	182	151	145	191	137	142	181	132	116	138
33132	MIAMI	50	48	93	53	46	52	57	51	60	58	77	61	59	81	57	61	77	55	49	57
33133	MIAMI	133	139	220	140	134	151	147	140	153	152	195	160	153	199	149	157	194	145	139	155
33134	MIAMI	101	114	191	110	109	122	119	113	125	122	160	128	124	170	122	130	161	117	110	122
33135	MIAMI	38	37	72	33	34	41	42	40	49	46	64	45	42	66	43	53	64	44	42	44
33136	MIAMI	34	31	48	29	29	35	36	34	41	37	51	39	36	51	36	43	50	37	37	39
33137	MIAMI	70	68	114	67	65	75	77	73	84	80	107	83	77	109	77	87	106	77	74	81
33138	MIAMI	73	77	116	74	74	84	81	78	85	82	108	88	83	111	83	89	107	81	79	86
33139	MIAMI BEACH	71	75	140	75	71	83	86	78	92	86	117	92	89	127	88	97	118	84	79	86
33140	MIAMI BEACH	138	145	198	141	144	163	146	146	152	150	191	161	151	189	152	157	188	149	152	162
33141	MIAMI BEACH	53	54	102	50	50	59	62	57	69	64	89	65	62	94	63	74	90	62	59	63
33142	MIAMI	40	36	56	33	34	41	41	40	47	43	59	44	41	58	41	50	59	43	44	45
33143	MIAMI	121	139	210	137	134	148	142	134	144	142	182	155	150	194	146	148	182	138	131	147
33144	MIAMI	59	58	113	52	54	64	67	63	77	72	100	70	66	103	68	83	101	68	66	69
33145	MIAMI	60	58	112	52	54	64	67	63	77	72	99	70	66	103	68	83	100	68	66	69
33146	MIAMI	202	252	370	253	243	262	236	227	227	241	288	262	261	306	246	229	291	225	210	248
33147	MIAMI	53	47	66	44	46	54	53	52	59	55	75	57	53	72	53	63	73	55	57	59
33149	KEY BISCAYNE	214	288	395	282	281	303	251	249	234	257	295	279	285	311	267	236	300	239	231	270
33150	MIAMI	51	46	61	42	44	52	51	50	56	53	70	55	50	68	50	59	69	52	54	57
33154	MIAMI BEACH	132	135	161	133	136	154	135	137	137	137	172	150	139	165	140	141	167	138	145	152
33155	MIAMI	79	83	134	78	79	88	88	85	95	93	123	95	90	128	90	100	123	89	84	92
33156	MIAMI	222	281	384	273	271	292	257	252	248	263	315	285	282	335	269	251	319	248	236	273
33157	MIAMI	101	113	146	109	109	117	110	108	112	114	142	122	115	147	112	113	142	109	104	118
33158	MIAMI	199	285	386	270	274	291	245	242	229	248	288	273	277	315	262	232	294	233	220	259
33160	NORTH MIAMI BEACH	95	97	125	94	98	113	98	100	102	100	128	107	101	123	103	106	124	101	108	110
33161	MIAMI	52	55	95	54	53	60	61	57	66	62	84	66	63	91	63	69	84	60	57	63
33162	MIAMI	56	60	88	58	57	63	63	60	66	64	83	68	65	88	64	67	84	62	59	66
33165	MIAMI	74	76	124	70	71	81	82	79	90	87	116	88	82	120	83	94	117	83	79	86
33166	MIAMI	82	87	140	81	82	92	92	89	99	97	128	99	93	133	93	104	129	93	88	96
33167	MIAMI	57	54	67	51	52	60	57	56	61	59	77	62	59	76	57	63	76	58	58	63
33168	MIAMI	63	65	74	62	62	67	65	65	66	68	84	72	66	85	65	66	84	66	62	71
33169	MIAMI	71	67	81	67	65	73	72	70	74	74	94	79	73	92	71	75	92	72	70	78
33170	MIAMI	66	61	71	57	60	68	65	65	70	67	86	73	65	83	64	72	84	67	69	74
33172	MIAMI	55	54	103	49	51	60	62	59	71	67	92	65	61	95	63	76	93	64	61	64
33173	MIAMI	91	97	141	92	92	102	100	97	106	104	135	109	103	142	102	109	136	101	94	105
33174	MIAMI	64	62	121	56	58	69	72	68	83	77	108	75	71	111	73	89	108	74	71	74
33175	MIAMI	84	88	134	82	83	93	92	90	99	97	127	100	93	132	93	103	128	93	88	97
33176	MIAMI	119	141	189	135	135	146	134	131	135	138	171	147	143	181	139	138	173	132	125	143
33177	MIAMI	84	92	108	92	88	90	89	87	87	92	111	100	91	113	88	85	111	88	80	95
33178	MIAMI	118	131	150	130	125	129	125	123	122	130	155	140	128	158	124	119	155	123	112	134
33179	MIAMI	76	76	96	77	74	81	82	78	83	82	104	91	83	104	81	82	102	81	77	86
33180	MIAMI	129	139	164	135	139	156	132	137	134	136	167	147	138	161	139	137	163	136	142	151
33181	MIAMI	82	86	128	88	83	92	95	88	96	93	122	105	96	127	95	97	121	93	86	97
33182	MIAMI	90	88	165	80	83	97	100	95	114	107	148	106	99	153	101	123	149	102	99	104
33183	MIAMI	78	80	133	74	76	86	86	83	95	92	122	92	87	127	88	100	123	88	84	90
33184	MIAMI	75	77	126	71	72	82	83	80	91	88	118	89	83	121	84	96	118	84	80	87
33185	MIAMI	113	126	135	127	120	122	118	117	113	123	144	134	121	146	117	109	143	116	104	127
33186	MIAMI	101	109	127	108	104	108	106	104	105	110	134	119	109	136	105	103	133	105	96	114
33187	MIAMI	119	125	115	127	121	121	115	117	109	119	138	136	115	136	113	104	135	115	105	132
33189	MIAMI	70	74	97	71	70	77	76	73	78	78	99	83	77	101	76	79	99	76	72	80
33190	MIAMI	86	92	123	91	87	91	91	89	93	97	120	102	92	122	91	94	120	91	83	97
33193	MIAMI	68	70	110	66	66	73	74	71	80	79	103	80	74	106	74	83	103	75	70	78
33196	MIAMI	95	103	127	101	98	103	101	99	101	106	129	112	103	132	100	101	129	100	92	108
33199	MIAMI	36	22	27	25	21	26	42	31	41	36	51	43	34	46	34	36	48	38	29	35
33301	FORT LAUDERDALE	139	154	228	161	150	164	159	149	155	159	196	176	168	201	160	153	195	153	140	164
33304	FORT LAUDERDALE	78	76	104	80	74	82	87	80	87	85	110	97	86	109	84	85	108	86	77	89
	FLORIDA	89	87	95	86	87	96	87	89	89	89	111	100	87	107	88	90	108	90	91	101
	UNITED STATES	100	100	100	100	100	100	100	100	100	100	100	100	100	100	100	100	100	100	100	100

# POST OFFICE NAME	COUNTY FIPS CODE	POPULATION 2000	2004	2009	2000-2004 ANNUAL RATE % Rate	State Centile	HOUSEHOLDS 2000	2004	2009	% Annual Rate 2000-2004	2004 Average HH Size	FAMILIES 2000	2004	% Annual Rate 2000-2004
33305 FORT LAUDERDALE	011	11531	11589	12246	0.1	6	6002	6047	6376	0.2	1.89	2283	2221	-0.7
33306 FORT LAUDERDALE	011	3809	3875	4116	0.4	12	1995	2029	2151	0.4	1.85	932	927	-0.1
33308 FORT LAUDERDALE	011	29792	30959	33247	0.9	26	16765	17442	18657	0.9	1.76	7427	7526	0.3
33309 FORT LAUDERDALE	011	35420	37758	40573	1.5	43	13500	14434	15493	1.6	2.51	7837	8183	1.0
33311 FORT LAUDERDALE	011	66088	67442	71478	0.5	14	21670	22151	23407	0.5	2.99	15098	15154	0.1
33312 FORT LAUDERDALE	011	45863	46614	49404	0.4	11	17370	17675	18679	0.4	2.62	10993	10995	0.0
33313 FORT LAUDERDALE	011	57379	60091	64293	1.1	30	21439	22253	23614	0.9	2.66	14122	14420	0.5
33314 FORT LAUDERDALE	011	23350	25168	27393	1.8	50	9549	10289	11147	1.8	2.44	5563	5887	1.3
33315 FORT LAUDERDALE	011	12996	13267	14127	0.5	14	6223	6351	6737	0.5	2.07	2954	2946	-0.1
33316 FORT LAUDERDALE	011	10718	11095	11858	0.8	23	5849	6154	6625	1.2	1.70	2312	2338	0.3
33317 FORT LAUDERDALE	011	34638	35357	37381	0.5	14	12292	12560	13229	0.5	2.79	9044	9093	0.1
33319 FORT LAUDERDALE	011	42727	43647	46177	0.5	15	20025	20335	21376	0.4	2.14	11157	11108	-0.1
33321 FORT LAUDERDALE	011	38929	41691	45177	1.6	46	19252	20714	22407	1.7	2.00	11316	11903	1.2
33322 FORT LAUDERDALE	011	40275	43952	48601	2.1	57	18538	19911	21728	1.7	2.21	10989	11629	1.3
33323 FORT LAUDERDALE	011	17652	19699	21845	2.6	68	5823	6538	7239	2.8	3.01	4728	5213	2.3
33324 FORT LAUDERDALE	011	38251	41746	45541	2.1	57	17444	18964	20567	2.0	2.19	10105	10760	1.5
33325 FORT LAUDERDALE	011	26722	28111	30003	1.2	34	9300	9770	10377	1.2	2.87	7158	7447	0.9
33326 FORT LAUDERDALE	011	28330	34027	38910	4.4	87	10159	12082	13682	4.2	2.81	7895	9309	4.0
33327 FORT LAUDERDALE	011	10763	13972	16569	6.3	95	3336	4312	5082	6.2	3.24	2985	3837	6.1
33328 FORT LAUDERDALE	011	22876	24459	26445	1.6	45	8264	8805	9461	1.5	2.78	6295	6620	1.2
33330 FORT LAUDERDALE	011	11381	12641	13920	2.5	66	3584	3960	4331	2.4	3.19	3118	3424	2.2
33331 FORT LAUDERDALE	011	21176	26613	31151	5.5	92	6570	8234	9584	5.5	3.23	5775	7190	5.3
33332 FORT LAUDERDALE	011	7550	9711	11464	6.1	94	2273	2883	3365	5.8	3.37	2041	2574	5.6
33334 FORT LAUDERDALE	011	30741	31962	34280	0.9	26	12865	13256	14095	0.7	2.38	7011	7066	0.2
33351 FORT LAUDERDALE	011	32810	34658	37222	1.3	36	11949	12619	13504	1.3	2.68	8389	8750	1.0
33401 WEST PALM BEACH	099	20985	22731	25261	1.9	53	9395	10249	11501	2.1	2.05	4208	4496	1.6
33403 WEST PALM BEACH	099	12662	13248	14324	1.1	30	5106	5361	5803	1.2	2.45	3025	3103	0.6
33404 WEST PALM BEACH	099	28177	29871	32829	1.4	39	11118	11962	13276	1.7	2.48	7082	7428	1.1
33405 WEST PALM BEACH	099	19802	20239	21719	0.5	15	7809	7924	8475	0.3	2.54	4804	4799	0.0
33406 WEST PALM BEACH	099	24749	25561	27500	0.8	21	8813	9096	9816	0.8	2.63	5939	6023	0.3
33407 WEST PALM BEACH	099	28287	29728	32258	1.2	33	10603	11238	12273	1.4	2.54	6377	6634	0.9
33408 NORTH PALM BEACH	099	17558	18896	20678	1.7	50	9008	9761	10716	1.9	1.93	4836	5100	1.3
33409 WEST PALM BEACH	099	21443	23708	26510	2.4	64	9257	10316	11580	2.6	2.24	4513	4887	1.9
33410 PALM BEACH GARDENS	099	27268	28819	31445	1.3	37	11900	12674	13876	1.5	2.25	7688	8001	0.9
33411 WEST PALM BEACH	099	41542	50223	58579	4.6	89	15173	18311	21328	4.5	2.69	11241	13457	4.3
33412 WEST PALM BEACH	099	8856	12193	15023	7.8	97	2919	4054	4983	8.0	3.01	2540	3510	7.9
33413 WEST PALM BEACH	099	9484	10793	12214	3.1	74	3604	4168	4747	3.5	2.57	2581	2926	3.0
33414 WEST PALM BEACH	099	38109	43658	49554	3.3	76	12895	14912	17012	3.5	2.93	10647	12207	3.3
33415 WEST PALM BEACH	099	39568	41414	45325	1.1	30	16030	16885	18535	1.2	2.45	10086	10410	0.8
33417 WEST PALM BEACH	099	28850	30148	32781	1.0	29	14458	15062	16380	1.0	1.98	7047	7230	0.6
33418 PALM BEACH GARDENS	099	27102	30924	35156	3.2	75	11346	13053	14902	3.4	2.35	8181	9281	3.0
33426 BOYNTON BEACH	099	14431	15408	16889	1.6	44	7006	7591	8374	1.9	2.01	4076	4290	1.2
33428 BOCA RATON	099	37404	41354	46035	2.4	64	14025	15470	17187	2.3	2.67	10329	11260	2.1
33430 BELLE GLADE	099	21147	21367	22747	0.2	8	6334	6434	6894	0.4	3.09	4542	4545	0.0
33431 BOCA RATON	099	16063	16880	18278	1.2	32	6052	6479	7132	1.6	2.28	3839	4056	1.3
33432 BOCA RATON	099	19223	19312	20629	0.1	6	9801	9935	10644	0.3	1.94	5101	5046	-0.3
33433 BOCA RATON	099	40754	42859	46644	1.2	33	19400	20607	22555	1.4	2.03	11447	11873	0.9
33434 BOCA RATON	099	20731	21904	23956	1.3	36	10337	11064	12205	1.6	1.98	6126	6438	1.2
33435 BOYNTON BEACH	099	30813	31335	33545	0.4	12	12622	12910	13876	0.5	2.38	7444	7473	0.1
33436 BOYNTON BEACH	099	36551	39987	44120	2.1	59	16918	18532	20456	2.2	2.13	10661	11446	1.7
33437 BOYNTON BEACH	099	39202	46885	54121	4.3	86	18239	21965	25426	4.5	2.12	13766	16411	4.2
33438 CANAL POINT	099	854	858	903	0.1	6	294	297	314	0.2	2.77	218	217	-0.1
33440 CLEWISTON	051	17615	17771	18379	0.2	8	5641	5687	5875	0.2	3.04	4328	4341	0.1
33441 DEERFIELD BEACH	011	26648	27851	29936	1.0	29	11730	12284	13158	1.1	2.26	6409	6540	0.5
33442 DEERFIELD BEACH	011	28707	31504	34495	2.2	59	15471	16959	18510	2.2	1.82	7420	8013	1.8
33444 DELRAY BEACH	099	21369	21889	23483	0.6	16	7747	8030	8669	0.9	2.70	4848	4914	0.3
33445 DELRAY BEACH	099	28061	29895	32692	1.5	42	13300	13996	15223	1.2	2.12	7592	7821	0.7
33446 DELRAY BEACH	099	15787	17517	19747	2.5	66	9202	10172	11467	2.4	1.70	5321	5904	2.5
33455 HOBE SOUND	085	18037	19290	21222	1.6	45	8217	8859	9830	1.8	2.14	5467	5875	1.7
33458 JUPITER	099	33858	37635	42018	2.5	67	13074	14614	16359	2.7	2.56	9261	10198	2.3
33460 LAKE WORTH	099	31885	32523	34648	0.5	14	12162	12271	13023	0.2	2.59	6852	6769	-0.3
33461 LAKE WORTH	099	36009	38137	41524	1.4	38	14121	14913	16216	1.3	2.51	8651	8944	0.8
33462 LAKE WORTH	099	26842	28627	31210	1.5	43	11321	12123	13247	1.6	2.32	7037	7412	1.2
33463 LAKE WORTH	099	40900	47093	53802	3.4	78	15315	17549	19991	3.3	2.67	10789	12374	3.3
33467 LAKE WORTH	099	39820	48472	56813	4.7	90	16626	19879	23095	4.3	2.44	11995	14455	4.5
33469 JUPITER	085	14171	14529	15469	0.6	17	6522	6776	7356	0.9	2.13	4373	4461	0.5
33470 LOXAHATCHEE	099	19493	24211	28492	5.2	91	6064	7550	8876	5.3	3.20	5143	6369	5.2
33471 MOORE HAVEN	043	7448	7684	7910	0.7	20	2531	2638	2743	1.0	2.58	1843	1909	0.8
33476 PAHOKEE	099	8264	8375	8850	0.3	10	2408	2452	2599	0.4	3.33	1822	1832	0.1
33477 JUPITER	099	11903	12404	13468	1.0	27	6325	6652	7247	1.2	1.86	3952	4078	0.7
33478 JUPITER	099	11252	12293	13680	2.1	57	3701	4076	4552	2.3	3.01	3184	3481	2.1
33480 PALM BEACH	099	11167	11768	12878	1.2	35	6242	6576	7196	1.2	1.79	3220	3309	0.6
33483 DELRAY BEACH	099	12515	12943	13898	0.8	22	6543	6786	7296	0.9	1.90	3208	3240	0.2
33484 DELRAY BEACH	099	23734	25139	27352	1.4	38	13433	14293	15580	1.5	1.73	7435	7738	0.9
33486 BOCA RATON	099	21961	22343	23963	0.4	12	8945	9176	9890	0.6	2.38	5725	5736	0.1
33487 BOCA RATON	099	16326	17550	19302	1.7	48	7967	8604	9487	1.8	2.02	4837	5160	1.5
33493 SOUTH BAY	099	4525	4451	4676	-0.4	2	1011	996	1064	-0.4	3.47	792	772	-0.6
33496 BOCA RATON	099	20673	23562	26584	3.1	75	9011	10320	11673	3.2	2.28	6686	7564	3.0
33498 BOCA RATON	099	14725	17897	20871	4.7	90	5286	6380	7415	4.5	2.79	4551	5459	4.4
33510 BRANDON	057	22405	24742	27933	2.4	63	8214	9181	10451	2.7	2.67	6175	6830	2.4
33511 BRANDON	057	45530	53014	61289	3.7	81	17129	20040	23292	3.8	2.63	12372	14253	3.4
33513 BUSHNELL	119	11095	12746	15828	3.3	77	3954	4704	6118	4.2	2.33	2751	3220	3.8
33514 CENTER HILL	119	1546	1820	2331	3.9	83	523	613	790	3.8	2.96	393	455	3.5
33523 DADE CITY	101	17421	18494	20621	1.4	40	6225	6675	7507	1.7	2.71	4553	4830	1.4
33525 DADE CITY	101	13816	15444	17740	2.7	68	5320	6096	7122	3.3	2.44	3781	4270	2.9
33527 DOVER	057	12066	13116	14644	2.0	55	3873	4222	4730	2.1	3.08	3072	3315	1.8
33534 GIBSONTON	057	7632	8437	9483	2.4	64	2664	2955	3332	2.5	2.85	1865	2041	2.1
33538 LAKE PANASOFFKEE	119	4732	5619	7226	4.1	85	2194	2615	3403	4.2	2.15	1435	1681	3.8
33540 ZEPHYRHILLS	101	8236	9633	11397	3.8	82	3261	3869	4618	4.1	2.48	2421	2832	3.8
33541 ZEPHYRHILLS	101	14966	17672	20833	4.0	83	6909	8334	9972	4.5	2.04	4639	5507	4.1
33542 ZEPHYRHILLS	101	18752	20543	23343	2.2	59	9092	10080	11559	2.5	2.01	5668	6157	2.0
33543 ZEPHYRHILLS	101	12019	15692	19470	6.5	95	4604	6009	7470	6.5	2.61	3574	4612	6.2
33544 ZEPHYRHILLS	101	8387	12509	16537	9.9	99	2973	4523	6050	10.4	2.76	2427	3647	10.1
33547 LITHIA	057	8016	10258	12539	6.0	94	2753	3571	4401	6.3	2.87	2232	2880	6.2
33548 LUTZ	057	5423	6065	6952	2.7	69	1957	2209	2545	2.9	2.74	1584	1771	2.7
FLORIDA					2.1					2.2	2.45			2.0
UNITED STATES					1.2					1.3	2.58			1.1

ZIP CODE #	POST OFFICE NAME	RACE (%) White 2000	White 2004	Black 2000	Black 2004	Asian/Pacific 2000	Asian/Pacific 2004	% Hispanic Origin 2000	% Hispanic Origin 2004	2004 AGE DISTRIBUTION (%) 0-4	5-9	10-14	15-19	20-24	25-44	45-64	65-84	85+	18+	MEDIAN AGE 2004	% 2004 Males	% 2004 Females
33305	FORT LAUDERDALE	85.1	83.4	8.2	9.2	1.4	1.6	7.9	9.5	3.9	3.5	3.9	3.9	4.9	31.9	31.8	14.0	2.2	86.4	44.1	55.6	44.4
33306	FORT LAUDERDALE	96.1	95.4	0.9	1.2	1.2	1.4	5.7	7.1	3.8	3.6	3.9	3.6	3.8	25.8	32.4	17.6	5.6	86.5	48.0	51.6	48.4
33308	FORT LAUDERDALE	96.1	95.3	1.0	1.2	1.1	1.3	6.7	8.2	2.5	2.6	3.1	3.1	3.2	21.0	32.2	27.0	5.4	89.9	54.3	48.6	51.4
33309	FORT LAUDERDALE	57.3	53.9	33.5	36.1	1.6	1.8	13.1	15.0	6.5	6.0	6.2	6.2	7.3	33.0	23.4	8.7	2.8	77.7	36.6	50.8	49.2
33311	FORT LAUDERDALE	11.1	10.0	82.0	83.1	0.5	0.6	3.4	3.8	8.4	7.9	9.0	8.6	7.7	25.8	21.8	9.3	1.5	69.3	31.9	47.7	52.4
33312	FORT LAUDERDALE	58.2	56.5	33.9	34.9	1.3	1.5	15.1	17.2	6.3	6.3	6.8	6.5	6.6	28.9	27.7	9.8	1.1	76.7	38.3	51.0	49.0
33313	FORT LAUDERDALE	25.5	22.8	66.3	68.8	1.7	1.7	7.9	8.7	8.2	7.8	8.2	7.6	7.8	28.7	20.3	8.9	2.6	71.3	32.7	46.2	53.8
33314	FORT LAUDERDALE	84.8	82.4	5.3	6.1	2.8	3.2	22.6	26.9	6.3	6.0	6.9	6.7	8.4	34.2	21.9	8.7	1.1	77.0	33.9	49.7	50.3
33315	FORT LAUDERDALE	85.7	83.4	7.2	8.2	1.7	2.0	16.1	19.4	4.6	4.5	5.0	4.7	6.3	33.1	29.5	10.8	1.5	83.2	40.8	52.1	48.0
33316	FORT LAUDERDALE	90.2	88.3	5.0	5.9	1.7	2.1	9.7	12.0	3.0	3.0	3.0	3.1	4.7	30.5	29.7	19.0	4.0	89.5	46.8	53.4	46.6
33317	FORT LAUDERDALE	70.2	67.0	20.5	22.8	2.6	2.9	17.7	20.1	6.4	6.7	7.3	6.7	6.4	27.3	26.1	11.4	1.7	75.5	38.3	48.8	51.2
33319	FORT LAUDERDALE	58.7	54.9	33.0	36.1	1.9	2.1	11.4	12.9	5.3	4.8	4.8	4.4	5.4	23.4	22.4	22.1	7.4	82.5	46.7	44.6	55.4
33321	FORT LAUDERDALE	85.9	83.7	7.3	8.4	1.5	1.7	14.0	16.7	4.0	3.8	3.6	3.1	3.5	21.4	21.8	31.6	7.2	86.8	55.0	44.3	55.7
33322	FORT LAUDERDALE	83.2	80.2	9.9	11.6	2.5	3.0	11.9	14.6	4.9	5.1	5.1	4.6	4.3	24.0	23.1	21.9	7.0	82.1	46.5	45.5	54.5
33323	FORT LAUDERDALE	80.0	76.7	10.8	12.5	3.5	4.2	18.1	21.8	7.0	7.4	8.5	7.4	5.8	33.6	24.4	5.5	0.5	72.3	35.0	49.3	50.7
33324	FORT LAUDERDALE	86.2	83.8	6.5	7.7	2.8	3.3	14.2	17.2	5.1	4.9	5.1	5.2	6.0	30.5	26.0	14.7	2.5	81.7	40.6	46.5	53.5
33325	FORT LAUDERDALE	88.3	86.2	4.0	4.8	2.2	2.6	17.2	20.8	6.9	7.2	8.3	7.6	6.4	30.5	25.8	6.7	0.6	72.7	35.8	48.9	51.1
33326	FORT LAUDERDALE	88.3	86.6	3.4	3.9	2.8	3.1	30.0	34.7	7.3	7.6	8.4	7.2	5.9	30.8	23.6	8.5	0.8	72.2	36.0	47.8	52.2
33327	FORT LAUDERDALE	88.4	86.6	3.6	4.2	3.3	3.7	28.1	32.9	10.6	10.8	9.9	6.8	4.4	32.2	21.2	3.8	0.2	64.3	32.7	49.2	50.8
33328	FORT LAUDERDALE	91.4	89.9	2.0	2.4	3.2	3.8	12.4	15.1	6.3	6.9	7.6	6.8	5.6	26.9	29.3	9.4	1.2	75.0	39.5	48.3	51.7
33330	FORT LAUDERDALE	89.2	87.6	3.9	4.6	3.4	3.8	18.7	22.3	6.6	8.7	9.8	7.9	4.5	27.5	27.9	6.5	0.5	69.5	37.8	48.9	51.1
33331	FORT LAUDERDALE	85.7	83.6	4.7	5.5	4.2	4.7	26.9	31.9	8.8	9.4	9.6	7.0	4.6	31.2	24.4	4.7	0.4	67.7	34.7	48.9	51.1
33332	FORT LAUDERDALE	90.8	89.4	3.0	3.6	2.1	2.3	24.2	28.7	8.9	9.7	9.6	6.9	4.4	28.0	26.5	5.8	0.3	67.4	36.2	49.4	50.6
33334	FORT LAUDERDALE	76.1	72.2	12.5	15.0	1.9	2.1	21.5	24.5	6.4	6.0	6.3	6.3	7.4	32.0	24.4	9.4	1.9	77.6	37.3	52.3	47.7
33351	FORT LAUDERDALE	69.1	65.4	18.5	20.9	4.0	4.4	19.7	22.7	6.9	6.8	7.7	7.4	7.5	32.7	21.9	6.9	2.3	74.1	34.2	47.4	52.6
33401	WEST PALM BEACH	49.8	45.4	42.1	46.1	1.2	1.2	10.1	11.5	5.6	5.1	5.4	6.2	7.5	26.3	21.8	16.1	6.1	80.6	40.6	46.8	53.2
33403	WEST PALM BEACH	55.0	52.0	36.2	38.5	2.9	3.2	5.7	6.9	6.7	6.4	6.9	6.8	7.0	30.0	22.9	11.2	2.3	76.1	36.8	48.7	51.3
33404	WEST PALM BEACH	27.0	27.5	69.4	68.9	0.5	0.6	3.6	4.0	6.9	7.0	8.3	7.4	6.0	22.4	23.7	16.0	2.2	73.2	38.6	47.3	52.7
33405	WEST PALM BEACH	81.9	79.4	4.8	5.4	1.0	1.1	46.3	53.0	6.0	5.9	6.3	6.1	6.5	30.3	24.6	12.4	2.0	78.2	38.6	51.6	48.4
33406	WEST PALM BEACH	81.9	78.8	7.4	8.4	1.6	1.8	28.8	35.1	6.2	6.1	6.0	6.3	7.0	32.6	23.9	10.5	1.5	78.1	36.7	52.0	48.0
33407	WEST PALM BEACH	31.5	27.4	59.3	62.8	1.4	1.4	9.2	10.4	7.5	7.1	7.6	7.7	7.6	28.1	23.5	9.4	1.5	73.0	34.6	49.2	50.8
33408	NORTH PALM BEACH	96.6	95.7	0.9	1.2	1.1	1.3	3.9	5.3	3.2	3.5	4.2	3.8	3.6	20.3	29.6	26.8	5.1	86.7	52.9	48.4	51.6
33409	WEST PALM BEACH	69.3	65.0	20.2	23.0	2.4	2.8	17.4	20.9	6.0	5.6	5.8	5.9	9.0	36.1	19.1	10.1	2.2	79.5	33.7	49.9	50.1
33410	PALM BEACH GARDENS	92.0	89.8	3.5	4.7	2.1	2.5	6.3	8.4	4.9	5.1	5.6	5.2	5.1	25.9	28.1	17.3	2.9	81.4	44.0	48.0	52.0
33411	WEST PALM BEACH	80.0	76.2	12.9	15.5	2.2	2.5	11.5	14.4	6.0	6.1	7.4	7.3	6.6	26.6	24.1	13.5	2.4	76.2	39.4	48.0	52.1
33412	WEST PALM BEACH	86.9	83.6	7.3	9.2	1.8	2.2	9.9	12.9	8.5	8.5	8.8	7.1	5.6	30.6	23.9	6.5	0.4	69.8	36.0	50.4	49.6
33413	WEST PALM BEACH	79.7	76.6	10.5	11.9	2.3	2.7	19.3	23.6	6.3	6.0	6.5	6.3	6.4	30.2	23.0	14.0	1.3	77.3	37.6	49.0	51.0
33414	WEST PALM BEACH	89.1	86.5	5.2	6.5	2.0	2.4	11.2	14.5	6.2	7.1	8.9	8.2	5.4	25.1	28.5	9.7	0.9	72.6	39.0	48.8	51.2
33415	WEST PALM BEACH	76.4	73.2	11.7	13.3	1.8	1.9	27.3	31.9	6.7	6.5	6.8	6.6	6.8	28.9	22.0	13.2	2.5	76.0	36.9	47.4	52.6
33417	WEST PALM BEACH	75.5	71.1	17.3	20.4	1.9	2.1	11.2	13.8	5.1	4.7	4.9	4.7	5.6	21.9	19.6	24.6	8.9	82.5	47.8	45.4	54.6
33418	PALM BEACH GARDENS	94.1	92.6	1.7	2.2	2.5	3.1	5.4	7.3	4.3	4.9	5.9	5.3	3.8	20.9	33.6	19.3	2.1	81.3	47.9	47.8	52.2
33426	BOYNTON BEACH	87.7	85.0	7.5	9.2	1.4	1.6	7.1	9.3	4.1	4.2	4.2	3.5	3.3	22.9	22.9	26.9	7.9	85.2	51.1	44.7	55.3
33428	BOCA RATON	89.1	86.7	3.5	4.4	3.0	3.5	12.1	15.6	6.6	6.9	7.5	6.7	5.4	27.1	24.2	13.5	2.3	74.8	39.4	48.2	51.8
33430	BELLE GLADE	28.9	27.2	54.3	55.3	0.3	0.3	26.0	28.4	9.1	8.7	9.4	8.7	8.3	27.7	20.8	6.9	0.5	67.3	29.2	53.2	46.8
33431	BOCA RATON	89.2	87.4	5.2	6.1	1.9	2.1	8.1	10.5	3.9	4.3	5.0	10.4	9.8	22.8	26.4	14.7	2.7	83.6	40.9	48.9	51.2
33432	BOCA RATON	88.4	86.4	5.5	6.5	2.1	2.3	9.8	12.3	3.8	3.7	4.1	3.8	4.7	23.7	27.2	24.4	4.5	86.2	49.6	48.4	51.6
33433	BOCA RATON	94.5	93.2	1.3	1.7	1.8	2.2	7.8	10.2	3.9	4.2	4.6	4.2	4.4	21.9	25.6	23.8	7.3	84.7	50.1	45.4	54.6
33434	BOCA RATON	95.6	94.6	1.2	1.5	1.4	1.7	5.1	6.7	3.0	3.5	4.1	3.9	2.9	12.9	22.6	35.7	11.4	87.0	62.6	43.8	56.3
33435	BOYNTON BEACH	57.9	54.5	34.8	37.4	0.8	0.9	10.2	12.0	5.9	5.8	6.4	6.2	5.7	23.9	24.0	17.4	4.8	78.1	42.3	47.7	52.3
33436	BOYNTON BEACH	86.2	83.3	8.5	10.3	2.0	2.3	7.6	9.9	5.3	4.6	4.3	3.5	4.2	24.2	21.4	27.7	4.9	83.7	48.5	46.3	53.8
33437	BOYNTON BEACH	92.7	91.0	3.5	4.4	1.8	2.1	5.8	7.6	3.6	3.7	4.0	3.1	2.5	15.0	20.5	44.7	3.0	86.8	63.3	46.8	53.2
33438	CANAL POINT	26.2	23.1	55.0	56.5	0.2	0.4	28.5	30.8	10.5	9.8	11.5	14.0	8.4	21.5	18.0	5.7	0.7	58.6	22.5	49.3	50.7
33440	CLEWISTON	63.8	62.2	21.8	21.9	0.7	0.8	35.3	40.1	8.6	7.9	8.8	9.1	8.8	27.5	20.1	8.3	0.9	69.0	30.1	52.1	47.9
33441	DEERFIELD BEACH	65.6	63.2	26.7	28.0	1.2	1.4	8.8	10.7	5.7	5.3	5.8	5.8	6.7	29.6	23.2	15.0	2.9	79.8	39.5	48.5	51.6
33442	DEERFIELD BEACH	90.9	89.0	4.1	5.0	1.7	2.0	7.4	9.3	3.6	3.3	3.2	2.6	2.8	22.6	21.2	27.9	12.9	88.3	56.4	44.0	56.0
33444	DELRAY BEACH	42.0	40.6	48.3	49.5	0.9	1.0	9.5	10.9	7.1	6.8	7.0	6.9	7.3	29.3	24.2	10.1	1.3	74.9	36.0	49.9	50.1
33445	DELRAY BEACH	77.6	74.0	17.3	20.2	1.5	1.7	5.8	7.3	4.2	4.3	4.4	4.0	3.8	21.9	22.8	27.0	7.6	84.5	50.9	45.5	54.5
33446	DELRAY BEACH	98.0	97.5	0.7	0.8	0.3	0.3	3.1	3.9	0.9	0.9	0.9	0.7	0.6	4.9	17.0	60.8	13.4	96.9	75.0	43.5	56.5
33455	HOBE SOUND	93.9	92.1	3.9	5.0	0.6	0.8	2.4	3.5	3.7	4.1	5.0	4.2	3.2	17.9	29.4	28.9	3.7	84.5	53.3	48.4	51.6
33458	JUPITER	91.8	89.9	3.5	4.5	1.5	1.7	8.8	11.0	6.1	6.8	7.5	6.5	5.3	28.3	26.9	11.4	1.4	75.5	39.6	49.8	50.2
33460	LAKE WORTH	63.0	59.1	20.1	21.8	0.8	0.8	31.5	36.3	7.6	6.9	6.2	5.9	7.8	32.3	21.4	9.5	2.5	75.9	34.6	52.4	47.6
33461	LAKE WORTH	75.1	71.1	9.6	11.1	1.2	1.3	30.2	35.7	7.6	6.9	6.7	6.4	7.6	30.5	20.3	11.8	2.2	75.3	34.7	50.5	49.5
33462	LAKE WORTH	80.0	76.7	11.4	13.2	1.2	1.4	14.8	18.1	5.8	5.8	6.0	5.6	5.3	26.5	25.3	15.8	4.0	78.9	41.8	49.2	50.8
33463	LAKE WORTH	78.7	75.1	9.0	10.6	2.3	2.6	22.0	26.0	7.2	7.1	7.3	6.1	5.7	28.6	22.0	14.1	2.0	74.6	37.4	48.6	51.5
33467	LAKE WORTH	93.0	90.5	3.0	4.1	1.4	1.9	8.2	11.0	6.0	6.4	5.9	4.8	3.1	22.3	22.3	24.5	4.7	78.7	46.1	47.7	52.3
33469	JUPITER	98.0	97.5	0.5	0.6	0.6	0.7	2.5	3.4	4.3	4.6	5.2	4.4	3.2	18.2	30.4	25.4	4.4	83.0	51.6	47.9	52.2
33470	LOXAHATCHEE	88.3	85.2	6.0	7.8	1.2	1.4	11.3	14.8	8.1	8.3	9.1	7.8	6.1	30.7	24.2	5.4	0.4	69.7	35.4	50.5	49.5
33471	MOORE HAVEN	75.7	72.9	14.8	15.9	0.4	0.5	18.3	22.0	5.8	5.6	7.0	5.8	6.8	28.9	24.1	14.9	1.1	78.1	38.1	56.7	43.3
33476	PAHOKEE	21.8	19.2	62.7	64.2	0.5	0.5	23.9	25.6	10.3	9.7	10.8	11.6	8.4	23.0	18.3	7.0	0.9	61.6	24.5	48.2	51.8
33477	JUPITER	98.2	97.7	0.2	0.3	0.6	0.8	2.0	2.7	1.9	2.1	2.3	2.0	1.9	12.9	36.2	37.7	3.1	92.5	60.9	47.6	52.4
33478	JUPITER	96.4	95.4	1.0	1.3	0.6	0.7	3.9	5.3	5.7	7.3	9.2	8.5	3.6	28.6	30.7	6.0	0.6	71.9	40.0	50.6	49.4
33480	PALM BEACH	96.2	95.1	2.4	3.2	0.6	0.7	2.5	3.5	2.2	2.4	2.8	2.7	1.3	9.8	27.3	40.5	11.2	91.1	66.0	43.9	56.1
33483	DELRAY BEACH	87.4	86.1	7.1	8.0	1.0	1.1	4.9	6.2	2.8	2.9	3.0	2.9	3.2	21.5	32.2	25.3	6.3	89.6	53.8	48.0	52.0
33484	DELRAY BEACH	95.7	94.2	2.4	3.2	0.6	0.8	3.1	4.2	1.5	1.4	1.4	1.2	1.2	8.1	16.2	54.4	14.6	95.0	75.1	42.6	57.4
33486	BOCA RATON	91.3	89.6	2.4	3.0	2.5	2.9	9.4	12.2	5.3	5.7	5.9	5.4	5.3	28.6	28.3	12.8	2.7	79.9	41.6	48.8	51.3
33487	BOCA RATON	94.0	92.8	2.6	3.2	1.0	1.2	6.5	8.5	3.6	3.5	3.4	3.2	2.6	18.8	31.1	28.9	5.0	87.5	55.0	47.5	52.5
33493	SOUTH BAY	27.7	25.1	61.0	63.0	0.5	0.5	23.2	24.8	7.2	7.1	8.6	8.2	8.6	34.1	20.2	5.8	0.4	71.9	31.4	59.8	40.2
33496	BOCA RATON	95.0	93.8	1.3	1.7	2.0	2.4	6.2	8.3	4.2	4.8	5.3	5.0	3.4	16.8	29.3	29.1	2.1	82.5	52.6	46.8	53.2
33498	BOCA RATON	92.5	90.6	1.8	2.3	3.3	3.9	8.9	11.8	6.4	7.5	7.8	6.1	3.7	22.7	28.1	16.1	1.7	74.4	42.8	48.9	51.1
33510	BRANDON	83.1	79.6	8.9	11.0	2.1	2.4	11.2	14.4	6.8	6.9	7.5	6.8	6.9	29.3	25.6	9.1	1.1	74.7	36.3	48.2	51.8
33511	BRANDON	81.5	77.8	9.5	11.4	2.7	3.1	12.8	16.2	7.2	6.9	7.4	6.9	7.8	31.9	23.2	7.6	1.0	74.3	34.0	48.6	51.4
33513	BUSHNELL	82.3	80.5	14.2	15.5	0.5	0.5	4.0	4.8	4.8	4.8	5.3	5.6	6.9	27.9	26.0	17.0	1.8	82.0	41.5	55.8	44.2
33514	CENTER HILL	83.8	80.9	5.7	6.7	1.5	1.6	18.7	22.8	9.2	8.8	9.1	7.3	6.1	25.4	21.5	11.9	0.8	67.8	33.4	52.8	47.3
33523	DADE CITY	76.6	74.4	11.3	11.9	0.3	0.3	21.1	23.9	7.9	7.5	7.5	7.3	7.3	25.2	22.8	12.7	1.9	72.8	35.7	50.7	49.3
33525	DADE CITY	84.6	83.2	7.6	7.6	0.7	0.7	11.1	13.3	5.8	5.8	6.5	7.5	7.2	22.7	25.0	17.1	2.5	77.8	41.2	49.0	51.0
33527	DOVER	85.2	82.5	1.2	1.5	0.7	0.8	25.4	30.5	7.8	7.6	8.0	7.7	7.2	28.7	23.4	8.5	1.0	71.9	33.6	51.7	48.3
33534	GIBSONTON	88.0	85.7	1.4	1.8	0.7	0.8	19.4	24.2	9.4	8.2	8.1	7.4	7.7	29.0	21.7	8.0	0.6	70.1	31.5	51.6	48.4
33538	LAKE PANASOFFKEE	93.2	92.1	4.5	5.1	0.4	0.5	1.3	1.7	5.2	5.0	4.9	4.0	4.2	19.7	27.7	26.6	2.7	82.4	50.6	48.9	51.1
33540	ZEPHYRHILLS	92.4	91.2	3.1	3.5	0.7	0.8	5.3	6.6	5.8	5.8	6.5	6.1	5.3	22.5	25.1	20.4	2.4	77.8	43.5	48.7	51.3
33541	ZEPHYRHILLS	95.3	94.5	2.0	2.2	0.7	0.8	2.9	3.8	3.5	3.5	3.9	3.6	3.5	17.4	25.0	35.1	4.5	87.0	57.7	48.9	51.1
33542	ZEPHYRHILLS	94.5	93.7	1.6	1.8	1.0	1.1	3.6	4.6	4.4	4.1	3.9	3.8	3.8	16.6	22.3	35.0	6.2	85.4	58.3	46.3	53.7
33543	ZEPHYRHILLS	87.3	84.8	4.7	5.6	3.6	4.3	8.8	11.2	8.4	8.0	6.6	5.2	4.5	31.9	23.9	10.7	0.9	73.8	37.4	48.5	51.5
33544	ZEPHYRHILLS	94.0	92.9	1.7	1.9	1.5	1.7	7.7	9.6	6.7	6.9	7.2	6.6	5.2	28.6	27.7	10.7	0.5	75.1	39.0	49.3	50.7
33547	LITHIA	93.4	91.8	1.5	2.2	0.5	0.7	6.7	8.5	7.5	7.7	8.1	6.8	6.0	29.7	25.8	7.6	0.7	72.5	35.7	49.7	50.3
33548	LUTZ	95.5	94.5	1.4	1.7	1.0	1.2	7.1	9.4	5.5	6.5	8.1	6.7	4.2	26.2	32.2	9.6	1.0	75.4	41.4	49.6	50.4
	FLORIDA	78.0	76.5	14.6	15.2	1.7	2.0	16.8	19.0	6.0	5.9	6.4	6.4	6.5	26.6	24.5	15.5	2.4	78.1	40.0	48.8	51.2
	UNITED STATES	75.1	73.6	12.3	12.5	3.8	4.2	12.5	14.1	6.9	6.7	7.2	7.0	7.3	28.6	23.8	10.8	1.7	75.1	36.0	49.1	50.9

#	POST OFFICE NAME	2004 Per Capita Income	2004 HH Income Base	2004 HOUSEHOLD INCOME DISTRIBUTION (%) Less than $25,000	$25,000 to $49,999	$50,000 to $99,999	$100,000 to $149,999	$150,000 or More	MEDIAN HOUSEHOLD INCOME 2004	2009	2004 National Centile	2004 State Centile	2004 Home Value Base	2004 HOME VALUE DISTRIBUTION (%) Less than $50,000	$50,000 to $89,999	$90,000 to $174,999	$175,000 to $399,999	$400,000 or More	2004 Median Home Value
33305	FORT LAUDERDALE	36477	6047	23.9	31.1	27.7	9.4	7.9	46131	54587	64	63	3265	1.6	6.5	35.7	38.9	17.3	199222
33306	FORT LAUDERDALE	48994	2029	17.8	21.4	31.3	13.2	16.3	62201	75252	86	89	1351	0.5	2.2	12.7	45.7	38.9	302922
33308	FORT LAUDERDALE	49325	17442	21.7	26.0	27.8	12.1	12.4	52448	62233	76	78	12421	1.3	9.7	23.2	43.0	22.8	233790
33309	FORT LAUDERDALE	20793	14434	24.6	33.4	32.9	7.4	1.8	43594	50896	58	56	8811	5.9	11.4	59.0	23.2	0.5	136827
33311	FORT LAUDERDALE	13303	22151	43.8	29.4	21.2	4.4	1.2	28850	34138	10	8	10844	8.4	15.6	63.5	11.7	0.7	120300
33312	FORT LAUDERDALE	22232	17675	28.2	29.5	30.0	8.6	3.8	42542	50135	55	52	11752	6.4	8.5	50.7	29.7	4.7	147572
33313	FORT LAUDERDALE	16493	22253	36.9	34.2	21.9	4.9	2.0	32748	37929	20	18	12271	21.2	22.5	41.6	14.3	0.4	107166
33314	FORT LAUDERDALE	21254	10289	29.7	31.3	27.8	8.5	2.7	40197	47728	47	45	5795	30.6	7.9	42.2	17.5	1.8	113978
33315	FORT LAUDERDALE	28832	6351	24.4	28.3	32.3	10.7	4.3	46996	56237	66	66	3401	4.3	3.1	37.5	47.3	7.7	186143
33316	FORT LAUDERDALE	63291	6154	21.9	24.6	23.4	10.3	19.9	53791	64865	78	79	3369	0.6	3.9	23.8	29.5	42.2	308160
33317	FORT LAUDERDALE	26233	12560	19.2	24.4	33.1	15.0	8.4	56794	65712	81	83	9845	2.9	7.3	30.5	54.7	4.6	200512
33319	FORT LAUDERDALE	23566	20335	31.7	33.2	25.8	6.7	2.7	37179	43277	36	33	14667	14.1	28.2	38.6	17.9	1.3	101242
33321	FORT LAUDERDALE	26591	20714	31.6	30.3	28.4	7.1	2.6	38678	45544	42	39	16830	4.5	12.8	54.0	27.7	0.9	142009
33322	FORT LAUDERDALE	26363	19911	30.5	26.4	27.8	10.9	4.4	42628	50829	55	53	16302	15.4	17.2	33.0	31.3	3.2	135384
33323	FORT LAUDERDALE	27872	6538	8.0	18.8	45.8	21.6	5.9	71874	83771	92	93	5298	0.6	1.0	22.5	68.1	7.8	211243
33324	FORT LAUDERDALE	33184	18964	18.8	28.8	31.8	12.7	7.9	52229	61586	76	77	12309	5.2	9.5	46.1	29.6	9.6	148792
33325	FORT LAUDERDALE	27493	9770	13.5	24.2	38.1	16.6	7.7	61515	71988	86	88	8518	26.9	8.1	14.9	39.5	10.6	175204
33326	FORT LAUDERDALE	33738	12082	13.7	18.1	34.7	19.5	13.9	73844	87254	93	94	9391	0.2	1.3	31.1	53.3	14.2	222115
33327	FORT LAUDERDALE	46545	4312	5.6	7.1	30.1	25.4	31.9	111031	130200	99	100	3942	0.2	0.0	6.3	56.1	37.4	332289
33328	FORT LAUDERDALE	30496	8805	13.0	18.8	37.9	20.3	10.0	69856	81513	91	93	7647	3.3	1.8	23.2	62.2	9.6	225847
33330	FORT LAUDERDALE	36549	3960	5.8	12.8	35.0	28.0	18.4	93457	107266	97	98	3728	0.8	0.2	14.3	48.8	35.9	293525
33331	FORT LAUDERDALE	40722	8234	5.0	10.4	34.4	28.1	22.1	100167	114426	98	99	7495	0.2	0.1	4.0	66.7	29.1	315746
33332	FORT LAUDERDALE	52610	2883	5.1	10.6	22.3	23.6	38.4	123593	141256	99	100	2737	0.4	0.4	1.8	36.4	61.1	472156
33334	FORT LAUDERDALE	21037	13256	28.8	33.4	27.7	7.8	2.4	39787	46680	45	43	6510	3.4	8.9	45.8	39.1	3.0	156472
33351	FORT LAUDERDALE	22020	12619	18.1	32.2	37.6	9.4	2.8	49778	57410	71	73	7594	0.8	10.5	43.1	45.1	0.5	166496
33401	WEST PALM BEACH	27657	10249	36.0	30.7	19.6	7.6	6.2	35036	41426	28	25	4706	4.6	16.2	43.2	22.7	13.3	130474
33403	WEST PALM BEACH	20196	5361	27.6	35.0	29.8	6.1	1.5	38616	46399	41	39	3082	10.5	12.8	61.2	15.1	0.5	125280
33404	WEST PALM BEACH	24397	11962	36.4	29.9	21.3	6.3	6.1	35256	42131	28	26	7044	11.1	17.4	37.3	24.9	9.3	124151
33405	WEST PALM BEACH	25649	7924	27.6	29.0	27.0	9.4	7.0	44293	51778	59	57	5103	1.5	9.8	51.6	25.6	11.5	139672
33406	WEST PALM BEACH	22899	9096	19.8	32.3	34.7	9.6	3.7	48141	56281	69	69	6364	3.1	12.0	54.7	29.0	1.3	133193
33407	WEST PALM BEACH	19969	11238	34.2	29.8	26.5	6.4	3.0	37306	44288	37	34	6132	6.3	15.8	59.7	16.0	2.2	115931
33408	NORTH PALM BEACH	56033	9761	17.5	23.4	30.7	13.5	15.0	61320	74051	86	88	7080	0.4	5.2	30.7	41.9	21.8	221674
33409	WEST PALM BEACH	26022	10316	25.9	32.2	29.3	7.9	4.7	43986	52164	59	57	4190	12.4	16.3	49.9	18.2	3.1	110308
33410	PALM BEACH GARDENS	40037	12674	17.7	26.2	31.4	14.4	10.3	57466	68036	82	84	9446	8.0	4.7	33.4	40.9	13.0	186589
33411	WEST PALM BEACH	27988	18311	16.9	23.4	37.8	15.0	6.9	59135	69382	84	85	15126	4.6	11.4	34.9	44.8	4.4	173359
33412	WEST PALM BEACH	33622	4054	5.4	15.5	47.7	20.4	11.0	76406	92339	94	95	3936	0.2	0.3	21.1	65.2	13.2	227080
33413	WEST PALM BEACH	28994	4168	15.7	27.7	39.9	10.6	6.1	56205	68990	81	82	2726	0.6	4.8	37.4	54.6	2.6	187342
33414	WEST PALM BEACH	37750	14912	9.6	17.3	34.8	22.1	16.3	80288	97918	95	96	12714	0.2	1.7	16.9	61.7	19.7	245089
33415	WEST PALM BEACH	20109	16885	31.3	33.6	27.8	5.5	1.9	37709	44629	38	36	11636	18.9	23.7	50.2	6.2	1.1	99251
33417	WEST PALM BEACH	20938	15062	41.2	31.6	20.7	4.9	1.6	30196	35681	13	10	10033	45.3	17.9	27.9	8.4	0.6	58736
33418	PALM BEACH GARDENS	55126	13053	9.5	18.3	29.9	19.6	22.7	83445	103448	96	97	11510	0.1	2.3	23.8	46.3	27.5	275083
33426	BOYNTON BEACH	26929	7591	24.3	29.4	35.1	9.3	1.9	45690	53420	63	62	6167	1.8	11.4	66.4	19.9	0.5	129037
33428	BOCA RATON	33905	15470	15.2	26.0	31.7	14.7	12.4	60695	72904	85	87	12244	1.4	9.2	31.6	42.8	15.1	196105
33430	BELLE GLADE	12065	6434	50.2	25.9	18.3	3.9	1.8	24881	28458	4	3	2725	19.5	24.0	45.6	10.2	0.8	99103
33431	BOCA RATON	51667	6479	12.6	21.5	30.1	15.0	20.9	69508	86632	91	93	4826	0.3	0.0	19.0	51.0	29.6	256004
33432	BOCA RATON	60300	9935	18.8	27.3	23.7	10.0	20.2	56022	68469	81	82	6437	1.3	7.9	22.2	30.0	38.8	293300
33433	BOCA RATON	47107	20607	13.6	22.8	32.7	17.0	14.0	66621	80408	90	91	14730	0.2	2.9	28.7	52.2	16.1	227227
33434	BOCA RATON	57272	11064	25.6	21.9	22.8	12.5	17.2	53865	65274	78	79	9745	6.0	23.5	22.0	25.6	23.0	167086
33435	BOYNTON BEACH	26448	12910	29.5	32.2	25.6	7.4	5.4	40570	47405	48	46	9300	12.3	20.9	42.9	15.0	8.9	112788
33436	BOYNTON BEACH	34196	18532	18.5	30.6	33.1	10.4	7.4	50820	60151	74	75	13908	9.3	9.8	36.3	37.1	7.5	160168
33437	BOYNTON BEACH	37824	21965	13.1	26.1	37.1	15.1	8.7	60445	71925	85	86	19611	1.1	0.8	25.9	66.4	5.8	220232
33438	CANAL POINT	13442	297	49.8	24.9	18.2	5.1	2.0	25087	28900	5	3	105	21.0	28.6	32.4	18.1	0.0	90556
33440	CLEWISTON	15317	5687	33.5	32.6	27.0	5.1	1.8	36858	41992	35	32	4092	25.8	30.3	35.5	6.7	1.7	83111
33441	DEERFIELD BEACH	24426	12284	30.4	29.8	28.0	7.9	3.9	38899	45520	42	40	6585	2.8	17.7	40.0	32.4	7.1	145248
33442	DEERFIELD BEACH	30442	16959	31.9	28.7	26.0	9.3	4.0	38300	45553	40	38	13610	16.9	23.1	33.1	25.1	1.9	112238
33444	DELRAY BEACH	21338	8030	30.8	26.7	29.0	8.6	4.9	41362	50020	51	49	4351	3.6	15.1	38.9	34.0	8.4	152295
33445	DELRAY BEACH	34284	13996	21.6	28.8	30.5	12.2	6.9	49634	59783	71	72	10562	4.3	26.6	34.9	27.0	7.2	128531
33446	DELRAY BEACH	42796	10172	28.2	27.5	28.0	7.2	9.1	43435	52685	57	55	9567	14.7	18.9	29.3	27.5	9.7	136382
33455	HOBE SOUND	34594	8859	21.2	31.7	28.5	12.5	6.1	47389	57006	67	66	7722	9.4	12.0	30.5	36.1	12.0	167500
33458	JUPITER	33487	14614	14.0	24.8	34.8	15.3	11.1	61175	73215	86	88	11149	1.0	2.9	36.8	43.8	15.7	205102
33460	LAKE WORTH	17023	12271	35.5	34.8	22.6	5.1	2.0	33962	39791	24	23	6027	6.5	20.7	52.7	16.9	3.2	115894
33461	LAKE WORTH	18746	14913	30.4	36.4	25.6	5.7	1.9	36508	42712	34	31	9111	18.9	19.3	52.2	9.6	0.1	106269
33462	LAKE WORTH	31360	12123	23.4	33.1	27.5	9.2	6.8	45020	52919	61	59	8706	10.6	11.5	45.8	19.9	12.2	135182
33463	LAKE WORTH	20943	17549	22.2	32.6	33.2	9.2	2.8	45954	54569	64	63	13796	14.4	15.4	45.7	23.3	1.2	125640
33467	LAKE WORTH	34775	19879	15.6	23.8	32.9	17.7	9.9	62690	77619	87	89	18775	2.2	13.6	26.1	48.7	9.4	203475
33469	JUPITER	48877	6776	15.4	21.4	30.9	16.7	15.6	66700	82288	90	91	5916	0.2	6.6	22.5	43.3	27.4	234552
33470	LOXAHATCHEE	28247	7550	7.3	18.4	47.0	19.0	8.3	71154	85246	92	93	7101	0.2	1.0	25.1	64.6	9.2	217138
33471	MOORE HAVEN	17477	2638	34.4	31.8	25.6	6.0	2.1	34354	39544	25	24	2118	20.5	30.6	36.6	10.3	2.0	88553
33476	PAHOKEE	11425	2452	48.7	26.8	17.9	4.7	1.8	25741	29223	5	4	1127	29.6	28.1	32.1	9.2	1.0	82731
33477	JUPITER	69550	6652	13.3	19.1	28.3	16.9	22.6	75243	94869	93	95	5812	1.1	1.1	19.7	53.7	24.5	268151
33478	JUPITER	31590	4076	5.8	15.2	45.0	24.1	9.9	79795	95258	95	96	3928	0.4	1.5	12.4	79.0	6.8	239758
33480	PALM BEACH	128432	6576	13.6	14.9	21.3	13.3	36.9	100613	123042	98	99	5629	0.2	1.9	12.0	26.8	59.2	564189
33483	DELRAY BEACH	63269	6786	17.9	22.6	26.9	12.9	19.8	61203	75640	86	88	5267	1.7	5.7	26.6	32.8	33.2	242594
33484	DELRAY BEACH	29985	14293	31.3	33.2	24.3	7.8	3.4	36824	43755	35	31	12859	10.3	30.8	40.7	16.3	1.9	105552
33486	BOCA RATON	40047	9176	14.3	22.1	31.5	17.0	15.1	68842	83575	91	92	6923	0.3	4.0	13.8	66.5	15.4	246345
33487	BOCA RATON	57196	8604	13.7	21.1	28.3	17.9	19.0	72161	89883	92	94	7342	0.3	1.6	22.0	52.3	23.8	263339
33493	SOUTH BAY	11484	996	45.5	32.6	16.7	4.2	1.0	27190	30875	7	5	512	25.4	26.0	46.5	2.2	0.0	88333
33496	BOCA RATON	75362	10320	11.7	17.1	24.4	16.1	30.6	90165	113426	97	98	9161	0.2	0.5	24.5	28.5	46.2	364197
33498	BOCA RATON	46457	6380	7.3	15.4	31.1	24.0	22.3	92056	111440	97	98	6148	0.0	0.2	11.2	57.3	31.4	311059
33510	BRANDON	24817	9181	14.0	26.5	43.6	12.1	3.8	57610	65928	82	84	6865	0.7	5.6	69.9	22.5	1.3	139074
33511	BRANDON	26725	20040	12.2	29.4	39.7	13.9	4.8	57236	66198	82	83	13504	1.4	4.1	61.2	31.5	1.9	152779
33513	BUSHNELL	18639	4704	40.1	32.4	21.5	4.4	1.5	30774	34071	14	12	3777	25.8	27.2	33.4	11.7	1.9	84512
33514	CENTER HILL	14258	613	41.9	31.0	22.0	2.8	2.3	30956	34389	15	13	476	27.3	24.8	33.2	14.3	0.4	86000
33523	DADE CITY	17573	6675	36.9	33.1	22.3	4.6	3.0	33325	36742	22	21	4842	19.7	32.0	30.9	15.4	2.1	87306
33525	DADE CITY	20326	6096	30.8	33.7	25.6	6.7	3.2	37350	41979	37	34	4774	18.1	22.5	40.9	15.9	2.5	105516
33527	DOVER	18975	4222	23.6	29.9	33.0	9.2	4.3	46226	52712	64	64	3433	14.3	20.4	40.1	23.7	1.5	116796
33534	GIBSONTON	17164	2955	31.7	33.1	28.5	3.9	2.9	37029	44104	36	32	1870	32.8	27.1	29.7	9.0	1.4	76000
33538	LAKE PANASOFFKEE	18958	2615	41.0	38.9	14.8	3.8	1.6	29230	32399	11	9	2150	29.8	32.6	31.1	5.8	0.8	73333
33540	ZEPHYRHILLS	18074	3869	29.6	35.3	30.6	3.8	0.8	37680	42466	38	35	3290	19.3	30.7	38.8	10.0	1.3	89961
33541	ZEPHYRHILLS	20008	8334	36.4	39.0	20.0	2.8	1.8	31599	35465	17	15	7423	29.5	35.5	25.2	8.4	1.4	68977
33542	ZEPHYRHILLS	19321	10080	41.4	36.3	18.5	2.3	1.6	29357	32703	11	9	7981	28.9	34.8	30.1	5.3	0.9	74176
33543	ZEPHYRHILLS	29986	6009	13.7	25.7	41.1	13.8	5.8	60450	67695	85	86	5645	6.4	14.9	33.0	42.2	3.5	167792
33544	ZEPHYRHILLS	25041	4523	13.3	22.5	46.5	14.6	3.0	61205	69632	86	88	4229	3.6	12.7	40.4	41.6	1.6	164267
33547	LITHIA	23134	3571	16.6	25.9	39.2	13.6	4.8	57969	67769	83	84	3163	7.6	16.6	33.9	33.9	8.1	152841
33548	LUTZ	41751	2209	12.0	14.8	32.5	21.3	19.4	82089	98900	96	96	2027	2.2	5.3	25.7	53.5	13.4	230585
	FLORIDA	25506		26.4	29.9	29.1	9.1	5.6	44138	51288				8.8	15.8	40.2	28.3	7.0	137042
	UNITED STATES	25866		24.7	27.1	30.8	10.9	6.5	48124	56710				10.9	15.0	33.7	30.1	10.4	145905

ZIP CODE		FINANCIAL SERVICES				THE HOME						ENTERTAINMENT						PERSONAL			
						Home Improvements		Furnishings													
#	POST OFFICE NAME	Auto Loan	Home Loan	Invest-ments	Retire-ment Plans	Home Repair	Lawn & Garden	Comput-ers & Hard-ware	Major Appli-ances	TV, Radio, Sound Equip-ment	Furni-ture	Dine out/ Carry out	Sports Equip-ment	Fees & Tickets	Toys & Games	Travel	Cable TV	Apparel & Services	Auto Repairs	Health Insur-ance	Pets & Supplies
33305	FORT LAUDERDALE	89	96	125	98	95	103	98	96	98	98	123	111	101	124	100	98	121	98	93	105
33306	FORT LAUDERDALE	125	134	154	134	135	147	130	132	128	132	161	147	134	155	134	129	156	131	133	146
33308	FORT LAUDERDALE	120	121	139	119	123	139	120	123	122	122	153	133	122	144	125	126	148	124	132	138
33309	FORT LAUDERDALE	74	71	81	74	69	73	76	73	75	77	95	86	75	91	73	72	93	76	68	81
33311	FORT LAUDERDALE	55	50	58	47	49	56	54	53	58	55	72	59	55	70	54	60	70	55	57	61
33312	FORT LAUDERDALE	77	81	96	79	79	86	82	81	82	83	104	91	84	104	82	83	102	82	80	89
33313	FORT LAUDERDALE	58	56	72	55	54	62	61	59	64	61	80	66	61	79	60	65	78	61	60	66
33314	FORT LAUDERDALE	73	69	75	72	68	72	75	72	73	74	92	86	72	89	72	70	90	75	68	81
33315	FORT LAUDERDALE	79	82	99	86	81	85	87	83	84	86	106	99	87	106	85	81	104	86	77	91
33316	FORT LAUDERDALE	148	145	175	148	146	163	153	151	152	153	192	171	153	181	153	152	186	155	153	168
33317	FORT LAUDERDALE	95	105	125	103	103	110	104	102	103	104	129	117	108	132	105	103	128	102	98	112
33319	FORT LAUDERDALE	69	66	79	66	66	75	70	70	72	71	90	77	70	85	71	73	87	72	73	78
33321	FORT LAUDERDALE	73	73	84	70	75	86	72	76	75	75	94	80	74	87	76	78	90	76	84	83
33322	FORT LAUDERDALE	82	86	91	84	86	94	80	85	80	84	101	90	83	94	83	81	97	83	87	93
33323	FORT LAUDERDALE	119	135	133	140	129	126	123	121	113	126	143	142	126	144	120	105	142	118	104	133
33324	FORT LAUDERDALE	100	102	119	105	100	108	104	103	102	106	129	118	104	124	103	99	125	105	99	113
33325	FORT LAUDERDALE	118	117	111	119	114	117	113	114	109	116	137	133	112	132	110	104	134	114	105	130
33326	FORT LAUDERDALE	136	143	148	150	139	141	137	135	129	142	165	157	140	159	134	123	161	135	122	150
33327	FORT LAUDERDALE	207	245	264	251	235	234	219	217	201	227	255	251	232	260	219	192	254	210	189	237
33328	FORT LAUDERDALE	114	129	140	133	125	126	123	120	115	124	146	142	126	148	122	110	144	119	108	132
33330	FORT LAUDERDALE	154	191	212	196	184	187	169	165	154	172	196	191	184	203	171	149	197	159	147	182
33331	FORT LAUDERDALE	182	215	218	223	206	202	192	188	175	197	222	219	203	227	190	166	222	183	163	207
33332	FORT LAUDERDALE	222	290	363	290	281	296	254	249	234	258	297	284	284	311	265	232	300	240	228	273
33334	FORT LAUDERDALE	65	68	86	68	66	72	71	68	72	71	90	80	72	92	71	72	89	70	66	76
33351	FORT LAUDERDALE	85	85	91	90	82	84	87	84	82	88	105	100	86	101	83	77	102	86	75	93
33401	WEST PALM BEACH	79	77	93	78	77	84	83	81	84	83	105	94	82	102	82	84	102	84	82	90
33403	WEST PALM BEACH	66	67	77	68	66	71	71	68	71	70	88	80	71	89	70	69	86	70	66	76
33404	WEST PALM BEACH	88	78	82	74	79	93	81	85	88	83	109	92	81	101	82	92	104	86	95	99
33405	WEST PALM BEACH	80	89	126	85	85	93	90	87	93	93	119	99	93	124	92	95	119	90	84	95
33406	WEST PALM BEACH	83	89	101	89	86	91	87	87	86	89	108	99	89	108	87	84	107	87	81	95
33407	WEST PALM BEACH	70	66	79	65	64	71	71	69	74	72	93	80	72	92	70	75	91	72	69	78
33408	NORTH PALM BEACH	149	154	172	152	156	174	150	155	151	153	189	168	153	178	156	154	182	154	163	172
33409	WEST PALM BEACH	85	78	85	81	76	82	84	83	84	86	106	96	81	99	81	81	103	86	79	92
33410	PALM BEACH GARDENS	119	132	156	133	130	138	130	128	125	130	157	148	134	158	131	123	155	128	122	140
33411	WEST PALM BEACH	102	112	119	114	109	113	106	105	102	108	129	121	109	128	106	100	126	104	99	116
33412	WEST PALM BEACH	145	163	157	170	156	151	147	147	135	154	172	171	152	172	144	127	170	143	126	160
33413	WEST PALM BEACH	109	105	104	102	108	123	101	109	105	105	130	114	102	116	106	108	124	108	119	123
33414	WEST PALM BEACH	151	178	184	183	173	172	160	158	147	163	187	183	170	190	160	141	186	153	141	175
33415	WEST PALM BEACH	70	68	74	68	68	74	69	70	69	71	87	79	69	83	69	69	84	71	69	78
33417	WEST PALM BEACH	60	56	63	56	57	65	58	60	59	60	74	64	57	66	58	59	70	61	62	66
33418	PALM BEACH GARDENS	185	193	203	191	196	216	179	189	178	186	224	203	186	207	188	182	216	185	198	212
33426	BOYNTON BEACH	75	78	86	76	79	88	75	79	76	77	95	84	77	89	78	77	91	78	82	86
33428	BOCA RATON	124	133	147	135	131	139	128	128	125	131	157	145	133	154	129	123	154	128	123	142
33430	BELLE GLADE	52	46	50	43	45	50	50	50	54	52	67	57	49	64	49	54	65	52	52	57
33431	BOCA RATON	172	194	225	192	194	209	182	186	177	185	223	207	191	219	189	179	218	183	183	204
33432	BOCA RATON	165	162	178	161	166	188	161	168	164	165	205	180	163	187	167	168	197	168	179	188
33433	BOCA RATON	138	139	151	141	141	154	136	140	134	140	169	154	138	157	139	135	163	140	143	156
33434	BOCA RATON	162	167	178	160	171	195	153	168	156	162	195	170	159	175	163	162	186	162	182	184
33435	BOYNTON BEACH	88	88	98	85	88	99	87	90	90	90	112	96	89	106	89	92	108	90	95	99
33436	BOYNTON BEACH	106	103	110	103	105	117	101	107	102	106	128	114	102	116	103	103	123	106	111	118
33437	BOYNTON BEACH	117	114	118	110	118	136	109	118	112	113	140	122	110	125	115	117	132	116	131	132
33438	CANAL POINT	51	45	49	44	45	51	52	50	55	50	68	59	50	66	50	55	65	52	52	56
33440	CLEWISTON	68	65	61	62	64	68	64	66	65	66	81	75	63	79	63	65	79	66	65	76
33441	DEERFIELD BEACH	74	74	90	75	72	80	78	76	79	79	99	87	79	96	77	78	97	78	75	84
33442	DEERFIELD BEACH	78	80	88	79	82	90	77	82	78	80	97	88	79	90	80	78	93	81	85	89
33444	DELRAY BEACH	77	75	94	75	74	82	81	78	83	81	104	90	81	103	80	84	102	81	79	88
33445	DELRAY BEACH	102	104	113	101	106	120	99	106	101	103	127	111	102	116	104	104	121	105	114	117
33446	DELRAY BEACH	108	104	106	97	109	130	96	110	102	103	127	105	98	107	105	109	119	106	129	122
33455	HOBE SOUND	110	105	102	99	110	129	99	111	105	104	129	112	100	114	106	111	121	108	127	125
33458	JUPITER	116	129	143	133	125	128	124	121	118	126	149	141	128	150	123	114	147	121	110	133
33460	LAKE WORTH	57	57	73	57	56	61	62	59	64	62	80	69	62	82	61	64	79	62	59	65
33461	LAKE WORTH	64	64	72	62	63	71	66	66	67	66	84	73	66	82	66	68	82	67	68	72
33462	LAKE WORTH	102	102	109	101	103	112	103	105	103	104	129	118	103	125	104	103	125	105	106	116
33463	LAKE WORTH	80	81	82	80	81	87	79	81	78	81	98	90	79	93	79	77	94	80	80	89
33467	LAKE WORTH	118	128	134	124	129	141	117	124	116	122	145	132	122	137	123	118	140	121	128	136
33469	JUPITER	148	151	160	147	155	176	142	152	144	147	181	159	146	164	151	150	173	149	165	170
33470	LOXAHATCHEE	127	147	144	152	140	136	132	131	121	136	154	153	137	156	130	114	152	127	112	143
33471	MOORE HAVEN	78	62	43	57	67	75	59	69	66	60	79	80	54	75	61	69	74	68	79	90
33476	PAHOKEE	51	47	55	45	45	52	52	50	55	52	69	57	52	68	51	57	67	52	53	57
33477	JUPITER	195	183	178	173	194	230	170	194	180	182	224	188	172	186	185	193	209	188	227	219
33478	JUPITER	132	155	157	160	149	147	138	136	127	142	161	158	146	163	138	121	160	132	120	150
33480	PALM BEACH	325	342	380	329	352	402	309	336	313	326	392	345	327	355	334	329	377	325	367	378
33483	DELRAY BEACH	173	171	182	166	177	203	162	175	167	170	209	181	166	187	172	174	199	173	193	197
33484	DELRAY BEACH	76	74	78	68	77	92	69	78	73	74	91	75	70	78	75	78	85	76	90	85
33486	BOCA RATON	125	144	172	146	141	148	139	136	132	139	167	157	145	170	141	130	166	135	126	148
33487	BOCA RATON	167	170	175	163	175	200	156	171	160	165	200	174	162	178	167	167	191	166	189	191
33493	SOUTH BAY	53	43	45	39	43	52	49	50	55	49	67	54	47	60	47	59	64	52	58	58
33496	BOCA RATON	221	269	339	262	265	288	241	246	232	249	292	269	263	296	255	236	291	238	239	267
33498	BOCA RATON	171	203	225	203	202	212	185	186	175	187	220	209	197	221	192	174	218	181	178	204
33510	BRANDON	91	98	106	101	96	98	96	94	92	97	115	111	98	116	95	88	114	94	86	104
33511	BRANDON	99	107	111	112	103	103	102	100	96	105	122	118	104	121	100	90	120	100	88	110
33513	BUSHNELL	73	56	39	49	61	72	53	64	61	55	73	71	49	67	56	66	67	63	78	83
33514	CENTER HILL	79	53	24	46	60	69	51	64	62	52	73	77	44	69	52	67	66	64	79	91
33523	DADE CITY	75	65	54	62	67	73	64	70	68	66	84	79	61	79	64	69	80	70	74	83
33525	DADE CITY	77	67	58	65	71	80	67	74	72	68	87	82	64	82	68	74	82	73	82	87
33527	DOVER	90	84	70	81	83	88	81	86	82	83	102	98	78	98	80	81	99	86	85	99
33534	GIBSONTON	79	70	53	67	71	75	67	73	69	69	84	84	63	80	66	68	81	72	73	87
33538	LAKE PANASOFFKEE	61	57	58	52	60	73	53	62	57	57	71	59	53	60	58	61	66	59	73	68
33540	ZEPHYRHILLS	69	63	56	59	66	75	60	67	63	62	78	71	58	70	62	65	73	66	74	78
33541	ZEPHYRHILLS	60	58	61	53	61	74	54	62	58	58	72	58	55	60	59	62	67	60	73	67
33542	ZEPHYRHILLS	56	54	56	50	56	67	51	58	55	54	68	56	52	60	55	58	64	56	67	63
33543	ZEPHYRHILLS	116	123	113	126	119	118	113	114	106	117	134	133	113	132	110	101	131	112	102	128
33544	ZEPHYRHILLS	100	109	102	110	106	105	99	101	94	102	118	117	101	118	98	90	116	98	91	113
33547	LITHIA	98	102	92	101	101	103	93	97	91	95	113	113	94	114	93	88	110	95	92	112
33548	LUTZ	149	186	200	188	181	182	165	163	152	166	192	189	178	202	169	148	193	157	147	180
	FLORIDA	89	87	95	86	87	96	87	89	89	89	111	100	87	107	88	90	108	90	91	101
	UNITED STATES	100	100	100	100	100	100	100	100	100	100	100	100	100	100	100	100	100	100	100	100

POPULATION CHANGE

#	POST OFFICE NAME	COUNTY FIPS CODE	POPULATION			2000-2004 ANNUAL RATE		HOUSEHOLDS					FAMILIES		
			2000	2004	2009	% Rate	State Centile	2000	2004	2009	% Annual Rate 2000-2004	2004 Average HH Size	2000	2004	% Annual Rate 2000-2004
33549	LUTZ	057	17033	18367	20504	1.8	51	6705	7314	8226	2.1	2.49	4574	4911	1.7
33556	ODESSA	057	18646	22599	26654	4.6	89	6603	8112	9648	5.0	2.79	5456	6643	4.7
33558	LUTZ	057	14263	17303	20469	4.7	89	5974	7161	8435	4.4	2.41	3880	4618	4.2
33559	LUTZ	057	8668	10115	11817	3.7	82	3270	3809	4452	3.7	2.65	2344	2736	3.7
33563	PLANT CITY	057	22497	23355	25413	0.9	24	8230	8561	9344	0.9	2.71	5717	5872	0.6
33565	PLANT CITY	057	15499	17055	19153	2.3	61	5696	6329	7153	2.5	2.67	4402	4840	2.3
33566	PLANT CITY	057	18009	20467	23391	3.1	74	6035	6965	8038	3.4	2.90	4794	5490	3.2
33567	PLANT CITY	057	8544	9458	10609	2.4	65	2735	3029	3404	2.4	3.07	2187	2401	2.2
33569	RIVERVIEW	057	34765	43597	52190	5.5	92	12847	16143	19384	5.5	2.67	9637	12005	5.3
33570	RUSKIN	057	12937	14839	17228	3.3	77	4951	5560	6399	2.8	2.65	3468	3868	2.6
33572	APOLLO BEACH	057	7551	8716	9989	3.4	79	3147	3690	4268	3.8	2.36	2372	2753	3.6
33573	SUN CITY CENTER	057	16377	19088	22016	3.7	81	9153	10912	12787	4.2	1.64	5442	6364	3.8
33576	SAN ANTONIO	101	2636	3173	3767	4.5	87	884	1107	1348	5.4	2.69	656	810	5.1
33584	SEFFNER	057	20282	21828	24264	1.7	50	7371	8003	8945	2.0	2.72	5538	5951	1.7
33585	SUMTERVILLE	119	778	889	1106	3.2	75	285	334	431	3.8	2.52	196	227	3.5
33592	THONOTOSASSA	057	9786	10549	11719	1.8	50	3629	3930	4387	1.9	2.65	2555	2734	1.6
33594	VALRICO	057	45427	54437	63678	4.4	87	15784	18986	22278	4.4	2.87	13033	15589	4.3
33597	WEBSTER	119	6802	8216	10550	4.5	88	2560	3119	4061	4.8	2.63	1879	2261	4.5
33598	WIMAUMA	057	8430	10173	11896	4.5	88	2099	2524	2951	4.4	3.96	1798	2147	4.3
33602	TAMPA	057	8809	10518	12357	4.3	86	3562	4469	5417	5.5	2.15	1769	2153	4.7
33603	TAMPA	057	20526	21063	22917	0.6	18	8100	8335	9097	0.7	2.51	4804	4853	0.2
33604	TAMPA	057	35928	36748	39930	0.5	16	14413	14792	16118	0.6	2.48	8607	8673	0.2
33605	TAMPA	057	17066	17445	19023	0.5	15	6151	6332	6952	0.7	2.67	3775	3801	0.2
33606	TAMPA	057	14717	15397	16815	1.1	30	7140	7586	8397	1.4	1.86	2837	2952	0.9
33607	TAMPA	057	22864	23741	26003	0.9	25	9390	9857	10870	1.2	2.41	5592	5744	0.6
33609	TAMPA	057	16697	17605	19410	1.3	35	7856	8339	9242	1.4	2.10	3954	4094	0.8
33610	TAMPA	057	32676	33614	36973	0.7	19	11871	12321	13643	0.9	2.68	8090	8271	0.5
33611	TAMPA	057	29984	31595	34750	1.2	35	14497	15375	16985	1.4	2.05	7310	7597	0.9
33612	TAMPA	057	45460	48802	54396	1.7	47	17596	19084	21505	1.9	2.37	10129	10676	1.3
33613	TAMPA	057	29170	30787	33921	1.3	36	13163	14108	15719	1.6	2.11	6097	6289	0.7
33614	TAMPA	057	44725	48907	54867	2.1	58	18398	20059	22530	2.1	2.40	10712	11568	1.8
33615	TAMPA	057	40963	43493	48099	1.4	40	16640	17802	19784	1.6	2.43	10380	10991	1.4
33616	TAMPA	057	12019	12501	13598	0.9	26	4927	5173	5658	1.2	2.42	3057	3153	0.7
33617	TAMPA	057	42725	45476	50121	1.5	42	17683	18854	20831	1.5	2.38	10391	10933	1.2
33618	TAMPA	057	20010	21708	24354	1.9	54	8259	8979	10094	2.0	2.40	5482	5903	1.8
33619	TAMPA	057	29835	31179	34088	1.0	29	9286	9860	10929	1.4	2.89	6779	7108	1.1
33621	TAMPA	057	2692	2603	2770	-0.8	1	608	582	626	-1.0	3.76	599	573	-1.0
33624	TAMPA	057	43103	45029	49281	1.0	28	17101	18021	19828	1.2	2.49	11764	12219	0.9
33625	TAMPA	057	18381	21153	24415	3.4	78	6465	7546	8790	3.7	2.77	4988	5745	3.4
33626	TAMPA	057	11116	15691	19792	8.5	98	4177	5872	7396	8.3	2.67	3208	4437	7.9
33629	TAMPA	057	22366	23021	25067	0.7	19	10339	10715	11726	0.8	2.14	5890	6000	0.4
33634	TAMPA	057	19798	22678	26300	3.3	76	7472	8533	9891	3.2	2.65	5174	5900	3.1
33635	TAMPA	057	12282	15342	18394	5.4	92	4986	6317	7653	5.7	2.43	3272	3990	4.8
33637	TAMPA	057	12531	13122	14377	1.1	30	5296	5651	6254	1.5	2.32	3065	3172	0.8
33647	TAMPA	057	26181	36470	46644	8.1	98	10249	14116	17994	7.8	2.58	6832	9399	7.8
33701	SAINT PETERSBURG	103	15229	14877	14968	-0.6	1	8086	7904	8002	-0.5	1.67	2355	2254	-1.0
33702	SAINT PETERSBURG	103	29057	29300	29914	0.2	8	13612	13789	14158	0.3	2.10	7693	7710	0.1
33703	SAINT PETERSBURG	103	25345	25832	26386	0.5	13	11226	11507	11819	0.6	2.24	6965	7048	0.3
33704	SAINT PETERSBURG	103	16639	16634	16847	0.0	4	7753	7801	7953	0.2	2.09	4165	4139	-0.2
33705	SAINT PETERSBURG	103	27958	27969	28442	0.0	5	11677	11760	12047	0.2	2.31	6625	6557	-0.2
33706	SAINT PETERSBURG	103	17376	17572	17893	0.3	9	9420	9640	9905	0.5	1.79	4785	4809	0.1
33707	SAINT PETERSBURG	103	26482	27143	27950	0.6	17	13470	14016	14593	0.9	1.89	6784	6888	0.4
33708	SAINT PETERSBURG	103	16640	17474	18114	1.2	32	8991	9553	9990	1.4	1.82	4571	4789	1.1
33709	SAINT PETERSBURG	103	26233	26172	26463	-0.1	4	12253	12319	12544	0.1	2.07	6857	6799	-0.2
33710	SAINT PETERSBURG	103	33273	33044	33419	-0.2	3	14564	14522	14765	-0.1	2.24	8985	8865	-0.3
33711	SAINT PETERSBURG	103	19867	19760	20034	-0.1	3	7383	7439	7623	0.2	2.47	4830	4809	-0.1
33712	SAINT PETERSBURG	103	26378	26795	27382	0.4	11	10615	10881	11204	0.6	2.42	6652	6728	0.3
33713	SAINT PETERSBURG	103	31157	31330	31794	0.1	6	13266	13352	13597	0.2	2.32	7730	7686	-0.1
33714	SAINT PETERSBURG	103	18695	18824	19131	0.2	7	8528	8617	8802	0.2	2.15	4545	4534	-0.1
33715	SAINT PETERSBURG	103	7403	7719	7956	1.0	27	3890	4108	4273	1.3	1.88	2419	2526	1.0
33716	SAINT PETERSBURG	103	12007	12625	13253	1.2	33	6793	7249	7693	1.5	1.69	2508	2653	1.3
33755	CLEARWATER	103	25734	26152	26711	0.4	11	10116	10306	10581	0.4	2.39	6055	6100	0.2
33756	CLEARWATER	103	28966	30258	31477	1.0	28	13014	13636	14263	1.1	2.14	7170	7363	0.6
33759	CLEARWATER	103	20454	20626	20963	0.2	8	8755	8910	9129	0.4	2.20	4880	4890	0.1
33760	CLEARWATER	103	17046	16879	17015	-0.2	3	6107	6087	6193	-0.1	2.24	3575	3521	-0.4
33761	CLEARWATER	103	17540	18113	18755	0.8	21	8214	8668	9091	1.3	2.08	5137	5350	1.0
33762	CLEARWATER	103	5667	6518	7073	3.4	78	2998	3483	3809	3.6	1.85	1379	1556	2.9
33763	CLEARWATER	103	19636	19750	20198	0.1	6	10301	10395	10704	0.2	1.88	5579	5616	0.2
33764	CLEARWATER	103	26718	27227	28275	0.5	13	12394	12724	13314	0.6	2.10	7252	7372	0.4
33765	CLEARWATER	103	11864	12044	12301	0.4	10	5362	5463	5606	0.4	2.17	2972	2988	0.1
33767	CLEARWATER BEACH	103	8750	9115	9397	1.0	27	4841	5101	5307	1.2	1.79	2680	2803	1.1
33770	LARGO	103	24576	25388	26237	0.8	21	11938	12368	12843	0.8	2.01	6426	6576	0.5
33771	LARGO	103	24681	24975	25616	0.3	9	12201	12508	12952	0.6	1.94	6610	6656	0.2
33772	SEMINOLE	103	23759	23757	24070	0.0	5	11088	11187	11424	0.2	2.09	6622	6617	0.0
33773	LARGO	103	18932	19436	19933	0.6	18	8451	8771	9073	0.9	2.17	5250	5393	0.6
33774	LARGO	103	19022	19744	20412	0.9	24	8604	8987	9356	1.0	2.17	5307	5532	1.0
33776	SEMINOLE	103	12913	13000	13206	0.2	7	5122	5222	5353	0.5	2.48	3801	3834	0.2
33777	SEMINOLE	103	17195	17611	18054	0.6	16	6867	7136	7395	0.9	2.43	4825	4967	0.7
33778	LARGO	103	13236	13104	13209	-0.2	2	5638	5654	5751	0.1	2.29	3686	3665	-0.1
33781	PINELLAS PARK	103	24619	24637	25062	0.0	5	10025	10120	10374	0.2	2.41	6329	6317	0.0
33782	PINELLAS PARK	103	19630	19876	20320	0.3	9	8345	8538	8801	0.5	2.26	5331	5385	0.2
33785	INDIAN ROCKS BEACH	103	6745	6981	7174	0.8	22	3658	3831	3972	1.1	1.82	1865	1925	0.8
33786	BELLEAIR BEACH	103	1751	1932	2048	2.3	62	825	923	988	2.7	2.09	522	577	2.4
33801	LAKELAND	105	31120	32668	35337	1.2	32	13164	13843	15039	1.2	2.30	7759	8094	1.0
33803	LAKELAND	105	26088	27389	29580	1.2	32	11456	12217	13356	1.5	2.14	7034	7396	1.2
33805	LAKELAND	105	19745	20502	22080	0.9	25	7429	7786	8457	1.1	2.57	5006	5194	0.9
33809	LAKELAND	105	26167	28605	31335	2.1	58	10072	11149	12330	2.4	2.50	7346	8030	2.1
33810	LAKELAND	105	30829	33699	36938	2.1	58	11832	13058	14420	2.4	2.56	9112	9973	2.2
33811	LAKELAND	105	16135	17577	19260	2.0	56	6202	6812	7510	2.2	2.58	4484	4863	1.9
33813	LAKELAND	105	35676	38472	42113	1.8	51	12866	13928	15308	1.9	2.75	10176	10963	1.8
33815	LAKELAND	105	13980	14570	15766	1.0	27	5633	5855	6350	0.9	2.46	3582	3665	0.5
33823	AUBURNDALE	105	26692	28604	31123	1.6	46	10048	10847	11876	1.8	2.62	7492	8030	1.7
33825	AVON PARK	055	21649	22430	23739	0.8	23	8689	9007	9540	0.9	2.46	6195	6377	0.7
33827	BABSON PARK	105	2434	2497	2657	0.6	18	875	901	966	0.7	2.65	623	636	0.5
33830	BARTOW	105	25451	25726	27299	0.3	9	9038	9191	9841	0.4	2.62	6477	6528	0.2
	FLORIDA					2.1					2.2	2.45			2.0
	UNITED STATES					1.2					1.3	2.58			1.1

ZIP CODE #	POST OFFICE NAME	RACE (%) White 2000	White 2004	Black 2000	Black 2004	Asian/Pacific 2000	Asian/Pacific 2004	% Hispanic Origin 2000	% Hispanic Origin 2004	2004 AGE DISTRIBUTION (%) 0-4	5-9	10-14	15-19	20-24	25-44	45-64	65-84	85+	18+	MEDIAN AGE 2004	% 2004 Males	% 2004 Females
33549	LUTZ	88.2	86.0	5.4	6.4	1.7	1.9	10.2	12.9	6.6	6.7	6.9	6.2	6.2	30.8	26.8	8.8	0.9	75.9	37.4	50.1	49.9
33556	ODESSA	91.3	89.7	3.7	4.5	2.1	2.5	8.5	11.0	6.9	7.7	7.6	6.3	4.0	29.8	28.9	8.3	0.6	73.9	39.2	50.0	50.0
33558	LUTZ	88.3	86.4	3.8	4.5	3.9	4.4	11.6	14.6	6.2	6.4	7.0	6.4	6.2	31.5	27.4	8.1	1.0	76.6	37.5	49.4	50.6
33559	LUTZ	88.2	86.5	5.6	6.3	2.4	2.6	11.4	14.4	7.6	7.5	7.6	7.0	6.7	31.9	23.9	7.3	0.6	73.0	34.6	48.4	51.6
33563	PLANT CITY	66.1	63.1	19.6	20.3	0.4	0.5	21.6	25.6	8.6	7.9	7.9	7.4	7.5	26.8	20.5	11.6	1.8	71.1	32.9	48.5	51.5
33565	PLANT CITY	92.3	90.3	1.4	1.9	0.5	0.6	8.7	11.2	6.9	7.0	7.0	6.2	5.8	26.1	24.5	15.2	1.3	75.2	39.2	49.3	50.7
33566	PLANT CITY	84.2	81.4	4.5	5.4	1.3	1.5	16.6	20.2	7.6	7.5	7.6	7.2	6.7	28.9	23.5	9.9	1.1	72.8	35.1	49.5	50.5
33567	PLANT CITY	73.3	68.4	12.2	14.2	0.3	0.3	22.5	27.5	8.2	7.7	8.2	7.6	8.1	28.6	22.3	8.5	0.9	71.3	32.1	50.8	49.2
33569	RIVERVIEW	85.4	81.8	7.5	9.7	1.4	1.6	10.8	14.1	7.5	7.6	7.6	7.4	6.0	30.0	23.8	9.3	0.8	73.0	35.5	49.8	50.2
33570	RUSKIN	84.2	81.1	1.0	1.2	0.6	0.6	32.2	39.5	7.2	6.7	6.9	6.1	6.1	23.9	22.9	18.2	1.9	75.5	39.2	50.8	49.3
33572	APOLLO BEACH	93.3	91.9	0.8	1.1	1.4	1.7	8.3	10.4	3.9	4.5	5.2	4.7	4.1	21.3	35.5	19.1	1.9	83.6	48.7	49.6	50.4
33573	SUN CITY CENTER	98.9	98.7	0.1	0.2	0.5	0.6	1.5	1.9	0.1	0.1	0.1	0.2	0.2	0.9	12.9	69.7	15.8	99.6	76.2	42.3	57.7
33576	SAN ANTONIO	93.9	92.9	1.9	2.1	0.9	1.0	7.6	9.5	5.9	6.1	6.7	9.1	8.6	24.9	25.9	11.5	1.3	77.2	38.0	49.7	50.3
33584	SEFFNER	86.4	83.5	7.3	8.9	1.0	1.2	9.0	11.7	7.1	7.0	7.8	7.2	6.8	29.4	25.0	8.9	0.9	73.6	35.8	49.7	50.3
33585	SUMTERVILLE	88.3	85.8	7.6	9.3	0.9	1.1	5.7	7.2	5.6	5.9	6.6	6.3	5.6	26.6	25.9	16.0	1.6	78.1	40.4	50.7	49.3
33592	THONOTOSASSA	83.3	80.1	11.5	13.8	0.6	0.7	6.4	8.2	6.9	6.8	7.8	7.1	6.6	27.9	25.3	10.5	1.1	74.2	36.7	50.5	49.5
33594	VALRICO	88.0	85.6	5.9	7.1	2.2	2.6	9.5	12.2	6.6	7.3	8.3	7.5	5.6	27.7	27.5	8.8	0.8	73.0	37.9	48.9	51.1
33597	WEBSTER	82.6	79.5	12.5	14.8	0.3	0.3	5.9	7.2	7.0	7.0	7.2	6.6	6.0	24.1	24.5	16.3	1.4	74.4	39.3	49.6	50.4
33598	WIMAUMA	61.2	58.0	4.1	4.3	0.7	0.7	58.0	63.3	11.0	10.0	10.1	8.3	8.3	28.7	17.3	6.0	0.5	63.9	26.5	52.3	47.7
33602	TAMPA	45.3	46.4	47.1	45.7	1.1	1.4	16.8	17.5	7.1	6.2	6.8	6.5	7.0	30.2	23.3	11.0	1.8	76.3	35.9	49.2	50.8
33603	TAMPA	60.9	58.1	28.2	29.8	0.7	0.7	28.7	33.2	7.3	7.2	7.6	7.1	7.2	30.2	21.8	9.8	1.8	73.7	34.6	48.8	51.2
33604	TAMPA	64.4	61.2	24.8	26.7	1.5	1.6	21.0	25.1	7.4	7.3	8.0	7.3	7.1	29.6	23.2	8.9	1.3	72.8	34.4	48.8	51.2
33605	TAMPA	27.6	27.0	62.3	62.4	0.2	0.2	26.3	28.5	7.2	7.3	8.2	7.9	6.8	25.3	22.9	12.5	2.0	72.3	35.9	49.8	50.2
33606	TAMPA	83.8	82.4	11.3	11.9	1.8	2.1	8.0	10.2	4.1	4.0	4.9	8.3	10.1	34.2	23.7	8.9	1.8	84.1	35.1	50.1	49.9
33607	TAMPA	50.3	49.6	38.4	38.6	1.4	1.4	40.9	43.8	6.8	6.6	7.0	6.1	6.5	27.1	21.5	15.8	2.8	76.0	37.3	47.7	52.3
33609	TAMPA	84.6	82.6	7.1	8.1	2.0	2.2	21.3	25.2	5.0	5.1	5.8	5.5	6.0	29.6	26.2	14.2	2.6	80.8	41.0	49.0	51.0
33610	TAMPA	37.5	35.9	56.7	57.9	0.6	0.7	9.1	10.6	7.8	7.7	8.4	7.6	7.1	25.4	23.5	11.2	1.4	71.4	34.9	47.1	52.9
33611	TAMPA	85.1	82.5	6.2	7.4	3.5	4.1	10.5	13.3	5.3	5.1	5.4	5.1	5.7	32.6	25.2	13.5	2.1	81.2	39.9	48.7	51.3
33612	TAMPA	60.2	56.1	29.1	32.0	2.3	2.4	17.2	20.3	7.7	6.7	7.1	9.6	10.3	28.1	19.4	9.3	1.8	74.7	30.6	47.8	52.2
33613	TAMPA	68.6	65.5	18.8	20.4	3.3	3.8	16.8	19.8	6.3	5.3	5.0	6.8	16.7	28.9	18.4	9.3	3.3	80.3	30.0	49.2	50.8
33614	TAMPA	74.4	72.4	9.1	9.8	3.6	3.7	47.0	53.1	6.6	6.0	6.3	6.7	8.8	33.3	21.0	10.0	1.3	77.2	33.9	49.5	50.5
33615	TAMPA	77.8	74.8	8.2	9.3	3.0	3.3	28.6	34.2	6.3	6.0	6.5	6.3	7.3	32.7	23.7	10.2	1.1	77.6	36.1	48.9	51.1
33616	TAMPA	67.1	62.7	17.8	20.6	6.4	7.0	13.6	16.6	6.8	6.3	7.3	7.5	8.6	31.9	22.4	8.6	0.6	75.0	33.5	50.3	49.7
33617	TAMPA	62.4	58.4	27.3	30.1	2.9	3.2	14.0	16.8	6.7	6.4	7.0	7.9	10.9	29.9	21.6	8.7	1.0	75.9	31.9	48.0	52.0
33618	TAMPA	87.3	84.9	4.5	5.5	3.1	3.4	15.3	19.7	5.8	5.8	6.5	6.7	6.7	28.3	28.6	10.5	1.1	77.9	39.0	48.0	52.0
33619	TAMPA	52.1	48.3	38.6	41.4	0.8	0.8	18.0	20.8	7.2	7.1	8.5	8.6	8.3	29.2	22.1	8.3	0.7	72.0	32.5	51.4	48.6
33621	TAMPA	61.9	56.6	24.5	28.2	3.3	3.5	12.0	14.7	13.5	12.7	9.3	8.1	17.8	35.1	3.2	0.2	0.0	60.5	21.8	53.3	46.7
33624	TAMPA	83.9	81.2	6.3	7.5	3.8	4.3	17.7	22.0	6.1	6.3	7.1	6.7	6.6	30.8	27.1	8.3	0.9	76.3	37.0	47.8	52.2
33625	TAMPA	81.1	78.9	7.5	8.3	3.4	3.7	21.7	26.0	7.3	7.3	7.4	6.9	6.2	32.3	24.7	6.9	1.0	73.6	35.5	48.6	51.4
33626	TAMPA	86.9	84.3	5.1	6.1	4.1	4.8	11.9	15.2	10.7	10.1	6.7	4.1	3.4	39.0	20.7	4.9	0.5	70.0	35.0	48.6	51.4
33629	TAMPA	95.5	94.6	1.2	1.4	1.3	1.5	8.4	11.0	6.2	6.1	5.7	5.0	4.1	29.8	26.4	13.9	2.8	78.8	41.3	47.7	52.3
33634	TAMPA	77.0	74.2	8.3	9.1	3.4	3.6	37.2	44.6	6.4	6.4	7.4	6.9	7.6	31.7	23.6	9.5	0.7	75.7	35.2	48.3	51.7
33635	TAMPA	83.5	80.9	5.8	7.0	4.5	4.9	16.3	20.1	7.2	7.1	6.8	5.2	5.3	35.2	23.1	9.3	0.8	75.5	36.4	49.2	50.9
33637	TAMPA	74.8	71.0	16.4	18.9	2.5	2.9	12.1	15.0	7.3	6.7	6.7	6.3	10.2	34.6	20.3	7.2	0.8	75.7	31.2	48.4	51.7
33647	TAMPA	82.7	79.2	6.0	7.4	6.9	8.1	9.3	12.0	8.3	8.0	7.7	6.2	6.4	37.3	21.2	4.6	0.3	72.2	32.3	49.2	50.8
33701	SAINT PETERSBURG	72.9	69.6	21.7	24.3	1.9	2.3	3.8	4.5	4.5	3.6	3.9	4.1	6.4	27.8	26.5	16.7	6.5	85.9	44.9	50.7	49.3
33702	SAINT PETERSBURG	89.4	87.4	2.8	3.5	3.3	4.0	5.2	6.4	4.7	4.7	5.3	5.3	5.4	26.4	27.5	17.6	3.2	82.0	44.0	48.3	51.7
33703	SAINT PETERSBURG	93.8	92.5	1.1	1.5	2.3	2.8	3.9	5.0	5.4	5.7	6.1	5.4	4.4	26.5	27.3	16.1	3.0	79.3	43.1	47.8	52.2
33704	SAINT PETERSBURG	93.5	92.2	1.9	2.5	1.7	2.1	3.9	5.0	5.5	5.5	5.7	5.3	5.0	29.2	29.0	11.7	3.0	79.8	41.8	47.9	52.1
33705	SAINT PETERSBURG	39.3	35.2	55.7	59.6	1.3	1.5	3.2	3.6	6.3	6.6	7.8	6.9	6.0	24.4	24.4	13.8	3.8	75.0	39.6	46.1	53.9
33706	SAINT PETERSBURG	97.7	97.2	0.5	0.6	0.6	0.7	2.4	3.1	2.3	2.5	2.7	2.3	2.3	19.0	39.0	26.2	3.7	91.1	55.1	49.7	50.3
33707	SAINT PETERSBURG	91.4	89.9	5.6	6.7	0.8	1.0	2.8	3.5	3.2	3.4	3.9	3.9	3.6	19.2	28.6	27.6	6.6	87.0	53.7	45.8	54.2
33708	SAINT PETERSBURG	97.3	96.8	0.3	0.5	0.7	0.9	2.6	3.3	2.4	2.5	2.7	2.8	2.8	18.5	35.4	28.5	4.3	90.7	55.6	49.1	50.9
33709	SAINT PETERSBURG	90.7	88.8	2.7	3.4	2.8	3.3	4.5	5.6	5.0	5.0	5.1	4.6	4.3	22.0	25.8	23.5	4.8	82.0	48.0	47.2	52.8
33710	SAINT PETERSBURG	92.4	90.8	2.0	2.5	2.7	3.2	4.6	5.8	5.3	5.5	6.0	5.5	5.3	26.4	26.8	15.9	3.4	79.9	42.7	47.4	52.6
33711	SAINT PETERSBURG	37.0	34.5	59.4	61.8	0.9	1.0	2.5	2.8	6.1	7.1	7.8	9.4	8.5	21.8	24.3	12.4	2.6	74.6	35.9	45.9	54.1
33712	SAINT PETERSBURG	26.1	23.6	69.6	72.0	0.9	0.9	2.9	3.2	7.0	6.7	7.5	7.3	8.4	25.0	23.9	12.5	1.9	74.6	36.3	45.9	54.1
33713	SAINT PETERSBURG	78.4	74.6	9.9	11.9	7.0	8.3	6.0	7.3	6.4	6.1	6.3	6.4	6.5	30.2	25.2	10.9	2.2	77.4	38.4	49.8	50.2
33714	SAINT PETERSBURG	88.1	85.8	2.9	3.7	5.1	6.1	4.4	5.5	5.3	5.2	5.9	5.6	5.7	26.3	26.6	16.6	2.9	80.2	42.5	49.7	50.3
33715	SAINT PETERSBURG	96.6	95.8	1.2	1.6	1.1	1.3	2.9	3.7	2.1	2.1	2.4	2.2	1.8	15.9	38.0	32.3	3.2	92.1	58.1	48.6	51.4
33716	SAINT PETERSBURG	86.5	84.0	5.0	6.3	3.9	4.5	7.4	8.9	4.2	3.3	3.2	3.3	9.5	47.5	19.8	7.2	2.1	87.8	33.9	50.2	49.8
33755	CLEARWATER	66.9	63.5	25.1	27.4	1.0	1.2	11.3	13.3	6.4	6.0	6.7	6.9	7.5	29.8	24.4	10.4	1.8	76.7	36.8	49.5	50.5
33756	CLEARWATER	88.5	86.4	6.3	7.6	1.0	1.1	8.3	10.3	5.4	5.3	5.6	4.9	5.1	24.6	25.3	18.5	5.2	80.7	44.4	47.6	52.4
33759	CLEARWATER	83.2	80.4	9.3	11.1	2.7	3.2	9.3	10.9	6.0	5.8	6.2	6.4	8.2	26.2	21.4	14.0	5.9	78.8	38.6	47.4	52.6
33760	CLEARWATER	76.8	72.7	15.4	18.3	3.3	3.8	7.6	9.1	5.9	5.2	5.1	6.6	8.4	36.3	21.8	9.4	1.3	80.3	35.7	55.1	44.9
33761	CLEARWATER	96.1	95.2	0.8	1.0	1.6	2.0	4.0	5.1	3.7	4.1	4.9	4.8	4.1	20.3	30.4	23.7	3.9	84.2	50.7	45.0	55.0
33762	CLEARWATER	90.5	88.3	3.4	4.3	3.2	3.9	4.3	5.5	3.3	2.9	2.6	2.6	4.2	35.1	23.8	21.6	3.9	89.7	44.4	47.9	52.1
33763	CLEARWATER	93.9	92.7	1.8	2.3	1.6	1.9	6.6	7.9	3.3	3.1	3.4	3.4	4.1	18.7	22.8	33.9	7.3	88.2	57.7	44.9	55.2
33764	CLEARWATER	92.7	90.6	2.8	3.9	1.7	2.1	5.0	6.5	4.5	4.6	5.3	4.8	4.9	23.5	27.2	21.6	3.6	82.6	46.6	48.2	51.8
33765	CLEARWATER	86.8	84.2	5.4	6.7	2.8	3.3	9.7	11.9	5.0	5.0	5.4	5.5	7.1	29.8	25.1	14.4	2.8	81.4	40.0	48.1	52.0
33767	CLEARWATER BEACH	97.8	97.3	0.3	0.3	0.8	1.0	2.6	3.3	1.9	2.1	2.0	2.0	2.2	15.1	38.6	31.9	4.2	92.8	58.9	49.7	50.3
33770	LARGO	93.3	91.7	2.6	3.4	1.4	1.7	3.7	4.7	4.3	4.3	4.9	4.5	5.0	23.3	26.1	22.0	5.8	83.8	47.6	47.3	52.7
33771	LARGO	92.0	90.2	2.6	3.3	2.3	2.8	4.7	5.9	4.4	4.2	4.1	3.7	4.4	23.6	24.7	25.3	5.5	85.1	49.6	46.6	53.4
33772	SEMINOLE	96.2	95.4	0.6	0.7	1.1	1.4	2.9	3.7	4.0	4.4	5.3	5.3	4.4	21.3	27.6	21.0	6.7	82.8	48.3	46.1	53.9
33773	LARGO	92.2	90.6	2.0	2.5	3.2	3.8	3.9	4.8	4.9	5.0	5.5	5.4	4.9	25.2	26.8	18.8	3.5	81.1	44.4	47.9	52.1
33774	LARGO	91.4	89.6	5.6	6.8	1.2	1.5	2.9	3.6	4.3	4.5	5.7	5.6	4.8	20.8	28.1	21.9	4.3	81.9	47.9	46.6	53.4
33776	SEMINOLE	96.9	96.2	0.4	0.5	1.3	1.7	2.3	3.0	3.8	4.8	6.7	6.5	4.9	19.0	32.2	19.0	3.2	80.2	47.5	47.0	53.0
33777	SEMINOLE	93.4	92.0	1.3	1.8	2.9	3.5	3.8	4.8	5.1	5.6	6.9	6.1	5.2	23.4	28.7	16.2	2.9	78.6	43.5	47.1	52.9
33778	LARGO	83.4	82.1	13.0	13.7	1.2	1.4	3.5	4.4	5.0	5.2	6.1	5.5	4.7	23.8	27.6	19.1	3.1	80.2	44.8	47.3	52.7
33781	PINELLAS PARK	89.0	86.8	2.3	2.9	3.9	4.7	7.2	8.8	6.4	6.0	6.8	6.6	6.7	29.1	24.6	11.7	2.0	76.5	38.1	49.0	51.0
33782	PINELLAS PARK	90.0	88.0	1.3	1.7	4.6	5.5	4.7	6.0	4.8	4.8	5.5	5.7	5.0	24.4	25.6	20.4	3.9	81.2	44.9	46.9	53.1
33785	INDIAN ROCKS BEACH	97.5	97.0	0.3	0.4	0.6	0.7	3.1	4.0	2.3	2.5	2.2	2.5	3.1	23.7	39.8	21.9	2.1	91.6	52.4	50.0	50.0
33786	BELLEAIR BEACH	97.5	97.0	0.1	0.2	1.2	1.6	2.7	3.4	1.8	2.0	1.6	1.5	2.1	12.7	42.3	33.2	2.7	93.8	59.8	49.1	50.9
33801	LAKELAND	81.3	78.6	12.5	14.2	1.1	1.3	7.2	8.9	7.1	6.3	6.2	6.2	8.2	28.7	21.8	13.4	2.2	77.2	35.8	48.7	51.3
33803	LAKELAND	89.8	87.8	4.9	5.8	1.5	1.8	7.6	9.7	5.7	5.5	5.6	6.8	7.9	26.1	23.1	16.1	3.2	79.8	39.3	46.9	53.1
33805	LAKELAND	43.7	41.4	50.7	52.4	0.5	0.5	7.5	8.7	8.4	7.8	8.0	7.2	7.1	24.3	21.3	13.4	2.5	71.5	34.8	47.0	53.0
33809	LAKELAND	91.0	89.2	4.3	5.2	1.4	1.7	5.1	6.5	5.8	6.0	6.7	6.6	5.6	25.8	24.7	15.6	3.2	77.3	40.8	47.9	52.1
33810	LAKELAND	89.4	87.4	6.8	8.1	0.7	0.9	4.7	5.9	6.8	6.6	6.7	6.2	5.8	25.5	23.8	17.3	1.4	76.1	39.8	49.0	51.0
33811	LAKELAND	88.4	85.6	6.8	8.5	0.6	0.7	6.6	8.3	7.0	7.0	7.1	6.4	6.4	29.0	25.5	10.5	1.0	74.9	36.9	49.4	50.6
33813	LAKELAND	90.2	88.1	4.6	5.6	2.6	3.2	5.3	6.7	6.1	6.8	8.1	7.3	5.1	25.9	27.5	12.1	1.3	74.3	39.7	48.6	51.4
33815	LAKELAND	65.5	62.4	26.3	27.8	0.5	0.6	10.8	13.3	8.1	7.3	6.6	6.0	6.2	22.3	21.7	19.2	2.7	74.4	39.4	48.4	51.6
33823	AUBURNDALE	85.9	83.5	8.2	9.4	0.6	0.7	7.5	9.1	6.9	6.7	7.1	6.3	6.0	25.7	24.7	15.1	1.5	75.6	39.0	49.2	50.8
33825	AVON PARK	73.5	71.1	16.1	16.8	1.9	2.2	15.8	18.9	6.0	5.5	6.0	6.4	6.3	19.5	23.2	24.0	3.1	78.7	45.3	49.0	51.0
33827	BABSON PARK	89.5	87.1	6.2	7.6	0.7	0.9	5.6	7.1	5.9	5.7	6.1	6.4	7.4	24.3	25.8	16.3	2.2	78.8	40.6	49.1	50.9
33830	BARTOW	69.3	66.4	23.1	24.7	0.7	0.8	11.0	13.2	7.0	6.8	7.2	7.8	7.2	27.4	22.4	12.6	1.6	74.2	35.8	50.2	49.8
	FLORIDA	78.0	76.5	14.6	15.2	1.7	2.0	16.8	19.0	6.0	5.9	6.4	6.4	6.5	26.6	24.5	15.5	2.4	78.1	40.0	48.8	51.2
	UNITED STATES	75.1	73.6	12.3	12.5	3.8	4.2	12.5	14.1	6.9	6.7	7.2	7.0	7.3	28.6	23.8	10.8	1.7	75.1	36.0	49.1	50.9

INCOME

ZIP CODE #	POST OFFICE NAME	2004 Per Capita Income	2004 HH Income Base	2004 HOUSEHOLD INCOME DISTRIBUTION (%) Less than $25,000	$25,000 to $49,999	$50,000 to $99,999	$100,000 to $149,999	$150,000 or More	MEDIAN HOUSEHOLD INCOME 2004	2009	2004 National Centile	2004 State Centile	2004 Home Value Base	2004 HOME VALUE DISTRIBUTION (%) Less than $50,000	$50,000 to $89,999	$90,000 to $174,999	$175,000 to $399,999	$400,000 or More	2004 Median Home Value
33549	LUTZ	26873	7314	19.2	28.6	32.4	13.5	6.4	52569	60328	76	78	5455	5.5	5.5	47.3	38.9	2.8	158875
33556	ODESSA	36704	8112	10.4	17.9	34.9	22.2	14.6	79522	92964	95	96	7620	2.3	6.2	18.0	59.2	14.3	235175
33558	LUTZ	36566	7161	15.7	26.4	31.6	14.4	11.9	60160	69984	84	86	4532	2.4	5.0	22.6	54.3	15.7	227748
33559	LUTZ	26379	3809	13.9	29.7	39.6	12.8	3.9	56056	63864	81	82	3083	3.8	13.5	57.2	24.6	1.0	143027
33563	PLANT CITY	16930	8561	32.5	36.0	25.6	4.2	1.7	35500	40615	29	27	5477	16.6	26.0	47.6	9.2	0.7	97482
33565	PLANT CITY	21206	6329	23.9	30.6	34.3	8.6	2.6	45251	52497	62	60	5483	17.7	21.2	35.4	22.7	3.0	114371
33566	PLANT CITY	24676	6965	19.7	24.0	37.1	11.7	7.5	55417	63724	80	81	5393	6.5	15.1	37.7	37.5	3.2	150174
33567	PLANT CITY	16398	3029	27.4	32.8	31.7	6.3	1.7	41409	48443	51	49	2394	19.0	20.2	38.3	21.6	1.0	109626
33569	RIVERVIEW	23839	16143	18.9	28.5	36.4	11.7	4.6	52291	60732	76	77	12804	12.9	13.3	37.9	33.5	2.4	144065
33570	RUSKIN	15465	5560	34.6	37.7	22.5	3.8	1.4	32634	37927	20	18	4443	29.8	23.9	35.0	10.4	0.8	84011
33572	APOLLO BEACH	35127	3690	17.1	24.4	32.9	16.3	9.2	58068	68122	83	84	3235	4.5	12.7	31.6	41.1	10.0	179092
33573	SUN CITY CENTER	30369	10912	25.4	35.4	30.8	6.0	2.4	41820	47666	52	51	10024	3.7	18.7	51.7	24.5	1.4	128490
33576	SAN ANTONIO	22044	1107	23.3	26.7	33.4	13.4	3.2	49956	55896	72	74	963	10.1	11.1	44.8	31.8	2.3	142763
33584	SEFFNER	21108	8003	21.2	30.6	36.3	9.1	2.8	48473	56371	69	70	6227	12.9	12.4	57.2	16.7	0.9	118887
33585	SUMTERVILLE	18533	334	35.0	31.1	27.0	5.1	1.8	34786	38489	27	25	272	23.9	28.7	26.5	19.1	1.8	85882
33592	THONOTOSASSA	19657	3930	26.6	29.7	33.9	7.8	2.0	44345	51883	60	58	2952	26.5	18.6	35.5	16.8	2.6	100297
33594	VALRICO	29718	18986	11.9	19.6	39.9	19.0	9.6	69192	80860	91	92	17151	5.8	6.9	36.7	46.0	4.6	176305
33597	WEBSTER	14425	3119	40.9	34.0	20.9	3.0	1.3	30126	33470	13	10	2582	28.7	33.3	27.5	9.4	1.1	76326
33598	WIMAUMA	14050	2524	31.9	26.0	29.2	9.0	3.8	42208	47739	54	52	1917	19.6	19.2	36.8	22.6	1.8	109592
33602	TAMPA	34583	4469	39.5	19.4	18.3	6.9	16.0	36005	47125	32	29	1682	3.4	18.7	42.3	22.8	12.8	134673
33603	TAMPA	16955	8335	36.7	32.9	23.9	4.8	1.7	33692	38830	23	21	5109	5.6	30.7	54.8	8.1	0.9	101829
33604	TAMPA	16743	14792	37.6	33.1	24.1	4.1	1.2	33553	38884	23	21	8867	7.5	30.6	56.0	5.2	0.7	99567
33605	TAMPA	12037	6332	54.3	28.4	13.5	2.4	1.4	22381	25782	3	2	3261	23.0	41.0	33.6	1.9	0.5	78464
33606	TAMPA	55208	7586	16.7	26.5	26.6	12.7	17.5	60179	74615	85	86	3412	1.4	5.3	16.5	41.2	35.6	302772
33607	TAMPA	20861	9857	41.8	28.8	21.1	5.2	3.2	30218	35345	13	11	5062	6.2	29.4	58.0	6.0	0.4	101421
33609	TAMPA	38171	8339	23.7	28.7	26.8	10.4	10.5	47888	56322	68	68	4975	1.2	11.2	40.9	26.6	20.1	163208
33610	TAMPA	15199	12321	40.0	34.4	20.3	3.6	1.7	30819	35896	14	12	8206	20.8	31.4	42.9	4.4	0.5	87643
33611	TAMPA	31941	15375	23.9	32.2	28.7	9.0	6.2	44280	51783	59	57	8808	6.1	15.5	50.0	18.8	9.6	128385
33612	TAMPA	17724	19084	40.7	33.4	19.8	4.4	1.8	30075	34362	12	10	8805	7.0	24.2	57.0	10.0	1.8	105869
33613	TAMPA	20487	14108	40.2	34.3	17.8	4.9	2.8	30847	35257	14	13	5036	21.8	13.9	40.4	19.5	4.4	116691
33614	TAMPA	19569	20059	30.1	36.5	25.9	5.6	1.9	36831	42222	35	31	8806	4.5	21.4	62.0	11.6	0.5	114206
33615	TAMPA	25154	17802	22.0	32.3	32.9	8.4	4.4	46089	52983	64	63	11014	5.8	12.9	61.4	16.5	3.4	121817
33616	TAMPA	20917	5173	29.0	35.1	29.5	5.2	1.3	38971	45198	43	40	2692	10.6	22.0	62.8	4.1	0.5	99936
33617	TAMPA	23534	18854	29.7	32.1	25.1	9.0	4.1	39321	45331	44	41	8821	2.7	17.4	50.2	26.6	3.1	125587
33618	TAMPA	35523	8979	15.8	27.7	33.5	12.5	10.5	56802	65845	81	83	6195	0.6	5.5	38.9	44.1	10.9	186329
33619	TAMPA	15074	9860	34.2	33.2	27.2	4.4	1.1	36146	41247	32	30	6917	12.1	38.0	41.2	8.0	0.7	89894
33621	TAMPA	12943	582	12.0	58.6	25.3	2.9	1.2	41852	47615	52	51	15	100.0	0.0	0.0	0.0	0.0	40625
33624	TAMPA	31586	18021	12.8	27.2	38.4	14.1	7.5	60649	68857	85	87	13088	1.1	5.1	52.8	38.1	2.9	160956
33625	TAMPA	24914	7546	11.6	26.1	43.6	15.2	3.5	60163	68808	84	86	6304	3.6	3.8	63.3	27.9	1.4	144271
33626	TAMPA	45334	5872	6.4	15.8	34.2	24.5	19.0	88174	104626	97	98	5309	0.2	6.6	17.0	63.5	12.7	234735
33629	TAMPA	52552	10715	14.0	20.5	31.3	15.9	18.3	70128	84348	91	93	8161	0.2	1.7	24.1	49.6	24.5	252021
33634	TAMPA	21632	8533	18.7	35.0	34.9	8.5	2.9	46777	53109	66	65	5623	1.2	18.0	62.4	15.9	2.5	116945
33635	TAMPA	26987	6317	18.1	27.7	36.9	12.7	4.6	53178	62474	77	79	4929	28.7	8.5	27.1	34.5	1.2	144203
33637	TAMPA	21232	5651	26.5	35.4	30.4	6.2	1.6	41652	47479	52	50	2796	12.3	17.9	58.6	10.5	0.7	109697
33647	TAMPA	39522	14116	12.0	16.7	36.8	19.5	15.1	76264	90417	94	95	8864	0.6	1.3	16.3	64.0	17.8	246810
33701	SAINT PETERSBURG	23843	7904	51.4	25.2	15.4	5.2	2.8	24078	27653	4	2	2582	12.4	16.2	32.3	30.8	8.2	142609
33702	SAINT PETERSBURG	25756	13789	28.1	32.7	28.6	7.1	3.6	40196	46765	47	44	9291	20.0	19.9	40.5	16.4	3.2	105577
33703	SAINT PETERSBURG	30412	11507	22.9	29.2	29.2	11.5	7.1	47591	55712	67	67	9610	9.0	20.6	37.7	24.3	8.4	121293
33704	SAINT PETERSBURG	36247	7801	22.0	26.5	29.5	12.9	9.1	51517	61890	75	76	5403	2.9	11.9	35.4	35.7	14.1	174119
33705	SAINT PETERSBURG	20414	11760	40.2	29.4	22.1	5.2	3.2	31393	36305	16	14	6443	9.9	28.4	45.3	14.4	2.0	104020
33706	SAINT PETERSBURG	43222	9640	22.5	25.0	30.6	10.3	11.6	52860	63505	77	78	7118	0.6	4.2	26.2	46.2	22.8	242154
33707	SAINT PETERSBURG	28650	14016	35.1	30.7	22.9	5.8	5.5	35045	40157	28	25	10076	4.9	25.5	42.6	20.5	6.6	116313
33708	SAINT PETERSBURG	34825	9553	29.6	28.9	26.4	8.7	6.6	40711	47973	49	47	7181	11.7	8.1	34.5	36.2	9.6	161665
33709	SAINT PETERSBURG	21499	12319	35.9	35.3	23.0	3.9	1.9	33044	37817	21	19	9584	24.6	29.1	40.5	5.4	0.4	85707
33710	SAINT PETERSBURG	25104	14522	25.0	32.5	32.1	7.3	3.2	43594	51218	58	56	11260	3.7	19.6	60.6	13.9	2.2	117085
33711	SAINT PETERSBURG	19497	7439	34.0	32.8	23.8	5.2	4.2	35145	40384	28	26	5232	11.6	35.3	31.7	16.0	5.5	93582
33712	SAINT PETERSBURG	17725	10881	36.2	34.4	23.2	4.5	1.8	32480	37396	19	17	5591	11.0	24.8	51.5	11.5	1.2	109646
33713	SAINT PETERSBURG	19954	13352	30.2	35.9	27.3	5.0	1.6	37154	43676	36	33	9292	6.0	36.7	52.8	4.2	0.3	95845
33714	SAINT PETERSBURG	17350	8617	40.8	37.0	17.9	3.5	0.9	29754	33859	12	10	5848	32.4	33.9	31.9	1.4	0.4	71609
33715	SAINT PETERSBURG	62929	4108	12.0	20.1	28.2	20.5	19.2	79833	98577	95	96	3642	0.3	0.9	33.1	43.4	22.3	229727
33716	SAINT PETERSBURG	37820	7249	16.7	35.5	33.3	9.0	5.5	48342	56539	69	69	1782	23.7	26.7	13.5	28.4	7.8	89439
33755	CLEARWATER	19636	10306	31.2	31.4	30.0	5.9	1.5	38029	44885	39	37	6223	4.7	20.5	61.2	12.1	1.6	116015
33756	CLEARWATER	27830	13636	32.4	30.3	25.2	6.9	5.2	37867	44048	39	36	8984	5.9	17.6	49.8	19.3	7.4	126644
33759	CLEARWATER	24712	8910	29.2	32.4	26.0	8.0	4.3	40787	46797	49	47	4933	18.4	17.1	39.0	20.3	5.2	116435
33760	CLEARWATER	22325	6087	28.6	35.6	24.7	7.6	3.5	39326	45135	44	41	3511	19.7	19.7	43.6	16.3	0.7	104173
33761	CLEARWATER	35511	8668	22.8	27.4	30.8	10.8	8.3	49833	57279	72	73	7258	11.3	17.7	31.8	34.5	4.7	136298
33762	CLEARWATER	40455	3483	18.9	31.3	31.0	11.2	7.5	49799	59416	72	73	2033	20.7	13.5	35.7	25.2	4.9	130391
33763	CLEARWATER	25737	10395	30.5	33.6	29.2	4.7	1.9	37537	43350	38	35	8464	8.7	32.2	49.5	9.5	0.2	103020
33764	CLEARWATER	28322	12724	26.4	30.8	29.6	8.3	4.8	43191	50323	56	54	9362	28.5	10.1	33.1	25.5	2.7	120493
33765	CLEARWATER	26888	5463	26.2	35.3	26.9	8.5	3.0	41761	48503	52	51	3111	14.1	12.9	51.4	18.6	3.1	123376
33767	CLEARWATER BEACH	53279	5101	19.9	23.3	28.4	13.4	15.1	58267	71359	83	85	3741	0.3	2.5	15.2	51.4	30.6	269433
33770	LARGO	26779	12368	32.0	32.1	26.3	5.9	3.8	37172	43077	36	33	8118	17.7	16.7	45.4	16.8	3.4	113296
33771	LARGO	22494	12508	32.6	38.1	24.7	3.1	1.4	34434	39278	26	24	8656	34.8	25.0	33.5	6.2	0.5	74026
33772	SEMINOLE	28775	11187	24.4	31.8	30.6	9.0	4.2	44345	51568	60	58	9058	11.3	11.8	46.5	27.5	2.9	132086
33773	LARGO	24318	8771	26.9	32.3	30.3	7.7	2.8	41648	47890	52	50	6665	21.4	24.7	36.7	16.3	0.9	96311
33774	LARGO	28352	8987	24.9	32.8	28.5	9.6	4.2	43798	51355	58	56	6589	4.9	15.7	48.7	27.3	3.3	136698
33776	SEMINOLE	30716	5222	14.0	23.8	38.2	16.7	7.3	62324	74428	87	89	4812	1.3	2.5	38.1	54.6	3.6	187102
33777	SEMINOLE	34243	7136	20.0	30.4	31.1	10.0	8.6	49644	57416	71	72	6106	2.3	24.3	48.6	17.2	7.6	119872
33778	LARGO	22858	5654	25.8	35.3	29.4	7.3	2.3	40778	47062	49	47	4716	19.2	21.8	44.9	12.9	1.2	104920
33781	PINELLAS PARK	20219	10120	28.1	36.7	28.9	4.9	1.5	39382	45745	44	41	6950	15.9	28.5	47.7	5.6	2.3	94523
33782	PINELLAS PARK	22624	8538	27.3	35.1	29.9	5.7	2.1	39574	45988	45	42	6971	12.0	25.1	54.1	7.8	1.0	104223
33785	INDIAN ROCKS BEACH	47726	3831	17.6	25.4	33.0	12.9	11.2	57137	68002	82	83	2719	1.3	2.3	19.8	55.1	21.7	244970
33786	BELLEAIR BEACH	62569	923	12.1	17.4	31.0	17.2	22.2	77055	94846	94	95	803	0.1	0.0	6.0	64.1	29.8	292188
33801	LAKELAND	18397	13843	36.5	35.1	22.2	4.5	1.7	33165	37576	21	20	8006	22.2	42.8	31.0	3.7	0.4	75594
33803	LAKELAND	27525	12217	26.0	33.1	28.0	7.2	5.6	42837	48882	56	54	8214	16.7	23.3	39.6	17.0	3.4	102754
33805	LAKELAND	15655	7786	42.0	30.4	22.7	3.1	1.8	29365	33002	11	9	4685	26.4	45.2	24.7	3.2	0.5	71387
33809	LAKELAND	24473	11149	20.0	31.1	35.8	9.7	3.4	48975	55156	70	71	8617	11.8	18.4	50.7	17.7	1.4	115762
33810	LAKELAND	21209	13058	23.8	33.0	33.0	7.6	2.6	43513	49686	57	55	10990	13.0	29.3	45.5	11.5	0.7	98577
33811	LAKELAND	23315	6812	20.5	31.2	35.4	9.6	3.4	48702	55015	70	70	5059	10.7	20.8	47.7	19.3	1.6	112918
33813	LAKELAND	29982	13928	13.2	24.7	39.2	13.2	9.7	61074	70242	85	87	11961	5.7	12.7	49.8	28.3	3.6	137924
33815	LAKELAND	15825	5855	45.0	35.4	14.4	3.1	2.0	27257	30934	7	5	4017	57.1	26.0	10.4	5.4	1.1	41250
33823	AUBURNDALE	18962	10847	29.4	31.8	30.3	6.1	2.3	39681	45305	45	42	8390	17.2	36.5	34.2	10.7	1.4	85532
33825	AVON PARK	17440	9007	38.4	33.8	20.5	5.0	2.3	31802	35688	17	16	6950	20.3	28.5	38.8	11.7	0.7	91680
33827	BABSON PARK	20219	901	28.4	31.5	32.1	4.3	3.7	44162	50412	59	57	753	21.7	28.7	38.1	9.0	2.5	89138
33830	BARTOW	19916	9191	30.2	31.4	29.1	6.3	3.1	40597	46685	48	46	6925	17.2	41.7	31.1	9.2	0.7	81949
	FLORIDA	25506		26.4	29.9	29.1	9.1	5.6	44138	51288				8.8	15.8	40.2	28.3	7.0	137042
	UNITED STATES	25866		24.7	27.1	30.8	10.9	6.5	48124	56710				10.9	15.0	33.7	30.1	10.4	145905

ZIP CODE #	POST OFFICE NAME	FINANCIAL SERVICES: Auto Loan	FINANCIAL SERVICES: Home Loan	FINANCIAL SERVICES: Investments	FINANCIAL SERVICES: Retirement Plans	THE HOME: Home Improvements: Home Repair	THE HOME: Home Improvements: Lawn & Garden	THE HOME: Furnishings: Computers & Hardware	THE HOME: Furnishings: Major Appliances	THE HOME: Furnishings: TV, Radio, Sound Equipment	THE HOME: Furnishings: Furniture	ENTERTAINMENT: Dine out/Carry out	ENTERTAINMENT: Sports Equipment	ENTERTAINMENT: Fees & Tickets	ENTERTAINMENT: Toys & Games	ENTERTAINMENT: Travel	ENTERTAINMENT: Cable TV	PERSONAL: Apparel & Services	PERSONAL: Auto Repairs	PERSONAL: Health Insurance	PERSONAL: Pets & Supplies
33549	LUTZ	94	98	105	102	95	97	98	95	93	99	117	113	98	116	95	88	115	96	85	105
33556	ODESSA	144	163	162	167	158	159	147	147	137	151	173	170	154	174	147	132	172	143	132	164
33558	LUTZ	123	129	141	136	125	127	128	124	121	130	154	148	129	152	124	115	152	126	111	138
33559	LUTZ	100	104	108	110	100	100	102	100	96	105	122	118	102	120	98	90	120	100	87	110
33563	PLANT CITY	66	61	60	59	61	68	63	65	66	64	82	73	62	79	63	66	79	66	67	73
33565	PLANT CITY	90	81	67	76	83	92	76	85	80	79	98	94	73	91	78	82	93	83	91	101
33566	PLANT CITY	108	109	97	109	107	109	102	105	99	105	123	122	101	121	100	95	120	104	99	121
33567	PLANT CITY	83	71	51	67	73	79	68	75	71	70	87	88	63	82	68	72	83	75	79	94
33569	RIVERVIEW	95	95	90	96	93	96	91	93	88	94	111	107	90	107	89	85	108	92	87	104
33570	RUSKIN	62	56	50	53	58	66	55	61	58	57	72	64	53	66	56	60	68	60	66	69
33572	APOLLO BEACH	109	126	140	123	126	136	116	120	113	118	142	131	122	140	122	114	139	116	119	130
33573	SUN CITY CENTER	75	72	76	66	76	92	67	78	72	72	89	72	68	75	73	77	83	75	91	84
33576	SAN ANTONIO	87	92	87	91	91	93	86	88	83	87	103	103	86	104	86	81	101	87	83	101
33584	SEFFNER	84	85	79	84	85	87	81	83	80	81	99	98	80	99	81	78	96	83	80	96
33585	SUMTERVILLE	82	55	25	47	62	72	53	66	64	54	75	79	45	71	54	69	68	66	82	94
33592	THONOTOSASSA	83	74	59	70	75	80	72	77	74	73	91	89	68	86	71	74	87	77	79	92
33594	VALRICO	119	134	135	135	131	133	121	123	115	125	145	140	127	144	122	112	143	120	114	137
33597	WEBSTER	70	49	24	42	54	62	47	58	55	48	65	68	40	62	47	59	60	57	69	80
33598	WIMAUMA	80	74	71	73	73	75	78	78	79	81	99	90	75	98	74	75	99	81	72	85
33602	TAMPA	102	94	143	98	91	104	109	102	115	110	145	119	111	145	107	117	142	108	103	114
33603	TAMPA	56	57	67	57	56	61	60	58	61	60	76	68	61	77	60	60	75	60	58	64
33604	TAMPA	56	54	64	54	53	58	59	56	60	58	75	66	59	75	58	59	73	58	56	63
33605	TAMPA	45	38	42	35	37	44	42	43	47	43	57	47	41	53	41	49	55	44	47	48
33606	TAMPA	141	139	218	151	135	149	157	144	158	157	199	173	161	203	154	156	197	152	138	160
33607	TAMPA	66	60	89	58	58	68	68	66	74	70	94	74	68	92	67	77	92	69	69	73
33609	TAMPA	104	113	143	114	111	120	115	111	112	115	142	129	118	143	115	111	140	113	106	121
33610	TAMPA	59	53	54	49	52	60	55	56	60	56	73	63	54	69	55	62	71	57	61	65
33611	TAMPA	87	90	108	93	89	95	94	91	92	93	116	107	95	116	93	90	114	93	87	100
33612	TAMPA	58	54	63	55	53	59	61	58	62	60	77	69	60	75	59	61	75	61	58	65
33613	TAMPA	60	55	65	57	54	59	64	59	63	62	79	71	61	76	60	61	77	63	57	66
33614	TAMPA	63	61	77	63	58	63	67	63	67	68	85	75	66	84	64	65	84	67	59	70
33615	TAMPA	86	84	91	88	83	88	88	86	86	88	109	102	87	106	85	83	106	88	81	96
33616	TAMPA	68	69	77	71	68	72	72	70	71	71	90	83	73	90	71	70	88	72	67	77
33617	TAMPA	78	74	86	78	73	78	81	78	80	81	101	93	80	98	78	77	99	81	73	86
33618	TAMPA	115	129	143	133	126	128	124	121	117	125	148	143	128	148	123	112	146	121	110	133
33619	TAMPA	63	59	58	58	59	65	60	61	62	61	77	71	60	76	60	63	75	62	63	71
33621	TAMPA	76	48	46	55	44	52	72	62	73	67	91	83	62	82	59	67	88	73	58	71
33624	TAMPA	110	117	126	123	113	114	115	112	108	117	137	132	116	136	111	102	135	112	99	123
33625	TAMPA	99	108	107	112	104	102	101	100	94	104	119	118	102	119	98	89	118	99	87	110
33626	TAMPA	173	197	190	205	187	181	177	175	162	184	206	205	183	207	173	151	204	171	149	192
33629	TAMPA	143	165	216	170	161	170	162	156	155	162	196	183	171	202	164	153	195	157	145	171
33634	TAMPA	77	82	94	83	80	83	82	80	80	83	101	93	83	103	81	78	100	81	74	87
33635	TAMPA	96	98	97	102	94	96	95	94	90	98	114	110	94	110	91	85	111	94	85	105
33637	TAMPA	71	64	71	68	63	67	72	68	70	71	89	83	68	85	68	67	86	72	64	77
33647	TAMPA	145	153	160	162	146	147	149	145	140	153	178	172	151	175	143	131	175	146	126	160
33701	SAINT PETERSBURG	56	49	65	52	49	55	60	56	61	58	77	67	58	74	57	60	74	60	56	62
33702	SAINT PETERSBURG	75	77	83	75	78	86	75	78	76	76	95	85	77	91	77	77	92	77	81	86
33703	SAINT PETERSBURG	92	98	107	96	99	108	95	97	95	95	118	108	98	118	98	96	115	96	99	108
33704	SAINT PETERSBURG	98	111	135	113	109	115	110	107	106	109	133	126	114	136	111	104	132	108	101	117
33705	SAINT PETERSBURG	64	61	73	59	60	68	66	64	69	66	86	73	66	84	65	71	83	66	68	72
33706	SAINT PETERSBURG	115	110	112	106	115	132	105	115	109	109	136	119	106	121	112	114	129	113	129	132
33707	SAINT PETERSBURG	77	75	80	72	77	89	74	79	78	76	96	83	75	89	78	81	91	78	88	88
33708	SAINT PETERSBURG	93	88	89	83	93	108	84	94	89	87	110	97	84	100	90	94	104	92	106	108
33709	SAINT PETERSBURG	65	62	61	58	64	74	61	66	64	62	79	69	61	73	63	67	74	65	74	74
33710	SAINT PETERSBURG	73	81	92	80	81	87	80	79	79	79	99	90	83	102	82	80	97	79	78	86
33711	SAINT PETERSBURG	69	66	71	63	66	75	66	68	70	68	87	74	67	82	68	72	84	69	74	78
33712	SAINT PETERSBURG	61	56	63	56	55	61	60	59	62	61	78	68	60	73	59	62	75	61	60	67
33713	SAINT PETERSBURG	60	63	72	63	63	68	66	64	66	64	82	75	67	84	66	65	80	65	63	70
33714	SAINT PETERSBURG	54	48	49	47	50	57	51	53	54	50	66	60	50	65	52	56	63	54	58	61
33715	SAINT PETERSBURG	168	175	180	171	180	201	161	173	161	168	202	181	167	184	171	167	194	168	186	194
33716	SAINT PETERSBURG	96	81	96	91	78	84	95	89	93	97	119	109	90	110	87	87	115	96	80	100
33755	CLEARWATER	64	63	73	63	63	68	67	66	68	66	85	77	67	85	67	68	83	67	65	73
33756	CLEARWATER	81	83	94	81	83	92	85	85	86	84	107	95	86	105	86	87	104	86	87	93
33759	CLEARWATER	74	77	90	78	76	82	79	78	78	78	98	91	80	97	79	77	95	79	76	85
33760	CLEARWATER	73	67	80	71	65	72	75	71	75	75	95	85	73	91	72	73	92	75	68	79
33761	CLEARWATER	103	104	115	100	107	123	100	107	103	104	129	111	103	118	106	107	123	106	117	118
33762	CLEARWATER	111	98	111	103	97	109	106	107	107	110	136	120	103	122	103	104	130	111	105	118
33763	CLEARWATER	68	69	74	65	71	82	66	72	68	69	85	72	67	77	70	71	80	70	79	78
33764	CLEARWATER	83	84	91	81	86	98	82	87	85	83	105	93	84	99	86	87	100	86	93	96
33765	CLEARWATER	78	81	96	82	80	87	83	82	83	83	104	94	85	103	84	82	102	83	80	89
33767	CLEARWATER BEACH	142	134	133	128	141	165	126	141	132	134	165	140	128	140	136	140	155	137	162	160
33770	LARGO	72	76	87	74	76	84	76	77	76	76	95	85	78	93	78	77	92	77	79	84
33771	LARGO	62	61	67	58	63	73	59	64	62	62	77	66	60	70	63	65	73	63	71	70
33772	SEMINOLE	80	88	99	85	88	97	84	86	84	85	105	94	88	104	88	86	102	85	89	94
33773	LARGO	76	76	76	73	78	88	73	78	74	75	92	83	73	86	75	76	87	77	84	87
33774	LARGO	85	87	98	85	88	99	85	88	86	87	108	96	87	102	89	88	104	88	93	97
33776	SEMINOLE	105	115	120	112	116	126	105	111	104	108	130	119	110	124	111	106	126	107	114	123
33777	SEMINOLE	111	124	138	124	124	131	119	119	115	119	145	136	123	145	122	114	142	118	116	131
33778	LARGO	72	76	83	72	77	86	71	76	73	74	91	79	74	87	75	76	88	74	81	83
33781	PINELLAS PARK	70	68	66	67	68	73	69	70	69	68	86	81	68	85	68	68	82	70	70	79
33782	PINELLAS PARK	74	74	73	72	75	82	71	75	72	73	90	82	72	86	73	73	86	74	78	84
33785	INDIAN ROCKS BEACH	128	123	124	120	129	143	117	127	121	120	149	140	117	140	123	125	143	126	137	150
33786	BELLEAIR BEACH	198	185	178	176	196	231	171	195	181	184	226	191	174	188	187	194	211	190	228	223
33801	LAKELAND	61	55	57	54	57	64	59	60	62	58	76	69	57	74	59	63	72	61	64	68
33803	LAKELAND	81	85	94	84	85	92	85	85	84	84	105	97	86	106	86	85	102	85	85	94
33805	LAKELAND	58	50	52	48	50	58	55	55	59	55	73	63	53	70	54	61	70	57	60	64
33809	LAKELAND	90	87	82	87	89	96	87	90	87	85	107	104	85	105	87	87	102	89	92	103
33810	LAKELAND	83	78	70	75	80	88	74	81	76	76	94	89	73	88	76	77	89	79	85	94
33811	LAKELAND	86	86	88	87	85	89	85	85	84	86	105	100	85	103	84	82	102	86	81	97
33813	LAKELAND	120	125	117	125	125	128	116	120	113	117	141	141	117	143	117	111	137	117	116	139
33815	LAKELAND	58	51	50	48	53	61	52	56	56	53	69	61	51	64	53	58	65	56	63	65
33823	AUBURNDALE	79	66	52	63	70	78	66	73	72	66	87	84	62	84	67	74	82	72	81	90
33825	AVON PARK	64	56	53	53	59	70	57	63	62	58	76	66	56	70	59	65	71	62	72	71
33827	BABSON PARK	93	71	48	65	78	91	69	82	78	71	94	91	63	86	72	84	86	80	98	105
33830	BARTOW	79	72	66	69	74	82	72	76	76	73	93	87	71	91	73	78	89	76	81	90
	FLORIDA	89	87	95	86	87	96	87	89	89	89	111	100	87	107	88	90	108	90	91	101
	UNITED STATES	100	100	100	100	100	100	100	100	100	100	100	100	100	100	100	100	100	100	100	100

FLORIDA

POPULATION CHANGE

A 33834-34209

#	POST OFFICE NAME	COUNTY FIPS CODE	POPULATION 2000	POPULATION 2004	POPULATION 2009	2000-2004 ANNUAL RATE % Rate	State Centile	HOUSEHOLDS 2000	HOUSEHOLDS 2004	HOUSEHOLDS 2009	% Annual Rate 2000-2004	2004 Average HH Size	FAMILIES 2000	FAMILIES 2004	% Annual Rate 2000-2004
33834	BOWLING GREEN	081	7272	7754	8398	1.5	43	1950	2115	2322	1.9	3.14	1538	1659	1.8
33837	DAVENPORT	105	12569	15044	17316	4.3	86	4825	5846	6782	4.6	2.55	3616	4343	4.4
33838	DUNDEE	105	2900	3114	3382	1.7	47	1079	1162	1266	1.8	2.66	790	841	1.5
33839	EAGLE LAKE	105	2304	2501	2730	2.0	54	889	968	1061	2.0	2.57	623	670	1.7
33841	FORT MEADE	105	8362	8689	9273	0.9	26	2920	3062	3291	1.1	2.81	2221	2306	0.9
33843	FROSTPROOF	105	11022	11704	12557	1.4	40	3274	3517	3833	1.7	2.76	2392	2543	1.5
33844	HAINES CITY	105	29490	32770	36421	2.5	67	11120	12546	14111	2.9	2.57	8174	9100	2.6
33849	KATHLEEN	105	986	1125	1261	3.2	75	347	400	452	3.4	2.81	277	317	3.2
33850	LAKE ALFRED	105	3931	4005	4266	0.4	12	1545	1587	1703	0.6	2.49	1125	1143	0.4
33852	LAKE PLACID	055	19902	21374	23015	1.7	47	8420	9027	9716	1.7	2.34	5850	6215	1.4
33853	LAKE WALES	105	10420	10804	11558	0.9	24	4146	4331	4666	1.0	2.43	2605	2694	0.8
33857	LORIDA	055	1801	2165	2466	4.4	87	808	972	1108	4.4	2.23	568	680	4.3
33859	LAKE WALES	105	7762	8373	9226	1.8	52	3097	3314	3654	1.6	2.48	2213	2341	1.3
33860	MULBERRY	105	17364	19145	21188	2.3	61	6235	6949	7754	2.6	2.74	4803	5313	2.4
33865	ONA	049	485	574	652	4.0	84	194	231	263	4.2	2.33	137	162	4.0
33868	POLK CITY	105	10844	12614	14271	3.6	80	3288	3854	4395	3.8	3.12	2640	3072	3.6
33870	SEBRING	055	17491	18090	19263	0.8	22	7360	7577	8069	0.7	2.30	4602	4703	0.5
33872	SEBRING	055	11323	12488	13638	2.3	62	5465	6048	6617	2.4	2.06	3746	4100	2.2
33873	WAUCHULA	049	14536	15426	16571	1.4	40	4521	4764	5090	1.2	3.07	3387	3547	1.1
33875	SEBRING	055	9933	10731	11564	1.8	52	4435	4834	5234	2.1	2.21	3206	3462	1.8
33876	SEBRING	055	4181	4471	4794	1.6	45	1860	2000	2151	1.7	2.22	1340	1426	1.5
33880	WINTER HAVEN	105	35185	37423	40751	1.5	41	13420	14341	15704	1.6	2.60	9180	9696	1.3
33881	WINTER HAVEN	105	28082	29162	31350	0.9	25	12140	12745	13817	1.2	2.24	7746	8055	0.9
33884	WINTER HAVEN	105	19641	21338	23414	2.0	55	8168	8945	9886	2.2	2.33	5905	6414	2.0
33890	ZOLFO SPRINGS	049	5159	5430	5807	1.2	34	1671	1752	1867	1.1	3.08	1329	1388	1.0
33896	DAVENPORT	097	3448	4357	5255	5.7	93	1364	1769	2163	6.3	2.32	1042	1338	6.1
33897	DAVENPORT	105	4921	5895	6738	4.3	87	2273	2858	3369	5.5	1.74	1754	2059	3.8
33898	LAKE WALES	105	16293	17964	19917	2.3	61	7061	7816	8705	2.4	2.27	5013	5503	2.2
33901	FORT MYERS	071	21095	22523	26166	1.6	44	9030	9623	11265	1.5	2.23	4710	4911	1.0
33903	NORTH FORT MYERS	071	22807	24535	28528	1.7	49	11064	12025	14104	2.0	2.03	7034	7485	1.5
33904	CAPE CORAL	071	32856	36375	42929	2.4	65	15007	16801	20012	2.7	2.15	10044	11069	2.3
33905	FORT MYERS	071	25864	28450	33493	2.3	60	9170	10170	12078	2.5	2.75	6461	7045	2.1
33907	FORT MYERS	071	20360	22249	26078	2.1	58	9110	10115	12027	2.5	2.12	4708	5090	1.9
33908	FORT MYERS	071	24365	31949	41265	6.6	96	11850	15559	20172	6.6	2.01	7572	9839	6.4
33909	CAPE CORAL	071	8806	10214	12332	3.6	80	3072	3602	4385	3.8	2.83	2366	2736	3.5
33912	FORT MYERS	071	33603	41724	52201	5.2	91	13369	16861	21331	5.6	2.47	10057	12547	5.3
33913	FORT MYERS	071	4001	5643	7464	8.4	98	1454	2120	2863	9.3	2.60	1231	1779	9.1
33914	CAPE CORAL	071	25515	32419	40991	5.8	93	9777	12490	15882	5.9	2.60	7683	9748	5.8
33916	FORT MYERS	071	20490	21856	25323	1.5	43	7326	8025	9498	2.2	2.62	4658	4937	1.4
33917	NORTH FORT MYERS	071	28757	31392	36810	2.1	57	13157	14570	17256	2.4	2.15	8645	9431	2.1
33919	FORT MYERS	071	26918	29447	34624	2.1	59	13218	14650	17397	2.5	2.00	8123	8846	2.0
33920	ALVA	071	4879	5533	6509	3.0	73	1895	2168	2564	3.2	2.55	1396	1574	2.9
33921	BOCA GRANDE	071	1028	1154	1369	2.8	70	533	607	728	3.1	1.90	375	421	2.8
33922	BOKEELIA	071	4172	4623	5453	2.4	65	1872	2093	2488	2.7	2.21	1305	1435	2.3
33924	CAPTIVA	071	6	8	10	7.0	96	4	5	7	5.4	1.60	3	3	0.0
33928	ESTERO	071	8734	12522	16709	8.9	99	4224	6105	8205	9.1	2.03	3061	4372	8.8
33931	FORT MYERS BEACH	071	11395	12756	15141	2.7	69	6118	6944	8326	3.0	1.83	3752	4191	2.6
33935	LABELLE	051	16939	18190	19317	1.7	47	5002	5343	5652	1.6	3.19	3689	3920	1.4
33936	LEHIGH ACRES	071	15890	18396	22179	3.5	79	6444	7416	8946	3.4	2.47	4345	4932	3.0
33946	PLACIDA	015	1617	1937	2272	4.3	87	825	999	1181	4.6	1.94	598	718	4.4
33947	ROTONDA WEST	015	5322	6002	6838	2.9	71	2405	2747	3162	3.2	2.17	1784	2025	3.0
33948	PORT CHARLOTTE	015	14535	15842	17520	2.1	56	5983	6601	7375	2.3	2.37	4384	4791	2.1
33950	PUNTA GORDA	015	19667	21113	23332	1.7	47	9785	10632	11871	2.0	1.95	6778	7316	1.8
33952	PORT CHARLOTTE	015	30822	32200	35115	1.0	28	14025	14716	16139	1.1	2.18	8880	9184	0.8
33953	PORT CHARLOTTE	015	3462	4412	5303	5.9	93	1552	2036	2492	6.6	2.17	1152	1493	6.3
33954	PORT CHARLOTTE	015	7257	8454	9699	3.7	81	2777	3272	3790	3.9	2.58	2225	2611	3.8
33955	PUNTA GORDA	015	6213	7368	8617	4.1	84	2855	3436	4071	4.5	2.14	2139	2546	4.2
33956	SAINT JAMES CITY	071	4095	4404	5185	1.7	49	2135	2317	2748	1.9	1.90	1419	1513	1.5
33957	SANIBEL	071	6522	7213	8563	2.4	64	3285	3690	4428	2.8	1.95	2289	2524	2.3
33960	VENUS	055	744	749	776	0.2	7	290	294	306	0.3	2.50	204	206	0.2
33971	LEHIGH ACRES	071	8825	12082	15913	7.7	97	2867	3983	5303	8.0	3.01	2334	3218	7.9
33972	LEHIGH ACRES	071	8045	8768	10248	2.1	56	3165	3464	4071	2.2	2.53	2395	2590	1.9
33980	PORT CHARLOTTE	015	9059	9743	10682	1.7	49	4360	4761	5291	2.1	1.94	2652	2854	1.7
33981	PORT CHARLOTTE	015	7230	8111	9107	2.7	70	3103	3508	3967	2.9	2.31	2316	2586	2.6
33982	PUNTA GORDA	015	8997	10024	11222	2.6	68	3552	4030	4598	3.0	2.21	2457	2768	2.8
33983	PUNTA GORDA	015	10960	12575	14347	3.3	77	4600	5317	6113	3.5	2.35	3462	3966	3.3
33990	CAPE CORAL	071	23207	28032	34486	4.5	88	8789	10775	13406	4.9	2.58	6741	8161	4.6
33991	CAPE CORAL	071	8638	11172	14227	6.2	95	3026	3956	5081	6.5	2.80	2449	3174	6.3
33993	CAPE CORAL	071	4240	5656	7408	7.0	97	1635	2163	2829	6.8	2.61	1218	1622	7.0
34102	NAPLES	021	11851	12076	13968	0.4	12	5999	6144	7146	0.6	1.94	3492	3517	0.2
34103	NAPLES	021	13110	14328	17127	2.1	58	6532	7278	8807	2.6	1.95	4152	4560	2.2
34104	NAPLES	021	18862	24664	32129	6.5	96	8382	11056	14481	6.7	2.23	5661	7384	6.5
34105	NAPLES	021	10037	11942	14918	4.2	86	4791	5786	7305	4.5	2.03	2932	3498	4.2
34108	NAPLES	021	16590	17558	20460	1.3	38	7690	8261	9725	1.7	2.10	5276	5597	1.4
34109	NAPLES	021	17741	22937	29540	6.2	94	7644	9995	12974	6.5	2.27	5230	6745	6.2
34110	NAPLES	021	15960	19952	25328	5.4	92	7479	9531	12255	5.9	2.03	5066	6342	5.4
34112	NAPLES	021	26604	31392	38752	4.0	83	12051	14302	17783	4.1	2.14	7524	8793	3.7
34113	NAPLES	021	14215	16546	20230	3.6	80	5634	6388	7724	3.0	2.56	3832	4318	2.9
34114	NAPLES	021	9040	10936	13549	4.6	89	3802	4647	5825	4.8	2.23	2568	3091	4.5
34116	NAPLES	021	25170	28951	35255	3.4	78	8137	9361	11423	3.4	3.09	6171	6964	2.9
34117	NAPLES	021	10266	12835	16238	5.4	92	3243	4078	5180	5.5	3.14	2737	3413	5.3
34119	NAPLES	021	10014	16130	23392	11.9	100	4110	6819	10006	12.7	2.36	3298	5414	12.4
34120	NAPLES	021	11982	16955	22778	8.5	99	3791	5390	7266	8.6	3.12	3208	4531	8.5
34134	BONITA SPRINGS	021	11844	15606	20198	6.7	96	6059	8032	10461	6.9	1.94	4139	5428	6.6
34135	BONITA SPRINGS	071	24785	32428	41908	6.5	96	10220	13453	17526	6.7	2.40	7151	9357	6.5
34141	OCHOPEE	021	1185	1289	1521	2.0	56	538	592	704	2.3	2.13	362	392	1.9
34142	IMMOKALEE	021	23863	25987	30619	2.0	56	5410	5905	7057	2.1	3.97	4221	4572	1.9
34145	MARCO ISLAND	021	14783	17560	21759	4.1	85	7084	8438	10488	4.2	2.08	5131	6043	3.9
34201	BRADENTON	081	663	1106	1525	12.8	100	335	565	782	13.1	1.96	220	363	12.5
34202	BRADENTON	081	7970	11438	15000	8.9	99	2850	4188	5554	9.5	2.73	2448	3547	9.1
34203	BRADENTON	081	26449	31427	37207	4.1	85	10627	12565	14842	4.0	2.46	7595	8938	3.9
34205	BRADENTON	081	31819	33427	37160	1.2	32	13832	14511	16130	1.1	2.24	7761	7945	0.6
34207	BRADENTON	081	31084	31984	35276	0.7	19	15118	15571	17162	0.7	2.05	8204	8226	0.1
34208	BRADENTON	081	30677	34679	40134	2.9	72	11029	12515	14501	3.0	2.73	7876	8793	2.6
34209	BRADENTON	081	33229	36368	41289	2.2	59	14578	15962	18120	2.2	2.23	9763	10533	1.8
	FLORIDA					2.1					2.2	2.45			2.0
	UNITED STATES					1.2					1.3	2.58			1.1

ZIP CODE # POST OFFICE NAME	RACE (%) White		Black		Asian/Pacific		% Hispanic Origin		2004 AGE DISTRIBUTION (%)										MEDIAN AGE		
	2000	2004	2000	2004	2000	2004	2000	2004	0-4	5-9	10-14	15-19	20-24	25-44	45-64	65-84	85+	18+	2004	% 2004 Males	% 2004 Females
33834 BOWLING GREEN	68.3	65.8	12.4	12.4	0.3	0.3	31.8	36.1	7.2	6.7	6.5	6.7	7.6	31.2	19.8	13.4	1.1	75.8	34.6	57.9	42.2
33837 DAVENPORT	84.9	82.9	6.4	7.2	0.7	0.9	16.0	19.0	6.8	6.6	6.0	4.7	4.3	26.6	25.1	18.4	1.4	77.6	41.5	49.6	50.4
33838 DUNDEE	69.0	64.5	23.8	27.3	0.7	0.7	10.7	12.9	6.3	6.5	7.8	6.7	5.7	23.0	21.6	19.8	2.8	75.5	40.6	48.3	51.7
33839 EAGLE LAKE	86.5	84.0	4.4	5.2	0.4	0.4	13.2	16.1	7.4	7.0	7.3	6.4	5.8	25.5	24.0	14.6	2.0	74.5	38.0	49.1	50.9
33841 FORT MEADE	71.2	67.8	15.7	16.9	0.1	0.2	21.1	25.0	7.1	7.5	8.1	7.8	6.6	25.8	21.7	13.8	1.7	72.6	35.4	50.0	50.0
33843 FROSTPROOF	68.1	63.2	14.0	16.3	0.3	0.3	21.0	24.5	5.4	5.3	6.2	6.6	8.6	30.2	20.6	15.2	2.0	79.5	37.1	59.4	40.6
33844 HAINES CITY	69.2	67.4	18.9	19.4	0.4	0.5	20.6	23.2	6.7	6.2	6.4	6.1	6.3	22.7	21.9	21.6	2.1	77.0	41.4	49.7	50.3
33849 KATHLEEN	95.1	94.1	0.8	1.0	0.6	0.7	5.1	6.5	5.2	5.2	5.7	5.2	4.4	18.6	29.3	25.5	0.9	81.0	49.4	49.6	50.4
33850 LAKE ALFRED	80.2	77.3	15.5	17.8	0.8	0.9	5.9	7.3	6.3	6.4	6.8	5.8	5.2	23.3	23.3	20.5	2.4	76.6	42.2	46.6	53.4
33852 LAKE PLACID	85.5	83.5	7.4	8.0	0.5	0.6	16.5	20.0	4.8	4.7	5.2	5.3	5.6	19.0	23.3	28.6	3.7	82.2	50.4	50.4	49.6
33853 LAKE WALES	59.5	57.2	34.0	35.5	0.6	0.7	10.5	12.4	7.5	6.9	7.4	6.9	7.1	24.0	21.2	15.8	3.4	73.8	36.8	47.7	52.3
33857 LORIDA	96.0	95.2	0.4	0.6	0.3	0.4	6.8	8.7	4.0	5.5	6.1	4.3	3.9	19.5	27.7	26.7	2.2	81.5	50.9	51.5	48.5
33859 LAKE WALES	82.3	77.9	10.5	13.2	0.5	0.6	11.5	14.7	5.8	5.8	6.1	6.2	6.5	22.0	23.2	22.2	2.2	78.7	42.9	50.2	49.8
33860 MULBERRY	81.5	79.1	11.6	12.7	0.6	0.7	12.0	14.5	7.5	7.4	7.9	7.1	6.6	28.5	23.5	10.7	0.9	72.9	35.1	50.4	49.7
33865 ONA	76.1	72.8	11.8	12.5	0.4	0.5	17.5	21.4	5.9	6.1	5.4	5.8	6.3	26.8	28.9	13.2	1.6	78.4	40.4	55.4	44.6
33868 POLK CITY	88.8	86.7	6.5	7.7	0.8	0.9	6.7	8.5	5.9	6.0	6.4	6.4	5.1	26.3	26.8	16.2	0.9	77.7	41.1	52.2	47.8
33870 SEBRING	77.2	73.7	14.5	16.8	0.8	0.9	10.9	13.0	5.4	5.2	5.5	5.6	6.1	20.5	21.5	25.1	5.1	80.5	46.5	48.7	51.4
33872 SEBRING	92.2	90.4	3.1	3.7	1.5	1.8	8.7	11.2	4.0	3.7	3.5	3.4	3.1	14.7	24.1	38.5	5.1	86.7	60.7	46.9	53.1
33873 WAUCHULA	69.5	66.3	8.3	8.6	0.3	0.4	37.0	42.5	8.3	7.3	7.3	7.4	8.3	28.3	20.2	11.6	1.4	72.9	32.5	53.0	47.0
33875 SEBRING	94.9	93.9	1.7	2.1	0.9	1.1	4.1	5.2	4.0	4.3	4.8	4.2	4.0	17.3	26.6	31.4	3.5	84.2	54.2	47.8	52.2
33876 SEBRING	92.5	90.9	2.5	3.0	0.4	0.5	8.3	10.5	3.9	3.8	4.4	4.6	4.3	16.8	28.3	30.9	3.0	85.1	55.2	48.9	51.1
33880 WINTER HAVEN	80.3	77.0	9.7	11.1	1.2	1.3	13.6	16.4	7.5	7.1	7.3	6.9	6.9	27.8	22.5	12.1	1.8	74.0	35.5	49.0	51.0
33881 WINTER HAVEN	67.7	65.6	26.9	28.5	0.8	0.9	4.8	5.8	5.5	5.3	5.9	5.9	5.3	19.7	23.8	24.3	4.4	79.8	47.1	47.2	52.9
33884 WINTER HAVEN	93.1	91.7	2.3	2.9	1.8	2.2	4.9	6.0	5.0	5.3	5.7	5.5	4.4	21.8	26.2	22.8	3.4	80.5	46.8	47.0	53.0
33890 ZOLFO SPRINGS	78.1	75.3	1.9	1.9	0.5	0.6	37.5	43.5	8.4	8.1	8.2	7.0	7.1	27.3	20.2	12.7	1.1	71.1	32.9	52.8	47.2
33896 DAVENPORT	84.5	82.0	8.1	9.2	1.1	1.4	13.0	16.1	6.0	6.0	5.6	5.4	4.0	27.4	27.0	17.9	0.9	79.0	42.2	52.5	47.5
33897 DAVENPORT	81.4	78.0	13.4	15.8	1.1	1.3	8.6	10.6	4.1	4.3	3.8	5.9	3.9	27.0	29.8	20.3	0.9	84.0	45.8	57.9	42.1
33898 LAKE WALES	85.2	83.7	10.8	11.5	0.6	0.7	4.6	5.8	4.9	5.0	5.9	5.5	5.0	20.2	26.3	24.8	2.6	80.9	47.8	49.4	50.6
33901 FORT MYERS	68.6	63.8	22.4	26.4	1.3	1.4	10.4	12.2	7.1	5.8	6.1	5.7	7.0	28.0	22.1	13.3	4.9	77.6	38.5	48.9	51.1
33903 NORTH FORT MYERS	94.7	93.3	1.6	2.1	0.9	1.1	4.9	6.3	3.6	3.6	3.9	3.9	3.7	15.3	24.2	37.5	4.4	86.5	59.2	47.3	52.7
33904 CAPE CORAL	94.9	93.5	1.2	1.7	0.8	1.0	6.7	8.8	3.7	3.9	4.7	4.2	3.6	19.0	30.0	26.8	4.0	85.1	52.9	47.8	52.2
33905 FORT MYERS	74.3	71.4	13.5	14.8	0.9	1.1	22.4	25.3	6.6	6.5	7.0	7.0	7.2	25.9	24.6	13.7	1.6	75.8	37.6	50.8	49.2
33907 FORT MYERS	85.8	82.9	6.4	7.9	1.3	1.5	15.3	18.4	5.9	5.1	4.6	4.6	8.1	29.6	19.0	17.4	5.6	82.0	38.8	49.0	51.0
33908 FORT MYERS	95.1	92.3	2.2	3.7	0.5	0.7	5.3	7.8	2.6	3.0	3.3	3.0	2.7	15.1	29.5	35.0	5.8	89.3	60.1	47.1	52.9
33909 CAPE CORAL	90.6	88.3	3.3	4.3	0.7	0.9	9.7	12.3	7.1	7.4	8.4	7.7	6.2	29.8	22.0	10.4	1.0	72.3	35.4	48.9	51.1
33912 FORT MYERS	95.1	93.7	1.1	1.6	1.1	1.4	5.5	7.0	6.2	6.4	6.4	5.6	4.7	25.4	25.9	18.0	1.6	77.6	42.3	49.2	50.8
33913 FORT MYERS	92.3	90.7	2.8	3.6	1.4	1.7	7.9	9.3	7.7	8.2	7.3	6.6	4.2	25.7	26.1	13.7	0.5	73.6	39.9	49.3	50.7
33914 CAPE CORAL	93.9	92.2	1.5	2.1	0.8	0.9	8.1	10.8	6.0	6.2	7.1	6.1	4.9	25.8	29.0	13.8	1.2	76.9	41.3	49.0	51.0
33916 FORT MYERS	29.7	27.7	58.6	60.0	0.7	0.7	17.1	18.6	9.9	8.3	8.6	9.1	10.4	27.5	17.3	7.6	1.2	68.2	27.3	49.9	50.1
33917 NORTH FORT MYERS	97.2	96.6	0.4	0.6	0.4	0.5	2.8	3.7	4.0	4.1	4.7	4.3	3.6	18.0	26.7	31.3	3.3	84.6	54.3	48.7	51.3
33919 FORT MYERS	95.4	94.1	1.6	2.2	1.1	1.3	4.0	5.2	3.6	3.7	3.9	3.8	4.1	18.2	28.8	29.2	4.8	86.6	54.5	46.4	53.6
33920 ALVA	86.0	83.3	8.6	10.3	0.4	0.5	7.5	9.0	6.1	6.5	6.8	6.4	4.7	23.6	29.2	15.2	1.5	76.5	42.4	50.1	49.9
33921 BOCA GRANDE	99.4	99.2	0.3	0.4	0.2	0.4	1.5	2.3	2.0	2.4	2.3	2.5	1.3	8.6	35.4	42.0	3.5	91.8	63.3	46.9	53.1
33922 BOKEELIA	97.6	97.1	0.1	0.2	0.2	0.3	7.1	9.7	4.3	4.3	4.8	4.0	3.7	19.2	31.6	26.1	2.1	84.1	51.9	51.6	48.4
33924 CAPTIVA	100.0	100.0	0.0	0.0	0.0	0.0	0.0	0.0	0.0	0.0	0.0	0.0	0.0	0.0	87.5	12.5	0.0	100.0	60.0	37.5	62.5
33928 ESTERO	97.7	96.9	0.4	0.6	0.4	0.5	4.0	5.3	2.2	2.2	2.3	3.1	2.6	10.7	28.4	45.7	2.8	92.1	64.3	48.4	51.7
33931 FORT MYERS BEACH	98.0	97.6	0.1	0.1	0.3	0.4	2.7	3.5	1.2	1.3	1.5	1.4	1.7	11.3	32.3	45.1	4.2	95.2	64.7	49.3	50.7
33935 LABELLE	69.6	66.6	5.3	5.7	0.3	0.3	46.4	51.7	8.4	7.6	7.5	7.6	9.8	30.1	17.9	10.2	1.1	72.2	30.3	56.5	43.5
33936 LEHIGH ACRES	83.9	80.0	8.3	10.7	0.9	1.1	15.5	18.9	6.5	6.1	6.7	6.1	5.4	23.2	21.6	21.0	3.5	77.0	42.1	47.5	52.5
33946 PLACIDA	98.7	98.6	0.3	0.4	0.2	0.3	0.8	0.9	1.3	1.5	2.1	2.1	1.8	6.7	35.7	45.5	3.3	93.8	64.5	48.1	51.9
33947 ROTONDA WEST	98.4	98.2	0.4	0.5	0.3	0.3	1.3	1.7	2.5	2.6	3.0	2.7	2.6	11.5	30.8	40.8	3.6	90.1	62.5	47.7	52.3
33948 PORT CHARLOTTE	90.0	88.6	6.5	7.3	1.1	1.3	4.2	5.3	4.5	4.8	5.5	5.4	4.8	20.4	28.8	22.6	3.3	81.9	48.2	47.6	52.4
33950 PUNTA GORDA	95.0	94.6	2.8	2.9	0.7	0.8	1.9	2.4	2.1	2.3	2.6	2.5	2.4	10.4	30.5	42.5	4.7	91.4	63.8	47.9	52.1
33952 PORT CHARLOTTE	89.9	88.4	5.5	6.2	1.2	1.4	5.5	7.0	4.5	4.5	5.1	5.0	4.6	19.4	24.8	26.5	5.7	82.9	50.7	46.3	53.7
33953 PORT CHARLOTTE	94.5	94.0	3.0	3.1	0.8	1.0	2.6	3.1	3.6	3.6	3.8	3.6	3.4	16.3	29.6	34.5	1.8	86.9	58.1	48.4	51.7
33954 PORT CHARLOTTE	86.4	84.8	9.3	10.2	1.3	1.5	4.6	5.8	5.4	5.9	7.0	6.0	4.8	22.6	27.0	19.7	1.5	78.0	43.9	47.7	52.4
33955 PUNTA GORDA	97.3	96.7	1.0	1.2	0.7	0.8	1.8	2.2	2.6	2.7	3.2	3.1	2.6	12.6	32.0	38.7	2.5	89.6	61.3	48.6	51.4
33956 SAINT JAMES CITY	99.0	98.6	0.1	0.1	0.3	0.3	0.8	1.1	1.3	1.5	1.8	1.9	1.5	8.3	35.1	44.9	3.7	94.1	64.4	49.6	50.4
33957 SANIBEL	98.0	97.5	0.9	1.2	0.4	0.5	1.4	1.7	1.6	2.1	2.7	2.4	1.5	9.6	37.0	39.8	3.4	92.0	62.5	47.8	52.2
33960 VENUS	92.6	90.9	3.5	4.1	0.4	0.5	9.4	11.9	3.9	4.1	5.9	7.2	4.9	21.2	27.8	23.5	1.5	81.6	47.0	51.3	48.7
33971 LEHIGH ACRES	82.7	78.3	10.4	13.9	0.9	0.9	15.0	18.1	9.2	8.8	9.2	7.7	5.8	32.5	19.2	6.4	1.2	67.8	31.5	49.7	50.4
33972 LEHIGH ACRES	86.4	82.5	8.6	11.3	0.7	0.8	7.8	10.0	5.4	5.5	6.7	6.6	4.9	21.4	27.3	19.5	2.7	78.4	44.7	48.8	51.3
33980 PORT CHARLOTTE	89.1	87.8	7.8	8.5	1.2	1.5	3.5	4.3	2.9	2.7	3.4	3.9	3.4	13.1	23.2	37.6	9.9	88.7	63.2	44.5	55.5
33981 PORT CHARLOTTE	95.6	94.9	1.6	1.8	0.7	0.8	2.5	3.1	4.9	4.8	5.2	4.7	3.9	19.6	27.3	27.4	2.3	82.2	50.6	49.1	50.9
33982 PUNTA GORDA	91.1	89.6	6.4	7.5	0.4	0.5	3.1	3.9	3.7	4.0	4.4	4.9	4.8	25.3	27.8	22.5	2.7	84.8	46.9	54.9	45.1
33983 PUNTA GORDA	89.7	88.2	6.6	7.5	1.4	1.7	3.3	4.2	3.9	4.0	4.8	4.9	3.6	16.2	27.5	31.9	3.2	84.2	54.6	46.0	54.0
33990 CAPE CORAL	90.9	88.4	2.8	3.8	1.5	1.8	10.5	13.6	5.8	5.9	6.8	6.4	5.7	25.5	26.2	15.3	2.5	77.5	41.2	48.2	51.8
33991 CAPE CORAL	92.4	90.4	2.5	3.4	1.1	1.2	7.4	9.7	6.9	7.3	8.0	6.6	5.3	28.9	23.9	11.6	1.6	73.5	37.6	49.1	50.9
33993 CAPE CORAL	94.5	93.0	1.9	2.4	0.6	0.7	4.7	6.1	7.0	6.2	7.5	6.9	4.5	27.2	26.8	12.8	1.1	75.0	39.4	50.4	49.6
34102 NAPLES	88.1	86.6	7.9	8.9	0.4	0.5	2.0	2.9	3.2	3.6	3.8	3.7	2.6	15.8	31.9	30.2	5.1	86.9	56.7	47.0	53.0
34103 NAPLES	96.4	95.3	0.7	0.8	0.5	0.6	7.9	10.4	2.8	2.9	3.1	2.5	2.5	13.7	28.1	38.7	5.9	89.7	62.2	46.8	53.2
34104 NAPLES	89.8	87.6	3.6	4.4	1.3	1.5	14.4	18.8	5.5	5.1	4.8	3.8	4.5	24.7	24.4	25.9	1.5	82.4	46.5	48.4	51.6
34105 NAPLES	96.2	94.7	0.8	1.2	1.1	1.3	6.3	9.4	3.5	3.5	4.0	3.6	3.2	18.4	26.5	31.9	5.4	86.7	56.3	46.3	53.7
34108 NAPLES	96.0	94.6	0.7	0.9	0.7	0.8	7.9	10.9	2.9	3.2	3.8	3.9	3.2	16.9	28.7	33.8	3.5	87.6	57.8	48.2	51.9
34109 NAPLES	95.5	93.9	1.2	1.7	1.1	1.3	6.6	9.6	4.5	5.0	6.1	5.3	4.2	22.6	29.2	20.7	2.4	80.7	46.5	47.4	52.7
34110 NAPLES	96.9	95.7	0.7	1.0	0.5	0.6	6.2	8.4	3.3	3.7	3.6	3.2	3.0	15.6	28.7	33.5	5.3	87.4	58.8	47.3	52.7
34112 NAPLES	87.7	84.8	5.5	6.7	0.6	0.7	16.6	21.2	4.3	4.1	3.8	3.4	4.4	22.0	24.6	30.1	3.2	85.8	52.2	50.5	49.5
34113 NAPLES	78.0	73.5	7.2	8.1	0.5	0.5	30.8	37.5	5.9	5.2	5.5	5.1	6.4	23.3	23.1	22.0	3.7	80.4	43.8	51.1	48.9
34114 NAPLES	88.1	83.9	1.7	2.1	0.6	0.6	26.9	35.5	4.9	4.7	4.7	4.0	4.2	23.6	24.5	27.3	2.2	83.6	49.2	52.9	47.1
34116 NAPLES	79.7	75.8	8.9	10.3	0.9	1.0	32.4	39.6	8.2	7.7	7.9	7.1	8.4	33.1	20.0	7.1	0.6	72.0	31.5	52.0	48.0
34117 NAPLES	89.4	85.6	1.8	2.4	0.6	0.7	20.3	28.2	7.6	7.5	8.4	7.0	6.5	32.0	24.3	6.3	0.4	72.2	35.1	51.5	48.5
34119 NAPLES	97.2	96.3	0.6	0.7	0.6	0.8	4.5	6.3	4.2	4.8	5.3	4.0	2.6	17.5	33.7	26.9	1.2	83.1	53.0	48.0	52.0
34120 NAPLES	88.7	84.6	3.0	4.0	0.4	0.4	22.4	31.2	8.4	8.2	8.3	7.3	6.5	31.0	22.7	7.5	0.3	70.5	33.8	51.3	48.7
34134 BONITA SPRINGS	97.9	97.3	0.4	0.5	0.5	0.6	2.6	3.4	2.1	2.2	2.1	1.7	1.8	12.5	36.3	38.7	2.5	92.5	61.9	48.9	51.1
34135 BONITA SPRINGS	85.7	83.4	0.4	0.5	0.4	0.5	26.7	30.9	5.5	5.1	4.9	4.2	5.2	22.8	24.8	25.6	2.1	82.1	47.3	52.1	47.9
34141 OCHOPEE	95.5	93.8	1.4	1.9	0.3	0.3	3.9	5.9	3.3	3.5	3.5	5.2	4.0	20.3	31.6	26.2	2.5	86.2	53.0	52.4	47.6
34142 IMMOKALEE	41.7	39.2	17.6	16.6	0.4	0.4	67.8	72.1	10.2	8.9	8.7	9.6	13.1	31.0	14.6	3.7	0.3	67.1	24.8	58.0	42.0
34145 MARCO ISLAND	98.1	97.4	0.3	0.4	0.6	0.7	4.0	6.0	2.4	2.8	2.9	2.6	2.3	13.1	32.3	38.7	2.9	90.1	61.4	49.2	50.9
34201 BRADENTON	95.9	94.9	1.4	1.8	1.5	1.8	2.1	3.1	1.8	1.9	1.7	1.1	1.5	19.3	33.7	37.2	1.8	93.9	60.3	48.0	52.0
34202 BRADENTON	95.5	94.0	1.4	1.9	1.7	2.1	3.5	4.7	7.1	8.2	8.3	5.8	2.7	26.3	28.6	12.7	0.4	72.5	41.0	49.6	50.4
34203 BRADENTON	84.5	82.2	8.6	9.9	1.1	1.3	12.3	14.8	6.8	6.3	6.0	5.2	5.1	22.4	23.1	21.9	3.2	77.8	43.6	49.0	51.0
34205 BRADENTON	84.8	82.2	8.2	9.4	0.9	1.1	12.3	15.5	6.0	5.7	6.0	6.1	6.4	26.1	23.0	16.0	4.7	78.7	40.7	48.3	51.7
34207 BRADENTON	89.2	86.6	5.1	6.4	1.3	1.5	7.9	10.4	5.4	4.8	4.9	4.9	5.8	23.7	22.3	24.0	4.3	82.1	45.5	47.1	52.9
34208 BRADENTON	65.9	63.7	25.7	27.1	0.6	0.7	15.1	17.2	8.1	7.7	8.1	7.2	7.0	26.2	21.7	12.1	1.9	71.6	34.5	49.1	50.9
34209 BRADENTON	96.6	95.6	0.9	1.2	1.0	1.2	2.6	3.7	3.7	4.1	5.3	5.4	4.2	18.3	28.4	25.0	5.5	83.4	50.9	46.4	53.6
FLORIDA	78.0	76.5	14.6	15.2	1.7	2.0	16.8	19.0	6.0	5.9	6.4	6.4	6.5	26.6	24.5	15.5	2.4	78.1	40.0	48.8	51.2
UNITED STATES	75.1	73.6	12.3	12.5	3.8	4.2	12.5	14.1	6.9	6.7	7.2	7.0	7.3	28.6	23.8	10.8	1.7	75.1	36.0	49.1	50.9

ZIP CODE #	POST OFFICE NAME	2004 Per Capita Income	2004 HH Income Base	2004 Household Income Distribution (%) Less than $25,000	$25,000 to $49,999	$50,000 to $99,999	$100,000 to $149,999	$150,000 or More	Median Household Income 2004	2009	2004 National Centile	2004 State Centile	2004 Home Value Base	2004 Home Value Distribution (%) Less than $50,000	$50,000 to $89,999	$90,000 to $174,999	$175,000 to $399,999	$400,000 or More	2004 Median Home Value
33834	BOWLING GREEN	14895	2115	34.9	34.8	23.0	3.5	3.9	32695	37254	20	18	1684	30.8	29.2	26.8	11.3	1.9	75294
33837	DAVENPORT	20495	5846	23.7	35.9	32.8	4.7	2.9	42486	48751	55	52	4947	23.3	22.6	42.2	11.5	0.3	96574
33838	DUNDEE	15724	1162	34.6	36.4	23.8	4.6	0.7	33136	37755	21	19	908	29.7	27.1	38.9	4.3	0.0	83673
33839	EAGLE LAKE	16983	968	34.3	32.9	26.8	5.1	1.0	34536	38971	26	24	726	26.7	38.3	26.0	7.4	1.5	72206
33841	FORT MEADE	18422	3062	32.4	33.5	26.7	4.8	2.6	37780	42938	38	36	2429	31.6	40.1	22.5	5.3	0.5	70665
33843	FROSTPROOF	15798	3517	36.7	36.7	21.1	3.1	2.4	32145	36886	18	17	2740	34.8	33.0	21.0	10.9	0.3	64306
33844	HAINES CITY	18457	12546	33.8	35.7	23.5	4.0	3.0	34505	38654	26	24	9582	26.1	36.9	26.6	9.4	1.0	73986
33849	KATHLEEN	20027	400	26.0	33.0	28.8	7.3	5.0	44005	49055	59	57	372	10.2	41.9	36.6	10.2	1.1	88261
33850	LAKE ALFRED	19016	1587	32.1	29.9	31.7	4.3	2.1	40407	45652	48	45	1223	21.0	32.1	41.1	5.8	0.0	86173
33852	LAKE PLACID	20441	9027	35.5	37.2	20.5	4.5	2.2	33293	37125	22	20	7553	14.0	25.9	39.9	17.6	2.7	105247
33853	LAKE WALES	18548	4331	42.1	31.5	18.2	4.7	3.5	29413	33581	11	9	2491	19.6	37.9	37.3	4.1	1.2	82580
33857	LORIDA	15748	972	46.0	38.9	9.9	2.9	2.4	26918	30411	7	5	800	28.8	18.5	30.5	18.8	3.5	94074
33859	LAKE WALES	18555	3314	36.9	34.8	20.9	3.9	3.5	34023	38028	24	23	2662	35.4	33.6	20.8	9.1	1.2	65385
33860	MULBERRY	21870	6949	17.7	32.6	38.4	7.5	3.9	49677	56257	71	72	5533	16.1	29.6	43.5	9.9	0.9	95699
33865	ONA	20387	231	33.3	29.4	29.0	5.2	3.0	37641	43696	38	35	174	14.4	28.7	39.1	12.6	5.2	102632
33868	POLK CITY	17157	3854	24.1	34.5	33.1	5.9	2.4	42836	48517	56	53	3395	17.6	36.4	35.2	10.0	0.9	85867
33870	SEBRING	17380	7577	44.5	32.1	17.5	3.9	2.1	28389	31733	9	7	5432	30.8	33.0	27.8	6.7	1.7	74078
33872	SEBRING	22926	6048	31.9	35.3	25.2	5.0	2.6	35679	40210	30	28	5136	11.5	37.6	36.1	14.4	0.4	91247
33873	WAUCHULA	14922	4764	36.4	32.8	23.5	4.5	2.8	33181	37616	21	20	3577	22.1	31.5	32.2	13.0	1.3	85241
33875	SEBRING	23893	4834	27.1	36.0	28.2	5.9	2.9	39217	44109	43	40	4228	14.6	25.1	41.8	16.7	1.8	105184
33876	SEBRING	21565	2000	28.7	37.2	27.3	4.0	2.9	37572	42206	38	35	1727	14.3	18.3	47.3	17.6	2.6	110132
33880	WINTER HAVEN	20158	14341	29.7	31.7	30.8	5.7	2.2	39610	45873	45	42	9760	16.3	38.5	35.5	8.5	1.2	85205
33881	WINTER HAVEN	20602	12745	36.3	32.7	23.0	5.8	2.2	33937	38398	24	23	8925	24.3	37.7	27.4	9.5	1.1	76544
33884	WINTER HAVEN	32082	8945	17.8	32.2	33.1	10.5	6.5	50005	56984	72	74	7491	8.5	14.5	52.7	20.9	3.5	119412
33890	ZOLFO SPRINGS	15952	1752	34.7	32.9	25.6	4.5	2.4	36164	41684	32	30	1406	24.9	32.4	27.6	12.9	2.2	79697
33896	DAVENPORT	25111	1769	18.0	35.7	35.6	7.1	3.7	46651	53104	65	65	1547	14.5	21.4	46.5	14.9	2.7	113860
33897	DAVENPORT	29403	2858	16.6	38.9	35.2	7.4	1.9	45683	51029	63	62	2662	10.7	27.0	46.7	15.4	0.2	110724
33898	LAKE WALES	20866	7816	33.2	35.8	23.0	5.4	2.7	34449	39029	26	24	6168	24.4	30.5	29.2	14.8	1.1	81784
33901	FORT MYERS	24550	9623	36.6	32.0	19.5	6.8	5.1	32983	37339	21	19	4405	4.7	17.5	46.6	24.4	6.8	131953
33903	NORTH FORT MYERS	25336	12025	30.0	35.9	25.1	6.0	3.1	37424	42219	37	35	9823	17.2	33.1	35.0	13.2	1.6	89709
33904	CAPE CORAL	26629	16801	23.2	33.2	31.8	7.5	4.3	45211	51667	62	60	13582	0.5	5.3	48.4	41.1	4.7	165284
33905	FORT MYERS	18054	10170	30.9	34.2	26.3	6.8	1.9	38462	43672	41	38	7629	11.0	24.1	42.6	19.4	2.9	107563
33907	FORT MYERS	22410	10115	28.5	37.0	27.5	5.1	1.9	38258	43291	40	38	5030	4.5	20.4	58.4	16.4	0.3	124749
33908	FORT MYERS	38803	15559	22.1	32.3	25.7	10.3	9.6	46276	52614	65	64	12567	7.2	13.0	31.0	33.7	15.2	170436
33909	CAPE CORAL	18667	3602	20.6	35.2	35.7	6.7	1.9	45629	51412	63	62	2819	1.3	9.6	71.3	16.5	1.4	123957
33912	FORT MYERS	31984	16861	13.4	26.6	38.5	13.4	8.1	59352	69106	84	85	14122	4.7	5.1	34.6	45.3	10.5	187169
33913	FORT MYERS	43951	2120	10.5	13.6	38.0	21.8	16.1	83000	100435	96	97	1888	0.0	1.6	11.2	72.1	15.0	255590
33914	CAPE CORAL	26926	12490	14.5	28.6	39.5	10.9	6.5	55519	64468	80	81	10370	0.3	2.7	41.5	45.0	10.5	186804
33916	FORT MYERS	13542	8025	46.0	34.4	15.2	3.4	1.1	27031	30488	7	5	2679	21.9	35.4	37.6	4.4	0.8	82519
33917	NORTH FORT MYERS	22191	14570	30.9	36.5	24.8	5.6	2.2	36974	42227	35	32	12644	23.9	29.3	26.5	18.9	1.5	85593
33919	FORT MYERS	35426	14650	21.1	31.2	30.2	9.9	7.6	47577	54145	67	67	11894	0.6	9.3	44.7	38.3	7.0	164241
33920	ALVA	25899	2168	22.9	29.1	33.5	7.8	6.7	47857	53322	68	67	1871	6.8	17.3	38.6	29.1	8.2	133396
33921	BOCA GRANDE	119422	607	13.0	9.9	18.3	8.6	50.3	150536	177420	100	100	523	0.0	1.9	0.6	9.8	87.8	1000001
33922	BOKEELIA	27540	2093	29.5	28.6	28.7	8.7	4.5	42147	47788	53	52	1772	10.4	15.0	33.4	35.2	6.0	145321
33924	CAPTIVA	31367	5	20.0	40.0	40.0	0.0	0.0	28290	77107	9	7	5	0.0	0.0	0.0	100.0	0.0	316667
33928	ESTERO	36284	6105	20.2	33.2	28.8	9.2	8.5	46504	53567	65	65	5578	11.5	17.1	26.6	36.6	8.2	157560
33931	FORT MYERS BEACH	36089	6944	24.4	30.9	29.0	9.5	6.3	45322	51894	62	61	5908	14.9	10.3	15.5	43.7	15.7	207031
33935	LABELLE	16322	5343	33.0	31.7	27.3	5.2	2.8	36923	41807	35	32	4018	21.7	32.1	33.3	11.6	1.4	85237
33936	LEHIGH ACRES	18042	7416	29.1	38.9	26.4	4.1	1.5	37225	42892	36	33	5793	2.4	26.9	57.3	13.1	0.4	110091
33946	PLACIDA	65992	999	15.6	26.9	22.9	12.8	21.7	63327	72224	87	90	902	1.3	6.1	19.6	20.2	52.8	432051
33947	ROTONDA WEST	24134	2747	23.0	35.9	31.0	7.6	2.5	44260	51218	59	57	2372	0.6	7.0	44.0	46.7	1.7	171953
33948	PORT CHARLOTTE	21805	6601	24.3	36.1	30.4	7.3	1.9	42938	49049	56	54	5491	0.3	13.1	61.1	24.4	1.1	134195
33950	PUNTA GORDA	34856	10632	24.3	29.0	30.7	8.5	7.5	46963	53551	66	66	9186	8.9	14.7	21.4	36.1	18.9	206287
33952	PORT CHARLOTTE	21221	14716	33.3	35.5	23.7	5.1	2.3	34776	39189	27	25	11331	1.7	27.3	54.1	15.3	1.6	116318
33953	PORT CHARLOTTE	30999	2036	25.3	31.6	29.2	8.3	5.6	43253	48544	57	54	1713	1.8	20.0	38.7	31.6	7.9	146536
33954	PORT CHARLOTTE	24994	3272	16.0	32.0	38.0	11.6	2.5	51372	58974	75	75	2929	0.2	8.6	47.7	42.5	1.0	161738
33955	PUNTA GORDA	31527	3436	22.1	32.7	30.6	7.5	7.2	46016	52492	64	63	3177	11.6	19.1	23.4	37.8	8.2	160482
33956	SAINT JAMES CITY	30619	2317	29.6	31.1	28.0	6.5	4.8	39886	46178	46	43	2140	4.5	11.6	47.9	31.8	4.3	140240
33957	SANIBEL	83091	3690	11.5	16.3	27.1	16.2	28.9	88824	108180	97	98	3224	0.4	2.3	5.1	17.2	75.1	606016
33960	VENUS	17797	294	45.6	35.0	15.7	0.7	3.1	26859	30639	7	5	254	44.9	13.4	20.5	21.3	0.0	70833
33971	LEHIGH ACRES	18965	3983	15.4	36.2	40.4	6.0	2.0	49064	55991	70	71	3493	1.5	17.3	59.3	21.3	0.6	125209
33972	LEHIGH ACRES	21666	3464	19.7	32.5	39.2	7.3	1.4	48398	54707	69	69	3019	0.6	16.2	58.0	23.9	1.3	135942
33980	PORT CHARLOTTE	24409	4761	31.9	36.9	23.0	5.0	3.2	36515	40888	34	31	3910	7.1	28.9	47.0	15.4	1.6	108345
33981	PORT CHARLOTTE	21668	3508	24.3	37.5	31.2	5.5	1.6	41319	46461	51	49	3041	3.1	16.7	50.5	26.8	2.9	128367
33982	PUNTA GORDA	23169	4030	27.4	37.0	25.6	5.1	4.9	37724	42557	38	36	3409	15.9	25.7	31.0	20.6	6.8	107577
33983	PUNTA GORDA	25532	5317	17.6	36.2	33.9	8.5	3.7	47296	53713	67	66	4599	1.2	11.8	43.5	42.1	1.4	165341
33990	CAPE CORAL	21075	10775	19.3	34.7	36.9	7.5	1.6	46617	53235	65	65	8335	0.2	3.5	57.8	37.7	0.9	156161
33991	CAPE CORAL	22922	3956	16.2	31.3	37.5	10.4	4.5	52189	59761	76	76	3389	1.7	3.5	52.7	40.8	1.4	159983
33993	CAPE CORAL	26081	2163	13.1	34.2	39.8	9.5	3.5	52407	61561	76	77	1860	4.2	4.7	51.0	38.3	1.7	151036
34102	NAPLES	68094	6144	15.9	21.0	26.7	16.2	20.3	69891	87495	91	93	4567	0.3	0.7	10.6	27.9	60.5	547657
34103	NAPLES	71680	7278	12.9	21.5	28.1	13.8	23.7	72609	91043	92	94	6181	0.7	0.5	14.0	28.2	56.6	486392
34104	NAPLES	28535	11056	16.4	32.0	36.6	10.8	4.2	51111	60232	74	75	8018	7.1	3.2	30.9	52.4	6.4	195710
34105	NAPLES	57935	5786	18.5	21.6	28.4	16.4	15.1	63709	77451	88	90	4427	0.0	3.6	25.5	39.3	31.7	244962
34108	NAPLES	67124	8261	12.6	21.3	27.5	14.8	23.8	72530	91874	92	94	6852	0.5	0.0	10.4	34.7	54.4	446189
34109	NAPLES	41800	9995	12.9	25.1	32.9	14.3	14.8	62621	77886	87	89	7327	0.4	0.9	12.8	59.1	26.8	294905
34110	NAPLES	51955	9531	16.5	22.5	29.5	16.6	14.9	64329	79751	88	91	7796	4.4	4.5	16.9	47.4	26.8	264320
34112	NAPLES	27967	14302	22.1	36.8	27.3	8.5	5.3	42476	49568	55	52	10631	5.9	9.4	45.2	33.6	5.9	147734
34113	NAPLES	29337	6388	23.8	26.6	33.5	9.4	6.8	49505	57303	71	72	4771	4.3	6.3	43.1	34.4	12.0	165791
34114	NAPLES	25166	4647	26.5	36.2	26.3	7.7	3.3	41474	47821	51	49	3805	10.9	18.7	37.5	22.9	10.0	126975
34116	NAPLES	20267	9361	18.8	33.7	35.3	8.6	3.7	48076	54121	68	68	5895	0.6	1.5	56.6	37.4	3.9	162240
34117	NAPLES	22857	4078	10.5	25.3	45.2	14.9	4.0	60931	72140	85	87	3749	0.9	1.4	28.4	62.9	6.5	209912
34119	NAPLES	52777	6819	8.2	15.6	35.2	19.7	21.3	84233	104339	96	97	6426	0.7	0.4	6.7	53.7	38.6	340358
34120	NAPLES	23787	5390	10.1	28.4	42.8	13.1	5.6	60133	70219	84	86	5029	1.2	2.0	30.0	62.6	4.3	203257
34134	BONITA SPRINGS	77200	8032	11.5	23.8	29.6	14.3	20.8	71015	83899	92	93	6889	3.0	3.7	13.2	45.1	35.0	285699
34135	BONITA SPRINGS	28749	13453	21.0	33.5	29.2	9.0	7.3	46485	53484	65	64	11004	10.7	13.7	29.6	36.6	9.4	160579
34141	OCHOPEE	23900	592	23.1	41.7	26.4	4.9	3.9	41190	46921	50	48	489	14.5	15.8	31.9	30.9	7.0	146394
34142	IMMOKALEE	9868	5905	45.8	31.9	18.5	2.7	1.1	27513	31208	8	5	2666	29.4	19.2	40.6	9.5	1.2	91667
34145	MARCO ISLAND	50868	8438	14.0	21.4	31.3	15.5	17.8	68822	85534	91	92	7381	0.5	0.4	6.8	38.0	54.3	435116
34201	BRADENTON	51347	565	12.0	17.4	36.3	18.6	15.8	74062	86481	93	94	397	0.0	0.8	16.9	47.1	35.3	330357
34202	BRADENTON	41817	4188	8.7	13.8	31.5	27.2	18.8	92453	109860	97	98	3806	2.3	0.0	3.5	61.9	32.3	319881
34203	BRADENTON	22498	12565	25.0	31.9	31.0	8.7	3.4	43300	50453	57	55	10106	13.5	16.2	31.4	37.6	1.3	142828
34205	BRADENTON	19349	14511	36.4	32.8	24.6	4.7	1.7	33193	37911	21	20	8947	11.7	22.9	53.5	10.6	1.4	112308
34207	BRADENTON	19612	15571	37.1	37.4	21.5	2.9	1.1	31397	35962	16	14	10490	30.7	21.2	42.2	5.5	0.4	86122
34208	BRADENTON	19114	12515	29.0	33.9	27.4	6.0	3.8	39277	45865	44	41	7738	9.4	17.7	44.7	24.8	3.5	123878
34209	BRADENTON	31621	15962	17.5	32.7	33.2	10.2	6.5	49876	57423	72	73	13358	1.7	7.5	44.5	41.0	5.4	167882
	FLORIDA	25506		26.4	29.9	29.1	9.1	5.6	44138	51288				8.8	15.8	40.2	28.3	7.0	137042
	UNITED STATES	25866		24.7	27.1	30.8	10.9	6.5	48124	56710				10.9	15.0	33.7	30.1	10.4	145905

ZIP CODE #	POST OFFICE NAME	FINANCIAL SERVICES: Auto Loan	FINANCIAL SERVICES: Home Loan	FINANCIAL SERVICES: Invest-ments	FINANCIAL SERVICES: Retire-ment Plans	THE HOME: Home Improvements: Home Repair	THE HOME: Home Improvements: Lawn & Garden	THE HOME: Furnishings: Comput-ers & Hard-ware	THE HOME: Furnishings: Major Appli-ances	THE HOME: Furnishings: TV, Radio, Sound Equip-ment	THE HOME: Furnishings: Furni-ture	ENTERTAINMENT: Dine out/ Carry out	ENTERTAINMENT: Sports Equip-ment	ENTERTAINMENT: Fees & Tickets	ENTERTAINMENT: Toys & Games	ENTERTAINMENT: Travel	ENTERTAINMENT: Cable TV	PERSONAL: Apparel & Services	PERSONAL: Auto Repairs	PERSONAL: Health Insur-ance	PERSONAL: Pets & Supplies
33834	BOWLING GREEN	69	63	59	58	64	73	61	68	64	65	80	69	59	70	63	66	77	67	74	74
33837	DAVENPORT	85	71	55	65	77	87	67	79	74	68	89	88	63	85	71	78	84	77	91	100
33838	DUNDEE	67	52	36	49	57	67	56	62	62	54	74	69	50	69	56	66	67	62	74	75
33839	EAGLE LAKE	66	53	45	51	56	65	60	62	65	57	78	71	55	75	59	68	73	63	71	72
33841	FORT MEADE	78	73	64	70	75	83	70	76	73	71	90	84	69	88	72	75	86	74	81	88
33843	FROSTPROOF	58	51	44	48	52	59	51	56	54	53	67	60	48	61	51	56	64	56	60	63
33844	HAINES CITY	73	63	58	58	66	77	63	70	68	66	84	74	61	75	65	72	79	70	79	81
33849	KATHLEEN	85	80	76	76	85	99	74	84	78	79	97	82	75	81	80	83	91	82	98	96
33850	LAKE ALFRED	75	62	48	60	66	77	64	70	70	63	84	77	60	80	64	72	77	69	80	83
33852	LAKE PLACID	73	65	59	61	68	81	63	71	69	66	84	73	62	74	67	73	78	70	83	82
33853	LAKE WALES	68	55	50	53	57	67	62	64	68	60	82	72	58	78	60	70	77	65	72	74
33857	LORIDA	58	47	38	42	51	61	44	53	50	47	61	56	42	54	47	54	56	52	64	65
33859	LAKE WALES	78	61	45	56	67	78	59	70	66	60	79	77	54	73	61	71	73	68	83	89
33860	MULBERRY	100	83	58	78	88	96	79	89	85	80	103	106	74	101	80	87	97	88	98	115
33865	ONA	86	57	26	50	65	75	55	69	67	57	79	83	47	74	56	72	71	69	86	99
33868	POLK CITY	91	74	52	68	78	87	70	81	77	72	93	92	65	87	72	80	87	80	90	103
33870	SEBRING	60	53	50	49	56	67	53	59	58	54	71	61	52	63	55	62	66	58	69	68
33872	SEBRING	68	66	71	63	69	82	63	71	66	67	82	69	64	71	68	70	77	69	80	77
33873	WAUCHULA	69	58	47	55	59	65	60	65	64	62	79	72	56	73	59	64	76	66	67	73
33875	SEBRING	81	74	69	70	79	93	69	79	74	73	91	79	69	77	75	79	85	77	93	92
33876	SEBRING	73	66	60	61	70	83	63	72	68	66	83	72	62	72	67	72	77	70	85	82
33880	WINTER HAVEN	76	72	68	71	73	78	73	75	75	72	92	87	71	91	72	74	89	76	76	86
33881	WINTER HAVEN	66	62	63	59	64	74	63	67	67	64	82	72	63	77	65	69	78	66	74	75
33884	WINTER HAVEN	103	111	116	106	113	125	104	109	105	105	131	118	108	127	109	108	126	106	115	122
33890	ZOLFO SPRINGS	77	70	56	66	69	73	68	73	69	71	86	82	64	79	66	68	83	73	71	83
33896	DAVENPORT	95	83	70	78	90	101	78	89	83	80	102	98	75	94	83	88	96	87	102	111
33897	DAVENPORT	85	79	76	75	84	99	73	83	77	78	96	81	74	80	80	83	90	81	97	95
33898	LAKE WALES	75	62	51	57	67	78	60	70	67	62	81	75	57	73	63	71	75	69	82	85
33901	FORT MYERS	72	72	88	73	72	79	77	75	78	77	98	86	78	96	77	78	95	77	75	82
33903	NORTH FORT MYERS	75	71	72	67	74	86	69	76	73	71	90	78	69	82	73	76	85	74	85	85
33904	CAPE CORAL	82	81	84	77	84	96	77	83	80	80	100	86	79	91	82	84	95	82	93	94
33905	FORT MYERS	70	70	71	67	70	77	69	71	70	70	87	79	69	85	70	71	85	71	73	79
33907	FORT MYERS	68	64	72	65	64	71	67	68	68	69	86	76	67	81	67	68	83	69	68	75
33908	FORT MYERS	119	110	106	104	117	139	104	118	111	110	137	116	104	116	112	118	128	115	139	134
33909	CAPE CORAL	76	78	74	79	77	80	75	77	73	76	92	89	75	91	74	71	89	76	73	86
33912	FORT MYERS	113	119	119	118	119	127	110	115	108	114	136	126	113	128	113	108	131	113	115	128
33913	FORT MYERS	157	184	196	190	179	182	168	164	155	169	196	191	179	201	169	150	197	160	148	183
33914	CAPE CORAL	101	106	103	107	105	109	99	102	95	102	120	115	101	116	99	93	117	100	97	113
33916	FORT MYERS	50	43	51	43	42	48	49	48	52	50	65	55	48	62	47	52	63	50	49	54
33917	NORTH FORT MYERS	71	67	65	63	70	82	63	71	67	66	83	73	64	74	67	70	78	69	80	81
33919	FORT MYERS	101	101	107	98	104	118	96	104	98	101	123	108	98	111	102	102	117	102	113	115
33920	ALVA	97	95	92	92	97	106	90	96	92	92	114	107	90	110	93	93	109	95	100	112
33921	BOCA GRANDE	312	344	400	332	350	396	309	330	308	324	386	344	331	360	333	321	375	319	350	368
33922	BOKEELIA	93	82	75	77	88	105	80	91	87	83	106	91	78	92	85	92	98	89	107	104
33924	CAPTIVA	85	67	46	60	75	84	63	76	71	62	84	89	56	83	67	76	79	75	90	104
33928	ESTERO	111	105	102	99	111	131	97	111	103	104	128	107	98	107	106	110	119	107	130	125
33931	FORT MYERS BEACH	100	93	91	87	99	117	86	99	92	92	114	98	87	98	94	99	107	96	116	113
33935	LABELLE	80	70	61	67	70	75	72	76	75	75	93	85	68	88	70	73	91	77	76	85
33936	LEHIGH ACRES	64	61	61	58	63	71	61	64	64	61	78	70	61	75	63	66	74	64	71	72
33946	PLACIDA	190	182	184	171	192	227	168	191	177	180	221	186	172	186	183	189	207	185	222	214
33947	ROTONDA WEST	79	74	73	70	78	93	69	79	73	74	91	76	70	76	75	78	85	76	92	88
33948	PORT CHARLOTTE	73	74	77	71	76	86	70	75	72	72	90	80	72	84	74	75	86	74	81	84
33950	PUNTA GORDA	103	96	94	90	102	121	90	103	96	96	119	100	91	100	98	103	111	100	121	115
33952	PORT CHARLOTTE	68	63	60	59	66	78	62	68	66	63	81	71	61	74	65	70	76	67	78	77
33953	PORT CHARLOTTE	102	94	87	91	99	115	89	100	94	94	116	102	89	101	95	99	109	97	114	114
33954	PORT CHARLOTTE	92	93	93	90	96	107	88	94	89	90	111	100	90	105	92	92	107	92	101	106
33955	PUNTA GORDA	100	95	96	89	101	120	88	102	94	95	117	97	90	98	96	101	109	98	119	113
33956	SAINT JAMES CITY	86	82	82	77	87	103	76	87	81	82	101	84	78	85	83	87	94	84	102	97
33957	SANIBEL	244	232	225	220	244	285	214	242	225	228	279	240	217	238	232	239	263	235	279	277
33960	VENUS	76	60	41	54	67	75	56	67	63	56	75	79	50	74	60	68	70	66	79	92
33971	LEHIGH ACRES	83	87	83	88	85	86	82	83	78	83	98	96	82	98	81	75	96	81	77	93
33972	LEHIGH ACRES	81	77	73	73	80	90	74	81	77	76	95	86	74	89	77	80	90	79	89	91
33980	PORT CHARLOTTE	69	69	72	64	71	85	64	72	68	68	84	70	66	74	69	72	79	70	82	78
33981	PORT CHARLOTTE	77	68	60	64	72	86	66	75	72	68	87	76	65	77	70	76	81	73	87	86
33982	PUNTA GORDA	80	74	73	69	79	94	70	80	75	74	93	78	70	79	76	81	87	78	95	90
33983	PUNTA GORDA	87	86	87	82	89	102	81	88	83	84	104	91	82	92	86	87	98	86	98	99
33990	CAPE CORAL	76	78	79	77	79	85	76	78	76	76	94	89	77	95	77	76	91	77	79	87
33991	CAPE CORAL	90	101	100	102	98	98	92	93	87	94	110	108	95	110	92	84	108	91	84	103
33993	CAPE CORAL	99	104	100	104	103	108	96	100	93	99	117	112	97	112	97	92	113	97	97	112
34102	NAPLES	190	193	208	186	199	227	180	194	184	189	230	201	187	208	192	192	220	190	213	218
34103	NAPLES	203	199	207	191	205	236	189	205	196	198	245	210	192	219	200	205	234	201	227	230
34104	NAPLES	97	86	82	85	90	103	86	93	90	89	112	100	84	99	88	92	105	93	102	108
34105	NAPLES	175	167	171	159	174	204	158	175	166	167	207	175	160	178	170	175	195	171	200	197
34108	NAPLES	210	203	204	196	212	241	191	209	197	197	244	223	193	225	202	206	233	204	230	243
34109	NAPLES	139	137	140	137	141	156	131	140	132	137	165	149	133	149	136	134	158	138	148	157
34110	NAPLES	157	154	157	150	161	183	145	159	149	152	186	164	148	164	154	155	176	155	176	179
34112	NAPLES	90	84	83	79	88	103	80	90	85	84	105	91	80	94	85	90	99	88	102	101
34113	NAPLES	111	103	104	99	107	123	101	111	106	108	133	113	101	117	106	109	127	110	121	123
34114	NAPLES	94	77	61	70	86	98	73	87	81	74	97	96	68	92	78	87	90	85	102	112
34116	NAPLES	85	91	99	90	88	92	89	88	87	91	110	101	90	110	88	85	109	89	82	97
34117	NAPLES	102	116	112	120	111	108	104	104	96	108	122	122	108	123	102	90	121	101	90	115
34119	NAPLES	185	182	179	175	189	217	166	184	171	176	214	186	171	186	179	180	203	179	207	209
34120	NAPLES	103	116	120	120	113	112	108	107	101	110	127	126	111	128	107	96	125	105	95	118
34134	BONITA SPRINGS	224	212	208	201	223	262	197	222	208	210	259	220	200	219	214	222	243	217	258	253
34135	BONITA SPRINGS	102	97	94	92	100	113	93	102	97	98	120	105	93	108	97	100	115	100	111	114
34141	OCHOPEE	87	68	47	62	77	86	64	78	73	64	86	91	58	85	69	78	80	76	92	106
34142	IMMOKALEE	54	47	44	46	46	47	51	52	53	55	67	59	49	65	48	50	68	55	48	55
34145	MARCO ISLAND	160	150	144	142	159	187	139	158	147	149	182	154	141	152	151	157	171	153	185	180
34201	BRADENTON	152	142	136	135	151	178	132	150	139	141	173	147	133	144	143	149	162	146	175	171
34202	BRADENTON	160	181	183	184	177	183	162	165	153	168	194	184	171	189	165	150	191	160	155	183
34203	BRADENTON	80	79	79	76	80	89	76	81	78	78	97	87	77	91	78	79	93	80	85	90
34205	BRADENTON	59	58	67	58	58	64	62	61	62	61	77	70	61	76	61	62	75	62	61	67
34207	BRADENTON	58	55	55	52	57	65	54	59	57	55	70	62	54	66	56	59	67	58	65	66
34208	BRADENTON	73	71	76	70	70	77	73	74	75	74	93	83	73	90	73	75	90	75	75	82
34209	BRADENTON	99	103	112	101	105	118	98	104	98	101	123	110	101	114	103	101	118	102	110	114
	FLORIDA	89	87	95	86	87	96	87	89	89	89	111	100	87	107	88	90	108	90	91	101
	UNITED STATES	100	100	100	100	100	100	100	100	100	100	100	100	100	100	100	100	100	100	100	100

POPULATION CHANGE

ZIP CODE			POPULATION			2000-2004 ANNUAL RATE		HOUSEHOLDS					FAMILIES		
# POST OFFICE NAME	COUNTY FIPS CODE		2000	2004	2009	% Rate	State Centile	2000	2004	2009	% Annual Rate 2000-2004	2004 Average HH Size	2000	2004	% Annual Rate 2000-2004
34210 BRADENTON	081		12993	14707	16992	3.0	72	6737	7629	8804	3.0	1.92	3965	4383	2.4
34211 BRADENTON	081		1884	2395	2923	5.8	93	713	892	1079	5.4	2.68	619	769	5.2
34212 BRADENTON	081		5511	7588	9628	7.8	98	1926	2671	3398	8.0	2.80	1604	2203	7.8
34215 CORTEZ	081		564	624	709	2.4	64	284	315	358	2.5	1.98	175	190	2.0
34217 BRADENTON BEACH	081		8262	8562	9409	0.8	23	4238	4403	4836	0.9	1.94	2445	2477	0.3
34219 PARRISH	081		5944	7803	9726	6.6	96	2334	3070	3829	6.7	2.51	1899	2473	6.4
34221 PALMETTO	081		32626	35446	40021	2.0	55	12135	13403	15314	2.4	2.47	8496	9182	1.8
34222 ELLENTON	081		8160	8917	10137	2.1	58	4353	4737	5366	2.0	1.88	2754	2955	1.7
34223 ENGLEWOOD	115		17664	18205	19548	0.7	19	8843	9177	9920	0.9	1.97	5677	5808	0.5
34224 ENGLEWOOD	015		14876	15831	17348	1.5	42	7173	7716	8539	1.7	2.04	4890	5187	1.4
34228 LONGBOAT KEY	115		7603	8172	9025	1.7	48	4280	4627	5130	1.9	1.77	2845	3032	1.5
34229 OSPREY	115		4882	5952	6949	4.8	90	2332	2880	3391	5.1	2.07	1642	2000	4.8
34231 SARASOTA	115		32639	33310	35814	0.5	14	15776	16216	17560	0.7	2.01	8649	8717	0.2
34232 SARASOTA	115		32042	33595	36440	1.1	31	13315	14151	15496	1.4	2.35	8814	9194	1.0
34233 SARASOTA	115		14717	16250	18159	2.4	63	6538	7289	8204	2.6	2.20	4254	4680	2.3
34234 SARASOTA	115		20104	21295	23299	1.4	38	8474	9136	10124	1.8	2.22	4856	5127	1.3
34235 SARASOTA	115		13462	14472	15887	1.7	48	6255	6785	7503	1.9	2.10	4091	4370	1.6
34236 SARASOTA	115		11982	12728	13835	1.4	41	6218	6667	7342	1.7	1.74	2567	2665	0.9
34237 SARASOTA	115		16995	17846	19401	1.2	32	7134	7544	8272	1.3	2.24	3852	3992	0.8
34238 SARASOTA	115		13415	17420	20947	6.3	95	6508	8430	10149	6.3	2.05	4334	5529	5.9
34239 SARASOTA	115		15456	16065	17341	0.9	26	7318	7673	8347	1.1	2.06	4081	4197	0.7
34240 SARASOTA	115		7240	8453	9668	3.7	82	2554	3015	3478	4.0	2.79	2150	2521	3.8
34241 SARASOTA	115		11617	13026	14561	2.7	70	4409	4979	5598	2.9	2.61	3544	3965	2.7
34242 SARASOTA	115		9581	9682	10391	0.3	9	5019	5115	5523	0.5	1.89	3035	3036	0.0
34243 SARASOTA	081		21726	25046	29271	3.4	78	9557	11241	13282	3.9	2.22	6562	7547	3.4
34251 MYAKKA CITY	081		4202	5138	6113	4.9	90	1257	1570	1893	5.4	2.96	1044	1294	5.2
34266 ARCADIA	027		28342	30068	32231	1.4	39	8920	9456	10150	1.4	2.84	6343	6674	1.2
34269 ARCADIA	027		3867	4403	4913	3.1	75	1826	2091	2337	3.2	2.08	1333	1514	3.0
34275 NOKOMIS	115		14938	16380	18237	2.2	59	7156	7893	8836	2.3	2.07	4821	5263	2.1
34285 VENICE	115		18150	18768	20302	0.8	22	9913	10353	11310	1.0	1.73	5406	5538	0.6
34286 NORTH PORT	115		7103	10490	13415	9.6	99	2488	3692	4743	9.7	2.83	2027	2997	9.6
34287 NORTH PORT	115		18999	21442	24085	2.9	72	8842	9983	11251	2.9	2.13	5940	6624	2.6
34288 NORTH PORT	115		1569	2401	3110	10.5	100	531	818	1065	10.7	2.94	450	688	10.5
34292 VENICE	115		7466	8573	9706	3.3	77	3668	4264	4874	3.6	1.97	2548	2931	3.4
34293 VENICE	115		31029	33346	36634	1.7	48	14334	15520	17157	1.9	2.15	10068	10765	1.6
34420 BELLEVIEW	083		14059	15536	17849	2.4	63	5847	6494	7518	2.5	2.38	4019	4407	2.2
34428 CRYSTAL RIVER	017		8920	9478	10362	1.4	41	3713	3983	4397	1.7	2.35	2571	2731	1.4
34429 CRYSTAL RIVER	017		8605	9254	10214	1.7	49	3885	4242	4748	2.1	2.11	2649	2880	2.0
34431 DUNNELLON	083		6664	7335	8389	2.3	61	3014	3356	3885	2.6	2.15	2061	2258	2.2
34432 DUNNELLON	083		9659	10917	12668	2.9	72	4211	4794	5613	3.1	2.26	3071	3467	2.9
34433 DUNNELLON	017		4246	4579	5030	1.8	51	1726	1874	2073	2.0	2.44	1277	1375	1.8
34434 DUNNELLON	017		4904	5441	6074	2.5	66	2172	2410	2702	2.5	2.24	1566	1726	2.3
34436 FLORAL CITY	017		8175	8732	9586	1.6	44	3616	3911	4341	1.9	2.21	2496	2667	1.6
34442 HERNANDO	017		11174	12023	13225	1.7	50	5107	5577	6213	2.1	2.11	3638	3949	2.0
34446 HOMOSASSA	017		12160	13522	15105	2.5	67	5541	6247	7058	2.9	2.15	4094	4585	2.7
34448 HOMOSASSA	017		10009	10769	11858	1.7	50	4507	4922	5486	2.1	2.18	3033	3269	1.8
34449 INGLIS	075		3908	3954	4241	0.3	9	1736	1784	1939	0.6	2.19	1143	1162	0.4
34450 INVERNESS	017		10064	10596	11562	1.2	34	4844	5138	5651	1.4	2.06	3161	3320	1.2
34452 INVERNESS	017		10627	11279	12265	1.4	40	4617	4950	5445	1.7	2.18	3113	3305	1.4
34453 INVERNESS	017		7903	8737	9716	2.4	64	3426	3836	4315	2.7	2.23	2286	2531	2.4
34461 LECANTO	017		8700	10100	11516	3.6	80	3206	3793	4387	4.0	2.60	2449	2871	3.8
34465 BEVERLY HILLS	017		12051	13580	15325	2.9	71	6028	6787	7701	2.8	1.95	3829	4279	2.7
34470 OCALA	083		18541	19391	21774	1.1	29	8397	8873	10070	1.3	2.16	5172	5386	1.0
34471 OCALA	083		21356	22322	24975	1.1	29	8498	8939	10108	1.2	2.41	5823	6067	1.0
34472 OCALA	083		18293	21007	24620	3.3	77	7398	8577	10148	3.5	2.44	5361	6148	3.3
34473 OCALA	083		8581	11500	14514	7.1	97	3247	4335	5485	7.0	2.65	2427	3213	6.8
34474 OCALA	083		15963	17937	20707	2.8	70	6630	7575	8913	3.2	2.18	4145	4694	3.0
34475 OCALA	083		12573	12988	14331	0.8	21	3715	3880	4390	1.0	2.82	2426	2507	0.8
34476 OCALA	083		12596	15805	19390	5.5	92	5967	7545	9337	5.7	2.09	4425	5577	5.6
34479 OCALA	083		11944	12967	14744	2.0	54	4574	5007	5748	2.2	2.56	3333	3613	1.9
34480 OCALA	083		10396	11522	13252	2.5	65	3782	4209	4875	2.6	2.71	2884	3177	1.9
34481 OCALA	083		13249	15383	18094	3.6	80	6814	8034	9576	4.0	1.89	4725	5504	3.7
34482 OCALA	083		16370	19211	22694	3.8	83	6311	7543	9055	4.3	2.46	4497	5308	4.0
34484 OXFORD	119		1973	2556	3434	6.3	95	755	990	1352	6.6	2.58	563	728	6.2
34488 SILVER SPRINGS	083		9034	9967	11429	2.3	62	3943	4383	5072	2.5	2.24	2688	2952	2.2
34491 SUMMERFIELD	083		16712	20872	25528	5.4	92	7006	8903	11036	5.8	2.34	5289	6662	5.6
34498 YANKEETOWN	075		574	572	615	-0.1	4	287	290	316	0.2	1.93	184	184	0.0
34601 BROOKSVILLE	053		20991	22612	25301	1.8	50	8768	9547	10787	2.0	2.32	5774	6244	1.9
34602 BROOKSVILLE	053		5883	6817	7873	3.5	79	2271	2639	3063	3.6	2.58	1705	1961	3.4
34604 BROOKSVILLE	053		6454	6856	7531	1.4	41	2164	2332	2611	1.8	2.56	1611	1717	1.5
34606 SPRING HILL	053		23990	25252	27917	1.2	34	11029	11735	13102	1.5	2.14	7724	8132	1.2
34607 SPRING HILL	053		7037	7625	8508	1.9	54	3154	3460	3895	2.2	2.20	2350	2545	1.9
34608 SPRING HILL	053		23102	25623	28904	2.5	66	9743	10911	12420	2.7	2.31	7203	7991	2.5
34609 SPRING HILL	053		21982	26030	30431	4.1	84	8712	10407	12259	4.3	2.49	6910	8212	4.2
34610 SPRING HILL	101		10644	11793	13486	2.4	65	3846	4339	5015	2.9	2.72	2894	3222	2.6
34613 BROOKSVILLE	053		13657	15414	17548	2.9	72	6521	7402	8481	3.0	2.07	4503	5060	2.8
34614 BROOKSVILLE	053		2938	3337	3812	3.0	74	1101	1263	1454	3.3	2.64	837	951	3.1
34639 LAND O LAKES	101		17691	23690	29827	7.1	97	6306	8568	10891	7.5	2.75	4957	6660	7.2
34652 NEW PORT RICHEY	101		24335	25777	28779	1.4	38	11616	12435	13993	1.6	2.05	6740	7061	1.1
34653 NEW PORT RICHEY	101		30903	33245	37493	1.7	49	13653	14937	17059	2.1	2.15	8570	9185	1.6
34654 NEW PORT RICHEY	101		16374	18205	21060	2.5	67	6446	7291	8523	2.9	2.48	4700	5284	2.8
34655 NEW PORT RICHEY	101		24211	27447	31787	3.0	73	10360	11889	13878	3.3	2.31	7662	8750	3.2
34667 HUDSON	101		30380	34225	39603	2.8	71	13980	15940	18606	3.1	2.11	9131	10257	2.8
34668 PORT RICHEY	101		42415	44027	48784	0.9	24	19785	20773	23209	1.2	2.10	12066	12408	0.7
34669 HUDSON	101		10280	11680	13529	3.1	74	4022	4660	5464	3.5	2.49	2950	3373	3.2
34677 OLDSMAR	103		19541	20963	21900	1.7	46	7896	8504	8928	1.8	2.45	5533	5902	1.5
34683 PALM HARBOR	103		34688	35563	36481	0.6	17	14113	14671	15198	0.9	2.42	9765	10031	0.6
34684 PALM HARBOR	103		26593	26933	27419	0.3	9	12253	12502	12824	0.5	2.07	7606	7692	0.3
34685 PALM HARBOR	103		17283	19317	20634	2.7	68	6777	7593	8146	2.7	2.54	5285	5872	2.5
34688 TARPON SPRINGS	103		5663	6952	7799	4.9	90	2185	2716	3077	5.3	2.54	1716	2123	5.1
34689 TARPON SPRINGS	103		23532	25918	27611	2.3	61	10228	11362	12185	2.5	2.24	6666	7358	2.4
34690 HOLIDAY	101		12799	13555	15232	1.4	38	5914	6303	7131	1.5	2.11	3570	3732	1.1
34691 HOLIDAY	101		18829	19943	22362	1.4	38	8850	9428	10622	1.5	2.12	5399	5640	1.0
34695 SAFETY HARBOR	103		18164	18171	18445	0.0	5	7553	7633	7816	0.3	2.32	5098	5112	0.1
34698 DUNEDIN	103		36896	37810	38736	0.6	17	17594	18209	18809	0.8	2.26	9966	10211	0.6
FLORIDA						2.1					2.2	2.45			2.0
UNITED STATES						1.2					1.3	2.58			1.1

ZIP CODE #	POST OFFICE NAME	RACE (%) White 2000	White 2004	Black 2000	Black 2004	Asian/Pacific 2000	Asian/Pacific 2004	% Hispanic Origin 2000	% Hispanic Origin 2004	2004 AGE DISTRIBUTION (%) 0-4	5-9	10-14	15-19	20-24	25-44	45-64	65-84	85+	18+	MEDIAN AGE 2004	% 2004 Males	% 2004 Females
34210	BRADENTON	94.9	93.4	1.7	2.3	1.7	2.0	3.4	4.9	3.1	3.0	3.5	4.0	4.7	19.6	25.5	32.5	4.2	88.0	55.4	47.1	52.9
34211	BRADENTON	96.3	95.2	0.8	1.2	0.9	1.1	2.9	4.3	4.3	6.1	8.2	6.2	2.3	23.8	33.1	15.2	0.9	77.0	44.6	50.8	49.2
34212	BRADENTON	94.5	92.4	1.8	2.4	1.0	1.2	5.1	7.6	7.7	8.0	7.6	6.3	4.3	28.1	26.1	11.0	1.0	72.5	39.1	48.9	51.1
34215	CORTEZ	98.4	98.1	0.4	0.5	0.9	1.1	1.4	2.1	1.4	1.8	2.1	2.1	1.8	11.7	37.2	37.3	4.7	93.4	61.6	49.5	50.5
34217	BRADENTON BEACH	98.5	98.1	0.2	0.3	0.3	0.3	1.8	2.7	2.2	2.6	3.6	3.3	2.6	16.4	37.1	28.4	3.8	89.6	55.8	48.4	51.6
34219	PARRISH	94.0	92.2	3.0	3.8	0.4	0.5	5.0	7.1	5.2	5.4	5.3	5.0	3.5	22.2	29.1	23.3	1.1	81.0	47.4	48.8	51.2
34221	PALMETTO	74.9	73.5	16.8	17.1	0.4	0.5	17.7	20.5	6.3	6.1	6.2	5.9	5.6	23.2	23.9	20.3	2.7	78.0	42.6	50.3	49.7
34222	ELLENTON	95.9	94.6	1.6	2.1	0.3	0.3	5.3	7.3	3.3	3.1	2.7	2.5	2.4	12.3	23.3	44.1	6.3	89.4	65.2	45.6	54.5
34223	ENGLEWOOD	98.4	98.0	0.2	0.2	0.5	0.6	1.5	2.0	2.2	2.4	3.1	3.0	2.9	12.0	29.1	39.2	6.0	90.4	62.4	47.3	52.7
34224	ENGLEWOOD	98.3	98.1	0.3	0.3	0.3	0.4	1.3	1.7	3.2	3.2	3.8	3.8	3.2	15.3	28.8	35.0	3.9	87.5	58.4	48.1	51.9
34228	LONGBOAT KEY	99.2	99.1	0.1	0.1	0.5	0.5	0.7	1.0	0.6	0.7	0.7	0.6	0.7	4.4	30.2	55.5	6.7	97.7	68.9	46.1	53.9
34229	OSPREY	97.7	97.2	0.2	0.2	1.0	1.2	1.4	1.9	3.3	3.8	4.0	3.3	2.7	14.9	34.6	29.9	3.5	86.8	56.5	48.5	51.6
34231	SARASOTA	96.5	95.6	0.6	0.9	0.9	1.1	3.5	4.7	3.6	3.7	4.5	4.7	4.7	21.9	28.3	22.6	5.9	85.3	49.5	47.0	53.0
34232	SARASOTA	94.7	93.4	1.5	1.9	0.9	1.1	5.4	7.1	5.0	5.4	6.2	5.9	5.2	25.4	27.2	16.5	3.3	79.7	43.2	47.8	52.2
34233	SARASOTA	96.7	95.8	0.7	0.9	1.1	1.3	3.1	4.2	3.7	4.2	5.7	5.3	4.0	17.9	28.8	24.8	5.6	82.9	51.1	45.9	54.1
34234	SARASOTA	55.3	53.1	39.6	41.1	0.7	0.9	6.7	8.2	6.1	5.7	6.0	7.1	8.0	23.0	23.6	17.7	2.8	78.7	40.2	47.6	52.4
34235	SARASOTA	92.5	90.7	3.6	4.5	1.1	1.4	5.1	6.6	4.0	4.1	4.1	3.8	3.2	19.8	26.5	29.6	4.9	85.5	53.6	46.2	53.8
34236	SARASOTA	79.3	76.9	12.1	13.7	0.9	1.0	14.2	15.8	3.6	3.1	3.0	3.3	4.9	22.0	26.5	26.1	7.5	88.5	53.0	49.9	50.1
34237	SARASOTA	86.0	83.6	5.7	6.8	1.1	1.2	18.1	21.6	5.8	5.3	5.3	5.4	7.1	30.7	22.0	14.7	3.6	80.3	38.8	49.7	50.4
34238	SARASOTA	97.1	96.2	0.9	1.3	1.3	1.7	2.5	3.3	2.9	3.0	3.7	3.5	3.1	15.1	30.3	34.5	3.9	88.1	58.8	46.5	53.5
34239	SARASOTA	95.5	94.4	0.9	1.2	1.3	1.6	5.2	6.9	4.3	4.5	4.8	4.6	4.0	23.8	28.9	20.7	4.4	83.5	47.5	46.8	53.2
34240	SARASOTA	97.6	97.1	0.6	0.8	0.6	0.8	2.8	3.7	4.9	6.1	8.1	7.0	3.9	22.9	32.8	13.1	1.4	76.4	43.6	49.5	50.5
34241	SARASOTA	97.1	96.3	0.5	0.7	0.7	0.9	2.8	3.8	4.2	5.3	7.2	6.9	4.4	20.4	32.2	17.9	1.6	78.7	45.9	49.2	50.8
34242	SARASOTA	98.5	98.1	0.2	0.2	0.5	0.7	1.5	2.0	1.9	2.3	2.7	2.6	1.8	13.0	34.8	36.3	4.6	91.5	61.0	47.9	52.2
34243	SARASOTA	92.0	90.3	3.8	4.7	1.7	2.0	4.8	6.3	4.5	4.7	4.5	3.8	3.7	23.7	29.6	23.3	2.3	84.1	48.8	48.3	51.7
34251	MYAKKA CITY	96.1	95.0	0.7	1.1	0.7	0.8	16.3	20.7	7.9	7.6	8.4	7.4	5.9	32.3	24.3	5.7	0.6	71.7	34.5	51.5	48.5
34266	ARCADIA	70.6	67.4	14.1	14.8	0.5	0.6	27.7	32.6	6.5	6.1	6.2	7.3	8.4	29.2	20.3	14.2	1.8	77.1	34.7	56.9	43.1
34269	ARCADIA	93.4	92.6	2.9	3.1	0.2	0.3	4.6	5.6	3.5	3.6	3.9	4.0	3.9	14.9	27.1	36.3	2.7	86.3	58.9	50.2	49.8
34275	NOKOMIS	96.8	96.2	1.3	1.5	0.6	0.8	1.4	1.9	2.7	3.0	3.8	3.6	3.1	14.4	32.2	32.7	4.5	88.2	58.0	48.5	51.5
34285	VENICE	98.2	97.8	0.5	0.7	0.4	0.5	1.1	1.5	1.3	1.4	1.9	2.0	1.7	8.1	24.7	46.4	12.6	94.2	68.9	43.6	56.4
34286	NORTH PORT	93.4	91.7	3.9	5.2	0.4	0.5	3.0	3.9	7.9	7.8	7.6	5.9	4.9	30.7	22.9	11.4	0.9	72.9	36.7	49.4	50.6
34287	NORTH PORT	93.8	92.0	3.5	4.7	0.5	0.6	2.6	3.6	4.1	4.2	4.9	4.2	3.5	17.5	20.9	35.6	5.0	84.0	57.0	46.4	53.6
34288	NORTH PORT	94.8	93.6	1.4	1.9	0.7	0.9	4.2	5.5	8.5	8.3	9.1	6.3	5.1	33.3	19.0	9.8	0.5	70.1	34.1	49.6	50.4
34292	VENICE	98.2	97.7	0.5	0.7	0.5	0.6	1.4	1.9	1.6	1.9	3.0	2.7	2.0	10.5	29.1	44.5	4.6	91.7	64.6	46.4	53.6
34293	VENICE	97.8	97.3	0.4	0.5	0.7	0.8	1.5	2.0	3.2	3.5	4.2	3.9	3.2	16.6	28.0	33.2	4.1	86.7	56.8	47.3	52.7
34420	BELLEVIEW	91.9	90.4	4.0	4.8	0.4	0.5	6.2	7.7	5.5	5.5	6.1	6.2	5.6	23.1	25.2	20.5	2.3	79.0	43.7	48.4	51.7
34428	CRYSTAL RIVER	92.8	91.9	3.8	4.2	1.0	1.2	2.8	3.5	4.6	4.8	6.0	5.5	4.6	20.6	30.6	21.1	2.3	80.8	47.4	48.5	51.5
34429	CRYSTAL RIVER	92.5	91.7	4.7	5.1	1.1	1.4	2.2	2.7	3.5	3.7	4.8	4.8	4.4	17.0	32.0	26.1	3.5	84.7	52.9	48.2	51.8
34431	DUNNELLON	92.6	90.9	4.5	5.7	0.6	0.7	3.9	4.7	3.6	3.7	5.4	5.3	4.1	18.5	27.1	28.3	4.1	83.9	52.6	47.1	52.9
34432	DUNNELLON	90.9	89.1	6.0	7.2	0.5	0.6	4.5	5.6	3.4	3.6	4.3	4.2	3.5	15.6	26.5	35.7	3.1	85.9	58.1	47.8	52.2
34433	DUNNELLON	95.6	95.0	2.1	2.3	0.6	0.6	2.5	3.2	4.2	4.5	5.9	5.5	4.7	20.0	30.6	22.6	2.1	81.9	48.8	49.2	50.8
34434	DUNNELLON	90.5	88.7	6.0	7.0	0.6	0.8	4.4	5.6	4.4	4.2	5.0	5.3	4.0	17.7	26.3	29.6	3.7	83.2	53.1	47.8	52.2
34436	FLORAL CITY	97.1	96.7	1.0	1.2	0.2	0.3	2.5	3.3	3.9	4.0	4.9	5.8	4.5	17.9	29.4	26.9	2.8	83.4	51.5	48.9	51.1
34442	HERNANDO	94.9	94.0	2.3	2.6	1.2	1.5	2.0	2.5	3.4	3.6	4.2	4.4	3.5	15.8	29.9	31.5	3.6	85.9	56.6	48.7	51.3
34446	HOMOSASSA	97.6	97.3	0.6	0.7	0.6	0.8	1.6	2.1	3.1	3.1	3.9	4.1	3.5	14.3	28.5	36.1	3.3	87.3	59.3	48.6	51.4
34448	HOMOSASSA	96.6	96.2	1.0	1.1	0.6	0.7	1.7	2.1	4.0	4.1	5.1	4.9	4.2	18.8	29.6	26.8	2.6	83.6	51.7	49.7	50.3
34449	INGLIS	97.1	96.7	1.2	1.4	0.3	0.4	1.5	1.9	3.8	3.9	5.1	5.9	4.7	18.6	33.6	22.3	2.2	83.4	50.4	49.9	50.1
34450	INVERNESS	95.2	94.7	2.5	2.8	0.5	0.5	2.4	3.0	3.6	3.8	4.5	4.8	4.0	15.8	30.4	29.3	3.9	85.1	55.1	47.5	52.6
34452	INVERNESS	95.0	94.3	2.3	2.6	0.6	0.7	4.7	6.0	4.1	4.2	5.2	5.5	4.8	19.6	25.6	27.0	4.1	83.1	50.2	47.7	52.3
34453	INVERNESS	94.4	93.6	3.2	3.5	0.9	1.1	2.3	2.8	4.5	4.4	5.0	4.7	4.8	18.3	27.7	26.6	4.0	83.1	51.5	47.7	52.3
34461	LECANTO	95.0	94.3	1.9	2.1	1.4	1.6	2.6	3.3	3.7	4.1	5.4	5.6	4.3	17.9	30.7	25.8	2.5	83.2	51.4	49.3	50.7
34465	BEVERLY HILLS	95.4	94.7	2.0	2.3	0.9	1.1	3.5	4.3	3.1	3.0	3.2	2.7	3.0	12.4	23.0	42.7	7.0	89.0	64.8	45.4	54.7
34470	OCALA	86.3	84.1	10.0	11.6	0.8	1.0	5.0	6.1	6.3	5.6	5.9	5.5	6.2	22.7	23.6	20.7	3.5	78.8	43.3	46.0	54.0
34471	OCALA	93.1	91.7	3.6	4.5	1.3	1.6	3.8	4.8	5.5	5.7	6.8	6.9	5.7	23.5	26.4	15.9	3.8	78.0	42.5	46.9	53.1
34472	OCALA	74.0	71.1	18.8	20.9	0.8	1.0	10.5	12.2	6.5	6.4	7.1	6.3	5.6	24.0	20.9	20.9	2.4	75.9	40.5	46.5	53.5
34473	OCALA	76.3	72.7	11.8	13.5	0.7	0.8	26.1	30.9	5.8	5.7	6.5	6.7	5.4	22.1	24.9	20.8	2.0	77.9	43.4	47.8	52.2
34474	OCALA	69.0	68.0	23.7	24.0	2.2	2.5	7.6	8.9	5.7	5.5	6.0	6.8	7.3	24.2	22.8	19.0	2.7	78.9	41.0	49.7	50.3
34475	OCALA	46.0	42.9	49.5	52.2	0.5	0.6	5.3	6.0	6.4	6.0	6.7	8.4	8.5	29.7	21.6	10.8	1.9	76.4	35.4	50.6	49.5
34476	OCALA	94.0	92.9	3.1	3.7	0.9	1.2	4.1	5.0	2.8	3.0	3.1	2.8	2.3	12.0	25.5	45.9	2.7	89.4	64.3	46.9	53.1
34479	OCALA	85.9	83.5	10.5	12.3	0.7	0.9	4.7	5.8	6.8	6.8	7.0	6.5	6.2	26.7	24.8	13.6	1.6	75.4	38.8	48.0	52.0
34480	OCALA	88.2	85.9	7.7	9.1	1.1	1.3	5.1	6.4	6.1	6.6	7.4	7.1	5.7	24.4	27.0	14.0	1.7	75.2	40.7	48.7	51.3
34481	OCALA	95.2	94.3	2.9	3.5	0.4	0.6	2.8	3.4	2.1	2.1	2.3	2.2	1.8	9.1	22.4	52.2	5.9	92.2	68.3	46.0	54.1
34482	OCALA	77.5	74.2	17.0	19.4	0.5	0.6	8.7	10.5	5.7	5.7	6.1	6.1	5.7	26.0	26.3	17.0	1.5	78.8	41.5	50.0	50.0
34484	OXFORD	80.3	79.1	16.3	16.6	0.4	0.5	3.9	4.9	6.4	6.5	7.1	6.9	6.3	26.0	24.9	14.4	1.6	75.9	38.4	48.4	51.6
34488	SILVER SPRINGS	94.4	93.5	3.1	3.6	0.4	0.4	2.3	2.8	5.0	4.9	5.9	5.9	5.0	21.8	27.0	22.0	2.5	80.3	46.1	49.5	50.5
34491	SUMMERFIELD	92.4	91.3	4.2	4.8	0.3	0.3	6.3	7.5	4.7	4.7	5.5	5.3	4.6	19.8	24.9	28.6	2.0	81.9	49.5	48.6	51.4
34498	YANKEETOWN	97.7	97.0	0.5	0.5	0.4	0.5	0.9	1.2	2.8	3.2	5.1	6.6	4.0	16.4	34.4	25.0	2.5	84.3	53.3	51.9	48.1
34601	BROOKSVILLE	85.0	84.1	11.7	12.1	0.7	0.8	3.0	3.6	5.8	5.6	6.2	6.0	5.6	21.7	26.0	19.6	3.5	78.7	44.4	47.3	52.7
34602	BROOKSVILLE	88.8	86.5	8.6	10.4	0.4	0.5	4.3	5.3	6.1	6.2	7.0	6.5	5.3	22.7	28.9	15.4	1.9	76.7	42.5	48.3	51.7
34604	BROOKSVILLE	89.2	87.8	7.1	8.0	0.6	0.7	5.3	6.5	4.9	5.3	6.5	7.3	7.8	28.4	25.6	12.9	1.3	78.8	38.9	49.1	50.9
34606	SPRING HILL	95.0	94.1	1.9	2.2	0.5	0.6	5.7	7.0	4.1	4.0	4.2	3.8	3.7	15.7	20.8	39.1	4.7	85.4	60.4	46.5	53.5
34607	SPRING HILL	95.3	94.6	1.8	2.1	1.3	1.6	2.7	3.3	2.7	3.0	4.1	3.9	3.5	13.5	37.5	29.6	2.3	87.7	56.8	48.9	51.1
34608	SPRING HILL	94.4	93.3	2.4	2.9	0.7	0.9	7.0	8.8	4.3	4.4	4.8	5.0	4.5	18.2	26.6	28.0	4.3	83.5	52.0	47.0	53.0
34609	SPRING HILL	94.0	92.9	2.8	3.3	0.8	1.0	6.8	8.3	4.7	4.8	5.8	5.8	4.9	19.2	28.4	24.4	2.0	80.9	48.4	47.8	52.2
34610	SPRING HILL	96.6	96.0	0.8	0.9	0.2	0.3	3.8	4.8	6.0	6.4	7.2	7.2	5.8	25.9	28.3	12.1	1.1	75.9	40.2	49.7	50.3
34613	BROOKSVILLE	97.6	97.1	0.6	0.7	0.5	0.6	2.8	3.7	2.9	2.9	3.4	3.4	2.9	12.7	25.7	41.2	4.9	88.6	62.7	47.2	52.8
34614	BROOKSVILLE	95.8	94.9	0.6	0.7	0.4	0.5	5.0	6.5	6.1	6.1	7.4	6.8	5.5	22.9	27.2	17.0	1.2	76.1	41.8	50.6	49.5
34639	LAND O LAKES	94.3	93.3	1.6	1.9	1.1	1.3	8.1	10.1	6.4	6.6	7.8	7.3	6.1	27.9	27.2	9.7	0.9	74.5	38.1	49.2	50.8
34652	NEW PORT RICHEY	95.4	94.5	0.7	0.9	1.0	1.2	4.1	5.2	4.7	4.6	4.9	4.4	4.4	21.3	26.4	24.2	5.2	83.2	49.5	47.4	52.6
34653	NEW PORT RICHEY	95.0	94.2	1.0	1.2	1.1	1.2	4.7	6.0	5.3	5.0	5.3	5.2	5.2	22.1	23.1	23.7	5.2	81.1	46.6	46.5	53.5
34654	NEW PORT RICHEY	96.7	96.1	0.6	0.7	0.8	1.0	2.5	3.3	5.3	5.5	6.3	6.8	5.5	22.5	27.8	18.1	2.3	78.3	43.8	49.6	50.5
34655	NEW PORT RICHEY	96.4	95.8	0.9	1.1	1.1	1.3	3.1	3.9	4.8	5.2	5.8	5.0	3.7	20.0	26.2	26.7	2.8	81.1	49.0	47.7	52.3
34667	HUDSON	96.6	96.1	0.5	0.6	0.8	0.9	2.8	3.6	3.8	3.9	4.5	4.3	4.0	17.6	27.7	29.0	5.2	85.1	54.4	48.2	51.9
34668	PORT RICHEY	95.5	94.7	1.1	1.3	0.9	1.0	4.9	6.1	4.8	4.6	4.9	4.5	4.5	20.7	23.3	27.1	5.7	83.1	50.2	46.8	53.2
34669	HUDSON	96.9	96.4	0.5	0.6	0.6	0.6	2.6	3.3	5.3	5.4	6.2	6.0	5.2	23.0	29.3	18.1	1.6	79.4	44.3	50.2	49.9
34677	OLDSMAR	91.6	89.7	2.6	3.3	2.7	3.2	6.0	7.5	5.9	6.6	7.0	6.1	5.0	28.8	25.2	14.0	1.5	76.7	39.9	48.0	52.0
34683	PALM HARBOR	96.2	95.4	0.8	1.1	1.1	1.4	3.4	4.4	4.5	5.2	6.9	6.7	5.0	24.7	30.3	14.7	2.0	78.9	43.4	48.0	52.1
34684	PALM HARBOR	95.4	94.3	1.1	1.5	1.5	1.9	3.5	4.4	4.2	4.4	5.1	4.4	3.4	22.0	22.8	26.4	7.2	83.5	49.9	45.4	54.7
34685	PALM HARBOR	94.8	93.7	1.1	1.5	2.3	2.9	3.7	4.7	5.5	6.4	8.0	6.5	3.9	24.1	29.5	14.9	1.4	75.8	42.8	48.8	51.2
34688	TARPON SPRINGS	95.0	93.9	1.0	1.3	2.4	3.0	3.2	4.0	5.1	5.7	7.3	5.6	4.0	21.1	30.9	18.7	1.6	78.2	45.7	48.4	51.6
34689	TARPON SPRINGS	90.3	88.8	5.9	6.6	1.1	1.4	4.2	5.3	5.1	5.0	5.3	5.0	5.0	21.6	27.9	21.9	3.1	81.6	47.0	47.9	52.1
34690	HOLIDAY	95.8	95.1	0.8	1.0	0.9	1.0	4.4	5.5	5.4	5.2	5.1	4.0	3.8	22.3	23.0	24.9	6.3	81.8	48.5	46.6	53.4
34691	HOLIDAY	94.8	93.9	1.6	1.9	1.0	1.2	3.7	4.7	5.0	4.8	4.8	4.2	4.1	22.2	23.4	26.7	4.9	82.8	49.4	47.1	52.9
34695	SAFETY HARBOR	92.2	90.5	4.2	5.2	1.6	2.0	3.5	4.5	4.7	5.4	6.3	5.8	4.4	23.7	30.8	16.0	2.9	79.8	44.8	47.7	52.3
34698	DUNEDIN	94.9	93.8	2.0	2.6	1.1	1.4	3.3	4.2	3.8	3.9	4.6	4.6	4.5	21.6	27.4	23.6	6.1	84.9	49.9	45.7	54.3
	FLORIDA	78.0	76.5	14.6	15.2	1.7	2.0	16.8	19.0	6.0	5.9	6.4	6.4	6.5	26.6	24.5	15.5	2.4	78.1	40.0	48.8	51.2
	UNITED STATES	75.1	73.6	12.3	12.5	3.8	4.2	12.5	14.1	6.9	6.7	7.2	7.0	7.3	28.6	23.8	10.8	1.7	75.1	36.0	49.1	50.9

ZIP CODE #	POST OFFICE NAME	2004 Per Capita Income	2004 HH Income Base	2004 Household Income Distribution (%) Less than $25,000	$25,000 to $49,999	$50,000 to $99,999	$100,000 to $149,999	$150,000 or More	Median Household Income 2004	2009	2004 National Centile	2004 State Centile	2004 Home Value Base	2004 Home Value Distribution (%) Less than $50,000	$50,000 to $89,999	$90,000 to $174,999	$175,000 to $399,999	$400,000 or More	2004 Median Home Value
34210	BRADENTON	30643	7629	22.6	33.9	31.4	8.4	3.7	44768	50907	61	58	5146	3.2	6.6	49.6	37.2	3.5	152523
34211	BRADENTON	33026	892	9.0	19.8	38.9	23.8	8.5	77258	89262	94	95	850	1.9	0.8	11.7	62.0	23.7	279927
34212	BRADENTON	28751	2671	12.7	17.9	44.0	19.5	5.9	67643	79398	90	92	2349	4.7	4.1	17.3	66.3	7.6	241323
34215	CORTEZ	33672	315	28.9	26.0	26.0	14.3	4.8	45141	53009	62	59	282	3.6	8.9	27.7	55.3	4.6	206731
34217	BRADENTON BEACH	34289	4403	24.9	28.6	31.1	8.0	7.4	46609	54387	65	65	3297	4.5	1.3	13.3	55.1	25.8	289051
34219	PARRISH	30191	3070	16.9	28.2	34.6	10.6	9.7	55117	62582	80	81	2841	1.6	13.0	38.1	33.0	14.4	164418
34221	PALMETTO	20507	13403	29.7	32.4	29.5	5.5	3.0	39544	45034	44	42	11033	22.3	18.6	40.1	16.2	2.8	104169
34222	ELLENTON	23525	4737	32.2	35.9	25.9	4.6	1.5	34183	38879	25	23	4246	37.8	24.4	27.3	9.7	0.9	67234
34223	ENGLEWOOD	29789	9177	27.2	34.5	27.1	6.4	4.9	39794	46035	45	43	7927	4.0	15.3	45.9	27.3	7.5	134901
34224	ENGLEWOOD	24258	7716	31.7	34.1	26.6	5.4	2.3	36504	40982	34	30	6444	3.7	15.9	54.1	23.3	3.0	127424
34228	LONGBOAT KEY	98986	4627	11.9	13.5	23.3	19.2	32.1	102630	122650	98	99	4272	0.5	0.5	4.3	31.8	63.0	540979
34229	OSPREY	59239	2880	18.6	21.4	28.5	13.4	18.1	64452	76969	88	91	2515	9.2	5.6	17.0	31.7	36.5	307973
34231	SARASOTA	34105	16216	23.1	31.8	29.3	9.3	6.6	45162	52410	62	59	11617	4.3	4.9	48.5	33.6	8.7	157226
34232	SARASOTA	27212	14151	19.2	30.3	36.5	9.1	4.9	50402	57447	73	74	11147	1.6	5.5	57.1	33.2	2.6	149192
34233	SARASOTA	31013	7289	18.4	27.5	34.9	12.9	6.4	53418	62094	78	79	6206	5.8	6.9	39.5	43.6	4.3	169183
34234	SARASOTA	19952	9136	39.1	30.3	23.8	4.6	2.2	33499	39229	22	21	5764	13.7	28.8	40.8	12.8	4.0	97522
34235	SARASOTA	35624	6785	15.7	27.8	36.7	13.3	6.6	55590	64368	80	81	5754	0.6	4.1	48.9	42.9	3.5	167798
34236	SARASOTA	40896	6667	31.7	26.3	22.6	9.1	10.3	41197	48536	50	48	3829	2.7	2.4	16.8	40.1	38.0	315688
34237	SARASOTA	19882	7544	30.7	39.3	24.7	4.1	1.2	35244	40956	28	26	4136	3.4	17.9	72.1	6.3	0.4	114989
34238	SARASOTA	44572	8430	15.8	20.3	34.7	15.5	13.6	65177	78646	89	91	6572	6.1	3.9	8.7	54.0	27.3	297965
34239	SARASOTA	32072	7673	23.2	31.1	29.8	10.6	5.4	46119	53803	64	63	5655	5.7	5.3	47.3	33.1	8.7	160211
34240	SARASOTA	42509	3015	6.8	16.2	34.6	24.4	18.0	85537	107885	96	97	2844	0.0	1.0	6.0	62.1	30.9	306713
34241	SARASOTA	39709	4979	10.6	23.4	35.6	18.0	12.3	67428	80301	90	92	4539	1.7	4.9	25.8	44.4	23.3	231241
34242	SARASOTA	69324	5115	12.0	20.2	28.3	17.5	22.0	79133	99577	95	96	4289	0.0	0.2	4.1	35.5	60.2	484922
34243	SARASOTA	36413	11241	14.6	23.5	39.2	14.1	8.6	61815	72403	86	88	8908	1.2	1.7	29.5	57.4	10.1	208211
34251	MYAKKA CITY	26122	1570	12.9	25.4	44.8	10.8	6.1	59259	68018	84	85	1391	3.0	5.6	28.9	49.7	12.8	204167
34266	ARCADIA	15366	9456	36.9	36.0	21.3	3.7	2.1	32498	36458	19	17	7082	25.5	32.7	28.5	10.8	2.6	79167
34269	ARCADIA	25836	2091	30.3	28.7	33.4	4.7	2.9	42962	47560	56	54	1825	18.4	21.5	32.0	23.0	5.2	109108
34275	NOKOMIS	39009	7893	22.5	28.8	29.0	9.1	10.5	48713	56418	70	70	6891	10.6	9.2	29.4	35.2	15.7	178067
34285	VENICE	32334	10353	26.6	34.8	25.5	8.4	4.7	40699	47135	49	47	8548	13.5	16.2	34.1	28.7	7.4	128518
34286	NORTH PORT	20156	3692	15.4	33.2	41.9	6.9	2.6	50740	58569	73	75	3394	0.0	6.5	61.7	30.6	1.1	145631
34287	NORTH PORT	20937	9983	32.4	37.2	24.7	3.6	2.0	35840	41466	31	29	8684	6.1	29.0	57.3	7.5	0.1	103346
34288	NORTH PORT	18775	818	13.1	38.4	41.6	4.4	2.6	49162	56499	70	71	763	1.1	0.8	64.2	29.8	4.2	151074
34292	VENICE	40537	4264	15.3	28.9	33.5	11.3	11.0	55258	65118	80	81	3645	3.6	2.4	27.7	51.1	15.3	239286
34293	VENICE	26160	15520	19.2	37.4	33.7	6.3	3.4	45376	51759	62	61	13717	1.7	5.8	56.6	33.6	2.3	146441
34420	BELLEVIEW	18293	6494	35.2	36.1	23.6	4.1	0.9	33342	37550	22	21	5104	24.5	36.1	30.9	7.5	1.1	78236
34428	CRYSTAL RIVER	22029	3983	32.2	32.7	23.8	7.7	3.6	35665	41058	30	28	3140	12.2	24.0	35.9	25.1	2.8	117795
34429	CRYSTAL RIVER	27267	4242	30.0	30.0	26.4	8.7	5.0	39032	45000	43	40	3547	8.4	15.2	43.6	26.8	6.0	129548
34431	DUNNELLON	19783	3356	37.8	32.5	24.4	3.5	1.8	31758	35262	17	15	2933	12.8	30.5	44.4	9.7	2.7	96422
34432	DUNNELLON	21626	4794	27.1	36.1	28.8	6.3	1.8	39082	44734	43	40	4286	13.6	23.2	39.8	22.2	1.3	109504
34433	DUNNELLON	18479	1874	34.6	34.1	24.0	4.4	2.9	33237	37303	22	20	1654	14.6	22.6	42.3	17.7	3.0	110242
34434	DUNNELLON	18800	2410	33.4	40.1	21.5	3.0	2.0	32925	36998	21	19	2186	7.0	29.0	49.2	14.4	0.4	108391
34436	FLORAL CITY	18160	3911	39.1	35.2	20.5	4.1	1.1	30469	34015	13	12	3510	22.0	24.5	38.8	13.5	1.2	94604
34442	HERNANDO	23282	5577	31.1	34.1	26.5	5.1	3.3	37960	43970	39	37	4727	14.8	21.5	31.3	30.3	2.2	123871
34446	HOMOSASSA	22528	6247	27.7	35.2	29.1	5.9	2.1	40193	45375	47	44	5589	12.1	19.0	38.6	29.3	1.1	125550
34448	HOMOSASSA	18419	4922	36.9	37.0	20.5	3.9	1.7	31644	35769	17	15	4121	25.5	28.0	28.4	14.5	3.7	83728
34449	INGLIS	18277	1784	44.8	29.6	20.2	3.5	1.9	28170	30842	9	7	1510	25.0	26.6	28.1	16.9	3.4	86190
34450	INVERNESS	23523	5138	36.9	35.0	19.9	5.4	2.8	32386	36270	19	17	4296	13.8	21.1	47.4	15.9	1.8	109927
34452	INVERNESS	20166	4950	35.5	38.8	20.1	4.1	1.5	31118	35025	15	13	4182	7.7	28.0	53.3	10.5	0.6	104281
34453	INVERNESS	18996	3836	37.6	34.7	21.0	4.8	2.0	32665	36667	20	18	3224	16.2	31.8	36.2	14.2	1.6	92941
34461	LECANTO	20702	3793	27.4	31.1	31.2	6.6	3.7	42689	49038	55	53	3308	12.8	18.8	35.7	29.2	3.5	130172
34465	BEVERLY HILLS	22361	6787	38.5	35.6	20.0	3.6	2.4	31212	35401	16	13	5919	7.8	36.8	39.5	14.3	1.6	96568
34470	OCALA	20065	8873	37.7	32.0	24.5	4.2	1.6	32752	36773	20	18	6023	20.8	29.8	43.6	5.5	0.3	89242
34471	OCALA	29409	8939	19.7	31.4	29.1	12.6	7.2	48935	56968	70	71	6583	2.9	18.4	45.7	28.7	4.2	136681
34472	OCALA	18121	8577	33.1	34.8	26.2	4.3	1.6	34737	39225	26	25	6860	15.6	37.9	41.0	5.2	0.3	85761
34473	OCALA	16361	4335	30.8	38.6	25.5	3.6	1.5	35169	39399	28	26	3591	10.6	38.6	43.0	6.6	1.1	90733
34474	OCALA	23164	7575	37.5	30.7	21.5	5.3	5.0	32858	37162	20	19	4505	26.6	23.8	23.7	19.6	6.5	89403
34475	OCALA	13312	3880	49.1	30.3	16.5	2.6	1.6	25531	28245	5	4	2359	29.2	39.5	24.6	5.4	1.3	70233
34476	OCALA	24707	7545	27.0	39.2	26.5	5.0	2.3	38081	43270	40	37	6979	9.7	20.1	50.8	17.2	2.2	116518
34479	OCALA	19991	5007	29.5	34.8	28.3	5.2	2.2	38544	44334	41	38	4021	14.0	36.2	39.3	9.8	0.8	89781
34480	OCALA	25015	4209	27.5	29.4	27.5	8.9	6.8	44823	50980	61	59	3470	15.6	16.8	42.5	18.3	6.8	114092
34481	OCALA	24228	8034	30.6	39.6	24.3	4.2	1.3	35117	39454	28	26	7617	6.3	36.6	46.5	9.8	0.7	96426
34482	OCALA	19244	7543	33.1	37.4	22.7	3.7	3.1	33984	38529	24	23	6014	21.3	28.7	27.8	18.4	3.8	89922
34484	OXFORD	21061	990	30.2	29.2	33.2	5.6	1.8	42137	47927	53	51	788	18.2	23.0	31.9	21.5	5.6	113462
34488	SILVER SPRINGS	17481	4383	39.9	35.6	19.6	3.3	1.6	30433	33883	13	11	3617	42.7	25.3	26.5	4.8	0.7	58312
34491	SUMMERFIELD	22068	8903	33.1	37.7	23.1	4.3	1.9	35169	39691	28	26	7977	19.9	24.3	45.2	9.6	1.0	95878
34498	YANKEETOWN	23352	290	41.0	28.6	24.8	3.8	1.7	31349	34117	16	14	248	17.7	31.5	27.4	21.4	2.0	91429
34601	BROOKSVILLE	19024	9547	36.5	33.4	24.4	3.6	2.1	32769	36590	20	18	7153	29.6	21.2	31.1	16.1	2.0	88420
34602	BROOKSVILLE	18946	2639	28.5	34.2	30.4	4.5	2.4	41056	46299	50	48	2301	10.8	34.8	28.7	20.5	5.2	97808
34604	BROOKSVILLE	17521	2332	28.9	40.0	25.3	3.8	2.0	38330	43779	41	38	1899	19.6	28.3	30.5	19.6	2.1	93000
34606	SPRING HILL	22868	11735	32.3	35.9	25.4	4.2	2.3	35403	39796	29	27	9820	3.1	18.4	53.7	24.4	0.4	127086
34607	SPRING HILL	29470	3460	25.5	30.5	28.8	8.6	6.6	43586	49856	58	56	3107	6.1	9.4	35.2	45.0	4.3	173299
34608	SPRING HILL	20143	10911	30.3	36.8	27.3	3.9	1.6	36411	40570	33	30	9371	0.9	18.1	63.6	17.4	0.0	119731
34609	SPRING HILL	20250	10407	22.5	40.0	30.2	5.5	1.8	40181	46383	47	44	9334	1.7	14.8	55.0	27.7	0.9	132086
34610	SPRING HILL	16983	4339	30.5	34.3	27.7	6.1	1.5	37312	42398	37	34	3649	13.6	23.4	41.3	20.0	1.7	106220
34613	BROOKSVILLE	21884	7402	36.8	37.2	18.9	4.4	2.7	30984	34388	15	13	6762	13.6	39.1	31.6	13.7	2.0	86565
34614	BROOKSVILLE	21089	1263	34.1	31.7	25.3	3.6	5.4	35705	39856	30	28	1077	18.0	27.6	41.9	12.1	0.5	100212
34639	LAND O LAKES	24773	8568	15.5	26.3	39.9	14.3	4.1	57834	64880	82	84	7289	6.1	9.3	42.8	38.9	3.0	161508
34652	NEW PORT RICHEY	20848	12435	38.9	35.3	19.7	3.5	2.6	30681	34456	14	12	9349	11.8	42.6	28.6	14.4	2.7	85244
34653	NEW PORT RICHEY	19731	14937	36.5	35.5	23.1	3.3	1.6	33299	37659	22	21	11169	15.8	30.5	45.4	8.1	0.3	94952
34654	NEW PORT RICHEY	21562	7291	28.1	33.2	29.2	6.3	3.2	40954	46660	50	48	6474	17.6	19.1	37.9	22.5	2.9	115483
34655	NEW PORT RICHEY	28354	11889	19.2	33.5	31.6	9.9	5.8	47607	55290	67	67	10823	2.1	16.1	37.4	42.1	2.4	159836
34667	HUDSON	20712	15940	34.4	35.9	24.1	3.7	1.9	34456	38438	26	24	13156	14.4	25.8	42.3	16.7	0.7	104404
34668	PORT RICHEY	17591	20773	40.1	37.4	19.3	2.5	0.8	30212	33531	13	11	16212	8.5	42.9	44.9	3.5	0.3	88909
34669	HUDSON	17430	4660	30.0	40.4	23.6	4.8	1.2	35543	40369	30	27	3935	8.7	27.7	50.8	11.6	1.2	106977
34677	OLDSMAR	30079	8504	16.4	26.5	37.4	12.0	7.7	57713	68078	82	84	6542	0.8	15.2	45.7	32.2	6.1	144391
34683	PALM HARBOR	32946	14671	17.6	25.5	33.8	13.2	9.9	57151	66516	82	83	11849	5.8	7.9	34.2	44.6	7.5	179638
34684	PALM HARBOR	29112	12502	21.5	34.4	29.9	9.0	5.2	45247	52364	62	60	9596	2.2	13.9	51.7	29.3	2.9	142390
34685	PALM HARBOR	43664	7593	11.3	15.9	33.3	20.4	19.1	81573	97398	95	96	6598	0.5	5.7	17.8	53.1	22.8	270743
34688	TARPON SPRINGS	45208	2716	11.8	17.4	30.0	20.3	20.5	82937	98972	96	97	2382	0.8	7.2	10.8	50.7	30.5	287903
34689	TARPON SPRINGS	25206	11362	27.7	30.5	29.4	8.1	4.2	42803	50225	55	53	9136	15.0	13.6	40.2	27.1	4.0	131331
34690	HOLIDAY	19627	6303	37.1	39.4	19.3	2.9	1.4	31424	35281	16	14	5205	9.1	60.1	27.5	3.2	0.3	77752
34691	HOLIDAY	19267	9428	38.0	36.5	21.9	2.6	1.1	30815	34586	14	12	7775	10.5	55.4	28.3	5.4	0.5	78393
34695	SAFETY HARBOR	32993	7633	18.5	26.0	32.9	14.1	8.6	55905	65412	81	82	6502	7.5	13.8	33.8	38.5	6.4	157922
34698	DUNEDIN	26892	18209	30.2	30.2	28.2	7.5	3.9	39565	46145	45	42	13636	12.2	16.1	48.6	20.5	2.7	122867
	FLORIDA	25506		26.4	29.9	29.1	9.1	5.6	44138	51288				8.8	15.8	40.2	28.3	7.0	137042
	UNITED STATES	25866		24.7	27.1	30.8	10.9	6.5	48124	56710				10.9	15.0	33.7	30.1	10.4	145905

#	POST OFFICE NAME	FINANCIAL SERVICES: Auto Loan	FINANCIAL SERVICES: Home Loan	FINANCIAL SERVICES: Invest-ments	FINANCIAL SERVICES: Retire-ment Plans	THE HOME: Home Improvements: Home Repair	THE HOME: Home Improvements: Lawn & Garden	THE HOME: Furnishings: Comput-ers & Hard-ware	THE HOME: Furnishings: Major Appli-ances	THE HOME: Furnishings: TV, Radio, Sound Equip-ment	THE HOME: Furnishings: Furni-ture	ENTERTAINMENT: Dine out/ Carry out	ENTERTAINMENT: Sports Equip-ment	ENTERTAINMENT: Fees & Tickets	ENTERTAINMENT: Toys & Games	ENTERTAINMENT: Travel	ENTERTAINMENT: Cable TV	PERSONAL: Apparel & Services	PERSONAL: Auto Repairs	PERSONAL: Health Insur-ance	PERSONAL: Pets & Supplies
34210	BRADENTON	84	80	90	79	81	94	80	85	83	84	104	89	81	93	83	85	99	85	92	94
34211	BRADENTON	132	132	127	131	134	148	121	131	121	128	152	137	124	136	126	124	145	127	138	147
34212	BRADENTON	125	122	105	121	124	127	112	120	111	114	137	140	109	137	113	110	132	117	118	144
34215	CORTEZ	101	94	91	90	100	118	87	100	92	94	115	97	89	96	95	99	108	97	116	114
34217	BRADENTON BEACH	106	92	79	86	100	116	86	100	93	90	114	105	83	101	93	100	106	98	117	123
34219	PARRISH	115	109	104	104	115	133	101	113	105	107	131	114	102	113	109	112	123	110	130	130
34221	PALMETTO	78	71	66	67	74	84	69	76	73	72	90	80	68	82	71	76	85	75	84	87
34222	ELLENTON	66	61	59	56	64	77	58	66	63	61	77	65	58	67	62	67	72	64	78	74
34223	ENGLEWOOD	87	82	81	77	86	101	78	88	83	82	102	88	78	89	83	87	96	85	101	98
34224	ENGLEWOOD	75	68	64	63	72	86	65	74	71	68	86	74	64	75	70	75	80	72	88	84
34228	LONGBOAT KEY	264	247	240	234	262	309	229	261	242	246	302	254	232	251	249	259	282	253	306	296
34229	OSPREY	186	173	166	165	184	216	160	183	170	172	211	179	163	175	174	181	197	177	214	208
34231	SARASOTA	95	97	107	95	98	109	96	99	97	97	121	109	98	116	99	99	117	99	103	109
34232	SARASOTA	87	94	104	93	94	101	90	92	89	92	111	103	93	109	93	88	108	91	92	101
34233	SARASOTA	96	100	107	97	102	113	94	100	95	97	118	107	97	111	99	97	114	98	105	111
34234	SARASOTA	62	59	68	57	59	67	62	63	64	63	80	69	62	75	62	65	77	64	66	69
34235	SARASOTA	105	111	116	109	112	122	105	109	104	106	130	120	108	125	109	106	126	107	113	122
34236	SARASOTA	108	104	112	101	107	122	103	110	106	107	132	115	103	120	107	109	126	109	119	121
34237	SARASOTA	61	62	72	62	61	67	64	63	64	64	80	72	64	78	64	63	78	64	62	69
34238	SARASOTA	139	130	125	123	138	162	120	137	127	129	158	134	122	132	131	136	148	133	160	156
34239	SARASOTA	88	95	110	93	95	105	93	94	93	93	116	103	96	114	96	95	113	93	97	103
34240	SARASOTA	156	189	211	188	188	191	169	171	159	170	200	198	181	211	175	157	199	165	158	191
34241	SARASOTA	147	155	157	152	158	171	143	152	142	148	178	163	147	166	150	144	171	148	157	170
34242	SARASOTA	189	192	199	184	199	228	176	193	180	185	225	197	182	199	189	189	214	187	214	218
34243	SARASOTA	115	118	119	115	120	133	111	118	112	114	140	126	114	131	116	115	134	115	125	132
34251	MYAKKA CITY	115	125	122	127	121	120	117	117	110	119	139	138	118	140	115	104	136	116	104	130
34266	ARCADIA	70	58	48	54	61	68	58	65	63	60	77	72	55	72	59	65	73	65	70	77
34269	ARCADIA	81	76	76	71	80	96	71	81	75	76	93	78	72	78	77	80	87	78	95	90
34275	NOKOMIS	120	114	112	107	120	142	106	121	113	113	140	118	108	120	115	121	131	117	140	135
34285	VENICE	84	81	84	75	85	102	75	86	80	81	100	82	77	84	82	86	93	83	101	95
34286	NORTH PORT	86	83	73	85	84	89	80	83	80	81	99	95	79	97	79	79	95	82	83	95
34287	NORTH PORT	67	61	59	57	65	77	59	67	64	61	78	67	59	69	63	68	73	65	78	75
34288	NORTH PORT	79	89	85	92	85	82	80	80	74	83	94	93	82	94	78	69	93	78	69	88
34292	VENICE	119	115	117	108	121	143	106	121	112	114	140	117	109	119	116	120	131	117	140	134
34293	VENICE	80	80	81	75	83	96	75	82	79	78	97	84	77	89	80	83	92	80	93	92
34420	BELLEVIEW	70	58	46	53	62	72	57	65	63	58	76	70	54	69	59	66	70	64	76	78
34428	CRYSTAL RIVER	80	71	61	67	75	88	69	77	74	71	90	80	67	79	72	78	84	76	90	90
34429	CRYSTAL RIVER	90	82	76	76	87	103	76	88	81	81	101	88	76	86	82	87	94	85	103	102
34431	DUNNELLON	62	60	61	56	63	75	56	64	60	60	74	62	57	64	61	64	69	62	74	70
34432	DUNNELLON	75	70	65	66	73	83	65	73	68	69	85	75	65	74	69	71	80	72	82	84
34433	DUNNELLON	69	62	55	58	65	76	60	67	64	62	79	69	58	70	63	67	73	66	77	77
34434	DUNNELLON	64	59	57	54	62	75	55	64	59	59	73	62	55	62	59	64	68	62	75	72
34436	FLORAL CITY	61	54	50	50	57	69	53	60	58	55	70	60	52	61	56	61	65	59	71	68
34442	HERNANDO	74	69	69	66	73	84	66	74	69	69	86	75	66	75	70	73	80	72	84	84
34446	HOMOSASSA	73	69	66	65	72	85	64	73	68	68	84	72	64	71	69	72	79	71	84	82
34448	HOMOSASSA	64	55	49	50	59	70	52	61	57	55	70	62	51	60	55	61	65	59	72	72
34449	INGLIS	64	53	44	48	57	68	52	60	58	53	70	63	49	62	54	62	64	59	72	72
34450	INVERNESS	71	68	71	64	71	85	64	72	68	68	84	70	65	71	69	72	79	70	84	80
34452	INVERNESS	68	59	53	55	63	76	59	66	64	60	78	68	57	69	62	68	72	65	78	75
34453	INVERNESS	63	59	58	55	62	74	56	64	60	59	74	63	56	64	60	64	69	62	75	71
34461	LECANTO	83	77	70	74	80	91	73	81	75	76	94	84	72	82	76	78	88	79	89	93
34465	BEVERLY HILLS	65	61	62	57	65	77	58	66	62	62	77	64	58	65	62	66	71	64	77	73
34470	OCALA	59	58	62	56	60	68	58	61	60	59	74	65	59	71	60	62	71	60	66	67
34471	OCALA	96	107	118	108	106	111	103	103	99	103	124	119	106	125	104	97	122	102	97	113
34472	OCALA	68	60	53	58	63	73	60	66	63	60	77	70	58	72	61	66	72	64	73	76
34473	OCALA	69	56	40	53	59	69	59	64	64	57	76	72	53	72	58	67	71	64	74	77
34474	OCALA	73	70	78	67	71	81	70	74	74	72	91	80	70	85	72	76	88	74	79	83
34475	OCALA	50	43	44	40	43	50	47	48	52	47	63	53	46	59	46	54	60	49	53	55
34476	OCALA	78	73	72	67	77	91	67	78	72	72	89	75	68	76	73	77	83	75	91	87
34479	OCALA	75	69	61	68	72	80	69	73	72	69	88	82	68	87	70	74	84	72	78	85
34480	OCALA	111	95	71	90	102	110	89	101	96	89	115	121	85	116	92	98	109	99	111	131
34481	OCALA	68	65	65	59	68	81	60	69	64	65	80	67	61	68	65	69	74	67	81	76
34482	OCALA	75	66	56	62	68	77	63	71	67	66	83	77	61	75	65	69	78	70	78	84
34484	OXFORD	93	73	47	69	80	88	71	83	77	71	93	97	63	89	72	80	86	82	92	108
34488	SILVER SPRINGS	66	51	37	46	56	66	50	59	57	51	68	65	46	62	52	61	63	58	71	75
34491	SUMMERFIELD	80	72	66	66	76	88	68	78	73	72	90	80	66	79	72	77	84	76	89	90
34498	YANKEETOWN	67	63	65	58	67	81	59	68	64	64	79	65	60	67	64	68	73	66	81	74
34601	BROOKSVILLE	70	60	52	56	63	72	59	65	63	60	77	72	56	72	60	66	73	65	73	79
34602	BROOKSVILLE	76	70	61	67	72	80	66	73	68	69	85	78	64	76	68	70	80	72	78	85
34604	BROOKSVILLE	64	57	44	55	58	63	56	60	57	56	70	69	52	66	55	57	67	60	62	71
34606	SPRING HILL	73	67	66	62	71	85	65	73	70	68	86	73	64	75	69	74	79	71	86	81
34607	SPRING HILL	100	91	83	86	97	114	84	97	90	90	112	98	84	95	92	97	104	94	114	114
34608	SPRING HILL	70	64	62	61	68	81	62	70	66	65	81	70	62	70	66	70	76	68	81	79
34609	SPRING HILL	76	71	67	66	75	88	66	75	71	70	87	75	67	76	71	75	82	73	88	86
34610	SPRING HILL	74	66	51	62	67	73	62	69	65	65	80	78	59	74	63	66	76	68	72	83
34613	BROOKSVILLE	69	63	62	59	67	80	59	68	64	63	79	67	59	67	64	68	73	66	80	77
34614	BROOKSVILLE	92	79	57	74	81	87	75	83	79	77	96	96	70	91	75	79	91	83	87	103
34639	LAND O LAKES	97	107	102	108	104	104	98	99	93	100	116	115	100	117	97	89	114	97	90	111
34652	NEW PORT RICHEY	66	56	49	53	60	72	57	64	62	58	75	66	54	67	59	66	69	63	75	73
34653	NEW PORT RICHEY	65	56	49	53	60	70	57	63	62	57	75	67	55	69	59	65	70	62	73	72
34654	NEW PORT RICHEY	85	74	63	70	78	88	71	81	76	73	92	89	68	85	74	78	87	79	89	97
34655	NEW PORT RICHEY	97	93	87	89	96	109	88	96	92	90	113	102	88	104	92	96	107	94	107	110
34667	HUDSON	67	60	57	56	63	74	58	65	62	60	76	69	57	69	61	65	71	64	74	76
34668	PORT RICHEY	56	49	44	46	52	63	49	55	53	50	65	56	47	58	51	57	60	54	65	63
34669	HUDSON	70	58	44	54	61	70	58	65	63	58	76	71	54	70	59	66	71	64	74	77
34677	OLDSMAR	100	111	120	112	109	113	106	105	101	106	127	123	108	129	106	99	125	105	98	117
34683	PALM HARBOR	106	121	133	121	120	126	113	114	109	113	136	129	118	138	116	108	134	111	109	126
34684	PALM HARBOR	85	86	96	87	88	96	86	88	85	87	107	98	87	101	88	86	103	88	90	97
34685	PALM HARBOR	144	177	194	177	174	178	159	159	148	160	187	182	171	194	164	146	187	154	146	174
34688	TARPON SPRINGS	158	179	185	177	179	189	161	167	156	165	196	184	170	192	168	157	191	162	166	187
34689	TARPON SPRINGS	78	82	88	79	83	92	78	82	79	80	99	88	81	95	82	81	95	80	86	90
34690	HOLIDAY	64	54	47	51	58	70	55	62	60	56	73	64	53	65	57	64	67	61	74	71
34691	HOLIDAY	63	54	47	50	57	69	54	61	59	55	71	62	52	63	56	63	66	60	72	70
34695	SAFETY HARBOR	102	117	133	118	116	122	110	111	106	111	133	126	116	133	113	105	131	109	106	121
34698	DUNEDIN	77	78	84	75	80	91	75	80	77	77	96	84	77	88	79	80	91	79	87	88
	FLORIDA	89	87	95	86	87	96	87	89	89	89	111	100	87	107	88	90	108	90	91	101
	UNITED STATES	100	100	100	100	100	100	100	100	100	100	100	100	100	100	100	100	100	100	100	100

# POST OFFICE NAME	COUNTY FIPS CODE	POPULATION			2000-2004 ANNUAL RATE		HOUSEHOLDS					FAMILIES		
		2000	2004	2009	% Rate	State Centile	2000	2004	2009	% Annual Rate 2000-2004	2004 Average HH Size	2000	2004	% Annual Rate 2000-2004
34705 ASTATULA	069	2137	2385	2859	2.6	68	820	925	1116	2.9	2.58	622	695	2.7
34711 CLERMONT	069	38598	53829	71709	8.1	98	14332	20112	26940	8.3	2.63	10875	15166	8.1
34731 FRUITLAND PARK	069	9305	10035	11843	1.8	51	3867	4204	4991	2.0	2.38	2837	3052	1.7
34734 GOTHA	095	3789	4953	6028	6.5	96	1372	1819	2229	6.9	2.67	918	1197	6.4
34736 GROVELAND	069	8415	10195	12693	4.6	89	3100	3870	4916	5.4	2.54	2412	2981	5.1
34737 HOWEY IN THE HILLS	069	1939	2241	2733	3.5	79	731	851	1043	3.6	2.63	570	655	3.3
34739 KENANSVILLE	097	825	943	1215	3.2	76	328	375	481	3.2	2.51	242	273	2.9
34741 KISSIMMEE	097	35274	41468	54252	3.9	83	13246	15555	20289	3.9	2.64	8483	9866	3.6
34743 KISSIMMEE	097	26358	33275	44870	5.6	93	8229	10385	13940	5.6	3.20	6826	8561	5.5
34744 KISSIMMEE	097	28401	35726	47995	5.6	92	9537	12184	16502	5.9	2.83	7391	9348	5.7
34746 KISSIMMEE	097	17975	23462	32142	6.5	95	6924	8880	12045	6.0	2.62	4772	6021	5.6
34747 KISSIMMEE	097	5227	10599	17368	18.1	100	1869	3751	6103	17.8	2.81	1387	2709	17.1
34748 LEESBURG	069	30512	34579	41962	3.0	73	13962	16092	19755	3.4	2.11	9410	10731	3.1
34753 MASCOTTE	069	2672	3020	3644	2.9	72	798	910	1105	3.1	3.31	637	723	3.0
34756 MONTVERDE	069	2405	2945	3692	4.9	90	909	1127	1423	5.2	2.60	732	900	5.0
34758 KISSIMMEE	097	13723	20004	28759	9.3	99	4466	6443	9188	9.0	3.10	3684	5283	8.9
34759 KISSIMMEE	105	7294	10043	13096	7.8	98	2450	3360	4351	7.7	2.99	1957	2664	7.5
34761 OCOEE	095	25921	30118	34718	3.6	80	8688	10200	11810	3.9	2.94	7058	8222	3.7
34762 OKAHUMPKA	069	989	1196	1493	4.6	89	443	541	680	4.8	2.21	327	395	4.6
34769 SAINT CLOUD	097	18534	22046	28864	4.2	86	7226	8641	11324	4.3	2.51	5081	6018	4.1
34771 SAINT CLOUD	097	9811	12047	16054	5.0	91	3632	4468	5938	5.0	2.69	2837	3465	4.8
34772 SAINT CLOUD	097	11232	13723	18216	4.8	90	3865	4743	6290	4.9	2.87	3036	3689	4.7
34773 SAINT CLOUD	097	1657	2063	2763	5.3	91	554	688	917	5.2	2.99	420	516	5.0
34785 WILDWOOD	119	16148	20077	24256	5.3	91	5040	6079	7978	4.5	2.32	3437	4089	4.2
34786 WINDERMERE	095	8194	10531	12790	6.1	94	2746	3532	4287	6.1	2.98	2341	3000	6.0
34787 WINTER GARDEN	095	23158	28005	33006	4.6	89	8435	10271	12138	4.7	2.67	5998	7246	4.6
34788 LEESBURG	069	15500	17448	21175	2.8	71	7444	8386	10208	2.8	2.08	5034	5596	2.5
34797 YALAHA	069	872	1003	1220	3.4	78	401	467	572	3.7	2.14	311	357	3.3
34945 FORT PIERCE	111	4087	4465	5056	2.1	57	1285	1434	1665	2.6	2.68	948	1048	2.4
34946 FORT PIERCE	111	6600	7068	8080	1.6	46	2527	2766	3214	2.2	2.54	1721	1853	1.8
34947 FORT PIERCE	111	10279	11050	12726	1.7	48	3296	3563	4138	1.9	3.00	2425	2590	1.6
34949 FORT PIERCE	111	6601	8420	10450	5.9	93	3531	4531	5661	6.0	1.85	2140	2738	6.0
34950 FORT PIERCE	111	18018	18708	21084	0.9	25	6424	6655	7541	0.8	2.77	3899	3987	0.5
34951 FORT PIERCE	111	12939	13962	15999	1.8	52	5845	6353	7340	2.0	2.19	4125	4449	1.8
34952 PORT SAINT LUCIE	111	31060	35947	42452	3.5	79	13691	15925	18960	3.6	2.22	8970	10333	3.4
34953 PORT SAINT LUCIE	111	25690	31856	38878	5.2	91	8903	11117	13665	5.4	2.87	7124	8822	5.2
34956 INDIANTOWN	085	9074	9225	9823	0.4	12	2303	2336	2521	0.3	3.37	1778	1791	0.2
34957 JENSEN BEACH	085	18854	21739	25178	3.4	79	9362	10900	12750	3.6	1.99	5649	6489	3.3
34972 OKEECHOBEE	093	17830	19030	20540	1.5	43	5250	5687	6238	1.9	2.98	3909	4211	1.8
34974 OKEECHOBEE	043	21382	22353	23672	1.1	29	8772	9264	9899	1.3	2.41	6091	6372	1.1
34981 FORT PIERCE	111	3927	4567	5392	3.6	80	1453	1713	2049	4.0	2.57	1022	1189	3.6
34982 FORT PIERCE	111	23110	25342	29274	2.2	59	9345	10227	11872	2.1	2.45	6307	6858	2.0
34983 PORT SAINT LUCIE	111	26616	29252	33629	2.3	60	9992	11036	12772	2.4	2.63	7584	8289	2.1
34984 PORT SAINT LUCIE	111	9775	10880	12576	2.6	67	3588	4030	4696	2.8	2.70	2872	3203	2.6
34986 PORT SAINT LUCIE	111	6126	8330	10591	7.5	97	2932	4028	5167	7.8	2.07	2310	3146	7.5
34987 PORT SAINT LUCIE	111	1146	1355	1617	4.0	83	387	462	556	4.3	2.93	318	375	4.0
34988 PORT SAINT LUCIE	111	70	76	86	2.0	54	25	27	31	1.8	2.81	21	23	2.2
34990 PALM CITY	085	23821	27010	30499	3.0	73	9890	11283	12823	3.2	2.37	7469	8465	3.0
34994 STUART	085	14897	16430	18474	2.3	62	7116	8060	9250	3.0	1.93	3713	4134	2.6
34996 STUART	085	10987	11734	12955	1.6	44	5504	5867	6480	1.5	1.97	3212	3417	1.5
34997 STUART	085	31793	34675	38430	2.1	57	13888	15261	17042	2.2	2.25	9446	10291	2.0
FLORIDA					2.1					2.2	2.45			2.0
UNITED STATES					1.2					1.3	2.58			1.1

#	POST OFFICE NAME	White 2000	White 2004	Black 2000	Black 2004	Asian/Pacific 2000	Asian/Pacific 2004	% Hispanic Origin 2000	% Hispanic Origin 2004	0-4	5-9	10-14	15-19	20-24	25-44	45-64	65-84	85+	18+	MEDIAN AGE 2004	% 2004 Males	% 2004 Females
34705	ASTATULA	88.1	85.8	1.1	1.4	0.2	0.3	14.3	17.2	6.1	6.6	7.3	5.5	4.4	25.5	28.7	14.3	1.7	76.5	41.7	48.9	51.1
34711	CLERMONT	87.4	85.8	6.5	6.9	1.3	1.5	9.3	11.5	7.4	7.1	6.8	5.6	5.3	31.6	23.7	11.5	1.1	75.3	37.4	49.4	50.6
34731	FRUITLAND PARK	91.7	89.9	5.5	6.9	0.9	1.1	2.1	2.6	4.8	4.9	5.8	5.8	4.9	20.8	27.0	23.7	2.3	80.9	47.2	48.6	51.4
34734	GOTHA	80.6	77.3	9.7	11.3	3.0	3.4	13.1	16.0	7.7	7.0	7.2	6.9	8.2	35.8	19.5	6.2	1.5	74.2	32.7	48.2	51.8
34736	GROVELAND	84.8	82.8	7.9	9.0	0.5	0.6	11.0	12.4	5.5	5.6	6.2	5.8	5.4	25.8	26.5	17.9	1.4	79.2	42.4	52.4	47.6
34737	HOWEY IN THE HILLS	93.9	92.7	2.8	3.4	0.8	1.0	4.0	5.0	4.2	4.6	4.9	5.0	3.3	18.3	28.4	29.0	2.4	83.2	52.0	49.1	50.9
34739	KENANSVILLE	95.0	94.1	0.1	0.2	0.1	0.1	8.5	10.8	4.4	4.2	5.6	6.4	6.6	24.4	27.6	19.7	1.2	82.1	43.8	52.9	47.1
34741	KISSIMMEE	69.1	65.5	8.3	8.7	3.6	4.0	40.0	46.7	8.0	6.7	7.4	7.7	10.8	33.7	17.9	6.8	0.8	73.6	29.8	49.7	50.3
34743	KISSIMMEE	61.8	59.6	11.2	11.1	2.7	2.8	57.9	63.8	7.1	7.1	8.4	8.1	8.2	28.9	22.1	9.3	0.9	72.4	32.8	48.3	51.7
34744	KISSIMMEE	77.2	75.3	9.8	9.7	1.9	2.1	24.7	29.5	6.2	6.5	7.5	7.2	6.9	28.9	26.2	9.8	0.9	75.5	36.9	50.3	49.7
34746	KISSIMMEE	84.1	81.1	3.1	3.6	3.5	4.1	20.6	25.8	6.0	5.9	6.2	5.8	6.2	27.7	25.3	13.9	3.0	78.4	40.0	49.0	51.1
34747	KISSIMMEE	88.0	86.8	2.9	3.2	4.2	4.6	11.6	14.2	6.2	6.7	8.6	7.5	5.8	28.5	28.0	8.1	0.6	73.1	37.2	49.9	50.1
34748	LEESBURG	78.6	76.8	18.1	19.5	1.0	1.1	3.2	3.8	4.6	4.4	5.1	4.6	4.5	17.0	22.8	32.2	4.9	83.1	54.8	46.8	53.2
34753	MASCOTTE	70.1	66.7	7.9	8.8	0.2	0.3	33.9	38.0	8.5	8.0	8.3	7.2	8.1	28.8	20.4	9.9	0.8	70.8	32.0	54.2	45.8
34756	MONTVERDE	94.7	93.6	0.9	1.1	0.6	0.7	5.5	6.9	5.4	6.1	7.0	6.5	4.7	27.2	29.9	12.2	1.1	77.4	41.9	49.5	50.5
34758	KISSIMMEE	68.4	65.2	15.7	16.8	1.2	1.3	34.4	40.4	7.5	8.0	9.0	7.9	6.7	26.9	22.7	10.5	0.8	70.3	34.1	48.7	51.3
34759	KISSIMMEE	69.0	66.1	14.1	15.0	1.3	1.3	37.8	43.6	8.4	8.1	7.5	6.4	6.5	29.2	23.1	10.1	0.8	72.1	34.1	48.5	51.5
34761	OCOEE	81.5	78.3	6.6	7.9	2.7	3.2	15.1	17.9	8.2	8.0	7.9	6.9	6.5	32.0	22.8	6.9	0.7	71.6	34.1	49.6	50.4
34762	OKAHUMPKA	88.6	87.1	8.9	10.1	0.3	0.3	1.8	2.2	3.7	3.6	3.5	3.3	2.8	14.2	26.2	39.8	2.8	87.1	61.3	48.0	52.0
34769	SAINT CLOUD	92.3	90.6	1.9	2.2	0.9	1.1	9.8	12.8	6.6	6.2	6.9	6.6	6.3	27.6	23.2	14.3	2.5	76.3	38.8	48.3	51.8
34771	SAINT CLOUD	95.2	94.3	1.5	1.7	0.7	0.9	5.6	7.4	5.9	6.5	7.5	6.6	5.5	27.8	27.9	11.5	0.8	75.8	39.8	50.2	49.8
34772	SAINT CLOUD	90.7	88.6	2.7	3.1	0.9	1.1	12.7	16.6	7.4	7.0	7.9	7.1	6.6	28.5	23.2	11.0	1.4	73.3	36.0	48.6	51.4
34773	SAINT CLOUD	94.0	92.8	0.8	1.0	0.1	0.2	6.3	8.2	4.9	5.1	8.0	9.4	8.1	26.6	26.6	10.7	0.6	76.4	36.7	51.8	48.2
34785	WILDWOOD	70.0	66.1	25.4	28.5	0.4	0.5	12.0	15.2	3.4	3.6	4.1	4.5	6.1	31.8	23.4	20.8	2.2	86.2	42.7	60.0	40.0
34786	WINDERMERE	90.2	88.4	2.8	3.4	4.4	5.2	5.0	6.5	7.2	8.3	9.3	6.6	3.6	26.7	30.0	7.6	0.7	70.7	39.5	49.8	50.2
34787	WINTER GARDEN	76.6	74.8	14.7	15.2	1.1	1.3	14.2	16.7	7.2	6.9	7.3	6.5	6.2	28.7	24.0	11.4	1.9	74.4	37.4	48.8	51.2
34788	LEESBURG	95.1	93.9	2.3	2.9	1.0	1.2	2.2	2.8	3.4	3.4	4.0	4.0	3.1	15.1	25.9	36.8	4.3	86.8	59.5	47.6	52.4
34797	YALAHA	91.9	90.1	4.9	6.0	0.7	0.8	3.4	4.3	2.7	2.9	3.5	3.3	2.6	14.0	26.0	42.9	2.2	88.8	62.3	49.1	51.0
34945	FORT PIERCE	86.9	83.7	9.5	11.9	0.5	0.5	6.3	8.1	3.0	3.1	3.6	5.0	6.5	23.5	25.9	27.7	1.8	87.7	49.0	54.7	45.3
34946	FORT PIERCE	44.8	41.3	54.9	54.9	0.3	0.3	3.6	4.1	5.6	6.0	7.7	7.8	6.3	21.3	26.6	16.7	2.0	75.7	41.2	48.9	51.1
34947	FORT PIERCE	30.0	28.3	61.9	62.6	0.7	0.8	11.4	13.5	9.0	8.4	9.3	8.9	9.3	25.2	19.8	8.7	1.5	68.1	28.9	48.7	51.3
34949	FORT PIERCE	97.6	96.9	0.7	1.0	0.8	1.0	2.2	3.0	1.7	1.8	2.0	2.2	2.6	12.7	31.1	42.1	3.9	93.2	63.0	48.8	51.3
34950	FORT PIERCE	32.4	29.3	55.9	58.1	0.5	0.6	18.3	20.1	8.1	7.3	8.3	8.3	8.4	25.9	21.2	10.7	2.0	71.4	32.7	50.8	49.3
34951	FORT PIERCE	92.5	90.5	4.7	6.0	0.7	0.8	2.9	3.9	4.7	4.6	5.2	5.0	4.9	19.7	24.8	28.1	3.0	82.5	49.5	48.6	51.4
34952	PORT SAINT LUCIE	88.1	85.0	6.8	8.9	1.3	1.5	7.4	9.5	4.6	4.5	5.1	4.8	4.9	19.2	24.0	27.8	5.2	82.9	50.6	46.7	53.3
34953	PORT SAINT LUCIE	88.1	84.7	7.1	9.5	1.2	1.4	7.2	9.4	6.5	6.8	7.8	6.9	5.1	27.7	23.7	14.5	1.0	74.5	39.2	49.1	51.0
34956	INDIANTOWN	50.0	44.6	22.2	23.5	0.8	0.9	41.1	46.3	8.1	7.0	7.7	7.3	8.6	33.2	17.0	10.4	0.8	73.0	31.6	60.5	39.5
34957	JENSEN BEACH	96.4	95.5	1.8	2.2	0.5	0.5	2.5	3.4	3.2	3.3	4.3	4.2	3.4	16.3	29.1	32.1	4.2	86.6	56.3	48.1	51.9
34972	OKEECHOBEE	68.8	65.7	14.3	14.9	0.3	0.4	25.6	30.0	7.1	6.9	7.6	8.9	8.3	30.7	20.4	9.2	1.1	73.0	32.1	56.8	43.3
34974	OKEECHOBEE	88.3	86.5	1.5	1.7	1.0	1.1	10.5	12.9	5.9	5.4	5.6	5.6	5.9	21.8	25.6	22.2	2.1	79.8	44.9	50.6	49.4
34981	FORT PIERCE	83.3	79.2	10.8	13.8	1.4	1.6	11.4	14.1	6.7	6.4	7.2	7.4	8.6	27.4	24.1	10.5	1.8	75.9	35.4	50.3	49.7
34982	FORT PIERCE	85.5	82.0	8.0	10.2	1.2	1.3	10.8	13.4	6.1	5.8	6.3	5.9	5.9	23.4	23.8	20.1	2.7	78.2	42.4	48.3	51.7
34983	PORT SAINT LUCIE	89.1	85.7	6.1	8.4	1.1	1.3	6.8	8.9	5.4	5.7	7.0	6.9	5.7	24.3	27.3	15.5	2.3	77.6	42.0	48.9	51.1
34984	PORT SAINT LUCIE	90.4	87.3	5.9	8.2	1.0	1.2	7.0	9.2	5.4	5.7	6.4	5.8	5.1	23.8	28.3	18.1	1.3	78.8	43.6	48.9	51.1
34986	PORT SAINT LUCIE	90.9	88.2	4.7	6.5	1.7	2.0	5.9	7.7	5.5	5.7	6.5	5.4	3.8	22.9	24.1	24.5	1.7	79.0	45.2	48.0	52.0
34987	PORT SAINT LUCIE	92.4	89.9	2.5	3.7	1.0	1.2	10.0	12.7	5.5	5.8	6.2	6.6	5.2	24.5	29.0	15.9	1.3	78.4	42.7	50.4	49.6
34988	PORT SAINT LUCIE	92.9	92.1	1.4	1.3	0.0	0.0	12.9	15.8	6.6	6.6	5.3	7.9	5.3	23.7	34.2	9.2	1.3	73.7	41.7	50.0	50.0
34990	PALM CITY	96.3	95.2	1.2	1.7	1.0	1.2	3.2	4.6	4.3	4.9	6.5	5.8	3.8	18.9	31.0	22.3	2.7	80.7	48.3	48.1	51.9
34994	STUART	84.3	83.0	11.9	12.4	0.7	0.7	6.3	8.2	3.9	4.0	4.8	4.7	4.9	22.1	26.0	23.9	5.7	84.3	49.1	47.8	52.2
34996	STUART	94.5	93.2	2.0	2.3	0.5	0.6	5.0	6.7	2.7	3.1	3.7	3.6	3.7	14.7	28.2	33.4	7.0	88.4	59.5	46.7	53.3
34997	STUART	91.5	89.7	4.3	5.0	0.7	0.8	8.2	10.7	4.7	4.8	5.3	5.0	4.4	20.3	28.0	24.4	3.1	82.1	48.9	48.6	51.4
	FLORIDA	78.0	76.5	14.6	15.2	1.7	2.0	16.8	19.0	6.0	5.9	6.4	6.4	6.5	26.6	24.5	15.5	2.4	78.1	40.0	48.8	51.2
	UNITED STATES	75.1	73.6	12.3	12.5	3.8	4.2	12.5	14.1	6.9	6.7	7.2	7.0	7.3	28.6	23.8	10.8	1.7	75.1	36.0	49.1	50.9

#	POST OFFICE NAME	2004 Per Capita Income	2004 HH Income Base	2004 HOUSEHOLD INCOME DISTRIBUTION (%)					MEDIAN HOUSEHOLD INCOME				2004 Home Value Base	2004 HOME VALUE DISTRIBUTION (%)					2004 Median Home Value
				Less than $25,000	$25,000 to $49,999	$50,000 to $99,999	$100,000 to $149,999	$150,000 or More	2004	2009	2004 National Centile	2004 State Centile		Less than $50,000	$50,000 to $89,999	$90,000 to $174,999	$175,000 to $399,999	$400,000 or More	
34705	ASTATULA	20317	925	25.7	39.0	26.5	6.4	2.4	40333	46125	47	45	782	13.8	27.1	40.0	16.4	2.7	102016
34711	CLERMONT	25235	20112	15.5	29.2	39.5	11.4	4.4	54145	61941	79	80	16355	5.3	5.5	45.9	38.5	4.8	164045
34731	FRUITLAND PARK	22478	4204	27.4	35.4	28.9	5.4	3.0	40120	45301	46	44	3536	24.9	21.4	36.3	16.2	1.2	96502
34734	GOTHA	22961	1819	14.4	36.1	36.2	10.1	3.2	49661	56785	71	72	957	3.1	2.5	49.8	36.7	7.8	159914
34736	GROVELAND	22301	3870	25.3	29.8	34.0	7.7	3.2	45875	51144	64	63	3204	17.3	16.4	32.9	30.6	2.8	123590
34737	HOWEY IN THE HILLS	24575	851	17.0	29.4	39.1	10.0	4.5	52069	58641	76	76	767	1.7	5.6	52.8	36.3	3.7	159744
34739	KENANSVILLE	21239	375	33.1	33.1	26.1	5.3	2.4	40383	45405	47	45	313	12.1	32.6	32.9	16.6	5.8	99167
34741	KISSIMMEE	16052	15555	32.9	40.8	22.4	2.7	1.3	33759	37874	23	22	5415	15.0	22.4	51.9	10.2	0.5	104677
34743	KISSIMMEE	15696	10385	24.9	36.4	31.6	5.3	1.8	41610	45633	52	50	7779	0.7	11.4	72.4	15.4	0.1	132151
34744	KISSIMMEE	21990	12184	21.2	29.2	34.5	11.0	4.2	49691	55518	71	73	9725	7.6	5.3	53.7	30.4	3.0	144686
34746	KISSIMMEE	22306	8880	25.6	35.5	28.9	6.6	3.4	41516	47357	51	50	6742	22.3	13.1	34.0	29.0	1.6	131179
34747	KISSIMMEE	31079	3751	13.9	23.7	36.6	15.6	10.2	62039	70157	86	89	2706	4.2	8.0	29.9	32.2	25.7	198253
34748	LEESBURG	23114	16092	33.3	33.1	25.8	5.0	2.9	36025	40604	32	29	12407	18.4	26.8	38.1	14.8	2.0	97866
34753	MASCOTTE	15892	910	28.8	36.0	27.4	5.8	2.0	38909	42312	42	40	664	15.7	27.7	41.1	12.8	2.7	96984
34756	MONTVERDE	28214	1127	15.0	23.7	41.1	12.4	7.8	58773	67548	83	85	1005	8.8	21.2	27.0	35.9	7.2	149617
34758	KISSIMMEE	14829	6443	28.2	36.2	30.7	3.9	1.1	38172	42254	40	37	5043	2.3	14.2	68.9	13.0	1.7	122161
34759	KISSIMMEE	16242	3360	21.8	34.8	39.1	4.1	0.3	45351	51035	62	61	2722	1.3	15.3	78.6	4.8	0.1	111916
34761	OCOEE	25361	10200	14.6	25.6	39.3	14.1	6.4	58991	67751	84	85	8531	2.0	10.4	48.2	34.2	5.3	147364
34762	OKAHUMPKA	23000	541	23.8	44.0	24.6	5.4	2.2	37757	42366	38	36	489	33.1	19.4	33.5	13.1	0.8	84318
34769	SAINT CLOUD	19263	8641	27.2	34.8	31.3	5.1	1.6	40996	46503	50	48	6488	5.6	16.9	63.5	13.4	0.7	118111
34771	SAINT CLOUD	22351	4468	18.5	30.8	37.4	10.3	3.1	50561	56546	73	75	3911	10.3	12.8	40.4	33.0	3.6	146274
34772	SAINT CLOUD	21362	4743	20.6	29.9	38.5	8.0	3.1	49702	55540	71	73	3694	2.9	10.3	58.1	27.2	1.5	145690
34773	SAINT CLOUD	14734	688	36.5	32.3	25.2	4.7	1.5	35817	41164	31	28	547	23.8	29.8	24.7	19.7	2.0	84091
34785	WILDWOOD	16292	6079	40.4	36.7	19.7	2.6	0.7	30428	33717	13	11	4926	30.5	29.2	30.8	8.5	1.0	77060
34786	WINDERMERE	52740	3532	8.0	12.0	26.6	21.5	32.0	106330	123397	99	99	3323	1.2	1.1	3.5	46.8	47.5	385871
34787	WINTER GARDEN	23461	10271	23.0	30.5	31.1	9.5	6.0	46917	54865	66	65	7563	9.3	25.2	33.1	25.1	7.3	122369
34788	LEESBURG	22611	8386	31.7	37.0	23.9	5.0	2.4	35674	40201	30	28	7647	29.7	22.1	32.3	14.4	1.5	85774
34797	YALAHA	23186	467	23.1	37.9	31.7	5.6	1.7	39756	44286	45	43	437	2.3	5.7	61.8	28.4	1.8	150702
34945	FORT PIERCE	19968	1434	26.2	36.1	26.2	7.0	4.5	42849	42541	40	38	1232	19.2	31.2	25.2	21.8	2.7	89487
34946	FORT PIERCE	15650	2766	40.4	34.3	19.9	3.9	1.6	30506	33833	14	12	2090	35.7	26.4	28.0	6.3	3.7	75612
34947	FORT PIERCE	11798	3563	48.6	30.0	17.6	2.7	1.2	25966	29172	6	4	1827	14.1	38.5	40.2	7.2	0.0	87738
34949	FORT PIERCE	36870	4531	23.3	29.7	29.9	10.1	7.1	46951	53507	66	65	3584	2.6	5.8	31.6	47.1	12.8	200934
34950	FORT PIERCE	13116	6655	53.1	27.0	15.5	2.4	2.0	22938	25362	3	2	2755	16.1	45.0	35.8	2.3	0.8	80826
34951	FORT PIERCE	23239	6353	29.3	34.5	28.4	5.1	2.8	39029	43619	43	40	5281	20.3	21.6	43.5	12.9	1.7	102753
34952	PORT SAINT LUCIE	22354	15925	28.6	36.1	25.7	6.5	3.1	37992	42977	39	37	12177	18.0	12.0	45.6	22.2	2.2	121006
34953	PORT SAINT LUCIE	19781	11117	17.0	34.7	38.2	8.0	2.1	48727	55675	70	70	9523	0.4	9.1	63.9	24.6	2.1	138273
34956	INDIANTOWN	13448	2336	35.7	31.7	27.6	3.8	1.3	34955	40703	27	25	1545	19.9	22.9	34.1	19.7	3.4	105260
34957	JENSEN BEACH	32612	10900	26.9	28.9	29.6	8.1	6.5	43926	50957	58	57	8939	10.4	14.8	35.7	32.1	7.0	142849
34972	OKEECHOBEE	15412	5687	35.2	35.6	22.4	4.7	2.0	33198	38027	21	20	4184	18.2	29.7	37.5	13.2	1.4	92623
34974	OKEECHOBEE	18984	9264	35.4	32.7	23.8	5.9	2.2	34055	38955	24	23	7565	16.1	27.1	41.0	14.2	1.5	97571
34981	FORT PIERCE	21022	1713	29.3	32.9	25.3	8.1	4.4	37995	41601	39	37	1133	1.9	23.9	44.0	28.3	1.8	137731
34982	FORT PIERCE	19685	10227	31.1	34.3	26.5	5.2	3.0	36607	40957	34	31	8013	11.9	25.1	46.0	15.7	1.4	109079
34983	PORT SAINT LUCIE	21161	11036	21.1	38.2	31.6	6.5	2.7	43134	49200	56	54	9154	0.4	12.7	70.4	15.8	0.6	128289
34984	PORT SAINT LUCIE	27918	4030	15.5	31.2	38.2	9.2	5.8	52199	60422	76	77	3523	0.6	6.1	61.8	24.5	7.1	145509
34986	PORT SAINT LUCIE	30957	4028	13.9	32.3	39.5	10.2	4.2	52557	61065	76	78	3766	0.2	2.6	51.8	39.5	5.9	165170
34987	PORT SAINT LUCIE	25753	462	9.1	30.5	43.9	10.2	6.3	56801	64929	81	83	367	0.0	3.0	35.7	52.3	9.0	205000
34988	PORT SAINT LUCIE	30534	27	3.7	29.6	48.2	7.4	11.1	61112	67631	85	87	18	0.0	0.0	16.7	72.2	11.1	258333
34990	PALM CITY	42617	11283	11.2	21.3	34.5	18.4	14.6	71367	87387	92	93	9773	0.5	1.2	20.9	55.0	22.5	259000
34994	STUART	27466	8060	31.9	32.3	24.3	7.5	4.1	37354	44499	37	34	5391	6.9	27.9	39.2	19.0	7.0	111952
34996	STUART	48494	5867	25.1	26.3	25.6	9.4	13.6	48372	58295	69	69	4983	3.1	18.5	30.3	24.7	23.5	166741
34997	STUART	36599	15261	20.6	29.6	29.9	10.7	9.3	49809	59877	72	73	12259	5.7	10.0	35.3	37.0	12.1	170765
	FLORIDA	25506		26.4	29.9	29.1	9.1	5.6	44138	51288				8.8	15.8	40.2	28.3	7.0	137042
	UNITED STATES	25866		24.7	27.1	30.8	10.9	6.5	48124	56710				10.9	15.0	33.7	30.1	10.4	145905

#	POST OFFICE NAME	Auto Loan	Home Loan	Invest-ments	Retire-ment Plans	Home Repair	Lawn & Garden	Comput-ers & Hard-ware	Major Appli-ances	TV, Radio, Sound Equip-ment	Furni-ture	Dine out/ Carry out	Sports Equip-ment	Fees & Tickets	Toys & Games	Travel	Cable TV	Apparel & Services	Auto Repairs	Health Insur-ance	Pets & Supplies
34705	ASTATULA	83	76	59	73	77	81	72	77	73	73	90	90	68	87	71	73	86	77	78	93
34711	CLERMONT	97	103	100	104	101	104	95	97	91	99	115	110	97	111	95	89	112	95	92	108
34731	FRUITLAND PARK	79	76	73	72	79	91	71	79	75	74	93	82	72	85	76	78	87	77	88	91
34734	GOTHA	90	79	92	88	76	81	90	85	88	92	112	103	87	104	84	82	109	91	76	95
34736	GROVELAND	89	80	68	76	84	95	77	85	81	79	99	91	75	89	79	84	93	84	94	100
34737	HOWEY IN THE HILLS	89	94	98	89	96	108	88	93	90	90	112	98	92	107	93	94	108	91	101	103
34739	KENANSVILLE	89	73	52	67	79	87	69	80	75	69	90	93	63	88	72	79	85	79	90	105
34741	KISSIMMEE	62	55	61	59	54	57	61	59	61	62	77	71	59	72	58	57	74	62	55	66
34743	KISSIMMEE	62	66	96	61	62	69	68	66	72	72	93	74	69	96	69	75	93	69	65	72
34744	KISSIMMEE	89	92	91	93	91	95	90	90	88	90	109	106	90	110	89	85	106	90	86	102
34746	KISSIMMEE	89	83	77	81	86	94	80	86	82	81	101	97	78	96	82	83	97	85	90	102
34747	KISSIMMEE	128	131	128	131	133	140	121	126	119	122	148	147	124	150	124	119	145	124	125	152
34748	LEESBURG	70	67	72	64	69	81	66	71	69	69	86	73	67	78	69	73	82	70	79	79
34753	MASCOTTE	83	76	61	73	77	82	72	78	74	75	91	88	69	84	72	73	87	78	80	92
34756	MONTVERDE	118	105	80	100	110	118	98	108	103	98	125	128	95	127	100	105	119	105	115	138
34758	KISSIMMEE	68	67	62	67	67	72	64	67	64	65	80	76	64	77	65	64	77	66	67	76
34759	KISSIMMEE	74	68	56	69	69	75	68	71	69	67	85	81	65	83	67	69	80	70	73	82
34761	OCOEE	105	115	115	118	111	110	109	107	102	111	129	126	110	128	106	96	127	106	94	118
34762	OKAHUMPKA	75	71	74	66	75	91	66	77	71	72	88	72	68	74	73	76	82	74	90	84
34769	SAINT CLOUD	72	65	59	64	68	76	67	71	70	66	85	79	64	81	67	71	80	70	76	81
34771	SAINT CLOUD	92	88	75	86	89	93	84	88	84	85	104	103	81	101	83	82	100	88	87	105
34772	SAINT CLOUD	95	87	73	85	89	96	85	91	87	86	107	103	82	102	85	87	102	90	93	106
34773	SAINT CLOUD	70	64	50	61	64	68	61	65	62	62	76	76	58	72	60	61	73	65	65	78
34785	WILDWOOD	54	47	44	43	50	59	45	52	49	48	61	53	44	53	48	53	56	51	61	61
34786	WINDERMERE	203	256	304	259	249	258	225	222	208	229	264	254	249	274	233	205	266	214	202	245
34787	WINTER GARDEN	92	91	85	90	91	96	88	91	88	89	110	106	87	108	88	87	106	91	90	105
34788	LEESBURG	69	66	67	61	69	82	62	71	66	66	81	69	62	71	67	70	76	68	82	79
34797	YALAHA	75	70	67	67	75	88	65	74	69	70	86	73	66	71	71	74	80	72	87	85
34945	FORT PIERCE	82	78	81	72	82	99	72	84	78	78	97	80	74	82	79	83	90	81	98	92
34946	FORT PIERCE	61	53	48	50	55	63	53	57	57	54	70	63	51	66	54	60	66	57	65	69
34947	FORT PIERCE	49	44	51	43	44	50	48	48	51	49	64	54	48	61	48	52	62	49	50	54
34949	FORT PIERCE	104	97	93	92	103	121	90	102	95	96	118	100	91	98	97	101	110	99	119	116
34950	FORT PIERCE	53	44	45	42	44	51	49	50	54	50	66	56	47	62	48	55	63	52	55	57
34951	FORT PIERCE	77	71	67	67	75	86	67	76	71	70	88	80	67	81	71	75	83	74	86	88
34952	PORT SAINT LUCIE	72	69	69	66	71	82	67	73	70	69	87	77	68	80	70	73	82	72	80	82
34953	PORT SAINT LUCIE	81	85	84	86	84	88	80	82	78	83	98	93	81	94	81	76	95	81	79	91
34956	INDIANTOWN	66	59	57	56	60	67	60	65	64	64	79	68	60	75	60	64	77	66	68	71
34957	JENSEN BEACH	93	93	95	88	96	111	87	96	91	91	112	98	89	102	93	95	106	93	107	107
34972	OKEECHOBEE	72	64	54	60	64	69	63	68	66	66	81	76	60	75	62	65	78	68	69	78
34974	OKEECHOBEE	70	63	57	59	66	77	60	68	65	63	79	71	59	72	63	68	74	67	78	79
34981	FORT PIERCE	77	76	79	77	75	82	77	77	77	77	96	89	77	96	76	76	93	78	76	87
34982	FORT PIERCE	70	67	66	64	69	78	66	70	68	67	84	76	66	80	68	70	80	69	76	79
34983	PORT SAINT LUCIE	78	79	77	77	80	88	78	80	79	76	97	90	79	99	79	80	94	78	82	90
34984	PORT SAINT LUCIE	110	108	103	107	110	121	104	110	105	106	131	121	105	126	106	106	125	108	114	124
34986	PORT SAINT LUCIE	97	91	87	86	96	113	84	96	89	90	110	93	85	92	91	95	103	93	112	109
34987	PORT SAINT LUCIE	118	108	91	102	114	126	100	111	105	103	129	123	99	122	105	110	122	108	124	136
34988	PORT SAINT LUCIE	138	123	93	116	130	139	113	126	120	113	146	150	111	149	117	123	139	122	136	162
34990	PALM CITY	144	149	154	146	153	169	139	149	139	144	174	158	143	160	147	143	167	145	158	166
34994	STUART	74	75	87	73	76	87	74	78	77	76	95	82	76	89	77	79	92	77	84	85
34996	STUART	138	139	149	132	144	166	129	142	134	136	166	144	134	150	139	140	158	138	157	158
34997	STUART	125	114	106	109	120	138	111	123	117	114	144	129	109	129	116	122	135	120	138	141
	FLORIDA	89	87	95	86	87	96	87	89	89	89	111	100	87	107	88	90	108	90	91	101
	UNITED STATES	100	100	100	100	100	100	100	100	100	100	100	100	100	100	100	100	100	100	100	100

GEORGIA

POPULATION CHANGE

A 30002-30165

# POST OFFICE NAME	COUNTY FIPS CODE	POPULATION 2000	2004	2009	2000-2004 ANNUAL RATE % Rate	State Centile	HOUSEHOLDS 2000	2004	2009	% Annual Rate 2000-2004	2004 Average HH Size	FAMILIES 2000	2004	% Annual Rate 2000-2004
30002 AVONDALE ESTATES	089	7474	7985	8683	1.6	49	3092	3264	3529	1.3	2.44	1774	1829	0.7
30004 ALPHARETTA	121	41604	50351	59716	4.6	90	15836	19233	22804	4.7	2.61	11318	13548	4.3
30005 ALPHARETTA	121	26622	31981	37070	4.4	89	9285	11118	12866	4.3	2.88	7132	8404	3.9
30008 MARIETTA	067	33188	36273	39810	2.1	60	10936	12049	13323	2.3	2.77	7275	7866	1.9
30011 AUBURN	013	11911	14497	18498	4.7	91	3996	4876	6223	4.8	2.96	3232	3889	4.5
30012 CONYERS	247	23686	25560	28780	1.8	53	8027	8693	9859	1.9	2.83	5807	6175	1.5
30013 CONYERS	247	18484	21390	25098	3.5	82	6630	7728	9129	3.7	2.77	5132	5915	3.4
30014 COVINGTON	217	26747	33413	45145	5.4	94	9633	12187	16687	5.7	2.69	7388	9232	5.4
30016 COVINGTON	217	26155	36364	51936	8.1	99	9292	13044	18799	8.3	2.79	7216	10010	8.0
30017 GRAYSON	135	9577	12983	16891	7.4	98	3139	4265	5541	7.5	3.04	2730	3665	7.2
30019 DACULA	135	19791	26904	35047	7.5	99	6625	9047	11773	7.6	2.97	5698	7693	7.3
30021 CLARKSTON	089	22433	24842	27390	2.4	67	7697	8383	9160	2.0	2.96	5042	5380	1.5
30022 ALPHARETTA	121	54977	63047	70592	3.3	79	19340	22054	24634	3.1	2.86	14621	16413	2.8
30024 SUWANEE	135	37473	50832	67389	7.4	99	12268	16691	22102	7.5	3.03	10480	14091	7.2
30025 SOCIAL CIRCLE	297	7031	8186	10152	3.6	84	2454	2889	3617	3.9	2.80	1952	2272	3.6
30030 DECATUR	089	24646	25585	27397	0.9	35	11291	11842	12763	1.1	2.06	5256	5290	0.2
30032 DECATUR	089	58321	59405	63139	0.4	21	18951	19427	20745	0.6	2.90	13483	13537	-0.1
30033 DECATUR	089	27884	28583	30447	0.6	27	13446	13902	14879	0.8	1.97	6310	6297	-0.1
30034 DECATUR	089	45045	49788	54928	2.4	66	14937	16675	18478	2.6	2.94	11469	12631	2.3
30035 DECATUR	089	19003	20908	23091	2.3	64	6534	7251	8029	2.5	2.88	4748	5157	2.0
30038 LITHONIA	089	23654	29091	34147	5.0	92	8190	10149	11950	5.2	2.87	6258	7658	4.9
30039 SNELLVILLE	135	29169	34261	41633	3.9	86	9580	11307	13734	4.0	3.01	7892	9206	3.7
30040 CUMMING	117	42181	55303	76139	6.6	96	14706	19327	26626	6.6	2.83	11880	15446	6.4
30041 CUMMING	117	31397	42629	59563	7.5	99	11263	15247	21239	7.4	2.79	8997	12054	7.1
30043 LAWRENCEVILLE	135	62763	77730	96847	5.2	93	19706	24610	30755	5.4	3.07	16451	20274	5.0
30044 LAWRENCEVILLE	135	64815	76397	93165	3.9	86	22154	26194	31895	4.0	2.90	16714	19330	3.5
30045 LAWRENCEVILLE	135	38951	52383	68247	7.2	98	13416	17946	23274	7.1	2.90	10264	13613	6.9
30047 LILBURN	135	54210	59726	70691	2.3	64	18319	20192	23841	2.3	2.94	14586	15785	1.9
30052 LOGANVILLE	297	32647	42153	53934	6.2	95	10990	14244	18259	6.3	2.96	9205	11805	6.0
30054 OXFORD	217	9266	10933	14189	4.0	87	3089	3717	4916	4.5	2.84	2542	3027	4.2
30055 MANSFIELD	217	2549	3196	4176	5.5	94	961	1212	1592	5.6	2.63	785	979	5.3
30056 NEWBORN	159	2222	2740	3479	5.1	93	722	900	1156	5.3	3.04	589	726	5.0
30058 LITHONIA	089	42867	50728	57892	4.0	87	14419	17092	19500	4.1	2.95	10911	12732	3.7
30060 MARIETTA	067	36193	38602	42009	1.5	48	13160	14010	15230	1.5	2.67	8159	8382	0.6
30062 MARIETTA	067	61375	63671	68089	0.9	34	21915	22863	24493	1.0	2.77	17098	17583	0.7
30064 MARIETTA	067	41033	44610	48878	2.0	58	15009	16331	17901	2.0	2.71	11479	12367	1.8
30066 MARIETTA	067	51683	55093	60020	1.5	48	18199	19554	21361	1.7	2.81	14210	15004	1.3
30067 MARIETTA	067	48357	50728	54308	1.1	40	20706	21615	23073	1.0	2.32	11106	11245	0.3
30068 MARIETTA	067	31812	32108	33977	0.2	16	11931	12105	12840	0.3	2.65	9203	9199	0.0
30069 MARIETTA	067	27	27	27	0.0	12	6	6	6	0.0	1.00	6	0	-100.0
30071 NORCROSS	135	21874	24899	29758	3.1	77	6711	7522	8914	2.7	3.22	4631	5062	2.1
30075 ROSWELL	121	46331	50780	55698	2.2	62	16548	18169	19951	2.2	2.77	12799	13848	1.9
30076 ROSWELL	121	39808	43325	47156	2.0	59	15030	16260	17651	1.9	2.65	10163	10798	1.4
30078 SNELLVILLE	135	29995	34085	40820	3.1	76	9912	11288	13499	3.1	3.00	8255	9274	2.8
30079 SCOTTDALE	089	3086	3172	3365	0.7	29	1149	1200	1284	1.0	2.62	664	671	0.3
30080 SMYRNA	067	43480	47890	53287	2.3	64	20293	22335	24843	2.3	2.14	9357	9853	1.2
30082 SMYRNA	067	23275	25540	28044	2.2	63	9320	10285	11325	2.4	2.45	6001	6423	1.6
30083 STONE MOUNTAIN	089	56816	58575	62454	0.7	31	20325	20915	22249	0.7	2.79	13553	13608	0.1
30084 TUCKER	089	29902	31926	35264	1.6	49	11953	12804	14126	1.6	2.47	7797	8127	1.0
30087 STONE MOUNTAIN	089	34974	38606	43868	2.4	66	12065	13324	15139	2.4	2.89	9683	10533	2.0
30088 STONE MOUNTAIN	089	28597	29622	31647	0.8	34	9920	10347	11075	1.0	2.86	7240	7416	0.6
30092 NORCROSS	135	31270	35543	42570	3.1	76	12382	13937	16550	2.8	2.54	7916	8704	2.3
30093 NORCROSS	135	50024	57600	69580	3.4	80	17372	19621	23401	2.9	2.93	11004	12070	2.2
30094 CONYERS	247	26527	29868	34284	2.8	73	8970	10212	11828	3.1	2.91	7537	8496	2.9
30096 DULUTH	135	57263	65379	78447	3.2	78	22623	25759	30767	3.1	2.53	14268	15703	2.3
30097 DULUTH	121	25134	31564	38215	5.5	94	8440	10487	12625	5.2	3.01	7174	8845	5.1
30101 ACWORTH	067	38175	47280	56535	5.2	93	13414	16616	19851	5.2	2.84	10676	13069	4.9
30102 ACWORTH	057	32399	36968	45068	3.2	78	10898	12494	15297	3.3	2.96	8529	9645	2.9
30103 ADAIRSVILLE	015	10539	12381	14892	3.9	86	3870	4570	5517	4.0	2.71	3042	3547	3.7
30104 ARAGON	233	4132	4624	5143	2.7	71	1515	1709	1911	2.9	2.71	1206	1345	2.6
30105 ARMUCHEE	115	2657	2908	3142	2.2	61	991	1096	1191	2.4	2.65	796	866	2.0
30106 AUSTELL	067	15940	17852	19719	2.7	71	5908	6653	7366	2.8	2.65	4294	4744	2.4
30107 BALL GROUND	057	8446	10331	13539	4.9	91	3021	3722	4904	5.0	2.78	2422	2948	4.7
30108 BOWDON	045	7617	8615	10508	2.9	75	3037	3467	4263	3.2	2.48	2225	2497	2.8
30110 BREMEN	143	10283	11181	12359	2.0	58	3938	4321	4818	2.2	2.54	2886	3118	1.8
30113 BUCHANAN	143	6212	6843	7581	2.3	64	2336	2597	2901	2.5	2.59	1739	1906	2.2
30114 CANTON	057	22125	31299	44236	8.5	100	7824	11130	15818	8.7	2.78	5955	8368	8.3
30115 CANTON	057	19706	26137	35893	6.9	97	6877	9166	12647	7.0	2.84	5605	7382	6.7
30116 CARROLLTON	045	18394	21294	26246	3.5	82	6488	7624	9519	3.9	2.74	5023	5827	3.6
30117 CARROLLTON	045	30485	35230	43265	3.5	82	11610	13609	16961	3.8	2.48	7653	8776	3.3
30118 CARROLLTON	045	2135	2320	2587	2.0	57	13	16	20	5.0	2.56	5	6	4.4
30120 CARTERSVILLE	015	29226	34396	41853	3.9	86	10549	12415	15131	3.9	2.75	8049	9355	3.6
30121 CARTERSVILLE	015	15758	18617	22678	4.0	87	5569	6675	8223	4.4	2.70	4235	5002	4.0
30122 LITHIA SPRINGS	097	17253	20117	24144	3.7	84	6741	8008	9758	4.1	2.51	4631	5377	3.6
30124 CAVE SPRING	115	2666	2795	2953	1.1	40	1040	1101	1170	1.4	2.53	802	835	1.0
30125 CEDARTOWN	233	22826	23983	25896	1.2	41	8267	8718	9459	1.3	2.67	6041	6277	0.9
30126 MABLETON	067	23700	27438	31111	3.5	82	8744	10130	11473	3.5	2.70	6474	7355	3.1
30127 POWDER SPRINGS	067	48005	55641	64384	3.5	83	15642	18201	21108	3.6	3.04	13241	15239	3.4
30132 DALLAS	223	16764	22535	32056	7.2	98	5965	8090	11587	7.4	2.74	4623	6211	7.2
30134 DOUGLASVILLE	097	31190	38598	49569	5.1	93	10859	13475	17373	5.2	2.82	8395	10395	5.2
30135 DOUGLASVILLE	097	43389	49446	58615	3.1	78	14781	16997	20362	3.3	2.89	11993	13680	3.2
30137 EMERSON	015	1490	1607	1871	1.8	53	512	554	647	1.9	2.90	412	441	1.6
30139 FAIRMOUNT	129	3570	4272	5099	4.3	88	1358	1640	1971	4.5	2.60	1046	1244	4.2
30141 HIRAM	223	12506	16797	23667	7.2	98	4257	5731	8086	7.3	2.93	3484	4641	7.0
30143 JASPER	227	15581	18493	22489	4.1	87	6098	7326	9017	4.4	2.50	4567	5413	4.1
30144 KENNESAW	067	38773	46584	53459	4.4	89	14542	17611	20271	4.6	2.64	10246	12161	4.1
30145 KINGSTON	015	5800	7079	8643	4.8	91	1981	2430	2975	4.9	2.91	1624	1971	4.7
30147 LINDALE	115	5062	5413	5803	1.6	50	1928	2072	2230	1.7	2.59	1459	1550	1.4
30148 MARBLE HILL	085	1041	1331	1679	6.0	95	447	580	742	6.3	2.29	354	453	6.0
30149 MOUNT BERRY	115	1230	1213	1223	-0.3	7	34	33	34	-0.7	2.55	16	14	-3.1
30152 KENNESAW	067	25280	29014	32588	3.3	80	8332	9674	10930	3.6	2.98	6884	7876	3.2
30153 ROCKMART	233	13794	15935	18645	3.5	82	5185	6016	7056	3.6	2.63	3866	4431	3.3
30157 DALLAS	223	30320	39490	54773	6.4	96	10278	13445	18733	6.5	2.93	8434	10910	6.2
30161 ROME	115	34411	35146	36816	0.5	24	13171	13540	14261	0.7	2.49	9064	9148	0.2
30165 ROME	115	35897	37904	40289	1.3	44	13736	14520	15485	1.3	2.51	9538	9900	0.9
GEORGIA					2.4					2.5	2.64			2.2
UNITED STATES					1.2					1.3	2.58			1.1

#	POST OFFICE NAME	RACE (%) White 2000	White 2004	Black 2000	Black 2004	Asian/Pacific 2000	Asian/Pacific 2004	% Hispanic Origin 2000	% Hispanic Origin 2004	2004 AGE DISTRIBUTION (%) 0-4	5-9	10-14	15-19	20-24	25-44	45-64	65-84	85+	18+	MEDIAN AGE 2004	% 2004 Males	% 2004 Females
30002	AVONDALE ESTATES	40.7	36.7	50.7	53.6	1.9	2.0	2.0	2.3	8.4	7.3	7.4	7.0	8.8	32.9	20.1	7.2	1.0	73.2	32.3	47.1	52.9
30004	ALPHARETTA	89.4	86.0	4.4	6.5	2.9	3.2	4.5	6.1	8.0	8.3	7.4	5.4	4.5	34.4	24.4	6.8	0.7	72.8	36.1	49.8	50.2
30005	ALPHARETTA	83.0	78.3	5.4	8.1	8.9	10.0	3.5	5.0	10.2	10.3	9.0	6.1	4.2	36.2	20.9	2.9	0.2	66.5	33.2	49.5	50.5
30008	MARIETTA	52.0	48.7	35.6	37.1	2.4	2.7	15.4	18.2	8.2	7.1	6.5	6.5	9.1	37.4	18.0	6.1	1.1	74.6	31.6	51.4	48.6
30011	AUBURN	90.3	88.7	3.4	3.9	3.0	3.5	3.2	4.0	9.7	8.8	8.2	6.3	5.9	37.0	18.3	5.3	0.5	69.4	31.6	50.6	49.4
30012	CONYERS	69.0	66.4	21.9	22.6	1.4	1.5	12.4	15.4	7.0	6.6	7.2	6.9	7.8	30.8	22.6	9.5	1.6	75.2	34.2	50.8	49.2
30013	CONYERS	72.6	70.3	21.3	22.8	3.4	3.8	3.9	5.0	6.7	6.8	7.7	7.3	7.2	29.0	26.4	8.3	0.6	74.2	36.0	49.3	50.7
30014	COVINGTON	70.9	68.5	26.8	28.8	0.7	0.8	1.9	2.4	7.7	7.4	7.7	7.1	6.7	29.1	23.0	9.9	1.4	73.0	34.7	48.3	51.7
30016	COVINGTON	78.9	76.2	18.4	20.7	0.7	0.8	2.0	2.5	9.0	8.3	7.5	6.2	5.8	34.3	20.5	7.6	0.7	71.3	33.0	48.9	51.1
30017	GRAYSON	91.3	89.3	4.5	5.4	1.8	2.3	3.0	4.2	7.7	7.8	8.4	7.5	6.2	30.4	24.9	6.5	0.5	70.8	35.0	49.5	50.6
30019	DACULA	91.6	89.8	4.7	5.4	1.6	2.1	3.1	4.4	8.9	8.6	8.2	6.6	5.8	33.7	22.2	5.5	0.5	70.1	34.0	49.4	50.6
30021	CLARKSTON	21.3	19.2	60.6	61.0	10.0	11.1	4.3	5.1	9.2	7.9	7.8	7.8	10.5	36.9	15.6	3.9	0.4	70.7	28.2	49.5	50.5
30022	ALPHARETTA	81.2	76.1	7.2	10.4	8.4	9.4	4.2	5.7	8.0	8.7	8.9	6.9	4.9	32.8	25.6	4.0	0.3	70.0	35.2	49.0	51.0
30024	SUWANEE	84.5	81.6	6.2	7.2	6.6	7.8	4.0	5.4	10.6	10.4	8.3	5.5	4.3	36.5	20.8	3.5	0.2	67.0	33.6	49.7	50.3
30025	SOCIAL CIRCLE	75.9	72.6	22.5	25.5	0.5	0.6	1.1	1.4	7.5	7.5	7.2	6.7	5.7	28.8	24.6	10.6	1.4	73.6	36.4	49.5	50.5
30030	DECATUR	64.3	61.4	30.7	32.6	2.6	3.1	1.8	2.4	5.5	4.8	5.4	6.7	7.2	34.0	22.7	10.7	3.1	80.8	37.4	43.2	56.8
30032	DECATUR	7.1	6.5	88.7	88.8	0.9	1.0	2.6	3.1	7.0	7.0	7.9	8.0	9.0	31.2	22.9	6.3	0.6	73.4	31.9	48.5	51.5
30033	DECATUR	79.1	76.1	10.2	11.2	7.7	9.1	3.6	4.7	4.6	3.9	3.8	4.8	9.5	32.7	22.5	14.7	3.5	85.3	39.0	46.0	54.0
30034	DECATUR	4.1	3.5	94.1	94.6	0.2	0.2	1.1	1.1	7.2	7.3	8.0	7.9	7.9	30.7	25.3	5.2	0.5	72.4	32.9	46.4	53.6
30035	DECATUR	6.9	6.0	89.9	90.6	1.1	1.1	1.7	1.8	7.8	7.7	8.6	8.0	8.2	32.3	22.2	4.7	0.4	71.0	31.3	45.7	54.3
30038	LITHONIA	9.2	10.0	88.6	87.6	0.2	0.2	1.3	1.5	8.2	8.1	8.2	7.3	6.8	33.4	22.5	5.1	0.5	71.0	32.7	46.7	53.3
30039	SNELLVILLE	76.4	72.8	18.0	20.4	1.9	2.3	4.1	5.4	6.4	6.9	8.2	7.8	6.8	30.3	27.9	5.1	0.6	73.5	35.8	49.6	50.4
30040	CUMMING	94.8	93.6	0.8	0.9	0.5	0.6	6.6	8.6	9.0	8.6	7.2	5.6	5.4	34.2	21.9	7.2	1.0	71.8	34.6	50.4	49.6
30041	CUMMING	95.1	94.1	0.5	0.6	0.8	0.9	5.4	6.9	8.9	8.9	7.2	5.1	4.3	33.3	24.8	6.9	0.6	71.7	36.3	51.0	49.0
30043	LAWRENCEVILLE	79.4	75.7	10.1	11.5	6.9	8.2	5.2	7.1	9.0	8.9	8.6	6.8	5.8	35.5	21.3	3.8	0.3	69.1	32.9	50.3	49.7
30044	LAWRENCEVILLE	68.1	63.9	16.2	17.6	9.1	10.5	10.0	12.9	8.3	7.9	7.5	6.7	7.2	35.2	22.2	4.4	0.5	72.2	32.6	49.4	50.6
30045	LAWRENCEVILLE	79.2	75.9	11.6	12.7	3.3	4.0	9.6	12.6	8.5	8.0	7.7	6.8	7.0	33.5	21.4	6.4	0.8	71.6	32.8	49.8	50.2
30047	LILBURN	77.2	73.4	9.7	10.8	7.9	9.3	8.6	11.4	6.1	6.5	7.5	7.4	6.6	28.4	29.7	7.1	0.8	75.3	37.5	49.5	50.5
30052	LOGANVILLE	93.5	92.0	3.2	3.9	1.0	1.2	2.8	3.8	8.6	8.2	7.9	6.7	6.1	32.7	22.5	6.8	0.6	71.2	34.0	49.2	50.8
30054	OXFORD	82.6	81.1	14.9	16.1	1.0	1.1	1.3	1.6	7.2	7.0	6.8	6.8	6.9	29.3	25.4	9.7	0.9	75.7	36.1	49.3	50.7
30055	MANSFIELD	87.7	85.5	10.9	12.8	0.4	0.5	1.1	1.4	7.1	7.5	7.9	6.2	5.3	29.5	26.1	9.5	0.9	73.5	36.4	49.8	50.2
30056	NEWBORN	76.2	73.0	21.4	24.3	0.2	0.2	2.4	3.0	8.0	8.1	7.9	7.2	6.9	28.1	24.1	8.8	1.0	71.6	34.5	50.4	49.6
30058	LITHONIA	8.8	8.0	88.1	88.6	0.6	0.6	2.1	2.5	8.8	8.6	9.2	8.0	7.1	35.2	18.8	3.8	0.6	68.4	30.8	46.2	53.9
30060	MARIETTA	51.9	48.5	31.0	31.6	2.6	2.7	21.3	25.8	8.2	7.0	6.7	7.2	10.4	33.1	17.4	8.6	1.5	74.6	30.8	51.5	48.6
30062	MARIETTA	83.9	81.6	8.0	8.8	4.8	5.6	4.5	5.8	6.3	7.1	7.7	6.8	5.5	29.1	30.5	6.5	0.6	74.7	38.0	49.9	50.1
30064	MARIETTA	80.3	78.0	14.6	15.7	1.6	1.9	4.9	6.3	6.9	7.4	8.0	6.7	5.7	29.2	27.4	7.7	1.1	73.5	37.1	49.1	50.9
30066	MARIETTA	86.0	83.6	7.1	8.1	3.7	4.3	3.9	5.2	6.3	6.9	7.6	7.1	6.1	30.5	28.3	6.7	0.6	74.8	36.9	49.4	50.6
30067	MARIETTA	60.7	58.1	26.0	26.9	5.4	6.1	10.4	12.4	6.4	5.7	6.2	6.7	10.1	39.0	19.8	5.6	0.6	77.8	31.9	50.5	49.6
30068	MARIETTA	89.3	87.6	4.1	4.6	4.3	5.2	2.6	3.5	5.1	6.2	7.4	6.9	5.3	24.4	34.0	9.9	0.8	76.8	41.9	48.9	51.1
30069	MARIETTA	59.3	59.3	33.3	33.3	0.0	0.0	11.1	11.1	7.4	3.7	0.0	7.4	40.7	37.0	3.7	0.0	0.0	88.9	23.9	81.5	18.5
30071	NORCROSS	50.7	48.3	22.6	22.1	8.3	8.8	36.6	42.0	8.2	7.0	6.4	6.6	10.4	40.1	16.6	4.3	0.4	74.8	29.9	55.2	44.8
30075	ROSWELL	88.3	84.6	5.6	7.9	2.8	3.2	5.6	7.6	6.6	7.3	7.5	6.6	5.2	28.5	29.8	7.4	1.1	74.3	38.7	49.9	50.1
30076	ROSWELL	77.2	72.2	9.5	12.8	4.0	4.3	16.5	19.4	6.9	6.6	6.1	6.5	8.5	34.0	24.1	6.3	1.0	76.6	34.0	51.3	48.7
30078	SNELLVILLE	86.4	83.5	7.0	8.1	3.0	3.8	4.6	6.3	6.8	7.2	8.2	7.6	6.3	28.4	26.9	7.6	1.0	72.7	36.4	48.9	51.1
30079	SCOTTDALE	33.3	31.9	57.5	57.5	5.3	6.2	3.4	4.2	8.0	7.9	7.9	6.8	7.8	33.1	18.7	8.2	1.7	72.3	32.0	46.9	53.1
30080	SMYRNA	59.0	54.2	27.3	29.9	3.6	3.9	14.7	17.7	6.3	5.2	4.7	4.9	11.2	42.9	18.2	5.9	0.7	81.2	31.8	50.2	49.8
30082	SMYRNA	62.5	59.5	26.8	28.4	3.2	3.6	11.0	13.1	7.2	6.5	5.7	5.2	7.3	36.3	21.1	9.1	1.6	77.5	34.7	48.5	51.5
30083	STONE MOUNTAIN	17.9	16.1	72.7	73.4	4.4	4.8	4.6	5.6	8.4	7.8	7.8	7.1	8.9	35.2	18.9	5.3	0.7	71.9	30.4	47.5	52.5
30084	TUCKER	65.5	61.9	20.1	21.3	8.2	9.4	9.6	12.2	6.6	6.2	5.6	5.3	6.3	32.6	24.0	12.0	1.5	78.4	37.5	48.6	51.5
30087	STONE MOUNTAIN	44.7	41.5	47.8	49.9	4.1	4.8	3.4	4.1	6.8	7.2	7.9	7.1	5.8	29.2	27.6	7.7	0.7	73.5	37.1	48.4	51.6
30088	STONE MOUNTAIN	8.5	7.5	87.4	88.0	1.3	1.4	2.2	2.5	7.4	7.5	8.6	7.9	8.2	33.2	22.7	4.1	0.3	71.7	31.7	46.3	53.7
30092	NORCROSS	65.6	61.8	20.3	21.4	7.6	8.9	9.3	11.7	7.7	7.6	7.3	6.3	7.7	35.3	23.2	4.6	0.4	73.7	32.9	50.4	49.6
30093	NORCROSS	43.1	40.7	26.7	26.3	13.6	14.1	29.6	34.4	8.6	7.3	6.6	6.5	10.3	40.9	16.3	3.3	0.2	73.8	29.6	52.7	47.3
30094	CONYERS	82.4	79.8	14.1	15.9	1.6	1.9	2.0	2.7	6.2	6.7	8.1	7.8	6.2	27.7	28.7	8.1	0.7	74.2	37.7	49.0	51.0
30096	DULUTH	64.5	59.9	14.0	15.0	13.0	14.8	13.1	16.4	7.4	6.6	6.2	6.1	8.7	39.3	20.7	4.6	0.4	76.4	32.4	50.6	49.4
30097	DULUTH	77.7	72.8	6.2	8.2	13.2	15.3	3.5	4.8	9.3	9.7	9.3	6.7	4.8	32.1	24.5	3.4	0.3	67.3	34.6	49.1	50.9
30101	ACWORTH	87.5	85.6	7.5	8.4	1.7	2.0	3.7	4.8	9.2	9.1	8.4	6.3	5.1	35.0	21.2	5.4	0.5	69.3	33.5	49.5	50.6
30102	ACWORTH	87.7	85.5	5.8	6.5	1.9	2.2	5.3	7.1	8.1	7.9	7.8	6.8	6.3	34.3	23.5	4.9	0.3	72.0	33.6	50.7	49.3
30103	ADAIRSVILLE	90.1	88.8	7.3	8.0	0.7	0.8	1.6	2.0	7.8	7.6	7.4	6.6	6.1	30.9	23.7	9.1	1.0	73.2	34.7	49.1	50.9
30104	ARAGON	90.9	89.8	7.7	8.5	0.2	0.2	1.6	2.2	8.1	7.7	6.9	6.5	6.6	30.0	24.3	9.2	0.9	73.5	35.2	50.3	49.7
30105	ARMUCHEE	96.6	95.7	1.9	2.4	0.5	0.5	0.6	0.9	6.2	6.7	7.3	6.4	5.4	28.0	27.9	11.0	1.1	75.9	39.3	50.5	49.6
30106	AUSTELL	62.3	58.5	31.9	34.6	1.6	1.9	4.3	5.4	7.7	7.1	6.8	6.2	6.6	33.4	21.4	9.4	1.4	74.6	35.0	47.9	52.1
30107	BALL GROUND	97.5	97.1	1.0	1.1	0.1	0.1	1.2	1.5	7.3	7.5	7.2	6.1	5.3	31.4	25.4	9.0	0.9	74.3	37.0	50.1	49.9
30108	BOWDON	85.7	84.2	12.4	13.5	0.1	0.2	1.6	2.0	6.8	6.9	7.2	6.2	6.1	28.2	25.2	11.9	1.5	75.3	37.9	49.7	50.4
30110	BREMEN	91.2	90.0	7.2	8.0	0.4	0.5	0.6	0.8	7.0	6.9	7.2	6.6	6.5	28.8	24.0	11.7	1.6	74.9	36.8	49.1	50.9
30113	BUCHANAN	95.9	95.3	3.1	3.5	0.1	0.1	0.5	0.7	6.6	6.8	6.8	6.2	6.0	28.6	25.4	12.2	1.4	75.9	38.1	50.0	50.1
30114	CANTON	88.7	86.8	3.6	3.9	0.6	0.7	10.0	12.2	8.2	7.6	6.6	6.1	6.5	32.9	22.5	8.4	1.4	74.1	34.7	50.5	49.6
30115	CANTON	95.5	94.5	0.9	1.0	0.3	0.4	4.3	5.6	7.8	8.0	7.5	6.2	5.4	32.0	25.0	7.5	0.7	72.9	35.9	50.3	49.7
30116	CARROLLTON	80.3	77.8	16.8	18.8	0.8	0.9	1.5	1.9	7.8	7.5	7.6	6.8	6.9	30.9	23.3	8.1	1.1	73.0	33.9	49.4	50.6
30117	CARROLLTON	73.0	70.5	22.7	24.4	0.8	0.9	4.3	5.5	6.7	6.5	6.7	8.6	10.7	28.7	20.8	9.6	1.7	76.1	32.0	48.5	51.5
30118	CARROLLTON	60.0	55.4	31.8	34.6	0.9	1.0	7.8	9.8	1.4	1.2	1.3	42.7	35.8	10.0	5.6	1.8	0.2	93.2	20.5	42.2	57.8
30120	CARTERSVILLE	83.4	81.6	12.3	13.3	0.5	0.5	4.7	5.9	7.9	7.6	7.7	6.6	6.4	30.3	22.5	9.6	1.3	72.7	34.6	48.8	51.2
30121	CARTERSVILLE	87.1	85.0	9.0	10.2	0.7	0.8	3.6	4.7	7.9	7.5	7.2	6.3	6.7	32.6	22.7	8.1	1.1	73.7	34.2	49.6	50.4
30122	LITHIA SPRINGS	70.0	67.2	25.1	27.1	1.5	1.7	3.6	4.5	7.4	7.0	6.9	6.3	7.1	34.0	22.1	8.2	1.0	74.9	33.9	48.8	51.2
30124	CAVE SPRING	92.8	91.1	4.8	6.0	0.5	0.6	1.5	2.0	6.1	6.4	6.9	6.4	4.9	27.2	27.8	12.9	1.4	76.8	40.6	49.7	50.3
30125	CEDARTOWN	77.9	74.8	13.0	13.8	0.4	0.4	11.9	15.1	7.2	6.9	6.7	7.0	7.4	28.4	22.9	11.9	1.7	75.1	35.5	50.9	49.1
30126	MABLETON	63.6	59.3	28.9	31.8	1.6	1.8	7.5	9.7	7.4	7.4	7.0	6.1	5.7	32.8	23.5	9.2	0.9	74.3	36.1	48.8	51.2
30127	POWDER SPRINGS	74.5	72.4	21.6	23.0	1.1	1.2	3.1	3.8	8.1	8.3	8.8	7.4	5.9	32.6	22.8	5.4	0.6	70.0	34.1	49.1	50.9
30132	DALLAS	92.6	91.8	5.0	5.3	0.4	0.5	1.6	2.1	9.5	8.9	7.7	6.2	6.0	34.9	19.1	7.0	0.7	70.0	32.1	49.8	50.2
30134	DOUGLASVILLE	75.8	74.3	20.4	21.4	0.7	0.7	3.0	3.6	9.3	8.7	8.2	6.6	6.3	34.9	19.2	6.2	0.7	69.9	32.0	49.4	50.6
30135	DOUGLASVILLE	83.1	81.3	13.1	14.2	1.4	1.6	2.3	2.9	6.8	7.0	7.8	7.1	6.8	31.0	26.2	6.5	0.7	74.0	35.6	48.9	51.1
30137	EMERSON	90.6	89.2	6.9	7.8	0.3	0.4	1.9	2.6	7.2	7.4	7.7	6.5	6.0	28.5	27.6	8.5	0.8	73.8	37.0	50.2	49.8
30139	FAIRMOUNT	97.7	97.1	1.2	1.4	0.1	0.1	1.2	1.6	6.7	6.8	7.4	6.7	6.1	29.8	25.5	9.9	1.1	75.0	36.8	50.4	49.6
30141	HIRAM	89.3	87.9	8.1	9.0	0.3	0.4	2.0	2.5	9.4	8.8	8.3	6.3	5.9	36.2	19.2	5.5	0.5	69.6	32.1	49.5	50.5
30143	JASPER	95.9	95.2	1.6	1.7	0.3	0.4	2.3	2.9	6.3	6.4	6.4	5.9	5.3	28.5	26.7	13.2	1.3	77.3	39.4	48.7	51.4
30144	KENNESAW	81.9	78.9	10.0	11.4	3.5	4.2	5.3	6.9	8.4	7.7	6.9	5.9	7.0	38.1	20.5	5.1	0.4	73.5	32.5	49.5	50.5
30145	KINGSTON	92.4	91.1	5.7	6.6	0.2	0.3	1.4	1.9	8.5	8.2	8.0	6.9	6.2	31.8	22.5	7.3	0.7	71.0	33.3	49.7	50.3
30147	LINDALE	95.2	94.2	2.3	2.8	0.5	0.6	1.9	2.5	6.4	6.5	7.0	6.4	6.3	27.6	26.1	12.5	1.4	76.3	38.5	50.3	49.8
30148	MARBLE HILL	98.1	97.6	0.1	0.2	0.1	0.1	0.5	0.8	4.9	5.0	5.2	4.4	4.1	20.7	33.9	21.2	0.8	82.3	49.4	49.4	50.6
30149	MOUNT BERRY	88.3	85.6	4.5	5.4	2.0	2.3	5.5	7.3	2.2	1.8	0.7	30.8	45.8	9.2	4.6	3.1	1.6	94.6	21.6	40.2	59.9
30152	KENNESAW	87.5	85.1	6.2	7.0	2.4	2.9	4.7	6.5	8.1	8.2	8.2	7.2	6.2	31.2	25.1	5.3	0.6	70.9	34.7	49.6	50.4
30153	ROCKMART	84.6	83.1	13.7	14.9	0.4	0.5	1.2	1.6	7.1	7.2	7.1	6.8	6.3	28.7	23.9	11.6	1.5	74.4	36.4	49.5	50.5
30157	DALLAS	92.3	91.3	5.2	5.8	0.5	0.5	1.6	2.1	9.0	8.6	8.3	6.8	6.1	35.5	19.9	5.3	0.5	69.9	32.3	49.9	50.1
30161	ROME	72.4	69.9	23.4	25.1	0.6	0.7	5.0	6.2	6.5	6.5	6.7	6.3	6.6	28.2	24.4	12.7	2.2	76.5	37.5	49.0	51.1
30165	ROME	82.2	79.1	9.6	11.0	1.8	2.1	8.2	10.5	7.0	6.9	6.9	7.1	7.4	27.6	22.3	13.0	1.8	75.4	35.8	47.7	52.3
	GEORGIA	65.1	63.4	28.7	29.4	2.2	2.5	5.3	6.6	7.3	7.1	7.2	7.0	7.6	31.0	23.0	8.6	1.1	74.3	34.2	49.3	50.7
	UNITED STATES	75.1	73.6	12.3	12.5	3.8	4.2	12.5	14.1	6.9	6.7	7.2	7.0	7.3	28.6	23.8	10.8	1.7	75.1	36.0	49.1	50.9

ZIP CODE #	POST OFFICE NAME	2004 Per Capita Income	2004 HH Income Base	2004 Household Income Distribution (%) Less than $25,000	$25,000 to $49,999	$50,000 to $99,999	$100,000 to $149,999	$150,000 or More	Median Household Income 2004	2009	2004 National Centile	2004 State Centile	2004 Home Value Base	2004 Home Value Distribution (%) Less than $50,000	$50,000 to $89,999	$90,000 to $174,999	$175,000 to $399,999	$400,000 or More	2004 Median Home Value
30002	AVONDALE ESTATES	31288	3264	26.6	26.6	27.5	12.3	7.0	45862	57027	63	67	1459	2.8	9.0	31.5	50.2	6.5	198665
30004	ALPHARETTA	50429	19233	7.3	15.6	31.5	21.6	24.0	91446	122596	97	98	15368	1.3	1.8	22.5	51.0	23.4	249794
30005	ALPHARETTA	52782	11118	5.2	8.8	28.0	26.6	31.5	113341	150053	99	100	8922	0.6	0.9	9.9	61.2	27.5	305454
30008	MARIETTA	23574	12049	16.6	30.6	36.6	11.5	4.7	52537	63089	76	78	7340	9.4	9.1	55.4	25.1	1.1	134681
30011	AUBURN	23462	4876	11.2	29.1	45.9	11.0	2.8	57750	63824	82	83	4227	3.1	8.0	70.1	15.8	3.1	136229
30012	CONYERS	19664	8693	25.1	29.1	32.6	9.6	3.6	45863	54822	64	67	5620	13.3	18.9	48.4	16.3	3.2	110149
30013	CONYERS	30543	7728	11.7	25.3	34.0	19.1	9.9	64840	78071	88	89	5595	2.2	4.3	47.5	41.4	4.7	166736
30014	COVINGTON	21491	12187	24.4	31.1	31.5	9.4	3.7	45388	51713	62	66	8780	6.6	17.6	51.3	21.0	3.6	121606
30016	COVINGTON	23655	13044	15.7	29.0	40.8	11.1	3.4	54042	62340	78	80	10633	6.6	10.0	65.8	16.4	1.3	132897
30017	GRAYSON	31316	4265	6.1	16.3	44.4	22.3	10.9	78642	92289	95	96	3981	0.6	1.2	41.1	49.4	7.8	186340
30019	DACULA	31220	9047	6.9	16.4	43.0	22.3	11.4	79028	94083	95	96	8569	1.4	2.3	38.1	49.8	8.3	189192
30021	CLARKSTON	17756	8383	25.1	34.0	31.3	7.3	2.3	42753	49804	55	60	2402	3.2	14.2	67.9	14.8	0.0	132426
30022	ALPHARETTA	53423	22054	5.0	10.6	27.0	26.0	31.4	111414	146635	99	99	17783	0.4	0.5	18.1	52.2	28.8	289476
30024	SUWANEE	40248	16691	4.4	11.1	35.1	27.8	21.5	98766	120504	98	99	15142	0.8	1.1	16.3	67.4	14.4	254527
30025	SOCIAL CIRCLE	24668	2889	20.0	27.0	35.0	12.1	5.9	52858	62273	77	78	2388	7.3	15.5	42.4	29.2	5.5	137749
30030	DECATUR	38442	11842	19.6	23.2	31.0	15.1	11.1	59027	77880	84	84	6552	0.7	4.0	23.8	56.2	15.3	246711
30032	DECATUR	17746	19427	27.4	33.4	29.5	7.3	2.5	40883	47154	49	55	10656	2.7	29.2	62.8	4.6	0.7	102634
30033	DECATUR	42119	13902	15.9	22.6	33.8	16.0	11.7	63839	83060	88	89	7980	0.7	1.7	26.2	59.8	11.7	230362
30034	DECATUR	23765	16675	14.9	25.1	38.4	16.9	4.8	60610	71694	85	86	12093	0.9	6.0	69.9	22.5	0.7	138868
30035	DECATUR	20518	7251	16.1	31.5	40.5	9.4	2.5	51468	59105	75	77	4419	0.8	12.1	74.3	12.0	0.8	121518
30038	LITHONIA	27734	10149	11.3	24.0	43.5	13.9	7.4	62663	74916	87	88	8285	1.2	6.4	67.6	20.7	4.1	142870
30039	SNELLVILLE	28758	11307	7.2	18.5	43.5	21.7	9.1	74680	87344	93	94	10070	3.0	1.3	49.6	41.3	4.8	169393
30040	CUMMING	30589	19327	12.7	18.7	38.6	19.6	10.5	72419	88336	92	93	16526	4.8	5.5	28.4	49.2	12.1	197563
30041	CUMMING	38491	15247	9.6	15.7	34.9	22.2	17.6	83058	102911	96	97	13669	4.0	3.7	20.3	56.4	15.7	246162
30043	LAWRENCEVILLE	31673	24610	5.8	15.1	41.4	25.9	11.8	82707	100872	96	97	21786	1.5	0.7	35.5	59.3	3.0	195211
30044	LAWRENCEVILLE	28135	26194	8.3	22.1	43.2	19.7	6.8	69071	81358	91	92	19635	1.8	1.5	56.3	39.4	1.1	165700
30045	LAWRENCEVILLE	26332	17946	13.9	23.7	40.4	15.6	6.5	62798	75449	87	88	13430	4.3	2.4	53.8	36.0	3.6	161953
30047	LILBURN	30735	20192	8.8	19.0	38.8	22.4	11.0	75920	88827	94	95	16441	1.3	1.2	45.1	50.0	2.4	179123
30052	LOGANVILLE	25892	14244	11.1	22.6	43.0	17.1	6.2	66386	77994	89	90	12718	6.1	3.5	49.4	36.0	4.9	162954
30054	OXFORD	25705	3717	14.1	28.5	37.0	13.7	6.7	57572	65799	82	83	3167	7.5	13.7	40.6	31.0	7.1	141901
30055	MANSFIELD	24898	1212	19.6	30.2	33.7	11.1	5.4	50148	58400	72	75	1038	7.5	12.1	47.3	27.1	6.0	131818
30056	NEWBORN	17531	900	21.9	38.8	31.1	5.0	3.2	42751	49119	55	60	744	15.5	19.9	43.7	17.7	3.2	108456
30058	LITHONIA	22642	17092	13.7	29.4	39.6	13.2	4.1	56478	66401	81	82	13083	2.6	5.5	70.1	20.9	0.9	136595
30060	MARIETTA	21013	14010	27.3	32.8	28.8	7.8	3.3	40658	49298	48	53	6174	5.7	13.0	65.0	14.3	2.1	119321
30062	MARIETTA	40719	22863	6.8	14.7	33.2	25.5	19.9	91452	112410	97	99	18971	0.7	0.9	26.3	61.6	10.5	221005
30064	MARIETTA	37936	16331	9.3	15.8	36.5	23.2	15.2	82063	102499	96	97	13499	2.6	2.1	33.1	53.3	8.9	205081
30066	MARIETTA	35507	19554	7.1	17.0	37.6	23.7	14.6	82176	100819	96	97	16270	0.2	1.2	45.1	47.2	6.4	181840
30067	MARIETTA	37625	21615	13.6	28.7	33.5	12.8	11.4	57897	71332	83	84	8527	0.8	4.1	37.5	32.9	24.7	208148
30068	MARIETTA	54686	12105	6.6	12.5	28.2	22.8	29.9	104485	129650	98	99	10563	0.5	0.5	13.1	65.8	20.2	276470
30069	MARIETTA	26624	6	0.0	0.0	100.0	0.0	0.0	75000	88047	93	94	0	0.0	0.0	0.0	0.0	0.0	0
30071	NORCROSS	20092	7522	16.7	28.6	38.9	12.0	3.8	53755	62925	78	79	3942	1.4	5.9	65.9	24.8	2.0	146761
30075	ROSWELL	47280	18169	6.8	13.5	27.2	23.9	28.7	103983	134688	98	99	15080	0.6	1.5	16.8	59.4	21.6	272585
30076	ROSWELL	43306	16260	8.6	17.8	33.4	21.6	18.7	82392	110676	96	97	10407	0.3	1.9	25.3	56.9	15.7	227020
30078	SNELLVILLE	30978	11288	7.6	19.9	40.0	21.2	11.2	75482	88386	93	95	9718	0.7	0.8	51.5	40.5	6.5	171370
30079	SCOTTDALE	20275	1200	33.6	31.3	24.0	7.3	3.8	36826	43772	35	42	515	5.2	26.2	43.3	25.1	0.2	128348
30080	SMYRNA	33701	22335	16.0	29.9	34.5	12.9	6.7	53604	65398	78	79	8304	1.0	7.6	51.7	26.7	13.1	148909
30082	SMYRNA	32747	10285	12.8	25.0	37.5	17.2	7.5	61897	77095	86	87	6370	3.7	3.7	49.2	40.8	2.8	164848
30083	STONE MOUNTAIN	22205	20915	16.2	33.5	37.0	9.5	3.8	50248	58486	72	75	10771	1.0	10.5	72.9	15.0	0.6	130611
30084	TUCKER	31839	12804	12.1	25.8	36.5	16.6	9.0	63005	77395	87	88	8346	1.4	3.1	44.5	48.3	2.7	176702
30087	STONE MOUNTAIN	33041	13324	8.5	18.1	39.6	20.6	13.2	76406	92539	94	95	12120	4.6	1.7	40.5	45.9	7.2	181680
30088	STONE MOUNTAIN	25272	10347	11.0	27.0	43.0	13.5	5.5	60974	72110	85	86	7337	0.1	4.2	78.0	17.4	0.3	137361
30092	NORCROSS	41493	13937	11.0	24.5	29.3	16.7	18.6	69012	82931	91	92	7370	0.6	2.8	16.5	57.7	22.5	295886
30093	NORCROSS	20910	19621	15.3	34.1	36.6	10.7	3.2	50458	59003	73	75	7714	4.2	4.7	69.7	20.8	0.7	140773
30094	CONYERS	30616	10212	8.2	19.3	42.3	21.0	9.2	73106	86210	92	93	9015	1.3	6.6	55.1	34.1	2.9	152190
30096	DULUTH	32514	25759	10.2	25.2	38.6	17.2	8.8	64505	77107	88	89	13273	2.8	1.6	44.0	45.9	5.7	177760
30097	DULUTH	52934	10487	4.1	7.4	27.0	28.6	33.0	115740	145111	99	100	9503	2.3	0.9	8.9	61.2	26.8	283572
30101	ACWORTH	32930	16616	9.9	17.8	37.4	22.6	12.4	77652	93759	94	95	14346	2.0	3.7	39.4	48.8	6.1	184691
30102	ACWORTH	26331	12494	10.5	22.1	42.1	19.1	6.3	67217	79391	90	91	10594	7.4	7.9	54.8	28.8	1.1	152587
30103	ADAIRSVILLE	19543	4570	26.4	31.9	32.9	6.1	2.8	42571	48646	55	60	3607	12.0	25.9	44.0	15.7	2.4	103659
30104	ARAGON	18344	1709	28.2	31.6	30.1	8.1	2.0	40967	47453	50	55	1416	21.5	34.7	29.9	12.6	1.3	83577
30105	ARMUCHEE	21919	1096	23.1	29.2	33.7	12.3	1.7	47944	55842	68	72	971	10.1	21.9	39.2	22.6	6.2	120630
30106	AUSTELL	25423	6653	15.2	27.7	39.9	13.8	3.4	55932	67652	81	82	4912	0.9	10.8	68.5	18.8	1.0	137072
30107	BALL GROUND	23405	3722	16.4	26.9	41.7	11.2	3.9	55448	65215	80	81	3240	7.3	11.1	41.0	32.3	8.4	158621
30108	BOWDON	20106	3467	32.5	32.9	27.0	5.2	2.5	38187	44236	40	46	2745	18.1	28.5	36.6	14.6	2.3	95870
30110	BREMEN	19657	4321	35.3	30.9	25.6	5.8	2.5	35144	40374	28	35	3305	16.7	30.2	39.7	12.2	1.2	94271
30113	BUCHANAN	18219	2597	35.1	31.5	25.5	4.9	3.0	35932	41215	31	38	2132	23.3	33.2	29.8	11.0	2.8	82634
30114	CANTON	26621	11130	17.9	22.5	37.3	14.4	8.0	60560	72439	85	86	8662	3.2	10.1	38.4	39.5	8.8	172070
30115	CANTON	28193	9166	13.1	21.6	38.1	18.9	8.4	66903	79961	90	91	7954	2.9	4.4	40.0	41.1	11.6	181744
30116	CARROLLTON	24026	7624	23.2	25.3	36.0	9.9	5.6	51243	60895	74	77	5905	12.8	17.5	45.2	19.8	4.6	115153
30117	CARROLLTON	21800	13609	34.1	27.2	26.6	7.9	4.2	39022	45745	43	49	8099	11.7	22.3	44.0	19.1	2.9	113073
30118	CARROLLTON	7995	16	43.8	31.3	18.8	6.3	0.0	27230	27261	7	6	4	50.0	0.0	0.0	50.0	0.0	155000
30120	CARTERSVILLE	23738	12415	21.1	29.6	34.7	9.9	4.7	49377	56456	71	74	9248	8.4	18.2	51.3	19.9	2.2	120072
30121	CARTERSVILLE	22570	6675	19.2	29.2	38.7	9.8	3.2	51189	58511	74	77	4892	12.8	13.8	55.1	17.1	1.2	117773
30122	LITHIA SPRINGS	24351	8008	20.4	30.0	36.2	10.1	3.3	49591	57068	71	74	5201	11.3	14.5	55.1	18.3	0.7	121084
30124	CAVE SPRING	22538	1101	24.4	30.2	34.5	7.6	3.3	46277	53317	65	69	930	13.7	30.8	32.9	16.9	5.8	99286
30125	CEDARTOWN	18331	8718	35.0	31.0	25.7	5.0	3.2	35691	40790	30	37	6275	17.4	31.9	40.3	9.9	0.5	90737
30126	MABLETON	26911	10130	15.2	24.1	37.4	17.2	6.1	61670	76938	86	87	8304	6.1	11.5	51.6	25.6	5.2	133238
30127	POWDER SPRINGS	28460	18201	9.4	18.6	41.4	21.8	8.8	75255	88711	93	94	16680	1.4	4.3	53.5	36.3	4.5	161202
30132	DALLAS	21682	8090	17.4	27.0	43.8	10.1	1.9	54068	61468	78	80	6378	6.7	10.4	54.8	26.5	1.6	134019
30134	DOUGLASVILLE	23227	13475	17.0	28.2	39.9	11.8	3.1	54049	62705	78	80	10510	6.9	9.8	63.8	19.2	0.4	130147
30135	DOUGLASVILLE	27295	16997	9.0	22.3	43.7	18.3	6.7	66855	78473	90	90	14340	2.5	6.1	61.9	26.3	3.3	138930
30137	EMERSON	23543	554	19.0	29.1	37.7	10.1	4.2	51636	59716	75	77	463	13.6	23.5	40.8	17.7	4.3	108994
30139	FAIRMOUNT	19502	1640	24.5	34.2	32.9	6.5	2.0	42798	48850	55	60	1376	22.7	25.9	34.5	13.2	3.9	91980
30141	HIRAM	22938	5731	14.1	24.0	46.1	12.2	3.6	60488	66780	85	85	5021	5.8	8.7	64.9	18.0	2.6	133205
30143	JASPER	23179	7326	24.3	28.8	34.2	8.8	4.0	47055	54016	66	70	5951	10.5	17.0	44.2	22.0	6.3	124097
30144	KENNESAW	31140	17611	8.6	19.6	44.3	19.1	8.3	70436	85749	91	92	12858	2.4	2.6	50.3	42.6	2.1	168271
30145	KINGSTON	21339	2430	20.7	28.5	38.7	8.1	4.0	50640	58012	73	76	2062	12.1	19.2	47.2	18.0	3.5	114363
30147	LINDALE	20837	2072	25.2	34.5	29.8	7.9	2.6	42192	49002	53	58	1631	12.5	28.0	44.3	13.4	1.8	99843
30148	MARBLE HILL	35912	580	17.2	26.9	31.7	11.4	12.8	56717	67815	81	82	526	11.2	12.4	21.9	36.3	18.3	205000
30149	MOUNT BERRY	10836	33	36.4	51.5	12.1	0.0	0.0	38629	40000	42	47	6	0.0	50.0	50.0	0.0	0.0	85000
30152	KENNESAW	36086	9674	5.3	16.0	39.7	23.9	15.2	83814	104121	96	98	8783	6.3	1.1	34.5	47.6	10.4	194717
30153	ROCKMART	18881	6016	29.7	33.1	30.2	5.4	1.7	39331	45109	44	50	4611	16.1	27.9	42.9	11.0	2.2	97380
30157	DALLAS	23780	13445	13.0	27.5	43.0	12.8	3.8	59866	65239	84	85	11522	5.1	8.9	61.7	22.3	2.1	136351
30161	ROME	21930	13540	33.4	30.1	25.2	7.3	4.1	37828	44587	39	45	9205	15.6	30.3	36.9	14.9	2.4	96140
30165	ROME	21882	14520	28.6	31.5	27.3	8.4	4.3	40353	47585	47	52	9610	12.3	27.0	42.2	16.0	2.5	104971
	GEORGIA	26143		23.6	26.3	31.4	11.6	7.0	50024	60470				12.5	17.5	39.3	24.8	6.0	125860
	UNITED STATES	25866		24.7	27.1	30.8	10.9	6.5	48124	56710				10.9	15.0	33.7	30.1	10.4	145905

#	POST OFFICE NAME	FINANCIAL SERVICES: Auto Loan	FINANCIAL SERVICES: Home Loan	FINANCIAL SERVICES: Investments	FINANCIAL SERVICES: Retirement Plans	THE HOME: Home Improvements: Home Repair	THE HOME: Home Improvements: Lawn & Garden	THE HOME: Furnishings: Computers & Hardware	THE HOME: Furnishings: Major Appliances	THE HOME: Furnishings: TV, Radio, Sound Equipment	THE HOME: Furnishings: Furniture	ENTERTAINMENT: Dine out/Carry out	ENTERTAINMENT: Sports Equipment	ENTERTAINMENT: Fees & Tickets	ENTERTAINMENT: Toys & Games	ENTERTAINMENT: Travel	ENTERTAINMENT: Cable TV	PERSONAL: Apparel & Services	PERSONAL: Auto Repairs	PERSONAL: Health Insurance	PERSONAL: Pets & Supplies
30002	AVONDALE ESTATES	104	103	125	109	100	106	110	105	108	111	137	126	110	134	106	104	134	109	97	117
30004	ALPHARETTA	182	205	218	215	198	197	192	187	178	196	226	220	200	228	189	169	225	185	164	206
30005	ALPHARETTA	212	233	247	246	224	226	221	215	205	226	262	253	229	260	216	194	259	213	188	237
30008	MARIETTA	95	93	101	99	90	92	97	93	93	98	118	111	95	113	92	87	115	96	84	103
30011	AUBURN	98	107	106	109	104	102	101	100	95	103	120	119	102	120	99	89	118	100	88	111
30012	CONYERS	83	77	72	76	77	83	79	81	80	79	99	93	76	97	77	79	96	81	81	92
30013	CONYERS	115	131	138	135	127	127	122	121	114	124	145	142	127	147	122	109	143	119	107	133
30014	COVINGTON	87	81	71	79	83	90	80	84	83	79	101	98	79	102	80	83	97	83	87	99
30016	COVINGTON	95	98	94	99	97	98	94	95	91	94	114	113	94	114	93	88	111	94	89	108
30017	GRAYSON	135	155	152	161	148	144	139	137	127	144	162	161	145	163	136	119	160	133	117	151
30019	DACULA	133	150	145	157	143	138	136	134	124	141	158	157	139	158	132	116	156	131	114	147
30021	CLARKSTON	76	68	77	73	66	69	76	73	75	78	95	87	73	90	71	70	93	77	66	80
30022	ALPHARETTA	211	240	255	250	230	230	222	217	206	228	262	254	232	262	219	195	260	214	190	239
30024	SUWANEE	174	199	193	207	189	183	179	177	164	186	208	207	185	209	175	153	206	172	151	194
30025	SOCIAL CIRCLE	106	100	84	98	103	110	95	101	97	95	119	118	94	120	96	98	114	99	104	123
30030	DECATUR	106	111	146	114	108	117	116	111	115	116	145	131	119	146	116	114	143	114	107	123
30032	DECATUR	72	68	78	67	65	74	72	70	75	74	95	79	73	92	71	76	92	72	72	80
30033	DECATUR	110	118	157	123	115	123	123	116	120	123	152	139	126	154	122	117	150	120	109	128
30034	DECATUR	98	102	110	105	99	102	101	99	97	103	123	116	103	123	99	94	121	99	90	110
30035	DECATUR	82	81	91	83	78	83	84	82	83	86	106	96	85	104	82	81	103	84	76	91
30038	LITHONIA	113	119	124	126	115	114	116	113	109	119	138	134	117	136	112	102	136	113	99	124
30039	SNELLVILLE	122	140	138	145	134	130	127	125	116	131	148	147	131	149	124	109	146	122	108	138
30040	CUMMING	126	136	128	140	132	131	125	126	118	128	149	148	127	150	123	113	146	123	114	142
30041	CUMMING	155	172	164	178	165	162	156	156	145	161	183	183	160	184	153	136	180	152	136	173
30043	LAWRENCEVILLE	142	160	155	167	152	147	145	143	132	150	168	167	149	169	141	123	166	139	121	157
30044	LAWRENCEVILLE	116	125	130	131	119	119	119	116	111	122	142	137	122	140	116	105	140	116	101	128
30045	LAWRENCEVILLE	109	117	116	121	114	114	111	110	104	113	132	129	112	132	108	99	130	109	98	122
30047	LILBURN	123	139	150	144	136	138	131	128	123	133	156	151	137	158	131	118	154	127	115	142
30052	LOGANVILLE	107	122	121	126	118	115	112	111	103	114	130	130	115	132	110	97	129	108	96	122
30054	OXFORD	108	112	103	110	114	117	103	107	102	103	126	126	105	131	105	101	122	104	106	128
30055	MANSFIELD	101	96	79	92	100	105	88	95	91	88	111	113	88	115	90	92	107	93	100	120
30056	NEWBORN	85	77	59	73	79	84	72	79	75	74	92	92	69	89	73	75	88	78	81	97
30058	LITHONIA	96	99	102	103	95	96	97	95	92	100	117	112	97	115	94	87	115	96	84	105
30060	MARIETTA	80	74	81	76	72	78	82	78	82	81	102	93	79	99	78	79	99	82	75	87
30062	MARIETTA	153	178	192	185	172	174	164	160	152	166	193	187	174	197	164	146	193	157	142	177
30064	MARIETTA	141	160	171	166	155	156	150	147	140	152	177	172	156	179	149	133	175	145	131	161
30066	MARIETTA	135	156	165	161	151	152	145	142	135	147	171	166	152	174	144	129	169	140	126	157
30067	MARIETTA	124	117	140	127	113	120	128	121	124	129	158	146	126	150	121	117	154	128	109	135
30068	MARIETTA	194	227	250	235	220	225	209	204	194	212	247	237	224	251	211	188	247	201	184	226
30069	MARIETTA	116	73	70	84	67	80	109	94	111	102	139	126	94	124	90	101	133	111	87	107
30071	NORCROSS	92	88	97	91	85	89	94	91	92	96	117	107	92	114	89	87	116	95	82	100
30075	ROSWELL	176	205	228	212	199	202	191	186	177	193	225	217	202	230	191	171	225	183	166	205
30076	ROSWELL	159	172	190	181	166	169	167	162	157	170	200	192	172	198	164	149	198	163	144	179
30078	SNELLVILLE	127	147	154	151	142	142	135	133	125	137	159	156	141	162	134	120	158	130	117	146
30079	SCOTTDALE	74	69	82	70	66	74	75	72	77	76	97	84	75	94	73	76	95	75	71	81
30080	SMYRNA	101	91	119	101	88	95	105	98	103	106	132	119	102	127	99	98	129	104	89	109
30082	SMYRNA	114	110	126	118	108	112	118	113	113	119	144	136	115	138	112	107	140	118	103	125
30083	STONE MOUNTAIN	88	86	94	92	83	86	90	87	87	91	110	105	89	107	86	81	108	90	78	97
30084	TUCKER	106	112	131	117	110	115	114	111	110	114	139	131	115	138	112	106	136	113	102	122
30087	STONE MOUNTAIN	132	150	155	155	145	145	139	137	129	142	163	160	144	165	137	123	162	134	121	150
30088	STONE MOUNTAIN	103	106	111	111	102	103	105	103	100	107	127	123	105	124	101	94	124	104	90	113
30092	NORCROSS	148	149	171	160	144	150	154	147	146	156	187	175	155	181	148	139	184	151	131	163
30093	NORCROSS	89	79	91	85	76	81	89	84	87	91	112	101	85	105	83	82	109	90	76	94
30094	CONYERS	121	141	143	143	138	138	128	129	120	129	151	150	134	157	129	117	150	125	117	143
30096	DULUTH	119	113	125	123	109	113	120	115	115	123	147	138	118	140	113	108	144	120	102	128
30097	DULUTH	219	260	267	270	249	246	232	228	211	238	269	265	247	275	231	201	269	220	198	250
30101	ACWORTH	133	147	145	152	142	141	135	135	127	139	160	158	139	161	133	120	158	132	120	150
30102	ACWORTH	113	121	114	123	118	117	112	113	106	115	133	133	113	132	110	101	131	111	101	127
30103	ADAIRSVILLE	86	74	54	70	78	85	70	78	75	70	91	92	67	90	71	77	86	76	85	99
30104	ARAGON	89	65	36	58	72	81	62	75	72	63	85	89	55	83	63	76	79	73	89	103
30105	ARMUCHEE	94	82	61	78	87	94	76	85	82	76	99	102	74	101	79	84	94	83	93	111
30106	AUSTELL	95	98	101	99	96	100	97	97	94	97	118	114	97	118	95	91	115	97	91	108
30107	BALL GROUND	99	95	81	93	98	103	88	95	90	89	111	112	88	113	90	91	107	92	97	116
30108	BOWDON	88	65	38	59	71	81	63	75	73	64	86	88	57	83	64	77	80	74	88	101
30110	BREMEN	92	64	33	57	72	82	62	76	73	63	87	90	55	83	63	78	79	75	91	105
30113	BUCHANAN	89	60	27	52	68	78	58	72	70	59	82	86	49	77	59	75	74	71	89	102
30114	CANTON	110	108	97	108	108	114	104	107	104	104	129	125	103	129	103	103	124	106	106	125
30115	CANTON	115	124	118	125	122	122	114	116	109	116	137	136	116	139	114	105	134	114	107	132
30116	CARROLLTON	104	93	74	91	96	104	91	97	94	91	115	113	87	113	90	94	109	96	101	117
30117	CARROLLTON	83	71	65	70	74	82	76	78	80	75	98	92	72	95	75	80	93	80	82	93
30118	CARROLLTON	54	33	41	37	32	39	63	46	61	53	77	65	52	69	51	54	72	57	43	53
30120	CARTERSVILLE	98	94	83	92	95	101	91	94	92	91	113	110	90	114	91	92	109	93	96	111
30121	CARTERSVILLE	97	87	68	84	90	98	83	90	87	84	107	105	81	106	84	88	101	89	96	111
30122	LITHIA SPRINGS	87	87	92	91	85	87	89	87	85	89	108	103	88	105	86	81	105	88	79	96
30124	CAVE SPRING	90	78	60	76	82	91	77	83	82	76	99	97	74	99	77	83	93	82	90	102
30125	CEDARTOWN	81	64	46	60	69	78	65	72	72	64	86	84	60	84	65	75	80	72	83	92
30126	MABLETON	101	110	110	111	108	110	104	104	100	105	125	121	106	128	104	97	123	103	97	116
30127	POWDER SPRINGS	122	139	137	144	134	130	126	125	116	130	148	147	130	149	124	110	146	122	108	138
30132	DALLAS	89	87	78	89	87	91	84	87	84	85	104	101	84	103	83	82	100	85	84	99
30134	DOUGLASVILLE	95	96	93	98	95	98	94	95	92	95	115	111	94	114	92	89	111	94	90	106
30135	DOUGLASVILLE	112	122	121	125	120	119	114	114	108	115	135	134	116	138	113	103	133	112	103	128
30137	EMERSON	109	98	75	93	102	109	91	100	96	92	117	118	88	117	93	97	111	98	106	126
30139	FAIRMOUNT	87	69	44	63	75	82	65	76	73	66	87	90	60	85	66	76	81	74	86	101
30141	HIRAM	99	104	95	106	102	102	96	98	92	98	115	114	97	116	94	88	112	95	90	111
30143	JASPER	95	80	60	76	84	94	77	86	83	78	101	98	73	96	78	86	95	85	95	107
30144	KENNESAW	116	126	130	131	121	120	120	118	112	123	142	139	122	141	116	105	140	117	102	129
30145	KINGSTON	99	91	73	89	94	98	84	91	86	86	106	108	83	106	85	86	102	89	93	113
30147	LINDALE	81	74	63	71	78	86	73	78	78	71	94	89	72	97	75	80	90	76	85	93
30148	MARBLE HILL	129	116	100	110	122	138	109	123	115	114	142	131	106	126	115	120	133	121	137	147
30149	MOUNT BERRY	47	29	36	32	28	34	55	41	54	47	67	57	45	60	44	47	63	50	38	46
30152	KENNESAW	152	175	173	183	167	163	157	155	144	163	183	181	164	185	155	135	182	151	133	170
30153	ROCKMART	85	65	42	59	71	81	64	74	72	63	86	87	58	84	65	76	80	73	86	97
30157	DALLAS	103	107	98	109	104	105	100	101	95	102	120	119	100	120	98	92	117	99	93	115
30161	ROME	81	74	71	71	75	84	76	78	80	75	98	90	74	97	76	82	94	79	85	92
30165	ROME	83	74	66	73	77	86	77	80	81	75	98	92	75	98	77	82	93	79	86	93
	GEORGIA	103	97	95	97	97	104	97	99	98	98	122	116	96	120	96	98	118	100	99	116
	UNITED STATES	100	100	100	100	100	100	100	100	100	100	100	100	100	100	100	100	100	100	100	100

ZIP CODE			POPULATION			2000-2004 ANNUAL RATE		HOUSEHOLDS					FAMILIES		
#	POST OFFICE NAME	COUNTY FIPS CODE	2000	2004	2009	% Rate	State Centile	2000	2004	2009	% Annual Rate 2000-2004	2004 Average HH Size	2000	2004	% Annual Rate 2000-2004
30168	AUSTELL	067	22672	25189	28180	2.5	68	8321	9208	10301	2.4	2.73	5475	5900	1.8
30170	ROOPVILLE	149	2833	3124	3651	2.3	65	1049	1166	1371	2.5	2.68	811	889	2.2
30171	RYDAL	015	2002	2295	2744	3.3	79	702	809	971	3.4	2.84	566	646	3.2
30173	SILVER CREEK	115	5858	6546	7163	2.7	70	2107	2374	2611	2.9	2.75	1719	1912	2.5
30175	TALKING ROCK	227	5493	6643	8289	4.6	90	2066	2516	3166	4.8	2.62	1579	1896	4.4
30176	TALLAPOOSA	143	6765	7083	7652	1.1	39	2668	2807	3050	1.2	2.52	1923	1993	0.8
30177	TATE	227	877	1140	1447	6.4	96	413	544	699	6.7	2.10	323	420	6.4
30178	TAYLORSVILLE	015	2832	3474	4303	4.9	92	969	1192	1481	5.0	2.91	802	978	4.8
30179	TEMPLE	045	9815	12615	16442	6.1	95	3540	4575	5999	6.2	2.76	2799	3572	5.9
30180	VILLA RICA	045	18024	24680	33068	7.7	99	6564	9061	12228	7.9	2.72	5122	6944	7.4
30182	WACO	045	2631	2928	3385	2.6	69	976	1096	1278	2.8	2.67	724	800	2.4
30183	WALESKA	057	3820	4563	5920	4.3	88	1337	1635	2169	4.9	2.61	1069	1293	4.6
30184	WHITE	015	5739	6742	8268	3.9	86	2049	2415	2971	3.9	2.78	1675	1953	3.7
30185	WHITESBURG	045	3844	4476	5535	3.7	84	1377	1621	2023	3.9	2.76	1071	1243	3.6
30187	WINSTON	097	6262	7479	9060	4.3	88	2196	2656	3254	4.6	2.82	1823	2189	4.4
30188	WOODSTOCK	057	37032	44932	59175	4.7	90	13091	16039	21283	4.9	2.79	10173	12304	4.6
30189	WOODSTOCK	057	33773	44449	60875	6.7	97	11522	15157	20789	6.7	2.93	9384	12248	6.5
30204	BARNESVILLE	171	11739	12563	13709	1.6	50	4160	4520	5011	2.0	2.60	3048	3260	1.6
30205	BROOKS	113	2590	2835	3102	2.2	61	902	999	1104	2.4	2.84	769	844	2.2
30206	CONCORD	231	2219	2560	3089	3.4	81	744	867	1056	3.7	2.93	605	698	3.4
30213	FAIRBURN	121	15918	18131	20252	3.1	78	5512	6328	7103	3.3	2.83	4102	4618	2.8
30214	FAYETTEVILLE	113	20984	22649	24845	1.8	53	7558	8259	9152	2.1	2.72	6094	6584	1.8
30215	FAYETTEVILLE	113	27466	31434	35808	3.2	79	9206	10593	12141	3.4	2.95	7821	8950	3.2
30216	FLOVILLA	035	2454	2775	3264	2.9	75	806	929	1111	3.4	2.99	646	736	3.1
30217	FRANKLIN	149	9501	10385	11555	2.1	61	3476	3830	4295	2.3	2.68	2609	2835	2.0
30218	GAY	199	2033	2109	2232	0.9	34	693	734	792	1.4	2.87	548	574	1.1
30220	GRANTVILLE	077	3177	3662	4308	3.4	81	1166	1355	1607	3.6	2.70	877	1006	3.3
30222	GREENVILLE	199	4445	4704	5033	1.3	45	1555	1678	1831	1.8	2.70	1139	1212	1.5
30223	GRIFFIN	255	35213	36966	39513	1.2	41	12724	13476	14538	1.4	2.73	9359	9775	1.0
30224	GRIFFIN	255	21749	23505	25511	1.8	54	8268	9024	9891	2.1	2.54	6036	6496	1.7
30228	HAMPTON	151	20640	26755	35362	6.3	96	6702	8886	11971	6.9	2.89	5410	7081	6.5
30230	HOGANSVILLE	285	7044	7502	8093	1.5	48	2654	2843	3089	1.6	2.61	1938	2051	1.3
30233	JACKSON	035	18003	20905	24795	3.6	83	6029	7195	8767	4.3	2.63	4547	5366	4.0
30234	JENKINSBURG	035	1458	1781	2175	4.8	91	495	616	765	5.3	2.88	374	459	4.9
30236	JONESBORO	063	44365	49155	56597	2.4	68	16096	17892	20596	2.5	2.71	11669	12749	2.1
30238	JONESBORO	063	32233	37093	42900	3.4	80	10711	12376	14308	3.5	3.00	8490	9676	3.1
30240	LAGRANGE	285	25929	28173	30627	2.0	57	9694	10653	11710	2.2	2.57	6877	7426	1.5
30241	LAGRANGE	285	20296	21065	22391	0.9	35	7503	7867	8444	1.1	2.59	5300	5475	0.8
30248	LOCUST GROVE	151	10896	14495	20571	7.0	98	3673	4918	7020	7.1	2.95	3073	4084	6.9
30251	LUTHERSVILLE	199	1969	2136	2316	1.9	57	692	762	839	2.3	2.80	541	589	2.0
30252	MCDONOUGH	151	18700	28644	43409	10.6	100	6328	9733	14822	10.7	2.94	5493	8356	10.4
30253	MCDONOUGH	151	25960	36249	52609	8.2	99	8945	12635	18523	8.5	2.83	6946	9631	8.0
30256	MEANSVILLE	231	2340	2558	2960	2.1	61	847	931	1084	2.3	2.72	667	724	2.0
30257	MILNER	171	3882	4374	4944	2.9	74	1423	1617	1842	3.1	2.71	1138	1279	2.9
30258	MOLENA	231	2368	2894	3482	4.8	91	809	1007	1228	5.3	2.80	649	798	5.0
30259	MORELAND	077	2472	2887	3488	3.7	85	866	1015	1229	3.8	2.84	694	803	3.5
30260	MORROW	063	23815	26147	29532	2.2	63	8372	9175	10334	2.2	2.82	5863	6291	1.7
30263	NEWNAN	077	42085	48888	58867	3.6	83	14922	17432	21111	3.7	2.76	11224	12925	3.4
30265	NEWNAN	077	17900	22105	27449	5.1	93	6325	7870	9820	5.3	2.81	5099	6249	4.9
30268	PALMETTO	121	7065	7833	8742	2.5	68	2555	2840	3172	2.5	2.74	1891	2066	2.1
30269	PEACHTREE CITY	113	31890	35848	40186	2.8	72	11021	12512	14151	3.0	2.85	8936	10032	2.8
30273	REX	063	11438	13275	15494	3.6	83	3867	4502	5249	3.6	2.95	3055	3506	3.3
30274	RIVERDALE	063	29318	33227	38064	3.0	75	10108	11463	13107	3.0	2.88	7247	8067	2.6
30276	SENOIA	077	8965	10328	12310	3.4	81	3092	3593	4313	3.6	2.87	2515	2893	3.4
30277	SHARPSBURG	077	15315	19413	24386	5.7	95	5264	6691	8427	5.8	2.90	4487	5647	5.6
30281	STOCKBRIDGE	151	46880	59842	82979	5.9	95	16714	21511	30032	6.1	2.77	13109	16693	5.9
30285	THE ROCK	293	464	487	507	1.1	41	172	183	192	1.5	2.65	139	146	1.2
30286	THOMASTON	293	23931	24589	25480	0.6	29	9359	9709	10160	0.9	2.49	6613	6752	0.5
30288	CONLEY	089	6374	7341	8397	3.4	81	2074	2392	2733	3.4	3.06	1573	1781	3.0
30290	TYRONE	113	5281	6230	7115	4.0	87	1830	2184	2518	4.3	2.85	1572	1860	4.0
30291	UNION CITY	121	12024	13527	15010	2.8	73	5134	5839	6520	3.1	2.30	3264	3632	2.6
30292	WILLIAMSON	231	4587	5115	5927	2.6	70	1583	1785	2089	2.9	2.79	1230	1369	2.6
30293	WOODBURY	199	3503	3637	3873	0.9	35	1289	1368	1486	1.4	2.65	931	971	1.0
30294	ELLENWOOD	089	25731	30991	38132	4.5	89	8322	10091	12499	4.6	3.02	6718	8056	4.4
30295	ZEBULON	231	3264	3832	4654	3.9	85	1189	1411	1732	4.1	2.62	926	1085	3.8
30296	RIVERDALE	063	22519	25937	29934	3.4	81	7748	8900	10235	3.3	2.91	5679	6415	2.9
30297	FOREST PARK	063	32084	34400	38299	1.7	51	10296	10945	12111	1.5	3.09	7354	7665	1.0
30303	ATLANTA	121	3001	3343	3649	2.6	69	1246	1481	1691	4.2	1.54	340	364	1.6
30305	ATLANTA	121	20669	22830	25208	2.4	66	11339	12544	13862	2.4	1.80	4298	4605	1.6
30306	ATLANTA	121	21141	22473	24262	1.5	47	11309	12150	13194	1.7	1.81	3681	3734	0.3
30307	ATLANTA	089	17132	18323	19845	1.6	50	7677	8307	9058	1.9	2.14	3342	3470	0.9
30308	ATLANTA	121	11568	12962	14321	2.7	71	6578	7519	8419	3.2	1.57	1293	1397	1.8
30309	ATLANTA	121	18838	20166	21988	1.6	50	11556	12493	13715	1.9	1.52	2492	2525	0.3
30310	ATLANTA	121	34376	33075	34497	-0.9	1	12133	11654	12188	-0.9	2.69	7247	6800	-1.5
30311	ATLANTA	121	33839	34506	36504	0.5	22	13164	13466	14279	0.5	2.56	8577	8610	0.1
30312	ATLANTA	121	21716	22280	23495	0.6	28	8896	9176	9747	0.7	2.18	3641	3600	-0.3
30313	ATLANTA	121	9385	9789	10218	1.0	37	1552	1810	2085	3.7	1.51	452	496	2.3
30314	ATLANTA	121	26737	27319	29040	0.5	24	9270	9476	10143	0.5	2.52	5036	4978	-0.3
30315	ATLANTA	121	39944	41565	44021	0.9	36	11824	12084	12842	0.5	3.13	8146	8194	0.1
30316	ATLANTA	089	32181	33060	35082	0.6	29	11433	11827	12606	0.8	2.73	7407	7490	0.3
30317	ATLANTA	089	13760	14134	15227	0.6	29	5027	5208	5632	0.8	2.70	3082	3129	0.4
30318	ATLANTA	121	54663	55936	59207	0.5	25	19093	19634	20952	0.7	2.52	10863	10884	0.1
30319	ATLANTA	089	39094	41444	44833	1.4	46	17192	18348	19941	1.5	2.21	8671	8899	0.6
30322	ATLANTA	089	1724	1688	1692	-0.5	4	3	3	3	0.0	2.67	0	0	0.0
30324	ATLANTA	121	20396	24274	27973	4.2	88	10593	12088	13590	3.2	2.01	3218	3536	2.2
30326	ATLANTA	121	2133	2472	2765	3.5	83	1323	1564	1772	4.0	1.43	395	441	2.6
30327	ATLANTA	121	21199	22359	24060	1.3	43	8844	9385	10122	1.4	2.37	5664	5856	0.8
30328	ATLANTA	121	27702	28649	30696	0.8	33	12802	13339	14353	1.0	2.14	6930	7027	0.3
30329	ATLANTA	089	22436	23521	25263	1.1	40	9631	9941	10630	0.8	2.22	3427	3422	0.0
30330	ATLANTA	121	294	266	270	-2.3	0	68	59	60	-3.3	3.02	65	56	-3.5
30331	ATLANTA	121	43362	44792	47893	0.8	32	15870	16513	17724	0.9	2.70	11167	11402	0.5
30334	ATLANTA	121	7	7	8	0.0	12	0	0	0	0.0	0.00	0	0	0.0
30336	ATLANTA	121	1067	970	1001	-2.2	0	328	298	308	-2.2	3.14	232	208	-2.5
30337	ATLANTA	121	16700	16366	17271	-0.5	4	6596	6423	6763	-0.6	2.53	3912	3714	-1.2
30338	ATLANTA	089	29675	31005	33477	1.0	38	12394	13161	14331	1.4	2.32	8061	8288	0.7
	GEORGIA					2.4					2.5	2.64			2.2
	UNITED STATES					1.2					1.3	2.58			1.1

60-A

ZIP CODE #	POST OFFICE NAME	RACE (%) White 2000	White 2004	Black 2000	Black 2004	Asian/Pacific 2000	Asian/Pacific 2004	% Hispanic Origin 2000	% Hispanic Origin 2004	2004 AGE DISTRIBUTION (%) 0-4	5-9	10-14	15-19	20-24	25-44	45-64	65-84	85+	18+	MEDIAN AGE 2004	% 2004 Males	% 2004 Females
30168	AUSTELL	35.5	34.1	54.2	53.8	0.8	0.9	13.4	16.3	8.8	7.8	8.0	7.1	8.9	36.7	17.3	4.9	0.6	71.4	29.8	49.1	50.9
30170	ROOPVILLE	92.7	91.6	6.1	7.1	0.1	0.2	0.8	1.1	8.3	8.2	7.9	6.5	5.8	29.0	24.1	9.0	1.1	71.5	34.3	50.0	50.0
30171	RYDAL	97.7	97.2	1.1	1.2	0.1	0.1	1.3	1.7	7.2	7.5	7.5	5.9	5.2	30.8	25.4	9.6	0.9	74.1	36.2	50.3	49.7
30173	SILVER CREEK	95.5	94.5	3.1	3.7	0.3	0.4	1.2	1.6	6.6	6.6	7.4	7.1	6.8	29.2	26.2	9.3	0.8	75.2	36.4	50.3	49.7
30175	TALKING ROCK	95.1	94.0	0.3	0.3	0.3	0.3	4.8	6.3	7.5	7.3	6.8	6.1	6.0	30.9	23.8	10.4	1.2	74.7	35.9	50.5	49.5
30176	TALLAPOOSA	94.6	93.8	3.3	3.7	0.5	0.6	0.6	0.7	7.1	7.1	7.6	6.5	5.7	28.0	24.4	12.3	1.5	74.2	36.9	48.5	51.6
30177	TATE	98.0	97.5	0.0	0.0	0.0	0.1	0.7	0.9	2.7	2.9	3.2	2.7	2.7	13.0	40.0	31.9	0.9	89.7	58.9	48.7	51.3
30178	TAYLORSVILLE	94.8	94.1	3.4	3.7	0.3	0.3	1.6	2.1	7.9	7.7	8.2	7.2	6.1	32.6	23.6	6.5	0.4	71.7	33.7	50.4	49.6
30179	TEMPLE	91.3	89.3	7.1	8.7	0.3	0.4	0.9	1.2	7.6	7.7	7.6	6.6	5.9	31.7	23.6	8.7	0.7	73.1	34.7	49.5	50.5
30180	VILLA RICA	86.6	84.2	10.8	12.7	0.7	0.8	1.6	2.1	7.7	7.6	7.6	6.4	6.0	30.8	24.0	9.2	0.8	73.2	35.2	49.3	50.7
30182	WACO	88.4	87.0	9.5	10.7	0.4	0.5	0.9	1.2	7.2	7.3	7.7	7.2	6.3	29.1	23.9	10.1	1.1	73.3	35.5	49.9	50.1
30183	WALESKA	97.2	96.7	0.8	0.8	0.5	0.6	1.4	1.9	5.0	5.5	6.5	9.0	8.0	26.7	27.7	11.1	0.6	79.6	38.2	50.2	49.8
30184	WHITE	95.8	95.1	1.6	1.8	0.5	0.6	1.6	2.2	6.9	7.3	7.6	6.6	4.9	31.6	25.8	8.5	0.7	73.7	36.4	50.2	49.8
30185	WHITESBURG	92.3	91.0	6.7	7.9	0.1	0.1	0.4	0.6	7.2	7.2	7.6	7.2	6.2	29.2	26.3	8.4	0.8	73.6	36.1	51.4	48.6
30187	WINSTON	89.9	88.6	7.8	8.6	0.4	0.5	1.6	2.0	7.2	7.5	7.4	6.1	5.2	29.5	27.8	8.5	0.7	74.1	37.8	49.1	50.9
30188	WOODSTOCK	92.6	91.5	2.8	2.9	1.0	1.1	4.7	6.0	7.9	7.9	7.4	6.4	5.7	33.6	24.5	5.9	0.6	72.8	34.9	49.4	50.6
30189	WOODSTOCK	91.6	90.3	3.0	3.3	1.4	1.6	5.0	6.3	9.6	9.5	8.7	6.2	4.9	34.8	22.0	4.0	0.3	68.3	33.5	49.9	50.1
30204	BARNESVILLE	63.0	60.1	35.1	37.9	0.4	0.5	1.2	1.5	6.4	6.4	7.0	7.9	8.0	27.4	23.9	11.4	1.7	76.6	35.8	47.4	52.6
30205	BROOKS	96.1	95.5	1.9	2.2	0.4	0.5	1.4	1.8	5.6	6.2	8.5	7.4	5.6	27.3	29.3	9.4	0.8	75.1	39.5	50.2	49.8
30206	CONCORD	74.2	71.2	24.4	27.2	0.1	0.0	1.1	1.4	7.3	7.5	7.9	7.0	6.3	28.1	24.7	10.2	1.2	73.0	36.2	49.7	50.4
30213	FAIRBURN	51.0	43.8	43.1	49.6	0.8	0.8	6.5	7.5	6.7	6.8	7.3	6.8	6.4	27.2	26.5	10.7	1.8	75.1	37.4	48.1	51.9
30214	FAYETTEVILLE	78.1	75.7	17.4	19.1	2.4	2.8	2.3	2.8	5.0	5.8	7.5	7.5	5.1	23.4	33.0	11.3	1.3	76.8	42.4	48.4	51.7
30215	FAYETTEVILLE	84.9	82.5	11.6	13.5	1.7	2.0	2.3	3.0	6.3	7.5	9.0	7.5	5.0	27.6	29.1	7.3	0.8	72.3	38.3	49.2	50.8
30216	FLOVILLA	64.7	60.9	33.7	37.4	0.2	0.2	1.0	1.3	6.5	6.6	7.1	7.0	7.0	28.1	27.3	9.6	0.9	75.6	36.8	50.1	49.9
30217	FRANKLIN	86.1	84.5	12.1	13.4	0.2	0.2	1.1	1.4	7.9	7.9	8.1	6.8	6.0	28.9	23.5	9.8	1.2	71.9	35.1	49.4	50.6
30218	GAY	57.3	53.3	41.8	45.6	0.0	0.0	0.5	0.5	7.4	7.4	7.3	6.3	6.2	29.5	25.5	9.4	1.2	74.2	36.2	50.3	49.7
30220	GRANTVILLE	68.4	65.7	29.8	32.2	0.3	0.3	1.5	1.7	7.9	7.9	7.8	6.5	6.1	28.8	24.2	9.7	1.2	72.4	35.4	48.6	51.4
30222	GREENVILLE	43.7	39.6	54.9	58.8	0.1	0.1	1.1	1.3	6.7	6.8	7.4	7.4	6.3	26.9	24.5	11.7	2.2	75.0	37.3	47.8	52.3
30223	GRIFFIN	60.7	58.3	36.7	38.6	0.6	0.8	1.9	2.3	7.9	7.7	7.8	7.1	7.0	28.7	23.1	9.6	1.2	72.4	34.0	48.1	51.9
30224	GRIFFIN	75.0	71.7	22.9	25.9	0.8	0.9	1.1	1.4	7.1	6.7	7.1	6.6	6.6	27.4	24.8	11.9	1.8	75.2	37.1	48.9	51.1
30228	HAMPTON	76.5	74.8	20.0	21.2	1.2	1.5	2.2	2.9	7.9	7.7	7.7	7.1	6.7	33.4	22.1	7.0	0.6	72.6	33.6	51.1	48.9
30230	HOGANSVILLE	72.6	68.7	25.7	29.3	0.3	0.3	1.0	1.3	7.2	7.3	7.7	6.9	6.5	27.1	24.6	11.2	1.6	73.4	36.4	48.6	51.5
30233	JACKSON	73.7	71.9	24.3	25.8	0.3	0.3	1.5	1.9	6.6	6.4	6.5	6.4	7.0	31.9	24.3	9.7	1.2	76.7	36.4	53.4	46.6
30234	JENKINSBURG	54.4	50.0	43.2	47.3	0.3	0.3	1.4	1.6	7.1	7.5	8.1	6.5	6.7	28.2	27.0	8.1	0.8	73.5	36.0	47.8	52.2
30236	JONESBORO	52.6	50.3	37.5	38.2	3.8	4.3	8.4	10.0	7.6	7.2	7.5	7.1	8.0	31.5	23.1	7.3	0.8	73.4	33.1	49.3	50.7
30238	JONESBORO	39.5	36.6	54.2	56.3	2.2	2.5	4.0	4.8	8.8	8.5	9.2	8.0	7.0	33.7	20.3	4.3	0.3	68.5	30.8	47.0	53.0
30240	LAGRANGE	73.0	69.9	24.5	27.1	0.8	0.9	1.9	2.3	7.2	7.2	7.7	7.0	7.0	27.5	24.0	10.5	1.9	73.7	35.3	47.2	52.8
30241	LAGRANGE	54.9	52.1	42.4	44.7	0.7	0.7	2.0	2.4	7.6	7.3	7.6	7.1	7.3	28.8	22.4	10.5	1.5	73.1	34.2	48.7	51.3
30248	LOCUST GROVE	86.7	85.2	10.9	11.9	0.3	0.4	1.9	2.5	9.0	8.7	8.0	6.4	5.8	34.1	21.1	6.4	0.5	70.3	32.8	50.0	50.0
30251	LUTHERSVILLE	63.5	59.6	34.2	37.8	0.1	0.1	0.9	1.0	7.6	7.5	8.2	7.6	6.9	27.9	24.4	8.9	0.9	72.1	34.5	48.4	51.6
30252	MCDONOUGH	92.2	90.6	5.9	7.2	0.6	0.7	1.2	1.6	7.9	8.1	8.2	6.3	5.1	32.0	24.2	7.8	0.6	71.9	35.9	49.8	50.2
30253	MCDONOUGH	75.6	72.6	19.9	22.0	2.0	2.3	3.0	3.8	8.8	8.3	8.0	6.6	6.7	33.7	20.3	6.8	0.9	71.1	32.4	48.4	51.6
30256	MEANSVILLE	89.7	87.8	8.6	10.2	0.3	0.4	1.4	1.8	6.3	6.8	7.5	7.3	5.0	27.7	26.3	11.8	1.3	74.7	38.5	51.5	48.5
30257	MILNER	83.4	81.2	14.9	16.7	0.3	0.4	0.7	0.9	6.6	6.9	7.3	6.1	5.3	28.9	27.3	10.6	0.9	75.5	38.0	49.3	50.7
30258	MOLENA	84.3	82.1	14.2	16.1	0.2	0.2	1.1	1.5	6.7	6.8	7.0	7.2	6.6	28.3	25.4	10.4	1.6	74.6	37.2	49.9	50.1
30259	MORELAND	87.4	85.4	11.3	13.0	0.1	0.2	0.7	0.9	7.3	7.9	8.5	6.0	4.9	29.9	25.0	9.5	1.1	72.6	36.1	50.0	50.1
30260	MORROW	44.6	41.0	40.6	42.2	8.7	9.6	6.5	8.0	7.4	6.8	7.8	8.1	9.7	30.5	20.1	8.7	1.1	73.5	31.5	48.1	51.9
30263	NEWNAN	70.6	67.9	26.6	28.8	0.5	0.6	3.1	3.8	7.8	7.6	7.8	6.9	6.5	29.7	23.4	9.0	1.4	72.8	34.6	48.9	51.1
30265	NEWNAN	85.6	83.2	10.2	11.7	1.3	1.5	3.7	4.8	8.6	8.3	8.1	6.7	5.7	33.5	22.7	5.9	0.5	70.8	33.9	49.7	50.3
30268	PALMETTO	66.9	58.9	27.5	34.6	0.4	0.4	7.1	8.6	7.6	7.5	7.7	7.1	5.8	29.1	24.2	10.0	1.1	72.5	35.6	48.9	51.1
30269	PEACHTREE CITY	88.1	86.1	5.8	6.7	3.7	4.3	3.7	4.6	6.2	7.2	9.1	8.4	5.7	25.6	29.2	7.6	1.0	71.8	38.1	48.7	51.3
30273	REX	49.1	45.7	44.1	46.6	2.7	3.0	4.1	5.1	8.3	8.3	8.7	7.1	6.4	33.9	22.0	5.0	0.4	70.4	32.6	47.8	52.2
30274	RIVERDALE	27.3	25.2	61.4	62.2	5.9	6.5	5.9	7.1	8.6	8.0	8.9	8.2	8.5	33.3	18.9	5.0	0.5	69.5	29.8	47.4	52.6
30276	SENOIA	84.2	81.9	13.4	15.3	0.4	0.5	1.4	1.7	8.7	8.6	7.7	6.1	5.5	33.4	21.9	7.6	0.7	71.2	33.6	50.1	49.9
30277	SHARPSBURG	89.4	87.6	7.2	8.3	0.9	1.0	3.3	4.4	8.7	8.5	7.7	6.0	5.3	33.1	23.7	6.7	0.4	71.4	35.2	50.2	49.8
30281	STOCKBRIDGE	80.5	78.3	14.5	15.8	2.5	3.0	2.7	3.4	7.7	7.5	7.7	6.9	6.5	31.8	24.1	7.2	0.7	72.7	35.1	49.3	50.7
30285	THE ROCK	85.1	83.0	13.6	15.4	0.2	0.4	0.9	1.0	6.4	6.8	7.8	6.8	6.0	27.5	26.5	11.3	1.0	75.0	37.9	50.9	49.1
30286	THOMASTON	69.7	66.9	28.8	31.3	0.4	0.5	1.3	1.6	6.6	6.6	7.2	6.7	6.3	27.0	24.1	13.2	2.2	75.5	37.9	47.5	52.5
30288	CONLEY	25.7	22.6	64.4	66.5	3.7	3.8	7.5	8.7	7.9	8.2	9.4	8.6	7.8	30.9	21.3	5.5	0.4	69.4	30.3	47.6	52.4
30290	TYRONE	90.1	88.1	7.2	8.6	1.2	1.4	1.7	2.3	5.6	6.8	8.1	7.0	5.4	25.3	32.6	8.6	0.7	75.1	40.5	49.2	50.9
30291	UNION CITY	22.7	16.2	71.6	78.3	1.0	0.8	6.2	6.2	7.7	7.8	8.5	7.6	7.8	32.1	20.9	6.3	1.3	71.3	31.4	46.2	53.8
30292	WILLIAMSON	81.5	79.0	16.9	19.1	0.4	0.5	1.2	1.5	7.2	7.3	7.1	6.6	6.0	30.0	25.1	9.7	1.0	74.5	36.4	49.5	50.5
30293	WOODBURY	50.6	47.5	48.1	51.0	0.1	0.2	0.8	0.9	6.5	6.6	7.2	6.7	6.5	25.3	26.8	13.1	1.4	75.7	38.5	48.3	51.7
30294	ELLENWOOD	30.9	30.5	64.9	64.7	1.8	2.0	2.3	2.8	7.6	7.6	8.5	7.6	7.2	33.1	22.9	5.2	0.4	71.7	32.7	48.3	51.7
30295	ZEBULON	82.1	80.5	16.1	17.3	0.6	0.7	1.4	1.8	6.6	6.9	7.4	7.4	6.0	29.2	25.0	10.3	1.2	74.5	37.0	50.8	49.2
30296	RIVERDALE	21.6	19.2	70.5	71.9	2.9	3.1	5.2	6.2	7.6	7.5	8.2	7.5	7.6	30.5	24.5	5.9	0.7	72.0	33.0	47.7	52.3
30297	FOREST PARK	41.8	39.2	40.6	41.0	6.6	7.0	18.3	21.7	8.9	8.0	8.0	7.3	9.5	33.0	17.5	7.1	0.6	70.8	29.4	50.6	49.5
30303	ATLANTA	22.5	17.5	67.6	73.0	1.1	1.0	11.0	10.8	4.6	3.4	3.3	10.7	12.5	45.7	16.4	2.9	0.5	83.0	31.0	59.2	40.8
30305	ATLANTA	91.8	89.0	3.7	5.5	2.1	2.3	4.9	6.5	4.6	3.7	3.4	3.2	5.6	39.1	23.9	12.9	3.9	86.5	39.0	48.7	51.3
30306	ATLANTA	90.1	86.7	5.6	8.0	1.9	2.2	3.4	4.7	4.1	3.4	3.2	3.2	6.8	49.7	22.9	5.7	1.3	87.3	35.1	52.2	47.8
30307	ATLANTA	70.0	66.3	24.5	27.4	2.5	2.9	2.3	3.0	5.7	4.8	5.2	4.9	8.9	42.8	21.4	5.3	1.1	81.6	33.4	49.6	50.5
30308	ATLANTA	51.0	42.1	44.3	52.9	1.8	1.8	3.0	3.6	3.5	2.7	2.8	3.5	9.3	51.4	18.5	7.3	1.2	89.2	34.0	56.4	43.7
30309	ATLANTA	78.8	71.7	15.4	21.5	3.2	3.4	3.5	4.7	2.9	1.9	1.6	2.6	10.3	52.6	21.6	5.4	1.1	92.4	34.4	55.8	44.2
30310	ATLANTA	3.7	2.5	93.1	94.8	1.5	1.2	1.3	1.2	6.6	6.9	8.0	10.0	8.4	26.9	22.9	9.2	1.3	74.1	33.2	49.7	50.3
30311	ATLANTA	2.8	2.0	95.5	96.5	0.1	0.1	2.2	2.0	7.3	7.3	7.6	7.0	6.6	27.8	24.0	11.1	1.3	73.6	34.9	44.4	55.6
30312	ATLANTA	24.4	19.0	70.5	76.0	1.0	0.9	4.6	4.9	7.5	6.7	6.3	6.7	8.5	36.7	19.3	7.1	1.3	75.8	32.7	50.4	49.7
30313	ATLANTA	53.3	45.5	31.2	38.5	13.5	13.9	3.0	3.7	2.5	1.8	1.4	32.5	32.2	19.5	7.2	2.5	0.4	93.0	21.8	58.0	42.0
30314	ATLANTA	1.4	0.9	97.0	97.6	0.2	0.2	1.0	1.0	6.4	6.3	6.6	13.4	11.3	24.0	19.2	10.2	2.6	77.0	29.8	44.0	56.0
30315	ATLANTA	13.3	10.7	77.8	80.9	2.9	2.5	9.6	9.8	8.8	8.5	9.1	8.0	8.3	30.5	19.0	6.9	1.0	68.9	29.5	51.8	48.2
30316	ATLANTA	17.2	14.5	79.6	82.0	0.4	0.4	3.2	3.6	7.2	7.3	7.8	7.0	7.3	32.5	23.0	7.3	0.7	73.5	33.1	47.1	52.9
30317	ATLANTA	11.7	10.7	85.9	86.7	0.2	0.3	3.6	4.3	6.5	6.8	7.5	6.5	6.4	31.5	22.5	11.0	1.3	75.5	35.3	48.2	51.8
30318	ATLANTA	25.2	22.3	68.5	71.0	3.1	3.4	4.3	4.7	7.0	6.6	6.6	8.2	12.3	32.4	17.8	8.0	1.1	76.1	30.0	51.0	49.0
30319	ATLANTA	70.4	67.6	13.7	14.5	4.4	4.9	18.0	20.8	5.9	5.0	4.2	4.9	8.3	41.2	20.6	8.3	1.6	82.6	34.4	52.2	47.8
30322	ATLANTA	75.2	71.5	7.5	8.2	14.2	16.5	3.3	4.3	0.1	0.0	0.0	55.9	31.5	1.2	0.5	4.6	6.2	99.3	19.5	46.1	53.9
30324	ATLANTA	69.5	61.5	9.8	13.1	4.4	4.5	20.6	27.0	4.0	2.8	2.5	3.9	11.2	49.0	18.3	7.0	1.4	89.0	33.5	56.8	43.2
30326	ATLANTA	87.2	82.1	7.9	11.9	2.7	3.0	4.1	5.7	2.5	2.0	2.0	3.5	5.5	29.6	18.7	16.9	19.3	92.4	50.4	42.9	57.1
30327	ATLANTA	93.3	90.7	3.3	5.0	2.0	2.4	2.1	3.0	5.2	6.4	7.0	6.4	4.5	24.8	32.0	11.5	2.2	77.2	42.4	48.8	51.2
30328	ATLANTA	82.9	78.0	10.6	14.6	3.1	3.3	6.3	8.0	5.2	4.9	4.6	4.5	6.6	34.4	24.7	12.6	2.5	82.7	38.3	47.4	52.6
30329	ATLANTA	69.2	66.3	14.1	14.2	6.9	7.6	18.6	23.0	4.7	3.4	3.7	5.5	12.4	45.5	14.6	7.4	2.8	86.1	31.3	52.8	47.3
30330	ATLANTA	50.7	39.5	40.8	50.8	1.0	1.1	9.2	10.5	10.2	8.3	3.8	4.5	17.7	42.9	12.8	0.0	0.0	74.8	27.0	57.9	42.1
30331	ATLANTA	2.6	1.9	95.4	96.3	0.3	0.3	1.6	1.4	7.5	7.9	8.3	7.1	6.8	28.0	24.6	8.9	0.9	72.1	33.9	45.1	54.9
30334	ATLANTA	14.3	14.3	71.4	85.7	0.0	0.0	0.0	0.0	0.0	0.0	0.0	0.0	14.3	85.7	0.0	0.0	0.0	100.0	36.3	100.0	0.0
30336	ATLANTA	5.3	4.0	81.5	83.6	1.7	1.4	15.2	14.3	8.4	8.3	7.4	6.6	7.0	33.9	19.6	8.4	0.5	72.9	31.7	49.8	50.2
30337	ATLANTA	14.5	11.3	80.1	83.2	0.6	0.5	6.6	7.0	8.4	7.5	8.6	7.9	9.9	33.1	18.8	5.1	0.8	70.9	29.0	48.5	51.5
30338	ATLANTA	84.8	82.4	4.6	5.2	7.7	8.9	4.8	6.1	6.2	6.2	5.4	4.1	5.7	32.8	26.0	12.1	1.4	79.7	38.8	48.9	51.1
	GEORGIA	65.1	63.4	28.7	29.4	2.2	2.5	5.3	6.6	7.3	7.1	7.2	7.0	7.6	31.0	23.0	8.6	1.1	74.3	34.2	49.3	50.7
	UNITED STATES	75.1	73.6	12.3	12.5	3.8	4.2	12.5	14.1	6.9	6.7	7.2	7.0	7.3	28.6	23.8	10.8	1.7	75.1	36.0	49.1	50.9

INCOME

#	POST OFFICE NAME	2004 Per Capita Income	2004 HH Income Base	2004 Household Income Distribution (%): Less than $25,000	$25,000 to $49,999	$50,000 to $99,999	$100,000 to $149,999	$150,000 or More	Median Household Income: 2004	2009	2004 National Centile	2004 State Centile	2004 Home Value Base	2004 Home Value Distribution (%): Less than $50,000	$50,000 to $89,999	$90,000 to $174,999	$175,000 to $399,999	$400,000 or More	2004 Median Home Value
30168	AUSTELL	19839	9208	22.2	33.1	34.9	7.5	2.3	45786	53786	63	67	4879	15.9	19.1	55.2	9.5	0.4	108433
30170	ROOPVILLE	21350	1166	26.2	33.3	31.2	5.8	3.5	41492	48554	51	56	979	18.5	28.5	32.7	17.9	2.5	94470
30171	RYDAL	21017	809	23.2	28.7	34.6	10.3	3.2	48517	55786	69	73	695	15.4	21.2	42.6	14.2	6.6	106810
30173	SILVER CREEK	20717	2374	23.9	31.4	35.0	7.4	2.4	46263	53668	64	69	1857	13.1	26.6	45.9	13.2	1.2	99871
30175	TALKING ROCK	20386	2516	22.7	37.4	30.1	6.6	3.3	42000	48350	53	58	2093	20.3	18.3	39.1	20.0	2.4	108717
30176	TALLAPOOSA	18560	2807	32.8	32.5	26.2	6.2	2.4	37527	42904	38	44	2173	21.7	30.8	38.1	7.2	2.3	86614
30177	TATE	45145	544	16.4	20.0	30.3	15.8	17.5	67031	86937	90	91	516	6.8	4.1	16.1	49.2	23.8	275000
30178	TAYLORSVILLE	21061	1192	14.4	31.2	39.7	11.0	3.8	52623	60733	76	78	1028	8.5	20.3	51.0	19.2	1.1	118173
30179	TEMPLE	19702	4575	23.9	32.9	33.9	6.9	2.4	44704	51256	60	65	3843	14.3	25.5	46.8	12.5	0.9	102649
30180	VILLA RICA	21426	9061	23.5	27.8	35.5	10.1	3.0	48832	55760	70	73	7178	10.3	18.6	48.2	21.0	2.0	118127
30182	WACO	18210	1096	31.5	34.9	27.6	3.9	2.2	37947	43870	39	45	875	21.6	32.6	33.8	9.8	2.2	84206
30183	WALESKA	26990	1635	14.6	22.5	40.6	16.2	6.2	60227	71986	85	85	1424	5.6	7.6	35.3	39.5	12.2	179323
30184	WHITE	25677	2415	17.4	27.2	36.7	13.8	5.0	55823	64283	80	82	2090	8.8	15.0	41.2	29.8	5.2	144249
30185	WHITESBURG	25032	1621	25.8	32.6	25.8	9.4	6.4	43278	50912	57	61	1355	17.9	27.6	34.0	17.6	2.9	99918
30187	WINSTON	27624	2656	12.5	25.5	40.0	16.4	5.7	63240	75441	87	88	2408	4.8	13.0	51.3	27.7	3.2	130527
30188	WOODSTOCK	31041	16039	8.0	21.2	42.4	19.5	8.9	71160	83724	92	93	13959	1.4	2.4	50.9	40.9	4.4	169455
30189	WOODSTOCK	35235	15157	6.7	15.0	37.8	24.0	16.5	85339	103895	96	98	13132	4.4	1.1	29.6	59.2	5.7	205685
30204	BARNESVILLE	19593	4520	29.6	34.0	27.5	6.1	2.9	39760	44938	45	50	3286	14.6	31.6	37.1	13.4	3.3	95299
30205	BROOKS	27699	999	12.0	23.4	38.0	18.7	7.8	65484	78438	89	90	913	1.4	7.9	41.4	37.1	12.2	173646
30206	CONCORD	19093	867	22.8	30.6	36.0	7.7	2.9	47669	53944	68	71	732	13.7	16.0	43.7	23.8	2.9	124779
30213	FAIRBURN	25354	6328	17.4	28.2	33.8	13.1	7.5	54442	68777	79	81	5000	13.5	9.7	51.2	20.3	5.2	121156
30214	FAYETTEVILLE	36402	8259	9.6	16.0	37.9	22.2	14.3	80035	99261	95	96	7322	3.9	2.2	31.8	52.4	9.7	196377
30215	FAYETTEVILLE	34557	10593	6.2	17.0	39.1	22.6	15.1	81447	99040	95	97	9561	2.5	1.0	28.3	57.2	11.1	213236
30216	FLOVILLA	18792	929	19.9	39.0	28.7	7.6	4.7	44039	50808	59	63	755	11.0	21.7	49.3	13.6	4.4	107635
30217	FRANKLIN	17725	3830	31.9	32.7	28.8	5.1	1.5	38237	43173	40	47	3000	26.8	29.7	35.3	7.8	0.4	81447
30218	GAY	23302	734	21.7	36.1	29.3	7.2	5.7	44442	52277	60	65	618	16.2	18.0	41.8	18.1	6.0	111194
30220	GRANTVILLE	19180	1355	30.8	30.0	30.4	5.6	3.3	38863	46865	42	48	1104	18.8	30.2	38.4	10.3	2.4	91791
30222	GREENVILLE	19255	1678	37.7	26.3	27.5	4.8	3.7	34596	41143	26	33	1306	27.8	27.3	29.1	14.0	1.8	82717
30223	GRIFFIN	17466	13476	32.6	30.9	28.3	6.3	1.9	38216	45000	40	46	8656	15.0	31.3	41.3	10.0	2.4	93306
30224	GRIFFIN	24406	9024	24.3	27.2	32.1	11.4	5.1	48396	56474	69	73	6387	5.1	16.1	55.4	20.8	2.7	124722
30228	HAMPTON	24011	8886	14.4	24.9	41.9	13.8	5.1	60108	68747	84	85	7813	11.2	10.9	48.9	27.1	2.0	138481
30230	HOGANSVILLE	18130	2843	32.9	31.5	28.0	5.0	2.6	37151	43331	36	42	2190	22.8	29.4	34.3	12.9	0.6	87363
30233	JACKSON	21001	7195	24.2	30.6	33.4	8.8	3.1	46217	53374	64	69	5697	10.4	17.2	53.9	16.1	2.4	114388
30234	JENKINSBURG	18136	616	23.1	30.8	37.5	5.7	2.9	45655	51697	63	67	468	12.2	28.2	42.7	16.2	0.6	103829
30236	JONESBORO	26195	17892	17.3	28.2	36.5	11.8	6.1	54583	62588	79	81	11176	7.0	11.0	51.7	26.4	4.0	132266
30238	JONESBORO	20172	12376	16.5	29.9	41.0	10.0	2.7	52522	59797	76	78	9936	5.6	17.4	65.8	10.6	0.7	114828
30240	LAGRANGE	25695	10653	26.7	25.7	29.6	11.0	7.0	47275	56976	67	71	7196	11.0	21.5	41.3	22.5	3.7	116937
30241	LAGRANGE	17277	7867	35.7	30.1	26.3	6.5	1.5	36002	42273	32	39	5007	18.1	31.1	42.0	8.0	0.8	90985
30248	LOCUST GROVE	27221	4918	10.2	27.1	44.6	12.7	5.5	60612	70090	85	86	4422	11.3	12.6	51.3	21.6	3.2	134756
30251	LUTHERSVILLE	17883	762	30.3	30.3	32.0	6.0	1.3	39655	46201	45	50	571	22.4	28.0	30.0	18.9	0.7	89359
30252	MCDONOUGH	28940	9733	7.6	18.6	46.9	18.8	8.1	71975	82014	92	93	9129	1.3	2.6	43.2	48.6	4.2	179791
30253	MCDONOUGH	27932	12635	12.5	25.7	40.1	15.7	6.1	61716	70031	86	87	9279	5.7	9.4	45.6	34.3	5.1	158137
30256	MEANSVILLE	20387	931	24.9	29.3	32.6	10.2	3.0	46471	52822	65	69	797	20.1	18.8	36.9	22.0	2.3	108854
30257	MILNER	22026	1617	20.0	32.0	35.9	9.4	2.7	47682	54676	68	71	1365	11.4	24.5	43.0	17.7	3.4	110353
30258	MOLENA	18954	1007	23.5	30.6	36.5	7.6	1.8	47111	54349	66	70	848	14.3	25.1	33.6	23.0	4.0	108557
30259	MORELAND	22621	1015	21.7	24.7	35.9	12.3	5.4	53494	62851	78	79	891	5.4	10.7	40.7	38.1	5.2	162500
30260	MORROW	19801	9175	21.8	32.8	36.1	7.4	1.9	45948	52291	64	68	5188	1.5	16.2	76.5	5.6	0.3	111893
30263	NEWNAN	24615	17432	23.1	25.0	33.6	12.1	6.3	51841	61046	75	78	12211	6.9	16.5	46.7	24.1	5.7	128055
30265	NEWNAN	30937	7870	8.7	17.3	46.2	18.8	9.1	72517	84942	92	93	6592	2.2	1.8	48.4	43.6	4.0	171904
30268	PALMETTO	24030	2840	21.9	29.6	34.1	9.9	4.5	48692	61476	70	73	2236	13.5	17.0	53.4	13.4	2.6	109920
30269	PEACHTREE CITY	39330	12512	7.9	14.0	34.9	24.8	18.5	88244	108504	97	98	10497	1.9	0.9	21.9	60.9	14.4	237340
30273	REX	23059	4502	12.4	26.3	46.1	11.7	3.6	56958	64634	82	83	3871	4.4	8.5	75.3	11.6	0.3	122096
30274	RIVERDALE	18754	11463	20.0	35.4	36.2	6.8	1.7	45796	51420	63	67	6435	1.4	21.6	73.2	3.5	0.3	108530
30276	SENOIA	23919	3593	11.8	28.1	42.5	12.9	4.7	59541	69490	84	84	3083	5.3	9.0	58.8	22.4	4.5	139686
30277	SHARPSBURG	29646	6691	6.4	16.6	47.5	21.5	8.1	76182	88046	94	95	6197	2.9	2.9	43.4	48.9	1.9	176421
30281	STOCKBRIDGE	27069	21511	10.6	23.1	43.9	17.4	5.1	64930	76205	88	90	17549	4.0	5.6	54.2	33.9	2.2	153269
30285	THE ROCK	19257	183	24.6	35.5	33.3	3.8	2.7	45508	50613	63	66	153	19.6	36.6	32.7	9.8	1.3	84063
30286	THOMASTON	20165	9709	37.0	30.7	24.6	4.8	3.1	34337	40180	25	31	6846	21.7	39.4	30.3	7.9	0.7	78177
30288	CONLEY	17432	2392	26.4	34.1	29.5	7.0	3.1	41110	47487	50	55	1492	3.6	31.0	60.1	5.4	0.0	98919
30290	TYRONE	36588	2184	6.3	18.3	37.7	23.4	14.2	81006	98800	95	96	1975	0.8	5.0	28.6	55.0	10.7	206595
30291	UNION CITY	22888	5839	24.6	33.7	32.1	7.4	2.2	43818	53962	58	63	2800	7.5	31.8	57.3	2.1	1.3	99967
30292	WILLIAMSON	22435	1785	21.6	27.7	35.2	9.8	5.8	50618	57935	73	76	1396	8.4	13.3	45.0	29.3	4.1	136196
30293	WOODBURY	17561	1368	36.5	30.4	25.5	5.4	2.2	34866	41084	27	34	1081	27.9	35.5	26.7	8.6	1.2	74802
30294	ELLENWOOD	23174	10091	11.3	24.5	46.0	13.9	4.3	61288	70744	86	87	8687	3.5	7.5	66.9	20.5	1.6	132860
30295	ZEBULON	23740	1411	23.8	27.9	32.8	9.0	6.5	48453	55063	69	73	1138	11.5	15.4	42.2	27.0	4.0	125641
30296	RIVERDALE	22716	8900	14.9	31.1	37.6	12.4	4.2	53900	61536	78	80	6451	5.8	6.2	69.7	17.4	1.0	126817
30297	FOREST PARK	15945	10945	29.1	35.7	27.4	5.8	2.1	37962	43171	39	45	5510	6.5	47.0	44.5	1.7	0.2	88042
30303	ATLANTA	24778	1481	43.8	23.2	21.9	7.2	3.9	31159	45692	15	18	282	1.4	13.8	43.6	28.4	12.8	150962
30305	ATLANTA	95615	12544	15.1	15.2	23.9	15.3	30.6	89727	138021	97	98	6666	0.0	0.4	8.3	28.1	63.1	506200
30306	ATLANTA	66050	12150	12.2	19.0	27.7	18.2	22.9	79977	117357	95	96	5786	1.0	0.5	3.9	41.2	53.4	413437
30307	ATLANTA	46120	8307	19.3	19.6	26.5	16.5	18.1	67230	92875	90	91	4206	1.6	2.8	10.2	50.3	35.2	339729
30308	ATLANTA	37219	7519	32.7	22.5	27.8	11.7	5.3	44204	65621	59	64	1776	0.1	8.4	30.4	43.9	17.3	211304
30309	ATLANTA	71904	12493	17.3	22.9	27.5	14.2	18.2	64281	98691	88	89	4471	0.0	0.8	19.1	39.9	40.3	316411
30310	ATLANTA	15585	11654	45.0	29.1	19.1	4.0	2.8	28008	35459	9	8	5468	10.1	48.9	35.7	4.6	0.8	82743
30311	ATLANTA	22092	13466	39.2	26.2	22.0	8.4	4.2	33578	44653	23	28	6623	3.8	23.4	57.2	14.4	1.3	110820
30312	ATLANTA	20139	9176	49.6	19.6	18.2	8.4	4.2	25374	36691	5	3	2623	5.2	8.7	28.9	49.9	7.3	191740
30313	ATLANTA	15367	1810	66.3	15.2	12.3	4.3	1.9	14285	19150	1	1	128	6.3	3.1	16.4	55.5	18.8	241667
30314	ATLANTA	13105	9476	55.6	27.4	12.6	3.2	1.4	21699	26987	2	2	3585	14.5	52.3	29.1	3.5	0.5	76845
30315	ATLANTA	11890	12084	51.3	24.9	17.2	5.1	1.6	24074	31912	4	3	4714	12.8	52.5	25.4	8.2	1.2	76935
30316	ATLANTA	19361	11827	31.8	31.0	27.0	7.4	2.8	38795	46562	42	48	6803	3.1	25.6	52.2	18.7	0.4	112334
30317	ATLANTA	17986	5208	38.6	30.7	21.9	5.7	3.1	32573	37982	20	23	2910	4.3	20.3	48.2	24.9	2.4	121117
30318	ATLANTA	22917	19634	39.6	24.5	20.5	8.3	7.1	34318	45165	25	31	8608	9.8	29.5	28.8	20.3	11.7	105306
30319	ATLANTA	53682	18348	13.2	19.6	29.7	17.7	19.9	74721	100692	93	94	8773	0.9	1.1	10.8	50.0	37.2	338256
30322	ATLANTA	12205	3	100.0	0.0	0.0	0.0	0.0	12500	17500	1	1	0	0.0	0.0	0.0	0.0	0.0	0
30324	ATLANTA	47386	12088	14.4	20.4	33.9	16.9	14.3	67553	97197	90	91	4015	1.2	0.9	8.9	56.9	32.1	301839
30326	ATLANTA	92299	1564	17.5	10.9	27.8	20.3	23.6	86361	132621	97	98	697	0.0	0.0	9.5	39.7	50.8	406044
30327	ATLANTA	115543	9385	7.1	10.2	18.6	16.7	47.5	141048	198723	100	100	7146	0.2	0.3	5.0	18.1	76.5	667923
30328	ATLANTA	62135	13339	11.4	17.4	29.6	18.3	23.3	83074	116713	96	98	7657	0.6	3.2	16.1	43.2	37.0	339886
30329	ATLANTA	34143	9941	18.7	25.5	32.9	13.6	9.3	56060	74235	81	82	2657	0.3	0.1	11.3	67.9	20.4	276752
30330	ATLANTA	22723	59	0.0	0.0	79.7	20.3	0.0	71108	86660	92	92	0	0.0	0.0	0.0	0.0	0.0	0
30331	ATLANTA	23885	16513	28.6	26.5	27.0	11.2	6.6	43634	57783	58	62	9919	2.5	20.5	53.4	18.7	5.0	117481
30334	ATLANTA	8952	0	0.0	0.0	0.0	0.0	0.0	0	0	0	0	0	0.0	0.0	0.0	0.0	0.0	0
30336	ATLANTA	17970	298	29.2	22.5	33.2	11.4	3.7	43925	60000	58	63	155	0.7	30.3	56.1	8.4	4.5	108430
30337	ATLANTA	18189	6423	35.0	32.0	24.4	6.3	2.3	34876	44978	27	34	1873	3.7	20.2	59.9	15.2	1.1	116675
30338	ATLANTA	54795	13161	7.6	13.6	29.1	22.6	27.0	99202	126979	98	99	8781	0.4	0.7	5.5	59.4	34.0	352367
	GEORGIA	26143		23.6	26.3	31.4	11.6	7.0	50024	60470				12.5	17.5	39.3	24.8	6.0	125860
	UNITED STATES	25866		24.7	27.1	30.8	10.9	6.5	48124	56710				10.9	15.0	33.7	30.1	10.4	145905

#	POST OFFICE NAME	FINANCIAL SERVICES: Auto Loan	FINANCIAL SERVICES: Home Loan	FINANCIAL SERVICES: Investments	FINANCIAL SERVICES: Retirement Plans	THE HOME: Home Improvements: Home Repair	THE HOME: Home Improvements: Lawn & Garden	THE HOME: Furnishings: Computers & Hardware	THE HOME: Furnishings: Major Appliances	THE HOME: Furnishings: TV, Radio, Sound Equipment	THE HOME: Furnishings: Furniture	ENTERTAINMENT: Dine out/Carry out	ENTERTAINMENT: Sports Equipment	ENTERTAINMENT: Fees & Tickets	ENTERTAINMENT: Toys & Games	ENTERTAINMENT: Travel	ENTERTAINMENT: Cable TV	PERSONAL: Apparel & Services	PERSONAL: Auto Repairs	PERSONAL: Health Insurance	PERSONAL: Pets & Supplies
30168	AUSTELL	78	73	78	77	71	76	78	76	77	79	97	90	76	93	75	73	94	79	70	85
30170	ROOPVILLE	96	80	55	74	84	92	75	85	81	76	98	100	70	96	76	83	92	83	93	110
30171	RYDAL	96	85	65	81	90	96	79	87	83	79	102	104	77	104	81	86	96	85	94	112
30173	SILVER CREEK	93	79	58	75	84	92	75	84	81	75	98	99	72	99	77	83	92	82	92	107
30175	TALKING ROCK	91	74	49	69	77	84	71	80	76	72	92	94	64	87	71	78	87	80	87	103
30176	TALLAPOOSA	81	59	35	53	66	76	59	70	69	59	81	82	53	78	60	73	75	69	84	93
30177	TATE	143	134	128	127	142	167	124	141	131	133	163	138	126	136	135	140	153	137	165	161
30178	TAYLORSVILLE	95	92	76	90	93	96	84	90	85	85	105	106	84	106	85	84	101	87	90	110
30179	TEMPLE	90	76	54	71	80	86	72	81	77	73	93	95	68	90	73	78	88	80	87	102
30180	VILLA RICA	92	82	66	78	85	91	79	85	82	79	101	100	76	99	79	83	96	85	90	105
30182	WACO	88	63	35	56	70	79	61	73	71	62	84	87	54	81	62	75	77	72	87	100
30183	WALESKA	104	112	106	110	112	114	102	106	99	103	124	124	105	127	104	98	121	103	101	123
30184	WHITE	113	103	81	99	107	114	96	105	100	96	122	124	94	123	98	101	117	102	110	132
30185	WHITESBURG	110	100	79	96	100	106	95	102	97	98	119	118	90	113	94	95	115	102	102	122
30187	WINSTON	109	120	116	118	120	122	109	112	106	109	132	132	113	137	111	104	129	109	107	130
30188	WOODSTOCK	123	138	135	143	132	129	126	125	117	130	148	147	129	149	123	110	146	123	108	137
30189	WOODSTOCK	147	161	159	167	156	154	150	149	140	154	177	175	152	176	147	132	174	147	132	164
30204	BARNESVILLE	82	69	56	65	72	82	69	75	75	69	91	86	66	90	69	78	86	74	84	93
30205	BROOKS	110	122	119	120	123	124	110	114	107	110	132	134	114	139	113	105	130	110	109	132
30206	CONCORD	100	74	43	67	82	92	70	84	81	71	96	100	63	94	72	86	89	83	99	116
30213	FAIRBURN	97	107	110	106	107	110	102	103	100	101	124	119	105	129	103	98	122	101	99	114
30214	FAYETTEVILLE	133	155	162	155	153	156	142	143	135	142	169	166	149	176	145	132	167	139	133	159
30215	FAYETTEVILLE	138	163	171	167	159	157	148	147	137	150	173	172	156	179	149	131	172	143	130	162
30216	FLOVILLA	103	73	37	64	81	92	69	85	82	70	97	101	61	93	71	87	88	84	102	118
30217	FRANKLIN	78	66	48	63	68	74	65	71	68	65	83	82	60	78	64	69	78	71	75	87
30218	GAY	117	90	55	81	98	109	85	100	96	85	115	119	77	113	87	101	107	98	116	136
30220	GRANTVILLE	91	68	43	62	75	84	66	78	75	67	89	92	60	86	67	79	83	77	90	104
30222	GREENVILLE	91	67	42	62	74	85	67	79	77	67	91	93	60	87	68	81	84	78	93	104
30223	GRIFFIN	75	62	51	59	65	73	64	69	69	64	84	80	60	81	63	71	80	69	76	85
30224	GRIFFIN	90	86	83	83	87	96	86	89	89	85	110	102	86	110	87	91	106	88	93	103
30228	HAMPTON	106	108	95	108	106	107	100	103	97	103	121	121	99	119	99	94	118	102	96	119
30230	HOGANSVILLE	77	64	48	59	68	76	62	70	68	62	82	81	59	82	63	71	77	68	79	88
30233	JACKSON	91	79	62	75	82	90	77	83	82	77	99	97	74	98	77	84	94	82	90	103
30234	JENKINSBURG	98	66	30	57	75	86	64	80	77	65	90	95	54	85	65	83	82	79	98	113
30236	JONESBORO	101	100	109	105	98	101	103	100	100	104	126	119	103	124	100	95	124	103	92	112
30238	JONESBORO	84	93	94	95	89	89	88	87	82	89	104	102	89	105	86	78	103	86	76	95
30240	LAGRANGE	93	94	97	93	95	102	93	94	94	92	117	110	94	119	94	95	113	94	96	109
30241	LAGRANGE	71	60	50	56	63	70	60	65	65	60	79	76	57	77	60	67	75	65	72	81
30248	LOCUST GROVE	125	119	98	117	120	125	110	118	111	112	137	138	108	136	110	110	132	115	117	142
30251	LUTHERSVILLE	89	65	40	59	72	81	63	75	73	64	86	90	56	83	64	77	80	75	88	102
30252	MCDONOUGH	120	137	135	141	131	128	124	123	114	127	145	144	128	147	122	108	143	120	106	135
30253	MCDONOUGH	115	118	120	124	113	115	115	113	110	119	139	132	116	136	111	104	137	114	101	125
30256	MEANSVILLE	97	75	46	68	82	91	70	83	80	71	95	99	65	94	72	84	89	82	96	113
30257	MILNER	95	85	66	81	89	95	80	88	83	81	102	103	77	101	81	84	97	86	92	110
30258	MOLENA	90	73	49	68	79	87	69	79	76	69	91	94	65	91	71	79	86	77	89	105
30259	MORELAND	104	91	68	86	97	104	84	94	90	85	110	112	82	112	87	93	104	92	103	122
30260	MORROW	77	79	85	81	77	80	81	79	78	80	99	93	81	99	79	75	96	80	73	87
30263	NEWNAN	101	94	89	93	96	103	94	98	97	94	120	115	93	119	94	97	115	98	100	116
30265	NEWNAN	126	139	133	145	133	130	126	126	117	131	148	148	129	148	123	109	146	123	109	139
30268	PALMETTO	94	94	88	92	95	103	92	94	93	91	115	108	92	117	93	94	111	93	97	108
30269	PEACHTREE CITY	154	182	186	188	175	172	163	161	150	167	190	188	172	195	163	142	189	156	140	177
30273	REX	96	106	105	110	102	100	99	98	92	102	117	116	101	117	97	86	115	97	85	108
30274	RIVERDALE	76	75	81	79	73	75	79	76	76	79	96	91	77	94	75	72	94	78	69	84
30276	SENOIA	100	104	97	103	103	105	97	100	94	98	118	118	97	119	97	92	115	98	94	116
30277	SHARPSBURG	124	138	132	144	132	129	125	125	115	130	146	146	128	147	122	108	144	121	107	138
30281	STOCKBRIDGE	104	119	121	122	115	113	109	108	101	111	128	127	113	131	108	96	127	106	95	119
30285	THE ROCK	96	64	29	56	73	84	62	78	75	63	88	93	53	83	63	81	80	77	96	110
30286	THOMASTON	84	65	45	59	70	81	65	74	74	65	88	86	60	85	66	78	82	73	87	97
30288	CONLEY	76	71	75	71	70	76	75	74	77	75	96	86	74	94	73	76	93	75	73	84
30290	TYRONE	137	170	182	173	165	165	151	148	138	152	175	173	163	183	153	134	176	143	132	164
30291	UNION CITY	75	73	79	77	72	75	76	75	74	76	93	89	75	91	74	71	91	77	70	83
30292	WILLIAMSON	98	88	72	84	91	99	85	91	90	84	110	108	83	111	86	92	104	90	98	113
30293	WOODBURY	83	61	35	55	67	76	59	70	68	59	80	83	53	78	60	72	74	69	83	95
30294	ELLENWOOD	100	109	107	112	105	104	102	102	96	105	121	120	103	121	100	90	119	101	90	113
30295	ZEBULON	102	88	66	84	93	101	84	93	90	83	109	109	81	109	85	92	103	90	101	118
30296	RIVERDALE	95	97	97	99	95	97	95	95	91	96	115	112	94	113	93	87	112	95	87	107
30297	FOREST PARK	68	65	70	66	64	69	70	68	71	70	89	80	69	88	68	69	87	70	66	75
30303	ATLANTA	37	29	38	32	29	32	41	36	40	38	51	45	37	47	36	37	49	40	33	40
30305	ATLANTA	220	242	361	257	235	254	248	235	243	251	307	278	263	317	251	240	305	239	220	258
30306	ATLANTA	153	154	270	173	147	162	174	157	175	177	223	191	182	233	172	174	221	166	146	174
30307	ATLANTA	129	129	206	138	123	137	144	131	145	145	184	158	149	189	142	144	182	139	124	146
30308	ATLANTA	82	71	111	79	69	77	91	80	92	89	116	100	88	114	85	88	113	89	76	90
30309	ATLANTA	146	137	251	158	130	146	165	145	168	166	214	180	170	222	160	166	212	157	136	163
30310	ATLANTA	58	53	62	50	51	60	57	56	62	58	77	62	58	74	57	64	75	58	61	65
30311	ATLANTA	77	72	85	68	70	81	76	75	82	79	103	83	79	100	77	85	100	77	80	86
30312	ATLANTA	62	53	71	55	51	58	65	60	67	64	84	72	63	81	61	66	82	65	60	67
30313	ATLANTA	40	32	44	35	32	37	45	39	45	42	56	49	41	53	41	43	54	44	38	43
30314	ATLANTA	47	38	43	35	37	45	45	44	50	45	61	49	43	56	43	51	59	46	49	51
30315	ATLANTA	51	44	53	41	43	50	50	49	54	51	68	55	49	64	48	56	66	51	52	55
30316	ATLANTA	72	69	80	67	67	76	73	71	76	74	96	80	75	93	73	78	93	73	74	81
30317	ATLANTA	68	61	70	58	60	70	65	65	71	67	89	71	67	84	65	74	86	67	71	75
30318	ATLANTA	83	73	96	73	71	83	84	80	90	85	112	92	84	107	82	91	108	84	84	91
30319	ATLANTA	158	157	234	170	152	165	173	161	172	175	218	193	177	221	169	168	216	168	149	177
30322	ATLANTA	16	14	21	15	14	17	18	16	19	17	23	19	17	23	17	19	22	18	18	18
30324	ATLANTA	122	116	197	130	111	123	136	123	138	138	176	150	140	181	133	135	174	131	114	136
30326	ATLANTA	192	196	254	209	195	207	206	200	202	206	254	237	208	252	205	196	248	205	191	220
30327	ATLANTA	337	421	613	426	408	443	391	378	373	399	472	434	435	496	409	374	477	373	351	413
30328	ATLANTA	177	187	247	197	182	195	192	184	186	194	235	217	198	234	190	180	232	188	170	203
30329	ATLANTA	103	98	158	110	94	103	113	103	114	115	144	125	115	147	110	111	143	110	96	114
30330	ATLANTA	132	84	80	96	77	91	125	108	127	117	159	143	107	142	103	116	152	127	100	123
30331	ATLANTA	88	85	99	82	83	94	88	87	93	91	117	97	91	115	88	96	114	88	90	99
30334	ATLANTA	0	0	0	0	0	0	0	0	0	0	0	0	0	0	0	0	0	0	0	0
30336	ATLANTA	77	74	88	71	71	80	78	76	83	80	104	86	80	103	77	85	102	78	78	87
30337	ATLANTA	64	58	69	59	56	62	65	62	67	65	84	73	64	82	63	66	82	66	61	70
30338	ATLANTA	157	184	284	190	177	191	183	173	179	186	227	203	198	241	188	179	228	175	160	189
	GEORGIA	103	97	95	97	97	104	97	99	98	98	122	116	96	120	96	98	118	100	99	116
	UNITED STATES	100	100	100	100	100	100	100	100	100	100	100	100	100	100	100	100	100	100	100	100

GEORGIA

A 30339-30566

POPULATION CHANGE

# POST OFFICE NAME	COUNTY FIPS CODE	POPULATION 2000	POPULATION 2004	POPULATION 2009	2000-2004 ANNUAL RATE % Rate	2000-2004 ANNUAL RATE State Centile	HOUSEHOLDS 2000	HOUSEHOLDS 2004	HOUSEHOLDS 2009	% Annual Rate 2000-2004	2004 Average HH Size	FAMILIES 2000	FAMILIES 2004	% Annual Rate 2000-2004
30339 ATLANTA	067	14931	14978	15928	0.1	13	8473	8588	9162	0.3	1.74	2660	2523	-1.2
30340 ATLANTA	089	27100	29830	33095	2.3	64	9987	10870	11970	2.0	2.73	5900	6190	1.1
30341 ATLANTA	089	32528	35057	38508	1.8	52	12078	12987	14261	1.7	2.68	6979	7237	0.9
30342 ATLANTA	121	25739	27849	30278	1.9	55	11455	12297	13322	1.7	2.24	5076	5236	0.7
30344 ATLANTA	121	38789	38304	40269	-0.3	7	14268	14029	14728	-0.4	2.70	9262	8918	-0.9
30345 ATLANTA	089	21828	22819	24557	1.1	38	8282	8548	9139	0.8	2.65	5210	5247	0.2
30346 ATLANTA	089	1452	1859	2196	6.0	95	827	1077	1282	6.4	1.68	284	370	6.4
30349 ATLANTA	121	54621	60792	68497	2.6	69	20654	22845	25674	2.4	2.65	13351	14510	2.0
30350 ATLANTA	121	31129	32538	34844	1.1	38	15170	15790	16876	1.0	2.06	6880	6957	0.3
30354 ATLANTA	121	17792	17962	18861	0.2	16	6145	6193	6500	0.2	2.88	4314	4270	-0.2
30360 ATLANTA	089	16511	18195	20335	2.3	64	6512	7136	7938	2.2	2.55	3850	4063	1.3
30401 SWAINSBORO	107	13766	13947	14296	0.3	18	5129	5253	5446	0.6	2.57	3648	3674	0.2
30410 AILEY	209	1093	1177	1280	1.8	52	417	453	499	2.0	2.59	298	318	1.5
30411 ALAMO	309	3910	4063	4159	0.9	36	1131	1211	1270	1.6	2.52	806	848	1.2
30413 BARTOW	163	1625	1611	1606	-0.2	8	594	597	603	0.1	2.65	439	435	-0.2
30415 BROOKLET	031	5961	6534	7249	2.2	62	2142	2366	2649	2.4	2.76	1625	1766	2.0
30417 CLAXTON	109	9963	10792	11925	1.9	56	3602	3944	4407	2.2	2.59	2542	2738	1.8
30420 COBBTOWN	267	1666	1747	1871	1.1	40	668	705	759	1.3	2.48	460	478	0.9
30421 COLLINS	267	1735	1811	1936	1.0	37	711	749	806	1.2	2.42	476	492	0.8
30425 GARFIELD	107	1337	1319	1331	-0.3	7	516	516	528	0.0	2.56	388	382	-0.4
30426 GIRARD	033	1074	1077	1096	0.1	13	397	404	416	0.4	2.67	281	282	0.1
30427 GLENNVILLE	267	9567	10077	10792	1.2	43	3168	3385	3679	1.6	2.57	2221	2335	1.2
30428 GLENWOOD	309	2614	2565	2564	-0.4	4	1020	1015	1029	-0.1	2.46	692	676	-0.6
30434 LOUISVILLE	163	6354	6524	6683	0.6	28	2268	2365	2428	1.0	2.61	1596	1638	0.6
30436 LYONS	279	11206	11542	11893	0.7	30	4142	4313	4491	1.0	2.64	2882	2950	0.6
30438 MANASSAS	267	962	1023	1107	1.5	47	363	387	421	1.5	2.63	255	266	1.0
30439 METTER	043	9372	9945	10666	1.4	47	3297	3495	3744	1.4	2.73	2369	2473	1.0
30441 MIDVILLE	033	1655	1661	1696	0.1	13	621	630	651	0.3	2.64	441	440	-0.1
30442 MILLEN	165	7549	7579	7563	0.1	13	2819	2864	2893	0.4	2.60	1975	1974	0.0
30445 MOUNT VERNON	209	3423	3467	3615	0.3	17	1033	1063	1134	0.7	2.56	703	710	0.2
30446 NEWINGTON	251	1549	1755	1924	3.0	75	599	687	762	3.3	2.55	443	500	2.9
30450 PORTAL	031	2922	3062	3317	1.1	39	1054	1122	1232	1.5	2.73	789	826	1.1
30452 REGISTER	031	2120	2133	2303	0.1	15	734	747	815	0.4	2.85	561	562	0.0
30453 REIDSVILLE	267	8090	8554	9121	1.3	45	2072	2244	2460	1.9	2.67	1410	1502	1.5
30454 ROCKLEDGE	175	632	784	893	5.2	93	267	336	388	5.6	2.33	200	246	5.0
30455 ROCKY FORD	251	764	774	794	0.3	18	294	302	314	0.6	2.53	218	221	0.3
30456 SARDIS	033	2074	2088	2126	0.2	15	731	742	763	0.4	2.81	524	524	0.0
30457 SOPERTON	283	6849	6975	7105	0.4	21	2531	2624	2719	0.9	2.51	1824	1863	0.5
30458 STATESBORO	031	32506	34996	38573	1.8	52	12122	13308	14982	2.2	2.37	5961	6370	1.6
30461 STATESBORO	031	9883	11245	12722	3.1	77	3753	4328	4959	3.4	2.57	2675	3005	2.8
30467 SYLVANIA	251	13149	13489	14025	0.6	27	4948	5132	5398	0.9	2.57	3477	3546	0.5
30470 TARRYTOWN	209	1285	1376	1491	1.6	50	532	577	632	1.9	2.38	377	402	1.5
30471 TWIN CITY	107	4509	4512	4573	0.0	12	1534	1550	1588	0.2	2.71	1100	1093	-0.2
30473 UVALDA	209	2738	2994	3263	2.1	61	1053	1166	1286	2.4	2.57	777	847	2.1
30474 VIDALIA	279	15232	15492	15903	0.4	20	5865	6030	6259	0.7	2.52	4025	4070	0.3
30477 WADLEY	163	3257	3122	3056	-1.0	1	1212	1178	1169	-0.7	2.58	845	807	-1.1
30501 GAINESVILLE	139	29306	33503	40254	3.2	79	9398	10550	12518	2.8	3.05	6195	6813	2.3
30504 GAINESVILLE	139	15595	17908	21586	3.3	80	5236	5932	7061	3.0	2.99	3802	4237	2.6
30506 GAINESVILLE	139	32150	39111	49481	4.7	90	11617	14101	17750	4.7	2.76	9189	10986	4.3
30507 GAINESVILLE	139	21218	24802	30153	3.7	85	6672	7734	9315	3.5	3.15	5343	6103	3.2
30510 ALTO	011	6456	7306	8407	3.0	75	1974	2301	2723	3.7	2.66	1509	1736	3.4
30511 BALDWIN	011	3566	3905	4436	2.2	62	1281	1408	1607	2.3	2.72	948	1027	1.9
30512 BLAIRSVILLE	291	15876	19042	23815	4.4	89	6549	8011	10222	4.9	2.32	4763	5738	4.5
30513 BLUE RIDGE	111	8967	11038	14649	5.0	92	3807	4773	6453	5.5	2.29	2707	3340	5.1
30516 BOWERSVILLE	147	2005	2013	2072	0.1	13	796	808	843	0.4	2.49	601	602	0.0
30517 BRASELTON	157	5218	6877	8973	6.7	97	1846	2445	3198	6.8	2.79	1494	1955	6.5
30518 BUFORD	135	29485	36926	46396	5.4	94	10699	13402	16788	5.4	2.74	7957	9823	5.1
30519 BUFORD	135	19404	25833	33274	7.0	98	6146	8292	10733	7.3	3.02	5128	6836	7.0
30520 CANON	147	3773	3960	4151	1.1	41	1483	1577	1671	1.5	2.50	1084	1134	1.1
30521 CARNESVILLE	119	4510	4731	4956	1.1	40	1711	1810	1910	1.3	2.59	1296	1353	1.0
30522 CHERRYLOG	123	1326	1646	2137	5.2	93	580	729	958	5.5	2.24	425	526	5.1
30523 CLARKESVILLE	137	11005	12833	15192	3.7	84	4387	5153	6139	3.9	2.47	3295	3812	3.5
30525 CLAYTON	241	7882	8804	10088	2.6	70	3344	3790	4408	3.0	2.30	2266	2522	2.6
30527 CLERMONT	139	3367	3785	4517	2.8	72	1210	1352	1598	2.7	2.80	1000	1103	2.3
30528 CLEVELAND	311	16227	19178	23250	4.0	87	6118	7302	8936	4.3	2.57	4629	5451	3.9
30529 COMMERCE	157	8976	10436	12840	3.6	83	3439	4052	5045	3.9	2.51	2486	2880	3.5
30530 COMMERCE	011	5052	5688	6585	2.8	73	1831	2078	2425	3.0	2.74	1403	1572	2.7
30531 CORNELIA	137	9469	10256	11703	1.9	56	3600	3910	4483	2.0	2.59	2583	2756	1.5
30533 DAHLONEGA	187	17995	21075	25645	3.8	85	6763	8026	9910	4.1	2.52	4802	5608	3.7
30534 DAWSONVILLE	085	17914	21574	26845	4.5	89	6801	8320	10520	4.9	2.56	5231	6321	4.6
30535 DEMOREST	137	5774	6661	7822	3.4	81	2186	2556	3040	3.8	2.47	1616	1864	3.4
30537 DILLARD	241	687	763	868	2.5	68	320	362	422	2.9	1.96	227	254	2.7
30538 EASTANOLLEE	257	1545	1687	1806	2.1	60	601	660	711	2.2	2.56	468	507	1.9
30539 EAST ELLIJAY	123	665	720	867	1.9	55	241	263	321	2.1	2.61	174	187	1.7
30540 ELLIJAY	123	19393	23861	30753	5.0	92	7486	9271	12023	5.2	2.56	5511	6727	4.8
30541 EPWORTH	111	1479	1948	2666	6.7	97	590	787	1092	7.0	2.48	453	596	6.7
30542 FLOWERY BRANCH	139	20373	25485	32081	5.4	94	7192	8936	11139	5.2	2.84	5734	7049	5.0
30543 GILLSVILLE	139	3317	3810	4572	3.3	80	1166	1331	1584	3.2	2.86	937	1056	2.9
30545 HELEN	311	678	769	915	3.0	76	328	375	449	3.2	2.05	216	242	2.7
30546 HIAWASSEE	281	6154	6915	7845	2.8	72	2762	3139	3599	3.1	2.16	1920	2147	2.7
30547 HOMER	011	2420	2683	3059	2.5	68	941	1053	1209	2.7	2.55	727	803	2.4
30548 HOSCHTON	157	5616	7339	9593	6.5	96	1999	2635	3465	6.7	2.75	1607	2090	6.4
30549 JEFFERSON	157	12754	15284	19188	4.4	88	4453	5398	6855	4.6	2.74	3396	4060	4.3
30552 LAKEMONT	241	1417	1603	1850	2.9	75	620	711	831	3.3	2.25	449	507	2.9
30553 LAVONIA	119	6820	6969	7260	0.5	24	2836	2928	3080	0.8	2.38	2046	2079	0.4
30554 LULA	139	6226	7293	8781	3.8	85	2271	2655	3181	3.7	2.75	1807	2084	3.4
30555 MC CAYSVILLE	111	1979	2595	3543	6.6	96	895	1187	1642	6.9	2.19	601	784	6.5
30557 MARTIN	257	5112	5639	6074	2.3	65	1974	2196	2383	2.5	2.57	1475	1616	2.2
30558 MAYSVILLE	011	5000	5637	6703	2.9	74	1809	2054	2455	3.0	2.74	1420	1593	2.7
30559 MINERAL BLUFF	111	3502	4602	6292	6.6	97	1431	1914	2660	7.1	2.40	1041	1370	6.7
30560 MORGANTON	111	3617	4448	5876	5.0	92	1516	1898	2551	5.4	2.34	1127	1391	5.1
30563 MOUNT AIRY	137	4104	4770	5643	3.6	83	1543	1805	2147	3.8	2.64	1200	1386	3.5
30564 MURRAYVILLE	139	3596	4139	5005	3.4	80	1326	1528	1846	3.4	2.71	1038	1179	3.0
30565 NICHOLSON	157	4213	4791	5845	3.1	77	1521	1731	2115	3.1	2.77	1188	1335	2.8
30566 OAKWOOD	139	6851	7723	9237	2.9	74	2402	2686	3180	2.7	2.87	1831	2027	2.4
GEORGIA					2.4					2.5	2.64			2.2
UNITED STATES					1.2					1.3	2.58			1.1

ZIP CODE #	POST OFFICE NAME	RACE (%) White 2000	White 2004	Black 2000	Black 2004	Asian/Pacific 2000	Asian/Pacific 2004	% Hispanic Origin 2000	% Hispanic Origin 2004	2004 AGE DISTRIBUTION (%) 0-4	5-9	10-14	15-19	20-24	25-44	45-64	65-84	85+	18+	MEDIAN AGE 2004	% 2004 Males	% 2004 Females
30339	ATLANTA	77.6	74.1	13.5	15.3	5.7	6.7	3.9	5.1	3.3	2.1	2.0	2.8	14.9	53.3	16.3	4.9	0.4	91.0	30.8	50.7	49.3
30340	ATLANTA	49.9	46.8	22.3	22.7	12.6	13.1	27.4	31.9	7.1	6.3	6.2	6.5	9.9	37.5	19.0	7.1	0.5	76.8	31.8	52.5	47.5
30341	ATLANTA	58.2	55.8	9.6	9.7	12.1	12.3	32.7	37.0	6.7	5.3	4.7	5.9	10.5	38.8	18.7	8.6	0.9	80.3	32.7	55.5	44.5
30342	ATLANTA	78.1	72.3	7.0	9.8	2.3	2.5	17.2	21.5	5.9	5.0	4.5	4.7	10.5	40.0	19.8	8.1	1.5	81.9	33.1	51.6	48.5
30344	ATLANTA	16.5	12.1	77.7	82.2	0.7	0.6	7.7	7.8	8.3	7.6	8.3	8.0	8.5	29.1	21.7	7.4	1.1	71.1	31.2	47.1	52.9
30345	ATLANTA	68.4	65.9	11.8	11.6	5.1	5.6	24.4	28.5	6.4	5.7	4.9	6.0	8.4	33.3	22.0	11.9	1.5	79.9	36.1	54.3	45.7
30346	ATLANTA	78.0	74.7	8.5	9.4	10.6	12.4	3.4	4.6	3.7	3.3	2.4	2.9	13.2	50.0	17.5	4.9	2.2	89.6	31.5	50.1	49.9
30349	ATLANTA	8.7	6.7	86.3	88.0	2.1	2.4	2.3	2.4	8.0	7.3	7.9	7.5	9.2	33.7	21.1	4.7	0.6	72.3	30.3	46.7	53.3
30350	ATLANTA	72.0	64.8	17.7	23.6	4.5	4.8	7.2	8.9	5.2	4.7	4.6	4.6	9.8	42.7	21.6	6.0	0.9	82.8	32.9	48.8	51.2
30354	ATLANTA	21.1	17.7	70.0	73.1	3.3	3.1	10.0	10.9	8.9	8.4	9.1	8.2	9.1	29.8	20.1	5.6	0.8	68.6	28.8	47.7	52.3
30360	ATLANTA	55.5	51.6	21.9	22.1	6.0	6.6	25.3	30.7	6.8	5.8	5.0	5.1	10.3	41.4	19.1	6.2	0.4	79.7	32.0	53.5	46.5
30401	SWAINSBORO	61.1	57.7	36.1	38.9	0.3	0.3	3.2	4.0	7.4	6.9	7.0	8.3	7.2	26.1	24.0	11.3	1.9	73.3	35.0	47.1	52.9
30410	AILEY	75.0	72.1	22.2	24.6	0.0	0.0	2.2	2.7	7.8	7.6	7.8	7.1	7.1	29.0	23.3	9.4	0.9	72.7	35.1	47.9	52.1
30411	ALAMO	60.5	59.4	38.4	39.4	0.1	0.1	2.2	2.2	5.4	5.4	5.7	5.8	8.5	35.5	23.4	8.9	1.4	80.3	35.9	60.8	39.2
30413	BARTOW	42.3	40.0	56.1	58.4	0.2	0.2	1.7	1.7	7.3	6.7	7.3	7.0	6.5	27.2	24.8	11.6	1.7	74.3	37.3	47.4	52.6
30415	BROOKLET	85.1	82.7	13.7	15.8	0.2	0.3	1.1	1.4	7.1	7.0	7.7	7.4	6.9	29.3	24.4	9.4	0.8	73.7	35.5	49.4	50.6
30417	CLAXTON	60.7	57.5	33.9	35.9	0.4	0.4	6.0	7.3	7.1	6.9	7.4	7.5	7.6	29.1	22.2	10.6	1.8	74.0	34.4	49.1	50.9
30420	COBBTOWN	77.0	73.7	11.6	12.5	0.1	0.1	12.8	15.6	7.1	6.5	6.0	6.0	6.5	27.3	23.8	15.1	1.8	76.9	38.0	50.7	49.3
30421	COLLINS	66.8	63.7	28.5	30.6	0.1	0.1	4.5	5.6	7.3	7.1	6.7	6.4	6.0	25.5	24.8	14.6	1.6	74.8	38.1	48.9	51.1
30425	GARFIELD	72.6	69.8	26.0	28.4	0.1	0.1	1.9	2.3	6.8	7.0	8.4	7.4	6.2	26.2	23.7	13.0	1.4	73.3	36.8	48.9	51.1
30426	GIRARD	44.4	41.4	54.2	57.0	0.6	0.7	1.5	1.8	7.9	8.6	8.5	7.0	6.1	27.9	22.8	10.2	1.0	70.7	34.3	50.6	49.4
30427	GLENNVILLE	64.1	60.8	29.9	32.0	0.6	0.6	6.2	7.6	6.4	6.1	6.3	6.7	8.4	32.1	21.5	10.7	1.9	77.2	34.9	54.7	45.4
30428	GLENWOOD	73.1	72.2	22.9	23.8	0.2	0.2	5.4	5.5	7.2	6.9	6.1	6.7	6.5	25.4	26.2	12.5	2.6	75.4	38.5	49.1	50.9
30434	LOUISVILLE	36.4	34.5	62.5	64.5	0.3	0.3	1.0	1.0	6.9	6.9	7.9	7.7	6.9	27.2	22.9	11.7	2.0	73.5	35.7	47.3	52.7
30436	LYONS	72.1	68.9	18.6	19.9	0.2	0.3	14.0	17.1	8.4	7.5	7.5	7.7	7.7	27.7	22.5	9.9	1.2	72.0	33.2	49.7	50.3
30438	MANASSAS	61.4	57.1	27.0	28.9	0.1	0.1	11.4	14.0	7.3	6.9	6.7	6.7	7.6	30.4	23.2	10.0	1.1	75.1	34.7	51.6	48.4
30439	METTER	65.4	62.2	27.3	28.9	0.3	0.4	9.1	11.1	7.2	7.0	7.4	7.2	6.5	26.3	23.4	12.5	2.4	74.0	36.2	50.5	49.5
30441	MIDVILLE	44.0	41.3	54.5	57.0	0.1	0.1	0.9	1.1	6.2	7.0	7.3	7.8	7.1	23.5	26.6	12.2	2.2	74.7	38.1	47.5	52.5
30442	MILLEN	54.2	52.7	42.8	44.4	0.3	0.3	3.1	3.1	7.3	7.2	8.1	7.2	7.1	25.6	24.2	11.7	1.7	73.1	35.9	48.2	51.8
30445	MOUNT VERNON	57.5	54.1	40.6	43.5	0.5	0.6	1.9	2.4	6.8	6.0	5.9	8.3	12.8	32.3	19.2	7.7	1.1	78.0	30.1	54.5	45.5
30446	NEWINGTON	51.7	48.5	46.4	49.4	0.4	0.4	1.7	2.0	6.7	7.0	8.3	7.5	6.0	26.0	24.6	12.8	1.2	73.4	37.1	49.1	50.9
30450	PORTAL	64.2	60.3	33.7	37.3	0.1	0.1	4.4	5.4	8.1	7.3	8.0	7.4	6.7	28.7	22.6	10.2	1.1	72.2	33.6	50.6	49.4
30452	REGISTER	68.4	65.5	28.3	30.4	0.1	0.2	3.6	4.6	7.6	7.6	8.7	6.8	6.6	30.4	22.5	8.9	0.9	71.9	33.2	50.2	49.8
30453	REIDSVILLE	51.5	47.9	39.0	40.5	0.3	0.4	10.1	12.3	5.6	5.3	5.6	5.9	10.3	40.6	19.4	6.5	0.9	80.4	32.9	64.9	35.1
30454	ROCKLEDGE	92.3	90.7	6.8	8.6	0.0	0.0	0.8	0.9	6.1	6.0	6.0	5.2	6.3	28.2	25.3	15.1	1.9	79.0	39.4	50.1	49.9
30455	ROCKY FORD	62.0	59.0	37.0	40.1	0.1	0.1	0.9	0.9	5.9	6.1	6.9	7.4	6.7	26.7	26.7	12.0	1.6	76.7	38.4	50.0	50.0
30456	SARDIS	51.6	48.7	47.7	50.6	0.1	0.1	0.9	1.0	9.2	9.2	9.4	7.2	6.3	25.4	22.3	9.8	1.3	67.8	31.9	47.3	52.7
30457	SOPERTON	65.6	63.0	33.1	35.6	0.3	0.3	1.2	1.4	7.3	7.3	6.7	7.5	7.7	26.9	23.4	11.6	1.6	74.8	34.7	50.1	49.9
30458	STATESBORO	62.1	59.2	34.7	37.1	1.2	1.3	2.2	2.7	5.1	4.6	5.0	16.0	22.6	22.5	15.7	7.3	1.3	82.7	24.3	48.7	51.3
30461	STATESBORO	76.4	73.3	21.7	24.3	0.7	0.9	1.1	1.5	7.3	6.7	7.7	7.5	8.1	29.9	22.4	9.3	1.2	73.8	33.8	48.6	51.4
30467	SYLVANIA	53.5	50.6	45.4	48.1	0.3	0.4	0.9	1.0	6.6	6.8	8.2	7.6	6.6	25.6	24.8	12.1	1.8	73.6	37.0	48.1	51.9
30470	TARRYTOWN	86.9	85.0	11.1	12.6	0.1	0.1	3.4	4.4	6.8	7.1	6.8	5.5	6.2	28.3	27.0	11.0	1.3	75.9	38.8	51.7	48.3
30471	TWIN CITY	61.1	57.4	35.8	38.9	0.2	0.2	3.5	4.3	6.0	6.5	7.3	7.9	8.0	28.1	23.8	11.2	1.3	75.6	35.5	52.3	47.7
30473	UVALDA	78.6	75.0	15.7	18.2	0.0	0.0	6.3	7.6	7.3	7.4	7.5	6.2	5.5	27.4	25.2	12.6	1.0	74.1	37.5	50.0	50.0
30474	VIDALIA	66.6	63.9	28.8	30.6	0.7	0.8	5.0	6.2	7.4	7.1	7.5	7.6	7.2	26.1	23.8	11.3	2.2	73.4	35.8	46.8	53.3
30477	WADLEY	31.7	30.3	66.1	67.5	0.1	0.1	2.4	2.3	7.5	7.1	7.9	7.7	7.1	25.8	22.4	12.1	2.6	72.9	35.2	46.3	53.7
30501	GAINESVILLE	66.7	63.6	12.5	12.5	1.7	1.9	40.0	46.7	8.8	7.4	6.2	6.7	10.2	32.2	17.0	9.7	1.7	74.2	30.3	52.2	47.8
30504	GAINESVILLE	70.6	66.5	5.3	5.5	4.8	5.1	34.8	41.9	8.2	7.4	6.9	6.6	9.1	32.7	20.1	8.2	1.0	73.9	31.3	52.3	47.7
30506	GAINESVILLE	94.5	92.9	1.0	1.1	0.5	0.6	6.7	9.5	7.3	7.4	6.9	5.9	5.3	30.2	26.3	9.9	1.0	74.8	37.1	50.4	49.6
30507	GAINESVILLE	70.4	66.2	15.6	16.4	1.4	1.7	22.0	28.3	9.2	8.5	7.7	6.5	7.3	32.8	20.0	7.1	1.0	70.7	31.3	50.9	49.1
30510	ALTO	79.5	76.6	14.4	15.7	1.7	2.1	5.8	7.7	6.7	6.6	5.9	8.7	10.1	32.5	21.0	7.8	0.7	76.4	32.1	58.4	41.6
30511	BALDWIN	91.4	90.1	2.1	2.2	1.5	1.6	12.9	15.7	7.5	6.8	6.3	6.2	7.0	28.3	24.6	11.2	2.2	76.0	36.1	50.8	49.2
30512	BLAIRSVILLE	97.9	97.6	0.6	0.7	0.3	0.3	0.9	1.2	5.0	5.2	5.7	5.0	4.8	23.0	28.9	20.2	2.3	81.2	46.0	49.2	50.8
30513	BLUE RIDGE	98.3	98.1	0.2	0.2	0.3	0.3	0.8	1.0	5.4	5.5	5.4	5.2	5.0	23.9	29.2	18.2	2.3	80.5	44.7	48.0	52.0
30516	BOWERSVILLE	90.3	88.8	8.0	9.2	0.3	0.3	0.8	1.1	7.1	7.3	7.3	6.2	5.4	28.7	25.4	11.5	1.3	74.6	37.5	50.0	50.0
30517	BRASELTON	93.1	91.6	2.9	3.4	1.5	1.7	3.4	4.7	8.1	7.8	7.5	6.5	5.9	33.1	23.3	7.2	0.7	72.6	34.6	51.1	48.9
30518	BUFORD	85.6	83.4	7.1	7.3	1.3	1.7	9.8	12.7	8.5	8.1	7.2	5.7	5.9	34.6	22.0	7.1	0.9	72.7	34.2	50.1	49.9
30519	BUFORD	89.7	87.6	5.7	6.5	1.4	1.8	4.8	6.6	8.4	8.1	7.7	6.3	6.0	34.7	22.5	5.9	0.4	71.8	34.0	51.3	48.7
30520	CANON	87.0	85.3	11.1	12.6	0.3	0.3	1.0	1.2	7.0	7.0	7.1	6.1	5.9	27.6	25.6	12.6	1.1	75.1	37.5	50.0	50.0
30521	CARNESVILLE	91.4	90.1	7.5	8.5	0.2	0.3	0.8	1.1	6.8	6.8	6.9	6.2	6.1	28.6	25.5	11.7	1.4	75.8	37.6	50.9	49.1
30522	CHERRYLOG	96.8	96.1	0.2	0.2	0.1	0.2	1.9	2.6	5.0	5.2	4.4	4.1	3.7	24.2	36.0	16.2	1.2	82.8	47.1	51.0	49.0
30523	CLARKESVILLE	95.7	94.5	1.3	1.6	0.3	0.4	3.4	4.8	5.9	5.9	6.1	6.1	5.5	25.8	27.8	15.3	1.6	78.5	41.5	49.2	50.8
30525	CLAYTON	94.0	92.7	0.8	0.9	0.5	0.6	5.5	7.1	5.8	6.0	6.0	4.9	4.7	25.8	28.2	16.7	2.0	79.2	42.8	49.9	50.1
30527	CLERMONT	97.1	96.1	0.5	0.6	0.3	0.4	2.2	3.3	7.2	7.5	7.8	6.5	5.5	29.2	25.2	10.1	1.1	73.5	36.5	49.8	50.2
30528	CLEVELAND	95.6	94.9	1.8	2.1	0.4	0.5	1.7	2.2	6.8	6.7	6.8	6.0	6.2	28.6	25.3	12.2	1.4	76.3	37.6	49.7	50.3
30529	COMMERCE	87.0	85.4	10.6	11.9	0.5	0.6	1.8	2.2	6.9	6.8	6.7	5.6	6.1	28.7	24.0	12.6	2.7	76.1	37.6	47.9	52.1
30530	COMMERCE	92.6	91.5	4.8	5.4	0.6	0.7	1.8	2.3	7.4	7.4	7.4	6.3	6.3	29.5	25.1	9.6	1.1	74.1	36.0	49.9	50.1
30531	CORNELIA	83.4	81.0	4.8	5.2	4.0	4.6	14.6	18.0	6.8	6.8	6.8	6.2	7.0	28.9	23.6	12.0	1.9	76.3	36.2	50.7	49.3
30533	DAHLONEGA	93.8	92.8	1.5	1.7	0.4	0.5	3.8	4.9	6.6	6.5	6.7	7.7	8.0	30.4	23.4	9.6	1.2	76.2	34.4	49.9	50.1
30534	DAWSONVILLE	97.2	96.6	0.4	0.4	0.4	0.4	1.7	2.2	7.1	7.2	7.0	5.8	5.2	31.2	26.4	9.4	0.6	75.5	37.3	50.2	49.9
30535	DEMOREST	94.9	93.5	1.3	1.6	1.6	2.0	2.9	4.2	6.0	6.1	6.2	7.6	7.7	26.5	25.7	12.4	1.8	78.2	38.3	49.2	50.8
30537	DILLARD	94.2	93.1	1.6	1.8	0.9	0.9	4.2	5.5	5.1	5.2	5.8	9.6	5.4	21.9	27.4	17.2	2.5	76.8	42.6	49.4	50.6
30538	EASTANOLLEE	94.9	94.0	3.6	4.3	0.1	0.2	0.7	0.9	7.0	7.2	7.8	6.6	5.8	29.2	24.5	10.6	1.4	74.0	36.8	50.6	49.4
30539	EAST ELLIJAY	86.5	83.1	0.2	0.1	1.2	1.4	15.0	19.3	6.9	6.7	6.1	5.3	6.4	29.6	21.4	14.3	3.3	77.2	37.6	50.0	50.0
30540	ELLIJAY	93.7	92.2	0.3	0.3	0.5	0.6	7.8	10.0	7.2	7.2	6.5	5.6	5.7	28.3	26.0	12.4	1.1	75.7	38.0	51.2	48.9
30541	EPWORTH	97.8	97.5	0.1	0.1	0.1	0.1	0.6	0.8	5.4	5.8	5.5	5.3	4.7	25.9	29.6	15.8	2.1	80.1	43.2	49.7	50.3
30542	FLOWERY BRANCH	90.1	88.0	5.2	5.9	0.8	1.1	6.5	8.9	8.9	8.3	7.3	6.0	5.7	34.5	22.4	6.4	0.5	71.8	33.8	50.2	49.8
30543	GILLSVILLE	86.3	83.0	6.0	6.9	0.7	0.8	11.2	15.6	8.3	8.0	7.5	7.0	6.5	31.1	22.5	8.4	0.8	72.1	33.8	50.7	49.3
30545	HELEN	88.2	86.9	7.2	7.8	3.5	4.3	1.2	1.3	4.7	4.9	5.1	4.3	3.5	23.5	32.4	19.8	1.8	82.7	47.4	48.9	51.1
30546	HIAWASSEE	98.8	98.6	0.0	0.0	0.3	0.4	0.9	1.1	4.5	4.6	4.6	3.9	3.5	20.5	29.7	25.4	3.3	83.9	51.5	48.4	51.6
30547	HOMER	92.7	91.7	4.8	5.3	0.2	0.2	2.0	2.5	7.3	7.3	6.9	6.2	6.4	28.6	26.1	10.3	0.9	74.7	36.6	51.7	48.3
30548	HOSCHTON	93.4	92.3	2.7	3.0	1.6	1.9	3.5	4.5	7.7	7.6	7.8	6.6	5.8	32.8	23.7	7.4	0.7	72.9	35.0	51.5	48.5
30549	JEFFERSON	85.5	83.6	11.5	12.7	1.1	1.3	3.0	3.8	7.2	7.2	7.5	6.2	6.4	31.7	24.0	8.8	1.0	74.3	35.6	51.2	48.8
30552	LAKEMONT	97.1	96.4	0.3	0.3	0.0	0.0	2.8	3.7	6.2	6.4	6.0	5.3	5.2	25.3	30.2	14.2	1.1	78.2	41.9	50.5	49.5
30553	LAVONIA	85.8	84.3	12.3	13.4	0.2	0.2	1.1	1.4	6.0	5.8	6.3	5.7	5.2	24.9	28.6	16.2	1.4	78.6	42.4	47.9	52.1
30554	LULA	95.1	93.8	2.5	3.2	0.5	0.6	2.6	3.6	7.5	7.4	7.1	6.4	5.8	31.1	23.9	9.9	0.9	74.1	35.3	49.7	50.3
30555	MC CAYSVILLE	97.5	97.2	0.1	0.0	0.4	0.5	0.9	1.2	6.1	6.2	6.4	5.9	5.0	24.6	25.2	18.2	2.5	77.7	41.9	46.9	53.1
30557	MARTIN	88.9	87.1	9.9	11.4	0.3	0.4	0.9	1.1	6.0	6.3	6.9	6.8	5.9	27.5	27.5	11.9	1.2	76.7	38.9	50.2	49.9
30558	MAYSVILLE	93.3	92.1	3.4	3.9	0.5	0.5	2.6	3.3	7.3	7.2	7.3	6.9	6.3	29.8	24.8	9.5	0.9	73.9	36.1	50.6	49.4
30559	MINERAL BLUFF	97.4	96.9	0.1	0.1	0.1	0.2	0.5	0.7	5.2	5.3	5.9	5.6	5.0	26.0	28.7	16.8	1.5	80.0	43.0	49.3	50.7
30560	MORGANTON	98.2	97.9	0.2	0.2	0.3	0.4	0.5	0.6	5.2	5.5	5.7	5.3	4.6	23.8	31.5	16.8	1.6	80.3	44.9	49.0	51.0
30563	MOUNT AIRY	92.4	90.6	1.1	1.1	2.0	2.5	5.4	7.3	6.8	6.8	6.7	5.9	5.8	28.8	26.1	12.1	1.2	76.3	38.0	50.5	49.5
30564	MURRAYVILLE	96.8	95.8	0.6	0.8	0.4	0.5	2.2	3.2	7.1	7.3	7.7	6.5	5.4	30.1	25.3	9.9	0.9	74.0	36.5	49.9	50.1
30565	NICHOLSON	93.5	92.4	3.2	3.7	0.2	0.3	3.6	4.4	8.2	8.0	7.7	6.8	6.0	31.6	23.0	8.0	0.9	72.0	34.1	51.1	49.0
30566	OAKWOOD	82.7	79.4	5.7	6.3	2.2	2.5	15.9	20.8	7.1	7.0	7.1	6.9	7.6	31.1	23.8	8.6	0.8	74.8	34.2	50.4	49.6
	GEORGIA	65.1	63.4	28.7	29.4	2.2	2.5	5.3	6.6	7.3	7.1	7.2	7.0	7.6	31.0	23.0	8.6	1.1	74.3	34.2	49.3	50.7
	UNITED STATES	75.1	73.6	12.3	12.5	3.8	4.2	12.5	14.1	6.9	6.7	7.2	7.0	7.3	28.6	23.8	10.8	1.7	75.1	36.0	49.1	50.9

ZIP CODE #	POST OFFICE NAME	2004 Per Capita Income	2004 HH Income Base	2004 HOUSEHOLD INCOME DISTRIBUTION (%) Less than $25,000	$25,000 to $49,999	$50,000 to $99,999	$100,000 to $149,999	$150,000 or More	MEDIAN HOUSEHOLD INCOME 2004	2009	2004 National Centile	2004 State Centile	2004 Home Value Base	2004 HOME VALUE DISTRIBUTION (%) Less than $50,000	$50,000 to $89,999	$90,000 to $174,999	$175,000 to $399,999	$400,000 or More	2004 Median Home Value
30339	ATLANTA	55344	8588	11.4	20.4	39.9	15.6	12.8	67844	88930	90	91	1635	1.9	1.7	10.8	41.0	44.7	364549
30340	ATLANTA	22715	10870	18.9	33.2	32.4	10.4	5.0	48143	57453	69	72	4945	1.5	10.6	53.2	33.2	1.4	151499
30341	ATLANTA	29430	12987	16.3	24.3	33.4	15.7	10.4	60714	77036	85	86	5837	1.1	3.5	27.1	61.9	6.4	217049
30342	ATLANTA	58319	12297	10.2	18.4	29.7	18.1	23.6	82013	123129	96	97	5859	0.1	1.5	10.8	41.7	46.0	381115
30344	ATLANTA	18440	14029	31.2	33.7	25.5	7.0	2.6	37501	47443	37	44	6593	3.9	29.4	58.4	7.8	0.4	103442
30345	ATLANTA	37339	8548	11.9	19.1	33.3	18.2	17.6	74345	96797	93	94	5392	0.7	0.7	9.4	68.9	20.3	294824
30346	ATLANTA	55442	1077	11.5	15.3	38.1	23.9	11.2	75168	103544	93	94	224	0.0	0.5	0.9	57.1	41.5	372059
30349	ATLANTA	21380	22845	20.8	35.2	32.5	8.7	2.8	45056	53549	61	65	10811	2.5	14.3	74.8	7.5	0.9	114653
30350	ATLANTA	51481	15790	11.5	25.1	34.5	12.8	16.1	63896	86062	88	89	5328	0.4	5.5	24.6	19.9	49.8	397909
30354	ATLANTA	14723	6193	37.3	33.5	23.0	4.8	1.3	32454	40968	19	23	2556	6.6	51.6	38.4	2.9	0.6	84583
30360	ATLANTA	29938	7136	15.1	28.5	32.7	14.1	9.6	57309	68067	82	83	3037	0.2	3.1	33.1	51.5	12.2	219467
30401	SWAINSBORO	17812	5253	46.1	25.6	19.6	6.0	2.8	28684	34165	10	10	3604	37.0	36.2	19.2	7.0	0.6	61979
30410	AILEY	17039	453	35.1	32.0	24.7	6.6	1.6	35579	41510	30	36	365	42.7	19.2	26.9	11.2	0.0	65323
30411	ALAMO	17522	1211	42.2	29.5	19.0	7.2	2.2	30321	36117	13	14	973	41.1	33.1	19.8	4.2	1.8	62368
30413	BARTOW	14975	597	40.5	31.0	23.0	4.0	1.5	30433	34775	13	15	485	41.4	27.4	20.8	8.9	1.4	58469
30415	BROOKLET	21256	2366	21.3	36.2	30.6	8.7	3.2	44126	52959	59	63	1941	25.7	28.9	31.2	12.5	1.8	84290
30417	CLAXTON	15205	3944	45.2	30.7	19.4	2.9	1.9	28004	31481	9	8	2934	37.6	29.9	23.3	7.3	1.9	67005
30420	COBBTOWN	15224	705	44.1	31.4	19.9	3.8	0.9	28770	33007	10	10	560	40.0	33.9	22.1	3.2	0.7	61194
30421	COLLINS	14773	749	48.5	29.2	17.9	3.2	1.2	26366	30684	6	5	601	45.8	33.6	17.5	3.0	0.2	55426
30425	GARFIELD	16669	516	45.5	24.6	22.7	3.7	3.5	28697	34553	10	10	420	38.1	26.0	25.0	6.2	4.8	66286
30426	GIRARD	13357	404	43.3	34.4	19.1	3.2	0.0	29103	33233	11	11	354	51.7	26.0	13.6	3.7	5.1	48421
30427	GLENNVILLE	17602	3385	37.1	25.8	28.8	6.0	2.3	35879	41377	31	38	2508	33.6	27.2	32.3	6.4	0.6	71053
30428	GLENWOOD	17904	1015	48.9	26.1	20.5	2.4	2.2	25663	29261	5	4	800	45.3	31.6	18.1	4.8	0.3	55205
30434	LOUISVILLE	17405	2365	45.5	25.0	21.8	3.5	4.2	29767	34739	12	13	1735	47.1	22.5	25.8	4.1	0.5	55316
30436	LYONS	15233	4313	44.6	26.9	21.3	5.2	2.0	29009	33926	10	11	3049	45.2	27.3	19.5	7.5	0.6	55347
30438	MANASSAS	16470	387	35.9	36.4	20.9	4.9	1.8	35801	41100	31	37	316	38.6	32.6	19.6	6.3	2.9	63590
30439	METTER	15038	3495	45.2	26.4	22.2	4.9	1.3	29126	33256	11	11	2708	39.2	28.8	24.0	6.5	1.6	60803
30441	MIDVILLE	14529	630	46.8	31.3	15.9	3.3	2.7	27594	32709	8	7	505	47.1	29.5	16.6	4.0	2.8	52900
30442	MILLEN	16269	2864	48.1	24.0	19.3	6.2	2.5	26335	31013	6	4	2184	44.7	28.4	19.1	6.6	1.3	56138
30445	MOUNT VERNON	17225	1063	40.3	28.6	21.4	5.7	4.1	32872	38495	21	25	761	42.2	28.1	23.7	4.1	2.0	62778
30446	NEWINGTON	14557	687	41.5	30.6	25.0	2.6	0.3	30737	34335	14	15	559	36.5	30.6	23.8	6.8	2.3	66944
30450	PORTAL	17117	1122	36.5	31.4	21.9	7.7	2.5	34014	40175	24	29	887	36.9	25.4	24.9	10.3	2.6	71032
30452	REGISTER	15612	747	32.4	33.2	27.4	5.2	1.7	36161	42545	32	39	602	40.2	21.9	27.7	9.3	0.8	67742
30453	REIDSVILLE	16607	2244	40.9	31.1	21.2	5.4	1.4	30965	36244	15	16	1619	35.2	35.8	23.8	4.3	0.9	65565
30454	ROCKLEDGE	19868	336	36.9	38.1	17.6	5.1	2.4	34291	39756	25	31	286	43.4	28.0	24.5	2.1	2.1	62593
30455	ROCKY FORD	17348	302	32.8	33.4	28.7	3.6	2.0	35000	39465	28	34	255	43.9	29.4	21.2	5.5	0.0	57045
30456	SARDIS	13954	742	41.1	28.7	25.5	3.6	1.1	31011	36222	15	17	591	47.4	35.9	13.9	2.0	0.9	53523
30457	SOPERTON	16630	2624	46.2	28.4	19.8	3.4	2.3	28239	32844	9	9	2037	48.0	26.2	19.6	5.8	0.4	54611
30458	STATESBORO	19662	13308	45.8	24.2	19.5	6.8	3.7	28132	33337	9	8	6485	21.5	19.1	39.3	17.7	2.4	106739
30461	STATESBORO	25563	4328	28.8	29.7	29.0	8.6	4.0	42401	52261	54	59	3150	14.1	22.0	40.7	21.4	1.8	110781
30467	SYLVANIA	16964	5132	38.0	32.9	23.6	3.0	2.5	32713	37077	20	24	4002	38.8	28.5	26.2	5.8	0.8	65377
30470	TARRYTOWN	19284	577	32.2	34.8	22.7	8.8	1.4	37838	44007	39	45	471	38.6	14.9	33.3	9.1	4.0	80294
30471	TWIN CITY	14687	1550	43.7	28.7	21.7	4.6	1.4	29071	34078	10	11	1247	45.1	31.0	17.8	4.5	1.6	55591
30473	UVALDA	17484	1166	38.0	31.1	23.5	4.7	2.7	33511	39374	22	27	985	45.7	27.6	20.7	6.0	0.0	54570
30474	VIDALIA	18736	6030	38.5	27.1	24.3	7.3	2.8	33895	40543	24	29	3968	29.4	29.5	32.6	7.9	0.6	81083
30477	WADLEY	14704	1178	51.4	28.3	16.2	2.0	2.2	23890	27069	4	3	860	58.4	24.0	11.9	5.6	0.2	43898
30501	GAINESVILLE	19826	10550	31.6	29.5	24.8	8.5	5.6	40163	47781	47	51	5010	6.3	16.3	43.8	24.8	8.8	141374
30504	GAINESVILLE	23100	5932	21.7	28.2	31.0	12.0	7.3	50224	59531	72	75	3581	5.9	11.1	52.8	22.4	7.8	136977
30506	GAINESVILLE	29760	14101	16.4	24.1	37.1	14.3	8.1	59734	72836	84	85	12036	6.6	8.0	38.8	33.6	13.0	167643
30507	GAINESVILLE	19278	7734	21.6	32.3	33.7	8.3	4.2	47000	53703	66	70	5973	12.8	14.3	51.9	18.4	2.8	119022
30510	ALTO	20241	2301	25.6	37.5	28.8	5.7	2.4	41232	46708	51	56	1849	21.4	23.3	39.8	13.5	2.0	96588
30511	BALDWIN	19326	1408	27.6	33.2	31.0	4.6	3.7	42498	47985	55	59	1107	19.3	26.3	35.6	15.4	3.4	96063
30512	BLAIRSVILLE	21139	8011	33.3	31.7	26.4	5.4	3.2	36425	42988	33	41	6689	8.8	16.4	41.8	27.9	5.2	135890
30513	BLUE RIDGE	20308	4773	35.8	34.8	21.9	4.6	3.0	34799	39568	27	33	3859	16.5	23.4	35.3	21.7	3.2	106276
30516	BOWERSVILLE	17471	808	33.8	33.7	26.9	4.3	1.4	35453	41647	29	36	682	19.2	30.2	30.4	16.3	4.0	91176
30517	BRASELTON	26808	2445	17.6	23.3	38.7	14.4	6.1	59420	69061	84	84	2124	9.5	8.6	42.4	34.0	5.6	153320
30518	BUFORD	27220	13402	15.2	25.3	38.7	14.5	6.3	61040	73135	85	87	10833	11.5	6.9	40.2	36.9	4.5	162378
30519	BUFORD	29815	8292	8.0	17.0	45.1	20.0	9.9	76438	88785	94	95	7700	4.4	3.0	38.0	48.1	6.5	181644
30520	CANON	17007	1577	38.9	30.5	23.8	4.8	1.9	31946	36680	18	20	1297	25.4	27.7	32.9	11.7	2.4	85063
30521	CARNESVILLE	18748	1810	29.5	34.8	29.8	3.0	2.9	40000	45470	46	51	1531	18.8	32.1	30.2	15.1	3.9	88875
30522	CHERRYLOG	25979	729	24.3	33.1	31.1	8.9	2.6	43940	51366	58	63	641	12.5	17.6	33.5	30.1	6.2	142763
30523	CLARKESVILLE	23050	5153	29.2	29.6	29.1	7.8	4.4	41666	48379	52	56	4210	9.1	17.1	42.7	24.8	6.4	127100
30525	CLAYTON	24666	3790	29.9	32.0	27.2	6.1	4.8	39771	47664	45	51	3023	14.3	18.1	37.4	21.4	8.8	120016
30527	CLERMONT	23674	1352	19.8	29.4	34.7	10.0	6.2	50623	59209	73	76	1157	7.1	13.2	42.3	27.1	10.4	151380
30528	CLEVELAND	19175	7302	26.8	35.9	29.8	5.5	1.9	40147	45307	47	51	5963	11.3	15.2	46.3	24.7	2.5	126202
30529	COMMERCE	22620	4052	31.0	30.3	26.6	7.4	4.8	40331	47361	47	52	2987	18.5	24.0	38.1	16.0	3.4	100952
30530	COMMERCE	19090	2078	29.5	31.3	30.9	5.5	2.8	40875	46560	49	55	1708	18.0	26.9	37.1	14.8	3.2	97521
30531	CORNELIA	20981	3910	30.5	31.7	27.9	6.5	3.5	40207	46398	47	51	2943	17.8	20.9	41.2	15.8	4.3	106573
30533	DAHLONEGA	22835	8026	27.7	28.1	31.9	8.9	3.4	44282	51884	59	64	6090	11.3	14.7	43.4	24.6	6.2	131662
30534	DAWSONVILLE	27728	8320	18.4	26.6	36.7	12.8	5.6	54136	63670	79	80	7005	7.0	12.4	35.8	33.2	11.6	163736
30535	DEMOREST	20630	2556	29.0	32.8	27.7	8.0	2.5	41203	47186	50	55	2003	14.1	24.9	39.0	20.7	1.4	106307
30537	DILLARD	29804	362	30.7	32.9	24.0	6.1	6.4	37320	43943	37	43	295	10.5	20.7	39.7	25.1	4.1	125962
30538	EASTANOLLEE	16729	660	35.5	33.3	24.7	5.0	1.5	33887	39344	24	29	556	29.9	33.1	25.9	9.2	2.0	73542
30539	EAST ELLIJAY	18539	263	27.4	33.8	32.7	4.9	1.1	43145	48817	56	61	194	11.3	15.5	52.1	20.1	1.0	119079
30540	ELLIJAY	20099	9271	30.5	33.2	27.2	6.0	3.2	38605	44054	41	47	7498	20.4	20.4	38.3	18.2	2.7	106463
30541	EPWORTH	19210	787	25.5	39.4	28.1	4.8	2.2	40270	45200	47	52	682	17.7	28.3	28.0	22.6	3.4	103226
30542	FLOWERY BRANCH	26316	8936	12.7	25.2	40.5	15.8	5.8	61994	74370	86	88	7620	8.4	9.1	47.4	29.6	5.5	152300
30543	GILLSVILLE	20879	1331	19.8	32.7	37.5	7.1	2.9	48650	55673	70	73	1111	9.2	23.0	51.0	13.5	3.3	108480
30545	HELEN	28372	375	29.6	31.7	25.9	6.4	6.4	40685	46519	49	53	293	5.1	14.7	35.2	33.1	12.0	162917
30546	HIAWASSEE	23194	3139	35.1	30.2	23.0	8.2	3.5	35854	41458	31	38	2667	16.1	10.6	33.6	31.4	8.4	140563
30547	HOMER	21618	1053	27.6	33.8	27.7	7.7	3.2	40967	46396	50	55	856	16.6	25.4	35.3	18.8	4.0	100000
30548	HOSCHTON	26678	2635	18.1	25.5	37.4	12.9	6.2	56594	65043	81	82	2248	10.8	8.7	41.4	31.4	7.7	153646
30549	JEFFERSON	20692	5398	26.9	27.0	33.7	8.7	3.7	47049	54450	66	70	4302	13.4	20.3	38.8	22.1	5.3	117687
30552	LAKEMONT	24075	711	27.3	38.5	25.3	3.7	5.2	35624	42710	30	37	598	18.6	19.4	35.3	17.4	9.4	109247
30553	LAVONIA	19874	2928	34.6	32.7	24.8	4.9	3.0	36233	42549	32	40	2296	19.8	22.3	33.5	21.1	3.4	102914
30554	LULA	21283	2655	22.1	31.8	35.2	7.0	3.9	47522	54685	67	71	2176	14.6	21.3	42.0	16.3	5.7	111201
30555	MC CAYSVILLE	15518	1187	46.9	30.8	18.9	3.0	0.5	27002	29806	7	5	926	16.4	35.2	33.6	12.6	2.2	88052
30557	MARTIN	18285	2196	33.3	33.1	25.8	5.7	2.1	35685	41655	30	37	1841	20.6	28.6	34.9	13.5	2.3	91133
30558	MAYSVILLE	21979	2054	25.5	33.6	30.2	6.6	4.1	43388	49258	57	61	1694	16.1	23.0	39.6	16.5	4.9	104766
30559	MINERAL BLUFF	17823	1914	38.4	36.3	18.7	3.3	3.3	31524	35380	16	19	1643	22.4	24.4	36.3	15.8	1.1	95899
30560	MORGANTON	19222	1898	33.6	33.3	27.1	4.9	1.2	35666	40133	30	37	1634	18.4	20.0	39.6	17.9	4.2	106194
30563	MOUNT AIRY	22627	1805	26.4	29.8	31.9	7.6	4.3	44260	50851	59	64	1501	13.3	20.6	38.7	24.1	3.3	117849
30564	MURRAYVILLE	24191	1528	19.6	27.2	38.2	9.1	5.9	53275	62295	77	79	1285	12.4	14.1	36.0	28.3	9.3	144929
30565	NICHOLSON	20910	1731	23.3	31.0	34.1	8.7	3.0	46473	53557	65	69	1431	17.5	26.6	34.4	19.7	1.8	102704
30566	OAKWOOD	22185	2686	17.6	27.8	38.3	13.0	3.4	54897	64465	80	81	1828	4.5	8.3	56.3	26.5	4.4	147467
	GEORGIA	26143		23.6	26.3	31.4	11.6	7.0	50024	60470				12.5	17.5	39.3	24.8	6.0	125860
	UNITED STATES	25866		24.7	27.1	30.8	10.9	6.5	48124	56710				10.9	15.0	33.7	30.1	10.4	145905

SPENDING POTENTIAL INDICES

GEORGIA

30339-30566 D

#	POST OFFICE NAME	FINANCIAL SERVICES: Auto Loan	FINANCIAL SERVICES: Home Loan	FINANCIAL SERVICES: Investments	FINANCIAL SERVICES: Retirement Plans	THE HOME: Home Improvements: Home Repair	THE HOME: Home Improvements: Lawn & Garden	THE HOME: Furnishings: Computers & Hardware	THE HOME: Furnishings: Major Appliances	THE HOME: Furnishings: TV, Radio, Sound Equipment	THE HOME: Furnishings: Furniture	ENTERTAINMENT: Dine out/Carry out	ENTERTAINMENT: Sports Equipment	ENTERTAINMENT: Fees & Tickets	ENTERTAINMENT: Toys & Games	ENTERTAINMENT: Travel	ENTERTAINMENT: Cable TV	PERSONAL: Apparel & Services	PERSONAL: Auto Repairs	PERSONAL: Health Insurance	PERSONAL: Pets & Supplies
30339	ATLANTA	122	116	218	134	110	123	138	122	141	140	179	150	143	188	135	140	178	131	114	136
30340	ATLANTA	86	84	97	86	81	86	89	86	88	91	111	100	88	109	85	84	110	89	79	94
30341	ATLANTA	103	111	141	111	107	114	113	109	111	115	141	126	116	144	112	109	140	112	100	118
30342	ATLANTA	170	169	278	188	162	178	189	172	189	192	240	208	196	247	186	185	238	181	159	191
30344	ATLANTA	68	63	74	61	62	71	69	67	73	69	91	75	70	89	68	74	89	69	70	76
30345	ATLANTA	134	141	163	143	138	145	142	139	138	145	175	161	144	175	140	134	174	142	128	151
30346	ATLANTA	120	115	216	132	108	121	135	120	139	138	177	148	141	185	133	138	175	129	112	134
30349	ATLANTA	80	76	85	79	73	79	81	78	81	82	102	93	80	98	78	77	99	82	73	88
30350	ATLANTA	148	139	179	152	134	144	154	145	150	156	191	175	152	184	146	143	187	153	132	161
30354	ATLANTA	57	53	63	51	52	58	59	57	62	59	78	65	59	77	58	63	76	59	58	64
30360	ATLANTA	108	101	122	109	97	103	111	105	108	113	138	127	109	131	105	102	135	111	94	117
30401	SWAINSBORO	78	58	40	53	62	72	60	68	68	60	81	78	54	77	59	72	75	68	79	87
30410	AILEY	72	63	47	60	64	68	60	66	62	62	76	76	56	72	60	62	73	65	67	80
30411	ALAMO	59	42	28	36	45	54	43	50	51	44	60	58	38	56	43	55	56	50	61	67
30413	BARTOW	73	49	23	42	55	64	47	59	57	48	67	70	41	63	48	62	61	58	73	83
30415	BROOKLET	94	85	66	82	85	90	81	87	82	83	101	101	77	96	80	81	97	87	87	104
30417	CLAXTON	67	51	34	46	54	62	51	58	58	52	69	68	46	65	51	61	65	59	67	75
30420	COBBTOWN	68	47	24	42	53	61	47	57	56	47	66	67	41	62	48	60	60	56	70	77
30421	COLLINS	65	45	23	40	50	58	45	54	53	45	62	64	39	58	45	56	56	54	65	74
30425	GARFIELD	80	54	25	47	61	70	52	65	63	53	73	78	44	69	53	67	67	64	80	92
30426	GIRARD	67	45	20	39	51	59	43	54	52	44	61	65	37	58	44	56	56	54	67	77
30427	GLENNVILLE	67	57	43	54	58	64	56	61	60	57	72	70	52	68	55	61	69	61	65	75
30428	GLENWOOD	83	56	25	48	63	73	54	67	65	55	76	80	46	72	55	70	69	67	83	96
30434	LOUISVILLE	79	56	38	49	61	72	58	67	69	59	81	78	52	75	58	74	75	68	82	90
30436	LYONS	67	52	37	48	55	62	53	59	59	53	71	69	48	68	52	61	66	59	67	76
30438	MANASSAS	69	62	48	60	63	67	60	64	61	61	75	74	56	71	59	60	72	64	65	76
30439	METTER	72	53	34	47	57	66	52	61	60	53	72	71	47	68	53	64	67	61	72	81
30441	MIDVILLE	72	48	22	42	55	63	47	58	56	47	66	70	40	62	47	61	60	58	72	83
30442	MILLEN	77	53	29	46	59	69	53	64	63	53	74	75	46	69	53	67	68	63	78	87
30445	MOUNT VERNON	82	58	32	52	64	75	60	70	69	59	81	81	52	77	60	74	74	69	85	92
30446	NEWINGTON	70	47	21	40	53	61	45	57	55	46	64	68	38	61	46	59	58	56	70	80
30450	PORTAL	87	59	28	52	67	77	57	71	68	58	80	85	49	76	58	73	73	70	87	101
30452	REGISTER	71	65	50	62	65	68	62	66	62	63	77	76	58	73	61	62	74	66	66	79
30453	REIDSVILLE	67	59	45	57	60	64	58	62	59	59	73	71	54	68	57	59	69	62	63	74
30454	ROCKLEDGE	83	61	35	55	67	75	59	70	67	60	80	83	52	76	59	70	74	69	81	94
30455	ROCKY FORD	83	56	25	48	63	72	54	67	65	55	76	80	46	72	55	70	69	66	83	95
30456	SARDIS	74	49	22	43	56	64	48	60	58	49	68	71	41	64	48	62	61	59	73	85
30457	SOPERTON	75	53	32	47	59	68	53	63	62	54	73	74	47	69	53	66	67	63	76	86
30458	STATESBORO	70	56	61	58	56	63	72	65	72	68	90	80	65	84	65	69	86	71	64	75
30461	STATESBORO	98	93	90	93	93	97	93	95	93	94	115	112	90	112	91	90	112	96	92	110
30467	SYLVANIA	80	55	29	49	62	71	54	66	64	55	76	78	47	71	55	69	70	66	80	91
30470	TARRYTOWN	79	63	40	58	66	73	60	69	66	61	79	81	54	75	60	68	74	69	76	90
30471	TWIN CITY	75	50	23	43	57	66	49	61	59	50	69	73	41	65	49	63	63	60	75	86
30473	UVALDA	85	57	26	49	64	74	55	68	66	56	77	82	46	73	56	71	70	68	84	97
30474	VIDALIA	69	65	63	63	65	71	66	67	68	66	83	78	64	81	65	68	80	68	70	78
30477	WADLEY	63	46	35	40	49	58	48	55	57	49	68	62	44	62	48	61	63	55	66	71
30501	GAINESVILLE	86	79	80	78	79	85	85	85	87	86	109	98	82	107	82	85	106	87	84	94
30504	GAINESVILLE	102	95	95	96	94	99	97	98	98	99	123	115	95	121	94	95	120	100	94	113
30506	GAINESVILLE	122	123	110	120	125	130	114	120	113	114	140	141	114	143	116	113	136	117	119	143
30507	GAINESVILLE	99	87	66	83	90	96	82	91	86	84	105	106	78	102	82	87	100	89	94	112
30510	ALTO	70	61	44	57	62	67	58	64	60	59	74	74	54	70	57	61	70	63	66	79
30511	BALDWIN	86	75	55	71	79	85	70	78	75	71	91	92	67	90	71	76	86	76	84	100
30512	BLAIRSVILLE	85	64	41	58	71	82	63	74	72	63	85	85	56	81	65	77	78	74	89	98
30513	BLUE RIDGE	80	60	37	55	67	76	59	70	68	59	80	82	53	78	61	72	74	69	83	93
30516	BOWERSVILLE	79	57	31	50	63	71	54	66	63	55	75	78	48	72	55	67	69	65	78	91
30517	BRASELTON	116	112	93	110	114	118	103	109	104	104	128	130	102	130	104	103	123	106	110	134
30518	BUFORD	107	114	112	116	111	112	108	108	102	110	129	126	109	128	106	98	127	106	97	120
30519	BUFORD	132	147	141	153	140	136	133	133	123	139	156	155	136	156	130	115	154	130	114	146
30520	CANON	76	55	30	49	61	69	54	64	62	54	74	76	47	70	54	66	68	63	76	87
30521	CARNESVILLE	91	62	29	53	69	80	59	74	71	61	84	88	51	79	60	77	76	73	91	105
30522	CHERRYLOG	99	78	53	70	87	98	73	88	83	73	98	103	66	97	78	88	91	87	104	120
30523	CLARKESVILLE	94	77	55	73	83	92	75	85	82	74	98	99	70	97	76	85	92	83	95	109
30525	CLAYTON	100	73	43	67	81	93	72	86	83	72	98	100	64	95	74	88	90	85	102	114
30527	CLERMONT	106	93	71	89	98	107	88	97	93	88	114	114	86	115	90	96	108	94	105	123
30528	CLEVELAND	80	70	52	67	72	78	67	73	70	68	85	86	63	83	67	71	81	73	77	91
30529	COMMERCE	91	77	59	75	81	90	77	84	83	77	100	96	74	99	77	84	94	83	91	101
30530	COMMERCE	88	73	51	68	75	82	70	78	74	72	90	91	64	85	69	75	85	78	83	98
30531	CORNELIA	86	74	58	71	78	86	73	80	78	73	95	93	70	94	74	80	90	79	87	98
30533	DAHLONEGA	92	80	66	78	82	89	81	85	83	80	102	100	76	99	79	83	97	86	88	103
30534	DAWSONVILLE	115	101	77	96	106	114	95	105	100	96	122	124	91	121	97	102	116	104	113	133
30535	DEMOREST	88	69	45	64	74	84	67	77	75	67	90	90	62	88	68	78	83	76	88	100
30537	DILLARD	110	79	44	69	89	101	75	92	88	76	104	109	65	100	78	95	95	91	112	129
30538	EASTANOLLEE	81	54	24	47	61	70	52	65	63	53	74	78	44	70	53	68	67	64	80	92
30539	EAST ELLIJAY	92	62	28	53	70	81	60	75	72	61	85	89	51	80	61	78	77	74	92	106
30540	ELLIJAY	92	68	39	61	75	84	65	78	75	66	89	92	58	85	66	79	82	77	91	106
30541	EPWORTH	79	66	46	61	71	78	61	70	67	61	81	84	58	81	63	70	76	69	79	93
30542	FLOWERY BRANCH	108	116	109	118	114	114	107	109	102	109	128	127	109	128	106	98	125	106	100	123
30543	GILLSVILLE	95	86	66	82	89	95	80	88	84	81	102	103	78	101	81	84	98	86	92	110
30545	HELEN	97	78	58	72	87	99	74	88	82	74	98	99	68	94	79	88	92	86	103	116
30546	HIAWASSEE	84	68	51	62	75	86	64	76	71	66	86	83	60	79	68	76	80	74	90	98
30547	HOMER	93	77	53	72	80	86	73	82	78	75	95	96	67	90	73	79	90	82	88	104
30548	HOSCHTON	116	108	87	105	111	116	100	108	103	101	126	128	98	127	101	103	121	106	111	133
30549	JEFFERSON	92	82	62	78	84	90	78	85	81	79	99	99	74	96	78	81	94	84	88	104
30552	LAKEMONT	94	71	44	65	81	91	68	83	77	67	91	98	60	90	72	82	84	81	98	114
30553	LAVONIA	80	61	41	55	66	76	60	70	69	60	82	81	54	78	62	73	76	70	83	93
30554	LULA	99	81	55	75	85	93	77	87	83	78	101	103	71	97	77	85	95	86	95	113
30555	MC CAYSVILLE	59	42	24	38	47	55	44	51	50	43	59	59	38	56	44	54	54	51	62	66
30557	MARTIN	85	61	33	54	67	76	59	71	68	60	81	84	52	77	60	72	74	70	84	97
30558	MAYSVILLE	98	86	64	82	87	93	82	90	85	84	104	104	77	98	81	85	99	89	92	109
30559	MINERAL BLUFF	81	54	24	47	61	70	52	65	63	53	74	78	44	70	53	68	67	64	80	92
30560	MORGANTON	82	57	30	52	66	74	56	69	65	56	77	82	48	74	57	70	70	68	83	96
30563	MOUNT AIRY	100	83	58	77	88	96	78	88	85	78	102	105	74	101	79	88	96	87	98	115
30564	MURRAYVILLE	102	96	78	92	98	103	89	96	91	90	112	113	87	111	90	91	108	94	98	117
30565	NICHOLSON	92	84	65	80	84	89	80	86	81	82	100	99	76	95	79	80	96	85	86	103
30566	OAKWOOD	91	92	91	94	92	96	90	91	89	90	111	107	90	111	89	87	107	91	88	104
	GEORGIA	103	97	95	97	97	104	97	99	98	98	122	116	96	120	96	98	118	100	99	116
	UNITED STATES	100	100	100	100	100	100	100	100	100	100	100	100	100	100	100	100	100	100	100	100

Copyright © 2004 ESRI BIS. All rights reserved. Reproduction by any method is prohibited.

POPULATION CHANGE

#	POST OFFICE NAME	COUNTY FIPS CODE	POPULATION 2000	2004	2009	2000-2004 ANNUAL RATE % Rate	State Centile	HOUSEHOLDS 2000	2004	2009	% Annual Rate 2000-2004	2004 Average HH Size	FAMILIES 2000	2004	% Annual Rate 2000-2004
30567	PENDERGRASS	157	2554	3217	4146	5.6	94	905	1147	1486	5.7	2.80	724	907	5.5
30568	RABUN GAP	241	2319	2563	2914	2.4	66	879	990	1148	2.8	2.46	622	689	2.4
30571	SAUTEE NACOOCHEE	311	2852	3342	4032	3.8	85	1220	1450	1771	4.2	2.24	889	1041	3.8
30572	SUCHES	291	1140	1295	1609	3.1	76	501	578	729	3.4	2.24	354	402	3.0
30575	TALMO	157	1358	1783	2330	6.6	97	448	588	769	6.6	3.02	359	466	6.3
30576	TIGER	241	2555	2862	3286	2.7	71	1015	1154	1343	3.1	2.47	720	805	2.7
30577	TOCCOA	257	21828	22695	23873	0.9	36	8539	8979	9551	1.2	2.42	6018	6226	0.8
30582	YOUNG HARRIS	281	3498	3830	4300	2.2	62	1383	1540	1763	2.6	2.25	1014	1114	2.2
30597	DAHLONEGA	187	1035	1107	1253	1.6	50	0	0	0	0.0	0.00	0	0	0.0
30601	ATHENS	059	17872	18950	20568	1.4	46	7100	7544	8223	1.4	2.50	3894	4061	1.0
30602	ATHENS	059	1400	1375	1396	-0.4	5	4	4	4	0.0	2.50	1	1	0.0
30605	ATHENS	059	39017	41411	44791	1.4	47	14753	15958	17621	1.9	2.22	6206	6548	1.3
30606	ATHENS	059	35383	38251	42131	1.9	54	14900	16252	18058	2.1	2.29	7733	8168	1.3
30607	ATHENS	157	8267	9407	10815	3.1	77	2887	3276	3788	3.0	2.83	2064	2299	2.6
30609	ATHENS	059	109	143	171	6.6	97	42	55	66	6.6	2.60	7	8	3.2
30619	ARNOLDSVILLE	221	1228	1429	1576	3.6	84	489	575	641	3.9	2.48	350	406	3.6
30620	BETHLEHEM	013	5480	7426	9934	7.4	98	1831	2483	3323	7.4	2.99	1507	2017	7.1
30621	BISHOP	219	3636	4027	4528	2.4	67	1255	1402	1587	2.6	2.81	1000	1103	2.3
30622	BOGART	219	7820	8832	10008	2.9	74	2851	3252	3708	3.1	2.70	2180	2450	2.8
30624	BOWMAN	105	3113	3529	3808	3.0	75	1214	1394	1522	3.3	2.52	890	1007	2.5
30625	BUCKHEAD	211	2097	2319	2598	2.4	67	806	906	1030	2.8	2.55	635	705	2.5
30627	CARLTON	221	2128	2150	2253	0.2	16	834	852	902	0.5	2.50	600	604	0.2
30628	COLBERT	195	6328	7150	8014	2.9	74	2372	2704	3060	3.1	2.64	1775	1997	2.8
30629	COMER	195	4057	4323	4705	1.5	48	1515	1630	1794	1.7	2.58	1105	1171	1.4
30630	CRAWFORD	221	1994	2163	2310	1.9	57	773	849	917	2.2	2.48	549	594	1.9
30631	CRAWFORDVILLE	265	2116	2071	2018	-0.5	4	877	878	876	0.0	2.33	566	557	-0.4
30633	DANIELSVILLE	195	7833	8268	9017	1.3	44	2992	3195	3522	1.6	2.58	2265	2387	1.2
30634	DEWY ROSE	105	1500	1684	1813	2.8	72	482	556	610	3.4	2.85	365	413	3.0
30635	ELBERTON	105	16873	16949	17261	0.1	14	6584	6678	6865	0.3	2.50	4726	4718	0.0
30641	GOOD HOPE	297	1382	1515	1773	2.2	62	523	580	685	2.5	2.60	416	456	2.2
30642	GREENSBORO	133	9043	10085	11195	2.6	70	3478	3972	4509	3.2	2.51	2635	2966	2.8
30643	HARTWELL	147	14831	15559	16376	1.1	40	5998	6386	6820	1.5	2.37	4283	4492	1.1
30646	HULL	195	5848	6368	7064	2.0	59	2221	2446	2743	2.3	2.60	1671	1816	2.0
30648	LEXINGTON	221	2433	2466	2528	0.3	19	923	947	981	0.6	2.59	686	695	0.3
30650	MADISON	211	10079	10933	12125	1.9	57	3580	3933	4421	2.2	2.74	2716	2943	2.0
30655	MONROE	297	18132	22248	27904	4.9	92	6674	8255	10431	5.1	2.65	4979	6076	4.8
30656	MONROE	297	10558	12617	15617	4.3	88	3695	4453	5552	4.5	2.81	2971	3541	4.2
30660	RAYLE	317	1189	1193	1204	0.1	13	469	477	488	0.4	2.48	329	329	0.0
30662	ROYSTON	119	8179	8421	8761	0.7	30	3107	3240	3412	1.0	2.43	2167	2224	0.6
30663	RUTLEDGE	211	2854	3385	3931	4.1	87	1012	1217	1432	4.4	2.78	809	961	4.1
30666	STATHAM	013	5361	6193	7617	3.5	82	1925	2237	2764	3.6	2.74	1486	1703	3.3
30667	STEPHENS	221	1121	1144	1173	0.5	22	396	409	425	0.8	2.76	289	294	0.4
30668	TIGNALL	317	2073	2053	2077	-0.2	8	869	874	899	0.1	2.34	600	593	-0.3
30669	UNION POINT	133	3636	3787	4046	1.0	36	1367	1451	1583	1.4	2.54	922	962	1.0
30673	WASHINGTON	317	8125	8234	8350	0.3	18	3265	3363	3467	0.7	2.41	2249	2278	0.3
30677	WATKINSVILLE	219	13781	15314	17270	2.5	68	4825	5374	6069	2.6	2.84	3901	4298	2.3
30678	WHITE PLAINS	133	1212	1310	1431	1.9	54	453	502	560	2.5	2.61	349	382	2.2
30680	WINDER	013	25090	30149	38289	4.4	89	9144	11031	14057	4.5	2.70	6777	8057	4.2
30683	WINTERVILLE	221	5197	5463	5794	1.2	42	2036	2175	2335	1.6	2.48	1417	1485	1.1
30701	CALHOUN	129	29873	33315	38174	2.6	70	10901	12211	14062	2.7	2.69	8126	8982	2.4
30705	CHATSWORTH	213	31021	34210	38037	2.3	65	11235	12468	13944	2.5	2.73	8670	9505	2.2
30707	CHICKAMAUGA	295	13948	14530	15087	1.0	37	5293	5580	5860	1.3	2.60	4126	4291	0.9
30708	CISCO	213	668	749	837	2.7	72	265	300	337	3.0	2.50	200	223	2.6
30710	COHUTTA	313	5389	6016	6776	2.6	70	1910	2126	2381	2.6	2.83	1581	1743	2.3
30711	CRANDALL	213	3419	3637	3953	1.5	47	1283	1376	1506	1.7	2.64	1002	1061	1.4
30720	DALTON	313	24292	25930	28673	1.6	49	8945	9508	10452	1.5	2.67	6231	6498	1.0
30721	DALTON	313	41833	46577	52485	2.6	69	14165	15614	17429	2.3	2.97	10853	11811	2.0
30725	FLINTSTONE	295	3332	3616	3833	1.9	57	1305	1432	1535	2.2	2.53	974	1051	1.8
30728	LA FAYETTE	295	17199	17520	17991	0.4	21	6648	6848	7112	0.7	2.48	4859	4932	0.4
30730	LYERLY	055	1913	1879	1885	-0.4	5	746	745	756	0.0	2.52	559	551	-0.3
30731	MENLO	055	2338	2534	2664	1.9	56	1007	1108	1180	2.3	2.29	742	805	1.9
30733	PLAINVILLE	129	1910	2090	2364	2.1	61	720	791	898	2.2	2.64	558	604	1.9
30734	RANGER	129	3039	3431	3973	2.9	74	1107	1263	1475	3.2	2.70	870	979	2.8
30735	RESACA	129	4722	5115	5750	1.9	56	1703	1855	2093	2.0	2.76	1334	1434	1.7
30736	RINGGOLD	047	34411	38338	42813	2.6	70	12695	14282	16096	2.8	2.67	10045	11163	2.5
30738	RISING FAWN	083	3420	3677	3857	1.7	51	1323	1446	1536	2.1	2.52	1036	1117	1.8
30739	ROCK SPRING	295	3609	3980	4281	2.3	65	1229	1389	1521	2.9	2.71	967	1078	2.6
30740	ROCKY FACE	313	7122	8022	9070	2.8	73	2617	2949	3317	2.9	2.72	2058	2292	2.6
30741	ROSSVILLE	295	28206	28797	30212	0.5	23	11508	11878	12601	0.8	2.40	8062	8168	0.3
30742	FORT OGLETHORPE	047	5744	6261	6934	2.1	60	2398	2675	3011	2.6	2.26	1564	1708	2.1
30746	SUGAR VALLEY	129	1054	1183	1359	2.8	72	387	438	506	3.0	2.70	304	339	2.6
30747	SUMMERVILLE	055	16209	16707	17149	0.7	31	5808	6070	6310	1.0	2.48	4168	4287	0.7
30750	LOOKOUT MOUNTAIN	083	4079	4126	4197	0.3	17	1305	1342	1386	0.7	2.63	979	993	0.3
30751	TENNGA	213	71	79	88	2.5	69	28	31	35	2.4	2.55	21	23	2.2
30752	TRENTON	083	8719	8949	9169	0.6	28	3352	3491	3619	1.0	2.53	2533	2602	0.6
30753	TRION	055	6619	6758	6910	0.5	23	2629	2722	2816	0.8	2.48	1846	1879	0.4
30755	TUNNEL HILL	313	8399	8949	9800	1.5	48	3081	3293	3608	1.6	2.72	2448	2586	1.5
30757	WILDWOOD	083	1778	1833	1877	0.7	31	720	747	770	0.9	2.43	516	527	0.5
30802	APPLING	073	5223	5635	6336	1.8	53	1761	1932	2209	2.2	2.81	1390	1496	1.7
30803	AVERA	163	679	727	747	1.6	50	291	315	329	1.9	2.30	207	220	1.4
30805	BLYTHE	245	2030	2166	2246	1.5	48	698	750	782	1.7	2.85	545	578	1.4
30808	DEARING	189	4277	4370	4484	0.5	24	1546	1597	1656	0.8	2.73	1192	1216	0.5
30809	EVANS	073	26156	31393	37345	4.4	89	8717	10587	12748	4.7	2.95	7501	9030	4.5
30810	GIBSON	125	1708	1683	1711	-0.4	6	656	655	676	0.0	2.42	461	453	-0.4
30813	GROVETOWN	073	16398	17984	20461	2.2	63	5395	6044	7017	2.7	2.92	4219	4672	2.4
30814	HARLEM	073	6943	7569	8572	2.1	60	2516	2775	3182	2.3	2.72	1962	2132	2.0
30815	HEPHZIBAH	245	36549	38422	39535	1.2	42	12031	12756	13223	1.4	3.00	9888	10366	1.1
30816	KEYSVILLE	033	1566	1618	1677	0.8	32	562	588	617	1.1	2.74	434	448	0.8
30817	LINCOLNTON	181	7919	8331	8823	1.2	42	3071	3290	3549	1.6	2.51	2250	2375	1.3
30818	MATTHEWS	163	568	576	580	0.3	19	196	201	204	0.6	2.87	148	149	0.2
30820	MITCHELL	125	844	948	1026	2.8	72	350	399	439	3.1	2.36	255	286	2.7
30821	NORWOOD	301	1162	1156	1149	-0.1	10	446	454	462	0.4	2.55	301	300	-0.1
30822	PERKINS	165	663	677	680	0.5	23	257	265	269	0.7	2.55	189	192	0.4
30823	STAPLETON	163	1415	1423	1424	0.1	15	495	503	509	0.4	2.81	379	380	0.1
30824	THOMSON	189	16836	17223	17698	0.5	25	6381	6603	6864	0.8	2.56	4633	4721	0.4
	GEORGIA					2.4					2.5	2.64			2.2
	UNITED STATES					1.2					1.3	2.58			1.1

ZIP CODE #	POST OFFICE NAME	RACE (%) White 2000	White 2004	Black 2000	Black 2004	Asian/Pacific 2000	Asian/Pacific 2004	% Hispanic Origin 2000	% Hispanic Origin 2004	2004 AGE DISTRIBUTION (%) 0-4	5-9	10-14	15-19	20-24	25-44	45-64	65-84	85+	18+	MEDIAN AGE 2004	% 2004 Males	% 2004 Females
30567	PENDERGRASS	93.4	92.4	2.3	2.5	1.1	1.3	4.9	6.3	7.9	7.8	7.8	6.6	6.1	31.6	23.3	8.1	0.8	72.4	34.6	50.9	49.1
30568	RABUN GAP	93.9	92.7	1.3	1.4	0.6	0.7	4.8	6.1	5.5	5.7	5.9	8.3	5.2	22.8	27.6	16.9	2.3	77.3	42.5	49.0	51.0
30571	SAUTEE NACOOCHEE	94.2	93.4	2.8	3.1	1.5	1.8	0.8	1.0	4.8	4.9	5.3	4.8	5.2	23.6	31.6	18.4	1.5	82.7	46.0	50.0	50.0
30572	SUCHES	97.9	97.6	0.4	0.4	0.4	0.5	0.5	0.5	3.6	4.1	5.1	4.7	3.7	21.6	33.6	21.7	1.9	84.4	49.9	49.8	50.2
30575	TALMO	87.6	85.9	3.2	3.4	1.7	1.9	14.4	17.6	8.9	8.4	8.0	6.2	6.4	33.9	20.7	6.8	0.7	70.9	32.5	51.6	48.4
30576	TIGER	97.2	96.6	0.4	0.4	0.1	0.1	2.7	3.5	5.6	5.8	5.8	5.1	4.9	23.9	31.3	16.2	1.4	79.5	44.2	50.3	49.7
30577	TOCCOA	85.4	83.9	12.2	13.4	0.7	0.8	1.0	1.3	6.1	6.2	6.5	6.7	7.4	25.8	24.9	14.2	2.3	77.8	38.6	48.2	51.8
30582	YOUNG HARRIS	98.7	98.5	0.3	0.3	0.3	0.4	0.4	0.6	4.4	4.6	4.3	9.5	7.2	19.7	27.1	21.3	2.0	84.4	45.3	46.2	53.8
30597	DAHLONEGA	95.0	94.2	1.5	1.6	0.7	0.7	2.6	3.4	5.4	4.8	5.4	17.6	18.0	23.7	18.9	5.6	0.6	81.9	24.7	44.2	55.8
30601	ATHENS	40.0	37.3	53.3	55.1	0.7	0.8	10.2	11.9	7.2	7.1	6.7	8.0	15.5	30.0	17.5	7.2	0.8	74.8	27.8	49.3	50.8
30602	ATHENS	71.2	67.2	12.5	13.8	13.4	15.6	2.9	3.7	1.8	1.1	0.6	49.0	32.4	13.0	1.6	0.5	0.1	96.2	19.8	45.2	54.8
30605	ATHENS	74.9	72.0	17.2	18.8	5.0	5.6	3.1	4.0	4.2	3.5	3.1	15.0	31.5	23.8	13.1	5.2	0.6	87.4	23.9	48.8	51.3
30606	ATHENS	70.5	67.9	22.7	24.3	2.5	2.9	5.5	6.7	5.1	4.9	5.1	6.9	19.5	27.9	19.5	9.6	1.8	82.0	29.6	48.4	51.6
30607	ATHENS	55.9	52.9	29.7	30.2	1.0	1.1	19.0	23.0	8.3	7.7	7.7	7.4	9.7	32.8	18.9	6.6	1.0	72.0	29.4	51.6	48.4
30609	ATHENS	86.2	83.9	9.2	11.2	1.8	2.1	1.8	4.2	1.4	1.4	0.7	11.2	69.2	10.5	4.9	0.7	0.0	96.5	22.6	46.9	53.2
30619	ARNOLDSVILLE	77.0	74.7	21.3	23.4	0.2	0.2	1.1	1.3	7.4	7.4	6.9	6.0	5.5	27.5	27.2	10.7	1.3	74.4	38.2	48.4	51.6
30620	BETHLEHEM	82.7	79.9	10.1	11.4	3.2	3.6	5.4	6.9	8.7	8.2	7.6	6.4	6.4	34.5	20.5	7.0	0.7	71.7	32.7	50.8	49.2
30621	BISHOP	89.6	87.8	8.7	10.1	0.5	0.6	2.0	2.7	6.2	7.3	8.7	7.6	5.5	28.5	26.1	8.6	1.6	72.8	36.8	49.5	50.5
30622	BOGART	80.5	79.1	15.2	15.8	2.3	2.7	3.0	3.8	6.7	7.4	7.8	6.5	5.9	29.8	25.9	8.9	1.1	73.9	36.4	48.9	51.1
30624	BOWMAN	79.8	77.2	18.3	20.6	0.1	0.2	1.0	1.3	6.9	7.0	7.0	6.4	6.1	28.6	25.8	11.1	1.2	75.3	36.9	49.7	50.3
30625	BUCKHEAD	79.3	76.4	18.6	21.1	0.4	0.5	2.2	2.7	6.2	6.5	6.8	6.0	5.9	26.6	29.6	11.4	1.0	76.5	40.2	49.9	50.2
30627	CARLTON	70.5	68.3	27.5	29.4	0.6	0.7	1.3	1.5	6.1	6.1	7.0	6.3	5.7	27.4	27.1	12.4	1.9	76.8	39.7	48.9	51.1
30628	COLBERT	87.8	86.2	9.6	10.8	0.3	0.3	1.9	2.5	8.1	8.1	7.9	6.2	5.5	30.9	23.7	8.8	0.9	72.1	35.0	49.3	50.7
30629	COMER	82.3	80.7	16.1	17.4	0.5	0.6	0.9	1.2	7.4	7.2	7.2	6.4	5.6	28.0	24.6	11.5	2.2	73.9	37.6	48.4	51.6
30630	CRAWFORD	81.3	78.9	16.8	19.0	0.3	0.3	1.4	1.6	7.3	7.2	6.4	5.6	5.5	27.5	25.5	12.6	2.4	75.4	39.0	47.4	52.6
30631	CRAWFORDVILLE	39.9	38.4	58.5	59.8	0.1	0.1	1.2	1.3	6.5	6.3	5.6	6.9	6.0	24.8	25.0	16.1	2.7	77.2	40.8	48.9	51.1
30633	DANIELSVILLE	95.9	95.3	2.3	2.6	0.2	0.2	1.7	2.2	6.5	6.8	7.2	6.5	6.1	29.7	25.9	10.2	1.0	75.4	37.2	49.5	50.5
30634	DEWY ROSE	72.9	70.4	25.7	27.9	0.1	0.2	0.8	0.9	7.1	7.0	6.3	6.2	6.1	31.2	26.0	9.4	0.8	75.8	36.7	53.2	46.8
30635	ELBERTON	63.9	60.7	33.9	36.6	0.3	0.3	2.7	3.4	6.3	6.5	6.9	6.8	6.5	26.1	25.0	13.9	2.2	76.0	38.5	48.0	52.0
30641	GOOD HOPE	87.1	85.0	11.2	12.9	0.4	0.5	0.9	1.1	6.2	6.4	6.3	6.7	5.2	27.3	28.9	11.4	1.5	77.1	39.4	51.2	48.8
30642	GREENSBORO	53.2	50.7	43.9	45.9	0.3	0.4	3.5	4.2	6.7	6.4	6.4	5.8	6.1	23.4	30.3	13.6	1.3	77.1	41.3	48.5	51.5
30643	HARTWELL	77.0	75.0	21.4	23.1	0.7	0.8	0.9	1.1	6.0	6.0	6.2	5.8	5.4	25.4	26.5	16.6	2.1	78.2	41.7	48.9	51.1
30646	HULL	85.0	83.0	11.3	12.5	0.3	0.4	3.0	3.8	6.8	7.0	7.5	6.6	6.3	30.0	25.5	9.6	0.8	74.8	36.0	49.5	50.5
30648	LEXINGTON	69.1	66.2	29.1	31.7	0.4	0.5	1.0	1.2	6.6	6.7	7.4	6.9	6.0	27.3	26.8	10.9	1.6	75.1	38.4	49.2	50.9
30650	MADISON	63.6	60.6	34.1	36.7	0.5	0.6	2.0	2.5	6.7	7.0	7.9	6.3	5.6	27.8	25.3	11.6	1.9	74.6	37.7	48.9	51.1
30655	MONROE	71.6	69.0	25.9	28.2	0.5	0.6	2.0	2.4	8.1	7.8	7.4	6.4	6.6	29.9	22.6	9.8	1.5	73.0	34.5	47.9	52.1
30656	MONROE	77.8	75.2	18.5	20.4	1.6	1.8	2.0	2.5	8.2	8.2	7.6	6.2	5.6	31.9	23.2	7.9	1.2	72.1	34.6	48.5	51.5
30660	RAYLE	68.4	65.1	28.1	30.8	0.3	0.3	4.0	5.0	6.5	6.4	6.5	6.3	6.7	27.3	24.9	13.8	1.7	76.7	39.1	51.3	48.7
30662	ROYSTON	88.3	87.1	9.7	10.6	0.6	0.6	1.0	1.3	6.1	6.4	6.6	7.6	8.1	25.9	23.0	13.9	2.6	77.3	37.4	48.2	51.8
30663	RUTLEDGE	79.4	76.8	19.5	22.1	0.3	0.3	1.0	1.2	7.3	7.5	7.6	6.5	5.7	27.6	26.1	10.7	1.0	73.6	37.1	48.2	51.8
30666	STATHAM	84.2	82.0	13.0	14.7	1.0	1.2	1.5	1.9	7.7	7.5	7.2	6.3	6.0	30.8	23.3	9.5	1.5	73.4	35.5	49.4	50.6
30667	STEPHENS	69.6	66.4	27.7	30.2	0.3	0.4	2.5	3.2	6.3	6.5	7.6	6.8	6.5	27.0	24.3	13.6	1.5	75.4	37.9	49.8	50.2
30668	TIGNALL	61.8	58.0	36.6	40.1	0.1	0.1	2.2	2.6	5.9	6.2	6.7	5.4	4.6	25.5	27.0	16.2	2.5	78.0	42.2	50.6	49.4
30669	UNION POINT	48.7	44.8	49.3	53.0	0.3	0.4	1.7	1.9	7.6	7.1	6.8	7.7	6.4	24.9	24.6	12.5	2.4	74.0	37.6	48.2	51.8
30673	WASHINGTON	52.7	50.1	45.7	48.1	0.3	0.4	1.6	2.0	5.9	5.9	6.7	6.4	6.6	25.5	25.7	15.1	2.4	77.7	40.5	47.2	52.8
30677	WATKINSVILLE	90.0	88.6	6.5	7.2	1.4	1.6	2.5	3.2	6.6	7.3	8.3	7.4	5.7	28.0	27.8	8.0	1.0	72.8	36.9	49.6	50.4
30678	WHITE PLAINS	54.5	50.9	43.9	47.3	0.3	0.3	2.2	2.8	6.1	6.0	6.1	6.0	6.0	23.9	29.8	14.7	1.5	78.1	41.7	48.8	51.2
30680	WINDER	83.4	81.5	11.6	12.6	1.9	2.2	2.9	3.7	7.8	7.5	7.6	6.6	6.6	32.2	21.6	8.8	1.4	73.0	33.9	49.4	50.6
30683	WINTERVILLE	81.9	79.4	14.6	16.4	0.6	0.6	2.9	3.8	6.7	6.5	7.0	6.4	9.8	30.5	23.3	8.6	1.1	75.6	34.0	49.6	50.4
30701	CALHOUN	86.7	84.2	4.5	4.9	0.8	0.9	9.7	12.4	7.3	7.0	7.1	6.3	6.9	31.3	22.8	10.1	1.2	74.8	35.0	49.8	50.2
30705	CHATSWORTH	95.0	93.9	0.7	0.7	0.3	0.4	6.0	7.6	8.1	7.7	7.6	6.7	6.8	32.1	23.0	7.5	0.7	72.5	33.4	50.2	49.8
30707	CHICKAMAUGA	94.1	93.2	4.5	5.2	0.2	0.3	0.5	0.7	6.5	6.7	7.0	6.4	6.4	29.1	26.4	10.7	1.0	76.0	37.2	49.7	50.3
30708	CISCO	97.5	96.9	0.2	0.3	0.2	0.3	2.3	3.2	7.1	7.2	8.0	6.0	5.9	31.9	23.9	9.1	0.9	74.0	35.6	51.4	48.6
30710	COHUTTA	95.6	94.5	1.4	1.7	0.2	0.3	2.2	3.1	7.2	7.4	7.8	7.1	6.2	29.8	26.4	7.7	0.6	73.3	35.8	49.7	50.3
30711	CRANDALL	98.0	97.6	0.3	0.4	0.1	0.1	1.4	1.9	7.6	7.5	7.5	6.4	5.9	31.5	23.8	8.8	1.0	73.5	35.4	50.3	49.7
30720	DALTON	79.8	76.3	3.9	4.2	2.0	2.3	23.0	28.3	7.9	7.3	6.7	6.3	7.3	30.0	22.1	10.3	2.1	74.3	34.6	50.3	49.7
30721	DALTON	75.8	72.3	4.7	4.7	0.5	0.5	29.5	35.3	8.9	8.3	7.4	6.5	7.1	31.0	21.1	8.9	0.9	71.7	32.3	51.1	48.9
30725	FLINTSTONE	94.7	93.9	3.5	3.9	0.5	0.6	0.7	0.9	6.7	6.7	6.6	5.8	5.9	28.7	25.6	12.6	1.4	76.4	38.0	49.2	50.8
30728	LA FAYETTE	93.6	92.7	4.7	5.3	0.3	0.4	1.1	1.4	6.7	6.6	6.8	6.3	6.4	28.1	25.2	12.2	1.7	76.0	37.7	49.0	51.0
30730	LYERLY	88.7	87.1	9.2	10.4	0.0	0.0	0.4	0.5	7.1	7.0	6.6	6.3	5.9	28.3	26.5	11.4	0.9	75.6	37.8	50.3	49.7
30731	MENLO	96.5	95.9	1.9	2.1	0.2	0.2	0.9	1.1	5.7	6.0	5.8	5.3	5.9	26.7	29.8	13.6	1.2	79.3	41.5	49.9	50.1
30733	PLAINVILLE	95.3	94.1	1.3	1.4	0.1	0.1	4.4	6.0	6.8	6.9	6.9	5.5	6.3	30.9	25.3	10.1	1.1	75.9	36.2	50.4	49.6
30734	RANGER	98.3	97.9	0.2	0.2	0.2	0.2	1.0	1.3	6.9	7.0	6.8	6.0	5.9	31.0	25.5	9.9	1.0	75.8	36.9	51.5	48.5
30735	RESACA	94.6	93.2	0.9	1.1	0.4	0.5	4.1	5.5	7.9	7.8	7.5	6.5	5.7	31.3	23.9	8.5	0.9	72.8	34.4	50.7	49.3
30736	RINGGOLD	96.7	96.2	1.3	1.4	0.5	0.6	1.2	1.6	7.2	7.3	7.5	6.4	5.8	30.8	24.8	9.4	0.8	74.0	36.0	49.2	50.8
30738	RISING FAWN	98.7	98.5	0.2	0.2	0.2	0.2	0.6	0.7	6.2	6.4	6.4	6.3	6.2	26.9	29.0	11.4	1.3	77.4	39.8	49.8	50.2
30739	ROCK SPRING	94.5	94.1	4.2	4.4	0.3	0.3	0.6	0.8	5.9	6.1	6.3	5.6	5.6	29.9	27.6	11.9	1.2	78.4	39.5	51.7	48.3
30740	ROCKY FACE	94.2	92.7	1.7	2.0	0.9	1.0	3.5	4.9	7.3	7.4	7.3	6.4	6.0	29.5	26.2	9.2	0.7	74.1	36.6	49.6	50.4
30741	ROSSVILLE	95.4	94.7	2.1	2.2	0.7	0.8	1.1	1.4	6.5	6.3	6.5	6.1	6.3	27.7	24.4	14.5	1.8	77.0	38.5	47.7	52.3
30742	FORT OGLETHORPE	92.8	92.1	3.3	3.5	1.6	1.9	1.4	1.7	6.4	5.6	5.9	5.7	6.5	23.7	24.3	18.5	3.5	78.5	41.9	44.9	55.2
30746	SUGAR VALLEY	92.6	90.8	3.0	3.7	0.3	0.3	3.8	5.0	6.2	6.6	7.5	6.8	5.8	30.9	26.4	9.0	0.9	75.5	37.0	50.8	49.2
30747	SUMMERVILLE	82.5	80.7	15.7	17.3	0.2	0.2	1.2	1.5	6.5	6.4	5.8	6.0	7.7	30.2	23.7	12.0	1.8	78.1	36.7	53.2	46.8
30750	LOOKOUT MOUNTAIN	97.9	97.4	0.3	0.3	0.4	0.5	1.2	1.7	5.7	5.8	7.4	11.7	13.5	23.2	22.7	8.9	1.2	77.2	31.3	47.9	52.1
30751	TENNGA	98.6	97.5	0.0	0.0	0.0	0.0	1.4	1.3	6.3	6.3	7.6	6.3	5.1	32.9	25.3	8.9	1.3	76.0	38.1	51.9	48.1
30752	TRENTON	97.9	97.6	0.3	0.3	0.3	0.4	0.9	1.2	6.4	6.6	7.2	6.2	6.2	27.9	26.3	12.0	1.3	76.1	37.9	49.8	50.2
30753	TRION	95.2	94.1	1.9	2.2	0.2	0.2	5.1	6.6	6.8	6.7	6.8	6.3	6.5	29.2	23.3	12.8	1.8	76.0	36.9	49.9	50.1
30755	TUNNEL HILL	95.9	95.0	1.4	1.7	0.4	0.5	2.7	3.6	6.6	7.1	7.9	6.6	6.0	30.9	25.2	8.9	0.8	74.3	36.0	50.3	49.7
30757	WILDWOOD	94.5	93.7	3.3	3.7	0.7	0.9	0.5	0.7	5.7	6.0	7.3	5.3	6.0	29.1	28.4	11.4	0.9	77.6	38.8	50.1	49.9
30802	APPLING	79.7	77.5	17.6	19.3	0.8	0.9	1.0	1.3	6.2	6.6	7.8	6.9	5.7	26.9	27.6	10.4	1.9	75.4	39.4	49.4	50.6
30803	AVERA	68.9	67.4	30.5	32.1	0.2	0.1	0.9	1.0	5.5	6.1	6.2	5.5	5.5	27.8	28.8	12.9	1.8	79.0	40.9	51.3	48.7
30805	BLYTHE	72.1	68.7	24.2	27.0	1.0	1.2	2.4	3.0	7.4	7.4	8.8	7.4	7.1	29.1	23.8	8.3	0.7	71.5	34.8	49.6	50.4
30808	DEARING	75.7	72.8	22.1	24.5	0.4	0.4	2.1	2.6	7.4	6.9	7.4	7.7	7.4	28.1	24.5	9.6	1.1	73.5	35.5	49.0	51.0
30809	EVANS	84.9	82.9	8.9	9.9	3.9	4.5	2.1	2.7	7.6	8.0	8.7	7.6	6.4	28.4	26.6	6.0	0.8	70.8	35.6	48.9	51.1
30810	GIBSON	92.2	91.9	7.1	7.4	0.0	0.0	0.5	0.4	7.2	6.8	6.4	5.8	6.0	25.2	23.3	15.9	3.5	76.1	39.9	47.2	52.8
30813	GROVETOWN	76.2	74.1	17.8	18.8	1.7	2.0	4.8	5.8	7.6	7.5	8.0	7.5	7.2	31.7	23.0	6.9	0.6	72.3	33.5	50.0	50.0
30814	HARLEM	78.7	76.5	17.9	19.6	0.8	0.9	2.1	2.7	6.9	6.9	7.7	7.2	6.7	29.5	24.7	9.4	0.9	74.0	35.8	49.2	50.8
30815	HEPHZIBAH	43.2	40.7	51.2	53.1	2.0	2.1	3.1	3.5	7.4	7.5	8.9	8.5	8.0	29.2	24.4	5.7	0.4	70.7	32.1	48.1	51.9
30816	KEYSVILLE	54.3	50.7	42.3	45.6	0.5	0.6	2.0	2.2	7.0	7.2	7.9	7.9	6.8	26.5	25.8	9.9	1.1	72.9	36.2	48.6	51.4
30817	LINCOLNTON	64.1	61.3	34.6	37.2	0.2	0.3	0.9	1.1	5.4	5.9	7.1	6.5	5.8	26.3	28.1	13.8	1.1	77.5	40.5	48.6	51.4
30818	MATTHEWS	65.9	65.5	31.0	31.4	0.2	0.2	3.2	3.0	7.3	7.5	7.8	6.4	6.6	29.3	23.3	10.6	1.2	73.4	35.2	50.2	49.8
30820	MITCHELL	82.7	82.7	15.3	15.5	0.0	0.0	0.5	0.5	6.0	6.3	5.9	4.6	5.9	26.0	30.2	12.8	2.3	79.1	41.5	50.5	49.5
30821	NORWOOD	35.5	34.1	63.6	65.0	0.2	0.2	0.3	0.4	6.8	6.9	6.7	6.1	6.8	25.4	26.9	12.7	1.7	76.0	39.5	47.2	52.8
30822	PERKINS	64.7	63.7	30.3	31.2	0.5	0.4	5.6	5.6	7.2	7.5	9.0	6.7	6.7	27.6	24.1	10.3	0.9	71.9	35.1	49.8	50.2
30823	STAPLETON	55.4	53.8	43.5	45.2	0.0	0.0	0.7	0.6	7.1	7.7	8.2	7.4	6.7	27.5	25.1	8.9	1.5	72.1	35.4	49.9	50.1
30824	THOMSON	56.8	53.9	41.7	44.4	0.4	0.4	1.2	1.3	7.2	7.1	7.6	7.3	6.8	26.8	24.9	10.9	1.5	73.7	36.1	47.2	52.8
	GEORGIA	65.1	63.4	28.7	29.4	2.2	2.5	5.3	6.6	7.3	7.1	7.2	7.0	7.6	31.0	23.0	8.6	1.1	74.3	34.2	49.3	50.7
	UNITED STATES	75.1	73.6	12.3	12.5	3.8	4.2	12.5	14.1	6.9	6.7	7.2	7.0	7.3	28.6	23.8	10.8	1.7	75.1	36.0	49.1	50.9

#	POST OFFICE NAME	2004 Per Capita Income	2004 HH Income Base	2004 HOUSEHOLD INCOME DISTRIBUTION (%) Less than $25,000	$25,000 to $49,999	$50,000 to $99,999	$100,000 to $149,999	$150,000 or More	MEDIAN HOUSEHOLD INCOME 2004	2009	2004 National Centile	2004 State Centile	2004 Home Value Base	2004 HOME VALUE DISTRIBUTION (%) Less than $50,000	$50,000 to $89,999	$90,000 to $174,999	$175,000 to $399,999	$400,000 or More	2004 Median Home Value
30567	PENDERGRASS	22816	1147	23.9	28.0	35.3	8.5	4.4	48025	55636	68	72	925	16.8	16.0	36.5	25.3	5.4	119940
30568	RABUN GAP	22044	990	30.6	34.6	24.6	5.7	4.7	37366	43648	37	43	814	13.5	21.3	37.6	23.6	4.1	118287
30571	SAUTEE NACOOCHEE	25064	1450	22.8	35.4	31.5	6.1	4.3	44098	50497	59	63	1217	3.9	11.3	40.4	36.1	8.2	161936
30572	SUCHES	48189	578	29.8	25.6	30.5	9.9	4.3	44234	50250	59	64	493	12.2	19.3	35.7	19.7	13.2	133036
30575	TALMO	19664	588	24.3	28.4	35.7	7.7	3.9	47021	55132	66	70	450	16.0	15.6	38.0	25.6	4.9	129891
30576	TIGER	22927	1154	26.7	36.7	25.3	5.2	6.2	37268	45342	36	43	970	14.6	17.7	35.5	19.2	13.0	118238
30577	TOCCOA	18508	8979	37.2	31.4	23.8	4.9	2.9	33065	38139	21	25	6611	19.0	29.2	37.7	11.8	2.4	92627
30582	YOUNG HARRIS	20642	1540	30.0	38.4	22.4	7.0	2.2	37163	42906	36	43	1323	18.5	12.0	35.5	28.1	5.9	127102
30597	DAHLONEGA	3863	0	0.0	0.0	0.0	0.0	0.0	0	0	0	0	0	0.0	0.0	0.0	0.0	0.0	0
30601	ATHENS	14850	7544	47.7	29.4	17.7	3.7	1.6	26469	32090	6	5	3263	38.0	25.4	28.3	7.6	0.7	67688
30602	ATHENS	9309	4	100.0	0.0	0.0	0.0	0.0	6667	6667	0	1	0	0.0	0.0	0.0	0.0	0.0	0
30605	ATHENS	19636	15958	45.5	22.5	20.6	8.0	3.5	29182	35911	11	12	5960	9.9	8.9	54.7	23.9	2.6	134972
30606	ATHENS	28732	16252	34.5	24.9	22.2	10.2	8.2	38952	49022	43	49	7855	5.3	9.6	42.1	34.3	8.8	160068
30607	ATHENS	18570	3276	31.0	32.3	27.2	5.1	4.4	40293	47940	47	52	1931	9.2	21.2	52.6	13.1	3.9	109625
30609	ATHENS	10185	55	69.1	18.2	9.1	3.6	0.0	16261	19222	1	1	5	20.0	0.0	80.0	0.0	0.0	97500
30619	ARNOLDSVILLE	19939	575	34.4	30.3	25.7	6.3	3.3	39426	45567	44	50	463	22.7	22.9	30.5	20.5	3.5	99762
30620	BETHLEHEM	21698	2483	14.9	25.7	45.5	10.4	3.6	56245	63333	81	82	2151	4.5	10.6	61.1	21.5	2.2	143667
30621	BISHOP	25987	1402	16.0	25.5	37.0	14.0	7.6	57785	70071	82	83	1218	9.1	13.5	37.6	30.3	9.5	141493
30622	BOGART	29434	3252	15.7	23.7	36.7	14.5	9.4	60814	76484	85	86	2579	7.1	8.9	40.5	35.9	7.6	157908
30624	BOWMAN	18378	1394	35.8	34.2	23.2	4.7	2.2	34320	39171	25	31	1145	28.8	35.2	27.6	6.7	1.7	71933
30625	BUCKHEAD	26534	906	19.9	25.9	36.3	9.9	8.0	52949	62822	77	78	763	13.4	19.8	34.9	25.0	7.0	120490
30627	CARLTON	22603	852	32.5	33.2	24.7	3.5	6.1	38233	43439	40	47	723	24.9	23.8	33.1	17.0	1.2	92639
30628	COLBERT	21322	2704	27.1	32.3	30.0	7.9	2.6	42965	49556	56	61	2261	17.7	25.3	39.7	14.8	2.6	99606
30629	COMER	19999	1630	34.5	30.4	27.0	4.6	3.6	36133	41324	32	39	1347	22.1	28.7	36.3	10.6	2.3	88765
30630	CRAWFORD	19513	849	35.2	32.2	23.8	5.3	3.5	37574	43181	38	45	661	24.1	21.9	35.3	17.1	1.7	98833
30631	CRAWFORDVILLE	18286	878	45.9	28.5	17.0	5.6	3.1	27148	31032	7	6	693	44.7	32.6	16.6	6.1	0.0	56636
30633	DANIELSVILLE	19444	3195	27.5	31.6	34.3	5.2	1.4	41945	47650	53	57	2666	20.7	22.5	40.2	13.6	3.0	99430
30634	DEWY ROSE	16154	556	26.3	36.5	30.6	5.4	1.3	39124	44279	43	49	488	28.5	28.5	32.0	9.4	1.6	78710
30635	ELBERTON	16720	6678	41.2	30.9	21.9	4.2	1.9	31346	35100	16	18	4972	31.0	30.7	27.3	8.8	2.2	73993
30641	GOOD HOPE	24238	580	19.1	26.0	40.7	9.7	4.5	54184	62850	79	80	499	5.8	12.6	45.5	23.5	12.6	133929
30642	GREENSBORO	37029	3972	32.0	22.5	22.2	10.1	13.1	43781	61584	58	62	3034	23.5	22.5	18.2	10.8	25.0	100658
30643	HARTWELL	20823	6386	33.1	29.6	28.3	6.1	3.0	37729	44351	38	45	5050	15.3	32.6	30.7	17.2	4.2	93484
30646	HULL	20782	2446	26.5	35.0	28.7	7.4	2.4	42016	48375	53	58	1938	18.7	25.8	42.4	10.6	2.5	95815
30648	LEXINGTON	20568	947	30.8	30.9	27.2	7.0	4.0	37415	43226	37	44	791	25.3	24.4	31.4	16.8	2.2	90455
30650	MADISON	23881	3933	26.7	27.6	31.1	8.5	6.1	45594	54537	63	66	3141	16.4	22.0	31.5	19.6	10.5	113582
30655	MONROE	22202	8255	27.9	27.7	30.2	9.7	4.5	43691	52194	58	62	5683	10.5	18.0	44.3	22.5	4.8	123938
30656	MONROE	23374	4453	19.9	26.3	36.2	11.9	5.7	53452	62948	78	79	3546	6.0	10.8	51.9	25.6	5.8	135368
30660	RAYLE	16905	477	39.2	31.2	24.7	2.1	2.7	32933	38632	21	25	396	33.1	30.1	25.0	10.9	1.0	74762
30662	ROYSTON	18591	3240	37.0	29.7	26.5	4.4	2.4	34603	39715	26	33	2508	25.8	30.6	29.7	12.4	1.4	81615
30663	RUTLEDGE	22062	1217	23.8	30.1	29.8	11.9	4.4	45625	55235	63	67	1015	7.3	16.6	43.4	29.7	3.2	124651
30666	STATHAM	20942	2237	24.9	30.1	33.0	7.8	4.2	46139	51702	64	69	1885	13.5	18.1	44.4	19.1	4.9	115270
30667	STEPHENS	16779	409	35.0	25.2	35.0	2.7	2.2	40396	45896	47	53	350	31.1	24.6	32.3	9.7	2.3	83103
30668	TIGNALL	16505	874	40.5	33.0	20.9	5.5	0.1	30903	35877	15	16	710	42.5	32.5	18.7	5.6	0.6	57794
30669	UNION POINT	19140	1451	38.4	34.1	19.6	5.7	2.2	32554	38433	19	23	1127	43.0	28.9	23.1	3.3	1.7	59937
30673	WASHINGTON	17946	3363	39.8	27.1	25.7	5.6	1.8	32697	38324	20	24	2521	25.8	34.8	28.2	9.8	1.4	74600
30677	WATKINSVILLE	30237	5374	13.6	22.1	37.9	15.8	10.6	65506	80349	89	90	4609	6.3	6.5	36.9	39.7	10.6	175743
30678	WHITE PLAINS	21207	502	31.3	24.3	29.3	12.2	3.0	44256	55533	59	64	423	32.2	19.4	17.7	18.9	11.8	86750
30680	WINDER	21403	11031	23.4	28.9	35.6	9.1	3.0	48183	53892	69	73	8068	9.0	13.6	56.5	18.4	2.5	123327
30683	WINTERVILLE	22522	2175	21.5	34.4	31.7	9.5	2.9	45183	54537	62	66	1674	15.1	18.0	49.1	14.7	3.1	110852
30701	CALHOUN	21653	12211	27.3	29.8	32.1	7.2	3.7	44576	50996	60	65	8834	11.3	24.4	44.9	17.0	2.3	105575
30705	CHATSWORTH	19381	12468	26.7	33.6	31.9	4.9	2.8	42502	47574	55	59	9675	26.5	24.9	37.1	10.3	1.2	88092
30707	CHICKAMAUGA	19748	5580	28.3	34.1	30.3	4.6	2.7	40804	45997	49	54	4574	18.4	33.8	36.8	9.8	1.3	87513
30708	CISCO	17598	300	33.3	32.3	28.7	4.7	1.0	35398	40087	29	35	247	48.6	17.0	26.7	5.7	2.0	58750
30710	COHUTTA	24377	2126	17.9	26.2	38.6	12.0	5.4	55113	64432	80	81	1850	14.1	18.0	38.4	27.8	1.8	119427
30711	CRANDALL	17614	1376	28.9	37.4	26.4	5.7	1.7	38018	42826	39	46	1128	36.3	19.9	33.2	7.6	3.0	77455
30720	DALTON	31598	9508	22.8	29.2	27.4	9.7	10.9	47915	58109	68	72	5754	8.3	16.6	37.3	29.3	8.5	138052
30721	DALTON	17499	15614	27.1	34.3	29.9	6.0	2.7	40758	47735	49	54	11062	17.5	27.0	44.9	8.5	2.0	97190
30725	FLINTSTONE	20436	1432	25.4	34.9	33.7	4.9	1.2	42081	46257	53	58	1120	12.5	39.7	39.3	8.0	0.5	88227
30728	LA FAYETTE	17191	6848	37.3	32.0	25.5	3.3	1.8	34659	39273	26	33	5137	22.0	36.3	31.4	8.1	2.2	80563
30730	LYERLY	18814	745	25.9	35.2	31.5	5.9	1.5	40580	45691	48	53	602	24.4	28.1	34.2	11.6	1.7	86667
30731	MENLO	21108	1108	29.8	36.6	26.9	4.4	2.3	38146	43442	40	46	925	23.8	29.4	32.9	12.7	1.3	85903
30733	PLAINVILLE	17725	791	28.8	32.5	33.0	4.4	1.3	40242	46074	47	52	647	13.0	33.7	38.5	13.1	1.7	92471
30734	RANGER	19118	1263	22.9	38.8	31.7	4.1	2.5	41677	47530	52	57	1069	28.9	22.6	34.5	10.6	3.4	87155
30735	RESACA	18546	1855	26.3	33.0	32.5	5.2	3.1	41843	47827	52	57	1537	26.5	20.9	35.0	15.0	2.7	92630
30736	RINGGOLD	22615	14282	20.8	29.4	36.5	10.4	2.9	49832	55737	72	74	11931	9.2	19.8	51.8	16.4	2.8	114560
30738	RISING FAWN	19088	1446	31.6	34.2	27.6	4.4	2.2	38050	43789	39	46	1208	24.9	26.0	34.4	12.8	1.9	88721
30739	ROCK SPRING	17935	1389	26.2	32.7	32.8	6.9	1.4	43195	47915	56	61	1194	14.2	31.2	39.7	13.7	1.1	94779
30740	ROCKY FACE	22946	2949	22.3	25.3	35.7	12.3	4.4	52276	62728	76	78	2444	13.7	18.5	45.2	18.0	4.7	113697
30741	ROSSVILLE	17402	11878	35.3	35.0	24.7	3.6	1.4	34451	39555	26	32	8879	23.7	43.5	29.3	3.4	0.1	73301
30742	FORT OGLETHORPE	17410	2675	39.4	32.9	22.2	4.2	1.3	32254	37105	18	21	1661	5.3	40.9	47.3	6.5	0.0	93079
30746	SUGAR VALLEY	20787	438	28.8	32.2	27.9	5.3	5.9	42779	48732	55	60	364	21.7	24.7	31.6	17.9	4.1	95652
30747	SUMMERVILLE	16910	6070	36.8	33.2	24.2	4.7	1.0	33962	38161	24	29	4659	30.0	33.0	28.1	8.1	0.9	73567
30750	LOOKOUT MOUNTAIN	30261	1342	18.6	24.5	31.7	13.9	11.3	58050	72460	83	84	1125	12.6	11.2	29.5	34.0	12.7	168750
30751	TENNGA	16698	31	38.7	32.3	22.6	6.5	0.0	31120	38632	15	17	26	53.9	15.4	23.1	7.7	0.0	40000
30752	TRENTON	18715	3491	33.2	32.6	28.5	3.1	2.6	37227	42204	36	43	2853	26.5	29.6	34.2	8.3	1.4	82159
30753	TRION	17311	2722	36.9	35.0	22.5	3.9	1.7	32648	36660	20	24	2109	33.6	39.7	19.7	4.6	2.4	66137
30755	TUNNEL HILL	19667	3293	24.6	31.7	34.5	7.2	2.0	45436	51839	62	66	2739	14.7	33.2	38.6	11.0	2.5	92614
30757	WILDWOOD	25792	747	23.6	32.4	33.6	4.8	5.6	45924	52674	64	68	612	27.6	23.5	35.6	11.8	1.5	89028
30802	APPLING	22671	1932	17.1	28.9	38.1	11.8	4.1	53173	61868	77	79	1627	19.0	27.0	29.8	18.6	5.5	97679
30803	AVERA	19770	315	34.0	33.3	24.4	5.4	2.9	34857	40150	27	34	268	35.8	33.2	20.9	6.7	3.4	63871
30805	BLYTHE	19850	750	26.5	31.6	30.3	8.3	3.3	43439	51186	57	61	625	32.2	25.8	36.3	5.1	0.6	82500
30808	DEARING	19641	1597	30.3	37.8	22.7	6.3	3.0	36602	43534	34	41	1305	32.9	38.2	22.1	5.8	1.1	66520
30809	EVANS	31709	10587	6.6	15.4	41.4	24.8	11.8	80874	97637	95	96	9498	1.5	4.1	48.7	41.2	4.5	168665
30810	GIBSON	15999	655	41.2	29.6	24.1	4.6	0.5	34219	38403	25	31	512	35.2	32.6	22.9	6.1	3.3	65849
30813	GROVETOWN	19928	6044	20.8	30.3	37.7	9.0	2.2	49005	58016	70	74	4815	20.2	23.0	44.7	10.9	1.3	98773
30814	HARLEM	21502	2775	25.9	31.9	31.6	7.4	3.1	43469	51692	57	62	2313	21.1	31.0	37.4	9.7	0.9	87660
30815	HEPHZIBAH	18048	12756	23.1	33.5	33.3	8.1	2.0	45158	51894	62	66	10222	16.1	34.0	44.9	4.4	0.5	89872
30816	KEYSVILLE	15320	588	40.3	29.8	22.3	5.3	2.4	31604	36556	17	20	476	35.5	34.0	21.6	7.6	1.3	65192
30817	LINCOLNTON	18418	3290	34.7	29.6	27.4	6.7	1.6	35997	41591	32	38	2716	27.9	25.4	28.5	14.9	3.2	82417
30818	MATTHEWS	15705	201	31.8	35.3	26.4	4.0	2.5	34463	39568	26	32	156	39.1	24.4	26.9	8.3	1.3	70000
30820	MITCHELL	18198	399	39.4	28.8	23.1	7.3	1.5	31768	36357	17	20	334	41.3	38.0	12.9	7.8	0.0	60652
30821	NORWOOD	17096	454	41.0	30.0	21.2	4.6	3.3	30466	35427	13	15	376	55.1	26.1	15.7	2.9	0.3	46200
30822	PERKINS	14211	265	44.2	32.8	20.8	2.3	0.0	29494	34357	11	12	218	54.1	20.6	17.9	6.4	0.9	47353
30823	STAPLETON	16518	503	36.6	38.2	17.1	6.2	2.0	33533	39586	22	27	417	39.3	31.2	24.7	4.8	0.0	63163
30824	THOMSON	23092	6603	36.6	26.3	26.3	7.0	3.9	36883	43684	35	42	4730	24.4	35.8	27.4	11.4	1.0	77358
	GEORGIA	26143		23.6	26.3	31.4	11.6	7.0	50024	60470				12.5	17.5	39.3	24.8	6.0	125860
	UNITED STATES	25866		24.7	27.1	30.8	10.9	6.5	48124	56710				10.9	15.0	33.7	30.1	10.4	145905

SPENDING POTENTIAL INDICES GEORGIA
30567-30824 D

#	ZIP CODE POST OFFICE NAME	FINANCIAL SERVICES Auto Loan	Home Loan	Investments	Retirement Plans	THE HOME Home Improvements Home Repair	Lawn & Garden	Furnishings Computers & Hardware	Major Appliances	TV, Radio, Sound Equipment	Furniture	ENTERTAINMENT Dine out/ Carry out	Sports Equipment	Fees & Tickets	Toys & Games	Travel	Cable TV	PERSONAL Apparel & Services	Auto Repairs	Health Insurance	Pets & Supplies
30567	PENDERGRASS	102	92	72	89	94	99	88	95	89	90	110	110	83	106	87	89	106	94	96	114
30568	RABUN GAP	100	71	38	62	80	91	68	84	81	69	95	99	59	91	70	86	87	83	102	117
30571	SAUTEE NACOOCHEE	95	77	56	72	85	96	73	86	80	74	97	96	68	91	77	85	90	84	101	111
30572	SUCHES	183	144	98	130	162	182	135	163	153	134	182	191	121	179	144	164	169	161	193	223
30575	TALMO	98	84	62	80	86	92	81	89	84	83	103	103	75	97	80	84	98	88	92	109
30576	TIGER	100	73	44	68	84	94	71	87	81	70	96	103	62	94	75	86	88	85	103	119
30577	TOCCOA	75	59	42	54	63	72	59	66	66	59	79	78	54	77	59	69	74	66	76	86
30582	YOUNG HARRIS	76	65	54	61	70	82	63	72	69	65	84	75	61	73	66	73	77	70	85	85
30597	DAHLONEGA	0	0	0	0	0	0	0	0	0	0	0	0	0	0	0	0	0	0	0	0
30601	ATHENS	54	45	48	44	45	51	52	51	55	52	68	59	49	64	50	55	65	53	53	59
30602	ATHENS	10	6	7	7	6	7	11	8	11	10	14	12	9	12	9	10	13	10	8	10
30605	ATHENS	63	47	59	52	47	53	72	58	70	64	87	77	63	81	62	63	83	67	54	66
30606	ATHENS	92	85	98	90	83	90	99	91	97	96	122	111	95	117	92	91	118	97	85	101
30607	ATHENS	75	71	71	69	70	76	74	74	76	74	94	85	72	92	73	76	92	76	74	83
30609	ATHENS	37	23	29	26	22	27	44	32	43	37	54	45	36	48	35	38	50	40	30	37
30619	ARNOLDSVILLE	78	69	53	67	71	77	68	73	71	68	86	84	64	84	67	71	82	72	77	87
30620	BETHLEHEM	99	96	81	95	95	99	91	95	90	93	112	110	89	109	90	88	108	94	92	110
30621	BISHOP	106	113	106	111	114	116	103	107	101	104	125	126	105	129	105	100	122	104	103	125
30622	BOGART	112	121	119	121	120	122	113	115	109	113	136	135	115	140	114	107	134	113	108	131
30624	BOWMAN	86	59	28	51	66	76	57	70	68	58	80	84	49	76	58	73	73	70	86	99
30625	BUCKHEAD	109	97	73	92	102	109	90	99	95	90	116	118	87	117	92	97	110	97	107	127
30627	CARLTON	104	73	38	65	81	92	71	86	83	72	98	102	61	92	71	88	90	85	103	119
30628	COLBERT	90	82	64	78	82	86	78	84	79	80	97	97	74	92	77	78	93	83	83	99
30629	COMER	91	70	43	64	75	83	67	78	75	69	90	92	60	85	67	78	84	78	88	103
30630	CRAWFORD	77	67	52	66	69	76	67	72	70	67	85	82	64	83	66	70	81	71	75	85
30631	CRAWFORDVILLE	81	54	24	47	61	70	52	65	63	53	74	78	44	70	53	68	67	64	80	92
30633	DANIELSVILLE	80	73	56	70	73	78	69	74	70	71	87	86	65	83	68	70	83	74	75	89
30634	DEWY ROSE	83	62	36	55	68	76	58	70	67	59	80	83	53	78	60	71	74	69	82	96
30635	ELBERTON	72	53	35	48	58	67	54	62	62	54	73	72	48	70	54	65	68	62	73	81
30641	GOOD HOPE	101	90	69	86	95	102	83	92	88	83	108	110	82	110	86	91	102	90	100	119
30642	GREENSBORO	148	123	103	115	131	152	123	137	135	125	164	151	117	151	127	142	154	136	158	167
30643	HARTWELL	87	65	39	58	72	82	63	75	72	63	86	87	56	81	65	77	79	74	90	101
30646	HULL	92	74	50	69	78	86	71	81	77	73	93	95	65	89	71	79	88	80	89	104
30648	LEXINGTON	96	69	38	62	76	86	67	81	78	68	92	95	59	87	68	82	85	80	95	110
30650	MADISON	111	91	62	84	97	106	86	98	94	87	113	116	80	111	87	97	106	96	109	128
30655	MONROE	94	81	65	78	84	91	80	86	85	80	103	101	76	102	79	86	98	85	92	107
30656	MONROE	95	98	92	97	98	101	93	95	91	92	113	112	93	115	93	90	110	94	92	110
30660	RAYLE	79	53	24	46	60	69	51	64	62	52	73	76	44	69	52	67	66	63	79	91
30662	ROYSTON	77	60	39	56	65	74	60	68	67	60	80	79	55	77	61	70	74	68	79	88
30663	RUTLEDGE	98	87	67	83	92	99	81	90	86	81	104	107	79	107	83	88	99	87	97	116
30666	STATHAM	93	81	62	77	84	90	78	85	81	79	100	99	73	96	78	83	95	84	90	105
30667	STEPHENS	87	59	27	51	66	76	57	71	68	58	80	84	48	76	57	73	73	70	87	100
30668	TIGNALL	71	49	25	43	56	64	47	59	56	48	66	70	41	63	49	61	60	58	72	83
30669	UNION POINT	92	62	29	54	70	81	60	74	72	61	84	89	51	80	61	77	77	74	91	105
30673	WASHINGTON	67	56	46	52	59	68	57	62	64	57	77	71	55	75	58	67	72	62	72	76
30677	WATKINSVILLE	116	137	140	137	135	133	123	124	115	124	145	145	129	152	125	112	144	120	112	139
30678	WHITE PLAINS	97	73	45	65	82	93	69	84	79	69	94	99	61	91	73	85	87	83	100	116
30680	WINDER	90	81	67	79	83	90	80	85	82	80	101	98	77	99	79	82	96	84	87	101
30683	WINTERVILLE	83	81	75	81	80	83	80	81	78	81	98	96	78	95	78	76	95	82	77	93
30701	CALHOUN	93	80	62	78	85	93	79	86	84	78	102	100	76	102	79	85	96	84	93	106
30705	CHATSWORTH	89	72	48	67	76	84	70	79	76	70	92	92	64	88	70	78	86	78	87	101
30707	CHICKAMAUGA	88	68	44	64	74	82	67	77	74	67	89	90	61	86	67	77	83	76	87	100
30708	CISCO	77	59	36	54	63	70	57	66	63	58	76	78	51	72	57	65	71	66	74	87
30710	COHUTTA	105	102	88	98	105	109	94	101	95	95	117	119	93	119	96	96	113	99	103	123
30711	CRANDALL	86	60	30	53	67	76	58	71	68	59	80	84	50	76	58	72	74	70	85	98
30720	DALTON	127	118	110	116	119	128	118	122	121	118	149	143	116	148	117	120	144	122	124	143
30721	DALTON	85	69	51	65	72	78	69	76	75	71	91	89	64	89	68	75	87	76	81	94
30725	FLINTSTONE	78	72	60	69	75	82	69	74	73	68	89	86	69	92	71	75	85	73	80	91
30728	LA FAYETTE	73	55	36	50	60	69	55	63	63	55	75	75	50	73	56	66	69	63	74	84
30730	LYERLY	89	60	27	52	68	78	58	72	70	59	82	86	49	77	59	75	74	71	89	103
30731	MENLO	89	61	30	54	69	79	59	73	71	60	83	87	51	79	60	76	76	72	89	102
30733	PLAINVILLE	84	61	34	55	68	77	58	70	68	59	80	84	52	78	60	72	74	69	84	97
30734	RANGER	96	66	32	58	74	85	64	79	76	65	89	94	55	84	65	81	81	78	95	110
30735	RESACA	93	66	34	58	74	84	63	77	74	64	88	92	55	84	64	79	81	76	93	108
30736	RINGGOLD	92	89	77	87	90	94	83	88	84	84	104	104	83	105	84	83	100	86	88	106
30738	RISING FAWN	82	64	41	59	69	78	62	72	70	62	83	84	57	82	63	73	77	71	82	94
30739	ROCK SPRING	85	66	43	61	72	80	63	73	71	64	85	87	58	83	64	74	79	72	84	98
30740	ROCKY FACE	99	90	72	86	93	99	84	92	87	85	107	108	82	107	85	88	102	90	96	114
30741	ROSSVILLE	66	56	43	52	59	66	56	61	61	55	73	71	53	73	56	63	69	60	68	76
30742	FORT OGLETHORPE	59	50	43	48	52	60	54	56	59	52	71	64	51	69	54	61	66	57	64	66
30746	SUGAR VALLEY	91	76	57	74	81	90	75	82	80	74	97	96	71	97	75	82	91	81	91	103
30747	SUMMERVILLE	73	50	25	43	56	65	48	60	58	49	68	71	42	65	49	62	62	59	73	84
30750	LOOKOUT MOUNTAIN	116	130	145	131	130	136	123	124	119	123	149	144	128	152	126	118	146	122	118	138
30751	TENNGA	80	54	24	46	61	70	52	65	63	53	73	77	44	69	53	67	67	64	80	92
30752	TRENTON	85	61	34	55	67	77	60	71	70	60	82	84	53	79	61	74	76	71	85	96
30753	TRION	75	56	34	50	62	70	54	64	63	54	74	76	49	73	55	67	69	63	76	87
30755	TUNNEL HILL	87	76	56	72	79	85	71	79	75	72	92	93	68	90	72	76	87	78	84	100
30757	WILDWOOD	98	84	65	83	88	99	86	92	91	84	111	105	82	110	85	93	104	90	100	109
30802	APPLING	104	92	71	88	95	101	88	96	91	90	111	112	82	106	88	91	106	96	99	118
30803	AVERA	86	58	26	50	65	75	55	69	67	57	79	83	47	74	56	72	71	69	86	99
30805	BLYTHE	92	81	61	78	82	88	78	85	80	80	98	98	73	93	77	80	94	84	86	102
30808	DEARING	90	75	53	70	77	84	72	80	76	74	93	93	66	88	71	77	88	80	85	100
30809	EVANS	131	150	151	156	144	142	137	135	126	141	160	158	142	161	135	118	158	132	117	148
30810	GIBSON	68	53	33	48	56	62	51	59	56	52	67	69	46	64	51	58	63	58	65	77
30813	GROVETOWN	90	87	74	85	87	90	82	86	81	84	101	100	80	97	81	80	98	85	84	101
30814	HARLEM	93	85	66	82	85	90	81	87	82	83	101	100	77	96	80	81	97	87	86	103
30815	HEPHZIBAH	81	81	72	80	79	81	77	79	75	78	94	93	75	91	76	72	91	79	75	91
30816	KEYSVILLE	73	55	35	50	59	66	54	62	61	55	73	73	48	70	54	64	68	62	72	83
30817	LINCOLNTON	81	59	34	53	66	76	58	70	68	58	80	82	51	76	60	72	73	69	84	94
30818	MATTHEWS	76	62	42	58	65	71	60	67	64	61	78	79	55	73	59	65	73	67	72	85
30820	MITCHELL	81	54	25	47	61	71	52	66	63	53	74	78	45	70	53	68	67	65	81	93
30821	NORWOOD	82	55	25	47	62	72	53	66	64	54	75	79	45	71	54	69	68	66	82	94
30822	PERKINS	68	46	21	39	52	60	44	55	53	45	63	66	38	59	45	57	57	55	68	78
30823	STAPLETON	86	59	29	52	66	76	57	70	68	58	80	84	49	76	58	73	73	70	85	99
30824	THOMSON	96	76	60	70	81	92	78	86	87	78	105	100	73	101	78	91	99	86	99	109
	GEORGIA	103	97	95	97	97	104	97	99	98	98	122	116	96	120	96	98	118	100	99	116
	UNITED STATES	100	100	100	100	100	100	100	100	100	100	100	100	100	100	100	100	100	100	100	100

# POST OFFICE NAME	COUNTY FIPS CODE	POPULATION 2000	2004	2009	2000-2004 ANNUAL RATE % Rate	State Centile	HOUSEHOLDS 2000	2004	2009	% Annual Rate 2000-2004	2004 Average HH Size	FAMILIES 2000	2004	% Annual Rate 2000-2004
30828 WARRENTON	301	4113	4098	4081	-0.1	11	1575	1600	1624	0.4	2.49	1083	1083	0.0
30830 WAYNESBORO	033	13656	14137	14760	0.8	33	4867	5100	5390	1.1	2.73	3530	3643	0.7
30833 WRENS	163	4088	4058	4034	-0.2	9	1550	1556	1564	0.1	2.61	1125	1113	-0.3
30901 AUGUSTA	245	20332	19728	19845	-0.7	2	7847	7718	7853	-0.4	2.41	4617	4405	-1.1
30904 AUGUSTA	245	29450	28495	28404	-0.8	2	12589	12269	12330	-0.6	2.21	7007	6625	-1.3
30905 AUGUSTA	245	7763	7620	7592	-0.4	4	864	835	835	-0.8	3.68	842	813	-0.8
30906 AUGUSTA	245	60383	61808	63047	0.6	26	20984	21616	22194	0.7	2.77	15611	15821	0.3
30907 AUGUSTA	073	45341	49340	55107	2.0	59	17010	18751	21143	2.3	2.61	12815	13936	2.1
30909 AUGUSTA	245	34134	34647	35286	0.4	19	14925	15333	15763	0.6	2.18	9076	9073	0.0
30912 AUGUSTA	245	1217	1199	1196	-0.4	6	712	694	693	-0.6	1.64	165	153	-1.8
31001 ABBEVILLE	315	3388	3423	3446	0.2	16	808	836	857	0.8	2.48	570	581	0.5
31002 ADRIAN	167	2844	3113	3315	2.2	61	1111	1234	1331	2.5	2.46	798	872	2.1
31003 ALLENTOWN	319	503	520	537	0.8	33	202	212	222	1.1	2.45	156	162	0.9
31005 BONAIRE	153	10548	12063	14115	3.2	79	3625	4191	4952	3.5	2.88	3149	3600	3.2
31006 BUTLER	269	5320	5391	5512	0.3	18	1908	1962	2038	0.7	2.57	1346	1364	0.3
31007 BYROMVILLE	093	1118	1096	1096	-0.5	4	363	357	361	-0.4	2.83	268	260	-0.7
31008 BYRON	225	13206	14771	16456	2.7	71	4845	5492	6191	3.0	2.69	3769	4215	2.7
31009 CADWELL	175	1310	1417	1504	1.9	54	522	573	617	2.2	2.47	380	410	1.8
31011 CHAUNCEY	091	1596	1531	1535	-1.0	1	611	596	606	-0.6	2.50	455	437	-1.0
31012 CHESTER	091	2030	2487	2808	4.9	91	402	588	726	9.4	2.52	292	422	9.1
31014 COCHRAN	023	12948	13563	14462	1.1	39	4862	5163	5585	1.4	2.50	3477	3635	1.1
31015 CORDELE	081	20933	21326	21690	0.4	21	7921	8161	8382	0.7	2.56	5573	5649	0.3
31016 CULLODEN	207	1379	1516	1665	2.3	63	512	570	634	2.6	2.65	383	420	2.2
31017 DANVILLE	289	1937	2122	2292	2.2	62	751	834	915	2.5	2.54	537	588	2.2
31018 DAVISBORO	303	2573	2630	2671	0.5	25	490	514	533	1.1	2.94	368	381	0.8
31019 DEXTER	175	1993	2081	2168	1.0	37	793	840	886	1.4	2.48	575	598	0.8
31020 DRY BRANCH	289	2998	3055	3183	0.4	21	1097	1136	1202	0.8	2.69	833	850	0.5
31021 DUBLIN	175	27033	27641	28784	0.5	25	10247	10615	11213	0.8	2.49	7095	7227	0.4
31022 DUDLEY	175	1113	1073	1096	-0.9	1	430	421	436	-0.5	2.55	324	312	-0.9
31023 EASTMAN	091	13164	13316	13587	0.3	17	5101	5228	5411	0.6	2.42	3452	3472	0.1
31024 EATONTON	237	17483	19174	21207	2.2	63	6867	7649	8588	2.6	2.47	5074	5573	2.2
31025 ELKO	153	1375	1723	2112	5.5	94	489	620	767	5.7	2.78	386	482	5.4
31027 EAST DUBLIN	175	9476	10288	11020	2.0	57	3534	3888	4219	2.3	2.65	2631	2847	1.9
31028 CENTERVILLE	153	3919	4330	5004	2.4	66	1458	1642	1924	2.8	2.63	1152	1276	2.4
31029 FORSYTH	207	13385	14138	15293	1.3	44	4692	5012	5489	1.6	2.71	3535	3723	1.2
31030 FORT VALLEY	225	15565	16511	17680	1.4	46	5470	5884	6392	1.7	2.63	3726	3942	1.3
31031 GORDON	319	6887	7052	7274	0.6	26	2578	2678	2804	0.9	2.63	1894	1938	0.5
31032 GRAY	169	9354	10330	11714	2.4	66	3374	3787	4361	2.8	2.66	2607	2890	2.5
31033 HADDOCK	169	2061	2253	2520	2.1	61	777	861	976	2.4	2.61	578	631	2.1
31035 HARRISON	303	1437	1558	1634	1.9	56	520	568	603	2.1	2.74	400	432	1.8
31036 HAWKINSVILLE	235	11042	11839	12732	1.7	51	3926	4267	4652	2.0	2.52	2743	2942	1.7
31037 HELENA	271	2767	2857	2944	0.8	31	674	722	771	1.6	2.54	470	495	1.2
31038 HILLSBORO	169	682	731	834	1.7	51	260	281	324	1.8	2.60	191	204	1.6
31041 IDEAL	193	1100	1126	1153	0.6	26	404	424	444	1.1	2.47	293	303	0.8
31042 IRWINTON	319	1564	1546	1574	-0.3	8	564	567	586	0.1	2.70	422	419	-0.2
31044 JEFFERSONVILLE	289	3384	3503	3686	0.8	33	1183	1250	1342	1.3	2.69	877	913	1.0
31045 JEWELL	301	987	979	972	-0.2	8	378	383	389	0.3	2.56	283	283	0.0
31046 JULIETTE	207	2807	2960	3212	1.3	43	1034	1101	1207	1.5	2.69	846	893	1.3
31047 KATHLEEN	153	5682	6976	8433	5.0	92	1913	2384	2917	5.3	2.88	1574	1929	4.9
31049 KITE	167	1447	1536	1603	1.4	47	578	620	656	1.7	2.44	425	450	1.4
31050 KNOXVILLE	079	3612	3931	4345	2.0	59	1221	1337	1489	2.2	2.94	965	1046	1.9
31052 LIZELLA	079	8540	9220	9740	1.8	53	3130	3417	3647	2.1	2.67	2472	2667	1.8
31054 MC INTYRE	319	1209	1215	1235	0.1	14	457	467	482	0.5	2.60	333	335	0.1
31055 MC RAE	271	5044	5172	5351	0.6	27	1934	2012	2115	0.9	2.47	1351	1383	0.6
31057 MARSHALLVILLE	193	2003	2034	2083	0.4	19	742	773	810	1.0	2.55	522	535	0.6
31058 MAUK	269	1640	1735	1803	1.3	45	619	663	698	1.6	2.60	460	485	1.3
31060 MILAN	271	1810	1820	1856	0.1	15	650	666	694	0.6	2.36	466	470	0.2
31061 MILLEDGEVILLE	009	43781	45001	46554	0.7	29	14436	15142	16008	1.1	2.46	9598	9889	0.7
31063 MONTEZUMA	193	6060	6129	6277	0.3	17	2134	2190	2281	0.6	2.76	1553	1572	0.3
31064 MONTICELLO	159	7651	8712	10362	3.1	77	2851	3277	3930	3.3	2.63	2077	2348	2.9
31065 MONTROSE	175	921	901	932	-0.5	3	340	336	351	-0.3	2.67	264	258	-0.5
31066 MUSELLA	079	1360	1545	1747	3.1	76	515	594	680	3.4	2.58	382	434	3.1
31068 OGLETHORPE	193	4530	4700	4847	0.9	34	1415	1503	1586	1.4	2.66	1015	1061	1.1
31069 PERRY	153	15190	17365	20233	3.2	79	5685	6578	7748	3.5	2.60	4210	4772	3.0
31070 PINEHURST	093	815	816	830	0.0	12	341	345	356	0.3	2.37	235	234	-0.1
31071 PINEVIEW	315	1212	1211	1213	0.0	12	443	449	454	0.3	2.55	321	320	-0.1
31072 PITTS	315	1235	1261	1280	0.5	23	484	503	516	0.9	2.44	339	347	0.6
31075 RENTZ	175	1867	2000	2113	1.6	51	737	802	859	2.0	2.49	548	587	1.6
31076 REYNOLDS	269	2956	3092	3232	1.1	38	1161	1238	1317	1.5	2.44	785	822	1.1
31077 RHINE	091	1042	1008	1014	-0.8	2	437	428	436	-0.5	2.35	306	295	-0.9
31078 ROBERTA	079	2476	2674	2940	1.8	53	911	1002	1120	2.3	2.57	676	734	2.0
31079 ROCHELLE	315	2863	2905	2932	0.3	19	1091	1121	1145	0.6	2.57	777	787	0.3
31081 RUPERT	269	200	210	218	1.2	41	88	93	98	1.3	2.26	63	65	0.6
31082 SANDERSVILLE	303	10526	10785	11075	0.6	26	3995	4163	4340	1.0	2.54	2859	2930	0.6
31085 SHADY DALE	159	851	1041	1281	4.9	91	284	350	433	5.0	2.97	227	276	4.7
31087 SPARTA	141	10039	10290	10602	0.6	27	3224	3395	3599	1.2	2.60	2302	2387	0.9
31088 WARNER ROBINS	153	36960	42050	49311	3.1	77	14167	16221	19148	3.2	2.58	10140	11449	2.9
31089 TENNILLE	303	4902	4784	4812	-0.6	3	1783	1755	1785	-0.4	2.68	1281	1242	-0.7
31090 TOOMSBORO	319	1157	1288	1384	2.6	69	415	468	511	2.9	2.63	303	336	2.5
31091 UNADILLA	093	3860	3824	3843	-0.2	8	1079	1078	1099	0.0	2.49	753	739	-0.4
31092 VIENNA	093	5775	6048	6266	1.1	39	2153	2284	2395	1.4	2.63	1531	1599	1.0
31093 WARNER ROBINS	153	27481	29593	33732	1.8	52	10925	11905	13715	2.0	2.45	7342	7835	1.5
31094 WARTHEN	303	1284	1275	1298	-0.2	9	492	496	512	0.2	2.56	358	354	-0.3
31096 WRIGHTSVILLE	167	6154	6257	6350	0.4	20	2173	2250	2325	0.8	2.54	1554	1583	0.4
31097 YATESVILLE	293	1241	1285	1330	0.8	33	468	490	512	1.1	2.62	374	387	0.8
31098 WARNER ROBINS	153	5402	5979	6764	2.4	67	1083	1249	1475	3.4	3.62	1029	1171	3.1
31201 MACON	021	9554	9407	9422	-0.4	6	4177	4148	4148	-0.4	2.09	1882	1810	-0.9
31204 MACON	021	32834	32113	32010	-0.5	3	13811	13646	13737	-0.3	2.32	8547	8232	-0.9
31206 MACON	021	31100	30643	30811	-0.4	6	11407	11303	11454	-0.2	2.66	7882	7651	-0.7
31207 MACON	021	1366	1347	1343	-0.3	7	2	2	2	0.0	2.50	0	0	0.0
31210 MACON	021	28128	29584	30533	1.2	42	11234	11996	12532	1.6	2.43	7816	8191	1.1
31211 MACON	169	16454	17410	18729	1.3	45	6764	7223	7821	1.6	2.40	4527	4749	1.1
31216 MACON	021	14189	14955	15390	1.2	43	5028	5392	5626	1.7	2.57	3919	4139	1.3
31217 MACON	289	20585	21215	22250	0.7	31	7261	7555	8017	0.9	2.74	5349	5496	0.6
31220 MACON	021	11153	11794	12150	1.3	45	4144	4449	4643	1.7	2.69	3172	3350	1.3
GEORGIA					2.4					2.5	2.64			2.2
UNITED STATES					1.2					1.3	2.58			1.1

ZIP CODE #	POST OFFICE NAME	RACE (%) White 2000	White 2004	Black 2000	Black 2004	Asian/Pacific 2000	Asian/Pacific 2004	% Hispanic Origin 2000	% Hispanic Origin 2004	2004 AGE DISTRIBUTION (%) 0-4	5-9	10-14	15-19	20-24	25-44	45-64	65-84	85+	18+	MEDIAN AGE 2004	% 2004 Males	% 2004 Females
30828	WARRENTON	40.6	39.2	58.3	59.7	0.2	0.2	0.9	0.9	6.9	7.2	7.4	6.7	6.2	24.6	25.2	12.9	2.9	74.5	38.2	46.8	53.2
30830	WAYNESBORO	43.4	40.6	54.6	57.2	0.2	0.2	1.4	1.6	8.2	8.2	8.8	8.2	7.4	25.7	23.0	9.0	1.5	69.5	32.6	47.4	52.6
30833	WRENS	47.6	46.5	50.2	51.2	0.1	0.1	1.6	1.6	7.7	7.9	8.1	7.4	6.5	27.0	23.1	11.0	1.3	71.5	34.8	46.8	53.2
30901	AUGUSTA	8.6	8.7	89.4	89.2	0.5	0.5	1.1	1.2	8.6	7.7	7.5	7.1	8.1	24.8	21.3	12.4	2.5	71.9	33.0	46.9	53.2
30904	AUGUSTA	53.5	50.5	42.7	45.2	1.4	1.7	1.9	2.3	6.7	6.2	5.9	6.4	8.2	28.8	22.1	13.5	2.2	77.9	35.5	46.5	53.5
30905	AUGUSTA	56.0	51.9	32.9	35.6	2.6	2.9	10.7	12.7	6.9	5.7	4.7	23.2	28.8	29.1	1.5	0.1	0.1	80.9	21.6	69.0	31.1
30906	AUGUSTA	41.9	38.2	53.8	57.0	1.3	1.4	2.7	3.1	7.3	7.3	8.5	8.3	7.5	27.7	23.2	9.4	0.8	71.7	33.5	47.2	52.8
30907	AUGUSTA	82.6	80.2	10.5	11.7	4.5	5.2	2.4	3.0	6.1	6.5	7.5	6.9	7.0	28.0	27.6	9.2	1.2	75.6	37.3	47.9	52.1
30909	AUGUSTA	59.1	55.6	36.0	38.9	1.9	2.2	2.8	3.3	6.8	6.1	5.8	5.9	8.5	32.0	22.0	11.3	1.6	77.8	34.4	48.3	51.7
30912	AUGUSTA	35.0	31.4	62.1	65.5	0.8	0.9	1.4	1.6	3.5	3.0	3.4	3.7	8.0	24.0	26.8	23.4	4.3	87.8	48.0	50.6	49.4
31001	ABBEVILLE	52.7	51.3	46.3	47.8	0.2	0.2	1.0	1.0	4.4	4.6	4.5	4.7	8.4	39.4	24.1	8.7	1.3	84.1	37.0	67.3	32.7
31002	ADRIAN	84.2	82.8	12.7	13.4	0.0	0.1	2.9	3.5	6.3	6.6	7.3	6.6	5.5	26.5	24.7	14.1	2.3	75.6	39.0	49.1	50.9
31003	ALLENTOWN	77.1	74.0	22.3	25.4	0.0	0.0	0.6	0.6	4.4	4.6	5.8	6.4	5.2	26.5	30.8	14.8	1.5	81.4	43.6	47.9	52.1
31005	BONAIRE	85.3	83.1	10.5	11.9	1.8	2.2	2.8	3.6	6.2	7.0	8.8	8.1	5.7	27.7	28.8	7.4	0.4	72.8	38.2	50.4	49.6
31006	BUTLER	52.1	48.8	45.2	48.0	0.1	0.1	2.6	3.2	7.9	7.7	7.3	6.3	6.8	28.7	22.9	10.5	1.9	73.3	34.8	50.0	50.1
31007	BYROMVILLE	40.8	37.4	51.8	53.6	1.0	1.1	9.2	11.3	7.8	7.4	7.3	6.9	6.5	25.5	21.8	13.5	3.4	72.5	36.4	46.2	53.8
31008	BYRON	84.8	81.8	12.4	14.8	0.7	0.8	2.0	2.7	7.5	7.5	7.9	6.7	6.0	31.3	24.0	8.4	0.6	73.0	35.1	49.1	50.9
31009	CADWELL	81.1	77.6	18.4	21.8	0.1	0.1	0.8	1.0	6.3	5.6	6.7	6.9	6.3	27.9	26.3	12.0	2.2	77.1	39.0	49.9	50.1
31011	CHAUNCEY	76.3	74.2	23.1	25.1	0.0	0.0	0.9	1.2	7.3	7.1	6.6	6.5	6.5	27.6	25.3	11.8	1.3	75.1	37.2	51.0	49.1
31012	CHESTER	56.1	52.9	42.8	45.8	0.1	0.1	1.1	1.3	3.5	3.7	4.3	4.7	8.6	45.0	22.4	7.3	0.5	86.3	37.1	70.1	29.9
31014	COCHRAN	73.3	70.8	24.6	26.8	0.9	1.0	0.9	1.1	6.5	6.7	7.3	8.7	7.4	26.1	23.3	12.5	1.6	75.0	36.2	48.4	51.6
31015	CORDELE	52.8	49.8	44.7	47.2	0.7	0.8	1.8	2.2	7.9	7.6	7.8	7.2	7.2	25.6	23.5	11.4	1.8	72.4	35.0	47.0	53.0
31016	CULLODEN	48.3	46.5	51.2	52.9	0.1	0.1	0.8	1.0	5.1	5.5	6.7	6.5	5.5	27.0	30.0	12.8	1.0	79.0	41.2	49.5	50.5
31017	DANVILLE	59.4	55.5	39.3	43.2	0.1	0.1	0.6	0.8	6.6	6.8	7.7	6.8	6.1	27.5	25.4	11.5	1.6	74.7	36.8	47.3	52.7
31018	DAVISBORO	44.7	40.8	53.8	57.6	0.2	0.2	1.1	1.2	4.7	4.5	4.7	6.1	9.3	45.1	20.2	4.6	1.0	83.1	35.2	31.9	68.1
31019	DEXTER	90.1	87.8	9.3	11.3	0.2	0.2	0.3	0.3	7.0	6.9	6.5	6.3	6.4	27.7	27.5	10.2	1.4	75.7	37.0	50.2	49.8
31020	DRY BRANCH	58.1	55.4	40.2	42.6	0.1	0.2	1.0	1.2	7.0	7.2	7.3	7.2	6.6	28.1	25.9	9.9	0.9	74.1	36.5	48.7	51.3
31021	DUBLIN	56.7	53.8	40.9	43.4	1.3	1.5	1.1	1.4	7.1	6.9	7.3	6.8	6.7	26.6	24.4	12.3	2.1	74.7	37.2	48.2	51.8
31022	DUDLEY	71.0	66.6	27.9	32.2	0.1	0.1	0.5	0.5	6.3	6.8	7.4	6.2	6.3	28.9	25.5	10.4	2.1	75.8	38.0	47.7	52.3
31023	EASTMAN	68.3	66.0	29.7	31.6	0.3	0.4	1.5	1.8	6.7	6.8	7.5	8.8	6.2	26.0	23.8	12.2	1.9	72.9	36.0	48.7	51.4
31024	EATONTON	66.5	63.8	31.0	33.2	0.7	0.8	2.1	2.6	6.1	6.1	6.0	5.8	5.6	25.8	28.9	14.6	1.2	78.4	41.4	49.5	50.5
31025	ELKO	58.5	56.1	40.3	42.5	0.4	0.4	1.4	1.6	6.2	6.3	8.0	8.8	6.8	27.2	26.8	9.1	1.0	74.2	37.3	48.3	51.7
31027	EAST DUBLIN	68.4	64.9	30.0	33.3	0.2	0.2	1.6	2.0	7.0	7.1	8.4	7.1	7.0	28.3	23.9	10.2	0.9	73.1	35.0	48.4	51.6
31028	CENTERVILLE	83.1	80.7	12.8	14.4	1.3	1.6	2.6	3.4	7.3	7.2	7.9	7.1	6.5	30.0	24.2	9.3	0.6	73.2	35.1	48.9	51.1
31029	FORSYTH	62.8	60.0	35.5	38.0	0.4	0.5	1.4	1.6	6.4	6.6	7.4	7.0	6.9	29.1	25.3	9.9	1.5	75.4	36.3	49.9	50.1
31030	FORT VALLEY	34.1	31.4	62.1	64.3	0.3	0.3	5.5	6.5	6.5	6.2	7.1	8.4	11.7	27.0	22.3	9.6	1.2	76.4	31.6	48.1	51.9
31031	GORDON	64.4	61.5	34.3	36.9	0.1	0.1	0.8	1.1	7.5	7.3	7.2	7.0	6.8	28.3	24.0	10.9	1.1	73.8	35.7	48.3	51.7
31032	GRAY	73.9	70.8	24.5	27.4	0.5	0.6	0.8	1.0	6.4	6.6	7.5	6.7	6.0	28.4	26.5	10.4	1.5	75.3	38.0	49.2	50.8
31033	HADDOCK	66.8	63.1	30.8	34.1	0.4	0.4	1.6	1.8	6.5	6.6	8.0	7.3	6.5	28.9	25.7	9.5	1.0	74.6	36.3	49.6	50.4
31035	HARRISON	55.2	51.4	44.1	47.9	0.1	0.1	1.0	1.2	6.6	6.5	7.6	7.2	6.0	26.9	27.0	10.9	1.4	74.6	38.4	49.9	50.1
31036	HAWKINSVILLE	64.9	62.3	32.5	34.7	0.4	0.5	2.7	3.2	6.3	6.3	6.6	6.4	6.7	29.7	25.4	11.0	1.7	76.9	37.5	44.4	55.6
31037	HELENA	46.0	43.1	51.3	53.7	0.3	0.4	2.8	3.3	4.6	4.7	5.1	5.4	9.8	40.4	21.1	7.6	1.5	83.0	34.3	64.6	35.4
31038	HILLSBORO	66.7	62.5	32.3	36.3	0.2	0.3	0.6	0.7	6.8	6.7	6.6	7.5	7.0	27.2	26.1	10.9	1.1	75.4	37.7	49.5	50.5
31041	IDEAL	44.6	41.1	54.2	57.6	0.1	0.2	0.5	0.4	6.2	6.7	7.4	6.8	5.4	23.5	25.0	16.1	3.0	75.4	40.4	45.1	54.9
31042	IRWINTON	30.8	28.1	67.1	69.3	0.0	0.0	2.6	3.0	7.4	7.2	8.2	7.3	7.6	28.0	22.8	10.2	1.2	72.8	35.2	47.8	52.2
31044	JEFFERSONVILLE	40.9	37.5	58.0	61.4	0.1	0.2	1.3	1.4	6.2	6.4	6.9	7.0	7.1	27.1	25.5	12.2	1.6	76.3	37.7	47.5	52.5
31045	JEWELL	38.0	36.7	60.8	62.2	0.2	0.2	0.9	0.8	6.0	6.1	7.3	7.2	6.7	26.1	25.3	13.5	1.8	76.1	38.5	46.5	53.5
31046	JULIETTE	81.7	79.2	16.9	19.2	0.3	0.3	0.8	1.1	6.8	7.1	7.4	6.4	6.0	28.2	28.6	8.7	0.9	74.8	38.2	49.4	50.6
31047	KATHLEEN	81.2	78.7	15.8	17.8	1.0	1.3	1.8	2.3	6.6	7.0	8.5	7.5	6.5	30.0	26.2	6.9	0.9	72.8	36.1	49.5	50.5
31049	KITE	89.4	88.5	10.1	10.8	0.0	0.1	1.2	1.4	7.6	7.1	7.1	6.4	6.0	24.8	25.6	13.7	1.8	74.2	38.0	47.9	52.2
31050	KNOXVILLE	72.8	69.4	20.3	22.3	0.3	0.3	5.5	6.9	6.7	7.3	8.2	7.8	6.5	31.1	24.6	7.1	0.7	73.0	34.8	51.5	48.5
31052	LIZELLA	81.3	77.5	17.2	20.8	0.5	0.6	0.9	1.2	6.4	6.7	6.6	6.0	5.2	29.5	29.0	9.9	0.7	76.6	38.9	50.6	49.4
31054	MC INTYRE	75.8	72.8	23.0	25.8	0.3	0.3	0.3	0.4	7.9	7.6	6.1	6.2	6.3	27.7	25.0	12.0	1.2	74.7	37.1	48.2	51.9
31055	MC RAE	61.1	58.4	37.2	39.5	0.3	0.3	1.6	1.9	6.7	6.7	6.6	6.3	6.5	26.6	24.4	13.8	2.4	76.0	38.4	47.8	52.2
31057	MARSHALLVILLE	28.6	25.7	70.7	73.7	0.1	0.1	0.3	0.3	7.0	7.1	7.6	6.9	7.2	23.0	26.0	12.5	2.8	74.1	37.7	44.6	55.4
31058	MAUK	84.9	82.5	11.7	13.6	0.4	0.4	1.5	2.0	5.9	6.3	8.1	7.0	6.6	26.2	29.2	9.5	1.2	75.3	38.7	50.6	49.4
31060	MILAN	76.0	73.3	22.7	25.1	0.1	0.1	1.0	1.3	4.8	4.8	5.4	6.3	8.2	30.7	24.8	13.4	1.6	81.8	39.4	57.0	43.0
31061	MILLEDGEVILLE	54.0	51.1	43.6	46.2	1.0	1.2	1.4	1.6	5.2	5.2	5.8	8.2	9.9	31.1	23.5	9.9	1.2	79.8	35.1	54.1	45.9
31063	MONTEZUMA	35.2	32.8	61.5	63.2	0.6	0.7	2.7	3.2	8.4	8.2	8.2	7.3	7.2	24.2	23.6	11.2	1.7	70.6	34.3	46.7	53.3
31064	MONTICELLO	67.3	64.8	30.9	33.2	0.2	0.2	2.1	2.6	6.7	6.9	7.5	6.4	5.6	26.9	26.4	12.1	1.5	75.0	38.4	49.1	50.9
31065	MONTROSE	48.9	44.3	49.2	53.4	0.5	0.8	0.7	1.0	6.2	6.3	7.9	7.7	7.0	27.5	25.2	10.5	1.7	74.5	36.9	47.6	52.4
31066	MUSELLA	57.3	54.1	40.2	43.0	0.2	0.3	1.3	1.6	6.0	6.3	6.9	7.1	6.4	25.9	28.0	11.8	1.5	76.4	39.8	49.6	50.4
31068	OGLETHORPE	41.5	38.3	54.1	56.6	1.1	1.2	4.0	4.8	5.7	6.0	6.9	6.7	7.5	33.2	24.5	8.4	1.0	77.2	35.9	57.0	43.0
31069	PERRY	66.8	63.9	30.4	32.9	1.0	1.2	1.5	1.9	7.0	6.7	7.1	7.1	7.2	27.9	24.9	10.7	1.5	74.9	36.7	48.1	51.9
31070	PINEHURST	56.3	52.8	40.1	43.0	0.4	0.4	3.6	4.3	5.5	5.5	6.9	7.2	6.5	25.7	27.0	13.7	2.0	77.8	39.6	48.7	51.4
31071	PINEVIEW	69.2	68.1	29.3	30.3	0.1	0.1	2.1	2.1	6.9	6.9	7.1	7.0	6.2	23.1	24.1	14.7	3.9	75.1	39.4	47.4	52.6
31072	PITTS	87.9	87.4	10.8	11.3	0.1	0.1	3.5	3.6	6.4	6.4	6.2	6.7	6.2	25.5	27.5	13.3	1.8	76.6	40.2	50.4	49.6
31075	RENTZ	83.5	80.0	15.2	18.3	0.2	0.2	1.2	1.6	7.1	6.7	6.7	6.5	6.6	29.2	24.8	11.5	1.3	75.7	36.9	49.9	50.1
31076	REYNOLDS	54.0	51.1	45.3	48.2	0.3	0.4	0.5	0.6	6.0	6.5	7.7	7.8	5.6	25.9	26.0	12.7	1.8	74.2	38.7	47.7	52.3
31077	RHINE	77.8	75.9	21.4	23.2	0.0	0.0	1.3	1.5	6.0	6.3	6.6	6.3	5.8	25.6	26.8	14.8	2.1	77.5	40.9	48.2	51.8
31078	ROBERTA	42.8	39.4	54.9	58.0	0.2	0.2	1.3	1.5	5.7	6.0	6.8	6.5	6.1	25.3	28.3	13.4	2.1	77.4	41.0	48.7	51.4
31079	ROCHELLE	61.6	59.8	37.1	38.9	0.3	0.3	1.4	1.3	8.0	7.8	7.5	6.9	6.4	25.1	24.9	11.7	1.7	72.5	35.8	47.3	52.7
31081	RUPERT	80.5	78.6	17.0	19.1	0.0	0.0	1.0	1.0	5.7	6.7	7.6	5.2	6.2	25.7	29.5	11.4	1.9	76.7	40.3	51.4	48.6
31082	SANDERSVILLE	45.9	43.6	53.0	55.2	0.5	0.5	0.3	0.4	6.6	7.2	8.0	7.1	6.3	26.3	24.9	11.9	2.0	73.9	37.3	46.4	53.6
31085	SHADY DALE	77.8	74.7	20.1	22.7	0.0	0.1	2.4	3.2	7.7	7.8	8.3	7.5	6.7	28.0	24.7	8.6	0.9	71.7	34.5	50.4	49.6
31087	SPARTA	21.7	19.9	77.5	79.3	0.1	0.1	0.5	0.6	5.8	5.9	6.7	6.9	7.6	30.2	24.7	10.9	1.4	77.4	36.7	53.5	46.5
31088	WARNER ROBINS	73.8	70.9	20.7	22.7	2.0	2.4	3.9	4.9	7.0	6.6	7.8	7.5	8.3	30.2	23.5	8.6	0.7	74.0	34.3	49.3	50.7
31089	TENNILLE	40.4	37.0	58.4	61.8	0.1	0.1	0.9	1.1	7.2	7.4	8.7	7.4	7.3	26.7	23.0	10.2	2.2	72.1	34.9	47.4	52.6
31090	TOOMSBORO	55.1	51.3	44.0	47.6	0.0	0.0	0.9	1.1	6.8	6.5	6.6	6.4	6.4	24.6	23.9	16.2	2.6	75.9	39.7	46.7	53.3
31091	UNADILLA	42.2	38.7	53.9	56.6	0.4	0.5	3.7	4.5	5.3	5.2	5.0	5.7	8.6	36.4	24.0	8.5	1.2	81.4	36.7	62.6	37.4
31092	VIENNA	48.5	45.8	47.1	49.1	0.6	0.6	4.5	5.3	8.0	7.5	7.7	7.3	7.6	26.2	24.4	9.9	1.4	72.4	34.2	48.0	52.0
31093	WARNER ROBINS	60.0	57.1	35.4	37.6	1.5	1.7	2.8	3.4	7.2	6.8	7.7	7.0	7.5	29.1	22.6	11.1	1.1	73.9	34.8	47.7	52.3
31094	WARTHEN	54.8	51.1	44.9	48.4	0.1	0.1	0.6	0.6	5.7	6.2	7.7	7.0	6.1	27.6	26.0	11.8	1.9	76.2	39.0	48.4	51.6
31096	WRIGHTSVILLE	52.3	50.9	47.0	48.5	0.2	0.2	0.9	0.9	7.2	7.1	7.2	12.4	6.5	23.6	22.0	12.0	2.0	69.4	33.6	50.0	50.0
31097	YATESVILLE	77.0	75.2	21.8	23.6	0.2	0.2	1.1	1.4	5.6	6.0	7.3	6.9	6.2	27.5	28.2	11.2	1.2	76.8	39.2	50.3	49.7
31098	WARNER ROBINS	59.1	55.1	31.1	34.0	2.8	3.0	5.2	6.4	11.6	9.7	7.8	12.8	20.4	34.2	3.0	0.3	0.0	67.9	22.0	55.3	44.7
31201	MACON	24.6	21.4	73.3	76.5	0.5	0.6	1.4	1.4	9.1	6.7	5.6	6.4	10.0	27.8	20.4	11.3	2.8	75.8	32.7	47.1	52.9
31204	MACON	39.5	36.6	58.6	61.4	0.6	0.6	1.1	1.2	7.4	7.0	6.8	6.6	6.4	26.4	23.6	13.2	2.6	74.8	37.1	44.4	55.6
31206	MACON	33.1	28.3	64.7	69.3	0.5	0.5	1.5	1.7	8.8	8.1	8.9	8.3	7.9	26.7	20.1	9.9	1.3	69.2	31.2	45.3	54.7
31207	MACON	68.1	62.1	25.7	31.3	4.8	5.1	0.2	0.2	0.2	0.1	0.3	52.5	42.5	2.2	1.6	0.6	0.2	99.0	19.7	5.0	95.0
31210	MACON	78.0	74.4	17.4	20.3	3.1	3.5	1.5	2.0	6.5	6.6	7.5	7.4	7.1	28.4	25.2	10.3	1.1	75.1	36.1	46.8	53.2
31211	MACON	52.4	50.8	45.8	47.2	0.6	0.7	0.9	1.1	6.5	6.6	7.1	6.6	6.6	28.7	24.9	11.4	1.6	75.8	37.3	46.6	53.4
31216	MACON	86.4	83.3	11.3	13.9	0.5	0.6	1.5	2.1	5.9	6.3	6.4	5.6	5.0	30.2	27.7	11.8	1.1	77.9	39.7	52.5	47.5
31217	MACON	37.1	36.2	61.4	62.1	0.3	0.3	1.0	1.0	7.6	7.4	8.5	8.0	6.8	25.9	23.7	10.5	1.7	71.5	34.8	46.5	53.5
31220	MACON	82.4	78.2	14.9	18.7	1.4	1.6	1.3	1.6	7.4	7.5	6.8	6.2	5.6	30.9	26.5	7.9	1.1	74.2	36.5	48.1	52.0
	GEORGIA	65.1	63.4	28.7	29.4	2.2	2.5	5.3	6.6	7.3	7.1	7.2	7.0	7.6	31.0	23.0	8.6	1.1	74.3	34.2	49.3	50.7
	UNITED STATES	75.1	73.6	12.3	12.5	3.8	4.2	12.5	14.1	6.9	6.7	7.2	7.0	7.3	28.6	23.8	10.8	1.7	75.1	36.0	49.1	50.9

#	ZIP CODE POST OFFICE NAME	2004 Per Capita Income	2004 HH Income Base	2004 HOUSEHOLD INCOME DISTRIBUTION (%) Less than $25,000	$25,000 to $49,999	$50,000 to $99,999	$100,000 to $149,999	$150,000 or More	MEDIAN HOUSEHOLD INCOME 2004	2009	2004 National Centile	2004 State Centile	2004 Home Value Base	2004 HOME VALUE DISTRIBUTION (%) Less than $50,000	$50,000 to $89,999	$90,000 to $174,999	$175,000 to $399,999	$400,000 or More	2004 Median Home Value
30828	WARRENTON	16223	1600	43.9	28.5	21.8	3.1	2.6	29717	34042	12	12	1226	40.3	31.7	21.3	5.6	1.1	62712
30830	WAYNESBORO	15745	5100	42.8	25.8	23.8	5.7	1.9	30936	35674	15	16	3631	31.1	36.0	25.5	6.6	0.8	69015
30833	WRENS	15495	1556	43.3	32.1	19.9	2.5	2.3	28822	32465	10	11	1094	38.0	29.1	27.7	4.8	0.5	67708
30901	AUGUSTA	12347	7718	64.6	21.3	10.1	2.3	1.8	15947	18744	1	1	2838	54.7	36.1	5.5	3.1	0.6	46138
30904	AUGUSTA	23980	12269	40.4	30.1	19.4	5.2	4.9	32370	38151	19	22	6472	19.5	39.6	30.4	7.3	3.2	80638
30905	AUGUSTA	13363	835	13.5	48.7	33.5	4.2	0.0	41667	47065	52	56	23	0.0	47.8	52.2	0.0	0.0	92500
30906	AUGUSTA	17070	21616	31.9	33.4	27.4	5.7	1.6	37773	43314	38	45	15078	15.4	53.1	30.1	0.8	0.6	75079
30907	AUGUSTA	31310	18751	12.7	23.8	40.6	13.8	9.1	62632	74083	87	88	14401	2.9	18.5	54.0	20.8	3.8	118491
30909	AUGUSTA	31648	15333	26.4	29.3	26.6	9.6	8.1	44406	52810	60	64	8498	7.2	24.2	46.5	19.0	3.1	114369
30912	AUGUSTA	25597	694	69.9	17.0	7.6	1.6	3.9	14412	17672	1	1	75	25.3	34.7	0.0	37.3	2.7	67941
31001	ABBEVILLE	16157	836	38.4	30.5	24.2	5.1	1.8	32139	37503	18	21	670	46.3	35.1	16.0	2.7	0.0	53472
31002	ADRIAN	15653	1234	47.5	24.4	22.4	4.1	1.6	26830	31332	7	5	1003	46.5	33.0	17.6	2.9	0.1	53660
31003	ALLENTOWN	18932	212	24.5	40.1	32.1	3.3	0.0	40715	46489	49	54	185	18.9	33.5	25.4	13.5	8.7	86250
31005	BONAIRE	31504	4191	6.5	19.1	42.9	21.3	10.3	75167	87213	93	94	3781	5.2	12.4	51.3	29.0	2.1	139315
31006	BUTLER	15997	1962	45.4	27.1	22.1	4.0	1.5	27558	31647	8	7	1531	40.9	31.8	21.4	5.3	0.6	60096
31007	BYROMVILLE	22722	357	40.9	27.2	17.1	2.8	12.0	34313	44149	25	31	281	38.1	42.7	13.9	4.6	0.7	62344
31008	BYRON	24349	5492	18.8	26.7	38.9	12.1	3.6	53838	63230	78	80	4686	18.6	24.0	44.8	11.1	1.5	99857
31009	CADWELL	18557	573	34.4	31.9	27.2	5.1	1.4	36182	41744	32	40	467	30.8	41.8	15.2	10.7	1.5	63571
31011	CHAUNCEY	16037	596	43.5	32.4	17.3	4.9	2.0	29127	33829	11	11	491	50.5	32.8	13.9	2.9	0.0	49479
31012	CHESTER	16157	588	42.0	25.0	26.4	3.6	3.1	30665	37436	14	15	479	41.3	36.5	17.1	4.2	0.8	56917
31014	COCHRAN	19430	5163	33.8	29.9	26.8	7.2	2.3	37102	43006	36	42	4061	33.7	29.5	29.4	6.2	1.1	73516
31015	CORDELE	17856	8161	43.3	25.3	22.2	6.6	2.6	30924	36784	15	16	5213	27.8	29.1	30.3	11.4	1.5	80733
31016	CULLODEN	27119	570	29.7	31.1	26.7	6.7	6.0	40757	48884	49	54	468	26.9	24.4	34.2	11.8	2.8	88537
31017	DANVILLE	17445	834	35.7	30.1	27.0	5.2	2.0	34467	40625	26	32	693	39.5	34.6	21.9	1.4	2.5	61458
31018	DAVISBORO	14923	514	36.2	30.4	24.7	5.8	2.9	36196	43058	32	40	414	31.2	38.2	21.7	7.5	1.5	71500
31019	DEXTER	24086	840	32.0	26.9	27.5	8.1	5.5	38898	45832	42	49	711	30.0	34.7	25.2	9.0	1.1	67115
31020	DRY BRANCH	18669	1136	31.0	28.4	30.5	8.8	1.3	41684	49308	52	57	933	39.3	34.1	24.2	1.9	0.4	62269
31021	DUBLIN	21346	10615	34.8	27.7	25.6	7.7	4.3	37400	44322	37	44	7387	23.0	28.6	35.8	11.0	1.7	88113
31022	DUDLEY	24664	421	25.9	22.8	37.8	9.5	4.0	50842	58968	74	76	362	16.6	36.5	33.7	12.2	1.1	87027
31023	EASTMAN	18578	5228	41.4	29.9	20.9	4.8	3.0	31645	36583	17	20	3788	42.6	28.8	19.7	7.7	1.3	59307
31024	EATONTON	25393	7649	29.4	27.6	28.2	8.8	6.1	42791	52074	55	60	6168	21.5	23.4	30.8	16.5	7.8	99844
31025	ELKO	19743	620	26.3	36.8	26.5	4.8	5.7	40875	47338	49	55	522	33.0	31.8	26.1	8.4	0.8	71429
31027	EAST DUBLIN	16852	3888	38.6	31.3	24.1	4.1	1.9	33876	39679	24	28	2994	41.8	31.6	22.8	3.6	0.3	59722
31028	CENTERVILLE	22727	1642	15.7	33.7	38.1	9.7	2.9	50494	57156	73	75	1314	11.0	40.0	45.0	3.7	0.4	89498
31029	FORSYTH	21421	5012	27.6	28.6	31.1	9.2	3.5	44133	51993	59	64	3876	19.0	28.5	34.4	16.3	1.8	93593
31030	FORT VALLEY	17065	5884	40.0	27.4	23.2	7.0	2.4	32917	40053	21	25	3865	25.4	35.7	31.6	6.6	0.7	77196
31031	GORDON	17878	2678	32.3	31.6	29.2	5.0	2.0	38885	44581	42	48	2187	35.4	33.7	25.1	5.2	0.6	66280
31032	GRAY	24129	3787	23.9	25.4	35.6	11.0	4.2	50544	57606	73	76	3239	19.2	25.4	40.9	13.4	1.2	97684
31033	HADDOCK	20568	861	30.3	28.8	29.6	8.5	2.8	41591	48572	52	56	730	26.9	33.4	29.9	9.3	0.6	76066
31035	HARRISON	16458	568	38.9	23.1	28.9	8.1	1.1	34339	41356	25	31	462	39.6	31.0	21.9	6.3	1.3	62222
31036	HAWKINSVILLE	20126	4267	33.1	30.6	27.0	5.1	4.3	37542	44854	38	44	3297	26.0	26.5	35.5	11.1	0.9	86267
31037	HELENA	14370	722	45.7	32.3	16.3	3.7	1.9	27508	31180	8	6	567	54.3	28.2	15.2	2.1	0.2	46938
31038	HILLSBORO	24471	281	33.1	24.2	28.5	9.3	5.0	42369	50000	54	59	236	27.1	41.1	19.1	12.3	0.4	76190
31041	IDEAL	17508	424	46.7	21.2	22.4	4.0	5.7	27614	32724	8	7	347	56.2	19.9	21.0	2.3	0.6	46161
31042	IRWINTON	15390	567	40.9	28.0	24.9	4.8	1.4	31131	35703	15	17	449	41.4	32.7	21.6	3.8	0.5	61809
31044	JEFFERSONVILLE	16298	1250	42.0	22.9	25.4	7.3	2.4	32351	38476	19	22	1004	39.0	32.5	25.1	1.7	1.7	63077
31045	JEWELL	25635	383	35.5	35.8	24.5	0.3	3.9	34023	39297	24	29	319	34.2	36.7	19.4	9.7	0.0	66714
31046	JULIETTE	27860	1101	15.9	21.7	40.2	17.1	5.1	63321	74458	87	89	973	14.6	16.0	29.5	35.5	4.4	147461
31047	KATHLEEN	24261	2384	13.3	28.4	38.5	15.3	4.5	58327	67233	83	84	2159	8.7	24.6	45.4	18.8	2.5	110668
31049	KITE	16346	620	48.4	21.5	24.7	2.1	3.4	26281	31011	6	4	508	52.4	24.8	21.7	1.0	0.2	48462
31050	KNOXVILLE	19106	1337	29.6	30.3	30.3	7.2	2.6	41778	46995	52	57	1145	22.5	30.0	39.1	8.0	0.5	86944
31052	LIZELLA	25336	3417	17.5	25.7	37.8	15.6	3.5	56900	67952	82	83	2967	11.4	22.2	50.2	14.2	2.0	109895
31054	MC INTYRE	16402	467	35.3	31.9	29.1	3.2	0.4	34034	39153	24	29	393	33.1	29.0	30.5	7.4	0.0	69625
31055	MC RAE	17314	2012	41.2	30.6	20.4	5.5	2.3	30220	34764	13	14	1582	47.0	32.3	16.8	3.0	1.0	53019
31057	MARSHALLVILLE	14402	773	46.4	29.0	20.2	2.9	1.6	27807	33596	8	7	602	37.4	36.5	17.9	7.6	0.5	64304
31058	MAUK	17022	663	34.7	31.5	26.1	5.9	1.8	35431	41609	29	36	571	37.8	29.3	24.3	6.8	1.8	68929
31060	MILAN	17464	666	42.3	28.5	21.5	4.5	3.2	32266	37355	18	22	548	40.9	33.0	21.2	0.9	4.0	60000
31061	MILLEDGEVILLE	21803	15142	30.6	29.1	27.6	7.9	4.8	40855	49004	49	54	10258	23.1	28.3	32.7	14.2	1.7	88345
31063	MONTEZUMA	13801	2190	47.7	25.5	21.6	4.6	0.6	26158	29955	6	4	1532	33.9	36.4	25.5	3.1	1.2	66429
31064	MONTICELLO	25483	3277	26.5	27.3	35.4	6.7	4.1	45971	52616	64	68	2631	15.8	19.8	41.2	19.4	3.8	107527
31065	MONTROSE	19549	336	28.6	29.2	33.0	7.1	2.1	42018	49566	53	58	282	31.6	26.2	34.0	7.8	0.4	75625
31066	MUSELLA	19744	594	30.1	31.7	28.0	7.6	2.7	41744	46648	52	57	477	26.8	31.0	32.9	9.0	0.2	81071
31068	OGLETHORPE	14638	1503	45.3	27.7	21.2	3.9	2.0	28212	33378	9	9	1125	50.1	26.7	20.7	1.9	0.6	49867
31069	PERRY	21784	6578	28.1	28.3	31.3	9.1	3.2	44879	51411	61	65	4748	15.3	27.8	43.9	11.9	1.1	97231
31070	PINEHURST	18659	345	39.7	24.6	30.7	2.9	2.0	34813	40000	27	33	274	38.7	27.7	25.2	7.7	0.7	65417
31071	PINEVIEW	18094	449	39.6	30.5	22.3	4.0	3.6	32233	37478	18	21	372	39.5	32.5	21.0	7.0	0.0	66364
31072	PITTS	18399	503	37.4	33.2	19.1	9.2	1.2	32447	38187	19	23	417	44.8	35.0	13.9	6.2	0.0	54300
31075	RENTZ	19098	802	32.0	32.9	27.9	5.0	2.1	37193	43536	36	43	675	38.8	36.0	21.0	3.7	0.4	63092
31076	REYNOLDS	16441	1238	44.8	27.8	19.7	6.2	1.5	28384	32370	9	9	989	34.3	30.8	30.1	4.0	0.7	67670
31077	RHINE	21768	428	44.2	24.5	22.7	5.4	3.3	31302	37238	16	18	359	50.7	25.4	20.9	3.1	0.0	49306
31078	ROBERTA	16181	1002	39.4	32.6	20.7	5.5	1.8	33503	38832	22	27	800	34.5	32.9	24.5	6.6	1.5	70411
31079	ROCHELLE	19380	1121	42.6	27.4	21.5	5.1	3.4	31132	36973	15	17	892	47.2	29.7	19.0	4.0	0.1	55102
31081	RUPERT	18118	93	41.9	24.7	25.8	5.4	2.2	31913	38647	18	20	81	45.7	27.2	21.0	3.7	2.5	62143
31082	SANDERSVILLE	20692	4163	36.8	26.1	25.9	8.7	2.6	35476	43594	29	36	3069	31.5	30.7	24.4	12.6	0.8	71841
31085	SHADY DALE	17184	350	22.0	39.1	32.6	3.7	2.6	43197	49598	56	61	289	14.5	22.5	46.7	14.9	1.4	102331
31087	SPARTA	13644	3395	50.5	26.8	18.2	2.9	1.6	24673	28034	4	3	2495	43.9	31.3	19.7	4.3	0.9	60425
31088	WARNER ROBINS	24348	16221	17.5	28.3	39.2	11.8	3.3	53149	61017	77	79	11310	9.0	27.9	53.3	9.4	0.4	102177
31089	TENNILLE	16838	1755	45.0	24.5	22.7	5.5	2.3	30189	36589	13	13	1314	45.1	24.9	22.2	7.1	0.7	56957
31090	TOOMSBORO	16457	468	40.2	25.0	30.3	3.4	1.1	32241	36800	18	21	375	43.2	37.9	17.6	0.8	0.5	60341
31091	UNADILLA	15023	1078	46.0	28.9	20.0	3.6	1.5	27553	32091	8	7	813	35.7	35.7	24.9	3.7	0.1	62443
31092	VIENNA	18598	2284	38.9	28.1	25.2	4.5	3.3	34171	40687	25	30	1691	33.2	30.8	28.3	6.9	0.8	68370
31093	WARNER ROBINS	19887	11905	30.0	31.0	30.3	6.9	1.8	40185	46354	47	51	7549	14.6	46.2	36.1	2.7	0.3	80139
31094	WARTHEN	17150	496	39.1	22.2	30.7	7.5	0.6	34171	40000	25	30	401	37.2	24.7	23.7	14.2	0.3	73250
31096	WRIGHTSVILLE	14305	2250	48.1	26.3	20.3	4.0	1.2	26244	30906	6	4	1778	51.5	26.3	18.7	2.9	0.7	48761
31097	YATESVILLE	20277	490	28.6	30.8	33.3	4.5	2.9	45179	51177	62	66	412	22.6	31.3	35.4	10.0	0.7	85429
31098	WARNER ROBINS	13106	1249	14.4	51.1	30.4	3.5	0.6	41473	46731	51	56	53	24.5	37.7	37.7	0.0	0.0	67500
31201	MACON	13620	4115	65.8	21.7	8.8	2.7	1.1	15361	18146	1	1	1106	49.5	26.6	9.9	12.5	1.6	50588
31204	MACON	20800	13646	40.0	26.3	23.4	6.7	3.6	33282	40779	22	26	7531	18.3	38.4	35.0	7.2	1.1	83195
31206	MACON	15169	11303	44.3	32.7	19.2	2.7	1.2	28661	33578	10	10	6171	33.7	54.9	10.9	0.3	0.2	61282
31207	MACON	12542	2	100.0	0.0	0.0	0.0	0.0	5000	5000	0	0	0	0.0	0.0	0.0	0.0	0.0	0
31210	MACON	39829	11996	14.0	21.9	35.0	15.8	13.3	66620	83424	90	90	7938	2.2	10.6	47.3	32.0	7.9	155788
31211	MACON	26572	7223	25.4	27.1	31.5	10.3	5.7	47259	56011	67	71	4960	14.3	30.9	40.7	12.5	1.7	95106
31216	MACON	25738	5392	17.0	23.8	41.3	14.2	3.8	59347	70759	84	84	4683	12.4	15.7	59.4	11.6	0.9	114758
31217	MACON	16853	7555	37.6	30.8	24.4	5.4	1.8	34177	41477	25	30	5104	34.8	43.7	19.0	2.3	0.3	63537
31220	MACON	29826	4449	9.6	24.7	43.2	16.6	5.9	64613	78269	88	89	3769	4.5	21.3	53.1	18.1	3.0	114725
	GEORGIA	26143		23.6	26.3	31.4	11.6	7.0	50024	60470				12.5	17.5	39.3	24.8	6.0	125860
	UNITED STATES	25866		24.7	27.1	30.8	10.9	6.5	48124	56710				10.9	15.0	33.7	30.1	10.4	145905

ZIP CODE #	POST OFFICE NAME	FINANCIAL SERVICES: Auto Loan	FINANCIAL SERVICES: Home Loan	FINANCIAL SERVICES: Invest-ments	FINANCIAL SERVICES: Retire-ment Plans	THE HOME: Home Improvements: Home Repair	THE HOME: Home Improvements: Lawn & Garden	THE HOME: Furnishings: Comput-ers & Hard-ware	THE HOME: Furnishings: Major Appli-ances	THE HOME: Furnishings: TV, Radio, Sound Equip-ment	THE HOME: Furnishings: Furni-ture	ENTERTAINMENT: Dine out/ Carry out	ENTERTAINMENT: Sports Equip-ment	ENTERTAINMENT: Fees & Tickets	ENTERTAINMENT: Toys & Games	ENTERTAINMENT: Travel	ENTERTAINMENT: Cable TV	PERSONAL: Apparel & Services	PERSONAL: Auto Repairs	PERSONAL: Health Insur-ance	PERSONAL: Pets & Supplies
30828	WARRENTON	71	50	31	43	55	64	51	60	60	52	71	70	45	66	51	65	66	60	73	81
30830	WAYNESBORO	67	56	51	51	57	65	57	61	63	58	77	70	55	74	57	66	73	62	68	75
30833	WRENS	66	51	38	47	54	63	53	59	60	53	71	67	49	66	53	63	67	59	68	73
30901	AUGUSTA	41	34	40	31	33	40	39	39	44	40	54	44	38	50	38	46	52	41	44	45
30904	AUGUSTA	73	70	82	69	69	77	76	74	78	76	98	85	76	95	75	79	95	76	75	82
30905	AUGUSTA	77	49	47	56	45	53	73	63	74	68	92	83	62	82	60	67	88	74	58	71
30906	AUGUSTA	67	66	67	64	65	71	66	66	68	67	84	75	66	83	66	68	82	67	68	76
30907	AUGUSTA	110	124	136	128	121	123	119	116	112	119	141	137	123	144	118	107	140	116	105	128
30909	AUGUSTA	99	95	105	98	94	102	100	98	100	100	125	115	99	122	98	97	121	101	96	110
30912	AUGUSTA	58	49	65	50	48	56	61	56	64	59	80	67	59	76	58	64	77	61	59	63
31001	ABBEVILLE	35	23	11	20	26	30	22	28	27	23	32	34	19	30	23	29	29	28	35	40
31002	ADRIAN	72	49	24	43	55	63	48	59	57	49	67	70	41	63	48	60	61	58	71	82
31003	ALLENTOWN	87	59	27	51	66	76	56	71	68	58	80	84	48	76	57	73	73	70	87	100
31005	BONAIRE	125	144	144	146	142	142	129	130	122	131	153	153	136	159	131	118	152	126	119	148
31006	BUTLER	78	52	24	45	59	68	51	63	61	52	72	76	43	68	51	66	65	63	78	90
31007	BYROMVILLE	120	83	46	73	93	107	83	99	98	84	116	118	72	110	84	104	106	99	120	137
31008	BYRON	101	97	81	95	97	101	91	96	91	93	112	112	89	110	90	89	108	95	94	114
31009	CADWELL	86	58	26	50	66	75	56	70	67	57	79	83	48	75	57	73	72	69	86	99
31011	CHAUNCEY	76	51	24	44	58	66	49	61	59	50	70	73	42	66	50	64	63	61	75	87
31012	CHESTER	8	5	2	5	6	7	5	6	6	5	7	8	4	7	5	7	7	6	8	9
31014	COCHRAN	87	64	37	57	70	80	62	74	72	63	86	87	55	82	63	77	79	73	88	100
31015	CORDELE	72	59	51	55	61	70	61	66	67	62	81	75	57	77	61	70	77	67	73	81
31016	CULLODEN	133	93	47	81	104	118	89	109	105	90	124	130	77	119	90	112	113	108	132	153
31017	DANVILLE	84	56	25	48	63	73	54	68	65	55	76	81	46	72	55	70	70	67	83	96
31018	DAVISBORO	32	21	10	18	24	28	21	26	25	21	29	31	18	28	21	27	27	26	32	37
31019	DEXTER	102	82	54	76	86	94	79	89	85	81	103	105	72	97	78	87	97	89	97	114
31020	DRY BRANCH	82	70	52	66	72	78	67	74	71	69	87	86	63	82	67	72	83	74	79	92
31021	DUBLIN	82	72	65	68	74	82	73	77	78	73	95	88	71	92	73	80	91	77	83	92
31022	DUDLEY	103	88	64	83	94	102	82	92	89	82	107	110	79	108	84	91	101	90	102	121
31023	EASTMAN	80	58	35	52	63	73	58	68	67	59	80	79	51	75	58	71	73	68	81	90
31024	EATONTON	108	83	56	75	92	104	80	95	91	80	108	111	72	105	83	96	100	94	111	128
31025	ELKO	92	77	54	72	79	86	73	82	78	75	95	96	68	89	73	79	90	82	87	103
31027	EAST DUBLIN	78	60	37	55	64	71	58	67	64	59	77	79	52	73	58	66	72	67	75	88
31028	CENTERVILLE	89	89	78	88	89	92	84	87	83	85	103	101	83	102	84	82	100	86	85	101
31029	FORSYTH	95	80	61	76	84	93	78	86	84	79	102	99	74	99	79	87	96	85	95	108
31030	FORT VALLEY	68	58	55	55	59	68	61	64	67	62	81	73	59	77	61	69	78	65	70	76
31031	GORDON	80	64	44	59	68	75	61	70	67	63	81	82	56	78	62	70	76	70	78	90
31032	GRAY	105	91	69	87	95	103	87	96	92	87	112	112	83	110	87	93	106	94	102	120
31033	HADDOCK	91	74	50	69	78	85	71	80	77	73	93	94	65	88	71	78	87	80	87	102
31035	HARRISON	85	57	26	49	64	74	55	69	66	56	78	82	47	74	56	71	71	68	84	97
31036	HAWKINSVILLE	79	63	45	59	67	76	63	71	70	63	84	82	58	80	63	73	78	70	80	89
31037	HELENA	37	25	12	22	28	33	25	30	29	25	35	36	21	33	25	32	31	30	37	42
31038	HILLSBORO	120	80	36	69	91	105	77	97	94	79	110	116	66	104	79	101	100	96	119	138
31041	IDEAL	83	55	25	48	63	72	53	67	65	54	76	80	45	72	54	69	69	66	82	95
31042	IRWINTON	78	52	24	45	59	68	51	63	61	52	72	76	43	68	51	66	65	63	78	90
31044	JEFFERSONVILLE	83	56	25	48	63	73	54	67	65	55	76	80	46	72	55	70	69	67	83	95
31045	JEWELL	123	83	37	71	94	108	80	100	96	81	113	119	68	107	81	104	103	99	123	142
31046	JULIETTE	113	111	97	108	115	120	102	109	103	102	127	129	102	131	104	104	123	106	111	134
31047	KATHLEEN	103	107	99	108	105	106	101	102	96	103	121	121	100	120	99	92	118	101	94	116
31049	KITE	75	50	23	44	57	66	49	61	59	50	69	73	41	65	50	63	63	60	75	87
31050	KNOXVILLE	89	82	64	78	82	86	78	83	79	80	97	96	73	92	77	78	93	83	83	99
31052	LIZELLA	100	102	92	99	103	107	94	99	94	95	116	116	95	117	96	93	113	97	98	117
31054	MC INTYRE	79	54	26	48	61	70	53	65	62	54	74	77	45	70	53	67	67	64	79	91
31055	MC RAE	75	52	27	47	58	68	53	63	62	52	73	73	46	69	53	66	66	62	77	84
31057	MARSHALLVILLE	62	45	33	39	48	57	47	53	55	48	65	61	42	60	46	59	61	54	65	70
31058	MAUK	75	61	41	57	64	70	59	66	63	60	77	78	54	72	58	64	72	66	72	84
31060	MILAN	75	53	29	48	59	69	54	64	63	53	74	74	47	70	54	68	68	64	78	85
31061	MILLEDGEVILLE	82	76	75	74	77	84	78	80	80	78	99	93	76	97	77	80	95	81	82	94
31063	MONTEZUMA	60	47	40	43	49	58	50	54	56	50	68	62	47	64	49	59	64	55	63	68
31064	MONTICELLO	111	93	66	87	99	109	88	99	96	88	116	117	84	116	90	99	109	97	110	128
31065	MONTROSE	92	70	42	63	77	85	66	78	75	67	90	93	60	88	67	79	83	77	91	107
31066	MUSELLA	94	66	34	58	73	83	63	77	74	65	88	92	55	83	64	79	81	77	93	107
31068	OGLETHORPE	71	49	28	42	54	63	49	59	58	50	69	69	43	64	49	63	63	59	72	81
31069	PERRY	80	81	81	79	81	87	79	81	80	79	99	93	80	100	80	80	97	80	81	93
31070	PINEHURST	80	57	31	50	63	71	55	67	64	56	76	79	48	72	56	68	70	66	79	91
31071	PINEVIEW	87	59	28	51	66	77	58	71	69	58	81	84	49	76	58	74	74	70	87	99
31072	PITTS	79	56	31	51	62	73	58	68	67	57	79	79	51	75	58	72	72	67	82	89
31075	RENTZ	85	63	37	57	68	76	61	72	69	62	82	85	54	78	61	72	76	71	83	96
31076	REYNOLDS	76	51	23	44	58	66	49	61	59	50	69	73	42	66	50	64	63	61	76	87
31077	RHINE	96	65	29	56	73	84	62	78	75	64	88	93	53	83	63	81	80	77	96	111
31078	ROBERTA	79	53	24	46	60	69	51	64	61	52	72	76	43	68	52	66	66	63	78	90
31079	ROCHELLE	87	61	38	53	67	79	62	73	74	63	87	85	55	81	62	79	81	73	89	99
31081	RUPERT	77	52	23	45	58	67	50	62	60	51	71	74	42	67	51	65	64	62	77	88
31082	SANDERSVILLE	83	69	57	65	72	82	70	76	77	71	93	86	67	88	70	80	88	76	85	93
31085	SHADY DALE	81	74	57	71	75	80	70	76	72	71	88	88	67	85	70	71	84	75	77	92
31087	SPARTA	50	39	34	34	40	48	41	45	47	42	56	50	38	52	41	51	53	46	54	56
31088	WARNER ROBINS	86	93	98	95	90	92	91	89	87	91	110	104	92	110	89	84	108	89	81	98
31089	TENNILLE	80	56	34	49	61	72	56	67	67	58	79	78	50	74	57	72	73	67	82	90
31090	TOOMSBORO	82	55	25	47	62	72	53	66	64	54	75	79	45	71	54	69	68	66	82	94
31091	UNADILLA	54	51	55	51	52	56	55	55	56	54	69	64	54	67	54	55	67	56	55	61
31092	VIENNA	83	65	44	59	69	76	64	73	71	65	85	85	58	81	64	73	80	73	81	93
31093	WARNER ROBINS	68	67	72	67	66	72	69	68	70	69	87	79	69	87	68	69	85	69	68	77
31094	WARTHEN	79	57	31	51	62	71	55	66	64	56	76	78	49	72	56	68	70	65	78	90
31096	WRIGHTSVILLE	65	45	26	40	50	59	46	54	54	46	64	63	40	60	46	58	58	54	66	73
31097	YATESVILLE	94	71	42	64	78	87	67	80	77	68	91	95	61	89	68	81	84	78	93	109
31098	WARNER ROBINS	75	48	46	55	44	52	71	61	72	66	90	82	61	81	59	66	86	72	57	70
31201	MACON	39	32	41	31	31	37	40	38	43	39	53	44	38	50	38	44	51	41	40	43
31204	MACON	66	62	73	60	61	70	67	66	71	67	88	74	67	85	66	73	85	68	70	74
31206	MACON	56	51	57	48	50	58	55	55	60	56	74	62	55	71	55	61	71	56	59	62
31207	MACON	7	4	5	5	4	5	8	6	8	7	10	9	7	9	7	7	9	8	6	7
31210	MACON	130	145	165	149	141	145	140	137	134	141	169	161	146	172	140	130	168	137	125	151
31211	MACON	92	89	90	87	89	96	89	91	90	89	112	106	88	111	89	90	108	91	92	106
31216	MACON	107	99	82	96	103	109	92	100	96	93	117	119	91	119	94	97	112	98	105	125
31217	MACON	69	61	59	57	61	70	62	65	67	64	83	73	61	78	62	69	79	66	70	77
31220	MACON	108	123	126	126	120	120	114	113	106	115	134	133	117	137	113	102	132	111	102	126
	GEORGIA	103	97	95	97	97	104	97	99	98	98	122	116	96	120	96	98	118	100	99	116
	UNITED STATES	100	100	100	100	100	100	100	100	100	100	100	100	100	100	100	100	100	100	100	100

GEORGIA

A 31301-31638

POPULATION CHANGE

#	POST OFFICE NAME	COUNTY FIPS CODE	POPULATION 2000	POPULATION 2004	POPULATION 2009	2000-2004 ANNUAL RATE % Rate	2000-2004 ANNUAL RATE State Centile	HOUSEHOLDS 2000	HOUSEHOLDS 2004	HOUSEHOLDS 2009	% Annual Rate 2000-2004	2004 Average HH Size	FAMILIES 2000	FAMILIES 2004	% Annual Rate 2000-2004
31301	ALLENHURST	179	3854	3994	4140	0.8	34	1342	1393	1450	0.9	2.84	960	984	0.6
31302	BLOOMINGDALE	103	8332	9011	10124	1.9	54	3055	3348	3806	2.2	2.69	2368	2554	1.8
31303	CLYO	103	1651	1875	2224	3.0	76	574	662	796	3.4	2.83	446	508	3.1
31304	CRESCENT	191	1770	1893	2045	1.6	50	651	708	777	2.0	2.67	460	492	1.6
31305	DARIEN	191	4489	4746	5090	1.3	45	1691	1816	1981	1.7	2.53	1201	1271	1.3
31308	ELLABELL	029	6327	7239	8591	3.2	79	2237	2599	3132	3.6	2.77	1747	2003	3.3
31309	FLEMING	179	655	713	757	2.0	59	235	260	279	2.4	2.55	175	191	2.1
31312	GUYTON	103	11103	13443	16461	4.6	90	3844	4699	5812	4.8	2.85	3089	3738	4.6
31313	HINESVILLE	179	35795	38013	40386	1.4	47	12384	13163	14035	1.5	2.88	9447	9950	1.2
31314	FORT STEWART	179	3048	2963	2994	-0.7	3	6	7	7	3.7	2.57	5	5	0.0
31315	FORT STEWART	179	10297	10010	10108	-0.7	3	2459	2376	2430	-0.8	2.76	2379	2295	-0.8
31316	LUDOWICI	183	9804	10617	11464	1.9	55	3384	3651	3924	1.8	2.91	2537	2699	1.5
31319	MERIDIAN	191	216	235	257	2.0	58	85	94	104	2.4	2.50	62	68	2.2
31320	MIDWAY	179	7119	8164	8911	3.3	79	2641	3060	3370	3.5	2.61	1941	2222	3.2
31321	PEMBROKE	031	5681	6352	7400	2.7	71	2015	2281	2689	3.0	2.77	1557	1737	2.6
31322	POOLER	051	6218	8443	10139	7.5	99	2241	3099	3774	7.9	2.69	1782	2425	7.5
31323	RICEBORO	179	1585	1567	1591	-0.3	8	561	559	572	-0.1	2.80	417	411	-0.3
31324	RICHMOND HILL	029	14502	17504	21570	4.5	90	4940	6040	7540	4.8	2.89	4064	4917	4.6
31326	RINCON	103	12219	14443	17473	4.0	87	4293	5111	6234	4.2	2.83	3457	4069	3.9
31327	SAPELO ISLAND	191	130	140	152	1.8	52	67	73	81	2.0	1.92	49	53	1.9
31328	TYBEE ISLAND	051	3696	3759	3875	0.4	20	1704	1764	1846	0.8	2.05	1003	1005	0.1
31329	SPRINGFIELD	103	7317	8232	9699	2.8	73	2541	2907	3477	3.2	2.77	1992	2252	2.9
31331	TOWNSEND	191	4242	4614	5029	2.0	58	1708	1887	2090	2.4	2.44	1241	1351	2.0
31401	SAVANNAH	051	21755	21884	22793	0.1	15	9020	9229	9752	0.5	2.19	4041	3990	-0.3
31404	SAVANNAH	051	32048	32471	33743	0.3	18	11977	12184	12764	0.4	2.62	7912	7844	-0.2
31405	SAVANNAH	051	31535	32158	33681	0.5	22	11906	12261	13018	0.7	2.44	7698	7760	0.2
31406	SAVANNAH	051	34480	35190	36706	0.5	22	13438	13873	14648	0.8	2.48	9193	9282	0.2
31407	SAVANNAH	051	3431	3311	3405	-0.8	1	1332	1281	1333	-0.9	2.11	937	883	-1.4
31408	SAVANNAH	051	11178	11020	11342	-0.3	7	3879	3856	4010	-0.1	2.70	2620	2536	-0.8
31409	SAVANNAH	051	1308	1388	1448	1.4	47	161	190	212	4.0	3.12	157	185	3.9
31410	SAVANNAH	051	22165	24934	27243	2.8	73	8721	9934	10972	3.1	2.51	6316	7043	2.6
31411	SAVANNAH	051	6958	7952	8710	3.2	78	3207	3734	4152	3.6	2.13	2714	3121	3.3
31415	SAVANNAH	051	12783	13031	13700	0.5	21	4803	4974	5295	0.8	2.62	3254	3276	0.2
31419	SAVANNAH	051	41312	44254	47438	1.6	51	16272	17654	19169	1.9	2.48	10906	11603	1.5
31501	WAYCROSS	299	14533	14434	14436	-0.2	10	6026	6056	6135	0.1	2.30	3866	3805	-0.4
31503	WAYCROSS	299	20891	21084	21349	0.2	16	7449	7633	7847	0.6	2.53	5406	5459	0.2
31510	ALMA	005	8754	8915	9149	0.4	21	3324	3433	3573	0.8	2.56	2438	2481	0.4
31512	AMBROSE	069	2254	2372	2539	1.2	42	856	913	987	1.5	2.60	644	677	1.2
31513	BAXLEY	001	15371	15748	16228	0.6	26	5792	5980	6212	0.8	2.59	4257	4332	0.4
31516	BLACKSHEAR	229	11967	12503	13185	1.0	38	4574	4845	5183	1.4	2.56	3399	3553	1.1
31518	BRISTOL	001	665	655	669	-0.4	6	266	266	276	0.0	2.46	198	195	-0.4
31519	BROXTON	069	3619	3634	3813	0.1	14	1371	1394	1477	0.4	2.60	1005	1007	0.1
31520	BRUNSWICK	127	21796	21638	22411	-0.2	9	8576	8642	9093	0.2	2.43	5431	5344	-0.4
31522	SAINT SIMONS ISLAND	127	14317	15504	16630	1.9	55	6557	7193	7821	2.2	2.14	4114	4422	1.7
31523	BRUNSWICK	127	8784	9511	10213	1.9	55	3327	3659	3988	2.3	2.60	2616	2831	1.9
31525	BRUNSWICK	127	21432	23208	24981	1.9	55	8093	8880	9696	2.2	2.56	5796	6254	1.8
31527	JEKYLL ISLAND	127	938	897	921	-1.1	1	485	471	491	-0.7	1.90	325	307	-1.3
31532	DENTON	161	916	913	950	-0.1	11	345	349	368	0.3	2.62	262	261	-0.1
31533	DOUGLAS	069	15557	16405	17680	1.3	43	5732	6098	6629	1.5	2.64	4037	4222	1.1
31535	DOUGLAS	069	9584	10932	12282	3.1	78	3379	3883	4398	3.3	2.79	2582	2926	3.0
31537	FOLKSTON	049	8187	8466	8815	0.8	33	2574	2710	2876	1.2	2.71	1910	1984	0.9
31539	HAZLEHURST	161	11921	12651	13595	1.4	47	4542	4884	5318	1.7	2.57	3374	3577	1.4
31542	HOBOKEN	025	2566	2830	3153	2.3	65	956	1075	1221	2.8	2.63	754	837	2.5
31543	HORTENSE	305	1620	1703	1827	1.2	42	619	664	726	1.7	2.55	462	488	1.3
31544	JACKSONVILLE	271	763	773	794	0.3	18	317	328	343	0.8	2.36	221	225	0.4
31545	JESUP	305	14200	14605	15269	0.7	30	5280	5492	5812	0.9	2.63	3962	4066	0.6
31546	JESUP	305	7108	7482	7637	1.2	42	2098	2117	2212	0.2	2.49	1505	1492	-0.2
31547	KINGS BAY	039	1329	1324	1373	-0.1	11	239	241	259	0.2	3.17	237	238	0.1
31548	KINGSLAND	039	14797	16195	18023	2.2	61	5070	5578	6243	2.3	2.90	3888	4224	2.0
31549	LUMBER CITY	271	1799	1791	1831	-0.1	10	706	719	750	0.4	2.38	468	468	0.0
31550	MANOR	299	807	825	830	0.5	25	312	323	329	0.8	2.50	243	248	0.5
31551	MERSHON	229	1073	1047	1071	-0.6	3	383	379	395	-0.3	2.74	293	286	-0.6
31552	MILLWOOD	299	814	848	861	1.0	37	300	317	327	1.3	2.66	238	249	1.1
31553	NAHUNTA	025	3638	3889	4258	1.6	49	1361	1487	1664	2.1	2.57	1015	1094	1.8
31554	NICHOLLS	069	5996	6177	6490	0.7	30	1884	1971	2108	1.1	2.61	1415	1458	0.7
31555	ODUM	305	2742	2869	2985	1.1	38	971	1032	1089	1.4	2.60	739	773	1.1
31557	PATTERSON	229	2650	2889	3116	2.1	60	1015	1125	1233	2.5	2.56	750	818	2.1
31558	SAINT MARYS	039	19627	22106	24757	2.8	73	6496	7405	8384	3.1	2.83	5078	5729	2.9
31560	SCREVEN	305	2211	2883	3443	6.4	96	861	1135	1374	6.7	2.54	648	842	6.4
31561	SEA ISLAND	127	368	445	505	4.6	90	196	240	276	4.9	1.85	140	168	4.4
31562	SAINT GEORGE	049	2287	2381	2486	1.0	36	835	880	930	1.2	2.71	642	668	0.9
31563	SURRENCY	001	1183	1310	1395	2.4	67	471	529	569	2.8	2.46	345	382	2.4
31565	WAVERLY	039	1370	1452	1567	1.4	46	551	592	645	1.7	2.45	399	419	1.2
31566	WAYNESVILLE	025	5177	5697	6338	2.3	64	1858	2079	2354	2.7	2.74	1438	1588	2.4
31567	WEST GREEN	069	803	881	963	2.2	63	308	342	378	2.5	2.57	231	254	2.3
31568	WHITE OAK	039	1411	2036	2564	9.0	100	508	739	937	9.2	2.75	385	550	8.8
31569	WOODBINE	039	4914	5004	5341	0.4	21	1767	1821	1963	0.7	2.69	1330	1348	0.3
31601	VALDOSTA	185	31015	31772	33779	0.6	26	11457	11925	12862	1.0	2.61	7507	7664	0.5
31602	VALDOSTA	185	28993	30559	32641	1.3	43	10652	11393	12382	1.6	2.42	6690	7014	1.1
31605	VALDOSTA	185	14626	17375	19703	4.1	88	5247	6328	7292	4.5	2.58	4038	4755	3.9
31606	VALDOSTA	185	3592	3707	3932	0.7	31	1301	1368	1472	1.2	2.70	1020	1055	0.8
31620	ADEL	075	11001	11373	11884	0.8	33	4068	4250	4489	1.0	2.62	2949	3037	0.7
31622	ALAPAHA	019	1520	1510	1562	-0.2	10	602	608	637	0.2	2.48	449	447	-0.1
31624	AXSON	003	1313	1376	1435	1.1	39	468	496	521	1.4	2.77	363	380	1.1
31625	BARNEY	027	966	959	978	-0.2	9	358	361	374	0.2	2.59	277	275	-0.2
31626	BOSTON	275	3428	3517	3680	0.6	27	1318	1374	1461	1.0	2.54	949	974	0.6
31629	DIXIE	027	974	959	975	-0.4	6	363	362	374	-0.1	2.65	267	262	-0.4
31630	DU PONT	065	658	681	704	0.8	33	242	255	268	1.2	2.62	190	198	1.2
31631	FARGO	065	527	524	534	-0.1	10	205	208	216	0.3	2.52	151	151	0.0
31632	HAHIRA	185	6640	7101	7618	1.6	50	2426	2599	2804	1.6	2.72	1846	1939	1.2
31634	HOMERVILLE	065	5695	5861	6051	0.7	30	2066	2164	2276	1.1	2.55	1482	1528	0.7
31635	LAKELAND	173	4971	5161	5407	0.9	35	1799	1893	2009	1.2	2.58	1313	1360	0.7
31636	LAKE PARK	101	7894	8505	9339	1.8	52	2946	3189	3512	1.9	2.65	2122	2256	1.5
31637	LENOX	075	2271	2256	2320	-0.2	10	889	897	933	0.2	2.51	640	636	-0.2
31638	MORVEN	027	1123	1136	1167	0.3	17	408	422	442	0.8	2.64	283	288	0.4
	GEORGIA					2.4					2.5	2.64			2.2
	UNITED STATES					1.2					1.3	2.58			1.1

ZIP CODE #	POST OFFICE NAME	RACE (%) White 2000	White 2004	Black 2000	Black 2004	Asian/Pacific 2000	Asian/Pacific 2004	% Hispanic Origin 2000	% Hispanic Origin 2004	2004 AGE DISTRIBUTION (%) 0-4	5-9	10-14	15-19	20-24	25-44	45-64	65-84	85+	18+	MEDIAN AGE 2004	% 2004 Males	% 2004 Females
31301	ALLENHURST	44.5	41.5	48.9	51.1	1.2	1.3	5.2	6.3	12.0	9.1	7.9	7.9	11.9	34.2	13.2	3.5	0.3	66.5	25.5	50.1	49.9
31302	BLOOMINGDALE	92.6	90.9	5.2	6.4	0.4	0.5	1.1	1.4	7.2	7.2	7.4	6.7	6.4	29.6	26.0	8.9	0.7	74.1	36.2	50.7	49.3
31303	CLYO	72.3	69.6	25.6	27.9	0.2	0.3	0.8	1.0	7.1	7.0	7.6	7.1	7.1	28.4	25.8	9.1	0.9	74.0	35.8	49.5	50.5
31304	CRESCENT	45.2	42.1	52.8	55.7	0.2	0.3	0.6	0.7	6.9	7.3	8.4	7.7	6.0	25.3	26.5	10.9	1.0	72.6	36.5	49.1	50.9
31305	DARIEN	64.5	61.5	33.6	36.3	0.5	0.6	1.2	1.4	6.8	7.5	8.6	9.2	6.1	26.1	24.3	10.1	1.3	70.4	34.7	49.8	50.2
31308	ELLABELL	83.3	81.3	15.0	16.8	0.2	0.3	0.8	0.9	7.2	7.1	7.8	7.7	7.4	28.0	25.6	8.6	0.7	73.4	35.2	50.2	49.8
31309	FLEMING	41.4	38.2	53.6	56.2	1.1	1.1	3.7	4.4	7.4	6.9	8.0	8.3	9.1	30.4	20.2	8.1	1.5	72.1	31.7	49.2	50.8
31312	GUYTON	88.4	86.9	9.7	10.8	0.3	0.4	1.3	1.7	8.0	7.9	7.9	7.2	6.8	30.7	23.7	7.2	0.7	71.9	34.0	50.1	49.9
31313	HINESVILLE	43.8	40.3	44.4	46.2	2.7	2.9	8.6	10.4	10.7	9.0	8.6	8.3	10.5	34.6	14.7	3.2	0.3	66.8	26.3	49.5	50.5
31314	FORT STEWART	49.8	46.4	36.9	38.2	2.2	2.5	12.0	14.5	12.8	8.5	6.2	11.9	26.5	32.7	1.3	0.1	0.0	70.2	22.0	64.2	35.8
31315	FORT STEWART	49.6	46.1	37.1	38.5	2.2	2.5	12.1	14.5	12.8	8.5	6.2	11.9	26.4	32.8	1.3	0.1	0.0	70.2	22.0	64.1	35.9
31316	LUDOWICI	68.4	65.6	23.7	25.2	0.8	0.9	9.3	11.3	11.2	9.4	8.2	7.2	9.3	32.0	16.5	5.6	0.5	67.0	27.3	50.9	49.1
31319	MERIDIAN	63.4	60.0	34.3	37.0	0.5	0.4	0.9	1.3	6.8	8.5	7.7	7.2	5.5	27.7	26.4	9.4	0.9	72.3	34.9	50.2	49.8
31320	MIDWAY	66.5	65.0	30.4	31.4	0.7	0.9	1.6	2.0	6.2	6.2	7.1	7.0	6.7	27.1	27.1	11.4	1.1	76.1	38.5	50.0	50.1
31321	PEMBROKE	77.7	75.3	20.5	22.7	0.3	0.4	1.0	1.3	7.3	7.2	7.9	8.0	7.6	27.3	24.8	9.3	0.8	72.9	34.3	48.9	51.1
31322	POOLER	88.7	86.1	7.2	8.9	1.9	2.1	1.2	1.9	7.5	7.3	7.9	6.1	5.6	32.1	23.9	8.6	1.1	73.3	34.7	48.5	51.6
31323	RICEBORO	12.5	11.1	87.0	88.3	0.1	0.1	0.8	0.8	5.9	7.0	9.4	8.6	6.2	25.0	25.9	10.5	1.6	72.8	36.9	49.4	50.6
31324	RICHMOND HILL	85.6	83.7	10.7	11.9	1.2	1.4	2.6	3.3	7.9	8.2	8.6	7.7	6.4	30.9	23.3	6.1	0.9	70.4	33.9	49.7	50.4
31326	RINCON	86.0	84.0	10.8	12.2	0.9	1.0	2.0	2.5	8.2	7.9	8.3	7.2	7.0	31.3	22.9	6.7	0.5	71.0	33.2	49.3	50.7
31327	SAPELO ISLAND	46.9	43.6	51.5	54.3	0.0	0.7	0.0	0.0	7.1	7.9	7.9	7.1	5.7	25.7	27.1	10.0	1.4	72.9	37.1	50.0	50.0
31328	TYBEE ISLAND	96.2	95.2	1.7	2.3	0.8	1.0	1.4	1.8	3.0	3.5	3.8	4.1	3.5	24.5	38.2	17.1	2.3	87.1	48.7	48.9	51.1
31329	SPRINGFIELD	73.5	71.3	24.9	26.8	0.2	0.2	1.1	1.4	7.7	7.6	7.8	7.4	7.0	28.8	23.5	8.8	1.4	72.3	34.6	49.0	51.0
31331	TOWNSEND	65.1	62.4	33.3	35.7	0.2	0.3	0.8	1.0	6.0	6.4	7.2	5.9	4.8	23.9	31.0	14.0	0.9	76.7	42.1	49.9	50.1
31401	SAVANNAH	32.1	29.6	64.7	66.8	1.4	1.6	1.5	1.8	7.0	6.3	6.2	8.8	14.3	27.3	19.3	9.4	1.5	77.2	29.3	48.3	51.7
31404	SAVANNAH	30.0	25.4	66.4	70.7	2.0	2.1	1.0	1.1	7.5	7.7	8.3	7.8	8.3	27.1	21.8	10.1	1.5	72.1	32.3	46.1	53.9
31405	SAVANNAH	46.1	42.2	50.9	54.5	0.7	0.8	2.1	2.5	6.4	6.2	6.6	7.2	8.4	28.3	22.7	11.7	2.4	76.7	35.5	49.0	51.0
31406	SAVANNAH	65.4	60.3	29.9	34.6	2.1	2.3	2.6	3.1	6.7	6.6	7.3	7.0	7.2	28.1	23.8	11.1	2.3	75.2	36.0	47.4	52.6
31407	SAVANNAH	76.1	72.2	20.4	23.7	1.2	1.4	2.5	3.1	5.5	5.2	5.1	4.9	7.9	34.0	22.4	13.2	1.8	81.6	37.7	56.7	43.3
31408	SAVANNAH	48.9	44.8	45.4	48.8	1.1	1.1	6.1	6.9	7.8	7.2	7.2	6.4	7.9	32.4	20.8	9.3	1.1	74.2	33.0	52.0	48.0
31409	SAVANNAH	53.9	47.7	37.2	42.3	1.9	2.0	10.5	12.3	8.3	5.2	3.5	12.0	34.8	29.3	0.8	2.5	3.8	82.3	23.0	67.1	32.9
31410	SAVANNAH	89.0	86.1	6.0	7.8	3.3	3.9	1.6	2.2	6.3	6.4	7.2	6.3	5.8	30.2	27.2	9.5	1.0	76.2	38.0	48.7	51.3
31411	SAVANNAH	97.6	97.0	0.5	0.6	1.4	1.6	0.8	1.1	1.8	2.1	2.9	3.1	2.3	7.3	36.2	42.6	1.8	90.9	63.0	48.4	51.6
31415	SAVANNAH	0.8	0.7	98.0	98.2	0.1	0.1	0.6	0.6	7.8	7.5	8.9	7.7	7.0	21.4	22.3	15.3	2.3	71.1	36.3	44.7	55.3
31419	SAVANNAH	65.9	60.1	27.5	32.5	2.7	3.0	4.0	4.9	7.4	6.4	6.7	6.9	9.3	33.1	21.4	7.9	0.9	75.6	32.2	48.2	51.9
31501	WAYCROSS	56.4	55.0	41.4	42.8	0.8	0.8	1.1	1.1	6.4	6.2	6.8	6.7	6.2	24.5	24.8	15.7	2.7	76.5	40.1	46.7	53.3
31503	WAYCROSS	79.3	78.3	18.5	19.5	0.3	0.3	2.2	2.3	6.5	6.5	6.8	6.5	7.3	29.9	23.8	11.0	1.8	76.3	36.0	51.4	48.6
31510	ALMA	80.1	78.1	17.1	18.6	0.3	0.4	3.4	4.2	7.5	7.4	6.6	6.4	6.8	28.3	23.9	11.8	1.4	74.6	35.9	49.1	50.9
31512	AMBROSE	73.9	70.4	19.3	21.3	0.3	0.3	8.8	10.7	7.6	7.6	7.9	6.6	7.2	30.1	23.8	8.4	0.9	73.0	33.8	49.5	50.5
31513	BAXLEY	76.1	73.6	20.1	21.7	0.3	0.4	4.8	6.1	7.6	7.3	7.1	7.0	7.3	27.7	24.4	10.4	1.3	73.6	35.2	49.7	50.3
31516	BLACKSHEAR	87.3	86.0	10.9	11.8	0.2	0.2	1.6	2.2	6.8	6.7	7.3	7.2	6.7	27.6	25.6	10.9	1.3	74.9	36.8	49.2	50.8
31518	BRISTOL	91.6	90.7	6.2	6.7	0.6	0.6	6.0	7.5	6.1	6.0	6.1	6.1	6.9	26.1	27.8	13.1	1.8	78.5	40.7	51.3	48.7
31519	BROXTON	73.2	70.0	22.4	24.7	0.2	0.3	4.6	5.7	8.2	7.8	7.4	6.8	6.4	28.0	24.0	10.1	1.3	72.5	35.2	48.7	51.3
31520	BRUNSWICK	44.5	41.0	52.1	55.1	0.4	0.5	5.2	6.2	7.8	7.2	7.4	7.3	7.5	26.3	22.0	12.3	2.3	73.5	35.0	47.7	52.3
31522	SAINT SIMONS ISLAND	94.2	92.6	3.9	5.0	0.9	1.1	1.8	2.6	4.2	4.8	5.6	5.1	3.9	21.8	32.6	19.0	3.2	82.1	48.0	46.7	53.3
31523	BRUNSWICK	88.2	84.9	9.9	12.7	0.3	0.4	1.1	1.6	6.3	6.7	7.2	6.3	5.8	27.8	28.7	10.4	0.9	75.8	38.9	49.5	50.5
31525	BRUNSWICK	72.9	68.8	23.7	27.3	0.9	0.9	2.4	3.1	7.3	7.0	7.4	8.2	7.8	28.1	24.6	8.9	0.8	73.4	34.3	48.5	51.5
31527	JEKYLL ISLAND	97.3	96.5	1.5	1.9	0.4	0.5	1.1	1.6	1.5	1.3	1.5	2.5	2.5	14.1	31.2	40.5	5.1	94.2	62.7	48.1	52.0
31532	DENTON	89.3	87.7	7.8	8.7	0.0	0.0	2.7	3.5	7.5	6.9	5.7	7.6	5.6	29.0	26.0	10.6	1.2	75.4	37.8	49.6	50.4
31533	DOUGLAS	65.0	61.7	27.7	29.6	0.9	1.1	8.4	10.3	7.9	7.7	7.5	7.2	7.8	28.1	21.9	10.1	1.8	72.7	33.2	48.0	52.0
31535	DOUGLAS	69.4	67.0	25.3	26.8	0.5	0.6	5.5	6.7	8.7	8.2	8.4	7.7	8.4	30.2	21.0	6.8	0.7	70.3	30.8	48.5	51.5
31537	FOLKSTON	61.2	58.0	36.7	39.8	0.3	0.3	0.8	0.9	6.5	6.4	7.3	8.5	8.4	31.3	21.5	8.9	1.1	74.9	33.8	53.6	46.4
31539	HAZLEHURST	80.6	78.5	15.7	17.0	0.5	0.6	5.3	6.7	7.8	7.5	7.2	6.6	6.8	27.6	24.3	11.1	1.2	73.5	35.5	49.6	50.5
31542	HOBOKEN	94.1	93.4	3.6	3.9	0.1	0.1	1.3	1.6	6.2	6.5	7.7	7.2	6.6	29.1	25.2	10.9	0.6	75.1	36.6	50.7	49.3
31543	HORTENSE	96.5	95.8	2.0	2.4	0.1	0.1	1.4	1.8	7.3	7.6	8.0	6.2	5.6	27.1	25.1	11.8	1.2	73.5	36.6	49.2	50.8
31544	JACKSONVILLE	75.6	72.7	23.3	26.0	0.0	0.0	0.9	1.2	7.2	6.9	6.6	6.2	6.5	24.8	26.4	13.2	2.2	75.4	38.4	47.2	52.8
31545	JESUP	77.4	75.9	19.1	19.9	0.5	0.6	3.6	4.5	7.7	7.2	7.8	7.7	7.4	27.5	23.6	10.0	1.1	72.5	34.4	48.7	51.3
31546	JESUP	67.8	65.5	29.6	31.4	0.6	0.7	6.1	7.7	4.7	4.9	5.2	5.7	7.0	37.4	24.6	9.6	1.0	81.9	37.2	62.1	37.9
31547	KINGS BAY	73.6	70.8	18.1	19.4	1.0	1.1	8.9	11.0	13.7	6.1	3.1	9.9	37.8	28.3	1.1	0.1	0.0	76.2	22.3	69.3	30.7
31548	KINGSLAND	76.1	73.5	19.4	21.3	1.1	1.3	3.0	3.8	9.2	8.6	9.0	7.9	7.4	34.6	18.8	4.3	0.3	68.1	29.9	50.4	49.6
31549	LUMBER CITY	56.9	53.2	41.7	45.2	0.0	0.0	2.0	2.3	7.7	7.3	6.3	5.7	6.6	23.9	25.4	13.6	3.6	75.1	39.5	47.4	52.7
31550	MANOR	93.1	92.6	2.7	3.0	0.1	0.1	5.0	5.1	6.6	7.4	7.5	6.9	4.4	27.5	24.9	13.8	1.1	74.9	38.0	50.8	49.2
31551	MERSHON	88.7	86.8	6.8	7.7	0.4	0.5	7.6	9.7	7.7	7.3	6.7	7.0	7.5	29.2	24.5	8.9	1.3	74.6	35.1	52.6	47.4
31552	MILLWOOD	91.3	90.6	3.2	3.7	0.1	0.1	6.4	6.6	7.7	7.4	7.6	6.4	5.9	29.1	25.6	9.4	0.9	73.6	35.0	50.5	49.5
31553	NAHUNTA	92.7	91.9	5.9	6.6	0.2	0.2	0.9	1.1	7.4	7.1	7.3	7.1	7.2	26.9	24.8	10.7	1.5	73.8	35.5	50.0	50.0
31554	NICHOLLS	71.6	69.3	25.4	26.9	0.2	0.2	4.4	5.8	6.6	6.5	6.5	6.2	8.4	35.7	22.0	7.5	0.6	76.9	33.8	57.6	42.5
31555	ODUM	89.5	88.1	8.1	9.0	0.2	0.2	1.6	2.1	6.7	6.9	7.0	5.9	5.5	31.3	24.8	10.8	1.2	75.7	37.0	53.7	46.3
31557	PATTERSON	84.5	82.2	12.7	14.4	0.3	0.4	2.2	2.7	6.9	6.9	7.4	6.5	6.5	26.5	25.6	12.2	1.6	74.8	37.3	49.9	50.1
31558	SAINT MARYS	76.4	74.1	17.7	19.0	1.4	1.6	4.7	5.8	9.7	8.0	7.8	8.1	11.4	34.7	15.6	4.3	0.4	69.8	27.4	52.0	48.0
31560	SCREVEN	82.0	74.3	16.7	24.0	0.1	0.0	1.1	1.6	6.7	6.7	7.7	6.8	6.1	26.3	25.9	12.1	1.7	74.8	37.6	50.5	49.5
31561	SEA ISLAND	94.8	93.5	3.8	4.9	1.1	1.4	0.5	0.9	1.8	2.3	3.2	4.0	3.6	8.5	35.3	36.4	4.9	90.1	61.0	46.3	53.7
31562	SAINT GEORGE	95.1	94.4	2.2	2.5	0.7	0.9	1.0	1.2	8.0	7.7	7.9	7.2	5.9	28.2	24.6	9.8	0.7	71.9	35.5	51.6	48.4
31563	SURRENCY	76.2	73.7	21.4	23.4	0.2	0.2	2.3	2.8	6.6	6.3	7.4	6.2	7.0	26.6	26.8	11.6	1.6	76.0	38.8	49.8	50.2
31565	WAVERLY	69.3	66.6	28.6	31.1	0.2	0.2	0.3	0.3	6.2	6.3	6.6	6.7	5.4	26.8	28.3	12.7	1.0	76.7	40.6	48.1	51.9
31566	WAYNESVILLE	93.6	92.6	4.9	5.4	0.1	0.1	0.7	0.8	8.2	7.3	7.9	8.3	7.3	29.6	23.0	8.0	0.5	71.5	33.5	51.4	48.6
31567	WEST GREEN	91.0	89.3	6.2	7.2	0.0	0.0	4.6	6.0	8.1	7.8	7.0	6.2	5.9	30.4	22.6	10.8	1.1	73.2	34.8	50.7	49.3
31568	WHITE OAK	68.3	65.5	30.3	33.0	0.1	0.1	0.8	1.0	5.6	6.7	8.1	8.5	5.1	27.4	27.2	10.5	1.0	73.6	38.7	48.6	51.4
31569	WOODBINE	70.5	68.4	26.9	28.7	0.6	0.6	1.7	2.1	6.2	6.8	9.0	8.2	6.5	28.3	26.7	7.6	0.7	72.4	36.7	48.9	51.1
31601	VALDOSTA	38.8	36.3	58.4	60.4	0.6	0.7	2.5	3.0	8.2	7.6	8.2	8.5	10.6	27.8	20.1	8.0	1.0	71.3	29.3	47.5	52.5
31602	VALDOSTA	70.1	66.6	25.8	28.9	1.6	1.7	2.1	2.5	6.4	5.8	5.7	8.5	13.0	29.9	19.8	9.4	1.6	78.9	30.8	49.5	50.6
31605	VALDOSTA	72.3	68.6	21.4	24.2	2.5	2.9	3.5	4.2	7.7	7.6	7.7	7.1	9.4	35.7	18.5	6.0	0.4	72.7	30.5	51.0	49.0
31606	VALDOSTA	84.3	80.5	13.5	16.9	0.2	0.2	1.8	2.3	7.5	7.4	8.3	7.2	6.2	29.2	24.3	9.6	0.5	72.5	35.6	49.3	50.7
31620	ADEL	64.2	62.0	32.7	34.5	0.5	0.6	3.3	4.1	8.0	7.7	7.6	7.0	6.6	27.8	21.7	11.8	1.8	72.4	34.4	47.8	52.2
31622	ALAPAHA	70.3	67.8	28.9	31.2	0.1	0.1	0.2	0.3	7.4	6.8	6.5	5.4	6.6	25.5	27.3	13.6	1.1	76.2	38.4	49.8	50.2
31624	AXSON	86.2	83.7	4.2	4.6	0.0	0.0	13.0	16.1	9.6	8.7	7.4	7.3	7.1	29.6	21.1	8.2	1.2	70.0	32.7	50.4	49.6
31625	BARNEY	66.8	62.9	27.5	30.3	0.1	0.1	6.7	8.6	6.3	6.3	6.9	6.2	7.0	26.7	26.4	12.7	1.7	77.0	37.8	52.0	48.0
31626	BOSTON	48.6	42.9	49.5	55.0	0.1	0.1	2.5	2.9	6.8	6.9	7.8	7.4	6.4	26.0	25.2	11.9	1.7	73.6	37.7	48.3	51.8
31629	DIXIE	42.7	38.6	56.6	60.8	0.1	0.1	0.8	0.8	5.3	5.9	9.0	6.9	7.5	23.5	26.9	12.6	2.4	75.6	38.9	50.1	50.0
31630	DU PONT	62.5	59.6	36.2	38.9	0.0	0.0	1.5	2.1	8.1	7.6	7.3	7.9	7.3	30.0	24.1	7.1	0.6	72.4	33.2	50.2	49.8
31631	FARGO	84.1	82.4	13.7	15.1	0.0	0.0	0.4	0.4	6.7	6.7	6.7	8.0	5.3	27.9	27.7	10.3	0.8	75.0	37.4	50.0	50.0
31632	HAHIRA	82.6	79.2	14.2	17.1	0.4	0.5	2.5	3.1	7.2	7.7	7.8	7.4	6.6	29.2	24.4	8.7	0.9	72.7	35.1	49.2	50.8
31634	HOMERVILLE	68.3	65.7	30.2	32.6	0.1	0.2	0.7	0.9	7.4	7.4	7.5	6.7	6.6	28.3	23.9	11.0	1.3	73.3	35.6	50.0	50.0
31635	LAKELAND	66.2	63.7	31.1	33.2	0.4	0.5	1.9	2.3	7.0	7.0	6.8	7.1	7.8	29.4	23.4	9.9	1.6	74.8	34.9	51.3	48.8
31636	LAKE PARK	82.6	79.0	8.7	10.3	0.4	0.5	10.1	12.8	7.3	6.7	7.1	7.2	8.2	29.2	23.0	10.2	1.2	74.7	34.5	50.9	49.1
31637	LENOX	79.3	76.3	17.0	19.2	0.1	0.1	3.5	4.4	7.1	6.9	6.5	6.3	5.8	26.9	26.2	12.6	1.6	75.6	37.9	50.8	49.3
31638	MORVEN	58.6	54.8	36.7	39.5	0.3	0.3	4.5	5.4	6.2	6.3	7.7	7.8	7.2	26.9	24.8	11.5	1.7	75.0	37.0	49.5	50.5
	GEORGIA	65.1	63.4	28.7	29.4	2.2	2.5	5.3	6.6	7.3	7.1	7.2	7.0	7.6	31.0	23.0	8.6	1.1	74.3	34.2	49.3	50.7
	UNITED STATES	75.1	73.6	12.3	12.5	3.8	4.2	12.5	14.1	6.9	6.7	7.2	7.0	7.3	28.6	23.8	10.8	1.7	75.1	36.0	49.1	50.9

#	POST OFFICE NAME	2004 Per Capita Income	2004 HH Income Base	2004 Household Income Distribution (%): Less than $25,000	$25,000 to $49,999	$50,000 to $99,999	$100,000 to $149,999	$150,000 or More	Median Household Income: 2004	2009	2004 National Centile	2004 State Centile	2004 Home Value Base	2004 Home Value Distribution (%): Less than $50,000	$50,000 to $89,999	$90,000 to $174,999	$175,000 to $399,999	$400,000 or More	2004 Median Home Value
31301	ALLENHURST	15581	1393	30.5	37.4	27.1	4.4	0.7	36568	41618	34	41	713	32.3	18.4	46.6	2.4	0.4	88548
31302	BLOOMINGDALE	23188	3348	21.3	30.9	37.1	7.3	3.4	47827	56032	68	72	2793	18.4	30.3	36.6	12.8	1.9	92039
31303	CLYO	18862	662	26.9	24.2	39.7	7.7	1.5	47846	54219	68	72	575	19.7	27.1	37.6	13.6	2.1	96607
31304	CRESCENT	14207	708	41.2	29.4	24.7	4.1	0.6	30521	33589	14	15	561	52.8	18.7	14.4	8.6	5.5	46026
31305	DARIEN	15858	1816	38.4	34.7	22.1	3.1	1.7	32906	36535	21	25	1405	40.9	28.2	21.1	6.8	3.1	64551
31308	ELLABELL	20152	2599	27.6	30.4	28.2	10.6	3.2	41399	52030	51	56	2205	33.1	27.4	27.7	10.5	1.4	75357
31309	FLEMING	18992	260	31.2	33.9	25.0	8.9	1.2	38898	44771	42	49	201	25.9	28.9	41.3	3.0	1.0	85476
31312	GUYTON	21987	4699	19.3	28.4	38.0	10.7	3.6	51803	60031	75	77	4050	16.8	25.3	38.5	18.3	1.2	103164
31313	HINESVILLE	16232	13163	28.7	36.4	28.4	4.9	1.6	38011	42674	39	46	6857	8.5	35.1	51.2	4.7	0.6	94479
31314	FORT STEWART	4844	7	14.3	0.0	85.7	0.0	0.0	62635	79274	87	88	5	0.0	0.0	100.0	0.0	0.0	112500
31315	FORT STEWART	13682	2376	27.8	53.1	17.3	1.8	0.0	33664	37147	23	28	135	48.2	19.3	23.0	3.0	6.7	60357
31316	LUDOWICI	14048	3651	35.3	37.0	23.3	3.4	1.0	33864	37166	24	28	2637	35.3	34.7	25.2	3.9	0.8	67303
31319	MERIDIAN	15566	94	35.1	37.2	23.4	3.2	1.1	32933	36708	21	25	72	34.7	23.6	27.8	12.5	1.4	74000
31320	MIDWAY	20150	3060	27.9	33.1	25.9	10.3	2.9	39367	45370	44	50	2496	24.0	24.2	35.0	15.9	0.9	92744
31321	PEMBROKE	19336	2281	29.4	28.3	30.3	9.6	2.3	41955	51099	53	58	1822	29.2	28.7	34.1	7.6	0.4	82000
31322	POOLER	24348	3099	17.1	27.8	37.3	13.9	3.9	54871	66678	80	81	2616	9.6	19.8	57.1	13.0	0.5	111375
31323	RICEBORO	14568	559	45.4	27.4	22.0	3.0	2.2	28728	31302	10	10	472	46.2	26.5	23.7	3.6	0.0	55455
31324	RICHMOND HILL	28164	6040	16.0	18.8	40.5	16.1	8.6	66881	79135	90	91	4479	5.8	8.3	46.7	34.8	4.4	152892
31326	RINCON	24999	5111	16.4	24.8	41.4	12.3	5.2	59682	67268	84	85	4249	7.7	14.1	48.4	27.5	2.3	131023
31327	SAPELO ISLAND	21007	73	38.4	26.0	28.8	5.5	1.4	36360	37370	33	40	58	46.6	20.7	12.1	10.3	10.3	55000
31328	TYBEE ISLAND	42185	1764	21.5	18.7	36.0	13.0	10.8	61022	79482	85	87	1267	2.8	2.6	30.2	47.2	17.1	214148
31329	SPRINGFIELD	20812	2907	25.5	25.1	36.4	10.3	2.8	49295	56352	71	74	2385	15.9	25.3	39.7	16.3	2.9	102670
31331	TOWNSEND	19159	1887	33.5	35.1	24.0	5.5	2.0	35656	40140	30	37	1679	34.7	27.4	19.4	16.2	2.3	72287
31401	SAVANNAH	21673	9229	55.9	24.0	12.0	3.6	4.5	21355	25535	2	2	2797	16.7	25.0	19.6	16.5	22.3	116830
31404	SAVANNAH	18567	12184	39.3	28.6	24.2	5.1	2.8	32652	39640	20	24	6982	10.8	51.7	33.1	3.7	0.7	80179
31405	SAVANNAH	24467	12261	31.2	30.9	25.4	7.4	5.1	38851	47208	42	48	8085	14.2	23.4	43.2	15.7	3.5	106464
31406	SAVANNAH	27852	13873	23.5	27.2	30.8	11.4	7.1	49223	59556	71	74	9382	4.0	18.9	52.7	19.3	5.2	117562
31407	SAVANNAH	25008	1281	22.3	26.7	39.0	9.7	2.3	50736	61052	73	76	1006	11.6	45.2	34.7	8.5	0.0	84651
31408	SAVANNAH	15799	3856	35.4	32.6	26.2	4.5	1.4	33332	39720	22	26	2193	32.9	28.4	33.4	4.5	0.7	76039
31409	SAVANNAH	12871	190	32.6	45.8	21.6	0.0	0.0	32043	36973	18	21	6	0.0	50.0	50.0	0.0	0.0	95000
31410	SAVANNAH	37116	9934	11.0	21.8	37.8	17.2	12.3	69664	87633	91	92	7641	0.3	3.1	54.9	34.1	7.7	161835
31411	SAVANNAH	85947	3734	4.9	9.8	27.3	18.1	39.9	117506	167669	99	100	3614	0.0	0.0	4.0	48.4	47.7	389147
31415	SAVANNAH	15365	4974	55.0	23.9	15.5	3.2	2.4	21603	25567	2	2	2645	31.8	43.8	22.1	1.6	0.6	65940
31419	SAVANNAH	25859	17654	21.1	29.0	34.2	11.1	4.6	49921	60284	72	74	10608	9.3	13.6	58.6	16.2	2.2	117239
31501	WAYCROSS	18557	6056	42.2	26.9	23.9	4.4	2.6	31419	35597	16	19	4030	29.6	34.5	29.6	5.9	0.5	73034
31503	WAYCROSS	16478	7633	38.5	32.2	23.5	4.0	1.7	32720	37148	20	24	5861	40.7	31.3	22.0	4.8	1.2	61062
31510	ALMA	17139	3433	43.8	28.2	21.0	4.3	2.8	29655	33814	12	12	2649	41.5	27.4	24.0	6.5	0.6	59239
31512	AMBROSE	18647	913	36.0	30.5	24.0	6.6	3.0	34202	40308	25	30	754	43.4	25.6	21.1	7.6	2.4	58929
31513	BAXLEY	18061	5980	38.3	27.4	25.1	6.5	2.7	34414	40966	25	32	4734	37.2	33.1	22.7	6.0	1.0	64298
31516	BLACKSHEAR	16851	4845	38.0	31.0	25.0	5.0	1.0	33274	37540	22	26	3853	40.7	28.8	21.8	8.0	0.8	63369
31518	BRISTOL	19338	266	38.4	30.1	19.2	8.7	3.8	34204	40000	25	30	225	23.6	29.8	34.7	10.7	1.3	86591
31519	BROXTON	22260	1394	35.2	31.9	21.9	6.1	5.0	35155	41033	28	35	1148	40.6	29.1	17.8	12.0	0.5	63737
31520	BRUNSWICK	16080	8642	46.2	27.9	19.4	4.2	2.3	27547	32469	8	7	4725	26.0	39.1	30.2	4.1	0.7	73345
31522	SAINT SIMONS ISLAND	49156	7193	12.3	19.7	34.3	18.7	15.0	73000	92957	92	93	5758	1.5	1.7	18.8	51.7	26.4	262350
31523	BRUNSWICK	23365	3659	21.8	27.6	37.0	10.5	3.2	50767	62074	73	76	3142	14.8	25.9	37.6	18.7	3.1	104430
31525	BRUNSWICK	22456	8880	25.7	28.8	31.6	11.2	2.7	46058	55242	64	68	6013	16.1	31.9	38.7	11.9	1.4	92233
31527	JEKYLL ISLAND	42137	471	8.1	25.5	37.2	21.7	7.6	68062	86944	90	92	365	0.0	3.3	9.3	84.9	2.5	245168
31532	DENTON	18257	349	43.6	30.4	16.1	5.7	4.3	29874	34307	12	13	294	48.6	25.5	18.4	7.5	0.0	51667
31533	DOUGLAS	20522	6098	36.6	31.3	22.3	5.6	4.2	34539	40402	26	32	4352	33.0	33.9	24.0	7.8	1.2	70231
31535	DOUGLAS	17748	3883	33.2	30.8	27.9	5.1	3.0	37020	43029	36	42	3120	41.6	29.1	21.8	6.4	1.2	59560
31537	FOLKSTON	15953	2710	41.1	28.4	23.2	5.3	2.0	31393	36471	16	19	2157	40.5	30.1	22.4	6.6	0.4	63644
31539	HAZLEHURST	16200	4884	40.8	31.6	20.4	4.9	2.3	30528	34965	14	15	3843	40.9	33.0	21.5	4.7	0.0	60924
31542	HOBOKEN	16378	1075	38.4	26.7	29.7	3.7	1.5	33535	37184	23	27	945	54.9	23.1	16.5	4.0	1.5	44655
31543	HORTENSE	16512	664	37.1	29.7	27.4	4.1	1.8	33523	37473	22	27	556	48.2	31.1	15.1	4.0	1.6	51852
31544	JACKSONVILLE	24643	328	44.2	29.9	20.7	3.7	1.5	27952	31407	9	8	296	57.8	23.7	17.6	1.0	0.0	37632
31545	JESUP	19162	5492	35.8	27.8	26.2	7.6	2.6	36361	43344	33	40	4200	35.5	27.8	26.3	9.9	0.6	72867
31546	JESUP	19199	2117	32.6	26.5	27.3	11.1	2.6	40558	48262	48	53	1612	32.8	30.3	25.3	10.6	0.9	69337
31547	KINGS BAY	12905	241	16.2	66.0	17.4	0.4	0.0	37500	42047	37	44	0	0.0	0.0	0.0	0.0	0.0	0
31548	KINGSLAND	18313	5578	22.0	33.5	36.3	6.4	1.9	45866	51409	64	67	3848	19.1	26.8	44.3	9.2	0.7	94104
31549	LUMBER CITY	18425	719	47.6	29.4	13.9	4.7	4.5	26764	30903	7	5	546	49.5	30.4	15.9	4.2	0.0	50714
31550	MANOR	16767	323	28.5	48.3	16.4	5.3	1.6	35288	40495	29	35	270	61.1	16.3	14.8	7.8	0.0	34286
31551	MERSHON	17194	379	40.1	29.3	19.8	8.7	2.1	31071	35463	15	17	315	26.0	36.2	30.8	3.8	3.2	75156
31552	MILLWOOD	15563	317	29.7	42.0	25.9	2.2	0.3	37338	42779	37	43	266	36.5	41.0	15.8	4.9	1.9	66000
31553	NAHUNTA	16192	1487	37.3	34.7	21.9	4.8	1.3	33402	37491	22	26	1230	46.8	30.0	16.5	5.5	1.2	53571
31554	NICHOLLS	15418	1971	39.4	31.5	23.6	3.3	2.2	32722	37513	20	25	1597	50.9	25.2	17.1	5.7	1.1	49262
31555	ODUM	19348	1032	30.4	28.2	31.0	7.5	2.9	41775	50113	52	57	879	37.1	26.4	25.5	10.1	0.9	69338
31557	PATTERSON	15959	1125	36.6	36.9	22.0	3.5	1.0	33927	38184	24	29	937	36.2	32.2	25.6	5.8	0.2	64655
31558	SAINT MARYS	19705	7405	18.8	36.5	33.0	8.8	2.8	46623	52457	65	70	4139	6.7	24.9	50.6	16.1	1.7	108765
31560	SCREVEN	19158	1135	33.1	35.2	24.9	4.5	2.3	35177	40815	28	35	949	42.2	33.5	19.0	3.8	1.6	57842
31561	SEA ISLAND	82060	240	15.0	18.8	17.9	24.2	24.2	95126	123877	98	99	223	0.0	0.9	3.6	50.2	45.3	379412
31562	SAINT GEORGE	15713	880	34.9	33.2	26.6	4.1	1.3	33544	39045	23	27	762	38.5	25.3	28.2	8.0	0.0	67619
31563	SURRENCY	18297	529	38.4	27.0	28.5	4.4	1.7	35493	41239	29	36	447	37.4	33.6	21.9	6.3	0.9	65000
31565	WAVERLY	20567	592	33.8	26.9	29.6	5.4	4.4	40671	45313	48	53	463	26.8	13.8	35.0	19.9	4.5	103984
31566	WAYNESVILLE	15270	2079	31.3	36.6	28.4	3.4	0.3	35944	40780	31	38	1727	51.9	29.7	14.1	4.3	0.0	47624
31567	WEST GREEN	17972	342	30.7	45.0	18.7	3.5	2.1	35613	41042	30	37	287	45.0	35.2	13.2	4.9	1.7	54833
31568	WHITE OAK	16802	739	35.9	24.4	32.2	4.7	2.8	40273	44355	47	52	649	41.1	20.3	23.1	14.2	1.2	69468
31569	WOODBINE	20121	1821	26.1	26.5	39.1	5.9	2.4	47702	52702	68	71	1462	23.1	22.0	40.8	13.3	0.8	96857
31601	VALDOSTA	13906	11925	49.1	28.8	17.6	2.9	1.5	25585	29833	5	3	6235	34.9	36.3	24.4	3.9	0.6	63378
31602	VALDOSTA	23768	11393	27.3	29.5	28.3	9.1	5.8	43674	50880	58	62	7111	8.5	20.8	48.6	21.0	1.1	115463
31605	VALDOSTA	25382	6328	19.6	30.2	34.9	9.3	6.0	50158	60119	72	75	4346	12.5	14.5	54.0	13.3	5.8	115991
31606	VALDOSTA	18028	1368	30.0	31.2	30.5	6.7	1.7	39070	46761	43	49	1166	19.8	36.6	32.3	10.0	1.2	83363
31620	ADEL	15291	4250	41.7	32.2	20.4	4.9	1.0	30240	34280	13	14	3118	31.7	34.7	24.2	8.6	0.7	68084
31622	ALAPAHA	16354	608	37.0	34.7	22.7	4.0	1.6	31509	35874	16	19	497	45.3	25.2	25.0	2.6	2.0	57121
31624	AXSON	12511	496	42.9	37.5	16.5	3.0	0.0	29686	33285	12	12	417	59.2	26.1	8.2	5.3	1.2	41250
31625	BARNEY	17408	361	30.8	28.8	35.7	3.1	1.7	40392	45977	47	53	306	36.6	29.1	23.9	7.8	2.6	66667
31626	BOSTON	15562	1374	45.0	30.6	18.7	2.9	2.8	28554	32686	10	10	1082	34.0	32.9	21.4	9.8	1.9	68261
31629	DIXIE	14500	362	40.1	34.3	21.6	4.1	0.0	35264	38913	28	35	299	38.8	26.8	22.4	11.4	0.7	65476
31630	DU PONT	17060	255	29.4	36.9	27.8	3.1	2.8	38746	43358	42	48	216	43.5	32.9	17.6	2.3	3.7	58750
31631	FARGO	14415	208	39.9	38.5	17.3	3.4	1.0	31395	35515	16	19	173	66.5	27.2	5.2	1.2	0.0	31406
31632	HAHIRA	20089	2599	28.1	29.2	30.9	9.4	2.5	42438	50813	54	59	2093	19.5	25.5	38.2	14.9	2.0	100049
31634	HOMERVILLE	14892	2164	45.4	30.8	17.5	4.1	2.3	28553	32042	10	10	1635	41.9	36.8	14.9	4.4	2.1	58548
31635	LAKELAND	16387	1893	38.3	31.5	24.5	3.5	2.3	32309	35968	19	22	1424	39.2	31.5	20.4	9.0	0.0	64744
31636	LAKE PARK	19427	3189	35.6	24.2	29.5	7.8	2.9	40301	47623	47	52	2379	19.0	24.8	39.8	15.6	0.9	98743
31637	LENOX	16665	897	41.4	26.4	27.0	2.7	2.6	31337	36090	16	18	740	42.3	28.7	23.4	2.7	3.0	60400
31638	MORVEN	14209	422	43.8	33.2	19.4	2.1	1.4	28544	32986	10	9	346	47.1	24.9	19.7	7.2	1.2	53704
	GEORGIA	26143		23.6	26.3	31.4	11.6	7.0	50024	60470				12.5	17.5	39.3	24.8	6.0	125860
	UNITED STATES	25866		24.7	27.1	30.8	10.9	6.5	48124	56710				10.9	15.0	33.7	30.1	10.4	145905

ZIP CODE #	POST OFFICE NAME	FINANCIAL SERVICES: Auto Loan	Home Loan	Invest-ments	Retire-ment Plans	THE HOME: Home Improvements: Home Repair	Lawn & Garden	Furnishings: Comput-ers & Hard-ware	Major Appli-ances	TV, Radio, Sound Equip-ment	Furni-ture	ENTERTAINMENT: Dine out/ Carry out	Sports Equip-ment	Fees & Tickets	Toys & Games	Travel	Cable TV	PERSONAL: Apparel & Services	Auto Repairs	Health Insur-ance	Pets & Supplies
31301	ALLENHURST	71	50	45	54	47	54	66	60	67	63	83	77	58	76	57	62	80	68	57	69
31302	BLOOMINGDALE	102	87	63	83	90	98	84	93	89	85	108	108	79	104	84	90	102	92	98	115
31303	CLYO	88	76	55	72	77	83	72	80	75	74	92	93	67	87	72	76	88	79	82	98
31304	CRESCENT	71	48	23	42	54	62	47	58	56	48	66	69	40	62	47	60	60	57	70	81
31305	DARIEN	65	54	40	52	56	63	55	60	58	55	70	68	51	66	54	59	66	60	64	71
31308	ELLABELL	89	81	63	78	81	86	77	83	78	80	97	96	73	91	76	77	93	83	82	98
31309	FLEMING	79	72	56	69	72	76	69	73	69	70	86	85	65	81	68	68	82	73	73	87
31312	GUYTON	99	92	75	90	92	96	87	93	87	90	108	107	84	103	86	85	104	92	90	109
31313	HINESVILLE	74	51	49	57	47	54	70	62	71	67	89	81	62	81	60	66	85	72	58	71
31314	FORT STEWART	98	87	71	86	86	91	86	89	87	88	108	106	81	102	83	85	103	91	87	106
31315	FORT STEWART	61	39	37	44	36	42	58	50	58	54	73	66	49	65	47	53	70	59	46	57
31316	LUDOWICI	64	53	45	53	52	57	58	58	59	58	74	70	54	69	54	57	71	61	57	67
31319	MERIDIAN	62	56	44	54	56	60	54	58	54	55	67	67	51	63	53	54	65	58	57	68
31320	MIDWAY	86	76	58	72	77	83	72	79	75	74	91	91	68	87	72	75	87	79	81	96
31321	PEMBROKE	88	75	55	71	77	84	73	80	76	74	93	93	68	89	72	77	88	79	84	98
31322	POOLER	96	98	91	98	99	102	92	95	91	92	113	113	93	115	93	89	110	94	93	111
31323	RICEBORO	77	51	23	44	58	67	50	62	60	51	70	74	42	67	51	65	64	62	77	88
31324	RICHMOND HILL	114	123	130	129	121	121	118	117	111	120	140	137	120	139	116	105	137	116	106	128
31326	RINCON	105	105	95	105	105	108	99	103	97	100	121	122	99	122	99	95	118	101	98	121
31327	SAPELO ISLAND	76	51	23	44	58	66	49	61	59	50	69	73	42	66	50	64	63	61	76	87
31328	TYBEE ISLAND	139	122	106	115	132	147	116	132	124	117	151	150	111	146	123	130	143	130	147	166
31329	SPRINGFIELD	93	83	64	80	85	90	79	86	82	81	100	100	75	97	79	82	96	85	88	104
31331	TOWNSEND	85	60	32	53	68	77	58	71	68	58	80	84	50	77	60	73	73	70	86	99
31401	SAVANNAH	67	56	72	56	55	64	69	65	73	68	91	76	66	86	65	73	88	70	68	73
31404	SAVANNAH	66	63	73	60	61	70	67	66	71	68	89	74	68	87	67	73	86	67	69	74
31405	SAVANNAH	84	82	88	80	81	89	83	83	86	84	106	95	84	104	83	87	103	84	86	95
31406	SAVANNAH	94	101	109	102	100	104	100	99	97	99	122	116	102	122	100	94	119	99	93	109
31407	SAVANNAH	86	80	70	74	83	92	78	82	84	76	102	94	78	106	80	87	97	81	92	99
31408	SAVANNAH	63	58	56	56	58	64	60	61	62	59	76	70	58	74	59	62	74	62	63	70
31409	SAVANNAH	59	38	36	43	34	41	56	48	57	52	71	65	48	64	46	52	68	57	45	55
31410	SAVANNAH	127	147	153	151	143	142	135	134	125	137	159	156	141	161	135	120	157	131	118	146
31411	SAVANNAH	277	259	248	246	275	323	240	273	253	257	316	267	243	262	261	271	295	265	319	312
31415	SAVANNAH	57	49	55	45	48	58	54	55	60	55	74	59	53	68	53	63	71	56	62	63
31419	SAVANNAH	91	92	98	95	90	93	93	91	90	94	113	108	93	111	90	86	111	93	84	101
31501	WAYCROSS	65	55	51	52	57	66	58	62	63	58	77	70	55	73	58	66	72	62	69	73
31503	WAYCROSS	66	53	38	49	56	63	52	59	57	53	69	69	48	66	52	59	65	59	66	75
31510	ALMA	78	57	34	51	62	70	56	66	64	57	76	78	49	72	56	67	71	66	77	88
31512	AMBROSE	87	64	35	57	69	78	61	73	70	62	84	87	54	79	62	74	77	73	86	100
31513	BAXLEY	81	63	40	58	67	74	61	70	68	62	82	83	55	77	61	70	76	70	79	91
31516	BLACKSHEAR	70	58	43	55	60	67	58	64	62	59	75	73	54	71	58	64	71	64	69	78
31518	BRISTOL	90	60	27	52	68	78	58	72	70	59	82	87	49	78	59	75	75	72	89	103
31519	BROXTON	102	78	47	71	83	92	75	87	83	76	100	103	67	94	75	86	93	86	98	115
31520	BRUNSWICK	57	49	49	46	49	57	53	54	58	53	71	61	51	67	52	60	68	56	61	63
31522	SAINT SIMONS ISLAND	145	155	169	153	158	171	147	152	145	148	181	171	151	177	153	147	176	150	155	173
31523	BRUNSWICK	99	86	64	82	89	96	82	90	85	83	104	106	77	101	82	86	99	89	94	112
31525	BRUNSWICK	86	82	77	82	81	86	82	83	81	83	101	98	80	98	80	79	98	84	80	96
31527	JEKYLL ISLAND	122	114	109	108	120	142	105	120	111	113	138	117	107	115	114	119	129	116	140	137
31532	DENTON	90	60	27	52	68	79	58	73	70	59	82	87	49	78	59	76	75	72	90	103
31533	DOUGLAS	88	72	56	68	76	85	73	80	79	73	95	92	67	91	72	81	90	80	88	99
31535	DOUGLAS	80	71	54	68	72	77	68	74	70	70	86	85	64	81	67	69	82	73	75	89
31537	FOLKSTON	83	56	26	48	63	73	54	67	65	55	76	80	46	72	55	70	69	67	82	95
31539	HAZLEHURST	75	53	30	48	59	67	52	63	61	53	72	74	46	68	53	65	67	62	75	85
31542	HOBOKEN	72	60	42	57	62	67	58	64	61	59	74	75	53	70	57	62	71	64	68	80
31543	HORTENSE	78	54	27	47	60	69	52	64	62	53	73	76	45	69	53	66	66	63	77	89
31544	JACKSONVILLE	109	73	33	63	83	96	71	88	85	72	100	106	60	95	72	92	91	87	109	126
31545	JESUP	81	70	54	66	72	78	69	74	72	70	88	86	64	84	68	73	84	74	79	90
31546	JESUP	73	62	49	57	64	72	61	67	66	62	80	76	58	77	61	69	76	66	74	83
31547	KINGS BAY	63	40	38	46	37	43	60	51	61	56	76	69	51	68	49	55	72	61	48	58
31548	KINGSLAND	85	70	57	70	69	75	76	76	77	75	95	91	69	88	71	75	91	80	75	89
31549	LUMBER CITY	84	56	25	48	63	73	54	68	65	55	77	81	46	72	55	70	70	67	83	96
31550	MANOR	79	53	24	46	60	69	51	64	62	52	73	76	44	69	52	67	66	63	79	91
31551	MERSHON	89	60	27	51	67	78	57	72	69	59	81	86	49	77	58	75	74	71	89	102
31552	MILLWOOD	78	52	24	45	59	68	51	63	61	52	71	75	43	68	51	65	65	62	77	89
31553	NAHUNTA	68	59	44	57	60	64	57	62	59	58	72	72	53	68	56	59	69	62	63	75
31554	NICHOLLS	72	56	35	51	59	65	54	62	59	55	71	73	48	67	54	61	66	61	69	81
31555	ODUM	84	73	54	69	74	80	70	76	72	72	89	89	65	84	69	72	85	76	79	93
31557	PATTERSON	77	52	24	45	58	67	50	62	60	51	71	74	43	67	51	64	64	62	76	88
31558	SAINT MARYS	89	64	62	71	62	70	84	77	85	80	106	98	75	98	73	80	101	86	73	88
31560	SCREVEN	92	61	28	53	69	80	59	74	71	60	84	88	50	79	60	77	76	73	91	105
31561	SEA ISLAND	231	216	206	205	228	269	199	227	211	214	262	222	202	218	217	225	245	220	266	259
31562	SAINT GEORGE	80	54	24	46	61	70	52	65	62	53	73	77	44	69	53	67	67	64	80	92
31563	SURRENCY	84	57	27	50	65	74	55	69	66	57	78	82	48	74	56	71	71	68	83	96
31565	WAVERLY	80	73	57	70	73	77	70	75	71	72	87	86	66	82	69	70	84	75	74	89
31566	WAYNESVILLE	67	61	47	58	61	64	58	62	59	60	72	72	55	68	57	58	69	62	62	74
31567	WEST GREEN	86	59	29	52	66	75	57	70	68	58	80	84	49	75	58	72	73	70	85	98
31568	WHITE OAK	85	60	30	52	66	75	57	70	67	59	80	83	50	75	58	72	73	69	84	97
31569	WOODBINE	80	80	74	80	79	82	78	79	76	78	95	93	77	94	76	74	92	79	75	89
31601	VALDOSTA	53	45	45	43	45	51	50	50	53	50	65	57	47	61	48	54	63	52	53	59
31602	VALDOSTA	83	81	90	84	80	85	87	83	85	85	107	100	86	105	84	82	104	86	79	93
31605	VALDOSTA	89	83	86	88	81	85	91	86	88	89	110	104	88	106	85	83	108	90	79	96
31606	VALDOSTA	78	71	55	68	71	75	67	72	68	69	84	84	64	80	66	67	81	72	72	86
31620	ADEL	64	53	42	50	55	62	54	58	58	54	71	67	51	67	54	60	67	59	64	71
31622	ALAPAHA	72	54	31	48	59	66	51	61	59	52	70	73	46	68	52	62	64	60	72	84
31624	AXSON	64	44	22	39	50	57	43	53	51	44	60	63	37	57	43	54	55	52	64	74
31625	BARNEY	85	57	26	49	65	75	55	69	67	56	78	83	47	74	56	72	71	68	85	98
31626	BOSTON	72	49	27	43	55	64	49	59	59	50	69	70	43	65	49	63	63	59	73	82
31629	DIXIE	72	48	22	42	55	63	47	58	56	48	66	70	40	63	48	61	60	58	72	83
31630	DU PONT	84	57	26	49	64	74	55	68	66	56	77	82	46	73	56	71	70	68	84	97
31631	FARGO	68	46	21	40	52	60	44	55	53	45	63	66	38	59	45	57	57	55	68	78
31632	HAHIRA	82	80	70	79	81	84	76	80	76	77	94	93	75	93	76	75	91	79	79	94
31634	HOMERVILLE	72	48	22	42	55	63	46	58	56	47	66	69	39	62	47	60	60	57	72	82
31635	LAKELAND	68	54	45	50	56	64	57	61	63	57	76	70	53	71	56	65	72	62	69	75
31636	LAKE PARK	82	73	59	71	75	80	71	76	72	71	89	89	67	86	70	72	85	76	79	93
31637	LENOX	77	54	26	47	60	68	52	63	61	53	72	76	44	68	52	65	66	63	77	89
31638	MORVEN	69	48	24	42	54	61	46	57	55	47	65	68	40	61	47	58	59	56	68	79
	GEORGIA	103	97	95	97	97	104	97	99	98	98	122	116	96	120	96	98	118	100	99	116
	UNITED STATES	100	100	100	100	100	100	100	100	100	100	100	100	100	100	100	100	100	100	100	100

GEORGIA

A 31639-39823

POPULATION CHANGE

# POST OFFICE NAME	COUNTY FIPS CODE	POPULATION 2000	2004	2009	2000-2004 ANNUAL RATE % Rate	State Centile	HOUSEHOLDS 2000	2004	2009	% Annual Rate 2000-2004	2004 Average HH Size	FAMILIES 2000	2004	% Annual Rate 2000-2004
31639 NASHVILLE	019	9164	9572	10140	1.0	37	3589	3804	4088	1.4	2.48	2540	2650	1.0
31641 NAYLOR	185	780	857	932	2.2	63	277	309	341	2.6	2.77	224	246	2.2
31642 PEARSON	003	4341	4553	4731	1.1	40	1531	1611	1681	1.2	2.81	1101	1141	0.8
31643 QUITMAN	027	9348	9578	9912	0.6	26	3449	3587	3775	0.9	2.59	2414	2472	0.6
31645 RAY CITY	019	3785	4076	4364	1.8	52	1374	1492	1614	2.0	2.72	1026	1098	1.6
31647 SPARKS	075	2431	2722	2964	2.7	71	894	1009	1109	2.9	2.68	665	737	2.5
31648 STATENVILLE	101	1251	1352	1530	1.8	54	440	475	534	1.8	2.85	335	357	1.5
31649 STOCKTON	173	1581	1625	1694	0.7	29	571	594	626	0.9	2.74	440	452	0.6
31650 WILLACOOCHEE	003	3138	3261	3405	0.9	36	1154	1209	1269	1.1	2.68	859	888	0.8
31699 MOODY A F B	185	3160	3141	3188	-0.1	10	19	19	20	0.0	2.58	15	14	-1.6
31701 ALBANY	095	22549	22157	22354	-0.4	5	8291	8208	8365	-0.2	2.56	5288	5172	-0.5
31704 ALBANY	095	987	939	926	-1.2	0	232	222	222	-1.0	3.41	221	210	-1.2
31705 ALBANY	095	37585	37890	38325	0.2	16	12394	12651	12977	0.5	2.76	9079	9117	0.1
31707 ALBANY	095	21781	22548	23133	0.8	33	9372	9786	10144	1.0	2.30	5922	6088	0.7
31709 AMERICUS	261	15986	16289	16609	0.4	21	6044	6223	6411	0.7	2.47	3958	4005	0.3
31711 ANDERSONVILLE	261	940	1083	1169	3.4	81	339	397	435	3.8	2.61	259	298	3.4
31712 ARABI	081	1034	1079	1104	1.0	37	402	425	440	1.3	2.54	289	301	1.0
31714 ASHBURN	287	7033	7087	7196	0.2	15	2569	2624	2696	0.5	2.66	1855	1865	0.1
31716 BACONTON	205	3091	3373	3591	2.1	60	1094	1215	1317	2.5	2.77	850	933	2.2
31719 AMERICUS	261	10857	10978	11141	0.3	17	3677	3773	3878	0.6	2.78	2837	2869	0.3
31721 ALBANY	095	18919	19566	20075	0.8	33	7299	7693	8008	1.2	2.53	5462	5656	0.8
31730 CAMILLA	205	11764	11959	12248	0.4	20	3617	3750	3924	0.9	2.75	2684	2740	0.5
31733 CHULA	277	1497	1554	1618	0.9	35	565	596	629	1.3	2.53	450	469	1.0
31735 COBB	261	842	911	951	1.9	55	355	389	409	2.2	2.34	254	274	1.8
31738 COOLIDGE	275	1876	1820	1853	-0.7	2	745	734	758	-0.4	2.48	526	510	-0.7
31743 DE SOTO	261	528	545	566	0.8	31	182	190	200	1.0	2.87	136	140	0.7
31744 DOERUN	071	2578	2484	2536	-0.9	1	1008	983	1017	-0.6	2.53	736	709	-0.9
31749 ENIGMA	019	3303	3495	3704	1.3	45	1219	1304	1396	1.6	2.68	942	995	1.3
31750 FITZGERALD	017	17555	17711	17974	0.2	16	6708	6842	7022	0.5	2.53	4653	4667	0.1
31756 HARTSFIELD	071	612	650	685	1.4	47	237	255	271	1.7	2.55	190	202	1.5
31757 THOMASVILLE	275	9238	10226	10976	2.4	67	3374	3797	4136	2.8	2.64	2517	2792	2.5
31760 IRWINVILLE	155	1034	1030	1046	-0.1	11	406	407	417	0.1	2.53	303	299	-0.3
31763 LEESBURG	177	20056	23522	28697	3.8	85	6657	7929	9824	4.2	2.87	5467	6446	4.0
31764 LESLIE	261	1496	1531	1566	0.6	26	512	528	544	0.7	2.90	391	398	0.4
31765 MEIGS	275	2491	2534	2629	0.4	20	926	957	1009	0.8	2.63	676	690	0.5
31768 MOULTRIE	071	22735	23446	24569	0.7	31	8822	9183	9705	1.0	2.52	6050	6193	0.6
31771 NORMAN PARK	071	5642	5845	6073	0.8	34	1888	1984	2084	1.2	2.78	1438	1488	0.8
31772 OAKFIELD	321	555	596	629	1.7	51	205	224	241	2.1	2.66	156	169	1.9
31773 OCHLOCKNEE	275	3204	3700	4054	3.4	82	1243	1453	1611	3.7	2.54	921	1060	3.4
31774 OCILLA	155	6709	7058	7394	1.2	42	2392	2549	2703	1.5	2.62	1765	1856	1.2
31775 OMEGA	277	2474	2532	2635	0.6	26	812	835	875	0.7	2.96	616	625	0.3
31778 PAVO	027	3794	3804	3887	0.1	13	1459	1483	1537	0.4	2.55	1036	1036	0.0
31779 PELHAM	205	8213	8461	8745	0.7	30	3044	3199	3371	1.2	2.55	2166	2243	0.8
31780 PLAINS	261	2511	2462	2458	-0.5	4	894	888	898	-0.2	2.65	648	633	-0.6
31781 POULAN	321	1640	1721	1797	1.1	41	610	651	692	1.5	2.64	469	493	1.2
31783 REBECCA	287	1344	1337	1353	-0.1	10	504	502	511	-0.1	2.66	381	375	-0.4
31784 SALE CITY	205	669	652	662	-0.6	3	260	258	267	-0.2	2.53	199	195	-0.5
31787 SMITHVILLE	177	1988	2162	2506	2.0	58	686	754	883	2.3	2.87	534	580	2.0
31788 MOULTRIE	071	10094	10958	11692	2.0	57	3382	3702	3985	2.2	2.80	2542	2733	1.7
31789 SUMNER	321	1722	1764	1828	0.6	26	651	677	714	0.9	2.60	498	511	0.6
31790 SYCAMORE	287	1769	1925	2024	2.0	59	609	667	707	2.2	2.81	485	524	1.8
31791 SYLVESTER	321	13059	13300	13676	0.4	21	4722	4877	5088	0.8	2.69	3542	3607	0.4
31792 THOMASVILLE	275	22874	23132	23786	0.3	17	8851	9073	9457	0.6	2.45	6001	6027	0.1
31793 TIFTON	277	6348	6589	6892	0.9	35	2297	2416	2559	1.2	2.57	1739	1799	0.8
31794 TIFTON	277	27093	28309	29907	1.0	38	9879	10444	11171	1.3	2.61	7010	7299	1.0
31795 TY TY	321	1958	2007	2085	0.6	27	729	759	799	1.0	2.64	560	576	0.7
31796 WARWICK	321	1274	1345	1406	1.3	44	510	547	581	1.7	2.46	372	394	1.4
31798 WRAY	155	1069	1055	1074	-0.3	7	411	411	423	0.0	2.57	304	300	-0.3
31801 BOX SPRINGS	263	2637	2866	3052	2.0	58	987	1101	1198	2.6	2.57	751	826	2.3
31803 BUENA VISTA	197	4890	4996	5085	0.5	24	1840	1908	1965	0.9	2.60	1275	1301	0.5
31804 CATAULA	145	4567	5258	6152	3.4	80	1645	1911	2254	3.6	2.75	1379	1588	3.4
31805 CUSSETA	053	2832	2744	2789	-0.7	2	1060	1052	1091	-0.2	2.61	790	760	-0.9
31806 ELLAVILLE	249	3735	3943	4169	1.3	44	1423	1519	1623	1.6	2.59	1033	1086	1.2
31807 ELLERSLIE	145	1462	1662	1932	3.1	76	523	599	701	3.2	2.77	435	493	3.0
31808 FORTSON	145	5068	5912	6901	3.7	84	1838	2167	2553	4.0	2.72	1515	1766	3.7
31811 HAMILTON	145	2723	2911	3279	1.6	49	1069	1158	1319	1.9	2.49	804	855	1.5
31812 JUNCTION CITY	263	378	607	781	11.8	100	151	247	324	12.3	2.46	103	167	12.0
31815 LUMPKIN	259	2024	2012	1978	-0.1	10	800	815	823	0.4	2.42	543	544	0.0
31816 MANCHESTER	199	5805	6305	6909	2.0	57	2308	2536	2815	2.2	2.49	1599	1725	1.8
31820 MIDLAND	215	5121	5776	6333	2.9	74	1801	2041	2252	3.0	2.83	1381	1558	2.9
31821 OMAHA	259	841	831	815	-0.3	7	334	339	342	0.4	2.45	224	223	-0.1
31822 PINE MOUNTAIN	145	4383	4842	5438	2.4	66	1641	1828	2071	2.6	2.65	1260	1386	2.3
31823 PINE MOUNTAIN VALLEY	145	1152	1265	1439	2.2	63	406	452	521	2.6	2.62	316	347	2.2
31824 PRESTON	307	1902	1942	2003	0.5	23	722	751	789	0.9	2.58	533	547	0.6
31825 RICHLAND	259	2389	2316	2257	-0.7	2	874	867	865	-0.2	2.41	583	568	-0.6
31826 SHILOH	145	1940	2026	2241	1.0	37	704	741	826	1.2	2.73	546	567	0.9
31827 TALBOTTON	263	2417	2390	2453	-0.3	8	933	935	975	0.1	2.54	655	646	-0.3
31829 UPATOI	215	768	830	874	1.8	54	262	283	300	1.8	2.93	230	247	1.7
31830 WARM SPRINGS	199	3016	2964	3093	-0.4	5	1105	1105	1178	0.0	2.45	777	763	-0.4
31831 WAVERLY HALL	145	2273	2646	3105	3.6	84	853	1009	1203	4.0	2.53	644	751	3.7
31832 WESTON	307	478	480	490	0.1	14	185	189	196	0.5	2.54	139	140	0.2
31833 WEST POINT	145	6550	6722	7217	0.6	28	2533	2616	2833	0.8	2.56	1824	1855	0.4
31836 WOODLAND	263	1837	1806	1850	-0.4	5	731	730	761	0.0	2.47	533	525	-0.4
31901 COLUMBUS	215	8291	8232	8376	-0.2	9	3604	3606	3712	0.0	1.97	1575	1523	-0.8
31903 COLUMBUS	215	22444	22172	22751	-0.3	7	8503	8436	8709	-0.2	2.63	5549	5372	-0.8
31904 COLUMBUS	215	29998	30996	32107	0.8	32	12053	12558	13128	1.0	2.42	8003	8199	0.6
31905 FORT BENNING	053	23530	23559	23921	0.0	12	3951	4026	4196	0.4	3.46	3772	3828	0.4
31906 COLUMBUS	215	24306	24276	24825	0.0	12	10329	10402	10729	0.2	2.33	6261	6144	-0.4
31907 COLUMBUS	215	56175	57649	59580	0.6	28	20444	21174	22091	0.8	2.62	14778	15036	0.4
31909 COLUMBUS	215	27889	30777	33062	2.4	66	10818	12123	13181	2.7	2.52	8023	8821	2.3
39813 ARLINGTON	037	1806	1855	1911	0.6	29	663	687	716	0.8	2.70	456	465	0.5
39815 ATTAPULGUS	087	2328	2339	2415	0.1	14	745	762	798	0.5	3.03	585	591	0.2
39817 BAINBRIDGE	087	11179	11865	12629	1.4	47	4034	4335	4671	1.7	2.64	2952	3129	1.4
39819 BAINBRIDGE	087	10890	11293	11858	0.9	34	4146	4336	4602	1.1	2.54	2881	2962	0.7
39823 BLAKELY	099	8627	8808	9053	0.5	23	3228	3348	3497	0.9	2.55	2265	2311	0.5
GEORGIA					2.4					2.5	2.64			2.2
UNITED STATES					1.2					1.3	2.58			1.1

ZIP CODE # POST OFFICE NAME	RACE (%) White 2000	White 2004	Black 2000	Black 2004	Asian/Pacific 2000	Asian/Pacific 2004	% Hispanic Origin 2000	% Hispanic Origin 2004	2004 AGE DISTRIBUTION (%) 0-4	5-9	10-14	15-19	20-24	25-44	45-64	65-84	85+	18+	MEDIAN AGE 2004	% 2004 Males	% 2004 Females
31639 NASHVILLE	85.4	83.6	11.8	13.2	0.3	0.3	2.2	2.7	6.5	6.5	7.2	6.6	6.5	27.3	25.1	12.3	2.0	75.7	37.5	49.1	50.9
31641 NAYLOR	72.1	67.2	26.0	31.0	0.1	0.1	0.6	0.9	7.5	7.2	8.9	8.5	6.8	29.4	22.8	8.5	0.5	71.4	34.5	50.1	49.9
31642 PEARSON	63.7	59.8	20.0	20.8	0.1	0.1	19.1	22.9	10.0	9.2	8.1	6.7	8.4	29.3	19.9	7.5	1.0	69.1	29.8	49.9	50.1
31643 QUITMAN	49.7	46.5	47.9	50.7	0.3	0.3	2.1	2.6	7.1	7.0	8.3	7.3	6.9	25.3	23.0	12.6	2.7	73.2	35.9	47.0	53.0
31645 RAY CITY	87.2	85.1	9.7	11.2	1.0	1.2	1.6	2.1	9.0	8.3	8.1	7.4	6.9	31.0	20.3	8.1	1.0	69.9	31.7	50.3	49.7
31647 SPARKS	75.2	70.7	21.8	25.9	0.5	0.7	2.6	3.2	7.9	7.5	8.3	7.9	6.7	28.7	21.6	10.2	1.3	71.5	33.9	48.6	51.4
31648 STATENVILLE	78.3	75.4	11.8	12.7	0.1	0.1	9.1	11.3	8.3	7.4	7.8	8.2	8.4	27.5	21.1	10.4	0.9	71.6	32.6	50.5	49.5
31649 STOCKTON	84.3	81.9	13.2	15.2	0.2	0.2	1.1	1.4	7.9	7.4	7.9	6.8	8.0	29.5	23.0	8.7	0.7	72.7	33.3	50.9	49.1
31650 WILLACOOCHEE	66.2	63.0	24.8	26.2	0.4	0.4	12.3	14.8	9.5	8.4	7.7	7.5	7.9	29.4	20.6	8.1	0.9	70.0	31.0	49.5	50.5
31699 MOODY A F B	70.5	65.4	22.6	26.6	1.8	2.0	5.7	7.1	3.1	2.6	2.8	5.1	20.1	56.8	7.8	1.5	0.2	90.0	29.3	72.8	27.2
31701 ALBANY	23.2	22.7	75.4	75.7	0.4	0.5	0.7	0.8	8.4	7.9	7.8	7.2	7.0	25.9	21.6	11.6	2.6	71.7	34.0	45.5	54.5
31704 ALBANY	54.8	49.8	38.8	43.1	1.7	1.8	7.0	8.3	15.6	9.1	5.8	6.4	18.0	40.2	4.5	0.6	0.0	67.0	23.7	58.8	41.2
31705 ALBANY	31.2	28.6	66.7	69.1	0.3	0.3	1.7	1.9	8.2	7.7	8.1	10.7	10.1	26.9	19.7	7.9	0.7	70.7	28.5	47.4	52.6
31707 ALBANY	56.8	53.1	41.0	44.3	0.9	1.0	1.4	1.6	6.3	6.2	6.5	6.6	7.1	28.3	23.5	13.7	1.8	77.1	36.8	46.4	53.7
31709 AMERICUS	52.3	49.1	44.0	46.7	1.1	1.2	3.3	3.9	7.7	6.7	6.8	7.9	9.6	27.9	20.5	10.3	2.7	74.9	32.4	46.0	54.0
31711 ANDERSONVILLE	63.2	59.5	33.9	37.1	0.3	0.5	3.6	4.4	7.7	7.5	6.8	6.2	6.5	29.2	26.0	9.1	1.0	74.2	37.0	52.5	47.5
31712 ARABI	80.6	76.0	17.8	22.2	0.8	0.8	0.0	0.1	5.8	6.1	7.2	7.4	5.8	28.0	24.8	13.4	1.4	76.4	39.6	51.3	48.7
31714 ASHBURN	47.3	44.3	50.2	52.8	0.4	0.4	2.5	3.0	8.4	7.4	8.1	7.9	7.6	25.8	22.0	11.1	1.8	71.7	33.3	47.5	52.5
31716 BACONTON	65.6	60.9	31.4	35.7	0.1	0.2	1.8	2.2	7.5	7.4	7.2	6.8	6.6	29.1	25.0	9.6	0.7	73.4	35.1	50.6	49.4
31719 AMERICUS	36.5	34.3	62.2	64.3	0.2	0.3	1.5	1.7	8.8	8.5	8.4	7.8	7.4	27.5	21.8	8.4	1.5	69.8	31.7	48.4	51.6
31721 ALBANY	59.6	55.9	38.3	41.6	1.1	1.2	1.2	1.4	6.4	6.8	7.2	6.7	6.7	28.6	27.7	9.2	0.8	75.5	36.5	47.7	52.3
31730 CAMILLA	41.0	37.4	56.6	59.8	0.4	0.4	2.1	2.5	6.9	6.9	7.1	6.8	8.1	32.1	21.8	9.0	1.4	75.3	33.6	53.3	46.7
31733 CHULA	87.5	84.4	7.4	9.1	0.3	0.3	5.5	7.3	6.8	6.8	6.1	6.1	6.1	27.9	29.2	10.2	1.0	76.8	38.8	51.1	48.9
31735 COBB	73.3	68.9	19.4	22.1	0.0	0.0	7.2	9.1	5.8	6.0	6.4	4.9	4.7	24.5	33.0	13.7	0.9	78.6	43.4	49.8	50.2
31738 COOLIDGE	71.2	66.4	26.0	30.2	0.6	0.7	2.2	2.8	6.3	6.6	7.6	6.4	6.2	25.9	26.9	12.1	1.9	75.5	39.3	48.2	51.8
31743 DE SOTO	58.5	55.1	37.7	40.4	0.0	0.0	4.0	5.1	5.9	6.2	7.2	6.1	5.7	25.1	30.1	12.5	1.3	77.1	40.5	48.4	51.6
31744 DOERUN	77.2	73.5	20.8	24.1	0.3	0.3	1.8	2.3	6.6	6.5	6.6	7.0	6.5	27.1	25.9	12.4	1.5	76.1	38.2	50.0	50.0
31749 ENIGMA	89.8	87.7	4.9	5.7	0.6	0.7	4.8	6.1	8.0	7.6	8.1	7.4	6.9	29.3	22.9	9.0	0.8	71.7	33.6	49.6	50.4
31750 FITZGERALD	63.3	60.3	32.6	34.8	0.3	0.3	4.6	5.6	7.4	7.1	7.3	7.1	6.9	26.9	23.8	11.6	1.9	73.8	35.5	48.3	51.7
31756 HARTSFIELD	92.3	90.6	4.9	6.0	0.2	0.3	3.3	4.2	6.6	6.9	8.0	7.5	6.0	27.9	24.9	11.2	0.9	73.9	36.8	52.6	47.4
31757 THOMASVILLE	73.4	69.7	24.5	27.9	0.4	0.5	1.5	2.0	6.9	6.8	7.8	7.4	6.8	28.5	24.6	10.0	1.2	73.8	36.0	47.9	52.1
31760 IRWINVILLE	95.8	94.8	2.1	2.6	0.1	0.1	2.1	2.7	7.1	7.0	7.0	6.3	5.9	28.9	24.5	11.8	1.6	75.2	36.7	49.9	50.1
31763 LEESBURG	83.8	81.9	13.8	15.3	0.9	1.0	1.2	1.6	7.1	7.3	8.3	8.0	7.1	31.5	24.0	6.1	0.6	72.3	33.6	50.7	49.3
31764 LESLIE	51.4	47.3	46.3	50.0	0.4	0.4	2.1	2.6	6.7	7.0	8.0	6.9	6.3	26.3	27.4	9.9	1.4	73.9	36.8	49.1	50.9
31765 MEIGS	58.8	56.1	36.7	38.9	0.8	0.8	5.1	5.9	7.1	7.2	8.0	7.1	7.4	26.3	24.4	11.2	1.2	73.3	35.5	48.1	51.9
31768 MOULTRIE	61.9	59.8	32.1	33.0	0.3	0.3	7.8	9.6	7.7	7.3	7.2	7.2	7.2	26.8	22.7	12.1	1.9	73.5	35.2	48.5	51.5
31771 NORMAN PARK	76.4	71.7	10.5	12.4	0.2	0.3	15.5	18.9	7.4	7.3	6.7	6.8	8.0	31.0	22.3	9.4	1.2	74.5	32.9	52.4	47.6
31772 OAKFIELD	79.6	77.0	18.6	21.0	0.2	0.2	0.7	0.8	6.4	6.5	7.1	7.4	6.4	27.9	27.0	10.7	0.7	75.5	37.9	50.3	49.7
31773 OCHLOCKNEE	88.4	85.6	9.2	11.4	0.4	0.5	1.5	1.9	6.6	6.6	7.0	6.5	6.2	28.7	26.6	10.6	1.2	75.8	37.9	48.9	51.1
31774 OCILLA	63.7	61.3	34.4	36.4	0.4	0.4	1.8	2.1	7.1	7.0	7.5	10.0	7.0	26.1	21.5	11.7	2.0	71.1	34.2	49.5	50.5
31775 OMEGA	66.5	60.5	11.3	12.6	0.2	0.2	27.2	33.2	9.0	8.5	7.9	7.0	7.0	29.7	20.6	9.2	1.2	70.4	31.9	50.9	49.1
31778 PAVO	73.0	68.5	21.0	24.1	0.5	0.6	6.0	7.4	6.2	6.2	6.3	6.2	6.6	25.6	27.8	13.1	2.0	77.5	40.1	50.1	49.9
31779 PELHAM	53.7	52.2	44.0	45.1	0.3	0.3	1.9	2.3	7.7	7.3	8.7	7.1	6.9	24.9	22.9	12.4	2.0	71.9	35.4	47.9	52.1
31780 PLAINS	54.6	51.0	43.6	47.0	0.1	0.1	2.8	3.4	7.1	7.2	7.4	6.7	6.1	25.6	23.0	14.1	2.8	74.3	37.3	48.1	52.0
31781 POULAN	75.7	72.4	22.7	25.7	0.1	0.1	1.0	1.2	7.3	7.2	7.7	7.2	7.6	25.7	25.2	10.6	1.4	73.5	36.0	49.1	50.9
31783 REBECCA	88.2	85.3	8.8	11.0	0.4	0.4	2.7	3.5	6.4	6.7	7.1	7.1	5.8	27.5	25.4	12.3	1.9	75.5	37.6	49.3	50.7
31784 SALE CITY	79.2	75.8	16.9	19.3	0.3	0.5	3.0	3.8	7.1	7.1	7.2	5.7	5.8	27.6	24.7	13.5	1.4	75.2	38.1	51.5	48.5
31787 SMITHVILLE	50.5	45.5	48.5	53.3	0.2	0.2	1.0	1.1	10.2	9.1	7.1	7.5	7.9	25.9	23.4	7.9	1.2	69.3	31.2	47.9	52.1
31788 MOULTRIE	71.6	66.7	14.4	16.7	0.3	0.4	17.3	20.6	8.7	8.0	7.4	6.9	8.4	30.3	20.3	8.7	1.3	72.1	31.5	51.4	48.6
31789 SUMNER	78.5	75.3	19.1	21.9	0.1	0.1	2.0	2.5	7.3	7.1	7.6	7.3	7.4	26.6	25.1	10.3	1.3	73.6	35.8	49.5	50.5
31790 SYCAMORE	80.9	76.5	16.2	20.0	0.1	0.2	2.6	3.3	7.8	7.5	8.3	6.7	6.8	28.1	23.4	10.3	1.3	72.4	34.5	52.4	47.6
31791 SYLVESTER	63.0	60.5	35.6	37.9	0.3	0.3	0.8	1.0	7.4	7.3	7.9	7.7	6.7	26.1	24.6	10.8	1.6	72.5	35.9	47.2	52.8
31792 THOMASVILLE	50.3	47.6	47.7	50.2	0.5	0.6	1.4	1.7	6.8	6.7	7.1	7.3	6.8	25.9	24.2	12.7	2.4	74.7	37.6	46.5	53.5
31793 TIFTON	76.1	71.6	14.6	17.1	1.0	1.2	11.3	14.2	7.3	7.0	6.8	7.9	8.4	30.2	23.3	8.5	0.8	75.4	33.2	51.3	48.7
31794 TIFTON	61.1	58.8	34.0	35.4	1.1	1.3	5.4	6.7	8.0	7.5	7.3	7.5	8.0	27.2	22.3	10.7	1.7	73.2	33.4	47.8	52.2
31795 TY TY	80.1	76.1	16.4	19.5	0.2	0.3	3.0	3.8	7.3	7.3	7.6	6.6	6.5	28.8	24.9	9.8	1.3	73.8	35.3	49.8	50.2
31796 WARWICK	68.1	64.5	29.5	32.7	0.2	0.2	1.1	1.3	6.3	6.7	7.8	6.6	5.7	21.6	29.9	14.1	1.3	75.2	41.1	48.4	51.6
31798 WRAY	77.6	73.7	18.3	21.1	0.4	0.5	4.2	5.2	6.4	6.2	6.4	6.6	6.3	25.5	27.3	13.7	1.7	77.2	40.1	49.6	50.4
31801 BOX SPRINGS	69.0	64.9	28.7	32.5	0.2	0.2	1.2	1.7	5.8	6.3	7.4	6.7	5.5	25.9	29.0	11.9	1.4	76.0	40.2	49.0	51.0
31803 BUENA VISTA	48.1	44.5	46.2	48.7	0.4	0.5	7.6	9.2	6.6	7.0	8.5	7.0	7.0	28.1	24.5	9.9	1.4	73.5	35.3	49.8	50.2
31804 CATAULA	84.8	82.9	13.3	14.9	0.5	0.6	0.9	1.1	6.3	7.0	7.6	6.1	5.1	28.2	29.8	9.1	0.9	75.3	39.4	49.3	50.7
31805 CUSSETA	63.4	60.8	33.2	35.2	1.2	1.4	1.5	1.8	7.8	7.3	8.3	7.7	7.3	30.0	22.1	9.0	0.5	71.8	33.5	48.7	51.3
31806 ELLAVILLE	65.6	62.7	31.4	33.8	0.2	0.3	2.4	2.9	8.5	8.2	7.6	7.2	6.3	27.2	23.8	9.9	1.2	71.0	35.1	48.0	52.0
31807 ELLERSLIE	83.2	81.0	14.5	16.3	0.8	0.8	1.9	2.4	6.0	7.0	8.1	6.0	4.8	27.7	29.2	10.2	0.9	75.1	39.8	49.9	50.1
31808 FORTSON	90.2	88.8	7.2	8.2	0.8	1.0	1.2	1.5	5.6	6.6	8.1	6.6	4.8	30.2	28.9	8.6	0.6	75.6	39.3	50.0	50.0
31811 HAMILTON	74.2	71.9	23.9	25.9	0.5	0.6	0.7	0.9	5.8	6.2	6.8	6.2	5.4	26.0	30.3	12.1	1.3	77.2	41.2	50.1	49.9
31812 JUNCTION CITY	35.2	32.5	63.5	66.2	0.3	0.3	1.3	1.3	6.3	6.8	6.8	4.6	4.1	24.9	28.8	15.5	2.3	77.3	42.9	49.6	50.4
31815 LUMPKIN	34.2	33.0	65.2	66.4	0.0	0.0	0.6	0.6	6.5	6.8	8.1	6.9	5.7	26.3	24.0	13.7	2.2	74.8	37.7	48.2	51.8
31816 MANCHESTER	62.6	62.1	35.5	35.7	0.8	0.9	0.8	1.0	7.0	7.0	8.0	7.1	6.2	25.3	24.6	12.7	2.2	73.8	37.5	47.2	52.9
31820 MIDLAND	78.9	75.5	15.8	18.5	2.8	3.1	3.0	3.7	5.6	6.3	7.8	7.2	6.5	30.2	28.4	7.6	0.6	75.4	37.7	50.4	49.6
31821 OMAHA	38.4	36.9	60.6	62.1	0.0	0.0	0.8	0.8	5.3	5.7	6.9	6.7	6.5	25.3	27.9	13.5	2.3	78.2	40.8	49.6	50.4
31822 PINE MOUNTAIN	72.7	69.8	25.8	28.6	0.1	0.1	1.1	1.4	6.7	7.1	7.6	6.2	5.4	25.6	28.2	11.5	1.7	74.7	39.1	48.5	51.6
31823 PINE MOUNTAIN VALLEY	87.2	85.4	10.6	12.0	0.0	0.0	1.2	1.6	5.7	6.0	6.5	6.8	5.9	28.5	26.6	12.5	1.6	77.6	40.2	53.8	46.3
31824 PRESTON	51.1	49.7	46.4	47.8	0.0	0.0	2.6	2.5	7.0	7.1	7.0	6.1	6.1	26.5	25.6	12.8	1.9	75.4	38.4	50.7	49.3
31825 RICHLAND	39.1	37.8	58.8	60.1	0.4	0.4	2.5	2.6	6.4	6.8	6.6	5.6	6.0	23.3	24.9	16.2	4.2	76.7	41.5	47.7	52.3
31826 SHILOH	66.2	63.5	31.4	33.7	0.2	0.2	1.2	1.5	6.1	6.5	8.1	7.7	6.6	26.4	26.9	10.6	1.1	74.5	37.8	47.7	52.3
31827 TALBOTTON	26.7	24.5	71.0	72.8	0.7	0.8	1.7	1.9	6.0	6.4	7.2	6.6	5.6	25.7	28.3	12.3	2.0	76.7	40.5	46.4	53.6
31829 UPATOI	83.3	79.4	14.2	17.7	1.2	1.3	0.9	1.2	4.6	7.2	9.2	8.1	3.5	24.7	33.4	8.9	0.5	73.4	41.4	50.7	49.3
31830 WARM SPRINGS	67.1	63.4	30.8	34.3	0.4	0.5	0.6	0.7	5.2	5.4	6.2	7.1	7.1	26.3	26.4	14.2	2.2	79.6	40.0	48.8	51.2
31831 WAVERLY HALL	71.1	68.1	26.8	29.6	0.6	0.7	1.1	1.4	5.0	5.6	7.5	5.7	5.7	25.1	29.3	14.3	1.9	78.0	42.1	49.1	50.9
31832 WESTON	48.1	46.5	49.8	51.3	0.0	0.0	3.4	3.5	6.5	6.7	6.9	5.8	5.8	26.5	27.9	11.5	2.5	76.3	39.5	52.1	47.9
31833 WEST POINT	56.6	53.4	42.2	45.2	0.6	0.6	0.7	0.8	6.6	7.0	8.3	6.8	5.7	24.8	26.2	12.8	1.8	73.6	38.6	47.2	52.8
31836 WOODLAND	41.1	38.4	57.7	60.4	0.0	0.0	1.2	1.4	5.9	6.3	7.1	6.2	5.7	25.0	29.4	12.8	1.7	77.0	40.5	46.7	53.3
31901 COLUMBUS	41.6	37.6	55.8	59.6	0.3	0.3	2.1	2.5	7.0	6.4	6.0	5.9	7.6	31.4	22.0	11.1	2.7	77.5	35.5	49.0	51.0
31903 COLUMBUS	21.5	18.7	70.4	72.3	1.6	1.7	7.6	8.8	8.7	8.7	9.0	7.8	7.9	27.4	20.0	9.7	0.9	68.8	30.5	46.9	53.1
31904 COLUMBUS	75.3	72.0	20.3	22.7	1.6	1.8	3.1	3.9	7.4	6.8	6.8	6.2	6.5	27.0	23.9	12.9	2.5	75.3	37.8	46.8	53.2
31905 FORT BENNING	57.2	52.6	27.8	30.1	2.5	2.7	13.7	16.5	10.6	8.0	5.6	14.2	27.9	32.0	1.6	0.2	0.0	73.3	22.1	68.6	31.4
31906 COLUMBUS	30.9	28.2	66.3	68.7	0.6	0.7	2.4	2.8	7.0	6.9	7.4	7.0	7.0	27.2	22.8	12.6	2.1	74.4	35.4	45.2	54.8
31907 COLUMBUS	38.0	34.2	56.7	59.9	1.6	1.7	3.8	4.5	6.4	6.3	7.6	7.9	8.6	28.7	23.2	10.1	1.3	75.0	34.4	47.8	52.2
31909 COLUMBUS	82.6	79.0	11.4	13.9	2.8	3.3	3.4	4.5	6.9	6.9	7.1	6.3	6.4	31.3	23.9	10.2	1.2	75.2	36.0	48.0	52.0
39813 ARLINGTON	34.8	33.1	64.2	65.8	0.3	0.3	1.0	1.1	8.3	8.7	8.1	7.7	6.1	26.2	21.1	12.3	1.6	70.2	35.0	47.3	52.7
39815 ATTAPULGUS	25.8	22.8	68.6	70.6	0.0	0.0	5.8	6.9	7.9	7.8	8.0	8.1	7.3	26.8	22.9	9.8	1.5	71.6	33.5	49.0	51.0
39817 BAINBRIDGE	55.7	52.7	42.7	45.4	0.1	0.1	1.8	2.2	8.3	8.1	7.9	7.4	7.0	28.6	22.1	9.4	1.2	71.2	33.2	48.9	51.1
39819 BAINBRIDGE	61.2	58.0	34.7	37.1	0.8	0.9	4.4	5.5	7.3	7.2	7.3	6.5	6.5	26.2	23.0	13.5	2.5	74.1	37.3	46.8	53.2
39823 BLAKELY	47.6	44.7	50.7	53.3	0.3	0.3	1.3	1.5	7.5	7.7	8.1	7.7	6.4	24.2	22.8	12.8	2.8	71.7	36.0	46.7	53.3
GEORGIA	65.1	63.4	28.7	29.4	2.2	2.5	5.3	6.6	7.3	7.1	7.2	7.0	7.6	31.0	23.0	8.6	1.1	74.3	34.2	49.3	50.7
UNITED STATES	75.1	73.6	12.3	12.5	3.8	4.2	12.5	14.1	6.9	6.7	7.2	7.0	7.3	28.6	23.8	10.8	1.7	75.1	36.0	49.1	50.9

#	POST OFFICE NAME	2004 Per Capita Income	2004 HH Income Base	2004 Household Income Distribution (%): Less than $25,000	$25,000 to $49,999	$50,000 to $99,999	$100,000 to $149,999	$150,000 or More	Median Household Income: 2004	2009	2004 National Centile	2004 State Centile	2004 Home Value Base	2004 Home Value Distribution (%): Less than $50,000	$50,000 to $89,999	$90,000 to $174,999	$175,000 to $399,999	$400,000 or More	2004 Median Home Value
31639	NASHVILLE	21292	3804	37.5	32.9	22.8	3.2	3.6	34123	38564	24	30	2890	36.2	25.5	30.0	7.9	0.5	69100
31641	NAYLOR	17748	309	36.9	27.2	27.5	6.5	1.9	35523	41846	30	36	264	26.1	50.4	15.5	6.1	1.9	70000
31642	PEARSON	15393	1611	41.8	28.6	23.4	3.4	2.9	31874	35977	17	20	1226	56.5	24.9	13.2	4.7	0.7	41919
31643	QUITMAN	15837	3587	45.9	28.7	19.0	4.1	2.3	27267	31048	8	6	2605	34.6	30.3	26.6	7.8	0.7	67520
31645	RAY CITY	17170	1492	31.7	40.6	22.7	3.9	1.1	36107	41571	32	39	1153	29.2	32.5	29.1	6.2	3.0	74610
31647	SPARKS	17230	1009	36.1	35.1	22.2	4.8	1.9	33534	38302	23	27	800	35.6	36.5	23.6	4.1	0.1	65500
31648	STATENVILLE	26333	475	38.7	35.8	16.0	4.6	4.8	29533	35125	11	12	381	42.8	30.7	21.8	4.7	0.0	58333
31649	STOCKTON	13614	594	40.1	34.3	22.2	3.4	0.0	30067	32670	12	13	499	49.1	26.5	22.2	1.2	1.0	51071
31650	WILLACOOCHEE	16083	1209	40.0	32.1	20.6	5.0	2.4	32257	37599	18	22	952	53.5	22.0	17.5	6.4	0.6	46796
31699	MOODY A F B	9408	19	36.8	26.3	36.8	0.0	0.0	33576	45000	23	28	15	20.0	6.7	73.3	0.0	0.0	110417
31701	ALBANY	14699	8208	52.1	25.0	17.4	3.6	2.0	23262	28848	3	2	3826	30.8	41.6	22.9	3.6	1.2	65077
31704	ALBANY	15269	222	7.2	48.2	35.6	9.0	0.0	44626	51208	60	65	25	44.0	56.0	0.0	0.0	0.0	65000
31705	ALBANY	15656	12651	41.9	28.6	22.5	5.4	1.6	31231	37249	16	18	7384	35.4	43.4	18.8	2.0	0.4	61926
31707	ALBANY	25156	9786	30.8	29.2	25.9	9.0	5.1	41042	49672	50	55	5993	9.9	44.1	38.8	6.9	0.3	86842
31709	AMERICUS	20049	6223	35.7	32.1	22.2	6.1	3.9	34869	40970	27	34	3622	22.8	34.1	34.2	8.4	0.6	80775
31711	ANDERSONVILLE	29180	397	29.5	24.7	30.7	6.6	8.6	44773	53009	61	65	331	30.2	34.7	22.1	7.3	5.7	76724
31712	ARABI	17527	425	39.1	29.4	26.1	3.8	1.7	32330	38046	19	22	350	39.1	30.9	19.7	9.1	1.1	57600
31714	ASHBURN	15560	2624	49.1	25.8	18.5	5.2	1.5	25592	29441	5	4	1765	43.5	31.1	19.3	4.8	1.5	58021
31716	BACONTON	17303	1215	30.0	34.1	28.6	5.9	1.4	38307	45360	40	47	1009	30.1	35.1	29.4	4.4	1.0	70616
31719	AMERICUS	15369	3773	39.1	30.6	23.7	4.3	2.4	32143	36545	18	21	2588	27.7	37.2	25.5	9.4	0.2	72188
31721	ALBANY	35903	7693	16.6	23.1	33.7	14.8	11.8	61988	77744	86	87	5578	8.8	19.3	44.7	23.0	4.2	121258
31730	CAMILLA	15686	3750	45.3	24.4	21.4	5.3	3.7	28452	33178	9	9	2595	33.2	31.3	27.0	7.4	1.2	67128
31733	CHULA	26389	596	23.8	26.0	33.1	10.6	6.5	50147	60489	72	75	509	19.3	31.6	24.2	22.4	2.6	88594
31735	COBB	21560	389	22.4	36.3	31.4	9.0	1.0	45965	53198	64	68	324	25.0	21.6	36.4	15.4	1.5	102000
31738	COOLIDGE	16712	734	40.7	30.0	23.3	4.8	1.2	30816	35596	14	16	599	38.6	23.9	27.7	9.4	0.5	66455
31743	DE SOTO	16690	190	32.1	31.1	25.8	9.0	2.1	36541	43217	34	41	154	30.5	33.1	24.7	10.4	1.3	72143
31744	DOERUN	18841	983	35.9	29.6	26.0	6.2	2.2	35042	41500	28	35	804	27.2	36.0	27.5	7.8	1.5	75303
31749	ENIGMA	19574	1304	34.8	33.2	22.7	5.8	3.5	35429	40791	29	36	1061	43.5	26.2	23.8	5.4	1.1	60172
31750	FITZGERALD	16808	6842	42.1	26.5	23.1	7.1	1.3	30739	36114	14	16	4791	35.6	35.0	23.2	6.0	0.3	65318
31756	HARTSFIELD	23858	255	21.6	31.4	38.0	4.7	4.3	47874	54164	68	72	216	37.0	16.7	35.2	7.4	3.7	81111
31757	THOMASVILLE	23214	3797	30.1	29.1	28.9	8.9	3.0	41947	50037	53	58	2998	27.4	22.1	36.5	12.4	1.7	90865
31760	IRWINVILLE	21621	407	31.7	34.6	24.8	4.7	4.2	38281	45193	40	47	343	30.6	35.0	26.2	6.4	1.8	69516
31763	LEESBURG	23980	7929	17.4	27.9	36.4	13.2	5.2	54767	64258	79	81	6462	16.0	20.6	49.9	12.8	0.8	106396
31764	LESLIE	17716	528	37.9	25.8	24.4	8.7	3.2	33728	38539	23	28	429	32.2	36.6	21.0	9.1	1.2	69896
31765	MEIGS	15782	957	46.5	27.9	18.4	4.9	2.3	27926	32893	9	8	744	43.3	27.3	19.2	8.7	1.5	57692
31768	MOULTRIE	17162	9183	42.3	29.8	20.9	4.4	2.6	30073	34725	12	13	6100	32.8	32.0	26.5	7.1	1.6	69910
31771	NORMAN PARK	16322	1984	34.8	33.2	26.0	4.3	1.8	34838	40568	27	34	1592	43.8	25.7	23.6	6.2	0.7	60727
31772	OAKFIELD	19018	224	36.2	33.9	17.4	7.6	4.9	34178	39528	25	30	192	38.0	32.8	26.6	2.6	0.0	66923
31773	OCHLOCKNEE	19293	1453	29.5	27.2	35.6	6.6	1.2	42262	49061	54	59	1209	24.6	27.6	34.5	11.3	2.0	86807
31774	OCILLA	16199	2549	38.7	30.5	23.6	4.9	2.4	32540	37928	19	23	1925	36.4	37.6	18.3	7.7	0.0	60955
31775	OMEGA	14032	835	38.0	31.7	24.8	4.4	1.1	33092	38295	21	26	650	40.8	31.1	22.6	4.0	1.5	59524
31778	PAVO	16965	1483	42.1	31.9	19.8	4.3	2.0	31033	36236	15	17	1238	35.3	30.7	22.9	10.0	1.1	67737
31779	PELHAM	15878	3199	44.8	31.2	18.1	3.7	2.2	28447	32591	9	9	2266	31.5	34.7	23.1	9.0	1.6	69916
31780	PLAINS	16668	888	35.4	32.1	26.7	5.0	0.9	35000	40258	28	34	716	39.1	30.0	23.5	6.8	0.6	60135
31781	POULAN	18811	651	35.9	30.4	26.9	4.6	2.2	36396	42234	33	41	517	34.2	33.5	23.4	7.5	1.4	69674
31783	REBECCA	17650	502	31.9	36.7	25.1	4.0	2.4	36122	43062	32	39	423	36.6	32.9	23.6	5.7	1.2	64032
31784	SALE CITY	21043	258	34.5	26.4	27.1	9.3	2.7	38180	46153	40	46	210	38.6	18.6	30.0	7.6	5.2	77500
31787	SMITHVILLE	16555	754	27.6	33.7	32.5	5.0	1.2	43613	49933	58	62	625	33.0	31.4	28.6	5.3	1.8	66948
31788	MOULTRIE	16232	3702	37.4	28.4	26.0	6.6	1.7	34601	40661	26	33	2686	32.8	29.6	26.4	10.2	1.0	69011
31789	SUMNER	18499	677	35.0	31.8	26.9	4.0	2.4	36371	42239	33	40	545	34.9	31.7	24.8	7.5	1.1	70357
31790	SYCAMORE	19693	667	31.2	30.1	26.1	7.8	4.8	38458	46327	41	47	557	30.0	33.2	25.9	10.6	0.4	69769
31791	SYLVESTER	19760	4877	34.9	27.5	28.1	5.9	3.7	37044	43362	36	42	3639	24.2	37.1	31.3	6.7	0.7	74329
31792	THOMASVILLE	20183	9073	35.4	30.1	23.9	6.7	3.8	36079	42429	32	39	6069	21.4	30.6	29.9	15.2	3.0	87334
31793	TIFTON	23343	2416	25.7	28.3	31.4	9.1	5.6	45972	54929	64	68	1846	27.1	24.4	31.2	14.9	2.4	87565
31794	TIFTON	20127	10444	35.8	29.1	23.8	7.5	3.8	36232	43039	32	40	6703	29.7	25.9	31.9	11.0	1.6	82910
31795	TY TY	23411	759	30.4	31.1	26.2	5.3	7.0	38696	46393	42	48	633	33.2	27.7	19.4	16.1	3.6	73214
31796	WARWICK	19418	547	31.4	32.0	28.7	6.6	1.3	39394	46042	44	50	450	26.9	31.8	34.9	6.4	0.0	82041
31798	WRAY	20760	411	34.1	31.1	22.9	9.3	2.7	34509	40580	26	32	349	49.9	25.8	12.6	9.2	2.6	50294
31801	BOX SPRINGS	17676	1101	32.0	34.2	26.7	6.3	0.9	37553	43301	38	44	922	36.2	28.3	24.5	9.5	1.4	68333
31803	BUENA VISTA	15813	1908	43.1	27.9	22.2	4.9	1.9	29828	34022	12	13	1420	36.0	28.9	24.9	8.0	2.3	70808
31804	CATAULA	28066	1911	13.9	23.4	35.4	20.4	6.9	65552	80775	89	90	1730	10.5	13.4	38.4	33.2	4.6	152637
31805	CUSSETA	16854	1052	39.0	32.6	23.4	3.7	1.3	32645	36384	20	24	859	34.3	39.1	20.4	3.8	2.3	65413
31806	ELLAVILLE	17870	1519	37.1	30.5	25.2	4.6	2.6	35943	40881	31	38	1216	38.7	32.4	20.6	6.6	1.6	62432
31807	ELLERSLIE	29575	599	12.4	26.0	39.4	16.7	5.5	60223	74881	85	85	538	8.4	11.0	48.5	29.0	3.2	140476
31808	FORTSON	30974	2167	12.8	14.4	44.3	21.0	7.6	73069	86921	92	93	2038	6.5	11.9	40.9	37.6	3.1	158651
31811	HAMILTON	28203	1158	25.5	23.1	30.1	13.0	8.2	51148	61929	74	77	978	11.4	22.2	34.5	22.3	9.7	124427
31812	JUNCTION CITY	14204	247	46.6	32.0	16.6	3.6	1.2	27462	33195	8	6	205	56.6	19.0	18.1	6.3	0.0	42059
31815	LUMPKIN	19866	815	46.5	29.2	19.3	1.6	3.4	27212	31405	7	6	603	56.7	27.2	11.1	4.3	0.7	43468
31816	MANCHESTER	18062	2536	37.6	30.6	23.5	6.5	1.7	32657	38024	20	24	1729	30.3	34.4	26.8	8.1	0.4	75516
31820	MIDLAND	33197	2041	13.1	22.9	32.8	22.1	9.1	68193	85156	90	92	1546	2.9	7.6	34.2	49.9	5.5	186351
31821	OMAHA	13902	339	44.0	37.8	14.2	4.1	0.0	27882	30332	8	7	273	47.3	21.3	18.0	5.5	8.1	62885
31822	PINE MOUNTAIN	23164	1828	24.8	28.3	28.4	13.4	5.0	47246	55571	67	71	1399	14.7	22.5	28.9	26.4	7.5	115494
31823	PINE MOUNTAIN VALLEY	22114	452	25.0	32.3	27.2	10.4	5.1	46258	54373	64	69	379	15.3	42.5	30.1	11.4	0.8	84914
31824	PRESTON	16995	751	40.5	30.4	23.2	2.9	3.1	31260	36441	16	18	608	47.5	31.4	16.1	3.3	1.6	53750
31825	RICHLAND	26994	867	45.0	28.1	17.9	3.6	5.4	28335	32954	9	9	660	51.2	27.6	18.5	2.6	0.2	48806
31826	SHILOH	17924	741	32.1	27.4	31.4	7.6	1.5	43662	50664	58	62	608	23.5	35.4	33.2	6.3	1.6	78592
31827	TALBOTTON	19148	935	43.5	25.6	23.0	3.7	4.2	32074	40048	18	21	748	44.9	23.1	24.6	6.0	1.3	59048
31829	UPATOI	38204	283	5.7	21.9	36.4	25.8	10.3	80887	101181	95	96	269	3.7	5.6	29.0	55.4	6.3	207456
31830	WARM SPRINGS	20166	1105	34.7	27.7	27.3	7.8	2.5	39963	46811	46	51	872	26.2	24.9	33.9	12.0	3.0	88767
31831	WAVERLY HALL	19551	1009	32.0	28.7	29.3	7.8	2.1	42532	49874	55	60	833	22.1	29.8	32.4	13.5	2.3	85156
31832	WESTON	19725	189	38.1	33.9	18.5	3.7	5.8	31838	37760	17	20	153	51.6	24.2	18.3	4.6	1.3	47222
31833	WEST POINT	20472	2616	32.4	31.0	24.6	7.6	4.3	39217	46562	43	49	1936	22.1	27.9	37.9	9.6	2.6	90000
31836	WOODLAND	17191	730	46.2	23.0	22.3	6.3	2.2	28005	33719	9	8	600	39.3	29.8	23.7	7.2	0.0	58421
31901	COLUMBUS	16654	3606	58.9	23.7	11.1	4.2	2.1	18404	21766	1	2	1020	24.3	27.2	34.4	11.9	2.3	87581
31903	COLUMBUS	13520	8436	48.8	30.7	16.5	2.3	1.7	25718	29662	5	4	3737	27.7	57.0	14.7	0.4	0.2	64760
31904	COLUMBUS	27515	12558	33.1	26.4	24.2	8.6	7.8	38874	46435	42	48	8085	10.9	29.5	38.6	15.2	5.8	102221
31905	FORT BENNING	13376	4026	21.3	46.8	27.3	3.7	0.9	36947	41742	35	42	115	34.8	31.3	23.5	4.4	6.1	66429
31906	COLUMBUS	24224	10402	38.1	31.2	18.7	6.0	6.0	32494	38053	19	23	5544	17.2	32.0	32.9	14.5	3.4	91163
31907	COLUMBUS	21867	21174	23.4	33.7	31.2	8.9	2.8	44027	51671	59	63	14705	7.5	43.7	42.2	6.4	0.3	89140
31909	COLUMBUS	26224	12123	15.3	26.9	40.9	13.4	3.5	56950	67392	82	83	9270	2.7	24.2	60.2	12.6	0.3	112772
39813	ARLINGTON	15414	687	44.4	29.8	19.1	5.4	1.3	29074	33267	10	11	532	52.8	26.9	16.4	4.0	0.0	47170
39815	ATTAPULGUS	17115	762	41.2	29.1	21.8	4.3	3.5	30678	35645	14	15	614	53.3	26.6	10.6	8.1	1.5	48077
39817	BAINBRIDGE	15071	4335	43.9	28.8	21.7	3.8	1.7	29219	33492	11	12	3133	30.2	34.4	27.7	6.5	1.1	72733
39819	BAINBRIDGE	20968	4336	36.5	28.3	23.9	7.4	3.8	36673	43151	34	41	3173	20.1	31.5	32.2	14.0	2.2	88138
39823	BLAKELY	16193	3348	46.0	26.6	18.6	6.8	2.1	28136	33259	9	8	2455	39.4	32.6	20.7	6.9	0.4	60365
	GEORGIA	26143		23.6	26.3	31.4	11.6	7.0	50024	60470				12.5	17.5	39.3	24.8	6.0	125860
	UNITED STATES	25866		24.7	27.1	30.8	10.9	6.5	48124	56710				10.9	15.0	33.7	30.1	10.4	145905

ZIP CODE		FINANCIAL SERVICES				THE HOME						ENTERTAINMENT						PERSONAL			
						Home Improvements		Furnishings													
#	POST OFFICE NAME	Auto Loan	Home Loan	Invest-ments	Retire-ment Plans	Home Repair	Lawn & Garden	Comput-ers & Hard-ware	Major Appli-ances	TV, Radio, Sound Equip-ment	Furni-ture	Dine out/ Carry out	Sports Equip-ment	Fees & Tickets	Toys & Games	Travel	Cable TV	Apparel & Services	Auto Repairs	Health Insur-ance	Pets & Supplies
31639	NASHVILLE	93	70	42	63	75	85	68	80	77	69	92	93	61	87	69	81	85	79	92	105
31641	NAYLOR	78	71	56	69	71	75	68	73	69	70	85	84	64	80	67	68	82	73	72	87
31642	PEARSON	82	55	25	47	62	71	53	66	64	54	75	79	45	71	54	69	68	65	81	94
31643	QUITMAN	69	53	37	48	56	64	53	60	61	54	73	70	48	68	53	63	68	61	70	78
31645	RAY CITY	77	66	49	63	68	72	64	70	66	65	81	81	59	76	63	66	77	69	72	85
31647	SPARKS	81	62	38	57	66	74	60	69	67	61	80	82	54	76	60	69	74	69	79	91
31648	STATENVILLE	119	109	85	105	109	115	104	111	105	107	130	128	98	122	102	103	124	111	110	132
31649	STOCKTON	65	50	31	46	54	59	48	56	54	49	64	66	43	61	48	56	60	56	63	74
31650	WILLACOOCHEE	77	57	33	52	62	69	55	65	62	56	74	77	49	70	55	65	69	65	75	87
31699	MOODY A F B	0	0	0	0	0	0	0	0	0	0	0	0	0	0	0	0	0	0	0	0
31701	ALBANY	53	47	53	44	46	53	51	51	56	52	69	57	51	65	50	58	66	53	56	59
31704	ALBANY	86	54	52	62	50	59	81	70	82	76	103	93	69	92	67	75	99	83	65	80
31705	ALBANY	64	57	57	54	56	63	59	61	63	60	78	70	58	75	59	65	75	62	64	72
31707	ALBANY	78	78	91	77	77	86	81	80	82	81	103	90	82	101	81	84	101	81	81	89
31709	AMERICUS	72	65	70	66	65	71	72	70	73	71	91	83	69	88	69	72	87	73	70	80
31711	ANDERSONVILLE	127	111	83	106	113	121	106	116	110	109	135	135	99	127	105	110	129	116	119	141
31712	ARABI	82	57	30	51	64	72	55	68	65	56	77	80	48	73	56	69	70	67	80	93
31714	ASHBURN	66	52	43	47	54	63	54	59	61	55	74	68	51	70	54	64	69	60	68	74
31716	BACONTON	84	65	40	59	69	76	62	72	69	64	83	85	56	78	62	71	77	72	81	95
31719	AMERICUS	68	56	48	51	57	65	56	61	63	57	76	70	54	73	56	65	72	61	68	76
31721	ALBANY	130	131	137	134	129	136	129	128	126	131	159	150	131	156	127	123	156	129	122	147
31730	CAMILLA	62	49	42	44	50	58	51	55	57	52	69	63	47	65	50	60	65	56	62	69
31733	CHULA	109	97	74	93	100	107	91	100	95	92	116	117	88	115	92	96	111	98	104	124
31735	COBB	86	67	46	61	76	85	63	76	72	63	85	89	57	84	68	77	79	75	90	104
31738	COOLIDGE	77	53	25	46	59	68	51	63	61	52	71	75	43	68	52	65	65	62	77	89
31743	DE SOTO	84	63	38	56	70	79	60	72	69	61	82	85	53	79	62	73	76	72	85	99
31744	DOERUN	85	62	35	56	68	77	60	72	69	61	82	85	53	78	61	73	76	71	84	97
31749	ENIGMA	84	76	59	73	76	81	73	78	73	74	91	90	69	86	72	73	87	77	77	93
31750	FITZGERALD	68	54	44	50	57	65	56	61	63	56	76	71	52	73	56	66	71	62	70	77
31756	HARTSFIELD	100	85	61	80	91	99	79	89	86	79	104	107	76	105	81	89	98	87	99	118
31757	THOMASVILLE	100	88	67	84	91	97	84	92	87	86	106	107	79	102	84	87	102	91	95	113
31760	IRWINVILLE	98	72	40	64	79	88	69	83	79	71	94	98	61	89	70	83	87	82	96	112
31763	LEESBURG	102	106	98	106	104	105	100	102	96	102	120	119	99	118	98	92	117	101	93	115
31764	LESLIE	88	71	47	65	74	81	68	77	73	69	89	90	61	84	67	75	83	77	84	99
31765	MEIGS	77	53	25	46	59	68	51	63	61	52	72	75	44	68	52	65	65	63	77	89
31768	MOULTRIE	68	55	46	52	58	66	58	62	64	57	77	72	54	74	57	66	72	63	70	77
31771	NORMAN PARK	74	65	50	62	66	70	63	68	65	64	79	79	59	75	62	64	76	68	69	82
31772	OAKFIELD	81	73	56	70	73	78	70	75	71	72	87	87	66	83	69	70	84	75	75	90
31773	OCHLOCKNEE	83	68	47	64	71	77	65	73	70	67	85	86	60	80	65	71	80	73	79	93
31774	OCILLA	69	55	41	53	58	67	57	63	63	57	76	71	53	73	57	65	70	62	71	77
31775	OMEGA	75	54	30	49	60	67	52	63	60	54	72	74	46	68	53	63	66	62	73	85
31778	PAVO	81	55	25	47	62	71	53	66	64	54	75	79	45	71	54	68	68	65	81	93
31779	PELHAM	68	50	36	45	54	63	53	59	61	53	72	67	48	67	52	65	67	60	71	75
31780	PLAINS	84	56	26	49	64	73	54	68	65	55	77	81	46	73	55	70	70	67	83	96
31781	POULAN	92	64	31	56	71	81	61	75	73	62	86	90	53	81	62	78	78	75	91	106
31783	REBECCA	88	60	28	52	67	77	57	71	69	58	81	85	49	77	58	74	74	71	88	101
31784	SALE CITY	98	67	33	61	77	88	66	82	77	66	91	98	56	87	67	82	82	81	99	115
31787	SMITHVILLE	77	68	52	65	69	73	65	71	67	67	82	82	61	77	64	66	78	70	72	85
31788	MOULTRIE	75	64	47	60	66	71	62	68	65	63	79	79	58	76	61	66	75	68	71	84
31789	SUMNER	88	62	32	55	69	78	60	73	70	61	83	87	52	79	61	75	76	72	87	101
31790	SYCAMORE	97	75	46	69	82	91	71	84	80	71	95	100	65	94	73	83	88	82	97	113
31791	SYLVESTER	84	72	58	68	74	82	72	77	77	73	94	89	68	90	72	78	89	77	83	94
31792	THOMASVILLE	71	68	68	64	68	76	68	70	72	69	88	80	68	87	69	74	85	71	75	81
31793	TIFTON	95	89	75	87	90	94	85	90	86	87	106	105	82	102	85	85	102	90	90	107
31794	TIFTON	77	71	72	68	71	78	73	75	77	74	95	86	72	92	73	78	91	76	78	86
31795	TY TY	103	87	61	81	91	98	82	92	88	84	106	108	77	103	83	89	101	91	99	117
31796	WARWICK	87	62	34	55	68	77	60	72	69	61	82	86	52	78	61	73	76	72	85	99
31798	WRAY	100	67	30	58	76	88	65	81	78	66	92	97	55	87	66	84	84	80	100	115
31801	BOX SPRINGS	79	62	39	57	66	73	59	68	65	60	79	81	53	75	59	68	73	68	77	90
31803	BUENA VISTA	75	53	27	47	59	67	51	62	60	52	71	74	44	67	52	64	65	62	74	86
31804	CATAULA	111	118	109	115	120	123	107	112	105	107	130	132	110	136	110	105	127	108	110	133
31805	CUSSETA	70	64	50	61	64	67	61	65	62	63	76	75	58	72	60	61	73	65	65	77
31806	ELLAVILLE	84	61	33	54	66	75	58	70	67	60	80	83	51	75	59	71	74	69	82	95
31807	ELLERSLIE	109	131	135	130	129	129	117	118	110	117	138	139	123	146	120	107	137	114	109	133
31808	FORTSON	123	133	126	136	130	129	121	123	114	124	143	144	123	145	120	109	141	119	111	139
31811	HAMILTON	113	97	73	93	103	114	93	104	100	93	121	121	89	121	96	103	114	102	115	132
31812	JUNCTION CITY	66	44	20	38	50	57	42	53	51	43	60	63	36	57	43	55	55	53	65	75
31815	LUMPKIN	75	58	49	53	60	73	64	69	73	64	87	76	59	80	63	78	81	70	82	82
31816	MANCHESTER	72	57	44	55	61	70	60	65	66	59	79	74	56	76	59	69	74	65	74	80
31820	MIDLAND	128	140	153	145	137	138	136	133	128	137	162	158	139	165	134	123	161	133	119	147
31821	OMAHA	64	43	19	37	49	56	41	52	50	42	59	62	35	56	42	54	53	51	64	74
31822	PINE MOUNTAIN	100	84	62	79	90	100	80	91	87	80	105	106	76	105	83	91	99	89	102	117
31823	PINE MOUNTAIN VALLEY	95	85	65	81	90	96	78	87	83	78	101	104	77	103	81	85	96	85	94	112
31824	PRESTON	83	55	25	48	63	72	53	67	65	54	76	80	45	72	54	69	69	66	82	95
31825	RICHLAND	129	86	39	75	98	113	83	104	101	85	118	125	71	112	85	108	107	103	129	148
31826	SHILOH	81	68	48	64	73	79	64	72	69	64	83	86	61	84	65	72	79	70	80	95
31827	TALBOTTON	92	61	28	53	70	80	59	74	72	60	84	89	50	79	60	77	76	73	91	105
31829	UPATOI	145	181	192	181	178	175	161	161	149	161	188	188	172	200	165	145	188	155	144	178
31830	WARM SPRINGS	91	63	34	57	71	83	65	77	76	64	89	89	56	84	65	81	81	76	93	103
31831	WAVERLY HALL	90	65	35	59	73	82	62	76	72	63	85	91	54	83	64	77	78	75	91	105
31832	WESTON	94	63	29	54	72	82	61	76	74	62	86	91	52	82	62	79	79	75	94	108
31833	WEST POINT	81	69	59	64	72	82	69	75	77	70	93	85	67	90	70	80	88	75	85	92
31836	WOODLAND	80	54	24	46	61	70	52	65	62	53	73	77	44	69	53	67	67	64	80	92
31901	COLUMBUS	46	40	49	38	39	46	46	45	50	46	61	51	45	58	45	51	59	47	48	51
31903	COLUMBUS	50	44	49	42	44	51	49	48	52	49	65	54	48	63	48	54	62	50	52	55
31904	COLUMBUS	90	92	105	91	92	100	95	93	95	94	119	107	96	119	94	95	116	94	93	103
31905	FORT BENNING	73	47	45	54	43	51	69	60	71	65	88	80	59	79	57	64	84	71	56	68
31906	COLUMBUS	78	72	84	70	71	81	78	77	82	79	102	87	78	98	77	84	99	79	80	87
31907	COLUMBUS	79	81	90	81	79	85	82	80	82	83	103	93	84	102	81	81	101	82	78	89
31909	COLUMBUS	89	101	106	102	98	100	96	94	91	96	114	110	98	117	95	88	113	93	86	104
39813	ARLINGTON	69	52	37	47	56	64	54	60	61	54	74	72	49	71	54	64	69	61	70	78
39815	ATTAPULGUS	98	66	30	57	74	86	63	79	76	65	90	95	54	85	64	82	82	78	97	112
39817	BAINBRIDGE	63	51	43	48	53	60	54	57	59	54	71	66	50	68	53	60	67	58	63	69
39819	BAINBRIDGE	81	71	64	68	74	82	73	77	78	72	94	90	70	92	73	79	90	78	84	93
39823	BLAKELY	72	52	34	46	57	66	52	61	61	53	73	71	47	68	53	66	67	61	74	82
	GEORGIA	103	97	95	97	97	104	97	99	98	98	122	116	96	120	96	98	118	100	99	116
	UNITED STATES	100	100	100	100	100	100	100	100	100	100	100	100	100	100	100	100	100	100	100	100

ZIP CODE		COUNTY FIPS CODE	POPULATION			2000-2004 ANNUAL RATE		HOUSEHOLDS					FAMILIES		
#	POST OFFICE NAME		2000	2004	2009	% Rate	State Centile	2000	2004	2009	% Annual Rate 2000-2004	2004 Average HH Size	2000	2004	% Annual Rate 2000-2004
39824	BLUFFTON	061	722	712	712	-0.3	7	275	279	285	0.3	2.55	200	200	0.0
39825	BRINSON	087	1483	1523	1599	0.6	29	570	596	635	1.1	2.55	439	452	0.7
39826	BRONWOOD	273	833	850	869	0.5	22	293	304	315	0.9	2.75	211	215	0.4
39827	CAIRO	131	3642	4032	4351	2.4	67	1334	1487	1617	2.6	2.70	1020	1117	2.2
39828	CAIRO	131	14613	14811	15323	0.3	19	5424	5536	5768	0.5	2.65	3959	3982	0.1
39834	CLIMAX	087	2107	2222	2358	1.3	43	788	844	907	1.6	2.63	610	644	1.3
39836	COLEMAN	243	345	339	339	-0.4	5	143	143	145	0.0	2.37	99	97	-0.5
39837	COLQUITT	201	6134	6127	6128	0.0	12	2360	2389	2422	0.3	2.51	1676	1671	-0.1
39840	CUTHBERT	243	5682	5714	5753	0.1	15	2124	2168	2216	0.5	2.50	1420	1423	0.1
39841	DAMASCUS	099	1256	1285	1320	0.5	25	486	504	525	0.9	2.55	341	349	0.6
39842	DAWSON	273	9756	9957	10221	0.5	22	3549	3665	3809	0.8	2.66	2584	2629	0.4
39845	DONALSONVILLE	253	8420	9294	10626	2.4	66	3237	3630	4222	2.7	2.48	2343	2588	2.4
39846	EDISON	037	1955	2029	2100	0.9	35	737	779	822	1.3	2.50	500	519	0.9
39851	FORT GAINES	061	2638	2676	2701	0.3	19	1073	1112	1144	0.8	2.36	729	742	0.4
39854	GEORGETOWN	239	1567	1640	1755	1.1	39	621	658	712	1.4	2.49	446	465	1.0
39859	IRON CITY	253	1258	1401	1618	2.6	69	483	547	641	3.0	2.56	359	401	2.6
39861	JAKIN	099	2060	2103	2156	0.5	23	847	877	912	0.8	2.40	589	600	0.4
39862	LEARY	037	987	993	1011	0.1	15	381	392	407	0.7	2.53	268	272	0.4
39866	MORGAN	037	2001	1994	2007	-0.1	11	322	326	338	0.3	2.33	226	225	-0.1
39867	MORRIS	239	1097	1188	1292	1.9	55	453	494	541	2.1	2.40	329	353	1.7
39870	NEWTON	007	3956	4063	4201	0.6	29	1473	1528	1596	0.9	2.65	1065	1089	0.5
39877	PARROTT	273	352	362	372	0.7	30	149	155	162	0.9	2.34	109	112	0.6
39886	SHELLMAN	243	1701	1696	1709	-0.1	11	616	623	636	0.3	2.72	435	433	-0.1
39897	WHIGHAM	131	3589	3795	3999	1.3	45	1321	1415	1509	1.6	2.60	1000	1058	1.3
	GEORGIA					2.4					2.5	2.64			2.2
	UNITED STATES					1.2					1.3	2.58			1.1

#	POST OFFICE NAME	White		Black		Asian/Pacific		% Hispanic Origin		0-4	5-9	10-14	15-19	20-24	25-44	45-64	65-84	85+	18+	MEDIAN AGE	% 2004 Males	% 2004 Females
		2000	2004	2000	2004	2000	2004	2000	2004											2004		
39824	BLUFFTON	50.3	49.0	48.5	49.9	1.1	1.1	0.1	0.1	4.1	4.6	7.4	8.2	6.7	20.4	31.6	14.5	2.5	78.8	43.6	48.7	51.3
39825	BRINSON	77.1	74.1	21.0	23.7	0.0	0.0	2.0	2.5	7.0	7.0	6.7	7.3	6.5	27.3	25.3	11.5	1.4	74.4	37.1	50.0	50.0
39826	BRONWOOD	47.3	43.4	51.9	55.7	0.2	0.2	1.6	1.9	7.3	7.7	8.2	7.3	6.6	23.8	25.7	11.7	1.9	71.9	37.1	48.8	51.2
39827	CAIRO	84.2	81.0	9.9	11.8	0.2	0.2	6.0	7.8	7.5	7.1	6.8	6.6	6.6	28.7	24.3	10.9	1.5	74.6	36.3	49.3	50.7
39828	CAIRO	54.9	51.5	39.6	41.9	0.4	0.5	6.0	7.2	7.4	7.5	7.5	6.9	7.1	27.2	23.6	11.1	1.7	73.3	34.9	47.3	52.7
39834	CLIMAX	61.9	58.9	35.6	38.2	0.2	0.2	2.3	2.8	7.3	7.3	7.9	7.4	6.4	26.0	24.9	11.5	1.3	73.0	36.6	48.0	52.0
39836	COLEMAN	27.8	26.6	70.4	71.7	0.0	0.0	1.5	1.5	6.8	7.4	8.0	8.0	7.4	25.4	25.1	10.3	1.8	72.9	36.8	50.7	49.3
39837	COLQUITT	69.6	68.3	29.5	30.8	0.1	0.1	0.8	0.8	6.2	6.4	7.4	7.0	5.9	25.2	24.8	14.3	2.7	75.5	39.5	47.6	52.4
39840	CUTHBERT	37.8	36.5	60.4	61.8	0.4	0.4	1.4	1.4	6.9	6.6	7.1	8.9	7.7	22.9	23.8	13.5	2.7	75.2	37.3	46.4	53.6
39841	DAMASCUS	39.6	36.3	59.2	62.3	0.2	0.2	1.4	1.6	6.7	7.4	7.6	7.7	6.9	26.5	23.9	11.7	1.7	73.6	37.1	47.7	52.3
39842	DAWSON	36.0	33.5	62.6	65.0	0.4	0.4	1.2	1.4	7.9	7.7	7.6	7.1	7.3	25.2	23.9	11.6	1.7	72.6	35.9	47.2	52.8
39845	DONALSONVILLE	61.7	58.7	34.4	36.6	0.2	0.2	3.9	4.8	7.2	7.0	7.1	6.5	6.3	25.0	24.9	14.2	1.9	74.8	38.4	48.4	51.6
39846	EDISON	39.2	37.9	59.6	60.9	0.0	0.0	1.6	1.6	7.5	7.5	7.3	7.1	7.2	23.6	23.8	12.7	3.3	73.1	37.2	45.1	55.0
39851	FORT GAINES	35.1	33.9	63.8	65.1	0.1	0.1	1.2	1.2	7.6	7.1	7.1	5.9	6.7	19.6	25.9	17.3	2.7	74.5	41.4	44.9	55.1
39854	GEORGETOWN	46.5	43.4	53.0	56.1	0.1	0.1	0.2	0.2	6.1	6.3	7.3	6.7	6.0	22.6	26.0	16.7	2.4	76.3	41.5	46.6	53.4
39859	IRON CITY	67.0	63.6	31.8	35.1	0.1	0.1	1.3	1.6	8.7	8.0	6.8	5.6	5.3	26.6	24.2	13.4	1.4	73.1	36.6	46.8	53.2
39861	JAKIN	70.6	67.5	28.1	31.0	0.0	0.0	0.8	1.0	6.0	6.1	6.8	6.1	5.4	25.0	27.2	15.6	1.9	77.5	41.5	48.0	52.0
39862	LEARY	38.5	37.2	59.4	60.7	0.0	0.0	2.0	2.0	7.4	7.3	6.9	6.8	6.3	25.5	27.2	11.6	1.2	74.6	37.7	46.8	53.2
39866	MORGAN	40.7	39.3	58.7	60.1	0.1	0.1	6.2	6.3	1.9	1.9	2.3	3.4	12.7	51.6	20.1	5.4	0.9	92.3	35.6	80.6	19.4
39867	MORRIS	58.3	55.5	39.9	42.6	0.0	0.0	1.0	1.0	6.7	6.6	6.7	5.0	5.1	22.2	28.9	17.4	1.5	77.0	43.4	48.2	51.8
39870	NEWTON	47.4	44.5	50.5	53.0	0.0	0.0	2.7	3.2	7.3	7.3	7.7	6.9	6.6	27.2	23.8	11.6	1.7	73.8	35.7	46.7	53.3
39877	PARROTT	67.3	63.8	31.0	34.3	0.6	0.6	2.0	2.2	6.9	6.6	5.5	6.1	5.0	25.7	27.9	14.9	1.4	77.6	41.0	48.3	51.7
39886	SHELLMAN	45.7	44.2	53.3	54.8	0.1	0.1	0.2	0.2	8.5	8.0	7.7	7.4	7.0	24.1	23.9	11.6	1.8	71.3	36.0	47.9	52.1
39897	WHIGHAM	74.4	70.5	21.4	24.9	0.2	0.2	2.1	2.6	6.6	6.6	6.7	6.6	6.0	26.0	26.5	12.8	2.2	76.1	39.4	48.1	51.9
	GEORGIA	65.1	63.4	28.7	29.4	2.2	2.5	5.3	6.6	7.3	7.1	7.2	7.0	7.6	31.0	23.0	8.6	1.1	74.3	34.2	49.3	50.7
	UNITED STATES	75.1	73.6	12.3	12.5	3.8	4.2	12.5	14.1	6.9	6.7	7.2	7.0	7.3	28.6	23.8	10.8	1.7	75.1	36.0	49.1	50.9

| ZIP CODE | | 2004 Per Capita Income | 2004 HH Income Base | 2004 HOUSEHOLD INCOME DISTRIBUTION (%) | | | | | MEDIAN HOUSEHOLD INCOME | | | | 2004 Home Value Base | 2004 HOME VALUE DISTRIBUTION (%) | | | | | 2004 Median Home Value |
#	POST OFFICE NAME			Less than $25,000	$25,000 to $49,999	$50,000 to $99,999	$100,000 to $149,999	$150,000 or More	2004	2009	2004 National Centile	2004 State Centile		Less than $50,000	$50,000 to $89,999	$90,000 to $174,999	$175,000 to $399,999	$400,000 or More	
39824	BLUFFTON	17244	279	38.7	28.7	25.1	3.6	3.9	35975	42012	31	38	225	48.4	23.1	21.8	5.3	1.3	51667
39825	BRINSON	17635	596	35.9	34.7	23.3	3.5	2.5	32399	37597	19	22	497	32.4	32.4	24.6	7.7	3.0	69478
39826	BRONWOOD	15710	304	53.6	30.3	10.9	3.3	2.0	22157	24876	3	2	236	37.3	38.6	16.1	8.1	0.0	61786
39827	CAIRO	20576	1487	32.7	27.4	29.5	7.9	2.6	40824	46921	49	54	1216	24.4	24.9	29.8	16.5	4.4	91067
39828	CAIRO	16050	5536	43.9	28.7	20.1	4.6	2.7	30322	35290	13	14	3948	29.7	30.4	28.0	9.4	2.5	73831
39834	CLIMAX	16985	844	37.9	28.0	27.0	5.2	1.9	34678	40517	26	33	711	30.1	33.8	24.3	8.7	3.1	68938
39836	COLEMAN	18296	143	42.0	28.0	23.8	4.2	2.1	30834	36874	14	16	114	50.9	31.6	12.3	5.3	0.0	48571
39837	COLQUITT	18318	2389	41.3	29.9	20.3	5.7	2.8	30284	34887	13	14	1904	39.8	29.9	22.5	7.3	0.6	62047
39840	CUTHBERT	14088	2168	51.9	23.7	19.4	3.6	1.5	23591	27471	4	3	1552	46.5	33.3	16.2	3.2	0.8	53986
39841	DAMASCUS	21743	504	40.1	25.2	21.2	8.3	5.2	36170	44056	32	39	399	37.3	34.3	21.3	7.0	0.0	62500
39842	DAWSON	16443	3665	41.9	28.7	21.9	4.3	3.1	31022	35387	15	17	2536	28.7	35.8	28.6	5.4	1.5	72205
39845	DONALSONVILLE	17975	3630	40.1	28.4	23.6	5.3	2.6	31161	37005	15	18	2931	31.9	36.4	24.7	6.0	0.9	68116
39846	EDISON	13270	779	52.0	28.1	15.8	3.1	1.0	23832	27053	4	3	572	42.8	35.5	18.4	3.3	0.0	59762
39851	FORT GAINES	22123	1112	53.1	25.9	14.1	2.0	5.0	22481	27414	3	2	850	48.5	29.1	14.5	6.9	1.1	53250
39854	GEORGETOWN	15444	658	45.9	32.2	16.6	3.7	1.7	27492	30723	8	6	521	46.6	35.5	14.4	3.5	0.0	53500
39859	IRON CITY	16589	547	42.4	29.1	19.9	6.4	2.2	30256	36592	13	14	447	47.2	30.9	16.8	5.2	0.0	53571
39861	JAKIN	24143	877	44.6	22.2	24.1	4.6	4.6	31405	37915	16	19	716	49.2	23.6	23.2	2.7	1.4	51200
39862	LEARY	18770	392	41.1	28.8	24.2	3.1	2.8	31348	35687	16	19	306	38.6	25.5	26.8	6.2	2.9	63462
39866	MORGAN	15628	326	35.3	33.1	24.9	4.0	2.8	33133	37923	21	26	261	33.3	48.7	12.3	5.8	0.0	62674
39867	MORRIS	19214	494	41.3	34.8	17.2	3.9	2.8	30000	34762	12	13	404	38.4	34.7	23.0	4.0	0.0	60476
39870	NEWTON	22805	1528	38.3	28.1	25.5	5.0	3.1	33769	39509	23	28	1216	40.9	30.6	24.0	4.3	0.3	63370
39877	PARROTT	35155	155	25.2	32.3	25.2	3.9	13.6	46765	54993	66	70	130	23.1	19.2	40.0	10.0	7.7	103333
39886	SHELLMAN	14342	623	46.6	28.4	17.8	5.6	1.6	26986	31593	7	5	464	53.5	23.7	16.4	4.7	1.7	43600
39897	WHIGHAM	15683	1415	38.0	33.6	23.2	4.5	0.9	33172	38662	21	26	1171	31.6	23.9	33.3	9.5	1.7	79750
	GEORGIA	26143		23.6	26.3	31.4	11.6	7.0	50024	60470				12.5	17.5	39.3	24.8	6.0	125860
	UNITED STATES	25866		24.7	27.1	30.8	10.9	6.5	48124	56710				10.9	15.0	33.7	30.1	10.4	145905

ZIP CODE		FINANCIAL SERVICES				THE HOME						ENTERTAINMENT						PERSONAL			
						Home Improvements		Furnishings													
#	POST OFFICE NAME	Auto Loan	Home Loan	Invest-ments	Retire-ment Plans	Home Repair	Lawn & Garden	Comput-ers & Hard-ware	Major Appli-ances	TV, Radio, Sound Equip-ment	Furni-ture	Dine out/ Carry out	Sports Equip-ment	Fees & Tickets	Toys & Games	Travel	Cable TV	Apparel & Services	Auto Repairs	Health Insur-ance	Pets & Supplies
39824	BLUFFTON	83	55	25	48	63	72	54	67	65	55	76	80	46	72	54	70	69	66	82	95
39825	BRINSON	80	60	35	54	65	72	57	68	65	59	78	80	51	73	58	68	72	67	78	91
39826	BRONWOOD	82	55	25	47	62	71	53	66	64	54	75	79	45	71	54	69	68	65	81	94
39827	CAIRO	94	77	52	72	80	87	74	83	79	76	96	97	67	91	73	81	91	83	90	106
39828	CAIRO	65	56	50	53	57	64	58	61	62	58	76	70	55	72	57	63	72	61	65	72
39834	CLIMAX	80	59	34	53	64	72	57	68	65	58	77	80	50	73	57	68	71	67	78	91
39836	COLEMAN	82	55	25	47	62	71	53	66	64	54	75	79	45	71	54	69	68	65	81	94
39837	COLQUITT	78	58	39	53	63	73	60	68	68	60	81	78	54	77	60	72	75	68	80	87
39840	CUTHBERT	59	43	30	38	46	55	45	52	53	45	62	59	40	58	45	56	58	52	62	66
39841	DAMASCUS	104	70	32	60	79	91	67	84	81	69	96	101	57	90	69	88	87	83	104	119
39842	DAWSON	71	56	44	51	58	68	58	64	65	58	78	72	53	73	57	68	73	64	73	79
39845	DONALSONVILLE	77	57	36	51	63	73	57	67	66	57	78	78	50	74	58	70	71	67	80	90
39846	EDISON	51	39	36	36	41	50	44	47	50	44	60	51	41	54	43	54	56	48	56	55
39851	FORT GAINES	91	66	43	58	72	84	66	78	78	67	92	90	59	86	66	83	85	77	93	104
39854	GEORGETOWN	72	49	24	42	55	63	47	59	56	48	66	70	40	63	48	61	60	58	72	83
39859	IRON CITY	79	54	26	47	61	70	52	65	62	53	73	77	44	69	53	67	66	64	79	91
39861	JAKIN	101	78	48	71	83	92	75	87	83	77	100	103	67	94	75	86	93	86	98	115
39862	LEARY	90	60	27	52	68	78	58	72	70	59	82	86	49	77	59	75	75	72	89	103
39866	MORGAN	0	0	0	0	0	0	0	0	0	0	0	0	0	0	0	0	0	0	0	0
39867	MORRIS	78	61	42	55	68	77	58	70	66	58	78	81	52	77	61	71	73	69	82	95
39870	NEWTON	114	76	35	66	86	100	74	92	89	75	104	110	63	99	75	96	95	91	114	131
39877	PARROTT	155	104	47	89	117	135	100	125	121	102	142	149	85	134	102	130	129	124	154	177
39886	SHELLMAN	73	49	22	42	56	64	47	59	57	48	67	71	40	63	48	62	61	59	73	84
39897	WHIGHAM	76	52	26	46	59	67	51	62	60	52	71	74	44	67	51	64	65	62	75	87
	GEORGIA	103	97	95	97	97	104	97	99	98	98	122	116	96	120	96	98	118	100	99	116
	UNITED STATES	100	100	100	100	100	100	100	100	100	100	100	100	100	100	100	100	100	100	100	100

# POST OFFICE NAME	COUNTY FIPS CODE	POPULATION 2000	2004	2009	2000-2004 ANNUAL RATE % Rate	State Centile	HOUSEHOLDS 2000	2004	2009	% Annual Rate 2000-2004	2004 Average HH Size	FAMILIES 2000	2004	% Annual Rate 2000-2004
96701 AIEA	003	45453	44621	44553	-0.4	20	14960	14879	15081	-0.1	2.89	11138	10964	-0.4
96704 CAPTAIN COOK	001	7578	7683	7869	0.3	43	2762	2891	3035	1.1	2.65	1898	1955	0.7
96705 ELEELE	007	1156	1191	1222	0.7	59	341	359	377	1.2	3.32	255	265	0.9
96706 EWA BEACH	003	43571	48635	51976	2.6	95	11710	13410	14606	3.2	3.60	9809	11088	2.9
96707 KAPOLEI	003	24150	26059	27309	1.8	80	6905	7526	7979	2.1	3.46	5875	6347	1.8
96708 HAIKU	009	8371	9134	9823	2.1	85	2968	3354	3701	2.9	2.68	1936	2154	2.5
96710 HAKALAU	001	263	255	259	-0.7	11	97	97	101	0.0	2.63	67	66	-0.4
96712 HALEIWA	003	7469	7266	7216	-0.7	16	2411	2390	2408	-0.2	3.02	1685	1652	-0.5
96713 HANA	009	1849	1816	1882	-0.4	22	589	591	625	0.1	3.07	404	400	-0.2
96716 HANAPEPE	007	4325	4723	4997	2.1	88	1401	1569	1699	2.7	3.01	1087	1203	2.4
96717 HAUULA	003	5155	5179	5219	0.1	36	1414	1429	1456	0.3	3.58	1089	1092	0.1
96718 HAWAII NATIONAL PARK	001	124	122	125	-0.4	24	54	55	57	0.4	2.20	39	39	0.0
96719 HAWI	001	3184	3279	3382	0.7	58	794	847	900	1.5	3.09	591	622	1.2
96720 HILO	001	43005	44075	45627	0.6	56	15219	16046	17008	1.3	2.66	10679	11088	0.9
96722 PRINCEVILLE	007	2694	2839	2926	1.2	72	1108	1214	1290	2.2	2.32	702	755	1.7
96725 HOLUALOA	001	3122	3220	3359	0.7	60	1167	1236	1316	1.4	2.60	783	817	1.0
96727 HONOKAA	001	4954	4995	5115	0.2	39	1695	1765	1853	1.0	2.76	1241	1276	0.7
96728 HONOMU	001	585	625	657	1.6	78	206	225	242	2.1	2.78	152	164	1.8
96729 HOOLEHUA	009	1104	1121	1166	0.4	45	297	312	332	1.2	3.59	241	251	1.0
96730 KAAAWA	003	1140	1320	1421	3.5	99	366	427	465	3.7	3.08	252	291	3.4
96731 KAHUKU	003	3149	3165	3192	0.1	38	839	857	876	0.5	3.52	642	647	0.2
96732 KAHULUI	009	19270	21173	22960	2.2	92	5639	6386	7095	3.0	3.20	4235	4732	2.7
96734 KAILUA	003	49653	50519	51327	0.4	48	15488	15953	16425	0.7	2.98	12300	12599	0.6
96738 WAIKOLOA	001	4855	5616	6150	3.5	98	1777	2084	2316	3.8	2.69	1250	1442	3.4
96740 KAILUA KONA	001	24646	26732	28824	1.9	84	9015	9999	11001	2.5	2.66	6213	6797	2.1
96741 KALAHEO	007	5907	5958	6061	0.2	40	2138	2247	2358	1.2	2.64	1579	1635	0.8
96742 KALAUPAPA	005	142	138	138	-0.7	15	111	112	112	0.2	1.23	21	20	-1.1
96743 KAMUELA	001	8620	8968	9288	0.9	66	3014	3238	3436	1.7	2.71	2205	2334	1.4
96744 KANEOHE	003	53208	52317	52547	-0.4	23	16495	16649	16781	0.0	3.14	13337	13201	-0.2
96746 KAPAA	007	18505	18944	19329	0.6	51	6277	6652	6981	1.4	2.82	4550	4755	1.0
96747 KAUMAKANI	007	105	98	98	-1.6	8	33	32	33	-0.7	3.06	26	25	-0.9
96748 KAUNAKAKAI	009	4668	4626	4791	-0.2	28	1519	1548	1641	0.5	2.98	1123	1129	0.1
96749 KEAAU	001	8727	9704	10435	2.5	94	2980	3405	3742	3.2	2.85	2160	2434	2.9
96750 KEALAKEKUA	001	1303	1294	1314	-0.2	32	448	459	478	0.6	2.79	329	334	0.4
96752 KEKAHA	007	3231	3119	3117	-0.8	10	1088	1093	1127	0.1	2.84	803	795	-0.2
96753 KIHEI	009	22696	25095	27327	2.4	93	8779	9913	11002	2.9	2.52	5402	5999	2.5
96754 KILAUEA	007	2971	3165	3281	1.5	75	1014	1120	1195	2.4	2.81	721	783	2.0
96755 KAPAAU	001	2510	2606	2709	0.9	64	814	869	924	1.6	2.94	597	629	1.2
96756 KOLOA	007	4312	4370	4440	0.3	41	1633	1723	1806	1.3	2.52	1162	1209	0.9
96757 KUALAPUU	009	856	878	914	0.6	57	277	294	313	1.4	2.99	227	239	1.2
96760 KURTISTOWN	001	5330	5834	6222	2.2	91	1768	1982	2158	2.7	2.94	1272	1407	2.4
96761 LAHAINA	009	15685	17902	19827	3.2	97	5014	5877	6640	3.8	3.04	3233	3711	3.3
96762 LAIE	003	4762	4877	4942	0.6	53	953	982	1006	0.7	4.42	773	791	0.5
96763 LANAI CITY	009	3189	3297	3447	0.8	61	1158	1237	1326	1.6	2.66	803	846	1.2
96764 LAUPAHOEHOE	001	1004	997	1020	-0.2	32	344	351	367	0.5	2.84	268	271	0.3
96766 LIHUE	007	12022	12572	13028	1.1	67	3978	4300	4586	1.9	2.86	2839	3033	1.6
96768 MAKAWAO	009	15861	16240	17075	0.6	53	5323	5631	6069	1.3	2.88	3990	4168	1.0
96769 MAKAWELI	007	627	559	549	-2.7	3	184	169	171	-2.0	3.31	151	137	-2.3
96770 MAUNALOA	009	624	620	644	-0.2	33	210	216	230	0.7	2.87	168	171	0.4
96771 MOUNTAIN VIEW	001	4858	5269	5593	1.9	84	1770	1978	2149	2.7	2.62	1195	1313	2.2
96772 NAALEHU	001	4201	4587	4895	2.1	88	1654	1873	2052	3.0	2.45	1037	1156	2.6
96773 NINOLE	001	57	60	63	1.2	68	25	27	29	1.8	2.22	18	20	2.5
96774 OOKALA	001	298	314	329	1.2	72	97	105	112	1.9	2.99	73	78	1.6
96776 PAAUILO	001	1196	1225	1258	0.6	55	398	421	444	1.3	2.91	301	314	1.0
96777 PAHALA	001	1467	1446	1473	-0.3	25	481	490	511	0.4	2.91	348	350	0.1
96778 PAHOA	001	8572	9274	9811	1.9	81	3102	3466	3757	2.7	2.68	2063	2267	2.2
96779 PAIA	009	2396	2220	2276	-1.8	7	723	688	721	-1.2	3.12	520	488	-1.5
96780 PAPAALOA	001	227	241	253	1.4	74	91	99	106	2.0	2.43	68	73	1.7
96781 PAPAIKOU	001	1651	1603	1629	-0.7	14	562	563	586	0.0	2.85	425	421	-0.2
96782 PEARL CITY	003	39904	39478	39707	-0.3	27	11873	11965	12232	0.2	3.06	9582	9539	-0.1
96783 PEPEEKEO	001	1895	1880	1919	-0.2	30	695	713	746	0.6	2.64	509	515	0.3
96785 VOLCANO	001	3231	3443	3612	1.5	76	1332	1464	1573	2.3	2.29	802	864	1.5
96786 WAHIAWA	003	41786	41033	41179	-0.4	20	11357	11305	11511	-0.1	3.21	9638	9488	-0.4
96789 MILILANI	003	44670	47316	49275	1.4	73	14601	15872	16870	2.0	2.98	11878	12734	1.7
96790 KULA	009	6384	6532	6783	0.5	50	2425	2572	2745	1.4	2.44	1649	1723	1.0
96791 WAIALUA	003	6270	6142	6161	-0.5	18	1938	1929	1962	-0.1	3.12	1448	1424	-0.4
96792 WAIANAE	003	42232	41250	41056	-0.6	17	10504	10380	10457	-0.3	3.93	8791	8624	-0.5
96793 WAILUKU	009	22385	24481	26590	2.1	90	7362	8170	9011	2.5	2.99	5284	5821	2.3
96795 WAIMANALO	003	11884	11273	11167	-1.2	9	3078	2988	3009	-0.7	3.70	2589	2500	-0.8
96796 WAIMEA	007	1894	1874	1886	-0.3	27	665	683	708	0.6	2.66	491	498	0.3
96797 WAIPAHU	003	64905	70240	73758	1.9	82	17773	19713	21121	2.5	3.49	14365	15755	2.2
96813 HONOLULU	003	29247	30339	31344	0.9	63	12742	13623	14397	1.6	2.07	6327	6539	0.8
96814 HONOLULU	003	21962	22262	22681	0.3	43	12361	12710	13136	0.7	1.72	4952	4951	0.0
96815 HONOLULU	003	19957	21821	23012	2.1	89	10243	11188	11873	2.1	1.94	4302	4689	2.1
96816 HONOLULU	003	45199	45983	47016	0.4	48	16033	16564	17192	0.8	2.73	11264	11529	0.6
96817 HONOLULU	003	53797	54010	55310	0.1	35	20143	20695	21593	0.6	2.53	12429	12451	0.0
96818 HONOLULU	003	47252	48319	49976	0.5	49	14813	15304	16031	0.8	3.13	12179	12395	0.4
96819 HONOLULU	003	49449	48014	48016	-0.7	14	11823	11506	11617	-0.6	3.99	9929	9572	-0.9
96821 HONOLULU	003	19841	19839	19978	0.0	34	6845	6949	7091	0.4	2.84	5465	5503	0.2
96822 HONOLULU	003	36362	36929	37480	0.4	45	15007	15501	15988	0.8	2.23	8296	8426	0.4
96825 HONOLULU	003	24634	25601	26318	0.9	65	8535	9009	9400	1.3	2.84	6898	7245	1.2
96826 HONOLULU	003	24713	26349	27488	1.5	77	11951	12879	13588	1.8	2.04	5784	6105	1.3
96844 HONOLULU	003	1348	1246	1227	-1.8	6	218	177	172	-4.8	2.19	108	85	-5.5
96853 HICKAM AFB	003	1265	1930	1983	10.5	100	216	245	262	3.0	3.99	212	240	3.0
96858 FORT SHAFTER	003	626	546	530	-3.2	1	203	173	169	-3.7	2.46	177	149	-4.0
96860 PEARL HARBOR	003	2092	1910	1876	-2.1	5	223	179	173	-5.0	4.24	205	165	-5.0
96862 BARBERS POINT	003	1200	1264	1291	1.2	69	370	384	391	0.9	3.29	359	372	0.8
96863 M C B H KANEOHE BAY	003	3897	3463	3383	-2.7	2	630	510	494	-4.9	3.20	618	500	-4.9
HAWAII					0.7					1.2	2.86			0.9
UNITED STATES					1.2					1.3	2.58			1.1

ZIP CODE #	POST OFFICE NAME	RACE (%) White 2000	White 2004	Black 2000	Black 2004	Asian/Pacific 2000	Asian/Pacific 2004	% Hispanic Origin 2000	% Hispanic Origin 2004	2004 AGE DISTRIBUTION (%) 0-4	5-9	10-14	15-19	20-24	25-44	45-64	65-84	85+	18+	MEDIAN AGE 2004	% 2004 Males	% 2004 Females
96701	AIEA	18.1	18.2	2.3	2.7	58.6	58.0	6.4	7.0	5.7	5.6	6.1	5.9	7.0	30.5	25.3	12.5	1.4	79.0	38.1	51.2	48.8
96704	CAPTAIN COOK	34.9	34.4	0.4	0.4	35.5	35.6	6.9	7.6	5.4	6.0	7.8	7.4	5.9	21.9	32.5	11.6	1.6	76.1	42.0	50.8	49.2
96705	ELEELE	18.4	18.0	0.3	0.3	53.8	54.0	11.3	12.1	7.0	7.1	7.6	7.1	7.5	25.9	22.6	13.0	2.3	74.1	36.1	48.9	51.1
96706	EWA BEACH	16.5	15.8	2.2	2.5	56.9	56.8	8.8	9.4	9.4	9.0	8.5	6.4	6.4	34.9	17.9	7.0	0.7	69.1	31.5	50.3	49.7
96707	KAPOLEI	19.7	19.6	2.0	2.4	49.9	49.3	9.4	10.2	8.9	8.7	9.2	7.2	6.0	33.2	20.8	5.7	0.4	68.7	32.3	50.1	49.9
96708	HAIKU	57.9	57.5	0.6	0.7	15.9	15.7	8.1	9.0	6.7	6.8	7.1	6.7	6.2	29.6	30.0	6.2	0.8	75.1	37.3	50.7	49.3
96710	HAKALAU	24.7	23.9	0.4	0.4	46.0	46.3	8.0	9.0	6.7	6.7	7.1	5.9	5.9	21.2	27.5	16.5	2.8	76.1	42.3	47.8	52.2
96712	HALEIWA	41.7	42.1	1.7	2.0	29.4	28.3	9.2	10.3	7.3	6.0	6.9	6.8	8.7	30.8	24.6	7.8	1.1	75.8	33.7	52.3	47.7
96713	HANA	26.2	26.1	0.1	0.1	41.6	41.0	5.1	5.7	7.2	7.1	9.0	7.7	6.1	22.4	30.2	9.3	1.2	71.4	36.5	48.2	51.8
96716	HANAPEPE	12.2	12.5	0.1	0.2	63.5	62.7	7.9	8.7	6.5	6.9	9.7	8.8	6.8	25.6	22.2	11.5	2.1	71.5	36.2	50.0	50.1
96717	HAUULA	21.8	22.3	0.6	0.7	40.2	39.1	8.2	8.9	8.8	9.2	9.4	8.5	7.9	25.5	22.0	7.6	1.2	67.2	29.9	48.8	51.3
96718	HAWAII NATIONAL PARK	14.5	14.8	0.0	0.0	53.2	53.3	6.5	5.7	4.9	4.9	6.6	8.2	9.0	20.5	27.1	15.6	3.3	78.7	41.9	50.8	49.2
96719	HAWI	37.8	37.4	0.9	1.0	32.1	31.9	10.4	11.4	5.0	5.5	6.6	7.4	7.4	27.2	28.1	11.3	1.6	78.7	39.4	51.1	48.9
96720	HILO	17.4	17.1	0.4	0.5	51.2	51.1	8.9	9.6	5.7	5.9	7.0	8.0	7.9	23.0	25.7	14.4	2.5	77.1	39.5	48.9	51.1
96722	PRINCEVILLE	71.9	71.9	0.2	0.3	14.6	14.4	4.1	4.8	5.6	5.9	6.4	6.6	4.8	23.6	34.9	11.3	1.0	78.0	43.3	50.8	49.2
96725	HOLUALOA	47.4	46.9	0.3	0.3	27.7	27.7	8.2	9.0	5.1	5.4	6.4	6.5	6.4	23.4	32.1	13.1	1.6	79.3	42.9	50.6	49.4
96727	HONOKAA	30.7	30.2	0.1	0.1	39.1	39.3	9.4	10.2	6.1	6.3	7.0	6.6	5.6	23.8	28.0	14.1	2.6	76.3	41.5	49.6	50.4
96728	HONOMU	23.4	22.9	0.0	0.0	36.1	35.7	12.0	12.5	5.4	6.2	8.0	5.8	4.5	22.9	26.6	18.4	2.2	77.0	42.6	47.4	52.6
96729	HOOLEHUA	12.1	12.0	0.2	0.2	56.5	55.8	4.5	4.8	8.2	8.2	10.1	8.3	6.6	23.5	22.1	11.9	1.2	68.4	33.3	50.1	49.9
96730	KAAAWA	35.0	35.7	0.4	0.5	31.9	30.9	8.1	9.1	7.3	7.2	7.2	7.0	6.1	26.6	27.8	9.9	1.0	73.9	37.2	48.8	51.2
96731	KAHUKU	18.7	19.7	0.6	0.7	51.2	50.0	7.7	8.3	7.7	7.5	9.0	9.4	8.7	24.8	21.5	9.6	1.9	69.9	31.3	50.7	49.4
96732	KAHULUI	10.2	10.4	0.2	0.3	63.5	62.8	8.7	9.4	7.1	6.4	6.8	6.9	8.0	26.2	21.8	14.1	2.8	75.6	36.2	49.1	50.9
96734	KAILUA	46.6	46.8	2.5	3.0	26.4	25.7	7.4	8.3	6.6	6.2	6.7	7.2	10.2	27.9	23.5	10.5	1.3	76.8	35.1	51.7	48.3
96738	WAIKOLOA	45.9	45.2	0.4	0.5	26.3	26.3	8.8	9.7	7.5	7.8	9.1	7.3	5.6	29.0	26.2	7.0	0.6	70.6	35.7	50.3	49.7
96740	KAILUA KONA	46.9	47.2	0.5	0.5	27.0	26.5	7.9	8.6	6.3	6.5	6.7	6.2	5.9	25.6	30.8	11.0	1.2	76.6	40.5	50.0	50.0
96741	KALAHEO	41.1	41.2	0.3	0.3	32.8	32.4	11.4	12.5	5.2	5.9	7.3	6.5	5.7	24.9	30.2	12.7	1.8	77.6	41.5	50.6	49.5
96742	KALAUPAPA	26.1	26.8	0.0	0.0	65.5	63.8	4.2	4.4	0.0	0.0	2.2	0.0	1.5	18.1	47.8	30.4	0.0	97.8	57.8	52.2	47.8
96743	KAMUELA	35.2	34.9	0.4	0.4	33.3	33.1	7.5	8.3	6.1	6.7	7.9	7.5	6.3	26.4	28.2	9.9	1.1	74.4	38.1	49.3	50.7
96744	KANEOHE	21.0	21.4	0.8	0.9	48.5	47.8	7.1	7.7	6.0	6.1	7.0	6.8	6.7	26.7	26.7	12.5	1.6	76.5	38.9	49.2	50.8
96746	KAPAA	29.9	29.7	0.4	0.5	40.7	40.4	8.9	9.7	6.6	6.8	8.2	7.6	6.7	25.6	27.4	9.7	1.5	73.5	37.4	49.6	50.4
96747	KAUMAKANI	3.8	4.1	0.0	0.0	80.0	79.6	4.8	5.1	4.1	4.1	8.2	8.2	8.2	22.5	25.5	17.4	2.0	77.6	42.2	52.0	48.0
96748	KAUNAKAKAI	14.4	14.3	0.1	0.1	52.8	52.0	5.3	5.7	7.3	7.0	10.1	9.0	6.7	20.4	25.4	12.2	1.9	69.9	36.2	48.4	51.6
96749	KEAAU	30.4	30.2	0.5	0.5	36.0	35.4	13.1	14.3	6.8	7.0	8.7	8.3	7.5	24.6	26.9	9.2	1.1	71.7	35.4	50.9	49.1
96750	KEALAKEKUA	34.5	33.5	0.4	0.5	37.8	38.2	7.7	8.4	5.0	5.8	6.3	6.0	4.2	22.2	31.5	17.2	1.9	79.0	45.4	49.1	50.9
96752	KEKAHA	17.1	17.3	0.2	0.2	55.2	54.6	8.7	9.4	5.3	5.5	7.3	7.0	6.4	23.6	29.3	13.6	2.2	77.5	41.4	49.9	50.1
96753	KIHEI	54.8	53.9	0.8	0.9	27.5	27.9	6.9	7.7	6.1	6.0	6.6	6.2	6.9	30.1	28.5	8.8	0.8	77.5	38.2	50.3	49.7
96754	KILAUEA	53.4	53.4	0.6	0.6	28.7	28.4	6.1	6.9	6.1	6.5	8.1	8.2	7.3	25.5	29.7	7.5	1.2	74.3	37.4	51.2	48.8
96755	KAPAAU	24.0	23.9	0.1	0.1	37.5	37.2	18.4	19.9	7.1	7.0	8.3	8.3	6.1	23.8	25.7	11.9	1.9	72.1	37.0	49.1	50.9
96756	KOLOA	36.8	37.4	0.2	0.3	39.5	38.8	9.3	10.1	5.4	5.6	6.4	6.5	6.7	23.1	29.5	14.3	2.6	78.3	42.4	50.4	49.6
96757	KUALAPUU	7.7	7.6	0.0	0.0	58.8	58.0	5.5	5.8	7.6	8.0	10.4	8.0	6.4	23.7	23.0	11.9	1.1	69.0	34.1	51.5	48.5
96760	KURTISTOWN	31.5	31.3	0.7	0.8	32.0	31.4	15.2	16.7	8.1	8.1	8.5	8.1	7.4	25.9	25.6	7.7	0.7	70.2	32.9	51.7	48.3
96761	LAHAINA	39.8	41.5	0.5	0.6	41.4	39.6	8.0	9.0	6.5	6.0	5.9	5.8	6.2	32.0	26.2	10.3	1.2	78.2	37.8	51.2	48.8
96762	LAIE	25.7	26.2	0.4	0.5	47.3	46.2	3.8	4.3	8.7	8.4	8.8	11.1	13.8	28.1	16.1	4.6	0.5	67.9	24.7	48.0	52.0
96763	LANAI CITY	13.6	13.5	0.1	0.2	64.9	64.4	7.7	8.2	7.2	6.9	8.0	7.1	6.6	27.5	21.8	12.6	2.3	73.0	35.8	50.4	49.7
96764	LAUPAHOEHOE	26.1	25.6	0.3	0.3	42.6	42.9	9.7	10.3	6.1	5.7	6.5	7.6	7.3	20.8	26.8	16.4	2.8	77.2	41.9	50.6	49.5
96766	LIHUE	16.8	16.7	0.3	0.3	59.7	59.4	6.9	7.5	6.3	6.1	7.0	6.5	6.7	25.5	25.0	14.5	2.4	76.4	39.1	49.0	51.0
96768	MAKAWAO	38.4	38.5	0.3	0.4	31.2	30.5	9.8	10.8	6.6	7.0	7.5	7.1	6.7	27.5	28.2	8.4	1.1	74.5	37.1	49.8	50.2
96769	MAKAWELI	9.4	9.3	0.2	0.2	68.7	68.3	5.7	5.7	7.0	5.4	10.9	8.4	7.5	23.4	21.3	14.5	1.6	71.0	35.1	53.5	46.5
96770	MAUNALOA	20.4	20.3	0.5	0.7	52.9	52.1	2.7	3.2	9.5	8.7	10.0	9.2	7.3	22.3	20.2	11.8	1.1	66.0	30.6	47.4	52.6
96771	MOUNTAIN VIEW	34.2	33.8	0.8	0.9	32.7	32.4	11.7	12.8	5.7	6.3	7.9	7.6	6.4	25.1	30.9	9.0	1.0	74.8	39.8	51.5	48.5
96772	NAALEHU	42.7	43.1	1.1	1.3	28.5	27.4	7.2	8.0	6.0	6.5	7.5	7.0	4.1	22.7	32.5	12.9	0.9	75.3	42.7	52.4	47.6
96773	NINOLE	29.8	30.0	0.0	0.0	36.8	38.3	10.5	8.3	6.7	6.7	8.3	6.7	6.7	23.3	25.0	13.3	3.3	75.0	37.5	51.7	48.3
96774	OOKALA	30.9	29.9	0.3	0.3	36.6	36.6	9.4	10.2	5.1	5.7	7.6	7.6	5.4	23.3	30.3	12.7	2.2	77.1	41.4	52.2	47.8
96776	PAAUILO	26.5	26.3	0.1	0.1	38.7	38.7	11.9	12.6	6.0	6.7	8.7	7.0	6.0	22.9	26.9	14.0	1.7	74.2	39.6	50.9	49.1
96777	PAHALA	14.9	14.4	0.2	0.2	53.2	53.4	6.3	6.7	5.2	5.2	6.2	7.6	8.4	21.0	27.6	16.0	2.8	77.8	42.1	49.7	50.4
96778	PAHOA	38.1	37.8	0.8	0.9	30.6	30.3	12.3	13.3	6.5	7.6	8.2	7.6	5.8	23.8	28.9	10.4	1.2	72.8	38.7	51.4	48.6
96779	PAIA	37.2	38.1	0.3	0.4	33.1	32.2	11.1	12.0	7.6	7.5	7.7	7.4	6.9	30.2	24.9	6.7	1.1	73.2	34.2	50.5	49.5
96780	PAPAALOA	31.3	30.3	0.4	0.4	36.1	36.5	9.7	10.8	5.0	5.8	7.9	7.5	5.4	23.7	29.9	12.5	2.5	76.4	41.1	51.9	48.1
96781	PAPAIKOU	16.6	16.2	0.5	0.6	54.0	54.1	7.0	7.5	6.2	6.2	6.7	6.9	5.9	23.6	24.8	16.7	3.0	76.6	41.3	49.3	50.7
96782	PEARL CITY	17.0	17.2	2.5	3.0	59.9	58.9	7.3	8.0	5.3	5.0	5.6	6.1	10.4	27.7	23.6	14.8	1.5	80.8	37.3	52.6	47.4
96783	PEPEEKEO	20.0	19.2	0.2	0.3	55.2	55.9	8.0	8.5	5.6	5.8	6.4	5.7	4.9	22.0	27.4	19.3	2.9	78.6	44.7	48.8	51.2
96785	VOLCANO	40.5	40.0	0.4	0.5	25.0	24.7	12.4	13.5	5.6	6.0	8.0	7.2	5.8	25.1	32.9	8.6	0.8	75.8	40.6	51.1	48.9
96786	WAHIAWA	32.0	30.2	11.1	12.0	33.7	33.9	12.9	13.8	10.9	7.7	6.9	7.5	15.0	30.5	12.4	7.9	1.2	71.1	25.9	53.5	46.5
96789	MILILANI	18.3	18.3	2.9	3.4	53.2	52.7	7.7	8.2	7.4	7.5	7.9	6.7	6.1	31.3	25.3	7.2	0.6	72.9	35.3	50.1	49.9
96790	KULA	56.5	56.2	0.2	0.2	24.4	24.3	5.3	6.0	4.3	5.0	6.5	7.0	5.8	21.2	36.3	11.5	2.5	79.5	45.1	48.3	51.7
96791	WAIALUA	22.4	22.8	1.0	1.2	48.6	47.8	7.1	7.8	6.7	6.0	6.8	7.3	8.5	27.5	23.1	12.2	2.0	76.1	35.6	51.8	48.2
96792	WAIANAE	11.3	11.6	1.1	1.4	45.5	44.3	13.9	15.0	9.1	8.5	10.0	9.2	8.5	26.5	20.1	7.4	0.7	66.6	28.5	49.9	50.1
96793	WAILUKU	17.6	17.2	0.3	0.3	55.3	55.2	7.6	8.4	6.8	6.6	7.4	7.3	7.3	26.6	25.6	10.8	1.6	74.6	37.2	50.1	49.9
96795	WAIMANALO	16.1	16.7	0.3	0.4	51.9	51.1	7.3	8.0	7.1	7.1	7.7	7.5	7.5	28.9	24.0	9.2	1.1	73.6	34.3	50.3	49.7
96796	WAIMEA	13.4	13.3	0.1	0.1	55.3	54.8	7.1	7.9	5.7	5.8	6.7	7.9	7.2	21.6	26.7	13.8	4.6	76.1	41.3	48.9	51.1
96797	WAIPAHU	8.8	9.2	1.6	1.9	70.5	69.4	6.3	6.7	7.5	7.3	7.5	6.6	6.7	31.0	22.5	9.7	1.3	73.5	34.7	49.9	50.2
96813	HONOLULU	22.5	22.6	1.0	1.2	59.7	59.2	3.9	4.4	4.1	3.9	4.4	4.7	5.9	29.8	28.6	15.9	2.8	85.0	43.3	49.1	50.9
96814	HONOLULU	25.8	26.2	1.4	1.6	60.9	60.0	3.5	3.9	3.4	3.0	3.2	3.6	5.9	30.4	27.8	19.2	3.6	88.6	45.4	47.9	52.1
96815	HONOLULU	36.9	36.8	1.5	1.7	48.3	47.9	4.4	4.8	3.6	3.3	3.1	3.6	5.6	32.0	28.5	17.1	3.2	88.1	44.3	50.9	49.1
96816	HONOLULU	16.9	17.2	0.3	0.4	65.7	65.1	3.4	3.8	3.9	4.2	5.3	5.7	6.1	25.6	27.3	17.9	4.1	83.3	44.5	48.7	51.4
96817	HONOLULU	10.9	11.5	0.7	0.8	73.3	72.5	4.0	4.4	4.3	4.5	5.4	5.6	6.2	25.9	26.3	18.2	3.6	82.3	43.7	48.0	52.0
96818	HONOLULU	31.3	30.1	7.8	8.8	45.3	45.3	7.1	7.8	9.5	8.5	8.1	5.9	7.8	36.0	16.2	7.2	0.7	70.2	30.6	49.6	50.4
96819	HONOLULU	7.6	7.4	1.4	1.6	75.6	75.4	5.1	5.5	6.8	6.7	7.3	6.7	7.1	27.8	21.4	14.1	2.2	75.2	35.9	50.3	49.7
96821	HONOLULU	25.3	25.6	0.2	0.2	59.0	58.5	2.7	3.0	4.0	4.9	6.0	5.6	4.6	22.4	31.7	18.3	2.6	81.4	46.4	49.2	50.8
96822	HONOLULU	20.9	21.1	0.9	1.1	61.8	61.2	4.1	4.5	3.9	3.8	4.3	6.4	8.4	29.2	25.8	15.2	3.0	85.4	40.9	47.7	52.4
96825	HONOLULU	31.2	30.7	0.5	0.5	51.0	51.1	3.4	3.8	4.9	5.4	6.1	5.8	5.0	25.1	32.0	14.3	1.5	79.9	43.6	49.2	50.9
96826	HONOLULU	15.3	15.7	1.1	1.2	65.5	64.8	4.6	5.1	4.7	4.3	4.9	5.2	8.2	32.8	25.9	12.2	1.9	83.2	38.7	49.5	50.5
96844	HONOLULU	18.3	18.5	1.6	1.9	60.0	59.3	4.6	5.0	2.8	1.5	2.6	16.3	44.7	20.6	8.4	3.0	0.2	91.7	23.0	52.7	47.4
96853	HICKAM AFB	64.1	62.1	13.8	16.0	8.6	8.2	9.6	10.7	9.6	8.2	10.1	8.0	22.8	37.8	3.1	0.3	0.1	70.2	23.1	56.9	43.1
96858	FORT SHAFTER	27.6	25.6	8.8	9.5	48.1	49.1	8.0	8.6	8.8	6.6	6.6	6.8	11.9	38.1	15.6	5.0	0.7	74.5	28.9	57.5	42.5
96860	PEARL HARBOR	63.2	61.6	15.7	17.9	11.7	11.1	6.4	7.2	4.6	3.2	3.6	10.4	28.6	40.2	8.6	0.7	0.1	86.9	24.9	71.0	29.0
96862	BARBERS POINT	62.0	60.8	11.3	13.1	10.5	10.1	8.4	9.3	17.3	11.6	8.5	2.5	9.7	47.5	2.3	0.6	0.1	60.7	25.1	48.8	51.2
96863	M C B H KANEOHE BAY	67.4	65.7	12.3	14.0	5.9	5.5	15.2	16.8	9.0	5.3	4.4	11.2	43.9	25.0	1.2	0.1	0.0	79.8	22.3	72.7	27.3
	HAWAII	24.3	24.4	1.8	2.1	51.0	50.4	7.2	7.9	6.5	6.3	6.8	6.6	7.5	28.4	24.5	11.7	1.7	76.5	36.9	50.1	49.9
	UNITED STATES	75.1	73.6	12.3	12.5	3.8	4.2	12.5	14.1	6.9	6.7	7.2	7.0	7.3	28.6	23.8	10.8	1.7	75.1	36.0	49.1	50.9

ZIP CODE #	POST OFFICE NAME	2004 Per Capita Income	2004 HH Income Base	2004 HOUSEHOLD INCOME DISTRIBUTION (%) Less than $25,000	$25,000 to $49,999	$50,000 to $99,999	$100,000 to $149,999	$150,000 or More	MEDIAN HOUSEHOLD INCOME 2004	2009	2004 National Centile	2004 State Centile	2004 Home Value Base	2004 HOME VALUE DISTRIBUTION (%) Less than $50,000	$50,000 to $89,999	$90,000 to $174,999	$175,000 to $399,999	$400,000 or More	2004 Median Home Value
96701	AIEA	28054	14879	12.3	22.2	36.8	19.2	9.6	66458	77522	89	90	8812	0.9	2.3	11.1	32.4	53.3	415344
96704	CAPTAIN COOK	23958	2891	26.2	26.6	30.3	10.8	6.1	46198	51612	64	42	1963	2.1	1.7	9.8	49.9	36.5	329841
96705	ELEELE	17777	359	21.7	27.6	37.9	9.8	3.1	50634	57377	73	56	254	0.8	0.0	8.3	76.0	15.0	272115
96706	EWA BEACH	21094	13410	10.1	20.7	46.2	18.5	4.5	65762	77823	89	89	9493	0.6	1.3	16.4	69.7	12.1	286756
96707	KAPOLEI	24102	7526	6.9	18.0	46.7	21.9	6.5	73830	85635	93	94	6001	1.5	0.3	19.5	60.4	18.3	301630
96708	HAIKU	26968	3354	22.5	26.3	33.8	9.5	8.0	51243	61095	74	57	2185	0.0	0.0	2.7	31.2	66.1	514038
96710	HAKALAU	21431	97	37.1	21.7	25.8	9.3	6.2	40571	48016	48	25	66	0.0	3.0	18.2	57.6	21.2	246429
96712	HALEIWA	25699	2390	23.4	22.1	29.8	15.4	9.3	55210	66159	80	73	1179	1.2	0.5	3.8	42.5	52.0	409671
96713	HANA	19009	591	25.9	29.8	28.6	9.8	5.9	42278	47911	54	28	384	3.1	2.6	9.4	29.2	55.7	433333
96716	HANAPEPE	18202	1569	26.4	25.6	37.0	8.5	2.6	48200	54201	69	45	916	0.4	0.0	6.9	77.0	15.7	269565
96717	HAUULA	16694	1429	23.8	28.3	33.1	10.9	3.9	46288	55077	65	43	655	2.8	3.5	6.6	55.0	32.2	331065
96718	HAWAII NATIONAL PARK	18390	55	40.0	30.9	23.6	5.5	0.0	31701	37963	17	7	40	5.0	20.0	60.0	15.0	0.0	121875
96719	HAWI	23206	847	21.5	21.6	37.3	12.2	7.4	55673	65663	80	74	622	0.8	0.0	8.8	58.2	32.2	295652
96720	HILO	21750	16046	28.9	26.4	30.3	10.3	4.1	44256	50304	59	35	10638	1.1	2.4	24.5	61.1	10.9	225392
96722	PRINCEVILLE	40742	1214	22.6	26.7	23.9	13.1	13.8	51455	63401	75	58	725	0.0	0.0	7.6	20.3	72.1	599390
96725	HOLUALOA	29207	1236	23.1	24.7	31.1	11.3	9.8	51986	61208	75	61	769	0.4	0.9	7.4	31.9	59.4	460924
96727	HONOKAA	22785	1765	23.1	34.3	28.6	7.9	6.2	44371	50193	60	38	1362	0.9	5.4	22.1	50.2	21.4	245602
96728	HONOMU	18347	225	36.9	31.1	20.0	7.1	4.9	34352	38822	25	13	164	0.0	11.6	43.3	34.2	11.0	155000
96729	HOOLEHUA	17032	312	28.2	34.0	27.9	6.1	3.9	38625	44721	42	19	234	8.1	9.8	26.9	38.9	16.2	190000
96730	KAAAWA	23456	427	17.1	21.6	41.7	13.4	6.3	59408	71925	84	80	249	0.8	1.6	4.4	35.7	57.4	423125
96731	KAHUKU	17533	857	24.9	26.5	32.9	12.3	3.5	48422	59157	69	48	482	1.5	0.4	15.2	63.5	19.5	280114
96732	KAHULUI	22057	6386	23.1	23.6	34.6	12.1	6.6	52638	60445	76	66	3648	2.0	1.0	2.8	64.4	29.8	333901
96734	KAILUA	32772	15953	11.2	18.6	33.0	21.5	15.8	77341	94199	94	98	10458	0.4	0.2	1.9	23.8	73.7	486678
96738	WAIKOLOA	26555	2084	14.8	28.6	35.6	16.2	4.9	56866	64623	82	77	1129	0.0	0.0	9.0	71.2	19.8	303541
96740	KAILUA KONA	28799	9999	18.3	26.8	33.8	11.7	9.3	54013	62894	78	70	6394	0.5	0.6	7.0	54.2	37.7	343033
96741	KALAHEO	27835	2247	15.7	23.5	36.5	17.9	6.5	62227	71510	86	83	1595	1.3	1.4	7.1	51.0	39.3	357018
96742	KALAUPAPA	12397	112	67.0	33.0	0.0	0.0	0.0	9180	9333	0	1	0	0.0	0.0	0.0	0.0	0.0	0
96743	KAMUELA	29843	3238	14.3	26.6	38.3	13.2	7.6	58807	67839	83	78	2074	2.8	0.8	10.8	50.1	35.5	320424
96744	KANEOHE	28726	16469	10.1	16.1	40.1	22.8	10.9	76595	88993	94	97	11774	0.2	0.3	4.9	43.4	51.2	404841
96746	KAPAA	22588	6652	24.7	27.2	33.6	9.0	5.6	48341	54240	69	47	3942	1.1	1.3	8.4	55.8	33.4	320848
96747	KAUMAKANI	14131	32	34.4	40.6	18.8	6.3	0.0	35000	38629	28	15	0	0.0	0.0	0.0	0.0	0.0	0
96748	KAUNAKAKAI	17216	1548	33.9	30.4	26.2	7.1	2.3	37620	42152	38	18	1071	2.7	4.6	16.6	61.7	14.4	233059
96749	KEAAU	18111	3405	30.7	29.9	29.1	7.5	2.8	40600	47268	48	26	2481	2.5	5.4	37.2	49.6	5.4	182695
96750	KEALAKEKUA	27850	459	20.3	29.2	34.6	7.4	8.5	50449	57165	73	55	288	0.0	1.0	10.4	62.5	26.0	315854
96752	KEKAHA	19945	1093	23.4	27.3	37.0	8.5	3.8	48478	54162	69	49	675	0.0	3.7	18.5	62.5	15.3	244173
96753	KIHEI	30098	9913	19.3	26.4	32.5	12.6	9.1	54044	61804	78	72	5177	0.2	0.4	14.1	40.5	44.8	373448
96754	KILAUEA	26543	1120	25.0	30.4	25.1	12.1	7.4	45906	51884	64	41	688	0.3	0.0	6.4	50.3	43.0	370732
96755	KAPAAU	20337	869	22.4	24.3	39.5	11.1	2.8	52181	60501	76	65	660	1.4	1.1	20.9	58.9	17.7	244800
96756	KOLOA	29017	1723	24.0	24.2	32.2	12.1	7.5	51617	58186	75	59	993	0.6	0.0	3.6	51.9	43.9	366201
96757	KUALAPUU	21564	294	24.2	34.0	33.0	5.1	3.7	42991	49454	56	31	244	9.8	9.8	26.6	41.4	12.3	185227
96760	KURTISTOWN	15161	1982	42.0	24.0	24.9	6.3	2.8	32340	36975	19	10	1428	5.7	9.1	50.0	30.3	4.9	140025
96761	LAHAINA	29188	5877	17.4	21.0	35.2	14.7	11.7	61496	71145	86	82	3340	0.8	0.8	4.8	38.5	55.2	430070
96762	LAIE	15641	982	21.4	22.3	34.6	16.6	5.1	56095	66584	81	76	418	1.4	0.7	3.1	44.5	50.2	401190
96763	LANAI CITY	22590	1237	22.5	28.2	38.7	7.7	2.9	49468	57665	71	52	623	1.3	2.3	28.6	58.4	9.5	215372
96764	LAUPAHOEHOE	16254	351	30.8	29.6	33.6	4.0	2.0	39116	44541	43	20	289	2.1	2.4	51.2	35.6	8.7	161694
96766	LIHUE	23616	4300	21.4	25.1	36.6	11.5	5.4	53158	59445	77	69	2615	0.5	1.3	14.5	54.7	29.0	290876
96768	MAKAWAO	27096	5631	16.8	21.2	40.4	14.6	7.0	62311	71787	87	84	3517	0.7	0.4	4.0	48.5	46.5	388091
96769	MAKAWELI	12878	169	39.1	28.4	27.8	3.6	1.2	28466	29876	9	3	25	0.0	0.0	8.0	72.0	20.0	240625
96770	MAUNALOA	19473	216	37.0	32.9	18.5	7.9	3.7	32300	37964	19	8	126	6.4	11.1	29.4	27.8	25.4	186111
96771	MOUNTAIN VIEW	18179	1978	36.4	27.2	25.2	8.5	2.7	34960	39028	27	14	1595	9.8	9.3	35.0	37.5	8.3	163125
96772	NAALEHU	18448	1873	41.1	29.3	21.7	4.7	3.2	31647	35364	17	6	1475	12.9	13.2	41.2	28.7	4.0	135559
96773	NINOLE	23375	27	22.2	33.3	33.3	11.1	0.0	44047	49057	59	34	22	0.0	0.0	27.3	36.4	36.4	250000
96774	OOKALA	19743	105	19.1	28.6	37.1	12.4	2.9	52159	60000	76	64	89	0.0	5.6	31.5	38.2	24.7	217308
96776	PAAUILO	17662	421	24.9	35.2	30.2	7.4	2.4	42364	49739	54	30	351	5.1	19.9	33.6	23.4	18.0	143611
96777	PAHALA	13884	490	38.0	32.5	24.5	4.3	0.8	32307	36926	19	9	357	7.0	17.9	58.8	15.4	0.8	120500
96778	PAHOA	14887	3466	42.2	29.3	22.5	4.9	1.2	30889	35146	15	5	2628	7.2	14.1	52.4	21.2	5.1	130619
96779	PAIA	28703	688	14.7	22.7	38.1	14.4	10.2	65590	77819	89	88	523	0.0	0.0	5.5	59.7	34.8	332627
96780	PAPAALOA	24740	99	19.2	28.3	37.4	13.1	2.0	52148	62049	76	63	84	0.0	6.0	29.8	36.9	27.4	225000
96781	PAPAIKOU	17474	563	31.3	28.2	32.9	5.7	2.0	40865	47885	49	27	438	0.9	6.6	36.3	48.0	8.2	188500
96782	PEARL CITY	26119	11965	12.5	21.0	37.3	20.4	8.7	68059	78948	90	92	8013	0.6	2.2	10.3	49.2	37.8	358481
96783	PEPEEKEO	23711	713	32.3	24.7	28.2	10.9	3.9	44260	50544	59	36	536	2.1	1.7	26.1	56.9	13.3	215455
96785	VOLCANO	19184	1464	37.6	33.4	21.0	6.3	1.8	33009	37005	21	11	1078	7.6	12.5	41.3	29.7	8.9	146825
96786	WAHIAWA	16953	11305	25.2	32.7	29.9	9.9	2.4	43028	50063	56	32	3779	2.1	0.8	4.7	67.0	25.4	328125
96789	MILILANI	28522	15872	7.8	17.0	43.3	24.4	7.6	76473	88394	94	95	12293	0.5	1.5	12.8	50.3	35.0	340358
96790	KULA	39192	2572	16.5	21.2	31.6	17.5	13.2	64518	79156	88	85	1662	0.0	0.0	2.4	15.6	82.0	620385
96791	WAIALUA	21546	1929	21.8	25.1	34.9	13.2	5.0	52683	60780	76	67	1072	1.0	1.8	7.7	62.4	27.2	320968
96792	WAIANAE	14996	10380	27.5	23.7	34.0	10.6	4.2	48575	55470	69	50	6201	3.4	5.7	22.8	57.3	10.9	218617
96793	WAILUKU	23493	8170	18.8	24.5	37.2	13.2	6.3	55751	62948	80	75	5336	0.9	0.9	10.6	55.1	32.5	321776
96795	WAIMANALO	23272	2988	12.1	21.1	36.8	20.6	9.5	71249	83371	92	93	2275	1.9	2.3	9.7	39.0	47.1	384024
96796	WAIMEA	22507	683	22.6	29.1	33.2	12.3	2.8	48579	53230	69	51	330	0.6	3.0	10.6	57.6	28.2	314286
96797	WAIPAHU	22563	19713	12.3	21.6	39.8	19.1	7.3	66461	77578	89	91	13096	0.6	2.0	11.4	58.5	27.5	329234
96813	HONOLULU	31825	13623	26.5	28.6	25.8	11.4	7.7	45160	51157	62	39	6136	1.8	1.0	14.9	40.5	41.8	346849
96814	HONOLULU	30340	12710	36.3	29.2	23.5	7.2	3.8	35495	40461	29	16	4335	3.0	3.1	16.6	52.1	25.3	273831
96815	HONOLULU	32306	11188	30.3	30.2	23.9	9.1	6.5	40243	46066	47	24	4940	4.4	1.3	14.3	41.5	38.5	319718
96816	HONOLULU	34000	16564	15.8	22.7	31.7	17.0	12.8	64873	76457	88	86	10652	0.7	0.7	2.1	23.4	73.1	520510
96817	HONOLULU	25872	20695	30.1	25.1	25.8	11.0	8.0	44034	50841	59	33	8130	1.7	1.2	9.5	33.6	54.0	421940
96818	HONOLULU	21505	15304	13.6	34.0	35.3	11.4	5.7	51703	60053	75	60	5402	3.9	1.0	17.1	42.3	35.7	315611
96819	HONOLULU	18454	11506	22.4	24.4	30.8	14.6	7.8	53145	61119	77	68	5866	1.1	1.5	9.6	30.1	57.6	432534
96821	HONOLULU	46753	6949	7.1	12.4	31.2	23.0	26.2	98437	117246	98	100	5785	0.4	0.4	0.8	10.3	88.2	645139
96822	HONOLULU	32815	15501	23.4	26.3	27.7	12.5	10.2	50344	58305	73	53	7485	2.4	0.8	9.4	26.8	60.6	505349
96825	HONOLULU	39793	9009	8.4	12.1	34.1	26.3	19.0	91511	109297	97	99	7111	0.8	0.4	1.0	24.0	73.7	488997
96826	HONOLULU	24042	12879	30.3	32.8	27.4	7.6	1.9	39871	45187	46	23	4187	3.0	5.0	18.5	52.8	20.7	234287
96844	HONOLULU	17038	177	70.1	10.2	17.0	2.8	0.0	14643	17287	1	2	0	0.0	0.0	0.0	0.0	0.0	0
96853	HICKAM AFB	16806	245	11.0	44.9	31.0	12.7	0.4	47016	54827	66	44	2	0.0	0.0	0.0	100.0	0.0	187500
96858	FORT SHAFTER	22232	173	23.1	33.0	31.8	9.3	2.9	45203	51754	62	40	35	0.0	0.0	48.6	11.4	40.0	187500
96860	PEARL HARBOR	18378	179	9.5	28.5	37.4	19.0	5.6	59723	70561	84	81	21	14.3	4.8	14.3	28.6	38.1	337500
96862	BARBERS POINT	16492	384	8.1	56.3	31.0	2.9	1.8	39504	44945	44	22	4	0.0	0.0	0.0	100.0	0.0	350000
96863	M C B H KANEOHE BAY	16758	510	26.1	43.7	24.1	6.1	0.0	35634	41059	30	17	12	0.0	0.0	8.3	91.7	0.0	188889
	HAWAII	25763		20.1	24.4	33.2	14.5	7.9	55724	64555				1.5	1.9	12.2	44.3	40.1	348617
	UNITED STATES	25866		24.7	27.1	30.8	10.9	6.5	48124	56710				10.9	15.0	33.7	30.1	10.4	145905

ZIP CODE #	POST OFFICE NAME	FINANCIAL SERVICES: Auto Loan	FINANCIAL SERVICES: Home Loan	FINANCIAL SERVICES: Invest-ments	FINANCIAL SERVICES: Retire-ment Plans	THE HOME: Home Improvements: Home Repair	THE HOME: Home Improvements: Lawn & Garden	THE HOME: Furnishings: Comput-ers & Hard-ware	THE HOME: Furnishings: Major Appli-ances	THE HOME: Furnishings: TV, Radio, Sound Equip-ment	THE HOME: Furnishings: Furni-ture	ENTERTAINMENT: Dine out/ Carry out	ENTERTAINMENT: Sports Equip-ment	ENTERTAINMENT: Fees & Tickets	ENTERTAINMENT: Toys & Games	ENTERTAINMENT: Travel	ENTERTAINMENT: Cable TV	PERSONAL: Apparel & Services	PERSONAL: Auto Repairs	PERSONAL: Health Insur-ance	PERSONAL: Pets & Supplies
96701	AIEA	101	112	156	127	115	110	123	119	110	118	139	153	117	134	121	99	137	127	97	125
96704	CAPTAIN COOK	81	96	115	99	96	94	93	92	86	92	108	110	94	111	94	81	108	92	80	99
96705	ELEELE	71	84	116	94	88	83	89	88	79	85	99	112	86	96	90	71	98	92	72	91
96706	EWA BEACH	101	113	132	123	112	107	114	111	102	113	129	138	111	126	111	93	128	114	92	119
96707	KAPOLEI	116	126	137	135	123	119	123	121	113	125	143	146	123	140	119	103	141	122	101	131
96708	HAIKU	101	111	111	113	107	106	106	105	99	107	125	124	106	126	104	93	123	104	92	115
96710	HAKALAU	68	80	113	91	84	78	86	84	75	82	94	110	82	91	86	66	93	90	67	87
96712	HALEIWA	99	110	140	118	110	110	115	111	107	112	134	137	113	134	113	100	133	115	96	119
96713	HANA	88	80	78	80	87	91	80	88	81	77	98	107	73	96	83	81	93	89	91	109
96716	HANAPEPE	66	78	110	89	82	76	84	82	73	80	91	107	79	88	84	64	91	87	65	85
96717	HAUULA	72	85	119	96	89	83	91	89	79	87	100	114	87	97	91	71	99	94	71	92
96718	HAWAII NATIONAL PARK	48	57	81	65	60	55	62	60	53	58	67	78	58	65	62	47	67	64	48	62
96719	HAWI	92	110	143	119	113	110	111	110	100	108	126	136	110	123	113	92	125	113	94	116
96720	HILO	72	78	108	88	81	78	89	84	80	83	100	109	83	96	87	72	98	91	70	89
96722	PRINCEVILLE	145	131	119	125	140	152	126	139	133	125	162	164	120	162	131	137	154	139	151	176
96725	HOLUALOA	99	110	131	112	110	115	108	107	105	107	131	126	111	135	110	103	129	107	101	118
96727	HONOKAA	77	92	122	100	94	90	95	93	84	91	106	118	92	105	95	76	105	97	77	98
96728	HONOMU	64	75	84	72	75	81	72	72	71	71	88	81	75	91	74	72	87	71	72	78
96729	HOOLEHUA	73	87	123	99	91	84	94	92	81	89	102	119	89	98	94	71	101	97	73	95
96730	KAAAWA	92	106	132	110	105	106	105	102	99	104	125	122	107	128	105	95	124	103	92	111
96731	KAHUKU	74	87	124	100	92	85	94	92	81	89	103	120	89	99	94	72	102	98	73	95
96732	KAHULUI	85	101	143	115	106	98	108	106	94	103	118	138	103	114	108	83	117	113	84	110
96734	KAILUA	120	153	200	150	148	154	145	141	137	143	172	167	153	183	149	134	173	142	125	150
96738	WAIKOLOA	103	116	111	120	110	107	104	104	96	109	122	121	107	122	102	89	120	101	88	114
96740	KAILUA KONA	108	112	115	110	113	119	107	110	106	107	132	128	107	134	109	106	129	109	109	128
96741	KALAHEO	93	113	132	116	113	111	107	106	99	105	124	128	111	128	109	94	123	106	93	115
96742	KALAUPAPA	19	17	25	18	17	20	22	20	23	20	28	23	21	28	21	23	27	22	21	22
96743	KAMUELA	110	120	137	124	121	121	118	118	111	117	139	143	117	139	118	106	137	120	107	132
96744	KANEOHE	110	132	181	144	135	130	136	133	121	131	153	167	133	152	137	111	152	139	110	139
96746	KAPAA	83	93	111	100	95	92	94	94	86	92	108	116	92	107	94	80	106	96	81	102
96747	KAUMAKANI	52	62	87	70	64	60	66	65	57	63	72	84	63	70	66	51	72	69	51	67
96748	KAUNAKAKAI	62	73	103	83	76	71	78	77	68	74	86	100	74	82	78	60	85	82	61	79
96749	KEAAU	71	78	82	81	76	75	76	75	70	76	89	90	75	89	74	66	87	75	65	82
96750	KEALAKEKUA	104	109	134	118	116	114	114	117	105	109	130	148	106	127	115	98	127	122	105	132
96752	KEKAHA	68	81	114	92	85	78	87	85	75	82	95	111	82	91	87	66	94	90	67	88
96753	KIHEI	111	102	109	107	107	112	107	111	106	105	131	137	100	126	107	102	126	115	108	132
96754	KILAUEA	97	108	129	106	104	109	106	103	104	108	132	118	108	135	106	102	131	105	96	112
96755	KAPAAU	72	86	120	97	89	83	91	90	79	87	100	116	87	97	92	70	99	95	72	93
96756	KOLOA	103	102	115	107	109	110	104	110	100	100	123	138	97	119	107	96	119	114	105	129
96757	KUALAPUU	77	92	130	104	96	89	99	97	85	94	107	126	93	104	99	75	107	102	76	100
96760	KURTISTOWN	62	68	70	70	66	65	65	65	61	66	77	77	65	77	64	57	76	65	56	71
96761	LAHAINA	126	120	138	128	126	128	127	130	123	125	153	162	119	146	127	117	148	136	122	150
96762	LAIE	81	95	135	109	100	93	103	101	89	98	112	131	97	108	103	78	111	107	80	104
96763	LANAI CITY	72	85	121	97	89	83	92	90	79	87	100	117	87	97	92	70	100	96	71	93
96764	LAUPAHOEHOE	56	66	90	73	69	66	70	68	62	66	78	87	67	76	70	56	77	72	57	71
96766	LIHUE	83	96	134	109	101	95	103	102	90	98	114	130	98	108	103	81	112	107	83	105
96768	MAKAWAO	104	119	132	125	117	114	115	113	105	115	133	137	115	134	114	98	132	114	97	123
96769	MAKAWELI	51	61	86	69	63	59	65	64	56	62	71	83	62	69	65	50	71	68	50	66
96770	MAUNALOA	67	79	113	91	83	77	86	84	74	81	93	109	81	90	86	65	93	89	66	87
96771	MOUNTAIN VIEW	68	69	68	70	69	71	69	69	66	68	82	82	67	81	67	64	80	70	65	77
96772	NAALEHU	70	56	46	56	61	70	62	67	67	59	79	77	56	75	62	68	73	68	75	79
96773	NINOLE	65	76	87	74	76	82	73	73	72	72	90	83	77	92	76	72	88	72	73	79
96774	OOKALA	75	87	98	84	86	93	83	83	82	82	102	94	87	106	86	83	100	82	83	90
96776	PAAUILO	63	76	95	80	77	76	76	75	69	73	87	91	76	88	77	65	86	76	65	79
96777	PAHALA	48	57	81	65	60	55	62	60	53	58	67	78	58	65	62	47	67	64	48	62
96778	PAHOA	58	54	51	55	55	60	56	57	57	55	70	67	54	70	55	56	67	57	58	65
96779	PAIA	117	133	162	129	128	136	127	125	125	131	159	141	133	165	129	125	160	126	117	136
96780	PAPAALOA	76	89	98	84	88	96	84	84	84	83	104	94	89	109	88	86	102	83	86	92
96781	PAPAIKOU	60	71	100	81	74	69	76	75	66	72	83	97	72	80	76	58	82	79	59	77
96782	PEARL CITY	100	115	160	130	119	112	124	121	109	118	137	157	118	132	123	97	136	129	97	126
96783	PEPEEKEO	75	89	126	101	93	86	96	94	83	91	104	122	90	101	96	73	104	99	74	97
96785	VOLCANO	63	57	54	57	59	65	62	63	64	59	77	73	59	76	61	64	74	64	66	72
96786	WAHIAWA	72	67	87	75	66	68	81	75	76	77	96	97	74	91	75	70	94	83	64	81
96789	MILILANI	110	126	155	139	127	120	128	125	113	126	144	157	124	140	126	102	142	129	102	133
96790	KULA	119	156	189	151	152	156	140	138	132	140	165	159	151	177	146	131	166	135	126	149
96791	WAIALUA	86	92	125	105	95	91	102	99	91	98	115	127	96	110	100	82	114	105	81	104
96792	WAIANAE	73	83	111	91	85	82	88	86	79	85	100	108	85	98	88	73	99	90	72	90
96793	WAILUKU	86	100	138	112	105	98	107	105	93	101	117	135	101	114	107	84	116	111	85	110
96795	WAIMANALO	104	123	174	140	129	119	132	129	114	126	144	168	125	139	132	101	143	137	102	134
96796	WAIMEA	72	86	121	98	90	83	92	90	80	88	101	117	87	97	92	70	100	96	71	93
96797	WAIPAHU	95	113	157	128	118	109	121	118	104	115	132	153	114	127	120	92	131	125	94	122
96813	HONOLULU	82	96	137	109	100	94	104	101	90	99	114	131	98	110	104	80	113	107	81	105
96814	HONOLULU	63	72	107	80	75	72	78	76	71	75	90	98	75	89	79	66	89	81	64	81
96815	HONOLULU	75	84	129	91	85	86	92	88	87	89	110	110	90	112	93	84	110	93	78	94
96816	HONOLULU	112	134	189	151	140	130	143	140	124	136	156	180	136	151	143	110	155	148	111	145
96817	HONOLULU	80	93	132	106	98	91	101	99	88	96	111	128	95	107	101	78	110	105	78	102
96818	HONOLULU	92	85	108	97	85	86	103	96	95	97	119	126	93	111	96	85	117	106	81	103
96819	HONOLULU	89	103	144	116	107	100	112	109	98	106	124	141	105	119	111	87	122	116	88	113
96821	HONOLULU	161	195	272	214	201	194	200	197	177	193	223	247	197	219	203	161	222	204	163	206
96822	HONOLULU	90	108	151	122	112	105	115	112	100	109	126	145	109	122	115	89	125	119	90	116
96825	HONOLULU	137	169	225	181	171	166	169	166	151	164	190	205	168	191	171	140	189	170	139	174
96826	HONOLULU	59	69	99	79	73	68	75	73	65	71	82	95	71	80	75	58	82	78	58	76
96844	HONOLULU	37	22	28	25	22	27	43	32	42	37	53	44	35	47	35	37	49	39	30	36
96853	HICKAM AFB	92	58	56	67	53	63	87	75	88	81	110	100	74	99	71	80	105	88	69	85
96858	FORT SHAFTER	76	73	93	83	73	73	87	81	79	82	100	106	79	94	81	71	98	89	68	87
96860	PEARL HARBOR	115	73	70	84	67	79	109	94	110	101	138	125	93	123	89	101	132	111	87	107
96862	BARBERS POINT	87	55	53	64	51	60	83	71	84	77	105	95	71	94	68	77	100	84	66	81
96863	M C B H KANEOHE BAY	71	45	43	52	41	49	67	58	68	63	85	77	57	76	55	62	82	68	54	66
	HAWAII	94	105	138	115	107	104	111	108	100	107	126	137	107	123	110	92	125	114	91	115
	UNITED STATES	100	100	100	100	100	100	100	100	100	100	100	100	100	100	100	100	100	100	100	100

IDAHO

POPULATION CHANGE

A 83201-83440

#	POST OFFICE NAME	COUNTY FIPS CODE	POPULATION 2000	2004	2009	2000-2004 ANNUAL RATE % Rate	State Centile	HOUSEHOLDS 2000	2004	2009	% Annual Rate 2000-2004	2004 Average HH Size	FAMILIES 2000	2004	% Annual Rate 2000-2004
83201	POCATELLO	005	35989	36441	36885	0.3	32	13110	13465	13784	0.6	2.59	8973	9068	0.3
83202	POCATELLO	005	16692	17254	17492	0.8	48	5541	5876	6058	1.4	2.92	4367	4559	1.0
83203	FORT HALL	005	132	143	149	1.9	78	40	44	47	2.3	3.25	33	36	2.1
83204	POCATELLO	077	17535	17370	17332	-0.2	15	6648	6685	6751	0.1	2.51	4402	4351	-0.3
83209	POCATELLO	005	1	1	1	0.0	24	1	1	1	0.0	1.00	1	0	-100.0
83210	ABERDEEN	011	3538	3565	3609	0.2	28	1125	1141	1165	0.3	3.11	870	866	-0.1
83211	AMERICAN FALLS	077	5960	5746	5534	-0.9	4	2030	1981	1931	-0.6	2.87	1548	1492	-0.9
83212	ARBON	077	122	118	114	-0.8	6	44	43	43	-0.5	2.74	35	34	-0.7
83213	ARCO	023	1817	1803	1794	-0.2	17	716	729	738	0.4	2.44	491	491	0.0
83214	ARIMO	005	603	594	589	-0.4	13	176	178	179	0.3	3.33	144	143	-0.2
83217	BANCROFT	029	835	817	799	-0.5	11	289	291	293	0.2	2.81	219	218	-0.1
83220	BERN	007	227	238	252	1.1	60	75	81	87	1.8	2.94	59	63	1.6
83221	BLACKFOOT	011	23508	24214	24857	0.7	44	7666	8034	8371	1.1	2.98	6103	6332	0.9
83226	CHALLIS	037	2530	2488	2429	-0.4	12	1032	1044	1048	0.3	2.38	717	715	-0.1
83227	CLAYTON	037	8	8	8	0.0	24	3	3	3	0.0	2.67	2	2	0.0
83228	CLIFTON	041	431	441	460	0.5	39	124	129	136	0.9	3.42	105	109	0.9
83230	CONDA	029	15	15	15	0.0	24	7	7	7	0.0	2.14	5	6	4.4
83232	DAYTON	041	715	745	783	1.0	55	208	221	235	1.4	3.37	178	187	1.2
83234	DOWNEY	005	1271	1236	1222	-0.7	9	455	454	457	-0.1	2.68	344	337	-0.5
83235	ELLIS	059	218	235	259	1.8	76	103	113	128	2.2	2.08	70	76	2.1
83236	FIRTH	011	4403	4566	4686	0.9	51	1364	1448	1512	1.4	3.13	1120	1178	1.2
83237	FRANKLIN	041	1119	1204	1287	1.7	74	330	358	385	1.9	3.36	281	303	1.8
83238	GENEVA	007	118	119	123	0.2	28	36	37	40	0.7	3.14	27	27	0.0
83241	GRACE	029	2009	1939	1884	-0.8	5	702	696	694	-0.2	2.79	555	544	-0.5
83243	HOLBROOK	071	202	210	211	0.9	53	60	64	65	1.5	3.28	51	53	0.9
83244	HOWE	023	206	204	203	-0.2	15	69	70	71	0.3	2.91	57	58	0.4
83245	INKOM	005	1656	1733	1773	1.1	58	551	593	618	1.7	2.92	460	488	1.4
83246	LAVA HOT SPRINGS	005	918	922	918	0.1	26	373	384	389	0.7	2.38	243	244	0.1
83250	MCCAMMON	005	1989	1929	1907	-0.7	8	683	680	685	-0.1	2.83	553	543	-0.4
83251	MACKAY	037	1255	1245	1219	-0.2	16	510	520	523	0.5	2.33	343	344	0.1
83252	MALAD CITY	071	3923	3914	3870	-0.1	21	1370	1392	1401	0.4	2.78	1042	1046	0.1
83253	MAY	059	269	292	326	2.0	80	119	132	150	2.5	2.21	80	88	2.3
83254	MONTPELIER	007	4733	4868	5084	0.7	43	1646	1731	1850	1.2	2.78	1237	1284	0.9
83255	MOORE	023	896	885	878	-0.3	13	310	315	320	0.4	2.80	257	259	0.2
83261	PARIS	007	877	932	991	1.4	67	313	341	371	2.0	2.73	244	263	1.8
83262	PINGREE	011	1297	1288	1299	-0.2	17	400	405	416	0.3	3.18	325	326	0.1
83263	PRESTON	041	8070	8561	9125	1.4	67	2526	2709	2916	1.7	3.13	2061	2189	1.4
83271	ROCKLAND	077	569	551	531	-0.8	7	175	172	169	-0.4	3.20	138	134	-0.7
83272	SAINT CHARLES	007	200	215	230	1.7	74	78	86	94	2.3	2.49	58	63	2.0
83274	SHELLEY	019	8621	8727	8852	0.3	32	2674	2774	2866	0.9	3.13	2224	2285	0.6
83276	SODA SPRINGS	029	4476	4531	4508	0.3	32	1569	1628	1660	0.9	2.74	1204	1235	0.6
83278	STANLEY	037	535	532	521	-0.1	19	221	225	225	0.4	2.24	134	134	0.0
83283	THATCHER	041	115	134	149	3.7	93	39	46	52	4.0	2.91	32	37	3.5
83285	WAYAN	019	117	119	123	0.4	35	45	47	50	1.0	2.53	35	36	0.7
83286	WESTON	041	879	953	1023	1.9	79	249	274	298	2.3	3.48	216	236	2.1
83287	FISH HAVEN	007	183	198	213	1.9	78	87	97	107	2.6	2.04	65	72	2.4
83301	TWIN FALLS	083	42152	43900	45868	1.0	54	15953	16849	17817	1.3	2.53	11019	11465	0.9
83302	ROGERSON	083	133	139	145	1.0	57	55	59	62	1.7	2.31	41	43	1.1
83313	BELLEVUE	013	3170	3573	4113	2.9	88	1181	1356	1583	3.3	2.63	863	973	2.9
83314	BLISS	047	921	979	1037	1.5	68	332	353	374	1.5	2.77	241	252	1.1
83316	BUHL	083	9358	9573	9918	0.5	39	3506	3632	3806	0.8	2.62	2583	2637	0.5
83318	BURLEY	031	15898	16139	16463	0.4	33	5297	5452	5628	0.7	2.90	4066	4131	0.4
83320	CAREY	013	950	1006	1122	1.4	65	310	334	378	1.8	3.01	242	258	1.5
83321	CASTLEFORD	083	370	391	408	1.3	64	141	151	160	1.6	2.59	103	109	1.3
83322	CORRAL	025	55	61	70	2.5	83	18	21	24	3.7	2.90	13	15	3.4
83323	DECLO	031	1778	2020	2183	3.1	90	546	634	694	3.6	3.19	447	515	3.4
83324	DIETRICH	063	540	582	639	1.8	76	172	188	208	2.1	3.10	133	144	1.9
83325	EDEN	053	1050	1054	1074	0.1	26	389	394	403	0.3	2.68	298	297	-0.1
83327	FAIRFIELD	025	936	1044	1190	2.6	86	378	431	501	3.1	2.42	274	307	2.7
83328	FILER	083	4434	4678	4897	1.3	63	1591	1694	1791	1.5	2.75	1181	1239	1.1
83330	GOODING	047	5920	6135	6411	0.8	50	2157	2235	2333	0.8	2.67	1548	1580	0.5
83332	HAGERMAN	083	2183	2204	2277	0.2	30	869	883	914	0.4	2.49	600	599	0.2
83333	HAILEY	013	9918	11460	13350	3.5	92	3892	4578	5417	3.9	2.47	2611	3004	3.4
83334	HANSEN	031	1950	2043	2132	1.1	59	660	701	741	1.4	2.90	511	535	1.1
83335	HAZELTON	053	1640	1691	1749	0.7	46	554	574	594	0.8	2.95	433	443	0.5
83336	HEYBURN	067	5116	5177	5241	0.3	31	1767	1833	1894	0.9	2.82	1384	1417	0.6
83338	JEROME	053	15486	16062	16679	0.9	51	5311	5525	5744	0.9	2.89	4041	4152	0.6
83340	KETCHUM	013	4947	5269	5876	1.5	69	2394	2597	2946	1.9	1.96	1122	1172	1.0
83341	KIMBERLY	083	4791	4956	5131	0.8	48	1613	1683	1757	1.0	2.92	1269	1307	0.7
83342	MALTA	031	2299	2297	2325	0.0	22	778	794	816	0.5	2.89	632	638	0.2
83343	MINIDOKA	067	240	261	275	2.0	81	65	71	75	2.1	3.62	56	61	2.0
83344	MURTAUGH	083	1115	1109	1134	-0.1	19	338	340	352	0.1	3.18	277	275	-0.2
83346	OAKLEY	031	1382	1486	1557	1.7	74	441	480	509	2.0	3.08	345	371	1.7
83347	PAUL	067	3245	3145	3153	-0.7	8	1164	1156	1181	-0.2	2.72	876	858	-0.5
83348	PICABO	013	6	7	7	3.7	93	3	3	4	0.0	2.33	2	3	10.0
83349	RICHFIELD	063	879	983	1100	2.7	87	311	352	398	3.0	2.79	230	257	2.7
83350	RUPERT	067	11603	11933	12258	0.7	43	3964	4125	4293	0.9	2.86	3031	3119	0.7
83352	SHOSHONE	063	2601	2781	3042	1.6	72	957	1032	1138	1.8	2.66	681	723	1.4
83355	WENDELL	047	5302	5571	5876	1.2	61	1739	1831	1931	1.2	3.02	1359	1414	0.9
83401	IDAHO FALLS	019	30239	31380	33395	0.9	52	10290	10942	11895	1.5	2.81	7689	8044	1.1
83402	IDAHO FALLS	019	24679	25636	27281	0.9	52	9018	9533	10324	1.3	2.66	6330	6557	0.8
83404	IDAHO FALLS	019	18263	19566	21129	1.6	72	6580	7168	7870	2.0	2.71	5027	5421	1.8
83406	IDAHO FALLS	019	8432	10366	11982	5.0	96	2504	3179	3764	5.8	3.22	2145	2684	5.4
83420	ASHTON	043	2606	2666	2792	0.5	39	899	938	1003	1.0	2.81	689	711	0.7
83422	DRIGGS	081	2149	2747	3799	6.0	100	732	950	1337	6.3	2.88	509	651	6.0
83423	DUBOIS	033	949	983	1023	0.8	49	310	317	323	0.5	3.10	236	238	0.2
83424	FELT	081	193	243	335	5.6	99	52	67	94	6.1	3.63	39	50	6.0
83425	HAMER	051	586	560	579	-1.1	4	162	158	166	-0.6	3.54	135	130	-0.9
83428	IRWIN	019	188	194	204	0.7	47	79	84	91	1.5	2.31	58	61	1.4
83429	ISLAND PARK	043	826	904	982	2.2	81	372	420	465	2.9	2.15	266	297	2.6
83431	LEWISVILLE	051	934	973	1033	1.0	55	301	322	349	1.6	3.02	253	268	1.4
83434	MENAN	051	1605	1680	1785	1.1	58	487	521	564	1.6	3.22	418	444	1.4
83435	MONTEVIEW	051	463	451	469	-0.6	9	139	138	146	-0.2	3.26	115	113	-0.4
83436	NEWDALE	065	447	454	478	0.4	34	121	126	136	1.0	3.60	98	101	0.7
83440	REXBURG	065	25440	28319	32390	2.6	84	6677	7621	8938	3.2	3.54	4461	5013	2.8
	IDAHO					1.8					2.1	2.65			1.8
	UNITED STATES					1.2					1.3	2.58			1.1

ZIP CODE #	POST OFFICE NAME	RACE (%) White 2000	White 2004	Black 2000	Black 2004	Asian/Pacific 2000	Asian/Pacific 2004	% Hispanic Origin 2000	% Hispanic Origin 2004	2004 AGE DISTRIBUTION (%) 0-4	5-9	10-14	15-19	20-24	25-44	45-64	65-84	85+	18+	MEDIAN AGE 2004	% 2004 Males	% 2004 Females
83201	POCATELLO	92.4	92.0	0.8	0.8	1.6	1.8	4.7	5.3	8.5	7.2	6.7	7.6	11.5	28.7	19.5	8.9	1.5	74.0	29.1	49.0	51.0
83202	POCATELLO	84.8	83.8	0.3	0.3	0.9	1.0	5.5	6.1	9.2	8.7	8.5	7.7	7.9	27.2	21.6	8.1	1.1	68.9	30.5	49.0	51.0
83203	FORT HALL	34.1	35.0	0.0	0.0	0.8	0.7	3.0	3.5	8.4	8.4	8.4	8.4	7.7	30.1	21.0	7.0	0.7	69.2	29.5	50.4	49.7
83204	POCATELLO	91.3	90.9	0.7	0.8	0.8	0.9	5.3	5.9	7.8	6.9	7.1	7.8	9.2	29.5	23.0	7.6	1.1	73.7	31.4	50.4	49.6
83209	POCATELLO	100.0	100.0	0.0	0.0	0.0	0.0	0.0	0.0	0.0	0.0	0.0	0.0	100.0	0.0	0.0	0.0	0.0	100.0	22.5	100.0	0.0
83210	ABERDEEN	76.8	74.9	0.1	0.1	0.4	0.5	28.8	31.3	10.4	9.3	10.0	8.4	6.2	24.5	19.6	10.0	1.5	64.5	30.4	50.3	49.7
83211	AMERICAN FALLS	84.1	82.8	0.1	0.1	0.3	0.4	25.8	28.4	9.3	7.9	9.3	8.2	7.8	24.9	22.0	9.4	1.3	68.0	31.3	50.2	49.8
83212	ARBON	95.9	96.6	0.0	0.0	0.0	0.0	4.1	3.4	8.5	8.5	10.2	8.5	6.8	18.6	27.1	11.0	0.9	67.8	33.3	50.9	49.2
83213	ARCO	94.4	94.3	0.4	0.4	0.2	0.2	4.3	4.3	6.1	6.7	8.2	7.1	5.7	20.9	28.7	14.6	2.1	74.5	41.4	49.4	50.6
83214	ARIMO	97.4	97.3	0.0	0.0	0.5	0.5	0.7	0.7	9.1	9.4	8.9	8.9	7.4	19.9	26.8	7.6	2.0	67.0	31.1	50.8	49.2
83217	BANCROFT	97.0	96.9	0.1	0.1	0.1	0.1	2.6	2.8	9.1	9.3	9.8	6.9	6.0	21.4	24.9	9.8	2.9	67.4	34.4	49.7	50.3
83220	BERN	98.7	98.7	0.4	0.4	0.0	0.0	0.9	1.3	8.0	7.6	8.8	8.4	7.6	19.3	24.8	14.3	1.3	70.6	36.0	48.7	51.3
83221	BLACKFOOT	86.3	85.1	0.2	0.2	0.8	0.9	13.4	14.9	9.2	8.3	8.6	8.4	8.8	24.6	21.6	9.4	1.3	68.6	30.1	50.1	49.9
83226	CHALLIS	97.7	97.7	0.0	0.0	0.1	0.1	4.8	4.9	5.4	6.2	7.8	6.8	3.7	24.1	31.2	13.1	1.7	75.6	42.7	51.1	48.9
83227	CLAYTON	100.0	100.0	0.0	0.0	0.0	0.0	0.0	0.0	0.0	0.0	0.0	0.0	25.0	12.5	62.5	0.0	0.0	100.0	51.0	87.5	12.5
83228	CLIFTON	95.4	95.0	0.2	0.2	0.0	0.0	4.6	5.2	11.8	10.4	9.3	7.7	7.3	24.0	19.7	8.4	1.4	63.7	27.8	51.9	48.1
83230	CONDA	93.3	100.0	0.0	0.0	0.0	0.0	0.0	0.0	13.3	13.3	13.3	13.3	13.3	26.7	6.7	0.0	0.0	60.0	18.8	53.3	46.7
83232	DAYTON	96.1	95.7	0.1	0.1	0.1	0.1	4.3	4.8	10.5	10.1	9.9	8.5	7.3	24.7	19.7	8.2	1.2	63.9	27.8	51.1	48.9
83234	DOWNEY	97.2	96.9	0.2	0.2	0.5	0.5	1.4	1.5	7.0	7.3	9.1	7.4	5.7	22.1	22.6	15.5	3.2	71.1	38.5	50.0	50.0
83235	ELLIS	95.4	95.3	0.0	0.0	0.0	0.0	2.8	3.0	4.3	4.3	5.5	6.0	4.7	13.6	36.2	23.8	1.7	82.1	54.0	53.2	46.8
83236	FIRTH	50.7	50.5	0.2	0.2	0.1	0.1	9.5	10.0	8.8	8.4	9.5	9.7	7.8	25.9	21.2	7.7	1.0	66.9	29.3	49.7	50.3
83237	FRANKLIN	90.0	89.1	0.0	0.0	0.1	0.1	10.2	11.3	11.3	10.8	11.0	8.7	6.9	25.1	17.2	7.8	1.3	61.5	26.2	50.4	49.6
83238	GENEVA	97.5	98.3	0.0	0.0	0.0	0.0	1.7	2.5	5.9	5.9	7.6	7.6	6.7	21.9	26.1	15.1	3.4	74.8	41.4	49.6	50.4
83241	GRACE	94.7	94.6	0.1	0.1	0.1	0.1	6.7	6.8	8.4	8.4	8.5	6.9	6.3	23.2	24.9	11.4	2.3	70.6	35.5	51.4	48.6
83243	HOLBROOK	96.5	96.7	0.0	0.0	0.0	0.0	3.0	2.9	8.1	8.1	8.6	9.1	7.6	22.9	25.2	9.1	1.4	70.5	32.7	54.8	45.2
83244	HOWE	94.7	94.6	0.0	0.0	0.5	0.5	5.3	4.9	9.8	10.8	8.8	4.9	4.9	26.5	21.6	11.8	1.0	67.7	33.3	48.5	51.5
83245	INKOM	96.5	96.3	0.4	0.5	0.2	0.3	2.1	2.3	6.2	6.6	8.5	9.2	7.0	24.1	28.5	9.2	0.8	73.1	37.1	50.3	49.7
83246	LAVA HOT SPRINGS	97.5	97.3	0.0	0.0	0.2	0.2	2.2	2.4	6.1	6.2	6.8	8.6	6.4	21.2	29.1	13.6	2.2	75.0	42.2	50.7	49.4
83250	MCCAMMON	96.7	96.6	0.3	0.3	0.4	0.4	1.7	1.9	5.7	6.3	8.3	8.5	7.6	21.3	29.3	11.9	1.2	74.5	38.8	50.3	49.7
83251	MACKAY	95.9	96.0	0.0	0.0	0.0	0.0	4.3	4.3	5.5	5.7	6.7	6.2	5.1	22.9	30.9	15.3	1.8	77.5	43.8	49.5	50.5
83252	MALAD CITY	97.6	97.6	0.1	0.1	0.2	0.2	2.3	2.3	8.1	7.3	7.8	7.4	8.0	21.7	23.8	13.6	2.4	72.1	36.5	50.8	49.2
83253	MAY	94.8	94.9	0.0	0.0	0.4	0.3	2.6	2.7	4.1	3.8	5.1	6.2	4.5	13.7	36.0	25.0	1.7	82.9	55.1	53.1	46.9
83254	MONTPELIER	97.3	97.1	0.1	0.1	0.2	0.2	2.8	3.2	7.6	7.4	8.4	9.0	7.9	21.8	23.2	12.6	2.1	70.6	34.7	49.5	50.5
83255	MOORE	95.2	95.3	0.0	0.0	0.2	0.2	3.7	3.7	6.6	7.1	8.7	7.6	5.8	22.2	26.7	13.9	1.6	72.8	39.4	50.4	49.6
83261	PARIS	98.9	98.9	0.2	0.2	0.0	0.0	0.9	0.9	7.4	7.2	8.5	8.6	6.7	18.2	26.0	15.3	2.2	71.7	39.8	49.5	50.5
83262	PINGREE	85.2	83.7	0.2	0.2	0.9	1.0	15.7	17.3	8.4	8.5	9.3	10.3	8.3	24.8	21.7	7.4	1.2	67.2	29.0	50.5	49.5
83263	PRESTON	95.4	94.9	0.1	0.2	0.2	0.2	4.9	5.5	10.6	9.8	9.4	8.1	7.1	24.8	18.6	9.7	2.1	65.0	28.7	49.7	50.3
83271	ROCKLAND	96.0	95.6	0.0	0.0	0.2	0.2	3.5	4.0	8.5	8.7	9.4	8.7	6.4	19.4	26.5	11.1	1.3	67.9	34.3	50.6	49.4
83272	SAINT CHARLES	98.5	98.1	0.0	0.0	0.0	0.0	2.0	1.9	7.0	7.0	7.9	8.4	5.6	18.1	26.5	16.7	2.8	73.0	42.2	51.2	48.8
83274	SHELLEY	92.1	91.4	0.1	0.1	0.4	0.5	8.6	9.6	9.5	8.9	9.2	8.8	7.9	24.9	21.1	8.7	1.1	66.8	29.4	50.2	49.8
83276	SODA SPRINGS	96.7	96.7	0.0	0.0	0.3	0.3	2.9	2.9	7.4	7.3	8.1	8.4	7.8	24.4	24.0	11.4	1.4	71.9	34.8	49.3	50.7
83278	STANLEY	98.3	98.3	0.0	0.0	0.0	0.0	0.9	0.9	5.8	6.2	6.0	4.5	2.8	26.5	40.8	7.0	0.4	79.3	43.9	53.6	46.4
83283	THATCHER	96.5	96.3	0.0	0.0	0.9	0.8	4.4	5.2	9.0	9.0	10.5	9.0	4.5	21.6	26.9	8.2	1.5	64.9	34.0	53.0	47.0
83285	WAYAN	95.7	96.6	0.0	0.0	0.0	0.0	2.6	3.4	5.0	6.7	7.6	6.7	5.9	18.5	32.8	15.1	1.7	75.6	44.7	50.4	49.6
83286	WESTON	97.6	97.6	0.0	0.0	0.3	0.4	3.3	3.7	10.1	9.2	11.2	10.0	6.9	24.6	19.6	7.4	1.1	62.1	26.7	50.8	49.2
83287	FISH HAVEN	98.4	98.5	0.0	0.0	0.0	0.0	1.1	1.5	7.1	7.1	8.1	8.1	5.6	16.7	27.8	17.2	2.5	73.2	43.1	50.5	49.5
83301	TWIN FALLS	92.4	91.8	0.2	0.3	1.1	1.3	8.4	9.4	7.7	7.0	7.0	7.2	8.5	25.9	22.7	11.5	2.5	74.2	34.6	48.6	51.4
83302	ROGERSON	93.2	92.8	0.0	0.0	0.0	0.0	12.0	12.2	5.8	7.2	8.6	8.6	5.0	29.5	25.2	8.6	1.4	71.9	35.8	53.2	46.8
83313	BELLEVUE	88.7	87.9	0.1	0.1	0.9	1.0	14.5	15.9	6.7	7.0	7.1	6.4	6.4	30.9	28.8	6.0	0.8	75.4	36.6	53.3	46.7
83314	BLISS	84.9	83.7	1.1	1.3	0.0	0.0	18.9	20.8	10.1	7.0	7.3	7.5	6.8	25.3	23.3	11.6	1.1	71.0	35.3	52.1	47.9
83316	BUHL	90.8	90.0	0.1	0.1	0.4	0.5	12.4	13.9	7.2	7.4	7.4	6.8	6.3	24.3	24.9	13.6	2.2	73.7	37.6	50.5	49.5
83318	BURLEY	83.3	82.0	0.2	0.2	0.5	0.6	20.3	22.4	9.2	8.3	9.0	7.8	8.0	24.1	21.0	10.6	2.1	68.8	31.2	49.9	50.2
83320	CAREY	88.6	87.8	0.1	0.1	0.3	0.4	13.6	14.7	8.7	9.1	9.0	7.3	7.6	24.4	23.9	8.8	1.6	68.9	31.9	52.7	47.3
83321	CASTLEFORD	90.8	90.3	0.0	0.0	0.5	0.5	20.5	22.5	6.1	6.7	8.4	6.9	5.6	26.3	26.6	11.8	1.5	74.2	37.4	49.4	50.6
83322	CORRAL	94.6	95.1	1.8	1.6	0.0	0.0	5.5	6.6	3.3	6.6	8.2	6.6	3.3	26.2	31.2	13.1	1.6	75.4	42.5	52.5	47.5
83323	DECLO	85.9	84.4	0.1	0.2	0.3	0.4	16.1	18.1	9.8	9.8	9.9	7.9	6.4	25.6	21.9	7.8	0.9	65.6	30.7	50.7	49.3
83324	DIETRICH	83.7	82.3	0.9	1.2	0.2	0.2	15.4	17.2	8.4	8.4	9.3	8.6	7.6	25.6	22.9	8.6	0.7	68.7	30.9	53.8	46.2
83325	EDEN	86.4	85.2	0.1	0.1	0.9	1.0	15.5	17.3	8.3	8.1	7.8	7.3	6.4	25.1	24.8	10.7	1.6	71.4	34.9	52.1	47.9
83327	FAIRFIELD	95.2	94.8	1.2	1.5	0.2	0.2	5.6	6.4	4.5	5.4	8.6	7.2	4.6	26.7	30.1	11.3	1.6	76.4	40.7	51.5	48.5
83328	FILER	95.6	95.3	0.2	0.2	0.2	0.2	7.6	8.6	7.4	7.4	8.0	7.6	6.9	25.9	23.9	10.9	2.0	72.4	35.6	50.8	49.3
83330	GOODING	90.4	89.6	0.1	0.2	0.3	0.3	14.0	15.6	7.3	7.3	8.0	7.6	6.4	24.9	22.2	13.3	3.0	72.4	36.6	50.9	49.1
83332	HAGERMAN	91.5	90.8	0.2	0.3	0.4	0.5	10.9	12.1	6.6	6.4	6.2	5.4	6.2	21.8	28.1	16.8	2.5	77.5	43.1	52.3	47.7
83333	HAILEY	90.3	89.4	0.2	0.2	0.9	1.0	11.3	12.6	6.6	7.0	7.4	6.8	5.8	29.7	29.4	6.5	0.7	74.8	37.4	50.9	49.1
83334	HANSEN	93.3	92.9	0.3	0.3	0.3	0.3	10.6	11.9	7.8	8.7	9.2	7.7	7.1	26.9	23.2	8.7	0.8	68.9	32.7	50.7	49.3
83335	HAZELTON	84.6	83.3	0.2	0.4	0.3	0.4	21.0	23.3	8.3	8.2	9.2	7.9	6.7	26.4	21.5	10.4	1.4	69.4	33.0	51.3	48.7
83336	HEYBURN	79.1	77.4	0.3	0.3	0.5	0.6	23.2	25.5	8.8	8.6	8.4	7.2	7.2	25.8	23.1	9.8	1.1	69.8	33.0	49.6	50.4
83338	JEROME	87.3	86.3	0.2	0.3	0.3	0.3	16.8	18.6	8.6	8.0	8.2	7.1	7.4	26.9	22.1	10.4	1.5	70.7	33.3	50.9	49.1
83340	KETCHUM	93.4	92.9	0.1	0.1	0.7	0.8	6.5	7.2	2.7	3.1	4.4	5.3	6.9	30.0	35.4	11.8	0.5	86.9	43.4	53.2	46.8
83341	KIMBERLY	95.3	94.9	0.1	0.1	0.4	0.4	7.2	8.3	7.4	8.0	8.8	8.4	6.4	26.3	23.1	10.0	1.7	70.5	34.5	49.7	50.3
83342	MALTA	90.2	89.2	0.2	0.2	0.1	0.1	13.0	14.5	9.1	9.1	8.7	8.5	6.7	22.2	22.9	11.6	1.3	67.6	33.7	52.6	47.4
83343	MINIDOKA	68.3	65.1	0.0	0.0	0.8	1.2	34.6	38.7	9.2	10.0	9.6	9.2	8.8	26.4	18.4	8.1	0.4	64.8	27.2	52.9	47.1
83344	MURTAUGH	81.7	79.9	0.3	0.5	0.2	0.2	29.1	32.3	9.4	9.3	9.6	7.4	7.3	27.8	20.7	7.4	1.2	66.7	30.4	52.1	47.9
83346	OAKLEY	90.2	89.0	0.0	0.0	0.1	0.1	12.4	14.1	9.1	9.2	9.6	7.8	7.1	22.6	22.3	10.6	1.8	67.0	31.5	51.8	48.2
83347	PAUL	81.4	79.7	0.1	0.1	0.5	0.5	19.0	21.1	7.6	7.4	7.8	7.0	6.9	24.8	24.6	12.5	1.5	72.9	36.0	51.7	48.3
83348	PICABO	83.3	85.7	0.0	0.0	0.0	0.0	0.0	14.3	0.0	0.0	0.0	0.0	28.6	71.4	0.0	0.0	0.0	100.0	28.8	57.1	42.9
83349	RICHFIELD	91.5	90.7	0.8	1.0	0.1	0.1	9.6	10.9	8.2	8.4	9.0	7.4	6.3	26.3	24.2	9.3	0.9	69.8	33.5	53.1	46.9
83350	RUPERT	76.8	75.2	0.3	0.4	0.4	0.4	28.2	30.5	8.6	8.3	8.4	7.9	7.4	24.0	22.2	11.7	1.5	69.6	33.2	50.1	49.9
83352	SHOSHONE	85.4	84.0	0.3	0.4	0.7	0.8	14.2	15.9	7.4	7.6	8.0	7.0	6.3	26.0	23.2	12.5	2.1	72.7	35.8	51.1	48.9
83355	WENDELL	83.7	82.6	0.2	0.3	0.3	0.4	23.0	25.2	9.1	8.9	8.5	7.0	7.0	27.5	20.5	9.8	1.6	69.1	31.5	51.5	48.5
83401	IDAHO FALLS	92.4	91.5	0.5	0.6	0.6	0.7	7.8	9.1	9.1	8.4	8.3	8.2	8.7	26.8	20.7	8.3	1.4	69.2	30.0	50.0	50.0
83402	IDAHO FALLS	90.4	89.6	0.5	0.5	1.0	1.1	10.1	11.1	8.6	8.2	8.2	7.8	8.0	27.8	22.1	8.3	1.0	70.2	31.7	50.8	49.2
83404	IDAHO FALLS	94.9	94.4	0.6	0.6	1.3	1.5	3.4	3.9	7.0	7.3	8.7	8.0	6.8	23.5	26.6	10.9	1.4	71.8	36.9	48.7	51.3
83406	IDAHO FALLS	96.0	95.5	0.2	0.3	0.7	0.8	3.1	3.6	9.6	9.2	9.9	9.2	6.7	26.2	20.9	7.5	1.0	65.3	29.6	49.3	50.7
83420	ASHTON	89.3	88.2	0.3	0.3	0.2	0.2	11.6	12.9	8.1	8.3	7.8	7.4	6.2	23.7	23.0	12.9	2.6	71.0	36.4	49.9	50.2
83422	DRIGGS	89.3	88.4	0.1	0.0	0.6	0.6	14.3	16.0	7.6	8.2	9.4	7.8	7.4	31.5	20.7	6.6	0.9	69.5	31.7	51.9	48.1
83423	DUBOIS	73.0	73.1	0.1	0.1	0.3	0.3	35.9	35.7	9.7	9.3	9.8	8.0	8.2	25.8	19.9	8.3	0.9	66.3	29.4	52.4	47.6
83424	FELT	91.7	90.5	0.0	0.0	0.5	0.4	14.5	16.1	8.6	9.5	8.6	7.0	6.2	30.5	21.8	7.4	0.4	68.3	32.3	53.1	46.9
83425	HAMER	85.3	83.6	0.2	0.2	0.5	0.5	15.0	17.0	10.5	8.9	12.1	8.8	9.1	22.9	19.6	7.3	0.7	62.1	25.4	54.6	45.4
83428	IRWIN	97.3	96.4	0.0	0.0	1.1	1.0	1.1	1.6	4.6	5.7	5.2	5.2	4.1	19.6	35.6	18.0	2.1	80.9	48.7	51.6	48.5
83429	ISLAND PARK	95.9	95.4	0.0	0.0	0.5	0.6	3.3	3.8	5.1	5.3	5.3	4.2	4.4	20.6	33.3	20.8	1.0	81.8	47.8	52.5	47.5
83431	LEWISVILLE	92.6	91.9	0.1	0.1	0.1	0.1	7.4	8.4	8.1	8.1	8.8	8.2	7.6	25.2	23.6	8.9	1.3	69.6	32.5	50.7	49.3
83434	MENAN	91.3	90.2	0.1	0.1	0.1	0.1	9.3	10.5	9.3	8.9	9.4	8.2	7.3	23.9	22.3	9.5	1.3	67.4	30.9	50.5	49.5
83435	MONTEVIEW	84.5	82.5	0.2	0.2	0.4	0.7	16.2	18.2	10.4	9.3	10.9	8.7	9.5	24.0	19.1	7.5	0.7	63.4	25.9	54.3	45.7
83436	NEWDALE	87.3	85.9	0.2	0.2	0.2	0.2	16.3	18.5	9.9	8.8	9.0	8.6	9.0	24.9	19.4	9.3	1.1	67.2	28.5	50.9	49.1
83440	REXBURG	95.4	95.0	0.2	0.3	0.8	0.9	4.1	4.6	7.9	6.4	7.2	19.6	23.2	18.5	11.7	4.8	0.7	74.8	21.9	46.3	53.7
	IDAHO	91.0	90.3	0.4	0.5	1.0	1.2	7.9	8.8	7.8	7.4	7.7	7.7	7.9	27.3	23.1	9.6	1.5	72.7	33.5	50.1	49.9
	UNITED STATES	75.1	73.6	12.3	12.5	3.8	4.2	12.5	14.1	6.9	6.7	7.2	7.0	7.3	28.6	23.8	10.8	1.7	75.1	36.0	49.1	50.9

ZIP CODE #	POST OFFICE NAME	2004 Per Capita Income	2004 HH Income Base	2004 Household Income Distribution (%): Less than $25,000	$25,000 to $49,999	$50,000 to $99,999	$100,000 to $149,999	$150,000 or More	Median Household Income: 2004	2009	2004 National Centile	2004 State Centile	2004 Home Value Base	2004 Home Value Distribution (%): Less than $50,000	$50,000 to $89,999	$90,000 to $174,999	$175,000 to $399,999	$400,000 or More	2004 Median Home Value
83201	POCATELLO	21407	13465	29.4	29.7	29.4	8.1	3.5	41721	49620	52	75	8853	7.7	33.1	48.4	10.4	0.3	96997
83202	POCATELLO	18310	5876	24.4	30.6	34.9	8.0	2.1	45150	52253	62	88	4676	17.1	22.1	51.0	9.4	0.4	98158
83203	FORT HALL	14038	44	29.6	36.4	27.3	6.8	0.0	38600	42955	41	60	38	13.2	34.2	47.4	5.3	0.0	92500
83204	POCATELLO	21781	6685	32.2	28.3	26.6	9.3	3.6	40198	47428	47	66	4486	14.5	28.3	41.7	14.6	0.9	99758
83209	POCATELLO	0	0	0.0	0.0	0.0	0.0	0.0	0	0	0	0	0	0.0	0.0	0.0	0.0	0.0	0
83210	ABERDEEN	14228	1141	34.1	44.9	15.3	3.9	1.8	32796	36596	20	15	890	23.6	33.3	31.0	11.2	0.9	84078
83211	AMERICAN FALLS	18596	1981	30.9	36.1	23.9	5.0	4.1	35842	41147	31	38	1532	21.3	24.6	41.2	11.2	1.7	94922
83212	ARBON	15402	43	37.2	32.6	25.6	4.7	0.0	34279	36689	25	25	36	19.4	33.3	41.7	5.6	0.0	85000
83213	ARCO	18155	729	37.3	30.0	25.7	4.9	2.1	33901	40651	24	24	569	27.8	33.9	31.1	5.8	1.4	74020
83214	ARIMO	17054	178	25.3	34.3	29.8	6.2	4.5	45238	51078	62	89	150	11.3	31.3	42.0	12.7	2.7	96875
83217	BANCROFT	16558	291	38.8	26.5	28.2	4.8	1.7	33131	37023	21	17	236	26.3	38.6	23.7	8.9	2.5	71176
83220	BERN	14650	81	32.1	35.8	28.4	3.7	0.0	37340	43376	37	52	69	15.9	46.4	33.3	4.4	0.0	81500
83221	BLACKFOOT	17987	8034	25.0	34.7	30.7	7.1	2.5	41451	47120	51	74	6430	10.7	31.1	45.1	12.2	0.9	97619
83226	CHALLIS	17373	1044	36.9	33.4	25.1	3.8	0.8	35137	39621	28	30	849	14.7	25.6	39.8	13.4	6.5	101673
83227	CLAYTON	0	0	0.0	0.0	0.0	0.0	0.0	0	0	0	0	0	0.0	0.0	0.0	0.0	0.0	0
83228	CLIFTON	13942	129	23.3	46.5	24.0	3.9	2.3	36428	39344	33	44	106	8.5	23.6	51.9	11.3	4.7	111458
83230	CONDA	26853	7	14.3	28.6	42.9	14.3	0.0	54416	79274	79	96	6	0.0	33.3	66.7	0.0	0.0	100000
83232	DAYTON	14547	221	21.7	45.7	26.7	3.6	2.3	37682	40615	38	54	182	7.1	23.6	54.4	11.5	3.3	111538
83234	DOWNEY	14862	454	38.1	31.5	27.8	1.1	1.5	35264	39622	28	31	377	18.3	30.2	45.9	5.6	0.0	92115
83235	ELLIS	14016	113	53.1	36.3	7.1	3.5	0.0	23312	27691	3	4	97	16.5	22.7	46.4	11.3	3.1	97000
83236	FIRTH	14244	1448	31.5	35.2	26.2	5.7	1.5	36924	42239	35	48	1129	24.5	32.3	34.7	7.3	1.2	81500
83237	FRANKLIN	14214	358	22.9	48.0	20.4	6.4	2.2	36806	40688	35	47	301	8.0	16.9	59.5	13.6	2.0	120474
83238	GENEVA	13865	37	32.4	32.4	32.4	2.7	0.0	35733	41519	31	37	30	6.7	46.7	33.3	10.0	3.3	88000
83241	GRACE	14654	696	31.9	40.4	24.0	3.2	0.6	35729	40684	30	36	563	17.2	38.5	32.3	8.5	3.4	83868
83243	HOLBROOK	14751	64	28.1	42.2	25.0	1.6	3.1	40000	41735	46	65	54	16.7	13.0	42.6	25.9	1.9	125000
83244	HOWE	13959	70	31.4	34.3	31.4	2.9	0.0	33388	38354	22	20	56	8.9	32.1	42.9	14.3	1.8	96250
83245	INKOM	20769	593	18.2	29.7	38.8	10.5	2.9	51679	60291	75	94	548	9.7	23.2	54.4	11.7	1.1	104545
83246	LAVA HOT SPRINGS	18524	384	34.4	33.6	26.6	4.2	1.3	35825	41192	31	37	299	13.0	23.4	50.2	12.0	1.3	99643
83250	MCCAMMON	19542	680	23.5	31.0	35.6	7.7	2.2	46499	52784	65	90	607	9.9	28.0	44.7	16.5	1.0	99800
83251	MACKAY	19835	520	35.4	30.8	25.4	5.8	2.7	35000	40074	28	29	427	15.7	27.4	39.8	12.7	4.5	97973
83252	MALAD CITY	15940	1392	29.0	40.3	26.0	3.2	1.5	37166	40729	36	50	1156	11.8	25.4	47.8	14.5	0.7	104113
83253	MAY	12672	132	54.6	36.4	6.1	3.0	0.0	22589	27428	3	3	114	14.9	21.9	49.1	11.4	2.6	97895
83254	MONTPELIER	15376	1731	30.8	35.6	29.8	3.6	0.2	35131	40079	28	30	1400	14.4	42.2	35.9	5.9	1.5	84038
83255	MOORE	16744	315	24.4	41.9	25.4	6.7	1.6	36992	42800	35	50	261	16.1	32.2	42.2	8.8	0.8	91667
83261	PARIS	16292	341	29.3	37.5	29.0	3.2	0.9	38314	43250	40	58	299	11.7	40.8	36.8	10.4	0.3	88125
83262	PINGREE	14462	405	22.2	41.7	31.6	3.7	0.7	38744	43766	42	61	338	12.4	21.9	43.8	20.7	1.2	109722
83263	PRESTON	16429	2709	23.1	38.3	30.5	5.6	2.6	41025	46859	50	72	2189	5.2	22.1	51.6	20.1	1.1	114638
83271	ROCKLAND	13118	172	34.9	33.1	26.7	5.2	0.0	36010	38995	32	41	142	21.8	32.4	39.4	4.9	1.4	80000
83272	SAINT CHARLES	18251	86	29.1	38.4	29.1	2.3	1.2	36517	42865	34	46	76	9.2	32.9	39.5	17.1	1.3	97500
83274	SHELLEY	16489	2774	23.3	34.8	33.9	5.9	2.1	45149	50958	62	87	2317	10.4	26.8	53.7	8.6	0.7	98703
83276	SODA SPRINGS	19552	1628	23.8	30.7	35.1	8.2	2.3	46752	52767	66	90	1329	14.4	30.4	45.6	7.9	1.7	95650
83278	STANLEY	21292	225	24.4	36.9	32.4	4.0	2.2	43335	47630	57	82	156	12.8	18.0	32.7	25.0	11.5	127632
83283	THATCHER	14552	46	28.3	34.8	32.6	4.4	0.0	33848	36806	24	23	38	2.6	21.1	39.5	34.2	2.6	135000
83285	WAYAN	21176	47	34.0	23.4	29.8	6.4	6.4	41156	45000	50	73	39	18.0	18.0	35.9	20.5	7.7	115625
83286	WESTON	15061	274	18.6	44.2	31.8	2.9	2.6	40172	43333	47	66	230	3.9	22.6	60.0	12.6	0.9	114674
83287	FISH HAVEN	22627	97	28.9	38.1	29.9	2.1	1.0	36928	43641	35	49	88	8.0	29.6	44.3	17.1	1.1	105769
83301	TWIN FALLS	20647	16849	30.3	33.9	26.5	6.2	3.1	38703	44359	42	60	11675	9.0	21.8	52.4	14.8	2.1	112643
83302	ROGERSON	19404	59	32.2	42.4	18.6	3.4	3.4	33579	36487	23	21	46	15.2	21.7	50.0	8.7	4.4	97500
83313	BELLEVUE	25532	1356	17.1	29.8	37.3	9.7	6.1	52497	62724	76	95	1032	3.3	4.2	26.1	45.2	21.3	221918
83314	BLISS	16673	353	31.7	39.4	22.1	2.8	4.0	35414	40000	29	33	255	27.1	17.3	36.9	12.6	6.3	101389
83316	BUHL	18221	3632	31.3	32.8	29.3	3.7	2.9	37625	42169	38	53	2777	11.4	28.3	42.0	15.2	3.2	99121
83318	BURLEY	16121	5452	33.0	33.8	26.4	5.0	1.9	36473	41834	33	44	4068	13.3	31.8	42.2	11.3	1.4	93776
83320	CAREY	19437	334	31.1	31.4	30.5	3.9	3.0	38286	44757	40	57	263	5.7	27.4	48.7	12.6	5.7	104830
83321	CASTLEFORD	18184	151	37.8	30.5	25.8	3.3	2.7	34715	39440	26	28	110	18.2	19.1	32.7	26.4	3.6	108333
83322	CORRAL	18156	21	28.6	28.6	33.3	4.8	4.8	42367	40000	54	78	17	5.9	23.5	47.1	23.5	0.0	112500
83323	DECLO	15244	634	34.4	32.3	27.1	3.6	2.5	35409	40238	29	32	511	19.2	22.1	32.5	24.7	1.6	99271
83324	DIETRICH	14490	188	24.5	41.0	29.8	4.3	0.5	39052	45318	43	63	152	9.9	39.5	42.1	6.6	2.0	90500
83325	EDEN	18527	394	34.3	39.1	17.8	6.6	2.3	35903	38716	31	39	266	11.7	23.3	46.2	17.3	1.5	104891
83327	FAIRFIELD	25232	431	29.2	33.2	28.1	5.1	4.4	39324	45419	44	63	352	11.7	25.9	37.8	17.9	6.8	108333
83328	FILER	16970	1694	29.2	35.1	29.2	4.8	1.8	37678	42578	38	54	1328	9.2	26.1	46.5	15.7	2.6	103953
83330	GOODING	16561	2235	33.0	33.9	26.7	4.3	2.2	34774	40227	27	28	1697	13.3	34.5	40.3	8.3	3.7	91921
83332	HAGERMAN	17811	883	33.9	32.4	27.9	4.2	1.7	36482	41287	33	45	715	8.7	19.7	43.8	21.5	6.3	116375
83333	HAILEY	36645	4578	14.6	24.4	35.4	14.8	10.8	62092	74671	86	99	3522	5.2	0.8	12.4	43.0	38.6	309663
83334	HANSEN	16793	701	29.8	38.1	24.3	5.7	2.1	37308	43344	37	51	541	22.0	31.4	30.9	12.9	2.8	86146
83335	HAZELTON	14454	574	38.0	36.1	20.0	4.5	1.4	32187	34874	18	13	378	16.9	29.4	35.7	13.5	4.5	94118
83336	HEYBURN	15586	1833	31.5	36.9	26.0	4.0	1.6	36285	40915	33	42	1466	16.6	38.5	37.0	7.2	0.7	85313
83338	JEROME	18133	5525	27.6	36.3	28.2	5.9	2.1	39197	44532	43	63	4224	12.3	27.4	40.7	16.7	2.9	103180
83340	KETCHUM	59886	2597	19.6	22.3	26.9	12.8	18.4	61135	78533	85	98	1670	2.9	0.5	5.3	23.2	68.1	612351
83341	KIMBERLY	18535	1683	27.3	35.0	28.6	6.4	2.7	40743	45779	49	70	1352	7.4	21.3	53.9	14.4	3.0	111935
83342	MALTA	18432	794	23.3	39.2	30.2	3.3	4.0	41547	46880	51	74	625	18.4	24.5	37.6	15.0	4.5	98091
83343	MINIDOKA	13449	71	28.2	36.6	31.0	1.4	2.8	36110	40308	32	41	51	13.7	17.7	49.0	9.8	9.8	108929
83344	MURTAUGH	13091	340	35.6	36.8	22.4	3.8	1.5	33353	36836	22	19	201	18.9	27.9	36.3	14.9	2.0	93611
83346	OAKLEY	15915	480	29.6	34.4	30.8	2.9	2.3	36955	41610	35	49	384	14.8	32.6	39.1	12.8	0.8	92941
83347	PAUL	17331	1156	33.0	35.6	25.5	3.6	2.4	35593	39891	30	35	927	12.4	32.3	46.3	7.8	1.3	96037
83348	PICABO	0	0	0.0	0.0	0.0	0.0	0.0	0	0	0	0	0	0.0	0.0	0.0	0.0	0.0	0
83349	RICHFIELD	14967	352	32.1	35.8	27.6	4.6	0.0	35553	40787	30	34	287	23.0	28.2	33.1	11.5	4.2	87308
83350	RUPERT	15593	4125	36.4	34.8	23.0	2.6	3.2	34041	38941	24	24	3180	16.7	35.9	37.0	8.9	1.5	87235
83352	SHOSHONE	18349	1032	30.9	34.4	27.8	4.8	2.1	35931	40852	31	40	812	11.2	33.1	45.8	9.4	0.5	94466
83355	WENDELL	16152	1831	29.4	38.8	24.9	4.8	2.1	36875	42739	35	48	1411	14.8	27.6	39.3	15.9	2.4	96361
83401	IDAHO FALLS	18423	10942	27.0	31.4	32.6	6.9	2.1	42511	49653	55	78	7926	14.7	27.2	48.8	8.7	0.6	96779
83402	IDAHO FALLS	20062	9533	25.8	32.3	31.3	8.4	2.3	43329	50686	57	81	6664	9.0	26.5	53.7	10.3	0.6	104014
83404	IDAHO FALLS	30175	7168	17.2	21.9	36.5	15.3	9.1	61078	72649	85	98	5909	2.9	18.7	48.7	27.1	2.7	132322
83406	IDAHO FALLS	21934	3179	16.5	23.9	42.7	12.7	4.3	57729	66587	82	97	2751	2.6	18.0	57.2	19.6	2.6	128567
83420	ASHTON	14981	938	34.5	35.5	25.1	3.7	1.2	33809	36768	23	23	790	24.3	25.8	39.4	10.0	0.5	89787
83422	DRIGGS	19576	950	20.8	37.8	34.3	3.9	3.2	44460	48330	60	84	726	15.6	6.5	36.1	36.0	5.9	150820
83423	DUBOIS	11338	317	36.6	46.1	16.1	0.6	0.6	34641	36697	26	27	222	38.7	32.4	26.6	1.4	0.9	68889
83424	FELT	13688	67	19.4	41.8	32.8	4.5	1.5	44525	47701	60	85	56	8.9	10.7	44.6	32.1	3.6	156818
83425	HAMER	12269	158	35.4	34.8	23.4	4.4	1.9	33161	37108	21	17	123	25.2	24.4	30.9	16.3	3.3	90455
83428	IRWIN	25042	84	26.2	31.0	32.1	6.0	4.8	43904	49451	58	83	72	18.1	13.9	37.5	23.6	6.9	116667
83429	ISLAND PARK	32825	420	27.4	39.5	25.0	2.1	6.0	40629	45729	48	68	357	10.1	14.9	41.2	31.7	2.2	130793
83431	LEWISVILLE	17013	322	20.8	37.9	32.3	6.5	2.5	43950	50081	58	83	270	11.5	23.3	47.4	12.2	5.6	109091
83434	MENAN	16270	521	23.4	32.4	39.0	3.3	1.9	45577	51535	63	89	448	15.0	21.7	49.8	11.2	2.5	102163
83435	MONTEVIEW	13165	138	35.5	35.5	23.9	3.6	1.5	32999	37331	21	17	108	25.0	25.0	33.3	14.8	1.9	90000
83436	NEWDALE	13205	126	27.0	42.9	23.0	4.8	2.4	40859	46913	49	71	109	18.4	28.4	47.7	4.6	0.9	93500
83440	REXBURG	13334	7621	33.4	33.0	26.8	4.2	2.6	35942	41199	31	40	4325	13.5	14.2	49.9	20.5	1.9	119556
	IDAHO	21160		26.4	31.8	30.4	7.9	3.5	42682	49896				9.8	16.8	49.1	20.6	3.6	122288
	UNITED STATES	25866		24.7	27.1	30.8	10.9	6.5	48124	56710				10.9	15.0	33.7	30.1	10.4	145905

#	POST OFFICE NAME	FINANCIAL SERVICES: Auto Loan	FINANCIAL SERVICES: Home Loan	FINANCIAL SERVICES: Invest-ments	FINANCIAL SERVICES: Retire-ment Plans	THE HOME: Home Improvements: Home Repair	THE HOME: Home Improvements: Lawn & Garden	THE HOME: Furnishings: Comput-ers & Hard-ware	THE HOME: Furnishings: Major Appli-ances	THE HOME: Furnishings: TV, Radio, Sound Equip-ment	THE HOME: Furnishings: Furni-ture	ENTERTAINMENT: Dine out/ Carry out	ENTERTAINMENT: Sports Equip-ment	ENTERTAINMENT: Fees & Tickets	ENTERTAINMENT: Toys & Games	ENTERTAINMENT: Travel	ENTERTAINMENT: Cable TV	PERSONAL: Apparel & Services	PERSONAL: Auto Repairs	PERSONAL: Health Insur-ance	PERSONAL: Pets & Supplies
83201	POCATELLO	76	75	83	78	75	79	82	78	80	79	100	94	80	100	79	76	97	80	73	86
83202	POCATELLO	80	78	71	77	78	81	75	78	74	76	92	92	73	91	74	73	89	78	76	91
83203	FORT HALL	73	66	52	64	66	70	63	68	64	65	79	78	60	74	62	63	76	67	67	80
83204	POCATELLO	76	77	81	79	76	79	80	78	77	78	97	93	79	97	78	74	95	79	73	86
83209	POCATELLO	0	0	0	0	0	0	0	0	0	0	0	0	0	0	0	0	0	0	0	0
83210	ABERDEEN	72	58	42	54	60	65	59	67	63	62	78	74	53	71	58	63	75	67	69	78
83211	AMERICAN FALLS	84	72	60	70	75	81	73	78	76	72	93	92	69	91	72	77	89	78	82	95
83212	ARBON	76	53	28	50	62	70	53	65	61	52	71	79	45	70	55	64	65	64	78	91
83213	ARCO	73	54	35	52	60	71	59	66	66	56	78	75	52	74	59	70	71	66	79	81
83214	ARIMO	103	72	38	68	84	94	71	88	82	70	96	106	61	94	74	86	87	86	104	122
83217	BANCROFT	84	59	31	55	68	77	58	72	67	57	78	86	50	77	60	70	71	71	85	100
83220	BERN	77	55	29	52	63	71	54	66	62	53	73	80	46	71	56	65	66	65	79	92
83221	BLACKFOOT	82	75	63	73	78	84	73	78	76	73	93	91	71	92	74	76	88	77	82	94
83226	CHALLIS	75	52	28	49	61	68	52	64	59	51	70	77	44	68	53	62	64	63	76	89
83227	CLAYTON	0	0	0	0	0	0	0	0	0	0	0	0	0	0	0	0	0	0	0	0
83228	CLIFTON	86	60	31	57	70	79	59	74	69	59	80	89	51	79	62	72	73	72	88	102
83230	CONDA	90	76	60	76	80	90	79	84	83	77	101	96	75	100	78	85	95	83	91	99
83232	DAYTON	89	62	32	59	72	81	61	76	70	60	83	91	52	81	63	74	75	75	90	105
83234	DOWNEY	72	50	26	47	59	66	50	61	57	49	67	74	42	66	51	60	61	60	73	85
83235	ELLIS	50	39	26	35	44	49	37	44	41	36	49	52	33	48	39	44	46	43	52	60
83236	FIRTH	68	61	52	59	62	68	61	64	64	61	78	75	59	77	61	64	75	64	67	77
83237	FRANKLIN	73	65	54	66	67	74	66	70	68	65	84	80	64	83	65	69	79	69	72	81
83238	GENEVA	73	57	38	52	64	72	54	65	61	53	72	76	48	71	57	65	67	64	77	89
83241	GRACE	74	52	27	49	60	67	51	63	59	50	69	76	43	67	53	62	63	62	75	88
83243	HOLBROOK	88	61	32	58	71	80	60	75	70	60	82	90	52	80	63	73	74	74	89	104
83244	HOWE	74	51	27	49	60	67	51	63	58	50	69	76	43	67	53	61	63	62	75	87
83245	INKOM	95	88	70	84	92	98	81	89	84	81	103	106	80	106	83	86	98	87	94	113
83246	LAVA HOT SPRINGS	80	56	29	53	65	73	55	68	63	54	74	82	47	73	57	67	68	67	81	95
83250	MCCAMMON	100	70	37	66	81	91	69	85	79	68	93	103	59	91	72	83	85	84	102	119
83251	MACKAY	79	62	42	56	70	78	58	70	66	58	78	82	52	77	62	70	73	69	83	96
83252	MALAD CITY	80	56	29	53	65	73	55	68	64	55	75	82	47	73	57	67	68	67	81	95
83253	MAY	48	37	25	34	42	47	35	42	40	35	47	50	31	47	37	43	44	42	50	58
83254	MONTPELIER	71	56	37	53	62	69	56	64	62	55	73	75	51	72	57	64	68	63	74	83
83255	MOORE	84	59	32	56	68	77	59	72	68	58	80	86	51	78	61	71	73	71	86	99
83261	PARIS	79	57	33	53	66	74	56	68	64	55	75	81	48	74	58	67	69	67	81	94
83262	PINGREE	83	58	30	55	68	76	57	71	66	57	77	85	49	76	59	69	71	70	84	99
83263	PRESTON	83	70	52	68	74	82	69	76	74	68	89	89	65	89	69	75	84	75	83	94
83271	ROCKLAND	76	53	28	50	62	69	52	65	60	52	71	78	45	69	54	63	65	64	77	90
83272	SAINT CHARLES	77	60	41	55	68	77	57	69	65	57	76	80	51	76	61	69	71	68	81	94
83274	SHELLEY	78	74	65	73	76	80	71	75	72	71	89	88	70	89	72	72	85	74	76	89
83276	SODA SPRINGS	91	70	45	67	78	87	70	81	78	69	92	95	63	91	71	80	85	80	93	106
83278	STANLEY	82	64	43	58	72	81	60	73	69	60	81	86	54	80	64	73	75	72	86	100
83283	THATCHER	77	54	28	51	62	70	53	65	61	52	71	79	45	70	55	64	65	64	78	91
83285	WAYAN	91	71	49	64	80	90	67	81	76	67	90	95	60	89	72	81	84	80	96	111
83286	WESTON	95	66	35	63	77	86	65	81	75	65	88	97	56	87	68	79	81	80	96	113
83287	FISH HAVEN	78	61	42	55	69	78	58	70	66	57	78	82	52	77	62	70	72	69	83	95
83301	TWIN FALLS	76	71	69	71	73	79	74	75	75	72	92	88	72	92	73	75	88	76	77	87
83302	ROGERSON	81	57	30	54	66	74	56	69	64	55	76	83	48	74	58	68	69	68	82	96
83313	BELLEVUE	100	101	92	101	101	103	94	98	92	96	114	116	93	114	94	90	111	97	94	116
83314	BLISS	84	58	31	55	68	76	58	71	66	57	78	86	49	76	60	70	71	70	85	99
83316	BUHL	81	61	39	59	68	77	62	72	69	61	82	85	56	81	63	72	76	71	83	94
83318	BURLEY	77	60	43	57	65	73	62	69	68	61	81	81	56	79	62	70	76	69	78	87
83320	CAREY	105	74	40	70	86	96	73	90	84	72	99	109	63	97	76	88	90	89	107	125
83321	CASTLEFORD	85	59	31	56	69	78	59	73	68	58	79	88	50	78	61	71	72	72	87	101
83322	CORRAL	89	70	48	63	79	89	66	80	75	66	89	93	59	88	71	80	82	78	94	109
83323	DECLO	87	62	33	58	71	80	61	75	70	60	82	90	52	80	63	73	75	74	88	103
83324	DIETRICH	71	65	51	62	65	69	62	66	63	64	78	77	59	74	61	62	74	66	66	79
83325	EDEN	90	63	33	59	73	82	62	76	71	61	84	92	53	82	64	75	76	75	91	106
83327	FAIRFIELD	103	81	55	73	91	103	77	92	87	76	103	108	68	101	82	93	95	91	109	126
83328	FILER	79	59	38	56	67	76	60	70	68	59	80	82	54	79	62	71	74	69	82	92
83330	GOODING	75	54	33	52	61	71	58	66	66	56	77	77	51	74	58	69	70	66	79	85
83332	HAGERMAN	76	55	33	52	62	72	58	67	65	56	77	78	50	74	58	69	70	67	80	87
83333	HAILEY	123	143	158	146	139	142	131	130	123	133	155	152	138	158	132	119	154	127	118	145
83334	HANSEN	78	69	55	67	71	75	67	72	68	68	84	85	63	81	66	68	80	72	74	88
83335	HAZELTON	77	54	28	51	63	70	53	66	61	52	72	79	45	70	55	64	65	65	78	91
83336	HEYBURN	71	60	45	59	63	69	60	65	63	60	76	75	56	74	59	64	72	65	70	79
83338	JEROME	86	70	49	67	75	83	69	78	75	69	90	92	63	88	70	77	84	78	87	99
83340	KETCHUM	180	155	185	156	163	182	160	169	172	161	211	201	156	215	165	178	203	172	182	213
83341	KIMBERLY	80	77	71	78	78	82	76	79	76	76	94	92	74	93	75	74	90	78	78	91
83342	MALTA	95	69	39	65	78	87	68	82	76	67	90	98	59	88	70	79	83	81	95	111
83343	MINIDOKA	81	60	42	58	66	72	63	72	70	64	84	85	56	82	63	70	80	73	78	91
83344	MURTAUGH	75	52	27	49	61	68	52	64	59	51	70	77	44	68	53	62	63	63	76	89
83346	OAKLEY	89	62	32	59	72	81	61	76	71	60	83	91	52	81	64	74	75	75	90	105
83347	PAUL	87	60	29	54	68	78	58	72	68	58	80	87	50	77	60	73	73	71	87	101
83348	PICABO	0	0	0	0	0	0	0	0	0	0	0	0	0	0	0	0	0	0	0	0
83349	RICHFIELD	65	55	43	55	58	66	57	61	61	56	74	70	55	73	57	62	69	60	66	72
83350	RUPERT	73	56	41	54	61	68	59	66	65	58	78	77	53	76	59	66	73	66	74	82
83352	SHOSHONE	82	65	43	62	70	78	64	73	70	64	84	86	58	82	65	72	78	73	82	94
83355	WENDELL	81	67	47	64	70	76	65	73	70	66	84	85	60	80	65	71	80	72	78	91
83401	IDAHO FALLS	71	76	78	76	75	77	74	74	72	74	90	87	75	91	74	70	88	74	70	82
83402	IDAHO FALLS	73	77	80	77	76	79	76	76	75	75	93	88	77	95	76	73	91	76	73	84
83404	IDAHO FALLS	107	124	139	126	123	126	118	116	112	117	140	135	123	144	119	109	139	114	108	127
83406	IDAHO FALLS	97	113	115	115	109	107	103	102	95	104	120	120	107	124	102	91	119	100	89	112
83420	ASHTON	73	53	31	51	60	68	54	64	61	53	72	75	47	70	55	64	66	63	75	84
83422	DRIGGS	86	82	72	82	83	86	79	83	78	79	97	99	76	97	78	76	93	83	81	99
83423	DUBOIS	56	51	40	49	51	54	49	52	49	50	61	60	46	57	48	49	58	52	52	62
83424	FELT	69	76	76	77	73	73	72	72	68	73	86	85	73	86	71	64	84	71	63	79
83425	HAMER	79	55	29	52	64	72	54	67	63	54	73	81	46	72	56	66	67	66	80	93
83428	IRWIN	98	77	52	69	87	97	73	87	82	72	97	102	65	96	77	88	90	86	103	120
83429	ISLAND PARK	120	94	64	85	106	119	89	107	100	88	119	125	79	117	94	107	110	105	126	146
83431	LEWISVILLE	93	65	34	61	76	85	64	79	74	63	87	95	55	85	66	77	79	78	94	110
83434	MENAN	86	73	53	70	78	85	69	78	74	69	89	93	65	90	71	76	84	76	85	101
83435	MONTEVIEW	76	55	31	52	63	70	54	66	61	54	73	79	47	71	56	64	67	65	76	90
83436	NEWDALE	76	63	47	62	67	75	64	70	69	63	83	80	61	82	64	70	78	69	77	84
83440	REXBURG	67	57	60	59	57	61	71	64	69	66	86	80	64	82	64	64	82	69	60	73
	IDAHO	84	79	73	78	80	85	79	81	79	78	98	96	76	97	78	78	94	81	82	96
	UNITED STATES	100	100	100	100	100	100	100	100	100	100	100	100	100	100	100	100	100	100	100	100

# POST OFFICE NAME	COUNTY FIPS CODE	POPULATION 2000	2004	2009	% Rate	State Centile	HOUSEHOLDS 2000	2004	2009	% Annual Rate 2000-2004	2004 Average HH Size	FAMILIES 2000	2004	% Annual Rate 2000-2004
83442 RIGBY	051	12796	13745	14775	1.7	73	4027	4411	4828	2.2	3.10	3302	3586	2.0
83443 RIRIE	019	547	564	598	0.7	46	180	191	207	1.4	2.95	148	155	1.1
83444 ROBERTS	051	1409	1503	1602	1.5	70	388	418	452	1.8	3.59	329	352	1.6
83445 SAINT ANTHONY	043	6796	7176	7651	1.3	63	2135	2302	2510	1.8	2.99	1681	1794	1.5
83446 SPENCER	033	73	65	66	-2.7	0	30	26	26	-3.3	2.50	21	18	-3.6
83448 SUGAR CITY	065	1984	2041	2250	0.7	43	547	579	655	1.4	3.53	476	502	1.3
83449 SWAN VALLEY	019	404	416	437	0.7	44	169	180	193	1.5	2.31	126	131	0.9
83450 TERRETON	051	1186	1242	1321	1.1	59	341	364	394	1.6	3.36	282	297	1.2
83451 TETON	043	743	760	795	0.5	37	242	253	270	1.1	3.00	195	202	0.8
83452 TETONIA	081	1192	1505	2071	5.6	99	418	539	758	6.2	2.79	313	399	5.9
83455 VICTOR	081	2465	3364	4784	7.6	100	876	1228	1789	8.3	2.72	604	833	7.9
83460 REXBURG	065	375	413	464	2.3	83	0	0	0	0.0	0.00	0	0	0.0
83462 CARMEN	059	271	301	339	2.5	84	110	124	143	2.9	2.41	71	79	2.5
83463 GIBBONSVILLE	059	191	206	230	1.8	76	87	96	109	2.3	2.13	59	63	1.6
83464 LEADORE	059	638	693	774	2.0	80	235	260	295	2.4	2.66	170	186	2.1
83466 NORTH FORK	059	457	511	580	2.7	86	202	230	266	3.1	2.21	128	143	2.6
83467 SALMON	059	5702	6167	6873	1.9	77	2387	2631	2986	2.3	2.34	1623	1760	1.9
83469 SHOUP	059	55	56	61	0.4	35	30	31	34	0.8	1.81	16	16	0.0
83501 LEWISTON	069	32659	32664	32757	0.0	24	13480	13647	13833	0.3	2.34	8793	8740	-0.1
83520 AHSAHKA	035	155	158	159	0.5	36	58	60	61	0.8	2.63	45	46	0.5
83522 COTTONWOOD	049	1777	1780	1761	0.0	25	644	657	659	0.5	2.29	464	466	0.1
83523 CRAIGMONT	061	821	798	796	-0.7	9	331	328	333	-0.2	2.43	239	233	-0.6
83524 CULDESAC	069	1161	1223	1252	1.2	61	451	484	503	1.7	2.52	342	361	1.3
83525 ELK CITY	049	585	547	526	-1.6	2	260	249	246	-1.0	2.16	174	164	-1.4
83526 FERDINAND	049	652	652	645	0.0	24	131	133	133	0.4	4.20	101	101	0.0
83530 GRANGEVILLE	049	5231	5207	5131	-0.1	19	2067	2095	2102	0.3	2.43	1438	1434	-0.1
83533 GREENCREEK	049	270	268	263	-0.2	17	94	95	95	0.3	2.80	74	74	0.0
83535 JULIAETTA	069	1070	1113	1137	0.9	53	440	462	476	1.2	2.41	314	326	0.9
83536 KAMIAH	049	3686	3728	3731	0.3	30	1514	1564	1599	0.8	2.37	1043	1059	0.4
83537 KENDRICK	057	1072	1103	1122	0.7	43	437	454	467	0.9	2.43	321	329	0.6
83539 KOOSKIA	049	2844	2834	2790	-0.1	20	1142	1161	1164	0.4	2.41	830	831	0.0
83540 LAPWAI	069	1946	2006	2026	0.7	46	648	685	704	1.3	2.93	498	518	0.9
83541 LENORE	035	1076	1099	1106	0.5	37	440	456	465	0.8	2.41	328	335	0.5
83542 LUCILE	049	250	248	244	-0.2	16	100	102	102	0.5	2.42	61	61	0.0
83543 NEZPERCE	061	698	691	692	-0.2	14	265	267	271	0.2	2.56	201	200	-0.1
83544 OROFINO	035	6094	6178	6247	0.3	33	2333	2414	2485	0.8	2.31	1616	1646	0.4
83545 PECK	069	538	536	530	-0.1	20	242	245	246	0.3	2.19	179	178	-0.1
83546 PIERCE	035	754	730	727	-0.8	7	313	310	315	-0.2	2.34	236	231	-0.5
83547 POLLOCK	049	417	416	412	-0.1	21	184	188	189	0.5	2.21	114	114	0.0
83548 REUBENS	069	180	177	176	-0.4	12	67	67	68	0.0	2.63	48	47	-0.5
83549 RIGGINS	049	747	741	729	-0.2	16	360	366	366	0.4	2.02	219	218	-0.1
83553 WEIPPE	035	1244	1245	1253	0.0	24	481	490	500	0.4	2.54	376	378	0.1
83554 WHITE BIRD	049	660	646	632	-0.5	11	286	285	285	-0.1	2.26	208	204	-0.5
83555 WINCHESTER	061	383	374	372	-0.6	10	167	166	170	-0.1	2.22	114	112	-0.4
83601 ATLANTA	039	245	273	301	2.6	85	123	139	156	2.9	1.96	77	86	2.6
83604 BRUNEAU	073	753	778	802	0.8	48	303	319	333	1.2	2.42	195	202	0.8
83605 CALDWELL	027	26067	29822	35451	3.2	91	9074	10461	12531	3.4	2.76	6382	7245	3.0
83607 CALDWELL	027	16715	20532	25341	5.0	96	5535	6859	8514	5.2	2.99	4527	5515	4.8
83610 CAMBRIDGE	087	977	944	930	-0.8	6	392	384	381	-0.5	2.46	283	274	-0.8
83611 CASCADE	085	2330	2493	2645	1.6	72	989	1084	1177	2.2	2.28	723	780	1.8
83612 COUNCIL	003	1876	1989	2147	1.4	66	772	842	933	2.1	2.32	555	596	1.7
83615 DONNELLY	085	569	584	607	0.6	41	251	264	280	1.2	2.21	186	193	0.9
83616 EAGLE	001	15218	18814	22126	5.1	98	5210	6511	7729	5.4	2.88	4196	5153	5.0
83617 EMMETT	045	14198	15131	16004	1.5	69	5192	5568	5910	1.7	2.68	3903	4131	1.3
83619 FRUITLAND	075	6000	6469	6903	1.8	76	2153	2335	2502	1.9	2.77	1660	1779	1.6
83622 GARDEN VALLEY	015	1820	2239	2919	5.0	97	726	909	1205	5.4	2.43	522	644	5.1
83623 GLENNS FERRY	039	2130	2182	2305	0.6	40	795	822	877	0.8	2.64	577	589	0.5
83624 GRAND VIEW	073	1548	1585	1631	0.6	39	546	569	592	1.0	2.78	413	424	0.6
83626 GREENLEAF	027	1339	1418	1623	1.4	65	424	454	524	1.6	3.12	345	364	1.3
83627 HAMMETT	039	456	485	523	1.5	68	141	152	166	1.8	3.14	110	117	1.5
83628 HOMEDALE	073	4050	4230	4386	1.0	56	1364	1426	1484	1.1	2.94	1011	1044	0.8
83629 HORSESHOE BEND	015	1622	1943	2498	4.3	94	606	741	972	4.9	2.57	443	534	4.5
83631 IDAHO CITY	015	1018	1258	1645	5.1	98	408	513	682	5.5	2.44	279	345	5.1
83632 INDIAN VALLEY	003	205	219	238	1.6	71	90	98	109	2.0	2.23	68	74	2.0
83633 KING HILL	039	334	352	378	1.2	62	115	123	134	1.6	2.81	90	96	1.5
83634 KUNA	001	13066	16047	18800	5.0	95	3403	4455	5435	6.5	3.06	2786	3585	6.1
83636 LETHA	045	50	54	57	1.8	77	20	22	23	2.3	2.45	16	17	1.4
83637 LOWMAN	015	192	236	308	5.0	96	90	113	150	5.5	2.06	65	80	5.0
83638 MCCALL	085	4763	4869	5055	0.5	37	1971	2059	2185	1.0	2.34	1346	1383	0.6
83639 MARSING	073	2780	2879	2974	0.8	49	949	996	1038	1.1	2.89	724	750	0.8
83641 MELBA	027	1787	2013	2369	2.8	88	604	686	812	3.0	2.86	463	518	2.7
83642 MERIDIAN	001	45437	55241	64432	4.7	95	15388	18982	22397	5.1	2.89	12497	15186	4.7
83643 MESA	003	119	128	139	1.7	74	53	58	65	2.1	2.21	41	44	1.7
83644 MIDDLETON	027	6281	7140	8476	3.1	91	2147	2468	2948	3.3	2.89	1692	1912	2.9
83645 MIDVALE	087	690	736	756	1.5	70	273	294	303	1.8	2.50	200	213	1.5
83647 MOUNTAIN HOME	039	16714	18134	19753	1.9	79	6333	6947	7657	2.2	2.59	4456	4828	1.9
83648 MOUNTAIN HOME A F B	039	9202	9272	9545	0.2	28	1566	1616	1726	0.7	3.34	1524	1570	0.7
83650 MURPHY	073	1513	1586	1647	1.1	59	548	584	613	1.5	2.67	414	436	1.2
83651 NAMPA	027	20718	24300	29371	3.8	93	7722	9162	11174	4.1	2.60	5305	6200	3.7
83654 NEW MEADOWS	003	1223	1298	1405	1.4	67	485	524	579	1.8	2.48	351	375	1.6
83655 NEW PLYMOUTH	075	3793	4175	4504	2.3	82	1317	1458	1578	2.4	2.85	1029	1126	2.1
83657 OLA	045	151	157	163	0.9	53	63	66	69	1.1	2.35	49	51	1.0
83660 PARMA	027	5397	6016	7007	2.6	85	1886	2111	2468	2.7	2.84	1472	1624	2.3
83661 PAYETTE	075	9650	9777	10102	0.3	33	3541	3610	3744	0.5	2.68	2598	2608	0.1
83669 STAR	001	2917	3309	3753	3.0	89	1035	1189	1361	3.3	2.77	820	921	2.8
83670 SWEET	045	485	503	524	0.9	51	164	172	181	1.1	2.90	128	133	0.9
83672 WEISER	087	8310	8321	8325	0.0	25	3097	3127	3139	0.2	2.61	2253	2243	-0.1
83676 WILDER	027	3781	4094	4742	1.9	78	1201	1306	1516	2.0	3.13	977	1048	1.7
83677 YELLOW PINE	085	25	23	23	-1.9	1	11	10	10	-2.2	2.30	6	6	0.1
83686 NAMPA	027	30879	36955	44977	4.3	94	10325	12476	15310	4.6	2.89	8078	9671	4.3
83687 NAMPA	027	19128	23721	29402	5.2	98	6312	7947	9956	5.6	2.92	4873	6062	5.3
83702 BOISE	001	21404	21655	23254	0.3	30	10149	10531	11527	0.9	2.00	4836	4771	-0.3
83703 BOISE	001	17011	18013	19644	1.4	65	6828	7379	8172	1.8	2.41	4353	4563	1.0
83704 BOISE	001	38953	40788	44265	1.1	59	14561	15649	17297	1.7	2.52	9905	10309	1.0
83705 BOISE	001	26282	27383	29772	1.0	55	11252	11979	13222	1.5	2.27	6563	6724	0.5
IDAHO					1.8					2.1	2.65			1.8
UNITED STATES					1.2					1.3	2.58			1.1

POPULATION COMPOSITION

IDAHO

83442-83705 B

ZIP CODE #	POST OFFICE NAME	RACE (%) White 2000	White 2004	Black 2000	Black 2004	Asian/Pacific 2000	Asian/Pacific 2004	% Hispanic Origin 2000	% Hispanic Origin 2004	2004 AGE DISTRIBUTION (%) 0-4	5-9	10-14	15-19	20-24	25-44	45-64	65-84	85+	18+	MEDIAN AGE 2004	% 2004 Males	% 2004 Females
83442	RIGBY	94.3	93.8	0.2	0.3	0.3	0.4	6.2	7.0	9.5	9.1	9.4	8.7	7.7	24.9	21.5	8.3	1.0	66.5	29.6	50.0	50.0
83443	RIRIE	96.0	95.6	0.4	0.5	0.0	0.0	2.9	3.6	9.2	8.2	9.8	8.3	7.3	24.5	22.9	8.7	1.2	67.4	31.9	50.4	49.7
83444	ROBERTS	73.1	70.4	1.4	1.7	0.4	0.4	30.2	33.5	9.0	8.7	10.5	10.5	9.0	24.0	20.8	6.9	0.9	65.5	27.1	53.4	46.6
83445	SAINT ANTHONY	92.8	92.3	0.2	0.2	0.5	0.6	9.1	10.2	9.3	9.0	7.9	9.3	7.6	24.9	21.3	9.5	1.2	67.7	30.4	52.0	48.0
83446	SPENCER	89.0	89.2	0.0	0.0	0.0	0.0	12.3	12.3	6.2	7.7	6.2	1.5	1.5	24.6	36.9	15.4	0.0	78.5	50.3	50.8	49.2
83448	SUGAR CITY	94.1	93.6	0.2	0.2	0.7	0.8	6.3	7.1	9.0	10.2	11.3	10.2	7.0	23.8	20.7	7.1	0.7	62.9	26.4	50.2	49.8
83449	SWAN VALLEY	97.3	97.4	0.0	0.0	0.5	0.5	1.2	1.2	5.3	5.8	5.3	5.3	4.3	19.5	35.3	17.3	1.9	80.8	47.9	51.0	49.0
83450	TERRETON	80.7	78.4	0.1	0.1	0.5	0.6	20.8	23.4	10.8	9.9	9.3	8.1	11.2	26.0	16.8	7.4	0.6	64.7	25.6	54.2	45.8
83451	TETON	86.5	85.0	0.1	0.1	0.1	0.1	17.9	20.0	9.9	9.0	8.4	8.4	9.6	25.3	19.1	9.3	1.1	68.0	28.8	50.4	49.6
83452	TETONIA	91.4	90.6	0.2	0.2	0.5	0.5	14.3	16.1	9.2	9.3	8.8	7.1	6.1	30.0	21.7	7.4	0.4	68.2	32.0	54.4	45.7
83455	VICTOR	92.9	92.2	0.3	0.3	0.3	0.4	8.1	9.2	9.0	8.5	7.6	6.4	6.8	34.0	21.9	5.3	0.7	70.9	32.4	52.1	47.9
83460	REXBURG	97.3	97.1	0.3	0.5	0.8	1.0	1.9	2.2	0.5	0.0	0.0	49.4	41.4	2.7	0.2	2.2	3.6	98.8	20.0	41.2	58.8
83462	CARMEN	97.1	97.3	0.0	0.0	0.0	0.0	1.9	2.0	5.7	6.0	5.7	6.0	4.7	20.9	34.2	14.6	2.3	78.7	45.7	49.8	50.2
83463	GIBBONSVILLE	95.8	95.6	0.0	0.5	0.0	0.0	2.6	2.9	4.9	6.8	6.3	6.8	3.4	21.4	34.0	14.6	1.9	77.7	45.3	49.5	50.5
83464	LEADORE	95.0	94.7	0.0	0.0	0.3	0.3	4.9	5.5	5.9	9.0	8.8	8.5	2.9	26.1	25.7	12.7	0.4	68.7	39.8	50.4	49.6
83466	NORTH FORK	97.4	97.3	0.0	0.0	0.2	0.2	1.5	1.8	5.9	5.9	5.3	5.9	5.1	21.1	33.7	14.5	2.7	78.9	45.5	49.9	50.1
83467	SALMON	96.9	96.8	0.1	0.1	0.2	0.3	1.9	2.2	5.1	6.2	7.5	6.9	4.4	21.2	32.0	14.6	1.9	76.7	44.0	49.7	50.3
83469	SHOUP	98.2	98.2	0.0	0.0	0.0	0.0	0.0	0.0	1.8	3.6	3.6	3.6	0.0	25.0	44.6	17.9	0.0	89.3	50.8	57.1	42.9
83501	LEWISTON	95.1	94.8	0.3	0.3	0.8	0.9	1.9	2.1	6.1	5.9	6.6	6.6	7.5	26.3	24.5	13.9	2.7	77.7	38.6	48.9	51.1
83520	AHSAHKA	91.0	91.1	0.0	0.0	0.7	0.6	1.9	0.6	6.3	7.0	7.0	5.7	4.4	21.5	31.7	15.2	1.3	76.0	43.5	51.3	48.7
83522	COTTONWOOD	96.1	95.7	0.3	0.3	0.3	0.3	2.2	2.5	5.5	5.6	7.2	9.3	8.9	25.3	22.7	13.0	2.5	76.4	37.0	54.6	45.4
83523	CRAIGMONT	96.4	96.2	0.0	0.0	0.2	0.3	0.7	0.8	5.0	5.5	5.9	7.1	5.4	23.3	31.1	14.7	2.0	79.2	43.6	53.0	47.0
83524	CULDESAC	64.7	65.0	0.3	0.3	0.2	0.2	2.3	2.4	7.4	7.3	7.5	7.0	5.9	23.2	26.7	13.6	1.5	73.6	39.1	50.1	49.9
83525	ELK CITY	96.4	96.5	0.0	0.0	0.2	0.2	1.4	1.7	4.9	5.5	4.9	4.6	2.9	22.3	40.6	13.7	0.6	81.2	47.6	55.0	45.0
83526	FERDINAND	94.8	94.3	0.3	0.3	0.3	0.3	2.2	2.5	5.4	6.0	8.0	8.3	8.3	27.2	22.9	12.4	1.7	75.8	36.7	54.5	45.6
83530	GRANGEVILLE	96.4	96.2	0.1	0.1	0.3	0.3	1.5	1.7	6.2	6.2	6.9	7.2	5.1	20.9	30.2	14.7	2.8	76.1	43.5	48.7	51.3
83533	GREENCREEK	95.2	95.2	0.0	0.0	0.0	0.0	0.7	0.4	6.3	7.1	9.3	6.7	5.2	23.9	26.1	14.2	1.1	72.0	39.5	47.8	52.2
83535	JULIAETTA	89.7	89.9	0.1	0.1	0.1	0.1	1.5	1.5	5.6	5.8	6.7	7.4	5.8	23.0	29.3	14.5	2.2	77.4	42.2	51.6	48.4
83536	KAMIAH	86.7	86.5	0.2	0.2	0.4	0.4	2.4	2.5	5.1	5.6	7.5	6.8	5.7	20.8	29.2	17.4	2.0	77.2	44.0	49.3	50.7
83537	KENDRICK	97.2	97.0	0.2	0.2	0.0	0.0	1.6	1.7	5.3	5.6	6.8	7.0	4.4	23.5	29.7	15.6	2.3	77.8	43.5	52.3	47.7
83539	KOOSKIA	93.1	92.9	0.0	0.0	0.3	0.4	1.1	1.3	4.9	5.2	6.9	7.1	4.8	20.6	32.2	16.5	1.8	78.2	45.3	52.0	48.0
83540	LAPWAI	50.9	50.9	0.3	0.4	0.2	0.2	3.1	3.1	8.9	8.6	8.0	7.1	5.9	24.9	24.4	11.1	1.0	70.1	34.8	49.9	50.2
83541	LENORE	92.1	92.0	0.0	0.0	0.4	0.4	1.7	1.7	5.4	6.0	5.8	5.1	3.6	19.7	35.9	16.8	1.6	79.7	47.6	52.2	47.8
83542	LUCILE	98.0	98.0	0.0	0.0	0.0	0.0	1.2	1.6	3.2	3.6	5.7	5.7	4.4	16.9	37.5	20.2	2.8	83.5	50.8	50.8	49.2
83543	NEZPERCE	92.1	92.0	1.0	1.0	0.9	0.9	0.6	0.6	5.1	5.8	9.0	8.1	5.1	19.7	29.4	16.6	1.3	75.3	43.3	54.4	45.6
83544	OROFINO	94.3	94.2	0.2	0.2	0.5	0.5	2.2	2.2	4.8	5.1	6.1	5.9	5.4	25.6	30.7	14.4	2.0	80.2	43.2	54.4	45.6
83545	PECK	94.8	94.6	0.0	0.0	0.0	0.0	0.6	0.8	4.5	5.0	5.6	6.0	4.9	23.0	30.2	18.1	2.8	81.0	45.7	50.8	49.3
83546	PIERCE	96.2	96.3	0.0	0.0	0.0	0.0	1.3	1.2	4.9	5.2	7.1	6.3	5.5	24.9	31.8	13.6	0.7	77.8	42.5	51.0	49.0
83547	POLLOCK	97.8	97.8	0.0	0.0	0.0	0.0	1.4	1.9	3.4	3.9	6.0	5.5	4.1	16.8	37.7	19.7	2.9	82.7	50.6	51.0	49.0
83548	REUBENS	93.9	93.8	0.0	0.0	0.0	0.0	0.6	0.6	4.0	4.5	6.2	6.2	5.1	21.5	32.2	18.1	2.3	81.4	46.5	51.4	48.6
83549	RIGGINS	98.0	97.8	0.0	0.0	0.0	0.0	1.3	1.8	3.2	3.8	5.8	5.4	4.3	16.5	38.1	19.8	3.1	83.1	51.0	51.0	49.0
83553	WEIPPE	98.2	98.2	0.1	0.1	0.0	0.0	0.8	0.8	5.1	6.2	8.2	7.3	5.1	21.0	30.5	14.8	1.9	75.5	42.9	50.9	49.1
83554	WHITE BIRD	96.1	95.8	0.2	0.2	0.5	0.5	2.3	2.8	5.7	6.0	7.0	7.0	4.8	20.1	33.6	13.9	1.9	76.3	44.6	50.3	49.7
83555	WINCHESTER	92.2	92.0	0.0	0.0	0.5	0.5	1.3	1.3	4.0	4.8	5.9	5.4	4.8	18.5	37.4	17.4	1.9	81.6	48.6	51.9	48.1
83601	ATLANTA	94.7	94.1	0.0	0.0	0.0	0.0	5.7	6.6	2.2	2.2	4.4	8.1	1.1	18.7	42.1	19.1	2.2	85.4	49.9	52.8	47.3
83604	BRUNEAU	87.3	86.4	0.0	0.0	0.0	0.0	20.5	22.6	5.1	5.3	6.3	8.4	6.9	27.8	27.3	12.0	1.0	76.9	38.5	56.7	43.3
83605	CALDWELL	76.3	74.3	0.4	0.5	1.0	1.1	26.2	28.8	9.6	8.3	8.0	7.4	8.7	27.6	19.3	9.2	1.9	69.8	30.0	49.0	51.0
83607	CALDWELL	83.7	82.1	0.2	0.2	0.7	0.8	18.3	20.7	8.1	8.2	8.5	7.5	6.3	26.3	23.9	10.0	1.1	70.5	33.7	50.5	49.5
83610	CAMBRIDGE	97.8	97.7	0.4	0.4	0.2	0.2	0.6	0.6	6.3	6.4	6.4	6.5	5.5	19.0	30.6	17.0	2.5	77.2	45.1	52.1	47.9
83611	CASCADE	96.3	96.1	0.0	0.0	0.5	0.6	1.6	1.8	3.9	4.4	6.1	6.6	4.5	19.0	34.5	19.4	1.6	80.4	48.2	50.6	49.4
83612	COUNCIL	96.3	96.2	0.0	0.0	0.3	0.3	1.5	1.7	3.8	4.9	6.8	7.2	3.4	17.9	37.3	16.6	2.0	79.3	48.1	51.4	48.6
83615	DONNELLY	96.0	95.9	0.0	0.0	0.4	0.3	1.8	1.7	4.6	6.7	6.9	6.2	2.6	25.2	37.0	10.5	0.5	77.2	43.9	52.9	47.1
83616	EAGLE	96.1	95.8	0.3	0.4	0.9	1.0	2.6	2.9	8.0	8.4	9.3	7.6	5.3	26.3	26.6	7.6	0.8	69.2	36.1	49.6	50.4
83617	EMMETT	93.7	93.2	0.1	0.1	0.4	0.5	7.1	8.0	7.3	7.3	7.7	6.9	6.4	24.4	24.5	13.2	2.4	73.4	37.7	49.4	50.6
83619	FRUITLAND	89.5	88.7	0.1	0.1	1.3	1.4	13.3	14.8	8.5	8.5	8.3	7.1	6.4	25.2	23.0	11.6	1.5	70.4	34.6	49.3	50.7
83622	GARDEN VALLEY	96.9	96.7	0.2	0.2	0.4	0.4	3.2	3.7	5.7	5.9	7.6	6.6	2.7	20.5	35.2	14.7	1.1	75.8	45.5	52.3	47.7
83623	GLENNS FERRY	84.5	83.6	0.1	0.1	0.3	0.3	27.6	30.0	7.4	7.8	8.3	8.5	6.1	22.4	24.6	13.2	1.8	71.3	37.3	51.1	48.9
83624	GRAND VIEW	76.1	75.2	0.2	0.3	0.5	0.4	14.2	15.7	7.5	9.0	8.8	8.7	7.0	27.1	20.8	10.2	1.0	69.0	32.7	51.8	48.2
83626	GREENLEAF	83.1	81.3	0.3	0.4	0.6	0.6	16.6	18.9	7.1	7.4	9.2	8.3	7.2	24.6	26.0	9.5	0.9	71.2	35.9	50.9	49.1
83627	HAMMETT	82.9	81.7	0.4	0.6	0.4	0.4	28.7	31.1	6.8	6.6	7.4	8.0	7.8	25.4	26.6	10.1	1.2	73.8	36.4	52.0	48.0
83628	HOMEDALE	71.5	69.3	0.2	0.2	0.9	1.1	30.1	32.8	9.8	9.2	9.2	7.4	6.4	25.6	19.6	10.8	2.1	67.0	31.5	50.3	49.7
83629	HORSESHOE BEND	94.4	94.1	0.0	0.0	0.1	0.1	5.6	6.2	6.7	7.3	7.3	6.4	6.0	25.1	29.4	10.6	1.2	73.9	38.8	51.5	48.5
83631	IDAHO CITY	94.1	94.0	0.1	0.1	0.5	0.6	3.4	3.9	6.1	6.4	8.7	6.6	3.4	26.7	33.3	8.3	0.5	73.5	40.7	50.6	49.4
83632	INDIAN VALLEY	98.1	97.7	0.0	0.0	0.5	0.5	0.0	0.0	3.2	5.0	8.2	7.8	0.5	16.0	41.6	15.5	2.3	78.1	50.7	53.4	46.6
83633	KING HILL	82.3	81.0	0.3	0.3	0.3	0.3	31.4	34.1	6.3	6.5	7.4	8.2	7.4	23.3	28.4	11.1	1.4	74.7	38.6	51.7	48.3
83634	KUNA	94.4	93.9	0.5	0.5	0.5	0.5	6.7	7.2	8.5	7.7	7.4	6.6	8.3	37.1	19.4	4.5	0.5	72.4	31.1	57.6	42.4
83636	LETHA	96.0	96.3	0.0	0.0	0.0	0.0	4.0	3.7	7.4	7.4	7.4	7.4	7.4	25.9	24.1	13.0	0.0	77.8	36.3	51.9	48.2
83637	LOWMAN	96.9	97.0	0.0	0.0	0.0	0.4	3.1	3.8	5.9	5.9	7.6	6.8	2.5	21.2	33.5	15.3	1.3	75.4	45.0	51.7	48.3
83638	MCCALL	96.6	96.5	0.0	0.0	0.3	0.3	2.2	2.5	4.6	5.6	6.9	6.8	3.6	24.1	35.1	12.1	1.3	77.9	44.1	51.8	48.2
83639	MARSING	77.0	75.4	0.2	0.2	0.2	0.2	24.6	26.5	8.6	8.3	8.3	6.8	6.8	28.6	22.1	9.3	1.2	70.6	32.6	53.5	46.5
83641	MELBA	81.4	79.0	0.3	0.3	0.5	0.6	18.7	21.4	8.1	7.9	8.5	7.4	8.4	28.2	21.9	8.7	1.1	71.1	32.8	53.9	46.1
83642	MERIDIAN	94.3	93.8	0.5	0.5	1.4	1.6	3.6	4.1	10.6	9.8	8.5	6.4	5.9	32.8	19.1	6.1	0.7	66.8	31.2	49.2	50.9
83643	MESA	96.6	96.9	0.0	0.0	0.0	0.0	1.7	2.3	2.3	4.7	7.0	5.5	2.3	14.1	45.3	17.2	1.6	81.3	51.4	51.6	48.4
83644	MIDDLETON	93.6	92.9	0.2	0.2	0.5	0.5	7.2	8.5	8.5	8.4	8.9	7.4	6.5	28.5	23.3	7.9	0.7	69.7	33.0	50.5	49.5
83645	MIDVALE	94.6	94.8	0.0	0.0	0.0	0.0	2.5	2.5	5.7	5.8	6.5	6.0	5.2	18.2	29.4	21.1	2.2	78.3	46.6	49.9	50.1
83647	MOUNTAIN HOME	86.7	85.7	1.9	2.2	1.7	1.9	12.0	13.3	8.1	7.1	7.9	8.2	7.9	29.2	21.8	8.8	1.1	71.8	32.6	51.0	49.0
83648	MOUNTAIN HOME A F B	83.2	81.8	6.7	7.5	2.7	3.0	7.1	7.9	10.2	7.8	4.8	5.5	21.1	47.6	2.6	0.3	0.0	75.2	25.2	63.2	36.8
83650	MURPHY	86.6	85.5	0.1	0.1	0.6	0.7	12.0	13.6	5.0	5.9	8.0	7.7	5.7	23.5	31.0	12.4	0.9	76.1	41.2	55.4	44.6
83651	NAMPA	83.7	82.0	0.3	0.4	1.2	1.3	16.8	19.1	9.0	8.2	7.9	6.9	7.5	27.9	18.7	11.5	2.4	70.8	32.0	48.7	51.3
83654	NEW MEADOWS	96.0	95.7	0.2	0.2	0.0	0.0	1.8	2.1	5.0	6.4	9.1	7.0	3.5	25.7	30.6	11.2	1.5	75.0	41.4	51.2	48.8
83655	NEW PLYMOUTH	93.4	92.9	0.2	0.2	0.3	0.4	7.8	8.7	7.6	7.8	8.9	7.1	6.1	25.0	24.6	11.4	1.6	71.2	35.2	50.0	50.0
83657	OLA	95.4	94.9	0.0	0.0	0.0	0.0	4.0	4.5	5.1	6.4	7.6	7.6	5.1	20.4	33.1	13.4	1.3	75.8	43.5	52.2	47.8
83660	PARMA	87.5	86.0	0.1	0.1	1.3	1.5	18.5	21.1	8.0	8.3	8.7	7.2	5.9	25.1	24.4	11.0	1.5	70.6	35.1	50.9	49.1
83661	PAYETTE	89.1	88.3	0.1	0.1	0.8	0.9	13.5	15.1	7.6	7.4	8.4	7.9	7.1	25.5	22.5	11.5	2.1	71.7	34.8	49.4	50.7
83669	STAR	95.0	94.7	0.2	0.2	0.4	0.4	3.8	4.4	9.7	9.0	7.6	6.2	6.1	31.0	22.8	6.8	0.9	69.7	32.5	49.6	50.4
83670	SWEET	95.3	95.0	0.0	0.0	0.0	0.0	3.9	4.4	5.6	6.6	7.2	7.4	5.0	20.7	31.8	14.1	1.8	75.4	43.5	52.7	47.3
83672	WEISER	85.8	85.9	0.1	0.1	1.3	1.3	16.2	16.2	7.0	7.3	8.0	6.7	6.3	23.2	24.5	14.4	2.6	73.6	38.6	49.0	51.0
83676	WILDER	65.3	63.0	0.2	0.2	0.9	1.0	39.6	42.5	8.7	8.7	9.3	8.3	6.6	25.3	22.5	9.8	0.9	68.2	32.0	50.2	49.8
83677	YELLOW PINE	88.0	82.6	0.0	0.0	4.0	4.4	0.0	0.0	0.0	8.7	4.4	0.0	0.0	17.4	52.2	17.4	0.0	87.0	49.5	56.5	43.5
83686	NAMPA	88.3	87.2	0.4	0.4	0.9	1.0	12.4	13.9	10.0	8.8	8.1	7.3	8.2	29.7	18.8	7.6	1.5	68.7	29.6	49.0	51.0
83687	NAMPA	82.2	81.5	0.3	0.4	1.0	1.1	19.8	20.5	11.2	9.6	8.0	6.8	7.1	33.6	17.2	5.8	0.8	67.1	28.7	51.1	49.0
83702	BOISE	93.9	93.4	0.6	0.7	1.4	1.6	3.6	4.2	5.7	5.1	5.2	5.9	9.0	34.4	24.7	8.4	1.7	81.0	35.2	51.0	49.0
83703	BOISE	93.3	92.8	0.6	0.7	1.2	1.4	4.8	5.4	6.8	6.6	6.4	6.7	8.4	29.4	25.8	8.3	1.7	76.3	35.4	49.5	50.5
83704	BOISE	92.1	91.3	0.7	0.8	2.4	2.9	4.5	5.1	6.8	6.5	7.4	7.5	8.3	28.4	23.0	9.9	2.2	74.8	34.5	48.9	51.1
83705	BOISE	90.7	89.9	1.0	1.1	1.9	2.1	6.3	7.1	7.2	6.4	6.3	6.2	8.9	32.2	20.7	9.9	2.3	76.7	33.1	49.4	50.6
	IDAHO	91.0	90.3	0.4	0.5	1.0	1.2	7.9	8.8	7.8	7.4	7.7	7.7	7.9	27.3	23.1	9.6	1.5	72.7	33.5	50.1	49.9
	UNITED STATES	75.1	73.6	12.3	12.5	3.8	4.2	12.5	14.1	6.9	6.7	7.2	7.0	7.3	28.6	23.8	10.8	1.7	75.1	36.0	49.1	50.9

ZIP CODE				2004 HOUSEHOLD INCOME DISTRIBUTION (%)					MEDIAN HOUSEHOLD INCOME					2004 HOME VALUE DISTRIBUTION (%)					
#	POST OFFICE NAME	2004 Per Capita Income	2004 HH Income Base	Less than $25,000	$25,000 to $49,999	$50,000 to $99,999	$100,000 to $149,999	$150,000 or More	2004	2009	2004 National Centile	2004 State Centile	2004 Home Value Base	Less than $50,000	$50,000 to $89,999	$90,000 to $174,999	$175,000 to $399,999	$400,000 or More	2004 Median Home Value
83442	RIGBY	16995	4411	25.4	33.7	31.5	7.2	2.3	42224	48478	54	77	3767	11.6	21.4	50.4	15.0	1.6	110111
83443	RIRIE	16824	191	24.6	39.8	25.7	8.4	1.6	38841	44823	42	61	159	16.4	24.5	48.4	9.4	1.3	98529
83444	ROBERTS	16318	418	27.0	30.4	34.5	5.0	3.1	44501	50755	60	84	351	18.2	30.2	45.3	5.1	1.1	91122
83445	SAINT ANTHONY	15261	2302	30.5	38.5	24.9	4.7	1.4	36351	40257	33	43	1905	18.4	32.6	38.0	10.6	0.5	88984
83446	SPENCER	19500	26	30.8	26.9	34.6	7.7	0.0	45000	40000	61	87	16	43.8	37.5	18.8	0.0	0.0	65000
83448	SUGAR CITY	16076	579	17.3	33.2	40.6	6.4	2.6	49634	56639	71	93	524	6.7	15.8	59.2	17.6	0.8	118846
83449	SWAN VALLEY	24733	180	26.7	32.8	29.4	6.1	5.0	42578	48289	55	78	154	16.9	14.3	39.0	22.7	7.1	117000
83450	TERRETON	12081	364	35.4	36.8	22.8	3.3	1.7	33305	38058	22	19	288	27.4	26.4	31.6	11.8	2.8	83529
83451	TETON	14834	253	28.5	43.1	22.5	5.1	0.8	39573	45181	45	65	220	22.3	31.4	43.2	2.7	0.5	83333
83452	TETONIA	18317	539	20.8	40.8	31.4	5.0	2.0	44576	47808	60	85	448	10.3	10.9	41.7	33.5	3.6	154577
83455	VICTOR	23017	1228	17.4	32.1	38.7	7.5	4.3	50337	57109	73	93	1002	7.4	5.4	39.6	38.5	9.1	170804
83460	REXBURG	3251	0	0.0	0.0	0.0	0.0	0.0	0	0	0	0	0	0.0	0.0	0.0	0.0	0.0	0
83462	CARMEN	17196	124	37.9	34.7	21.8	4.0	1.6	31711	36261	17	11	92	12.0	16.3	48.9	21.7	1.1	114706
83463	GIBBONSVILLE	23832	96	38.5	31.3	22.9	3.1	4.2	33416	38816	22	20	76	10.5	25.0	43.4	17.1	4.0	106250
83464	LEADORE	16005	260	41.2	37.3	15.0	4.6	1.9	31341	34136	16	10	191	26.2	17.8	31.4	14.1	10.5	100781
83466	NORTH FORK	17089	230	38.3	36.5	20.0	5.2	0.0	30632	34581	14	9	165	12.7	13.3	49.1	24.2	0.6	118304
83467	SALMON	19769	2631	35.0	34.2	23.0	5.7	2.1	35683	40058	30	36	2137	11.8	24.6	44.5	15.8	3.4	105362
83469	SHOUP	11007	31	67.7	32.3	0.0	0.0	0.0	12711	15000	1	2	27	33.3	0.0	0.0	48.2	18.5	322727
83501	LEWISTON	22421	13647	28.5	29.9	31.7	7.2	2.7	41644	49207	52	74	9639	6.7	14.3	60.8	17.3	0.8	124583
83520	AHSAHKA	19516	60	23.3	33.3	36.7	5.0	1.7	45893	49095	64	89	52	15.4	11.5	46.2	23.1	3.9	127500
83522	COTTONWOOD	20000	657	27.4	38.7	27.1	4.4	2.4	36887	41167	35	48	513	10.3	31.6	44.4	12.3	1.4	96288
83523	CRAIGMONT	19368	328	35.7	34.2	23.2	4.9	2.1	35526	39413	30	33	269	15.6	34.2	39.8	9.7	0.7	90179
83524	CULDESAC	17203	484	33.9	30.8	29.8	4.3	1.2	36330	41141	33	42	389	18.8	25.2	37.5	16.2	2.3	99400
83525	ELK CITY	16237	249	33.3	49.8	15.3	1.6	0.0	31821	36040	17	12	202	25.7	23.3	39.6	9.9	1.5	90870
83526	FERDINAND	11783	133	27.8	42.1	23.3	3.8	3.0	37313	40666	37	51	110	11.8	14.6	45.5	20.9	7.3	119048
83530	GRANGEVILLE	16956	2095	36.0	35.9	22.6	4.9	0.7	34186	37659	25	25	1656	15.6	24.2	42.1	15.6	2.5	103451
83533	GREENCREEK	16411	95	29.5	44.2	21.1	3.2	2.1	35825	38945	31	37	79	13.9	11.4	43.0	22.8	8.9	124107
83535	JULIAETTA	20425	462	32.0	33.8	27.9	3.7	2.6	37739	43499	38	55	384	21.6	23.7	41.2	12.5	1.0	96667
83536	KAMIAH	16146	1564	41.8	32.5	22.0	2.3	1.4	30429	33844	13	9	1205	16.5	22.1	37.8	19.9	3.7	103646
83537	KENDRICK	21052	454	23.6	39.7	29.1	5.1	2.6	41877	47529	53	76	372	14.5	16.9	39.8	23.1	5.7	117647
83539	KOOSKIA	14324	1161	43.9	36.3	16.7	2.5	0.6	27896	31129	8	4	924	22.1	21.8	28.1	21.7	6.4	101250
83540	LAPWAI	15010	685	34.2	30.8	29.3	4.4	1.3	36501	41609	34	45	551	18.0	22.9	37.8	18.2	3.3	103734
83541	LENORE	19928	456	29.0	33.6	30.3	5.7	1.5	40698	45730	49	70	390	13.9	15.4	35.9	27.7	7.2	135326
83542	LUCILE	15829	102	42.2	38.2	15.7	2.9	1.0	30000	31966	12	7	80	13.8	25.0	36.3	17.5	7.5	99000
83543	NEZPERCE	19029	267	28.8	34.5	29.6	4.9	2.3	40610	45110	48	67	222	18.9	32.9	40.5	5.4	2.3	87333
83544	OROFINO	18368	2414	33.1	37.2	24.7	3.9	1.1	35498	39213	29	33	1934	19.1	26.3	39.1	14.2	1.2	94757
83545	PECK	20425	245	32.7	32.7	27.4	6.5	0.8	36381	40845	33	43	203	14.3	23.7	32.0	23.7	6.4	115341
83546	PIERCE	18144	310	34.8	36.1	26.5	1.3	1.3	35884	39844	31	39	261	43.7	39.1	13.0	4.2	0.0	54024
83547	POLLOCK	17660	188	42.0	38.3	16.0	3.2	0.5	30249	33102	13	7	149	14.1	24.2	37.6	16.8	7.4	99722
83548	REUBENS	17460	67	31.3	32.8	29.9	6.0	0.0	37323	41141	37	52	56	12.5	32.1	35.7	16.1	3.6	97500
83549	RIGGINS	19081	366	42.1	38.3	15.6	2.7	1.4	30257	32703	13	8	289	13.5	24.9	38.4	16.3	6.9	99306
83553	WEIPPE	16417	490	33.9	38.0	24.7	2.2	1.2	32951	37512	21	16	403	35.2	29.0	24.6	9.4	1.7	68500
83554	WHITE BIRD	18305	285	35.8	33.7	25.3	4.9	0.4	35381	38799	29	31	232	10.3	21.6	42.2	23.7	2.2	114535
83555	WINCHESTER	21500	166	29.5	32.5	28.9	8.4	0.6	40501	44388	48	67	140	12.9	39.3	35.7	11.4	0.7	88000
83601	ATLANTA	17052	139	24.5	67.6	6.5	1.4	0.0	35384	40315	29	32	116	33.6	16.4	11.2	31.0	7.8	95000
83604	BRUNEAU	24782	319	41.7	37.9	10.7	3.5	6.3	30109	32325	13	7	184	23.9	20.7	34.8	13.0	7.6	94545
83605	CALDWELL	16295	10461	33.9	35.0	23.9	5.5	1.8	34980	39881	27	28	7066	11.4	27.8	51.6	8.8	0.5	98392
83607	CALDWELL	17930	6859	25.1	34.5	30.5	7.5	2.6	41922	46282	53	76	5730	9.0	14.4	49.5	24.7	2.4	124784
83610	CAMBRIDGE	15720	384	42.2	34.4	17.7	4.2	1.6	29315	32792	11	6	308	12.7	22.7	42.5	16.6	5.5	106132
83611	CASCADE	21153	1084	27.8	39.0	25.6	4.9	2.8	37772	43275	38	56	914	11.3	19.0	43.5	23.1	3.1	122772
83612	COUNCIL	17428	842	40.7	36.2	17.9	3.9	1.2	29450	32776	11	6	693	13.1	29.0	32.0	20.2	5.6	99237
83615	DONNELLY	26692	264	26.5	30.3	33.0	7.2	3.0	43204	49579	56	81	227	3.5	18.1	30.8	40.5	7.1	168125
83616	EAGLE	31691	6511	13.4	21.2	34.5	19.0	11.9	69947	81352	91	100	5629	7.7	3.4	27.6	46.6	14.6	199178
83617	EMMETT	17894	5568	31.0	33.9	26.8	7.0	1.4	38411	43612	41	59	4455	8.0	17.2	55.4	17.2	2.4	117602
83619	FRUITLAND	17745	2335	28.2	37.9	26.9	4.2	2.8	38776	44334	42	61	1902	11.0	22.4	51.9	14.0	0.6	103438
83622	GARDEN VALLEY	22957	909	26.7	31.0	29.0	10.0	3.2	42810	50779	55	79	761	9.5	10.3	40.6	34.0	5.7	147995
83623	GLENNS FERRY	17221	822	38.8	31.8	24.7	2.9	1.8	31740	34446	17	11	569	23.9	33.9	30.1	10.4	1.8	81759
83624	GRAND VIEW	14826	569	41.0	31.8	21.6	3.0	2.6	30505	35143	14	9	346	28.3	28.6	29.8	9.5	3.8	81429
83626	GREENLEAF	18814	454	25.8	33.0	31.1	9.0	1.1	40873	44651	49	71	377	10.1	19.9	48.8	18.8	2.4	114358
83627	HAMMETT	17039	152	27.6	35.5	29.6	4.6	2.6	39439	41376	44	64	104	21.2	18.3	29.8	26.0	4.8	112500
83628	HOMEDALE	14021	1426	41.3	33.9	18.7	4.3	1.9	29086	33495	10	5	1105	17.9	33.2	35.4	11.6	1.9	88984
83629	HORSESHOE BEND	17162	741	32.0	32.4	29.8	5.5	0.3	37097	43459	36	50	618	25.4	17.2	38.0	15.5	3.9	97541
83631	IDAHO CITY	17692	513	29.4	38.0	26.9	5.1	0.6	37643	43922	38	54	411	22.1	17.0	40.6	17.3	2.9	106840
83632	INDIAN VALLEY	20476	98	32.7	34.7	22.5	7.1	3.1	35546	40242	30	34	93	7.5	14.0	39.8	28.0	10.8	141250
83633	KING HILL	19068	123	28.5	35.8	28.5	4.1	3.3	38294	40000	40	57	83	24.1	20.5	24.1	25.3	6.0	101563
83634	KUNA	19213	4455	16.5	33.5	37.1	11.6	1.2	49976	58494	72	93	3888	3.1	4.6	60.8	25.2	6.3	133344
83636	LETHA	23519	22	22.7	31.8	31.8	9.1	4.6	45000	48618	61	87	19	0.0	10.5	47.4	42.1	0.0	162500
83637	LOWMAN	27101	113	26.6	31.0	29.2	9.7	3.5	43074	50597	56	80	95	9.5	10.5	39.0	34.7	6.3	151389
83638	MCCALL	23629	2059	25.7	31.8	32.7	7.0	2.7	42793	49583	55	79	1665	3.4	11.1	36.5	38.4	10.6	172602
83639	MARSING	15727	996	28.5	41.3	22.8	5.7	1.7	35869	41124	31	39	812	12.2	25.4	43.6	16.0	2.8	101815
83641	MELBA	17142	686	29.9	34.1	27.1	5.8	3.1	38044	42375	39	57	518	10.6	19.7	40.7	25.5	3.5	123973
83642	MERIDIAN	25726	18982	13.1	24.3	42.0	15.6	5.0	61654	72895	86	98	16383	3.8	2.5	59.4	30.6	3.7	149521
83643	MESA	18561	58	36.2	34.5	22.4	5.2	1.7	32318	35557	19	15	51	5.9	21.6	33.3	31.4	7.8	140625
83644	MIDDLETON	17236	2468	22.9	36.4	34.4	4.7	1.6	42121	47368	53	76	2042	5.5	19.2	52.1	21.5	1.7	122149
83645	MIDVALE	19312	294	38.1	31.3	20.4	3.7	6.5	33767	37025	23	22	238	16.8	12.2	38.2	19.8	13.0	125893
83647	MOUNTAIN HOME	19318	6947	26.5	36.9	28.8	6.7	1.1	40792	45332	49	70	5146	13.5	20.4	55.1	9.9	1.1	107544
83648	MOUNTAIN HOME A F B	13748	1616	24.7	55.8	17.2	2.2	0.2	34327	37674	25	26	84	21.4	16.7	39.3	22.6	0.0	121875
83650	MURPHY	16464	584	37.5	31.2	22.6	6.9	1.9	31827	36409	17	12	469	18.1	14.1	33.1	23.5	11.3	133864
83651	NAMPA	17311	9162	32.2	33.9	28.0	4.8	1.2	36519	41391	34	46	6531	13.6	21.0	58.3	6.8	0.4	102378
83654	NEW MEADOWS	17171	524	33.2	37.8	23.7	4.2	1.2	33989	38957	24	24	416	14.9	16.6	42.8	19.2	6.5	113953
83655	NEW PLYMOUTH	16467	1458	29.6	38.6	22.8	6.7	2.3	37642	42859	38	53	1173	12.5	20.0	48.0	16.0	3.5	110239
83657	OLA	20172	66	33.3	33.3	27.3	4.6	1.5	35000	40442	28	29	56	3.6	8.9	37.5	39.3	10.7	175000
83660	PARMA	16061	2111	34.5	33.6	25.7	3.2	3.0	35241	38279	28	30	1650	15.8	24.2	43.0	14.9	2.2	104775
83661	PAYETTE	16666	3610	34.7	32.3	27.3	3.1	2.5	34630	39572	26	26	2639	9.0	26.4	51.8	11.9	1.0	99199
83669	STAR	23415	1189	17.6	28.8	36.3	13.2	4.2	52881	61975	77	95	1020	2.5	8.8	51.1	28.2	9.4	148655
83670	SWEET	16423	172	31.4	33.7	27.3	5.2	2.3	35679	39829	30	35	145	4.1	8.3	39.3	38.6	9.7	167188
83672	WEISER	18522	3127	34.5	35.7	23.1	4.0	2.7	34417	39760	25	26	2408	8.9	23.4	49.9	16.1	1.7	109133
83676	WILDER	13987	1306	34.8	36.8	21.7	4.9	1.9	33217	35832	22	18	972	13.4	28.8	36.1	18.9	2.8	102119
83677	YELLOW PINE	13717	10	60.0	10.0	20.0	10.0	0.0	20000	25000	2	3	8	25.0	50.0	25.0	0.0	0.0	73333
83686	NAMPA	19739	12476	21.5	34.8	33.1	7.1	3.5	45215	52041	62	88	9655	2.3	10.3	65.3	20.6	1.5	125797
83687	NAMPA	17438	7947	22.6	36.4	33.9	5.4	1.7	42846	49660	56	80	6107	11.5	15.1	55.6	16.1	1.7	113971
83702	BOISE	34010	10531	31.4	26.7	24.8	9.1	8.2	40645	48854	48	69	5482	1.6	5.5	44.1	41.6	7.2	172621
83703	BOISE	29098	7379	21.8	26.8	32.5	11.0	7.9	51312	61776	74	94	4802	2.8	4.9	64.7	23.3	4.3	138858
83704	BOISE	24427	15649	19.9	32.0	33.8	10.8	3.5	48164	55526	69	91	10599	8.0	6.2	65.2	19.3	1.3	134039
83705	BOISE	22341	11979	27.0	34.2	30.3	6.7	1.8	41048	49117	50	72	7077	3.7	12.4	72.3	10.2	1.4	117899
	IDAHO	21160		26.4	31.8	30.4	7.9	3.5	42682	49896				9.8	16.8	49.1	20.6	3.6	122288
	UNITED STATES	25866		24.7	27.1	30.8	10.9	6.5	48124	56710				10.9	15.0	33.7	30.1	10.4	145905

ZIP CODE		FINANCIAL SERVICES				THE HOME						ENTERTAINMENT						PERSONAL			
						Home Improvements		Furnishings													
#	POST OFFICE NAME	Auto Loan	Home Loan	Invest-ments	Retire-ment Plans	Home Repair	Lawn & Garden	Comput-ers & Hard-ware	Major Appli-ances	TV, Radio, Sound Equip-ment	Furni-ture	Dine out/ Carry out	Sports Equip-ment	Fees & Tickets	Toys & Games	Travel	Cable TV	Apparel & Services	Auto Repairs	Health Insur-ance	Pets & Supplies
83442	RIGBY	83	73	59	72	76	82	72	78	75	72	91	92	68	90	72	75	86	77	81	95
83443	RIRIE	81	68	51	67	73	78	67	74	70	66	85	88	62	84	67	71	80	74	79	94
83444	ROBERTS	82	90	89	91	87	86	85	85	80	86	101	100	86	101	83	76	99	84	75	93
83445	SAINT ANTHONY	79	59	36	56	66	73	59	69	66	58	78	82	52	75	60	68	72	68	79	92
83446	SPENCER	83	65	44	59	73	82	61	74	69	61	82	86	55	81	65	74	76	73	87	101
83448	SUGAR CITY	83	85	78	84	84	86	80	82	78	81	97	98	80	98	79	76	95	81	78	96
83449	SWAN VALLEY	97	76	51	69	86	96	72	86	81	71	96	101	64	95	76	87	89	85	102	118
83450	TERRETON	67	57	41	54	59	63	54	61	57	55	69	71	50	66	54	57	66	60	63	75
83451	TETON	70	59	46	59	62	70	61	65	65	60	78	74	58	78	60	66	73	64	71	77
83452	TETONIA	73	77	75	78	76	76	74	74	70	74	88	88	73	88	72	67	86	74	67	83
83455	VICTOR	88	96	96	98	93	92	91	91	86	92	108	107	92	109	89	81	106	90	80	100
83460	REXBURG	0	0	0	0	0	0	0	0	0	0	0	0	0	0	0	0	0	0	0	0
83462	CARMEN	69	51	32	49	56	67	55	62	62	53	73	70	49	69	55	65	66	62	74	77
83463	GIBBONSVILLE	89	63	36	60	73	83	65	77	74	63	87	91	56	84	66	78	79	77	92	104
83464	LEADORE	77	54	28	51	63	70	53	66	61	52	72	79	45	70	55	64	65	65	78	91
83466	NORTH FORK	61	46	30	44	50	60	51	56	57	48	67	63	45	63	50	60	61	56	67	67
83467	SALMON	81	58	32	55	66	75	59	70	67	57	79	83	51	77	60	71	72	70	84	95
83469	SHOUP	34	26	18	24	30	33	25	30	28	25	33	35	22	33	27	30	31	30	36	41
83501	LEWISTON	76	71	68	70	73	80	74	75	76	72	93	88	72	92	73	76	89	76	79	87
83520	AHSAHKA	93	65	34	61	76	85	64	79	74	63	87	96	55	85	67	78	79	78	94	110
83522	COTTONWOOD	85	60	31	56	69	78	59	73	68	58	80	88	50	78	61	71	73	72	87	101
83523	CRAIGMONT	85	59	31	56	69	78	59	73	68	58	79	87	50	78	61	71	72	72	87	101
83524	CULDESAC	76	56	33	52	62	70	56	65	63	56	75	77	50	73	56	66	69	64	76	86
83525	ELK CITY	60	46	31	42	52	59	44	53	50	44	59	63	39	58	47	53	55	52	63	73
83526	FERDINAND	84	58	31	55	68	76	58	71	66	57	78	86	49	76	60	70	71	70	85	99
83530	GRANGEVILLE	71	52	31	50	59	67	53	62	60	52	71	73	47	69	54	63	65	62	73	82
83533	GREENCREEK	83	58	30	55	68	76	57	71	66	57	77	85	49	76	59	69	71	70	84	99
83535	JULIAETTA	80	61	40	59	67	79	66	73	73	63	87	83	59	83	65	77	79	73	86	90
83536	KAMIAH	67	47	26	43	53	62	49	58	57	48	67	67	43	63	49	60	61	57	70	76
83537	KENDRICK	92	65	34	61	75	84	64	79	74	63	86	95	55	85	66	77	79	78	94	110
83539	KOOSKIA	61	43	23	40	49	56	44	52	50	43	59	61	38	57	44	54	54	52	63	70
83540	LAPWAI	73	57	39	55	62	70	58	65	64	58	77	75	54	75	58	66	71	64	73	82
83541	LENORE	86	61	33	57	71	79	60	74	69	59	81	89	51	79	62	73	74	73	88	103
83542	LUCILE	62	47	31	45	51	61	52	57	58	49	68	64	46	64	51	61	62	57	68	68
83543	NEZPERCE	88	62	32	58	72	80	61	75	70	60	82	91	52	81	63	74	75	74	90	105
83544	OROFINO	66	48	29	46	54	63	50	58	57	49	67	68	44	64	51	60	61	58	70	76
83545	PECK	81	56	30	53	66	74	56	69	64	55	75	83	48	74	58	67	69	68	82	96
83546	PIERCE	79	54	27	47	61	70	52	65	62	53	73	77	45	70	53	67	67	64	79	91
83547	POLLOCK	63	48	31	45	52	62	52	58	58	50	69	65	46	65	52	62	63	58	69	70
83548	REUBENS	83	58	30	55	67	76	57	71	66	57	77	85	49	76	59	69	70	70	84	99
83549	RIGGINS	62	47	31	45	51	61	52	57	58	49	68	64	46	64	51	61	62	57	68	69
83553	WEIPPE	78	53	24	46	60	69	51	64	61	52	72	76	43	68	52	66	65	63	78	90
83554	WHITE BIRD	75	52	27	49	61	68	52	64	59	51	70	77	44	68	53	62	64	63	76	89
83555	WINCHESTER	87	61	32	57	71	79	60	74	69	59	81	89	51	79	62	72	74	73	88	103
83601	ATLANTA	57	45	30	40	50	56	42	51	48	42	56	59	38	56	45	51	52	50	60	69
83604	BRUNEAU	102	80	54	72	90	101	75	91	85	75	101	106	67	100	80	91	94	90	107	124
83605	CALDWELL	67	60	55	59	61	66	63	64	65	62	79	75	60	77	61	64	76	65	66	74
83607	CALDWELL	84	76	61	73	78	83	73	79	76	74	93	91	70	91	73	76	89	78	81	95
83610	CAMBRIDGE	70	49	26	46	57	64	48	60	56	48	65	72	41	64	50	58	59	59	71	83
83611	CASCADE	82	64	44	58	72	81	61	73	69	60	81	85	54	80	65	73	76	72	86	100
83612	COUNCIL	68	51	32	48	57	66	52	61	59	51	70	70	46	67	53	63	64	60	72	79
83615	DONNELLY	100	79	54	71	88	99	74	89	84	73	99	104	66	98	79	90	92	88	105	122
83616	EAGLE	130	148	145	153	142	138	133	132	122	138	155	155	138	157	131	115	154	128	114	145
83617	EMMETT	76	64	50	62	68	76	64	70	69	63	83	82	61	83	65	71	79	69	77	87
83619	FRUITLAND	77	66	51	65	69	78	67	72	71	66	86	82	64	86	67	72	81	71	78	86
83622	GARDEN VALLEY	95	75	51	67	84	94	70	85	80	70	94	99	63	93	75	85	88	83	100	116
83623	GLENNS FERRY	74	60	43	59	64	72	61	67	66	60	79	78	57	78	61	67	74	66	75	83
83624	GRAND VIEW	67	56	42	54	59	64	56	61	59	56	71	72	51	69	55	59	68	61	65	76
83626	GREENLEAF	94	84	64	80	89	95	77	86	82	77	100	102	76	102	80	84	95	84	93	111
83627	HAMMETT	95	66	38	64	75	84	69	81	78	67	92	99	59	89	69	80	84	82	94	110
83628	HOMEDALE	67	54	39	51	56	60	55	62	59	58	72	69	49	66	54	58	70	62	64	72
83629	HORSESHOE BEND	70	64	50	62	64	68	61	65	62	63	76	76	58	72	60	61	73	65	65	78
83631	IDAHO CITY	73	58	40	53	65	72	55	65	61	54	73	76	49	72	58	65	68	64	76	88
83632	INDIAN VALLEY	83	58	30	55	67	75	57	71	66	56	77	85	49	76	59	69	70	70	84	98
83633	KING HILL	97	68	36	64	79	89	67	83	77	66	91	100	57	89	70	81	83	82	99	115
83634	KUNA	74	78	75	79	77	77	74	74	70	75	88	88	74	89	73	67	86	73	67	84
83636	LETHA	93	82	63	78	87	93	76	84	81	76	98	100	75	100	78	83	93	82	91	109
83637	LOWMAN	95	75	51	67	84	95	70	85	80	70	94	99	63	93	75	85	88	84	100	116
83638	MCCALL	94	74	50	67	83	93	70	84	79	69	93	98	62	92	74	84	87	83	99	115
83639	MARSING	71	64	51	60	63	66	63	67	64	66	80	75	58	73	61	63	78	68	65	75
83641	MELBA	74	67	53	65	67	71	64	69	65	66	80	79	61	76	63	64	77	68	68	82
83642	MERIDIAN	105	118	117	123	114	111	109	108	100	112	127	126	112	129	106	94	126	105	93	118
83643	MESA	71	54	35	49	61	69	51	62	58	51	69	73	45	68	54	62	64	61	74	85
83644	MIDDLETON	77	71	60	70	73	78	68	73	70	68	86	86	67	87	69	70	82	71	75	88
83645	MIDVALE	88	61	32	58	71	80	60	75	69	60	82	90	51	80	63	73	74	74	89	104
83647	MOUNTAIN HOME	72	68	67	69	68	72	72	71	71	70	88	85	70	87	69	69	86	73	68	80
83648	MOUNTAIN HOME A F B	63	41	38	46	38	44	59	52	60	55	75	68	51	67	49	55	72	60	48	59
83650	MURPHY	80	56	29	53	65	73	55	68	63	54	74	82	47	73	57	66	68	67	81	95
83651	NAMPA	62	63	66	64	63	66	64	64	63	63	79	75	64	79	63	62	77	64	62	71
83654	NEW MEADOWS	70	56	41	53	62	69	55	63	61	55	73	73	51	72	57	64	68	62	72	81
83655	NEW PLYMOUTH	78	62	43	60	68	75	62	70	67	61	81	82	57	80	63	69	75	69	79	90
83657	OLA	86	60	31	57	70	78	59	73	68	59	80	88	51	79	62	72	73	72	87	102
83660	PARMA	74	62	46	60	65	72	61	68	65	62	79	78	58	77	61	66	75	67	73	83
83661	PAYETTE	66	60	54	58	61	68	61	64	64	60	79	74	60	79	61	65	75	64	67	76
83669	STAR	95	97	89	97	97	99	92	94	89	92	112	112	91	113	91	87	108	93	90	110
83670	SWEET	86	60	31	57	70	78	59	73	68	59	80	88	51	79	62	72	73	72	87	102
83672	WEISER	81	62	41	60	68	78	64	72	71	62	84	84	58	82	64	74	78	71	84	93
83676	WILDER	72	57	41	53	60	66	57	64	63	59	77	75	53	75	57	64	73	65	69	81
83677	YELLOW PINE	54	42	29	38	47	53	40	48	45	39	53	56	35	52	42	48	49	47	56	65
83686	NAMPA	84	82	77	82	82	86	81	82	80	80	99	97	80	100	80	78	96	82	80	95
83687	NAMPA	75	76	70	77	74	75	73	74	70	75	88	86	72	87	71	67	87	74	67	82
83702	BOISE	91	92	113	98	91	95	102	95	98	99	123	116	100	122	98	93	121	100	87	104
83703	BOISE	94	103	115	107	101	102	103	99	97	102	123	118	104	125	101	93	121	100	89	108
83704	BOISE	83	91	101	93	90	92	90	88	86	89	108	104	92	109	89	82	106	88	81	97
83705	BOISE	66	71	81	73	70	73	74	71	71	72	89	85	74	91	73	68	88	72	66	77
	IDAHO	84	79	73	78	80	85	79	81	79	78	98	96	76	97	78	78	94	81	82	96
	UNITED STATES	100	100	100	100	100	100	100	100	100	100	100	100	100	100	100	100	100	100	100	100

ZIP CODE		COUNTY FIPS CODE	POPULATION			2000-2004 ANNUAL RATE		HOUSEHOLDS					FAMILIES		
#	POST OFFICE NAME		2000	2004	2009	% Rate	State Centile	2000	2004	2009	% Annual Rate 2000-2004	2004 Average HH Size	2000	2004	% Annual Rate 2000-2004
83706	BOISE	001	29730	31305	34207	1.2	61	12781	13858	15455	1.9	2.17	7124	7402	0.9
83709	BOISE	001	34742	38972	43958	2.7	87	12070	13818	15826	3.2	2.80	9563	10836	3.0
83712	BOISE	001	7571	8024	8744	1.4	66	3372	3627	4001	1.7	2.19	1975	2045	0.8
83713	BOISE	001	22311	25344	28588	3.0	89	7568	8807	10095	3.6	2.87	5948	6777	3.1
83714	GARDEN CITY	015	16927	19660	22474	3.6	92	6688	7882	9109	3.9	2.49	4474	5145	3.3
83716	BOISE	015	11388	14005	16778	5.0	97	4148	5210	6347	5.5	2.69	3130	3847	5.0
83725	BOISE	001	780	779	817	0.0	22	0	0	0	0.0	0.00	0	0	0.0
83801	ATHOL	055	5305	5964	6621	2.8	87	1925	2174	2425	2.9	2.74	1474	1639	2.5
83802	AVERY	079	105	100	95	-1.1	3	46	45	44	-0.5	2.18	30	29	-0.8
83803	BAYVIEW	055	288	308	336	1.6	72	148	160	176	1.9	1.93	95	100	1.2
83804	BLANCHARD	017	1057	1138	1189	1.8	75	414	454	480	2.2	2.51	306	330	1.8
83805	BONNERS FERRY	021	5963	6156	6367	0.8	47	2246	2375	2513	1.3	2.53	1612	1679	1.0
83809	CAREYWOOD	017	239	252	260	1.3	62	85	92	96	1.9	2.74	66	70	1.4
83810	CATALDO	055	1386	1455	1569	1.2	60	552	590	645	1.6	2.45	408	429	1.2
83811	CLARK FORK	017	1153	1164	1174	0.2	29	490	502	512	0.6	2.32	326	328	0.1
83812	CLARKIA	079	103	98	93	-1.2	3	38	37	36	-0.6	2.62	25	24	-1.0
83813	COCOLALLA	017	1035	1097	1135	1.4	66	399	430	452	1.8	2.55	302	322	1.5
83814	COEUR D ALENE	055	22609	23150	24860	0.6	39	9310	9635	10449	0.8	2.31	5733	5782	0.2
83815	COEUR D ALENE	055	21887	24877	28014	3.1	91	8555	9851	11200	3.4	2.49	6037	6850	3.0
83821	COOLIN	017	197	200	202	0.4	34	97	101	103	1.0	1.96	62	63	0.4
83822	OLDTOWN	017	2492	2563	2611	0.7	43	960	1001	1031	1.0	2.56	679	695	0.6
83823	DEARY	057	1653	1646	1654	-0.1	20	636	640	651	0.2	2.57	475	473	-0.1
83824	DESMET	009	253	255	258	0.2	28	87	89	91	0.5	2.84	65	66	0.4
83827	ELK RIVER	035	99	103	106	0.9	54	46	49	51	1.5	2.10	35	37	1.3
83830	FERNWOOD	009	431	414	417	-0.9	4	169	166	171	-0.4	2.49	122	118	-0.8
83832	GENESEE	057	1455	1433	1433	-0.4	13	551	548	554	-0.1	2.61	421	415	-0.3
83833	HARRISON	055	1539	1625	1761	1.3	63	664	709	774	1.6	2.29	474	496	1.1
83834	HARVARD	057	254	248	248	-0.6	10	100	99	101	-0.2	2.51	78	76	-0.6
83835	HAYDEN	055	15599	17140	19043	2.2	82	5791	6454	7236	2.6	2.65	4505	4949	2.2
83836	HOPE	017	1112	1186	1232	1.5	70	483	522	548	1.8	2.27	349	371	1.5
83837	KELLOGG	079	4679	4626	4479	-0.3	14	2030	2041	2014	0.1	2.23	1255	1237	-0.3
83839	KINGSTON	079	871	840	804	-0.9	5	345	342	335	-0.2	2.46	245	240	-0.5
83842	MEDIMONT	055	84	95	107	2.9	89	35	40	46	3.2	2.35	26	29	2.6
83843	MOSCOW	057	24865	25303	25820	0.4	35	9128	9492	9884	0.9	2.25	4858	4932	0.4
83845	MOYIE SPRINGS	021	2158	2258	2355	1.1	57	815	870	924	1.6	2.59	604	637	1.3
83846	MULLAN	079	926	863	813	-1.6	1	399	380	366	-1.1	2.27	254	237	-1.6
83847	NAPLES	021	1650	1702	1760	0.7	46	608	645	684	1.4	2.54	452	473	1.1
83848	NORDMAN	017	266	267	269	0.1	26	133	137	141	0.7	1.86	84	85	0.3
83850	PINEHURST	079	2033	1932	1836	-1.2	2	876	855	833	-0.6	2.26	623	599	-0.9
83851	PLUMMER	009	1605	1649	1702	0.6	41	554	574	602	0.8	2.86	425	437	0.7
83853	PORTHILL	021	100	102	105	0.5	36	38	40	42	1.2	2.55	31	32	0.8
83854	POST FALLS	055	27068	30951	34996	3.2	91	9888	11456	13067	3.5	2.70	7372	8401	3.1
83855	POTLATCH	057	2008	1997	2003	-0.1	19	801	806	819	0.2	2.48	564	559	-0.2
83856	PRIEST RIVER	017	6086	6244	6355	0.6	40	2374	2480	2557	1.0	2.52	1695	1744	0.7
83857	PRINCETON	057	869	854	855	-0.4	11	319	318	324	-0.1	2.69	247	244	-0.3
83858	RATHDRUM	055	10315	11358	12595	2.3	83	3535	3921	4374	2.5	2.89	2845	3116	2.2
83860	SAGLE	017	5135	5330	5471	0.9	52	1991	2101	2183	1.3	2.53	1509	1571	1.0
83861	SAINT MARIES	009	6707	6917	7177	0.7	46	2704	2848	3012	1.2	2.38	1872	1940	0.8
83864	SANDPOINT	017	16492	16935	17373	0.6	41	6679	7000	7286	1.1	2.38	4441	4578	0.7
83868	SMELTERVILLE	079	292	276	262	-1.3	2	131	127	123	-0.7	2.17	85	81	-1.1
83869	SPIRIT LAKE	055	2853	3181	3514	2.6	85	1031	1146	1266	2.5	2.77	791	867	2.2
83870	TENSED	009	469	472	479	0.2	27	177	180	185	0.4	2.61	133	133	0.0
83871	TROY	057	1762	1778	1817	0.2	29	688	704	730	0.5	2.53	511	517	0.3
83872	VIOLA	057	615	641	657	1.0	56	242	256	265	1.3	2.50	185	193	1.0
83873	WALLACE	079	4533	4394	4222	-0.7	8	1948	1922	1884	-0.3	2.23	1274	1237	-0.7
83876	WORLEY	055	1252	1361	1496	2.0	80	440	481	532	2.1	2.83	338	364	1.8
	IDAHO					1.8					2.1	2.65			1.8
	UNITED STATES					1.2					1.3	2.58			1.1

#	POST OFFICE NAME	White 2000	White 2004	Black 2000	Black 2004	Asian/Pacific 2000	Asian/Pacific 2004	% Hispanic Origin 2000	% Hispanic Origin 2004	0-4	5-9	10-14	15-19	20-24	25-44	45-64	65-84	85+	18+	MEDIAN AGE 2004	% 2004 Males	% 2004 Females
83706	BOISE	91.5	90.7	1.0	1.1	2.5	2.9	4.5	5.1	6.0	5.3	5.9	8.0	12.3	30.7	22.8	7.6	1.6	79.1	32.2	49.8	50.2
83709	BOISE	92.9	92.2	0.5	0.5	2.5	2.9	4.0	4.5	7.0	7.2	7.7	7.3	7.0	28.1	26.5	8.3	1.0	73.4	35.5	49.8	50.2
83712	BOISE	94.3	93.9	0.6	0.7	1.7	1.9	2.7	3.1	5.1	5.3	5.7	5.5	8.8	29.1	29.6	9.3	1.8	80.5	38.6	48.0	52.0
83713	BOISE	92.7	92.0	0.7	0.7	2.6	3.1	3.8	4.3	9.1	8.8	8.8	7.4	6.7	30.3	22.6	5.9	0.6	68.5	32.1	49.3	50.7
83714	GARDEN CITY	91.5	91.0	0.4	0.5	1.3	1.5	7.4	8.1	8.2	7.7	6.9	5.9	6.6	31.5	22.7	9.3	1.2	73.7	34.7	50.0	50.0
83716	BOISE	92.0	91.3	1.0	1.2	2.7	3.1	3.9	4.4	9.6	9.2	8.1	6.1	4.9	36.7	20.7	4.5	0.3	69.3	32.6	51.0	49.1
83725	BOISE	84.5	83.2	1.9	2.1	4.1	4.8	8.0	8.9	5.3	2.4	1.5	27.7	37.4	19.0	5.0	1.4	0.3	90.0	21.7	48.3	51.7
83801	ATHOL	96.2	96.0	0.1	0.1	0.2	0.2	1.9	2.2	5.5	6.1	7.9	7.2	5.8	25.3	30.5	11.0	0.7	75.9	40.4	51.2	48.8
83802	AVERY	94.3	94.0	0.0	0.0	1.9	2.0	1.9	1.0	6.0	6.0	6.0	5.0	4.0	23.0	35.0	14.0	1.0	77.0	45.0	55.0	45.0
83803	BAYVIEW	95.5	95.8	0.4	0.3	0.0	0.0	1.4	1.6	2.9	3.3	4.2	3.9	3.6	14.9	40.6	25.0	1.6	87.7	54.7	52.6	47.4
83804	BLANCHARD	95.7	95.7	0.0	0.0	0.0	0.0	1.0	1.1	4.6	5.3	8.9	7.5	4.2	24.0	33.7	11.4	0.5	76.5	42.2	52.2	47.8
83805	BONNERS FERRY	94.6	94.1	0.2	0.3	0.7	0.8	3.6	4.1	7.0	6.9	7.3	7.4	7.2	22.1	27.5	12.6	2.0	73.8	38.9	49.9	50.1
83809	CAREYWOOD	95.8	95.6	0.0	0.0	0.0	0.0	2.1	2.0	5.2	5.6	8.3	6.0	3.6	25.0	35.3	10.7	0.4	76.6	43.1	52.0	48.0
83810	CATALDO	96.4	96.3	0.2	0.2	0.4	0.5	1.3	1.4	5.2	5.5	5.4	6.7	5.8	21.8	34.1	14.1	1.4	79.7	44.7	51.1	48.9
83811	CLARK FORK	95.6	95.3	0.4	0.4	0.3	0.3	1.3	1.6	4.6	5.2	6.9	5.7	4.8	18.8	36.1	16.3	1.6	79.6	47.3	50.3	49.7
83812	CLARKIA	94.2	93.9	0.0	0.0	1.9	2.0	1.9	1.0	6.1	6.1	6.1	5.1	4.1	23.5	33.7	14.3	1.0	76.5	44.4	56.1	43.9
83813	COCOLALLA	96.5	96.4	0.1	0.1	0.3	0.4	1.5	1.6	4.6	6.6	8.7	6.3	4.3	22.8	36.9	9.0	1.0	75.6	43.3	50.9	49.1
83814	COEUR D ALENE	95.9	95.7	0.2	0.2	0.7	0.7	2.5	2.8	6.2	5.8	6.1	7.0	8.6	26.7	25.5	11.6	2.6	78.1	37.2	49.5	50.5
83815	COEUR D ALENE	96.4	96.2	0.2	0.2	0.6	0.7	2.5	2.8	6.8	6.7	7.0	6.8	6.8	26.3	24.6	12.8	2.2	75.4	37.6	48.3	51.7
83821	COOLIN	96.5	97.0	0.0	0.0	0.0	0.0	1.0	0.5	3.5	6.0	4.0	5.0	3.5	21.5	39.5	16.5	0.5	82.5	49.3	52.5	47.5
83822	OLDTOWN	96.2	96.0	0.1	0.2	0.3	0.3	1.3	1.5	7.0	6.7	7.1	7.8	5.3	24.4	28.1	12.5	1.1	74.3	39.6	50.2	49.8
83823	DEARY	96.2	95.9	0.0	0.0	0.5	0.7	1.9	2.2	6.0	6.7	8.9	7.4	3.9	25.6	28.9	11.7	1.0	74.1	39.1	51.0	49.0
83824	DESMET	62.9	62.0	0.0	0.0	0.4	0.4	2.8	3.1	10.6	8.2	7.5	7.5	4.7	22.0	25.9	12.9	0.8	67.5	36.7	49.4	50.6
83827	ELK RIVER	97.0	97.1	0.0	0.0	0.0	0.0	1.0	1.0	3.9	4.9	2.9	4.9	3.9	13.6	42.7	21.4	1.9	85.4	53.3	55.3	44.7
83830	FERNWOOD	96.8	96.4	0.0	0.2	0.2	0.5	0.7	0.7	5.1	5.8	6.8	6.8	5.3	22.2	32.6	14.5	1.0	78.0	43.8	52.2	47.8
83832	GENESEE	96.7	96.6	0.1	0.1	0.6	0.7	0.9	0.9	7.5	8.2	8.2	5.7	4.1	28.5	27.1	9.7	1.1	72.4	37.8	51.9	48.2
83833	HARRISON	95.0	94.7	0.1	0.1	0.7	0.7	1.3	1.4	4.2	5.7	5.9	5.3	3.2	18.6	37.7	17.9	1.5	80.7	49.7	52.1	47.9
83834	HARVARD	97.6	97.2	0.4	0.4	0.4	0.8	2.0	2.0	5.2	5.7	6.9	7.3	7.3	23.8	30.2	12.1	1.6	77.4	41.4	53.2	46.8
83835	HAYDEN	96.9	96.7	0.1	0.2	0.6	0.7	2.1	2.4	6.2	6.8	7.9	7.1	5.5	24.8	28.4	12.1	1.3	74.7	39.8	49.6	50.4
83836	HOPE	97.6	97.4	0.5	0.5	0.4	0.5	2.1	2.3	3.8	4.4	5.6	5.1	4.5	16.6	38.5	19.3	2.2	83.1	50.5	50.1	49.9
83837	KELLOGG	95.4	95.2	0.1	0.1	0.4	0.4	1.9	2.1	6.1	6.2	6.9	6.0	5.7	24.6	26.2	15.7	2.6	77.0	41.2	49.5	50.5
83839	KINGSTON	96.0	96.0	0.0	0.0	0.3	0.4	1.3	1.4	5.1	5.6	5.6	5.4	5.0	21.3	33.5	17.1	1.4	80.0	46.2	51.9	48.1
83842	MEDIMONT	94.1	93.7	0.0	0.0	1.2	1.1	2.4	2.1	5.3	6.3	6.3	7.4	4.2	22.1	33.7	12.6	2.1	76.8	43.9	52.6	47.4
83843	MOSCOW	92.8	92.2	0.8	0.9	2.9	3.3	2.3	2.6	5.0	4.3	5.0	16.3	16.9	27.3	17.4	6.2	1.7	82.4	26.2	51.8	48.2
83845	MOYIE SPRINGS	97.4	97.3	0.1	0.0	0.4	0.5	1.4	1.6	6.2	6.9	8.9	7.1	5.4	22.8	30.8	11.5	0.6	73.3	39.7	50.0	50.0
83846	MULLAN	96.3	96.2	0.0	0.0	0.3	0.4	2.7	3.0	4.5	4.9	7.1	7.1	6.1	22.7	29.0	15.9	2.8	79.1	43.4	50.9	49.1
83847	NAPLES	94.9	94.5	0.2	0.2	0.7	0.8	5.4	6.1	7.7	7.5	7.9	7.1	6.2	23.2	29.9	9.9	0.7	72.4	38.0	52.5	47.5
83848	NORDMAN	97.4	97.4	0.4	0.4	0.0	0.0	1.1	1.1	2.3	2.6	3.0	3.4	3.0	19.1	41.2	24.0	1.5	90.3	52.0	51.7	48.3
83850	PINEHURST	96.7	96.6	0.1	0.1	0.2	0.2	1.6	1.8	5.6	5.6	6.0	5.4	5.6	23.5	30.0	16.6	1.8	79.6	43.9	48.9	51.1
83851	PLUMMER	68.3	67.0	0.5	0.5	0.3	0.3	2.5	2.6	9.0	9.0	8.6	6.9	6.8	25.2	22.9	10.6	1.0	69.1	32.6	49.3	50.7
83853	PORTHILL	96.0	96.1	0.0	0.0	1.0	1.0	2.0	2.0	7.8	7.8	8.8	6.9	5.9	22.6	29.4	10.8	0.0	69.6	37.0	48.0	52.0
83854	POST FALLS	96.2	96.0	0.2	0.2	0.6	0.7	2.3	2.7	8.4	8.4	8.3	6.7	6.3	29.5	22.8	8.7	1.0	70.7	33.5	49.5	50.5
83855	POTLATCH	96.6	96.3	0.1	0.1	0.4	0.4	2.4	2.8	5.7	6.1	8.1	7.5	6.2	25.6	26.6	12.3	1.9	75.5	39.1	50.4	49.6
83856	PRIEST RIVER	96.5	96.4	0.0	0.0	0.2	0.2	1.4	1.5	6.3	6.5	7.5	6.8	5.0	23.4	32.3	11.3	1.0	75.3	41.3	51.1	48.9
83857	PRINCETON	97.5	97.3	0.2	0.4	0.5	0.6	1.8	2.2	5.2	5.7	6.9	7.0	6.8	24.1	30.4	12.1	1.8	78.0	41.7	52.2	47.8
83858	RATHDRUM	96.1	95.9	0.2	0.2	0.4	0.5	2.6	3.0	7.6	7.8	8.7	8.0	6.6	28.0	25.6	7.2	0.5	70.9	34.4	50.6	49.4
83860	SAGLE	97.1	97.0	0.1	0.1	0.5	0.6	1.6	1.9	5.2	6.3	8.2	7.1	4.3	22.6	33.7	11.6	1.0	75.2	42.7	50.0	50.0
83861	SAINT MARIES	95.9	95.7	0.0	0.0	0.2	0.2	1.3	1.4	5.7	6.4	7.2	6.8	5.2	23.8	29.8	13.1	2.1	76.2	41.7	51.7	48.3
83864	SANDPOINT	96.6	96.5	0.1	0.1	0.4	0.4	1.9	2.1	6.0	6.2	7.2	7.1	5.8	24.3	30.4	11.1	1.9	76.0	41.0	49.3	50.7
83868	SMELTERVILLE	96.6	96.4	0.0	0.0	0.3	0.4	1.7	2.2	7.3	5.8	5.1	5.1	6.9	20.7	26.8	19.6	2.9	78.3	44.3	46.0	54.0
83869	SPIRIT LAKE	96.0	95.9	0.1	0.1	0.4	0.4	1.9	2.2	6.2	6.5	8.1	7.6	5.2	26.5	29.6	9.7	0.6	74.2	39.0	50.6	49.4
83870	TENSED	62.7	62.1	0.0	0.0	0.2	0.2	3.0	2.8	9.1	8.5	7.6	7.2	5.1	22.3	26.5	12.9	0.9	69.1	37.6	49.8	50.2
83871	TROY	96.9	96.8	0.1	0.1	0.4	0.5	0.9	1.0	6.6	7.3	8.0	5.9	4.5	26.4	29.3	10.6	1.5	74.4	39.6	51.6	48.4
83872	VIOLA	95.3	95.0	0.0	0.0	0.5	0.6	2.9	3.4	5.5	6.7	8.4	6.2	4.2	24.8	32.1	10.9	1.1	75.7	41.6	51.2	48.8
83873	WALLACE	95.8	95.7	0.2	0.2	0.2	0.3	2.2	2.5	5.0	5.3	6.0	6.2	5.7	22.5	31.1	15.8	2.3	79.5	44.5	50.2	49.8
83876	WORLEY	62.9	62.3	0.2	0.2	0.4	0.4	1.6	1.5	8.5	8.7	7.7	5.5	4.1	24.8	28.0	11.7	1.0	71.5	38.5	50.8	49.2
	IDAHO	91.0	90.3	0.4	0.5	1.0	1.2	7.9	8.8	7.8	7.4	7.7	7.7	7.9	27.3	23.1	9.6	1.5	72.7	33.5	50.1	49.9
	UNITED STATES	75.1	73.6	12.3	12.5	3.8	4.2	12.5	14.1	6.9	6.7	7.2	7.0	7.3	28.6	23.8	10.8	1.7	75.1	36.0	49.1	50.9

C   83706-83876

#	POST OFFICE NAME	2004 Per Capita Income	2004 HH Income Base	2004 HOUSEHOLD INCOME DISTRIBUTION (%)					MEDIAN HOUSEHOLD INCOME				2004 Home Value Base	2004 HOME VALUE DISTRIBUTION (%)					2004 Median Home Value
				Less than $25,000	$25,000 to $49,999	$50,000 to $99,999	$100,000 to $149,999	$150,000 or More	2004	2009	2004 National Centile	2004 State Centile		Less than $50,000	$50,000 to $89,999	$90,000 to $174,999	$175,000 to $399,999	$400,000 or More	
83706	BOISE	31138	13858	25.1	30.3	27.4	9.8	7.4	44562	52327	60	85	7526	3.6	7.3	54.1	30.4	4.7	145431
83709	BOISE	25147	13818	13.3	24.8	43.1	14.1	4.6	60774	70959	85	97	11739	2.3	3.4	61.8	30.6	2.0	152024
83712	BOISE	36675	3627	21.1	23.0	30.2	16.2	9.6	56427	65855	81	96	2319	0.1	1.5	32.7	56.6	9.1	201452
83713	BOISE	28080	8807	12.4	23.2	40.5	16.4	7.5	64068	76255	88	99	7338	8.4	3.5	48.7	36.3	3.2	154733
83714	GARDEN CITY	26701	7882	20.1	31.0	32.5	11.0	5.5	48896	59276	70	92	5757	14.7	8.5	44.2	27.6	4.9	139065
83716	BOISE	29269	5210	10.2	22.9	44.4	15.5	7.0	64689	76622	88	100	4516	8.1	6.2	51.4	29.9	4.4	145647
83725	BOISE	5920	0	0.0	0.0	0.0	0.0	0.0	0	0	0	0	0	0.0	0.0	0.0	0.0	0.0	0
83801	ATHOL	17676	2174	28.7	35.3	28.8	4.5	2.7	38898	44259	42	62	1859	10.9	14.3	45.7	26.5	2.7	132078
83802	AVERY	18412	45	40.0	33.3	20.0	6.7	0.0	32320	35000	19	15	32	31.3	21.9	28.1	18.8	0.0	80000
83803	BAYVIEW	25930	160	31.3	26.9	33.8	3.8	4.4	41149	46159	50	73	133	12.8	15.0	33.8	35.3	3.0	149167
83804	BLANCHARD	14815	454	35.9	35.5	26.7	1.3	0.7	33728	38401	23	22	390	13.1	26.7	44.6	15.6	0.0	105903
83805	BONNERS FERRY	17322	2375	37.0	34.1	23.5	2.9	2.5	32842	37084	20	16	1829	11.1	19.0	43.9	22.1	3.9	115492
83809	CAREYWOOD	20075	92	26.1	33.7	33.7	2.2	4.4	40633	46302	48	68	79	2.5	7.6	43.0	31.7	15.2	166071
83810	CATALDO	19006	590	29.8	31.5	31.4	7.0	0.3	39438	43984	44	64	502	14.9	20.3	35.5	18.5	10.8	117188
83811	CLARK FORK	17100	502	42.4	27.5	24.5	3.6	2.0	28800	33573	10	5	410	15.6	31.5	29.5	18.1	5.4	93158
83812	CLARKIA	15562	37	37.8	35.1	21.6	5.4	0.0	32302	37347	19	14	26	38.5	19.2	23.1	19.2	0.0	75000
83813	COCOLALLA	18404	430	28.6	32.1	33.7	4.2	1.4	38935	45361	43	62	366	6.8	11.8	43.2	30.6	7.7	147826
83814	COEUR D ALENE	21964	9635	31.5	33.7	25.7	5.7	3.4	37732	43726	38	55	5948	2.8	11.0	53.5	25.8	6.9	136234
83815	COEUR D ALENE	22151	9851	25.6	31.7	31.0	8.3	3.4	42910	50148	56	90	7361	9.1	8.0	53.6	27.3	2.0	140757
83821	COOLIN	27889	101	31.7	24.8	31.7	5.9	5.9	39446	44450	44	65	84	7.1	9.5	40.5	35.7	7.1	153571
83822	OLDTOWN	14441	1001	38.7	37.2	21.0	3.0	0.2	31699	36649	17	11	841	18.1	20.2	42.1	17.6	2.0	104360
83823	DEARY	20382	640	27.7	30.2	31.9	8.6	1.7	43367	50878	57	82	551	23.8	20.5	29.2	23.2	3.3	101907
83824	DESMET	13280	89	37.1	38.2	21.4	3.4	0.0	31983	34590	18	13	71	25.4	19.7	33.8	15.5	5.6	95000
83827	ELK RIVER	17917	49	32.7	46.9	18.4	2.0	0.0	33560	37245	23	21	41	22.0	17.1	39.0	17.1	4.9	112500
83830	FERNWOOD	15995	166	34.3	34.3	29.5	0.6	1.2	32283	36319	19	14	143	32.9	21.0	36.4	9.1	0.7	83889
83832	GENESEE	23153	548	21.2	31.0	36.5	6.0	5.3	48328	54826	69	91	452	15.3	11.5	55.3	16.2	1.8	123529
83833	HARRISON	22283	709	22.7	37.8	30.3	6.4	2.8	41814	48526	52	75	609	7.1	8.9	28.9	35.5	19.7	197500
83834	HARVARD	21157	99	33.3	32.3	31.3	1.0	2.0	36758	43066	35	46	86	20.9	16.3	41.9	18.6	2.3	107500
83835	HAYDEN	24301	6454	21.9	30.5	33.2	9.8	4.7	47701	54842	68	91	5565	6.5	4.6	48.3	33.5	7.2	158099
83836	HOPE	22167	522	36.0	29.5	22.4	7.7	4.4	36816	42275	35	47	441	3.4	12.5	29.9	42.9	11.3	187171
83837	KELLOGG	18159	2041	41.3	33.6	20.9	2.5	1.7	30271	34253	13	8	1380	26.4	37.8	30.7	4.6	0.6	75535
83839	KINGSTON	18698	342	36.6	30.1	26.3	4.7	2.3	33620	37187	23	22	287	22.7	25.4	41.1	8.0	2.8	91719
83842	MEDIMONT	19381	40	27.5	32.5	32.5	7.5	0.0	42301	46120	54	77	35	20.0	11.4	31.4	28.6	8.6	134375
83843	MOSCOW	20204	9492	38.4	25.5	26.2	7.6	2.4	34708	42016	26	27	4560	14.6	5.2	46.3	32.0	1.9	150202
83845	MOYIE SPRINGS	18339	870	28.4	34.0	32.1	2.8	2.8	38332	43545	41	58	736	7.3	19.8	45.1	23.6	4.1	124385
83846	MULLAN	17810	380	31.6	39.7	25.3	3.4	0.0	35630	40716	30	35	292	34.3	41.1	21.6	3.1	0.0	67143
83847	NAPLES	18116	645	29.3	35.2	31.0	3.3	1.2	37778	42758	38	56	541	10.9	17.9	42.0	24.4	4.8	120964
83848	NORDMAN	34394	137	32.1	26.3	27.7	9.5	4.4	35844	40851	31	38	116	8.6	15.5	25.9	33.6	16.4	175000
83850	PINEHURST	18165	855	39.0	27.4	28.4	4.7	0.6	33245	37210	22	18	699	21.6	33.6	39.2	5.6	0.0	83814
83851	PLUMMER	14186	574	34.8	34.3	26.3	3.7	0.9	33512	38219	22	20	453	24.7	23.0	33.8	15.7	2.9	93000
83853	PORTHILL	19559	40	37.5	27.5	25.0	2.5	7.5	37354	50000	37	52	34	11.8	14.7	38.2	23.5	11.8	133333
83854	POST FALLS	20475	11456	22.9	35.8	32.4	6.3	2.7	43434	50013	57	83	9078	11.1	7.9	57.0	21.1	3.0	132266
83855	POTLATCH	19850	806	25.9	33.6	34.6	4.0	1.9	40893	49101	49	72	636	22.2	25.0	31.8	20.0	1.1	95455
83856	PRIEST RIVER	17353	2480	33.6	34.8	26.2	4.0	1.4	36042	41513	32	41	2065	12.5	21.5	42.4	19.7	4.0	116105
83857	PRINCETON	19896	318	30.8	31.5	34.3	1.9	1.6	38506	45000	41	59	275	20.7	15.3	41.8	20.0	2.2	110662
83858	RATHDRUM	17957	3921	22.0	34.2	35.4	6.5	1.9	45027	51119	61	87	3324	7.8	12.3	54.7	22.1	3.1	131032
83860	SAGLE	19454	2101	29.7	30.6	28.6	9.9	1.2	40653	46950	48	69	1803	11.6	9.0	33.6	36.2	9.7	164742
83861	SAINT MARIES	19113	2848	32.5	34.8	26.0	5.4	1.4	36335	41448	33	43	2339	24.1	22.3	36.0	15.4	2.2	95182
83864	SANDPOINT	21701	7000	32.2	30.4	28.2	6.6	2.6	38500	44958	41	59	5156	7.8	15.6	41.6	30.2	4.8	135323
83868	SMELTERVILLE	16460	127	48.8	29.1	17.3	3.9	0.8	25724	29707	5	4	92	10.9	50.0	34.8	4.4	0.0	80000
83869	SPIRIT LAKE	16808	1146	29.3	34.2	30.3	4.1	2.1	40483	45954	48	67	972	9.0	15.6	42.4	30.5	2.6	137277
83870	TENSED	14589	180	38.3	36.7	21.1	3.3	0.6	31682	35935	17	10	144	24.3	20.1	33.3	16.0	6.3	96154
83871	TROY	22352	704	18.9	32.2	37.5	9.7	1.7	48695	56492	70	92	593	4.4	9.3	47.6	37.1	1.7	148645
83872	VIOLA	24081	256	16.8	26.2	46.1	8.2	2.7	57146	63979	82	96	228	11.8	2.6	46.5	33.3	5.7	148780
83873	WALLACE	18084	1922	37.9	35.3	21.0	4.9	0.8	31964	36443	18	13	1484	23.3	38.1	32.6	5.9	0.2	77640
83876	WORLEY	20815	481	27.7	27.9	29.1	11.2	4.2	44587	52560	60	86	382	8.4	11.3	31.9	32.5	16.0	168750
	IDAHO	21160		26.4	31.8	30.4	7.9	3.5	42682	49896				9.8	16.8	49.1	20.6	3.6	122288
	UNITED STATES	25866		24.7	27.1	30.8	10.9	6.5	48124	56710				10.9	15.0	33.7	30.1	10.4	145905

ZIP CODE #	POST OFFICE NAME	FINANCIAL SERVICES				THE HOME						ENTERTAINMENT						PERSONAL			
						Home Improvements		Furnishings													
		Auto Loan	Home Loan	Invest-ments	Retire-ment Plans	Home Repair	Lawn & Garden	Comput-ers & Hard-ware	Major Appli-ances	TV, Radio, Sound Equip-ment	Furni-ture	Dine out/ Carry out	Sports Equip-ment	Fees & Tickets	Toys & Games	Travel	Cable TV	Apparel & Services	Auto Repairs	Health Insur-ance	Pets & Supplies
83706	BOISE	95	92	105	98	90	95	102	96	98	100	123	116	99	120	96	92	120	100	87	105
83709	BOISE	96	110	114	111	106	106	102	101	95	103	120	118	105	124	101	91	119	99	90	111
83712	BOISE	107	109	132	116	107	112	119	111	114	116	143	135	118	142	114	108	141	116	101	122
83713	BOISE	115	126	122	129	122	120	117	117	109	120	138	137	119	138	115	103	136	115	103	129
83714	GARDEN CITY	96	102	99	104	100	100	96	96	91	98	114	113	96	113	94	86	112	95	88	108
83716	BOISE	111	127	124	130	122	119	114	114	105	117	133	133	118	136	113	100	132	111	99	126
83725	BOISE	0	0	0	0	0	0	0	0	0	0	0	0	0	0	0	0	0	0	0	0
83801	ATHOL	77	70	56	67	71	76	66	72	68	68	84	81	63	78	67	68	80	71	74	85
83802	AVERY	68	54	37	48	60	68	51	61	57	50	68	71	45	67	54	61	63	60	72	83
83803	BAYVIEW	76	71	68	67	75	88	65	74	69	70	86	73	66	72	71	74	81	72	87	85
83804	BLANCHARD	70	47	21	40	53	61	45	57	55	46	64	68	38	61	46	59	58	56	70	80
83805	BONNERS FERRY	76	57	34	54	64	71	56	67	63	55	75	79	50	73	58	66	69	66	78	89
83809	CAREYWOOD	88	78	59	74	83	89	72	80	77	72	94	96	71	96	75	79	89	78	87	104
83810	CATALDO	79	61	39	58	68	76	60	70	67	59	80	83	55	79	62	70	74	69	81	93
83811	CLARK FORK	64	49	32	46	53	63	53	59	59	50	70	66	47	66	53	63	64	59	70	72
83812	CLARKIA	69	54	37	49	61	68	51	61	58	50	68	72	45	67	54	61	63	60	72	84
83813	COCOLALLA	82	62	38	59	70	77	60	71	67	59	79	85	54	79	62	70	73	70	82	97
83814	COEUR D ALENE	68	70	81	72	70	73	74	71	72	72	90	85	74	91	73	70	89	73	67	78
83815	COEUR D ALENE	77	81	83	81	80	83	79	79	77	79	96	92	79	96	79	75	94	79	75	89
83821	COOLIN	93	73	50	66	82	92	69	83	78	68	92	97	62	91	73	83	86	82	98	114
83822	OLDTOWN	61	52	37	49	53	58	50	55	53	51	64	64	46	61	49	53	60	55	58	69
83823	DEARY	84	75	57	71	79	85	69	77	73	69	89	91	68	91	71	75	85	75	83	99
83824	DESMET	68	48	25	45	56	62	47	58	54	47	64	70	40	62	49	57	58	57	69	81
83827	ELK RIVER	64	50	34	45	56	63	47	57	53	47	63	67	42	63	50	57	59	56	67	78
83830	FERNWOOD	75	50	23	43	57	66	49	61	59	49	69	73	41	65	49	63	63	60	75	86
83832	GENESEE	110	77	40	72	89	100	76	93	87	75	102	112	65	100	78	92	93	92	111	130
83833	HARRISON	88	67	43	61	76	85	64	78	73	63	86	92	56	85	68	77	79	76	92	107
83834	HARVARD	85	76	58	72	80	86	70	77	74	70	90	92	68	92	72	76	86	75	84	100
83835	HAYDEN	93	95	89	94	96	102	90	93	89	90	111	107	91	111	91	89	107	91	94	107
83836	HOPE	86	67	45	60	75	85	63	76	72	63	85	89	56	84	67	76	79	75	90	104
83837	KELLOGG	65	50	33	47	54	65	54	60	61	51	71	67	48	68	54	64	65	60	72	73
83839	KINGSTON	77	57	36	53	63	74	60	68	68	58	80	78	53	76	61	72	73	68	82	87
83842	MEDIMONT	83	58	30	55	67	75	57	70	66	56	77	85	49	76	59	69	70	69	84	98
83843	MOSCOW	65	55	65	59	54	59	72	63	70	67	88	80	66	83	65	65	84	69	58	70
83845	MOYIE SPRINGS	80	65	43	62	69	75	63	72	67	63	81	85	57	78	63	68	76	71	78	92
83846	MULLAN	65	49	32	47	54	64	54	60	61	52	72	67	48	68	54	64	65	60	72	72
83847	NAPLES	78	63	42	60	68	74	60	69	65	60	78	82	55	77	61	67	74	68	76	90
83848	NORDMAN	111	87	59	79	98	110	82	99	93	81	110	116	73	109	88	99	102	97	117	135
83850	PINEHURST	66	53	39	49	57	66	54	60	60	53	72	69	50	69	55	63	67	60	70	75
83851	PLUMMER	66	54	39	51	58	64	54	60	58	54	70	69	49	67	54	60	66	60	67	75
83853	PORTHILL	90	63	33	60	73	82	62	77	72	61	84	93	53	82	65	75	77	76	92	107
83854	POST FALLS	82	80	73	80	81	84	77	80	77	78	95	94	76	95	77	76	92	80	79	94
83855	POTLATCH	80	65	47	64	70	79	66	73	71	65	85	85	61	84	66	72	79	72	81	91
83856	PRIEST RIVER	74	59	40	55	64	71	57	65	62	57	75	77	52	73	58	64	70	64	73	85
83857	PRINCETON	85	77	60	73	81	86	71	78	75	71	91	93	70	93	73	76	87	76	84	100
83858	RATHDRUM	78	77	68	76	77	79	73	76	72	74	89	89	71	88	72	70	86	75	73	89
83860	SAGLE	81	68	49	64	74	81	64	73	69	64	84	87	60	84	66	72	79	72	82	97
83861	SAINT MARIES	78	59	37	55	65	74	59	68	66	58	79	80	53	77	60	69	73	67	80	90
83864	SANDPOINT	81	70	57	68	74	81	70	76	74	69	89	90	66	88	71	75	85	76	82	94
83868	SMELTERVILLE	56	45	33	43	48	57	48	52	53	46	63	59	44	60	48	56	58	52	62	63
83869	SPIRIT LAKE	77	65	47	61	68	74	62	70	66	63	80	81	57	76	63	67	76	69	75	88
83870	TENSED	69	48	25	45	56	63	47	59	55	47	64	71	41	63	49	57	58	58	70	82
83871	TROY	90	80	62	77	86	91	75	85	79	74	95	101	71	97	77	80	90	83	91	108
83872	VIOLA	79	97	103	97	96	94	87	87	80	86	101	101	92	108	89	78	101	83	78	96
83873	WALLACE	65	49	33	47	54	64	54	60	61	51	71	67	48	67	54	64	65	60	71	73
83876	WORLEY	100	78	54	71	88	99	74	89	84	73	99	104	66	98	79	89	92	88	105	122
IDAHO		84	79	73	78	80	85	79	81	79	78	98	96	76	97	78	78	94	81	82	96
UNITED STATES		100	100	100	100	100	100	100	100	100	100	100	100	100	100	100	100	100	100	100	100

ILLINOIS

A 60002-60146

POPULATION CHANGE

#	POST OFFICE NAME	COUNTY FIPS CODE	POPULATION 2000	2004	2009	% Rate	State Centile	HOUSEHOLDS 2000	2004	2009	% Annual Rate 2000-2004	2004 Average HH Size	FAMILIES 2000	2004	% Annual Rate 2000-2004
60002	ANTIOCH	097	19450	21089	22978	1.9	88	7382	8037	8776	2.0	2.62	5342	5732	1.7
60004	ARLINGTON HEIGHTS	031	52064	51729	51963	-0.2	34	19942	20030	20269	0.1	2.56	14029	13846	-0.3
60005	ARLINGTON HEIGHTS	031	29197	29432	29808	0.2	51	12660	12805	13030	0.3	2.27	7741	7772	0.1
60007	ELK GROVE VILLAGE	031	35531	35115	35119	-0.3	26	13556	13608	13739	0.1	2.57	9467	9352	-0.3
60008	ROLLING MEADOWS	031	23243	23363	23454	0.1	48	8388	8477	8556	0.3	2.73	5767	5747	-0.1
60010	BARRINGTON	031	41472	42740	44758	0.7	72	14544	15131	15939	0.9	2.82	11973	12340	0.7
60012	CRYSTAL LAKE	111	9620	11128	12883	3.5	95	3106	3651	4279	3.9	3.02	2583	3010	3.7
60013	CARY	111	23834	26376	29965	2.4	91	7684	8558	9793	2.6	3.08	6288	6925	2.3
60014	CRYSTAL LAKE	111	44904	50466	58332	2.8	94	15301	17318	20166	3.0	2.91	11754	13152	2.7
60015	DEERFIELD	097	25987	26928	28795	0.8	75	8760	9182	9891	1.1	2.83	7060	7302	0.8
60016	DES PLAINES	031	58529	59588	60294	0.4	63	23485	23935	24275	0.5	2.46	15029	15061	0.1
60018	DES PLAINES	031	29738	30405	30865	0.5	66	10326	10584	10791	0.6	2.82	7232	7320	0.3
60020	FOX LAKE	097	7169	7704	8378	1.7	86	3255	3524	3848	1.9	2.19	1895	2005	1.3
60021	FOX RIVER GROVE	111	5679	6046	6716	1.5	84	1989	2138	2396	1.7	2.82	1524	1616	1.4
60022	GLENCOE	031	8527	8440	8413	-0.2	28	2988	2970	2976	-0.1	2.84	2484	2448	-0.3
60025	GLENVIEW	031	50555	52691	54006	1.0	77	18953	19879	20489	1.1	2.61	14121	14634	0.8
60029	GOLF	031	67	66	65	-0.4	22	23	23	23	0.0	2.87	19	18	-1.3
60030	GRAYSLAKE	097	31645	35426	39333	2.7	93	11326	12689	14112	2.7	2.79	8687	9616	2.4
60031	GURNEE	097	36289	41635	46737	3.3	95	13301	15291	17206	3.3	2.72	9835	11187	3.1
60033	HARVARD	111	13120	14037	15618	1.6	85	4397	4737	5308	1.8	2.95	3302	3504	1.4
60034	HEBRON	111	1914	2217	2571	3.5	96	702	827	971	3.9	2.68	520	604	3.6
60035	HIGHLAND PARK	097	30644	31476	33574	0.6	70	11321	11706	12532	0.8	2.67	8755	8944	0.5
60037	FORT SHERIDAN	097	944	1313	1614	8.1	100	259	360	443	8.1	3.65	226	311	7.8
60040	HIGHWOOD	097	4111	4264	4580	0.9	75	1545	1592	1709	0.7	2.62	927	935	0.2
60041	INGLESIDE	097	9260	10930	12585	4.0	96	3417	4071	4709	4.2	2.68	2532	2993	4.0
60042	ISLAND LAKE	111	8549	9398	10515	2.3	90	2969	3297	3718	2.5	2.84	2233	2440	2.1
60043	KENILWORTH	031	2610	2511	2482	-0.9	5	830	800	794	-0.9	3.14	722	691	-1.0
60044	LAKE BLUFF	097	10648	10942	11571	0.6	70	4206	4343	4609	0.8	2.47	2893	2939	0.4
60045	LAKE FOREST	097	21875	22580	24061	0.8	73	7279	7612	8188	1.1	2.74	5827	6023	0.8
60046	LAKE VILLA	097	30240	33846	37437	2.7	93	10346	11632	12908	2.8	2.88	8272	9219	2.6
60047	LAKE ZURICH	097	35425	38284	41635	1.8	87	11086	12048	13146	2.0	3.14	9618	10379	1.8
60048	LIBERTYVILLE	097	29098	30575	33018	1.2	80	9961	10481	11351	1.2	2.84	7585	7929	1.1
60050	MCHENRY	111	35203	37941	42749	1.8	87	12598	13804	15741	2.2	2.73	9308	10036	1.8
60051	MCHENRY	111	12733	13873	15739	2.0	89	4559	5064	5816	2.5	2.74	3490	3810	2.1
60053	MORTON GROVE	031	22101	22807	23268	0.7	73	7944	8263	8486	0.9	2.75	6173	6332	0.6
60056	MOUNT PROSPECT	031	57125	58312	59142	0.5	66	21815	22269	22652	0.5	2.61	15301	15458	0.2
60060	MUNDELEIN	097	36392	39451	42969	1.9	88	11648	12584	13689	1.8	3.12	9091	9707	1.5
60061	VERNON HILLS	097	20899	22560	24636	1.8	87	7774	8410	9192	1.9	2.68	5567	5952	1.6
60062	NORTHBROOK	031	40565	40781	41179	0.1	48	15048	15282	15547	0.4	2.60	11626	11666	0.1
60064	NORTH CHICAGO	097	15080	15602	16657	0.8	74	4670	4790	5096	0.6	3.21	3348	3389	0.3
60067	PALATINE	031	36666	37847	38579	0.8	73	14506	15222	15682	1.1	2.46	9746	10017	0.7
60068	PARK RIDGE	031	37797	37907	38214	0.1	45	14236	14473	14726	0.4	2.58	10523	10554	0.1
60069	LINCOLNSHIRE	097	7346	7900	8618	1.7	86	2621	2853	3135	2.0	2.74	2236	2406	1.7
60070	PROSPECT HEIGHTS	031	16652	16909	17058	0.4	61	6241	6317	6379	0.3	2.68	3902	3868	-0.2
60071	RICHMOND	111	3210	3692	4264	3.4	95	1142	1337	1563	3.8	2.76	878	1012	3.4
60072	RINGWOOD	111	590	692	808	3.8	96	217	259	305	4.3	2.67	184	217	4.0
60073	ROUND LAKE	097	39399	45659	51728	3.5	96	11856	13901	15869	3.8	3.27	9351	10808	3.5
60074	PALATINE	031	39013	40648	41867	1.0	77	14756	15278	15719	0.8	2.66	9750	9922	0.4
60076	SKOKIE	031	33955	34963	35863	0.7	71	11601	11995	12361	0.8	2.84	9050	9273	0.6
60077	SKOKIE	031	24691	24806	24898	0.1	47	9908	9993	10068	0.2	2.45	6676	6618	-0.2
60081	SPRING GROVE	111	7675	8790	10074	3.2	95	2590	2986	3440	3.4	2.94	2001	2292	3.3
60082	TECHNY	031	91	110	121	4.6	98	37	45	50	4.7	2.42	31	38	4.9
60083	WADSWORTH	097	5445	6198	6912	3.1	94	1908	2193	2458	3.3	2.83	1446	1630	2.9
60084	WAUCONDA	097	12921	13797	14881	1.6	85	4841	5187	5606	1.6	2.63	3384	3581	1.3
60085	WAUKEGAN	097	72877	77577	84018	1.5	84	23026	24294	26235	1.3	3.11	15565	16136	0.9
60087	WAUKEGAN	097	24776	27266	29998	2.3	91	8496	9382	10345	2.4	2.89	6300	6845	2.0
60088	GREAT LAKES	097	19527	19039	19931	-0.6	13	2183	2056	2149	-1.4	3.39	2012	1885	-1.5
60089	BUFFALO GROVE	097	44319	47114	50628	1.5	84	16257	17267	18528	1.4	2.71	12240	12932	1.3
60090	WHEELING	031	36869	37780	38375	0.6	68	14296	14646	14909	0.6	2.55	9385	9458	0.2
60091	WILMETTE	031	27745	27990	28239	0.2	53	10068	10203	10345	0.3	2.72	7732	7761	0.1
60093	WINNETKA	031	19627	19821	19985	0.2	54	6957	7046	7134	0.3	2.81	5489	5504	0.1
60096	WINTHROP HARBOR	097	6740	6923	7349	0.6	70	2393	2474	2636	0.8	2.80	1878	1922	0.6
60097	WONDER LAKE	111	10015	11005	12423	2.2	90	3527	3940	4500	2.6	2.79	2730	3004	2.3
60098	WOODSTOCK	111	27484	29796	33344	1.9	88	9787	10791	12247	2.3	2.69	6922	7477	1.8
60099	ZION	097	30166	31431	33626	1.0	77	10263	10774	11579	1.2	2.87	7600	7863	0.8
60101	ADDISON	043	37872	39201	40921	0.8	74	12317	12813	13465	0.9	3.04	9542	9820	0.7
60102	ALGONQUIN	111	25361	30020	35595	4.1	97	8495	10070	11968	4.1	2.98	6910	8208	3.8
60103	BARTLETT	043	37214	39476	41337	1.4	83	12367	13319	14093	1.8	2.96	10097	10770	1.5
60104	BELLWOOD	031	20517	20270	20254	-0.3	26	6434	6425	6470	0.0	3.14	5095	5031	-0.3
60106	BENSENVILLE	043	22766	23697	24833	1.0	77	7589	7888	8298	0.9	2.95	5233	5364	0.6
60107	STREAMWOOD	031	36087	36428	36774	0.2	53	11929	12209	12435	0.6	2.96	9138	9248	0.3
60108	BLOOMINGDALE	043	21977	23078	24199	1.2	80	8318	8869	9460	1.6	2.51	5804	6118	1.3
60110	CARPENTERSVILLE	089	32171	37088	44098	3.4	95	9338	10740	12730	3.4	3.45	7754	8828	3.1
60111	CLARE	037	325	364	404	2.7	93	119	135	151	3.0	2.70	92	103	2.7
60112	CORTLAND	037	2098	2343	2593	2.6	92	721	809	901	2.8	2.90	535	591	2.4
60115	DEKALB	037	41919	45064	48913	1.7	86	14358	15776	17504	2.2	2.39	7261	7820	1.8
60118	DUNDEE	089	14779	17620	21271	4.2	97	5427	6441	7741	4.1	2.73	4080	4780	3.8
60119	ELBURN	089	7720	9568	11770	5.2	99	2692	3332	4086	5.2	2.87	2195	2680	4.8
60120	ELGIN	031	48945	52137	57246	1.5	84	15556	16524	18021	1.4	3.14	11324	11851	1.1
60123	ELGIN	089	55173	61829	72325	2.7	93	19262	21513	25129	2.6	2.80	13859	15281	2.3
60126	ELMHURST	043	45196	45901	47657	0.4	61	16477	16953	17806	0.7	2.63	11966	12170	0.4
60129	ESMOND	141	373	413	451	2.4	92	131	147	162	2.8	2.81	100	111	2.5
60130	FOREST PARK	031	15688	15432	15369	-0.4	20	7632	7534	7537	-0.3	2.02	3477	3344	-0.9
60131	FRANKLIN PARK	031	19090	18947	18945	-0.2	32	6381	6344	6363	-0.1	2.96	4665	4576	-0.5
60133	HANOVER PARK	043	38329	38911	39785	0.4	61	11081	11301	11632	0.5	3.44	9035	9137	0.3
60134	GENEVA	089	21601	25699	30995	4.2	97	7346	8684	10438	4.0	2.90	5609	6547	3.7
60135	GENOA	037	6012	6339	6809	1.3	81	2193	2336	2530	1.5	2.71	1657	1741	1.2
60136	GILBERTS	089	1588	2062	2593	6.3	99	495	645	810	6.4	3.20	435	562	6.2
60137	GLEN ELLYN	043	38594	39696	41496	0.7	71	14320	14837	15636	0.8	2.67	10274	10552	0.6
60139	GLENDALE HEIGHTS	043	31912	32692	33875	0.6	68	10834	11231	11753	0.9	2.91	7752	7903	0.5
60140	HAMPSHIRE	089	7507	9081	11031	4.6	98	2578	3123	3789	4.6	2.90	2096	2508	4.3
60142	HUNTLEY	111	7619	10937	14140	8.9	100	2943	4255	5540	9.1	2.57	2358	3350	8.6
60143	ITASCA	043	9456	9510	9812	0.1	48	3604	3680	3844	0.5	2.54	2673	2703	0.3
60145	KINGSTON	037	2314	2483	2695	1.7	85	774	841	921	2.0	2.93	636	682	1.7
60146	KIRKLAND	037	2070	2134	2266	0.7	72	753	782	836	0.9	2.93	572	586	0.6
	ILLINOIS					0.7					0.9	2.61			0.6
	UNITED STATES					1.2					1.3	2.58			1.1

ZIP CODE #	POST OFFICE NAME	RACE (%) White 2000	White 2004	Black 2000	Black 2004	Asian/Pacific 2000	Asian/Pacific 2004	% Hispanic Origin 2000	% Hispanic Origin 2004	2004 AGE DISTRIBUTION (%) 0-4	5-9	10-14	15-19	20-24	25-44	45-64	65-84	85+	18+	MEDIAN AGE 2004	% 2004 Males	% 2004 Females
60002	ANTIOCH	96.4	95.5	0.7	0.9	0.8	1.0	3.0	4.1	6.6	6.9	7.4	6.6	6.0	28.0	27.8	9.6	1.1	74.9	38.3	50.1	49.9
60004	ARLINGTON HEIGHTS	90.2	87.5	1.2	1.4	5.2	6.4	6.3	8.6	6.3	6.4	6.8	6.4	5.8	26.9	26.3	12.9	2.3	76.5	39.7	48.4	51.7
60005	ARLINGTON HEIGHTS	86.8	84.7	1.3	1.5	7.9	9.2	6.7	8.1	6.0	6.1	6.3	5.4	5.5	28.9	24.5	14.0	3.3	78.2	40.1	48.3	51.7
60007	ELK GROVE VILLAGE	86.2	82.9	1.5	1.8	8.6	10.5	6.3	8.5	5.9	6.1	6.9	6.5	6.1	28.8	26.9	11.4	1.3	77.0	39.0	48.8	51.2
60008	ROLLING MEADOWS	82.6	79.9	2.7	3.0	6.3	7.3	19.9	22.9	7.0	6.7	7.1	6.1	6.7	32.3	22.8	10.3	1.1	75.5	35.5	50.6	49.4
60010	BARRINGTON	93.6	92.1	0.6	0.7	4.4	5.4	2.1	2.8	5.9	7.4	8.8	7.2	4.2	20.9	33.7	10.8	1.2	73.2	42.5	49.3	50.8
60012	CRYSTAL LAKE	95.3	94.5	0.4	0.5	1.4	1.7	5.5	6.8	6.2	7.9	9.6	8.3	5.2	25.9	29.0	6.6	1.3	70.6	37.9	50.5	49.5
60013	CARY	95.9	95.1	0.4	0.4	1.1	1.3	5.8	7.3	8.2	9.5	9.7	7.1	4.5	30.5	23.7	6.0	0.8	68.1	35.4	50.2	49.8
60014	CRYSTAL LAKE	94.4	93.3	0.6	0.6	1.9	2.3	6.2	7.6	8.3	8.4	8.5	7.0	5.7	30.5	23.4	7.1	1.0	70.3	34.8	49.6	50.4
60015	DEERFIELD	94.1	92.7	0.7	0.8	3.6	4.4	2.2	3.0	7.1	8.3	8.6	7.5	5.0	22.9	29.0	10.3	1.3	71.5	39.8	49.1	50.9
60016	DES PLAINES	75.2	71.4	2.6	2.9	15.9	18.0	10.4	13.3	6.0	5.8	5.9	5.5	6.4	29.5	25.0	13.3	2.6	79.0	39.0	47.9	52.2
60018	DES PLAINES	80.2	77.0	1.0	1.0	7.3	8.5	24.0	28.3	6.4	6.3	7.1	6.8	7.1	27.6	23.9	12.2	2.6	76.1	37.6	49.8	50.2
60020	FOX LAKE	95.5	94.3	0.6	0.8	0.8	0.9	6.0	8.0	6.6	6.3	6.1	5.8	5.7	31.3	24.9	10.4	2.8	77.4	38.0	50.2	49.8
60021	FOX RIVER GROVE	95.6	94.8	0.6	0.6	1.7	2.0	3.8	4.7	7.0	7.6	8.3	6.8	5.4	29.7	26.8	7.4	1.0	72.6	37.8	51.1	48.9
60022	GLENCOE	95.0	93.7	2.0	2.5	1.7	2.2	1.3	1.7	6.9	9.0	10.6	7.2	3.3	17.1	30.9	13.2	1.9	68.7	42.6	48.9	51.1
60025	GLENVIEW	83.6	80.0	1.7	2.0	11.7	14.2	5.1	6.9	6.2	6.7	7.1	6.4	5.0	23.9	27.9	14.5	2.4	75.9	41.7	48.1	51.9
60029	GOLF	97.0	95.5	0.0	0.0	3.0	3.0	0.0	1.5	6.1	7.6	9.1	6.1	3.0	16.7	30.3	18.2	3.0	77.3	45.8	51.5	48.5
60030	GRAYSLAKE	92.0	90.0	1.4	1.7	3.6	4.5	4.7	6.4	9.9	9.7	8.2	6.0	4.7	32.6	21.3	6.9	0.7	68.4	34.7	49.1	50.9
60031	GURNEE	82.8	79.4	5.0	6.0	7.5	9.0	6.1	7.8	9.2	9.3	8.3	6.0	4.9	32.6	22.8	6.3	0.6	69.3	34.9	48.6	51.5
60033	HARVARD	84.2	81.6	0.6	0.6	1.2	1.4	25.4	29.8	8.2	7.7	7.4	6.9	7.7	29.5	22.9	8.4	1.4	72.6	32.8	52.4	47.7
60034	HEBRON	98.0	97.6	0.3	0.3	0.1	0.1	3.7	4.7	6.9	7.0	7.6	7.6	6.3	26.4	26.8	9.9	1.4	73.8	37.8	50.5	49.5
60035	HIGHLAND PARK	91.4	89.4	1.5	1.8	2.2	2.7	9.2	11.6	7.1	8.0	7.8	6.3	4.1	22.5	28.4	14.1	1.8	73.0	41.6	48.9	51.1
60037	FORT SHERIDAN	80.1	76.2	11.1	13.5	3.0	3.4	6.1	7.5	10.4	14.1	13.6	5.7	2.3	40.2	11.3	2.1	0.4	58.0	27.6	49.7	50.3
60040	HIGHWOOD	74.5	69.4	2.2	2.4	2.2	2.4	36.1	44.0	7.5	6.5	6.0	5.9	8.2	33.5	18.5	10.9	3.0	76.6	34.0	50.3	49.7
60041	INGLESIDE	96.1	94.9	0.4	0.5	0.8	1.1	4.9	6.6	7.0	7.3	7.2	6.3	5.2	31.6	26.6	7.9	0.8	74.4	37.1	50.4	49.6
60042	ISLAND LAKE	93.8	92.4	0.7	0.7	1.5	1.8	8.3	10.6	9.4	9.1	8.9	6.1	5.3	36.7	19.3	4.9	0.4	68.6	33.1	49.6	50.4
60043	KENILWORTH	97.1	96.3	0.2	0.2	2.3	3.0	1.4	1.9	7.1	9.3	11.4	8.6	4.2	16.4	30.0	11.7	1.4	66.8	40.9	47.2	52.9
60044	LAKE BLUFF	90.9	88.8	2.1	2.6	4.9	5.9	2.8	3.8	7.0	7.6	7.7	7.0	5.3	25.9	27.7	10.6	1.2	72.8	38.8	49.0	51.0
60045	LAKE FOREST	93.6	92.2	1.4	1.7	3.6	4.3	2.1	2.9	5.6	7.1	8.6	9.1	6.9	17.1	30.2	13.0	2.3	73.6	42.0	47.7	52.3
60046	LAKE VILLA	92.3	90.4	2.0	2.5	2.4	3.0	4.5	6.1	9.1	9.0	8.1	6.6	5.2	33.0	22.5	5.9	0.7	69.5	34.4	49.6	50.4
60047	LAKE ZURICH	93.0	91.2	0.8	1.0	3.9	4.8	4.1	5.5	7.5	8.8	9.9	7.4	4.3	25.2	29.6	6.4	0.9	68.8	38.3	49.9	50.1
60048	LIBERTYVILLE	91.6	89.5	1.2	1.5	5.1	6.4	2.8	3.7	6.7	7.7	8.4	7.0	4.7	24.8	29.3	9.5	1.8	72.4	39.9	48.7	51.3
60050	MCHENRY	95.7	94.8	0.3	0.3	0.7	0.8	5.5	6.9	6.7	7.1	8.1	7.2	6.3	29.5	24.8	8.7	1.5	73.5	36.0	49.5	50.5
60051	MCHENRY	96.2	95.4	0.4	0.4	0.8	1.0	4.3	5.5	6.9	7.4	8.0	6.7	5.3	31.1	26.5	7.3	0.8	73.4	36.7	51.4	48.6
60053	MORTON GROVE	73.9	69.1	0.7	0.8	22.2	26.3	4.6	5.9	4.7	5.2	6.3	6.0	5.5	22.4	28.6	18.8	2.6	80.1	45.0	47.6	52.4
60056	MOUNT PROSPECT	80.6	77.5	1.9	2.1	11.3	13.1	12.0	14.5	6.6	6.4	6.5	5.9	6.4	29.6	23.7	13.3	1.6	76.9	37.8	49.8	50.2
60060	MUNDELEIN	80.0	76.3	1.6	1.8	6.2	7.2	22.2	26.7	8.6	8.7	8.5	6.9	6.4	32.0	22.0	6.4	0.6	69.9	33.1	50.9	49.1
60061	VERNON HILLS	82.5	79.4	1.7	1.9	10.9	12.6	8.4	10.5	7.7	8.6	8.1	6.6	5.7	32.5	24.4	5.3	1.0	71.1	35.2	49.0	51.0
60062	NORTHBROOK	87.6	84.8	0.7	0.8	10.1	12.4	2.1	2.9	5.4	6.4	7.2	6.3	4.3	19.5	30.2	17.5	3.2	76.9	45.5	48.2	51.8
60064	NORTH CHICAGO	22.6	21.5	58.9	58.6	0.9	0.9	29.2	31.7	10.1	9.7	9.1	8.4	8.3	27.8	18.5	7.5	0.8	66.2	28.0	50.2	49.8
60067	PALATINE	89.0	86.2	1.3	1.5	6.8	8.3	4.9	6.7	6.0	6.4	6.8	6.1	5.5	29.7	28.3	9.8	1.3	76.9	39.0	49.1	50.9
60068	PARK RIDGE	95.1	93.8	0.3	0.4	3.0	3.8	2.8	3.9	5.7	6.4	7.3	6.4	4.6	21.8	27.8	16.9	3.1	76.4	43.6	47.5	52.5
60069	LINCOLNSHIRE	91.1	88.9	0.6	0.8	6.8	8.6	2.9	4.0	6.7	8.5	9.3	6.9	3.4	22.9	30.4	10.9	0.9	70.8	41.2	49.1	51.0
60070	PROSPECT HEIGHTS	77.3	73.1	2.1	2.3	5.7	6.6	25.5	30.7	7.0	6.5	6.1	5.4	6.4	32.8	22.7	11.7	1.5	77.3	35.9	49.9	50.1
60071	RICHMOND	98.1	97.8	0.3	0.3	0.4	0.5	3.0	3.8	6.4	6.9	7.6	7.8	5.6	25.6	29.3	9.7	1.2	74.3	39.5	49.6	50.4
60072	RINGWOOD	98.5	98.4	0.0	0.1	0.3	0.4	2.2	2.6	5.5	6.5	8.1	8.0	6.4	26.5	30.5	8.0	0.7	75.0	38.1	50.6	49.4
60073	ROUND LAKE	77.1	73.7	2.6	2.9	1.6	1.8	28.8	33.7	10.5	9.7	8.5	6.6	6.9	34.3	18.0	4.9	0.5	67.2	29.9	50.7	49.3
60074	PALATINE	78.7	74.8	2.9	3.3	8.3	9.3	20.8	25.9	8.0	7.3	6.8	6.1	7.4	35.2	20.9	7.5	0.8	74.3	32.9	50.6	49.4
60076	SKOKIE	67.1	62.4	4.8	5.4	22.3	25.6	6.0	7.4	5.2	5.7	7.1	7.2	6.0	23.0	27.6	15.2	3.0	77.4	42.0	48.2	51.8
60077	SKOKIE	69.8	64.4	2.8	3.2	22.6	26.7	5.6	7.2	4.6	4.6	5.7	6.4	6.9	23.5	25.9	18.5	4.0	81.2	43.9	46.3	53.7
60081	SPRING GROVE	97.5	97.0	0.2	0.2	0.6	0.7	2.3	3.0	7.5	8.3	9.1	6.5	4.5	29.3	25.9	7.9	1.2	71.0	37.5	50.7	49.3
60082	TECHNY	91.2	89.1	0.0	0.0	6.6	8.2	0.0	0.9	3.6	5.5	7.3	6.4	2.7	13.6	29.1	30.0	1.8	78.2	52.9	48.2	51.8
60083	WADSWORTH	87.5	84.4	5.2	6.6	2.4	3.0	5.3	7.1	6.6	7.0	7.5	6.4	6.4	28.2	29.6	7.8	0.6	75.1	37.8	50.2	49.9
60084	WAUCONDA	91.7	89.5	0.4	0.5	1.5	1.8	10.5	13.7	7.1	7.2	7.2	5.7	5.2	31.2	25.1	9.9	1.5	74.9	37.8	50.7	49.3
60085	WAUKEGAN	48.2	45.6	19.2	19.0	3.7	4.1	48.7	52.9	9.9	8.7	8.0	7.1	8.7	33.8	16.7	6.1	1.0	69.3	28.9	51.2	48.9
60087	WAUKEGAN	64.6	60.4	13.2	14.0	3.6	3.9	28.9	34.0	8.3	7.9	7.8	6.9	7.1	30.2	22.1	8.7	1.0	71.8	33.1	49.5	50.5
60088	GREAT LAKES	65.5	60.8	20.6	23.3	5.3	5.9	10.6	13.2	6.6	5.0	3.6	28.8	29.8	21.9	2.4	1.6	0.2	82.9	21.0	70.5	29.5
60089	BUFFALO GROVE	89.1	86.6	0.8	0.9	8.0	9.9	3.4	4.4	6.3	7.3	8.3	7.3	5.1	26.9	29.1	8.6	1.2	73.3	39.1	48.4	51.6
60090	WHEELING	76.5	71.9	2.4	2.7	8.8	10.2	21.7	27.0	6.6	6.3	6.4	6.0	7.1	32.5	23.8	9.9	1.5	77.1	35.6	49.5	50.5
60091	WILMETTE	89.6	87.3	0.6	0.7	8.2	10.0	2.1	2.9	6.8	8.3	9.1	7.3	3.9	17.7	29.7	14.7	2.6	70.9	43.1	48.0	52.0
60093	WINNETKA	94.1	92.6	0.4	0.5	3.6	4.5	3.0	4.1	7.1	8.9	10.0	7.6	3.7	17.8	29.1	14.0	1.7	68.8	41.9	48.7	51.4
60096	WINTHROP HARBOR	92.1	90.3	1.8	2.1	1.9	2.3	5.2	6.9	6.5	6.9	7.7	6.9	6.1	28.9	28.1	8.3	0.6	74.5	37.1	49.9	50.1
60097	WONDER LAKE	96.4	95.7	0.2	0.2	0.6	0.7	4.8	6.1	7.2	7.4	7.9	7.5	6.2	30.8	24.8	7.4	0.9	72.8	35.5	51.1	48.9
60098	WOODSTOCK	90.0	88.4	0.8	0.9	1.7	1.9	14.9	17.8	7.3	7.1	7.5	7.0	7.3	29.3	24.0	8.7	1.9	73.8	35.0	50.5	49.5
60099	ZION	65.0	60.9	22.2	24.3	1.9	2.1	14.1	17.2	8.5	8.3	8.8	7.7	7.4	28.8	21.6	7.8	1.1	69.7	31.8	48.7	51.3
60101	ADDISON	76.9	74.2	2.4	2.4	7.4	8.5	27.1	30.9	7.6	7.1	7.0	6.8	7.9	30.8	22.9	9.1	0.8	74.3	33.4	50.5	49.6
60102	ALGONQUIN	94.2	92.8	0.9	1.0	2.4	3.0	4.2	5.7	9.6	9.7	8.5	6.1	4.5	33.0	22.9	5.3	0.5	68.4	34.4	49.6	50.4
60103	BARTLETT	86.7	84.1	2.2	2.4	7.8	9.5	5.8	7.2	9.9	9.9	8.2	5.6	4.6	33.3	22.5	5.4	0.5	68.4	34.6	49.4	50.7
60104	BELLWOOD	11.8	10.1	81.7	82.9	1.0	1.0	8.0	8.8	7.4	7.9	8.9	7.8	6.9	27.4	25.5	7.3	0.9	70.9	33.2	46.6	53.4
60106	BENSENVILLE	72.9	70.4	2.6	2.6	6.0	6.5	33.8	38.3	7.4	6.9	6.7	6.7	8.1	31.6	21.2	9.6	1.9	75.1	33.6	51.3	48.7
60107	STREAMWOOD	77.8	73.4	3.7	4.3	8.6	10.3	17.0	21.0	8.6	8.2	7.3	5.9	6.0	35.3	21.7	6.3	0.6	72.2	33.6	49.9	50.1
60108	BLOOMINGDALE	85.3	82.5	2.5	2.7	9.0	10.9	5.1	6.3	5.5	5.7	6.3	5.7	6.4	30.3	27.4	10.7	2.0	79.0	38.6	48.3	51.7
60110	CARPENTERSVILLE	68.3	63.8	5.5	5.7	1.9	2.1	39.5	46.4	10.7	9.8	9.5	7.5	7.9	32.6	16.9	4.8	0.2	65.4	27.9	51.2	48.8
60111	CLARE	95.7	95.1	0.3	0.3	0.0	0.0	1.5	1.9	8.0	7.7	7.1	6.0	5.2	28.6	25.8	10.2	1.4	73.4	37.4	50.3	49.7
60112	CORTLAND	95.5	94.5	1.0	1.2	1.1	1.3	5.2	6.5	8.5	8.2	9.8	7.2	5.9	32.1	20.1	7.2	1.1	68.9	32.8	49.1	50.9
60115	DEKALB	80.3	78.0	8.6	9.1	4.6	5.5	8.7	10.2	5.6	4.7	4.5	16.0	22.2	25.4	13.8	6.5	1.4	82.5	24.3	49.5	50.5
60118	DUNDEE	92.9	90.8	1.0	1.2	2.2	2.8	4.6	6.7	7.6	7.6	7.4	5.9	5.3	30.4	26.3	8.5	1.0	73.7	37.1	49.3	50.7
60119	ELBURN	97.4	96.5	0.2	0.2	0.7	0.9	2.4	3.7	8.0	8.6	8.8	6.5	5.1	28.7	26.8	6.8	0.8	70.4	36.4	49.2	50.8
60120	ELGIN	64.7	60.6	6.6	6.8	4.8	5.1	44.0	50.3	9.9	9.1	8.2	6.9	7.5	33.6	18.7	5.4	0.8	68.7	30.2	50.8	49.3
60123	ELGIN	80.3	76.6	5.5	6.0	3.2	3.8	19.8	25.1	8.2	7.6	7.2	6.2	7.0	31.1	22.6	8.6	1.5	73.4	34.1	49.3	50.7
60126	ELMHURST	93.1	91.8	1.0	1.0	3.9	4.7	4.1	5.1	6.8	7.1	7.3	6.9	5.7	25.2	25.6	13.0	2.5	74.7	39.8	48.4	51.6
60129	ESMOND	96.3	95.4	0.3	0.5	0.3	0.2	1.9	2.4	7.3	7.3	7.8	6.5	5.1	27.9	26.4	10.7	1.2	73.4	38.0	51.6	48.4
60130	FOREST PARK	56.1	50.6	31.2	34.8	6.9	7.8	7.8	9.8	6.3	5.7	5.5	5.3	6.0	35.9	23.2	10.0	2.2	79.4	37.1	47.5	52.5
60131	FRANKLIN PARK	79.5	76.1	0.8	0.9	2.4	2.7	37.9	44.3	7.3	6.8	7.1	7.1	7.8	29.6	21.4	11.0	1.9	74.6	34.3	50.1	49.9
60133	HANOVER PARK	69.7	65.8	5.6	5.9	11.9	13.6	25.2	28.9	8.7	8.5	8.5	7.2	7.5	33.8	20.8	4.7	0.4	70.0	30.9	51.1	48.9
60134	GENEVA	96.3	95.2	1.1	1.4	1.2	1.5	3.0	4.5	7.7	8.8	9.2	7.4	5.0	27.8	25.0	7.6	1.6	69.4	36.6	49.8	50.3
60135	GENOA	95.9	95.0	0.2	0.2	0.3	0.4	8.7	10.7	8.6	8.1	8.1	6.6	6.5	30.5	21.9	8.8	0.9	71.2	33.6	50.0	50.0
60136	GILBERTS	95.5	94.0	0.4	0.5	1.6	1.9	2.8	4.3	6.0	7.1	9.3	7.1	6.4	24.5	32.3	6.8	0.5	73.2	39.4	50.0	50.1
60137	GLEN ELLYN	88.1	86.2	2.6	2.7	5.3	6.4	5.5	6.8	7.3	7.8	7.9	6.6	5.5	27.8	26.1	10.0	1.2	73.0	37.6	49.0	51.1
60139	GLENDALE HEIGHTS	65.9	61.8	4.5	4.5	19.0	21.6	17.3	19.9	8.0	7.3	6.9	6.6	8.5	35.4	21.4	5.4	0.5	73.9	31.7	50.9	49.1
60140	HAMPSHIRE	97.9	97.2	0.1	0.2	0.4	0.5	2.9	4.4	5.9	6.3	7.5	7.0	5.1	24.7	28.2	14.0	1.2	75.8	41.0	49.4	50.6
60142	HUNTLEY	95.1	94.1	0.6	0.7	1.9	2.2	4.4	5.7	8.9	8.3	7.1	5.6	5.0	31.5	22.1	10.6	0.8	72.2	35.7	49.7	50.3
60143	ITASCA	89.6	87.8	1.1	1.2	5.1	6.2	5.9	7.2	6.0	6.0	6.3	6.1	6.0	28.3	27.9	11.6	1.8	77.9	39.9	48.4	51.6
60145	KINGSTON	96.5	95.7	0.4	0.4	0.3	0.3	4.7	6.0	7.9	7.9	8.3	7.2	6.2	30.5	24.2	7.2	0.6	71.3	34.8	50.1	49.9
60146	KIRKLAND	97.4	96.9	0.4	0.5	0.1	0.2	2.3	3.0	7.4	6.9	7.3	8.0	7.2	28.0	24.9	9.1	1.2	73.7	36.0	51.1	48.9
	ILLINOIS	73.5	71.8	15.1	15.2	3.5	4.0	12.3	14.2	7.1	7.0	7.3	7.0	7.3	29.0	23.2	10.4	1.7	74.5	35.2	49.0	51.0
	UNITED STATES	75.1	73.6	12.3	12.5	3.8	4.2	12.5	14.1	6.9	6.7	7.2	7.0	7.3	28.6	23.8	10.8	1.7	75.1	36.0	49.1	50.9

#	POST OFFICE NAME	2004 Per Capita Income	2004 HH Income Base	2004 HOUSEHOLD INCOME DISTRIBUTION (%) Less than $25,000	$25,000 to $49,999	$50,000 to $99,999	$100,000 to $149,999	$150,000 or More	MEDIAN HOUSEHOLD INCOME 2004	2009	2004 National Centile	2004 State Centile	2004 Home Value Base	2004 HOME VALUE DISTRIBUTION (%) Less than $50,000	$50,000 to $89,999	$90,000 to $174,999	$175,000 to $399,999	$400,000 or More	2004 Median Home Value
60002	ANTIOCH	32761	8037	13.4	22.8	37.5	16.2	10.2	64928	79095	88	86	6610	0.8	0.9	27.3	60.0	11.1	217335
60004	ARLINGTON HEIGHTS	37048	20030	10.9	19.7	34.6	21.4	13.4	76638	87936	94	94	16034	0.2	0.9	14.1	65.8	19.0	280416
60005	ARLINGTON HEIGHTS	38133	12805	13.5	25.4	31.8	16.2	13.1	64086	75809	88	86	9195	2.9	0.6	22.4	56.2	18.0	262011
60007	ELK GROVE VILLAGE	32906	13608	11.7	21.1	40.5	17.8	8.9	68189	79388	90	89	10784	0.7	0.3	18.6	74.9	5.6	228234
60008	ROLLING MEADOWS	28900	8477	11.1	24.7	39.3	16.1	8.9	64567	76275	88	86	6785	0.8	3.0	28.6	59.2	8.4	203638
60010	BARRINGTON	65825	15131	7.8	10.4	22.8	20.7	38.4	119329	141692	99	99	14035	0.4	0.3	3.0	34.4	61.8	482334
60012	CRYSTAL LAKE	37547	3651	9.6	13.9	32.7	20.0	23.9	88505	98878	97	97	3239	0.6	0.4	8.0	63.9	27.3	315247
60013	CARY	32961	8558	7.1	17.1	39.8	21.9	14.0	80665	90067	95	95	7924	0.6	1.1	18.1	65.5	14.7	240095
60014	CRYSTAL LAKE	30892	17318	9.2	18.4	41.5	19.7	11.2	75504	83353	93	93	14744	0.8	0.7	21.8	68.6	8.2	222530
60015	DEERFIELD	62043	9182	6.6	9.2	24.0	22.4	37.9	120385	148179	99	99	8293	0.3	0.1	3.3	39.4	57.0	444664
60016	DES PLAINES	27483	23935	17.0	26.5	37.7	13.6	5.2	55828	64741	81	75	16852	1.5	2.7	31.5	59.7	4.7	203129
60018	DES PLAINES	23185	10584	19.2	25.7	37.0	13.6	4.4	54845	64012	79	73	8137	15.6	2.0	15.0	64.1	3.3	208289
60020	FOX LAKE	28817	3524	19.8	28.6	36.7	12.2	2.8	51484	62734	75	67	2418	1.1	6.5	45.8	42.4	4.3	168189
60021	FOX RIVER GROVE	34008	2138	11.1	20.7	38.3	18.1	11.9	71917	79997	92	91	1845	0.0	1.6	14.9	66.9	16.6	237986
60022	GLENCOE	99680	2970	4.8	5.9	19.8	13.4	56.1	178047	212407	100	100	2782	0.0	0.3	2.2	10.8	86.7	786706
60025	GLENVIEW	45589	19879	9.8	19.4	31.6	17.1	22.2	80096	93429	95	95	16423	1.5	0.6	11.3	45.0	41.6	357933
60029	GOLF	68120	23	13.0	4.4	47.8	8.7	26.1	73310	97105	93	92	23	0.0	0.0	0.0	21.7	78.3	652778
60030	GRAYSLAKE	34247	12689	8.5	16.6	39.6	22.5	12.9	79589	95014	95	95	10876	0.7	0.3	19.7	71.0	8.3	228833
60031	GURNEE	37846	15291	9.7	15.6	34.4	24.7	15.6	83652	102254	96	96	12702	0.4	0.8	19.9	64.2	14.6	247880
60033	HARVARD	22515	4737	15.9	27.3	41.8	10.3	4.7	56037	64376	81	76	3410	2.1	2.4	41.7	44.4	9.4	183101
60034	HEBRON	24551	827	13.2	26.0	45.5	11.9	3.5	57074	66289	82	78	646	2.0	2.9	31.0	49.4	14.7	198698
60035	HIGHLAND PARK	70043	11706	8.2	13.7	21.5	19.0	37.6	115525	143797	99	99	9842	0.3	0.2	3.0	33.7	62.8	496634
60037	FORT SHERIDAN	26446	360	7.2	30.3	40.3	8.3	13.9	61861	75099	86	83	127	0.0	0.0	0.0	22.1	78.0	636905
60040	HIGHWOOD	28296	1592	16.1	33.6	31.1	9.9	9.3	50351	62875	73	63	826	0.0	0.0	9.1	61.7	29.2	296087
60041	INGLESIDE	29884	4071	12.3	18.1	43.1	18.8	7.7	69116	83811	91	90	3530	0.7	2.2	31.4	58.3	7.4	205457
60042	ISLAND LAKE	28338	3297	7.8	20.8	47.9	16.7	6.8	68201	77837	90	89	3009	0.2	3.0	39.5	54.4	3.0	187014
60043	KENILWORTH	112260	800	3.8	4.9	9.6	14.4	67.4	221071	259035	100	100	760	0.0	0.0	0.0	4.1	95.9	1000001
60044	LAKE BLUFF	59419	4343	10.6	15.3	28.0	17.4	28.8	89444	112488	97	98	3375	0.8	2.8	3.0	34.0	59.4	465670
60045	LAKE FOREST	94823	7612	6.2	10.6	16.9	15.0	51.3	155037	195856	100	100	6806	0.0	0.0	1.3	11.8	86.9	820778
60046	LAKE VILLA	31416	11632	7.8	15.1	45.2	22.4	9.5	77204	90929	94	94	10371	0.3	0.9	23.2	69.4	6.2	212757
60047	LAKE ZURICH	49535	12048	5.3	10.3	26.9	23.7	33.8	112255	135997	99	99	11342	0.3	0.3	4.5	46.5	48.4	391174
60048	LIBERTYVILLE	50961	10481	7.6	11.6	28.7	21.7	30.5	103696	128214	98	98	9042	0.2	0.3	6.5	51.3	41.7	363711
60050	MCHENRY	27230	13804	12.3	23.8	43.3	15.0	5.6	63190	71968	87	85	11393	0.7	1.3	34.0	58.0	6.0	194551
60051	MCHENRY	30211	5064	11.7	18.5	46.5	16.9	6.3	68664	78859	91	89	4438	1.1	2.1	30.3	57.5	9.0	198797
60053	MORTON GROVE	30564	8263	12.1	20.2	38.3	19.9	9.5	71575	83102	92	91	7814	0.9	0.4	7.9	82.7	8.2	263087
60056	MOUNT PROSPECT	30668	22269	14.3	22.0	37.7	17.1	8.9	65002	77141	89	87	16402	0.4	1.6	16.4	72.6	9.1	257466
60060	MUNDELEIN	31346	12584	8.5	17.8	38.5	21.1	14.1	78626	93995	95	94	10436	1.0	0.5	25.8	60.2	12.5	213880
60061	VERNON HILLS	38336	8410	8.7	18.4	34.0	21.5	17.4	81140	97408	95	96	6725	0.7	1.3	25.4	51.4	21.2	255112
60062	NORTHBROOK	54609	15282	8.8	16.4	26.9	18.7	29.2	94583	109986	98	98	13561	0.7	0.4	4.3	39.1	55.6	429493
60064	NORTH CHICAGO	15928	4790	30.6	31.9	28.9	6.1	2.5	39035	47122	43	26	2483	1.7	12.1	67.7	17.8	0.6	130448
60067	PALATINE	45264	15222	9.6	17.9	33.9	19.7	18.9	81235	94893	95	96	11719	0.6	1.0	15.5	53.9	29.1	289830
60068	PARK RIDGE	41468	14473	10.2	18.3	34.0	20.2	17.3	80208	93409	95	95	12996	0.3	0.3	5.8	52.8	40.9	365743
60069	LINCOLNSHIRE	64712	2853	6.0	9.4	21.2	21.7	41.7	129205	157494	100	99	2712	0.6	0.2	2.3	31.5	65.5	498126
60070	PROSPECT HEIGHTS	27981	6317	15.1	27.5	38.1	11.2	8.2	56628	64899	81	77	4336	1.0	5.9	35.5	46.6	11.1	208618
60071	RICHMOND	30261	1337	12.4	20.1	38.1	18.3	11.1	67945	77088	90	89	1134	0.4	1.2	19.0	61.6	17.8	257911
60072	RINGWOOD	31430	259	7.7	15.1	49.4	20.9	7.0	75944	83296	94	94	235	0.0	0.9	24.7	59.2	15.3	239634
60073	ROUND LAKE	21939	13901	12.8	22.3	45.1	15.0	4.8	63185	75841	87	85	11488	6.3	3.2	51.1	38.0	1.5	157043
60074	PALATINE	30797	15278	12.6	22.6	39.0	16.4	9.5	65713	76868	89	87	10482	0.5	4.7	29.4	57.7	7.8	211966
60076	SKOKIE	32262	11995	12.5	20.6	35.1	18.7	13.2	71394	83433	92	91	9890	1.0	0.3	8.4	78.6	11.7	268644
60077	SKOKIE	28330	9993	20.4	24.7	35.0	13.4	6.5	54328	63013	79	72	6753	1.6	1.1	19.0	70.9	7.4	241075
60081	SPRING GROVE	28597	2986	12.9	16.3	40.3	21.0	9.5	74222	83729	93	92	2676	0.6	2.8	19.5	63.0	14.1	260336
60082	TECHNY	122283	45	11.1	8.9	11.1	15.6	53.3	157028	191030	100	100	44	0.0	0.0	2.3	2.3	95.5	1000001
60083	WADSWORTH	35929	2193	8.3	16.7	36.8	22.3	16.0	79330	96449	95	95	1710	0.0	1.0	12.3	61.2	25.6	303464
60084	WAUCONDA	31059	5187	15.0	20.9	38.8	16.2	9.2	66221	79322	89	88	4304	3.4	3.5	25.9	54.9	12.5	208559
60085	WAUKEGAN	18337	24294	25.1	31.2	33.2	7.8	2.8	44797	53128	61	47	13299	10.6	5.5	56.6	26.2	1.1	141800
60087	WAUKEGAN	23866	9382	14.4	26.4	38.9	16.1	4.2	60286	71652	85	81	7179	3.4	1.3	50.2	43.3	1.8	168785
60088	GREAT LAKES	15394	2056	13.5	48.4	29.1	5.4	3.7	44780	51104	61	47	210	32.4	5.2	11.9	10.5	40.0	250000
60089	BUFFALO GROVE	45296	17267	6.3	15.0	33.3	23.1	22.3	91250	111261	97	98	15697	0.3	1.1	13.4	63.4	21.8	274596
60090	WHEELING	30272	14646	13.5	23.4	40.4	14.7	8.0	62722	74427	87	84	10063	3.0	2.8	31.1	56.7	6.5	196411
60091	WILMETTE	64974	10203	7.2	12.5	23.2	19.8	37.4	117723	140132	99	99	9075	0.4	0.9	3.0	24.9	70.8	549147
60093	WINNETKA	91605	7046	6.6	11.1	17.4	16.3	48.6	145110	172570	100	100	6524	2.2	0.5	2.3	13.0	81.9	759361
60096	WINTHROP HARBOR	27891	2474	12.2	19.7	41.8	19.9	6.5	68033	81276	90	89	2091	1.9	0.1	39.6	55.1	3.4	186308
60097	WONDER LAKE	25850	3940	10.9	27.8	42.6	14.0	4.7	60803	69061	85	82	3439	0.4	2.1	45.2	45.5	6.8	178681
60098	WOODSTOCK	28146	10791	17.3	24.1	38.1	12.9	7.6	58283	66582	83	79	7493	0.3	1.1	29.4	55.5	13.7	209435
60099	ZION	22568	10774	20.7	25.5	36.7	12.9	4.2	54124	65070	79	72	7348	6.2	3.7	51.2	36.1	2.8	158121
60101	ADDISON	24662	12813	14.5	25.3	37.6	15.3	7.3	60220	70174	85	81	9070	0.7	2.3	19.5	71.7	5.8	221631
60102	ALGONQUIN	34000	10070	5.6	14.0	41.9	24.2	14.4	83777	94591	96	96	9547	0.5	0.1	14.3	74.6	10.6	244074
60103	BARTLETT	34940	13319	6.4	14.6	38.4	26.2	14.4	86354	100508	97	97	12503	2.0	0.8	14.3	73.1	9.8	247400
60104	BELLWOOD	22331	6425	17.0	24.4	40.6	13.7	4.3	57875	66932	83	78	5077	0.6	3.3	72.3	23.6	0.3	147562
60106	BENSENVILLE	23581	7888	13.7	25.0	41.5	15.1	4.8	60829	70962	85	82	4921	0.0	1.2	28.0	67.6	3.2	210502
60107	STREAMWOOD	27848	12209	7.4	19.0	47.0	19.1	7.6	72231	82451	92	92	11100	0.3	0.9	42.1	54.1	2.7	182692
60108	BLOOMINGDALE	36240	8898	9.0	18.6	38.7	20.6	13.1	77256	88504	94	94	6566	0.4	0.1	18.6	66.9	14.1	263222
60110	CARPENTERSVILLE	20818	10740	13.6	25.2	41.2	14.0	6.0	60758	70190	85	82	8744	0.5	1.7	61.2	33.3	3.3	158233
60111	CLARE	25275	135	14.1	26.7	43.0	11.1	5.2	58736	64345	83	79	101	3.0	1.0	34.7	56.4	5.0	186058
60112	CORTLAND	21270	809	15.0	26.6	45.5	10.9	2.1	56870	63651	82	77	689	11.9	2.2	41.2	43.1	1.6	167926
60115	DEKALB	20304	15776	34.6	25.3	29.1	8.4	2.7	39285	45178	44	27	7479	1.9	4.0	47.1	44.8	2.3	170569
60118	DUNDEE	33916	6441	10.5	18.9	36.1	21.5	13.0	75869	87207	94	93	5302	0.5	0.4	14.5	72.1	12.5	247693
60119	ELBURN	37436	3332	6.9	12.6	37.6	26.5	16.3	88545	102971	97	97	2962	0.5	0.5	10.6	67.1	21.4	297500
60120	ELGIN	23191	16524	14.7	27.0	39.2	13.5	5.6	57875	66185	83	78	11446	2.5	1.7	47.0	44.5	4.3	173492
60123	ELGIN	27633	21513	13.7	22.5	40.3	16.8	6.8	64433	75643	88	86	16430	1.8	1.7	33.0	58.3	5.2	197655
60126	ELMHURST	38167	16953	10.9	17.2	35.2	20.1	16.6	78726	91772	95	95	14507	1.1	1.1	9.1	67.6	21.2	272081
60129	ESMOND	24079	147	14.3	29.9	38.8	11.6	5.4	54814	62777	79	73	113	1.8	8.9	37.2	45.1	7.1	177717
60130	FOREST PARK	30242	7534	18.8	31.5	36.7	8.6	4.4	49700	58455	71	62	3634	0.4	11.7	42.7	43.3	1.9	167474
60131	FRANKLIN PARK	19917	6344	20.5	28.4	38.1	10.8	2.2	50864	57558	74	65	4538	0.1	1.0	38.5	59.8	0.5	184227
60133	HANOVER PARK	23337	11301	9.5	21.9	43.4	18.0	7.3	69271	79850	91	90	9592	0.4	1.2	39.6	56.5	2.3	186271
60134	GENEVA	35695	8684	9.1	15.3	36.1	22.3	17.3	82825	94952	96	96	7453	0.2	0.7	10.9	69.8	18.3	282898
60135	GENOA	23880	2336	15.4	26.9	41.1	13.3	3.3	56825	64268	82	77	1891	5.5	2.9	46.5	43.1	2.1	168916
60136	GILBERTS	34563	645	5.3	11.5	36.6	29.6	17.1	94587	106958	98	98	605	0.2	0.5	7.4	71.6	20.3	314115
60137	GLEN ELLYN	41922	14837	10.3	19.6	32.5	18.6	19.0	78118	90239	94	94	11759	0.1	0.9	13.2	58.2	27.6	295808
60139	GLENDALE HEIGHTS	25675	11231	10.2	24.0	44.3	15.9	5.6	63676	74240	88	85	7940	0.5	3.3	37.3	58.0	0.9	186692
60140	HAMPSHIRE	28744	3123	10.5	22.0	41.3	18.0	8.2	69764	79660	91	90	2704	0.8	0.4	17.3	65.0	16.5	249379
60142	HUNTLEY	32712	4255	8.7	19.4	46.4	16.7	8.8	71411	80292	92	91	3500	0.6	0.3	11.6	77.4	10.1	254050
60143	ITASCA	41438	3680	8.6	15.5	39.4	22.3	14.3	80488	94517	95	95	2943	1.0	2.2	9.2	71.7	16.0	271670
60145	KINGSTON	24972	841	10.8	20.9	47.3	15.7	5.2	63662	71934	88	85	739	2.3	1.2	43.0	47.6	5.8	180543
60146	KIRKLAND	24021	782	15.9	25.5	42.6	11.6	4.5	56552	65098	81	76	647	0.5	1.9	52.4	39.7	5.6	166974
	ILLINOIS	27033		22.1	25.9	32.9	11.9	7.3	52039	60941				7.7	12.8	34.0	36.6	8.9	162771
	UNITED STATES	25866		24.7	27.1	30.8	10.9	6.5	48124	56710				10.9	15.0	33.7	30.1	10.4	145905

ZIP CODE #	POST OFFICE NAME	Financial Services: Auto Loan	Financial Services: Home Loan	Financial Services: Investments	Financial Services: Retirement Plans	The Home: Home Improvements: Home Repair	The Home: Home Improvements: Lawn & Garden	The Home: Furnishings: Computers & Hardware	The Home: Furnishings: Major Appliances	The Home: Furnishings: TV, Radio, Sound Equipment	The Home: Furnishings: Furniture	Entertainment: Dine out/Carry out	Entertainment: Sports Equipment	Entertainment: Fees & Tickets	Entertainment: Toys & Games	Entertainment: Travel	Entertainment: Cable TV	Personal: Apparel & Services	Personal: Auto Repairs	Personal: Health Insurance	Personal: Pets & Supplies
60002	ANTIOCH	115	132	140	133	129	130	124	123	117	124	147	144	128	152	124	113	146	121	111	135
60004	ARLINGTON HEIGHTS	123	144	169	145	141	147	136	134	130	137	164	155	144	168	139	128	163	133	125	147
60005	ARLINGTON HEIGHTS	114	127	152	129	124	131	125	122	121	125	152	142	129	154	126	118	150	123	114	134
60007	ELK GROVE VILLAGE	112	126	141	127	123	127	121	119	116	122	147	138	126	150	122	114	145	119	111	131
60008	ROLLING MEADOWS	105	115	130	116	112	116	113	111	110	114	139	129	117	141	113	106	138	112	102	121
60010	BARRINGTON	239	297	356	298	291	306	265	263	247	270	313	298	290	321	275	246	314	255	245	289
60012	CRYSTAL LAKE	152	181	194	186	176	177	165	162	152	167	193	189	175	198	166	147	192	158	145	179
60013	CARY	140	162	164	166	156	153	148	146	136	151	173	171	153	176	146	129	171	143	127	160
60014	CRYSTAL LAKE	123	142	147	145	137	136	130	129	121	132	153	151	136	156	130	116	152	126	114	142
60015	DEERFIELD	221	290	378	286	282	298	258	254	241	261	304	290	286	321	270	240	307	246	233	276
60016	DES PLAINES	88	96	118	97	94	100	97	94	95	97	120	110	99	121	97	93	118	96	89	103
60018	DES PLAINES	89	95	104	94	94	99	93	93	91	94	115	107	95	116	93	90	113	93	89	103
60020	FOX LAKE	91	88	82	88	89	96	89	91	89	87	110	105	87	110	88	89	106	90	91	103
60021	FOX RIVER GROVE	134	152	152	156	146	143	140	139	130	143	164	163	143	166	138	122	162	136	121	152
60022	GLENCOE	343	462	633	452	450	486	402	399	375	411	474	448	457	499	429	378	481	383	370	433
60025	GLENVIEW	148	189	236	182	182	192	171	169	163	173	205	193	185	218	178	163	207	166	155	182
60029	GOLF	251	303	342	301	302	317	278	280	263	279	331	316	296	336	289	262	328	272	267	304
60030	GRAYSLAKE	134	149	151	153	144	144	138	137	129	142	164	159	142	163	136	123	161	135	123	151
60031	GURNEE	143	160	167	166	155	153	150	147	139	153	177	174	154	179	147	132	175	145	129	162
60033	HARVARD	92	99	100	98	96	97	95	96	92	97	115	111	96	115	94	88	114	95	87	104
60034	HEBRON	90	103	105	104	100	98	96	95	89	96	112	112	98	115	95	85	111	93	84	104
60035	HIGHLAND PARK	229	298	393	288	289	311	266	264	253	271	319	297	294	337	281	256	322	257	247	286
60037	FORT SHERIDAN	152	104	105	117	96	112	146	127	147	137	184	167	128	167	123	135	177	148	118	144
60040	HIGHWOOD	99	104	128	105	101	108	107	103	105	108	133	120	108	134	106	103	132	106	97	113
60041	INGLESIDE	108	124	129	125	122	122	115	115	109	115	137	136	119	142	116	105	135	113	104	128
60042	ISLAND LAKE	115	130	126	135	124	120	118	117	108	122	137	137	121	138	115	101	136	114	99	128
60043	KENILWORTH	426	574	787	563	560	604	500	496	466	512	589	557	568	620	533	470	599	476	461	539
60044	LAKE BLUFF	194	232	268	235	227	234	214	212	201	217	254	245	227	260	218	196	252	208	193	231
60045	LAKE FOREST	347	441	578	432	434	470	392	394	372	401	468	440	435	481	416	376	470	381	376	430
60046	LAKE VILLA	126	142	146	147	137	136	132	131	123	135	156	154	136	157	130	116	154	129	115	144
60047	LAKE ZURICH	207	254	282	260	245	248	227	222	208	230	264	258	245	274	230	201	265	216	198	245
60048	LIBERTYVILLE	182	239	288	237	230	236	212	208	197	214	249	240	232	266	220	194	252	202	185	225
60050	MCHENRY	102	114	116	115	112	113	107	107	102	107	128	125	110	131	107	98	126	105	98	119
60051	MCHENRY	114	128	131	129	125	125	119	119	112	120	141	141	122	145	119	108	139	117	108	133
60053	MORTON GROVE	102	132	162	126	129	136	119	119	114	120	143	134	129	152	125	115	143	116	112	128
60056	MOUNT PROSPECT	102	117	144	116	115	121	114	112	111	115	140	129	119	144	116	110	139	113	105	122
60060	MUNDELEIN	134	151	159	154	146	147	141	139	133	144	169	161	146	171	140	128	168	137	125	153
60061	VERNON HILLS	141	158	170	165	153	155	149	146	139	151	176	171	155	177	147	132	175	144	130	161
60062	NORTHBROOK	185	226	273	224	223	237	205	207	195	208	245	233	221	248	215	195	244	201	197	225
60064	NORTH CHICAGO	70	65	74	63	63	71	71	69	74	72	93	78	71	91	69	75	91	72	70	77
60067	PALATINE	147	167	200	173	163	168	162	157	153	163	194	184	169	198	162	149	193	157	142	172
60068	PARK RIDGE	135	170	202	164	167	177	153	154	146	154	183	172	165	191	161	147	183	149	147	166
60069	LINCOLNSHIRE	222	293	370	290	284	297	256	252	237	261	300	287	286	316	268	235	304	243	229	274
60070	PROSPECT HEIGHTS	104	101	108	101	100	105	105	105	106	108	133	120	105	131	103	101	132	108	99	113
60071	RICHMOND	108	135	143	135	132	131	120	120	111	120	140	140	128	149	123	108	140	116	107	133
60072	RINGWOOD	112	134	137	133	132	132	120	121	113	119	141	142	126	150	123	110	140	117	111	136
60073	ROUND LAKE	102	110	108	111	106	106	104	104	98	106	124	122	104	124	102	94	122	103	93	115
60074	PALATINE	114	114	130	119	110	115	118	114	114	120	145	136	118	142	114	109	143	118	104	126
60076	SKOKIE	108	145	196	140	140	146	133	131	126	133	159	151	143	172	140	126	161	130	118	139
60077	SKOKIE	88	101	127	99	100	107	99	98	97	99	122	111	102	123	102	97	120	99	95	106
60081	SPRING GROVE	117	130	128	132	128	129	121	121	115	121	144	141	124	148	121	111	141	118	112	135
60082	TECHNY	361	487	667	477	475	512	424	420	395	434	500	472	482	526	452	399	507	404	390	457
60083	WADSWORTH	140	152	167	160	147	150	147	143	138	149	176	169	152	176	144	132	174	143	127	158
60084	WAUCONDA	113	123	127	125	121	124	118	117	113	118	142	138	120	144	117	109	139	116	109	131
60085	WAUKEGAN	81	74	80	75	72	77	80	79	81	83	103	91	78	100	77	78	102	82	74	86
60087	WAUKEGAN	92	100	111	100	97	100	98	97	96	100	121	112	101	124	98	93	121	97	89	106
60088	GREAT LAKES	89	60	58	68	55	64	85	74	86	80	108	98	74	97	72	79	104	87	69	84
60089	BUFFALO GROVE	161	195	218	199	190	194	177	174	165	179	209	201	190	216	181	161	209	170	159	192
60090	WHEELING	105	110	128	113	107	112	111	108	108	113	137	127	113	137	110	105	135	110	100	119
60091	WILMETTE	216	289	379	282	281	298	254	251	237	258	299	284	283	317	268	237	303	242	230	271
60093	WINNETKA	318	416	552	408	407	438	365	364	342	373	432	410	410	451	387	345	437	351	340	397
60096	WINTHROP HARBOR	103	122	128	122	119	118	113	112	106	113	133	131	117	139	113	102	132	109	100	122
60097	WONDER LAKE	100	111	111	111	110	111	103	104	98	103	123	123	106	127	103	95	121	102	96	118
60098	WOODSTOCK	106	112	116	114	111	114	110	109	106	110	133	128	111	135	108	103	131	109	102	121
60099	ZION	90	94	98	94	92	96	93	92	91	93	114	107	94	115	92	88	112	92	87	102
60101	ADDISON	102	106	118	106	103	108	106	105	105	109	133	120	108	134	105	102	133	107	97	114
60102	ALGONQUIN	141	163	164	169	157	153	148	146	136	152	172	171	153	175	146	128	171	142	126	160
60103	BARTLETT	143	163	169	169	156	155	151	148	139	154	177	174	156	179	148	132	175	145	129	162
60104	BELLWOOD	94	97	110	93	94	104	97	96	99	99	125	107	101	125	98	101	123	96	97	108
60106	BENSENVILLE	95	98	109	98	96	102	99	98	98	100	124	113	100	124	98	97	122	99	94	108
60107	STREAMWOOD	115	130	132	133	125	123	120	119	112	123	142	139	124	144	118	106	141	117	104	130
60108	BLOOMINGDALE	123	139	159	143	137	140	134	131	127	135	160	154	139	162	134	122	158	131	119	144
60110	CARPENTERSVILLE	101	103	104	104	99	100	103	102	100	106	127	118	102	127	99	94	127	103	91	110
60111	CLARE	86	105	116	102	103	105	97	96	93	96	117	111	104	124	100	91	116	94	89	105
60112	CORTLAND	87	92	90	94	90	91	89	89	85	89	107	105	89	107	87	81	104	88	81	99
60115	DEKALB	71	62	70	65	62	67	78	69	76	72	95	86	72	91	71	71	91	74	65	77
60118	DUNDEE	123	145	157	147	141	141	134	132	125	135	158	155	140	164	135	120	157	129	118	145
60119	ELBURN	140	174	186	176	170	169	155	153	143	155	180	179	167	191	158	138	181	148	137	170
60120	ELGIN	102	102	107	103	99	101	104	102	102	107	129	118	103	129	100	97	129	105	92	111
60123	ELGIN	106	116	125	118	113	115	113	110	108	114	136	129	116	138	111	104	135	110	101	121
60126	ELMHURST	124	162	201	158	157	163	146	144	138	147	173	166	158	187	152	137	175	141	131	155
60129	ESMOND	93	102	102	99	102	106	94	97	93	94	115	113	98	121	97	92	113	94	94	111
60130	FOREST PARK	82	81	99	85	80	85	89	84	87	88	110	101	88	109	86	84	108	88	79	93
60131	FRANKLIN PARK	77	84	97	81	81	86	83	82	83	85	105	92	85	108	83	82	105	83	78	89
60133	HANOVER PARK	112	120	125	123	115	116	116	114	110	119	140	133	117	140	113	105	139	114	101	125
60134	GENEVA	139	165	180	168	160	161	151	149	141	153	178	174	159	183	152	136	177	146	134	164
60135	GENOA	94	93	86	94	94	99	91	94	91	91	113	109	91	113	91	90	108	92	92	107
60136	GILBERTS	147	167	186	172	166	169	159	158	150	159	189	184	165	191	160	145	186	156	146	173
60137	GLEN ELLYN	145	171	201	173	166	172	161	157	152	162	193	182	171	198	163	149	192	155	144	172
60139	GLENDALE HEIGHTS	104	104	119	108	100	104	108	104	105	110	133	123	107	130	104	100	131	108	94	115
60140	HAMPSHIRE	113	130	135	129	128	131	119	120	113	120	142	138	124	144	121	110	140	117	113	133
60142	HUNTLEY	119	132	131	134	129	130	120	122	113	124	143	139	124	141	121	110	141	119	112	135
60143	ITASCA	141	163	179	165	160	162	153	151	145	153	182	177	160	188	154	140	181	149	137	167
60145	KINGSTON	101	114	115	115	112	111	106	106	100	106	125	125	108	129	106	95	124	104	95	118
60146	KIRKLAND	96	94	85	94	96	103	91	95	92	90	113	109	91	115	92	92	109	93	96	110
	ILLINOIS	98	100	111	99	99	106	100	99	101	100	126	115	102	127	100	100	123	100	98	112
	UNITED STATES	100	100	100	100	100	100	100	100	100	100	100	100	100	100	100	100	100	100	100	100

# POST OFFICE NAME	COUNTY FIPS CODE	POPULATION 2000	2004	2009	2000-2004 ANNUAL RATE % Rate	State Centile	HOUSEHOLDS 2000	2004	2009	% Annual Rate 2000-2004	2004 Average HH Size	FAMILIES 2000	2004	% Annual Rate 2000-2004
60148 LOMBARD	043	51068	53596	56595	1.1	80	19520	20786	22220	1.5	2.51	13123	13748	1.1
60150 MALTA	037	1676	1668	1756	-0.1	36	629	635	676	0.2	2.63	457	453	-0.2
60151 MAPLE PARK	089	3661	4282	5088	3.8	96	1267	1486	1763	3.8	2.88	1013	1171	3.5
60152 MARENGO	111	10963	11899	13338	2.0	88	3951	4346	4924	2.3	2.72	3022	3275	1.9
60153 MAYWOOD	031	27340	26548	26467	-0.7	9	7985	7790	7809	-0.6	3.38	6180	5972	-0.8
60154 WESTCHESTER	031	16692	16357	16277	-0.5	17	6943	6884	6908	-0.2	2.36	4842	4737	-0.5
60155 BROADVIEW	031	8183	8099	8085	-0.2	28	3162	3151	3164	-0.1	2.51	2111	2070	-0.5
60156 LAKE IN THE HILLS	111	23147	29466	35958	5.8	99	7650	9746	11936	5.9	3.02	6395	8110	5.8
60157 MEDINAH	043	2953	3019	3140	0.5	66	999	1037	1092	0.9	2.85	693	714	0.7
60160 MELROSE PARK	031	23098	23451	23766	0.4	61	7596	7670	7775	0.2	3.05	5422	5403	-0.1
60162 HILLSIDE	031	8326	8265	8292	-0.2	33	3061	3042	3062	-0.2	2.64	2125	2082	-0.5
60163 BERKELEY	031	5240	5270	5291	0.1	48	1876	1892	1908	0.2	2.68	1383	1377	-0.1
60164 MELROSE PARK	031	21919	22707	23224	0.8	75	7026	7317	7524	1.0	3.07	5170	5318	0.7
60165 STONE PARK	031	5127	5073	5063	-0.3	27	1265	1231	1221	-0.6	4.12	1060	1023	-0.8
60171 RIVER GROVE	031	10699	10484	10419	-0.5	17	4381	4296	4279	-0.5	2.43	2772	2669	-0.9
60172 ROSELLE	043	25037	25161	25879	0.1	48	9106	9338	9734	0.6	2.68	6806	6899	0.3
60173 SCHAUMBURG	031	11654	11943	12129	0.6	68	5715	5817	5905	0.4	2.05	2625	2629	0.0
60174 SAINT CHARLES	089	30321	34634	40880	3.2	95	11139	12760	15088	3.3	2.62	8057	9085	2.9
60175 SAINT CHARLES	089	18042	21974	26827	4.8	98	5511	6720	8190	4.8	3.27	4898	5911	4.5
60176 SCHILLER PARK	031	11774	11667	11615	-0.2	30	4220	4190	4184	-0.2	2.78	3025	2963	-0.5
60177 SOUTH ELGIN	089	16630	20196	24615	4.7	98	5765	6992	8509	4.6	2.86	4521	5437	4.4
60178 SYCAMORE	037	16397	17641	19156	1.7	86	6247	6801	7457	2.0	2.57	4413	4739	1.7
60180 UNION	111	1612	1710	1896	1.4	83	549	593	665	1.8	2.88	455	486	1.6
60181 VILLA PARK	043	30018	31189	32653	0.9	76	11269	11740	12354	1.0	2.64	7665	7872	0.6
60184 WAYNE	043	2174	2456	2753	2.9	94	730	824	926	2.9	2.97	641	720	2.8
60185 WEST CHICAGO	043	33368	35532	37562	1.5	84	9780	10415	11061	1.5	3.38	7926	8340	1.2
60187 WHEATON	043	62396	65414	68853	1.1	79	21414	22776	24283	1.5	2.70	15677	16511	1.2
60188 CAROL STREAM	043	42941	43850	45488	0.5	66	14673	15016	15655	0.6	2.91	10880	10981	0.2
60190 WINFIELD	043	10596	11168	11719	1.2	81	3505	3742	3972	1.6	2.92	2891	3067	1.4
60191 WOOD DALE	043	14015	14205	14719	0.3	59	5289	5415	5665	0.6	2.62	3870	3917	0.3
60192 SCHAUMBURG	031	1762	2159	2392	4.9	98	510	625	694	4.9	3.45	405	492	4.7
60193 SCHAUMBURG	031	40864	41090	41416	0.1	48	16380	16719	17015	0.5	2.44	11315	11367	0.1
60194 SCHAUMBURG	031	40753	41714	42523	0.6	67	15374	15853	16254	0.7	2.60	10492	10612	0.3
60195 SCHAUMBURG	031	29992	29459	29385	-0.4	19	10886	10764	10799	-0.3	2.74	7642	7483	-0.5
60201 EVANSTON	031	40213	41051	41786	0.5	66	15950	16485	16952	0.8	2.20	8188	8307	0.3
60202 EVANSTON	031	32208	32760	33197	0.4	62	13704	14036	14309	0.6	2.29	7781	7818	0.1
60203 EVANSTON	031	4589	4445	4406	-0.8	8	1679	1646	1643	-0.5	2.70	1310	1269	-0.8
60208 EVANSTON	031	1857	1831	1825	-0.3	23	9	9	10	0.0	2.56	4	4	0.0
60301 OAK PARK	031	2357	2402	2415	0.5	64	1493	1539	1560	0.7	1.56	460	460	0.0
60302 OAK PARK	031	32285	32788	33296	0.4	61	14680	15115	15495	0.7	2.15	7895	7970	0.2
60304 OAK PARK	031	17882	17939	18132	0.1	45	6906	7004	7140	0.3	2.56	4625	4618	0.0
60305 RIVER FOREST	031	11635	11597	11633	-0.1	37	4092	4122	4168	0.2	2.59	2909	2893	-0.1
60401 BEECHER	197	5390	6305	7692	3.8	96	2123	2534	3142	4.3	2.45	1599	1867	3.7
60402 BERWYN	031	60382	61913	62779	0.6	69	22227	22496	22714	0.3	2.73	14638	14592	-0.1
60406 BLUE ISLAND	031	25277	25284	25348	0.0	42	9060	9075	9122	0.0	2.78	5930	5837	-0.4
60407 BRACEVILLE	063	1751	1936	2180	2.4	91	625	700	797	2.7	2.76	464	511	2.3
60408 BRAIDWOOD	197	4986	5760	7000	3.5	95	1701	2001	2467	3.9	2.87	1337	1544	3.5
60409 CALUMET CITY	031	39147	39699	40154	0.3	59	15162	15333	15527	0.3	2.58	10072	10045	-0.1
60410 CHANNAHON	197	7776	10480	13680	7.3	99	2440	3343	4418	7.7	3.13	2092	2827	7.3
60411 CHICAGO HEIGHTS	031	59399	59556	59929	0.1	45	19829	20047	20304	0.3	2.93	14620	14605	0.0
60415 CHICAGO RIDGE	031	14086	14260	14437	0.3	58	5650	5778	5897	0.5	2.40	3461	3494	0.2
60416 COAL CITY	063	7251	7676	8204	1.4	82	2811	3023	3277	1.7	2.54	2024	2143	1.4
60417 CRETE	197	15274	16396	19246	1.7	86	5463	5983	7138	2.2	2.70	4295	4619	1.7
60419 DOLTON	031	25116	24896	24801	-0.2	30	8341	8276	8267	-0.2	2.99	6334	6209	-0.5
60420 DWIGHT	105	6307	6360	6427	0.2	52	1999	2044	2096	0.5	2.66	1360	1370	0.2
60421 ELWOOD	197	3471	4241	5294	4.8	98	1274	1590	2016	5.4	2.67	992	1213	4.9
60422 FLOSSMOOR	031	9598	9980	10188	0.9	77	3434	3603	3704	1.1	2.77	2684	2778	0.8
60423 FRANKFORT	197	22671	28305	35780	5.4	99	7264	9223	11817	5.8	3.04	6224	7808	5.5
60424 GARDNER	063	2969	2985	3126	0.1	48	1172	1195	1270	0.5	2.50	817	818	0.0
60425 GLENWOOD	031	9743	9645	9689	-0.2	31	3647	3660	3700	0.1	2.64	2696	2671	-0.2
60426 HARVEY	031	47687	47715	48099	0.0	42	14427	14566	14784	0.2	3.25	11036	11001	-0.1
60429 HAZEL CREST	031	16208	16286	16499	0.1	47	5591	5690	5814	0.4	2.84	4167	4178	0.1
60430 HOMEWOOD	031	20333	20260	20334	-0.1	37	7815	7881	7974	0.2	2.53	5498	5457	-0.2
60431 JOLIET	197	22947	28368	35603	5.1	98	7742	9750	12421	5.6	2.87	6174	7654	5.2
60432 JOLIET	197	21121	22673	26517	1.7	86	5639	6123	7301	2.0	3.42	4367	4653	1.5
60433 JOLIET	197	17882	18775	21654	1.2	80	5818	6200	7273	1.5	2.89	4195	4364	0.9
60435 JOLIET	197	52701	58917	70645	2.7	93	21011	23866	28961	2.9	2.42	13485	14812	2.2
60436 JOLIET	197	16959	17958	20882	1.4	83	6415	6904	8148	1.7	2.54	4094	4281	1.1
60437 KINSMAN	063	204	204	214	0.0	42	82	83	88	0.3	2.46	66	67	0.4
60438 LANSING	031	28892	29161	29471	0.2	53	11621	11870	12098	0.5	2.46	7927	7963	0.1
60439 LEMONT	031	19957	21782	22829	2.1	89	6628	7310	7727	2.3	2.90	5307	5796	2.1
60440 BOLINGBROOK	197	46889	52075	63665	2.9	94	14602	16770	20431	3.3	3.14	11611	13142	3.0
60441 LOCKPORT	197	26985	30810	36977	3.2	94	8728	10309	12767	4.0	2.70	6541	7587	3.6
60442 MANHATTAN	197	6171	7261	8906	3.9	96	2002	2390	2967	4.3	3.04	1638	1925	3.9
60443 MATTESON	031	14976	16121	16734	1.8	87	5507	6021	6314	2.1	2.65	4115	4438	1.8
60444 MAZON	063	1559	1578	1646	0.3	58	576	594	630	0.7	2.66	452	461	0.5
60445 MIDLOTHIAN	031	26079	26030	26101	0.0	39	10022	10144	10269	0.3	2.56	6663	6604	-0.2
60446 ROMEOVILLE	197	20926	26213	33323	5.4	99	6678	8563	11081	6.0	2.97	5202	6580	5.7
60447 MINOOKA	093	7199	9337	11712	6.3	99	2439	3197	4047	6.6	2.92	1991	2593	6.4
60448 MOKENA	197	19647	24121	30248	5.0	98	6323	7856	9955	5.2	3.07	5337	6551	4.9
60449 MONEE	197	6072	7205	8869	4.1	97	2244	2715	3392	4.6	2.65	1739	2064	4.1
60450 MORRIS	063	18998	20209	21697	1.5	84	7318	7914	8630	1.9	2.51	5096	5435	1.5
60451 NEW LENOX	197	27083	32422	40114	4.3	97	8787	10643	13308	4.6	3.04	7385	8830	4.3
60452 OAK FOREST	031	27677	28055	28360	0.3	59	9663	9898	10082	0.6	2.78	7258	7351	0.3
60453 OAK LAWN	031	55392	55206	55497	-0.1	37	22292	22566	22922	0.3	2.42	14573	14500	-0.1
60455 BRIDGEVIEW	031	15198	14806	14694	-0.6	12	5567	5457	5447	-0.5	2.64	3767	3640	-0.8
60456 HOMETOWN	031	4467	4321	4277	-0.8	7	1895	1855	1852	-0.5	2.33	1172	1126	-0.9
60457 HICKORY HILLS	031	13887	13739	13713	-0.3	27	5195	5188	5214	0.0	2.64	3711	3656	-0.4
60458 JUSTICE	031	14013	13899	13848	-0.2	31	5154	5133	5133	-0.1	2.70	3536	3472	-0.4
60459 BURBANK	031	27912	28392	28756	0.4	62	9339	9590	9784	0.6	2.95	7307	7428	0.4
60460 ODELL	105	1733	1723	1730	-0.1	34	676	687	702	0.4	2.21	497	499	0.1
60461 OLYMPIA FIELDS	031	4772	4724	4709	-0.3	27	1708	1714	1725	0.1	2.72	1375	1367	-0.1
60462 ORLAND PARK	031	38356	38780	39085	0.3	55	14330	14695	14946	0.6	2.62	10857	11021	0.4
60463 PALOS HEIGHTS	031	12998	13224	13372	0.4	63	4803	4948	5046	0.7	2.54	3587	3653	0.4
60464 PALOS PARK	031	9997	9965	10000	-0.1	37	3681	3705	3744	0.2	2.63	2717	2702	-0.1
ILLINOIS					0.7					0.9	2.61			0.6
UNITED STATES					1.2					1.3	2.58			1.1

#	POST OFFICE NAME	RACE (%) White 2000	White 2004	Black 2000	Black 2004	Asian/Pacific 2000	Asian/Pacific 2004	% Hispanic Origin 2000	% Hispanic Origin 2004	2004 AGE DISTRIBUTION (%) 0-4	5-9	10-14	15-19	20-24	25-44	45-64	65-84	85+	18+	MEDIAN AGE 2004	% 2004 Males	% 2004 Females
60148	LOMBARD	86.4	84.1	2.9	3.0	6.9	8.4	6.2	7.5	6.2	6.2	6.7	6.3	6.3	30.6	23.6	11.4	2.6	76.9	37.6	48.9	51.1
60150	MALTA	96.6	96.0	0.7	0.8	0.2	0.3	1.6	2.0	6.8	7.1	7.4	6.8	5.5	29.3	24.2	11.0	1.9	74.5	37.7	50.0	50.0
60151	MAPLE PARK	98.0	97.4	0.3	0.4	0.3	0.4	2.2	3.2	5.8	7.2	8.4	7.7	6.0	26.8	28.5	8.8	0.9	73.7	38.4	51.6	48.4
60152	MARENGO	94.1	92.9	0.3	0.3	0.4	0.4	9.1	11.3	7.0	7.3	8.1	7.3	6.1	27.3	25.6	10.1	1.4	73.1	37.0	50.3	49.7
60153	MAYWOOD	9.9	9.0	82.6	82.9	0.3	0.3	10.5	11.4	8.1	8.3	9.1	8.2	7.6	27.0	21.7	9.2	1.0	69.5	31.4	46.6	53.4
60154	WESTCHESTER	84.9	81.7	7.9	9.4	3.9	4.7	5.8	7.7	5.5	5.8	5.4	4.3	3.5	24.9	26.2	20.5	3.9	80.5	45.4	46.7	53.3
60155	BROADVIEW	23.8	20.2	71.5	74.7	1.4	1.4	3.8	4.4	6.4	6.7	7.0	6.3	5.9	28.8	26.8	10.8	1.4	76.1	37.9	46.8	53.2
60156	LAKE IN THE HILLS	92.2	90.8	1.4	1.5	3.1	3.8	6.0	7.5	12.6	11.2	8.2	5.0	3.9	39.5	15.8	3.5	0.3	64.7	31.5	50.0	50.0
60157	MEDINAH	89.1	87.7	2.8	2.9	4.5	5.3	6.3	7.4	6.2	6.1	6.3	5.8	7.1	28.7	26.7	12.1	1.1	77.7	38.9	50.6	49.4
60160	MELROSE PARK	71.6	68.0	2.9	3.2	2.0	2.2	53.8	60.0	9.0	8.1	7.5	6.4	7.9	32.3	18.5	8.9	1.4	71.6	31.2	50.1	49.9
60162	HILLSIDE	52.3	47.1	34.9	38.3	4.4	4.8	12.7	15.3	6.5	6.5	7.6	6.5	6.1	28.9	22.4	13.2	2.3	75.5	37.8	47.9	52.2
60163	BERKELEY	60.8	55.1	26.8	30.0	3.7	4.3	14.9	18.4	6.4	6.9	7.8	6.0	5.0	27.9	23.6	13.1	3.3	75.3	39.2	48.9	51.1
60164	MELROSE PARK	74.6	70.4	3.0	3.2	4.1	4.5	35.5	42.3	6.9	6.8	7.7	7.3	7.6	28.5	22.3	10.3	2.6	74.1	35.1	49.9	50.1
60165	STONE PARK	54.3	51.6	1.8	1.8	2.1	2.0	78.6	83.2	10.6	9.4	9.0	7.9	9.5	32.8	15.2	5.2	0.5	66.4	27.0	53.3	46.7
60171	RIVER GROVE	91.8	89.4	0.4	0.4	2.1	2.6	10.4	13.9	5.8	5.5	6.1	6.4	7.6	28.8	24.5	12.8	2.6	78.9	37.9	48.4	51.6
60172	ROSELLE	87.6	85.2	1.7	2.0	7.1	8.6	5.8	7.3	6.7	6.7	6.9	6.6	6.5	30.9	26.5	8.2	1.0	75.6	36.8	48.8	51.2
60173	SCHAUMBURG	66.0	60.9	5.3	5.9	24.8	28.6	5.7	6.9	5.2	4.5	4.8	4.9	8.4	43.3	22.0	6.3	0.6	82.5	33.9	50.9	49.1
60174	SAINT CHARLES	93.3	91.5	2.1	2.4	1.7	2.2	5.5	7.9	6.0	6.6	7.8	9.2	5.7	27.0	27.3	8.9	1.5	73.1	37.5	50.5	49.5
60175	SAINT CHARLES	96.0	94.7	0.8	1.0	1.6	2.1	2.5	3.8	7.6	8.9	9.9	7.8	4.3	26.8	28.9	5.4	0.4	68.4	37.0	50.7	49.3
60176	SCHILLER PARK	80.9	76.7	2.0	2.3	5.2	6.1	22.0	27.8	6.6	6.3	6.7	6.4	7.8	32.9	22.5	9.8	1.0	76.6	34.3	50.8	49.2
60177	SOUTH ELGIN	85.6	82.5	3.8	4.2	4.6	5.6	10.9	14.4	9.9	9.2	7.5	5.7	5.6	34.9	20.7	5.7	0.9	70.0	32.9	49.6	50.4
60178	SYCAMORE	94.3	93.3	2.2	2.5	0.8	1.0	3.9	4.8	6.8	6.8	7.8	7.6	6.5	28.0	25.3	9.8	1.4	74.0	36.5	49.0	51.0
60180	UNION	97.5	97.0	0.1	0.2	0.5	0.6	4.5	5.6	6.0	7.2	7.5	7.1	4.3	27.7	29.0	9.9	1.4	74.9	40.2	49.3	50.7
60181	VILLA PARK	85.8	83.8	2.8	2.8	5.7	6.7	13.1	15.7	6.7	6.4	7.1	6.6	7.3	30.6	22.8	10.7	2.0	75.9	36.1	49.8	50.2
60184	WAYNE	92.3	90.4	1.1	1.2	4.1	5.0	4.3	5.7	8.8	9.4	8.1	6.0	4.0	28.4	27.9	6.9	0.6	69.9	37.3	48.7	51.3
60185	WEST CHICAGO	82.0	79.9	1.6	1.6	2.0	2.3	35.5	39.9	8.9	8.3	7.8	6.8	7.9	31.9	21.4	6.2	0.7	70.9	31.1	52.0	48.0
60187	WHEATON	90.5	88.8	2.6	2.7	4.6	5.7	3.7	4.6	6.4	7.1	7.8	8.1	7.9	25.9	26.0	9.2	1.7	74.1	36.5	49.1	51.0
60188	CAROL STREAM	79.0	76.0	4.0	4.1	11.0	13.1	9.7	11.6	8.2	8.3	8.7	7.2	7.2	33.6	21.2	4.8	1.0	70.3	32.2	49.4	50.6
60190	WINFIELD	92.5	91.1	1.5	1.5	2.9	3.6	6.2	7.6	7.3	8.0	8.3	6.9	4.8	28.0	28.0	7.8	0.9	71.7	37.6	50.1	49.9
60191	WOOD DALE	87.7	85.4	0.6	0.6	3.6	4.4	15.5	18.6	6.1	6.2	6.6	5.9	5.8	28.3	26.7	13.2	1.3	77.6	39.5	49.8	50.2
60192	SCHAUMBURG	78.4	73.9	3.6	4.2	10.8	12.8	12.3	16.0	10.2	10.1	8.1	4.8	3.8	36.6	21.2	4.9	0.5	68.6	34.6	48.8	51.2
60193	SCHAUMBURG	85.5	82.1	2.0	2.5	9.2	11.3	5.3	7.1	6.1	6.0	6.2	6.1	6.3	30.4	27.7	9.8	1.3	78.0	38.3	48.3	51.8
60194	SCHAUMBURG	72.4	68.0	4.7	5.3	16.4	18.9	11.1	14.0	6.9	6.6	7.1	6.9	7.5	31.2	24.2	7.3	2.4	75.1	35.0	48.9	51.1
60195	SCHAUMBURG	76.3	71.8	4.5	5.2	14.4	17.1	7.2	9.2	6.8	6.9	7.4	6.7	7.5	33.1	25.3	5.9	0.5	74.7	33.8	50.1	49.9
60201	EVANSTON	69.5	66.1	18.7	19.9	7.4	8.9	4.3	5.5	5.3	5.4	5.2	9.9	13.3	27.2	20.7	10.1	2.9	81.0	32.4	47.5	52.5
60202	EVANSTON	59.7	55.2	28.2	30.7	4.0	4.6	8.4	10.4	6.3	6.0	6.3	6.4	6.9	34.5	24.7	7.6	1.3	77.3	35.7	46.8	53.2
60203	EVANSTON	77.3	73.3	11.6	13.5	7.9	9.4	3.9	4.9	7.2	8.3	7.9	6.3	4.0	20.1	28.6	15.4	2.3	72.7	42.5	47.6	52.4
60208	EVANSTON	71.5	66.3	5.5	6.5	18.7	22.1	4.6	6.0	0.5	0.4	0.6	50.6	36.9	4.4	3.4	2.7	0.4	98.0	19.8	46.8	53.2
60301	OAK PARK	72.6	67.4	16.1	19.1	7.9	9.4	4.2	5.5	3.4	2.6	2.9	4.7	7.7	37.7	24.2	11.5	5.3	88.5	39.6	42.4	57.6
60302	OAK PARK	68.7	64.2	23.2	26.5	3.9	4.7	4.1	5.2	6.1	6.1	6.4	6.6	6.8	30.4	27.3	8.4	1.9	77.2	37.5	46.5	53.6
60304	OAK PARK	68.4	63.5	21.8	25.1	4.1	4.8	5.4	6.9	7.8	7.6	7.5	7.2	6.5	30.2	25.8	6.6	0.9	72.6	35.4	47.6	52.4
60305	RIVER FOREST	89.4	86.7	4.8	6.0	3.2	3.9	4.0	5.4	6.1	7.0	8.2	9.2	7.2	20.8	27.4	11.9	2.1	74.4	39.4	45.9	54.1
60401	BEECHER	97.4	96.8	0.5	0.7	0.2	0.3	2.3	3.1	4.7	5.1	6.3	6.3	5.6	23.1	30.1	16.3	2.6	80.3	44.4	47.9	52.2
60402	BERWYN	75.3	70.5	1.2	1.3	2.5	2.7	36.1	43.7	7.8	7.2	7.4	6.4	7.0	30.3	20.9	10.7	2.3	73.8	34.4	49.0	51.0
60406	BLUE ISLAND	52.8	48.7	26.0	27.0	0.4	0.5	35.6	40.9	8.9	8.2	8.4	7.5	8.0	30.5	19.3	8.0	1.2	70.0	30.8	49.0	51.0
60407	BRACEVILLE	98.0	97.5	0.1	0.2	0.2	0.3	2.3	3.1	8.3	7.9	8.2	6.6	6.6	29.5	23.6	8.7	0.7	71.5	33.9	49.5	50.5
60408	BRAIDWOOD	97.6	96.9	0.3	0.4	0.3	0.4	2.9	4.0	7.5	7.5	8.0	7.3	7.1	30.4	23.1	8.1	1.0	72.5	34.5	50.5	49.5
60409	CALUMET CITY	38.9	34.3	52.7	56.0	0.6	0.6	10.9	13.0	7.8	8.0	8.5	7.0	6.5	29.1	21.1	10.6	1.5	71.5	34.0	46.6	53.4
60410	CHANNAHON	97.3	96.5	0.4	0.5	0.3	0.4	3.6	4.9	7.5	7.6	8.8	7.8	6.1	29.3	26.2	6.4	0.3	71.2	35.3	50.8	49.2
60411	CHICAGO HEIGHTS	50.1	46.6	37.4	39.1	0.7	0.8	17.2	20.1	8.8	8.4	8.9	7.4	7.1	27.7	20.9	9.7	1.2	69.4	31.8	48.8	51.2
60415	CHICAGO RIDGE	89.3	86.9	2.6	3.0	1.4	1.7	6.3	8.5	8.0	7.2	6.3	5.4	6.8	34.5	19.4	10.6	2.0	75.4	34.1	48.5	51.5
60416	COAL CITY	98.1	97.8	0.1	0.1	0.1	0.1	2.3	2.9	6.8	6.6	7.4	7.2	7.1	29.5	24.2	9.8	1.5	74.9	36.0	49.0	51.0
60417	CRETE	84.6	80.8	12.0	15.1	0.8	0.9	4.0	5.2	5.3	6.3	7.2	6.0	5.1	23.7	31.5	13.1	1.9	77.5	42.8	49.0	51.0
60419	DOLTON	14.5	12.0	82.1	84.5	0.6	0.6	3.2	3.6	7.3	8.0	9.7	8.3	6.7	26.9	23.9	8.0	1.2	69.9	33.9	46.4	53.6
60420	DWIGHT	90.0	89.0	7.7	8.2	0.3	0.3	3.0	3.6	5.9	6.0	7.0	6.4	7.3	31.9	22.9	10.6	2.1	77.4	36.7	42.9	57.1
60421	ELWOOD	96.6	95.7	1.3	1.6	0.5	0.7	3.5	4.8	7.6	7.9	7.0	5.3	4.5	29.7	26.7	10.5	0.9	74.3	37.6	49.8	50.3
60422	FLOSSMOOR	66.0	60.3	27.8	32.5	3.7	4.4	2.5	3.2	5.2	6.5	8.0	8.1	5.2	19.9	31.7	13.8	1.6	75.2	43.1	47.9	52.1
60423	FRANKFORT	94.6	93.2	1.8	2.3	1.8	2.2	3.1	4.2	7.9	8.9	9.1	7.2	4.8	27.8	26.2	7.2	0.9	69.4	36.4	49.0	51.0
60424	GARDNER	97.9	97.5	0.1	0.1	0.3	0.3	2.7	3.4	7.1	6.8	7.1	6.2	6.0	29.0	23.8	12.0	1.9	74.9	37.0	49.5	50.5
60425	GLENWOOD	50.9	46.8	44.5	47.9	0.7	0.7	5.3	6.5	6.4	6.6	8.0	6.8	6.0	26.4	26.5	11.9	1.4	74.8	38.3	46.5	53.5
60426	HARVEY	12.7	11.1	79.2	80.3	0.4	0.5	9.7	10.4	9.0	9.0	9.9	8.5	7.4	25.8	20.3	9.3	1.0	66.9	29.9	47.4	52.6
60429	HAZEL CREST	27.7	23.9	67.7	71.0	1.1	1.1	3.9	4.6	7.1	7.5	8.8	8.0	6.6	26.2	25.5	8.7	1.6	71.6	35.2	45.9	54.1
60430	HOMEWOOD	73.7	69.6	22.0	25.1	1.6	2.0	3.0	3.9	5.6	6.3	8.1	7.5	5.4	23.4	27.8	13.4	2.7	75.2	41.3	46.2	53.9
60431	JOLIET	90.4	88.3	4.4	5.2	1.6	1.9	5.5	7.3	7.7	7.9	8.2	7.6	6.1	29.4	24.2	7.6	1.3	71.4	34.9	49.6	50.4
60432	JOLIET	42.4	40.3	30.4	30.0	0.3	0.3	46.6	50.4	10.1	8.9	8.4	8.1	10.4	31.9	15.8	5.8	0.6	68.2	27.1	54.6	45.4
60433	JOLIET	48.6	44.8	42.6	45.0	0.2	0.2	15.0	17.5	7.9	7.8	8.8	8.1	7.4	26.9	19.9	10.1	3.1	70.6	32.3	47.7	52.3
60435	JOLIET	81.8	78.5	9.2	10.6	1.5	1.7	11.5	14.3	7.7	6.9	6.5	6.1	7.4	30.3	21.2	11.7	2.2	75.4	35.2	48.3	51.7
60436	JOLIET	66.2	62.0	22.7	24.4	0.7	0.8	14.5	18.0	8.0	7.4	6.9	7.1	7.0	29.2	20.5	11.6	2.2	73.4	34.0	49.3	50.7
60437	KINSMAN	98.5	98.0	0.0	0.0	0.0	0.0	4.9	5.9	6.4	6.9	8.3	8.3	6.4	25.5	24.5	12.3	1.5	73.0	39.3	50.0	50.0
60438	LANSING	85.4	82.9	11.2	12.7	0.7	0.9	5.7	7.5	6.4	6.5	6.8	6.4	6.1	27.3	25.2	13.5	1.9	76.4	38.9	47.6	52.4
60439	LEMONT	97.1	96.2	0.4	0.4	1.1	1.4	3.0	4.1	6.6	7.5	8.4	6.6	4.6	24.9	28.3	10.2	3.0	73.2	40.5	48.4	51.6
60440	BOLINGBROOK	64.2	58.9	20.8	23.8	5.9	6.5	14.0	16.9	8.8	8.6	8.4	7.2	7.2	32.0	22.5	4.7	0.7	69.9	31.6	49.8	50.2
60441	LOCKPORT	81.9	80.9	13.8	14.0	0.7	0.8	6.1	7.6	7.1	6.9	6.7	6.3	7.8	34.4	21.6	8.3	1.0	75.7	34.2	54.2	45.8
60442	MANHATTAN	97.6	96.8	0.3	0.5	0.2	0.2	2.4	3.3	7.8	8.1	8.7	7.6	6.6	29.2	24.4	6.8	0.9	70.7	34.8	51.0	49.0
60443	MATTESON	39.2	36.4	56.4	58.7	1.5	1.6	3.2	4.0	5.9	6.4	7.5	7.0	5.9	25.2	28.3	12.3	1.5	75.8	40.0	46.2	53.8
60444	MAZON	96.5	96.0	0.2	0.2	0.1	0.1	2.8	3.6	6.6	7.1	7.9	6.8	5.9	28.8	25.0	10.7	1.2	74.2	36.7	50.7	49.3
60445	MIDLOTHIAN	90.4	88.2	5.3	6.2	1.2	1.5	5.4	7.2	6.7	6.6	7.0	6.1	6.2	29.5	23.7	12.1	2.0	75.9	37.6	47.9	52.1
60446	ROMEOVILLE	86.2	82.9	4.8	5.9	2.2	2.7	11.8	14.9	9.0	8.1	7.1	5.9	6.9	34.8	17.7	9.8	0.7	72.6	32.8	49.6	50.4
60447	MINOOKA	97.8	97.1	0.3	0.4	0.3	0.4	3.0	3.9	7.9	7.8	8.3	7.3	6.6	29.9	24.9	6.6	0.6	71.5	34.2	50.3	49.7
60448	MOKENA	96.7	95.7	0.6	0.8	1.3	1.6	3.0	4.1	7.6	8.1	8.8	7.3	6.0	29.2	26.1	6.2	0.7	71.0	35.5	50.3	49.8
60449	MONEE	90.6	89.1	5.8	6.3	0.5	0.6	3.3	4.5	7.1	7.4	6.9	5.5	4.4	30.0	25.4	12.1	1.2	75.1	38.6	50.4	49.6
60450	MORRIS	96.3	95.6	0.3	0.3	0.5	0.6	5.5	6.6	6.5	6.5	6.8	6.8	7.0	27.5	25.3	11.2	2.3	75.9	37.9	49.7	50.3
60451	NEW LENOX	97.6	96.8	0.4	0.5	0.4	0.5	3.1	4.3	8.3	8.6	8.8	7.2	5.8	29.7	24.5	6.6	0.6	69.8	35.1	49.2	50.8
60452	OAK FOREST	90.3	88.1	3.7	4.4	2.7	3.3	5.9	7.9	6.6	6.8	7.1	6.6	6.6	30.0	26.3	9.0	1.0	75.5	36.6	49.8	50.3
60453	OAK LAWN	93.3	91.6	1.2	1.5	1.7	2.2	5.3	7.3	5.5	5.5	6.2	6.0	5.7	24.6	24.4	18.6	3.3	79.1	42.6	46.8	53.2
60455	BRIDGEVIEW	87.2	84.2	0.9	1.1	2.2	2.7	9.3	12.5	7.1	6.8	6.8	6.1	6.3	28.3	23.7	12.8	2.2	75.7	37.5	49.5	50.5
60456	HOMETOWN	97.3	96.5	0.0	0.0	0.3	0.4	3.8	5.3	6.2	6.0	6.5	6.4	6.2	28.0	22.2	15.8	2.8	77.5	39.3	45.7	54.3
60457	HICKORY HILLS	86.0	83.4	6.3	7.0	2.2	2.7	7.6	10.2	6.7	6.4	6.7	6.6	6.9	29.2	24.7	11.5	1.3	76.3	36.5	49.4	50.6
60458	JUSTICE	79.4	76.3	12.3	13.4	1.6	1.9	7.6	10.0	8.0	7.4	7.5	6.7	7.7	31.6	22.6	7.7	0.9	73.1	32.8	49.2	50.8
60459	BURBANK	90.3	87.7	0.3	0.3	1.8	2.2	11.7	15.6	6.2	6.3	7.1	6.9	7.1	27.7	24.5	12.6	1.6	76.4	37.3	48.9	51.1
60460	ODELL	90.4	89.4	7.6	8.2	0.3	0.4	1.9	2.3	5.9	6.1	7.1	7.3	6.8	30.4	23.7	11.4	1.3	76.6	37.4	43.4	56.6
60461	OLYMPIA FIELDS	42.2	37.0	53.2	57.8	2.8	3.1	2.2	2.8	5.5	6.5	7.0	6.2	4.6	19.8	31.1	17.3	2.0	77.3	45.3	47.0	53.0
60462	ORLAND PARK	93.3	91.5	0.6	0.8	3.6	4.6	3.9	5.4	5.0	5.5	6.8	6.6	6.0	23.4	29.8	14.7	2.1	78.6	42.7	47.6	52.4
60463	PALOS HEIGHTS	96.3	95.2	0.6	0.7	1.7	2.2	1.7	2.4	4.8	5.2	6.2	6.5	6.2	19.1	28.5	20.6	3.0	80.4	46.4	47.4	52.7
60464	PALOS PARK	95.9	94.7	0.3	0.4	2.5	3.2	2.4	3.3	4.0	5.1	6.8	6.8	4.9	18.5	33.5	16.9	3.6	79.6	47.2	47.8	52.2
	ILLINOIS	73.5	71.8	15.1	15.2	3.5	4.0	12.3	14.2	7.1	7.0	7.3	7.0	7.3	29.0	23.2	10.4	1.7	74.5	35.2	49.0	51.0
	UNITED STATES	75.1	73.6	12.3	12.5	3.8	4.2	12.5	14.1	6.9	6.7	7.2	7.0	7.3	28.6	23.8	10.8	1.7	75.1	36.0	49.1	50.9

ZIP CODE #	POST OFFICE NAME	2004 Per Capita Income	2004 HH Income Base	2004 Household Income Distribution (%): Less than $25,000	$25,000 to $49,999	$50,000 to $99,999	$100,000 to $149,999	$150,000 or More	Median Household Income: 2004	2009	2004 National Centile	2004 State Centile	2004 Home Value Base	2004 Home Value Distribution (%): Less than $50,000	$50,000 to $89,999	$90,000 to $174,999	$175,000 to $399,999	$400,000 or More	2004 Median Home Value
60148	LOMBARD	32827	20786	12.1	21.2	39.9	17.9	8.9	67362	79023	90	88	16218	0.3	2.1	23.0	69.6	5.0	217131
60150	MALTA	25098	635	13.4	30.6	38.9	12.9	4.3	55655	62908	80	75	502	1.2	2.4	51.2	38.7	6.6	167683
60151	MAPLE PARK	28819	1486	12.3	17.6	45.8	17.4	6.8	69131	79320	91	90	1284	0.7	0.5	23.3	62.4	13.2	231518
60152	MARENGO	29355	4346	12.2	23.5	40.6	14.7	9.1	64979	74789	89	87	3383	0.6	0.6	26.5	59.5	12.7	216727
60153	MAYWOOD	16862	7790	25.3	28.6	33.1	9.3	3.7	46259	53359	64	53	5236	1.0	6.3	69.8	22.8	0.1	138594
60154	WESTCHESTER	34321	6884	12.2	24.2	38.1	17.5	8.0	64621	75705	88	86	6344	0.4	0.1	19.5	74.5	5.5	216925
60155	BROADVIEW	24928	3151	20.2	28.6	35.3	13.0	2.9	51129	60807	74	66	2294	3.6	2.4	64.4	29.5	0.2	153143
60156	LAKE IN THE HILLS	31660	9746	4.9	14.5	46.7	23.0	10.8	81411	92075	95	96	9189	0.4	0.4	20.1	70.9	8.3	230667
60157	MEDINAH	32159	1037	13.9	17.4	38.7	18.4	11.7	71510	84186	92	91	770	0.4	4.0	14.3	62.3	19.0	282710
60160	MELROSE PARK	18505	7670	25.6	29.5	33.0	8.8	3.1	45449	52672	62	50	4415	6.6	1.6	27.6	63.4	0.7	195789
60162	HILLSIDE	24460	3042	16.2	26.4	41.6	11.4	4.3	56745	65996	81	77	2263	0.4	1.9	48.6	48.9	0.2	174095
60163	BERKELEY	28730	1892	14.2	22.5	39.0	18.5	5.9	64682	76196	88	86	1666	0.6	0.5	48.1	50.5	0.3	175787
60164	MELROSE PARK	19876	7317	18.9	25.1	42.2	11.3	2.6	54738	62713	79	73	5683	1.1	3.1	45.9	49.5	0.5	174899
60165	STONE PARK	13592	1231	26.7	34.3	30.9	5.4	2.7	43140	48589	56	42	785	9.9	0.4	53.5	35.3	0.9	156421
60171	RIVER GROVE	22954	4296	23.0	32.9	33.1	8.4	2.7	44870	52072	61	48	2617	0.5	1.8	40.4	54.5	2.9	183370
60172	ROSELLE	33311	9338	8.5	19.0	43.1	19.9	9.5	72024	83460	92	92	7787	0.5	0.2	22.0	71.4	5.9	221621
60173	SCHAUMBURG	42730	5817	11.8	20.4	41.6	15.3	11.0	67153	78999	90	88	2603	0.4	1.9	40.7	36.0	21.1	196726
60174	SAINT CHARLES	38097	12760	11.1	18.7	36.0	18.5	15.7	75247	85858	93	93	10055	0.4	0.2	14.5	63.6	21.3	244119
60175	SAINT CHARLES	42506	6720	4.6	11.0	29.9	24.8	29.8	106813	124616	99	98	6401	0.1	0.4	5.2	49.5	44.9	379145
60176	SCHILLER PARK	20391	4190	20.8	34.4	32.7	9.6	2.4	46043	53187	64	52	2513	1.1	1.6	25.4	69.0	2.9	204813
60177	SOUTH ELGIN	31407	6992	9.8	15.6	46.3	18.0	10.4	75920	85690	94	93	5976	0.5	0.4	29.1	59.1	10.8	208923
60178	SYCAMORE	27836	6801	13.8	25.0	42.7	13.4	5.1	61069	68643	85	83	5364	5.5	1.1	37.8	49.8	5.7	183790
60180	UNION	29829	593	10.1	18.6	41.2	21.6	8.6	71511	81042	92	91	520	0.2	3.1	19.8	58.7	18.3	250781
60181	VILLA PARK	29483	11740	12.8	25.2	40.3	15.0	6.6	61763	72827	86	83	8942	0.3	0.6	32.3	62.3	4.5	199228
60184	WAYNE	60247	824	5.1	7.2	32.2	22.3	33.3	108602	125402	99	99	795	0.3	0.0	3.7	44.4	51.7	416265
60185	WEST CHICAGO	27474	10415	10.6	18.6	38.7	20.2	11.9	75409	85348	93	93	8111	1.8	1.2	22.0	57.7	17.2	226918
60187	WHEATON	41449	22776	7.7	16.4	34.2	20.9	20.8	84885	99368	96	97	17998	0.2	0.4	13.7	60.7	25.0	284320
60188	CAROL STREAM	29379	15016	10.8	18.6	39.6	21.6	9.4	73755	84229	93	92	11301	0.6	1.8	23.9	67.4	6.3	219691
60190	WINFIELD	40140	3742	4.7	12.8	38.7	25.2	18.6	89389	102712	97	97	3504	0.1	0.0	13.4	70.7	15.8	254775
60191	WOOD DALE	30257	5415	11.4	22.3	40.2	18.1	8.0	66023	77718	89	88	4522	1.0	0.7	21.5	68.9	8.0	221873
60192	SCHAUMBURG	33507	625	6.1	14.4	35.5	26.6	17.4	89168	103896	97	97	602	0.5	0.7	24.1	51.3	23.4	227966
60193	SCHAUMBURG	34797	16719	10.5	21.5	40.1	18.9	9.1	69481	81077	91	90	14000	0.3	1.8	30.9	63.0	4.0	208199
60194	SCHAUMBURG	30343	15853	11.7	22.4	40.9	17.1	8.0	65994	76891	89	88	11631	0.7	4.4	32.0	57.6	5.3	197815
60195	SCHAUMBURG	33665	10764	6.9	19.2	41.3	21.4	11.2	76770	88183	94	94	7639	0.8	1.4	20.8	69.2	7.9	228497
60201	EVANSTON	45068	16485	22.8	18.9	24.3	14.6	19.4	63994	77948	88	85	9139	0.4	2.4	12.8	38.8	45.6	369664
60202	EVANSTON	38589	14036	14.7	21.7	35.9	15.0	12.7	64390	79719	88	86	7916	0.5	1.3	23.3	55.9	19.0	238154
60203	EVANSTON	46385	1646	10.6	14.2	31.3	20.3	23.7	89180	106106	97	97	1543	0.6	0.0	5.6	56.6	37.1	347763
60208	EVANSTON	12752	9	11.1	0.0	22.2	22.2	44.4	136237	137500	100	100	7	0.0	0.0	0.0	14.3	85.7	812500
60301	OAK PARK	51746	1539	17.0	23.9	37.4	12.2	9.5	60400	72718	85	82	456	2.4	7.5	51.1	31.8	7.2	156061
60302	OAK PARK	47284	15115	14.6	22.6	30.1	14.6	18.1	65991	79944	89	87	8472	1.1	2.8	16.4	49.0	30.8	290523
60304	OAK PARK	33440	7004	13.4	21.1	35.9	19.0	10.7	68994	80544	91	90	4910	0.6	0.9	15.9	74.1	8.6	236882
60305	RIVER FOREST	54494	4122	11.0	17.8	22.1	14.9	34.2	97314	114691	98	98	3561	0.0	2.7	13.6	27.2	56.4	437034
60401	BEECHER	26388	2534	17.1	25.3	40.6	13.3	3.7	56669	64207	81	77	2197	12.7	6.8	26.0	48.8	5.7	184641
60402	BERWYN	22099	22496	20.9	30.5	35.5	9.6	3.4	48570	56468	69	59	14801	1.0	1.6	47.3	49.6	0.5	175080
60406	BLUE ISLAND	18212	9075	28.5	34.3	28.7	7.0	1.6	39448	45688	44	28	5293	13.2	9.6	57.1	19.2	0.8	127548
60407	BRACEVILLE	21204	700	18.0	28.9	41.1	10.1	1.9	52530	61328	76	69	573	9.3	12.2	57.8	19.6	1.2	133068
60408	BRAIDWOOD	23016	2001	17.8	24.5	39.1	14.2	4.3	58565	66082	83	79	1713	2.4	7.1	61.9	28.0	0.6	145981
60409	CALUMET CITY	20645	15333	24.8	32.2	32.7	8.3	2.0	44180	51484	59	46	9917	5.3	16.6	66.2	11.2	0.7	115562
60410	CHANNAHON	26448	3343	5.8	18.6	47.4	21.4	6.9	76600	83466	94	94	3058	1.2	1.4	28.1	66.0	3.2	201493
60411	CHICAGO HEIGHTS	19689	20047	26.4	27.7	33.4	9.5	3.1	46110	53972	64	52	14342	11.6	17.0	55.5	15.2	0.7	113940
60415	CHICAGO RIDGE	23766	5778	20.8	29.8	36.9	10.7	1.9	49512	57427	71	61	3466	0.6	5.7	56.1	36.6	1.0	157633
60416	COAL CITY	26571	3023	16.6	25.8	38.8	15.0	3.8	58011	65287	83	79	2326	9.5	4.5	49.6	33.4	3.0	154265
60417	CRETE	31758	5983	10.0	21.5	38.5	19.4	10.6	71411	79549	92	91	5420	4.9	2.8	26.0	59.1	7.3	209598
60419	DOLTON	20475	8276	18.5	28.7	38.6	11.7	2.7	52425	60549	76	68	6791	0.9	14.8	74.4	9.6	0.4	119668
60420	DWIGHT	20986	2044	22.8	36.2	28.1	9.7	3.2	44288	49236	59	46	1528	9.2	12.1	60.5	17.3	0.9	121409
60421	ELWOOD	28180	1590	13.3	24.0	40.2	16.7	5.9	65526	75000	89	87	1404	2.4	2.4	37.4	54.6	3.2	183786
60422	FLOSSMOOR	47934	3603	9.7	13.5	29.6	22.7	24.5	94213	110876	98	98	3450	0.3	1.3	20.4	59.9	18.0	247680
60423	FRANKFORT	31751	9223	8.1	14.9	41.7	23.0	12.2	80699	89390	95	95	8688	0.3	0.5	15.7	67.1	16.5	249918
60424	GARDNER	22130	1195	21.6	33.0	34.9	8.9	1.7	46580	53551	65	54	958	12.9	11.0	58.0	16.7	1.4	120964
60425	GLENWOOD	26831	3660	16.1	24.5	37.8	15.1	6.6	59081	69518	84	80	3017	0.6	10.0	56.8	31.8	0.7	150714
60426	HARVEY	14495	14566	33.5	31.5	27.0	6.1	1.9	37687	42865	38	21	9992	10.8	36.2	48.5	4.0	0.6	91968
60429	HAZEL CREST	23557	5690	15.6	28.2	39.2	12.2	4.8	55611	64755	80	75	4740	1.3	13.3	62.9	21.1	1.4	125190
60430	HOMEWOOD	30322	7881	15.3	22.3	37.6	16.9	8.0	63457	74917	87	85	6914	0.7	5.3	50.3	42.2	1.5	166023
60431	JOLIET	30310	9750	10.6	18.1	42.5	20.1	8.8	74145	81300	93	92	8816	3.3	1.3	29.4	62.6	3.4	192279
60432	JOLIET	13366	6123	31.4	34.2	28.7	4.6	1.1	38093	44115	40	23	3453	9.4	33.5	49.5	6.8	0.8	96792
60433	JOLIET	18467	6200	25.1	31.9	32.9	7.2	2.9	44248	51087	59	46	4118	5.1	25.5	57.0	11.4	1.0	110174
60435	JOLIET	24543	23866	20.9	29.3	36.3	10.5	3.0	49790	57706	72	62	15981	0.8	6.9	61.7	30.0	0.6	147628
60436	JOLIET	20949	6904	27.2	29.9	32.4	8.2	2.3	42662	50507	55	40	4608	2.2	14.0	70.9	12.2	0.7	117987
60437	KINSMAN	25909	83	16.9	22.9	47.0	8.4	4.8	56589	64075	81	77	70	1.4	12.9	37.1	41.4	7.1	171875
60438	LANSING	25928	11870	18.5	28.4	38.4	11.1	3.7	52885	62211	77	69	9124	0.9	6.8	62.4	29.2	0.9	147025
60439	LEMONT	37261	7310	9.7	15.0	35.5	22.0	17.8	84857	100561	96	96	6545	0.0	1.0	9.8	59.2	30.1	311431
60440	BOLINGBROOK	25961	16770	9.0	19.1	45.7	19.3	6.9	70124	79582	91	91	13833	0.5	3.5	47.2	46.3	2.5	173497
60441	LOCKPORT	25906	10309	13.2	26.1	42.6	12.7	5.4	60271	68327	85	81	8419	2.4	4.1	38.8	51.3	3.4	182827
60442	MANHATTAN	25770	2390	12.8	18.6	42.9	17.9	7.9	67613	75425	90	89	2102	0.1	1.1	25.6	65.8	7.4	220337
60443	MATTESON	28578	6021	16.5	23.3	37.3	15.9	7.0	61137	69710	85	83	5196	6.8	9.4	45.6	36.2	2.0	156158
60444	MAZON	25022	594	14.7	23.7	44.6	14.3	2.7	61869	69097	86	83	500	2.6	3.4	61.2	30.6	2.2	149779
60445	MIDLOTHIAN	24583	10144	17.2	28.0	39.9	11.9	3.0	53854	63395	78	71	8292	0.4	3.7	62.3	32.7	1.0	150183
60446	ROMEOVILLE	23955	8563	8.2	23.5	50.4	14.4	3.4	64387	75523	88	86	7316	0.7	1.2	56.9	40.6	0.7	160733
60447	MINOOKA	26069	3197	10.8	20.2	45.2	17.8	5.9	67379	75393	90	89	2857	9.8	3.5	22.7	60.9	3.1	199969
60448	MOKENA	30535	7856	5.6	18.3	41.7	23.9	10.5	79406	87303	95	95	7130	0.2	0.9	15.2	72.2	11.5	258714
60449	MONEE	31808	2715	13.0	20.7	39.0	17.8	9.6	69211	78051	91	90	2384	0.9	6.4	24.7	52.9	15.2	214649
60450	MORRIS	26363	7914	17.9	25.5	38.8	13.6	4.3	57465	64315	82	78	5787	2.5	3.3	44.7	44.8	4.9	174428
60451	NEW LENOX	28687	10643	7.7	15.9	46.0	22.4	8.1	76557	84989	94	94	9683	0.0	0.2	20.4	74.2	5.2	229180
60452	OAK FOREST	27456	9898	13.6	21.9	41.9	16.5	6.1	64957	75886	88	87	8151	0.9	1.5	38.2	57.6	1.9	184873
60453	OAK LAWN	27268	22566	18.7	29.1	33.9	13.3	4.9	52101	60720	76	68	18738	1.3	3.7	37.2	56.1	1.8	186012
60455	BRIDGEVIEW	21765	5457	23.5	29.2	34.2	10.3	2.9	47425	54777	67	56	4203	15.8	3.5	36.0	44.2	0.6	166057
60456	HOMETOWN	22403	1855	23.8	33.1	32.5	8.7	1.8	44809	52727	61	48	1393	3.0	2.6	89.1	5.3	0.0	121388
60457	HICKORY HILLS	27339	5188	14.7	24.2	40.7	14.5	5.9	60400	70237	85	82	3860	0.5	0.9	27.0	67.6	4.0	203749
60458	JUSTICE	23371	5133	19.9	27.0	39.7	10.3	3.2	52576	60762	76	69	3354	21.5	4.4	30.5	42.0	1.5	163077
60459	BURBANK	21484	9590	17.5	27.9	37.8	13.4	3.4	54017	63130	78	71	8118	0.5	1.2	49.1	47.8	1.4	174012
60460	ODELL	23880	687	20.2	32.6	37.9	7.7	1.6	47087	51663	66	56	552	10.0	20.5	55.1	12.3	2.2	112879
60461	OLYMPIA FIELDS	48009	1714	10.5	13.0	30.2	23.6	22.7	92586	109298	97	98	1560	0.4	1.0	14.6	62.7	21.4	271895
60462	ORLAND PARK	34197	14695	11.2	20.1	37.2	19.8	11.7	72625	83468	92	92	13003	0.4	0.3	21.9	69.9	7.6	233631
60463	PALOS HEIGHTS	36006	4948	14.6	19.3	34.5	17.7	14.0	71960	81734	92	92	4604	0.1	1.1	9.5	78.5	10.8	255084
60464	PALOS PARK	41147	3705	10.7	18.0	30.9	22.0	18.4	81744	93257	95	96	3474	1.0	0.2	7.2	57.5	34.0	332769
	ILLINOIS	27033		22.1	25.9	32.9	11.9	7.3	52039	60941				7.7	12.8	34.0	36.6	8.9	162771
	UNITED STATES	25866		24.7	27.1	30.8	10.9	6.5	48124	56710				10.9	15.0	33.7	30.1	10.4	145905

ZIP CODE #	POST OFFICE NAME	FINANCIAL SERVICES: Auto Loan	Home Loan	Invest-ments	Retire-ment Plans	THE HOME: Home Improvements: Home Repair	Lawn & Garden	Furnishings: Comput-ers & Hard-ware	Major Appli-ances	TV, Radio, Sound Equip-ment	Furni-ture	ENTERTAINMENT: Dine out/ Carry out	Sports Equip-ment	Fees & Tickets	Toys & Games	Travel	Cable TV	PERSONAL: Apparel & Services	Auto Repairs	Health Insur-ance	Pets & Supplies
60148	LOMBARD	108	124	145	125	121	126	120	117	115	119	145	136	125	150	121	113	144	117	109	128
60150	MALTA	88	101	106	99	99	100	94	94	90	94	113	110	98	118	95	88	112	92	87	104
60151	MAPLE PARK	114	130	130	129	130	131	117	120	112	117	140	141	123	147	120	110	138	116	112	137
60152	MARENGO	112	122	119	123	120	122	115	116	110	115	138	136	117	140	114	106	135	114	107	129
60153	MAYWOOD	78	74	86	71	72	83	78	76	82	80	103	84	80	101	78	84	101	78	80	87
60154	WESTCHESTER	107	119	131	114	119	131	113	115	113	113	141	126	118	141	118	116	137	113	119	126
60155	BROADVIEW	84	86	99	83	84	95	87	86	90	88	113	94	91	112	88	92	110	86	89	97
60156	LAKE IN THE HILLS	136	154	150	160	147	143	140	139	128	145	163	162	144	164	137	120	161	135	118	152
60157	MEDINAH	124	134	155	138	132	138	133	130	128	134	162	153	136	160	133	124	159	132	121	143
60160	MELROSE PARK	79	77	79	74	75	78	79	80	80	82	101	89	77	99	76	77	101	81	75	86
60162	HILLSIDE	83	95	108	95	94	97	94	91	90	92	113	107	97	119	94	88	112	91	86	99
60163	BERKELEY	99	119	132	116	117	122	111	110	107	110	135	126	118	142	115	107	134	108	105	120
60164	MELROSE PARK	80	87	102	85	85	89	86	84	86	87	108	97	88	112	86	85	107	85	81	92
60165	STONE PARK	82	69	67	69	68	70	78	78	81	82	103	89	74	100	72	75	103	83	71	83
60171	RIVER GROVE	71	81	95	80	79	84	79	77	78	79	98	90	83	101	81	77	97	78	74	84
60172	ROSELLE	120	137	149	140	134	135	129	127	122	130	154	149	134	158	129	117	152	126	115	140
60173	SCHAUMBURG	122	120	147	130	116	121	127	121	123	130	157	146	127	153	122	117	154	126	108	134
60174	SAINT CHARLES	137	156	171	160	152	154	147	145	139	148	175	170	153	178	147	133	173	143	131	159
60175	SAINT CHARLES	184	226	245	233	219	221	201	196	184	204	234	228	219	242	204	177	235	190	174	217
60176	SCHILLER PARK	74	82	96	78	78	83	79	78	79	82	101	87	81	104	79	79	101	79	73	85
60177	SOUTH ELGIN	127	141	141	145	136	136	131	129	122	133	155	152	134	156	129	116	153	127	115	144
60178	SYCAMORE	97	109	113	109	107	108	103	103	98	103	123	121	106	127	103	95	122	102	94	113
60180	UNION	111	135	146	134	132	133	123	122	116	123	146	142	131	155	126	113	145	119	112	134
60181	VILLA PARK	99	114	136	113	112	117	111	109	108	111	136	126	116	141	113	106	135	109	102	118
60184	WAYNE	240	291	329	296	280	284	259	257	239	267	303	296	278	311	262	230	303	249	226	280
60185	WEST CHICAGO	127	137	149	138	132	136	133	131	129	136	163	151	136	164	131	124	162	132	120	144
60187	WHEATON	150	176	213	181	171	177	168	162	159	168	201	190	178	209	169	155	200	161	148	178
60188	CAROL STREAM	120	129	135	135	125	125	124	122	117	127	149	144	126	148	121	111	146	122	108	134
60190	WINFIELD	156	187	205	190	183	186	171	169	159	172	202	195	182	209	173	155	201	164	154	186
60191	WOOD DALE	102	119	136	118	117	122	113	111	109	113	137	128	118	142	115	107	136	110	105	122
60192	SCHAUMBURG	166	188	181	196	178	172	169	168	155	176	197	196	174	197	165	144	195	163	142	183
60193	SCHAUMBURG	113	130	143	132	127	128	123	121	116	124	147	143	128	151	123	112	145	120	109	133
60194	SCHAUMBURG	108	118	130	121	114	116	114	112	109	116	138	131	117	139	113	104	137	112	101	123
60195	SCHAUMBURG	127	137	150	143	133	135	134	130	126	135	160	154	137	160	131	120	158	131	115	144
60201	EVANSTON	140	141	193	146	137	150	159	144	155	154	196	174	159	197	153	151	193	152	135	159
60202	EVANSTON	115	118	175	126	114	123	127	119	127	129	161	142	131	166	126	126	160	124	111	132
60203	EVANSTON	150	203	258	195	198	208	178	178	167	180	211	200	197	226	189	169	213	171	164	190
60208	EVANSTON	192	191	255	196	186	208	227	196	215	212	271	242	222	264	212	203	265	210	182	217
60301	OAK PARK	107	108	149	116	107	114	116	111	114	116	144	132	118	144	115	111	141	114	105	122
60302	OAK PARK	129	142	208	149	137	148	146	138	143	147	182	163	154	188	147	142	181	141	128	151
60304	OAK PARK	109	127	157	130	125	128	124	120	117	123	148	142	129	153	125	114	147	120	109	130
60305	RIVER FOREST	182	239	309	233	232	245	214	211	202	216	254	240	235	270	225	202	256	205	195	228
60401	BEECHER	93	96	90	92	97	103	90	94	90	90	112	108	91	113	92	91	108	92	95	109
60402	BERWYN	79	85	99	83	83	89	85	84	85	86	107	94	87	110	85	85	106	84	81	91
60406	BLUE ISLAND	71	68	71	67	67	72	71	71	72	72	90	82	70	88	70	71	88	73	69	78
60407	BRACEVILLE	94	83	64	79	87	94	78	86	82	78	100	101	76	101	80	84	95	84	92	109
60408	BRAIDWOOD	95	99	94	97	99	102	93	95	91	93	113	112	94	116	93	90	111	94	92	111
60409	CALUMET CITY	71	72	82	70	71	78	74	73	76	74	95	83	76	97	75	77	93	74	74	81
60410	CHANNAHON	110	132	138	132	129	127	120	119	111	120	140	140	125	147	121	107	139	116	106	132
60411	CHICAGO HEIGHTS	80	81	85	79	80	85	81	81	82	82	102	93	82	103	81	81	100	82	79	90
60415	CHICAGO RIDGE	78	79	93	82	77	82	83	80	81	83	103	95	84	102	81	78	101	82	74	88
60416	COAL CITY	98	98	90	97	98	104	95	98	94	95	117	113	94	117	94	93	113	96	96	112
60417	CRETE	113	135	146	135	133	135	124	123	117	124	147	143	131	154	126	114	146	120	113	135
60419	DOLTON	83	87	95	84	84	91	85	84	86	87	108	95	89	108	86	87	106	85	84	95
60420	DWIGHT	85	75	63	74	79	87	77	81	81	75	98	95	74	98	77	82	93	81	88	97
60421	ELWOOD	111	113	102	110	116	120	103	109	103	103	127	129	105	132	106	103	124	106	109	132
60422	FLOSSMOOR	164	212	254	206	208	217	189	189	178	190	224	215	205	236	198	178	225	183	175	204
60423	FRANKFORT	131	156	163	158	151	151	140	139	130	143	164	161	148	169	141	125	163	135	124	153
60424	GARDNER	82	76	67	74	78	86	76	79	79	75	97	90	75	98	76	80	92	78	84	92
60425	GLENWOOD	94	105	115	103	103	108	100	99	98	101	123	113	104	125	102	97	121	98	96	110
60426	HARVEY	65	62	69	59	60	69	64	64	68	66	85	70	66	82	64	70	83	65	67	72
60429	HAZEL CREST	88	97	112	96	95	101	95	93	93	95	117	108	99	120	96	93	116	93	89	103
60430	HOMEWOOD	97	116	138	114	114	120	110	109	106	110	133	125	116	138	113	106	132	108	103	118
60431	JOLIET	118	138	145	141	135	135	126	125	118	128	149	146	133	153	127	114	148	122	113	138
60432	JOLIET	64	58	60	57	57	60	63	63	66	65	82	72	61	80	61	63	81	66	60	68
60433	JOLIET	72	71	81	69	70	78	75	73	77	75	97	83	76	97	75	79	94	74	75	82
60435	JOLIET	79	84	94	84	82	88	85	83	84	84	106	97	87	108	85	83	104	84	80	91
60436	JOLIET	70	74	83	72	73	80	75	74	76	74	95	84	77	98	76	77	93	74	75	82
60437	KINSMAN	83	97	104	95	96	99	90	90	87	89	109	105	95	115	92	86	108	88	86	100
60438	LANSING	81	93	105	92	92	97	91	89	88	89	111	103	95	116	92	87	109	88	86	97
60439	LEMONT	142	174	194	175	170	173	158	156	147	159	186	181	169	194	161	144	186	152	142	171
60440	BOLINGBROOK	113	124	130	127	120	120	118	117	112	120	141	137	121	143	117	106	139	116	104	128
60441	LOCKPORT	98	107	111	107	105	108	103	102	99	103	125	119	105	127	102	96	122	101	95	113
60442	MANHATTAN	104	124	130	125	122	120	113	113	105	113	132	132	118	139	114	101	132	110	100	124
60443	MATTESON	101	115	126	114	114	120	108	109	104	108	130	123	112	132	111	103	128	107	105	120
60444	MAZON	105	95	75	91	100	107	88	97	93	88	113	115	87	116	91	95	108	94	104	124
60445	MIDLOTHIAN	80	89	102	89	88	92	89	86	87	87	109	101	92	112	89	85	107	87	82	94
60446	ROMEOVILLE	99	108	113	110	106	109	103	103	99	105	124	118	106	124	103	96	122	102	95	113
60447	MINOOKA	106	120	118	120	118	117	109	110	103	110	129	129	112	132	110	99	127	107	100	124
60448	MOKENA	128	150	154	154	145	143	136	135	126	138	159	158	142	164	136	120	158	131	118	148
60449	MONEE	127	125	108	121	129	134	115	123	116	115	143	145	115	148	118	117	138	119	125	151
60450	MORRIS	96	96	90	96	97	102	94	96	93	93	115	112	93	117	94	92	111	95	95	110
60451	NEW LENOX	121	139	138	142	134	134	126	126	118	129	148	146	131	152	125	113	147	122	112	139
60452	OAK FOREST	101	116	128	117	114	116	111	109	105	110	133	127	115	138	111	102	132	108	100	119
60453	OAK LAWN	85	98	112	95	96	104	93	93	92	93	115	105	98	118	96	93	113	92	92	101
60455	BRIDGEVIEW	79	86	89	84	84	88	82	83	80	82	101	95	83	102	82	79	99	82	79	92
60456	HOMETOWN	66	71	83	69	70	78	73	71	75	71	93	80	76	97	74	76	90	72	74	78
60457	HICKORY HILLS	94	104	120	105	102	107	103	101	100	103	126	118	106	129	104	98	125	101	95	110
60458	JUSTICE	90	87	90	88	85	90	90	89	89	91	112	105	88	110	87	86	109	91	85	100
60459	BURBANK	82	95	104	92	93	97	89	89	87	89	110	102	94	116	92	87	109	87	85	98
60460	ODELL	70	63	48	59	66	71	58	64	61	58	75	76	57	76	60	63	71	62	69	83
60461	OLYMPIA FIELDS	172	195	224	198	195	204	188	188	180	188	226	217	195	226	192	177	222	186	179	205
60462	ORLAND PARK	117	138	154	137	137	143	128	128	122	128	153	145	135	157	132	121	152	125	122	140
60463	PALOS HEIGHTS	124	142	161	139	142	154	132	135	129	134	161	149	139	160	138	130	158	132	134	148
60464	PALOS PARK	148	165	181	166	166	176	155	158	149	157	188	177	162	183	160	149	184	155	155	174
	ILLINOIS	98	100	111	99	99	106	100	99	101	100	126	115	102	127	100	100	123	100	98	112
	UNITED STATES	100	100	100	100	100	100	100	100	100	100	100	100	100	100	100	100	100	100	100	100

POPULATION CHANGE

# POST OFFICE NAME	COUNTY FIPS CODE	POPULATION 2000	2004	2009	2000-2004 ANNUAL RATE % Rate	State Centile	HOUSEHOLDS 2000	2004	2009	% Annual Rate 2000-2004	2004 Average HH Size	FAMILIES 2000	2004	% Annual Rate 2000-2004
60465 PALOS HILLS	031	17690	17558	17494	-0.2	32	7340	7383	7424	0.1	2.36	4773	4725	-0.2
60466 PARK FOREST	197	30184	31493	33900	1.0	78	11423	12058	13055	1.3	2.58	7958	8270	0.9
60467 ORLAND PARK	031	21022	23339	24898	2.5	92	6894	7789	8365	2.9	2.98	5850	6553	2.7
60468 PEOTONE	197	5306	6309	7771	4.2	97	1905	2301	2869	4.5	2.74	1452	1718	4.0
60469 POSEN	031	4701	4836	4891	0.7	71	1620	1666	1688	0.7	2.90	1177	1198	0.4
60470 RANSOM	099	670	644	645	-0.9	5	238	233	236	-0.5	2.60	186	179	-0.9
60471 RICHTON PARK	031	12853	12709	12653	-0.3	27	4697	4675	4681	-0.1	2.65	3297	3241	-0.4
60472 ROBBINS	031	6645	6282	6191	-1.3	1	1992	1905	1892	-1.1	3.07	1488	1405	-1.3
60473 SOUTH HOLLAND	031	22569	22311	22258	-0.3	26	7818	7802	7840	-0.1	2.79	6111	6031	-0.3
60475 STEGER	031	9984	10471	11620	1.1	80	3977	4248	4795	1.6	2.46	2586	2675	0.8
60476 THORNTON	031	2596	2487	2458	-1.0	4	1013	985	984	-0.7	2.52	690	661	-1.0
60477 TINLEY PARK	031	56762	59736	61788	1.2	81	20198	21545	22467	1.5	2.74	15002	15867	1.3
60478 COUNTRY CLUB HILLS	031	16622	17052	17372	0.6	69	5447	5650	5798	0.9	2.99	4236	4360	0.7
60479 VERONA	063	689	713	752	0.8	74	233	245	262	1.2	2.91	189	197	1.0
60480 WILLOW SPRINGS	031	4666	5048	5266	1.9	88	1794	1934	2018	1.8	2.61	1312	1408	1.7
60481 WILMINGTON	197	11692	12951	15359	2.4	92	4402	4981	6012	3.0	2.53	3148	3484	2.4
60482 WORTH	031	10983	11147	11300	0.4	60	4411	4555	4666	0.8	2.45	2818	2847	0.2
60490 BOLINGBROOK	197	9264	12109	15612	6.5	99	2776	3699	4837	7.0	3.27	2525	3336	6.8
60491 LOCKPORT	197	21434	25101	30751	3.8	96	6503	7762	9645	4.3	3.23	5781	6829	4.0
60501 SUMMIT ARGO	031	11190	11459	11602	0.6	68	3559	3643	3698	0.6	3.14	2575	2600	0.2
60504 AURORA	043	45219	55430	64470	4.9	98	16253	20072	23511	5.1	2.76	12025	14706	4.9
60505 AURORA	089	56104	61676	71508	2.3	90	15888	17250	19839	2.0	3.54	11924	12724	1.5
60506 AURORA	089	50891	57020	66786	2.7	93	17519	19627	22972	2.7	2.85	12693	14040	2.4
60510 BATAVIA	089	26625	31480	37808	4.0	97	9364	11053	13251	4.0	2.79	7087	8237	3.6
60511 BIG ROCK	089	1895	2238	2687	4.0	96	661	782	939	4.0	2.86	550	645	3.8
60512 BRISTOL	093	1059	1529	2090	9.0	100	364	538	749	9.6	2.81	304	442	9.2
60513 BROOKFIELD	031	19119	20026	20535	1.1	79	7552	7983	8243	1.3	2.48	5042	5243	0.9
60514 CLARENDON HILLS	043	9183	9630	10076	1.1	79	3532	3746	3962	1.4	2.53	2456	2550	0.9
60515 DOWNERS GROVE	043	27188	27243	28153	0.1	44	11050	11223	11729	0.4	2.38	7123	7101	-0.1
60516 DOWNERS GROVE	043	33036	33434	34616	0.3	57	12354	12662	13243	0.6	2.63	9221	9365	0.4
60517 WOODRIDGE	043	29416	31847	34065	1.9	88	10718	11747	12690	2.2	2.70	7594	8206	1.8
60518 EARLVILLE	099	3711	3847	3975	0.9	75	1370	1437	1500	1.1	2.68	1051	1088	0.8
60520 HINCKLEY	037	2849	3002	3224	1.2	81	1026	1094	1186	1.5	2.74	793	834	1.2
60521 HINSDALE	043	18375	18216	18608	-0.2	31	6382	6343	6516	-0.1	2.85	5030	4956	-0.4
60523 OAK BROOK	043	9456	9432	9694	-0.1	38	3431	3481	3629	0.3	2.59	2550	2557	0.1
60525 LA GRANGE	031	31719	31941	32233	0.2	50	12498	12733	12961	0.4	2.45	8448	8453	0.0
60526 LA GRANGE PARK	031	13296	13077	13012	-0.4	20	5433	5377	5380	-0.2	2.37	3596	3505	-0.6
60527 WILLOWBROOK	043	27684	29096	30627	1.2	80	10910	11639	12406	1.5	2.46	7321	7678	1.1
60530 LEE	103	609	619	637	0.4	61	215	223	233	0.9	2.77	166	169	0.4
60531 LELAND	099	1979	2049	2114	0.8	75	711	747	779	1.2	2.74	546	566	0.9
60532 LISLE	043	27212	28822	30525	1.4	83	11428	12343	13248	1.8	2.28	6410	6751	1.2
60534 LYONS	031	10129	9968	9896	-0.4	20	3974	3928	3916	-0.3	2.54	2548	2476	-0.7
60538 MONTGOMERY	089	14261	15993	19333	2.7	94	5241	5954	7260	3.1	2.68	3951	4441	2.8
60540 NAPERVILLE	043	42928	44138	46146	0.7	71	15116	15797	16736	1.0	2.72	11468	11834	0.7
60541 NEWARK	093	3034	3296	3933	2.0	88	1032	1135	1371	2.3	2.90	835	908	2.0
60542 NORTH AURORA	089	10892	13160	16031	4.6	98	4140	4999	6076	4.5	2.61	2975	3539	4.2
60543 OSWEGO	093	18734	23220	29705	5.2	99	6382	8000	10352	5.5	2.89	5099	6329	5.2
60544 PLAINFIELD	197	44373	61632	81864	8.0	100	15041	21078	28252	8.3	2.92	12536	17355	8.0
60545 PLANO	093	7667	8167	9699	1.5	84	2597	2797	3358	1.8	2.92	2023	2155	1.5
60546 RIVERSIDE	031	15810	15378	15261	-0.7	11	6575	6450	6441	-0.5	2.32	4237	4087	-0.8
60548 SANDWICH	037	11062	11843	12677	1.6	85	3998	4319	4662	1.8	2.70	2999	3204	1.6
60549 SERENA	099	496	522	540	1.2	81	181	193	202	1.5	2.70	143	151	1.3
60550 SHABBONA	037	1344	1348	1410	0.1	45	477	483	511	0.3	2.66	342	341	-0.1
60551 SHERIDAN	099	5156	5279	5367	0.6	68	1212	1270	1313	1.1	2.90	952	981	0.8
60552 SOMONAUK	037	3651	4007	4307	2.2	90	1310	1458	1585	2.6	2.75	1028	1132	2.3
60553 STEWARD	103	755	788	802	1.0	78	262	279	289	1.5	2.82	209	219	1.1
60554 SUGAR GROVE	089	4926	6800	8853	7.9	100	1627	2221	2868	7.6	3.06	1325	1791	7.4
60555 WARRENVILLE	043	13979	14042	14449	0.1	47	5152	5230	5434	0.4	2.67	3620	3620	0.0
60556 WATERMAN	037	1881	1915	2025	0.4	63	686	708	756	0.8	2.70	521	531	0.5
60558 WESTERN SPRINGS	031	12396	12297	12304	-0.2	31	4281	4267	4293	-0.1	2.88	3504	3457	-0.3
60559 WESTMONT	043	26041	26520	27501	0.4	64	10399	10681	11182	0.6	2.40	6622	6692	0.3
60560 YORKVILLE	093	11061	13815	17711	5.4	99	3873	4904	6368	5.7	2.80	3070	3844	5.4
60561 DARIEN	043	23570	23687	24451	0.1	48	8907	9087	9493	0.5	2.58	6523	6547	0.1
60563 NAPERVILLE	043	31062	33846	36322	2.0	89	12780	14108	15315	2.4	2.34	7991	8638	1.9
60564 NAPERVILLE	197	32066	41211	52157	6.1	99	9516	12372	15791	6.4	3.33	8416	10857	6.2
60565 NAPERVILLE	043	40843	43794	48702	1.7	85	12832	13863	15488	1.8	3.15	10921	11749	1.7
60601 CHICAGO	031	5624	5686	5785	0.3	55	3512	3582	3679	0.5	1.58	1339	1330	-0.2
60602 CHICAGO	031	67	133	194	17.5	100	21	35	46	12.8	3.57	8	12	10.0
60603 CHICAGO	031	380	439	479	3.5	95	14	20	24	8.8	2.55	7	10	8.8
60604 CHICAGO	031	85	105	118	5.1	98	36	50	60	8.0	1.66	22	30	7.6
60605 CHICAGO	031	12639	14845	16188	3.9	96	6773	8116	8917	4.4	1.61	2258	2698	4.3
60606 CHICAGO	031	1374	1879	2200	7.6	100	838	1144	1339	7.6	1.57	321	422	6.7
60607 CHICAGO	031	15555	18410	20278	4.0	97	7034	8591	9638	4.8	2.00	2865	3358	3.8
60608 CHICAGO	031	82795	83214	83875	0.1	48	24687	25026	25382	0.3	3.28	17748	17778	0.0
60609 CHICAGO	031	78995	76493	76082	-0.8	8	22683	22082	22057	-0.6	3.45	16903	16241	-0.9
60610 CHICAGO	031	47212	50845	53202	1.8	87	28493	30902	32475	1.9	1.60	8215	8656	1.2
60611 CHICAGO	031	25717	26347	26806	0.6	68	17067	17645	18075	0.8	1.46	5338	5327	-0.1
60612 CHICAGO	031	38672	39518	40237	0.5	66	12557	12992	13338	0.8	2.72	7486	7587	0.3
60613 CHICAGO	031	50003	49685	50057	-0.2	34	28990	29055	29483	0.1	1.69	7986	7769	-0.7
60614 CHICAGO	031	64631	65534	66426	0.3	59	35969	36691	37396	0.5	1.69	10456	10357	-0.2
60615 CHICAGO	031	45077	44993	45383	0.0	39	21330	21546	21919	0.2	2.00	9260	9080	-0.5
60616 CHICAGO	031	47548	49663	51286	1.0	78	19454	20738	21713	1.5	2.26	10179	10497	0.7
60617 CHICAGO	031	96552	94101	93420	-0.6	13	31699	31114	31085	-0.4	3.02	23619	22900	-0.7
60618 CHICAGO	031	99028	99923	100338	0.2	53	35257	35502	35716	0.2	2.80	22145	21919	-0.2
60619 CHICAGO	031	74868	74850	75214	0.0	40	29824	30001	30321	0.1	2.49	18623	18448	-0.2
60620 CHICAGO	031	85806	82650	81772	-0.9	5	28500	27769	27701	-0.6	2.96	21129	20327	-0.9
60621 CHICAGO	031	47762	45403	44860	-1.2	2	15043	14403	14312	-1.0	3.10	10345	9760	-1.4
60622 CHICAGO	031	75799	77122	78239	0.4	63	30900	32058	32906	0.9	2.38	14986	15069	0.1
60623 CHICAGO	031	117211	116921	117122	0.0	39	27641	27768	27971	0.1	3.82	22543	22465	-0.1
60624 CHICAGO	031	45650	43516	43053	-1.1	3	13744	13204	13144	-0.9	3.22	9907	9401	-1.2
60625 CHICAGO	031	91185	89076	88474	-0.6	14	30523	29885	29794	-0.5	2.92	19723	18996	-0.9
60626 CHICAGO	031	60494	60394	60668	0.0	39	24386	24467	24653	0.1	2.36	11687	11378	-0.6
60628 CHICAGO	031	87487	84023	83110	-1.0	4	26920	26192	26136	-0.6	3.18	20476	19689	-0.9
60629 CHICAGO	031	114837	116564	117348	0.4	60	32675	32526	32502	-0.1	3.57	25284	24891	-0.4
60630 CHICAGO	031	54836	55494	55989	0.3	57	21539	21759	21975	0.2	2.55	13925	13848	-0.1
ILLINOIS					0.7					0.9	2.61			0.6
UNITED STATES					1.2					1.3	2.58			1.1

ZIP CODE #	POST OFFICE NAME	RACE (%) White 2000	White 2004	Black 2000	Black 2004	Asian/Pacific 2000	Asian/Pacific 2004	% Hispanic Origin 2000	% Hispanic Origin 2004	2004 AGE DISTRIBUTION (%) 0-4	5-9	10-14	15-19	20-24	25-44	45-64	65-84	85+	18+	MEDIAN AGE 2004	% 2004 Males	% 2004 Females
60465	PALOS HILLS	87.4	84.7	5.2	6.2	2.6	3.2	5.0	6.7	4.9	4.9	5.1	5.2	6.0	27.3	27.9	16.4	2.3	82.0	42.4	46.7	53.3
60466	PARK FOREST	48.3	42.3	46.7	52.2	0.8	0.9	4.4	5.4	7.4	7.4	8.0	7.1	7.0	27.8	24.5	9.7	1.1	72.8	35.0	46.6	53.4
60467	ORLAND PARK	94.8	93.5	0.8	1.0	2.9	3.6	3.1	4.2	6.4	7.4	8.6	6.8	5.0	23.2	29.0	12.5	1.2	73.2	40.9	48.7	51.3
60468	PEOTONE	97.2	96.3	0.9	1.2	0.4	0.5	1.9	2.6	6.2	6.5	8.0	7.7	6.8	26.3	27.6	9.4	1.5	74.6	38.1	49.0	51.0
60469	POSEN	74.5	70.5	13.1	14.2	0.3	0.4	21.8	27.5	8.5	8.0	8.1	6.8	7.0	30.3	20.3	10.0	1.0	71.3	33.3	50.0	50.0
60470	RANSOM	98.7	98.1	0.3	0.3	0.3	0.5	1.6	2.0	5.8	6.2	7.5	6.8	5.3	25.0	25.8	13.7	4.0	75.9	41.0	49.7	50.3
60471	RICHTON PARK	38.6	33.1	56.1	61.0	1.5	1.7	4.1	4.9	7.4	7.2	8.0	7.3	7.2	29.9	24.4	7.5	1.2	72.8	33.9	45.9	54.1
60472	ROBBINS	7.9	7.2	87.9	88.4	0.2	0.2	7.4	8.0	8.4	8.1	8.8	8.0	7.5	25.9	20.7	11.2	1.4	69.5	32.8	47.1	52.9
60473	SOUTH HOLLAND	43.4	38.1	52.4	57.1	0.9	1.0	3.8	4.6	6.1	6.6	7.5	6.8	5.4	23.7	25.4	15.5	3.1	75.6	41.1	47.0	53.0
60475	STEGER	85.1	81.2	8.6	10.8	0.6	0.7	8.2	10.8	7.5	6.9	6.8	6.1	7.2	31.6	22.7	10.1	1.2	75.3	34.8	49.8	50.2
60476	THORNTON	93.1	91.2	4.0	5.2	0.5	0.6	3.9	5.4	5.4	5.7	6.3	5.6	5.2	23.6	26.7	18.9	2.5	79.1	43.9	45.9	54.1
60477	TINLEY PARK	91.9	89.7	2.9	3.7	2.4	3.1	4.3	5.8	6.8	7.0	7.7	6.7	6.3	29.6	25.8	8.9	1.2	74.3	36.4	48.6	51.4
60478	COUNTRY CLUB HILLS	19.0	16.6	77.4	79.7	1.0	1.1	1.9	2.2	6.5	7.3	8.7	7.7	6.3	26.6	26.8	9.0	1.1	72.7	36.5	45.6	54.4
60479	VERONA	97.2	96.6	0.0	0.0	0.3	0.4	4.9	6.2	6.9	7.3	9.1	7.2	6.0	26.8	25.0	10.7	1.1	71.4	37.9	50.8	49.2
60480	WILLOW SPRINGS	91.8	90.3	3.0	3.2	1.8	2.3	5.1	7.1	5.6	6.4	7.4	6.6	5.0	25.2	31.3	11.2	1.4	76.5	41.4	50.1	49.9
60481	WILMINGTON	96.2	95.2	1.6	2.0	0.3	0.3	2.0	2.8	6.4	6.4	7.1	6.9	6.4	28.4	27.2	9.6	1.6	75.7	38.3	49.2	50.8
60482	WORTH	92.7	90.8	1.4	1.6	1.2	1.6	6.1	8.3	6.6	6.3	6.6	6.0	7.0	30.4	23.6	12.1	1.4	76.9	36.9	49.2	50.8
60490	BOLINGBROOK	71.5	66.1	15.8	19.1	7.8	8.8	6.9	8.9	11.6	11.5	9.1	5.8	3.8	37.1	18.8	2.2	0.2	64.0	32.1	49.9	50.1
60491	LOCKPORT	96.5	95.6	0.4	0.5	1.6	1.9	3.4	4.6	7.0	7.8	8.7	7.2	5.7	27.5	29.0	6.4	0.7	71.8	36.8	50.2	49.8
60501	SUMMIT ARGO	65.1	61.7	11.5	11.3	1.4	1.4	46.3	53.0	8.7	7.8	8.1	7.4	8.6	29.7	19.2	9.0	1.4	71.0	30.8	51.4	48.7
60504	AURORA	80.6	77.5	7.2	7.7	7.0	8.3	7.8	9.9	11.2	10.3	8.0	5.3	5.1	40.2	17.2	2.6	0.2	67.1	31.2	49.5	50.5
60505	AURORA	57.6	54.6	10.2	9.9	0.7	0.6	60.8	67.5	10.9	9.5	8.6	7.6	9.1	32.0	15.7	5.8	0.9	66.7	27.3	51.9	48.1
60506	AURORA	72.2	68.7	13.2	13.9	1.4	1.6	23.5	28.9	8.7	8.1	7.8	6.9	7.2	29.4	21.6	8.6	1.6	71.3	32.9	49.4	50.6
60510	BATAVIA	92.8	90.7	2.6	3.2	1.5	1.9	5.3	7.7	7.8	8.5	8.7	7.2	5.3	27.7	25.9	7.3	1.5	70.1	36.3	49.3	50.7
60511	BIG ROCK	96.6	95.5	0.7	0.9	0.2	0.3	2.7	4.0	4.4	6.4	8.2	8.0	5.1	24.9	33.1	8.8	1.1	75.6	41.2	51.1	48.9
60512	BRISTOL	96.3	95.8	0.7	0.7	0.8	0.9	3.7	4.8	7.3	7.5	6.7	6.1	4.8	31.8	26.2	9.1	0.6	74.7	37.5	51.9	48.1
60513	BROOKFIELD	93.5	91.6	0.9	1.1	1.3	1.6	8.1	11.0	6.5	6.5	6.6	6.2	5.6	29.1	25.3	11.5	2.8	76.7	39.0	47.7	52.3
60514	CLARENDON HILLS	93.4	92.1	0.9	1.0	3.9	4.9	2.7	3.4	8.2	8.9	8.1	5.9	4.2	27.4	25.2	10.1	2.0	70.6	38.3	47.6	52.4
60515	DOWNERS GROVE	93.7	92.5	1.3	1.3	3.2	3.9	3.0	3.7	6.0	6.5	6.9	6.1	5.1	26.0	27.1	13.2	3.2	76.7	41.2	47.3	52.7
60516	DOWNERS GROVE	83.5	81.0	3.1	3.1	10.3	12.3	5.1	6.0	6.4	7.0	7.5	6.6	5.9	28.1	28.3	9.3	1.1	75.1	38.3	49.6	50.4
60517	WOODRIDGE	77.4	74.9	7.9	8.0	9.3	11.0	8.8	10.3	7.2	6.9	7.0	6.7	7.4	33.0	25.0	6.2	0.5	74.8	34.1	49.7	50.3
60518	EARLVILLE	97.3	96.9	0.1	0.1	0.4	0.4	2.5	3.1	7.4	7.5	7.8	7.8	5.7	27.0	24.2	11.4	1.3	72.4	37.4	50.4	49.6
60520	HINCKLEY	97.6	97.1	0.3	0.3	0.1	0.2	2.6	3.3	6.4	7.0	8.2	6.8	5.0	29.0	27.7	8.8	1.2	74.2	38.3	50.5	49.5
60521	HINSDALE	92.5	91.1	0.8	0.8	5.2	6.4	2.4	3.1	7.7	9.3	9.9	7.5	4.2	20.4	28.8	10.3	1.9	68.2	40.1	48.1	51.9
60523	OAK BROOK	79.7	76.4	1.8	1.8	16.6	19.6	2.8	3.4	3.0	3.9	5.5	5.6	4.4	16.4	32.6	23.4	5.1	84.0	52.9	45.8	54.2
60525	LA GRANGE	91.9	90.1	3.6	4.0	1.3	1.6	6.9	9.2	6.5	7.0	6.7	6.0	4.9	24.5	27.9	14.2	2.3	76.0	41.7	48.7	51.3
60526	LA GRANGE PARK	93.2	91.5	3.1	3.8	1.7	2.1	3.6	5.0	6.9	6.9	6.6	5.6	4.6	24.9	24.1	15.4	5.0	76.0	41.6	46.1	53.9
60527	WILLOWBROOK	81.9	78.6	4.7	5.3	10.3	12.5	4.1	5.2	5.2	5.9	6.6	6.5	5.7	25.6	29.7	12.7	2.2	78.2	41.4	47.9	52.1
60530	LEE	98.2	98.2	0.2	0.2	0.2	0.2	3.0	3.2	7.0	7.8	9.1	8.1	4.5	28.0	24.4	10.0	1.3	70.9	36.5	51.5	48.5
60531	LELAND	97.5	96.9	0.1	0.1	0.2	0.2	2.9	3.7	6.6	7.1	8.2	8.1	5.0	27.7	25.9	10.0	1.4	72.9	37.7	50.6	49.4
60532	LISLE	83.6	80.8	3.5	3.6	9.6	11.6	5.1	6.2	6.1	5.9	6.4	6.0	9.1	34.3	24.3	6.5	1.5	78.2	34.1	51.0	49.0
60534	LYONS	87.1	83.7	1.0	1.2	1.4	1.7	15.9	21.0	7.6	7.1	6.5	5.7	6.8	30.9	22.7	10.8	1.9	75.4	36.0	49.9	50.1
60538	MONTGOMERY	89.0	86.9	3.5	3.7	0.9	1.0	11.3	14.7	8.1	8.0	7.5	6.3	6.1	29.3	24.1	9.5	1.2	72.6	35.3	48.9	51.1
60540	NAPERVILLE	87.5	85.2	2.0	2.1	8.3	10.1	3.5	4.3	7.5	8.1	8.2	7.3	5.7	28.0	26.7	7.4	1.2	71.9	36.6	49.2	50.8
60541	NEWARK	98.4	98.1	0.2	0.2	0.3	0.3	1.4	1.8	6.5	7.1	7.9	6.6	6.9	26.6	27.2	9.6	1.7	74.6	37.6	51.9	48.1
60542	NORTH AURORA	87.2	84.9	4.7	5.3	2.7	2.9	10.3	13.5	8.7	8.5	7.7	5.9	5.1	31.4	22.6	8.6	1.6	71.3	35.4	49.4	50.6
60543	OSWEGO	92.8	91.5	2.0	2.1	1.3	1.6	6.0	7.7	8.6	8.5	8.1	6.4	5.4	32.7	22.8	6.5	0.9	70.7	34.4	49.4	50.6
60544	PLAINFIELD	91.6	89.4	2.3	2.8	2.2	2.6	6.7	9.0	11.4	10.6	8.5	5.7	4.4	36.2	16.9	5.8	0.5	65.9	32.0	49.7	50.3
60545	PLANO	86.0	83.2	0.4	0.3	0.4	0.5	20.3	24.5	8.1	8.0	8.5	7.2	6.8	28.7	23.3	8.6	0.9	71.1	33.7	49.4	50.6
60546	RIVERSIDE	92.7	90.8	1.8	2.2	2.0	2.5	7.0	9.5	5.6	5.8	5.9	5.3	5.1	25.1	27.2	16.4	3.7	79.5	43.4	48.0	52.0
60548	SANDWICH	96.5	95.8	0.2	0.2	0.3	0.4	5.8	7.0	6.8	7.1	8.1	7.1	6.0	28.3	23.9	10.9	1.9	73.4	37.1	49.4	50.6
60549	SERENA	98.2	97.5	0.0	0.0	0.4	0.6	1.8	2.7	8.1	7.9	7.3	6.1	6.1	27.6	26.8	9.0	1.2	73.0	37.1	52.1	47.9
60550	SHABBONA	98.4	98.2	0.2	0.2	0.1	0.1	1.1	1.3	6.5	6.9	8.2	8.1	5.8	24.2	22.6	13.1	4.6	73.0	40.1	45.2	54.8
60551	SHERIDAN	77.1	75.3	17.5	18.4	0.2	0.3	5.6	6.7	5.9	5.8	5.6	6.3	10.6	39.7	19.4	6.1	0.6	79.8	32.8	65.3	34.7
60552	SOMONAUK	97.4	96.9	0.1	0.2	0.4	0.6	1.9	2.4	7.3	7.5	8.4	7.8	5.8	27.9	24.5	9.6	1.2	71.9	36.4	49.6	50.4
60553	STEWARD	97.8	97.8	0.1	0.1	0.0	0.0	3.6	3.6	7.2	8.0	8.5	7.4	4.8	28.9	23.9	10.2	1.1	71.6	36.6	52.8	47.2
60554	SUGAR GROVE	95.2	93.2	1.7	2.1	0.6	0.8	4.2	6.6	7.3	7.8	8.2	6.7	5.2	29.1	26.9	8.3	0.6	72.5	37.3	50.8	49.2
60555	WARRENVILLE	88.7	86.8	2.5	2.6	3.5	4.3	11.2	13.6	7.6	7.5	7.5	7.2	6.1	33.7	24.0	5.8	0.7	72.9	34.2	49.2	50.8
60556	WATERMAN	98.4	98.1	0.4	0.4	0.1	0.1	1.4	1.8	7.2	7.6	8.8	7.6	5.4	26.0	25.3	10.1	2.2	71.7	37.2	49.0	51.0
60558	WESTERN SPRINGS	98.4	98.0	0.2	0.2	0.7	0.9	1.7	2.3	7.5	8.8	9.7	6.4	3.5	20.4	27.6	13.4	2.5	69.7	41.4	47.9	52.1
60559	WESTMONT	80.2	77.4	4.4	4.4	11.3	13.6	6.2	7.4	6.6	6.2	6.2	5.8	6.3	30.5	23.6	11.5	3.4	77.5	37.6	47.4	52.6
60560	YORKVILLE	97.0	96.3	0.5	0.5	0.5	0.6	3.0	3.9	7.6	7.6	8.1	7.0	6.1	29.1	25.0	8.2	1.3	72.3	36.0	50.2	49.8
60561	DARIEN	84.2	81.4	2.3	2.3	11.1	13.4	4.1	4.9	5.4	6.0	6.6	6.0	5.2	25.4	30.6	12.8	2.0	78.1	42.1	48.5	51.5
60563	NAPERVILLE	82.7	79.8	4.4	4.7	10.2	12.4	4.4	5.3	6.8	6.7	6.3	6.1	6.4	34.6	23.6	7.8	1.8	76.5	35.2	48.4	51.6
60564	NAPERVILLE	84.7	81.5	4.8	5.9	7.6	9.1	4.2	5.5	11.5	11.9	10.1	6.0	3.2	36.7	18.3	2.1	0.2	62.3	31.9	49.6	50.4
60565	NAPERVILLE	85.6	82.9	2.4	2.7	10.3	12.3	2.4	3.1	7.9	9.3	10.4	8.1	4.7	26.3	28.5	4.5	0.4	67.1	36.0	49.2	50.8
60601	CHICAGO	74.5	69.0	11.1	13.2	10.6	13.2	5.8	7.6	2.9	2.7	1.5	1.5	2.4	33.8	37.3	16.3	1.6	92.1	47.8	47.8	52.2
60602	CHICAGO	62.7	53.4	4.5	3.0	25.4	36.1	20.9	21.1	3.8	3.0	2.3	1.5	8.3	24.1	36.8	20.3	0.0	91.0	48.7	63.2	36.8
60603	CHICAGO	65.0	59.9	8.4	9.3	17.9	20.5	13.7	16.6	2.3	1.1	1.1	29.6	31.4	18.9	13.2	2.3	0.0	94.3	22.5	48.1	51.9
60604	CHICAGO	43.5	38.1	12.9	14.3	31.8	35.2	18.8	21.9	4.8	2.9	1.9	15.2	16.2	29.5	25.7	2.9	1.0	88.6	31.4	54.3	45.7
60605	CHICAGO	53.7	48.0	33.8	37.4	7.8	9.0	4.9	6.1	3.8	3.2	2.5	4.1	12.5	43.1	23.0	6.9	1.0	89.6	35.2	51.4	48.6
60606	CHICAGO	72.7	68.2	5.8	6.8	16.5	19.1	8.2	9.9	2.7	1.4	1.7	2.5	7.8	54.9	24.5	4.5	0.1	93.7	34.0	53.9	46.1
60607	CHICAGO	47.4	42.4	33.4	37.3	13.7	14.1	8.3	9.5	4.6	3.7	3.9	4.5	13.2	43.4	18.8	7.2	0.8	85.5	32.0	51.3	48.7
60608	CHICAGO	37.8	35.3	12.0	12.3	5.6	5.9	68.6	70.9	10.2	9.1	9.1	8.1	9.5	31.7	15.9	5.9	0.7	66.9	27.2	51.7	48.3
60609	CHICAGO	34.6	34.0	39.1	37.0	1.3	1.4	43.1	47.4	11.1	10.3	10.2	9.0	9.0	28.7	15.5	5.7	0.6	63.1	25.3	49.5	50.6
60610	CHICAGO	65.8	62.4	26.9	28.8	4.4	5.3	4.0	5.1	4.7	3.9	3.7	3.8	8.9	42.9	22.4	8.5	1.1	85.8	34.6	47.1	52.9
60611	CHICAGO	82.7	79.0	5.1	6.1	9.5	11.5	3.6	4.8	2.2	1.4	1.4	1.3	5.5	41.7	29.5	15.0	2.0	94.3	42.7	46.5	53.6
60612	CHICAGO	19.3	17.5	65.1	65.3	5.8	6.2	14.1	16.2	7.7	7.8	8.5	11.5	10.9	27.5	17.2	7.9	1.0	70.2	27.4	47.8	52.2
60613	CHICAGO	76.9	72.6	8.7	10.0	5.8	6.7	13.1	16.7	3.7	2.4	2.6	3.3	10.1	50.9	18.1	7.7	1.4	89.6	33.4	51.2	48.8
60614	CHICAGO	87.6	84.8	4.8	5.7	3.7	4.6	5.4	7.2	4.3	2.6	2.2	3.7	12.7	50.5	17.3	5.6	1.2	89.7	31.9	48.9	51.1
60615	CHICAGO	23.1	20.2	67.5	69.5	5.8	6.4	2.9	3.4	5.8	5.2	5.9	7.1	10.0	32.8	21.9	9.8	1.5	79.6	33.4	46.1	53.9
60616	CHICAGO	26.7	23.3	37.6	39.7	29.2	29.8	9.6	10.8	6.2	5.8	6.0	6.7	8.7	31.5	20.9	12.2	2.0	78.8	34.9	47.8	52.2
60617	CHICAGO	23.6	22.4	54.7	54.0	0.2	0.3	34.2	37.2	8.3	8.2	8.7	7.5	7.1	26.6	21.5	10.9	1.1	70.1	32.6	46.7	53.4
60618	CHICAGO	59.3	55.0	3.1	3.2	5.1	5.4	49.1	55.6	7.9	6.8	6.9	6.8	8.8	35.5	19.6	6.9	0.9	74.5	31.8	50.3	49.7
60619	CHICAGO	0.6	0.5	98.1	98.2	0.1	0.1	0.7	0.7	6.7	7.3	7.8	6.4	5.8	25.4	24.2	14.4	2.1	74.3	38.3	44.0	56.1
60620	CHICAGO	3.3	3.0	95.6	95.8	0.1	0.1	0.8	0.8	7.3	7.7	8.5	7.2	6.2	25.4	23.8	12.8	1.2	72.1	36.0	44.9	55.1
60621	CHICAGO	0.6	0.6	98.2	98.3	0.1	0.1	0.8	0.9	9.6	9.7	10.3	8.7	7.3	24.5	18.2	10.3	1.6	65.0	28.8	45.2	54.9
60622	CHICAGO	58.9	55.2	11.0	11.3	2.0	2.1	45.2	50.5	6.7	5.5	6.1	6.3	9.9	42.4	16.0	6.2	0.8	78.1	31.0	52.0	48.0
60623	CHICAGO	20.8	19.9	38.2	38.3	0.2	0.2	58.9	59.6	10.0	9.0	9.4	9.1	10.7	32.1	14.4	4.9	0.5	66.6	26.0	53.7	46.3
60624	CHICAGO	0.8	0.7	98.1	98.2	0.1	0.1	1.0	1.1	9.3	9.3	10.6	9.5	7.7	25.7	18.3	8.7	0.9	64.9	27.9	45.9	54.1
60625	CHICAGO	55.5	51.7	3.9	4.1	17.3	18.3	37.7	42.5	7.8	6.7	6.7	6.9	9.3	35.1	19.2	7.2	1.2	75.0	31.5	50.8	49.2
60626	CHICAGO	46.8	43.1	28.9	30.1	7.8	8.5	27.2	30.6	7.7	6.2	6.0	7.4	12.1	35.5	17.5	6.3	1.2	76.6	30.3	51.1	48.9
60628	CHICAGO	2.6	2.4	94.8	94.8	0.1	0.1	3.1	3.4	7.6	7.9	9.1	7.8	6.8	25.5	22.9	11.5	1.0	70.6	33.7	45.5	54.5
60629	CHICAGO	43.1	40.2	26.1	25.7	0.8	0.8	48.5	53.4	9.6	9.0	9.3	8.4	8.8	29.5	17.4	6.7	1.2	67.0	28.1	48.8	51.2
60630	CHICAGO	81.5	77.5	0.5	0.6	7.5	8.9	16.6	21.2	6.4	6.1	6.1	5.3	6.0	30.5	24.8	12.6	2.2	78.3	38.6	48.4	51.6
	ILLINOIS	73.5	71.8	15.1	15.2	3.5	4.0	12.3	14.2	7.1	7.0	7.3	7.0	7.3	29.0	23.2	10.4	1.7	74.5	35.2	49.0	51.0
	UNITED STATES	75.1	73.6	12.3	12.5	3.8	4.2	12.5	14.1	6.9	6.7	7.2	7.0	7.3	28.6	23.8	10.8	1.7	75.1	36.0	49.1	50.9

INCOME

ZIP CODE				2004 HOUSEHOLD INCOME DISTRIBUTION (%)					MEDIAN HOUSEHOLD INCOME					2004 HOME VALUE DISTRIBUTION (%)					
#	POST OFFICE NAME	2004 Per Capita Income	2004 HH Income Base	Less than $25,000	$25,000 to $49,999	$50,000 to $99,999	$100,000 to $149,999	$150,000 or More	2004	2009	2004 National Centile	2004 State Centile	2004 Home Value Base	Less than $50,000	$50,000 to $89,999	$90,000 to $174,999	$175,000 to $399,999	$400,000 or More	2004 Median Home Value
60465	PALOS HILLS	29207	7383	15.1	27.3	38.9	14.4	4.2	57978	66097	83	78	6029	0.9	1.6	36.2	56.4	4.9	194686
60466	PARK FOREST	24832	12058	17.4	28.1	39.1	12.0	3.5	53735	62726	78	71	8878	16.8	14.1	57.7	10.9	0.5	109991
60467	ORLAND PARK	39044	7789	7.5	14.0	35.8	24.5	18.3	88420	103544	97	97	7595	0.2	0.0	5.2	73.4	21.2	286733
60468	PEOTONE	27485	2301	10.8	18.6	50.2	15.5	5.0	64209	74164	88	86	1821	1.5	1.1	22.1	70.8	4.5	214266
60469	POSEN	20455	1666	17.4	27.3	42.1	11.7	1.5	54175	63639	79	72	1347	4.8	10.6	71.9	12.5	0.2	119424
60470	RANSOM	22669	233	20.6	24.9	42.5	9.0	3.0	53402	60349	78	70	202	10.9	24.3	43.6	19.3	2.0	110811
60471	RICHTON PARK	25636	4675	15.0	30.2	34.7	15.4	4.8	54375	63651	79	72	3220	2.1	11.1	48.7	36.4	1.7	154130
60472	ROBBINS	11624	1905	46.1	30.5	19.4	3.7	0.4	28005	31760	9	3	1110	22.2	44.7	25.4	6.4	1.4	73446
60473	SOUTH HOLLAND	28451	7802	14.1	23.2	37.8	17.8	7.1	64813	76375	88	86	7170	0.8	2.0	52.9	42.7	1.6	167702
60475	STEGER	22644	4248	25.9	26.1	35.3	10.6	2.2	47017	53956	66	55	2848	1.9	7.7	69.2	20.7	0.5	128592
60476	THORNTON	26404	985	17.3	32.2	33.4	12.4	4.8	50510	57792	73	64	878	0.8	4.9	82.4	11.5	0.5	133672
60477	TINLEY PARK	28840	21545	12.1	20.4	42.4	18.0	7.1	68406	79103	91	89	18644	0.3	0.5	29.7	65.8	3.7	201408
60478	COUNTRY CLUB HILLS	23879	5650	11.1	26.9	40.6	16.1	5.2	62110	72882	86	84	5164	0.7	10.3	63.5	24.3	1.3	138045
60479	VERONA	20826	245	13.9	27.4	47.8	9.4	1.6	56725	64435	81	77	213	7.0	15.0	40.4	31.0	6.6	148828
60480	WILLOW SPRINGS	35389	1934	13.9	22.6	36.4	16.1	11.1	66845	78471	90	88	1684	0.2	0.1	18.1	61.5	20.0	267930
60481	WILMINGTON	26289	4981	16.3	28.2	39.1	12.4	4.1	55076	63623	80	74	3971	2.7	6.4	50.7	37.9	2.4	154605
60482	WORTH	23008	4555	23.5	29.1	35.2	9.7	2.6	47659	54947	68	57	3289	6.2	3.7	44.9	43.3	1.9	168203
60490	BOLINGBROOK	35178	3699	3.2	7.7	37.7	35.0	16.4	101164	112982	98	98	3635	0.2	0.5	5.8	78.1	15.5	254894
60491	LOCKPORT	33370	7762	5.9	13.2	42.1	24.0	14.9	84965	93857	96	97	7528	0.7	0.2	6.1	75.5	17.5	295600
60501	SUMMIT ARGO	16542	3643	30.0	29.1	29.8	8.3	2.9	42794	48734	55	41	2167	0.6	4.8	64.6	29.4	0.7	148103
60504	AURORA	39032	20072	5.2	15.5	39.9	23.4	16.0	83755	97473	96	96	16285	0.5	2.1	24.8	55.6	17.0	233185
60505	AURORA	14641	17250	24.1	33.9	33.4	7.0	1.6	44552	50724	60	47	10996	3.3	9.8	72.0	14.8	0.2	123331
60506	AURORA	24690	19627	16.9	25.8	37.5	13.0	6.7	56894	66527	82	77	14300	0.9	4.4	46.0	44.6	4.2	173312
60510	BATAVIA	32938	11053	10.8	16.8	37.3	21.3	13.7	77600	87773	94	94	9132	0.8	0.3	15.3	70.7	13.0	251848
60511	BIG ROCK	35181	782	7.9	15.1	45.5	21.7	9.7	75465	86390	93	93	691	0.0	0.1	11.7	69.0	19.1	249381
60512	BRISTOL	31717	538	8.0	19.1	41.1	22.3	9.5	76009	83073	94	94	504	1.2	0.0	20.4	68.1	10.3	233465
60513	BROOKFIELD	28134	7983	14.3	26.2	38.5	16.0	5.0	59020	69477	84	80	6262	0.4	0.5	29.4	68.4	1.3	195359
60514	CLARENDON HILLS	47178	3746	6.7	18.7	31.7	19.7	23.2	85865	100755	96	97	3061	0.0	1.3	7.2	48.5	43.0	368603
60515	DOWNERS GROVE	36967	11223	16.4	20.0	32.6	17.9	13.1	66564	78212	89	88	9184	0.4	4.3	16.7	61.9	16.6	244444
60516	DOWNERS GROVE	36676	12662	8.6	17.5	36.8	24.1	13.0	79697	92669	95	95	10288	0.4	0.4	16.4	70.2	12.6	259429
60517	WOODRIDGE	31642	11747	9.7	22.5	38.7	20.2	9.0	69727	81387	91	90	8399	0.8	5.7	24.7	61.9	6.9	210293
60518	EARLVILLE	22240	1437	21.8	27.0	40.4	8.6	2.2	50866	56899	74	65	1163	9.0	13.2	50.1	24.9	2.8	132634
60520	HINCKLEY	25940	1094	10.4	23.9	46.3	15.8	3.6	64356	74414	88	86	939	0.0	1.0	27.2	69.1	2.8	202289
60521	HINSDALE	75475	6343	9.1	12.8	22.2	16.1	39.8	116062	134992	99	99	5503	0.4	0.4	2.9	23.9	72.5	638830
60523	OAK BROOK	72200	3481	11.2	12.8	22.3	15.3	38.5	109349	126155	99	99	3115	0.6	0.9	3.1	27.1	68.3	620484
60525	LA GRANGE	37521	12733	15.4	21.7	30.2	18.5	14.2	69073	79947	91	90	10499	6.2	2.7	13.4	53.5	24.2	260763
60526	LA GRANGE PARK	35886	5377	14.8	23.4	33.8	17.2	10.8	65671	77474	89	87	4120	0.2	0.6	11.0	71.4	17.0	257368
60527	WILLOWBROOK	48558	11639	9.1	21.8	32.2	16.0	20.9	75809	87640	94	93	9220	0.2	7.6	17.5	38.0	36.7	285557
60530	LEE	22517	223	16.6	25.1	43.1	11.2	4.0	55863	61454	81	75	185	2.2	8.7	44.3	35.1	9.7	163125
60531	LELAND	21710	747	17.5	28.4	43.1	8.2	2.8	52776	59521	77	69	612	1.6	6.5	51.6	35.1	5.1	159694
60532	LISLE	41290	12343	10.7	19.7	38.9	16.9	13.8	69490	81176	91	90	6949	0.7	1.7	19.1	63.1	15.4	249031
60534	LYONS	23763	3928	18.4	31.2	38.2	8.7	3.4	50267	59474	72	63	2600	0.3	1.8	54.4	39.5	4.2	167694
60538	MONTGOMERY	26446	5954	13.2	22.7	45.2	14.5	4.3	63110	71847	87	84	5016	1.5	1.6	52.9	43.3	0.8	168838
60540	NAPERVILLE	43366	15797	7.8	12.1	30.0	27.1	23.0	100049	113969	98	98	13174	1.1	0.3	5.2	71.8	21.6	312855
60541	NEWARK	24614	1135	10.4	22.3	48.0	14.3	5.0	63220	71137	87	85	955	2.5	2.8	35.2	42.7	16.8	194504
60542	NORTH AURORA	31386	4999	10.8	23.1	39.8	16.7	9.6	65572	76675	89	87	4034	0.2	1.1	31.6	56.6	10.5	199503
60543	OSWEGO	30774	8000	9.1	17.1	44.4	20.5	9.0	75498	82580	93	93	7166	0.3	2.3	20.1	71.2	6.2	223866
60544	PLAINFIELD	30587	21078	5.7	15.0	48.2	22.7	8.4	77981	87065	94	94	19948	0.3	0.3	19.4	73.8	6.2	222988
60545	PLANO	23949	2797	14.8	28.4	42.5	10.4	4.0	56299	63624	81	76	2214	1.0	3.4	46.5	43.6	5.6	173791
60546	RIVERSIDE	35395	6450	14.9	24.8	36.2	13.7	10.4	61439	71661	86	83	4926	0.2	0.5	19.0	62.7	17.6	232070
60548	SANDWICH	22941	4319	16.7	26.7	42.2	12.2	2.3	57312	63891	82	78	3599	5.5	4.1	36.8	51.9	1.7	180100
60549	SERENA	24161	193	18.1	21.2	43.5	13.5	3.6	56293	63431	81	76	155	5.8	10.3	39.4	37.4	7.1	161719
60550	SHABBONA	24730	483	16.4	25.5	41.6	12.6	3.9	55974	64540	81	76	380	0.8	0.8	61.3	33.2	4.0	158219
60551	SHERIDAN	19581	1270	16.9	26.2	42.1	11.8	3.0	55074	61702	80	74	1082	3.4	12.2	48.2	33.4	2.9	147283
60552	SOMONAUK	23298	1458	11.9	28.6	46.0	11.1	2.3	58980	65455	84	79	1236	1.4	2.8	39.4	54.2	2.2	182776
60553	STEWARD	21770	279	15.1	28.7	42.3	10.0	3.9	54459	60387	79	73	238	3.8	10.9	47.1	31.9	6.3	151667
60554	SUGAR GROVE	33329	2221	7.1	15.4	44.4	19.2	13.9	79551	89227	95	95	1932	0.0	0.7	16.5	67.0	15.8	234095
60555	WARRENVILLE	34584	5230	6.6	19.7	46.2	18.3	9.2	72142	83061	92	92	4366	0.4	1.1	39.0	53.4	6.1	190965
60556	WATERMAN	23301	708	19.6	24.3	41.5	10.2	4.4	54867	62603	80	74	567	2.5	1.9	40.7	48.0	6.9	181740
60558	WESTERN SPRINGS	49210	4267	5.8	12.9	26.5	22.7	32.1	107887	129314	99	99	4026	0.2	0.3	2.4	43.4	53.7	416297
60559	WESTMONT	34683	10681	15.8	22.6	36.0	14.7	11.0	62669	74547	87	84	6997	0.2	2.1	21.7	59.7	16.4	231394
60560	YORKVILLE	29140	4904	10.6	20.0	44.4	17.2	7.8	69736	77328	91	90	4110	1.3	0.1	20.5	69.1	9.1	227556
60561	DARIEN	38357	9087	10.3	16.4	36.6	22.1	14.6	79101	91955	95	95	7877	0.7	0.2	12.6	74.7	11.8	266157
60563	NAPERVILLE	41030	14108	9.9	19.4	35.9	20.9	13.9	75566	87909	93	93	9267	0.6	2.0	18.7	62.6	16.2	250105
60564	NAPERVILLE	39507	12372	2.9	7.6	33.2	29.4	27.0	107757	122881	99	99	11968	0.8	0.3	5.8	55.4	37.8	341637
60565	NAPERVILLE	41343	13863	5.4	10.0	29.1	28.4	26.9	107139	124032	99	99	12944	0.5	1.1	7.3	60.1	31.0	330624
60601	CHICAGO	86832	3582	14.8	16.0	27.2	13.7	28.4	81981	96031	96	96	2193	1.0	0.1	14.1	47.2	37.7	333538
60602	CHICAGO	25127	35	25.7	22.9	20.0	11.4	20.0	52229	66919	76	68	15	0.0	0.0	46.7	53.3	0.0	176563
60603	CHICAGO	12546	20	5.0	10.0	65.0	0.0	20.0	78668	92153	95	94	11	0.0	0.0	0.0	100.0	0.0	204167
60604	CHICAGO	66693	50	12.0	26.0	0.0	0.0	62.0	168085	205602	100	100	32	0.0	0.0	0.0	100.0	0.0	218000
60605	CHICAGO	50398	8116	26.1	16.0	27.7	13.7	16.5	60120	73269	84	81	3558	0.2	0.7	9.7	64.7	24.7	274861
60606	CHICAGO	93679	1144	4.1	3.7	41.8	26.2	24.2	100604	126842	98	98	837	0.0	0.0	8.1	64.3	27.6	338119
60607	CHICAGO	37431	8591	33.9	17.2	24.9	11.0	13.0	48079	60848	68	58	3442	2.0	0.8	9.6	56.7	30.9	301940
60608	CHICAGO	12975	25026	40.5	32.0	20.9	4.9	1.7	31127	35895	15	5	8929	3.4	6.2	48.2	39.5	2.6	160365
60609	CHICAGO	12514	22082	44.6	27.7	20.8	5.1	1.9	29043	33716	10	3	8115	7.0	19.2	48.8	22.7	2.3	120127
60610	CHICAGO	66141	30902	23.7	17.9	28.2	12.2	18.0	61622	78178	86	83	12200	0.5	1.3	15.5	44.8	37.9	318571
60611	CHICAGO	99923	17645	14.0	16.7	28.6	14.5	26.2	81347	103632	95	96	8941	0.4	1.6	13.9	40.0	44.2	353083
60612	CHICAGO	16240	12992	46.1	25.3	19.9	5.4	3.4	28601	35046	10	3	3630	5.0	7.5	32.4	43.2	11.9	192096
60613	CHICAGO	46974	29055	19.8	24.7	31.7	13.6	10.1	55945	69999	81	75	10610	0.6	4.4	22.7	43.9	28.5	258454
60614	CHICAGO	81908	36691	14.7	15.8	27.9	15.6	26.0	81347	104396	95	96	15234	0.2	0.6	8.3	33.7	57.3	457224
60615	CHICAGO	28538	21546	37.6	25.0	24.1	7.4	6.0	36602	44713	34	18	6039	4.0	9.7	28.7	42.5	15.1	194609
60616	CHICAGO	22104	20738	39.1	24.6	24.5	7.4	4.3	35672	42707	30	15	5966	4.7	3.5	26.8	57.0	8.1	209941
60617	CHICAGO	17221	31114	32.6	29.1	28.0	7.6	2.8	39177	44859	43	27	19893	3.4	17.0	65.3	13.8	0.5	116266
60618	CHICAGO	22744	35502	22.2	30.0	32.9	9.9	5.1	47997	58524	68	58	14136	0.5	1.4	15.4	65.6	17.1	249008
60619	CHICAGO	19709	30001	32.7	30.2	27.1	7.5	2.5	38389	45474	41	24	15684	2.6	13.2	59.8	23.0	1.5	126369
60620	CHICAGO	18292	27769	31.4	28.5	28.1	8.5	3.5	40552	47316	48	32	16922	1.9	11.1	66.8	18.1	2.1	121612
60621	CHICAGO	10886	14403	53.9	25.9	16.2	2.9	1.2	22159	26674	3	1	4969	14.1	35.6	41.8	7.9	0.5	90237
60622	CHICAGO	27630	32058	29.7	23.9	27.8	10.5	8.1	45920	58316	64	52	10155	1.1	1.6	10.0	52.4	35.0	336952
60623	CHICAGO	10990	27768	41.1	31.5	21.5	4.7	1.2	31378	36318	16	5	10613	3.7	10.0	54.7	30.6	1.0	145708
60624	CHICAGO	11793	13204	49.0	27.1	18.6	3.7	1.7	25802	31738	6	2	4335	3.3	13.0	52.3	30.0	1.4	134845
60625	CHICAGO	20813	29885	24.6	29.1	31.9	9.7	4.7	46471	56682	65	54	10591	1.3	1.5	20.0	61.6	15.7	247237
60626	CHICAGO	20191	24467	34.7	33.9	22.6	5.8	3.0	35733	42149	31	15	5786	3.0	11.9	30.6	43.2	11.3	186881
60628	CHICAGO	16481	26192	29.8	28.9	29.9	9.1	2.4	42013	48078	53	37	17792	4.7	20.6	64.0	9.9	0.9	110744
60629	CHICAGO	15062	32526	25.8	30.5	32.7	8.6	2.4	44115	50390	59	45	21070	0.9	5.5	66.5	26.3	0.7	145010
60630	CHICAGO	26044	21759	20.5	25.7	34.5	13.9	5.5	53792	63934	78	71	14232	0.7	0.7	19.3	74.1	5.4	227216
	ILLINOIS	27033		22.1	25.9	32.9	11.9	7.3	52039	60941				7.7	12.8	34.0	36.6	8.9	162771
	UNITED STATES	25866		24.7	27.1	30.8	10.9	6.5	48124	56710				10.9	15.0	33.7	30.1	10.4	145905

SPENDING POTENTIAL INDICES

ZIP CODE		FINANCIAL SERVICES				THE HOME						ENTERTAINMENT						PERSONAL			
						Home Improvements		Furnishings													
#	POST OFFICE NAME	Auto Loan	Home Loan	Invest-ments	Retire-ment Plans	Home Repair	Lawn & Garden	Comput-ers & Hard-ware	Major Appli-ances	TV, Radio, Sound Equip-ment	Furni-ture	Dine out/ Carry out	Sports Equip-ment	Fees & Tickets	Toys & Games	Travel	Cable TV	Apparel & Services	Auto Repairs	Health Insur-ance	Pets & Supplies
60465	PALOS HILLS	90	99	115	99	97	104	98	96	96	98	121	111	102	123	99	96	119	97	93	105
60466	PARK FOREST	84	93	105	93	91	95	92	90	89	91	112	105	95	116	92	88	111	90	85	98
60467	ORLAND PARK	153	190	202	192	185	184	168	167	155	169	196	195	181	207	172	150	196	161	149	184
60468	PEOTONE	97	119	128	117	116	117	108	107	102	107	128	125	115	136	111	100	127	104	98	118
60469	POSEN	81	87	89	86	86	89	84	84	82	84	103	97	86	106	84	81	101	83	80	93
60470	RANSOM	97	86	65	82	91	97	79	88	84	79	103	105	78	105	82	86	98	86	95	114
60471	RICHTON PARK	96	98	104	103	95	97	100	97	95	101	121	117	99	119	96	90	118	99	87	107
60472	ROBBINS	51	42	46	38	41	50	47	48	53	48	64	52	46	59	46	56	62	49	54	55
60473	SOUTH HOLLAND	104	121	132	118	120	125	114	114	110	113	138	130	120	143	117	110	136	111	110	125
60475	STEGER	76	77	82	78	77	82	79	78	79	78	99	91	80	100	78	78	96	79	76	87
60476	THORNTON	85	98	109	94	98	106	93	93	93	92	115	104	99	120	97	95	113	91	95	101
60477	TINLEY PARK	106	123	133	124	120	122	114	113	108	115	136	131	119	139	115	105	135	111	103	124
60478	COUNTRY CLUB HILLS	97	108	114	109	107	109	103	103	98	103	123	119	106	125	103	95	121	101	95	113
60479	VERONA	97	87	66	82	91	98	80	89	85	80	103	105	79	105	82	87	98	86	96	114
60480	WILLOW SPRINGS	120	141	156	141	139	141	132	131	126	132	158	152	139	165	134	123	157	129	121	144
60481	WILMINGTON	100	97	86	94	99	106	92	97	94	92	116	114	92	119	94	95	112	95	100	117
60482	WORTH	73	79	90	79	79	84	80	78	79	78	99	91	82	102	81	78	97	79	76	86
60490	BOLINGBROOK	165	187	180	195	178	171	168	167	154	175	196	195	173	196	164	143	194	162	141	182
60491	LOCKPORT	146	169	179	175	165	165	156	154	145	158	183	180	163	186	156	139	182	151	138	170
60501	SUMMIT ARGO	76	70	66	66	68	71	72	75	74	77	93	81	68	87	69	71	93	77	70	79
60504	AURORA	156	163	165	173	156	155	157	154	147	163	187	182	158	183	151	137	184	154	133	170
60505	AURORA	74	67	68	66	66	69	73	72	74	75	94	83	70	91	69	71	93	75	68	78
60506	AURORA	94	104	116	104	101	106	101	99	98	102	123	114	104	126	101	96	123	99	93	108
60510	BATAVIA	125	144	154	148	140	141	135	133	126	136	159	156	140	163	134	121	158	131	118	146
60511	BIG ROCK	131	162	172	163	160	157	145	145	134	144	169	169	154	180	148	130	169	139	130	160
60512	BRISTOL	116	145	154	145	142	140	129	129	120	129	150	151	137	160	132	116	150	124	115	142
60513	BROOKFIELD	91	104	117	103	102	107	100	98	97	99	121	113	104	126	101	96	120	97	94	107
60514	CLARENDON HILLS	152	188	227	189	182	187	174	169	163	175	206	198	186	216	177	160	207	167	152	184
60515	DOWNERS GROVE	116	132	152	133	131	137	127	126	122	127	153	144	132	154	129	120	151	125	120	138
60516	DOWNERS GROVE	128	147	168	151	144	147	140	136	131	140	166	160	146	170	140	127	165	136	123	150
60517	WOODRIDGE	118	127	139	132	123	125	124	121	117	126	149	144	127	149	122	112	147	122	108	134
60518	EARLVILLE	94	85	67	81	90	96	79	87	83	79	101	103	78	104	81	85	97	84	93	111
60520	HINCKLEY	100	109	108	110	107	106	103	103	97	103	122	122	104	124	101	93	120	102	93	115
60521	HINSDALE	270	344	437	343	336	354	309	305	289	313	365	349	340	381	323	287	367	297	281	332
60523	OAK BROOK	250	299	369	297	296	319	274	276	261	279	329	310	296	331	287	262	327	269	266	302
60525	LA GRANGE	124	138	157	135	136	146	131	132	128	133	161	149	136	161	134	129	159	131	129	146
60526	LA GRANGE PARK	111	126	149	127	124	132	123	120	119	122	150	138	129	153	125	119	148	120	116	132
60527	WILLOWBROOK	163	176	209	180	173	185	172	170	166	175	210	196	178	206	173	163	207	171	161	188
60530	LEE	103	86	60	82	93	101	81	93	88	81	106	110	77	107	84	91	100	90	103	122
60531	LELAND	93	86	70	82	90	96	79	87	83	79	101	103	79	104	82	85	97	84	92	109
60532	LISLE	129	135	170	145	131	136	138	132	133	140	169	157	142	170	136	128	166	135	120	146
60534	LYONS	77	87	99	87	86	91	86	84	84	84	105	98	89	110	87	83	103	84	81	92
60538	MONTGOMERY	94	109	115	109	106	107	102	101	97	102	122	118	106	127	102	94	121	99	92	110
60540	NAPERVILLE	161	187	206	193	181	184	174	170	162	176	205	198	183	209	174	156	204	168	153	187
60541	NEWARK	93	114	121	113	112	111	103	102	96	102	121	119	109	128	105	94	120	99	93	113
60542	NORTH AURORA	113	126	132	130	122	122	119	117	112	121	142	137	122	143	117	107	140	116	104	128
60543	OSWEGO	122	141	143	144	137	135	129	128	120	131	152	150	134	156	129	115	150	125	113	141
60544	PLAINFIELD	127	141	138	145	137	137	129	130	121	133	153	148	132	151	128	115	150	126	117	142
60545	PLANO	98	106	104	106	105	108	100	101	96	99	120	118	102	123	100	94	117	99	95	114
60546	RIVERSIDE	106	124	145	121	122	131	118	117	115	117	144	134	124	149	122	116	142	116	114	128
60548	SANDWICH	89	91	86	90	93	98	87	90	87	86	107	104	88	110	88	87	104	87	90	104
60549	SERENA	89	103	104	102	103	103	92	94	88	92	110	111	97	116	95	87	109	91	88	108
60550	SHABBONA	105	89	69	89	94	106	91	98	97	90	118	112	87	117	91	99	110	97	107	117
60551	SHERIDAN	67	65	55	63	67	70	59	64	61	59	75	76	60	77	61	61	72	62	66	79
60552	SOMONAUK	98	91	77	89	95	102	87	93	90	86	110	109	86	112	88	91	105	91	97	113
60553	STEWARD	99	88	67	83	93	99	81	90	86	81	105	107	79	107	83	88	100	87	97	116
60554	SUGAR GROVE	137	165	171	169	160	158	148	146	136	150	172	171	156	179	149	130	171	142	129	161
60555	WARRENVILLE	129	144	148	149	139	137	135	133	126	138	159	157	138	161	132	119	157	131	116	146
60556	WATERMAN	98	85	69	85	90	99	86	92	90	85	110	106	83	110	86	92	104	90	99	110
60558	WESTERN SPRINGS	179	228	263	226	222	230	203	201	189	205	239	230	221	250	211	187	240	195	184	219
60559	WESTMONT	115	121	140	126	118	123	123	119	118	123	149	141	124	147	120	113	146	121	109	131
60560	YORKVILLE	109	129	135	130	126	125	118	117	110	118	139	138	123	145	119	106	138	114	105	129
60561	DARIEN	124	157	185	154	153	157	143	141	134	143	169	163	153	179	147	133	169	138	129	153
60563	NAPERVILLE	137	138	156	147	133	139	142	136	135	144	172	162	142	167	137	128	169	140	122	151
60564	NAPERVILLE	189	213	206	223	203	196	192	191	176	200	224	223	198	224	187	164	221	185	162	208
60565	NAPERVILLE	172	211	231	217	204	205	189	184	173	191	220	215	204	228	191	167	221	179	164	203
60601	CHICAGO	167	160	298	183	151	170	189	167	193	192	246	206	197	257	186	192	244	179	157	187
60602	CHICAGO	17	16	30	18	15	17	19	17	19	19	24	20	20	26	18	19	24	18	15	18
60603	CHICAGO	96	103	128	108	101	105	108	102	103	106	130	124	108	131	106	99	128	106	93	112
60604	CHICAGO	62	49	65	56	49	54	69	60	68	64	85	77	63	79	61	62	83	68	56	67
60605	CHICAGO	113	113	189	126	108	119	127	115	128	128	163	139	132	169	126	127	161	121	108	128
60606	CHICAGO	36	38	59	42	37	39	41	38	41	42	52	46	43	54	41	40	51	40	35	42
60607	CHICAGO	97	86	133	95	83	93	106	95	108	105	136	118	105	135	101	104	133	104	91	106
60608	CHICAGO	59	53	59	52	52	55	59	58	61	61	77	67	57	76	56	59	78	62	55	63
60609	CHICAGO	61	53	58	52	52	57	59	59	63	62	79	67	58	77	57	62	78	62	58	65
60610	CHICAGO	137	128	232	144	121	137	152	136	158	155	200	166	157	207	149	157	198	146	130	153
60611	CHICAGO	187	179	338	206	170	190	212	187	217	216	276	231	221	290	208	215	274	201	175	210
60612	CHICAGO	57	52	75	51	51	59	60	57	65	61	81	66	60	81	60	67	80	61	60	65
60613	CHICAGO	101	97	178	111	92	103	114	102	117	116	148	124	119	155	112	116	147	109	95	113
60614	CHICAGO	183	174	323	199	165	185	207	183	212	210	270	225	215	282	203	210	267	197	172	205
60615	CHICAGO	77	70	106	74	67	77	82	76	86	83	108	91	83	107	80	86	105	81	76	86
60616	CHICAGO	65	66	91	70	66	69	74	70	72	73	91	86	72	89	72	69	89	75	65	76
60617	CHICAGO	73	68	72	64	66	74	71	72	75	74	94	78	71	89	70	76	92	73	73	80
60618	CHICAGO	80	81	121	82	78	85	89	84	92	91	117	97	90	123	88	93	118	88	80	91
60619	CHICAGO	67	64	73	61	62	73	66	66	71	68	89	71	69	86	67	74	86	67	71	75
60620	CHICAGO	74	72	82	68	70	81	73	73	78	76	98	79	76	94	74	81	95	74	78	83
60621	CHICAGO	47	39	46	36	39	47	45	45	51	46	62	49	44	58	44	53	60	47	50	52
60622	CHICAGO	79	77	142	81	73	84	91	82	97	92	123	98	93	130	91	99	123	89	81	91
60623	CHICAGO	58	49	53	48	48	52	56	55	59	58	74	62	54	72	53	58	74	58	54	60
60624	CHICAGO	53	45	53	42	44	53	51	50	56	52	70	56	50	66	50	59	67	52	56	58
60625	CHICAGO	71	75	133	76	71	80	85	77	89	85	114	91	87	124	86	92	115	83	75	85
60626	CHICAGO	61	54	86	58	53	59	70	62	72	67	91	77	67	92	66	70	90	69	59	69
60628	CHICAGO	72	69	78	65	67	78	71	70	75	73	95	76	74	91	72	78	92	72	76	81
60629	CHICAGO	76	70	74	68	68	73	74	75	77	78	98	84	73	95	72	75	97	77	72	81
60630	CHICAGO	85	94	113	92	92	99	93	91	93	94	117	103	96	121	94	93	116	92	88	99
	ILLINOIS	98	100	111	99	99	106	100	99	101	100	126	115	102	127	100	100	123	100	98	112
	UNITED STATES	100	100	100	100	100	100	100	100	100	100	100	100	100	100	100	100	100	100	100	100

# ZIP CODE / POST OFFICE NAME	COUNTY FIPS CODE	POPULATION 2000	2004	2009	2000-2004 ANNUAL RATE % Rate	State Centile	HOUSEHOLDS 2000	2004	2009	% Annual Rate 2000-2004	2004 Average HH Size	FAMILIES 2000	2004	% Annual Rate 2000-2004
60631 CHICAGO	031	28822	28576	28591	-0.2	31	11929	11995	12120	0.1	2.33	7555	7467	-0.3
60632 CHICAGO	031	87331	90486	91927	0.8	75	24463	24653	24754	0.2	3.66	18976	18924	-0.1
60633 CHICAGO	031	13100	12676	12547	-0.8	7	5024	4900	4881	-0.6	2.52	3279	3142	-1.0
60634 CHICAGO	031	74348	75497	76174	0.4	61	26272	26684	27013	0.4	2.81	18832	18797	0.0
60636 CHICAGO	031	51073	50378	50342	-0.3	24	13907	13903	14020	0.0	3.59	10982	10857	-0.3
60637 CHICAGO	031	57346	56566	56626	-0.3	24	21811	21633	21779	-0.2	2.48	12317	11935	-0.7
60638 CHICAGO	031	55834	56067	56351	0.1	47	20771	21024	21267	0.3	2.66	14453	14413	-0.1
60639 CHICAGO	031	91999	94057	95146	0.5	66	25155	25362	25530	0.2	3.70	20143	20123	0.0
60640 CHICAGO	031	75890	76343	77165	0.1	49	36207	36796	37472	0.4	1.97	13934	13770	-0.3
60641 CHICAGO	031	73507	74761	75337	0.4	62	25241	25330	25413	0.1	2.93	17014	16827	-0.3
60643 CHICAGO	031	52251	51447	51409	-0.4	21	17415	17380	17525	-0.1	2.94	13154	12965	-0.3
60644 CHICAGO	031	59210	59612	60255	0.2	50	17946	18226	18553	0.4	3.19	13051	13067	0.0
60645 CHICAGO	031	43685	43451	43403	-0.1	35	15994	15827	15806	-0.3	2.69	10245	9958	-0.7
60646 CHICAGO	031	25968	26160	26327	0.2	51	10319	10471	10602	0.3	2.50	7176	7176	0.0
60647 CHICAGO	031	97584	98040	98633	0.1	47	32989	33537	34056	0.4	2.90	20173	20129	-0.1
60649 CHICAGO	031	54520	53937	53874	-0.3	27	23411	23369	23501	0.0	2.27	12745	12456	-0.5
60651 CHICAGO	031	78000	77885	77965	0.0	40	21305	21442	21602	0.2	3.62	17308	17260	-0.1
60652 CHICAGO	031	39212	39257	39333	0.0	43	12901	12895	12936	0.0	3.04	10127	10024	-0.2
60653 CHICAGO	031	34503	34277	34754	-0.2	34	12898	12928	13189	0.1	2.57	7553	7380	-0.5
60655 CHICAGO	031	29145	28350	28091	-0.7	11	10758	10576	10568	-0.4	2.64	7472	7237	-0.8
60656 CHICAGO	031	27971	27694	27789	-0.2	29	12483	12420	12495	-0.1	2.23	7564	7433	-0.4
60657 CHICAGO	031	68573	69980	71118	0.5	65	40870	42112	43083	0.7	1.64	10211	10206	0.0
60659 CHICAGO	031	39606	39116	39019	-0.3	25	13254	13063	13047	-0.3	2.95	9364	9097	-0.7
60660 CHICAGO	031	46822	47320	47776	0.3	54	22115	22513	22872	0.4	2.01	9116	9024	-0.2
60661 CHICAGO	031	4276	5104	5624	4.3	97	2874	3357	3658	3.7	1.52	798	916	3.3
60706 HARWOOD HEIGHTS	031	22329	22422	22551	0.1	47	8906	9036	9161	0.3	2.43	5940	5933	0.0
60707 ELMWOOD PARK	031	42586	42251	42174	-0.2	31	15820	15630	15606	-0.3	2.69	10786	10504	-0.6
60712 LINCOLNWOOD	031	12372	12207	12152	-0.3	24	4488	4466	4474	-0.1	2.72	3450	3396	-0.4
60714 NILES	031	29988	30182	30380	0.2	50	11708	11942	12136	0.5	2.39	7942	7935	0.0
60803 ALSIP	031	23204	23396	23555	0.2	51	9066	9260	9403	0.5	2.52	5885	5903	0.1
60804 CICERO	031	86096	88475	89557	0.6	70	23117	23094	23098	0.0	3.82	18110	17917	-0.3
60805 EVERGREEN PARK	031	20911	20547	20448	-0.4	19	7503	7425	7433	-0.3	2.71	5328	5200	-0.6
60827 RIVERDALE	031	33371	31856	31458	-1.1	3	10843	10351	10239	-1.1	3.07	8166	7699	-1.4
60901 KANKAKEE	091	37089	36795	37200	-0.2	31	13614	13635	13945	0.0	2.58	9054	8911	-0.4
60911 ASHKUM	075	1478	1501	1520	0.4	61	578	598	614	0.8	2.45	428	437	0.5
60912 BEAVERVILLE	075	647	649	652	0.1	45	253	256	260	0.3	2.54	174	174	0.0
60913 BONFIELD	091	1692	1702	1725	0.1	49	588	602	619	0.6	2.83	492	499	0.3
60914 BOURBONNAIS	091	22068	22807	23500	0.8	74	8058	8536	8976	1.4	2.50	5753	6009	1.0
60915 BRADLEY	091	10699	10838	11044	0.3	58	4179	4304	4452	0.7	2.46	2789	2820	0.3
60917 BUCKINGHAM	091	481	450	449	-1.6	1	162	154	156	-1.2	2.92	132	124	-1.5
60918 BUCKLEY	075	955	971	984	0.4	62	399	411	422	0.7	2.36	293	298	0.4
60919 CABERY	053	486	474	476	-0.6	13	187	184	185	-0.4	2.58	134	130	-0.7
60921 CHATSWORTH	105	1733	1733	1740	0.0	42	692	704	718	0.4	2.46	473	468	-0.3
60922 CHEBANSE	075	2424	2492	2553	0.7	71	893	937	975	1.1	2.65	668	691	0.8
60924 CISSNA PARK	075	1867	1856	1866	-0.1	34	735	740	753	0.2	2.49	522	517	-0.2
60927 CLIFTON	075	2250	2213	2222	-0.4	20	841	842	860	0.0	2.56	623	615	-0.3
60928 CRESCENT CITY	075	802	809	817	0.2	52	325	332	338	0.5	2.43	243	245	0.2
60929 CULLOM	105	750	746	749	-0.1	35	321	325	331	0.3	2.30	206	205	-0.1
60930 DANFORTH	075	909	969	1007	1.5	84	319	347	367	2.0	2.58	233	250	1.7
60931 DONOVAN	075	699	699	703	0.0	42	258	261	265	0.3	2.68	188	188	0.0
60934 EMINGTON	105	290	287	288	-0.2	28	115	116	118	0.2	2.47	89	89	0.0
60935 ESSEX	091	847	918	966	1.9	88	303	333	355	2.3	2.76	244	265	2.0
60936 GIBSON CITY	053	4532	4517	4559	-0.1	37	1909	1928	1970	0.2	2.29	1276	1270	-0.1
60938 GILMAN	075	2145	2163	2181	0.2	52	863	881	899	0.5	2.39	590	593	0.1
60940 GRANT PARK	091	3200	3492	3693	2.1	89	1129	1254	1347	2.5	2.71	893	979	2.2
60941 HERSCHER	091	2171	2253	2317	0.9	76	758	799	833	1.3	2.81	623	650	1.0
60942 HOOPESTON	183	6828	6584	6412	-0.9	6	2626	2564	2531	-0.6	2.42	1754	1682	-1.0
60946 KEMPTON	053	404	401	403	-0.2	32	140	140	141	0.0	2.85	101	100	-0.2
60948 LODA	075	1422	1538	1610	1.9	87	582	636	673	2.1	2.42	436	470	1.8
60949 LUDLOW	019	759	761	780	0.1	45	312	321	335	0.7	2.37	213	215	0.2
60950 MANTENO	091	8832	9599	10112	2.0	89	3402	3761	4022	2.4	2.50	2440	2655	2.0
60951 MARTINTON	075	926	906	906	-0.5	16	343	339	343	-0.3	2.62	270	264	-0.5
60952 MELVIN	053	705	722	736	0.6	68	278	288	296	0.8	2.51	197	201	0.5
60953 MILFORD	075	2630	2605	2617	-0.2	29	1108	1119	1142	0.2	2.33	781	777	-0.1
60954 MOMENCE	091	7117	7191	7329	0.2	54	2549	2601	2681	0.5	2.68	1806	1812	0.1
60955 ONARGA	075	2085	2099	2116	0.2	50	685	696	708	0.4	2.84	491	491	0.0
60957 PAXTON	053	5638	5691	5752	0.2	53	2173	2228	2283	0.6	2.45	1501	1516	0.2
60959 PIPER CITY	053	1171	1162	1168	-0.2	32	437	437	443	0.0	2.52	318	314	-0.3
60960 RANKIN	183	1322	1264	1231	-1.1	3	499	484	478	-0.7	2.56	352	336	-1.1
60961 REDDICK	091	861	868	889	0.2	51	318	326	339	0.6	2.66	255	258	0.3
60962 ROBERTS	053	578	645	689	2.6	92	246	278	300	2.9	2.32	171	190	2.5
60963 ROSSVILLE	183	1930	1886	1846	-0.5	14	807	801	796	-0.2	2.35	554	542	-0.5
60964 SAINT ANNE	091	7948	8113	8305	0.5	65	2799	2907	3023	0.9	2.68	2043	2086	0.5
60966 SHELDON	075	1925	1945	1965	0.2	54	736	752	769	0.5	2.54	535	540	0.2
60968 THAWVILLE	075	335	337	340	0.1	49	134	137	140	0.5	2.46	98	99	0.2
60970 WATSEKA	075	7906	7888	7920	-0.1	39	3193	3230	3286	0.3	2.37	2140	2130	-0.1
60973 WELLINGTON	075	483	472	473	-0.5	15	200	200	204	0.0	2.36	151	149	-0.3
61001 APPLE RIVER	085	1059	1104	1136	1.0	77	469	503	532	1.7	2.19	337	356	1.3
61006 ASHTON	103	1833	1885	1908	0.7	71	685	716	736	1.1	2.61	517	533	0.7
61007 BAILEYVILLE	141	569	560	561	-0.4	21	205	206	211	0.1	2.72	170	169	-0.1
61008 BELVIDERE	007	28274	31051	34807	2.2	90	10087	11150	12559	2.4	2.76	7508	8192	2.1
61010 BYRON	141	6830	7686	8288	2.8	94	2362	2687	2925	3.1	2.83	1855	2079	2.7
61011 CALEDONIA	007	2593	2908	3241	2.7	94	906	1022	1145	2.9	2.85	766	853	2.6
61012 CAPRON	007	1983	2217	2507	2.7	93	681	769	874	2.9	2.88	534	593	2.5
61014 CHADWICK	015	1193	1251	1278	1.1	79	464	496	513	1.6	2.52	352	371	1.2
61015 CHANA	141	1043	1146	1221	2.2	90	377	421	454	2.6	2.72	309	340	2.3
61016 CHERRY VALLEY	201	4222	4596	4891	2.0	89	1560	1705	1821	2.1	2.70	1252	1349	1.8
61018 DAKOTA	177	1019	1016	1009	-0.1	38	389	396	399	0.4	2.57	300	301	0.1
61019 DAVIS	177	3409	3553	3640	1.0	77	1313	1389	1440	1.3	2.55	1052	1102	1.1
61020 DAVIS JUNCTION	141	1492	1649	1757	2.4	91	504	564	609	2.7	2.92	417	462	2.4
61021 DIXON	103	23298	23110	23083	-0.2	31	8556	8630	8759	0.2	2.36	5698	5653	-0.2
61024 DURAND	201	2589	2687	2771	0.9	76	949	994	1033	1.1	2.59	711	732	0.7
61025 EAST DUBUQUE	085	4832	4881	4961	0.2	54	1887	1957	2039	0.9	2.49	1336	1366	0.5
61028 ELIZABETH	085	1994	2029	2075	0.4	63	841	879	922	1.1	2.25	555	570	0.6
61030 FORRESTON	141	2360	2401	2464	0.4	63	926	954	989	0.7	2.52	689	700	0.4
ILLINOIS					0.7					0.9	2.61			0.6
UNITED STATES					1.2					1.3	2.58			1.1

ZIP CODE		RACE (%)						% Hispanic Origin		2004 AGE DISTRIBUTION (%)										MEDIAN AGE		
		White		Black		Asian/Pacific																
#	POST OFFICE NAME	2000	2004	2000	2004	2000	2004	2000	2004	0-4	5-9	10-14	15-19	20-24	25-44	45-64	65-84	85+	18+	2004	% 2004 Males	% 2004 Females
60631	CHICAGO	94.6	93.1	1.0	1.3	2.2	2.7	5.1	7.0	5.7	5.8	5.5	4.8	4.2	26.2	25.8	17.7	4.3	79.9	43.6	46.5	53.5
60632	CHICAGO	54.7	51.2	1.1	1.1	2.0	2.0	70.5	76.1	10.5	9.2	8.8	7.8	8.8	31.1	16.0	6.8	1.1	66.8	27.7	51.1	48.9
60633	CHICAGO	66.7	62.5	18.0	18.9	0.6	0.7	23.1	28.6	6.8	6.9	7.4	6.2	5.5	27.6	23.7	13.8	2.2	75.1	38.5	48.6	51.4
60634	CHICAGO	83.7	80.0	0.7	0.9	3.9	4.5	19.6	24.8	6.0	5.9	6.1	5.5	6.3	29.5	25.4	12.9	2.5	78.8	38.8	48.3	51.7
60636	CHICAGO	0.8	0.8	97.8	97.9	0.1	0.1	1.2	1.2	8.7	8.9	10.0	8.9	7.6	25.1	20.5	9.4	0.8	66.9	29.6	46.4	53.6
60637	CHICAGO	12.6	12.0	82.3	82.2	3.2	3.8	1.3	1.6	8.2	7.9	8.8	8.7	9.0	26.5	19.0	10.1	1.9	70.7	30.3	45.1	54.9
60638	CHICAGO	82.8	80.4	8.0	7.8	0.8	0.9	15.3	19.9	6.3	6.4	6.8	5.7	5.9	27.9	24.1	14.6	2.4	77.0	39.0	48.2	51.8
60639	CHICAGO	42.0	40.1	18.0	17.5	1.4	1.4	66.5	70.5	9.6	8.8	9.2	8.3	9.1	30.9	17.9	5.5	0.7	67.4	27.9	49.7	50.3
60640	CHICAGO	52.9	48.3	19.2	20.2	13.5	14.8	21.2	25.2	5.3	4.5	4.8	5.2	8.1	39.2	21.3	9.8	1.9	82.6	35.6	51.1	48.9
60641	CHICAGO	70.9	66.4	1.4	1.5	4.0	4.4	39.0	46.0	7.2	6.7	7.0	6.6	7.8	31.7	23.2	8.6	1.2	75.2	34.0	49.7	50.3
60643	CHICAGO	20.1	18.5	77.5	79.0	0.3	0.3	1.8	2.1	6.2	6.8	8.1	7.4	6.2	24.8	26.0	12.9	1.6	74.3	38.4	46.0	54.0
60644	CHICAGO	2.5	2.1	95.3	95.5	0.3	0.4	2.2	2.5	9.1	9.0	9.7	8.5	7.9	26.2	20.2	8.6	0.8	67.0	29.3	45.8	54.3
60645	CHICAGO	60.9	56.5	10.6	11.4	16.2	18.1	15.6	18.7	7.4	6.9	7.2	6.6	6.8	28.0	22.3	11.8	3.1	74.5	36.2	48.9	51.1
60646	CHICAGO	89.8	87.3	0.4	0.5	6.1	7.5	6.6	8.9	6.5	6.7	6.0	5.2	4.4	25.8	27.2	15.2	3.0	77.5	42.2	48.1	51.9
60647	CHICAGO	45.7	42.4	6.6	6.5	1.4	1.5	67.7	72.5	8.8	7.6	8.1	7.6	9.3	37.1	16.0	5.0	0.6	71.1	29.0	50.9	49.1
60649	CHICAGO	1.4	1.1	96.8	97.1	0.2	0.2	1.1	1.3	7.8	7.6	7.7	6.7	7.0	29.0	22.9	10.1	1.2	72.9	34.2	43.6	56.4
60651	CHICAGO	11.1	10.7	70.0	69.4	0.5	0.5	27.3	28.7	9.5	9.2	10.3	9.1	9.1	27.4	19.6	5.5	0.4	65.6	26.9	46.7	53.3
60652	CHICAGO	44.5	40.3	41.8	43.6	1.1	1.2	17.4	20.8	7.5	7.7	8.9	7.5	6.5	28.4	22.1	9.9	1.4	71.2	34.5	47.6	52.4
60653	CHICAGO	0.8	0.7	97.9	98.0	0.2	0.2	0.8	0.9	9.6	9.6	10.0	8.2	6.8	24.5	18.4	10.4	2.5	65.8	30.0	43.5	56.5
60655	CHICAGO	91.9	90.1	5.5	6.5	0.5	0.6	3.6	4.9	7.0	7.0	7.6	6.7	6.2	28.6	24.1	10.7	2.1	74.4	36.7	48.9	51.1
60656	CHICAGO	89.6	87.2	1.1	1.3	5.6	6.8	6.6	8.8	5.3	4.8	4.5	4.0	5.9	30.6	25.3	17.0	2.7	83.1	41.5	48.1	51.9
60657	CHICAGO	86.1	82.8	3.4	4.1	5.2	6.4	8.0	10.6	3.5	1.7	1.5	1.6	13.1	55.1	15.4	6.1	2.0	92.5	31.8	49.8	50.2
60659	CHICAGO	54.4	49.5	5.0	5.4	27.1	30.0	15.9	19.0	7.4	6.7	7.1	6.7	7.4	29.8	22.5	10.5	2.0	74.8	34.7	49.3	50.7
60660	CHICAGO	54.1	48.9	18.1	19.8	12.6	14.0	20.9	24.5	5.8	4.7	4.4	6.4	8.9	37.5	21.2	9.5	1.7	82.5	34.9	50.4	49.6
60661	CHICAGO	63.0	59.2	16.1	18.3	17.1	18.1	4.8	6.0	2.9	1.3	1.2	1.7	10.2	63.6	17.2	1.7	0.2	93.9	32.6	53.1	46.9
60706	HARWOOD HEIGHTS	93.8	92.0	0.2	0.3	3.4	4.3	4.6	6.3	4.0	4.1	4.9	5.3	5.7	24.9	25.9	21.5	3.9	83.9	45.8	46.6	53.4
60707	ELMWOOD PARK	79.7	76.2	6.8	7.4	2.6	3.0	19.0	23.8	6.2	6.1	6.7	6.4	7.0	29.0	24.2	12.2	2.3	77.1	37.9	48.2	51.8
60712	LINCOLNWOOD	74.5	69.8	0.4	0.4	21.1	25.1	4.2	5.4	5.3	5.8	6.8	6.5	5.0	19.1	27.0	19.5	5.0	78.1	46.0	46.7	53.3
60714	NILES	82.5	79.1	0.6	0.7	13.0	15.4	5.3	6.9	4.0	4.1	4.8	5.2	5.5	23.2	25.3	22.5	5.4	83.9	47.3	46.8	53.3
60803	ALSIP	83.0	79.4	9.3	11.0	1.9	2.2	8.4	11.1	7.0	6.7	7.3	6.7	6.9	30.4	22.7	10.8	1.6	75.0	35.8	48.4	51.6
60804	CICERO	48.5	45.1	1.1	1.1	1.0	1.0	77.2	82.2	11.2	9.8	9.5	8.0	9.0	31.4	14.7	5.4	1.0	64.7	26.4	51.5	48.5
60805	EVERGREEN PARK	88.4	85.7	7.9	9.5	1.2	1.5	4.0	5.3	6.8	7.1	8.0	7.2	6.0	26.3	22.4	13.2	3.0	73.5	37.9	47.6	52.4
60827	RIVERDALE	8.3	7.1	88.6	89.6	0.2	0.2	3.5	4.0	10.0	10.5	11.1	8.8	7.1	27.8	18.4	5.7	0.7	62.8	27.0	45.3	54.7
60901	KANKAKEE	62.1	59.2	31.6	33.7	0.3	0.4	7.2	8.3	7.5	7.4	7.9	7.2	6.9	26.9	22.8	11.2	2.3	72.7	35.0	48.2	51.8
60911	ASHKUM	98.4	97.9	0.1	0.1	0.0	0.1	1.0	1.4	5.5	6.1	6.4	5.9	5.5	25.5	28.3	13.6	3.3	78.4	41.9	50.3	49.7
60912	BEAVERVILLE	87.6	86.6	10.7	11.7	0.2	0.2	0.5	0.5	7.1	7.4	7.9	5.9	5.6	23.6	25.6	15.4	1.7	74.1	39.8	50.9	49.2
60913	BONFIELD	98.8	98.5	0.0	0.1	0.2	0.2	0.8	1.1	6.2	6.6	7.5	7.2	5.9	27.6	27.1	10.9	1.0	75.2	38.7	51.0	49.0
60914	BOURBONNAIS	92.2	90.5	3.5	4.2	2.0	2.4	2.5	3.3	7.1	6.6	7.1	7.4	9.6	27.9	23.8	9.6	1.0	75.5	33.5	47.9	52.1
60915	BRADLEY	95.5	94.4	1.3	1.6	0.7	0.8	3.9	5.0	7.8	7.1	7.1	6.4	7.5	30.6	20.7	10.8	1.9	74.4	33.9	48.1	52.0
60917	BUCKINGHAM	96.9	96.2	0.0	0.0	0.0	0.0	1.0	1.3	7.1	7.1	8.2	6.7	5.6	26.7	25.3	12.0	1.3	73.6	37.3	49.8	50.2
60918	BUCKLEY	98.0	97.5	0.2	0.2	0.2	0.2	2.9	3.6	6.1	6.2	6.8	6.2	4.8	23.8	26.9	17.3	2.0	77.1	42.5	50.7	49.3
60919	CABERY	97.5	97.3	0.0	0.0	0.2	0.2	2.1	2.3	8.0	8.4	8.9	7.0	5.9	25.7	23.6	10.8	1.7	70.3	34.4	50.8	49.2
60921	CHATSWORTH	98.4	98.2	0.3	0.4	0.1	0.2	1.6	1.9	6.4	6.2	8.3	8.7	6.0	23.2	25.2	13.9	2.3	74.0	39.3	50.4	49.6
60922	CHEBANSE	94.4	93.3	3.4	4.1	0.5	0.5	2.1	2.6	6.3	6.4	7.7	7.9	6.5	27.1	24.6	12.0	1.4	74.5	37.5	49.5	50.5
60924	CISSNA PARK	98.9	98.7	0.2	0.2	0.3	0.4	1.0	1.4	6.2	6.5	7.7	6.9	5.5	21.7	26.4	16.0	3.3	75.1	42.1	48.6	51.4
60927	CLIFTON	99.1	98.8	0.0	0.0	0.3	0.4	0.7	1.0	6.3	6.4	7.6	7.1	6.0	24.9	26.3	13.0	2.6	75.2	39.6	48.4	51.6
60928	CRESCENT CITY	97.8	97.3	0.0	0.0	0.6	0.7	1.5	2.1	6.8	7.2	7.1	5.4	4.2	27.6	25.5	14.0	2.4	75.4	39.7	51.4	48.6
60929	CULLOM	98.8	98.7	0.5	0.7	0.1	0.1	0.3	0.3	6.2	6.6	7.6	6.3	4.8	26.9	22.4	16.0	3.2	75.6	40.2	49.2	50.8
60930	DANFORTH	98.2	97.8	0.2	0.3	0.2	0.2	1.2	1.4	5.7	6.2	6.0	5.9	5.8	23.7	27.7	13.2	5.9	77.8	42.8	49.1	50.9
60931	DONOVAN	95.7	95.1	2.6	2.9	0.1	0.1	1.6	2.0	6.4	6.9	8.0	6.2	5.0	25.8	27.5	12.2	2.2	75.0	40.4	49.6	50.4
60934	EMINGTON	98.6	98.3	0.0	0.0	0.3	0.4	0.7	1.4	6.3	8.0	9.1	7.0	5.9	27.2	24.4	11.2	1.1	71.8	38.0	53.3	46.7
60935	ESSEX	97.6	97.1	0.1	0.1	0.1	0.1	0.6	0.8	6.2	6.5	7.3	7.2	6.8	27.5	26.5	11.3	0.8	75.7	38.0	52.0	48.0
60936	GIBSON CITY	98.3	98.0	0.5	0.5	0.4	0.5	0.7	0.9	5.9	6.0	6.6	6.5	5.3	23.8	25.5	16.4	3.9	77.0	42.2	47.3	52.7
60938	GILMAN	92.9	91.1	0.3	0.3	0.3	0.4	8.5	10.6	5.5	5.6	7.3	6.8	6.0	25.3	24.2	15.7	3.7	77.4	40.8	48.8	51.2
60940	GRANT PARK	97.1	96.4	0.2	0.3	0.3	0.4	2.6	3.4	6.2	6.6	7.7	6.8	5.6	27.5	28.3	10.2	1.2	75.5	38.7	50.7	49.3
60941	HERSCHER	97.6	97.0	0.3	0.4	0.5	0.6	1.2	1.6	7.2	7.3	7.3	7.6	7.5	25.7	24.9	11.1	1.5	73.6	36.2	50.0	50.0
60942	HOOPESTON	92.4	90.8	0.8	0.8	0.3	0.4	7.6	9.4	7.0	6.8	6.3	6.3	6.3	23.4	24.2	16.8	2.9	75.8	40.7	50.3	49.7
60946	KEMPTON	98.3	98.3	0.0	0.0	0.3	0.3	1.7	2.0	7.5	8.0	9.2	6.7	6.0	24.4	24.2	12.0	2.0	71.1	36.1	51.4	48.6
60948	LODA	97.4	97.0	0.8	0.9	0.3	0.4	1.9	2.4	4.9	5.1	5.9	5.6	5.0	22.1	31.1	18.7	1.8	80.8	45.9	50.3	49.7
60949	LUDLOW	93.8	92.9	1.7	2.0	0.3	0.4	4.0	4.9	8.9	8.7	6.8	6.4	5.5	28.7	23.4	10.4	1.2	71.6	35.0	49.5	50.5
60950	MANTENO	96.1	95.0	1.6	2.0	0.3	0.4	2.9	3.8	6.9	7.0	7.7	7.2	5.8	28.3	23.7	12.5	1.1	74.1	36.9	50.1	49.9
60951	MARTINTON	97.8	97.6	0.9	1.0	0.1	0.1	1.2	1.6	7.2	7.7	7.8	6.8	5.3	26.6	24.9	11.6	2.0	72.9	37.4	50.0	50.0
60952	MELVIN	99.2	99.2	0.0	0.0	0.0	0.0	1.1	1.5	8.6	8.5	7.2	5.3	4.9	27.0	21.9	14.4	2.4	72.4	37.3	49.7	50.3
60953	MILFORD	98.1	97.8	0.2	0.2	0.1	0.1	2.7	3.3	4.9	5.2	6.0	6.0	6.2	24.1	28.5	16.7	2.5	80.3	43.3	50.4	49.6
60954	MOMENCE	81.4	79.0	13.7	15.1	0.1	0.2	7.6	9.4	6.7	6.6	7.3	7.1	6.6	25.8	24.8	12.9	2.3	75.1	38.1	49.7	50.3
60955	ONARGA	79.2	76.0	1.6	1.6	0.2	0.2	25.8	30.1	6.6	6.7	8.7	10.4	6.2	24.1	22.4	12.4	2.4	71.4	35.0	51.5	48.5
60957	PAXTON	98.0	97.6	0.3	0.3	0.3	0.4	1.5	1.9	6.7	6.5	7.0	7.2	6.5	25.6	22.7	14.5	3.3	75.4	39.1	48.3	51.7
60959	PIPER CITY	97.8	97.5	0.1	0.1	0.6	0.7	1.1	1.3	5.8	5.7	6.5	7.3	5.9	20.6	25.7	18.5	4.1	77.5	43.8	47.8	52.2
60960	RANKIN	95.6	94.8	0.5	0.6	0.4	0.5	3.4	4.3	6.7	7.0	8.2	5.9	5.5	24.3	25.2	14.9	2.4	74.2	40.2	50.6	49.5
60961	REDDICK	97.4	96.8	0.1	0.1	0.1	0.1	0.7	1.0	6.5	6.9	8.0	6.9	6.1	27.1	26.0	11.4	1.2	74.4	37.8	51.4	48.6
60962	ROBERTS	99.3	99.4	0.0	0.0	0.0	0.0	0.5	0.8	7.1	7.6	7.4	5.6	4.5	23.7	26.7	14.9	2.5	74.4	41.7	47.4	52.6
60963	ROSSVILLE	97.9	97.6	0.2	0.2	0.2	0.2	1.7	2.1	6.0	6.2	7.1	5.8	6.5	25.5	25.9	15.3	1.8	77.3	40.8	48.5	51.5
60964	SAINT ANNE	67.1	63.9	28.2	30.6	0.4	0.4	4.7	5.8	6.4	7.0	7.8	7.3	5.9	22.9	26.2	14.7	1.8	74.3	39.6	51.8	48.2
60966	SHELDON	97.3	96.9	0.4	0.4	0.5	0.7	1.7	2.1	7.7	6.9	7.5	6.3	5.9	24.0	25.0	14.2	2.5	73.9	39.5	49.4	50.6
60968	THAWVILLE	97.9	97.3	0.0	0.0	0.3	0.3	3.0	3.9	6.2	6.5	7.1	6.2	5.0	24.0	26.4	16.3	2.1	76.6	41.6	50.7	49.3
60970	WATSEKA	96.9	96.3	0.6	0.7	0.5	0.6	2.3	2.9	6.6	6.3	6.4	6.3	6.2	23.9	24.5	16.5	3.3	76.9	41.1	48.2	51.8
60973	WELLINGTON	98.8	98.7	0.2	0.2	0.0	0.0	1.7	2.3	7.4	7.4	6.4	5.5	4.0	25.9	29.2	12.5	1.7	75.0	41.0	51.3	48.7
61001	APPLE RIVER	99.3	99.3	0.2	0.2	0.2	0.2	0.7	0.8	5.8	6.1	7.3	5.7	4.4	21.9	27.2	19.6	2.2	77.2	44.2	51.7	48.3
61006	ASHTON	97.6	97.6	0.8	0.9	0.5	0.5	2.6	2.8	6.9	6.7	7.9	7.6	7.3	26.1	23.8	12.3	1.5	73.7	37.3	49.1	50.9
61007	BAILEYVILLE	98.2	97.9	0.2	0.2	0.4	0.5	0.7	1.1	4.8	6.8	8.9	6.8	3.9	25.4	30.0	12.5	0.9	75.0	41.0	50.4	49.6
61008	BELVIDERE	87.6	85.5	1.0	1.0	0.6	0.7	15.8	18.8	7.6	7.5	8.4	7.1	6.5	28.2	23.3	9.8	1.5	72.1	35.3	49.9	50.2
61010	BYRON	97.9	97.4	0.3	0.4	0.4	0.5	1.2	1.5	6.8	7.8	10.1	9.1	5.2	27.9	23.3	8.3	1.5	68.9	35.8	49.3	50.8
61011	CALEDONIA	94.6	93.3	1.4	1.7	1.2	1.6	4.1	5.3	7.9	8.2	9.3	7.5	5.9	28.9	24.9	7.1	0.5	69.9	34.7	50.5	49.6
61012	CAPRON	91.7	89.7	0.5	0.5	0.3	0.4	12.8	16.2	8.0	7.9	7.9	6.5	6.0	28.7	24.2	10.0	0.8	72.0	35.0	50.7	49.4
61014	CHADWICK	98.2	98.1	0.1	0.1	0.4	0.4	1.6	1.8	6.2	6.5	6.7	6.5	5.4	26.6	26.5	13.9	1.8	76.7	40.3	51.7	48.3
61015	CHANA	98.4	98.0	0.3	0.4	0.4	0.4	1.2	1.5	5.7	6.9	8.3	6.5	4.8	25.6	31.9	9.5	0.9	75.0	40.5	51.9	48.1
61016	CHERRY VALLEY	96.1	95.0	1.2	1.5	1.6	2.0	2.1	2.9	5.2	6.0	7.2	7.1	5.8	26.0	33.9	8.3	0.6	77.2	41.0	50.6	49.4
61018	DAKOTA	98.3	97.9	0.3	0.4	0.4	0.5	0.5	0.7	5.5	6.2	7.8	7.3	5.8	26.9	28.2	10.9	1.5	76.1	39.2	50.4	49.6
61019	DAVIS	98.7	98.3	0.3	0.5	0.2	0.3	0.7	1.0	5.3	5.7	7.2	6.7	4.9	21.8	27.5	19.6	1.4	77.6	44.0	49.1	50.9
61020	DAVIS JUNCTION	96.0	94.9	0.1	0.2	0.3	0.4	4.2	5.4	7.3	7.8	9.1	7.1	5.4	30.0	24.5	8.0	0.8	71.3	35.4	49.1	50.9
61021	DIXON	89.9	89.4	7.3	7.7	0.7	0.8	3.6	3.7	5.1	5.1	6.2	6.5	6.7	30.1	26.0	12.1	2.2	79.6	39.4	52.1	47.9
61024	DURAND	97.6	97.0	0.7	1.0	0.1	0.2	1.1	1.5	5.7	6.2	7.2	8.1	6.0	23.6	27.7	12.8	2.8	75.4	40.9	49.2	50.8
61025	EAST DUBUQUE	98.9	98.7	0.2	0.3	0.2	0.3	0.8	1.0	6.5	6.8	7.3	6.5	6.1	26.0	28.1	11.8	1.0	75.5	39.2	51.3	48.7
61028	ELIZABETH	98.5	98.2	0.3	0.3	0.2	0.2	1.2	1.4	4.9	5.3	5.9	4.6	4.0	21.2	30.2	19.6	4.4	80.9	48.0	49.3	50.7
61030	FORRESTON	98.9	98.8	0.0	0.0	0.3	0.3	1.0	1.3	6.6	7.0	8.2	7.1	5.1	26.2	24.6	13.0	2.2	73.5	39.0	49.2	50.9
	ILLINOIS	73.5	71.8	15.1	15.2	3.5	4.0	12.3	14.2	7.1	7.0	7.3	7.0	7.3	29.0	23.2	10.4	1.7	74.5	35.2	49.0	51.0
	UNITED STATES	75.1	73.6	12.3	12.5	3.8	4.2	12.5	14.1	6.9	6.7	7.2	7.0	7.3	28.6	23.8	10.8	1.7	75.1	36.0	49.1	50.9

ZIP CODE #	POST OFFICE NAME	2004 Per Capita Income	2004 HH Income Base	2004 HOUSEHOLD INCOME DISTRIBUTION (%) Less than $25,000	$25,000 to $49,999	$50,000 to $99,999	$100,000 to $149,999	$150,000 or More	MEDIAN HOUSEHOLD INCOME 2004	2009	2004 National Centile	2004 State Centile	2004 Home Value Base	2004 HOME VALUE DISTRIBUTION (%) Less than $50,000	$50,000 to $89,999	$90,000 to $174,999	$175,000 to $399,999	$400,000 or More	2004 Median Home Value
60631	CHICAGO	32842	11995	16.4	23.4	35.4	16.5	8.2	62006	72298	86	83	9618	0.3	0.3	15.2	74.5	9.7	260328
60632	CHICAGO	14370	24653	27.9	32.0	30.7	7.6	1.8	41414	47043	51	35	14650	0.8	4.5	56.1	37.9	0.7	160011
60633	CHICAGO	21865	4900	24.8	29.8	33.1	10.2	2.1	45324	52563	62	49	3932	8.0	14.1	68.3	8.7	0.9	115274
60634	CHICAGO	23338	26684	18.7	25.9	37.2	13.8	4.4	55066	64191	80	74	20159	0.4	0.7	23.1	73.4	2.3	210206
60636	CHICAGO	11514	13903	42.8	27.9	22.9	5.4	1.1	30518	35388	14	4	7912	7.1	34.9	50.9	6.4	0.8	95303
60637	CHICAGO	18690	21633	47.5	23.8	19.3	5.1	4.4	27151	33581	7	2	5776	4.8	13.5	42.4	28.9	10.4	141770
60638	CHICAGO	22837	21024	24.5	25.3	34.1	12.7	3.5	50192	58593	72	63	16701	0.7	3.1	46.1	49.2	1.0	175222
60639	CHICAGO	14840	25362	25.0	31.6	32.8	7.8	2.9	44653	51341	60	47	12874	0.8	1.6	35.8	60.2	1.6	189850
60640	CHICAGO	28373	36796	34.3	26.0	25.9	8.3	5.5	39264	48925	44	27	10186	1.9	6.2	23.6	47.3	21.0	236327
60641	CHICAGO	20350	25330	21.7	30.8	33.4	10.0	4.1	47732	56370	68	57	12548	0.6	0.8	21.1	70.5	7.1	221163
60643	CHICAGO	25057	17380	20.3	24.3	33.2	14.8	7.4	55840	65181	81	75	13886	1.6	10.1	50.9	33.6	3.8	143900
60644	CHICAGO	14351	18226	41.9	27.4	23.3	5.3	2.1	31387	38650	16	5	6380	3.0	10.2	55.2	27.9	3.8	143684
60645	CHICAGO	22643	15827	25.5	28.6	30.7	10.0	5.3	46069	53953	64	52	8184	1.5	6.8	27.0	56.2	8.5	215441
60646	CHICAGO	36898	10471	14.3	21.3	34.0	16.2	14.1	67966	80575	90	89	8510	0.7	0.3	5.7	63.8	29.6	313553
60647	CHICAGO	19605	33537	30.6	29.3	27.2	7.9	5.0	40700	48479	49	32	12477	1.4	2.5	22.9	53.9	19.4	231912
60649	CHICAGO	18618	23369	39.4	32.3	21.1	5.3	1.9	31905	38316	18	6	6654	3.7	16.4	44.4	29.4	6.0	139355
60651	CHICAGO	13616	21442	34.5	29.9	26.9	6.4	2.4	37002	43955	35	20	10170	1.8	6.9	61.1	28.5	1.7	140329
60652	CHICAGO	22092	12895	16.5	24.3	42.0	13.5	3.7	59627	68188	84	80	11859	0.9	2.7	67.1	28.4	0.8	149981
60653	CHICAGO	13015	12928	60.3	19.3	14.1	4.2	2.2	17138	21370	1	0	2076	2.5	9.2	16.7	55.8	15.8	240346
60655	CHICAGO	30408	10576	14.0	18.9	43.2	17.9	6.0	66446	78102	89	88	9361	0.4	1.3	47.6	49.1	1.5	175736
60656	CHICAGO	29857	12420	19.9	25.8	36.0	13.8	4.5	53538	62461	78	70	8409	0.6	1.1	21.9	70.6	5.8	229234
60657	CHICAGO	61795	42112	15.1	22.6	31.2	15.9	15.3	65546	82019	89	87	13881	0.5	1.2	10.7	44.3	43.3	363599
60659	CHICAGO	21578	13063	25.3	26.0	32.1	11.0	5.6	48625	57652	70	60	5980	1.7	5.0	18.0	64.7	10.6	246897
60660	CHICAGO	25754	22513	31.0	31.2	27.1	7.1	3.6	39635	47352	45	28	7899	4.1	11.0	33.4	38.7	12.8	179333
60661	CHICAGO	61967	3357	16.2	21.5	29.2	17.4	15.8	68340	83219	90	89	1219	0.0	0.0	0.7	76.6	22.6	293325
60706	HARWOOD HEIGHTS	26111	9036	20.1	28.3	35.7	12.1	3.9	51405	60220	75	66	7047	0.4	0.5	10.8	84.8	3.6	243500
60707	ELMWOOD PARK	24438	15630	19.2	27.2	35.4	13.8	4.4	53339	62849	77	70	11110	0.5	1.9	23.1	70.9	3.7	213296
60712	LINCOLNWOOD	41416	4466	11.4	16.6	33.0	17.8	21.1	81010	95062	95	96	4096	0.8	0.6	3.4	53.6	41.6	370713
60714	NILES	27104	11942	19.4	25.7	36.2	13.3	5.4	54339	63376	79	72	9161	0.7	0.6	12.3	78.3	8.2	247844
60803	ALSIP	23978	9260	19.7	28.7	37.7	11.0	3.0	51241	59263	74	66	6347	4.9	5.5	46.3	42.8	0.5	165806
60804	CICERO	13325	23094	26.3	33.9	32.0	6.2	1.6	41649	47001	52	36	13041	1.0	3.7	63.2	31.8	0.4	152900
60805	EVERGREEN PARK	26572	7425	17.3	23.5	37.6	15.2	6.4	59853	70063	84	81	6362	0.6	1.1	51.4	46.0	0.9	171537
60827	RIVERDALE	14843	10351	35.3	28.8	27.9	6.5	1.5	36757	42199	35	19	5565	3.7	22.7	68.8	4.6	0.1	107690
60901	KANKAKEE	19454	13635	32.4	28.7	29.7	6.4	2.8	39727	45228	45	29	8955	11.0	30.9	48.1	8.8	1.2	97089
60911	ASHKUM	22543	598	29.1	28.6	30.4	7.2	4.7	43022	47755	56	42	501	6.0	16.0	56.9	17.2	4.0	121413
60912	BEAVERVILLE	17821	256	30.1	35.9	28.9	4.3	0.8	40207	44605	47	30	216	12.0	31.9	49.5	5.6	0.9	101667
60913	BONFIELD	24346	602	13.0	27.9	41.0	13.3	4.8	59015	65374	84	79	535	4.1	15.3	43.4	33.1	4.1	144572
60914	BOURBONNAIS	25793	8536	19.3	27.9	38.1	10.1	4.6	52149	58462	76	68	6388	14.3	8.5	52.9	22.2	2.1	131640
60915	BRADLEY	20886	4304	24.8	32.9	34.0	6.7	1.6	42221	48802	54	38	3161	3.8	26.5	65.0	4.5	0.2	103618
60917	BUCKINGHAM	23199	154	15.6	26.0	39.6	14.9	3.9	61529	66239	86	83	137	5.1	28.5	53.3	13.1	0.0	105288
60918	BUCKLEY	23750	411	18.3	36.3	37.0	5.6	2.9	46669	51893	65	55	349	7.2	31.2	43.3	16.3	2.0	106836
60919	CABERY	23140	184	20.1	34.8	32.6	9.8	2.7	46141	52361	64	53	148	15.5	26.4	48.0	10.1	0.0	100926
60921	CHATSWORTH	18435	704	31.7	29.1	33.1	5.4	0.7	38515	42069	41	25	526	18.1	49.8	25.5	6.3	0.4	77049
60922	CHEBANSE	19476	937	22.8	32.2	37.1	7.3	0.5	45947	51678	64	52	797	23.5	9.4	48.9	17.6	0.6	114621
60924	CISSNA PARK	19491	740	28.5	31.4	34.6	3.4	2.2	41041	45953	50	34	622	9.8	27.8	48.6	13.0	0.8	107480
60927	CLIFTON	23572	842	21.7	27.9	37.7	10.1	2.6	50265	56392	72	63	681	3.4	11.6	59.0	22.9	3.1	135216
60928	CRESCENT CITY	22110	332	19.3	32.5	41.6	5.1	1.5	47882	52644	68	57	283	6.0	22.6	55.1	15.6	0.7	112364
60929	CULLOM	19362	325	29.5	34.8	30.2	4.6	0.9	38272	41713	40	24	264	22.4	27.3	42.4	8.0	0.0	90455
60930	DANFORTH	19608	347	27.1	34.3	31.4	5.5	1.7	43277	48096	57	43	280	7.1	23.9	51.4	9.6	7.9	112705
60931	DONOVAN	20875	261	22.2	40.2	29.5	5.8	2.3	43054	48503	56	42	215	15.8	31.6	43.3	7.9	1.4	94583
60934	EMINGTON	22900	116	13.8	37.1	40.5	6.0	2.6	48667	50762	70	60	94	13.8	18.1	41.5	24.5	2.1	123333
60935	ESSEX	21340	333	17.1	26.4	45.4	9.6	1.5	54215	61285	79	72	295	18.6	13.6	47.1	20.0	0.7	116898
60936	GIBSON CITY	21360	1928	29.1	35.1	28.0	6.1	1.9	38322	42314	40	24	1483	13.8	30.6	44.0	11.3	0.3	97877
60938	GILMAN	20231	881	28.5	32.5	33.6	3.2	2.3	39936	43925	46	29	695	13.0	23.0	53.2	9.6	1.2	106811
60940	GRANT PARK	24209	1254	17.9	24.4	40.9	13.6	3.1	56580	63531	81	77	1083	5.7	9.3	49.8	33.5	1.7	153427
60941	HERSCHER	21199	799	19.0	28.2	40.1	11.3	1.5	52505	58862	76	68	667	0.8	13.0	63.3	21.9	1.1	132964
60942	HOOPESTON	17856	2564	32.8	35.5	25.8	4.6	1.4	35554	39176	30	14	1917	27.8	45.3	23.4	3.1	0.3	66190
60946	KEMPTON	20703	140	17.1	36.4	33.6	10.0	2.9	47078	52407	66	56	110	11.8	20.9	58.2	9.1	0.0	109483
60948	LODA	27155	636	14.5	29.6	45.8	6.5	3.8	53220	59566	77	70	553	10.7	23.9	40.0	25.1	0.4	121140
60949	LUDLOW	21808	321	20.6	40.5	30.8	6.2	1.9	41834	48512	52	37	263	38.4	23.2	24.7	13.7	0.0	72368
60950	MANTENO	25128	3761	19.8	27.2	37.5	10.6	4.9	52624	58123	76	69	3034	11.5	15.6	41.8	29.1	2.0	132311
60951	MARTINTON	21618	339	21.5	31.9	37.5	6.5	2.7	47708	52818	68	57	284	9.9	18.3	50.7	16.2	4.9	117672
60952	MELVIN	19320	288	27.8	29.2	36.1	6.3	0.7	42671	45000	55	40	244	34.0	43.9	20.1	2.1	0.0	65806
60953	MILFORD	21495	1119	30.5	34.1	28.8	4.4	2.2	38173	42430	40	23	881	21.6	29.6	37.3	9.9	1.6	88333
60954	MOMENCE	20156	2601	23.4	32.2	34.6	7.3	2.5	44036	50086	59	45	2022	9.8	21.9	51.8	15.7	0.8	112234
60955	ONARGA	16582	696	27.9	32.6	33.5	3.9	2.2	39336	43162	44	28	574	17.6	32.4	40.8	7.5	1.7	90000
60957	PAXTON	20340	2228	23.3	37.3	31.6	7.1	0.9	42286	46926	54	38	1805	9.8	37.0	45.8	7.5	0.0	93162
60959	PIPER CITY	21143	437	20.8	39.4	30.4	5.7	3.7	43094	47688	56	42	344	11.3	21.8	59.9	6.4	0.6	104524
60960	RANKIN	17419	484	31.6	38.0	25.8	3.7	0.8	36627	40700	34	18	395	32.9	29.1	30.6	6.3	1.0	73800
60961	REDDICK	23155	326	16.3	27.3	43.3	10.7	2.5	55340	61125	80	74	286	13.3	20.3	48.3	17.5	0.7	112000
60962	ROBERTS	22131	278	21.9	33.5	37.4	6.8	0.4	45753	49167	63	51	233	23.2	22.8	45.9	7.3	0.9	93393
60963	ROSSVILLE	19557	801	29.3	32.5	33.8	3.3	1.1	42353	46666	54	39	640	27.8	34.5	32.5	4.7	0.5	74468
60964	SAINT ANNE	18922	2907	29.7	29.4	31.7	7.4	2.0	41923	47612	53	37	2313	16.0	24.0	41.6	16.6	1.8	102004
60966	SHELDON	19872	752	27.1	36.0	30.2	5.1	1.6	40875	45437	49	33	597	15.6	34.5	41.2	7.9	0.8	89921
60968	THAWVILLE	21973	137	19.7	36.5	35.0	5.8	2.9	45247	50000	62	49	116	8.6	32.8	42.2	13.8	2.6	102381
60970	WATSEKA	20919	3230	32.8	31.5	27.4	4.9	3.4	36361	41075	33	17	2482	12.1	34.7	40.7	12.0	0.5	93922
60973	WELLINGTON	23974	200	21.5	43.0	23.5	5.5	6.5	39567	42931	45	28	164	26.8	29.9	39.0	4.3	0.0	78462
61001	APPLE RIVER	24951	503	19.7	37.8	33.8	5.6	3.2	44474	49296	60	47	414	12.1	18.8	35.8	28.0	5.3	122388
61006	ASHTON	23156	716	17.2	35.6	37.3	7.5	2.4	48031	54409	68	58	557	4.5	21.4	56.4	16.3	1.4	114227
61007	BAILEYVILLE	27545	206	18.0	28.6	40.3	7.8	5.3	52911	59154	77	69	170	8.2	19.4	42.9	25.3	4.1	128704
61008	BELVIDERE	23973	11150	20.1	26.5	37.8	10.0	5.7	53208	60841	77	70	8668	8.1	9.6	56.3	22.4	3.6	128932
61010	BYRON	23942	2687	17.5	24.8	37.9	14.4	5.4	59752	65181	84	81	2151	2.9	5.7	53.0	37.4	1.0	156288
61011	CALEDONIA	31572	1022	9.7	17.8	45.5	16.7	10.3	71083	79106	92	91	936	3.9	3.6	53.9	32.4	6.3	163117
61012	CAPRON	24020	769	14.7	24.3	44.1	10.8	6.1	60360	66605	85	82	641	7.8	4.8	56.2	27.2	4.1	144318
61014	CHADWICK	21164	496	25.2	29.0	37.1	5.7	3.0	46149	48944	64	53	405	11.1	31.6	34.6	14.3	8.4	101458
61015	CHANA	27721	421	7.8	21.6	49.2	17.3	4.0	63980	73396	88	85	369	3.5	12.5	42.3	36.9	4.9	159115
61016	CHERRY VALLEY	30657	1705	10.9	18.2	45.5	19.7	5.8	74199	80692	93	92	1533	3.3	4.6	69.8	21.5	0.9	142243
61018	DAKOTA	22002	396	16.4	35.6	38.6	6.3	3.0	47970	52491	68	58	330	10.9	23.0	43.3	19.4	3.3	109722
61019	DAVIS	26410	1389	15.5	23.7	43.3	13.6	3.9	59429	65618	84	80	1289	2.3	8.5	58.1	29.0	2.1	144372
61020	DAVIS JUNCTION	23800	564	9.0	28.2	47.0	12.1	3.7	59357	67331	84	80	512	13.1	12.3	45.3	26.2	3.1	138014
61021	DIXON	22210	8630	25.5	31.8	32.1	7.6	3.1	43828	48387	58	45	6651	7.9	25.5	49.0	16.0	1.7	106992
61024	DURAND	26064	994	16.8	25.1	43.3	9.9	5.0	56279	64043	81	76	807	2.5	18.6	51.4	25.7	1.9	130540
61025	EAST DUBUQUE	25049	1957	23.2	31.5	35.8	7.0	2.6	46162	51423	64	53	1612	11.0	20.3	47.0	19.5	2.2	117430
61028	ELIZABETH	23135	879	27.3	37.1	25.7	4.8	5.1	39595	43828	45	28	699	10.9	19.2	36.6	23.8	9.6	126096
61030	FORRESTON	21277	954	25.3	34.5	32.6	6.0	1.7	42562	48022	55	40	777	12.4	30.1	46.5	9.4	1.7	95735
	ILLINOIS	27033		22.1	25.9	32.9	11.9	7.3	52039	60941				7.7	12.8	34.0	36.6	8.9	162771
	UNITED STATES	25866		24.7	27.1	30.8	10.9	6.5	48124	56710				10.9	15.0	33.7	30.1	10.4	145905

ZIP CODE #	POST OFFICE NAME	FINANCIAL SERVICES				THE HOME						ENTERTAINMENT						PERSONAL			
						Home Improvements		Furnishings													
		Auto Loan	Home Loan	Invest-ments	Retire-ment Plans	Home Repair	Lawn & Garden	Comput-ers & Hard-ware	Major Appli-ances	TV, Radio, Sound Equip-ment	Furni-ture	Dine out/ Carry out	Sports Equip-ment	Fees & Tickets	Toys & Games	Travel	Cable TV	Apparel & Services	Auto Repairs	Health Insur-ance	Pets & Supplies
60631	CHICAGO	98	113	134	111	111	120	109	108	107	109	135	123	115	139	113	108	133	107	106	117
60632	CHICAGO	77	67	65	66	66	68	73	74	76	77	96	83	70	92	69	72	96	77	68	79
60633	CHICAGO	74	76	80	73	77	85	77	77	79	75	98	87	79	102	78	81	95	76	81	86
60634	CHICAGO	86	95	110	91	92	99	92	91	92	94	116	101	95	119	93	92	115	91	88	99
60636	CHICAGO	58	52	57	48	51	60	55	55	60	57	75	60	56	70	55	63	72	57	62	64
60637	CHICAGO	64	56	76	54	54	63	64	61	70	66	87	70	64	85	63	72	85	65	65	70
60638	CHICAGO	78	87	99	84	86	93	85	84	85	85	107	95	89	111	87	86	105	84	84	92
60639	CHICAGO	77	70	74	68	68	72	76	75	79	80	100	85	74	98	73	76	100	79	71	82
60640	CHICAGO	67	68	128	73	65	74	80	72	84	80	107	86	82	115	81	86	107	77	70	80
60641	CHICAGO	76	82	108	79	78	84	83	80	85	85	108	92	85	113	84	85	108	83	77	88
60643	CHICAGO	99	104	118	100	101	113	102	101	104	104	130	111	107	128	104	106	128	101	104	114
60644	CHICAGO	63	56	66	52	54	64	62	61	68	63	84	68	62	81	61	70	82	63	66	70
60645	CHICAGO	71	79	130	78	76	85	85	79	89	85	112	92	88	122	87	92	113	83	78	86
60646	CHICAGO	112	141	176	135	137	146	130	129	126	130	158	146	140	169	136	128	158	127	122	139
60647	CHICAGO	73	68	105	70	66	72	79	74	83	81	106	86	79	110	77	83	107	79	71	81
60649	CHICAGO	58	53	65	50	51	59	58	56	62	59	78	63	59	76	57	64	76	58	60	64
60651	CHICAGO	67	62	76	59	59	68	67	65	72	69	91	73	68	90	66	73	89	68	67	73
60652	CHICAGO	88	99	109	96	97	102	95	94	93	95	117	107	99	121	96	93	116	93	90	103
60653	CHICAGO	45	38	51	36	37	44	45	43	50	46	62	49	45	59	44	51	60	46	47	49
60655	CHICAGO	103	122	136	120	120	124	115	114	111	114	139	132	122	147	118	110	138	112	107	124
60656	CHICAGO	89	93	107	94	91	99	95	92	93	95	118	107	97	117	94	92	115	94	89	102
60657	CHICAGO	129	125	228	143	119	132	146	130	149	148	189	160	152	198	144	147	188	139	122	145
60659	CHICAGO	74	83	136	82	80	88	89	83	92	89	117	97	92	127	91	95	118	87	80	90
60660	CHICAGO	61	61	116	63	58	67	74	65	78	73	100	79	75	108	74	81	100	72	65	73
60661	CHICAGO	108	103	193	118	97	109	122	108	125	124	158	133	127	166	120	123	157	116	101	121
60706	HARWOOD HEIGHTS	82	92	108	89	90	98	90	89	90	90	112	100	94	116	92	91	111	89	88	97
60707	ELMWOOD PARK	84	95	112	92	93	99	93	91	92	93	116	103	96	119	94	92	115	91	88	99
60712	LINCOLNWOOD	135	181	231	175	176	184	162	161	152	162	191	184	176	204	170	152	192	157	146	172
60714	NILES	86	96	112	94	95	102	94	93	92	94	116	106	97	118	96	93	114	93	91	101
60803	ALSIP	79	88	100	88	86	89	87	85	84	86	105	99	89	108	87	82	104	85	79	92
60804	CICERO	74	64	63	63	63	65	71	71	73	75	92	81	67	89	66	69	93	75	65	76
60805	EVERGREEN PARK	94	109	121	106	108	113	103	103	100	102	125	117	108	131	106	100	124	101	99	113
60827	RIVERDALE	62	58	69	55	56	64	62	61	66	64	83	69	63	81	62	68	81	63	63	69
60901	KANKAKEE	68	69	76	67	68	75	71	70	73	70	90	81	72	92	71	73	88	71	71	79
60911	ASHKUM	101	70	37	67	82	92	70	86	80	69	94	104	59	92	72	84	86	85	102	120
60912	BEAVERVILLE	58	63	66	60	64	71	62	62	65	60	80	69	66	87	64	67	77	60	66	68
60913	BONFIELD	107	100	81	96	104	111	92	100	96	92	117	119	91	120	95	97	112	98	106	127
60914	BOURBONNAIS	93	96	100	98	94	97	96	95	92	96	116	113	95	115	94	88	113	96	87	106
60915	BRADLEY	70	72	75	72	72	77	74	73	73	72	91	85	74	94	73	72	89	73	72	80
60917	BUCKINGHAM	86	104	115	102	102	104	97	96	92	96	116	110	103	123	99	91	116	93	89	104
60918	BUCKLEY	99	72	43	68	83	93	71	86	80	71	95	101	62	91	74	84	87	85	102	117
60919	CABERY	89	82	71	81	85	93	82	86	85	81	104	99	81	105	82	86	99	85	91	100
60921	CHATSWORTH	60	64	65	60	65	71	62	62	65	60	80	70	65	86	64	67	77	61	67	70
60922	CHEBANSE	78	73	62	71	74	80	71	75	73	71	90	87	70	89	71	73	86	74	77	88
60924	CISSNA PARK	73	67	59	64	71	79	65	71	69	64	83	82	63	84	67	71	79	70	78	87
60927	CLIFTON	109	77	42	74	89	100	77	94	88	76	103	112	66	101	79	92	94	92	111	129
60928	CRESCENT CITY	87	76	56	72	81	87	71	79	76	71	92	94	68	93	73	78	87	77	86	103
60929	CULLOM	80	56	29	53	65	73	55	69	64	55	75	83	47	73	58	67	68	68	82	95
60930	DANFORTH	94	65	34	62	76	85	64	80	74	64	87	96	55	85	67	78	79	79	95	111
60931	DONOVAN	95	73	47	69	82	91	71	84	80	70	95	100	65	96	74	84	88	83	98	112
60934	EMINGTON	91	81	62	77	85	92	75	83	79	75	96	99	73	99	77	81	92	81	90	107
60935	ESSEX	94	84	64	80	89	95	78	86	82	78	100	102	76	102	80	84	95	84	93	111
60936	GIBSON CITY	77	64	49	61	68	78	66	72	72	64	86	82	62	86	67	75	80	71	82	87
60938	GILMAN	78	61	43	60	66	77	66	72	72	63	86	81	60	83	65	75	79	71	83	86
60940	GRANT PARK	106	95	72	90	100	107	87	97	93	87	113	115	86	115	90	95	107	94	105	125
60941	HERSCHER	88	87	79	84	90	95	81	86	83	81	102	101	82	106	83	83	99	84	88	104
60942	HOOPESTON	66	58	49	57	61	69	60	63	63	58	77	72	57	76	60	65	72	63	70	75
60946	KEMPTON	96	77	55	76	84	94	79	88	86	78	103	102	74	102	79	88	96	86	98	109
60948	LODA	109	88	67	83	98	112	84	100	93	87	112	109	79	101	89	98	103	97	118	126
60949	LUDLOW	81	69	53	68	73	82	70	75	75	69	90	87	67	90	70	76	85	74	82	91
60950	MANTENO	95	94	86	91	94	101	88	93	88	91	109	104	87	104	89	87	105	91	94	107
60951	MARTINTON	96	78	52	74	85	93	74	85	81	73	97	102	69	97	76	84	90	83	96	113
60952	MELVIN	88	61	32	58	71	80	60	75	70	60	82	90	52	80	63	73	74	74	89	104
60953	MILFORD	80	64	47	61	71	80	66	74	73	64	87	85	61	87	67	76	81	73	86	93
60954	MOMENCE	83	73	60	68	76	86	73	78	79	71	96	89	71	96	74	82	90	77	88	95
60955	ONARGA	76	63	47	60	64	70	64	71	68	66	83	78	58	78	62	68	80	71	73	81
60957	PAXTON	78	67	54	66	71	80	68	73	73	67	88	84	66	89	69	75	83	72	81	88
60959	PIPER CITY	91	67	41	64	74	87	71	81	80	68	94	93	62	90	71	85	86	81	97	103
60960	RANKIN	73	57	38	55	63	72	59	66	65	57	78	77	54	75	60	68	72	66	77	84
60961	REDDICK	90	91	82	87	93	98	84	89	85	84	105	104	85	109	86	86	102	86	91	107
60962	ROBERTS	93	65	34	61	76	85	64	79	74	63	86	95	55	85	66	77	79	78	94	110
60963	ROSSVILLE	64	65	62	61	66	73	63	64	65	61	80	73	64	85	65	67	77	63	69	75
60964	SAINT ANNE	78	69	61	66	71	79	69	73	74	69	90	83	67	87	69	76	85	73	80	88
60966	SHELDON	87	65	41	62	72	82	65	76	74	65	88	89	59	85	66	77	81	75	88	99
60968	THAWVILLE	97	69	38	65	80	90	68	83	78	67	91	99	59	89	70	81	83	82	99	115
60970	WATSEKA	76	66	54	62	70	79	67	72	73	65	87	83	64	87	68	76	82	72	82	88
60973	WELLINGTON	102	71	37	68	83	93	71	87	81	70	95	105	60	94	73	85	87	86	104	122
61001	APPLE RIVER	91	75	54	69	82	91	70	82	77	70	93	96	66	93	74	81	87	80	93	109
61006	ASHTON	96	84	65	81	88	97	81	89	86	80	105	104	79	105	82	88	99	87	96	110
61007	BAILEYVILLE	117	108	87	104	114	121	100	109	104	100	127	130	99	131	103	106	122	106	116	138
61008	BELVIDERE	97	94	86	92	96	102	92	95	93	91	115	111	91	117	92	94	111	94	97	112
61010	BYRON	93	105	108	107	102	101	99	97	92	99	117	115	101	119	98	88	115	96	86	107
61011	CALEDONIA	129	143	137	147	139	137	129	130	121	133	153	152	133	154	128	115	150	126	116	146
61012	CAPRON	106	102	85	98	106	111	93	101	96	93	118	120	93	121	96	97	113	98	105	126
61014	CHADWICK	86	75	55	71	79	86	70	78	75	70	91	93	68	92	72	77	86	77	86	101
61015	CHANA	117	110	91	106	115	121	101	110	105	101	128	131	101	132	104	106	123	107	115	138
61016	CHERRY VALLEY	111	131	135	131	129	128	118	119	111	118	139	140	124	147	120	108	138	115	108	133
61018	DAKOTA	90	81	62	77	85	91	75	82	79	75	96	98	73	98	77	81	91	80	89	106
61019	DAVIS	106	96	81	92	102	112	89	99	94	91	115	111	88	110	93	98	109	97	110	123
61020	DAVIS JUNCTION	111	100	77	95	105	112	92	102	97	92	118	121	90	121	95	100	113	99	109	131
61021	DIXON	72	72	70	70	73	79	71	73	73	69	89	84	72	93	72	74	86	72	76	84
61024	DURAND	99	101	94	101	102	108	97	100	96	95	118	115	98	121	97	95	114	97	99	114
61025	EAST DUBUQUE	95	89	74	84	93	100	83	90	88	82	107	105	83	112	86	90	103	87	97	112
61028	ELIZABETH	88	66	42	62	74	86	68	79	77	66	91	91	60	88	70	82	83	78	94	102
61030	FORRESTON	95	70	41	65	79	88	68	81	77	68	91	97	60	90	70	81	84	80	95	111
	ILLINOIS	98	100	111	99	99	106	100	99	101	100	126	115	102	127	100	100	123	100	98	112
	UNITED STATES	100	100	100	100	100	100	100	100	100	100	100	100	100	100	100	100	100	100	100	100

ILLINOIS

A 61031-61320

POPULATION CHANGE

#	POST OFFICE NAME	COUNTY FIPS CODE	POPULATION 2000	2004	2009	% Rate	State Centile	HOUSEHOLDS 2000	2004	2009	% Annual Rate 2000-2004	2004 Average HH Size	FAMILIES 2000	2004	% Annual Rate 2000-2004
61031	FRANKLIN GROVE	103	1871	1862	1861	-0.1	36	657	670	683	0.5	2.59	473	476	0.2
61032	FREEPORT	177	33093	32702	32444	-0.3	26	13814	13845	13896	0.1	2.31	8909	8770	-0.4
61036	GALENA	085	6268	6391	6507	0.5	64	2670	2795	2920	1.1	2.25	1746	1802	0.8
61038	GARDEN PRAIRIE	007	1309	1477	1679	2.9	94	470	538	618	3.2	2.72	383	436	3.1
61039	GERMAN VALLEY	177	867	854	848	-0.4	22	319	321	323	0.2	2.66	252	251	-0.1
61041	HANOVER	085	1322	1326	1339	0.1	45	601	618	639	0.7	2.15	386	388	0.1
61042	HARMON	103	523	505	500	-0.8	6	195	193	195	-0.2	2.62	153	150	-0.5
61044	KENT	177	206	227	239	2.3	91	70	79	85	2.9	2.68	53	59	2.6
61046	LANARK	015	2864	2877	2880	0.1	47	1172	1195	1209	0.5	2.39	852	857	0.1
61047	LEAF RIVER	141	1720	1742	1780	0.3	58	658	677	701	0.7	2.57	511	517	0.3
61048	LENA	177	4512	4502	4482	-0.1	39	1706	1731	1745	0.3	2.58	1256	1255	0.0
61049	LINDENWOOD	141	447	492	524	2.3	91	168	188	203	2.7	2.62	128	141	2.3
61050	MC CONNELL	177	464	468	467	0.2	52	178	183	186	0.7	2.56	142	144	0.3
61051	MILLEDGEVILLE	015	1623	1602	1591	-0.3	24	663	664	667	0.0	2.41	478	471	-0.4
61052	MONROE CENTER	141	1562	1657	1730	1.4	83	558	600	634	1.7	2.76	446	474	1.4
61053	MOUNT CARROLL	015	3172	3221	3235	0.4	61	1260	1298	1318	0.7	2.41	875	887	0.3
61054	MOUNT MORRIS	141	4175	4151	4213	-0.1	34	1732	1751	1801	0.3	2.33	1174	1167	-0.1
61060	ORANGEVILLE	177	1488	1499	1497	0.2	51	576	591	598	0.6	2.54	428	432	0.2
61061	OREGON	141	7534	7658	7878	0.4	61	2987	3079	3206	0.7	2.40	2108	2138	0.3
61062	PEARL CITY	177	2051	2116	2140	0.7	73	745	784	805	1.2	2.66	592	615	0.9
61063	PECATONICA	201	4068	4385	4622	1.8	87	1576	1713	1817	2.0	2.56	1209	1293	1.6
61064	POLO	141	4036	3955	4004	-0.5	17	1588	1584	1625	-0.1	2.53	1115	1093	-0.5
61065	POPLAR GROVE	007	7044	8216	9489	3.7	96	2238	2627	3048	3.8	3.12	1888	2192	3.6
61067	RIDOTT	177	915	897	885	-0.5	17	355	354	354	-0.1	2.53	275	270	-0.4
61068	ROCHELLE	141	14693	14862	15197	0.3	56	5496	5650	5850	0.7	2.61	3879	3920	0.3
61070	ROCK CITY	177	1200	1227	1235	0.5	66	429	447	456	1.0	2.74	330	339	0.6
61071	ROCK FALLS	195	14895	14627	14396	-0.4	18	5936	5942	5950	0.0	2.44	4157	4104	-0.3
61072	ROCKTON	201	8993	9608	10092	1.6	85	3224	3435	3607	1.5	2.77	2536	2664	1.2
61073	ROSCOE	201	15851	17303	18440	2.1	89	5399	5921	6334	2.2	2.92	4571	4954	1.9
61074	SAVANNA	015	4977	4835	4792	-0.7	10	2118	2092	2097	-0.3	2.26	1313	1272	-0.7
61075	SCALES MOUND	085	1003	1035	1067	0.7	73	383	407	431	1.4	2.54	292	306	1.1
61078	SHANNON	015	1404	1464	1491	1.0	78	532	566	586	1.5	2.53	393	412	1.1
61080	SOUTH BELOIT	201	8585	8921	9280	0.9	76	3384	3524	3676	1.0	2.51	2354	2403	0.5
61081	STERLING	195	23052	23059	22916	0.0	42	8978	9117	9198	0.4	2.48	6194	6193	0.0
61084	STILLMAN VALLEY	141	3206	3467	3662	1.9	87	1144	1255	1341	2.2	2.75	923	1002	2.0
61085	STOCKTON	085	3622	3682	3760	0.4	62	1485	1542	1610	0.9	2.35	1033	1056	0.5
61087	WARREN	085	1878	1846	1854	-0.4	19	781	785	809	0.1	2.35	525	518	-0.3
61088	WINNEBAGO	201	4879	5170	5401	1.4	83	1699	1805	1890	1.4	2.86	1398	1467	1.1
61089	WINSLOW	177	908	909	904	0.0	43	323	329	331	0.4	2.76	246	247	0.1
61101	ROCKFORD	201	23904	24337	25097	0.4	63	8296	8482	8779	0.5	2.73	5761	5785	0.1
61102	ROCKFORD	201	20211	19727	20035	-0.6	13	6890	6733	6849	-0.5	2.88	5038	4841	-0.9
61103	ROCKFORD	201	24128	24139	24736	0.0	42	10184	10191	10464	0.0	2.28	5869	5757	-0.5
61104	ROCKFORD	201	19759	19704	20138	-0.1	38	7983	7916	8074	-0.2	2.47	4357	4200	-0.9
61107	ROCKFORD	201	30765	31572	32693	0.6	69	12732	13105	13607	0.7	2.34	8207	8269	0.2
61108	ROCKFORD	201	27572	28280	29276	0.6	69	11472	11830	12292	0.7	2.34	7542	7617	0.2
61109	ROCKFORD	201	26262	27851	29478	1.4	83	10526	11163	11833	1.4	2.49	7069	7413	1.1
61111	LOVES PARK	201	20453	21609	22666	1.3	82	8318	8802	9271	1.3	2.45	5538	5763	0.9
61112	ROCKFORD	201	13	15	17	3.4	95	4	5	5	5.4	3.00	3	3	0.1
61114	ROCKFORD	201	15233	16264	17197	1.6	85	5890	6315	6699	1.7	2.50	4270	4498	1.2
61115	MACHESNEY PARK	201	20242	20458	21001	0.3	54	7612	7742	7976	0.4	2.63	5748	5757	0.0
61201	ROCK ISLAND	161	39241	38426	37598	-0.5	16	15998	15888	15753	-0.2	2.26	9406	9148	-0.7
61230	ALBANY	195	1195	1203	1197	0.2	50	465	478	483	0.7	2.52	354	359	0.3
61231	ALEDO	131	5683	5670	5677	-0.1	39	2253	2286	2324	0.3	2.39	1592	1593	0.0
61234	ANNAWAN	073	1226	1209	1190	-0.3	23	490	491	491	0.1	2.41	350	345	-0.3
61235	ATKINSON	073	1488	1468	1446	-0.3	24	612	616	617	0.2	2.32	428	424	-0.2
61238	CAMBRIDGE	073	3600	3581	3540	-0.1	35	1394	1411	1415	0.3	2.47	1030	1027	-0.1
61240	COAL VALLEY	161	5976	6145	6141	0.7	71	2155	2262	2299	1.2	2.65	1701	1767	0.9
61241	COLONA	073	7183	7073	6963	-0.4	21	2699	2715	2722	0.1	2.61	2086	2075	-0.1
61242	CORDOVA	161	1201	1203	1185	0.0	43	461	470	470	0.5	2.53	345	346	0.1
61243	DEER GROVE	195	266	257	251	-0.8	7	93	92	91	-0.3	2.79	77	75	-0.6
61244	EAST MOLINE	161	24099	23778	23315	-0.3	24	10010	9996	9926	0.0	2.34	6407	6286	-0.5
61250	ERIE	195	2676	2737	2749	0.5	67	998	1042	1066	1.0	2.62	766	792	0.8
61251	FENTON	195	377	389	392	0.7	73	137	144	148	1.2	2.70	110	114	0.8
61252	FULTON	195	5772	5729	5663	-0.2	32	2280	2304	2315	0.3	2.43	1635	1629	-0.1
61254	GENESEO	073	11102	11076	10968	-0.1	38	4260	4309	4325	0.3	2.53	3153	3157	0.0
61256	HAMPTON	161	1279	1286	1276	0.1	48	483	496	501	0.6	2.57	382	385	0.2
61257	HILLSDALE	161	1350	1333	1306	-0.3	25	500	500	495	0.0	2.63	377	372	-0.3
61259	ILLINOIS CITY	161	1427	1495	1505	1.1	79	513	544	554	1.4	2.74	425	446	1.1
61260	JOY	131	844	836	835	-0.2	29	339	341	346	0.1	2.45	254	252	-0.2
61261	LYNDON	195	880	874	864	-0.2	33	344	346	348	0.1	2.53	260	258	-0.2
61262	LYNN CENTER	073	1209	1154	1124	-1.1	3	419	407	403	-0.7	2.84	345	331	-1.0
61263	MATHERVILLE	131	784	793	798	0.3	56	293	299	304	0.5	2.65	221	223	0.2
61264	MILAN	161	12811	12645	12399	-0.3	24	4825	4853	4830	0.1	2.39	3381	3354	-0.2
61265	MOLINE	161	45389	43993	42757	-0.7	8	19149	18790	18497	-0.4	2.32	12054	11581	-0.9
61270	MORRISON	195	7729	7639	7549	-0.3	26	2986	2999	3009	0.1	2.42	2153	2132	-0.2
61272	NEW BOSTON	131	1508	1525	1538	0.3	55	616	633	648	0.6	2.41	434	440	0.3
61273	ORION	073	3252	3221	3187	-0.2	29	1250	1262	1268	0.2	2.52	957	954	-0.1
61274	OSCO	073	416	433	438	1.0	77	149	158	163	1.4	2.74	121	127	1.2
61275	PORT BYRON	161	4631	4758	4743	0.6	70	1788	1866	1887	1.0	2.54	1347	1387	0.7
61277	PROPHETSTOWN	195	3744	3605	3529	-0.9	5	1439	1411	1404	-0.5	2.44	1044	1009	-0.8
61279	REYNOLDS	161	990	975	958	-0.4	21	396	396	395	0.0	2.46	306	303	-0.2
61281	SHERRARD	131	2611	2629	2634	0.2	50	956	978	995	0.6	2.69	774	785	0.3
61282	SILVIS	161	8486	8500	8390	0.0	43	3495	3576	3591	0.5	2.35	2282	2291	0.1
61283	TAMPICO	011	1674	1615	1584	-0.8	6	590	578	575	-0.5	2.79	445	430	-0.8
61284	TAYLOR RIDGE	161	3527	3496	3429	-0.2	30	1327	1342	1338	0.3	2.60	1065	1067	0.0
61285	THOMSON	015	1729	1752	1761	0.3	58	703	727	740	0.8	2.41	512	520	0.4
61301	LA SALLE	099	10528	10515	10646	0.0	40	4457	4498	4604	0.2	2.30	2721	2694	-0.2
61310	AMBOY	103	4241	4269	4280	0.2	50	1608	1646	1678	0.6	2.53	1141	1148	0.1
61311	ANCONA	105	475	461	461	-0.7	9	182	180	183	-0.3	2.56	139	137	-0.3
61312	ARLINGTON	011	1074	1069	1069	-0.1	36	421	426	432	0.3	2.51	311	310	-0.1
61313	BLACKSTONE	105	231	229	230	-0.2	31	89	90	92	0.3	2.46	72	73	0.3
61314	BUDA	011	926	984	1019	1.4	84	359	386	405	1.7	2.55	269	285	1.4
61318	COMPTON	103	695	718	727	0.8	73	263	276	284	1.1	2.60	203	211	0.9
61319	CORNELL	105	730	741	750	0.4	60	278	287	295	0.8	2.58	203	207	0.5
61320	DALZELL	011	949	953	956	0.1	47	369	376	383	0.4	2.51	271	273	0.2
	ILLINOIS					0.7					0.9	2.61			0.6
	UNITED STATES					1.2					1.3	2.58			1.1

# ZIP CODE	POST OFFICE NAME	RACE (%) White 2000	White 2004	Black 2000	Black 2004	Asian/Pacific 2000	Asian/Pacific 2004	% Hispanic Origin 2000	% Hispanic Origin 2004	2004 AGE DISTRIBUTION (%) 0-4	5-9	10-14	15-19	20-24	25-44	45-64	65-84	85+	18+	MEDIAN AGE 2004	% 2004 Males	% 2004 Females
61031	FRANKLIN GROVE	98.1	98.1	0.5	0.5	0.3	0.3	1.4	1.5	6.1	6.2	7.3	7.8	6.9	24.1	23.2	13.1	5.5	75.5	39.3	48.1	51.9
61032	FREEPORT	84.8	83.3	11.3	12.2	1.0	1.2	1.8	2.2	6.4	6.1	6.6	6.6	6.6	25.6	25.1	14.3	2.8	76.9	39.8	47.5	52.5
61036	GALENA	98.1	97.8	0.3	0.3	0.2	0.3	3.2	3.9	5.2	5.5	5.6	5.3	5.4	23.1	30.6	16.7	2.5	80.3	44.8	49.9	50.1
61038	GARDEN PRAIRIE	96.3	95.4	0.5	0.6	0.5	0.7	4.1	5.2	5.8	6.3	8.1	6.8	5.4	25.2	30.8	10.0	1.6	75.4	40.7	49.9	50.1
61039	GERMAN VALLEY	99.2	99.1	0.0	0.0	0.5	0.6	1.0	1.4	4.7	5.5	8.6	7.9	5.7	27.8	26.1	12.2	1.6	76.5	39.3	50.6	49.4
61041	HANOVER	98.0	97.8	0.2	0.2	0.2	0.2	1.3	1.6	5.5	5.3	5.4	6.3	5.6	22.3	30.0	17.3	2.4	80.0	44.8	49.6	50.4
61042	HARMON	97.7	97.6	0.4	0.4	0.0	0.0	3.1	3.2	5.7	6.1	7.7	6.3	5.5	24.8	29.7	12.7	1.4	76.4	41.5	51.3	48.7
61044	KENT	99.0	99.6	0.0	0.0	0.0	0.0	1.0	0.9	5.7	6.6	7.9	6.6	5.3	24.7	23.8	13.7	5.7	74.9	40.7	49.3	50.7
61046	LANARK	97.9	97.9	0.1	0.1	0.7	0.7	0.5	0.6	4.8	5.2	6.8	6.7	5.6	24.1	27.7	17.0	2.2	78.9	43.2	50.9	49.1
61047	LEAF RIVER	98.4	98.2	0.5	0.6	0.1	0.2	0.9	1.3	5.5	6.7	8.0	7.5	4.0	27.2	28.1	12.2	0.8	74.9	40.1	50.4	49.6
61048	LENA	98.8	98.6	0.2	0.2	0.1	0.1	1.1	1.3	5.7	6.0	7.6	7.4	6.4	23.8	26.3	14.2	2.7	76.1	40.4	49.3	50.7
61049	LINDENWOOD	96.9	96.1	0.2	0.4	0.2	0.2	3.1	4.1	6.7	7.3	8.7	6.9	5.1	28.9	25.8	9.4	1.2	73.2	37.5	51.6	48.4
61050	MC CONNELL	98.9	98.7	0.2	0.2	0.2	0.2	0.9	1.1	5.6	6.0	7.5	6.8	5.6	25.9	28.6	13.3	0.9	77.1	40.3	51.5	48.5
61051	MILLEDGEVILLE	97.6	97.6	0.1	0.1	0.3	0.3	1.5	1.6	5.7	6.1	7.1	6.8	6.5	26.0	26.5	13.2	2.2	77.0	39.6	48.9	51.1
61052	MONROE CENTER	97.3	96.4	0.1	0.1	0.1	0.2	3.2	4.3	7.0	7.4	8.7	6.9	5.4	31.0	23.6	8.8	1.2	72.6	35.9	50.1	49.9
61053	MOUNT CARROLL	98.1	98.0	0.2	0.2	0.2	0.2	1.4	1.4	6.6	6.6	6.5	6.0	5.4	23.8	25.7	16.2	3.3	76.8	41.7	49.3	50.7
61054	MOUNT MORRIS	97.3	96.7	0.1	0.1	0.4	0.5	2.4	3.1	6.7	6.7	6.7	6.1	5.7	25.3	25.1	14.6	3.1	76.2	39.9	48.7	51.3
61060	ORANGEVILLE	98.8	98.5	0.3	0.4	0.1	0.1	0.8	1.0	5.1	8.3	7.9	6.7	5.3	26.8	26.8	11.7	1.5	74.4	38.0	50.2	49.8
61061	OREGON	97.0	96.5	0.6	0.6	0.5	0.6	1.8	2.4	5.3	5.7	7.0	6.5	5.9	24.9	27.5	14.7	2.5	77.7	41.8	49.6	50.4
61062	PEARL CITY	98.6	98.5	0.3	0.4	0.2	0.1	0.6	0.6	6.8	7.2	7.8	6.5	5.7	26.4	26.2	11.2	2.2	74.1	38.8	49.7	50.3
61063	PECATONICA	98.4	97.9	0.3	0.3	0.2	0.2	0.8	1.1	6.2	6.6	7.2	6.7	6.0	25.8	28.0	12.0	1.6	75.8	40.3	49.5	50.5
61064	POLO	98.4	98.1	0.1	0.1	0.3	0.4	1.6	2.1	5.6	5.7	7.3	7.4	6.3	24.1	27.0	13.7	3.0	76.7	41.1	49.2	50.8
61065	POPLAR GROVE	95.6	94.6	0.9	1.0	0.4	0.5	4.7	6.1	8.9	8.7	9.3	7.8	6.2	29.1	21.8	7.5	0.7	68.2	32.7	50.5	49.5
61067	RIDOTT	98.1	97.9	0.3	0.3	0.3	0.3	0.9	1.1	5.2	6.1	8.4	7.5	4.7	25.4	28.3	12.8	1.6	75.6	40.7	50.6	49.4
61068	ROCHELLE	89.4	87.4	0.9	0.9	0.7	0.8	16.8	20.4	7.6	7.4	7.8	7.3	7.2	28.0	22.5	10.5	1.6	72.6	34.5	50.0	50.0
61070	ROCK CITY	98.0	97.6	0.2	0.2	0.6	0.7	0.7	0.7	6.0	6.9	9.0	7.9	3.9	26.6	26.1	12.0	1.8	72.8	38.6	50.0	50.0
61071	ROCK FALLS	93.0	91.6	0.8	0.9	0.2	0.3	9.7	11.9	6.9	6.4	6.6	6.4	6.4	26.0	25.7	14.0	1.6	76.3	38.7	48.6	51.4
61072	ROCKTON	96.9	96.2	0.8	1.0	0.8	0.9	1.9	2.5	6.4	7.0	8.4	8.1	5.7	26.8	27.5	9.1	1.0	72.9	38.1	50.0	50.0
61073	ROSCOE	96.4	95.4	1.1	1.4	1.0	1.2	1.8	2.5	6.8	7.5	8.6	7.6	5.5	27.5	29.2	6.8	0.5	72.2	37.5	50.3	49.7
61074	SAVANNA	95.0	94.8	1.3	1.3	0.3	0.3	4.3	4.4	5.8	5.7	6.6	6.0	5.9	23.4	26.3	16.8	3.5	78.0	42.5	48.6	51.4
61075	SCALES MOUND	98.7	98.6	0.3	0.3	0.3	0.3	1.2	1.6	4.6	5.4	6.6	6.5	5.1	21.4	30.0	18.7	1.8	79.0	45.3	52.7	47.3
61078	SHANNON	97.4	97.3	0.3	0.3	1.1	1.1	1.0	1.0	4.7	5.3	6.2	6.4	4.8	21.4	30.1	18.9	2.3	79.1	45.8	50.4	49.6
61080	SOUTH BELOIT	90.0	87.8	3.5	4.1	0.8	0.9	6.9	8.8	7.3	7.3	7.6	6.4	6.3	30.0	23.6	10.3	1.1	73.9	35.8	50.5	49.5
61081	STERLING	87.4	85.5	1.8	1.9	0.8	1.0	15.5	18.3	6.8	6.7	7.0	6.6	6.8	26.1	24.4	13.1	2.5	75.6	38.2	48.7	51.3
61084	STILLMAN VALLEY	97.8	97.5	0.3	0.3	0.4	0.5	0.8	1.0	5.3	7.4	9.4	7.3	4.7	26.6	28.5	9.8	1.1	72.8	38.5	50.5	49.5
61085	STOCKTON	99.1	99.0	0.1	0.1	0.1	0.1	0.6	0.8	6.0	6.1	7.6	5.8	4.5	25.4	25.4	16.8	2.4	76.3	41.6	49.5	50.5
61087	WARREN	99.3	99.4	0.2	0.2	0.0	0.0	1.1	1.3	5.3	5.7	6.8	5.9	6.3	24.4	26.2	16.6	2.8	78.6	41.8	49.2	50.8
61088	WINNEBAGO	97.8	97.3	1.1	1.3	0.4	0.5	1.4	1.8	6.5	7.4	8.6	7.5	5.2	28.3	26.2	9.3	1.0	72.7	37.6	49.7	50.3
61089	WINSLOW	98.2	98.1	0.1	0.2	0.2	0.2	1.3	1.3	6.2	6.5	9.8	7.3	5.6	28.1	24.3	11.3	1.0	72.3	37.1	50.8	49.2
61101	ROCKFORD	56.7	53.9	35.3	36.9	0.4	0.4	9.2	10.7	7.9	7.8	8.5	8.2	7.7	27.1	21.4	9.8	1.6	70.8	32.5	48.3	51.7
61102	ROCKFORD	48.1	46.6	37.8	38.1	0.4	0.4	18.9	20.7	8.6	8.3	8.7	7.7	7.1	27.4	21.4	9.6	1.2	69.8	32.5	50.0	50.0
61103	ROCKFORD	79.8	77.1	14.0	15.6	0.8	1.0	6.3	7.8	7.1	6.8	7.1	6.9	6.5	28.1	22.6	11.9	3.1	74.9	36.6	47.2	52.8
61104	ROCKFORD	70.0	66.2	14.2	15.5	4.2	4.7	16.5	19.8	9.8	8.1	7.6	7.2	8.1	32.1	18.9	7.1	1.1	70.3	30.4	50.2	49.8
61107	ROCKFORD	89.5	87.3	4.4	5.3	2.4	2.9	5.7	7.2	5.9	5.9	6.1	6.4	6.1	25.6	25.9	15.2	3.0	78.5	40.8	48.2	51.8
61108	ROCKFORD	87.6	85.2	5.3	6.1	2.4	2.8	6.5	8.2	6.6	6.3	5.8	5.6	5.7	27.2	24.8	15.4	2.7	77.9	40.3	48.1	51.9
61109	ROCKFORD	83.4	80.5	8.0	9.1	3.1	3.7	7.5	9.4	7.6	7.1	7.0	6.2	7.4	30.4	24.7	9.3	0.6	74.7	34.6	49.8	50.2
61111	LOVES PARK	93.2	91.5	2.2	2.8	1.7	2.2	3.1	4.1	7.0	6.8	7.4	6.4	6.3	31.8	23.2	10.2	1.0	74.9	35.6	48.8	51.3
61112	ROCKFORD	92.3	100.0	0.0	0.0	0.0	0.0	0.0	6.7	6.7	6.7	0.0	0.0	6.7	33.3	46.7	0.0	0.0	86.7	43.8	46.7	53.3
61114	ROCKFORD	88.9	86.5	4.8	5.7	3.8	4.7	2.7	3.5	5.8	5.9	6.9	6.6	5.3	22.1	29.7	13.7	3.9	77.1	43.2	47.2	52.8
61115	MACHESNEY PARK	95.3	94.1	1.4	1.7	1.0	1.2	2.9	3.8	6.6	6.8	7.7	6.9	5.9	29.9	26.1	9.4	0.7	74.7	36.9	49.7	50.3
61201	ROCK ISLAND	76.8	75.1	17.5	18.4	0.8	1.0	5.9	7.1	6.3	5.9	6.0	7.8	9.0	25.1	23.7	13.3	3.0	78.3	37.2	47.5	52.5
61230	ALBANY	98.7	98.3	0.5	0.6	0.1	0.1	0.8	1.1	6.4	6.7	7.6	6.7	4.8	26.4	27.1	12.6	1.7	75.3	39.7	49.2	50.8
61231	ALEDO	98.3	98.3	0.4	0.4	0.3	0.3	0.9	0.9	5.7	5.7	6.4	6.2	5.8	24.1	26.4	15.6	4.1	78.3	42.4	48.0	52.0
61234	ANNAWAN	99.5	99.3	0.1	0.1	0.0	0.1	1.3	1.5	6.8	6.9	7.0	6.6	5.9	23.2	24.1	16.5	3.1	75.4	40.7	47.6	52.4
61235	ATKINSON	98.6	98.4	0.3	0.3	0.1	0.1	1.2	1.5	5.7	5.9	6.7	6.3	5.8	24.7	24.9	16.4	3.7	77.7	41.8	49.2	50.8
61238	CAMBRIDGE	98.4	98.2	0.5	0.5	0.3	0.4	0.6	0.8	5.4	5.6	6.8	7.1	7.1	25.9	26.9	13.0	2.2	77.9	39.8	50.9	49.1
61240	COAL VALLEY	97.0	96.4	1.0	1.2	0.4	0.5	2.5	3.1	5.7	6.3	6.8	7.3	5.5	25.9	30.5	10.7	1.2	76.3	40.0	50.4	49.6
61241	COLONA	97.1	96.5	0.3	0.4	0.2	0.2	3.6	4.4	6.4	6.6	7.5	6.6	6.3	28.7	27.6	9.6	0.7	75.4	37.2	50.2	49.8
61242	CORDOVA	97.3	96.7	0.3	0.3	0.3	0.3	1.9	2.5	5.5	6.0	7.0	6.7	5.2	23.4	30.8	14.2	1.3	76.6	42.7	52.0	48.1
61243	DEER GROVE	96.6	95.7	0.4	0.4	0.0	0.0	3.0	3.9	10.5	9.7	8.2	5.8	4.7	28.8	21.0	10.5	0.8	67.7	32.1	49.8	50.2
61244	EAST MOLINE	82.5	80.2	6.5	6.9	1.9	2.3	13.3	15.9	6.9	6.4	6.5	6.6	7.2	25.8	24.5	13.8	2.3	76.4	38.0	48.2	51.8
61250	ERIE	98.4	98.1	0.2	0.2	0.1	0.1	1.1	1.4	6.0	6.4	7.4	6.5	6.3	25.3	27.6	12.7	1.8	76.2	40.2	49.1	50.9
61251	FENTON	98.7	98.5	0.3	0.3	0.0	0.0	1.1	1.3	5.9	6.4	8.0	5.9	5.7	24.9	30.6	11.3	1.3	75.8	40.9	50.1	49.9
61252	FULTON	98.1	97.8	0.5	0.5	0.4	0.5	1.1	1.5	6.0	5.9	6.2	6.7	6.4	24.7	26.7	14.4	3.0	77.8	41.3	50.1	49.9
61254	GENESEO	98.6	98.3	0.2	0.3	0.3	0.4	1.2	1.5	5.6	6.3	7.3	7.2	5.0	23.7	28.8	13.3	2.9	76.1	41.9	49.0	51.0
61256	HAMPTON	95.2	94.0	0.6	0.7	0.1	0.1	5.1	6.5	5.4	5.9	6.1	6.5	5.7	24.5	33.2	11.8	0.9	78.2	42.1	49.0	51.0
61257	HILLSDALE	96.2	95.5	0.6	0.6	0.4	0.5	2.2	2.8	6.1	6.3	7.6	7.4	5.9	27.7	28.4	9.6	1.1	75.5	38.9	49.3	50.7
61259	ILLINOIS CITY	98.4	98.1	0.1	0.2	0.1	0.1	1.6	2.1	5.8	6.6	8.0	6.5	4.3	28.2	28.8	10.6	1.2	75.3	40.7	50.8	49.2
61260	JOY	99.1	99.0	0.0	0.0	0.1	0.1	0.6	0.7	6.6	6.7	6.9	5.5	6.0	27.2	26.3	13.3	1.6	76.4	38.7	50.5	49.5
61261	LYNDON	96.6	95.8	0.1	0.1	0.3	0.3	1.5	2.1	6.2	7.0	7.4	5.7	5.0	24.8	30.8	11.7	1.4	75.7	40.3	51.4	48.6
61262	LYNN CENTER	98.4	98.1	0.2	0.2	0.4	0.5	1.2	1.4	4.9	6.2	8.3	6.4	5.5	23.0	30.8	13.6	1.4	76.8	42.5	50.7	49.3
61263	MATHERVILLE	98.5	98.4	0.0	0.0	0.3	0.3	0.9	1.0	9.8	6.7	7.4	6.9	6.1	29.9	21.9	9.7	1.5	71.0	33.7	48.9	51.1
61264	MILAN	88.8	87.5	8.2	8.9	0.3	0.4	3.1	3.8	6.0	6.1	6.1	5.8	6.3	29.6	27.0	11.7	1.5	78.3	38.6	53.1	46.9
61265	MOLINE	88.6	86.7	3.0	3.3	1.4	1.7	11.7	13.9	6.5	6.2	6.5	6.4	6.9	26.6	25.6	13.2	2.3	77.1	38.6	47.9	52.1
61270	MORRISON	98.1	97.7	0.5	0.5	0.1	0.2	1.9	2.5	5.4	5.8	7.0	6.9	6.5	24.7	27.0	13.6	3.2	77.9	41.0	49.5	50.5
61272	NEW BOSTON	99.1	99.2	0.1	0.1	0.0	0.0	0.8	0.8	5.6	5.6	5.6	6.3	7.5	24.7	27.7	15.5	1.4	79.4	41.6	51.7	48.3
61273	ORION	98.9	98.6	0.2	0.3	0.1	0.2	1.5	1.8	5.5	5.8	7.0	7.2	6.4	23.9	29.7	12.6	2.1	77.5	41.5	49.9	50.1
61274	OSCO	98.3	98.4	0.0	0.0	0.2	0.2	0.7	0.5	5.8	6.0	6.2	6.2	5.8	24.3	31.6	12.9	1.2	78.3	42.2	53.6	46.4
61275	PORT BYRON	97.5	97.0	0.4	0.4	0.2	0.3	2.0	2.5	5.9	6.3	6.5	6.5	5.8	25.6	31.0	11.1	1.3	77.1	41.0	51.1	48.9
61277	PROPHETSTOWN	98.1	97.8	0.5	0.6	0.1	0.2	1.5	1.9	6.1	5.7	5.9	6.5	5.3	23.6	27.8	15.5	3.7	78.2	43.0	49.5	50.5
61279	REYNOLDS	98.8	98.8	0.2	0.2	0.2	0.2	1.2	1.4	6.0	6.2	7.0	6.0	6.1	26.1	28.0	13.4	1.4	77.3	40.9	49.7	50.3
61281	SHERRARD	98.4	98.3	0.3	0.4	0.2	0.2	1.5	1.6	4.8	6.2	7.9	7.6	5.8	26.5	31.3	8.8	1.1	76.4	40.3	50.1	49.9
61282	SILVIS	86.4	84.1	3.5	3.9	0.8	0.9	13.6	16.4	7.1	6.6	6.5	6.8	7.6	25.6	24.0	13.1	2.7	75.6	37.5	48.1	51.9
61283	TAMPICO	98.2	98.0	0.4	0.4	0.2	0.3	1.9	2.4	8.2	7.8	8.2	7.1	6.1	25.2	24.1	11.9	1.4	71.3	36.1	50.5	49.5
61284	TAYLOR RIDGE	97.9	97.4	0.7	0.8	0.2	0.3	1.4	1.7	5.0	5.7	7.4	6.4	5.2	25.4	32.1	11.8	1.1	78.0	42.2	50.2	49.8
61285	THOMSON	97.1	97.0	0.8	0.9	0.5	0.5	1.2	1.2	5.8	6.0	6.6	6.6	5.7	23.9	27.7	16.2	1.6	77.7	42.1	50.6	49.4
61301	LA SALLE	93.9	92.8	1.2	1.3	0.6	0.7	7.8	9.5	6.8	6.3	6.1	6.2	7.3	26.9	23.9	13.8	2.7	77.2	38.2	49.9	50.1
61310	AMBOY	98.1	98.0	0.6	0.6	0.1	0.1	2.2	2.3	6.3	6.3	7.9	7.2	6.5	25.1	23.9	14.7	2.1	75.1	39.1	49.8	50.2
61311	ANCONA	98.3	98.1	0.2	0.2	0.0	0.0	1.9	2.4	5.9	5.9	6.1	5.9	6.1	25.0	30.4	13.7	1.3	79.0	42.2	51.2	48.8
61312	ARLINGTON	97.4	96.9	0.1	0.1	0.4	0.4	2.2	2.9	6.8	6.8	7.0	6.1	5.3	26.4	28.2	11.4	2.0	75.3	40.1	49.0	51.0
61313	BLACKSTONE	95.2	95.2	3.0	3.1	0.0	0.0	1.7	2.2	5.2	6.1	8.3	7.0	4.8	25.8	27.5	13.1	2.2	76.0	40.4	48.9	51.1
61314	BUDA	98.8	98.7	0.0	0.0	0.5	0.7	0.9	1.2	6.8	6.8	8.5	6.8	6.6	24.8	23.5	14.4	1.7	73.7	37.7	47.4	52.6
61318	COMPTON	98.4	98.6	0.0	0.0	0.6	0.6	1.6	1.5	7.4	7.8	8.9	7.2	4.2	25.8	26.6	11.0	1.1	71.3	37.9	50.7	49.3
61319	CORNELL	98.8	98.5	0.4	0.4	0.1	0.1	1.2	1.5	6.5	7.2	8.2	6.2	7.0	24.0	28.5	10.5	1.9	74.2	38.8	49.5	50.5
61320	DALZELL	97.9	97.2	0.2	0.3	0.2	0.4	3.2	4.2	5.9	6.3	6.9	6.2	5.6	25.6	27.0	14.1	2.5	76.6	40.5	48.3	51.7
	ILLINOIS	73.5	71.8	15.1	15.2	3.5	4.0	12.3	14.2	7.1	7.0	7.3	7.0	7.3	29.0	23.2	10.4	1.7	74.5	35.2	49.0	51.0
	UNITED STATES	75.1	73.6	12.3	12.5	3.8	4.2	12.5	14.1	6.9	6.7	7.2	7.0	7.3	28.6	23.8	10.8	1.7	75.1	36.0	49.1	50.9

#	POST OFFICE NAME	2004 Per Capita Income	2004 HH Income Base	2004 Household Income Distribution (%): Less than $25,000	$25,000 to $49,999	$50,000 to $99,999	$100,000 to $149,999	$150,000 or More	Median Household Income: 2004	2009	2004 National Centile	2004 State Centile	2004 Home Value Base	2004 Home Value Distribution (%): Less than $50,000	$50,000 to $89,999	$90,000 to $174,999	$175,000 to $399,999	$400,000 or More	2004 Median Home Value
61031	FRANKLIN GROVE	20764	670	20.3	32.5	37.3	6.4	3.4	48055	54569	68	58	515	7.8	17.7	57.5	15.2	1.9	113879
61032	FREEPORT	22568	13845	29.1	30.7	31.2	6.6	2.4	41642	46410	52	36	10221	17.9	27.5	41.6	12.4	0.6	96489
61036	GALENA	26170	2795	25.9	29.7	32.0	6.5	6.0	45547	50086	63	51	2205	4.7	15.7	41.6	31.2	6.8	151379
61038	GARDEN PRAIRIE	27769	538	10.6	22.1	44.4	16.5	6.3	65800	75283	89	87	472	0.0	1.1	47.9	46.4	4.7	176894
61039	GERMAN VALLEY	23054	321	19.0	30.8	37.1	9.7	3.4	50105	54375	72	63	275	5.8	20.4	45.1	25.5	3.3	118202
61041	HANOVER	23561	618	29.6	34.8	27.4	4.9	3.4	38647	42282	42	25	480	14.6	32.7	35.0	10.2	7.5	94063
61042	HARMON	21977	193	10.9	44.0	36.3	5.7	3.1	47033	52660	66	56	160	5.6	30.6	44.4	18.1	1.3	109677
61044	KENT	19131	79	22.8	35.4	34.2	5.1	2.5	43370	49449	57	43	63	11.1	25.4	41.3	19.1	3.2	120313
61046	LANARK	25166	1195	23.5	31.5	36.0	5.9	3.1	45383	48515	62	49	993	10.2	31.6	38.0	15.3	4.9	101201
61047	LEAF RIVER	23153	677	18.3	32.8	34.7	11.8	2.4	49307	56076	71	61	571	4.2	19.3	43.8	25.9	6.8	132656
61048	LENA	21015	1731	23.3	31.6	36.1	7.2	1.9	45734	50318	63	51	1434	3.9	19.4	55.5	20.3	0.9	121661
61049	LINDENWOOD	25038	188	11.7	32.5	42.0	10.6	3.2	54251	61703	79	72	154	6.5	20.1	46.1	21.4	5.8	130556
61050	MC CONNELL	22070	183	33.3	24.6	35.0	4.4	2.7	40462	43213	48	32	154	5.8	32.5	39.0	18.8	3.9	111250
61051	MILLEDGEVILLE	22563	664	21.1	39.9	32.1	3.3	3.6	42124	46446	53	38	563	13.1	33.8	45.5	6.4	1.2	93125
61052	MONROE CENTER	25719	600	13.2	25.7	44.8	11.8	4.5	59164	66266	84	80	534	9.2	8.1	54.1	23.2	5.4	142763
61053	MOUNT CARROLL	20182	1298	27.6	36.8	28.7	4.7	2.2	39607	44391	45	28	1042	15.7	26.4	39.6	15.2	3.1	102632
61054	MOUNT MORRIS	24107	1751	24.6	29.5	35.6	7.3	3.0	46459	52697	65	54	1361	12.9	25.8	51.1	9.6	0.6	100495
61060	ORANGEVILLE	20153	591	23.0	34.2	37.4	4.7	0.7	44704	50238	60	47	495	6.1	27.3	45.7	18.2	2.8	110069
61061	OREGON	24033	3079	25.0	28.9	31.2	10.5	4.4	46203	52096	64	53	2385	4.2	17.2	54.6	21.8	2.3	119261
61062	PEARL CITY	21021	784	20.2	32.0	38.5	7.5	1.8	48233	53652	69	59	665	12.6	16.2	49.5	20.0	1.7	118545
61063	PECATONICA	24866	1713	16.6	26.4	42.9	11.4	2.7	55657	63335	80	75	1469	4.0	19.3	55.7	19.0	2.0	119089
61064	POLO	21468	1584	22.9	31.8	36.5	7.1	1.6	46774	52951	66	55	1258	7.0	33.2	48.6	10.2	1.0	97278
61065	POPLAR GROVE	23222	2627	12.0	21.5	46.3	15.0	5.3	63360	70474	87	85	2396	5.5	4.1	58.8	29.2	2.5	155946
61067	RIDOTT	24911	354	17.2	27.1	40.4	12.4	2.8	55247	60767	80	74	302	9.9	18.5	38.4	29.1	4.0	126613
61068	ROCHELLE	21355	5650	22.5	32.6	33.7	8.6	2.6	45966	51530	64	52	4036	7.7	14.5	63.7	12.9	1.2	116708
61070	ROCK CITY	21983	447	22.2	30.0	33.1	9.8	4.9	48682	54028	70	60	377	7.7	12.7	49.6	28.4	1.6	127035
61071	ROCK FALLS	20329	5942	27.0	32.6	33.5	5.1	1.9	42105	46556	53	38	4467	11.3	38.5	43.0	6.8	0.5	90218
61072	ROCKTON	25644	3435	11.6	25.5	43.1	13.9	5.8	61739	68644	86	83	2953	1.0	8.4	61.0	28.2	1.4	141798
61073	ROSCOE	31309	5921	7.9	17.1	46.7	18.0	10.4	73881	82450	93	92	5366	1.1	5.6	60.4	29.4	3.5	153598
61074	SAVANNA	18978	2092	37.0	35.3	22.1	3.7	1.9	34106	37207	24	10	1560	31.0	33.7	23.6	9.7	2.0	70909
61075	SCALES MOUND	22178	407	18.7	36.4	35.9	5.7	3.4	45962	51416	64	52	357	6.2	13.5	40.3	33.6	6.4	147500
61078	SHANNON	26174	566	19.3	31.8	37.5	7.4	4.1	49007	52760	70	61	485	8.7	27.2	39.2	19.2	5.8	110031
61080	SOUTH BELOIT	22821	3524	24.4	29.1	33.9	9.5	3.0	45489	50553	63	50	2696	16.3	21.4	50.2	10.9	1.2	105829
61081	STERLING	22859	9117	25.6	31.4	33.3	6.8	3.0	43944	48161	58	45	6635	7.0	31.3	45.5	15.2	1.1	102685
61084	STILLMAN VALLEY	26719	1255	13.2	24.1	42.2	14.8	5.7	62227	70240	86	84	1103	2.3	4.0	64.2	26.6	3.0	152629
61085	STOCKTON	22085	1542	25.0	35.6	31.5	5.6	2.2	42677	48119	55	40	1223	10.8	26.7	42.9	15.6	4.1	107826
61087	WARREN	24598	785	25.9	32.2	33.8	6.4	1.8	42408	46941	54	39	651	14.8	30.1	45.9	7.2	2.0	95678
61088	WINNEBAGO	25298	1805	13.9	21.3	44.8	16.3	3.7	63955	72886	88	85	1608	2.4	10.1	63.6	22.4	1.6	136632
61089	WINSLOW	18678	329	22.2	25.5	46.8	4.6	0.9	50814	55063	73	65	270	4.4	30.0	48.5	12.6	4.4	105128
61101	ROCKFORD	16321	8482	35.3	31.8	26.4	4.9	1.6	35440	40313	29	14	5344	24.4	43.9	26.6	4.9	0.3	70218
61102	ROCKFORD	16941	6733	33.4	32.2	25.7	6.7	2.0	37277	41969	36	20	4752	37.5	33.0	22.7	6.2	0.6	61925
61103	ROCKFORD	22946	10191	30.1	29.9	29.8	6.9	3.3	41941	47996	53	37	6311	5.7	47.4	39.4	6.5	1.1	88091
61104	ROCKFORD	15488	7916	40.7	32.5	23.2	2.7	0.9	30972	35766	15	5	3463	19.2	66.1	14.2	0.4	0.2	67980
61107	ROCKFORD	31053	13105	19.2	28.6	32.4	10.7	9.0	51951	58814	75	67	9502	1.6	21.1	61.5	13.8	2.1	115587
61108	ROCKFORD	24621	11830	19.2	32.0	36.8	9.4	2.7	48985	55514	70	60	8934	1.2	27.8	64.2	6.6	0.2	104062
61109	ROCKFORD	22468	11163	22.9	31.7	33.9	8.6	2.8	46264	52424	64	53	7653	13.3	24.5	56.4	5.6	0.3	100473
61111	LOVES PARK	23763	8802	20.4	29.6	39.5	8.3	2.3	50028	57030	72	63	6566	9.4	25.8	56.8	7.5	0.6	102948
61112	ROCKFORD	29000	5	0.0	0.0	60.0	40.0	0.0	85357	110555	96	97	4	0.0	0.0	100.0	0.0	0.0	125000
61114	ROCKFORD	36052	6315	13.8	20.7	33.6	18.0	14.0	70165	79062	91	91	5046	0.4	6.6	63.0	27.5	2.5	147824
61115	MACHESNEY PARK	23000	7742	16.7	29.8	43.2	8.5	1.9	52770	60581	77	69	6511	3.7	31.9	59.0	4.9	0.5	103426
61201	ROCK ISLAND	22288	15888	31.5	31.5	27.8	6.5	2.7	38466	43745	41	25	10820	18.5	37.2	37.9	6.1	0.3	83701
61230	ALBANY	23330	478	18.6	30.8	38.9	9.6	2.1	50434	53719	73	64	423	15.6	19.9	55.8	8.8	0.0	104808
61231	ALEDO	20623	2286	29.0	33.2	30.2	5.5	2.1	40269	44541	47	31	1807	11.8	32.9	39.6	13.3	2.4	96325
61234	ANNAWAN	22122	491	25.9	31.2	35.0	6.1	1.8	43385	48502	57	43	410	13.4	35.6	42.0	8.1	1.0	91143
61235	ATKINSON	22275	616	27.1	30.0	35.6	5.7	1.6	42701	47827	55	41	479	18.2	35.5	37.0	8.6	0.8	85732
61238	CAMBRIDGE	21386	1411	23.3	31.8	36.4	6.6	1.8	45423	51242	62	50	1157	14.1	31.9	43.3	9.4	1.3	93974
61240	COAL VALLEY	24778	2262	20.0	25.6	37.6	12.0	4.9	54602	61821	79	73	2105	18.4	15.4	43.5	21.2	1.6	114262
61241	COLONA	22234	2715	20.9	30.2	36.9	8.9	3.1	49043	55302	70	61	2308	16.8	27.6	44.5	10.1	1.0	97303
61242	CORDOVA	26949	470	16.6	24.3	42.1	10.6	6.4	58558	65517	83	79	408	7.6	18.4	45.8	23.3	4.9	124074
61243	DEER GROVE	20166	92	14.1	39.1	38.0	5.4	3.3	48329	53349	69	59	73	6.9	23.3	48.0	17.8	4.1	114844
61244	EAST MOLINE	21025	9996	30.0	31.6	29.4	7.0	2.1	40259	45349	47	31	7129	15.5	33.2	42.8	8.2	0.4	91537
61250	ERIE	22172	1042	19.1	32.5	36.8	8.5	3.1	48841	53525	70	60	889	8.2	24.6	55.2	10.5	1.5	109261
61251	FENTON	24735	144	16.0	29.9	38.2	10.4	5.6	52860	58029	77	69	125	4.0	18.4	64.8	11.2	1.6	114338
61252	FULTON	21441	2304	22.4	37.6	31.8	5.2	3.0	43083	48774	56	42	1904	9.5	29.7	45.4	13.8	1.7	102278
61254	GENESEO	23789	4309	18.9	29.3	38.0	10.7	3.2	51711	57320	75	67	3656	4.5	17.2	51.9	24.9	1.6	129091
61256	HAMPTON	25808	496	19.4	25.8	38.1	12.1	4.6	55007	60621	80	74	450	4.4	28.4	54.2	10.2	2.7	107955
61257	HILLSDALE	25363	500	16.6	27.8	42.8	7.6	5.2	53701	61616	78	71	430	15.1	24.4	37.9	20.0	2.6	107463
61259	ILLINOIS CITY	23509	544	21.0	23.9	37.0	14.2	4.0	53864	61018	78	71	481	8.1	10.6	53.6	27.7	0.0	140489
61260	JOY	20488	341	22.9	36.4	34.6	3.2	2.9	42149	47416	53	38	271	24.4	30.3	32.8	10.0	2.6	84565
61261	LYNDON	18813	346	24.6	36.7	32.4	6.1	0.3	40938	45213	49	33	303	20.8	35.6	39.6	4.0	0.0	84091
61262	LYNN CENTER	21832	407	15.2	28.5	42.0	12.8	1.5	54676	61910	79	73	360	8.9	22.5	50.6	16.9	1.1	114063
61263	MATHERVILLE	17731	299	30.4	32.8	30.8	5.4	0.7	41613	47448	52	35	231	17.3	39.0	39.0	4.8	0.0	81944
61264	MILAN	22582	4853	25.9	27.0	35.4	9.2	2.5	46802	52731	66	55	3876	20.3	28.4	36.8	13.8	0.8	91527
61265	MOLINE	24330	18790	26.6	31.0	31.4	7.7	3.4	43186	48678	56	43	13472	9.5	36.8	39.6	12.8	1.4	93966
61270	MORRISON	23153	2999	19.8	32.3	38.1	6.6	3.1	48098	53035	69	58	2526	5.8	28.2	49.8	15.7	0.6	108648
61272	NEW BOSTON	18926	633	29.4	34.6	30.5	4.4	1.1	39289	43976	44	27	534	37.8	25.1	21.9	8.6	6.6	71463
61273	ORION	26071	1262	15.1	26.5	43.7	11.3	3.4	56897	63592	82	77	1069	4.0	16.3	57.1	20.3	2.3	123836
61274	OSCO	20005	158	24.7	26.0	43.7	3.2	2.5	48931	52583	70	60	117	2.6	29.1	38.5	16.2	13.7	129688
61275	PORT BYRON	28437	1866	19.4	24.1	37.0	12.1	7.5	56618	63782	81	77	1660	9.5	16.1	43.6	27.7	3.1	121368
61277	PROPHETSTOWN	21700	1411	23.3	36.6	30.1	7.1	3.0	42019	46548	53	38	1168	9.7	30.8	47.4	10.6	1.5	99823
61279	REYNOLDS	25109	396	24.0	27.3	34.9	10.9	3.0	49198	55522	71	61	340	8.2	30.0	42.4	14.4	5.0	111111
61281	SHERRARD	26078	978	10.8	21.2	52.4	11.8	3.9	62506	68744	87	84	870	8.3	20.6	44.3	26.0	0.9	128604
61282	SILVIS	19422	3576	29.5	36.6	26.8	5.9	1.2	39343	45107	44	28	2329	10.2	43.0	42.3	4.5	0.0	87597
61283	TAMPICO	17840	578	22.8	36.9	33.4	4.8	2.1	43437	47893	57	44	452	8.6	37.6	43.6	6.9	3.3	93469
61284	TAYLOR RIDGE	28252	1342	16.5	24.3	39.5	16.0	3.7	60450	68575	85	82	1212	5.9	21.9	50.7	19.0	2.6	121711
61285	THOMSON	21667	727	23.3	38.2	29.9	5.2	3.4	41712	46390	52	36	603	15.6	25.2	43.5	10.6	5.1	105671
61301	LA SALLE	21616	4498	33.4	28.5	30.6	5.1	2.4	37156	42074	36	20	3177	9.8	32.0	43.4	13.6	1.2	98413
61310	AMBOY	20468	1646	24.4	36.6	31.2	5.7	2.3	42189	47454	53	38	1322	16.9	20.7	48.5	10.7	3.3	104377
61311	ANCONA	25468	180	13.9	27.2	42.2	16.1	0.6	57668	62521	82	78	150	10.0	22.7	50.0	17.3	0.0	107895
61312	ARLINGTON	21706	426	16.9	36.2	39.4	5.6	1.9	47931	54093	68	58	363	10.2	33.9	40.5	13.0	2.5	98958
61313	BLACKSTONE	25611	90	16.7	27.8	44.4	7.8	3.3	54495	60000	79	73	70	8.6	21.4	55.7	11.4	2.9	113333
61314	BUDA	18665	386	25.9	36.0	33.2	3.9	1.0	40714	46803	49	33	312	26.3	32.4	34.6	3.5	3.2	78636
61318	COMPTON	20577	276	22.8	27.9	41.3	7.6	0.4	49313	53054	71	61	237	9.3	17.7	40.5	23.2	9.3	131500
61319	CORNELL	20867	287	23.0	26.8	41.1	7.3	1.7	50107	53849	72	63	241	29.1	28.6	37.3	3.3	1.7	79750
61320	DALZELL	23486	376	17.8	30.9	40.2	8.5	2.7	50887	57135	74	65	325	6.5	25.9	52.0	14.5	1.2	114718
	ILLINOIS	27033		22.1	25.9	32.9	11.9	7.3	52039	60941				7.7	12.8	34.0	36.6	8.9	162771
	UNITED STATES	25866		24.7	27.1	30.8	10.9	6.5	48124	56710				10.9	15.0	33.7	30.1	10.4	145905

ZIP CODE #	POST OFFICE NAME	FINANCIAL SERVICES: Auto Loan	FINANCIAL SERVICES: Home Loan	FINANCIAL SERVICES: Invest-ments	FINANCIAL SERVICES: Retire-ment Plans	THE HOME: Home Improvements: Home Repair	THE HOME: Home Improvements: Lawn & Garden	THE HOME: Furnishings: Comput-ers & Hard-ware	THE HOME: Furnishings: Major Appli-ances	THE HOME: Furnishings: TV, Radio, Sound Equip-ment	THE HOME: Furnishings: Furni-ture	ENTERTAINMENT: Dine out/ Carry out	ENTERTAINMENT: Sports Equip-ment	ENTERTAINMENT: Fees & Tickets	ENTERTAINMENT: Toys & Games	ENTERTAINMENT: Travel	ENTERTAINMENT: Cable TV	PERSONAL: Apparel & Services	PERSONAL: Auto Repairs	PERSONAL: Health Insur-ance	PERSONAL: Pets & Supplies
61031	FRANKLIN GROVE	79	77	78	78	79	84	77	79	77	76	95	93	76	94	77	76	91	79	79	91
61032	FREEPORT	75	72	70	70	74	81	72	75	75	71	92	86	72	93	73	76	88	74	78	86
61036	GALENA	88	82	76	79	85	94	80	86	84	79	102	99	78	103	83	87	98	85	92	104
61038	GARDEN PRAIRIE	110	116	107	113	117	120	105	110	104	105	128	130	107	134	107	103	125	106	108	131
61039	GERMAN VALLEY	109	79	45	75	91	101	77	94	88	76	104	113	67	102	80	92	95	92	110	129
61041	HANOVER	86	63	38	60	71	82	66	76	74	63	87	88	58	84	67	78	80	76	91	99
61042	HARMON	97	78	52	74	86	94	74	86	81	74	98	103	69	98	77	84	91	84	97	115
61044	KENT	77	71	72	73	74	80	72	76	73	72	90	90	70	88	73	72	86	76	77	89
61046	LANARK	93	84	69	78	89	98	80	87	85	78	104	102	78	107	83	89	98	86	97	110
61047	LEAF RIVER	90	84	71	83	87	94	82	87	84	81	103	100	81	104	82	85	98	85	91	103
61048	LENA	82	77	65	73	80	87	73	78	76	72	93	92	73	96	75	78	89	76	84	97
61049	LINDENWOOD	105	93	71	89	99	106	86	96	92	86	112	114	85	114	89	94	106	93	104	124
61050	MC CONNELL	90	80	61	76	85	91	74	82	79	74	96	98	73	98	77	81	91	80	89	106
61051	MILLEDGEVILLE	91	71	48	69	78	87	71	81	78	70	94	95	66	93	72	81	87	80	92	104
61052	MONROE CENTER	114	101	77	96	107	115	94	104	99	94	121	124	92	123	96	102	115	101	112	134
61053	MOUNT CARROLL	81	63	43	59	70	79	64	73	71	62	85	85	58	84	65	75	78	72	85	94
61054	MOUNT MORRIS	84	78	71	78	80	87	78	82	80	77	99	96	77	99	78	80	94	81	84	96
61060	ORANGEVILLE	82	73	56	69	77	83	67	75	72	67	87	89	66	89	69	73	83	73	81	96
61061	OREGON	88	81	71	79	85	93	80	85	83	78	101	99	78	102	81	85	96	84	91	102
61062	PEARL CITY	87	80	66	77	84	89	75	82	78	75	96	97	74	97	77	80	91	80	87	103
61063	PECATONICA	102	91	70	87	96	103	84	93	89	84	108	111	82	111	87	91	103	90	100	120
61064	POLO	76	74	68	70	77	84	72	75	75	70	92	86	73	98	74	78	89	73	82	89
61065	POPLAR GROVE	106	114	106	116	112	111	103	105	98	106	123	124	106	125	102	94	121	102	96	120
61067	RIDOTT	103	88	64	84	95	102	82	93	89	82	107	111	79	109	85	91	101	91	103	122
61068	ROCHELLE	84	77	66	76	79	87	77	81	80	75	97	93	75	98	77	81	93	80	85	95
61070	ROCK CITY	105	79	48	75	89	99	77	92	86	76	102	110	68	101	79	90	94	90	106	125
61071	ROCK FALLS	71	68	65	66	70	77	69	71	71	67	87	81	68	89	69	72	84	70	74	82
61072	ROCKTON	101	110	105	111	108	110	101	103	98	102	122	120	104	125	101	95	119	100	97	117
61073	ROSCOE	129	143	141	145	141	142	130	132	123	132	155	155	135	159	131	120	153	128	121	150
61074	SAVANNA	69	56	41	53	60	69	57	63	63	56	76	72	54	75	58	66	70	62	73	78
61075	SCALES MOUND	93	77	56	72	85	93	72	84	80	72	95	99	68	96	76	83	90	82	96	112
61078	SHANNON	107	90	69	86	97	108	89	99	96	87	115	114	83	115	91	99	108	97	110	124
61080	SOUTH BELOIT	87	80	68	78	82	89	79	83	82	78	100	97	77	101	79	83	96	82	87	99
61081	STERLING	79	80	82	79	81	87	80	81	80	78	100	94	80	102	80	80	96	80	82	92
61084	STILLMAN VALLEY	106	113	106	110	114	117	102	107	101	102	124	126	105	130	105	100	122	103	105	127
61085	STOCKTON	83	69	52	66	75	84	69	77	75	67	90	89	65	91	70	78	84	75	86	96
61087	WARREN	78	81	81	77	83	91	79	80	82	77	102	90	83	109	82	85	98	78	86	91
61088	WINNEBAGO	112	106	87	103	110	116	97	106	100	98	123	125	97	126	100	102	118	103	110	132
61089	WINSLOW	83	74	56	70	78	83	68	75	72	68	88	90	67	90	70	74	84	73	82	97
61101	ROCKFORD	58	58	66	56	58	64	61	60	63	60	79	68	62	80	61	64	77	60	61	66
61102	ROCKFORD	73	65	60	61	65	72	66	69	71	67	87	79	64	85	66	72	84	70	73	81
61103	ROCKFORD	68	72	82	72	72	76	74	72	74	72	92	84	76	95	74	73	90	73	70	79
61104	ROCKFORD	51	49	56	49	48	53	55	52	56	53	69	61	54	69	53	55	67	54	52	57
61107	ROCKFORD	97	106	120	106	104	111	105	103	103	104	129	119	108	130	106	101	127	103	99	113
61108	ROCKFORD	77	81	90	81	81	87	82	81	82	81	102	94	84	105	83	81	99	82	81	90
61109	ROCKFORD	81	79	78	79	79	83	78	80	79	79	98	94	78	98	78	77	95	80	78	92
61111	LOVES PARK	83	85	81	85	84	88	82	83	81	83	101	97	83	102	82	80	98	83	81	94
61112	ROCKFORD	121	133	133	136	129	127	127	126	119	128	150	149	127	151	124	112	148	125	110	138
61114	ROCKFORD	122	138	152	140	137	142	131	131	125	131	157	151	136	160	133	123	155	129	124	144
61115	MACHESNEY PARK	86	90	86	89	90	93	85	87	84	85	105	101	87	108	86	83	102	85	85	99
61201	ROCK ISLAND	67	69	79	68	69	76	72	70	73	71	91	81	74	93	73	74	89	72	72	78
61230	ALBANY	94	84	64	80	88	95	77	86	82	77	100	102	76	102	80	84	95	84	93	111
61231	ALEDO	74	67	57	64	70	79	68	72	72	65	87	82	65	87	69	75	82	71	80	85
61234	ANNAWAN	97	68	36	64	79	89	67	83	77	66	91	100	57	89	70	81	83	82	99	116
61235	ATKINSON	88	64	39	61	72	84	68	78	77	66	91	90	60	87	69	81	83	78	93	99
61238	CAMBRIDGE	79	74	65	70	77	85	72	76	76	71	92	88	71	95	74	78	88	75	83	92
61240	COAL VALLEY	93	102	100	101	102	103	94	96	90	94	113	112	96	116	95	89	111	93	91	110
61241	COLONA	79	85	84	83	86	91	81	82	81	79	100	94	84	105	83	81	97	80	83	93
61242	CORDOVA	87	105	116	103	103	106	98	97	93	97	117	112	104	125	100	92	117	94	90	105
61243	DEER GROVE	90	80	61	76	85	91	74	82	79	74	96	98	73	98	76	81	91	80	89	106
61244	EAST MOLINE	68	67	72	68	67	73	70	69	70	69	88	80	70	87	69	70	85	70	69	77
61250	ERIE	93	83	63	79	88	94	77	85	81	77	99	101	75	101	79	84	94	83	92	110
61251	FENTON	107	95	73	90	101	108	88	98	94	88	114	116	86	116	91	96	108	95	106	126
61252	FULTON	75	74	69	71	76	84	72	75	74	71	91	86	73	94	73	76	87	73	80	88
61254	GENESEO	89	86	79	84	90	95	83	88	85	82	104	103	82	107	85	85	100	86	91	106
61256	HAMPTON	85	102	112	99	100	104	94	94	91	94	114	107	100	121	97	91	113	92	90	102
61257	HILLSDALE	101	98	85	94	101	107	90	97	93	90	114	115	91	118	93	94	110	94	101	120
61259	ILLINOIS CITY	97	96	82	93	99	103	87	94	89	87	109	111	88	113	90	90	106	91	96	116
61260	JOY	76	67	56	63	72	81	66	73	72	65	87	84	64	90	69	75	82	71	82	90
61261	LYNDON	76	68	52	64	72	77	63	69	67	63	81	83	61	83	65	68	77	68	75	90
61262	LYNN CENTER	93	90	78	86	93	99	84	90	86	83	105	107	83	109	86	87	101	88	94	111
61263	MATHERVILLE	73	62	49	62	65	74	64	69	68	63	83	78	62	82	64	69	77	68	74	81
61264	MILAN	85	76	62	74	79	88	76	81	80	74	97	93	73	97	76	82	91	79	88	97
61265	MOLINE	74	80	88	79	79	85	80	79	80	79	100	91	82	102	81	80	98	79	78	87
61270	MORRISON	85	81	72	78	84	91	78	82	80	77	98	96	77	101	79	82	94	81	87	100
61272	NEW BOSTON	80	61	37	55	67	74	58	68	66	58	78	81	53	77	59	69	73	67	79	92
61273	ORION	86	102	108	99	100	103	93	94	90	93	113	108	99	119	96	90	112	91	89	104
61274	OSCO	88	78	60	74	83	89	72	80	77	72	93	95	71	95	74	79	89	78	87	103
61275	PORT BYRON	114	104	82	99	109	117	96	105	101	96	123	125	95	126	99	103	118	103	113	135
61277	PROPHETSTOWN	85	73	56	69	78	87	71	79	77	70	93	92	68	92	73	80	87	78	89	99
61279	REYNOLDS	86	92	90	89	93	97	86	89	85	85	105	104	87	110	88	85	103	87	89	104
61281	SHERRARD	91	111	119	111	109	109	100	100	94	100	118	117	107	126	103	92	118	97	91	110
61282	SILVIS	68	62	54	61	64	72	63	66	66	61	80	75	62	81	63	68	76	65	71	76
61283	TAMPICO	83	65	45	64	71	80	66	74	72	65	86	87	61	85	66	74	80	73	83	94
61284	TAYLOR RIDGE	94	116	126	115	114	114	105	105	99	105	125	122	112	133	108	97	124	101	95	115
61285	THOMSON	86	71	49	67	76	84	68	77	75	68	90	91	65	89	69	77	84	76	86	99
61301	LA SALLE	66	69	77	68	69	74	71	69	71	69	88	80	72	91	71	71	86	70	69	76
61310	AMBOY	79	71	59	67	76	83	69	75	74	68	90	87	68	93	71	77	85	74	83	93
61311	ANCONA	105	93	71	88	98	105	86	95	91	86	111	114	84	113	89	94	106	93	103	123
61312	ARLINGTON	86	78	61	74	82	88	72	79	76	72	93	94	71	95	74	78	88	77	86	102
61313	BLACKSTONE	97	86	65	82	91	97	79	88	84	79	103	105	78	105	82	86	97	86	95	114
61314	BUDA	75	64	50	63	67	75	65	69	69	64	83	80	62	83	65	70	78	68	75	83
61318	COMPTON	86	76	58	72	81	87	71	78	75	71	91	93	69	93	73	77	87	76	85	101
61319	CORNELL	85	72	56	72	76	85	73	79	78	72	94	90	70	94	73	79	88	77	85	94
61320	DALZELL	78	89	94	87	88	92	84	84	82	83	102	97	88	107	85	81	100	82	81	93
	ILLINOIS	98	100	111	99	99	106	100	99	101	100	126	115	102	127	100	100	123	100	98	112
	UNITED STATES	100	100	100	100	100	100	100	100	100	100	100	100	100	100	100	100	100	100	100	100

A 61321-61483

# POST OFFICE NAME	COUNTY FIPS CODE	POPULATION 2000	2004	2009	ANNUAL RATE % Rate	State Centile	HOUSEHOLDS 2000	2004	2009	% Annual Rate 2000-2004	2004 Average HH Size	FAMILIES 2000	2004	% Annual Rate 2000-2004
61321 DANA	099	352	344	346	-0.5	15	128	127	130	-0.2	2.71	93	91	-0.5
61325 GRAND RIDGE	099	976	1024	1056	1.1	80	363	388	406	1.6	2.64	280	295	1.2
61326 GRANVILLE	155	2978	3151	3397	1.3	82	1193	1279	1398	1.7	2.46	834	881	1.3
61327 HENNEPIN	155	1202	1293	1406	1.7	86	469	515	571	2.2	2.50	339	368	2.0
61329 LADD	011	1231	1225	1225	-0.1	36	527	533	541	0.3	2.29	349	347	-0.1
61330 LA MOILLE	011	1617	1622	1625	0.1	45	612	624	633	0.5	2.60	470	472	0.1
61333 LONG POINT	105	542	540	542	-0.1	37	199	201	205	0.2	2.63	159	159	0.0
61334 LOSTANT	099	723	708	710	-0.5	16	290	289	294	-0.1	2.45	204	200	-0.5
61335 MC NABB	155	690	730	787	1.3	82	273	294	322	1.8	2.48	209	223	1.5
61336 MAGNOLIA	155	521	551	595	1.3	82	192	207	227	1.8	2.66	148	158	1.6
61337 MALDEN	011	872	863	862	-0.2	28	304	306	310	0.2	2.82	243	242	-0.1
61341 MARSEILLES	099	7821	7993	8143	0.5	66	2994	3106	3205	0.9	2.54	2167	2214	0.5
61342 MENDOTA	099	9353	9407	9524	0.1	49	3507	3566	3650	0.4	2.57	2485	2484	0.0
61344 MINERAL	011	440	429	427	-0.6	13	176	175	176	-0.1	2.45	129	126	-0.6
61345 NEPONSET	011	785	775	774	-0.3	25	310	312	316	0.2	2.48	228	226	-0.2
61346 NEW BEDFORD	011	156	165	170	1.3	82	64	69	72	1.8	2.29	47	50	1.5
61348 OGLESBY	099	4505	4559	4637	0.3	57	1945	1999	2060	0.7	2.27	1259	1270	0.2
61349 OHIO	011	1201	1205	1208	0.1	46	463	474	482	0.6	2.54	347	351	0.3
61350 OTTAWA	099	24265	24485	24882	0.2	53	9747	9960	10243	0.5	2.41	6562	6595	0.1
61353 PAW PAW	103	1265	1267	1266	0.0	43	490	497	505	0.3	2.55	344	344	0.0
61354 PERU	099	10815	10941	11216	0.3	56	4507	4646	4837	0.7	2.29	2942	2969	0.4
61356 PRINCETON	011	12914	13112	13265	0.4	61	5315	5491	5638	0.8	2.34	3492	3552	0.4
61358 RUTLAND	123	514	505	508	-0.4	19	207	207	211	0.0	2.44	153	151	-0.3
61360 SENECA	099	3119	3266	3371	1.1	79	818	820	831	1.4	2.71	878	921	1.1
61361 SHEFFIELD	011	2036	2013	2013	-0.3	26	818	820	831	0.1	2.45	581	574	-0.3
61362 SPRING VALLEY	011	5601	5610	5638	0.0	43	2252	2287	2328	0.4	2.39	1540	1541	0.0
61364 STREATOR	099	20903	20877	21151	0.0	40	8447	8573	8803	0.4	2.41	5618	5600	-0.1
61367 SUBLETTE	103	865	869	871	0.1	47	340	349	356	0.6	2.49	247	249	0.2
61368 TISKILWA	011	1463	1461	1470	0.0	40	568	578	592	0.4	2.53	430	432	0.1
61369 TOLUCA	123	1814	1847	1888	0.4	64	754	780	810	0.8	2.26	481	489	0.4
61370 TONICA	099	1242	1253	1271	0.2	53	531	546	562	0.7	2.29	361	365	0.3
61373 UTICA	099	1800	2016	2154	2.7	93	711	808	875	3.1	2.41	495	553	2.6
61375 VARNA	123	1511	1550	1591	0.6	69	615	643	672	1.1	2.41	491	506	0.7
61376 WALNUT	011	2108	2164	2202	0.6	70	812	845	872	0.9	2.50	584	600	0.6
61377 WENONA	099	1334	1338	1357	0.1	45	545	556	573	0.5	2.41	346	346	0.0
61378 WEST BROOKLYN	103	545	551	552	0.3	55	208	213	217	0.6	2.59	155	156	0.3
61379 WYANET	011	1591	1610	1624	0.3	57	628	647	662	0.7	2.49	450	456	0.3
61401 GALESBURG	095	37341	37065	36543	-0.2	33	14778	14882	14872	0.2	2.21	9072	8983	-0.2
61410 ABINGDON	095	4097	3989	3891	-0.6	11	1620	1605	1591	-0.2	2.45	1130	1102	-0.6
61411 ADAIR	109	461	516	559	2.7	93	191	220	242	3.4	2.35	144	163	3.0
61412 ALEXIS	131	1587	1625	1643	0.6	68	650	679	695	1.0	2.39	476	489	0.6
61413 ALPHA	073	1122	1074	1044	-1.0	4	445	433	428	-0.6	2.48	335	321	-1.0
61414 ALTONA	095	926	899	876	-0.7	9	348	342	337	-0.4	2.63	271	263	-0.7
61415 AVON	057	2085	2069	2053	-0.2	32	832	842	849	0.3	2.42	623	622	0.0
61417 BERWICK	187	338	346	348	0.6	67	140	146	149	1.0	2.36	110	113	0.6
61418 BIGGSVILLE	071	586	609	631	0.9	76	246	261	275	1.4	2.33	176	184	1.1
61420 BLANDINSVILLE	109	1243	1245	1267	0.0	43	520	527	544	0.3	2.36	365	364	-0.1
61421 BRADFORD	175	1884	1907	1925	0.3	58	728	747	766	0.6	2.55	534	541	0.3
61422 BUSHNELL	109	3633	3701	3806	0.4	64	1487	1532	1596	0.7	2.41	1012	1024	0.3
61423 CAMERON	187	726	726	724	0.0	42	276	280	282	0.3	2.59	223	224	0.1
61425 CARMAN	071	370	372	380	0.1	48	161	165	171	0.6	2.25	118	119	0.2
61427 CUBA	057	2300	2314	2306	0.1	49	908	928	938	0.5	2.44	662	668	0.2
61428 DAHINDA	095	823	812	796	-0.3	24	366	370	371	0.3	2.19	289	289	0.0
61431 ELLISVILLE	057	374	397	406	1.4	83	154	167	175	1.9	2.38	119	127	1.5
61432 FAIRVIEW	057	662	644	632	-0.7	11	266	262	260	-0.4	2.46	196	190	-0.7
61433 FIATT	057	44	52	56	4.0	97	16	19	20	4.1	2.74	12	14	3.7
61434 GALVA	073	3727	3640	3566	-0.6	14	1551	1534	1521	-0.3	2.36	1031	1002	-0.7
61435 GERLAW	187	161	160	159	-0.2	34	68	69	69	0.3	2.32	55	55	0.0
61436 GILSON	095	1049	1008	977	-0.9	5	397	390	385	-0.4	2.58	308	299	-0.7
61437 GLADSTONE	071	1165	1180	1206	0.3	58	492	507	527	0.7	2.33	351	357	0.4
61438 GOOD HOPE	109	732	770	805	1.2	81	302	323	342	1.6	2.38	220	231	1.2
61440 INDUSTRY	109	884	878	895	-0.2	33	340	344	356	0.3	2.55	264	264	0.0
61441 IPAVA	057	1063	1067	1065	0.1	46	443	450	453	0.4	2.37	316	317	0.1
61442 KEITHSBURG	131	851	853	855	0.1	45	342	347	352	0.3	2.46	250	250	0.0
61443 KEWANEE	073	14391	14189	13982	-0.3	23	5899	5893	5886	0.0	2.37	3799	3721	-0.5
61447 KIRKWOOD	187	1001	976	962	-0.6	13	381	378	377	-0.2	2.58	294	287	-0.6
61448 KNOXVILLE	095	4564	4513	4430	-0.3	27	1743	1755	1751	0.2	2.48	1274	1262	-0.2
61449 LA FAYETTE	175	520	506	499	-0.6	11	204	201	202	-0.4	2.52	152	148	-0.6
61450 LA HARPE	067	1835	1770	1716	-0.8	6	725	707	693	-0.6	2.44	510	489	-1.0
61451 LAURA	143	415	457	479	2.3	91	151	170	181	2.8	2.69	113	125	2.4
61452 LITTLETON	169	372	368	365	-0.3	27	140	141	141	0.2	2.61	107	106	-0.2
61453 LITTLE YORK	187	493	496	496	0.1	49	195	199	201	0.5	2.49	147	148	0.2
61454 LOMAX	071	992	1004	1023	0.3	57	397	409	424	0.7	2.38	277	281	0.3
61455 MACOMB	109	21735	22137	22727	0.4	64	7864	8194	8607	1.0	2.13	3904	3964	0.4
61458 MAQUON	095	898	868	842	-0.8	7	385	379	375	-0.4	2.29	268	259	-0.8
61459 MARIETTA	057	403	449	472	2.6	92	156	177	189	3.0	2.54	116	130	2.7
61460 MEDIA	071	468	472	481	0.2	52	180	184	190	0.5	2.57	140	141	0.2
61462 MONMOUTH	187	12041	11792	11654	-0.5	16	4523	4466	4442	-0.3	2.39	2970	2878	-0.7
61465 NEW WINDSOR	131	1153	1158	1163	0.1	47	466	476	484	0.5	2.43	341	344	0.2
61466 NORTH HENDERSON	131	338	337	338	-0.1	38	134	136	138	0.4	2.48	104	104	0.0
61467 ONEIDA	095	1275	1242	1210	-0.6	11	502	497	493	-0.2	2.50	384	375	-0.6
61469 OQUAWKA	071	2640	2693	2762	0.5	65	1098	1136	1180	0.8	2.35	732	746	0.5
61470 PRAIRIE CITY	109	595	667	719	2.7	93	204	233	256	3.2	2.74	161	181	2.8
61471 RARITAN	071	322	324	331	0.2	50	124	126	131	0.4	2.57	97	97	0.0
61472 RIO	095	575	548	529	-1.1	2	229	222	218	-0.7	2.47	176	169	-1.0
61473 ROSEVILLE	187	1791	1859	1888	0.9	76	711	751	773	1.3	2.38	510	530	0.9
61474 SAINT AUGUSTINE	095	344	351	350	0.5	65	138	145	147	1.2	2.42	100	104	0.9
61475 SCIOTA	109	243	241	246	-0.2	31	90	90	93	0.0	2.68	69	68	-0.3
61476 SEATON	071	735	734	740	0.0	40	291	295	302	0.3	2.49	223	224	0.1
61477 SMITHFIELD	057	621	687	717	2.4	91	248	279	296	2.8	2.46	188	208	2.4
61478 SMITHSHIRE	187	320	332	338	0.9	75	126	133	137	1.3	2.50	97	102	1.2
61479 SPEER	175	509	510	513	0.1	44	186	189	193	0.4	2.70	144	145	0.2
61480 STRONGHURST	071	1164	1184	1211	0.4	62	448	463	482	0.8	2.51	326	333	0.5
61482 TABLE GROVE	057	607	652	673	1.7	86	245	268	281	2.1	2.43	177	190	1.7
61483 TOULON	175	2312	2261	2241	-0.5	16	909	904	909	-0.1	2.37	619	605	-0.5
ILLINOIS					0.7					0.9	2.61			0.6
UNITED STATES					1.2					1.3	2.58			1.1

ZIP CODE #	POST OFFICE NAME	RACE (%) White 2000	White 2004	Black 2000	Black 2004	Asian/Pacific 2000	Asian/Pacific 2004	% Hispanic Origin 2000	% Hispanic Origin 2004	2004 AGE DISTRIBUTION (%) 0-4	5-9	10-14	15-19	20-24	25-44	45-64	65-84	85+	18+	MEDIAN AGE 2004	% 2004 Males	% 2004 Females
61321	DANA	99.4	99.4	0.0	0.0	0.0	0.0	1.4	1.5	6.7	6.4	6.4	7.3	7.0	27.3	25.0	12.5	1.5	76.2	37.8	51.7	48.3
61325	GRAND RIDGE	99.4	99.2	0.2	0.2	0.1	0.1	2.1	2.5	7.6	7.5	7.0	6.7	6.0	23.7	26.4	12.8	2.3	73.6	39.9	49.5	50.5
61326	GRANVILLE	98.0	97.6	0.2	0.3	0.2	0.3	3.8	4.7	6.4	6.6	7.7	7.0	5.7	25.8	26.1	12.4	2.4	74.9	39.3	47.7	52.3
61327	HENNEPIN	97.4	97.1	0.9	1.0	0.4	0.5	2.6	3.1	5.7	5.9	5.9	6.5	6.2	24.9	28.3	14.9	1.7	78.7	42.0	51.0	49.0
61329	LADD	97.6	97.0	0.2	0.2	0.0	0.1	3.2	4.2	6.6	6.5	6.2	5.2	6.2	27.6	22.6	15.6	3.5	77.5	39.4	48.4	51.6
61330	LA MOILLE	98.2	97.8	0.2	0.2	0.0	0.0	2.9	3.8	7.0	7.2	7.6	6.2	5.4	26.0	27.5	11.5	1.8	74.5	38.3	50.9	49.1
61333	LONG POINT	97.6	97.0	0.7	0.9	0.6	0.7	0.6	0.7	5.0	5.7	7.4	8.2	5.6	22.4	30.9	12.4	2.4	76.7	42.1	49.6	50.4
61334	LOSTANT	98.3	98.3	0.3	0.3	0.1	0.1	0.8	1.1	6.2	6.5	6.6	6.1	5.5	26.7	26.7	13.1	2.5	76.8	40.0	49.4	50.6
61335	MC NABB	97.4	97.1	1.3	1.4	0.1	0.3	0.6	0.7	6.3	6.4	7.3	7.4	5.5	26.3	26.4	12.6	1.8	75.3	39.5	50.6	49.5
61336	MAGNOLIA	97.3	96.9	1.3	1.5	0.2	0.4	0.4	0.5	6.4	6.5	7.1	7.4	5.6	26.3	26.3	12.7	1.6	75.5	39.4	50.8	49.2
61337	MALDEN	97.4	96.9	0.2	0.2	0.5	0.6	1.8	2.4	7.1	7.4	7.2	6.6	6.4	24.6	27.2	12.3	1.3	74.2	39.0	52.7	47.3
61341	MARSEILLES	98.0	97.7	0.2	0.2	0.2	0.3	1.6	2.0	6.5	6.6	7.1	6.5	6.4	26.2	26.5	12.2	1.9	75.6	39.1	49.3	50.7
61342	MENDOTA	90.5	88.8	0.3	0.4	0.7	0.9	15.1	18.0	7.2	6.9	7.0	7.0	6.8	24.6	23.4	13.9	3.3	74.7	38.2	48.4	51.6
61344	MINERAL	98.0	97.4	0.5	0.7	0.2	0.2	1.4	1.4	6.8	6.8	5.8	5.1	5.1	24.7	26.3	17.5	1.9	77.2	41.6	51.1	49.0
61345	NEPONSET	98.2	98.2	0.4	0.4	0.9	1.0	1.8	2.3	3.6	3.9	6.2	6.7	6.6	23.6	30.3	16.9	2.2	82.5	44.6	50.2	49.8
61346	NEW BEDFORD	98.7	98.8	0.6	0.6	0.0	0.0	1.3	1.2	7.3	7.3	7.9	6.7	4.9	25.5	21.2	15.8	3.6	73.3	39.0	49.1	50.9
61348	OGLESBY	98.2	97.8	0.4	0.5	0.3	0.4	2.7	3.3	5.7	5.9	6.6	6.0	5.5	25.7	24.8	16.7	3.1	78.2	41.4	48.5	51.5
61349	OHIO	98.8	98.7	0.3	0.3	0.1	0.1	1.8	2.1	6.3	6.6	7.3	7.1	5.4	24.9	25.9	15.0	1.5	75.5	40.0	49.5	50.5
61350	OTTAWA	95.9	95.3	1.1	1.2	0.8	1.0	4.5	5.5	6.3	6.2	6.9	6.8	6.7	25.7	24.8	13.9	2.7	76.4	39.5	48.3	51.7
61353	PAW PAW	98.7	98.7	0.0	0.0	0.6	0.6	1.1	1.1	6.6	7.0	8.3	7.2	5.4	25.1	26.5	12.3	1.6	73.6	39.9	50.8	49.2
61354	PERU	96.5	95.8	0.3	0.4	1.1	1.4	4.0	4.9	5.4	5.3	6.0	6.3	6.2	24.9	25.2	16.6	4.1	79.6	42.4	47.5	52.5
61356	PRINCETON	95.4	94.7	0.3	0.3	0.9	1.1	8.4	9.7	5.7	5.6	6.3	6.5	6.7	23.7	26.3	15.7	3.4	78.2	41.9	48.3	51.7
61358	RUTLAND	98.8	98.6	0.2	0.2	0.2	0.2	1.4	1.8	6.5	6.3	6.9	6.7	6.5	27.7	25.7	12.1	1.4	76.0	38.0	51.7	48.3
61360	SENECA	98.5	98.2	0.1	0.2	0.1	0.1	1.7	2.2	6.5	6.9	8.5	7.9	6.0	26.3	26.0	10.7	1.2	73.0	37.8	49.8	50.2
61361	SHEFFIELD	98.1	97.8	0.3	0.4	0.3	0.4	1.4	1.8	6.0	6.3	7.7	7.0	5.9	24.8	24.7	15.4	2.3	75.4	40.1	48.6	51.4
61362	SPRING VALLEY	95.9	95.1	0.7	0.8	0.5	0.6	6.5	8.5	6.1	5.9	6.5	6.5	7.1	25.5	25.0	13.8	3.7	77.8	39.8	48.4	51.6
61364	STREATOR	95.5	94.7	1.5	1.6	0.4	0.5	5.4	6.7	6.4	6.4	6.9	6.5	6.5	24.7	24.5	15.5	2.8	76.3	40.2	48.7	51.3
61367	SUBLETTE	98.2	98.2	0.5	0.5	0.0	0.0	2.9	3.0	5.6	6.0	7.5	6.7	5.5	25.4	26.7	15.3	1.3	76.6	40.5	50.8	49.3
61368	TISKILWA	97.8	97.5	0.2	0.2	0.5	0.6	0.8	1.0	6.1	6.6	7.3	6.0	5.5	24.2	27.7	14.6	2.1	76.5	41.4	49.3	50.7
61369	TOLUCA	97.9	97.6	0.1	0.1	0.3	0.4	1.4	1.7	5.5	5.7	6.8	5.2	4.8	24.8	24.1	18.6	4.6	78.8	43.1	47.0	53.0
61370	TONICA	98.5	98.4	0.2	0.2	0.4	0.4	2.8	3.6	5.9	6.4	6.9	5.4	4.8	25.5	25.6	16.0	3.4	77.6	42.1	48.8	51.2
61373	UTICA	97.9	97.4	0.2	0.3	0.3	0.4	2.2	2.8	6.6	6.8	7.0	5.9	5.0	27.0	25.5	12.9	3.4	76.0	40.7	47.5	52.5
61375	VARNA	98.6	98.5	0.1	0.1	0.1	0.2	1.3	1.6	5.5	6.1	7.0	5.2	5.0	24.2	30.3	15.2	1.6	78.1	42.8	49.7	50.3
61376	WALNUT	98.9	98.7	0.3	0.3	0.1	0.1	1.0	1.3	6.4	6.6	7.4	7.4	5.4	23.6	23.7	16.0	3.6	75.1	40.5	48.9	51.1
61377	WENONA	97.9	97.7	0.4	0.4	0.2	0.2	1.1	1.5	6.1	6.1	7.3	7.1	5.8	23.3	24.6	17.0	2.8	76.2	40.9	48.4	51.6
61378	WEST BROOKLYN	97.1	97.3	0.2	0.2	0.6	0.5	2.8	2.9	6.4	7.1	8.7	7.1	4.5	27.0	26.0	12.0	1.3	73.5	38.5	49.0	51.0
61379	WYANET	98.9	98.6	0.0	0.0	0.4	0.6	0.8	1.1	5.9	6.2	7.8	7.1	6.8	26.6	25.5	12.5	1.7	75.7	38.0	49.5	50.5
61401	GALESBURG	85.6	84.1	9.3	9.9	1.0	1.2	4.6	5.5	5.6	5.6	5.8	6.8	8.2	25.8	24.4	14.6	3.3	79.5	39.3	50.3	49.7
61410	ABINGDON	98.2	98.0	0.5	0.6	0.1	0.1	1.0	1.2	5.9	6.6	7.2	6.7	5.8	26.1	25.1	14.1	2.5	75.9	39.7	48.1	51.9
61411	ADAIR	98.9	98.6	0.4	0.4	0.2	0.4	0.9	1.2	5.2	5.2	5.8	5.4	5.0	24.8	28.5	18.0	1.9	80.8	44.1	49.6	50.4
61412	ALEXIS	99.2	99.3	0.1	0.1	0.1	0.1	1.3	1.4	5.1	5.2	5.4	7.1	5.7	25.2	28.8	15.6	2.0	80.1	43.0	50.6	49.4
61413	ALPHA	98.2	98.0	0.2	0.2	0.2	0.2	1.3	1.5	5.2	5.7	8.8	6.5	6.4	23.6	26.8	14.3	2.7	76.4	40.9	51.5	48.5
61414	ALTONA	99.2	99.2	0.0	0.0	0.1	0.1	0.8	0.9	6.8	7.3	7.6	6.9	5.6	24.5	27.4	12.1	1.9	74.0	39.8	49.4	50.6
61415	AVON	99.0	98.8	0.1	0.1	0.1	0.2	0.4	0.5	5.1	5.3	5.8	5.5	5.3	23.6	28.7	17.7	3.0	80.8	44.6	49.9	50.1
61417	BERWICK	99.4	99.4	0.0	0.0	0.3	0.3	0.6	0.6	6.1	6.4	6.7	5.8	5.2	26.3	27.2	15.0	1.5	77.5	41.1	50.3	49.7
61418	BIGGSVILLE	98.5	98.2	0.7	0.8	0.2	0.2	0.9	1.2	5.3	5.3	4.8	5.1	6.9	25.8	29.4	14.9	2.6	82.1	43.0	50.6	49.4
61420	BLANDINSVILLE	99.0	98.9	0.0	0.0	0.1	0.1	0.6	0.8	5.3	5.6	6.7	5.9	5.9	24.3	28.0	15.8	2.7	78.8	42.4	49.6	50.4
61421	BRADFORD	98.6	98.5	0.2	0.2	0.3	0.3	0.7	0.8	7.0	7.5	7.5	5.7	4.9	25.3	27.0	13.3	2.1	74.6	39.8	50.2	49.8
61422	BUSHNELL	98.8	98.6	0.1	0.1	0.1	0.2	0.6	0.8	6.2	6.7	7.4	6.3	5.8	26.8	24.2	14.2	2.4	76.0	38.1	48.2	51.8
61423	CAMERON	99.2	99.0	0.0	0.0	0.6	0.7	0.6	0.6	3.9	4.7	6.9	7.0	5.7	23.8	32.0	15.2	1.0	80.2	43.7	51.8	48.2
61425	CARMAN	98.4	98.7	0.0	0.0	0.0	0.0	1.1	1.1	4.6	4.6	4.6	5.1	5.4	23.7	35.5	15.9	0.8	83.1	46.2	50.0	50.0
61427	CUBA	98.5	98.2	0.2	0.2	0.3	0.3	0.5	0.7	5.8	6.0	6.3	6.6	5.9	24.3	27.7	14.4	3.1	77.7	41.6	48.7	51.3
61428	DAHINDA	98.4	98.2	0.6	0.6	0.4	0.5	1.3	1.7	4.1	4.3	4.2	4.6	3.8	19.6	38.4	19.8	1.2	84.7	51.1	53.2	46.8
61431	ELLISVILLE	99.2	99.2	0.3	0.3	0.0	0.0	0.5	0.3	4.5	5.0	6.1	5.5	4.3	25.9	29.2	17.4	2.0	81.4	44.3	53.4	46.6
61432	FAIRVIEW	99.2	99.1	0.2	0.2	0.2	0.3	0.2	0.2	4.8	5.4	7.3	5.8	6.2	25.6	28.0	14.4	2.5	78.7	41.6	53.3	46.7
61433	FIATT	100.0	100.0	0.0	0.0	0.0	0.0	0.0	0.0	5.8	5.8	7.7	5.8	5.8	28.9	23.1	15.4	1.9	80.8	38.8	57.7	42.3
61434	GALVA	98.2	98.0	0.5	0.5	0.1	0.1	1.8	2.3	5.9	6.0	7.0	6.6	6.0	24.5	26.0	15.0	3.1	77.0	41.1	48.6	51.4
61435	GERLAW	98.8	98.1	0.0	0.0	0.0	0.0	1.2	1.3	5.0	5.0	6.9	6.9	6.3	24.4	29.4	15.0	1.3	78.8	42.3	50.6	49.4
61436	GILSON	98.8	98.5	0.0	0.1	0.1	0.1	1.0	1.2	5.1	5.5	6.3	5.3	4.9	24.4	32.1	15.1	1.5	80.1	44.1	51.7	48.3
61437	GLADSTONE	98.5	98.1	0.2	0.2	0.3	0.3	0.8	0.9	4.7	5.0	5.8	5.5	5.8	23.9	34.1	14.2	1.2	81.3	44.6	50.6	49.4
61438	GOOD HOPE	99.3	99.2	0.0	0.0	0.3	0.4	0.3	0.3	6.6	7.0	6.8	5.1	4.7	26.2	26.9	15.5	1.3	76.5	40.9	51.3	48.7
61440	INDUSTRY	98.3	97.8	0.1	0.1	0.8	1.0	0.7	1.0	6.2	6.4	6.7	6.2	5.1	25.4	27.5	14.6	2.1	77.0	41.5	49.3	50.7
61441	IPAVA	98.8	98.8	0.0	0.0	0.1	0.1	0.9	0.8	5.8	6.1	6.7	5.0	5.8	24.2	28.8	14.8	2.9	78.4	42.5	50.8	49.2
61442	KEITHSBURG	98.1	98.1	0.4	0.4	0.0	0.0	0.4	0.4	6.5	8.1	6.5	5.6	5.7	25.0	25.9	15.8	0.9	75.6	39.6	48.9	51.1
61443	KEWANEE	90.9	89.5	3.3	3.6	0.4	0.4	5.8	7.1	7.0	6.4	6.4	6.4	7.3	24.3	23.1	15.6	3.5	76.5	39.1	47.7	52.3
61447	KIRKWOOD	98.1	97.6	0.1	0.1	0.2	0.2	1.6	2.2	7.2	6.7	5.3	6.7	6.4	25.2	27.9	13.1	1.6	76.8	40.7	48.9	51.1
61448	KNOXVILLE	98.2	97.9	0.4	0.5	0.1	0.2	1.0	1.3	5.8	5.8	6.2	6.3	5.8	22.7	28.2	15.4	3.9	78.3	43.2	47.8	52.2
61449	LA FAYETTE	98.5	98.6	0.0	0.0	0.2	0.2	1.0	1.0	5.3	5.9	7.1	7.1	6.7	24.7	28.3	13.2	1.6	77.5	40.6	50.2	49.8
61450	LA HARPE	99.3	99.2	0.0	0.0	0.0	0.0	0.1	0.1	5.3	5.8	7.4	6.4	6.1	22.8	26.2	16.1	3.8	77.2	42.3	47.5	52.5
61451	LAURA	96.9	96.1	0.0	0.0	0.0	0.2	2.7	3.7	7.0	7.0	7.2	5.7	5.7	26.3	26.3	12.9	2.0	75.1	39.0	50.1	49.9
61452	LITTLETON	98.1	98.4	0.8	0.8	0.0	0.0	0.5	0.5	6.3	6.5	6.8	5.4	5.7	25.3	28.3	13.9	1.9	77.5	41.5	51.6	48.4
61453	LITTLE YORK	99.0	99.0	0.0	0.0	0.2	0.2	0.8	1.0	5.7	6.1	8.5	6.9	6.5	24.0	29.0	11.5	2.0	75.8	39.6	51.0	49.0
61454	LOMAX	98.9	98.6	0.1	0.1	0.2	0.3	0.9	1.2	6.3	6.5	7.2	6.3	5.8	24.4	24.8	15.1	3.7	76.1	40.7	47.8	52.2
61455	MACOMB	89.8	88.4	5.2	5.6	3.0	3.7	1.9	2.3	3.8	3.5	4.2	15.6	20.8	21.2	17.9	10.5	2.5	85.9	26.3	48.4	51.6
61458	MAQUON	99.0	98.7	0.0	0.0	0.3	0.5	1.5	1.7	6.9	6.6	5.8	5.9	5.1	25.7	27.8	14.3	2.1	77.3	41.0	48.5	51.5
61459	MARIETTA	98.8	98.7	0.0	0.0	0.0	0.0	1.0	0.9	5.1	6.0	7.1	5.4	4.9	27.2	29.0	14.0	1.3	78.2	40.6	51.5	48.6
61460	MEDIA	97.0	96.4	1.1	1.3	0.0	0.0	0.6	0.9	6.1	6.1	6.6	6.8	6.6	23.5	27.1	15.9	1.3	76.9	41.4	50.2	49.8
61462	MONMOUTH	93.6	92.6	2.4	2.7	0.6	0.7	3.8	4.7	6.0	5.8	6.1	9.1	11.1	23.4	23.6	12.6	2.4	78.2	35.8	48.0	52.0
61465	NEW WINDSOR	98.5	98.6	0.1	0.1	0.2	0.2	2.3	2.3	5.3	5.8	6.7	6.5	5.3	25.0	26.6	16.2	2.8	78.2	42.4	49.7	50.3
61466	NORTH HENDERSON	98.8	99.1	0.0	0.0	0.0	0.0	2.1	2.1	5.3	5.3	5.3	7.1	6.2	24.6	28.8	15.1	2.1	79.8	42.3	49.9	50.2
61467	ONEIDA	98.6	98.5	0.1	0.1	0.4	0.5	1.1	1.3	6.2	6.4	6.7	6.0	5.4	25.2	27.4	14.7	2.1	76.9	41.2	50.2	49.8
61469	OQUAWKA	98.5	98.2	0.1	0.2	0.1	0.2	0.9	1.2	6.5	6.4	6.1	5.2	5.4	25.1	27.7	15.7	1.8	77.9	41.7	50.0	50.0
61470	PRAIRIE CITY	98.2	97.9	0.0	0.0	0.7	0.9	0.7	0.8	4.7	5.6	8.1	6.6	4.8	27.0	26.4	12.4	4.5	77.2	40.5	49.8	50.2
61471	RARITAN	96.9	96.6	1.2	1.2	0.0	0.0	0.9	0.9	6.2	6.2	6.5	6.8	6.8	24.1	26.5	15.7	1.2	77.5	41.0	50.0	50.0
61472	RIO	99.1	99.1	0.0	0.0	0.0	0.0	1.2	1.5	5.7	6.2	7.1	6.6	4.4	24.6	29.0	15.0	1.5	76.8	42.2	50.9	49.1
61473	ROSEVILLE	99.6	99.6	0.1	0.1	0.1	0.1	0.4	0.5	5.3	5.7	6.5	5.3	5.5	22.9	25.9	18.0	4.8	79.1	43.9	47.6	52.5
61474	SAINT AUGUSTINE	98.8	98.6	0.0	0.0	0.0	0.0	0.6	0.6	6.6	6.0	6.3	6.3	6.6	23.9	28.5	14.8	1.1	77.5	41.6	48.4	51.6
61475	SCIOTA	99.2	98.8	0.4	0.4	0.4	0.4	0.4	0.4	5.8	5.8	7.5	6.6	4.6	23.7	29.9	14.1	2.1	76.8	42.6	49.0	51.0
61476	SEATON	98.4	98.4	1.1	1.1	0.0	0.0	0.3	0.3	7.0	7.2	7.2	5.7	4.8	25.8	27.5	13.5	1.4	74.9	40.0	50.1	49.9
61477	SMITHFIELD	98.6	98.5	0.0	0.0	0.0	0.0	0.8	1.0	5.1	6.0	7.3	5.2	4.8	26.8	29.3	14.0	1.6	78.5	41.1	52.6	47.5
61478	SMITHSHIRE	99.7	99.7	0.0	0.0	0.0	0.0	0.6	0.6	6.9	7.2	6.3	5.1	4.5	27.4	26.8	14.2	1.5	76.2	40.5	49.7	50.3
61479	SPEER	98.2	98.2	0.0	0.0	0.0	0.0	2.6	2.6	7.1	7.3	7.3	5.7	5.3	26.3	26.1	13.1	2.0	74.7	39.7	52.0	48.0
61480	STRONGHURST	99.1	99.1	0.1	0.1	0.2	0.2	0.9	1.1	5.8	6.0	6.5	6.4	6.0	23.6	28.2	14.8	2.7	77.6	42.3	48.9	51.1
61482	TABLE GROVE	99.5	99.5	0.0	0.0	0.2	0.2	0.0	0.0	4.9	5.5	7.5	6.4	4.9	24.4	27.9	16.0	2.5	78.2	42.7	50.9	49.1
61483	TOULON	98.4	98.4	0.1	0.1	0.1	0.1	0.9	0.9	5.8	6.0	6.9	6.0	5.6	24.1	24.5	16.2	5.0	77.7	42.1	46.7	53.3
	ILLINOIS	73.5	71.8	15.1	15.2	3.5	4.0	12.3	14.2	7.1	7.0	7.3	7.0	7.3	29.0	23.2	10.4	1.7	74.5	35.2	49.0	51.0
	UNITED STATES	75.1	73.6	12.3	12.5	3.8	4.2	12.5	14.1	6.9	6.7	7.2	7.0	7.3	28.6	23.8	10.8	1.7	75.1	36.0	49.1	50.9

#	POST OFFICE NAME	2004 Per Capita Income	2004 HH Income Base	2004 Household Income Distribution (%): Less than $25,000	$25,000 to $49,999	$50,000 to $99,999	$100,000 to $149,999	$150,000 or More	Median Household Income: 2004	2009	2004 National Centile	2004 State Centile	2004 Home Value Base	2004 Home Value Distribution (%): Less than $50,000	$50,000 to $89,999	$90,000 to $174,999	$175,000 to $399,999	$400,000 or More	2004 Median Home Value
61321	DANA	18212	127	33.9	33.9	23.6	7.1	1.6	37569	43190	38	21	107	36.5	32.7	24.3	6.5	0.0	70556
61325	GRAND RIDGE	22470	388	18.8	32.0	36.1	9.3	3.9	48990	53532	70	61	332	9.9	19.9	42.5	21.7	6.0	119545
61326	GRANVILLE	20916	1279	24.5	31.4	35.4	7.9	0.9	46346	50689	65	54	1068	13.3	26.5	46.6	13.1	0.5	103222
61327	HENNEPIN	24442	515	19.4	29.9	37.5	9.9	3.3	50439	53634	73	64	442	5.7	15.2	50.2	26.7	2.3	134274
61329	LADD	24386	533	21.4	33.6	35.8	7.3	1.9	45781	52292	63	51	434	4.8	35.9	50.7	8.1	0.5	100266
61330	LA MOILLE	20805	624	20.5	35.9	35.6	5.6	2.4	43748	48666	58	44	500	7.0	29.2	44.4	17.4	2.0	110795
61333	LONG POINT	23145	201	18.9	26.4	42.3	9.0	3.5	53298	57874	77	70	171	20.5	19.9	38.6	16.4	4.7	109583
61334	LOSTANT	22214	289	18.0	36.7	36.3	8.3	0.7	46327	51989	65	53	249	14.1	27.7	49.0	6.8	2.4	102500
61335	MC NABB	23273	294	17.7	30.3	40.8	9.9	1.4	51579	55479	75	67	252	13.9	19.8	50.8	15.5	0.0	113830
61336	MAGNOLIA	21998	207	16.9	30.9	40.6	10.6	1.0	51733	56120	75	67	178	14.6	18.5	50.6	16.3	0.0	115625
61337	MALDEN	21088	306	18.0	26.1	46.7	7.5	1.6	54074	60695	78	72	257	12.1	28.0	45.5	13.2	1.2	101944
61341	MARSEILLES	21946	3106	22.8	29.8	36.7	8.7	2.1	47604	53297	67	57	2554	9.6	19.9	45.1	23.5	1.8	119400
61342	MENDOTA	21229	3566	23.2	31.4	35.8	7.0	2.6	46428	52356	65	54	2850	6.4	16.7	58.5	17.9	0.5	118666
61344	MINERAL	23898	175	17.1	38.9	34.3	6.3	3.4	43933	48198	58	45	144	21.5	27.8	33.3	12.5	4.9	91667
61345	NEPONSET	21869	312	23.4	32.7	34.6	8.3	1.0	43018	47514	56	42	268	29.9	33.2	28.0	7.8	1.1	78571
61346	NEW BEDFORD	25672	69	27.5	29.0	33.3	4.4	5.8	42372	48228	54	39	57	17.5	29.8	40.4	8.8	3.5	92500
61348	OGLESBY	22473	1999	31.9	27.8	30.8	7.2	2.4	40770	45618	49	33	1617	9.8	29.0	45.9	13.7	1.7	102351
61349	OHIO	21267	474	16.9	37.8	37.1	5.9	2.3	47205	53199	67	56	399	13.8	29.6	46.9	8.5	1.3	95096
61350	OTTAWA	22524	9960	28.6	29.6	30.4	8.3	3.0	42737	48234	55	41	7459	4.9	20.2	51.7	21.7	1.5	119394
61353	PAW PAW	20479	497	22.7	33.6	37.2	5.2	1.2	42827	47131	55	41	431	3.3	19.0	51.5	22.7	3.5	129303
61354	PERU	23192	4646	27.7	31.2	32.1	6.1	3.0	42364	47960	54	39	3626	4.1	24.8	56.1	13.8	1.3	112256
61356	PRINCETON	22808	5491	28.2	29.5	32.4	6.9	3.2	43310	47932	57	43	4271	12.0	20.3	49.0	18.0	0.8	113510
61358	RUTLAND	20472	207	30.4	33.8	28.0	6.3	1.5	39821	45128	45	29	174	32.8	29.9	27.0	9.8	0.6	76000
61360	SENECA	22679	1203	19.4	25.7	41.4	10.5	3.1	54085	60790	78	72	1051	9.1	10.6	49.8	28.5	2.0	140887
61361	SHEFFIELD	20668	820	21.2	39.5	32.0	6.5	0.9	41817	46732	52	36	672	18.2	39.0	33.0	6.0	3.9	82836
61362	SPRING VALLEY	22529	2287	27.8	28.0	33.3	7.9	3.0	42987	48192	56	41	1740	8.1	32.2	47.4	12.1	0.3	100561
61364	STREATOR	19397	8573	31.7	29.9	32.2	5.2	1.1	39146	44069	43	27	6689	22.8	35.8	34.3	6.8	0.3	80295
61367	SUBLETTE	27231	349	17.8	28.9	39.0	9.7	4.6	52461	55441	76	68	283	10.6	15.6	49.1	24.4	0.4	121272
61368	TISKILWA	20949	578	21.6	34.6	36.2	5.4	2.3	43103	48111	56	42	488	10.3	25.8	42.2	18.7	3.1	110119
61369	TOLUCA	21242	780	26.2	33.7	34.2	4.2	1.7	42530	47780	55	40	614	20.9	35.7	32.7	10.3	0.5	82857
61370	TONICA	25200	546	22.7	31.7	36.3	7.0	2.4	46035	51455	64	52	461	9.8	26.7	50.5	10.4	2.6	106057
61373	UTICA	26088	808	18.4	31.7	39.6	6.2	4.1	49871	55207	72	62	694	16.3	15.1	37.2	27.5	3.9	130405
61375	VARNA	22644	643	18.0	34.1	38.9	5.6	3.4	47888	52707	68	58	558	10.2	19.2	47.1	22.0	1.4	117568
61376	WALNUT	23053	845	26.3	33.3	30.1	6.2	4.3	42402	47420	54	39	712	11.5	35.3	44.2	7.4	1.5	93382
61377	WENONA	19256	556	34.4	27.2	32.9	4.3	1.3	39813	43182	45	29	435	17.7	38.2	39.3	4.6	0.2	85952
61378	WEST BROOKLYN	23843	213	17.4	25.8	45.5	9.4	1.9	54432	60177	79	73	176	7.4	20.5	41.5	23.3	7.4	121875
61379	WYANET	21129	647	21.0	35.9	36.9	4.8	1.4	45407	51719	62	50	525	10.5	34.3	43.8	9.5	1.9	95288
61401	GALESBURG	20846	14882	33.5	32.6	26.2	5.3	2.4	35793	39408	31	15	10377	20.6	37.6	33.6	7.5	0.7	81588
61410	ABINGDON	18119	1605	28.5	36.2	30.7	4.2	0.4	39692	44422	45	29	1290	27.8	39.9	30.3	1.9	0.0	68365
61411	ADAIR	22425	220	27.3	30.0	33.6	6.8	2.3	43818	49199	58	45	188	29.8	38.8	20.7	9.0	1.6	72143
61412	ALEXIS	21029	679	21.5	35.4	36.5	5.5	1.2	44925	49044	61	48	566	24.2	35.9	30.4	6.7	2.8	79038
61413	ALPHA	20391	433	21.5	35.6	37.2	4.2	1.6	43376	49589	57	43	376	23.4	38.3	31.9	4.8	1.6	78913
61414	ALTONA	17504	342	20.8	43.9	31.3	3.5	0.6	39668	45084	45	29	296	26.0	38.5	30.4	1.4	3.7	73750
61415	AVON	20387	842	26.1	34.9	30.8	5.7	2.5	40979	45786	50	34	692	29.1	33.1	26.6	9.4	1.9	75800
61417	BERWICK	22200	146	23.3	33.6	32.9	8.2	2.1	44441	47601	60	47	116	20.7	25.0	38.8	12.1	3.5	97143
61418	BIGGSVILLE	21373	261	24.9	34.5	34.9	3.5	2.3	42901	46249	56	41	217	39.2	31.3	20.7	8.8	0.0	60294
61420	BLANDINSVILLE	18544	527	31.5	34.9	29.4	3.2	1.0	37377	42275	37	21	420	33.1	37.9	22.9	5.5	0.7	66170
61421	BRADFORD	19515	747	25.3	34.7	32.3	5.6	2.1	41618	45514	52	35	621	16.9	33.3	36.1	10.1	3.5	89688
61422	BUSHNELL	19071	1532	32.8	37.5	25.1	3.0	1.6	35800	40143	31	15	1196	46.3	35.4	15.3	2.6	0.4	53667
61423	CAMERON	22338	280	15.0	34.3	39.6	10.0	1.1	50528	56612	73	64	243	13.6	31.7	39.5	14.0	1.2	103250
61425	CARMAN	21928	165	19.4	41.8	33.3	4.9	0.6	45110	50429	61	49	139	42.5	33.8	20.1	3.6	0.0	57500
61427	CUBA	19151	928	30.6	36.5	25.0	5.9	1.9	36666	41075	34	18	771	26.9	32.7	29.7	10.4	0.4	76351
61428	DAHINDA	29439	370	16.0	30.3	40.5	9.2	4.1	52245	58007	76	68	339	7.4	24.2	36.9	25.7	5.9	122750
61431	ELLISVILLE	19212	167	31.1	37.7	24.6	4.2	2.4	36345	40904	33	17	139	23.0	35.3	28.8	11.5	1.4	85400
61432	FAIRVIEW	19196	262	26.0	39.3	28.2	5.7	0.8	38729	43481	42	25	221	24.9	34.8	38.0	2.3	0.0	77500
61433	FIATT	20227	19	21.1	26.3	47.4	5.3	0.0	51328	50000	74	66	16	18.8	25.0	37.5	18.8	0.0	100000
61434	GALVA	20198	1534	30.8	31.2	30.6	5.8	1.6	38622	42987	41	25	1211	25.0	35.2	32.3	6.0	1.5	75840
61435	GERLAW	19516	69	23.2	42.0	31.9	2.9	0.0	37729	41907	38	22	57	10.5	17.5	52.6	17.5	1.8	115179
61436	GILSON	21140	390	16.4	38.5	36.4	6.9	1.8	45619	50487	63	51	337	12.2	31.8	38.6	13.4	4.2	102394
61437	GLADSTONE	21061	507	23.7	38.5	31.2	5.9	0.8	44702	47743	60	47	428	33.9	34.6	26.2	4.4	0.9	68611
61438	GOOD HOPE	20417	323	20.7	37.2	39.0	1.9	1.2	45894	51022	64	52	268	26.1	30.2	32.5	8.2	3.0	81905
61440	INDUSTRY	19376	344	25.0	31.7	36.6	5.8	0.9	45000	49747	61	48	291	24.7	34.0	25.8	14.1	1.4	77885
61441	IPAVA	18542	450	32.0	32.2	31.3	2.7	1.8	37770	41209	38	22	379	39.8	33.3	15.0	10.3	1.6	59167
61442	KEITHSBURG	17899	347	30.8	38.0	28.2	1.7	1.2	35801	40155	31	15	295	48.1	29.2	17.6	5.1	0.0	52500
61443	KEWANEE	18101	5893	35.7	35.0	23.2	4.5	1.7	33727	37518	23	9	4415	38.6	38.2	18.0	4.8	0.5	59592
61447	KIRKWOOD	17562	378	22.5	43.1	31.2	2.4	0.8	39642	45342	45	29	317	36.3	30.3	28.4	4.1	1.0	68200
61448	KNOXVILLE	23465	1755	18.0	30.1	40.7	7.6	3.5	51079	57969	74	65	1461	12.9	28.8	43.9	12.8	1.6	98796
61449	LA FAYETTE	18834	201	27.4	35.8	31.3	3.5	2.0	42145	46259	53	38	163	24.5	39.3	25.2	9.2	1.8	72143
61450	LA HARPE	18558	707	27.3	41.3	25.6	3.8	2.0	37534	42360	38	21	578	30.8	40.5	23.0	5.7	0.0	70857
61451	LAURA	21945	170	18.8	29.4	38.8	10.0	2.9	51055	57749	74	65	144	9.0	33.3	35.4	18.8	3.5	105208
61452	LITTLETON	21647	141	23.4	27.7	38.3	5.0	5.7	48660	49655	70	60	118	29.7	22.9	25.4	17.0	5.1	85714
61453	LITTLE YORK	19574	199	29.7	31.7	31.7	4.5	2.5	43330	46292	57	43	161	29.2	31.7	26.1	7.5	5.6	70500
61454	LOMAX	19087	409	28.4	34.2	31.8	4.7	1.0	38088	41816	40	23	341	32.0	36.7	23.2	7.6	0.6	65811
61455	MACOMB	19249	8194	42.3	27.2	22.7	5.6	2.1	31822	35073	17	6	4630	19.5	29.5	39.7	10.7	0.7	91536
61458	MAQUON	20456	379	20.8	45.7	28.0	5.0	0.5	40329	46081	47	31	305	27.2	34.4	28.9	7.5	2.0	75345
61459	MARIETTA	19369	177	22.6	40.1	31.1	4.5	1.7	38993	43957	43	26	152	36.2	27.0	25.0	11.2	0.7	68182
61460	MEDIA	18170	184	20.1	45.1	28.3	3.8	2.7	37944	41763	39	22	150	28.7	30.7	39.3	1.3	0.0	82632
61462	MONMOUTH	18967	4466	30.6	34.1	28.4	5.4	1.5	37936	41970	39	22	3280	27.2	35.6	29.7	6.8	0.7	74085
61465	NEW WINDSOR	21018	476	24.8	31.1	38.5	4.8	0.8	44364	47874	60	46	402	15.2	40.1	33.6	6.5	4.7	85116
61466	NORTH HENDERSON	20612	136	20.6	34.6	36.0	8.1	0.7	46369	50843	65	54	119	26.1	36.1	28.6	5.0	4.2	74091
61467	ONEIDA	21713	497	21.1	33.4	38.2	5.2	2.0	44912	49082	61	48	418	16.8	36.1	41.6	3.8	1.7	87209
61469	OQUAWKA	19086	1136	33.7	34.8	25.2	5.2	1.1	36287	39162	33	17	924	30.5	34.0	27.9	6.7	0.9	71443
61470	PRAIRIE CITY	19636	233	25.3	30.0	34.3	6.9	3.4	45991	50291	64	52	200	56.5	19.0	18.5	2.0	4.0	46061
61471	RARITAN	18166	126	20.6	45.2	27.8	4.0	2.4	37536	42521	38	21	102	27.5	31.4	39.2	2.0	0.0	83077
61472	RIO	23700	222	10.4	40.1	44.1	3.2	2.3	49686	54612	71	62	188	12.2	22.9	56.4	6.9	1.6	106667
61473	ROSEVILLE	19841	751	28.9	33.3	30.4	5.6	1.9	39245	43821	44	27	612	25.8	37.4	28.3	7.8	0.7	76557
61474	SAINT AUGUSTINE	18006	145	22.8	42.8	31.7	2.8	0.0	41154	45786	50	34	122	32.0	40.2	22.1	4.9	0.8	64667
61475	SCIOTA	20904	90	16.7	38.9	34.4	6.7	3.3	47510	52850	67	57	71	22.5	25.4	32.4	16.9	2.8	93750
61476	SEATON	22414	295	27.1	35.6	28.5	5.4	3.4	40401	44128	48	31	242	23.6	30.6	38.4	7.4	0.0	82857
61477	SMITHFIELD	19396	279	26.2	36.6	31.5	3.9	1.8	37704	42308	38	22	234	29.9	26.9	25.6	16.2	1.3	82000
61478	SMITHSHIRE	20158	133	27.8	32.3	30.1	7.5	2.3	40747	43399	49	33	100	24.0	22.0	40.0	11.0	3.0	95000
61479	SPEER	19377	189	18.0	40.2	33.9	6.9	1.1	44831	49175	61	48	153	5.9	32.7	39.9	17.7	3.9	106019
61480	STRONGHURST	18977	463	26.1	34.3	33.9	4.8	0.9	40770	44843	49	33	390	29.7	35.9	26.4	6.9	1.0	70625
61482	TABLE GROVE	21390	268	25.4	28.4	38.8	4.9	2.6	46323	50844	65	53	231	43.3	33.8	19.9	3.0	0.0	56458
61483	TOULON	19042	904	28.4	36.8	29.1	4.2	1.4	38711	42220	42	25	718	20.1	37.6	31.9	9.1	1.4	79306
	ILLINOIS	27033		22.1	25.9	32.9	11.9	7.3	52039	60941				7.7	12.8	34.0	36.6	8.9	162771
	UNITED STATES	25866		24.7	27.1	30.8	10.9	6.5	48124	56710				10.9	15.0	33.7	30.1	10.4	145905

# POST OFFICE NAME	FINANCIAL SERVICES: Auto Loan	FINANCIAL SERVICES: Home Loan	FINANCIAL SERVICES: Investments	FINANCIAL SERVICES: Retirement Plans	THE HOME: Home Improvements: Home Repair	THE HOME: Home Improvements: Lawn & Garden	THE HOME: Furnishings: Computers & Hardware	THE HOME: Furnishings: Major Appliances	THE HOME: Furnishings: TV, Radio, Sound Equipment	THE HOME: Furnishings: Furniture	ENTERTAINMENT: Dine out/ Carry out	ENTERTAINMENT: Sports Equipment	ENTERTAINMENT: Fees & Tickets	ENTERTAINMENT: Toys & Games	ENTERTAINMENT: Travel	ENTERTAINMENT: Cable TV	PERSONAL: Apparel & Services	PERSONAL: Auto Repairs	PERSONAL: Health Insurance	PERSONAL: Pets & Supplies
61321 DANA	79	70	54	67	74	80	65	72	69	65	84	86	64	86	67	71	80	70	78	93
61325 GRAND RIDGE	101	79	51	76	88	97	76	90	84	76	100	108	69	100	79	87	93	88	102	120
61326 GRANVILLE	82	72	55	69	76	83	68	75	73	68	88	89	67	89	70	74	84	73	81	95
61327 HENNEPIN	101	85	61	81	92	100	80	91	86	80	104	108	76	105	82	89	98	89	101	119
61329 LADD	72	81	87	78	81	87	78	77	79	76	98	87	83	105	81	80	96	76	79	85
61330 LA MOILLE	93	72	45	68	80	88	69	82	77	69	92	98	62	91	71	80	85	80	94	111
61333 LONG POINT	100	86	64	82	92	100	80	90	86	80	104	108	78	106	83	89	99	88	99	118
61334 LOSTANT	87	78	59	74	82	88	72	80	76	72	93	95	70	95	74	78	88	77	86	103
61335 MC NABB	96	80	55	76	86	94	75	86	82	75	98	103	71	99	77	84	92	84	96	113
61336 MAGNOLIA	98	80	54	76	87	95	76	87	83	75	99	105	71	100	78	86	93	85	98	116
61337 MALDEN	95	85	65	81	90	96	78	87	83	78	101	104	77	103	81	85	96	85	94	112
61341 MARSEILLES	84	80	70	78	83	89	76	81	79	76	96	95	76	98	78	80	92	79	85	98
61342 MENDOTA	82	75	65	73	79	88	74	79	78	73	96	91	73	97	76	81	91	78	86	95
61344 MINERAL	96	82	60	78	88	95	77	86	82	77	100	103	74	101	79	85	94	84	95	113
61345 NEPONSET	87	77	59	74	82	88	72	79	76	72	93	95	70	94	74	78	88	77	86	102
61346 NEW BEDFORD	109	76	40	72	88	99	75	93	86	74	101	112	64	99	78	91	92	91	110	129
61348 OGLESBY	75	68	60	65	71	81	70	73	74	67	90	82	68	90	71	77	85	72	82	85
61349 OHIO	97	69	38	65	80	89	68	83	78	67	91	100	59	90	70	81	84	82	98	115
61350 OTTAWA	76	77	76	75	79	85	76	77	77	74	95	89	77	98	77	79	92	76	81	89
61353 PAW PAW	84	74	57	71	79	84	69	76	73	69	89	91	67	91	71	75	84	74	83	98
61354 PERU	75	75	77	74	76	82	75	76	76	74	94	89	75	95	76	76	90	76	78	87
61356 PRINCETON	76	77	75	74	78	84	74	76	75	74	93	88	75	95	76	76	90	75	78	88
61358 RUTLAND	80	71	54	68	75	81	66	73	70	66	85	87	65	87	68	72	81	71	79	94
61360 SENECA	92	90	79	86	93	98	83	89	85	83	105	105	84	109	86	87	101	87	92	110
61361 SHEFFIELD	78	68	55	64	73	81	67	73	73	65	88	85	65	91	69	75	83	72	83	92
61362 SPRING VALLEY	79	75	68	73	77	85	75	78	78	73	95	89	74	97	76	79	90	77	83	90
61364 STREATOR	65	64	61	60	66	73	64	65	67	62	83	74	65	86	65	70	79	65	72	76
61367 SUBLETTE	112	94	67	89	102	110	88	100	96	88	115	120	84	117	91	98	108	98	111	132
61368 TISKILWA	72	75	74	72	77	84	72	74	75	71	92	84	75	98	75	77	89	72	79	85
61369 TOLUCA	66	68	68	65	70	77	67	68	69	65	86	76	69	92	69	72	83	66	73	77
61370 TONICA	100	76	47	72	86	95	74	87	82	73	98	105	66	97	76	86	91	86	101	119
61373 UTICA	101	86	64	82	91	102	85	93	92	83	110	108	81	109	86	95	103	92	105	116
61375 VARNA	89	76	56	71	82	89	71	81	77	70	92	96	67	93	74	80	87	79	90	106
61376 WALNUT	105	74	38	69	86	96	73	90	84	72	98	108	62	96	75	88	89	89	107	125
61377 WENONA	75	58	39	56	63	74	62	68	69	59	81	77	56	78	62	72	75	68	80	83
61378 WEST BROOKLYN	99	88	67	84	93	100	81	90	86	81	105	107	80	107	84	89	100	88	98	116
61379 WYANET	83	71	56	70	75	84	71	77	75	70	91	89	68	91	71	77	86	76	84	94
61401 GALESBURG	63	62	63	61	63	70	64	65	66	62	81	74	64	82	64	67	78	65	68	73
61410 ABINGDON	60	63	64	60	64	70	61	62	63	60	78	71	64	83	63	65	75	61	65	71
61411 ADAIR	95	66	35	63	77	87	66	81	76	65	89	98	56	87	68	79	81	80	97	113
61412 ALEXIS	83	68	48	65	75	81	65	75	71	65	85	90	61	86	67	73	80	74	84	99
61413 ALPHA	92	64	33	60	74	83	63	78	73	62	85	94	54	84	65	76	78	77	93	109
61414 ALTONA	83	58	30	55	68	76	57	71	66	57	78	86	49	76	60	69	71	70	85	99
61415 AVON	70	70	67	67	72	79	67	70	70	66	86	80	69	90	70	72	83	69	75	82
61417 BERWICK	92	69	42	65	78	86	67	80	75	66	89	96	60	88	69	78	82	78	92	108
61418 BIGGSVILLE	63	74	82	70	73	80	70	70	69	69	86	78	74	90	73	71	85	68	71	76
61420 BLANDINSVILLE	72	57	40	56	62	70	58	65	63	57	76	76	54	75	59	65	71	64	73	81
61421 BRADFORD	84	66	44	63	73	81	65	75	71	64	85	88	60	85	66	74	79	73	84	97
61422 BUSHNELL	74	59	42	57	63	73	62	68	68	60	81	77	57	78	62	70	75	67	77	82
61423 CAMERON	93	82	62	78	87	94	76	85	81	76	99	101	75	101	79	83	94	83	92	110
61425 CARMAN	83	67	47	62	74	82	63	74	70	63	83	87	58	83	66	74	78	73	85	100
61427 CUBA	67	64	59	62	67	75	64	67	67	62	82	76	64	83	66	70	78	66	74	78
61428 DAHINDA	108	86	60	79	95	107	82	97	92	81	110	113	75	108	87	97	102	95	113	129
61431 ELLISVILLE	79	59	37	56	67	75	58	69	65	57	77	83	51	77	60	68	71	68	81	94
61432 FAIRVIEW	61	66	69	62	67	74	65	64	67	63	84	72	69	91	67	70	81	63	69	71
61433 FIATT	76	81	81	78	82	87	77	79	77	76	95	92	78	99	79	77	93	78	80	92
61434 GALVA	71	65	58	62	69	77	64	69	68	62	83	79	63	85	66	71	79	68	76	84
61435 GERLAW	81	58	31	54	67	75	57	70	65	56	76	84	49	75	59	68	70	69	82	97
61436 GILSON	84	78	65	75	81	87	73	79	76	73	93	93	72	95	75	78	89	78	84	99
61437 GLADSTONE	80	69	51	64	74	80	64	72	69	64	83	86	61	84	66	72	79	71	80	95
61438 GOOD HOPE	88	62	32	58	72	80	61	75	70	60	82	90	52	80	63	73	75	74	89	104
61440 INDUSTRY	89	63	33	59	73	81	62	76	71	61	83	92	53	82	64	75	76	75	91	106
61441 IPAVA	66	59	51	56	63	70	58	63	63	57	76	73	57	80	60	66	72	62	71	77
61442 KEITHSBURG	78	57	34	51	63	72	55	66	64	56	76	78	49	73	56	68	70	65	79	90
61443 KEWANEE	58	59	61	56	60	67	59	60	61	58	76	67	61	79	61	63	73	59	64	67
61447 KIRKWOOD	65	62	56	58	65	72	61	64	65	59	79	73	61	84	63	68	75	63	71	76
61448 KNOXVILLE	81	85	85	83	86	92	83	84	83	81	102	97	84	104	84	83	99	83	85	95
61449 LA FAYETTE	86	60	31	57	70	78	59	73	68	58	80	88	51	78	61	72	73	72	87	102
61450 LA HARPE	74	57	38	55	62	73	61	67	68	58	80	77	55	77	61	71	73	67	79	83
61451 LAURA	95	83	62	79	89	95	77	87	83	77	100	103	75	102	80	85	95	84	94	112
61452 LITTLETON	102	71	37	67	83	93	70	87	81	70	95	105	60	93	73	85	87	86	104	121
61453 LITTLE YORK	88	62	32	58	72	80	61	75	70	60	82	91	52	81	63	74	75	74	90	105
61454 LOMAX	72	61	48	61	64	72	62	67	66	61	80	77	60	80	62	67	75	66	72	80
61455 MACOMB	62	52	57	55	53	58	65	59	65	61	80	74	60	77	60	61	77	64	58	68
61458 MAQUON	66	66	62	62	68	74	63	66	66	62	82	75	65	87	66	69	79	64	71	78
61459 MARIETTA	81	68	48	65	74	80	64	73	69	64	83	87	61	84	66	71	79	71	81	96
61460 MEDIA	84	59	32	56	69	77	58	72	67	58	79	86	50	77	61	70	72	71	85	99
61462 MONMOUTH	67	61	59	59	64	71	64	66	67	62	82	76	62	83	64	68	78	66	71	78
61465 NEW WINDSOR	68	75	79	71	75	82	71	72	71	70	88	82	74	92	74	73	86	71	74	81
61466 NORTH HENDERSON	81	73	56	69	77	82	67	75	71	67	87	89	66	89	70	73	83	73	80	96
61467 ONEIDA	98	69	36	65	80	89	68	84	78	67	91	101	58	90	70	82	83	83	100	117
61469 OQUAWKA	78	57	34	52	63	73	58	67	66	57	78	78	51	75	58	70	72	67	80	88
61470 PRAIRIE CITY	87	78	59	74	82	88	72	80	76	72	93	95	70	95	74	78	88	78	86	103
61471 RARITAN	85	59	31	56	69	77	58	72	67	58	79	87	50	77	60	70	72	71	86	100
61472 RIO	100	77	49	73	86	95	75	89	83	74	99	106	67	98	77	87	92	87	102	119
61473 ROSEVILLE	73	63	52	60	67	77	64	70	69	62	83	80	61	82	65	72	78	69	79	85
61474 SAINT AUGUSTINE	80	56	28	49	63	71	54	66	64	55	75	79	47	72	55	68	69	65	80	92
61475 SCIOTA	97	74	47	71	83	91	72	85	80	71	94	102	64	94	74	82	87	84	98	115
61476 SEATON	79	78	75	76	80	89	77	80	79	76	97	90	78	99	78	81	93	78	84	91
61477 SMITHFIELD	81	65	43	61	71	78	62	71	68	61	81	85	57	81	64	70	76	70	81	95
61478 SMITHSHIRE	90	64	34	60	74	83	63	77	72	62	85	93	54	83	65	76	78	76	92	107
61479 SPEER	94	66	35	62	77	86	65	81	75	64	88	97	56	86	68	79	80	79	96	112
61480 STRONGHURST	76	66	51	64	69	76	64	70	68	64	83	81	62	83	65	70	78	68	76	86
61482 TABLE GROVE	94	66	35	62	77	86	65	80	75	64	88	97	56	86	67	79	80	79	95	112
61483 TOULON	79	57	33	54	65	74	59	69	67	57	79	81	51	76	60	70	72	69	82	92
ILLINOIS	98	100	111	99	99	106	100	99	101	100	126	115	102	127	100	100	123	100	98	112
UNITED STATES	100	100	100	100	100	100	100	100	100	100	100	100	100	100	100	100	100	100	100	100

POPULATION CHANGE

#	POST OFFICE NAME	COUNTY FIPS CODE	POPULATION 2000	POPULATION 2004	POPULATION 2009	2000-2004 ANNUAL RATE % Rate	2000-2004 ANNUAL RATE State Centile	HOUSEHOLDS 2000	HOUSEHOLDS 2004	HOUSEHOLDS 2009	% Annual Rate 2000-2004	2004 Average HH Size	FAMILIES 2000	FAMILIES 2004	% Annual Rate 2000-2004
61484	VERMONT	057	958	947	938	-0.3	26	376	376	377	0.0	2.52	268	265	-0.3
61485	VICTORIA	095	641	608	586	-1.2	2	237	227	222	-1.0	2.68	183	173	-1.3
61486	VIOLA	131	1591	1601	1608	0.2	50	618	630	640	0.5	2.54	467	469	0.1
61488	WATAGA	095	1224	1193	1163	-0.6	13	479	479	475	0.0	2.49	372	367	-0.3
61489	WILLIAMSFIELD	095	1006	913	865	-2.3	0	390	359	346	-1.9	2.53	286	260	-2.2
61490	WOODHULL	073	1172	1160	1145	-0.2	28	488	489	489	0.1	2.37	348	344	-0.3
61491	WYOMING	175	1592	1626	1649	0.5	66	691	720	743	1.0	2.26	466	479	0.7
61501	ASTORIA	057	2022	2000	1976	-0.3	27	829	835	836	0.2	2.35	586	581	-0.2
61516	BENSON	203	855	865	897	0.3	56	316	325	343	0.7	2.65	237	240	0.3
61517	BRIMFIELD	143	3198	3314	3376	0.8	75	1161	1228	1271	1.3	2.70	924	965	1.0
61519	BRYANT	057	19	19	19	0.0	42	9	9	9	0.0	2.11	6	6	0.0
61520	CANTON	057	19398	19102	18884	-0.4	21	7282	7253	7249	-0.1	2.32	4842	4747	-0.5
61523	CHILLICOTHE	143	11037	11100	11158	0.1	48	4373	4475	4568	0.5	2.45	3186	3216	0.2
61524	DUNFERMLINE	057	21	21	20	0.0	42	11	11	11	0.0	1.91	8	8	0.0
61525	DUNLAP	143	5408	5740	5909	1.4	83	1895	2052	2147	1.9	2.80	1551	1659	1.6
61526	EDELSTEIN	143	915	985	1019	1.8	87	301	328	344	2.0	3.00	249	269	1.8
61528	EDWARDS	143	1729	1802	1834	1.0	77	635	670	691	1.3	2.68	490	509	0.9
61529	ELMWOOD	143	2677	2742	2766	0.6	68	1050	1095	1121	1.0	2.48	784	804	0.6
61530	EUREKA	203	6149	6367	6700	0.8	75	2147	2265	2431	1.3	2.53	1502	1558	0.9
61531	FARMINGTON	057	3483	3470	3448	-0.1	37	1389	1401	1408	0.2	2.41	985	979	-0.1
61532	FOREST CITY	125	588	581	576	-0.3	26	209	209	208	0.0	2.78	161	159	-0.3
61533	GLASFORD	143	2054	2072	2073	0.2	53	789	811	825	0.7	2.55	611	621	0.4
61534	GREEN VALLEY	179	1800	1806	1815	0.1	46	643	656	669	0.5	2.73	512	516	0.2
61535	GROVELAND	179	1526	1549	1563	0.4	60	571	592	609	0.9	2.62	456	467	0.6
61536	HANNA CITY	143	2948	3088	3154	1.1	79	1042	1121	1167	1.7	2.53	823	875	1.5
61537	HENRY	123	3217	3207	3253	-0.1	38	1269	1287	1329	0.3	2.43	863	861	-0.1
61540	LACON	123	2792	2871	2949	0.7	71	1112	1164	1215	1.1	2.37	797	822	0.7
61542	LEWISTOWN	057	3970	3907	3855	-0.4	20	1639	1636	1634	0.0	2.33	1096	1073	-0.5
61543	LIVERPOOL	057	176	172	169	-0.5	15	71	70	70	-0.3	2.46	54	53	-0.4
61544	LONDON MILLS	057	770	755	743	-0.5	17	286	286	284	0.0	2.64	221	218	-0.3
61545	LOWPOINT	203	890	970	1054	2.1	89	324	362	401	2.6	2.68	260	287	2.4
61546	MANITO	179	4411	4370	4355	-0.2	29	1691	1705	1722	0.2	2.56	1315	1311	-0.1
61547	MAPLETON	143	3803	3966	4036	1.0	78	1334	1417	1466	1.4	2.79	1125	1184	1.2
61548	METAMORA	203	9177	10099	10962	2.3	91	3226	3622	4002	2.8	2.75	2595	2889	2.6
61550	MORTON	179	16807	16841	17022	0.1	44	6617	6735	6917	0.4	2.43	4766	4796	0.2
61552	MOSSVILLE	143	197	216	226	2.2	90	79	88	94	2.8	2.43	65	72	2.4
61554	PEKIN	179	44686	45712	46514	0.5	67	17404	18131	18795	1.0	2.39	11993	12290	0.6
61559	PRINCEVILLE	143	3020	3135	3189	0.9	76	1151	1216	1257	1.3	2.58	871	905	0.9
61560	PUTNAM	155	814	860	922	1.3	82	341	368	401	1.8	2.33	263	280	1.5
61561	ROANOKE	203	2723	2740	2838	0.2	50	976	999	1054	0.6	2.68	745	753	0.3
61563	SAINT DAVID	057	14	14	14	0.0	42	5	5	5	0.0	2.80	4	4	0.0
61565	SPARLAND	123	1749	1778	1816	0.4	62	636	661	688	0.9	2.69	508	522	0.6
61567	TOPEKA	125	1116	1160	1180	0.9	76	435	458	466	1.2	2.53	321	333	0.9
61568	TREMONT	179	4300	4275	4285	-0.1	34	1554	1570	1598	0.2	2.71	1220	1219	0.0
61569	TRIVOLI	143	1291	1319	1333	0.5	66	496	518	533	1.0	2.54	410	424	0.8
61570	WASHBURN	203	1853	1848	1908	-0.1	38	694	704	739	0.3	2.63	522	521	-0.1
61571	WASHINGTON	179	19684	20045	20379	0.4	64	7731	8018	8295	0.9	2.48	5612	5744	0.6
61572	YATES CITY	095	1163	1132	1103	-0.6	11	476	472	467	-0.2	2.40	347	340	-0.5
61602	PEORIA	143	722	693	685	-1.0	4	339	324	322	-1.1	1.67	139	128	-1.9
61603	PEORIA	143	18930	18229	18016	-0.9	5	7206	7001	6997	-0.7	2.51	4280	4056	-1.3
61604	PEORIA	143	32916	32606	32487	-0.2	29	13217	13265	13390	0.1	2.35	8294	8131	-0.5
61605	PEORIA	143	18645	17921	17754	-0.9	5	6952	6775	6801	-0.6	2.61	4442	4208	-1.3
61606	PEORIA	143	7914	7727	7679	-0.6	14	2859	2806	2812	-0.4	2.34	1293	1233	-1.1
61607	PEORIA	143	10248	10282	10311	0.1	46	4133	4226	4306	0.5	2.43	3011	3027	0.1
61610	CREVE COEUR	179	5459	5380	5383	-0.3	22	2223	2229	2269	0.1	2.41	1494	1474	-0.3
61611	EAST PEORIA	179	24905	25088	25521	0.2	51	10241	10515	10883	0.6	2.35	7186	7277	0.3
61614	PEORIA	143	27478	27591	27742	0.1	47	12151	12391	12643	0.5	2.16	7363	7356	0.0
61615	PEORIA	143	19435	20876	21653	1.7	86	8237	8994	9463	2.1	2.27	5425	5824	1.7
61616	PEORIA HEIGHTS	143	6783	6590	6521	-0.7	10	3201	3158	3170	-0.3	2.06	1699	1628	-1.0
61625	PEORIA	143	1751	1744	1740	-0.1	37	6	6	6	0.0	2.50	3	3	0.0
61635	PEORIA	179	108	111	114	0.7	71	10	10	11	0.0	2.60	8	8	0.0
61701	BLOOMINGTON	113	37118	37337	39017	0.1	49	16175	16601	17697	0.6	2.11	8377	8360	-0.1
61704	BLOOMINGTON	113	35518	40352	44934	3.1	94	13287	15233	17150	3.3	2.64	9608	10930	3.1
61720	ANCHOR	113	356	347	360	-0.6	13	117	116	123	-0.2	2.91	88	86	-0.5
61721	ARMINGTON	179	658	657	659	0.0	39	238	240	243	0.2	2.74	193	192	-0.1
61722	ARROWSMITH	113	724	726	760	0.1	45	245	250	267	0.5	2.88	195	196	0.1
61723	ATLANTA	107	2462	2436	2404	-0.3	27	968	976	980	0.2	2.32	703	700	-0.1
61724	BELLFLOWER	113	659	650	677	-0.3	24	250	252	268	0.2	2.58	190	189	-0.1
61725	CARLOCK	113	1114	1218	1319	2.1	89	424	475	525	2.7	2.56	344	380	2.4
61726	CHENOA	113	2966	2999	3157	0.3	55	1105	1139	1221	0.7	2.57	828	839	0.3
61727	CLINTON	039	10425	10434	10461	0.0	42	4226	4292	4363	0.4	2.39	2839	2840	0.0
61728	COLFAX	113	1482	1484	1542	0.0	43	571	581	613	0.4	2.47	394	394	0.0
61729	CONGERVILLE	203	891	942	1001	1.3	82	315	340	368	1.8	2.77	268	288	1.7
61730	COOKSVILLE	113	439	428	446	-0.6	13	183	182	193	-0.1	2.30	139	136	-0.5
61731	CROPSEY	113	236	232	242	-0.4	19	80	80	85	0.0	2.90	65	65	0.0
61732	DANVERS	113	2105	2171	2279	0.7	73	753	794	850	1.3	2.73	597	621	0.9
61733	DEER CREEK	203	1683	1759	1833	1.0	78	602	639	675	1.4	2.75	477	502	1.2
61734	DELAVAN	179	2897	2867	2868	-0.2	28	1080	1078	1092	0.0	2.65	833	821	-0.3
61735	DEWITT	039	465	474	477	0.5	64	179	185	190	0.8	2.56	137	141	0.7
61736	DOWNS	113	1624	1606	1673	-0.3	27	572	577	611	0.2	2.78	474	472	-0.1
61737	ELLSWORTH	113	622	620	648	-0.1	37	216	219	233	0.3	2.83	177	177	0.0
61738	EL PASO	203	3819	3936	4121	0.7	72	1384	1451	1546	1.1	2.60	1028	1062	0.8
61739	FAIRBURY	105	4765	4808	4880	0.2	53	1797	1841	1900	0.6	2.54	1261	1274	0.2
61740	FLANAGAN	105	1533	1548	1565	0.2	54	580	598	615	0.7	2.41	400	407	0.4
61741	FORREST	105	1811	1838	1866	0.4	60	644	658	674	0.5	2.79	494	499	0.2
61742	GOODFIELD	203	633	727	806	3.3	95	209	243	272	3.6	2.99	175	201	3.3
61743	GRAYMONT	105	240	238	239	-0.2	31	88	88	90	0.0	2.70	71	70	-0.3
61744	GRIDLEY	113	2147	2141	2211	-0.1	38	801	813	853	0.4	2.60	595	582	-0.5
61745	HEYWORTH	113	3717	3835	4029	0.7	73	1367	1435	1531	1.2	2.67	1078	1114	0.8
61747	HOPEDALE	179	1501	1568	1606	1.0	78	530	562	585	1.4	2.64	424	445	1.1
61748	HUDSON	113	2587	2595	2711	0.1	45	955	977	1037	0.5	2.66	771	765	-0.2
61749	KENNEY	039	797	799	800	0.1	45	331	338	344	0.5	2.36	244	245	0.1
61752	LE ROY	113	4047	4094	4274	0.3	56	1564	1613	1714	0.7	2.50	1142	1157	0.3
61753	LEXINGTON	113	3004	3034	3195	0.2	54	1180	1218	1306	0.8	2.46	880	889	0.2
61754	MC LEAN	113	1332	1362	1440	0.5	67	498	520	560	1.0	2.58	389	400	0.7
	ILLINOIS					0.7					0.9	2.61			0.6
	UNITED STATES					1.2					1.3	2.58			1.1

ZIP CODE #	POST OFFICE NAME	RACE (%) White 2000	White 2004	Black 2000	Black 2004	Asian/Pacific 2000	Asian/Pacific 2004	% Hispanic Origin 2000	% Hispanic Origin 2004	2004 AGE DISTRIBUTION (%) 0-4	5-9	10-14	15-19	20-24	25-44	45-64	65-84	85+	18+	MEDIAN AGE 2004	% 2004 Males	% 2004 Females
61484	VERMONT	98.0	97.6	0.0	0.0	0.3	0.3	0.8	1.3	6.8	6.8	7.6	7.2	6.0	25.0	24.8	13.9	1.9	74.5	38.5	52.0	48.1
61485	VICTORIA	99.2	99.0	0.0	0.0	0.0	0.0	0.6	1.0	6.6	6.9	6.6	6.3	4.6	25.0	28.1	14.1	1.8	76.2	41.5	52.1	47.9
61486	VIOLA	97.3	97.3	0.4	0.4	0.1	0.1	2.8	2.9	6.0	6.8	8.2	7.1	4.9	27.8	25.2	12.5	1.4	74.5	38.8	49.7	50.3
61488	WATAGA	98.2	97.9	0.4	0.4	0.2	0.2	1.2	1.4	6.0	6.4	6.5	6.2	6.9	24.9	29.9	11.9	1.3	77.4	40.5	48.1	51.9
61489	WILLIAMSFIELD	99.1	98.7	0.0	0.0	0.0	0.0	0.8	1.1	6.6	6.7	6.5	5.6	5.5	28.0	25.6	13.6	2.0	76.7	39.5	50.7	49.3
61490	WOODHULL	98.9	98.7	0.3	0.3	0.2	0.2	1.2	1.6	4.7	5.3	7.7	6.6	5.7	25.8	26.8	15.3	2.2	78.4	41.6	50.8	49.2
61491	WYOMING	98.9	98.9	0.1	0.1	0.2	0.2	0.3	0.2	6.4	6.7	7.1	5.7	5.7	23.8	26.2	15.9	2.6	76.2	40.7	48.0	52.0
61501	ASTORIA	98.6	98.3	0.0	0.0	0.2	0.3	1.0	1.4	5.2	5.5	7.4	5.9	6.1	25.3	23.9	17.8	3.2	78.4	41.4	49.0	51.0
61516	BENSON	99.3	99.2	0.1	0.1	0.1	0.1	0.2	0.2	7.4	7.6	8.0	6.6	5.6	25.1	23.0	14.8	2.0	72.7	38.0	50.1	49.9
61517	BRIMFIELD	98.0	97.5	0.3	0.4	0.1	0.2	1.3	1.7	6.3	6.9	7.8	6.3	5.3	25.2	30.0	10.9	1.3	74.7	40.3	51.2	48.8
61519	BRYANT	100.0	100.0	0.0	0.0	0.0	0.0	0.0	0.0	5.3	5.3	10.5	10.5	10.5	36.8	21.1	0.0	0.0	79.0	31.3	47.4	52.6
61520	CANTON	91.5	90.6	7.0	7.7	0.4	0.5	1.8	2.1	5.5	5.3	5.6	6.1	7.5	29.3	23.2	14.7	2.9	80.2	38.8	53.5	46.5
61523	CHILLICOTHE	97.7	97.2	0.3	0.3	0.4	0.5	2.3	2.9	6.1	6.6	7.1	6.4	5.7	25.8	28.2	12.2	2.0	76.3	39.9	49.1	50.9
61524	DUNFERMLINE	100.0	100.0	0.0	0.0	0.0	0.0	0.0	0.0	4.8	4.8	4.8	9.5	4.8	38.1	33.3	0.0	0.0	85.7	36.3	47.6	52.4
61525	DUNLAP	96.2	95.3	0.7	0.9	2.0	2.5	0.9	1.2	6.2	6.9	8.0	7.3	5.2	23.7	32.3	9.5	0.9	74.3	40.4	50.0	50.0
61526	EDELSTEIN	98.5	98.2	0.2	0.3	0.4	0.5	0.9	1.1	5.6	6.4	7.6	7.2	5.7	23.5	32.9	9.8	1.4	76.0	41.5	50.5	49.5
61528	EDWARDS	94.3	92.8	3.0	3.7	1.7	2.2	1.3	1.7	7.1	7.1	6.9	6.2	5.2	26.2	30.2	9.5	1.6	74.5	39.6	50.6	49.5
61529	ELMWOOD	98.0	97.6	0.7	0.8	0.2	0.2	0.9	1.1	6.9	6.6	7.2	6.3	5.3	26.2	25.2	13.6	2.8	75.0	40.0	48.5	51.5
61530	EUREKA	97.9	97.6	0.5	0.6	0.4	0.5	1.0	1.2	6.5	6.9	6.9	8.5	10.4	23.0	19.8	12.8	5.3	76.0	34.8	47.2	52.8
61531	FARMINGTON	98.8	98.6	0.1	0.2	0.1	0.2	0.8	1.1	6.5	6.5	6.4	5.5	5.6	25.7	24.4	15.8	3.7	77.2	40.7	48.5	51.5
61532	FOREST CITY	98.8	98.6	0.2	0.3	0.0	0.2	0.7	0.5	7.1	7.4	7.9	6.9	4.8	26.5	26.0	11.9	1.6	73.2	38.1	50.3	49.7
61533	GLASFORD	98.9	98.7	0.0	0.0	0.0	0.1	0.7	1.0	5.2	5.5	6.9	6.5	7.1	27.2	28.4	11.8	1.4	78.6	39.4	48.9	51.1
61534	GREEN VALLEY	99.2	99.2	0.1	0.1	0.1	0.1	0.6	0.7	6.9	7.1	8.0	7.6	6.4	27.1	26.1	9.4	1.4	73.4	37.1	48.7	51.3
61535	GROVELAND	98.2	97.9	0.1	0.1	0.6	0.8	1.0	1.2	4.7	6.4	7.4	5.8	3.7	23.5	36.0	11.2	1.3	77.4	44.1	49.3	50.7
61536	HANNA CITY	91.5	89.7	6.4	7.7	0.6	0.8	1.1	1.5	5.9	6.4	6.1	5.9	5.7	30.0	27.0	11.4	1.7	77.7	39.2	52.9	47.2
61537	HENRY	97.6	97.2	0.6	0.7	0.3	0.4	0.7	0.9	6.1	6.1	7.1	6.1	6.1	23.8	25.4	15.9	3.5	76.9	41.3	48.6	51.4
61540	LACON	99.2	99.0	0.1	0.1	0.2	0.2	0.9	1.1	5.2	5.5	6.8	5.7	5.6	23.7	26.5	16.8	4.3	79.1	43.4	48.8	51.2
61542	LEWISTOWN	99.0	98.8	0.1	0.1	0.2	0.2	0.9	1.2	5.1	5.3	6.1	6.5	6.2	24.5	25.9	17.0	3.4	79.4	42.5	48.6	51.5
61543	LIVERPOOL	98.9	98.3	0.0	0.0	0.6	0.6	1.1	1.7	4.7	5.2	5.8	6.4	5.8	25.6	31.4	14.0	1.2	80.2	42.9	52.3	47.7
61544	LONDON MILLS	99.4	99.3	0.1	0.1	0.0	0.0	0.4	0.4	7.2	7.0	5.2	7.4	5.2	25.8	25.8	14.2	2.3	76.0	40.7	48.5	51.5
61545	LOWPOINT	97.5	97.0	0.5	0.5	0.7	0.8	1.4	1.8	5.5	6.1	6.9	7.6	6.4	25.0	29.8	11.2	1.6	77.1	40.6	51.9	48.1
61546	MANITO	98.6	98.4	0.3	0.3	0.3	0.3	0.4	0.5	6.1	6.4	6.7	5.9	5.7	26.8	29.1	11.9	1.4	77.2	40.5	51.4	48.6
61547	MAPLETON	97.6	97.0	0.6	0.7	0.4	0.5	1.0	1.3	6.5	6.8	6.6	6.1	5.5	27.3	31.3	9.3	0.8	76.6	39.8	50.4	49.7
61548	METAMORA	98.5	98.2	0.3	0.3	0.4	0.5	0.6	0.8	6.4	7.4	8.0	7.0	5.2	24.6	28.2	11.0	2.1	73.7	39.5	48.6	51.4
61550	MORTON	97.9	97.5	0.1	0.1	1.1	1.4	0.8	1.0	5.8	6.2	6.9	6.4	5.8	24.4	27.4	14.2	3.0	77.1	41.3	48.6	51.4
61552	MOSSVILLE	94.9	94.4	1.0	0.9	2.5	3.2	1.0	1.4	5.1	6.5	8.3	7.4	5.6	21.3	34.7	10.2	0.9	74.5	42.4	50.0	50.0
61554	PEKIN	96.4	96.1	2.0	2.1	0.4	0.5	1.2	1.5	6.4	6.1	6.4	6.2	6.8	28.7	24.4	12.9	2.0	77.3	38.0	49.5	50.6
61559	PRINCEVILLE	97.8	97.1	0.1	0.1	0.2	0.2	1.9	2.6	7.4	7.5	7.5	6.3	5.6	25.3	26.6	12.2	1.9	73.5	38.6	49.7	50.3
61560	PUTNAM	96.9	96.5	0.5	0.5	0.1	0.1	2.5	3.3	5.0	5.5	4.7	4.4	5.1	21.4	33.5	19.0	1.5	82.4	47.5	54.1	45.9
61561	ROANOKE	99.2	99.1	0.1	0.1	0.1	0.1	0.2	0.2	7.2	7.4	7.6	6.4	5.7	24.1	23.2	15.2	3.3	73.6	38.7	48.8	51.2
61563	SAINT DAVID	100.0	100.0	0.0	0.0	0.0	0.0	0.0	0.0	0.0	0.0	0.0	0.0	0.0	21.4	78.6	0.0	0.0	100.0	53.3	28.6	71.4
61565	SPARLAND	98.2	98.0	0.7	0.8	0.2	0.3	1.3	1.6	5.5	6.1	7.3	6.0	5.8	26.3	31.3	10.5	1.2	77.3	40.2	52.1	47.9
61567	TOPEKA	98.8	98.8	0.0	0.1	0.1	0.1	0.5	0.5	5.5	5.8	7.1	6.8	6.3	26.0	29.8	11.6	1.1	77.6	40.2	51.6	48.4
61568	TREMONT	99.1	99.1	0.1	0.1	0.2	0.2	0.7	0.9	6.5	7.0	7.5	7.4	5.7	25.6	26.8	11.7	1.8	74.5	38.7	49.9	50.2
61569	TRIVOLI	97.7	97.1	0.5	0.6	0.2	0.2	0.9	1.1	4.9	5.6	7.1	6.2	5.2	24.6	31.4	13.7	1.4	78.7	42.8	51.1	48.9
61570	WASHBURN	97.3	97.0	0.2	0.2	0.2	0.2	0.9	1.1	5.9	6.2	7.9	7.0	6.5	27.0	25.7	11.7	2.1	75.6	37.8	51.0	49.0
61571	WASHINGTON	98.2	97.9	0.3	0.3	0.5	0.6	0.7	0.8	6.5	6.6	7.1	6.3	6.3	27.4	25.7	12.6	1.8	76.1	38.5	48.7	51.4
61572	YATES CITY	98.9	98.9	0.3	0.3	0.0	0.0	0.4	0.5	5.7	6.3	7.0	5.8	4.8	27.7	26.5	14.5	1.8	77.6	40.1	50.8	49.2
61602	PEORIA	48.5	43.7	40.0	43.0	1.9	2.2	9.7	11.5	6.4	5.9	6.4	6.6	8.4	32.6	22.4	9.7	1.7	78.2	34.9	54.7	45.3
61603	PEORIA	60.9	57.6	32.3	34.7	1.0	1.1	4.8	5.5	8.4	8.1	8.4	7.5	7.5	29.5	20.7	8.4	1.5	70.4	31.8	48.7	51.3
61604	PEORIA	76.8	73.7	19.0	21.4	1.2	1.4	1.7	2.1	7.4	7.0	6.6	6.2	6.1	27.0	23.2	13.3	3.3	75.4	37.5	46.8	53.2
61605	PEORIA	37.9	34.3	57.4	60.6	0.2	0.2	3.2	3.7	10.3	9.4	9.8	7.8	7.2	23.9	19.3	10.9	1.4	65.8	29.5	46.3	53.7
61606	PEORIA	71.5	68.8	21.3	22.8	2.9	3.4	2.3	2.9	5.1	4.2	4.8	13.5	28.7	22.3	15.1	5.6	0.7	83.1	23.9	49.9	50.1
61607	PEORIA	97.7	97.2	0.6	0.7	0.5	0.6	1.0	1.3	5.7	5.9	6.6	5.7	5.9	26.1	28.7	14.0	1.6	78.4	41.1	48.8	51.2
61610	CREVE COEUR	97.2	96.7	0.4	0.5	0.2	0.2	1.9	2.4	6.8	6.5	7.0	6.1	6.6	29.4	24.0	12.2	1.4	76.1	36.8	49.3	50.7
61611	EAST PEORIA	97.5	97.1	0.4	0.5	0.7	0.8	1.3	1.6	5.5	5.7	6.4	5.9	5.8	26.2	28.1	14.1	2.2	78.8	41.4	49.0	51.0
61614	PEORIA	87.8	85.6	6.3	7.3	4.2	5.1	1.3	1.7	5.2	5.1	5.6	5.8	6.3	25.4	26.1	16.9	3.7	80.5	42.4	47.3	52.7
61615	PEORIA	83.9	81.6	10.4	11.5	3.4	4.1	1.6	2.0	6.7	6.5	7.0	6.3	6.1	27.3	27.1	11.4	1.6	75.6	38.1	48.5	51.5
61616	PEORIA HEIGHTS	92.7	91.4	3.6	4.2	1.1	1.3	1.9	2.4	5.7	5.4	5.7	5.3	6.6	30.7	24.4	13.8	2.5	80.1	38.7	48.0	52.0
61625	PEORIA	88.7	86.4	5.7	6.7	2.8	3.5	2.8	3.6	1.2	1.0	1.3	45.2	40.8	5.3	3.7	1.3	0.1	95.9	20.2	48.0	52.0
61635	PEORIA	97.2	97.3	0.0	0.0	0.9	0.9	0.9	0.9	5.4	6.3	7.2	6.3	5.4	27.9	27.9	10.8	2.7	75.7	40.7	49.6	50.5
61701	BLOOMINGTON	84.8	83.2	9.9	10.7	1.5	1.8	3.7	4.6	6.4	5.9	5.8	7.8	10.0	31.0	20.3	10.5	2.3	78.5	33.4	47.9	52.1
61704	BLOOMINGTON	87.6	86.2	5.6	6.0	4.1	4.9	2.9	3.3	8.0	8.2	8.4	6.8	6.4	31.8	24.1	5.8	0.5	71.0	33.7	49.6	50.4
61720	ANCHOR	98.6	98.6	0.3	0.3	0.0	0.0	0.0	0.0	4.6	5.8	7.5	6.9	6.1	25.4	30.3	12.1	1.4	77.5	41.4	47.0	53.0
61721	ARMINGTON	99.1	99.1	0.3	0.3	0.3	0.3	1.2	1.4	6.7	7.5	8.8	6.5	5.0	26.3	26.3	11.4	1.4	72.8	39.3	53.1	46.9
61722	ARROWSMITH	97.7	97.1	0.6	0.6	0.1	0.3	0.7	0.8	7.0	7.2	7.4	7.2	6.1	27.3	26.0	9.9	1.9	74.0	37.8	49.3	50.7
61723	ATLANTA	98.6	98.4	0.7	0.7	0.2	0.2	0.6	0.7	5.9	5.9	6.7	8.7	9.2	26.0	24.1	11.7	1.8	77.5	36.1	48.3	51.7
61724	BELLFLOWER	96.4	96.0	2.4	2.6	0.2	0.2	0.2	0.2	5.1	5.2	7.1	8.3	6.2	26.0	28.3	11.9	2.0	77.4	39.6	50.8	49.2
61725	CARLOCK	98.3	98.0	0.3	0.3	0.8	1.1	0.5	0.7	5.4	6.3	8.2	7.1	4.7	27.7	31.2	8.3	1.1	75.5	40.0	51.0	49.0
61726	CHENOA	97.8	97.4	0.3	0.3	0.3	0.4	2.0	2.5	7.0	7.3	7.6	6.6	5.1	26.2	24.8	12.0	3.4	74.0	38.7	49.6	50.4
61727	CLINTON	97.3	97.2	0.7	0.7	0.4	0.4	1.8	1.8	6.5	6.6	6.8	6.4	6.4	27.0	24.5	13.4	2.4	76.1	38.6	48.1	51.9
61728	COLFAX	98.9	98.7	0.1	0.1	0.1	0.1	1.2	1.5	5.2	5.7	7.2	7.8	5.8	25.1	23.6	15.4	4.3	76.3	40.4	48.9	51.1
61729	CONGERVILLE	98.4	98.2	0.0	0.0	0.3	0.4	0.2	0.2	6.8	7.0	7.1	6.6	5.7	25.7	31.7	8.5	0.9	74.8	38.8	51.6	48.4
61730	COOKSVILLE	98.4	98.1	0.2	0.2	0.0	0.0	0.2	0.2	5.1	6.1	7.5	7.0	5.8	26.2	29.4	11.2	1.6	77.1	40.5	47.4	52.6
61731	CROPSEY	98.3	97.8	0.4	0.4	0.4	0.4	1.3	1.7	6.0	6.9	8.6	6.9	6.5	24.6	28.5	11.2	0.9	74.1	38.5	51.3	48.7
61732	DANVERS	98.2	97.9	0.6	0.6	0.1	0.2	0.7	0.9	7.1	7.6	9.0	7.2	6.2	28.0	24.9	9.0	1.0	71.7	36.1	48.8	51.2
61733	DEER CREEK	98.2	98.0	0.2	0.2	0.4	0.5	0.2	0.2	7.9	8.0	7.4	6.2	6.1	27.0	26.0	10.6	0.9	73.0	36.4	51.2	48.8
61734	DELAVAN	98.5	98.3	0.4	0.4	0.1	0.1	0.4	0.5	7.1	7.3	7.7	6.6	6.1	25.3	25.3	13.1	1.7	73.9	38.1	49.7	50.3
61735	DEWITT	98.5	98.3	0.2	0.4	0.2	0.2	0.4	0.2	6.1	6.3	6.5	5.9	4.9	28.5	26.8	13.3	1.7	77.2	40.1	50.6	49.4
61736	DOWNS	98.4	98.2	0.5	0.6	0.2	0.2	0.6	0.8	6.9	7.7	8.9	6.9	5.5	28.9	26.6	8.1	0.5	72.2	37.6	50.9	49.1
61737	ELLSWORTH	97.4	96.9	0.5	0.5	0.2	0.3	0.5	0.7	7.4	7.6	7.6	7.3	6.1	26.5	26.9	9.2	1.5	72.7	37.5	49.4	50.7
61738	EL PASO	98.7	98.5	0.2	0.3	0.2	0.3	0.7	0.9	7.8	7.5	6.8	6.6	6.0	27.3	24.3	11.4	2.4	74.0	37.2	49.2	50.8
61739	FAIRBURY	96.8	96.1	0.5	0.5	0.4	0.5	2.5	3.0	7.0	6.8	7.5	7.5	7.0	23.7	22.4	14.1	4.2	73.6	38.3	48.5	51.5
61740	FLANAGAN	98.5	98.2	0.4	0.5	0.1	0.2	0.6	0.7	5.2	5.9	6.7	6.7	5.6	21.8	25.7	16.7	5.8	77.2	43.6	46.3	53.7
61741	FORREST	96.5	96.1	0.6	0.7	0.2	0.2	2.2	2.6	7.5	7.5	8.7	8.4	5.9	24.2	23.7	12.5	1.6	71.1	36.5	49.9	50.1
61742	GOODFIELD	98.7	98.5	0.2	0.1	0.0	0.0	0.0	0.0	11.3	10.5	8.8	5.9	5.8	28.2	21.1	7.7	0.8	65.9	31.4	51.0	49.0
61743	GRAYMONT	99.2	99.6	0.0	0.0	0.0	0.0	0.8	0.8	8.8	8.8	8.0	6.7	6.3	22.7	28.2	9.7	0.8	69.3	36.4	50.0	50.0
61744	GRIDLEY	97.9	97.5	0.4	0.4	0.4	0.5	0.8	0.9	7.4	7.4	8.6	6.9	5.1	24.4	25.9	12.1	2.2	72.2	38.2	50.3	49.7
61745	HEYWORTH	98.1	97.8	0.2	0.2	0.3	0.3	0.7	0.9	8.6	8.7	8.1	6.1	5.4	28.8	24.2	9.0	1.2	70.9	35.8	49.4	50.6
61747	HOPEDALE	99.4	99.2	0.1	0.1	0.1	0.1	0.4	0.5	6.8	7.2	6.8	6.3	5.0	26.1	23.8	13.5	4.5	75.5	39.5	48.8	51.2
61748	HUDSON	98.6	98.3	0.1	0.2	0.5	0.6	0.7	0.9	7.7	7.8	7.3	6.5	5.7	27.6	27.8	8.8	0.9	73.3	37.5	49.4	50.6
61749	KENNEY	98.9	98.8	0.3	0.3	0.4	0.4	0.8	0.8	4.5	5.0	6.0	5.3	6.3	27.7	31.9	11.8	1.6	81.5	42.2	50.8	49.2
61752	LE ROY	98.8	98.6	0.3	0.4	0.1	0.1	1.2	1.5	7.0	7.1	7.6	6.6	5.7	29.0	22.6	12.2	2.2	73.9	37.2	48.6	51.4
61753	LEXINGTON	98.6	98.4	0.3	0.3	0.1	0.1	0.6	0.7	6.2	6.6	7.6	6.5	5.7	26.3	28.1	10.4	2.7	75.6	39.5	49.4	50.6
61754	MC LEAN	98.2	98.0	0.5	0.4	0.7	0.8	0.1	0.2	6.2	6.1	6.7	7.1	6.0	26.8	26.4	12.3	2.5	76.7	40.0	49.9	50.2
	ILLINOIS	73.5	71.8	15.1	15.2	3.5	4.0	12.3	14.2	7.1	7.0	7.3	7.0	7.3	29.0	23.2	10.4	1.7	74.5	35.2	49.0	51.0
	UNITED STATES	75.1	73.6	12.3	12.5	3.8	4.2	12.5	14.1	6.9	6.7	7.2	7.0	7.3	28.6	23.8	10.8	1.7	75.1	36.0	49.1	50.9

ZIP CODE #	POST OFFICE NAME	2004 Per Capita Income	2004 HH Income Base	2004 HOUSEHOLD INCOME DISTRIBUTION (%) Less than $25,000	$25,000 to $49,999	$50,000 to $99,999	$100,000 to $149,999	$150,000 or More	MEDIAN HOUSEHOLD INCOME 2004	2009	2004 National Centile	2004 State Centile	2004 Home Value Base	2004 HOME VALUE DISTRIBUTION (%) Less than $50,000	$50,000 to $89,999	$90,000 to $174,999	$175,000 to $399,999	$400,000 or More	2004 Median Home Value
61484	VERMONT	15646	376	38.6	35.6	22.3	2.7	0.8	33560	36835	23	9	316	55.4	23.4	17.7	3.5	0.0	44848
61485	VICTORIA	16635	227	25.6	41.9	26.9	4.9	0.9	35263	38854	28	13	189	22.2	20.6	37.6	10.1	9.5	99643
61486	VIOLA	19391	630	24.8	32.1	36.4	6.0	0.8	43086	47844	56	42	527	15.9	37.0	35.5	10.6	1.0	86477
61488	WATAGA	22089	479	23.4	34.7	34.5	4.2	3.3	44884	50581	61	48	387	19.6	35.1	36.4	5.9	2.8	85488
61489	WILLIAMSFIELD	19693	359	22.3	35.4	36.2	4.5	1.7	44072	49215	59	45	311	20.6	36.3	33.1	7.1	2.9	82321
61490	WOODHULL	19838	489	30.5	34.4	30.5	3.7	1.0	40150	45074	47	30	370	18.7	40.8	33.5	6.5	0.5	82045
61491	WYOMING	19121	720	34.2	32.2	28.5	4.2	1.0	35317	38539	29	13	574	19.5	36.8	39.0	4.0	0.7	85443
61501	ASTORIA	16916	835	33.8	36.1	27.3	2.6	0.2	33393	37369	22	9	652	46.9	31.9	16.9	3.1	1.2	53030
61516	BENSON	21938	325	16.3	32.9	38.8	11.4	0.6	50725	56541	73	64	285	8.8	27.0	42.5	20.7	1.1	106127
61517	BRIMFIELD	25928	1228	12.5	25.6	40.6	17.0	4.3	59373	67824	84	80	1105	7.3	20.0	44.2	26.7	1.8	130371
61519	BRYANT	12895	9	44.4	55.6	0.0	0.0	0.0	27247	27247	7	2	8	12.5	37.5	50.0	0.0	0.0	85000
61520	CANTON	20002	7253	34.9	32.1	25.2	5.5	2.3	35916	39442	31	16	5409	19.6	38.1	34.6	7.5	0.3	81268
61523	CHILLICOTHE	26283	4475	18.9	29.2	36.4	12.1	3.4	51424	59124	75	66	3776	11.7	26.7	47.6	12.7	1.3	101669
61524	DUNFERMLINE	28119	11	36.4	18.2	27.3	18.2	0.0	47321	47321	67	56	9	11.1	44.4	22.2	22.2	0.0	85000
61525	DUNLAP	37294	2052	10.5	19.5	37.4	17.9	14.6	74932	86365	93	93	1823	5.5	9.0	36.8	39.1	9.7	172783
61526	EDELSTEIN	25639	328	10.4	23.8	39.6	21.0	5.2	64016	75000	88	85	305	10.8	16.1	40.0	31.5	1.6	143534
61528	EDWARDS	33792	670	13.6	22.4	33.6	19.4	11.0	67269	77941	90	88	549	7.8	8.9	34.6	41.4	7.3	172321
61529	ELMWOOD	23397	1095	19.2	29.5	39.2	10.9	1.3	51041	57517	74	65	946	9.4	33.7	46.0	10.3	0.6	98125
61530	EUREKA	24313	2265	21.2	29.3	36.3	8.7	4.6	49544	54399	71	61	1740	5.9	18.2	59.5	15.1	1.3	117291
61531	FARMINGTON	21834	1401	27.6	32.8	31.3	6.3	2.1	40218	44322	47	30	1164	18.8	35.6	41.0	4.3	0.3	86531
61532	FOREST CITY	17313	209	22.0	41.6	30.6	3.8	1.9	40609	45596	48	32	178	33.7	18.5	38.2	8.4	1.1	85556
61533	GLASFORD	21921	811	19.9	31.8	36.6	10.4	1.4	46967	54775	66	55	681	12.2	29.8	46.0	11.8	0.3	100658
61534	GREEN VALLEY	21856	656	17.1	26.8	42.5	11.9	1.7	55699	62615	80	75	564	6.0	27.7	52.3	13.5	0.5	109223
61535	GROVELAND	32940	592	10.5	21.3	41.2	17.1	10.0	67629	76177	90	89	568	9.2	4.4	46.8	36.6	3.0	162174
61536	HANNA CITY	27197	1121	17.0	24.6	40.5	13.4	4.5	58718	66060	83	79	989	7.8	20.5	47.4	22.2	2.0	122402
61537	HENRY	21018	1287	25.5	31.9	34.7	5.7	2.3	44884	49018	61	48	1052	12.7	32.9	46.3	6.8	1.3	95610
61540	LACON	21445	1164	21.1	34.5	36.6	6.1	1.7	46260	50588	64	53	985	9.5	27.6	51.2	11.4	0.3	106595
61542	LEWISTOWN	19496	1636	31.4	31.8	30.5	4.6	1.7	38074	42053	40	23	1203	24.5	38.5	29.9	7.0	0.1	77574
61543	LIVERPOOL	22065	70	30.0	30.0	31.4	7.1	1.4	44187	50000	59	46	59	23.7	35.6	32.2	8.5	0.0	73750
61544	LONDON MILLS	19167	286	25.9	35.7	30.8	4.6	3.2	40798	46372	49	33	247	30.4	31.6	24.3	8.9	4.9	73000
61545	LOWPOINT	21529	362	17.7	22.9	49.7	9.4	0.3	56962	62604	82	78	315	10.8	21.0	41.9	25.4	1.0	124085
61546	MANITO	24361	1705	19.7	31.0	38.7	7.1	3.6	49390	54931	71	61	1474	10.9	31.5	51.1	6.0	0.5	99262
61547	MAPLETON	27624	1417	9.4	20.2	48.5	16.4	5.5	66496	76465	89	88	1314	3.6	12.6	53.1	29.7	1.1	145114
61548	METAMORA	26954	3622	13.7	21.4	44.4	14.9	5.6	63444	70376	87	85	3252	5.4	9.9	48.3	33.0	3.4	148584
61550	MORTON	30568	6735	15.6	24.7	38.7	13.7	7.3	59954	65717	84	81	5474	6.7	6.3	55.5	29.5	2.0	150462
61552	MOSSVILLE	52305	89	6.7	15.7	38.2	19.1	20.2	85273	101646	96	97	80	2.5	6.3	32.5	45.0	13.8	196875
61554	PEKIN	22272	18131	26.4	30.2	33.3	7.2	3.0	44442	50222	60	47	13600	9.9	37.9	43.6	8.1	0.5	92042
61559	PRINCEVILLE	24749	1216	16.5	28.0	40.3	11.8	3.4	53761	61443	78	71	1046	8.4	25.9	45.9	16.7	3.1	114158
61560	PUTNAM	23664	368	13.0	35.1	43.5	7.1	1.4	52729	55785	73	64	319	3.1	10.0	48.3	33.5	5.0	153779
61561	ROANOKE	24269	999	19.3	29.7	37.4	9.6	3.9	50733	55870	73	64	856	7.9	20.0	55.5	15.4	1.2	114418
61563	SAINT DAVID	23052	5	0.0	20.0	80.0	0.0	0.0	69801	87500	91	91	5	0.0	0.0	60.0	40.0	0.0	162500
61565	SPARLAND	20623	661	21.5	30.9	35.7	10.6	1.4	46909	50540	66	55	564	8.0	21.6	49.7	18.3	2.5	115238
61567	TOPEKA	20254	458	24.9	36.5	30.8	6.6	1.3	40953	45287	49	33	388	33.8	22.2	32.2	11.6	0.3	84651
61568	TREMONT	26054	1570	13.6	25.8	43.4	13.5	3.7	60229	65802	85	81	1345	1.9	15.8	55.3	26.2	0.7	132796
61569	TRIVOLI	27611	518	11.4	25.9	44.4	14.3	4.1	60000	68958	84	81	464	5.4	20.7	48.1	21.6	4.3	128774
61570	WASHBURN	21732	704	16.1	34.1	38.8	9.2	1.9	49878	55885	72	62	578	13.5	27.9	44.3	13.8	0.5	98333
61571	WASHINGTON	26726	8018	18.4	26.7	39.3	11.3	4.3	54234	61510	79	72	6451	4.4	21.6	55.6	17.4	1.0	114798
61572	YATES CITY	20127	472	22.5	41.3	29.0	5.7	1.5	41125	45951	50	34	410	15.4	38.3	38.5	6.1	1.7	87500
61602	PEORIA	16853	324	58.6	23.5	15.4	1.9	0.6	20830	23956	2	1	124	42.7	33.9	16.1	4.8	2.4	55294
61603	PEORIA	16432	7001	38.4	31.9	24.6	4.2	0.9	32884	37816	21	8	4234	31.4	47.1	19.8	1.0	0.7	65000
61604	PEORIA	21025	13265	30.1	31.8	29.4	6.7	2.0	39542	45465	44	28	9678	14.4	38.4	43.4	3.6	0.1	87486
61605	PEORIA	10975	6775	58.2	27.3	12.4	1.5	0.6	20487	22924	2	1	3237	67.0	25.5	5.9	1.1	0.5	39874
61606	PEORIA	18615	2806	43.0	26.6	21.1	5.9	3.5	30868	34295	14	4	1260	13.5	35.6	39.6	9.9	1.4	91528
61607	PEORIA	24958	4226	18.2	31.4	38.8	8.6	3.0	50336	57799	73	63	3591	8.1	32.9	50.0	8.6	0.4	99802
61610	CREVE COEUR	19581	2229	27.5	34.0	35.0	3.0	0.5	41042	48679	50	34	1734	16.3	50.5	31.8	1.4	0.0	73411
61611	EAST PEORIA	24755	10515	22.8	28.0	36.7	9.4	3.1	49248	54946	71	61	8603	9.2	20.8	52.5	16.8	0.8	113884
61614	PEORIA	34637	12391	18.0	25.9	35.0	13.1	8.0	55555	63477	80	75	8632	2.4	12.9	58.2	24.2	2.4	135658
61615	PEORIA	33156	8994	20.6	24.1	33.2	13.5	8.6	55346	63108	80	74	6432	9.3	16.0	42.2	27.3	5.2	132790
61616	PEORIA HEIGHTS	24144	3158	27.9	37.7	28.0	4.6	1.8	36637	42697	34	18	2085	18.9	51.2	24.8	3.3	1.8	73746
61625	PEORIA	12125	6	0.0	0.0	50.0	50.0	0.0	100000	100000	98	98	4	0.0	0.0	100.0	0.0	0.0	125000
61635	PEORIA	6985	10	10.0	20.0	50.0	20.0	0.0	75000	84899	93	93	9	11.1	0.0	44.4	44.4	0.0	168750
61701	BLOOMINGTON	24850	16601	29.2	30.0	30.2	7.3	3.3	41743	48892	52	36	9758	10.4	25.9	53.4	9.2	1.2	102998
61704	BLOOMINGTON	33216	15233	11.7	19.6	36.9	19.7	12.1	72329	83168	92	92	11917	10.3	3.6	41.2	40.8	4.1	167424
61720	ANCHOR	20417	116	15.5	32.8	39.7	10.3	1.7	51938	61298	75	67	97	10.3	24.7	56.7	8.3	0.0	108929
61721	ARMINGTON	22129	240	13.3	36.3	37.9	10.8	1.7	50420	55416	73	64	204	16.2	27.9	34.8	13.2	7.8	98571
61722	ARROWSMITH	24417	250	12.4	23.6	45.2	14.0	4.8	61646	70286	86	83	217	6.0	27.2	46.5	17.1	3.2	109936
61723	ATLANTA	22931	976	24.2	29.2	36.2	8.7	1.7	47235	52852	67	56	800	10.4	24.6	55.3	8.5	1.3	104773
61724	BELLFLOWER	22602	252	18.7	29.8	39.3	10.3	2.0	51057	58292	74	65	214	23.8	33.6	38.3	4.2	0.0	81111
61725	CARLOCK	27499	475	12.2	23.2	44.8	14.1	5.7	62248	71445	86	84	427	1.4	16.4	42.6	35.8	3.8	147545
61726	CHENOA	23476	1139	18.4	30.0	39.0	10.0	2.6	51221	59113	74	66	936	13.7	33.7	40.0	11.1	1.6	92551
61727	CLINTON	22907	4292	27.8	28.3	31.3	9.0	3.6	43840	49692	58	45	3201	14.1	29.1	41.3	13.8	1.6	99025
61728	COLFAX	21565	581	21.9	28.4	41.7	7.1	1.0	49733	56734	71	62	491	16.9	35.2	42.0	5.3	0.6	88158
61729	CONGERVILLE	27730	340	7.1	25.6	46.5	13.8	7.1	63045	70803	87	84	305	2.3	5.3	46.9	42.0	3.6	165878
61730	COOKSVILLE	26290	182	14.8	31.9	39.6	11.5	2.2	53588	62976	78	70	153	9.8	24.8	57.5	7.8	0.0	108446
61731	CROPSEY	23339	80	20.0	26.3	37.5	11.3	5.0	53307	61828	77	70	65	15.4	26.2	33.9	20.0	4.6	99167
61732	DANVERS	24100	794	13.5	27.0	42.7	13.1	3.8	60000	68072	84	81	686	1.3	19.4	62.0	16.6	0.7	122826
61733	DEER CREEK	25306	639	11.7	29.0	43.2	10.8	5.3	58379	63586	83	79	551	4.2	10.7	54.3	26.9	4.0	133167
61734	DELAVAN	22372	1078	18.3	32.8	37.4	8.4	3.1	48819	55115	70	60	907	10.9	35.0	39.5	12.8	1.9	93827
61735	DEWITT	26557	185	17.3	22.2	42.2	13.5	4.9	58192	65486	83	79	159	15.1	19.5	33.3	28.3	3.8	120500
61736	DOWNS	29123	577	8.3	21.0	48.0	15.9	6.8	67942	77395	90	89	520	4.8	14.4	41.9	36.2	2.7	147959
61737	ELLSWORTH	26156	219	11.0	23.3	45.2	15.1	5.5	62189	72672	86	84	192	4.7	27.6	43.8	19.3	4.7	111765
61738	EL PASO	24909	1451	15.6	29.0	40.3	11.7	3.4	53761	60746	78	71	1193	7.8	22.2	52.0	14.9	3.1	111182
61739	FAIRBURY	21380	1841	24.5	29.5	35.7	8.3	2.0	47487	51832	67	57	1414	6.4	19.4	54.0	18.9	1.4	116328
61740	FLANAGAN	22272	598	22.1	33.1	34.3	8.9	1.7	45398	49372	62	50	492	5.1	28.5	56.1	9.4	1.0	106364
61741	FORREST	19603	658	18.8	34.7	37.5	7.1	1.8	47584	53537	67	57	528	9.3	29.0	50.0	11.7	0.0	100605
61742	GOODFIELD	22240	243	13.6	22.6	46.9	13.2	3.7	61997	67441	86	83	212	10.9	10.9	50.5	24.5	3.3	131731
61743	GRAYMONT	27250	88	17.1	26.1	38.6	12.5	5.7	55505	62224	80	75	71	7.0	29.6	40.9	22.5	0.0	111458
61744	GRIDLEY	22276	813	16.5	32.2	39.9	9.6	1.9	50790	58009	73	65	650	8.5	25.7	56.0	9.1	0.8	104636
61745	HEYWORTH	26754	1435	14.6	23.8	44.3	12.1	5.2	60759	68566	85	82	1257	10.0	14.8	53.0	20.3	1.9	119575
61747	HOPEDALE	23461	562	20.1	25.4	39.0	11.2	4.3	53620	60073	78	70	488	4.5	18.7	54.5	20.9	1.4	122059
61748	HUDSON	30051	977	9.1	24.5	43.0	17.7	5.7	64412	71835	88	86	871	3.2	11.7	57.9	22.9	4.4	136960
61749	KENNEY	26476	338	18.9	31.4	34.3	9.5	5.9	49582	55298	71	62	291	25.1	22.3	27.8	21.7	3.1	94412
61752	LE ROY	24931	1613	16.2	27.9	41.4	11.5	3.0	54713	63993	79	73	1350	6.3	19.9	59.5	13.9	0.4	115644
61753	LEXINGTON	27198	1218	17.8	28.4	36.7	12.4	4.7	53423	61562	78	70	1032	8.8	18.7	53.5	15.8	3.2	116707
61754	MC LEAN	24589	520	13.1	28.5	46.2	9.6	2.7	56408	66316	81	76	425	8.2	35.8	47.3	8.7	0.0	94397
	ILLINOIS	27033		22.1	25.9	32.9	11.9	7.3	52039	60941				7.7	12.8	34.0	36.6	8.9	162771
	UNITED STATES	25866		24.7	27.1	30.8	10.9	6.5	48124	56710				10.9	15.0	33.7	30.1	10.4	145905

ZIP CODE #	POST OFFICE NAME	FINANCIAL SERVICES: Auto Loan	Home Loan	Invest-ments	Retire-ment Plans	THE HOME: Home Improvements: Home Repair	Lawn & Garden	Furnishings: Comput-ers & Hard-ware	Major Appli-ances	TV, Radio, Sound Equip-ment	Furni-ture	ENTERTAINMENT: Dine out/ Carry out	Sports Equip-ment	Fees & Tickets	Toys & Games	Travel	Cable TV	PERSONAL: Apparel & Services	Auto Repairs	Health Insur-ance	Pets & Supplies
61484	VERMONT	74	50	23	43	56	65	48	60	58	49	68	72	41	64	49	62	62	59	74	85
61485	VICTORIA	80	57	30	53	66	74	56	69	64	55	75	82	48	74	58	67	69	68	82	95
61486	VIOLA	77	68	54	67	72	78	66	72	70	66	85	84	65	86	67	71	81	70	77	88
61488	WATAGA	91	76	54	72	82	89	72	82	78	71	93	97	68	95	74	80	88	80	90	107
61489	WILLIAMSFIELD	80	66	49	65	71	79	67	73	72	66	87	85	63	86	67	74	81	72	81	90
61490	WOODHULL	67	64	59	60	67	75	63	66	67	61	82	76	64	87	65	70	78	65	74	79
61491	WYOMING	72	53	33	51	59	70	57	65	64	54	75	74	50	72	57	68	69	64	77	82
61501	ASTORIA	64	50	34	48	55	64	53	59	59	51	70	67	49	67	53	62	64	58	69	72
61516	BENSON	100	77	49	73	86	95	75	88	83	74	99	105	67	98	77	86	91	86	101	118
61517	BRIMFIELD	105	100	86	99	103	111	96	102	98	95	120	118	95	123	97	99	115	99	105	121
61519	BRYANT	35	38	40	36	38	43	38	37	39	36	48	41	40	52	39	40	47	36	40	41
61520	CANTON	62	61	58	58	62	70	61	63	64	59	78	71	61	80	62	66	75	62	68	72
61523	CHILLICOTHE	86	97	100	94	97	102	91	91	90	89	112	105	95	119	93	90	109	89	91	103
61524	DUNFERMLINE	86	77	58	73	81	87	71	78	75	71	91	93	69	93	73	77	87	76	85	101
61525	DUNLAP	136	166	176	166	164	163	149	149	140	149	176	175	158	187	153	137	175	144	136	166
61526	EDELSTEIN	106	120	118	118	120	121	108	111	104	108	130	130	113	137	111	103	128	107	106	128
61528	EDWARDS	122	147	151	148	143	140	131	131	121	132	153	153	138	160	132	116	152	126	116	144
61529	ELMWOOD	80	85	85	84	86	91	81	83	81	81	100	96	84	104	83	81	98	81	82	94
61530	EUREKA	94	90	82	88	92	99	89	93	91	88	112	108	87	111	89	91	107	93	96	108
61531	FARMINGTON	68	76	81	72	76	84	74	73	75	72	93	82	78	100	76	77	91	72	77	81
61532	FOREST CITY	77	68	52	65	72	78	63	70	67	63	82	84	62	84	65	69	78	69	76	91
61533	GLASFORD	87	77	61	76	80	89	76	82	80	75	97	95	74	98	76	81	92	80	88	99
61534	GREEN VALLEY	88	90	81	88	92	95	82	87	82	82	101	103	83	105	84	82	98	85	88	106
61535	GROVELAND	117	136	137	134	135	135	122	125	116	122	145	146	127	153	125	114	143	120	116	142
61536	HANNA CITY	90	111	120	109	109	109	101	100	96	100	120	116	108	128	104	94	120	97	92	110
61537	HENRY	69	73	75	69	74	81	71	72	73	69	90	81	74	95	73	75	87	70	76	81
61540	LACON	69	74	76	70	75	82	71	72	72	69	90	81	74	94	74	75	87	71	76	82
61542	LEWISTOWN	67	62	54	59	65	73	62	66	66	60	80	75	61	81	63	68	76	65	73	78
61543	LIVERPOOL	87	77	59	73	82	88	71	79	76	71	92	94	70	94	74	78	88	77	86	102
61544	LONDON MILLS	88	65	40	62	74	83	64	77	73	63	86	92	57	85	67	76	79	76	90	104
61545	LOWPOINT	89	84	69	80	87	92	77	84	80	77	98	99	77	101	79	82	94	82	88	105
61546	MANITO	100	89	68	85	94	101	82	91	87	82	106	109	81	108	85	90	101	89	99	118
61547	MAPLETON	102	121	126	120	120	120	110	111	104	110	131	129	116	138	113	102	130	107	102	123
61548	METAMORA	104	113	109	112	113	117	105	107	102	104	127	125	107	132	106	102	124	105	104	123
61550	MORTON	101	114	121	111	113	119	106	107	103	106	129	123	111	133	109	103	127	105	105	120
61552	MOSSVILLE	165	205	218	205	201	198	183	182	169	182	213	213	195	227	187	164	213	176	163	201
61554	PEKIN	70	74	80	73	74	79	75	74	75	73	93	85	76	96	75	75	90	73	74	81
61559	PRINCEVILLE	90	95	91	92	97	101	88	92	88	88	109	107	91	114	90	88	106	89	91	108
61560	PUTNAM	93	74	52	68	83	92	70	83	78	69	93	98	63	92	74	83	87	82	97	113
61561	ROANOKE	92	94	90	90	95	103	91	94	92	89	113	107	92	116	93	94	110	92	98	108
61563	SAINT DAVID	83	100	113	99	100	105	92	92	87	92	109	104	98	111	96	87	108	90	88	101
61565	SPARLAND	89	79	60	75	84	90	73	81	78	73	94	97	72	96	75	80	90	79	88	105
61567	TOPEKA	82	73	56	69	77	83	68	75	72	68	87	89	66	89	70	74	83	73	81	97
61568	TREMONT	96	108	109	108	108	110	100	102	97	100	120	118	104	126	102	95	118	99	96	114
61569	TRIVOLI	99	104	100	99	105	112	96	100	97	96	120	116	99	125	100	99	117	98	103	118
61570	WASHBURN	84	81	72	79	83	90	78	82	80	78	99	95	78	101	79	81	95	81	85	97
61571	WASHINGTON	89	98	103	96	98	103	94	94	92	93	115	109	97	119	95	92	112	93	92	106
61572	YATES CITY	67	68	65	64	70	76	66	67	69	64	84	77	68	90	68	71	81	66	73	78
61602	PEORIA	39	34	43	34	34	39	41	39	44	40	54	45	40	53	40	44	52	41	41	43
61603	PEORIA	55	53	62	53	53	58	59	56	60	57	75	66	58	75	58	60	73	58	57	62
61604	PEORIA	67	66	70	65	67	73	69	69	70	67	87	80	69	88	69	71	84	70	70	77
61605	PEORIA	40	34	40	32	34	40	39	38	43	39	53	43	38	50	38	45	51	40	42	44
61606	PEORIA	62	49	63	54	48	55	68	59	68	64	85	75	62	80	61	63	82	67	56	66
61607	PEORIA	77	90	97	87	89	94	85	84	84	84	105	96	91	113	88	85	104	82	84	93
61610	CREVE COEUR	61	67	71	63	67	74	65	65	67	63	83	72	69	90	68	69	81	63	69	71
61611	EAST PEORIA	79	84	87	82	85	91	82	82	82	80	102	94	84	106	83	83	99	81	84	93
61614	PEORIA	97	109	130	109	108	116	108	106	106	107	133	122	112	136	110	106	131	106	103	116
61615	PEORIA	103	115	122	116	113	115	109	108	105	109	131	126	112	135	109	102	129	107	101	120
61616	PEORIA HEIGHTS	64	69	81	69	69	74	71	69	70	69	88	80	73	91	72	70	86	70	68	75
61625	PEORIA	141	86	109	98	85	103	167	123	162	141	202	171	136	182	133	143	190	150	114	140
61635	PEORIA	117	104	79	99	110	118	96	107	102	96	124	127	94	127	99	105	118	104	116	138
61701	BLOOMINGTON	71	72	85	74	71	76	78	74	76	76	96	88	77	96	76	74	94	77	71	81
61704	BLOOMINGTON	123	129	139	136	125	128	127	124	121	129	153	146	129	151	124	115	151	125	111	138
61720	ANCHOR	108	76	40	72	88	99	75	92	86	74	101	111	64	99	78	90	92	91	110	129
61721	ARMINGTON	110	77	40	72	89	100	76	93	87	75	102	113	65	100	78	91	93	92	111	130
61722	ARROWSMITH	95	106	108	103	106	110	99	100	97	98	121	117	103	127	101	96	119	98	98	114
61723	ATLANTA	83	77	64	75	80	87	74	79	77	74	94	93	73	96	75	78	90	78	84	96
61724	BELLFLOWER	93	83	63	79	88	94	77	85	82	77	99	101	75	101	79	84	94	83	92	110
61725	CARLOCK	90	110	120	108	108	109	101	100	95	100	120	116	107	128	103	94	120	97	92	109
61726	CHENOA	99	83	61	80	90	98	80	90	86	80	104	106	76	105	82	89	98	88	99	115
61727	CLINTON	80	76	69	74	79	87	75	79	78	74	96	90	75	98	77	80	91	78	84	92
61728	COLFAX	76	74	68	70	77	85	73	76	77	70	94	87	73	100	75	80	90	75	84	90
61729	CONGERVILLE	117	113	96	109	117	123	104	112	106	104	130	133	104	135	107	107	126	108	116	139
61730	COOKSVILLE	107	79	47	75	90	100	77	93	87	76	103	112	68	102	80	91	95	92	109	127
61731	CROPSEY	122	85	45	81	100	112	84	104	97	83	114	126	72	112	88	102	104	103	124	145
61732	DANVERS	90	103	105	104	100	99	96	95	89	96	113	112	98	115	95	85	111	93	84	105
61733	DEER CREEK	94	106	108	104	105	107	99	99	95	98	119	116	102	124	100	94	118	97	94	112
61734	DELAVAN	87	83	75	81	87	94	81	86	84	80	103	100	80	104	83	85	98	85	91	102
61735	DEWITT	119	89	54	85	101	111	86	103	97	86	115	124	77	114	89	101	106	101	120	141
61736	DOWNS	108	130	135	130	128	127	116	116	108	116	136	136	123	144	118	106	136	112	106	130
61737	ELLSWORTH	94	115	127	113	112	115	106	104	100	105	127	121	113	134	108	99	126	102	97	114
61738	EL PASO	89	95	99	95	95	99	94	93	92	92	115	109	96	119	94	91	112	93	90	104
61739	FAIRBURY	85	74	59	74	77	86	75	80	79	74	96	92	72	95	75	80	90	79	85	94
61740	FLANAGAN	88	73	55	72	78	87	74	81	79	73	96	93	70	95	74	81	90	80	89	99
61741	FORREST	90	73	51	71	79	88	72	82	78	72	94	96	67	93	73	80	88	80	91	104
61742	GOODFIELD	93	102	102	104	98	97	97	96	91	98	115	114	97	115	95	86	113	96	84	105
61743	GRAYMONT	118	105	81	100	111	119	97	108	103	97	125	128	95	128	100	106	119	105	116	139
61744	GRIDLEY	97	76	52	72	85	95	75	87	83	73	99	103	69	100	77	87	92	86	100	115
61745	HEYWORTH	105	107	98	106	108	111	100	104	98	100	122	123	100	125	100	97	119	102	100	122
61747	HOPEDALE	81	97	105	94	95	98	90	89	86	89	108	103	95	115	92	85	108	87	84	98
61748	HUDSON	110	128	130	131	123	123	116	115	107	119	136	133	121	137	115	102	134	112	102	126
61749	KENNEY	96	92	77	88	95	100	84	91	87	84	106	108	84	110	87	88	102	88	95	114
61752	LE ROY	93	90	80	88	92	99	86	91	88	85	108	106	86	111	87	89	104	89	94	108
61753	LEXINGTON	100	98	88	95	102	107	92	98	93	91	114	116	92	118	94	94	111	96	101	119
61754	MC LEAN	89	96	94	93	96	100	89	91	88	88	109	107	92	114	91	88	107	89	90	106
	ILLINOIS	98	100	111	99	99	106	100	99	101	100	126	115	102	127	100	100	123	100	98	112
	UNITED STATES	100	100	100	100	100	100	100	100	100	100	100	100	100	100	100	100	100	100	100	100

ZIP CODE			POPULATION			2000-2004 ANNUAL RATE		HOUSEHOLDS					FAMILIES		
#	POST OFFICE NAME	COUNTY FIPS CODE	2000	2004	2009	% Rate	State Centile	2000	2004	2009	% Annual Rate 2000-2004	2004 Average HH Size	2000	2004	% Annual Rate 2000-2004
61755	MACKINAW	179	3894	3933	3968	0.2	54	1402	1436	1472	0.6	2.74	1118	1135	0.4
61756	MAROA	115	1968	1982	1980	0.2	51	779	800	811	0.6	2.48	578	586	0.3
61759	MINIER	179	1550	1567	1576	0.3	55	616	632	646	0.6	2.48	458	464	0.3
61760	MINONK	203	2661	2646	2740	-0.1	35	1030	1038	1091	0.2	2.49	729	723	-0.2
61761	NORMAL	113	43733	47149	50845	1.8	87	14689	16479	18376	2.7	2.35	8016	8761	2.1
61764	PONTIAC	105	14757	14896	15055	0.2	53	5214	5348	5489	0.6	2.38	3441	3472	0.2
61769	SAUNEMIN	105	669	670	672	0.0	43	237	237	240	0.0	2.83	189	187	-0.3
61770	SAYBROOK	113	1132	1106	1151	-0.6	14	458	458	486	0.0	2.41	328	321	-0.5
61771	SECOR	203	1006	1021	1060	0.4	60	351	362	382	0.7	2.82	285	291	0.5
61772	SHIRLEY	113	451	473	505	1.1	80	171	183	199	1.6	2.52	134	141	1.2
61773	SIBLEY	053	594	602	608	0.3	59	221	226	230	0.5	2.66	172	174	0.3
61774	STANFORD	113	1085	1097	1153	0.3	55	387	399	427	0.7	2.73	309	313	0.3
61775	STRAWN	105	242	293	326	4.6	98	87	108	122	5.2	2.71	71	86	4.6
61776	TOWANDA	113	1092	1121	1195	0.6	70	406	424	460	1.0	2.64	324	330	0.4
61777	WAPELLA	039	1004	989	983	-0.4	22	391	393	398	0.1	2.47	289	287	-0.2
61778	WAYNESVILLE	039	687	673	669	-0.5	17	271	271	274	0.0	2.48	197	194	-0.4
61790	NORMAL	113	1932	2101	2263	2.0	89	576	638	700	2.4	2.97	261	272	1.0
61801	URBANA	019	29281	29529	30479	0.2	52	11168	11513	12178	0.7	2.10	4526	4445	-0.4
61802	URBANA	019	16766	17555	18449	1.1	79	7236	7721	8261	1.5	2.20	4293	4473	1.0
61810	ALLERTON	183	366	356	349	-0.7	11	139	137	136	-0.3	2.60	111	108	-0.6
61811	ALVIN	183	760	794	801	1.0	78	265	282	289	1.5	2.82	209	220	1.2
61812	ARMSTRONG	183	291	279	270	-1.0	4	116	113	111	-0.6	2.43	89	85	-1.1
61813	BEMENT	147	2047	2074	2125	0.3	58	787	814	849	0.8	2.46	560	571	0.5
61814	BISMARCK	183	1107	1062	1031	-1.0	4	417	408	404	-0.5	2.60	334	324	-0.7
61816	BROADLANDS	019	455	447	458	-0.4	19	180	180	188	0.0	2.48	140	139	-0.2
61817	CATLIN	183	2987	2898	2825	-0.7	9	1106	1096	1088	-0.2	2.62	837	819	-0.5
61818	CERRO GORDO	147	2019	2010	2037	-0.1	36	782	792	815	0.3	2.54	589	589	0.0
61820	CHAMPAIGN	019	33760	34474	35626	0.5	66	12691	13203	13963	0.9	2.08	3594	3572	-0.1
61821	CHAMPAIGN	019	30545	32128	33950	1.2	81	12998	13980	15061	1.7	2.28	7916	8311	1.2
61822	CHAMPAIGN	019	13738	15118	16271	2.3	91	5502	6125	6680	2.6	2.46	3935	4317	2.2
61830	CISCO	147	482	492	502	0.5	65	188	196	203	1.0	2.51	151	156	0.8
61831	COLLISON	183	360	383	392	1.5	84	138	149	155	1.8	2.57	109	117	1.7
61832	DANVILLE	183	38197	37482	36756	-0.4	18	15882	15811	15727	-0.1	2.32	10011	9788	-0.5
61833	TILTON	183	2602	2527	2465	-0.7	9	1158	1149	1141	-0.2	2.14	720	701	-0.5
61834	DANVILLE	183	8724	8831	8818	0.3	58	2782	2882	2926	0.8	2.44	1933	1976	0.5
61839	DE LAND	147	707	710	719	0.1	47	275	281	289	0.5	2.53	219	221	0.2
61840	DEWEY	019	692	711	738	0.6	70	255	266	280	1.0	2.67	197	202	0.6
61841	FAIRMOUNT	183	1342	1303	1271	-0.7	9	537	530	525	-0.3	2.46	406	395	-0.6
61842	FARMER CITY	039	2913	2940	2956	0.2	53	1159	1186	1209	0.5	2.43	817	823	0.2
61843	FISHER	019	2079	2097	2142	0.2	52	789	811	848	0.7	1.86	603	608	0.2
61844	FITHIAN	183	1139	1097	1066	-0.9	5	447	438	433	-0.5	2.50	336	325	-0.8
61845	FOOSLAND	019	1842	1850	1872	0.1	47	145	149	156	0.6	6.49	111	112	0.2
61846	GEORGETOWN	183	5169	5048	4938	-0.6	14	2071	2059	2047	-0.1	2.45	1457	1427	-0.5
61847	GIFFORD	019	1188	1175	1204	-0.3	27	437	440	460	0.2	2.49	330	327	-0.1
61849	HOMER	019	1729	1701	1739	-0.4	20	691	695	724	0.1	2.45	501	495	-0.3
61850	INDIANOLA	183	520	507	495	-0.6	13	198	197	195	-0.1	2.57	153	150	-0.5
61851	IVESDALE	019	496	494	509	-0.1	36	197	201	211	0.5	2.46	147	147	0.0
61852	LONGVIEW	019	343	335	341	-0.6	14	124	123	128	-0.2	2.72	97	95	-0.5
61853	MAHOMET	019	10522	11435	12198	2.0	89	3696	4094	4443	2.4	2.79	2966	3244	2.1
61854	MANSFIELD	147	1466	1489	1517	0.4	61	600	620	643	0.8	2.40	458	467	0.5
61855	MILMINE	147	163	163	165	0.0	42	60	61	63	0.4	2.67	45	46	0.5
61856	MONTICELLO	147	6649	6815	6994	0.6	68	2686	2798	2915	1.0	2.39	1883	1934	0.6
61858	OAKWOOD	183	2663	2703	2691	0.4	60	1085	1126	1143	0.9	2.40	795	814	0.6
61859	OGDEN	019	1422	1441	1481	0.3	58	545	561	585	0.7	2.57	416	422	0.4
61862	PENFIELD	019	500	516	538	0.7	73	175	185	196	1.3	2.79	138	144	1.0
61863	PESOTUM	019	775	769	789	-0.2	32	312	317	332	0.4	2.43	235	234	-0.1
61864	PHILO	019	1596	1705	1802	1.6	85	573	624	672	2.0	2.73	463	497	1.7
61865	POTOMAC	183	1406	1392	1372	-0.2	28	514	515	514	0.1	2.68	394	389	-0.3
61866	RANTOUL	019	14218	14312	14887	0.2	50	5858	6047	6423	0.8	2.37	3734	3766	0.2
61870	RIDGE FARM	183	1418	1387	1356	-0.5	16	564	565	562	0.0	2.45	411	405	-0.4
61872	SADORUS	019	746	745	767	0.0	40	279	284	299	0.4	2.62	209	208	-0.1
61873	SAINT JOSEPH	019	5045	5193	5385	0.7	71	1901	1998	2110	1.2	2.60	1470	1522	0.8
61874	SAVOY	019	4017	4240	4470	1.3	81	1753	1898	2044	1.9	2.19	1113	1172	1.2
61875	SEYMOUR	019	788	816	847	0.8	75	275	287	302	1.0	2.84	217	224	0.8
61876	SIDELL	183	779	759	741	-0.6	12	296	291	288	-0.4	2.61	227	220	-0.7
61877	SIDNEY	019	1560	1578	1620	0.3	56	602	621	650	0.7	2.54	445	451	0.3
61878	THOMASBORO	019	1454	1457	1491	0.1	44	582	595	620	0.5	2.45	399	401	0.1
61880	TOLONO	019	3324	3372	3478	0.3	59	1315	1367	1438	0.9	2.46	898	913	0.4
61882	WELDON	039	579	572	570	-0.3	25	237	238	241	0.1	2.40	178	176	-0.3
61883	WESTVILLE	183	4411	4417	4372	0.0	43	1898	1928	1936	0.4	2.29	1224	1220	-0.1
61884	WHITE HEATH	147	1298	1433	1529	2.4	91	453	510	554	2.8	2.81	372	415	2.6
61910	ARCOLA	041	4281	4348	4403	0.4	61	1456	1488	1523	0.5	2.87	1114	1128	0.3
61911	ARTHUR	139	4134	4231	4314	0.6	67	1396	1447	1495	0.9	2.88	1038	1058	0.5
61912	ASHMORE	029	1426	1354	1312	-1.2	2	553	533	525	-0.9	2.54	407	388	-1.1
61913	ATWOOD	041	2007	1998	2012	-0.1	36	793	803	823	0.3	2.49	574	572	-0.1
61914	BETHANY	139	1898	1855	1862	-0.5	15	769	767	783	-0.1	2.42	579	569	-0.4
61917	BROCTON	045	703	692	682	-0.4	21	286	287	287	0.1	2.41	204	202	-0.2
61919	CAMARGO	041	875	965	1023	2.3	91	348	391	422	2.8	2.47	272	302	2.5
61920	CHARLESTON	029	24511	24742	24727	0.2	53	9008	9279	9433	0.7	2.24	4369	4369	0.0
61924	CHRISMAN	045	2478	2466	2443	-0.1	36	945	953	955	0.2	2.39	654	649	-0.2
61925	DALTON CITY	115	1044	1042	1050	-0.1	39	373	380	389	0.4	2.74	303	306	0.2
61928	GAYS	139	681	708	727	0.9	77	265	278	289	1.1	2.55	210	218	0.8
61929	HAMMOND	147	933	926	937	-0.2	32	391	394	404	0.2	2.35	279	276	-0.3
61930	HINDSBORO	041	529	501	496	-1.3	1	203	197	198	-0.7	2.48	150	144	-1.0
61931	HUMBOLDT	029	862	846	832	-0.4	18	327	326	326	-0.1	2.60	246	243	-0.3
61932	HUME	045	547	535	525	-0.5	16	242	240	239	-0.2	2.23	176	173	-0.4
61933	KANSAS	045	1101	1090	1077	-0.2	28	434	434	433	0.0	2.51	297	292	-0.4
61937	LOVINGTON	139	2006	2036	2076	0.4	60	782	808	836	0.8	2.50	576	587	0.5
61938	MATTOON	029	23111	22872	22609	-0.2	28	9940	10012	10068	0.2	2.24	6146	6111	-0.1
61940	METCALF	045	428	418	411	-0.6	14	160	159	158	-0.2	2.63	117	114	-0.6
61942	NEWMAN	041	1378	1311	1299	-1.2	2	563	545	547	-0.8	2.30	385	367	-1.1
61943	OAKLAND	029	1824	1740	1695	-1.1	3	683	659	650	-0.8	2.44	499	477	-1.1
61944	PARIS	045	14331	14112	13911	-0.4	21	5762	5750	5738	-0.1	2.35	3842	3773	-0.4
61951	SULLIVAN	139	7274	7492	7676	0.7	72	2807	2929	3038	1.0	2.43	1997	2059	0.6
61953	TUSCOLA	041	6403	6446	6505	0.2	50	2540	2600	2663	0.6	2.43	1777	1794	0.2
	ILLINOIS					0.7					0.9	2.61			0.6
	UNITED STATES					1.2					1.3	2.58			1.1

ZIP CODE #	POST OFFICE NAME	RACE (%) White 2000	White 2004	Black 2000	Black 2004	Asian/Pacific 2000	Asian/Pacific 2004	% Hispanic Origin 2000	% Hispanic Origin 2004	2004 AGE DISTRIBUTION (%) 0-4	5-9	10-14	15-19	20-24	25-44	45-64	65-84	85+	18+	MEDIAN AGE 2004	% 2004 Males	% 2004 Females
61755	MACKINAW	97.3	96.8	0.6	0.6	0.5	0.6	0.9	1.0	7.9	7.5	7.4	6.8	7.5	29.1	23.9	8.9	1.1	73.2	34.8	50.4	49.6
61756	MAROA	99.1	98.9	0.2	0.2	0.2	0.3	0.7	0.9	6.4	6.7	7.4	7.0	5.9	25.5	28.4	11.8	1.1	75.4	39.3	50.8	49.2
61759	MINIER	98.8	98.6	0.3	0.3	0.1	0.2	1.0	1.3	6.3	6.9	7.2	6.2	5.3	27.6	24.4	14.4	1.7	75.9	39.8	49.3	50.7
61760	MINONK	99.0	98.9	0.1	0.1	0.1	0.1	1.1	1.2	6.8	7.0	7.5	6.5	5.2	25.7	22.7	15.0	3.7	74.8	39.8	48.2	51.8
61761	NORMAL	88.4	87.0	7.2	7.7	2.1	2.5	2.5	3.0	4.9	4.6	4.8	13.8	26.2	22.8	15.0	6.8	1.2	83.0	24.2	47.1	52.9
61764	PONTIAC	87.3	86.0	9.3	10.0	0.4	0.5	3.8	4.6	6.0	5.9	6.3	6.6	7.8	30.7	23.3	11.1	2.3	78.1	36.5	53.4	46.6
61769	SAUNEMIN	98.8	98.7	0.2	0.2	0.0	0.0	1.5	1.8	6.9	7.5	9.6	8.8	5.1	25.7	25.2	10.5	0.9	70.5	36.0	53.4	46.6
61770	SAYBROOK	98.9	98.7	0.2	0.2	0.1	0.1	0.3	0.4	5.9	6.3	7.4	6.2	5.3	28.1	24.6	14.2	1.9	76.6	40.1	48.7	51.3
61771	SECOR	99.2	99.2	0.1	0.1	0.1	0.1	0.3	0.3	7.6	7.2	5.9	6.8	5.7	25.6	30.2	10.1	1.1	75.3	39.4	50.5	49.5
61772	SHIRLEY	97.8	97.5	0.2	0.2	0.7	0.6	1.8	2.3	5.5	6.1	7.6	6.1	5.3	25.8	29.0	12.3	2.3	77.0	41.3	51.0	49.1
61773	SIBLEY	97.1	96.5	0.0	0.0	0.0	0.0	2.5	3.2	7.6	7.8	6.6	6.6	6.0	25.1	25.3	12.5	2.5	73.6	37.1	52.3	47.7
61774	STANFORD	98.4	98.3	0.0	0.0	0.2	0.2	1.0	1.3	7.6	7.4	7.5	8.2	7.6	26.4	25.2	8.7	1.6	72.6	35.6	49.1	50.9
61775	STRAWN	97.9	97.3	1.2	1.4	0.4	0.3	0.4	0.3	8.2	8.2	9.9	6.8	6.5	25.9	23.2	10.6	0.7	69.6	32.9	50.5	49.5
61776	TOWANDA	97.7	97.1	0.7	1.0	0.6	1.0	0.6	0.8	7.0	7.8	6.7	5.8	4.7	26.9	30.9	9.6	0.8	74.8	39.6	48.9	51.1
61777	WAPELLA	98.4	98.4	0.1	0.1	0.3	0.3	0.6	0.6	6.6	7.4	6.1	5.6	5.6	28.2	26.6	11.9	2.1	76.5	38.9	50.6	49.4
61778	WAYNESVILLE	98.5	98.5	0.4	0.5	0.0	0.0	0.9	0.9	6.5	6.8	7.4	5.7	5.5	25.6	27.9	13.1	1.5	75.6	40.3	48.9	51.1
61790	NORMAL	70.0	67.4	19.9	21.0	5.7	6.7	4.6	5.4	8.4	6.0	6.5	8.2	18.4	38.6	8.1	3.8	2.0	75.6	25.6	45.6	54.4
61801	URBANA	66.6	63.2	13.0	13.0	15.9	18.8	3.8	4.4	3.5	3.4	3.5	17.7	24.3	25.8	13.3	7.3	1.3	87.7	24.5	54.4	45.6
61802	URBANA	78.7	75.9	13.0	14.1	4.9	6.1	2.1	2.6	6.9	6.4	6.5	5.9	7.1	32.3	22.8	9.6	2.4	76.6	34.3	48.0	52.0
61810	ALLERTON	99.2	98.9	0.0	0.0	0.0	0.0	0.6	0.8	5.1	5.6	6.7	6.7	5.6	25.8	28.9	13.2	2.3	79.2	42.1	49.7	50.3
61811	ALVIN	99.0	98.6	0.1	0.1	0.1	0.3	0.3	0.4	6.1	6.3	8.6	6.6	5.9	28.8	25.6	11.2	1.0	75.1	38.2	50.1	49.9
61812	ARMSTRONG	96.2	96.1	1.4	1.4	0.3	0.4	1.0	1.1	5.7	7.2	7.2	7.5	4.7	26.9	25.8	14.0	1.1	75.6	39.4	52.7	47.3
61813	BEMENT	98.4	98.2	0.7	0.8	0.2	0.2	0.3	0.4	6.0	6.3	7.0	6.0	5.7	27.3	24.8	14.7	2.3	77.1	39.7	49.7	50.3
61814	BISMARCK	98.0	97.8	0.3	0.3	0.2	0.2	0.8	0.9	6.7	6.8	7.6	6.9	5.6	26.6	28.5	10.3	1.1	74.6	39.2	49.0	51.0
61816	BROADLANDS	98.2	98.2	0.4	0.5	0.0	0.0	0.0	0.0	6.7	7.2	6.9	6.7	4.7	24.2	29.5	11.9	2.2	75.2	41.5	49.2	50.8
61817	CATLIN	99.0	98.8	0.1	0.1	0.1	0.1	0.5	0.6	6.5	6.1	6.8	6.7	6.4	25.6	26.6	13.6	1.8	76.5	39.8	47.8	52.2
61818	CERRO GORDO	99.2	99.2	0.3	0.3	0.1	0.1	0.5	0.6	6.8	6.5	7.7	7.4	7.4	25.7	24.6	12.1	1.8	74.5	38.1	48.8	51.2
61820	CHAMPAIGN	69.3	66.0	16.3	16.9	9.1	11.0	5.5	6.5	3.1	2.6	3.0	19.7	33.3	22.7	9.9	4.6	1.2	89.7	23.3	53.6	46.5
61821	CHAMPAIGN	76.0	72.7	16.3	17.9	4.3	5.4	2.6	3.2	6.6	6.3	6.8	6.6	7.9	30.2	23.3	10.8	1.4	76.3	34.7	48.6	51.4
61822	CHAMPAIGN	85.3	82.5	6.1	6.7	6.1	7.8	1.7	2.2	7.1	7.3	7.7	6.2	4.9	29.5	28.2	8.3	0.9	73.8	37.4	49.1	50.9
61830	CISCO	97.9	97.6	0.0	0.0	0.0	0.0	0.6	1.0	7.3	6.9	5.5	4.9	5.3	25.6	29.7	13.2	1.6	77.2	41.0	49.2	50.8
61831	COLLISON	97.5	97.7	0.8	0.8	0.3	0.3	0.6	0.8	5.2	6.3	7.1	7.3	4.7	25.9	29.2	13.3	1.0	77.0	41.1	51.4	48.6
61832	DANVILLE	76.5	74.3	18.8	20.2	1.0	1.2	3.7	4.4	7.4	7.0	7.1	6.5	6.7	24.6	24.0	14.4	2.4	74.7	37.8	47.4	52.7
61833	TILTON	98.1	97.6	0.3	0.3	0.2	0.3	1.2	1.5	6.0	5.9	6.0	5.3	5.8	24.4	26.4	17.4	2.9	78.9	42.6	46.7	53.3
61834	DANVILLE	79.4	78.5	17.2	17.6	1.0	1.2	3.4	3.9	4.9	5.0	5.1	5.3	8.7	32.8	25.2	11.6	1.5	82.3	37.6	59.2	40.8
61839	DE LAND	98.4	98.0	0.3	0.3	0.3	0.3	0.9	0.9	6.1	6.8	7.8	5.9	5.9	26.1	28.3	12.1	1.1	75.8	40.1	49.6	50.4
61840	DEWEY	97.8	97.5	0.3	0.4	0.3	0.3	1.3	1.6	6.1	6.8	8.0	7.2	5.5	26.3	27.4	11.4	1.4	74.8	39.4	49.4	50.6
61841	FAIRMOUNT	98.9	98.7	0.2	0.2	0.1	0.1	0.6	0.8	5.8	6.1	6.8	6.4	5.5	25.6	28.9	12.7	2.2	77.4	41.0	49.4	50.7
61842	FARMER CITY	99.2	99.1	0.2	0.3	0.0	0.0	0.4	0.4	5.8	5.9	6.8	6.9	6.1	25.3	25.4	14.8	3.0	77.1	40.8	49.4	50.6
61843	FISHER	90.1	88.6	4.6	5.0	2.7	3.4	2.0	2.4	4.6	5.3	6.8	18.1	9.4	22.4	20.6	10.0	3.0	79.3	31.6	46.0	54.0
61844	FITHIAN	99.0	98.9	0.3	0.3	0.0	0.0	0.4	0.5	6.1	7.0	8.3	5.9	4.1	30.5	26.2	10.5	1.4	74.8	38.5	52.3	47.7
61845	FOOSLAND	84.9	82.4	7.5	8.2	4.5	5.7	2.6	3.2	3.6	4.1	6.1	26.0	12.2	20.0	15.6	8.6	4.0	82.4	24.2	43.4	56.6
61846	GEORGETOWN	96.2	95.6	2.2	2.4	0.1	0.1	1.0	1.4	6.8	6.6	7.4	6.8	7.0	25.3	25.3	13.2	1.7	75.1	38.0	48.5	51.6
61847	GIFFORD	97.5	97.2	1.1	1.2	0.4	0.5	0.8	0.9	6.0	6.7	6.3	6.1	5.2	25.5	24.6	14.3	5.3	76.8	41.2	47.6	52.4
61849	HOMER	99.0	98.8	0.1	0.1	0.4	0.5	0.2	0.2	6.9	7.1	7.1	6.1	5.1	26.7	26.2	13.2	1.7	75.1	39.3	50.3	49.7
61850	INDIANOLA	98.7	98.4	0.2	0.2	0.6	0.8	0.4	0.4	5.3	5.9	7.3	6.5	6.3	24.1	29.4	13.6	1.6	77.5	41.4	49.5	50.5
61851	IVESDALE	97.8	97.4	0.2	0.2	0.0	0.0	0.0	0.2	5.3	7.1	7.9	6.1	3.2	32.4	26.7	10.1	1.2	76.1	38.7	53.0	47.0
61852	LONGVIEW	98.0	97.9	0.6	0.6	0.3	0.3	1.2	0.9	7.2	7.8	7.8	6.9	5.4	25.4	27.8	10.8	1.2	73.1	38.7	51.9	48.1
61853	MAHOMET	97.8	97.3	0.4	0.5	0.6	0.7	0.9	1.1	7.6	7.9	8.8	8.0	6.6	27.5	26.0	7.1	0.6	70.8	35.1	48.9	51.1
61854	MANSFIELD	98.8	98.5	0.1	0.1	0.3	0.4	0.7	0.8	6.4	6.6	6.9	6.3	6.1	25.5	28.9	12.2	1.1	76.3	40.6	50.1	49.9
61855	MILMINE	97.6	97.6	0.6	0.6	0.0	0.0	0.0	0.0	7.4	6.8	6.1	5.5	4.9	23.3	29.5	14.7	1.8	76.1	42.7	49.7	50.3
61856	MONTICELLO	99.0	98.8	0.1	0.1	0.2	0.2	0.8	0.9	6.1	6.3	6.8	6.2	5.6	23.7	27.5	14.8	3.0	77.0	42.1	47.9	52.1
61858	OAKWOOD	99.3	99.2	0.1	0.1	0.0	0.0	0.4	0.5	6.6	6.6	6.9	6.0	6.2	27.0	27.0	12.7	1.0	76.1	38.7	49.2	50.8
61859	OGDEN	98.2	97.9	0.2	0.2	0.4	0.6	0.6	0.8	6.5	6.8	8.3	7.2	5.7	27.3	24.4	12.1	1.7	74.0	38.0	49.2	50.8
61862	PENFIELD	96.6	96.1	0.8	1.0	0.4	0.6	1.8	2.1	6.0	8.9	8.1	7.2	3.3	25.2	28.1	12.0	1.2	72.3	38.5	50.8	49.2
61863	PESOTUM	99.1	99.0	0.0	0.0	0.4	0.5	0.3	0.3	5.1	5.3	6.5	6.8	6.1	25.5	29.5	13.1	2.1	79.3	42.0	51.0	49.0
61864	PHILO	99.1	99.0	0.3	0.3	0.0	0.0	0.3	0.3	6.9	7.4	7.6	7.0	5.2	27.0	25.5	11.5	1.8	73.8	37.9	51.3	48.7
61865	POTOMAC	97.3	96.8	0.4	0.5	0.3	0.4	1.5	1.9	6.5	7.0	7.7	6.9	5.5	26.2	26.1	12.4	1.8	74.6	38.8	50.6	49.4
61866	RANTOUL	77.8	75.8	15.7	16.7	1.8	2.3	2.8	3.4	8.7	7.8	7.6	6.9	7.1	30.6	20.5	9.6	1.2	71.7	32.6	47.9	52.1
61870	RIDGE FARM	99.5	99.4	0.0	0.0	0.1	0.1	0.6	0.8	6.3	6.5	7.4	6.8	5.8	25.0	27.8	12.9	1.5	75.6	39.7	49.6	50.4
61872	SADORUS	98.0	97.6	0.1	0.1	0.1	0.1	0.3	0.3	5.1	7.0	7.9	6.3	3.6	31.8	27.0	10.1	1.2	76.1	38.8	52.8	47.3
61873	SAINT JOSEPH	98.9	98.7	0.1	0.2	0.2	0.3	0.8	1.0	7.0	7.2	7.6	7.1	5.9	28.3	26.4	9.2	1.3	73.5	37.4	48.7	51.3
61874	SAVOY	83.4	80.3	4.1	4.4	9.6	12.0	2.1	2.5	7.8	7.1	6.2	5.4	5.6	31.0	23.5	10.5	2.9	75.5	35.6	46.5	53.5
61875	SEYMOUR	97.1	96.6	0.3	0.3	0.5	0.7	1.0	1.6	7.5	8.3	8.6	7.1	5.5	26.7	26.2	9.2	0.9	71.1	35.8	48.8	51.2
61876	SIDELL	99.4	99.5	0.1	0.1	0.0	0.0	0.5	0.7	6.2	6.5	7.8	7.1	5.1	27.1	26.0	12.8	1.5	75.1	39.4	50.6	49.4
61877	SIDNEY	97.8	97.5	0.3	0.3	0.6	0.8	0.3	0.4	7.7	8.0	7.3	6.3	5.2	27.6	25.1	11.0	2.0	73.3	38.2	49.2	50.8
61878	THOMASBORO	95.5	94.7	1.3	1.4	0.8	1.0	1.1	1.4	6.8	6.9	7.3	7.3	5.9	29.0	24.4	10.8	1.7	74.5	36.3	49.1	50.9
61880	TOLONO	97.2	96.8	0.8	0.8	0.5	0.6	0.9	1.1	7.2	7.0	6.4	6.3	5.8	30.3	25.4	10.6	1.1	75.7	37.0	51.2	48.8
61882	WELDON	97.4	97.4	0.0	0.0	0.5	0.5	0.2	0.2	6.8	7.0	6.5	5.2	4.9	26.4	28.5	13.1	1.6	76.2	40.4	51.2	48.8
61883	WESTVILLE	98.2	97.9	0.3	0.3	0.1	0.1	0.8	1.0	6.0	6.0	6.6	6.8	5.9	26.4	25.2	15.0	2.2	77.3	39.9	48.2	51.8
61884	WHITE HEATH	99.1	99.0	0.1	0.1	0.1	0.1	0.8	1.0	6.4	7.1	7.5	6.8	5.5	25.8	30.9	9.2	0.8	74.7	40.2	50.5	49.6
61910	ARCOLA	92.5	91.1	0.3	0.3	0.5	0.6	13.0	15.6	8.8	8.4	7.7	6.8	6.6	26.3	22.0	12.0	1.5	71.0	34.6	49.6	50.4
61911	ARTHUR	99.5	99.4	0.0	0.0	0.1	0.1	0.5	0.6	8.6	7.8	8.4	7.4	7.5	23.7	21.5	12.3	2.7	70.4	33.6	48.1	51.9
61912	ASHMORE	97.8	97.5	0.4	0.4	0.9	1.1	0.5	0.6	6.1	6.4	7.1	6.8	6.2	27.8	27.6	10.8	1.3	76.3	38.3	48.9	51.1
61913	ATWOOD	99.1	99.0	0.2	0.2	0.1	0.1	1.0	1.3	7.0	7.0	7.4	7.4	5.9	25.7	24.7	13.4	1.7	74.2	38.7	48.7	51.3
61914	BETHANY	98.8	98.7	0.1	0.1	0.0	0.0	0.4	0.5	5.6	6.0	6.9	5.8	5.2	25.7	28.7	14.0	2.2	78.1	41.8	49.7	50.4
61917	BROCTON	99.3	98.8	0.0	0.0	0.1	0.1	0.4	0.9	5.5	5.9	7.1	6.4	5.6	23.7	29.5	14.5	1.9	77.6	42.5	50.0	50.0
61919	CAMARGO	98.4	98.3	0.6	0.6	0.0	0.0	0.2	0.2	5.5	6.0	6.7	7.1	5.6	25.1	28.5	14.2	1.4	77.6	41.5	50.2	49.8
61920	CHARLESTON	93.2	92.3	3.7	4.0	1.3	1.6	1.7	2.1	4.1	3.9	4.7	16.1	21.9	21.8	17.5	8.7	1.5	84.4	24.9	47.0	53.0
61924	CHRISMAN	99.0	98.9	0.4	0.5	0.2	0.2	0.2	0.2	5.3	6.5	6.2	6.0	5.9	23.4	24.7	16.1	6.1	78.3	42.8	48.2	51.8
61925	DALTON CITY	98.5	98.3	0.6	0.6	0.2	0.2	0.9	1.2	6.7	6.8	8.7	7.1	5.1	27.5	29.1	8.5	0.6	73.0	38.1	49.7	50.3
61928	GAYS	97.9	97.7	0.4	0.4	0.7	0.9	0.3	0.3	5.5	6.5	6.9	6.4	4.7	24.7	29.8	14.4	1.1	77.3	42.1	50.6	49.4
61929	HAMMOND	98.6	98.5	0.4	0.4	0.1	0.1	0.2	0.3	6.5	6.9	7.9	6.6	5.7	26.0	26.2	12.3	1.8	74.6	39.2	51.6	48.4
61930	HINDSBORO	99.4	99.4	0.0	0.0	0.2	0.2	1.5	1.6	7.0	7.2	6.4	5.2	4.4	23.6	28.9	15.0	2.4	76.1	42.3	50.1	49.9
61931	HUMBOLDT	98.7	98.6	0.0	0.0	0.0	0.0	2.7	3.2	8.3	7.9	7.6	6.3	5.4	28.1	23.3	11.6	1.5	72.5	34.9	48.7	51.3
61932	HUME	99.6	99.6	0.0	0.0	0.0	0.0	0.9	1.1	5.8	5.8	6.2	6.0	6.4	24.5	28.0	15.1	2.2	78.7	41.9	49.9	50.1
61933	KANSAS	98.7	98.5	0.3	0.3	0.2	0.2	1.4	1.6	5.6	6.0	8.4	7.5	6.2	23.1	26.3	14.0	2.8	75.2	39.3	47.6	52.4
61937	LOVINGTON	98.9	98.7	0.3	0.3	0.3	0.3	0.5	0.6	6.3	6.6	7.8	6.6	6.7	27.7	24.8	12.1	1.5	75.2	37.8	50.1	50.0
61938	MATTOON	97.1	96.7	1.2	1.3	0.4	0.5	1.1	1.4	6.6	6.0	6.1	6.2	6.7	27.3	24.0	14.3	2.6	77.5	38.3	48.1	51.9
61940	METCALF	99.5	99.5	0.0	0.0	0.0	0.0	0.9	1.2	5.7	6.0	6.0	6.0	6.5	24.9	27.8	15.1	2.2	79.2	41.6	50.2	49.8
61942	NEWMAN	98.1	97.9	0.9	0.9	0.1	0.1	0.4	0.5	5.7	5.6	5.6	6.3	5.6	22.4	26.5	17.9	4.4	79.3	44.1	46.9	53.1
61943	OAKLAND	98.1	97.9	0.7	0.8	0.1	0.1	1.0	1.2	5.9	5.6	6.2	7.7	9.4	23.2	25.6	14.2	2.3	78.6	39.0	49.9	50.1
61944	PARIS	96.4	96.0	2.4	2.6	0.2	0.3	0.8	1.0	6.1	5.9	6.5	6.4	6.5	26.6	25.1	14.3	2.6	77.7	39.7	49.2	50.8
61951	SULLIVAN	99.0	98.8	0.2	0.2	0.1	0.2	0.4	0.5	6.4	6.5	6.5	6.0	6.0	24.3	24.5	15.6	4.2	76.9	41.1	48.1	51.9
61953	TUSCOLA	98.2	97.9	0.3	0.4	0.4	0.5	1.1	1.4	6.5	6.4	6.6	6.9	6.1	26.4	24.1	14.4	2.5	76.2	39.3	48.5	51.5
	ILLINOIS	73.5	71.8	15.1	15.2	3.5	4.0	12.3	14.2	7.1	7.0	7.3	7.0	7.3	29.0	23.2	10.4	1.7	74.5	35.2	49.0	51.0
	UNITED STATES	75.1	73.6	12.3	12.5	3.8	4.2	12.5	14.1	6.9	6.7	7.2	7.0	7.3	28.6	23.8	10.8	1.7	75.1	36.0	49.1	50.9

ZIP CODE #	POST OFFICE NAME	2004 Per Capita Income	2004 HH Income Base	2004 HOUSEHOLD INCOME DISTRIBUTION (%) Less than $25,000	$25,000 to $49,999	$50,000 to $99,999	$100,000 to $149,999	$150,000 or More	MEDIAN HOUSEHOLD INCOME 2004	2009	2004 National Centile	2004 State Centile	2004 Home Value Base	2004 HOME VALUE DISTRIBUTION (%) Less than $50,000	$50,000 to $89,999	$90,000 to $174,999	$175,000 to $399,999	$400,000 or More	2004 Median Home Value
61755	MACKINAW	24103	1436	15.3	24.9	41.9	13.7	4.3	58404	65120	83	79	1241	4.9	14.7	57.9	21.4	1.1	127455
61756	MAROA	22589	800	20.8	33.6	35.9	6.0	3.8	46172	52148	64	53	659	22.9	36.1	30.5	8.8	1.7	78077
61759	MINIER	21476	632	21.4	33.7	36.2	5.7	3.0	46390	52306	65	54	528	13.5	23.9	55.3	7.4	0.0	100600
61760	MINONK	21114	1038	24.7	27.5	38.3	8.0	1.5	47585	52104	67	57	867	13.2	33.3	44.1	9.3	0.1	93050
61761	NORMAL	22769	16479	27.2	27.1	30.9	11.1	3.8	45242	51693	62	49	9504	6.1	8.3	65.2	19.7	0.6	137124
61764	PONTIAC	20746	5348	26.5	32.1	31.6	7.2	2.7	43694	48410	58	44	3983	16.3	26.7	42.9	13.8	0.4	99022
61769	SAUNEMIN	21962	237	13.1	30.0	45.6	8.9	2.5	54591	61174	79	73	206	16.0	32.0	37.4	9.7	4.9	93077
61770	SAYBROOK	19894	458	23.8	32.8	38.4	5.0	0.0	45143	51624	62	49	382	19.4	36.1	31.2	13.4	0.0	84324
61771	SECOR	25224	362	16.9	29.3	37.3	9.7	6.9	53234	58434	77	70	310	7.7	23.9	38.1	26.5	3.9	116981
61772	SHIRLEY	30469	183	11.5	26.2	39.9	14.8	7.7	63732	74597	88	85	150	9.3	22.0	39.3	28.0	1.3	117857
61773	SIBLEY	23908	226	30.5	23.5	35.0	4.9	6.2	47194	50603	67	56	187	36.9	29.4	21.9	7.0	4.8	63000
61774	STANFORD	23438	399	13.8	29.3	43.1	10.8	3.0	54428	63839	79	72	330	10.6	36.7	43.9	5.5	3.3	92308
61775	STRAWN	23678	108	9.3	27.8	51.9	8.3	2.8	61045	63648	85	82	89	11.2	21.4	50.6	16.9	0.0	113125
61776	TOWANDA	32047	424	9.9	26.2	39.9	15.3	8.7	65313	75221	89	87	369	7.3	13.3	45.0	28.2	6.2	139803
61777	WAPELLA	23932	393	17.6	31.8	37.4	9.2	4.1	50374	56059	73	63	338	16.3	28.7	33.7	16.6	4.7	95152
61778	WAYNESVILLE	20106	271	24.0	35.4	31.7	7.0	1.9	45082	50403	61	49	237	27.0	32.1	29.1	10.6	1.3	78500
61790	NORMAL	10497	638	50.9	33.9	13.3	1.6	0.3	24429	27543	4	1	131	66.4	22.1	11.5	0.0	0.0	18750
61801	URBANA	19322	11513	45.7	26.2	19.2	5.3	3.7	28355	31782	9	3	4492	5.6	23.9	52.8	16.1	1.5	114498
61802	URBANA	23043	7721	27.4	35.1	28.1	5.8	3.6	39307	45749	44	27	4979	24.2	26.2	34.8	12.3	2.5	89472
61810	ALLERTON	21688	137	18.3	32.1	38.7	8.0	2.9	49654	52686	71	62	115	18.3	33.9	33.0	14.8	0.0	86875
61811	ALVIN	18321	282	23.1	34.0	37.9	3.2	1.8	45577	50718	63	51	236	24.6	34.3	32.6	8.1	0.4	77647
61812	ARMSTRONG	21335	113	20.4	38.9	32.7	7.1	0.9	45832	48649	63	51	92	18.5	20.7	45.7	10.9	4.4	104167
61813	BEMENT	20808	814	19.7	35.9	38.3	4.1	2.1	45530	50898	63	50	680	17.9	36.0	39.7	6.0	0.3	86301
61814	BISMARCK	23349	408	20.3	24.5	39.7	13.0	2.5	53683	59169	78	71	353	13.6	31.2	35.7	18.4	1.1	99250
61816	BROADLANDS	20263	180	18.3	45.0	28.9	3.9	3.9	41092	46485	50	34	149	19.5	36.2	28.9	15.4	0.0	84688
61817	CATLIN	20720	1096	20.3	30.8	39.8	7.5	1.7	48916	53096	70	60	898	10.5	36.3	44.9	8.0	0.3	93053
61818	CERRO GORDO	19738	792	26.0	28.0	38.9	6.6	0.5	46009	50880	64	52	643	12.0	37.0	44.6	5.6	0.8	90985
61820	CHAMPAIGN	15716	13203	56.3	22.9	15.9	3.3	1.7	20997	23757	2	1	3880	17.3	30.9	42.5	8.4	1.0	92517
61821	CHAMPAIGN	27792	13980	21.3	29.3	34.7	9.4	5.3	49459	56766	71	61	9575	4.5	29.9	49.5	14.9	1.3	107646
61822	CHAMPAIGN	37067	6125	11.9	22.0	36.9	15.4	13.8	68411	78945	91	89	4997	4.3	8.7	40.3	41.4	5.4	168326
61830	CISCO	22148	196	16.3	33.2	42.9	6.1	1.5	50305	54968	72	63	160	10.6	21.9	41.9	22.5	3.1	108824
61831	COLLISON	21035	149	18.8	33.6	39.6	6.7	1.3	48113	52623	69	59	123	11.4	23.6	48.0	13.8	3.3	110119
61832	DANVILLE	19074	15811	36.9	32.5	24.1	4.7	1.9	33955	37009	24	10	10658	35.4	32.5	24.4	7.5	0.3	66800
61833	TILTON	18248	1149	34.3	37.5	25.3	2.4	0.4	35259	38721	28	13	886	36.7	47.3	14.9	1.1	0.0	61043
61834	DANVILLE	19917	2882	28.9	28.4	33.1	7.0	2.6	42369	45937	54	39	2280	21.2	25.8	37.9	14.6	0.5	95738
61839	DE LAND	24544	281	21.0	26.0	41.3	6.8	5.0	51472	56966	75	66	236	7.2	35.2	29.2	19.5	8.9	103906
61840	DEWEY	27234	266	14.3	24.1	44.7	10.9	6.0	59621	69150	84	80	229	7.4	14.4	53.3	22.7	2.2	130208
61841	FAIRMOUNT	21468	530	22.1	30.2	39.6	6.2	1.9	47932	52332	68	58	454	24.2	37.0	30.4	8.4	0.0	77143
61842	FARMER CITY	23986	1186	20.2	32.0	34.9	10.1	2.8	48111	55004	69	59	960	11.2	31.2	45.0	12.2	0.5	100962
61843	FISHER	28653	811	14.9	33.2	38.8	9.9	3.2	51442	59467	75	66	702	12.4	26.2	47.9	12.0	1.6	103650
61844	FITHIAN	20928	438	16.7	32.9	44.3	5.5	0.7	50248	53399	72	63	364	22.8	30.0	37.6	9.1	0.6	86667
61845	FOOSLAND	11583	149	16.1	38.9	35.6	8.7	0.7	47457	54388	67	56	129	14.0	32.6	44.2	8.5	0.8	93462
61846	GEORGETOWN	17317	2059	30.6	35.9	29.0	3.8	0.7	37209	41591	36	20	1594	33.5	38.1	25.0	3.0	0.4	64049
61847	GIFFORD	22686	440	13.2	33.4	44.6	6.4	2.5	52167	59792	76	68	384	6.0	27.9	56.3	9.9	0.0	103893
61849	HOMER	22005	695	18.1	42.2	32.4	5.5	1.9	44144	51105	59	46	605	14.6	40.8	35.2	8.8	0.7	85000
61850	INDIANOLA	19631	197	24.9	36.6	28.9	7.6	2.0	42160	47338	53	38	170	42.4	16.5	34.1	7.1	0.0	75000
61851	IVESDALE	27500	201	9.5	31.8	45.3	10.5	3.0	55705	63647	80	75	173	15.6	42.2	29.5	10.4	2.3	85000
61852	LONGVIEW	21735	123	13.0	34.2	44.7	6.5	1.6	52534	59148	76	69	106	17.0	24.5	32.1	26.4	0.0	106818
61853	MAHOMET	26110	4094	14.6	27.1	38.9	13.3	6.1	59661	68210	84	80	3672	13.8	7.7	53.9	22.4	2.2	130995
61854	MANSFIELD	25184	620	14.8	34.2	40.8	7.4	2.7	50639	56666	73	64	510	9.8	25.5	50.6	14.1	0.0	105819
61855	MILMINE	18484	61	26.2	29.5	37.7	6.6	0.0	44305	47988	59	46	51	15.7	35.3	31.4	15.7	2.0	89000
61856	MONTICELLO	26602	2798	19.3	30.2	36.1	9.5	4.8	50405	54772	73	63	2301	9.2	14.6	46.8	27.2	2.3	126764
61858	OAKWOOD	21624	1126	20.5	34.0	38.2	5.4	1.9	47091	52346	66	56	948	27.5	31.4	31.8	8.8	0.5	80000
61859	OGDEN	24770	561	12.3	34.4	42.3	7.8	3.2	52477	60981	76	68	497	4.4	26.6	56.7	10.5	1.8	108226
61862	PENFIELD	22824	185	10.8	34.6	41.1	10.3	3.2	52766	59221	77	69	154	16.2	22.1	51.3	10.4	0.0	105645
61863	PESOTUM	24957	317	12.0	29.0	47.6	11.4	0.0	55947	63765	81	76	294	7.1	40.1	43.2	7.1	2.4	92500
61864	PHILO	25983	624	9.1	26.0	48.7	12.0	4.2	62829	73012	87	84	569	3.0	16.3	65.6	15.1	0.0	119554
61865	POTOMAC	18683	515	23.5	36.1	34.4	4.5	1.6	45206	49369	62	49	434	29.0	34.6	28.8	6.5	1.2	72727
61866	RANTOUL	20842	6047	25.6	35.9	30.7	5.9	2.0	41255	47713	51	35	3561	20.5	31.3	41.4	6.5	0.4	88277
61870	RIDGE FARM	18819	565	24.6	37.7	31.5	5.8	0.4	41098	45882	50	34	459	36.4	39.4	23.5	0.7	0.0	66563
61872	SADORUS	26413	284	9.2	31.3	45.8	10.9	2.8	56429	64601	81	76	245	14.7	42.5	29.4	11.0	2.5	85395
61873	SAINT JOSEPH	25940	1998	17.7	21.6	45.1	11.6	4.1	59515	68362	84	80	1752	1.9	14.9	64.6	17.8	0.9	126567
61874	SAVOY	36543	1898	19.1	21.2	36.4	11.9	11.4	59808	69648	84	81	1238	3.9	6.7	36.3	48.0	5.2	179733
61875	SEYMOUR	27997	287	10.1	18.5	44.6	21.3	5.6	70087	81237	91	91	243	6.2	21.0	38.3	32.1	2.5	128289
61876	SIDELL	17062	291	29.9	40.9	24.7	3.4	1.0	37841	42073	39	22	247	38.9	33.6	20.2	6.5	0.8	62143
61877	SIDNEY	25786	621	18.4	24.0	43.5	11.1	3.1	57043	65607	82	78	516	10.5	18.0	54.8	14.7	1.9	112190
61878	THOMASBORO	21622	595	17.8	36.0	39.0	6.6	0.7	46823	55545	66	55	474	9.7	39.7	44.1	5.9	0.6	90411
61880	TOLONO	23711	1367	17.2	29.6	42.4	8.6	2.3	52013	60160	75	67	1084	9.1	25.8	56.0	7.4	1.7	102019
61882	WELDON	26829	238	16.0	32.4	37.4	9.2	5.0	51285	55791	74	66	204	20.1	32.4	30.9	16.2	0.5	87917
61883	WESTVILLE	19710	1928	32.1	33.7	30.0	3.2	1.0	36728	40370	34	18	1515	27.8	44.3	24.6	3.4	0.0	69158
61884	WHITE HEATH	26163	510	11.2	27.3	45.1	11.8	4.7	58411	64035	83	79	454	5.5	16.3	40.1	37.4	0.7	152119
61910	ARCOLA	19832	1488	22.7	34.5	31.6	8.5	2.8	42493	47186	55	40	1235	18.6	27.3	39.9	13.0	1.2	96645
61911	ARTHUR	18297	1447	22.5	37.9	31.0	6.5	2.1	42667	46907	55	40	1173	11.9	31.4	43.1	12.0	1.6	96795
61912	ASHMORE	18604	533	22.9	38.3	34.9	2.4	1.5	44175	50626	59	46	451	22.8	33.9	37.5	4.4	1.3	79907
61913	ATWOOD	19853	803	29.8	33.0	30.3	4.7	2.2	40900	45358	49	33	685	19.3	33.0	38.0	9.6	0.2	87933
61914	BETHANY	21787	767	23.0	33.6	34.8	7.0	1.6	44559	47835	60	47	660	12.3	33.5	45.3	8.6	0.3	95957
61917	BROCTON	20797	287	34.5	33.5	27.2	3.1	1.7	36755	40090	35	19	238	45.8	37.0	13.5	2.9	0.8	56667
61919	CAMARGO	24675	391	17.4	29.2	40.9	9.5	3.1	53127	59408	77	70	342	16.7	17.3	44.4	19.6	2.1	113559
61920	CHARLESTON	18946	9279	44.4	25.5	20.9	6.4	2.9	29950	32658	12	4	4862	16.3	23.0	43.5	15.8	1.4	105343
61924	CHRISMAN	19730	953	27.3	35.4	31.2	4.2	2.0	41074	44723	50	34	759	29.9	29.5	27.5	11.5	1.6	80467
61925	DALTON CITY	23478	380	14.5	25.8	46.3	10.8	2.6	56640	63498	81	77	339	9.4	26.0	48.4	16.2	0.0	104464
61928	GAYS	22725	278	13.3	36.7	40.7	7.6	1.8	50000	55274	72	62	242	19.0	33.1	43.8	4.1	0.0	88387
61929	HAMMOND	22619	394	21.6	31.0	39.6	6.6	1.3	48132	52857	69	59	314	17.2	30.9	43.6	8.0	0.3	91875
61930	HINDSBORO	19620	197	30.0	31.5	30.0	6.6	2.0	38213	41407	40	24	166	21.1	35.5	28.3	9.6	5.4	82143
61931	HUMBOLDT	22018	326	21.5	36.5	32.5	7.7	1.8	42575	48451	55	40	274	18.3	39.4	36.5	5.8	0.0	85532
61932	HUME	22682	240	28.3	35.0	27.1	6.7	2.9	40206	43689	47	30	195	43.1	24.1	23.1	7.7	2.1	60357
61933	KANSAS	16550	434	37.8	34.3	23.7	2.1	2.1	32809	36555	20	8	327	35.5	38.8	24.8	0.9	0.0	64091
61937	LOVINGTON	21380	808	21.9	35.6	33.2	6.3	3.0	43398	48277	57	43	666	20.3	31.5	39.9	8.3	0.0	88209
61938	MATTOON	21996	10012	31.5	31.5	28.9	5.5	2.6	38266	43608	40	24	7217	15.5	37.5	36.2	9.7	1.1	87064
61940	METCALF	19192	159	28.3	35.2	26.4	6.3	3.8	40154	43310	47	30	129	42.6	24.0	22.5	8.5	2.3	60556
61942	NEWMAN	21589	545	30.5	34.3	27.9	5.0	2.4	36027	39162	32	16	438	35.4	40.4	18.5	5.3	0.5	64286
61943	OAKLAND	18353	659	29.3	38.4	26.6	3.5	2.3	38113	43396	40	23	551	29.0	36.1	24.7	8.0	2.2	75000
61944	PARIS	20398	5750	31.9	34.3	27.6	3.6	2.6	37247	40877	36	20	4369	25.0	35.7	30.8	7.6	0.9	74958
61951	SULLIVAN	21037	2929	23.8	34.6	32.6	6.8	2.3	43182	48161	56	43	2350	13.3	28.8	44.5	12.3	1.1	99487
61953	TUSCOLA	21805	2600	19.9	37.2	34.5	6.0	2.4	44824	49677	61	48	2081	16.3	24.8	46.4	12.1	0.5	101337
	ILLINOIS	27033		22.1	25.9	32.9	11.9	7.3	52039	60941				7.7	12.8	34.0	36.6	8.9	162771
	UNITED STATES	25866		24.7	27.1	30.8	10.9	6.5	48124	56710				10.9	15.0	33.7	30.1	10.4	145905

ZIP CODE #	POST OFFICE NAME	FINANCIAL SERVICES: Auto Loan	FINANCIAL SERVICES: Home Loan	FINANCIAL SERVICES: Invest-ments	FINANCIAL SERVICES: Retire-ment Plans	THE HOME: Home Improvements: Home Repair	THE HOME: Home Improvements: Lawn & Garden	THE HOME: Furnishings: Comput-ers & Hard-ware	THE HOME: Furnishings: Major Appli-ances	THE HOME: Furnishings: TV, Radio, Sound Equip-ment	THE HOME: Furnishings: Furni-ture	ENTERTAINMENT: Dine out/ Carry out	ENTERTAINMENT: Sports Equip-ment	ENTERTAINMENT: Fees & Tickets	ENTERTAINMENT: Toys & Games	ENTERTAINMENT: Travel	ENTERTAINMENT: Cable TV	PERSONAL: Apparel & Services	PERSONAL: Auto Repairs	PERSONAL: Health Insur-ance	PERSONAL: Pets & Supplies
61755	MACKINAW	93	98	93	98	99	103	93	95	91	92	113	111	95	117	94	91	110	93	94	109
61756	MAROA	93	73	49	71	80	90	74	84	81	73	97	98	67	95	74	83	90	82	95	107
61759	MINIER	83	71	55	71	74	84	73	78	77	71	94	89	70	93	72	78	88	77	84	92
61760	MINONK	80	69	56	67	73	84	72	76	77	69	93	86	69	93	72	80	87	76	86	90
61761	NORMAL	79	76	86	80	74	78	86	79	83	83	104	97	83	101	81	77	101	83	72	87
61764	PONTIAC	64	59	54	58	61	66	60	62	62	59	76	73	58	76	60	62	73	62	65	74
61769	SAUNEMIN	99	89	67	84	94	100	82	91	87	82	106	108	80	108	84	89	100	88	98	117
61770	SAYBROOK	75	64	50	64	67	76	66	70	70	64	84	80	63	84	65	71	79	69	76	83
61771	SECOR	97	102	114	106	103	107	102	102	98	101	123	120	103	122	102	95	119	102	97	113
61772	SHIRLEY	118	115	99	112	119	125	105	113	107	105	132	134	106	136	108	108	127	110	116	140
61773	SIBLEY	115	80	42	76	94	105	79	98	92	78	107	118	68	105	82	96	98	97	117	137
61774	STANFORD	103	92	70	87	97	104	85	94	90	85	109	112	83	112	87	92	104	91	102	121
61775	STRAWN	90	98	98	100	95	94	94	93	88	94	111	110	94	111	92	83	109	92	81	102
61776	TOWANDA	109	134	145	133	131	131	121	120	114	121	144	140	130	152	124	112	143	117	110	132
61777	WAPELLA	95	85	65	81	90	96	79	87	83	79	101	104	77	104	81	85	96	85	94	112
61778	WAYNESVILLE	80	71	54	68	75	81	66	73	70	66	85	87	64	87	68	72	81	71	79	94
61790	NORMAL	41	32	42	37	32	36	45	39	44	42	56	51	41	52	40	41	54	45	37	44
61801	URBANA	58	49	60	51	48	54	65	56	64	60	80	71	60	76	59	60	77	62	53	63
61802	URBANA	72	69	74	72	69	73	74	72	73	73	91	86	72	89	72	70	88	75	69	81
61810	ALLERTON	91	80	60	76	85	91	74	83	79	74	96	99	72	98	76	81	91	81	90	107
61811	ALVIN	83	74	56	70	78	83	68	75	72	68	88	90	67	90	70	74	83	73	82	97
61812	ARMSTRONG	90	69	43	66	78	85	67	79	74	66	88	95	60	88	69	77	82	77	91	107
61813	BEMENT	82	69	53	68	73	82	70	76	75	69	91	87	67	90	70	76	85	75	83	91
61814	BISMARCK	91	90	78	87	93	97	82	88	84	82	103	104	83	106	85	84	99	86	90	109
61816	BROADLANDS	87	65	40	62	74	82	64	77	72	63	85	92	57	84	66	75	78	76	89	104
61817	CATLIN	71	84	90	83	83	85	77	77	74	77	93	90	82	98	79	73	92	75	73	86
61818	CERRO GORDO	81	66	48	65	71	80	67	74	72	66	87	85	63	86	67	74	81	73	82	91
61820	CHAMPAIGN	46	36	44	39	35	40	51	43	51	47	63	56	46	59	45	47	61	49	41	49
61821	CHAMPAIGN	85	88	102	91	86	90	93	88	89	91	112	106	93	112	90	85	110	91	82	97
61822	CHAMPAIGN	128	139	145	145	134	134	133	130	124	136	158	153	136	157	130	117	156	130	115	143
61830	CISCO	99	71	40	68	82	91	70	85	80	69	94	103	61	93	72	83	86	84	100	118
61831	COLLISON	92	73	49	69	81	88	70	81	77	69	92	97	65	92	72	79	86	79	92	108
61832	DANVILLE	63	58	59	56	59	67	61	62	64	60	79	71	60	79	61	66	76	63	67	71
61833	TILTON	50	55	58	52	55	61	54	54	56	52	70	60	57	75	56	58	67	52	58	59
61834	DANVILLE	76	67	58	64	71	77	66	71	70	66	85	84	64	85	67	72	81	71	77	89
61839	DE LAND	99	89	69	85	94	100	82	91	87	82	106	108	81	108	84	89	100	88	97	116
61840	DEWEY	94	115	123	114	112	112	104	104	98	104	124	120	111	131	106	96	123	101	94	113
61841	FAIRMOUNT	83	76	61	73	80	85	70	77	74	70	90	92	69	92	72	75	86	75	82	98
61842	FARMER CITY	88	82	70	78	86	94	79	84	83	78	102	98	79	105	81	86	97	82	91	103
61843	FISHER	92	91	84	90	93	99	89	92	89	87	110	105	89	112	89	89	106	90	93	105
61844	FITHIAN	85	74	55	70	79	85	69	77	74	69	89	92	67	91	71	75	85	75	84	100
61845	FOOSLAND	88	77	62	77	81	90	78	83	82	77	100	95	75	100	78	83	94	82	89	98
61846	GEORGETOWN	64	58	49	53	61	68	56	61	61	55	74	70	56	77	58	64	70	59	68	75
61847	GIFFORD	94	82	61	78	87	94	76	85	81	76	99	102	74	100	78	84	93	83	93	111
61849	HOMER	71	79	82	76	79	84	75	76	75	73	93	87	78	99	77	76	91	74	76	85
61850	INDIANOLA	81	72	55	68	76	82	67	74	71	67	86	88	65	88	69	73	82	72	80	95
61851	IVESDALE	88	104	112	102	101	103	97	96	92	96	116	111	102	122	98	90	115	94	88	105
61852	LONGVIEW	80	89	92	86	89	92	83	85	81	82	101	98	86	106	85	81	100	83	82	96
61853	MAHOMET	103	114	111	115	110	110	105	106	99	107	125	124	107	126	104	94	123	104	94	118
61854	MANSFIELD	90	91	81	88	93	96	83	88	83	82	102	104	84	106	85	83	99	85	89	107
61855	MILMINE	89	62	33	59	73	81	62	76	71	61	83	92	53	82	64	75	76	75	91	106
61856	MONTICELLO	88	93	97	93	94	99	90	92	89	90	111	106	92	112	92	88	108	91	91	103
61858	OAKWOOD	82	75	58	72	77	82	70	76	73	70	89	90	68	88	71	73	85	75	80	95
61859	OGDEN	99	91	76	90	94	98	88	94	89	88	109	113	83	108	87	87	104	93	94	115
61862	PENFIELD	113	82	47	78	94	105	80	97	91	79	108	117	70	106	83	95	99	96	114	134
61863	PESOTUM	77	93	103	91	91	93	86	85	82	86	104	99	92	110	89	81	103	83	79	93
61864	PHILO	91	111	121	109	109	110	102	101	96	101	121	117	108	129	104	94	120	98	93	110
61865	POTOMAC	81	71	53	67	75	81	66	74	70	66	85	88	64	87	68	72	81	72	80	96
61866	RANTOUL	68	69	73	69	69	74	70	70	69	69	87	81	70	87	70	69	84	70	69	78
61870	RIDGE FARM	73	63	49	62	66	73	62	67	66	62	80	78	60	80	63	68	76	66	73	82
61872	SADORUS	90	107	115	105	104	105	99	98	94	99	119	114	104	125	101	92	118	96	90	107
61873	SAINT JOSEPH	92	103	105	104	101	101	97	97	92	97	115	114	99	118	97	88	114	96	88	108
61874	SAVOY	115	119	125	126	115	116	118	115	112	120	141	137	118	138	114	105	139	117	102	127
61875	SEYMOUR	109	125	129	128	121	120	116	114	107	117	136	134	120	138	115	102	135	112	100	126
61876	SIDELL	80	57	31	54	66	73	56	68	64	55	75	82	48	74	58	67	69	67	81	95
61877	SIDNEY	84	103	112	101	101	102	94	93	89	93	111	108	100	119	96	87	111	90	85	102
61878	THOMASBORO	81	72	60	72	75	83	73	77	76	72	93	88	71	93	73	77	88	76	82	90
61880	TOLONO	82	86	84	86	86	89	83	84	81	83	101	98	84	103	83	79	98	83	80	94
61882	WELDON	117	81	43	77	95	106	80	99	93	79	109	120	69	107	83	97	99	98	118	139
61883	WESTVILLE	63	62	59	60	63	71	62	63	65	60	80	71	63	84	63	67	76	62	68	72
61884	WHITE HEATH	96	118	125	119	116	115	106	106	98	105	123	124	112	131	108	95	123	102	95	117
61910	ARCOLA	93	76	54	73	81	91	76	84	83	75	100	98	72	98	76	85	93	83	94	105
61911	ARTHUR	89	70	47	67	76	85	69	79	76	68	91	93	64	90	70	79	85	78	89	102
61912	ASHMORE	75	65	50	63	69	75	63	69	67	63	82	81	61	82	64	69	77	68	75	86
61913	ATWOOD	89	64	35	58	72	81	62	75	71	62	84	90	54	82	63	75	77	74	89	104
61914	BETHANY	77	74	66	71	77	84	71	75	74	70	91	87	72	96	73	77	87	73	81	91
61917	BROCTON	91	63	33	60	74	83	63	77	72	62	85	93	53	83	65	76	77	76	92	108
61919	CAMARGO	100	85	61	81	91	99	79	90	86	79	104	107	76	105	82	88	98	88	99	118
61920	CHARLESTON	62	51	58	55	52	57	67	59	66	62	82	75	61	79	61	62	79	65	57	68
61924	CHRISMAN	82	62	38	59	69	78	62	73	70	61	83	86	56	81	64	73	76	72	85	96
61925	DALTON CITY	96	96	84	93	99	103	88	93	89	87	109	111	89	113	90	89	105	91	95	115
61928	GAYS	93	83	63	78	87	94	76	85	81	76	99	101	75	101	79	83	94	82	92	109
61929	HAMMOND	86	74	55	71	80	86	70	78	75	70	90	93	67	92	72	77	85	76	86	102
61930	HINDSBORO	89	62	32	58	72	81	61	76	70	60	83	91	52	81	63	74	75	75	90	105
61931	HUMBOLDT	92	75	56	74	80	90	77	84	83	76	100	96	73	99	77	85	94	83	92	102
61932	HUME	92	64	33	60	74	83	63	78	73	62	85	94	54	84	65	76	78	77	93	109
61933	KANSAS	65	55	42	55	58	65	57	61	60	56	73	70	54	72	56	61	68	60	66	72
61937	LOVINGTON	85	74	57	72	78	86	72	78	76	71	93	92	70	93	73	78	87	77	85	97
61938	MATTOON	69	68	68	66	69	76	69	69	71	67	87	80	69	90	69	72	84	69	73	80
61940	METCALF	91	64	33	60	74	83	63	78	73	62	85	94	54	83	65	76	78	77	93	108
61942	NEWMAN	85	62	38	59	69	81	66	75	74	63	88	87	58	84	66	79	80	75	90	96
61943	OAKLAND	77	59	39	57	65	73	60	68	66	59	78	80	54	77	60	68	73	67	78	88
61944	PARIS	71	65	57	62	69	77	65	69	70	63	85	79	65	87	67	73	80	68	77	83
61951	SULLIVAN	80	70	56	68	74	82	70	75	75	69	90	87	68	91	71	77	85	74	83	91
61953	TUSCOLA	76	74	71	72	76	83	73	76	76	72	93	87	74	96	74	77	89	74	80	88
	ILLINOIS	98	100	111	99	99	106	100	99	101	100	126	115	102	127	100	100	123	100	98	112
	UNITED STATES	100	100	100	100	100	100	100	100	100	100	100	100	100	100	100	100	100	100	100	100

ZIP CODE		POPULATION			2000-2004 ANNUAL RATE		HOUSEHOLDS					FAMILIES		
# POST OFFICE NAME	COUNTY FIPS CODE	2000	2004	2009	% Rate	State Centile	2000	2004	2009	% Annual Rate 2000-2004	2004 Average HH Size	2000	2004	% Annual Rate 2000-2004
61956 VILLA GROVE	041	2886	2830	2822	-0.5	17	1145	1151	1168	0.1	2.45	824	813	-0.3
61957 WINDSOR	173	2077	2078	2101	0.0	42	818	827	846	0.3	2.48	596	595	0.0
62001 ALHAMBRA	119	1602	1635	1664	0.5	65	568	588	607	0.8	2.57	441	449	0.4
62002 ALTON	119	34108	34110	34645	0.0	42	13851	14037	14436	0.3	2.36	8774	8712	-0.2
62006 BATCHTOWN	013	677	688	697	0.4	61	249	256	263	0.7	2.68	183	185	0.3
62009 BENLD	117	1857	1919	1952	0.8	74	795	830	857	1.0	2.31	509	524	0.7
62010 BETHALTO	119	10803	11122	11417	0.7	71	4175	4355	4524	1.0	2.53	3056	3143	0.7
62011 BINGHAM	051	500	492	488	-0.4	20	196	196	198	0.0	2.51	141	140	-0.2
62012 BRIGHTON	083	6664	6975	7194	1.1	78	2407	2575	2705	1.6	2.68	1936	2049	1.3
62013 BRUSSELS	013	1225	1230	1235	0.1	47	481	491	502	0.5	2.51	349	351	0.1
62014 BUNKER HILL	117	3997	3973	3950	-0.1	34	1498	1515	1530	0.3	2.59	1142	1140	0.0
62015 BUTLER	135	597	582	569	-0.6	13	238	237	237	-0.1	2.46	187	185	-0.3
62016 CARROLLTON	061	3151	3149	3120	0.0	40	1262	1280	1285	0.3	2.41	886	885	0.0
62017 COFFEEN	135	1296	1349	1358	1.0	77	530	562	575	1.4	2.40	381	398	1.0
62018 COTTAGE HILLS	119	4320	4311	4375	-0.1	39	1615	1634	1679	0.3	2.55	1175	1169	-0.1
62019 DONNELLSON	005	646	638	633	-0.3	25	273	275	277	0.2	2.32	195	194	-0.1
62021 DORSEY	119	863	946	1000	2.2	90	331	369	396	2.6	2.56	273	300	2.2
62022 DOW	083	918	959	1005	1.0	78	330	352	375	1.5	2.72	263	278	1.3
62024 EAST ALTON	119	12539	12180	12241	-0.7	10	5247	5158	5244	-0.4	2.36	3502	3380	-0.8
62025 EDWARDSVILLE	119	30593	32411	33758	1.4	83	10932	11737	12385	1.7	2.51	7508	7942	1.3
62027 ELDRED	061	758	728	708	-1.0	4	296	289	286	-0.6	2.52	212	205	-0.8
62028 ELSAH	083	1642	1679	1731	0.5	67	437	457	483	1.1	3.00	323	333	0.7
62030 FIDELITY	083	137	143	149	1.0	78	55	58	62	1.3	2.47	43	45	1.1
62031 FIELDON	083	1292	1339	1392	0.8	75	487	514	543	1.3	2.60	372	387	0.9
62032 FILLMORE	135	801	829	832	0.8	74	310	325	330	1.1	2.52	228	236	0.8
62033 GILLESPIE	117	5865	5718	5638	-0.6	13	2407	2391	2395	-0.2	2.35	1629	1592	-0.5
62034 GLEN CARBON	119	11593	12460	13040	1.7	86	4481	4877	5163	2.0	2.53	3221	3454	1.7
62035 GODFREY	119	15099	15525	15889	0.7	71	6056	6315	6546	1.0	2.37	4413	4531	0.6
62036 GOLDEN EAGLE	013	249	249	250	0.0	42	106	108	110	0.4	2.31	77	77	0.0
62037 GRAFTON	083	1974	2042	2125	0.8	74	730	771	818	1.3	2.56	541	564	1.0
62040 GRANITE CITY	119	46080	45472	45899	-0.3	24	18437	18395	18775	-0.1	2.45	12610	12362	-0.5
62044 GREENFIELD	061	1761	1851	1885	1.2	80	713	759	784	1.5	2.44	502	529	1.2
62045 HAMBURG	013	393	393	395	0.0	42	161	164	167	0.4	2.40	117	118	0.2
62047 HARDIN	013	1133	1132	1136	0.0	40	453	460	470	0.4	2.35	297	297	0.0
62048 HARTFORD	119	1431	1419	1430	-0.2	31	609	612	623	0.1	2.32	406	401	-0.3
62049 HILLSBORO	135	7002	6955	6873	-0.2	33	2832	2861	2871	0.2	2.34	1931	1921	-0.1
62050 HILLVIEW	061	644	621	605	-0.9	6	233	228	226	-0.5	2.72	184	178	-0.8
62051 IRVING	135	2905	2869	2841	-0.3	25	348	343	340	-0.3	2.98	263	256	-0.6
62052 JERSEYVILLE	083	11707	12114	12643	0.8	74	4598	4847	5154	1.3	2.43	3161	3278	0.9
62053 KAMPSVILLE	013	545	542	543	-0.1	35	236	240	246	0.4	2.26	161	162	0.2
62054 KANE	061	1131	1112	1095	-0.4	19	419	418	417	-0.1	2.66	324	319	-0.4
62056 LITCHFIELD	135	8963	8642	8407	-0.9	6	3564	3501	3464	-0.4	2.40	2415	2338	-0.8
62060 MADISON	119	5842	5670	5704	-0.7	9	2404	2343	2374	-0.6	2.42	1487	1416	-1.1
62061 MARINE	119	1224	1325	1392	1.9	88	483	530	563	2.2	2.50	360	390	1.9
62062 MARYVILLE	119	4490	5080	5468	3.0	94	1675	1925	2100	3.3	2.56	1273	1443	3.0
62063 MEDORA	083	1326	1336	1351	0.2	51	471	481	493	0.5	2.78	354	357	0.2
62065 MICHAEL	013	325	323	324	-0.2	34	130	132	136	0.4	2.45	88	89	0.3
62067 MORO	119	2464	2654	2784	1.8	87	1052	1145	1213	2.0	2.32	716	769	1.7
62069 MOUNT OLIVE	117	3789	3836	3851	0.3	58	1550	1589	1616	0.6	2.41	1085	1094	0.2
62070 MOZIER	013	236	234	234	-0.2	31	99	100	102	0.2	2.34	72	72	0.0
62074 NEW DOUGLAS	119	1725	1650	1652	-1.0	3	705	682	691	-0.8	2.42	504	479	-1.2
62075 NOKOMIS	135	3857	3942	3989	0.5	66	1580	1624	1657	0.7	2.34	1037	1045	0.2
62079 PIASA	117	270	272	275	0.2	51	98	100	103	0.5	2.72	75	76	0.3
62080 RAMSEY	051	3063	3025	3010	-0.3	25	1212	1213	1223	0.0	2.49	886	878	-0.2
62081 ROCKBRIDGE	061	706	692	678	-0.5	17	273	271	269	-0.2	2.55	202	197	-0.6
62082 ROODHOUSE	061	3105	2999	2924	-0.8	7	1162	1132	1114	-0.6	2.51	821	789	-0.9
62083 ROSAMOND	021	173	185	193	1.6	85	68	74	79	2.0	2.12	49	53	1.9
62084 ROXANA	119	1433	1489	1529	0.9	76	613	644	669	1.2	2.31	402	413	0.6
62086 SORENTO	005	1713	1731	1784	0.3	54	664	681	712	0.6	2.54	497	503	0.3
62087 SOUTH ROXANA	119	1896	1993	2058	1.2	80	710	755	789	1.5	2.64	519	544	1.1
62088 STAUNTON	117	6818	6714	6667	-0.4	21	2734	2730	2749	0.0	2.42	1894	1861	-0.4
62090 VENICE	119	1589	1467	1458	-1.9	0	574	539	543	-1.5	2.72	413	382	-1.8
62091 WALSHVILLE	135	426	411	400	-0.8	6	162	160	159	-0.3	2.57	123	120	-0.6
62092 WHITE HALL	061	3611	3472	3377	-0.9	5	1444	1407	1385	-0.6	2.39	981	941	-1.0
62094 WITT	135	1269	1229	1198	-0.8	8	543	537	532	-0.3	2.17	343	333	-0.7
62095 WOOD RIVER	119	10519	10295	10348	-0.5	16	4432	4380	4448	-0.3	2.32	2808	2719	-0.8
62097 WORDEN	119	2593	2750	2858	1.4	83	995	1070	1125	1.7	2.56	765	811	1.4
62201 EAST SAINT LOUIS	163	9154	9130	9282	-0.1	38	3392	3417	3526	0.2	2.65	2171	2153	-0.2
62203 EAST SAINT LOUIS	163	10278	9715	9628	-1.3	1	3272	3170	3212	-0.7	2.86	2408	2297	-1.1
62204 EAST SAINT LOUIS	163	10717	10096	10016	-1.4	1	3427	3307	3352	-0.8	3.04	2476	2357	-1.2
62205 EAST SAINT LOUIS	163	10202	9575	9532	-1.5	1	3769	3631	3699	-0.9	2.61	2473	2338	-1.3
62206 EAST SAINT LOUIS	163	18329	17596	17537	-1.0	4	6302	6136	6219	-0.6	2.83	4692	4502	-1.0
62207 EAST SAINT LOUIS	163	9890	9632	9661	-0.6	11	3553	3545	3633	-0.1	2.70	2480	2436	-0.4
62208 FAIRVIEW HEIGHTS	163	14700	14902	15109	0.3	59	5941	6163	6378	0.9	2.40	4084	4155	0.4
62214 ADDIEVILLE	189	1300	1440	1529	2.4	92	479	542	585	3.0	2.66	373	415	2.5
62215 ALBERS	027	991	1023	1046	0.8	73	321	341	357	1.4	2.96	245	256	1.0
62217 BALDWIN	157	4109	4165	4188	0.3	59	352	376	390	1.6	3.40	253	267	1.3
62218 BARTELSO	027	1529	1576	1609	0.7	72	511	541	566	1.4	2.91	420	441	1.2
62220 BELLEVILLE	163	18531	18758	19013	0.3	58	7379	7590	7825	0.7	2.39	4666	4727	0.3
62221 BELLEVILLE	163	22553	23998	24950	1.5	84	9096	9821	10381	1.8	2.42	6262	6663	1.5
62223 BELLEVILLE	163	17398	17750	18119	0.5	65	7249	7560	7874	1.0	2.31	4784	4903	0.6
62225 SCOTT AIR FORCE BASE	163	5684	6319	6773	2.5	92	1444	1634	1784	3.0	3.75	1366	1532	2.7
62226 BELLEVILLE	163	28468	28798	29127	0.3	56	11787	12102	12449	0.6	2.29	7331	7401	0.2
62230 BREESE	027	5988	6264	6466	1.1	78	2160	2303	2424	1.5	2.67	1599	1684	1.2
62231 CARLYLE	027	8632	8641	8729	0.0	42	3334	3416	3527	0.6	2.48	2362	2384	0.2
62232 CASEYVILLE	163	7025	7023	7059	0.0	40	2723	2782	2854	0.5	2.48	1927	1936	0.1
62233 CHESTER	157	6642	6731	6803	0.3	58	2595	2673	2746	0.7	2.34	1707	1727	0.3
62234 COLLINSVILLE	119	32517	33152	33892	0.5	64	13335	13760	14238	0.7	2.40	8897	9024	0.3
62236 COLUMBIA	133	10248	10858	11823	1.4	83	3917	4212	4650	1.7	2.55	2895	3069	1.4
62237 COULTERVILLE	145	2944	2997	3041	0.4	63	1177	1222	1263	0.9	2.45	863	884	0.6
62238 CUTLER	145	818	813	815	-0.1	34	299	301	307	0.2	2.70	227	226	-0.1
62239 DUPO	163	4768	4710	4710	-0.3	25	1888	1901	1937	0.2	2.48	1303	1290	-0.2
62240 EAST CARONDELET	163	2020	2028	2044	0.1	46	733	749	769	0.5	2.71	530	534	0.2
62241 ELLIS GROVE	157	1116	1097	1085	-0.4	19	423	424	427	0.1	2.55	319	316	-0.2
62242 EVANSVILLE	157	1611	1625	1634	0.2	52	636	659	678	0.8	2.24	447	456	0.5
ILLINOIS					0.7					0.9	2.61			0.6
UNITED STATES					1.2					1.3	2.58			1.1

ZIP CODE		RACE (%)						% Hispanic Origin		2004 AGE DISTRIBUTION (%)										MEDIAN AGE		
#	POST OFFICE NAME	White		Black		Asian/Pacific																
		2000	2004	2000	2004	2000	2004	2000	2004	0-4	5-9	10-14	15-19	20-24	25-44	45-64	65-84	85+	18+	2004	% 2004 Males	% 2004 Females
61956	VILLA GROVE	98.2	97.9	0.3	0.3	0.1	0.2	0.8	1.0	6.5	6.6	7.1	7.1	6.7	26.6	24.3	13.1	2.0	75.3	38.7	49.1	51.0
61957	WINDSOR	99.2	99.1	0.0	0.0	0.0	0.0	0.2	0.3	5.8	6.3	8.0	5.9	5.7	25.0	25.5	14.5	3.3	76.3	40.8	48.7	51.3
62001	ALHAMBRA	98.8	98.5	0.0	0.1	0.1	0.1	0.8	1.0	4.8	5.4	6.6	6.1	4.9	24.5	27.4	15.5	5.0	79.9	43.8	49.2	50.8
62002	ALTON	75.6	73.7	21.7	23.4	0.4	0.5	1.4	1.7	6.9	6.6	6.9	6.6	6.4	27.5	23.2	13.2	2.6	75.5	37.3	47.5	52.5
62006	BATCHTOWN	98.8	98.8	0.2	0.2	0.0	0.0	0.6	0.6	7.4	7.3	6.4	5.5	5.5	27.6	25.0	12.9	2.3	75.9	38.7	52.3	47.7
62009	BENLD	98.2	98.0	0.5	0.6	0.0	0.0	1.0	1.2	6.8	6.5	7.2	5.8	6.2	27.6	21.7	13.9	4.2	76.0	38.3	48.8	51.2
62010	BETHALTO	97.9	97.4	0.8	0.9	0.4	0.5	0.9	1.2	6.1	6.1	7.1	7.0	7.2	27.6	25.6	11.5	1.8	76.5	37.9	48.8	51.2
62011	BINGHAM	98.8	98.2	0.2	0.2	0.2	0.4	0.2	0.6	6.3	6.5	7.3	5.9	6.3	24.8	26.8	14.2	1.8	76.2	40.4	51.2	48.8
62012	BRIGHTON	98.0	97.6	0.7	0.9	0.4	0.5	0.8	1.0	6.3	6.7	7.3	6.6	6.2	27.7	26.9	11.0	1.3	75.4	38.5	49.7	50.3
62013	BRUSSELS	99.1	99.0	0.0	0.0	0.1	0.1	0.5	0.6	5.1	5.3	6.3	6.0	5.9	25.9	27.4	15.6	2.5	79.8	41.9	50.9	49.1
62014	BUNKER HILL	97.1	96.9	1.9	2.1	0.1	0.1	0.4	0.5	6.2	6.4	7.1	6.8	6.3	26.0	25.9	13.9	1.5	76.3	39.6	48.6	51.4
62015	BUTLER	99.0	98.8	0.2	0.2	0.3	0.5	0.3	0.5	4.6	5.3	6.0	6.2	5.5	25.4	30.4	14.3	2.2	80.4	42.9	51.4	48.6
62016	CARROLLTON	98.7	98.4	0.0	0.0	0.3	0.4	0.4	0.6	6.6	6.5	6.4	6.5	6.7	23.9	24.1	15.7	3.6	76.3	40.2	48.3	51.7
62017	COFFEEN	98.6	98.3	0.0	0.0	0.5	0.7	0.6	0.8	5.5	5.6	7.4	6.9	5.3	25.1	26.1	15.2	3.0	77.3	41.1	49.2	50.8
62018	COTTAGE HILLS	93.8	92.7	4.0	4.7	0.3	0.4	1.0	1.3	6.8	7.0	7.8	6.8	7.2	30.0	23.5	10.2	0.9	74.4	34.5	51.1	48.9
62019	DONNELLSON	97.7	97.5	0.9	0.9	0.2	0.2	0.5	0.6	5.5	5.6	6.9	6.3	6.1	24.8	27.0	15.8	2.0	77.9	41.9	50.9	49.1
62021	DORSEY	97.7	97.3	0.9	1.1	0.4	0.4	0.6	0.9	4.9	5.6	7.1	6.7	5.3	24.6	32.6	12.3	1.1	78.3	42.6	50.6	49.4
62022	DOW	98.6	98.3	0.3	0.3	0.1	0.2	0.4	0.5	5.7	6.1	6.9	7.2	6.8	27.1	28.5	11.2	0.6	77.0	39.8	50.0	50.1
62024	EAST ALTON	97.4	97.0	0.7	0.9	0.4	0.5	0.9	1.1	6.1	6.1	6.9	6.3	6.5	26.5	25.0	14.6	2.0	77.2	39.4	48.0	52.0
62025	EDWARDSVILLE	89.3	87.8	7.6	8.6	1.4	1.6	0.9	1.1	5.8	5.6	6.2	8.1	10.8	28.6	23.5	9.9	1.6	78.8	34.5	47.5	52.5
62027	ELDRED	98.9	99.0	0.0	0.0	0.3	0.3	0.1	0.3	4.4	5.4	7.0	6.6	5.4	23.8	30.4	15.3	1.9	79.4	43.5	49.0	51.0
62028	ELSAH	96.2	95.7	1.2	1.3	0.5	0.6	1.3	1.5	5.9	5.7	5.9	11.4	17.3	22.8	22.8	7.7	0.6	79.0	29.6	49.4	50.6
62030	FIDELITY	98.5	98.6	0.0	0.0	0.0	0.7	0.7	0.7	5.6	6.3	8.4	7.0	5.6	27.3	25.2	13.3	1.4	75.5	39.8	50.4	49.7
62031	FIELDON	98.6	98.4	0.2	0.2	0.6	0.8	0.9	1.0	6.7	7.0	7.4	6.4	5.6	27.6	27.2	11.1	1.1	74.9	38.9	52.1	48.0
62032	FILLMORE	98.0	97.6	0.6	0.7	0.1	0.1	0.9	1.1	6.8	6.5	6.9	7.2	7.1	23.9	25.3	14.2	2.1	75.6	39.2	51.5	48.5
62033	GILLESPIE	98.2	98.0	0.3	0.4	0.1	0.2	0.7	0.8	5.8	5.7	6.0	6.0	6.7	25.2	26.4	15.0	3.3	78.9	41.4	48.0	52.0
62034	GLEN CARBON	90.6	89.0	5.9	6.8	1.9	2.3	1.4	1.7	6.8	6.7	7.4	6.7	6.6	29.7	25.4	9.2	1.6	74.9	36.0	49.1	51.0
62035	GODFREY	93.6	92.6	4.4	5.1	0.7	0.9	1.0	1.2	5.5	5.8	6.2	6.6	6.0	23.6	27.8	16.6	1.9	78.5	42.6	48.5	51.5
62036	GOLDEN EAGLE	99.2	99.2	0.0	0.0	0.0	0.0	0.4	0.4	4.8	4.8	6.4	6.0	6.0	25.7	27.3	16.1	2.8	80.3	42.2	49.8	50.2
62037	GRAFTON	96.4	96.2	2.2	2.4	0.2	0.2	1.0	1.2	5.6	5.9	7.2	8.8	6.9	25.3	28.1	11.2	1.0	75.1	38.6	51.4	48.6
62040	GRANITE CITY	94.0	93.2	2.9	3.3	0.5	0.6	2.4	3.0	6.4	6.1	6.8	6.8	7.0	27.5	24.6	13.3	1.6	76.7	38.1	48.4	51.6
62044	GREENFIELD	99.0	98.9	0.1	0.2	0.1	0.1	0.3	0.4	6.1	6.0	6.2	7.1	7.3	25.7	24.2	15.1	2.3	77.5	39.2	48.8	51.2
62045	HAMBURG	98.5	98.7	0.0	0.0	0.3	0.3	0.5	0.5	5.3	5.3	5.9	5.6	5.9	23.9	29.5	16.3	2.3	80.4	44.0	51.2	48.9
62047	HARDIN	99.4	99.4	0.0	0.0	0.2	0.2	0.7	0.7	5.8	5.7	6.5	6.2	5.7	26.3	22.0	17.2	4.4	78.1	40.1	48.2	51.8
62048	HARTFORD	98.4	98.2	0.1	0.1	0.4	0.4	0.8	0.9	6.1	5.9	6.6	6.3	5.7	27.1	25.0	15.9	1.5	77.7	40.0	50.7	49.3
62049	HILLSBORO	97.5	97.0	1.2	1.3	0.3	0.4	1.0	1.2	6.4	6.1	6.9	6.7	6.4	25.5	24.3	14.5	3.3	76.5	39.7	48.4	51.6
62050	HILLVIEW	98.3	98.1	0.0	0.0	0.0	0.0	1.1	1.3	5.5	6.4	9.2	6.4	4.5	26.6	25.6	14.5	1.3	74.9	39.6	49.8	50.2
62051	IRVING	63.4	60.2	33.0	35.6	0.0	0.0	4.6	5.4	2.0	2.1	2.9	5.2	14.5	51.9	16.6	4.3	0.7	91.0	33.3	82.3	17.7
62052	JERSEYVILLE	98.8	98.6	0.1	0.1	0.2	0.3	0.5	0.7	6.3	6.3	6.9	6.8	6.4	26.2	23.6	14.3	3.0	76.1	39.2	47.4	52.6
62053	KAMPSVILLE	98.0	97.8	0.0	0.0	0.4	0.4	0.9	0.7	5.5	5.4	6.5	6.3	6.3	23.8	25.5	18.8	2.0	79.2	43.0	50.2	49.8
62054	KANE	98.9	98.5	0.1	0.1	0.1	0.2	0.2	0.2	6.3	6.9	7.6	7.1	5.5	26.8	25.3	13.0	1.5	74.6	38.7	50.7	49.3
62056	LITCHFIELD	98.4	98.1	0.4	0.4	0.3	0.4	0.9	1.1	6.4	6.4	7.1	6.7	6.0	25.0	24.0	15.1	3.3	75.9	40.0	47.6	52.4
62060	MADISON	46.3	42.7	51.1	54.5	0.2	0.2	2.3	2.6	7.4	7.9	8.5	7.0	6.9	25.9	21.4	13.1	2.0	71.9	34.9	48.4	51.6
62061	MARINE	98.0	97.7	0.3	0.3	0.1	0.1	0.7	0.8	6.5	6.3	6.6	7.6	7.2	27.5	25.7	11.3	1.4	76.2	37.4	49.9	50.1
62062	MARYVILLE	95.3	94.5	2.4	2.8	0.7	0.9	1.7	2.2	6.9	7.1	7.1	6.1	5.4	29.6	25.1	10.6	2.3	74.9	38.1	48.2	51.8
62063	MEDORA	98.1	97.8	0.2	0.2	0.2	0.2	0.8	0.9	5.5	7.0	9.0	7.6	6.2	26.1	24.3	12.8	1.7	73.7	37.9	49.9	50.2
62065	MICHAEL	97.9	97.8	0.0	0.0	0.3	0.3	1.2	0.9	5.6	5.6	6.8	6.5	6.2	23.5	24.5	19.2	2.2	78.3	42.4	49.9	50.2
62067	MORO	97.8	97.3	0.7	0.8	0.1	0.2	0.7	0.9	5.2	5.4	7.2	7.5	5.9	25.1	27.0	13.8	3.1	77.6	41.4	48.5	51.5
62069	MOUNT OLIVE	98.7	98.5	0.0	0.1	0.1	0.2	0.6	0.8	5.5	6.0	7.2	6.2	6.5	26.4	24.1	15.0	3.1	77.5	39.9	49.9	50.1
62070	MOZIER	98.3	98.3	0.0	0.0	0.4	0.4	0.4	0.4	4.3	4.7	5.6	6.0	6.0	20.9	32.1	18.4	2.1	82.9	46.7	49.6	50.4
62074	NEW DOUGLAS	98.6	98.6	0.1	0.1	0.1	0.1	1.0	1.2	5.5	5.7	7.0	6.4	5.9	26.6	25.0	15.0	2.8	78.0	41.0	50.5	49.5
62075	NOKOMIS	98.5	98.3	0.5	0.6	0.1	0.1	0.3	0.4	5.8	5.9	7.2	6.5	5.8	24.1	24.6	16.1	4.0	76.9	41.1	49.0	51.0
62079	PIASA	98.2	97.8	0.7	1.1	0.4	0.4	0.7	0.7	5.9	6.3	7.7	6.6	6.3	27.2	26.5	11.8	1.8	75.7	38.5	51.1	48.9
62080	RAMSEY	98.8	98.5	0.2	0.3	0.1	0.2	0.4	0.5	7.2	7.2	7.7	6.4	6.4	25.5	25.4	12.2	2.0	74.0	37.7	50.3	49.8
62081	ROCKBRIDGE	98.9	98.6	0.0	0.0	0.1	0.3	0.3	0.3	7.2	7.4	7.1	6.4	5.6	26.6	24.7	13.2	1.9	74.3	37.9	50.3	49.7
62082	ROODHOUSE	95.6	95.1	3.3	3.6	0.1	0.1	0.5	0.6	7.0	6.7	7.6	7.8	8.9	26.9	21.9	11.6	1.7	74.8	34.2	51.7	48.4
62083	ROSAMOND	89.0	89.2	8.7	8.7	0.6	0.5	2.3	2.7	5.4	6.0	6.0	5.4	6.5	28.1	27.0	13.5	2.2	79.5	41.0	56.2	43.8
62084	ROXANA	98.5	98.3	0.1	0.1	0.2	0.3	0.7	0.9	6.7	6.5	6.7	6.0	5.5	29.2	23.2	14.0	2.3	76.6	37.7	47.4	52.6
62086	SORENTO	98.1	97.8	0.1	0.1	0.4	0.4	0.7	0.9	6.5	6.6	6.6	6.1	6.2	26.0	27.4	13.1	1.5	76.6	40.0	49.7	50.3
62087	SOUTH ROXANA	97.7	97.3	0.3	0.4	0.3	0.4	0.8	1.1	6.6	6.5	8.4	7.4	7.6	28.1	24.4	10.3	0.7	74.0	35.1	49.3	50.7
62088	STAUNTON	98.7	98.5	0.1	0.2	0.3	0.4	0.7	0.8	5.8	6.0	7.5	6.9	6.4	26.4	23.5	14.4	3.1	76.5	39.3	48.6	51.4
62090	VENICE	8.1	7.0	91.2	92.4	0.0	0.0	0.7	0.8	11.0	9.9	10.6	8.7	7.6	23.9	20.5	7.2	0.7	63.1	26.8	42.7	57.3
62091	WALSHVILLE	98.8	98.8	0.2	0.2	0.2	0.2	0.2	0.2	4.9	6.1	9.0	6.8	5.4	25.8	27.7	12.4	2.0	75.7	39.8	50.6	49.4
62092	WHITE HALL	98.7	98.5	0.1	0.1	0.0	0.0	0.9	1.0	6.1	6.3	7.1	5.9	5.7	25.1	23.6	16.4	3.8	76.7	40.8	48.1	51.9
62094	WITT	96.9	96.6	2.6	2.9	0.1	0.1	0.6	0.8	6.1	6.4	6.4	6.2	5.6	27.0	24.0	15.8	2.5	77.4	40.0	50.7	49.3
62095	WOOD RIVER	97.8	97.4	0.5	0.6	0.4	0.5	1.3	1.6	6.8	6.3	6.4	6.1	7.4	28.2	22.0	14.1	2.6	76.9	37.0	47.6	52.4
62097	WORDEN	98.5	98.3	0.4	0.5	0.3	0.3	0.7	0.8	5.7	6.1	6.8	6.1	5.3	26.9	29.8	11.8	1.5	77.7	40.9	49.5	50.5
62201	EAST SAINT LOUIS	18.9	18.8	71.9	70.8	0.1	0.1	15.3	17.4	12.3	10.4	8.8	7.8	8.0	24.0	17.3	9.7	1.7	63.8	26.8	44.5	55.5
62203	EAST SAINT LOUIS	6.6	5.3	92.0	93.3	0.1	0.1	1.0	1.0	6.5	7.1	8.6	8.6	8.3	27.2	24.4	8.7	0.7	72.6	32.8	49.5	50.5
62204	EAST SAINT LOUIS	3.6	2.9	94.8	95.5	0.1	0.1	1.6	1.6	9.5	9.3	10.8	9.6	8.0	24.0	21.0	7.2	0.6	64.4	27.1	45.7	54.3
62205	EAST SAINT LOUIS	1.1	0.9	98.0	98.2	0.0	0.0	0.6	0.7	6.4	6.6	8.3	7.8	6.1	23.8	23.5	15.3	2.2	73.9	38.3	46.4	53.7
62206	EAST SAINT LOUIS	56.0	49.6	41.1	47.3	0.4	0.4	2.1	2.4	8.2	8.3	10.0	9.0	7.8	27.1	19.1	9.7	1.0	68.0	30.6	46.7	53.3
62207	EAST SAINT LOUIS	2.0	1.5	96.9	97.4	0.1	0.1	0.5	0.6	9.3	9.6	9.6	8.0	6.8	24.7	19.7	10.7	1.7	66.5	30.7	45.1	54.9
62208	FAIRVIEW HEIGHTS	78.6	73.9	16.9	20.9	2.0	2.3	2.1	2.5	5.7	5.8	6.3	6.3	5.9	27.5	25.6	14.7	2.1	78.2	40.4	48.0	52.0
62214	ADDIEVILLE	99.2	99.1	0.0	0.0	0.1	0.1	0.7	0.8	5.1	5.5	6.8	7.1	6.5	26.0	28.5	13.3	1.2	78.3	41.3	51.8	48.2
62215	ALBERS	94.5	93.3	0.3	0.4	0.2	0.4	5.3	6.4	6.9	6.9	7.6	6.7	7.1	32.1	22.1	9.8	0.7	74.3	35.4	51.0	49.0
62217	BALDWIN	47.3	45.8	47.1	48.6	0.2	0.2	6.3	6.4	2.0	2.0	2.2	4.8	15.9	54.2	14.9	3.6	0.4	92.5	32.1	85.6	14.5
62218	BARTELSO	98.5	98.2	0.4	0.4	0.2	0.3	0.8	1.0	7.6	7.7	8.5	7.2	6.4	30.0	22.8	9.0	0.8	71.8	34.7	51.6	48.4
62220	BELLEVILLE	84.9	81.6	11.8	14.7	0.9	1.0	1.9	2.3	6.8	6.3	7.1	7.3	7.4	28.9	22.7	10.7	2.8	75.3	36.1	48.1	51.9
62221	BELLEVILLE	78.2	73.0	17.0	21.6	1.9	2.2	2.5	2.9	7.5	7.1	7.2	6.6	7.1	31.3	23.3	9.0	1.1	74.2	34.6	48.0	52.0
62223	BELLEVILLE	84.7	81.8	13.4	16.0	0.6	0.6	1.1	1.3	5.2	5.5	6.3	6.5	5.7	24.9	27.1	16.2	2.8	79.0	42.4	47.2	52.8
62225	SCOTT AIR FORCE BASE	80.1	75.8	12.3	15.4	2.5	2.8	4.6	5.6	11.9	11.5	10.9	7.3	6.2	38.0	11.4	2.6	0.2	60.7	26.2	49.6	50.4
62226	BELLEVILLE	82.3	78.2	14.7	18.3	1.2	1.4	1.6	1.9	6.1	6.0	6.6	6.5	6.7	28.0	23.6	13.5	3.0	77.4	38.9	47.2	52.9
62230	BREESE	98.7	98.4	0.1	0.1	0.3	0.4	1.1	1.4	7.3	7.3	8.0	7.0	6.4	28.1	21.7	12.1	2.1	73.0	36.2	49.5	50.5
62231	CARLYLE	96.6	96.1	2.2	2.5	0.4	0.5	0.9	1.1	6.1	6.3	7.0	6.7	6.6	25.6	24.6	14.4	2.7	76.5	39.5	49.6	50.5
62232	CASEYVILLE	90.3	87.8	6.4	8.2	0.6	0.8	3.1	3.8	6.2	6.2	6.6	6.1	6.2	27.7	25.4	13.5	2.1	77.3	39.4	49.1	50.9
62233	CHESTER	95.9	95.8	2.8	2.9	0.2	0.2	0.7	0.7	5.6	5.7	6.0	6.5	6.4	26.8	24.8	14.8	3.5	78.3	40.5	51.6	48.4
62234	COLLINSVILLE	92.6	91.3	4.7	5.5	0.6	0.7	2.5	3.0	6.2	6.2	6.6	6.3	6.6	28.9	25.2	12.1	1.9	77.2	37.8	48.9	51.1
62236	COLUMBIA	98.6	98.4	0.1	0.1	0.3	0.4	0.9	1.1	6.7	7.1	7.4	6.7	5.1	27.7	25.1	12.2	2.0	74.4	39.2	48.8	51.2
62237	COULTERVILLE	97.3	97.1	1.1	1.1	0.3	0.3	0.6	0.8	5.7	6.0	7.5	7.2	6.0	26.6	27.2	12.4	1.4	76.4	39.7	50.0	50.0
62238	CUTLER	98.3	98.3	0.1	0.1	0.1	0.1	0.7	0.7	8.7	7.8	7.3	6.5	7.4	28.0	23.3	9.6	1.5	72.6	34.1	49.6	50.4
62239	DUPO	97.4	96.7	1.1	1.4	0.2	0.3	0.7	1.0	6.4	6.2	6.7	7.3	7.5	29.3	24.5	11.0	1.1	76.4	36.2	48.9	51.1
62240	EAST CARONDELET	96.9	96.2	1.4	1.9	0.2	0.2	0.4	0.5	6.6	6.6	7.6	8.4	6.9	27.9	25.0	10.2	0.9	74.3	36.1	49.7	50.4
62241	ELLIS GROVE	98.7	98.6	0.4	0.4	0.1	0.1	0.3	0.3	7.0	7.2	7.8	7.1	5.7	26.3	26.2	11.3	1.5	73.6	38.3	49.7	50.3
62242	EVANSVILLE	93.9	93.7	4.8	5.0	0.3	0.3	1.2	1.2	6.0	6.1	5.9	5.9	6.2	29.1	24.9	13.4	2.5	78.3	39.4	53.2	46.8
	ILLINOIS	73.5	71.8	15.1	15.2	3.5	4.0	12.3	14.2	7.1	7.0	7.3	7.0	7.3	29.0	23.2	10.4	1.7	74.5	35.2	49.0	51.0
	UNITED STATES	75.1	73.6	12.3	12.5	3.8	4.2	12.5	14.1	6.9	6.7	7.2	7.0	7.3	28.6	23.8	10.8	1.7	75.1	36.0	49.1	50.9

INCOME

ZIP CODE #	POST OFFICE NAME	2004 Per Capita Income	2004 HH Income Base	2004 Household Income Distribution (%): Less than $25,000	$25,000 to $49,999	$50,000 to $99,999	$100,000 to $149,999	$150,000 or More	Median Household Income: 2004	2009	2004 National Centile	2004 State Centile	2004 Home Value Base	2004 Home Value Distribution (%): Less than $50,000	$50,000 to $89,999	$90,000 to $174,999	$175,000 to $399,999	$400,000 or More	2004 Median Home Value
61956	VILLA GROVE	19646	1151	26.1	34.8	33.5	5.1	0.5	41667	47165	52	36	928	15.0	44.0	35.9	5.2	0.0	82906
61957	WINDSOR	18604	827	26.5	35.7	32.2	4.2	1.5	41218	45098	50	35	697	20.2	38.9	33.7	6.6	0.6	82701
62001	ALHAMBRA	21211	588	18.7	30.1	41.3	7.7	2.2	50731	56024	73	64	517	9.7	20.5	42.6	23.6	3.7	114559
62002	ALTON	20185	14037	34.6	29.8	28.1	5.6	1.9	37979	43009	39	23	9938	22.6	41.3	28.9	6.4	0.9	76962
62006	BATCHTOWN	18246	256	27.3	30.5	35.9	4.7	1.6	45000	44447	61	48	219	14.2	26.5	42.5	13.7	3.2	99318
62009	BENLD	17536	830	37.2	33.1	25.1	4.0	0.6	33516	36450	22	9	670	35.5	40.8	18.4	5.1	0.3	61842
62010	BETHALTO	22021	4355	23.1	29.1	36.4	9.5	1.9	47604	53817	67	57	3447	8.2	28.2	50.6	12.4	0.7	101676
62011	BINGHAM	16183	196	31.1	38.8	28.1	2.0	0.0	35369	39249	29	14	167	31.1	29.3	30.5	8.4	0.6	79444
62012	BRIGHTON	21425	2575	20.1	32.5	35.2	9.5	2.6	47931	53321	68	58	2272	6.6	29.0	41.4	20.9	2.1	108480
62013	BRUSSELS	19476	491	26.5	32.8	34.0	4.5	2.2	42181	46958	53	38	417	13.9	25.9	46.0	13.7	0.5	103382
62014	BUNKER HILL	20422	1515	24.2	30.2	36.0	7.7	1.9	46544	50253	65	54	1278	14.6	31.7	39.0	14.8	0.0	96000
62015	BUTLER	21270	237	22.8	37.1	32.1	5.9	2.1	44725	46926	60	47	203	31.0	26.1	31.5	10.3	1.0	82368
62016	CARROLLTON	19577	1280	31.3	35.5	26.3	3.9	3.0	36352	39701	33	17	991	23.0	30.8	34.9	11.0	0.3	84932
62017	COFFEEN	17265	562	36.8	29.0	30.4	3.4	0.4	36949	40297	35	19	455	43.1	23.7	28.4	4.2	0.7	58750
62018	COTTAGE HILLS	18161	1634	28.7	33.8	30.9	5.4	1.2	40434	45520	48	31	1330	40.8	33.2	19.3	6.7	0.0	61667
62019	DONNELLSON	21819	275	26.6	37.5	28.4	5.5	2.2	40313	45558	47	31	238	36.6	21.4	30.3	10.1	1.7	70000
62021	DORSEY	26979	369	11.4	26.0	43.9	13.3	5.4	60686	66938	85	82	346	2.9	15.9	50.6	29.2	1.5	141279
62022	DOW	20482	352	22.2	29.8	38.6	6.5	2.8	48416	53411	69	59	306	10.1	26.1	44.8	17.0	2.0	112879
62024	EAST ALTON	20545	5158	31.3	30.2	31.0	5.7	1.9	39672	44511	45	29	3772	17.4	40.4	36.1	5.4	0.7	83059
62025	EDWARDSVILLE	27772	11737	19.1	25.7	34.8	13.0	7.4	55354	62294	80	75	9194	5.2	20.0	44.1	27.7	3.0	127867
62027	ELDRED	18941	289	27.7	33.2	31.1	6.9	1.0	38162	42218	40	23	240	31.7	27.5	23.3	10.0	7.5	78947
62028	ELSAH	20885	457	15.8	32.2	37.0	8.5	6.6	51464	58562	75	66	374	11.0	19.8	44.9	20.9	3.5	111111
62030	FIDELITY	20080	58	22.4	34.5	36.2	5.2	1.7	43209	50000	57	43	51	15.7	11.8	43.1	23.5	5.9	131944
62031	FIELDON	19255	514	23.4	33.5	35.8	6.6	0.8	45828	51020	63	51	437	17.6	19.2	40.1	18.5	4.6	108627
62032	FILLMORE	17690	325	36.9	26.2	31.7	3.7	1.5	38645	40417	42	25	269	30.9	32.7	26.8	9.3	0.4	68333
62033	GILLESPIE	20267	2391	31.7	35.5	25.0	6.4	1.5	37344	41389	37	21	1899	26.8	35.4	27.8	9.0	1.1	73282
62034	GLEN CARBON	31378	4877	15.5	23.0	35.6	16.9	9.1	62866	70376	87	84	3813	4.3	7.7	51.9	33.3	2.9	156277
62035	GODFREY	29871	6315	18.1	27.3	38.0	10.8	5.8	53699	60757	78	71	5355	2.8	23.6	50.0	20.4	3.2	117938
62036	GOLDEN EAGLE	21155	108	25.9	33.3	34.3	4.6	1.9	41992	47343	53	37	92	15.2	27.2	43.5	14.1	0.0	101471
62037	GRAFTON	26085	771	24.4	30.5	32.8	8.7	3.6	45386	50343	62	49	636	17.9	21.4	44.5	14.0	2.2	101157
62040	GRANITE CITY	20381	18395	27.4	33.1	31.9	5.9	1.8	41441	47109	51	35	13822	24.3	41.7	31.1	2.7	0.3	74679
62044	GREENFIELD	17907	759	31.8	36.8	27.4	3.2	0.9	36367	39756	33	17	593	29.2	43.5	21.9	4.1	1.4	67338
62045	HAMBURG	18591	164	31.1	29.9	34.8	3.1	1.2	37989	42057	39	23	141	19.9	26.2	34.8	17.0	2.1	94583
62047	HARDIN	19977	460	35.9	33.3	26.3	3.5	1.1	35713	40619	30	15	346	25.1	37.9	31.5	5.2	0.3	75938
62048	HARTFORD	18538	612	33.7	32.2	28.8	4.4	1.0	36534	41326	34	18	482	41.5	45.9	11.8	0.8	0.0	54940
62049	HILLSBORO	19691	2861	32.6	32.3	28.3	4.7	2.1	36608	40102	34	18	2187	28.6	30.8	32.7	7.6	0.4	75422
62050	HILLVIEW	14845	228	34.7	36.4	26.3	2.6	0.0	34449	36715	26	11	193	57.0	28.5	11.4	2.1	1.0	44600
62051	IRVING	14520	343	33.5	32.9	29.5	3.5	0.6	35214	38630	28	13	291	37.8	25.8	22.7	13.8	0.0	72647
62052	JERSEYVILLE	22585	4847	30.0	27.0	32.4	6.9	3.7	43526	48607	57	44	3764	9.8	29.8	43.4	15.6	1.5	101021
62053	KAMPSVILLE	17946	240	39.2	30.0	27.5	1.7	1.7	32955	36540	21	8	190	24.7	36.3	30.0	7.9	1.1	78636
62054	KANE	17398	418	28.0	33.7	32.5	5.3	0.5	38933	43626	43	26	352	27.8	29.6	28.1	9.9	4.6	80370
62056	LITCHFIELD	18555	3501	35.5	32.9	24.1	5.1	2.3	35454	38970	29	14	2725	26.8	32.0	28.8	11.2	1.2	78209
62060	MADISON	14499	2343	46.9	29.5	19.9	3.0	0.7	26921	30057	7	2	1395	55.5	37.1	5.2	2.2	0.0	46988
62061	MARINE	23077	530	22.6	30.6	33.8	9.1	4.0	47033	54057	66	56	414	7.7	20.1	54.1	17.4	0.7	108908
62062	MARYVILLE	31866	1925	12.5	21.6	44.1	15.5	6.3	65885	75128	89	87	1592	3.2	13.9	58.2	24.2	0.5	140378
62063	MEDORA	17532	481	24.7	37.6	32.4	3.3	1.9	41095	45338	50	34	415	25.3	26.3	30.1	12.8	5.5	87969
62065	MICHAEL	16490	132	40.2	30.3	26.5	1.5	1.5	32328	35644	19	7	103	25.2	35.9	30.1	7.8	1.0	79500
62067	MORO	21741	1145	28.0	31.7	31.0	7.1	2.2	42934	49093	56	41	835	8.0	26.7	47.1	17.4	0.8	108742
62069	MOUNT OLIVE	18731	1589	30.2	34.8	29.9	3.7	1.5	37757	41339	38	22	1322	29.1	37.8	26.3	6.7	0.2	69577
62070	MOZIER	18354	100	33.0	30.0	35.0	1.0	1.0	35909	40000	31	16	86	22.1	25.6	32.6	18.6	1.2	92857
62074	NEW DOUGLAS	21910	682	25.2	32.6	33.4	7.8	1.0	44860	50052	61	48	570	26.0	33.5	30.9	9.3	0.4	78293
62075	NOKOMIS	18463	1624	33.9	34.9	26.5	3.8	1.1	34708	38144	26	12	1316	34.8	38.6	22.3	3.7	0.5	63444
62079	PIASA	20947	100	20.0	35.0	34.0	8.0	3.0	45756	50414	63	51	87	14.9	29.9	33.3	20.7	1.2	99000
62080	RAMSEY	16803	1213	32.5	38.5	24.6	3.4	1.1	34217	37912	25	11	1030	32.3	28.5	28.8	9.8	0.5	73621
62081	ROCKBRIDGE	16364	271	34.3	36.2	25.1	3.3	1.1	33752	36954	23	9	223	33.2	35.0	22.9	6.3	2.7	67174
62082	ROODHOUSE	15236	1132	34.7	39.1	23.4	2.5	0.4	32780	35209	20	8	860	43.8	36.3	16.7	2.2	0.9	55096
62083	ROSAMOND	23523	74	28.4	32.4	28.4	6.8	4.1	39062	43622	43	26	62	16.1	24.2	37.1	21.0	1.6	105769
62084	ROXANA	22335	644	23.5	37.7	28.9	8.7	1.2	43184	49337	56	43	494	22.1	58.1	18.8	0.2	0.8	67600
62086	SORENTO	19066	681	25.7	37.9	30.3	4.6	1.6	39177	44093	43	27	598	37.5	26.3	23.4	12.4	0.5	68571
62087	SOUTH ROXANA	17080	755	31.9	33.5	29.4	3.6	1.6	36936	42127	35	19	568	36.1	44.4	18.1	1.4	0.0	57596
62088	STAUNTON	19963	2730	27.6	35.0	31.0	4.3	2.2	40235	45285	47	31	2182	17.0	33.3	42.5	6.9	0.3	89751
62090	VENICE	12303	539	55.8	25.4	13.2	3.7	1.9	19195	21311	2	1	231	74.0	22.9	3.0	0.0	0.0	40263
62091	WALSHVILLE	20784	160	28.8	29.4	30.0	9.4	2.5	43371	46620	57	43	140	29.3	27.1	28.6	11.4	3.6	82500
62092	WHITE HALL	16118	1407	40.2	34.8	20.4	3.1	1.6	30468	32978	13	4	1083	44.5	32.0	16.7	4.7	2.0	55721
62094	WITT	17813	537	41.5	31.1	23.7	2.1	1.7	30532	33171	14	4	435	46.4	27.4	18.9	7.4	0.0	54306
62095	WOOD RIVER	19915	4380	30.2	35.5	27.2	5.9	1.3	37701	43866	38	22	3192	15.9	56.1	27.0	1.1	0.0	74746
62097	WORDEN	22978	1070	22.3	25.3	41.4	7.9	3.0	51456	57578	75	66	921	15.0	25.4	39.2	19.0	1.4	103716
62201	EAST SAINT LOUIS	9840	3417	65.4	22.1	10.6	1.3	0.6	15267	17240	1	0	1476	59.4	30.5	8.3	1.8	0.1	43252
62203	EAST SAINT LOUIS	14508	3170	38.4	30.4	26.0	4.2	1.0	32470	36161	19	7	2303	35.7	47.2	15.6	1.5	0.0	57563
62204	EAST SAINT LOUIS	10630	3307	56.4	26.7	13.8	2.3	0.9	19946	22057	2	1	1817	61.7	31.1	6.9	0.3	0.0	43787
62205	EAST SAINT LOUIS	14639	3631	45.3	30.3	18.3	5.0	1.1	27685	30545	8	2	2381	48.7	34.8	14.2	1.9	0.5	51003
62206	EAST SAINT LOUIS	15478	6136	38.5	30.9	26.0	3.7	1.0	32467	36202	19	7	4106	56.9	33.6	8.7	0.6	0.3	46732
62207	EAST SAINT LOUIS	10563	3545	55.9	28.4	13.8	1.3	0.6	20868	23338	2	1	1863	54.4	33.3	10.8	1.5	0.0	46590
62208	FAIRVIEW HEIGHTS	25138	6163	19.9	28.2	37.9	10.3	3.7	51396	58406	75	66	4939	7.5	28.5	52.5	10.9	0.5	101020
62214	ADDIEVILLE	19609	542	26.6	31.0	33.4	7.4	1.7	45390	49615	62	50	470	11.9	24.3	41.7	18.9	3.2	112931
62215	ALBERS	22373	341	17.9	23.2	42.8	12.3	3.8	57462	62543	82	78	285	8.1	23.5	52.3	15.4	0.7	114643
62217	BALDWIN	14118	376	29.5	38.8	25.3	5.1	1.3	37324	41090	37	20	324	30.6	35.2	27.2	7.1	0.0	70000
62218	BARTELSO	23393	541	14.1	24.6	47.5	10.5	3.3	60056	65375	84	81	488	8.4	16.2	54.9	18.2	2.3	121809
62220	BELLEVILLE	20875	7590	27.7	32.4	30.5	7.2	2.3	41175	47631	50	35	5012	14.4	37.9	36.9	10.3	0.5	87844
62221	BELLEVILLE	26104	9821	21.7	28.3	34.2	10.5	5.2	49981	56731	72	62	6912	6.7	21.6	49.6	18.9	3.2	120990
62223	BELLEVILLE	29154	7560	21.4	26.8	35.8	9.5	6.6	51524	58557	75	67	6073	7.0	27.9	49.1	13.9	2.1	106403
62225	SCOTT AIR FORCE BASE	18362	1634	9.7	37.5	38.6	9.5	4.7	52209	58633	76	68	5	17.8	8.5	22.6	37.8	13.3	180556
62226	BELLEVILLE	24496	12102	26.0	30.8	31.4	8.2	3.6	44384	50872	60	46	8428	11.6	32.0	42.8	12.8	0.8	96597
62230	BREESE	22773	2303	14.4	29.0	45.0	7.8	3.8	53884	61096	78	71	1919	5.3	19.8	55.0	19.0	0.9	118198
62231	CARLYLE	20431	3416	27.2	31.6	32.9	6.8	1.5	43504	48827	57	44	2809	24.9	28.5	37.3	7.8	1.5	85952
62232	CASEYVILLE	21015	2782	22.7	36.5	32.0	6.8	2.0	42739	49419	55	41	2325	21.9	33.7	35.8	7.7	1.0	84921
62233	CHESTER	26314	2673	27.4	30.3	32.2	6.4	3.7	43102	47172	56	42	2118	21.6	34.8	33.9	9.5	0.3	83266
62234	COLLINSVILLE	24404	13760	23.6	28.6	34.9	9.9	3.0	48041	54092	68	58	10340	10.7	26.6	49.4	12.5	0.8	103609
62236	COLUMBIA	30414	4212	11.8	17.9	48.4	15.6	6.3	66606	75235	90	88	3635	1.2	3.9	51.6	40.9	2.5	164573
62237	COULTERVILLE	20002	1222	30.4	33.4	28.7	5.7	1.7	39419	42551	44	28	1039	32.2	32.1	27.4	8.1	0.2	72905
62238	CUTLER	19201	301	29.6	37.5	26.6	2.7	3.7	37519	41361	38	21	252	53.2	32.1	11.5	2.0	1.2	47647
62239	DUPO	23020	1901	18.7	31.8	40.0	8.1	1.4	49571	57552	71	61	1499	23.0	35.1	35.5	6.3	0.2	81268
62240	EAST CARONDELET	20513	749	22.4	32.3	36.2	6.9	2.1	45610	51849	63	51	619	33.1	30.9	26.8	8.7	0.5	68534
62241	ELLIS GROVE	21506	424	22.2	30.2	38.0	6.8	2.8	48611	53370	69	59	367	16.4	32.4	39.0	11.4	0.8	91607
62242	EVANSVILLE	21644	659	27.8	35.7	31.4	3.8	1.4	39798	43938	45	29	547	24.5	36.6	30.9	6.6	1.5	77444
	ILLINOIS	27033		22.1	25.9	32.9	11.9	7.3	52039	60941				7.7	12.8	34.0	36.6	8.9	162771
	UNITED STATES	25866		24.7	27.1	30.8	10.9	6.5	48124	56710				10.9	15.0	33.7	30.1	10.4	145905

ZIP CODE #	POST OFFICE NAME	FINANCIAL SERVICES: Auto Loan	FINANCIAL SERVICES: Home Loan	FINANCIAL SERVICES: Investments	FINANCIAL SERVICES: Retirement Plans	THE HOME: Home Improvements: Home Repair	THE HOME: Home Improvements: Lawn & Garden	THE HOME: Furnishings: Computers & Hardware	THE HOME: Furnishings: Major Appliances	THE HOME: Furnishings: TV, Radio, Sound Equipment	THE HOME: Furnishings: Furniture	ENTERTAINMENT: Dine out/ Carry out	ENTERTAINMENT: Sports Equipment	ENTERTAINMENT: Fees & Tickets	ENTERTAINMENT: Toys & Games	ENTERTAINMENT: Travel	ENTERTAINMENT: Cable TV	PERSONAL: Apparel & Services	PERSONAL: Auto Repairs	PERSONAL: Health Insurance	PERSONAL: Pets & Supplies
61956	VILLA GROVE	72	65	56	61	69	77	64	69	69	62	84	80	63	87	66	72	79	68	78	85
61957	WINDSOR	75	64	47	61	68	74	61	68	66	61	80	80	59	80	62	67	75	66	74	86
62001	ALHAMBRA	89	80	62	76	84	90	74	82	78	74	95	97	73	97	76	80	90	79	88	105
62002	ALTON	65	65	69	63	65	72	67	66	69	66	86	76	68	87	67	70	83	67	69	74
62006	BATCHTOWN	88	62	33	58	72	80	61	75	71	60	83	90	52	81	63	74	75	74	90	104
62009	BENLD	57	54	50	51	56	64	55	57	59	53	72	64	55	74	56	62	68	56	64	65
62010	BETHALTO	76	81	83	79	80	85	79	79	78	78	98	91	81	101	79	78	95	78	78	88
62011	BINGHAM	71	52	31	48	57	66	52	61	59	52	71	71	47	68	52	62	65	60	71	80
62012	BRIGHTON	91	82	63	78	86	93	77	84	81	76	99	100	75	100	79	83	94	82	91	107
62013	BRUSSELS	88	62	32	58	72	80	61	75	70	60	82	91	52	81	63	74	75	74	90	105
62014	BUNKER HILL	85	74	56	71	78	85	70	78	75	70	91	92	68	92	72	77	86	76	85	99
62015	BUTLER	94	66	35	62	77	86	65	81	75	64	88	97	56	86	68	79	80	79	96	112
62016	CARROLLTON	78	60	39	57	66	76	62	71	70	60	82	82	56	80	63	73	76	70	84	90
62017	COFFEEN	66	51	36	49	56	66	56	61	62	53	73	69	50	70	55	65	67	61	72	74
62018	COTTAGE HILLS	64	68	67	65	68	72	65	66	65	65	81	75	66	83	66	66	79	65	66	75
62019	DONNELLSON	86	68	45	61	73	82	64	75	73	65	87	89	59	85	66	77	81	74	88	100
62021	DORSEY	96	105	104	103	106	109	96	99	95	96	118	116	100	124	99	94	115	96	96	115
62022	DOW	89	80	61	76	84	90	74	82	78	74	95	97	72	97	76	80	90	79	88	105
62024	EAST ALTON	65	67	70	64	68	76	67	68	69	66	85	76	69	88	69	71	82	67	72	75
62025	EDWARDSVILLE	95	106	121	108	104	107	106	102	101	104	127	122	108	131	105	97	125	103	94	112
62027	ELDRED	77	64	47	62	68	76	64	70	69	63	83	82	60	82	64	70	77	69	78	88
62028	ELSAH	100	96	89	94	99	105	91	96	93	91	115	115	91	117	93	94	110	95	99	118
62030	FIDELITY	89	63	35	60	73	81	62	76	71	61	84	91	54	82	64	74	77	75	90	105
62031	FIELDON	82	69	51	65	75	82	65	74	71	65	85	88	61	86	68	74	80	73	83	98
62032	FILLMORE	79	56	31	53	65	72	55	68	63	55	74	81	48	73	57	66	68	67	80	93
62033	GILLESPIE	72	63	52	59	67	77	64	69	69	62	84	78	62	85	65	73	79	68	79	84
62034	GLEN CARBON	110	117	125	119	118	122	113	114	110	112	137	135	115	139	114	108	134	113	110	130
62035	GODFREY	97	106	110	102	106	115	101	102	101	99	125	116	104	128	104	102	121	101	105	115
62036	GOLDEN EAGLE	88	62	32	58	72	80	61	75	70	60	82	91	52	81	63	74	75	74	90	105
62037	GRAFTON	109	93	68	88	99	109	90	99	97	89	117	116	86	117	91	100	110	98	111	126
62040	GRANITE CITY	67	70	73	68	71	77	70	70	71	68	88	80	71	91	71	72	85	70	72	79
62044	GREENFIELD	74	54	33	51	61	70	57	66	64	55	76	76	50	73	57	68	69	65	78	84
62045	HAMBURG	80	56	30	53	65	73	56	69	64	55	75	82	48	74	58	67	69	68	82	95
62047	HARDIN	77	58	38	55	63	76	64	70	71	60	84	79	56	79	63	75	76	70	84	85
62048	HARTFORD	55	60	63	57	61	67	59	59	61	57	76	65	63	83	61	64	74	57	63	65
62049	HILLSBORO	67	61	57	59	64	72	63	65	67	61	81	75	62	82	64	69	77	65	71	76
62050	HILLVIEW	76	51	23	44	58	67	49	62	59	50	70	74	42	66	50	64	63	61	76	87
62051	IRVING	11	8	5	8	9	11	9	10	10	9	12	11	8	11	9	11	11	10	12	12
62052	JERSEYVILLE	81	76	67	73	79	88	75	79	79	73	97	91	75	99	77	82	92	78	87	94
62053	KAMPSVILLE	67	50	31	47	55	65	54	60	60	51	71	69	47	68	54	64	65	60	72	75
62054	KANE	81	60	36	57	68	76	59	70	66	58	78	85	52	77	61	69	72	69	82	96
62056	LITCHFIELD	67	59	52	57	62	70	61	64	65	59	78	74	58	78	61	66	74	64	71	77
62060	MADISON	49	44	45	42	45	52	48	48	52	47	63	54	47	63	48	54	60	49	54	55
62061	MARINE	87	79	68	79	82	90	80	84	83	78	101	96	78	101	80	83	96	82	88	97
62062	MARYVILLE	113	130	132	132	127	125	120	119	112	121	141	141	124	145	120	107	140	117	106	132
62063	MEDORA	80	64	44	62	70	78	64	72	70	63	84	85	60	83	65	72	78	71	81	92
62065	MICHAEL	66	49	32	47	54	64	54	60	60	51	71	68	48	67	53	64	65	60	72	74
62067	MORO	66	74	83	75	74	76	72	72	69	72	87	84	74	88	73	67	85	71	67	78
62069	MOUNT OLIVE	64	62	58	58	64	72	61	63	65	59	79	72	62	84	63	68	76	62	70	75
62070	MOZIER	77	54	29	51	63	71	54	66	62	53	73	80	46	71	56	65	66	65	79	92
62074	NEW DOUGLAS	78	75	66	71	78	85	71	75	75	70	92	88	72	96	73	77	88	74	81	92
62075	NOKOMIS	68	55	41	53	60	69	57	63	63	55	75	72	53	74	58	66	69	62	73	77
62079	PIASA	91	81	62	77	86	92	75	83	80	75	97	99	74	99	77	82	92	81	90	107
62080	RAMSEY	75	54	29	48	60	68	52	63	61	53	72	75	46	69	53	65	66	62	75	86
62081	ROCKBRIDGE	72	53	33	50	61	68	53	63	60	52	71	75	47	71	55	63	65	62	74	85
62082	ROODHOUSE	64	49	33	46	54	62	50	57	56	49	67	66	45	66	51	59	62	56	67	73
62083	ROSAMOND	73	51	27	48	59	66	50	62	58	50	68	75	43	67	52	61	62	61	74	87
62084	ROXANA	66	72	76	68	73	81	71	70	74	69	92	79	75	99	74	77	88	69	76	78
62086	SORENTO	89	63	32	55	70	79	60	73	71	61	83	87	52	80	61	75	76	72	88	102
62087	SOUTH ROXANA	70	60	47	60	63	71	62	66	65	60	79	75	59	79	61	66	74	65	71	78
62088	STAUNTON	72	66	57	63	69	77	66	69	70	64	85	79	65	87	67	72	81	68	76	82
62090	VENICE	46	39	51	36	37	44	45	44	50	47	63	50	45	61	44	52	61	46	47	50
62091	WALSHVILLE	91	73	48	67	79	87	68	79	76	69	91	95	64	91	70	79	85	78	90	106
62092	WHITE HALL	59	50	39	47	53	62	52	56	57	50	68	64	49	68	52	60	63	56	65	68
62094	WITT	59	45	29	43	49	59	49	54	55	47	65	61	44	61	49	58	59	54	65	66
62095	WOOD RIVER	61	64	68	62	65	72	65	64	66	62	82	73	67	86	66	68	79	64	68	71
62097	WORDEN	83	86	81	82	87	93	81	83	82	79	102	96	83	108	83	84	98	81	87	98
62201	EAST SAINT LOUIS	38	31	34	28	30	35	35	36	39	37	48	39	34	44	34	40	47	37	38	40
62203	EAST SAINT LOUIS	56	54	60	51	52	61	54	54	58	56	73	58	57	70	55	60	71	55	59	62
62204	EAST SAINT LOUIS	46	38	45	35	37	45	43	43	48	44	60	47	42	55	42	51	57	45	48	50
62205	EAST SAINT LOUIS	54	48	52	44	48	57	51	52	56	53	69	56	51	64	51	59	67	53	58	60
62206	EAST SAINT LOUIS	59	57	63	55	56	63	61	59	64	60	79	68	61	80	60	65	77	61	62	67
62207	EAST SAINT LOUIS	41	34	38	31	33	41	38	39	43	39	52	42	37	48	37	46	50	40	44	45
62208	FAIRVIEW HEIGHTS	77	89	101	87	88	93	86	85	84	85	105	97	90	109	88	84	103	84	82	92
62214	ADDIEVILLE	88	71	48	67	78	85	67	78	74	67	88	93	63	89	69	76	83	76	88	103
62215	ALBERS	100	93	80	93	96	104	92	97	94	91	116	111	91	116	92	95	110	95	100	112
62217	BALDWIN	1	1	0	0	1	1	0	1	0	0	1	1	0	1	0	1	1	0	1	1
62218	BARTELSO	99	103	96	102	102	103	97	99	94	97	117	117	97	118	96	91	114	97	93	114
62220	BELLEVILLE	67	70	78	70	70	74	72	70	71	71	89	83	73	91	72	70	87	71	68	77
62221	BELLEVILLE	86	92	97	93	91	94	91	90	88	90	111	105	92	113	90	86	108	90	84	99
62223	BELLEVILLE	88	99	113	98	99	105	96	95	94	96	118	108	100	120	98	94	116	94	94	104
62225	SCOTT AIR FORCE BASE	111	71	68	81	65	77	105	91	107	98	134	121	90	120	87	98	128	107	84	103
62226	BELLEVILLE	77	81	87	80	80	86	80	80	80	80	100	92	82	101	81	80	98	80	79	88
62230	BREESE	86	90	87	89	91	95	86	88	85	85	106	102	88	109	87	85	103	86	86	100
62231	CARLYLE	76	71	63	69	74	81	69	74	72	68	88	85	68	90	71	74	84	72	79	89
62232	CASEYVILLE	76	74	68	70	76	82	71	75	74	71	91	86	71	93	73	75	87	74	79	89
62233	CHESTER	92	87	80	85	90	100	87	91	91	85	111	104	86	113	88	93	106	90	98	106
62234	COLLINSVILLE	79	84	89	83	85	90	83	83	82	81	102	96	85	105	84	82	100	82	82	92
62236	COLUMBIA	101	123	132	122	121	121	112	111	105	111	132	129	119	140	114	103	131	108	101	122
62237	COULTERVILLE	84	67	44	61	72	80	63	73	70	63	84	87	59	83	64	73	78	71	83	98
62238	CUTLER	96	66	31	58	75	85	64	79	76	64	89	94	54	85	65	81	81	78	96	111
62239	DUPO	82	79	72	77	81	89	79	81	81	77	100	92	79	102	79	83	96	80	86	93
62240	EAST CARONDELET	90	77	58	72	80	88	74	82	79	74	96	96	70	94	74	81	91	81	89	103
62241	ELLIS GROVE	91	77	56	74	83	90	72	82	78	72	94	98	69	95	75	80	89	80	90	107
62242	EVANSVILLE	67	62	55	59	66	72	61	65	64	59	79	75	60	82	63	67	75	63	71	79
	ILLINOIS	98	100	111	99	99	106	100	99	101	100	126	115	102	127	100	100	123	100	98	112
	UNITED STATES	100	100	100	100	100	100	100	100	100	100	100	100	100	100	100	100	100	100	100	100

POPULATION CHANGE

ZIP CODE		POPULATION			2000-2004 ANNUAL RATE		HOUSEHOLDS					FAMILIES		
#	POST OFFICE NAME	COUNTY FIPS CODE	2000	2004	2009	% Rate	State Centile	2000	2004	2009	% Annual Rate 2000-2004	2004 Average HH Size	2000	2004	% Annual Rate 2000-2004
62243	FREEBURG	163	5427	5664	5812	1.0	78	1958	2084	2178	1.5	2.65	1528	1613	1.3
62244	FULTS	133	1117	1201	1326	1.7	86	385	424	476	2.3	2.83	312	340	2.0
62245	GERMANTOWN	027	2091	2096	2118	0.1	45	758	780	807	0.7	2.68	581	590	0.4
62246	GREENVILLE	005	10064	10474	10824	0.9	77	3178	3324	3516	1.1	2.37	2171	2235	0.7
62248	HECKER	133	475	568	659	4.3	97	188	229	270	4.8	2.48	146	176	4.5
62249	HIGHLAND	119	13797	14482	14995	1.2	80	5247	5570	5828	1.4	2.57	3794	3970	1.1
62253	KEYESPORT	005	745	750	770	0.2	50	324	332	347	0.6	2.26	230	231	0.1
62254	LEBANON	163	5548	5676	5773	0.5	67	1997	2090	2171	1.1	2.51	1405	1447	0.7
62255	LENZBURG	163	1227	1254	1268	0.5	66	438	457	471	1.0	2.74	339	349	0.7
62257	MARISSA	163	3751	3648	3640	-0.7	11	1491	1482	1509	-0.1	2.46	1069	1044	-0.6
62258	MASCOUTAH	163	7302	7275	7291	-0.1	37	2725	2772	2833	0.4	2.57	2024	2031	0.1
62260	MILLSTADT	163	6260	6365	6437	0.4	62	2392	2488	2568	0.9	2.54	1794	1836	0.6
62261	MODOC	157	195	214	223	2.2	90	79	89	94	2.8	2.29	58	64	2.3
62262	MULBERRY GROVE	005	2091	2308	2491	2.4	91	839	944	1034	2.8	2.44	601	666	2.5
62263	NASHVILLE	189	5165	5242	5356	0.4	60	2093	2147	2217	0.6	2.43	1479	1498	0.3
62264	NEW ATHENS	163	3335	3386	3436	0.4	61	1272	1315	1356	0.8	2.54	942	959	0.4
62265	NEW BADEN	027	4562	4671	4750	0.6	68	1681	1764	1836	1.1	2.60	1237	1280	0.8
62268	OAKDALE	189	854	938	995	2.2	90	316	352	378	2.6	2.66	253	278	2.2
62269	O FALLON	163	25299	27397	28650	1.9	88	9619	10603	11288	2.3	2.56	6990	7570	1.9
62271	OKAWVILLE	189	2009	2051	2082	0.5	66	819	849	873	0.9	2.42	567	578	0.5
62272	PERCY	157	1362	1348	1343	-0.2	28	551	555	563	0.2	2.40	370	367	-0.2
62274	PINCKNEYVILLE	145	8384	8433	8503	0.1	49	2589	2659	2734	0.6	2.53	1782	1803	0.3
62275	POCAHONTAS	005	3648	3786	3965	0.9	76	1386	1459	1549	1.2	2.59	1031	1071	0.9
62277	PRAIRIE DU ROCHER	157	1445	1444	1471	0.0	40	562	573	595	0.5	2.50	409	412	0.2
62278	RED BUD	133	6462	6687	6910	0.8	74	2413	2537	2660	1.2	2.57	1753	1823	0.9
62280	ROCKWOOD	077	436	471	490	1.8	87	166	183	194	2.3	2.54	127	139	2.2
62281	SAINT JACOB	119	1709	1864	1967	2.1	89	626	689	733	2.3	2.71	497	542	2.1
62284	SMITHBORO	005	618	637	665	0.7	72	233	243	258	1.0	2.62	180	186	0.8
62285	SMITHTON	163	3050	3334	3499	2.1	89	1059	1185	1269	2.7	2.74	826	913	2.4
62286	SPARTA	157	7211	7051	6998	-0.5	15	2858	2849	2879	-0.1	2.38	1964	1927	-0.5
62288	STEELEVILLE	157	2933	2879	2867	-0.4	18	1211	1210	1225	0.0	2.36	824	811	-0.4
62293	TRENTON	027	5669	5726	5794	0.2	54	2146	2222	2299	0.8	2.54	1623	1661	0.6
62294	TROY	119	12020	12780	13300	1.5	84	4279	4601	4843	1.7	2.76	3345	3551	1.4
62295	VALMEYER	133	941	991	1081	1.2	81	334	357	394	1.6	2.78	259	273	1.3
62297	WALSH	157	399	389	386	-0.6	13	155	155	157	0.0	2.01	117	116	-0.2
62298	WATERLOO	133	13941	15469	17244	2.5	92	5122	5768	6519	2.8	2.64	3924	4367	2.6
62301	QUINCY	001	34919	34392	34295	-0.4	21	14339	14306	14456	-0.1	2.25	8676	8462	-0.6
62305	QUINCY	001	17347	17752	18046	0.5	67	6620	6919	7155	1.0	2.55	4887	5021	0.6
62311	AUGUSTA	067	906	890	871	-0.4	19	364	357	352	-0.5	2.48	234	226	-0.8
62312	BARRY	149	2497	2453	2401	-0.4	19	986	984	976	-0.1	2.41	698	688	-0.3
62313	BASCO	067	378	367	357	-0.7	9	154	151	149	-0.5	2.43	116	113	-0.6
62314	BAYLIS	149	579	566	552	-0.5	15	214	211	207	-0.3	2.68	157	153	-0.6
62316	BOWEN	067	727	762	767	1.1	79	277	293	299	1.3	2.56	194	202	1.0
62319	CAMDEN	169	270	264	261	-0.5	15	111	111	111	0.0	2.38	81	80	-0.3
62320	CAMP POINT	001	2344	2372	2382	0.3	57	858	880	894	0.6	2.59	629	634	0.2
62321	CARTHAGE	067	4448	4350	4255	-0.5	16	1840	1817	1796	-0.3	2.34	1213	1183	-0.6
62323	CHAMBERSBURG	149	200	194	189	-0.7	9	82	81	79	-0.3	2.40	55	54	-0.4
62324	CLAYTON	001	1630	1657	1671	0.4	62	569	587	599	0.7	2.57	391	395	0.2
62325	COATSBURG	001	498	499	500	0.1	44	192	196	199	0.5	2.55	141	141	0.0
62326	COLCHESTER	109	2718	2789	2882	0.6	69	1109	1156	1214	1.0	2.39	771	792	0.6
62330	DALLAS CITY	067	2035	2114	2131	0.9	76	843	893	914	1.4	2.35	599	623	0.9
62334	ELVASTON	067	151	145	140	-1.0	4	66	64	63	-0.7	2.27	53	51	-0.9
62338	FOWLER	001	1455	1493	1523	0.6	69	530	554	574	1.1	2.69	421	436	0.8
62339	GOLDEN	001	916	910	908	-0.2	34	355	357	360	0.1	2.48	264	262	-0.2
62340	GRIGGSVILLE	149	1587	1509	1454	-1.2	2	623	598	584	-1.0	2.51	457	434	-1.2
62341	HAMILTON	067	3627	3459	3339	-1.1	3	1437	1393	1364	-0.7	2.41	986	942	-1.1
62343	HULL	149	665	612	581	-1.9	0	272	255	245	-1.5	2.40	186	171	-2.0
62344	HUNTSVILLE	169	160	156	154	-0.6	13	70	69	69	-0.3	2.26	50	49	-0.5
62345	KINDERHOOK	149	370	354	341	-1.0	3	151	147	144	-0.6	2.41	110	106	-0.9
62346	LA PRAIRIE	001	168	166	166	-0.3	26	63	63	63	0.0	2.63	47	47	0.0
62347	LIBERTY	001	2049	2371	2578	3.5	95	767	911	1011	4.1	2.60	609	712	3.8
62348	LIMA	001	415	428	434	0.7	73	147	154	159	1.1	2.78	109	113	0.9
62349	LORAINE	001	703	695	692	-0.3	26	262	263	266	0.1	2.63	203	200	-0.4
62351	MENDON	001	1848	1837	1832	-0.1	34	658	665	672	0.3	2.59	482	479	-0.2
62352	MILTON	149	541	536	524	-0.2	29	212	212	210	0.0	2.50	157	155	-0.3
62353	MOUNT STERLING	009	5182	5247	5298	0.3	58	1406	1456	1497	0.8	2.25	887	902	0.4
62354	NAUVOO	067	1588	1551	1514	-0.6	14	623	619	613	-0.2	2.41	448	439	-0.5
62355	NEBO	013	936	921	905	-0.4	20	379	379	378	0.0	2.43	271	267	-0.4
62356	NEW CANTON	149	673	660	644	-0.5	17	274	272	269	-0.2	2.43	208	204	-0.5
62357	NEW SALEM	149	295	293	287	-0.2	33	112	112	111	0.0	2.60	84	83	-0.3
62358	NIOTA	067	652	652	645	0.0	42	252	255	256	0.3	2.51	185	184	-0.1
62359	PALOMA	001	154	155	156	0.2	50	63	65	66	0.7	2.38	46	46	0.0
62360	PAYSON	001	1936	1926	1937	-0.1	35	700	708	723	0.3	2.72	537	536	0.0
62361	PEARL	149	355	350	343	-0.3	23	149	149	147	0.0	2.35	105	103	-0.5
62362	PERRY	149	636	613	594	-0.9	5	276	270	263	-0.5	2.27	190	183	-0.9
62363	PITTSFIELD	149	6457	6422	6313	-0.1	35	2514	2536	2521	0.2	2.30	1665	1651	-0.1
62365	PLAINVILLE	001	763	921	1015	4.5	98	277	341	381	5.0	2.70	220	268	4.8
62366	PLEASANT HILL	149	1456	1418	1379	-0.6	11	602	593	583	-0.4	2.35	415	404	-0.6
62367	PLYMOUTH	169	1498	1545	1564	0.7	73	579	606	620	1.1	2.51	412	424	0.7
62370	ROCKPORT	149	655	640	623	-0.5	15	243	240	236	-0.3	2.67	182	178	-0.5
62373	SUTTER	067	308	293	282	-1.2	2	107	103	100	-0.9	2.84	86	82	-1.1
62374	TENNESSEE	067	280	276	279	-0.3	22	121	121	124	0.0	2.28	87	85	-0.6
62375	TIMEWELL	009	530	531	531	0.0	43	200	204	207	0.5	2.60	143	145	0.3
62376	URSA	001	988	1023	1041	0.8	75	407	429	443	1.3	2.38	296	307	0.9
62378	VERSAILLES	009	1134	1122	1120	-0.3	27	462	467	473	0.3	2.40	321	320	-0.1
62379	WARSAW	067	2292	2165	2081	-1.3	1	922	887	865	-0.9	2.44	654	620	-1.3
62380	WEST POINT	067	505	503	494	-0.1	37	190	191	190	0.1	2.63	142	140	-0.3
62401	EFFINGHAM	049	19575	20137	20919	0.7	71	7846	8237	8726	1.2	2.40	5248	5426	0.8
62410	ALLENDALE	185	1085	1055	1036	-0.7	10	399	393	392	-0.4	2.64	307	299	-0.6
62411	ALTAMONT	049	3956	4003	4120	0.3	57	1485	1528	1601	0.7	2.56	1077	1090	0.3
62413	ANNAPOLIS	033	340	312	292	-2.0	0	123	115	109	-1.6	2.71	96	88	-2.0
62414	BEECHER CITY	051	1915	2027	2131	1.4	82	763	820	876	1.7	2.47	566	599	1.3
62417	BRIDGEPORT	101	3589	3610	3573	0.1	49	1453	1487	1496	0.6	2.40	1008	1013	0.1
62418	BROWNSTOWN	051	2533	2584	2606	0.5	65	998	1027	1046	0.7	2.51	707	720	0.4
62419	CALHOUN	159	630	631	625	0.0	43	239	244	246	0.5	2.59	181	182	0.1
	ILLINOIS					0.7					0.9	2.61			0.6
	UNITED STATES					1.2					1.3	2.58			1.1

#	POST OFFICE NAME	RACE (%) White 2000	White 2004	Black 2000	Black 2004	Asian/Pacific 2000	Asian/Pacific 2004	% Hispanic Origin 2000	% Hispanic Origin 2004	2004 AGE DISTRIBUTION (%) 0-4	5-9	10-14	15-19	20-24	25-44	45-64	65-84	85+	18+	MEDIAN AGE 2004	% 2004 Males	% 2004 Females
62243	FREEBURG	97.3	96.3	0.9	1.5	0.4	0.5	1.6	2.1	6.1	6.5	7.8	7.6	6.1	27.4	25.4	10.7	2.6	74.9	38.7	48.8	51.2
62244	FULTS	99.0	98.9	0.0	0.0	0.3	0.3	0.5	0.6	7.1	7.1	7.6	7.1	6.3	27.3	27.4	9.1	1.1	73.9	38.0	52.0	48.0
62245	GERMANTOWN	99.0	98.6	0.1	0.1	0.1	0.2	0.8	1.1	6.8	7.0	7.4	6.3	6.4	29.5	23.0	12.5	1.1	74.8	37.3	50.4	49.6
62246	GREENVILLE	86.9	85.9	11.1	11.9	0.4	0.4	1.9	2.4	5.1	5.0	5.3	6.7	10.0	31.5	21.9	12.1	2.5	81.8	36.2	57.3	42.7
62248	HECKER	99.2	99.3	0.0	0.0	0.0	0.0	0.2	0.2	6.9	6.9	6.5	6.5	6.2	28.4	25.9	12.2	0.7	76.1	38.0	51.2	48.8
62249	HIGHLAND	98.8	98.5	0.1	0.1	0.4	0.5	1.0	1.2	6.5	6.7	7.4	7.0	6.6	26.4	24.6	12.4	2.4	75.0	38.4	48.5	51.5
62253	KEYESPORT	98.7	98.5	0.4	0.4	0.1	0.1	0.4	0.7	5.5	5.9	6.3	5.2	4.7	25.2	27.9	17.9	1.6	79.3	43.1	50.0	50.0
62254	LEBANON	84.0	80.1	12.9	16.4	0.7	0.9	1.4	1.7	6.2	5.9	7.1	7.7	9.4	26.3	23.9	11.4	2.2	77.0	36.1	48.0	52.0
62255	LENZBURG	98.8	98.6	0.3	0.5	0.1	0.1	0.6	0.7	6.9	6.8	7.3	7.4	6.9	28.2	22.7	12.7	1.0	74.4	37.6	50.7	49.3
62257	MARISSA	98.7	98.5	0.4	0.5	0.2	0.2	0.7	0.8	6.1	6.1	7.0	6.9	6.9	25.6	25.9	13.9	1.6	76.6	38.9	48.9	51.2
62258	MASCOUTAH	93.2	91.6	3.3	4.3	0.9	1.0	1.6	2.0	5.5	5.7	7.8	7.9	6.6	27.4	25.0	11.9	2.3	75.9	38.8	48.8	51.2
62260	MILLSTADT	98.0	97.6	0.6	0.8	0.2	0.2	0.7	0.9	6.1	6.6	7.0	6.2	5.4	26.0	27.8	12.7	2.3	76.6	40.8	49.2	50.8
62261	MODOC	99.0	98.6	0.0	0.0	0.5	0.5	0.0	0.5	6.5	6.5	5.6	5.6	6.1	23.8	28.0	14.5	3.3	78.0	42.4	50.5	49.5
62262	MULBERRY GROVE	91.0	89.5	7.6	8.8	0.2	0.3	0.6	0.7	6.6	6.7	7.2	7.1	5.7	24.7	25.7	14.4	2.0	75.2	39.4	50.1	49.9
62263	NASHVILLE	98.8	98.6	0.2	0.2	0.3	0.4	0.8	1.0	5.8	6.1	7.2	6.8	6.2	25.7	25.8	14.0	2.4	76.7	40.0	48.2	51.8
62264	NEW ATHENS	98.4	98.1	0.5	0.6	0.4	0.4	0.6	0.8	6.4	6.3	6.5	7.1	6.9	26.6	25.5	12.4	2.4	76.6	39.4	48.8	51.2
62265	NEW BADEN	95.7	94.8	1.3	1.5	0.7	0.9	2.3	2.9	6.6	6.8	7.6	7.2	6.7	29.2	23.7	10.8	1.4	74.6	36.8	49.4	50.6
62268	OAKDALE	98.6	98.3	0.0	0.0	0.2	0.2	0.6	0.6	6.5	6.5	6.6	6.9	6.2	26.2	26.0	13.8	1.3	76.1	40.2	50.1	49.9
62269	O FALLON	83.7	79.8	11.2	14.3	2.4	2.8	2.3	2.7	6.5	6.6	7.4	7.3	7.1	29.2	26.3	8.5	1.1	75.1	36.5	48.6	51.4
62271	OKAWVILLE	98.6	98.4	0.3	0.3	0.1	0.2	0.6	0.6	6.1	6.1	6.9	6.8	5.9	27.3	24.1	14.4	2.3	76.7	39.1	50.2	49.8
62272	PERCY	99.3	99.3	0.2	0.2	0.1	0.1	1.3	1.3	6.8	6.7	6.2	5.8	5.7	26.9	25.5	13.8	2.7	76.9	38.6	48.3	51.7
62274	PINCKNEYVILLE	84.3	83.8	12.8	13.2	0.3	0.3	2.7	2.8	4.3	4.6	5.6	6.1	8.6	33.2	23.3	12.0	2.4	82.2	37.7	58.3	41.7
62275	POCAHONTAS	97.8	97.5	0.3	0.3	0.3	0.3	1.0	1.3	7.0	7.0	7.2	6.7	6.9	27.9	25.4	10.9	1.1	74.8	37.2	51.4	48.6
62277	PRAIRIE DU ROCHER	98.7	98.6	0.0	0.0	0.1	0.1	0.5	0.5	7.3	7.3	6.9	6.5	6.7	27.7	25.6	10.3	1.8	74.7	37.3	49.0	51.0
62278	RED BUD	98.6	98.6	0.2	0.2	0.3	0.3	0.7	0.7	6.4	6.4	6.4	6.4	5.9	26.8	25.4	13.6	2.8	76.9	39.9	49.3	50.7
62280	ROCKWOOD	98.9	99.2	0.0	0.0	0.2	0.2	0.2	0.0	6.8	6.8	6.4	6.8	6.2	25.1	26.5	13.4	2.1	75.6	39.4	51.4	48.6
62281	SAINT JACOB	98.3	98.0	0.1	0.1	0.2	0.3	1.6	2.0	6.0	6.3	7.1	7.0	6.0	29.4	26.3	10.8	1.1	76.3	38.5	50.5	49.5
62284	SMITHBORO	96.8	96.6	1.8	1.9	0.0	0.0	0.8	0.8	6.1	6.9	8.2	6.1	4.7	25.4	27.6	13.2	1.7	75.0	40.3	50.9	49.1
62285	SMITHTON	97.7	97.2	0.6	0.8	0.6	0.7	0.4	0.6	6.8	7.2	7.5	6.7	6.0	28.2	25.6	11.1	1.0	74.8	37.7	49.0	51.1
62286	SPARTA	86.0	85.5	11.7	12.2	0.4	0.4	1.4	1.4	6.0	6.1	7.0	6.8	6.9	24.5	26.1	14.0	2.8	76.8	40.0	48.5	51.5
62288	STEELEVILLE	98.8	98.7	0.1	0.2	0.4	0.4	0.8	0.8	5.5	5.8	6.8	5.9	5.5	25.7	25.8	15.5	3.4	78.2	41.4	48.4	51.6
62293	TRENTON	98.3	97.9	0.5	0.6	0.5	0.6	1.1	1.4	6.2	6.6	7.4	6.4	5.8	27.8	25.3	12.4	2.3	75.7	38.7	49.4	50.6
62294	TROY	96.0	95.3	1.4	1.6	0.6	0.7	1.4	1.8	7.0	6.9	8.1	7.8	6.6	30.4	24.2	8.1	1.1	72.9	35.4	49.3	50.7
62295	VALMEYER	98.6	98.5	0.2	0.2	0.4	0.5	0.6	0.7	7.6	7.5	7.1	6.7	6.6	26.9	26.7	9.7	1.3	74.3	37.7	49.2	50.8
62297	WALSH	84.5	83.8	13.3	14.1	0.0	0.0	2.3	2.3	5.1	5.1	5.1	6.2	8.5	33.4	24.9	10.3	1.3	81.5	37.4	61.2	38.8
62298	WATERLOO	98.8	98.6	0.0	0.0	0.3	0.4	0.7	0.9	6.7	6.8	7.3	6.7	6.1	27.9	25.1	11.5	2.0	75.2	38.4	49.0	51.0
62301	QUINCY	92.7	91.9	5.0	5.5	0.5	0.6	0.9	1.1	6.2	5.8	6.5	7.0	7.9	25.6	22.0	15.0	4.0	77.6	38.3	47.5	52.5
62305	QUINCY	97.0	96.5	1.2	1.4	0.6	0.7	0.8	1.0	6.2	6.3	7.1	6.6	5.7	23.6	27.6	15.0	1.9	76.2	41.3	48.4	51.6
62311	AUGUSTA	99.6	99.6	0.0	0.0	0.1	0.1	0.6	0.8	5.7	5.5	6.5	5.8	6.6	24.3	25.1	17.4	3.0	78.8	42.0	47.1	52.9
62312	BARRY	99.0	98.7	0.0	0.0	0.3	0.5	0.7	0.9	6.3	6.4	7.1	5.9	5.3	24.0	25.2	15.8	4.1	76.8	41.4	48.1	51.9
62313	BASCO	99.7	99.7	0.0	0.0	0.0	0.0	0.3	0.3	5.5	6.0	6.8	6.3	6.3	28.6	24.8	14.2	1.6	78.5	39.7	51.0	49.1
62314	BAYLIS	98.6	98.4	0.0	0.0	0.4	0.5	0.4	0.4	6.5	6.7	9.0	6.7	5.1	25.1	25.8	12.9	2.1	73.7	38.7	51.1	48.9
62316	BOWEN	98.6	98.3	0.1	0.1	0.3	0.5	0.3	0.3	7.0	7.5	7.4	7.0	5.6	27.4	22.3	14.0	1.8	73.2	36.9	49.6	50.4
62319	CAMDEN	98.9	98.9	0.4	0.4	0.0	0.0	0.7	0.4	7.2	6.8	6.4	4.9	4.6	26.5	27.3	14.8	1.5	76.1	40.3	52.7	47.4
62320	CAMP POINT	99.0	98.7	0.0	0.0	0.1	0.2	0.4	0.6	6.3	6.5	8.3	7.5	5.5	25.1	22.8	14.3	3.6	73.7	39.0	48.4	51.6
62321	CARTHAGE	98.6	98.4	0.3	0.4	0.4	0.5	0.4	0.4	5.9	6.0	7.0	6.6	5.7	24.4	25.0	15.9	3.5	77.0	41.3	48.3	51.7
62323	CHAMBERSBURG	99.0	98.5	0.0	0.0	0.0	0.0	0.0	0.0	6.2	6.7	5.7	6.2	5.2	23.7	25.3	17.0	4.1	77.3	42.3	48.5	51.6
62324	CLAYTON	91.5	90.3	7.0	7.9	0.0	0.0	1.5	2.0	6.9	6.8	6.9	5.9	5.9	30.0	22.8	12.3	2.5	75.6	37.3	53.8	46.2
62325	COATSBURG	99.2	99.0	0.0	0.0	0.0	0.0	0.8	1.0	7.0	7.2	7.8	6.2	5.2	27.5	26.3	11.6	1.2	74.2	38.3	49.1	50.9
62326	COLCHESTER	99.0	98.9	0.1	0.1	0.1	0.1	0.6	0.8	5.6	5.7	6.3	6.6	5.9	25.4	28.0	14.3	2.2	78.5	41.5	48.8	51.2
62330	DALLAS CITY	98.5	98.2	0.1	0.1	0.1	0.1	0.4	0.6	5.4	5.9	7.1	5.8	5.4	23.6	29.8	14.7	2.4	78.2	42.9	48.5	51.5
62334	ELVASTON	99.3	99.3	0.0	0.0	0.0	0.7	0.0	0.7	5.5	6.2	5.5	6.2	6.2	24.1	30.3	13.8	2.1	78.6	41.9	49.7	50.3
62338	FOWLER	98.0	97.7	0.7	0.8	0.1	0.3	0.4	0.5	7.0	7.4	7.7	6.8	5.6	26.0	27.4	11.3	0.8	73.6	38.9	49.8	50.2
62339	GOLDEN	99.1	99.0	0.0	0.0	0.1	0.1	1.0	1.1	7.1	7.3	7.9	6.7	4.7	24.4	22.9	15.4	3.6	74.0	40.2	48.0	52.0
62340	GRIGGSVILLE	99.2	99.1	0.1	0.1	0.1	0.1	0.2	0.3	6.7	7.0	7.5	7.1	6.1	24.9	24.7	14.4	1.8	74.3	38.5	48.2	51.8
62341	HAMILTON	98.4	98.3	0.5	0.5	0.4	0.5	0.7	0.8	4.9	5.5	6.9	6.0	5.9	25.3	27.9	14.6	3.0	78.9	41.7	48.4	51.6
62343	HULL	98.4	98.2	0.0	0.0	0.3	0.3	0.5	0.5	5.9	6.1	5.7	6.5	6.4	27.0	27.1	12.8	2.6	78.1	39.9	51.0	49.0
62344	HUNTSVILLE	99.4	99.4	0.0	0.0	0.0	0.0	0.0	0.6	6.4	8.3	5.8	4.5	4.5	26.9	26.3	15.4	1.9	75.6	40.0	53.2	46.8
62345	KINDERHOOK	98.7	98.3	0.3	0.3	0.0	0.0	1.1	1.1	5.9	6.2	6.2	6.8	6.5	26.6	27.4	13.3	1.1	77.4	38.8	52.3	47.7
62346	LA PRAIRIE	100.0	100.0	0.0	0.0	0.0	0.0	0.0	0.6	7.2	7.8	8.4	6.6	4.2	25.3	22.9	15.1	2.4	72.3	38.9	51.2	48.8
62347	LIBERTY	99.1	99.0	0.1	0.0	0.1	0.1	0.4	0.5	6.2	6.7	7.6	6.4	5.3	27.4	27.6	11.7	1.1	75.5	38.3	51.3	48.7
62348	LIMA	99.0	98.8	0.0	0.0	0.2	0.2	1.0	1.6	6.8	6.8	6.8	7.5	6.1	25.2	25.5	13.6	1.9	75.5	39.3	47.9	52.1
62349	LORAINE	99.4	99.6	0.0	0.0	0.0	0.0	0.3	0.4	6.6	7.1	8.2	6.0	5.5	25.3	26.6	13.1	1.6	74.4	39.1	49.9	50.1
62351	MENDON	99.6	99.5	0.1	0.1	0.0	0.0	0.4	0.5	7.6	7.4	6.7	5.9	5.4	25.6	23.2	13.2	5.0	75.0	39.0	47.5	52.5
62352	MILTON	99.3	99.3	0.0	0.0	0.0	0.0	0.2	0.4	8.8	8.0	7.3	6.0	4.7	27.1	21.6	14.0	2.6	72.8	36.8	49.8	50.2
62353	MOUNT STERLING	73.9	73.2	24.4	25.1	0.2	0.2	5.1	5.1	3.7	3.5	4.2	5.2	11.6	41.0	18.7	9.8	2.3	86.0	34.8	67.8	32.3
62354	NAUVOO	98.1	97.9	0.2	0.2	0.1	0.2	1.1	1.4	6.2	6.3	6.5	5.2	5.7	21.7	28.3	17.4	2.7	77.8	43.9	49.3	50.7
62355	NEBO	98.6	98.6	0.0	0.0	0.1	0.1	0.9	0.9	5.8	6.0	6.7	7.2	6.3	23.8	28.9	14.0	1.4	77.2	41.6	52.2	47.8
62356	NEW CANTON	99.7	99.7	0.0	0.0	0.0	0.0	0.2	0.2	4.7	5.3	8.6	7.4	5.5	27.7	22.1	17.3	1.4	76.8	40.3	48.5	51.5
62357	NEW SALEM	98.3	98.0	0.0	0.0	0.3	0.3	0.3	0.7	6.1	6.8	10.6	7.2	5.1	24.9	25.9	11.3	2.1	71.7	37.7	51.2	48.8
62358	NIOTA	98.6	98.5	0.0	0.0	0.2	0.2	0.5	0.5	6.0	6.1	6.0	5.4	5.5	23.3	29.9	15.6	2.2	79.0	43.3	50.0	50.0
62359	PALOMA	99.4	99.4	0.0	0.0	0.0	0.0	1.3	1.3	7.1	7.1	7.7	5.8	5.2	29.7	25.8	10.3	1.3	74.2	38.5	48.4	51.6
62360	PAYSON	98.6	98.4	0.4	0.4	0.1	0.1	0.4	0.5	6.7	6.8	8.5	7.5	7.7	25.7	25.4	10.7	1.1	73.6	36.3	50.3	49.7
62361	PEARL	98.3	98.0	0.0	0.0	0.3	0.3	0.3	0.3	6.6	6.3	7.1	6.6	4.9	24.3	25.7	15.7	2.9	76.6	41.4	51.4	48.6
62362	PERRY	98.9	98.7	0.0	0.0	0.3	0.3	0.0	0.0	6.5	6.5	6.7	5.7	5.2	24.0	25.0	17.0	3.4	76.7	41.5	49.6	50.4
62363	PITTSFIELD	94.8	94.3	4.0	4.3	0.4	0.5	0.6	0.8	5.3	5.5	6.0	5.6	6.8	25.3	24.5	16.5	4.6	79.7	41.8	50.6	49.4
62365	PLAINVILLE	99.0	98.7	0.0	0.0	0.0	0.0	0.3	0.2	6.6	6.6	7.4	7.1	6.2	26.5	25.5	12.8	1.3	75.1	38.5	51.8	48.2
62366	PLEASANT HILL	98.8	98.7	0.0	0.0	0.1	0.2	0.5	0.5	6.6	6.9	7.1	6.1	5.6	24.6	24.1	15.8	3.2	75.1	39.3	50.7	49.3
62367	PLYMOUTH	98.5	98.1	0.1	0.1	0.3	0.5	0.6	0.7	7.5	7.3	7.1	6.4	5.5	26.0	24.5	14.0	1.7	73.8	38.1	50.6	49.4
62370	ROCKPORT	99.2	99.4	0.2	0.2	0.0	0.0	0.6	0.6	5.5	5.9	7.2	7.7	7.0	24.8	28.8	11.4	1.7	76.6	39.8	50.2	49.8
62373	SUTTER	99.0	99.3	0.0	0.0	0.0	0.0	0.7	0.3	7.2	7.5	7.9	5.5	4.8	23.9	26.3	14.7	2.4	73.7	41.8	50.2	49.8
62374	TENNESSEE	98.6	98.9	0.0	0.0	0.0	0.0	0.0	0.0	5.1	5.4	6.5	5.8	5.8	25.4	28.6	15.6	1.8	78.6	42.6	50.4	49.6
62375	TIMEWELL	98.3	98.1	0.2	0.2	0.2	0.2	1.1	1.3	5.3	5.7	7.7	7.0	6.0	27.5	25.8	13.8	1.3	77.4	39.9	53.3	46.7
62376	URSA	99.1	98.7	0.0	0.0	0.2	0.3	1.1	1.5	7.1	6.8	6.7	7.4	5.9	25.6	25.5	13.0	2.0	75.0	39.0	47.2	52.8
62378	VERSAILLES	99.4	99.4	0.1	0.1	0.2	0.2	0.3	0.2	5.4	5.9	7.0	5.7	6.5	25.0	28.4	13.3	2.7	78.1	41.3	50.8	49.2
62379	WARSAW	98.8	98.5	0.1	0.1	0.2	0.2	0.8	1.0	5.6	5.8	7.0	7.1	6.5	24.0	28.3	13.5	2.2	77.3	41.1	49.6	50.4
62380	WEST POINT	99.4	99.4	0.2	0.2	0.0	0.0	0.0	0.0	6.0	7.4	8.0	7.2	6.0	26.8	23.5	13.3	2.0	73.8	37.7	50.7	49.3
62401	EFFINGHAM	98.2	97.8	0.3	0.3	0.5	0.6	1.0	1.2	7.2	6.9	7.5	6.8	6.9	26.3	23.8	12.3	2.3	74.3	37.2	49.3	50.7
62410	ALLENDALE	98.3	98.1	0.5	0.5	0.1	0.1	0.7	1.0	4.9	5.8	8.6	8.3	6.6	23.8	28.6	11.8	1.5	75.7	40.3	51.6	48.4
62411	ALTAMONT	99.4	99.3	0.1	0.1	0.0	0.1	0.4	0.4	6.7	6.7	7.4	7.2	6.7	24.5	24.4	13.0	3.3	74.5	38.7	49.1	50.9
62413	ANNAPOLIS	97.7	97.1	0.3	0.3	0.3	0.3	0.9	1.3	6.7	6.4	6.4	6.4	6.7	26.6	27.2	11.5	1.9	76.6	40.3	51.3	48.7
62414	BEECHER CITY	99.5	99.5	0.0	0.0	0.0	0.0	0.4	0.4	6.9	7.0	7.0	7.0	5.7	26.2	25.8	12.8	1.6	74.8	38.6	50.1	49.9
62417	BRIDGEPORT	98.5	98.2	0.3	0.4	0.0	0.0	0.6	0.8	6.2	6.2	7.1	6.5	5.9	27.1	24.5	14.0	2.5	76.6	39.1	48.4	51.6
62418	BROWNSTOWN	98.9	98.7	0.2	0.4	0.1	0.1	0.4	0.5	6.4	6.7	7.7	6.7	6.0	26.3	26.3	11.9	2.1	75.1	38.8	48.1	51.9
62419	CALHOUN	98.4	98.3	0.0	0.0	1.0	1.1	0.2	0.2	6.0	6.0	7.0	6.3	6.5	27.9	26.3	12.4	1.6	77.0	38.8	51.0	49.0
	ILLINOIS	73.5	71.8	15.1	15.2	3.5	4.0	12.3	14.2	7.1	7.0	7.3	7.0	7.3	29.0	23.2	10.4	1.7	74.5	35.2	49.0	51.0
	UNITED STATES	75.1	73.6	12.3	12.5	3.8	4.2	12.5	14.1	6.9	6.7	7.2	7.0	7.3	28.6	23.8	10.8	1.7	75.1	36.0	49.1	50.9

#	POST OFFICE NAME	2004 Per Capita Income	2004 HH Income Base	2004 Household Income Distribution (%): Less than $25,000	$25,000 to $49,999	$50,000 to $99,999	$100,000 to $149,999	$150,000 or More	Median Household Income: 2004	2009	2004 National Centile	2004 State Centile	2004 Home Value Base	2004 Home Value Distribution (%): Less than $50,000	$50,000 to $89,999	$90,000 to $174,999	$175,000 to $399,999	$400,000 or More	2004 Median Home Value
62243	FREEBURG	24587	2084	18.0	25.2	40.8	11.4	4.6	56630	63825	81	77	1715	12.4	11.0	45.0	29.5	2.2	124888
62244	FULTS	19778	424	17.2	28.8	44.3	9.2	0.5	52322	58742	76	68	383	11.2	13.6	43.6	30.0	1.6	139031
62245	GERMANTOWN	24079	780	19.4	25.4	40.3	12.8	2.2	55160	59167	80	74	683	8.4	22.0	53.6	15.2	0.9	113504
62246	GREENVILLE	20999	3324	28.7	31.3	30.4	7.0	2.5	41734	45921	52	36	2538	16.2	28.9	41.9	12.5	0.4	95668
62248	HECKER	27451	229	16.2	26.6	41.9	10.5	4.8	57985	61977	83	78	206	6.3	9.2	51.9	26.2	6.3	147059
62249	HIGHLAND	25251	5570	20.2	27.3	37.2	10.2	5.1	52350	59549	76	68	4466	2.5	17.9	56.2	22.4	1.1	121584
62253	KEYESPORT	18887	332	36.1	29.2	29.8	4.5	0.3	36955	41905	35	19	276	28.6	29.0	29.7	9.1	3.6	82222
62254	LEBANON	22456	2090	25.0	29.6	31.2	9.9	4.4	46544	52407	65	54	1573	11.8	20.1	44.6	21.3	2.2	112610
62255	LENZBURG	18450	457	23.2	34.6	34.6	6.6	1.1	43615	50506	58	44	389	29.1	25.7	33.4	11.8	0.0	82600
62257	MARISSA	19736	1482	27.6	32.5	32.9	6.1	0.8	40186	45562	47	30	1224	31.9	30.2	29.2	8.5	0.3	71579
62258	MASCOUTAH	24275	2772	18.4	29.3	40.2	8.6	3.5	51782	59890	75	67	2246	8.7	30.9	45.7	12.3	2.4	100062
62260	MILLSTADT	26861	2488	17.0	25.8	39.5	13.2	4.5	57165	64473	82	78	2142	6.7	13.9	49.3	27.2	2.9	136795
62261	MODOC	21128	89	25.8	37.1	29.2	6.7	1.1	42005	46300	53	37	77	20.8	22.1	41.6	13.0	2.6	100893
62262	MULBERRY GROVE	19075	944	28.2	35.9	30.7	4.0	1.2	39329	43590	44	28	773	31.3	29.8	26.8	10.7	1.4	73642
62263	NASHVILLE	23844	2147	21.2	33.0	34.1	7.7	3.9	46426	51502	65	54	1730	10.1	29.0	44.4	15.3	1.3	103163
62264	NEW ATHENS	22549	1315	21.2	31.8	35.9	8.0	3.1	47557	54880	67	57	1111	15.2	31.0	39.8	12.8	1.3	94250
62265	NEW BADEN	22854	1764	20.6	26.9	40.0	9.8	2.7	52083	57364	76	68	1441	9.9	25.1	51.0	13.0	1.0	105910
62268	OAKDALE	22606	352	17.6	38.4	32.1	8.5	3.4	46818	52059	66	55	306	13.7	21.6	42.5	20.3	2.0	119022
62269	O FALLON	28260	10603	15.5	25.5	36.9	15.1	7.0	59920	67210	84	81	8250	8.9	17.5	41.3	30.8	1.5	133918
62271	OKAWVILLE	21974	849	29.2	28.7	34.3	5.9	1.9	42583	47314	55	40	691	19.0	25.5	43.7	11.1	0.7	97000
62272	PERCY	17130	555	35.3	35.9	25.4	2.5	0.9	34931	38405	27	12	456	34.0	36.6	26.8	2.6	0.0	65319
62274	PINCKNEYVILLE	17165	2659	31.0	34.2	29.7	3.4	1.8	38308	41550	40	24	2132	21.6	36.6	32.8	8.0	0.9	82072
62275	POCAHONTAS	19981	1459	24.0	33.8	34.7	5.9	1.6	43272	47613	57	43	1283	24.6	24.1	36.9	13.5	0.9	92037
62277	PRAIRIE DU ROCHER	20020	573	21.5	34.2	38.2	5.4	0.7	44649	50184	60	47	489	19.8	29.7	35.6	13.1	1.8	90610
62278	RED BUD	21936	2537	23.2	28.6	37.7	8.3	2.2	48409	52714	69	59	2150	11.4	17.4	45.7	22.1	3.4	120917
62280	ROCKWOOD	19154	183	20.2	37.2	38.3	3.3	1.1	43527	49338	57	44	165	26.7	27.3	35.8	10.3	0.0	85357
62281	SAINT JACOB	25788	689	12.9	28.7	41.1	10.2	7.1	56565	63843	81	76	599	7.4	21.5	44.6	24.5	2.0	120869
62284	SMITHBORO	24138	243	23.1	28.8	32.1	10.7	5.4	48005	51971	68	58	207	15.5	17.9	38.2	27.1	1.5	120089
62285	SMITHTON	23428	1185	21.5	24.0	40.9	10.2	3.4	55146	61425	80	74	1061	8.4	18.3	56.4	15.6	1.4	118689
62286	SPARTA	18342	2849	31.8	35.2	27.2	4.6	1.2	36871	40810	35	19	2209	30.1	35.6	28.8	4.7	0.8	72598
62288	STEELEVILLE	20464	1210	28.6	33.7	30.8	5.5	1.4	40000	44135	46	30	1019	19.5	30.4	43.8	6.3	0.0	90051
62293	TRENTON	24683	2222	19.5	23.5	42.2	11.3	3.5	55113	61344	80	74	1921	6.2	18.4	53.2	19.7	2.6	120811
62294	TROY	25988	4601	12.9	25.8	42.3	12.3	6.7	62102	68946	86	84	3668	5.5	10.3	59.0	24.3	1.0	135625
62295	VALMEYER	21413	357	18.5	28.3	39.2	11.2	2.8	52972	58702	77	69	319	6.0	11.3	48.9	32.6	1.3	151591
62297	WALSH	21722	155	23.2	38.7	32.9	3.9	1.3	41806	46619	52	36	135	20.7	31.9	37.0	10.4	0.0	86500
62298	WATERLOO	24411	5768	15.9	27.1	41.5	11.4	4.2	56473	62370	81	76	4873	2.2	10.7	46.1	38.4	2.6	159415
62301	QUINCY	20017	14306	36.1	33.1	24.6	3.9	2.3	33889	37869	24	10	9717	15.3	38.5	36.1	9.6	0.5	86741
62305	QUINCY	23676	6919	24.2	30.6	32.1	8.4	4.7	45502	49845	63	50	5946	16.8	12.2	46.4	22.0	2.5	121472
62311	AUGUSTA	17002	357	36.1	35.9	23.5	3.6	0.8	35571	38408	30	14	301	53.5	23.9	17.6	3.0	2.0	46719
62312	BARRY	19207	984	38.3	30.9	25.3	3.1	2.4	32897	36268	21	8	795	36.1	29.6	27.8	6.0	0.5	69609
62313	BASCO	19731	151	22.5	38.4	35.1	4.0	0.0	40672	44763	48	32	129	38.0	34.1	24.8	3.1	0.0	61071
62314	BAYLIS	17513	211	30.8	35.6	28.9	2.8	1.9	37630	42180	38	21	170	40.6	21.8	31.2	4.1	2.4	68000
62316	BOWEN	15766	293	35.5	33.5	29.0	1.0	1.0	34017	37203	24	10	240	49.6	28.8	15.0	2.5	4.2	50385
62319	CAMDEN	18498	111	36.0	35.1	22.5	4.5	1.8	35964	39536	31	16	92	35.9	32.6	17.4	12.0	2.2	72500
62320	CAMP POINT	17701	880	31.3	35.0	27.5	4.6	1.7	38269	42306	40	24	710	23.2	31.8	35.6	9.2	0.1	82653
62321	CARTHAGE	20445	1817	28.7	31.9	32.3	5.9	1.2	40670	44087	48	32	1395	20.8	36.6	36.3	5.7	0.6	81977
62323	CHAMBERSBURG	17793	81	42.0	28.4	24.7	3.7	1.2	31111	32974	15	5	68	45.6	30.9	17.7	5.9	0.0	54286
62324	CLAYTON	16261	587	38.2	31.7	24.4	3.8	2.0	33310	35831	22	9	471	46.9	30.2	15.3	4.9	2.8	53816
62325	COATSBURG	17366	196	31.1	36.2	27.0	4.1	1.5	40372	43986	47	31	166	19.9	27.1	33.1	14.5	5.4	98333
62326	COLCHESTER	20348	1156	28.8	34.0	30.2	4.5	2.5	39116	44141	43	26	937	34.6	32.2	24.4	8.0	0.8	67289
62330	DALLAS CITY	19210	893	29.8	35.1	29.1	4.8	1.2	37506	41801	37	21	741	30.6	32.5	27.9	8.6	0.3	73431
62334	ELVASTON	24562	64	18.8	31.3	45.3	3.1	1.6	50000	49096	72	62	55	27.3	20.0	43.6	7.3	1.8	95000
62338	FOWLER	19726	554	21.7	30.0	41.0	5.6	1.8	48524	52337	69	59	492	10.2	26.2	41.3	21.3	1.0	113333
62339	GOLDEN	18785	357	25.5	37.5	28.9	7.8	0.3	38786	43056	42	25	303	22.4	31.0	30.7	13.9	2.0	83824
62340	GRIGGSVILLE	16922	598	30.4	36.3	29.3	3.2	0.8	36739	41173	34	19	476	35.5	31.7	30.3	1.7	0.8	68333
62341	HAMILTON	21554	1393	25.5	30.0	37.6	4.3	2.6	45544	50389	63	50	1176	20.6	34.2	34.6	9.7	0.9	85556
62343	HULL	18108	255	34.1	36.9	25.9	3.1	0.0	34525	38364	26	11	211	37.0	32.7	22.3	5.7	2.4	61875
62344	HUNTSVILLE	16528	69	42.0	39.1	14.5	4.4	0.0	29513	31718	11	4	57	40.4	35.1	14.0	10.5	0.0	63750
62345	KINDERHOOK	21614	147	25.2	37.4	31.3	4.1	2.0	41830	46237	52	36	126	44.4	31.0	19.8	3.2	1.6	56364
62346	LA PRAIRIE	16406	63	27.0	38.1	31.8	3.2	0.0	39520	42327	44	28	53	18.9	50.9	22.6	5.7	1.9	72143
62347	LIBERTY	19826	911	22.0	39.5	32.6	3.8	2.1	44194	48983	59	46	788	19.8	24.6	41.5	12.1	2.0	101078
62348	LIMA	17384	154	26.0	35.1	33.8	3.9	1.3	42851	47607	56	41	131	19.1	33.6	35.9	9.9	1.5	87308
62349	LORAINE	21176	263	20.5	36.9	34.6	6.1	1.9	45501	50488	63	50	227	30.4	27.3	30.8	10.1	1.3	76786
62351	MENDON	18289	665	29.2	34.9	29.5	4.2	2.3	40504	44371	48	32	565	18.6	36.1	36.5	7.1	1.8	86103
62352	MILTON	18676	212	28.3	40.6	25.9	1.9	3.3	36197	40735	32	17	181	34.8	28.2	23.8	9.9	3.3	73182
62353	MOUNT STERLING	17264	1456	36.6	31.7	26.7	3.5	1.5	34877	38082	27	12	1071	33.6	34.9	24.3	6.4	0.8	67548
62354	NAUVOO	21097	619	24.6	30.5	37.3	5.8	1.8	44094	47548	59	45	530	16.8	29.3	39.4	12.8	1.7	95250
62355	NEBO	18232	379	34.6	35.4	25.6	3.2	1.3	35507	39243	30	14	327	44.3	24.8	19.0	9.5	2.5	55606
62356	NEW CANTON	16456	272	40.1	33.1	23.2	2.6	1.1	31777	34013	17	6	228	52.6	31.6	11.8	4.0	0.0	47500
62357	NEW SALEM	19003	112	30.4	34.8	28.6	3.6	2.7	38138	43469	40	23	91	44.0	15.4	36.3	2.2	2.2	66250
62358	NIOTA	19170	255	24.7	36.5	32.2	5.5	1.2	41063	45000	50	34	219	23.7	34.7	31.1	10.1	0.5	79688
62359	PALOMA	17586	65	30.8	40.0	24.6	3.1	1.5	40561	41552	48	32	55	18.2	27.3	32.7	14.6	7.3	101389
62360	PAYSON	18136	708	27.4	33.8	32.1	4.9	1.8	43741	48823	58	44	593	17.9	34.7	33.6	12.8	1.0	87281
62361	PEARL	21070	149	38.3	32.9	22.2	2.0	4.7	32830	34648	20	8	127	50.4	18.9	13.4	5.5	11.8	49375
62362	PERRY	18852	270	37.8	31.5	25.9	3.0	1.9	33822	36198	24	10	223	41.3	30.5	21.1	6.3	0.9	59750
62363	PITTSFIELD	17712	2536	38.1	28.4	30.1	2.6	0.9	33698	35941	23	9	1967	19.5	35.8	33.5	10.6	0.6	85024
62365	PLAINVILLE	17230	341	22.3	41.9	30.5	5.3	0.0	41857	46442	52	37	300	23.3	23.7	36.3	15.7	1.0	94737
62366	PLEASANT HILL	15544	593	41.2	33.7	22.4	2.7	0.0	30453	33336	13	4	479	37.2	37.0	19.6	5.9	0.4	63229
62367	PLYMOUTH	17800	606	32.7	33.8	28.7	2.6	2.2	36585	39476	34	18	500	45.4	23.8	21.0	8.4	1.4	56970
62370	ROCKPORT	15851	240	33.3	34.2	27.5	5.0	0.0	36344	39625	33	17	203	32.5	23.2	31.0	13.3	0.0	79667
62373	SUTTER	17327	103	21.4	36.9	34.0	5.8	1.9	42366	43871	54	39	87	14.9	33.3	37.9	11.5	2.3	95000
62374	TENNESSEE	19474	121	27.3	37.2	32.2	2.5	0.8	40661	44306	48	32	105	36.2	24.8	22.9	12.4	3.8	64375
62375	TIMEWELL	18781	204	16.7	46.6	31.4	3.4	2.0	42931	45697	56	41	165	29.7	34.6	24.9	10.9	0.0	71190
62376	URSA	19889	429	26.8	34.5	33.6	3.7	1.4	43584	47920	58	44	363	18.2	35.0	35.0	10.2	1.7	86892
62378	VERSAILLES	20034	467	27.4	34.3	32.1	4.5	1.7	43941	47472	58	45	395	40.0	30.9	23.3	4.8	1.0	60417
62379	WARSAW	21154	887	26.5	36.6	30.3	4.1	2.5	39132	43562	43	26	736	22.8	37.4	34.1	5.2	0.5	80964
62380	WEST POINT	16497	191	30.4	33.5	33.5	2.1	0.5	38406	41867	41	24	160	34.4	35.0	23.8	0.6	6.3	62941
62401	EFFINGHAM	22521	8237	27.6	31.1	31.4	6.1	3.7	42308	47113	54	38	6108	10.6	21.0	47.3	19.9	1.2	115236
62410	ALLENDALE	17752	393	28.5	37.9	29.3	3.6	0.8	38869	43581	42	26	344	32.6	34.9	27.0	5.2	0.3	69091
62411	ALTAMONT	19797	1528	28.0	35.3	30.6	4.3	1.8	40787	46005	49	33	1252	16.1	30.3	43.5	9.4	0.8	94286
62413	ANNAPOLIS	17845	115	30.4	31.3	29.6	7.8	0.9	39064	42649	43	26	102	42.2	27.5	24.5	5.9	0.0	57273
62414	BEECHER CITY	17426	820	31.1	39.4	25.0	3.3	1.2	36307	40164	33	17	686	30.6	23.8	29.3	13.3	3.1	82105
62417	BRIDGEPORT	16825	1487	37.4	35.9	23.2	2.2	1.3	32800	35765	20	8	1204	40.7	36.8	19.9	1.2	1.5	59573
62418	BROWNSTOWN	17471	1027	32.7	38.0	23.8	3.3	2.2	33237	36761	22	9	858	27.0	31.9	28.6	11.3	1.2	78667
62419	CALHOUN	16769	244	35.3	32.4	27.1	4.1	1.2	36143	40000	32	16	210	41.9	27.1	23.8	7.1	0.0	59444
	ILLINOIS	27033		22.1	25.9	32.9	11.9	7.3	52039	60941				7.7	12.8	34.0	36.6	8.9	162771
	UNITED STATES	25866		24.7	27.1	30.8	10.9	6.5	48124	56710				10.9	15.0	33.7	30.1	10.4	145905

ZIP CODE		FINANCIAL SERVICES				THE HOME						ENTERTAINMENT						PERSONAL			
						Home Improvements		Furnishings													
#	POST OFFICE NAME	Auto Loan	Home Loan	Invest-ments	Retire-ment Plans	Home Repair	Lawn & Garden	Comput-ers & Hard-ware	Major Appli-ances	TV, Radio, Sound Equip-ment	Furni-ture	Dine out/ Carry out	Sports Equip-ment	Fees & Tickets	Toys & Games	Travel	Cable TV	Apparel & Services	Auto Repairs	Health Insur-ance	Pets & Supplies
62243	FREEBURG	92	98	97	97	98	101	93	94	91	92	113	111	95	117	94	89	111	93	90	108
62244	FULTS	94	77	52	73	84	91	72	84	79	72	95	100	68	96	75	82	89	82	94	111
62245	GERMANTOWN	85	98	103	97	97	99	92	92	88	91	111	106	96	116	93	87	109	90	86	102
62246	GREENVILLE	75	70	62	67	73	81	69	74	72	68	88	84	67	88	70	74	83	72	80	88
62248	HECKER	86	105	116	102	103	105	97	96	93	96	117	111	103	124	100	91	116	94	89	105
62249	HIGHLAND	93	94	88	92	96	102	90	94	91	89	112	109	91	116	92	92	108	92	96	110
62253	KEYESPORT	70	54	36	50	59	69	56	64	63	54	74	72	50	71	57	67	68	63	76	81
62254	LEBANON	82	84	83	84	84	89	82	83	81	81	100	97	82	102	82	80	97	82	82	95
62255	LENZBURG	90	67	39	60	74	83	64	76	73	64	87	90	58	85	65	77	80	75	89	104
62257	MARISSA	75	68	56	63	71	78	64	70	69	64	84	81	63	86	66	72	80	69	78	87
62258	MASCOUTAH	86	96	97	93	95	97	89	90	86	89	108	105	92	112	90	85	106	88	86	102
62260	MILLSTADT	91	104	110	103	104	106	97	98	93	96	117	114	101	122	99	92	115	95	93	110
62261	MODOC	81	69	50	65	74	80	64	73	69	64	84	87	62	85	66	71	79	71	80	95
62262	MULBERRY GROVE	75	62	46	61	66	74	62	69	67	62	81	80	59	81	63	69	76	67	76	85
62263	NASHVILLE	94	77	57	74	84	94	77	86	83	75	100	100	72	99	78	86	93	85	97	109
62264	NEW ATHENS	84	83	76	81	85	90	79	83	81	79	99	96	79	101	80	81	95	81	85	97
62265	NEW BADEN	84	86	83	85	88	93	83	86	84	82	103	99	84	106	85	84	100	84	87	98
62268	OAKDALE	97	86	65	82	91	97	79	88	84	79	103	105	78	105	82	86	97	86	95	114
62269	O FALLON	102	112	110	113	109	110	104	105	99	106	125	122	106	126	103	96	122	103	96	117
62271	OKAWVILLE	86	68	47	66	74	85	71	79	78	69	93	90	65	90	71	81	86	78	90	97
62272	PERCY	74	52	28	47	58	67	52	62	61	52	71	73	45	68	52	65	65	61	75	84
62274	PINCKNEYVILLE	66	58	46	55	61	69	57	62	62	56	74	71	55	76	58	64	70	61	70	76
62275	POCAHONTAS	88	71	48	67	76	83	68	78	74	69	89	92	62	86	69	76	84	77	85	100
62277	PRAIRIE DU ROCHER	81	72	55	68	76	81	66	73	70	66	86	87	65	87	68	72	81	71	79	95
62278	RED BUD	82	82	76	79	84	90	77	81	79	77	97	95	79	100	79	80	94	79	83	97
62280	ROCKWOOD	78	68	51	65	71	78	65	72	69	65	84	84	63	83	66	71	80	71	77	90
62281	SAINT JACOB	109	101	82	97	106	112	93	102	97	93	119	121	93	122	96	99	113	99	107	128
62284	SMITHBORO	98	88	75	86	95	103	85	94	89	84	107	109	82	107	88	91	102	92	102	116
62285	SMITHTON	100	95	79	91	99	104	87	94	90	87	110	112	87	113	90	91	106	92	98	118
62286	SPARTA	69	57	43	53	60	69	57	63	63	56	75	73	53	74	58	65	70	62	72	79
62288	STEELEVILLE	74	67	56	64	71	78	65	70	69	64	83	81	64	84	67	71	79	69	77	86
62293	TRENTON	85	96	98	94	96	99	88	90	86	88	107	105	92	113	91	86	106	88	87	103
62294	TROY	100	112	111	114	109	108	104	104	98	105	123	122	106	125	103	93	121	102	93	115
62295	VALMEYER	96	84	63	80	89	96	78	87	83	78	101	104	76	103	80	86	96	85	95	113
62297	WALSH	57	45	29	43	50	55	43	50	47	43	57	60	39	57	44	49	53	49	57	67
62298	WATERLOO	93	96	91	95	97	101	90	93	90	90	111	109	92	114	92	89	108	91	92	109
62301	QUINCY	60	63	69	61	63	68	64	63	65	63	81	73	65	83	65	65	79	64	64	70
62305	QUINCY	95	85	69	81	90	98	81	89	85	80	103	104	78	103	83	87	98	87	97	111
62311	AUGUSTA	56	59	60	56	60	66	58	58	60	56	75	65	61	80	60	63	72	57	63	65
62312	BARRY	77	59	40	57	65	75	62	69	68	60	81	80	56	79	62	71	75	69	80	87
62313	BASCO	85	61	34	58	70	79	60	74	69	60	81	88	52	80	62	72	74	72	87	101
62314	BAYLIS	85	59	31	56	69	77	58	72	67	58	79	87	50	77	61	71	72	71	86	101
62316	BOWEN	63	54	42	53	56	63	55	59	59	54	71	67	53	70	55	60	67	58	64	70
62319	CAMDEN	80	56	29	53	65	73	55	68	63	54	74	82	47	73	57	66	68	67	81	95
62320	CAMP POINT	74	62	46	61	66	74	62	68	66	61	80	79	59	80	62	68	75	67	75	84
62321	CARTHAGE	76	64	48	61	68	77	64	70	70	63	84	81	61	84	65	72	79	69	79	86
62323	CHAMBERSBURG	69	52	34	50	57	68	57	63	64	54	75	71	51	71	57	68	69	63	75	76
62324	CLAYTON	71	52	32	50	58	68	55	63	62	53	73	73	48	70	55	66	67	63	76	81
62325	COATSBURG	79	57	32	54	65	73	56	68	63	55	75	81	49	74	58	66	69	67	79	93
62326	COLCHESTER	68	69	65	65	71	77	66	69	69	65	85	79	68	90	68	71	82	67	74	81
62330	DALLAS CITY	72	61	46	60	64	72	61	66	65	60	79	77	58	79	61	67	74	65	73	81
62334	ELVASTON	89	79	60	75	84	90	73	81	78	73	95	97	72	97	76	80	90	79	88	105
62338	FOWLER	85	76	57	72	80	86	70	78	74	70	90	93	69	92	72	76	86	76	84	100
62339	GOLDEN	85	59	31	56	69	77	58	72	67	58	79	87	50	77	61	71	72	71	86	101
62340	GRIGGSVILLE	77	54	28	51	62	70	53	65	61	52	72	79	45	70	55	64	65	65	78	91
62341	HAMILTON	84	73	56	71	78	84	70	77	74	69	90	90	68	91	71	76	85	75	83	97
62343	HULL	75	57	35	54	65	71	55	66	62	55	74	79	50	73	57	64	68	65	76	89
62344	HUNTSVILLE	68	47	25	45	55	62	47	58	54	46	63	69	40	62	48	56	57	57	69	80
62345	KINDERHOOK	84	74	56	70	78	84	68	76	73	68	89	91	67	90	71	75	84	74	83	99
62346	LA PRAIRIE	78	55	29	52	64	71	54	67	62	53	73	80	46	71	56	65	66	66	79	93
62347	LIBERTY	84	73	54	69	78	84	68	76	72	68	88	91	65	89	70	74	83	74	83	99
62348	LIMA	87	61	32	58	71	80	60	75	69	60	81	90	51	80	63	73	74	73	89	104
62349	LORAINE	92	77	55	74	84	91	73	83	79	72	95	99	69	96	75	81	89	81	91	108
62351	MENDON	79	63	44	62	68	77	64	71	69	63	83	83	59	82	64	71	77	70	80	90
62352	MILTON	76	61	43	60	66	75	62	69	68	61	81	81	58	80	63	69	76	68	78	86
62353	MOUNT STERLING	54	44	33	42	48	55	45	50	50	44	60	58	42	60	46	53	56	50	58	63
62354	NAUVOO	81	71	55	69	75	82	69	75	73	68	89	88	67	89	70	75	84	74	81	93
62355	NEBO	82	56	27	50	64	73	54	68	65	55	76	81	46	73	56	69	69	67	82	96
62356	NEW CANTON	72	50	26	48	59	66	50	62	57	49	67	74	43	66	52	60	61	61	73	86
62357	NEW SALEM	90	63	33	59	73	82	62	76	71	61	84	92	53	82	64	75	76	75	91	106
62358	NIOTA	77	67	52	65	71	77	65	71	69	64	84	83	63	84	66	70	79	69	77	88
62359	PALOMA	76	53	28	50	62	69	52	65	60	52	71	78	45	69	54	63	64	64	77	90
62360	PAYSON	78	67	52	66	71	78	66	72	71	66	85	84	64	86	67	72	80	71	79	89
62361	PEARL	90	63	33	59	73	82	62	76	71	61	83	92	53	82	64	75	76	75	91	106
62362	PERRY	72	53	32	50	59	69	56	64	63	54	74	74	49	71	56	67	68	64	77	82
62363	PITTSFIELD	68	52	34	50	57	66	55	62	61	53	73	70	49	70	55	64	66	61	72	77
62365	PLAINVILLE	84	59	31	56	69	77	58	72	67	57	78	87	50	77	60	70	72	71	85	100
62366	PLEASANT HILL	63	45	26	43	51	59	47	55	54	46	63	64	41	61	48	57	58	55	66	72
62367	PLYMOUTH	73	60	43	58	65	72	59	66	64	59	77	78	56	77	60	66	72	65	74	84
62370	ROCKPORT	77	53	28	50	62	70	53	65	61	52	71	79	45	70	55	64	65	64	78	91
62373	SUTTER	89	62	33	59	73	81	62	76	71	61	83	91	53	82	64	74	76	75	90	106
62374	TENNESSEE	79	57	32	54	66	73	56	68	64	55	75	82	49	74	58	66	69	67	80	94
62375	TIMEWELL	88	62	32	58	72	81	61	75	70	60	82	91	52	81	63	74	75	74	90	105
62376	URSA	86	60	31	57	70	78	59	73	68	58	80	88	51	78	61	72	73	72	87	102
62378	VERSAILLES	87	61	32	57	71	79	60	74	69	59	81	90	51	80	62	73	74	73	88	103
62379	WARSAW	77	72	62	68	75	82	69	74	73	68	89	85	69	93	71	76	85	72	81	90
62380	WEST POINT	69	57	43	57	61	69	59	64	63	58	76	74	55	75	59	64	71	63	70	77
62401	EFFINGHAM	83	75	64	73	78	85	74	79	77	73	94	92	71	94	75	79	89	78	85	95
62410	ALLENDALE	75	67	51	64	71	76	62	69	66	62	80	82	61	82	64	67	76	67	74	89
62411	ALTAMONT	77	71	60	68	73	81	69	74	73	68	89	85	68	89	70	74	84	72	79	88
62413	ANNAPOLIS	78	69	52	65	73	78	64	71	68	64	82	84	62	84	66	70	78	69	77	92
62414	BEECHER CITY	78	56	29	49	62	71	53	65	63	54	74	78	47	71	54	67	68	64	78	91
62417	BRIDGEPORT	66	51	34	49	56	65	54	60	59	52	71	69	49	68	54	62	65	60	70	75
62418	BROWNSTOWN	77	56	33	53	63	71	56	66	64	56	76	78	50	74	57	67	70	65	77	88
62419	CALHOUN	70	62	47	59	65	70	57	63	61	57	74	76	56	75	59	62	70	62	69	82
	ILLINOIS	98	100	111	99	99	106	100	99	101	100	126	115	102	127	100	100	123	100	98	112
	UNITED STATES	100	100	100	100	100	100	100	100	100	100	100	100	100	100	100	100	100	100	100	100

ILLINOIS

POPULATION CHANGE

A 62420-62601

ZIP CODE #	POST OFFICE NAME	COUNTY FIPS CODE	POPULATION 2000	2004	2009	2000-2004 ANNUAL RATE % Rate	State Centile	HOUSEHOLDS 2000	2004	2009	% Annual Rate 2000-2004	2004 Average HH Size	FAMILIES 2000	2004	% Annual Rate 2000-2004
62420	CASEY	023	5237	5197	5174	-0.2	32	2148	2156	2157	0.1	2.35	1437	1419	-0.3
62421	CLAREMONT	159	918	973	993	1.4	83	342	369	383	1.8	2.63	273	291	1.5
62422	COWDEN	051	1518	1504	1510	-0.2	29	576	578	588	0.1	2.60	422	418	-0.2
62423	DENNISON	023	643	695	723	1.9	87	249	273	286	2.2	2.55	186	201	1.8
62424	DIETERICH	049	1936	2029	2122	1.1	79	632	673	714	1.5	3.01	516	544	1.3
62425	DUNDAS	159	558	606	627	2.0	88	205	228	240	2.5	2.63	156	171	2.2
62426	EDGEWOOD	025	742	754	774	0.4	61	311	322	337	0.8	2.34	235	240	0.5
62427	FLAT ROCK	033	2223	2174	2096	-0.5	16	849	842	825	-0.2	2.58	650	637	-0.5
62428	GREENUP	035	3083	3054	3058	-0.2	29	1302	1311	1331	0.2	2.28	852	842	-0.3
62431	HERRICK	173	687	699	712	0.4	63	262	271	279	0.8	2.58	188	191	0.4
62432	HIDALGO	079	555	565	580	0.4	63	225	235	246	1.0	2.39	162	166	0.6
62433	HUTSONVILLE	033	1057	1030	989	-0.6	12	400	397	386	-0.2	2.37	286	279	-0.6
62434	INGRAHAM	025	916	925	943	0.2	54	302	311	323	0.7	2.80	233	237	0.4
62436	JEWETT	035	495	501	507	0.3	57	183	189	193	0.8	2.63	134	136	0.4
62438	LAKEWOOD	173	409	410	414	0.1	45	161	164	168	0.4	2.50	125	126	0.2
62439	LAWRENCEVILLE	101	7456	7300	7133	-0.5	16	3144	3124	3097	-0.2	2.21	2006	1960	-0.5
62440	LERNA	029	1376	1377	1369	0.0	42	524	533	539	0.4	2.58	405	409	0.2
62441	MARSHALL	023	7605	7724	7770	0.4	61	3124	3225	3267	0.8	2.36	2149	2184	0.4
62442	MARTINSVILLE	023	2016	1997	1984	-0.2	29	835	837	836	0.1	2.39	605	598	-0.3
62443	MASON	049	2090	2139	2207	0.6	67	713	742	780	0.9	2.88	555	571	0.7
62445	MONTROSE	035	1286	1295	1315	0.2	50	434	448	464	0.8	2.89	341	347	0.4
62446	MOUNT ERIE	191	419	408	402	-0.6	11	169	168	168	-0.1	2.42	131	129	-0.4
62447	NEOGA	035	3696	3795	3865	0.6	70	1370	1431	1478	1.0	2.62	1012	1042	0.7
62448	NEWTON	079	5979	6086	6279	0.4	63	2377	2458	2577	0.8	2.45	1651	1684	0.5
62449	OBLONG	033	3335	3179	3028	-1.1	3	1335	1291	1246	-0.8	2.41	955	908	-1.2
62450	OLNEY	159	11552	11363	11197	-0.4	20	4901	4901	4907	0.0	2.29	3200	3144	-0.4
62451	PALESTINE	033	2169	2095	2008	-0.8	7	946	934	908	-0.3	2.00	637	618	-0.7
62452	PARKERSBURG	159	423	421	416	-0.1	36	182	185	186	0.4	2.28	139	139	0.0
62454	ROBINSON	033	11877	11526	11062	-0.7	9	4418	4320	4177	-0.5	2.39	2996	2887	-0.9
62458	SAINT ELMO	051	1964	1914	1896	-0.6	13	755	747	750	-0.3	2.50	547	535	-0.5
62460	SAINT FRANCISVILLE	101	1739	1699	1655	-0.6	14	690	685	678	-0.2	2.48	505	494	-0.5
62461	SHUMWAY	049	506	562	606	2.5	92	179	203	223	3.0	2.77	137	153	2.6
62462	SIGEL	035	1354	1371	1386	0.3	58	438	452	464	0.7	3.03	340	347	0.5
62463	STEWARDSON	173	1267	1275	1289	0.2	50	501	512	526	0.5	2.49	354	356	0.1
62465	STRASBURG	173	901	912	925	0.3	58	315	323	332	0.6	2.59	228	231	0.3
62466	SUMNER	101	1982	1932	1883	-0.6	13	742	732	724	-0.3	2.45	521	506	-0.6
62467	TEUTOPOLIS	049	3120	3166	3254	0.3	59	998	1039	1090	1.0	3.04	773	793	0.6
62468	TOLEDO	035	2630	2647	2669	0.2	50	1053	1078	1101	0.6	2.44	742	748	0.2
62469	TRILLA	035	588	612	623	1.0	77	206	219	227	1.5	2.75	145	152	1.1
62471	VANDALIA	051	10209	10397	10626	0.4	64	3570	3709	3864	0.9	2.35	2352	2397	0.5
62473	WATSON	049	1209	1242	1283	0.6	70	416	435	458	1.1	2.85	332	343	0.8
62474	WESTFIELD	023	1063	1051	1041	-0.3	26	423	425	424	0.1	2.47	306	304	-0.2
62475	WEST LIBERTY	079	282	281	287	-0.1	37	100	102	106	0.5	2.75	77	77	0.0
62476	WEST SALEM	047	2060	2173	2230	1.3	81	833	895	931	1.7	2.39	598	634	1.4
62477	WEST UNION	023	1043	1032	1024	-0.3	27	427	427	427	0.0	2.42	303	299	-0.3
62478	WEST YORK	023	484	479	467	-0.2	28	190	191	189	0.1	2.51	140	139	-0.2
62479	WHEELER	079	863	867	889	0.1	47	310	319	333	0.7	2.72	249	253	0.4
62480	WILLOW HILL	079	1250	1340	1420	1.7	85	481	524	566	2.0	2.56	368	397	1.8
62481	YALE	079	432	434	443	0.1	47	160	164	171	0.6	2.65	124	126	0.4
62501	ARGENTA	115	2623	2596	2571	-0.2	28	1013	1023	1031	0.2	2.54	800	797	-0.1
62510	ASSUMPTION	021	1854	1905	1944	0.6	70	770	805	833	1.1	2.37	535	550	0.7
62512	BEASON	107	471	465	458	-0.3	25	161	161	161	0.0	2.89	133	132	-0.2
62513	BLUE MOUND	115	1748	1697	1669	-0.7	9	689	684	685	-0.2	2.48	518	507	-0.5
62514	BOODY	115	159	155	153	-0.6	13	59	59	59	0.0	2.63	47	46	-0.5
62515	BUFFALO	167	942	943	946	0.0	42	360	368	377	0.5	2.56	274	275	0.1
62517	BULPITT	021	206	208	210	0.2	54	96	99	101	0.7	2.10	66	66	0.0
62518	CHESTNUT	107	462	453	446	-0.5	17	183	181	180	-0.3	2.50	146	143	-0.5
62520	DAWSON	167	1376	1387	1395	0.2	51	542	559	573	0.7	2.47	426	432	0.3
62521	DECATUR	115	37567	37025	36619	-0.3	22	15403	15460	15528	0.1	2.37	10783	10653	-0.3
62522	DECATUR	115	18863	18456	18220	-0.5	16	7272	7197	7190	-0.2	2.31	4246	4110	-0.8
62523	DECATUR	115	548	526	516	-1.0	4	135	124	120	-2.0	1.76	36	32	-2.7
62526	DECATUR	115	37068	37180	37145	0.1	45	15917	16276	16521	0.5	2.22	9822	9860	0.1
62530	DIVERNON	167	1519	1496	1495	-0.4	21	607	610	620	0.1	2.45	451	445	-0.3
62531	EDINBURG	021	2133	2157	2180	0.3	55	859	888	915	0.8	2.43	615	626	0.4
62533	FARMERSVILLE	135	1054	1022	995	-0.7	8	422	418	415	-0.2	2.44	298	292	-0.5
62534	FINDLAY	173	1358	1345	1357	-0.2	29	568	573	588	0.2	2.35	415	413	-0.1
62535	FORSYTH	115	2069	2109	2114	0.5	64	750	784	802	1.1	2.68	585	604	0.8
62536	GLENARM	167	1012	1027	1035	0.4	60	347	360	368	0.9	2.85	295	302	0.6
62538	HARVEL	135	452	431	419	-1.1	3	175	171	169	-0.5	2.52	133	128	-0.9
62539	ILLIOPOLIS	167	1288	1254	1249	-0.6	11	502	499	506	-0.1	2.51	372	363	-0.6
62543	LATHAM	107	513	489	476	-1.1	3	209	203	201	-0.7	2.41	160	154	-0.9
62544	MACON	115	1723	1712	1697	-0.2	34	661	671	677	0.4	2.49	497	498	0.1
62545	MECHANICSBURG	167	1119	1105	1105	-0.3	25	433	437	445	0.2	2.53	324	321	-0.2
62546	MORRISONVILLE	021	1632	1621	1625	-0.2	33	646	652	665	0.2	2.49	472	469	-0.2
62547	MOUNT AUBURN	021	717	706	707	-0.4	21	310	312	319	0.2	2.26	234	233	-0.1
62548	MOUNT PULASKI	107	2485	2436	2397	-0.5	17	996	990	988	-0.1	2.33	704	691	-0.4
62549	MT ZION	115	5585	5654	5651	0.3	58	2098	2167	2203	0.8	2.58	1647	1680	0.5
62550	MOWEAQUA	173	3189	3184	3215	0.0	39	1222	1239	1270	0.3	2.50	913	914	0.0
62551	NIANTIC	115	896	874	859	-0.6	13	328	326	326	-0.1	2.68	245	240	-0.5
62553	OCONEE	173	877	899	918	0.6	68	325	339	350	1.0	2.65	267	275	0.7
62554	OREANA	115	1701	1742	1750	0.6	68	624	652	667	1.0	2.67	504	520	0.7
62555	OWANECO	021	555	561	565	0.3	54	205	215	223	1.1	1.26	165	69	-18.6
62556	PALMER	021	461	465	471	0.2	52	162	166	170	0.6	2.80	127	128	0.2
62557	PANA	021	7252	7307	7401	0.2	51	2930	2998	3082	0.5	2.33	1913	1925	0.2
62558	PAWNEE	167	3345	3288	3283	-0.4	19	1279	1278	1297	0.2	2.57	939	921	-0.5
62560	RAYMOND	135	1489	1449	1413	-0.6	11	589	582	576	-0.3	2.47	428	417	-0.6
62561	RIVERTON	167	4616	4846	4978	1.2	80	1788	1914	1998	1.6	2.53	1298	1362	1.1
62563	ROCHESTER	167	4990	5123	5211	0.6	70	1843	1935	2005	1.2	2.65	1511	1564	0.8
62565	SHELBYVILLE	173	7565	7802	8019	0.7	73	3159	3318	3467	1.2	2.32	2123	2194	0.8
62567	STONINGTON	021	1231	1216	1218	-0.3	25	494	498	508	0.2	2.44	369	367	-0.1
62568	TAYLORVILLE	021	18218	18400	18591	0.2	54	7024	7203	7389	0.6	2.39	4669	4713	0.2
62571	TOWER HILL	173	1575	1574	1589	0.0	40	604	614	631	0.4	2.56	457	460	0.2
62572	WAGGONER	135	452	434	421	-1.0	4	171	167	165	-0.6	2.60	133	129	-0.7
62573	WARRENSBURG	115	1875	1861	1844	-0.2	32	718	726	730	0.3	2.55	547	546	0.0
62601	ALEXANDER	137	471	532	561	2.9	94	184	212	226	3.4	2.51	142	160	2.9
	ILLINOIS					0.7					0.9	2.61			0.6
	UNITED STATES					1.2					1.3	2.58			1.1

POPULATION COMPOSITION ILLINOIS
62420-62601 B

ZIP CODE #	POST OFFICE NAME	RACE (%) White 2000	White 2004	Black 2000	Black 2004	Asian/Pacific 2000	Asian/Pacific 2004	% Hispanic Origin 2000	% Hispanic Origin 2004	2004 AGE DISTRIBUTION (%) 0-4	5-9	10-14	15-19	20-24	25-44	45-64	65-84	85+	18+	MEDIAN AGE 2004	% 2004 Males	% 2004 Females
62420	CASEY	98.9	98.8	0.3	0.3	0.0	0.0	0.3	0.3	6.0	6.5	7.4	6.4	5.8	24.7	24.5	15.1	3.7	76.1	40.4	47.4	52.6
62421	CLAREMONT	98.4	98.2	0.0	0.0	0.7	0.8	0.4	0.4	6.1	6.1	8.7	7.0	4.3	27.0	26.2	12.7	1.9	74.1	39.2	50.6	49.4
62422	COWDEN	99.0	98.9	0.2	0.2	0.0	0.0	0.1	0.2	6.9	6.9	8.3	7.1	6.8	25.1	25.1	12.4	1.5	73.6	36.7	50.3	49.7
62423	DENNISON	99.1	99.1	0.0	0.0	0.0	0.0	0.2	0.1	5.5	5.9	7.3	5.6	5.9	26.0	29.9	12.2	1.6	78.0	41.4	51.4	48.6
62424	DIETERICH	99.3	99.3	0.1	0.1	0.1	0.1	0.3	0.3	8.7	8.8	9.6	8.5	6.8	27.6	20.2	9.1	0.7	67.7	31.6	52.0	48.1
62425	DUNDAS	99.1	99.0	0.0	0.0	0.4	0.5	1.4	2.0	6.3	6.8	7.4	7.1	5.6	26.6	25.4	11.9	3.0	74.8	39.6	48.4	51.7
62426	EDGEWOOD	99.1	98.8	0.0	0.0	0.1	0.3	0.8	1.1	7.3	6.9	8.1	7.0	6.8	28.1	24.3	10.2	1.3	73.6	35.6	50.9	49.1
62427	FLAT ROCK	97.0	96.6	1.2	1.4	0.3	0.3	0.4	0.4	5.7	6.1	7.6	6.4	5.3	25.3	27.6	14.6	1.3	76.5	40.8	49.6	50.4
62428	GREENUP	99.1	99.0	0.1	0.1	0.2	0.2	0.3	0.4	5.7	5.4	6.2	6.4	6.6	23.9	25.4	16.2	4.4	79.0	42.0	48.9	51.2
62431	HERRICK	99.6	99.4	0.0	0.0	0.0	0.1	0.4	0.6	8.9	8.4	7.7	7.4	6.2	25.9	19.6	13.7	2.2	70.7	34.4	52.9	47.1
62432	HIDALGO	99.3	99.1	0.0	0.0	0.2	0.2	0.2	0.2	4.8	5.0	6.9	6.4	5.8	26.6	27.6	14.0	3.0	78.8	41.5	50.3	49.7
62433	HUTSONVILLE	98.2	98.0	0.9	0.9	0.1	0.1	0.8	1.0	4.7	4.8	6.1	7.1	6.8	23.0	29.3	15.5	2.7	80.2	43.3	51.9	48.1
62434	INGRAHAM	99.2	99.1	0.1	0.1	0.1	0.2	0.3	0.2	6.0	6.1	6.6	6.3	5.6	24.7	25.7	14.7	4.4	77.4	41.4	50.0	50.1
62436	JEWETT	99.2	99.0	0.0	0.2	0.0	0.0	0.4	0.4	6.2	6.2	7.6	7.2	7.6	27.7	24.6	11.2	1.8	75.1	36.8	49.3	50.7
62438	LAKEWOOD	99.0	99.0	0.5	0.5	0.0	0.0	0.5	0.5	5.4	5.9	8.1	6.6	6.1	25.6	27.3	12.9	2.2	76.6	40.6	52.7	47.3
62439	LAWRENCEVILLE	97.8	97.6	0.9	1.0	0.2	0.3	1.3	1.6	5.7	5.4	5.9	5.6	5.7	23.3	24.5	18.5	5.4	79.8	43.9	46.7	53.3
62440	LERNA	98.1	97.8	0.4	0.4	0.5	0.7	0.8	1.0	5.8	6.9	7.4	7.7	5.2	27.5	28.8	9.6	1.1	74.7	39.0	51.2	48.8
62441	MARSHALL	98.6	98.6	0.2	0.2	0.3	0.3	0.5	0.5	6.3	6.2	7.2	6.1	5.7	26.1	25.2	14.4	2.7	76.6	40.0	48.3	51.7
62442	MARTINSVILLE	99.3	99.4	0.1	0.1	0.1	0.1	0.2	0.2	6.7	6.5	6.7	6.4	6.1	24.5	25.0	15.7	2.5	76.4	40.5	48.9	51.1
62443	MASON	99.1	98.9	0.1	0.1	0.2	0.3	0.6	0.8	7.3	7.6	8.8	7.2	6.2	28.3	23.5	10.0	1.2	71.8	35.2	51.1	48.9
62445	MONTROSE	99.3	99.2	0.0	0.0	0.1	0.2	0.5	0.6	7.9	7.7	8.3	7.6	7.3	27.6	22.9	9.3	1.4	71.4	34.4	50.9	49.1
62446	MOUNT ERIE	98.3	98.0	0.2	0.3	0.5	0.5	1.0	1.0	5.4	5.4	5.6	6.6	5.6	27.9	26.0	15.4	2.0	79.4	41.4	53.7	46.3
62447	NEOGA	98.5	98.3	0.2	0.2	0.2	0.3	0.8	1.0	7.5	7.5	7.5	6.5	6.0	26.7	24.1	12.8	1.6	73.6	37.0	49.9	50.1
62448	NEWTON	99.1	99.0	0.1	0.1	0.2	0.3	0.5	0.6	6.0	6.2	6.9	6.7	6.4	25.9	24.8	14.2	2.9	76.9	39.9	48.6	51.4
62449	OBLONG	98.5	98.2	0.5	0.5	0.1	0.2	0.5	0.6	5.6	5.8	6.6	7.0	6.2	25.8	24.6	15.1	3.2	77.2	40.8	49.0	51.0
62450	OLNEY	97.9	97.5	0.4	0.4	0.7	0.9	0.9	1.0	6.2	6.1	6.4	6.5	6.5	24.7	24.6	16.1	3.0	77.4	40.6	47.7	52.4
62451	PALESTINE	91.8	91.0	6.8	7.4	0.3	0.3	2.0	2.5	5.7	5.9	5.5	5.7	6.8	28.6	25.0	14.5	2.2	79.8	39.1	54.6	45.4
62452	PARKERSBURG	98.6	98.6	0.0	0.0	0.7	1.0	0.0	0.0	6.2	6.2	6.7	6.7	6.4	26.6	26.6	13.1	1.7	76.7	39.5	50.8	49.2
62454	ROBINSON	91.4	90.5	6.2	6.7	0.5	0.6	2.3	2.8	5.6	5.5	6.0	6.3	7.2	28.9	24.1	14.1	2.4	79.3	38.8	52.9	47.1
62458	SAINT ELMO	98.9	98.8	0.1	0.1	0.2	0.2	0.1	0.1	7.6	7.6	6.9	6.4	5.5	25.1	22.5	15.8	2.5	73.9	38.8	48.1	51.9
62460	SAINT FRANCISVILLE	98.8	98.6	0.1	0.1	0.1	0.1	0.3	0.4	5.5	5.7	7.1	5.8	7.1	25.8	27.8	13.5	1.7	78.2	40.4	49.8	50.2
62461	SHUMWAY	98.2	97.7	0.2	0.4	0.2	0.4	0.0	0.2	7.5	7.8	8.2	6.6	5.7	26.2	26.3	10.3	1.4	72.2	37.3	52.3	47.7
62462	SIGEL	98.8	98.5	0.0	0.0	0.3	0.5	0.7	1.0	7.4	8.2	10.1	8.4	6.6	27.2	20.6	10.5	1.0	69.2	33.5	51.4	48.7
62463	STEWARDSON	99.5	99.4	0.0	0.0	0.1	0.2	0.2	0.2	7.1	6.8	6.6	6.2	7.3	24.9	24.8	13.8	2.6	76.1	38.3	50.4	49.6
62465	STRASBURG	99.3	99.3	0.2	0.2	0.1	0.1	0.1	0.1	4.4	5.4	7.7	6.7	5.6	22.4	25.4	16.1	6.4	78.3	43.6	47.5	52.5
62466	SUMNER	98.0	97.8	1.1	1.2	0.0	0.0	0.6	0.7	5.3	5.6	6.6	6.4	6.1	25.5	26.7	15.3	2.5	78.7	41.2	49.0	51.0
62467	TEUTOPOLIS	99.7	99.7	0.0	0.0	0.1	0.1	0.5	0.6	7.9	7.7	9.0	8.8	7.1	26.7	21.5	10.0	1.5	69.7	33.2	51.5	48.6
62468	TOLEDO	99.1	98.9	0.0	0.1	0.0	0.1	0.5	0.6	6.0	6.1	7.6	7.3	6.8	27.2	24.6	12.2	2.2	75.6	37.8	48.9	51.1
62469	TRILLA	97.5	97.2	1.4	1.5	0.5	0.7	0.9	1.0	6.7	6.1	6.2	7.0	10.1	28.4	23.7	10.3	1.5	76.8	34.9	50.5	49.5
62471	VANDALIA	88.4	87.5	10.3	10.9	0.2	0.3	1.4	1.7	6.1	5.8	5.7	6.2	8.1	31.3	21.5	12.8	2.5	79.1	36.6	55.3	44.7
62473	WATSON	98.9	98.7	0.0	0.0	0.3	0.4	0.5	0.6	7.6	7.7	8.6	7.0	6.8	29.0	24.2	8.1	1.1	71.9	34.2	50.8	49.2
62474	WESTFIELD	98.1	98.0	0.4	0.4	0.3	0.3	0.4	0.4	6.5	6.9	7.8	6.3	5.7	25.6	26.2	13.5	1.6	75.0	39.7	50.3	49.7
62475	WEST LIBERTY	100.0	100.0	0.0	0.0	0.0	0.0	0.4	0.4	6.1	6.8	6.4	8.2	5.7	27.1	23.8	13.5	2.5	75.4	39.0	48.8	51.3
62476	WEST SALEM	98.6	98.6	0.3	0.3	0.3	0.4	0.3	0.3	5.8	6.3	7.0	5.7	5.5	25.9	27.0	14.9	2.0	77.4	40.5	50.0	50.0
62477	WEST UNION	99.1	99.1	0.1	0.1	0.0	0.0	0.1	0.1	6.0	6.1	6.8	6.4	5.9	24.7	27.5	14.3	2.2	77.3	40.9	52.3	47.7
62478	WEST YORK	98.4	98.3	0.4	0.4	0.2	0.4	0.8	0.8	4.6	5.4	7.7	6.5	6.1	25.7	30.7	11.7	1.7	77.9	41.3	52.6	47.4
62479	WHEELER	99.4	99.3	0.0	0.0	0.1	0.1	0.5	0.7	6.5	6.6	7.2	7.4	6.9	28.1	24.1	11.9	1.4	75.2	37.3	52.3	47.8
62480	WILLOW HILL	98.8	98.5	0.0	0.0	0.5	0.7	0.5	0.5	6.0	6.1	7.4	8.2	6.0	25.8	24.9	13.7	1.9	75.3	39.2	50.5	49.6
62481	YALE	98.8	98.6	0.2	0.2	0.0	0.0	1.2	1.4	5.3	5.3	8.1	6.9	6.5	28.1	27.0	11.1	1.8	76.7	39.9	50.9	49.1
62501	ARGENTA	98.3	98.1	0.5	0.5	0.2	0.2	0.3	0.5	5.3	5.9	8.1	7.8	5.0	25.7	29.6	11.6	1.1	75.7	40.7	50.0	50.0
62510	ASSUMPTION	99.6	99.6	0.1	0.1	0.2	0.2	0.2	0.2	6.0	6.2	7.7	6.8	6.3	26.0	24.1	13.9	3.0	75.9	39.9	47.6	52.4
62512	BEASON	99.6	99.6	0.2	0.2	0.0	0.0	0.2	0.4	6.0	6.9	8.8	7.1	6.0	26.0	26.7	11.0	1.5	73.8	38.8	50.5	49.5
62513	BLUE MOUND	99.5	99.3	0.1	0.1	0.0	0.0	0.2	0.4	6.3	6.7	7.3	5.6	5.5	28.0	26.3	12.6	1.8	76.2	39.2	48.7	51.3
62514	BOODY	99.4	100.0	0.0	0.0	0.0	0.0	0.6	0.7	5.2	5.8	7.7	5.8	4.5	26.5	31.0	12.3	1.3	77.4	41.7	51.6	48.4
62515	BUFFALO	98.0	97.7	0.4	0.4	0.2	0.3	0.5	0.6	6.0	6.5	7.0	6.9	5.8	27.6	29.2	10.2	0.9	76.0	39.4	49.2	50.8
62517	BULPITT	99.5	100.0	0.0	0.0	0.0	0.0	0.0	0.0	7.2	10.1	7.2	4.8	4.3	24.5	25.5	13.9	2.4	72.6	39.2	50.0	50.0
62518	CHESTNUT	98.7	98.2	0.4	0.7	0.0	0.0	0.7	0.7	6.0	6.4	7.7	6.2	6.2	24.1	27.8	13.9	1.8	75.9	41.0	50.6	49.5
62520	DAWSON	98.0	97.7	0.4	0.5	0.2	0.3	0.6	0.7	5.6	6.1	6.9	7.0	5.7	26.0	31.7	10.2	0.9	76.8	40.9	49.1	50.9
62521	DECATUR	83.0	81.8	14.6	15.5	0.6	0.7	0.9	1.1	6.3	6.4	7.0	6.5	5.7	24.7	27.3	14.3	1.8	76.3	40.5	47.9	52.1
62522	DECATUR	73.2	71.3	23.8	25.4	0.5	0.7	1.0	1.2	5.9	5.9	6.2	11.1	14.0	22.8	22.0	10.1	2.0	78.5	31.4	47.0	53.1
62523	DECATUR	42.5	38.6	54.4	58.0	0.2	0.2	1.8	1.9	4.0	4.6	3.0	7.6	12.0	35.4	18.4	12.6	2.5	84.4	33.6	65.4	34.6
62526	DECATUR	81.5	79.5	15.5	17.0	0.8	0.9	1.3	1.6	6.7	6.5	6.6	6.1	6.1	25.4	25.0	14.8	2.8	76.5	39.4	46.6	53.5
62530	DIVERNON	98.7	98.5	0.3	0.4	0.1	0.1	1.4	1.7	6.7	6.6	7.2	6.2	6.2	29.8	25.3	10.9	1.1	75.9	38.1	48.7	51.3
62531	EDINBURG	99.0	98.7	0.1	0.3	0.1	0.2	0.5	0.6	6.3	6.8	7.4	5.3	5.1	26.1	28.0	13.3	1.9	76.2	40.7	49.3	50.7
62533	FARMERSVILLE	97.8	97.5	0.6	0.7	1.0	1.2	0.5	0.6	8.1	7.8	6.9	5.3	5.8	28.2	25.1	11.4	1.6	74.1	37.5	48.4	51.6
62534	FINDLAY	98.7	98.7	0.4	0.5	0.2	0.2	0.7	0.8	5.5	6.0	7.1	6.1	5.7	24.5	27.6	16.1	1.5	77.7	41.5	49.2	50.8
62535	FORSYTH	96.6	95.9	1.7	2.0	1.3	1.6	0.8	1.0	5.6	6.9	8.8	6.5	4.0	22.4	31.5	13.0	1.4	74.2	42.6	48.8	51.2
62536	GLENARM	98.6	98.4	0.4	0.5	0.1	0.1	0.9	1.1	6.1	5.7	8.7	7.0	4.2	26.7	34.8	6.1	0.7	75.2	40.6	52.2	47.8
62538	HARVEL	98.7	98.8	0.2	0.2	0.2	0.2	0.4	0.7	5.6	6.0	6.7	6.5	6.5	24.4	30.2	12.3	1.9	77.7	41.3	50.8	49.2
62539	ILLIOPOLIS	98.7	98.5	0.5	0.5	0.0	0.0	0.2	0.2	6.4	6.3	7.0	6.1	6.9	28.2	26.6	11.7	0.6	76.6	37.6	48.7	51.3
62543	LATHAM	99.6	99.6	0.0	0.0	0.2	0.2	0.2	0.2	5.1	5.7	7.8	6.3	5.5	25.4	28.8	13.7	1.6	77.5	41.2	49.5	50.5
62544	MACON	99.0	98.8	0.2	0.2	0.3	0.4	0.5	0.6	5.4	6.0	7.4	6.7	6.0	24.8	26.8	13.5	3.5	76.8	41.0	48.5	51.5
62545	MECHANICSBURG	98.4	98.1	0.5	0.5	0.3	0.4	0.3	0.4	6.5	7.1	7.7	6.6	5.9	28.0	26.4	11.0	0.8	74.7	38.1	50.4	49.6
62546	MORRISONVILLE	98.5	98.3	0.2	0.2	0.5	0.6	0.9	1.0	5.7	6.0	7.6	7.4	6.1	23.8	26.2	15.1	2.1	76.1	40.7	50.3	49.7
62547	MOUNT AUBURN	98.7	98.3	0.0	0.0	0.3	0.3	0.3	0.4	4.1	5.1	7.1	5.7	4.4	27.8	30.6	13.6	1.7	80.3	42.5	48.7	51.3
62548	MOUNT PULASKI	98.5	98.4	1.1	1.1	0.0	0.0	0.5	0.7	6.0	6.2	6.7	6.4	5.6	23.8	24.0	16.6	4.7	77.1	41.7	47.9	52.1
62549	MT ZION	98.2	97.8	0.2	0.3	0.7	0.9	0.3	0.4	5.6	6.2	8.0	7.1	5.7	26.4	30.0	9.8	1.3	75.4	39.7	50.4	49.6
62550	MOWEAQUA	98.7	98.5	0.2	0.2	0.2	0.3	0.5	0.5	6.1	6.4	7.3	6.0	5.3	25.3	26.0	14.1	3.3	76.5	40.9	47.7	52.3
62551	NIANTIC	99.1	99.0	0.3	0.3	0.0	0.0	0.3	0.6	7.7	7.3	7.7	8.1	6.2	26.4	23.8	10.8	2.1	72.4	36.3	48.9	51.1
62553	OCONEE	98.6	98.3	0.1	0.1	0.8	1.0	0.5	0.6	5.8	6.2	8.3	6.3	5.7	25.6	26.1	14.5	1.5	75.8	40.0	50.7	49.3
62554	OREANA	98.4	98.2	0.4	0.4	0.2	0.3	0.5	0.6	5.7	6.2	7.0	6.4	5.4	25.5	31.2	11.5	1.1	77.0	41.5	50.9	49.1
62555	OWANECO	66.1	63.3	28.1	30.3	0.4	0.4	7.0	8.2	3.0	3.2	3.4	5.2	9.5	47.6	21.4	6.1	0.7	88.1	36.8	76.7	23.4
62556	PALMER	97.8	97.6	0.2	0.2	0.4	0.7	0.4	0.2	6.2	6.9	7.5	6.9	5.8	24.3	26.9	14.0	1.5	75.1	39.8	51.4	48.6
62557	PANA	98.5	98.2	0.6	0.6	0.3	0.4	0.6	0.8	6.6	6.3	6.8	6.3	6.3	23.9	23.7	16.3	3.8	76.2	40.6	48.2	51.8
62558	PAWNEE	98.7	98.4	0.3	0.3	0.2	0.2	0.3	0.4	6.7	6.7	7.5	7.2	6.1	29.7	24.8	9.7	1.5	74.7	37.2	48.7	51.3
62560	RAYMOND	99.3	99.3	0.2	0.2	0.1	0.1	0.2	0.2	6.6	7.0	6.8	6.1	6.1	25.9	24.6	14.3	2.6	76.0	39.5	48.7	51.4
62561	RIVERTON	98.7	98.4	0.3	0.3	0.1	0.1	0.8	1.0	6.0	7.0	7.6	7.5	6.2	28.7	27.0	8.9	1.1	74.5	37.3	49.3	50.7
62563	ROCHESTER	98.0	97.6	0.6	0.7	0.4	0.5	0.5	0.6	4.5	6.3	9.0	7.9	4.7	24.3	33.0	9.3	1.1	74.9	41.4	49.9	50.1
62565	SHELBYVILLE	98.7	98.5	0.2	0.2	0.3	0.4	0.7	0.9	5.7	5.9	6.5	6.4	5.8	24.9	25.2	16.7	3.0	78.0	41.6	48.9	51.1
62567	STONINGTON	99.3	99.1	0.2	0.3	0.1	0.1	0.7	0.8	7.9	8.0	7.2	6.5	4.0	25.5	24.2	14.5	2.2	72.8	38.8	48.7	51.3
62568	TAYLORVILLE	95.2	94.6	2.9	3.1	0.5	0.6	1.2	1.4	6.0	6.1	6.6	6.3	6.1	27.6	24.7	13.7	2.9	77.3	39.5	50.7	49.3
62571	TOWER HILL	99.1	99.0	0.1	0.1	0.1	0.1	0.3	0.3	6.4	6.5	7.5	6.6	6.0	26.4	25.0	14.2	1.4	75.4	39.0	50.0	50.0
62572	WAGGONER	99.3	99.5	0.0	0.0	0.0	0.0	0.0	0.0	7.6	8.3	7.6	5.5	6.9	27.2	25.4	10.1	1.4	72.8	35.9	51.8	48.2
62573	WARRENSBURG	97.8	97.4	0.7	0.8	0.2	0.3	0.4	0.6	6.5	6.5	8.1	7.9	5.6	27.9	27.8	8.8	1.0	73.5	36.8	49.9	50.1
62601	ALEXANDER	97.9	97.6	0.4	0.6	0.0	0.0	0.9	0.9	5.1	6.6	7.9	8.1	5.3	27.8	26.7	11.1	1.5	75.2	39.6	49.6	50.4
	ILLINOIS	73.5	71.8	15.1	15.2	3.5	4.0	12.3	14.2	7.1	7.0	7.3	7.0	7.3	29.0	23.2	10.4	1.7	74.5	35.2	49.0	51.0
	UNITED STATES	75.1	73.6	12.3	12.5	3.8	4.2	12.5	14.1	6.9	6.7	7.2	7.0	7.3	28.6	23.8	10.8	1.7	75.1	36.0	49.1	50.9

Copyright © 2004 ESRI BIS. All rights reserved. Reproduction by any method is prohibited.

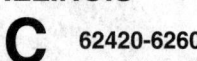

ZIP CODE #	POST OFFICE NAME	2004 Per Capita Income	2004 HH Income Base	2004 Household Income Distribution (%): Less than $25,000	$25,000 to $49,999	$50,000 to $99,999	$100,000 to $149,999	$150,000 or More	Median Household Income: 2004	2009	2004 National Centile	2004 State Centile	2004 Home Value Base	2004 Home Value Distribution (%): Less than $50,000	$50,000 to $89,999	$90,000 to $174,999	$175,000 to $399,999	$400,000 or More	2004 Median Home Value
62420	CASEY	18598	2156	35.1	31.9	26.4	5.7	1.0	36747	40405	34	19	1716	27.7	30.5	36.4	5.4	0.0	79516
62421	CLAREMONT	15016	369	33.6	39.8	23.9	2.4	0.3	35077	39219	28	13	319	30.4	20.4	34.8	13.8	0.6	88077
62422	COWDEN	15205	578	40.1	31.1	24.4	2.9	1.4	31935	34676	18	7	495	41.0	32.1	23.6	3.2	0.0	58241
62423	DENNISON	19449	273	19.1	43.6	31.1	5.1	1.1	39905	45000	46	29	239	18.8	20.9	39.8	18.4	2.1	109583
62424	DIETERICH	17865	673	18.4	34.9	38.8	6.2	1.6	47827	53091	68	57	587	13.6	24.9	47.4	13.8	0.3	103726
62425	DUNDAS	12848	228	43.4	39.9	14.9	1.8	0.0	27893	31413	8	3	198	32.3	40.9	19.7	4.0	3.0	69091
62426	EDGEWOOD	17752	322	32.0	36.0	28.6	2.2	1.2	35708	39413	30	15	276	43.5	22.8	23.9	8.3	1.5	62143
62427	FLAT ROCK	17636	842	31.0	36.2	26.3	4.2	2.4	36693	40289	34	18	750	35.7	31.2	26.9	5.2	0.9	67576
62428	GREENUP	19115	1311	34.8	36.0	25.3	2.1	1.8	35593	38863	30	14	1055	22.5	37.5	33.8	6.0	0.2	82518
62431	HERRICK	15885	271	38.0	34.7	22.9	2.6	1.9	32189	35122	18	7	230	42.6	34.4	17.4	4.4	1.3	60526
62432	HIDALGO	19033	235	22.1	44.3	30.6	1.3	1.7	37789	43547	38	22	201	31.8	25.4	30.9	11.0	1.0	78077
62433	HUTSONVILLE	19564	397	30.0	35.3	27.2	5.5	2.0	38076	42234	40	23	322	38.2	29.2	28.0	4.4	0.3	63182
62434	INGRAHAM	16571	311	28.9	33.4	30.2	6.1	1.3	38419	41834	41	24	282	36.2	20.2	32.3	11.4	0.0	76667
62436	JEWETT	17346	189	30.7	31.8	32.3	4.2	1.1	36326	39064	33	17	158	22.8	32.3	34.8	8.9	1.3	83333
62438	LAKEWOOD	20454	164	23.8	33.5	33.5	6.1	3.1	43902	47127	58	45	144	25.7	24.3	36.1	13.2	0.7	90000
62439	LAWRENCEVILLE	21583	3124	38.7	30.9	22.9	4.5	3.1	32524	35412	19	7	2297	38.7	31.1	23.6	5.9	0.8	60587
62440	LERNA	25899	533	20.8	25.3	37.7	10.7	5.4	52802	59128	77	69	487	18.7	13.1	37.4	28.5	2.3	120673
62441	MARSHALL	22283	3225	29.5	31.1	31.2	5.0	3.2	41524	45419	51	35	2484	18.9	28.1	41.2	10.9	0.9	93606
62442	MARTINSVILLE	17632	837	34.2	34.8	25.7	4.4	1.0	35347	38590	29	13	689	35.9	31.9	26.1	6.1	0.0	68750
62443	MASON	16143	742	26.6	36.5	31.5	3.9	1.5	40715	45391	49	33	637	29.8	22.0	36.6	10.7	0.9	86618
62445	MONTROSE	18135	448	25.0	28.1	38.4	6.0	2.5	46701	50583	66	55	385	15.3	25.2	36.4	19.2	3.9	107598
62446	MOUNT ERIE	16317	168	38.7	31.0	27.4	3.0	0.0	31904	35000	18	6	141	35.5	26.2	26.2	8.5	3.6	71667
62447	NEOGA	19920	1431	22.9	35.0	35.4	4.9	1.8	45202	49037	62	49	1230	16.8	25.9	44.3	12.2	0.9	99192
62448	NEWTON	18520	2458	33.2	29.5	31.6	4.8	0.9	37004	41060	35	20	2001	23.4	31.4	37.7	7.2	0.4	84212
62449	OBLONG	17257	1291	33.6	36.3	25.6	4.1	0.5	34436	38020	26	11	1071	34.9	34.0	26.6	3.6	0.8	66308
62450	OLNEY	20222	4901	36.9	30.2	25.6	5.0	2.4	34020	37896	24	10	3797	25.6	30.7	32.6	9.2	1.9	82660
62451	PALESTINE	19757	934	35.2	36.9	23.1	3.8	1.0	34615	37506	26	12	763	39.6	36.0	20.8	3.0	0.5	61250
62452	PARKERSBURG	20642	185	35.1	30.8	28.1	4.3	1.6	36808	40000	35	19	160	38.1	25.6	27.5	8.8	0.0	67500
62454	ROBINSON	19105	4320	32.3	34.0	25.8	5.4	2.5	35621	40157	30	15	3441	26.0	37.3	28.7	7.0	0.9	75251
62458	SAINT ELMO	16211	747	37.4	30.7	28.8	2.4	0.8	34377	36943	25	11	620	36.3	33.9	23.2	6.5	0.2	65085
62460	SAINT FRANCISVILLE	17173	685	31.7	39.7	23.4	3.4	1.9	33879	37985	24	10	567	48.2	27.9	20.8	3.2	0.0	52561
62461	SHUMWAY	22344	203	27.6	35.0	28.6	4.4	4.4	41744	46922	52	36	173	16.2	20.2	28.9	27.8	6.9	119643
62462	SIGEL	17131	452	23.0	35.8	32.5	6.2	2.4	44355	48843	60	46	383	14.4	22.5	41.0	17.2	5.0	111806
62463	STEWARDSON	18538	512	27.2	37.1	30.5	3.3	2.0	40000	44389	46	30	412	23.5	33.3	33.5	8.7	1.0	82432
62465	STRASBURG	18776	323	23.8	34.7	35.0	4.6	1.9	45077	46569	61	49	293	11.3	25.3	51.9	11.6	0.0	101372
62466	SUMNER	16108	732	36.5	34.7	24.7	2.7	1.4	33852	37086	24	10	606	45.2	32.8	17.0	4.5	0.5	54915
62467	TEUTOPOLIS	21378	1039	20.5	26.4	39.0	8.3	5.9	51994	58052	75	67	888	7.0	18.8	52.4	19.8	2.0	120859
62468	TOLEDO	19144	1078	28.9	34.9	31.5	3.3	1.5	38670	42514	42	25	911	21.7	29.1	37.4	11.3	0.4	89038
62469	TRILLA	19342	219	27.4	32.0	33.3	4.1	3.2	41873	47352	53	37	178	20.2	28.1	33.7	18.0	0.0	93000
62471	VANDALIA	17541	3709	35.5	32.9	26.2	3.7	1.8	35187	37668	28	13	2888	22.1	37.0	33.1	7.2	0.6	82202
62473	WATSON	18464	435	19.1	37.0	37.2	4.4	2.3	45992	50892	64	52	382	14.1	30.1	43.7	11.0	1.1	97097
62474	WESTFIELD	17874	425	26.4	42.1	26.8	3.5	1.2	39113	43442	43	26	361	33.0	28.0	32.7	5.8	0.6	72143
62475	WEST LIBERTY	16586	102	22.6	42.2	30.4	3.9	1.0	40986	45994	50	34	91	20.9	31.9	35.2	11.0	1.1	86429
62476	WEST SALEM	18116	895	30.3	38.7	26.6	3.5	1.0	35976	39309	31	16	768	41.0	34.5	20.7	2.6	1.2	59857
62477	WEST UNION	17903	427	31.9	30.2	32.8	4.9	0.2	35919	38876	31	16	366	42.6	29.5	25.7	2.2	0.0	61500
62478	WEST YORK	23384	191	24.1	28.3	34.6	10.0	3.1	47375	49612	67	56	169	27.8	27.2	34.9	9.5	0.6	85000
62479	WHEELER	18321	319	27.6	26.3	37.6	8.2	0.3	46741	50803	66	55	276	21.0	19.9	43.1	15.2	0.7	103889
62480	WILLOW HILL	19176	524	31.1	35.7	27.7	3.4	2.1	37540	42685	38	21	457	30.2	25.0	33.9	10.1	0.9	83088
62481	YALE	22495	164	28.7	35.4	31.7	1.2	3.1	38502	41618	41	25	141	29.8	27.7	38.3	4.3	0.0	75909
62501	ARGENTA	24594	1023	15.1	28.4	43.7	10.2	2.7	55373	63052	80	75	901	10.1	34.7	33.6	20.1	1.4	96940
62510	ASSUMPTION	22849	805	28.2	34.8	30.6	4.0	2.5	41228	46437	51	35	641	26.5	42.3	26.5	4.5	0.2	66802
62512	BEASON	19273	161	19.9	31.7	38.5	9.9	0.0	48852	54478	70	60	129	14.7	31.0	35.7	12.4	6.2	94583
62513	BLUE MOUND	23423	684	20.3	27.8	41.1	8.5	2.3	50886	57216	74	65	581	23.8	40.3	27.4	7.8	0.9	76554
62514	BOODY	24458	59	18.6	20.3	44.1	11.9	5.1	60558	67521	85	82	53	22.6	17.0	30.2	24.5	5.7	112500
62515	BUFFALO	23736	368	20.7	23.9	41.9	10.9	2.7	54778	63034	79	73	314	18.5	28.0	41.7	10.5	1.3	93667
62517	BULPITT	20568	99	36.4	31.3	28.3	4.0	0.0	35270	40316	29	13	82	31.7	31.7	32.9	3.7	0.0	70000
62518	CHESTNUT	23441	181	17.7	24.9	46.4	9.4	1.7	53713	61050	78	71	152	11.2	34.2	44.7	5.3	4.6	98750
62520	DAWSON	26457	559	15.9	24.7	43.8	12.3	3.2	59065	65586	84	80	482	14.9	21.6	45.2	16.6	1.7	109848
62521	DECATUR	24652	15460	25.5	31.1	31.7	7.7	3.9	44346	50508	60	46	12099	24.8	33.8	31.8	8.4	1.2	80505
62522	DECATUR	20955	7197	37.1	27.7	27.1	6.0	2.2	35087	39592	28	13	4544	29.3	37.5	27.9	4.3	1.0	70864
62523	DECATUR	12606	124	75.0	21.8	3.2	0.0	0.0	12728	15329	1	0	20	70.0	30.0	0.0	0.0	0.0	47143
62526	DECATUR	21886	16276	33.7	31.4	25.8	6.3	2.8	36278	41225	33	17	11168	33.5	32.9	27.8	5.6	0.3	71461
62530	DIVERNON	24926	610	13.4	34.6	38.5	10.2	3.3	51478	59691	75	66	501	11.0	33.1	47.9	7.2	0.8	94338
62531	EDINBURG	21578	888	21.6	37.6	33.2	5.5	2.0	42664	47056	55	40	751	19.4	28.1	40.5	11.3	0.7	93190
62533	FARMERSVILLE	21025	418	25.1	32.5	32.8	7.7	1.9	40589	44423	48	32	349	14.9	40.7	35.8	8.0	0.6	85125
62534	FINDLAY	20349	573	27.6	36.3	28.8	5.8	1.6	38716	42799	42	25	463	26.6	31.8	34.6	5.8	1.3	81047
62535	FORSYTH	38955	784	15.3	19.4	32.3	16.1	17.0	74300	84552	93	93	707	1.1	11.9	42.2	40.3	4.5	162500
62536	GLENARM	28602	360	6.7	21.4	45.3	19.2	7.5	71698	82247	92	91	338	1.5	9.5	62.1	24.0	3.0	138806
62538	HARVEL	19039	171	22.8	45.6	22.8	7.6	1.2	36425	41170	33	18	143	23.8	19.6	44.1	10.5	2.1	102404
62539	ILLIOPOLIS	24777	499	12.6	29.9	46.1	7.8	3.6	55324	63442	80	74	414	16.2	46.1	33.1	4.4	0.2	78000
62543	LATHAM	25006	203	20.7	22.7	42.4	11.8	2.5	54867	61003	80	74	169	9.5	42.6	39.6	7.1	1.2	88833
62544	MACON	23157	671	21.9	30.6	36.1	8.6	2.8	46940	55468	66	55	560	18.4	41.4	33.4	6.1	0.7	79481
62545	MECHANICSBURG	22288	437	23.6	28.2	37.3	8.7	2.3	48591	54413	69	59	381	22.1	30.7	36.5	10.5	0.3	87237
62546	MORRISONVILLE	21769	652	25.5	33.1	31.3	7.2	2.9	42574	45825	55	40	538	19.5	35.5	39.0	4.3	1.7	84490
62547	MOUNT AUBURN	22978	312	14.1	39.1	40.1	6.1	0.6	46330	52251	65	54	271	27.3	31.0	30.3	10.3	1.1	77941
62548	MOUNT PULASKI	21905	990	22.8	33.5	35.3	7.3	1.1	45715	50775	63	51	807	8.8	32.7	50.6	7.3	0.6	97611
62549	MT ZION	26623	2167	17.9	22.1	42.5	13.9	3.7	61370	68779	86	83	1855	2.5	22.9	61.3	12.5	0.8	108675
62550	MOWEAQUA	22225	1239	20.7	31.5	37.0	8.6	2.3	48030	52125	68	58	1032	18.4	24.5	45.3	9.8	2.0	98795
62551	NIANTIC	22131	326	19.0	32.8	39.9	6.1	2.2	48770	56499	70	60	273	16.9	42.5	33.0	7.3	0.4	83108
62553	OCONEE	17536	339	23.0	39.8	34.8	1.2	1.2	42228	47313	54	38	301	20.6	31.2	33.9	13.0	1.3	88036
62554	OREANA	24761	652	15.2	25.5	42.5	13.5	3.4	58069	65775	83	79	574	8.7	36.6	40.6	13.4	0.7	94821
62555	OWANECO	29267	215	18.1	30.7	40.9	8.4	1.9	50859	56347	74	65	182	20.3	28.6	35.7	12.1	3.3	92500
62556	PALMER	21622	166	26.5	28.9	32.5	7.2	4.8	43790	48655	58	45	135	20.7	30.4	35.6	9.6	3.7	88125
62557	PANA	18372	2998	34.8	38.4	21.2	3.5	2.1	34583	38124	26	12	2244	31.8	35.4	26.0	6.7	0.1	67822
62558	PAWNEE	24318	1278	17.2	27.3	41.2	10.6	3.8	54993	63424	80	74	1070	13.6	36.2	44.6	5.3	0.3	90134
62560	RAYMOND	19631	582	26.0	37.3	28.5	6.5	1.7	40262	44737	47	31	485	28.0	33.0	31.8	6.8	0.4	75119
62561	RIVERTON	25359	1914	17.7	27.2	38.6	11.7	4.8	54056	61724	78	72	1594	13.7	25.7	52.4	7.8	0.4	98848
62563	ROCHESTER	31305	1935	11.0	24.1	40.4	15.5	8.9	66014	76654	89	88	1773	1.8	11.5	57.3	26.1	3.4	139140
62565	SHELBYVILLE	21261	3318	26.6	35.4	30.4	5.2	2.4	40022	44501	46	30	2634	18.6	28.7	41.9	9.7	1.1	93859
62567	STONINGTON	22098	498	25.7	30.3	33.7	7.8	2.4	45527	49788	63	50	403	25.3	30.3	35.5	7.2	1.7	81346
62568	TAYLORVILLE	20147	7203	29.7	32.4	29.9	6.1	2.0	40024	43665	46	30	5537	18.9	38.7	34.7	7.4	0.3	83404
62571	TOWER HILL	17071	614	29.6	37.1	29.0	3.3	1.0	36838	40585	35	19	524	38.9	28.6	26.0	6.3	0.2	65641
62572	WAGGONER	18357	167	23.4	40.1	30.5	6.0	0.0	41140	44745	50	34	142	40.9	35.2	21.8	1.4	0.7	61250
62573	WARRENSBURG	24735	726	13.6	28.5	44.6	9.9	3.3	54380	62515	79	72	600	8.8	35.8	42.3	12.0	1.0	95818
62601	ALEXANDER	20734	212	24.5	30.2	37.3	5.7	2.4	46309	49651	65	53	172	13.4	30.8	37.8	12.2	5.8	97143
	ILLINOIS	27033		22.1	25.9	32.9	11.9	7.3	52039	60941				7.7	12.8	34.0	36.6	8.9	162771
	UNITED STATES	25866		24.7	27.1	30.8	10.9	6.5	48124	56710				10.9	15.0	33.7	30.1	10.4	145905

ZIP CODE #	POST OFFICE NAME	FINANCIAL SERVICES: Auto Loan	Home Loan	Invest-ments	Retire-ment Plans	THE HOME: Home Improvements: Home Repair	Lawn & Garden	Furnishings: Comput-ers & Hard-ware	Major Appli-ances	TV, Radio, Sound Equip-ment	Furni-ture	ENTERTAINMENT: Dine out/ Carry out	Sports Equip-ment	Fees & Tickets	Toys & Games	Travel	Cable TV	PERSONAL: Apparel & Services	Auto Repairs	Health Insur-ance	Pets & Supplies
62420	CASEY	73	56	36	53	61	71	58	65	64	56	76	76	52	74	58	67	70	65	76	83
62421	CLAREMONT	70	49	27	47	57	65	50	60	57	49	67	72	43	65	51	60	61	60	72	82
62422	COWDEN	73	50	25	44	57	65	49	60	58	49	68	72	42	65	49	62	62	59	73	84
62423	DENNISON	79	71	54	67	75	80	65	72	69	65	84	86	64	86	67	71	80	70	78	93
62424	DIETERICH	79	80	74	80	80	82	76	78	74	76	92	93	76	93	75	72	90	77	74	91
62425	DUNDAS	55	41	26	39	45	54	45	50	50	43	59	56	40	56	45	53	54	50	60	61
62426	EDGEWOOD	67	55	40	54	58	66	56	61	60	55	73	70	53	72	56	62	68	60	68	75
62427	FLAT ROCK	80	60	35	55	67	74	57	69	65	57	77	82	51	76	59	69	71	68	80	94
62428	GREENUP	66	60	50	58	62	69	60	63	63	58	77	72	59	78	60	64	73	62	68	75
62431	HERRICK	56	58	65	60	58	61	59	59	57	58	71	69	59	70	58	55	69	59	57	65
62432	HIDALGO	82	58	31	55	67	75	57	70	65	56	77	84	49	75	59	69	70	69	83	97
62433	HUTSONVILLE	77	60	42	58	65	76	64	70	70	61	83	80	58	80	63	74	77	69	82	86
62434	INGRAHAM	79	64	43	60	69	76	60	69	67	61	80	83	57	80	62	69	75	68	78	92
62436	JEWETT	83	59	32	53	66	75	57	69	67	58	79	82	50	76	58	71	72	68	83	96
62438	LAKEWOOD	81	73	57	69	77	82	68	75	72	68	87	89	66	89	70	73	83	73	80	96
62439	LAWRENCEVILLE	75	62	49	60	67	77	65	71	71	63	85	81	61	83	66	74	79	71	81	86
62440	LERNA	101	99	85	96	102	107	91	97	92	91	113	115	91	117	93	93	109	94	100	120
62441	MARSHALL	83	72	57	68	77	85	70	77	75	69	91	90	68	92	72	78	86	76	86	97
62442	MARTINSVILLE	73	53	30	49	59	68	54	63	62	53	73	74	47	70	54	66	67	63	76	84
62443	MASON	73	64	49	62	67	74	62	68	66	62	81	79	60	81	63	68	76	66	74	84
62445	MONTROSE	85	74	55	70	79	85	69	77	74	69	89	91	67	91	71	76	85	75	84	100
62446	MOUNT ERIE	74	50	23	43	56	65	48	60	58	49	68	72	41	64	49	62	62	59	74	85
62447	NEOGA	84	74	56	71	78	84	69	77	74	69	90	91	68	91	71	76	85	75	83	97
62448	NEWTON	72	60	45	58	65	73	60	67	66	59	79	77	57	78	61	68	74	66	75	83
62449	OBLONG	64	57	46	52	60	67	55	60	60	54	73	69	54	74	56	63	69	59	68	75
62450	OLNEY	78	58	36	55	64	75	61	69	69	59	81	80	54	78	61	72	74	69	83	89
62451	PALESTINE	54	43	31	42	46	53	46	49	50	44	59	56	42	58	45	51	55	49	56	59
62452	PARKERSBURG	75	67	51	64	71	76	62	69	66	62	80	82	61	82	64	67	76	67	74	89
62454	ROBINSON	65	61	55	58	64	70	60	63	64	59	78	73	60	81	62	65	74	62	69	76
62458	SAINT ELMO	66	54	39	48	58	65	52	59	59	52	71	69	49	71	54	62	66	58	69	76
62460	SAINT FRANCISVILLE	64	59	50	56	62	68	57	61	60	56	74	71	56	77	59	63	70	60	67	75
62461	SHUMWAY	112	78	41	74	91	102	77	95	89	76	104	115	66	102	80	93	95	94	114	133
62462	SIGEL	83	74	56	70	78	84	68	76	73	68	88	90	67	90	70	75	84	74	82	98
62463	STEWARDSON	73	62	48	61	66	73	62	67	66	61	80	78	60	80	62	67	76	66	73	82
62465	STRASBURG	87	65	39	61	73	81	63	75	71	62	84	91	56	83	65	74	77	74	88	103
62466	SUMNER	66	51	34	49	55	64	53	59	58	51	69	68	48	67	53	61	64	59	68	74
62467	TEUTOPOLIS	103	93	72	89	98	104	86	95	91	86	111	113	85	113	89	93	106	93	102	121
62468	TOLEDO	79	62	41	58	67	75	61	69	68	61	81	81	56	79	61	70	75	68	79	90
62469	TRILLA	85	74	57	72	78	85	72	78	76	71	93	91	70	93	73	78	87	76	85	97
62471	VANDALIA	66	55	43	52	58	67	57	61	62	55	75	70	54	74	57	65	70	61	70	75
62473	WATSON	84	75	57	71	79	85	69	77	74	69	90	92	68	92	72	76	85	75	83	99
62474	WESTFIELD	80	56	30	53	65	73	55	68	63	55	75	82	47	73	57	67	68	67	81	95
62475	WEST LIBERTY	79	57	33	54	64	74	59	69	67	57	79	81	51	76	60	70	72	69	83	91
62476	WEST SALEM	71	58	42	53	62	70	56	63	63	56	76	74	53	76	57	66	71	62	73	82
62477	WEST UNION	78	57	32	51	63	71	54	65	63	55	74	78	48	72	55	66	68	64	77	90
62478	WEST YORK	94	84	64	79	88	95	77	86	82	77	100	102	76	102	80	84	95	83	93	111
62479	WHEELER	80	71	54	67	75	80	66	73	70	66	85	87	64	87	68	71	81	71	79	94
62480	WILLOW HILL	79	66	48	63	71	79	65	72	70	64	85	84	62	84	66	73	79	71	81	91
62481	YALE	96	85	64	80	90	96	78	87	83	78	101	104	77	103	81	86	96	85	95	113
62501	ARGENTA	95	91	77	87	94	100	84	90	87	84	106	107	84	110	86	88	102	88	95	112
62510	ASSUMPTION	84	71	55	70	76	86	73	79	79	71	95	90	69	93	73	81	88	78	88	95
62512	BEASON	89	79	60	75	84	90	73	81	78	73	95	97	72	97	76	80	90	79	88	105
62513	BLUE MOUND	92	83	65	80	88	94	77	85	81	77	99	101	76	101	79	83	94	83	91	109
62514	BOODY	83	104	110	104	102	100	93	92	86	92	108	108	98	115	95	83	108	89	83	102
62515	BUFFALO	81	95	98	93	94	95	86	87	82	86	103	101	91	109	88	81	102	84	81	98
62517	BULPITT	56	60	64	57	61	68	60	59	62	57	77	66	63	83	62	64	74	58	63	65
62518	CHESTNUT	94	84	64	79	88	95	77	86	82	77	100	102	76	102	80	84	95	83	93	111
62520	DAWSON	84	104	112	102	102	102	94	93	88	93	111	108	100	118	96	86	111	90	85	102
62521	DECATUR	79	82	86	79	82	90	81	82	83	80	103	93	84	106	83	85	100	81	85	92
62522	DECATUR	68	65	73	65	65	72	71	68	73	69	90	80	71	90	70	72	87	71	69	77
62523	DECATUR	22	19	28	20	19	23	24	22	25	23	32	26	24	31	24	26	31	24	24	24
62526	DECATUR	65	68	74	66	68	74	69	68	70	68	86	78	70	89	70	70	84	68	69	76
62530	DIVERNON	78	96	104	95	94	95	88	87	83	87	104	101	93	110	90	81	103	84	79	95
62531	EDINBURG	91	69	42	65	77	86	67	79	75	66	89	95	60	88	69	78	82	78	92	108
62533	FARMERSVILLE	82	68	50	67	72	81	69	76	74	68	90	87	65	89	69	76	84	75	84	92
62534	FINDLAY	77	62	43	59	66	76	64	70	70	62	83	81	59	81	64	73	77	70	81	87
62535	FORSYTH	136	169	179	169	166	163	151	150	140	150	175	176	160	187	154	135	175	145	134	166
62536	GLENARM	106	132	140	132	129	128	117	117	109	117	137	137	125	146	120	106	137	113	105	129
62538	HARVEL	86	61	32	57	70	79	60	74	69	59	81	89	51	79	62	73	74	73	88	102
62539	ILLIOPOLIS	88	89	84	88	90	97	87	89	88	86	108	103	88	111	88	88	104	88	91	102
62543	LATHAM	96	86	66	82	91	97	79	88	84	79	103	105	78	105	82	86	98	86	95	113
62544	MACON	82	81	76	79	83	91	80	82	83	78	102	94	81	106	81	85	98	81	87	94
62545	MECHANICSBURG	86	83	69	80	86	90	76	82	78	76	96	97	76	99	78	79	92	80	85	102
62546	MORRISONVILLE	98	68	36	65	80	89	68	84	78	67	91	101	58	89	70	82	83	82	99	116
62547	MOUNT AUBURN	83	74	56	70	78	84	69	76	73	69	89	91	67	90	71	75	84	74	82	98
62548	MOUNT PULASKI	70	72	72	69	74	81	70	72	72	68	89	81	72	93	72	74	86	70	76	83
62549	MT ZION	89	111	118	111	109	108	99	99	92	99	116	116	106	124	102	90	116	96	89	109
62550	MOWEAQUA	92	74	51	71	81	91	74	84	81	72	96	98	68	95	75	84	90	83	95	107
62551	NIANTIC	93	80	62	79	85	94	80	87	85	79	103	100	77	103	80	87	97	85	94	105
62553	OCONEE	75	66	51	63	70	75	61	68	65	61	79	81	60	81	63	67	75	66	74	88
62554	OREANA	94	98	94	95	100	104	91	95	91	91	113	111	94	118	94	92	110	92	95	112
62555	OWANECO	10	7	4	7	9	10	7	9	8	7	10	11	6	10	7	9	9	9	11	12
62556	PALMER	104	78	49	74	89	99	77	92	87	76	103	109	69	103	80	91	95	90	107	123
62557	PANA	65	54	44	52	58	67	57	61	62	55	75	70	54	75	58	65	70	61	70	74
62558	PAWNEE	87	93	92	93	94	98	88	90	86	87	107	104	91	111	89	86	105	88	87	102
62560	RAYMOND	86	63	37	60	72	80	61	74	70	61	82	89	54	81	64	73	76	73	87	102
62561	RIVERTON	85	100	105	99	97	98	92	92	87	92	110	107	96	114	93	84	109	90	83	101
62563	ROCHESTER	108	133	140	133	130	129	119	119	111	119	139	140	126	148	122	107	139	115	106	131
62565	SHELBYVILLE	73	67	58	64	70	79	67	71	71	65	87	81	66	88	68	74	82	70	79	84
62567	STONINGTON	83	71	55	69	75	85	74	79	79	71	94	90	69	92	74	82	88	78	89	94
62568	TAYLORVILLE	69	67	63	65	69	76	67	69	70	65	85	79	67	87	68	71	81	68	74	80
62571	TOWER HILL	75	59	39	54	64	71	56	65	63	56	75	78	52	74	57	65	70	64	74	87
62572	WAGGONER	78	67	49	64	71	77	63	70	67	62	81	84	60	82	64	69	77	69	77	91
62573	WARRENSBURG	85	96	98	93	95	99	88	90	87	88	108	105	92	114	91	86	106	88	87	103
62601	ALEXANDER	94	66	34	62	77	86	65	80	75	64	88	97	55	86	67	79	80	79	96	112
	ILLINOIS	98	100	111	99	99	106	100	99	101	100	126	115	102	127	100	100	123	100	98	112
	UNITED STATES	100	100	100	100	100	100	100	100	100	100	100	100	100	100	100	100	100	100	100	100

# POST OFFICE NAME	COUNTY FIPS CODE	POPULATION			2000-2004 ANNUAL RATE		HOUSEHOLDS					FAMILIES		
		2000	2004	2009	% Rate	State Centile	2000	2004	2009	% Annual Rate 2000-2004	2004 Average HH Size	2000	2004	% Annual Rate 2000-2004
62611 ARENZVILLE	017	1099	1068	1054	-0.7	10	426	419	416	-0.4	2.52	314	306	-0.6
62612 ASHLAND	017	2023	2013	2010	-0.1	35	803	807	811	0.1	2.49	584	580	-0.2
62613 ATHENS	129	3455	3696	3918	1.6	85	1326	1444	1556	2.0	2.56	980	1056	1.8
62615 AUBURN	167	5873	5813	5813	-0.2	28	2178	2196	2232	0.2	2.62	1634	1616	-0.3
62617 BATH	125	1014	1022	1024	0.2	51	438	449	456	0.6	2.28	310	313	0.2
62618 BEARDSTOWN	017	7654	7647	7643	0.0	40	2902	2916	2920	0.1	2.58	1994	1974	-0.2
62621 BLUFFS	171	1076	1061	1058	-0.3	23	439	440	445	0.1	2.41	308	304	-0.3
62624 BROWNING	169	628	600	587	-1.1	3	264	258	256	-0.5	2.33	191	184	-0.9
62625 CANTRALL	167	1021	1038	1048	0.4	62	358	371	380	0.8	2.80	297	303	0.5
62626 CARLINVILLE	117	8174	8137	8104	-0.1	36	3068	3092	3121	0.2	2.43	2127	2111	-0.2
62627 CHANDLERVILLE	017	1016	1007	1004	-0.2	30	419	422	423	0.2	2.39	294	292	-0.2
62628 CHAPIN	137	1020	981	957	-0.9	5	384	377	374	-0.4	2.60	296	286	-0.8
62629 CHATHAM	167	9570	10323	10755	1.8	87	3455	3806	4034	2.3	2.71	2773	3012	2.0
62630 CHESTERFIELD	117	679	716	733	1.3	81	265	285	296	1.7	2.51	200	212	1.4
62631 CONCORD	137	286	277	271	-0.8	8	107	106	105	-0.2	2.60	86	84	-0.6
62633 EASTON	125	1022	1011	1006	-0.3	27	410	413	417	0.2	2.45	317	316	-0.1
62634 ELKHART	107	1035	1047	1046	0.3	56	402	412	417	0.6	2.17	295	299	0.3
62635 EMDEN	107	828	804	788	-0.7	9	320	314	311	-0.4	2.56	236	229	-0.7
62638 FRANKLIN	137	1186	1244	1268	1.1	80	443	475	493	1.7	2.62	335	353	1.2
62639 FREDERICK	169	731	723	718	-0.3	27	300	302	305	0.2	2.39	229	229	0.0
62640 GIRARD	117	4080	4045	4016	-0.2	31	1594	1608	1622	0.2	2.48	1139	1133	-0.1
62642 GREENVIEW	129	1598	1574	1615	-0.4	21	627	626	652	0.0	2.51	463	458	-0.3
62643 HARTSBURG	107	580	569	559	-0.5	18	210	209	208	-0.1	2.72	164	162	-0.3
62644 HAVANA	125	5508	5460	5435	-0.2	30	2220	2228	2239	0.1	2.39	1551	1535	-0.2
62649 HETTICK	117	381	373	369	-0.5	16	152	152	153	0.0	2.45	107	106	-0.2
62650 JACKSONVILLE	137	28143	27928	27734	-0.2	32	10715	10786	10862	0.2	2.28	6806	6731	-0.3
62655 KILBOURNE	125	607	602	598	-0.2	31	240	243	246	0.3	2.48	171	171	0.0
62656 LINCOLN	107	20810	20713	20548	-0.1	36	7093	7161	7193	0.2	2.36	4607	4572	-0.2
62661 LOAMI	167	1316	1299	1298	-0.3	24	507	510	519	0.1	2.55	392	388	-0.2
62664 MASON CITY	125	3087	3045	3021	-0.3	24	1230	1231	1236	0.0	2.41	830	819	-0.3
62665 MEREDOSIA	171	1882	1865	1851	-0.2	30	773	779	785	0.2	2.39	536	532	-0.2
62666 MIDDLETOWN	107	579	569	560	-0.4	19	218	217	217	-0.1	2.62	166	164	-0.3
62667 MODESTO	117	540	530	524	-0.4	18	207	207	208	0.0	2.56	159	157	-0.3
62668 MURRAYVILLE	137	1612	1694	1723	1.2	80	601	647	671	1.8	2.62	472	502	1.5
62670 NEW BERLIN	167	2651	2938	3108	2.5	92	1043	1175	1262	2.8	2.50	781	865	2.4
62671 NEW HOLLAND	107	623	610	600	-0.5	16	237	235	234	-0.2	2.60	182	179	-0.4
62672 NILWOOD	117	352	351	349	-0.1	38	141	143	144	0.3	2.34	107	107	0.0
62673 OAKFORD	129	595	575	584	-0.8	7	229	225	232	-0.4	2.56	165	161	-0.6
62674 PALMYRA	117	1525	1496	1478	-0.5	18	667	667	671	0.0	2.24	471	464	-0.4
62675 PETERSBURG	129	5329	5635	5973	1.3	82	2122	2283	2461	1.7	2.39	1496	1584	1.4
62677 PLEASANT PLAINS	167	2586	2720	2801	1.2	81	957	1026	1075	1.7	2.65	773	817	1.3
62681 RUSHVILLE	169	4662	4651	4637	-0.1	38	1945	1969	1981	0.3	2.31	1307	1302	-0.1
62682 SAN JOSE	125	975	963	954	-0.3	25	362	362	362	0.0	2.66	275	271	-0.3
62683 SCOTTVILLE	117	231	228	225	-0.3	24	86	86	86	0.0	2.65	66	65	-0.4
62684 SHERMAN	167	3614	3960	4165	2.2	89	1267	1413	1508	2.6	2.69	1024	1127	2.3
62685 SHIPMAN	117	2124	2093	2074	-0.4	22	806	808	813	0.1	2.59	614	608	-0.2
62688 TALLULA	129	1666	1666	1712	0.0	42	622	631	657	0.3	2.64	485	487	0.1
62690 VIRDEN	117	4196	4141	4107	-0.3	24	1715	1728	1742	0.2	2.31	1133	1121	-0.3
62691 VIRGINIA	017	2485	2537	2568	0.5	66	1021	1062	1085	0.9	2.33	680	696	0.6
62692 WAVERLY	137	2201	2114	2070	-0.9	4	894	874	869	-0.5	2.42	609	581	-1.1
62693 WILLIAMSVILLE	167	1623	1724	1781	1.4	83	605	654	686	1.9	2.64	474	504	1.5
62694 WINCHESTER	171	3817	3797	3791	-0.1	35	1553	1573	1596	0.3	2.38	1086	1085	0.0
62701 SPRINGFIELD	167	1159	1121	1115	-0.8	7	696	677	683	-0.7	1.25	107	97	-2.3
62702 SPRINGFIELD	167	38892	38229	38348	-0.4	19	17055	17094	17432	0.1	2.20	9727	9463	-0.7
62703 SPRINGFIELD	167	31030	30530	30718	-0.4	20	12783	12779	13049	0.0	2.32	7708	7514	-0.6
62704 SPRINGFIELD	167	41046	40271	40322	-0.5	18	19401	19395	19735	0.0	2.05	10384	10051	-0.8
62707 SPRINGFIELD	167	28174	31206	33111	2.4	92	10649	12094	13087	3.0	2.53	7875	8754	2.5
62801 CENTRALIA	121	24315	23550	22960	-0.8	8	9213	9027	8908	-0.5	2.34	6061	5834	-0.9
62803 HOYLETON	189	1082	1125	1153	0.9	77	386	408	424	1.3	2.61	285	297	1.0
62806 ALBION	047	2939	2846	2793	-0.8	8	1252	1230	1220	-0.4	2.28	835	806	-0.8
62807 ALMA	121	858	837	809	-0.6	13	348	345	338	-0.2	2.43	256	250	-0.6
62808 ASHLEY	189	1253	1214	1216	-0.7	8	488	478	485	-0.5	2.51	341	328	-0.9
62809 BARNHILL	191	182	181	180	-0.1	35	78	79	80	0.3	2.29	60	60	0.0
62810 BELLE RIVE	081	1004	1003	1010	0.0	40	364	369	377	0.3	2.72	291	292	0.1
62812 BENTON	055	11924	11937	11865	0.0	43	4963	5040	5076	0.4	2.31	3309	3298	-0.1
62814 BLUFORD	081	2333	2373	2409	0.4	62	858	889	917	0.8	2.66	676	691	0.5
62815 BONE GAP	047	492	483	476	-0.4	18	178	177	176	-0.1	2.73	149	147	-0.3
62816 BONNIE	081	1194	1208	1221	0.3	56	475	487	499	0.6	2.48	355	358	0.2
62817 BROUGHTON	065	655	638	624	-0.6	11	262	258	255	-0.4	2.47	197	191	-0.7
62818 BROWNS	047	374	362	355	-0.8	7	153	151	150	-0.3	2.40	116	113	-0.6
62819 BUCKNER	055	487	480	470	-0.3	22	219	221	220	0.2	2.17	141	140	-0.2
62820 BURNT PRAIRIE	193	207	202	199	-0.6	13	90	90	89	0.0	2.23	63	61	-0.8
62821 CARMI	193	8187	8027	7907	-0.5	17	3518	3502	3495	-0.1	2.20	2288	2238	-0.5
62822 CHRISTOPHER	055	3086	2985	2905	-0.8	7	1395	1371	1353	-0.4	2.17	891	858	-0.9
62823 CISNE	191	1413	1400	1386	-0.2	29	576	580	584	0.2	2.36	403	399	-0.2
62824 CLAY CITY	025	1767	1801	1845	0.5	64	731	755	783	0.8	2.39	503	512	0.5
62827 CROSSVILLE	193	1311	1293	1277	-0.3	24	560	563	564	0.1	2.29	389	385	-0.2
62828 DAHLGREN	065	1632	1601	1568	-0.5	18	633	628	620	-0.2	2.55	478	468	-0.5
62829 DALE	065	549	532	520	-0.7	8	208	205	202	-0.3	2.58	163	159	-0.6
62830 DIX	081	1622	1699	1751	1.1	79	685	729	762	1.5	2.33	459	479	1.0
62831 DU BOIS	189	994	972	972	-0.5	15	329	325	329	-0.3	2.50	229	222	-0.7
62832 DU QUOIN	145	9678	9672	9748	0.0	40	3974	4051	4165	0.5	2.29	2616	2622	0.1
62833 ELLERY	047	158	153	149	-0.8	8	64	63	63	-0.4	2.43	49	48	-0.5
62835 ENFIELD	193	1199	1180	1165	-0.4	20	493	494	496	0.1	2.30	345	341	-0.3
62836 EWING	055	699	778	808	2.6	92	255	286	301	2.7	2.72	193	214	2.5
62837 FAIRFIELD	191	8711	8739	8710	0.1	46	3754	3831	3880	0.5	2.24	2460	2470	0.1
62838 FARINA	051	987	1045	1075	1.4	82	404	436	454	1.8	2.36	273	291	1.5
62839 FLORA	025	6883	7028	7234	0.5	66	2850	2950	3079	0.8	2.30	1843	1874	0.4
62842 GEFF	191	697	698	694	0.0	43	279	283	285	0.3	2.47	205	205	0.0
62843 GOLDEN GATE	191	696	690	683	-0.2	31	281	284	286	0.3	2.43	215	215	0.0
62844 GRAYVILLE	193	2343	2311	2286	-0.3	24	986	987	988	0.0	2.27	665	655	-0.4
62845 HERALD	193	74	78	79	1.3	81	30	32	33	1.5	2.41	24	26	1.9
62846 INA	081	2787	2793	2799	0.1	44	322	328	334	0.4	2.52	237	237	0.0
62849 IUKA	121	2228	2296	2276	0.7	72	842	880	884	1.0	2.61	660	681	0.8
62850 JOHNSONVILLE	191	1251	1241	1229	-0.2	31	491	496	500	0.2	2.50	380	379	-0.1
ILLINOIS					0.7					0.9	2.61			0.6
UNITED STATES					1.2					1.3	2.58			1.1

ZIP CODE		RACE (%)						% Hispanic Origin		2004 AGE DISTRIBUTION (%)										MEDIAN AGE		
#	POST OFFICE NAME	White		Black		Asian/Pacific																
		2000	2004	2000	2004	2000	2004	2000	2004	0-4	5-9	10-14	15-19	20-24	25-44	45-64	65-84	85+	18+	2004	% 2004 Males	% 2004 Females
62611	ARENZVILLE	99.3	99.3	0.2	0.2	0.0	0.0	0.9	0.9	6.2	6.5	6.7	6.4	5.4	24.2	28.1	14.1	2.5	76.6	41.6	50.8	49.3
62612	ASHLAND	98.7	98.6	0.3	0.3	0.1	0.2	0.2	0.3	5.9	6.3	6.9	6.9	5.3	28.0	27.1	12.3	1.3	76.6	39.5	49.8	50.2
62613	ATHENS	98.6	98.3	0.3	0.3	0.2	0.2	1.1	1.3	6.7	7.4	8.4	6.6	5.6	28.1	27.3	8.7	1.2	73.3	37.7	48.8	51.2
62615	AUBURN	98.6	98.4	0.2	0.3	0.2	0.3	0.8	1.0	8.3	8.2	8.2	6.8	6.2	30.8	20.9	8.8	1.9	71.1	34.1	48.1	51.9
62617	BATH	98.1	98.1	0.1	0.1	0.0	0.0	0.4	0.4	6.0	6.5	7.1	5.6	4.2	26.1	27.7	15.2	1.8	77.3	40.6	49.2	50.8
62618	BEARDSTOWN	92.3	92.1	0.7	0.7	0.4	0.4	14.5	14.9	7.5	7.1	6.8	6.0	7.0	28.2	22.7	12.6	2.2	74.9	35.9	50.1	49.9
62621	BLUFFS	99.4	99.4	0.0	0.0	0.2	0.2	0.2	0.1	7.4	6.9	6.4	6.1	7.4	26.9	25.5	11.8	1.8	75.5	37.6	49.0	51.0
62624	BROWNING	98.6	98.5	0.0	0.0	0.0	0.0	0.8	0.8	6.0	6.2	5.5	4.5	6.2	23.7	29.8	16.0	2.2	79.8	43.5	53.3	46.7
62625	CANTRALL	98.4	98.4	0.1	0.1	0.5	0.5	0.3	0.4	5.8	7.0	9.0	6.9	4.4	27.2	29.4	9.8	0.5	73.7	40.0	50.2	49.8
62626	CARLINVILLE	97.2	96.8	1.4	1.6	0.3	0.4	0.7	0.9	5.6	5.7	6.1	7.8	8.3	23.2	25.2	14.4	3.7	78.5	40.1	48.6	51.4
62627	CHANDLERVILLE	97.2	97.1	0.2	0.2	0.5	0.5	1.1	1.2	6.3	6.4	7.2	6.0	6.0	27.8	25.6	13.0	1.9	76.4	39.1	50.2	49.9
62628	CHAPIN	99.1	98.9	0.0	0.0	0.0	0.0	0.5	0.6	7.1	6.9	7.7	6.1	5.1	26.9	26.7	11.7	1.7	74.2	38.5	51.7	48.3
62629	CHATHAM	97.3	96.6	1.0	1.2	0.9	1.1	0.8	1.0	6.8	7.7	8.9	8.3	6.2	28.5	25.9	7.0	0.8	71.2	35.9	49.2	50.8
62630	CHESTERFIELD	97.6	97.2	1.2	1.4	0.0	0.1	0.3	0.4	5.5	6.4	7.4	7.5	6.6	25.7	27.1	12.3	1.5	75.8	39.2	49.7	50.3
62631	CONCORD	99.7	99.6	0.0	0.0	0.0	0.0	0.0	0.4	5.4	5.4	5.8	7.2	5.8	23.5	31.4	14.4	1.1	79.1	42.6	52.4	47.7
62633	EASTON	99.2	99.2	0.1	0.1	0.1	0.1	0.1	0.1	4.8	5.3	7.3	5.8	5.3	23.9	31.3	14.3	1.9	78.9	43.5	51.6	48.4
62634	ELKHART	89.0	88.4	10.1	10.5	0.1	0.2	1.9	2.4	4.7	6.1	7.6	6.8	5.8	33.7	23.9	9.9	1.4	77.0	37.4	52.6	47.4
62635	EMDEN	98.7	98.5	0.0	0.0	0.5	0.6	0.6	0.9	7.0	6.6	7.1	7.5	7.3	24.0	21.9	16.0	2.6	75.3	39.0	46.6	53.4
62638	FRANKLIN	98.6	98.2	0.3	0.3	0.0	0.0	1.0	1.4	5.6	6.7	8.4	8.0	5.2	27.6	26.3	10.9	1.4	73.9	38.5	50.6	49.4
62639	FREDERICK	98.9	98.8	0.1	0.1	0.4	0.4	0.6	0.7	6.0	6.2	6.6	6.2	4.6	25.6	32.1	12.0	0.7	77.7	41.8	51.0	49.0
62640	GIRARD	98.7	98.5	0.3	0.3	0.3	0.3	0.8	1.0	6.1	6.2	7.4	6.7	6.4	24.2	26.4	14.0	2.5	76.2	40.4	49.4	50.6
62642	GREENVIEW	99.1	99.0	0.3	0.4	0.2	0.2	0.6	0.8	5.6	7.0	9.2	6.6	5.1	28.7	24.5	11.5	1.8	74.1	37.7	51.5	48.5
62643	HARTSBURG	98.3	97.9	0.0	0.0	0.2	0.2	1.4	1.8	7.6	7.4	6.7	6.9	6.9	24.8	26.4	11.8	1.8	74.2	38.3	50.8	49.2
62644	HAVANA	98.8	98.8	0.1	0.1	0.4	0.4	0.5	0.5	5.8	5.7	7.0	6.2	6.0	25.0	25.4	15.9	3.2	77.9	41.2	47.8	52.2
62649	HETTICK	99.5	99.2	0.3	0.3	0.0	0.0	0.3	0.3	5.9	6.4	6.4	5.9	5.9	25.2	27.4	15.3	1.6	78.0	40.7	52.0	48.0
62650	JACKSONVILLE	90.3	89.3	6.9	7.5	0.6	0.7	1.6	2.0	5.6	5.2	5.9	7.8	9.0	26.2	24.4	13.2	2.8	79.6	38.2	49.8	50.2
62655	KILBOURNE	98.5	98.3	0.2	0.2	0.2	0.2	0.5	0.5	5.3	5.7	7.6	6.5	5.2	25.6	27.6	15.1	1.5	77.4	40.7	52.7	47.3
62656	LINCOLN	88.7	87.6	9.1	9.8	0.8	1.0	2.0	2.5	5.2	5.1	5.5	8.0	8.8	29.9	23.4	11.8	2.5	80.7	36.7	50.6	49.4
62661	LOAMI	98.2	98.1	0.4	0.4	0.9	0.9	1.5	1.7	6.8	7.0	7.5	5.9	6.5	28.1	27.7	9.7	0.8	75.1	38.3	49.0	51.0
62664	MASON CITY	99.1	99.1	0.1	0.1	0.2	0.2	0.6	0.6	5.9	5.9	7.2	6.6	6.0	23.7	24.4	16.4	4.0	76.8	41.6	47.9	52.1
62665	MEREDOSIA	99.4	99.4	0.2	0.2	0.0	0.0	0.2	0.2	5.8	5.8	7.6	6.3	6.5	25.7	26.1	14.1	2.0	77.0	40.1	49.5	50.5
62666	MIDDLETOWN	98.5	98.1	0.2	0.2	0.2	0.2	0.7	1.1	6.7	6.7	7.4	7.9	6.0	25.5	28.1	10.5	1.2	74.2	38.6	51.0	49.0
62667	MODESTO	99.8	99.8	0.0	0.0	0.2	0.2	0.4	0.4	4.9	4.9	8.1	7.9	5.7	24.5	27.6	14.5	1.9	76.4	41.5	49.8	50.2
62668	MURRAYVILLE	98.8	98.8	0.2	0.2	0.1	0.1	0.1	0.1	6.0	6.4	7.4	6.9	5.5	28.1	28.2	10.6	0.9	75.7	39.0	50.7	49.3
62670	NEW BERLIN	98.5	98.2	0.4	0.5	0.3	0.4	0.7	0.9	6.9	7.1	7.5	6.5	5.1	27.5	26.9	11.2	1.3	74.3	39.1	49.7	50.3
62671	NEW HOLLAND	98.6	98.4	0.2	0.2	0.0	0.0	0.8	1.0	7.7	7.7	7.4	7.2	5.9	25.9	24.6	12.0	1.6	72.8	37.9	50.0	50.0
62672	NILWOOD	98.3	98.3	0.6	0.6	0.3	0.3	0.9	1.1	7.1	7.1	7.1	6.6	7.7	25.1	24.2	13.4	1.7	75.2	36.9	52.1	47.9
62673	OAKFORD	98.5	98.6	0.2	0.2	0.2	0.2	0.8	0.9	6.1	5.4	9.4	7.1	4.7	29.2	25.9	11.1	1.0	74.1	37.5	50.4	49.6
62674	PALMYRA	99.2	99.1	0.2	0.2	0.3	0.3	0.4	0.5	5.2	5.4	6.5	5.9	5.6	24.8	27.9	16.2	2.5	79.1	42.8	50.1	49.9
62675	PETERSBURG	98.4	98.3	0.5	0.6	0.2	0.2	0.7	0.8	5.6	5.7	7.5	6.9	6.0	24.8	26.4	13.9	3.3	77.1	41.4	48.2	51.8
62677	PLEASANT PLAINS	97.8	97.4	1.0	1.2	0.2	0.3	0.7	0.9	6.4	6.8	7.3	7.4	5.7	24.7	30.0	10.5	1.2	75.0	40.4	49.6	50.4
62681	RUSHVILLE	98.9	98.8	0.2	0.2	0.1	0.1	0.5	0.5	5.6	5.7	6.3	5.9	5.6	24.7	25.6	16.7	3.9	78.7	42.3	49.0	51.0
62682	SAN JOSE	98.3	98.0	0.2	0.2	0.1	0.1	1.3	1.4	7.7	7.6	8.0	6.1	5.4	27.2	22.5	13.8	1.7	72.9	37.7	48.7	51.3
62683	SCOTTVILLE	99.6	99.6	0.0	0.0	0.4	0.4	0.9	0.9	5.3	4.8	8.3	9.2	4.8	26.3	24.6	14.0	2.6	74.1	40.5	49.6	50.4
62684	SHERMAN	98.0	97.5	0.4	0.5	0.8	1.0	0.5	0.6	5.8	6.9	8.2	7.1	4.8	26.2	28.2	9.6	3.4	74.5	40.1	48.9	51.1
62685	SHIPMAN	93.0	92.5	5.6	5.9	0.1	0.1	0.6	0.7	5.8	6.1	7.3	6.6	5.7	26.9	26.6	13.4	1.6	76.7	40.0	51.1	48.9
62688	TALLULA	98.6	98.4	0.2	0.2	0.1	0.2	0.4	0.5	5.1	6.1	8.6	7.5	5.5	25.7	30.5	9.5	1.5	75.6	40.7	51.5	48.5
62690	VIRDEN	99.0	98.9	0.1	0.2	0.1	0.1	0.4	0.5	6.3	5.8	6.4	6.2	6.3	25.7	23.6	15.5	4.2	77.3	40.4	47.8	52.2
62691	VIRGINIA	98.1	98.0	0.1	0.1	0.3	0.3	1.1	1.2	5.6	5.6	6.2	6.2	6.0	24.8	26.5	15.8	3.3	78.2	42.1	48.5	51.5
62692	WAVERLY	99.4	99.4	0.1	0.1	0.1	0.1	0.5	0.7	5.8	6.2	7.2	6.9	5.6	25.9	26.5	13.4	2.5	76.5	40.2	48.9	51.1
62693	WILLIAMSVILLE	98.3	97.8	0.5	0.6	0.2	0.2	0.7	0.9	6.3	6.9	8.5	7.1	5.7	27.7	24.1	12.3	1.4	73.8	38.4	47.7	52.3
62694	WINCHESTER	99.5	99.5	0.1	0.1	0.1	0.1	0.2	0.2	6.4	6.4	6.9	6.2	5.8	25.1	25.2	15.0	3.1	76.3	40.8	48.2	51.8
62701	SPRINGFIELD	72.7	68.8	22.9	26.1	2.1	2.5	1.3	1.4	2.1	1.7	1.8	3.5	6.9	40.8	25.3	15.2	2.9	93.3	41.5	60.6	39.4
62702	SPRINGFIELD	87.0	84.9	9.8	11.4	0.8	1.0	1.2	1.5	6.5	6.4	6.7	6.2	6.6	28.5	24.0	13.0	2.2	76.7	37.8	47.5	52.5
62703	SPRINGFIELD	63.6	61.4	32.8	34.6	0.9	1.1	1.2	1.5	7.4	7.2	7.8	6.8	7.1	28.6	22.1	11.2	1.9	73.4	34.9	46.8	53.2
62704	SPRINGFIELD	88.6	86.7	7.3	8.5	2.1	2.5	1.3	1.6	5.7	5.5	5.7	5.9	6.8	27.7	25.7	14.1	2.9	79.5	39.8	46.6	53.5
62707	SPRINGFIELD	94.6	93.4	2.6	3.2	1.5	2.0	0.9	1.1	6.0	6.6	7.2	6.4	5.4	26.4	30.2	10.2	1.6	76.2	40.6	48.5	51.5
62801	CENTRALIA	86.2	84.8	10.8	11.8	0.6	0.7	1.6	2.0	6.1	6.0	6.6	6.4	7.2	28.1	24.1	13.1	2.5	77.6	38.2	51.2	48.8
62803	HOYLETON	97.0	96.8	2.0	2.1	0.3	0.4	0.7	0.9	6.8	7.0	6.9	8.0	6.0	25.6	24.6	12.0	2.9	74.7	37.0	49.1	50.9
62806	ALBION	98.9	98.8	0.1	0.1	0.5	0.5	0.5	0.5	5.7	5.9	6.4	5.8	5.3	24.8	25.1	17.0	3.9	78.4	42.1	47.2	52.8
62807	ALMA	99.2	99.2	0.2	0.2	0.0	0.0	0.4	0.5	6.1	6.3	6.9	6.2	6.1	26.1	27.8	12.8	1.7	76.7	40.0	50.8	49.2
62808	ASHLEY	98.6	98.5	0.2	0.2	0.1	0.1	0.8	0.8	5.3	5.6	8.0	7.2	6.3	26.4	25.2	13.7	2.4	76.7	39.8	50.4	49.6
62809	BARNHILL	99.5	99.5	0.0	0.0	0.0	0.0	0.0	0.6	5.0	5.5	6.6	7.7	6.6	25.4	29.3	12.7	1.1	78.5	40.2	51.9	48.1
62810	BELLE RIVE	98.0	97.8	0.9	1.0	0.0	0.0	0.0	0.1	5.4	5.9	7.2	7.6	6.6	25.4	27.1	13.1	1.8	77.0	40.2	51.4	48.7
62812	BENTON	98.6	98.4	0.2	0.2	0.2	0.3	0.6	0.7	5.3	5.6	6.6	6.1	5.8	24.6	26.4	16.1	3.4	78.7	42.1	48.3	51.7
62814	BLUFORD	99.0	98.9	0.0	0.0	0.1	0.1	0.9	1.1	6.1	7.0	8.2	7.6	5.8	27.4	24.7	11.7	1.6	74.3	36.9	50.4	49.6
62815	BONE GAP	99.6	99.4	0.0	0.0	0.2	0.2	0.2	0.2	7.0	7.0	6.6	6.6	6.8	25.5	27.5	11.4	1.5	75.6	37.8	50.5	49.5
62816	BONNIE	97.7	97.4	0.5	0.6	0.2	0.3	0.8	0.8	5.9	6.4	6.8	5.4	5.6	28.5	28.3	11.7	1.6	77.7	39.2	50.8	49.3
62817	BROUGHTON	98.9	98.8	0.2	0.2	0.2	0.2	0.5	0.5	5.5	5.8	6.6	6.0	6.6	23.4	29.0	15.7	1.6	78.7	42.5	50.0	50.0
62818	BROWNS	98.9	99.2	0.0	0.0	0.5	0.6	0.5	0.6	4.4	5.0	6.6	6.4	5.5	27.1	28.7	14.4	1.9	80.7	41.9	50.0	50.0
62819	BUCKNER	98.6	98.3	0.0	0.0	0.0	0.0	1.0	1.3	4.6	5.0	6.7	7.7	5.4	25.6	26.5	16.0	2.5	79.0	41.3	51.3	48.8
62820	BURNT PRAIRIE	98.6	99.0	0.0	0.0	0.5	0.5	1.0	0.5	5.0	5.0	5.5	5.0	6.9	23.3	30.7	16.8	2.0	81.7	44.7	49.5	50.5
62821	CARMI	97.9	97.6	0.4	0.5	0.2	0.2	0.8	1.0	5.0	5.1	5.9	5.9	5.9	23.8	26.0	17.8	4.5	80.4	43.9	47.7	52.3
62822	CHRISTOPHER	98.4	98.2	0.1	0.1	0.3	0.4	0.6	0.7	5.6	5.5	5.7	5.9	5.7	24.7	26.8	17.0	3.2	79.8	42.7	47.3	52.7
62823	CISNE	99.0	99.0	0.2	0.2	0.2	0.2	0.7	0.6	6.0	6.0	6.7	6.1	5.4	25.8	23.6	16.9	3.4	77.4	40.9	49.1	50.9
62824	CLAY CITY	98.8	98.7	0.1	0.1	0.2	0.3	0.3	0.3	5.8	5.9	7.0	6.3	5.9	26.7	25.2	14.6	2.6	77.4	40.2	49.5	50.5
62827	CROSSVILLE	98.3	98.1	0.0	0.0	0.0	0.0	0.9	1.2	5.2	5.3	6.3	5.7	5.1	25.4	29.0	15.2	2.8	79.7	43.4	50.9	49.1
62828	DAHLGREN	98.9	98.6	0.1	0.1	0.1	0.1	1.0	1.4	6.1	6.4	6.9	5.8	5.8	25.9	27.5	13.6	2.2	76.9	40.4	51.0	49.0
62829	DALE	98.5	98.3	0.4	0.4	0.2	0.2	0.7	0.9	5.3	5.8	7.0	5.5	5.5	25.4	29.5	14.7	1.5	78.6	42.1	49.6	50.4
62830	DIX	97.0	96.4	0.7	0.9	0.7	0.9	0.9	1.2	5.3	5.8	7.5	7.1	5.4	24.8	27.6	14.1	2.4	77.0	40.9	48.7	51.3
62831	DU BOIS	98.5	98.4	0.6	0.6	0.0	0.0	1.0	1.3	5.3	5.6	6.3	5.6	4.4	22.3	21.9	19.7	9.1	79.0	45.4	49.5	50.5
62832	DU QUOIN	92.0	91.6	5.7	6.1	0.4	0.4	1.2	1.2	5.9	5.8	6.4	6.7	7.0	25.0	24.8	15.4	3.0	78.0	40.2	49.2	50.9
62833	ELLERY	99.4	99.4	0.0	0.0	0.6	0.7	0.0	0.7	4.6	5.2	5.9	6.5	5.9	26.8	28.8	14.4	2.0	80.4	41.9	49.7	50.3
62835	ENFIELD	99.0	98.8	0.1	0.1	0.1	0.2	0.3	0.3	5.8	5.7	5.8	6.0	6.1	22.8	28.1	16.4	3.5	78.6	43.6	48.1	51.9
62836	EWING	99.3	99.2	0.0	0.0	0.0	0.0	1.1	1.4	7.8	7.5	7.6	7.5	5.9	25.5	24.4	11.6	2.3	72.5	36.9	48.5	51.5
62837	FAIRFIELD	98.7	98.6	0.1	0.1	0.5	0.5	0.5	0.6	5.9	5.9	5.9	6.0	6.0	24.4	25.0	17.5	3.5	78.8	42.2	47.6	52.4
62838	FARINA	99.2	99.1	0.0	0.0	0.0	0.0	0.1	0.1	4.4	5.7	6.6	7.7	5.0	23.7	27.8	15.1	4.0	77.9	42.9	48.0	52.0
62839	FLORA	97.9	97.5	0.2	0.2	1.0	1.2	0.7	0.9	6.0	6.0	7.0	6.1	6.1	25.1	23.8	16.4	3.6	77.4	40.6	46.9	53.1
62842	GEFF	98.4	98.4	0.6	0.6	0.1	0.1	1.3	1.3	7.7	7.9	7.3	7.2	6.0	23.6	25.8	12.6	1.9	72.8	37.7	49.7	50.3
62843	GOLDEN GATE	99.1	99.3	0.0	0.0	0.1	0.1	1.3	1.5	5.5	5.7	7.0	7.8	6.5	26.7	28.3	11.3	1.3	77.0	39.5	53.8	46.2
62844	GRAYVILLE	98.6	98.4	0.1	0.1	0.3	0.4	0.4	0.4	5.5	5.3	5.4	5.6	5.7	24.9	26.3	18.0	3.4	80.1	43.5	47.1	52.9
62845	HERALD	98.7	98.7	0.0	0.0	0.0	0.0	0.0	1.3	5.1	5.1	5.1	7.7	5.1	25.6	33.3	12.8	0.0	76.9	42.9	48.7	51.3
62846	INA	60.4	56.2	36.8	40.5	0.2	0.3	5.8	6.8	2.2	2.4	2.5	4.6	13.1	52.5	18.0	4.3	0.5	91.8	33.9	85.3	14.8
62849	IUKA	98.9	98.7	0.0	0.0	0.2	0.3	0.6	0.7	6.9	7.0	7.5	7.1	6.1	26.7	24.9	11.9	1.9	74.2	38.3	50.0	50.0
62850	JOHNSONVILLE	98.0	98.1	0.2	0.2	0.5	0.5	0.7	0.7	6.0	6.4	6.9	5.3	5.8	26.4	28.1	13.6	1.5	77.6	40.7	51.0	49.0
	ILLINOIS	73.5	71.8	15.1	15.2	3.5	4.0	12.3	14.2	7.1	7.0	7.3	7.0	7.3	29.0	23.2	10.4	1.7	74.5	35.2	49.0	51.0
	UNITED STATES	75.1	73.6	12.3	12.5	3.8	4.2	12.5	14.1	6.9	6.7	7.2	7.0	7.3	28.6	23.8	10.8	1.7	75.1	36.0	49.1	50.9

ZIP CODE #	POST OFFICE NAME	2004 Per Capita Income	2004 HH Income Base	2004 Household Income Distribution (%) Less than $25,000	$25,000 to $49,999	$50,000 to $99,999	$100,000 to $149,999	$150,000 or More	Median Household Income 2004	2009	2004 National Centile	2004 State Centile	2004 Home Value Base	2004 Home Value Distribution (%) Less than $50,000	$50,000 to $89,999	$90,000 to $174,999	$175,000 to $399,999	$400,000 or More	2004 Median Home Value
62611	ARENZVILLE	20577	419	19.3	37.2	36.8	5.3	1.4	45502	49638	63	50	350	21.4	27.7	39.7	7.7	3.4	91500
62612	ASHLAND	22133	807	22.1	33.2	36.4	5.3	3.0	45599	49480	63	51	672	17.3	29.8	44.6	6.7	1.6	93390
62613	ATHENS	23354	1444	18.8	28.7	39.1	11.4	1.9	51993	57562	75	67	1215	9.5	23.6	51.4	15.1	0.4	111534
62615	AUBURN	21358	2196	21.5	29.8	39.0	6.8	2.9	48803	54439	70	60	1810	11.4	36.1	44.4	7.3	0.8	91642
62617	BATH	19402	449	34.7	31.9	28.7	3.1	1.6	36050	39736	32	16	382	41.9	25.1	26.7	6.0	0.3	60303
62618	BEARDSTOWN	16122	2916	34.2	35.4	26.2	3.5	0.8	34672	38371	26	12	2169	35.6	35.5	25.6	3.0	0.4	63721
62621	BLUFFS	23253	440	28.4	30.2	30.9	7.5	3.0	42430	45079	54	39	372	29.6	33.6	21.5	12.6	2.7	70714
62624	BROWNING	17819	258	29.1	39.5	28.3	2.7	0.4	34781	38199	27	12	223	57.4	16.6	20.2	5.8	0.0	43654
62625	CANTRALL	23695	371	14.8	23.2	43.1	16.4	2.4	59116	67450	84	80	334	7.5	20.7	49.4	19.8	2.7	120625
62626	CARLINVILLE	20391	3092	29.4	33.6	27.4	6.1	3.5	39142	42778	43	27	2362	12.7	30.6	41.6	14.1	1.0	97085
62627	CHANDLERVILLE	18453	422	35.8	28.2	29.9	5.5	0.7	36927	40279	35	19	355	39.4	31.8	25.6	2.5	0.6	60167
62628	CHAPIN	19952	377	22.3	33.4	37.9	4.8	1.6	46673	52056	65	55	330	18.8	35.2	38.8	5.8	1.5	86579
62629	CHATHAM	27701	3806	11.9	21.8	45.6	15.5	5.3	65745	75644	89	87	3341	6.5	12.5	60.3	19.5	1.2	123280
62630	CHESTERFIELD	22310	285	26.3	30.5	33.7	5.6	3.9	43701	47223	58	44	241	19.5	23.2	37.8	14.5	5.0	99211
62631	CONCORD	20391	106	32.1	25.5	34.9	4.7	2.8	40639	41762	48	32	90	21.1	21.1	40.0	13.3	4.4	100000
62633	EASTON	18525	413	32.0	29.3	33.4	4.4	1.0	39878	42118	46	29	347	18.2	36.9	32.9	11.0	1.2	84697
62634	ELKHART	25502	412	17.2	32.3	39.3	9.2	1.9	50439	56932	73	64	340	13.8	29.7	40.9	12.7	2.9	98462
62635	EMDEN	20262	314	24.2	38.2	28.0	7.6	1.9	42444	49649	54	40	244	7.8	41.8	44.7	5.7	0.0	90556
62638	FRANKLIN	21713	475	22.3	28.0	39.4	8.2	2.1	49693	53612	71	62	398	14.1	28.6	38.2	14.8	4.3	101515
62639	FREDERICK	23120	302	23.5	36.1	32.8	4.3	3.3	45000	49866	61	48	264	31.8	17.8	43.6	6.8	0.0	90476
62640	GIRARD	19088	1608	29.6	33.2	29.9	5.7	1.6	39262	42986	44	27	1284	16.9	34.0	34.7	13.5	1.0	88922
62642	GREENVIEW	23789	626	20.3	32.0	39.1	6.2	2.4	47684	53197	68	57	489	17.6	32.5	39.9	9.0	1.0	89861
62643	HARTSBURG	23298	209	17.7	31.6	38.8	9.1	2.9	50703	56744	73	64	173	6.4	32.4	48.0	13.3	0.0	106071
62644	HAVANA	19354	2228	29.6	37.1	26.4	5.0	1.9	36769	40848	35	19	1715	26.0	41.2	27.1	5.5	0.3	70601
62649	HETTICK	20452	152	23.7	39.5	28.3	5.3	3.3	42672	46896	55	40	129	27.9	18.6	34.9	14.7	3.9	99000
62650	JACKSONVILLE	21374	10786	28.5	33.9	28.6	6.0	3.0	39478	44116	44	28	7700	13.7	27.5	45.0	12.4	1.5	101156
62655	KILBOURNE	20226	243	28.0	30.9	32.5	5.4	3.3	38585	43423	41	25	205	37.1	41.0	19.0	2.0	1.0	63261
62656	LINCOLN	19941	7161	29.5	31.1	31.0	6.3	2.1	40457	45263	48	32	5264	14.3	27.4	46.5	10.9	0.9	98220
62661	LOAMI	23494	510	14.1	34.3	41.2	8.4	2.0	50759	56968	73	65	435	29.4	30.1	32.4	7.6	0.5	79853
62664	MASON CITY	20644	1231	29.7	29.7	33.9	4.8	2.0	41272	45426	51	35	972	21.6	39.2	35.2	4.0	0.0	80278
62665	MEREDOSIA	20349	779	30.0	34.9	31.5	2.3	1.3	37601	41807	38	21	641	34.3	40.6	21.7	3.3	0.2	63716
62666	MIDDLETOWN	20539	217	21.2	30.4	41.0	5.5	1.8	48972	54629	70	60	174	23.0	30.5	34.5	12.1	0.0	84000
62667	MODESTO	21343	207	20.3	32.9	39.1	5.8	1.9	48126	52617	69	59	177	24.3	23.7	35.6	15.3	1.1	94375
62668	MURRAYVILLE	19755	647	19.5	36.8	37.3	5.3	1.2	46124	51076	64	53	561	15.7	35.7	38.9	8.4	1.4	88529
62670	NEW BERLIN	25106	1175	16.9	30.7	39.7	9.5	3.3	52053	59673	76	67	999	7.5	24.6	50.6	15.0	2.3	107214
62671	NEW HOLLAND	23295	235	20.0	33.6	35.7	7.7	3.0	46610	51153	65	55	194	16.5	29.4	46.4	7.2	0.5	95333
62672	NILWOOD	22502	143	27.3	37.8	25.2	7.0	2.8	40428	43989	48	31	123	28.5	26.0	29.3	14.6	1.6	82143
62673	OAKFORD	21775	225	26.7	34.7	33.3	2.7	2.7	41974	47188	53	37	186	31.7	37.1	27.4	3.8	0.0	62273
62674	PALMYRA	19285	667	33.9	34.3	26.5	4.1	1.2	36506	39373	34	18	530	37.6	24.2	27.7	8.7	1.9	68788
62675	PETERSBURG	26609	2283	22.8	26.2	36.9	9.1	5.0	50708	56129	73	64	1804	11.2	24.0	43.0	21.3	0.5	109796
62677	PLEASANT PLAINS	27847	1026	13.2	25.2	39.5	15.2	6.9	60843	69771	85	82	920	8.3	18.8	52.9	17.4	2.6	114148
62681	RUSHVILLE	19236	1969	33.3	34.6	26.0	3.1	3.0	37189	40702	36	20	1539	33.7	31.4	28.6	5.5	0.8	69211
62682	SAN JOSE	19737	362	23.2	32.6	36.7	6.1	1.4	45203	50408	62	49	299	25.4	34.1	37.5	2.7	0.3	80172
62683	SCOTTVILLE	18069	86	27.9	34.9	31.4	5.8	0.0	40000	40000	46	30	72	38.9	23.6	29.2	5.6	2.8	70000
62684	SHERMAN	29990	1413	6.9	19.2	47.4	20.2	6.3	73520	81014	93	92	1264	2.9	10.7	61.5	23.8	1.1	136017
62685	SHIPMAN	18584	808	24.9	36.0	33.2	4.6	1.4	41849	46096	52	37	693	19.1	27.3	36.4	15.9	1.4	94722
62688	TALLULA	23956	631	17.9	27.1	43.9	7.1	4.0	53422	60379	78	70	552	22.1	25.9	41.1	10.5	0.4	92157
62690	VIRDEN	20030	1728	30.4	33.1	30.3	4.9	1.3	38918	43072	42	26	1337	18.6	36.4	39.6	5.2	0.3	85791
62691	VIRGINIA	20577	1062	29.2	31.6	32.3	5.1	1.8	41436	45622	51	35	817	25.5	33.9	33.9	6.4	0.4	79044
62692	WAVERLY	21184	874	25.9	33.9	33.3	4.8	2.2	42745	47654	55	41	742	18.7	39.9	32.2	8.1	1.1	80725
62693	WILLIAMSVILLE	23198	654	16.7	26.6	43.1	11.3	2.3	56125	63929	81	76	562	4.1	27.9	53.7	13.5	0.7	108636
62694	WINCHESTER	18641	1573	32.7	33.0	29.8	3.5	1.0	39029	42713	43	26	1247	26.7	33.7	31.8	6.8	1.0	75896
62701	SPRINGFIELD	20890	677	66.6	15.8	13.9	1.9	1.8	16587	19536	1	0	40	12.5	22.5	50.0	0.0	15.0	96000
62702	SPRINGFIELD	20934	17094	32.6	34.4	26.6	4.8	1.6	37078	42252	36	20	11798	31.9	42.8	21.5	3.5	0.3	66879
62703	SPRINGFIELD	18763	12779	35.3	31.8	27.2	4.7	1.0	35140	39964	28	13	8216	25.9	44.6	27.7	1.4	0.4	70883
62704	SPRINGFIELD	32280	19395	22.7	31.1	30.4	9.8	6.0	46563	52796	65	54	12245	4.7	26.2	53.9	13.1	2.2	110469
62707	SPRINGFIELD	35835	12094	9.1	23.8	38.9	16.8	11.5	69039	79098	91	90	10430	7.3	9.8	47.8	30.8	4.4	145858
62801	CENTRALIA	19491	9027	33.3	34.3	25.2	4.8	2.5	36651	40457	34	18	6748	36.0	34.8	23.2	5.8	0.2	65095
62803	HOYLETON	20901	408	24.0	32.4	35.5	4.9	3.2	44736	48771	60	47	340	14.7	44.7	32.1	6.2	2.4	81351
62806	ALBION	17718	1230	36.8	37.2	22.4	2.2	1.5	32854	35595	20	8	974	43.7	29.7	21.1	4.4	1.1	59385
62807	ALMA	20012	345	30.1	36.2	22.9	7.5	3.2	36175	40712	32	16	302	27.2	27.5	39.4	6.0	0.0	85758
62808	ASHLEY	18639	478	30.1	33.3	29.5	4.2	2.9	40390	45189	47	31	401	38.7	28.4	23.9	8.5	0.5	63194
62809	BARNHILL	22479	79	24.1	38.0	31.7	5.1	1.3	42752	45909	55	41	69	33.3	29.0	34.8	2.9	0.0	78750
62810	BELLE RIVE	15950	369	31.2	35.5	30.4	2.4	0.5	41689	46496	52	36	321	32.4	34.9	20.3	12.5	0.0	70897
62812	BENTON	17741	5040	40.5	33.2	21.2	3.7	1.5	31347	34293	16	5	3922	34.3	36.3	23.1	5.9	0.4	65238
62814	BLUFORD	19408	889	23.3	36.9	32.4	5.2	2.3	43030	47260	56	42	818	32.4	31.9	28.4	6.6	0.7	69610
62815	BONE GAP	22612	177	28.8	34.5	31.1	1.1	4.5	40678	43524	48	32	156	41.7	16.7	37.8	3.9	0.0	60000
62816	BONNIE	18418	487	25.9	36.8	33.3	3.7	0.4	41713	46411	52	36	425	34.6	33.9	25.9	5.4	0.2	70357
62817	BROUGHTON	13539	258	46.1	33.3	18.2	1.6	0.8	28165	29493	9	3	226	46.9	31.0	15.0	7.1	0.0	55385
62818	BROWNS	21078	151	25.2	36.4	30.5	4.6	3.3	41887	47117	53	37	138	34.8	23.9	33.3	8.0	0.0	75714
62819	BUCKNER	16833	221	41.2	38.0	17.7	0.5	2.7	29332	32165	11	3	183	72.7	16.9	3.3	7.1	0.0	33654
62820	BURNT PRAIRIE	18599	90	36.7	34.4	23.3	4.4	1.1	32320	34637	19	7	76	48.7	27.6	14.5	9.2	0.0	52000
62821	CARMI	18181	3502	41.3	31.8	22.0	3.6	1.4	30742	33651	14	4	2679	42.3	29.4	23.5	4.6	0.2	58327
62822	CHRISTOPHER	16840	1371	44.7	30.4	21.1	2.9	0.9	28235	30300	9	3	1055	53.4	28.9	14.7	3.0	0.0	47601
62823	CISNE	15913	580	41.4	33.1	22.8	2.1	0.7	30752	33542	14	4	470	42.3	30.9	22.3	3.8	0.6	57826
62824	CLAY CITY	16726	755	38.8	34.6	23.4	1.9	1.3	32366	34798	19	7	633	42.0	32.7	19.0	5.1	1.3	59528
62827	CROSSVILLE	21057	563	33.0	35.0	27.4	2.8	1.8	36417	40203	33	17	467	45.0	33.2	16.1	5.8	0.0	56184
62828	DAHLGREN	20374	628	26.1	40.0	24.4	5.1	4.5	40000	43614	46	30	548	39.1	23.5	26.8	8.8	1.8	66750
62829	DALE	17651	205	25.4	37.1	33.2	4.4	0.0	37931	42979	39	22	181	37.0	21.0	34.3	7.7	0.0	73500
62830	DIX	19206	729	40.9	23.6	28.9	5.2	1.4	35466	37455	29	14	576	22.9	28.7	37.2	9.9	1.4	87907
62831	DU BOIS	18721	325	28.6	29.2	36.6	2.8	2.8	43062	46683	56	42	291	27.8	35.1	25.1	11.0	1.0	72115
62832	DU QUOIN	17892	4051	36.5	34.2	24.3	3.8	1.2	34555	37078	26	11	3166	33.0	37.0	25.8	3.7	0.5	67609
62833	ELLERY	21218	63	23.8	38.1	30.2	4.8	3.2	42327	47335	54	39	58	36.2	22.4	34.5	6.9	0.0	75000
62835	ENFIELD	20120	494	33.2	40.3	18.2	4.3	4.1	35210	38617	28	13	424	40.1	33.3	17.9	7.8	0.9	61556
62836	EWING	15577	286	39.2	27.6	27.3	4.9	1.1	33468	35993	22	9	245	31.4	30.6	30.2	6.9	0.8	76591
62837	FAIRFIELD	18876	3831	38.1	33.0	23.6	3.5	1.8	32664	35760	20	8	2983	37.1	33.5	24.9	4.1	0.4	63571
62838	FARINA	18064	436	33.3	33.7	25.9	6.4	0.7	34721	37845	26	12	382	44.5	32.7	21.5	1.3	0.0	56774
62839	FLORA	18757	2950	37.8	36.5	20.0	3.5	2.2	31653	34491	17	6	2255	34.4	34.6	25.1	5.1	0.8	66176
62842	GEFF	15907	283	33.9	41.0	20.1	4.2	0.7	32975	37454	21	8	240	50.8	26.7	16.7	5.0	0.8	49286
62843	GOLDEN GATE	16064	284	33.5	41.6	21.5	3.2	0.4	35730	40180	30	15	245	45.7	22.9	24.1	6.5	0.8	56563
62844	GRAYVILLE	18232	987	37.4	36.4	21.1	3.6	1.6	34312	37299	25	11	780	46.9	28.7	20.5	3.3	0.5	53333
62845	HERALD	18632	32	34.4	28.1	34.4	3.1	0.0	42348	42389	54	39	28	35.7	32.1	28.6	3.6	0.0	70000
62846	INA	15052	328	38.7	33.2	24.7	3.1	0.3	32060	34574	18	7	276	37.0	36.6	18.8	6.5	1.1	64000
62849	IUKA	17054	880	28.9	36.6	29.9	3.9	0.8	37210	41275	36	20	766	32.6	33.6	24.5	8.0	1.3	71600
62850	JOHNSONVILLE	17409	496	26.2	38.9	30.2	4.2	0.4	38212	42494	40	24	448	37.1	33.9	22.5	5.8	0.7	64783
	ILLINOIS	27033		22.1	25.9	32.9	11.9	7.3	52039	60941				7.7	12.8	34.0	36.6	8.9	162771
	UNITED STATES	25866		24.7	27.1	30.8	10.9	6.5	48124	56710				10.9	15.0	33.7	30.1	10.4	145905

#	POST OFFICE NAME	FINANCIAL SERVICES: Auto Loan	Home Loan	Invest-ments	Retire-ment Plans	THE HOME: Home Improvements: Home Repair	Lawn & Garden	Furnishings: Comput-ers & Hard-ware	Major Appli-ances	TV, Radio, Sound Equip-ment	Furni-ture	ENTERTAINMENT: Dine out/ Carry out	Sports Equip-ment	Fees & Tickets	Toys & Games	Travel	Cable TV	PERSONAL: Apparel & Services	Auto Repairs	Health Insur-ance	Pets & Supplies
62611	ARENZVILLE	94	66	35	62	77	86	65	80	75	64	88	97	56	86	67	78	80	79	95	111
62612	ASHLAND	92	72	48	70	79	89	72	83	80	71	95	97	66	94	73	82	88	81	93	106
62613	ATHENS	85	88	84	89	88	91	85	86	83	85	103	101	85	104	84	81	100	85	83	98
62615	AUBURN	79	82	81	82	82	84	80	81	78	79	97	95	80	99	79	76	95	80	76	91
62617	BATH	71	55	37	53	60	70	59	65	66	57	78	74	53	74	59	69	71	65	77	79
62618	BEARDSTOWN	66	53	42	51	57	64	56	60	61	54	73	70	52	72	56	63	69	60	68	74
62621	BLUFFS	99	73	41	69	83	92	71	86	80	70	95	103	62	94	73	84	87	84	100	118
62624	BROWNING	55	58	59	54	59	65	57	57	59	55	73	64	59	79	59	62	71	56	62	64
62625	CANTRALL	95	101	95	99	103	105	92	96	90	92	112	113	94	117	94	90	109	93	94	114
62626	CARLINVILLE	80	67	52	64	73	82	67	75	73	65	87	86	63	87	69	76	82	74	85	93
62627	CHANDLERVILLE	77	56	33	53	64	72	56	67	64	55	75	80	49	74	58	67	69	66	79	90
62628	CHAPIN	85	72	52	69	78	84	68	77	73	68	88	92	65	89	70	75	83	75	85	101
62629	CHATHAM	102	118	121	119	114	114	109	108	101	110	128	126	113	131	108	97	127	106	96	118
62630	CHESTERFIELD	94	73	48	71	80	90	74	84	81	72	97	98	67	95	74	83	90	83	95	108
62631	CONCORD	96	67	35	63	78	88	66	82	76	66	90	99	57	88	69	80	82	81	98	114
62633	EASTON	81	58	32	55	67	75	57	69	65	56	77	84	50	75	59	68	70	68	82	96
62634	ELKHART	84	59	31	56	69	77	58	72	67	58	79	87	50	77	60	70	72	71	86	100
62635	EMDEN	94	66	34	62	76	86	65	80	75	64	87	96	55	86	67	78	80	79	95	111
62638	FRANKLIN	98	76	48	72	85	93	73	86	81	72	96	103	66	96	75	84	89	84	98	116
62639	FREDERICK	94	75	49	71	82	90	71	83	79	71	94	99	66	94	74	81	88	81	94	111
62640	GIRARD	77	62	44	59	68	76	62	70	69	61	82	82	58	82	64	71	76	69	80	89
62642	GREENVIEW	88	82	76	83	84	92	83	87	85	82	105	100	81	103	83	85	99	86	89	99
62643	HARTSBURG	104	88	63	84	95	103	83	94	89	82	108	112	79	109	85	92	102	92	104	123
62644	HAVANA	73	61	45	58	65	74	62	68	68	60	81	78	59	80	63	71	76	67	78	83
62649	HETTICK	94	63	29	55	72	83	61	76	74	62	86	91	52	82	62	79	79	76	94	108
62650	JACKSONVILLE	70	67	66	66	69	75	68	70	70	67	86	81	67	87	69	71	83	70	73	81
62655	KILBOURNE	81	63	43	60	68	80	67	74	74	64	88	84	61	84	67	78	81	73	87	91
62656	LINCOLN	67	67	65	65	68	74	67	68	69	65	84	78	67	86	68	70	81	67	71	77
62661	LOAMI	87	89	83	89	89	90	85	87	82	85	103	104	84	103	84	79	100	87	82	101
62664	MASON CITY	72	69	63	66	71	79	68	71	72	67	87	81	68	90	70	74	83	70	77	84
62665	MEREDOSIA	89	63	33	56	70	80	60	74	71	61	84	88	53	80	62	76	77	73	89	103
62666	MIDDLETOWN	97	68	36	64	79	89	67	83	77	66	91	100	57	89	70	81	83	82	99	116
62667	MODESTO	98	70	38	66	81	90	68	84	78	68	92	101	59	91	71	82	84	83	100	117
62668	MURRAYVILLE	85	72	51	68	78	84	67	76	73	67	88	91	64	89	70	75	83	75	85	100
62670	NEW BERLIN	107	85	56	82	94	102	81	95	89	81	106	114	74	105	83	91	99	93	106	126
62671	NEW HOLLAND	109	76	40	72	89	100	75	93	87	75	102	112	64	100	78	91	93	92	111	130
62672	NILWOOD	92	70	45	67	79	88	68	82	76	68	91	97	61	89	71	80	84	80	94	109
62673	OAKFORD	101	70	37	66	82	92	69	86	80	69	94	103	59	92	72	84	86	85	102	120
62674	PALMYRA	74	53	31	50	60	70	56	65	64	54	75	75	49	72	56	68	69	65	78	85
62675	PETERSBURG	93	91	84	89	94	102	90	94	91	88	111	107	88	111	91	92	107	92	98	108
62677	PLEASANT PLAINS	99	114	118	112	113	115	104	106	100	104	125	124	109	132	107	99	124	103	100	120
62681	RUSHVILLE	73	56	37	54	62	71	59	66	66	57	78	76	54	75	59	69	72	66	77	83
62682	SAN JOSE	76	71	65	67	75	83	70	74	75	68	92	85	71	97	73	78	87	73	83	89
62683	SCOTTVILLE	87	61	32	57	71	79	60	74	69	59	81	89	51	79	62	72	74	73	88	103
62684	SHERMAN	107	131	142	131	130	130	118	118	110	118	139	137	126	146	121	108	138	114	108	130
62685	SHIPMAN	80	67	46	62	72	78	62	71	68	63	82	85	59	82	64	71	77	69	80	94
62688	TALLULA	96	93	81	91	97	101	86	94	87	85	106	111	85	110	88	88	102	91	96	115
62690	VIRDEN	75	59	41	58	64	74	63	69	69	61	82	79	57	79	62	72	76	68	80	84
62691	VIRGINIA	72	64	54	61	67	77	65	69	70	63	85	78	63	86	66	73	80	68	78	82
62692	WAVERLY	82	68	51	64	74	83	67	75	73	65	88	88	63	90	69	76	82	74	86	97
62693	WILLIAMSVILLE	78	94	103	92	92	94	87	86	83	86	105	100	92	111	89	82	104	84	81	95
62694	WINCHESTER	73	57	38	54	62	71	59	66	65	57	77	76	53	75	59	68	71	65	77	83
62701	SPRINGFIELD	37	32	46	34	32	37	41	37	42	39	53	44	39	52	39	42	51	41	39	41
62702	SPRINGFIELD	62	64	69	63	63	68	65	64	66	64	82	74	66	83	65	66	80	65	64	71
62703	SPRINGFIELD	58	58	67	57	58	63	61	60	63	61	78	69	62	78	61	63	76	61	61	67
62704	SPRINGFIELD	87	93	112	95	92	97	96	92	93	95	117	109	98	118	95	91	115	94	87	101
62707	SPRINGFIELD	126	143	147	145	140	141	132	132	124	133	156	154	136	159	132	120	154	129	120	147
62801	CENTRALIA	70	62	53	59	65	72	62	66	66	61	80	76	60	80	62	68	76	66	73	81
62803	HOYLETON	100	70	37	66	82	91	69	86	80	68	93	103	59	92	72	84	85	84	102	119
62806	ALBION	72	52	29	47	57	66	51	61	59	51	70	72	45	67	52	63	64	60	73	82
62807	ALMA	77	66	51	65	70	77	65	71	69	65	84	82	63	84	66	71	79	69	77	87
62808	ASHLEY	87	60	30	53	68	77	58	71	68	58	81	85	50	77	59	73	74	71	87	100
62809	BARNHILL	86	71	49	67	77	84	67	77	73	67	87	92	63	88	69	75	82	75	85	101
62810	BELLE RIVE	69	62	47	59	65	70	57	63	61	58	74	75	56	75	59	62	70	62	68	81
62812	BENTON	65	52	38	49	56	66	55	60	61	53	72	68	51	70	55	64	67	60	71	73
62814	BLUFORD	88	70	46	64	76	84	66	77	74	67	89	92	62	87	68	77	83	75	88	103
62815	BONE GAP	99	88	67	84	93	100	81	90	86	81	105	107	80	107	84	89	100	88	98	116
62816	BONNIE	73	66	50	63	67	72	62	67	64	63	78	79	59	77	62	64	75	66	70	83
62817	BROUGHTON	54	42	29	40	46	53	45	49	50	43	59	56	41	56	45	52	54	49	58	60
62818	BROWNS	82	71	52	67	76	82	66	74	71	66	86	89	64	87	68	73	81	73	82	97
62819	BUCKNER	59	44	29	43	49	58	49	54	55	47	65	61	44	61	49	58	59	54	65	65
62820	BURNT PRAIRIE	77	52	25	46	59	68	51	63	61	52	72	75	44	68	52	66	65	63	77	88
62821	CARMI	65	52	38	49	56	65	53	59	59	52	70	68	49	69	54	62	65	59	69	74
62822	CHRISTOPHER	56	47	36	45	50	58	50	53	54	48	65	60	47	64	50	57	60	53	61	63
62823	CISNE	64	47	28	43	52	61	49	56	56	48	66	65	43	63	49	59	60	56	68	72
62824	CLAY CITY	75	50	23	43	57	66	49	61	59	49	69	73	41	65	49	63	63	60	75	86
62827	CROSSVILLE	83	60	35	57	68	78	63	73	71	61	84	85	55	80	63	75	76	72	87	95
62828	DAHLGREN	93	66	36	63	77	85	65	80	74	64	88	96	56	86	67	78	80	78	94	110
62829	DALE	74	65	49	61	69	74	60	67	64	60	78	80	58	79	62	66	74	65	73	87
62830	DIX	72	58	41	56	63	72	60	66	65	58	78	76	55	76	60	68	72	65	76	82
62831	DU BOIS	91	62	29	54	70	80	60	74	71	60	84	89	51	80	61	76	76	74	91	105
62832	DU QUOIN	62	54	44	51	57	65	55	59	59	53	72	67	52	71	55	62	67	58	67	71
62833	ELLERY	84	72	53	69	77	83	67	76	72	67	88	91	65	89	70	74	83	74	83	99
62835	ENFIELD	81	58	33	55	66	76	60	71	68	58	80	83	52	78	61	72	73	70	85	94
62836	EWING	66	56	44	56	59	67	58	62	61	57	75	71	55	74	57	62	70	61	67	73
62837	FAIRFIELD	71	54	36	50	59	68	55	63	62	54	74	73	50	72	56	66	68	62	74	81
62838	FARINA	80	54	25	47	61	70	52	65	63	53	73	78	44	70	53	67	67	64	80	92
62839	FLORA	70	55	37	53	59	69	58	64	64	56	77	73	53	74	58	67	70	64	75	78
62842	GEFF	74	49	22	43	56	65	48	60	58	49	68	71	41	64	49	62	61	59	74	85
62843	GOLDEN GATE	71	51	28	45	57	64	49	59	57	49	67	70	43	65	50	60	62	58	70	81
62844	GRAYVILLE	69	51	32	49	57	67	55	62	62	53	73	71	48	69	55	65	67	62	74	78
62845	HERALD	73	65	50	62	66	70	62	67	64	64	78	78	59	74	62	63	75	67	68	81
62846	INA	0	0	0	0	0	0	0	0	0	0	0	0	0	0	0	0	0	0	0	0
62849	IUKA	71	62	47	60	65	71	60	65	63	59	77	76	58	77	60	65	73	64	70	81
62850	JOHNSONVILLE	74	60	40	55	65	71	56	64	62	56	74	77	53	74	57	65	70	63	73	86
	ILLINOIS	98	100	111	99	99	106	100	99	101	100	126	115	102	127	100	100	123	100	98	112
	UNITED STATES	100	100	100	100	100	100	100	100	100	100	100	100	100	100	100	100	100	100	100	100

POPULATION CHANGE

ZIP CODE			POPULATION			2000-2004 ANNUAL RATE		HOUSEHOLDS					FAMILIES		
#	POST OFFICE NAME	COUNTY FIPS CODE	2000	2004	2009	% Rate	State Centile	2000	2004	2009	% Annual Rate 2000-2004	2004 Average HH Size	2000	2004	% Annual Rate 2000-2004
62851	KEENES	191	1028	1029	1023	0.0	42	379	386	389	0.4	2.67	301	303	0.2
62853	KELL	121	1017	1049	1041	0.7	73	383	403	407	1.2	2.60	309	321	0.9
62854	KINMUNDY	121	1850	1775	1703	-1.0	4	729	710	691	-0.6	2.50	534	511	-1.0
62855	LANCASTER	185	69	69	69	0.0	42	26	26	27	0.0	2.65	20	20	0.0
62858	LOUISVILLE	025	3861	3907	3990	0.3	57	1500	1545	1603	0.7	2.41	1082	1099	0.4
62859	MC LEANSBORO	065	4513	4424	4339	-0.5	17	1881	1850	1821	-0.4	2.29	1227	1186	-0.8
62860	MACEDONIA	065	1382	1376	1359	-0.1	36	516	520	519	0.2	2.61	397	395	-0.1
62862	MILL SHOALS	193	367	357	350	-0.7	11	166	165	164	-0.1	2.16	115	112	-0.6
62863	MOUNT CARMEL	185	11612	11534	11429	-0.2	33	4704	4757	4795	0.3	2.39	3214	3197	-0.1
62864	MOUNT VERNON	081	24565	24622	24957	0.1	44	10207	10393	10694	0.4	2.31	6641	6644	0.0
62865	MULKEYTOWN	055	1830	1816	1787	-0.2	32	750	759	760	0.3	2.38	537	535	-0.1
62866	NASON	081	11	13	15	4.0	97	6	7	8	3.7	1.86	4	5	5.4
62867	NEW HAVEN	059	622	618	615	-0.2	34	267	270	270	0.3	2.29	179	178	-0.1
62868	NOBLE	159	2098	2026	1977	-0.8	6	803	792	787	-0.3	2.56	595	577	-0.7
62869	NORRIS CITY	193	2497	2553	2567	0.5	66	1048	1087	1108	0.9	2.35	726	741	0.5
62870	ODIN	121	2086	2052	1989	-0.4	20	785	785	772	0.0	2.52	567	558	-0.4
62871	OMAHA	059	715	763	788	1.5	85	302	326	339	1.8	2.33	205	217	1.4
62872	OPDYKE	081	862	888	906	0.7	72	290	303	314	1.0	2.91	237	246	0.9
62875	PATOKA	121	1068	1022	980	-1.0	3	444	431	419	-0.7	2.37	303	288	-1.2
62877	RICHVIEW	189	1018	986	988	-0.8	8	389	383	390	-0.4	2.57	291	283	-0.7
62878	RINARD	191	362	358	354	-0.3	27	153	155	156	0.3	2.31	114	114	0.0
62880	SAINT PETER	051	702	679	672	-0.8	7	289	284	285	-0.4	2.39	208	203	-0.6
62881	SALEM	121	11790	11603	11275	-0.4	20	4678	4675	4606	0.0	2.40	3187	3138	-0.4
62882	SANDOVAL	121	2678	2589	2492	-0.8	7	1040	1021	996	-0.4	2.54	774	749	-0.8
62883	SCHELLER	081	751	847	909	2.9	94	289	337	369	3.7	2.50	204	233	3.2
62884	SESSER	055	3035	2952	2878	-0.7	11	1279	1266	1253	-0.2	2.31	868	845	-0.6
62885	SHOBONIER	051	220	216	214	-0.4	18	77	77	77	0.0	2.81	54	53	-0.4
62886	SIMS	191	817	806	796	-0.3	24	317	318	319	0.1	2.53	239	237	-0.2
62887	SPRINGERTON	065	511	494	483	-0.8	7	206	203	201	-0.3	2.41	149	145	-0.6
62888	TAMAROA	145	2203	2169	2166	-0.4	21	871	872	887	0.0	2.12	633	624	-0.3
62889	TEXICO	081	1259	1309	1340	0.9	77	493	522	543	1.4	2.51	376	393	1.1
62890	THOMPSONVILLE	055	2474	2476	2466	0.0	42	937	956	966	0.5	2.59	729	735	0.2
62892	VERNON	121	323	307	293	-1.2	2	132	127	124	-0.9	2.42	99	94	-1.2
62893	WALNUT HILL	081	1165	1184	1182	0.4	61	442	457	464	0.8	2.59	354	361	0.5
62894	WALTONVILLE	081	1073	1111	1138	0.8	75	415	437	455	1.2	2.54	307	319	0.9
62895	WAYNE CITY	191	1467	1448	1431	-0.3	24	622	622	623	0.0	2.33	432	426	-0.3
62896	WEST FRANKFORT	055	12675	12329	12055	-0.7	11	5374	5296	5247	-0.3	2.30	3553	3451	-0.7
62897	WHITTINGTON	055	421	538	597	5.9	99	176	229	259	6.4	2.35	128	164	6.0
62898	WOODLAWN	081	2262	2340	2393	0.8	74	829	872	906	1.2	2.68	657	683	0.9
62899	XENIA	025	1231	1261	1297	0.6	68	491	510	531	0.9	2.47	372	381	0.6
62901	CARBONDALE	077	22298	22571	22722	0.3	58	10707	11048	11302	0.7	1.97	3920	3937	0.1
62902	CARBONDALE	199	3830	3892	3907	0.4	61	1684	1732	1760	0.7	2.23	975	979	0.1
62903	CARBONDALE	077	3441	3482	3491	0.3	57	1453	1461	1471	0.1	2.38	869	860	-0.2
62905	ALTO PASS	181	743	738	740	-0.2	33	305	309	315	0.3	2.38	229	228	-0.1
62906	ANNA	181	8031	7946	8000	-0.3	27	3257	3255	3318	0.0	2.23	2051	2013	-0.4
62907	AVA	077	1995	2046	2063	0.6	69	774	810	831	1.1	2.51	567	585	0.7
62908	BELKNAP	087	229	265	287	3.5	96	87	102	112	3.8	2.60	64	73	3.1
62910	BROOKPORT	127	2348	2410	2423	0.6	70	970	1013	1034	1.0	2.38	707	725	0.6
62912	BUNCOMBE	087	993	992	1005	0.0	40	379	382	392	0.2	2.58	292	291	-0.1
62914	CAIRO	003	4050	3775	3507	-1.6	1	1756	1667	1578	-1.2	2.21	1013	939	-1.8
62916	CAMPBELL HILL	077	861	876	881	0.4	63	323	333	339	0.7	2.63	244	248	0.4
62917	CARRIER MILLS	165	2811	2882	2972	0.6	69	1136	1181	1231	0.9	2.36	775	791	0.5
62918	CARTERVILLE	199	9791	9898	9959	0.3	55	4128	4252	4331	0.7	2.32	2688	2728	0.4
62919	CAVE IN ROCK	069	2105	2052	1987	-0.6	13	819	815	806	-0.1	2.37	596	585	-0.4
62920	COBDEN	181	2942	3229	3431	2.2	90	1147	1289	1393	2.8	2.44	822	910	2.4
62922	CREAL SPRINGS	199	2842	2878	2886	0.3	58	1168	1206	1226	0.8	2.36	875	892	0.5
62923	CYPRESS	087	432	500	542	3.5	96	185	218	239	3.9	2.29	136	157	3.4
62924	DE SOTO	077	3005	2902	2852	-0.8	6	1232	1209	1203	-0.4	2.40	822	793	-0.8
62926	DONGOLA	181	2330	2379	2415	0.5	66	939	973	1001	0.9	2.41	673	687	0.5
62928	EDDYVILLE	151	721	716	721	-0.2	33	310	314	323	0.3	2.06	225	225	0.0
62930	ELDORADO	165	6778	6734	6842	-0.2	34	2864	2891	2978	0.2	2.25	1827	1801	-0.3
62931	ELIZABETHTOWN	069	772	758	736	-0.4	18	366	366	362	0.0	1.99	233	230	-0.3
62932	ELKVILLE	077	2052	2006	1976	-0.5	15	831	827	828	-0.1	2.41	598	586	-0.5
62933	ENERGY	199	1150	1266	1323	2.3	91	454	515	548	3.0	2.26	314	351	2.7
62934	EQUALITY	059	1283	1303	1318	0.4	61	533	549	560	0.7	2.36	384	391	0.4
62935	GALATIA	165	2039	2281	2482	2.7	93	822	939	1039	3.2	2.36	573	645	2.8
62938	GOLCONDA	151	2866	2917	2975	0.4	63	1205	1250	1299	0.9	2.25	811	828	0.5
62939	GOREVILLE	087	2750	2825	2868	0.6	70	1135	1183	1217	1.0	2.36	848	875	0.7
62940	GORHAM	077	514	513	509	-0.1	39	205	208	210	0.3	2.38	150	150	0.0
62941	GRAND CHAIN	153	821	823	803	0.1	45	321	326	323	0.4	2.52	225	226	0.1
62942	GRAND TOWER	077	735	691	670	-1.4	1	308	296	293	-0.9	2.33	216	205	-1.2
62943	GRANTSBURG	087	3210	3326	3395	0.8	75	226	258	278	3.2	4.93	168	188	2.7
62946	HARRISBURG	165	13922	14056	14434	0.2	54	5698	5828	6064	0.5	2.28	3712	3737	0.2
62947	HEROD	151	896	901	913	0.1	48	276	283	294	0.6	2.76	202	205	0.4
62948	HERRIN	199	11951	11864	11868	-0.2	33	5112	5145	5200	0.2	2.24	3230	3202	-0.2
62950	JACOB	077	230	232	231	0.2	52	92	94	95	0.4	2.33	67	67	0.0
62951	JOHNSTON CITY	199	5616	5418	5337	-0.8	6	2355	2310	2303	-0.5	2.35	1616	1562	-0.8
62952	JONESBORO	181	3471	3485	3520	0.1	46	1352	1379	1411	0.5	2.44	959	959	0.0
62953	JOPPA	127	272	267	263	-0.4	18	109	109	109	0.0	2.44	89	88	-0.3
62954	JUNCTION	059	614	606	603	-0.3	24	245	247	248	0.2	2.43	161	159	-0.3
62955	KARBERS RIDGE	069	640	624	604	-0.6	13	269	267	264	-0.2	2.19	179	174	-0.7
62956	KARNAK	153	988	984	954	-0.1	36	401	404	396	0.2	2.43	288	286	-0.2
62957	MC CLURE	003	1221	1158	1084	-1.2	2	506	488	465	-0.9	2.37	351	334	-1.2
62958	MAKANDA	181	1901	1947	1966	0.6	68	805	839	860	1.0	2.32	554	568	0.6
62959	MARION	199	24561	24745	24734	0.2	51	9981	10163	10277	0.4	2.31	6764	6775	0.0
62960	METROPOLIS	127	12040	11865	11719	-0.3	22	5002	5006	5017	0.0	2.30	3380	3333	-0.3
62961	MILLCREEK	181	76	79	81	0.9	77	29	31	32	1.6	2.55	23	24	1.0
62962	MILLER CITY	003	104	97	91	-1.6	1	46	44	42	-1.0	2.20	30	28	-1.6
62963	MOUND CITY	153	730	677	635	-1.8	1	297	280	266	-1.4	2.41	187	174	-1.7
62964	MOUNDS	153	1756	1644	1547	-1.5	1	658	626	598	-1.2	2.54	444	415	-1.6
62966	MURPHYSBORO	077	20544	20297	20143	-0.3	26	6688	6716	6764	0.1	2.25	4173	4111	-0.4
62967	NEW BURNSIDE	087	461	400	391	-3.3	0	175	154	153	-3.0	2.60	137	120	-3.1
62970	OLMSTED	153	749	726	691	-0.7	8	324	318	307	-0.4	2.28	222	214	-0.9
62972	OZARK	087	1075	1020	1015	-1.2	2	432	421	427	-0.6	2.16	330	318	-0.9
62974	PITTSBURG	199	1117	1147	1154	0.6	70	427	449	458	1.2	2.55	329	342	0.9
	ILLINOIS					0.7					0.9	2.61			0.6
	UNITED STATES					1.2					1.3	2.58			1.1

ZIP CODE #	POST OFFICE NAME	RACE (%) White 2000	White 2004	Black 2000	Black 2004	Asian/Pacific 2000	Asian/Pacific 2004	% Hispanic Origin 2000	% Hispanic Origin 2004	2004 AGE DISTRIBUTION (%) 0-4	5-9	10-14	15-19	20-24	25-44	45-64	65-84	85+	18+	MEDIAN AGE 2004	% 2004 Males	% 2004 Females
62851	KEENES	98.5	98.5	0.3	0.3	0.1	0.1	0.1	0.1	6.9	7.1	7.2	6.5	6.3	25.9	26.3	12.4	1.4	74.8	38.3	49.1	50.9
62853	KELL	99.4	99.3	0.0	0.0	0.1	0.1	0.3	0.4	6.9	7.1	7.2	6.7	5.7	24.5	28.3	11.8	1.8	74.8	40.0	50.5	49.5
62854	KINMUNDY	98.7	98.4	0.2	0.2	0.0	0.0	0.6	0.9	5.9	6.1	7.4	6.7	5.9	25.9	25.2	14.9	1.9	76.4	40.0	49.4	50.7
62855	LANCASTER	98.6	98.6	0.0	0.0	0.0	0.0	0.0	0.0	5.8	5.8	7.3	5.8	5.8	27.5	29.0	11.6	1.5	81.2	40.4	50.7	49.3
62858	LOUISVILLE	99.2	99.1	0.1	0.1	0.1	0.1	0.3	0.3	6.8	6.0	6.5	5.9	6.1	25.1	25.4	14.6	3.6	77.1	40.5	49.8	50.2
62859	MC LEANSBORO	98.3	98.1	0.6	0.6	0.2	0.3	0.5	0.6	6.1	5.9	6.6	5.7	6.3	23.3	23.8	18.1	4.3	78.0	42.3	47.0	53.1
62860	MACEDONIA	96.8	96.6	2.0	2.2	0.1	0.1	0.7	0.8	6.7	6.8	6.8	6.7	5.6	25.1	27.5	13.3	1.5	75.2	40.1	49.4	50.7
62862	MILL SHOALS	98.9	98.9	0.0	0.0	0.8	0.8	0.3	0.3	5.0	5.0	5.0	5.0	7.0	23.3	29.4	18.5	1.7	82.1	44.7	49.3	50.7
62863	MOUNT CARMEL	97.8	97.5	0.4	0.4	0.5	0.7	0.7	0.9	6.1	6.0	6.6	6.3	6.8	25.7	25.5	14.1	2.9	77.4	39.9	48.8	51.2
62864	MOUNT VERNON	88.8	87.7	8.4	9.1	0.7	0.8	1.2	1.5	6.3	6.4	6.9	6.7	6.2	24.7	25.5	14.7	2.8	76.4	39.9	47.7	52.3
62865	MULKEYTOWN	98.9	98.8	0.1	0.1	0.1	0.1	0.7	0.8	4.4	4.7	6.3	5.4	5.8	26.0	30.8	15.0	1.6	81.4	43.3	49.0	51.1
62866	NASON	100.0	100.0	0.0	0.0	0.0	0.0	0.0	0.0	0.0	0.0	15.4	0.0	0.0	38.5	46.2	0.0	0.0	84.6	34.5	84.6	15.4
62867	NEW HAVEN	99.0	99.0	0.2	0.3	0.0	0.0	0.6	0.7	5.7	6.0	6.2	4.7	5.2	24.4	27.8	17.0	3.1	79.5	43.3	50.0	50.0
62868	NOBLE	99.1	98.8	0.1	0.2	0.1	0.2	0.6	0.7	6.6	6.7	6.8	7.3	6.1	28.6	24.1	11.9	1.9	75.3	37.3	50.9	49.1
62869	NORRIS CITY	98.6	98.4	0.1	0.1	0.2	0.2	0.5	0.7	5.9	5.9	5.8	6.0	5.8	26.3	27.9	14.3	2.3	78.9	41.5	47.8	52.2
62870	ODIN	97.8	97.4	0.9	1.0	0.2	0.3	1.2	1.5	6.6	6.7	7.2	6.8	6.0	25.6	24.3	13.6	3.3	75.4	39.0	48.1	51.9
62871	OMAHA	99.3	99.3	0.0	0.0	0.3	0.3	0.0	0.0	5.4	4.5	6.6	7.9	4.5	28.3	23.2	17.2	2.6	79.3	41.2	50.6	49.4
62872	OPDYKE	98.4	98.2	0.4	0.5	0.0	0.0	0.7	0.9	7.3	7.2	7.6	7.8	6.4	26.5	25.3	10.6	1.4	73.2	36.3	49.3	50.7
62875	PATOKA	98.8	98.5	0.2	0.2	0.4	0.4	1.0	1.2	5.8	5.9	7.6	6.4	6.0	25.8	25.7	14.2	2.6	76.9	40.6	50.0	50.0
62877	RICHVIEW	97.6	97.4	0.4	0.4	0.4	0.4	0.8	1.1	6.7	6.9	7.9	6.9	6.3	27.0	26.4	10.6	1.4	74.2	36.8	51.4	48.6
62878	RINARD	100.0	100.0	0.0	0.0	0.0	0.0	1.4	1.4	5.9	5.9	6.7	6.7	5.6	26.3	26.5	14.8	1.7	77.1	40.7	50.6	49.4
62880	SAINT PETER	99.3	99.3	0.0	0.0	0.1	0.2	0.1	0.3	5.7	6.0	6.8	6.0	5.5	25.2	25.5	16.5	2.8	77.6	41.8	51.3	48.8
62881	SALEM	97.6	97.1	0.5	0.6	0.8	1.0	0.6	0.8	6.4	6.3	6.8	6.4	6.5	25.6	24.6	14.3	3.1	76.7	39.5	48.3	51.7
62882	SANDOVAL	98.3	98.0	0.4	0.5	0.3	0.4	0.7	0.9	6.9	7.5	8.0	7.3	6.3	25.8	25.7	11.1	1.5	73.4	36.6	49.3	50.8
62883	SCHELLER	98.9	98.7	0.1	0.2	0.1	0.2	0.4	0.5	6.5	6.5	6.3	5.9	5.3	26.9	26.7	13.5	2.5	77.0	39.7	51.2	48.8
62884	SESSER	98.7	98.4	0.1	0.1	0.1	0.1	0.9	1.1	6.9	6.8	6.5	5.4	5.8	25.5	25.7	15.0	2.4	76.3	39.6	47.6	52.4
62885	SHOBONIER	98.2	97.7	0.0	0.0	0.5	0.5	0.9	1.4	5.6	6.5	8.3	7.9	5.1	25.0	27.3	13.0	1.4	74.1	40.0	50.5	49.5
62886	SIMS	98.9	98.8	0.4	0.4	0.1	0.1	0.6	0.6	6.1	6.5	7.1	6.5	6.3	27.3	25.8	12.7	1.9	76.3	38.6	50.0	50.0
62887	SPRINGERTON	99.0	98.8	0.0	0.0	0.2	0.2	0.6	0.6	6.3	6.3	6.3	6.3	5.9	25.5	25.7	15.8	2.0	77.3	41.3	49.0	51.0
62888	TAMAROA	87.4	86.8	9.8	10.3	0.3	0.3	1.8	1.8	5.2	5.4	5.4	5.7	8.2	33.2	24.4	11.1	1.4	80.9	37.0	57.6	42.4
62889	TEXICO	98.7	98.2	0.3	0.4	0.2	0.2	0.5	0.7	5.2	5.7	7.5	7.4	5.9	26.1	29.1	11.6	1.5	77.0	40.6	51.6	48.4
62890	THOMPSONVILLE	98.3	98.2	0.2	0.2	0.0	0.0	0.7	0.8	6.5	6.7	6.5	6.1	5.9	27.8	27.1	12.2	1.4	76.7	38.7	49.6	50.4
62892	VERNON	97.8	97.7	0.0	0.0	1.2	1.6	0.9	1.3	5.9	5.9	5.9	6.5	7.5	24.4	29.3	12.7	2.0	78.2	41.3	53.8	46.3
62893	WALNUT HILL	98.0	97.6	0.6	0.8	0.3	0.3	0.3	0.3	5.7	6.5	7.5	7.1	6.5	26.2	28.9	10.3	1.4	76.2	38.9	50.2	49.8
62894	WALTONVILLE	99.2	99.2	0.1	0.1	0.1	0.1	0.5	0.5	6.1	7.5	7.7	6.3	4.5	29.2	24.9	12.0	1.8	74.6	37.5	50.1	50.0
62895	WAYNE CITY	99.0	99.0	0.1	0.1	0.1	0.1	0.4	0.4	7.3	6.8	6.2	6.8	6.9	23.6	23.4	15.8	3.3	75.3	38.5	48.6	51.5
62896	WEST FRANKFORT	98.5	98.2	0.2	0.2	0.2	0.3	0.7	0.8	5.8	5.9	6.3	6.2	6.0	25.6	25.6	15.8	2.9	78.2	41.1	48.1	51.9
62897	WHITTINGTON	99.8	99.8	0.0	0.0	0.0	0.0	0.5	0.4	5.6	5.4	6.3	6.5	5.4	23.8	28.6	16.4	2.0	78.8	43.2	49.8	50.2
62898	WOODLAWN	98.7	98.5	0.3	0.3	0.1	0.2	0.4	0.6	6.3	7.1	8.1	7.7	6.1	28.4	25.2	9.7	1.4	73.9	36.6	50.3	49.7
62899	XENIA	98.8	98.7	0.0	0.0	0.2	0.2	1.6	1.9	5.5	6.0	8.3	6.3	5.1	27.0	26.8	13.6	1.4	76.1	40.3	50.0	50.0
62901	CARBONDALE	69.2	67.0	21.4	22.1	5.4	6.4	3.2	3.8	4.7	4.2	4.9	9.9	20.5	30.5	15.7	7.8	1.8	82.8	27.2	51.7	48.3
62902	CARBONDALE	90.2	89.0	5.0	5.4	2.6	3.1	2.2	2.7	5.2	5.3	6.7	6.9	8.5	31.8	25.8	9.0	0.7	79.0	35.2	51.4	48.6
62903	CARBONDALE	75.5	72.3	11.4	12.2	8.4	10.1	3.3	4.0	8.5	7.0	6.0	7.0	10.4	35.9	18.2	6.4	0.7	74.5	29.3	51.6	48.4
62905	ALTO PASS	95.6	94.7	0.1	0.3	0.0	0.0	5.7	6.8	5.3	5.6	6.2	6.8	6.1	26.0	29.4	13.0	1.6	78.6	41.2	51.1	48.9
62906	ANNA	96.4	95.9	1.4	1.5	0.3	0.4	1.6	2.0	5.0	5.1	6.2	6.2	5.5	25.2	26.5	16.4	4.0	79.9	43.0	48.2	51.8
62907	AVA	98.7	98.3	0.5	0.5	0.2	0.2	0.6	0.8	6.8	6.6	6.1	7.3	5.3	27.4	26.3	12.5	1.8	75.9	39.2	50.2	49.8
62908	BELKNAP	96.9	97.0	0.4	0.8	0.0	0.0	0.9	0.4	7.2	7.2	6.4	4.9	5.7	28.3	26.0	12.8	1.5	75.9	38.5	49.4	50.6
62910	BROOKPORT	91.0	90.0	6.9	7.6	0.3	0.3	1.2	1.4	6.8	6.7	6.9	6.3	6.3	27.8	25.2	12.7	1.2	75.8	38.0	50.0	50.0
62912	BUNCOMBE	98.6	98.3	0.2	0.3	0.0	0.0	0.4	0.6	7.1	6.9	6.1	5.3	5.5	26.8	28.4	12.3	1.6	76.6	39.4	50.6	49.4
62914	CAIRO	37.9	34.8	59.8	62.7	0.7	0.8	0.7	0.7	7.7	7.6	7.9	7.0	6.5	21.4	24.3	14.3	3.3	72.3	38.0	44.9	55.1
62916	CAMPBELL HILL	98.3	98.1	1.2	1.4	0.2	0.2	0.1	0.2	6.6	6.5	7.3	7.2	7.4	24.7	26.3	12.2	1.8	75.2	38.4	51.4	48.6
62917	CARRIER MILLS	90.2	89.2	8.1	8.9	0.1	0.2	0.9	1.1	6.0	6.2	6.5	5.8	5.5	25.2	25.8	15.2	4.0	77.8	41.4	47.5	52.5
62918	CARTERVILLE	94.8	94.3	3.0	3.2	0.5	0.6	0.9	1.1	6.8	6.4	6.5	6.7	7.2	28.0	24.8	12.0	1.7	76.3	36.9	48.0	52.0
62919	CAVE IN ROCK	93.2	92.4	4.5	4.9	0.7	0.8	1.1	1.3	5.7	5.8	5.3	5.1	6.0	26.8	29.9	14.0	1.5	80.4	42.2	52.3	47.7
62920	COBDEN	93.9	93.1	0.7	0.8	0.2	0.3	7.2	8.3	5.1	5.5	7.0	6.7	6.0	24.2	30.4	13.4	1.7	78.3	42.1	49.3	50.7
62922	CREAL SPRINGS	98.1	97.7	0.3	0.3	0.1	0.2	1.3	1.6	5.1	5.3	6.1	5.6	5.1	24.8	30.1	16.1	1.8	80.0	43.7	50.2	49.8
62923	CYPRESS	97.2	96.8	0.7	1.0	0.0	0.0	0.0	0.2	7.8	7.8	6.6	4.8	5.8	27.2	25.4	13.4	1.2	75.0	38.0	50.4	49.6
62924	DE SOTO	97.0	96.2	1.0	1.1	0.6	0.8	1.5	1.8	7.1	6.7	6.5	5.7	7.1	30.9	24.4	10.3	1.2	76.0	35.8	48.8	51.2
62926	DONGOLA	93.1	92.9	4.3	4.2	0.3	0.3	0.4	0.5	6.6	6.8	7.7	6.6	5.9	25.4	25.7	13.4	1.9	74.9	38.7	49.5	50.5
62928	EDDYVILLE	90.3	89.9	6.4	6.7	0.4	0.4	1.3	1.4	4.2	4.2	4.9	8.4	8.1	24.3	29.8	15.1	1.1	82.1	42.3	53.1	46.9
62930	ELDORADO	98.2	97.9	0.3	0.4	0.1	0.1	0.9	1.2	5.5	5.7	6.2	6.6	5.9	23.3	25.3	17.9	3.7	78.5	42.7	47.4	52.6
62931	ELIZABETHTOWN	95.5	95.0	3.6	4.0	0.0	0.1	0.8	0.9	4.9	4.6	4.6	4.5	5.7	23.0	32.7	17.3	2.8	83.4	46.8	51.2	48.8
62932	ELKVILLE	96.4	95.9	1.6	1.7	0.1	0.1	1.1	1.6	6.5	6.3	7.0	5.9	6.3	26.9	24.7	14.3	2.1	76.6	38.3	49.0	51.0
62933	ENERGY	97.4	97.0	0.9	1.0	0.8	1.0	1.0	1.1	5.5	5.1	5.2	5.8	6.2	23.3	27.3	18.3	3.3	80.7	44.1	46.4	53.6
62934	EQUALITY	98.8	98.8	0.2	0.3	0.0	0.0	0.8	0.8	5.3	5.6	6.8	5.8	5.9	25.3	28.9	14.0	2.4	78.9	41.8	49.2	50.8
62935	GALATIA	98.7	98.5	0.1	0.1	0.1	0.1	0.5	0.6	6.8	6.4	6.1	5.5	5.9	24.6	24.8	15.8	4.1	77.5	41.1	46.6	53.4
62938	GOLCONDA	96.0	95.9	1.4	1.5	0.2	0.2	0.6	0.6	5.3	5.6	5.9	6.3	5.5	24.2	26.9	17.2	3.1	79.6	43.2	49.4	50.6
62939	GOREVILLE	98.1	97.6	0.6	0.7	0.2	0.2	1.0	1.3	5.7	6.2	6.5	5.2	5.0	25.8	27.8	16.3	1.5	78.3	42.1	50.7	49.3
62940	GORHAM	98.3	98.1	0.2	0.2	0.0	0.0	0.4	0.4	6.4	6.2	6.2	7.6	7.2	27.5	23.2	13.7	2.0	75.8	37.4	50.3	49.7
62941	GRAND CHAIN	88.7	87.6	9.6	10.5	0.1	0.1	1.2	1.5	6.7	6.7	7.2	6.8	5.8	24.4	24.4	15.9	2.1	75.3	40.0	48.4	51.6
62942	GRAND TOWER	97.6	97.3	0.1	0.1	0.0	0.0	0.7	0.7	6.1	5.9	6.7	7.7	8.0	26.5	26.8	12.3	0.1	76.6	37.9	48.3	51.7
62943	GRANTSBURG	53.5	50.8	43.3	45.5	0.2	0.2	6.3	7.3	2.1	2.2	2.7	5.6	15.1	50.2	16.5	4.9	0.7	91.5	32.7	80.0	20.0
62946	HARRISBURG	92.0	91.1	5.8	6.3	0.3	0.4	1.2	1.4	5.8	5.8	6.1	9.1	6.3	24.2	25.1	15.1	2.7	76.5	40.1	49.1	50.9
62947	HEROD	87.6	87.1	8.9	9.3	0.3	0.3	1.7	1.7	4.2	4.1	4.7	9.3	9.7	23.5	29.6	13.9	1.0	82.2	41.1	53.7	46.3
62948	HERRIN	96.7	96.3	0.9	1.0	0.7	0.9	1.0	1.2	6.3	5.9	6.0	5.5	6.2	26.1	24.4	16.2	3.5	78.6	40.8	46.3	53.7
62950	JACOB	98.7	98.7	0.0	0.0	0.0	0.0	0.4	0.4	6.5	6.0	6.0	7.3	6.9	28.9	20.7	15.1	2.6	76.3	37.2	50.4	49.6
62951	JOHNSTON CITY	98.7	98.6	0.2	0.2	0.1	0.2	1.0	1.2	5.6	6.4	6.5	6.1	5.1	26.5	26.7	14.5	2.6	77.7	40.7	47.8	52.2
62952	JONESBORO	97.1	96.6	0.4	0.5	0.4	0.6	2.0	2.5	5.6	5.8	7.3	6.3	6.0	25.6	26.3	14.6	2.4	77.5	40.8	48.8	51.2
62953	JOPPA	96.3	96.3	1.8	1.9	0.4	0.4	0.7	0.4	6.4	6.4	6.7	6.0	5.2	27.7	26.6	13.1	1.9	76.4	39.6	53.2	46.8
62954	JUNCTION	96.9	96.9	0.5	0.5	0.0	0.0	1.8	1.7	5.5	5.5	6.4	6.1	6.3	25.4	27.6	14.5	2.8	79.2	41.5	48.8	51.2
62955	KARBERS RIDGE	98.4	98.2	0.2	0.2	0.6	0.6	1.3	1.4	5.6	5.3	4.8	4.8	6.9	23.2	26.6	19.2	3.5	81.3	44.6	49.2	50.8
62956	KARNAK	93.8	93.0	5.2	5.8	0.1	0.1	2.2	2.9	8.7	7.7	6.8	6.4	5.4	24.0	22.7	16.2	2.1	72.7	38.2	47.3	52.7
62957	MC CLURE	97.4	96.9	0.7	0.8	0.4	0.6	1.2	1.5	5.0	5.4	6.8	5.9	5.9	25.3	28.1	16.1	1.6	79.2	42.2	49.3	50.7
62958	MAKANDA	94.2	93.2	1.6	1.8	1.7	2.1	1.5	1.8	5.0	5.5	6.9	6.9	6.0	27.5	30.8	10.4	1.0	77.8	40.2	51.5	48.5
62959	MARION	93.7	92.9	4.0	4.3	0.7	0.8	1.6	1.9	5.7	5.7	6.2	6.1	5.9	27.0	25.8	15.0	2.7	78.7	40.6	49.7	50.3
62960	METROPOLIS	92.7	92.0	5.4	5.8	0.3	0.3	0.8	0.9	6.2	6.0	6.4	5.4	6.2	25.8	25.3	15.7	3.2	78.3	41.2	47.5	52.5
62961	MILLCREEK	98.7	100.0	0.0	0.0	0.0	0.0	1.3	1.3	7.6	7.6	6.3	6.3	5.1	27.9	26.6	11.4	1.3	74.7	37.5	51.9	48.1
62962	MILLER CITY	79.8	77.3	18.3	20.6	0.0	0.0	1.0	1.0	4.1	4.1	6.2	5.2	5.2	23.7	29.9	18.6	3.1	80.4	46.1	48.5	51.6
62963	MOUND CITY	50.8	47.4	48.2	51.6	0.1	0.2	1.1	1.3	7.2	7.1	10.0	8.9	8.0	25.7	21.3	10.0	1.8	70.8	32.6	43.0	57.0
62964	MOUNDS	48.6	45.8	49.1	51.7	0.1	0.2	0.7	0.9	7.3	7.0	8.2	8.7	6.5	22.1	23.0	13.9	3.3	71.8	37.1	47.0	53.0
62966	MURPHYSBORO	85.0	83.3	11.2	12.3	1.0	1.3	2.2	2.6	4.1	4.1	4.8	17.9	15.3	22.3	19.3	10.1	2.0	83.8	27.9	50.8	49.2
62967	NEW BURNSIDE	96.8	96.0	0.9	1.0	0.4	0.5	0.9	1.5	5.8	6.5	7.3	6.5	4.8	27.3	27.8	12.5	1.8	76.0	39.1	50.8	49.3
62970	OLMSTED	83.2	81.3	15.1	16.7	0.3	0.4	0.8	0.8	5.2	5.8	7.2	7.0	6.2	24.4	26.5	15.4	2.3	77.8	41.3	46.8	53.2
62972	OZARK	90.3	89.0	7.4	8.5	0.4	0.4	2.0	2.5	4.8	5.2	6.0	5.5	6.2	29.5	27.8	13.6	1.4	80.9	40.1	56.8	43.2
62974	PITTSBURG	98.4	98.3	0.6	0.7	0.1	0.1	0.5	0.6	5.8	5.6	6.6	7.2	6.2	28.1	28.0	11.5	1.1	77.7	38.8	50.3	49.7
	ILLINOIS	73.5	71.8	15.1	15.2	3.5	4.0	12.3	14.2	7.1	7.0	7.3	7.0	7.3	29.0	23.2	10.4	1.7	74.5	35.2	49.0	51.0
	UNITED STATES	75.1	73.6	12.3	12.5	3.8	4.2	12.5	14.1	6.9	6.7	7.2	7.0	7.3	28.6	23.8	10.8	1.7	75.1	36.0	49.1	50.9

#	POST OFFICE NAME	2004 Per Capita Income	2004 HH Income Base	2004 Household Income Distribution (%): Less than $25,000	$25,000 to $49,999	$50,000 to $99,999	$100,000 to $149,999	$150,000 or More	Median Household Income: 2004	2009	2004 National Centile	2004 State Centile	2004 Home Value Base	2004 Home Value Distribution (%): Less than $50,000	$50,000 to $89,999	$90,000 to $174,999	$175,000 to $399,999	$400,000 or More	2004 Median Home Value
62851	KEENES	15144	386	38.3	28.2	30.8	2.1	0.5	34166	35886	25	11	334	46.4	25.8	20.4	5.1	2.4	56316
62853	KELL	20487	403	21.1	33.0	37.7	6.2	2.0	45802	50533	63	51	362	23.8	27.4	37.0	10.5	1.4	88788
62854	KINMUNDY	17493	710	30.1	34.7	30.9	3.8	0.6	37966	41478	39	23	584	44.4	27.9	22.1	5.7	0.0	56875
62855	LANCASTER	16739	26	23.1	42.3	30.8	3.9	0.0	42330	48630	54	39	23	26.1	30.4	39.1	0.0	4.4	75000
62858	LOUISVILLE	16776	1545	34.6	38.1	22.8	3.6	0.9	33661	36325	23	9	1312	38.4	30.6	24.9	5.8	0.3	65385
62859	MC LEANSBORO	18143	1850	43.8	28.5	21.8	4.2	1.6	28725	31731	10	3	1442	42.2	29.7	23.9	4.3	0.0	60172
62860	MACEDONIA	17086	520	29.0	33.5	32.3	4.8	0.4	38433	42499	41	24	454	34.6	28.0	30.4	7.1	0.0	69722
62862	MILL SHOALS	18387	165	37.6	33.9	24.2	3.6	0.6	31437	34613	16	6	140	52.1	25.7	13.6	8.6	0.0	47500
62863	MOUNT CARMEL	19122	4757	32.1	32.9	27.5	5.4	2.1	37225	41246	36	20	3696	34.4	30.3	27.2	7.0	1.1	66104
62864	MOUNT VERNON	19660	10393	36.1	32.4	24.0	5.0	2.6	34413	38108	25	11	7588	31.7	28.1	30.5	8.9	0.7	77202
62865	MULKEYTOWN	18586	759	36.0	31.0	26.4	3.8	2.9	33263	36326	22	9	647	39.3	28.8	25.7	6.3	0.0	66574
62866	NASON	13462	7	57.1	42.9	0.0	0.0	0.0	22183	30000	3	1	6	16.7	33.3	50.0	0.0	0.0	90000
62867	NEW HAVEN	20297	270	36.3	33.0	25.6	2.6	2.6	33876	38705	24	10	226	38.9	32.3	25.7	3.1	0.0	60800
62868	NOBLE	17656	792	33.6	33.7	26.9	4.6	1.3	35893	39945	31	15	670	27.5	29.9	32.5	8.2	1.9	78750
62869	NORRIS CITY	17517	1087	41.1	28.7	24.8	4.0	1.4	30637	33559	14	4	902	46.2	25.5	23.2	4.6	0.6	55667
62870	ODIN	20197	785	29.8	32.6	30.1	5.4	2.2	39190	43338	43	27	640	38.3	32.2	23.4	4.8	1.3	62830
62871	OMAHA	17108	326	42.6	31.3	19.6	5.5	0.9	29355	33693	11	3	266	40.6	23.7	26.7	9.0	0.0	72083
62872	OPDYKE	17292	303	22.8	38.6	30.7	6.3	1.7	43650	47924	58	44	277	27.1	32.9	34.3	4.3	1.4	75870
62875	PATOKA	17771	431	36.0	33.0	26.5	3.9	0.7	34577	38142	26	11	358	36.3	34.4	22.4	6.7	0.3	66774
62877	RICHVIEW	18446	383	24.8	37.6	32.4	3.9	1.3	41005	45870	50	34	317	29.3	33.8	33.8	3.2	0.0	74600
62878	RINARD	17436	155	34.2	35.5	25.8	4.5	0.0	34792	38498	27	12	135	36.3	29.6	27.4	5.9	0.7	66818
62880	SAINT PETER	17728	284	35.6	33.8	23.6	4.6	2.5	34432	36481	25	11	246	32.9	36.2	26.0	3.7	1.2	71000
62881	SALEM	19630	4675	29.8	33.0	30.0	5.6	1.7	39177	43308	43	27	3661	24.8	34.4	34.6	5.7	0.6	78736
62882	SANDOVAL	18402	1021	35.6	29.3	30.3	3.1	1.8	37672	41008	38	21	825	48.2	29.8	18.9	3.0	0.0	52302
62883	SCHELLER	18126	337	37.1	30.0	26.1	3.9	3.0	37834	41060	39	22	290	27.2	32.1	30.3	8.6	1.7	83415
62884	SESSER	18195	1266	38.6	32.9	22.6	4.1	1.7	31527	34525	16	6	1028	38.0	37.8	21.7	2.4	0.0	61078
62885	SHOBONIER	15739	77	33.8	29.9	31.2	3.9	1.3	37740	40446	38	22	66	22.7	33.3	33.3	10.6	0.0	85000
62886	SIMS	15358	318	37.4	34.9	24.2	2.8	0.6	31834	35394	17	6	269	42.4	33.5	15.2	7.4	1.5	59318
62887	SPRINGERTON	22558	203	33.0	35.5	22.7	3.9	4.9	35135	38276	28	13	175	36.6	35.4	24.6	3.4	0.0	68438
62888	TAMAROA	19773	872	33.0	34.2	28.7	3.3	0.8	36280	37246	33	17	757	36.2	30.8	25.6	6.7	0.7	67881
62889	TEXICO	21242	522	24.7	34.7	32.8	5.4	2.5	44068	49254	59	45	469	24.5	26.0	37.3	12.2	0.0	88684
62890	THOMPSONVILLE	18681	956	32.0	31.1	31.0	4.3	1.7	39631	43767	45	28	833	28.2	27.4	35.9	7.9	0.6	81058
62892	VERNON	21744	127	28.4	27.6	38.6	4.7	0.8	43082	47888	56	42	110	32.7	30.0	23.6	12.7	0.9	73333
62893	WALNUT HILL	25944	457	17.9	32.2	38.3	7.0	4.6	49921	55053	72	62	414	16.9	31.4	37.4	13.0	1.2	92500
62894	WALTONVILLE	18565	437	26.8	35.2	30.9	5.3	1.8	41823	46559	52	36	377	25.5	28.4	34.2	11.1	0.8	85323
62895	WAYNE CITY	16454	622	40.7	30.9	24.9	3.1	0.5	31636	35063	17	6	493	44.6	32.1	19.9	3.3	0.2	58548
62896	WEST FRANKFORT	17168	5296	40.7	31.8	22.6	3.8	1.2	31254	34023	16	5	4141	38.9	35.1	21.1	4.6	0.3	61096
62897	WHITTINGTON	21859	229	29.7	28.4	32.8	5.7	3.5	41877	46069	53	37	194	13.4	26.8	38.7	19.1	2.1	106818
62898	WOODLAWN	21763	872	22.0	35.4	34.2	6.0	2.4	45314	50076	62	49	763	20.2	28.6	37.6	13.0	0.7	92021
62899	XENIA	20951	510	23.5	45.5	22.9	3.9	4.1	37640	42079	38	21	450	26.2	30.2	32.9	10.7	0.0	76667
62901	CARBONDALE	16791	11048	59.2	20.4	15.0	3.6	1.9	18574	20421	1	0	4001	19.5	26.5	41.5	11.7	0.9	94969
62902	CARBONDALE	25300	1732	35.5	27.2	25.7	6.8	4.9	38756	43706	42	25	1200	31.8	11.1	32.3	22.8	2.0	101101
62903	CARBONDALE	18256	1461	51.1	20.7	18.9	4.8	4.5	24298	27309	4	1	691	30.8	13.3	32.7	21.1	2.0	102872
62905	ALTO PASS	21113	309	29.8	35.0	28.8	4.5	1.9	38814	43387	42	26	266	34.2	20.3	30.8	12.4	2.3	82500
62906	ANNA	19147	3255	40.7	30.8	22.2	4.6	1.7	31484	34156	16	6	2381	26.5	32.6	29.0	11.2	0.7	80787
62907	AVA	19128	810	32.1	32.0	28.8	4.2	3.0	40779	46570	49	33	706	27.3	30.3	25.6	15.3	1.4	81563
62908	BELKNAP	16771	102	34.3	34.3	29.4	2.0	0.0	35633	38618	30	15	88	51.1	21.6	22.7	4.6	0.0	48571
62910	BROOKPORT	16994	1013	36.5	33.9	25.8	2.9	1.0	34732	38259	26	12	838	34.0	31.5	27.9	6.1	0.5	68986
62912	BUNCOMBE	17405	382	29.3	37.4	29.1	3.7	0.5	38161	42516	40	23	334	33.8	27.8	28.1	10.2	0.0	74615
62914	CAIRO	18106	1667	52.3	29.6	13.2	2.0	2.8	22907	25328	3	1	1023	78.5	14.9	3.6	1.3	1.8	33094
62916	CAMPBELL HILL	18537	333	22.8	34.2	37.5	5.4	0.0	43686	49604	58	44	299	31.4	26.8	25.4	14.1	2.3	75526
62917	CARRIER MILLS	17655	1181	37.9	34.3	22.1	5.0	0.7	32356	35457	19	7	967	42.1	27.1	25.2	5.3	0.3	58793
62918	CARTERVILLE	19878	4252	36.7	28.0	26.3	6.9	2.1	35808	40183	31	15	3103	26.4	30.4	32.8	10.2	0.1	81000
62919	CAVE IN ROCK	17350	815	39.6	34.4	21.5	3.9	0.6	30712	33752	14	4	684	38.5	29.4	27.3	4.8	0.0	64426
62920	COBDEN	19003	1289	31.4	35.3	26.2	5.4	1.7	36284	40449	33	17	1086	29.8	25.1	34.2	9.8	1.1	78462
62922	CREAL SPRINGS	21800	1206	33.1	32.8	26.0	4.6	3.5	35419	39881	29	14	1057	30.9	23.0	32.2	12.2	1.7	84610
62923	CYPRESS	18979	218	33.9	34.4	28.9	1.4	1.4	35590	38914	30	14	186	53.8	20.4	19.4	5.9	0.5	45625
62924	DE SOTO	17347	1209	35.5	32.7	28.1	2.9	0.8	34614	40936	26	12	909	38.7	35.1	22.7	3.2	0.3	64195
62926	DONGOLA	17457	973	38.0	32.8	23.5	4.2	1.4	33135	36811	21	8	793	34.1	29.6	26.9	9.0	0.5	67500
62928	EDDYVILLE	21794	314	30.9	38.2	26.4	3.2	1.3	35349	38953	29	14	276	24.3	26.5	33.7	12.7	2.9	89048
62930	ELDORADO	16321	2891	44.2	30.4	21.7	3.0	0.7	28367	30881	9	3	2198	48.3	27.8	20.7	2.8	0.5	51872
62931	ELIZABETHTOWN	19739	366	47.5	30.1	17.2	3.6	1.6	27325	27823	8	2	304	42.8	26.0	25.0	6.3	0.0	61429
62932	ELKVILLE	16915	827	33.4	38.2	24.4	2.7	1.3	32990	38489	21	8	661	44.6	28.4	21.8	4.8	0.3	55145
62933	ENERGY	23278	515	29.7	28.5	32.2	6.4	3.1	41455	45652	51	35	373	7.5	23.9	53.4	13.7	1.6	113167
62934	EQUALITY	16287	549	42.3	33.2	21.1	2.4	1.1	29556	32938	11	4	460	42.6	28.7	22.6	3.9	2.2	60882
62935	GALATIA	16775	939	40.8	29.8	24.7	3.9	0.8	31546	34583	16	6	767	29.7	37.4	27.3	5.5	0.1	66649
62938	GOLCONDA	18596	1250	40.5	30.6	24.2	2.8	2.0	31103	33598	15	5	1012	33.9	29.4	26.6	7.3	2.9	71970
62939	GOREVILLE	23522	1183	32.4	30.4	29.0	5.5	2.8	39130	43139	43	26	1021	21.9	25.2	37.1	13.8	2.0	95364
62940	GORHAM	18139	208	37.0	30.8	26.4	4.3	1.4	34564	40000	26	11	177	50.3	28.3	18.1	3.4	0.0	49773
62941	GRAND CHAIN	16014	326	38.3	33.7	24.5	3.4	0.0	33352	36400	22	9	266	46.6	32.7	18.1	2.3	0.4	53333
62942	GRAND TOWER	17429	296	34.1	37.2	24.7	3.7	0.3	34250	39430	25	11	246	57.3	27.2	15.5	0.0	0.0	43077
62943	GRANTSBURG	12524	258	33.0	30.6	30.2	5.4	0.8	37993	40603	39	23	233	25.8	27.5	38.6	8.2	0.0	85588
62946	HARRISBURG	19348	5828	39.1	32.2	22.4	4.2	2.2	32195	35458	18	7	4442	38.9	29.6	24.9	5.6	1.0	64524
62947	HEROD	16266	283	27.9	39.9	25.8	4.6	1.8	36097	40413	32	16	254	22.8	25.2	35.0	13.8	3.2	92000
62948	HERRIN	18996	5145	39.9	31.0	22.4	5.3	1.4	31848	35454	17	6	3811	32.8	37.1	25.0	5.1	0.1	65000
62950	JACOB	17202	94	43.6	28.7	22.3	5.3	0.0	29181	36376	11	3	79	54.4	26.6	17.7	1.3	0.0	46500
62951	JOHNSTON CITY	16748	2310	40.9	34.6	20.8	2.4	1.3	32168	35916	18	7	1852	46.8	28.9	20.3	3.7	0.3	55085
62952	JONESBORO	18034	1379	34.8	32.1	27.4	3.9	1.8	35343	38725	29	13	1105	29.6	33.5	26.7	9.3	0.9	73961
62953	JOPPA	20546	109	18.4	41.3	33.9	4.6	1.8	42323	45974	54	39	92	28.3	21.7	39.1	10.9	0.0	90000
62954	JUNCTION	16672	247	48.2	28.3	20.2	1.2	2.0	26036	28268	6	2	194	50.0	30.4	16.5	2.6	0.5	50000
62955	KARBERS RIDGE	20662	267	41.2	34.5	18.0	3.4	3.0	31053	33694	15	5	207	44.9	30.9	18.4	4.4	1.5	55833
62956	KARNAK	17648	404	36.9	35.4	23.3	2.7	1.7	33997	37238	24	10	317	46.7	28.1	19.6	4.4	1.3	53889
62957	MC CLURE	18598	488	39.1	35.0	19.7	4.1	2.1	32796	36334	20	8	418	48.8	30.4	16.0	2.9	1.9	51316
62958	MAKANDA	26970	839	26.9	26.8	30.6	8.3	7.3	46237	52301	64	53	690	19.4	17.3	33.9	26.1	3.3	117308
62959	MARION	21783	10163	33.1	31.7	25.2	6.3	3.7	36803	41585	35	19	7611	21.5	27.6	35.5	13.2	2.3	91355
62960	METROPOLIS	18440	5006	37.8	30.3	25.8	5.0	1.1	33850	36867	24	10	3901	27.1	29.9	35.7	6.7	0.6	81462
62961	MILLCREEK	15967	31	35.5	35.5	22.6	6.5	0.0	31120	30000	15	5	27	29.6	25.9	29.6	14.8	0.0	85000
62962	MILLER CITY	22676	44	27.3	31.8	31.8	4.6	4.6	38182	40000	40	24	38	44.7	29.0	21.1	5.3	0.0	60000
62963	MOUND CITY	11495	280	61.4	22.1	12.1	4.3	0.0	17107	17303	1	0	161	71.4	23.6	5.0	0.0	0.0	35625
62964	MOUNDS	12723	626	51.8	27.8	17.3	2.7	0.5	23631	25690	4	1	449	68.8	22.3	7.4	1.6	0.0	34097
62966	MURPHYSBORO	19767	6716	36.9	30.0	24.2	6.0	2.9	35734	41403	31	15	4931	29.8	32.1	27.9	8.9	1.3	75257
62967	NEW BURNSIDE	18907	154	26.6	37.7	27.3	5.8	2.6	36019	40465	32	16	137	41.6	21.2	29.2	3.7	4.4	71667
62970	OLMSTED	16837	318	39.3	28.9	27.4	3.8	0.6	30730	33714	14	4	264	48.1	27.3	18.9	5.7	0.0	52174
62972	OZARK	24934	421	30.6	33.5	25.2	6.4	4.3	37030	41445	36	20	380	29.2	22.6	32.4	13.2	2.6	86957
62974	PITTSBURG	23389	449	27.4	31.9	29.0	4.7	7.1	43004	48686	56	42	405	30.4	26.4	31.6	10.6	1.0	80517
	ILLINOIS	27033		22.1	25.9	32.9	11.9	7.3	52039	60941				7.7	12.8	34.0	36.6	8.9	162771
	UNITED STATES	25866		24.7	27.1	30.8	10.9	6.5	48124	56710				10.9	15.0	33.7	30.1	10.4	145905

ZIP CODE #	POST OFFICE NAME	FINANCIAL SERVICES: Auto Loan	Home Loan	Investments	Retirement Plans	THE HOME: Home Improvements: Home Repair	Lawn & Garden	Furnishings: Computers & Hardware	Major Appliances	TV, Radio, Sound Equipment	Furniture	ENTERTAINMENT: Dine out/ Carry out	Sports Equipment	Fees & Tickets	Toys & Games	Travel	Cable TV	PERSONAL: Apparel & Services	Auto Repairs	Health Insurance	Pets & Supplies
62851	KEENES	76	51	23	44	58	66	49	61	59	50	70	73	42	66	50	64	63	61	76	87
62853	KELL	85	76	58	72	80	86	70	78	75	70	91	93	69	93	72	77	86	76	84	101
62854	KINMUNDY	77	58	35	53	64	71	55	65	63	56	75	78	50	73	56	66	70	64	76	89
62855	LANCASTER	71	63	48	60	67	72	59	65	62	59	76	77	57	77	60	64	72	63	70	84
62858	LOUISVILLE	69	52	32	48	57	66	53	61	60	52	71	71	47	68	53	63	65	60	72	79
62859	MC LEANSBORO	68	53	35	50	57	67	56	62	62	54	74	71	51	71	56	65	68	62	73	76
62860	MACEDONIA	79	57	32	54	65	73	56	68	64	56	76	81	49	74	58	67	70	67	80	93
62862	MILL SHOALS	75	50	23	43	57	65	48	61	58	49	69	72	41	65	49	63	62	60	75	86
62863	MOUNT CARMEL	71	61	48	58	65	73	61	67	66	60	80	77	59	80	62	69	75	66	75	82
62864	MOUNT VERNON	68	60	56	58	63	70	62	65	66	61	80	75	60	80	63	68	76	65	71	78
62865	MULKEYTOWN	65	59	52	56	61	71	61	64	65	58	78	71	59	77	61	67	73	63	72	74
62866	NASON	47	32	14	27	36	41	30	38	37	31	43	45	26	41	31	40	39	38	47	54
62867	NEW HAVEN	76	57	37	54	62	74	62	69	70	59	82	78	55	77	61	73	75	69	82	85
62868	NOBLE	73	60	43	59	65	72	60	67	65	59	78	78	56	78	61	67	73	66	74	84
62869	NORRIS CITY	69	53	34	50	58	66	54	62	60	53	71	71	49	68	55	62	66	61	71	78
62870	ODIN	89	68	42	62	74	83	66	77	75	66	89	90	60	87	67	78	82	76	89	101
62871	OMAHA	64	48	32	46	53	63	54	59	60	51	71	66	48	67	53	63	64	59	71	71
62872	OPDYKE	79	72	58	70	74	79	69	74	71	70	87	87	66	85	69	71	83	73	76	90
62875	PATOKA	68	53	37	51	58	67	56	62	62	54	74	71	51	71	56	65	68	62	72	76
62877	RICHVIEW	77	67	49	64	71	77	62	70	67	62	81	83	60	82	64	69	76	68	76	91
62878	RINARD	76	51	24	44	58	66	49	61	59	50	69	73	42	66	50	64	63	61	75	87
62880	SAINT PETER	77	54	28	50	62	70	53	65	61	52	72	79	45	70	55	64	65	64	78	91
62881	SALEM	75	64	50	61	68	76	63	69	68	62	83	80	61	82	64	71	78	68	77	85
62882	SANDOVAL	79	62	41	58	67	74	61	70	67	62	81	81	56	78	61	70	75	69	78	89
62883	SCHELLER	85	57	26	49	65	75	55	69	67	56	78	82	47	74	56	72	71	68	85	98
62884	SESSER	69	53	37	50	58	68	55	62	62	54	74	71	50	71	56	66	68	62	73	78
62885	SHOBONIER	79	57	32	54	65	73	56	68	63	55	75	81	48	74	58	66	68	67	80	93
62886	SIMS	73	49	22	42	56	64	47	59	57	48	67	71	40	63	48	62	61	59	73	84
62887	SPRINGERTON	89	72	51	69	78	88	72	80	79	71	94	93	67	93	73	82	88	79	91	101
62888	TAMAROA	54	47	38	43	50	56	46	50	50	45	61	58	45	62	47	53	57	49	57	63
62889	TEXICO	85	75	57	71	79	86	70	78	75	70	91	92	68	92	72	77	86	76	85	100
62890	THOMPSONVILLE	85	64	38	58	70	79	61	72	70	62	83	86	56	81	62	74	77	71	85	98
62892	VERNON	84	75	57	71	79	85	69	77	74	69	89	92	68	91	71	75	85	75	83	99
62893	WALNUT HILL	108	96	73	91	101	108	88	98	94	88	114	117	87	117	91	96	109	95	106	127
62894	WALTONVILLE	84	62	36	56	69	77	59	71	68	60	81	84	53	79	60	72	75	70	83	97
62895	WAYNE CITY	66	47	27	44	53	62	50	57	57	48	67	66	43	63	50	61	61	57	69	74
62896	WEST FRANKFORT	61	51	41	48	54	63	53	57	58	51	69	65	50	68	53	60	65	57	66	69
62897	WHITTINGTON	89	65	38	62	73	84	66	78	75	64	88	92	58	86	67	78	80	77	92	104
62898	WOODLAWN	94	83	63	79	88	94	77	85	82	77	99	102	75	101	79	84	94	83	92	110
62899	XENIA	84	68	49	67	73	82	69	76	75	68	90	89	65	89	69	77	84	75	85	94
62901	CARBONDALE	46	36	44	39	35	40	52	43	51	47	63	56	46	59	45	47	61	49	41	49
62902	CARBONDALE	76	75	86	79	74	77	84	78	81	80	101	96	82	100	80	76	99	82	72	86
62903	CARBONDALE	60	53	64	57	52	57	64	59	63	61	79	74	61	76	60	59	77	64	55	66
62905	ALTO PASS	91	64	34	60	74	83	63	77	72	62	85	93	54	83	65	76	78	76	92	108
62906	ANNA	71	55	37	53	60	70	58	65	64	56	76	74	52	73	58	68	70	64	76	80
62907	AVA	85	62	36	59	71	78	61	74	69	61	81	88	53	79	63	72	75	73	85	100
62908	BELKNAP	70	53	35	51	58	69	59	64	66	55	77	72	52	73	58	69	70	64	77	78
62910	BROOKPORT	63	54	42	54	57	64	55	59	58	54	71	67	53	70	55	59	67	58	64	70
62912	BUNCOMBE	80	56	31	53	65	74	57	69	65	56	76	82	49	74	58	68	70	68	82	94
62914	CAIRO	57	49	53	45	49	59	54	55	60	54	73	60	53	70	53	64	70	56	62	63
62916	CAMPBELL HILL	78	69	53	66	73	79	64	71	68	65	83	85	63	84	66	70	79	70	77	92
62917	CARRIER MILLS	69	52	33	49	57	67	56	62	62	53	74	71	50	70	55	66	67	62	74	77
62918	CARTERVILLE	70	61	52	60	64	71	63	67	67	62	81	78	60	79	63	68	76	67	72	79
62919	CAVE IN ROCK	73	51	28	46	57	67	53	62	62	52	72	73	46	68	53	66	66	62	76	83
62920	COBDEN	80	60	37	57	67	76	60	70	67	59	80	83	54	78	61	70	73	69	82	93
62922	CREAL SPRINGS	86	66	44	61	72	85	67	77	76	66	90	87	61	84	69	80	82	76	92	97
62923	CYPRESS	70	53	35	51	58	69	58	64	65	55	77	72	52	73	58	69	70	64	77	78
62924	DE SOTO	66	54	41	54	57	65	57	61	61	55	73	69	53	71	56	62	68	60	67	72
62926	DONGOLA	72	52	31	50	59	68	55	63	62	53	73	74	48	70	55	66	67	63	76	82
62928	EDDYVILLE	77	60	40	55	66	76	60	70	68	58	80	80	54	77	62	72	74	69	83	91
62930	ELDORADO	58	46	35	44	50	58	49	54	54	47	65	61	45	64	49	57	60	53	63	66
62931	ELIZABETHTOWN	66	48	30	46	53	64	52	59	59	50	70	67	46	66	52	63	64	59	71	74
62932	ELKVILLE	64	54	42	54	57	64	56	59	59	55	72	68	53	71	55	60	67	59	65	70
62933	ENERGY	76	75	71	71	77	87	75	78	78	73	95	87	74	95	76	81	91	77	85	88
62934	EQUALITY	63	47	30	45	52	62	51	57	58	49	68	65	45	64	51	61	62	57	69	71
62935	GALATIA	66	49	30	47	54	64	52	59	59	50	70	68	46	66	52	62	63	59	71	75
62938	GOLCONDA	71	52	32	50	58	68	55	63	62	53	73	73	49	70	56	66	67	63	76	81
62939	GOREVILLE	96	71	43	66	80	92	71	85	81	69	95	99	62	92	73	85	87	84	101	113
62940	GORHAM	71	55	37	53	60	69	58	64	64	56	76	73	52	72	58	67	70	64	75	80
62941	GRAND CHAIN	65	50	35	49	54	64	55	59	60	52	71	67	50	68	54	63	66	59	69	71
62942	GRAND TOWER	77	51	23	44	58	67	50	62	60	50	70	74	42	66	50	64	64	61	76	88
62943	GRANTSBURG	64	48	31	46	53	63	52	58	59	50	69	66	46	66	52	62	63	58	70	72
62946	HARRISBURG	74	56	35	53	62	72	59	67	66	57	78	77	52	75	59	69	71	66	79	84
62947	HEROD	77	60	40	55	67	76	58	69	65	57	77	80	51	76	61	70	72	68	82	93
62948	HERRIN	65	55	44	53	58	68	58	62	63	56	75	70	54	73	58	66	70	62	71	73
62950	JACOB	65	50	33	48	54	64	55	60	61	52	72	67	49	68	54	64	65	60	71	72
62951	JOHNSTON CITY	64	50	34	47	54	63	52	58	58	50	69	66	48	66	52	61	63	58	68	71
62952	JONESBORO	74	56	35	52	61	71	58	66	66	56	77	76	52	74	58	69	71	65	78	83
62953	JOPPA	88	64	38	62	73	82	64	76	72	63	85	91	56	84	66	75	78	75	89	103
62954	JUNCTION	71	50	28	46	56	66	52	61	60	51	71	70	45	67	52	64	64	60	74	80
62955	KARBERS RIDGE	75	56	36	54	62	74	62	68	69	59	82	77	55	77	61	73	74	68	82	84
62956	KARNAK	70	53	34	51	58	69	57	64	64	55	76	72	51	72	57	68	69	64	76	78
62957	MC CLURE	83	56	26	48	63	73	54	67	65	55	76	80	46	72	55	70	69	66	82	95
62958	MAKANDA	83	92	105	94	92	94	89	89	86	89	108	106	91	111	90	84	106	89	83	100
62959	MARION	79	68	57	66	73	81	69	75	74	68	89	86	66	87	70	76	84	74	83	91
62960	METROPOLIS	66	57	44	54	60	68	57	62	62	56	74	71	55	74	58	64	70	61	70	76
62961	MILLCREEK	77	51	23	44	58	67	50	62	60	50	70	74	42	66	50	64	64	61	76	88
62962	MILLER CITY	81	61	40	58	66	80	67	74	75	64	88	83	60	83	66	79	81	74	88	89
62963	MOUND CITY	41	32	34	29	32	40	37	38	42	38	51	41	35	45	36	45	48	39	45	44
62964	MOUNDS	49	39	36	35	40	47	43	45	48	43	58	51	40	54	42	51	55	46	52	54
62966	MURPHYSBORO	71	63	60	62	66	73	67	69	70	65	86	80	64	85	67	71	81	69	74	81
62967	NEW BURNSIDE	89	62	32	59	72	81	61	76	71	61	83	91	52	81	64	74	75	75	90	106
62970	OLMSTED	71	48	23	42	54	63	47	58	57	48	66	69	40	63	48	61	60	58	72	82
62972	OZARK	84	61	36	57	70	79	59	73	68	59	80	87	52	78	62	72	73	72	86	100
62974	PITTSBURG	96	85	65	81	90	97	79	87	84	79	102	104	77	104	81	86	97	85	95	113
	ILLINOIS	98	100	111	99	99	106	100	99	101	100	126	115	102	127	100	100	123	100	98	112
	UNITED STATES	100	100	100	100	100	100	100	100	100	100	100	100	100	100	100	100	100	100	100	100

A 62975-62999

ZIP CODE			POPULATION			2000-2004 ANNUAL RATE		HOUSEHOLDS					FAMILIES		
#	POST OFFICE NAME	COUNTY FIPS CODE	2000	2004	2009	% Rate	State Centile	2000	2004	2009	% Annual Rate 2000-2004	2004 Average HH Size	2000	2004	% Annual Rate 2000-2004
62975	POMONA	077	334	319	311	-1.1	3	124	121	120	-0.6	2.64	90	86	-1.1
62976	PULASKI	153	497	473	451	-1.2	2	202	193	185	-1.1	1.92	132	124	-1.5
62977	RALEIGH	165	661	711	750	1.7	86	269	296	317	2.3	2.40	193	209	1.9
62979	RIDGWAY	059	1381	1370	1366	-0.2	31	594	598	601	0.2	2.22	396	392	-0.2
62982	ROSICLARE	069	1283	1235	1189	-0.9	5	533	522	511	-0.5	2.28	360	346	-0.9
62983	ROYALTON	055	1550	1511	1476	-0.6	13	684	679	673	-0.2	2.22	437	424	-0.7
62984	SHAWNEETOWN	059	2060	2012	1994	-0.6	14	876	872	872	-0.1	2.29	585	572	-0.5
62985	SIMPSON	087	555	563	567	0.3	59	216	231	241	1.6	1.25	164	78	-16.0
62987	STONEFORT	165	737	846	914	3.3	95	287	334	365	3.6	2.53	215	246	3.2
62988	TAMMS	003	2429	2395	2294	-0.3	23	771	772	744	0.0	2.46	553	544	-0.4
62990	THEBES	003	1822	1771	1670	-0.7	10	744	736	706	-0.3	2.41	539	524	-0.7
62992	ULLIN	153	1097	1003	938	-2.1	0	385	354	333	-2.0	2.49	241	217	-2.4
62994	VERGENNES	077	878	989	1044	2.8	94	279	325	351	3.7	2.66	209	240	3.3
62995	VIENNA	087	3126	3223	3317	0.7	72	1305	1368	1428	1.1	2.15	885	916	0.8
62996	VILLA RIDGE	153	757	730	694	-0.9	6	295	289	280	-0.5	2.53	217	210	-0.8
62997	WILLISVILLE	145	983	1000	1010	0.4	62	374	384	392	0.6	2.60	281	285	0.3
62998	WOLF LAKE	181	532	513	512	-0.9	6	204	201	203	-0.4	2.55	153	147	-0.9
62999	ZEIGLER	055	1672	1635	1598	-0.5	15	713	708	700	-0.2	2.26	447	434	-0.7
	ILLINOIS					0.7					0.9	2.61			0.6
	UNITED STATES					1.2					1.3	2.58			1.1

ZIP CODE		RACE (%)								2004 AGE DISTRIBUTION (%)										MEDIAN AGE		
		White		Black		Asian/Pacific		% Hispanic Origin													% 2004 Males	% 2004 Females
#	POST OFFICE NAME	2000	2004	2000	2004	2000	2004	2000	2004	0-4	5-9	10-14	15-19	20-24	25-44	45-64	65-84	85+	18+	2004		
62975	POMONA	97.6	97.2	0.3	0.3	0.0	0.0	0.9	1.3	6.3	6.3	6.6	7.2	6.9	28.5	26.7	11.0	0.6	76.8	37.7	50.5	49.5
62976	PULASKI	52.9	49.9	38.6	40.4	6.4	7.6	4.6	5.3	5.1	5.1	5.5	5.9	8.7	30.7	24.5	12.9	1.7	80.6	38.4	57.5	42.5
62977	RALEIGH	99.1	99.3	0.2	0.1	0.2	0.1	0.2	0.1	6.6	6.6	6.5	5.9	5.6	25.0	28.8	13.2	1.7	76.4	41.2	50.6	49.4
62979	RIDGWAY	99.1	99.1	0.4	0.4	0.1	0.1	0.5	0.6	5.4	5.7	6.5	5.0	4.8	24.7	26.1	17.9	3.9	79.6	43.4	49.1	51.0
62982	ROSICLARE	97.7	97.2	0.6	0.7	1.0	1.2	1.1	1.3	5.9	5.7	5.7	5.4	6.4	24.1	25.4	18.2	3.2	79.4	42.8	47.0	53.0
62983	ROYALTON	99.4	99.3	0.0	0.0	0.1	0.1	0.3	0.4	6.0	6.7	6.5	5.2	5.5	23.8	27.0	16.9	2.4	77.6	42.2	47.9	52.2
62984	SHAWNEETOWN	97.4	97.3	0.3	0.3	0.2	0.2	1.1	1.2	5.3	5.3	6.8	6.7	6.9	24.9	27.1	14.6	2.6	78.7	41.1	47.9	52.1
62985	SIMPSON	63.6	60.8	33.3	35.9	0.4	0.4	5.6	6.8	2.8	3.0	3.6	5.7	12.4	45.1	20.1	6.6	0.7	88.8	34.1	74.1	25.9
62987	STONEFORT	96.2	95.7	3.0	3.4	0.0	0.0	1.2	1.3	5.8	6.3	7.5	6.5	5.4	25.1	28.8	13.2	1.4	76.6	41.3	48.4	51.7
62988	TAMMS	70.1	67.1	27.5	30.1	0.1	0.1	3.6	4.2	4.5	4.7	5.3	6.0	6.7	34.5	23.8	12.7	1.8	81.6	38.3	58.1	41.9
62990	THEBES	85.8	84.2	12.6	14.1	0.1	0.1	0.6	0.7	6.6	6.6	7.0	7.4	6.0	24.2	26.3	13.8	2.1	75.2	39.6	49.2	50.8
62992	ULLIN	61.9	58.7	33.6	36.0	2.6	3.1	2.1	2.4	5.3	6.2	7.5	7.1	7.1	25.8	23.7	14.7	2.7	76.5	39.5	51.1	49.0
62994	VERGENNES	87.6	86.1	9.7	11.0	0.2	0.3	2.1	2.2	4.8	6.2	7.0	23.3	2.4	26.6	19.7	8.9	1.2	62.8	31.3	58.3	41.7
62995	VIENNA	92.6	91.8	4.9	5.2	0.2	0.2	2.5	3.2	5.7	5.7	5.9	6.1	6.7	28.1	24.5	14.7	2.6	79.2	39.4	52.0	48.0
62996	VILLA RIDGE	76.1	73.6	22.7	24.9	0.1	0.3	0.5	0.7	5.8	6.2	7.4	6.0	6.6	24.5	27.4	14.3	1.9	77.0	40.2	49.3	50.7
62997	WILLISVILLE	99.5	99.6	0.1	0.1	0.0	0.0	0.6	0.7	7.8	7.5	7.4	6.5	7.2	25.7	24.5	12.2	1.2	73.4	36.0	48.9	51.1
62998	WOLF LAKE	97.7	97.5	0.2	0.2	0.2	0.2	1.9	2.3	5.5	5.7	7.8	7.4	6.0	27.9	25.3	13.1	1.4	76.4	38.3	51.1	48.9
62999	ZEIGLER	98.9	98.6	0.1	0.1	0.2	0.2	0.5	0.7	6.1	6.0	6.1	6.0	5.8	27.7	24.5	15.1	2.8	78.2	40.1	48.4	51.6
	ILLINOIS	73.5	71.8	15.1	15.2	3.5	4.0	12.3	14.2	7.1	7.0	7.3	7.0	7.3	29.0	23.2	10.4	1.7	74.5	35.2	49.0	51.0
	UNITED STATES	75.1	73.6	12.3	12.5	3.8	4.2	12.5	14.1	6.9	6.7	7.2	7.0	7.3	28.6	23.8	10.8	1.7	75.1	36.0	49.1	50.9

#	POST OFFICE NAME	2004 Per Capita Income	2004 HH Income Base	2004 HOUSEHOLD INCOME DISTRIBUTION (%)					MEDIAN HOUSEHOLD INCOME				2004 Home Value Base	2004 HOME VALUE DISTRIBUTION (%)					2004 Median Home Value
				Less than $25,000	$25,000 to $49,999	$50,000 to $99,999	$100,000 to $149,999	$150,000 or More	2004	2009	2004 National Centile	2004 State Centile		Less than $50,000	$50,000 to $89,999	$90,000 to $174,999	$175,000 to $399,999	$400,000 or More	
62975	POMONA	22003	121	29.8	28.9	29.8	5.0	6.6	39684	46170	45	29	102	34.3	18.6	30.4	11.8	4.9	82500
62976	PULASKI	17889	193	47.2	30.6	18.1	2.6	1.6	27890	29714	8	2	158	53.8	21.5	22.2	2.5	0.0	45714
62977	RALEIGH	19169	296	34.5	29.4	30.4	3.4	2.4	35000	37334	28	12	252	27.8	29.0	31.8	9.9	1.6	72727
62979	RIDGWAY	20228	598	37.5	31.1	24.8	3.9	2.8	34018	38323	24	10	489	39.5	31.9	26.0	2.7	0.0	61979
62982	ROSICLARE	16946	522	46.2	32.4	17.1	2.3	2.1	27662	30643	8	2	403	55.3	31.0	10.4	2.5	0.7	46838
62983	ROYALTON	16673	679	46.2	33.3	16.8	2.7	1.0	27063	30042	7	2	539	51.2	32.7	14.1	2.0	0.0	49156
62984	SHAWNEETOWN	18308	872	49.4	27.0	18.7	1.7	3.2	25386	27883	5	2	676	50.7	32.3	14.8	1.3	0.9	49038
62985	SIMPSON	28212	231	31.6	30.7	28.1	6.9	2.6	40293	43295	47	31	207	21.3	27.5	36.2	14.0	1.0	92273
62987	STONEFORT	19542	334	26.4	36.2	30.5	5.7	1.2	40000	44675	46	30	289	35.6	27.7	29.4	6.6	0.7	70333
62988	TAMMS	17277	772	41.5	33.9	20.1	2.9	1.7	31072	33972	15	5	658	45.3	30.1	20.4	4.0	0.3	60000
62990	THEBES	21187	736	40.0	33.2	22.2	2.5	2.3	31097	34615	15	5	621	47.2	26.3	22.4	4.2	0.0	57292
62992	ULLIN	13600	354	49.4	28.5	19.2	2.5	0.3	25436	27946	5	2	277	55.6	23.5	16.3	4.0	0.7	44038
62994	VERGENNES	16712	325	25.5	41.9	28.0	3.1	1.5	42253	48884	54	38	283	35.7	26.9	30.0	7.4	0.0	65476
62995	VIENNA	19667	1368	38.8	30.3	24.6	4.2	2.1	33138	36048	21	9	1089	29.0	27.5	32.8	10.6	0.2	79557
62996	VILLA RIDGE	15043	289	38.1	33.9	24.6	3.5	0.0	31393	35000	16	6	242	46.7	28.5	19.4	5.4	0.0	53636
62997	WILLISVILLE	18956	384	25.8	43.5	27.3	1.8	1.6	35527	38780	30	14	321	45.2	31.2	23.1	0.3	0.3	55962
62998	WOLF LAKE	17232	201	32.8	38.8	22.9	2.5	3.0	35896	40106	31	16	164	27.4	37.8	27.4	7.3	0.0	81379
62999	ZEIGLER	15286	708	46.9	31.9	17.8	3.3	0.1	26729	29591	7	2	552	61.8	28.1	8.7	1.1	0.4	40972
	ILLINOIS	27033		22.1	25.9	32.9	11.9	7.3	52039	60941				7.7	12.8	34.0	36.6	8.9	162771
	UNITED STATES	25866		24.7	27.1	30.8	10.9	6.5	48124	56710				10.9	15.0	33.7	30.1	10.4	145905

# ZIP CODE / POST OFFICE NAME	FINANCIAL SERVICES				THE HOME — Home Improvements		THE HOME — Furnishings				ENTERTAINMENT						PERSONAL			
	Auto Loan	Home Loan	Investments	Retirement Plans	Home Repair	Lawn & Garden	Computers & Hardware	Major Appliances	TV, Radio, Sound Equipment	Furniture	Dine out/ Carry out	Sports Equipment	Fees & Tickets	Toys & Games	Travel	Cable TV	Apparel & Services	Auto Repairs	Health Insurance	Pets & Supplies
62975 POMONA	101	78	49	71	85	95	74	86	83	74	99	103	68	98	75	87	92	85	100	117
62976 PULASKI	60	44	27	41	49	58	47	53	54	46	63	61	42	60	47	57	58	53	64	67
62977 RALEIGH	83	58	30	55	68	76	57	71	66	57	78	86	49	76	60	69	71	70	85	99
62979 RIDGWAY	73	55	36	53	60	72	61	67	68	58	80	75	54	76	60	72	73	67	80	81
62982 ROSICLARE	63	47	31	45	51	62	52	57	58	49	69	64	46	65	52	62	63	57	69	69
62983 ROYALTON	59	45	30	43	49	59	50	55	56	47	65	61	45	62	49	59	60	54	65	66
62984 SHAWNEETOWN	75	52	28	47	58	68	53	63	62	53	73	74	46	69	53	67	67	63	77	85
62985 SIMPSON	31	22	11	20	25	28	21	26	25	21	29	32	18	28	22	26	26	26	31	37
62987 STONEFORT	85	61	35	56	68	80	64	74	74	62	87	85	56	82	64	79	79	74	90	96
62988 TAMMS	74	54	33	51	60	71	58	66	66	56	78	75	51	73	58	70	71	66	79	83
62990 THEBES	89	63	35	58	70	82	66	76	76	64	89	88	57	84	66	81	81	76	93	100
62992 ULLIN	54	41	27	39	44	53	45	49	50	43	59	55	40	56	44	53	54	49	59	60
62994 VERGENNES	81	57	31	54	66	74	57	70	65	56	76	84	49	75	59	68	70	69	83	96
62995 VIENNA	66	48	30	46	54	63	52	59	59	50	69	67	46	66	52	62	63	59	70	74
62996 VILLA RIDGE	71	48	22	41	54	62	46	58	56	47	66	69	39	62	47	60	60	57	71	82
62997 WILLISVILLE	93	62	28	54	71	81	60	75	72	61	85	90	51	80	61	78	77	74	92	107
62998 WOLF LAKE	83	55	25	48	63	72	54	67	65	55	76	80	46	72	54	70	69	66	82	95
62999 ZEIGLER	49	45	41	43	47	54	47	49	51	45	61	55	46	63	48	53	58	48	55	56
ILLINOIS	98	100	111	99	99	106	100	99	101	100	126	115	102	127	100	100	123	100	98	112
UNITED STATES	100	100	100	100	100	100	100	100	100	100	100	100	100	100	100	100	100	100	100	100

INDIANA

POPULATION CHANGE

A 46001-46204

#	POST OFFICE NAME	COUNTY FIPS CODE	POPULATION 2000	POPULATION 2004	POPULATION 2009	2000-2004 ANNUAL RATE % Rate	State Centile	HOUSEHOLDS 2000	HOUSEHOLDS 2004	HOUSEHOLDS 2009	% Annual Rate 2000-2004	2004 Average HH Size	FAMILIES 2000	FAMILIES 2004	% Annual Rate 2000-2004
46001	ALEXANDRIA	095	12356	11936	11674	-0.8	3	4809	4746	4733	-0.3	2.49	3473	3305	-1.2
46011	ANDERSON	095	17511	17483	17349	0.0	24	6975	7131	7221	0.5	2.39	5127	5060	-0.3
46012	ANDERSON	095	20925	20848	20717	-0.1	22	8426	8568	8675	0.4	2.29	5699	5577	-0.5
46013	ANDERSON	095	17250	17537	17574	0.4	45	8004	8322	8503	0.9	2.10	4849	4786	-0.3
46016	ANDERSON	095	21872	21209	20790	-0.7	3	8973	8837	8802	-0.4	2.34	5309	4948	-1.6
46017	ANDERSON	095	6419	6257	6141	-0.6	5	2609	2598	2599	-0.1	2.36	1861	1785	-1.0
46030	ARCADIA	057	3252	3487	4084	1.7	82	1129	1234	1475	2.1	2.70	869	916	1.3
46031	ATLANTA	057	2107	2255	2600	1.6	82	755	823	964	2.1	2.69	604	638	1.3
46032	CARMEL	057	34857	41837	52064	4.4	98	12683	15459	19519	4.8	2.68	9399	11112	4.0
46033	CARMEL	057	28827	33740	41614	3.8	97	9453	11291	14157	4.3	2.98	8347	9816	3.9
46034	CICERO	057	6678	7294	8671	2.1	90	2572	2869	3466	2.6	2.54	1959	2109	1.8
46035	COLFAX	023	1119	1166	1187	1.0	64	422	450	463	1.5	2.59	311	320	0.7
46036	ELWOOD	095	13075	12812	12624	-0.5	8	5177	5172	5191	0.0	2.45	3687	3547	-0.9
46038	FISHERS	057	39903	52745	68946	6.8	100	14790	19783	26154	7.1	2.67	10954	14236	6.4
46039	FOREST	023	778	765	755	-0.4	9	292	292	291	0.0	2.62	229	223	-0.6
46040	FORTVILLE	059	6339	7136	8192	2.8	95	2463	2826	3306	3.3	2.52	1841	2041	2.5
46041	FRANKFORT	023	25180	25140	25130	0.0	24	9371	9474	9519	0.3	2.59	6657	6487	-0.6
46044	FRANKTON	095	2901	2831	2781	-0.6	6	1135	1133	1134	0.0	2.50	868	838	-0.8
46048	INGALLS	095	1154	1246	1284	1.8	86	413	453	474	2.2	2.75	330	353	1.6
46049	KEMPTON	159	820	802	793	-0.5	7	302	301	303	-0.1	2.66	234	227	-0.7
46050	KIRKLIN	023	1774	1839	1904	0.9	61	660	693	724	1.2	2.65	501	511	0.5
46051	LAPEL	095	2574	2586	2570	0.1	32	1009	1035	1049	0.6	2.50	737	729	-0.3
46052	LEBANON	011	21166	22256	24309	1.2	71	8251	8836	9812	1.6	2.47	5771	5939	0.7
46055	MC CORDSVILLE	059	3595	4684	5874	6.4	99	1199	1580	2006	6.7	2.96	1020	1314	6.1
46056	MARKLEVILLE	095	2532	2589	2613	0.5	50	942	977	1002	0.9	2.65	754	761	0.2
46057	MICHIGANTOWN	023	1075	1188	1243	2.4	93	387	435	460	2.8	2.73	306	334	2.1
46058	MULBERRY	023	1980	1921	1896	-0.7	4	711	701	697	-0.3	2.54	527	502	-1.1
46060	NOBLESVILLE	057	41769	51145	64416	4.9	99	15343	19093	24411	5.3	2.65	11814	14321	4.6
46064	PENDLETON	095	13120	13315	13376	0.4	43	3948	4100	4199	0.9	2.59	3045	3071	0.2
46065	ROSSVILLE	023	3118	3201	3252	0.6	52	1097	1141	1166	0.9	2.74	854	864	0.3
46068	SHARPSVILLE	159	3072	3069	3059	0.0	26	1105	1126	1142	0.4	2.73	907	902	-0.1
46069	SHERIDAN	057	6795	7363	8600	1.9	88	2420	2668	3165	2.3	2.71	1850	1941	1.1
46070	SUMMITVILLE	095	2500	2478	2450	-0.2	17	942	951	957	0.2	2.57	722	705	-0.6
46071	THORNTOWN	011	3312	3473	3782	1.1	69	1220	1304	1442	1.6	2.66	961	994	0.8
46072	TIPTON	159	9714	9585	9509	-0.3	13	3912	3943	3991	0.2	2.38	2719	2633	-0.8
46074	WESTFIELD	057	10364	14495	19479	8.2	100	3691	5229	7110	8.5	2.75	2768	3800	7.7
46075	WHITESTOWN	011	1683	1806	1992	1.7	83	630	691	776	2.2	2.61	493	523	1.4
46076	WINDFALL	159	1753	1830	1870	1.0	66	678	721	751	1.5	2.54	517	533	0.7
46077	ZIONSVILLE	011	16225	19098	22086	3.9	98	5625	6751	7938	4.4	2.77	4508	5261	3.7
46104	ARLINGTON	139	1188	1161	1155	-0.5	6	411	410	416	-0.1	2.83	331	321	-0.7
46105	BAINBRIDGE	133	1949	2093	2179	1.7	83	734	806	852	2.2	2.60	583	622	1.5
46106	BARGERSVILLE	081	4642	5332	6026	3.3	97	1665	1947	2235	3.8	2.74	1332	1515	3.1
46107	BEECH GROVE	097	13591	13308	13339	-0.5	8	5515	5552	5706	0.2	2.31	3556	3388	-1.1
46110	BOGGSTOWN	145	411	408	409	-0.2	19	155	158	162	0.5	2.58	123	122	-0.2
46112	BROWNSBURG	063	25449	31521	39964	5.2	99	9113	11578	15004	5.8	2.70	7228	8933	5.1
46113	CAMBY	109	6415	7248	8062	2.9	95	2289	2660	3033	3.6	2.70	1904	2159	3.0
46115	CARTHAGE	139	2073	2158	2202	1.0	64	798	846	880	1.4	2.55	613	631	0.7
46117	CHARLOTTESVILLE	059	564	650	753	3.4	97	198	234	278	4.0	2.78	167	193	3.5
46118	CLAYTON	063	4418	5007	6073	3.0	95	1623	1885	2334	3.6	2.66	1329	1504	3.0
46120	CLOVERDALE	133	6616	6728	6809	0.4	45	1952	2020	2071	0.8	2.80	1460	1457	-0.1
46121	COATESVILLE	063	4985	5741	6613	3.4	97	1835	2157	2524	3.9	2.66	1486	1701	3.2
46122	DANVILLE	063	12328	14808	18480	4.4	98	4408	5415	6912	5.0	2.67	3404	4053	4.2
46123	AVON	063	19340	23521	29601	4.7	99	6780	8400	10765	5.2	2.79	5637	6817	4.6
46124	EDINBURGH	145	7665	7581	7818	-0.3	15	2916	2946	3096	0.2	2.55	2068	2004	-0.7
46126	FAIRLAND	145	4878	5026	5092	0.7	55	1699	1794	1851	1.3	2.80	1387	1426	0.7
46127	FALMOUTH	139	399	391	390	-0.5	8	156	157	160	0.2	2.49	121	118	-0.6
46128	FILLMORE	133	1610	1637	1658	0.4	45	581	603	619	0.9	2.70	466	470	0.2
46130	FOUNTAINTOWN	145	2444	2601	2750	1.5	79	862	934	1002	1.9	2.78	716	757	1.3
46131	FRANKLIN	081	27030	29563	32607	2.1	90	9434	10575	11937	2.7	2.58	7013	7587	1.9
46133	GLENWOOD	139	965	965	963	0.0	27	351	360	367	0.6	2.68	272	271	-0.1
46135	GREENCASTLE	133	18148	18552	18892	0.5	50	6227	6502	6723	1.0	2.36	4365	4393	0.2
46140	GREENFIELD	059	32760	36709	42080	2.7	94	12523	14411	16944	3.4	2.52	9608	10750	2.7
46142	GREENWOOD	081	30958	33602	37042	2.0	88	11665	12930	14511	2.5	2.57	8664	9299	1.7
46143	GREENWOOD	081	31587	35405	39661	2.7	94	12315	14049	15992	3.2	2.51	8823	9731	2.3
46147	JAMESTOWN	011	3106	3351	3721	1.8	86	1137	1254	1417	2.3	2.67	890	950	1.6
46148	KNIGHTSTOWN	065	4892	4832	4791	-0.3	14	1940	1958	1977	0.2	2.47	1423	1385	-0.6
46149	LIZTON	063	1795	2132	2653	4.1	98	672	818	1040	4.7	2.61	525	620	4.0
46150	MANILLA	139	913	919	927	0.2	34	339	348	358	0.6	2.64	265	264	-0.1
46151	MARTINSVILLE	109	32147	33452	35306	0.9	63	11928	12688	13672	1.5	2.60	9093	9388	0.8
46156	MILROY	139	1610	1620	1627	0.2	34	539	554	567	0.7	2.91	424	422	-0.1
46157	MONROVIA	109	2911	3038	3215	1.0	65	1040	1109	1198	1.5	2.74	843	876	0.9
46158	MOORESVILLE	109	24027	25832	27894	1.7	84	8750	9618	10596	2.3	2.67	6905	7377	1.6
46160	MORGANTOWN	013	5969	6413	7005	1.7	84	2207	2417	2690	2.2	2.63	1737	1851	1.5
46161	MORRISTOWN	145	2602	2670	2722	0.6	51	944	985	1019	1.0	2.67	721	729	0.3
46162	NEEDHAM	081	271	285	303	1.2	71	109	117	126	1.7	2.44	88	92	1.1
46163	NEW PALESTINE	059	9451	10360	11694	2.2	91	3280	3677	4247	2.7	2.80	2706	2962	2.2
46164	NINEVEH	013	4774	5176	5660	1.9	88	1627	1816	2042	2.6	2.50	1267	1369	1.8
46165	NORTH SALEM	063	1565	1877	2345	4.4	98	583	713	907	4.9	2.63	452	534	4.0
46166	PARAGON	109	2096	2168	2275	0.8	59	731	772	826	1.3	2.81	580	596	0.6
46167	PITTSBORO	063	4748	5785	7283	4.8	99	1675	2088	2682	5.3	2.76	1393	1695	4.7
46168	PLAINFIELD	063	23375	26675	32275	3.2	96	8360	9855	12348	4.0	2.47	6013	6862	3.2
46171	REELSVILLE	133	1878	1847	1847	-0.4	10	701	704	712	0.1	2.51	568	555	-0.5
46172	ROACHDALE	133	2593	2567	2571	-0.2	16	962	964	975	0.1	2.66	720	697	-0.8
46173	RUSHVILLE	139	11384	11300	11304	-0.2	19	4416	4474	4562	0.3	2.47	3095	3017	-0.6
46175	RUSSELLVILLE	133	662	668	671	0.2	37	261	267	271	0.5	2.50	182	178	-0.5
46176	SHELBYVILLE	145	27422	27324	27399	-0.1	23	10809	10995	11214	0.4	2.43	7450	7278	-0.6
46180	STILESVILLE	109	1120	1286	1531	3.3	97	433	509	618	3.9	2.53	341	390	3.2
46181	TRAFALGAR	081	4193	4807	5430	3.3	96	1490	1738	1994	3.7	2.76	1227	1394	3.1
46182	WALDRON	145	1904	1916	1921	0.2	34	691	715	731	0.8	2.58	534	534	0.0
46184	WHITELAND	081	9342	10051	10986	1.7	84	3194	3502	3891	2.2	2.87	2646	2830	1.6
46186	WILKINSON	059	2243	2537	2917	2.9	95	830	958	1125	3.4	2.65	651	728	2.7
46201	INDIANAPOLIS	097	38717	36708	36373	-1.3	1	14895	14473	14667	-0.7	2.50	8580	7816	-2.2
46202	INDIANAPOLIS	097	15268	15148	15256	-0.2	18	7885	8076	8351	0.6	1.69	2474	2284	-1.9
46203	INDIANAPOLIS	097	41711	40633	40703	-0.6	5	16095	16153	16596	0.1	2.48	10360	9876	-1.1
46204	INDIANAPOLIS	097	6491	6525	6566	0.1	32	1701	1715	1752	0.2	1.47	265	234	-2.9
	INDIANA					0.8					1.2	2.48			0.3
	UNITED STATES					1.2					1.3	2.58			1.1

ZIP CODE #	POST OFFICE NAME	RACE (%) White		Black		Asian/Pacific		% Hispanic Origin		2004 AGE DISTRIBUTION (%)										MEDIAN AGE	%	%
		2000	2004	2000	2004	2000	2004	2000	2004	0-4	5-9	10-14	15-19	20-24	25-44	45-64	65-84	85+	18+	2004	2004 Males	2004 Females
46001	ALEXANDRIA	98.3	98.0	0.5	0.5	0.2	0.2	0.9	1.1	6.6	6.5	7.2	6.8	6.4	26.1	25.3	13.3	1.9	75.5	38.5	48.9	51.1
46011	ANDERSON	86.5	85.0	11.7	13.0	0.3	0.4	1.0	1.2	5.8	6.1	6.7	6.2	5.5	24.7	27.7	14.8	2.5	77.5	41.5	48.0	52.0
46012	ANDERSON	93.6	92.8	4.2	4.7	0.6	0.7	1.2	1.4	5.6	5.3	5.6	7.6	9.5	23.7	26.0	14.4	2.3	80.3	39.2	47.8	52.2
46013	ANDERSON	92.6	91.4	5.1	5.8	0.8	1.0	1.3	1.6	6.4	6.2	5.9	5.0	5.2	27.3	24.1	17.4	2.5	78.4	40.8	47.2	52.8
46016	ANDERSON	71.3	70.0	24.6	25.5	0.2	0.2	3.4	3.9	8.0	7.5	7.3	6.4	7.1	30.1	21.6	10.1	1.9	73.4	33.9	49.1	50.9
46017	ANDERSON	96.9	96.4	1.8	2.1	0.3	0.4	1.1	1.3	6.3	6.7	6.5	6.0	5.1	25.9	28.2	13.8	1.4	76.5	40.2	48.2	51.8
46030	ARCADIA	97.5	97.2	0.5	0.5	0.2	0.3	0.8	1.0	6.9	6.9	7.6	7.1	6.1	29.5	25.2	9.5	1.1	73.9	37.1	50.5	49.5
46031	ATLANTA	97.5	97.2	0.3	0.3	0.2	0.3	1.2	1.4	6.7	6.9	7.9	7.1	6.3	29.5	26.2	8.5	1.0	73.6	37.3	50.4	49.6
46032	CARMEL	92.7	91.4	1.6	1.7	4.0	5.0	1.9	2.2	8.4	9.2	9.0	7.0	4.7	29.1	24.0	7.1	1.6	68.8	35.8	48.9	51.1
46033	CARMEL	93.4	92.0	1.3	1.3	4.1	5.2	1.6	1.9	8.3	9.5	9.7	7.2	4.3	24.3	28.9	7.2	0.5	67.6	37.9	49.6	50.4
46034	CICERO	97.9	97.6	0.3	0.3	0.4	0.5	1.0	1.3	6.5	7.0	7.5	6.2	5.7	29.3	28.3	8.6	0.8	75.1	38.2	49.7	50.3
46035	COLFAX	99.2	99.1	0.0	0.0	0.1	0.1	2.1	2.0	8.0	8.3	8.3	5.9	5.5	28.9	22.4	11.5	1.2	71.8	35.9	50.1	49.9
46036	ELWOOD	98.4	98.2	0.1	0.1	0.3	0.3	1.5	1.8	6.2	6.2	7.0	7.1	6.4	26.3	25.8	13.2	1.8	76.3	39.1	49.0	51.0
46038	FISHERS	92.7	91.6	2.8	3.0	2.9	3.6	1.9	2.2	10.8	10.2	8.3	5.7	5.0	37.8	18.2	3.9	0.2	67.1	31.9	48.8	51.3
46039	FOREST	98.8	98.8	0.4	0.4	0.0	0.0	1.0	1.2	6.3	6.9	8.4	6.5	5.4	28.5	23.5	12.9	1.6	74.5	37.9	48.4	51.6
46040	FORTVILLE	98.1	97.8	0.4	0.4	0.3	0.3	1.2	1.4	7.5	7.9	7.9	6.6	5.7	30.3	23.9	9.0	1.3	72.5	36.1	49.4	50.6
46041	FRANKFORT	92.9	92.8	0.3	0.4	0.3	0.3	9.5	9.7	7.3	6.9	7.3	7.0	7.1	27.2	22.9	12.3	2.1	74.4	35.9	49.6	50.4
46044	FRANKTON	97.9	97.6	0.1	0.1	0.3	0.4	1.3	1.6	6.3	6.3	7.2	6.3	6.6	27.9	25.1	12.8	1.5	76.4	37.8	48.7	51.3
46048	INGALLS	97.8	97.4	0.3	0.3	0.3	0.2	1.0	1.2	8.4	8.1	8.0	6.6	6.6	31.3	21.3	8.8	1.0	71.4	34.2	50.6	49.4
46049	KEMPTON	98.5	98.6	0.0	0.0	0.1	0.1	1.0	1.0	6.0	6.7	7.6	7.2	4.9	26.8	28.3	10.7	1.8	75.2	38.8	50.1	49.9
46050	KIRKLIN	97.4	97.4	0.3	0.3	0.3	0.3	1.5	1.6	7.2	7.8	7.5	6.8	5.6	27.5	26.7	9.7	1.3	73.4	37.3	51.6	48.5
46051	LAPEL	98.8	98.7	0.2	0.2	0.1	0.1	0.4	0.5	7.0	7.0	7.5	7.1	5.8	28.1	24.4	11.7	1.4	74.2	37.0	48.5	51.6
46052	LEBANON	97.9	97.6	0.3	0.3	0.3	0.4	1.4	1.6	7.6	7.3	7.3	6.6	6.2	28.8	23.4	10.9	1.8	73.5	36.3	48.7	51.3
46055	MC CORDSVILLE	97.3	96.8	1.0	1.2	0.5	0.7	0.8	1.0	7.7	8.2	7.9	6.4	4.8	28.1	27.8	8.4	0.7	72.1	38.3	49.2	50.9
46056	MARKLEVILLE	98.7	98.6	0.1	0.1	0.1	0.2	0.6	0.7	5.5	7.4	7.0	6.9	4.3	27.2	29.9	10.7	1.0	75.4	39.7	50.1	49.9
46057	MICHIGANTOWN	98.8	98.9	0.0	0.0	0.1	0.1	0.8	0.8	6.6	6.9	8.3	6.6	6.1	28.3	24.5	11.2	1.6	74.2	37.5	50.1	49.9
46058	MULBERRY	99.0	99.1	0.1	0.1	0.2	0.2	0.6	0.6	5.9	5.9	7.0	6.5	6.2	26.8	22.8	13.7	5.2	77.2	39.8	47.5	52.5
46060	NOBLESVILLE	96.6	96.2	1.1	1.1	0.9	1.1	1.3	1.5	9.0	8.7	7.9	6.4	5.9	31.5	22.7	7.1	0.8	70.3	34.0	49.2	50.8
46064	PENDLETON	89.2	88.3	8.7	9.3	0.4	0.6	1.2	1.4	5.5	5.9	6.2	5.8	7.4	34.1	25.5	8.6	1.1	79.0	37.2	58.7	41.3
46065	ROSSVILLE	98.6	98.5	0.3	0.3	0.2	0.2	0.9	1.0	7.4	8.0	8.5	6.7	5.4	29.1	22.4	10.0	2.7	71.7	36.0	47.5	52.5
46068	SHARPSVILLE	98.5	98.6	0.2	0.2	0.3	0.3	1.2	1.1	6.2	6.6	7.5	7.3	6.1	27.1	28.8	9.4	1.0	75.2	38.4	50.3	49.7
46069	SHERIDAN	97.8	97.5	0.5	0.5	0.3	0.4	1.0	1.2	6.8	7.0	8.3	7.4	6.2	28.4	24.6	9.7	1.7	73.3	36.7	48.7	51.3
46070	SUMMITVILLE	99.2	99.1	0.2	0.3	0.1	0.1	0.6	0.7	6.5	6.9	8.1	6.1	5.1	26.9	25.5	13.0	1.9	74.4	38.5	49.3	50.7
46071	THORNTOWN	98.3	98.1	0.1	0.1	0.1	0.1	1.2	1.4	7.0	7.4	8.3	7.1	5.3	27.5	25.6	10.7	1.2	73.0	38.1	49.2	50.9
46072	TIPTON	98.2	98.2	0.2	0.2	0.4	0.4	1.2	1.3	6.3	6.3	6.6	6.1	5.8	26.4	25.9	13.8	2.8	77.0	39.9	48.4	51.6
46074	WESTFIELD	95.2	94.6	0.8	0.8	1.7	2.2	2.0	2.2	9.3	8.9	8.5	6.5	6.7	32.2	20.7	6.1	1.1	69.1	32.8	49.0	51.0
46075	WHITESTOWN	98.1	97.9	0.5	0.5	0.4	0.5	0.5	0.7	6.0	7.7	7.7	6.6	4.6	29.0	27.9	9.5	1.1	74.8	38.9	50.8	49.2
46076	WINDFALL	98.7	98.6	0.1	0.1	0.1	0.1	0.8	0.8	6.6	6.8	7.2	6.3	5.3	28.3	26.7	11.4	1.4	75.5	38.5	50.6	49.4
46077	ZIONSVILLE	97.2	96.8	0.8	0.8	1.0	1.3	1.0	1.2	7.2	8.3	9.1	7.2	4.6	24.4	28.4	8.7	2.1	70.8	39.1	48.7	51.3
46104	ARLINGTON	98.5	98.5	0.1	0.1	0.2	0.2	0.4	0.3	5.9	7.3	9.0	7.2	4.7	29.5	24.4	10.6	1.4	72.9	37.5	51.1	48.9
46105	BAINBRIDGE	98.7	98.5	0.3	0.3	0.2	0.3	0.6	0.8	7.0	7.3	7.1	6.4	5.2	28.0	26.2	11.8	1.1	74.6	38.6	50.3	49.7
46106	BARGERSVILLE	98.9	98.8	0.1	0.1	0.3	0.3	0.6	0.7	7.1	7.6	8.0	6.3	5.3	28.7	27.6	8.5	0.9	73.3	37.1	50.7	49.3
46107	BEECH GROVE	96.2	95.4	1.0	1.2	0.8	1.0	2.1	2.6	6.9	6.3	6.5	6.6	7.0	28.0	21.8	13.6	3.2	76.2	37.5	47.1	52.9
46110	BOGGSTOWN	98.8	98.8	0.0	0.0	0.0	0.0	0.7	0.5	6.9	7.8	7.6	6.4	5.2	28.2	27.7	9.6	0.7	73.5	38.7	50.0	50.0
46112	BROWNSBURG	97.5	97.1	0.3	0.3	0.8	1.0	1.0	1.2	7.8	7.9	8.3	6.7	5.5	29.9	23.9	8.9	1.2	71.7	36.0	48.9	51.1
46113	CAMBY	97.6	97.2	0.4	0.4	0.5	0.7	0.9	1.1	8.1	8.2	7.6	6.4	5.2	30.1	24.6	9.1	0.8	72.0	35.9	49.9	50.2
46115	CARTHAGE	98.0	98.1	0.0	0.0	0.0	0.0	0.9	0.9	6.5	6.9	7.5	6.1	5.0	29.7	25.0	12.0	1.3	75.3	38.6	51.1	48.9
46117	CHARLOTTESVILLE	98.2	98.0	0.2	0.3	0.2	0.2	1.1	1.2	6.9	7.1	6.5	6.5	5.4	29.1	27.2	10.2	1.2	75.7	38.9	51.4	48.6
46118	CLAYTON	98.8	98.7	0.1	0.0	0.1	0.1	0.7	0.8	5.8	6.5	8.2	6.6	5.0	27.1	29.1	10.9	0.7	75.3	40.0	49.4	50.6
46120	CLOVERDALE	91.7	90.9	6.0	6.5	0.2	0.2	1.4	1.7	6.0	6.0	6.4	6.6	8.1	33.0	23.6	9.3	1.1	78.0	36.2	57.1	42.9
46121	COATESVILLE	98.6	98.5	0.3	0.4	0.1	0.2	0.6	0.6	7.4	7.7	7.6	6.1	4.7	28.3	26.3	10.8	1.1	73.4	38.1	50.7	49.4
46122	DANVILLE	98.6	98.4	0.3	0.3	0.2	0.3	0.9	1.0	6.9	7.3	7.7	6.9	5.9	28.2	25.7	10.1	1.4	73.5	37.4	50.1	49.9
46123	AVON	97.1	96.6	0.3	0.4	1.0	1.3	1.4	1.6	8.5	8.6	8.2	6.4	5.4	30.0	25.5	6.6	0.7	70.6	35.7	49.7	50.3
46124	EDINBURGH	98.6	98.4	0.6	0.6	0.1	0.1	1.0	1.2	6.9	6.8	7.3	6.9	6.7	29.0	25.6	10.1	0.8	74.9	36.7	49.6	50.4
46126	FAIRLAND	98.5	98.2	0.1	0.1	0.1	0.1	0.8	1.0	6.5	7.4	7.9	6.8	5.4	27.9	28.2	9.2	0.8	73.9	38.4	50.4	49.6
46127	FALMOUTH	99.5	99.5	0.3	0.3	0.0	0.0	0.0	0.0	7.7	7.7	7.7	6.4	5.1	29.2	24.3	10.7	1.3	72.9	36.5	51.4	48.6
46128	FILLMORE	98.3	98.2	0.3	0.4	0.1	0.1	0.9	1.0	6.7	7.3	8.7	6.4	4.6	28.8	24.4	12.0	1.0	73.1	38.0	50.2	49.9
46130	FOUNTAINTOWN	98.7	98.5	0.1	0.1	0.3	0.3	1.0	1.2	7.5	7.7	7.7	6.4	5.5	29.1	27.4	8.0	0.7	73.0	37.4	50.4	49.6
46131	FRANKLIN	97.0	96.5	1.1	1.2	0.5	0.6	1.2	1.5	7.7	7.1	7.0	7.1	7.4	28.3	20.6	11.7	3.2	74.3	35.0	48.3	51.7
46133	GLENWOOD	98.8	98.9	0.3	0.3	0.0	0.0	0.2	0.2	6.5	7.2	8.2	6.5	5.5	26.4	26.6	11.8	1.2	74.0	38.8	50.5	49.5
46135	GREENCASTLE	94.0	93.3	3.3	3.5	0.9	1.2	1.3	1.6	6.0	5.8	5.9	9.5	11.8	26.2	21.3	11.4	2.2	78.8	33.7	50.9	49.1
46140	GREENFIELD	98.4	98.2	0.1	0.1	0.5	0.6	1.1	1.3	6.9	7.0	7.0	6.2	5.7	28.2	26.6	10.9	1.5	75.2	38.2	49.4	50.6
46142	GREENWOOD	96.9	96.3	0.3	0.4	1.3	1.7	2.0	2.3	7.5	7.5	7.5	6.9	6.8	28.4	25.0	9.2	1.4	73.4	36.2	49.1	51.0
46143	GREENWOOD	97.2	96.7	0.3	0.4	1.2	1.5	1.2	1.4	7.6	7.4	7.5	6.6	5.7	30.1	24.5	9.2	1.4	73.3	35.7	48.4	51.6
46147	JAMESTOWN	98.9	98.9	0.1	0.1	0.1	0.1	1.0	1.1	6.7	7.1	7.7	6.5	5.4	29.2	25.8	10.5	1.1	74.3	38.0	49.4	50.6
46148	KNIGHTSTOWN	99.2	99.1	0.4	0.4	0.1	0.1	0.3	0.4	6.6	6.9	7.3	6.4	5.5	27.0	25.7	13.0	1.7	75.3	39.0	48.8	51.2
46149	LIZTON	98.6	98.4	0.1	0.2	0.3	0.4	0.7	0.8	6.3	6.7	8.0	6.2	5.5	28.9	28.1	9.4	1.0	75.1	38.7	49.2	50.8
46150	MANILLA	98.6	98.6	0.1	0.1	0.4	0.4	0.7	0.7	7.9	8.3	8.3	7.0	4.9	26.6	25.1	10.3	1.6	71.2	36.8	50.0	50.1
46151	MARTINSVILLE	98.7	98.5	0.1	0.1	0.3	0.3	0.8	0.9	6.9	7.0	7.2	6.4	6.0	28.3	26.7	10.4	1.3	75.0	37.7	50.3	49.7
46156	MILROY	98.0	97.9	0.1	0.1	0.4	0.4	1.1	1.2	8.2	8.5	8.3	6.4	5.3	26.9	23.6	11.7	1.2	70.9	35.9	49.6	50.4
46157	MONROVIA	98.9	98.8	0.0	0.0	0.2	0.3	0.5	0.6	6.2	7.0	7.8	6.9	5.2	28.3	28.0	9.6	1.0	74.3	38.6	50.3	49.7
46158	MOORESVILLE	98.4	98.3	0.1	0.1	0.3	0.4	0.7	0.8	7.8	7.6	7.5	6.9	6.3	29.0	24.8	9.2	0.9	72.9	36.1	49.2	50.9
46160	MORGANTOWN	98.7	98.6	0.1	0.1	0.1	0.1	0.9	1.0	5.9	6.6	7.5	6.6	5.2	26.6	29.2	11.2	1.4	76.0	40.0	50.6	49.5
46161	MORRISTOWN	98.9	98.8	0.1	0.1	0.2	0.2	0.9	1.1	7.0	7.3	7.7	7.2	6.1	28.2	23.6	11.1	1.8	73.7	37.2	49.3	50.7
46162	NEEDHAM	99.3	99.3	0.0	0.0	0.0	0.0	0.7	0.7	7.4	7.7	7.7	6.7	4.9	26.3	28.8	9.5	1.1	73.0	38.9	49.1	50.9
46163	NEW PALESTINE	98.7	98.5	0.1	0.1	0.4	0.5	0.6	0.7	6.5	7.6	7.7	7.0	4.1	26.3	30.5	9.4	1.0	73.3	40.3	49.3	50.7
46164	NINEVEH	89.5	89.7	8.0	7.8	0.2	0.3	2.1	2.2	4.8	5.5	6.2	12.1	8.0	25.1	28.4	9.6	0.4	76.5	37.3	53.6	46.4
46165	NORTH SALEM	98.4	98.2	0.1	0.1	0.5	0.6	0.5	0.6	6.6	7.3	7.5	7.8	5.0	26.7	27.5	10.1	1.6	73.5	38.3	48.6	51.4
46166	PARAGON	99.0	99.0	0.0	0.0	0.1	0.1	0.5	0.6	7.5	7.8	8.4	6.9	5.4	28.2	25.0	10.1	0.9	72.1	36.6	50.2	49.8
46167	PITTSBORO	98.4	98.2	0.1	0.1	0.3	0.4	0.6	0.7	7.9	7.9	7.9	6.5	5.3	28.6	25.8	9.4	0.8	72.3	36.7	48.6	51.4
46168	PLAINFIELD	93.6	92.8	3.8	4.2	0.8	1.0	1.4	1.6	6.4	6.4	6.8	7.7	6.5	30.8	24.1	9.9	1.4	75.4	36.4	52.4	47.7
46171	REELSVILLE	96.5	96.2	2.2	2.4	0.0	0.0	0.5	0.6	5.7	6.5	7.0	7.1	5.4	28.9	28.3	10.5	0.8	75.9	39.1	51.4	48.6
46172	ROACHDALE	98.7	98.6	0.2	0.2	0.1	0.2	0.3	0.4	7.0	7.6	7.2	7.3	5.5	28.0	23.9	12.1	1.6	73.4	37.5	50.3	49.7
46173	RUSHVILLE	97.3	97.3	0.9	0.9	0.7	0.7	0.4	0.4	6.7	6.8	7.4	6.5	6.1	26.8	23.9	13.5	2.4	75.0	38.0	48.7	51.3
46175	RUSSELLVILLE	98.0	97.8	0.0	0.0	0.3	0.5	1.2	1.5	7.2	7.2	8.2	7.3	5.1	27.4	23.2	13.0	1.4	72.8	37.6	50.3	49.7
46176	SHELBYVILLE	96.4	95.9	1.1	1.2	0.9	1.2	1.4	1.6	7.0	6.9	7.1	6.7	6.5	29.1	23.9	11.1	1.7	74.9	36.5	49.4	50.6
46180	STILESVILLE	98.6	98.4	0.1	0.1	0.1	0.1	0.5	0.5	6.8	6.8	6.1	5.7	5.6	27.0	27.0	13.5	1.6	77.0	40.4	50.4	49.6
46181	TRAFALGAR	98.7	98.5	0.2	0.3	0.2	0.3	0.6	0.7	6.2	6.7	8.2	6.8	5.3	27.6	28.3	10.1	0.9	74.6	38.6	50.9	49.1
46182	WALDRON	98.7	98.7	0.2	0.2	0.1	0.1	0.4	0.5	6.0	6.1	7.2	6.5	6.6	26.6	24.8	12.9	3.3	76.6	39.9	49.0	51.0
46184	WHITELAND	98.6	98.4	0.1	0.1	0.3	0.5	1.1	1.3	8.4	8.1	8.3	7.2	6.4	31.8	21.2	8.1	0.4	70.6	33.2	49.1	50.9
46186	WILKINSON	99.1	98.9	0.0	0.0	0.1	0.2	0.5	0.6	7.0	7.1	6.9	6.2	5.7	28.5	26.0	11.4	1.2	75.3	37.9	50.7	49.3
46201	INDIANAPOLIS	72.5	69.4	19.0	20.9	0.4	0.5	9.2	10.7	8.6	7.8	7.6	7.2	7.8	32.0	20.6	7.5	0.9	71.7	31.9	49.6	50.4
46202	INDIANAPOLIS	43.4	40.4	50.8	53.1	2.5	3.0	2.9	3.3	5.2	4.2	3.9	5.6	11.8	35.7	22.1	9.9	1.8	84.5	34.5	52.8	47.2
46203	INDIANAPOLIS	85.3	83.5	9.6	10.6	0.5	0.6	5.3	6.3	8.2	7.6	7.5	6.9	6.7	30.2	21.6	10.2	1.2	72.4	33.9	49.9	50.1
46204	INDIANAPOLIS	48.0	43.7	47.8	51.7	1.4	1.8	2.5	2.9	0.9	0.5	0.5	5.5	15.7	51.8	18.7	5.4	1.1	97.1	34.2	76.3	23.8
	INDIANA	87.5	86.7	8.4	8.7	1.0	1.3	3.5	4.1	7.0	6.9	7.1	7.1	7.4	28.1	24.0	10.8	1.6	75.0	35.9	49.2	50.8
	UNITED STATES	75.1	73.6	12.3	12.5	3.8	4.2	12.5	14.1	6.9	6.7	7.2	7.0	7.3	28.6	23.8	10.8	1.7	75.1	36.0	49.1	50.9

INCOME

ZIP CODE #	POST OFFICE NAME	2004 Per Capita Income	2004 HH Income Base	2004 Household Income Distribution (%): Less than $25,000	$25,000 to $49,999	$50,000 to $99,999	$100,000 to $149,999	$150,000 or More	Median Household Income: 2004	2009	2004 National Centile	2004 State Centile	2004 Home Value Base	2004 Home Value Distribution (%): Less than $50,000	$50,000 to $89,999	$90,000 to $174,999	$175,000 to $399,999	$400,000 or More	2004 Median Home Value
46001	ALEXANDRIA	21307	4746	25.0	32.9	33.0	7.2	2.0	43391	49721	57	40	3665	12.9	37.7	39.7	8.5	1.3	89633
46011	ANDERSON	28904	7131	17.8	26.9	37.9	12.3	5.1	54373	61803	79	86	5894	6.2	28.4	51.2	12.6	1.6	107372
46012	ANDERSON	25937	8568	22.3	30.5	33.4	9.8	4.1	47297	53423	67	63	6419	8.2	34.3	47.7	9.4	0.5	98712
46013	ANDERSON	24578	8322	28.5	35.2	28.0	6.7	1.7	39745	45117	45	22	6009	14.3	36.4	45.5	3.1	0.8	89345
46016	ANDERSON	16257	8837	45.1	31.4	18.9	3.4	1.2	27763	30731	8	3	4887	43.2	45.2	10.3	1.1	0.2	55698
46017	ANDERSON	25300	2598	18.2	31.2	36.3	11.1	3.2	50474	58138	73	74	2193	11.7	31.2	50.3	6.3	0.6	95534
46030	ARCADIA	22705	1234	17.0	25.9	42.7	11.2	3.2	55707	65049	80	87	966	5.2	20.4	53.0	16.2	5.3	113589
46031	ATLANTA	23435	823	19.9	25.9	38.2	13.2	2.8	53546	62567	78	83	683	6.2	20.6	47.7	19.6	5.9	118225
46032	CARMEL	47923	15459	9.2	17.8	31.4	20.2	21.4	83602	99326	96	100	11390	0.6	1.3	27.9	48.7	21.5	236574
46033	CARMEL	50640	11291	4.2	8.5	28.3	28.6	30.4	112073	127966	99	100	10686	0.7	0.2	11.4	67.6	20.1	269806
46034	CICERO	28768	2869	13.6	22.4	44.3	13.6	6.1	63076	74295	87	95	2351	4.4	10.2	51.5	27.6	6.3	140440
46035	COLFAX	19697	450	26.2	29.6	36.4	6.7	1.1	45464	50562	62	53	367	16.6	39.0	32.2	11.4	0.8	85816
46036	ELWOOD	18909	5172	32.0	32.5	27.2	6.9	1.5	37141	42573	36	15	3972	17.0	42.6	34.8	5.2	0.5	79780
46038	FISHERS	38421	19783	5.4	15.4	40.3	25.5	13.4	83734	99616	96	100	15446	0.5	0.6	38.6	51.7	8.6	192793
46039	FOREST	22116	292	23.6	29.5	33.6	9.9	3.4	42349	46579	54	36	252	9.1	26.2	54.0	6.8	4.0	95873
46040	FORTVILLE	26323	2826	20.8	24.5	36.5	12.8	5.3	54313	64202	79	85	2250	5.7	10.0	59.2	18.6	6.5	132561
46041	FRANKFORT	19130	9474	28.1	29.9	33.0	7.8	1.3	42497	48155	55	37	6771	10.1	34.1	45.3	9.9	0.6	94227
46044	FRANKTON	21679	1133	24.4	29.5	35.8	8.5	1.9	46092	51845	64	57	957	15.6	28.9	47.2	7.1	1.2	94038
46048	INGALLS	20181	453	17.9	36.2	35.8	8.8	1.3	47845	54520	68	66	379	9.2	39.3	48.6	2.9	0.0	91058
46049	KEMPTON	25781	301	20.6	27.2	41.2	7.3	3.7	51660	58138	75	79	256	16.8	25.0	47.7	10.2	0.4	94375
46050	KIRKLIN	21644	693	21.2	30.9	35.2	9.1	3.6	48683	54728	70	70	578	10.7	31.7	43.1	9.9	4.7	95116
46051	LAPEL	22068	1035	18.2	36.2	34.8	9.1	1.7	46222	52552	64	58	812	4.7	30.4	54.3	10.0	0.6	100902
46052	LEBANON	22038	8836	23.3	29.9	35.8	8.3	2.7	46652	54073	65	60	6519	6.5	13.8	59.7	17.8	2.2	119528
46055	MC CORDSVILLE	31999	1580	10.1	16.7	37.9	22.7	12.8	77818	88151	94	99	1463	2.6	4.2	40.6	40.1	12.5	180596
46056	MARKLEVILLE	23173	977	17.6	28.7	38.2	14.0	1.5	54195	61449	79	85	890	9.6	19.2	48.7	19.8	2.8	113172
46057	MICHIGANTOWN	21422	435	23.2	28.3	34.3	10.1	4.1	47397	51118	67	64	355	11.6	29.3	41.1	12.1	5.9	98553
46058	MULBERRY	23362	701	18.1	23.3	44.8	10.7	3.1	57396	63330	82	90	565	4.4	19.8	54.7	19.8	1.2	112841
46060	NOBLESVILLE	33074	19093	13.7	18.5	39.2	18.8	9.9	68959	80889	91	97	14912	5.1	6.2	41.7	40.0	7.1	170225
46064	PENDLETON	25478	4100	17.1	26.4	36.4	14.7	5.4	57443	64316	82	90	3411	7.5	8.4	56.3	25.3	2.6	139613
46065	ROSSVILLE	20327	1141	16.4	30.8	42.6	9.3	1.0	51605	57412	75	79	979	10.4	16.5	55.7	16.7	0.8	116390
46068	SHARPSVILLE	27363	1126	11.6	19.9	45.2	18.2	5.2	66827	75800	90	97	985	9.5	21.8	54.0	13.8	0.8	111422
46069	SHERIDAN	21267	2668	22.7	25.8	36.8	12.0	2.7	51183	58590	74	78	2103	8.3	9.8	62.2	18.0	1.8	131361
46070	SUMMITVILLE	20088	951	26.6	29.6	34.2	8.1	1.6	44553	49813	60	47	791	20.6	31.2	45.6	2.5	0.0	88407
46071	THORNTOWN	22033	1304	18.2	33.3	36.3	9.1	3.1	48517	55725	69	69	1112	8.9	18.9	53.4	15.0	3.8	119406
46072	TIPTON	23859	3943	23.7	25.6	37.3	11.6	1.7	50519	56700	73	74	3087	11.0	30.4	45.6	12.4	0.7	96966
46074	WESTFIELD	28696	5229	17.6	19.0	35.9	19.1	8.4	65269	77338	89	96	4136	8.9	4.9	35.1	44.4	6.8	177842
46075	WHITESTOWN	25237	691	14.2	30.8	40.2	11.0	3.8	54600	62160	79	86	598	3.5	9.7	57.9	24.1	4.9	148986
46076	WINDFALL	22710	721	20.3	34.0	32.0	11.1	2.6	46969	53782	66	61	605	20.0	30.7	39.2	8.9	1.2	89182
46077	ZIONSVILLE	38413	6751	15.3	18.1	27.2	17.6	21.9	77248	92602	94	99	5788	4.2	2.0	23.4	45.4	25.1	245590
46104	ARLINGTON	17431	410	24.9	34.4	31.5	9.3	0.0	42009	45509	53	34	351	8.3	38.2	37.9	15.7	0.0	95682
46105	BAINBRIDGE	20352	806	20.6	35.5	34.5	7.2	2.2	44738	50216	61	48	687	9.3	16.9	46.4	24.5	2.9	121472
46106	BARGERSVILLE	27009	1947	13.3	22.7	41.6	17.0	5.6	62872	71418	87	95	1642	2.6	8.3	51.2	32.2	5.9	140278
46107	BEECH GROVE	23933	5552	21.1	31.6	35.5	9.3	2.6	47658	54744	68	65	3704	0.3	22.4	72.2	4.5	0.6	107156
46110	BOGGSTOWN	23349	158	13.3	38.0	33.5	12.0	3.2	49465	56805	71	71	138	5.1	14.5	39.9	37.7	2.9	150000
46112	BROWNSBURG	27969	11578	11.2	24.1	40.7	18.5	5.4	63857	71989	88	95	9834	2.9	2.5	55.4	35.1	4.2	158833
46113	CAMBY	24204	2660	17.3	21.7	44.1	12.9	4.2	58793	65231	83	92	2368	4.0	6.8	60.9	26.1	2.2	141427
46115	CARTHAGE	22279	846	23.9	28.1	33.9	11.7	2.4	46511	49765	65	60	694	9.1	23.5	47.1	16.6	3.8	116284
46117	CHARLOTTESVILLE	27793	234	15.0	17.1	44.9	15.8	7.3	64183	75000	88	96	206	0.0	10.2	49.0	37.4	3.4	162500
46118	CLAYTON	23655	1885	16.9	28.1	40.1	12.8	2.1	53746	60992	78	83	1639	2.7	15.3	45.3	32.2	4.6	144299
46120	CLOVERDALE	17115	2020	25.3	34.4	31.3	7.8	1.2	43881	49593	58	43	1617	11.6	24.4	48.5	14.0	1.5	106684
46121	COATESVILLE	22845	2157	17.8	28.6	39.4	11.9	2.3	52569	58821	76	81	1919	4.7	12.5	45.3	34.6	2.9	152397
46122	DANVILLE	24931	5415	15.3	26.9	38.6	14.6	4.5	57624	64216	82	90	4415	1.7	8.4	54.6	32.2	3.2	158004
46123	AVON	29471	8400	8.8	19.5	45.0	21.1	5.7	69968	79450	91	98	7348	3.8	1.4	47.9	43.6	3.2	171257
46124	EDINBURGH	19211	2946	29.1	31.3	32.1	5.7	1.8	40976	47035	50	28	2137	21.1	15.0	49.5	12.6	1.9	104710
46126	FAIRLAND	24958	1794	16.4	26.2	35.2	16.9	5.3	56579	63343	81	89	1585	2.3	20.1	51.1	23.8	2.7	129099
46127	FALMOUTH	21706	157	19.1	31.2	40.8	7.0	1.9	49745	55153	71	71	130	9.2	26.2	46.2	12.3	6.2	108333
46128	FILLMORE	21264	603	24.9	31.8	31.8	8.5	3.0	45773	51063	63	55	518	8.9	18.2	46.3	23.0	3.7	122549
46130	FOUNTAINTOWN	26819	934	12.3	23.5	41.5	17.5	5.3	64438	72652	88	96	822	0.4	7.2	62.4	27.7	2.3	148319
46131	FRANKLIN	22561	10575	20.4	26.0	39.2	11.8	2.7	53325	61128	77	83	7540	11.3	10.4	58.3	18.4	1.6	124258
46133	GLENWOOD	19545	360	25.0	28.9	37.8	6.7	1.7	46687	51700	65	60	302	11.6	27.2	44.7	14.6	2.0	98947
46135	GREENCASTLE	19736	6502	29.3	31.8	29.3	6.9	2.6	38831	43554	42	19	4701	12.6	18.9	49.5	16.8	2.1	111280
46140	GREENFIELD	28780	14411	14.5	25.5	38.4	16.1	5.5	59881	68332	84	93	11637	3.0	9.2	53.7	31.1	3.1	153202
46142	GREENWOOD	27683	12930	15.9	22.5	39.5	16.8	5.3	60716	67848	85	93	9656	5.3	3.7	56.9	33.0	1.1	156554
46143	GREENWOOD	30338	14049	16.9	23.5	35.4	16.3	8.0	60463	67950	85	93	10445	8.3	7.4	45.1	33.7	5.7	156710
46147	JAMESTOWN	24506	1254	14.6	28.4	39.2	13.7	4.2	54275	62996	79	85	1030	7.6	13.5	62.4	14.3	2.2	124885
46148	KNIGHTSTOWN	23573	1958	25.3	29.6	33.6	9.6	2.0	43690	49224	58	42	1588	6.4	23.9	51.8	15.3	2.6	109838
46149	LIZTON	25216	818	20.3	28.1	36.8	9.9	4.9	51502	57947	75	78	685	2.6	8.3	51.8	33.9	3.4	147650
46150	MANILLA	19974	348	19.5	38.2	30.8	11.2	0.3	43467	47852	57	41	294	10.2	19.7	37.1	27.2	5.8	125000
46151	MARTINSVILLE	23311	12688	22.4	27.0	37.8	9.1	3.7	50550	56147	73	74	9934	8.4	13.7	49.2	24.4	4.3	133154
46156	MILROY	18846	554	23.1	29.1	35.7	11.7	0.4	48104	52612	69	67	460	10.4	23.7	44.4	15.0	6.5	102244
46157	MONROVIA	24354	1109	20.9	22.5	40.5	12.4	3.8	56459	62241	81	89	946	5.9	14.9	53.5	23.4	2.3	123718
46158	MOORESVILLE	25041	9618	17.6	27.1	38.7	12.8	3.8	54383	61010	79	86	7958	10.9	7.2	53.7	24.6	3.6	138752
46160	MORGANTOWN	20587	2417	28.2	28.3	31.6	9.1	2.7	42253	47919	54	35	2033	10.6	14.2	43.4	28.3	3.4	129018
46161	MORRISTOWN	22354	985	19.7	29.1	37.1	11.6	2.5	50640	57089	73	75	800	10.5	22.9	48.4	16.3	2.0	108462
46162	NEEDHAM	26585	117	12.8	29.1	41.0	13.7	3.4	57589	64938	82	90	103	4.9	10.7	45.6	35.0	3.9	146094
46163	NEW PALESTINE	29993	3677	13.4	19.8	37.2	19.6	10.0	71182	80419	92	98	3313	3.4	2.8	37.5	53.0	3.3	183195
46164	NINEVEH	22920	1816	16.2	30.3	39.7	10.1	3.6	52245	59285	76	80	1658	2.1	10.4	57.1	28.7	1.9	147786
46165	NORTH SALEM	26326	713	18.2	25.3	38.2	12.9	5.5	55824	62528	80	87	614	4.9	23.5	50.2	17.8	3.8	122222
46166	PARAGON	18652	772	21.9	33.8	36.0	7.6	0.7	46150	52658	64	58	625	14.4	21.0	43.4	17.6	3.7	111037
46167	PITTSBORO	24966	2088	12.7	24.1	43.3	15.9	3.9	61445	69187	86	94	1846	0.6	3.1	50.7	41.7	3.9	167819
46168	PLAINFIELD	24764	9855	19.6	25.4	38.4	12.6	3.9	54186	61827	79	85	7416	6.0	3.3	58.9	30.7	1.1	153652
46171	REELSVILLE	20280	704	26.0	28.4	35.5	9.1	1.0	47203	52124	67	62	631	6.8	22.0	48.5	20.9	1.7	115213
46172	ROACHDALE	19750	964	23.1	33.8	33.3	7.6	2.2	44325	49530	60	46	792	8.7	28.8	41.2	19.4	1.9	99900
46173	RUSHVILLE	19861	4474	29.3	36.4	26.7	5.6	2.1	39087	43091	43	20	3202	10.8	31.0	46.9	8.8	2.6	97892
46175	RUSSELLVILLE	16449	267	30.0	40.5	25.1	4.5	0.0	35925	40995	31	11	223	21.1	34.1	35.9	9.0	0.0	80417
46176	SHELBYVILLE	22793	10995	24.5	30.8	33.6	8.6	2.6	44964	50518	61	49	7616	7.2	24.3	54.8	12.0	1.7	109649
46180	STILESVILLE	22986	509	16.5	35.6	34.6	11.8	1.6	48413	54618	69	68	431	4.9	12.3	55.9	26.5	0.5	130048
46181	TRAFALGAR	24889	1738	15.3	26.1	41.1	12.3	5.2	57291	64691	82	90	1503	2.9	8.5	50.2	32.8	5.6	155525
46182	WALDRON	21013	715	22.7	32.0	33.9	9.0	2.5	45429	50483	62	53	601	5.5	23.3	54.1	13.8	3.3	111409
46184	WHITELAND	23151	3502	9.1	27.9	46.7	14.4	1.9	61163	69701	85	94	3034	0.0	9.8	76.1	12.5	1.6	119465
46186	WILKINSON	24581	958	17.8	23.5	42.4	13.5	2.9	58327	66326	83	91	816	4.9	14.1	58.6	21.0	1.5	133772
46201	INDIANAPOLIS	15076	14473	40.4	34.8	21.0	3.2	0.7	30587	35031	14	5	6989	29.2	58.2	11.0	1.4	0.3	64290
46202	INDIANAPOLIS	23970	8076	49.0	24.7	18.1	5.3	3.0	25558	30125	5	2	2198	21.8	31.4	23.0	19.9	3.9	85625
46203	INDIANAPOLIS	17630	16153	35.1	34.0	25.0	4.7	1.3	34842	39612	27	9	10040	23.3	51.6	22.2	2.4	0.4	71240
46204	INDIANAPOLIS	22239	1715	44.7	21.9	20.6	7.4	5.4	29269	36571	11	4	241	2.1	3.3	33.6	44.0	17.0	207353
	INDIANA	23565		24.7	29.6	32.4	9.4	3.9	45964	52146				12.3	23.5	44.9	16.9	2.4	109048
	UNITED STATES	25866		24.7	27.1	30.8	10.9	6.5	48124	56710				10.9	15.0	33.7	30.1	10.4	145905

#	ZIP CODE POST OFFICE NAME	FINANCIAL SERVICES: Auto Loan	FINANCIAL SERVICES: Home Loan	FINANCIAL SERVICES: Invest-ments	FINANCIAL SERVICES: Retire-ment Plans	THE HOME: Home Improvements: Home Repair	THE HOME: Home Improvements: Lawn & Garden	THE HOME: Furnishings: Comput-ers & Hard-ware	THE HOME: Furnishings: Major Appli-ances	THE HOME: Furnishings: TV, Radio, Sound Equip-ment	THE HOME: Furnishings: Furni-ture	ENTERTAINMENT: Dine out/ Carry out	ENTERTAINMENT: Sports Equip-ment	ENTERTAINMENT: Fees & Tickets	ENTERTAINMENT: Toys & Games	ENTERTAINMENT: Travel	ENTERTAINMENT: Cable TV	PERSONAL: Apparel & Services	PERSONAL: Auto Repairs	PERSONAL: Health Insur-ance	PERSONAL: Pets & Supplies
46001	ALEXANDRIA	72	76	76	73	76	83	74	75	75	72	93	85	76	97	76	77	90	74	78	85
46011	ANDERSON	96	101	106	100	102	108	98	100	97	97	121	116	100	123	100	97	118	99	99	114
46012	ANDERSON	81	87	96	86	87	93	87	86	86	85	107	99	89	110	88	86	105	86	85	94
46013	ANDERSON	74	69	68	67	72	80	71	73	74	69	91	83	70	91	72	76	87	73	80	85
46016	ANDERSON	53	49	51	48	50	56	53	53	56	52	69	61	52	68	53	57	66	54	56	60
46017	ANDERSON	83	87	86	84	88	95	84	86	85	82	105	97	86	109	86	87	102	84	88	97
46030	ARCADIA	96	89	73	86	92	100	85	91	88	84	108	107	84	109	86	90	103	89	96	111
46031	ATLANTA	95	95	84	93	96	99	88	92	88	88	109	110	88	111	89	87	105	91	91	110
46032	CARMEL	171	199	231	205	193	200	186	182	175	189	222	212	197	225	188	170	221	180	166	200
46033	CARMEL	199	246	271	252	239	242	218	214	200	222	254	247	238	262	222	194	255	207	192	236
46034	CICERO	98	114	118	114	112	112	105	105	99	105	124	124	109	130	106	96	123	102	95	117
46035	COLFAX	82	73	55	69	77	82	67	75	71	67	87	89	66	89	69	73	83	73	81	96
46036	ELWOOD	66	64	60	60	66	73	63	65	67	61	82	74	64	86	65	69	78	64	71	76
46038	FISHERS	147	166	160	173	158	152	150	148	137	156	174	174	154	175	146	128	172	144	126	162
46039	FOREST	93	83	63	78	87	94	76	85	81	76	99	101	75	101	79	83	94	82	92	109
46040	FORTVILLE	98	95	85	95	97	103	92	96	93	91	115	112	91	116	92	93	110	94	97	113
46041	FRANKFORT	77	67	55	64	70	78	67	72	72	66	87	84	65	88	68	74	83	71	79	88
46044	FRANKTON	82	74	62	69	78	86	72	78	77	71	94	90	71	96	74	81	89	77	86	96
46048	INGALLS	89	79	60	75	84	90	73	81	78	73	95	97	72	97	75	80	90	79	88	105
46049	KEMPTON	110	98	75	93	104	111	91	100	96	91	117	120	89	119	93	99	111	98	109	130
46050	KIRKLIN	93	81	59	77	86	93	75	85	81	75	98	101	73	99	78	83	92	82	93	110
46051	LAPEL	82	76	66	73	79	87	75	79	79	73	96	90	75	99	76	81	92	77	85	93
46052	LEBANON	79	77	72	76	79	85	76	79	78	75	96	92	76	97	77	78	92	78	81	92
46055	MC CORDSVILLE	127	153	159	155	149	146	137	136	127	138	160	160	145	167	138	122	159	132	120	150
46056	MARKLEVILLE	98	88	68	84	93	99	81	90	86	81	104	107	80	107	84	88	100	87	96	115
46057	MICHIGANTOWN	94	83	64	79	88	95	77	85	82	77	100	102	76	102	79	84	95	83	93	110
46058	MULBERRY	97	85	67	83	89	98	83	90	88	82	107	105	81	107	84	89	101	88	97	110
46060	NOBLESVILLE	127	135	128	139	132	134	126	127	121	128	151	148	129	152	124	116	148	124	117	143
46064	PENDLETON	113	107	93	104	111	118	101	108	104	101	128	128	100	129	103	105	122	106	112	132
46065	ROSSVILLE	89	79	60	76	83	90	75	82	79	74	97	97	73	98	76	81	91	80	89	103
46068	SHARPSVILLE	120	106	81	101	112	121	98	109	104	98	127	130	96	130	101	107	121	106	118	141
46069	SHERIDAN	80	86	85	85	86	89	82	83	80	81	100	97	84	104	83	79	98	81	81	95
46070	SUMMITVILLE	74	73	68	69	75	82	70	73	74	69	90	84	72	96	73	76	87	71	79	87
46071	THORNTOWN	94	84	64	79	88	95	77	86	82	77	100	102	76	102	80	84	95	83	93	111
46072	TIPTON	85	80	71	78	83	91	78	82	81	77	100	95	78	102	79	83	95	81	88	98
46074	WESTFIELD	109	122	128	126	119	119	115	114	107	116	136	133	118	137	114	102	134	112	101	125
46075	WHITESTOWN	104	95	76	92	100	106	88	96	92	88	112	114	87	115	90	93	107	93	102	122
46076	WINDFALL	92	82	63	78	87	93	76	84	81	76	98	100	74	100	78	83	93	82	91	109
46077	ZIONSVILLE	141	173	191	176	169	170	156	153	144	157	182	177	168	189	159	140	182	148	138	169
46104	ARLINGTON	79	70	53	67	74	80	65	72	69	65	84	86	64	86	67	71	80	70	78	92
46105	BAINBRIDGE	86	72	52	69	76	85	70	78	76	70	92	91	67	91	71	78	86	76	86	98
46106	BARGERSVILLE	109	111	101	109	113	116	102	107	101	102	126	127	104	129	104	101	122	104	106	129
46107	BEECH GROVE	75	78	85	78	78	84	80	79	80	78	99	92	81	102	80	79	96	79	78	87
46110	BOGGSTOWN	97	86	65	82	91	97	79	88	84	79	103	105	78	105	82	87	98	86	95	114
46112	BROWNSBURG	106	118	116	118	116	116	108	109	103	109	129	129	111	133	108	100	127	107	101	124
46113	CAMBY	96	97	91	96	98	102	91	95	91	91	112	112	92	114	92	90	109	93	94	113
46115	CARTHAGE	90	78	59	76	82	91	76	83	81	75	98	97	73	99	77	83	93	82	90	103
46117	CHARLOTTESVILLE	101	124	131	124	122	121	111	111	103	110	130	130	118	138	113	100	129	107	100	123
46118	CLAYTON	94	94	83	91	97	100	86	91	86	86	106	108	87	110	88	87	103	88	93	112
46120	CLOVERDALE	78	69	54	67	71	77	67	72	70	67	85	84	64	84	67	70	81	71	76	88
46121	COATESVILLE	97	87	67	83	91	98	81	89	85	81	104	105	79	106	83	87	99	86	95	113
46122	DANVILLE	99	99	89	97	102	106	93	98	93	92	115	115	93	119	94	93	111	95	98	117
46123	AVON	117	132	127	135	127	124	119	119	111	123	140	140	123	141	117	105	138	116	105	132
46124	EDINBURGH	80	66	49	63	70	77	65	72	71	65	85	84	61	84	65	72	81	71	79	90
46126	FAIRLAND	103	103	92	100	105	111	96	101	97	96	120	118	97	123	98	98	116	98	103	120
46127	FALMOUTH	87	77	59	73	81	87	71	79	76	71	92	94	70	94	73	78	87	77	86	102
46128	FILLMORE	91	80	61	77	84	92	77	84	82	76	99	98	75	100	78	84	94	82	91	105
46130	FOUNTAINTOWN	107	114	108	112	116	118	104	108	102	103	126	127	107	132	106	101	123	105	106	128
46131	FRANKLIN	88	87	81	86	88	93	85	87	85	84	105	101	84	105	85	84	101	86	87	100
46133	GLENWOOD	88	71	48	67	78	85	67	78	74	67	89	94	63	89	70	77	83	77	88	105
46135	GREENCASTLE	75	63	50	60	66	74	64	69	69	63	83	81	60	82	64	71	78	69	77	86
46140	GREENFIELD	101	109	109	109	110	113	103	105	100	103	125	123	106	129	104	99	122	103	101	119
46142	GREENWOOD	98	108	112	110	107	108	103	102	98	103	123	120	105	125	102	95	121	101	95	114
46143	GREENWOOD	108	113	116	115	111	115	109	109	105	110	132	127	110	131	108	102	129	108	102	123
46147	JAMESTOWN	104	94	74	90	99	106	87	96	91	87	111	114	86	114	89	93	106	93	102	122
46148	KNIGHTSTOWN	85	82	73	77	85	93	78	82	82	77	101	95	79	106	81	85	97	81	89	99
46149	LIZTON	103	95	75	91	100	106	87	96	92	87	112	114	86	115	90	93	107	93	102	122
46150	MANILLA	85	75	57	71	79	85	70	77	74	70	90	92	68	92	72	76	85	75	83	99
46151	MARTINSVILLE	92	87	74	84	90	97	83	88	86	82	105	103	82	107	84	88	100	86	93	107
46156	MILROY	88	78	60	74	83	89	72	80	77	72	93	96	71	95	75	79	89	78	87	104
46157	MONROVIA	107	95	72	90	101	108	88	97	93	88	114	116	86	116	91	96	108	95	106	126
46158	MOORESVILLE	96	100	94	99	100	104	94	97	93	94	115	112	95	118	95	92	112	94	95	112
46160	MORGANTOWN	90	74	52	70	79	88	71	80	78	71	94	95	67	93	72	80	88	79	90	104
46161	MORRISTOWN	95	84	65	81	88	96	81	88	85	80	104	103	79	105	82	87	98	86	95	109
46162	NEEDHAM	104	92	70	88	98	105	85	95	91	85	110	113	84	113	88	93	105	92	102	122
46163	NEW PALESTINE	112	136	144	138	133	133	121	120	112	121	142	140	130	149	124	109	141	116	109	135
46164	NINEVEH	100	84	61	79	92	100	79	91	86	79	103	107	74	104	82	90	97	89	102	120
46165	NORTH SALEM	101	105	97	103	107	110	96	100	95	95	117	119	98	122	98	95	114	97	99	120
46166	PARAGON	90	71	45	65	77	85	67	78	75	67	90	93	62	89	68	79	84	76	90	105
46167	PITTSBORO	97	107	104	106	106	107	98	100	94	98	117	118	101	121	99	91	115	97	93	114
46168	PLAINFIELD	90	94	93	94	94	98	90	92	89	90	111	107	91	112	91	88	107	91	90	105
46171	REELSVILLE	77	69	52	65	73	78	64	71	68	64	82	84	62	84	66	69	78	69	76	91
46172	ROACHDALE	79	74	63	70	77	84	70	75	74	69	91	88	70	94	72	77	87	73	82	93
46173	RUSHVILLE	79	66	49	62	71	79	65	72	71	64	86	84	62	86	66	74	80	71	82	92
46175	RUSSELLVILLE	77	52	24	45	59	68	50	63	60	51	71	75	43	67	51	65	64	62	77	89
46176	SHELBYVILLE	84	76	68	75	78	85	77	80	80	76	98	94	75	98	77	81	94	80	84	96
46180	STILESVILLE	93	83	63	79	88	94	77	85	81	77	99	101	75	101	79	83	94	83	92	110
46181	TRAFALGAR	110	98	75	93	104	111	91	100	96	91	117	120	89	120	93	99	111	98	109	130
46182	WALDRON	88	79	60	75	83	89	73	80	77	73	94	96	71	96	75	79	89	78	87	104
46184	WHITELAND	90	103	107	104	100	100	96	95	90	97	114	111	99	116	96	86	112	93	86	104
46186	WILKINSON	89	98	99	98	98	101	92	93	89	91	111	108	95	116	94	88	109	91	90	105
46201	INDIANAPOLIS	51	47	53	47	47	52	54	51	55	52	69	60	53	68	52	55	66	53	52	56
46202	INDIANAPOLIS	57	47	65	50	46	53	61	55	63	59	78	67	58	75	56	61	76	60	55	62
46203	INDIANAPOLIS	60	57	61	56	57	64	62	60	64	60	79	70	61	80	61	65	76	61	63	68
46204	INDIANAPOLIS	70	60	92	67	59	67	77	69	79	75	99	85	75	97	73	76	96	76	67	77
	INDIANA	86	83	80	82	84	90	82	84	84	82	103	98	82	104	82	84	100	84	86	98
	UNITED STATES	100	100	100	100	100	100	100	100	100	100	100	100	100	100	100	100	100	100	100	100

INDIANA

POPULATION CHANGE

A 46205-46534

ZIP CODE # / POST OFFICE NAME	COUNTY FIPS CODE	POPULATION 2000	2004	2009	2000-2004 ANNUAL RATE % Rate	State Centile	HOUSEHOLDS 2000	2004	2009	% Annual Rate 2000-2004	2004 Average HH Size	FAMILIES 2000	2004	% Annual Rate 2000-2004
46205 INDIANAPOLIS	097	30742	29836	29845	-0.7	4	12789	12815	13160	0.1	2.30	6926	6476	-1.6
46208 INDIANAPOLIS	097	24447	23686	23674	-0.7	3	9888	9910	10198	0.1	2.17	5221	4840	-1.8
46214 INDIANAPOLIS	097	22210	22824	23205	0.6	52	10400	10976	11432	1.3	2.05	5258	5216	-0.2
46216 INDIANAPOLIS	097	342	803	1191	22.2	100	154	389	604	24.4	2.06	89	212	22.7
46217 INDIANAPOLIS	097	19223	22717	24902	4.0	98	7306	8874	9966	4.7	2.56	5513	6494	3.9
46218 INDIANAPOLIS	097	35005	33427	33143	-1.1	1	13527	13381	13652	-0.3	2.46	8901	8357	-1.5
46219 INDIANAPOLIS	097	36213	35702	35723	-0.3	11	15793	16059	16491	0.4	2.18	9261	8852	-1.1
46220 INDIANAPOLIS	097	35199	34796	34878	-0.3	14	16585	16869	17336	0.4	2.04	8560	8121	-1.2
46221 INDIANAPOLIS	097	24398	25125	25767	0.7	54	9045	9594	10093	1.4	2.60	6475	6614	0.5
46222 INDIANAPOLIS	097	36273	34553	34208	-1.1	1	13786	13461	13638	-0.6	2.49	8414	7753	-1.9
46224 INDIANAPOLIS	097	34766	34182	34068	-0.4	9	15278	15291	15542	0.0	2.21	8470	7901	-1.6
46225 INDIANAPOLIS	097	8140	7665	7572	-1.4	0	3048	2954	2993	-0.7	2.46	1782	1621	-2.2
46226 INDIANAPOLIS	097	44714	43516	43354	-0.6	5	17820	17819	18190	0.0	2.44	11643	11047	-1.2
46227 INDIANAPOLIS	097	52839	52130	52167	-0.3	12	22516	22881	23487	0.4	2.21	13238	12648	-1.1
46228 INDIANAPOLIS	097	14929	15524	15909	0.9	62	5829	6211	6516	1.5	2.48	4093	4182	0.5
46229 INDIANAPOLIS	097	24178	25155	25825	0.9	63	9359	10011	10529	1.6	2.51	6594	6743	0.5
46231 INDIANAPOLIS	063	5173	6867	8218	6.9	100	1833	2505	3078	7.6	2.70	1460	1939	6.9
46234 INDIANAPOLIS	063	18697	20489	22370	2.2	91	7184	8082	9017	2.8	2.50	4969	5333	1.7
46235 INDIANAPOLIS	097	23745	24598	25144	0.8	60	8979	9505	9922	1.4	2.57	6181	6241	0.2
46236 INDIANAPOLIS	097	26881	30158	32010	2.7	94	9367	10644	11487	3.1	2.82	7440	8258	2.5
46237 INDIANAPOLIS	097	28228	31552	33640	2.7	94	10724	12382	13567	3.4	2.54	7677	8585	2.7
46239 INDIANAPOLIS	097	12603	14738	16028	3.8	97	4694	5646	6293	4.4	2.60	3601	4184	3.6
46240 INDIANAPOLIS	097	18093	18706	19110	0.8	58	9125	9722	10192	1.5	1.90	4364	4326	-0.2
46241 INDIANAPOLIS	097	30587	30381	30592	-0.2	20	11945	12203	12599	0.5	2.48	8111	7905	-0.6
46250 INDIANAPOLIS	097	17242	17543	17963	0.4	46	8501	8958	9446	1.2	1.93	3919	3894	-0.2
46254 INDIANAPOLIS	097	34885	37670	39198	1.8	86	15314	16808	17816	2.2	2.23	8472	8678	0.6
46256 INDIANAPOLIS	097	24340	25184	26043	0.8	59	9629	10209	10774	1.4	2.45	6515	6655	0.5
46259 INDIANAPOLIS	097	6738	8115	9042	4.5	99	2237	2732	3097	4.8	2.97	1927	2318	4.4
46260 INDIANAPOLIS	097	31825	31785	32044	0.0	25	13579	13933	14397	0.6	2.22	7951	7689	-0.8
46268 INDIANAPOLIS	097	22629	23750	24403	1.1	70	10163	10847	11362	1.5	2.13	5307	5360	0.2
46278 INDIANAPOLIS	097	6930	7541	7933	2.0	89	2465	2752	2959	2.6	2.73	1943	2089	1.7
46280 INDIANAPOLIS	057	6504	7441	9049	3.2	96	2548	2991	3705	3.8	2.49	1831	2056	2.8
46290 INDIANAPOLIS	057	189	229	286	4.6	99	86	106	134	5.0	2.15	64	76	4.1
46303 CEDAR LAKE	089	11587	12169	12554	1.2	71	4191	4435	4612	1.3	2.74	3180	3261	0.6
46304 CHESTERTON	127	21893	22681	23780	0.8	60	8243	8713	9331	1.3	2.58	5900	6005	0.4
46307 CROWN POINT	089	49065	52581	54959	1.6	82	17580	19048	20129	1.9	2.65	13172	13812	1.1
46310 DEMOTTE	073	12250	13159	14183	1.7	84	4312	4748	5224	2.3	2.74	3439	3684	1.6
46311 DYER	089	16436	17691	18465	1.8	85	5674	6165	6488	2.0	2.81	4580	4846	1.3
46312 EAST CHICAGO	089	32385	32106	32545	-0.2	18	11692	11648	11879	-0.1	2.74	7931	7560	-1.1
46319 GRIFFITH	089	19243	19607	19982	0.4	47	7502	7672	7866	0.5	2.55	5310	5234	-0.3
46320 HAMMOND	089	16664	16766	17117	0.1	34	6165	6266	6448	0.4	2.65	3813	3660	-1.0
46321 MUNSTER	089	21463	21990	22513	0.6	51	8076	8289	8529	0.6	2.61	6131	6115	-0.1
46322 HIGHLAND	089	23506	23729	24055	0.2	38	9605	9784	9996	0.4	2.42	6666	6505	-0.6
46323 HAMMOND	089	23669	23584	23789	-0.1	23	9284	9284	9413	0.0	2.54	6146	5875	-1.1
46324 HAMMOND	089	23377	23126	23275	-0.3	16	9068	9020	9136	-0.1	2.56	6114	5815	-1.2
46327 HAMMOND	089	11971	11965	12134	0.0	26	4365	4339	4408	-0.1	2.73	2913	2766	-1.2
46340 HANNA	091	1113	1153	1164	0.8	60	403	429	438	1.5	2.69	300	308	0.6
46341 HEBRON	127	9408	9993	10580	1.4	78	3460	3767	4076	2.0	2.65	2648	2791	1.3
46342 HOBART	089	29635	31096	32137	1.1	70	11566	12221	12727	1.3	2.53	8078	8180	0.3
46347 KOUTS	127	3899	4325	4688	2.5	93	1413	1607	1783	3.1	2.65	1112	1229	2.4
46348 LA CROSSE	091	1056	1081	1085	0.6	50	413	435	443	1.2	2.49	298	301	0.2
46349 LAKE VILLAGE	111	3457	3638	3796	1.2	72	1216	1308	1392	1.7	2.78	949	993	1.1
46350 LA PORTE	091	44246	44461	44545	0.1	32	16980	17376	17548	0.5	2.52	12008	11870	-0.3
46356 LOWELL	089	15238	15981	16436	1.1	69	5412	5718	5924	1.3	2.77	4204	4305	0.6
46360 MICHIGAN CITY	091	46684	46318	46254	-0.2	18	18058	18314	18477	0.3	2.38	11964	11597	-0.7
46365 MILL CREEK	091	1176	1186	1190	0.2	36	422	434	439	0.7	2.73	344	344	0.0
46366 NORTH JUDSON	149	6198	6325	6654	0.5	48	2261	2354	2522	1.0	2.68	1682	1698	0.2
46368 PORTAGE	127	34827	36499	38651	1.1	69	13244	14238	15446	1.7	2.54	9512	9842	0.8
46371 ROLLING PRAIRIE	091	3133	3220	3237	0.7	52	1159	1213	1229	1.1	2.65	903	918	0.4
46373 SAINT JOHN	089	8646	9701	10356	2.8	95	2893	3262	3504	2.9	2.97	2475	2739	2.4
46374 SAN PIERRE	149	1086	1155	1223	1.5	79	365	400	435	2.2	2.56	257	270	1.2
46375 SCHERERVILLE	089	19031	19781	20242	0.9	62	7329	7642	7860	1.0	2.58	5283	5312	0.1
46382 UNION MILLS	091	2079	2211	2273	1.5	79	742	803	832	1.9	2.52	576	604	1.1
46383 VALPARAISO	127	35879	37487	39461	1.0	67	13636	14600	15754	1.6	2.39	9025	9274	0.6
46385 VALPARAISO	127	33516	35439	37754	1.3	75	11858	12848	14005	1.9	2.74	9327	9836	1.3
46390 WANATAH	091	2438	2390	2369	-0.5	8	921	916	912	-0.1	2.01	729	706	-0.8
46391 WESTVILLE	091	7598	7933	8152	1.0	66	1735	1918	2041	2.4	2.90	1286	1371	1.5
46392 WHEATFIELD	073	6765	7241	7848	1.6	82	2286	2496	2755	2.1	2.87	1882	2008	1.5
46394 WHITING	089	12533	12346	12445	-0.4	11	5250	5188	5258	-0.3	2.37	3201	2998	-1.5
46402 GARY	089	8972	8566	8539	-1.1	1	3477	3336	3348	-1.0	2.50	2044	1864	-2.2
46403 GARY	089	14620	14465	14642	-0.3	16	5872	5860	5943	-0.1	2.46	3792	3600	-1.2
46404 GARY	089	20818	20517	20742	-0.3	11	7825	7761	7903	-0.2	2.63	5464	5206	-1.1
46405 LAKE STATION	089	13224	13133	13271	-0.2	20	4708	4710	4795	0.0	2.77	3364	3234	-0.9
46406 GARY	089	12308	11800	11787	-1.0	2	4354	4206	4230	-0.8	2.78	3112	2888	-1.7
46407 GARY	089	18045	17079	16993	-1.3	0	7089	6753	6762	-1.1	2.50	4388	3970	-2.3
46408 GARY	089	20337	19880	19987	-0.5	7	7364	7241	7327	-0.4	2.73	5085	4782	-1.4
46409 GARY	089	12724	12389	12401	-0.6	5	4101	4011	4042	-0.5	3.07	3019	2845	-1.4
46410 MERRILLVILLE	089	32787	34127	35219	1.0	64	12560	13192	13725	1.2	2.53	8700	8749	0.1
46501 ARGOS	099	3740	3761	3826	0.1	32	1358	1392	1439	0.6	2.70	1047	1042	-0.1
46504 BOURBON	099	3386	3397	3462	0.1	30	1215	1238	1281	0.4	2.74	906	893	-0.3
46506 BREMEN	099	10120	10291	10518	0.4	45	3575	3687	3819	0.7	2.76	2732	2731	0.0
46507 BRISTOL	039	9055	9535	10052	1.2	72	3318	3544	3777	1.6	2.68	2557	2647	0.8
46508 BURKET	085	195	207	221	1.4	77	76	82	89	1.8	2.52	60	63	1.2
46510 CLAYPOOL	085	3643	3825	4066	1.2	70	1284	1376	1487	1.6	2.78	1003	1043	0.9
46511 CULVER	099	4209	4271	4390	0.3	42	1642	1694	1767	0.7	2.47	1156	1149	-0.1
46514 ELKHART	039	38761	40356	42475	1.0	64	15347	16194	17228	1.3	2.48	10641	10781	0.3
46516 ELKHART	039	33426	34098	35548	0.5	48	12051	12414	13061	0.7	2.73	8114	8005	-0.3
46517 ELKHART	039	20507	21556	22763	1.2	71	7665	8146	8694	1.4	2.58	5308	5436	0.6
46524 ETNA GREEN	085	1998	2213	2419	2.4	93	619	688	757	2.5	3.20	477	515	1.8
46526 GOSHEN	039	27737	29080	30646	1.1	69	9986	10604	11305	1.4	2.60	6965	7113	0.5
46528 GOSHEN	039	23177	24342	25610	1.2	71	7699	8164	8667	1.4	2.96	6061	6255	0.7
46530 GRANGER	141	27440	29768	31265	1.9	88	8967	9940	10616	2.5	2.99	7863	8556	2.0
46531 GROVERTOWN	149	1376	1438	1520	1.0	67	486	519	559	1.6	2.77	389	404	0.9
46532 HAMLET	149	2149	2110	2159	-0.4	9	804	808	841	0.1	2.61	622	606	-0.6
46534 KNOX	149	10828	11308	11999	1.0	66	4049	4307	4651	1.5	2.59	2960	3047	0.7
INDIANA					0.8					1.2	2.48			0.3
UNITED STATES					1.2					1.3	2.58			1.1

Copyright © 2004 ESRI BIS. All rights reserved. Reproduction by any method is prohibited.   86-A

ZIP CODE #	POST OFFICE NAME	RACE (%) White 2000	White 2004	Black 2000	Black 2004	Asian/Pacific 2000	Asian/Pacific 2004	% Hispanic Origin 2000	% Hispanic Origin 2004	2004 AGE DISTRIBUTION (%) 0-4	5-9	10-14	15-19	20-24	25-44	45-64	65-84	85+	18+	MEDIAN AGE 2004	% 2004 Males	% 2004 Females
46205	INDIANAPOLIS	28.4	26.2	68.6	70.6	0.5	0.5	1.5	1.6	7.5	7.0	7.6	7.3	8.0	29.5	22.7	9.3	1.2	73.4	33.5	47.2	52.8
46208	INDIANAPOLIS	29.3	27.9	68.4	69.6	0.6	0.7	0.9	1.0	5.9	5.8	6.6	11.0	10.6	24.3	21.7	12.0	2.2	77.9	34.2	45.6	54.4
46214	INDIANAPOLIS	81.3	78.5	12.8	14.6	2.4	3.0	2.7	3.2	6.2	5.7	5.8	7.0	8.9	34.3	21.1	9.2	1.9	78.2	33.7	47.5	52.5
46216	INDIANAPOLIS	73.1	68.2	19.9	24.8	2.3	3.0	0.9	1.0	3.7	6.1	7.9	4.7	4.5	32.6	24.4	12.1	4.0	78.8	40.0	42.8	57.2
46217	INDIANAPOLIS	97.1	96.4	0.4	0.4	1.1	1.4	1.3	1.8	6.4	6.7	7.1	6.5	5.8	28.1	27.4	11.1	0.9	75.6	38.4	49.0	51.0
46218	INDIANAPOLIS	23.7	22.4	73.5	74.7	0.2	0.2	2.1	2.3	7.3	7.6	8.4	7.9	6.3	26.1	22.4	12.4	1.7	71.6	35.3	46.4	53.6
46219	INDIANAPOLIS	85.1	83.1	11.3	12.8	0.7	0.9	2.4	2.9	6.8	6.6	6.3	5.9	5.9	28.4	23.4	14.2	2.7	76.9	39.2	47.4	52.6
46220	INDIANAPOLIS	85.4	82.8	10.9	12.7	1.4	1.7	2.2	2.7	5.7	5.0	5.4	5.4	7.1	34.5	23.9	11.0	2.1	80.6	36.6	48.4	51.7
46221	INDIANAPOLIS	94.7	93.9	1.9	2.1	0.4	0.5	3.9	4.7	8.1	7.5	7.6	7.2	7.1	30.8	21.7	9.2	0.9	72.4	33.5	49.8	50.2
46222	INDIANAPOLIS	53.5	50.4	38.5	40.6	1.6	1.9	7.4	8.6	7.6	7.5	7.8	8.3	8.8	30.5	19.7	8.6	1.1	72.4	31.2	49.7	50.3
46224	INDIANAPOLIS	66.6	63.0	23.0	25.2	2.6	3.0	8.8	10.0	7.9	6.8	6.5	6.2	9.0	33.0	19.2	9.9	1.5	75.6	32.3	48.7	51.3
46225	INDIANAPOLIS	84.9	82.5	8.6	9.8	0.2	0.2	7.0	8.4	7.9	7.2	6.8	6.0	8.1	32.3	21.0	9.2	1.4	74.7	33.6	52.3	47.7
46226	INDIANAPOLIS	43.5	40.2	51.7	54.5	1.1	1.3	3.8	4.4	7.3	7.2	7.9	7.5	7.7	27.9	23.5	10.2	0.9	73.1	34.1	47.3	52.7
46227	INDIANAPOLIS	93.5	92.3	2.5	2.8	1.1	1.4	3.3	4.1	7.2	6.3	6.3	6.8	9.1	29.0	21.2	11.9	2.2	76.8	34.1	47.7	52.3
46228	INDIANAPOLIS	50.5	46.3	44.1	47.8	2.0	2.4	1.7	1.9	6.2	6.5	7.4	6.4	6.0	27.2	26.8	12.2	1.5	75.9	39.2	47.6	52.4
46229	INDIANAPOLIS	75.1	71.7	19.5	22.1	1.9	2.2	2.8	3.3	7.8	7.6	8.2	7.3	7.1	30.0	22.3	9.0	0.8	72.0	33.7	47.2	52.8
46231	INDIANAPOLIS	93.0	91.3	3.3	4.1	2.0	2.6	1.4	1.7	7.0	7.5	8.2	6.7	5.7	29.2	26.7	7.9	1.1	73.0	36.5	48.6	51.4
46234	INDIANAPOLIS	92.8	91.6	3.7	4.2	1.4	1.8	1.9	2.3	7.3	6.9	7.0	6.5	6.7	31.8	24.1	8.4	1.4	74.8	35.4	48.3	51.7
46235	INDIANAPOLIS	39.2	36.1	55.2	57.9	1.0	1.2	4.4	4.9	11.5	9.6	8.7	8.2	9.2	29.6	17.1	5.2	0.8	65.3	26.7	45.2	54.8
46236	INDIANAPOLIS	86.1	83.2	9.5	11.6	2.2	2.7	2.1	2.5	9.6	9.7	9.0	6.8	4.9	31.8	22.9	4.8	0.6	67.4	33.8	49.5	50.5
46237	INDIANAPOLIS	95.6	94.6	0.9	1.1	1.7	2.2	1.8	2.2	8.4	7.8	7.4	6.3	6.8	34.1	21.6	6.9	0.8	72.7	32.6	49.3	50.7
46239	INDIANAPOLIS	93.9	92.7	3.5	4.2	1.1	1.4	1.0	1.3	6.8	7.1	7.6	6.7	5.5	28.1	26.4	11.0	0.8	74.2	38.2	48.7	51.3
46240	INDIANAPOLIS	91.3	89.8	3.9	4.6	2.0	2.4	2.6	3.2	4.4	4.7	5.0	5.0	7.5	30.3	25.4	15.0	2.7	82.8	40.4	47.9	52.1
46241	INDIANAPOLIS	92.2	90.6	4.0	4.8	0.6	0.8	2.8	3.6	8.0	7.3	7.7	7.1	7.2	30.2	22.6	9.0	0.9	72.7	33.9	49.3	50.7
46250	INDIANAPOLIS	86.3	84.0	7.8	9.0	2.7	3.3	3.4	4.2	5.1	4.6	4.8	5.5	11.5	34.5	21.3	10.6	2.1	82.2	34.0	48.1	51.9
46254	INDIANAPOLIS	49.5	45.4	38.8	41.7	3.9	4.5	7.7	8.5	9.0	7.6	6.9	6.2	8.6	39.2	17.8	4.3	0.4	72.8	30.5	47.4	52.6
46256	INDIANAPOLIS	84.9	82.6	8.9	10.1	2.8	3.5	2.9	3.5	7.0	7.4	7.7	6.6	6.7	29.6	26.0	8.2	0.8	73.7	36.1	49.2	50.8
46259	INDIANAPOLIS	98.2	97.6	0.2	0.2	0.6	0.9	0.8	1.1	8.7	8.4	8.8	7.4	4.3	30.2	24.9	6.8	0.5	69.1	35.1	50.1	49.9
46260	INDIANAPOLIS	64.7	61.7	27.8	29.9	1.9	2.3	6.7	7.7	6.4	5.9	6.6	7.0	8.3	28.4	23.2	12.0	2.1	76.9	35.6	47.5	52.5
46268	INDIANAPOLIS	64.3	59.8	28.1	31.5	3.4	4.1	4.2	4.9	6.9	6.3	6.1	6.2	7.8	34.7	19.5	8.3	4.3	76.8	34.6	46.6	53.4
46278	INDIANAPOLIS	78.6	74.7	14.9	17.6	4.5	5.5	1.9	2.3	7.2	8.1	8.2	6.2	4.2	27.0	29.1	8.3	1.8	72.5	39.6	49.3	50.7
46280	INDIANAPOLIS	94.6	93.9	1.1	1.1	2.1	2.7	1.7	2.0	7.8	7.8	6.8	5.4	4.2	29.4	25.1	12.4	1.1	74.1	39.0	47.5	52.5
46290	INDIANAPOLIS	93.7	93.0	2.1	2.2	2.7	3.5	1.1	1.3	7.4	7.9	7.0	5.2	3.5	27.1	27.5	13.1	1.3	74.2	40.6	47.2	52.8
46303	CEDAR LAKE	97.5	96.8	0.1	0.2	0.2	0.3	3.3	4.4	7.1	7.3	7.9	7.0	6.3	30.0	25.3	8.4	0.8	73.5	35.8	50.9	49.1
46304	CHESTERTON	96.4	95.9	0.5	0.5	0.9	1.2	3.7	4.3	7.0	7.0	7.0	6.7	6.5	27.3	27.6	9.8	1.2	74.9	37.6	49.2	50.8
46307	CROWN POINT	94.1	92.2	2.0	2.9	1.1	1.4	4.9	6.3	6.0	6.1	6.7	6.7	6.9	27.7	27.1	11.0	1.8	77.2	38.7	49.1	50.9
46310	DEMOTTE	98.2	97.9	0.1	0.2	0.2	0.3	2.2	2.7	7.0	7.4	8.0	6.6	5.7	27.3	25.5	10.9	1.7	73.6	37.3	49.6	50.4
46311	DYER	95.7	94.5	0.6	0.9	1.5	1.8	4.8	6.4	6.1	6.5	7.2	6.7	6.1	25.9	28.8	11.2	1.6	75.9	40.0	49.0	51.0
46312	EAST CHICAGO	36.5	33.3	36.1	38.4	0.3	0.3	51.6	52.4	9.3	8.6	7.9	7.2	8.6	25.9	19.7	11.4	1.5	70.0	30.9	47.9	52.2
46319	GRIFFITH	85.0	82.2	9.3	10.9	0.9	1.0	8.3	10.5	6.5	6.6	7.1	6.5	6.8	29.9	25.0	10.4	1.2	75.9	36.6	48.6	51.5
46320	HAMMOND	43.2	37.6	40.0	44.0	0.4	0.4	23.8	26.2	9.6	8.8	8.8	7.6	7.4	28.0	19.7	9.1	1.1	68.1	30.6	48.6	51.4
46321	MUNSTER	92.3	90.0	1.0	1.6	4.5	5.7	4.9	6.3	4.9	5.7	7.2	6.6	5.0	21.3	29.8	16.6	3.0	78.1	44.6	47.9	52.1
46322	HIGHLAND	94.4	92.7	1.3	1.9	1.1	1.4	6.6	8.7	5.3	5.4	6.0	5.8	6.1	27.7	26.4	15.6	1.8	79.9	41.1	48.0	52.0
46323	HAMMOND	79.7	75.3	11.2	13.6	0.7	0.8	16.6	20.4	8.0	7.2	6.9	6.3	7.5	29.6	22.5	10.8	1.3	74.3	34.4	49.2	50.8
46324	HAMMOND	79.9	75.2	10.0	12.6	0.6	0.6	16.9	20.5	8.0	7.6	7.5	6.1	6.6	29.7	22.3	10.4	1.7	73.2	34.9	48.4	51.6
46327	HAMMOND	72.0	66.3	3.8	4.9	0.6	0.7	37.4	44.1	8.2	7.9	8.2	7.2	7.7	28.6	20.5	10.0	1.8	71.5	32.4	50.3	49.7
46340	HANNA	98.2	97.9	0.5	0.6	0.5	0.6	0.4	0.4	6.4	6.3	6.1	6.1	7.0	27.2	27.9	11.5	1.5	77.5	40.0	51.3	48.7
46341	HEBRON	97.3	96.9	0.4	0.4	0.3	0.4	3.0	3.5	6.8	6.7	7.4	7.0	6.6	27.3	26.9	10.2	1.1	74.7	37.4	49.2	50.8
46342	HOBART	92.9	90.7	1.3	1.9	0.5	0.6	9.3	12.1	6.5	6.4	6.6	6.2	6.6	28.8	24.7	12.3	1.9	76.7	37.5	48.6	51.4
46347	KOUTS	98.6	98.5	0.3	0.3	0.2	0.2	1.2	1.5	7.3	7.4	7.1	7.2	6.2	27.7	25.6	10.2	1.3	73.3	36.8	50.4	49.6
46348	LA CROSSE	97.9	97.7	0.3	0.4	0.6	0.7	1.5	1.8	5.7	5.8	6.3	6.9	6.6	27.5	27.2	11.7	2.3	78.0	40.2	49.4	50.6
46349	LAKE VILLAGE	96.4	96.0	0.1	0.1	0.2	0.3	2.4	2.9	6.2	6.6	8.0	7.4	6.5	29.3	25.2	10.1	0.6	74.7	37.1	50.5	49.5
46350	LA PORTE	94.5	93.7	1.7	1.9	0.4	0.5	4.1	4.8	6.5	6.5	7.1	6.6	6.3	27.0	26.2	12.0	1.9	75.8	38.4	49.3	50.7
46356	LOWELL	97.4	96.7	0.1	0.2	0.3	0.3	3.0	4.0	6.6	7.0	7.9	7.2	6.4	28.0	26.0	9.8	1.2	74.0	37.1	50.2	49.8
46360	MICHIGAN CITY	77.0	75.3	19.1	20.4	0.6	0.8	2.7	3.1	6.8	6.4	6.5	6.1	6.8	27.4	25.4	12.9	1.8	76.7	38.3	50.4	49.6
46365	MILL CREEK	96.4	96.0	0.9	0.9	0.1	0.2	1.6	1.9	6.8	7.0	7.9	6.5	5.5	28.6	25.6	11.1	1.0	74.3	38.2	51.0	49.0
46366	NORTH JUDSON	97.8	97.5	0.1	0.1	0.1	0.1	3.4	4.0	7.1	7.1	8.1	7.6	6.5	26.8	24.3	11.2	1.4	73.0	36.0	49.0	51.0
46368	PORTAGE	92.9	91.9	1.4	1.5	0.7	0.8	9.4	11.0	7.2	7.0	7.0	6.4	6.7	28.6	25.2	10.4	1.5	74.9	36.2	48.6	51.4
46371	ROLLING PRAIRIE	97.5	97.1	0.3	0.4	0.2	0.3	2.5	3.0	6.4	6.8	7.2	6.7	5.7	27.6	28.1	10.6	1.0	75.5	39.0	51.0	49.0
46373	SAINT JOHN	97.4	96.7	0.1	0.3	0.6	0.7	4.0	5.3	5.5	6.7	7.9	7.2	5.6	25.3	31.8	9.1	0.9	75.1	40.5	50.3	49.7
46374	SAN PIERRE	98.6	98.4	0.2	0.2	0.0	0.0	0.9	1.1	4.8	4.9	5.5	5.8	6.1	22.3	28.5	17.8	4.3	80.7	45.3	50.9	49.1
46375	SCHERERVILLE	93.0	90.9	1.4	2.1	2.4	3.0	5.5	7.2	5.9	6.1	6.5	6.2	6.8	27.4	29.1	11.0	1.1	77.8	39.3	49.3	50.7
46382	UNION MILLS	92.9	92.6	5.1	5.1	0.4	0.5	1.1	1.4	6.2	6.6	7.5	6.7	7.0	29.9	26.4	8.7	1.1	75.8	36.9	55.6	44.4
46383	VALPARAISO	95.5	94.9	1.2	1.3	1.2	1.5	2.9	3.5	5.7	6.0	6.3	8.1	9.8	26.5	25.3	10.3	2.0	78.2	36.0	48.6	51.4
46385	VALPARAISO	95.7	95.0	0.7	0.7	1.3	1.7	4.0	4.8	6.3	6.6	7.5	7.0	7.0	27.1	28.8	8.8	0.9	75.3	37.6	49.4	50.6
46390	WANATAH	87.5	86.3	10.0	11.0	0.3	0.3	1.9	2.2	4.8	5.3	5.3	5.2	8.2	35.9	25.5	8.7	1.0	81.7	37.0	61.7	38.3
46391	WESTVILLE	82.4	81.7	14.1	14.6	0.3	0.4	2.5	2.9	4.5	4.8	5.5	5.4	9.5	37.1	25.4	7.0	0.8	82.3	36.2	65.0	35.0
46392	WHEATFIELD	97.9	97.6	0.4	0.4	0.1	0.1	2.8	3.4	7.8	7.4	7.6	7.1	6.6	28.6	25.1	9.0	0.8	72.6	34.8	50.6	49.5
46394	WHITING	89.7	87.0	0.4	0.5	0.5	0.6	19.8	24.6	5.9	5.8	6.6	6.2	6.4	27.8	24.2	14.2	3.0	77.9	39.6	48.1	51.9
46402	GARY	5.6	4.3	89.0	90.8	0.1	0.1	6.6	6.2	7.9	8.0	7.8	7.0	6.6	23.2	23.0	14.4	2.0	72.2	36.3	46.1	53.9
46403	GARY	20.7	15.9	73.8	78.9	0.3	0.2	5.8	5.8	8.2	7.8	7.3	6.8	7.6	25.6	27.6	8.3	0.7	72.4	33.9	46.5	53.5
46404	GARY	1.8	1.5	96.4	96.9	0.1	0.1	1.5	1.5	8.0	7.7	7.6	7.2	6.6	22.8	23.4	15.3	1.5	72.4	36.8	44.4	55.6
46405	LAKE STATION	84.1	80.5	2.8	3.1	0.4	0.4	20.5	25.7	7.7	7.4	7.2	6.7	7.7	28.8	23.8	9.7	1.1	73.8	33.8	49.9	50.1
46406	GARY	30.6	28.8	63.1	64.6	0.2	0.2	11.4	12.2	8.0	8.0	8.7	7.4	6.9	25.6	22.9	11.6	0.9	70.8	33.9	46.7	53.3
46407	GARY	1.2	0.9	97.2	97.7	0.1	0.1	1.3	1.3	8.9	8.2	7.8	7.0	6.8	22.4	21.4	15.0	2.5	71.0	35.3	44.7	55.3
46408	GARY	38.8	36.4	55.7	57.8	0.3	0.4	7.5	8.4	7.9	7.6	7.9	7.8	7.9	25.9	24.9	9.0	1.0	71.9	33.1	47.4	52.6
46409	GARY	10.2	7.6	85.0	87.9	0.1	0.2	5.5	5.3	9.0	9.4	9.9	8.5	8.0	24.9	22.9	6.7	0.6	66.4	28.5	46.4	53.6
46410	MERRILLVILLE	67.7	61.0	24.9	30.6	1.4	1.6	9.5	11.3	6.7	6.5	6.6	6.6	7.3	28.2	24.0	11.8	2.4	76.2	36.9	48.2	51.9
46501	ARGOS	98.8	98.6	0.2	0.3	0.1	0.2	1.2	1.5	7.6	7.6	8.4	7.4	6.4	28.4	22.8	9.8	1.5	71.8	34.6	50.6	49.4
46504	BOURBON	97.0	96.6	0.3	0.3	0.4	0.5	3.7	4.4	8.6	8.1	8.3	7.4	6.4	28.5	21.8	9.7	1.2	70.2	33.6	49.7	50.3
46506	BREMEN	95.0	94.2	0.1	0.1	0.3	0.4	6.3	7.4	7.9	8.0	8.1	7.0	6.3	26.3	23.8	10.9	1.9	71.4	35.6	50.0	50.0
46507	BRISTOL	93.6	92.4	1.2	1.3	1.2	1.4	4.0	4.9	8.1	8.3	7.7	6.4	5.5	29.1	25.9	8.3	0.8	72.0	35.6	50.7	49.3
46508	BURKET	98.0	97.6	0.5	0.5	0.0	0.0	1.5	2.4	7.7	7.3	8.7	6.8	5.3	30.0	22.7	10.1	1.5	71.5	35.4	52.2	47.8
46510	CLAYPOOL	97.9	97.7	0.2	0.2	0.1	0.1	1.4	1.7	7.4	7.4	7.7	6.9	6.0	29.2	24.4	10.0	1.1	73.4	35.9	51.4	48.7
46511	CULVER	96.0	95.7	1.1	1.1	0.4	0.5	2.5	2.9	6.2	6.3	7.1	6.3	5.8	25.0	25.5	15.1	2.7	76.4	40.8	49.2	50.8
46514	ELKHART	90.9	89.4	3.7	4.2	1.2	1.5	4.3	5.3	7.5	7.2	7.2	6.4	6.1	28.8	24.3	11.0	1.6	74.2	36.4	48.5	51.5
46516	ELKHART	70.8	68.6	16.0	16.6	0.9	1.1	14.8	16.8	9.1	8.2	8.1	7.1	7.5	30.1	20.9	8.0	1.0	70.4	31.3	50.2	49.8
46517	ELKHART	79.7	77.5	9.4	10.0	1.0	1.2	11.2	12.9	7.4	7.2	7.3	7.0	6.9	29.0	23.4	10.0	1.9	73.8	35.3	48.8	51.2
46524	ETNA GREEN	96.9	96.3	0.2	0.2	0.3	0.4	3.5	4.3	9.9	9.7	9.9	8.4	7.0	27.8	19.4	7.0	0.9	64.8	29.7	51.7	48.3
46526	GOSHEN	88.8	86.8	1.4	1.5	1.1	1.4	12.4	14.8	7.5	7.2	7.0	7.0	7.9	28.5	20.8	11.4	2.9	74.4	34.1	49.6	50.4
46528	GOSHEN	87.8	85.8	1.2	1.3	1.0	1.2	12.8	15.0	8.7	8.8	9.0	7.7	6.5	30.5	21.6	6.6	0.7	68.7	31.5	51.4	48.6
46530	GRANGER	94.0	92.7	1.8	2.1	2.7	3.4	1.3	1.7	7.0	8.1	9.3	7.7	5.3	24.5	30.0	7.5	0.6	70.8	38.3	49.3	50.7
46531	GROVERTOWN	98.0	97.7	0.2	0.1	0.2	0.1	2.7	3.2	6.7	7.4	8.3	7.3	5.4	27.6	25.2	11.1	1.0	73.0	37.1	50.9	49.1
46532	HAMLET	97.3	97.0	0.8	0.9	0.5	0.6	1.2	1.4	7.0	7.9	8.0	6.7	5.6	28.3	24.8	10.6	1.1	73.0	36.2	51.7	48.3
46534	KNOX	97.3	96.9	0.2	0.2	0.3	0.4	1.8	2.2	6.5	6.8	7.6	7.0	6.2	26.6	25.1	12.7	1.5	74.7	37.7	49.6	50.4
	INDIANA	87.5	86.7	8.4	8.7	1.0	1.3	3.5	4.1	7.0	6.9	7.1	7.1	7.4	28.1	24.0	10.8	1.6	75.0	35.9	49.2	50.8
	UNITED STATES	75.1	73.6	12.3	12.5	3.8	4.2	12.5	14.1	6.9	6.7	7.2	7.0	7.3	28.6	23.8	10.8	1.7	75.1	36.0	49.1	50.9

#	POST OFFICE NAME	2004 Per Capita Income	2004 HH Income Base	2004 Household Income Distribution (%): Less than $25,000	$25,000 to $49,999	$50,000 to $99,999	$100,000 to $149,999	$150,000 or More	Median Household Income: 2004	2009	2004 National Centile	2004 State Centile	2004 Home Value Base	2004 Home Value Distribution (%): Less than $50,000	$50,000 to $89,999	$90,000 to $174,999	$175,000 to $399,999	$400,000 or More	2004 Median Home Value
46205	INDIANAPOLIS	20442	12815	37.2	29.8	23.6	6.3	3.1	34295	38163	25	8	6112	12.6	41.3	30.8	13.4	2.0	85761
46208	INDIANAPOLIS	21320	9910	41.7	27.5	20.8	5.8	4.3	30748	34134	14	5	5158	22.5	36.0	22.2	16.3	3.0	77373
46214	INDIANAPOLIS	28399	10976	19.8	32.9	35.7	9.3	2.4	47916	53637	68	66	5174	1.4	9.9	76.2	12.2	0.4	125278
46216	INDIANAPOLIS	54398	389	16.7	8.5	34.2	20.1	20.6	82358	95274	96	99	282	3.2	5.7	42.2	48.9	0.0	173770
46217	INDIANAPOLIS	29356	8874	11.0	25.3	40.4	17.6	5.6	63037	71632	87	95	7725	1.2	8.6	67.2	21.6	1.5	135015
46218	INDIANAPOLIS	15601	13381	42.6	33.4	20.0	3.0	1.1	29179	32595	11	3	8162	26.7	63.9	8.9	0.4	0.1	64217
46219	INDIANAPOLIS	23773	16059	26.5	33.1	31.0	7.4	2.1	42214	48490	54	34	10610	8.8	33.2	54.3	3.4	0.3	96797
46220	INDIANAPOLIS	40313	16869	15.6	25.5	34.6	14.3	10.0	59636	68867	84	93	10863	0.5	5.1	54.6	34.0	5.7	159117
46221	INDIANAPOLIS	20131	9594	27.2	28.2	34.3	8.8	1.5	44738	51320	61	48	6914	12.8	29.1	52.4	5.1	0.7	99655
46222	INDIANAPOLIS	16978	13461	33.9	37.5	23.3	4.2	1.2	34133	38610	24	7	7228	28.1	57.2	14.2	0.4	0.2	66164
46224	INDIANAPOLIS	21272	15291	29.0	35.5	28.0	6.1	1.3	38022	42626	39	17	6186	5.2	32.4	59.8	2.5	0.2	98552
46225	INDIANAPOLIS	15055	2954	41.7	34.2	21.0	2.8	0.3	30296	34734	13	4	1522	30.4	52.6	16.4	0.7	0.0	64639
46226	INDIANAPOLIS	21326	17819	25.5	35.2	29.5	7.4	2.6	41049	46450	50	29	10666	9.9	49.8	35.4	4.2	0.8	83646
46227	INDIANAPOLIS	23643	22881	27.0	33.6	29.3	7.5	2.7	40411	45915	48	26	11874	5.9	16.8	68.8	7.8	0.8	115881
46228	INDIANAPOLIS	29941	6211	18.4	23.0	35.1	16.0	7.6	58737	67288	83	92	5124	1.4	8.7	63.8	22.2	3.9	137762
46229	INDIANAPOLIS	24470	10011	17.9	32.4	35.9	10.8	3.0	49734	57193	71	71	6041	1.0	12.5	75.5	10.4	0.6	120946
46231	INDIANAPOLIS	25854	2505	12.5	25.8	41.8	16.1	3.9	61261	69733	86	94	2224	7.4	8.8	66.4	17.1	0.3	121485
46234	INDIANAPOLIS	28404	8082	15.5	26.1	39.5	13.5	5.5	58003	65612	83	91	6493	20.7	7.2	53.2	17.3	1.7	119953
46235	INDIANAPOLIS	17730	9505	34.8	31.9	26.2	5.6	1.5	35333	39679	29	10	4761	20.3	32.0	44.5	2.2	1.0	87380
46236	INDIANAPOLIS	38993	10644	8.2	17.9	36.6	20.4	16.9	78776	92490	95	99	9992	10.3	3.1	42.4	32.6	11.6	163549
46237	INDIANAPOLIS	28243	12382	11.9	24.7	44.2	14.9	4.2	61156	71926	85	94	9396	2.5	8.1	73.8	14.3	1.4	128406
46239	INDIANAPOLIS	27381	5646	13.8	25.4	39.4	16.2	5.1	61609	69861	86	94	4995	10.5	5.7	62.1	21.0	0.8	139004
46240	INDIANAPOLIS	41034	9722	19.7	29.4	29.4	11.7	9.8	50975	57146	74	77	5145	1.3	5.3	44.8	38.1	10.5	172770
46241	INDIANAPOLIS	18931	12203	28.3	35.0	29.9	5.4	1.4	39607	45424	45	22	8401	22.5	43.6	32.4	1.2	0.3	77001
46250	INDIANAPOLIS	35258	8958	12.6	32.6	35.7	13.3	5.7	53890	61352	78	84	4139	0.0	1.4	58.9	35.9	3.9	160864
46254	INDIANAPOLIS	26751	16808	20.5	32.3	34.5	9.5	3.3	47550	53978	67	64	7973	1.4	16.6	70.5	9.5	1.9	121911
46256	INDIANAPOLIS	36013	10209	14.8	21.1	33.8	17.7	12.5	68979	78831	91	97	7441	0.2	2.6	51.1	39.3	6.9	170306
46259	INDIANAPOLIS	30276	2732	7.2	16.9	44.5	23.4	8.1	76824	88133	94	98	2581	3.5	6.0	45.7	41.0	3.9	167681
46260	INDIANAPOLIS	35619	13933	19.3	29.7	29.4	11.6	10.0	50878	57492	74	76	7219	0.9	8.7	51.1	31.0	8.3	158229
46268	INDIANAPOLIS	28259	10847	21.9	29.5	32.6	10.9	5.0	48546	54431	69	69	5826	1.2	7.7	70.3	20.8	0.0	140717
46278	INDIANAPOLIS	41648	2752	6.9	20.2	31.4	22.0	19.5	82068	93736	96	99	2552	0.3	4.6	29.7	51.4	14.1	203500
46280	INDIANAPOLIS	38016	2991	8.9	20.6	42.7	17.5	10.3	70009	81676	91	98	2459	1.1	2.7	56.9	34.6	4.8	161437
46290	INDIANAPOLIS	63255	106	4.7	18.9	40.6	16.0	19.8	73935	85043	93	98	93	0.0	3.2	47.3	28.0	21.5	174038
46303	CEDAR LAKE	22517	4435	17.6	28.6	38.6	12.8	2.5	53115	60829	77	82	3599	4.1	17.0	50.5	25.3	3.1	128533
46304	CHESTERTON	28979	8713	15.9	24.4	39.2	13.8	6.7	58884	65619	83	92	6788	10.2	6.7	46.7	30.4	6.0	153628
46307	CROWN POINT	27763	19048	14.3	23.0	40.7	15.7	6.3	63304	71574	87	95	15503	1.8	5.0	55.6	34.0	3.6	160532
46310	DEMOTTE	22320	4748	19.0	30.7	38.0	9.3	3.1	50220	55573	72	72	4067	8.0	9.2	56.1	25.0	1.7	139124
46311	DYER	29732	6165	12.3	20.3	40.5	19.9	7.0	67858	76347	90	97	5543	0.9	3.6	53.3	37.0	5.2	166282
46312	EAST CHICAGO	15241	11648	43.0	29.2	21.4	4.6	1.9	29352	34391	11	4	5219	15.8	48.7	33.1	2.2	0.2	78909
46319	GRIFFITH	24927	7672	17.7	27.5	39.3	12.1	3.4	53961	61907	78	84	5391	1.4	9.2	75.9	13.2	0.4	121841
46320	HAMMOND	13934	6266	44.6	31.0	20.5	2.7	1.2	28209	32281	9	3	2740	25.0	53.2	19.5	2.0	0.3	67768
46321	MUNSTER	35257	8289	13.9	20.6	34.6	17.4	13.6	67035	74934	90	97	7382	1.0	3.4	38.1	49.7	7.8	185382
46322	HIGHLAND	28078	9784	15.9	26.9	40.5	12.7	4.1	55929	63602	81	88	7735	1.2	6.4	72.0	19.4	1.0	140779
46323	HAMMOND	20220	9284	24.6	32.9	33.9	7.1	1.5	44810	51600	61	48	6155	3.2	42.6	52.3	1.7	0.3	92449
46324	HAMMOND	19668	9020	27.6	31.8	32.6	6.3	1.7	42057	49307	53	34	6349	3.8	41.1	50.9	3.8	0.4	93086
46327	HAMMOND	15345	4339	34.5	34.2	26.0	4.5	0.8	34242	39963	25	8	2862	18.2	51.4	29.3	1.0	0.1	76352
46340	HANNA	19972	429	16.8	37.3	39.6	4.7	1.6	47262	53272	67	63	366	6.0	18.3	54.1	19.1	2.5	114535
46341	HEBRON	24501	3767	17.9	23.7	42.7	12.8	2.8	56852	63894	82	89	3130	8.8	5.3	56.9	26.1	3.0	141306
46342	HOBART	23645	12221	20.5	29.0	38.7	9.3	2.4	50289	57286	72	73	9760	10.1	19.9	59.2	10.4	0.4	108521
46347	KOUTS	24655	1607	13.9	24.6	48.2	11.1	2.3	60413	67018	85	93	1337	1.1	7.9	58.7	30.7	1.7	152172
46348	LA CROSSE	21270	435	19.8	34.5	40.0	4.4	1.4	46328	51993	65	59	371	7.0	26.2	53.1	12.4	1.4	102287
46349	LAKE VILLAGE	19218	1308	22.9	32.1	37.5	6.0	1.5	44810	48306	61	48	1110	9.2	15.8	59.8	13.9	1.4	118672
46350	LA PORTE	22630	17376	23.6	28.4	35.9	9.1	2.9	47966	53342	68	66	13285	7.1	19.4	54.6	17.6	1.4	116232
46356	LOWELL	24496	5718	15.4	25.0	42.4	13.3	3.9	58530	66338	83	92	4724	3.1	7.5	61.7	25.7	2.0	140333
46360	MICHIGAN CITY	22342	18314	27.7	31.3	30.7	7.2	3.2	42195	47741	53	34	12715	9.3	26.7	44.8	16.3	3.0	104252
46365	MILL CREEK	22204	434	14.5	34.1	38.9	9.9	2.5	50967	57096	74	77	390	9.0	21.5	50.8	15.4	3.3	112963
46366	NORTH JUDSON	17110	2354	30.1	35.5	27.5	5.6	1.3	39068	42704	43	20	1892	14.3	28.4	46.9	9.0	1.3	97173
46368	PORTAGE	24435	14238	20.8	25.3	40.8	10.0	3.1	53139	60374	77	83	10581	15.3	9.0	61.0	13.5	1.3	122232
46371	ROLLING PRAIRIE	22693	1213	18.4	29.4	38.3	11.8	2.1	51611	56594	75	79	1067	10.6	13.7	52.8	19.6	3.4	121761
46373	SAINT JOHN	28994	3262	10.4	18.9	41.3	20.6	8.8	73381	80920	93	98	3078	0.6	1.6	34.1	59.9	3.8	191746
46374	SAN PIERRE	18187	400	24.8	33.3	34.8	7.0	0.3	42345	46402	54	36	343	16.0	35.6	45.5	2.9	0.0	88333
46375	SCHERERVILLE	32855	7642	12.8	22.5	39.3	16.4	9.0	64199	73025	88	96	5986	0.7	4.2	44.0	45.8	5.4	176672
46382	UNION MILLS	20748	803	17.7	33.6	40.1	6.9	1.7	48022	52945	68	67	706	10.5	23.7	50.3	13.0	2.6	108125
46383	VALPARAISO	27336	14600	21.3	23.8	37.0	12.3	5.7	54827	61149	79	87	9944	6.0	5.1	53.7	30.7	4.5	154521
46385	VALPARAISO	31346	12848	12.3	20.1	43.8	15.9	7.9	66243	75852	89	96	10989	3.6	7.2	47.5	36.1	5.7	158959
46390	WANATAH	26261	916	17.6	25.9	43.9	10.8	1.9	57055	61750	82	90	802	1.4	13.5	66.6	16.8	1.8	122149
46391	WESTVILLE	19653	1918	20.0	22.9	41.1	11.6	4.4	56600	62447	81	89	1649	21.0	8.7	34.8	29.6	6.0	135813
46392	WHEATFIELD	21816	2496	15.2	29.7	43.2	10.2	1.8	53831	60972	78	84	2117	7.4	13.9	54.8	20.9	3.0	130071
46394	WHITING	21046	5188	28.5	30.8	31.2	7.4	2.1	41819	48378	52	32	3337	4.8	23.0	66.5	5.5	0.2	107855
46402	GARY	13744	3336	54.2	22.8	19.1	3.1	0.9	21874	25293	3	2	1428	50.7	36.2	12.1	0.6	0.4	49592
46403	GARY	21425	5860	30.8	29.4	28.2	8.0	3.6	39892	44621	46	23	3454	18.8	33.3	36.5	9.8	1.6	86712
46404	GARY	15819	7761	43.7	27.0	21.3	6.2	1.9	29076	32678	10	3	4662	35.0	42.7	20.9	1.1	0.3	61180
46405	LAKE STATION	17381	4710	28.5	34.1	30.1	5.8	1.4	41207	47312	50	29	3534	18.4	46.1	33.6	1.7	0.2	79255
46406	GARY	14129	4206	43.5	29.3	21.2	4.5	1.4	29250	32925	11	3	2596	46.6	41.6	10.0	1.9	0.0	53397
46407	GARY	14123	6753	55.4	23.9	15.8	3.0	2.0	21561	24882	2	2	3134	53.4	33.9	12.3	0.3	0.2	47643
46408	GARY	17443	7241	32.4	31.6	27.1	7.6	1.3	39202	44735	43	21	4910	33.4	43.4	22.2	1.0	0.0	68427
46409	GARY	13993	4011	40.0	30.4	22.6	5.3	1.6	31008	34766	15	5	2241	47.0	42.8	10.2	0.0	0.0	52254
46410	MERRILLVILLE	25150	13192	16.7	29.8	39.4	11.4	2.7	52977	61083	77	82	9234	1.7	16.4	73.2	8.5	0.3	115332
46501	ARGOS	19238	1392	22.2	37.1	33.1	6.1	1.5	44301	49606	59	45	1128	10.8	28.6	47.1	10.4	3.1	99754
46504	BOURBON	19767	1238	20.5	33.4	36.4	8.3	1.3	46938	52485	66	61	988	10.0	26.6	50.6	12.0	0.7	101604
46506	BREMEN	21591	3687	16.0	34.0	38.7	8.8	2.6	50009	55651	72	72	3033	4.1	18.7	53.3	20.5	3.4	119608
46507	BRISTOL	26384	3544	19.6	25.9	37.6	9.7	7.2	53882	59473	78	84	2941	16.2	11.2	40.3	27.4	5.0	128163
46508	BURKET	22146	82	22.0	36.6	34.2	4.9	2.4	43185	48636	56	39	71	15.5	25.4	43.7	12.7	2.8	104464
46510	CLAYPOOL	20371	1376	19.8	35.3	33.7	8.2	3.1	44904	49842	61	49	1174	16.7	24.6	45.3	11.8	1.6	100503
46511	CULVER	21005	1694	25.0	33.2	33.2	5.8	2.8	43738	47682	58	42	1356	11.6	28.9	44.5	12.0	3.0	98165
46514	ELKHART	26009	16194	19.7	30.1	35.5	9.6	5.1	50144	55574	72	72	12184	12.3	21.2	51.4	12.8	2.4	109501
46516	ELKHART	19181	12414	27.9	34.1	28.9	5.9	3.2	40006	45407	46	24	7636	9.8	34.9	45.6	8.4	1.3	94352
46517	ELKHART	22162	8146	24.1	30.0	34.1	8.5	3.3	46023	51226	64	57	5525	7.7	24.8	54.1	12.6	0.9	106207
46524	ETNA GREEN	16247	688	18.8	41.3	33.3	4.5	2.2	44413	50393	60	46	572	22.7	23.6	38.8	14.5	0.4	94565
46526	GOSHEN	23481	10604	22.6	30.4	35.8	6.9	4.3	47131	51928	66	62	7740	11.9	17.1	54.1	15.2	1.6	115545
46528	GOSHEN	22161	8164	16.1	31.0	38.4	10.2	4.4	52040	57640	76	80	6394	10.6	13.9	51.6	21.2	2.8	125980
46530	GRANGER	36112	9940	6.2	15.0	39.7	23.4	15.8	83170	96427	96	99	9384	2.3	3.9	46.9	41.6	5.3	170462
46531	GROVERTOWN	19211	519	24.5	32.2	33.9	7.7	1.7	45965	48815	64	56	446	11.4	22.2	55.4	10.8	0.2	104427
46532	HAMLET	18550	808	25.9	34.0	33.5	5.1	1.5	43060	47163	56	39	665	17.1	35.2	37.7	8.7	1.2	87847
46534	KNOX	18593	4307	30.3	32.7	29.2	5.5	2.3	40154	44057	47	25	3390	11.5	31.1	47.1	8.8	1.5	96562
	INDIANA	23565		24.7	29.6	32.4	9.4	3.9	45964	52146				12.3	23.5	44.9	16.9	2.4	109048
	UNITED STATES	25866		24.7	27.1	30.8	10.9	6.5	48124	56710				10.9	15.0	33.7	30.1	10.4	145905

ZIP CODE		FINANCIAL SERVICES				THE HOME						ENTERTAINMENT						PERSONAL			
						Home Improvements		Furnishings													
#	POST OFFICE NAME	Auto Loan	Home Loan	Investments	Retirement Plans	Home Repair	Lawn & Garden	Computers & Hardware	Major Appliances	TV, Radio, Sound Equipment	Furniture	Dine out/ Carry out	Sports Equipment	Fees & Tickets	Toys & Games	Travel	Cable TV	Apparel & Services	Auto Repairs	Health Insurance	Pets & Supplies
46205	INDIANAPOLIS	64	61	74	61	60	66	66	64	68	66	85	74	66	83	65	68	83	66	64	72
46208	INDIANAPOLIS	67	61	71	58	60	69	67	66	71	67	87	74	66	83	65	73	84	68	70	74
46214	INDIANAPOLIS	81	82	94	86	80	84	85	82	82	85	104	97	85	101	82	78	101	84	76	91
46216	INDIANAPOLIS	150	161	190	167	161	170	161	160	155	161	194	187	164	191	162	151	190	161	153	175
46217	INDIANAPOLIS	99	117	124	117	116	117	108	107	102	107	128	125	113	134	110	99	126	105	99	119
46218	INDIANAPOLIS	53	48	54	45	48	56	52	52	57	53	70	57	52	67	52	59	67	53	57	59
46219	INDIANAPOLIS	68	73	83	72	72	77	74	72	74	73	92	84	76	94	75	73	90	73	71	80
46220	INDIANAPOLIS	106	117	153	123	115	121	119	114	115	119	146	136	123	149	120	112	144	116	106	125
46221	INDIANAPOLIS	74	73	71	73	73	78	74	74	75	73	92	86	74	93	73	74	89	74	74	83
46222	INDIANAPOLIS	57	54	62	54	53	59	61	58	62	59	77	68	60	76	59	61	75	60	58	64
46224	INDIANAPOLIS	65	63	72	66	61	65	68	65	67	68	85	78	67	82	65	64	83	68	61	72
46225	INDIANAPOLIS	49	47	52	46	47	52	52	50	54	50	66	58	51	66	51	54	64	51	52	55
46226	INDIANAPOLIS	70	72	80	71	70	76	73	72	74	73	92	83	75	92	73	73	90	73	71	80
46227	INDIANAPOLIS	71	71	83	74	71	75	77	73	75	75	94	88	76	94	75	72	92	76	69	81
46228	INDIANAPOLIS	100	113	123	113	110	113	107	105	102	108	129	121	111	131	107	100	127	104	98	115
46229	INDIANAPOLIS	82	91	97	92	89	90	89	87	85	88	106	103	90	108	88	81	105	87	80	95
46231	INDIANAPOLIS	96	108	112	108	106	107	101	101	96	101	120	119	104	123	101	93	118	99	93	113
46234	INDIANAPOLIS	100	109	111	110	107	109	102	103	98	104	123	120	105	123	102	94	121	102	95	115
46235	INDIANAPOLIS	63	59	69	61	58	63	65	63	66	65	83	74	64	81	63	64	81	65	60	70
46236	INDIANAPOLIS	157	177	174	182	170	168	160	159	148	165	188	185	166	188	158	140	186	155	140	176
46237	INDIANAPOLIS	101	108	110	111	104	105	104	102	99	105	125	121	105	125	102	94	122	102	92	113
46239	INDIANAPOLIS	99	110	109	108	110	112	100	103	97	100	121	120	104	126	102	96	119	100	98	118
46240	INDIANAPOLIS	108	108	128	114	106	112	114	110	110	114	140	130	113	135	111	106	136	113	101	121
46241	INDIANAPOLIS	66	65	65	64	66	70	66	66	67	65	83	78	66	84	66	66	80	67	67	76
46250	INDIANAPOLIS	96	93	108	100	91	96	99	96	96	100	122	114	98	117	96	91	119	100	88	106
46254	INDIANAPOLIS	86	79	90	86	76	81	87	83	85	89	108	100	85	102	82	80	105	87	74	92
46256	INDIANAPOLIS	120	135	150	141	130	134	128	124	120	130	153	146	135	153	127	115	152	124	111	137
46259	INDIANAPOLIS	123	145	147	147	140	137	130	130	120	132	152	152	136	157	130	115	151	126	114	143
46260	INDIANAPOLIS	109	111	133	117	109	115	116	112	112	117	142	133	116	139	113	108	140	115	104	124
46268	INDIANAPOLIS	85	86	96	91	84	87	88	86	85	89	107	102	88	104	86	81	105	88	80	95
46278	INDIANAPOLIS	150	181	198	185	177	179	164	162	152	165	192	188	176	199	167	148	192	157	147	179
46280	INDIANAPOLIS	126	148	161	151	144	145	137	135	128	138	161	158	143	165	138	123	160	132	121	148
46290	INDIANAPOLIS	173	215	256	212	213	225	194	194	183	196	231	220	210	236	203	183	230	189	184	212
46303	CEDAR LAKE	95	89	74	86	91	97	84	90	86	84	106	106	83	107	85	87	101	88	93	110
46304	CHESTERTON	105	113	110	111	113	117	105	108	103	105	128	126	108	133	107	102	125	106	105	124
46307	CROWN POINT	99	116	125	115	114	117	108	107	102	107	129	124	113	133	110	101	127	105	100	118
46310	DEMOTTE	93	87	77	86	90	96	84	89	86	84	106	105	82	105	85	87	101	88	93	108
46311	DYER	110	136	145	136	134	133	122	121	113	121	142	142	130	151	124	110	142	117	109	134
46312	EAST CHICAGO	60	54	55	50	52	58	57	58	61	60	76	64	55	71	56	61	74	60	59	64
46319	GRIFFITH	85	94	103	95	93	95	91	90	88	91	110	105	94	113	91	85	109	89	83	100
46320	HAMMOND	51	47	53	46	46	51	51	50	54	52	67	57	51	65	50	54	65	52	51	56
46321	MUNSTER	120	142	159	141	140	148	132	132	126	132	159	150	140	163	136	126	157	129	126	144
46322	HIGHLAND	87	101	114	98	99	106	96	95	94	95	118	109	101	123	99	94	116	94	93	104
46323	HAMMOND	67	72	77	70	72	77	73	71	73	70	91	82	75	95	73	73	88	71	72	78
46324	HAMMOND	65	70	77	68	70	76	71	69	72	69	89	79	73	93	72	72	87	69	70	76
46327	HAMMOND	57	57	57	54	56	62	58	58	61	58	75	65	59	77	58	61	73	58	61	64
46340	HANNA	86	77	58	73	81	87	71	78	75	71	91	93	69	93	73	77	87	76	85	101
46341	HEBRON	93	95	88	94	97	102	90	94	90	89	111	109	91	115	92	91	108	91	94	110
46342	HOBART	81	87	90	85	87	92	84	85	84	83	104	98	86	108	85	84	102	84	84	95
46347	KOUTS	96	100	90	97	102	105	90	96	90	90	111	113	92	116	93	90	108	93	95	115
46348	LA CROSSE	83	73	56	71	77	84	71	77	75	70	92	90	69	92	72	77	86	76	83	95
46349	LAKE VILLAGE	85	74	57	72	78	85	72	78	76	71	92	91	69	93	73	78	87	76	85	97
46350	LA PORTE	80	82	81	80	83	88	80	81	81	78	100	95	81	103	81	81	97	80	83	94
46356	LOWELL	99	102	94	100	103	106	95	99	94	95	117	116	96	120	96	93	113	96	97	116
46360	MICHIGAN CITY	76	74	73	71	75	83	74	76	77	73	95	87	74	96	75	78	91	76	80	88
46365	MILL CREEK	100	85	60	79	91	98	79	89	86	79	104	107	75	104	81	89	98	87	99	118
46366	NORTH JUDSON	77	61	41	56	67	74	59	68	66	59	79	80	55	79	60	70	74	66	78	90
46368	PORTAGE	92	91	83	89	91	96	87	90	87	87	108	105	86	107	87	86	104	89	89	105
46371	ROLLING PRAIRIE	96	86	66	82	91	97	79	88	84	79	103	105	78	105	82	86	98	86	95	113
46373	SAINT JOHN	116	135	139	134	135	137	122	124	116	122	145	145	128	152	125	115	144	120	117	141
46374	SAN PIERRE	79	69	51	65	73	79	64	71	68	64	83	85	62	84	66	70	78	69	78	93
46375	SCHERERVILLE	112	129	142	131	127	130	122	120	115	122	146	141	127	149	123	112	144	119	111	133
46382	UNION MILLS	78	68	51	65	73	78	63	71	68	63	82	84	62	84	65	70	78	69	77	92
46383	VALPARAISO	92	95	106	98	95	99	98	95	95	96	119	115	98	120	97	92	116	97	90	107
46385	VALPARAISO	117	134	141	134	130	132	124	123	117	125	147	145	128	152	124	113	146	121	112	137
46390	WANATAH	68	60	46	57	64	68	56	62	59	56	72	74	55	73	57	61	68	60	67	80
46391	WESTVILLE	95	93	80	90	96	101	86	92	88	86	108	108	86	111	88	88	104	89	95	112
46392	WHEATFIELD	98	90	72	87	94	101	84	92	88	84	108	108	83	110	86	90	103	89	98	115
46394	WHITING	65	68	73	65	69	76	69	68	72	67	89	76	72	94	71	74	86	68	72	75
46402	GARY	47	42	51	40	41	49	47	46	51	47	63	51	47	60	46	53	61	48	51	52
46403	GARY	71	71	82	69	69	76	73	71	75	74	95	81	76	95	73	76	93	73	72	80
46404	GARY	58	54	61	51	52	61	56	56	60	58	75	61	58	72	57	63	73	57	61	64
46405	LAKE STATION	66	68	67	65	68	74	67	68	68	66	85	76	68	88	68	69	82	67	70	76
46406	GARY	55	50	54	47	50	58	53	53	57	54	71	59	53	69	53	60	68	54	58	62
46407	GARY	50	43	49	40	42	51	47	48	53	49	65	52	47	60	47	56	62	49	54	55
46408	GARY	67	63	66	60	63	72	65	65	69	65	85	72	66	84	65	71	83	66	70	75
46409	GARY	59	54	65	51	52	60	58	57	63	60	79	64	60	78	58	65	77	58	60	65
46410	MERRILLVILLE	86	93	103	93	92	96	92	91	89	91	112	106	94	114	92	87	110	91	86	100
46501	ARGOS	82	72	55	70	76	83	70	76	74	69	90	89	68	90	70	75	85	74	82	94
46504	BOURBON	86	74	57	73	78	86	73	79	77	72	94	92	71	94	74	79	89	78	86	97
46506	BREMEN	94	84	67	82	88	96	80	87	84	80	103	102	79	104	82	86	98	85	93	108
46507	BRISTOL	109	103	87	101	105	112	97	103	99	98	122	121	96	121	98	99	117	101	105	125
46508	BURKET	90	80	61	76	84	90	74	82	78	74	95	97	72	97	76	80	90	80	88	105
46510	CLAYPOOL	93	80	58	75	85	92	74	83	80	74	97	99	72	98	76	82	91	81	91	109
46511	CULVER	83	71	55	69	75	84	70	77	75	70	91	88	68	90	71	77	86	75	84	93
46514	ELKHART	99	90	77	87	93	101	88	94	91	88	112	110	86	112	89	92	107	93	98	113
46516	ELKHART	76	69	66	68	71	78	72	74	76	71	93	86	71	93	72	76	89	75	77	86
46517	ELKHART	85	78	76	79	79	86	81	82	83	80	102	97	79	100	80	82	98	83	84	96
46524	ETNA GREEN	82	71	55	70	75	83	70	76	75	69	90	88	68	91	71	76	85	75	82	93
46526	GOSHEN	95	85	75	83	88	96	86	90	89	85	109	106	83	109	86	90	104	90	96	109
46528	GOSHEN	100	94	81	92	97	103	90	95	92	89	113	112	89	116	91	93	109	94	98	116
46530	GRANGER	149	173	178	177	167	168	156	155	145	160	183	180	164	186	156	139	182	151	138	172
46531	GROVERTOWN	93	71	43	65	78	87	67	80	76	68	91	95	61	89	69	81	85	78	93	108
46532	HAMLET	84	66	42	60	71	79	62	72	69	62	83	86	57	82	63	73	77	71	83	97
46534	KNOX	75	66	54	63	70	77	64	70	69	63	84	81	63	85	66	71	79	69	77	87
	INDIANA	86	83	80	82	84	90	82	84	84	82	103	98	82	104	82	84	100	84	86	98
	UNITED STATES	100	100	100	100	100	100	100	100	100	100	100	100	100	100	100	100	100	100	100	100

POPULATION CHANGE

ZIP CODE			POPULATION			2000-2004 ANNUAL RATE		HOUSEHOLDS					FAMILIES		
#	POST OFFICE NAME	COUNTY FIPS CODE	2000	2004	2009	% Rate	State Centile	2000	2004	2009	% Annual Rate 2000-2004	2004 Average HH Size	2000	2004	% Annual Rate 2000-2004
46536	LAKEVILLE	141	2911	2997	3055	0.7	54	1104	1159	1202	1.2	2.59	827	838	0.3
46538	LEESBURG	085	4418	4709	5048	1.5	80	1762	1925	2106	2.1	2.45	1306	1378	1.3
46539	MENTONE	085	2190	2309	2460	1.3	73	796	851	919	1.6	2.71	583	601	0.7
46540	MIDDLEBURY	039	10285	11083	11833	1.8	85	3246	3548	3832	2.1	3.12	2699	2883	1.6
46542	MILFORD	085	3854	3939	4122	0.5	49	1374	1434	1528	1.0	2.71	1047	1058	0.3
46543	MILLERSBURG	039	2708	2905	3099	1.7	83	789	856	921	1.9	3.39	670	712	1.4
46544	MISHAWAKA	141	30117	29918	30202	-0.2	20	12043	12150	12439	0.2	2.43	7855	7566	-0.9
46545	MISHAWAKA	141	25937	26780	27606	0.8	56	11515	12127	12707	1.2	2.13	6426	6358	-0.3
46550	NAPPANEE	039	12086	12340	12845	0.5	48	4030	4171	4389	0.8	2.95	3096	3105	0.1
46552	NEW CARLISLE	141	6075	6407	6582	1.3	74	2263	2438	2540	1.8	2.52	1605	1657	0.8
46553	NEW PARIS	039	2969	3134	3302	1.3	74	1003	1074	1146	1.6	2.92	824	861	1.0
46554	NORTH LIBERTY	141	4134	4212	4267	0.4	47	1579	1639	1686	0.9	2.57	1206	1211	0.1
46555	NORTH WEBSTER	085	2685	2830	3013	1.3	73	1093	1181	1284	1.8	2.38	771	801	0.9
46556	NOTRE DAME	141	6846	6826	6823	-0.1	23	0	0	0	0.0	0.00	0	0	0.0
46561	OSCEOLA	141	10117	11162	11869	2.3	92	3555	3985	4296	2.7	2.80	2854	3126	2.2
46562	PIERCETON	085	3837	3976	4212	0.8	60	1428	1510	1628	1.3	2.63	1080	1106	0.6
46563	PLYMOUTH	099	22840	23931	24900	1.1	68	8447	8993	9493	1.5	2.61	6134	6320	0.7
46565	SHIPSHEWANA	087	6350	6729	7220	1.4	77	1810	1942	2110	1.7	3.46	1507	1582	1.2
46566	SIDNEY	085	160	182	201	3.1	95	59	69	77	3.8	2.64	46	52	2.9
46567	SYRACUSE	085	9614	10244	10975	1.5	80	3814	4154	4537	2.0	2.45	2714	2849	1.2
46570	TIPPECANOE	099	1074	1064	1077	-0.2	17	390	394	406	0.2	2.70	301	296	-0.4
46571	TOPEKA	087	5660	5996	6432	1.4	77	1528	1636	1775	1.6	3.67	1281	1344	1.1
46573	WAKARUSA	039	3318	3497	3675	1.2	73	1161	1248	1332	1.7	2.70	908	945	0.9
46574	WALKERTON	091	7996	8141	8346	0.4	46	3008	3113	3236	0.8	2.58	2218	2209	-0.1
46580	WARSAW	085	21140	21957	23312	0.9	62	7727	8165	8826	1.3	2.57	5493	5614	0.5
46582	WARSAW	085	10618	11400	12266	1.7	83	3946	4302	4701	2.1	2.64	2918	3070	1.2
46590	WINONA LAKE	085	3855	3980	4193	0.8	56	1328	1396	1498	1.2	2.70	940	952	0.3
46601	SOUTH BEND	141	5966	6260	6547	1.1	70	2560	2682	2825	1.1	2.02	1029	988	-1.0
46613	SOUTH BEND	141	11597	11290	11341	-0.6	5	4236	4159	4219	-0.4	2.69	2734	2551	-1.6
46614	SOUTH BEND	141	30020	30524	31133	0.4	45	12346	12820	13288	0.9	2.33	8308	8229	-0.2
46615	SOUTH BEND	141	15709	15362	15378	-0.5	7	6824	6769	6867	-0.2	2.25	3910	3654	-1.6
46616	SOUTH BEND	141	7154	6907	6900	-0.8	2	2778	2722	2754	-0.5	2.52	1669	1535	-2.0
46617	SOUTH BEND	141	11227	11253	11422	0.1	29	4295	4372	4508	0.4	2.34	2544	2431	-1.1
46619	SOUTH BEND	141	21025	21167	21364	0.2	35	7576	7693	7846	0.4	2.73	5399	5259	-0.6
46628	SOUTH BEND	141	26865	26511	26728	-0.3	13	10501	10540	10785	0.1	2.50	7087	6796	-1.0
46635	SOUTH BEND	141	6452	6477	6545	0.1	31	2474	2544	2619	0.7	2.42	1735	1719	-0.1
46637	SOUTH BEND	141	15539	15498	15649	-0.1	24	6058	6163	6328	0.4	2.28	3682	3534	-1.0
46701	ALBION	113	7543	7919	8272	1.2	70	2753	2938	3113	1.5	2.64	2047	2116	0.8
46702	ANDREWS	069	2457	2430	2425	-0.3	15	901	907	920	0.2	2.62	706	691	-0.5
46703	ANGOLA	151	17929	18899	20308	1.3	73	6832	7345	8053	1.7	2.45	4579	4725	0.7
46705	ASHLEY	033	1694	1710	1773	0.2	38	661	681	720	0.7	2.51	458	452	-0.3
46706	AUBURN	033	17261	17747	18337	0.7	53	6703	7041	7420	1.2	2.48	4673	4727	0.3
46710	AVILLA	113	4133	4354	4547	1.2	72	1514	1636	1741	1.8	2.55	1101	1150	1.0
46711	BERNE	001	7513	7558	7568	0.1	34	2538	2595	2642	0.5	2.85	1890	1868	-0.3
46714	BLUFFTON	179	14726	15101	15619	0.6	51	5734	5996	6318	1.1	2.46	3987	4011	0.1
46721	BUTLER	033	5142	5223	5386	0.4	43	1840	1906	2005	0.8	2.69	1369	1369	0.0
46723	CHURUBUSCO	183	7107	7425	7764	1.0	67	2598	2771	2954	1.5	2.67	1987	2059	0.8
46725	COLUMBIA CITY	183	20979	22175	23519	1.3	75	8119	8782	9521	1.9	2.48	5927	6196	1.1
46730	CORUNNA	033	1433	1542	1624	1.7	84	487	536	578	2.3	2.87	387	414	1.6
46731	CRAIGVILLE	179	635	694	740	2.1	90	219	243	265	2.5	2.86	180	195	1.9
46732	CROMWELL	113	3603	3796	3999	1.2	73	1216	1302	1391	1.6	2.92	949	988	1.0
46733	DECATUR	001	19175	19010	18900	-0.2	18	7258	7364	7473	0.3	2.55	5201	5092	-0.5
46737	FREMONT	151	6452	7006	7654	2.0	89	2538	2818	3139	2.5	2.49	1848	1980	1.6
46738	GARRETT	033	7551	7642	7831	0.3	39	2845	2945	3080	0.8	2.58	1995	1986	-0.1
46740	GENEVA	001	3854	3870	3865	0.1	31	1212	1240	1261	0.5	3.09	883	871	-0.3
46741	GRABILL	003	4283	4620	4844	1.8	86	1232	1349	1434	2.2	3.42	1015	1078	1.4
46742	HAMILTON	151	3488	3773	4084	1.9	87	1315	1451	1600	2.3	2.60	989	1055	1.5
46743	HARLAN	003	1942	2100	2226	1.9	87	658	728	785	2.4	2.88	543	583	1.7
46745	HOAGLAND	003	1532	1687	1781	2.3	92	535	604	651	2.9	2.79	421	458	2.0
46746	HOWE	087	4711	4904	5212	1.0	64	1621	1712	1845	1.3	2.86	1278	1314	0.7
46747	HUDSON	151	2661	2786	2981	1.1	68	1046	1117	1218	1.6	2.49	780	804	0.7
46748	HUNTERTOWN	003	3243	3502	3673	1.8	86	1147	1263	1346	2.3	2.77	948	1014	1.6
46750	HUNTINGTON	069	27835	28187	28501	0.3	40	10453	10808	11127	0.8	2.51	7455	7436	-0.1
46755	KENDALLVILLE	113	15192	15756	16449	0.9	61	5904	6234	6603	1.3	2.50	4062	4121	0.3
46759	KEYSTONE	179	707	705	721	-0.1	23	268	273	285	0.4	2.58	209	207	-0.2
46760	KIMMELL	113	1619	1758	1867	2.0	89	584	645	694	2.4	2.73	446	478	1.6
46761	LAGRANGE	087	10478	10981	11721	1.1	69	3480	3714	4030	1.5	2.90	2601	2689	0.8
46763	LAOTTO	113	1662	1678	1721	0.2	38	608	627	654	0.7	2.64	482	486	0.2
46764	LARWILL	183	1544	1652	1768	1.6	81	533	583	636	2.1	2.81	428	457	1.6
46765	LEO	003	4092	4444	4673	2.0	89	1364	1502	1600	2.3	2.94	1156	1241	1.7
46766	LIBERTY CENTER	179	653	678	704	0.9	62	227	240	254	1.3	2.83	183	188	0.6
46767	LIGONIER	113	8411	8648	8937	0.7	53	2568	2642	2746	0.7	3.24	1985	1986	0.0
46770	MARKLE	179	2105	2150	2207	0.5	49	778	809	845	0.9	2.63	596	601	0.2
46772	MONROE	001	2826	2869	2880	0.4	43	742	768	785	0.8	3.74	632	640	0.3
46773	MONROEVILLE	003	3719	3973	4130	1.6	81	1318	1438	1522	2.1	2.76	1013	1066	1.2
46774	NEW HAVEN	003	14702	15250	15652	0.9	61	5486	5846	6124	1.5	2.59	4040	4129	0.5
46776	ORLAND	151	1488	1632	1790	2.2	91	590	660	736	2.7	2.47	426	460	1.8
46777	OSSIAN	179	6338	6595	6853	0.9	63	2328	2470	2612	1.4	2.64	1763	1811	0.6
46779	PLEASANT LAKE	151	1896	1967	2097	0.9	61	732	773	837	1.3	2.54	543	554	0.5
46781	PONETO	179	642	646	663	0.2	34	223	229	239	0.6	2.82	175	175	0.0
46783	ROANOKE	069	5555	5739	5885	0.8	57	2050	2160	2252	1.2	2.64	1588	1624	0.5
46784	ROME CITY	113	2574	2594	2654	0.2	36	955	982	1019	0.7	2.64	751	752	0.0
46785	SAINT JOE	033	1371	1469	1543	1.6	82	468	513	549	2.2	2.86	382	408	1.6
46787	SOUTH WHITLEY	183	4095	4173	4366	0.4	47	1536	1599	1709	1.0	2.60	1128	1133	0.1
46788	SPENCERVILLE	033	2741	2917	3048	1.5	79	848	922	982	2.0	3.14	711	753	1.4
46791	UNIONDALE	179	930	963	999	0.8	59	335	354	374	1.3	2.72	263	269	0.5
46792	WARREN	069	4196	4280	4342	0.5	48	1486	1547	1598	1.0	2.54	1115	1125	0.2
46793	WATERLOO	033	4143	4223	4357	0.5	47	1532	1598	1685	1.0	2.64	1172	1183	0.2
46794	WAWAKA	113	1487	1537	1590	0.8	58	532	559	586	1.2	2.75	427	437	0.6
46795	WOLCOTTVILLE	087	6221	6724	7307	1.9	87	2320	2566	2838	2.4	2.62	1800	1930	1.7
46797	WOODBURN	003	4041	4240	4365	1.1	70	1415	1518	1592	1.7	2.79	1163	1211	1.0
46798	YODER	003	1797	1943	2036	1.9	87	691	769	822	2.6	2.53	536	574	1.6
46802	FORT WAYNE	003	11270	10938	10980	-0.7	4	4850	4814	4926	-0.2	2.08	1991	1819	-2.1
46803	FORT WAYNE	003	10492	10365	10500	-0.3	14	3903	3929	4046	0.2	2.55	2425	2305	-1.2
46804	FORT WAYNE	003	26143	27502	28579	1.2	72	10505	11280	11915	1.7	2.42	7290	7482	0.6
	INDIANA					0.8					1.2	2.48			0.3
	UNITED STATES					1.2					1.3	2.58			1.1

ZIP CODE #	POST OFFICE NAME	RACE (%) White 2000	White 2004	Black 2000	Black 2004	Asian/Pacific 2000	Asian/Pacific 2004	% Hispanic Origin 2000	% Hispanic Origin 2004	2004 AGE DISTRIBUTION (%) 0-4	5-9	10-14	15-19	20-24	25-44	45-64	65-84	85+	18+	MEDIAN AGE 2004	% 2004 Males	% 2004 Females
46536	LAKEVILLE	98.3	98.0	0.1	0.1	0.1	0.1	1.3	1.6	5.1	5.8	7.7	7.5	5.9	24.8	28.5	13.5	1.2	76.4	40.3	49.9	50.2
46538	LEESBURG	96.7	96.2	0.1	0.1	0.7	0.9	2.5	3.0	6.6	6.7	6.2	5.8	5.4	26.3	28.7	13.2	1.3	77.0	40.7	50.2	49.8
46539	MENTONE	95.9	95.2	0.2	0.2	0.1	0.1	4.6	5.5	7.8	7.5	8.2	7.7	7.5	28.1	21.4	10.3	1.7	72.0	33.7	50.2	49.8
46540	MIDDLEBURY	97.7	97.3	0.2	0.2	0.6	0.8	0.9	1.2	8.4	8.5	9.7	8.9	6.4	26.9	23.3	7.2	0.8	67.8	32.1	50.6	49.4
46542	MILFORD	94.9	94.0	0.5	0.5	0.2	0.2	7.4	8.8	7.4	7.4	8.0	7.6	6.5	26.8	24.1	10.5	1.8	72.3	35.4	49.5	50.5
46543	MILLERSBURG	98.7	98.5	0.1	0.1	0.0	0.1	1.8	2.2	11.1	10.2	9.9	9.0	7.0	27.4	18.1	6.6	0.6	63.2	27.4	52.2	47.9
46544	MISHAWAKA	95.6	94.8	1.6	1.9	0.5	0.6	1.9	2.4	7.0	6.7	7.2	7.2	7.1	27.9	23.3	11.5	2.1	74.5	36.0	48.3	51.7
46545	MISHAWAKA	89.0	87.2	4.7	5.3	2.4	3.1	3.2	3.9	6.7	5.9	5.8	6.9	9.5	30.7	21.2	11.0	2.4	78.2	33.9	47.6	52.4
46550	NAPPANEE	96.5	95.8	0.2	0.2	0.4	0.6	3.5	4.4	9.6	9.1	8.8	7.7	7.4	28.0	19.6	8.5	1.2	67.6	30.2	50.0	50.0
46552	NEW CARLISLE	97.3	96.8	1.0	1.2	0.2	0.2	1.3	1.6	5.1	5.5	7.3	7.0	5.8	26.4	26.3	12.5	4.0	77.4	41.2	48.4	51.6
46553	NEW PARIS	98.3	98.1	0.1	0.1	0.1	0.2	1.5	1.8	7.4	7.9	9.2	7.6	5.7	26.9	24.3	9.8	1.2	70.7	35.9	49.8	50.2
46554	NORTH LIBERTY	97.8	97.4	0.3	0.4	0.3	0.3	1.0	1.3	6.2	6.4	7.6	6.5	5.8	24.9	28.6	12.5	1.5	75.8	40.4	50.4	49.6
46555	NORTH WEBSTER	97.9	97.5	0.1	0.1	0.4	0.5	1.4	1.8	6.6	6.6	6.4	5.4	5.9	27.6	27.6	11.8	1.9	76.8	39.2	49.0	51.0
46556	NOTRE DAME	89.5	87.6	2.9	3.4	2.4	2.8	6.6	8.2	0.0	0.0	0.1	44.5	45.7	2.5	2.1	3.7	1.5	99.7	20.6	52.4	47.6
46561	OSCEOLA	96.7	96.0	0.8	0.9	1.1	1.5	1.0	1.3	7.1	7.4	7.9	7.1	6.2	27.5	26.4	9.7	0.9	73.2	37.1	49.5	50.5
46562	PIERCETON	95.3	94.6	0.4	0.4	0.6	0.7	4.0	4.7	7.5	7.6	8.0	6.9	6.5	28.7	24.6	9.4	0.9	72.7	35.5	51.4	48.6
46563	PLYMOUTH	94.7	93.9	0.3	0.4	0.4	0.5	7.6	8.9	7.3	7.2	7.3	6.7	6.9	27.5	24.1	11.2	1.9	74.1	36.1	49.9	50.1
46565	SHIPSHEWANA	98.4	98.2	0.1	0.2	0.2	0.2	1.4	1.7	12.4	11.2	10.2	8.6	8.0	26.5	16.1	6.3	0.7	60.9	24.7	51.5	48.5
46566	SIDNEY	98.1	98.4	0.0	0.0	0.0	0.0	1.3	1.7	7.1	7.1	7.1	5.5	6.0	27.5	25.8	12.1	1.7	75.3	38.6	51.1	48.9
46567	SYRACUSE	96.0	95.4	0.5	0.5	0.4	0.5	3.1	3.7	6.3	6.5	7.2	6.5	5.6	25.9	27.6	12.8	1.8	76.0	39.5	50.8	49.2
46570	TIPPECANOE	98.9	98.8	0.4	0.4	0.2	0.3	1.0	1.2	7.2	7.5	7.5	7.2	5.5	25.6	28.4	9.8	1.3	73.3	38.5	50.9	49.1
46571	TOPEKA	98.7	98.5	0.1	0.1	0.2	0.2	1.1	1.3	12.8	11.0	10.5	9.7	9.0	24.8	15.5	5.9	0.8	59.9	23.3	51.2	48.8
46573	WAKARUSA	97.5	97.1	0.3	0.4	0.5	0.6	1.4	1.7	7.3	7.6	8.2	7.1	5.2	25.8	23.9	11.9	3.1	72.9	37.3	48.1	51.9
46574	WALKERTON	96.7	96.1	0.3	0.3	0.2	0.2	2.7	3.4	6.1	6.5	7.6	6.5	6.0	26.6	25.7	12.9	2.1	75.8	39.1	49.6	50.4
46580	WARSAW	92.7	91.6	1.1	1.1	0.8	1.0	7.0	8.2	7.2	7.1	7.1	6.7	6.9	27.5	24.2	11.1	2.1	74.4	36.1	49.5	50.5
46582	WARSAW	93.0	91.7	0.7	0.8	1.0	1.3	6.2	7.4	8.6	8.2	7.5	6.3	6.3	29.8	23.4	9.0	1.0	71.8	34.0	50.4	49.6
46590	WINONA LAKE	91.2	89.5	0.7	0.8	0.8	1.0	8.5	10.2	8.4	7.9	8.2	6.8	7.3	29.4	20.2	8.3	3.4	71.1	32.3	49.1	50.9
46601	SOUTH BEND	43.0	38.7	48.5	52.1	0.8	0.9	7.7	8.6	8.4	7.1	6.8	6.9	9.6	30.0	19.4	9.5	2.2	73.6	32.0	49.4	50.6
46613	SOUTH BEND	63.5	59.7	22.8	24.4	0.8	1.0	14.3	16.8	9.4	8.7	8.5	8.0	7.8	30.7	18.0	7.7	1.2	68.5	29.8	49.4	50.6
46614	SOUTH BEND	91.2	89.8	5.0	5.6	0.9	1.1	2.5	3.1	6.7	6.4	6.7	6.1	5.6	25.8	25.2	14.5	3.0	76.3	39.9	47.9	52.1
46615	SOUTH BEND	82.9	80.3	9.4	10.8	2.8	3.4	4.1	5.1	7.5	6.8	6.8	6.1	7.9	29.8	20.8	11.9	2.4	75.4	34.2	46.9	53.1
46616	SOUTH BEND	66.1	63.7	25.2	26.7	1.1	1.3	6.7	7.8	8.7	7.7	7.6	7.3	8.0	30.9	20.4	8.1	1.5	71.6	31.5	48.2	51.8
46617	SOUTH BEND	66.8	64.2	26.8	28.5	1.9	2.3	3.9	4.6	6.6	6.9	6.3	8.9	11.4	25.6	19.8	11.8	2.8	76.3	32.4	49.8	50.2
46619	SOUTH BEND	60.3	57.7	24.4	25.2	0.4	0.4	18.2	20.6	8.4	8.0	8.0	6.8	6.6	26.3	21.4	12.5	1.9	71.4	34.4	49.1	50.9
46628	SOUTH BEND	63.3	61.6	31.0	32.1	0.7	0.9	4.6	5.2	8.4	7.9	7.8	6.6	6.5	28.1	22.5	10.8	1.4	71.8	34.5	48.0	52.0
46635	SOUTH BEND	90.2	88.4	4.7	5.4	2.5	3.1	2.5	3.1	5.6	6.1	6.4	6.1	6.7	22.0	26.4	17.3	3.4	77.9	43.0	46.9	53.1
46637	SOUTH BEND	89.0	87.0	5.5	6.4	2.2	2.7	2.6	3.3	5.0	5.1	5.5	8.7	13.9	24.8	22.3	12.8	1.9	80.9	34.6	45.2	54.8
46701	ALBION	98.1	97.8	0.4	0.4	0.1	0.1	1.1	1.4	7.1	7.3	7.8	6.9	6.1	29.7	24.5	9.5	1.2	73.7	35.9	52.2	47.8
46702	ANDREWS	97.6	97.4	0.1	0.1	0.2	0.3	1.3	1.5	6.8	7.0	7.7	6.6	5.6	27.9	25.6	10.9	1.9	74.2	38.2	50.5	49.5
46703	ANGOLA	96.2	95.7	0.6	0.6	0.7	0.8	2.7	3.2	7.0	6.6	6.8	7.2	8.6	28.4	24.1	9.6	1.7	75.9	34.6	50.7	49.3
46705	ASHLEY	97.5	97.2	0.2	0.2	0.5	0.5	1.5	1.8	8.1	8.0	7.7	6.4	6.6	29.9	22.9	9.1	1.3	72.4	34.6	51.1	48.9
46706	AUBURN	97.8	97.4	0.3	0.4	0.5	0.6	1.5	1.8	7.6	7.6	7.5	6.6	6.1	28.7	23.9	10.2	1.9	73.1	35.7	49.2	50.8
46710	AVILLA	97.2	97.0	0.7	0.7	0.3	0.4	0.8	1.1	6.6	7.0	8.2	6.6	5.1	30.7	22.7	10.5	2.6	74.1	36.3	50.2	49.8
46711	BERNE	98.1	98.1	0.1	0.1	0.2	0.2	1.5	1.5	9.8	9.0	9.4	8.2	7.0	23.4	18.6	11.3	3.4	66.6	30.8	49.0	51.1
46714	BLUFFTON	98.0	97.8	0.2	0.3	0.3	0.4	1.9	2.2	6.9	6.4	7.2	6.6	7.2	26.0	24.1	13.0	2.6	75.5	37.8	48.8	51.2
46721	BUTLER	97.9	97.6	0.1	0.1	0.1	0.2	1.9	2.3	8.1	8.1	8.6	7.3	6.1	29.7	22.6	8.1	1.4	70.6	33.7	50.8	49.2
46723	CHURUBUSCO	98.4	98.1	0.2	0.2	0.2	0.3	0.8	0.9	6.5	6.6	7.8	7.4	6.4	27.9	26.6	9.7	1.2	74.5	37.2	49.9	50.1
46725	COLUMBIA CITY	98.3	98.1	0.2	0.2	0.2	0.3	0.9	1.1	6.9	6.9	7.0	6.4	6.0	27.4	25.8	11.6	2.0	75.3	38.2	49.6	50.5
46730	CORUNNA	98.6	98.5	0.1	0.1	0.0	0.0	2.1	2.4	7.3	7.5	8.0	6.7	6.2	26.4	27.7	9.3	0.8	73.0	37.4	50.9	49.1
46731	CRAIGVILLE	98.9	98.7	0.0	0.0	0.0	0.1	1.1	1.2	6.6	7.1	8.8	7.6	6.3	25.8	26.7	9.9	1.2	72.6	37.3	51.4	48.6
46732	CROMWELL	92.3	91.1	0.3	0.3	0.3	0.4	15.7	18.2	9.4	9.0	8.5	6.9	6.7	30.2	22.1	6.7	0.6	68.8	31.2	51.9	48.1
46733	DECATUR	96.5	96.4	0.2	0.2	0.3	0.3	4.9	5.0	7.0	7.2	8.0	6.9	6.6	27.5	23.7	11.1	2.1	73.5	36.0	49.7	50.3
46737	FREMONT	98.5	98.3	0.2	0.2	0.1	0.2	1.3	1.5	5.9	6.4	7.7	6.6	5.7	26.7	28.5	11.4	1.1	75.9	39.5	50.0	50.0
46738	GARRETT	97.6	97.2	0.3	0.3	0.7	0.9	1.7	2.0	7.5	7.3	7.7	6.8	6.5	30.0	22.8	9.9	1.5	73.3	34.8	49.5	50.5
46740	GENEVA	98.4	98.4	0.2	0.2	0.4	0.3	0.9	0.9	9.0	8.3	9.2	8.5	7.3	24.1	20.5	10.3	3.0	68.2	31.2	50.3	49.7
46741	GRABILL	98.4	98.2	0.1	0.2	0.4	0.4	0.7	0.9	9.8	9.7	9.9	8.2	6.9	27.2	19.9	7.5	1.0	65.5	29.8	49.6	50.5
46742	HAMILTON	98.7	98.5	0.1	0.1	0.1	0.1	1.1	1.4	7.1	7.4	7.9	6.5	5.1	26.3	26.8	11.6	1.3	73.5	37.9	50.0	50.0
46743	HARLAN	98.7	98.3	0.3	0.3	0.1	0.1	0.6	1.0	9.7	9.5	8.8	7.3	6.5	27.3	22.1	8.1	0.9	67.5	31.5	51.0	49.1
46745	HOAGLAND	98.8	98.6	0.2	0.2	0.3	0.4	1.0	1.4	6.4	6.9	8.0	6.7	6.0	25.7	29.0	10.4	1.0	74.6	39.2	49.8	50.2
46746	HOWE	92.8	91.6	0.3	0.3	0.5	0.6	7.7	9.2	8.7	8.5	7.8	6.9	6.7	27.4	23.7	9.3	1.1	70.9	33.5	51.2	48.8
46747	HUDSON	98.4	98.1	0.1	0.1	0.1	0.1	0.9	1.1	7.2	7.4	7.3	6.2	5.4	29.7	24.4	11.4	0.9	74.2	37.0	51.2	48.8
46748	HUNTERTOWN	97.8	97.3	0.5	0.6	0.6	0.8	0.9	1.2	6.4	7.6	8.7	7.1	5.3	27.3	29.0	7.9	0.7	72.7	37.9	49.6	50.4
46750	HUNTINGTON	98.1	97.8	0.2	0.2	0.4	0.5	0.9	1.1	7.0	6.9	7.0	7.5	8.1	26.9	23.4	11.3	1.8	74.9	35.5	48.7	51.3
46755	KENDALLVILLE	96.6	95.9	0.5	0.5	0.6	0.8	2.7	3.5	8.2	7.2	6.9	6.7	7.3	28.9	22.9	10.2	1.7	73.7	34.6	48.6	51.4
46759	KEYSTONE	98.2	98.0	0.1	0.1	0.1	0.1	1.4	1.3	5.5	6.1	8.2	6.8	6.0	26.2	28.2	11.5	1.4	75.9	39.7	51.5	48.5
46760	KIMMELL	98.2	98.0	0.2	0.2	0.3	0.3	1.9	2.5	6.2	6.5	8.2	6.8	5.7	28.4	26.5	10.6	1.0	74.9	38.3	51.7	48.3
46761	LAGRANGE	95.2	94.3	0.3	0.3	0.3	0.4	4.8	5.8	9.3	8.6	8.0	7.2	6.7	26.7	21.2	10.5	1.8	69.7	32.4	50.2	49.8
46763	LAOTTO	97.7	97.3	0.7	0.8	0.2	0.4	0.9	1.2	7.0	7.5	7.4	6.0	5.2	30.0	26.3	9.8	0.7	74.3	37.3	51.7	48.3
46764	LARWILL	98.1	97.9	0.2	0.2	0.2	0.2	1.0	1.2	6.9	7.5	8.3	7.5	5.9	27.6	25.4	9.9	1.0	72.5	36.5	51.5	48.5
46765	LEO	97.9	97.4	0.4	0.5	0.5	0.7	0.8	1.0	7.4	8.2	9.2	7.4	5.4	26.5	26.3	8.6	1.1	70.5	37.0	49.4	50.6
46766	LIBERTY CENTER	97.2	96.9	0.2	0.2	0.3	0.4	1.2	1.5	6.1	6.6	8.0	7.4	6.1	25.1	28.0	11.5	1.3	74.6	39.7	50.4	49.6
46767	LIGONIER	80.6	77.4	0.3	0.4	0.5	0.5	25.4	29.6	10.4	9.6	8.7	7.6	8.0	28.8	19.0	7.1	1.0	66.6	28.8	51.7	48.3
46770	MARKLE	99.1	99.0	0.1	0.1	0.1	0.2	0.9	1.0	6.7	6.9	8.2	7.0	6.3	27.2	25.5	10.7	1.5	73.8	37.3	50.3	49.7
46772	MONROE	99.0	99.0	0.0	0.0	0.0	0.0	1.1	1.1	11.4	10.8	10.5	8.5	7.5	25.0	17.2	8.0	1.1	61.9	26.0	51.2	48.8
46773	MONROEVILLE	97.9	97.5	0.2	0.2	0.1	0.1	1.4	1.8	7.4	7.7	8.1	6.5	5.9	28.2	24.0	10.6	1.5	72.6	36.3	49.8	50.2
46774	NEW HAVEN	97.7	97.2	0.7	0.9	0.3	0.4	1.3	1.7	6.8	6.8	7.4	6.9	6.5	26.7	25.4	12.0	1.6	74.8	37.4	49.1	50.9
46776	ORLAND	98.0	97.7	0.1	0.1	0.2	0.2	1.1	1.3	5.9	6.2	7.5	6.1	5.6	29.0	26.1	12.4	1.2	76.7	38.8	51.8	48.2
46777	OSSIAN	98.5	98.3	0.1	0.1	0.2	0.2	1.0	1.2	7.1	7.7	8.2	7.3	5.6	27.6	24.0	10.6	1.8	72.5	36.4	49.7	50.3
46779	PLEASANT LAKE	97.5	97.0	0.1	0.2	0.3	0.5	2.5	3.1	6.8	6.9	7.0	6.3	6.0	27.6	26.9	11.5	1.1	75.4	38.2	50.6	49.4
46781	PONETO	98.3	98.1	0.0	0.0	0.2	0.2	0.8	0.9	6.4	6.7	7.9	7.0	6.4	27.1	27.1	10.4	1.2	74.9	38.1	50.3	49.7
46783	ROANOKE	98.2	97.7	0.3	0.4	0.4	0.5	1.0	1.3	6.0	6.6	7.7	7.1	5.7	25.8	30.7	9.0	1.3	75.2	40.0	50.0	50.0
46784	ROME CITY	98.3	98.2	0.2	0.2	0.2	0.3	1.1	1.3	7.8	7.8	7.6	6.8	5.9	28.0	25.0	10.3	0.9	72.6	35.9	50.0	50.0
46785	SAINT JOE	98.2	97.8	0.2	0.3	0.0	0.0	1.8	2.2	7.8	8.0	8.4	7.0	6.2	28.9	23.6	9.2	1.0	71.5	35.3	52.0	48.0
46787	SOUTH WHITLEY	98.6	98.4	0.1	0.1	0.2	0.3	0.9	1.1	7.8	7.8	7.8	6.9	6.1	27.2	24.6	10.0	1.8	72.4	35.2	49.8	50.2
46788	SPENCERVILLE	98.5	98.2	0.3	0.4	0.0	0.1	0.7	1.0	8.0	8.5	9.5	7.5	6.1	25.9	25.5	8.0	1.0	69.2	34.6	51.3	48.8
46791	UNIONDALE	99.7	99.7	0.0	0.0	0.1	0.1	0.2	0.2	6.3	6.9	8.2	7.7	6.1	27.2	25.7	10.7	1.3	73.8	37.8	52.3	47.7
46792	WARREN	98.9	98.8	0.1	0.1	0.1	0.1	1.0	1.1	5.3	6.0	6.9	6.0	5.0	23.9	24.3	15.5	7.2	78.1	42.9	47.6	52.5
46793	WATERLOO	96.9	96.6	0.2	0.2	0.2	0.2	2.3	2.7	7.7	7.6	7.5	7.1	5.9	28.5	25.9	8.9	1.0	72.8	35.8	51.5	48.5
46794	WAWAKA	97.5	97.0	0.2	0.2	0.2	0.3	2.3	2.9	8.1	7.9	7.9	7.6	6.1	27.8	24.0	10.0	0.9	71.5	35.2	51.2	48.8
46795	WOLCOTTVILLE	98.5	98.3	0.2	0.2	0.2	0.2	0.9	1.0	7.7	7.7	7.1	6.6	5.7	26.4	25.3	12.6	1.0	73.5	37.4	51.0	49.0
46797	WOODBURN	98.6	98.3	0.3	0.4	0.1	0.1	1.3	1.8	8.0	7.8	8.1	8.0	7.1	25.9	24.7	9.4	1.0	70.9	34.0	50.1	50.0
46798	YODER	96.4	95.6	0.8	1.0	0.5	0.6	1.8	2.4	5.6	6.3	7.7	6.7	6.1	25.4	30.8	10.5	1.0	76.4	40.3	50.1	49.9
46802	FORT WAYNE	72.6	68.6	15.4	17.6	1.8	2.0	12.3	14.6	6.6	5.8	5.8	6.7	10.0	34.3	21.7	7.9	1.2	78.2	33.1	55.0	45.0
46803	FORT WAYNE	40.3	36.2	51.0	54.6	1.3	1.3	9.1	9.9	10.1	9.5	8.5	8.2	8.9	27.2	18.5	8.4	0.8	67.4	28.2	49.6	50.4
46804	FORT WAYNE	92.7	90.8	2.7	3.3	2.1	2.7	2.4	3.1	6.8	6.8	6.8	6.8	6.6	27.8	26.5	10.5	1.5	75.6	37.8	48.6	51.4
	INDIANA	87.5	86.7	8.4	8.7	1.0	1.3	3.5	4.1	7.0	6.9	7.1	7.1	7.4	28.1	24.0	10.8	1.6	75.0	35.9	49.2	50.8
	UNITED STATES	75.1	73.6	12.3	12.5	3.8	4.2	12.5	14.1	6.9	6.7	7.2	7.0	7.3	28.6	23.8	10.8	1.7	75.1	36.0	49.1	50.9

INCOME

ZIP CODE #	POST OFFICE NAME	2004 Per Capita Income	2004 HH Income Base	2004 HOUSEHOLD INCOME DISTRIBUTION (%) Less than $25,000	$25,000 to $49,999	$50,000 to $99,999	$100,000 to $149,999	$150,000 or More	MEDIAN HOUSEHOLD INCOME 2004	2009	2004 National Centile	2004 State Centile	2004 Home Value Base	2004 HOME VALUE DISTRIBUTION (%) Less than $50,000	$50,000 to $89,999	$90,000 to $174,999	$175,000 to $399,999	$400,000 or More	2004 Median Home Value
46536	LAKEVILLE	22071	1159	22.3	29.9	36.6	8.5	2.8	48434	54304	69	68	958	8.7	22.7	47.9	18.2	2.6	112847
46538	LEESBURG	26290	1925	17.8	31.0	36.4	10.9	4.0	50912	55644	74	76	1638	14.3	16.8	38.3	22.9	7.7	119106
46539	MENTONE	19894	851	23.2	34.4	33.4	6.4	2.7	44698	49349	60	47	680	20.0	32.2	38.5	8.1	1.2	87619
46540	MIDDLEBURY	22800	3548	14.0	27.6	41.0	11.9	5.5	56472	62734	81	89	3036	7.2	8.3	49.4	31.4	3.7	149562
46542	MILFORD	21172	1434	18.6	33.9	35.2	9.2	3.1	48159	53026	69	67	1151	11.9	22.3	45.8	19.2	0.8	111149
46543	MILLERSBURG	18999	856	12.4	32.6	43.2	7.9	3.9	52536	60107	76	81	710	4.1	20.0	47.0	24.4	4.5	124775
46544	MISHAWAKA	20733	12150	27.5	32.0	31.9	7.0	1.6	41563	47761	52	31	8685	12.4	37.8	43.0	6.2	0.6	89826
46545	MISHAWAKA	22894	12127	28.8	34.0	29.0	6.0	2.2	38633	44121	42	18	6262	11.9	35.7	40.2	11.4	0.9	92838
46550	NAPPANEE	21243	4171	18.0	27.5	41.4	9.8	3.4	52789	59435	77	82	3185	12.1	17.4	49.4	18.8	2.3	111870
46552	NEW CARLISLE	21660	2438	22.5	27.7	39.1	8.7	2.1	49757	54600	71	71	2018	4.3	28.9	49.0	15.6	2.3	111513
46553	NEW PARIS	21418	1074	15.3	29.6	41.7	9.4	4.0	53377	59918	77	83	902	4.2	17.1	64.3	11.8	2.7	119500
46554	NORTH LIBERTY	23442	1639	20.6	28.1	37.2	11.3	2.9	50930	57648	74	77	1385	5.2	26.7	47.4	18.1	2.5	108863
46555	NORTH WEBSTER	22762	1181	21.9	32.8	34.2	9.6	1.6	45960	50833	64	56	990	7.9	22.3	49.2	18.5	2.1	113293
46556	NOTRE DAME	11690	0	0.0	0.0	0.0	0.0	0.0	0	0	0	0	0	0.0	0.0	0.0	0.0	0.0	0
46561	OSCEOLA	23419	3985	12.2	29.4	43.8	11.7	2.9	55932	63745	81	88	3560	2.6	20.1	66.4	10.7	0.2	117267
46562	PIERCETON	19963	1510	23.8	33.4	35.0	5.2	2.6	44039	49168	59	44	1253	23.6	23.6	34.5	17.5	0.8	93966
46563	PLYMOUTH	21170	8993	23.8	31.6	33.8	7.7	3.2	45650	49919	63	55	6683	10.5	25.5	47.8	14.3	1.8	104285
46565	SHIPSHEWANA	17158	1942	19.4	32.7	36.8	7.5	3.7	48463	53239	69	68	1621	6.9	9.3	43.6	35.9	4.3	155671
46566	SIDNEY	21533	69	29.0	26.1	34.8	7.3	2.9	45566	50515	63	54	60	13.3	28.3	38.3	20.0	0.0	98333
46567	SYRACUSE	27744	4154	18.0	29.9	36.6	10.3	5.2	51322	55769	74	78	3284	7.6	19.3	40.5	24.6	8.0	134773
46570	TIPPECANOE	18907	394	19.5	38.1	35.3	5.8	1.3	45517	50137	63	54	340	18.8	22.9	47.7	8.2	2.4	95833
46571	TOPEKA	15372	1636	18.2	34.2	38.0	6.8	2.8	48208	53314	69	67	1194	9.2	13.2	35.5	35.9	6.2	154741
46573	WAKARUSA	23365	1248	17.6	29.3	39.6	8.7	5.0	52533	58578	76	81	1059	8.0	12.0	56.3	19.3	4.4	125530
46574	WALKERTON	20889	3113	24.0	33.3	32.8	7.2	2.6	44739	50293	61	48	2567	7.4	33.1	45.1	12.9	1.5	98795
46580	WARSAW	21912	8165	24.0	31.8	32.4	7.9	3.8	45245	50332	62	51	6114	13.1	26.3	45.8	13.4	1.4	102387
46582	WARSAW	22546	4302	18.8	30.8	37.3	10.2	2.9	50287	55237	72	73	3539	21.3	13.7	44.3	19.9	0.8	114023
46590	WINONA LAKE	22292	1396	17.8	32.9	37.6	7.6	4.2	49381	54666	71	70	1027	9.8	23.2	44.7	18.3	4.0	109592
46601	SOUTH BEND	13916	2682	60.8	23.5	11.9	3.3	0.5	18968	21416	2	1	684	29.8	42.5	25.6	1.6	0.4	68875
46613	SOUTH BEND	14484	4159	37.9	37.2	21.9	2.2	0.8	32315	36386	19	6	2622	42.0	51.7	5.6	0.7	0.0	54372
46614	SOUTH BEND	26471	12820	23.7	28.7	33.3	10.1	4.2	47425	53211	67	64	10012	6.4	29.7	49.5	12.4	1.9	104003
46615	SOUTH BEND	20909	6769	29.8	37.2	25.3	5.4	2.3	37417	42989	37	15	4111	10.0	55.2	29.6	4.9	0.4	79580
46616	SOUTH BEND	18594	2722	32.4	33.5	25.1	6.8	2.3	36839	42460	35	14	1484	23.6	45.7	29.1	1.6	0.1	72644
46617	SOUTH BEND	22228	4372	31.1	27.8	28.6	8.7	3.8	40657	44756	48	27	2826	11.5	29.6	49.5	8.2	1.2	96829
46619	SOUTH BEND	16265	7693	31.6	34.3	27.7	5.7	0.8	36310	41169	33	12	5896	28.3	41.4	26.6	3.5	0.3	68612
46628	SOUTH BEND	20003	10540	28.6	33.0	30.2	6.4	1.9	40716	46262	49	27	7131	17.6	38.8	36.1	6.5	1.1	80330
46635	SOUTH BEND	29972	2544	18.4	25.1	35.5	14.2	6.9	57961	65334	83	91	2108	3.6	18.0	58.5	18.8	1.1	118352
46637	SOUTH BEND	23882	6163	26.4	25.9	34.3	10.0	3.5	47664	53411	68	65	4193	6.8	25.9	58.3	8.2	0.8	106192
46701	ALBION	21149	2938	19.3	31.3	39.2	8.0	2.2	49434	53759	71	70	2512	11.8	23.7	45.1	17.4	2.0	107356
46702	ANDREWS	22453	907	19.3	36.9	32.8	8.5	2.5	45396	50513	62	52	750	13.9	27.9	44.1	12.9	1.2	103472
46703	ANGOLA	22879	7345	20.6	32.7	35.4	7.9	3.5	47352	52049	67	63	5340	14.1	15.6	43.5	21.9	4.9	120957
46705	ASHLEY	21943	681	24.7	31.3	35.8	5.1	3.1	45356	49873	62	52	529	14.6	33.3	41.2	8.7	2.3	91474
46706	AUBURN	23942	7041	20.0	29.5	37.3	10.0	3.3	50370	54766	73	73	5550	14.1	20.5	47.9	15.6	2.0	109263
46710	AVILLA	22318	1636	21.3	28.2	37.5	10.9	2.1	50395	55018	73	73	1306	7.5	14.5	55.4	20.7	1.9	120242
46711	BERNE	16494	2595	29.5	34.5	28.5	5.9	1.6	38566	42770	41	18	1921	9.9	34.6	44.0	10.4	1.0	94378
46714	BLUFFTON	21473	5996	24.0	34.1	31.8	7.9	2.1	43506	48219	57	41	4586	16.2	30.5	41.5	11.3	0.6	93256
46721	BUTLER	19308	1906	20.6	35.6	35.4	6.8	1.6	45878	50825	64	56	1543	17.4	35.6	39.3	7.4	0.3	86987
46723	CHURUBUSCO	21243	2771	19.1	27.6	39.0	11.4	2.9	52374	57793	76	80	2407	14.5	20.7	47.1	16.5	1.2	104796
46725	COLUMBIA CITY	23789	8782	19.3	29.8	38.4	9.2	3.3	50646	55695	73	75	7209	9.7	21.2	50.0	17.4	1.7	114827
46730	CORUNNA	20122	536	20.0	33.8	33.0	9.9	3.4	47215	51138	67	63	470	6.2	22.1	48.9	17.0	5.7	114691
46731	CRAIGVILLE	23979	243	13.2	28.0	39.9	15.6	3.3	57978	61588	83	91	220	6.4	20.9	41.8	30.0	0.9	134783
46732	CROMWELL	20316	1302	19.4	30.8	39.3	8.4	2.2	49850	54116	72	72	1056	23.7	19.9	43.9	11.3	1.2	98947
46733	DECATUR	21694	7364	22.1	33.2	34.0	8.2	2.5	46003	50999	64	56	5803	12.4	28.8	46.1	11.7	1.0	98428
46737	FREMONT	25376	2818	20.2	31.7	37.1	7.8	3.2	48483	52741	69	69	2398	11.5	16.0	39.4	26.6	6.5	127157
46738	GARRETT	21305	2945	20.4	33.1	39.0	5.7	1.8	46504	51333	65	60	2362	16.1	40.0	38.8	5.0	0.1	85185
46740	GENEVA	15235	1240	31.1	30.6	32.2	4.7	1.5	40000	43322	46	24	968	18.5	35.5	36.4	8.9	0.7	86723
46741	GRABILL	17835	1349	15.7	32.5	38.4	10.2	3.3	51189	57226	74	78	1184	11.3	14.4	54.3	16.7	3.2	113410
46742	HAMILTON	22544	1451	20.5	32.5	33.6	9.7	3.6	47018	51094	66	62	1247	10.8	21.4	41.0	23.1	3.7	115987
46743	HARLAN	21484	728	14.0	29.8	40.9	12.8	2.5	54186	61612	79	85	623	10.0	13.6	57.8	15.4	3.2	120389
46745	HOAGLAND	23164	604	16.7	24.8	42.1	13.3	3.2	58250	64498	83	91	551	9.6	23.6	48.3	18.2	0.4	112500
46746	HOWE	18190	1712	20.1	37.2	34.5	6.8	1.5	44431	47515	60	46	1452	9.2	19.6	51.9	18.1	1.2	114088
46747	HUDSON	22515	1117	16.4	37.8	38.7	5.6	1.6	47625	52441	67	65	967	9.3	29.2	45.2	14.9	1.5	101875
46748	HUNTERTOWN	27754	1263	12.0	22.4	41.2	17.5	7.0	64028	71085	88	96	1114	3.4	17.8	50.8	24.0	4.0	130201
46750	HUNTINGTON	22094	10808	24.4	31.9	33.9	7.0	2.8	44601	49451	60	47	8232	12.6	37.0	40.0	10.0	0.5	90403
46755	KENDALLVILLE	20813	6234	25.1	33.3	33.1	6.6	1.9	43214	48530	57	40	4566	12.5	26.0	45.9	14.7	0.9	101775
46759	KEYSTONE	19509	273	22.0	34.4	37.0	6.2	0.4	43928	48640	58	43	237	11.4	19.4	62.9	6.3	0.0	107750
46760	KIMMELL	19888	645	19.4	34.9	36.0	8.2	1.6	45515	50443	63	54	560	10.0	31.6	42.5	14.8	1.1	99216
46761	LAGRANGE	18401	3714	24.4	34.4	32.6	7.0	1.6	42837	46585	56	38	2970	9.9	19.8	46.7	21.7	1.9	115109
46763	LAOTTO	24343	627	18.8	27.1	39.2	12.0	2.9	53127	57905	77	82	571	4.2	9.6	53.8	27.9	4.6	151297
46764	LARWILL	23194	583	15.6	30.5	40.8	10.1	2.9	52507	58226	76	81	509	11.6	22.6	43.6	21.4	0.8	110518
46765	LEO	25890	1502	10.9	21.2	43.2	19.3	5.3	67540	75252	90	97	1384	1.2	12.8	50.0	34.3	1.7	149171
46766	LIBERTY CENTER	19903	240	22.9	24.6	41.3	7.9	3.3	51600	53174	75	78	215	11.6	23.7	45.1	18.6	0.9	104942
46767	LIGONIER	16654	2642	19.8	35.8	35.3	7.5	1.6	44248	49319	59	45	2003	13.1	30.2	43.3	12.0	1.4	95925
46770	MARKLE	22452	809	19.0	26.3	41.9	11.4	1.4	52874	57752	77	82	670	10.9	30.2	48.1	10.0	0.9	98219
46772	MONROE	14263	768	19.3	37.6	35.3	4.8	3.0	45237	50435	62	51	660	5.3	26.8	54.2	12.3	1.4	106376
46773	MONROEVILLE	20507	1438	21.8	27.3	39.5	9.4	2.1	50620	56753	73	75	1226	14.2	25.7	45.7	12.2	2.2	100820
46774	NEW HAVEN	23427	5846	17.0	32.0	38.5	10.2	2.3	50781	57974	73	76	4738	7.8	38.0	44.5	8.9	0.8	93401
46776	ORLAND	24382	660	16.4	33.2	39.7	8.0	2.7	50266	55078	72	72	567	14.3	20.1	45.2	16.8	3.7	106766
46777	OSSIAN	22398	2470	15.6	28.8	44.5	9.9	1.3	53724	60083	78	83	2070	11.2	24.8	46.7	16.2	1.1	105145
46779	PLEASANT LAKE	23807	773	18.6	37.1	33.6	6.9	3.8	46698	51908	65	60	660	18.0	17.6	45.9	16.4	2.1	110263
46781	PONETO	17076	229	20.1	39.3	35.8	3.9	0.9	45280	50508	62	51	197	11.2	24.4	51.8	12.7	0.0	105523
46783	ROANOKE	26578	2160	13.0	27.5	39.6	16.1	3.8	57602	63621	82	90	1902	9.4	16.4	49.1	21.8	3.3	123889
46784	ROME CITY	20574	982	19.6	35.0	36.5	6.4	2.6	45454	50566	62	53	792	12.6	24.4	40.2	20.8	2.0	108763
46785	SAINT JOE	20120	513	18.7	34.5	35.5	7.6	3.7	47198	52570	67	62	453	18.1	22.5	45.9	12.6	0.9	97328
46787	SOUTH WHITLEY	20828	1599	23.6	33.7	33.1	7.6	2.0	44078	49917	59	44	1281	11.1	32.9	44.2	10.5	1.3	96483
46788	SPENCERVILLE	20476	922	15.6	25.5	42.8	12.8	3.3	58395	63347	83	91	850	5.9	15.3	51.8	25.2	1.9	135000
46791	UNIONDALE	21365	354	17.2	30.5	41.5	9.6	1.1	51635	56304	75	79	320	12.2	32.8	45.6	9.1	0.3	94571
46792	WARREN	20657	1547	20.8	33.5	35.9	7.6	2.3	46594	51839	65	60	1271	16.1	32.0	41.7	6.9	3.4	91944
46793	WATERLOO	21465	1598	18.3	30.5	40.0	9.5	1.8	50657	54756	73	75	1337	15.3	30.5	35.9	17.4	1.0	94669
46794	WAWAKA	21880	559	15.2	31.1	43.3	7.3	3.0	51920	57230	75	79	505	11.1	15.8	52.7	19.0	1.4	122685
46795	WOLCOTTVILLE	21848	2566	19.4	32.9	37.5	7.2	3.0	48033	51618	68	67	2195	4.3	16.4	50.4	24.2	4.7	129049
46797	WOODBURN	23144	1518	16.5	26.6	43.5	10.7	2.8	54801	62502	79	86	1242	11.5	29.1	44.6	13.5	1.4	100350
46798	YODER	25153	769	10.4	34.3	38.8	14.3	2.2	53988	60997	78	84	715	20.0	22.9	38.7	16.9	1.4	99182
46802	FORT WAYNE	17660	4814	44.9	32.2	17.7	3.6	1.6	28063	31936	9	3	1814	44.1	33.0	19.7	3.0	0.2	55625
46803	FORT WAYNE	13989	3929	46.6	31.1	17.6	3.6	1.1	27341	30827	8	3	2018	63.8	28.1	7.1	0.9	0.0	39663
46804	FORT WAYNE	33732	11280	14.4	21.9	38.6	16.5	8.7	63661	71791	88	95	8572	0.9	8.4	66.1	22.5	2.1	138139
	INDIANA	23565		24.7	29.6	32.4	9.4	3.9	45964	52146				12.3	23.5	44.9	16.9	2.4	109048
	UNITED STATES	25866		24.7	27.1	30.8	10.9	6.5	48124	56710				10.9	15.0	33.7	30.1	10.4	145905

ZIP CODE #	POST OFFICE NAME	FINANCIAL SERVICES: Auto Loan	Home Loan	Invest-ments	Retire-ment Plans	THE HOME: Home Improvements: Home Repair	Lawn & Garden	Furnishings: Comput-ers & Hard-ware	Major Appli-ances	TV, Radio, Sound Equip-ment	Furni-ture	ENTERTAINMENT: Dine out/ Carry out	Sports Equip-ment	Fees & Tickets	Toys & Games	Travel	Cable TV	PERSONAL: Apparel & Services	Auto Repairs	Health Insur-ance	Pets & Supplies
46536	LAKEVILLE	78	84	84	81	85	90	79	81	79	78	98	93	82	104	81	80	96	79	81	93
46538	LEESBURG	102	90	72	86	96	104	85	94	90	85	110	112	82	110	88	93	104	92	103	121
46539	MENTONE	85	74	57	72	78	86	72	79	77	72	93	92	70	94	73	78	88	77	85	97
46540	MIDDLEBURY	112	104	83	101	107	113	96	104	99	97	121	123	95	123	97	100	116	101	108	130
46542	MILFORD	97	80	55	74	86	94	75	85	82	75	99	102	71	99	77	85	93	83	96	113
46543	MILLERSBURG	103	92	70	87	97	104	85	94	90	85	110	112	83	112	88	93	104	92	102	122
46544	MISHAWAKA	70	70	70	69	71	77	71	72	72	69	89	82	71	90	71	72	86	71	74	81
46545	MISHAWAKA	69	65	74	67	65	70	71	68	71	70	89	81	70	88	69	69	86	71	67	77
46550	NAPPANEE	101	88	66	84	92	100	84	92	89	84	108	108	80	108	85	91	102	90	99	116
46552	NEW CARLISLE	87	77	60	74	81	88	74	81	79	73	96	95	72	96	76	81	91	80	88	101
46553	NEW PARIS	100	89	68	85	94	101	82	91	87	82	106	109	81	109	85	90	101	89	99	118
46554	NORTH LIBERTY	89	88	79	86	90	95	83	87	84	82	103	102	83	106	84	84	99	85	89	104
46555	NORTH WEBSTER	87	74	56	71	79	87	72	80	78	72	94	93	69	94	74	80	88	78	88	100
46556	NOTRE DAME	0	0	0	0	0	0	0	0	0	0	0	0	0	0	0	0	0	0	0	0
46561	OSCEOLA	100	97	82	95	99	103	90	95	91	90	112	112	90	114	91	91	108	93	97	116
46562	PIERCETON	83	75	59	72	77	82	72	77	74	72	91	90	69	89	72	74	86	76	80	94
46563	PLYMOUTH	86	76	63	74	80	88	75	81	80	74	97	94	73	97	76	81	92	80	87	99
46565	SHIPSHEWANA	95	83	64	80	87	95	79	87	84	79	102	102	77	103	81	86	97	85	94	109
46566	SIDNEY	91	81	62	77	86	92	75	83	80	75	97	99	73	99	77	82	92	81	90	107
46567	SYRACUSE	110	96	72	91	102	110	90	100	96	90	116	118	87	118	92	99	110	98	109	129
46570	TIPPECANOE	82	73	55	69	77	83	67	75	71	67	87	89	66	89	69	73	83	73	81	96
46571	TOPEKA	89	78	60	76	82	90	75	82	80	75	97	96	73	98	76	82	92	80	89	103
46573	WAKARUSA	99	94	78	90	97	103	86	94	89	86	109	111	86	113	89	91	105	91	98	117
46574	WALKERTON	87	74	56	70	79	86	72	80	77	71	93	94	68	93	73	79	88	78	87	102
46580	WARSAW	89	80	64	77	83	91	78	84	82	77	100	98	76	100	79	83	95	82	89	102
46582	WARSAW	96	84	63	80	88	95	80	88	84	80	102	103	76	101	81	85	97	86	93	110
46590	WINONA LAKE	84	91	94	93	89	89	90	88	85	89	107	105	90	108	88	81	105	89	79	96
46601	SOUTH BEND	38	34	44	34	33	39	40	38	42	40	53	44	40	52	39	43	52	40	40	43
46613	SOUTH BEND	52	50	56	50	50	55	56	53	57	54	70	63	55	71	54	56	68	55	54	58
46614	SOUTH BEND	84	90	94	88	90	96	88	88	87	86	108	102	90	111	89	87	106	87	88	98
46615	SOUTH BEND	62	65	74	65	65	69	68	65	67	66	83	77	68	85	67	65	81	66	64	72
46616	SOUTH BEND	62	64	73	64	63	68	67	65	67	66	83	76	68	84	66	66	82	66	63	71
46617	SOUTH BEND	72	70	84	71	70	76	78	74	78	76	98	88	77	96	76	77	95	77	73	82
46619	SOUTH BEND	61	60	61	58	60	65	62	62	64	61	79	71	62	80	61	64	77	62	63	69
46628	SOUTH BEND	69	68	74	67	67	73	70	69	72	70	89	80	71	90	69	72	87	70	70	79
46635	SOUTH BEND	103	107	109	105	108	117	106	107	105	104	130	122	107	130	107	105	126	106	107	120
46637	SOUTH BEND	75	79	91	79	78	84	82	79	81	80	101	93	83	103	82	80	99	80	77	87
46701	ALBION	93	79	56	74	84	91	73	83	79	73	96	99	70	97	75	82	91	81	92	109
46702	ANDREWS	95	85	65	81	90	96	78	87	83	78	101	104	77	103	81	85	96	85	94	112
46703	ANGOLA	90	78	64	76	82	89	77	83	82	77	99	98	74	99	78	83	94	83	89	103
46705	ASHLEY	87	75	58	74	79	88	74	80	79	73	96	94	72	96	75	80	90	79	87	99
46706	AUBURN	89	86	76	85	88	93	83	87	84	82	103	102	82	104	83	83	99	85	88	103
46710	AVILLA	92	80	62	78	84	93	78	85	83	77	100	99	75	101	79	84	95	83	92	105
46711	BERNE	75	63	49	61	67	75	63	70	68	62	82	81	59	80	64	70	77	69	77	86
46714	BLUFFTON	78	75	69	72	77	83	73	76	75	72	93	88	73	94	74	77	89	75	80	90
46721	BUTLER	85	71	51	68	76	84	69	77	75	69	91	90	66	90	70	77	85	75	85	98
46723	CHURUBUSCO	95	90	76	86	94	100	84	90	87	83	107	107	84	111	86	89	103	88	96	112
46725	COLUMBIA CITY	91	83	70	81	87	94	81	86	84	80	103	101	79	104	82	85	98	85	91	105
46730	CORUNNA	93	82	63	78	87	93	76	84	81	76	99	101	75	101	78	83	94	82	91	109
46731	CRAIGVILLE	101	103	92	100	105	109	94	99	94	94	116	118	95	120	96	94	112	96	100	121
46732	CROMWELL	95	85	66	81	88	93	80	87	83	81	102	102	77	100	81	84	97	86	91	108
46733	DECATUR	84	78	66	75	81	88	75	80	79	74	96	93	75	99	77	81	92	78	86	97
46737	FREMONT	103	86	63	80	93	103	82	94	90	81	108	110	77	107	85	93	101	92	106	122
46738	GARRETT	87	76	60	74	80	87	75	81	78	74	95	94	72	95	75	79	90	79	86	98
46740	GENEVA	75	63	49	62	67	75	63	69	68	63	82	80	60	81	63	69	77	68	76	85
46741	GRABILL	96	85	68	83	89	97	82	89	86	82	105	104	80	106	83	88	100	87	95	109
46742	HAMILTON	94	84	64	79	88	95	77	86	82	77	100	102	76	102	80	84	95	83	93	111
46743	HARLAN	99	88	67	84	93	100	82	91	87	82	106	108	80	108	84	89	100	88	98	117
46745	HOAGLAND	95	98	88	95	100	103	89	94	89	89	109	111	90	114	91	89	106	91	94	114
46746	HOWE	83	74	57	71	78	84	69	76	73	69	89	91	67	91	71	75	84	74	82	98
46747	HUDSON	92	78	58	73	84	92	73	83	79	73	95	98	70	96	76	82	90	81	92	109
46748	HUNTERTOWN	108	119	115	117	120	122	108	111	104	107	130	131	112	136	110	103	127	108	107	130
46750	HUNTINGTON	82	79	73	76	82	88	77	81	80	76	98	94	77	101	78	81	94	80	84	96
46755	KENDALLVILLE	83	71	54	69	75	83	70	76	75	69	91	89	67	91	70	76	85	75	83	95
46759	KEYSTONE	81	72	55	68	76	81	66	74	71	66	86	88	65	88	68	72	82	72	80	95
46760	KIMMELL	87	77	59	73	82	88	71	79	76	71	92	94	70	94	74	78	88	77	86	102
46761	LAGRANGE	88	73	52	69	79	87	70	79	77	70	93	93	67	92	72	79	87	78	88	102
46763	LAOTTO	104	92	70	88	97	105	85	95	91	85	110	113	84	112	88	93	105	92	102	122
46764	LARWILL	105	93	71	89	99	106	86	96	92	86	112	114	85	114	89	94	106	93	104	124
46765	LEO	104	119	124	121	115	115	110	109	103	112	131	128	114	133	110	99	129	107	98	120
46766	LIBERTY CENTER	91	80	59	76	85	91	74	82	79	74	96	98	72	97	76	81	91	80	90	107
46767	LIGONIER	84	73	60	71	76	81	73	78	77	74	95	91	71	95	72	77	92	78	80	94
46770	MARKLE	91	87	74	84	91	95	80	86	82	80	101	102	80	104	82	83	97	84	89	107
46772	MONROE	85	76	58	72	80	86	70	78	75	70	91	93	69	93	72	76	86	76	84	100
46773	MONROEVILLE	90	79	61	76	84	91	75	83	80	75	97	97	73	98	77	82	92	81	90	104
46774	NEW HAVEN	87	90	84	88	91	95	84	88	84	84	104	102	86	108	86	84	101	85	87	102
46776	ORLAND	101	82	57	75	90	101	77	90	85	76	102	106	70	101	81	90	95	89	105	122
46777	OSSIAN	87	88	80	87	88	92	83	86	82	84	102	101	83	103	83	81	99	85	84	100
46779	PLEASANT LAKE	100	85	61	79	91	98	79	89	85	79	103	106	76	104	81	88	97	87	99	117
46781	PONETO	83	64	41	61	72	79	62	73	68	61	82	87	56	81	64	71	76	71	83	98
46783	ROANOKE	106	105	90	101	108	113	96	102	97	96	119	121	96	123	98	98	115	99	105	126
46784	ROME CITY	94	73	46	67	80	89	69	81	78	70	93	97	64	92	71	82	87	79	93	109
46785	SAINT JOE	92	82	63	78	87	93	76	84	81	76	98	100	74	100	78	83	93	82	91	109
46787	SOUTH WHITLEY	91	73	50	69	79	88	71	80	78	71	94	95	66	93	72	81	87	79	91	104
46788	SPENCERVILLE	99	92	79	89	96	102	87	94	90	87	110	111	86	111	89	91	105	92	99	117
46791	UNIONDALE	91	84	68	81	88	93	77	85	81	77	99	101	77	101	80	82	94	82	90	107
46792	WARREN	87	74	54	71	78	87	73	80	78	71	94	93	69	94	73	81	88	78	89	100
46793	WATERLOO	90	79	61	76	84	91	76	83	80	75	97	98	74	99	77	82	92	81	90	104
46794	WAWAKA	96	86	65	81	91	97	79	88	84	79	102	105	78	105	82	86	97	86	95	113
46795	WOLCOTTVILLE	92	80	60	76	85	92	76	84	81	75	98	99	73	99	78	83	93	82	92	107
46797	WOODBURN	99	91	76	90	95	102	88	94	91	87	111	109	87	113	89	92	106	92	99	113
46798	YODER	99	93	76	89	95	100	86	93	88	87	109	109	85	108	87	89	104	91	95	114
46802	FORT WAYNE	50	45	54	46	44	50	54	50	55	52	69	60	52	67	51	54	67	54	50	55
46803	FORT WAYNE	50	44	48	42	43	50	49	48	52	49	65	55	48	63	48	53	62	50	51	55
46804	FORT WAYNE	109	120	135	122	119	123	118	116	113	117	142	137	121	143	118	110	139	116	109	128
	INDIANA	86	83	80	82	84	90	82	84	84	82	103	98	82	104	82	84	100	84	86	98
	UNITED STATES	100	100	100	100	100	100	100	100	100	100	100	100	100	100	100	100	100	100	100	100

ZIP CODE		COUNTY FIPS CODE	POPULATION			2000-2004 ANNUAL RATE		HOUSEHOLDS			% Annual Rate 2000-2004	2004 Average HH Size	FAMILIES		% Annual Rate 2000-2004
#	POST OFFICE NAME		2000	2004	2009	% Rate	State Centile	2000	2004	2009			2000	2004	
46805	FORT WAYNE	003	22204	21463	21523	-0.8	3	9639	9459	9632	-0.4	2.16	5051	4604	-2.2
46806	FORT WAYNE	003	26639	25443	25500	-1.1	1	9444	9160	9313	-0.7	2.77	6695	6197	-1.8
46807	FORT WAYNE	003	17253	17180	17391	-0.1	21	6605	6685	6870	0.3	2.52	4133	3942	-1.1
46808	FORT WAYNE	003	18989	18918	19169	-0.1	22	8141	8282	8542	0.4	2.24	4655	4429	-1.2
46809	FORT WAYNE	003	8688	8680	8770	0.0	26	3779	3880	4000	0.6	2.22	2327	2248	-0.8
46814	FORT WAYNE	003	7488	8321	8834	2.5	93	2388	2708	2925	3.0	3.07	2179	2435	2.7
46815	FORT WAYNE	003	26128	26139	26600	0.0	28	10184	10481	10895	0.7	2.46	7162	7020	-0.5
46816	FORT WAYNE	003	17527	17152	17243	-0.5	7	7255	7234	7391	-0.1	2.33	4424	4151	-1.5
46818	FORT WAYNE	003	13921	15565	16703	2.7	94	5353	6085	6634	3.1	2.51	3767	4153	2.3
46819	FORT WAYNE	003	9278	9342	9496	0.2	35	3816	3934	4077	0.7	2.36	2530	2479	-0.5
46825	FORT WAYNE	003	25155	27053	28476	1.7	84	10081	11056	11834	2.2	2.41	6643	6937	1.0
46835	FORT WAYNE	003	30998	32111	33070	0.8	60	12209	12946	13582	1.4	2.44	8302	8455	0.4
46845	FORT WAYNE	003	15576	17554	18782	2.9	95	5193	5932	6434	3.2	2.96	4511	5040	2.6
46901	KOKOMO	067	39858	39493	39414	-0.2	17	16185	16370	16511	0.3	2.37	10693	10365	-0.7
46902	KOKOMO	067	35570	36058	36252	0.3	41	15166	15765	16037	0.9	2.27	10133	10096	-0.1
46910	AKRON	049	3183	3242	3286	0.4	46	1159	1193	1214	0.7	2.72	880	876	-0.1
46911	AMBOY	103	1496	1522	1552	0.4	46	556	580	605	1.0	2.62	444	451	0.4
46913	BRINGHURST	015	1391	1535	1659	2.3	92	487	549	602	2.9	2.80	398	437	2.2
46914	BUNKER HILL	103	2532	2567	2614	0.3	41	984	1019	1058	0.8	2.52	739	741	0.1
46917	CAMDEN	015	2022	2147	2273	1.4	77	777	836	897	1.7	2.57	579	603	1.0
46919	CONVERSE	053	2193	2222	2246	0.3	41	860	894	924	0.9	2.48	656	660	0.1
46920	CUTLER	015	1354	1399	1469	0.8	57	532	558	594	1.1	2.51	399	404	0.3
46923	DELPHI	015	8504	8613	8913	0.3	40	3172	3264	3428	0.7	2.60	2293	2276	-0.2
46926	DENVER	103	1819	1862	1905	0.6	50	656	686	717	1.1	2.71	527	537	0.4
46928	FAIRMOUNT	053	5146	5007	4941	-0.2	20	2023	2058	2073	0.4	2.43	1488	1461	-0.4
46929	FLORA	015	3260	3328	3453	0.5	48	1277	1324	1394	0.9	2.45	932	934	0.1
46932	GALVESTON	017	3629	3669	3680	0.3	39	1394	1436	1455	0.7	2.56	1081	1080	0.0
46933	GAS CITY	053	6131	6016	5901	-0.4	8	2471	2485	2492	0.1	2.40	1756	1697	-0.8
46936	GREENTOWN	067	6333	6315	6273	-0.1	23	2327	2364	2371	0.4	2.64	1823	1795	-0.4
46938	JONESBORO	053	3540	3427	3346	-0.8	3	1409	1398	1395	-0.2	2.45	1038	994	-1.0
46939	KEWANNA	049	2210	2187	2173	-0.3	16	904	911	913	0.2	2.40	631	611	-0.8
46940	LA FONTAINE	169	3192	3293	3340	0.7	56	1246	1317	1363	1.3	2.41	930	947	0.4
46941	LAGRO	169	1533	1514	1506	-0.3	14	556	560	569	0.2	2.69	440	431	-0.5
46947	LOGANSPORT	017	30432	30547	30643	0.1	31	11751	11937	12055	0.4	2.47	7887	7685	-0.6
46950	LUCERNE	017	757	795	811	1.2	71	300	320	330	1.5	2.48	239	248	0.9
46951	MACY	103	2767	2783	2820	0.1	34	1022	1046	1076	0.6	2.66	789	785	-0.1
46952	MARION	053	22300	22077	21796	-0.2	16	9352	9462	9536	0.3	2.28	6305	6131	-0.7
46953	MARION	053	26145	25727	25329	-0.4	10	9838	9885	9922	0.1	2.38	6520	6275	-0.9
46960	MONTEREY	131	1365	1423	1497	1.0	64	501	532	569	1.4	2.67	373	382	0.6
46962	NORTH MANCHESTER	169	10197	10296	10370	0.2	38	3613	3728	3835	0.7	2.42	2526	2515	-0.1
46970	PERU	103	25835	26419	27125	0.5	50	9898	10386	10923	1.1	2.40	6825	6885	0.2
46974	ROANN	169	1319	1332	1334	0.2	38	489	504	514	0.7	2.63	389	390	0.1
46975	ROCHESTER	049	14489	14552	14579	0.1	31	5745	5854	5897	0.4	2.46	4035	3961	-0.4
46978	ROYAL CENTER	017	2102	2104	2099	0.0	28	808	826	834	0.5	2.55	606	599	-0.3
46979	RUSSIAVILLE	067	4448	4598	4643	0.8	58	1610	1701	1736	1.3	2.70	1301	1339	0.7
46982	SILVER LAKE	085	2615	2687	2805	0.6	52	976	1021	1085	1.1	2.63	760	772	0.4
46985	STAR CITY	131	1437	1481	1541	0.7	55	514	540	570	1.2	2.74	408	417	0.5
46986	SWAYZEE	053	2018	1971	1930	-0.6	6	789	787	787	-0.1	2.50	616	596	-0.8
46988	TWELVE MILE	017	1089	1091	1086	0.0	29	355	363	365	0.5	2.66	268	266	-0.2
46989	UPLAND	053	5976	6007	5982	0.1	32	1580	1615	1634	0.5	2.66	1204	1194	-0.2
46990	URBANA	169	678	672	670	-0.2	17	241	243	247	0.2	2.74	192	189	-0.4
46991	VAN BUREN	053	1697	1717	1712	0.3	39	647	670	682	0.8	2.54	493	493	0.0
46992	WABASH	169	17964	17766	17712	-0.3	15	7059	7137	7266	0.3	2.41	4905	4765	-0.7
46994	WALTON	017	2862	2857	2845	0.0	24	1073	1091	1096	0.4	2.62	817	805	-0.4
46996	WINAMAC	131	7399	7703	8053	1.0	64	2877	3044	3232	1.3	2.47	2053	2097	0.5
47001	AURORA	029	10298	10699	11358	0.9	62	3884	4120	4460	1.4	2.59	2855	2929	0.6
47003	WEST COLLEGE CORNER	161	1010	1053	1112	1.0	64	376	398	427	1.4	2.63	272	277	0.4
47006	BATESVILLE	137	10570	11442	12522	1.9	87	3789	4197	4692	2.4	2.66	2849	3060	1.7
47010	BATH	047	143	148	154	0.8	59	53	56	60	1.3	2.36	42	43	0.6
47011	BENNINGTON	155	1149	1324	1548	3.4	97	388	453	537	3.7	2.92	307	351	3.2
47012	BROOKVILLE	047	10231	10672	11259	1.0	65	3750	3992	4298	1.5	2.63	2801	2888	0.7
47016	CEDAR GROVE	047	844	899	958	1.5	80	304	331	360	2.0	2.72	243	258	1.4
47017	CROSS PLAINS	137	624	673	740	1.8	85	253	279	314	2.3	2.41	182	194	1.5
47018	DILLSBORO	029	4068	4280	4575	1.2	72	1515	1630	1780	1.7	2.55	1121	1160	0.8
47020	FLORENCE	155	1094	1157	1296	1.3	75	406	437	498	1.8	2.65	315	330	1.1
47022	GUILFORD	029	2444	2616	2809	1.6	82	851	930	1018	2.1	2.81	697	741	1.5
47023	HOLTON	137	1648	1726	1872	1.1	68	578	621	688	1.7	2.77	447	465	0.9
47024	LAUREL	047	3381	3426	3583	0.3	41	1195	1238	1322	0.8	2.77	959	968	0.2
47025	LAWRENCEBURG	029	20508	21689	23160	1.3	75	7585	8179	8895	1.8	2.61	5630	5879	1.0
47030	METAMORA	047	1424	1455	1534	0.5	49	507	528	567	1.0	2.76	405	410	0.3
47031	MILAN	137	4720	5089	5600	1.8	85	1735	1913	2149	2.3	2.62	1299	1382	1.5
47032	MOORES HILL	029	3245	3550	3859	2.1	91	1079	1207	1339	2.7	2.93	888	969	2.1
47036	OLDENBURG	047	1011	1101	1186	2.0	89	300	336	370	2.7	3.13	241	263	2.1
47037	OSGOOD	137	4486	4891	5416	2.1	89	1673	1860	2099	2.5	2.59	1233	1324	1.7
47038	PATRIOT	155	1265	1348	1517	1.5	80	447	488	561	2.1	2.75	353	376	1.5
47040	RISING SUN	115	4908	5238	5697	1.5	80	1947	2125	2361	2.1	2.44	1384	1457	1.2
47041	SUNMAN	137	5108	5581	6139	2.1	90	1799	2006	2250	2.6	2.78	1434	1556	1.9
47042	VERSAILLES	137	4080	4308	4692	1.3	74	1594	1719	1911	1.8	2.49	1157	1204	0.9
47043	VEVAY	155	4701	5394	6303	3.3	96	1874	2190	2608	3.7	2.42	1314	1479	2.8
47060	WEST HARRISON	029	6063	6513	6996	1.7	84	2152	2362	2588	2.2	2.76	1732	1851	1.6
47102	AUSTIN	143	7712	7904	8190	0.6	51	2883	3035	3218	1.2	2.60	2198	2244	0.5
47106	BORDEN	019	4749	5262	5720	2.4	93	1780	2015	2237	3.0	2.60	1409	1547	2.2
47108	CAMPBELLSBURG	175	2392	2349	2362	-0.4	9	900	905	926	0.1	2.60	655	636	-0.7
47110	CENTRAL	061	301	300	311	-0.1	23	111	114	121	0.6	2.63	81	80	-0.3
47111	CHARLESTOWN	019	11941	12437	13167	1.0	64	4451	4734	5120	1.5	2.60	3381	3473	0.6
47112	CORYDON	061	13664	14473	15384	1.4	76	5243	5684	6183	1.9	2.49	3765	3941	1.1
47114	CRANDALL	061	370	381	398	0.7	54	143	151	162	1.3	2.52	115	118	0.6
47115	DEPAUW	061	2478	2552	2705	0.7	54	940	994	1080	1.3	2.57	713	730	0.6
47116	ECKERTY	025	1012	1068	1140	1.3	74	392	424	464	1.9	2.52	286	298	1.0
47117	ELIZABETH	061	4168	4339	4562	1.0	64	1523	1627	1752	1.6	2.67	1203	1250	0.9
47118	ENGLISH	025	3654	3836	4067	1.2	70	1422	1530	1660	1.7	2.48	1024	1064	0.9
47119	FLOYDS KNOBS	043	9489	9914	10199	1.0	67	3307	3537	3707	1.6	2.80	2791	2913	1.0
47120	FREDERICKSBURG	175	964	1061	1120	2.3	92	354	397	426	2.7	2.67	276	300	2.0
47122	GEORGETOWN	043	8915	9337	9690	1.1	68	3154	3382	3580	1.7	2.76	2628	2746	1.0
47123	GRANTSBURG	025	84	89	95	1.4	77	40	43	47	1.7	2.05	30	31	0.8
	INDIANA					0.8					1.2	2.48			0.3
	UNITED STATES					1.2					1.3	2.58			1.1

ZIP CODE #	POST OFFICE NAME	RACE (%) White 2000	White 2004	Black 2000	Black 2004	Asian/Pacific 2000	Asian/Pacific 2004	% Hispanic Origin 2000	% Hispanic Origin 2004	2004 AGE DISTRIBUTION (%) 0-4	5-9	10-14	15-19	20-24	25-44	45-64	65-84	85+	18+	MEDIAN AGE 2004	% 2004 Males	% 2004 Females
46805	FORT WAYNE	89.3	87.1	4.4	5.4	1.7	2.1	5.0	6.2	7.5	6.5	6.1	6.0	7.5	31.4	19.8	11.4	3.9	76.4	34.7	47.8	52.2
46806	FORT WAYNE	30.9	27.8	58.8	61.3	0.9	1.0	10.5	11.5	9.8	9.3	9.9	8.6	8.3	26.7	19.8	6.9	0.8	65.8	28.1	47.3	52.7
46807	FORT WAYNE	79.7	76.3	10.4	12.2	1.5	1.8	9.1	10.9	9.2	8.3	7.6	7.0	8.1	30.7	19.9	7.7	1.4	70.8	31.3	48.2	51.8
46808	FORT WAYNE	92.3	90.7	2.2	2.8	1.2	1.5	4.2	5.4	6.9	6.6	6.7	7.1	7.9	31.4	22.1	9.9	1.4	75.9	33.9	50.0	50.0
46809	FORT WAYNE	91.3	89.4	3.9	4.9	0.5	0.6	4.6	5.8	7.0	6.5	6.5	6.1	6.8	28.0	24.5	12.5	2.1	76.2	37.8	48.8	51.2
46814	FORT WAYNE	94.1	92.4	1.5	1.9	2.9	3.7	1.6	2.1	6.6	8.2	10.1	8.5	5.4	21.6	33.3	6.1	0.4	69.8	39.5	50.0	50.0
46815	FORT WAYNE	91.0	88.9	4.9	6.1	1.3	1.7	2.3	3.0	6.9	6.8	7.3	7.0	6.6	25.5	24.7	12.7	2.5	74.7	37.6	47.4	52.6
46816	FORT WAYNE	58.0	53.8	33.7	37.1	1.4	1.6	6.0	6.9	8.2	7.4	7.3	6.9	8.6	27.4	21.7	10.0	2.6	73.2	33.1	47.7	52.3
46818	FORT WAYNE	94.6	93.2	1.7	2.2	1.4	1.9	1.9	2.4	7.6	7.7	7.5	5.9	5.2	31.8	23.6	9.8	0.9	73.4	35.7	49.8	50.2
46819	FORT WAYNE	91.0	89.2	5.2	6.3	0.4	0.6	3.4	4.3	6.7	6.5	6.6	6.5	6.9	26.3	25.2	13.3	2.1	76.3	38.3	49.2	50.8
46825	FORT WAYNE	89.0	86.7	4.4	5.3	3.3	4.2	2.6	3.3	8.2	7.7	7.0	5.8	7.0	31.6	21.8	9.3	1.6	73.6	33.7	48.4	51.6
46835	FORT WAYNE	92.2	90.4	3.6	4.5	1.8	2.3	2.0	2.5	7.3	7.1	6.9	6.4	7.5	29.2	24.4	9.9	1.4	75.0	34.9	49.4	50.6
46845	FORT WAYNE	96.4	95.5	1.0	1.2	1.3	1.6	0.9	1.2	7.7	8.5	9.2	7.4	5.1	26.4	27.9	7.4	0.5	69.9	37.0	49.7	50.3
46901	KOKOMO	87.8	87.0	8.8	9.2	0.4	0.5	2.3	2.7	7.1	7.0	7.2	6.8	6.1	27.1	25.0	11.9	1.9	74.4	37.1	48.6	51.5
46902	KOKOMO	89.8	88.5	5.7	6.3	1.9	2.4	2.0	2.3	7.0	6.5	6.5	5.9	6.3	27.1	26.4	12.8	1.6	76.5	38.4	48.1	51.9
46910	AKRON	94.9	94.8	0.1	0.1	0.0	0.0	7.9	8.1	6.7	6.9	8.1	7.2	6.6	28.4	23.1	11.4	1.7	74.0	36.6	50.6	49.4
46911	AMBOY	98.3	98.0	0.5	0.5	0.1	0.2	2.3	2.8	5.7	6.4	7.9	7.0	5.5	27.1	26.7	12.2	1.6	75.6	39.6	51.0	49.0
46913	BRINGHURST	98.4	98.2	0.1	0.2	0.1	0.1	1.3	1.6	6.5	6.9	7.5	6.6	5.5	25.5	28.3	12.0	1.2	75.1	39.4	51.2	48.8
46914	BUNKER HILL	96.6	96.1	0.9	1.0	0.3	0.4	1.0	1.3	6.8	6.7	8.0	7.1	6.2	25.9	27.2	10.8	1.3	73.9	37.4	50.1	49.9
46917	CAMDEN	99.1	99.1	0.3	0.3	0.0	0.0	0.6	0.8	7.5	7.6	7.5	6.3	4.9	28.3	24.3	11.7	2.0	73.5	37.8	49.5	50.5
46919	CONVERSE	97.6	97.3	0.1	0.2	0.3	0.4	2.6	3.1	5.9	6.1	7.4	7.0	6.1	25.7	27.3	12.8	1.7	76.2	39.7	49.3	50.7
46920	CUTLER	99.0	99.0	0.1	0.1	0.0	0.0	1.0	1.2	7.0	7.2	7.4	6.2	5.4	27.6	25.8	11.9	1.6	74.6	38.5	50.5	49.5
46923	DELPHI	96.5	95.9	0.2	0.2	0.1	0.1	5.0	5.9	7.2	7.2	7.4	6.6	5.9	27.5	25.2	11.4	1.6	74.2	37.1	50.4	49.6
46926	DENVER	97.1	96.9	0.1	0.1	0.1	0.1	0.7	0.8	6.4	7.0	8.3	7.0	5.7	27.9	26.1	10.6	1.0	74.0	37.6	51.2	48.8
46928	FAIRMOUNT	98.4	98.2	0.4	0.4	0.1	0.2	0.6	0.8	5.9	6.3	7.8	6.3	5.6	26.5	26.9	13.2	1.5	76.0	39.6	48.7	51.3
46929	FLORA	98.4	98.2	0.4	0.4	0.1	0.1	1.8	2.2	6.5	6.7	7.2	6.6	6.1	25.8	24.1	13.8	3.2	75.5	38.8	47.7	52.3
46932	GALVESTON	98.3	98.0	0.3	0.3	0.2	0.3	1.3	1.6	6.5	6.8	7.4	6.7	5.9	27.0	27.9	10.4	1.3	75.1	37.8	49.3	50.7
46933	GAS CITY	97.2	96.7	0.4	0.5	0.2	0.3	1.7	2.1	6.6	6.5	6.8	6.7	6.7	27.8	25.5	12.0	1.5	75.8	37.4	48.2	51.8
46936	GREENTOWN	97.7	97.3	0.5	0.6	0.3	0.4	1.0	1.3	6.2	6.6	7.6	7.3	6.2	24.8	28.0	11.3	2.0	75.0	39.7	49.1	50.9
46938	JONESBORO	97.7	97.5	0.3	0.3	0.2	0.2	1.4	1.7	5.8	6.2	7.6	6.3	5.6	27.0	26.8	13.5	1.3	76.5	39.8	48.4	51.6
46939	KEWANNA	97.6	97.6	1.0	1.0	0.1	0.1	0.5	0.5	6.5	6.7	7.7	6.1	5.2	25.1	25.8	14.6	2.3	75.4	40.5	49.3	50.7
46940	LA FONTAINE	97.8	97.8	0.3	0.2	0.1	0.1	1.1	1.2	5.5	6.0	6.9	7.3	5.6	25.4	27.9	12.9	2.6	76.7	40.7	50.0	50.0
46941	LAGRO	98.4	98.4	0.1	0.2	0.2	0.2	0.4	0.5	6.3	6.8	7.9	7.3	5.5	26.4	27.3	11.2	1.3	74.4	38.8	50.9	49.1
46947	LOGANSPORT	92.4	91.3	1.5	1.6	0.7	0.9	8.8	10.4	7.1	6.7	6.5	7.1	6.9	27.3	23.8	12.5	2.1	75.1	36.9	50.5	49.5
46950	LUCERNE	99.5	99.5	0.0	0.0	0.1	0.1	0.1	0.1	7.2	7.4	7.3	6.2	4.0	28.3	24.7	13.6	1.4	74.2	38.6	50.9	49.1
46951	MACY	97.9	97.7	0.1	0.1	0.0	0.0	0.8	0.9	6.3	6.9	8.4	7.1	5.5	26.5	26.8	11.8	0.7	74.1	38.9	52.2	47.8
46952	MARION	91.4	90.3	4.4	4.8	1.2	1.5	2.5	3.0	5.8	6.0	6.7	6.0	5.7	24.4	27.6	15.5	2.4	77.8	41.7	48.1	51.9
46953	MARION	79.8	78.4	16.0	16.9	0.3	0.4	3.4	3.9	6.5	6.2	6.7	7.6	8.7	25.1	23.5	13.7	2.0	77.0	36.5	47.7	52.3
46960	MONTEREY	93.6	93.2	3.4	3.6	0.6	0.8	1.3	1.5	6.7	6.9	7.1	6.3	6.5	25.8	26.6	12.5	1.6	75.2	37.8	51.2	48.8
46962	NORTH MANCHESTER	97.0	97.0	0.7	0.7	0.6	0.6	1.5	1.5	5.7	5.6	5.8	8.6	10.6	23.5	22.1	14.0	4.3	79.4	36.8	47.2	52.8
46970	PERU	92.2	91.6	4.0	4.3	0.4	0.5	1.3	1.5	6.4	6.4	7.0	6.5	6.7	28.6	25.3	11.6	1.7	76.4	37.6	51.0	49.0
46974	ROANN	97.5	97.5	0.1	0.1	0.2	0.2	0.8	0.8	5.9	6.1	7.1	7.2	6.2	26.6	26.8	12.5	1.7	76.4	39.1	49.4	50.6
46975	ROCHESTER	96.4	96.3	0.8	0.8	0.5	0.5	1.4	1.5	6.8	6.7	7.2	6.2	6.1	26.3	25.2	13.5	2.1	75.6	38.8	49.4	50.6
46978	ROYAL CENTER	98.5	98.4	0.3	0.4	0.1	0.1	0.4	0.5	7.1	7.0	7.3	7.3	6.5	25.4	23.8	14.4	1.4	74.2	37.9	50.8	49.2
46979	RUSSIAVILLE	97.6	97.3	0.7	0.8	0.5	0.6	0.9	1.1	6.7	7.2	8.1	7.2	5.2	26.9	28.4	9.3	1.0	73.2	38.4	49.8	50.2
46982	SILVER LAKE	97.2	96.7	0.2	0.2	0.0	0.0	2.5	2.9	6.7	6.7	7.3	7.2	6.9	28.0	25.2	10.9	1.1	75.0	36.3	49.8	50.2
46985	STAR CITY	99.0	98.9	0.1	0.1	0.1	0.1	0.7	0.7	6.3	6.8	8.4	7.2	5.7	27.2	26.3	11.0	1.3	74.1	38.2	51.2	48.8
46986	SWAYZEE	96.8	96.5	0.4	0.5	0.2	0.2	1.7	2.1	5.2	5.7	7.2	6.9	5.1	26.5	28.6	13.2	1.5	77.6	41.1	48.3	51.7
46988	TWELVE MILE	96.1	95.8	2.8	2.9	0.1	0.2	0.8	1.0	6.7	6.7	5.8	6.3	5.1	27.2	29.3	11.4	1.5	76.5	40.4	53.9	46.1
46989	UPLAND	95.9	95.4	1.0	1.1	1.0	1.3	1.7	2.0	4.0	4.5	5.9	15.9	22.5	18.4	19.2	8.5	1.2	82.4	24.4	49.3	50.7
46990	URBANA	98.2	98.2	0.0	0.2	0.2	0.2	0.6	0.7	6.3	6.7	8.0	7.3	5.7	26.5	26.3	11.6	1.6	74.4	38.4	51.3	48.7
46991	VAN BUREN	98.1	98.0	0.2	0.2	0.1	0.2	1.1	1.2	6.4	6.6	7.7	6.5	5.5	24.9	27.1	13.1	2.2	75.3	39.5	49.0	51.0
46992	WABASH	97.4	97.3	0.4	0.4	0.5	0.5	1.2	1.2	6.3	6.3	6.8	7.0	6.5	26.3	25.7	13.2	1.9	76.2	38.7	49.0	51.0
46994	WALTON	95.5	94.8	0.3	0.4	0.2	0.3	5.3	6.3	6.4	6.7	7.8	7.1	5.5	26.4	26.7	11.9	1.5	74.6	38.9	49.1	50.9
46996	WINAMAC	97.9	97.6	0.6	0.6	0.2	0.3	1.2	1.4	6.0	6.4	7.6	6.8	6.2	25.3	26.0	13.4	2.3	75.9	39.7	50.1	49.9
47001	AURORA	98.7	98.5	0.1	0.1	0.3	0.4	0.5	0.6	6.7	6.7	7.2	7.2	6.2	28.9	25.3	10.8	1.0	74.8	37.2	49.5	50.5
47003	WEST COLLEGE CORNER	98.5	98.6	0.1	0.1	0.1	0.1	0.2	0.2	9.0	8.7	8.2	7.3	5.9	28.3	23.0	8.3	1.3	69.6	33.2	50.9	49.1
47006	BATESVILLE	97.8	97.4	0.0	0.1	0.8	1.0	1.0	1.2	7.5	7.7	8.3	6.6	5.4	27.2	24.0	11.0	2.3	72.3	37.0	48.9	51.1
47010	BATH	99.3	99.3	0.0	0.0	0.0	0.0	0.0	0.7	6.8	6.8	6.1	6.1	4.7	25.0	25.7	12.2	6.8	75.7	41.0	48.7	51.4
47011	BENNINGTON	98.9	98.8	0.0	0.0	0.1	0.1	0.8	1.0	7.2	7.3	7.8	6.7	6.3	28.3	24.8	10.9	0.7	73.4	35.7	51.5	48.5
47012	BROOKVILLE	99.1	99.0	0.0	0.0	0.2	0.3	0.5	0.5	6.9	7.1	7.7	6.6	6.0	27.1	24.5	12.2	1.9	74.1	37.6	49.8	50.2
47016	CEDAR GROVE	99.5	99.6	0.0	0.0	0.1	0.1	0.4	0.4	6.6	6.8	7.3	7.0	6.7	28.3	26.4	9.8	1.2	75.1	37.3	50.5	49.5
47017	CROSS PLAINS	99.5	99.6	0.0	0.0	0.0	0.0	0.5	0.6	5.7	5.8	6.8	5.9	5.8	29.1	25.6	13.4	1.9	78.2	39.8	53.2	46.8
47018	DILLSBORO	99.0	98.8	0.1	0.1	0.2	0.2	0.6	0.7	6.2	6.4	7.1	7.0	5.9	26.3	25.4	13.3	2.4	76.0	40.0	48.7	51.3
47020	FLORENCE	99.2	99.0	0.4	0.4	0.2	0.3	1.1	1.4	7.7	7.6	7.3	5.5	6.6	28.8	25.9	9.9	0.8	74.2	36.2	51.5	48.5
47022	GUILFORD	99.4	99.3	0.0	0.0	0.1	0.1	0.2	0.2	6.5	7.2	8.1	7.5	5.7	27.2	27.0	10.1	0.8	73.3	37.9	51.0	49.0
47023	HOLTON	99.3	99.3	0.0	0.0	0.1	0.1	0.6	0.7	6.8	7.1	7.7	6.8	6.3	27.6	25.5	11.0	1.1	74.2	37.1	50.5	49.5
47024	LAUREL	98.8	98.7	0.1	0.1	0.1	0.1	0.5	0.6	7.9	7.8	8.1	6.8	6.5	29.7	22.8	9.9	0.6	72.0	34.4	50.7	49.3
47025	LAWRENCEBURG	97.2	96.9	1.3	1.4	0.4	0.5	0.7	0.8	7.1	7.2	7.6	6.8	6.0	28.3	25.3	10.2	1.5	74.0	37.2	48.9	51.1
47030	METAMORA	99.0	98.9	0.1	0.1	0.2	0.2	0.5	0.6	7.2	7.8	8.9	6.4	5.9	29.5	24.2	9.6	0.6	72.2	35.4	51.6	48.5
47031	MILAN	98.2	98.0	0.1	0.1	0.3	0.3	0.6	0.7	7.2	7.4	8.0	6.9	6.0	27.7	24.4	10.9	1.6	73.1	36.3	50.3	49.7
47032	MOORES HILL	97.8	97.5	0.1	0.1	0.3	0.4	0.8	1.0	7.3	7.5	8.1	7.8	6.9	27.6	24.9	8.9	1.0	72.3	35.3	50.5	49.6
47036	OLDENBURG	98.9	98.8	0.1	0.1	0.3	0.4	0.3	0.4	5.5	6.6	8.5	6.5	5.0	26.3	25.2	13.8	2.5	74.9	39.9	49.9	50.1
47037	OSGOOD	99.0	98.9	0.1	0.1	0.1	0.2	0.6	0.7	8.0	7.8	8.0	6.9	5.5	28.1	21.8	11.8	2.2	71.7	35.9	49.3	50.8
47038	PATRIOT	97.6	97.5	0.7	0.8	0.0	0.0	1.2	1.3	6.0	6.4	8.6	8.0	6.3	30.3	25.6	8.2	0.5	74.0	35.8	52.8	47.2
47040	RISING SUN	98.6	98.5	0.5	0.6	0.2	0.2	0.5	0.6	6.2	6.1	6.6	6.8	6.1	27.2	26.2	12.9	1.8	77.1	39.3	49.6	50.4
47041	SUNMAN	98.3	98.0	0.0	0.0	0.1	0.2	1.5	1.8	8.2	8.1	8.1	6.6	5.5	29.0	23.6	9.9	1.1	71.4	35.8	50.6	49.4
47042	VERSAILLES	99.1	99.0	0.0	0.0	0.1	0.1	0.4	0.5	7.1	6.8	7.0	6.7	7.1	25.7	25.6	12.4	1.6	75.0	37.6	48.1	51.9
47043	VEVAY	99.0	98.9	0.2	0.2	0.1	0.1	0.7	0.9	5.9	6.3	7.5	6.5	5.8	26.5	26.3	13.2	2.2	76.1	39.6	49.5	50.5
47060	WEST HARRISON	99.1	99.0	0.1	0.1	0.3	0.3	0.5	0.6	6.7	7.2	8.0	6.9	6.0	29.5	26.8	8.2	0.8	73.9	36.9	50.8	49.2
47102	AUSTIN	98.7	98.5	0.1	0.1	0.2	0.2	1.3	1.6	7.8	7.3	7.1	6.5	6.6	29.3	24.5	9.9	0.9	73.7	35.5	49.9	50.1
47106	BORDEN	97.8	97.5	0.2	0.3	0.3	0.3	1.2	1.4	6.5	6.9	6.9	6.2	5.8	28.9	28.3	9.9	0.7	75.9	38.7	50.9	49.1
47108	CAMPBELLSBURG	98.6	98.5	0.3	0.3	0.1	0.1	0.5	0.5	7.6	7.3	6.8	6.8	6.7	28.0	25.2	10.5	1.2	74.1	35.9	51.6	48.5
47110	CENTRAL	98.3	98.3	0.0	0.0	0.3	0.3	1.0	1.0	7.7	7.0	6.3	6.3	6.7	30.7	26.7	8.0	0.7	75.0	36.4	51.3	48.7
47111	CHARLESTOWN	94.7	93.9	1.9	2.2	0.3	0.4	3.1	3.7	7.6	7.5	7.3	6.3	6.4	29.7	24.6	9.7	1.0	73.7	35.8	49.3	50.8
47112	CORYDON	98.1	97.9	0.6	0.6	0.2	0.3	1.1	1.2	6.5	6.4	6.9	6.6	6.6	28.3	25.8	11.3	1.8	76.3	38.2	49.5	50.5
47114	CRANDALL	98.7	98.2	0.5	0.8	0.0	0.0	1.1	1.1	6.3	6.6	6.8	6.3	6.6	27.0	30.2	9.2	1.1	76.4	39.6	50.7	49.3
47115	DEPAUW	98.8	98.8	0.2	0.2	0.2	0.2	0.1	0.1	6.4	6.5	6.9	6.6	6.6	28.2	27.1	10.3	1.4	76.1	38.4	49.4	50.6
47116	ECKERTY	98.8	98.4	0.1	0.1	0.3	0.5	0.7	0.9	6.1	6.3	7.8	7.0	6.1	26.8	26.9	11.8	1.3	75.7	39.2	52.3	47.7
47117	ELIZABETH	98.4	98.2	0.2	0.3	0.1	0.1	0.5	0.6	6.0	6.4	7.2	6.5	6.0	28.3	28.5	10.0	1.2	76.4	39.1	49.5	50.5
47118	ENGLISH	98.2	97.9	0.2	0.2	0.2	0.3	1.0	1.2	6.2	6.4	6.9	6.6	6.1	27.5	27.1	11.9	1.4	76.9	38.9	50.0	50.1
47119	FLOYDS KNOBS	98.6	98.4	0.3	0.3	0.4	0.6	0.6	0.7	5.5	6.8	8.2	7.5	5.5	26.2	30.7	9.0	0.7	74.7	39.8	49.5	50.5
47120	FREDERICKSBURG	98.2	98.0	0.5	0.6	0.2	0.2	0.5	0.7	6.5	6.5	7.2	7.1	7.3	29.5	25.9	9.3	0.8	75.6	36.3	53.2	46.8
47122	GEORGETOWN	98.5	98.3	0.4	0.5	0.2	0.3	0.6	0.7	6.2	6.8	8.3	6.9	5.7	28.9	28.8	7.7	0.7	74.5	38.0	50.6	49.4
47123	GRANTSBURG	97.6	97.8	0.0	0.0	0.0	0.0	1.2	0.0	6.7	6.7	6.7	6.7	6.7	28.1	25.8	11.2	1.1	74.2	37.1	49.4	50.6
	INDIANA	87.5	86.7	8.4	8.7	1.0	1.3	3.5	4.1	7.0	6.9	7.1	7.1	7.4	28.1	24.0	10.8	1.6	75.0	35.9	49.2	50.8
	UNITED STATES	75.1	73.6	12.3	12.5	3.8	4.2	12.5	14.1	6.9	6.7	7.2	7.0	7.3	28.6	23.8	10.8	1.7	75.1	36.0	49.1	50.9

INCOME

ZIP CODE #	POST OFFICE NAME	2004 Per Capita Income	2004 HH Income Base	2004 Household Income Distribution (%) Less than $25,000	$25,000 to $49,999	$50,000 to $99,999	$100,000 to $149,999	$150,000 or More	Median Household Income 2004	2009	2004 National Centile	2004 State Centile	2004 Home Value Base	2004 Home Value Distribution (%) Less than $50,000	$50,000 to $89,999	$90,000 to $174,999	$175,000 to $399,999	$400,000 or More	2004 Median Home Value
46805	FORT WAYNE	22248	9459	29.2	37.9	26.4	4.8	1.8	36819	42344	35	14	5342	13.5	60.7	23.6	1.6	0.5	74630
46806	FORT WAYNE	13657	9160	40.0	36.1	19.1	4.1	0.7	30401	33855	13	5	5426	47.0	43.8	8.6	0.4	0.2	52194
46807	FORT WAYNE	20700	6685	27.3	33.2	30.8	5.8	3.0	41366	47275	51	30	4280	24.1	49.3	22.2	4.0	0.5	70403
46808	FORT WAYNE	19384	8282	31.7	35.3	28.1	4.2	0.7	36894	42108	35	14	5107	25.6	54.1	18.4	2.0	0.1	68421
46809	FORT WAYNE	21865	3880	27.9	34.8	30.5	4.9	1.9	40287	46149	47	25	2688	17.1	52.6	27.6	2.3	0.3	75956
46814	FORT WAYNE	61080	2708	6.3	7.5	23.9	24.3	38.0	121409	137693	99	100	2643	1.6	1.7	14.9	52.5	29.3	276136
46815	FORT WAYNE	26554	10481	18.6	26.2	38.4	12.4	4.4	54305	61539	79	85	7921	0.9	22.6	69.6	6.7	0.2	107644
46816	FORT WAYNE	20615	7234	31.4	31.4	29.5	6.3	1.4	38898	44135	42	19	4103	18.8	44.0	32.0	4.3	0.9	79193
46818	FORT WAYNE	22977	6085	18.7	31.9	37.8	9.7	1.9	49398	56903	71	70	5323	31.2	16.6	40.0	11.6	0.6	93098
46819	FORT WAYNE	23301	3934	21.1	32.6	35.8	8.2	2.3	47202	52587	67	62	2723	11.1	35.1	45.5	8.0	0.3	92459
46825	FORT WAYNE	25038	11056	19.5	33.4	33.7	10.0	3.5	47977	54623	68	67	7397	9.8	27.7	50.6	10.9	1.1	102141
46835	FORT WAYNE	27649	12946	15.8	27.1	39.9	12.9	4.4	56751	63932	81	89	9430	1.7	23.4	61.7	11.5	1.7	107658
46845	FORT WAYNE	35487	5932	6.6	16.0	41.4	24.4	11.7	80323	91196	95	99	5672	1.9	5.9	49.2	38.1	5.1	164774
46901	KOKOMO	23315	16370	28.3	27.7	30.9	10.3	2.8	43250	50466	57	40	11762	16.7	34.4	38.3	9.7	1.0	88633
46902	KOKOMO	27477	15765	22.5	27.1	35.3	10.9	4.3	50361	57206	73	73	11102	6.7	32.5	45.2	14.2	1.4	100946
46910	AKRON	17489	1193	27.0	36.6	30.5	5.2	0.8	40708	45366	49	27	992	15.9	31.4	44.6	7.5	0.7	92547
46911	AMBOY	22687	580	19.3	29.7	38.3	9.8	2.9	50786	55182	73	76	501	14.6	35.7	37.3	11.6	0.8	89516
46913	BRINGHURST	24357	549	14.9	29.9	38.8	12.9	3.5	54092	59222	78	85	500	10.8	14.4	49.6	21.2	4.0	121467
46914	BUNKER HILL	20450	1019	25.2	33.6	31.0	8.9	1.3	45250	49089	62	51	836	23.2	26.0	41.5	8.9	0.5	90854
46917	CAMDEN	20045	836	22.3	33.9	35.3	7.8	0.8	45607	50430	63	54	705	16.7	35.0	37.6	9.4	1.3	88047
46919	CONVERSE	21973	894	24.2	31.3	32.2	9.2	3.1	45176	50000	62	50	738	13.1	42.4	34.2	9.4	1.0	84533
46920	CUTLER	23385	558	21.0	29.8	36.6	11.5	1.3	49501	54363	71	71	456	15.1	20.2	45.4	18.6	0.7	109770
46923	DELPHI	20861	3264	24.4	29.0	36.5	7.9	2.1	46980	51364	66	61	2538	9.2	27.7	45.7	15.9	1.5	101460
46926	DENVER	18902	686	19.7	39.7	33.1	6.0	1.6	43196	48231	56	39	599	19.4	32.2	39.4	8.5	0.5	88100
46928	FAIRMOUNT	20628	2058	24.5	32.6	36.2	5.3	1.5	43054	48434	56	39	1670	24.3	36.7	32.8	5.9	0.4	77188
46929	FLORA	22821	1324	23.8	33.1	33.5	7.3	2.3	45273	50934	62	51	1047	11.8	29.0	49.2	9.1	1.0	97423
46932	GALVESTON	26078	1436	15.1	29.9	36.6	14.8	3.6	54347	59965	79	86	1229	12.0	23.4	55.7	8.2	0.8	101398
46933	GAS CITY	22425	2485	27.3	32.8	31.6	6.8	1.5	41235	47841	51	30	1909	16.6	49.8	30.4	3.1	0.1	77959
46936	GREENTOWN	25618	2364	15.7	24.9	39.6	14.6	5.2	58554	66542	83	92	1988	9.2	17.3	52.3	19.6	1.8	121222
46938	JONESBORO	20500	1398	23.7	32.9	36.0	6.8	0.6	44842	50599	61	48	1137	26.8	41.4	27.5	4.1	0.1	72218
46939	KEWANNA	18857	911	31.0	31.5	32.4	4.4	0.8	38180	41898	40	17	739	18.4	34.5	34.5	9.6	3.0	85700
46940	LA FONTAINE	22929	1317	18.9	31.9	38.6	8.7	1.9	49480	54403	71	71	1090	17.2	26.2	39.2	16.1	1.4	97129
46941	LAGRO	19529	560	18.8	37.1	37.0	5.4	1.8	45590	50264	63	54	492	16.1	26.8	44.5	11.0	1.6	97778
46947	LOGANSPORT	20390	11937	26.8	34.4	30.0	7.1	1.9	40296	45039	47	25	8401	18.8	40.3	33.4	6.9	0.7	80762
46950	LUCERNE	20322	320	17.8	45.6	27.5	7.8	1.3	41438	46458	51	30	273	13.6	35.9	42.5	6.6	1.5	90484
46951	MACY	18666	1046	20.8	40.1	32.3	5.0	1.8	43137	47811	56	39	889	18.7	27.3	42.5	9.6	1.9	95071
46952	MARION	24900	9462	28.0	31.6	27.7	8.6	4.1	41717	46790	52	32	6918	13.1	33.8	39.9	12.3	1.0	93854
46953	MARION	17978	9885	36.5	31.3	25.6	5.5	1.2	34678	38328	26	8	6828	32.8	36.3	26.8	3.4	0.7	67639
46960	MONTEREY	17460	532	35.2	32.5	22.9	5.6	3.8	35815	39116	31	11	443	22.8	37.5	24.2	14.7	0.9	76848
46962	NORTH MANCHESTER	20050	3728	22.2	36.3	33.4	6.9	1.2	42794	47124	55	38	2829	13.2	30.2	44.6	11.3	0.8	97431
46970	PERU	20373	10386	28.1	32.6	31.2	6.4	1.8	41629	45833	52	32	7623	23.9	34.8	33.2	7.4	0.8	80112
46974	ROANN	19287	504	20.2	38.5	34.5	5.4	1.4	45443	50095	62	53	427	22.0	30.0	37.2	10.5	0.2	87821
46975	ROCHESTER	20724	5854	26.3	32.2	33.5	5.8	2.2	42299	46888	54	35	4559	17.4	32.1	37.8	10.9	1.9	90679
46978	ROYAL CENTER	21032	826	20.8	32.9	36.1	9.2	1.0	46368	51113	65	59	692	19.5	38.0	34.4	6.7	1.5	81333
46979	RUSSIAVILLE	27340	1701	14.2	22.1	41.0	17.5	5.2	62399	71835	87	94	1530	5.9	18.8	51.1	22.0	2.2	123118
46982	SILVER LAKE	18075	1021	22.9	37.6	34.5	3.5	1.5	41912	46777	53	33	857	18.6	34.2	40.4	6.5	0.4	86987
46985	STAR CITY	17618	540	23.7	41.1	28.0	6.5	0.7	40866	45517	49	28	457	32.6	22.8	36.1	7.0	1.5	82344
46986	SWAYZEE	21647	787	22.1	28.6	38.8	9.9	0.6	48546	53753	69	69	676	17.0	31.5	44.7	6.5	0.3	91493
46988	TWELVE MILE	20346	363	16.0	36.9	36.1	8.3	2.8	44913	51750	61	49	307	10.4	37.1	40.4	10.8	1.3	91923
46989	UPLAND	18294	1615	23.3	32.4	34.6	7.7	2.0	45792	51611	63	55	1292	13.5	32.0	45.4	8.8	0.2	94914
46990	URBANA	18622	243	17.7	38.3	37.5	5.8	0.8	46400	50998	65	59	211	21.8	29.4	37.4	10.4	1.0	87917
46991	VAN BUREN	20131	670	24.5	32.4	34.8	7.0	1.3	45184	51190	62	50	538	23.4	35.7	32.9	7.6	0.4	78704
46992	WABASH	20894	7137	26.2	33.8	32.0	5.8	2.3	41793	45732	52	32	5244	14.8	35.0	38.8	10.8	0.8	90276
46994	WALTON	23830	1091	18.6	29.2	38.4	11.0	2.8	51923	57094	75	80	910	16.9	27.3	48.0	7.4	0.4	94862
46996	WINAMAC	19842	3044	28.1	36.3	26.9	5.3	3.5	38276	42285	40	17	2414	16.9	34.3	36.3	10.7	1.8	88707
47001	AURORA	21775	4120	22.4	30.9	36.3	8.3	2.1	46863	53161	66	61	3173	7.4	18.5	52.7	19.9	1.5	120275
47003	WEST COLLEGE CORNER	18000	398	24.1	45.0	23.1	5.8	2.0	38456	42185	41	18	295	18.0	37.3	34.6	5.4	4.8	84655
47006	BATESVILLE	24451	4197	18.6	25.7	39.3	10.8	5.6	54339	60217	79	86	3326	2.6	9.5	52.2	30.3	5.5	146682
47010	BATH	21143	56	21.4	32.1	37.5	3.6	5.4	46550	50000	65	60	43	4.7	27.9	48.8	16.3	2.3	108750
47011	BENNINGTON	16818	453	28.3	31.6	34.0	4.2	2.0	40876	45060	49	28	391	10.7	19.4	48.9	17.7	3.3	110096
47012	BROOKVILLE	20248	3992	24.7	31.4	33.6	7.9	2.4	45193	50844	62	51	3207	11.1	20.7	45.5	20.7	2.1	114096
47016	CEDAR GROVE	22394	331	18.7	30.5	39.0	9.1	2.7	50608	56984	73	75	285	13.3	14.7	41.1	25.3	5.6	126953
47017	CROSS PLAINS	20167	279	24.7	34.4	33.3	7.5	0.0	45521	50000	63	54	238	11.8	15.1	40.8	29.8	2.5	121739
47018	DILLSBORO	20511	1630	21.9	35.1	33.7	7.8	1.5	45038	50494	61	50	1279	9.3	13.1	47.2	27.8	2.7	129139
47020	FLORENCE	29312	437	23.6	33.9	33.2	4.8	4.6	44016	49078	59	44	353	18.1	24.4	43.3	13.0	1.1	97162
47022	GUILFORD	22432	930	13.8	33.7	37.5	11.5	3.6	52461	58368	76	81	854	4.3	9.8	42.6	41.0	2.2	164716
47023	HOLTON	18167	621	24.8	33.7	31.9	8.2	1.5	43258	47863	57	40	527	14.8	22.6	41.9	19.5	1.1	106807
47024	LAUREL	17947	1238	27.8	34.9	31.6	4.4	1.4	41188	46718	50	29	1026	25.2	24.3	35.3	12.5	2.8	90845
47025	LAWRENCEBURG	24491	8179	18.8	25.9	38.3	12.9	4.2	54521	60709	79	86	6355	3.6	9.6	49.3	34.8	2.7	155093
47030	METAMORA	18863	528	22.0	32.4	36.9	7.0	1.7	46395	52392	65	59	441	10.9	17.2	47.6	22.7	1.6	117139
47031	MILAN	18897	1913	24.8	34.6	33.1	6.2	1.3	43955	48328	58	43	1544	13.5	23.3	43.3	17.5	2.5	105807
47032	MOORES HILL	20359	1207	20.0	28.1	40.4	9.0	2.5	51121	56723	74	77	1021	9.6	19.5	45.1	22.7	3.1	115972
47036	OLDENBURG	20120	336	22.6	24.4	38.1	9.8	5.1	52466	58763	76	81	290	8.3	13.5	38.6	35.5	4.1	148684
47037	OSGOOD	18395	1860	27.5	34.5	32.0	5.0	1.0	41556	45812	52	31	1476	13.6	22.4	45.7	16.6	1.8	106766
47038	PATRIOT	19031	488	23.0	34.6	34.6	5.1	2.7	46084	50348	64	57	403	23.1	20.8	40.2	13.4	2.5	97000
47040	RISING SUN	23107	2125	26.3	27.8	37.1	6.8	2.0	46315	51367	65	58	1598	10.5	14.5	48.3	22.8	3.9	118316
47041	SUNMAN	20338	2006	19.9	27.8	41.2	9.4	1.6	51504	56211	75	78	1730	6.8	14.3	40.6	36.1	2.2	143864
47042	VERSAILLES	18756	1719	28.0	35.7	29.8	5.0	1.5	40834	45498	49	28	1303	11.5	25.5	45.7	15.4	2.0	104200
47043	VEVAY	18642	2190	35.6	31.1	27.6	3.6	2.2	37548	41374	38	16	1699	11.8	28.0	41.5	16.2	2.5	99225
47060	WEST HARRISON	25349	2362	15.3	23.8	41.6	14.1	5.2	60034	65582	84	93	2051	6.3	12.0	39.3	36.2	6.2	160494
47102	AUSTIN	16561	3035	37.3	33.8	22.6	5.0	1.2	33992	37157	24	7	2219	22.0	38.4	33.3	6.1	0.2	79824
47106	BORDEN	22658	2015	17.1	30.4	37.1	11.2	4.1	51787	56976	75	79	1754	8.6	18.7	42.4	25.8	4.5	122194
47108	CAMPBELLSBURG	17424	905	34.9	29.1	31.1	3.5	1.4	36426	40081	33	13	744	22.2	35.1	33.9	8.6	0.3	81692
47110	CENTRAL	18839	114	18.4	43.0	35.1	1.8	1.8	41348	45918	51	30	96	16.7	32.3	29.2	21.9	0.0	91667
47111	CHARLESTOWN	19100	4734	29.2	30.6	30.7	7.3	2.3	41963	46393	53	33	3501	12.4	28.3	41.4	15.8	2.0	99863
47112	CORYDON	22522	5684	23.6	32.1	33.2	8.4	2.7	46052	50612	64	57	4458	12.2	19.1	49.0	18.6	1.0	114239
47114	CRANDALL	25419	151	12.6	30.5	40.4	14.6	2.0	54988	61541	80	87	136	18.4	15.4	44.1	20.6	1.5	111458
47115	DEPAUW	23086	994	26.2	33.9	28.1	8.3	3.6	44246	48965	59	45	848	18.0	21.8	45.3	13.1	1.8	103600
47116	ECKERTY	22510	424	32.1	33.0	29.0	4.0	1.9	40220	43276	47	25	366	27.3	29.2	32.8	5.5	5.2	80000
47117	ELIZABETH	23469	1627	16.5	33.6	38.5	8.5	2.8	49802	53632	72	72	1446	13.2	23.2	40.0	20.9	2.6	108882
47118	ENGLISH	16524	1530	39.9	29.9	24.8	4.0	1.4	33966	37185	24	7	1251	32.9	31.2	26.5	7.8	1.7	73922
47119	FLOYDS KNOBS	32979	3537	11.6	22.2	37.4	17.1	11.7	67721	77404	90	97	3281	2.7	5.0	50.3	35.6	6.4	163575
47120	FREDERICKSBURG	15109	397	34.5	35.8	26.2	2.8	0.8	37239	41135	36	15	339	25.7	22.1	37.2	13.0	2.1	93261
47122	GEORGETOWN	25549	3382	13.6	25.3	41.3	15.4	4.4	59595	67247	84	92	3107	6.4	13.2	49.3	29.3	1.8	139364
47123	GRANTSBURG	19882	43	39.5	30.2	25.6	2.3	2.3	34062	37337	24	7	35	37.1	31.4	22.9	8.6	0.0	68333
	INDIANA	23565		24.7	29.6	32.4	9.4	3.9	45964	52146				12.3	23.5	44.9	16.9	2.4	109048
	UNITED STATES	25866		24.7	27.1	30.8	10.9	6.5	48124	56710				10.9	15.0	33.7	30.1	10.4	145905

ZIP CODE #	POST OFFICE NAME	FINANCIAL SERVICES: Auto Loan	Home Loan	Investments	Retirement Plans	THE HOME: Home Improvements: Home Repair	Lawn & Garden	Furnishings: Computers & Hardware	Major Appliances	TV, Radio, Sound Equipment	Furniture	ENTERTAINMENT: Dine out/Carry out	Sports Equipment	Fees & Tickets	Toys & Games	Travel	Cable TV	PERSONAL: Apparel & Services	Auto Repairs	Health Insurance	Pets & Supplies
46805	FORT WAYNE	66	64	73	65	64	70	70	68	71	68	88	80	69	88	69	69	85	70	67	75
46806	FORT WAYNE	51	49	55	47	48	53	53	51	55	52	69	58	53	69	52	56	67	52	53	57
46807	FORT WAYNE	70	72	80	73	71	76	75	73	74	74	93	86	75	93	74	73	91	75	71	80
46808	FORT WAYNE	60	59	62	59	59	64	62	61	63	60	78	71	62	79	61	62	75	61	61	68
46809	FORT WAYNE	65	68	71	66	68	74	69	68	69	67	86	78	70	89	69	70	83	68	69	75
46814	FORT WAYNE	247	308	335	318	298	301	272	264	247	275	314	306	299	327	276	239	317	255	235	293
46815	FORT WAYNE	87	98	107	98	97	101	94	94	90	94	113	108	97	115	95	89	111	93	89	103
46816	FORT WAYNE	68	66	68	65	65	70	68	68	69	67	86	79	68	86	67	68	83	69	67	76
46818	FORT WAYNE	89	87	74	85	87	90	81	85	80	82	100	100	79	99	81	79	96	84	83	101
46819	FORT WAYNE	73	82	89	81	82	86	78	78	76	77	95	90	81	98	80	75	93	77	76	87
46825	FORT WAYNE	87	89	88	91	87	89	87	87	84	88	106	103	87	105	85	81	103	87	80	98
46835	FORT WAYNE	93	102	110	105	100	101	98	97	93	99	117	114	101	118	97	89	116	96	87	107
46845	FORT WAYNE	142	170	176	174	165	163	152	150	140	154	177	175	161	183	153	134	177	145	133	166
46901	KOKOMO	81	76	70	74	78	86	77	79	80	75	98	92	75	98	77	81	93	79	84	93
46902	KOKOMO	85	90	95	89	90	95	88	88	87	87	109	103	90	112	89	87	107	88	86	99
46910	AKRON	78	65	47	62	69	76	63	70	68	62	82	82	60	82	64	70	77	68	77	89
46911	AMBOY	95	85	65	81	90	96	78	87	83	78	101	104	77	104	81	85	96	85	94	112
46913	BRINGHURST	109	97	74	92	103	110	90	100	95	90	116	119	88	118	92	98	110	97	108	128
46914	BUNKER HILL	82	71	55	69	75	82	69	75	73	69	89	88	67	89	70	75	84	74	81	93
46917	CAMDEN	83	73	56	70	78	83	68	75	72	68	88	90	67	90	70	74	83	73	81	97
46919	CONVERSE	87	76	58	73	80	87	73	80	77	72	94	94	71	95	74	79	89	78	86	100
46920	CUTLER	94	84	64	79	88	95	77	86	82	77	100	102	76	102	80	84	95	83	93	111
46923	DELPHI	87	76	57	72	80	88	72	80	78	72	94	94	70	94	74	80	88	78	88	101
46926	DENVER	82	73	56	69	77	83	68	75	72	68	87	89	66	89	70	74	83	73	81	97
46928	FAIRMOUNT	77	68	56	67	71	79	68	72	72	67	88	83	67	89	69	74	83	71	79	87
46929	FLORA	81	80	73	75	82	90	76	80	80	75	98	92	78	104	79	83	94	78	86	95
46932	GALVESTON	107	95	72	90	100	108	88	97	93	88	113	116	86	116	90	96	108	95	105	125
46933	GAS CITY	81	76	66	72	80	86	72	77	76	71	93	90	73	97	75	78	89	75	83	95
46936	GREENTOWN	98	101	96	100	103	107	94	98	94	94	116	116	96	119	96	93	112	96	98	117
46938	JONESBORO	82	70	51	66	74	81	66	74	71	66	86	87	63	87	67	73	81	72	81	95
46939	KEWANNA	80	60	36	55	66	74	57	68	65	57	77	81	52	76	59	68	71	67	79	93
46940	LA FONTAINE	89	79	60	76	83	90	75	82	79	74	97	97	73	98	76	81	91	80	89	104
46941	LAGRO	84	75	57	71	79	85	69	77	74	69	90	92	68	92	71	76	85	75	83	99
46947	LOGANSPORT	74	70	65	67	72	79	70	72	73	68	90	84	69	91	71	74	86	72	77	86
46950	LUCERNE	87	65	40	63	73	82	65	76	73	64	86	90	58	85	66	76	80	75	88	101
46951	MACY	83	69	47	64	74	81	64	73	70	64	85	87	61	85	66	73	80	72	82	97
46952	MARION	84	79	72	76	82	90	78	82	82	77	100	94	78	102	80	84	96	81	88	97
46953	MARION	67	57	50	54	60	67	59	63	64	58	78	73	57	77	59	66	74	63	69	76
46960	MONTEREY	78	61	41	58	66	75	61	69	68	61	81	80	57	79	62	70	75	68	79	88
46962	NORTH MANCHESTER	80	69	55	66	73	81	69	74	74	68	89	86	66	89	69	76	84	74	83	92
46970	PERU	76	66	55	64	69	77	66	71	71	65	86	83	64	86	67	72	81	71	77	87
46974	ROANN	85	71	49	66	76	83	66	75	72	66	87	89	63	87	68	75	82	73	84	99
46975	ROCHESTER	80	70	57	68	74	82	69	75	73	68	88	87	66	89	70	75	84	73	81	92
46978	ROYAL CENTER	87	75	55	71	80	87	70	79	75	70	91	94	68	93	72	77	86	77	87	103
46979	RUSSIAVILLE	109	108	97	107	111	117	102	107	103	101	126	125	103	130	103	103	122	104	108	127
46982	SILVER LAKE	76	65	49	63	68	76	64	70	68	63	83	81	61	83	64	70	78	68	76	86
46985	STAR CITY	80	67	47	63	72	78	63	72	68	63	82	86	60	83	65	70	77	70	80	94
46986	SWAYZEE	87	77	59	73	82	88	71	79	76	71	92	94	70	94	74	78	88	77	86	102
46988	TWELVE MILE	90	79	61	77	83	91	76	83	81	76	98	98	74	99	77	83	93	81	90	104
46989	UPLAND	86	72	59	71	75	83	77	78	80	74	98	95	72	97	75	80	92	79	83	97
46990	URBANA	82	73	56	69	77	83	68	75	72	68	87	89	66	89	70	74	83	73	81	97
46991	VAN BUREN	81	70	54	68	74	82	69	75	73	68	89	87	67	89	70	75	84	73	81	92
46992	WABASH	78	70	57	66	73	81	68	74	73	67	89	86	67	90	70	75	84	72	81	90
46994	WALTON	101	89	67	84	94	101	82	91	88	82	106	109	80	108	84	90	101	89	99	118
46996	WINAMAC	84	64	41	61	71	80	64	74	72	63	85	87	58	83	65	75	79	73	86	97
47001	AURORA	84	79	70	76	81	88	77	80	80	75	98	95	76	101	78	81	94	79	85	98
47003	WEST COLLEGE CORNER	75	64	50	63	67	75	64	69	68	63	83	80	62	83	64	69	78	68	75	84
47006	BATESVILLE	100	94	80	91	98	105	89	95	93	88	113	111	89	117	91	94	108	93	100	116
47010	BATH	84	75	57	71	79	85	69	77	74	69	90	92	68	91	71	75	85	75	83	99
47011	BENNINGTON	84	67	43	61	73	80	63	73	70	63	84	87	58	83	64	73	79	72	83	98
47012	BROOKVILLE	83	75	60	72	79	86	72	78	76	71	92	91	70	94	73	78	87	76	84	97
47016	CEDAR GROVE	97	87	66	82	92	98	80	89	85	80	104	106	79	106	83	87	98	87	96	115
47017	CROSS PLAINS	78	69	53	66	73	79	64	71	68	64	83	85	63	85	66	70	79	69	77	92
47018	DILLSBORO	84	74	56	71	77	85	71	77	75	70	91	91	69	92	72	77	86	76	84	97
47020	FLORENCE	146	98	44	84	111	128	94	118	114	96	134	141	80	126	96	123	122	117	146	168
47022	GUILFORD	93	95	85	92	97	101	86	92	87	86	107	108	88	111	89	87	104	89	92	111
47023	HOLTON	84	70	48	65	75	82	65	74	71	65	86	89	62	86	67	74	81	73	84	99
47024	LAUREL	87	67	41	61	73	81	63	74	71	64	85	88	58	84	64	75	79	73	86	100
47025	LAWRENCEBURG	92	94	90	94	94	99	91	92	90	90	111	108	91	113	91	89	108	91	91	106
47030	METAMORA	89	71	46	65	77	85	66	77	74	67	89	92	62	88	68	78	83	76	88	104
47031	MILAN	79	70	54	67	74	80	66	73	70	66	86	86	65	87	68	72	81	71	79	92
47032	MOORES HILL	94	82	63	80	86	95	80	87	85	80	104	102	78	104	81	87	98	86	95	107
47036	OLDENBURG	103	91	70	87	97	104	85	94	90	85	109	112	83	112	87	92	104	91	101	121
47037	OSGOOD	80	65	45	61	70	77	62	71	69	62	83	84	59	82	64	71	77	69	80	92
47038	PATRIOT	97	67	34	59	76	86	65	79	77	66	90	95	56	86	66	82	83	78	96	111
47040	RISING SUN	87	77	62	74	81	90	76	82	81	75	99	95	74	100	77	84	93	80	90	100
47041	SUNMAN	89	80	62	77	84	91	75	83	80	75	97	97	74	99	77	81	92	81	89	104
47042	VERSAILLES	76	62	45	60	66	75	62	69	68	61	81	80	59	80	63	70	76	68	77	86
47043	VEVAY	74	58	40	55	63	73	60	67	67	58	79	77	55	77	61	70	73	66	78	83
47060	WEST HARRISON	104	105	93	102	107	111	95	101	96	95	118	120	97	123	98	97	115	98	103	124
47102	AUSTIN	76	57	34	52	63	70	54	65	62	55	74	77	49	72	56	65	69	64	75	88
47106	BORDEN	105	103	89	100	106	111	94	101	96	94	118	120	95	122	97	97	114	98	103	124
47108	CAMPBELLSBURG	81	59	34	53	66	74	57	68	65	57	78	81	51	75	58	69	72	67	80	94
47110	CENTRAL	79	72	56	69	72	76	69	74	69	71	86	85	65	81	68	68	82	73	73	87
47111	CHARLESTOWN	77	68	56	66	70	78	68	72	72	67	87	84	65	87	68	73	82	72	78	87
47112	CORYDON	90	77	58	74	81	90	76	83	81	75	98	96	73	98	77	83	92	81	91	102
47114	CRANDALL	103	91	70	87	97	104	85	94	90	85	109	112	83	112	87	92	104	91	101	121
47115	DEPAUW	95	84	64	80	89	96	78	87	83	78	101	103	76	103	80	85	96	84	94	112
47116	ECKERTY	107	71	32	62	81	93	69	86	83	70	98	103	59	92	70	90	89	85	106	123
47117	ELIZABETH	100	89	68	85	94	101	82	91	88	83	107	109	81	109	85	90	101	89	99	118
47118	ENGLISH	75	53	28	47	59	67	51	62	60	52	71	74	45	68	52	64	65	61	75	86
47119	FLOYDS KNOBS	127	145	145	144	144	147	130	133	125	131	156	155	137	162	133	123	154	128	125	153
47120	FREDERICKSBURG	64	58	46	56	59	62	56	60	57	57	70	69	53	66	55	56	67	60	60	71
47122	GEORGETOWN	102	108	101	106	109	112	98	102	96	98	119	120	100	124	100	96	116	99	100	121
47123	GRANTSBURG	77	52	23	45	59	67	50	62	60	51	71	75	42	67	51	65	64	62	77	89
	INDIANA	86	83	80	82	84	90	82	84	84	82	103	98	82	104	82	84	100	84	86	98
	UNITED STATES	100	100	100	100	100	100	100	100	100	100	100	100	100	100	100	100	100	100	100	100

POPULATION CHANGE

ZIP CODE			POPULATION			2000-2004 ANNUAL RATE		HOUSEHOLDS					FAMILIES		
#	POST OFFICE NAME	COUNTY FIPS CODE	2000	2004	2009	% Rate	State Centile	2000	2004	2009	% Annual Rate 2000-2004	2004 Average HH Size	2000	2004	% Annual Rate 2000-2004
47124	GREENVILLE	043	3576	3867	4061	1.9	87	1239	1371	1466	2.4	2.82	1036	1118	1.8
47125	HARDINSBURG	117	1929	1828	1824	-1.3	1	718	697	709	-0.7	2.62	545	513	-1.4
47126	HENRYVILLE	019	3539	3717	3939	1.2	71	1287	1387	1505	1.8	2.63	1011	1056	1.0
47129	CLARKSVILLE	019	20587	20778	21771	0.2	38	8718	8995	9639	0.7	2.25	5297	5159	-0.6
47130	JEFFERSONVILLE	019	38750	41203	44256	1.5	78	16067	17582	19373	2.1	2.31	10543	11059	1.1
47135	LACONIA	061	1167	1206	1265	0.8	58	450	475	509	1.3	2.54	342	350	0.6
47136	LANESVILLE	061	3818	4039	4250	1.3	75	1389	1502	1614	1.9	2.69	1113	1173	1.2
47137	LEAVENWORTH	025	1472	1536	1630	1.0	65	557	594	644	1.5	2.52	421	435	0.8
47138	LEXINGTON	077	4312	4633	4883	1.7	84	1609	1772	1908	2.3	2.61	1270	1355	1.5
47140	MARENGO	117	2388	2497	2646	1.1	67	938	1003	1086	1.6	2.49	661	681	0.7
47141	MARYSVILLE	019	1623	1906	2145	3.9	98	587	704	808	4.4	2.70	477	556	3.7
47142	MAUCKPORT	061	823	820	852	-0.1	22	327	335	357	0.6	2.45	237	235	-0.2
47143	MEMPHIS	019	2722	3003	3272	2.3	92	1011	1143	1274	2.9	2.63	824	906	2.3
47145	MILLTOWN	025	2079	2177	2314	1.1	68	788	843	916	1.6	2.56	608	631	0.9
47147	NABB	019	947	1052	1146	2.5	93	366	415	462	3.0	2.52	282	309	2.2
47150	NEW ALBANY	043	47096	47332	48070	0.1	32	19257	19760	20417	0.6	2.35	12762	12498	-0.5
47160	NEW MIDDLETOWN	061	134	134	138	0.0	27	51	52	55	0.5	2.58	41	40	-0.6
47161	NEW SALISBURY	061	3326	3586	3846	1.8	85	1199	1327	1459	2.4	2.70	932	1003	1.7
47162	NEW WASHINGTON	019	719	791	862	2.3	92	240	271	303	2.9	2.87	182	198	2.0
47163	OTISCO	019	1688	1816	1955	1.7	84	614	676	745	2.3	2.68	511	547	1.6
47164	PALMYRA	061	3324	3484	3692	1.1	69	1223	1309	1415	1.6	2.65	944	980	0.9
47165	PEKIN	175	5957	6288	6544	1.3	74	2190	2351	2483	1.7	2.67	1669	1735	0.9
47166	RAMSEY	061	1230	1326	1422	1.8	85	457	506	556	2.4	2.62	355	381	1.7
47167	SALEM	175	14375	14579	14822	0.3	42	5517	5699	5887	0.8	2.50	3968	3959	-0.1
47170	SCOTTSBURG	143	13583	14232	14894	1.1	68	5313	5691	6082	1.6	2.46	3796	3925	0.8
47172	SELLERSBURG	019	10962	11962	12914	2.1	90	4219	4702	5185	2.6	2.51	3112	3341	1.7
47174	SULPHUR	025	65	69	73	1.4	77	24	26	28	1.9	2.65	19	20	1.2
47175	TASWELL	025	733	773	825	1.3	74	292	317	346	2.0	2.44	217	228	1.2
47177	UNDERWOOD	143	1073	1162	1244	1.9	87	400	444	487	2.5	2.59	324	349	1.8
47201	COLUMBUS	005	37694	38042	38451	0.2	38	15050	15460	15861	0.6	2.43	10494	10407	-0.2
47203	COLUMBUS	005	25051	25469	25745	0.4	45	9753	10092	10355	0.8	2.49	7111	7086	-0.1
47220	BROWNSTOWN	071	5379	5343	5402	-0.2	20	2051	2085	2153	0.4	2.50	1522	1494	-0.4
47223	BUTLERVILLE	079	1743	1779	1848	0.5	48	530	553	587	1.0	2.93	408	412	0.2
47224	CANAAN	077	569	624	688	2.2	91	202	224	249	2.5	2.79	163	176	1.8
47227	COMMISKEY	079	1232	1245	1287	0.3	38	462	479	505	0.9	2.59	364	365	0.1
47229	CROTHERSVILLE	071	3257	3238	3273	-0.1	21	1276	1298	1340	0.4	2.49	970	954	-0.4
47230	DEPUTY	077	2107	2290	2424	2.0	89	791	876	944	2.4	2.61	622	667	1.7
47231	DUPONT	077	1149	1153	1173	0.1	30	401	411	427	0.6	2.79	309	307	-0.2
47232	ELIZABETHTOWN	005	2468	2453	2473	-0.1	21	944	960	986	0.4	2.56	761	754	-0.2
47234	FLAT ROCK	145	1260	1362	1413	1.9	87	478	530	560	2.5	2.57	377	406	1.8
47235	FREETOWN	071	1517	1521	1555	0.1	29	589	608	637	0.8	2.48	439	437	-0.1
47236	GRAMMER	005	125	126	126	0.2	36	50	51	52	0.5	2.47	42	42	0.0
47240	GREENSBURG	031	20004	20639	21297	0.7	56	7699	8151	8625	1.4	2.50	5595	5725	0.5
47243	HANOVER	077	6140	6337	6495	0.8	56	1926	2045	2147	1.4	2.56	1427	1460	0.5
47244	HARTSVILLE	005	744	739	741	-0.2	20	260	262	266	0.2	2.82	208	203	-0.6
47246	HOPE	005	4749	4674	4646	-0.4	10	1664	1666	1681	0.0	2.76	1307	1270	-0.7
47250	MADISON	077	20841	21005	21430	0.2	36	8485	8747	9109	0.7	2.32	5643	5575	-0.3
47260	MEDORA	071	1844	1837	1852	-0.1	22	698	712	733	0.5	2.58	537	531	-0.3
47264	NORMAN	071	1546	1540	1558	-0.1	22	609	624	646	0.6	2.47	469	465	-0.2
47265	NORTH VERNON	079	19698	20852	22246	1.4	76	7381	7952	8633	1.8	2.58	5439	5675	1.0
47270	PARIS CROSSING	079	891	917	960	0.7	53	326	344	367	1.3	2.67	263	269	0.5
47272	SAINT PAUL	031	1985	1967	1978	-0.2	17	703	713	732	0.3	2.76	554	546	-0.3
47273	SCIPIO	079	2047	2133	2249	1.0	64	722	768	824	1.5	2.78	573	592	0.7
47274	SEYMOUR	071	28150	29030	29880	0.7	55	10962	11538	12108	1.2	2.48	7726	7845	0.4
47281	VALLONIA	071	1461	1517	1561	0.9	62	557	589	617	1.3	2.57	443	456	0.7
47282	VERNON	079	317	351	381	2.4	93	113	128	141	3.0	2.66	80	87	2.0
47283	WESTPORT	031	3533	3508	3553	-0.2	19	1321	1344	1395	0.4	2.61	998	985	-0.3
47302	MUNCIE	035	30498	29502	28911	-0.8	3	12772	12616	12604	-0.3	2.32	8480	8005	-1.4
47303	MUNCIE	035	31434	31220	31001	-0.2	20	11087	11226	11347	0.3	2.29	5874	5628	-1.0
47304	MUNCIE	035	28589	29363	29618	0.6	52	11967	12546	12900	1.1	2.29	7666	7655	0.0
47305	MUNCIE	035	4912	4730	4633	-0.9	2	2239	2193	2184	-0.5	2.04	922	830	-2.4
47306	MUNCIE	035	256	266	269	0.9	62	153	156	157	0.5	1.64	41	38	-1.8
47320	ALBANY	035	4307	4301	4266	0.0	25	1702	1732	1748	0.4	2.45	1238	1210	-0.5
47325	BROWNSVILLE	161	717	722	739	0.2	35	256	263	275	0.6	2.73	208	208	0.0
47326	BRYANT	075	2024	2022	2020	0.0	26	609	612	617	0.1	3.30	485	475	-0.5
47327	CAMBRIDGE CITY	177	5445	5350	5273	-0.4	9	2160	2164	2170	0.0	2.45	1583	1529	-0.8
47330	CENTERVILLE	177	5437	5361	5288	-0.3	11	2050	2068	2080	0.2	2.54	1599	1564	-0.5
47331	CONNERSVILLE	041	25019	24828	24636	-0.2	19	9979	10115	10230	0.3	2.41	6979	6809	-0.6
47334	DALEVILLE	035	3075	2963	2895	-0.4	2	1213	1190	1182	-0.5	2.49	901	851	-1.3
47336	DUNKIRK	075	4048	3986	3967	-0.4	11	1640	1643	1659	0.0	2.40	1176	1135	-0.8
47338	EATON	035	2972	2950	2921	-0.2	19	1151	1169	1180	0.4	2.52	878	861	-0.5
47339	ECONOMY	177	708	734	741	0.9	61	250	263	271	1.2	2.79	200	205	0.5
47340	FARMLAND	135	3149	3241	3253	0.7	53	1211	1272	1301	1.2	2.54	908	920	0.3
47341	FOUNTAIN CITY	177	2101	2118	2112	0.2	36	787	813	827	0.8	2.61	626	628	0.1
47342	GASTON	035	2810	2856	2856	0.4	44	1035	1072	1091	0.9	2.60	802	805	0.1
47345	GREENS FORK	177	1398	1405	1397	0.1	32	506	518	524	0.6	2.71	400	397	-0.2
47346	HAGERSTOWN	177	3950	3939	3909	-0.1	23	1611	1634	1649	0.4	2.41	1161	1133	-0.6
47348	HARTFORD CITY	009	10866	10871	10869	0.0	28	4382	4481	4549	0.6	2.39	3101	3058	-0.3
47352	LEWISVILLE	065	821	810	802	-0.3	12	317	320	324	0.2	2.53	251	246	-0.5
47353	LIBERTY	161	5849	6103	6444	1.0	65	2241	2380	2554	1.4	2.53	1656	1701	0.5
47354	LOSANTVILLE	135	1147	1180	1188	0.7	53	457	481	494	1.2	2.45	355	362	0.5
47355	LYNN	135	3037	2973	2910	-0.5	7	1206	1207	1206	0.0	2.46	887	854	-0.9
47356	MIDDLETOWN	065	6034	6120	6140	0.3	42	2339	2412	2460	0.7	2.50	1738	1731	-0.1
47357	MILTON	177	1234	1215	1197	-0.4	11	467	471	473	0.2	2.58	367	359	-0.5
47358	MODOC	135	1059	1034	1012	-0.6	6	396	396	396	0.0	2.61	302	292	-0.8
47359	MONTPELIER	009	3360	3348	3354	-0.1	23	1338	1359	1383	0.4	2.46	955	935	-0.5
47360	MOORELAND	065	1466	1495	1505	0.5	47	542	565	580	1.0	2.65	429	434	0.3
47362	NEW CASTLE	065	29534	29286	29107	-0.2	18	12115	12250	12403	0.3	2.34	8391	8161	-0.7
47368	PARKER CITY	135	2826	2792	2749	-0.3	14	1100	1111	1116	0.2	2.45	805	781	-0.7
47369	PENNVILLE	075	1269	1310	1332	0.8	56	496	519	534	1.1	2.52	354	356	0.1
47371	PORTLAND	075	12358	12518	12653	0.3	40	4859	5000	5127	0.7	2.47	3435	3409	-0.2
47373	REDKEY	075	2318	2288	2279	-0.3	13	936	945	958	0.2	2.42	669	651	-0.6
47374	RICHMOND	177	50124	49646	49163	-0.2	16	20452	20670	20848	0.3	2.30	13205	12762	-0.8
47380	RIDGEVILLE	135	2140	2070	2019	-0.8	3	818	808	803	-0.3	2.56	614	586	-1.1
47381	SALAMONIA	075	506	484	479	-1.0	2	177	171	171	-0.8	2.83	143	136	-1.2
	INDIANA					0.8					1.2	2.48			0.3
	UNITED STATES					1.2					1.3	2.58			1.1

ZIP CODE #	POST OFFICE NAME	RACE (%) White 2000	White 2004	Black 2000	Black 2004	Asian/Pacific 2000	Asian/Pacific 2004	% Hispanic Origin 2000	% Hispanic Origin 2004	2004 AGE DISTRIBUTION (%) 0-4	5-9	10-14	15-19	20-24	25-44	45-64	65-84	85+	18+	MEDIAN AGE 2004	% 2004 Males	% 2004 Females
47124	GREENVILLE	98.0	97.7	0.5	0.5	0.4	0.4	0.7	0.9	6.4	7.0	8.5	7.5	5.9	29.5	27.3	7.3	0.8	73.5	36.8	49.9	50.1
47125	HARDINSBURG	98.9	98.7	0.2	0.2	0.2	0.2	0.8	1.0	5.7	6.1	8.4	7.8	6.8	28.1	27.0	9.7	0.6	75.1	36.9	50.7	49.3
47126	HENRYVILLE	98.2	98.0	0.8	0.9	0.1	0.2	0.5	0.7	6.3	6.6	6.9	6.1	5.8	31.7	27.0	8.7	0.8	76.4	37.4	51.7	48.3
47129	CLARKSVILLE	90.1	88.9	6.0	6.6	0.9	1.1	2.9	3.5	6.4	6.0	6.3	6.0	7.3	28.7	23.4	13.4	2.6	77.9	37.4	47.9	52.2
47130	JEFFERSONVILLE	84.0	82.7	12.5	13.3	0.8	1.1	1.6	1.9	6.7	6.5	6.4	6.0	6.6	29.6	26.0	10.9	1.3	76.9	37.2	48.4	51.6
47135	LACONIA	99.1	98.8	0.1	0.1	0.5	0.6	0.8	1.0	6.2	6.8	7.8	6.9	6.2	27.3	26.6	10.7	1.5	75.0	38.4	51.1	48.9
47136	LANESVILLE	98.3	98.0	0.5	0.5	0.4	0.5	0.5	0.6	6.4	6.9	7.5	6.2	5.6	27.8	28.6	10.1	1.0	75.5	39.1	50.1	49.9
47137	LEAVENWORTH	98.0	97.7	0.2	0.3	0.3	0.3	1.3	1.6	6.5	6.7	6.8	6.0	5.7	26.0	27.0	13.7	1.6	76.3	39.8	51.4	48.6
47138	LEXINGTON	98.3	98.0	0.2	0.2	0.1	0.2	0.8	0.9	6.1	6.6	7.5	6.8	5.8	29.4	27.0	10.0	0.8	75.6	37.9	51.1	49.0
47140	MARENGO	98.7	98.5	0.2	0.2	0.3	0.3	0.8	0.9	6.5	6.7	7.8	6.8	6.8	29.0	24.8	10.5	1.1	74.8	35.7	51.0	49.0
47141	MARYSVILLE	98.6	98.5	0.2	0.2	0.1	0.2	0.6	0.7	7.1	7.1	6.8	6.0	6.1	29.4	26.4	9.9	1.2	75.4	37.5	49.9	50.1
47142	MAUCKPORT	98.4	98.1	0.1	0.1	0.2	0.4	0.9	1.1	7.6	7.2	6.5	6.3	6.6	30.1	26.6	8.4	0.7	74.9	36.4	51.0	49.0
47143	MEMPHIS	98.4	98.2	0.2	0.2	0.2	0.3	0.3	0.3	4.7	6.3	8.2	6.6	5.1	28.3	30.1	9.9	0.9	76.7	40.7	50.1	49.9
47145	MILLTOWN	98.2	98.0	0.1	0.1	0.2	0.3	0.8	0.9	6.3	6.4	7.2	7.5	6.2	27.9	26.9	10.5	1.2	75.0	37.7	50.1	49.9
47147	NABB	98.9	98.7	0.2	0.3	0.1	0.1	0.4	0.7	6.2	6.5	6.7	5.9	6.4	28.7	27.9	10.4	1.5	77.5	38.8	49.2	50.8
47150	NEW ALBANY	90.7	89.8	6.4	6.9	0.6	0.7	1.3	1.6	6.8	6.3	6.6	6.3	6.8	28.5	24.2	12.3	2.1	76.4	37.3	47.4	52.6
47160	NEW MIDDLETOWN	97.8	97.0	0.8	0.8	0.0	0.0	1.5	1.5	6.7	7.5	7.5	6.7	6.0	27.6	25.4	11.2	1.5	73.9	37.5	49.3	50.8
47161	NEW SALISBURY	98.5	98.3	0.4	0.4	0.2	0.2	2.2	2.5	6.9	6.8	7.1	6.8	6.8	30.8	25.4	8.7	0.8	75.1	36.3	50.8	49.2
47162	NEW WASHINGTON	97.6	97.4	0.8	0.9	0.0	0.1	0.7	1.0	6.8	6.8	6.6	5.7	6.3	29.1	27.4	9.7	1.5	76.5	37.7	49.7	50.3
47163	OTISCO	98.1	97.8	0.3	0.3	0.3	0.3	0.9	1.1	6.9	6.9	6.5	6.0	5.8	29.1	27.8	10.2	0.9	75.9	38.3	50.9	49.1
47164	PALMYRA	98.7	98.5	0.2	0.1	0.2	0.3	0.9	1.1	6.8	6.7	7.3	7.2	7.2	30.2	25.2	8.6	0.9	74.8	35.9	49.9	50.1
47165	PEKIN	98.6	98.4	0.1	0.1	0.2	0.3	1.2	1.5	6.7	7.0	8.0	7.2	6.6	30.9	24.6	8.3	0.7	73.9	35.4	50.5	49.5
47166	RAMSEY	98.7	98.6	0.2	0.3	0.2	0.2	1.7	2.0	6.6	6.6	7.0	6.7	6.9	29.8	26.5	8.9	1.0	75.6	36.9	50.2	49.8
47167	SALEM	98.9	98.8	0.1	0.1	0.2	0.2	0.6	0.7	6.7	6.7	6.9	6.3	6.2	27.9	25.1	12.2	2.0	75.8	37.8	49.4	50.6
47170	SCOTTSBURG	98.6	98.4	0.1	0.1	0.2	0.3	0.8	0.9	7.3	7.1	7.0	6.5	6.5	29.6	24.1	10.5	1.4	74.7	35.9	49.6	50.4
47172	SELLERSBURG	97.7	97.2	0.7	0.8	0.6	0.8	1.0	1.2	7.2	7.0	6.7	6.0	6.0	30.0	25.0	10.8	1.4	75.5	37.5	48.2	51.8
47174	SULPHUR	96.9	98.6	0.0	0.0	0.0	0.0	3.1	1.5	5.8	7.3	5.8	5.8	5.8	29.0	29.0	11.6	0.0	81.2	39.4	47.8	52.2
47175	TASWELL	98.8	98.5	0.1	0.1	0.4	0.7	0.4	0.7	6.2	6.5	7.0	6.7	5.6	26.1	28.5	12.3	1.2	76.3	40.3	53.0	47.0
47177	UNDERWOOD	98.5	98.4	0.4	0.3	0.1	0.2	0.6	0.7	6.4	6.7	7.0	6.1	5.8	29.7	28.5	9.2	0.7	76.0	38.4	51.7	48.3
47201	COLUMBUS	93.4	92.5	2.1	2.2	2.1	2.7	2.7	3.1	7.3	7.2	7.3	6.2	5.8	29.2	24.9	10.8	1.4	74.3	36.5	49.7	50.3
47203	COLUMBUS	93.9	92.9	1.9	2.1	2.3	2.9	1.9	2.2	7.2	7.5	7.5	6.3	5.4	26.4	25.8	12.0	1.9	73.8	38.2	48.3	51.7
47220	BROWNSTOWN	98.9	98.7	0.1	0.1	0.3	0.3	0.5	0.6	6.7	7.1	7.1	6.8	5.6	27.5	23.8	13.1	2.2	74.7	37.9	48.4	51.6
47223	BUTLERVILLE	97.3	96.9	0.9	0.9	0.3	0.5	0.7	0.9	6.6	7.2	7.6	5.5	5.3	31.3	27.4	8.0	1.0	74.9	37.1	51.7	48.3
47224	CANAAN	98.2	98.1	0.4	0.3	0.4	0.3	1.1	1.6	7.9	7.9	8.7	7.4	6.6	27.1	23.9	10.1	0.6	71.2	34.4	50.8	49.2
47227	COMMISKEY	98.9	98.8	0.3	0.3	0.2	0.2	0.3	0.5	6.6	6.8	7.6	6.9	6.2	28.6	26.1	10.3	0.9	74.7	36.7	50.6	49.4
47229	CROTHERSVILLE	98.7	98.5	0.1	0.1	0.4	0.4	1.1	1.3	6.8	6.8	7.0	6.3	5.9	28.4	25.8	11.9	1.1	75.5	37.8	50.3	49.7
47230	DEPUTY	98.2	98.1	0.1	0.2	0.1	0.2	1.0	1.1	6.4	6.7	7.6	6.8	5.7	29.0	26.7	10.4	0.9	75.2	37.8	50.5	49.5
47231	DUPONT	97.3	97.0	0.8	0.9	0.5	0.7	0.8	0.8	7.7	7.5	8.4	7.4	6.5	29.0	24.5	8.2	0.9	71.8	34.3	51.6	48.4
47232	ELIZABETHTOWN	97.7	97.4	0.7	0.8	0.1	0.1	2.5	3.0	6.5	6.9	7.0	6.1	5.4	28.5	28.7	10.0	0.9	75.9	38.4	50.6	49.5
47234	FLAT ROCK	99.4	99.3	0.1	0.1	0.1	0.1	0.4	0.4	5.9	6.2	6.7	6.5	6.0	28.6	27.6	10.8	1.8	77.3	39.9	51.0	49.0
47235	FREETOWN	98.4	98.1	0.1	0.1	0.1	0.1	0.9	1.1	5.6	5.9	5.7	6.1	6.4	27.3	28.6	12.6	1.8	79.2	40.8	50.8	49.2
47236	GRAMMER	96.8	96.0	2.4	2.4	0.0	0.0	0.0	0.0	5.6	6.4	7.1	4.8	4.8	28.6	27.8	13.5	1.6	76.2	40.5	51.6	48.4
47240	GREENSBURG	98.3	98.0	0.1	0.1	0.9	1.1	0.6	0.7	7.3	7.1	7.0	6.2	6.3	28.4	23.9	11.9	1.9	74.9	36.7	49.7	50.3
47243	HANOVER	96.3	95.8	1.4	1.6	0.9	1.1	1.2	1.3	6.2	6.0	6.9	10.3	14.0	25.7	20.5	9.3	1.2	77.7	29.7	48.2	51.8
47244	HARTSVILLE	98.5	98.5	0.4	0.4	0.5	0.5	0.5	0.4	6.8	7.3	7.9	7.0	5.1	27.6	26.9	10.4	1.0	73.8	37.8	51.3	48.7
47246	HOPE	98.6	98.4	0.4	0.5	0.1	0.2	1.1	1.3	7.4	7.6	8.3	7.5	5.7	27.9	24.2	9.6	1.7	72.1	35.7	50.2	49.8
47250	MADISON	95.8	95.3	1.7	1.8	0.6	0.8	1.1	1.3	6.3	6.2	6.5	6.2	6.1	27.4	26.3	13.0	1.9	77.1	39.6	49.6	50.4
47260	MEDORA	99.0	99.1	0.0	0.0	0.3	0.3	1.0	1.2	7.1	7.2	7.1	6.6	5.8	28.1	25.4	11.5	1.4	74.6	37.0	50.8	49.2
47264	NORMAN	98.7	98.6	0.0	0.0	0.2	0.3	0.7	0.9	6.8	7.0	7.3	6.7	5.8	28.1	26.5	10.8	1.1	74.9	38.2	51.7	48.3
47265	NORTH VERNON	97.1	96.9	0.9	1.0	0.3	0.4	0.8	0.9	8.0	7.8	8.0	6.5	6.2	29.1	23.2	10.0	1.2	72.2	34.8	49.5	50.5
47270	PARIS CROSSING	99.4	99.5	0.0	0.0	0.0	0.0	0.1	0.1	5.7	6.4	7.7	6.7	5.6	28.1	29.1	9.7	1.0	76.0	38.9	52.1	47.9
47272	SAINT PAUL	98.8	98.7	0.1	0.1	0.2	0.2	0.8	0.8	8.5	8.2	8.3	7.8	6.3	28.3	22.9	9.2	0.4	70.4	34.0	49.2	50.8
47273	SCIPIO	98.1	97.9	0.2	0.2	0.1	0.1	0.7	0.8	7.1	7.1	7.9	6.7	6.1	28.9	26.6	9.0	0.7	73.8	36.6	49.7	50.3
47274	SEYMOUR	94.9	94.0	0.8	0.8	1.1	1.4	3.6	4.2	7.4	7.1	6.9	5.9	6.4	30.1	23.5	10.8	1.8	75.0	35.9	49.6	50.5
47281	VALLONIA	99.3	99.3	0.1	0.1	0.1	0.1	0.3	0.4	5.9	6.3	8.0	6.7	5.9	28.5	24.9	12.1	1.7	75.6	38.5	52.1	47.9
47282	VERNON	98.1	98.0	1.3	1.4	0.0	0.0	0.0	0.3	6.6	7.4	7.7	6.0	5.4	29.3	25.4	10.3	2.0	74.4	36.6	52.1	47.9
47283	WESTPORT	99.2	99.1	0.1	0.1	0.1	0.1	0.2	0.2	8.0	8.0	7.2	6.1	5.5	29.4	23.9	10.7	1.3	73.0	35.8	50.4	49.6
47302	MUNCIE	88.0	87.7	9.8	10.0	0.2	0.3	1.1	1.2	7.1	7.0	7.0	7.0	5.4	27.6	24.4	13.0	1.5	74.5	37.4	47.9	52.1
47303	MUNCIE	88.0	87.0	9.5	10.1	0.6	0.8	1.3	1.6	4.7	4.3	4.4	18.3	18.3	21.2	17.1	9.9	1.8	83.8	25.0	47.2	52.8
47304	MUNCIE	92.8	91.4	3.9	4.7	1.6	2.0	1.2	1.5	5.7	5.7	6.0	6.2	9.0	25.3	24.9	14.6	2.6	79.2	38.7	47.7	52.3
47305	MUNCIE	79.3	76.3	16.0	18.6	0.7	0.8	1.6	1.8	6.5	5.6	6.1	7.5	9.8	35.2	20.8	7.1	1.3	77.3	31.6	51.8	48.2
47306	MUNCIE	62.5	57.5	5.9	6.4	26.2	30.5	2.0	2.3	3.8	1.1	1.5	4.1	36.1	44.7	6.4	2.3	0.0	92.9	25.6	50.0	50.0
47320	ALBANY	98.2	98.0	0.5	0.6	0.1	0.1	0.4	0.4	5.3	5.5	6.8	6.7	6.1	26.1	27.5	13.9	2.2	78.3	40.8	48.5	51.5
47325	BROWNSVILLE	98.9	98.8	0.3	0.3	0.3	0.4	0.4	0.6	6.4	6.5	7.3	6.4	5.8	28.7	26.7	11.1	1.1	75.9	38.7	51.3	48.8
47326	BRYANT	97.3	97.2	0.2	0.2	0.5	0.5	1.3	1.3	11.7	10.7	9.2	6.9	5.5	25.6	20.3	9.3	0.9	63.8	30.5	51.3	48.7
47327	CAMBRIDGE CITY	99.3	99.2	0.2	0.2	0.2	0.2	0.7	0.8	6.7	6.8	6.8	6.6	6.1	26.2	25.1	14.0	1.8	75.8	38.8	48.4	51.6
47330	CENTERVILLE	98.7	98.5	0.3	0.3	0.2	0.3	0.8	0.9	5.8	6.5	7.9	7.7	5.8	26.4	25.8	12.2	1.9	75.0	38.6	48.7	51.3
47331	CONNERSVILLE	97.1	96.8	1.7	1.8	0.3	0.4	0.5	0.6	6.5	6.5	6.9	5.9	6.3	26.5	25.6	13.7	2.0	76.5	38.9	48.7	51.3
47334	DALEVILLE	98.4	98.1	0.3	0.4	0.4	0.5	0.7	0.9	6.3	6.6	7.2	6.5	5.5	25.9	28.8	12.0	1.3	75.9	40.1	48.6	51.4
47336	DUNKIRK	98.1	98.0	0.3	0.3	0.4	0.4	0.6	0.7	6.4	6.2	7.0	6.3	5.8	25.1	26.4	14.9	2.0	76.8	40.4	49.0	51.0
47338	EATON	98.8	98.7	0.1	0.2	0.1	0.1	0.6	0.7	6.2	6.6	8.1	7.0	5.5	27.3	25.5	12.4	1.4	74.7	38.4	50.4	49.6
47339	ECONOMY	98.3	98.2	0.0	0.0	0.4	0.5	0.6	0.5	5.5	5.9	7.1	7.5	5.7	27.5	27.0	12.7	1.2	77.1	40.0	51.0	49.1
47340	FARMLAND	98.7	98.6	0.1	0.1	0.1	0.1	0.3	0.3	6.8	7.4	7.5	7.2	5.7	27.1	25.1	11.7	1.6	73.9	37.3	49.7	50.3
47341	FOUNTAIN CITY	98.1	97.9	0.6	0.7	0.1	0.1	0.2	0.2	5.1	5.5	7.4	7.9	6.2	25.5	28.1	12.7	1.5	77.1	40.5	50.7	49.3
47342	GASTON	98.7	98.6	0.2	0.3	0.0	0.0	0.5	0.6	6.0	6.4	7.0	6.7	6.1	26.7	28.5	11.2	1.4	76.0	39.5	50.1	49.9
47345	GREENS FORK	98.0	97.7	0.4	0.6	0.1	0.1	0.4	0.4	6.5	6.8	7.3	7.1	5.5	26.6	27.2	11.9	1.2	75.2	39.5	50.0	50.0
47346	HAGERSTOWN	99.0	98.9	0.1	0.1	0.1	0.2	0.3	0.3	5.7	5.9	7.0	6.8	5.6	27.2	26.1	13.9	1.8	77.2	40.1	48.9	51.1
47348	HARTFORD CITY	98.5	98.5	0.1	0.1	0.2	0.2	0.5	0.5	6.2	6.3	6.9	6.3	5.7	26.0	26.5	14.0	2.1	76.6	39.8	49.3	50.7
47352	LEWISVILLE	98.5	98.3	0.1	0.1	0.0	0.0	0.9	1.0	5.6	6.3	6.8	6.5	5.9	25.3	28.6	13.3	1.6	77.4	41.3	51.0	49.0
47353	LIBERTY	98.7	98.6	0.3	0.3	0.2	0.3	0.3	0.4	7.1	7.0	7.2	6.4	6.1	27.1	25.0	12.4	1.8	74.7	38.1	49.6	50.4
47354	LOSANTVILLE	98.5	98.3	0.2	0.3	0.1	0.1	1.0	1.4	6.4	6.7	7.2	5.7	5.9	26.1	27.8	12.6	1.7	76.4	39.9	50.3	49.8
47355	LYNN	98.3	98.1	0.2	0.2	0.3	0.4	0.2	0.2	7.0	7.1	7.5	5.9	5.9	27.5	23.9	13.6	1.7	74.8	37.9	49.5	50.6
47356	MIDDLETOWN	98.7	98.5	0.4	0.4	0.3	0.4	0.5	0.5	6.4	6.7	7.3	6.6	5.5	27.3	25.6	12.8	1.7	75.5	38.7	48.5	51.5
47357	MILTON	99.1	99.0	0.2	0.3	0.0	0.1	0.1	0.1	5.5	6.5	8.5	7.0	5.1	27.6	25.8	12.9	1.2	75.1	39.0	51.0	49.1
47358	MODOC	98.6	98.6	0.2	0.3	0.0	0.0	0.4	0.5	6.7	7.0	7.1	5.9	5.9	26.1	27.0	12.6	1.8	75.7	39.4	51.0	49.0
47359	MONTPELIER	98.2	98.2	0.1	0.1	0.0	0.0	0.9	0.9	7.7	7.5	6.9	6.5	5.4	27.4	24.9	12.2	1.6	73.9	37.4	50.0	50.0
47360	MOORELAND	99.1	98.9	0.1	0.1	0.3	0.3	1.0	1.2	7.1	7.4	7.8	6.1	4.7	27.2	27.6	10.6	1.7	73.9	38.2	49.6	50.4
47362	NEW CASTLE	97.4	97.1	1.2	1.3	0.2	0.3	0.9	1.1	6.1	6.1	6.4	6.1	5.9	26.3	25.8	14.9	2.5	77.6	40.4	48.0	52.0
47368	PARKER CITY	99.1	98.9	0.1	0.1	0.1	0.1	0.3	0.4	5.8	6.4	7.4	6.6	5.5	26.4	26.9	12.5	2.5	76.2	40.1	49.0	51.0
47369	PENNVILLE	98.7	98.6	0.3	0.3	0.0	0.0	1.6	1.5	7.0	7.3	9.2	7.0	5.7	26.6	22.1	13.4	1.7	72.1	36.7	50.1	49.9
47371	PORTLAND	97.3	97.2	0.3	0.3	0.3	0.3	2.4	2.4	6.9	7.0	7.2	6.2	5.7	26.4	25.4	12.9	2.2	74.9	38.2	49.0	51.0
47373	REDKEY	98.9	98.9	0.1	0.1	0.0	0.0	0.9	0.8	7.0	7.4	7.8	5.9	5.2	27.1	24.9	13.1	1.4	74.0	37.5	49.5	50.5
47374	RICHMOND	89.2	88.3	7.1	7.6	0.7	0.9	1.7	2.0	6.3	6.2	6.4	6.9	7.2	26.2	24.5	14.1	2.3	77.3	38.4	47.7	52.3
47380	RIDGEVILLE	99.3	99.2	0.0	0.0	0.1	0.1	0.6	0.7	6.7	7.2	7.8	6.3	5.4	27.7	26.3	11.6	1.1	74.5	37.6	50.7	49.3
47381	SALAMONIA	97.0	96.7	0.0	0.0	1.6	1.7	1.2	1.2	7.2	7.4	8.9	7.4	6.0	28.3	25.0	8.7	1.0	71.7	35.4	51.2	48.8
	INDIANA	87.5	86.7	8.4	8.7	1.0	1.3	3.5	4.1	7.0	6.9	7.1	7.1	7.4	28.1	24.0	10.8	1.6	75.0	35.9	49.2	50.8
	UNITED STATES	75.1	73.6	12.3	12.5	3.8	4.2	12.5	14.1	6.9	6.7	7.2	7.0	7.3	28.6	23.8	10.8	1.7	75.1	36.0	49.1	50.9

ZIP CODE #	POST OFFICE NAME	2004 Per Capita Income	2004 HH Income Base	2004 HOUSEHOLD INCOME DISTRIBUTION (%) Less than $25,000	$25,000 to $49,999	$50,000 to $99,999	$100,000 to $149,999	$150,000 or More	MEDIAN HOUSEHOLD INCOME 2004	2009	2004 National Centile	2004 State Centile	2004 Home Value Base	2004 HOME VALUE DISTRIBUTION (%) Less than $50,000	$50,000 to $89,999	$90,000 to $174,999	$175,000 to $399,999	$400,000 or More	2004 Median Home Value
47124	GREENVILLE	27091	1371	12.3	27.9	36.5	16.8	6.6	59783	67887	84	93	1251	5.2	9.8	44.3	37.8	2.9	155051
47125	HARDINSBURG	19959	697	29.8	36.6	25.3	5.2	3.2	35502	39557	29	10	599	28.1	26.4	35.4	8.4	1.8	83026
47126	HENRYVILLE	21135	1387	19.5	29.8	40.7	8.7	1.3	50626	55070	73	75	1141	13.5	21.2	45.1	17.1	3.2	108018
47129	CLARKSVILLE	21671	8995	31.5	33.8	27.0	5.4	2.4	36535	40934	34	13	5315	16.2	24.8	54.4	4.1	0.5	97508
47130	JEFFERSONVILLE	23679	17582	25.1	30.5	33.3	8.6	2.5	44690	50510	60	47	11902	8.3	24.3	55.0	11.4	0.9	105123
47135	LACONIA	20178	475	31.2	25.9	34.3	6.1	2.5	44049	48394	59	44	410	19.0	22.4	43.4	11.2	3.9	103646
47136	LANESVILLE	24494	1502	17.2	22.5	42.4	14.1	3.7	59409	66317	84	92	1368	6.5	16.5	48.1	27.6	1.3	126741
47137	LEAVENWORTH	18788	594	39.2	27.4	25.3	4.6	3.5	33970	37644	24	7	493	27.2	34.7	25.4	10.3	2.4	75288
47138	LEXINGTON	18537	1772	21.1	37.8	35.1	5.4	0.7	42322	47253	54	35	1509	17.9	25.5	42.5	12.2	1.9	99387
47140	MARENGO	15369	1003	36.8	40.0	19.8	2.8	0.6	32368	36695	19	6	798	33.2	33.0	29.5	2.8	1.6	69753
47141	MARYSVILLE	19916	704	21.5	36.4	32.2	6.4	3.6	45365	50598	62	52	620	14.2	23.4	42.1	17.6	2.7	108250
47142	MAUCKPORT	20300	335	18.5	42.4	35.2	2.1	1.8	41582	46614	52	31	281	18.2	32.4	29.5	19.2	0.7	89118
47143	MEMPHIS	28726	1143	18.1	28.2	36.2	11.9	5.6	53998	58771	78	84	1020	9.5	12.9	42.9	30.3	4.3	137838
47145	MILLTOWN	17605	843	32.2	32.7	29.1	5.1	1.0	41087	44778	50	29	729	23.9	30.7	38.8	5.5	1.1	84924
47147	NABB	19562	415	24.6	38.1	27.7	8.2	1.5	41535	46242	51	31	350	19.1	30.3	35.7	12.0	2.9	90833
47150	NEW ALBANY	22953	19760	27.6	31.4	30.0	8.1	3.0	42677	48701	55	37	12865	6.3	23.6	53.7	15.5	0.9	109747
47160	NEW MIDDLETOWN	23654	52	17.3	28.9	44.2	7.7	1.9	52404	55922	76	80	46	10.9	26.1	52.2	10.9	0.0	100000
47161	NEW SALISBURY	21779	1327	19.3	31.1	37.6	8.7	3.2	49619	54220	71	71	1115	16.7	21.2	43.1	16.5	2.5	106618
47162	NEW WASHINGTON	18027	271	24.7	33.6	31.0	8.5	2.2	44509	49837	60	46	226	17.7	28.8	37.2	13.7	2.7	95714
47163	OTISCO	21157	676	20.4	32.7	33.6	10.5	2.8	47660	52719	68	65	613	10.9	21.2	45.2	19.9	2.8	115188
47164	PALMYRA	20051	1309	23.2	34.6	33.2	7.0	2.0	45411	50152	62	53	1095	13.9	22.3	52.2	11.0	0.7	105380
47165	PEKIN	20109	2351	27.0	30.1	34.3	6.2	2.4	42886	47069	56	38	1944	17.4	30.4	41.0	10.0	1.2	92529
47166	RAMSEY	22019	506	23.7	28.9	35.0	9.1	3.4	47764	52310	68	66	431	15.8	20.7	50.1	11.8	1.6	105417
47167	SALEM	18845	5699	31.6	32.4	28.9	4.9	2.1	38650	42489	42	18	4560	17.5	30.8	40.0	10.4	1.3	92073
47170	SCOTTSBURG	19212	5691	30.1	34.7	27.2	6.0	2.0	38977	42711	43	20	4318	19.1	28.0	42.7	9.6	0.6	93342
47172	SELLERSBURG	23906	4702	18.0	33.6	33.8	11.3	3.3	48406	54274	69	68	3818	14.4	15.9	48.3	20.1	1.3	113520
47174	SULPHUR	17948	26	42.3	26.9	23.1	3.9	3.9	32308	40000	19	6	22	22.7	36.4	27.3	13.6	0.0	83333
47175	TASWELL	26680	317	30.3	30.6	31.2	5.4	2.5	42359	44634	54	36	282	26.6	26.2	35.5	7.1	4.6	84286
47177	UNDERWOOD	21635	444	18.2	34.9	35.8	8.6	2.5	47517	53110	67	64	389	17.5	21.9	39.6	18.8	2.3	106750
47201	COLUMBUS	24170	15460	24.6	29.6	32.7	9.4	3.8	46118	52222	64	57	11097	11.7	17.1	46.9	20.8	3.6	114145
47203	COLUMBUS	25822	10092	19.7	27.2	35.9	12.5	4.8	52928	59867	77	82	7852	13.1	6.1	55.2	24.0	1.5	133025
47220	BROWNSTOWN	19999	2085	25.7	35.9	29.7	6.3	2.3	42264	46282	54	35	1662	17.5	23.2	43.3	13.6	2.5	102737
47223	BUTLERVILLE	17957	553	19.7	45.2	27.3	5.4	2.4	42762	46594	55	37	462	22.3	26.8	41.8	7.8	1.3	90816
47224	CANAAN	17008	224	25.5	38.8	29.9	4.9	0.9	41513	45370	51	31	191	11.0	17.8	46.6	22.5	2.1	114643
47227	COMMISKEY	19807	479	20.5	39.0	32.4	6.7	1.5	43135	46971	56	39	401	15.7	28.4	41.7	12.7	1.5	96351
47229	CROTHERSVILLE	20329	1298	23.6	39.3	28.6	7.2	1.4	39030	42984	43	20	1066	18.7	31.6	40.8	8.0	0.9	89722
47230	DEPUTY	18773	876	21.5	40.5	31.3	6.1	0.7	39941	44944	46	23	757	19.2	27.5	43.6	8.5	1.3	93110
47231	DUPONT	16488	411	23.1	41.1	31.1	3.7	1.0	41419	46406	51	30	339	26.0	33.0	35.1	4.7	1.2	76304
47232	ELIZABETHTOWN	23563	960	18.0	35.0	33.5	11.2	2.3	47859	53330	68	66	844	19.9	14.0	48.3	16.1	1.7	110833
47234	FLAT ROCK	21617	530	15.9	40.9	32.8	9.3	1.1	46439	52775	65	59	450	3.3	29.8	48.2	14.7	4.0	109333
47235	FREETOWN	22635	608	21.7	38.3	30.6	6.6	2.8	43764	48706	58	42	512	15.8	21.1	42.4	17.8	2.9	110417
47236	GRAMMER	24120	51	5.9	52.9	27.5	9.8	3.9	47213	54194	67	63	47	4.3	14.9	53.2	25.5	2.1	122115
47240	GREENSBURG	21824	8151	23.6	34.0	32.9	7.1	2.4	43995	48513	59	43	6043	9.0	23.3	49.7	16.1	1.9	109202
47243	HANOVER	18300	2045	23.9	33.7	34.5	6.8	1.2	43680	48592	58	42	1551	12.0	35.1	41.5	9.7	1.7	92697
47244	HARTSVILLE	22702	262	14.1	30.5	39.7	11.5	4.2	54910	61210	80	87	224	4.9	21.9	49.6	20.5	3.1	116489
47246	HOPE	19997	1666	20.7	30.6	37.9	8.9	2.0	48975	55093	70	70	1366	9.7	27.7	49.5	12.7	0.4	103507
47250	MADISON	21004	8747	29.5	31.3	30.3	6.9	2.1	41075	45157	50	29	6432	13.3	25.2	44.6	15.0	2.0	104315
47260	MEDORA	16494	712	32.7	38.1	24.3	3.9	1.0	35241	39444	28	10	599	33.4	29.2	28.7	7.9	0.8	72283
47264	NORMAN	20571	624	22.8	40.1	29.3	6.6	1.3	42059	46541	53	34	523	21.4	20.1	39.6	15.9	3.1	100801
47265	NORTH VERNON	19155	7952	24.8	37.5	29.8	6.2	1.8	41982	45514	53	33	6151	22.3	29.6	38.4	8.5	1.2	88045
47270	PARIS CROSSING	19355	344	18.0	41.6	32.6	5.8	2.0	39808	42077	45	22	295	13.9	23.4	45.1	16.3	1.4	107598
47272	SAINT PAUL	18600	713	21.2	38.3	34.5	4.5	1.5	44952	49578	61	49	579	20.9	28.0	39.6	10.5	1.0	91048
47273	SCIPIO	18873	768	23.2	34.5	31.0	10.2	1.2	43894	46806	58	43	652	23.0	19.2	45.3	11.0	1.5	102941
47274	SEYMOUR	21570	11538	25.1	32.7	33.1	6.4	2.8	44268	48395	59	45	8547	15.8	23.3	47.4	12.4	1.2	101901
47281	VALLONIA	19094	589	23.3	35.5	34.8	5.1	1.4	44139	48044	59	45	508	12.6	23.8	48.4	11.6	3.5	107009
47282	VERNON	20605	128	24.2	39.1	24.2	10.2	2.3	40396	43391	47	26	106	15.1	24.5	49.1	11.3	0.0	101000
47283	WESTPORT	18992	1344	22.9	36.7	33.9	4.8	1.7	42482	46516	55	36	1107	11.9	28.3	43.3	14.5	2.1	98611
47302	MUNCIE	19003	12616	39.2	31.9	22.6	4.5	1.8	31954	36125	18	5	8637	31.6	43.4	20.3	4.3	0.4	65168
47303	MUNCIE	17729	11226	39.6	30.4	23.4	5.0	1.6	31770	36030	17	5	6165	24.2	37.8	33.5	4.2	0.3	76417
47304	MUNCIE	30245	12546	23.7	25.8	32.8	12.1	5.6	50477	57624	73	74	8749	3.9	23.6	54.8	16.1	1.5	113488
47305	MUNCIE	14588	2193	58.0	28.3	11.6	1.4	0.7	20685	23771	2	1	676	58.3	28.7	10.2	1.5	1.3	45333
47306	MUNCIE	8345	156	96.8	0.0	0.0	3.2	0.0	8298	9128	0	1	6	0.0	0.0	100.0	0.0	0.0	162500
47320	ALBANY	20726	1732	22.8	38.2	30.4	6.5	2.1	41031	47378	50	29	1393	14.3	37.7	37.8	9.3	1.0	88259
47325	BROWNSVILLE	31140	263	20.2	26.2	41.1	10.3	2.3	52730	59435	77	82	224	14.3	26.3	42.9	16.5	0.0	103659
47326	BRYANT	14684	612	23.2	40.7	31.5	3.6	1.0	41992	45414	53	33	525	23.2	28.2	39.4	6.5	2.7	88295
47327	CAMBRIDGE CITY	19377	2164	26.9	35.4	30.3	6.2	1.3	38824	43467	42	19	1654	13.2	33.1	42.7	10.0	1.0	93935
47330	CENTERVILLE	19911	2068	23.4	35.2	32.2	7.4	1.8	41949	47325	53	33	1639	10.3	24.1	49.1	14.9	1.7	106428
47331	CONNERSVILLE	21157	10115	28.1	31.7	30.3	7.6	2.3	41745	46764	52	32	7347	12.9	33.5	42.5	9.9	1.1	93323
47334	DALEVILLE	25128	1190	18.0	30.4	37.2	10.3	4.1	51387	59014	75	78	1001	4.9	25.7	54.9	14.0	0.6	108423
47336	DUNKIRK	18064	1643	27.0	40.0	28.3	4.4	0.4	39364	42528	44	21	1256	31.9	39.6	22.9	4.4	1.3	68241
47338	EATON	21189	1169	24.7	32.9	33.1	7.6	1.6	41882	47741	53	32	995	22.9	34.8	32.9	8.6	0.8	79737
47339	ECONOMY	17933	263	27.8	35.4	25.5	10.3	1.1	40754	45487	49	28	228	14.0	19.7	45.2	19.3	1.8	112838
47340	FARMLAND	21917	1272	23.0	33.5	35.7	5.9	2.0	44055	48372	59	44	1042	17.5	36.0	36.2	8.7	1.6	85263
47341	FOUNTAIN CITY	20489	813	24.0	30.5	35.4	7.8	2.3	45398	50262	62	52	672	9.8	23.5	51.8	14.6	0.3	105629
47342	GASTON	22116	1072	16.7	36.2	33.3	12.2	1.6	46303	53687	65	58	892	11.2	37.0	38.1	10.9	2.8	92254
47345	GREENS FORK	19565	518	21.0	33.8	37.1	6.8	1.4	47530	53175	67	64	441	20.2	19.5	44.9	12.0	3.4	101051
47346	HAGERSTOWN	21611	1634	24.5	32.9	33.5	7.7	1.4	44013	49653	59	44	1341	12.5	23.7	49.8	13.3	0.7	105345
47348	HARTFORD CITY	18398	4481	29.2	37.7	28.5	3.6	1.0	37713	41172	38	16	3461	25.1	39.4	29.7	4.8	1.0	73406
47352	LEWISVILLE	24840	320	20.6	28.4	33.4	11.6	5.9	51075	58021	74	77	267	10.5	28.1	45.7	12.7	3.0	99839
47353	LIBERTY	21351	2380	26.0	36.5	28.8	6.6	2.1	40025	43437	46	24	1876	11.9	29.2	40.2	16.0	2.7	101930
47354	LOSANTVILLE	19800	481	25.6	38.9	28.5	5.8	1.3	39924	44519	46	23	413	26.6	29.3	32.7	11.4	0.0	81552
47355	LYNN	18353	1207	30.1	34.1	30.7	4.4	0.8	37668	41520	38	16	978	20.4	35.7	39.2	3.9	0.9	83723
47356	MIDDLETOWN	22099	2412	22.5	31.8	32.6	11.2	2.0	46200	52603	64	58	2010	12.6	20.6	48.5	16.7	1.6	112109
47357	MILTON	20221	471	20.8	37.4	31.6	8.3	1.9	42259	46777	54	35	385	18.4	25.2	35.8	19.0	1.6	97903
47358	MODOC	17676	396	29.8	33.8	31.1	4.3	1.0	39292	43068	44	21	331	24.8	28.1	36.6	10.0	0.6	85250
47359	MONTPELIER	17974	1359	31.4	32.6	31.2	4.3	0.5	38339	41792	41	18	1063	31.0	34.4	30.5	4.1	0.1	72207
47360	MOORELAND	20243	565	19.8	38.1	31.9	8.7	1.6	44937	50829	61	49	487	18.5	25.5	40.7	15.0	0.4	97375
47362	NEW CASTLE	21467	12250	30.1	32.2	27.3	8.2	2.1	39692	44481	45	22	8958	15.0	30.7	44.9	8.0	1.4	95092
47368	PARKER CITY	19959	1111	26.1	39.6	26.6	5.9	1.8	39566	43476	45	22	898	19.4	35.1	37.9	6.9	0.8	84366
47369	PENNVILLE	17042	519	27.2	42.0	26.6	2.7	1.5	35729	40089	30	11	403	37.0	29.3	25.6	5.5	2.7	67167
47371	PORTLAND	19800	5000	27.4	36.9	29.4	4.4	1.9	39125	42256	43	21	3909	19.5	34.6	36.3	8.5	1.2	85800
47373	REDKEY	17160	945	31.8	38.8	25.5	3.4	0.5	36858	39502	35	14	706	30.6	40.8	24.9	3.1	0.6	68382
47374	RICHMOND	20242	20670	34.1	31.1	26.9	5.6	2.2	36258	40405	33	12	13481	17.4	30.5	42.4	8.7	0.9	92193
47380	RIDGEVILLE	17803	808	28.2	37.9	29.5	3.3	1.1	38405	42157	41	18	666	29.1	34.4	27.3	7.4	1.8	67573
47381	SALAMONIA	15955	171	26.3	42.1	26.9	4.1	0.6	39858	44206	45	23	146	31.5	31.5	15.8	15.8	5.5	74500
	INDIANA	23565		24.7	29.6	32.4	9.4	3.9	45964	52146				12.3	23.5	44.9	16.9	2.4	109048
	UNITED STATES	25866		24.7	27.1	30.8	10.9	6.5	48124	56710				10.9	15.0	33.7	30.1	10.4	145905

#	POST OFFICE NAME	FINANCIAL SERVICES: Auto Loan	FINANCIAL SERVICES: Home Loan	FINANCIAL SERVICES: Invest-ments	FINANCIAL SERVICES: Retire-ment Plans	THE HOME: Home Improvements: Home Repair	THE HOME: Home Improvements: Lawn & Garden	THE HOME: Furnishings: Comput-ers & Hard-ware	THE HOME: Furnishings: Major Appli-ances	THE HOME: Furnishings: TV, Radio, Sound Equip-ment	THE HOME: Furnishings: Furni-ture	ENTERTAINMENT: Dine out/ Carry out	ENTERTAINMENT: Sports Equip-ment	ENTERTAINMENT: Fees & Tickets	ENTERTAINMENT: Toys & Games	ENTERTAINMENT: Travel	ENTERTAINMENT: Cable TV	PERSONAL: Apparel & Services	PERSONAL: Auto Repairs	PERSONAL: Health Insur-ance	PERSONAL: Pets & Supplies
47124	GREENVILLE	109	119	113	119	118	119	108	111	104	109	129	130	111	134	109	101	127	107	104	128
47125	HARDINSBURG	91	68	41	63	74	84	67	78	76	67	91	92	61	88	68	80	84	77	91	103
47126	HENRYVILLE	90	80	61	76	84	90	74	82	78	74	95	97	72	97	76	80	91	80	89	106
47129	CLARKSVILLE	66	68	75	68	68	74	70	69	70	69	87	80	71	88	70	69	84	69	69	76
47130	JEFFERSONVILLE	75	77	83	78	77	81	78	77	77	77	96	91	79	98	78	76	94	78	75	86
47135	LACONIA	82	73	56	69	77	83	68	75	72	68	87	89	66	89	70	73	83	73	81	96
47136	LANESVILLE	92	100	97	97	100	104	91	94	90	91	112	111	95	117	94	90	110	92	93	110
47137	LEAVENWORTH	81	65	44	59	71	79	61	72	68	61	81	85	56	80	64	72	76	70	83	97
47138	LEXINGTON	82	67	45	62	72	79	62	72	69	63	83	86	59	83	64	72	78	70	81	96
47140	MARENGO	72	48	22	42	55	63	47	58	56	47	66	70	40	62	47	60	60	58	72	83
47141	MARYSVILLE	85	77	60	73	81	86	71	79	75	71	92	93	70	93	73	77	87	77	84	100
47142	MAUCKPORT	79	72	56	69	72	76	69	74	70	71	86	85	65	81	68	69	82	73	73	88
47143	MEMPHIS	113	113	99	109	116	121	103	110	104	103	128	130	104	133	106	105	124	106	112	134
47145	MILLTOWN	84	58	28	50	65	74	55	69	66	56	78	82	48	74	56	71	71	68	84	97
47147	NABB	75	70	62	69	73	78	67	72	69	67	85	85	66	85	68	70	81	71	75	88
47150	NEW ALBANY	73	77	81	76	76	82	77	76	77	76	95	88	78	98	77	77	93	76	76	85
47160	NEW MIDDLETOWN	98	87	66	83	92	99	80	89	85	80	104	106	79	106	83	87	99	87	96	115
47161	NEW SALISBURY	94	84	64	80	88	94	78	86	82	79	100	102	76	101	80	84	96	84	92	110
47162	NEW WASHINGTON	78	74	67	73	77	82	71	75	73	71	89	89	70	90	72	73	85	74	78	92
47163	OTISCO	91	80	61	77	85	91	75	83	80	75	97	98	73	99	77	82	92	81	90	106
47164	PALMYRA	85	76	58	73	79	85	71	78	74	72	91	92	69	91	72	75	87	76	82	98
47165	PEKIN	90	75	52	70	79	86	71	80	76	72	92	94	66	90	71	78	87	79	87	103
47166	RAMSEY	92	82	63	78	87	93	77	85	81	77	98	100	75	99	78	82	94	83	90	108
47167	SALEM	78	63	45	59	68	76	62	70	69	62	83	81	58	82	63	72	77	69	79	89
47170	SCOTTSBURG	77	65	47	60	69	76	63	70	68	62	82	81	59	82	64	71	77	69	78	89
47172	SELLERSBURG	87	89	84	88	89	94	85	87	84	85	104	101	86	105	85	83	101	85	86	99
47174	SULPHUR	90	60	27	52	68	78	58	72	70	59	82	87	49	78	59	75	75	72	89	103
47175	TASWELL	123	82	37	71	93	107	79	99	96	81	112	118	67	106	81	103	102	98	122	141
47177	UNDERWOOD	90	80	61	76	85	91	74	82	79	74	96	98	73	98	76	81	91	80	89	106
47201	COLUMBUS	86	83	78	81	84	91	82	84	83	81	103	98	82	104	82	84	99	83	87	98
47203	COLUMBUS	91	96	96	95	97	101	90	93	89	90	111	108	92	113	92	89	108	91	91	107
47220	BROWNSTOWN	79	68	53	67	72	80	68	74	72	67	88	85	66	88	68	74	83	72	80	89
47223	BUTLERVILLE	92	71	46	67	76	87	71	81	79	71	95	94	65	92	71	82	88	79	92	103
47224	CANAAN	82	64	41	59	70	77	60	70	68	61	81	84	56	80	62	71	76	69	81	95
47227	COMMISKEY	82	72	55	69	76	83	68	75	73	68	88	89	67	89	70	74	84	73	81	95
47229	CROTHERSVILLE	91	67	38	60	74	83	63	76	73	64	87	91	57	85	65	78	80	75	90	105
47230	DEPUTY	88	64	36	58	71	80	61	74	71	62	84	88	55	82	63	75	78	73	87	102
47231	DUPONT	75	62	45	60	65	73	62	68	66	62	80	79	58	78	62	68	75	67	74	84
47232	ELIZABETHTOWN	96	86	65	82	91	97	79	88	84	79	103	105	78	105	82	86	97	86	95	114
47234	FLAT ROCK	89	79	60	75	84	90	73	81	78	73	95	97	72	97	75	80	90	79	88	105
47235	FREETOWN	98	74	46	68	81	91	72	84	81	72	97	100	65	95	73	86	90	83	98	113
47236	GRAMMER	96	85	65	81	90	96	79	87	83	79	101	104	77	104	81	86	96	85	94	112
47240	GREENSBURG	85	75	60	73	79	87	74	80	78	73	95	93	72	95	75	80	90	78	86	97
47243	HANOVER	78	69	58	67	73	79	67	73	71	67	87	86	65	87	68	72	82	72	78	90
47244	HARTSVILLE	101	92	73	88	97	103	85	93	89	85	109	111	84	112	88	91	104	91	99	119
47246	HOPE	86	79	65	77	83	89	75	81	78	75	95	95	74	97	76	79	91	79	85	100
47250	MADISON	75	68	58	66	70	78	67	71	71	66	86	82	66	86	68	72	82	71	77	85
47260	MEDORA	78	55	28	48	61	70	53	64	62	53	73	77	46	70	54	66	67	64	78	90
47264	NORMAN	86	70	47	64	75	82	65	75	72	66	87	90	61	86	67	75	81	74	85	100
47265	NORTH VERNON	80	69	53	66	73	79	66	73	70	66	86	85	64	85	67	72	81	72	79	92
47270	PARIS CROSSING	83	74	56	70	78	83	68	75	72	68	88	90	67	90	70	74	83	73	82	97
47272	SAINT PAUL	82	73	56	69	77	83	68	75	72	68	87	89	66	89	70	74	83	73	81	97
47273	SCIPIO	84	75	57	71	78	84	70	77	73	70	90	91	68	90	71	75	85	75	82	97
47274	SEYMOUR	82	74	63	72	77	84	73	78	77	72	93	91	71	94	74	78	89	77	83	95
47281	VALLONIA	84	67	44	62	73	80	63	73	70	63	84	87	59	83	64	73	79	71	83	98
47282	VERNON	89	79	60	75	84	90	73	81	78	73	95	97	72	97	75	80	90	79	88	105
47283	WESTPORT	81	67	48	64	71	79	66	73	71	65	86	85	62	85	66	73	80	72	81	92
47302	MUNCIE	62	59	59	56	60	67	61	62	64	59	78	70	61	80	61	66	75	61	66	71
47303	MUNCIE	63	53	54	53	53	60	63	59	64	59	79	72	59	77	59	63	76	62	61	69
47304	MUNCIE	93	99	110	99	98	104	101	98	99	99	123	116	102	124	100	96	120	99	94	109
47305	MUNCIE	41	35	41	36	35	40	43	40	45	41	55	48	41	54	41	44	54	43	41	45
47306	MUNCIE	19	12	15	13	11	14	23	16	22	19	27	23	18	24	18	19	26	20	15	19
47320	ALBANY	70	72	73	70	73	79	71	71	72	69	89	82	73	93	72	73	86	70	75	81
47325	BROWNSVILLE	137	122	93	115	128	138	112	125	119	112	145	148	110	148	116	122	138	121	135	161
47326	BRYANT	77	67	52	65	71	77	65	71	69	64	84	83	63	84	66	70	79	69	77	88
47327	CAMBRIDGE CITY	68	67	62	64	69	76	65	67	68	63	83	77	66	88	67	70	80	66	72	79
47330	CENTERVILLE	77	71	60	68	74	81	69	73	73	68	89	85	68	91	70	74	84	72	79	89
47331	CONNERSVILLE	77	69	61	66	72	80	69	73	74	68	90	85	68	91	70	76	85	72	80	89
47334	DALEVILLE	93	87	76	86	89	98	87	90	89	85	109	104	85	110	87	90	104	89	94	105
47336	DUNKIRK	70	59	44	54	63	70	56	63	62	56	75	74	54	76	58	66	71	62	72	82
47338	EATON	81	76	65	74	78	84	73	77	75	72	92	90	72	94	74	76	88	76	81	94
47339	ECONOMY	80	71	54	68	75	81	66	73	70	66	85	87	65	87	68	72	81	71	79	94
47340	FARMLAND	85	77	64	74	80	89	75	80	80	74	97	93	74	99	77	82	92	79	87	97
47341	FOUNTAIN CITY	86	76	58	72	80	86	70	78	75	70	91	93	69	93	72	77	86	76	84	101
47342	GASTON	88	81	69	79	84	93	79	84	82	78	101	97	78	102	80	84	96	82	90	101
47345	GREENS FORK	85	76	58	72	80	86	70	78	74	70	90	92	69	92	72	76	86	75	84	100
47346	HAGERSTOWN	80	73	59	70	77	83	70	75	74	69	90	88	69	92	71	76	85	73	81	94
47348	HARTFORD CITY	67	62	52	58	64	71	59	63	63	58	76	73	59	79	61	65	73	62	69	78
47352	LEWISVILLE	99	89	70	85	94	101	83	91	88	83	107	108	82	110	86	91	102	89	99	116
47353	LIBERTY	83	75	61	71	79	87	73	78	78	71	94	91	71	96	74	80	89	77	87	97
47354	LOSANTVILLE	78	69	53	66	73	78	64	71	68	64	83	84	63	84	66	70	79	69	77	91
47355	LYNN	76	62	42	57	67	73	58	67	64	58	77	80	55	77	60	67	72	65	76	89
47356	MIDDLETOWN	89	77	58	74	81	89	74	81	79	73	96	95	71	96	75	81	90	80	89	102
47357	MILTON	83	74	57	71	78	84	69	76	73	69	89	90	68	91	71	75	84	74	82	98
47358	MODOC	74	65	50	62	69	74	61	67	65	61	79	80	60	80	63	67	75	66	73	86
47359	MONTPELIER	71	60	45	55	64	71	58	64	64	57	77	75	55	78	59	67	72	63	73	83
47360	MOORELAND	86	76	58	73	81	87	71	78	75	71	91	93	69	93	73	77	87	76	85	101
47362	NEW CASTLE	72	71	67	68	73	79	70	72	72	68	89	82	70	92	71	74	85	71	76	83
47368	PARKER CITY	72	68	60	66	71	78	67	70	71	66	87	81	67	90	68	73	82	69	76	83
47369	PENNVILLE	77	57	32	51	63	70	54	65	62	54	74	77	48	72	55	66	68	64	76	89
47371	PORTLAND	72	67	59	64	70	77	67	70	70	65	86	81	66	88	68	72	82	69	76	84
47373	REDKEY	74	55	31	49	60	68	52	62	60	53	71	75	47	69	53	64	66	61	74	86
47374	RICHMOND	68	63	59	60	65	72	64	66	68	63	83	77	63	84	65	69	79	66	72	78
47380	RIDGEVILLE	72	63	48	61	66	73	61	67	65	61	79	78	59	79	62	66	75	65	72	82
47381	SALAMONIA	72	64	49	61	68	73	60	66	63	60	77	79	58	79	61	65	73	64	71	85
	INDIANA	86	83	80	82	84	90	82	84	84	82	103	98	82	104	82	84	100	84	86	98
	UNITED STATES	100	100	100	100	100	100	100	100	100	100	100	100	100	100	100	100	100	100	100	100

INDIANA

POPULATION CHANGE

A 47382-47610

#	POST OFFICE NAME	COUNTY FIPS CODE	POPULATION 2000	2004	2009	% Rate	State Centile	HOUSEHOLDS 2000	2004	2009	% Annual Rate 2000-2004	2004 Average HH Size	FAMILIES 2000	2004	% Annual Rate 2000-2004
47382	SARATOGA	135	15	15	15	0.0	27	8	8	8	0.0	1.88	6	6	0.0
47383	SELMA	035	2718	2683	2648	-0.3	13	1038	1045	1051	0.2	2.55	803	783	-0.6
47384	SHIRLEY	065	1835	1876	1923	0.5	50	680	709	740	1.0	2.64	522	527	0.2
47385	SPICELAND	065	1794	1767	1747	-0.4	11	719	726	734	0.2	2.43	539	526	-0.6
47386	SPRINGPORT	065	1317	1311	1303	-0.1	21	501	511	519	0.5	2.57	416	414	-0.1
47387	STRAUGHN	065	837	866	878	0.8	59	316	335	347	1.4	2.59	246	253	0.7
47390	UNION CITY	135	5440	5434	5396	0.0	25	2257	2294	2319	0.4	2.35	1509	1476	-0.5
47392	WEBSTER	177	68	68	68	0.0	27	20	20	21	0.0	3.40	16	16	0.0
47393	WILLIAMSBURG	177	1189	1196	1189	0.1	34	391	400	404	0.5	2.99	326	326	0.0
47394	WINCHESTER	135	8934	8815	8696	-0.3	12	3641	3653	3666	0.1	2.36	2524	2447	-0.7
47396	YORKTOWN	035	6434	6536	6547	0.4	43	2449	2538	2590	0.8	2.55	1835	1837	0.0
47401	BLOOMINGTON	105	33122	35031	36713	1.3	75	14458	15652	16762	1.9	2.17	7474	7598	0.4
47403	BLOOMINGTON	105	25489	26740	28013	1.1	69	10725	11531	12366	1.7	2.26	6472	6519	0.2
47404	BLOOMINGTON	105	18057	18369	18911	0.4	45	7474	7754	8154	0.9	2.30	4242	4127	-0.6
47405	BLOOMINGTON	105	833	825	824	-0.2	16	1	1	1	0.0	3.00	0	0	0.0
47406	BLOOMINGTON	105	4211	4096	4085	-0.7	4	456	402	406	-2.9	1.63	139	109	-5.6
47408	BLOOMINGTON	105	29087	28982	29439	-0.1	22	10078	10297	10775	0.5	2.05	3700	3569	-0.8
47421	BEDFORD	093	28058	29026	30236	0.8	59	11500	12216	13053	1.4	2.33	7934	8098	0.5
47424	BLOOMFIELD	055	9829	9919	10157	0.2	37	4021	4138	4315	0.7	2.37	2841	2826	-0.1
47427	COAL CITY	119	1748	1854	2017	1.4	77	637	685	756	1.7	2.71	499	523	1.1
47429	ELLETTSVILLE	105	7057	7086	7219	0.1	31	2658	2740	2857	0.7	2.58	1951	1919	-0.4
47431	FREEDOM	119	1155	1209	1306	1.1	67	450	481	529	1.6	2.51	357	373	1.0
47432	FRENCH LICK	117	4194	4256	4368	0.4	43	1711	1772	1854	0.8	2.34	1162	1160	0.0
47433	GOSPORT	119	4444	4726	5113	1.5	79	1651	1789	1970	1.9	2.60	1251	1307	1.0
47436	HELTONVILLE	093	1603	1662	1725	0.9	61	645	689	733	1.6	2.41	485	501	0.8
47438	JASONVILLE	021	4577	4781	4976	1.0	66	1773	1880	1986	1.4	2.49	1241	1267	0.5
47441	LINTON	055	10146	10635	11187	1.1	69	4198	4490	4812	1.6	2.31	2831	2895	0.5
47443	LYONS	055	1746	1752	1786	0.1	30	653	666	690	0.5	2.55	478	472	-0.3
47446	MITCHELL	093	10001	10120	10406	0.3	39	3986	4125	4338	0.8	2.42	2885	2888	0.0
47448	NASHVILLE	013	7442	7930	8699	1.5	80	3063	3340	3740	2.1	2.35	2216	2332	1.2
47449	NEWBERRY	055	392	392	398	0.0	27	159	163	168	0.6	2.40	118	117	-0.2
47451	OOLITIC	093	1203	1220	1251	0.3	42	525	546	573	0.9	2.23	355	353	-0.1
47452	ORLEANS	117	4602	4660	4753	0.3	40	1758	1809	1879	0.7	2.58	1248	1240	-0.2
47453	OWENSBURG	055	1327	1375	1423	0.8	60	526	557	586	1.4	2.47	393	403	0.6
47454	PAOLI	117	7274	7484	7680	0.7	53	2872	3025	3173	1.2	2.41	1995	2016	0.3
47456	QUINCY	119	2097	2234	2439	1.5	80	806	871	965	1.8	2.56	618	649	1.0
47459	SOLSBERRY	055	2365	2410	2470	0.4	47	907	947	990	1.0	2.54	682	691	0.3
47460	SPENCER	119	10047	10851	11940	1.8	86	3860	4272	4804	2.4	2.49	2841	3040	1.6
47462	SPRINGVILLE	093	3639	3876	4078	1.5	80	1330	1448	1556	2.0	2.68	1031	1087	1.3
47465	SWITZ CITY	055	879	880	897	0.0	28	338	345	358	0.5	2.50	250	247	-0.3
47468	UNIONVILLE	105	1107	1189	1260	1.7	84	466	512	553	2.2	2.32	346	364	1.2
47469	WEST BADEN SPRINGS	117	1803	1795	1825	-0.1	21	725	738	767	0.4	2.43	516	507	-0.4
47470	WILLIAMS	093	2901	2991	3093	0.7	55	1085	1143	1207	1.2	2.62	827	845	0.5
47471	WORTHINGTON	055	2447	2425	2469	-0.2	17	1020	1029	1066	0.2	2.35	707	687	-0.7
47501	WASHINGTON	027	16151	16417	16846	0.4	45	6444	6644	6905	0.7	2.41	4305	4254	-0.3
47512	BICKNELL	083	4647	4459	4315	-1.0	2	1898	1850	1817	-0.6	2.38	1294	1209	-1.6
47513	BIRDSEYE	037	1695	1792	1875	1.3	75	657	709	756	1.8	2.53	471	491	1.0
47514	BRANCHVILLE	123	1130	1143	1147	0.3	39	84	88	90	1.1	2.56	70	71	0.3
47515	BRISTOW	123	989	1000	999	0.3	39	353	369	375	1.1	2.60	278	283	0.4
47516	BRUCEVILLE	083	1160	1141	1115	-0.4	10	466	468	466	0.1	2.44	353	343	-0.7
47519	CANNELBURG	027	1568	1617	1665	0.7	55	446	467	487	1.1	3.38	377	386	0.6
47520	CANNELTON	123	2551	2711	2814	1.4	78	1020	1118	1184	2.2	2.39	693	727	1.1
47521	CELESTINE	037	970	977	993	0.2	35	328	339	352	0.8	2.88	262	264	0.2
47522	CRANE	101	223	218	216	-0.5	7	99	99	100	0.0	2.20	74	71	-1.0
47523	DALE	173	2946	2985	3100	0.3	41	1109	1147	1214	0.8	2.54	809	807	-0.1
47524	DECKER	083	562	548	533	-0.6	6	217	216	215	-0.1	2.54	158	152	-0.9
47525	DERBY	123	633	634	631	0.0	29	256	265	268	0.8	2.39	198	198	0.0
47527	DUBOIS	037	1784	1985	2132	2.5	94	674	768	843	3.1	2.58	493	544	2.3
47528	EDWARDSPORT	083	534	520	506	-0.6	5	214	212	210	-0.2	2.45	155	148	-1.1
47529	ELNORA	027	2424	2468	2523	0.4	46	792	816	844	0.7	3.02	616	617	0.0
47531	EVANSTON	147	596	586	598	-0.4	9	216	216	225	0.0	2.71	169	165	-0.4
47532	FERDINAND	037	4729	4740	4857	0.1	29	1593	1631	1708	0.6	2.75	1225	1214	-0.2
47537	GENTRYVILLE	173	783	800	837	0.5	49	280	291	309	0.9	2.75	229	232	0.3
47541	HOLLAND	037	1336	1351	1387	0.3	39	499	515	539	0.8	2.62	374	373	-0.1
47542	HUNTINGBURG	037	8690	8939	9229	0.7	53	3220	3373	3548	1.1	2.59	2317	2346	0.3
47546	JASPER	037	19404	19744	20269	0.4	46	7450	7753	8132	0.9	2.50	5284	5301	0.1
47550	LAMAR	147	150	147	150	-0.5	8	57	57	59	0.0	2.58	45	44	-0.5
47551	LEOPOLD	123	872	879	879	0.2	36	309	323	328	1.1	2.23	245	249	0.4
47552	LINCOLN CITY	147	301	321	339	1.5	80	101	110	118	2.0	2.92	81	86	1.4
47553	LOOGOOTEE	101	6163	6263	6344	0.4	44	2473	2581	2675	1.0	2.40	1680	1683	0.0
47556	MARIAH HILL	147	250	267	282	1.6	80	87	94	101	1.8	2.74	69	73	1.3
47557	MONROE CITY	083	1304	1281	1251	-0.4	9	519	520	517	0.1	2.46	381	368	-0.8
47558	MONTGOMERY	027	3298	3405	3510	0.8	56	1012	1061	1107	1.1	3.19	825	842	0.5
47561	OAKTOWN	083	2243	2187	2130	-0.6	6	877	871	863	-0.2	2.44	636	609	-1.0
47562	ODON	027	4753	4854	4980	0.5	49	1581	1633	1692	0.8	2.94	1229	1233	0.1
47564	OTWELL	125	1391	1478	1578	1.4	78	563	610	662	1.9	2.42	400	417	0.8
47567	PETERSBURG	125	6133	6338	6674	0.8	58	2472	2599	2782	1.2	2.37	1744	1767	0.3
47568	PLAINVILLE	027	930	940	959	0.3	38	372	383	396	0.7	2.43	281	280	-0.1
47574	ROME	123	221	222	221	0.1	32	87	90	91	0.8	2.47	68	69	0.3
47575	SAINT ANTHONY	037	1471	1609	1713	2.1	90	534	601	655	2.8	2.63	420	459	2.1
47576	SAINT CROIX	123	416	423	424	0.4	45	150	158	161	1.2	2.68	118	121	0.6
47577	SAINT MEINRAD	147	949	938	954	-0.3	14	311	315	327	0.3	2.68	241	236	-0.5
47578	SANDBORN	083	886	860	836	-0.7	4	375	370	365	-0.3	2.31	253	238	-1.4
47579	SANTA CLAUS	147	2601	2836	3019	2.1	90	934	1035	1119	2.5	2.74	758	817	1.8
47580	SCHNELLVILLE	037	260	278	292	1.6	81	94	103	110	2.2	2.70	74	79	1.6
47581	SHOALS	101	4439	4388	4355	-0.3	14	1776	1798	1826	0.3	2.41	1255	1226	-0.6
47585	STENDAL	125	447	499	548	2.6	94	182	206	229	3.0	2.42	137	150	2.2
47586	TELL CITY	123	11010	10831	10741	-0.4	10	4577	4628	4659	0.3	2.26	3074	2983	-0.7
47588	TROY	123	554	554	550	0.0	27	236	243	246	0.7	2.27	171	170	-0.1
47590	VELPEN	125	672	736	799	2.2	91	243	271	298	2.6	2.72	183	197	1.8
47591	VINCENNES	083	26809	26568	26158	-0.2	17	10546	10647	10661	0.2	2.27	6581	6343	-0.9
47597	WHEATLAND	083	1111	1089	1062	-0.5	8	440	440	437	0.0	2.47	325	314	-0.8
47598	WINSLOW	125	3482	3672	3910	1.3	74	1364	1460	1576	1.6	2.51	992	1025	0.8
47601	BOONVILLE	173	14076	14269	14961	0.3	41	5426	5621	6025	0.8	2.49	4004	4007	0.0
47610	CHANDLER	173	5314	5393	5674	0.4	43	1977	2055	2213	0.9	2.60	1526	1540	0.2
	INDIANA					0.8					1.2	2.48			0.3
	UNITED STATES					1.2					1.3	2.58			1.1

ZIP CODE #	POST OFFICE NAME	RACE (%) White 2000	White 2004	Black 2000	Black 2004	Asian/Pacific 2000	Asian/Pacific 2004	% Hispanic Origin 2000	% Hispanic Origin 2004	2004 AGE DISTRIBUTION (%) 0-4	5-9	10-14	15-19	20-24	25-44	45-64	65-84	85+	18+	MEDIAN AGE 2004	% 2004 Males	% 2004 Females
47382	SARATOGA	100.0	100.0	0.0	0.0	0.0	0.0	0.0	0.0	0.0	0.0	6.7	6.7	0.0	26.7	60.0	0.0	0.0	93.3	47.5	40.0	60.0
47383	SELMA	98.4	98.1	0.4	0.5	0.1	0.2	0.4	0.5	6.1	6.2	7.6	7.4	4.8	26.8	27.4	12.2	1.5	75.3	39.6	49.2	50.8
47384	SHIRLEY	98.9	98.8	0.1	0.1	0.3	0.3	0.5	0.8	7.0	7.5	7.6	6.6	5.4	28.0	24.6	12.2	1.0	73.7	37.4	49.7	50.3
47385	SPICELAND	98.9	98.8	0.1	0.1	0.1	0.1	1.3	1.6	6.1	6.3	6.0	5.9	5.6	28.5	27.4	12.5	1.8	78.2	39.7	48.4	51.6
47386	SPRINGPORT	98.9	98.9	0.5	0.5	0.2	0.2	0.6	0.6	5.9	6.6	6.8	5.6	5.0	24.9	33.0	11.3	1.1	77.3	41.9	51.8	48.2
47387	STRAUGHN	99.2	99.1	0.2	0.2	0.1	0.1	0.8	0.9	3.6	4.3	7.3	6.5	6.7	26.4	29.7	13.9	1.7	80.8	42.0	48.4	51.6
47390	UNION CITY	95.7	95.1	0.7	0.8	0.2	0.3	3.4	4.1	7.3	6.6	6.5	6.6	6.4	25.2	24.5	14.9	2.1	75.6	38.5	49.1	50.9
47392	WEBSTER	98.5	97.1	0.0	1.5	0.0	0.0	0.0	0.0	4.4	5.9	8.8	8.8	4.4	29.4	30.9	7.4	0.0	72.1	38.3	51.5	48.5
47393	WILLIAMSBURG	98.0	97.7	0.2	0.2	0.0	0.0	1.3	1.6	6.7	7.3	9.0	8.0	6.2	26.7	25.3	9.8	1.1	71.9	36.3	52.4	47.6
47394	WINCHESTER	98.6	98.4	0.2	0.2	0.3	0.3	1.1	1.3	6.5	6.4	6.2	6.2	6.0	25.5	26.0	14.9	2.4	77.0	40.4	48.7	51.3
47396	YORKTOWN	98.0	97.7	0.7	0.8	0.2	0.3	0.7	0.9	6.5	6.6	7.2	6.7	5.4	25.6	27.9	12.4	1.7	75.5	40.0	48.1	51.9
47401	BLOOMINGTON	91.3	89.6	2.1	2.2	3.9	5.1	1.9	2.3	5.1	4.8	5.0	6.4	17.8	27.5	21.8	10.2	1.3	82.1	31.8	48.7	51.4
47403	BLOOMINGTON	93.1	92.3	3.3	3.6	1.2	1.5	1.4	1.7	7.1	6.5	6.2	6.1	8.7	32.4	21.9	9.9	1.3	76.7	34.1	48.8	51.2
47404	BLOOMINGTON	91.9	90.8	3.7	4.0	1.2	1.6	1.7	2.1	6.9	5.9	5.4	7.2	15.9	28.4	21.4	8.0	1.0	78.1	30.7	50.1	49.9
47405	BLOOMINGTON	81.2	78.1	8.2	8.6	8.0	10.3	2.8	3.4	0.1	0.1	0.0	58.7	34.6	5.6	0.7	0.0	0.2	99.5	19.2	44.6	55.4
47406	BLOOMINGTON	76.2	73.5	6.2	6.4	14.0	16.4	3.0	3.4	1.3	0.8	0.5	37.9	43.7	13.7	1.6	0.4	0.2	97.1	21.1	47.1	52.9
47408	BLOOMINGTON	88.0	86.3	3.4	3.6	5.6	7.0	2.5	2.8	2.2	2.3	2.4	21.5	32.0	19.2	12.8	6.2	1.5	91.6	23.4	49.7	50.3
47421	BEDFORD	97.7	97.4	0.5	0.5	0.4	0.5	1.1	1.3	6.2	6.4	6.6	5.8	5.7	26.7	26.2	14.4	2.2	77.3	40.3	48.7	51.4
47424	BLOOMFIELD	98.5	98.3	0.1	0.1	0.2	0.3	0.7	0.9	6.3	6.5	6.7	6.1	5.7	28.1	26.7	12.4	1.7	76.7	39.2	50.4	49.6
47427	COAL CITY	98.5	98.4	0.0	0.0	0.1	0.1	1.1	1.4	6.5	6.7	8.3	7.5	6.4	25.2	26.0	12.2	1.2	73.9	38.3	50.4	49.6
47429	ELLETTSVILLE	96.6	96.2	1.1	1.2	0.6	0.7	0.8	1.0	6.8	7.1	8.2	7.2	6.4	29.6	25.4	8.4	1.0	73.4	36.0	49.2	50.8
47431	FREEDOM	98.3	98.1	0.4	0.3	0.3	0.3	1.6	1.9	5.5	6.1	6.9	6.3	6.3	25.7	29.2	13.1	0.9	77.6	41.0	51.9	48.1
47432	FRENCH LICK	96.5	96.2	1.9	2.0	0.2	0.3	0.3	0.4	5.9	6.1	6.6	5.9	5.8	25.5	26.2	15.7	2.4	77.9	41.4	49.6	50.4
47433	GOSPORT	98.4	98.3	0.4	0.4	0.2	0.3	0.6	0.7	6.0	6.4	7.6	6.8	5.6	27.3	26.9	12.0	1.5	75.7	39.5	49.9	50.2
47436	HELTONVILLE	98.9	98.7	0.0	0.0	0.3	0.4	0.7	0.8	6.6	7.0	6.2	5.1	4.6	28.9	28.6	12.0	1.0	77.0	39.5	50.7	49.3
47438	JASONVILLE	98.7	98.5	0.1	0.1	0.2	0.2	0.8	1.0	6.6	6.4	7.3	7.2	6.9	26.7	23.3	13.4	2.4	75.3	38.0	48.4	51.6
47441	LINTON	98.5	98.4	0.1	0.1	0.3	0.4	1.0	1.1	6.3	6.3	6.3	6.3	5.5	25.5	25.6	15.6	2.7	77.3	40.7	48.2	51.8
47443	LYONS	99.1	99.0	0.0	0.0	0.2	0.2	0.5	0.6	6.9	6.7	7.4	6.4	5.8	25.9	25.2	13.0	2.8	74.7	38.8	49.7	50.3
47446	MITCHELL	98.4	98.3	0.3	0.3	0.1	0.1	0.6	0.7	6.7	6.9	7.3	6.2	5.8	27.0	25.9	12.5	1.8	75.3	38.3	48.9	51.1
47448	NASHVILLE	98.1	97.9	0.3	0.3	0.3	0.3	0.8	0.9	5.2	5.8	6.1	5.4	4.8	25.2	33.1	13.0	1.6	79.4	43.5	49.7	50.3
47449	NEWBERRY	99.0	99.2	0.0	0.0	0.0	0.0	0.8	0.8	6.9	6.9	6.9	6.4	5.6	26.3	27.8	11.7	1.5	75.0	39.1	52.0	48.0
47451	OOLITIC	98.8	98.7	0.0	0.0	0.1	0.1	0.3	0.3	6.6	6.5	6.0	5.3	6.1	26.8	27.5	13.5	1.7	77.7	40.2	47.3	52.7
47452	ORLEANS	98.3	98.2	0.2	0.3	0.1	0.1	0.6	0.6	8.3	7.7	7.9	6.9	5.8	26.2	23.4	11.9	1.9	71.9	35.8	49.0	51.0
47453	OWENSBURG	98.9	98.8	0.0	0.0	0.0	0.0	1.1	1.3	6.0	6.3	6.9	6.8	5.5	31.5	26.8	9.3	0.9	76.5	37.5	52.0	48.0
47454	PAOLI	98.5	98.3	0.2	0.2	0.2	0.2	0.5	0.6	6.9	6.8	7.0	6.4	5.8	27.4	25.1	12.6	2.0	75.4	38.2	49.1	50.9
47456	QUINCY	98.2	98.0	0.4	0.5	0.1	0.2	0.5	0.6	6.0	6.4	7.3	7.0	6.1	27.0	27.8	11.7	0.8	76.0	39.4	50.5	49.5
47459	SOLSBERRY	98.9	98.7	0.1	0.1	0.1	0.2	0.5	0.6	6.8	7.1	7.9	6.1	5.5	31.2	26.0	8.6	0.9	74.1	36.9	50.7	49.3
47460	SPENCER	98.3	98.1	0.2	0.2	0.2	0.3	0.7	0.8	6.7	6.6	7.0	6.8	6.6	26.7	26.0	12.0	1.6	75.5	38.4	48.7	51.3
47462	SPRINGVILLE	97.6	97.3	0.1	0.2	0.3	0.4	1.1	1.3	6.6	7.0	7.4	6.2	5.7	30.3	26.7	9.4	0.8	75.2	36.8	51.2	48.8
47465	SWITZ CITY	98.2	97.7	0.1	0.1	0.3	0.5	0.9	1.1	6.5	6.9	6.9	6.8	5.5	25.6	27.5	12.6	1.7	75.3	39.3	49.6	50.5
47468	UNIONVILLE	98.4	98.1	0.0	0.0	0.4	0.4	0.8	1.0	5.2	6.1	7.0	6.2	5.1	27.6	32.0	10.1	0.8	78.0	41.2	50.8	49.2
47469	WEST BADEN SPRINGS	97.0	96.7	1.0	1.1	0.4	0.5	1.5	1.7	6.5	6.4	6.1	6.6	6.1	26.5	27.2	13.3	1.3	77.1	39.6	49.0	51.0
47470	WILLIAMS	98.1	97.9	0.1	0.1	0.2	0.2	0.6	0.7	6.3	6.7	7.5	6.5	6.1	26.1	29.3	10.4	1.0	75.5	39.0	50.2	49.9
47471	WORTHINGTON	98.7	98.6	0.0	0.0	0.2	0.2	0.4	0.4	5.5	5.6	6.6	6.7	5.9	25.8	25.4	16.5	2.0	78.3	41.5	48.5	51.5
47501	WASHINGTON	96.3	95.7	0.8	0.8	0.4	0.5	3.2	3.9	6.6	6.5	6.9	6.7	6.6	25.2	24.8	14.0	2.7	75.9	39.0	48.7	51.3
47512	BICKNELL	98.4	98.3	0.4	0.4	0.2	0.2	0.5	0.5	7.1	6.2	6.8	6.7	6.3	25.5	24.4	14.8	2.2	75.8	39.1	47.7	52.3
47513	BIRDSEYE	99.1	99.0	0.0	0.0	0.1	0.2	1.5	1.6	7.8	7.7	7.3	7.0	5.8	29.6	23.9	9.7	1.2	72.9	36.0	51.0	49.0
47514	BRANCHVILLE	85.3	85.0	12.7	13.0	0.1	0.1	1.2	1.2	3.9	3.9	4.8	6.9	13.3	44.4	17.7	4.5	0.6	84.3	32.7	73.3	26.7
47515	BRISTOW	98.4	98.4	1.1	1.1	0.0	0.0	0.7	0.7	5.6	5.7	6.7	6.7	7.4	29.2	26.1	11.5	1.1	77.8	38.4	53.8	46.2
47516	BRUCEVILLE	98.9	98.8	0.2	0.2	0.1	0.2	0.5	0.5	6.2	6.3	6.9	7.0	6.1	25.9	27.2	13.1	1.3	76.3	40.4	49.6	50.4
47519	CANNELBURG	99.2	99.1	0.0	0.0	0.1	0.1	0.6	0.7	11.3	10.6	10.6	7.5	7.4	25.2	17.7	8.2	1.5	63.0	26.9	50.1	49.9
47520	CANNELTON	98.8	98.8	0.1	0.2	0.0	0.0	0.5	0.4	6.5	6.6	6.8	5.9	7.2	28.2	26.0	11.4	1.4	76.4	37.9	50.5	49.5
47521	CELESTINE	99.9	99.9	0.0	0.0	0.1	0.1	0.3	0.4	8.6	8.5	7.4	6.4	6.1	29.0	24.2	8.3	1.6	71.9	35.8	51.8	48.2
47522	CRANE	98.2	98.2	0.0	0.0	0.5	0.5	0.5	0.5	6.4	6.9	7.3	5.5	5.5	22.5	29.8	15.1	0.9	75.7	42.0	49.5	50.5
47523	DALE	95.5	94.7	0.5	0.6	0.1	0.1	5.2	6.1	6.6	6.5	7.2	6.9	6.6	26.9	25.6	11.7	2.0	75.4	37.7	48.9	51.1
47524	DECKER	99.3	99.1	0.5	0.6	0.0	0.0	0.4	0.7	5.7	7.7	9.1	8.2	4.7	26.5	26.8	9.7	1.6	72.8	37.4	52.0	48.0
47525	DERBY	99.4	99.4	0.0	0.0	0.0	0.0	0.2	0.3	4.9	5.5	6.6	6.9	5.7	26.8	32.2	9.9	1.4	78.4	41.1	51.9	48.1
47527	DUBOIS	99.2	99.1	0.0	0.0	0.2	0.2	0.5	0.6	6.9	7.0	7.4	7.0	6.9	29.2	24.6	10.0	1.2	74.4	35.8	51.1	48.9
47528	EDWARDSPORT	97.6	97.1	0.4	0.4	0.2	0.2	1.5	1.7	4.8	4.8	5.6	7.3	7.1	27.9	30.2	11.0	1.4	80.2	40.6	50.4	49.6
47529	ELNORA	98.9	98.7	0.0	0.1	0.1	0.2	0.7	0.8	8.8	8.4	8.8	7.2	6.9	24.9	22.2	11.2	1.5	69.5	33.3	50.8	49.2
47531	EVANSTON	98.7	98.5	0.3	0.3	0.2	0.2	1.7	2.1	6.5	7.0	8.0	6.1	5.5	26.8	27.8	11.3	1.0	74.7	39.1	52.1	48.0
47532	FERDINAND	99.2	99.0	0.1	0.1	0.2	0.3	0.6	0.7	7.0	7.5	8.1	6.9	5.6	28.4	22.7	11.8	2.0	72.9	37.0	49.0	51.0
47537	GENTRYVILLE	98.6	98.5	0.0	0.0	0.1	0.1	0.9	0.9	5.6	6.3	7.3	7.0	6.8	25.8	29.5	10.9	1.0	76.5	40.2	49.9	50.1
47541	HOLLAND	98.7	98.6	0.0	0.0	0.2	0.3	1.2	1.4	6.7	6.9	7.9	7.2	5.9	27.6	24.5	11.8	1.4	74.0	37.1	50.6	49.4
47542	HUNTINGBURG	94.7	93.9	0.1	0.1	0.2	0.2	6.6	7.8	7.1	7.0	7.5	6.8	6.6	27.4	24.0	11.8	1.8	74.0	36.9	49.1	50.9
47546	JASPER	97.8	97.4	0.2	0.3	0.3	0.4	2.3	2.8	7.2	7.4	7.5	6.5	5.9	28.3	24.3	11.0	2.0	73.8	37.3	49.8	50.2
47550	LAMAR	98.7	99.3	0.0	0.0	0.0	0.0	0.0	0.0	6.1	7.5	8.2	5.4	4.8	29.9	27.9	10.2	0.0	74.2	39.8	52.4	47.6
47551	LEOPOLD	93.7	93.6	5.2	5.2	0.0	0.0	0.6	0.6	4.3	4.7	6.0	7.4	8.8	34.2	25.9	7.6	1.0	80.7	36.7	60.5	39.5
47552	LINCOLN CITY	98.0	97.2	0.3	0.3	0.3	0.6	2.3	2.5	7.8	7.5	7.5	6.9	5.3	29.6	24.6	10.0	0.9	73.5	36.4	50.2	49.8
47553	LOOGOOTEE	98.9	98.9	0.1	0.1	0.2	0.2	0.4	0.4	6.5	6.7	7.3	6.5	5.7	25.8	26.8	13.0	1.8	75.5	39.4	50.2	49.8
47556	MARIAH HILL	98.8	98.5	0.0	0.0	0.4	0.4	1.2	1.5	6.4	7.1	7.9	7.5	5.6	29.2	24.7	10.5	1.1	74.2	37.1	52.1	47.9
47557	MONROE CITY	99.4	99.2	0.1	0.1	0.1	0.1	0.4	0.6	6.1	6.1	6.3	6.9	5.9	25.9	28.3	12.5	2.0	77.3	40.7	50.6	49.4
47558	MONTGOMERY	99.2	99.0	0.0	0.0	0.2	0.2	0.6	0.6	9.3	9.0	8.9	7.8	7.0	26.6	21.7	8.6	1.0	68.2	31.4	50.7	49.3
47561	OAKTOWN	99.0	98.9	0.1	0.1	0.2	0.3	0.9	1.0	6.0	6.0	6.5	6.3	5.8	25.0	26.2	14.8	3.4	77.6	41.5	49.3	50.7
47562	ODON	98.9	98.7	0.1	0.1	0.2	0.3	0.8	0.9	9.2	8.8	9.0	7.2	6.7	25.0	21.4	10.9	1.7	68.6	32.1	50.4	49.6
47564	OTWELL	99.2	99.0	0.1	0.1	0.1	0.2	0.6	0.8	6.8	7.0	7.2	6.2	5.8	26.8	25.6	12.8	1.8	75.1	38.3	50.6	49.4
47567	PETERSBURG	99.3	99.1	0.1	0.1	0.2	0.2	0.4	0.4	5.8	6.0	6.2	5.9	5.8	26.1	26.5	15.1	2.6	78.5	41.4	50.0	50.0
47568	PLAINVILLE	98.8	98.8	0.1	0.1	0.1	0.1	1.5	1.7	7.1	7.3	7.1	5.9	5.2	27.5	22.0	15.6	2.2	74.7	38.6	50.1	49.9
47574	ROME	99.6	99.6	0.0	0.0	0.0	0.0	0.0	0.5	6.3	6.3	6.8	6.3	6.8	26.6	29.3	10.8	0.9	77.5	39.4	50.9	49.1
47575	SAINT ANTHONY	99.5	99.3	0.0	0.0	0.1	0.2	0.5	0.6	7.8	7.9	7.7	6.6	5.8	28.4	25.1	9.5	1.2	72.3	36.7	49.7	50.3
47576	SAINT CROIX	99.8	99.8	0.0	0.0	0.0	0.0	0.5	0.2	6.4	6.4	7.8	8.0	7.1	29.3	25.3	9.0	0.7	74.7	36.0	51.1	48.9
47577	SAINT MEINRAD	98.8	98.5	0.3	0.3	0.4	0.6	1.2	1.4	5.5	6.0	7.0	6.8	6.0	29.3	25.3	12.2	1.9	76.9	39.4	55.5	44.5
47578	SANDBORN	98.3	98.3	0.2	0.2	0.1	0.1	0.5	0.4	4.4	4.7	6.6	7.1	6.4	22.6	28.3	17.2	2.8	80.0	43.9	49.0	51.1
47579	SANTA CLAUS	98.7	98.5	0.0	0.0	0.4	0.5	1.0	1.2	7.5	7.5	7.8	7.1	5.4	29.4	24.3	10.2	0.8	72.9	36.3	50.7	49.3
47580	SCHNELLVILLE	99.6	100.0	0.0	0.0	0.0	0.0	0.4	0.4	8.6	8.6	7.2	6.5	6.1	28.8	24.5	8.3	1.4	71.2	35.4	50.4	49.6
47581	SHOALS	98.9	98.9	0.2	0.2	0.1	0.1	0.5	0.5	6.1	6.2	6.6	6.8	6.8	26.6	27.4	12.3	1.3	77.1	38.9	51.8	48.2
47585	STENDAL	99.1	99.2	0.2	0.2	0.0	0.0	0.5	0.6	6.2	6.4	8.0	6.6	6.0	29.5	24.5	11.8	1.0	75.4	37.1	50.7	49.3
47586	TELL CITY	98.4	98.4	0.6	0.7	0.2	0.2	0.8	0.8	5.5	5.6	6.3	6.0	6.5	26.5	25.9	15.0	2.6	79.0	40.8	49.4	50.6
47588	TROY	99.6	99.6	0.0	0.0	0.0	0.0	0.7	0.7	5.6	5.8	6.9	6.9	6.7	31.2	25.6	10.7	0.7	77.8	38.1	52.0	48.0
47590	VELPEN	99.4	99.2	0.2	0.1	0.0	0.0	0.6	1.0	6.5	7.1	8.0	6.5	6.0	28.4	25.7	10.7	1.1	74.5	36.9	51.1	48.9
47591	VINCENNES	95.3	94.8	2.6	2.8	0.8	1.0	0.9	1.1	5.8	5.6	5.8	9.7	10.8	23.6	23.5	12.8	2.4	79.1	36.0	50.0	50.0
47597	WHEATLAND	99.0	98.9	0.2	0.2	0.2	0.2	0.3	0.5	5.8	5.9	6.9	6.3	5.6	27.3	28.0	12.4	1.8	77.4	40.6	49.7	50.3
47598	WINSLOW	98.8	98.7	0.1	0.1	0.3	0.3	1.0	1.2	6.6	6.8	7.2	6.1	5.9	27.0	26.3	12.9	1.4	75.7	38.7	50.7	49.3
47601	BOONVILLE	98.7	98.6	0.5	0.5	0.2	0.2	0.4	0.5	6.2	6.5	6.7	6.3	6.3	27.6	27.1	11.6	1.8	76.5	39.1	49.3	50.7
47610	CHANDLER	98.7	98.5	0.4	0.4	0.2	0.2	0.6	0.7	6.7	6.6	7.5	6.4	6.4	28.5	26.5	10.5	0.9	74.9	37.2	49.6	50.4
	INDIANA	87.5	86.7	8.4	8.7	1.0	1.3	3.5	4.1	7.0	6.9	7.1	7.1	7.4	28.1	24.0	10.8	1.6	75.0	35.9	49.2	50.8
	UNITED STATES	75.1	73.6	12.3	12.5	3.8	4.2	12.5	14.1	6.9	6.7	7.2	7.0	7.3	28.6	23.8	10.8	1.7	75.1	36.0	49.1	50.9

ZIP CODE #	POST OFFICE NAME	2004 Per Capita Income	2004 HH Income Base	2004 Household Income Distribution (%): Less than $25,000	$25,000 to $49,999	$50,000 to $99,999	$100,000 to $149,999	$150,000 or More	Median Household Income: 2004	2009	2004 National Centile	2004 State Centile	2004 Home Value Base	2004 Home Value Distribution (%): Less than $50,000	$50,000 to $89,999	$90,000 to $174,999	$175,000 to $399,999	$400,000 or More	2004 Median Home Value
47382	SARATOGA	22167	8	12.5	62.5	25.0	0.0	0.0	40000	40000	46	24	7	0.0	14.3	57.1	28.6	0.0	131250
47383	SELMA	23883	1045	20.2	26.7	38.5	9.9	4.8	52224	60491	76	80	863	10.8	29.7	49.9	9.0	0.6	97301
47384	SHIRLEY	19585	709	23.7	31.0	36.1	7.9	1.3	45315	51458	62	52	601	10.3	23.5	53.4	10.2	2.7	107560
47385	SPICELAND	22755	726	25.9	26.5	33.5	13.0	1.2	46748	52381	66	61	602	7.0	33.9	46.8	10.3	2.0	100682
47386	SPRINGPORT	25085	511	16.4	25.8	43.1	9.8	4.9	56108	63388	81	88	463	6.7	18.4	62.9	11.9	0.2	119977
47387	STRAUGHN	22341	335	26.6	25.1	33.7	11.6	3.0	48439	54578	69	68	288	13.9	31.3	39.2	12.9	2.8	96087
47390	UNION CITY	17528	2294	39.1	31.3	26.0	2.4	1.3	33620	37105	23	7	1639	26.5	40.3	27.9	4.4	0.9	73571
47392	WEBSTER	13640	20	25.0	40.0	25.0	10.0	0.0	40000	48610	46	24	17	5.9	17.7	64.7	11.8	0.0	114583
47393	WILLIAMSBURG	19331	400	18.8	35.0	36.3	7.3	2.8	47340	53080	67	63	345	13.0	23.2	48.4	13.3	2.0	105616
47394	WINCHESTER	20278	3653	32.4	33.8	27.3	4.3	2.1	37082	40579	36	14	2693	20.6	37.1	33.4	7.6	1.4	81612
47396	YORKTOWN	29703	2538	16.3	27.3	37.3	12.5	6.6	56126	64792	81	88	2101	5.7	27.4	47.8	15.6	3.6	111296
47401	BLOOMINGTON	28489	15652	32.0	23.7	26.0	11.9	6.5	43427	50989	57	40	8646	3.4	9.4	48.1	34.4	4.7	156521
47403	BLOOMINGTON	21425	11531	30.0	33.7	29.1	5.2	2.0	37909	44342	39	17	7128	17.0	18.8	52.3	10.6	1.3	103214
47404	BLOOMINGTON	20238	7754	35.7	30.0	24.4	7.7	2.2	35028	40416	28	9	4439	18.0	16.7	48.7	15.7	0.9	106666
47405	BLOOMINGTON	11244	1	100.0	0.0	0.0	0.0	0.0	5000	5000	0	0	0	0.0	0.0	0.0	0.0	0.0	0
47406	BLOOMINGTON	11724	402	82.3	12.9	4.2	0.5	0.0	10803	11903	1	1	6	0.0	0.0	100.0	0.0	0.0	95000
47408	BLOOMINGTON	18511	10297	47.8	23.6	18.7	7.2	2.8	26654	30622	7	2	3903	5.4	9.5	54.2	27.0	3.9	143940
47421	BEDFORD	20582	12216	30.5	32.1	29.3	6.6	1.5	39387	43095	44	21	9363	18.7	32.5	39.5	8.9	0.5	88660
47424	BLOOMFIELD	20264	4138	29.6	32.4	29.8	7.0	1.2	40599	45088	48	27	3350	22.6	29.4	38.6	8.7	0.7	87444
47427	COAL CITY	15938	685	32.4	36.4	27.6	2.8	0.9	36833	41229	35	14	577	24.3	32.4	27.9	8.8	6.6	77745
47429	ELLETTSVILLE	21647	2740	20.6	32.7	35.0	9.5	2.2	47133	55912	66	62	2221	7.7	22.3	60.4	9.2	0.4	107400
47431	FREEDOM	20322	481	27.4	35.8	31.4	1.7	3.7	37422	41862	37	15	407	11.6	28.8	49.6	7.6	2.5	102006
47432	FRENCH LICK	18720	1772	33.9	33.6	26.3	3.8	2.3	37136	41391	36	15	1369	30.4	28.9	27.8	11.8	1.0	79040
47433	GOSPORT	20694	1789	23.3	32.8	32.6	9.1	2.3	44040	49211	59	44	1473	13.0	23.4	47.3	16.0	0.5	109194
47436	HELTONVILLE	24230	689	19.6	33.4	33.5	10.2	3.3	46121	50976	64	57	590	19.7	23.7	40.5	15.1	1.0	95909
47438	JASONVILLE	14866	1880	42.0	31.3	23.6	2.7	0.4	29847	33163	12	4	1383	39.7	31.5	23.6	4.8	0.4	62465
47441	LINTON	18897	4490	34.6	32.4	26.4	5.5	1.1	35000	38903	28	9	3476	31.1	32.7	29.6	6.2	0.4	72611
47443	LYONS	16142	666	33.3	38.0	24.2	2.7	1.8	36107	39632	32	12	529	43.3	33.7	21.6	1.5	0.0	57100
47446	MITCHELL	18181	4125	29.4	36.4	29.0	4.3	0.9	37433	41512	37	16	3332	25.9	29.3	35.1	9.2	0.5	83593
47448	NASHVILLE	25428	3340	21.5	30.5	35.1	9.6	3.3	48348	54233	69	68	2733	5.3	9.4	48.8	32.8	3.7	147270
47449	NEWBERRY	18808	163	36.8	31.3	22.7	4.9	4.3	34159	37629	25	8	141	25.5	29.1	31.2	14.2	0.0	81875
47451	OOLITIC	18903	546	37.7	35.5	20.0	5.1	1.7	33574	36898	23	6	388	20.1	34.3	39.7	5.2	0.8	84516
47452	ORLEANS	17750	1809	33.9	36.6	22.6	4.7	2.3	35451	39273	29	10	1421	21.5	39.1	32.9	6.1	0.5	77226
47453	OWENSBURG	19055	557	28.6	38.2	25.9	5.0	2.3	35215	39704	28	10	502	23.3	22.9	45.8	8.0	0.0	94872
47454	PAOLI	18168	3025	37.5	33.8	22.6	4.4	1.6	32044	35486	18	5	2381	29.8	34.8	28.1	6.7	0.6	71553
47456	QUINCY	19688	871	23.9	36.9	30.7	7.1	1.5	41930	46631	53	33	749	17.4	22.8	40.3	19.1	0.4	105449
47459	SOLSBERRY	19268	947	24.9	38.0	29.4	7.4	0.3	41942	47002	53	33	798	30.8	22.1	33.8	11.7	1.6	86290
47460	SPENCER	20097	4272	26.9	34.6	30.3	6.1	2.1	40310	44408	47	26	3431	15.7	24.3	46.8	12.5	0.8	100473
47462	SPRINGVILLE	21074	1448	21.8	33.5	34.9	7.5	2.4	44921	51173	61	49	1263	21.4	25.7	42.5	7.4	2.9	92589
47465	SWITZ CITY	19148	345	29.3	28.7	35.7	5.5	0.9	41785	46762	52	32	291	27.2	31.3	34.7	6.5	0.3	79405
47468	UNIONVILLE	27075	512	20.3	27.5	35.9	10.7	5.5	51884	60426	75	79	446	9.2	20.2	43.3	25.8	1.6	117813
47469	WEST BADEN SPRINGS	22957	738	35.0	30.5	27.4	3.7	3.5	38200	42334	40	17	598	37.3	24.4	27.8	10.2	0.3	69512
47470	WILLIAMS	19945	1143	24.6	36.9	31.9	5.2	1.4	43477	48493	57	41	999	25.2	25.0	39.2	8.1	2.4	89603
47471	WORTHINGTON	20922	1029	33.5	32.7	27.6	3.5	2.7	37864	42193	39	16	829	31.7	35.0	27.6	4.6	1.1	67833
47501	WASHINGTON	19425	6644	35.3	32.2	25.6	4.3	2.8	34852	38901	27	9	4829	20.7	36.0	34.4	8.1	0.8	81523
47512	BICKNELL	15947	1850	44.1	29.8	20.9	4.2	1.0	29390	32931	11	4	1298	46.7	34.8	16.3	2.2	0.0	52251
47513	BIRDSEYE	19429	709	29.1	29.6	35.0	5.4	1.0	42223	46604	54	34	591	25.0	26.2	35.7	10.8	2.2	88295
47514	BRANCHVILLE	9750	88	17.1	36.4	38.6	4.6	3.4	47956	52582	68	66	85	7.1	29.4	54.1	8.2	1.2	104167
47515	BRISTOW	18937	369	22.2	35.8	34.2	5.7	2.2	43438	47236	57	41	331	20.9	19.6	44.1	10.6	4.8	102052
47516	BRUCEVILLE	18414	468	33.1	34.6	25.6	4.9	1.7	37250	42142	36	15	399	29.3	32.8	27.6	6.5	3.8	74271
47519	CANNELBURG	13101	467	30.4	32.6	33.0	2.1	1.9	38951	43383	43	19	398	13.3	26.6	38.9	19.6	1.5	103509
47520	CANNELTON	18112	1118	31.5	32.9	31.1	3.8	0.7	37988	42137	39	17	888	26.6	39.8	28.0	5.2	0.5	76569
47521	CELESTINE	19888	339	13.0	26.3	54.6	6.2	0.0	55328	62272	80	87	293	8.9	18.1	48.8	20.1	4.1	115441
47522	CRANE	23757	99	15.2	42.4	33.3	9.1	0.0	42652	47706	55	37	81	30.9	34.6	23.5	11.1	0.0	69286
47523	DALE	19633	1147	21.4	37.5	35.1	4.9	1.2	44795	50000	61	48	903	15.7	35.0	36.7	9.9	2.8	89156
47524	DECKER	17427	216	36.1	36.1	21.3	3.2	3.2	33369	36816	22	6	177	54.2	23.7	13.0	6.2	2.8	46429
47525	DERBY	20246	265	22.3	38.1	34.3	4.9	0.4	42638	47588	55	37	240	22.9	24.6	42.1	10.0	0.4	92500
47527	DUBOIS	19061	768	17.6	40.0	38.5	2.6	1.3	43207	48610	57	40	666	19.7	26.9	46.0	7.4	0.2	94035
47528	EDWARDSPORT	18705	212	33.5	25.9	32.6	8.0	0.0	40343	43525	47	26	173	45.7	22.5	27.8	3.5	0.6	58333
47529	ELNORA	15362	816	34.0	34.1	24.3	4.4	3.3	35725	39779	30	11	691	28.9	26.9	33.4	9.8	0.9	81383
47531	EVANSTON	21022	216	16.2	32.9	40.3	10.7	0.0	50890	57017	74	76	189	11.6	18.0	50.3	15.3	4.8	114236
47532	FERDINAND	20954	1631	17.8	30.5	40.2	9.0	2.5	51142	55859	74	77	1384	10.1	21.2	48.3	18.5	1.8	112066
47537	GENTRYVILLE	18190	291	22.3	30.9	39.9	5.8	1.0	47353	52343	67	64	256	21.5	27.3	34.4	13.7	3.1	91500
47541	HOLLAND	22010	515	21.9	33.0	35.0	5.4	4.7	45404	50581	62	52	443	14.2	36.8	39.5	8.8	0.7	88846
47542	HUNTINGBURG	20803	3373	24.9	33.1	33.1	6.1	2.7	42501	47324	55	37	2493	13.2	30.8	41.2	13.4	1.4	96939
47546	JASPER	25711	7753	19.5	29.8	36.8	9.5	4.4	50522	55697	73	74	5953	6.4	20.3	49.1	21.8	2.3	119616
47550	LAMAR	22226	57	19.3	33.3	35.1	10.5	1.8	47368	53096	67	64	49	12.2	20.4	44.9	20.4	2.0	107955
47551	LEOPOLD	20882	323	20.1	38.1	35.6	5.0	1.2	44280	49416	59	45	304	14.8	28.0	47.7	9.2	0.3	98462
47552	LINCOLN CITY	23126	110	15.5	25.5	42.7	11.8	4.6	56155	61290	81	89	98	5.1	12.2	51.0	27.6	4.1	137500
47553	LOOGOOTEE	20030	2581	30.4	31.9	30.8	4.9	2.0	40101	43924	46	25	2044	25.3	35.5	29.9	8.6	0.7	77098
47556	MARIAH HILL	23980	94	17.0	25.5	40.4	12.8	4.3	55877	60412	81	88	83	12.1	15.7	47.0	21.7	3.6	120833
47557	MONROE CITY	20015	520	26.7	31.0	34.2	6.9	1.2	42941	47952	56	39	424	24.8	37.0	26.7	8.7	2.8	78293
47558	MONTGOMERY	15855	1061	23.9	32.3	35.3	6.3	2.2	44654	49346	60	47	907	10.7	24.9	49.3	12.5	2.7	104120
47561	OAKTOWN	18296	871	35.8	29.6	26.4	6.4	1.7	36103	40288	32	12	675	32.6	36.2	25.3	4.0	1.9	65494
47562	ODON	17057	1633	26.9	37.2	27.9	5.6	2.3	39852	44669	45	23	1358	20.8	31.3	35.7	11.6	0.5	87752
47564	OTWELL	19838	610	25.7	33.1	34.9	5.4	0.8	39421	43866	44	21	515	27.4	31.8	31.7	8.7	0.4	79490
47567	PETERSBURG	17850	2599	34.0	33.0	29.1	3.1	0.9	35740	39239	31	11	2059	35.8	32.3	27.4	4.3	0.2	65692
47568	PLAINVILLE	20915	383	26.1	30.6	36.0	5.7	1.6	44324	49384	60	46	321	23.4	37.1	33.3	4.7	1.6	78171
47574	ROME	20424	90	22.2	33.3	37.8	5.6	1.1	45752	51121	63	55	76	25.0	25.0	40.8	7.9	1.3	90000
47575	SAINT ANTHONY	23234	601	17.3	31.1	38.4	10.2	3.0	51019	55572	74	77	528	11.0	21.0	42.8	23.5	1.7	117941
47576	SAINT CROIX	18573	158	24.7	32.3	34.8	7.0	1.3	45954	50542	64	56	139	14.4	34.5	41.7	7.9	1.4	91667
47577	SAINT MEINRAD	21586	315	19.1	30.8	33.3	13.7	3.2	50143	53508	72	72	272	23.2	21.7	38.2	14.3	2.6	97778
47578	SANDBORN	20821	370	36.5	23.8	33.0	4.3	2.4	36077	39392	32	12	304	45.7	36.5	12.2	2.0	3.6	53939
47579	SANTA CLAUS	25364	1035	15.4	23.9	43.1	12.5	5.2	57861	63566	83	91	932	6.3	10.8	50.1	27.9	4.8	140870
47580	SCHNELLVILLE	20681	103	16.5	26.2	49.5	6.8	1.0	53783	59187	78	84	89	10.1	22.5	46.1	20.2	1.1	110156
47581	SHOALS	18662	1798	29.9	36.9	27.5	4.1	1.6	38998	42877	43	20	1457	37.8	28.7	27.1	4.7	1.7	64628
47585	STENDAL	21089	206	26.7	32.0	30.6	7.3	3.4	40733	44530	49	28	174	35.6	38.5	19.5	4.6	1.7	69231
47586	TELL CITY	20507	4628	32.4	32.2	28.4	4.8	2.3	37497	41196	37	16	3456	16.7	36.9	37.2	8.5	0.8	86372
47588	TROY	20242	243	27.2	37.0	30.0	5.4	0.4	40449	44483	48	26	199	22.6	34.2	29.2	12.1	2.0	82500
47590	VELPEN	18692	271	22.9	36.9	31.0	7.4	1.9	41474	45609	51	30	231	29.0	35.1	25.1	10.0	0.9	75833
47591	VINCENNES	18831	10647	38.4	30.0	23.7	5.9	2.0	33725	37974	23	7	6948	22.4	32.9	33.8	9.6	1.3	83119
47597	WHEATLAND	21556	440	23.4	30.9	36.1	6.8	2.7	45955	51519	64	56	354	29.9	33.6	25.1	7.9	3.4	74000
47598	WINSLOW	17795	1460	30.0	37.1	27.3	4.4	1.2	37050	40676	36	14	1192	33.7	35.1	25.8	5.3	0.2	70902
47601	BOONVILLE	20405	5621	25.9	32.5	31.4	8.5	1.7	42477	48127	55	36	4523	17.4	35.8	33.5	11.8	1.5	86351
47610	CHANDLER	20387	2055	21.5	34.1	36.2	7.1	1.2	45795	52010	63	55	1737	17.3	40.0	34.2	7.4	1.2	83411
	INDIANA	23565		24.7	29.6	32.4	9.4	3.9	45964	52146				12.3	23.5	44.9	16.9	2.4	109048
	UNITED STATES	25866		24.7	27.1	30.8	10.9	6.5	48124	56710				10.9	15.0	33.7	30.1	10.4	145905

ZIP CODE #	POST OFFICE NAME	FINANCIAL SERVICES: Auto Loan	FINANCIAL SERVICES: Home Loan	FINANCIAL SERVICES: Invest-ments	FINANCIAL SERVICES: Retire-ment Plans	THE HOME: Home Improvements: Home Repair	THE HOME: Home Improvements: Lawn & Garden	THE HOME: Furnishings: Comput-ers & Hard-ware	THE HOME: Furnishings: Major Appli-ances	THE HOME: Furnishings: TV, Radio, Sound Equip-ment	THE HOME: Furnishings: Furni-ture	ENTERTAINMENT: Dine out/ Carry out	ENTERTAINMENT: Sports Equip-ment	ENTERTAINMENT: Fees & Tickets	ENTERTAINMENT: Toys & Games	ENTERTAINMENT: Travel	ENTERTAINMENT: Cable TV	PERSONAL: Apparel & Services	PERSONAL: Auto Repairs	PERSONAL: Health Insur-ance	PERSONAL: Pets & Supplies
47382	SARATOGA	67	59	45	56	63	67	55	61	58	55	71	72	54	72	56	60	67	59	66	78
47383	SELMA	85	88	85	84	90	97	83	86	86	82	106	99	86	111	86	88	102	84	91	101
47384	SHIRLEY	82	70	54	69	74	82	70	76	74	69	90	87	68	90	70	76	85	74	82	92
47385	SPICELAND	84	79	65	75	82	89	74	80	78	73	95	93	74	99	76	80	91	78	86	99
47386	SPRINGPORT	103	92	70	87	97	104	85	94	90	85	110	112	83	112	87	92	104	92	102	121
47387	STRAUGHN	91	80	61	77	84	92	77	84	82	77	100	99	75	100	78	84	94	83	91	105
47390	UNION CITY	58	57	55	54	58	64	57	57	59	55	73	66	58	76	58	61	70	57	62	67
47392	WEBSTER	74	66	50	63	70	75	61	68	65	61	79	81	60	81	63	67	75	66	73	87
47393	WILLIAMSBURG	93	82	63	78	87	93	76	84	81	76	98	101	75	100	78	83	94	82	91	109
47394	WINCHESTER	72	66	57	62	69	77	65	69	69	63	84	79	64	87	66	72	80	67	76	83
47396	YORKTOWN	107	110	107	109	111	118	107	109	107	105	132	127	108	135	108	106	128	108	109	124
47401	BLOOMINGTON	88	79	90	83	79	86	93	86	91	89	114	106	88	111	87	87	110	91	82	98
47403	BLOOMINGTON	71	65	66	67	66	70	70	69	70	68	87	83	67	85	68	68	84	71	68	80
47404	BLOOMINGTON	64	61	69	63	60	64	71	64	68	67	86	79	68	84	66	64	83	68	60	71
47405	BLOOMINGTON	7	4	5	5	4	5	8	6	8	7	10	9	7	9	7	7	10	8	6	7
47406	BLOOMINGTON	22	14	17	15	13	16	26	19	26	22	32	27	22	29	21	23	30	24	18	22
47408	BLOOMINGTON	59	48	56	51	48	53	67	56	65	60	81	73	60	77	59	60	78	63	53	64
47421	BEDFORD	73	66	56	63	69	76	65	69	69	63	84	80	64	86	66	72	80	68	76	84
47424	BLOOMFIELD	78	65	48	63	69	77	65	71	69	64	84	82	61	82	65	71	79	70	78	88
47427	COAL CITY	81	54	25	47	62	71	53	66	63	53	74	79	45	70	53	68	68	65	81	93
47429	ELLETTSVILLE	86	80	67	78	83	88	76	81	78	76	96	96	75	97	77	79	92	80	84	100
47431	FREEDOM	96	64	29	56	73	84	62	78	75	63	88	93	53	83	63	81	80	77	96	110
47432	FRENCH LICK	70	60	47	57	64	71	58	64	63	58	76	75	57	77	60	65	72	63	71	81
47433	GOSPORT	90	75	54	71	81	88	70	80	77	71	92	96	67	93	72	79	87	79	89	106
47436	HELTONVILLE	93	84	65	80	88	94	77	85	82	77	99	102	76	102	80	84	95	83	92	110
47438	JASONVILLE	66	49	28	44	54	61	47	56	54	47	64	66	42	62	48	57	59	55	66	76
47441	LINTON	72	56	39	53	61	71	58	65	65	56	77	75	53	75	59	68	71	64	76	81
47443	LYONS	72	52	30	49	59	67	54	63	61	52	72	74	47	69	54	64	65	62	75	83
47446	MITCHELL	71	60	45	56	63	70	58	64	63	58	77	75	56	77	59	66	72	63	72	82
47448	NASHVILLE	95	83	64	80	88	97	80	88	85	79	103	103	77	104	82	87	97	86	96	111
47449	NEWBERRY	85	57	26	49	65	74	55	69	66	56	78	82	47	74	56	72	71	68	85	98
47451	OOLITIC	57	59	59	56	60	67	58	58	60	56	74	66	60	80	60	62	72	57	63	67
47452	ORLEANS	80	60	36	53	66	74	57	68	66	58	79	80	52	77	59	71	73	67	81	92
47453	OWENSBURG	83	63	37	57	69	77	59	70	68	60	81	84	54	79	61	71	75	69	82	96
47454	PAOLI	77	58	35	52	63	72	56	66	64	56	77	77	51	75	57	68	71	65	77	88
47456	QUINCY	82	72	53	68	76	82	66	74	71	66	86	88	65	88	68	73	82	72	81	96
47459	SOLSBERRY	78	71	56	68	71	75	68	73	69	70	85	84	64	80	67	68	81	72	72	86
47460	SPENCER	82	69	50	66	74	81	66	74	72	66	87	87	63	87	68	74	81	73	82	95
47462	SPRINGVILLE	90	81	63	77	85	91	75	83	79	74	96	98	73	98	77	81	91	80	89	106
47465	SWITZ CITY	78	67	49	64	72	78	63	71	68	63	82	84	61	83	65	70	78	69	78	92
47468	UNIONVILLE	99	88	71	84	92	100	85	93	89	84	108	109	80	107	86	90	102	92	99	115
47469	WEST BADEN SPRINGS	102	72	38	64	80	91	69	84	81	70	96	100	61	92	70	87	88	83	101	117
47470	WILLIAMS	90	68	42	63	74	84	67	78	76	67	91	91	61	88	68	79	84	77	90	102
47471	WORTHINGTON	81	62	41	59	68	79	65	73	73	63	86	84	59	83	65	76	79	73	86	92
47501	WASHINGTON	71	62	53	60	65	73	64	68	68	62	83	78	62	83	64	70	78	67	75	81
47512	BICKNELL	58	48	41	47	51	58	52	54	56	50	67	63	49	67	52	57	64	55	61	65
47513	BIRDSEYE	87	65	38	58	72	80	62	74	71	62	84	88	56	82	63	75	78	72	87	101
47514	BRANCHVILLE	89	79	60	75	84	90	73	81	78	73	94	97	72	96	75	80	90	79	88	105
47515	BRISTOW	80	71	54	68	75	81	66	73	70	66	85	87	65	87	68	72	81	71	79	94
47516	BRUCEVILLE	81	57	30	54	66	74	56	69	65	55	76	83	48	74	58	68	69	68	82	96
47519	CANNELBURG	82	56	28	51	65	73	55	68	64	55	75	82	47	73	56	68	69	67	82	96
47520	CANNELTON	75	57	35	53	62	70	56	65	63	56	75	76	51	73	57	66	70	64	75	86
47521	CELESTINE	92	82	62	78	86	93	76	84	80	76	98	100	74	100	78	82	93	82	91	108
47522	CRANE	84	75	57	71	79	85	69	76	73	69	89	91	68	91	71	75	85	74	83	99
47523	DALE	79	69	53	67	72	80	68	73	72	67	88	85	66	88	68	74	82	72	80	90
47524	DECKER	80	56	29	53	65	73	55	68	64	54	75	82	47	73	57	67	68	67	81	95
47525	DERBY	78	69	53	66	73	78	64	71	68	64	82	84	63	84	66	70	78	69	77	91
47527	DUBOIS	79	70	54	67	74	80	65	72	69	65	84	86	64	86	67	71	80	70	78	93
47528	EDWARDSPORT	72	61	47	61	64	72	63	67	67	62	81	77	60	80	62	68	76	66	73	79
47529	ELNORA	79	60	37	56	66	75	60	70	68	59	80	82	54	78	61	71	74	69	82	91
47531	EVANSTON	91	81	62	77	86	92	75	83	80	75	97	99	74	99	77	82	92	81	90	108
47532	FERDINAND	94	83	64	80	88	95	78	86	83	78	101	102	76	103	80	85	96	84	93	110
47537	GENTRYVILLE	80	71	54	68	75	81	66	73	70	66	85	87	65	87	68	72	81	71	79	94
47541	HOLLAND	91	78	60	77	82	91	78	84	83	77	101	97	75	101	78	85	95	83	91	101
47542	HUNTINGBURG	88	73	55	70	78	86	72	79	78	72	94	94	68	94	73	80	89	78	88	101
47546	JASPER	98	92	79	90	95	102	89	94	92	88	112	109	88	114	90	92	107	92	98	112
47550	LAMAR	92	82	62	78	86	93	76	84	80	76	98	100	74	100	78	82	93	82	91	108
47551	LEOPOLD	81	72	55	69	77	82	67	74	71	67	87	88	66	88	69	73	82	72	80	96
47552	LINCOLN CITY	90	107	110	107	105	106	97	97	91	96	114	113	102	120	98	89	113	94	89	108
47553	LOOGOOTEE	81	64	43	59	70	78	62	71	70	62	83	84	58	83	64	73	78	70	82	93
47556	MARIAH HILL	97	102	94	100	104	106	92	97	92	92	113	115	95	118	95	91	110	94	96	116
47557	MONROE CITY	88	63	35	60	73	81	62	76	71	61	83	91	54	82	64	74	76	74	89	104
47558	MONTGOMERY	84	70	49	66	76	82	66	75	72	66	86	90	62	87	68	74	81	73	84	99
47561	OAKTOWN	77	58	36	56	65	73	58	68	65	57	77	80	52	76	59	67	71	67	78	89
47562	ODON	83	68	48	63	74	82	65	74	72	65	87	87	61	87	67	75	81	73	85	97
47564	OTWELL	89	61	30	54	69	79	59	73	70	60	83	87	51	79	60	75	76	72	89	103
47567	PETERSBURG	74	54	32	50	60	69	55	64	63	54	74	75	49	71	55	67	68	63	77	84
47568	PLAINVILLE	81	69	53	68	73	81	69	75	73	68	89	86	66	89	69	75	84	73	81	91
47574	ROME	81	72	55	68	76	81	66	74	71	66	86	88	65	88	68	72	82	72	80	95
47575	SAINT ANTHONY	99	88	67	83	93	100	81	90	86	81	105	107	80	107	84	88	100	88	97	116
47576	SAINT CROIX	80	71	54	67	75	80	66	73	70	66	85	87	64	86	68	71	80	71	79	94
47577	SAINT MEINRAD	96	87	68	83	92	98	80	89	85	80	103	105	79	106	83	87	98	86	95	114
47578	SANDBORN	77	64	47	63	68	76	65	71	70	64	84	82	61	83	65	71	79	70	78	86
47579	SANTA CLAUS	93	111	114	110	109	109	99	100	93	99	117	117	105	124	101	91	116	96	92	112
47580	SCHNELLVILLE	89	80	61	76	84	90	74	82	78	74	95	97	72	97	76	80	90	79	88	105
47581	SHOALS	83	58	29	51	65	74	56	68	66	57	78	82	48	74	57	71	71	68	83	96
47585	STENDAL	82	73	55	69	77	83	67	75	72	67	87	89	66	89	69	73	83	73	81	96
47586	TELL CITY	70	65	55	61	68	75	63	67	67	62	82	77	63	85	65	70	78	66	74	82
47588	TROY	75	65	47	61	69	75	60	68	65	60	79	81	58	79	62	67	74	66	74	88
47590	VELPEN	88	69	44	63	75	82	65	76	73	65	87	90	60	86	66	76	81	74	87	102
47591	VINCENNES	63	58	57	57	60	67	62	62	64	60	78	72	60	78	61	65	75	63	67	72
47597	WHEATLAND	96	67	35	64	78	88	67	82	77	66	90	99	57	88	69	80	82	81	98	114
47598	WINSLOW	80	58	33	52	64	73	56	67	65	57	77	79	50	75	57	69	71	66	80	91
47601	BOONVILLE	76	72	63	70	75	81	70	74	72	69	89	85	69	91	71	74	85	72	78	89
47610	CHANDLER	79	79	70	76	80	84	73	77	74	73	91	90	74	93	74	74	88	75	78	92
	INDIANA	86	83	80	82	84	90	82	84	84	82	103	98	82	104	82	84	100	84	86	98
	UNITED STATES	100	100	100	100	100	100	100	100	100	100	100	100	100	100	100	100	100	100	100	100

INDIANA

POPULATION CHANGE

A 47611-47955

# ZIP CODE	POST OFFICE NAME	COUNTY FIPS CODE	POPULATION 2000	2004	2009	2000-2004 ANNUAL RATE % Rate	State Centile	HOUSEHOLDS 2000	2004	2009	% Annual Rate 2000-2004	2004 Average HH Size	FAMILIES 2000	2004	% Annual Rate 2000-2004
47611	CHRISNEY	147	1885	1903	1966	0.2	38	709	727	763	0.6	2.62	535	532	-0.1
47612	CYNTHIANA	129	997	996	1002	0.0	26	364	367	374	0.2	2.71	280	275	-0.4
47613	ELBERFELD	051	3615	3687	3809	0.5	48	1384	1441	1518	1.0	2.56	1064	1074	0.2
47615	GRANDVIEW	147	1792	1777	1811	-0.2	18	674	681	706	0.2	2.61	511	501	-0.5
47616	GRIFFIN	129	327	322	322	-0.4	11	134	135	137	0.2	2.39	99	96	-0.7
47619	LYNNVILLE	173	1381	1463	1559	1.4	77	572	624	680	2.1	2.34	415	436	1.2
47620	MOUNT VERNON	129	14682	14684	14837	0.0	27	5652	5762	5926	0.5	2.52	4156	4100	-0.3
47630	NEWBURGH	173	27499	30240	33131	2.3	91	9928	11193	12547	2.9	2.67	8021	8807	2.2
47631	NEW HARMONY	129	1959	1972	1991	0.2	35	794	817	840	0.7	2.29	551	543	-0.3
47633	POSEYVILLE	129	2537	2678	2781	1.3	74	944	1014	1071	1.7	2.61	697	723	0.9
47634	RICHLAND	147	2386	2536	2684	1.4	78	939	1022	1102	2.0	2.48	732	773	1.3
47635	ROCKPORT	147	5593	5780	6018	0.8	58	2133	2241	2372	1.2	2.52	1563	1592	0.4
47637	TENNYSON	173	1608	1702	1821	1.4	76	595	644	705	1.9	2.64	479	505	1.3
47638	WADESVILLE	129	3308	3329	3373	0.2	34	1180	1213	1253	0.7	2.74	935	935	0.0
47639	HAUBSTADT	051	3766	3929	4046	1.0	65	1349	1436	1507	1.5	2.73	1053	1089	0.8
47640	HAZLETON	051	1297	1282	1300	-0.3	14	496	499	515	0.1	2.57	384	376	-0.5
47647	BUCKSKIN	051	233	234	236	0.1	31	100	102	105	0.5	2.29	75	74	-0.3
47648	FORT BRANCH	051	3954	3969	4020	0.1	31	1567	1604	1654	0.6	2.47	1127	1111	-0.3
47649	FRANCISCO	051	1478	1487	1505	0.1	34	590	607	627	0.7	2.45	437	435	-0.1
47660	OAKLAND CITY	125	4811	4840	4933	0.1	34	1878	1923	1994	0.6	2.36	1295	1274	-0.4
47665	OWENSVILLE	051	3751	3842	3924	0.6	51	1409	1463	1516	0.9	2.59	1053	1058	0.1
47666	PATOKA	051	1334	1369	1407	0.6	51	547	576	604	1.2	2.38	409	418	0.5
47670	PRINCETON	051	11493	11614	11816	0.3	38	4752	4902	5083	0.7	2.30	3147	3111	-0.3
47708	EVANSVILLE	163	946	935	929	-0.3	14	231	227	227	-0.4	1.38	60	53	-2.9
47710	EVANSVILLE	163	20589	19586	19141	-1.2	1	8607	8344	8296	-0.7	2.23	5162	4766	-1.9
47711	EVANSVILLE	163	29402	30102	30402	0.6	51	12440	12950	13289	1.0	2.30	8253	8213	-0.1
47712	EVANSVILLE	163	25042	24852	24719	-0.2	19	9482	9582	9688	0.3	2.37	5969	5749	-0.9
47713	EVANSVILLE	163	12306	11344	10908	-1.9	0	5151	4826	4711	-1.5	2.27	2739	2390	-3.2
47714	EVANSVILLE	163	34924	34118	33677	-0.6	6	14835	14770	14830	-0.1	2.21	8951	8393	-1.5
47715	EVANSVILLE	163	24418	25304	25770	0.8	60	11127	11732	12141	1.3	2.14	6361	6309	-0.2
47720	EVANSVILLE	163	16846	17347	17550	0.7	54	6392	6719	6922	1.2	2.55	4869	4946	0.4
47722	EVANSVILLE	163	1008	987	979	-0.5	8	15	14	13	-1.6	2.57	5	4	-5.1
47725	EVANSVILLE	163	9344	10300	10748	2.3	92	3362	3767	3991	2.7	2.73	2875	3153	2.2
47802	TERRE HAUTE	167	31182	31692	32082	0.4	44	11972	12465	12732	1.0	2.36	7841	7800	-0.1
47803	TERRE HAUTE	167	19970	19970	19956	0.0	27	8201	8361	8414	0.5	2.28	5179	5012	-0.8
47804	TERRE HAUTE	167	11054	10746	10601	-0.7	4	4574	4521	4486	-0.3	2.27	2750	2568	-1.6
47805	TERRE HAUTE	167	12612	12688	12713	0.1	34	4952	5070	5118	0.6	2.39	3573	3510	-0.4
47807	TERRE HAUTE	167	17337	16617	16311	-1.0	2	6141	5912	5805	-0.9	2.22	2913	2621	-2.5
47809	TERRE HAUTE	167	151	150	149	-0.2	20	72	72	72	0.0	2.08	31	29	-1.6
47832	BLOOMINGDALE	121	748	761	784	0.4	46	299	308	321	0.7	2.46	222	221	-0.1
47833	BOWLING GREEN	021	1156	1206	1275	1.0	65	427	452	486	1.4	2.67	329	338	0.6
47834	BRAZIL	021	19767	20176	20628	0.5	48	7639	7915	8193	0.8	2.51	5499	5498	0.0
47836	BRIDGETON	121	722	726	744	0.1	32	272	279	291	0.6	2.60	219	219	0.0
47837	CARBON	121	949	936	949	-0.3	12	347	349	360	0.1	2.68	269	263	-0.5
47838	CARLISLE	153	4251	4311	4359	0.3	42	859	894	925	0.9	2.65	648	653	0.2
47840	CENTERPOINT	021	1640	1878	2036	3.2	96	593	691	758	3.7	2.68	456	514	2.9
47841	CLAY CITY	021	2351	2349	2375	0.0	26	961	978	1002	0.4	2.40	685	673	-0.4
47842	CLINTON	165	10635	10626	10657	0.0	26	4330	4389	4464	0.3	2.36	2928	2851	-0.6
47846	CORY	021	735	742	752	0.2	38	297	305	313	0.6	2.43	209	206	-0.4
47847	DANA	165	1154	1155	1157	0.0	28	435	441	447	0.3	2.60	329	323	-0.4
47848	DUGGER	153	1340	1438	1502	1.7	83	560	613	651	2.2	2.35	410	433	1.3
47849	FAIRBANKS	153	321	323	325	0.2	34	117	119	122	0.4	2.71	93	92	-0.3
47850	FARMERSBURG	153	2773	2799	2833	0.2	38	1069	1095	1122	0.6	2.55	797	790	-0.2
47854	HILLSDALE	165	863	841	836	-0.6	5	329	326	329	-0.2	2.55	255	246	-0.8
47858	LEWIS	021	624	623	625	0.0	24	232	236	239	0.4	2.64	183	181	-0.3
47859	MARSHALL	121	793	835	878	1.2	72	295	315	335	1.6	2.63	228	236	0.8
47861	MEROM	153	668	668	671	0.0	27	248	252	258	0.4	2.65	195	193	-0.2
47862	MONTEZUMA	121	1515	1538	1583	0.4	43	600	620	648	0.8	2.45	440	440	0.0
47866	PIMENTO	167	418	432	438	0.8	58	172	181	185	1.2	2.39	135	138	0.5
47868	POLAND	119	3429	3647	3961	1.5	79	1280	1379	1519	1.8	2.64	938	978	1.0
47872	ROCKVILLE	121	9388	9709	10079	0.8	58	3355	3537	3741	1.3	2.42	2330	2366	0.4
47874	ROSEDALE	121	3761	3766	3823	0.0	28	1461	1490	1532	0.5	2.52	1109	1094	-0.3
47879	SHELBURN	153	3935	3925	3950	-0.1	24	1533	1552	1584	0.3	2.52	1128	1104	-0.5
47882	SULLIVAN	153	8750	8824	8944	0.2	36	3528	3619	3726	0.6	2.35	2379	2341	-0.4
47885	WEST TERRE HAUTE	167	10608	10629	10630	0.1	29	3968	4056	4086	0.5	2.51	2900	2847	-0.4
47901	LAFAYETTE	157	3345	3520	3756	1.2	72	1746	1872	2033	1.7	1.85	601	587	-0.6
47904	LAFAYETTE	157	16112	15935	16697	-0.3	15	6776	6828	7285	0.2	2.25	3609	3380	-1.5
47905	LAFAYETTE	157	36232	38473	41493	1.4	77	14854	16098	17691	1.9	2.36	9535	9839	0.7
47906	WEST LAFAYETTE	157	57394	61413	66058	1.6	82	18142	20251	22662	2.6	2.34	8949	9419	1.2
47907	WEST LAFAYETTE	157	1	1	1	0.0	27	1	1	1	0.0	1.00	0	0	0.0
47909	LAFAYETTE	157	30255	32845	35986	2.0	88	11666	12856	14305	2.3	2.55	8126	8599	1.3
47917	AMBIA	171	465	479	492	0.7	54	184	194	204	1.3	2.47	143	146	0.5
47918	ATTICA	045	6702	6786	6883	0.3	40	2597	2660	2732	0.6	2.53	1852	1834	-0.2
47920	BATTLE GROUND	157	2041	2106	2222	0.7	56	774	819	882	1.3	2.55	588	600	0.5
47921	BOSWELL	007	1160	1151	1145	-0.2	19	457	460	463	0.2	2.50	324	313	-0.8
47922	BROOK	111	1742	1875	1984	1.8	85	627	687	738	2.2	2.64	461	487	1.3
47923	BROOKSTON	181	3599	3676	3820	0.5	49	1379	1434	1511	0.9	2.56	1078	1089	0.2
47926	BURNETTSVILLE	181	1115	1104	1142	-0.2	16	413	417	437	0.2	2.65	319	313	-0.5
47928	CAYUGA	165	2593	2558	2551	-0.3	12	1047	1055	1070	0.2	2.40	744	721	-0.7
47929	CHALMERS	181	857	860	891	0.1	30	309	313	327	0.3	2.75	241	237	-0.4
47930	CLARKS HILL	157	1375	1428	1512	0.9	62	484	510	547	1.2	2.80	374	378	0.3
47932	COVINGTON	045	5609	5599	5591	0.0	24	2227	2266	2299	0.4	2.42	1608	1582	-0.4
47933	CRAWFORDSVILLE	107	26869	27442	28012	0.5	49	10496	10869	11217	0.8	2.42	7158	7125	-0.1
47940	DARLINGTON	107	2037	2067	2086	0.3	42	755	775	789	0.6	2.67	583	581	-0.1
47942	EARL PARK	007	907	909	902	0.1	29	321	329	332	0.6	2.61	232	230	-0.2
47943	FAIR OAKS	073	796	832	887	1.1	67	279	297	321	1.5	2.80	231	240	0.9
47944	FOWLER	007	3819	3756	3698	-0.4	10	1453	1452	1452	0.0	2.51	1017	979	-0.9
47946	FRANCESVILLE	131	1998	2056	2139	0.7	53	731	763	806	1.0	2.62	546	552	0.3
47948	GOODLAND	111	1513	1565	1623	0.8	59	575	601	631	1.1	2.60	422	427	0.3
47949	HILLSBORO	045	1318	1319	1308	0.0	28	504	514	518	0.5	2.57	380	375	-0.3
47950	IDAVILLE	181	833	855	894	0.6	52	334	350	372	1.1	2.44	246	249	0.3
47951	KENTLAND	111	2325	2300	2340	-0.3	16	935	941	973	0.2	2.40	637	613	-0.9
47952	KINGMAN	045	3085	3103	3107	0.1	34	1196	1219	1236	0.5	2.55	865	851	-0.4
47954	LADOGA	107	2454	2493	2531	0.4	43	900	927	951	0.7	2.63	695	694	-0.1
47955	LINDEN	107	1076	1109	1130	0.7	55	438	459	473	1.1	2.42	310	312	0.2
	INDIANA					0.8					1.2	2.48			0.3
	UNITED STATES					1.2					1.3	2.58			1.1

ZIP CODE #	POST OFFICE NAME	RACE (%) White 2000	White 2004	Black 2000	Black 2004	Asian/Pacific 2000	Asian/Pacific 2004	% Hispanic Origin 2000	% Hispanic Origin 2004	2004 AGE DISTRIBUTION (%) 0-4	5-9	10-14	15-19	20-24	25-44	45-64	65-84	85+	18+	MEDIAN AGE 2004	% 2004 Males	% 2004 Females
47611	CHRISNEY	98.5	98.4	0.2	0.2	0.1	0.1	0.9	1.1	6.6	7.1	7.8	6.3	5.6	27.2	26.5	11.7	1.3	74.5	38.4	50.1	49.9
47612	CYNTHIANA	98.9	98.8	0.0	0.0	0.2	0.3	0.3	0.3	7.2	7.3	8.0	7.0	5.6	26.9	25.1	11.5	1.3	73.1	37.7	48.9	51.1
47613	ELBERFELD	99.3	99.2	0.1	0.1	0.1	0.1	0.3	0.3	5.7	6.4	7.5	6.7	5.3	27.5	27.2	12.4	1.4	76.2	39.7	50.5	49.5
47615	GRANDVIEW	98.1	97.9	0.9	1.0	0.2	0.3	0.4	0.5	6.1	6.6	8.1	6.5	5.9	28.9	25.4	11.7	0.8	75.3	38.3	51.0	49.0
47616	GRIFFIN	99.1	99.4	0.0	0.0	0.3	0.3	0.0	0.0	5.6	6.2	6.5	6.2	4.7	24.5	29.5	15.2	1.6	78.0	42.9	51.2	48.8
47619	LYNNVILLE	99.3	99.2	0.0	0.0	0.1	0.1	0.0	0.0	6.0	6.1	5.3	5.3	5.4	28.6	29.7	12.1	1.4	79.5	40.9	50.7	49.3
47620	MOUNT VERNON	97.2	96.9	1.5	1.6	0.2	0.2	0.6	0.7	6.6	6.8	7.5	7.2	6.1	27.0	26.5	10.9	1.4	74.7	38.2	49.6	50.4
47630	NEWBURGH	96.2	95.8	1.6	1.7	1.1	1.4	0.9	1.0	6.9	7.3	8.0	6.7	5.6	27.0	28.1	8.9	1.4	73.5	38.1	48.8	51.2
47631	NEW HARMONY	98.8	98.7	0.1	0.1	0.2	0.2	0.3	0.4	5.2	5.5	6.4	6.3	5.0	22.9	28.6	16.4	3.6	78.5	44.0	48.1	51.9
47633	POSEYVILLE	99.1	99.1	0.1	0.1	0.0	0.1	0.1	0.1	6.1	6.8	8.6	7.2	5.4	25.4	24.4	14.2	2.1	73.6	39.8	50.3	49.7
47634	RICHLAND	98.5	98.3	0.2	0.2	0.1	0.1	0.7	0.9	6.0	6.3	7.2	6.2	5.8	28.1	27.5	11.7	1.2	76.7	39.1	50.2	49.8
47635	ROCKPORT	97.3	97.1	1.3	1.5	0.2	0.2	0.7	0.8	6.3	6.6	7.2	6.1	5.4	26.7	27.2	12.5	2.0	75.9	39.9	49.4	50.6
47637	TENNYSON	99.3	99.2	0.1	0.1	0.1	0.1	0.4	0.4	6.4	6.4	7.3	6.8	7.3	27.7	27.7	9.8	0.7	75.9	38.1	50.0	50.0
47638	WADESVILLE	98.8	98.6	0.2	0.2	0.2	0.2	0.3	0.5	6.5	6.9	8.1	7.3	5.7	27.7	27.9	9.1	0.8	73.7	38.1	50.2	49.8
47639	HAUBSTADT	99.5	99.4	0.1	0.1	0.2	0.2	0.3	0.3	7.2	7.4	7.7	7.1	5.8	27.1	25.5	10.7	1.4	72.7	37.7	50.6	49.4
47640	HAZLETON	98.2	98.1	0.6	0.6	0.2	0.2	0.2	0.2	5.5	6.2	7.3	6.2	6.1	26.2	28.9	12.2	1.5	77.3	40.5	50.3	49.7
47647	BUCKSKIN	98.7	98.7	0.4	0.4	0.0	0.0	0.9	0.9	7.3	7.3	6.8	5.1	4.3	28.6	25.6	12.4	2.6	75.2	38.4	50.4	49.6
47648	FORT BRANCH	98.9	98.8	0.3	0.3	0.2	0.3	0.5	0.6	6.4	6.8	7.4	6.0	5.7	28.1	25.7	12.5	1.5	75.7	38.8	49.3	50.7
47649	FRANCISCO	98.4	98.2	0.8	0.9	0.1	0.1	0.3	0.3	5.2	5.6	6.1	5.7	6.3	27.5	28.7	13.6	1.3	79.7	41.0	50.0	50.0
47660	OAKLAND CITY	98.3	98.1	0.4	0.5	0.3	0.4	1.1	1.2	5.7	5.7	6.3	7.8	8.0	24.8	23.9	14.8	3.0	78.4	39.2	48.4	51.6
47665	OWENSVILLE	98.5	98.4	0.5	0.6	0.1	0.2	0.9	1.0	6.5	6.7	7.2	7.1	6.6	26.5	25.1	12.0	2.3	75.1	38.5	49.7	50.3
47666	PATOKA	96.1	95.7	2.9	3.1	0.3	0.4	0.3	0.3	6.5	6.7	6.2	5.6	5.8	25.9	30.0	11.8	1.5	77.2	40.8	51.2	48.8
47670	PRINCETON	92.7	91.9	4.4	4.8	1.1	1.5	0.9	1.1	6.8	6.3	6.4	5.5	6.7	26.4	24.5	14.6	2.9	77.2	39.5	48.2	51.8
47708	EVANSVILLE	73.2	71.0	24.0	26.1	0.7	0.8	1.6	1.6	0.9	1.3	0.9	2.7	6.4	38.7	21.3	19.4	8.6	96.6	44.6	61.3	38.7
47710	EVANSVILLE	93.5	93.1	4.5	4.8	0.5	0.5	0.9	0.9	6.1	5.9	6.5	6.0	6.3	26.2	24.2	15.8	3.1	77.8	40.3	47.4	52.6
47711	EVANSVILLE	95.2	95.0	2.5	2.7	0.7	0.7	1.0	1.0	6.5	6.3	6.7	5.9	5.9	28.1	25.6	13.1	2.0	77.0	39.2	48.0	52.0
47712	EVANSVILLE	97.0	96.8	1.4	1.5	0.6	0.6	0.7	0.7	5.1	5.3	5.8	11.1	11.3	26.2	22.6	10.8	1.9	80.3	33.7	48.0	52.0
47713	EVANSVILLE	47.0	45.0	49.7	51.8	0.3	0.3	1.2	1.2	7.3	6.8	7.5	7.2	7.1	27.2	22.7	11.7	2.5	74.1	35.5	47.2	52.8
47714	EVANSVILLE	85.7	84.5	11.3	12.5	0.6	0.6	1.2	1.2	6.8	6.4	6.0	6.3	8.2	28.8	22.3	12.5	2.6	77.3	35.8	46.5	53.5
47715	EVANSVILLE	89.6	89.1	6.4	6.9	1.8	1.8	1.4	1.4	6.2	5.9	6.0	6.6	7.8	27.0	24.6	13.6	2.4	78.1	37.8	47.2	52.8
47720	EVANSVILLE	98.3	98.3	0.5	0.6	0.3	0.2	0.4	0.5	6.3	6.6	7.1	6.8	5.5	26.2	27.0	12.9	1.7	75.6	39.9	48.9	51.1
47722	EVANSVILLE	91.4	91.1	3.0	3.2	3.9	3.8	1.7	1.7	0.4	0.5	0.3	36.1	52.2	5.7	2.5	1.7	0.6	98.1	21.2	33.9	66.1
47725	EVANSVILLE	97.2	97.1	1.0	1.1	1.1	1.1	0.6	0.6	6.0	6.8	7.8	6.6	4.1	25.7	30.2	11.8	1.0	75.1	41.1	50.4	49.6
47802	TERRE HAUTE	89.0	88.1	6.6	6.9	2.0	2.5	1.7	1.9	6.5	6.0	6.1	5.8	7.8	28.8	24.6	12.2	2.2	78.0	37.5	50.6	49.4
47803	TERRE HAUTE	93.5	92.7	4.1	4.5	0.9	1.2	1.1	1.3	5.8	5.9	6.2	7.2	7.6	25.7	25.6	13.8	2.3	78.6	38.9	48.9	51.1
47804	TERRE HAUTE	92.8	92.1	5.1	5.7	0.3	0.3	0.9	1.1	6.2	6.1	6.8	6.2	6.7	25.6	23.2	15.3	3.9	77.2	39.1	46.1	53.9
47805	TERRE HAUTE	96.8	96.3	1.7	2.0	0.4	0.5	0.8	0.9	6.2	6.2	6.7	8.5	7.4	26.2	25.7	11.9	1.2	76.4	37.2	50.3	49.7
47807	TERRE HAUTE	78.6	76.1	15.3	16.9	2.3	2.9	1.5	1.8	6.0	5.4	5.6	14.2	23.3	23.7	13.4	7.3	1.2	80.1	24.0	49.1	50.9
47809	TERRE HAUTE	73.5	70.0	19.2	21.3	2.0	2.7	2.7	2.0	8.7	7.3	5.3	7.3	23.3	26.7	16.0	4.7	0.7	76.0	24.6	51.3	48.7
47832	BLOOMINGDALE	98.8	98.6	0.4	0.4	0.1	0.1	0.4	0.5	7.2	7.4	8.3	7.4	6.7	26.7	24.3	10.5	1.6	72.7	35.8	51.0	49.0
47833	BOWLING GREEN	98.2	98.1	0.1	0.1	0.2	0.2	1.0	1.2	6.8	7.0	8.0	7.5	6.7	26.1	27.0	9.9	1.1	73.6	37.3	50.8	49.2
47834	BRAZIL	98.3	98.1	0.4	0.5	0.1	0.2	0.6	0.7	6.6	6.7	7.1	6.6	6.4	26.7	24.9	12.8	2.1	75.5	38.1	48.7	51.3
47836	BRIDGETON	98.8	98.6	0.1	0.1	0.4	0.6	0.4	0.6	5.0	5.4	6.3	7.6	5.5	27.1	30.9	11.0	1.2	78.8	41.2	50.0	50.0
47837	CARBON	98.7	98.6	0.3	0.4	0.0	0.0	0.6	0.9	6.5	6.8	7.6	6.4	6.2	27.7	26.5	11.1	1.2	75.1	38.3	49.4	50.6
47838	CARLISLE	77.2	75.5	19.9	21.3	0.1	0.1	1.6	1.8	3.5	3.5	3.8	4.9	11.5	43.7	21.4	6.9	0.8	86.7	35.3	72.4	27.6
47840	CENTERPOINT	98.3	98.1	0.1	0.1	0.1	0.2	0.5	0.5	7.6	7.7	6.6	6.9	5.6	27.0	24.7	11.7	2.2	73.3	37.7	49.2	50.9
47841	CLAY CITY	98.9	98.8	0.0	0.0	0.0	0.0	0.6	0.8	6.2	6.2	6.6	6.1	5.6	26.2	24.9	15.8	2.5	77.4	40.1	48.5	51.6
47842	CLINTON	98.3	98.3	0.3	0.3	0.1	0.1	0.7	0.7	6.4	6.4	6.5	5.8	5.7	27.0	26.1	13.4	2.8	77.2	39.7	48.1	51.9
47846	CORY	99.5	99.3	0.0	0.0	0.4	0.5	0.3	0.3	5.9	6.1	7.1	6.7	6.7	28.3	25.7	10.9	2.4	76.8	37.9	50.3	49.7
47847	DANA	98.0	98.1	0.4	0.4	0.3	0.3	1.1	1.2	6.9	7.1	7.5	7.1	5.4	26.3	27.0	11.3	1.5	73.9	38.0	50.1	49.9
47848	DUGGER	98.9	98.8	0.0	0.0	0.2	0.3	0.8	1.0	5.2	5.6	6.4	6.6	5.6	27.3	28.1	13.8	1.5	78.9	40.7	49.9	50.1
47849	FAIRBANKS	99.4	99.4	0.0	0.0	0.0	0.0	0.6	0.6	5.6	6.5	8.4	5.9	5.0	27.6	26.6	13.0	1.6	75.9	39.9	52.0	48.0
47850	FARMERSBURG	98.2	98.0	0.1	0.1	0.2	0.3	0.7	0.9	6.6	6.8	7.4	6.0	6.1	26.4	26.0	13.1	1.7	75.4	38.8	50.3	49.7
47854	HILLSDALE	98.6	98.7	0.1	0.1	0.2	0.2	0.4	0.5	5.5	6.0	7.0	6.8	5.1	26.6	29.9	11.9	1.3	77.3	41.2	50.7	49.4
47858	LEWIS	98.9	98.7	0.2	0.2	0.3	0.5	0.8	1.0	5.9	6.1	6.4	5.8	5.9	27.0	27.6	13.6	1.6	78.2	40.6	49.9	50.1
47859	MARSHALL	98.6	98.3	0.4	0.4	0.1	0.1	0.3	0.5	6.2	6.5	7.2	7.7	5.8	25.9	27.9	11.3	1.7	75.2	38.9	51.9	48.1
47861	MEROM	99.3	99.3	0.2	0.2	0.0	0.0	0.2	0.3	6.0	6.1	6.7	6.4	7.0	27.4	27.5	11.5	1.2	77.5	39.4	50.9	49.1
47862	MONTEZUMA	96.4	96.4	1.9	2.0	0.1	0.1	0.8	0.9	7.0	6.8	6.8	6.7	6.8	26.2	26.3	11.8	1.7	75.2	37.5	50.3	49.7
47866	PIMENTO	98.3	98.4	0.2	0.2	0.7	0.9	1.0	0.9	5.8	5.8	5.3	5.6	5.6	25.9	30.3	14.1	1.6	79.6	42.5	49.1	50.9
47868	POLAND	97.5	97.3	0.5	0.5	0.1	0.1	0.7	0.8	6.3	6.5	7.3	7.7	6.5	26.8	27.7	10.3	1.0	75.3	38.5	51.3	48.7
47872	ROCKVILLE	94.7	94.3	3.5	3.7	0.2	0.3	0.8	0.9	5.2	5.4	6.2	6.1	5.9	27.7	27.0	14.5	2.0	79.3	41.0	45.9	54.2
47874	ROSEDALE	98.9	98.7	0.4	0.4	0.2	0.3	0.4	0.4	5.7	6.0	7.4	7.1	6.5	27.4	27.0	11.8	1.2	76.4	39.1	49.1	50.9
47879	SHELBURN	98.5	98.3	0.2	0.2	0.1	0.1	0.4	0.4	7.5	6.9	6.7	5.8	6.8	27.2	26.7	11.0	1.5	75.3	37.1	50.7	49.4
47882	SULLIVAN	97.9	97.7	0.8	0.8	0.2	0.3	0.7	0.9	5.9	5.9	6.4	6.2	6.3	25.8	25.8	14.9	2.8	78.0	40.5	48.0	52.0
47885	WEST TERRE HAUTE	98.7	98.5	0.1	0.1	0.3	0.4	0.5	0.6	6.0	6.1	7.1	6.9	6.8	26.3	25.9	12.8	2.2	76.8	38.8	47.4	52.6
47901	LAFAYETTE	86.8	85.2	4.6	4.9	1.6	2.2	9.4	11.1	5.5	4.5	5.5	5.9	15.1	37.7	18.1	6.7	1.0	81.8	29.4	54.1	45.9
47904	LAFAYETTE	89.6	88.1	3.2	3.5	1.1	1.4	8.0	9.4	6.4	6.0	6.0	5.8	9.3	33.3	19.8	11.1	2.4	78.6	33.3	50.4	49.6
47905	LAFAYETTE	91.2	89.8	2.3	2.5	1.6	2.1	6.8	8.0	6.7	6.6	6.9	6.2	7.0	30.9	24.3	9.9	1.5	76.1	35.1	49.8	50.2
47906	WEST LAFAYETTE	84.8	82.2	2.5	2.6	9.9	12.1	3.1	3.6	3.8	3.6	4.0	19.5	26.0	21.9	13.7	6.2	1.3	86.2	23.7	53.6	46.4
47907	WEST LAFAYETTE	100.0	100.0	0.0	0.0	0.0	0.0	0.0	0.0	0.0	0.0	0.0	0.0	100.0	0.0	0.0	0.0	0.0	100.0	22.5	100.0	0.0
47909	LAFAYETTE	91.9	90.8	2.6	2.8	0.8	1.0	6.5	7.6	8.6	7.8	7.5	6.6	8.1	32.8	20.4	7.6	0.7	72.2	31.4	49.3	50.7
47917	AMBIA	94.8	94.4	0.2	0.2	0.0	0.0	6.9	7.7	6.1	6.3	7.5	6.3	5.4	24.2	29.9	12.9	1.5	76.4	40.7	51.4	48.6
47918	ATTICA	98.3	98.2	0.1	0.1	0.2	0.3	1.1	1.2	6.9	7.3	7.8	6.6	5.6	26.9	24.0	12.7	2.2	73.8	37.9	50.2	49.8
47920	BATTLE GROUND	97.3	96.9	0.4	0.5	0.2	0.2	1.6	2.0	5.9	7.2	8.1	6.7	4.8	28.8	28.3	9.5	0.8	74.6	38.1	50.2	49.8
47921	BOSWELL	93.6	92.6	0.2	0.2	0.2	0.3	7.5	9.0	7.6	6.8	6.6	7.2	6.5	25.6	22.3	14.6	2.8	74.6	37.2	48.1	52.0
47922	BROOK	96.3	95.8	0.2	0.2	0.3	0.4	5.5	6.3	6.5	6.8	7.2	6.5	5.9	25.6	24.5	13.7	3.5	75.3	39.5	48.0	52.0
47923	BROOKSTON	98.6	98.5	0.1	0.1	0.3	0.4	1.1	1.3	6.9	7.4	8.1	6.5	5.3	28.4	26.9	9.5	1.1	73.6	37.5	49.5	50.5
47926	BURNETTSVILLE	98.9	98.6	0.0	0.0	0.0	0.0	1.3	1.5	5.8	6.5	7.7	6.3	5.8	27.1	28.3	11.6	1.0	76.1	39.1	51.5	48.5
47928	CAYUGA	98.5	98.4	0.2	0.2	0.2	0.2	0.7	0.7	6.0	6.0	6.3	6.7	6.3	26.2	26.9	13.8	1.9	77.7	40.2	50.8	49.2
47929	CHALMERS	98.5	98.6	0.0	0.0	0.0	0.0	1.1	1.3	7.2	7.7	7.9	5.6	5.5	29.8	24.5	10.8	1.1	73.8	37.6	49.1	50.9
47930	CLARKS HILL	97.8	97.5	0.3	0.3	0.4	0.6	1.5	1.8	8.4	8.8	9.4	6.8	6.0	28.2	23.5	8.3	0.8	69.3	34.0	48.7	51.3
47932	COVINGTON	98.7	98.5	0.3	0.3	0.3	0.4	0.5	0.6	5.8	6.1	6.4	6.7	5.9	25.2	27.5	14.2	2.3	77.5	41.0	49.8	50.2
47933	CRAWFORDSVILLE	95.9	95.4	1.0	1.1	0.6	0.8	2.1	2.5	6.6	6.6	7.2	7.1	7.3	26.4	24.2	12.5	2.0	75.7	37.4	49.9	50.1
47940	DARLINGTON	99.2	98.9	0.1	0.1	0.2	0.2	0.4	0.6	7.5	8.0	9.2	6.1	4.3	28.4	24.7	10.5	1.5	71.4	37.3	49.7	50.3
47942	EARL PARK	98.0	97.7	0.1	0.1	0.1	0.1	2.2	2.8	6.7	6.9	7.8	7.0	5.7	26.8	22.6	12.8	3.6	74.2	37.6	49.7	50.3
47943	FAIR OAKS	97.6	97.5	0.6	0.6	0.3	0.2	3.5	4.1	8.3	8.2	7.7	6.6	6.1	27.4	26.2	8.7	0.8	71.6	35.3	51.0	49.0
47944	FOWLER	97.3	97.0	0.3	0.4	0.1	0.1	2.0	2.4	6.8	7.4	7.8	7.3	5.9	25.0	24.3	13.2	2.4	73.2	38.1	50.5	49.5
47946	FRANCESVILLE	98.5	98.4	0.1	0.1	0.2	0.2	1.3	1.6	6.8	7.4	8.4	6.4	5.1	24.8	23.2	14.8	3.2	72.9	39.2	49.9	50.2
47948	GOODLAND	97.6	97.3	0.1	0.1	0.1	0.2	3.3	3.8	7.0	7.3	7.6	6.8	6.7	27.6	23.5	11.8	1.7	73.8	36.9	49.1	50.9
47949	HILLSBORO	99.3	99.4	0.0	0.0	0.2	0.2	0.4	0.5	6.8	7.1	8.4	6.7	5.5	27.4	23.9	12.7	1.7	73.6	37.8	49.7	50.3
47950	IDAVILLE	98.4	98.3	0.1	0.1	0.2	0.4	0.8	1.1	6.6	6.9	7.4	6.3	5.7	27.4	25.9	12.8	1.2	75.3	38.5	50.9	49.1
47951	KENTLAND	98.2	98.0	0.2	0.2	0.3	0.3	2.9	3.4	5.4	5.7	7.4	6.4	7.1	24.6	27.1	14.2	2.3	77.8	41.1	49.3	50.7
47952	KINGMAN	99.2	99.1	0.0	0.0	0.1	0.1	0.5	0.6	6.3	6.5	8.3	7.0	6.2	26.5	24.6	13.4	1.4	74.4	38.5	52.4	47.6
47954	LADOGA	99.2	99.0	0.1	0.1	0.2	0.3	0.5	0.5	7.1	7.3	7.7	7.0	5.3	27.2	24.8	11.1	2.5	73.5	38.1	50.6	49.4
47955	LINDEN	98.1	98.0	0.5	0.5	0.1	0.1	0.7	0.8	6.2	6.3	7.1	7.2	6.1	27.0	26.4	12.3	1.4	76.0	39.2	50.4	49.6
	INDIANA	87.5	86.7	8.4	8.7	1.0	1.3	3.5	4.1	7.0	6.9	7.1	7.1	7.4	28.1	24.0	10.8	1.6	75.0	35.9	49.2	50.8
	UNITED STATES	75.1	73.6	12.3	12.5	3.8	4.2	12.5	14.1	6.9	6.7	7.2	7.0	7.3	28.6	23.8	10.8	1.7	75.1	36.0	49.1	50.9

ZIP CODE #	POST OFFICE NAME	2004 Per Capita Income	2004 HH Income Base	2004 Household Income Distribution (%) Less than $25,000	$25,000 to $49,999	$50,000 to $99,999	$100,000 to $149,999	$150,000 or More	Median Household Income 2004	2009	2004 National Centile	2004 State Centile	2004 Home Value Base	2004 Home Value Distribution (%) Less than $50,000	$50,000 to $89,999	$90,000 to $174,999	$175,000 to $399,999	$400,000 or More	2004 Median Home Value
47611	CHRISNEY	20144	727	22.0	32.6	36.7	7.3	1.4	45315	50858	62	52	616	17.2	26.6	37.5	15.6	3.1	96441
47612	CYNTHIANA	18510	367	23.7	37.9	33.8	3.5	1.1	42341	48420	54	35	306	30.4	31.4	34.3	3.9	0.0	72727
47613	ELBERFELD	20564	1441	19.4	39.1	32.9	6.9	1.7	45343	50366	62	52	1233	16.0	32.4	36.9	14.0	0.7	91614
47615	GRANDVIEW	19305	681	25.1	33.2	33.5	7.2	1.0	42794	47367	55	38	567	21.2	28.0	37.7	11.3	1.8	90865
47616	GRIFFIN	19615	135	23.0	36.3	35.6	5.2	0.0	42343	49654	54	36	115	35.7	39.1	21.7	3.5	0.0	66538
47619	LYNNVILLE	21900	624	20.5	37.2	34.3	7.2	0.8	44792	50610	61	48	528	23.1	33.9	33.0	9.5	0.6	82128
47620	MOUNT VERNON	22495	5762	26.1	26.4	35.0	10.2	2.4	47107	53332	66	62	4558	14.8	27.5	45.4	11.6	0.7	98886
47630	NEWBURGH	29441	11193	13.6	22.6	40.7	16.2	6.9	63681	71207	88	95	9421	4.2	8.6	55.4	28.3	3.5	145675
47631	NEW HARMONY	21227	817	31.1	30.7	29.6	5.9	2.7	40554	46005	48	27	641	22.8	28.2	38.5	8.6	1.9	88088
47633	POSEYVILLE	21031	1014	22.7	29.7	36.5	8.5	2.7	47647	53872	68	65	854	22.7	38.1	32.2	6.8	0.2	78676
47634	RICHLAND	19945	1022	22.4	36.2	34.2	6.8	0.5	43941	49370	58	43	870	19.4	27.9	41.4	10.8	0.5	93151
47635	ROCKPORT	19221	2241	28.9	31.5	30.5	8.0	1.2	40942	45701	49	28	1847	14.9	32.3	42.1	10.4	0.3	93084
47637	TENNYSON	19129	644	20.2	35.3	38.8	5.0	0.8	45660	51188	63	55	545	22.6	32.3	35.6	8.1	1.5	82838
47638	WADESVILLE	23140	1213	15.8	27.5	41.6	12.0	3.1	55669	62638	80	87	1061	4.9	16.1	61.6	16.0	1.3	118938
47639	HAUBSTADT	24633	1436	17.0	26.3	42.6	10.7	3.4	55944	61669	81	88	1247	6.1	14.2	52.5	26.2	1.0	127747
47640	HAZLETON	18218	499	29.7	34.3	30.1	5.0	1.0	38334	42990	41	17	445	39.8	24.7	30.6	4.9	0.0	68939
47647	BUCKSKIN	20250	102	25.5	36.3	32.4	5.9	0.0	40000	44773	46	24	84	33.3	21.4	28.6	14.3	2.4	76667
47648	FORT BRANCH	22809	1604	20.0	31.4	37.2	8.9	2.6	48573	53093	69	69	1287	11.9	28.0	47.3	12.7	0.1	100637
47649	FRANCISCO	22395	607	19.8	32.5	39.0	6.6	2.1	48398	53471	69	68	527	25.1	32.5	34.7	7.8	0.0	83305
47660	OAKLAND CITY	17823	1923	32.2	35.7	25.9	5.7	0.5	36265	40227	33	12	1462	28.7	36.7	29.1	5.5	0.0	71136
47665	OWENSVILLE	19825	1463	23.0	32.1	36.2	7.4	1.4	45030	50055	61	50	1223	26.3	31.4	34.8	6.1	1.4	79056
47666	PATOKA	23983	576	29.9	31.3	30.9	5.2	2.8	40469	44479	48	26	489	36.6	22.9	32.5	6.5	1.4	68026
47670	PRINCETON	19595	4902	37.3	31.3	24.2	6.3	0.9	34177	38010	25	8	3414	26.6	36.0	31.8	5.0	0.6	73618
47708	EVANSVILLE	16830	227	56.0	22.9	11.5	6.2	3.5	18164	20591	1	1	31	0.0	0.0	100.0	0.0	0.0	157386
47710	EVANSVILLE	19490	8344	39.2	31.5	22.4	5.1	1.9	32222	36648	18	6	5030	24.5	40.7	27.5	6.7	0.6	75941
47711	EVANSVILLE	25036	12950	27.6	32.1	29.4	8.0	2.9	41533	47430	51	31	9707	14.7	38.8	35.7	10.0	0.8	85908
47712	EVANSVILLE	23469	9582	28.4	28.6	32.2	7.2	3.6	42828	48506	56	38	6653	14.7	32.2	41.1	10.7	1.4	93658
47713	EVANSVILLE	15608	4826	50.9	29.0	15.9	2.8	1.5	24451	26859	4	2	2145	48.4	32.6	13.7	4.5	0.8	51414
47714	EVANSVILLE	20940	14770	33.2	34.9	25.2	4.8	2.0	35723	40734	30	11	8961	11.6	53.5	30.9	3.6	0.4	78843
47715	EVANSVILLE	28321	11732	25.1	30.5	31.6	7.4	5.5	44667	50032	60	47	6393	4.3	17.8	60.1	15.7	2.1	114726
47720	EVANSVILLE	26307	6719	19.3	26.2	37.5	12.2	4.8	53719	60722	78	83	6057	18.4	18.9	42.3	18.3	2.1	108338
47722	EVANSVILLE	9996	14	50.0	28.6	14.3	7.1	0.0	22500	37321	3	2	5	0.0	80.0	0.0	20.0	0.0	72500
47725	EVANSVILLE	37337	3767	8.9	18.6	42.4	17.2	13.0	75056	84668	93	98	3547	0.7	7.7	48.1	34.3	9.1	162659
47802	TERRE HAUTE	22054	12465	29.3	32.5	27.8	7.2	3.3	39691	44794	45	22	8324	14.7	31.9	38.1	13.3	2.0	93939
47803	TERRE HAUTE	25596	8361	27.1	28.6	31.1	8.3	4.9	43947	49339	58	43	6207	14.1	34.0	37.0	13.6	1.3	92064
47804	TERRE HAUTE	17012	4521	41.9	31.8	21.1	4.1	1.2	30094	33918	12	4	2871	35.9	45.2	17.9	0.9	0.1	60590
47805	TERRE HAUTE	21537	5070	27.9	30.6	31.4	8.0	2.1	43595	49431	58	41	4076	15.2	34.9	42.4	6.6	0.9	89924
47807	TERRE HAUTE	13261	5912	56.6	28.5	12.6	1.8	0.6	21357	23847	2	1	2211	57.1	31.2	9.8	1.6	0.3	46038
47809	TERRE HAUTE	10482	72	66.7	23.6	6.9	2.8	0.0	15000	15574	1	1	20	65.0	35.0	0.0	0.0	0.0	30000
47832	BLOOMINGDALE	19754	308	29.2	31.5	30.5	6.2	2.6	37352	41298	37	15	257	37.4	35.4	18.7	4.7	3.9	65893
47833	BOWLING GREEN	17909	452	26.1	38.5	28.1	6.2	1.1	40147	43910	47	25	386	27.2	16.3	34.5	17.1	4.9	102727
47834	BRAZIL	18923	7915	30.0	32.9	29.1	6.3	1.7	40051	43658	46	24	6143	20.9	33.9	36.1	8.6	0.6	84492
47836	BRIDGETON	18336	279	32.3	30.1	28.3	9.0	0.4	39051	43656	43	20	242	27.3	21.1	33.1	15.3	3.3	92353
47837	CARBON	17367	349	29.5	33.5	29.8	6.9	0.3	39890	43523	46	23	298	28.9	26.9	37.6	6.4	0.3	84138
47838	CARLISLE	15254	894	30.1	36.2	26.3	4.9	2.5	40145	43695	47	25	741	34.6	33.6	26.7	4.6	0.5	64333
47840	CENTERPOINT	20109	691	21.0	35.5	33.9	6.5	3.2	46102	50839	64	57	590	23.2	18.5	48.0	9.2	1.2	97313
47841	CLAY CITY	18740	978	29.0	41.2	24.0	4.2	1.5	37614	41598	38	16	775	24.4	34.2	37.3	3.0	1.2	80634
47842	CLINTON	21081	4389	33.5	32.3	26.4	4.9	2.9	36696	41092	34	13	3368	31.9	35.7	26.5	5.5	0.4	70028
47846	CORY	18125	305	24.9	47.5	23.0	3.6	1.0	39092	43120	43	21	259	26.6	18.2	42.5	12.7	0.0	96429
47847	DANA	21074	441	24.0	38.1	29.7	5.9	2.3	41367	46590	51	30	370	31.1	38.4	24.6	6.0	0.0	68611
47848	DUGGER	17592	613	34.8	34.1	26.8	3.9	0.5	35160	38258	28	9	519	39.1	33.7	23.5	3.5	0.2	60319
47849	FAIRBANKS	20450	119	24.4	28.6	34.5	9.2	3.4	47665	52375	68	66	103	23.3	24.3	37.9	14.6	0.0	92500
47850	FARMERSBURG	17472	1095	33.9	32.5	26.7	5.5	1.5	36535	40407	34	13	911	29.8	38.1	25.3	6.5	0.4	72135
47854	HILLSDALE	28270	326	19.9	32.5	31.9	10.4	5.2	48042	54793	68	67	281	21.4	28.5	39.9	10.3	0.0	90185
47858	LEWIS	22449	236	25.0	32.2	32.2	5.5	5.1	38730	43384	42	19	203	23.2	26.6	38.4	11.3	0.5	90455
47859	MARSHALL	19764	315	23.5	27.3	39.7	9.5	0.0	49035	52770	70	70	259	23.6	29.0	29.7	15.4	2.3	85000
47861	MEROM	19291	252	25.0	34.1	31.8	7.9	1.2	42106	45928	53	34	217	26.7	39.6	30.9	2.8	0.0	72679
47862	MONTEZUMA	16766	620	34.7	37.4	22.9	4.5	0.5	34694	39103	26	9	484	43.6	32.6	17.8	5.0	1.0	55962
47866	PIMENTO	28625	181	25.4	23.8	34.8	8.3	7.7	50433	49612	73	74	154	10.4	26.0	50.7	11.0	2.0	110577
47868	POLAND	18439	1379	26.3	36.5	29.7	6.1	1.5	40684	45066	49	27	1177	28.6	21.1	34.8	14.1	1.5	90570
47872	ROCKVILLE	19772	3537	29.9	33.8	27.9	5.9	2.5	38436	42890	41	18	2713	22.9	29.5	35.8	9.6	2.3	85932
47874	ROSEDALE	20046	1490	24.2	33.0	35.3	6.5	0.9	45080	50444	61	50	1244	24.9	34.2	34.2	5.8	0.9	78065
47879	SHELBURN	16881	1552	34.8	35.3	23.7	4.8	1.5	34589	38283	26	8	1261	37.5	32.2	25.5	4.4	0.5	63515
47882	SULLIVAN	19787	3619	34.7	33.0	24.3	6.7	1.4	35516	39307	30	11	2725	28.6	36.5	28.6	5.9	0.4	72171
47885	WEST TERRE HAUTE	18249	4056	32.8	32.3	26.7	6.6	1.7	36320	40729	33	13	3209	29.0	27.7	32.6	10.2	0.6	79434
47901	LAFAYETTE	19850	1872	50.5	28.2	16.1	3.9	1.4	24693	28101	4	2	438	9.4	34.5	41.6	12.1	2.5	97941
47904	LAFAYETTE	19594	6828	31.8	37.4	24.9	4.3	1.6	35401	41329	29	10	3745	9.0	45.1	41.8	3.9	0.2	87803
47905	LAFAYETTE	26162	16098	22.9	28.8	33.4	10.9	4.1	48491	55839	69	69	10491	6.2	13.6	58.1	19.2	2.9	127879
47906	WEST LAFAYETTE	21332	20251	39.1	23.4	22.1	9.2	6.2	34362	39722	25	8	9250	10.5	5.4	49.4	30.4	4.4	149259
47907	WEST LAFAYETTE	0	0	0.0	0.0	0.0	0.0	0.0	0	0	0	0	0	0.0	0.0	0.0	0.0	0.0	0
47909	LAFAYETTE	23394	12856	17.1	32.0	37.7	10.7	2.5	50616	58605	73	75	8630	3.3	13.9	65.4	16.0	1.4	120080
47917	AMBIA	18559	194	24.7	37.1	32.5	5.2	0.5	42513	46928	55	37	158	26.0	34.8	35.4	3.8	0.0	74000
47918	ATTICA	19183	2660	27.4	34.6	30.7	6.0	1.3	39669	43842	45	22	2050	16.7	32.1	38.7	10.9	1.6	91171
47920	BATTLE GROUND	22937	819	18.1	34.9	32.6	11.4	3.1	47663	54094	68	65	695	9.4	17.3	46.5	24.2	2.7	124399
47921	BOSWELL	17510	460	32.0	35.0	27.6	5.0	0.4	39064	42911	43	20	362	21.3	42.3	32.6	3.6	0.3	76531
47922	BROOK	17140	687	28.4	34.9	31.3	4.2	1.2	40477	44108	48	26	541	9.4	38.5	44.4	6.1	1.7	91742
47923	BROOKSTON	22112	1434	17.5	31.4	41.9	7.3	1.9	50659	54143	73	76	1191	5.4	15.2	59.2	18.4	1.9	118413
47926	BURNETTSVILLE	21587	417	24.9	28.8	35.7	8.6	1.9	46987	51218	66	61	355	12.4	35.5	44.5	7.0	0.6	91744
47928	CAYUGA	19326	1055	30.7	33.7	28.7	4.6	2.3	36630	40534	34	13	885	31.3	42.3	22.5	3.8	0.1	67500
47929	CHALMERS	21345	313	21.4	26.8	41.9	7.7	2.2	50840	53281	74	76	268	7.8	24.3	50.0	13.4	4.5	108929
47930	CLARKS HILL	18335	510	22.4	33.3	36.1	7.1	1.2	46160	53048	64	58	425	17.4	29.4	39.3	12.0	1.9	92935
47932	COVINGTON	23308	2266	23.0	32.3	34.3	7.6	2.8	45882	50367	64	56	1849	16.7	32.4	42.2	7.8	0.8	90948
47933	CRAWFORDSVILLE	21834	10869	26.2	31.3	32.4	7.4	2.8	43760	48379	58	42	7834	8.8	24.1	52.0	13.8	1.3	109413
47940	DARLINGTON	20690	775	21.2	33.0	36.9	7.5	1.4	46490	51512	65	59	662	9.5	22.1	50.0	16.8	1.7	109643
47942	EARL PARK	16412	329	24.3	39.8	32.5	2.1	1.2	35079	39165	28	9	250	20.4	31.6	40.8	7.2	0.0	88214
47943	FAIR OAKS	20710	297	13.8	33.7	42.8	8.8	1.0	52420	57408	76	80	249	4.8	6.4	51.4	33.3	4.0	157500
47944	FOWLER	20026	1452	23.6	32.6	35.2	7.7	0.9	44438	48937	60	46	1119	14.0	29.9	49.2	6.7	0.1	94963
47946	FRANCESVILLE	18752	763	26.7	32.9	33.4	4.7	2.2	43360	48004	57	40	635	13.7	37.8	37.6	10.4	0.5	88443
47948	GOODLAND	17289	601	26.6	39.4	29.1	4.0	0.8	41090	45315	50	29	458	14.9	47.4	33.6	3.3	0.9	79483
47949	HILLSBORO	19939	514	23.7	31.9	38.1	4.1	2.1	45421	50259	62	53	436	23.4	39.5	31.0	6.2	0.0	78136
47950	IDAVILLE	23486	350	20.3	39.7	32.6	5.4	2.0	43650	47935	58	41	293	31.4	20.5	34.1	9.9	4.1	86333
47951	KENTLAND	20932	941	27.4	33.6	31.7	5.2	2.1	41492	45212	51	31	721	10.7	40.5	41.3	7.5	0.0	88712
47952	KINGMAN	16034	1219	33.6	39.8	22.8	2.6	1.2	33012	37004	21	6	998	40.7	36.8	18.2	3.4	0.9	62931
47954	LADOGA	20123	927	20.2	31.1	41.4	6.4	1.0	48949	53437	70	70	768	7.9	27.0	57.0	8.1	0.0	106875
47955	LINDEN	20587	459	24.0	34.6	34.9	6.3	0.2	44086	50607	59	45	359	14.2	30.1	46.2	8.1	1.4	95857
	INDIANA	23565		24.7	29.6	32.4	9.4	3.9	45964	52146				12.3	23.5	44.9	16.9	2.4	109048
	UNITED STATES	25866		24.7	27.1	30.8	10.9	6.5	48124	56710				10.9	15.0	33.7	30.1	10.4	145905

ZIP CODE #	POST OFFICE NAME	FINANCIAL SERVICES: Auto Loan	FINANCIAL SERVICES: Home Loan	FINANCIAL SERVICES: Invest-ments	FINANCIAL SERVICES: Retire-ment Plans	THE HOME: Home Improvements: Home Repair	THE HOME: Home Improvements: Lawn & Garden	THE HOME: Furnishings: Comput-ers & Hard-ware	THE HOME: Furnishings: Major Appli-ances	THE HOME: Furnishings: TV, Radio, Sound Equip-ment	THE HOME: Furnishings: Furni-ture	ENTERTAINMENT: Dine out/ Carry out	ENTERTAINMENT: Sports Equip-ment	ENTERTAINMENT: Fees & Tickets	ENTERTAINMENT: Toys & Games	ENTERTAINMENT: Travel	ENTERTAINMENT: Cable TV	PERSONAL: Apparel & Services	PERSONAL: Auto Repairs	PERSONAL: Health Insur-ance	PERSONAL: Pets & Supplies
47611	CHRISNEY	85	75	56	70	79	85	69	77	74	69	90	92	67	91	71	76	85	75	85	100
47612	CYNTHIANA	81	71	54	68	76	81	66	74	70	66	86	88	65	87	68	72	81	72	80	95
47613	ELBERFELD	84	75	58	72	79	85	69	77	74	70	89	91	68	91	72	75	85	75	83	99
47615	GRANDVIEW	81	72	55	68	76	81	66	74	71	66	86	88	65	88	68	72	82	72	80	95
47616	GRIFFIN	85	59	31	56	69	77	58	72	67	58	79	87	50	77	61	71	72	71	86	101
47619	LYNNVILLE	82	73	56	70	77	83	68	75	72	68	87	89	66	89	70	74	83	73	81	97
47620	MOUNT VERNON	85	80	69	78	83	90	78	82	81	77	99	95	77	100	79	82	94	81	87	98
47630	NEWBURGH	109	123	125	125	121	120	114	114	107	115	135	134	117	138	114	103	133	111	103	127
47631	NEW HARMONY	84	63	40	60	70	80	65	75	73	63	86	87	58	83	66	76	79	74	88	97
47633	POSEYVILLE	99	70	38	66	81	91	69	85	79	68	93	102	60	92	72	83	85	84	101	118
47634	RICHLAND	83	66	45	63	71	80	65	73	71	65	86	86	61	85	65	74	80	72	83	94
47635	ROCKPORT	78	66	50	64	70	78	66	71	70	65	85	83	63	85	66	72	80	70	79	88
47637	TENNYSON	82	72	54	68	76	82	66	74	71	66	86	88	65	88	68	73	82	72	81	96
47638	WADESVILLE	102	91	69	86	96	103	84	93	89	84	108	111	82	110	86	91	103	90	100	120
47639	HAUBSTADT	107	95	72	91	100	108	89	98	95	89	115	116	87	117	91	97	109	96	107	125
47640	HAZLETON	83	62	36	56	68	77	59	70	67	59	80	84	53	78	60	71	74	69	83	97
47647	BUCKSKIN	74	66	50	63	70	75	61	68	65	61	79	81	60	81	63	67	75	66	73	88
47648	FORT BRANCH	81	81	74	79	82	89	78	81	80	77	98	93	79	101	79	80	94	79	83	93
47649	FRANCISCO	88	78	60	74	83	89	72	80	77	72	93	96	71	95	74	79	89	78	87	103
47660	OAKLAND CITY	70	55	37	52	59	69	57	63	63	56	75	73	52	73	57	66	69	63	74	79
47665	OWENSVILLE	79	73	60	69	77	83	69	74	73	68	89	88	68	92	71	75	84	72	80	93
47666	PATOKA	100	76	46	69	83	93	72	85	82	73	98	102	66	96	74	86	91	84	99	116
47670	PRINCETON	69	60	51	57	62	70	62	65	66	60	80	75	59	80	62	68	76	65	72	78
47708	EVANSVILLE	0	0	0	0	0	0	0	0	0	0	0	0	0	0	0	0	0	0	0	0
47710	EVANSVILLE	61	58	62	56	58	66	62	61	64	60	79	70	61	78	62	66	76	63	65	69
47711	EVANSVILLE	78	81	84	79	82	89	81	81	82	79	102	92	83	106	82	83	99	80	84	91
47712	EVANSVILLE	80	80	83	79	81	87	82	81	83	80	102	95	82	105	82	82	99	82	82	92
47713	EVANSVILLE	49	43	51	42	42	49	50	48	53	49	66	55	49	63	48	53	63	50	50	54
47714	EVANSVILLE	62	64	71	63	64	69	67	65	67	65	84	75	68	86	67	67	82	66	65	71
47715	EVANSVILLE	81	85	98	87	84	89	87	85	85	87	107	100	88	107	86	83	105	86	81	94
47720	EVANSVILLE	96	102	97	100	102	106	94	98	93	94	115	113	96	118	96	92	112	95	95	113
47722	EVANSVILLE	46	28	36	32	28	34	55	40	53	46	66	56	45	59	44	47	62	49	37	46
47725	EVANSVILLE	141	160	160	159	159	163	144	146	138	144	172	171	151	179	147	136	170	142	139	169
47802	TERRE HAUTE	75	74	77	74	75	80	75	76	76	74	95	89	75	96	75	76	92	76	76	87
47803	TERRE HAUTE	82	82	85	81	83	91	84	84	85	82	105	97	84	107	84	86	102	84	87	95
47804	TERRE HAUTE	54	51	55	51	52	58	55	54	56	53	70	63	54	70	55	57	67	55	57	61
47805	TERRE HAUTE	77	73	65	71	76	83	72	75	75	71	91	87	72	94	73	76	87	74	80	89
47807	TERRE HAUTE	40	35	43	37	35	39	44	40	44	41	55	48	41	54	41	43	53	43	40	44
47809	TERRE HAUTE	30	24	31	27	24	26	33	29	33	31	41	37	30	38	30	30	40	33	27	32
47832	BLOOMINGDALE	78	68	51	65	73	78	63	71	68	63	82	84	62	84	65	70	78	69	77	92
47833	BOWLING GREEN	90	60	28	52	68	79	58	73	70	59	82	87	50	78	59	75	75	72	89	103
47834	BRAZIL	75	65	53	61	69	76	63	69	68	63	83	81	61	84	65	71	78	68	76	87
47836	BRIDGETON	76	68	52	65	72	77	63	70	67	63	81	83	62	83	65	68	77	68	75	90
47837	CARBON	74	63	48	61	67	75	62	68	67	61	81	79	59	80	63	69	76	67	75	85
47838	CARLISLE	23	17	10	16	20	22	17	20	19	17	22	24	15	22	17	20	21	20	23	28
47840	CENTERPOINT	87	77	58	73	82	88	71	79	76	71	92	95	70	94	74	78	88	77	86	103
47841	CLAY CITY	77	56	33	53	63	73	58	68	66	57	78	79	51	75	59	70	71	67	81	88
47842	CLINTON	74	68	58	65	71	80	68	72	73	66	88	82	67	90	69	75	83	71	80	85
47846	CORY	69	59	46	58	62	69	60	64	64	59	77	74	58	77	60	65	73	63	70	76
47847	DANA	87	75	58	73	79	87	74	80	79	73	96	93	72	96	75	80	90	79	87	98
47848	DUGGER	63	52	40	50	56	66	56	60	61	53	73	67	52	72	56	64	68	59	70	71
47849	FAIRBANKS	97	73	43	69	82	91	70	84	79	70	94	101	63	93	73	83	87	83	98	115
47850	FARMERSBURG	73	59	43	58	64	71	59	66	64	59	77	77	56	77	60	66	72	65	73	82
47854	HILLSDALE	116	104	79	98	109	117	96	106	102	96	124	126	94	126	99	104	117	103	115	137
47858	LEWIS	90	83	72	78	87	96	79	86	83	79	102	100	78	103	82	86	97	84	94	106
47859	MARSHALL	84	74	57	71	79	84	69	76	73	69	89	91	67	91	71	75	84	74	83	98
47861	MEROM	82	73	56	69	77	83	67	75	72	67	87	89	66	89	69	73	83	73	81	96
47862	MONTEZUMA	76	51	23	44	58	66	49	61	59	50	70	73	42	66	50	64	63	61	76	87
47866	PIMENTO	96	99	96	94	101	110	93	97	95	93	117	112	96	121	97	98	114	95	102	115
47868	POLAND	85	65	40	59	72	80	62	73	70	62	84	87	57	82	63	74	78	71	84	99
47872	ROCKVILLE	76	61	42	57	66	76	62	69	69	60	82	80	57	79	63	72	76	69	81	87
47874	ROSEDALE	79	71	56	68	74	81	68	74	72	67	87	86	66	88	69	73	83	72	79	91
47879	SHELBURN	79	54	27	48	61	70	52	65	62	53	73	77	45	70	53	67	67	64	78	91
47882	SULLIVAN	67	62	59	59	64	72	63	65	67	61	81	75	62	82	64	69	78	65	71	77
47885	WEST TERRE HAUTE	73	63	49	60	67	74	62	68	67	61	81	79	60	81	63	69	76	67	75	84
47901	LAFAYETTE	50	43	53	46	42	47	55	49	54	52	68	61	51	65	50	51	66	54	47	55
47904	LAFAYETTE	58	59	68	59	59	65	64	61	64	61	80	71	64	82	63	64	78	62	61	67
47905	LAFAYETTE	84	89	97	91	88	92	89	87	87	88	108	103	90	110	88	84	106	88	83	97
47906	WEST LAFAYETTE	78	70	81	74	69	74	85	76	82	80	103	95	80	99	78	77	100	82	70	85
47907	WEST LAFAYETTE	0	0	0	0	0	0	0	0	0	0	0	0	0	0	0	0	0	0	0	0
47909	LAFAYETTE	84	84	87	86	83	87	86	84	84	85	105	100	85	105	84	81	102	85	80	95
47917	AMBIA	83	58	30	55	67	76	57	71	66	56	77	85	49	76	59	69	70	70	84	98
47918	ATTICA	75	66	53	64	70	77	65	70	70	64	85	81	64	86	66	72	80	69	77	86
47920	BATTLE GROUND	97	80	56	77	86	95	77	87	83	77	100	103	72	100	79	86	94	86	97	113
47921	BOSWELL	69	58	44	58	61	69	59	64	63	58	77	74	57	76	59	65	72	63	70	77
47922	BROOK	73	64	49	61	67	73	61	67	65	61	79	78	59	80	62	66	75	65	72	84
47923	BROOKSTON	84	82	73	80	84	89	78	81	79	77	98	96	78	101	79	80	94	80	83	98
47926	BURNETTSVILLE	94	80	57	75	85	93	74	84	81	75	98	100	71	98	76	84	92	82	93	111
47928	CAYUGA	83	62	36	55	68	76	58	70	67	59	80	83	53	78	60	71	74	69	82	96
47929	CHALMERS	94	84	64	79	88	95	77	86	82	77	100	102	76	102	80	84	95	83	93	111
47930	CLARKS HILL	81	70	54	69	74	82	69	75	73	68	89	87	67	89	70	75	84	73	81	92
47932	COVINGTON	88	78	62	74	82	91	76	82	81	75	99	96	74	100	77	84	93	81	91	102
47933	CRAWFORDSVILLE	82	74	63	71	76	84	73	77	77	72	94	91	71	95	74	78	89	77	83	94
47940	DARLINGTON	88	79	60	75	83	89	73	81	77	73	94	96	71	96	75	79	89	78	87	104
47942	EARL PARK	68	58	45	58	61	68	60	64	63	58	77	73	57	76	59	64	72	63	69	75
47943	FAIR OAKS	93	83	63	79	87	94	76	85	81	76	99	101	75	101	79	83	94	83	92	109
47944	FOWLER	82	67	49	64	73	82	67	75	73	65	88	88	62	89	68	76	82	74	85	96
47946	FRANCESVILLE	84	68	45	64	74	81	64	74	70	64	84	89	60	85	66	73	79	73	84	99
47948	GOODLAND	72	62	47	60	66	72	60	66	64	60	78	77	58	78	61	65	73	64	72	82
47949	HILLSBORO	86	70	48	65	76	83	66	76	73	66	87	90	62	87	68	76	82	74	86	101
47950	IDAVILLE	93	76	55	74	81	91	76	84	83	76	100	98	72	99	77	85	93	83	94	105
47951	KENTLAND	79	67	52	67	70	80	69	74	73	68	89	84	66	88	69	75	83	73	80	87
47952	KINGMAN	76	52	24	45	58	67	50	62	60	51	70	74	43	67	51	64	64	61	76	88
47954	LADOGA	86	76	58	72	80	86	70	78	75	70	91	93	69	93	72	77	86	76	84	101
47955	LINDEN	78	67	52	66	70	79	68	73	72	67	87	83	65	87	67	73	82	71	79	87
	INDIANA	86	83	80	82	84	90	82	84	84	82	103	98	82	104	82	84	100	84	86	98
	UNITED STATES	100	100	100	100	100	100	100	100	100	100	100	100	100	100	100	100	100	100	100	100

ZIP CODE		COUNTY FIPS CODE	POPULATION			2000-2004 ANNUAL RATE		HOUSEHOLDS					FAMILIES		
#	POST OFFICE NAME		2000	2004	2009	% Rate	State Centile	2000	2004	2009	% Annual Rate 2000-2004	2004 Average HH Size	2000	2004	% Annual Rate 2000-2004
47957	MEDARYVILLE	131	1999	2031	2095	0.4	43	698	725	764	0.9	2.63	517	519	0.1
47959	MONON	181	2738	2859	3008	1.0	66	1020	1077	1146	1.3	2.63	721	733	0.4
47960	MONTICELLO	181	15744	16426	17300	1.0	65	6286	6656	7103	1.4	2.42	4451	4542	0.5
47963	MOROCCO	111	2287	2280	2324	-0.1	23	904	916	948	0.3	2.49	628	611	-0.6
47967	NEW RICHMOND	107	1073	1111	1140	0.8	59	408	429	444	1.2	2.59	313	319	0.5
47968	NEW ROSS	107	1128	1144	1155	0.3	42	432	446	455	0.8	2.57	325	324	-0.1
47970	OTTERBEIN	171	2051	2121	2195	0.8	58	775	814	855	1.2	2.61	579	589	0.4
47971	OXFORD	007	1869	1845	1819	-0.3	13	709	712	712	0.1	2.54	514	497	-0.8
47974	PERRYSVILLE	165	1175	1179	1181	0.1	30	464	476	486	0.6	2.47	335	330	-0.4
47975	PINE VILLAGE	171	646	676	725	1.1	67	263	281	308	1.6	2.40	192	199	0.9
47977	REMINGTON	073	2342	2413	2553	0.7	55	883	921	987	1.0	2.62	642	644	0.1
47978	RENSSELAER	073	11046	11706	12634	1.4	77	3970	4291	4729	1.9	2.54	2890	3016	1.0
47980	REYNOLDS	181	1241	1328	1422	1.6	82	439	472	509	1.7	2.81	341	357	1.1
47981	ROMNEY	157	741	798	878	1.8	85	265	289	323	2.1	2.76	211	223	1.3
47987	VEEDERSBURG	045	4453	4398	4331	-0.3	14	1721	1727	1725	0.1	2.54	1274	1236	-0.7
47989	WAVELAND	107	1028	1050	1065	0.5	49	395	410	420	0.9	2.56	290	290	0.0
47990	WAYNETOWN	107	1485	1486	1493	0.0	28	584	590	598	0.2	2.48	433	423	-0.6
47991	WEST LEBANON	171	1009	1063	1146	1.2	72	391	421	463	1.8	2.52	308	323	1.1
47992	WESTPOINT	157	1312	1495	1667	3.1	96	478	557	634	3.7	2.68	379	428	2.9
47993	WILLIAMSPORT	171	3863	4100	4430	1.4	77	1478	1601	1765	1.9	2.50	1078	1128	1.1
47994	WINGATE	107	572	582	588	0.4	46	218	225	229	0.8	2.59	163	162	-0.1
47995	WOLCOTT	181	1701	1848	1988	2.0	89	643	708	771	2.3	2.60	482	514	1.5
	INDIANA					0.8					1.2	2.48			0.3
	UNITED STATES					1.2					1.3	2.58			1.1

#	POST OFFICE NAME	White 2000	White 2004	Black 2000	Black 2004	Asian/Pacific 2000	Asian/Pacific 2004	% Hispanic Origin 2000	% Hispanic Origin 2004	0-4	5-9	10-14	15-19	20-24	25-44	45-64	65-84	85+	18+	MEDIAN AGE 2004	% 2004 Males	% 2004 Females
47957	MEDARYVILLE	95.8	95.4	2.4	2.5	0.1	0.2	2.7	3.2	6.3	6.3	7.4	7.3	7.2	28.2	25.0	10.9	1.5	75.5	36.9	53.1	46.9
47959	MONON	88.5	86.7	0.0	0.1	0.2	0.3	12.6	14.7	6.0	6.2	7.8	7.1	7.3	29.4	23.6	11.0	1.6	75.8	35.3	50.6	49.4
47960	MONTICELLO	95.1	94.3	0.2	0.2	0.3	0.4	5.8	6.8	6.0	6.1	6.5	6.0	6.0	25.5	27.0	14.9	2.0	77.7	40.8	49.7	50.4
47963	MOROCCO	98.4	98.2	0.2	0.2	0.4	0.5	1.6	1.9	6.1	6.5	7.1	6.1	6.3	26.5	27.2	12.3	2.1	76.8	39.3	50.3	49.7
47967	NEW RICHMOND	98.8	98.7	0.6	0.6	0.1	0.1	0.3	0.4	7.2	7.6	8.0	6.2	5.8	28.4	24.6	11.2	1.2	73.5	36.4	50.5	49.5
47968	NEW ROSS	98.9	98.7	0.1	0.1	0.0	0.0	0.8	1.0	6.5	6.8	7.7	7.0	5.2	29.9	25.1	10.5	1.3	74.7	37.4	51.5	48.5
47970	OTTERBEIN	98.5	98.3	0.1	0.1	0.1	0.1	0.7	0.8	6.9	7.3	8.2	7.4	7.2	28.5	23.5	10.0	1.1	72.8	35.4	50.3	49.7
47971	OXFORD	97.3	96.9	0.1	0.2	0.1	0.1	1.0	1.0	6.7	6.9	7.5	6.7	5.3	27.3	24.6	12.4	2.7	74.5	38.5	50.8	49.2
47974	PERRYSVILLE	99.0	99.0	0.1	0.1	0.2	0.2	0.2	0.3	5.9	6.6	7.1	5.2	5.8	23.9	30.1	13.7	1.6	77.1	41.3	51.3	48.7
47975	PINE VILLAGE	99.2	99.1	0.0	0.0	0.0	0.0	0.3	0.3	5.8	7.0	7.3	5.5	4.4	29.3	26.6	12.9	1.3	76.3	40.0	49.9	50.2
47977	REMINGTON	98.8	98.6	0.3	0.3	0.5	0.6	1.1	1.2	7.4	7.4	7.5	7.2	6.5	27.1	23.3	12.0	1.7	73.1	36.1	49.2	50.8
47978	RENSSELAER	97.5	97.2	0.6	0.6	0.2	0.3	2.7	3.2	6.4	6.3	7.1	8.4	9.8	25.5	22.8	11.6	2.1	76.3	35.2	49.5	50.5
47980	REYNOLDS	95.1	94.2	0.2	0.2	0.2	0.2	4.7	5.7	8.1	8.1	8.1	7.1	6.3	27.6	23.2	10.5	1.1	71.5	35.5	49.2	50.8
47981	ROMNEY	98.9	98.9	0.0	0.0	0.0	0.0	0.3	0.3	6.9	8.2	9.7	7.3	4.8	29.0	24.6	8.8	1.0	70.6	36.1	50.1	49.9
47987	VEEDERSBURG	99.0	98.8	0.1	0.1	0.1	0.1	1.8	2.2	6.8	6.9	7.3	6.6	5.8	26.6	25.1	13.3	1.6	74.9	38.1	49.8	50.3
47989	WAVELAND	98.0	97.6	0.1	0.1	0.2	0.3	0.7	0.9	6.6	7.0	9.1	7.0	5.2	29.0	23.9	11.0	1.4	73.1	37.0	50.5	49.5
47990	WAYNETOWN	99.1	99.0	0.2	0.2	0.1	0.1	0.3	0.4	7.5	7.5	7.9	5.8	5.4	27.6	23.4	12.5	2.4	73.2	36.8	48.7	51.3
47991	WEST LEBANON	98.9	98.8	0.0	0.0	0.2	0.2	0.7	0.9	7.1	7.2	7.3	6.6	5.1	26.0	26.9	12.7	1.1	74.3	38.8	51.6	48.5
47992	WESTPOINT	99.2	99.1	0.1	0.1	0.3	0.4	0.9	1.1	5.6	6.5	8.2	7.6	6.0	27.0	27.9	9.6	1.7	77.1	38.3	50.4	49.6
47993	WILLIAMSPORT	99.3	99.1	0.1	0.1	0.2	0.3	0.4	0.4	6.2	6.5	7.4	6.9	5.2	26.2	25.6	14.0	2.0	75.4	39.5	50.3	49.7
47994	WINGATE	99.7	99.7	0.0	0.0	0.2	0.2	0.5	0.7	6.4	7.4	8.9	6.0	5.8	26.6	24.4	13.4	1.0	73.5	39.0	49.0	51.0
47995	WOLCOTT	98.0	97.8	0.7	0.8	0.0	0.0	1.3	1.5	8.4	7.8	6.6	6.7	6.9	26.9	23.2	11.8	1.7	73.4	36.1	48.2	51.8
	INDIANA	87.5	86.7	8.4	8.7	1.0	1.3	3.5	4.1	7.0	6.9	7.1	7.1	7.4	28.1	24.0	10.8	1.6	75.0	35.9	49.2	50.8
	UNITED STATES	75.1	73.6	12.3	12.5	3.8	4.2	12.5	14.1	6.9	6.7	7.2	7.0	7.3	28.6	23.8	10.8	1.7	75.1	36.0	49.1	50.9

#	ZIP CODE POST OFFICE NAME	2004 Per Capita Income	2004 HH Income Base	2004 HOUSEHOLD INCOME DISTRIBUTION (%)					MEDIAN HOUSEHOLD INCOME				2004 Home Value Base	2004 HOME VALUE DISTRIBUTION (%)					2004 Median Home Value
				Less than $25,000	$25,000 to $49,999	$50,000 to $99,999	$100,000 to $149,999	$150,000 or More	2004	2009	2004 National Centile	2004 State Centile		Less than $50,000	$50,000 to $89,999	$90,000 to $174,999	$175,000 to $399,999	$400,000 or More	
47957	MEDARYVILLE	15897	725	34.2	34.8	25.2	4.7	1.1	35219	39172	28	10	607	22.1	31.0	38.9	7.7	0.3	85132
47959	MONON	16208	1077	30.9	38.8	25.0	4.2	1.1	36793	41023	35	13	826	24.7	34.9	32.9	6.2	1.3	78415
47960	MONTICELLO	21009	6656	25.7	33.5	31.9	7.0	1.9	43502	47621	57	41	5180	10.2	23.3	47.6	16.7	2.2	107599
47963	MOROCCO	19428	916	28.8	35.8	28.1	4.8	2.5	39854	43275	45	23	707	11.5	34.9	41.9	11.6	0.1	93355
47967	NEW RICHMOND	21033	429	17.3	31.9	42.4	6.5	1.9	50426	54539	73	73	358	9.8	27.7	53.6	7.8	1.1	103846
47968	NEW ROSS	21401	446	18.6	35.0	35.0	11.2	0.2	46901	50931	66	61	385	9.1	36.9	45.5	7.8	0.8	93298
47970	OTTERBEIN	20523	814	20.6	34.2	35.0	8.6	1.6	46332	51378	65	59	639	10.5	26.5	46.6	14.1	2.4	102394
47971	OXFORD	19798	712	22.1	35.4	34.7	6.9	1.0	45000	49592	61	49	592	9.3	41.6	44.9	4.1	0.2	89180
47974	PERRYSVILLE	19655	476	30.0	33.8	27.7	5.7	2.7	38741	43631	42	19	359	27.3	34.5	29.3	8.9	0.0	75875
47975	PINE VILLAGE	22330	281	21.7	32.7	33.8	11.0	0.7	44385	49630	60	46	233	14.2	31.3	39.5	7.7	7.3	98750
47977	REMINGTON	21530	921	22.0	30.9	35.5	7.9	3.6	47315	52510	67	63	686	8.8	24.6	58.3	8.2	0.2	103571
47978	RENSSELAER	21047	4291	26.2	33.9	29.4	7.6	2.9	42882	47744	56	38	3135	4.8	20.9	55.1	16.8	2.5	115818
47980	REYNOLDS	18560	472	27.8	29.9	35.0	5.5	1.9	45802	49904	63	55	366	11.5	32.5	42.6	11.5	1.9	95500
47981	ROMNEY	23207	289	12.8	36.7	32.2	15.2	3.1	50552	56966	73	74	244	4.5	9.4	54.5	27.5	4.1	140625
47987	VEEDERSBURG	20284	1727	25.0	35.8	32.8	4.5	1.9	42788	46704	55	38	1397	22.7	42.2	27.1	7.4	0.6	75820
47989	WAVELAND	19923	410	22.9	29.5	41.2	5.9	0.5	48667	53209	70	69	338	9.8	42.3	39.4	8.3	0.3	88000
47990	WAYNETOWN	20317	590	22.0	33.9	37.3	5.6	1.2	45560	50435	63	54	464	8.8	32.1	49.8	8.2	1.1	97000
47991	WEST LEBANON	21720	421	26.6	26.4	35.4	7.8	3.8	45177	48455	62	50	346	17.3	39.6	35.0	7.8	0.3	84667
47992	WESTPOINT	26677	557	7.4	29.1	44.3	13.6	5.6	61400	70761	86	94	478	1.7	14.4	62.6	17.8	3.6	120085
47993	WILLIAMSPORT	20174	1601	25.6	30.9	34.3	7.8	1.4	45475	50120	63	53	1255	18.3	35.9	34.6	9.2	2.0	86023
47994	WINGATE	18029	225	27.1	33.3	32.9	5.8	0.9	42378	47320	54	36	191	17.8	23.0	50.3	6.8	2.1	98750
47995	WOLCOTT	20208	708	24.0	31.4	36.6	5.8	2.3	43828	48086	58	42	556	12.2	31.5	44.1	10.1	2.2	97292
	INDIANA	23565		24.7	29.6	32.4	9.4	3.9	45964	52146				12.3	23.5	44.9	16.9	2.4	109048
	UNITED STATES	25866		24.7	27.1	30.8	10.9	6.5	48124	56710				10.9	15.0	33.7	30.1	10.4	145905

#	POST OFFICE NAME	FINANCIAL SERVICES				THE HOME						ENTERTAINMENT						PERSONAL			
						Home Improvements		Furnishings													
		Auto Loan	Home Loan	Invest-ments	Retire-ment Plans	Home Repair	Lawn & Garden	Comput-ers & Hard-ware	Major Appli-ances	TV, Radio, Sound Equip-ment	Furni-ture	Dine out/ Carry out	Sports Equip-ment	Fees & Tickets	Toys & Games	Travel	Cable TV	Apparel & Services	Auto Repairs	Health Insur-ance	Pets & Supplies
47957	MEDARYVILLE	79	54	25	47	61	70	52	65	62	53	73	77	44	70	53	67	67	64	79	91
47959	MONON	74	56	35	51	61	69	55	64	62	55	74	75	50	72	56	65	68	63	74	84
47960	MONTICELLO	84	70	51	66	75	83	67	76	73	67	88	89	63	88	69	76	82	75	85	98
47963	MOROCCO	76	65	51	64	69	77	66	71	70	65	84	81	63	84	66	71	79	69	76	85
47967	NEW RICHMOND	87	78	59	74	82	88	72	80	76	72	93	95	70	95	74	78	88	77	86	103
47968	NEW ROSS	88	78	60	74	83	89	72	80	77	72	93	96	71	95	75	79	89	78	87	104
47970	OTTERBEIN	82	75	61	74	78	85	73	78	76	72	92	91	71	93	73	77	88	76	82	94
47971	OXFORD	81	70	54	68	74	81	68	74	72	67	87	87	66	88	69	73	82	72	80	93
47974	PERRYSVILLE	86	65	38	58	71	79	61	73	70	62	83	87	56	81	63	74	77	72	85	99
47975	PINE VILLAGE	86	77	58	73	81	87	71	78	75	71	91	93	69	93	73	77	87	76	85	101
47977	REMINGTON	89	76	59	75	80	89	76	82	81	75	98	95	73	98	76	83	92	81	89	99
47978	RENSSELAER	82	76	67	74	79	87	75	79	78	74	96	92	74	97	76	80	91	78	85	95
47980	REYNOLDS	83	72	55	70	76	83	70	76	74	69	90	89	68	91	71	76	85	75	83	95
47981	ROMNEY	103	91	70	87	97	104	84	94	90	84	109	112	83	111	87	92	104	91	101	121
47987	VEEDERSBURG	81	70	54	69	74	82	70	75	74	69	90	87	67	90	70	76	85	74	82	92
47989	WAVELAND	82	73	55	69	77	82	67	75	71	67	87	89	66	89	69	73	83	73	81	96
47990	WAYNETOWN	80	69	53	68	72	80	69	74	73	68	88	86	66	88	69	74	83	73	80	90
47991	WEST LEBANON	94	74	48	70	82	90	70	82	78	70	93	99	64	93	73	81	86	81	94	111
47992	WESTPOINT	114	103	80	98	108	116	95	104	100	95	122	124	94	124	98	102	116	102	112	134
47993	WILLIAMSPORT	83	67	47	65	73	82	67	75	74	66	88	88	63	87	68	76	82	74	85	95
47994	WINGATE	75	66	51	63	70	75	61	68	65	61	79	81	60	81	63	67	75	66	74	88
47995	WOLCOTT	83	73	57	71	77	84	70	77	75	70	91	90	68	92	71	76	86	75	83	96
	INDIANA	86	83	80	82	84	90	82	84	84	82	103	98	82	104	82	84	100	84	86	98
	UNITED STATES	100	100	100	100	100	100	100	100	100	100	100	100	100	100	100	100	100	100	100	100

POPULATION CHANGE

ZIP CODE		POPULATION			2000-2004 ANNUAL RATE		HOUSEHOLDS					FAMILIES		
# POST OFFICE NAME	COUNTY FIPS CODE	2000	2004	2009	% Rate	State Centile	2000	2004	2009	% Annual Rate 2000-2004	2004 Average HH Size	2000	2004	% Annual Rate 2000-2004
50001 ACKWORTH	181	609	646	689	1.4	85	215	231	249	1.7	2.80	175	188	1.7
50002 ADAIR	077	1367	1304	1291	-1.1	5	581	560	557	-0.9	2.31	376	362	-0.9
50003 ADEL	049	6095	6588	7435	1.9	90	2293	2509	2861	2.1	2.58	1649	1798	2.1
50005 ALBION	127	817	789	785	-0.8	11	308	301	301	-0.5	2.62	243	236	-0.7
50006 ALDEN	083	1902	1792	1731	-1.4	2	738	702	684	-1.2	2.55	543	515	-1.2
50007 ALLEMAN	153	489	537	580	2.2	93	159	177	193	2.6	3.03	139	154	2.4
50008 ALLERTON	185	888	863	828	-0.7	16	356	348	336	-0.5	2.48	249	243	-0.6
50009 ALTOONA	153	11965	13340	14538	2.6	94	4434	4969	5435	2.7	2.66	3357	3736	2.6
50010 AMES	169	24969	26837	29050	1.7	88	10787	11712	12805	2.0	2.26	6225	6752	1.9
50011 AMES	169	1347	1348	1348	0.0	51	0	0	0	0.0	0.00	0	0	0.0
50013 AMES	169	1118	1118	1119	0.0	51	0	0	0	0.0	0.00	0	0	0.0
50014 AMES	169	27080	28723	30531	1.4	85	8737	9457	10274	1.9	2.38	3901	4255	2.1
50020 ANITA	029	1361	1344	1341	-0.3	33	573	572	577	0.0	2.32	381	378	-0.2
50021 ANKENY	153	31278	35466	39065	3.0	96	11808	13513	14962	3.2	2.58	8494	9693	3.2
50022 ATLANTIC	029	8734	8645	8645	-0.2	37	3670	3670	3705	0.0	2.26	2376	2366	-0.1
50025 AUDUBON	009	3840	3828	3841	-0.1	45	1559	1571	1590	0.2	2.36	1076	1079	0.1
50026 BAGLEY	077	698	764	823	2.2	92	281	310	336	2.3	2.45	207	227	2.2
50027 BARNES CITY	123	340	324	315	-1.1	4	150	145	142	-0.8	2.23	109	105	-0.9
50028 BAXTER	099	1597	1568	1563	-0.4	26	656	651	655	-0.2	2.37	458	451	-0.4
50029 BAYARD	077	780	819	864	1.2	82	308	327	349	1.4	2.45	217	230	1.4
50033 BEVINGTON	121	18	20	21	2.5	94	5	5	6	0.0	3.80	4	4	0.0
50034 BLAIRSBURG	079	474	470	468	-0.2	38	179	179	179	0.0	2.62	137	136	-0.2
50035 BONDURANT	153	2995	3546	3989	4.1	99	1048	1251	1415	4.3	2.83	833	990	4.2
50036 BOONE	015	16244	16566	17097	0.5	68	6628	6817	7089	0.7	2.37	4367	4472	0.6
50038 BOONEVILLE	049	6	6	7	0.0	51	3	3	3	0.0	2.00	2	2	0.0
50039 BOUTON	049	422	426	465	0.2	59	169	172	190	0.4	2.48	120	122	0.4
50040 BOXHOLM	015	250	255	263	0.5	68	116	119	124	0.6	2.14	79	81	0.6
50041 BRADFORD	069	106	106	107	0.0	51	42	43	43	0.6	2.47	31	31	0.0
50042 BRAYTON	009	434	461	474	1.4	86	170	180	186	1.4	2.56	129	136	1.3
50044 BUSSEY	125	868	855	869	-0.4	30	342	341	349	-0.1	2.51	253	251	-0.2
50046 CAMBRIDGE	169	1382	1369	1430	-0.2	37	522	523	552	0.1	2.62	375	374	-0.1
50047 CARLISLE	181	5337	5662	6009	1.4	85	2029	2180	2342	1.7	2.56	1526	1634	1.6
50048 CASEY	077	977	947	964	-0.7	15	397	389	400	-0.5	2.38	291	285	-0.5
50049 CHARITON	117	7097	7129	7217	0.1	54	2857	2864	2893	0.1	2.42	1889	1883	-0.1
50050 CHURDAN	073	751	717	706	-1.1	5	320	308	305	-0.9	2.33	222	213	-1.0
50051 CLEMONS	127	349	342	342	-0.5	24	146	145	145	-0.2	2.36	111	110	-0.2
50052 CLIO	185	153	153	148	0.0	51	69	69	68	0.0	2.22	48	48	0.0
50054 COLFAX	099	3573	3580	3589	0.1	52	1343	1358	1374	0.3	2.58	983	990	0.2
50055 COLLINS	169	943	932	961	-0.3	34	379	378	393	-0.1	2.45	282	280	-0.2
50056 COLO	169	1342	1320	1370	-0.4	28	511	507	530	-0.2	2.60	376	371	-0.3
50057 COLUMBIA	125	257	270	281	1.2	82	98	104	110	1.4	2.60	81	85	1.1
50058 COON RAPIDS	027	1984	1960	1933	-0.3	33	811	812	812	0.0	2.34	540	539	0.0
50059 COOPER	073	44	52	55	4.0	98	15	18	19	4.4	2.89	11	13	4.0
50060 CORYDON	185	2747	2667	2566	-0.7	16	1149	1121	1082	-0.6	2.30	751	730	-0.7
50061 CUMMING	121	1184	1241	1354	1.1	81	420	447	493	1.5	2.76	359	381	1.4
50062 DALLAS	125	1601	1589	1618	-0.2	39	628	633	651	0.2	2.51	454	454	0.0
50063 DALLAS CENTER	049	2256	2437	2746	1.8	90	829	907	1034	2.1	2.57	626	683	2.1
50064 DANA	073	138	142	143	0.7	73	49	50	50	0.5	2.84	34	35	0.7
50065 DAVIS CITY	053	802	806	818	0.1	55	313	316	321	0.2	2.49	229	230	0.1
50066 DAWSON	049	339	343	374	0.3	62	135	138	152	0.5	2.49	109	111	0.4
50067 DECATUR	053	425	445	462	1.1	81	175	185	192	1.3	2.41	119	125	1.2
50068 DERBY	117	359	367	374	0.5	70	138	140	142	0.3	2.62	104	106	0.5
50069 DE SOTO	049	1051	1064	1162	0.3	62	389	399	439	0.6	2.67	300	307	0.5
50070 DEXTER	121	1497	1574	1711	1.2	82	587	621	679	1.3	2.50	441	464	1.2
50071 DOWS	197	1295	1306	1307	0.2	59	558	566	571	0.3	2.26	369	372	0.2
50072 EARLHAM	121	2347	2517	2761	1.7	88	877	948	1046	1.9	2.63	674	726	1.8
50073 ELKHART	153	890	1059	1193	4.2	99	361	435	494	4.5	2.43	266	318	4.3
50074 ELLSTON	159	545	549	556	0.2	58	240	244	249	0.4	2.25	173	175	0.3
50075 ELLSWORTH	079	934	919	915	-0.4	28	352	352	353	-0.2	2.61	261	258	-0.3
50076 EXIRA	009	1626	1665	1701	0.6	70	682	699	718	0.6	2.30	452	463	0.6
50101 GALT	197	34	40	42	3.9	98	17	20	21	3.9	2.00	12	14	3.7
50102 GARDEN CITY	083	43	44	44	0.5	70	16	17	17	1.4	2.59	11	12	2.1
50103 GARDEN GROVE	053	689	695	706	0.2	59	263	266	272	0.3	2.61	204	206	0.2
50104 GIBSON	107	167	189	201	3.0	96	63	72	77	3.2	2.63	45	51	3.0
50105 GILBERT	169	1037	1043	1076	0.1	57	356	360	374	0.3	2.90	273	273	0.0
50106 GILMAN	127	1118	1111	1109	-0.2	42	462	464	466	0.1	2.39	326	325	-0.1
50107 GRAND JUNCTION	073	1215	1203	1201	-0.2	37	467	458	456	-0.5	2.63	328	321	-0.5
50108 GRAND RIVER	053	524	553	576	1.3	84	224	238	248	1.4	2.32	152	160	1.2
50109 GRANGER	049	1762	1813	1971	0.7	73	649	678	747	1.0	2.60	497	517	0.9
50111 GRIMES	153	5625	6513	7241	3.5	98	2067	2412	2698	3.7	2.70	1589	1819	3.2
50112 GRINNELL	157	11410	11595	11792	0.4	66	4362	4501	4653	0.7	2.28	2754	2832	0.7
50115 GUTHRIE CENTER	077	2766	2765	2874	0.0	48	1128	1133	1185	0.1	2.36	749	749	0.0
50116 HAMILTON	125	305	295	299	-0.8	13	114	112	114	-0.4	2.63	84	82	-0.6
50117 HAMLIN	009	220	215	213	-0.5	21	86	84	84	-0.6	2.56	61	60	-0.4
50118 HARTFORD	181	906	943	992	1.0	79	330	349	372	1.3	2.70	261	276	1.3
50119 HARVEY	125	498	528	551	1.4	85	194	209	220	1.8	2.53	146	156	1.6
50120 HAVERHILL	127	395	391	389	-0.2	37	136	136	136	0.0	2.88	102	101	-0.2
50122 HUBBARD	083	1536	1474	1430	-1.0	7	617	593	577	-0.9	2.39	434	416	-1.0
50123 HUMESTON	185	793	779	755	-0.4	26	374	369	358	-0.3	2.10	262	258	-0.4
50124 HUXLEY	169	2812	3057	3289	2.0	91	1094	1208	1315	2.4	2.51	793	872	2.3
50125 INDIANOLA	181	17266	17773	18561	0.7	73	6221	6479	6861	1.0	2.52	4493	4668	0.9
50126 IOWA FALLS	083	7001	6939	6835	-0.2	38	2945	2943	2917	0.0	2.24	1858	1850	-0.1
50127 IRA	099	33	34	34	0.7	74	14	14	15	0.0	2.43	12	12	0.0
50128 JAMAICA	077	398	446	487	2.7	95	163	184	202	2.9	2.42	121	135	2.6
50129 JEFFERSON	073	5679	5622	5612	-0.2	37	2326	2306	2301	-0.2	2.33	1530	1511	-0.3
50130 JEWELL	079	1697	1672	1665	-0.4	30	657	649	650	-0.3	2.56	481	473	-0.4
50131 JOHNSTON	153	8935	11006	12610	5.0	100	3327	4127	4752	5.2	2.61	2445	3009	5.0
50132 KAMRAR	079	402	398	397	-0.2	37	155	155	155	0.0	2.57	120	119	-0.2
50133 KELLERTON	159	649	662	675	0.5	68	250	256	263	0.6	2.59	171	174	0.4
50134 KELLEY	169	646	739	816	3.2	97	236	274	306	3.6	2.69	163	189	3.5
50135 KELLOGG	099	1569	1711	1794	2.1	91	632	698	741	2.4	2.45	471	518	2.3
50136 KESWICK	107	610	651	670	1.5	87	240	259	269	1.8	2.51	180	193	1.7
50138 KNOXVILLE	125	11718	12164	12598	0.9	78	4638	4861	5075	1.1	2.41	3144	3284	1.0
50139 LACONA	181	1115	1104	1141	-0.2	37	417	419	440	0.1	2.63	315	315	0.0
50140 LAMONI	053	2828	2844	2891	0.1	56	953	967	993	0.3	2.24	523	529	0.3
IOWA					0.5					0.7	2.43			0.6
UNITED STATES					1.2					1.3	2.58			1.1

ZIP CODE #	POST OFFICE NAME	RACE (%) White 2000	White 2004	Black 2000	Black 2004	Asian/Pacific 2000	Asian/Pacific 2004	% Hispanic Origin 2000	% Hispanic Origin 2004	2004 AGE DISTRIBUTION (%) 0-4	5-9	10-14	15-19	20-24	25-44	45-64	65-84	85+	18+	MEDIAN AGE 2004	% 2004 Males	% 2004 Females
50001	ACKWORTH	98.5	98.5	0.3	0.3	0.2	0.2	0.8	1.1	6.4	7.0	7.9	7.3	5.4	25.9	28.5	10.7	1.1	74.2	40.0	50.2	49.9
50002	ADAIR	98.8	98.6	0.1	0.1	0.3	0.4	1.2	1.3	5.4	5.5	6.3	6.5	5.8	23.9	26.1	17.0	3.5	78.8	42.7	49.7	50.3
50003	ADEL	98.2	97.7	0.2	0.2	0.4	0.6	1.0	1.4	6.3	7.1	7.9	7.1	6.3	25.3	27.1	10.5	2.5	74.0	39.2	49.2	50.8
50005	ALBION	98.7	98.5	0.0	0.0	0.5	0.5	1.2	1.4	7.0	7.4	7.6	6.3	5.5	23.6	28.8	12.8	1.1	74.1	39.5	51.3	48.7
50006	ALDEN	98.4	97.9	0.0	0.0	0.2	0.3	3.1	3.7	6.4	7.4	7.7	6.3	5.9	26.0	25.8	13.2	1.5	74.7	39.1	49.7	50.3
50007	ALLEMAN	99.6	99.4	0.0	0.0	0.0	0.2	0.4	0.6	8.0	8.4	7.8	6.5	3.9	30.0	26.6	8.2	0.6	71.5	38.4	52.9	47.1
50008	ALLERTON	99.3	99.4	0.0	0.0	0.1	0.1	0.7	0.8	5.6	6.0	7.7	7.0	6.0	24.0	24.5	16.3	3.0	76.4	41.0	48.4	51.6
50009	ALTOONA	96.2	95.2	0.8	1.1	0.8	1.1	1.6	2.1	8.5	8.2	8.4	7.1	6.5	30.4	22.8	7.4	0.8	70.4	33.5	47.9	52.1
50010	AMES	88.0	85.2	2.5	2.6	7.5	10.0	1.7	2.0	5.9	5.2	5.2	6.1	15.0	29.7	21.2	9.8	1.9	80.3	31.9	49.2	50.8
50011	AMES	90.7	88.7	3.9	4.2	3.3	4.6	1.7	2.0	0.1	0.0	0.0	52.3	46.6	1.0	0.0	0.0	0.0	99.7	19.8	56.7	43.3
50013	AMES	90.7	88.6	3.9	4.3	3.2	4.7	1.7	2.0	0.0	0.0	0.0	52.3	46.8	0.9	0.0	0.0	0.0	99.8	19.8	56.7	43.3
50014	AMES	87.8	84.5	2.4	2.6	7.5	10.4	2.2	2.5	3.5	3.2	3.5	14.8	36.9	19.9	13.0	4.5	0.7	87.8	23.4	54.7	45.3
50020	ANITA	99.3	99.3	0.0	0.0	0.1	0.1	0.3	0.4	4.9	5.2	6.4	6.4	6.3	22.8	27.2	16.9	3.8	79.5	43.7	50.2	49.9
50021	ANKENY	97.0	96.1	0.8	1.0	0.9	1.4	1.0	1.3	8.3	7.8	7.1	6.3	7.9	31.8	22.3	7.2	1.1	73.1	33.2	48.7	51.3
50022	ATLANTIC	98.6	98.6	0.2	0.2	0.3	0.3	0.8	0.8	5.6	5.8	6.3	6.3	6.2	23.0	25.4	17.3	4.3	78.4	42.9	48.1	52.0
50025	AUDUBON	99.3	99.4	0.2	0.2	0.1	0.1	0.4	0.5	6.4	5.8	7.3	6.1	5.6	20.4	23.9	19.3	5.3	76.9	43.9	47.4	52.6
50026	BAGLEY	97.9	97.8	0.3	0.4	0.0	0.0	2.2	2.5	6.3	6.8	6.4	5.1	4.8	23.3	29.7	15.7	1.8	77.2	43.3	50.0	50.0
50027	BARNES CITY	99.4	99.4	0.3	0.3	0.0	0.0	0.3	0.3	5.9	6.5	7.4	7.1	5.6	24.1	28.4	13.9	1.2	75.6	41.4	54.9	45.1
50028	BAXTER	98.9	98.7	0.6	0.6	0.3	0.5	0.0	0.0	6.6	6.6	7.1	5.7	6.1	27.1	25.1	13.1	2.5	76.2	39.1	49.4	50.6
50029	BAYARD	98.3	97.9	0.0	0.0	0.4	0.5	1.2	1.7	5.1	5.7	7.3	6.4	6.6	22.3	27.7	15.4	3.4	77.5	42.8	51.5	48.5
50033	BEVINGTON	100.0	100.0	0.0	0.0	0.0	0.0	0.0	0.0	10.0	10.0	10.0	5.0	5.0	35.0	25.0	0.0	0.0	70.0	32.5	55.0	45.0
50034	BLAIRSBURG	98.1	98.1	0.0	0.0	0.4	0.4	1.7	1.9	5.5	6.4	7.7	6.4	4.9	24.3	28.3	14.9	1.7	76.4	42.1	50.9	49.2
50035	BONDURANT	98.5	98.1	0.1	0.1	0.2	0.4	0.8	1.0	7.5	8.1	9.5	7.6	5.3	30.0	24.4	7.0	0.8	70.2	35.5	49.8	50.2
50036	BOONE	98.4	98.1	0.3	0.4	0.2	0.3	0.9	1.0	6.2	6.2	6.7	6.9	6.7	26.2	24.8	13.3	3.1	76.7	39.0	48.2	51.8
50038	BOONEVILLE	100.0	100.0	0.0	0.0	0.0	0.0	0.0	0.0	0.0	0.0	0.0	0.0	33.3	66.7	0.0	0.0	0.0	100.0	27.5	50.0	50.0
50039	BOUTON	98.8	98.6	0.2	0.2	0.2	0.2	1.4	2.1	5.9	6.3	7.0	7.0	5.2	24.9	31.2	10.8	1.6	76.5	41.5	52.1	47.9
50040	BOXHOLM	99.6	100.0	0.0	0.0	0.0	0.0	0.4	0.4	4.7	5.9	7.8	6.3	4.7	22.8	30.6	15.3	2.0	77.3	43.7	53.3	46.7
50041	BRADFORD	99.1	100.0	0.0	0.0	0.0	0.0	0.0	0.0	2.8	6.6	8.5	7.6	4.7	24.5	28.3	16.0	0.9	76.4	42.2	52.8	47.2
50042	BRAYTON	99.5	99.4	0.0	0.0	0.2	0.2	0.7	0.7	6.9	7.4	8.7	6.9	4.3	22.1	23.0	18.4	2.2	72.7	40.9	50.5	49.5
50044	BUSSEY	98.4	98.3	0.2	0.2	0.2	0.4	0.4	0.5	6.7	6.7	7.1	6.9	6.2	26.6	25.3	13.0	1.6	75.3	39.1	53.1	46.9
50046	CAMBRIDGE	96.6	96.1	0.7	0.7	0.5	0.7	1.9	2.3	7.5	7.5	7.4	6.6	6.0	30.0	24.7	8.8	1.7	73.6	36.1	48.9	51.1
50047	CARLISLE	97.8	97.3	0.3	0.4	0.4	0.6	1.4	1.7	7.2	7.5	7.5	6.4	5.9	27.3	25.6	11.1	1.7	74.0	37.4	48.5	51.5
50048	CASEY	98.7	98.5	0.1	0.1	0.2	0.2	1.1	1.3	5.8	5.9	7.1	5.6	4.7	23.7	26.4	18.1	2.9	77.6	43.5	49.7	50.3
50049	CHARITON	98.5	98.2	0.2	0.2	0.3	0.4	0.9	1.0	6.1	6.3	7.3	6.8	5.8	23.5	24.3	16.0	3.9	76.0	40.9	48.6	51.4
50050	CHURDAN	99.2	99.2	0.1	0.1	0.0	0.0	0.8	0.8	6.6	6.4	6.1	5.4	6.1	19.5	26.4	20.8	2.7	77.4	44.8	51.1	49.0
50051	CLEMONS	97.7	97.4	0.3	0.3	0.0	0.0	1.4	1.8	5.9	6.4	7.0	5.9	5.3	26.0	28.4	13.7	1.5	76.6	41.1	52.6	47.4
50052	CLIO	99.4	100.0	0.0	0.0	0.0	0.0	0.7	0.7	5.9	5.9	5.9	6.5	5.9	20.3	25.5	20.3	3.9	78.4	44.7	50.3	49.7
50054	COLFAX	98.4	98.2	0.3	0.3	0.1	0.2	0.9	1.1	6.6	7.0	8.1	7.2	5.6	27.2	25.6	11.3	1.4	73.6	37.6	51.0	49.0
50055	COLLINS	98.6	98.4	0.1	0.1	0.4	0.6	0.3	0.4	6.6	6.9	7.4	6.8	6.0	23.5	27.9	12.9	2.2	75.1	39.9	50.5	49.5
50056	COLO	97.9	97.5	0.7	0.8	0.5	0.8	0.3	0.3	6.1	6.4	7.4	7.7	7.1	26.9	23.4	13.2	1.7	75.5	37.3	50.5	49.6
50057	COLUMBIA	98.1	97.4	0.0	0.4	0.4	0.7	0.0	0.0	5.6	6.7	8.5	7.0	6.3	25.9	27.8	11.1	1.1	75.2	38.7	52.2	47.8
50058	COON RAPIDS	98.9	98.8	0.5	0.5	0.1	0.1	1.5	1.8	5.9	6.0	6.5	6.4	6.2	21.9	25.2	17.5	4.5	77.8	43.1	49.7	50.3
50059	COOPER	95.5	96.2	0.0	0.0	0.0	0.0	0.0	0.0	5.8	5.8	7.7	7.7	5.8	23.1	28.9	15.4	0.0	80.8	41.3	55.8	44.2
50060	CORYDON	99.1	99.0	0.1	0.1	0.2	0.3	0.4	0.4	5.2	5.4	6.8	5.6	5.6	20.2	25.6	20.0	5.7	78.9	45.9	47.0	53.0
50061	CUMMING	98.1	97.7	0.3	0.2	0.6	0.8	1.0	1.1	6.4	7.6	7.9	7.1	4.9	25.5	32.8	7.3	0.6	73.6	40.3	51.0	49.0
50062	DALLAS	98.6	98.4	0.1	0.1	0.4	0.6	0.2	0.3	5.2	5.5	7.4	7.9	7.1	23.5	25.9	15.4	2.0	76.2	40.1	49.8	50.2
50063	DALLAS CENTER	98.8	98.5	0.3	0.3	0.1	0.2	0.5	0.8	6.2	7.0	7.7	6.8	5.3	25.0	27.1	12.2	2.8	74.6	40.4	50.4	49.6
50064	DANA	97.8	98.6	0.0	0.0	0.0	0.0	2.9	2.8	7.8	7.8	7.8	6.3	5.6	24.7	24.7	12.7	2.8	72.5	38.3	50.0	50.0
50065	DAVIS CITY	97.1	96.7	0.6	0.7	0.3	0.5	1.1	1.5	7.2	7.3	8.1	6.1	5.6	22.3	26.2	15.1	2.1	74.2	39.8	49.8	50.3
50066	DAWSON	98.8	99.1	0.0	0.0	0.0	0.0	0.6	0.6	5.0	5.8	7.0	6.4	6.1	23.0	31.8	13.4	1.5	78.7	43.2	49.6	50.4
50067	DECATUR	97.4	96.9	0.2	0.5	0.2	0.2	1.9	2.3	7.2	7.2	7.2	5.8	4.7	24.3	25.4	16.4	1.8	74.4	40.6	50.3	49.7
50068	DERBY	96.4	95.6	0.0	0.0	1.1	1.6	1.4	1.9	7.4	7.4	8.2	7.9	6.0	22.6	25.1	13.6	1.9	72.2	38.8	50.1	49.9
50069	DE SOTO	98.6	98.2	0.1	0.1	0.6	0.9	0.6	0.8	8.2	8.2	7.3	6.5	5.5	29.5	26.8	7.3	0.8	72.3	35.2	50.9	49.2
50070	DEXTER	98.3	98.2	0.1	0.1	0.7	0.9	0.8	1.0	6.9	7.1	8.0	5.7	5.7	26.3	26.4	11.9	2.0	74.3	39.2	51.1	48.9
50071	DOWS	95.3	94.4	0.1	0.1	0.4	0.5	7.2	8.4	4.8	5.2	6.1	5.7	5.7	25.1	26.7	17.1	3.8	80.4	43.5	50.3	49.7
50072	EARLHAM	98.8	98.6	0.1	0.2	0.2	0.3	0.7	0.9	7.8	8.0	7.9	6.6	5.5	27.6	24.7	9.9	1.9	72.0	36.9	50.2	49.8
50073	ELKHART	98.9	98.6	0.5	0.6	0.3	0.5	0.5	0.5	7.1	7.4	6.9	6.0	4.3	28.2	27.1	10.8	2.2	74.9	38.8	51.5	48.5
50074	ELLSTON	98.9	98.9	0.2	0.2	0.2	0.2	0.2	0.2	4.6	5.1	5.5	4.9	4.6	18.2	31.9	23.1	2.2	82.2	50.4	51.4	48.6
50075	ELLSWORTH	95.1	95.0	0.3	0.3	0.4	0.4	5.9	6.0	6.4	7.0	7.6	7.0	5.6	26.3	24.8	13.5	1.9	74.5	38.5	50.5	49.5
50076	EXIRA	98.7	98.7	0.1	0.1	0.5	0.5	0.5	0.5	5.1	5.3	6.7	6.9	5.0	20.1	25.5	20.1	5.4	78.2	45.6	47.6	52.4
50101	GALT	94.1	97.5	0.0	0.0	0.0	0.0	2.9	5.0	5.0	5.0	5.0	5.0	7.5	25.0	27.5	17.5	2.5	85.0	43.8	50.0	50.0
50102	GARDEN CITY	97.7	97.7	0.0	0.0	0.0	0.0	4.7	4.6	4.6	4.6	4.6	4.6	6.8	20.5	31.8	18.2	4.6	86.4	47.0	47.7	52.3
50103	GARDEN GROVE	99.1	99.0	0.0	0.0	0.2	0.1	0.4	0.4	5.0	5.9	8.6	9.1	4.0	24.6	28.4	14.1	0.3	74.5	41.1	54.1	45.9
50104	GIBSON	98.8	99.5	0.0	0.0	0.0	0.0	1.2	0.5	4.2	4.8	6.4	6.9	6.9	24.9	27.0	16.9	2.1	80.4	42.8	49.2	50.8
50105	GILBERT	96.7	95.9	0.5	0.6	1.7	2.6	1.0	1.2	7.0	7.1	8.4	7.5	7.6	29.2	25.1	7.2	0.9	72.9	34.2	50.4	49.6
50106	GILMAN	94.7	93.9	0.1	0.1	0.1	0.2	3.9	4.9	6.0	6.5	8.0	7.5	6.7	24.0	27.6	11.7	2.0	75.0	38.7	50.1	49.9
50107	GRAND JUNCTION	98.2	98.3	0.1	0.1	0.1	0.1	1.2	1.2	7.3	7.1	8.3	8.2	6.3	26.4	20.3	14.1	2.2	72.2	36.0	52.1	47.9
50108	GRAND RIVER	97.3	96.6	0.2	0.4	0.2	0.4	1.9	2.2	7.4	7.2	7.2	6.0	4.9	24.2	25.5	15.7	1.8	74.5	40.2	50.6	49.4
50109	GRANGER	98.9	98.6	0.2	0.2	0.4	0.6	0.5	0.7	6.8	7.5	7.9	7.0	5.2	26.6	27.3	10.0	1.8	73.0	38.8	50.6	49.4
50111	GRIMES	97.2	96.3	0.4	0.5	0.9	1.4	1.1	1.4	10.3	9.5	8.1	6.2	5.7	35.7	18.6	5.3	0.6	68.2	31.7	48.6	51.4
50112	GRINNELL	95.6	94.7	0.9	1.0	1.8	2.5	1.3	1.6	5.6	5.4	6.0	9.8	10.9	22.3	22.8	13.9	3.4	79.1	36.9	47.3	52.7
50115	GUTHRIE CENTER	98.5	98.2	0.1	0.1	0.1	0.1	1.2	1.5	5.7	6.0	7.3	5.6	5.5	22.6	25.1	17.6	4.6	77.2	43.2	48.2	51.8
50116	HAMILTON	98.4	98.0	0.3	0.3	0.3	0.3	0.3	0.7	7.1	6.8	7.5	6.8	6.4	26.4	24.1	13.2	1.7	74.6	37.9	53.6	46.4
50117	HAMLIN	99.1	100.0	0.0	0.0	0.0	0.0	0.5	0.5	6.5	7.4	9.3	6.5	4.2	25.1	27.0	12.1	1.9	72.1	38.9	50.7	49.3
50118	HARTFORD	96.4	95.9	0.0	0.0	0.0	0.0	2.9	3.6	6.3	6.8	7.7	6.4	5.8	28.5	26.4	11.4	0.7	75.1	37.9	51.0	49.0
50119	HARVEY	99.8	99.8	0.2	0.2	0.0	0.0	0.0	0.0	7.8	7.2	6.4	6.1	6.4	27.7	26.1	11.6	0.8	75.0	37.3	51.1	48.9
50120	HAVERHILL	98.0	98.0	0.0	0.0	0.8	0.8	1.3	1.5	6.4	6.9	7.7	7.2	6.1	24.3	27.4	12.8	1.3	74.4	40.6	50.1	49.9
50122	HUBBARD	99.0	98.8	0.0	0.0	0.1	0.3	0.8	1.0	5.9	6.6	6.1	5.0	5.6	22.6	22.5	20.8	5.0	78.2	43.7	49.3	50.8
50123	HUMESTON	98.9	98.6	0.1	0.1	0.3	0.5	0.6	0.6	6.7	6.7	6.9	5.8	5.4	23.0	27.0	16.1	2.6	75.7	42.4	48.9	51.1
50124	HUXLEY	97.8	97.4	0.2	0.2	0.4	0.6	1.0	1.2	7.5	7.4	7.6	6.3	7.0	30.1	24.7	7.9	1.4	73.7	34.5	48.8	51.2
50125	INDIANOLA	98.1	97.8	0.4	0.4	0.5	0.7	0.8	1.0	6.5	6.4	6.8	8.0	9.0	25.6	23.8	11.5	2.5	76.4	36.2	47.6	52.4
50126	IOWA FALLS	97.6	97.2	1.0	1.1	0.3	0.4	1.1	1.3	5.7	5.3	5.7	6.9	8.9	22.6	24.7	16.0	4.2	79.9	41.1	48.9	51.1
50127	IRA	100.0	100.0	0.0	0.0	0.0	0.0	0.0	0.0	5.9	5.9	5.9	5.9	5.9	26.5	26.5	14.7	2.9	82.4	41.7	50.0	50.0
50128	JAMAICA	97.7	97.5	0.3	0.5	0.0	0.0	2.0	2.5	6.3	6.5	6.5	4.9	5.2	23.1	29.6	15.9	2.0	77.6	43.4	50.2	49.8
50129	JEFFERSON	98.2	98.1	0.1	0.1	0.3	0.3	1.6	1.7	5.6	5.8	6.8	6.7	6.1	20.9	25.0	17.7	5.5	77.6	43.8	47.2	52.8
50130	JEWELL	96.8	96.7	0.2	0.2	1.5	1.5	1.6	1.7	7.1	7.3	8.6	6.9	5.7	26.6	24.3	11.8	1.8	72.1	37.8	52.3	47.7
50131	JOHNSTON	96.3	94.9	0.6	0.7	1.9	2.9	1.5	2.0	7.3	8.3	8.5	7.0	4.5	30.6	24.5	7.7	1.7	70.8	36.6	49.4	50.7
50132	KAMRAR	98.3	98.5	0.0	0.0	0.3	0.3	1.2	1.3	5.5	6.5	7.8	7.0	5.0	24.1	28.1	14.3	1.5	75.6	41.5	51.5	48.5
50133	KELLERTON	98.9	98.9	0.0	0.0	0.0	0.0	0.3	0.3	8.2	7.1	6.2	8.9	8.6	21.5	21.6	15.3	2.7	73.3	36.7	47.7	52.3
50134	KELLEY	97.2	96.6	0.5	0.4	1.1	1.5	1.1	1.2	6.6	7.2	7.7	6.5	7.2	27.1	25.0	10.6	2.2	74.3	36.9	50.2	49.8
50135	KELLOGG	98.3	97.8	0.3	0.4	0.5	0.8	0.7	0.9	5.2	5.7	7.2	6.6	5.7	23.3	30.4	14.6	1.4	77.9	42.9	50.5	49.5
50136	KESWICK	99.2	99.1	0.0	0.0	0.2	0.2	0.5	0.6	6.3	6.6	8.0	7.1	5.2	24.0	25.2	15.7	2.0	74.8	40.7	49.6	50.4
50138	KNOXVILLE	97.4	97.1	0.9	1.0	0.4	0.6	0.8	1.0	6.5	6.5	7.0	6.6	6.0	24.9	26.0	14.0	2.5	75.9	40.2	50.5	49.5
50139	LACONA	98.4	98.2	0.0	0.0	0.3	0.5	0.4	0.4	5.8	6.3	7.2	7.1	6.0	25.8	28.1	11.7	2.2	76.3	39.9	50.8	49.2
50140	LAMONI	92.6	91.5	2.6	2.8	1.7	2.4	2.6	3.1	4.2	3.2	4.6	15.5	21.7	16.7	18.0	12.7	3.5	84.4	25.7	48.3	51.7
	IOWA	93.9	93.0	2.1	2.3	1.3	1.8	2.8	3.2	6.5	6.5	6.9	7.2	7.6	26.4	24.2	12.3	2.4	76.0	37.2	49.2	50.8
	UNITED STATES	75.1	73.6	12.3	12.5	3.8	4.2	12.5	14.1	6.9	6.7	7.2	7.0	7.3	28.6	23.8	10.8	1.7	75.1	36.0	49.1	50.9

#	POST OFFICE NAME	2004 Per Capita Income	2004 HH Income Base	2004 Household Income Distribution (%): Less than $25,000	$25,000 to $49,999	$50,000 to $99,999	$100,000 to $149,999	$150,000 or More	Median Household Income: 2004	2009	2004 National Centile	2004 State Centile	2004 Home Value Base	2004 Home Value Distribution (%): Less than $50,000	$50,000 to $89,999	$90,000 to $174,999	$175,000 to $399,999	$400,000 or More	2004 Median Home Value
50001	ACKWORTH	21465	231	13.0	33.8	42.9	9.1	1.3	53339	61406	77	88	206	9.7	10.2	40.8	36.4	2.9	153846
50002	ADAIR	20434	560	29.5	35.7	29.6	3.8	1.4	37642	43750	38	20	435	33.6	37.9	22.5	4.4	1.6	66413
50003	ADEL	25899	2509	15.8	29.3	37.0	13.1	4.9	53982	64905	78	90	1971	11.6	14.8	42.1	24.2	7.3	128811
50005	ALBION	19997	301	16.6	37.2	38.2	7.3	0.7	46677	54199	65	71	257	27.2	32.7	24.1	14.4	1.6	79800
50006	ALDEN	19467	702	24.4	34.9	32.8	6.1	1.9	41942	47182	53	48	557	31.2	31.2	27.5	7.5	2.5	72714
50007	ALLEMAN	22794	177	11.9	22.0	50.3	13.0	2.8	63106	76739	87	97	154	7.1	19.5	37.7	35.1	0.7	150000
50008	ALLERTON	16513	348	36.8	35.3	22.1	4.9	0.9	32414	38366	19	4	281	68.3	18.2	8.9	3.9	0.7	35543
50009	ALTOONA	24615	4969	15.3	23.6	43.7	14.7	2.8	59608	72628	84	94	3595	5.0	9.1	58.0	27.0	0.9	134481
50010	AMES	27108	11712	27.5	26.8	30.2	10.3	5.2	45697	55772	63	66	6470	9.8	5.9	50.0	32.0	2.3	147528
50011	AMES	11821	0	0.0	0.0	0.0	0.0	0.0	0	0	0	0	0	0.0	0.0	0.0	0.0	0.0	0
50013	AMES	11829	0	0.0	0.0	0.0	0.0	0.0	0	0	0	0	0	0.0	0.0	0.0	0.0	0.0	0
50014	AMES	23826	9457	30.7	24.1	28.1	10.6	6.5	43660	54587	58	57	3978	5.0	2.7	38.1	48.5	5.8	184941
50020	ANITA	17965	572	38.1	31.1	25.5	4.4	0.9	33325	38973	22	6	439	36.9	35.1	21.0	6.4	0.7	62843
50021	ANKENY	30658	13513	13.7	22.0	39.3	18.3	6.8	65180	79536	89	98	9788	5.7	6.0	52.4	33.7	2.3	151127
50022	ATLANTIC	20341	3670	29.2	38.1	24.5	6.2	2.0	37705	43570	38	21	2707	20.4	36.2	34.7	8.5	0.3	84077
50025	AUDUBON	24428	1571	29.7	35.2	25.3	5.4	4.4	39975	46492	46	34	1205	28.9	36.1	25.7	6.7	2.6	73098
50026	BAGLEY	23557	310	25.2	29.7	31.9	9.0	4.2	46458	54229	65	70	252	20.2	25.8	27.0	21.0	6.0	97143
50027	BARNES CITY	22131	145	24.8	33.1	33.8	5.5	2.8	43744	48646	58	58	106	32.1	20.8	32.1	8.5	6.6	82500
50028	BAXTER	22207	651	22.0	32.4	37.9	6.5	1.2	46693	55056	65	71	489	12.7	25.0	50.1	10.0	2.3	103381
50029	BAYARD	26274	327	33.0	31.8	23.9	6.7	4.6	37608	44837	38	20	260	36.5	25.8	25.8	11.5	0.4	65769
50033	BEVINGTON	18145	5	0.0	0.0	100.0	0.0	0.0	69801	84511	91	99	4	0.0	0.0	0.0	100.0	0.0	225000
50034	BLAIRSBURG	19148	179	21.8	34.6	39.1	3.4	1.1	46046	52000	64	68	139	28.1	25.9	32.4	10.1	3.6	83125
50035	BONDURANT	25228	1251	15.3	19.7	46.3	13.4	5.4	62858	77275	87	96	1075	5.2	12.7	56.9	24.6	0.7	120654
50036	BOONE	23048	6817	25.1	30.6	34.6	6.8	2.9	45352	52598	62	65	4944	21.1	31.5	34.3	12.0	1.0	86888
50038	BOONEVILLE	0	0	0.0	0.0	0.0	0.0	0.0	0	87500	0	0	0	0.0	0.0	0.0	0.0	0.0	0
50039	BOUTON	23212	172	19.8	38.4	25.6	13.4	2.9	43150	52574	56	54	138	21.0	21.7	39.1	15.9	2.2	105263
50040	BOXHOLM	21435	119	26.1	38.7	29.4	5.9	0.0	41118	46361	50	42	97	32.0	24.7	33.0	8.3	2.1	77500
50041	BRADFORD	24903	43	20.9	27.9	34.9	14.0	2.3	50819	60974	74	84	34	17.7	38.2	26.5	8.8	8.8	85000
50042	BRAYTON	18117	180	24.4	46.1	23.9	2.8	2.8	33279	38315	22	5	143	33.6	25.2	24.5	9.8	7.0	71667
50044	BUSSEY	21301	341	27.0	34.0	31.7	6.7	0.6	41420	47509	51	44	286	40.6	30.4	21.3	7.7	0.0	61905
50046	CAMBRIDGE	23401	523	18.2	28.7	37.7	12.8	2.7	52303	62681	76	87	445	13.9	23.4	38.4	20.9	3.4	109448
50047	CARLISLE	24256	2180	19.0	25.6	41.8	10.4	3.2	54310	63192	79	91	1856	15.6	17.1	47.2	17.6	2.5	114883
50048	CASEY	24812	389	26.0	32.7	33.4	4.6	3.3	41896	48694	53	47	313	34.2	30.7	24.6	6.7	3.8	72407
50049	CHARITON	17148	2864	36.8	31.6	27.0	3.0	1.6	34208	39515	25	7	2113	33.7	31.0	25.9	8.0	1.5	70578
50050	CHURDAN	18688	308	37.7	34.4	23.4	1.6	2.9	31260	36181	16	3	233	59.7	20.6	11.6	3.9	4.3	41667
50051	CLEMONS	21873	145	17.2	33.8	43.5	4.8	0.7	49349	55708	71	80	121	36.4	21.5	29.8	12.4	0.0	78125
50052	CLIO	20474	69	39.1	29.0	20.3	10.1	1.5	35439	42840	29	11	53	54.7	18.9	9.4	11.3	5.7	43750
50054	COLFAX	20735	1358	24.3	29.8	34.7	9.8	1.5	46927	53817	66	72	1125	16.6	28.1	41.3	13.8	0.2	96761
50055	COLLINS	23988	378	16.1	34.4	41.3	6.6	1.6	49666	58274	71	81	315	21.0	14.9	37.5	21.9	4.8	117448
50056	COLO	22486	507	16.8	33.9	39.8	7.7	1.8	49531	60716	71	81	404	15.8	32.2	41.6	9.2	1.2	92581
50057	COLUMBIA	19319	104	18.3	40.4	35.6	5.8	0.0	45792	52230	63	67	88	21.6	25.0	40.9	10.2	2.3	95000
50058	COON RAPIDS	20680	812	28.6	37.7	28.0	4.1	1.7	37728	44901	38	21	630	33.7	34.6	26.7	4.8	0.3	68462
50059	COOPER	17437	18	27.8	27.8	38.9	5.6	0.0	45000	47368	61	63	14	28.6	28.6	42.9	0.0	0.0	80000
50060	CORYDON	19022	1121	37.1	33.5	21.9	5.7	1.7	33738	39399	23	6	856	40.8	34.8	18.7	4.7	1.1	60870
50061	CUMMING	39983	447	5.4	15.7	45.2	19.9	13.9	77676	91893	94	99	411	1.5	6.3	34.8	41.6	15.8	195066
50062	DALLAS	19131	633	28.1	32.2	34.1	4.1	1.4	43909	50829	58	58	525	33.7	37.9	23.2	4.8	0.4	66489
50063	DALLAS CENTER	25155	907	16.0	23.9	42.6	14.0	3.5	60270	72302	85	95	773	8.3	14.1	52.3	23.4	1.9	127996
50064	DANA	18791	50	20.0	42.0	30.0	6.0	2.0	41122	48207	50	42	40	55.0	27.5	10.0	5.0	2.5	47778
50065	DAVIS CITY	15911	316	34.8	44.6	16.1	2.9	1.6	31615	36145	17	4	252	43.7	26.2	21.8	7.9	0.4	59412
50066	DAWSON	28570	138	18.1	25.4	37.7	13.0	5.8	57159	67813	82	93	116	22.4	17.2	41.4	12.9	6.0	110938
50067	DECATUR	16383	185	36.8	41.1	16.8	2.7	2.7	31511	35000	16	3	147	42.2	25.9	18.4	12.2	1.4	60455
50068	DERBY	16013	140	30.7	37.1	29.3	2.9	0.0	37652	42898	38	20	118	23.7	25.4	28.8	18.6	3.4	91429
50069	DE SOTO	24314	399	13.8	27.8	46.9	9.0	2.5	56069	67186	81	92	350	32.9	17.7	33.4	10.6	5.4	88750
50070	DEXTER	21741	621	21.9	30.4	38.3	7.9	1.5	48494	58167	69	78	509	18.9	28.9	40.9	8.8	2.6	93194
50071	DOWS	19196	566	28.8	35.5	31.6	2.8	1.2	38205	43694	40	23	443	43.3	30.7	14.7	9.5	1.8	55784
50072	EARLHAM	24923	948	19.3	25.7	39.9	11.3	3.8	53893	63197	78	90	795	8.6	15.9	47.2	23.5	4.9	126310
50073	ELKHART	27315	435	18.2	21.8	44.1	13.6	2.3	62292	76070	86	96	370	14.3	15.4	35.4	31.6	3.2	133871
50074	ELLSTON	19280	244	34.4	32.8	24.2	7.8	0.8	32991	37747	21	5	204	33.8	24.0	22.6	16.2	3.4	77143
50075	ELLSWORTH	19285	352	24.2	37.2	30.4	5.4	2.8	41122	45887	50	42	272	18.0	25.0	38.6	17.3	1.1	98261
50076	EXIRA	16829	699	37.9	37.1	21.2	2.9	1.0	31473	35971	16	3	561	42.8	24.8	23.7	7.1	1.6	59000
50101	GALT	21393	20	25.0	40.0	35.0	0.0	0.0	42301	43604	54	50	16	43.8	25.0	18.8	12.5	0.0	60000
50102	GARDEN CITY	18068	17	23.5	35.3	35.3	5.9	0.0	42353	52117	54	50	14	14.3	35.7	50.0	0.0	0.0	90000
50103	GARDEN GROVE	21539	266	36.8	30.5	24.4	3.0	5.3	34010	40000	24	7	219	37.9	24.2	24.2	10.1	3.7	71154
50104	GIBSON	18823	72	27.8	33.3	33.3	4.2	1.4	40899	47353	49	40	57	31.6	29.8	24.6	8.8	5.3	69000
50105	GILBERT	21580	360	21.7	26.1	33.9	15.6	2.8	52988	65235	77	88	294	26.5	9.5	43.2	18.7	2.0	119886
50106	GILMAN	19871	464	27.2	32.8	34.3	5.2	0.7	42661	50306	55	52	367	28.9	34.1	28.3	7.1	1.6	73966
50107	GRAND JUNCTION	15697	458	38.0	28.4	29.3	3.1	1.3	34312	39599	25	8	339	55.8	32.5	7.1	3.8	0.9	45851
50108	GRAND RIVER	16617	238	38.2	40.8	16.4	2.5	2.1	30857	34697	14	3	189	42.9	25.4	18.0	12.7	1.1	59643
50109	GRANGER	30152	678	12.8	25.2	36.0	19.6	6.3	62423	75906	87	96	588	5.6	13.4	48.3	27.0	5.6	139326
50111	GRIMES	28433	2412	12.0	25.5	39.4	17.2	5.9	64170	77721	88	97	2000	10.8	17.7	52.3	16.5	2.8	126467
50112	GRINNELL	22125	4501	26.5	31.6	30.5	8.2	3.3	42634	50499	55	52	2993	11.9	25.9	44.7	16.1	1.3	107526
50115	GUTHRIE CENTER	21110	1133	31.8	29.7	30.3	6.3	2.0	38389	45515	41	25	867	33.8	35.2	23.6	5.8	1.6	67048
50116	HAMILTON	19478	112	28.6	33.0	31.3	7.1	0.0	41306	45761	51	43	94	42.6	31.9	19.2	6.4	0.0	58750
50117	HAMLIN	16875	84	32.1	38.1	22.6	6.0	1.2	35624	40000	30	12	69	37.7	30.4	27.5	4.4	0.0	70714
50118	HARTFORD	22680	349	14.0	30.1	45.0	8.0	2.9	53810	62226	78	90	330	19.4	26.4	40.0	14.2	0.0	95185
50119	HARVEY	18925	209	23.0	37.3	33.5	6.2	0.0	42686	48705	55	52	173	38.7	28.9	22.0	8.7	1.7	62083
50120	HAVERHILL	18924	136	14.7	35.3	44.1	5.9	0.0	50000	57250	72	82	115	18.3	32.2	38.3	11.3	0.0	89500
50122	HUBBARD	24306	593	22.8	38.5	29.7	6.1	3.0	41430	47515	51	45	484	23.6	39.7	31.4	5.2	0.2	78409
50123	HUMESTON	20434	369	37.9	35.2	21.1	4.9	0.8	32202	37228	18	4	298	45.3	29.5	17.5	6.4	1.3	54667
50124	HUXLEY	26444	1208	17.8	23.5	40.1	14.2	4.5	59888	73340	84	94	939	21.1	8.3	45.6	24.4	0.6	123772
50125	INDIANOLA	23390	6479	19.6	26.3	40.7	10.5	3.0	53456	62741	78	89	4697	8.4	12.3	52.9	24.9	1.4	129349
50126	IOWA FALLS	21488	2943	29.4	34.3	27.7	6.6	1.9	38275	44054	40	24	2150	24.2	34.8	28.9	10.4	1.7	79167
50127	IRA	19779	14	35.7	28.6	21.4	14.3	0.0	37500	52087	37	19	13	0.0	7.7	38.5	53.9	0.0	181250
50128	JAMAICA	24219	184	24.5	29.9	32.1	9.2	4.4	46778	54525	66	72	151	19.2	25.2	28.5	21.2	6.0	99444
50129	JEFFERSON	19783	2306	30.7	30.8	32.1	5.1	1.3	40383	46892	47	38	1715	25.1	39.8	29.3	3.8	2.0	76165
50130	JEWELL	22253	649	19.3	32.8	38.2	6.9	2.8	47699	55791	68	75	507	12.2	27.0	51.1	9.3	0.4	102789
50131	JOHNSTON	42504	4127	10.9	17.0	28.9	21.8	21.4	85222	103187	96	100	3153	0.5	2.3	28.0	58.7	10.4	217563
50132	KAMRAR	19896	155	20.7	34.2	40.0	3.9	1.3	46949	53240	66	72	120	24.2	25.0	37.5	9.2	4.2	91667
50133	KELLERTON	12869	256	39.8	43.8	15.2	0.4	0.8	30353	35138	13	2	186	59.1	19.4	5.4	11.8	4.3	43929
50134	KELLEY	25277	274	17.5	23.4	43.8	10.2	5.1	60217	72076	85	94	206	5.3	13.6	56.3	21.4	3.4	129054
50135	KELLOGG	23455	698	19.5	33.1	36.4	9.2	1.9	48056	55294	68	77	599	14.5	23.5	36.6	24.2	1.2	105339
50136	KESWICK	23284	259	27.4	32.8	33.6	3.1	3.1	40992	46939	50	41	209	34.9	25.4	28.2	8.1	3.4	70625
50138	KNOXVILLE	21033	4861	25.5	31.5	33.6	7.4	2.0	44835	51803	61	62	3634	18.2	33.8	38.8	8.8	0.5	87879
50139	LACONA	19066	419	21.2	34.6	38.0	6.0	0.2	44699	52437	60	61	345	20.3	30.7	32.2	15.1	1.7	89000
50140	LAMONI	17204	967	44.7	25.1	21.5	5.3	3.4	28635	33678	10	1	533	29.1	28.9	34.5	7.1	0.4	79848
	IOWA	23554		24.6	30.5	32.9	8.4	3.7	45622	53985				17.5	26.2	39.3	15.0	2.1	98835
	UNITED STATES	25866		24.7	27.1	30.8	10.9	6.5	48124	56710				10.9	15.0	33.7	30.1	10.4	145905

ZIP CODE #	POST OFFICE NAME	FINANCIAL SERVICES: Auto Loan	FINANCIAL SERVICES: Home Loan	FINANCIAL SERVICES: Invest-ments	FINANCIAL SERVICES: Retire-ment Plans	THE HOME: Home Improvements: Home Repair	THE HOME: Home Improvements: Lawn & Garden	THE HOME: Furnishings: Comput-ers & Hard-ware	THE HOME: Furnishings: Major Appli-ances	THE HOME: Furnishings: TV, Radio, Sound Equip-ment	THE HOME: Furnishings: Furni-ture	ENTERTAINMENT: Dine out/ Carry out	ENTERTAINMENT: Sports Equip-ment	ENTERTAINMENT: Fees & Tickets	ENTERTAINMENT: Toys & Games	ENTERTAINMENT: Travel	ENTERTAINMENT: Cable TV	PERSONAL: Apparel & Services	PERSONAL: Auto Repairs	PERSONAL: Health Insur-ance	PERSONAL: Pets & Supplies
50001	ACKWORTH	87	90	82	87	92	95	82	87	83	82	102	102	84	106	85	83	99	84	87	104
50002	ADAIR	80	58	35	56	65	76	62	71	70	60	82	82	54	79	62	74	75	71	85	91
50003	ADEL	106	92	73	91	98	108	91	100	96	90	116	116	87	115	92	98	109	98	108	122
50005	ALBION	85	74	54	70	79	85	69	77	74	69	89	92	66	91	71	76	84	75	84	100
50006	ALDEN	90	63	33	59	73	82	62	77	71	61	84	92	53	82	64	75	76	76	91	107
50007	ALLEMAN	90	112	119	112	110	108	100	99	92	99	116	116	106	124	102	90	116	96	89	110
50008	ALLERTON	68	50	31	48	56	66	54	61	61	52	72	70	48	68	54	64	65	61	73	76
50009	ALTOONA	92	101	101	103	98	97	96	95	90	97	113	112	97	114	94	85	111	94	84	105
50010	AMES	82	80	96	84	79	84	92	84	89	88	111	103	89	109	87	84	109	89	78	93
50011	AMES	0	0	0	0	0	0	0	0	0	0	0	0	0	0	0	0	0	0	0	0
50013	AMES	0	0	0	0	0	0	0	0	0	0	0	0	0	0	0	0	0	0	0	0
50014	AMES	88	72	89	78	71	78	101	84	98	92	122	109	91	115	89	89	118	95	77	94
50020	ANITA	70	51	32	49	57	67	55	63	62	53	73	71	49	70	55	66	67	62	75	78
50021	ANKENY	112	118	123	122	114	117	116	114	110	117	139	134	116	138	113	105	137	114	103	126
50022	ATLANTIC	74	60	46	58	65	73	62	69	68	61	81	80	58	80	63	70	76	68	77	85
50025	AUDUBON	98	72	45	69	80	94	77	88	87	74	102	100	68	98	77	92	93	87	105	111
50026	BAGLEY	104	74	40	70	85	95	73	89	83	72	98	107	63	96	75	87	89	87	105	123
50027	BARNES CITY	79	71	54	67	75	80	65	72	69	65	84	86	64	86	67	71	80	70	78	93
50028	BAXTER	87	69	49	68	75	85	70	79	77	69	92	92	65	91	71	79	85	78	88	99
50029	BAYARD	118	82	43	78	96	107	81	101	94	80	110	121	69	108	84	98	100	99	120	140
50033	BEVINGTON	114	102	77	97	107	115	94	104	100	94	121	124	92	124	97	102	115	101	113	134
50034	BLAIRSBURG	91	63	33	60	74	83	63	77	72	62	85	93	53	83	65	76	77	76	92	108
50035	BONDURANT	97	112	115	113	109	108	104	103	97	104	122	121	107	126	103	92	121	101	91	113
50036	BOONE	83	75	64	74	78	87	76	80	79	74	96	92	73	97	76	81	91	79	86	95
50038	BOONEVILLE	0	0	0	0	0	0	0	0	0	0	0	0	0	0	0	0	0	0	0	0
50039	BOUTON	104	73	38	69	85	95	72	89	83	71	97	107	61	95	74	87	88	87	106	124
50040	BOXHOLM	83	58	30	55	68	76	57	71	66	57	77	85	49	76	59	69	71	70	84	99
50041	BRADFORD	111	78	41	73	90	101	77	95	88	76	104	114	65	101	79	93	94	93	113	132
50042	BRAYTON	84	59	31	55	68	76	58	72	67	57	78	86	49	77	60	70	71	71	85	100
50044	BUSSEY	97	69	36	61	77	88	66	81	78	67	92	96	58	88	67	83	84	80	97	112
50046	CAMBRIDGE	93	84	71	83	87	96	84	89	88	83	107	102	82	107	84	88	101	87	94	104
50047	CARLISLE	89	91	87	90	92	98	87	90	87	86	108	104	89	111	88	87	104	88	90	103
50048	CASEY	108	75	39	71	88	98	75	92	86	74	101	111	64	99	77	90	92	91	110	128
50049	CHARITON	70	52	34	50	58	68	55	63	61	53	73	72	49	71	55	65	67	62	74	80
50050	CHURDAN	72	53	34	51	59	70	58	65	65	55	76	74	51	73	58	68	70	65	77	81
50051	CLEMONS	84	72	53	69	77	84	67	76	73	67	88	91	65	89	70	75	83	74	84	99
50052	CLIO	74	55	36	53	61	72	61	67	68	58	80	76	54	76	60	72	73	67	81	82
50054	COLFAX	86	76	58	73	80	87	72	79	76	71	93	93	70	94	73	78	88	77	85	100
50055	COLLINS	107	74	39	70	87	97	74	91	85	73	99	110	63	97	76	89	91	90	108	127
50056	COLO	84	85	81	82	88	92	80	85	81	80	100	99	81	104	83	82	97	83	86	101
50057	COLUMBIA	80	72	54	68	76	81	66	73	70	66	85	87	65	87	68	72	81	71	79	95
50058	COON RAPIDS	86	61	35	58	70	80	63	75	72	61	84	88	54	81	64	75	77	74	89	100
50059	COOPER	91	64	33	60	74	83	63	78	72	62	85	94	54	83	65	76	77	77	93	108
50060	CORYDON	74	54	34	52	61	71	58	66	66	56	77	76	51	74	58	69	70	66	79	84
50061	CUMMING	145	180	193	182	176	175	160	158	147	160	186	184	172	196	163	143	186	152	141	175
50062	DALLAS	65	67	67	64	69	76	66	66	68	64	84	75	68	90	68	71	81	65	72	76
50063	DALLAS CENTER	106	94	73	91	101	107	88	99	92	87	111	118	84	113	91	94	106	97	106	127
50064	DANA	97	67	35	64	79	88	67	82	77	66	90	99	57	88	69	81	82	81	98	115
50065	DAVIS CITY	71	50	28	48	58	65	50	61	57	49	68	74	43	66	52	60	62	61	72	84
50066	DAWSON	129	90	47	85	105	117	89	110	102	88	120	132	76	117	92	107	109	108	130	153
50067	DECATUR	71	50	27	47	58	65	49	61	57	49	67	73	42	65	51	59	61	60	72	84
50068	DERBY	76	53	28	50	62	69	52	65	60	52	71	78	45	69	54	63	65	64	77	90
50069	DE SOTO	90	99	99	101	96	95	95	94	88	95	112	111	95	112	92	83	110	93	82	103
50070	DEXTER	97	70	39	66	80	90	69	84	78	68	92	101	60	91	71	82	84	83	99	116
50071	DOWS	79	55	29	52	64	72	55	67	63	54	74	81	47	72	57	66	67	66	80	94
50072	EARLHAM	109	90	64	87	99	107	86	99	93	85	111	119	79	111	89	95	104	98	110	130
50073	ELKHART	84	103	113	101	101	103	95	94	90	94	114	109	101	121	97	89	113	91	87	103
50074	ELLSTON	74	58	39	52	65	73	54	66	62	54	73	77	49	72	58	66	68	65	78	90
50075	ELLSWORTH	91	64	33	60	74	83	63	78	72	62	85	94	54	83	65	76	77	77	93	108
50076	EXIRA	68	49	28	46	56	64	50	59	57	49	67	70	43	65	51	60	61	59	71	79
50101	GALT	77	54	28	51	63	71	53	66	62	53	72	80	46	71	55	65	66	65	79	92
50102	GARDEN CITY	85	59	31	56	69	77	58	72	67	58	79	87	50	77	61	71	72	71	86	100
50103	GARDEN GROVE	76	79	91	83	80	84	81	80	78	80	98	94	81	95	80	76	95	81	77	88
50104	GIBSON	89	62	33	59	73	81	62	76	71	61	83	92	53	82	64	75	76	75	91	106
50105	GILBERT	87	96	96	97	92	92	91	90	85	92	108	107	91	108	89	80	106	90	79	99
50106	GILMAN	75	65	50	64	68	76	64	69	68	63	83	81	62	83	65	69	78	68	75	85
50107	GRAND JUNCTION	68	51	32	48	56	66	55	61	61	52	72	70	48	69	55	65	66	61	73	76
50108	GRAND RIVER	70	49	26	46	57	64	48	60	56	48	65	72	41	64	50	58	59	59	71	83
50109	GRANGER	130	111	83	108	121	129	105	120	112	104	134	143	99	135	108	114	127	117	131	155
50111	GRIMES	112	122	114	126	117	115	111	112	103	115	131	130	113	130	109	98	129	109	98	124
50112	GRINNELL	85	68	52	66	73	83	73	78	78	70	94	91	66	91	72	81	88	79	88	96
50115	GUTHRIE CENTER	85	62	38	59	70	81	66	76	75	64	88	87	58	84	67	79	80	75	91	96
50116	HAMILTON	96	65	31	57	73	84	63	78	75	64	88	93	54	84	64	81	81	77	95	110
50117	HAMLIN	78	55	29	52	64	71	54	67	62	53	73	80	46	71	56	65	66	66	79	93
50118	HARTFORD	98	87	67	83	92	99	81	90	86	81	104	107	79	107	83	88	99	87	97	116
50119	HARVEY	77	68	52	65	72	77	63	70	67	63	81	83	62	83	65	69	77	68	76	90
50120	HAVERHILL	89	76	56	72	82	88	71	80	76	71	92	96	68	94	73	79	87	78	88	105
50122	HUBBARD	100	73	44	70	82	96	77	89	88	75	103	103	68	99	78	92	94	88	106	114
50123	HUMESTON	76	55	32	52	63	70	54	66	62	54	73	79	47	71	56	64	67	65	77	90
50124	HUXLEY	93	102	103	104	99	98	97	96	91	98	115	114	98	116	95	86	113	96	85	106
50125	INDIANOLA	82	89	97	89	89	93	87	87	85	86	107	101	90	110	88	84	105	86	84	97
50126	IOWA FALLS	75	66	57	64	71	78	66	72	70	65	85	84	63	86	68	72	81	71	79	88
50127	IRA	77	68	52	65	72	78	63	70	67	63	82	84	62	84	65	69	78	68	76	91
50128	JAMAICA	106	74	39	70	86	97	73	91	84	72	99	109	63	97	76	89	90	89	108	126
50129	JEFFERSON	72	61	48	58	65	75	63	68	69	61	83	77	60	82	64	72	77	67	78	82
50130	JEWELL	103	72	38	68	84	94	71	88	82	70	96	106	61	94	74	86	88	87	105	123
50131	JOHNSTON	158	180	179	187	173	169	164	162	151	169	192	190	170	194	161	142	190	158	140	178
50132	KAMRAR	92	65	34	61	75	84	64	79	73	63	86	95	54	84	66	77	79	78	94	110
50133	KELLERTON	54	40	27	39	44	53	45	49	50	42	59	55	40	56	44	53	54	49	59	59
50134	KELLEY	93	104	108	106	101	100	99	98	93	100	117	116	100	119	98	88	116	97	86	107
50135	KELLOGG	97	78	53	74	86	94	74	86	81	74	98	103	69	98	77	84	91	84	97	114
50136	KESWICK	106	74	39	70	86	96	73	90	84	72	99	109	62	97	76	88	90	89	108	126
50138	KNOXVILLE	81	69	53	66	74	82	69	75	74	67	90	87	66	90	69	77	84	74	84	93
50139	LACONA	86	66	42	63	74	82	64	76	71	64	85	91	58	85	66	74	79	75	87	102
50140	LAMONI	59	52	61	56	53	57	61	58	61	59	76	72	58	74	58	58	74	62	56	67
	IOWA	87	79	73	79	82	89	80	84	83	79	102	98	78	102	80	83	97	84	88	100
	UNITED STATES	100	100	100	100	100	100	100	100	100	100	100	100	100	100	100	100	100	100	100	100

POPULATION CHANGE

ZIP CODE		POPULATION			2000-2004 ANNUAL RATE		HOUSEHOLDS					FAMILIES		
#	POST OFFICE NAME	COUNTY FIPS CODE	2000	2004	2009	% Rate	State Centile	2000	2004	2009	% Annual Rate 2000-2004	2004 Average HH Size	2000	2004	% Annual Rate 2000-2004
50141	LAUREL	127	595	589	587	-0.2	37	231	230	231	-0.1	2.56	171	170	-0.1
50143	LEIGHTON	123	678	670	660	-0.3	34	237	236	234	-0.1	2.78	199	198	-0.1
50144	LEON	053	2577	2630	2701	0.5	69	1068	1093	1127	0.6	2.34	676	689	0.5
50146	LINDEN	049	477	484	529	0.3	64	190	194	213	0.5	2.49	148	151	0.5
50147	LINEVILLE	185	403	402	391	-0.1	46	174	174	171	0.0	2.31	121	121	0.0
50148	LISCOMB	127	426	423	423	-0.2	39	176	176	177	0.0	2.40	127	126	-0.2
50149	LORIMOR	175	895	895	914	0.0	51	364	367	378	0.2	2.43	257	260	0.3
50150	LOVILIA	135	1073	1096	1117	0.5	69	414	427	438	0.7	2.57	311	320	0.7
50151	LUCAS	117	769	869	938	2.9	95	316	358	387	3.0	2.43	233	263	2.9
50152	LUTHER	015	21	22	23	1.1	81	9	9	10	0.0	2.44	8	8	0.0
50153	LYNNVILLE	099	778	843	882	1.9	91	283	311	331	2.2	2.71	223	245	2.2
50154	MC CALLSBURG	169	527	505	521	-1.0	7	202	196	205	-0.7	2.58	157	152	-0.8
50155	MACKSBURG	121	267	319	368	4.3	99	100	121	140	4.6	2.64	81	97	4.3
50156	MADRID	015	4224	4430	4667	1.1	81	1583	1673	1775	1.3	2.55	1174	1237	1.2
50157	MALCOM	157	796	798	807	0.1	53	320	326	336	0.4	2.40	248	251	0.3
50158	MARSHALLTOWN	127	31445	31747	32015	0.2	60	12229	12377	12518	0.3	2.47	8211	8290	0.2
50161	MAXWELL	153	1940	2205	2439	3.1	96	719	821	913	3.2	2.69	562	642	3.2
50162	MELBOURNE	127	1249	1248	1245	0.0	48	493	495	495	0.1	2.52	350	350	0.0
50164	MENLO	077	649	646	660	-0.1	43	272	273	280	0.1	2.37	198	198	0.0
50165	MILLERTON	185	57	55	53	-0.8	10	24	23	23	-1.0	2.39	18	17	-1.3
50166	MILO	181	1542	1610	1705	1.0	80	560	592	636	1.3	2.72	442	465	1.2
50167	MINBURN	049	761	782	860	0.6	72	293	304	337	0.9	2.57	213	220	0.8
50168	MINGO	099	721	729	733	0.3	61	287	293	297	0.5	2.45	223	227	0.4
50169	MITCHELLVILLE	153	2734	2869	3030	1.1	82	909	969	1038	1.5	2.57	671	710	1.3
50170	MONROE	099	2775	2756	2762	-0.2	41	1092	1096	1111	0.1	2.51	810	807	-0.1
50171	MONTEZUMA	157	2909	2881	2904	-0.2	37	1202	1211	1242	0.2	2.33	845	849	0.1
50173	MONTOUR	171	787	786	781	0.0	47	291	294	294	0.2	2.65	216	217	0.1
50174	MURRAY	039	1409	1401	1383	-0.1	42	550	549	544	0.0	2.55	412	409	-0.2
50201	NEVADA	169	8304	8251	8518	-0.2	42	3301	3313	3453	0.1	2.43	2251	2246	-0.1
50206	NEW PROVIDENCE	083	506	489	477	-0.8	11	201	196	192	-0.6	2.48	146	141	-0.8
50207	NEW SHARON	123	2648	2617	2580	-0.3	34	1017	1012	1006	-0.1	2.54	767	759	-0.3
50208	NEWTON	099	20901	21004	21196	0.1	55	8344	8470	8640	0.4	2.32	5522	5590	0.3
50210	NEW VIRGINIA	181	1753	1848	1931	1.3	83	669	715	757	1.6	2.54	525	558	1.4
50211	NORWALK	181	9133	9787	10518	1.6	88	3138	3417	3724	2.0	2.81	2547	2755	1.9
50212	OGDEN	015	3298	3513	3717	1.5	86	1303	1391	1479	1.6	2.48	958	1018	1.4
50213	OSCEOLA	039	6346	6325	6253	-0.1	45	2535	2521	2486	-0.1	2.46	1694	1679	-0.2
50214	OTLEY	125	879	936	980	1.5	86	310	332	349	1.6	2.82	265	282	1.5
50216	PANORA	077	2714	2927	3135	1.8	90	1125	1225	1324	2.0	2.32	777	844	2.0
50217	PATON	073	645	683	699	1.4	84	266	281	288	1.3	2.43	189	199	1.2
50218	PATTERSON	121	106	115	126	1.9	91	44	48	53	2.1	2.33	34	37	2.0
50219	PELLA	125	12825	13475	14071	1.2	82	4477	4766	5037	1.5	2.52	3204	3411	1.5
50220	PERRY	049	8986	9489	10537	1.3	84	3327	3513	3918	1.3	2.62	2328	2451	1.2
50222	PERU	121	587	682	774	3.6	98	208	243	278	3.7	2.81	169	197	3.7
50223	PILOT MOUND	015	464	474	489	0.5	69	194	199	207	0.6	2.38	133	135	0.4
50225	PLEASANTVILLE	125	2606	2632	2694	0.2	60	1018	1037	1070	0.4	2.50	727	730	0.1
50226	POLK CITY	153	3408	3601	3863	1.3	84	1204	1288	1392	1.6	2.76	984	1046	1.5
50227	POPEJOY	069	23	22	22	-1.0	6	10	10	10	0.0	2.20	7	7	0.0
50228	PRAIRIE CITY	099	2120	2128	2134	0.1	54	831	846	859	0.4	2.46	611	619	0.3
50229	PROLE	181	1388	1423	1493	0.6	71	518	540	574	1.0	2.62	407	423	0.9
50230	RADCLIFFE	083	1229	1252	1249	0.4	67	488	502	505	0.7	2.49	357	366	0.6
50231	RANDALL	079	148	147	146	-0.2	41	68	68	68	0.0	2.16	54	53	-0.4
50232	REASNOR	099	554	571	585	0.7	74	206	225	238	2.1	1.93	172	187	2.0
50233	REDFIELD	049	1358	1392	1524	0.6	71	551	570	629	0.8	2.43	384	395	0.7
50234	RHODES	127	498	496	495	-0.1	44	202	203	203	0.1	2.44	148	148	0.0
50235	RIPPEY	073	536	613	650	3.2	97	208	238	251	3.2	2.58	154	175	3.1
50236	ROLAND	169	1587	1599	1653	0.2	58	576	586	610	0.4	2.73	440	447	0.4
50237	RUNNELLS	153	2448	2678	2887	2.1	92	854	937	1013	2.2	2.86	729	795	2.1
50238	RUSSELL	117	874	868	873	-0.2	41	372	371	373	-0.1	2.34	238	236	-0.2
50239	SAINT ANTHONY	127	226	216	216	-1.1	6	84	81	82	-0.9	2.67	64	62	-0.7
50240	SAINT CHARLES	121	2029	2102	2244	0.8	77	777	816	880	1.2	2.57	596	623	1.1
50242	SEARSBORO	157	465	554	612	4.2	99	191	230	258	4.5	2.41	146	175	4.4
50244	SLATER	153	1714	1780	1869	0.9	78	684	720	764	1.2	2.47	487	511	1.1
50246	STANHOPE	079	893	883	880	-0.3	35	344	341	342	-0.2	2.59	249	247	-0.2
50247	STATE CENTER	127	2104	2073	2067	-0.4	30	838	834	836	-0.1	2.44	577	571	-0.3
50248	STORY CITY	169	4351	4554	4792	1.1	81	1715	1819	1939	1.4	2.38	1129	1190	1.3
50249	STRATFORD	079	1410	1385	1379	-0.4	26	544	537	537	-0.3	2.45	365	360	-0.3
50250	STUART	001	2420	2678	2859	2.4	94	976	1092	1174	2.7	2.39	679	755	2.5
50251	SULLY	099	1476	1448	1450	-0.5	25	553	548	554	-0.2	2.64	448	443	-0.3
50252	SWAN	125	461	482	501	1.1	80	154	162	170	1.2	2.98	126	132	1.1
50254	THAYER	175	363	379	387	1.0	80	146	154	159	1.3	2.39	109	115	1.3
50256	TRACY	125	476	490	505	0.7	73	189	197	206	1.0	2.48	142	148	1.0
50257	TRURO	121	900	958	1034	1.5	86	332	357	389	1.7	2.68	257	274	1.5
50258	UNION	083	1016	1030	1024	0.3	64	411	419	419	0.5	2.45	303	308	0.4
50261	VAN METER	121	1895	1973	2167	1.0	79	713	751	832	1.2	2.63	537	565	1.2
50262	VAN WERT	053	414	416	426	0.1	54	170	172	177	0.3	2.42	121	122	0.2
50263	WAUKEE	049	7146	8799	10627	5.0	100	2639	3271	3972	5.2	2.69	2023	2503	5.1
50264	WELDON	053	526	514	515	-0.5	21	210	207	208	-0.3	2.48	155	152	-0.5
50265	WEST DES MOINES	153	30144	31901	33960	1.3	84	12662	13477	14404	1.5	2.34	7905	8334	1.3
50266	WEST DES MOINES	153	16610	19993	23008	4.5	99	7286	8777	10135	4.5	2.28	4146	5043	4.7
50268	WHAT CHEER	107	1023	1021	1022	-0.1	46	447	450	454	0.2	2.27	283	284	0.1
50271	WILLIAMS	079	776	769	766	-0.2	38	312	312	313	0.0	2.46	241	241	0.0
50272	WILLIAMSON	117	512	515	521	0.1	57	203	204	207	0.1	2.50	154	154	0.0
50273	WINTERSET	121	7501	7926	8560	1.3	84	2879	3058	3324	1.4	2.51	2024	2142	1.3
50274	WIOTA	029	538	538	538	0.0	51	215	217	220	0.2	2.36	158	159	0.2
50275	WOODBURN	039	721	695	677	-0.9	10	260	253	247	-0.6	2.72	201	195	-0.7
50276	WOODWARD	015	2597	2667	2867	0.6	72	899	938	1030	1.0	2.57	621	645	0.9
50277	YALE	077	479	542	598	3.0	96	204	233	259	3.2	2.33	153	174	3.1
50278	ZEARING	169	904	866	892	-1.0	6	331	320	332	-0.8	2.60	242	233	-0.9
50309	DES MOINES	153	5011	4957	5076	-0.3	36	2272	2251	2337	-0.2	1.56	575	559	-0.7
50310	DES MOINES	153	31624	31463	32656	-0.1	42	13538	13573	14184	0.1	2.28	8279	8211	-0.2
50311	DES MOINES	153	18294	18281	19025	0.0	48	7365	7421	7808	0.2	2.20	3762	3729	-0.2
50312	DES MOINES	153	16304	16453	17156	0.2	59	7616	7762	8152	0.5	2.07	3790	3813	0.1
50313	DES MOINES	153	16399	16734	17557	0.5	69	6680	6851	7224	0.6	2.43	4352	4423	0.4
50314	DES MOINES	153	12318	12228	12694	-0.2	39	4427	4368	4539	-0.3	2.68	2569	2516	-0.5
50315	DES MOINES	153	37457	37704	39253	0.2	57	15137	15412	16178	0.4	2.41	9822	9892	0.2
	IOWA					0.5					0.7	2.43			0.6
	UNITED STATES					1.2					1.3	2.58			1.1

ZIP CODE #	POST OFFICE NAME	RACE (%) White		Black		Asian/Pacific		% Hispanic Origin		2004 AGE DISTRIBUTION (%)										MEDIAN AGE	% 2004 Males	% 2004 Females
		2000	2004	2000	2004	2000	2004	2000	2004	0-4	5-9	10-14	15-19	20-24	25-44	45-64	65-84	85+	18+	2004		
50141	LAUREL	98.2	97.8	0.0	0.0	0.5	0.7	1.2	1.5	6.8	7.0	7.5	7.1	6.1	23.9	27.3	12.6	1.7	74.4	40.2	49.6	50.4
50143	LEIGHTON	99.3	99.1	0.0	0.0	0.3	0.5	0.2	0.2	7.8	7.9	8.7	6.3	5.7	26.3	25.1	11.3	1.0	71.8	37.0	50.2	49.9
50144	LEON	98.6	98.3	0.2	0.2	0.4	0.6	1.4	1.6	6.6	6.8	7.5	6.2	5.9	23.7	23.0	16.2	4.3	75.0	40.3	47.5	52.6
50146	LINDEN	99.0	98.8	0.0	0.0	0.2	0.2	0.8	1.0	6.2	7.9	7.9	7.0	4.1	24.6	28.1	13.0	1.2	73.4	40.3	52.3	47.7
50147	LINEVILLE	99.5	99.3	0.0	0.0	0.5	0.5	0.7	1.0	5.2	5.2	5.7	6.5	5.7	19.2	27.1	21.6	3.7	79.4	46.5	48.0	52.0
50148	LISCOMB	98.6	98.6	0.0	0.0	0.2	0.2	0.5	0.5	5.4	5.9	7.3	6.2	5.4	24.8	29.6	13.7	1.7	77.3	41.6	50.4	49.7
50149	LORIMOR	97.7	97.5	0.0	0.0	0.2	0.3	0.8	1.0	6.5	6.5	7.0	6.7	5.8	26.3	26.4	13.7	1.1	75.5	39.1	50.5	49.5
50150	LOVILIA	98.9	98.9	0.1	0.1	0.1	0.1	0.2	0.2	8.0	8.1	8.5	6.8	5.6	26.6	21.9	13.2	1.4	71.1	36.2	50.4	49.6
50151	LUCAS	98.8	98.7	0.0	0.0	0.3	0.4	1.2	1.3	6.3	6.3	7.0	6.2	5.3	24.7	27.2	15.3	1.6	76.6	41.5	49.3	50.8
50152	LUTHER	100.0	100.0	0.0	0.0	0.0	0.0	0.0	0.0	4.6	9.1	9.1	9.1	9.1	27.3	31.8	0.0	0.0	77.3	35.0	50.0	50.0
50153	LYNNVILLE	99.9	99.8	0.0	0.0	0.1	0.2	0.8	0.8	6.6	7.1	9.5	6.9	5.6	24.1	26.2	12.5	1.5	72.5	38.6	51.5	48.5
50154	MC CALLSBURG	99.1	99.2	0.4	0.4	0.2	0.2	0.2	0.2	4.6	5.4	7.3	7.3	5.9	24.8	29.3	14.1	1.4	78.2	41.7	52.7	47.3
50155	MACKSBURG	97.4	96.9	0.0	0.0	0.4	0.3	1.9	1.9	6.9	7.2	7.2	6.0	5.0	24.8	28.8	12.5	1.6	74.9	39.9	50.5	49.5
50156	MADRID	99.0	98.7	0.2	0.2	0.3	0.4	0.8	1.1	6.7	6.8	7.2	6.3	5.7	25.7	25.0	13.2	3.5	75.3	39.3	48.8	51.2
50157	MALCOM	98.7	98.5	0.1	0.1	0.3	0.4	0.4	0.5	6.0	6.5	7.8	6.1	5.0	25.1	27.9	13.7	1.9	75.8	41.3	52.3	47.7
50158	MARSHALLTOWN	88.5	86.5	1.1	1.2	1.0	1.4	10.8	12.8	6.6	6.3	6.8	6.6	6.8	24.7	25.4	14.2	2.6	76.3	39.2	49.8	50.2
50161	MAXWELL	98.8	98.5	0.0	0.1	0.4	0.6	0.4	0.5	7.1	7.9	8.3	7.0	5.4	27.3	25.4	10.3	1.3	72.3	37.4	50.8	49.2
50162	MELBOURNE	99.1	99.0	0.1	0.1	0.2	0.3	0.5	0.7	6.8	7.1	7.5	6.0	6.3	29.6	24.8	10.4	1.6	75.1	37.1	50.2	49.8
50164	MENLO	98.6	98.9	0.0	0.0	0.0	0.0	0.9	0.9	5.6	4.6	8.1	6.4	6.2	25.2	27.4	15.0	1.6	77.1	41.5	51.2	48.8
50165	MILLERTON	96.5	98.2	0.0	0.0	0.0	0.0	0.0	0.0	3.6	5.5	7.3	7.3	3.6	20.0	27.3	23.6	1.8	80.0	46.9	43.6	56.4
50166	MILO	98.9	98.7	0.1	0.1	0.2	0.3	0.4	0.4	7.2	7.3	8.1	7.3	5.5	28.5	23.3	11.1	1.6	72.8	37.0	50.8	49.3
50167	MINBURN	99.1	98.9	0.1	0.1	0.0	0.0	0.9	1.2	6.4	7.2	7.9	6.4	4.6	26.5	28.1	11.4	1.5	74.3	39.8	50.3	49.7
50168	MINGO	98.5	98.4	0.1	0.1	0.1	0.3	1.1	1.2	5.9	6.6	7.8	6.5	4.8	26.8	28.4	11.4	1.9	75.7	40.6	49.8	50.2
50169	MITCHELLVILLE	94.0	92.6	2.9	3.7	0.6	0.9	1.5	1.9	6.3	6.5	7.0	7.3	7.1	32.5	22.7	8.8	1.9	76.0	35.7	43.9	56.1
50170	MONROE	98.1	97.7	0.1	0.2	0.5	0.6	1.0	1.2	6.6	7.5	7.9	6.2	5.6	27.3	25.6	11.9	1.4	74.0	38.1	49.6	50.4
50171	MONTEZUMA	98.9	98.8	0.1	0.1	0.3	0.4	0.3	0.4	5.1	5.4	6.0	6.3	5.6	22.4	29.2	17.2	2.8	79.6	44.4	49.9	50.1
50173	MONTOUR	77.9	77.0	0.1	0.1	0.0	0.0	2.5	2.7	7.1	7.6	7.5	7.0	5.6	26.2	24.8	13.0	1.2	73.3	37.5	52.5	47.5
50174	MURRAY	98.7	98.6	0.4	0.4	0.1	0.1	0.8	0.8	5.7	6.0	7.6	7.4	7.4	25.2	25.2	13.9	1.7	76.2	39.7	51.0	49.0
50201	NEVADA	97.2	96.6	0.5	0.6	0.7	1.1	0.9	1.1	6.7	6.3	6.8	6.8	7.5	28.5	24.2	10.9	2.4	76.0	36.3	48.8	51.2
50206	NEW PROVIDENCE	98.6	98.6	0.0	0.0	0.2	0.2	1.0	1.2	6.8	7.2	7.2	5.9	5.5	24.3	26.2	14.9	2.0	75.1	40.2	53.2	46.8
50207	NEW SHARON	99.1	98.8	0.1	0.1	0.3	0.4	0.5	0.6	6.4	6.9	7.9	7.2	5.7	25.6	24.1	13.1	3.1	73.9	39.1	49.6	50.4
50208	NEWTON	96.9	96.4	1.2	1.3	0.6	0.9	1.2	1.5	6.2	6.1	6.4	5.9	6.4	27.6	24.3	14.3	2.8	77.3	39.4	50.5	49.5
50210	NEW VIRGINIA	98.8	98.8	0.1	0.1	0.2	0.2	0.6	0.7	6.0	6.4	6.2	6.2	5.3	25.0	30.6	12.3	2.2	77.5	42.1	51.3	48.7
50211	NORWALK	97.8	97.3	0.2	0.3	0.6	0.8	1.4	1.6	8.1	8.2	8.4	7.4	5.9	29.4	24.1	7.2	1.4	70.2	35.2	48.1	51.9
50212	OGDEN	99.1	99.0	0.1	0.1	0.2	0.2	0.6	0.8	6.1	6.5	7.3	7.0	5.2	25.0	26.8	13.7	2.4	75.6	40.6	49.0	51.0
50213	OSCEOLA	96.2	96.1	0.1	0.1	0.5	0.5	5.0	5.2	6.6	6.6	7.0	7.2	6.1	24.7	24.7	13.9	3.4	75.4	39.3	48.8	51.2
50214	OTLEY	98.0	97.3	0.2	0.3	1.0	1.4	0.5	0.4	8.2	9.1	9.3	6.4	4.7	29.7	23.3	8.6	0.8	69.3	36.0	51.5	48.5
50216	PANORA	98.6	98.4	0.3	0.3	0.3	0.4	0.9	1.1	5.8	5.9	6.3	5.8	5.2	22.8	26.2	18.3	3.7	78.0	43.8	49.7	50.3
50217	PATON	97.8	98.0	0.2	0.2	0.3	0.3	2.2	2.3	6.6	6.7	7.6	6.3	5.6	25.0	25.6	14.1	2.5	75.1	40.2	51.8	48.2
50218	PATTERSON	99.1	98.3	0.0	0.0	0.0	0.0	0.0	0.0	6.1	7.0	7.0	6.1	4.4	27.0	30.4	11.3	0.9	75.7	40.3	52.2	47.8
50219	PELLA	96.8	95.9	0.2	0.2	2.0	2.9	0.9	1.1	6.0	6.2	6.6	9.7	10.2	23.6	21.8	12.4	3.5	77.1	35.5	48.5	51.6
50220	PERRY	85.2	81.9	1.0	1.0	0.8	1.0	21.0	25.9	7.8	7.1	7.1	6.9	7.2	27.1	21.7	12.5	2.8	73.8	36.0	50.2	49.8
50222	PERU	97.8	97.5	0.0	0.0	0.2	0.2	1.4	1.5	6.5	7.0	7.9	6.5	4.8	24.6	29.2	12.0	1.5	74.5	39.9	50.4	49.6
50223	PILOT MOUND	99.6	100.0	0.0	0.0	0.0	0.0	0.2	0.2	4.9	5.7	7.8	6.1	5.1	22.6	31.0	15.0	1.9	77.6	43.8	53.4	46.6
50225	PLEASANTVILLE	98.8	98.6	0.1	0.1	0.4	0.6	1.3	1.5	6.9	7.0	8.5	7.7	5.4	26.0	24.3	11.7	2.7	72.6	38.0	49.4	50.6
50226	POLK CITY	98.4	98.0	0.3	0.4	0.3	0.4	0.7	0.9	7.9	8.6	7.6	6.6	4.3	29.0	27.7	7.3	1.0	71.5	37.2	51.1	48.9
50227	POPEJOY	95.7	100.0	0.0	0.0	0.0	0.0	0.0	0.0	9.1	9.1	9.1	9.1	9.1	36.4	18.2	0.0	0.0	72.7	27.5	50.0	50.0
50228	PRAIRIE CITY	98.4	98.1	0.3	0.3	0.3	0.4	0.9	1.0	6.4	7.1	7.0	5.8	5.0	26.9	25.1	13.6	3.0	75.8	40.0	49.3	50.7
50229	PROLE	98.5	98.1	0.0	0.0	0.4	0.5	1.0	1.2	6.1	7.0	7.9	7.0	5.5	25.5	30.0	10.0	1.0	74.6	40.0	50.2	49.8
50230	RADCLIFFE	97.7	97.4	0.0	0.0	0.1	0.1	2.9	3.5	5.9	6.6	7.2	6.5	5.8	24.4	26.8	13.9	2.9	76.4	40.8	50.9	49.1
50231	RANDALL	98.0	98.0	0.7	0.7	0.0	0.0	1.4	1.4	5.4	6.8	8.2	6.1	4.8	25.2	30.6	11.6	1.4	75.5	41.8	53.7	46.3
50232	REASNOR	94.0	93.5	4.5	4.9	0.4	0.5	1.4	1.8	5.3	5.6	5.6	6.0	7.7	34.0	25.0	9.1	1.8	80.0	37.4	61.8	38.2
50233	REDFIELD	98.8	98.6	0.0	0.0	0.1	0.1	0.7	0.9	5.6	6.3	7.3	6.6	5.5	25.6	27.3	13.7	2.2	76.7	40.8	51.7	48.4
50234	RHODES	98.2	97.6	0.0	0.0	0.4	0.6	0.8	1.2	6.3	6.7	7.5	6.9	5.9	23.6	29.2	13.3	0.8	75.4	40.5	50.4	49.6
50235	RIPPEY	97.6	97.6	0.4	0.3	0.2	0.2	1.9	2.1	6.7	6.9	7.7	6.9	5.7	25.6	24.8	13.5	2.3	74.4	39.4	53.2	46.8
50236	ROLAND	99.0	98.9	0.1	0.1	0.3	0.4	0.7	0.8	7.4	7.9	9.0	7.9	5.0	28.1	23.7	9.4	1.5	70.7	36.2	49.2	50.8
50237	RUNNELLS	98.2	97.7	0.1	0.2	0.3	0.4	0.9	1.2	6.3	7.2	8.3	6.9	5.2	25.5	30.3	9.4	0.9	73.8	40.2	49.8	50.2
50238	RUSSELL	98.3	98.3	0.0	0.0	0.3	0.5	0.6	0.7	6.9	6.3	7.3	5.5	6.5	21.9	25.2	16.7	3.7	76.0	41.6	48.9	51.2
50239	SAINT ANTHONY	97.4	97.2	0.4	0.5	0.0	0.0	1.3	1.9	5.6	6.0	6.9	6.5	5.6	25.5	28.2	14.4	1.4	76.9	41.4	52.3	47.7
50240	SAINT CHARLES	98.5	98.5	0.0	0.0	0.1	0.1	1.0	1.1	6.6	7.4	7.4	6.7	4.9	27.1	28.6	10.1	1.2	74.4	39.2	51.0	49.1
50242	SEARSBORO	98.9	98.7	0.0	0.0	0.2	0.4	0.2	0.2	6.7	6.9	6.3	5.8	5.4	23.8	31.1	13.0	1.1	76.4	42.0	51.8	48.2
50244	SLATER	99.4	99.3	0.2	0.3	0.2	0.2	0.2	0.2	7.2	7.4	7.0	6.9	5.7	26.5	26.5	10.6	2.2	74.0	38.1	49.6	50.5
50246	STANHOPE	99.1	99.1	0.0	0.0	0.0	0.0	0.7	0.8	5.7	6.2	7.7	6.5	5.2	24.7	27.0	14.8	2.3	76.4	41.8	51.2	48.8
50247	STATE CENTER	98.0	97.6	0.0	0.0	0.2	0.3	1.7	2.1	5.8	6.2	8.0	6.4	5.2	26.0	24.9	14.4	3.1	76.0	40.3	49.2	50.8
50248	STORY CITY	98.4	98.1	0.5	0.5	0.4	0.6	0.6	0.8	6.1	6.7	6.6	6.4	5.2	24.6	24.0	14.1	6.4	76.7	41.4	48.0	52.0
50249	STRATFORD	99.2	99.1	0.0	0.0	0.1	0.1	0.5	0.5	5.6	5.9	6.7	6.3	5.1	23.1	25.1	17.7	4.6	77.7	43.3	50.8	49.2
50250	STUART	98.6	98.6	0.0	0.0	0.1	0.2	0.9	0.9	6.8	6.7	6.6	6.1	6.1	24.4	24.9	14.9	3.7	76.2	40.7	50.0	50.0
50251	SULLY	99.8	99.6	0.0	0.0	0.2	0.4	0.3	0.4	6.8	7.0	7.4	7.3	5.9	23.8	25.8	14.2	1.9	74.2	39.8	51.0	49.0
50252	SWAN	99.4	99.2	0.0	0.2	0.2	0.2	0.9	0.8	6.6	7.1	8.1	7.3	5.0	27.2	26.4	11.0	1.5	73.4	38.9	50.0	50.0
50254	THAYER	99.2	99.2	0.0	0.0	0.3	0.3	0.6	0.3	5.0	5.3	6.3	6.1	4.8	25.9	27.7	16.1	2.9	79.2	43.0	50.7	49.3
50256	TRACY	99.2	99.0	0.4	0.6	0.0	0.2	0.2	0.2	7.4	7.1	6.9	6.3	6.1	26.7	26.1	12.2	1.0	74.7	37.8	51.2	48.8
50257	TRURO	97.9	97.6	0.1	0.1	0.2	0.3	0.9	0.9	7.1	7.7	9.2	6.9	5.5	24.7	26.0	11.4	1.5	71.6	37.9	49.6	50.4
50258	UNION	98.7	98.5	0.1	0.1	0.2	0.4	0.8	1.0	6.2	6.9	7.7	5.5	6.1	21.7	28.3	15.8	1.8	75.8	41.6	50.4	49.6
50261	VAN METER	98.1	97.5	0.3	0.4	0.5	0.8	1.2	1.6	6.5	7.2	7.8	7.3	5.6	26.9	28.8	9.2	0.7	74.0	38.4	49.7	50.3
50262	VAN WERT	98.8	98.8	0.0	0.0	0.0	0.0	1.2	1.2	6.3	6.5	7.7	5.8	5.5	23.8	27.9	14.9	1.7	76.2	40.9	50.5	49.5
50263	WAUKEE	98.0	97.4	0.5	0.6	0.7	1.0	0.8	1.1	9.2	8.9	7.6	6.2	5.7	31.3	23.6	6.9	0.6	70.4	34.4	50.0	50.0
50264	WELDON	98.1	98.1	0.0	0.0	0.0	0.0	1.9	2.0	6.2	6.4	7.6	5.8	5.8	24.3	28.2	14.0	1.6	76.1	40.7	51.8	48.3
50265	WEST DES MOINES	93.1	91.0	1.5	1.8	2.7	4.0	3.1	3.8	7.1	6.7	6.7	6.1	7.0	32.6	23.1	9.3	1.4	75.6	34.8	48.0	52.0
50266	WEST DES MOINES	92.0	90.1	2.4	2.7	2.9	4.2	2.8	3.4	8.7	7.7	7.1	5.6	6.9	36.8	19.7	6.9	0.6	73.1	32.1	48.1	52.0
50268	WHAT CHEER	98.6	98.6	0.0	0.0	0.0	0.0	0.5	0.6	5.4	5.8	7.2	6.1	6.0	22.9	26.3	17.6	2.8	78.2	42.6	48.6	51.4
50271	WILLIAMS	98.3	98.3	0.1	0.1	0.4	0.4	1.0	1.2	5.6	6.5	7.7	6.8	4.9	24.2	28.1	14.7	1.6	76.1	41.8	51.5	48.5
50272	WILLIAMSON	98.4	98.3	0.2	0.2	0.2	0.2	0.6	0.8	5.1	6.0	7.6	7.4	4.9	23.7	30.1	14.2	1.2	76.5	42.1	50.5	49.5
50273	WINTERSET	98.7	98.5	0.1	0.1	0.2	0.3	0.7	0.8	6.9	7.0	7.1	6.8	6.2	24.6	24.4	13.0	3.9	74.5	38.9	48.4	51.6
50274	WIOTA	99.4	99.4	0.0	0.0	0.0	0.0	0.2	0.2	6.3	6.5	6.7	4.8	5.2	22.1	26.2	18.0	4.1	77.1	43.9	50.4	49.6
50275	WOODBURN	95.3	95.1	0.0	0.0	0.1	0.1	4.0	4.3	7.6	7.3	6.8	6.0	6.0	25.2	26.9	12.7	1.4	74.5	39.8	52.4	47.6
50276	WOODWARD	97.7	97.2	0.8	0.9	0.6	0.8	0.9	1.1	5.2	5.5	6.9	9.8	6.7	25.7	27.5	10.8	2.0	75.4	39.6	50.8	49.2
50277	YALE	99.2	98.9	0.2	0.2	0.2	0.4	0.6	0.7	5.2	5.5	5.5	5.2	4.6	21.8	31.7	18.3	2.2	80.4	46.5	50.4	49.6
50278	ZEARING	98.0	97.7	0.1	0.1	0.6	0.8	0.4	0.5	7.2	6.7	6.2	7.2	7.4	24.4	24.0	13.9	3.1	75.1	38.7	47.2	52.8
50309	DES MOINES	72.2	67.7	15.3	17.4	3.4	4.6	9.1	10.8	5.2	3.4	3.1	5.5	6.8	31.7	24.4	14.8	5.3	85.5	41.6	56.4	43.6
50310	DES MOINES	87.0	84.3	5.9	6.8	2.7	3.9	3.0	3.7	7.0	6.5	6.1	5.8	6.5	32.6	22.2	10.9	2.5	76.8	36.1	47.6	52.4
50311	DES MOINES	81.2	78.4	9.3	10.1	3.3	4.5	5.8	6.7	6.7	5.7	5.1	10.1	14.9	29.6	19.5	7.2	1.3	79.2	29.7	47.9	52.1
50312	DES MOINES	89.4	87.6	5.9	6.6	1.5	2.1	2.7	3.4	5.4	5.3	5.5	5.8	6.8	28.1	25.6	12.6	5.0	80.2	40.4	47.4	52.6
50313	DES MOINES	87.9	85.0	4.2	4.9	3.0	4.3	5.1	6.3	7.1	7.1	6.9	6.3	5.7	29.6	24.2	11.6	1.5	75.1	37.2	49.6	50.4
50314	DES MOINES	37.6	32.9	37.0	38.2	11.1	13.7	15.4	17.1	9.6	9.0	8.7	7.5	7.8	29.0	18.8	8.6	1.2	68.3	29.9	48.8	51.2
50315	DES MOINES	89.2	86.5	3.0	3.6	2.4	3.5	6.9	8.5	7.5	7.1	6.8	6.4	7.4	30.8	22.3	10.4	1.4	74.8	34.7	48.6	51.4
	IOWA	93.9	93.0	2.1	2.3	1.3	1.8	2.8	3.2	6.5	6.5	6.9	7.2	7.6	26.4	24.2	12.3	2.4	76.0	37.2	49.2	50.8
	UNITED STATES	75.1	73.6	12.3	12.5	3.8	4.2	12.5	14.1	6.9	6.7	7.2	7.0	7.3	28.6	23.8	10.8	1.7	75.1	36.0	49.1	50.9

ZIP CODE #	POST OFFICE NAME	2004 Per Capita Income	2004 HH Income Base	2004 HOUSEHOLD INCOME DISTRIBUTION (%) Less than $25,000	$25,000 to $49,999	$50,000 to $99,999	$100,000 to $149,999	$150,000 or More	MEDIAN HOUSEHOLD INCOME 2004	2009	2004 National Centile	2004 State Centile	2004 Home Value Base	2004 HOME VALUE DISTRIBUTION (%) Less than $50,000	$50,000 to $89,999	$90,000 to $174,999	$175,000 to $399,999	$400,000 or More	2004 Median Home Value
50141	LAUREL	21781	230	16.5	33.5	43.0	6.1	0.9	50000	58461	72	82	194	16.5	30.9	38.1	13.9	0.5	94167
50143	LEIGHTON	20113	236	15.7	37.7	39.0	5.9	1.7	47006	53228	66	73	194	12.9	20.6	44.9	16.0	5.7	109028
50144	LEON	15113	1093	41.4	37.4	18.9	1.4	0.9	29732	33709	12	2	788	45.8	31.0	19.8	2.8	0.6	55323
50146	LINDEN	24168	194	15.5	30.4	41.2	10.3	2.6	54262	63947	79	90	156	17.3	18.6	43.6	17.3	3.2	117105
50147	LINEVILLE	23601	174	36.2	27.6	22.4	10.9	2.9	38181	42805	40	23	133	56.4	18.1	9.0	11.3	5.3	42273
50148	LISCOMB	20443	176	22.7	33.5	38.6	5.1	0.0	46200	52645	64	69	139	18.0	22.3	42.5	13.7	3.6	106771
50149	LORIMOR	16759	367	33.8	37.1	24.8	3.8	0.5	35676	40881	30	12	300	46.3	22.3	23.3	7.0	1.0	55238
50150	LOVILIA	16013	427	32.3	33.5	30.4	3.8	0.0	36338	41155	33	15	362	41.4	36.7	15.2	3.6	3.0	56889
50151	LUCAS	23842	358	29.1	31.3	33.0	3.9	2.8	40961	46614	50	41	308	38.3	13.3	33.1	15.3	0.0	85833
50152	LUTHER	30857	9	0.0	22.2	55.6	22.2	0.0	65822	80896	89	98	8	0.0	0.0	37.5	62.5	0.0	200000
50153	LYNNVILLE	21949	311	12.2	34.4	41.8	9.0	2.6	52345	60118	76	87	257	10.1	26.1	46.7	13.2	3.9	105637
50154	MC CALLSBURG	19343	196	26.5	29.6	37.8	5.6	0.5	45640	54443	63	66	156	16.7	25.6	43.0	12.2	2.6	98000
50155	MACKSBURG	18194	121	25.6	35.5	31.4	6.6	0.8	41952	49222	53	48	101	31.7	19.8	34.7	13.9	0.0	86250
50156	MADRID	26554	1673	15.2	31.6	39.0	10.6	3.5	52270	61315	76	87	1333	12.0	25.6	44.2	14.5	3.8	108057
50157	MALCOM	22828	326	19.6	31.3	39.6	7.7	1.8	48984	56517	70	79	267	15.7	24.3	36.0	22.1	1.9	104934
50158	MARSHALLTOWN	21034	12377	26.0	32.2	31.8	7.4	2.6	43207	51002	57	54	8908	19.3	34.3	35.7	10.2	0.5	85856
50161	MAXWELL	26139	821	17.1	25.8	42.4	9.4	5.4	56200	67715	81	93	699	12.2	20.5	40.5	24.9	2.0	115940
50162	MELBOURNE	22661	495	16.2	29.3	45.3	7.5	1.8	52810	61429	77	88	415	20.5	35.4	36.6	6.8	0.7	84302
50164	MENLO	20606	273	31.9	37.4	25.6	3.7	1.5	37594	43640	38	19	224	30.8	38.8	27.2	3.1	0.0	73333
50165	MILLERTON	15667	23	34.8	39.1	26.1	0.0	0.0	33593	33593	23	6	19	42.1	26.3	26.3	0.0	5.3	57500
50166	MILO	20886	592	15.7	32.3	43.2	7.9	0.8	51525	60000	75	85	508	10.0	24.8	44.9	20.1	0.2	109184
50167	MINBURN	22830	304	20.7	27.6	37.5	11.8	2.3	51266	61814	74	85	249	13.7	18.1	52.6	13.3	2.4	116033
50168	MINGO	25019	293	17.4	31.1	38.6	10.2	2.7	51023	60132	74	84	252	10.3	15.9	47.6	24.6	1.6	122549
50169	MITCHELLVILLE	22516	969	18.7	24.7	43.3	10.2	3.1	55307	66942	80	91	737	8.8	18.7	54.1	17.6	0.7	115557
50170	MONROE	21521	1096	21.5	32.2	36.8	8.3	1.2	47479	54571	67	74	884	13.9	29.0	43.4	12.3	1.4	96495
50171	MONTEZUMA	25006	1211	23.3	31.7	35.6	7.0	2.4	45829	53271	63	68	941	16.5	29.3	37.1	16.4	0.7	95643
50173	MONTOUR	16384	294	28.9	35.0	32.0	3.1	1.0	35646	40605	30	12	238	29.0	30.3	29.0	9.2	2.5	78571
50174	MURRAY	17668	549	28.4	37.2	27.9	6.2	0.4	38590	45734	41	26	446	29.4	37.9	22.2	8.3	2.2	71628
50201	NEVADA	24628	3313	18.5	31.6	36.8	10.5	2.6	49924	61636	72	82	2335	16.9	20.6	47.0	13.7	1.9	105208
50206	NEW PROVIDENCE	24977	196	19.4	40.8	32.1	2.6	5.1	42976	49256	56	53	155	25.2	32.9	29.0	12.3	0.7	83056
50207	NEW SHARON	19422	1012	23.4	33.4	36.6	5.9	0.7	45562	51575	63	66	796	17.2	31.3	35.3	13.2	3.0	92182
50208	NEWTON	23083	8470	24.2	29.9	35.6	7.5	2.8	46550	54323	65	71	6147	11.2	30.3	41.4	16.0	1.1	99026
50210	NEW VIRGINIA	21655	715	19.4	30.1	40.7	7.0	2.8	50240	57890	72	83	626	11.0	25.4	39.5	22.4	1.8	116000
50211	NORWALK	26741	3417	11.3	19.5	47.8	15.6	5.9	66921	78214	90	98	2952	2.4	9.2	58.3	27.5	2.5	134683
50212	OGDEN	22511	1391	21.0	33.4	36.4	6.2	3.0	46835	53740	66	72	1173	19.9	25.0	39.7	14.3	1.1	96798
50213	OSCEOLA	19179	2521	31.7	29.3	31.3	6.5	1.3	39253	47125	44	30	1792	19.6	32.1	36.9	10.2	1.2	87687
50214	OTLEY	22973	332	16.9	20.5	47.3	12.7	2.7	62039	72719	86	96	301	2.0	16.0	47.5	29.6	5.0	136574
50216	PANORA	24614	1225	28.5	29.3	29.6	7.2	5.4	42647	51463	55	52	968	17.9	29.0	27.2	20.4	5.6	95455
50217	PATON	21538	281	23.1	38.1	29.2	6.8	2.9	41209	47997	50	43	224	46.4	27.7	17.0	6.3	2.7	55333
50218	PATTERSON	27606	48	12.5	27.1	45.8	10.4	4.2	58025	67753	83	93	42	16.7	11.9	28.6	33.3	9.5	156250
50219	PELLA	23683	4766	18.2	27.6	40.3	10.9	3.0	53502	62668	78	89	3575	4.7	9.6	51.1	30.3	4.3	144995
50220	PERRY	19889	3513	24.3	32.0	33.5	8.1	2.1	44029	54669	59	59	2488	20.5	37.6	33.3	7.9	0.7	82126
50222	PERU	17950	243	24.7	33.7	32.9	7.0	1.7	44256	51718	59	60	203	24.6	22.2	35.5	15.8	2.0	97222
50223	PILOT MOUND	19286	199	26.1	40.2	27.6	6.0	0.0	40384	46753	47	38	162	32.1	24.1	34.0	8.0	1.9	78000
50225	PLEASANTVILLE	21940	1037	22.0	29.4	38.2	9.4	1.1	48817	56180	70	79	820	20.6	23.1	42.0	12.3	2.1	97536
50226	POLK CITY	31655	1288	8.1	19.6	40.5	22.1	9.7	73974	88783	93	99	1149	1.7	8.2	48.3	36.6	5.3	152306
50227	POPEJOY	16136	10	30.0	50.0	20.0	0.0	0.0	35000	45000	28	10	8	25.0	25.0	50.0	0.0	0.0	85000
50228	PRAIRIE CITY	23890	846	19.4	29.6	37.6	10.6	2.8	50818	58955	74	84	691	8.0	19.4	57.0	14.2	1.5	114505
50229	PROLE	26559	540	13.7	25.6	41.5	14.4	4.8	60448	68955	85	95	476	7.1	14.1	46.6	28.6	3.6	138934
50230	RADCLIFFE	21650	502	20.1	33.9	36.9	6.6	2.6	46435	52516	65	70	400	19.5	36.5	35.5	7.8	0.8	83514
50231	RANDALL	30412	68	22.1	32.4	32.4	7.4	5.9	46147	52941	64	69	56	7.1	21.4	42.9	25.0	3.6	122727
50232	REASNOR	30727	225	11.6	32.9	38.2	13.3	4.0	55216	62548	80	91	198	5.1	19.7	44.4	28.8	2.0	128846
50233	REDFIELD	21466	570	23.0	33.9	34.6	7.4	1.2	45000	54566	61	63	445	35.7	29.9	24.7	7.6	2.0	68721
50234	RHODES	24086	203	19.7	27.1	39.4	9.9	3.9	52006	60182	75	86	172	18.0	24.4	36.6	17.4	3.5	97647
50235	RIPPEY	20789	238	23.1	37.4	29.0	6.3	4.2	41429	47187	51	45	189	45.5	29.1	14.3	6.4	4.8	55313
50236	ROLAND	23361	586	11.4	26.6	49.0	10.8	2.2	56693	69217	81	93	521	3.5	17.7	60.5	18.4	0.0	124885
50237	RUNNELLS	26860	937	13.3	14.9	48.7	17.7	5.3	71806	85974	92	99	847	1.4	10.2	39.4	43.2	5.8	173032
50238	RUSSELL	17494	371	32.1	40.2	22.1	5.1	0.5	34421	40254	25	8	285	50.9	26.0	20.7	2.1	0.4	49324
50239	SAINT ANTHONY	19180	81	21.0	32.1	40.7	4.9	1.2	48054	54895	68	77	67	38.8	22.4	28.4	10.5	0.0	73750
50240	SAINT CHARLES	26881	816	13.9	24.5	43.8	13.9	4.0	59510	68182	84	94	716	9.4	13.4	47.9	26.4	2.9	136875
50242	SEARSBORO	22546	230	22.6	33.9	33.9	6.5	3.0	43529	50346	57	56	187	23.0	20.9	33.2	19.3	3.7	99583
50244	SLATER	24457	720	16.1	28.5	42.8	11.0	1.7	54941	66696	80	91	617	13.0	15.4	59.6	12.0	0.0	112645
50246	STANHOPE	21451	341	18.8	32.8	38.7	7.6	2.1	48054	53755	68	77	269	23.8	32.0	33.5	9.7	1.1	84259
50247	STATE CENTER	23728	834	22.8	30.8	33.8	10.0	2.6	46684	54046	65	71	655	14.8	29.6	40.8	14.2	0.6	95448
50248	STORY CITY	25239	1819	20.7	27.3	39.7	8.7	3.6	51626	63304	75	85	1364	5.9	16.9	55.6	19.7	1.9	118560
50249	STRATFORD	19218	537	26.8	35.2	31.1	4.8	2.1	38412	43819	41	25	407	21.9	36.1	32.7	6.1	3.2	81875
50250	STUART	20316	1092	25.4	36.2	31.6	5.5	1.4	41303	49679	51	43	810	22.1	25.1	43.8	6.2	2.8	93833
50251	SULLY	22980	548	10.8	35.2	42.0	9.9	2.2	52820	60691	77	88	460	7.0	27.0	50.4	14.1	1.5	110142
50252	SWAN	20771	162	20.4	23.5	42.0	13.0	1.2	58954	68049	84	94	144	12.5	17.4	44.4	21.5	4.2	125000
50254	THAYER	19935	154	26.6	34.4	31.8	6.5	0.7	40652	47685	48	39	128	29.7	25.0	26.6	16.4	2.3	80000
50256	TRACY	19423	197	24.9	37.6	31.5	6.1	0.0	41537	48898	51	45	164	39.0	30.5	20.7	8.5	1.2	62857
50257	TRURO	21329	357	25.5	23.3	40.1	7.3	3.9	50668	58644	73	83	297	13.1	35.7	35.4	9.1	6.7	92188
50258	UNION	18961	419	21.7	42.5	30.8	4.1	1.0	38800	44069	42	27	342	38.9	35.1	17.5	7.3	1.2	58261
50261	VAN METER	28374	751	15.9	25.2	41.3	12.3	5.5	57290	68049	82	93	649	20.2	11.3	39.3	25.4	3.9	120504
50262	VAN WERT	19609	172	32.0	36.6	24.4	3.5	3.5	35335	41728	29	11	141	45.4	31.2	14.2	7.8	1.4	55417
50263	WAUKEE	31787	3271	10.9	20.4	43.4	15.3	10.0	68520	83191	91	99	2824	8.8	6.8	44.9	27.8	11.7	152778
50264	WELDON	24049	207	29.5	33.8	27.1	4.4	5.3	37874	44571	39	22	170	42.9	28.2	18.8	8.8	1.2	61111
50265	WEST DES MOINES	36948	13477	10.3	26.3	37.8	16.3	9.3	63427	78209	87	97	9023	4.2	8.6	49.9	32.7	4.6	156507
50266	WEST DES MOINES	39477	8777	15.0	24.5	31.5	15.8	13.3	63102	76840	87	97	4926	0.6	4.2	37.0	51.6	6.6	193036
50268	WHAT CHEER	20759	450	38.7	32.9	23.8	2.9	1.8	34566	41184	26	8	374	57.8	26.2	11.2	2.7	2.1	43256
50271	WILLIAMS	20635	312	21.2	34.0	39.7	3.5	1.6	46969	53396	66	73	243	27.2	25.5	34.2	9.1	4.1	85357
50272	WILLIAMSON	17319	204	29.9	32.8	33.8	2.9	0.5	38812	44310	42	27	172	21.5	27.9	31.4	14.5	4.7	90769
50273	WINTERSET	21406	3058	24.9	31.6	32.6	7.6	3.3	44131	52964	59	59	2277	12.1	20.5	45.5	19.0	3.0	112578
50274	WIOTA	19248	217	33.6	34.1	24.0	6.0	2.3	38625	42778	42	26	175	32.0	19.4	26.9	18.3	3.4	86875
50275	WOODBURN	19535	253	27.7	33.6	28.1	5.5	5.1	38970	46301	43	28	206	31.1	16.5	36.9	15.5	0.0	96250
50276	WOODWARD	21932	938	21.3	30.7	35.1	10.5	2.5	48206	58383	69	77	732	17.5	28.6	39.2	14.2	0.6	98529
50277	YALE	29719	233	25.3	30.9	27.0	7.7	9.0	44786	53523	61	62	191	15.2	23.6	23.6	29.8	7.9	129167
50278	ZEARING	19817	320	19.1	35.3	36.3	9.4	0.0	46536	57980	65	71	249	20.1	31.3	37.8	9.6	1.2	88250
50309	DES MOINES	18976	2251	59.8	23.2	12.8	1.7	2.5	20594	25075	2	1	384	29.2	22.1	31.5	13.5	3.7	88649
50310	DES MOINES	27780	13573	16.6	29.3	39.8	11.2	3.0	53110	64405	77	88	9168	3.1	22.1	67.4	6.8	0.5	112342
50311	DES MOINES	23389	7421	25.1	29.0	35.5	8.2	2.2	45738	55106	63	67	4033	5.7	19.8	65.0	9.2	0.3	113177
50312	DES MOINES	38012	7762	19.9	27.9	29.8	11.8	10.7	52266	63427	76	87	4720	5.7	17.1	42.9	27.2	7.1	133728
50313	DES MOINES	20937	6851	23.7	32.8	35.8	6.4	1.4	43847	54005	58	58	5103	11.3	49.7	33.8	5.2	0.0	82576
50314	DES MOINES	13026	4368	44.6	34.3	17.4	3.1	0.7	27745	33627	8	1	1601	39.7	39.2	18.6	2.3	0.2	58568
50315	DES MOINES	21602	15412	23.9	31.1	36.3	7.5	1.3	46242	55915	64	69	10136	10.6	40.3	45.9	3.1	0.2	89358
	IOWA	23554		24.6	30.5	32.9	8.4	3.7	45622	53985				17.5	26.2	39.3	15.0	2.1	98835
	UNITED STATES	25866		24.7	27.1	30.8	10.9	6.5	48124	56710				10.9	15.0	33.7	30.1	10.4	145905

ZIP CODE #	POST OFFICE NAME	FINANCIAL SERVICES: Auto Loan	Home Loan	Invest-ments	Retire-ment Plans	THE HOME: Home Improvements: Home Repair	Lawn & Garden	Furnishings: Comput-ers & Hard-ware	Major Appli-ances	TV, Radio, Sound Equip-ment	Furni-ture	ENTERTAINMENT: Dine out/ Carry out	Sports Equip-ment	Fees & Tickets	Toys & Games	Travel	Cable TV	PERSONAL: Apparel & Services	Auto Repairs	Health Insur-ance	Pets & Supplies
50141	LAUREL	90	79	60	75	84	90	73	82	78	73	95	97	72	97	76	80	90	80	89	106
50143	LEIGHTON	94	77	53	73	84	92	73	84	80	73	96	101	69	96	75	82	90	82	94	111
50144	LEON	58	44	29	42	48	57	48	53	53	45	63	60	43	60	47	56	57	53	63	64
50146	LINDEN	109	76	40	72	89	99	75	93	87	74	102	112	64	100	78	91	93	92	111	130
50147	LINEVILLE	89	66	43	64	73	87	73	81	82	69	96	91	65	91	72	86	88	81	97	98
50148	LISCOMB	89	62	32	59	72	81	61	76	71	61	83	91	52	81	64	74	76	75	90	106
50149	LORIMOR	67	54	38	53	58	65	54	60	59	53	71	70	51	70	55	60	66	60	67	75
50150	LOVILIA	64	55	42	54	57	65	56	60	60	55	72	68	54	72	56	61	68	59	65	71
50151	LUCAS	102	74	43	71	85	95	73	89	83	72	98	107	64	96	76	87	90	87	104	122
50152	LUTHER	98	122	129	122	120	118	109	108	101	108	127	127	116	135	111	98	126	104	97	120
50153	LYNNVILLE	96	85	64	80	90	96	78	87	83	78	101	104	76	103	81	86	96	85	95	113
50154	MC CALLSBURG	90	63	33	59	73	82	62	77	72	61	84	93	53	82	64	75	77	76	92	107
50155	MACKSBURG	87	61	32	57	71	79	60	74	69	59	81	89	51	79	62	72	74	73	88	103
50156	MADRID	104	96	81	95	100	109	95	101	99	93	120	116	92	120	96	100	114	99	107	119
50157	MALCOM	89	78	59	74	83	89	73	81	78	72	94	96	71	96	75	80	89	79	89	104
50158	MARSHALLTOWN	75	72	69	71	74	80	73	75	75	72	93	86	73	93	73	76	89	75	77	86
50161	MAXWELL	106	104	91	101	108	112	95	102	97	95	119	121	96	123	98	98	115	99	104	126
50162	MELBOURNE	95	79	55	75	86	93	74	85	81	74	97	102	70	98	76	83	91	83	95	112
50164	MENLO	88	62	32	58	72	80	61	75	70	60	82	91	52	81	63	74	75	74	90	105
50165	MILLERTON	68	47	25	45	55	62	47	58	54	46	63	70	40	62	48	57	58	57	69	80
50166	MILO	93	77	56	73	84	92	74	85	80	73	96	101	69	97	77	83	90	84	95	111
50167	MINBURN	106	74	39	70	86	97	73	91	84	72	99	109	63	97	76	89	90	89	108	126
50168	MINGO	103	85	59	81	92	101	80	92	87	80	105	110	75	106	83	90	98	90	103	122
50169	MITCHELLVILLE	90	90	83	90	91	95	88	90	87	87	107	105	86	107	87	85	103	89	89	103
50170	MONROE	85	73	57	72	77	86	73	79	78	72	94	91	71	94	73	79	89	78	86	96
50171	MONTEZUMA	96	77	55	73	84	95	77	87	85	76	102	101	71	100	79	89	95	86	100	110
50173	MONTOUR	70	57	42	56	61	69	58	64	63	57	76	74	55	75	58	64	71	63	71	79
50174	MURRAY	74	63	45	59	68	73	59	67	63	59	77	80	56	78	61	65	72	65	74	88
50201	NEVADA	88	85	81	85	87	93	85	87	85	84	105	102	83	105	85	85	101	87	88	101
50206	NEW PROVIDENCE	112	79	43	75	92	102	78	96	89	77	105	115	67	103	81	93	96	94	113	132
50207	NEW SHARON	82	66	46	64	72	80	65	74	71	65	86	87	61	85	66	73	80	73	83	94
50208	NEWTON	82	77	67	75	79	87	76	79	79	74	96	92	75	98	77	80	92	78	85	94
50210	NEW VIRGINIA	89	79	60	75	84	90	73	81	78	73	94	97	72	96	75	80	90	79	88	105
50211	NORWALK	103	119	122	120	116	114	110	109	103	111	129	129	113	133	110	98	128	107	97	121
50212	OGDEN	97	75	48	71	84	92	72	85	80	72	95	102	65	95	74	83	89	83	97	115
50213	OSCEOLA	77	61	42	59	66	76	64	70	70	61	83	80	58	81	64	73	77	70	81	87
50214	OTLEY	104	92	70	88	98	105	85	95	91	85	110	113	84	113	88	93	105	92	102	122
50216	PANORA	99	72	42	68	81	94	75	88	85	73	100	102	65	96	76	90	91	87	105	114
50217	PATON	94	66	35	62	77	86	65	81	75	65	88	97	56	87	68	79	81	80	96	112
50218	PATTERSON	105	93	71	88	98	106	86	95	91	86	111	114	84	114	89	94	106	93	103	123
50219	PELLA	93	90	85	90	92	98	88	91	89	87	109	107	87	111	89	88	105	90	92	107
50220	PERRY	81	69	57	69	73	81	72	77	76	70	93	89	69	92	72	77	87	76	83	91
50222	PERU	88	66	39	62	75	83	64	77	72	63	85	92	57	84	66	75	79	75	89	105
50223	PILOT MOUND	83	58	30	55	68	76	57	71	66	57	77	85	49	76	59	69	71	70	84	99
50225	PLEASANTVILLE	87	75	58	74	79	88	75	81	79	74	96	93	72	96	75	81	90	79	87	98
50226	POLK CITY	118	141	145	141	139	138	126	127	118	126	148	149	133	156	129	115	147	123	115	142
50227	POPEJOY	64	45	23	42	52	59	44	55	51	44	60	66	38	59	46	54	55	54	65	76
50228	PRAIRIE CITY	93	80	62	79	85	94	80	87	85	79	104	100	77	103	81	87	97	85	94	105
50229	PROLE	95	110	112	109	110	110	99	101	94	99	117	118	104	124	101	92	116	97	94	115
50230	RADCLIFFE	98	68	36	64	79	89	67	83	78	67	91	100	58	89	70	81	83	82	99	116
50231	RANDALL	119	83	43	78	97	108	82	101	95	81	111	122	70	109	85	99	101	100	121	141
50232	REASNOR	113	101	77	96	107	114	93	103	99	93	120	123	91	123	96	102	114	101	112	133
50233	REDFIELD	72	73	70	69	75	83	71	73	74	69	91	84	73	97	74	77	88	72	80	86
50234	RHODES	107	74	39	70	87	97	73	91	85	73	99	109	63	97	76	89	90	90	108	126
50235	RIPPEY	97	68	35	64	79	88	67	83	77	66	90	100	57	89	69	81	82	81	98	115
50236	ROLAND	90	97	96	99	94	94	93	92	87	93	110	109	93	110	91	82	108	92	82	102
50237	RUNNELLS	101	123	129	123	121	120	110	110	103	110	129	129	117	137	113	100	128	106	100	123
50238	RUSSELL	67	50	32	48	55	65	55	61	61	52	72	68	48	68	54	65	66	61	73	74
50239	SAINT ANTHONY	84	72	52	68	77	83	67	75	72	67	87	90	64	88	69	74	82	74	83	99
50240	SAINT CHARLES	104	103	89	99	106	111	94	101	95	94	117	119	95	121	96	96	113	98	103	124
50242	SEARSBORO	98	69	37	65	80	90	68	84	78	67	92	101	58	90	70	82	84	82	100	116
50244	SLATER	77	93	102	92	91	93	86	85	82	86	103	99	92	110	88	81	103	83	79	93
50246	STANHOPE	101	70	37	66	82	92	69	86	80	68	94	103	59	92	72	84	85	84	102	119
50247	STATE CENTER	99	76	49	73	84	94	76	88	84	75	100	104	69	99	77	87	93	87	100	115
50248	STORY CITY	101	79	54	76	86	99	82	92	90	80	107	106	74	104	82	94	99	91	106	115
50249	STRATFORD	81	60	36	57	67	78	63	72	71	61	83	84	55	80	63	75	76	72	86	93
50250	STUART	79	63	44	61	68	78	66	73	72	64	86	83	60	84	66	75	79	72	83	89
50251	SULLY	97	87	66	82	92	98	80	89	85	80	103	106	78	106	82	87	98	86	96	115
50252	SWAN	99	88	67	84	93	100	81	90	87	81	105	108	80	107	84	89	100	88	98	117
50254	THAYER	81	66	45	63	72	78	62	72	68	62	82	86	59	82	64	71	77	70	81	95
50256	TRACY	79	67	48	63	72	78	63	71	68	63	82	85	60	83	65	70	77	69	78	93
50257	TRURO	103	73	39	69	84	94	72	88	82	71	97	106	61	95	74	86	88	87	105	122
50258	UNION	75	61	45	60	65	74	63	69	67	61	81	79	59	80	63	69	76	68	76	84
50261	VAN METER	103	115	117	117	112	111	108	107	101	109	128	127	110	130	107	96	126	106	95	119
50262	VAN WERT	77	62	45	61	67	75	64	70	69	62	83	81	59	82	64	70	77	69	78	87
50263	WAUKEE	120	133	133	137	129	128	124	123	116	126	146	145	127	147	122	109	144	121	108	136
50264	WELDON	94	81	64	80	85	95	81	87	86	80	104	101	78	104	81	87	98	86	94	105
50265	WEST DES MOINES	119	131	140	135	127	129	127	124	119	128	151	146	129	151	124	114	149	123	111	136
50266	WEST DES MOINES	130	122	136	133	118	122	131	125	126	134	161	151	128	153	124	118	157	131	111	139
50268	WHAT CHEER	68	64	58	60	67	75	63	67	67	61	82	76	63	87	65	70	78	66	74	80
50271	WILLIAMS	92	64	34	61	75	84	63	78	73	63	86	95	54	84	66	77	78	77	93	109
50272	WILLIAMSON	79	55	29	52	64	72	54	67	63	54	73	81	46	72	56	66	67	66	80	94
50273	WINTERSET	92	70	45	67	78	88	71	82	79	69	94	96	64	92	72	83	86	81	95	107
50274	WIOTA	84	59	31	55	68	76	58	71	67	57	78	86	49	77	60	70	71	70	85	100
50275	WOODBURN	86	76	58	72	80	86	70	78	75	70	91	93	69	93	72	77	86	76	84	101
50276	WOODWARD	91	80	66	78	84	92	80	86	84	79	102	102	77	103	81	85	97	85	92	105
50277	YALE	125	87	46	83	102	114	86	107	99	85	117	129	74	114	89	104	106	105	127	149
50278	ZEARING	95	66	35	62	77	86	65	81	75	65	88	97	56	87	68	79	80	80	96	112
50309	DES MOINES	44	39	55	40	39	45	48	44	51	46	63	52	47	62	47	51	61	48	48	49
50310	DES MOINES	84	90	105	92	88	92	92	89	89	91	112	106	93	113	91	86	110	91	83	97
50311	DES MOINES	72	72	89	76	71	75	80	75	78	77	97	91	79	96	77	74	95	79	69	82
50312	DES MOINES	105	111	136	115	109	116	116	110	112	114	141	131	117	141	114	109	138	113	104	121
50313	DES MOINES	66	72	80	72	72	75	73	71	72	71	90	83	75	94	73	71	88	71	69	77
50314	DES MOINES	48	41	50	41	40	47	49	46	52	48	65	54	48	63	47	52	63	49	48	52
50315	DES MOINES	69	73	82	74	73	77	75	73	74	73	92	85	76	95	75	72	90	73	70	80
	IOWA	87	79	73	79	82	89	80	84	83	79	102	98	78	102	80	83	97	84	88	100
	UNITED STATES	100	100	100	100	100	100	100	100	100	100	100	100	100	100	100	100	100	100	100	100

IOWA

ZIP CODE			POPULATION			2000-2004 ANNUAL RATE		HOUSEHOLDS					FAMILIES		
#	POST OFFICE NAME	COUNTY FIPS CODE	2000	2004	2009	% Rate	State Centile	2000	2004	2009	% Annual Rate 2000-2004	2004 Average HH Size	2000	2004	% Annual Rate 2000-2004
50316	DES MOINES	153	16586	16419	17068	-0.2	37	6023	5980	6246	-0.2	2.65	3852	3777	-0.5
50317	DES MOINES	153	35143	35748	37459	0.4	66	13734	14090	14865	0.6	2.52	9480	9639	0.4
50320	DES MOINES	153	13947	14992	16072	1.7	88	5271	5681	6116	1.8	2.64	3798	4071	1.7
50321	DES MOINES	153	7227	7585	8042	1.1	82	2839	3029	3250	1.5	2.38	1741	1817	1.0
50322	URBANDALE	153	33174	34432	36194	0.9	78	13436	14071	14892	1.1	2.42	9109	9462	0.9
50323	URBANDALE	153	955	2011	2933	19.2	100	317	666	973	19.1	3.02	281	586	18.9
50325	CLIVE	153	12616	14222	15800	2.9	95	4656	5213	5773	2.7	2.73	3567	3981	2.6
50327	DES MOINES	153	6187	7120	7879	3.4	97	2277	2642	2941	3.6	2.67	1770	2039	3.4
50401	MASON CITY	033	31548	31628	31498	0.1	53	13279	13435	13488	0.3	2.27	8209	8282	0.2
50420	ALEXANDER	069	450	458	466	0.4	67	186	191	195	0.6	2.40	134	137	0.5
50421	BELMOND	197	3257	3191	3130	-0.5	24	1376	1355	1333	-0.4	2.30	878	862	-0.4
50423	BRITT	081	3113	3099	3109	-0.1	43	1255	1262	1278	0.1	2.40	826	827	0.0
50424	BUFFALO CENTER	189	1574	1556	1551	-0.3	35	665	662	666	-0.1	2.26	443	437	-0.3
50428	CLEAR LAKE	033	10034	9698	9474	-0.8	11	4188	4073	4008	-0.7	2.31	2800	2713	-0.7
50430	CORWITH	081	669	694	705	0.9	78	262	276	284	1.2	2.51	184	193	1.1
50432	CRYSTAL LAKE	081	292	292	292	0.0	51	127	129	130	0.4	2.26	90	91	0.3
50433	DOUGHERTY	033	264	256	251	-0.7	15	102	100	98	-0.5	2.56	77	75	-0.6
50434	FERTILE	195	509	501	499	-0.4	29	204	202	203	-0.2	2.48	156	154	-0.3
50435	FLOYD	067	847	934	968	2.3	93	314	350	365	2.6	2.67	254	282	2.5
50436	FOREST CITY	189	6204	6124	6118	-0.3	33	2360	2353	2375	-0.1	2.43	1607	1598	-0.1
50438	GARNER	081	4111	4153	4181	0.2	61	1618	1652	1679	0.5	2.48	1160	1180	0.4
50439	GOODELL	081	423	486	523	3.3	97	169	197	214	3.7	2.47	126	146	3.5
50440	GRAFTON	195	493	494	494	0.1	52	194	196	198	0.2	2.52	143	144	0.2
50441	HAMPTON	069	5660	5723	5823	0.3	61	2350	2392	2452	0.4	2.33	1539	1562	0.4
50444	HANLONTOWN	195	349	343	342	-0.4	27	137	136	136	-0.2	2.52	105	103	-0.5
50446	JOICE	195	621	612	610	-0.3	31	246	245	247	-0.1	2.50	184	183	-0.1
50447	KANAWHA	081	1290	1262	1260	-0.5	22	512	503	507	-0.4	2.43	352	345	-0.5
50448	KENSETT	195	843	833	831	-0.3	34	343	342	344	-0.1	2.43	244	243	-0.1
50449	KLEMME	081	817	839	850	0.6	72	326	337	344	0.8	2.49	239	246	0.7
50450	LAKE MILLS	189	2924	2893	2883	-0.3	36	1258	1262	1273	0.1	2.23	819	818	0.0
50451	LAKOTA	109	698	675	646	-0.8	12	286	280	272	-0.5	2.41	202	197	-0.6
50452	LATIMER	069	1128	1129	1145	0.0	51	434	436	444	0.1	2.59	315	315	0.0
50453	LELAND	189	595	594	596	0.0	47	234	236	240	0.2	2.52	182	183	0.1
50454	LITTLE CEDAR	131	154	155	153	0.2	57	63	64	63	0.4	2.36	46	46	0.0
50455	MC INTIRE	131	470	467	459	-0.2	42	157	157	155	0.0	2.96	120	119	-0.2
50456	MANLY	195	1788	1784	1781	-0.1	46	732	735	739	0.1	2.39	494	494	0.0
50457	MESERVEY	033	351	337	330	-1.0	7	161	156	153	-0.7	2.16	110	106	-0.9
50458	NORA SPRINGS	067	2019	1957	1906	-0.7	15	777	758	744	-0.6	2.47	553	537	-0.7
50459	NORTHWOOD	195	3066	3113	3145	0.4	64	1331	1365	1392	0.6	2.22	872	891	0.5
50460	ORCHARD	131	378	410	421	1.9	91	134	147	152	2.2	2.74	103	112	2.0
50461	OSAGE	131	5724	5662	5570	-0.3	35	2345	2331	2304	-0.1	2.38	1597	1583	-0.2
50464	PLYMOUTH	195	620	604	592	-0.6	18	243	239	236	-0.4	2.53	183	180	-0.4
50465	RAKE	189	259	246	243	-1.2	3	124	119	118	-1.0	2.07	76	72	-1.3
50466	RICEVILLE	089	1773	1709	1673	-0.9	10	665	643	633	-0.8	2.61	469	452	-0.9
50467	ROCK FALLS	033	41	41	41	0.0	51	13	13	13	0.0	3.15	10	10	0.0
50468	ROCKFORD	067	1646	1607	1571	-0.6	20	631	623	615	-0.3	2.57	434	427	-0.4
50469	ROCKWELL	033	1581	1580	1565	0.0	48	583	586	584	0.1	2.61	430	430	0.0
50470	ROWAN	197	325	378	402	3.6	98	138	161	173	3.7	2.35	100	117	3.8
50471	RUDD	067	777	802	804	0.8	75	307	321	326	1.1	2.43	225	234	0.9
50472	SAINT ANSGAR	131	2322	2241	2179	-0.8	10	893	866	847	-0.7	2.49	632	609	-0.9
50473	SCARVILLE	189	335	332	331	-0.2	38	130	131	132	0.2	2.53	100	100	0.0
50475	SHEFFIELD	069	1564	1554	1571	-0.2	42	615	616	627	0.0	2.43	443	444	0.1
50476	STACYVILLE	131	781	794	791	0.4	66	314	323	323	0.7	2.36	212	216	0.4
50477	SWALEDALE	033	419	408	400	-0.6	18	155	152	150	-0.5	2.68	117	114	-0.6
50478	THOMPSON	189	1028	1125	1177	2.1	92	428	472	499	2.3	2.38	306	336	2.2
50479	THORNTON	033	744	713	695	-1.0	7	314	303	297	-0.8	2.35	215	206	-1.0
50480	TITONKA	109	1120	1070	1021	-1.1	5	452	436	420	-0.8	2.39	321	308	-1.0
50482	VENTURA	033	893	860	840	-0.9	9	368	355	349	-0.8	2.42	266	256	-0.9
50483	WESLEY	109	961	957	931	-0.1	44	360	362	357	0.1	2.64	262	262	0.0
50484	WODEN	081	534	522	524	-0.5	22	210	207	209	-0.3	2.52	151	148	-0.5
50501	FORT DODGE	187	30389	30564	30727	0.1	57	12001	12186	12346	0.4	2.31	7524	7615	0.3
50510	ALBERT CITY	021	1139	1102	1091	-0.8	13	452	441	439	-0.6	2.42	317	309	-0.6
50511	ALGONA	109	7447	7225	6935	-0.7	16	3052	3001	2919	-0.4	2.35	2044	2002	-0.5
50514	ARMSTRONG	063	1520	1479	1434	-0.6	17	634	628	619	-0.2	2.28	420	413	-0.4
50515	AYRSHIRE	147	376	370	367	-0.4	28	155	155	156	0.0	2.39	115	114	-0.2
50516	BADGER	187	773	795	802	0.7	73	292	305	310	1.0	2.61	226	234	0.8
50517	BANCROFT	109	1140	1063	1005	-1.6	1	456	431	412	-1.3	2.38	300	282	-1.5
50518	BARNUM	187	388	415	428	1.6	88	142	153	159	1.8	2.71	111	119	1.7
50519	BODE	091	731	751	759	0.6	72	300	312	318	0.9	2.39	229	237	0.8
50520	BRADGATE	091	291	289	290	-0.2	41	122	123	125	0.2	2.35	93	93	0.0
50521	BURNSIDE	187	47	45	44	-1.0	6	15	15	15	0.0	3.00	11	11	0.0
50522	BURT	109	929	880	837	-1.3	3	361	344	330	-1.1	2.41	250	238	-1.2
50523	CALLENDER	187	806	794	788	-0.4	30	311	309	309	-0.2	2.57	231	229	-0.2
50524	CLARE	187	696	746	769	1.7	88	247	267	277	1.9	2.79	192	207	1.8
50525	CLARION	197	3952	3949	3910	0.0	48	1646	1648	1636	0.0	2.33	1081	1078	-0.1
50527	CURLEW	147	283	276	272	-0.6	20	115	114	114	-0.2	2.42	82	81	-0.3
50528	CYLINDER	147	524	530	531	0.3	61	199	203	206	0.5	2.61	157	159	0.3
50529	DAKOTA CITY	091	905	904	910	0.0	47	351	355	361	0.3	2.55	252	254	0.2
50530	DAYTON	187	1261	1226	1211	-0.7	17	492	483	482	-0.4	2.45	340	332	-0.6
50531	DOLLIVER	063	240	229	221	-1.1	5	105	102	100	-0.7	2.03	80	77	-0.9
50532	DUNCOMBE	187	1032	999	985	-0.8	14	405	398	397	-0.4	2.51	284	278	-0.5
50533	EAGLE GROVE	197	4320	4121	3997	-1.1	5	1734	1660	1618	-1.0	2.42	1164	1110	-1.1
50535	EARLY	161	996	965	945	-0.7	14	402	394	390	-0.5	2.45	287	280	-0.6
50536	EMMETSBURG	147	4643	4583	4543	-0.3	32	1872	1875	1879	0.0	2.27	1135	1132	-0.1
50538	FARNHAMVILLE	025	563	543	515	-0.9	10	251	245	234	-0.6	2.22	177	172	-0.7
50539	FENTON	109	655	610	576	-1.7	1	282	267	256	-1.3	2.28	188	177	-1.4
50540	FONDA	151	1239	1186	1121	-1.0	6	505	489	468	-0.8	2.35	330	318	-0.9
50541	GILMORE CITY	151	962	920	894	-1.0	6	399	385	379	-0.8	2.38	280	269	-0.9
50542	GOLDFIELD	197	963	949	934	-0.3	31	402	401	397	-0.1	2.37	275	274	-0.1
50543	GOWRIE	187	1506	1482	1472	-0.4	28	600	595	595	-0.2	2.42	405	399	-0.4
50544	HARCOURT	187	562	590	604	1.2	82	226	240	248	1.4	2.46	159	167	1.2
50545	HARDY	091	296	296	300	0.0	51	109	109	110	0.0	2.72	78	78	0.0
50546	HAVELOCK	151	534	498	466	-1.6	1	212	200	190	-1.4	2.49	155	146	-1.4
50548	HUMBOLDT	091	5672	5740	5814	0.3	62	2409	2468	2528	0.6	2.26	1532	1563	0.5
50551	JOLLEY	025	193	184	173	-1.1	4	85	82	78	-0.8	2.24	65	62	-1.1
	IOWA					0.5					0.7	2.43			0.6
	UNITED STATES					1.2					1.3	2.58			1.1

ZIP CODE		RACE (%)						% Hispanic Origin		2004 AGE DISTRIBUTION (%)										MEDIAN AGE		
#	POST OFFICE NAME	White 2000	White 2004	Black 2000	Black 2004	Asian/Pacific 2000	Asian/Pacific 2004	2000	2004	0-4	5-9	10-14	15-19	20-24	25-44	45-64	65-84	85+	18+	2004	% 2004 Males	% 2004 Females
50316	DES MOINES	67.3	63.1	15.7	16.5	6.4	8.5	12.6	14.7	8.4	7.5	7.8	7.9	7.7	28.5	20.4	9.5	2.4	71.7	32.7	48.4	51.6
50317	DES MOINES	91.9	89.7	2.3	2.7	2.1	3.1	4.2	5.3	7.1	6.8	6.9	6.3	6.5	28.5	24.4	11.9	1.6	75.3	36.8	48.6	51.4
50320	DES MOINES	83.9	80.2	5.6	6.5	4.1	5.9	9.2	10.9	10.1	9.0	7.6	5.8	6.7	32.5	20.4	7.4	0.5	69.9	31.7	49.3	50.7
50321	DES MOINES	90.7	88.1	4.0	4.8	1.7	2.5	3.5	4.7	6.4	5.7	6.3	7.3	11.2	28.3	24.1	9.8	0.9	78.3	32.9	47.2	52.8
50322	URBANDALE	95.0	93.5	1.6	2.0	1.8	2.7	1.8	2.2	6.4	6.6	7.1	6.3	5.9	28.6	26.7	11.0	1.5	75.9	38.4	48.1	51.9
50323	URBANDALE	94.4	92.4	1.2	1.3	3.4	5.1	1.4	1.8	11.7	11.8	8.6	4.6	3.9	32.6	23.5	3.3	0.0	64.9	33.4	50.5	49.5
50325	CLIVE	93.1	91.2	1.2	1.4	2.9	4.2	2.6	3.1	8.6	9.0	8.0	6.2	4.9	29.2	27.5	6.4	0.2	70.3	36.1	49.5	50.5
50327	DES MOINES	95.6	94.2	0.6	0.7	1.7	2.4	2.3	2.9	7.6	7.7	7.1	5.9	5.6	28.7	27.2	9.0	1.3	74.0	37.3	48.7	51.4
50401	MASON CITY	95.6	94.9	1.1	1.2	0.8	1.1	3.3	3.9	6.1	6.1	6.5	7.0	7.3	25.3	24.1	14.6	3.0	77.5	39.2	47.7	52.3
50420	ALEXANDER	96.9	96.5	0.0	0.0	0.0	0.0	2.9	3.5	5.0	5.2	6.6	7.6	5.9	22.9	29.3	15.1	2.4	78.6	43.1	52.4	47.6
50421	BELMOND	94.9	94.0	0.2	0.3	0.3	0.3	5.2	6.2	5.6	5.9	6.4	6.2	5.9	21.3	27.0	16.5	5.1	78.1	44.0	48.5	51.5
50423	BRITT	95.8	95.6	0.0	0.0	0.2	0.2	4.6	4.8	6.3	6.5	6.9	6.3	5.9	22.1	25.7	16.7	3.6	76.2	42.2	48.9	51.1
50424	BUFFALO CENTER	98.2	98.1	0.0	0.0	0.3	0.3	2.4	2.5	6.3	6.4	6.0	5.7	5.0	19.9	23.8	21.1	5.9	77.6	45.6	49.2	50.8
50428	CLEAR LAKE	97.2	96.5	0.2	0.3	0.9	1.2	1.8	2.3	5.7	5.9	6.4	6.0	6.2	23.7	28.3	15.2	2.6	78.2	42.5	48.5	51.5
50430	CORWITH	98.1	98.0	0.0	0.0	0.3	0.3	2.5	2.7	5.5	7.5	8.7	7.2	3.9	25.2	24.9	15.0	2.2	72.8	39.8	50.7	49.3
50432	CRYSTAL LAKE	98.3	98.0	0.0	0.0	0.3	0.3	1.7	2.1	5.5	5.8	6.5	6.2	6.5	24.3	28.8	14.7	1.7	78.1	42.0	50.7	49.3
50433	DOUGHERTY	99.2	99.6	0.0	0.0	0.0	0.0	0.8	0.4	5.1	7.8	10.2	7.0	4.7	25.0	27.3	12.1	0.8	71.9	38.6	50.4	49.6
50434	FERTILE	97.6	97.6	0.2	0.2	0.2	0.2	1.8	1.8	6.4	7.2	7.4	5.2	4.8	25.6	27.5	13.6	2.4	75.9	41.1	48.9	51.1
50435	FLOYD	99.1	98.8	0.0	0.0	0.5	0.8	0.2	0.2	6.3	6.8	7.0	7.3	5.6	23.3	29.7	12.3	1.8	75.4	41.0	51.4	48.6
50436	FOREST CITY	96.7	96.6	0.4	0.4	1.0	1.1	2.4	2.5	5.9	6.2	7.4	9.5	7.7	24.0	24.9	11.8	2.6	76.1	37.3	49.7	50.3
50438	GARNER	98.8	98.7	0.1	0.1	0.4	0.4	1.1	1.1	6.1	6.4	7.5	7.8	5.9	23.8	26.2	13.1	3.2	75.0	40.4	48.6	51.4
50439	GOODELL	97.6	97.7	0.5	0.4	0.5	0.4	2.6	2.7	5.1	6.6	8.0	8.4	5.1	27.2	28.4	10.1	1.0	74.1	40.0	52.5	47.5
50440	GRAFTON	99.6	99.4	0.0	0.0	0.2	0.2	0.4	0.2	5.7	6.1	6.7	7.5	5.5	25.9	27.5	13.2	2.0	77.3	41.3	52.4	47.6
50441	HAMPTON	92.7	91.2	0.1	0.1	0.2	0.3	8.8	10.5	6.2	6.0	6.5	6.0	6.6	23.1	25.1	16.6	3.8	77.7	41.6	48.5	51.5
50444	HANLONTOWN	97.7	97.4	0.3	0.3	0.3	0.3	2.0	2.0	6.4	7.0	7.6	5.3	4.7	24.8	28.0	13.7	2.6	75.5	41.3	48.1	51.9
50446	JOICE	98.6	98.5	0.2	0.2	0.2	0.2	1.1	1.1	6.1	6.9	7.4	5.9	5.1	26.1	26.1	14.7	1.8	76.0	41.0	50.5	49.5
50447	KANAWHA	97.8	97.5	0.1	0.1	0.3	0.3	1.9	2.0	6.8	6.7	6.6	6.7	5.1	21.9	24.1	17.8	4.5	75.6	42.7	49.8	50.2
50448	KENSETT	99.3	99.3	0.0	0.0	0.2	0.2	1.3	1.3	4.8	5.5	6.6	5.8	5.4	24.0	30.3	15.6	2.0	79.5	43.6	52.6	47.4
50449	KLEMME	98.9	98.9	0.0	0.0	0.1	0.1	2.2	2.3	7.8	7.9	6.9	5.6	5.7	27.1	21.9	14.2	3.0	73.8	36.4	49.8	50.2
50450	LAKE MILLS	98.3	98.2	0.0	0.0	0.6	0.6	1.7	1.8	4.9	5.1	6.6	6.8	6.6	21.9	27.5	15.5	5.0	78.9	43.6	47.5	52.5
50451	LAKOTA	99.0	98.8	0.1	0.2	0.0	0.0	1.6	1.9	6.4	6.2	6.4	7.0	5.0	20.7	27.9	18.1	2.4	76.4	43.9	51.1	48.9
50452	LATIMER	94.3	93.2	0.0	0.0	0.1	0.1	7.7	9.3	6.3	6.4	6.9	6.4	6.0	23.3	25.5	16.6	2.7	76.6	41.5	50.6	49.4
50453	LELAND	98.0	98.2	0.0	0.0	0.3	0.3	1.2	1.2	5.4	6.4	7.7	7.7	5.4	23.4	29.0	13.6	1.4	75.4	41.3	51.2	48.8
50454	LITTLE CEDAR	98.7	99.4	0.7	0.7	0.0	0.0	0.0	0.7	7.1	7.7	11.0	7.7	4.5	21.9	21.3	15.5	3.2	69.0	37.8	51.0	49.0
50455	MC INTIRE	98.5	98.3	1.3	1.3	0.2	0.2	0.6	0.9	9.2	9.4	9.6	9.9	5.1	23.1	21.2	10.9	1.5	65.3	32.0	53.8	46.3
50456	MANLY	97.8	97.8	0.8	0.8	0.2	0.2	1.5	1.5	6.8	6.9	7.9	6.3	5.9	25.3	23.4	14.3	3.2	74.3	39.1	48.4	51.6
50457	MESERVEY	98.9	98.5	0.0	0.0	0.0	0.0	1.7	2.1	4.5	5.0	5.9	6.5	5.6	23.7	27.9	18.1	2.7	80.7	44.2	49.9	50.2
50458	NORA SPRINGS	99.6	99.4	0.1	0.1	0.0	0.0	0.8	1.1	6.6	7.0	6.9	5.9	5.7	25.3	27.4	12.4	2.8	75.8	40.0	50.3	49.7
50459	NORTHWOOD	98.3	98.3	0.1	0.1	0.2	0.2	2.0	2.1	5.2	5.4	6.5	5.3	5.6	24.1	26.2	16.8	4.9	79.4	43.6	49.8	50.2
50460	ORCHARD	100.0	100.0	0.0	0.0	0.0	0.0	0.5	0.7	7.8	7.8	8.5	7.3	5.6	24.4	24.9	12.0	1.7	70.5	38.2	51.5	48.5
50461	OSAGE	99.3	99.1	0.1	0.1	0.2	0.3	0.6	0.8	6.0	6.7	7.5	6.7	5.1	22.9	23.6	17.6	3.9	75.4	41.7	48.5	51.5
50464	PLYMOUTH	98.9	98.8	0.0	0.0	0.3	0.3	1.0	1.0	4.8	5.1	6.3	7.3	6.1	25.5	29.3	13.7	1.8	79.5	42.3	51.2	48.8
50465	RAKE	96.9	96.8	0.0	0.0	0.0	0.0	4.3	4.5	4.9	5.3	5.7	5.7	5.3	27.6	26.4	15.9	3.3	80.5	42.3	52.4	47.6
50466	RICEVILLE	99.3	99.2	0.3	0.3	0.1	0.1	0.2	0.2	7.4	6.5	7.9	8.3	6.3	21.2	24.6	14.5	3.3	72.7	39.5	51.0	49.0
50467	ROCK FALLS	100.0	100.0	0.0	0.0	0.0	0.0	2.4	2.4	4.9	7.3	9.8	9.8	4.9	26.8	26.8	9.8	0.0	73.2	37.5	51.2	48.8
50468	ROCKFORD	98.8	98.7	0.2	0.2	0.1	0.2	0.7	0.8	6.6	6.8	8.1	7.5	6.1	24.2	24.5	13.8	2.4	73.9	38.5	50.2	49.8
50469	ROCKWELL	98.2	98.0	0.1	0.1	0.3	0.3	1.3	1.7	6.2	6.7	7.5	7.3	6.1	22.2	25.3	15.6	3.0	74.5	40.8	49.5	50.5
50470	ROWAN	95.1	94.7	0.6	0.5	0.3	0.5	4.6	5.8	5.8	6.4	6.4	5.3	6.6	20.1	32.0	14.8	2.7	78.0	44.7	51.6	48.4
50471	RUDD	99.1	99.0	0.0	0.0	0.0	0.0	1.4	1.8	6.9	7.2	7.7	6.5	5.2	24.3	27.2	12.5	2.5	74.1	40.1	50.3	49.8
50472	SAINT ANSGAR	99.4	99.1	0.0	0.0	0.3	0.6	0.7	0.9	5.6	6.2	7.7	6.5	5.4	21.4	26.4	16.1	4.6	76.4	43.1	48.1	51.9
50473	SCARVILLE	97.9	97.6	0.0	0.0	0.3	0.3	1.5	1.5	5.1	5.4	6.3	8.1	6.3	22.6	29.2	14.8	2.1	78.6	42.2	51.8	48.2
50475	SHEFFIELD	98.5	98.1	0.1	0.1	0.3	0.5	1.5	1.9	6.3	6.4	6.4	5.5	5.7	20.7	26.1	18.4	4.4	77.3	44.1	49.0	51.0
50476	STACYVILLE	99.4	99.2	0.1	0.1	0.1	0.1	0.3	0.3	5.8	6.1	6.9	6.2	4.7	22.9	24.1	18.5	4.9	76.8	43.5	51.0	49.0
50477	SWALEDALE	99.1	98.8	0.2	0.3	0.2	0.3	0.5	0.5	4.7	7.6	10.5	6.9	4.9	25.0	27.2	12.3	1.0	72.6	38.9	50.5	49.5
50478	THOMPSON	97.8	97.7	0.0	0.0	0.3	0.4	1.4	1.4	6.6	6.7	7.0	6.6	5.5	24.7	25.3	15.5	2.1	75.6	40.1	52.3	47.7
50479	THORNTON	98.9	98.6	0.0	0.0	0.0	0.0	1.6	1.8	4.5	4.9	5.9	6.3	5.5	23.8	28.3	18.1	2.7	80.9	44.5	50.6	49.4
50480	TITONKA	99.1	99.0	0.1	0.1	0.1	0.1	0.6	0.8	6.2	6.5	6.6	6.3	4.6	20.8	26.1	19.5	3.6	76.1	44.4	48.9	51.1
50482	VENTURA	98.9	98.7	0.1	0.1	0.3	0.5	0.9	1.1	4.5	5.5	7.2	5.9	4.3	21.9	33.4	15.6	1.7	79.0	45.4	50.6	49.4
50483	WESLEY	99.0	98.9	0.0	0.0	0.1	0.1	0.5	0.6	7.0	7.3	8.4	6.5	4.6	23.5	25.3	15.5	2.0	73.3	40.4	50.8	49.2
50484	WODEN	98.3	98.5	0.0	0.0	0.0	0.0	0.9	1.0	7.3	7.1	8.6	7.1	4.6	24.1	25.9	13.2	2.1	72.4	39.5	50.2	49.8
50501	FORT DODGE	91.7	90.7	4.4	4.8	0.8	1.2	2.8	3.4	6.5	6.3	6.4	7.5	8.5	24.8	23.0	14.0	3.1	77.0	37.3	50.1	49.9
50510	ALBERT CITY	98.7	98.8	0.0	0.0	0.1	0.1	1.0	1.0	5.4	6.3	7.3	6.0	5.4	22.7	26.6	16.3	4.1	77.0	43.1	49.9	50.1
50511	ALGONA	98.6	98.2	0.1	0.1	0.7	1.0	0.7	0.9	5.3	5.3	6.9	7.4	6.8	21.7	26.8	16.1	3.8	77.8	42.7	47.9	52.1
50514	ARMSTRONG	99.0	99.0	0.1	0.1	0.1	0.1	0.3	0.4	5.5	5.5	5.5	6.2	5.9	20.8	28.3	18.5	4.0	79.8	45.5	48.8	51.3
50515	AYRSHIRE	98.9	98.9	0.0	0.0	0.3	0.3	0.5	0.5	6.2	6.8	8.1	6.0	4.9	22.7	25.1	18.7	1.6	75.1	42.3	50.8	49.2
50516	BADGER	98.6	98.4	0.7	0.8	0.1	0.1	0.7	1.0	8.4	8.2	7.6	6.9	6.0	25.2	25.8	10.7	1.3	71.7	36.9	51.1	48.9
50517	BANCROFT	99.3	99.3	0.1	0.1	0.0	0.0	1.1	1.3	6.3	6.8	7.2	7.2	4.6	21.8	22.8	18.3	5.1	74.3	42.2	47.2	52.8
50518	BARNUM	98.7	98.3	0.0	0.0	0.0	0.2	1.0	1.2	6.8	7.5	9.2	7.5	4.8	23.6	28.7	10.8	1.2	71.8	39.3	52.3	47.7
50519	BODE	98.0	97.6	0.0	0.0	1.2	1.5	0.8	0.9	6.0	6.0	6.8	7.2	5.7	23.6	26.8	15.3	2.7	76.8	41.3	51.8	48.2
50520	BRADGATE	99.0	99.0	0.0	0.0	0.3	0.4	0.0	0.0	5.9	5.5	5.5	6.6	7.3	20.4	32.9	13.8	2.1	78.9	44.2	51.6	48.4
50521	BURNSIDE	97.9	100.0	0.0	0.0	0.0	0.0	0.0	0.0	6.7	6.7	4.4	6.7	6.7	24.4	31.1	13.3	0.0	82.2	42.5	48.9	51.1
50522	BURT	99.1	99.0	0.2	0.2	0.2	0.3	0.5	0.5	5.5	5.9	7.1	7.1	5.5	24.8	26.5	15.2	2.6	77.2	41.2	48.4	51.6
50523	CALLENDER	99.1	99.0	0.1	0.3	0.0	0.0	0.9	1.0	6.1	6.3	7.4	6.9	6.2	23.6	26.5	15.2	1.9	75.8	41.4	50.5	49.5
50524	CLARE	98.7	98.4	0.0	0.0	0.1	0.1	0.9	1.2	6.6	7.4	9.1	7.2	5.0	23.6	28.7	11.3	1.2	72.5	39.6	52.0	48.0
50525	CLARION	94.5	93.5	0.2	0.2	0.2	0.2	8.1	9.6	5.9	6.1	7.4	6.2	5.6	23.3	24.8	16.1	4.7	76.6	41.9	48.9	51.1
50527	CURLEW	98.9	98.9	0.0	0.0	0.4	0.4	0.4	0.4	5.4	5.8	7.6	6.5	5.1	21.4	25.4	19.6	3.3	76.8	43.8	50.0	50.0
50528	CYLINDER	98.5	98.7	0.2	0.2	0.2	0.2	0.8	0.8	6.0	7.4	8.5	7.2	4.5	24.0	27.9	13.4	1.1	73.0	40.5	51.3	48.7
50529	DAKOTA CITY	98.7	98.6	0.1	0.1	0.1	0.1	1.4	1.8	6.5	6.3	7.5	8.4	8.5	27.9	23.9	9.7	1.2	74.8	34.7	51.2	48.8
50530	DAYTON	98.5	98.3	0.1	0.1	0.3	0.5	0.5	0.5	6.1	6.0	6.9	7.1	6.5	22.8	23.5	16.7	4.3	76.9	41.2	49.5	50.5
50531	DOLLIVER	97.9	97.4	0.8	0.9	0.4	0.4	2.5	3.1	5.7	7.0	7.0	11.4	4.4	21.8	26.6	14.4	1.8	71.6	38.9	50.2	49.8
50532	DUNCOMBE	97.8	97.5	0.0	0.0	0.2	0.2	1.6	1.7	6.5	6.6	7.2	7.0	6.2	26.8	24.7	13.0	1.9	75.5	38.9	49.2	50.9
50533	EAGLE GROVE	97.5	97.0	0.2	0.2	0.1	0.2	1.9	2.3	6.2	6.3	7.5	6.7	6.1	23.1	24.8	16.0	3.4	76.0	41.1	49.0	51.0
50535	EARLY	96.8	96.3	0.5	0.5	0.0	0.0	2.9	3.6	6.2	6.5	8.3	6.7	4.9	24.9	25.2	15.2	2.1	74.7	40.3	49.3	50.7
50536	EMMETSBURG	98.6	98.6	0.1	0.1	0.5	0.6	0.8	0.8	5.8	5.3	5.7	6.6	8.8	22.8	23.7	17.0	4.4	80.1	41.1	48.8	51.2
50538	FARNHAMVILLE	98.8	98.5	0.0	0.0	0.0	0.0	1.1	1.1	5.7	6.3	6.1	5.3	6.8	19.5	28.9	18.6	2.8	78.3	45.2	47.9	52.1
50539	FENTON	98.8	98.9	0.0	0.0	0.0	0.0	0.2	0.2	5.6	6.2	7.7	7.1	4.1	22.6	24.9	17.9	3.9	75.9	43.2	47.9	52.1
50540	FONDA	98.9	98.8	0.2	0.2	0.0	0.0	1.4	1.6	5.0	5.2	6.2	8.0	5.7	19.8	26.7	18.9	4.4	77.9	45.0	51.2	48.8
50541	GILMORE CITY	98.9	98.7	0.1	0.1	0.1	0.1	0.5	0.7	5.3	6.0	7.6	7.8	6.0	22.9	27.5	14.8	2.1	75.8	41.7	51.0	49.0
50542	GOLDFIELD	99.0	98.7	0.0	0.0	0.0	0.1	1.8	2.1	5.2	5.9	7.6	6.5	5.6	23.1	25.3	18.3	2.5	77.3	42.3	52.0	48.1
50543	GOWRIE	98.6	98.2	0.2	0.2	0.3	0.5	0.9	1.2	5.3	5.4	7.4	7.2	6.8	21.5	24.5	17.7	4.2	77.2	42.4	48.4	51.6
50544	HARCOURT	98.8	98.3	0.2	0.2	0.5	0.9	1.1	1.0	5.8	5.8	5.4	5.6	8.3	24.1	29.0	14.1	2.0	80.0	42.0	52.4	47.6
50545	HARDY	98.7	98.3	0.0	0.0	0.3	0.3	1.0	1.0	5.7	7.8	8.8	7.4	3.7	25.0	24.7	14.5	2.4	73.7	40.4	51.7	48.3
50546	HAVELOCK	97.9	97.6	0.2	0.2	0.4	0.4	0.8	0.8	4.4	5.4	7.8	7.4	5.6	20.5	29.5	17.5	1.8	76.7	44.2	49.6	50.4
50548	HUMBOLDT	98.6	98.3	0.2	0.2	0.2	0.3	1.3	1.5	5.9	5.8	6.1	6.4	5.9	21.3	24.7	19.3	4.6	78.1	44.0	47.7	52.3
50551	JOLLEY	99.5	100.0	0.0	0.0	0.0	0.0	1.0	0.5	4.9	5.4	8.2	7.6	6.5	21.2	31.0	14.1	1.1	76.6	42.8	51.6	48.4
	IOWA	93.9	93.0	2.1	2.3	1.3	1.8	2.8	3.2	6.5	6.5	6.9	7.2	7.6	26.4	24.2	12.3	2.4	76.0	37.2	49.2	50.8
	UNITED STATES	75.1	73.6	12.3	12.5	3.8	4.2	12.5	14.1	6.9	6.7	7.2	7.0	7.3	28.6	23.8	10.8	1.7	75.1	36.0	49.1	50.9

#	POST OFFICE NAME	2004 Per Capita Income	2004 HH Income Base	2004 HOUSEHOLD INCOME DISTRIBUTION (%) Less than $25,000	$25,000 to $49,999	$50,000 to $99,999	$100,000 to $149,999	$150,000 or More	MEDIAN HOUSEHOLD INCOME 2004	2009	2004 National Centile	2004 State Centile	2004 Home Value Base	2004 HOME VALUE DISTRIBUTION (%) Less than $50,000	$50,000 to $89,999	$90,000 to $174,999	$175,000 to $399,999	$400,000 or More	2004 Median Home Value
50316	DES MOINES	16964	5980	31.3	33.9	28.3	5.1	1.4	38219	48094	40	23	3703	23.0	52.4	23.5	1.1	0.0	72732
50317	DES MOINES	20690	14090	24.7	32.2	34.5	6.9	1.6	44015	53383	59	58	10623	16.3	43.5	36.6	3.1	0.6	82404
50320	DES MOINES	22762	5681	21.0	29.0	38.0	9.8	2.2	49990	59589	72	82	4001	24.2	15.3	50.0	9.4	1.0	105902
50321	DES MOINES	34673	3029	14.6	27.5	29.0	16.7	12.2	58524	68730	83	94	1908	14.4	2.8	35.4	41.9	5.4	170900
50322	URBANDALE	33069	14071	12.2	22.5	40.1	16.9	8.4	65088	78883	89	98	10903	2.2	5.6	59.1	32.0	1.2	148836
50323	URBANDALE	57950	666	7.7	9.8	38.1	5.6	38.9	89010	102857	97	100	648	3.7	0.0	11.0	59.7	25.6	303067
50325	CLIVE	46828	5213	7.4	15.4	35.0	18.8	23.4	86737	105659	97	100	4174	1.6	3.0	26.3	55.6	13.5	211448
50327	DES MOINES	27210	2642	11.6	21.2	44.7	18.9	3.6	68025	81490	90	98	2129	5.5	8.3	58.9	25.6	1.8	140593
50401	MASON CITY	22976	13435	30.5	29.2	30.2	6.9	3.2	40884	49178	49	40	9230	15.3	35.3	36.4	12.3	0.7	89500
50420	ALEXANDER	20212	191	23.0	38.7	31.4	5.2	1.6	42113	49253	53	49	153	37.9	37.3	18.3	5.2	1.3	62917
50421	BELMOND	19871	1355	29.0	33.5	30.9	5.8	0.8	38750	44706	42	27	1012	19.2	41.2	33.0	5.7	0.9	81102
50423	BRITT	18004	1262	27.5	40.5	27.7	3.3	1.0	38899	44271	42	28	971	32.4	38.9	23.1	4.8	0.7	69267
50424	BUFFALO CENTER	19663	662	31.3	33.4	28.9	4.4	2.1	36332	42134	33	15	536	49.4	31.0	15.5	2.6	1.5	50714
50428	CLEAR LAKE	23823	4073	30.1	27.7	31.7	7.1	3.4	42767	50214	55	52	3052	11.0	25.6	40.9	17.2	5.2	106885
50430	CORWITH	17763	276	33.0	35.5	24.3	6.5	0.7	36834	41662	35	17	221	47.1	27.2	17.7	6.8	1.4	53095
50432	CRYSTAL LAKE	21520	129	22.5	38.8	30.2	7.8	0.8	44604	50000	60	61	105	30.5	30.5	28.6	10.5	0.0	71000
50433	DOUGHERTY	19569	100	20.0	36.0	39.0	4.0	1.0	45000	52108	61	63	78	37.2	20.5	30.8	10.3	1.3	76667
50434	FERTILE	19036	202	27.2	37.6	31.2	2.5	1.5	38686	43466	42	27	168	28.0	42.9	22.0	6.6	0.6	67727
50435	FLOYD	21338	350	23.1	35.4	31.1	6.6	3.7	43702	49902	58	57	299	18.7	27.1	41.5	12.4	0.3	94167
50436	FOREST CITY	22013	2353	21.7	33.1	37.1	6.0	2.1	46232	53350	64	69	1764	19.5	36.3	37.4	6.5	0.2	83312
50438	GARNER	22692	1652	21.5	33.6	35.5	5.5	3.9	46315	52053	65	70	1327	14.5	35.0	39.8	10.1	0.6	90533
50439	GOODELL	19341	197	16.8	46.7	32.0	3.1	1.5	42174	47054	53	49	159	35.9	27.0	23.3	11.3	2.5	71364
50440	GRAFTON	17955	196	23.5	39.3	34.7	2.6	0.0	40000	44399	46	35	159	23.9	33.3	28.3	8.8	5.7	79500
50441	HAMPTON	22346	2392	30.3	31.1	30.6	6.0	2.0	39173	47333	43	29	1704	27.9	37.0	27.2	7.0	0.8	71538
50444	HANLONTOWN	18919	136	27.9	37.5	30.2	2.9	1.5	38602	43707	41	26	113	27.4	40.7	23.9	7.1	0.9	68929
50446	JOICE	20754	245	22.5	39.6	31.0	5.3	1.6	42981	49267	56	53	206	30.1	33.5	25.2	10.7	0.5	72632
50447	KANAWHA	19472	503	22.5	40.6	31.8	4.2	1.0	40065	45403	46	36	385	46.8	26.5	17.9	6.8	2.1	54464
50448	KENSETT	18239	342	28.7	32.8	35.7	2.3	0.6	41897	45964	53	48	284	31.3	28.2	26.8	10.6	3.2	72353
50449	KLEMME	18658	337	26.4	35.9	31.5	5.3	0.9	38868	44110	42	28	264	51.9	32.2	10.6	3.4	1.9	48889
50450	LAKE MILLS	23261	1262	25.8	31.2	33.4	7.8	1.9	43203	50094	56	54	929	13.6	32.7	41.3	11.0	1.4	93876
50451	LAKOTA	19210	280	35.0	30.4	25.4	7.1	2.1	34713	40321	26	9	227	53.7	20.7	17.2	5.7	2.6	45000
50452	LATIMER	19000	436	24.8	37.2	30.3	5.5	2.3	41519	48724	51	45	348	35.1	28.7	26.7	7.5	2.0	73571
50453	LELAND	22705	236	11.9	40.7	37.7	8.1	1.7	48743	55327	70	78	199	21.1	25.6	41.7	10.1	1.5	93421
50454	LITTLE CEDAR	19117	64	26.6	42.2	25.0	4.7	1.6	39053	44523	43	29	53	41.5	24.5	20.8	9.4	3.8	61667
50455	MC INTIRE	15560	157	27.4	40.1	27.4	3.8	1.3	40103	45434	46	36	130	43.1	22.3	20.8	10.8	3.1	57500
50456	MANLY	18506	735	28.2	36.6	31.2	3.8	0.3	40112	45349	46	36	560	32.7	39.3	23.9	3.0	1.1	66515
50457	MESERVEY	19321	156	25.6	46.2	24.4	3.9	0.0	38300	44298	40	24	124	41.9	33.9	18.6	4.8	0.8	57143
50458	NORA SPRINGS	19578	758	27.0	34.6	31.7	5.2	1.6	41065	46817	50	42	625	25.1	27.2	38.2	5.6	3.8	87100
50459	NORTHWOOD	21636	1365	27.9	36.0	28.6	5.4	2.2	40560	45505	48	39	1078	21.6	36.1	32.3	8.7	1.3	81531
50460	ORCHARD	20403	147	21.1	38.8	29.3	6.8	4.1	43223	49532	57	54	121	18.2	29.8	26.5	15.7	9.9	95000
50461	OSAGE	19798	2331	29.9	34.9	28.8	4.6	1.8	38358	43884	41	24	1831	15.6	34.6	38.3	9.9	1.6	89855
50464	PLYMOUTH	18387	239	21.3	41.0	33.9	3.4	0.4	40953	47174	49	41	203	24.1	36.0	29.6	8.9	1.5	81458
50465	RAKE	22769	119	34.5	31.1	27.7	5.9	0.8	34216	40000	25	7	94	58.5	12.8	17.0	11.7	0.0	38750
50466	RICEVILLE	20540	643	31.6	31.7	30.2	4.4	2.2	39922	45602	46	34	519	32.0	31.6	24.9	10.4	1.2	69324
50467	ROCK FALLS	19123	13	7.7	23.1	61.5	7.7	0.0	60797	62902	85	95	11	9.1	18.2	63.6	9.1	0.0	118750
50468	ROCKFORD	18523	623	30.2	33.6	30.5	3.7	2.1	39569	45497	45	31	470	30.9	33.6	26.2	8.1	1.3	74390
50469	ROCKWELL	19750	586	22.0	33.3	37.2	6.1	1.4	46418	54430	65	70	487	25.3	33.3	33.7	6.6	1.2	81863
50470	ROWAN	18377	161	28.6	37.3	30.4	3.1	0.6	40729	46126	49	40	127	49.6	22.1	20.5	7.9	0.0	50500
50471	RUDD	21033	321	29.6	35.8	28.0	3.7	2.8	40801	46600	49	40	258	33.3	32.2	29.5	3.5	1.6	67895
50472	SAINT ANSGAR	18300	866	30.1	31.2	33.3	4.9	0.6	39075	44375	43	29	706	21.1	27.8	40.9	9.5	0.7	91081
50473	SCARVILLE	20815	131	13.7	45.8	34.4	5.3	0.8	46488	53237	65	71	109	33.9	22.9	33.0	5.5	4.6	79167
50475	SHEFFIELD	20564	616	25.7	32.1	32.3	8.1	1.8	44169	51819	59	60	509	25.9	38.1	27.3	7.1	1.6	76020
50476	STACYVILLE	19005	323	25.7	46.1	22.9	3.7	1.6	37594	42817	38	19	262	35.9	34.4	21.8	6.1	1.9	66552
50477	SWALEDALE	18749	152	19.7	36.8	38.8	4.0	0.7	44638	50449	60	61	119	38.7	20.2	31.1	9.2	0.8	73000
50478	THOMPSON	21102	472	23.5	40.0	29.9	4.0	2.5	41160	46923	50	43	365	47.1	26.6	20.6	4.7	1.1	53889
50479	THORNTON	18074	303	25.7	45.9	24.1	4.3	0.0	37717	44646	38	21	240	40.8	32.9	19.2	5.4	1.7	58800
50480	TITONKA	21057	436	26.4	36.7	30.1	4.4	2.5	41008	47042	50	42	360	41.1	32.2	18.9	4.7	3.1	56531
50482	VENTURA	26591	355	20.3	29.9	35.5	9.9	4.5	49847	56547	72	81	300	7.3	18.3	38.0	30.0	6.3	135000
50483	WESLEY	20749	362	23.5	33.2	34.0	7.2	2.2	44756	51373	61	61	293	31.7	35.2	25.3	7.5	0.3	67051
50484	WODEN	18054	207	26.1	41.1	28.0	4.4	0.5	39497	44849	44	31	161	45.3	32.9	13.7	6.8	1.2	54412
50501	FORT DODGE	21181	12186	30.0	33.3	28.0	5.7	3.1	39319	45938	44	30	8396	22.8	36.7	30.7	8.8	1.1	81452
50510	ALBERT CITY	17528	441	31.3	40.6	23.4	3.4	1.4	36253	41203	33	15	354	52.0	29.1	13.8	2.5	2.5	48727
50511	ALGONA	20697	3001	29.1	33.6	28.5	6.7	2.0	38945	45956	43	28	2266	20.5	33.7	36.1	9.7	0.1	85388
50514	ARMSTRONG	19987	628	30.1	33.8	29.3	5.4	1.4	39862	45641	45	33	510	42.9	32.6	19.2	3.5	1.8	57660
50515	AYRSHIRE	18008	155	31.0	36.8	27.7	2.6	1.9	36443	41372	33	16	124	34.7	30.7	21.0	10.5	3.2	67500
50516	BADGER	22567	305	15.4	33.1	41.6	7.5	2.3	51881	59591	75	86	256	10.9	21.5	55.5	12.1	0.0	111066
50517	BANCROFT	17578	431	34.6	35.3	23.9	4.6	1.6	35837	41418	31	13	324	40.7	34.6	20.7	3.1	0.9	60000
50518	BARNUM	20699	153	27.5	32.0	30.7	3.3	6.5	45634	50912	63	66	125	20.0	33.6	27.2	14.4	4.8	87000
50519	BODE	21104	312	22.4	40.7	29.2	5.1	2.6	41943	48520	53	48	247	41.3	25.1	22.7	8.5	2.4	60238
50520	BRADGATE	20182	123	26.8	36.6	30.1	4.9	1.6	40976	47907	50	41	99	47.5	22.2	20.2	6.1	4.0	53571
50521	BURNSIDE	15500	15	26.7	33.3	40.0	0.0	0.0	42343	47351	54	50	12	8.3	33.3	58.3	0.0	0.0	95000
50522	BURT	17663	344	33.7	33.7	27.9	3.8	0.9	35814	41455	31	13	278	51.8	29.9	12.2	4.3	1.8	48810
50523	CALLENDER	19879	309	27.8	31.4	32.4	4.9	3.6	41618	48882	52	46	251	19.5	36.3	33.9	6.4	4.0	85323
50524	CLARE	19703	267	27.3	33.0	29.2	3.8	6.7	45481	50953	63	66	217	18.0	35.0	27.7	14.8	4.6	87759
50525	CLARION	21592	1648	26.5	33.3	31.8	5.5	3.0	42856	50145	56	53	1253	27.9	35.3	30.4	4.2	2.2	71685
50527	CURLEW	18433	114	34.2	35.1	22.8	4.4	3.5	34472	40000	26	8	92	51.1	27.2	15.2	6.5	0.0	49000
50528	CYLINDER	27402	203	21.2	30.1	34.5	4.9	9.4	49220	56764	71	80	142	19.0	35.9	27.5	9.2	8.5	86111
50529	DAKOTA CITY	19065	355	24.2	36.3	33.2	5.4	0.9	41036	49908	50	42	285	17.2	45.6	34.7	2.5	0.0	80641
50530	DAYTON	18468	483	29.4	34.4	31.7	2.9	1.7	40429	46268	48	38	354	36.4	32.2	26.6	4.0	0.9	66757
50531	DOLLIVER	24603	102	21.6	42.2	24.5	8.8	2.9	40915	48207	49	41	82	25.6	31.7	36.6	3.7	2.4	82500
50532	DUNCOMBE	21189	398	22.6	40.5	32.4	3.5	1.0	39284	44812	44	30	325	32.6	24.9	35.7	4.9	1.9	79688
50533	EAGLE GROVE	23487	1660	27.4	33.5	29.8	5.2	4.2	41843	49090	52	47	1237	46.6	32.4	17.5	3.2	0.3	53400
50535	EARLY	19090	394	31.5	33.3	30.2	4.1	1.0	39142	44280	43	29	320	39.4	33.4	20.6	4.1	2.5	65429
50536	EMMETSBURG	21109	1875	30.5	34.1	28.8	4.7	2.0	37603	44378	38	20	1346	24.1	37.2	31.4	6.3	1.0	77190
50538	FARNHAMVILLE	26158	245	25.3	36.3	28.6	4.9	4.9	40280	46623	47	37	186	43.0	39.3	14.5	1.6	1.6	57647
50539	FENTON	18328	267	33.0	40.8	21.7	2.6	1.9	36171	41065	32	15	212	54.3	30.2	9.4	4.7	1.4	45909
50540	FONDA	19005	489	32.5	35.4	27.2	3.1	1.8	36819	42994	35	16	391	56.0	24.6	16.1	2.1	1.3	45204
50541	GILMORE CITY	20507	385	28.8	32.5	29.4	6.8	2.6	39589	46377	45	32	301	43.5	29.9	16.3	9.3	1.0	55270
50542	GOLDFIELD	18907	401	29.4	34.4	30.9	4.0	1.3	39895	46150	46	34	302	45.4	32.5	16.9	4.3	1.0	56667
50543	GOWRIE	19682	595	32.3	30.4	30.3	5.0	2.0	39924	45766	46	34	439	24.2	36.5	31.4	7.3	0.7	80700
50544	HARCOURT	25123	240	22.9	30.8	38.3	5.0	2.9	45000	53067	61	63	190	34.7	26.3	31.1	6.8	1.1	76000
50545	HARDY	18606	109	22.9	34.9	33.9	8.3	0.0	43389	49213	57	55	89	40.5	22.5	16.9	14.6	5.6	65000
50546	HAVELOCK	18560	200	27.0	40.0	26.5	3.5	3.0	36042	41773	32	14	162	50.6	24.7	21.6	0.6	2.5	49333
50548	HUMBOLDT	23409	2468	26.5	28.9	33.8	8.1	2.7	45734	53309	63	67	1848	15.0	23.7	47.4	12.9	1.0	101609
50551	JOLLEY	25686	82	17.1	46.3	26.8	4.9	4.9	45632	50930	63	66	64	29.7	26.6	21.9	20.3	1.6	82000
	IOWA	23554		24.6	30.5	32.9	8.4	3.7	45622	53985				17.5	26.2	39.3	15.0	2.1	98835
	UNITED STATES	25866		24.7	27.1	30.8	10.9	6.5	48124	56710				10.9	15.0	33.7	30.1	10.4	145905

#	POST OFFICE NAME	FINANCIAL SERVICES: Auto Loan	FINANCIAL SERVICES: Home Loan	FINANCIAL SERVICES: Invest-ments	FINANCIAL SERVICES: Retire-ment Plans	THE HOME: Home Improvements: Home Repair	THE HOME: Home Improvements: Lawn & Garden	THE HOME: Furnishings: Comput-ers & Hard-ware	THE HOME: Furnishings: Major Appli-ances	THE HOME: Furnishings: TV, Radio, Sound Equip-ment	THE HOME: Furnishings: Furni-ture	ENTERTAINMENT: Dine out/ Carry out	ENTERTAINMENT: Sports Equip-ment	ENTERTAINMENT: Fees & Tickets	ENTERTAINMENT: Toys & Games	ENTERTAINMENT: Travel	ENTERTAINMENT: Cable TV	PERSONAL: Apparel & Services	PERSONAL: Auto Repairs	PERSONAL: Health Insur-ance	PERSONAL: Pets & Supplies
50316	DES MOINES	60	60	66	59	60	65	65	62	66	62	81	73	65	83	64	65	79	64	63	68
50317	DES MOINES	71	73	74	72	74	80	73	73	74	71	92	84	74	95	74	75	89	73	75	82
50320	DES MOINES	87	85	86	87	83	87	86	86	84	87	106	101	84	102	83	80	103	87	79	97
50321	DES MOINES	115	115	134	120	113	120	124	118	121	122	152	143	122	150	120	116	149	123	110	132
50322	URBANDALE	107	121	135	125	119	121	116	114	110	117	139	134	121	141	116	106	137	113	104	125
50323	URBANDALE	234	287	305	297	276	276	254	248	231	259	294	287	275	303	256	222	295	239	218	274
50325	CLIVE	173	197	215	206	191	193	185	180	172	188	219	212	194	222	184	165	218	179	160	199
50327	DES MOINES	96	113	124	114	111	112	105	104	99	105	124	123	109	129	106	96	123	102	95	115
50401	MASON CITY	74	73	73	71	74	81	74	75	76	72	93	86	74	95	74	77	90	75	78	85
50420	ALEXANDER	88	61	32	58	71	80	60	75	70	60	82	90	52	80	63	73	75	74	89	104
50421	BELMOND	75	59	41	57	64	73	62	68	68	60	81	78	57	78	62	70	75	68	78	84
50423	BRITT	67	57	46	55	61	70	58	63	63	56	76	72	56	77	59	66	71	62	72	77
50424	BUFFALO CENTER	73	56	37	54	61	72	60	67	67	58	79	76	54	76	60	71	73	67	79	82
50428	CLEAR LAKE	90	75	56	73	80	90	74	83	80	73	97	96	70	96	76	83	90	81	92	103
50430	CORWITH	81	56	30	53	66	74	56	69	64	55	75	83	48	74	58	67	69	68	82	96
50432	CRYSTAL LAKE	78	69	53	66	73	79	64	71	68	64	83	85	63	85	66	70	79	69	77	92
50433	DOUGHERTY	91	63	33	60	74	83	63	77	72	62	84	93	53	83	65	76	77	76	92	108
50434	FERTILE	85	60	32	56	70	78	59	73	68	58	80	88	51	78	61	71	73	72	87	101
50435	FLOYD	93	80	58	76	85	92	74	84	80	74	97	100	71	98	77	82	91	82	93	110
50436	FOREST CITY	87	74	56	73	78	88	74	81	80	73	96	93	71	96	75	81	90	79	89	98
50438	GARNER	83	78	74	78	81	88	78	81	80	77	99	94	78	99	79	81	94	80	85	95
50439	GOODELL	76	68	52	65	72	77	63	70	67	63	81	83	62	83	65	69	77	68	75	90
50440	GRAFTON	82	57	30	54	67	75	56	70	65	56	76	84	48	75	59	68	70	69	83	97
50441	HAMPTON	82	68	55	68	73	82	72	77	76	70	92	90	67	91	71	78	86	77	84	93
50444	HANLONTOWN	86	61	33	58	70	79	60	73	68	59	81	88	52	79	62	72	74	72	87	102
50446	JOICE	87	71	49	68	78	84	67	77	73	67	88	92	63	89	69	76	83	75	86	102
50447	KANAWHA	86	61	33	58	71	79	60	74	69	59	81	89	52	80	62	72	74	72	87	102
50448	KENSETT	79	57	33	54	66	73	56	68	63	55	75	81	49	74	58	66	69	67	79	93
50449	KLEMME	73	62	48	62	65	73	63	68	67	62	82	78	61	81	63	68	76	67	74	81
50450	LAKE MILLS	80	71	63	72	74	82	72	76	75	71	91	89	70	90	72	75	87	76	81	91
50451	LAKOTA	84	58	31	55	68	76	58	71	67	57	78	86	49	77	60	70	71	70	85	100
50452	LATIMER	89	62	33	59	72	81	61	76	71	61	83	91	52	81	64	74	76	75	90	106
50453	LELAND	95	79	54	74	85	93	74	85	81	74	97	102	70	98	76	83	91	83	95	113
50454	LITTLE CEDAR	83	58	30	55	67	75	57	70	66	56	77	85	49	75	59	69	70	69	84	98
50455	MC INTIRE	84	58	31	55	68	76	58	71	66	57	78	86	49	76	60	70	71	70	85	99
50456	MANLY	71	59	44	58	62	70	60	65	64	59	78	75	57	77	60	66	73	64	72	79
50457	MESERVEY	75	53	28	50	61	69	52	64	60	51	70	78	45	69	54	63	64	63	77	90
50458	NORA SPRINGS	78	65	49	65	69	78	67	72	71	66	86	83	63	85	67	73	81	71	79	87
50459	NORTHWOOD	80	63	43	61	69	78	64	72	71	63	84	84	59	82	65	73	78	71	83	92
50460	ORCHARD	101	71	38	67	82	93	71	87	81	70	95	104	61	93	73	85	87	85	103	119
50461	OSAGE	79	59	38	57	66	76	63	71	70	60	83	82	56	80	63	73	76	70	83	89
50464	PLYMOUTH	84	59	31	55	68	77	58	72	67	57	78	86	49	77	60	70	71	71	85	100
50465	RAKE	74	62	49	62	66	74	64	69	68	63	83	78	62	82	64	69	78	68	74	81
50466	RICEVILLE	93	67	39	64	76	88	69	82	79	67	93	96	60	90	71	83	85	81	98	108
50467	ROCK FALLS	109	76	40	72	89	99	75	93	87	74	102	112	64	100	78	91	93	92	111	130
50468	ROCKFORD	79	62	43	61	68	76	63	71	69	62	83	83	58	82	64	71	77	70	80	90
50469	ROCKWELL	94	66	36	62	77	86	65	80	75	65	88	97	56	86	68	79	81	79	96	112
50470	ROWAN	78	54	29	51	64	71	54	67	62	53	73	80	46	71	56	65	66	66	79	93
50471	RUDD	90	66	39	63	75	84	66	79	74	65	88	94	58	87	68	78	81	78	92	105
50472	SAINT ANSGAR	79	57	34	54	65	75	60	70	68	58	80	81	52	77	61	72	73	69	83	90
50473	SCARVILLE	94	67	37	64	77	86	67	81	76	66	89	97	58	88	69	79	82	80	95	111
50475	SHEFFIELD	86	63	38	60	70	82	66	76	75	64	88	88	58	84	67	79	80	76	91	98
50476	STACYVILLE	82	57	30	54	67	75	57	70	65	56	77	85	48	75	59	69	70	69	84	98
50477	SWALEDALE	91	64	34	60	74	83	63	77	72	62	85	93	54	83	65	76	77	76	92	108
50478	THOMPSON	81	71	53	67	75	81	66	74	71	66	86	87	65	87	68	73	81	72	80	94
50479	THORNTON	77	54	28	51	63	70	53	66	61	52	72	79	45	70	55	64	65	65	78	91
50480	TITONKA	92	64	34	61	75	84	64	79	73	63	86	95	54	84	66	77	78	77	94	109
50482	VENTURA	108	87	60	79	97	108	81	97	91	81	109	114	74	108	86	97	101	95	113	131
50483	WESLEY	99	69	36	65	81	90	68	85	79	68	92	102	58	91	71	83	84	83	101	118
50484	WODEN	81	59	33	55	67	75	57	70	65	57	77	84	50	76	59	68	71	69	82	96
50501	FORT DODGE	69	67	67	65	68	75	68	69	70	66	87	80	68	89	69	72	83	69	73	80
50510	ALBERT CITY	78	54	28	51	63	71	54	66	62	53	72	80	46	71	55	65	66	65	79	92
50511	ALGONA	86	61	34	58	70	80	63	75	72	61	84	88	54	81	64	75	77	74	89	100
50514	ARMSTRONG	67	63	56	59	66	74	62	66	66	60	81	75	62	85	64	69	77	64	73	79
50515	AYRSHIRE	78	54	28	51	63	71	54	66	62	53	72	80	46	71	56	65	66	65	79	92
50516	BADGER	95	83	62	79	88	95	77	86	83	77	100	103	75	102	80	85	95	84	94	112
50517	BANCROFT	70	52	32	50	58	68	56	63	63	53	74	72	49	71	56	66	68	63	76	79
50518	BARNUM	102	71	37	67	83	93	70	87	81	69	95	104	60	93	73	85	86	85	103	121
50519	BODE	92	64	33	60	74	83	63	78	73	62	85	94	54	84	65	76	78	77	93	109
50520	BRADGATE	86	60	31	57	70	78	59	73	68	58	80	88	51	78	61	72	73	72	87	102
50521	BURNSIDE	84	59	31	56	68	77	58	72	67	57	78	86	50	77	60	70	71	71	85	100
50522	BURT	64	59	52	55	62	69	58	62	62	56	76	71	57	79	60	65	72	61	69	75
50523	CALLENDER	92	65	34	61	75	84	64	79	73	63	86	95	54	84	66	77	79	78	94	110
50524	CLARE	100	70	36	66	81	91	69	85	79	68	93	102	59	91	71	83	85	84	101	118
50525	CLARION	86	66	47	65	74	82	66	77	73	66	87	92	59	85	68	75	80	76	87	101
50527	CURLEW	76	55	33	52	62	72	58	67	66	56	77	78	51	74	59	69	71	67	80	86
50528	CYLINDER	129	90	47	85	105	118	89	110	103	88	121	133	76	118	93	108	110	109	131	154
50529	DAKOTA CITY	78	69	51	65	73	79	64	71	68	64	83	85	62	84	66	70	78	69	78	92
50530	DAYTON	76	56	35	54	62	73	61	68	68	58	80	78	54	76	61	72	73	68	82	85
50531	DOLLIVER	95	66	35	63	77	87	66	81	76	65	89	98	56	87	68	79	81	80	97	113
50532	DUNCOMBE	83	71	55	71	75	84	72	78	77	71	93	89	69	93	72	78	87	76	84	93
50533	EAGLE GROVE	95	73	49	71	81	92	76	86	84	74	100	99	69	98	77	87	92	85	99	108
50535	EARLY	76	61	45	61	66	74	63	69	68	62	82	80	59	81	63	69	76	68	77	85
50536	EMMETSBURG	82	61	38	58	68	79	65	74	74	62	86	85	57	82	65	78	79	74	88	93
50538	FARNHAMVILLE	105	73	38	69	85	96	72	89	83	71	98	108	62	96	75	87	89	88	107	125
50539	FENTON	69	51	32	49	57	67	55	62	62	53	73	71	49	70	55	66	67	62	75	78
50540	FONDA	77	56	34	53	63	73	59	68	67	57	78	79	52	75	59	70	72	68	81	88
50541	GILMORE CITY	87	61	33	58	71	80	62	75	71	61	83	89	53	81	64	74	76	74	89	102
50542	GOLDFIELD	81	57	30	53	66	74	56	69	64	55	75	83	48	74	58	68	69	68	82	96
50543	GOWRIE	79	59	37	56	65	77	64	72	72	61	84	81	56	80	64	76	77	71	86	89
50544	HARCOURT	112	78	41	74	91	102	77	95	89	76	104	115	66	102	80	93	95	94	113	133
50545	HARDY	91	64	33	60	74	83	63	78	73	62	85	94	54	84	65	76	78	77	93	109
50546	HAVELOCK	84	58	31	55	68	76	58	71	66	57	78	86	49	76	60	70	71	70	85	99
50548	HUMBOLDT	89	67	44	65	74	86	71	80	79	69	94	92	63	90	71	83	86	79	94	101
50551	JOLLEY	104	73	38	69	85	95	72	89	83	71	97	107	61	95	75	87	89	88	106	124
	IOWA	87	79	73	79	82	89	80	84	83	79	102	98	78	102	80	83	97	84	88	100
	UNITED STATES	100	100	100	100	100	100	100	100	100	100	100	100	100	100	100	100	100	100	100	100

POPULATION CHANGE

ZIP CODE			POPULATION			2000-2004 ANNUAL RATE		HOUSEHOLDS					FAMILIES		
#	POST OFFICE NAME	COUNTY FIPS CODE	2000	2004	2009	% Rate	State Centile	2000	2004	2009	% Annual Rate 2000-2004	2004 Average HH Size	2000	2004	% Annual Rate 2000-2004
50552	KNIERIM	025	129	126	122	-0.6	21	61	59	56	-0.8	1.10	46	11	-28.6
50554	LAURENS	151	1887	1765	1652	-1.6	1	821	777	735	-1.3	2.22	523	493	-1.4
50556	LEDYARD	109	368	354	339	-0.9	9	164	160	155	-0.6	2.21	115	112	-0.6
50557	LEHIGH	187	891	876	867	-0.4	27	387	386	385	-0.1	2.27	255	252	-0.3
50558	LIVERMORE	091	735	784	814	1.5	87	287	307	321	1.6	2.55	197	211	1.6
50559	LONE ROCK	109	344	323	305	-1.5	1	146	139	134	-1.2	2.32	100	95	-1.2
50560	LU VERNE	109	639	628	608	-0.4	27	267	266	262	-0.1	2.36	194	193	-0.1
50561	LYTTON	025	256	248	237	-0.7	14	98	97	94	-0.2	2.54	73	72	-0.3
50562	MALLARD	147	605	602	600	-0.1	42	238	240	241	0.2	2.51	172	172	0.0
50563	MANSON	025	2591	2445	2300	-1.4	2	1083	1026	969	-1.3	2.33	740	699	-1.3
50565	MARATHON	021	561	540	535	-0.9	9	242	235	234	-0.7	2.30	177	171	-0.8
50566	MOORLAND	187	447	458	461	0.6	70	182	188	191	0.8	2.44	144	149	0.8
50567	NEMAHA	161	293	284	278	-0.7	15	115	113	112	-0.4	2.51	86	84	-0.6
50568	NEWELL	021	1437	1408	1399	-0.5	24	554	547	546	-0.3	2.48	390	384	-0.4
50569	OTHO	187	907	935	944	0.7	74	369	386	393	1.1	2.42	260	270	0.9
50570	OTTOSEN	091	308	316	320	0.6	71	100	104	106	0.9	3.02	76	79	0.9
50571	PALMER	151	639	636	609	-0.1	43	259	261	253	0.2	2.44	187	188	0.1
50573	PLOVER	151	58	54	51	-1.7	1	22	21	20	-1.1	2.57	16	15	-1.5
50574	POCAHONTAS	151	2519	2385	2243	-1.3	3	1084	1037	985	-1.0	2.24	719	685	-1.1
50575	POMEROY	025	976	934	884	-1.0	6	426	412	392	-0.8	2.16	272	261	-1.0
50576	REMBRANDT	021	426	461	479	1.9	90	167	182	190	2.0	2.50	121	131	1.9
50577	RENWICK	091	547	551	558	0.2	58	226	227	230	0.1	2.43	163	163	0.0
50578	RINGSTED	063	723	743	738	0.6	72	318	334	337	1.2	2.22	219	229	1.1
50579	ROCKWELL CITY	025	3048	2932	2787	-0.9	9	1124	1087	1034	-0.8	2.35	735	709	-0.8
50581	ROLFE	151	1194	1159	1102	-0.7	16	483	474	456	-0.4	2.40	332	324	-0.6
50582	RUTLAND	091	330	328	330	-0.1	42	125	126	128	0.2	2.60	95	95	0.0
50583	SAC CITY	161	3499	3472	3445	-0.2	39	1530	1535	1540	0.1	2.20	971	970	-0.1
50585	SIOUX RAPIDS	041	1218	1210	1214	-0.2	42	511	511	515	0.0	2.32	338	337	-0.1
50586	SOMERS	025	515	484	455	-1.5	2	187	176	166	-1.4	2.45	132	124	-1.5
50588	STORM LAKE	021	12527	12485	12488	-0.1	45	4393	4362	4351	-0.2	2.58	2924	2895	-0.2
50590	SWEA CITY	109	1133	1079	1026	-1.1	4	475	458	441	-0.9	2.36	314	301	-1.0
50591	THOR	091	370	370	372	0.0	51	153	153	155	0.0	2.42	110	110	0.0
50594	VINCENT	187	310	293	288	-1.3	2	130	125	125	-0.9	2.34	98	94	-1.0
50595	WEBSTER CITY	079	9339	9467	9553	0.3	64	3949	4051	4131	0.6	2.31	2584	2642	0.5
50597	WEST BEND	147	1397	1419	1418	0.4	65	548	563	568	0.6	2.41	371	379	0.5
50598	WHITTEMORE	109	1034	1020	988	-0.3	32	414	415	409	0.1	2.45	293	293	0.0
50599	WOOLSTOCK	197	389	361	347	-1.7	1	170	159	154	-1.6	2.27	129	121	-1.5
50601	ACKLEY	083	2708	2710	2691	0.0	51	1055	1055	1051	0.0	2.47	744	742	-0.1
50602	ALLISON	023	1587	1568	1546	-0.3	34	634	636	636	0.1	2.35	444	445	0.1
50603	ALTA VISTA	037	585	590	586	0.2	59	225	229	230	0.4	2.57	168	171	0.4
50604	APLINGTON	023	1763	1707	1673	-0.8	14	709	696	690	-0.4	2.38	520	509	-0.5
50605	AREDALE	069	229	248	257	1.9	91	84	91	95	1.9	2.73	63	69	2.2
50606	ARLINGTON	065	1025	1003	991	-0.7	23	412	409	409	-0.2	2.45	294	290	-0.3
50607	AURORA	019	520	504	501	-0.7	15	203	199	200	-0.5	2.53	152	149	-0.5
50608	AUSTINVILLE	023	116	115	113	-0.2	38	51	51	51	0.0	2.25	41	41	0.0
50609	BEAMAN	075	440	438	449	-0.1	43	173	174	179	0.1	2.52	132	133	0.2
50611	BRISTOW	023	451	478	488	1.4	85	168	180	186	1.6	2.66	133	141	1.4
50612	BUCKINGHAM	171	538	528	524	-0.4	26	203	200	200	-0.4	2.64	151	149	-0.3
50613	CEDAR FALLS	013	38456	39444	40294	0.6	71	13710	14233	14706	0.9	2.44	8279	8545	0.8
50614	CEDAR FALLS	013	2	2	2	0.0	51	1	1	1	0.0	2.00	1	0	-100.0
50616	CHARLES CITY	067	10605	10401	10186	-0.5	25	4390	4341	4285	-0.3	2.31	2934	2890	-0.4
50619	CLARKSVILLE	023	2660	2595	2542	-0.6	20	1029	1018	1010	-0.3	2.49	767	756	-0.3
50621	CONRAD	075	1526	1556	1607	0.5	68	622	640	666	0.7	2.38	434	444	0.5
50622	DENVER	017	2931	3209	3414	2.2	93	1112	1231	1323	2.4	2.58	883	976	2.4
50624	DIKE	075	1607	1683	1764	1.1	81	623	658	694	1.3	2.56	472	497	1.2
50625	DUMONT	023	1147	1150	1145	0.1	53	457	460	461	0.2	2.42	313	313	0.0
50626	DUNKERTON	013	1740	1788	1824	0.6	72	605	629	648	0.9	2.84	484	503	0.9
50627	ELDORA	083	3765	3709	3647	-0.4	30	1480	1466	1449	-0.2	2.29	954	942	-0.3
50628	ELMA	089	1656	1621	1613	-0.5	23	648	641	644	-0.3	2.42	453	447	-0.3
50629	FAIRBANK	019	2456	2555	2615	0.9	79	862	913	949	1.4	2.80	661	698	1.3
50630	FREDERICKSBURG	037	1767	1712	1674	-0.7	14	693	681	674	-0.4	2.47	503	493	-0.5
50632	GARWIN	171	1042	1038	1030	-0.1	44	411	413	413	0.1	2.51	304	305	0.1
50633	GENEVA	069	431	481	516	2.6	94	166	187	203	2.8	2.57	116	130	2.7
50635	GLADBROOK	171	1845	1802	1772	-0.6	21	744	727	717	-0.5	2.40	516	502	-0.7
50636	GREENE	023	2014	1972	1935	-0.5	23	875	870	865	-0.1	2.24	605	599	-0.2
50638	GRUNDY CENTER	075	3401	3448	3559	0.3	64	1406	1436	1493	0.5	2.34	963	980	0.4
50641	HAZLETON	019	1809	1887	1932	1.0	79	625	662	688	1.4	2.85	437	461	1.3
50642	HOLLAND	075	495	500	514	0.2	61	195	199	207	0.5	2.51	155	158	0.5
50643	HUDSON	013	2624	2639	2658	0.1	56	973	993	1012	0.5	2.66	769	783	0.4
50644	INDEPENDENCE	019	8831	8664	8643	-0.5	25	3405	3379	3410	-0.2	2.45	2326	2299	-0.3
50645	IONIA	037	1216	1215	1205	0.0	48	456	462	464	0.3	2.60	342	346	0.3
50647	JANESVILLE	017	1867	2038	2164	2.1	92	736	816	879	2.5	2.49	570	629	2.3
50648	JESUP	019	3502	3406	3392	-0.7	17	1305	1288	1300	-0.3	2.64	976	959	-0.4
50649	KESLEY	023	46	45	44	-0.5	22	18	18	18	0.0	2.50	15	15	0.0
50650	LAMONT	019	845	891	918	1.3	83	340	364	380	1.6	2.45	240	256	1.5
50651	LA PORTE CITY	013	3974	4038	4129	0.4	66	1526	1562	1610	0.6	2.56	1125	1149	0.5
50652	LINCOLN	171	32	31	31	-0.7	14	12	12	12	0.0	2.58	9	9	0.0
50653	MARBLE ROCK	067	717	684	661	-1.1	5	300	290	285	-0.8	2.36	220	212	-0.9
50654	MASONVILLE	019	584	636	669	2.0	91	210	232	248	2.4	2.74	165	181	2.2
50655	MAYNARD	065	791	802	802	0.3	64	330	340	345	0.7	2.35	229	234	0.5
50658	NASHUA	037	2469	2436	2394	-0.3	32	1010	1006	1000	-0.1	2.42	717	713	-0.1
50659	NEW HAMPTON	037	5805	5723	5632	-0.3	31	2324	2322	2315	0.0	2.39	1565	1557	-0.1
50660	NEW HARTFORD	023	1411	1412	1402	0.0	51	554	564	569	0.4	2.50	431	437	0.3
50662	OELWEIN	065	7558	7351	7281	-0.7	17	3138	3086	3090	-0.4	2.32	2072	2028	-0.5
50665	PARKERSBURG	023	3211	3190	3169	-0.2	42	1293	1301	1309	0.2	2.45	949	952	0.1
50666	PLAINFIELD	017	1033	1031	1040	-0.1	46	423	429	438	0.3	2.40	305	308	0.2
50667	RAYMOND	013	59	61	62	0.8	76	24	25	26	1.0	2.44	19	20	1.2
50668	READLYN	017	1425	1393	1410	-0.5	22	557	553	566	-0.2	2.52	415	410	-0.3
50669	REINBECK	075	2613	2828	3011	1.9	90	1057	1150	1233	2.0	2.42	759	823	1.9
50670	SHELL ROCK	023	1811	1776	1745	-0.5	25	731	729	726	-0.1	2.37	530	527	-0.1
50671	STANLEY	065	333	323	320	-0.7	16	116	114	115	-0.4	2.83	87	86	-0.3
50672	STEAMBOAT ROCK	083	664	649	634	-0.5	21	274	269	264	-0.4	2.41	185	181	-0.5
50674	SUMNER	017	3939	3962	4036	0.1	57	1562	1590	1638	0.4	2.44	1111	1127	0.3
50675	TRAER	171	2281	2295	2289	0.1	57	940	952	956	0.3	2.33	644	650	0.3
50676	TRIPOLI	017	2072	2029	2057	-0.5	23	821	809	827	-0.4	2.47	578	566	-0.5
	IOWA					0.5					0.7	2.43			0.6
	UNITED STATES					1.2					1.3	2.58			1.1

ZIP CODE #	POST OFFICE NAME	RACE (%) White 2000	White 2004	Black 2000	Black 2004	Asian/Pacific 2000	Asian/Pacific 2004	% Hispanic Origin 2000	% Hispanic Origin 2004	2004 AGE DISTRIBUTION (%) 0-4	5-9	10-14	15-19	20-24	25-44	45-64	65-84	85+	18+	MEDIAN AGE 2004	% 2004 Males	% 2004 Females
50552	KNIERIM	87.6	86.5	7.8	7.9	0.0	0.8	3.9	4.0	3.2	2.4	3.2	2.4	8.7	48.4	23.8	7.1	0.8	90.5	37.8	73.0	27.0
50554	LAURENS	98.7	98.6	0.0	0.0	0.4	0.6	1.0	1.1	4.7	5.0	6.8	7.1	5.6	22.3	25.7	18.4	4.4	78.8	44.1	48.5	51.5
50556	LEDYARD	98.9	98.6	0.0	0.0	0.3	0.3	1.4	1.7	5.9	5.9	6.8	7.1	5.7	21.5	26.6	18.6	2.0	77.4	43.3	50.6	49.4
50557	LEHIGH	98.3	98.4	0.2	0.2	0.2	0.2	0.3	0.3	5.1	5.4	6.3	7.4	6.2	20.1	29.6	17.9	2.1	79.0	44.7	52.1	48.0
50558	LIVERMORE	99.6	99.6	0.0	0.0	0.1	0.1	0.3	0.3	3.8	5.4	8.0	8.9	5.9	23.5	27.3	15.1	2.2	76.5	42.5	50.4	49.6
50559	LONE ROCK	98.8	98.5	0.3	0.3	0.0	0.0	0.0	0.0	5.9	6.5	7.4	7.4	4.3	22.3	25.4	17.0	3.7	75.5	42.8	48.6	51.4
50560	LU VERNE	98.9	98.6	0.0	0.0	0.2	0.3	0.6	0.8	5.7	6.4	6.9	6.4	4.8	24.2	26.3	17.2	2.2	76.9	42.6	53.0	47.0
50561	LYTTON	99.2	99.2	0.0	0.0	0.0	0.0	0.8	0.8	5.2	5.7	8.1	6.9	6.1	20.6	30.7	14.5	2.4	77.0	43.5	52.4	47.6
50562	MALLARD	98.8	98.8	0.2	0.2	0.2	0.2	0.2	0.2	5.8	6.2	7.6	7.1	5.3	21.6	26.4	17.1	2.8	75.8	42.4	51.0	49.0
50563	MANSON	98.7	98.5	0.2	0.3	0.2	0.4	0.5	0.6	5.5	5.6	6.3	6.8	5.8	20.9	27.3	17.6	4.2	78.0	44.4	48.0	52.0
50565	MARATHON	98.4	98.0	0.2	0.2	0.0	0.0	2.1	2.2	4.4	5.4	7.8	6.9	4.4	22.6	29.4	17.0	2.0	78.3	44.0	52.4	47.6
50566	MOORLAND	98.9	98.7	0.5	0.4	0.2	0.2	0.9	1.1	5.7	6.3	7.4	6.3	5.5	22.3	27.1	17.5	2.0	76.6	42.8	50.9	49.1
50567	NEMAHA	97.6	97.5	0.0	0.0	0.7	0.7	0.7	1.1	6.7	7.0	7.0	6.3	3.9	24.7	26.1	16.9	1.4	75.0	41.5	53.5	46.5
50568	NEWELL	97.6	97.7	0.2	0.2	0.6	0.6	2.1	2.1	6.3	7.1	7.1	6.9	5.4	22.7	24.0	16.6	3.9	75.0	41.5	49.2	50.9
50569	OTHO	98.1	98.0	0.7	0.8	0.1	0.2	0.6	0.5	6.5	6.7	6.7	6.3	6.5	24.6	28.7	12.5	1.4	76.4	40.2	50.6	49.4
50570	OTTOSEN	97.7	97.5	0.0	0.0	1.6	1.6	0.7	1.0	6.0	6.3	6.7	7.0	6.0	23.7	25.6	15.8	2.9	76.9	40.9	51.6	48.4
50571	PALMER	98.3	98.1	1.1	1.3	0.2	0.2	0.6	0.8	4.9	5.8	7.6	7.6	5.4	21.5	29.7	15.6	2.0	76.7	43.5	52.4	47.6
50573	PLOVER	98.3	98.2	0.0	0.0	0.0	0.0	0.0	0.0	3.7	5.6	7.4	9.3	5.6	20.4	31.5	16.7	0.0	77.8	43.8	48.2	51.9
50574	POCAHONTAS	98.4	98.1	0.3	0.3	0.1	0.1	0.8	1.0	5.3	5.6	7.0	6.7	5.2	19.7	27.6	19.0	4.0	77.7	45.3	47.7	52.3
50575	POMEROY	99.6	99.6	0.0	0.0	0.0	0.0	0.4	0.4	5.6	5.5	5.4	6.6	5.6	19.3	25.9	20.5	5.8	78.9	46.4	47.4	52.6
50576	REMBRANDT	97.4	97.4	0.0	0.0	0.2	0.2	2.6	2.8	5.6	6.1	5.9	8.0	6.3	21.7	32.1	12.8	1.5	77.4	42.6	51.8	48.2
50577	RENWICK	98.5	98.6	0.0	0.0	0.2	0.4	0.7	0.9	5.3	7.3	8.5	7.6	4.4	23.8	26.3	14.9	2.0	74.2	41.2	51.9	48.1
50578	RINGSTED	99.7	99.7	0.0	0.0	0.1	0.1	0.0	0.0	4.4	5.0	6.3	6.9	5.9	23.0	29.3	16.2	3.0	79.8	44.0	51.1	48.9
50579	ROCKWELL CITY	96.4	95.9	1.6	1.8	0.3	0.3	1.3	1.5	4.5	4.8	5.9	5.8	5.9	27.0	26.0	16.3	3.7	80.6	42.5	52.8	47.2
50581	ROLFE	98.3	98.0	0.3	0.3	0.2	0.3	0.8	1.0	5.7	5.9	7.5	7.4	5.5	21.1	25.5	17.8	3.7	76.1	43.1	49.9	50.1
50582	RUTLAND	98.8	98.8	0.0	0.0	0.3	0.6	0.3	0.3	5.8	5.8	5.5	6.4	7.0	20.7	32.0	14.6	2.1	79.3	44.2	51.5	48.5
50583	SAC CITY	98.7	98.6	0.2	0.3	0.1	0.2	0.8	0.9	4.8	5.1	6.3	6.0	5.6	21.7	26.0	19.4	5.1	79.7	45.3	47.8	52.2
50585	SIOUX RAPIDS	98.8	98.8	0.2	0.2	0.1	0.1	1.3	1.3	5.3	5.6	7.0	7.0	5.7	20.6	28.2	16.5	4.1	77.8	44.1	49.3	50.7
50586	SOMERS	96.7	96.1	1.8	1.9	0.2	0.2	1.2	1.7	4.8	6.2	7.6	6.6	6.0	30.4	24.6	12.0	1.9	76.9	38.0	56.4	43.6
50588	STORM LAKE	82.6	82.1	0.4	0.4	6.8	6.9	17.9	18.5	6.3	6.4	7.1	8.2	10.1	26.3	20.9	11.8	2.8	76.4	34.3	50.3	49.7
50590	SWEA CITY	97.9	97.6	0.0	0.0	0.2	0.3	1.9	2.3	6.6	5.9	6.2	6.9	5.8	21.9	25.4	18.7	2.7	77.1	43.0	49.9	50.1
50591	THOR	98.9	98.9	0.0	0.0	0.5	0.5	0.5	0.5	6.2	7.0	7.6	6.8	5.1	23.2	27.6	13.8	2.7	75.1	40.8	53.5	46.5
50594	VINCENT	97.4	96.6	0.0	0.0	0.3	0.7	1.9	2.7	4.8	4.8	8.2	7.9	3.8	22.5	29.7	16.4	2.1	77.5	43.6	50.2	49.8
50595	WEBSTER CITY	95.9	95.8	0.3	0.3	2.2	2.2	1.2	1.3	6.9	6.5	6.5	6.4	6.5	25.2	23.7	15.0	3.3	76.2	39.3	48.6	51.4
50597	WEST BEND	99.2	99.2	0.1	0.1	0.1	0.1	0.8	0.7	5.1	5.3	7.3	7.5	6.1	20.3	26.0	17.6	4.7	77.6	43.9	48.8	51.2
50598	WHITTEMORE	98.9	98.7	0.6	0.6	0.1	0.1	0.5	0.6	6.3	6.7	7.7	7.7	6.2	23.1	24.7	15.2	2.6	74.7	40.5	51.7	48.3
50599	WOOLSTOCK	98.5	98.6	0.0	0.0	0.3	0.3	1.3	1.4	5.0	5.5	7.2	5.8	4.7	21.3	32.4	16.1	1.9	79.0	45.2	51.0	49.0
50601	ACKLEY	95.4	94.5	0.2	0.3	0.4	0.5	5.7	6.9	6.1	6.1	6.3	6.8	5.7	21.6	25.0	18.1	4.4	77.2	43.4	47.9	52.1
50602	ALLISON	99.2	99.0	0.0	0.0	0.3	0.3	0.5	0.6	5.1	5.7	7.0	6.2	5.2	22.8	24.2	18.9	4.9	78.2	43.4	48.9	51.1
50603	ALTA VISTA	99.2	99.2	0.0	0.0	0.2	0.2	0.3	0.5	7.3	7.3	7.3	6.4	5.8	26.3	24.9	12.7	2.0	74.4	38.4	52.7	47.3
50604	APLINGTON	99.0	98.8	0.0	0.0	0.2	0.4	0.5	0.6	5.7	6.0	7.3	6.3	4.9	22.2	24.4	18.9	4.5	76.9	43.5	48.5	51.6
50605	AREDALE	98.3	98.4	0.0	0.0	0.0	0.0	0.4	0.8	6.1	6.9	9.3	6.5	5.7	25.4	24.6	14.5	1.2	73.0	38.1	50.4	49.6
50606	ARLINGTON	98.8	98.9	0.1	0.1	0.1	0.1	0.2	0.2	6.1	6.6	8.0	5.8	5.8	21.8	28.3	14.8	2.9	75.7	42.3	48.9	51.2
50607	AURORA	97.1	97.0	0.8	0.8	0.0	0.0	0.2	0.2	7.5	7.5	7.1	7.9	5.2	24.4	25.4	13.1	1.8	72.6	38.6	50.4	49.6
50608	AUSTINVILLE	98.3	98.3	0.0	0.0	0.9	0.9	0.0	0.0	7.8	7.8	7.8	7.0	4.4	20.9	28.7	13.9	1.7	71.3	40.4	51.3	48.7
50609	BEAMAN	98.4	98.2	0.0	0.0	0.7	0.9	0.2	0.0	6.2	6.9	7.8	7.1	5.0	23.7	28.8	13.0	1.6	75.1	41.7	51.1	48.9
50611	BRISTOW	98.5	98.3	0.0	0.0	0.0	0.0	1.1	1.3	5.9	6.7	8.6	6.5	5.9	25.3	25.1	14.9	1.3	75.1	38.5	50.6	49.4
50612	BUCKINGHAM	99.1	99.1	0.2	0.2	0.2	0.2	0.7	0.6	5.5	5.9	6.3	7.0	5.9	21.8	30.1	14.8	2.8	78.0	43.2	51.1	48.9
50613	CEDAR FALLS	95.3	94.2	1.5	1.8	1.6	2.2	1.1	1.3	4.5	4.5	5.3	12.5	17.1	22.6	21.5	9.9	2.1	82.1	28.9	47.2	52.8
50614	CEDAR FALLS	100.0	100.0	0.0	0.0	0.0	0.0	0.0	0.0	0.0	0.0	0.0	100.0	0.0	0.0	0.0	0.0	0.0	100.0	17.5	0.0	100.0
50616	CHARLES CITY	97.4	96.9	0.3	0.4	0.7	1.0	1.7	2.1	6.2	6.1	6.6	6.3	5.9	23.2	24.7	16.8	4.3	77.1	41.9	47.4	52.6
50619	CLARKSVILLE	99.1	98.8	0.0	0.0	0.3	0.5	0.3	0.3	6.5	6.6	6.8	6.1	5.6	24.4	26.2	14.3	3.4	76.1	40.8	49.6	50.4
50621	CONRAD	98.6	98.5	0.0	0.0	0.3	0.3	0.5	0.5	6.9	6.8	7.3	6.4	6.1	20.8	27.3	14.4	4.0	74.6	42.0	48.5	51.5
50622	DENVER	98.7	98.6	0.1	0.1	0.1	0.2	0.7	0.8	6.2	6.6	7.0	6.4	6.1	23.3	30.7	11.5	2.2	75.8	41.3	49.3	50.7
50624	DIKE	98.8	98.7	0.1	0.1	0.3	0.3	0.8	0.9	5.7	6.2	7.6	7.0	6.0	26.0	27.0	13.1	1.3	76.1	39.0	50.6	49.4
50625	DUMONT	98.8	98.6	0.2	0.2	0.3	0.4	1.1	1.2	5.0	5.3	7.4	6.5	5.6	22.3	24.3	18.9	4.9	78.1	43.4	48.6	51.4
50626	DUNKERTON	98.0	97.7	0.0	0.0	1.2	1.5	0.8	1.0	6.7	6.9	8.5	8.3	6.7	28.4	25.3	8.6	0.8	72.9	35.6	51.0	49.1
50627	ELDORA	96.0	95.3	1.1	1.2	0.9	1.2	2.5	3.0	5.4	5.6	6.1	12.2	5.8	20.0	25.5	15.3	4.1	73.3	41.4	49.9	50.1
50628	ELMA	99.5	99.5	0.1	0.1	0.1	0.1	0.1	0.1	5.7	5.7	6.9	5.9	5.8	23.2	26.3	16.7	3.8	77.9	42.9	50.2	49.9
50629	FAIRBANK	98.4	98.4	0.3	0.3	0.7	0.7	0.9	0.9	9.2	8.8	9.2	8.1	7.0	24.1	22.7	9.7	1.1	67.8	31.3	51.3	48.7
50630	FREDERICKSBURG	97.4	96.9	0.2	0.2	0.4	0.5	1.6	2.0	7.1	7.0	6.8	7.1	5.9	23.5	25.8	13.8	3.0	74.5	40.0	49.9	50.1
50632	GARWIN	97.1	97.1	0.1	0.1	0.0	0.0	1.9	1.9	6.3	6.8	7.0	7.9	5.8	24.3	28.8	11.7	1.5	75.1	39.4	50.4	49.6
50633	GENEVA	98.8	98.5	0.0	0.0	0.2	0.2	0.9	1.3	4.6	6.4	7.7	8.3	5.8	24.7	27.7	12.7	2.1	75.5	40.7	50.3	49.7
50635	GLADBROOK	99.0	98.9	0.1	0.1	0.0	0.0	0.9	1.1	5.2	5.8	7.9	6.6	5.1	22.5	24.4	18.4	4.1	76.6	42.8	47.7	52.3
50636	GREENE	99.3	99.1	0.2	0.2	0.3	0.4	0.9	1.0	4.4	4.7	6.0	6.6	5.8	21.4	27.7	19.7	3.7	80.2	45.7	49.4	50.6
50638	GRUNDY CENTER	99.1	99.0	0.1	0.1	0.2	0.3	0.7	0.8	5.3	5.6	6.8	6.5	5.3	22.8	24.5	18.6	4.6	78.3	43.5	47.6	52.4
50641	HAZLETON	98.2	98.2	0.1	0.1	0.2	0.2	1.6	1.6	9.2	8.8	8.1	8.0	6.7	27.2	21.5	9.8	0.7	69.0	31.6	51.9	48.1
50642	HOLLAND	99.0	98.8	0.2	0.2	0.4	0.4	0.4	0.6	5.6	6.2	7.6	7.0	5.2	25.8	26.6	13.8	2.2	76.2	40.4	51.2	48.8
50643	HUDSON	98.6	98.1	0.1	0.1	0.6	0.8	0.5	0.7	5.7	6.5	8.3	7.5	5.8	23.6	29.4	12.0	1.3	74.8	40.9	48.7	51.3
50644	INDEPENDENCE	98.1	98.1	0.3	0.3	0.6	0.6	0.6	0.6	6.2	6.4	7.1	7.3	6.3	24.8	25.2	13.7	3.1	75.4	39.6	49.0	51.1
50645	IONIA	98.9	98.9	0.0	0.0	0.2	0.3	0.5	0.5	6.2	7.2	8.1	6.8	5.2	24.2	28.2	13.0	1.1	74.2	40.6	52.0	48.0
50647	JANESVILLE	98.6	98.2	0.2	0.2	0.5	0.7	0.4	0.5	5.1	5.5	6.3	6.5	5.2	24.5	33.1	12.5	1.2	79.0	43.0	49.9	50.1
50648	JESUP	99.1	99.1	0.1	0.1	0.1	0.1	0.5	0.6	6.7	6.5	8.0	7.6	7.0	25.5	24.8	12.2	1.8	74.0	37.6	49.7	50.4
50649	KESLEY	97.8	100.0	0.0	0.0	0.0	0.0	0.0	0.0	4.4	6.7	8.9	8.9	6.7	24.4	24.4	15.6	0.0	80.0	37.5	57.8	42.2
50650	LAMONT	99.2	99.1	0.2	0.2	0.2	0.2	0.4	0.3	7.2	7.4	7.7	6.0	5.4	25.9	25.1	12.9	2.4	74.1	38.8	52.2	47.8
50651	LA PORTE CITY	99.1	98.9	0.1	0.1	0.2	0.3	0.3	0.4	7.0	6.6	7.5	6.8	5.8	24.5	24.9	14.4	2.6	74.7	39.0	48.9	51.1
50652	LINCOLN	100.0	100.0	0.0	0.0	0.0	0.0	0.0	0.0	6.5	6.5	6.5	6.5	6.5	25.8	22.6	19.4	0.0	80.7	38.8	51.6	48.4
50653	MARBLE ROCK	99.2	99.0	0.0	0.0	0.6	0.7	0.6	0.6	5.4	6.3	8.2	6.7	5.7	22.7	29.1	13.6	2.3	75.9	41.3	51.9	48.1
50654	MASONVILLE	99.1	98.9	0.2	0.2	0.2	0.2	0.5	0.6	7.2	7.6	8.7	6.9	5.8	25.8	24.7	11.8	1.6	72.3	37.4	50.9	49.1
50655	MAYNARD	99.8	99.8	0.0	0.0	0.0	0.0	0.3	0.3	7.0	7.2	6.5	5.7	5.4	26.3	26.6	13.5	1.9	75.6	40.4	53.1	46.9
50658	NASHUA	99.3	99.1	0.1	0.1	0.2	0.3	0.2	0.3	5.3	5.9	7.4	7.1	6.1	23.0	25.7	17.5	2.2	77.3	41.9	49.7	50.3
50659	NEW HAMPTON	98.9	98.6	0.0	0.0	0.3	0.5	0.4	0.5	5.9	6.1	7.1	6.3	6.3	24.1	25.0	15.5	3.9	76.9	41.3	49.6	50.4
50660	NEW HARTFORD	98.9	98.8	0.1	0.1	0.1	0.1	1.1	1.3	5.7	6.3	6.8	5.4	6.4	26.1	30.0	11.4	1.9	78.1	40.8	50.3	49.7
50662	OELWEIN	97.4	97.3	0.4	0.4	0.4	0.4	2.2	2.3	6.5	6.3	6.4	6.2	6.6	23.0	24.1	17.1	3.9	76.8	41.3	47.4	52.6
50665	PARKERSBURG	99.1	99.1	0.1	0.1	0.1	0.1	0.5	0.5	5.9	6.0	7.1	7.9	5.5	24.1	26.2	15.0	2.3	76.0	40.8	48.8	51.2
50666	PLAINFIELD	99.5	99.5	0.0	0.0	0.1	0.1	0.5	0.6	5.7	6.2	7.3	5.9	6.0	26.0	27.8	13.3	1.8	77.3	40.2	51.2	48.8
50667	RAYMOND	98.3	100.0	0.0	0.0	0.0	0.0	0.0	1.6	6.6	6.6	6.6	8.2	4.9	26.2	31.2	9.8	0.0	75.4	38.1	50.8	49.2
50668	READLYN	98.7	98.4	0.3	0.3	0.6	0.7	0.4	0.6	5.7	6.2	8.1	7.1	5.7	23.6	27.9	13.4	2.4	75.5	40.9	50.3	49.8
50669	REINBECK	99.3	99.0	0.1	0.1	0.3	0.6	0.5	0.6	5.1	5.7	7.3	6.7	5.7	23.5	26.1	16.0	4.1	77.5	42.7	49.6	50.4
50670	SHELL ROCK	98.6	98.5	0.2	0.2	0.3	0.5	0.3	0.3	5.4	6.0	6.5	5.7	6.0	25.3	29.7	12.1	3.3	78.5	41.9	50.7	49.3
50671	STANLEY	97.6	97.8	0.6	0.6	0.0	0.0	0.3	0.3	7.4	7.7	7.1	8.4	5.3	23.8	25.7	13.0	1.6	72.8	38.7	50.8	49.2
50672	STEAMBOAT ROCK	96.8	96.3	0.3	0.3	0.3	0.5	3.0	3.7	6.3	6.2	5.9	7.1	5.7	23.0	25.9	17.6	2.5	77.5	42.2	51.2	48.8
50674	SUMNER	98.9	98.7	0.1	0.1	0.5	0.6	0.7	0.8	6.0	6.5	7.4	6.7	5.8	23.5	25.6	14.6	4.0	75.9	40.8	49.4	50.6
50675	TRAER	98.8	98.8	0.4	0.4	0.1	0.1	0.4	0.4	6.6	6.6	6.1	5.6	4.8	22.5	24.7	18.2	5.0	77.0	43.3	48.2	51.9
50676	TRIPOLI	98.9	98.9	0.1	0.2	0.1	0.2	0.3	0.4	7.0	7.0	8.1	6.3	5.6	24.4	24.4	14.1	3.2	74.0	39.4	49.4	50.6
	IOWA	93.9	93.0	2.1	2.3	1.3	1.8	2.8	3.2	6.5	6.5	6.9	7.2	7.6	26.4	24.2	12.3	2.4	76.0	37.2	49.2	50.8
	UNITED STATES	75.1	73.6	12.3	12.5	3.8	4.2	12.5	14.1	6.9	6.7	7.2	7.0	7.3	28.6	23.8	10.8	1.7	75.1	36.0	49.1	50.9

ZIP CODE #	POST OFFICE NAME	2004 Per Capita Income	2004 HH Income Base	2004 Household Income Distribution (%) Less than $25,000	$25,000 to $49,999	$50,000 to $99,999	$100,000 to $149,999	$150,000 or More	Median Household Income 2004	2009	2004 National Centile	2004 State Centile	2004 Home Value Base	2004 Home Value Distribution (%) Less than $50,000	$50,000 to $89,999	$90,000 to $174,999	$175,000 to $399,999	$400,000 or More	2004 Median Home Value
50552	KNIERIM	22435	59	39.0	33.9	27.1	0.0	0.0	30747	36535	14	2	47	27.7	31.9	34.0	2.1	4.3	77500
50554	LAURENS	21424	777	31.3	33.7	27.7	3.9	3.5	37288	43766	36	18	602	39.7	35.6	20.4	3.7	0.7	60615
50556	LEDYARD	22153	160	33.1	31.9	25.0	8.8	1.3	37071	43492	36	17	127	52.8	20.5	16.5	6.3	3.9	47667
50557	LEHIGH	19517	386	32.4	33.7	29.0	3.1	1.8	37869	43630	39	22	312	41.4	24.0	28.2	4.8	1.6	64167
50558	LIVERMORE	18715	307	29.0	38.1	26.7	4.2	2.0	37743	44096	38	21	251	42.6	31.5	19.1	4.4	2.4	60179
50559	LONE ROCK	17831	139	32.4	38.9	23.7	2.9	2.2	36435	41528	33	15	110	48.2	30.0	13.6	6.4	1.8	51667
50560	LU VERNE	18577	266	30.1	40.2	23.7	4.9	1.1	35196	40494	28	10	208	51.0	28.4	15.9	2.4	2.4	48889
50561	LYTTON	21570	97	20.6	44.3	26.8	4.1	4.1	44060	50000	59	59	74	31.1	27.0	23.0	17.6	1.4	80000
50562	MALLARD	19655	240	34.2	32.9	23.8	2.9	6.3	35000	40768	28	10	188	56.9	23.9	16.0	2.1	1.1	45000
50563	MANSON	21259	1026	33.2	29.8	27.7	6.8	2.4	40508	46827	48	39	795	19.0	43.3	28.2	7.9	1.6	78467
50565	MARATHON	16694	235	35.7	40.9	20.4	2.1	0.9	34048	39110	24	7	181	50.3	16.0	20.4	8.8	4.4	49688
50566	MOORLAND	25077	188	21.8	27.7	37.8	4.3	8.5	50434	59020	73	83	154	20.1	32.5	36.4	5.8	5.2	87895
50567	NEMAHA	22614	113	24.8	27.4	41.6	5.3	0.9	39646	47412	45	32	82	26.8	31.7	28.1	8.5	4.9	82222
50568	NEWELL	16982	547	29.8	39.7	25.2	5.3	0.0	37359	43096	37	18	417	38.1	32.4	22.8	4.8	1.9	65119
50569	OTHO	19433	386	24.1	36.8	33.7	4.4	1.0	39839	47911	45	33	293	34.1	38.6	25.3	1.0	1.0	62813
50570	OTTOSEN	16327	104	23.1	41.4	27.9	4.8	2.9	41124	47608	50	42	82	42.7	26.8	19.5	7.3	3.7	56667
50571	PALMER	19124	261	31.4	28.0	34.1	5.4	1.2	40419	47168	48	38	202	55.9	22.8	12.4	6.4	2.5	46129
50573	PLOVER	14583	21	23.8	52.4	23.8	0.0	0.0	34226	40000	25	7	17	58.8	23.5	17.7	0.0	0.0	32500
50574	POCAHONTAS	22046	1037	30.4	33.9	26.7	5.7	3.4	38391	45317	41	25	820	40.4	32.9	20.9	4.6	1.2	59634
50575	POMEROY	19780	412	35.9	38.1	19.2	4.6	2.2	31451	37805	16	3	314	45.2	29.3	20.4	4.1	1.0	60333
50576	REMBRANDT	18916	182	26.9	38.5	30.2	3.3	1.1	38148	42872	40	23	140	50.0	20.0	22.9	7.1	0.0	50000
50577	RENWICK	20781	227	24.2	33.9	33.9	7.1	0.9	42824	50000	55	53	186	37.1	23.7	20.4	12.9	5.9	70000
50578	RINGSTED	20826	334	35.3	34.1	22.2	5.7	2.7	35000	39802	28	10	248	42.3	27.4	19.8	8.9	1.6	59048
50579	ROCKWELL CITY	18878	1087	31.1	33.9	27.6	5.2	2.3	37176	43505	36	17	823	30.3	39.6	24.3	4.7	1.1	68133
50581	ROLFE	17089	474	35.4	34.8	23.8	4.2	1.7	34577	39822	26	9	365	59.7	24.9	13.4	0.3	1.6	39741
50582	RUTLAND	18431	126	26.2	36.5	29.4	5.6	2.4	41313	48196	51	44	101	46.5	21.8	20.8	6.9	4.0	55000
50583	SAC CITY	19932	1535	34.7	36.2	23.3	3.8	2.0	35749	41064	31	13	1136	40.5	34.5	21.0	2.9	1.1	59730
50585	SIOUX RAPIDS	20054	511	31.1	37.0	26.4	3.9	1.6	36201	41968	32	15	386	50.8	30.1	14.3	3.4	1.6	49455
50586	SOMERS	16433	176	36.4	30.1	29.0	4.0	0.6	34187	39068	25	7	145	48.3	25.5	25.5	0.0	0.7	51563
50588	STORM LAKE	19176	4362	29.5	31.0	30.1	6.4	3.0	41173	48049	50	43	3125	14.6	36.0	35.1	12.0	2.3	89391
50590	SWEA CITY	18070	458	33.6	34.7	25.6	5.2	0.9	35274	40943	29	11	346	54.9	26.6	12.4	3.8	2.3	46304
50591	THOR	20923	153	22.2	29.4	39.9	8.5	0.0	47393	53703	67	74	125	36.0	23.2	24.0	15.2	1.6	63889
50594	VINCENT	23381	125	23.2	23.2	48.8	4.8	0.0	53317	61037	77	88	105	18.1	20.0	40.0	16.2	5.7	109868
50595	WEBSTER CITY	23367	4051	26.2	32.0	33.3	6.0	2.5	43547	50920	57	56	2921	18.5	37.3	36.6	6.2	1.5	84487
50597	WEST BEND	22999	563	27.7	36.8	25.8	4.4	5.3	39792	46944	45	33	470	34.7	30.2	29.2	5.1	0.9	67027
50598	WHITTEMORE	19392	415	27.0	37.6	30.1	3.9	1.5	40205	46271	47	37	329	38.9	27.1	27.4	4.6	2.1	59865
50599	WOOLSTOCK	25262	159	13.8	35.9	40.3	8.2	1.9	50188	55666	72	82	127	32.3	29.1	26.0	10.2	2.4	66250
50601	ACKLEY	19688	1055	27.9	35.1	29.8	5.6	1.7	41511	47280	51	45	824	31.8	43.1	20.6	3.2	1.3	65632
50602	ALLISON	19761	636	26.4	36.8	30.4	5.2	1.3	41393	47894	51	44	494	20.9	47.0	23.7	6.5	2.0	74407
50603	ALTA VISTA	21523	229	20.1	43.2	29.7	4.4	2.6	43235	47662	57	55	189	33.3	26.5	29.1	9.0	2.1	76818
50604	APLINGTON	20683	696	26.0	36.4	31.9	3.9	1.9	40206	46022	47	37	572	24.0	34.3	33.9	6.8	1.1	81296
50605	AREDALE	17303	91	26.4	39.6	28.6	3.3	2.2	38942	46391	43	28	73	41.1	23.3	23.3	9.6	2.7	59286
50606	ARLINGTON	18211	409	37.4	31.8	22.7	3.9	4.2	34152	39275	25	7	326	39.3	26.7	23.0	7.4	3.7	59211
50607	AURORA	21258	199	32.7	31.7	23.1	6.0	6.5	39245	46393	44	30	163	29.5	28.8	28.8	8.6	4.3	75000
50608	AUSTINVILLE	19941	51	21.6	47.1	27.5	2.0	2.0	40431	44298	48	38	41	31.7	34.2	24.4	9.8	0.0	73750
50609	BEAMAN	21657	174	16.7	37.9	39.1	4.6	1.7	45913	51652	64	68	130	18.5	26.9	41.5	12.3	0.8	95455
50611	BRISTOW	17146	180	22.8	43.9	30.0	2.2	1.1	40000	45637	46	35	145	37.9	25.5	26.2	7.6	2.8	69000
50612	BUCKINGHAM	21802	200	22.5	29.0	34.5	13.5	0.5	48391	55538	69	77	158	10.8	31.7	36.7	16.5	4.4	99231
50613	CEDAR FALLS	24179	14233	26.1	26.2	32.3	9.9	5.6	47454	56695	67	74	9228	11.6	15.1	49.9	21.5	1.9	118731
50614	CEDAR FALLS	0	0	0.0	0.0	0.0	0.0	0.0	0	0	0	0	0	0.0	0.0	0.0	0.0	0.0	0
50616	CHARLES CITY	19779	4341	32.9	31.4	29.9	4.2	1.7	37975	43686	39	22	3213	15.7	39.0	36.0	8.7	0.6	85386
50619	CLARKSVILLE	18981	1018	28.7	33.2	31.3	5.6	1.2	39576	45083	45	32	789	27.4	30.7	33.6	6.6	1.8	80662
50621	CONRAD	24834	640	21.7	28.4	39.2	8.4	2.2	49842	57721	72	81	484	14.7	30.8	41.5	12.8	0.2	95000
50622	DENVER	27174	1231	15.0	29.1	36.9	14.4	4.7	55311	65101	80	92	1056	8.1	10.1	51.7	27.9	2.2	130952
50624	DIKE	23404	658	18.7	31.0	38.3	8.8	3.2	50197	57581	72	82	548	10.4	24.3	47.8	15.0	2.6	111480
50625	DUMONT	17308	460	33.5	35.4	27.0	2.8	1.3	34521	40052	26	8	355	51.8	29.3	14.1	3.7	1.1	48673
50626	DUNKERTON	19762	629	16.2	34.0	42.0	5.4	2.4	49800	58682	72	81	522	17.6	25.3	44.4	11.3	1.3	99487
50627	ELDORA	18704	1466	30.2	36.1	29.1	3.6	1.0	38596	44724	41	26	1063	36.9	36.8	20.8	5.1	0.5	66856
50628	ELMA	18107	641	30.4	35.1	28.2	5.5	0.8	39569	45631	45	31	518	39.8	27.0	20.5	10.0	2.7	66140
50629	FAIRBANK	17656	913	30.7	31.0	30.8	6.5	1.1	40994	47472	50	41	741	19.8	25.8	38.1	13.6	2.7	95804
50630	FREDERICKSBURG	19002	681	26.1	36.4	32.2	3.7	1.6	39319	44449	44	30	540	17.2	36.5	38.0	7.4	0.9	86429
50632	GARWIN	21200	413	20.3	33.7	39.0	6.1	1.0	47005	55057	66	73	325	22.5	43.1	24.3	10.2	0.0	74091
50633	GENEVA	21777	187	20.3	32.1	36.9	7.5	3.2	47374	54777	67	74	151	39.1	32.5	10.6	13.9	4.0	61000
50635	GLADBROOK	21349	727	21.5	38.4	31.2	6.7	2.2	43409	50473	57	55	594	24.8	38.9	29.0	5.1	2.4	77818
50636	GREENE	20614	870	28.3	34.9	30.3	5.2	1.3	40726	46438	49	40	704	28.0	33.2	30.1	7.4	1.3	76607
50638	GRUNDY CENTER	21878	1436	22.7	35.2	33.4	7.3	1.4	44063	51110	59	59	1148	15.9	32.5	43.1	7.3	1.1	91475
50641	HAZLETON	15913	662	30.7	32.6	32.0	3.0	1.7	37948	44111	39	22	540	43.7	22.6	25.4	8.2	0.2	60909
50642	HOLLAND	21175	199	19.6	40.2	32.7	5.0	2.5	42307	47465	54	50	157	21.0	36.3	31.9	6.4	4.5	81154
50643	HUDSON	27696	993	11.9	26.7	40.8	14.3	6.3	63053	76575	87	97	848	4.6	16.2	50.8	25.1	3.3	130088
50644	INDEPENDENCE	24726	3379	24.2	33.1	31.5	6.7	4.5	43814	52119	58	58	2630	13.6	31.8	43.3	8.6	2.8	94940
50645	IONIA	18232	462	24.5	36.6	34.0	3.7	1.3	43202	47948	56	54	387	23.3	24.8	34.4	12.1	5.4	92586
50647	JANESVILLE	27828	816	16.3	27.7	41.4	10.1	4.5	55285	64208	80	91	698	9.3	15.8	41.6	28.8	4.6	130625
50648	JESUP	21118	1288	21.3	30.7	39.4	6.8	1.9	48011	55935	68	76	1074	17.6	28.3	44.0	8.9	1.3	96471
50649	KESLEY	21954	18	16.7	38.9	38.9	5.6	0.0	45000	50000	61	63	14	7.1	28.6	42.9	21.4	0.0	108333
50650	LAMONT	19828	364	34.9	28.9	27.8	6.0	2.5	35264	40326	28	11	283	33.2	29.7	23.0	11.7	2.5	72826
50651	LA PORTE CITY	22747	1562	21.1	30.6	38.1	7.8	2.4	48532	57628	69	78	1258	17.6	30.3	41.6	9.5	1.1	92755
50652	LINCOLN	15645	12	25.0	50.0	25.0	0.0	0.0	40000	50000	46	35	10	10.0	50.0	40.0	0.0	0.0	85000
50653	MARBLE ROCK	23084	290	24.1	34.1	33.1	5.2	3.5	45174	51243	62	64	233	21.0	27.9	30.9	15.5	4.7	91471
50654	MASONVILLE	20039	232	22.8	34.1	31.5	8.6	3.0	44304	51627	59	60	187	18.2	20.3	34.2	21.9	5.4	111500
50655	MAYNARD	19265	340	31.2	32.9	30.3	5.0	0.6	40642	45566	48	39	275	21.5	39.6	25.5	10.2	3.3	81286
50658	NASHUA	18681	1006	28.9	40.1	25.6	4.8	0.7	37297	42773	36	18	783	29.0	31.3	30.4	7.7	1.7	76905
50659	NEW HAMPTON	23035	2322	23.3	33.4	34.6	6.6	2.2	45245	51373	62	65	1834	15.8	30.2	41.3	12.2	0.5	94124
50660	NEW HARTFORD	21442	564	24.1	32.6	33.0	8.7	1.6	45324	51280	62	65	471	22.9	29.3	28.5	16.8	2.6	87162
50662	OELWEIN	20563	3086	37.2	32.8	25.3	2.9	1.9	33004	39168	21	5	2227	32.8	39.6	23.4	3.1	1.0	67475
50665	PARKERSBURG	21475	1301	27.9	32.2	31.1	6.5	2.2	41125	47224	50	43	1014	15.2	31.0	44.7	7.8	1.4	94333
50666	PLAINFIELD	21671	429	21.5	31.7	40.8	4.9	1.2	47797	54836	68	75	362	16.3	31.2	41.4	9.1	1.9	91875
50667	RAYMOND	25159	25	20.0	24.0	44.0	12.0	0.0	54473	63023	79	91	22	18.2	18.2	54.6	9.1	0.0	104167
50668	READLYN	21709	553	22.1	28.8	39.1	9.2	0.9	49471	57633	71	80	463	7.6	27.9	49.2	13.4	1.9	104036
50669	REINBECK	22378	1150	21.4	37.2	31.9	7.3	2.2	43577	50805	57	57	952	20.4	31.6	35.2	10.0	2.8	87816
50670	SHELL ROCK	21737	729	22.1	34.0	34.6	8.2	1.1	46106	53103	64	69	587	11.1	31.0	42.1	14.0	1.9	99300
50671	STANLEY	19095	114	31.6	31.6	22.8	7.0	7.0	40000	44540	46	35	93	26.9	29.0	30.1	8.6	5.4	79167
50672	STEAMBOAT ROCK	17677	269	32.3	39.0	23.1	4.1	1.5	35550	40245	30	12	201	35.3	31.3	24.4	5.0	4.0	63571
50674	SUMNER	19788	1590	27.3	33.5	32.6	4.8	1.8	40253	47706	47	37	1279	14.4	37.9	35.8	9.5	2.4	87893
50675	TRAER	19903	952	25.3	35.3	32.8	6.3	0.3	41813	48526	52	47	761	20.0	32.2	38.0	7.4	2.5	87911
50676	TRIPOLI	22207	809	22.7	32.9	35.4	6.7	2.4	43556	52016	57	56	652	17.6	34.8	37.3	9.2	1.1	87377
	IOWA	23554		24.6	30.5	32.9	8.4	3.7	45622	53985				17.5	26.2	39.3	15.0	2.1	98835
	UNITED STATES	25866		24.7	27.1	30.8	10.9	6.5	48124	56710				10.9	15.0	33.7	30.1	10.4	145905

ZIP CODE #	POST OFFICE NAME	FINANCIAL SERVICES: Auto Loan	Home Loan	Investments	Retirement Plans	THE HOME: Home Improvements: Home Repair	Lawn & Garden	Furnishings: Computers & Hardware	Major Appliances	TV, Radio, Sound Equipment	Furniture	ENTERTAINMENT: Dine out/Carry out	Sports Equipment	Fees & Tickets	Toys & Games	Travel	Cable TV	PERSONAL: Apparel & Services	Auto Repairs	Health Insurance	Pets & Supplies
50552	KNIERIM	57	43	28	41	47	57	48	53	54	45	63	59	43	59	47	57	58	53	63	64
50554	LAURENS	82	59	35	57	67	78	62	72	71	60	83	84	54	80	63	74	76	72	87	94
50556	LEDYARD	89	62	32	58	72	81	61	76	70	60	83	91	52	81	63	74	75	75	90	105
50557	LEHIGH	62	61	57	57	63	70	60	62	63	58	78	71	61	82	62	66	74	61	69	73
50558	LIVERMORE	86	60	32	57	70	79	60	74	69	59	80	89	51	79	62	72	73	73	88	103
50559	LONE ROCK	71	51	30	49	58	67	54	63	61	52	72	73	47	69	54	64	65	62	75	81
50560	LU VERNE	79	55	29	52	64	72	55	68	63	54	74	81	47	72	57	66	67	67	80	94
50561	LYTTON	95	70	44	68	80	89	70	84	78	69	93	100	62	91	72	81	86	83	97	113
50562	MALLARD	83	61	37	58	68	79	65	74	73	62	86	85	57	82	65	77	78	73	88	94
50563	MANSON	77	66	53	62	70	81	67	73	73	65	87	83	63	85	68	76	81	72	84	89
50565	MARATHON	69	48	25	46	56	63	48	59	55	47	65	71	41	63	50	58	59	58	70	82
50566	MOORLAND	111	77	40	73	90	101	76	94	88	75	103	114	65	101	79	92	94	93	112	131
50567	NEMAHA	103	72	38	68	84	94	71	88	82	70	96	106	61	94	74	86	87	86	104	122
50568	NEWELL	71	52	33	50	58	68	56	64	63	54	75	73	50	71	56	67	68	63	76	80
50569	OTHO	76	67	50	63	71	76	62	69	66	62	80	82	60	82	64	68	76	67	75	90
50570	OTTOSEN	89	62	33	59	73	81	62	76	71	61	83	92	53	82	64	75	76	75	91	106
50571	PALMER	84	59	31	56	69	77	58	72	67	57	79	87	50	77	60	70	72	71	86	100
50573	PLOVER	68	47	25	45	55	62	47	58	54	46	63	70	40	62	49	57	58	57	69	81
50574	POCAHONTAS	86	62	36	59	71	81	64	76	73	63	86	89	56	83	65	77	79	75	91	100
50575	POMEROY	72	54	34	51	59	70	58	65	65	55	76	74	51	73	58	69	70	65	78	81
50576	REMBRANDT	86	60	31	57	70	78	59	73	68	59	80	88	51	78	61	72	73	72	87	102
50577	RENWICK	91	64	33	60	74	83	63	78	73	62	85	94	54	83	65	76	78	77	93	108
50578	RINGSTED	84	58	31	55	68	76	58	71	67	57	78	86	49	77	60	70	71	70	85	99
50579	ROCKWELL CITY	77	57	37	55	64	75	62	70	70	59	82	79	55	78	62	74	75	69	83	87
50581	ROLFE	68	50	32	48	56	66	55	61	62	52	72	70	48	69	55	65	66	61	74	77
50582	RUTLAND	87	61	32	57	70	79	60	74	69	59	81	89	51	79	62	73	74	73	88	103
50583	SAC CITY	70	56	43	55	61	70	60	65	65	58	77	75	55	74	60	67	72	65	74	79
50585	SIOUX RAPIDS	79	58	36	55	64	76	62	70	70	59	82	81	54	78	62	74	75	70	84	89
50586	SOMERS	73	52	29	49	60	68	53	64	60	52	71	75	46	69	54	64	65	63	76	86
50588	STORM LAKE	76	71	65	70	73	79	71	75	73	71	90	86	69	89	71	73	86	74	77	86
50590	SWEA CITY	72	52	32	50	59	69	56	64	63	54	74	74	49	71	56	66	68	64	76	82
50591	THOR	91	64	34	61	75	83	63	78	73	63	85	94	54	84	66	76	78	77	92	108
50594	VINCENT	88	78	60	74	83	89	72	80	77	72	93	95	71	95	74	79	89	78	87	103
50595	WEBSTER CITY	80	73	65	72	76	84	75	78	78	73	95	90	73	96	75	79	90	77	83	91
50597	WEST BEND	96	70	42	67	78	91	74	85	84	71	99	98	65	94	75	88	90	85	102	109
50598	WHITTEMORE	86	60	31	57	70	78	59	73	68	59	80	88	51	79	62	72	73	72	87	102
50599	WOOLSTOCK	103	73	40	69	85	94	72	88	82	71	97	106	62	95	74	86	88	87	104	122
50601	ACKLEY	81	62	41	60	68	79	66	73	73	63	86	84	59	83	66	76	79	73	85	91
50602	ALLISON	79	58	36	55	65	76	62	71	70	60	83	81	55	79	62	74	75	70	85	89
50603	ALTA VISTA	100	70	37	66	81	91	69	85	80	68	93	103	59	92	72	84	85	84	102	119
50604	APLINGTON	84	61	38	58	68	80	65	75	74	63	87	86	57	83	66	78	79	74	89	95
50605	AREDALE	85	60	31	56	69	78	59	73	68	58	80	88	50	78	61	71	72	72	87	101
50606	ARLINGTON	81	56	30	53	66	74	56	69	64	55	75	83	48	74	58	67	69	68	82	96
50607	AURORA	97	68	36	64	79	89	67	83	77	66	91	100	57	89	70	81	83	82	99	116
50608	AUSTINVILLE	81	57	30	54	66	74	56	69	65	55	76	84	48	74	58	68	69	68	83	97
50609	BEAMAN	99	69	36	65	80	90	68	84	78	67	92	101	58	90	71	82	84	83	100	117
50611	BRISTOW	82	58	30	54	67	75	57	70	65	56	77	85	48	75	59	69	70	69	84	98
50612	BUCKINGHAM	102	74	42	70	85	94	72	88	82	72	97	106	63	96	75	86	89	87	104	121
50613	CEDAR FALLS	84	85	100	88	83	89	93	86	90	90	113	104	91	112	89	86	110	90	81	96
50614	CEDAR FALLS	0	0	0	0	0	0	0	0	0	0	0	0	0	0	0	0	0	0	0	0
50616	CHARLES CITY	73	60	45	57	64	74	62	68	68	60	81	77	58	79	63	71	75	67	78	83
50619	CLARKSVILLE	81	59	36	56	66	77	62	72	70	60	83	83	55	79	63	74	76	71	86	92
50621	CONRAD	108	75	40	71	88	98	75	92	86	74	101	111	64	99	77	90	92	91	110	128
50622	DENVER	111	100	81	98	108	114	94	105	98	93	119	125	90	121	97	100	113	103	112	133
50624	DIKE	105	78	46	74	89	98	76	91	85	75	101	110	67	100	78	89	93	90	106	125
50625	DUMONT	71	52	32	50	58	68	55	63	63	53	74	73	49	70	56	66	67	63	76	81
50626	DUNKERTON	91	79	59	75	84	91	74	82	79	74	96	98	72	97	76	81	91	80	90	107
50627	ELDORA	72	56	38	54	61	71	60	66	66	57	78	75	54	75	59	69	72	65	77	80
50628	ELMA	76	55	33	52	62	72	58	67	65	56	77	78	50	74	58	69	70	67	80	87
50629	FAIRBANK	81	65	45	63	70	79	66	73	71	64	86	86	61	85	66	73	80	72	82	93
50630	FREDERICKSBURG	75	65	50	63	68	75	63	69	67	63	82	81	61	82	64	69	77	68	75	85
50632	GARWIN	87	70	50	69	76	85	71	79	77	70	92	92	66	92	71	79	86	78	88	99
50633	GENEVA	101	71	37	67	82	92	70	86	81	69	94	104	60	93	72	85	86	85	103	120
50635	GLADBROOK	94	66	35	62	76	86	65	80	75	64	88	97	56	86	67	78	80	79	95	111
50636	GREENE	73	61	47	58	66	75	62	69	67	60	80	79	58	79	63	70	75	68	78	85
50638	GRUNDY CENTER	83	68	50	64	74	84	68	77	75	67	89	89	63	88	70	78	83	76	88	97
50641	HAZLETON	71	60	47	60	63	71	62	66	66	61	80	76	59	79	61	67	75	65	72	78
50642	HOLLAND	96	67	35	63	78	88	66	82	76	66	90	99	57	88	69	80	82	81	98	114
50643	HUDSON	95	118	126	118	116	115	106	105	99	105	124	123	113	132	108	96	124	102	95	116
50644	INDEPENDENCE	95	84	67	81	88	99	83	90	89	82	108	103	81	109	84	92	102	88	99	109
50645	IONIA	83	63	38	59	71	78	60	72	68	60	80	87	54	80	62	71	74	71	84	98
50647	JANESVILLE	107	102	84	98	106	111	93	101	96	93	118	120	93	121	96	98	113	98	106	127
50648	JESUP	91	79	58	75	84	90	73	82	78	73	95	98	71	96	75	81	90	80	90	107
50649	KESLEY	99	69	36	66	81	90	68	85	79	68	93	102	58	91	71	83	84	83	101	118
50650	LAMONT	88	61	32	58	71	80	61	75	70	60	82	90	52	80	63	73	75	74	89	104
50651	LA PORTE CITY	86	82	73	79	85	93	80	84	83	79	101	97	79	103	81	84	97	83	90	100
50652	LINCOLN	73	51	27	48	60	67	50	62	58	50	68	75	43	67	52	61	62	61	74	87
50653	MARBLE ROCK	99	69	36	65	80	90	68	84	78	67	92	101	58	90	70	82	84	83	100	117
50654	MASONVILLE	99	70	37	66	81	91	69	85	79	68	93	102	59	91	71	83	85	83	101	118
50655	MAYNARD	82	57	30	54	67	75	57	70	65	56	77	84	48	75	59	68	70	69	83	98
50658	NASHUA	67	60	51	57	63	72	61	65	66	58	79	74	59	81	62	69	75	64	74	78
50659	NEW HAMPTON	87	74	57	71	79	89	75	82	81	73	97	94	71	96	76	84	91	81	92	100
50660	NEW HARTFORD	86	76	58	73	81	87	71	79	75	71	91	94	69	93	73	77	87	76	85	101
50662	OELWEIN	70	63	54	60	67	76	65	69	70	63	85	77	64	87	66	74	80	68	78	80
50665	PARKERSBURG	83	68	51	64	74	84	70	77	77	67	92	89	65	92	71	80	85	76	89	96
50666	PLAINFIELD	85	73	53	69	78	84	68	77	73	68	89	92	66	90	70	75	84	75	84	100
50667	RAYMOND	98	88	67	83	93	99	81	90	86	81	105	107	79	107	83	88	99	87	97	116
50668	READLYN	99	69	36	65	80	90	68	84	79	67	92	102	58	90	71	83	84	83	100	117
50669	REINBECK	98	69	37	66	80	90	68	84	78	67	92	101	59	90	71	82	84	83	100	117
50670	SHELL ROCK	83	72	55	70	76	83	70	76	74	69	90	89	68	91	71	76	85	75	83	95
50671	STANLEY	98	68	36	65	80	89	68	83	78	67	91	100	58	90	70	82	83	82	99	116
50672	STEAMBOAT ROCK	76	54	29	51	62	70	54	65	61	53	72	78	46	71	55	64	66	65	78	90
50674	SUMNER	82	65	41	60	69	78	64	73	71	63	84	85	58	82	65	74	78	72	84	93
50675	TRAER	68	65	61	62	68	75	63	67	67	62	81	77	63	84	66	69	78	66	74	80
50676	TRIPOLI	95	69	40	65	78	90	71	84	81	69	95	98	62	92	72	85	87	83	100	110
	IOWA	87	79	73	79	82	89	80	84	83	79	102	98	78	102	80	83	97	84	88	100
	UNITED STATES	100	100	100	100	100	100	100	100	100	100	100	100	100	100	100	100	100	100	100	100

ZIP CODE		COUNTY FIPS CODE	POPULATION			2000-2004 ANNUAL RATE		HOUSEHOLDS					FAMILIES		
#	POST OFFICE NAME		2000	2004	2009	% Rate	State Centile	2000	2004	2009	% Annual Rate 2000-2004	2004 Average HH Size	2000	2004	% Annual Rate 2000-2004
50677	WAVERLY	017	11261	11481	11734	0.5	68	4100	4236	4387	0.8	2.40	2831	2909	0.6
50680	WELLSBURG	075	1216	1225	1258	0.2	58	521	528	546	0.3	2.32	348	352	0.3
50681	WESTGATE	065	524	599	641	3.2	97	191	222	241	3.6	2.70	147	170	3.5
50682	WINTHROP	019	1662	1721	1753	0.8	76	631	661	682	1.1	2.60	452	473	1.1
50701	WATERLOO	013	30199	30367	30661	0.1	56	12622	12845	13115	0.4	2.33	8082	8202	0.4
50702	WATERLOO	013	19861	19837	19991	0.0	47	8321	8379	8517	0.2	2.27	5099	5110	0.1
50703	WATERLOO	013	21309	21031	21097	-0.3	32	8117	8060	8147	-0.2	2.56	5352	5306	-0.2
50706	WATERLOO	013	872	860	861	-0.3	31	334	333	338	-0.1	2.58	263	262	-0.1
50707	EVANSDALE	013	8128	8209	8308	0.2	60	3187	3257	3330	0.5	2.51	2266	2309	0.4
50801	CRESTON	175	9408	9348	9300	-0.2	42	4031	4066	4092	0.2	2.24	2510	2522	0.1
50830	AFTON	175	1663	1681	1686	0.3	61	669	683	691	0.5	2.40	468	475	0.4
50833	BEDFORD	173	2591	2573	2587	-0.2	41	1050	1044	1051	-0.1	2.41	688	680	-0.3
50835	BENTON	159	175	172	174	-0.4	27	72	72	73	0.0	2.39	53	53	0.0
50836	BLOCKTON	173	480	547	589	3.1	96	206	238	258	3.5	2.30	149	170	3.2
50837	BRIDGEWATER	001	426	486	517	3.2	96	190	220	235	3.5	2.21	139	160	3.4
50840	CLEARFIELD	173	491	483	481	-0.4	28	210	208	209	-0.2	2.18	141	139	-0.3
50841	CORNING	003	3066	3032	2997	-0.3	35	1292	1284	1276	-0.2	2.28	807	799	-0.2
50843	CUMBERLAND	029	623	734	799	3.9	98	263	312	343	4.1	2.35	188	222	4.0
50845	DIAGONAL	159	766	792	815	0.8	76	322	335	347	0.9	2.36	221	230	0.9
50846	FONTANELLE	001	1327	1293	1284	-0.6	18	543	529	525	-0.6	2.37	377	367	-0.6
50847	GRANT	137	44	48	50	2.1	92	20	22	23	2.3	2.18	15	17	3.0
50848	GRAVITY	173	604	600	599	-0.2	41	235	235	236	0.0	2.55	183	183	0.0
50849	GREENFIELD	001	2957	2935	2900	-0.2	39	1233	1230	1217	-0.1	2.32	810	806	-0.1
50851	LENOX	173	2141	2110	2096	-0.3	31	849	842	843	-0.2	2.39	564	556	-0.3
50853	MASSENA	029	766	807	829	1.2	83	325	347	360	1.6	2.33	227	241	1.4
50854	MOUNT AYR	159	2499	2513	2549	0.1	56	1028	1038	1058	0.2	2.30	678	683	0.2
50857	NODAWAY	003	457	439	429	-0.9	8	176	170	167	-0.8	2.46	121	116	-1.0
50858	ORIENT	001	962	912	891	-1.3	3	371	354	347	-1.1	2.55	284	272	-1.0
50859	PRESCOTT	003	596	633	646	1.4	86	250	269	277	1.7	2.35	185	198	1.6
50860	REDDING	159	453	449	454	-0.2	38	168	167	170	-0.1	2.53	122	122	0.0
50861	SHANNON CITY	175	268	255	249	-1.2	4	122	118	117	-0.8	2.16	89	85	-1.1
50862	SHARPSBURG	173	169	162	161	-1.0	7	65	63	64	-0.7	2.57	52	50	-0.9
50863	TINGLEY	159	308	311	315	0.2	60	141	144	146	0.5	2.16	101	103	0.5
50864	VILLISCA	137	2119	2086	2066	-0.4	29	881	873	869	-0.2	2.32	583	576	-0.3
51001	AKRON	149	2280	2310	2308	0.3	63	935	957	966	0.6	2.41	644	657	0.5
51002	ALTA	021	2703	2711	2723	0.1	53	1028	1036	1041	0.2	2.60	748	752	0.1
51003	ALTON	167	1616	1579	1570	-0.5	21	597	588	589	-0.4	2.69	420	411	-0.5
51004	ANTHON	193	1187	1159	1146	-0.6	20	493	486	485	-0.3	2.38	338	332	-0.4
51005	AURELIA	035	1675	1661	1647	-0.2	38	649	650	650	0.0	2.46	469	468	-0.1
51006	BATTLE CREEK	093	1216	1191	1180	-0.5	23	487	486	487	-0.1	2.36	316	313	-0.2
51007	BRONSON	193	655	638	631	-0.6	18	247	243	243	-0.4	2.63	191	188	-0.4
51009	CALUMET	141	198	191	184	-0.8	10	84	82	80	-0.6	2.33	65	63	-0.7
51010	CASTANA	133	539	499	491	-1.8	0	227	213	211	-1.5	2.32	152	142	-1.6
51012	CHEROKEE	035	6970	6891	6828	-0.3	35	2979	2990	3002	0.1	2.21	1874	1873	0.0
51014	CLEGHORN	035	531	541	544	0.4	67	212	220	225	0.9	2.46	159	164	0.7
51016	CORRECTIONVILLE	193	1515	1479	1464	-0.6	20	592	584	582	-0.3	2.47	409	402	-0.4
51018	CUSHING	193	403	394	392	-0.5	22	165	163	163	-0.3	2.42	119	118	-0.2
51019	DANBURY	193	830	770	754	-1.8	0	337	316	311	-1.5	2.43	238	222	-1.6
51020	GALVA	093	575	577	577	0.1	53	243	247	250	0.4	2.34	182	184	0.3
51022	GRANVILLE	141	856	864	861	0.2	59	308	313	315	0.4	2.76	232	235	0.3
51023	HAWARDEN	167	3135	2999	2964	-1.0	6	1270	1229	1228	-0.8	2.39	850	818	-0.9
51024	HINTON	149	2041	2101	2119	0.7	73	722	754	771	1.0	2.79	576	601	1.0
51025	HOLSTEIN	093	2269	2300	2314	0.3	64	920	944	958	0.6	2.38	636	650	0.5
51026	HORNICK	193	934	910	901	-0.6	18	352	346	346	-0.4	2.63	259	254	-0.5
51027	IRETON	167	1195	1234	1256	0.8	75	442	463	478	1.1	2.67	357	375	1.2
51028	KINGSLEY	149	2017	2034	2030	0.2	59	789	807	816	0.5	2.47	560	570	0.4
51029	LARRABEE	035	356	349	344	-0.5	24	149	148	148	-0.2	2.36	113	113	0.0
51030	LAWTON	193	1459	1539	1574	1.3	83	515	548	564	1.5	2.78	414	440	1.4
51031	LE MARS	149	12215	12267	12238	0.1	54	4644	4711	4746	0.3	2.55	3263	3299	0.3
51033	LINN GROVE	021	699	756	784	1.9	90	266	290	302	2.1	2.57	191	207	1.9
51034	MAPLETON	133	2134	2080	2065	-0.6	19	848	834	837	-0.4	2.30	548	537	-0.5
51035	MARCUS	035	1835	1820	1804	-0.2	39	711	716	719	0.2	2.47	480	481	0.1
51036	MAURICE	167	693	708	714	0.5	69	237	245	250	0.8	2.89	196	203	0.8
51037	MERIDEN	035	411	419	422	0.5	67	174	181	184	0.9	2.31	132	136	0.7
51038	MERRILL	149	1483	1489	1480	0.1	54	550	559	562	0.4	2.66	429	435	0.3
51039	MOVILLE	193	2435	2473	2481	0.4	65	922	943	951	0.5	2.62	692	704	0.4
51040	ONAWA	133	3973	3979	3979	0.0	52	1678	1691	1704	0.2	2.29	1040	1043	0.1
51041	ORANGE CITY	167	6657	6714	6739	0.2	59	2030	2072	2101	0.5	2.69	1559	1589	0.5
51044	OTO	193	271	267	265	-0.4	30	107	107	107	0.0	2.50	79	79	0.0
51046	PAULLINA	141	1828	1770	1713	-0.8	14	767	748	731	-0.6	2.31	528	514	-0.6
51047	PETERSON	041	645	664	670	0.7	73	296	309	315	1.0	2.15	209	219	1.1
51048	PIERSON	193	665	654	648	-0.4	28	259	256	255	-0.3	2.50	193	190	-0.4
51049	QUIMBY	035	606	604	600	-0.1	45	245	247	248	0.2	2.45	179	180	0.1
51050	REMSEN	149	2812	2665	2590	-1.3	3	1016	972	955	-1.0	2.67	757	721	-1.1
51051	RODNEY	133	114	104	102	-2.1	0	52	48	47	-1.9	2.15	35	32	-2.1
51052	SALIX	193	1026	1011	1003	-0.4	30	397	395	394	-0.1	2.56	288	285	-0.3
51053	SCHALLER	161	1302	1251	1221	-0.9	8	502	487	480	-0.7	2.57	364	352	-0.8
51054	SERGEANT BLUFF	193	4002	4302	4432	1.7	89	1382	1504	1553	2.0	2.85	1093	1187	2.0
51055	SLOAN	193	1409	1379	1365	-0.5	23	581	575	574	-0.2	2.40	396	390	-0.4
51056	SMITHLAND	193	498	497	494	-0.1	46	207	209	210	0.2	2.38	155	156	0.2
51058	SUTHERLAND	141	1104	1055	1016	-1.1	6	474	456	442	-0.9	2.25	324	311	-1.0
51060	UTE	133	598	612	618	0.6	70	272	282	288	0.9	2.17	186	192	0.8
51061	WASHTA	035	517	511	506	-0.3	35	209	210	210	0.1	2.43	156	155	-0.2
51062	WESTFIELD	149	761	822	851	1.8	90	283	309	324	2.1	2.66	219	239	2.1
51063	WHITING	133	1073	1101	1116	0.6	71	430	447	458	0.9	2.46	286	296	0.8
51101	SIOUX CITY	193	803	811	815	0.2	60	364	364	363	0.0	1.88	146	146	0.0
51103	SIOUX CITY	193	17525	17504	17536	0.0	47	6135	6147	6179	0.1	2.75	4218	4211	0.0
51104	SIOUX CITY	193	21818	21916	21957	0.1	54	8409	8499	8561	0.3	2.54	5520	5533	0.1
51105	SIOUX CITY	193	11480	11260	11165	-0.5	25	4118	4002	3960	-0.7	2.74	2499	2413	-0.8
51106	SIOUX CITY	193	27188	27177	27276	0.0	48	10383	10456	10559	0.2	2.50	7113	7142	0.1
51108	SIOUX CITY	193	6412	6407	6403	0.0	48	2536	2558	2575	0.2	2.44	1740	1757	0.2
51109	SIOUX CITY	149	2844	2858	2854	0.1	55	1184	1204	1210	0.4	2.37	762	773	0.3
51111	SIOUX CITY	193	143	132	129	-1.9	0	49	45	44	-2.0	2.69	37	34	-2.0
51201	SHELDON	141	6199	6120	5985	-0.3	33	2400	2401	2373	0.0	2.42	1632	1624	-0.1
51230	ALVORD	119	532	530	527	-0.1	44	166	168	170	0.3	3.15	136	138	0.3
	IOWA					0.5					0.7	2.43			0.6
	UNITED STATES					1.2					1.3	2.58			1.1

ZIP CODE #	POST OFFICE NAME	RACE (%) White 2000	White 2004	Black 2000	Black 2004	Asian/Pacific 2000	Asian/Pacific 2004	% Hispanic Origin 2000	% Hispanic Origin 2004	2004 AGE DISTRIBUTION (%) 0-4	5-9	10-14	15-19	20-24	25-44	45-64	65-84	85+	18+	MEDIAN AGE 2004	% 2004 Males	% 2004 Females
50677	WAVERLY	97.5	97.0	0.9	1.0	0.8	1.1	0.6	0.7	5.2	5.1	6.3	11.0	10.9	22.1	23.5	13.1	2.8	79.6	36.3	47.5	52.5
50680	WELLSBURG	98.9	98.7	0.1	0.1	0.4	0.6	0.3	0.2	5.6	5.7	6.8	6.7	5.1	21.1	27.4	17.3	4.3	77.7	44.3	48.5	51.5
50681	WESTGATE	99.2	99.3	0.2	0.2	0.0	0.0	1.3	1.3	7.2	7.2	7.5	6.5	5.0	25.4	27.1	12.9	1.3	74.1	40.1	52.1	47.9
50682	WINTHROP	98.9	99.0	0.2	0.2	0.1	0.1	0.5	0.5	7.2	7.2	7.7	7.1	6.1	26.4	24.5	12.0	1.9	73.6	37.8	51.2	48.8
50701	WATERLOO	92.6	91.2	4.1	4.8	1.0	1.4	1.8	2.2	6.7	6.4	6.1	5.9	7.0	27.9	25.9	12.1	1.8	77.4	37.3	48.6	51.5
50702	WATERLOO	91.4	90.0	4.4	5.1	1.0	1.4	1.8	2.1	6.7	6.2	6.0	5.7	6.7	27.4	21.4	15.3	4.7	77.9	38.1	47.7	52.3
50703	WATERLOO	62.6	60.1	32.2	34.2	0.4	0.6	3.9	4.5	7.3	7.2	8.2	7.6	7.3	26.6	23.1	11.1	1.5	72.7	34.2	48.4	51.7
50706	WATERLOO	99.3	99.1	0.1	0.1	0.2	0.2	0.6	0.7	6.6	7.0	7.3	5.7	6.4	25.1	29.7	11.6	0.6	75.7	39.7	49.3	50.7
50707	EVANSDALE	88.0	86.5	7.8	8.4	0.9	1.2	2.4	2.9	7.0	7.0	7.3	6.9	6.5	26.6	25.9	11.6	1.2	74.2	36.3	49.5	50.5
50801	CRESTON	98.3	98.3	0.3	0.3	0.3	0.3	1.1	1.1	6.2	6.0	6.2	6.5	7.4	24.3	25.4	14.8	3.2	78.1	40.6	47.5	52.5
50830	AFTON	99.0	99.0	0.0	0.0	0.1	0.1	1.3	1.3	5.9	6.1	6.8	6.0	5.7	24.2	27.5	15.1	2.8	77.3	41.7	49.3	50.7
50833	BEDFORD	98.3	98.3	0.0	0.0	0.2	0.2	1.4	1.4	6.0	6.1	6.5	6.7	6.2	22.2	23.7	17.9	4.6	77.3	42.3	47.8	52.2
50835	BENTON	99.4	99.4	0.0	0.0	0.6	0.6	0.0	0.0	4.1	5.2	7.0	5.8	5.8	23.8	26.7	19.2	2.3	79.7	43.9	52.3	47.7
50836	BLOCKTON	99.2	99.5	0.0	0.0	0.4	0.4	0.2	0.2	5.7	5.5	5.3	6.8	6.6	22.3	26.3	18.8	2.7	79.3	43.5	49.7	50.3
50837	BRIDGEWATER	99.3	99.6	0.0	0.0	0.2	0.2	0.2	0.2	5.6	6.0	7.2	6.0	5.1	23.5	28.0	16.7	2.1	77.4	43.0	52.7	47.3
50840	CLEARFIELD	98.0	97.7	0.0	0.0	0.0	0.0	1.6	1.7	4.4	4.1	5.6	5.8	7.9	17.6	28.2	21.5	5.0	82.4	47.7	44.5	55.5
50841	CORNING	99.0	99.0	0.1	0.1	0.2	0.2	0.6	0.6	5.7	5.7	6.6	6.3	5.1	22.8	25.3	18.5	3.9	77.6	43.5	48.6	51.5
50843	CUMBERLAND	98.4	98.4	0.5	0.4	0.2	0.1	1.6	1.8	4.5	5.2	7.9	7.5	5.2	25.3	27.0	15.4	2.0	77.8	41.8	52.2	47.8
50845	DIAGONAL	99.6	99.8	0.0	0.0	0.0	0.0	0.1	0.1	7.1	6.7	5.4	5.6	6.7	24.9	26.6	14.4	2.7	77.7	40.5	50.8	49.2
50846	FONTANELLE	99.3	99.2	0.1	0.1	0.1	0.1	0.5	0.5	5.8	5.7	6.2	6.2	5.6	21.0	25.4	19.6	4.6	77.9	44.7	48.9	51.1
50847	GRANT	100.0	100.0	0.0	0.0	0.0	0.0	0.0	0.0	4.2	6.3	6.3	4.2	4.2	22.9	35.4	14.6	2.1	83.3	46.3	50.0	50.0
50848	GRAVITY	98.7	98.7	0.2	0.2	0.3	0.3	1.2	1.2	4.8	5.8	8.3	7.0	6.0	24.8	26.2	14.8	2.2	76.7	41.1	52.2	47.8
50849	GREENFIELD	99.1	99.1	0.1	0.1	0.3	0.3	0.4	0.4	5.1	5.3	7.3	6.4	5.9	23.1	23.9	17.7	5.4	78.2	43.1	47.9	52.1
50851	LENOX	96.1	96.0	0.1	0.1	0.6	0.6	9.5	9.9	6.4	6.4	6.5	5.7	6.3	22.3	25.8	16.3	4.4	77.4	42.3	49.7	50.3
50853	MASSENA	99.9	99.9	0.0	0.0	0.0	0.0	0.1	0.1	5.2	5.6	6.1	5.2	5.8	22.8	30.5	15.7	3.1	80.2	44.5	52.3	47.7
50854	MOUNT AYR	99.0	99.0	0.1	0.1	0.2	0.2	0.3	0.4	5.9	5.8	6.2	5.9	6.1	19.9	23.1	21.3	5.9	78.3	45.2	47.0	53.0
50857	NODAWAY	98.5	98.4	0.0	0.0	0.2	0.2	0.7	0.7	4.1	5.0	8.2	6.2	3.9	22.6	27.3	20.5	2.3	78.4	45.1	51.0	49.0
50858	ORIENT	99.0	98.9	0.0	0.0	0.1	0.1	0.8	0.9	5.6	5.9	7.9	6.7	6.4	23.9	27.7	14.1	1.8	76.4	41.2	53.4	46.6
50859	PRESCOTT	98.7	98.6	0.0	0.0	0.2	0.2	0.7	0.6	6.0	6.3	6.6	5.5	5.4	23.7	29.2	15.3	1.9	77.7	42.8	51.8	48.2
50860	REDDING	98.9	98.9	0.4	0.5	0.0	0.0	0.0	0.0	7.6	7.6	7.6	5.8	4.9	21.6	24.3	15.8	4.9	73.9	41.4	50.3	49.7
50861	SHANNON CITY	99.6	100.0	0.0	0.0	0.0	0.0	0.0	0.0	5.1	5.1	5.1	5.1	4.7	23.9	29.8	18.8	2.4	81.2	45.6	51.8	48.2
50862	SHARPSBURG	98.2	98.2	0.0	0.0	1.2	1.2	0.0	0.0	6.2	6.2	6.8	8.0	5.6	22.2	25.9	16.7	2.5	75.9	41.7	50.0	50.0
50863	TINGLEY	99.0	98.7	0.3	0.3	0.3	0.3	0.0	0.0	4.8	5.1	5.5	4.8	4.8	18.7	31.2	22.8	2.3	81.4	49.6	51.8	48.2
50864	VILLISCA	99.1	98.9	0.1	0.1	0.1	0.1	0.5	0.6	5.1	5.4	7.1	6.7	5.7	21.9	26.1	18.2	3.8	78.1	43.8	48.0	52.0
51001	AKRON	98.7	98.7	0.2	0.2	0.1	0.2	0.7	0.8	5.7	6.1	7.7	6.7	6.1	23.5	25.1	16.3	2.9	76.5	40.7	49.6	50.4
51002	ALTA	93.8	93.7	0.5	0.5	1.1	1.1	8.1	8.4	6.2	6.6	8.1	8.0	5.6	25.4	24.6	13.4	2.2	74.0	38.6	49.9	50.1
51003	ALTON	99.0	98.7	0.1	0.1	0.2	0.3	1.2	1.3	6.5	6.6	8.1	7.9	7.6	24.5	25.0	12.2	1.8	74.0	37.5	49.7	50.3
51004	ANTHON	99.2	99.1	0.0	0.0	0.1	0.1	1.0	1.0	6.0	6.2	7.6	6.6	5.3	22.4	26.0	16.6	3.4	76.3	42.4	49.1	50.9
51005	AURELIA	98.8	98.6	0.1	0.1	0.2	0.3	1.0	1.1	5.8	5.9	6.0	7.1	6.1	21.5	24.4	19.0	4.2	77.2	43.4	49.8	50.2
51006	BATTLE CREEK	99.3	99.2	0.0	0.0	0.1	0.1	0.7	0.7	4.5	4.7	6.9	6.7	6.1	20.1	27.0	19.5	4.5	79.5	45.7	49.2	50.8
51007	BRONSON	98.8	98.9	0.0	0.0	0.5	0.5	0.8	0.8	5.3	6.6	8.9	7.7	4.9	29.5	27.6	8.6	0.9	74.0	38.4	53.1	46.9
51009	CALUMET	98.5	98.4	0.0	0.0	0.0	0.5	0.0	0.0	5.2	6.3	8.4	6.3	5.2	23.6	29.3	14.1	1.6	75.9	41.8	53.9	46.1
51010	CASTANA	98.9	98.6	0.0	0.0	0.2	0.2	0.7	0.8	5.4	6.6	8.4	5.8	4.6	24.1	27.3	15.2	2.6	75.8	41.5	50.9	49.1
51012	CHEROKEE	97.8	97.4	0.5	0.5	0.6	0.8	1.3	1.6	5.4	5.8	6.6	6.8	6.1	21.8	27.6	16.6	3.4	78.0	43.3	48.9	51.1
51014	CLEGHORN	99.6	99.5	0.2	0.2	0.2	0.2	0.0	0.2	5.9	6.1	5.7	6.7	5.4	23.8	29.2	15.3	1.9	78.0	42.9	50.3	49.7
51016	CORRECTIONVILLE	98.3	98.3	0.0	0.0	0.2	0.2	2.6	2.6	6.7	6.8	7.2	6.2	5.1	23.8	24.1	16.4	3.7	75.7	41.1	49.6	50.4
51018	CUSHING	99.0	99.0	0.0	0.0	0.0	0.0	1.7	2.0	6.4	6.9	8.4	5.8	5.3	25.6	25.9	13.7	2.0	74.6	39.3	49.8	50.3
51019	DANBURY	99.5	99.5	0.0	0.0	0.1	0.1	0.2	0.3	6.1	6.6	8.2	5.8	5.3	24.9	26.9	13.5	2.6	75.6	40.3	51.3	48.7
51020	GALVA	99.3	99.3	0.0	0.0	0.4	0.4	0.2	0.2	5.6	5.9	6.6	5.7	5.4	23.7	26.5	18.0	2.6	78.3	43.3	49.4	50.6
51022	GRANVILLE	97.9	97.8	0.5	0.5	0.2	0.2	1.4	1.6	6.7	7.4	9.4	7.6	5.9	23.5	24.1	13.3	2.1	71.8	38.1	52.0	48.0
51023	HAWARDEN	94.7	93.5	0.3	0.4	0.4	0.5	5.4	6.6	5.7	5.9	7.4	7.2	6.5	23.7	25.1	15.5	2.9	76.6	40.4	48.7	51.3
51024	HINTON	98.5	98.2	0.3	0.4	0.4	0.5	0.7	0.8	6.1	6.9	7.7	7.4	6.3	25.2	28.6	10.6	1.2	74.6	39.0	51.2	48.8
51025	HOLSTEIN	99.2	99.2	0.0	0.0	0.3	0.3	0.3	0.4	6.4	6.2	6.1	6.7	6.1	22.4	23.6	18.6	3.9	76.6	42.2	47.5	52.5
51026	HORNICK	97.6	97.5	0.2	0.2	0.2	0.2	0.5	0.6	6.8	7.3	7.4	5.9	6.0	24.2	28.7	12.3	1.4	75.0	40.3	51.4	48.6
51027	IRETON	98.8	98.5	0.0	0.0	0.5	0.7	0.8	1.0	6.5	6.9	8.4	7.5	6.7	25.6	25.8	11.8	0.9	73.7	37.5	51.1	48.9
51028	KINGSLEY	98.5	98.3	0.2	0.3	0.5	0.6	0.5	0.6	6.8	6.9	7.2	7.0	6.4	22.9	22.7	16.4	3.7	74.4	40.0	49.8	50.2
51029	LARRABEE	99.4	99.4	0.3	0.3	0.0	0.0	0.0	0.0	5.4	6.6	8.0	6.6	5.2	21.5	31.2	13.8	1.7	75.6	43.1	52.2	47.9
51030	LAWTON	98.7	98.7	0.1	0.1	0.6	0.6	0.2	0.1	7.3	7.9	8.6	7.0	5.3	27.8	24.4	10.5	1.4	71.7	36.6	49.5	50.5
51031	LE MARS	97.6	97.2	0.4	0.4	0.4	0.5	2.0	2.4	7.4	7.2	7.3	7.1	7.2	25.1	23.8	12.2	2.6	73.6	37.0	49.2	50.8
51033	LINN GROVE	97.6	97.6	0.0	0.0	0.1	0.1	2.3	2.4	5.7	6.1	5.6	7.7	6.4	21.6	31.9	13.6	1.6	77.9	43.0	52.1	47.9
51034	MAPLETON	98.7	98.8	0.1	0.1	0.1	0.1	0.4	0.4	4.9	5.0	6.2	6.2	5.7	19.8	23.7	20.9	7.8	80.1	46.9	47.6	52.5
51035	MARCUS	98.6	98.3	0.1	0.1	0.5	0.8	0.4	0.5	5.1	5.6	6.9	6.8	5.5	21.7	25.2	18.9	4.3	77.5	43.9	49.5	50.6
51036	MAURICE	98.4	97.9	0.0	0.0	0.7	1.0	1.6	1.8	7.1	7.2	8.2	7.5	7.8	24.9	25.7	10.6	1.1	72.9	36.2	51.1	48.9
51037	MERIDEN	99.5	99.3	0.2	0.2	0.0	0.2	0.0	0.2	6.0	6.4	6.0	6.4	5.3	24.3	29.4	14.6	1.7	77.3	42.5	50.6	49.4
51038	MERRILL	98.8	98.6	0.2	0.2	0.2	0.3	1.0	1.3	6.4	7.3	9.1	7.1	5.8	25.1	25.3	12.0	1.9	72.5	37.8	52.2	47.8
51039	MOVILLE	98.4	98.4	0.2	0.2	0.4	0.4	0.9	0.9	7.9	7.8	8.6	6.9	5.9	26.0	22.3	12.9	1.7	71.2	36.5	50.1	49.9
51040	ONAWA	98.0	98.0	0.1	0.1	0.2	0.2	1.0	1.0	5.9	5.9	6.6	5.7	5.3	23.0	24.2	18.4	5.0	77.8	43.3	48.0	52.0
51041	ORANGE CITY	97.7	97.2	0.4	0.5	0.9	1.2	1.1	1.3	7.2	6.4	6.7	10.4	13.6	23.0	18.9	11.3	2.6	75.9	28.9	47.2	52.8
51044	OTO	98.5	98.5	0.0	0.0	0.4	0.4	0.7	0.4	5.2	6.0	7.5	6.7	4.5	25.1	28.5	14.2	2.3	76.8	41.8	52.8	47.2
51046	PAULLINA	99.2	99.0	0.1	0.1	0.2	0.2	0.7	0.9	5.2	5.5	6.5	5.9	6.1	19.9	26.6	20.3	4.0	79.0	45.6	49.0	51.0
51047	PETERSON	99.4	99.4	0.0	0.0	0.2	0.2	0.6	0.5	5.0	5.3	5.6	5.6	5.3	22.1	29.7	18.8	2.7	80.7	45.6	52.1	47.9
51048	PIERSON	98.1	98.0	0.2	0.2	0.5	0.5	1.2	1.1	7.3	6.7	6.9	6.4	5.4	25.5	24.6	14.7	2.5	74.9	39.9	49.9	50.2
51049	QUIMBY	98.7	98.5	0.3	0.3	0.2	0.2	1.0	1.2	6.5	7.0	7.6	7.0	5.1	24.0	28.3	13.3	1.3	74.7	39.9	51.0	49.0
51050	REMSEN	99.3	99.2	0.1	0.1	0.1	0.2	0.5	0.5	7.3	7.7	8.5	7.5	6.0	23.7	23.5	12.3	3.5	71.6	37.6	50.6	49.4
51051	RODNEY	99.1	99.0	0.0	0.0	0.0	0.0	0.9	0.0	5.8	6.7	11.5	5.8	4.8	25.0	26.0	12.5	1.9	70.2	37.5	49.0	51.0
51052	SALIX	98.5	98.5	0.0	0.0	0.3	0.3	0.7	0.8	5.1	8.4	9.4	7.6	3.7	28.4	25.5	10.4	1.5	71.6	37.1	50.7	49.3
51053	SCHALLER	97.5	97.0	0.2	0.2	0.2	0.4	2.5	3.0	6.5	6.9	8.1	7.8	5.5	23.6	25.5	13.9	2.2	73.4	39.8	51.6	48.4
51054	SERGEANT BLUFF	95.1	95.0	0.8	0.8	1.6	1.7	1.7	1.7	8.0	8.1	9.3	7.7	7.3	27.8	23.6	7.7	0.6	70.0	32.8	49.9	50.1
51055	SLOAN	97.7	97.6	0.1	0.1	0.2	0.2	0.8	0.9	6.7	7.1	6.8	6.9	6.3	24.4	26.3	13.3	2.2	75.1	40.2	48.2	51.8
51056	SMITHLAND	98.4	98.4	0.2	0.2	0.2	0.2	0.4	0.6	5.2	5.6	7.7	7.0	4.0	24.8	29.0	14.5	2.2	77.3	42.3	52.5	47.5
51058	SUTHERLAND	98.6	98.4	0.2	0.2	0.1	0.1	0.4	0.4	4.8	5.3	7.0	6.3	5.7	20.3	26.8	18.9	4.9	78.6	45.4	50.0	50.1
51060	UTE	99.3	99.4	0.2	0.2	0.0	0.0	0.2	0.2	4.9	5.4	6.4	4.6	4.7	19.1	27.6	23.9	3.4	80.4	47.8	49.2	50.8
51061	WASHTA	99.0	98.6	0.2	0.2	0.4	0.6	0.4	0.6	6.1	6.5	7.1	7.4	5.1	21.7	29.2	15.7	1.4	76.3	42.4	51.7	48.3
51062	WESTFIELD	97.4	97.1	0.1	0.1	0.4	0.5	0.8	1.2	5.1	5.8	7.1	7.4	6.6	24.3	30.5	11.8	1.3	77.6	41.6	50.6	49.4
51063	WHITING	98.0	97.9	0.0	0.0	0.0	0.0	1.1	1.1	5.9	6.1	6.6	6.9	6.7	22.3	26.3	15.9	3.3	77.0	42.1	49.8	50.2
51101	SIOUX CITY	58.9	58.3	6.9	6.8	7.2	7.2	30.9	31.3	7.4	7.0	5.6	7.5	8.5	34.9	19.1	8.9	1.1	77.1	32.2	60.2	39.8
51103	SIOUX CITY	77.5	77.1	4.8	4.8	3.6	3.7	15.3	15.8	8.6	7.7	7.9	7.5	8.3	27.3	20.9	10.1	1.9	71.8	32.3	49.0	51.0
51104	SIOUX CITY	88.9	88.5	1.8	1.8	2.9	3.1	7.8	8.2	7.4	7.2	7.4	6.8	7.0	27.7	23.0	11.2	2.4	73.8	35.5	48.3	51.7
51105	SIOUX CITY	67.6	66.6	3.9	3.9	6.5	6.6	26.1	27.2	9.7	8.6	8.1	6.9	8.2	30.2	18.7	8.4	1.2	69.6	29.7	51.4	48.6
51106	SIOUX CITY	93.6	93.4	0.9	0.9	1.1	1.2	4.9	5.0	7.3	6.8	6.8	7.2	8.3	27.2	22.5	11.6	2.2	75.2	34.6	48.0	52.0
51108	SIOUX CITY	95.5	95.4	0.6	0.6	0.8	0.8	3.5	3.6	6.8	6.8	7.1	6.4	7.1	26.3	25.6	11.9	2.1	75.4	37.6	49.0	51.0
51109	SIOUX CITY	94.1	94.0	1.4	1.5	0.6	0.6	4.0	4.1	6.0	6.1	7.1	6.7	6.7	29.4	24.1	12.3	1.6	76.8	37.1	50.8	49.2
51111	SIOUX CITY	86.7	86.4	0.0	0.0	2.8	3.0	7.0	6.8	9.1	6.1	9.9	4.6	9.9	31.8	26.5	2.3	0.0	72.0	31.7	54.6	45.5
51201	SHELDON	97.6	97.1	0.4	0.4	0.7	1.0	2.2	2.6	6.9	6.6	6.8	6.5	7.2	26.0	23.0	13.9	3.1	76.0	37.9	49.9	50.1
51230	ALVORD	99.6	99.6	0.0	0.0	0.0	0.0	0.2	0.2	9.6	9.3	9.1	7.4	6.0	27.7	20.0	10.2	0.8	67.4	31.8	52.5	47.6
	IOWA	93.9	93.0	2.1	2.3	1.3	1.8	2.8	3.2	6.5	6.5	6.9	7.2	7.6	26.4	24.2	12.3	2.4	76.0	37.2	49.2	50.8
	UNITED STATES	75.1	73.6	12.3	12.5	3.8	4.2	12.5	14.1	6.9	6.7	7.2	7.0	7.3	28.6	23.8	10.8	1.7	75.1	36.0	49.1	50.9

INCOME

ZIP CODE #	POST OFFICE NAME	2004 Per Capita Income	2004 HH Income Base	2004 Household Income Distribution (%): Less than $25,000	$25,000 to $49,999	$50,000 to $99,999	$100,000 to $149,999	$150,000 or More	Median Household Income: 2004	2009	2004 National Centile	2004 State Centile	2004 Home Value Base	2004 Home Value Distribution (%): Less than $50,000	$50,000 to $89,999	$90,000 to $174,999	$175,000 to $399,999	$400,000 or More	2004 Median Home Value
50677	WAVERLY	22982	4236	21.4	30.8	35.7	8.5	3.6	47878	56576	68	75	3190	6.7	19.1	51.4	20.9	1.9	119192
50680	WELLSBURG	19940	528	27.3	42.2	26.3	3.0	1.1	37035	42690	36	17	427	47.3	33.7	14.3	3.0	1.6	52347
50681	WESTGATE	20338	222	23.9	35.6	31.1	8.1	1.4	42478	47942	55	51	183	23.0	32.2	29.0	12.0	3.8	85682
50682	WINTHROP	22309	661	25.6	31.8	33.1	5.9	3.6	45374	51920	62	65	533	17.1	29.1	34.9	15.0	3.9	95125
50701	WATERLOO	27641	12845	22.8	29.2	33.0	9.5	5.6	47988	57964	68	76	9119	16.3	26.3	42.8	13.0	1.7	97936
50702	WATERLOO	21257	8379	28.1	33.7	31.2	5.5	1.5	40004	48981	46	35	5554	14.6	49.2	33.9	2.1	0.2	79414
50703	WATERLOO	16589	8060	37.2	33.4	23.9	4.3	1.3	32462	39144	19	4	5308	47.4	32.8	15.1	4.1	0.6	51822
50706	WATERLOO	21807	333	16.5	30.9	44.4	7.2	0.9	51592	60233	75	85	288	11.8	42.7	33.3	9.7	2.4	86389
50707	EVANSDALE	18348	3257	28.8	35.0	30.2	5.4	0.6	38036	45884	39	22	2411	27.2	44.1	25.9	2.9	0.0	70556
50801	CRESTON	20259	4066	32.7	32.8	27.4	5.4	1.8	36727	42924	34	16	2902	28.6	31.6	33.1	5.6	1.1	76651
50830	AFTON	17067	683	34.6	36.9	24.0	4.0	0.6	36100	41139	32	14	523	38.2	34.4	18.7	7.7	1.0	60319
50833	BEDFORD	16926	1044	36.5	34.4	25.4	2.6	1.2	34580	39399	26	9	788	47.0	29.4	17.4	5.5	0.8	53478
50835	BENTON	23607	72	33.3	27.8	29.2	6.9	2.8	35893	40564	31	13	58	43.1	12.1	22.4	17.2	5.2	70000
50836	BLOCKTON	23245	238	30.7	36.6	26.5	2.1	4.2	37715	42902	38	21	182	41.8	35.2	15.9	6.0	1.1	62727
50837	BRIDGEWATER	19902	220	30.5	37.7	26.8	4.6	0.5	37303	42470	36	18	175	51.4	21.1	19.4	6.9	1.1	48529
50840	CLEARFIELD	16539	208	42.3	35.1	18.3	2.9	1.4	28846	32290	10	2	155	64.5	17.4	16.1	1.9	0.0	34722
50841	CORNING	17811	1284	36.2	31.6	27.1	4.5	0.6	33854	40000	24	6	976	38.4	31.4	23.8	5.6	0.8	63684
50843	CUMBERLAND	18602	312	35.6	35.3	23.7	3.2	2.2	34503	38819	26	8	249	34.5	32.5	20.9	10.8	1.2	74130
50845	DIAGONAL	19739	335	34.6	37.3	22.4	3.9	1.8	33004	37901	21	5	269	51.7	17.8	16.0	13.8	0.7	48333
50846	FONTANELLE	18766	529	26.1	39.3	30.6	2.8	1.1	39021	44639	43	29	425	35.3	31.1	24.7	7.5	1.4	70152
50847	GRANT	24589	22	27.3	27.3	31.8	13.6	0.0	45000	57159	61	63	18	33.3	22.2	27.8	16.7	0.0	80000
50848	GRAVITY	16240	235	40.9	23.4	31.9	2.6	1.3	35203	38736	28	11	190	59.5	23.2	15.8	1.6	0.0	44706
50849	GREENFIELD	22019	1230	30.6	31.4	29.5	5.8	2.8	40961	46838	50	41	899	20.6	41.1	30.6	6.9	0.9	78032
50851	LENOX	17364	842	32.5	37.8	24.8	3.3	1.5	34925	40036	27	9	622	40.7	30.4	21.5	5.0	2.4	60233
50853	MASSENA	18889	347	37.5	33.4	24.5	3.2	1.4	31920	36026	18	4	276	44.6	22.5	17.0	8.7	7.3	56250
50854	MOUNT AYR	17110	1038	39.5	31.7	24.1	3.8	1.0	31438	36036	16	3	765	35.4	35.8	22.4	5.8	0.7	64383
50857	NODAWAY	17254	170	35.9	30.0	30.0	4.1	0.0	34437	40325	26	8	135	46.7	29.6	20.0	2.2	1.5	55625
50858	ORIENT	19711	354	21.8	33.9	36.4	7.3	0.6	45213	51569	62	64	276	29.7	32.6	26.1	10.5	1.1	75714
50859	PRESCOTT	18672	269	31.6	33.8	28.6	4.8	1.1	35129	41489	28	10	217	35.5	22.1	24.4	14.3	3.7	72143
50860	REDDING	15482	167	37.1	35.3	24.6	2.4	0.6	33322	37749	22	6	133	37.6	31.6	20.3	10.5	0.0	69000
50861	SHANNON CITY	18801	118	39.8	32.2	23.7	2.5	1.7	30000	33063	12	2	98	34.7	37.8	17.4	10.2	0.0	64118
50862	SHARPSBURG	14476	63	34.9	41.3	22.2	1.6	0.0	34515	40000	26	8	51	43.1	31.4	25.5	0.0	0.0	55000
50863	TINGLEY	20066	144	34.7	32.6	24.3	7.6	0.7	33012	38016	21	5	120	34.2	23.3	21.7	16.7	4.2	77500
50864	VILLISCA	19518	873	33.6	32.8	26.2	5.4	2.1	35801	41054	31	13	677	45.4	27.6	18.9	6.9	1.2	54500
51001	AKRON	22752	957	25.8	35.0	30.6	5.9	2.7	40178	47856	47	37	745	13.7	31.4	42.8	9.3	2.8	94867
51002	ALTA	20519	1036	25.5	33.6	32.1	6.3	2.6	41404	50404	51	44	792	23.5	29.6	32.2	12.6	2.2	86842
51003	ALTON	18261	588	20.2	39.1	35.0	4.4	1.2	43629	48626	58	57	491	15.9	34.4	39.7	9.8	0.2	89732
51004	ANTHON	23988	486	35.2	30.3	26.8	4.1	3.7	34848	41447	27	9	399	35.3	29.6	23.3	9.8	2.0	68036
51005	AURELIA	20792	650	24.9	32.2	35.2	5.5	2.2	44353	51446	60	60	533	24.2	36.6	33.8	3.6	1.9	79222
51006	BATTLE CREEK	19964	486	28.4	38.7	26.5	3.7	2.7	37439	43306	37	18	377	45.4	31.3	17.2	4.5	1.6	54375
51007	BRONSON	22637	243	18.5	29.2	40.3	11.1	0.8	51717	60955	75	86	211	7.1	18.5	51.2	19.0	4.3	123929
51009	CALUMET	22474	82	24.4	40.2	26.8	4.9	3.7	43423	48190	57	56	62	27.4	33.9	21.0	11.3	6.5	75714
51010	CASTANA	16941	213	37.6	33.8	24.4	2.8	1.4	31664	36357	17	4	170	51.2	22.9	19.4	4.1	2.4	49048
51012	CHEROKEE	21481	2990	30.7	35.1	26.9	5.3	2.0	37130	43098	36	17	2170	27.7	40.5	23.0	7.8	1.1	71416
51014	CLEGHORN	19739	220	26.8	36.8	32.3	2.7	1.4	41424	48027	51	45	174	29.9	28.2	34.5	5.8	1.7	79000
51016	CORRECTIONVILLE	19686	584	33.6	31.2	26.5	6.0	2.7	37097	42645	36	17	448	40.6	32.1	20.1	5.4	1.8	59333
51018	CUSHING	20534	163	28.8	32.5	32.5	4.3	1.8	40183	45250	47	37	125	46.4	28.0	19.2	4.8	1.6	54091
51019	DANBURY	20180	316	32.6	36.1	25.0	4.1	2.2	37620	42773	38	20	243	24.7	30.9	29.2	14.4	0.8	82500
51020	GALVA	26557	247	28.3	44.1	18.2	4.9	4.5	36106	41686	32	14	204	46.1	20.6	16.7	16.2	0.5	54211
51022	GRANVILLE	17761	313	28.4	38.0	23.6	7.7	2.2	40939	45944	49	41	251	24.7	31.9	25.9	15.5	2.0	80833
51023	HAWARDEN	20341	1229	27.8	33.6	29.9	6.8	1.9	39449	45104	44	31	930	29.8	33.3	28.1	6.3	2.5	76750
51024	HINTON	25825	754	14.6	22.8	43.6	12.2	6.8	62056	73471	86	96	650	5.2	14.8	43.5	30.3	6.2	141327
51025	HOLSTEIN	19619	944	30.1	32.3	30.7	5.7	1.2	40000	45917	46	35	703	27.2	34.7	29.3	6.7	2.1	75900
51026	HORNICK	22543	346	20.8	32.1	35.8	5.5	5.8	46760	54394	66	72	293	25.3	22.5	34.5	14.3	3.4	92708
51027	IRETON	18304	463	20.7	41.9	32.0	3.7	1.7	43508	48926	57	56	376	17.6	28.7	39.6	10.9	3.2	93415
51028	KINGSLEY	21503	807	20.5	36.8	33.6	6.0	3.2	43000	51849	56	53	654	13.5	27.5	45.3	10.2	3.5	100746
51029	LARRABEE	22686	148	21.0	34.5	37.8	5.4	1.4	45905	52359	64	68	117	28.2	17.1	36.8	10.3	7.7	95500
51030	LAWTON	23001	548	18.1	25.7	41.6	13.3	1.3	55381	65251	80	92	477	9.9	17.0	52.8	19.5	0.8	118811
51031	LE MARS	22813	4711	24.0	29.4	35.2	7.6	3.8	46911	55860	66	72	3525	10.3	22.3	48.2	17.8	1.4	109990
51033	LINN GROVE	18493	290	26.2	39.3	29.7	3.5	1.4	38213	43226	40	23	225	48.0	21.3	23.1	7.1	0.4	52368
51034	MAPLETON	19901	834	34.2	34.3	25.7	3.0	2.9	36165	41658	32	14	632	31.5	36.7	26.0	5.1	0.8	68525
51035	MARCUS	20917	716	27.1	34.1	31.4	4.6	2.8	42023	48512	53	49	580	27.1	34.5	28.3	8.1	2.1	77600
51036	MAURICE	19535	245	11.8	39.2	42.0	6.5	0.4	49449	55841	71	80	201	16.4	30.9	39.3	12.9	0.5	93056
51037	MERIDEN	22404	181	26.0	35.9	33.7	2.8	1.7	42337	47588	54	50	142	26.1	28.2	38.0	4.9	2.8	84545
51038	MERRILL	23508	559	17.0	30.2	39.4	8.2	5.2	51981	60874	75	86	481	11.6	24.3	47.2	15.0	1.9	107827
51039	MOVILLE	22612	943	23.0	27.8	39.7	6.3	3.3	48882	55528	70	79	766	16.3	25.6	44.1	13.1	0.9	98986
51040	ONAWA	20986	1691	32.2	34.2	27.2	3.8	2.7	39057	44607	43	29	1272	27.8	42.1	26.3	3.1	0.8	72464
51041	ORANGE CITY	21346	2072	19.1	36.2	34.9	6.9	3.1	46424	53596	65	70	1596	6.8	22.7	53.5	15.3	1.8	116246
51044	OTO	19012	107	30.8	30.8	31.8	6.5	0.0	41390	46770	51	44	87	32.2	25.3	28.7	11.5	2.3	77000
51046	PAULLINA	20071	748	27.5	38.2	27.5	4.7	2.0	38689	43661	42	27	592	33.8	40.0	21.1	3.7	1.4	65000
51047	PETERSON	21874	309	23.0	45.3	27.2	2.9	1.6	40250	44633	47	37	248	41.9	23.0	25.4	6.9	2.8	59524
51048	PIERSON	20439	256	18.4	40.2	35.6	3.9	2.0	42901	49815	56	53	204	33.8	28.9	27.5	8.3	1.5	68571
51049	QUIMBY	17303	247	34.0	34.8	26.7	3.6	0.8	35293	40000	29	11	195	38.5	28.2	23.1	9.7	0.5	65357
51050	REMSEN	19599	972	20.0	34.3	37.6	6.1	2.2	45824	53930	63	68	806	8.3	29.2	50.7	10.2	1.6	102399
51051	RODNEY	18331	48	41.7	31.3	25.0	2.1	0.0	28840	35745	10	1	39	51.3	20.5	20.5	2.6	5.1	48750
51052	SALIX	24023	395	17.5	34.2	32.2	13.9	2.3	48473	57643	69	78	337	18.4	23.2	41.5	16.3	0.6	104688
51053	SCHALLER	17874	487	24.0	40.7	31.4	3.5	0.4	39658	45269	45	32	380	31.8	35.8	25.3	6.1	1.1	70278
51054	SERGEANT BLUFF	25212	1504	16.0	25.7	39.4	14.8	4.1	59723	70410	84	94	1182	18.8	17.0	41.9	21.8	0.5	118197
51055	SLOAN	21411	575	26.3	29.2	35.7	8.5	0.4	45330	52540	62	65	450	16.2	31.6	46.4	5.6	0.2	92381
51056	SMITHLAND	20162	209	30.1	30.1	31.6	8.1	0.0	42373	49232	54	51	172	33.1	25.0	27.9	10.5	3.5	76000
51058	SUTHERLAND	19870	456	30.3	35.5	29.4	3.5	1.3	39817	44424	45	33	362	51.1	31.2	13.3	3.0	1.4	49298
51060	UTE	19848	282	30.5	39.4	25.9	2.1	2.1	35840	40885	31	13	228	42.1	36.8	15.4	3.5	2.2	56207
51061	WASHTA	18331	210	28.1	40.5	26.7	3.8	1.0	40000	45242	46	35	156	28.2	28.9	28.9	10.9	3.2	80833
51062	WESTFIELD	29013	309	19.7	19.4	38.2	12.9	9.7	61744	74007	86	95	265	12.8	13.6	32.1	27.9	13.6	143534
51063	WHITING	19565	447	30.4	32.7	28.9	7.4	0.7	38580	43984	41	25	336	36.9	30.1	25.3	6.0	1.8	66129
51101	SIOUX CITY	15909	364	54.4	27.5	16.2	0.8	1.1	21710	25579	2	1	38	52.6	36.8	10.5	0.0	0.0	46667
51103	SIOUX CITY	17749	6147	31.2	34.2	28.1	4.8	1.8	38025	45415	39	22	4023	25.2	50.1	20.8	3.5	0.4	71003
51104	SIOUX CITY	29268	8499	19.3	27.9	35.7	9.5	7.6	52576	62500	76	88	5790	6.8	33.0	44.7	13.4	2.2	101411
51105	SIOUX CITY	14820	4002	39.2	35.8	20.4	2.7	1.9	30930	37474	15	3	1896	53.4	37.9	6.6	2.1	0.0	47059
51106	SIOUX CITY	24051	10456	20.6	30.0	35.8	10.6	3.0	49467	59279	71	80	7759	9.1	34.2	46.1	10.3	0.4	95757
51108	SIOUX CITY	23310	2558	22.4	34.3	32.5	7.5	3.3	44960	52805	61	62	1975	31.8	27.0	25.0	14.3	2.0	77545
51109	SIOUX CITY	21726	1204	33.1	26.4	28.8	9.9	1.8	41518	48949	51	45	883	18.7	53.8	21.4	4.6	1.5	73989
51111	SIOUX CITY	19590	45	6.7	33.3	57.8	2.2	0.0	54272	63960	79	90	4	0.0	0.0	0.0	100.0	0.0	250000
51201	SHELDON	19448	2401	27.2	35.9	30.0	5.8	1.0	40013	45128	46	36	1773	14.3	33.7	39.4	12.1	0.5	92634
51230	ALVORD	15576	168	17.9	41.7	35.1	5.4	0.0	42915	50000	56	53	140	20.0	32.1	37.1	10.0	0.7	87000
	IOWA	23554		24.6	30.5	32.9	8.4	3.7	45622	53985				17.5	26.2	39.3	15.0	2.1	98835
	UNITED STATES	25866		24.7	27.1	30.8	10.9	6.5	48124	56710				10.9	15.0	33.7	30.1	10.4	145905

SPENDING POTENTIAL INDICES IOWA

50677-51230 D

ZIP CODE		FINANCIAL SERVICES				THE HOME						ENTERTAINMENT						PERSONAL			
						Home Improvements		Furnishings													
#	POST OFFICE NAME	Auto Loan	Home Loan	Invest-ments	Retire-ment Plans	Home Repair	Lawn & Garden	Comput-ers & Hard-ware	Major Appli-ances	TV, Radio, Sound Equip-ment	Furni-ture	Dine out/ Carry out	Sports Equip-ment	Fees & Tickets	Toys & Games	Travel	Cable TV	Apparel & Services	Auto Repairs	Health Insur-ance	Pets & Supplies
50677	WAVERLY	88	80	73	79	83	91	80	84	83	79	102	99	78	102	81	84	97	84	89	102
50680	WELLSBURG	77	57	35	54	63	74	61	69	69	58	81	79	54	77	61	72	74	69	83	87
50681	WESTGATE	99	69	36	65	81	90	68	85	79	68	93	102	58	91	71	83	84	83	101	118
50682	WINTHROP	104	74	41	70	86	95	73	89	83	72	98	107	63	96	76	87	90	88	105	123
50701	WATERLOO	86	93	101	92	93	99	92	91	91	90	113	105	94	116	93	90	111	91	90	101
50702	WATERLOO	65	68	75	68	68	73	70	69	70	68	87	80	71	89	70	69	84	69	69	76
50703	WATERLOO	61	56	57	53	57	64	58	59	62	58	76	67	58	76	58	64	73	60	64	69
50706	WATERLOO	71	87	96	85	85	87	80	79	77	80	96	92	86	103	82	76	96	77	74	86
50707	EVANSDALE	67	62	56	60	65	72	63	65	66	61	81	74	63	84	63	68	77	64	71	77
50801	CRESTON	70	60	49	58	63	71	62	67	67	61	80	77	59	79	62	68	76	67	73	80
50830	AFTON	66	55	41	54	59	66	55	61	59	54	72	71	52	71	56	61	67	60	67	75
50833	BEDFORD	64	53	40	50	57	66	55	60	60	53	72	68	51	72	56	63	67	59	69	73
50835	BENTON	102	71	37	67	83	93	70	87	81	70	95	105	60	93	73	85	87	86	104	121
50836	BLOCKTON	97	67	35	64	79	88	67	82	77	66	90	99	57	88	69	81	82	81	98	115
50837	BRIDGEWATER	80	56	29	52	65	72	55	68	63	54	74	82	47	73	57	66	68	67	81	94
50840	CLEARFIELD	60	45	29	43	49	59	49	54	55	47	65	61	44	61	49	58	59	54	65	66
50841	CORNING	69	51	31	48	57	66	54	62	61	52	72	71	47	68	54	64	65	61	74	79
50843	CUMBERLAND	79	55	29	52	64	72	55	68	63	54	74	81	47	72	57	66	67	67	80	94
50845	DIAGONAL	84	59	31	56	69	77	58	72	67	58	79	87	50	77	60	70	72	71	86	100
50846	FONTANELLE	81	57	30	54	66	74	56	69	65	55	76	84	48	74	58	68	69	68	83	97
50847	GRANT	97	68	35	64	79	88	67	83	77	66	90	100	57	89	69	81	82	82	99	115
50848	GRAVITY	65	55	42	55	58	65	56	61	60	55	73	69	54	72	56	61	68	60	66	72
50849	GREENFIELD	87	65	40	62	72	83	68	78	76	65	90	90	60	86	68	80	82	77	92	99
50851	LENOX	70	54	35	52	59	68	56	63	62	54	73	73	50	71	56	64	67	62	73	79
50853	MASSENA	80	55	29	52	65	72	55	68	63	54	74	82	47	73	57	66	68	67	81	94
50854	MOUNT AYR	65	49	32	47	54	64	53	59	60	51	70	67	47	67	53	63	64	59	71	73
50857	NODAWAY	78	54	29	51	63	71	54	67	62	53	73	80	46	71	56	65	66	66	79	93
50858	ORIENT	88	66	40	63	75	83	64	77	72	64	85	92	57	85	66	75	79	75	89	105
50859	PRESCOTT	80	56	29	52	65	72	55	68	63	54	74	82	47	73	57	66	68	67	81	94
50860	REDDING	65	49	31	46	54	64	53	59	59	50	70	67	47	66	53	63	64	59	71	73
50861	SHANNON CITY	74	51	27	48	60	67	51	63	58	50	69	76	43	67	53	61	62	62	75	87
50862	SHARPSBURG	67	47	25	45	55	61	47	57	54	46	63	69	40	62	48	56	57	57	68	80
50863	TINGLEY	74	58	39	52	65	73	54	66	62	54	73	77	48	72	58	66	68	65	78	90
50864	VILLISCA	76	56	35	54	63	74	60	69	68	58	80	78	53	76	60	72	73	68	82	86
51001	AKRON	95	69	40	65	78	89	71	83	80	69	94	97	62	91	72	84	86	82	99	109
51002	ALTA	84	72	56	71	76	85	72	78	77	71	93	90	69	92	73	78	87	77	85	95
51003	ALTON	76	66	54	66	69	77	67	71	70	66	86	82	65	85	67	71	81	71	76	85
51004	ANTHON	96	70	43	67	78	92	75	86	85	72	100	98	66	95	75	90	91	85	102	108
51005	AURELIA	94	66	34	62	77	86	65	80	75	64	88	97	55	86	67	78	80	79	96	112
51006	BATTLE CREEK	80	59	36	56	66	77	63	72	71	60	84	82	55	80	63	75	76	71	86	90
51007	BRONSON	96	84	63	80	89	96	78	87	83	78	101	104	76	103	80	86	96	85	95	113
51009	CALUMET	95	66	35	62	77	86	65	81	75	65	88	97	56	87	68	79	80	80	96	112
51010	CASTANA	69	49	27	47	57	64	50	60	57	49	67	71	43	65	51	60	61	60	72	81
51012	CHEROKEE	73	64	54	62	68	76	66	70	70	64	85	80	63	84	66	73	80	70	78	84
51014	CLEGHORN	88	61	32	58	71	80	61	75	70	60	82	90	52	80	63	73	75	74	89	104
51016	CORRECTIONVILLE	83	61	37	58	68	79	64	74	73	62	85	85	56	82	65	77	78	73	88	95
51018	CUSHING	90	63	33	59	73	82	62	77	71	61	84	92	53	82	64	75	76	75	91	107
51019	DANBURY	89	62	33	59	72	81	61	76	71	61	83	91	52	81	64	74	76	75	90	105
51020	GALVA	112	79	42	74	91	102	77	96	89	77	105	115	66	103	80	94	95	94	114	133
51022	GRANVILLE	73	67	65	68	70	75	68	72	69	67	84	85	65	82	68	68	80	72	74	86
51023	HAWARDEN	79	64	47	64	69	78	66	72	71	65	86	83	62	85	66	73	80	71	80	88
51024	HINTON	99	112	112	112	113	113	102	104	97	101	121	123	105	127	104	95	119	101	98	120
51025	HOLSTEIN	79	58	36	55	65	76	62	71	70	59	82	81	54	78	62	74	75	70	84	89
51026	HORNICK	107	75	39	71	87	98	74	91	85	73	100	110	63	98	77	89	91	90	109	127
51027	IRETON	88	62	32	58	72	80	61	75	70	60	82	91	52	81	63	74	75	74	90	105
51028	KINGSLEY	90	66	41	63	74	86	70	80	79	68	93	92	62	89	71	84	85	80	96	102
51029	LARRABEE	97	68	35	64	79	88	67	83	77	66	90	99	57	88	69	81	82	81	98	115
51030	LAWTON	102	92	72	88	97	104	85	94	90	85	109	112	84	112	88	92	104	91	101	120
51031	LE MARS	97	77	54	74	84	94	77	88	84	76	101	104	70	99	78	87	94	87	99	113
51033	LINN GROVE	86	60	32	57	70	79	60	74	69	59	81	89	51	79	62	72	74	73	88	102
51034	MAPLETON	77	57	38	55	63	75	63	70	71	60	84	79	56	79	63	75	76	70	84	85
51035	MARCUS	88	64	40	61	72	84	69	78	78	66	91	90	60	87	69	82	83	78	94	99
51036	MAURICE	94	78	54	74	84	92	73	84	80	73	96	100	69	97	76	82	90	82	94	111
51037	MERIDEN	94	66	34	62	76	85	65	80	75	64	87	96	55	86	67	78	80	79	95	111
51038	MERRILL	108	83	53	79	93	102	80	95	89	79	105	115	72	105	83	92	98	94	109	128
51039	MOVILLE	97	78	55	76	84	94	79	88	86	78	103	102	74	102	79	88	96	86	98	109
51040	ONAWA	72	65	55	62	68	77	66	70	70	64	85	80	64	86	67	73	80	69	78	83
51041	ORANGE CITY	99	85	70	84	91	99	84	92	89	83	108	110	79	107	85	90	102	91	99	115
51044	OTO	86	60	31	57	70	78	59	73	68	58	80	88	51	78	61	72	73	72	87	102
51046	PAULLINA	79	58	35	55	64	75	62	70	69	59	82	81	54	78	62	73	75	70	84	89
51047	PETERSON	85	59	31	56	69	77	59	73	68	58	79	87	50	78	61	71	72	71	86	101
51048	PIERSON	93	65	35	61	75	85	65	79	74	64	87	95	55	85	67	78	80	78	95	110
51049	QUIMBY	77	53	28	50	62	70	53	65	61	52	71	79	45	70	55	64	65	64	78	91
51050	REMSEN	94	68	38	64	78	87	67	81	76	66	89	98	58	88	69	79	82	80	95	112
51051	RODNEY	71	50	26	47	58	65	50	61	57	49	67	73	42	65	51	60	61	60	73	84
51052	SALIX	100	86	64	82	92	100	81	90	86	80	105	108	78	106	83	89	99	88	99	118
51053	SCHALLER	76	60	42	59	65	73	61	68	66	60	80	79	56	79	61	68	74	67	77	86
51054	SERGEANT BLUFF	101	110	110	112	107	106	104	104	98	105	124	123	105	125	103	93	122	103	92	115
51055	SLOAN	82	68	51	67	72	81	69	75	74	68	90	87	66	89	69	76	84	74	83	92
51056	SMITHLAND	87	61	32	57	71	79	60	74	69	59	81	89	51	79	62	72	74	73	88	103
51058	SUTHERLAND	75	56	36	54	62	73	60	67	67	57	79	77	53	76	60	70	72	67	80	85
51060	UTE	70	52	34	50	57	69	58	64	65	55	76	71	51	72	57	68	70	64	76	77
51061	WASHTA	81	56	29	53	66	74	56	69	64	55	75	83	48	74	58	67	69	68	82	96
51062	WESTFIELD	101	124	130	124	122	121	111	111	103	110	130	130	118	138	113	101	129	107	100	123
51063	WHITING	80	59	37	56	66	77	64	72	72	61	84	82	56	80	64	76	77	72	86	91
51101	SIOUX CITY	40	36	39	35	35	40	42	40	44	40	54	46	40	53	40	44	52	42	41	44
51103	SIOUX CITY	66	66	71	65	66	73	70	68	71	67	88	79	70	90	69	71	85	69	69	76
51104	SIOUX CITY	99	108	119	108	107	113	107	105	104	105	130	123	109	134	107	103	128	105	102	116
51105	SIOUX CITY	58	53	53	51	52	57	57	57	59	57	74	65	56	73	55	59	72	58	57	63
51106	SIOUX CITY	80	88	97	88	87	91	88	86	86	86	107	100	90	110	88	84	105	86	82	94
51108	SIOUX CITY	81	83	84	82	83	88	81	82	80	80	100	95	82	102	81	80	97	81	81	94
51109	SIOUX CITY	75	71	64	68	74	82	70	73	74	68	90	83	70	94	71	76	86	72	80	86
51111	SIOUX CITY	76	84	85	86	81	81	79	79	74	80	94	93	80	95	78	70	93	78	69	86
51201	SHELDON	79	62	42	60	68	77	64	72	70	62	83	83	58	81	64	72	77	71	81	90
51230	ALVORD	76	71	59	69	74	77	67	72	68	67	84	85	66	85	68	69	81	70	74	89
	IOWA	87	79	73	79	82	89	80	84	83	79	102	98	78	102	80	83	97	84	88	100
	UNITED STATES	100	100	100	100	100	100	100	100	100	100	100	100	100	100	100	100	100	100	100	100

#	POST OFFICE NAME	COUNTY FIPS CODE	POPULATION 2000	2004	2009	2000-2004 ANNUAL RATE % Rate	State Centile	HOUSEHOLDS 2000	2004	2009	% Annual Rate 2000-2004	2004 Average HH Size	FAMILIES 2000	2004	% Annual Rate 2000-2004
51231	ARCHER	141	274	285	285	0.9	79	106	113	114	1.5	2.52	89	95	1.6
51232	ASHTON	143	1029	995	985	-0.8	12	385	375	373	-0.6	2.64	286	278	-0.7
51234	BOYDEN	167	1235	1230	1232	-0.1	44	456	460	466	0.2	2.65	361	362	0.1
51235	DOON	119	1006	998	992	-0.2	39	341	344	347	0.2	2.90	277	279	0.2
51237	GEORGE	119	1808	1785	1768	-0.3	33	752	751	753	0.0	2.31	515	512	-0.1
51238	HOSPERS	167	1233	1220	1217	-0.3	36	442	443	447	0.1	2.75	344	343	-0.1
51239	HULL	167	2962	3071	3125	0.9	77	973	1023	1053	1.2	2.95	781	817	1.1
51240	INWOOD	119	1864	1849	1837	-0.2	39	636	641	645	0.2	2.81	490	492	0.1
51241	LARCHWOOD	119	1888	1883	1873	-0.1	46	701	713	720	0.4	2.64	540	547	0.3
51243	LITTLE ROCK	119	814	866	889	1.5	86	313	338	351	1.8	2.56	230	247	1.7
51245	PRIMGHAR	141	1427	1402	1365	-0.4	26	577	573	563	-0.2	2.34	384	379	-0.3
51246	ROCK RAPIDS	119	3795	3733	3695	-0.4	28	1497	1489	1491	-0.1	2.44	1061	1052	-0.2
51247	ROCK VALLEY	167	4435	4366	4351	-0.4	29	1613	1617	1631	0.1	2.62	1185	1181	-0.1
51248	SANBORN	141	1909	1873	1825	-0.5	25	740	736	725	-0.1	2.43	528	522	-0.3
51249	SIBLEY	143	3795	3750	3738	-0.3	34	1532	1528	1538	-0.1	2.38	1041	1035	-0.1
51250	SIOUX CENTER	167	7220	7443	7550	0.7	74	2196	2295	2354	1.0	2.72	1679	1750	1.0
51301	SPENCER	041	12872	13002	13124	0.2	61	5438	5555	5676	0.5	2.29	3464	3522	0.4
51331	ARNOLDS PARK	059	975	995	1027	0.5	69	481	494	514	0.6	2.00	305	310	0.4
51333	DICKENS	041	648	625	618	-0.9	10	236	231	231	-0.5	2.71	179	176	-0.4
51334	ESTHERVILLE	063	8397	8165	7936	-0.7	17	3323	3269	3218	-0.4	2.36	2140	2098	-0.5
51338	EVERLY	041	1039	981	964	-1.3	2	415	398	397	-1.0	2.46	297	284	-1.1
51342	GRAETTINGER	147	1296	1308	1308	0.2	59	541	553	559	0.5	2.34	348	355	0.5
51343	GREENVILLE	041	332	382	409	3.4	97	142	165	179	3.6	2.32	101	118	3.7
51345	HARRIS	143	448	449	449	0.1	52	173	175	176	0.3	2.57	130	132	0.4
51346	HARTLEY	141	2722	2600	2509	-1.1	5	1069	1024	995	-1.0	2.46	731	698	-1.1
51347	LAKE PARK	059	1398	1352	1376	-0.8	13	574	560	576	-0.6	2.33	400	389	-0.7
51350	MELVIN	143	451	497	523	2.3	93	189	210	223	2.5	2.36	132	146	2.4
51351	MILFORD	059	4376	4617	4868	1.3	83	1891	2020	2154	1.6	2.26	1246	1328	1.5
51354	OCHEYEDAN	143	1259	1285	1299	0.5	69	488	504	514	0.8	2.55	351	362	0.7
51355	OKOBOJI	059	929	939	963	0.3	61	488	497	514	0.4	1.89	291	292	0.1
51357	ROYAL	041	808	779	770	-0.9	10	321	314	314	-0.5	2.48	221	216	-0.5
51358	RUTHVEN	147	1419	1365	1339	-0.9	9	605	591	586	-0.6	2.31	413	403	-0.6
51360	SPIRIT LAKE	059	7755	8139	8528	1.1	82	3287	3490	3699	1.4	2.28	2232	2365	1.4
51363	SUPERIOR	059	185	188	193	0.4	66	76	78	81	0.6	2.41	57	58	0.4
51364	TERRIL	059	809	774	789	-1.0	6	310	298	307	-0.9	2.58	232	223	-0.9
51365	WALLINGFORD	063	233	246	249	1.3	84	102	109	112	1.6	2.17	76	81	1.5
51366	WEBB	041	445	434	434	-0.6	20	179	176	178	-0.4	2.47	134	132	-0.4
51401	CARROLL	027	12479	12246	11949	-0.4	26	4965	4955	4918	-0.1	2.42	3268	3249	-0.1
51430	ARCADIA	027	908	905	887	-0.1	45	324	330	330	0.4	2.74	245	249	0.4
51431	ARTHUR	093	460	454	451	-0.3	32	187	188	189	0.1	2.41	139	139	0.0
51432	ASPINWALL	047	52	56	58	1.8	89	17	18	20	1.4	3.11	14	15	1.6
51433	AUBURN	161	767	740	718	-0.8	10	302	295	289	-0.6	2.51	213	208	-0.6
51436	BREDA	027	840	833	815	-0.2	38	337	341	341	0.3	2.44	234	236	0.2
51439	CHARTER OAK	047	1144	1150	1173	0.1	55	489	495	508	0.3	2.32	334	336	0.1
51440	DEDHAM	027	455	440	426	-0.8	12	174	171	169	-0.4	2.57	123	121	-0.4
51441	DELOIT	047	362	345	346	-1.1	4	141	136	138	-0.9	2.54	101	97	-1.0
51442	DENISON	047	8941	9136	9332	0.5	69	3257	3337	3421	0.6	2.56	2204	2252	0.5
51443	GLIDDEN	027	1855	1802	1752	-0.7	16	712	704	697	-0.3	2.38	484	476	-0.4
51444	HALBUR	027	181	175	169	-0.8	12	58	57	57	-0.4	3.07	44	44	0.0
51445	IDA GROVE	093	3221	3187	3171	-0.3	36	1335	1342	1349	0.1	2.33	881	882	0.0
51446	IRWIN	165	669	647	633	-0.8	13	279	273	271	-0.5	2.37	203	198	-0.6
51447	KIRKMAN	165	292	292	290	0.0	51	113	115	115	0.4	2.54	86	87	0.3
51448	KIRON	047	652	644	649	-0.3	33	278	279	285	0.1	2.31	197	197	0.0
51449	LAKE CITY	025	2421	2314	2189	-1.1	6	1023	983	936	-0.9	2.27	656	629	-1.0
51450	LAKE VIEW	161	1777	1833	1848	0.7	75	767	801	817	1.0	2.24	512	533	1.0
51451	LANESBORO	027	59	57	56	-0.8	11	21	21	20	0.0	2.71	16	16	0.0
51452	LIDDERDALE	027	282	274	266	-0.7	16	108	107	105	-0.2	2.56	82	81	-0.3
51453	LOHRVILLE	025	647	604	565	-1.6	1	266	250	235	-1.5	2.42	186	174	-1.6
51454	MANILLA	047	1527	1528	1548	0.0	51	568	574	586	0.3	2.56	401	404	0.2
51455	MANNING	027	2231	2181	2134	-0.5	22	905	895	886	-0.3	2.36	587	579	-0.3
51458	ODEBOLT	161	1753	1698	1664	-0.8	14	684	669	664	-0.5	2.42	462	451	-0.6
51460	RICKETTS	047	54	52	52	-0.9	9	20	19	20	-1.2	2.74	14	14	0.0
51461	SCHLESWIG	047	1134	1116	1126	-0.4	28	480	477	485	-0.2	2.34	331	328	-0.2
51462	SCRANTON	073	1138	1081	1061	-1.2	3	464	443	436	-1.1	2.44	325	309	-1.2
51463	TEMPLETON	027	609	581	561	-1.1	5	240	234	230	-0.6	2.48	172	167	-0.7
51465	VAIL	047	905	884	892	-0.6	21	343	340	345	-0.2	2.60	252	249	-0.3
51466	WALL LAKE	161	1216	1181	1158	-0.7	16	470	459	453	-0.6	2.43	326	318	-0.6
51467	WESTSIDE	047	580	565	569	-0.6	18	238	235	239	-0.3	2.40	175	172	-0.4
51501	COUNCIL BLUFFS	155	33982	34056	34866	0.1	52	13125	13269	13698	0.3	2.55	8778	8817	0.1
51503	COUNCIL BLUFFS	155	34914	37214	39241	1.5	87	13544	14575	15523	1.7	2.47	9477	10190	1.7
51510	CARTER LAKE	155	3248	3290	3362	0.3	63	1221	1254	1296	0.6	2.62	914	933	0.5
51520	ARION	047	269	317	349	3.9	98	98	117	130	4.3	2.71	80	94	3.9
51521	AVOCA	155	2152	2142	2168	-0.1	43	858	860	877	0.1	2.38	618	616	-0.1
51523	BLENCOE	133	338	333	332	-0.4	30	158	158	158	0.0	2.11	113	113	0.0
51525	CARSON	155	1086	1122	1158	0.8	76	441	460	480	1.0	2.44	321	333	0.9
51526	CRESCENT	155	1400	1473	1534	1.2	83	518	552	581	1.5	2.52	412	436	1.3
51527	DEFIANCE	165	627	637	637	0.4	65	220	226	229	0.6	2.80	169	174	0.7
51528	DOW CITY	047	1139	1191	1238	1.1	80	450	475	497	1.3	2.51	331	347	1.1
51529	DUNLAP	085	1771	1814	1865	0.6	70	715	739	765	0.8	2.38	474	490	0.8
51530	EARLING	165	1113	1095	1079	-0.4	28	408	407	406	-0.1	2.57	282	280	-0.2
51531	ELK HORN	165	973	949	932	-0.6	20	368	360	356	-0.5	2.37	271	265	-0.5
51532	ELLIOTT	137	799	811	814	0.4	64	314	321	325	0.5	2.53	237	241	0.4
51533	EMERSON	137	1091	1061	1063	-0.7	17	411	403	407	-0.5	2.63	302	296	-0.5
51534	GLENWOOD	129	8668	8944	9211	0.8	75	3031	3156	3278	1.0	2.64	2230	2314	0.9
51535	GRISWOLD	029	2052	2101	2133	0.6	70	811	835	856	0.7	2.45	571	588	0.7
51536	HANCOCK	155	556	542	558	-0.6	19	218	213	221	-0.5	2.54	162	157	-0.7
51537	HARLAN	165	6854	6743	6652	-0.4	28	2761	2741	2729	-0.2	2.41	1949	1928	-0.2
51540	HASTINGS	129	430	420	425	-0.6	21	171	169	173	-0.3	2.49	128	126	-0.4
51541	HENDERSON	129	398	388	392	-0.6	19	169	167	171	-0.3	2.32	125	123	-0.4
51542	HONEY CREEK	155	1121	1150	1184	0.6	71	417	433	450	0.9	2.66	328	339	0.8
51543	KIMBALLTON	009	525	511	506	-0.6	17	211	206	206	-0.6	2.48	155	152	-0.5
51544	LEWIS	029	787	795	802	0.2	61	324	330	337	0.4	2.41	240	244	0.4
51545	LITTLE SIOUX	085	473	534	569	2.9	95	190	215	230	3.0	2.48	129	144	2.6
51546	LOGAN	085	3152	3166	3185	0.1	54	1191	1205	1220	0.3	2.57	847	853	0.2
51548	MC CLELLAND	155	541	684	785	5.7	100	199	255	295	6.0	2.68	155	196	5.7
	IOWA					0.5					0.7	2.43			0.6
	UNITED STATES					1.2					1.3	2.58			1.1

ZIP CODE #	POST OFFICE NAME	RACE (%) White 2000	White 2004	Black 2000	Black 2004	Asian/Pacific 2000	Asian/Pacific 2004	% Hispanic Origin 2000	% Hispanic Origin 2004	2004 AGE DISTRIBUTION (%) 0-4	5-9	10-14	15-19	20-24	25-44	45-64	65-84	85+	18+	MEDIAN AGE 2004	% 2004 Males	% 2004 Females
51231	ARCHER	98.9	98.6	0.0	0.0	0.7	1.1	1.5	1.4	7.4	7.7	8.8	7.7	6.3	24.2	24.9	11.6	1.4	71.6	36.4	51.6	48.4
51232	ASHTON	99.3	99.3	0.1	0.1	0.1	0.1	0.6	0.6	6.9	6.9	7.3	7.6	5.7	25.5	24.6	13.3	2.0	73.8	38.5	50.7	49.4
51234	BOYDEN	98.7	98.4	0.2	0.2	0.3	0.5	1.9	2.2	8.5	8.4	7.7	6.8	6.3	26.0	22.4	12.4	1.7	71.3	35.7	53.1	46.9
51235	DOON	99.8	99.8	0.0	0.0	0.0	0.0	0.2	0.2	8.4	8.7	9.0	7.4	5.9	26.7	21.9	11.1	0.8	69.0	33.3	52.8	47.2
51237	GEORGE	99.2	99.1	0.2	0.2	0.1	0.1	0.3	0.4	5.1	5.5	6.7	6.2	5.5	21.2	24.0	21.2	4.6	78.6	44.9	49.0	51.0
51238	HOSPERS	97.3	97.0	0.0	0.0	0.4	0.5	1.1	1.3	8.0	7.9	7.7	7.1	6.4	23.9	23.2	14.2	1.7	72.1	37.1	50.7	49.3
51239	HULL	95.7	94.7	0.1	0.1	0.8	1.2	4.6	5.6	8.7	8.5	8.8	7.6	6.6	25.2	21.1	10.9	2.6	69.3	33.0	50.4	49.6
51240	INWOOD	98.2	98.2	0.2	0.2	0.1	0.1	1.2	1.2	7.9	8.0	8.2	7.8	6.5	24.5	21.4	12.6	3.2	71.0	35.2	49.5	50.5
51241	LARCHWOOD	99.1	99.0	0.0	0.0	0.2	0.2	0.2	0.2	7.5	7.7	7.5	6.6	6.5	26.3	24.4	11.3	2.1	73.3	36.3	51.0	49.0
51243	LITTLE ROCK	99.5	99.5	0.0	0.0	0.3	0.2	0.3	0.2	6.0	6.9	8.4	6.7	5.3	23.3	23.4	16.9	3.0	74.8	40.3	49.3	50.7
51245	PRIMGHAR	98.0	97.4	0.4	0.4	1.0	1.4	0.9	1.2	5.1	5.4	6.4	7.1	6.1	21.2	25.8	19.4	3.4	78.5	44.0	49.4	50.6
51246	ROCK RAPIDS	99.3	99.3	0.1	0.1	0.3	0.3	0.2	0.2	6.2	6.6	7.7	6.6	6.0	22.6	23.8	16.7	3.8	75.4	40.9	48.5	51.5
51247	ROCK VALLEY	98.7	98.4	0.1	0.1	0.3	0.4	1.2	1.4	7.5	7.5	7.8	7.6	6.5	24.6	21.8	13.9	2.7	72.4	35.9	49.0	51.0
51248	SANBORN	99.1	98.9	0.2	0.2	0.2	0.2	0.6	0.7	5.1	5.3	6.8	6.6	5.8	21.4	23.7	20.3	5.0	78.3	44.3	48.0	52.0
51249	SIBLEY	97.7	97.6	0.2	0.2	0.3	0.3	2.1	2.2	6.3	6.0	6.5	7.0	6.2	23.4	24.3	15.9	4.5	76.9	41.5	47.6	52.5
51250	SIOUX CENTER	96.9	96.2	0.1	0.1	0.8	1.2	4.0	4.8	6.8	6.2	6.8	11.4	14.8	23.5	18.1	10.4	2.2	76.3	27.9	48.7	51.3
51301	SPENCER	97.7	97.7	0.2	0.2	1.1	1.1	1.3	1.4	6.2	6.1	6.8	6.3	6.7	25.8	24.6	14.4	3.3	77.1	39.8	47.5	52.5
51331	ARNOLDS PARK	97.4	97.0	0.5	0.7	0.2	0.3	0.3	0.5	5.7	6.5	6.0	3.8	3.3	27.3	28.9	16.2	2.1	79.2	43.0	49.9	50.2
51333	DICKENS	99.2	99.4	0.0	0.0	0.5	0.5	0.2	0.2	5.8	6.2	8.3	6.6	5.0	23.8	29.6	13.1	1.6	75.4	41.5	50.6	49.4
51334	ESTHERVILLE	96.9	96.2	0.3	0.3	0.4	0.5	5.5	6.5	5.8	5.9	6.4	8.5	8.3	23.1	23.7	14.9	3.5	77.1	38.9	48.7	51.3
51338	EVERLY	99.1	99.2	0.1	0.1	0.1	0.1	0.1	0.1	6.0	6.5	7.9	7.1	5.2	25.7	27.0	12.8	1.7	75.1	39.4	51.3	48.7
51342	GRAETTINGER	98.8	98.7	0.1	0.1	0.2	0.2	0.9	1.0	6.4	6.7	7.3	7.3	5.7	24.7	23.1	16.2	2.8	74.4	39.6	48.0	52.0
51343	GREENVILLE	98.2	98.2	1.2	1.1	0.0	0.0	1.5	1.6	4.7	6.0	9.4	6.5	3.9	25.1	31.4	11.5	1.3	75.1	41.9	51.3	48.7
51345	HARRIS	98.0	97.8	0.2	0.2	0.5	0.5	1.6	1.6	4.7	8.5	8.5	7.1	5.8	25.4	27.2	11.4	1.6	73.5	39.0	51.9	48.1
51346	HARTLEY	97.4	97.1	0.8	0.8	0.3	0.4	3.2	3.8	6.5	6.3	7.4	7.0	5.7	23.1	24.5	15.2	4.2	75.0	40.9	49.5	50.5
51347	LAKE PARK	99.1	99.0	0.1	0.1	0.1	0.1	0.8	0.9	5.0	5.2	6.1	6.4	5.3	24.9	24.7	18.3	4.2	79.5	43.2	50.4	49.6
51350	MELVIN	96.9	97.0	0.0	0.0	0.0	0.0	2.7	2.8	5.0	5.4	6.0	5.8	5.2	22.5	30.2	17.9	1.8	79.9	44.9	50.1	49.9
51351	MILFORD	98.8	98.6	0.2	0.2	0.3	0.5	0.9	1.0	5.5	5.4	6.4	5.9	5.4	23.7	27.5	17.5	2.8	79.0	43.5	49.1	50.9
51354	OCHEYEDAN	98.8	98.8	0.0	0.0	0.2	0.2	1.3	1.3	6.4	7.9	8.1	5.9	5.8	25.4	25.4	13.5	1.7	73.9	39.3	51.3	48.7
51355	OKOBOJI	99.0	98.9	0.1	0.1	0.0	0.0	0.5	0.5	3.8	4.1	3.5	3.8	3.8	21.8	32.8	24.3	2.0	86.2	51.0	50.1	50.0
51357	ROYAL	99.6	99.6	0.0	0.0	0.0	0.0	1.1	1.2	6.3	6.7	7.6	6.6	4.8	29.0	24.5	12.8	1.8	75.4	37.9	51.9	48.1
51358	RUTHVEN	98.0	98.0	0.0	0.0	0.3	0.3	0.9	1.0	6.2	5.9	6.2	5.6	6.3	23.5	25.2	18.0	3.2	78.5	42.3	48.6	51.4
51360	SPIRIT LAKE	99.1	99.0	0.1	0.2	0.1	0.2	0.6	0.8	5.2	5.6	6.2	5.9	5.1	21.7	30.1	16.9	3.3	79.2	45.2	48.1	51.9
51363	SUPERIOR	99.5	99.5	0.0	0.0	0.5	0.5	0.5	1.1	3.7	4.3	4.3	4.3	4.8	17.6	36.2	22.3	2.7	84.6	51.7	50.0	50.0
51364	TERRIL	98.6	98.5	0.4	0.4	0.4	0.5	0.6	0.7	5.7	6.5	7.5	6.3	4.8	25.6	29.1	13.2	1.4	76.5	41.0	51.3	48.7
51365	WALLINGFORD	97.9	98.0	0.4	0.4	0.0	0.0	2.6	2.9	4.5	6.5	8.1	10.2	4.5	23.6	27.6	13.4	1.6	73.2	40.5	50.4	49.6
51366	WEBB	98.9	98.9	0.2	0.2	0.7	0.7	0.5	0.2	6.2	6.7	8.3	6.9	4.4	24.9	27.9	13.1	1.6	74.2	40.9	50.2	49.8
51401	CARROLL	98.7	98.4	0.2	0.2	0.5	0.7	0.5	0.7	6.3	6.3	7.7	7.2	7.0	24.1	23.6	14.6	3.2	75.2	39.1	48.6	51.5
51430	ARCADIA	99.7	99.7	0.0	0.0	0.2	0.3	0.1	0.1	7.9	7.9	7.6	7.4	6.3	24.9	21.8	14.5	1.9	72.2	37.1	52.5	47.5
51431	ARTHUR	98.9	98.7	0.0	0.0	0.2	0.2	0.9	0.7	6.4	6.2	7.9	7.9	6.0	23.8	27.3	12.8	1.8	74.5	39.6	52.6	47.4
51432	ASPINWALL	98.1	100.0	0.0	0.0	0.0	0.0	0.0	0.0	7.1	7.1	10.7	8.9	3.6	26.8	26.8	8.9	0.0	66.1	36.3	53.6	46.4
51433	AUBURN	99.4	99.3	0.0	0.0	0.1	0.1	0.3	0.4	7.2	7.2	7.0	6.0	6.5	26.0	24.7	13.5	2.0	75.0	39.1	53.0	47.0
51436	BREDA	99.3	99.2	0.2	0.2	0.4	0.5	0.4	0.4	6.1	6.5	7.8	7.8	5.8	23.4	25.3	13.8	3.5	74.6	39.7	52.5	47.5
51439	CHARTER OAK	99.2	99.0	0.0	0.0	0.2	0.3	0.6	0.9	6.6	7.0	7.5	5.8	5.0	23.0	27.5	15.1	2.4	75.0	41.7	52.1	47.9
51440	DEDHAM	98.0	98.0	0.9	0.9	0.0	0.0	1.1	1.4	8.0	7.7	7.1	6.4	5.9	26.4	23.6	13.0	2.1	73.2	37.1	53.2	46.8
51441	DELOIT	96.4	95.4	0.3	0.3	0.3	0.3	3.0	3.8	4.9	7.8	9.3	6.7	4.1	24.6	29.0	12.5	1.2	73.6	40.5	51.9	48.1
51442	DENISON	88.5	86.5	1.3	1.4	0.8	1.1	15.4	18.0	7.2	6.5	6.7	7.6	7.5	26.4	22.8	12.1	3.1	74.8	36.0	50.0	50.0
51443	GLIDDEN	99.4	99.2	0.1	0.1	0.1	0.2	0.2	0.2	4.5	5.3	7.7	7.2	6.1	26.4	28.2	12.8	1.9	77.8	41.0	49.4	50.6
51444	HALBUR	99.5	99.4	0.0	0.0	0.0	0.0	0.0	0.0	8.0	8.0	7.4	8.0	6.9	26.9	22.9	10.9	1.1	72.0	35.2	52.0	48.0
51445	IDA GROVE	98.7	98.7	0.2	0.2	0.3	0.3	0.6	0.6	5.7	5.9	7.3	7.1	5.6	21.8	26.9	16.5	3.2	76.5	42.7	48.5	51.5
51446	IRWIN	99.0	98.9	0.2	0.2	0.0	0.0	1.1	1.2	6.7	6.8	7.1	6.0	4.5	23.3	26.7	16.9	2.0	75.7	41.9	48.8	51.2
51447	KIRKMAN	98.6	99.0	0.0	0.0	0.0	0.0	1.4	1.4	6.5	6.9	7.9	7.5	4.5	24.7	26.7	14.0	1.4	73.6	40.0	52.1	48.0
51448	KIRON	97.6	96.9	0.2	0.2	0.2	0.3	1.8	2.5	5.8	7.1	7.6	6.1	5.1	23.9	28.7	13.8	1.9	75.6	41.4	51.2	48.8
51449	LAKE CITY	99.0	98.8	0.0	0.0	0.2	0.3	0.9	1.1	5.8	6.1	6.8	6.1	5.8	19.7	25.5	19.0	5.1	77.2	44.7	46.9	53.1
51450	LAKE VIEW	99.2	99.1	0.3	0.3	0.1	0.1	0.3	0.3	5.6	5.7	5.8	5.8	4.9	19.5	27.6	21.2	4.0	79.1	47.0	48.6	51.4
51451	LANESBORO	98.3	100.0	0.0	0.0	0.0	0.0	0.0	0.0	7.0	7.0	7.0	7.0	7.0	28.1	22.8	12.3	1.8	75.4	36.9	52.6	47.4
51452	LIDDERDALE	98.9	98.9	0.0	0.0	0.0	0.0	0.7	0.4	6.2	6.9	9.9	7.3	6.2	25.9	25.2	11.3	1.1	72.6	36.8	51.5	48.5
51453	LOHRVILLE	99.2	98.8	0.2	0.2	0.2	0.2	0.8	1.0	5.3	7.1	8.9	7.5	5.3	25.0	25.3	13.4	2.2	73.7	38.5	50.5	49.5
51454	MANILLA	98.4	98.2	0.1	0.1	0.1	0.1	0.5	0.6	6.9	6.7	7.1	6.7	4.8	23.1	24.1	16.8	3.8	74.7	41.4	50.1	49.9
51455	MANNING	98.9	98.7	0.0	0.1	0.5	0.6	0.4	0.4	5.8	6.1	7.3	7.3	5.4	22.1	23.2	18.1	4.7	75.8	42.5	47.7	52.3
51458	ODEBOLT	98.9	98.7	0.4	0.4	0.2	0.4	0.5	0.7	5.8	6.1	7.1	6.4	5.3	22.7	24.2	17.4	5.0	76.4	42.6	48.5	51.5
51460	RICKETTS	100.0	100.0	0.0	0.0	0.0	0.0	0.0	0.0	7.7	7.7	7.7	5.8	5.8	25.0	26.9	13.5	0.0	76.9	37.5	53.9	46.2
51461	SCHLESWIG	99.6	99.6	0.0	0.0	0.1	0.1	1.0	1.2	6.0	6.1	6.8	6.4	5.2	21.8	24.3	19.7	3.8	77.2	43.5	49.8	50.2
51462	SCRANTON	98.1	97.8	0.2	0.2	0.2	0.2	2.3	2.4	6.0	6.4	7.2	6.4	5.4	22.0	27.1	16.9	2.6	76.4	42.8	50.7	49.3
51463	TEMPLETON	99.0	99.0	0.2	0.2	0.0	0.0	0.2	0.2	6.9	7.2	9.1	7.6	4.7	26.3	23.4	13.9	0.9	71.4	38.0	51.5	48.5
51465	VAIL	98.5	98.2	0.3	0.3	0.1	0.1	1.3	1.8	5.7	6.6	8.0	6.8	5.0	24.4	26.8	15.1	1.7	75.2	41.2	51.2	48.8
51466	WALL LAKE	98.6	98.4	0.1	0.1	0.2	0.3	0.3	0.4	6.6	6.4	6.2	6.5	6.8	21.4	23.2	17.4	5.6	76.4	41.2	49.7	50.3
51467	WESTSIDE	98.5	98.2	0.3	0.4	0.2	0.2	1.4	1.6	5.7	6.6	8.0	6.7	5.1	24.4	26.2	15.6	1.8	75.6	41.2	50.8	49.2
51501	COUNCIL BLUFFS	93.8	92.8	1.2	1.3	0.6	0.9	5.5	6.6	7.7	7.1	7.3	6.9	7.6	29.8	22.2	10.4	1.0	73.8	34.1	49.0	51.0
51503	COUNCIL BLUFFS	96.9	96.3	0.6	0.7	0.5	0.8	2.3	2.8	6.1	6.2	7.1	7.4	7.0	25.4	26.0	12.7	2.3	76.3	39.0	48.3	51.8
51510	CARTER LAKE	96.7	96.2	0.3	0.3	0.3	0.4	2.9	3.5	6.4	6.6	7.6	6.6	6.3	28.2	25.9	11.8	0.7	75.4	38.1	50.2	49.8
51520	ARION	95.9	95.0	0.4	0.3	0.4	0.3	4.1	5.4	6.9	7.3	7.6	6.3	6.0	24.6	30.6	10.4	0.3	73.8	40.1	53.6	46.4
51521	AVOCA	99.1	98.8	0.1	0.1	0.1	0.1	1.2	1.6	5.9	6.1	6.8	5.8	5.6	25.3	25.2	16.0	3.5	77.2	41.5	49.7	50.3
51523	BLENCOE	98.2	98.2	0.0	0.0	0.0	0.0	0.9	0.9	4.5	5.1	6.6	6.3	4.8	21.0	31.8	17.4	2.4	79.6	45.9	52.6	47.5
51525	CARSON	98.8	98.6	0.1	0.1	0.3	0.5	0.2	0.1	5.9	6.6	7.4	5.4	5.8	24.5	28.3	13.9	2.2	76.8	41.3	48.4	51.6
51526	CRESCENT	98.4	98.0	0.6	0.8	0.2	0.3	2.1	2.5	4.3	5.2	6.7	6.5	6.0	26.5	33.3	10.8	0.8	79.9	41.9	52.9	47.1
51527	DEFIANCE	98.4	98.3	0.0	0.0	0.2	0.2	1.4	1.7	6.6	7.1	8.0	7.9	4.2	24.8	26.2	13.5	1.7	72.8	39.6	52.3	47.7
51528	DOW CITY	97.1	96.3	0.1	0.1	0.7	1.1	1.7	2.2	5.6	6.5	7.8	6.7	5.6	24.7	29.3	12.9	0.8	75.6	40.8	51.6	48.5
51529	DUNLAP	98.3	98.0	0.1	0.2	0.2	0.2	0.8	1.1	4.9	5.3	7.1	7.4	5.5	23.3	25.6	17.7	3.3	77.9	42.7	50.0	50.0
51530	EARLING	99.1	98.9	0.0	0.0	0.0	0.0	0.7	1.0	7.1	7.4	7.8	6.0	5.1	23.7	22.0	17.5	3.3	73.5	40.4	50.1	49.9
51531	ELK HORN	99.2	99.0	0.0	0.0	0.5	0.7	0.2	0.3	3.5	3.9	7.4	6.6	4.6	17.9	23.8	22.7	9.6	80.0	49.8	47.0	53.0
51532	ELLIOTT	98.9	98.6	0.0	0.1	0.3	0.4	0.0	0.0	6.8	6.7	6.3	6.2	5.6	25.8	26.0	14.7	2.1	76.5	40.9	52.4	47.6
51533	EMERSON	99.3	99.2	0.1	0.1	0.1	0.1	0.6	0.5	5.1	5.8	7.9	7.5	5.1	22.9	30.3	13.1	2.5	76.7	42.1	50.4	49.6
51534	GLENWOOD	97.6	97.2	0.4	0.5	0.3	0.5	1.4	1.7	6.8	6.6	7.6	7.5	6.6	26.6	26.4	10.2	1.6	74.3	37.6	50.2	49.8
51535	GRISWOLD	98.8	98.8	0.3	0.4	0.1	0.1	0.8	0.8	6.0	6.6	7.5	6.4	3.9	23.7	24.8	18.0	3.3	76.0	42.5	49.1	50.9
51536	HANCOCK	98.2	98.0	0.7	0.9	0.4	0.4	0.4	0.4	5.4	5.9	7.4	6.5	5.4	23.8	28.8	15.3	1.7	77.5	42.3	50.4	49.6
51537	HARLAN	98.5	98.2	0.1	0.2	0.4	0.6	0.7	0.8	5.8	6.0	7.2	7.4	6.1	22.2	25.5	16.2	3.7	76.2	42.0	48.4	51.7
51540	HASTINGS	99.1	99.3	0.0	0.0	0.0	0.0	0.9	1.2	6.4	7.1	7.1	5.2	4.8	22.6	31.7	13.3	1.7	76.4	42.6	50.7	49.3
51541	HENDERSON	99.5	99.2	0.0	0.0	0.3	0.3	1.0	1.3	4.1	5.2	7.0	7.7	5.2	22.7	32.5	13.7	2.1	79.1	43.9	52.8	47.2
51542	HONEY CREEK	98.1	97.8	0.3	0.3	0.3	0.4	0.7	1.0	5.2	6.1	7.2	6.4	4.9	23.9	34.0	11.5	0.9	77.6	43.0	52.1	47.9
51543	KIMBALLTON	99.2	99.2	0.2	0.2	0.2	0.2	0.6	0.4	6.5	7.1	8.4	6.7	4.7	24.1	28.2	12.9	1.6	73.8	40.1	51.3	48.7
51544	LEWIS	99.2	99.4	0.1	0.1	0.0	0.0	0.3	0.3	5.5	6.7	7.6	7.6	3.5	23.4	30.3	14.2	1.3	75.0	42.5	50.1	49.9
51545	LITTLE SIOUX	98.7	98.7	0.2	0.2	0.2	0.2	0.9	0.8	5.6	5.8	7.7	8.2	5.6	22.5	24.5	17.0	3.0	75.8	41.8	48.5	51.5
51546	LOGAN	98.6	98.5	0.1	0.1	0.2	0.3	0.8	0.9	6.6	7.2	7.9	6.7	5.3	25.6	24.3	13.6	2.7	73.8	39.3	50.3	49.7
51548	MC CLELLAND	98.3	97.8	0.2	0.2	0.4	0.4	0.9	1.0	7.5	7.6	7.8	6.9	5.4	26.3	27.6	10.1	0.9	73.0	38.7	52.2	47.8
	IOWA	93.9	93.0	2.1	2.3	1.3	1.8	2.8	3.2	6.5	6.5	6.9	7.2	7.6	26.4	24.2	12.3	2.4	76.0	37.2	49.2	50.8
	UNITED STATES	75.1	73.6	12.3	12.5	3.8	4.2	12.5	14.1	6.9	6.7	7.2	7.0	7.3	28.6	23.8	10.8	1.7	75.1	36.0	49.1	50.9

#	POST OFFICE NAME	2004 Per Capita Income	2004 HH Income Base	2004 Household Income Distribution (%) Less than $25,000	$25,000 to $49,999	$50,000 to $99,999	$100,000 to $149,999	$150,000 or More	Median Household Income 2004	2009	2004 National Centile	2004 State Centile	2004 Home Value Base	2004 Home Value Distribution (%) Less than $50,000	$50,000 to $89,999	$90,000 to $174,999	$175,000 to $399,999	$400,000 or More	2004 Median Home Value
51231	ARCHER	19549	113	15.9	40.7	38.1	4.4	0.9	45743	50494	63	67	87	29.9	37.9	26.4	4.6	1.2	67000
51232	ASHTON	19082	375	26.4	33.3	32.0	5.3	2.9	41939	50268	53	48	309	34.0	39.2	21.4	4.9	0.7	66034
51234	BOYDEN	18812	460	20.0	38.5	35.0	5.9	0.7	45819	50789	63	67	389	14.9	36.5	39.9	6.7	2.1	88472
51235	DOON	16915	344	17.7	40.7	36.3	5.2	0.0	44142	50787	59	59	288	23.3	33.3	35.8	5.9	1.7	82083
51237	GEORGE	18593	751	32.1	35.8	26.8	4.1	1.2	37233	42815	36	17	595	34.0	40.2	20.2	3.0	2.7	64041
51238	HOSPERS	18983	443	21.4	39.1	32.1	5.6	1.8	42385	47466	54	51	366	23.5	34.2	29.0	9.8	3.6	80968
51239	HULL	17654	1023	20.2	37.4	35.0	5.1	2.3	45949	51464	64	68	867	10.7	32.6	46.3	9.3	1.0	96845
51240	INWOOD	16996	641	24.8	35.7	32.1	7.3	0.0	41712	48722	52	46	528	15.2	28.6	41.5	12.9	1.9	97174
51241	LARCHWOOD	21060	713	18.5	35.6	36.5	7.6	1.8	46293	52441	65	70	603	11.8	26.5	42.3	16.8	2.7	103966
51243	LITTLE ROCK	17406	338	28.1	36.7	30.2	3.3	1.8	39547	44867	44	31	272	46.0	30.2	20.6	2.6	0.7	53548
51245	PRIMGHAR	19925	573	29.8	37.0	26.5	3.0	3.7	38797	43722	42	27	455	47.0	31.9	16.7	3.3	1.1	54219
51246	ROCK RAPIDS	19868	1489	25.1	34.1	32.1	7.3	1.5	42165	49127	53	49	1156	20.9	34.5	34.7	8.5	1.4	83942
51247	ROCK VALLEY	20348	1617	23.9	34.5	32.2	6.5	2.9	44764	50435	61	61	1312	9.6	30.3	47.8	11.9	0.5	102371
51248	SANBORN	20008	736	22.0	41.0	31.0	3.9	2.0	41699	47193	52	46	571	25.2	34.5	33.8	5.4	1.1	79043
51249	SIBLEY	19658	1528	31.8	30.9	28.8	6.9	1.6	39308	47125	44	30	1148	28.9	33.1	31.7	5.4	0.9	77045
51250	SIOUX CENTER	20468	2295	22.1	29.5	37.8	7.0	3.6	48837	55477	70	79	1837	6.8	15.0	54.3	23.1	0.8	125436
51301	SPENCER	23306	5555	29.6	33.5	27.3	6.4	3.2	39834	46019	45	33	3804	13.0	30.1	42.6	12.6	1.7	97982
51331	ARNOLDS PARK	29325	494	26.1	35.0	27.9	6.9	4.1	40148	46960	47	36	379	17.9	26.1	28.2	22.4	5.3	99000
51333	DICKENS	19506	231	23.8	35.1	34.2	4.3	2.6	43426	48952	57	56	184	31.5	28.3	26.6	11.4	2.2	70000
51334	ESTHERVILLE	19423	3269	28.4	36.6	27.0	6.0	2.0	37446	43889	37	18	2385	27.8	41.8	25.3	4.2	0.8	69979
51338	EVERLY	20660	398	18.6	43.0	34.4	3.5	0.5	43114	48990	56	54	326	26.4	33.7	31.0	6.1	2.8	80000
51342	GRAETTINGER	19249	553	34.2	33.6	24.8	5.8	1.6	35751	41905	31	13	418	41.2	34.7	20.3	2.9	1.0	62381
51343	GREENVILLE	33199	165	30.3	35.8	25.5	3.0	5.5	38396	43853	41	25	131	40.5	18.3	28.2	6.9	6.1	64375
51345	HARRIS	18775	175	23.4	37.1	32.0	6.9	0.6	40557	48198	48	39	136	36.0	30.9	27.9	5.2	0.0	65455
51346	HARTLEY	18591	1024	30.4	35.0	28.9	3.6	2.2	38746	43509	42	27	788	36.6	39.3	20.4	2.8	0.9	59636
51347	LAKE PARK	20522	560	26.1	35.0	32.0	5.2	1.8	41772	49452	52	47	446	19.7	37.7	30.9	10.1	1.6	83125
51350	MELVIN	23033	210	30.0	31.4	25.7	8.1	4.8	40639	47831	48	39	173	55.5	27.2	12.1	5.2	0.0	45476
51351	MILFORD	24801	2020	24.3	33.3	32.7	6.2	3.4	44458	52821	60	61	1536	13.2	25.6	39.1	15.2	6.9	103782
51354	OCHEYEDAN	16723	504	31.0	39.5	23.4	5.2	1.0	35979	41944	31	14	405	44.7	36.5	16.5	2.2	0.0	55000
51355	OKOBOJI	35957	497	23.5	31.2	28.6	10.3	6.4	45436	53121	62	65	421	19.0	6.9	27.3	38.0	8.8	160326
51357	ROYAL	22340	314	32.5	27.4	28.0	7.6	4.5	44270	49225	59	60	245	24.5	43.7	18.8	9.4	3.7	70200
51358	RUTHVEN	19906	591	30.6	37.1	26.9	3.4	2.0	37036	42664	36	17	457	39.4	32.8	20.8	5.7	1.3	62614
51360	SPIRIT LAKE	27178	3490	23.4	30.5	32.2	8.6	5.4	46672	55341	65	71	2735	9.5	16.3	38.4	29.5	6.3	128637
51363	SUPERIOR	26675	78	25.6	29.5	30.8	7.7	6.4	45000	53769	61	63	66	9.1	15.2	31.8	39.4	4.6	150000
51364	TERRIL	21810	298	16.4	37.6	38.6	4.7	2.7	47601	54655	67	74	242	27.3	22.3	31.0	16.9	2.5	90667
51365	WALLINGFORD	22271	109	24.8	38.5	29.4	6.4	0.9	41422	48632	51	44	87	24.1	33.3	32.2	8.1	2.3	82778
51366	WEBB	19395	176	26.7	38.6	29.0	4.0	1.7	39325	43884	44	30	140	42.1	27.1	20.7	7.9	2.1	56875
51401	CARROLL	23525	4955	25.2	28.7	35.2	7.7	3.3	46074	54136	64	68	3616	10.5	24.3	48.8	14.6	1.7	105455
51430	ARCADIA	17899	330	26.4	34.9	31.2	3.9	3.6	39369	45808	44	31	270	20.0	31.9	32.6	8.2	7.4	87368
51431	ARTHUR	25226	188	29.3	32.5	29.3	4.8	4.3	39620	45252	45	32	149	29.5	34.2	24.8	9.4	2.0	68077
51432	ASPINWALL	14876	18	27.8	33.3	33.3	5.6	0.0	45000	50000	61	63	13	15.4	38.5	46.2	0.0	0.0	85000
51433	AUBURN	22907	295	24.4	32.5	28.8	7.5	6.8	45481	51981	63	66	232	37.5	24.6	27.2	8.6	2.2	71429
51436	BREDA	20294	341	28.2	40.2	23.5	3.2	5.0	38731	45633	42	27	279	21.5	28.7	36.2	8.6	5.0	89706
51439	CHARTER OAK	19386	495	30.9	36.4	27.9	3.2	1.6	37779	43008	38	21	392	47.7	32.7	12.5	5.4	1.8	52727
51440	DEDHAM	15969	171	29.2	40.4	28.7	1.8	0.0	39780	47153	45	33	139	36.0	25.2	27.3	11.5	0.0	71667
51441	DELOIT	19647	136	29.4	39.0	25.7	3.7	2.2	37786	43297	38	21	110	40.9	23.6	30.0	4.6	0.9	67143
51442	DENISON	18266	3337	29.4	35.2	28.5	4.7	2.2	38170	43891	40	23	2365	17.8	35.5	36.9	9.4	0.3	86807
51443	GLIDDEN	21362	704	25.6	32.4	33.5	6.7	1.9	43112	50965	56	54	536	24.4	34.7	34.5	5.6	0.8	81091
51444	HALBUR	18108	57	17.5	35.1	36.8	7.0	3.5	46169	55932	64	69	47	14.9	29.8	21.3	17.0	17.0	102500
51445	IDA GROVE	23701	1342	30.0	31.7	29.8	5.0	3.4	40485	47333	48	39	986	27.1	33.1	31.4	7.4	1.0	77308
51446	IRWIN	18363	273	30.8	32.6	32.2	3.7	0.7	36141	41243	32	14	202	31.7	32.2	20.3	13.9	2.0	73182
51447	KIRKMAN	17600	115	27.8	33.9	33.0	4.4	0.9	39683	45458	45	32	92	28.3	28.3	30.4	13.0	0.0	80000
51448	KIRON	20118	279	30.8	36.6	26.9	3.9	1.8	38299	43341	40	24	222	30.6	38.7	22.1	7.2	1.4	66190
51449	LAKE CITY	19258	983	32.6	34.1	26.6	6.0	0.8	37192	43358	36	17	753	34.7	30.7	27.0	5.8	1.9	70397
51450	LAKE VIEW	20553	801	34.7	32.8	25.2	4.5	2.8	33732	38931	23	6	628	27.2	33.4	30.1	8.9	0.3	80290
51451	LANESBORO	16711	21	23.8	38.1	33.3	4.8	0.0	38596	50000	41	26	17	23.5	29.4	23.5	23.5	0.0	85000
51452	LIDDERDALE	21595	107	26.2	39.3	27.1	3.7	3.7	39060	44600	43	29	87	27.6	29.9	25.3	13.8	3.5	79167
51453	LOHRVILLE	18419	250	35.6	30.4	27.6	5.2	1.2	34736	40227	26	9	206	52.4	23.3	21.8	1.9	0.5	48214
51454	MANILLA	15991	574	30.8	38.7	27.0	2.8	0.7	36230	41565	32	15	456	43.9	38.4	13.2	4.0	0.7	56222
51455	MANNING	19955	895	32.0	33.4	26.9	5.3	2.5	38360	45568	41	24	682	27.3	40.8	23.0	6.9	2.1	69146
51458	ODEBOLT	18229	669	35.0	32.6	25.7	5.7	1.1	35589	41424	30	12	515	38.8	36.3	21.0	3.3	0.6	61122
51460	RICKETTS	16990	19	21.1	42.1	31.6	5.3	0.0	42361	45000	54	51	14	42.9	35.7	21.4	0.0	0.0	55000
51461	SCHLESWIG	18412	477	32.9	36.3	26.6	2.7	1.5	36023	41157	32	14	381	39.1	38.9	18.9	2.6	0.5	57981
51462	SCRANTON	16568	443	31.8	40.9	24.4	2.5	0.5	34366	39172	25	8	349	39.5	28.1	24.1	5.4	2.9	65952
51463	TEMPLETON	24400	234	29.5	31.2	28.2	6.4	4.7	40296	46551	47	37	187	16.0	35.3	35.8	8.0	4.8	88810
51465	VAIL	18741	340	25.9	42.4	28.2	2.7	0.9	38364	43230	41	24	274	36.1	32.9	28.1	2.2	0.7	69231
51466	WALL LAKE	18757	459	28.3	37.0	28.8	5.0	0.9	38417	44690	41	25	364	33.5	34.1	26.4	4.4	1.7	67941
51467	WESTSIDE	20337	235	26.0	42.6	28.1	2.6	0.9	38122	43138	40	23	190	36.8	33.2	27.4	2.1	0.5	68333
51501	COUNCIL BLUFFS	19090	13269	27.7	34.6	31.2	5.4	1.2	39779	47614	45	33	8905	19.6	46.2	32.2	1.4	0.5	77540
51503	COUNCIL BLUFFS	26337	14575	20.4	29.3	33.4	11.6	5.4	50365	59947	73	83	10553	4.7	18.3	50.7	24.3	2.0	124758
51510	CARTER LAKE	21816	1254	22.9	34.5	33.3	5.6	3.8	43850	52102	58	58	1053	26.5	43.2	24.1	5.9	0.3	76528
51520	ARION	15773	117	32.5	33.3	30.8	2.6	0.9	36419	40561	33	15	92	32.6	21.7	22.8	18.5	4.4	85556
51521	AVOCA	22662	860	17.6	41.3	32.2	7.3	1.6	45716	52694	63	67	665	17.4	29.8	41.8	9.6	1.4	92721
51523	BLENCOE	27187	158	27.2	24.7	35.4	9.5	3.2	48514	53305	69	78	126	27.0	24.6	34.1	11.9	2.4	87778
51525	CARSON	21950	460	23.3	29.4	39.4	6.5	1.5	47790	54802	68	75	376	13.6	29.3	45.7	10.4	1.1	98710
51526	CRESCENT	30059	552	8.3	24.1	44.6	16.5	6.5	65899	78734	89	98	494	3.0	11.5	49.6	33.8	2.0	146711
51527	DEFIANCE	16260	226	28.3	35.4	31.4	4.4	0.4	39401	44850	44	31	186	26.9	26.9	32.3	12.4	1.6	83636
51528	DOW CITY	17284	475	29.9	39.2	27.2	3.2	0.6	37782	43114	38	21	375	38.7	34.1	14.4	10.4	2.4	60161
51529	DUNLAP	21651	739	29.4	34.6	28.6	3.8	3.7	38836	45123	42	28	586	32.1	31.6	23.4	11.4	1.5	72000
51530	EARLING	17742	407	24.1	38.3	32.7	4.4	0.5	40670	46137	48	39	330	17.0	30.6	37.9	11.2	3.3	92963
51531	ELK HORN	20975	360	21.4	37.2	32.5	5.3	3.6	42343	49518	54	50	300	18.3	38.0	36.3	3.3	4.0	84571
51532	ELLIOTT	18827	321	32.1	27.4	32.4	6.5	1.6	41878	47227	53	47	264	41.3	28.0	23.5	4.2	3.0	68667
51533	EMERSON	19711	403	24.3	37.0	28.8	8.2	1.7	41264	48844	51	43	331	25.1	31.4	33.5	8.8	1.2	81042
51534	GLENWOOD	22046	3156	21.2	28.0	37.4	10.7	2.8	50652	60480	73	83	2346	7.3	13.9	49.6	27.4	1.8	124952
51535	GRISWOLD	19095	835	26.2	36.1	32.0	4.9	0.8	39797	46098	45	33	657	23.6	39.1	27.7	8.8	0.8	76509
51536	HANCOCK	20389	213	26.8	31.0	32.4	6.6	3.3	41341	47575	51	44	168	18.5	25.0	36.3	13.7	6.6	96471
51537	HARLAN	21092	2741	25.9	31.2	32.7	7.9	2.3	44023	51348	59	59	2116	14.0	29.7	41.3	13.5	1.5	98261
51540	HASTINGS	19621	169	29.0	32.5	31.4	5.3	1.8	41578	48246	52	46	128	32.8	22.7	25.8	14.8	3.9	82222
51541	HENDERSON	25518	167	20.4	36.5	32.9	7.2	3.0	45511	52214	63	66	131	17.6	26.7	32.1	21.4	2.3	97500
51542	HONEY CREEK	26111	433	11.3	25.2	46.0	13.6	3.9	61148	72057	85	95	386	10.1	9.3	42.0	34.7	3.9	148438
51543	KIMBALLTON	18913	206	30.1	39.3	23.8	4.9	1.9	36805	42317	35	16	168	33.9	26.8	29.2	7.1	3.0	75714
51544	LEWIS	20731	330	25.2	36.7	30.3	6.1	1.8	38632	44705	42	26	266	35.3	38.4	19.2	6.8	0.4	65926
51545	LITTLE SIOUX	15634	215	37.7	38.1	20.5	2.8	0.9	31678	37178	17	4	155	46.5	32.3	14.2	6.5	0.7	53438
51546	LOGAN	21831	1205	23.7	34.3	33.1	6.5	2.4	44401	50973	60	60	969	15.4	25.8	42.8	14.3	1.7	101588
51548	MC CLELLAND	24504	255	18.8	22.4	41.2	12.9	4.7	57100	66022	82	93	207	3.9	8.2	37.7	44.4	5.8	175735
	IOWA	23554		24.6	30.5	32.9	8.4	3.7	45622	53985				17.5	26.2	39.3	15.0	2.1	98835
	UNITED STATES	25866		24.7	27.1	30.8	10.9	6.5	48124	56710				10.9	15.0	33.7	30.1	10.4	145905

ZIP CODE		FINANCIAL SERVICES				THE HOME						ENTERTAINMENT						PERSONAL			
						Home Improvements		Furnishings													
#	POST OFFICE NAME	Auto Loan	Home Loan	Investments	Retirement Plans	Home Repair	Lawn & Garden	Computers & Hardware	Major Appliances	TV, Radio, Sound Equipment	Furniture	Dine out/ Carry out	Sports Equipment	Fees & Tickets	Toys & Games	Travel	Cable TV	Apparel & Services	Auto Repairs	Health Insurance	Pets & Supplies
51231	ARCHER	87	64	38	61	73	80	63	75	70	62	83	91	55	82	65	73	77	74	87	102
51232	ASHTON	91	64	34	61	74	83	63	78	72	62	85	94	54	83	65	76	78	77	92	108
51234	BOYDEN	79	67	51	66	70	79	68	73	72	67	87	84	65	87	68	74	82	72	80	88
51235	DOON	81	68	49	65	74	80	64	73	69	64	83	87	61	84	66	71	79	71	80	95
51237	GEORGE	73	53	33	51	60	70	57	65	64	55	76	75	50	72	57	68	69	65	78	83
51238	HOSPERS	94	66	36	63	77	86	65	80	75	65	88	97	56	87	68	79	81	79	95	111
51239	HULL	93	67	38	64	77	86	66	80	75	66	89	97	58	87	68	78	81	79	94	110
51240	INWOOD	78	62	44	60	67	76	65	72	70	63	84	83	59	81	64	73	78	71	81	89
51241	LARCHWOOD	99	71	41	68	82	91	70	85	80	70	94	103	61	92	73	83	86	84	100	117
51243	LITTLE ROCK	81	56	29	53	66	73	56	69	64	55	75	83	48	74	58	67	69	68	82	96
51245	PRIMGHAR	80	58	36	56	65	76	63	71	71	60	83	82	55	79	63	74	76	71	85	90
51246	ROCK RAPIDS	85	62	36	59	70	79	63	74	71	62	84	88	55	81	64	75	77	74	88	98
51247	ROCK VALLEY	92	68	42	65	77	87	70	81	79	68	93	95	62	90	71	82	85	81	95	106
51248	SANBORN	79	62	44	60	67	78	67	73	73	64	87	83	60	83	66	77	80	73	85	89
51249	SIBLEY	76	62	47	60	68	76	62	70	68	61	82	81	59	83	64	71	76	69	79	88
51250	SIOUX CENTER	93	82	69	81	86	94	82	88	85	81	104	104	78	104	82	86	98	88	94	108
51301	SPENCER	84	71	59	70	76	84	73	79	77	72	94	93	69	93	73	78	88	79	86	96
51331	ARNOLDS PARK	100	78	53	71	88	99	74	89	84	73	99	104	66	98	79	89	92	88	105	122
51333	DICKENS	96	67	35	63	78	87	66	81	76	65	89	98	56	87	68	80	81	80	97	113
51334	ESTHERVILLE	73	60	48	59	64	73	64	68	68	62	82	79	59	80	63	70	77	68	76	82
51338	EVERLY	92	64	34	61	75	84	64	79	73	63	86	95	54	84	66	77	78	77	94	109
51342	GRAETTINGER	75	55	35	53	62	73	60	67	67	57	79	77	53	75	60	71	72	67	81	85
51343	GREENVILLE	139	97	51	92	113	127	96	119	110	95	130	143	82	127	99	116	118	117	141	165
51345	HARRIS	87	61	32	57	71	79	60	74	69	59	81	90	51	80	62	73	74	73	89	103
51346	HARTLEY	75	60	42	58	65	74	62	68	67	60	81	79	57	79	62	70	75	67	78	85
51347	LAKE PARK	80	59	37	57	66	78	64	72	72	61	85	83	57	81	64	76	78	72	87	90
51350	MELVIN	98	69	36	65	80	90	68	84	78	67	92	101	58	90	71	82	84	83	100	117
51351	MILFORD	93	74	53	71	81	91	74	84	81	73	97	98	68	96	76	84	90	83	95	107
51354	OCHEYEDAN	72	53	32	50	59	69	56	64	63	54	74	74	49	71	56	66	67	64	77	83
51355	OKOBOJI	115	90	62	82	102	114	85	103	96	84	114	120	76	113	91	103	106	101	121	140
51357	ROYAL	100	70	37	66	82	91	69	86	80	68	93	103	59	92	72	84	85	84	102	119
51358	RUTHVEN	78	57	34	54	64	74	60	69	68	58	80	80	53	76	60	72	73	69	83	89
51360	SPIRIT LAKE	108	80	50	75	91	103	80	95	91	78	107	111	70	104	83	96	98	94	113	127
51363	SUPERIOR	109	86	58	77	96	108	81	97	91	80	108	114	72	107	86	98	101	96	115	133
51364	TERRIL	101	72	39	67	83	93	70	87	81	70	95	104	61	93	73	85	87	86	103	121
51365	WALLINGFORD	89	62	33	59	72	81	61	76	71	61	83	91	52	81	64	74	76	75	90	106
51366	WEBB	87	60	32	57	70	79	60	74	69	59	81	89	51	79	62	72	74	73	88	103
51401	CARROLL	83	80	75	78	82	89	79	83	81	77	100	96	78	101	80	82	96	82	87	97
51430	ARCADIA	89	62	32	59	72	81	61	76	71	61	83	91	52	81	64	74	75	75	90	105
51431	ARTHUR	110	77	40	73	90	100	76	94	88	75	103	113	65	101	79	92	94	93	112	131
51432	ASPINWALL	84	58	31	55	68	76	58	71	67	57	78	86	49	77	60	70	71	70	85	99
51433	AUBURN	104	73	38	69	85	95	72	89	83	71	97	107	61	95	74	87	88	87	106	123
51436	BREDA	90	63	33	59	73	82	62	76	71	61	84	92	53	82	64	75	76	75	91	107
51439	CHARTER OAK	76	55	34	53	62	73	59	68	67	57	78	78	52	75	59	70	71	67	81	86
51440	DEDHAM	74	52	28	49	61	68	51	63	59	51	69	76	44	68	53	62	63	62	75	88
51441	DELOIT	90	63	33	59	73	82	62	77	72	61	84	93	53	82	65	75	77	76	92	107
51442	DENISON	74	62	51	60	65	74	65	69	70	63	84	80	61	84	65	72	79	69	77	83
51443	GLIDDEN	83	71	54	70	75	83	71	77	75	70	91	89	68	91	71	77	86	75	84	94
51444	HALBUR	101	70	37	66	82	92	69	86	80	69	94	103	59	92	72	84	85	85	102	119
51445	IDA GROVE	93	71	46	69	79	90	73	84	81	72	97	97	66	94	74	84	89	83	96	107
51446	IRWIN	79	55	29	52	64	72	54	67	63	54	73	81	46	72	56	66	67	66	80	94
51447	KIRKMAN	81	56	30	53	66	74	56	69	64	55	75	83	48	74	58	67	69	68	82	96
51448	KIRON	84	59	31	55	68	77	58	72	67	57	78	86	49	77	60	70	71	71	85	100
51449	LAKE CITY	73	54	34	52	60	71	59	66	66	56	78	75	52	74	59	70	71	66	79	83
51450	LAKE VIEW	78	59	38	55	66	76	60	70	68	58	80	81	53	77	62	72	73	69	83	92
51451	LANESBORO	82	57	30	54	67	75	57	70	65	56	76	84	48	75	59	68	70	69	83	97
51452	LIDDERDALE	100	70	37	66	81	91	69	85	79	68	93	103	59	91	72	83	85	84	102	119
51453	LOHRVILLE	81	56	29	53	66	73	56	69	64	55	75	83	47	74	58	67	68	68	82	96
51454	MANILLA	70	51	31	49	57	67	54	62	61	52	72	71	48	69	54	65	66	62	74	79
51455	MANNING	80	58	36	56	65	77	63	71	71	60	83	82	55	79	63	75	76	71	85	90
51458	ODEBOLT	77	56	33	53	63	73	58	68	66	56	77	79	50	74	59	69	71	67	81	89
51460	RICKETTS	84	59	31	55	68	77	58	72	67	57	78	86	50	77	60	70	71	71	85	100
51461	SCHLESWIG	71	53	33	50	58	69	57	64	64	54	76	73	50	72	57	68	69	64	77	80
51462	SCRANTON	73	51	27	48	59	67	50	62	58	50	68	75	43	67	52	61	62	61	74	86
51463	TEMPLETON	110	77	40	72	89	100	76	93	87	75	102	113	65	100	78	91	93	92	111	130
51465	VAIL	88	62	32	58	72	80	61	75	70	60	82	91	52	81	63	74	75	74	90	105
51466	WALL LAKE	77	57	36	55	63	75	61	69	69	59	81	79	54	77	61	73	74	69	83	87
51467	WESTSIDE	88	62	32	58	72	81	61	75	70	60	82	91	52	81	63	74	75	74	90	105
51501	COUNCIL BLUFFS	67	67	69	66	67	73	69	68	70	67	86	79	69	88	69	70	84	68	69	76
51503	COUNCIL BLUFFS	87	95	104	95	95	100	95	93	92	93	115	109	97	118	95	91	113	93	90	103
51510	CARTER LAKE	81	86	82	83	86	89	80	82	79	80	98	96	81	101	81	78	96	81	80	95
51520	ARION	77	54	28	51	63	70	53	66	61	53	72	79	46	71	55	64	66	65	79	92
51521	AVOCA	84	74	60	70	79	88	73	80	79	71	96	93	70	99	75	82	90	78	90	100
51523	BLENCOE	104	72	38	68	84	94	71	88	82	71	97	107	61	95	74	86	88	87	105	123
51525	CARSON	95	69	39	65	79	88	67	82	77	67	90	99	58	89	70	80	83	81	97	113
51526	CRESCENT	102	124	131	123	122	122	112	112	105	112	132	131	119	141	115	103	132	108	103	125
51527	DEFIANCE	83	58	30	54	67	75	57	70	66	56	77	85	49	75	59	69	70	69	84	98
51528	DOW CITY	72	56	39	55	62	69	57	65	63	56	75	75	53	74	58	64	70	64	73	82
51529	DUNLAP	75	71	64	68	74	83	71	74	75	69	92	84	71	96	72	78	87	73	81	87
51530	EARLING	84	58	31	55	68	76	58	71	67	57	78	86	49	76	60	70	71	70	85	99
51531	ELK HORN	85	63	41	61	69	83	70	77	78	66	92	87	62	87	69	83	84	77	92	94
51532	ELLIOTT	86	60	31	57	70	78	59	73	68	59	80	88	51	79	62	72	73	72	87	102
51533	EMERSON	94	66	35	62	76	85	65	80	75	64	88	96	56	86	67	78	80	79	95	111
51534	GLENWOOD	83	80	72	80	82	86	78	82	79	77	97	97	76	98	78	78	93	81	82	97
51535	GRISWOLD	82	59	34	56	67	77	61	72	69	59	81	84	53	78	62	73	74	71	86	95
51536	HANCOCK	93	66	36	63	76	85	65	80	74	65	88	96	56	86	67	78	80	79	94	110
51537	HARLAN	81	67	52	65	72	81	69	76	74	67	89	88	64	88	69	76	83	75	85	93
51540	HASTINGS	88	62	32	58	72	80	61	75	70	60	82	91	52	81	63	74	75	74	90	105
51541	HENDERSON	107	75	39	71	87	98	74	91	85	73	100	110	63	98	77	89	91	90	109	127
51542	HONEY CREEK	99	106	100	104	108	110	96	100	94	96	117	118	99	123	99	94	115	97	98	119
51543	KIMBALLTON	85	59	31	56	69	77	58	72	67	58	79	87	50	77	61	71	72	71	86	101
51544	LEWIS	90	63	33	60	74	82	62	77	72	62	84	93	53	83	65	75	77	76	92	107
51545	LITTLE SIOUX	63	47	31	45	52	62	52	57	58	50	69	64	47	65	52	62	63	57	69	69
51546	LOGAN	97	72	44	69	81	92	73	86	82	71	97	101	65	95	75	86	89	84	100	113
51548	MC CLELLAND	90	102	103	103	99	98	96	95	89	96	113	112	97	115	94	85	111	94	84	104
	IOWA	87	79	73	79	82	89	80	84	83	79	102	98	78	102	80	83	97	84	88	100
	UNITED STATES	100	100	100	100	100	100	100	100	100	100	100	100	100	100	100	100	100	100	100	100

ZIP CODE		POPULATION			2000-2004 ANNUAL RATE		HOUSEHOLDS					FAMILIES		
# POST OFFICE NAME	COUNTY FIPS CODE	2000	2004	2009	% Rate	State Centile	2000	2004	2009	% Annual Rate 2000-2004	2004 Average HH Size	2000	2004	% Annual Rate 2000-2004
51549 MACEDONIA	155	513	501	507	-0.6	20	199	196	200	-0.4	2.56	150	147	-0.5
51551 MALVERN	129	1880	1884	1911	0.1	52	725	736	754	0.4	2.46	512	518	0.3
51552 MARNE	029	283	279	278	-0.3	31	107	107	108	0.0	2.60	83	83	0.0
51553 MINDEN	155	927	955	987	0.7	74	357	373	389	1.0	2.56	270	280	0.9
51555 MISSOURI VALLEY	085	5311	5197	5191	-0.5	23	2073	2045	2059	-0.3	2.48	1451	1431	-0.3
51556 MODALE	085	531	545	552	0.6	71	224	231	235	0.7	2.36	170	175	0.7
51557 MONDAMIN	085	854	999	1083	3.8	98	337	398	435	4.0	2.51	248	291	3.8
51558 MOORHEAD	133	520	573	603	2.3	93	225	252	269	2.7	2.27	161	179	2.5
51559 NEOLA	155	1775	1739	1774	-0.5	24	671	667	688	-0.1	2.61	508	502	-0.3
51560 OAKLAND	155	2124	2204	2302	0.9	78	843	886	936	1.2	2.42	593	621	1.1
51561 PACIFIC JUNCTION	129	1494	1633	1730	2.1	92	568	628	671	2.4	2.60	449	494	2.3
51562 PANAMA	165	476	467	460	-0.5	25	186	185	184	-0.1	2.52	135	133	-0.4
51563 PERSIA	085	867	866	865	0.0	47	312	315	317	0.2	2.75	253	254	0.1
51564 PISGAH	085	676	769	822	3.1	96	279	319	343	3.2	2.41	194	220	3.0
51565 PORTSMOUTH	165	622	606	595	-0.6	18	235	231	228	-0.4	2.62	178	174	-0.5
51566 RED OAK	137	7468	7343	7252	-0.4	27	3163	3123	3097	-0.3	2.30	2047	2011	-0.4
51570 SHELBY	165	1201	1213	1213	0.2	60	459	469	472	0.5	2.57	327	332	0.4
51571 SILVER CITY	129	632	607	612	-1.0	7	250	242	246	-0.8	2.51	196	188	-1.0
51572 SOLDIER	133	546	553	556	0.3	63	241	247	250	0.6	2.24	158	161	0.4
51573 STANTON	137	1168	1187	1191	0.4	66	451	464	470	0.7	2.46	329	336	0.5
51575 TREYNOR	155	15	15	16	0.0	51	4	4	4	0.0	3.75	3	3	0.0
51576 UNDERWOOD	155	1534	1589	1668	0.8	76	548	568	599	0.9	2.80	420	433	0.7
51577 WALNUT	155	1209	1144	1149	-1.3	2	475	455	462	-1.0	2.51	351	335	-1.1
51578 WESTPHALIA	165	232	230	227	-0.2	38	85	85	85	0.0	2.71	60	60	0.0
51579 WOODBINE	085	2386	2324	2322	-0.6	18	929	909	915	-0.5	2.48	644	626	-0.7
51601 SHENANDOAH	145	6297	6104	5924	-0.7	15	2717	2661	2611	-0.5	2.23	1714	1671	-0.6
51630 BLANCHARD	145	194	204	205	1.2	82	81	87	89	1.7	2.34	60	64	1.5
51631 BRADDYVILLE	145	400	387	375	-0.8	13	157	154	152	-0.5	2.51	121	119	-0.4
51632 CLARINDA	145	7554	7422	7264	-0.4	27	2749	2719	2677	-0.3	2.28	1809	1781	-0.4
51636 COIN	145	471	533	557	3.0	96	194	224	237	3.4	2.38	141	162	3.3
51637 COLLEGE SPRINGS	145	279	270	261	-0.8	13	103	101	99	-0.5	2.67	79	78	-0.3
51638 ESSEX	145	1495	1420	1365	-1.2	3	597	575	559	-0.9	2.47	452	433	-1.0
51639 FARRAGUT	071	1016	1053	1084	0.9	77	416	435	452	1.1	2.42	299	312	1.0
51640 HAMBURG	071	1816	1898	1970	1.0	80	761	805	843	1.3	2.35	517	543	1.2
51645 IMOGENE	071	262	253	254	-0.8	11	109	107	108	-0.4	2.36	78	76	-0.6
51646 NEW MARKET	173	822	820	819	-0.1	46	357	359	361	0.1	2.28	254	255	0.1
51647 NORTHBORO	145	253	270	276	1.5	87	103	112	116	2.0	2.41	75	81	1.8
51648 PERCIVAL	071	278	299	312	1.7	89	114	124	131	2.0	2.41	82	89	2.0
51649 RANDOLPH	071	430	416	417	-0.8	13	162	158	160	-0.6	2.61	115	112	-0.6
51650 RIVERTON	071	398	386	388	-0.7	15	167	164	166	-0.4	2.35	114	111	-0.6
51651 SHAMBAUGH	145	31	30	29	-0.8	13	12	12	12	0.0	2.50	9	9	0.0
51652 SIDNEY	071	1972	1958	1971	-0.2	39	756	754	763	-0.1	2.47	535	532	-0.1
51653 TABOR	071	1370	1370	1384	0.0	51	529	532	543	0.1	2.45	376	378	0.1
51654 THURMAN	071	532	575	602	1.9	90	209	228	241	2.1	2.52	151	165	2.1
51656 YORKTOWN	145	67	65	62	-0.7	16	24	23	23	-1.0	2.83	19	19	0.0
52001 DUBUQUE	061	43992	43320	43380	-0.4	29	17340	17363	17691	0.0	2.28	10653	10581	-0.2
52002 DUBUQUE	061	11681	12408	12873	1.4	86	4284	4632	4891	1.9	2.65	3246	3502	1.8
52003 DUBUQUE	061	13446	14160	14613	1.2	83	4960	5317	5583	1.7	2.57	3718	3971	1.6
52030 ANDREW	097	435	441	442	0.3	64	157	162	164	0.7	2.67	123	126	0.6
52031 BELLEVUE	097	5018	5037	5054	0.1	54	1875	1911	1946	0.5	2.59	1388	1410	0.4
52032 BERNARD	097	1320	1404	1450	1.5	86	497	544	574	2.2	2.58	362	393	2.0
52033 CASCADE	105	3024	3078	3112	0.4	67	1119	1160	1192	0.9	2.59	809	835	0.8
52035 COLESBURG	043	1039	1060	1074	0.5	68	402	418	430	0.9	2.54	311	323	0.9
52036 DELAWARE	055	51	50	51	-0.5	25	19	19	19	0.0	2.63	15	15	0.0
52037 DELMAR	045	1371	1415	1426	0.8	75	505	526	536	1.0	2.68	394	409	0.9
52038 DUNDEE	055	525	589	632	2.7	95	195	222	242	3.1	2.65	157	178	3.0
52039 DURANGO	061	947	926	926	-0.5	22	320	321	328	0.1	2.88	265	265	0.0
52040 DYERSVILLE	055	5242	5187	5183	-0.3	36	1971	1976	2004	0.1	2.60	1457	1452	-0.1
52041 EARLVILLE	055	1756	1768	1793	0.2	57	604	617	633	0.5	2.86	458	466	0.4
52042 EDGEWOOD	043	1678	1695	1703	0.2	61	590	601	612	0.4	2.73	450	457	0.4
52043 ELKADER	043	2416	2365	2323	-0.5	23	995	987	982	-0.2	2.29	672	663	-0.3
52044 ELKPORT	043	238	262	273	2.3	93	95	107	113	2.8	2.45	64	71	2.5
52045 EPWORTH	061	2181	2283	2341	1.1	81	716	769	804	1.7	2.82	565	602	1.5
52046 FARLEY	061	2144	2089	2080	-0.6	18	739	737	748	-0.1	2.82	564	558	-0.3
52047 FARMERSBURG	043	675	665	655	-0.4	30	266	266	265	0.0	2.50	202	201	-0.1
52048 GARBER	043	342	368	378	1.7	89	143	158	165	2.4	2.33	102	113	2.4
52049 GARNAVILLO	043	1323	1241	1202	-1.5	1	552	525	514	-1.2	2.28	368	347	-1.4
52050 GREELEY	055	621	608	612	-0.5	23	230	229	234	-0.1	2.65	180	179	-0.1
52052 GUTTENBERG	043	3420	3431	3420	0.1	53	1365	1389	1402	0.4	2.37	937	950	0.3
52053 HOLY CROSS	061	1229	1161	1142	-1.3	2	434	419	420	-0.8	2.77	352	338	-1.0
52054 LA MOTTE	097	1064	1181	1246	2.5	94	373	422	453	3.0	2.64	301	340	2.9
52057 MANCHESTER	055	8409	8528	8710	0.3	64	3234	3321	3437	0.6	2.52	2257	2312	0.6
52060 MAQUOKETA	097	8714	8680	8674	-0.1	44	3581	3610	3656	0.2	2.35	2336	2344	0.1
52064 MILES	097	820	838	846	0.5	69	314	327	337	1.0	2.56	229	238	0.9
52065 NEW VIENNA	061	1200	1134	1126	-1.3	2	434	418	423	-0.9	2.71	344	330	-1.0
52068 PEOSTA	061	2299	2544	2682	2.4	94	776	879	945	3.0	2.87	659	743	2.9
52069 PRESTON	097	1561	1509	1494	-0.8	12	637	629	633	-0.3	2.38	426	418	-0.5
52070 SABULA	097	1172	1156	1151	-0.3	32	525	529	536	0.2	2.19	350	351	0.1
52071 SAINT DONATUS	097	105	106	107	0.2	59	42	43	44	0.6	2.47	33	34	0.7
52072 SAINT OLAF	043	395	385	377	-0.6	19	147	145	144	-0.3	2.61	116	114	-0.4
52073 SHERRILL	061	1373	1349	1344	-0.4	27	469	471	477	0.1	2.86	395	394	-0.1
52074 SPRAGUEVILLE	097	355	342	338	-0.9	9	131	129	130	-0.4	2.64	106	104	-0.5
52076 STRAWBERRY POINT	043	2325	2292	2262	-0.3	31	848	844	842	-0.1	2.57	596	592	-0.2
52077 VOLGA	043	462	444	433	-0.9	8	177	172	170	-0.7	2.58	128	124	-0.7
52078 WORTHINGTON	061	950	907	901	-1.1	5	310	302	305	-0.6	2.97	244	237	-0.7
52079 ZWINGLE	097	851	864	869	0.4	64	316	329	337	1.0	2.63	241	249	0.8
52101 DECORAH	191	13792	13941	14126	0.3	61	4854	4966	5098	0.5	2.35	3158	3224	0.5
52132 CALMAR	191	2553	2537	2538	-0.2	42	1047	1060	1075	0.3	2.39	703	707	0.1
52133 CASTALIA	191	687	713	725	0.9	78	254	270	279	1.5	2.63	188	198	1.2
52134 CHESTER	089	513	500	496	-0.6	19	194	191	191	-0.4	2.62	142	139	-0.5
52135 CLERMONT	065	908	953	972	1.1	82	374	397	409	1.4	2.40	253	266	1.2
52136 CRESCO	089	6053	6095	6122	0.2	57	2430	2466	2498	0.4	2.40	1562	1581	0.3
52140 DORCHESTER	005	698	702	723	0.1	56	272	278	289	0.5	2.52	201	204	0.4
52141 ELGIN	065	1526	1499	1482	-0.4	26	619	615	616	-0.2	2.43	407	402	-0.3
52142 FAYETTE	065	1949	1983	1995	0.4	66	595	617	629	0.9	2.46	394	406	0.7
IOWA					0.5					0.7	2.43			0.6
UNITED STATES					1.2					1.3	2.58			1.1

#	POST OFFICE NAME	RACE (%) White 2000	White 2004	Black 2000	Black 2004	Asian/Pacific 2000	Asian/Pacific 2004	% Hispanic Origin 2000	% Hispanic Origin 2004	2004 AGE DISTRIBUTION (%) 0-4	5-9	10-14	15-19	20-24	25-44	45-64	65-84	85+	18+	MEDIAN AGE 2004	% 2004 Males	% 2004 Females
51549	MACEDONIA	98.3	98.2	0.0	0.0	0.2	0.2	0.4	0.4	5.2	5.6	7.6	7.0	6.6	24.4	28.1	13.8	1.8	77.5	41.4	51.1	48.9
51551	MALVERN	98.7	98.6	0.1	0.1	0.1	0.2	0.6	0.8	5.9	6.1	7.1	7.1	5.7	22.7	27.1	15.1	3.2	76.0	41.8	49.5	50.5
51552	MARNE	98.9	98.9	0.0	0.0	0.4	0.4	0.0	0.4	5.0	5.0	7.5	6.5	5.7	22.9	33.0	12.5	1.8	78.1	43.6	51.6	48.4
51553	MINDEN	99.2	99.2	0.0	0.0	0.1	0.1	0.5	0.6	6.3	6.7	7.6	7.3	6.0	26.6	26.5	11.6	1.4	74.8	38.2	50.4	49.6
51555	MISSOURI VALLEY	98.9	98.7	0.0	0.0	0.1	0.2	0.8	0.9	6.2	6.2	7.2	6.5	6.2	26.5	25.1	13.4	2.7	76.5	39.5	48.7	51.3
51556	MODALE	98.1	97.8	0.0	0.0	0.2	0.4	0.2	0.4	6.8	7.0	7.2	6.2	5.7	24.4	27.9	13.4	1.5	75.2	40.4	52.5	47.5
51557	MONDAMIN	98.2	98.1	0.0	0.0	0.2	0.3	1.3	1.6	5.4	5.9	7.5	7.2	5.1	25.6	28.9	13.0	1.3	76.6	41.5	50.8	49.3
51558	MOORHEAD	99.0	99.3	0.0	0.0	0.6	0.5	0.0	0.0	5.2	5.9	7.5	5.6	4.9	22.7	28.5	18.0	1.8	77.7	43.8	51.3	48.7
51559	NEOLA	98.7	98.3	0.2	0.2	0.4	0.6	0.7	0.9	7.1	7.4	7.4	6.7	6.2	26.7	25.1	11.6	1.8	74.0	37.6	48.7	51.3
51560	OAKLAND	98.5	98.2	0.3	0.4	0.2	0.3	0.4	0.5	5.6	6.0	7.3	7.0	5.9	24.4	24.6	15.4	3.7	76.7	41.1	48.6	51.4
51561	PACIFIC JUNCTION	98.1	97.8	0.1	0.1	0.5	0.7	1.1	1.4	5.8	6.6	7.8	7.1	5.5	25.8	31.6	8.8	1.1	75.1	39.9	52.0	48.0
51562	PANAMA	99.2	99.1	0.0	0.0	0.2	0.2	0.2	0.2	6.6	8.4	8.8	6.4	3.2	27.0	21.4	16.3	1.9	71.7	38.9	49.5	50.5
51563	PERSIA	99.4	99.3	0.4	0.4	0.1	0.2	0.7	0.9	6.9	7.4	8.1	7.3	5.8	24.5	26.1	12.2	1.7	73.1	39.3	50.9	49.1
51564	PISGAH	98.7	98.6	0.3	0.3	0.2	0.3	0.9	1.0	5.6	5.7	7.5	7.9	5.9	23.5	24.8	16.4	2.6	76.2	41.4	49.2	50.9
51565	PORTSMOUTH	99.2	99.2	0.0	0.0	0.2	0.2	0.3	0.3	8.1	8.1	7.6	5.6	5.3	26.2	22.1	16.0	1.0	72.6	39.3	51.0	49.0
51566	RED OAK	97.7	97.2	0.1	0.1	0.4	0.5	1.9	2.2	6.7	6.3	6.9	6.5	6.1	23.7	24.9	15.3	3.7	76.1	40.4	46.7	53.3
51570	SHELBY	98.7	98.4	0.0	0.0	0.2	0.3	0.8	0.9	6.5	6.8	7.8	6.2	5.4	25.4	26.0	14.1	1.9	74.9	40.1	50.7	49.3
51571	SILVER CITY	98.4	98.0	0.3	0.3	0.5	0.5	1.1	1.3	6.9	7.3	8.1	6.6	5.3	25.5	28.5	10.5	1.3	73.5	39.7	51.2	48.8
51572	SOLDIER	98.2	98.2	0.6	0.5	0.0	0.0	0.4	0.4	5.2	5.6	6.5	5.4	5.2	22.4	29.5	17.4	2.7	79.8	44.7	51.4	48.6
51573	STANTON	99.1	99.1	0.0	0.0	0.1	0.1	0.4	0.6	4.6	6.8	8.3	7.2	3.9	24.3	25.1	15.1	4.9	75.4	41.9	48.5	51.5
51575	TREYNOR	100.0	100.0	0.0	0.0	0.0	0.0	0.0	0.0	6.7	13.3	13.3	13.3	0.0	26.7	26.7	0.0	0.0	66.7	36.3	46.7	53.3
51576	UNDERWOOD	98.4	98.2	0.1	0.1	0.3	0.5	0.9	1.1	7.4	7.6	8.1	6.7	6.2	26.9	26.1	10.2	1.0	72.9	37.6	49.7	50.4
51577	WALNUT	98.3	98.0	0.4	0.4	0.3	0.4	0.8	1.0	6.4	6.8	7.6	6.6	4.9	22.7	27.7	15.3	2.0	75.2	41.8	49.9	50.1
51578	WESTPHALIA	99.1	99.1	0.0	0.0	0.0	0.0	0.0	0.0	6.1	8.7	9.6	7.0	2.2	27.4	21.7	15.2	2.2	70.4	38.5	48.7	51.3
51579	WOODBINE	98.4	98.1	0.1	0.1	0.3	0.5	0.7	0.7	6.5	7.0	7.1	6.7	5.9	24.0	22.2	16.1	4.4	75.0	40.3	48.8	51.3
51601	SHENANDOAH	97.9	97.5	0.1	0.2	0.2	0.3	2.5	3.0	6.2	6.1	6.2	5.9	6.0	23.2	24.6	17.7	4.1	77.9	42.3	47.2	52.8
51630	BLANCHARD	97.9	98.0	0.0	0.0	0.5	0.5	1.6	1.5	4.9	5.9	6.4	6.9	5.9	25.0	26.5	16.7	2.0	78.4	42.1	52.0	48.0
51631	BRADDYVILLE	99.3	99.0	0.0	0.0	0.3	0.3	0.3	0.3	6.7	7.5	7.8	6.5	5.2	22.5	28.9	14.0	1.0	73.6	40.8	50.4	49.6
51632	CLARINDA	93.6	92.7	3.6	3.9	0.9	1.3	1.2	1.5	4.9	5.0	6.1	8.0	7.1	27.2	23.5	14.7	3.7	78.2	39.4	54.0	46.0
51636	COIN	99.6	99.6	0.0	0.0	0.0	0.0	0.4	0.6	3.8	4.3	6.6	7.1	6.2	24.4	28.1	17.3	2.3	80.9	43.6	49.2	50.8
51637	COLLEGE SPRINGS	99.3	99.6	0.0	0.0	0.0	0.0	0.0	0.0	7.0	7.0	7.4	6.7	5.6	21.5	30.0	14.1	0.7	74.1	41.3	51.1	48.9
51638	ESSEX	98.1	98.0	0.1	0.1	0.0	0.0	0.5	0.6	6.7	7.0	6.5	5.8	4.7	24.4	28.9	13.9	2.1	76.2	41.6	50.5	49.5
51639	FARRAGUT	98.1	98.0	0.0	0.0	0.3	0.4	1.1	1.2	4.1	5.0	8.0	7.3	5.3	22.5	27.3	17.5	3.0	78.2	43.7	49.6	50.4
51640	HAMBURG	97.1	96.5	0.1	0.1	0.4	0.6	4.0	4.7	6.1	6.3	6.8	6.0	5.4	23.9	25.6	17.1	2.9	77.1	41.8	48.8	51.2
51645	IMOGENE	98.5	98.0	0.0	0.0	0.0	0.4	0.8	0.8	6.7	6.7	7.5	6.7	5.1	23.3	27.7	14.2	2.0	74.3	41.1	51.8	48.2
51646	NEW MARKET	98.5	98.3	0.0	0.0	0.2	0.2	1.3	1.5	5.5	6.2	8.5	6.6	5.1	24.9	24.5	16.2	2.4	75.5	40.0	49.3	50.7
51647	NORTHBORO	97.6	97.4	0.0	0.0	0.4	0.4	1.6	1.9	4.4	5.2	6.7	7.0	5.6	24.8	26.3	17.4	2.6	79.3	42.8	52.2	47.8
51648	PERCIVAL	97.1	96.3	0.0	0.0	0.4	0.3	3.2	3.7	5.4	6.7	8.0	6.4	3.7	27.1	29.4	12.4	1.0	75.6	41.5	50.8	49.2
51649	RANDOLPH	98.6	98.1	0.0	0.0	0.2	0.2	0.7	1.0	6.5	6.7	7.5	7.2	5.5	23.3	26.7	14.4	2.2	75.0	40.8	51.0	49.0
51650	RIVERTON	99.0	99.0	0.0	0.0	0.3	0.3	2.0	2.1	4.2	6.7	7.8	8.3	8.0	22.5	25.1	15.3	2.1	75.9	41.1	53.4	46.6
51651	SHAMBAUGH	96.8	100.0	0.0	0.0	0.0	0.0	0.0	0.0	6.7	6.7	6.7	6.7	6.7	26.7	26.7	13.3	0.0	80.0	37.5	50.0	50.0
51652	SIDNEY	98.3	98.1	0.1	0.1	0.2	0.3	2.0	2.4	6.4	6.6	7.0	6.5	5.6	22.8	25.6	15.9	3.7	75.8	41.7	49.1	50.9
51653	TABOR	98.9	98.8	0.0	0.0	0.1	0.2	1.2	1.4	5.4	6.0	6.5	6.4	5.5	21.4	27.5	16.9	4.6	77.7	44.2	47.4	52.6
51654	THURMAN	97.0	96.5	0.0	0.0	0.2	0.4	3.2	3.7	5.4	6.8	8.2	6.4	3.7	26.6	29.6	12.4	1.0	74.8	41.4	50.6	49.4
51656	YORKTOWN	97.0	98.5	0.0	0.0	0.0	0.0	0.0	0.0	6.2	6.2	6.2	4.6	4.6	26.2	29.2	13.9	3.1	81.5	42.5	50.8	49.2
52001	DUBUQUE	95.9	95.2	1.4	1.5	0.6	0.9	1.9	2.3	6.2	5.9	6.2	7.5	9.2	25.7	22.7	13.5	3.1	78.0	36.9	47.5	52.5
52002	DUBUQUE	97.2	96.5	0.6	0.6	1.3	1.8	0.8	0.9	7.3	7.6	8.0	6.8	5.9	26.9	26.7	9.6	1.3	72.8	37.0	49.2	50.9
52003	DUBUQUE	98.3	98.0	0.4	0.4	0.5	0.6	0.6	0.6	6.5	6.9	7.7	6.7	5.6	24.8	27.0	12.8	2.0	74.4	40.0	48.2	51.8
52030	ANDREW	99.3	99.3	0.0	0.0	0.0	0.0	0.9	1.4	6.4	6.6	8.2	7.3	5.9	26.5	25.6	12.2	1.4	73.9	38.5	49.7	50.3
52031	BELLEVUE	99.5	99.5	0.0	0.0	0.1	0.1	0.3	0.3	6.0	6.5	7.9	7.0	5.7	24.8	25.3	14.5	2.3	74.9	40.2	50.3	49.7
52032	BERNARD	99.6	99.7	0.1	0.1	0.0	0.0	0.1	0.1	5.4	6.6	8.4	7.2	4.9	25.4	29.1	11.9	1.2	74.8	40.6	53.6	46.4
52033	CASCADE	99.4	99.3	0.0	0.0	0.1	0.1	0.5	0.7	7.5	7.9	7.7	6.3	5.7	26.8	24.0	11.9	2.3	72.8	37.0	51.7	48.3
52035	COLESBURG	99.5	99.4	0.0	0.0	0.1	0.1	0.6	0.7	7.1	7.3	8.5	6.6	5.7	25.3	25.9	12.5	1.3	72.8	38.2	51.0	49.0
52036	DELAWARE	100.0	100.0	0.0	0.0	0.0	0.0	0.0	0.0	8.0	8.0	8.0	8.0	8.0	28.0	18.0	14.0	0.0	76.0	32.5	50.0	50.0
52037	DELMAR	99.1	98.9	0.1	0.1	0.1	0.1	0.4	0.6	5.9	7.6	9.1	7.7	4.5	26.2	25.4	12.4	1.4	72.4	38.3	50.0	50.0
52038	DUNDEE	99.1	98.8	0.0	0.0	0.0	0.2	0.8	0.9	6.6	7.1	9.2	7.0	5.8	25.5	25.5	11.9	1.5	72.5	38.2	49.9	50.1
52039	DURANGO	98.9	98.9	0.4	0.4	0.1	0.1	0.5	0.5	7.3	7.8	8.9	8.1	5.4	26.7	25.7	9.5	0.7	70.8	36.5	53.7	46.3
52040	DYERSVILLE	99.0	98.8	0.4	0.4	0.2	0.3	0.4	0.5	8.2	7.7	7.7	6.7	6.2	26.1	22.0	13.4	2.1	72.2	36.7	49.3	50.7
52041	EARLVILLE	99.2	99.1	0.1	0.1	0.1	0.2	0.8	0.9	6.8	7.1	8.4	8.0	6.6	26.9	23.3	11.7	1.2	72.7	36.6	51.0	49.0
52042	EDGEWOOD	99.3	99.2	0.0	0.0	0.2	0.2	0.4	0.5	6.3	6.7	8.3	7.0	6.1	24.0	25.3	13.3	3.2	74.0	39.7	49.0	51.0
52043	ELKADER	99.1	99.0	0.2	0.2	0.0	0.0	0.1	0.1	4.7	5.0	6.6	6.3	5.4	21.1	28.7	17.7	4.5	79.5	45.5	47.7	52.3
52044	ELKPORT	98.3	98.5	0.0	0.0	0.4	0.8	0.4	0.4	7.3	8.0	7.6	5.3	5.0	27.5	26.3	11.1	1.9	74.1	38.0	53.1	47.0
52045	EPWORTH	95.3	93.8	0.4	0.4	3.4	4.8	0.5	0.6	7.2	7.7	8.1	6.8	7.3	29.7	23.2	9.4	0.7	72.5	34.7	52.7	47.3
52046	FARLEY	99.0	98.8	0.1	0.1	0.3	0.4	0.7	0.8	8.1	8.3	8.0	7.3	6.1	27.7	22.6	10.7	1.3	70.8	34.4	50.8	49.2
52047	FARMERSBURG	99.3	99.3	0.0	0.0	0.2	0.2	0.7	0.9	6.5	7.4	8.4	6.6	5.0	26.3	25.3	12.9	1.7	73.2	39.1	52.5	47.5
52048	GARBER	98.8	98.6	0.0	0.0	0.3	0.5	0.3	0.3	7.3	8.2	8.4	6.0	5.4	26.6	26.1	10.3	1.6	72.3	36.8	52.5	47.6
52049	GARNAVILLO	99.7	99.6	0.3	0.3	0.0	0.0	0.5	0.7	4.3	4.6	5.5	6.6	5.8	21.7	28.9	18.9	3.9	81.4	46.0	50.9	49.1
52050	GREELEY	99.4	99.3	0.3	0.3	0.0	0.0	0.5	0.7	6.9	7.1	8.1	6.9	6.7	27.6	24.0	11.5	1.2	73.7	36.9	51.2	48.9
52052	GUTTENBERG	99.0	98.9	0.3	0.3	0.2	0.2	0.5	0.6	5.3	5.8	6.4	6.0	4.9	22.9	27.5	17.4	3.9	78.7	44.2	49.2	50.8
52053	HOLY CROSS	99.1	99.0	0.2	0.3	0.1	0.1	0.7	0.9	6.9	7.8	8.9	7.6	5.6	25.8	26.4	10.1	1.0	71.4	37.2	53.4	46.6
52054	LA MOTTE	98.8	98.9	0.0	0.0	0.0	0.1	0.0	0.1	7.2	7.4	7.6	6.6	5.9	26.0	26.3	12.0	1.0	73.7	38.8	51.9	48.1
52057	MANCHESTER	99.2	99.1	0.1	0.1	0.2	0.3	0.8	0.9	6.4	6.6	7.9	7.3	6.6	25.0	23.5	14.1	2.6	74.5	38.6	48.4	51.6
52060	MAQUOKETA	98.4	98.3	0.1	0.1	0.4	0.4	1.0	1.0	6.1	6.3	7.1	6.9	6.3	24.2	24.7	15.0	3.5	76.3	40.4	48.0	52.0
52064	MILES	98.9	99.1	0.1	0.1	0.0	0.0	0.0	0.0	6.7	7.0	6.9	6.0	4.9	25.9	27.3	13.5	1.8	75.9	41.0	50.6	49.4
52065	NEW VIENNA	99.9	99.7	0.0	0.0	0.1	0.1	0.1	0.3	7.0	7.9	7.7	6.2	5.7	25.7	25.1	13.0	1.8	73.4	38.1	52.8	47.2
52068	PEOSTA	99.3	99.1	0.1	0.2	0.2	0.3	0.4	0.6	8.7	9.2	8.9	6.1	5.0	28.0	25.4	8.2	0.5	69.2	35.7	50.2	49.8
52069	PRESTON	99.6	99.5	0.2	0.2	0.2	0.2	0.2	0.2	6.0	5.8	6.4	6.4	6.5	28.0	25.0	13.5	2.3	77.5	39.5	50.3	49.7
52070	SABULA	99.3	99.3	0.0	0.0	0.0	0.0	0.7	0.7	6.0	6.1	6.2	4.8	5.5	23.5	28.6	17.0	2.4	79.1	43.6	49.7	50.4
52071	SAINT DONATUS	100.0	100.0	0.0	0.0	0.0	0.0	0.0	0.0	6.6	6.6	8.5	6.6	6.6	24.5	26.4	14.2	0.0	72.6	40.0	54.7	45.3
52072	SAINT OLAF	99.8	100.0	0.0	0.0	0.0	0.0	0.3	0.0	6.8	7.3	8.1	7.3	5.2	23.6	27.8	12.7	1.3	73.8	39.5	53.3	46.8
52073	SHERRILL	99.1	99.0	0.3	0.3	0.0	0.0	0.7	0.8	7.3	7.4	7.6	6.8	5.6	27.4	26.0	11.2	0.7	73.6	37.9	52.6	47.4
52074	SPRAGUEVILLE	99.2	99.4	0.3	0.3	0.0	0.0	0.3	0.3	6.1	6.7	7.6	7.3	5.6	25.4	26.6	13.5	1.2	74.6	40.0	52.3	47.7
52076	STRAWBERRY POINT	98.9	98.8	0.0	0.1	0.0	0.0	0.6	0.7	6.6	6.9	7.5	7.0	5.9	23.3	24.0	14.2	4.6	74.2	39.8	48.2	51.8
52077	VOLGA	97.0	96.9	0.0	0.0	0.0	0.0	0.7	0.9	7.4	7.7	8.3	6.8	4.7	23.4	27.7	11.9	2.0	71.9	39.2	49.6	50.5
52078	WORTHINGTON	99.7	99.8	0.0	0.0	0.0	0.0	0.3	0.3	7.1	6.6	8.2	9.7	5.1	25.8	25.6	10.4	1.7	71.6	36.9	51.3	48.7
52079	ZWINGLE	99.2	99.2	0.1	0.1	0.2	0.2	0.5	0.5	6.6	6.7	8.7	8.0	5.2	26.5	28.2	9.1	0.9	72.6	38.3	52.3	47.7
52101	DECORAH	97.2	96.5	0.7	0.8	1.1	1.6	0.9	1.1	4.7	4.8	5.7	10.8	15.0	21.1	22.6	12.3	3.1	81.3	34.7	47.9	52.1
52132	CALMAR	98.9	98.7	0.1	0.1	0.4	0.5	0.5	0.6	6.9	6.8	7.7	6.5	6.7	27.4	23.1	12.9	2.0	74.5	37.4	52.0	48.0
52133	CASTALIA	98.5	98.3	0.0	0.0	0.4	0.6	1.3	1.4	5.8	6.6	7.4	6.3	5.1	26.4	27.8	13.0	1.7	76.2	40.5	53.2	46.8
52134	CHESTER	99.4	99.2	0.0	0.0	0.2	0.2	0.4	0.4	5.6	5.8	9.4	7.0	6.4	24.4	25.0	14.4	2.0	74.8	39.7	51.0	49.0
52135	CLERMONT	97.9	98.1	0.0	0.0	0.0	0.0	2.5	2.6	6.1	6.6	7.7	6.4	5.8	25.4	24.6	15.3	2.2	75.8	40.0	51.3	48.7
52136	CRESCO	98.9	98.9	0.2	0.2	0.2	0.2	0.7	0.7	6.6	6.6	7.4	6.4	5.5	24.9	23.4	15.5	3.7	75.2	40.0	49.1	50.9
52140	DORCHESTER	98.7	98.6	0.0	0.0	0.1	0.1	0.7	0.9	5.8	6.7	7.7	7.1	4.6	24.4	31.5	11.0	1.3	74.9	41.1	53.0	47.0
52141	ELGIN	99.3	99.2	0.1	0.1	0.1	0.1	0.8	0.8	6.1	6.5	7.1	6.5	5.5	23.3	25.4	16.3	3.4	76.0	41.6	50.1	49.9
52142	FAYETTE	92.3	92.3	3.5	3.5	1.7	1.8	2.1	2.2	5.5	4.9	5.2	9.3	19.7	19.8	19.8	12.8	3.0	81.4	30.2	52.7	47.3
	IOWA	93.9	93.0	2.1	2.3	1.3	1.8	2.8	3.2	6.5	6.5	6.9	7.2	7.6	26.4	24.2	12.3	2.4	76.0	37.2	49.2	50.8
	UNITED STATES	75.1	73.6	12.3	12.5	3.8	4.2	12.5	14.1	6.9	6.7	7.2	7.0	7.3	28.6	23.8	10.8	1.7	75.1	36.0	49.1	50.9

ZIP CODE #	POST OFFICE NAME	2004 Per Capita Income	2004 HH Income Base	2004 Household Income Distribution (%): Less than $25,000	$25,000 to $49,999	$50,000 to $99,999	$100,000 to $149,999	$150,000 or More	Median Household Income: 2004	2009	2004 National Centile	2004 State Centile	2004 Home Value Base	2004 Home Value Distribution (%): Less than $50,000	$50,000 to $89,999	$90,000 to $174,999	$175,000 to $399,999	$400,000 or More	2004 Median Home Value
51549	MACEDONIA	18880	196	28.6	30.6	33.7	6.1	1.0	41518	46993	51	45	156	14.7	25.6	43.0	16.0	0.6	107813
51551	MALVERN	21041	736	28.8	29.5	32.1	6.8	2.9	43164	50985	56	54	562	18.5	31.1	37.0	11.7	1.6	90417
51552	MARNE	19340	107	19.6	43.0	29.9	7.5	0.0	42298	49304	54	50	87	16.1	27.6	39.1	16.1	1.2	96111
51553	MINDEN	23008	373	20.6	26.8	39.7	10.7	2.1	52356	59860	76	87	307	7.2	13.7	53.8	24.1	1.3	122575
51555	MISSOURI VALLEY	21961	2045	22.8	30.0	36.8	8.1	2.3	47677	56130	68	75	1517	14.4	24.7	40.7	18.8	1.5	104346
51556	MODALE	24260	231	17.8	39.4	31.2	9.1	2.6	45582	51575	63	66	192	17.7	24.5	33.3	23.4	1.0	105000
51557	MONDAMIN	23539	398	21.1	33.7	35.7	6.5	3.0	47183	54011	67	73	333	19.8	29.4	33.3	14.7	2.7	91087
51558	MOORHEAD	21059	252	31.8	35.7	21.4	7.1	4.0	37536	43056	38	19	200	47.5	27.5	11.0	11.0	3.0	53846
51559	NEOLA	22495	667	18.4	26.4	44.5	8.0	2.7	53586	62004	78	89	554	5.1	26.0	49.1	19.0	0.9	112963
51560	OAKLAND	23250	886	22.0	33.5	34.7	7.1	2.7	45765	53181	63	67	719	10.7	31.9	44.7	11.8	1.0	96948
51561	PACIFIC JUNCTION	25231	628	16.7	29.3	36.2	13.9	4.0	53452	62500	78	89	553	17.5	15.9	31.1	32.4	3.1	128795
51562	PANAMA	18595	185	23.2	40.0	30.8	5.4	0.5	40971	47539	50	41	152	16.5	34.2	30.9	13.2	5.3	89231
51563	PERSIA	20164	315	19.4	28.6	42.2	9.5	0.3	51262	59847	74	85	263	11.0	16.4	50.2	17.1	5.3	117634
51564	PISGAH	17613	319	36.4	35.1	23.8	3.1	1.6	33392	39151	22	6	234	40.2	28.2	19.2	10.7	1.7	60588
51565	PORTSMOUTH	19741	231	22.5	33.8	34.2	8.7	0.9	43336	50000	57	55	190	13.2	33.7	32.1	21.1	0.0	94000
51566	RED OAK	18718	3123	33.0	36.7	24.2	4.9	1.3	36031	41202	32	14	2197	29.6	34.2	29.7	5.6	0.9	73750
51570	SHELBY	18482	469	23.7	37.1	33.9	4.9	0.4	42060	48325	53	49	373	16.1	29.5	42.1	11.5	0.8	95500
51571	SILVER CITY	27729	242	19.4	31.0	35.5	9.1	5.0	49671	57837	71	81	208	7.2	14.9	38.5	31.3	8.2	150000
51572	SOLDIER	16693	247	34.8	44.5	17.4	2.8	0.4	32563	37594	19	4	193	45.6	23.8	15.5	13.0	2.1	59444
51573	STANTON	19677	464	25.2	31.5	36.4	6.5	0.4	43645	50398	58	57	381	26.3	36.0	29.1	7.6	1.1	77581
51575	TREYNOR	19489	4	0.0	0.0	100.0	0.0	0.0	75000	100000	93	99	3	0.0	0.0	0.0	100.0	0.0	262500
51576	UNDERWOOD	22874	568	16.0	26.8	42.4	10.9	3.9	56158	64653	81	92	486	5.6	13.0	51.7	26.3	3.5	130500
51577	WALNUT	19219	455	22.0	38.7	34.1	4.6	0.7	41740	47757	52	46	371	17.8	37.5	35.3	8.1	1.4	85851
51578	WESTPHALIA	16755	85	23.5	42.4	29.4	3.5	1.2	41086	47331	50	42	70	17.1	34.3	30.0	11.4	7.1	88333
51579	WOODBINE	17899	909	34.2	29.5	30.4	4.8	1.1	37980	43715	39	22	670	13.6	31.0	40.2	13.9	1.3	96667
51601	SHENANDOAH	19337	2661	35.6	32.4	25.4	4.9	1.9	35256	41291	28	11	1795	33.1	33.5	27.6	5.4	0.4	69414
51630	BLANCHARD	20782	87	23.0	36.8	32.2	4.6	3.5	42626	48283	55	52	71	29.6	29.6	28.2	8.5	4.2	80714
51631	BRADDYVILLE	19661	154	18.8	40.3	35.1	5.8	0.0	44313	50422	59	60	131	35.9	30.5	26.7	6.9	0.0	63125
51632	CLARINDA	20420	2719	28.5	31.7	31.0	6.4	2.4	42147	49222	53	49	1958	22.6	34.5	34.6	7.8	0.5	82872
51636	COIN	20197	224	27.7	33.0	33.5	4.5	1.3	40520	46393	48	39	182	41.8	30.2	21.4	6.0	0.6	57500
51637	COLLEGE SPRINGS	18351	101	17.8	40.6	36.6	5.0	0.0	45241	48823	62	64	86	37.2	30.2	26.7	5.8	0.0	60000
51638	ESSEX	22191	575	19.8	32.7	39.5	5.7	2.3	47999	54434	68	76	463	27.9	38.2	26.6	7.1	0.2	70758
51639	FARRAGUT	22788	435	29.0	29.9	34.0	3.9	3.2	42355	49214	54	51	347	28.2	35.2	26.2	9.8	0.6	77500
51640	HAMBURG	20431	805	32.8	29.9	29.6	4.8	2.9	38486	46582	41	25	619	26.5	33.0	31.0	8.1	1.5	79063
51645	IMOGENE	26855	107	20.6	32.7	34.6	6.5	5.6	46952	54092	66	73	79	27.9	26.6	32.9	11.4	1.3	84167
51646	NEW MARKET	20256	359	29.5	33.7	32.9	3.1	0.8	39391	44396	44	31	276	39.5	31.2	20.3	6.9	2.2	63333
51647	NORTHBORO	20503	112	25.9	35.7	31.3	3.6	3.6	41638	47544	52	46	90	28.9	31.1	28.9	7.8	3.3	80000
51648	PERCIVAL	24430	124	22.6	32.3	33.9	8.1	3.2	46841	54144	66	72	103	22.3	25.2	36.9	12.6	2.9	92273
51649	RANDOLPH	25221	158	19.0	33.5	33.5	7.0	7.0	47642	54215	68	75	115	25.2	28.7	33.0	12.2	0.9	85500
51650	RIVERTON	18298	164	33.5	28.7	33.5	4.3	0.0	41674	48908	52	46	132	50.8	24.2	14.4	10.6	0.0	49167
51651	SHAMBAUGH	17250	12	25.0	41.7	33.3	0.0	0.0	40000	45000	46	35	10	20.0	40.0	40.0	0.0	0.0	80000
51652	SIDNEY	19349	754	26.4	28.9	39.0	4.0	1.7	46047	52024	64	68	572	20.6	35.3	34.1	7.7	2.3	83704
51653	TABOR	22130	532	28.0	24.4	37.0	7.5	3.0	47276	54616	67	73	394	13.2	26.4	44.4	15.5	0.5	102299
51654	THURMAN	23473	228	22.8	31.6	34.2	8.3	3.1	47199	54389	67	73	190	23.2	24.7	35.8	13.2	3.2	92000
51656	YORKTOWN	15962	23	26.1	34.8	34.8	4.4	0.0	41115	47380	50	42	18	38.9	27.8	16.7	16.7	0.0	60000
52001	DUBUQUE	21998	17363	28.7	34.2	28.4	6.1	2.6	39193	46822	43	29	11305	8.8	30.6	50.1	9.2	1.2	99345
52002	DUBUQUE	25104	4632	16.7	26.7	41.6	11.5	3.5	55607	64915	80	92	3635	3.2	6.9	65.1	23.4	1.5	132844
52003	DUBUQUE	29262	5317	16.3	29.4	35.1	10.3	8.9	53852	63649	78	90	4628	18.5	12.5	41.0	22.8	5.3	120120
52030	ANDREW	23522	162	19.1	38.9	32.7	6.2	3.1	45000	52434	61	63	138	10.9	18.8	48.6	18.1	3.6	112000
52031	BELLEVUE	20406	1911	27.6	31.6	31.9	6.5	2.3	44110	50828	59	59	1563	12.9	21.3	47.1	15.9	2.8	110775
52032	BERNARD	24015	544	29.8	22.1	38.2	6.6	3.3	48266	54458	69	77	449	16.7	16.9	32.3	28.5	5.6	117383
52033	CASCADE	20876	1160	25.0	28.2	40.2	4.7	1.9	47142	53451	66	73	907	9.0	25.6	51.5	10.0	3.9	106576
52035	COLESBURG	21281	418	25.1	37.8	29.4	4.6	3.1	43648	50000	58	57	342	23.4	26.6	31.0	12.0	7.0	90000
52036	DELAWARE	17034	19	21.1	36.8	42.1	0.0	0.0	42361	47368	54	51	15	13.3	26.7	40.0	6.7	13.3	104167
52037	DELMAR	18843	526	25.7	29.5	37.1	6.5	1.3	44146	50523	59	59	434	18.9	27.4	41.7	9.5	2.5	94324
52038	DUNDEE	20034	222	21.2	38.3	30.2	7.7	2.7	42451	50000	54	51	181	16.6	18.2	37.0	23.8	4.4	114453
52039	DURANGO	27215	321	12.2	31.2	38.3	9.7	8.7	55861	64982	81	92	275	6.6	12.4	43.6	31.6	5.8	143534
52040	DYERSVILLE	20646	1976	21.2	35.0	35.7	6.0	2.1	45400	53202	62	65	1605	5.6	20.6	50.3	21.0	2.6	116515
52041	EARLVILLE	17227	617	21.7	35.5	37.3	4.4	1.1	45143	51342	62	64	507	18.0	30.0	36.9	8.9	6.3	93182
52042	EDGEWOOD	19731	601	26.1	38.9	25.1	5.7	4.2	41125	47288	50	43	491	19.1	28.5	36.3	11.0	5.1	93026
52043	ELKADER	19510	987	28.7	37.7	28.5	3.4	1.7	38439	44585	41	25	776	18.6	37.5	34.2	8.1	1.7	84891
52044	ELKPORT	24720	107	42.1	29.0	18.7	6.5	3.7	30211	34643	13	2	88	31.8	26.1	25.0	17.1	0.0	81250
52045	EPWORTH	20898	769	18.9	32.9	34.6	10.1	3.5	48382	56265	69	77	641	6.7	20.9	52.0	16.9	3.6	113644
52046	FARLEY	20025	737	19.7	33.4	36.6	7.6	2.7	47122	54381	66	73	610	4.9	22.8	52.5	16.1	3.8	111986
52047	FARMERSBURG	17531	266	24.4	45.9	24.8	3.8	1.1	38007	42762	39	22	216	19.4	37.5	27.3	13.4	2.3	83478
52048	GARBER	26353	158	37.3	33.5	19.6	5.7	3.8	33289	38396	22	5	130	28.5	25.4	28.5	17.7	0.0	85455
52049	GARNAVILLO	22756	525	26.3	37.1	29.5	5.3	1.7	38513	44424	41	25	396	21.2	41.4	27.5	6.8	3.0	80566
52050	GREELEY	17146	229	23.1	43.2	30.6	2.2	0.9	38929	46538	42	28	181	24.9	26.5	27.1	10.5	11.1	87917
52052	GUTTENBERG	20261	1389	32.2	34.3	25.1	6.0	2.5	35748	41230	31	12	1091	13.7	26.4	45.5	12.7	1.8	102761
52053	HOLY CROSS	22615	419	17.7	34.4	38.2	5.5	4.3	48659	55700	70	78	350	9.1	22.3	42.9	20.0	5.7	117500
52054	LA MOTTE	19660	422	23.5	28.7	37.9	8.5	1.4	48070	54768	68	77	357	12.6	17.1	42.9	22.4	5.0	121780
52057	MANCHESTER	21544	3321	30.7	28.9	30.3	6.9	3.3	40385	48591	47	38	2565	11.3	30.4	43.6	12.3	2.4	98333
52060	MAQUOKETA	19406	3610	32.2	35.2	26.9	4.3	1.5	36126	42409	32	14	2614	19.0	33.1	36.7	10.1	1.2	88078
52064	MILES	19284	327	31.8	30.0	32.4	4.3	1.5	38217	43632	40	23	263	23.2	31.9	34.6	6.5	3.8	85345
52065	NEW VIENNA	19768	418	24.4	34.2	32.5	6.9	1.9	45000	50979	61	63	350	10.0	23.7	40.3	18.6	7.4	113636
52068	PEOSTA	25959	879	11.5	19.3	49.7	13.9	5.6	65107	77287	89	98	791	5.9	5.1	44.5	40.7	3.8	165705
52069	PRESTON	21330	629	27.7	32.1	34.2	4.5	1.6	41896	48452	53	47	475	12.8	31.6	38.7	13.7	3.2	96795
52070	SABULA	24394	529	31.8	36.1	24.6	5.1	2.5	35444	41599	29	12	427	24.8	26.9	32.6	11.9	3.8	87857
52071	SAINT DONATUS	23137	43	18.6	37.2	37.2	4.7	2.3	47966	56003	68	76	38	7.9	18.4	44.7	29.0	0.0	125000
52072	SAINT OLAF	17668	145	26.9	42.1	25.5	4.1	1.4	37693	43501	38	20	116	23.3	25.9	31.9	16.4	2.6	91000
52073	SHERRILL	23249	471	16.8	28.5	38.9	10.8	5.1	53593	62808	78	89	411	10.0	10.2	50.1	28.0	1.7	125255
52074	SPRAGUEVILLE	22013	129	23.3	34.9	34.1	5.4	2.3	43735	48782	58	57	105	13.3	15.2	43.8	22.9	4.8	120395
52076	STRAWBERRY POINT	20498	844	28.4	34.1	30.8	4.2	2.5	39591	45000	45	32	676	19.7	37.3	32.7	8.7	1.6	84125
52077	VOLGA	16537	172	33.1	34.3	28.5	2.3	1.7	34279	39529	25	7	142	27.5	21.1	26.8	23.2	1.4	92500
52078	WORTHINGTON	15832	302	26.5	34.4	35.4	3.3	0.3	39234	44560	44	30	249	6.0	24.5	37.4	18.9	13.3	116761
52079	ZWINGLE	21836	329	23.4	33.1	32.5	7.0	4.0	43350	49313	57	55	270	13.0	17.0	32.2	35.6	2.2	142857
52101	DECORAH	21340	4966	23.1	33.2	33.5	7.3	2.9	45124	52382	62	64	3595	7.9	21.2	47.3	21.1	2.6	120245
52132	CALMAR	22424	1060	27.7	33.2	31.9	5.0	2.2	39930	45996	46	34	830	15.2	34.0	35.3	14.1	1.5	90986
52133	CASTALIA	17855	270	26.3	34.8	33.3	5.6	0.0	41600	47207	52	46	218	28.0	29.8	18.8	19.7	3.7	80556
52134	CHESTER	18785	191	28.8	32.5	30.9	6.8	1.1	41733	46913	52	46	154	34.4	26.0	25.3	11.7	2.6	72727
52135	CLERMONT	19405	397	28.2	41.8	26.2	2.5	1.3	37594	42952	38	19	324	20.7	31.5	38.9	8.3	0.6	86957
52136	CRESCO	21321	2466	28.6	34.4	28.7	5.0	3.3	38924	45550	42	28	1927	19.5	36.7	31.7	10.7	1.4	83379
52140	DORCHESTER	17862	278	19.1	50.7	28.4	1.4	0.4	40480	45799	48	38	231	26.4	28.1	28.1	14.7	2.6	83000
52141	ELGIN	17518	615	33.8	32.5	30.1	2.9	0.7	37569	42633	38	19	467	24.4	32.8	31.5	9.9	1.5	82024
52142	FAYETTE	17964	617	33.6	32.3	23.7	7.5	3.1	38634	45287	42	26	448	22.1	33.9	31.5	9.4	3.1	82500
	IOWA	23554		24.6	30.5	32.9	8.4	3.7	45622	53985				17.5	26.2	39.3	15.0	2.1	98835
	UNITED STATES	25866		24.7	27.1	30.8	10.9	6.5	48124	56710				10.9	15.0	33.7	30.1	10.4	145905

ZIP CODE #	POST OFFICE NAME	FINANCIAL SERVICES: Auto Loan	FINANCIAL SERVICES: Home Loan	FINANCIAL SERVICES: Investments	FINANCIAL SERVICES: Retirement Plans	THE HOME: Home Improvements: Home Repair	THE HOME: Home Improvements: Lawn & Garden	THE HOME: Furnishings: Computers & Hardware	THE HOME: Furnishings: Major Appliances	THE HOME: Furnishings: TV, Radio, Sound Equipment	THE HOME: Furnishings: Furniture	ENTERTAINMENT: Dine out/Carry out	ENTERTAINMENT: Sports Equipment	ENTERTAINMENT: Fees & Tickets	ENTERTAINMENT: Toys & Games	ENTERTAINMENT: Travel	ENTERTAINMENT: Cable TV	PERSONAL: Apparel & Services	PERSONAL: Auto Repairs	PERSONAL: Health Insurance	PERSONAL: Pets & Supplies
51549	MACEDONIA	85	62	36	59	72	79	61	74	69	60	81	89	53	80	63	72	75	73	86	101
51551	MALVERN	84	70	53	69	75	84	71	78	76	70	92	90	67	91	71	77	86	76	85	95
51552	MARNE	91	63	33	60	74	83	63	78	72	62	85	93	54	83	65	76	77	76	92	108
51553	MINDEN	103	77	47	73	87	96	75	90	84	75	100	108	66	98	77	87	92	89	103	121
51555	MISSOURI VALLEY	81	77	70	75	79	86	76	79	78	75	96	92	75	97	77	79	92	78	83	93
51556	MODALE	103	73	39	69	84	94	72	88	82	71	97	106	62	95	74	86	88	87	104	122
51557	MONDAMIN	94	84	64	80	88	95	78	86	83	78	101	102	76	103	80	85	96	84	94	110
51558	MOORHEAD	86	60	32	57	70	79	60	74	69	59	81	89	51	79	62	72	74	73	88	102
51559	NEOLA	80	88	88	85	88	91	82	84	81	81	100	98	84	105	84	80	98	82	82	97
51560	OAKLAND	101	73	42	70	84	93	72	87	82	71	96	105	63	95	74	85	88	86	102	120
51561	PACIFIC JUNCTION	94	97	90	97	98	103	92	95	91	91	113	110	93	116	93	91	109	93	94	109
51562	PANAMA	85	59	31	56	69	77	58	72	67	58	79	87	50	77	61	71	72	71	86	101
51563	PERSIA	100	70	37	66	82	91	69	86	80	68	93	103	59	92	72	84	85	84	102	119
51564	PISGAH	68	53	37	51	57	67	57	62	63	55	75	70	52	72	57	66	69	62	73	75
51565	PORTSMOUTH	94	65	34	62	76	85	65	80	74	64	87	96	55	86	67	78	80	79	95	111
51566	RED OAK	65	56	48	54	59	67	59	62	64	57	77	71	56	76	59	66	72	62	69	73
51570	SHELBY	85	61	34	57	70	78	60	73	68	59	81	88	52	80	62	72	74	72	86	100
51571	SILVER CITY	118	93	63	89	104	113	90	106	98	89	117	126	81	117	93	102	109	104	119	140
51572	SOLDIER	61	46	29	44	50	60	50	56	56	47	66	63	44	62	49	59	60	55	67	69
51573	STANTON	88	63	34	59	72	81	62	75	71	61	83	91	54	82	64	74	76	74	89	104
51575	TREYNOR	95	118	125	118	116	114	105	105	98	105	123	123	112	131	108	95	122	101	94	116
51576	UNDERWOOD	101	91	73	89	96	102	86	95	89	86	108	114	82	109	88	90	103	94	100	120
51577	WALNUT	87	61	32	58	71	79	60	74	69	59	81	90	51	80	62	73	74	73	89	104
51578	WESTPHALIA	82	57	30	54	67	75	57	70	65	56	76	84	48	75	59	68	70	69	83	97
51579	WOODBINE	72	57	39	54	61	71	60	66	66	58	79	75	55	76	60	69	72	66	77	81
51601	SHENANDOAH	67	56	46	54	60	68	59	63	64	57	77	73	55	76	59	66	72	63	71	76
51630	BLANCHARD	87	63	36	59	72	80	61	75	70	61	82	90	54	81	64	73	76	73	88	103
51631	BRADDYVILLE	79	70	54	67	74	80	65	72	69	65	84	86	64	86	67	71	80	70	78	93
51632	CLARINDA	77	66	53	63	70	80	67	73	73	65	88	83	65	88	68	76	82	72	82	88
51636	COIN	87	61	32	57	71	79	60	74	69	59	81	89	51	79	62	73	74	73	88	103
51637	COLLEGE SPRINGS	79	70	53	66	74	79	65	72	69	65	84	85	63	85	67	70	79	70	78	93
51638	ESSEX	92	75	51	71	82	89	71	82	78	70	93	98	66	93	73	80	87	80	92	109
51639	FARRAGUT	100	70	36	66	81	91	69	85	79	68	93	103	59	91	71	83	85	84	101	119
51640	HAMBURG	83	60	34	57	68	78	62	73	70	60	83	86	54	80	63	74	75	72	87	96
51645	IMOGENE	115	80	42	76	93	105	79	98	91	78	107	118	68	105	82	96	98	97	117	136
51646	NEW MARKET	84	58	31	55	68	76	58	71	67	57	78	86	49	76	60	70	71	70	85	99
51647	NORTHBORO	89	62	33	59	73	81	62	76	71	61	83	92	53	82	64	75	76	75	91	106
51648	PERCIVAL	107	74	39	70	87	97	74	91	85	73	99	110	63	97	76	89	91	90	108	127
51649	RANDOLPH	118	83	45	79	97	109	83	102	96	82	112	122	72	110	86	100	102	100	121	140
51650	RIVERTON	78	54	29	51	63	71	54	66	62	53	73	80	46	71	56	65	66	65	79	92
51651	SHAMBAUGH	69	61	47	58	65	70	57	63	60	57	73	75	56	75	59	62	70	61	68	81
51652	SIDNEY	82	63	41	61	70	78	64	73	70	63	84	86	58	83	65	73	78	72	83	94
51653	TABOR	88	70	50	68	76	88	75	82	82	72	97	93	68	93	75	86	90	81	95	99
51654	THURMAN	107	75	39	71	87	98	74	91	85	73	100	110	63	98	77	89	91	90	109	127
51656	YORKTOWN	82	57	30	54	66	74	56	70	65	56	76	84	48	75	58	68	69	69	83	97
52001	DUBUQUE	71	71	75	70	72	78	74	73	75	72	92	85	74	94	74	75	90	74	75	82
52002	DUBUQUE	92	101	106	102	100	102	95	96	91	96	115	112	98	117	96	89	113	94	89	107
52003	DUBUQUE	111	113	106	110	114	121	107	111	107	107	132	128	107	133	108	107	128	109	112	129
52030	ANDREW	102	90	69	86	96	103	84	93	89	84	108	110	82	110	86	91	103	90	100	120
52031	BELLEVUE	87	71	50	67	77	86	70	79	77	68	92	92	65	90	71	80	85	78	90	101
52032	BERNARD	104	84	58	78	93	102	79	93	88	79	105	110	73	105	83	92	98	91	106	125
52033	CASCADE	94	73	45	69	81	89	70	83	78	69	93	99	63	92	72	81	86	81	95	112
52035	COLESBURG	93	72	45	68	80	88	69	82	77	68	91	98	62	91	71	80	85	80	94	110
52036	DELAWARE	78	58	35	55	65	73	58	68	65	57	77	81	51	75	59	67	70	67	79	90
52037	DELMAR	88	67	41	63	75	83	64	76	72	64	85	92	58	85	67	75	79	75	88	104
52038	DUNDEE	96	67	35	63	78	88	66	82	76	66	90	99	57	88	69	80	82	81	98	114
52039	DURANGO	125	113	88	107	119	127	104	115	110	104	134	136	102	137	107	112	127	112	123	147
52040	DYERSVILLE	85	74	60	72	79	85	72	80	76	71	92	95	68	93	73	77	87	79	85	101
52041	EARLVILLE	80	65	47	64	70	79	66	73	71	65	86	85	61	85	66	73	80	72	81	91
52042	EDGEWOOD	97	70	39	66	80	90	69	84	78	68	92	100	60	91	71	82	85	82	98	115
52043	ELKADER	79	56	33	54	64	74	59	69	67	57	78	81	51	76	60	70	71	68	82	91
52044	ELKPORT	96	80	61	80	85	95	82	89	88	81	106	102	78	105	82	89	99	87	97	106
52045	EPWORTH	95	82	64	81	86	95	82	88	86	80	105	102	78	105	82	88	99	87	95	107
52046	FARLEY	91	76	56	74	81	90	76	83	81	75	98	96	72	98	76	83	92	82	91	102
52047	FARMERSBURG	79	55	30	53	64	72	55	67	63	54	74	81	47	73	57	66	68	67	80	93
52048	GARBER	97	83	64	82	87	97	83	90	88	82	107	104	80	107	83	90	101	88	97	109
52049	GARNAVILLO	87	66	44	62	73	86	69	79	78	67	92	89	62	88	70	83	84	78	94	99
52050	GREELEY	81	58	32	55	67	75	57	70	65	56	77	84	49	75	59	68	70	69	82	96
52052	GUTTENBERG	80	62	41	58	68	79	64	73	72	62	85	83	58	82	65	76	78	72	86	92
52053	HOLY CROSS	105	86	59	81	94	102	81	93	89	81	106	112	76	107	84	92	100	91	105	124
52054	LA MOTTE	89	78	58	74	83	89	72	81	77	72	94	96	70	95	74	79	89	79	88	105
52057	MANCHESTER	90	71	50	68	78	87	72	81	79	71	95	95	66	93	73	82	88	80	92	104
52060	MAQUOKETA	73	61	47	58	66	73	61	67	66	60	79	79	57	79	62	68	75	66	76	85
52064	MILES	81	69	51	66	74	80	65	73	69	65	84	87	62	85	67	71	79	71	80	95
52065	NEW VIENNA	97	68	35	64	79	88	67	83	77	66	90	100	57	89	69	81	82	82	99	115
52068	PEOSTA	102	117	118	117	117	117	106	108	101	106	126	127	111	132	108	99	125	105	100	123
52069	PRESTON	74	69	63	66	73	81	68	72	73	66	89	83	68	94	71	76	85	71	80	87
52070	SABULA	98	68	34	60	77	87	66	81	78	67	92	97	57	88	67	83	84	80	98	113
52071	SAINT DONATUS	97	76	52	68	85	96	72	86	81	71	96	101	64	95	76	87	89	85	102	118
52072	SAINT OLAF	84	59	31	55	68	76	58	72	67	57	78	86	50	77	60	70	72	71	85	99
52073	SHERRILL	107	95	72	90	100	108	88	97	93	88	113	116	86	116	90	96	108	95	105	126
52074	SPRAGUEVILLE	101	77	48	73	87	95	74	88	83	74	99	106	67	98	77	86	91	87	102	120
52076	STRAWBERRY POINT	87	72	53	71	78	86	72	80	78	71	93	93	68	93	73	79	87	78	88	100
52077	VOLGA	77	54	28	51	63	70	53	66	61	53	72	79	45	70	55	64	65	65	78	92
52078	WORTHINGTON	79	64	44	61	70	77	61	70	67	61	80	84	57	80	63	69	75	69	79	93
52079	ZWINGLE	97	78	51	74	86	93	74	86	81	73	97	103	68	98	76	84	91	84	97	115
52101	DECORAH	83	74	66	72	78	86	73	79	78	72	94	93	71	94	75	79	89	79	86	97
52132	CALMAR	91	70	46	68	78	87	70	80	77	69	92	95	64	91	71	80	85	79	92	105
52133	CASTALIA	68	65	67	67	67	72	66	68	66	65	81	81	64	79	66	65	78	69	69	79
52134	CHESTER	89	62	32	59	72	81	61	76	71	61	83	91	52	81	64	74	76	75	90	106
52135	CLERMONT	84	59	31	56	69	77	58	72	67	57	79	87	50	77	60	70	72	71	86	100
52136	CRESCO	83	69	51	66	74	83	68	76	75	67	90	88	65	90	70	78	84	75	86	96
52140	DORCHESTER	82	57	30	54	66	74	56	70	65	56	76	84	48	74	58	68	69	69	83	97
52141	ELGIN	72	52	32	50	59	69	56	64	63	53	74	74	49	71	56	66	67	64	76	82
52142	FAYETTE	76	62	49	61	67	75	66	71	71	64	85	83	61	83	66	73	80	72	80	86
	IOWA	87	79	73	79	82	89	80	84	83	79	102	98	78	102	80	83	97	84	88	100
	UNITED STATES	100	100	100	100	100	100	100	100	100	100	100	100	100	100	100	100	100	100	100	100

#	POST OFFICE NAME	COUNTY FIPS CODE	POPULATION 2000	POPULATION 2004	POPULATION 2009	2000-2004 ANNUAL RATE % Rate	State Centile	HOUSEHOLDS 2000	HOUSEHOLDS 2004	HOUSEHOLDS 2009	% Annual Rate 2000-2004	2004 Average HH Size	FAMILIES 2000	FAMILIES 2004	% Annual Rate 2000-2004
52144	FORT ATKINSON	191	1424	1401	1396	-0.4	28	520	522	529	0.1	2.68	363	362	-0.1
52146	HARPERS FERRY	005	985	1062	1139	1.8	90	398	437	476	2.2	2.30	287	314	2.1
52147	HAWKEYE	065	1160	1155	1150	-0.1	44	464	466	470	0.1	2.48	332	332	0.0
52151	LANSING	005	2233	2272	2363	0.4	66	894	922	970	0.7	2.40	612	628	0.6
52154	LAWLER	037	1176	1134	1105	-0.9	10	454	444	438	-0.5	2.55	331	323	-0.6
52155	LIME SPRINGS	089	1125	1134	1137	0.2	58	443	449	454	0.3	2.50	316	319	0.2
52156	LUANA	043	650	670	682	0.7	74	249	259	267	0.9	2.59	189	196	0.9
52157	MC GREGOR	043	2180	2231	2235	0.6	70	918	958	977	1.0	2.27	579	602	0.9
52158	MARQUETTE	043	18	18	18	0.0	51	6	6	6	0.0	3.00	4	4	0.0
52159	MONONA	005	2360	2373	2384	0.1	56	951	965	980	0.3	2.45	659	668	0.3
52160	NEW ALBIN	005	901	913	948	0.3	63	370	380	400	0.6	2.40	250	256	0.6
52161	OSSIAN	191	1394	1445	1471	0.9	77	517	547	566	1.3	2.58	382	400	1.1
52162	POSTVILLE	005	3377	3527	3693	1.0	80	1214	1268	1334	1.0	2.72	870	903	0.9
52164	RANDALIA	065	304	340	359	2.7	95	109	124	132	3.1	2.73	87	99	3.1
52165	RIDGEWAY	191	1095	1171	1213	1.6	88	420	461	486	2.2	2.54	299	327	2.1
52166	SAINT LUCAS	065	128	124	122	-0.7	14	55	54	54	-0.4	2.30	42	41	-0.6
52169	WADENA	065	451	445	441	-0.3	32	188	189	190	0.1	2.35	138	138	0.0
52170	WATERVILLE	005	571	639	700	2.7	95	205	232	257	3.0	2.74	160	181	2.9
52171	WAUCOMA	065	1241	1216	1201	-0.5	24	477	474	475	-0.2	2.57	339	334	-0.4
52172	WAUKON	005	6288	6477	6781	0.7	74	2517	2627	2783	1.0	2.38	1655	1720	0.9
52175	WEST UNION	065	3605	3565	3546	-0.3	35	1494	1498	1510	0.1	2.27	957	953	-0.1
52201	AINSWORTH	183	1249	1287	1308	0.7	74	467	486	498	0.9	2.65	363	375	0.8
52202	ALBURNETT	113	1023	1091	1149	1.5	87	367	397	423	1.9	2.74	300	322	1.7
52203	AMANA	095	1916	1926	1960	0.1	55	767	778	798	0.3	2.38	539	545	0.3
52205	ANAMOSA	105	8374	8594	8720	0.6	71	2853	2990	3088	1.1	2.41	1995	2082	1.0
52206	ATKINS	011	1555	1729	1873	2.5	94	549	615	671	2.7	2.81	437	486	2.5
52207	BALDWIN	097	436	433	437	-0.2	41	175	177	182	0.3	2.45	121	122	0.2
52208	BELLE PLAINE	011	3262	3230	3331	-0.2	37	1358	1355	1408	-0.1	2.33	865	859	-0.2
52209	BLAIRSTOWN	011	974	1000	1051	0.6	72	392	406	430	0.8	2.46	284	293	0.7
52210	BRANDON	019	725	732	737	0.2	60	282	289	295	0.6	2.53	218	222	0.4
52211	BROOKLYN	157	2635	2724	2807	0.8	76	1068	1123	1176	1.2	2.38	721	755	1.1
52212	CENTER JUNCTION	105	359	350	349	-0.6	19	150	148	150	-0.3	2.36	105	104	-0.2
52213	CENTER POINT	113	3534	3593	3711	0.4	66	1315	1353	1411	0.7	2.65	1005	1027	0.5
52214	CENTRAL CITY	113	2982	3156	3314	1.3	84	1197	1281	1359	1.6	2.46	864	919	1.5
52215	CHELSEA	171	916	927	931	0.3	62	331	337	340	0.4	2.75	259	262	0.3
52216	CLARENCE	031	1424	1436	1473	0.2	59	580	589	609	0.4	2.36	393	397	0.2
52217	CLUTIER	171	629	662	674	1.2	83	266	283	290	1.5	2.34	191	202	1.3
52218	COGGON	113	1902	1975	2059	0.9	78	686	720	758	1.1	2.74	532	554	1.0
52219	PRAIRIEBURG	113	175	187	197	1.6	87	69	75	80	2.0	2.49	54	59	2.1
52220	CONROY	095	17	17	17	0.0	51	9	9	9	0.0	1.89	7	7	0.0
52221	GUERNSEY	157	139	131	131	-1.4	2	60	58	59	-0.8	2.26	43	41	-1.1
52222	DEEP RIVER	157	807	767	766	-1.2	3	313	303	307	-0.8	2.53	225	217	-0.9
52223	DELHI	055	1367	1386	1409	0.3	64	525	540	556	0.7	2.49	413	422	0.5
52224	DYSART	171	2017	1950	1929	-0.8	12	794	769	763	-0.8	2.47	574	554	-0.8
52225	ELBERON	171	376	401	412	1.5	87	138	149	154	1.8	2.69	105	113	1.7
52226	ELWOOD	045	33	35	36	1.4	85	11	12	12	2.1	2.92	8	9	2.8
52227	ELY	113	1844	2076	2253	2.8	95	683	779	856	3.1	2.65	509	579	3.1
52228	FAIRFAX	113	1988	2091	2194	1.2	83	724	771	819	1.5	2.71	588	624	1.4
52229	GARRISON	011	823	833	869	0.3	62	319	325	341	0.4	2.56	237	239	0.2
52231	HARPER	107	390	370	361	-1.2	3	148	142	140	-1.0	2.61	114	109	-1.1
52232	HARTWICK	157	231	255	272	2.4	93	98	110	118	2.8	2.32	71	79	2.5
52233	HIAWATHA	113	6433	6636	6872	0.7	75	2852	2984	3127	1.1	2.20	1691	1757	0.9
52236	HOMESTEAD	095	502	499	503	-0.1	42	190	191	194	0.1	2.61	152	152	0.0
52237	HOPKINTON	055	1663	1652	1659	-0.2	41	603	607	622	0.2	2.70	451	452	0.1
52240	IOWA CITY	103	32283	34271	37388	1.4	85	13136	14144	15660	1.8	2.28	6210	6668	1.7
52241	CORALVILLE	103	13726	15663	17797	3.2	96	6184	7056	8062	3.2	2.20	3120	3515	2.8
52242	IOWA CITY	103	802	802	802	0.0	51	1	1	1	0.0	6.00	0	0	0.0
52245	IOWA CITY	103	20464	21063	22584	0.7	73	7212	7546	8275	1.1	2.37	3704	3846	0.9
52246	IOWA CITY	103	19655	21354	23695	2.0	91	8793	9691	10923	2.3	2.11	4073	4467	2.2
52247	KALONA	183	5061	5001	5098	-0.3	34	1731	1721	1760	-0.1	2.85	1250	1239	-0.2
52248	KEOTA	183	1827	1759	1729	-0.9	9	727	707	700	-0.7	2.42	487	471	-0.8
52249	KEYSTONE	011	1096	1125	1171	0.6	72	430	447	469	0.9	2.43	297	305	0.6
52251	LADORA	095	522	509	511	-0.6	20	207	204	207	-0.3	2.50	152	149	-0.5
52253	LISBON	031	2796	2935	3075	1.2	82	1040	1106	1172	1.5	2.65	763	807	1.3
52254	LOST NATION	045	1037	1040	1033	0.1	53	426	430	430	0.2	2.42	303	304	0.1
52255	LOWDEN	031	1298	1293	1330	-0.1	44	531	534	556	0.1	2.42	381	381	0.0
52257	LUZERNE	011	337	400	448	4.1	99	118	142	161	4.5	2.82	96	114	4.1
52301	MARENGO	095	4535	4475	4506	-0.3	32	1821	1812	1836	-0.1	2.42	1225	1214	-0.2
52302	MARION	113	28918	31153	33249	1.8	89	11242	12270	13253	2.1	2.49	7857	8538	2.0
52305	MARTELLE	105	619	646	659	1.0	79	243	259	268	1.5	2.49	186	197	1.4
52306	MECHANICSVILLE	031	1810	1846	1906	0.5	68	684	705	735	0.7	2.53	497	510	0.6
52307	MIDDLE AMANA	095	6	6	6	0.0	51	2	2	2	0.0	3.00	1	1	0.0
52308	MILLERSBURG	095	237	234	236	-0.3	33	100	100	101	0.0	2.34	74	74	0.0
52309	MONMOUTH	097	479	476	481	-0.2	42	184	187	192	0.4	2.54	128	130	0.4
52310	MONTICELLO	105	6225	6102	6061	-0.5	24	2468	2448	2465	-0.2	2.43	1728	1709	-0.3
52313	MOUNT AUBURN	011	435	518	581	4.2	99	161	193	217	4.4	2.68	133	158	4.1
52314	MOUNT VERNON	113	4739	4937	5144	1.0	79	1612	1712	1813	1.4	2.54	1188	1252	1.2
52315	NEWHALL	011	1127	1122	1160	-0.1	44	448	449	468	0.1	2.50	325	324	-0.1
52316	NORTH ENGLISH	095	1561	1631	1684	1.0	80	616	648	671	1.2	2.43	418	438	1.1
52317	NORTH LIBERTY	103	6600	7964	9269	4.5	99	2731	3356	3957	5.0	2.37	1820	2205	4.6
52318	NORWAY	011	1900	2077	2230	2.1	92	642	704	760	2.2	2.95	530	577	2.0
52320	OLIN	105	1180	1165	1165	-0.3	33	469	469	475	0.0	2.48	326	325	-0.1
52321	ONSLOW	105	430	423	423	-0.4	28	176	176	179	0.0	2.39	127	126	-0.2
52322	OXFORD	103	2350	2528	2777	1.7	89	916	1000	1111	2.1	2.53	672	726	1.8
52323	OXFORD JUNCTION	105	971	927	915	-1.1	5	392	379	379	-0.8	2.45	258	248	-0.9
52324	PALO	113	1794	1997	2158	2.6	94	683	771	842	2.9	2.59	546	613	2.8
52325	PARNELL	095	742	949	1094	6.0	100	272	353	411	6.3	2.65	216	276	5.9
52326	QUASQUETON	019	486	486	486	0.0	51	192	194	197	0.2	2.51	151	153	0.3
52327	RIVERSIDE	183	2881	2987	3101	0.9	77	1069	1118	1168	1.1	2.66	739	766	0.9
52328	ROBINS	113	1529	1804	2006	4.0	98	497	595	670	4.3	3.01	400	475	4.1
52329	ROWLEY	019	908	972	1008	1.6	88	339	367	385	1.9	2.65	275	296	1.8
52330	RYAN	055	958	1003	1037	1.1	81	340	361	378	1.4	2.78	258	273	1.3
52332	SHELLSBURG	011	1700	1897	2059	2.6	94	628	710	779	2.9	2.65	469	527	2.8
52333	SOLON	103	6081	6481	7036	1.5	87	1891	2065	2294	2.1	2.72	1531	1656	1.9
52334	SOUTH AMANA	095	224	225	229	0.1	54	85	87	89	0.6	2.59	65	66	0.4
	IOWA					0.5					0.7	2.43			0.6
	UNITED STATES					1.2					1.3	2.58			1.1

#	POST OFFICE NAME	White 2000	White 2004	Black 2000	Black 2004	Asian/Pacific 2000	Asian/Pacific 2004	% Hispanic Origin 2000	% Hispanic Origin 2004	0-4	5-9	10-14	15-19	20-24	25-44	45-64	65-84	85+	18+	MEDIAN AGE 2004	% 2004 Males	% 2004 Females
52144	FORT ATKINSON	99.2	99.0	0.0	0.0	0.4	0.5	0.4	0.5	6.2	6.4	8.6	6.6	5.4	26.1	23.1	15.8	1.9	74.4	39.4	51.7	48.3
52146	HARPERS FERRY	98.1	97.8	0.8	0.9	0.0	0.0	0.8	0.9	5.6	5.7	5.7	5.3	4.1	22.6	29.9	19.5	1.7	79.4	45.8	53.4	46.6
52147	HAWKEYE	99.2	99.2	0.0	0.0	0.2	0.2	0.5	0.5	5.9	6.6	8.7	5.6	5.0	25.7	25.7	14.4	2.4	75.3	40.9	52.3	47.7
52151	LANSING	99.2	99.1	0.1	0.1	0.2	0.3	0.6	0.7	5.9	6.1	6.3	6.7	5.0	21.9	28.0	16.8	3.4	77.1	43.7	50.2	49.8
52154	LAWLER	99.2	99.0	0.0	0.0	0.1	0.2	0.9	1.2	4.8	6.3	8.1	7.1	6.4	23.9	27.4	14.4	1.8	75.8	40.8	51.5	48.5
52155	LIME SPRINGS	98.8	98.8	0.0	0.0	0.3	0.3	1.3	1.4	7.1	7.1	7.1	7.0	5.6	25.0	24.4	14.2	2.6	74.3	39.8	51.2	48.8
52156	LUANA	97.7	97.6	0.2	0.2	0.0	0.0	4.0	4.5	6.3	7.2	8.1	7.3	6.1	28.5	24.5	11.2	0.9	73.9	36.7	51.8	48.2
52157	MC GREGOR	99.3	99.2	0.1	0.1	0.1	0.0	0.9	1.1	6.6	6.4	5.9	5.5	6.0	25.6	27.0	14.4	2.7	77.6	41.1	50.6	49.4
52158	MARQUETTE	100.0	100.0	0.0	0.0	0.0	0.0	0.0	0.0	11.1	11.1	0.0	5.6	11.1	44.4	16.7	0.0	0.0	77.8	30.0	50.0	50.0
52159	MONONA	98.6	98.4	0.1	0.1	0.3	0.4	0.6	0.7	5.7	6.4	7.5	7.1	5.8	25.0	23.8	15.7	3.0	75.7	40.4	49.3	50.7
52160	NEW ALBIN	97.2	96.7	0.0	0.0	0.2	0.3	1.4	1.8	7.0	6.9	6.7	7.0	5.5	24.8	25.6	13.9	2.6	75.3	39.5	50.3	49.7
52161	OSSIAN	99.6	99.5	0.1	0.1	0.1	0.1	0.7	0.8	6.9	7.0	8.7	7.0	5.7	26.4	22.8	12.8	2.8	72.5	37.8	51.6	48.4
52162	POSTVILLE	86.2	83.4	0.1	0.1	0.6	0.8	13.7	16.4	6.6	6.8	7.0	6.6	6.6	28.4	23.4	12.2	2.5	75.4	37.0	51.8	48.2
52164	RANDALIA	99.7	99.7	0.0	0.0	0.0	0.0	0.3	0.6	6.5	6.8	7.1	7.1	5.9	24.7	28.8	11.8	1.5	75.3	39.8	52.4	47.7
52165	RIDGEWAY	99.1	99.0	0.2	0.3	0.4	0.4	0.7	0.9	5.9	5.9	7.2	5.9	5.9	27.1	27.4	13.2	1.6	77.4	40.9	52.9	47.1
52166	SAINT LUCAS	100.0	100.0	0.0	0.0	0.0	0.0	0.8	0.8	4.0	5.7	8.1	5.7	6.5	25.0	27.4	16.1	1.6	77.4	42.3	54.8	45.2
52169	WADENA	98.9	98.9	0.2	0.2	0.2	0.2	0.2	0.2	7.0	7.6	8.5	6.5	4.9	22.5	27.6	13.9	1.4	72.8	41.0	50.1	49.9
52170	WATERVILLE	99.1	99.1	0.2	0.2	0.0	0.2	0.9	0.9	5.0	7.8	9.4	7.8	5.8	26.5	26.3	10.6	0.8	72.3	37.9	53.7	46.3
52171	WAUCOMA	99.4	99.4	0.0	0.0	0.1	0.1	0.5	0.5	6.0	6.6	7.9	6.2	5.6	25.4	25.7	15.0	1.7	75.7	40.5	51.0	49.0
52172	WAUKON	98.8	98.6	0.1	0.1	0.2	0.4	0.6	0.8	6.0	6.2	7.2	6.7	6.1	23.8	24.6	15.7	3.7	76.4	41.0	48.7	51.3
52175	WEST UNION	97.6	97.6	0.3	0.3	0.6	0.7	1.4	1.4	5.7	5.9	6.6	6.7	6.1	25.3	24.5	15.2	4.1	77.6	40.8	50.4	49.7
52201	AINSWORTH	96.2	95.3	0.0	0.0	0.1	0.2	5.6	6.7	9.2	8.9	7.0	6.1	4.4	28.5	23.8	10.8	1.4	71.2	36.8	52.9	47.1
52202	ALBURNETT	99.3	99.2	0.0	0.0	0.2	0.3	0.3	0.3	7.0	7.6	8.5	6.9	5.7	27.5	25.9	9.7	1.2	72.6	36.4	51.1	49.0
52203	AMANA	99.1	98.8	0.2	0.2	0.3	0.4	0.5	0.6	5.3	6.0	7.2	5.8	3.8	24.1	27.8	15.6	4.4	77.8	43.7	47.7	52.3
52205	ANAMOSA	93.5	93.6	4.0	4.0	0.4	0.4	1.6	1.7	5.4	5.5	6.3	6.0	7.7	31.6	24.2	11.3	2.1	79.4	37.7	56.6	43.4
52206	ATKINS	98.9	98.7	0.5	0.5	0.1	0.2	0.8	1.0	9.0	9.0	8.0	7.0	5.2	29.7	22.3	8.9	0.9	69.6	35.7	51.0	49.0
52207	BALDWIN	99.3	99.5	0.0	0.0	0.0	0.0	0.5	0.2	4.6	6.5	9.5	6.7	4.9	25.9	27.5	13.2	1.4	75.1	39.9	52.0	48.0
52208	BELLE PLAINE	98.9	98.8	0.1	0.1	0.3	0.4	0.7	0.9	5.6	5.7	7.7	7.2	6.4	25.5	22.9	14.8	4.3	76.4	40.1	49.8	50.2
52209	BLAIRSTOWN	99.3	99.2	0.0	0.0	0.0	0.0	0.4	0.5	5.8	6.4	8.1	6.5	5.0	26.7	26.2	13.0	2.3	75.6	39.8	50.0	50.0
52210	BRANDON	99.3	99.5	0.0	0.0	0.0	0.0	0.0	0.0	6.2	6.4	7.2	6.3	6.8	27.3	26.1	11.8	1.9	76.4	38.2	50.8	49.2
52211	BROOKLYN	98.1	97.8	0.1	0.1	0.1	0.2	1.4	1.7	5.7	6.0	7.2	6.7	5.9	24.3	26.6	14.6	3.0	76.9	41.4	49.2	50.8
52212	CENTER JUNCTION	98.9	99.1	0.0	0.0	0.0	0.0	0.0	0.0	6.3	6.6	7.4	5.4	5.7	25.4	26.6	14.9	1.7	76.3	41.0	50.9	49.1
52213	CENTER POINT	98.5	98.2	0.4	0.5	0.1	0.2	0.5	0.7	7.8	8.2	8.3	6.7	5.0	29.7	23.9	8.7	1.6	71.5	36.0	50.4	49.6
52214	CENTRAL CITY	98.9	98.8	0.0	0.1	0.2	0.2	0.5	0.5	6.5	6.7	7.3	6.0	5.5	25.7	27.2	13.0	2.2	75.9	40.4	49.7	50.3
52215	CHELSEA	91.3	90.9	0.0	0.1	0.2	0.2	10.2	10.5	8.3	8.2	8.3	5.6	5.5	24.5	25.4	12.2	2.1	71.7	37.7	52.4	47.6
52216	CLARENCE	99.0	98.8	0.1	0.1	0.1	0.2	0.4	0.6	6.3	6.8	6.8	5.4	4.5	24.4	24.3	16.5	5.0	76.2	42.3	47.7	52.3
52217	CLUTIER	98.4	98.3	0.2	0.2	0.2	0.2	0.5	0.5	6.8	7.3	7.0	6.0	4.4	23.3	25.8	16.9	2.6	75.4	42.0	51.5	48.5
52218	COGGON	99.5	99.4	0.1	0.1	0.1	0.2	0.3	0.4	7.5	7.6	8.5	6.8	5.8	26.3	23.9	12.2	1.5	72.3	37.2	49.5	50.5
52219	PRAIRIEBURG	100.0	100.0	0.0	0.0	0.0	0.0	0.0	0.5	5.9	6.4	7.0	5.9	5.9	26.7	29.4	11.8	1.1	77.0	40.2	52.4	47.6
52220	CONROY	100.0	100.0	0.0	0.0	0.0	0.0	0.0	0.0	11.8	11.8	11.8	11.8	0.0	41.2	11.8	0.0	0.0	64.7	27.5	47.1	52.9
52221	GUERNSEY	97.8	98.5	0.0	0.0	0.0	0.0	2.2	2.3	6.9	6.9	6.9	6.1	3.8	26.0	26.0	15.3	2.3	74.8	41.1	50.4	49.6
52222	DEEP RIVER	98.3	97.9	0.0	0.0	0.0	0.0	1.9	2.4	6.7	6.8	7.4	6.0	4.4	25.6	27.3	14.1	1.8	75.2	41.0	51.0	49.0
52223	DELHI	99.5	99.4	0.1	0.1	0.2	0.3	0.2	0.1	5.8	6.3	7.5	6.6	6.1	24.7	28.8	13.0	1.2	75.8	41.3	50.4	49.6
52224	DYSART	98.7	98.6	0.2	0.2	0.4	0.4	0.6	0.6	6.6	6.9	7.7	6.4	5.0	22.2	25.5	16.0	3.7	75.0	41.6	50.2	49.9
52225	ELBERON	97.9	97.3	0.3	0.3	0.3	0.3	1.6	1.8	7.5	7.7	6.5	5.7	6.7	24.7	28.2	11.7	1.3	74.6	38.2	52.4	47.6
52226	ELWOOD	100.0	100.0	0.0	0.0	0.0	0.0	0.0	0.0	5.7	5.7	14.3	8.6	2.9	25.7	22.9	14.3	0.0	74.3	34.4	48.6	51.4
52227	ELY	98.0	97.7	0.4	0.5	0.2	0.3	1.0	1.2	7.9	7.8	7.6	6.6	6.8	30.1	25.2	6.7	1.3	73.0	35.2	50.6	49.4
52228	FAIRFAX	97.9	97.6	0.5	0.5	0.4	0.6	0.8	1.0	7.3	7.7	7.5	6.3	4.8	27.9	25.3	12.2	1.0	73.5	38.3	49.9	50.1
52229	GARRISON	98.7	98.3	0.1	0.1	0.4	0.6	0.7	1.1	5.9	6.2	7.3	6.5	5.4	24.9	29.4	12.9	1.6	76.5	41.4	50.3	49.7
52231	HARPER	99.2	98.9	0.0	0.0	0.5	0.5	0.5	0.5	6.8	7.0	8.4	7.3	4.9	23.5	27.6	13.0	1.6	73.2	40.5	51.1	48.9
52232	HARTWICK	98.7	98.0	0.0	0.4	0.0	0.4	0.9	1.2	5.1	5.9	6.7	6.3	4.7	23.5	31.4	14.9	1.6	78.0	43.6	52.6	47.5
52233	HIAWATHA	94.2	93.0	2.2	2.5	1.7	2.4	1.3	1.5	7.4	6.8	6.8	5.7	8.2	33.2	22.2	8.5	1.2	75.8	32.9	48.9	51.1
52236	HOMESTEAD	99.0	98.8	0.0	0.0	0.4	0.6	0.0	0.0	6.4	7.0	8.0	7.4	4.8	27.3	27.7	10.2	1.2	74.0	38.6	49.5	50.5
52237	HOPKINTON	99.0	99.0	0.1	0.1	0.1	0.2	0.4	0.4	6.8	7.5	9.1	7.1	6.0	26.0	24.2	12.1	1.2	71.6	37.6	51.3	48.7
52240	IOWA CITY	90.0	88.1	3.4	3.6	3.0	4.3	3.4	4.0	5.4	5.0	5.1	9.7	18.8	29.5	19.5	6.1	0.9	81.6	28.3	50.5	49.5
52241	CORALVILLE	86.5	84.1	4.5	4.6	5.5	7.6	3.0	3.4	7.5	6.5	6.1	6.1	10.3	38.4	18.9	5.3	1.0	76.5	30.5	49.0	51.1
52242	IOWA CITY	93.1	91.5	2.5	2.6	2.7	3.9	1.5	1.8	0.1	0.3	0.0	78.7	19.5	1.4	0.0	0.0	0.1	99.4	18.2	45.3	54.7
52245	IOWA CITY	92.7	91.0	2.3	2.6	2.7	3.9	2.2	2.7	4.0	3.8	4.3	14.2	19.1	24.5	21.0	8.0	1.3	85.1	28.0	48.9	51.1
52246	IOWA CITY	81.3	77.0	4.5	4.7	11.0	14.9	2.6	3.0	5.8	4.7	4.7	7.6	13.5	40.1	16.7	5.6	1.4	82.1	28.9	49.6	50.4
52247	KALONA	98.1	97.8	0.2	0.3	0.3	0.5	1.2	1.4	8.0	8.1	8.6	6.9	5.8	24.5	23.3	12.1	2.7	70.9	36.0	47.5	52.5
52248	KEOTA	98.8	98.7	0.0	0.0	0.4	0.4	0.6	0.7	5.9	6.1	7.8	6.2	5.7	24.5	25.2	14.5	4.0	76.5	41.1	48.9	51.1
52249	KEYSTONE	99.4	99.4	0.1	0.1	0.1	0.1	0.3	0.3	5.2	5.6	7.6	7.5	6.0	23.2	24.2	15.6	5.2	76.8	41.8	48.8	51.2
52251	LADORA	99.4	99.2	0.2	0.4	0.0	0.0	1.2	1.4	5.9	5.9	7.7	7.9	5.9	25.3	27.5	12.4	1.6	75.4	40.7	52.9	47.2
52253	LISBON	98.1	97.8	0.3	0.3	0.1	0.2	0.8	1.0	7.6	7.8	7.9	7.2	6.4	26.7	25.7	9.5	1.2	72.2	36.8	51.1	48.9
52254	LOST NATION	98.8	98.7	0.0	0.0	0.5	0.6	0.7	1.0	6.9	7.1	7.0	7.2	5.9	24.3	25.8	13.9	1.9	74.5	38.9	48.7	51.4
52255	LOWDEN	98.9	98.8	0.2	0.2	0.1	0.1	1.1	1.4	6.3	6.6	6.8	6.3	4.6	22.8	28.2	15.1	3.3	76.4	42.9	49.8	50.2
52257	LUZERNE	99.7	99.5	0.3	0.3	0.0	0.0	0.0	0.0	4.8	5.5	7.3	6.8	7.0	22.8	31.0	13.3	1.8	78.0	42.3	53.3	46.8
52301	MARENGO	98.5	98.3	0.2	0.2	0.4	0.6	0.9	1.0	6.2	6.5	7.3	7.0	5.7	25.7	25.4	13.3	3.0	75.6	40.0	49.1	50.9
52302	MARION	97.0	96.2	0.6	0.7	1.1	1.5	1.0	1.3	7.2	7.0	7.4	6.6	6.4	29.3	24.2	10.4	1.6	74.2	36.2	48.9	51.1
52305	MARTELLE	99.0	99.1	0.2	0.2	0.2	0.2	0.2	0.2	6.2	6.2	7.7	6.7	3.7	27.6	28.5	12.2	1.2	75.5	40.2	51.1	48.9
52306	MECHANICSVILLE	98.5	98.3	0.1	0.1	0.1	0.2	1.0	1.0	6.3	6.5	7.3	6.8	6.3	25.4	25.3	13.1	3.1	75.7	39.5	49.2	50.8
52307	MIDDLE AMANA	100.0	100.0	0.0	0.0	0.0	0.0	0.0	0.0	0.0	0.0	0.0	0.0	33.3	66.7	0.0	0.0	0.0	100.0	27.5	50.0	50.0
52308	MILLERSBURG	99.2	99.2	0.0	0.0	0.0	0.0	1.3	1.7	6.0	6.8	8.6	6.8	5.6	25.6	25.2	13.7	1.7	73.5	39.7	50.9	49.2
52309	MONMOUTH	99.4	99.6	0.0	0.0	0.0	0.0	0.4	0.2	4.4	6.5	9.2	6.7	4.8	25.8	27.3	13.5	1.7	75.0	40.3	51.9	48.1
52310	MONTICELLO	99.1	99.0	0.1	0.1	0.1	0.1	0.9	0.9	6.1	6.4	7.4	6.5	5.4	24.8	25.4	15.2	3.0	75.8	40.8	48.5	51.5
52313	MOUNT AUBURN	97.9	97.7	0.0	0.0	0.2	0.4	0.5	0.8	7.0	7.3	8.5	6.4	5.2	24.5	28.6	11.4	1.2	73.2	39.7	50.8	49.2
52314	MOUNT VERNON	97.5	96.9	0.6	0.7	0.6	0.9	0.8	1.0	5.6	6.1	7.5	9.7	13.2	23.2	25.1	8.3	1.4	76.4	33.0	48.4	51.6
52315	NEWHALL	99.6	99.5	0.0	0.0	0.1	0.1	0.5	0.7	6.3	6.7	8.4	7.5	6.4	24.8	23.4	13.8	2.8	73.8	38.8	48.9	51.1
52316	NORTH ENGLISH	99.0	98.8	0.3	0.3	0.1	0.1	1.0	1.2	7.3	7.2	6.9	6.1	5.3	24.2	21.5	16.5	5.0	74.9	40.4	47.9	52.1
52317	NORTH LIBERTY	95.7	94.7	1.2	1.3	1.4	2.0	2.0	2.4	8.5	7.8	7.3	6.5	7.5	35.4	21.4	5.1	0.6	72.6	32.0	49.6	50.4
52318	NORWAY	98.9	98.7	0.3	0.3	0.1	0.1	0.3	0.3	9.2	8.6	9.2	7.6	6.5	31.6	19.1	7.6	0.8	67.9	32.6	51.2	48.8
52320	OLIN	98.2	98.2	0.7	0.7	0.2	0.2	0.9	0.9	6.6	6.6	7.5	6.4	5.7	26.8	24.7	13.5	2.2	75.5	39.2	51.0	49.0
52321	ONSLOW	99.1	99.1	0.0	0.0	0.0	0.0	0.0	0.0	6.2	6.4	7.1	6.2	5.9	25.3	26.7	14.4	1.9	76.1	41.2	51.3	48.7
52322	OXFORD	98.0	97.5	0.3	0.4	0.4	0.6	0.9	1.1	5.7	6.4	8.0	6.9	5.7	28.7	27.7	9.8	1.2	75.8	39.0	51.0	49.0
52323	OXFORD JUNCTION	98.0	98.0	0.1	0.1	0.1	0.1	0.4	0.4	5.4	5.7	7.0	6.9	7.3	22.3	25.8	15.9	3.7	78.0	41.8	48.9	51.1
52324	PALO	97.7	97.1	0.7	0.8	0.7	1.2	0.6	0.7	5.9	7.7	9.8	7.7	4.3	28.6	28.3	6.9	0.8	71.3	37.6	51.2	48.8
52325	PARNELL	98.8	98.5	0.1	0.2	0.5	0.6	1.2	1.4	7.4	7.7	8.8	6.9	4.9	26.3	24.2	12.5	1.4	71.9	38.2	50.4	49.6
52326	QUASQUETON	97.3	97.3	0.6	0.6	0.8	0.8	0.4	0.4	6.0	6.8	7.8	7.6	5.1	25.7	28.2	10.9	1.9	74.5	38.9	51.9	48.2
52327	RIVERSIDE	96.7	96.1	0.7	0.9	0.4	0.6	1.5	1.8	8.0	7.8	7.6	6.5	6.6	29.9	23.8	8.5	1.3	72.7	34.7	49.7	50.4
52328	ROBINS	95.8	94.7	1.2	1.4	1.2	1.9	1.6	1.8	8.9	9.2	8.8	6.3	5.6	29.3	24.5	6.5	1.1	69.2	34.8	50.2	49.8
52329	ROWLEY	99.3	99.4	0.1	0.1	0.3	0.3	0.2	0.1	6.4	6.6	8.1	7.6	6.5	26.0	25.0	12.2	1.5	74.6	38.6	51.3	48.7
52330	RYAN	99.6	99.4	0.0	0.0	0.0	0.0	0.6	0.8	8.2	8.0	7.7	7.0	5.8	27.9	23.9	10.0	1.6	71.9	35.9	51.7	48.3
52332	SHELLSBURG	99.3	99.2	0.1	0.2	0.1	0.2	0.6	0.6	6.4	7.0	7.9	6.8	4.6	28.2	28.0	9.9	1.2	73.9	39.4	52.7	47.3
52333	SOLON	98.5	98.2	0.4	0.4	0.2	0.3	0.8	1.1	6.0	6.6	6.9	15.7	5.8	22.7	27.1	8.0	1.2	76.4	35.5	51.5	48.5
52334	SOUTH AMANA	99.1	99.1	0.0	0.0	0.5	0.4	0.0	0.0	6.2	7.1	8.0	7.6	4.9	26.7	26.7	11.1	1.8	73.3	39.2	50.7	49.3
	IOWA	93.9	93.0	2.1	2.3	1.3	1.8	2.8	3.2	6.5	6.5	6.9	7.2	7.6	26.4	24.2	12.3	2.4	76.0	37.2	49.2	50.8
	UNITED STATES	75.1	73.6	12.3	12.5	3.8	4.2	12.5	14.1	6.9	6.7	7.2	7.0	7.3	28.6	23.8	10.8	1.7	75.1	36.0	49.1	50.9

ZIP CODE #	POST OFFICE NAME	2004 Per Capita Income	2004 HH Income Base	2004 HOUSEHOLD INCOME DISTRIBUTION (%) Less than $25,000	$25,000 to $49,999	$50,000 to $99,999	$100,000 to $149,999	$150,000 or More	MEDIAN HOUSEHOLD INCOME 2004	2009	2004 National Centile	2004 State Centile	2004 Home Value Base	2004 HOME VALUE DISTRIBUTION (%) Less than $50,000	$50,000 to $89,999	$90,000 to $174,999	$175,000 to $399,999	$400,000 or More	2004 Median Home Value
52144	FORT ATKINSON	19459	522	29.1	35.1	27.6	5.9	2.3	41351	47176	51	44	432	22.0	28.9	39.8	7.6	1.6	88889
52146	HARPERS FERRY	19396	437	30.4	37.1	25.4	6.6	0.5	35936	41533	31	13	372	16.7	36.6	36.0	10.2	0.5	86571
52147	HAWKEYE	22465	466	28.3	42.9	22.5	3.0	3.2	37234	42968	36	18	380	29.5	32.1	24.7	10.8	2.9	76000
52151	LANSING	20393	922	24.5	40.8	27.1	6.2	1.4	38624	44587	42	26	738	26.3	26.4	32.5	12.5	2.3	86552
52154	LAWLER	23771	444	24.3	39.0	31.5	2.9	2.3	42331	47633	54	50	371	23.2	28.6	34.0	14.0	0.3	88194
52155	LIME SPRINGS	18610	449	27.8	37.2	28.7	5.1	1.1	40888	47268	49	40	376	25.5	37.2	23.4	12.5	1.3	77857
52156	LUANA	16510	259	29.3	42.1	25.1	2.3	1.2	37555	42870	38	19	189	16.9	28.0	30.7	19.1	5.3	95000
52157	MC GREGOR	20295	958	29.9	38.4	25.5	4.8	1.5	37453	43440	37	19	720	27.9	29.6	27.6	12.6	2.2	79362
52158	MARQUETTE	13056	6	16.7	50.0	33.3	0.0	0.0	36994	53930	35	17	4	0.0	0.0	100.0	0.0	0.0	112500
52159	MONONA	20337	965	26.4	38.3	27.5	5.1	2.7	40162	46025	47	36	746	19.6	40.0	31.6	7.5	1.3	81744
52160	NEW ALBIN	24904	380	29.2	34.2	29.0	4.5	3.2	40000	45565	46	35	319	39.5	28.5	21.0	10.0	0.9	64474
52161	OSSIAN	18617	547	25.8	36.4	30.5	6.2	1.1	42260	48025	54	50	438	15.5	28.8	38.1	13.0	4.6	96944
52162	POSTVILLE	17225	1268	30.4	34.2	28.4	4.8	2.2	38255	43837	40	24	956	19.0	38.3	29.7	9.8	3.1	82857
52164	RANDALIA	18111	124	26.6	33.9	32.3	4.8	2.4	40000	45000	46	35	97	22.7	32.0	30.9	8.3	6.2	81000
52165	RIDGEWAY	20209	461	23.4	36.2	32.5	5.0	2.8	43813	49688	58	58	371	20.5	21.8	38.0	15.6	4.0	99500
52166	SAINT LUCAS	22641	54	31.5	35.2	25.9	1.9	5.6	40000	50000	46	35	43	27.9	16.3	34.9	16.3	4.7	105357
52169	WADENA	20977	189	30.7	37.6	21.2	6.4	4.2	35556	40824	30	12	149	31.5	23.5	29.5	12.1	3.4	82500
52170	WATERVILLE	18773	232	20.3	47.0	22.8	5.6	4.3	39766	45782	45	32	189	22.8	25.9	32.8	15.9	2.7	91786
52171	WAUCOMA	23362	474	27.9	40.9	24.7	3.2	3.4	38823	44751	42	28	389	34.7	22.9	28.8	11.3	2.3	78958
52172	WAUKON	19766	2627	32.5	33.8	27.6	4.8	1.4	37588	43649	38	19	1914	20.4	30.6	36.5	10.7	1.8	88795
52175	WEST UNION	20453	1498	30.6	32.7	29.7	5.1	1.9	40712	46380	49	39	1120	25.1	31.8	32.1	10.3	0.7	83362
52201	AINSWORTH	19482	486	17.9	38.1	37.7	5.4	1.0	44890	50617	61	62	388	17.0	24.2	37.1	21.4	0.3	104911
52202	ALBURNETT	24633	397	16.4	19.1	47.4	14.1	3.0	62901	75886	87	97	339	3.2	14.5	55.5	26.0	0.9	130357
52203	AMANA	25680	778	21.1	27.4	36.5	11.1	4.0	51209	58921	74	85	660	9.7	4.2	38.0	40.9	7.1	171615
52205	ANAMOSA	20949	2990	24.8	31.1	33.4	8.5	2.3	44286	51759	59	60	2329	15.6	25.4	41.1	16.4	1.5	102872
52206	ATKINS	24051	615	13.8	22.3	49.8	11.7	2.4	62734	73850	87	96	536	4.7	8.8	48.7	33.8	4.1	153333
52207	BALDWIN	18391	177	28.8	37.3	27.7	5.1	1.1	36441	42008	33	16	142	44.4	16.9	23.2	10.6	4.9	62222
52208	BELLE PLAINE	19962	1355	27.8	29.8	37.6	4.3	0.5	43659	51187	58	57	1037	29.5	34.9	29.6	5.3	0.7	73611
52209	BLAIRSTOWN	21526	406	19.7	31.8	40.6	7.6	0.3	48225	55771	69	77	335	8.7	29.6	44.8	13.1	3.9	103935
52210	BRANDON	31689	289	21.1	31.8	34.6	6.2	6.2	46844	54658	66	72	239	18.0	25.5	34.7	15.9	5.9	96739
52211	BROOKLYN	22141	1123	24.0	36.2	30.9	6.8	2.1	43212	50557	57	54	891	18.2	34.3	32.9	12.4	2.2	87857
52212	CENTER JUNCTION	18412	148	27.0	41.2	27.0	4.7	0.0	37659	42849	38	20	118	29.7	28.0	31.4	6.8	4.2	81000
52213	CENTER POINT	24776	1353	15.2	25.4	45.9	11.3	2.3	58584	67412	83	94	1157	6.0	19.1	51.9	20.3	2.7	120506
52214	CENTRAL CITY	22354	1281	21.9	32.9	36.3	6.6	2.2	46325	54390	65	70	1014	10.3	25.3	40.7	20.2	3.6	109000
52215	CHELSEA	18913	337	19.9	37.1	35.9	5.9	1.2	46713	53094	66	72	287	31.0	23.3	34.5	10.1	1.1	84318
52216	CLARENCE	20369	589	24.8	34.3	32.6	7.8	0.5	42799	49682	55	53	439	13.9	37.1	39.6	8.0	1.4	89063
52217	CLUTIER	20858	283	27.9	31.1	32.9	6.0	2.1	37878	43163	39	22	223	21.5	24.7	23.8	22.4	7.6	105729
52218	COGGON	22497	720	15.8	29.7	41.1	10.8	2.5	53624	63749	78	89	581	12.1	21.3	46.3	16.9	3.4	109712
52219	PRAIRIEBURG	22989	75	18.7	32.0	36.0	10.7	2.7	49532	58681	71	81	62	11.3	19.4	41.9	24.2	3.2	117500
52220	CONROY	33757	9	0.0	33.3	55.6	11.1	0.0	62826	66667	87	96	8	0.0	0.0	62.5	37.5	0.0	150000
52221	GUERNSEY	20029	58	27.6	32.8	36.2	3.5	0.0	42383	48668	54	51	48	25.0	27.1	29.2	14.6	4.2	86667
52222	DEEP RIVER	18382	303	27.1	34.0	35.0	3.3	0.7	41931	47768	53	48	250	25.6	25.6	29.2	15.6	4.0	87857
52223	DELHI	22643	540	20.9	29.8	36.5	10.7	2.0	49415	57861	71	80	456	9.9	17.1	44.3	24.1	4.6	121471
52224	DYSART	23275	769	20.0	30.3	37.3	10.5	1.8	49749	57618	71	81	613	11.1	25.6	45.2	13.5	4.6	106196
52225	ELBERON	17946	149	20.1	45.0	28.2	5.4	1.3	41886	47573	53	47	122	33.6	25.4	30.3	6.6	4.1	78889
52226	ELWOOD	14286	12	33.3	25.0	41.7	0.0	0.0	35000	35000	28	10	10	10.0	40.0	50.0	0.0	0.0	90000
52227	ELY	26522	779	17.7	19.0	43.3	14.1	5.9	64291	77629	88	97	622	5.5	9.0	49.2	31.4	5.0	144892
52228	FAIRFAX	27223	771	12.5	21.1	43.8	17.4	5.2	65885	78647	89	98	692	2.2	10.6	46.1	38.4	2.8	155696
52229	GARRISON	20119	325	22.5	34.5	34.2	7.7	1.2	43281	49817	57	55	258	20.5	17.8	38.8	20.2	2.7	111364
52231	HARPER	18270	142	23.9	36.6	33.8	4.9	0.7	44131	49069	59	59	109	16.5	33.0	35.8	11.9	2.8	91667
52232	HARTWICK	24483	110	20.0	29.1	41.8	7.3	1.8	50574	56487	73	83	93	19.4	32.3	32.3	15.1	1.1	88333
52233	HIAWATHA	30751	2984	14.1	36.4	32.8	11.8	4.9	49528	58713	71	80	1795	34.2	7.3	34.9	21.3	2.3	107722
52236	HOMESTEAD	24294	191	8.9	33.5	49.2	7.9	0.5	56121	62380	81	92	165	4.2	12.7	57.0	24.9	1.2	135776
52237	HOPKINTON	17264	607	27.0	33.8	32.6	6.3	0.3	41221	47919	50	43	496	15.7	22.6	37.3	17.9	6.5	106159
52240	IOWA CITY	24982	14144	32.4	26.7	26.7	9.3	5.0	40314	51662	47	38	7192	19.4	8.9	43.8	23.9	4.1	126471
52241	CORALVILLE	28075	7056	22.6	32.0	29.3	11.2	5.0	45174	58754	62	64	3028	3.7	8.1	56.3	28.4	3.5	143852
52242	IOWA CITY	11799	0	0.0	0.0	0.0	0.0	0.0	0	0	0	0	0	0.0	0.0	0.0	0.0	0.0	0
52245	IOWA CITY	28635	7546	24.5	22.1	30.7	13.0	9.6	53935	68474	78	90	4411	5.8	4.6	53.2	32.4	4.0	153564
52246	IOWA CITY	30025	9691	31.6	23.9	25.2	11.9	7.5	43316	58709	57	55	4134	6.1	7.6	38.7	43.4	4.1	170375
52247	KALONA	19923	1721	24.5	33.9	31.7	6.1	3.7	42031	49372	53	49	1342	11.4	13.3	50.9	21.4	3.1	124544
52248	KEOTA	19728	707	25.2	36.2	30.7	6.9	1.0	41879	48786	53	47	561	20.1	39.2	33.3	5.9	1.4	81923
52249	KEYSTONE	21119	447	19.5	34.7	38.0	6.7	1.1	46197	54209	64	69	365	10.4	40.6	40.6	6.3	2.2	89222
52251	LADORA	21325	204	22.1	28.9	42.7	5.9	0.5	49010	52845	70	79	169	26.6	26.0	29.0	16.0	2.4	85000
52253	LISBON	23472	1106	21.3	26.5	38.5	10.1	3.5	51924	60989	75	86	922	7.7	21.2	48.8	20.3	2.1	117143
52254	LOST NATION	18105	430	25.4	39.3	31.6	3.3	0.5	38690	45653	42	27	322	27.0	29.2	32.6	9.3	1.9	80476
52255	LOWDEN	21269	534	25.3	32.6	32.6	7.7	1.9	43395	50000	57	55	414	16.4	30.2	40.6	11.4	1.5	93415
52257	LUZERNE	19376	142	19.0	28.9	43.0	8.5	0.7	51991	60236	75	86	117	13.7	20.5	45.3	16.2	4.3	105978
52301	MARENGO	20774	1812	25.4	30.1	38.9	4.8	0.8	45720	51670	63	67	1403	16.7	27.4	43.3	12.1	0.6	96157
52302	MARION	28796	12270	16.4	24.6	39.0	13.8	6.2	58334	69507	83	94	9540	13.2	12.0	53.7	19.1	2.0	119177
52305	MARTELLE	24238	259	18.5	29.0	40.2	9.7	2.7	52149	59526	76	87	210	7.6	25.2	47.6	16.7	2.9	116026
52306	MECHANICSVILLE	20917	705	23.1	33.9	33.1	8.4	1.6	45130	52278	62	64	563	13.5	30.9	39.8	14.6	1.2	97326
52307	MIDDLE AMANA	0	0	0.0	0.0	0.0	0.0	0.0	0	0	0	0	0	0.0	0.0	0.0	0.0	0.0	0
52308	MILLERSBURG	19701	100	21.0	40.0	34.0	5.0	0.0	41986	47026	53	49	81	17.3	29.6	29.6	18.5	4.9	95000
52309	MONMOUTH	17908	187	29.4	35.8	28.3	5.4	1.1	36727	42637	34	16	151	41.7	18.5	23.8	10.6	5.3	66500
52310	MONTICELLO	19780	2448	23.1	36.8	33.9	5.1	1.2	43745	50250	58	58	1893	11.9	26.2	45.2	14.2	2.5	105662
52313	MOUNT AUBURN	21136	193	14.0	38.9	38.3	4.7	4.2	48396	54439	69	78	159	12.0	22.0	42.1	21.4	2.5	124405
52314	MOUNT VERNON	25812	1712	16.7	21.2	43.0	14.5	4.6	61110	72265	85	95	1413	7.9	9.4	54.1	26.2	2.4	137196
52315	NEWHALL	24105	449	16.0	31.4	40.5	9.6	2.5	51950	60173	75	86	373	3.8	14.8	64.6	14.2	2.7	118382
52316	NORTH ENGLISH	20241	648	23.8	38.0	31.9	5.1	1.2	42342	48354	54	50	503	20.9	35.6	35.8	6.2	1.6	81667
52317	NORTH LIBERTY	36175	3356	14.0	27.1	36.1	12.5	10.4	60582	76749	85	95	2490	17.9	11.0	37.6	26.4	7.1	133306
52318	NORWAY	23658	704	11.1	23.4	48.3	14.9	2.3	63633	74820	88	97	608	5.9	11.2	41.6	40.3	1.0	156849
52320	OLIN	19815	469	27.5	34.1	31.3	5.3	1.7	40890	47179	49	40	377	25.5	30.5	34.0	8.5	1.6	83750
52321	ONSLOW	19352	176	25.6	39.8	28.4	5.7	0.6	39287	45616	44	30	141	22.7	27.0	37.6	8.5	4.3	90500
52322	OXFORD	25502	1000	17.1	26.5	39.1	13.4	3.9	56820	71008	82	93	831	21.1	16.0	35.1	19.9	7.9	126103
52323	OXFORD JUNCTION	15786	379	34.3	39.3	22.4	3.7	0.3	33063	38191	21	5	283	38.5	36.4	15.9	7.1	2.1	65741
52324	PALO	30876	771	11.5	19.7	43.6	18.8	6.4	68348	79421	90	99	680	9.7	7.7	40.0	39.3	3.4	159375
52325	PARNELL	24084	353	12.5	34.0	43.6	6.8	3.1	52122	58401	76	86	292	13.0	15.8	46.2	20.2	4.8	129245
52326	QUASQUETON	26492	194	20.1	35.1	35.1	6.7	3.1	46523	53506	65	71	166	16.3	28.9	39.2	14.5	1.2	96667
52327	RIVERSIDE	20409	1118	21.6	32.6	36.4	7.8	1.7	46753	54490	66	72	860	18.5	15.6	47.4	17.7	0.8	111826
52328	ROBINS	31724	595	7.2	18.3	41.9	23.2	9.4	77842	88899	94	99	491	0.2	4.7	43.4	47.3	4.1	177664
52329	ROWLEY	21299	367	17.4	34.1	39.0	8.5	1.1	49040	55984	70	79	308	12.7	25.7	42.9	12.3	6.5	108537
52330	RYAN	18720	361	18.8	35.2	38.8	5.8	1.4	47802	54735	68	75	288	11.1	13.9	56.3	11.5	7.3	111940
52332	SHELLSBURG	20889	710	18.3	35.2	37.0	8.7	0.7	47393	54368	67	74	615	21.0	11.1	44.4	20.8	2.8	120612
52333	SOLON	32951	2065	8.7	17.0	40.6	23.9	9.9	79320	100308	95	99	1788	1.6	5.5	38.6	44.5	9.9	185656
52334	SOUTH AMANA	22866	87	14.9	32.2	46.0	6.9	0.0	52395	57535	76	87	73	8.2	13.7	52.1	24.7	1.4	128750
	IOWA	23554		24.6	30.5	32.9	8.4	3.7	45622	53985				17.5	26.2	39.3	15.0	2.1	98835
	UNITED STATES	25866		24.7	27.1	30.8	10.9	6.5	48124	56710				10.9	15.0	33.7	30.1	10.4	145905

ZIP CODE #	POST OFFICE NAME	FINANCIAL SERVICES: Auto Loan	FINANCIAL SERVICES: Home Loan	FINANCIAL SERVICES: Invest-ments	FINANCIAL SERVICES: Retire-ment Plans	THE HOME: Home Improvements: Home Repair	THE HOME: Home Improvements: Lawn & Garden	THE HOME: Furnishings: Comput-ers & Hard-ware	THE HOME: Furnishings: Major Appli-ances	THE HOME: Furnishings: TV, Radio, Sound Equip-ment	THE HOME: Furnishings: Furni-ture	ENTERTAINMENT: Dine out/ Carry out	ENTERTAINMENT: Sports Equip-ment	ENTERTAINMENT: Fees & Tickets	ENTERTAINMENT: Toys & Games	ENTERTAINMENT: Travel	ENTERTAINMENT: Cable TV	PERSONAL: Apparel & Services	PERSONAL: Auto Repairs	PERSONAL: Health Insur-ance	PERSONAL: Pets & Supplies
52144	FORT ATKINSON	94	66	35	62	77	86	65	80	75	64	88	97	56	86	68	79	80	79	96	112
52146	HARPERS FERRY	78	61	41	55	68	77	57	69	65	57	77	81	51	76	61	69	71	68	82	94
52147	HAWKEYE	100	71	38	67	82	92	70	86	80	69	94	103	60	92	72	84	86	84	102	118
52151	LANSING	86	62	35	59	70	81	63	75	72	62	85	89	55	82	65	76	77	75	90	100
52154	LAWLER	109	77	42	73	89	100	76	93	87	75	102	112	65	101	79	91	94	92	111	129
52155	LIME SPRINGS	85	59	31	56	69	77	58	72	67	58	79	87	50	77	60	70	72	71	86	100
52156	LUANA	70	56	40	55	60	68	57	63	62	56	74	73	53	73	57	63	69	62	71	79
52157	MC GREGOR	76	62	44	59	67	75	61	69	67	60	80	80	57	79	63	69	75	68	78	88
52158	MARQUETTE	61	52	41	52	55	62	54	57	57	53	69	65	51	68	53	58	65	56	62	67
52159	MONONA	81	66	48	65	70	79	67	74	72	66	87	85	63	86	67	74	81	73	82	90
52160	NEW ALBIN	108	76	40	71	88	99	75	92	86	74	101	111	64	99	77	90	92	91	110	129
52161	OSSIAN	87	62	34	59	71	79	61	75	70	60	82	90	53	80	63	73	75	74	88	103
52162	POSTVILLE	74	63	49	62	66	74	64	69	68	63	83	79	61	82	64	69	77	68	75	83
52164	RANDALIA	90	63	33	59	73	82	62	76	71	61	84	92	53	82	64	75	76	75	91	106
52165	RIDGEWAY	82	73	55	69	77	83	68	75	72	68	88	89	66	89	70	74	83	73	82	97
52166	SAINT LUCAS	94	66	34	62	77	86	65	80	75	64	88	97	55	86	67	78	80	79	96	112
52169	WADENA	89	62	33	59	73	81	62	76	71	61	83	92	53	82	64	75	76	75	91	106
52170	WATERVILLE	93	65	35	62	76	85	64	79	74	64	87	96	55	85	67	78	79	78	95	111
52171	WAUCOMA	99	79	55	77	85	96	79	89	86	78	104	104	74	103	80	89	96	88	100	112
52172	WAUKON	81	59	36	56	66	77	62	72	71	60	83	83	55	79	63	74	76	71	86	92
52175	WEST UNION	73	64	52	62	67	75	64	69	68	63	82	80	61	82	65	70	78	68	76	84
52201	AINSWORTH	93	65	34	62	76	85	64	80	74	64	87	96	55	85	67	78	79	78	95	111
52202	ALBURNETT	109	96	73	91	102	109	89	99	95	89	115	118	87	117	92	97	109	96	107	128
52203	AMANA	89	89	92	90	91	95	88	90	86	87	107	106	88	107	88	85	104	89	89	103
52205	ANAMOSA	80	66	49	63	71	78	65	73	70	64	84	86	61	84	66	72	79	72	80	93
52206	ATKINS	94	103	104	105	100	99	99	98	92	99	117	116	99	117	96	87	115	97	86	107
52207	BALDWIN	80	58	33	54	67	75	56	69	64	56	76	82	49	74	59	68	70	68	82	96
52208	BELLE PLAINE	74	61	46	58	66	75	62	69	68	60	82	79	58	82	63	72	76	68	79	85
52209	BLAIRSTOWN	85	76	58	72	80	86	70	77	74	70	90	92	68	92	72	76	86	75	84	100
52210	BRANDON	129	114	87	109	121	130	106	117	112	106	137	140	104	140	109	115	130	114	127	151
52211	BROOKLYN	86	69	49	66	75	86	70	79	78	68	92	90	64	90	71	81	86	78	91	99
52212	CENTER JUNCTION	79	55	29	52	64	72	54	67	63	54	73	81	46	72	56	66	67	66	80	94
52213	CENTER POINT	105	94	71	89	99	106	87	96	92	87	112	115	85	114	89	94	106	94	104	124
52214	CENTRAL CITY	84	75	62	71	80	88	73	79	78	72	95	93	72	99	75	81	90	78	88	99
52215	CHELSEA	84	73	55	69	78	85	68	76	73	68	88	91	66	90	70	75	84	75	84	100
52216	CLARENCE	81	60	37	57	66	78	64	73	72	62	85	83	57	81	64	76	78	72	87	91
52217	CLUTIER	88	62	32	58	72	80	61	75	70	60	82	91	52	81	63	74	75	74	90	105
52218	COGGON	102	86	62	82	93	100	80	91	87	80	105	109	77	106	83	90	99	89	101	120
52219	PRAIRIEBURG	92	82	62	78	86	93	76	84	80	76	98	100	74	100	78	82	93	82	91	108
52220	CONROY	102	91	69	86	96	103	84	93	89	84	109	111	82	111	87	92	103	91	101	120
52221	GUERNSEY	82	57	30	54	67	75	56	70	65	56	76	84	48	75	59	68	70	69	83	97
52222	DEEP RIVER	84	59	31	56	69	77	58	72	67	57	78	86	50	77	60	70	72	71	85	100
52223	DELHI	102	73	42	68	85	95	72	88	82	71	96	105	62	95	75	86	88	87	104	122
52224	DYSART	105	74	39	70	86	96	73	90	84	72	98	108	62	96	75	88	90	89	107	125
52225	ELBERON	78	68	51	65	73	78	63	71	68	63	82	84	62	84	65	70	78	69	77	92
52226	ELWOOD	75	53	28	50	61	69	52	64	60	51	70	78	44	69	54	63	64	63	77	90
52227	ELY	93	113	118	113	111	110	101	102	94	101	119	119	107	125	103	92	118	98	92	113
52228	FAIRFAX	102	117	116	116	115	115	105	107	100	105	125	125	109	130	106	97	123	103	98	121
52229	GARRISON	93	65	34	62	76	85	64	80	74	64	87	96	55	85	67	78	79	78	95	111
52231	HARPER	86	60	31	57	70	78	59	73	68	59	80	89	51	79	62	72	73	72	87	102
52232	HARTWICK	95	76	53	69	85	95	72	85	80	71	96	100	65	95	76	85	89	84	100	116
52233	HIAWATHA	100	96	94	99	95	99	97	97	95	98	120	115	95	116	94	92	116	99	92	111
52236	HOMESTEAD	101	90	70	86	95	102	84	93	89	84	108	110	82	110	86	91	103	90	100	119
52237	HOPKINTON	78	61	40	59	67	75	61	70	67	60	81	82	56	79	62	70	75	69	79	90
52240	IOWA CITY	83	74	83	79	72	78	88	80	86	85	108	99	83	103	81	80	104	86	74	90
52241	CORALVILLE	86	81	95	87	79	84	91	86	88	90	112	104	88	107	86	83	109	91	79	95
52242	IOWA CITY	0	0	0	0	0	0	0	0	0	0	0	0	0	0	0	0	0	0	0	0
52245	IOWA CITY	100	97	117	102	96	102	113	102	108	107	136	126	109	133	106	101	132	108	93	113
52246	IOWA CITY	90	76	92	83	76	83	98	88	96	92	120	110	91	113	89	89	116	96	82	98
52247	KALONA	97	75	48	72	83	93	74	86	82	73	98	102	67	97	76	85	91	85	98	113
52248	KEOTA	82	60	36	57	67	78	63	73	71	61	84	84	55	80	64	75	77	72	87	93
52249	KEYSTONE	94	66	35	62	77	86	65	80	75	64	88	97	56	86	68	79	80	79	96	112
52251	LADORA	87	74	54	71	80	86	69	78	75	69	90	94	67	92	72	77	85	77	87	103
52253	LISBON	97	85	68	84	89	98	85	91	89	84	109	105	82	109	85	91	102	89	97	109
52254	LOST NATION	78	56	32	53	65	72	55	67	63	55	74	81	48	73	57	66	68	66	79	92
52255	LOWDEN	75	70	62	66	74	82	69	73	74	67	90	84	68	94	71	77	85	72	82	89
52257	LUZERNE	87	78	59	74	82	88	72	80	76	72	93	95	71	95	74	78	88	78	86	103
52301	MARENGO	80	69	53	68	73	81	68	74	73	68	88	86	66	88	69	74	83	73	80	91
52302	MARION	101	110	111	110	108	110	103	104	99	104	125	121	106	127	103	97	122	102	97	116
52305	MARTELLE	97	86	66	82	91	98	80	88	85	80	103	105	78	105	82	87	98	86	96	114
52306	MECHANICSVILLE	86	73	55	71	77	86	72	79	77	71	93	92	69	93	73	79	88	77	86	97
52307	MIDDLE AMANA	0	0	0	0	0	0	0	0	0	0	0	0	0	0	0	0	0	0	0	0
52308	MILLERSBURG	83	58	30	55	68	76	58	71	66	57	78	86	49	76	60	70	71	70	85	99
52309	MONMOUTH	81	58	33	54	67	75	57	70	65	56	77	83	50	75	60	69	71	69	83	96
52310	MONTICELLO	75	66	53	64	70	78	65	70	69	64	84	82	63	85	66	72	79	69	78	87
52313	MOUNT AUBURN	103	72	37	68	84	93	71	88	82	70	96	105	60	94	73	86	87	86	104	122
52314	MOUNT VERNON	94	105	116	107	103	105	101	100	97	101	121	119	103	124	101	94	119	100	92	111
52315	NEWHALL	107	77	43	73	89	99	76	93	86	75	102	111	66	100	78	90	93	91	109	127
52316	NORTH ENGLISH	80	66	50	65	71	79	67	73	72	66	87	85	64	86	67	73	81	72	80	90
52317	NORTH LIBERTY	119	132	134	135	128	127	125	124	117	126	148	146	127	149	123	110	146	123	109	136
52318	NORWAY	100	113	109	118	108	104	102	101	93	106	119	118	105	119	99	87	117	98	86	111
52320	OLIN	80	64	46	63	69	78	66	73	71	65	86	84	61	85	66	73	80	72	81	90
52321	ONSLOW	84	59	31	55	68	76	58	72	67	57	78	86	49	77	60	70	71	71	85	100
52322	OXFORD	98	93	79	91	96	102	88	94	90	87	110	110	87	113	89	91	106	92	97	113
52323	OXFORD JUNCTION	63	47	30	45	52	62	51	57	58	49	68	65	46	64	51	61	62	57	69	71
52324	PALO	109	126	127	125	125	125	113	115	108	113	135	135	119	142	116	106	133	111	107	131
52325	PARNELL	103	92	69	87	97	104	85	94	90	85	110	112	83	112	87	92	104	92	102	122
52326	QUASQUETON	106	95	72	90	100	107	87	97	93	87	113	116	86	115	90	95	107	94	105	125
52327	RIVERSIDE	83	80	68	78	80	83	76	80	75	76	93	94	73	92	75	74	90	79	78	95
52328	ROBINS	129	155	159	157	151	147	139	138	128	140	162	162	146	169	140	123	161	134	121	152
52329	ROWLEY	92	79	57	75	85	91	74	83	79	74	96	99	71	97	76	82	90	81	92	109
52330	RYAN	94	66	35	62	77	86	65	80	75	64	88	97	56	86	67	78	80	79	95	112
52332	SHELLSBURG	89	79	60	75	84	90	73	81	78	73	95	97	72	97	75	80	90	79	88	105
52333	SOLON	131	157	165	159	153	152	142	141	132	143	166	166	150	174	144	127	166	137	126	156
52334	SOUTH AMANA	95	84	64	80	89	96	78	86	83	78	101	103	76	103	80	85	96	84	94	112
	IOWA	87	79	73	79	82	89	80	84	83	79	102	98	78	102	80	83	97	84	88	100
	UNITED STATES	100	100	100	100	100	100	100	100	100	100	100	100	100	100	100	100	100	100	100	100

ZIP CODE #	POST OFFICE NAME	COUNTY FIPS CODE	POPULATION 2000	2004	2009	2000-2004 ANNUAL RATE % Rate	State Centile	HOUSEHOLDS 2000	2004	2009	% Annual Rate 2000-2004	2004 Average HH Size	FAMILIES 2000	2004	% Annual Rate 2000-2004
52335	SOUTH ENGLISH	107	658	629	615	-1.1	6	264	255	252	-0.8	2.47	192	185	-0.9
52336	SPRINGVILLE	113	2202	2228	2297	0.3	62	828	850	887	0.6	2.61	612	624	0.5
52337	STANWOOD	031	901	901	927	0.0	51	366	369	384	0.2	2.44	265	266	0.1
52338	SWISHER	103	2713	2896	3165	1.6	87	966	1045	1156	1.9	2.77	793	851	1.7
52339	TAMA	171	4029	4004	3973	-0.2	42	1491	1483	1473	-0.1	2.64	1046	1040	-0.1
52340	TIFFIN	103	1148	1378	1600	4.4	99	486	595	701	4.9	2.32	322	389	4.6
52341	TODDVILLE	113	1432	1442	1474	0.2	57	506	519	537	0.6	2.78	412	420	0.5
52342	TOLEDO	171	3576	3563	3539	-0.1	44	1377	1380	1377	0.1	2.43	936	935	0.0
52345	URBANA	011	1011	1088	1157	1.7	89	369	401	431	2.0	2.71	282	305	1.9
52346	VAN HORNE	011	1182	1174	1212	-0.2	41	439	440	457	0.1	2.66	320	317	-0.2
52347	VICTOR	095	1476	1458	1468	-0.3	33	583	582	590	0.0	2.49	415	412	-0.2
52348	VINING	171	186	196	200	1.2	83	76	81	83	1.5	2.42	58	62	1.6
52349	VINTON	011	7644	7858	8201	0.7	73	3064	3184	3351	0.9	2.41	2138	2213	0.8
52352	WALKER	113	1755	1832	1907	1.0	80	644	682	718	1.4	2.69	497	524	1.3
52353	WASHINGTON	183	9198	9403	9514	0.5	70	3670	3775	3842	0.7	2.40	2488	2553	0.6
52354	WATKINS	011	473	471	486	-0.1	44	172	173	180	0.1	2.72	123	122	-0.2
52355	WEBSTER	107	362	355	352	-0.5	25	128	127	127	-0.2	2.80	93	92	-0.3
52356	WELLMAN	183	2600	2620	2645	0.2	58	977	994	1010	0.4	2.56	703	712	0.3
52358	WEST BRANCH	031	3743	4170	4527	2.6	94	1429	1612	1768	2.9	2.54	1021	1151	2.9
52359	WEST CHESTER	183	258	253	252	-0.5	25	112	111	112	-0.2	2.26	83	82	-0.3
52361	WILLIAMSBURG	095	3984	4239	4428	1.5	86	1547	1648	1725	1.5	2.54	1058	1119	1.3
52362	WYOMING	105	1130	1093	1080	-0.8	13	479	471	473	-0.4	2.32	321	313	-0.6
52401	CEDAR RAPIDS	113	2135	2068	2107	-0.8	14	1103	1066	1095	-0.8	1.76	382	365	-1.1
52402	CEDAR RAPIDS	113	38827	40228	42154	0.8	77	15790	16556	17559	1.1	2.33	9844	10279	1.0
52403	CEDAR RAPIDS	113	25691	25322	25919	-0.3	31	10483	10424	10783	-0.1	2.37	6699	6624	-0.3
52404	CEDAR RAPIDS	113	33126	35055	37139	1.3	84	13972	15013	16113	1.7	2.28	8314	8876	1.6
52405	CEDAR RAPIDS	113	24273	25154	26321	0.8	77	9664	10146	10747	1.2	2.44	6595	6898	1.1
52411	CEDAR RAPIDS	113	5146	5615	5992	2.1	92	1704	1872	2014	2.2	3.00	1405	1536	2.1
52501	OTTUMWA	179	31181	30955	30753	-0.2	39	12790	12780	12777	0.0	2.34	8374	8338	-0.1
52530	AGENCY	179	960	944	934	-0.4	28	404	401	400	-0.2	2.35	299	296	-0.2
52531	ALBIA	135	6229	6271	6339	0.2	57	2525	2564	2613	0.4	2.38	1680	1700	0.3
52533	BATAVIA	101	1183	1154	1133	-0.6	20	463	457	454	-0.3	2.51	328	322	-0.4
52534	BEACON	123	460	459	454	-0.1	46	187	189	189	0.3	2.42	148	149	0.2
52535	BIRMINGHAM	177	1022	1041	1059	0.4	67	425	438	450	0.7	2.37	300	309	0.7
52536	BLAKESBURG	179	734	705	691	-0.9	8	310	301	298	-0.7	2.34	228	221	-0.7
52537	BLOOMFIELD	051	6419	6518	6612	0.4	64	2441	2494	2543	0.5	2.56	1707	1738	0.4
52540	BRIGHTON	101	1538	1536	1541	0.0	47	620	627	636	0.3	2.45	437	441	0.2
52542	CANTRIL	177	476	475	482	-0.1	46	203	205	210	0.2	2.32	143	143	0.0
52543	CEDAR	123	257	263	264	0.5	70	90	93	94	0.8	2.83	71	73	0.7
52544	CENTERVILLE	007	8251	8116	7995	-0.4	28	3507	3480	3459	-0.2	2.27	2219	2192	-0.3
52548	CHILLICOTHE	179	90	93	94	0.8	76	38	40	40	1.2	2.33	30	31	0.8
52549	CINCINNATI	007	760	792	802	1.0	79	306	322	330	1.2	2.46	212	223	1.2
52550	DELTA	107	679	728	750	1.7	88	283	305	317	1.8	2.39	187	201	1.7
52551	DOUDS	177	332	334	338	0.1	57	137	139	143	0.3	2.40	98	99	0.2
52552	DRAKESVILLE	051	1085	1103	1119	0.4	66	392	401	409	0.5	2.65	287	293	0.5
52553	EDDYVILLE	123	1595	1598	1598	0.0	52	624	631	636	0.3	2.53	441	445	0.2
52554	ELDON	179	1429	1428	1422	0.0	48	607	612	613	0.2	2.33	405	406	0.1
52555	EXLINE	007	372	365	359	-0.5	25	147	145	144	-0.3	2.52	110	109	-0.2
52556	FAIRFIELD	101	11808	11548	11330	-0.5	22	5008	4947	4903	-0.3	2.23	3112	3059	-0.4
52557	FAIRFIELD	101	606	629	635	0.9	78	158	168	172	1.5	3.11	96	101	1.2
52560	FLORIS	051	488	496	503	0.4	66	189	194	198	0.6	2.56	147	150	0.5
52561	FREMONT	123	1002	999	989	-0.1	45	391	393	391	0.1	2.54	283	283	0.0
52563	HEDRICK	107	1746	1733	1728	-0.2	39	682	682	683	0.0	2.52	501	500	-0.1
52565	KEOSAUQUA	177	2070	2090	2126	0.2	60	845	862	886	0.5	2.28	549	557	0.3
52566	KIRKVILLE	179	218	225	228	0.8	75	73	76	78	1.0	2.96	58	60	0.8
52567	LIBERTYVILLE	101	559	605	623	1.9	90	223	246	257	2.3	2.39	166	182	2.2
52569	MELROSE	135	644	645	648	0.0	52	270	273	278	0.3	2.36	203	205	0.2
52570	MILTON	177	893	903	919	0.3	61	321	326	334	0.4	2.77	238	241	0.3
52571	MORAVIA	007	1272	1268	1256	-0.1	45	550	557	559	0.3	2.28	384	387	0.2
52572	MOULTON	007	1149	1130	1113	-0.4	28	490	487	485	-0.1	2.32	322	318	-0.3
52573	MOUNT STERLING	177	240	240	243	0.0	51	95	96	98	0.3	2.50	67	67	0.0
52574	MYSTIC	007	1058	1067	1061	0.2	59	421	430	432	0.5	2.48	287	292	0.4
52576	OLLIE	107	574	629	655	2.2	93	236	262	274	2.5	2.40	169	186	2.3
52577	OSKALOOSA	123	15068	14850	14644	-0.3	31	6132	6101	6068	-0.1	2.35	4051	4016	-0.2
52580	PACKWOOD	101	530	508	493	-1.0	7	218	213	210	-0.5	2.38	156	151	-0.8
52581	PLANO	007	405	413	412	0.5	68	180	186	187	0.8	2.22	132	135	0.5
52583	PROMISE CITY	185	401	388	373	-0.8	13	161	157	151	-0.6	2.46	117	114	-0.6
52584	PULASKI	051	477	475	479	-0.1	44	162	162	165	0.0	2.85	128	128	0.0
52585	RICHLAND	107	991	1083	1128	2.1	92	408	451	473	2.4	2.40	291	320	2.3
52586	ROSE HILL	123	590	586	579	-0.2	41	233	234	234	0.1	2.50	181	181	0.0
52588	SELMA	177	496	499	506	0.1	57	210	214	219	0.4	2.33	153	155	0.3
52590	SEYMOUR	185	1195	1147	1099	-1.0	7	475	457	439	-0.9	2.43	327	314	-1.0
52591	SIGOURNEY	107	3237	3134	3082	-0.8	14	1285	1249	1234	-0.7	2.40	864	836	-0.8
52593	UDELL	007	129	124	121	-0.9	8	49	48	47	-0.5	2.58	38	38	0.0
52594	UNIONVILLE	007	399	387	379	-0.7	15	152	150	148	-0.3	2.58	116	114	-0.4
52601	BURLINGTON	057	31005	29943	28907	-0.8	11	12756	12456	12159	-0.6	2.35	8321	8087	-0.7
52619	ARGYLE	111	929	918	903	-0.3	34	322	322	320	0.0	2.79	249	248	-0.1
52620	BONAPARTE	177	875	999	1087	3.2	97	343	394	432	3.3	2.54	234	269	3.3
52621	CRAWFORDSVILLE	183	663	656	654	-0.3	36	248	246	246	-0.2	2.67	188	185	-0.4
52623	DANVILLE	057	1919	1868	1812	-0.6	17	725	713	699	-0.4	2.57	561	550	-0.5
52624	DENMARK	111	497	548	568	2.3	93	185	207	217	2.7	2.65	144	161	2.7
52625	DONNELLSON	111	2472	2422	2373	-0.5	24	962	954	945	-0.2	2.47	726	717	-0.3
52626	FARMINGTON	111	1333	1282	1283	-0.9	9	559	543	550	-0.7	2.36	363	351	-0.8
52627	FORT MADISON	111	13694	13551	13323	-0.3	34	5484	5469	5434	-0.1	2.29	3539	3511	-0.2
52630	HILLSBORO	111	440	425	414	-0.8	11	173	169	167	-0.6	2.51	124	120	-0.8
52631	HOUGHTON	111	61	59	58	-0.8	13	18	18	18	0.0	3.28	14	13	-1.7
52632	KEOKUK	111	13797	13606	13419	-0.3	31	5655	5634	5615	-0.1	2.37	3703	3681	-0.1
52635	LOCKRIDGE	101	758	772	771	0.4	67	285	296	299	0.9	2.61	209	216	0.8
52637	MEDIAPOLIS	057	2563	2568	2521	0.1	52	990	1002	994	0.3	2.45	702	708	0.2
52638	MIDDLETOWN	057	683	706	701	0.8	76	244	255	255	1.0	2.74	191	199	1.0
52639	MONTROSE	111	2181	2090	2032	-1.0	7	802	777	763	-0.7	2.48	577	556	-0.9
52640	MORNING SUN	115	1413	1449	1469	0.6	71	541	557	567	0.7	2.53	403	414	0.6
52641	MOUNT PLEASANT	087	12229	12049	11903	-0.4	30	4462	4415	4384	-0.3	2.40	2974	2932	-0.3
52644	MOUNT UNION	087	454	468	470	0.7	74	175	183	186	1.1	2.56	139	145	1.0
52645	NEW LONDON	087	3225	3260	3246	0.3	61	1272	1302	1310	0.6	2.47	925	942	0.4
	IOWA					0.5					0.7	2.43			0.6
	UNITED STATES					1.2					1.3	2.58			1.1

POPULATION COMPOSITION

IOWA

52335-52645 B

ZIP CODE #	POST OFFICE NAME	RACE (%) White 2000	White 2004	Black 2000	Black 2004	Asian/Pacific 2000	Asian/Pacific 2004	% Hispanic Origin 2000	% Hispanic Origin 2004	2004 AGE DISTRIBUTION (%) 0-4	5-9	10-14	15-19	20-24	25-44	45-64	65-84	85+	18+	MEDIAN AGE 2004	% 2004 Males	% 2004 Females
52335	SOUTH ENGLISH	99.4	99.2	0.0	0.0	0.3	0.3	0.3	0.3	7.2	7.6	7.5	7.0	6.0	23.7	26.6	12.4	2.1	73.5	40.1	50.9	49.1
52336	SPRINGVILLE	98.7	98.3	0.1	0.2	0.4	0.6	0.5	0.5	6.7	7.1	7.4	6.7	5.9	27.2	27.1	10.2	1.7	74.7	38.2	50.5	49.6
52337	STANWOOD	98.1	98.0	0.2	0.2	0.3	0.4	0.2	0.2	6.1	6.8	6.9	5.1	5.4	26.4	28.2	13.2	1.9	77.0	40.5	51.5	48.5
52338	SWISHER	98.2	97.7	0.2	0.2	0.7	1.0	0.4	0.5	6.4	7.4	7.8	6.7	3.6	28.6	30.8	8.1	0.5	74.2	39.3	51.0	49.0
52339	TAMA	78.6	78.1	0.4	0.4	0.3	0.3	8.4	8.6	8.7	7.7	7.5	7.1	7.3	23.5	21.6	13.5	3.1	71.4	35.8	48.5	51.5
52340	TIFFIN	96.2	95.4	1.1	1.2	1.1	1.5	2.0	2.5	8.1	7.5	7.5	6.8	7.6	35.3	21.2	5.4	0.7	72.9	32.1	50.0	50.0
52341	TODDVILLE	97.6	97.0	0.6	0.6	0.9	1.3	0.7	0.9	5.3	6.2	7.5	6.7	5.6	24.8	33.5	9.4	1.0	76.8	41.3	51.7	48.3
52342	TOLEDO	87.0	86.6	0.4	0.4	0.3	0.3	4.2	4.5	6.5	6.3	6.0	8.3	6.5	23.5	24.6	14.9	3.5	75.4	39.7	48.6	51.5
52345	URBANA	99.2	99.0	0.4	0.4	0.1	0.2	0.8	0.9	7.9	7.8	8.6	6.8	5.9	35.7	18.2	7.8	1.3	71.4	33.9	51.1	48.9
52346	VAN HORNE	98.2	98.0	0.5	0.5	0.3	0.3	0.5	0.6	7.1	7.2	8.2	6.3	5.7	26.5	25.0	11.8	2.3	73.0	38.6	51.2	48.8
52347	VICTOR	98.6	98.4	0.1	0.1	0.3	0.5	1.0	1.1	5.9	6.3	7.4	6.5	5.9	22.7	27.1	14.8	3.4	76.3	42.3	49.6	50.4
52348	VINING	96.2	96.4	0.0	0.0	0.0	0.0	3.8	3.1	7.7	7.7	6.6	5.6	6.6	25.0	28.6	11.2	1.0	74.5	38.2	53.1	46.9
52349	VINTON	98.5	98.3	0.2	0.2	0.3	0.3	0.8	0.9	6.4	6.5	7.1	6.7	5.9	26.1	24.3	14.1	2.9	76.0	39.9	49.7	50.3
52352	WALKER	99.0	98.9	0.2	0.2	0.1	0.1	0.2	0.2	7.0	7.1	7.9	6.6	6.2	26.8	25.6	11.2	1.8	74.1	37.7	50.7	49.3
52353	WASHINGTON	95.6	94.9	0.5	0.5	0.4	0.5	4.2	5.0	6.4	6.4	6.7	6.2	5.9	24.0	24.8	15.4	4.2	76.6	41.2	47.7	52.3
52354	WATKINS	99.2	99.2	0.0	0.0	0.0	0.0	0.4	0.6	6.2	6.8	8.5	6.8	4.7	27.8	24.2	12.7	2.3	74.3	38.5	49.3	50.7
52355	WEBSTER	99.5	99.4	0.0	0.0	0.0	0.0	0.6	0.3	7.0	7.3	7.6	7.0	6.2	23.9	25.6	13.0	2.3	73.8	39.9	51.0	49.0
52356	WELLMAN	98.6	98.4	0.1	0.1	0.1	0.2	1.0	1.2	7.0	7.0	8.1	6.8	5.5	24.4	24.0	13.8	3.6	73.4	39.2	50.0	50.0
52358	WEST BRANCH	97.3	96.8	0.4	0.4	0.7	0.9	1.6	1.9	6.5	6.6	7.0	6.6	6.4	27.1	27.1	10.4	2.3	75.7	39.2	48.6	51.4
52359	WEST CHESTER	98.1	98.0	0.0	0.0	0.0	0.0	0.8	0.8	6.7	6.7	8.3	7.5	4.7	26.1	28.5	10.3	1.2	72.7	39.6	51.4	48.6
52361	WILLIAMSBURG	98.3	97.9	0.1	0.2	0.4	0.5	1.5	1.7	6.7	6.9	9.0	7.6	5.8	26.0	22.6	13.1	2.4	72.4	37.8	48.3	51.7
52362	WYOMING	98.9	98.9	0.4	0.4	0.0	0.0	0.4	0.4	5.3	5.4	7.0	7.0	6.5	23.8	25.6	16.8	2.6	78.1	42.2	48.9	51.1
52401	CEDAR RAPIDS	70.4	66.5	17.9	19.6	6.4	8.5	3.4	3.9	6.5	6.0	6.8	6.0	6.3	29.1	20.8	13.4	5.0	77.5	37.1	48.1	51.9
52402	CEDAR RAPIDS	92.9	91.5	2.8	3.2	2.0	2.9	1.7	2.0	7.3	7.1	6.8	6.8	8.2	30.5	22.0	9.7	1.6	75.4	34.2	48.8	51.2
52403	CEDAR RAPIDS	89.5	88.3	6.2	6.7	1.3	1.8	1.8	2.1	6.5	6.8	7.2	6.8	6.2	26.4	25.4	12.1	2.6	75.5	38.4	48.5	51.5
52404	CEDAR RAPIDS	92.6	91.4	2.9	3.3	1.6	2.3	1.8	2.1	7.3	6.6	6.6	6.5	9.4	30.1	21.2	10.6	1.8	76.0	33.4	49.3	50.7
52405	CEDAR RAPIDS	94.9	93.9	1.7	1.9	1.5	2.1	1.3	1.6	6.7	6.9	7.1	5.9	6.0	29.7	24.0	11.5	2.2	75.7	37.3	49.0	51.0
52411	CEDAR RAPIDS	96.9	96.1	0.5	0.5	1.3	1.8	1.1	1.3	6.6	7.7	8.8	6.7	4.4	23.8	31.7	9.6	0.7	72.7	40.8	49.5	50.5
52501	OTTUMWA	95.9	95.2	1.1	1.2	0.7	1.0	2.5	2.9	6.0	6.1	6.5	6.4	6.9	25.4	25.0	14.7	3.0	77.8	39.7	48.8	51.2
52530	AGENCY	99.0	98.6	0.1	0.2	0.3	0.5	0.3	0.5	5.2	5.9	6.5	6.0	4.8	21.8	31.8	16.0	2.0	78.7	44.9	49.9	50.1
52531	ALBIA	98.2	98.2	0.2	0.2	0.5	0.5	0.6	0.6	6.4	6.5	6.9	6.5	6.0	23.9	24.2	16.1	3.6	76.1	40.6	48.5	51.5
52533	BATAVIA	97.9	97.3	0.1	0.1	1.1	1.6	1.0	1.2	6.0	6.3	6.7	6.4	4.9	24.0	32.2	11.9	1.7	77.2	42.2	50.6	49.4
52534	BEACON	98.5	98.3	0.2	0.2	0.0	0.2	0.0	0.2	6.5	6.5	6.8	6.5	6.1	25.9	28.3	12.4	0.9	75.8	39.4	50.5	49.5
52535	BIRMINGHAM	99.0	98.9	0.0	0.0	0.3	0.4	0.9	1.1	5.2	5.5	6.9	6.0	5.1	25.1	28.7	15.5	2.1	78.5	42.6	52.3	47.7
52536	BLAKESBURG	99.1	99.0	0.1	0.1	0.4	0.4	0.4	0.3	6.8	6.7	5.1	5.3	5.0	28.5	26.8	14.2	1.7	78.3	40.3	50.1	49.9
52537	BLOOMFIELD	98.3	98.1	0.2	0.2	0.3	0.4	0.7	0.9	7.3	6.8	7.2	6.4	5.8	24.2	25.1	14.1	3.2	74.7	39.6	49.9	50.1
52540	BRIGHTON	99.0	98.8	0.4	0.5	0.4	0.6	0.3	0.4	6.1	6.6	7.3	6.3	5.8	26.2	27.9	12.8	1.2	76.2	39.7	50.5	49.5
52542	CANTRIL	98.3	98.3	0.2	0.2	0.2	0.4	0.4	0.4	5.5	6.1	7.4	6.1	4.8	24.2	28.2	16.0	1.7	77.7	42.1	54.1	45.9
52543	CEDAR	98.1	98.1	0.4	0.4	0.4	0.4	0.8	0.8	6.1	6.5	7.6	7.6	4.9	28.1	27.4	11.0	0.8	74.9	39.6	54.4	45.6
52544	CENTERVILLE	97.7	97.4	0.6	0.7	0.4	0.5	1.3	1.6	6.1	5.9	6.8	6.5	6.3	24.6	23.6	16.3	4.0	77.2	40.9	46.9	53.1
52548	CHILLICOTHE	98.9	98.9	0.0	0.0	0.0	1.1	0.0	1.1	4.3	7.5	9.7	7.5	3.2	29.0	26.9	10.8	1.1	72.0	40.6	50.5	49.5
52549	CINCINNATI	98.6	98.5	0.0	0.0	0.0	0.0	0.7	0.8	6.6	6.8	7.2	6.2	5.8	24.2	27.4	13.5	2.3	75.5	40.4	50.8	49.2
52550	DELTA	98.2	98.4	0.3	0.3	0.4	0.4	1.0	1.1	5.6	5.6	8.7	6.2	6.3	25.0	23.5	16.5	2.6	76.2	39.4	47.3	52.8
52551	DOUDS	98.2	97.9	0.0	0.0	0.6	0.9	0.6	0.9	5.7	5.1	8.7	6.0	4.5	24.0	29.6	14.7	1.8	76.1	41.9	50.0	50.0
52552	DRAKESVILLE	98.9	98.6	0.0	0.1	0.2	0.3	0.6	0.6	7.6	7.6	7.5	6.7	6.2	23.8	23.7	13.4	3.5	73.1	38.1	49.5	50.5
52553	EDDYVILLE	99.0	98.8	0.1	0.1	0.3	0.4	0.7	0.7	6.9	7.1	6.9	7.0	6.5	26.9	26.1	11.3	1.4	74.9	37.6	49.9	50.1
52554	ELDON	98.4	98.1	0.1	0.1	0.1	0.1	1.2	1.5	6.1	6.4	7.6	6.3	5.0	25.5	26.6	14.2	2.4	75.9	40.6	49.1	50.9
52555	EXLINE	98.9	98.9	0.3	0.3	0.3	0.6	0.8	1.1	4.4	5.2	8.2	6.6	4.7	22.7	31.8	14.5	1.9	78.1	43.7	51.2	48.8
52556	FAIRFIELD	95.4	94.2	0.8	0.8	2.1	2.9	2.1	2.5	5.2	5.6	6.7	7.1	6.5	22.3	32.9	11.1	2.7	78.0	42.5	48.7	51.3
52557	FAIRFIELD	92.2	90.1	1.8	2.1	3.3	4.9	3.5	4.1	4.0	4.3	5.7	8.1	8.0	17.7	45.6	5.9	0.8	81.4	45.6	49.1	50.9
52560	FLORIS	99.0	98.8	0.0	0.0	0.2	0.4	0.8	1.0	6.5	6.7	5.7	6.3	4.8	25.0	27.8	15.3	2.0	77.6	41.7	51.6	48.4
52561	FREMONT	99.3	99.2	0.1	0.1	0.1	0.1	0.3	0.4	7.6	8.5	7.6	6.2	5.7	27.8	21.1	12.7	2.7	72.3	36.3	49.8	50.3
52563	HEDRICK	98.7	98.6	0.1	0.1	0.2	0.2	0.6	0.6	6.5	6.9	7.7	6.6	5.5	23.9	26.4	14.1	2.4	74.4	39.5	49.6	50.4
52565	KEOSAUQUA	98.6	98.3	0.1	0.1	0.4	0.6	0.2	0.3	4.7	5.1	6.6	6.2	5.4	21.6	26.8	18.6	5.2	79.7	45.3	47.2	52.8
52566	KIRKVILLE	99.1	99.1	0.0	0.0	0.5	0.4	0.5	0.4	4.0	7.6	9.8	7.6	3.1	25.3	29.8	12.0	0.9	73.8	41.3	52.4	47.6
52567	LIBERTYVILLE	98.8	98.5	0.2	0.2	0.2	0.3	0.4	0.3	5.3	5.8	7.8	6.9	5.8	26.1	29.3	11.9	1.2	77.2	40.6	49.8	50.3
52569	MELROSE	99.2	99.2	0.2	0.2	0.3	0.3	0.0	0.2	5.4	5.7	5.9	5.6	5.3	21.9	30.2	18.1	1.9	79.7	45.2	52.3	47.8
52570	MILTON	98.1	98.0	0.1	0.1	0.2	0.3	1.5	1.8	8.1	9.0	7.9	7.2	7.3	22.0	19.8	14.8	3.9	70.0	35.9	52.7	47.3
52571	MORAVIA	99.1	99.1	0.1	0.1	0.1	0.1	0.3	0.3	5.7	5.4	5.4	6.4	6.6	21.9	27.8	17.6	3.3	79.7	44.1	48.1	51.9
52572	MOULTON	98.4	98.1	0.3	0.3	0.2	0.2	0.4	0.4	5.2	5.2	6.6	6.4	6.6	23.3	26.3	17.8	2.7	78.9	42.5	49.6	50.4
52573	MOUNT STERLING	98.3	98.3	0.0	0.0	0.4	0.4	0.0	0.0	5.4	6.3	7.5	5.8	5.0	25.4	26.7	15.8	2.1	76.7	41.4	53.3	46.7
52574	MYSTIC	99.2	99.1	0.1	0.2	0.1	0.1	0.3	0.3	5.2	5.6	7.2	6.1	5.4	26.2	28.0	14.3	2.0	78.1	41.0	49.8	50.2
52576	OLLIE	99.3	99.4	0.0	0.0	0.0	0.2	0.5	0.3	6.0	6.7	8.1	5.6	4.9	25.8	25.8	14.6	2.5	75.7	40.7	50.7	49.3
52577	OSKALOOSA	96.4	95.6	0.9	1.0	1.2	1.7	1.1	1.3	6.8	6.3	6.8	6.9	8.1	25.6	23.2	13.8	2.7	76.4	37.3	49.6	50.4
52580	PACKWOOD	98.7	98.6	0.0	0.0	0.2	0.2	1.3	1.6	6.5	6.9	7.5	5.5	5.7	27.8	26.8	11.0	2.4	75.6	39.4	49.8	50.2
52581	PLANO	98.8	98.6	0.3	0.2	0.3	0.2	0.7	1.0	5.1	5.3	5.6	5.3	5.3	23.0	31.5	16.7	2.2	81.1	45.2	50.1	49.9
52583	PROMISE CITY	97.5	97.2	0.0	0.0	0.3	0.5	0.8	1.0	4.1	4.6	7.5	7.2	5.4	23.7	27.6	17.8	2.1	79.1	43.5	49.5	50.5
52584	PULASKI	97.1	96.8	1.1	1.1	0.0	0.0	1.3	1.5	7.2	7.8	9.1	7.0	5.1	22.5	24.2	14.7	2.5	71.2	39.0	49.7	50.3
52585	RICHLAND	99.2	99.3	0.1	0.1	0.1	0.1	0.5	0.5	6.1	6.8	7.9	5.2	4.9	26.4	26.0	14.3	2.4	75.9	40.9	50.8	49.2
52586	ROSE HILL	98.5	98.0	0.3	0.5	0.2	0.3	0.5	1.0	6.0	6.7	7.9	7.5	5.1	26.3	27.8	11.8	1.0	74.6	39.9	53.9	46.1
52588	SELMA	98.2	97.6	0.0	0.0	0.6	1.0	0.6	0.6	5.8	5.4	7.8	6.0	4.6	24.5	29.5	14.6	1.8	76.8	41.8	49.1	50.9
52590	SEYMOUR	98.1	97.8	0.0	0.0	0.0	0.0	1.4	1.8	5.2	5.5	6.6	7.3	5.3	23.0	24.6	18.2	4.2	78.3	43.1	47.9	52.1
52591	SIGOURNEY	99.0	99.0	0.1	0.1	0.4	0.4	0.6	0.6	6.0	6.1	7.4	6.5	5.8	22.3	23.2	17.2	5.5	76.2	41.9	46.8	53.2
52593	UDELL	98.5	99.2	0.0	0.0	0.0	0.0	1.6	1.6	4.8	4.8	8.1	6.5	5.7	22.6	29.0	16.9	1.6	77.4	43.5	50.8	49.2
52594	UNIONVILLE	98.8	98.5	0.0	0.0	0.3	0.3	0.8	1.0	5.2	5.4	7.0	6.5	6.2	22.7	28.7	16.0	2.3	78.0	43.2	50.4	49.6
52601	BURLINGTON	92.4	91.5	4.5	4.9	0.7	1.0	1.9	2.3	6.5	6.2	6.6	6.4	7.1	25.3	25.3	14.0	2.6	76.8	39.3	48.2	51.8
52619	ARGYLE	98.6	98.4	0.3	0.3	0.1	0.1	0.9	1.0	5.5	6.4	7.7	7.2	5.1	25.2	30.5	11.1	1.3	75.3	40.8	51.9	48.2
52620	BONAPARTE	99.1	99.0	0.0	0.0	0.5	0.6	1.7	1.9	6.2	6.3	7.5	8.2	7.0	24.3	24.8	13.3	2.3	75.1	38.1	49.5	50.6
52621	CRAWFORDSVILLE	98.6	98.3	0.2	0.2	0.0	0.0	1.7	2.0	6.9	7.0	8.2	6.3	5.3	26.5	28.1	10.5	1.2	74.1	40.2	51.7	48.3
52623	DANVILLE	98.1	97.7	0.5	0.5	0.3	0.4	0.6	0.9	5.9	6.3	7.4	5.8	5.7	25.4	28.2	12.5	2.7	76.6	40.8	49.7	50.3
52624	DENMARK	99.2	98.9	0.0	0.0	0.0	0.2	0.6	0.9	6.2	6.4	7.3	7.1	5.8	23.2	29.2	13.1	1.6	75.9	40.9	49.1	50.9
52625	DONNELLSON	98.8	98.5	0.2	0.3	0.2	0.3	1.0	1.2	5.2	5.8	7.3	6.9	5.9	24.3	27.5	14.2	2.9	76.8	41.6	48.9	51.1
52626	FARMINGTON	99.2	99.0	0.1	0.1	0.1	0.1	0.5	0.6	5.5	5.9	7.2	6.7	6.5	22.4	27.3	15.9	2.7	77.5	42.4	48.4	51.6
52627	FORT MADISON	91.6	90.4	4.1	4.4	0.7	0.9	4.7	5.6	5.7	5.6	6.1	6.3	6.6	26.2	27.1	13.8	2.7	78.9	40.8	51.2	48.9
52630	HILLSBORO	98.9	98.8	0.0	0.0	0.2	0.5	0.5	0.5	7.3	7.3	6.8	6.6	5.7	27.1	26.4	11.1	1.9	73.9	38.8	49.9	50.1
52631	HOUGHTON	98.4	100.0	0.0	0.0	0.0	0.0	0.0	0.0	6.8	6.8	6.8	6.8	5.1	25.4	27.1	13.6	1.7	76.3	40.5	52.5	47.5
52632	KEOKUK	93.8	93.1	3.4	3.6	0.5	0.7	1.0	1.2	6.6	6.5	7.2	6.6	6.5	24.4	25.6	14.2	2.5	75.7	39.4	48.1	52.0
52635	LOCKRIDGE	99.6	99.6	0.0	0.0	0.3	0.3	0.4	0.5	6.5	6.9	7.0	6.6	4.5	27.6	27.5	12.3	1.2	75.3	39.2	50.7	49.4
52637	MEDIAPOLIS	99.0	98.7	0.2	0.3	0.3	0.4	0.6	0.7	6.9	7.2	7.5	5.5	5.7	23.6	24.5	15.2	3.9	75.0	40.2	48.3	51.7
52638	MIDDLETOWN	95.8	94.8	1.3	1.6	0.7	1.1	1.8	2.1	5.2	7.4	7.8	7.2	6.5	26.9	28.5	9.4	1.1	74.8	38.9	50.6	49.4
52639	MONTROSE	96.2	95.7	1.5	1.7	0.1	0.2	2.2	2.7	5.0	5.6	6.6	6.5	5.7	25.6	29.3	13.2	2.7	78.5	42.2	51.8	48.2
52640	MORNING SUN	97.4	96.9	0.1	0.2	0.4	0.6	4.6	5.5	7.8	7.5	6.8	5.9	5.3	26.6	23.0	14.0	3.1	73.9	38.6	48.4	51.6
52641	MOUNT PLEASANT	92.4	90.8	2.4	2.6	2.9	4.1	1.5	1.8	6.1	5.9	6.4	6.8	8.1	29.8	23.8	10.7	2.4	77.6	36.7	52.1	47.9
52644	MOUNT UNION	98.5	98.3	0.2	0.2	0.4	0.4	0.7	0.9	6.4	6.8	7.7	6.0	5.8	28.6	27.6	10.0	1.1	75.4	39.1	51.3	48.7
52645	NEW LONDON	98.5	98.1	0.2	0.2	0.4	0.6	0.6	0.8	6.2	6.4	7.2	6.5	5.8	27.6	26.3	11.9	2.2	76.3	38.8	48.8	51.2
	IOWA	93.9	93.0	2.1	2.3	1.3	1.8	2.8	3.2	6.5	6.5	6.9	7.2	7.6	26.4	24.2	12.3	2.4	76.0	37.2	49.2	50.8
	UNITED STATES	75.1	73.6	12.3	12.5	3.8	4.2	12.5	14.1	6.9	6.7	7.2	7.0	7.3	28.6	23.8	10.8	1.7	75.1	36.0	49.1	50.9

ZIP CODE #	POST OFFICE NAME	2004 Per Capita Income	2004 HH Income Base	2004 Household Income Distribution (%): Less than $25,000	$25,000 to $49,999	$50,000 to $99,999	$100,000 to $149,999	$150,000 or More	Median Household Income: 2004	2009	2004 National Centile	2004 State Centile	2004 Home Value Base	2004 Home Value Distribution (%): Less than $50,000	$50,000 to $89,999	$90,000 to $174,999	$175,000 to $399,999	$400,000 or More	2004 Median Home Value
52335	SOUTH ENGLISH	19855	255	23.9	35.3	34.5	5.9	0.4	44298	50858	59	60	203	30.1	33.0	25.6	6.9	4.4	72059
52336	SPRINGVILLE	23497	850	16.1	26.9	44.0	10.8	2.1	55206	64259	80	91	716	10.5	18.7	48.5	19.3	3.1	114715
52337	STANWOOD	23059	369	20.6	30.6	39.3	5.7	3.8	49010	54787	70	79	299	13.0	33.4	42.1	10.4	1.0	94200
52338	SWISHER	33887	1045	7.5	13.3	47.3	23.4	8.6	79366	98885	95	100	933	0.5	5.0	39.0	46.2	9.2	185434
52339	TAMA	17567	1483	31.2	31.8	31.0	4.3	1.8	39046	45319	43	29	1086	25.4	37.8	32.5	3.4	0.9	77981
52340	TIFFIN	33525	595	14.8	28.7	37.0	12.3	7.2	57557	73931	82	93	435	20.7	12.0	38.2	23.0	6.2	126651
52341	TODDVILLE	31394	519	16.0	20.2	39.3	17.3	7.1	64510	77126	88	97	470	1.5	13.2	39.2	39.4	6.8	163158
52342	TOLEDO	19584	1380	27.0	34.5	30.7	5.7	2.2	39832	46204	45	33	1052	21.4	37.6	31.6	8.8	0.8	81754
52345	URBANA	22410	401	16.7	31.9	39.7	8.0	3.7	50875	59275	74	84	344	8.7	20.6	50.9	17.7	2.0	116518
52346	VAN HORNE	20321	440	17.5	28.9	46.6	6.4	0.7	51702	60050	75	86	355	7.3	21.4	53.0	13.0	5.4	111250
52347	VICTOR	20519	582	24.2	32.3	36.6	5.8	1.0	45114	50351	61	64	481	15.0	41.0	37.2	5.6	1.3	84818
52348	VINING	19911	81	19.8	45.7	28.4	4.9	1.2	41923	49535	53	48	67	34.3	22.4	32.8	7.5	3.0	81000
52349	VINTON	21737	3184	26.0	32.4	33.4	6.1	2.1	43468	50875	57	56	2401	14.4	29.6	41.6	13.2	1.3	95196
52352	WALKER	21514	682	16.1	34.5	37.7	9.8	1.9	49517	58655	71	80	569	9.8	19.9	46.9	21.4	1.9	115448
52353	WASHINGTON	20592	3775	25.8	32.5	34.6	5.5	1.7	43448	50346	57	56	2841	13.0	28.8	45.7	12.1	0.4	99340
52354	WATKINS	19887	173	19.1	32.4	41.0	7.5	0.0	48505	56482	69	78	143	7.0	29.4	46.2	14.0	3.5	107813
52355	WEBSTER	18948	127	25.2	32.3	33.9	7.1	1.6	43305	50268	57	55	104	36.5	28.9	22.1	8.7	3.9	68000
52356	WELLMAN	20282	994	20.0	39.9	32.9	5.0	2.1	43578	50454	57	57	776	17.0	26.2	41.4	13.4	2.1	100321
52358	WEST BRANCH	23516	1612	16.6	30.0	42.9	8.8	1.7	53196	60761	77	88	1280	14.8	19.7	42.9	18.7	3.9	114167
52359	WEST CHESTER	24128	111	17.1	41.4	36.9	3.6	0.9	46413	52810	65	70	89	13.5	20.2	46.1	19.1	1.1	111184
52361	WILLIAMSBURG	24038	1648	20.3	36.2	36.0	5.3	2.2	44834	51064	61	62	1223	10.4	15.2	55.9	16.4	2.1	121245
52362	WYOMING	19965	471	29.3	35.0	27.2	7.6	0.9	39779	46401	45	33	355	31.6	38.9	21.1	7.0	1.4	67833
52401	CEDAR RAPIDS	17544	1066	59.6	20.7	16.5	1.9	1.3	20727	25620	2	1	277	45.1	41.9	11.6	0.0	1.4	54091
52402	CEDAR RAPIDS	28796	16556	16.6	26.9	38.3	13.2	5.0	55919	66874	81	92	11064	4.5	15.6	58.1	20.5	1.4	121089
52403	CEDAR RAPIDS	32733	10424	19.6	26.8	32.3	12.2	9.1	54086	64896	78	90	7661	4.3	21.5	48.2	19.8	6.2	116144
52404	CEDAR RAPIDS	23342	15013	24.5	31.8	35.0	6.9	1.9	45215	54165	62	64	9662	19.0	26.7	46.8	7.1	0.4	94371
52405	CEDAR RAPIDS	25414	10146	16.2	26.8	42.4	12.7	2.0	55672	66347	80	92	7858	3.7	22.5	62.5	11.0	0.4	111397
52411	CEDAR RAPIDS	38698	1872	8.4	15.5	38.0	21.8	16.2	82210	96919	96	100	1806	8.1	3.4	26.3	52.6	9.6	203909
52501	OTTUMWA	19374	12780	33.5	34.4	25.3	4.4	2.4	35814	41346	31	13	9452	38.5	31.2	22.2	7.1	1.1	62780
52530	AGENCY	21455	401	24.2	34.9	32.7	7.2	1.0	44586	50872	60	61	332	20.8	38.3	28.0	12.4	0.6	82683
52531	ALBIA	20716	2564	30.5	33.0	28.7	5.3	2.5	39014	45017	43	28	1967	29.2	34.1	28.4	8.0	0.3	74636
52533	BATAVIA	25568	457	21.9	33.7	29.8	9.6	5.0	43501	55047	57	56	368	37.5	21.2	26.1	12.5	2.7	69688
52534	BEACON	22981	189	13.2	43.4	33.3	7.4	2.7	46186	52432	64	69	166	25.3	32.5	31.9	10.2	0.0	79286
52535	BIRMINGHAM	17862	438	33.1	35.2	27.4	3.2	1.1	34850	39317	27	9	366	40.4	32.8	20.0	5.7	1.1	62500
52536	BLAKESBURG	21569	301	20.3	40.2	31.2	7.0	1.3	40797	47342	49	40	245	36.7	22.9	37.1	3.3	0.0	66481
52537	BLOOMFIELD	17849	2494	32.9	30.0	31.5	4.5	1.1	38306	44980	40	24	1983	31.8	31.8	25.8	9.1	1.5	73780
52540	BRIGHTON	18788	627	28.2	41.3	25.8	3.0	1.6	36812	42379	35	16	500	33.2	31.8	24.0	8.6	2.4	72571
52542	CANTRIL	23326	205	30.2	35.6	25.4	4.9	3.9	36557	41125	34	16	170	38.2	24.1	28.2	8.8	0.6	65385
52543	CEDAR	21356	93	20.4	31.2	38.7	6.5	3.2	48819	53531	70	79	78	21.8	19.2	37.2	20.5	1.3	103846
52544	CENTERVILLE	16861	3480	40.5	33.2	21.9	3.1	1.3	31451	35561	16	3	2315	40.7	30.8	22.0	5.9	0.5	60024
52548	CHILLICOTHE	22859	40	20.0	35.0	35.0	7.5	2.5	45000	52150	61	63	35	34.3	31.4	20.0	11.4	2.9	75000
52549	CINCINNATI	16931	322	31.7	41.0	21.7	5.3	0.3	33925	38884	24	6	279	47.3	34.1	9.3	9.3	0.0	58333
52550	DELTA	20589	305	33.4	32.8	26.2	4.9	2.6	34247	41078	25	7	229	59.0	20.5	10.5	7.9	2.2	41087
52551	DOUDS	16122	139	33.1	41.7	20.9	4.3	0.0	35163	37580	28	10	116	41.4	25.9	25.0	6.0	1.7	63333
52552	DRAKESVILLE	17164	401	32.4	36.4	25.7	4.0	1.5	35289	42021	29	11	331	26.9	36.3	21.8	13.6	1.5	77500
52553	EDDYVILLE	21864	631	28.7	31.5	30.3	7.0	2.5	41327	46562	51	44	487	32.7	34.9	21.8	10.1	0.6	70119
52554	ELDON	17517	612	37.1	34.0	24.8	3.3	0.8	33461	38660	22	6	494	54.9	30.0	9.1	4.7	1.4	45789
52555	EXLINE	14690	145	37.2	41.4	17.9	1.4	2.1	30120	33711	13	2	120	34.2	30.0	23.3	11.7	0.8	73000
52556	FAIRFIELD	24442	4947	31.2	28.6	26.6	9.2	4.4	38676	48793	42	26	3411	20.3	30.2	34.3	13.1	2.1	89395
52557	FAIRFIELD	15255	168	38.1	23.8	25.6	10.7	1.8	35000	42383	28	10	73	9.6	46.6	28.8	9.6	5.5	82500
52560	FLORIS	17184	194	34.0	30.9	32.0	1.6	1.6	37638	45000	38	20	164	36.6	16.5	36.0	7.3	3.7	82857
52561	FREMONT	20733	393	26.5	29.3	34.6	8.1	1.5	45449	51153	62	65	333	27.9	42.9	22.8	6.0	0.3	71029
52563	HEDRICK	20227	682	30.4	32.3	28.6	6.0	2.8	40093	46448	46	36	532	40.0	29.5	18.8	7.1	4.5	63590
52565	KEOSAUQUA	18382	862	33.3	38.8	22.3	3.8	1.9	35143	39805	28	10	657	37.9	29.8	25.9	6.2	0.2	65746
52566	KIRKVILLE	18151	76	22.4	40.8	26.3	5.3	5.3	40000	46861	46	35	66	36.4	28.8	24.2	9.1	1.5	74000
52567	LIBERTYVILLE	23270	246	19.9	40.2	31.3	3.3	5.3	42728	51895	55	52	205	25.9	21.5	32.7	14.6	5.4	93235
52569	MELROSE	19335	273	22.3	47.6	24.2	4.8	1.1	40176	45814	47	36	233	34.8	27.9	27.0	6.9	3.4	67632
52570	MILTON	12974	326	42.3	39.0	16.6	0.9	1.2	29377	32892	11	2	267	61.8	20.6	13.5	4.1	0.0	39875
52571	MORAVIA	18030	557	36.5	39.0	20.8	2.3	1.4	32869	37477	21	5	438	38.8	34.0	18.3	8.0	0.9	61000
52572	MOULTON	16569	487	42.1	37.4	17.7	1.9	1.0	29643	32996	12	2	369	49.3	26.0	17.9	6.0	0.8	51250
52573	MOUNT STERLING	21605	96	29.2	34.4	28.1	5.2	3.1	37685	41297	38	20	80	37.5	23.8	30.0	8.8	0.0	66667
52574	MYSTIC	15986	430	38.8	36.1	20.9	2.6	1.6	31918	35440	18	4	357	50.4	28.9	15.4	4.5	0.8	49634
52576	OLLIE	18547	262	34.0	30.5	30.2	4.2	1.2	38194	44217	40	23	211	28.9	35.1	31.3	4.7	0.0	75952
52577	OSKALOOSA	22048	6101	28.6	32.7	30.9	5.2	2.7	40354	47290	47	38	4206	21.3	36.1	32.0	9.6	1.0	82488
52580	PACKWOOD	22735	213	21.6	38.0	27.7	10.8	1.9	41939	51811	53	48	173	33.5	27.2	35.8	3.5	0.0	73571
52581	PLANO	18912	186	31.2	41.9	22.0	2.7	2.2	35222	40603	28	11	156	32.7	26.3	28.9	9.6	2.6	80000
52583	PROMISE CITY	14975	157	36.3	41.4	19.1	1.9	1.3	32689	36705	20	5	131	36.6	27.5	26.7	5.3	3.8	66875
52584	PULASKI	16450	162	31.5	32.7	27.2	6.8	1.9	40000	46622	46	35	136	31.6	27.2	26.5	11.8	2.9	80000
52585	RICHLAND	18532	451	32.8	31.5	31.0	4.0	0.7	38227	44016	40	24	363	30.0	34.4	30.9	4.1	0.6	75571
52586	ROSE HILL	22615	234	22.2	31.2	37.2	6.4	3.0	47349	53915	67	74	188	26.1	20.7	31.9	18.6	2.7	95455
52588	SELMA	16737	214	33.2	43.9	19.6	3.3	0.0	34708	39499	26	9	180	42.8	23.9	26.1	6.1	1.1	62857
52590	SEYMOUR	16467	457	40.0	33.5	19.7	5.3	1.5	30903	36296	15	3	344	62.2	22.7	8.7	5.5	0.9	36563
52591	SIGOURNEY	19933	1249	33.3	30.2	28.3	5.3	2.9	37275	44251	36	18	933	27.1	38.7	25.4	8.4	0.4	72253
52593	UDELL	18283	48	31.3	37.5	27.1	2.1	2.1	36525	41156	34	16	40	30.0	22.5	32.5	15.0	0.0	86667
52594	UNIONVILLE	17656	150	31.3	37.3	26.7	2.7	2.0	36362	41146	33	15	124	29.0	23.4	32.3	14.5	0.8	86250
52601	BURLINGTON	23129	12456	29.4	31.5	30.5	5.4	3.2	40046	47728	46	36	8955	20.6	37.5	31.2	9.6	1.2	80982
52619	ARGYLE	18847	322	23.0	33.9	34.2	6.5	2.5	45000	52712	61	63	280	22.1	23.9	40.7	11.1	2.1	96471
52620	BONAPARTE	17930	394	31.7	34.3	28.9	3.3	1.8	37328	43017	37	18	297	47.1	26.9	19.9	6.1	0.0	53542
52621	CRAWFORDSVILLE	21451	246	16.3	32.1	39.8	10.6	1.2	50802	54135	73	84	199	14.6	29.2	35.2	16.1	5.0	98333
52623	DANVILLE	24113	713	17.5	26.2	45.3	8.3	2.7	53702	61813	78	89	611	16.0	27.0	43.5	11.6	1.8	98019
52624	DENMARK	22439	207	10.6	39.1	42.5	3.9	3.9	50153	58216	72	82	180	10.0	33.3	47.8	8.9	0.0	102049
52625	DONNELLSON	20913	954	20.4	35.5	36.0	6.6	1.5	44764	52249	61	61	788	19.3	33.6	34.3	10.9	1.9	87262
52626	FARMINGTON	21686	543	33.2	32.4	28.9	3.1	2.4	35664	41094	30	12	417	43.2	27.1	22.1	7.4	0.2	62742
52627	FORT MADISON	21810	5469	28.3	32.1	31.5	5.5	2.7	40232	47569	47	37	3953	30.9	38.7	24.2	5.2	1.0	69698
52630	HILLSBORO	21540	169	22.5	32.0	38.5	3.6	3.6	46147	52641	64	69	137	26.3	22.6	35.0	14.6	1.5	91500
52631	HOUGHTON	15127	18	22.2	33.3	38.9	5.6	0.0	47295	60000	67	74	14	7.1	21.4	64.3	7.1	0.0	110000
52632	KEOKUK	20847	5634	31.4	33.5	25.8	6.3	3.1	37694	44261	38	21	4025	37.5	30.9	24.5	6.2	1.0	64986
52635	LOCKRIDGE	17684	296	24.0	38.9	32.1	4.7	0.3	41985	50513	53	48	241	31.1	23.2	22.4	17.0	6.2	84474
52637	MEDIAPOLIS	22127	1002	25.1	29.8	34.7	7.3	3.1	45637	53572	63	66	812	19.7	28.5	40.5	10.3	1.0	91613
52638	MIDDLETOWN	19939	255	21.2	29.8	40.8	6.3	2.0	48957	55167	70	79	219	27.9	21.9	39.7	9.1	1.4	90294
52639	MONTROSE	20122	777	27.5	31.9	30.9	7.9	1.8	41549	48019	51	45	627	28.7	33.3	30.3	7.0	0.6	74352
52640	MORNING SUN	24021	557	23.5	33.0	34.5	5.9	3.1	45761	52227	63	67	429	39.4	33.1	19.4	6.5	1.6	62361
52641	MOUNT PLEASANT	20975	4415	27.6	30.2	31.2	8.7	2.2	43992	51192	59	58	3128	18.4	22.8	43.3	14.2	1.4	98818
52644	MOUNT UNION	23572	183	15.3	27.3	48.1	7.1	2.2	54833	61482	79	91	154	18.2	24.0	44.2	13.6	0.0	98571
52645	NEW LONDON	22277	1302	20.0	32.0	38.4	7.5	2.1	48491	55512	69	78	1053	24.4	30.8	36.9	7.7	0.3	84011
	IOWA	23554		24.6	30.5	32.9	8.4	3.7	45622	53985				17.5	26.2	39.3	15.0	2.1	98835
	UNITED STATES	25866		24.7	27.1	30.8	10.9	6.5	48124	56710				10.9	15.0	33.7	30.1	10.4	145905

ZIP CODE #	POST OFFICE NAME	FINANCIAL SERVICES: Auto Loan	Home Loan	Invest-ments	Retire-ment Plans	THE HOME: Home Improvements: Home Repair	Lawn & Garden	Furnishings: Comput-ers & Hard-ware	Major Appli-ances	TV, Radio, Sound Equip-ment	Furni-ture	ENTERTAINMENT: Dine out/ Carry out	Sports Equip-ment	Fees & Tickets	Toys & Games	Travel	Cable TV	PERSONAL: Apparel & Services	Auto Repairs	Health Insur-ance	Pets & Supplies
52335	SOUTH ENGLISH	83	66	44	63	73	80	63	73	69	63	83	88	59	83	65	72	78	72	83	98
52336	SPRINGVILLE	99	88	67	83	92	99	81	90	86	81	105	107	79	106	83	88	100	88	97	116
52337	STANWOOD	102	71	38	67	83	93	70	87	81	70	95	104	60	93	73	85	87	85	103	120
52338	SWISHER	122	152	161	152	149	147	135	135	125	135	158	158	144	168	138	122	157	130	121	149
52339	TAMA	71	62	54	62	65	73	64	68	67	63	82	78	61	80	64	68	77	68	73	80
52340	TIFFIN	109	119	118	120	115	115	113	112	106	113	134	133	113	135	111	100	131	111	100	124
52341	TODDVILLE	117	139	142	138	137	137	124	126	117	124	147	147	131	155	127	115	145	121	116	142
52342	TOLEDO	73	66	58	64	69	77	66	71	70	65	85	81	64	84	67	72	80	70	77	84
52345	URBANA	97	87	66	82	92	98	80	89	85	80	104	106	79	106	83	87	98	86	96	115
52346	VAN HORNE	98	69	36	65	80	89	68	83	78	67	91	101	58	90	70	82	83	82	99	116
52347	VICTOR	90	66	38	63	75	84	65	78	74	64	87	93	57	86	67	77	80	77	91	105
52348	VINING	77	69	52	65	73	78	63	70	67	64	82	84	62	84	65	69	78	69	76	91
52349	VINTON	77	73	68	71	76	83	73	76	75	71	92	88	72	93	74	76	88	75	80	89
52352	WALKER	94	82	60	77	87	94	76	85	81	76	98	101	73	100	78	83	93	83	93	110
52353	WASHINGTON	76	68	57	65	71	80	68	73	72	67	88	83	66	88	69	75	83	72	80	87
52354	WATKINS	87	77	58	73	82	87	71	80	76	71	92	95	69	94	73	78	87	78	86	103
52355	WEBSTER	89	73	50	69	79	86	69	79	75	68	90	94	64	91	71	77	84	77	88	105
52356	WELLMAN	86	69	49	68	75	84	70	78	76	69	91	91	65	90	70	78	85	77	87	98
52358	WEST BRANCH	92	87	73	85	89	95	83	88	84	83	104	103	81	103	83	85	99	87	90	105
52359	WEST CHESTER	99	69	36	65	81	90	68	84	79	67	92	102	58	90	71	83	84	83	101	118
52361	WILLIAMSBURG	102	81	56	79	89	99	81	92	88	80	106	108	75	105	82	91	98	90	103	118
52362	WYOMING	83	58	31	55	68	76	58	71	67	57	78	86	50	77	60	70	71	70	85	99
52401	CEDAR RAPIDS	42	37	47	38	36	42	46	42	48	44	59	51	44	57	44	47	57	46	43	47
52402	CEDAR RAPIDS	93	100	110	103	98	101	99	97	95	99	120	114	101	121	98	92	118	97	90	106
52403	CEDAR RAPIDS	102	114	130	115	113	118	113	110	109	111	137	129	116	140	114	107	135	111	105	121
52404	CEDAR RAPIDS	75	74	79	75	74	78	77	76	76	76	95	89	76	94	75	74	93	77	73	85
52405	CEDAR RAPIDS	83	92	100	92	90	94	89	88	86	89	108	103	92	112	90	84	107	88	83	97
52411	CEDAR RAPIDS	152	190	206	195	184	185	168	164	153	170	195	190	184	203	171	148	196	158	146	182
52501	OTTUMWA	66	62	59	59	64	71	63	65	66	61	81	75	62	82	64	68	77	65	70	76
52530	AGENCY	91	64	33	60	74	83	63	78	73	62	85	94	54	83	65	76	78	77	93	109
52531	ALBIA	78	66	50	63	70	79	67	72	72	65	87	83	63	87	67	75	81	71	82	88
52533	BATAVIA	104	91	69	87	97	104	85	94	90	85	110	112	82	112	87	93	104	92	103	122
52534	BEACON	89	79	61	75	84	90	73	81	78	73	95	97	72	97	76	80	90	79	88	105
52535	BIRMINGHAM	76	54	30	51	63	70	53	65	61	53	72	78	46	70	55	64	66	64	77	90
52536	BLAKESBURG	81	72	55	68	76	82	67	74	71	67	86	88	65	88	69	73	82	72	80	95
52537	BLOOMFIELD	78	59	38	57	66	74	60	69	67	59	79	81	54	78	61	70	73	68	80	90
52540	BRIGHTON	77	60	39	58	66	74	60	69	66	59	79	81	55	78	61	69	73	68	79	89
52542	CANTRIL	98	68	36	65	80	89	67	83	78	67	91	101	58	89	70	82	83	82	99	116
52543	CEDAR	107	78	45	74	89	99	76	92	86	76	102	111	67	101	79	90	94	91	108	126
52544	CENTERVILLE	60	50	38	48	53	61	52	56	56	50	68	64	49	67	52	59	63	56	65	68
52548	CHILLICOTHE	85	76	58	72	80	86	70	78	74	70	90	93	69	92	72	76	86	76	84	100
52549	CINCINNATI	56	57	57	54	59	66	57	58	60	55	73	65	59	78	59	62	70	57	63	66
52550	DELTA	68	67	65	64	70	78	67	69	70	64	86	78	68	92	69	73	83	67	76	80
52551	DOUDS	68	50	30	48	57	63	49	59	55	49	65	71	43	65	51	58	60	58	69	80
52552	DRAKESVILLE	83	58	30	55	68	76	57	71	66	57	78	86	49	76	60	69	71	70	85	99
52553	EDDYVILLE	88	76	59	74	80	88	74	81	79	74	96	94	72	96	75	81	90	79	88	100
52554	ELDON	67	54	38	53	58	65	55	61	59	54	71	70	51	70	55	61	66	60	67	75
52555	EXLINE	65	47	27	44	54	61	47	57	53	46	63	68	40	62	48	56	57	56	67	78
52556	FAIRFIELD	79	80	79	79	82	87	78	80	78	77	96	93	78	98	79	79	93	79	81	93
52557	FAIRFIELD	63	73	90	75	72	73	72	69	68	71	86	83	74	88	72	66	85	70	63	76
52560	FLORIS	76	58	36	55	65	72	56	66	63	56	74	80	50	74	58	65	69	65	77	90
52561	FREMONT	85	69	51	69	74	84	71	78	76	70	92	90	67	91	71	78	86	77	86	95
52563	HEDRICK	86	66	43	64	73	82	67	77	74	66	88	90	61	87	68	76	81	76	88	99
52565	KEOSAUQUA	70	54	36	52	59	69	57	64	63	55	75	73	51	72	57	66	69	63	75	80
52566	KIRKVILLE	86	77	58	73	81	87	71	79	75	71	91	94	69	93	73	77	87	76	85	101
52567	LIBERTYVILLE	90	80	61	76	85	91	74	82	79	74	96	98	73	98	77	81	91	80	89	106
52569	MELROSE	85	58	27	51	66	75	56	70	67	57	79	83	48	75	57	72	71	69	85	98
52570	MILTON	59	44	28	42	48	57	48	53	54	46	63	60	43	60	48	57	58	53	64	65
52571	MORAVIA	69	51	31	48	56	66	54	61	61	52	72	71	47	68	54	64	65	61	73	78
52572	MOULTON	64	47	29	45	53	62	51	58	57	48	67	66	44	64	51	60	61	57	69	73
52573	MOUNT STERLING	98	68	36	64	80	89	67	83	78	67	91	100	58	89	70	81	83	82	99	116
52574	MYSTIC	74	50	24	45	57	65	49	61	58	49	68	73	41	65	50	62	62	60	74	86
52576	OLLIE	81	56	29	53	66	73	56	69	64	55	75	83	47	74	58	67	68	68	82	96
52577	OSKALOOSA	83	69	54	67	74	83	71	77	76	69	92	89	67	91	71	78	86	76	86	95
52580	PACKWOOD	98	69	37	65	80	89	68	83	78	67	91	101	58	90	70	82	84	82	99	116
52581	PLANO	76	53	28	50	62	69	52	65	60	52	71	78	45	69	54	63	65	64	77	90
52583	PROMISE CITY	67	47	25	44	54	61	46	57	53	46	62	69	39	61	48	56	57	56	68	79
52584	PULASKI	86	60	31	56	70	78	59	73	68	58	80	88	50	78	61	71	73	72	87	102
52585	RICHLAND	81	56	29	53	66	73	56	69	64	55	75	83	47	74	58	67	68	68	82	96
52586	ROSE HILL	99	74	45	70	84	93	72	86	81	71	96	103	64	95	74	84	88	84	100	117
52588	SELMA	68	52	32	49	58	64	50	59	56	49	66	71	45	66	51	58	61	58	68	80
52590	SEYMOUR	67	49	31	47	55	65	53	60	60	51	71	69	47	67	53	63	64	60	72	76
52591	SIGOURNEY	80	60	38	57	66	78	64	73	72	62	85	83	57	82	64	76	78	72	87	91
52593	UDELL	85	60	31	56	70	78	59	73	68	58	80	88	50	78	61	71	73	72	87	101
52594	UNIONVILLE	81	57	31	54	66	75	58	70	66	56	78	83	50	75	59	69	71	69	83	95
52601	BURLINGTON	76	75	75	73	76	84	76	77	79	74	97	89	77	99	77	80	93	77	81	88
52619	ARGYLE	85	76	58	72	80	86	70	77	74	70	90	92	68	92	72	76	86	75	84	100
52620	BONAPARTE	62	62	61	59	64	72	62	63	65	60	80	71	64	85	64	68	77	62	69	72
52621	CRAWFORDSVILLE	103	73	40	69	84	94	72	88	82	71	97	106	62	95	74	86	88	87	104	122
52623	DANVILLE	100	89	68	85	94	101	82	91	88	82	106	109	81	109	85	90	101	89	99	118
52624	DENMARK	95	85	65	80	90	96	78	87	83	78	101	103	77	103	81	85	96	84	94	112
52625	DONNELLSON	83	72	55	70	76	84	70	76	74	69	90	90	67	91	71	76	85	75	83	96
52626	FARMINGTON	82	64	44	62	70	82	68	75	76	66	90	86	62	86	68	80	83	75	88	92
52627	FORT MADISON	72	69	66	68	71	77	70	72	72	68	88	83	70	90	70	73	85	71	75	82
52630	HILLSBORO	91	74	51	70	81	88	70	81	77	70	92	96	66	93	72	79	86	79	90	107
52631	HOUGHTON	90	63	33	59	73	82	62	76	71	61	84	92	53	82	64	75	76	75	91	107
52632	KEOKUK	72	68	64	66	70	77	68	71	71	67	87	82	68	89	69	73	83	70	76	83
52635	LOCKRIDGE	74	66	50	62	69	75	61	67	65	61	79	80	60	80	63	66	75	66	73	87
52637	MEDIAPOLIS	94	73	48	70	81	90	72	83	79	71	95	98	66	94	73	82	88	82	94	109
52638	MIDDLETOWN	88	78	60	74	83	89	72	80	77	72	93	95	71	95	74	79	89	78	87	103
52639	MONTROSE	82	70	53	68	74	82	70	75	74	69	90	87	67	90	70	76	84	74	83	92
52640	MORNING SUN	99	83	62	81	88	98	83	91	88	82	107	105	79	107	83	90	100	89	99	112
52641	MOUNT PLEASANT	83	72	57	70	76	85	72	78	77	71	93	90	69	93	73	79	87	77	85	94
52644	MOUNT UNION	100	83	58	79	90	98	78	89	85	78	102	107	74	103	81	88	96	87	100	118
52645	NEW LONDON	88	77	59	75	82	89	74	81	78	73	95	95	72	96	75	80	90	79	88	102
	IOWA	87	79	73	79	82	89	80	84	83	79	102	98	78	102	80	83	97	84	88	100
	UNITED STATES	100	100	100	100	100	100	100	100	100	100	100	100	100	100	100	100	100	100	100	100

POPULATION CHANGE

#	POST OFFICE NAME	COUNTY FIPS CODE	POPULATION			2000-2004 ANNUAL RATE		HOUSEHOLDS					FAMILIES		
			2000	2004	2009	% Rate	State Centile	2000	2004	2009	% Annual Rate 2000-2004	2004 Average HH Size	2000	2004	% Annual Rate 2000-2004
52646	OAKVILLE	115	815	794	788	-0.6	18	311	305	304	-0.5	2.60	223	218	-0.5
52647	OLDS	087	224	217	212	-0.7	14	93	91	90	-0.5	2.38	72	71	-0.3
52649	SALEM	087	1015	1160	1230	3.2	97	409	475	508	3.6	2.44	297	343	3.5
52650	SPERRY	057	840	868	862	0.8	76	304	318	320	1.1	2.73	237	247	1.0
52651	STOCKPORT	177	519	522	529	0.1	57	214	218	223	0.4	2.39	152	154	0.3
52653	WAPELLO	115	4511	4566	4621	0.3	62	1696	1725	1753	0.4	2.61	1230	1248	0.3
52654	WAYLAND	087	1674	1680	1676	0.1	53	628	637	641	0.3	2.57	478	484	0.3
52655	WEST BURLINGTON	057	4661	4633	4521	-0.1	42	1998	2004	1974	0.1	2.27	1329	1328	0.0
52656	WEST POINT	111	2528	2454	2397	-0.7	16	1000	986	975	-0.3	2.44	717	704	-0.4
52657	SAINT PAUL	111	174	168	164	-0.8	11	74	73	72	-0.3	2.30	55	54	-0.4
52658	WEVER	111	1190	1211	1208	0.4	66	455	469	473	0.7	2.57	368	378	0.6
52659	WINFIELD	087	1744	1699	1668	-0.6	18	671	659	653	-0.4	2.51	463	453	-0.5
52660	YARMOUTH	057	306	354	372	3.5	97	114	134	142	3.9	2.64	88	103	3.8
52701	ANDOVER	045	32	33	34	0.7	75	11	12	12	2.1	2.75	9	9	0.0
52720	ATALISSA	139	983	969	977	-0.3	31	376	375	381	-0.1	2.51	271	270	-0.1
52721	BENNETT	031	871	861	885	-0.3	35	343	344	358	0.1	2.50	270	269	-0.1
52722	BETTENDORF	163	33322	34361	35365	0.7	75	13252	13882	14474	1.1	2.45	9296	9636	0.9
52726	BLUE GRASS	163	5241	5240	5280	0.0	51	1891	1921	1962	0.4	2.73	1548	1568	0.3
52727	BRYANT	045	439	445	444	0.3	64	155	159	160	0.6	2.80	117	119	0.4
52729	CALAMUS	045	802	772	754	-0.9	9	324	316	312	-0.6	2.44	242	235	-0.7
52730	CAMANCHE	045	4748	4773	4748	0.1	55	2004	2046	2062	0.5	2.33	1396	1419	0.4
52731	CHARLOTTE	045	1067	1041	1022	-0.6	20	345	341	339	-0.3	2.76	265	261	-0.4
52732	CLINTON	045	29663	29211	28802	-0.4	29	12114	12060	12016	-0.1	2.36	7908	7847	-0.2
52738	COLUMBUS JUNCTION	115	4195	4262	4325	0.4	65	1516	1544	1570	0.4	2.73	1117	1134	0.4
52739	CONESVILLE	139	653	671	677	0.6	72	224	233	237	0.9	2.70	170	177	1.0
52742	DE WITT	045	7473	7416	7324	-0.2	39	2907	2914	2907	0.1	2.52	2047	2045	0.0
52745	DIXON	163	701	746	773	1.5	86	267	288	303	1.8	2.59	210	226	1.7
52746	DONAHUE	163	838	872	896	0.9	79	299	316	329	1.3	2.75	243	256	1.2
52747	DURANT	031	2092	2137	2203	0.5	69	817	843	877	0.7	2.52	599	616	0.7
52748	ELDRIDGE	163	7116	8006	8554	2.8	95	2526	2887	3127	3.2	2.77	1982	2260	3.1
52750	GOOSE LAKE	045	628	628	623	0.0	51	233	236	237	0.3	2.66	181	182	0.1
52751	GRAND MOUND	045	1012	1006	995	-0.1	42	374	376	376	0.1	2.68	301	301	0.0
52753	LE CLAIRE	163	4239	4525	4708	1.6	87	1645	1782	1878	1.9	2.54	1256	1352	1.8
52754	LETTS	139	1333	1350	1362	0.3	63	504	515	524	0.5	2.54	383	390	0.4
52755	LONE TREE	103	1847	1987	2178	1.7	89	708	769	851	2.0	2.54	516	557	1.8
52756	LONG GROVE	163	2285	2372	2435	0.9	78	813	858	893	1.3	2.74	673	708	1.2
52760	MOSCOW	139	656	654	656	-0.1	45	246	249	252	0.3	2.63	187	189	0.3
52761	MUSCATINE	139	30643	30568	30572	-0.1	46	11758	11848	11949	0.2	2.53	8295	8342	0.1
52765	NEW LIBERTY	163	465	482	493	0.9	77	164	173	179	1.3	2.79	129	136	1.3
52766	NICHOLS	139	871	950	991	2.1	91	341	373	392	2.1	2.55	253	274	1.9
52768	PRINCETON	163	1455	1432	1435	-0.4	29	542	540	548	-0.1	2.65	410	407	-0.2
52769	STOCKTON	139	759	749	748	-0.3	32	283	283	286	0.0	2.65	225	224	-0.1
52772	TIPTON	031	4999	5101	5272	0.5	69	2026	2087	2179	0.7	2.40	1414	1452	0.6
52773	WALCOTT	163	2280	2310	2343	0.3	63	897	921	944	0.6	2.51	656	670	0.5
52774	WELTON	045	59	59	59	0.0	51	19	19	19	0.0	3.11	16	16	0.0
52776	WEST LIBERTY	139	4140	4256	4299	0.7	73	1438	1483	1506	0.7	2.83	1040	1067	0.6
52777	WHEATLAND	045	1434	1367	1328	-1.1	4	551	529	518	-1.0	2.50	398	381	-1.0
52778	WILTON	031	3748	3732	3741	-0.1	44	1436	1443	1459	0.1	2.57	1047	1048	0.0
52801	DAVENPORT	163	1048	1070	1085	0.5	69	587	607	624	0.8	1.37	92	96	1.0
52802	DAVENPORT	163	11896	11427	11389	-0.9	8	4408	4257	4279	-0.8	2.60	2775	2665	-1.0
52803	DAVENPORT	163	24400	23879	23917	-0.5	23	9785	9647	9760	-0.3	2.34	5558	5452	-0.5
52804	DAVENPORT	163	25391	25445	25754	0.1	52	10001	10125	10356	0.3	2.46	6786	6840	0.2
52806	DAVENPORT	163	27044	27467	27872	0.4	65	10363	10667	10957	0.7	2.54	7371	7550	0.6
52807	DAVENPORT	163	10988	11419	11771	0.9	78	4903	5120	5322	1.0	2.22	2915	3031	0.9
	IOWA					0.5					0.7	2.43			0.6
	UNITED STATES					1.2					1.3	2.58			1.1

#	POST OFFICE NAME	White 2000	White 2004	Black 2000	Black 2004	Asian/Pacific 2000	Asian/Pacific 2004	% Hispanic Origin 2000	% Hispanic Origin 2004	0-4	5-9	10-14	15-19	20-24	25-44	45-64	65-84	85+	18+	MEDIAN AGE 2004	% 2004 Males	% 2004 Females
52646	OAKVILLE	99.0	98.9	0.3	0.3	0.4	0.5	0.6	0.8	8.2	8.3	7.9	5.9	5.7	26.5	23.8	11.8	1.9	71.9	36.3	50.8	49.2
52647	OLDS	97.8	97.2	0.5	0.5	0.5	0.5	1.8	2.3	7.4	7.4	7.8	5.1	4.6	27.7	24.0	14.3	1.8	74.2	39.5	50.2	49.8
52649	SALEM	98.3	98.0	0.1	0.1	0.5	0.8	0.4	0.4	6.3	6.5	6.4	6.9	5.4	24.3	29.4	13.0	1.8	76.6	41.5	50.3	49.7
52650	SPERRY	99.2	99.0	0.0	0.0	0.1	0.1	0.4	0.5	6.1	6.8	7.7	6.5	5.8	24.3	30.3	11.2	1.4	75.4	40.6	51.2	48.9
52651	STOCKPORT	97.9	97.3	0.0	0.0	0.4	0.6	1.4	1.7	5.4	5.9	7.1	5.9	4.8	25.1	30.5	13.0	2.3	77.8	41.2	52.1	47.9
52653	WAPELLO	96.6	95.9	0.2	0.2	0.2	0.3	6.7	8.2	7.2	7.1	7.1	6.8	6.6	27.4	23.8	11.9	2.3	74.6	36.9	49.6	50.4
52654	WAYLAND	98.3	97.8	0.0	0.0	0.4	0.6	0.9	1.2	5.7	6.0	7.4	6.9	6.5	24.3	25.1	15.4	2.8	76.1	40.5	48.6	51.4
52655	WEST BURLINGTON	95.5	94.7	2.2	2.4	0.8	1.0	2.4	2.8	5.3	5.6	6.4	6.3	6.4	24.7	28.5	14.5	2.4	79.2	42.0	49.1	50.9
52656	WEST POINT	99.5	99.4	0.0	0.0	0.0	0.1	0.6	0.7	5.7	6.1	7.1	6.4	5.4	24.5	28.3	13.7	2.9	76.7	41.8	48.7	51.3
52657	SAINT PAUL	98.9	98.2	0.0	0.0	0.6	0.6	0.0	0.0	7.7	7.7	6.6	6.6	5.4	26.8	25.0	12.5	1.8	73.8	38.8	49.4	50.6
52658	WEVER	98.5	98.1	0.2	0.2	0.3	0.3	1.2	1.6	5.6	6.3	7.5	6.3	5.5	23.8	31.3	12.2	1.6	76.6	42.1	49.8	50.2
52659	WINFIELD	98.0	97.7	0.3	0.4	0.3	0.4	1.7	2.0	6.7	6.7	7.8	7.4	5.9	24.9	23.2	13.7	3.8	73.5	39.0	49.4	50.6
52660	YARMOUTH	98.4	98.0	0.3	0.3	0.7	1.1	0.3	0.3	6.2	6.8	7.9	5.9	5.7	23.7	28.3	13.3	2.3	75.7	41.2	50.3	49.7
52701	ANDOVER	100.0	100.0	0.0	0.0	0.0	0.0	0.0	0.0	6.1	6.1	6.1	6.1	6.1	24.2	27.3	18.2	0.0	81.8	41.3	51.5	48.5
52720	ATALISSA	97.8	97.6	0.6	0.6	0.2	0.3	2.6	2.9	6.5	6.5	6.6	6.7	6.3	27.6	27.9	10.5	1.4	76.2	39.6	52.7	47.3
52721	BENNETT	98.9	98.7	0.0	0.0	0.1	0.1	1.0	1.3	5.9	6.5	7.3	6.0	5.2	27.3	27.0	12.7	2.1	76.4	40.2	51.2	48.8
52722	BETTENDORF	95.2	94.1	1.5	1.7	1.4	2.0	2.4	3.0	6.0	6.6	7.6	7.2	5.6	25.5	29.0	11.0	1.8	75.2	40.0	48.7	51.3
52726	BLUE GRASS	97.7	97.2	0.5	0.6	0.2	0.3	2.0	2.4	5.4	6.2	7.4	7.0	5.5	26.2	31.6	9.8	0.9	76.6	40.3	50.3	49.7
52727	BRYANT	99.1	99.1	0.0	0.0	0.0	0.0	0.9	1.1	7.4	7.6	8.1	8.3	6.1	26.3	23.8	11.5	0.9	71.5	36.6	51.7	48.3
52729	CALAMUS	99.0	99.0	0.0	0.0	0.0	0.0	0.9	1.2	6.0	6.5	7.6	7.1	4.8	28.9	24.9	12.3	1.9	75.3	38.8	49.2	50.8
52730	CAMANCHE	98.0	97.7	0.5	0.6	0.2	0.3	0.6	0.8	5.7	6.0	6.1	6.1	6.0	25.1	30.2	13.4	1.5	78.8	41.7	49.4	50.6
52731	CHARLOTTE	98.5	98.0	0.4	0.4	0.4	0.5	1.1	1.4	6.2	6.2	6.8	7.7	6.6	26.4	25.5	13.5	1.3	76.1	39.6	51.3	48.7
52732	CLINTON	94.1	93.3	3.0	3.3	0.8	1.1	1.6	1.9	6.6	6.3	6.6	6.8	7.1	24.9	25.1	14.0	2.6	76.4	39.3	48.1	51.9
52738	COLUMBUS JUNCTION	88.3	86.5	0.4	0.4	0.1	0.2	25.4	29.1	7.3	7.8	8.6	7.2	5.8	28.1	22.1	11.2	1.8	71.4	35.6	50.4	49.7
52739	CONESVILLE	93.3	92.7	0.2	0.3	0.3	0.3	15.3	16.1	5.7	6.6	8.1	6.3	5.2	25.6	25.3	12.7	4.6	75.6	40.7	49.3	50.7
52742	DE WITT	98.4	98.1	0.2	0.2	0.5	0.7	0.9	1.0	6.8	6.9	7.7	7.8	6.4	25.9	23.8	12.1	2.6	73.5	37.8	48.8	51.2
52745	DIXON	98.6	98.4	0.4	0.4	0.1	0.1	0.4	0.5	6.2	6.8	7.2	6.8	5.2	26.1	29.2	11.3	1.1	75.6	40.6	51.3	48.7
52746	DONAHUE	98.8	98.6	0.2	0.3	0.0	0.1	0.4	0.5	5.7	7.1	8.3	7.2	4.6	26.6	29.8	9.8	0.9	74.1	39.9	51.7	48.3
52747	DURANT	98.8	98.5	0.1	0.2	0.2	0.3	1.0	1.2	6.6	6.2	7.9	6.4	7.3	26.2	24.1	13.3	2.1	75.3	38.1	49.0	51.1
52748	ELDRIDGE	98.1	97.6	0.4	0.5	0.3	0.5	1.4	1.7	7.3	7.5	8.9	8.0	6.8	29.1	24.8	6.9	0.7	71.4	34.2	49.5	50.5
52750	GOOSE LAKE	99.0	98.9	0.0	0.0	0.0	0.0	1.0	1.3	6.5	7.5	8.3	8.6	6.1	25.2	26.1	11.0	0.8	72.0	37.6	52.7	47.3
52751	GRAND MOUND	98.1	97.8	0.2	0.2	0.2	0.4	0.6	0.8	7.4	7.5	7.2	7.2	5.8	25.8	26.8	11.0	1.5	73.6	38.3	49.8	50.2
52753	LE CLAIRE	97.6	97.1	0.2	0.2	0.5	0.7	2.0	2.4	6.2	6.5	6.6	6.4	5.9	25.5	31.3	10.9	0.8	76.9	40.6	50.0	50.0
52754	LETTS	93.9	93.0	0.3	0.4	0.4	0.5	12.4	13.6	6.5	6.8	7.6	7.0	5.9	25.9	25.4	11.9	3.0	74.7	39.4	49.4	50.6
52755	LONE TREE	98.5	98.3	0.5	0.5	0.2	0.2	1.0	1.1	7.3	7.4	7.5	6.0	5.8	27.0	24.8	11.8	2.4	73.8	38.4	50.4	49.6
52756	LONG GROVE	99.0	98.9	0.2	0.2	0.1	0.2	0.5	0.6	6.2	7.2	8.1	7.5	4.7	27.0	29.8	8.6	0.8	73.7	39.1	51.4	48.6
52760	MOSCOW	97.6	97.4	0.2	0.2	0.5	0.5	1.4	1.5	5.4	6.0	7.0	6.4	6.4	24.0	32.0	11.8	1.1	78.0	41.9	50.8	49.2
52761	MUSCATINE	91.9	91.8	0.9	0.9	0.6	0.6	10.5	10.6	7.1	6.9	7.4	6.6	6.8	27.0	25.5	11.0	1.8	74.7	36.9	49.4	50.6
52765	NEW LIBERTY	98.7	98.6	0.4	0.4	0.2	0.2	0.4	0.4	6.4	6.9	7.5	7.3	4.8	26.6	28.0	11.6	1.0	74.5	40.2	51.0	49.0
52766	NICHOLS	89.1	88.6	0.7	0.6	2.0	2.0	13.7	14.5	6.0	6.8	7.6	6.4	5.3	29.4	27.7	9.6	1.3	75.7	37.8	52.6	47.4
52768	PRINCETON	98.4	98.2	0.1	0.1	0.1	0.2	1.0	1.2	6.0	6.6	7.8	7.4	5.9	26.3	29.1	10.0	0.9	75.1	39.9	52.1	47.9
52769	STOCKTON	99.2	99.2	0.3	0.3	0.1	0.1	0.8	0.8	5.3	8.0	8.1	6.4	5.2	26.6	29.2	10.3	0.8	74.1	39.5	50.9	49.1
52772	TIPTON	98.7	98.6	0.3	0.3	0.3	0.5	0.8	0.9	6.1	6.2	6.8	6.2	6.0	25.7	25.9	13.9	3.2	76.9	40.4	50.3	49.7
52773	WALCOTT	97.6	97.2	0.4	0.4	0.4	0.5	1.0	1.2	6.6	7.0	7.6	6.4	6.0	28.1	26.2	10.7	1.5	74.8	38.0	49.3	50.7
52774	WELTON	98.3	98.3	0.0	0.0	0.0	0.0	0.0	0.0	6.8	6.8	6.8	6.8	6.8	22.0	30.5	11.9	1.7	79.7	40.6	45.8	54.2
52776	WEST LIBERTY	73.2	72.3	0.2	0.2	3.0	3.1	32.8	34.1	7.7	7.2	7.8	7.6	7.7	29.4	21.2	9.3	2.3	72.4	33.6	50.2	49.8
52777	WHEATLAND	98.4	98.3	0.2	0.2	0.1	0.1	0.6	0.7	6.4	6.7	8.0	6.8	5.1	23.0	26.9	13.2	3.8	74.3	40.5	50.9	50.9
52778	WILTON	97.7	97.5	0.2	0.2	0.4	0.5	2.1	2.2	6.8	6.7	7.8	7.4	6.7	28.3	24.1	10.3	1.9	74.2	36.1	49.0	51.0
52801	DAVENPORT	73.6	70.8	20.7	22.7	0.6	0.8	5.3	6.4	2.4	2.0	1.5	3.9	8.6	35.5	26.9	16.3	2.9	92.9	42.7	60.8	39.3
52802	DAVENPORT	82.3	79.8	6.8	7.4	1.7	2.3	10.5	12.5	7.4	6.9	7.8	7.9	7.8	29.8	20.6	10.0	1.9	73.1	33.4	50.5	49.5
52803	DAVENPORT	79.2	77.0	13.9	14.8	1.7	2.3	5.3	6.3	7.4	6.9	6.7	8.0	9.7	30.0	20.6	9.0	1.7	74.8	32.2	48.7	51.3
52804	DAVENPORT	87.5	85.4	5.8	6.4	2.2	3.1	5.1	6.1	6.9	6.7	6.8	6.5	6.7	27.6	23.9	12.8	2.2	75.7	37.1	48.3	51.7
52806	DAVENPORT	84.8	82.5	9.2	10.2	2.1	3.0	4.0	4.8	8.2	7.7	7.4	6.6	7.0	28.9	23.1	9.3	1.7	72.7	33.9	48.1	52.0
52807	DAVENPORT	87.6	85.8	6.8	7.3	2.2	3.1	2.9	3.5	6.8	6.3	6.6	7.1	9.6	27.3	26.2	9.0	1.1	75.9	34.0	48.9	51.1
	IOWA	93.9	93.0	2.1	2.3	1.3	1.8	2.8	3.2	6.5	6.5	6.9	7.2	7.6	26.4	24.2	12.3	2.4	76.0	37.2	49.2	50.8
	UNITED STATES	75.1	73.6	12.3	12.5	3.8	4.2	12.5	14.1	6.9	6.7	7.2	7.0	7.3	28.6	23.8	10.8	1.7	75.1	36.0	49.1	50.9

ZIP CODE #	POST OFFICE NAME	2004 Per Capita Income	2004 HH Income Base	2004 HOUSEHOLD INCOME DISTRIBUTION (%)					MEDIAN HOUSEHOLD INCOME				2004 Home Value Base	2004 HOME VALUE DISTRIBUTION (%)					2004 Median Home Value
				Less than $25,000	$25,000 to $49,999	$50,000 to $99,999	$100,000 to $149,999	$150,000 or More	2004	2009	2004 National Centile	2004 State Centile		Less than $50,000	$50,000 to $89,999	$90,000 to $174,999	$175,000 to $399,999	$400,000 or More	
52646	OAKVILLE	20102	305	25.6	33.1	32.8	4.6	3.9	42636	50000	55	52	242	47.1	27.7	20.3	4.6	0.4	55385
52647	OLDS	24707	91	17.6	36.3	37.4	6.6	2.2	47639	52312	67	75	72	20.8	18.1	43.1	15.3	2.8	104167
52649	SALEM	20133	475	26.1	36.6	31.6	4.2	1.5	44770	50624	61	61	396	30.1	26.5	27.5	14.1	1.8	82121
52650	SPERRY	24894	318	13.5	30.5	40.6	11.0	4.4	56389	65317	81	93	274	13.5	17.9	40.9	23.7	4.0	116837
52651	STOCKPORT	16777	218	29.4	42.2	24.8	3.7	0.0	35000	39287	28	10	180	42.2	20.0	32.8	3.3	1.7	60909
52653	WAPELLO	20063	1725	25.6	33.2	33.6	6.2	1.5	42481	49402	55	51	1371	25.5	31.7	33.3	8.2	1.3	83367
52654	WAYLAND	18439	637	25.0	36.0	33.6	3.9	1.6	41852	47691	52	47	506	20.8	33.4	35.6	8.9	1.4	85625
52655	WEST BURLINGTON	25277	2004	23.9	31.9	34.1	7.4	2.7	46384	54220	65	70	1570	23.3	29.2	37.2	8.8	1.6	86752
52656	WEST POINT	27473	986	19.4	30.8	37.6	8.5	3.7	49833	59570	72	81	825	13.0	23.8	46.2	16.4	0.7	105548
52657	SAINT PAUL	24283	73	21.9	31.5	37.0	5.5	4.1	48043	56180	68	76	58	12.1	29.3	46.6	12.1	0.0	100000
52658	WEVER	31060	469	16.6	28.8	40.5	9.2	4.9	53732	62624	78	89	409	13.2	25.9	41.1	19.1	0.7	105984
52659	WINFIELD	21160	659	28.1	29.6	34.9	6.1	1.4	42936	48309	56	53	494	25.1	30.8	36.4	6.5	1.2	83958
52660	YARMOUTH	21278	134	15.7	38.8	33.6	9.7	2.2	47802	54769	68	75	107	14.0	39.3	29.0	15.0	2.8	86500
52701	ANDOVER	17468	12	25.0	33.3	33.3	8.3	0.0	42500	45000	55	52	10	0.0	30.0	60.0	10.0	0.0	125000
52720	ATALISSA	24921	375	17.3	32.3	37.9	8.0	4.5	50268	59102	72	83	309	15.9	27.5	37.5	18.1	1.0	102744
52721	BENNETT	23180	344	16.6	30.8	45.1	5.8	1.7	51698	58253	75	85	275	10.6	28.0	39.3	15.6	6.6	108750
52722	BETTENDORF	33813	13882	16.0	21.7	38.3	15.6	8.4	62424	75464	87	96	10817	4.0	14.2	47.9	29.9	4.0	131004
52726	BLUE GRASS	29947	1921	13.4	20.8	44.0	14.7	7.0	65118	77800	89	98	1684	7.0	16.5	41.8	32.0	2.9	132143
52727	BRYANT	19064	159	16.4	31.5	45.9	5.7	0.6	50781	57418	73	84	134	8.2	23.1	50.8	9.7	8.2	115385
52729	CALAMUS	21875	316	16.8	32.0	43.4	7.3	0.6	50446	56865	73	83	266	19.2	27.4	42.1	7.1	4.1	93750
52730	CAMANCHE	22895	2046	23.2	30.2	37.9	7.1	1.6	47513	54517	67	74	1638	19.7	27.1	45.2	7.6	0.4	92755
52731	CHARLOTTE	17831	341	23.8	33.7	34.6	6.7	1.2	44877	51175	61	62	265	14.3	25.7	37.4	16.6	6.0	106419
52732	CLINTON	20182	12060	30.7	31.9	30.8	4.9	1.7	39411	46665	44	31	8485	25.1	35.9	31.1	6.6	1.3	77738
52738	COLUMBUS JUNCTION	20633	1544	23.0	32.0	35.0	7.9	2.1	45822	53114	63	68	1166	21.4	31.1	37.7	8.4	1.4	87364
52739	CONESVILLE	22809	233	23.2	22.8	36.5	13.3	4.3	52409	61459	76	87	197	13.2	22.3	39.1	21.8	3.6	113672
52742	DE WITT	23179	2914	22.1	23.9	41.7	9.7	2.6	53430	61873	78	89	2145	4.3	19.4	60.1	15.0	1.3	114151
52745	DIXON	24110	288	20.8	22.9	42.0	11.5	2.8	54182	64788	79	90	239	13.4	16.7	38.1	26.4	5.4	129911
52746	DONAHUE	26648	316	16.1	21.2	42.1	15.5	5.1	61011	74361	85	95	284	11.3	13.7	41.6	30.6	2.8	141176
52747	DURANT	22911	843	19.0	29.5	38.9	10.2	2.4	51131	58463	74	84	665	6.5	20.2	54.3	17.3	1.6	115872
52748	ELDRIDGE	24816	2887	14.9	23.7	42.7	14.5	4.2	60639	73607	85	95	2244	4.8	7.5	57.6	29.6	0.5	140741
52750	GOOSE LAKE	20401	236	17.4	30.5	44.1	6.8	1.3	50914	57455	74	84	197	8.6	22.3	49.8	10.2	9.1	117045
52751	GRAND MOUND	20656	376	18.6	31.1	41.0	8.0	1.3	50138	56241	72	82	318	13.2	24.2	45.9	14.2	2.5	103169
52753	LE CLAIRE	28884	1782	14.1	28.5	38.6	13.5	5.3	58411	71575	83	94	1502	3.5	21.8	47.1	23.4	4.2	118404
52754	LETTS	22100	515	20.4	31.8	35.2	10.1	2.5	47951	54728	68	76	432	18.8	26.4	36.3	16.0	2.6	99545
52755	LONE TREE	24085	769	19.4	23.5	45.0	9.1	3.0	55145	70102	80	91	574	8.4	22.5	49.3	18.3	1.6	114831
52756	LONG GROVE	28664	858	15.3	21.3	43.7	13.3	6.4	62629	75248	87	96	785	12.2	15.9	40.8	28.5	2.6	136574
52760	MOSCOW	19527	249	20.1	29.3	45.8	4.4	0.4	50305	57898	72	83	209	12.0	25.8	46.9	14.8	0.5	104044
52761	MUSCATINE	22424	11848	23.9	28.3	34.4	9.7	3.9	47952	56833	68	76	8925	17.5	27.0	37.9	16.3	1.3	97600
52765	NEW LIBERTY	19720	173	26.0	23.1	41.0	8.1	1.7	50690	59552	73	83	134	7.5	19.4	36.6	26.9	9.7	142857
52766	NICHOLS	21342	373	19.0	31.9	40.5	7.0	1.6	49433	57373	71	80	316	14.9	32.6	38.6	12.0	1.9	93810
52768	PRINCETON	23059	540	19.3	28.5	37.6	11.9	2.8	52276	61880	76	87	463	17.9	16.4	38.7	25.1	1.9	116136
52769	STOCKTON	20861	283	21.9	31.1	36.8	7.4	2.8	47913	55978	68	76	225	11.1	20.0	32.0	30.7	6.2	127206
52772	TIPTON	21668	2087	23.0	34.0	36.0	5.7	1.4	44403	51284	60	61	1659	12.7	20.7	48.4	15.6	2.6	111615
52773	WALCOTT	24578	921	17.7	27.0	42.1	10.9	2.3	53135	63049	77	88	759	21.2	16.7	47.0	13.0	2.0	105321
52774	WELTON	18511	19	21.1	26.3	42.1	10.5	0.0	51328	52140	74	85	16	6.3	25.0	50.0	18.8	0.0	106250
52776	WEST LIBERTY	18937	1483	18.3	34.8	39.2	6.0	1.6	47949	57556	68	76	1084	7.2	24.5	52.8	14.1	1.4	107589
52777	WHEATLAND	17789	529	26.7	37.8	30.1	5.5	0.0	40837	47500	49	40	409	20.1	36.7	31.3	11.0	1.0	83889
52778	WILTON	21406	1443	18.0	30.4	43.0	7.7	0.9	51062	61336	74	84	1119	15.2	22.9	51.1	10.3	0.5	102944
52801	DAVENPORT	14776	607	77.4	12.0	7.6	3.0	0.0	12721	15912	1	1	25	72.0	28.0	0.0	0.0	0.0	46944
52802	DAVENPORT	15194	4257	33.7	39.8	22.7	3.1	0.6	34005	41329	24	6	2656	39.6	49.4	9.3	1.4	0.3	55188
52803	DAVENPORT	22258	9647	29.6	29.1	31.1	7.4	3.0	42196	52463	53	49	5773	10.9	35.9	42.7	9.8	0.8	92843
52804	DAVENPORT	22761	10125	23.3	30.8	35.2	7.9	2.8	46530	56314	65	71	7651	12.4	38.1	44.0	5.1	0.4	89654
52806	DAVENPORT	22905	10667	22.0	28.0	37.8	10.1	2.1	49974	60603	72	82	7678	10.8	27.6	50.7	10.5	0.5	100918
52807	DAVENPORT	32532	5120	25.5	23.4	29.5	12.8	8.8	51263	62230	74	85	2940	0.8	8.4	37.2	47.4	6.2	183550
	IOWA	23554		24.6	30.5	32.9	8.4	3.7	45622	53985				17.5	26.2	39.3	15.0	2.1	98835
	UNITED STATES	25866		24.7	27.1	30.8	10.9	6.5	48124	56710				10.9	15.0	33.7	30.1	10.4	145905

# ZIP CODE / POST OFFICE NAME	Auto Loan	Home Loan	Invest-ments	Retire-ment Plans	Home Repair	Lawn & Garden	Comput-ers & Hard-ware	Major Appli-ances	TV, Radio, Sound Equip-ment	Furni-ture	Dine out/ Carry out	Sports Equip-ment	Fees & Tickets	Toys & Games	Travel	Cable TV	Apparel & Services	Auto Repairs	Health Insur-ance	Pets & Supplies
52646 OAKVILLE	82	70	55	70	74	83	71	76	75	70	91	88	68	91	71	77	86	75	83	92
52647 OLDS	107	74	39	70	87	97	74	91	85	73	99	110	63	97	76	89	91	90	108	127
52649 SALEM	79	70	52	66	74	80	65	72	69	65	84	86	63	85	67	71	79	70	79	94
52650 SPERRY	109	97	74	92	102	110	90	99	95	90	116	118	88	118	92	98	110	97	108	128
52651 STOCKPORT	72	51	27	48	59	66	50	62	58	50	68	75	43	67	52	60	62	61	73	86
52653 WAPELLO	83	71	55	70	75	83	71	77	76	70	92	89	69	92	71	77	86	75	83	93
52654 WAYLAND	85	61	34	58	71	79	60	73	69	60	81	88	52	80	62	72	74	72	86	101
52655 WEST BURLINGTON	89	79	65	75	83	92	78	83	83	76	101	97	76	103	79	86	96	82	92	102
52656 WEST POINT	111	88	60	84	96	109	89	100	99	87	117	117	82	115	90	103	109	99	116	127
52657 SAINT PAUL	101	71	37	67	82	92	70	86	80	69	94	104	60	92	72	84	86	85	103	120
52658 WEVER	128	113	86	108	120	129	105	116	111	105	136	139	103	138	108	114	129	113	126	150
52659 WINFIELD	88	71	51	70	76	86	72	80	78	71	93	93	67	92	72	80	87	78	89	99
52660 YARMOUTH	100	73	42	69	83	92	71	86	80	70	95	103	62	94	73	84	87	84	101	118
52701 ANDOVER	87	61	32	57	71	79	60	74	69	59	81	89	51	79	62	72	74	73	88	103
52720 ATALISSA	98	93	78	90	97	102	86	93	88	86	108	110	86	111	88	89	104	90	96	115
52721 BENNETT	105	73	38	69	85	96	72	90	83	72	98	108	62	96	75	88	89	88	107	125
52722 BETTENDORF	108	127	141	127	125	128	119	117	114	119	143	136	126	149	121	112	142	115	109	129
52726 BLUE GRASS	108	128	133	127	127	128	116	117	110	116	138	137	122	146	119	108	137	113	108	132
52727 BRYANT	87	75	56	71	80	86	70	78	75	70	91	94	68	92	72	77	86	76	86	102
52729 CALAMUS	97	68	36	64	79	88	67	82	77	66	90	99	57	88	69	81	82	81	98	115
52730 CAMANCHE	80	77	67	75	78	84	73	77	75	73	92	90	73	93	74	75	89	76	79	92
52731 CHARLOTTE	82	73	55	69	77	82	67	75	71	67	87	89	66	89	69	73	82	73	81	96
52732 CLINTON	67	66	66	64	67	73	67	68	69	65	85	78	67	87	67	69	81	68	71	78
52738 COLUMBUS JUNCTION	88	76	62	74	79	86	76	82	81	77	99	95	74	99	76	81	95	81	86	98
52739 CONESVILLE	102	91	69	86	96	103	84	93	89	84	108	111	82	110	86	91	103	90	100	120
52742 DE WITT	87	83	75	82	86	91	81	85	82	80	101	99	80	103	82	83	97	83	87	101
52745 DIXON	105	86	59	81	93	102	81	93	88	80	106	111	76	107	83	91	99	91	104	124
52746 DONAHUE	108	111	99	108	113	117	101	106	101	100	124	126	102	129	103	101	121	103	107	129
52747 DURANT	93	80	60	77	85	93	77	85	82	77	100	100	74	100	78	84	94	83	92	106
52748 ELDRIDGE	94	107	108	108	105	104	99	99	93	100	117	117	102	121	99	89	116	97	89	110
52750 GOOSE LAKE	87	77	59	74	82	88	72	79	76	72	92	95	70	94	74	78	88	77	86	102
52751 GRAND MOUND	91	77	55	73	83	90	72	82	78	72	94	98	69	95	74	80	89	80	90	107
52753 LE CLAIRE	105	109	102	106	110	115	102	105	101	101	126	123	104	131	103	101	122	103	105	123
52754 LETTS	90	79	60	76	83	91	76	83	81	76	98	97	74	99	77	83	93	81	90	103
52755 LONE TREE	88	91	85	91	92	97	87	89	86	86	106	103	88	109	87	85	103	87	88	102
52756 LONG GROVE	117	118	105	115	121	126	108	115	109	108	134	136	109	139	111	109	130	111	116	140
52760 MOSCOW	82	73	56	69	77	83	68	75	72	68	87	89	66	89	70	74	83	73	81	97
52761 MUSCATINE	90	87	81	85	89	96	86	89	88	85	108	102	86	109	86	88	104	88	91	103
52765 NEW LIBERTY	99	69	36	66	81	91	69	85	79	68	93	102	59	91	71	83	84	84	101	118
52766 NICHOLS	87	78	59	74	82	88	72	79	76	72	93	95	70	95	74	78	88	77	86	102
52768 PRINCETON	98	87	66	83	92	99	81	89	86	81	104	106	79	106	83	88	99	87	97	115
52769 STOCKTON	93	75	51	71	82	90	71	82	78	71	94	99	67	94	74	81	88	81	93	110
52772 TIPTON	85	71	52	67	76	85	69	77	75	68	90	91	65	91	71	77	84	76	87	99
52773 WALCOTT	97	84	66	82	88	98	83	90	88	82	107	104	80	107	84	90	101	88	97	109
52774 WELTON	92	82	62	78	87	93	76	84	80	76	98	100	74	100	78	83	93	82	91	108
52776 WEST LIBERTY	86	72	54	70	75	83	73	80	78	73	94	90	68	91	72	78	89	79	85	94
52777 WHEATLAND	77	56	33	53	63	73	58	68	66	56	78	79	51	75	59	70	71	67	81	88
52778 WILTON	87	74	57	73	78	87	75	81	79	74	96	93	72	96	75	81	91	79	87	97
52801 DAVENPORT	27	24	35	25	24	28	30	27	32	29	39	32	29	39	30	32	38	30	30	30
52802 DAVENPORT	55	51	52	49	52	58	55	55	58	53	72	63	54	72	55	60	69	55	59	62
52803 DAVENPORT	71	71	82	73	71	76	77	74	76	75	95	88	77	96	75	74	93	76	71	81
52804 DAVENPORT	78	79	79	77	80	87	79	80	80	77	99	92	80	101	80	81	96	79	82	93
52806 DAVENPORT	81	85	87	86	84	88	84	84	81	83	102	98	84	103	83	79	99	83	79	93
52807 DAVENPORT	99	100	116	106	99	103	105	101	101	105	128	121	105	126	102	97	125	104	93	112
IOWA	87	79	73	79	82	89	80	84	83	79	102	98	78	102	80	83	97	84	88	100
UNITED STATES	100	100	100	100	100	100	100	100	100	100	100	100	100	100	100	100	100	100	100	100

KANSAS

POPULATION CHANGE

A 66002-66219

# POST OFFICE NAME	COUNTY FIPS CODE	POPULATION 2000	2004	2009	2000-2004 ANNUAL RATE % Rate	State Centile	HOUSEHOLDS 2000	2004	2009	% Annual Rate 2000-2004	2004 Average HH Size	FAMILIES 2000	2004	% Annual Rate 2000-2004
66002 ATCHISON	005	13362	13235	13134	-0.2	38	4988	4994	5005	0.0	2.44	3312	3286	-0.2
66006 BALDWIN CITY	045	6179	6647	7115	1.7	88	2084	2280	2479	2.1	2.65	1588	1716	1.8
66007 BASEHOR	103	4117	4696	5215	3.1	96	1499	1748	1975	3.7	2.69	1225	1408	3.3
66008 BENDENA	043	294	296	300	0.2	55	108	109	112	0.2	2.72	85	85	0.0
66010 BLUE MOUND	107	622	620	625	-0.1	45	258	259	263	0.1	2.39	181	181	0.0
66012 BONNER SPRINGS	103	9438	9867	10173	1.1	79	3471	3663	3797	1.3	2.68	2619	2768	1.3
66013 BUCYRUS	121	1731	1872	2030	1.9	90	588	647	708	2.3	2.89	505	549	2.0
66014 CENTERVILLE	107	351	357	362	0.4	64	148	152	155	0.6	2.35	111	113	0.4
66015 COLONY	003	712	665	639	-1.6	0	277	262	255	-1.3	2.54	213	200	-1.5
66016 CUMMINGS	005	628	633	631	0.2	57	213	217	219	0.4	2.92	171	173	0.3
66017 DENTON	043	349	353	359	0.3	61	138	142	146	0.7	2.49	94	96	0.5
66018 DE SOTO	091	4837	5163	5666	1.6	86	1732	1864	2057	1.7	2.77	1364	1444	1.4
66020 EASTON	103	1802	1958	2125	2.0	91	636	705	778	2.5	2.71	519	568	2.2
66021 EDGERTON	091	2287	2470	2714	1.8	89	798	878	975	2.3	2.80	651	707	2.0
66023 EFFINGHAM	005	1374	1350	1332	-0.4	28	544	541	540	-0.1	2.50	399	393	-0.4
66025 EUDORA	045	5772	6558	7240	3.1	95	2139	2468	2759	3.4	2.62	1562	1777	3.1
66026 FONTANA	121	661	715	767	1.9	90	258	285	309	2.4	2.51	202	221	2.1
66027 FORT LEAVENWORTH	103	8940	9337	9731	1.0	79	1545	1625	1754	1.2	3.81	1504	1573	1.1
66030 GARDNER	091	11092	13174	15254	4.1	98	3946	4713	5481	4.3	2.75	2980	3493	3.8
66032 GARNETT	003	5030	4942	4874	-0.4	28	2036	2015	2002	-0.2	2.39	1353	1326	-0.5
66033 GREELEY	003	839	883	901	1.2	82	320	342	353	1.6	2.58	253	267	1.3
66035 HIGHLAND	043	1303	1291	1303	-0.2	38	446	450	462	0.2	2.15	264	264	0.0
66039 KINCAID	003	698	667	647	-1.1	5	268	260	255	-0.7	2.57	202	194	-1.0
66040 LA CYGNE	107	3157	3311	3433	1.1	80	1252	1324	1384	1.3	2.48	919	966	1.2
66041 LANCASTER	005	800	901	952	2.8	95	299	341	365	3.1	2.64	229	259	2.9
66042 LANE	059	685	730	776	1.5	86	258	278	298	1.8	2.63	204	218	1.6
66043 LANSING	103	8938	9849	10761	2.3	93	2445	2800	3165	3.2	2.76	1905	2164	3.0
66044 LAWRENCE	045	29444	29765	31093	0.3	60	11394	11742	12526	0.7	2.13	4692	4711	0.1
66045 LAWRENCE	045	2907	2908	2957	0.0	50	543	548	580	0.2	1.80	156	151	-0.8
66046 LAWRENCE	045	17642	18598	19926	1.3	82	7120	7611	8267	1.6	2.32	4035	4275	1.4
66047 LAWRENCE	045	16234	17936	19552	2.4	93	6522	7308	8067	2.7	2.42	3721	4058	2.1
66048 LEAVENWORTH	103	31918	32510	34414	0.4	65	12325	12749	13717	0.8	2.44	8286	8465	0.5
66049 LAWRENCE	045	20142	21604	23445	1.7	87	8130	8815	9668	1.9	2.43	4987	5358	1.7
66050 LECOMPTON	045	1802	1821	1895	0.3	59	646	663	698	0.6	2.75	498	504	0.3
66052 LINWOOD	103	1753	2030	2271	3.5	97	648	764	868	4.0	2.66	516	600	3.6
66053 LOUISBURG	121	5418	5948	6415	2.2	93	1906	2120	2306	2.5	2.75	1494	1642	2.3
66054 MC LOUTH	087	2701	2803	2964	0.9	76	999	1048	1118	1.1	2.67	788	821	1.0
66056 MOUND CITY	107	1763	1821	1867	0.8	73	710	742	768	1.0	2.39	511	530	0.9
66058 MUSCOTAH	005	381	379	376	-0.1	42	150	151	152	0.2	2.51	110	109	-0.2
66060 NORTONVILLE	087	1041	1070	1113	0.7	71	379	392	411	0.8	2.63	282	289	0.6
66061 OLATHE	091	42265	47087	53213	2.6	94	15196	17157	19577	2.9	2.71	11014	12295	2.6
66062 OLATHE	091	54409	65919	77996	4.6	99	18294	22540	26940	5.0	2.88	14603	17803	4.8
66064 OSAWATOMIE	121	6206	6215	6471	0.0	51	2366	2393	2516	0.3	2.47	1591	1583	-0.1
66066 OSKALOOSA	087	2683	2779	2919	0.8	75	991	1038	1101	1.1	2.58	727	755	0.9
66067 OTTAWA	059	15442	15768	16377	0.5	67	5984	6167	6465	0.7	2.47	4069	4158	0.5
66070 OZAWKIE	087	2272	2385	2527	1.2	81	854	906	967	1.4	2.63	660	695	1.2
66071 PAOLA	121	11783	12111	12690	0.7	71	4351	4513	4767	0.9	2.61	3242	3336	0.7
66072 PARKER	107	990	996	1006	0.1	55	366	371	377	0.3	2.68	281	283	0.2
66073 PERRY	087	2331	2449	2596	1.2	82	859	910	973	1.4	2.69	655	689	1.2
66075 PLEASANTON	107	2375	2394	2421	0.2	57	953	969	986	0.4	2.45	674	679	0.2
66076 POMONA	059	2212	2545	2809	3.4	97	823	958	1065	3.6	2.66	617	710	3.4
66078 PRINCETON	059	924	950	986	0.7	72	339	351	367	0.8	2.69	270	277	0.6
66079 RANTOUL	059	835	854	885	0.5	67	293	302	314	0.7	2.83	231	236	0.5
66080 RICHMOND	059	1080	1129	1175	1.1	79	375	396	416	1.3	2.77	295	310	1.2
66083 SPRING HILL	121	6359	7440	8461	3.8	98	2201	2615	3003	4.1	2.82	1821	2137	3.8
66085 STILWELL	091	5560	6381	7303	3.3	96	1867	2172	2507	3.6	2.94	1655	1913	3.5
66086 TONGANOXIE	103	6829	7953	8918	3.7	97	2447	2906	3311	4.1	2.71	1941	2271	3.8
66087 TROY	043	2321	2372	2426	0.5	67	915	945	978	0.8	2.50	657	673	0.6
66088 VALLEY FALLS	087	2478	2670	2865	1.8	89	912	990	1070	2.0	2.62	649	699	1.8
66090 WATHENA	043	3356	3453	3544	0.7	72	1313	1371	1427	1.0	2.49	916	947	0.8
66091 WELDA	003	347	353	354	0.4	64	138	141	142	0.5	2.50	105	106	0.2
66092 WELLSVILLE	059	3536	3749	3962	1.4	84	1324	1420	1516	1.7	2.60	1001	1066	1.5
66093 WESTPHALIA	003	562	634	670	2.9	95	210	240	255	3.2	2.64	162	183	2.9
66094 WHITE CLOUD	043	558	544	547	-0.6	18	227	226	230	-0.1	2.39	154	151	-0.5
66095 WILLIAMSBURG	059	928	962	1004	0.9	76	358	375	395	1.1	2.57	276	286	0.8
66097 WINCHESTER	087	1134	1206	1287	1.5	85	403	434	469	1.8	2.68	311	333	1.6
66101 KANSAS CITY	209	14791	14051	13552	-1.2	2	5443	5131	4936	-1.4	2.64	3071	2856	-1.7
66102 KANSAS CITY	209	28471	27844	27180	-0.5	22	10307	10044	9803	-0.6	2.75	6729	6474	-0.9
66103 KANSAS CITY	209	14497	13933	13483	-0.9	9	6636	6433	6265	-0.7	2.17	3104	2945	-1.2
66104 KANSAS CITY	209	27410	26725	26051	-0.6	18	10266	10104	9913	-0.4	2.61	6921	6739	-0.6
66105 KANSAS CITY	209	3212	3066	2959	-1.1	5	985	934	899	-1.2	3.28	703	660	-1.5
66106 KANSAS CITY	209	24220	23988	23527	-0.2	37	8751	8735	8621	0.0	2.74	6355	6285	-0.3
66109 KANSAS CITY	209	15859	16063	15993	0.3	62	5708	5835	5832	0.5	2.74	4540	4620	0.4
66111 KANSAS CITY	209	9501	9472	9320	-0.1	46	3612	3652	3624	0.3	2.54	2525	2525	0.0
66112 KANSAS CITY	209	12085	11997	11777	-0.2	39	4984	5008	4954	0.1	2.35	3119	3082	-0.3
66113 EDWARDSVILLE	209	1472	1561	1580	1.4	84	578	618	629	1.6	2.53	404	428	1.4
66118 KANSAS CITY	209	1	1	1	0.0	50	1	1	1	0.0	1.00	0	0	0.0
66202 MISSION	091	17219	17368	18879	0.2	58	8495	8778	9668	0.8	1.96	4298	4230	-0.4
66203 SHAWNEE	091	20007	20155	21872	0.2	56	8569	8800	9655	0.6	2.27	5377	5347	-0.1
66204 OVERLAND PARK	091	18794	18861	20348	0.1	53	8519	8686	9472	0.5	2.13	4722	4670	-0.3
66205 MISSION	091	13548	13388	14439	-0.3	35	6060	6093	6632	0.1	2.19	3644	3553	-0.6
66206 LEAWOOD	091	9937	9896	10611	-0.1	43	4095	4144	4495	0.3	2.34	2932	2902	-0.2
66207 OVERLAND PARK	091	13232	13390	14529	0.3	61	5359	5510	6043	0.7	2.39	3889	3913	0.1
66208 PRAIRIE VILLAGE	091	21220	21048	22686	-0.2	38	9139	9210	10027	0.2	2.26	5996	5888	-0.4
66209 LEAWOOD	091	18873	21607	24826	3.2	96	6616	7757	9033	3.8	2.73	5192	5944	3.2
66210 OVERLAND PARK	091	17116	18507	20616	1.9	90	7177	7893	8885	2.3	2.34	4542	4840	1.5
66211 LEAWOOD	091	3425	3900	4423	3.1	95	1425	1672	1928	3.8	2.30	1016	1175	3.5
66212 OVERLAND PARK	091	33848	34047	36804	0.1	55	14846	15164	16532	0.5	2.23	8909	8836	-0.2
66213 OVERLAND PARK	091	26140	31796	37605	4.7	99	9554	11590	13742	4.7	2.74	6905	8299	4.4
66214 OVERLAND PARK	091	12185	12224	13209	0.1	53	5438	5566	6077	0.6	2.20	3133	3104	-0.2
66215 LENEXA	091	26710	27343	29844	0.6	68	10542	10936	12064	0.9	2.43	6918	7006	0.3
66216 SHAWNEE	091	23728	25156	27701	1.4	84	8437	9073	10087	1.7	2.75	6650	7065	1.4
66217 SHAWNEE	091	3533	4498	5415	5.9	99	1413	1827	2219	6.2	2.46	1051	1334	5.8
66218 SHAWNEE	091	3250	4808	6249	9.7	100	1107	1668	2190	10.1	2.88	965	1439	9.9
66219 LENEXA	091	8022	9342	10870	3.7	97	3101	3780	4519	4.8	2.47	2006	2299	3.3
KANSAS					0.7					1.0	2.49			0.8
UNITED STATES					1.2					1.3	2.58			1.1

# ZIP CODE	POST OFFICE NAME	RACE (%) White 2000	White 2004	Black 2000	Black 2004	Asian/Pacific 2000	Asian/Pacific 2004	% Hispanic Origin 2000	% Hispanic Origin 2004	2004 AGE DISTRIBUTION (%) 0-4	5-9	10-14	15-19	20-24	25-44	45-64	65-84	85+	18+	MEDIAN AGE 2004	% 2004 Males	% 2004 Females
66002	ATCHISON	90.2	89.9	6.5	6.7	0.5	0.5	2.3	2.4	6.9	6.5	6.9	8.6	8.8	24.3	21.9	13.3	2.8	75.1	35.3	47.9	52.1
66006	BALDWIN CITY	95.5	95.1	0.8	0.8	0.5	0.6	1.5	1.8	6.1	6.1	7.6	9.2	8.7	25.8	25.1	9.5	1.9	75.5	35.5	50.0	50.0
66007	BASEHOR	97.1	96.6	0.4	0.5	0.5	0.7	1.8	2.3	5.6	6.4	7.6	8.1	6.0	25.9	28.0	11.4	1.1	75.4	40.0	49.0	51.0
66008	BENDENA	98.3	98.7	0.0	0.0	0.3	0.3	0.0	0.3	7.8	7.8	7.8	6.1	6.1	23.3	28.4	10.8	2.0	72.6	39.2	48.3	51.7
66010	BLUE MOUND	99.0	99.0	0.0	0.0	0.2	0.3	1.0	1.1	5.3	5.8	6.8	7.4	6.0	21.8	28.7	16.3	1.9	77.3	42.8	51.8	48.2
66012	BONNER SPRINGS	92.0	91.1	3.1	3.2	0.4	0.5	5.2	6.3	7.0	6.9	7.5	7.6	6.9	27.5	25.5	9.6	1.4	74.1	36.1	49.1	50.9
66013	BUCYRUS	97.1	96.7	0.3	0.3	0.4	0.5	1.7	2.1	6.5	7.6	8.4	7.4	5.1	26.4	29.4	8.4	0.6	72.8	39.3	50.1	49.9
66014	CENTERVILLE	97.4	97.2	0.3	0.3	0.0	0.0	0.9	0.8	5.3	5.6	5.9	6.4	5.3	21.3	31.4	17.1	1.7	79.0	45.1	52.7	47.3
66015	COLONY	97.5	97.4	0.6	0.6	0.1	0.2	0.8	1.1	5.1	5.6	7.7	7.7	5.6	21.1	26.9	17.4	3.0	77.0	43.2	50.4	49.6
66016	CUMMINGS	97.0	96.7	1.6	1.7	0.2	0.2	1.1	1.1	7.1	7.1	7.1	7.4	6.6	22.9	27.8	12.3	1.6	74.1	39.7	50.4	49.6
66017	DENTON	98.9	99.2	0.0	0.0	0.0	0.0	0.3	0.0	7.1	7.4	9.1	6.5	5.4	23.2	25.8	13.6	2.0	72.2	37.4	51.6	48.4
66018	DE SOTO	95.1	94.3	0.2	0.2	0.6	0.7	6.3	7.9	8.3	8.8	8.8	6.2	5.2	30.0	24.5	7.4	0.9	70.3	34.7	50.8	49.2
66020	EASTON	96.2	95.6	0.8	0.9	0.9	1.2	1.2	1.6	5.5	6.1	7.8	7.9	6.1	25.2	27.3	12.3	1.9	75.5	40.1	50.9	49.1
66021	EDGERTON	96.3	96.0	0.4	0.4	0.2	0.2	2.0	2.4	8.7	8.7	8.1	6.8	5.8	32.3	23.0	6.3	0.4	70.7	32.6	51.9	48.1
66023	EFFINGHAM	98.0	98.0	0.2	0.2	0.2	0.2	0.5	0.5	6.2	6.4	7.5	6.7	6.4	23.1	27.6	14.6	1.6	75.8	40.8	49.9	50.1
66025	EUDORA	95.4	94.8	0.5	0.6	0.5	0.6	2.3	2.9	7.9	7.5	8.4	7.7	7.1	30.3	21.0	8.5	1.7	71.4	33.2	47.8	52.2
66026	FONTANA	98.3	98.3	0.3	0.3	0.0	0.0	0.9	1.0	4.6	6.0	7.4	7.1	5.0	25.6	30.6	12.0	1.5	77.3	41.9	50.8	49.2
66027	FORT LEAVENWORTH	68.8	66.3	23.0	24.5	1.8	2.2	7.7	9.3	10.8	11.7	7.6	4.5	8.5	47.2	9.4	0.4	0.0	67.0	28.4	66.1	33.9
66030	GARDNER	94.5	93.6	1.4	1.4	1.0	1.2	2.7	3.4	10.1	9.2	8.0	6.8	6.2	34.8	17.9	6.0	0.9	68.4	31.2	49.5	50.5
66032	GARNETT	97.3	97.2	0.3	0.3	0.3	0.3	1.2	1.3	6.9	6.9	7.1	6.8	5.4	23.7	23.1	16.3	4.0	75.1	40.3	48.7	51.3
66033	GREELEY	98.1	98.0	0.1	0.1	0.2	0.3	1.0	0.9	5.6	6.9	7.0	8.0	4.0	24.7	26.8	15.7	1.3	75.4	41.0	50.4	49.6
66035	HIGHLAND	90.6	89.7	4.5	4.7	0.5	0.6	1.5	1.7	3.3	3.8	4.7	21.1	11.3	16.8	19.5	16.0	3.5	84.9	32.3	49.4	50.6
66039	KINCAID	96.3	96.3	0.4	0.5	0.3	0.3	1.0	1.2	4.7	5.0	7.4	7.2	6.3	23.1	28.5	15.6	2.4	78.9	43.1	51.3	48.7
66040	LA CYGNE	96.8	96.5	0.5	0.5	0.4	0.4	1.1	1.3	6.9	7.1	6.8	6.0	4.9	24.7	27.6	14.5	1.6	75.4	40.8	50.2	49.8
66041	LANCASTER	97.9	98.1	0.4	0.3	0.0	0.0	0.3	0.3	6.1	6.4	7.3	7.1	6.3	24.9	27.5	12.5	1.8	75.8	39.5	51.7	48.3
66042	LANE	96.8	96.4	0.4	0.6	0.2	0.3	0.9	1.0	6.2	6.7	6.9	7.5	6.3	25.6	28.2	11.6	1.0	75.6	39.7	50.8	49.2
66043	LANSING	82.6	81.4	11.2	11.6	1.4	1.9	3.8	4.6	4.9	5.3	6.7	7.6	7.2	32.9	26.7	7.3	1.5	78.3	37.8	59.2	40.8
66044	LAWRENCE	84.1	82.6	5.6	5.8	2.9	3.6	4.0	4.8	4.5	3.9	4.1	17.3	21.5	28.9	14.1	5.1	0.7	85.0	24.7	49.3	50.7
66045	LAWRENCE	76.1	72.8	7.2	7.3	12.1	14.8	4.5	5.3	1.3	0.7	0.7	53.1	27.3	13.9	2.0	0.9	0.1	96.5	19.5	47.5	52.5
66046	LAWRENCE	79.5	77.5	5.1	5.5	4.4	5.4	4.1	4.9	6.8	5.9	5.9	8.1	12.7	35.2	17.6	7.0	0.8	77.9	29.3	50.1	50.0
66047	LAWRENCE	88.5	86.9	3.3	3.5	3.3	4.2	2.6	3.3	5.5	5.1	6.2	8.3	12.5	32.3	20.8	7.6	1.8	78.8	29.7	49.3	50.7
66048	LEAVENWORTH	81.8	80.1	12.3	13.2	1.4	1.8	3.8	4.6	6.9	6.5	6.9	7.1	7.4	27.2	25.8	10.7	1.5	75.5	37.4	49.6	50.4
66049	LAWRENCE	88.0	86.8	4.3	4.5	3.0	3.8	2.9	3.4	6.1	6.2	7.0	7.4	10.1	30.7	23.9	7.8	1.0	76.8	32.6	49.6	50.5
66050	LECOMPTON	94.0	93.3	1.0	1.1	0.8	1.0	1.8	2.2	7.0	7.5	8.8	7.5	5.6	26.4	26.8	9.5	0.8	72.0	37.2	49.6	50.4
66052	LINWOOD	95.8	95.1	0.6	0.7	0.2	0.2	3.5	4.4	7.1	7.2	6.9	6.7	5.5	25.9	29.4	10.4	0.8	74.6	39.7	50.2	49.8
66053	LOUISBURG	97.6	97.3	0.3	0.3	0.2	0.2	1.1	1.4	7.5	7.8	7.7	6.8	5.5	27.9	25.4	9.2	2.3	72.7	37.2	49.3	50.7
66054	MC LOUTH	96.3	96.0	0.7	0.7	0.2	0.2	1.1	1.4	6.7	6.9	7.5	7.0	5.5	27.6	26.9	10.9	1.1	74.6	38.8	50.5	49.6
66056	MOUND CITY	97.8	97.5	0.9	1.0	0.1	0.2	0.7	0.9	5.6	5.8	6.7	7.0	5.2	21.8	27.3	17.7	3.1	77.4	43.6	49.2	50.9
66058	MUSCOTAH	95.8	96.0	1.1	1.1	0.0	0.0	1.1	0.8	6.6	6.6	7.4	6.1	6.1	26.1	26.4	13.2	1.6	75.5	38.9	50.9	49.1
66060	NORTONVILLE	97.7	97.6	0.4	0.4	0.0	0.0	1.2	1.4	6.6	7.0	8.2	6.3	5.5	23.9	22.4	15.7	4.3	74.3	40.2	50.3	49.7
66061	OLATHE	86.7	85.2	4.0	4.2	2.4	3.0	7.7	9.0	8.6	8.4	7.6	6.8	7.2	33.1	21.5	6.0	0.9	71.2	32.1	50.1	49.9
66062	OLATHE	90.6	89.3	3.2	3.4	2.9	3.7	3.5	4.3	9.9	9.0	8.2	7.4	6.5	35.3	19.8	3.4	0.5	68.5	30.9	49.7	50.3
66064	OSAWATOMIE	93.6	92.9	3.1	3.4	0.2	0.2	2.2	2.8	7.6	7.3	7.3	6.8	7.2	28.2	22.5	11.2	1.8	73.6	35.6	48.6	51.4
66066	OSKALOOSA	96.4	96.0	0.5	0.6	0.2	0.2	2.0	2.5	5.9	6.3	7.0	7.1	6.8	25.4	28.1	11.4	2.0	76.4	40.1	51.7	48.3
66067	OTTAWA	93.8	93.1	1.9	2.0	0.4	0.6	3.5	4.3	7.2	7.0	7.4	7.5	7.5	26.8	22.5	11.5	2.6	74.1	35.5	49.6	50.5
66070	OZAWKIE	96.9	96.7	0.5	0.6	0.1	0.1	0.9	1.1	5.8	6.3	7.0	7.3	5.7	24.7	30.9	11.2	0.9	76.3	41.2	51.2	48.8
66071	PAOLA	95.7	95.3	1.8	1.9	0.2	0.2	1.7	2.0	6.5	6.9	7.8	7.7	6.2	26.2	26.4	10.6	1.8	74.0	38.3	49.5	50.5
66072	PARKER	97.3	97.2	0.9	0.9	0.0	0.0	0.6	0.8	7.5	7.3	6.5	7.0	5.8	24.4	26.7	13.0	1.7	74.3	40.3	50.7	49.3
66073	PERRY	94.6	94.2	0.4	0.5	0.4	0.5	1.2	1.4	5.9	6.3	7.2	7.4	6.8	24.8	29.3	11.0	1.4	76.1	39.7	50.1	49.9
66075	PLEASANTON	97.9	97.8	0.6	0.5	0.0	0.0	0.8	1.0	6.6	6.6	6.6	6.0	6.5	23.1	26.8	15.3	2.6	76.5	41.3	49.8	50.2
66076	POMONA	96.4	96.1	0.1	0.0	0.1	0.0	1.5	1.8	6.4	7.0	8.2	7.9	5.6	26.3	26.0	11.4	1.3	73.4	37.9	51.0	49.0
66078	PRINCETON	95.7	95.3	0.2	0.2	0.2	0.3	1.0	1.3	6.4	7.1	7.9	7.6	5.8	25.4	27.5	11.2	1.3	73.9	39.1	50.8	49.2
66079	RANTOUL	97.3	97.0	0.1	0.1	0.1	0.1	2.0	2.3	6.3	7.4	7.4	7.3	4.5	26.8	28.2	10.9	1.3	74.2	39.8	51.1	49.0
66080	RICHMOND	97.1	96.9	0.1	0.1	0.4	0.5	0.9	1.2	7.3	7.2	7.5	7.7	6.7	26.7	22.3	12.3	2.3	72.9	37.0	48.6	51.4
66083	SPRING HILL	96.8	96.5	0.6	0.7	0.2	0.3	2.1	2.7	7.8	8.1	8.1	7.1	5.4	30.2	25.4	7.0	0.9	71.4	35.4	50.7	49.3
66085	STILWELL	96.6	95.8	0.7	0.8	1.2	1.6	1.7	2.2	7.7	8.8	9.6	7.6	4.4	26.3	29.1	6.1	0.4	68.8	37.7	50.2	49.8
66086	TONGANOXIE	96.2	95.7	1.0	1.2	0.4	0.5	1.9	2.3	7.3	7.3	7.4	6.9	6.6	27.1	25.8	10.0	1.5	73.8	36.9	50.0	50.0
66087	TROY	98.5	98.4	0.2	0.2	0.3	0.3	1.1	1.3	7.1	7.3	7.2	7.0	5.8	24.6	25.3	13.5	2.3	74.1	38.6	50.5	49.5
66088	VALLEY FALLS	97.7	97.4	0.5	0.5	0.2	0.3	0.9	1.1	7.5	7.5	7.9	6.3	6.5	25.3	23.6	13.0	2.4	73.2	37.9	50.8	49.2
66090	WATHENA	94.3	93.7	2.7	2.9	0.2	0.2	1.2	1.5	7.2	7.4	6.6	6.9	6.8	25.0	25.9	11.7	2.5	74.5	37.8	49.0	51.0
66091	WELDA	97.1	97.2	0.3	0.3	0.3	0.3	0.9	0.9	6.8	6.8	7.7	7.1	6.0	23.5	25.8	13.9	2.6	74.8	40.1	50.7	49.3
66092	WELLSVILLE	97.9	97.8	0.2	0.2	0.1	0.1	1.0	1.3	7.0	7.4	7.9	6.9	5.6	28.0	25.0	10.5	1.7	73.2	37.2	49.8	50.2
66093	WESTPHALIA	98.4	98.4	0.2	0.2	0.0	0.0	0.7	0.6	9.9	9.2	7.9	6.2	5.2	25.2	21.9	12.0	2.5	69.2	35.5	52.4	47.6
66094	WHITE CLOUD	83.7	82.7	2.0	2.0	0.4	0.6	1.8	2.4	5.9	6.3	6.8	8.5	6.4	24.1	28.9	12.1	1.1	77.2	39.0	51.7	48.4
66095	WILLIAMSBURG	97.5	97.4	0.1	0.1	0.0	0.0	0.7	0.8	7.1	7.3	6.9	6.7	5.4	25.7	26.2	13.7	1.1	74.6	39.1	50.6	49.4
66097	WINCHESTER	97.6	97.4	0.3	0.3	0.1	0.1	1.3	1.7	7.4	7.1	6.7	7.1	6.5	23.8	24.5	13.4	3.5	73.6	39.5	49.3	50.8
66101	KANSAS CITY	35.7	34.6	40.4	38.5	2.8	3.2	30.1	34.4	9.9	8.5	7.7	7.5	8.1	28.4	18.7	9.4	1.9	69.6	30.5	50.4	49.6
66102	KANSAS CITY	48.8	46.2	32.0	31.9	2.3	2.7	24.3	28.4	9.6	8.3	8.1	7.5	8.2	29.2	19.7	8.3	1.2	69.5	30.4	49.8	50.2
66103	KANSAS CITY	67.1	63.7	12.6	12.6	4.1	5.0	24.9	29.4	7.9	6.2	6.2	6.2	12.2	36.5	17.8	6.2	0.8	76.2	29.4	50.5	49.5
66104	KANSAS CITY	32.4	31.0	61.3	61.7	1.1	1.4	5.4	6.4	7.2	7.4	8.1	7.9	7.4	25.3	22.9	11.7	2.1	72.5	35.0	47.1	52.9
66105	KANSAS CITY	59.6	55.3	1.3	1.2	1.3	1.5	50.6	56.9	10.9	10.7	7.7	7.4	8.2	29.8	17.6	7.1	0.7	66.6	28.0	51.3	48.7
66106	KANSAS CITY	77.5	75.4	7.7	7.6	1.4	1.7	19.3	22.7	8.7	7.9	7.8	7.4	7.4	28.2	21.8	9.9	1.0	71.2	32.5	49.0	51.0
66109	KANSAS CITY	76.3	75.0	19.1	19.8	0.6	0.7	3.7	4.7	6.0	6.3	7.5	7.3	6.6	25.8	28.1	11.3	1.2	75.8	39.1	49.6	50.4
66111	KANSAS CITY	80.0	78.3	14.1	14.9	0.4	0.5	5.4	6.8	7.4	6.8	7.0	6.7	7.1	27.5	24.5	11.5	1.6	74.9	36.6	48.7	51.3
66112	KANSAS CITY	54.7	52.0	37.0	38.5	1.0	1.2	7.3	8.9	7.3	6.5	6.7	6.9	7.8	27.2	22.2	12.5	2.9	75.5	35.7	46.1	54.0
66113	EDWARDSVILLE	92.5	91.2	1.2	1.2	0.5	0.6	6.3	8.0	9.5	8.6	8.0	6.8	7.4	31.6	18.0	9.5	0.7	69.9	31.1	47.7	52.3
66118	KANSAS CITY	100.0	100.0	100.0	0.0	0.0	0.0	0.0	0.0	0.0	0.0	0.0	0.0	100.0	0.0	0.0	0.0	0.0	100.0	22.5	100.0	0.0
66202	MISSION	88.7	87.0	3.8	3.9	2.5	3.2	5.8	7.2	5.7	5.1	4.9	5.1	10.6	33.2	22.2	11.4	1.9	81.4	35.6	47.9	52.1
66203	SHAWNEE	89.1	87.5	3.7	3.9	1.7	2.2	6.0	7.7	6.5	6.1	6.1	5.8	6.8	30.3	24.2	12.3	1.8	77.9	37.5	48.1	52.0
66204	OVERLAND PARK	90.3	89.0	2.9	3.0	2.3	2.8	5.7	7.1	6.4	6.0	5.7	5.5	7.6	33.7	21.6	11.3	2.3	78.6	35.7	47.7	52.3
66205	MISSION	94.0	93.2	1.4	1.5	1.5	1.8	4.8	6.0	6.2	6.2	5.9	5.5	4.8	30.7	26.1	12.2	2.5	78.4	39.6	47.3	52.7
66206	LEAWOOD	97.3	96.9	0.3	0.3	1.1	1.4	1.2	1.5	5.1	6.1	6.4	6.1	3.5	18.6	30.1	19.1	5.1	78.2	47.4	47.1	52.9
66207	OVERLAND PARK	95.7	95.0	1.0	1.0	1.9	2.4	1.8	2.3	4.5	5.7	6.7	6.6	3.9	16.8	31.5	21.0	3.3	78.8	48.5	46.6	53.4
66208	PRAIRIE VILLAGE	96.6	96.1	0.7	0.7	0.8	1.0	2.3	2.9	5.8	6.3	6.8	6.5	4.3	25.8	26.7	14.8	3.0	76.7	41.5	46.6	53.4
66209	LEAWOOD	94.7	93.6	1.6	1.7	2.8	3.5	1.3	1.6	5.3	7.2	9.3	8.2	4.5	19.5	32.4	10.7	2.9	72.6	42.6	48.2	51.8
66210	OVERLAND PARK	89.7	88.1	2.6	2.7	4.8	5.9	3.3	4.1	5.9	6.2	6.3	6.5	7.7	32.1	28.3	6.6	0.5	77.7	35.8	49.4	50.6
66211	LEAWOOD	94.1	93.1	1.5	1.6	3.1	3.9	1.3	1.6	3.4	5.0	7.6	7.5	4.8	18.4	36.3	15.2	1.9	79.2	46.8	49.4	50.6
66212	OVERLAND PARK	88.3	86.6	3.2	3.3	4.6	5.6	5.7	7.0	5.5	5.5	6.0	6.3	6.6	28.8	25.0	14.3	2.1	79.2	39.2	48.2	51.8
66213	OVERLAND PARK	90.1	88.4	2.5	2.6	5.5	6.9	2.3	2.9	8.9	9.8	9.3	6.5	4.7	34.0	22.5	4.0	0.5	67.7	33.4	49.1	50.9
66214	OVERLAND PARK	86.6	84.8	3.9	4.0	4.9	6.0	5.4	6.6	5.7	5.3	6.1	6.8	8.7	31.6	25.4	9.7	0.7	79.0	35.0	50.2	49.8
66215	LENEXA	90.2	88.8	3.1	3.3	3.1	3.8	4.0	5.0	5.8	6.2	6.7	6.7	7.3	27.6	27.1	9.4	3.3	77.3	38.5	47.9	52.1
66216	SHAWNEE	89.3	88.0	3.3	3.3	4.1	4.9	3.7	4.5	6.5	7.2	7.9	7.4	5.9	26.8	29.9	7.7	0.8	73.7	38.4	48.8	51.2
66217	SHAWNEE	92.6	91.7	2.4	2.4	2.0	2.4	3.3	4.2	5.8	6.5	7.1	7.3	6.5	28.1	30.7	7.7	0.4	76.3	37.9	50.5	49.5
66218	SHAWNEE	94.2	93.1	1.4	1.4	1.0	1.3	3.8	4.9	10.5	8.9	7.3	5.4	4.0	37.6	22.4	3.6	0.3	69.7	33.2	51.4	48.6
66219	LENEXA	90.9	88.7	2.8	3.2	3.5	4.6	2.6	3.6	7.1	7.0	7.5	7.0	9.6	36.2	22.7	2.7	0.1	74.3	30.8	50.6	49.4
	KANSAS	86.1	84.9	5.7	5.8	1.8	2.2	7.0	8.1	7.1	7.0	7.2	7.5	7.6	27.3	23.4	10.9	2.0	74.4	35.6	49.5	50.5
	UNITED STATES	75.1	73.6	12.3	12.5	3.8	4.2	12.5	14.1	6.9	6.7	7.2	7.0	7.3	28.6	23.8	10.8	1.7	75.1	36.0	49.1	50.9

INCOME

#	POST OFFICE NAME	2004 Per Capita Income	2004 HH Income Base	2004 Household Income Distribution (%): Less than $25,000	$25,000 to $49,999	$50,000 to $99,999	$100,000 to $149,999	$150,000 or More	Median Household Income: 2004	2009	2004 National Centile	2004 State Centile	2004 Home Value Base	2004 Home Value Distribution (%): Less than $50,000	$50,000 to $89,999	$90,000 to $174,999	$175,000 to $399,999	$400,000 or More	2004 Median Home Value
66002	ATCHISON	18240	4994	31.6	36.2	25.0	5.6	1.6	37211	42598	36	34	3545	33.1	35.1	25.9	5.7	0.3	68987
66006	BALDWIN CITY	27654	2280	14.3	24.9	40.7	13.8	6.4	60871	74289	85	91	1830	7.6	9.7	48.4	28.9	5.4	142490
66007	BASEHOR	27042	1748	12.5	24.2	42.0	16.6	4.8	65393	76380	89	93	1537	1.2	8.5	62.7	26.2	1.4	148007
66008	BENDENA	19124	109	16.5	33.9	45.0	4.6	0.0	49603	53689	71	80	88	29.6	27.3	31.8	10.2	1.1	82500
66010	BLUE MOUND	26418	259	32.8	25.5	31.7	5.4	4.6	45454	51246	62	70	222	34.2	18.9	30.6	14.4	1.8	83000
66012	BONNER SPRINGS	25352	3663	19.2	24.3	37.7	14.4	4.4	56403	67543	81	87	2824	11.1	18.1	45.9	23.5	1.4	120966
66013	BUCYRUS	32145	647	9.6	16.2	38.5	24.4	11.3	79328	95916	95	97	586	3.6	8.7	25.3	46.6	15.9	205102
66014	CENTERVILLE	21541	152	28.3	36.2	27.6	5.3	2.6	38931	46674	43	44	131	42.8	16.0	29.0	10.7	1.5	60833
66015	COLONY	16465	262	34.4	35.5	26.7	1.9	1.5	35462	40138	29	24	216	38.4	29.6	25.5	4.6	1.9	62105
66016	CUMMINGS	18539	217	18.0	35.0	37.3	8.8	0.9	48291	55453	69	79	194	25.3	24.2	34.5	15.5	0.5	90714
66017	DENTON	16659	142	39.4	31.7	23.2	4.2	1.4	32099	37735	18	6	115	53.9	28.7	8.7	7.8	0.9	46538
66018	DE SOTO	31680	1864	12.8	25.9	38.9	16.0	6.4	60354	74598	85	90	1358	4.4	8.6	47.8	35.4	3.8	147478
66020	EASTON	22563	705	15.6	29.9	42.0	9.4	3.1	54633	63484	79	86	594	18.9	10.1	46.1	23.2	1.7	125321
66021	EDGERTON	25391	878	9.9	24.3	47.8	14.0	4.0	62040	74941	86	92	749	5.7	12.8	61.2	17.0	3.3	115894
66023	EFFINGHAM	19054	541	23.7	37.9	33.3	4.3	0.9	43519	48644	57	63	455	30.3	36.0	24.4	9.2	0.0	72717
66025	EUDORA	23136	2468	16.5	29.9	41.3	9.9	2.4	52941	64163	77	85	1719	8.1	10.6	60.3	19.1	1.9	122375
66026	FONTANA	25724	285	15.8	26.7	48.8	6.7	2.1	55632	65299	80	87	252	15.5	12.3	38.1	27.4	6.8	135417
66027	FORT LEAVENWORTH	15597	1625	7.8	24.6	58.3	8.7	0.6	61417	69020	86	91	28	0.0	0.0	57.1	42.9	0.0	166667
66030	GARDNER	26795	4713	11.4	26.0	45.2	13.3	4.2	60980	74158	85	91	3716	15.0	8.7	53.7	21.3	1.4	133766
66032	GARNETT	19926	2015	30.5	35.8	27.4	4.6	1.7	37596	42785	38	37	1555	33.1	28.4	32.7	5.5	0.3	74618
66033	GREELEY	21328	342	20.8	32.5	39.8	5.9	1.2	48061	53560	68	78	295	27.1	23.1	36.6	11.9	1.4	89500
66035	HIGHLAND	17895	450	39.3	31.1	23.6	4.4	1.6	33931	39117	24	15	321	39.3	36.1	21.2	3.4	0.0	60147
66039	KINCAID	16558	260	35.8	36.5	22.3	3.1	2.3	34401	39850	25	17	221	43.4	20.4	25.3	10.4	0.5	60882
66040	LA CYGNE	21833	1324	21.1	32.1	38.6	6.7	1.5	47326	53939	67	77	1114	20.7	23.7	36.9	16.3	2.4	98750
66041	LANCASTER	19107	341	21.4	36.1	37.5	2.6	2.4	45244	50720	62	69	288	34.0	31.9	20.8	12.9	0.4	65500
66042	LANE	22912	278	14.0	35.6	39.9	8.3	2.2	50244	57379	72	81	246	24.0	24.0	37.8	12.6	1.6	93571
66043	LANSING	25283	2800	7.4	21.9	48.7	16.1	5.9	68902	79368	91	95	2323	9.9	12.2	53.9	23.1	1.0	131194
66044	LAWRENCE	20114	11742	41.0	31.1	20.7	4.4	2.7	31307	38489	16	5	4683	16.9	25.0	41.1	15.4	1.6	102234
66045	LAWRENCE	13215	548	72.3	18.4	8.9	0.4	0.0	16782	19318	1	0	20	0.0	0.0	60.0	40.0	0.0	120833
66046	LAWRENCE	22004	7611	25.5	33.6	32.3	6.6	2.0	43076	52696	56	61	4150	10.3	9.5	68.7	10.4	1.1	117699
66047	LAWRENCE	30583	7308	22.6	25.0	32.6	11.7	8.1	52701	65649	76	84	4007	7.6	4.2	46.2	34.5	7.4	159693
66048	LEAVENWORTH	24326	12749	21.8	30.2	34.5	10.3	3.2	48026	57738	68	78	8512	12.2	29.8	43.1	14.3	0.6	102211
66049	LAWRENCE	34540	8815	20.0	20.6	32.8	15.9	10.7	61393	77871	86	91	5527	0.7	3.6	46.7	45.0	4.0	173207
66050	LECOMPTON	24164	663	13.9	28.7	41.8	12.5	3.2	57536	68541	82	88	572	21.2	8.9	49.0	18.9	2.1	116886
66052	LINWOOD	25238	764	13.0	28.0	44.0	11.4	3.7	58262	66904	83	89	664	5.7	18.1	47.3	24.3	4.7	135227
66053	LOUISBURG	27451	2120	13.3	25.1	41.6	14.8	5.2	61125	72112	85	91	1777	8.2	10.2	40.1	33.5	8.0	153743
66054	MC LOUTH	22853	1048	19.5	28.9	38.6	10.2	2.9	51245	59046	74	83	915	12.2	16.6	48.0	20.2	3.0	118581
66056	MOUND CITY	20082	742	32.8	33.7	25.7	4.7	3.1	37843	44432	39	39	622	41.3	27.3	26.5	4.3	0.5	60244
66058	MUSCOTAH	18660	151	29.8	32.5	33.1	2.7	2.0	40984	45655	50	54	124	53.2	21.8	14.5	10.5	0.0	46667
66060	NORTONVILLE	22364	392	21.4	38.3	32.1	5.6	2.6	45408	51113	62	70	327	24.5	39.1	31.2	5.2	0.0	75132
66061	OLATHE	28177	17157	12.5	25.3	40.5	14.9	6.8	62161	76034	86	92	11569	4.5	7.1	54.4	29.2	4.8	148342
66062	OLATHE	31526	22540	6.7	16.4	44.4	23.9	8.6	78490	95306	95	97	17771	0.5	0.6	40.9	56.5	1.5	183721
66064	OSAWATOMIE	20038	2393	27.8	35.9	27.2	7.0	2.2	38934	46089	43	44	1690	37.2	27.6	25.5	8.6	1.1	68095
66066	OSKALOOSA	21768	1038	21.6	32.7	34.2	8.9	2.7	46675	52852	65	74	884	16.3	25.5	41.7	14.6	1.9	101510
66067	OTTAWA	20089	6167	26.6	31.5	33.7	5.8	2.4	42324	49706	54	59	4362	20.3	31.2	39.2	8.9	0.4	88270
66070	OZAWKIE	26668	906	12.4	28.2	46.1	9.9	3.4	58251	64950	83	89	835	11.4	21.6	52.6	13.7	0.8	111163
66071	PAOLA	27029	4513	17.8	27.3	36.9	12.4	5.6	54270	64560	79	86	3590	8.8	17.3	40.6	29.9	3.4	133668
66072	PARKER	18367	371	23.2	35.6	35.0	5.9	0.3	44895	50921	61	68	335	26.6	21.5	33.7	17.9	0.3	92708
66073	PERRY	24025	910	21.5	28.1	39.5	7.3	3.6	50216	56131	72	81	746	13.7	19.8	45.7	17.3	3.5	110764
66075	PLEASANTON	17272	969	36.3	33.9	23.4	5.2	1.2	34724	40201	26	19	756	36.4	26.3	29.1	7.0	1.2	67188
66076	POMONA	18368	958	21.8	37.4	35.0	4.9	0.9	42813	49261	55	60	790	24.7	25.1	42.8	7.5	0.0	90345
66078	PRINCETON	21158	351	14.3	34.8	40.7	9.7	0.6	50642	57057	73	82	308	26.0	20.1	30.5	22.1	1.3	101163
66079	RANTOUL	20249	302	21.5	28.2	37.4	11.6	1.3	50230	56743	72	81	265	18.9	17.7	44.2	17.7	1.5	109115
66080	RICHMOND	18995	396	21.0	36.6	36.6	3.3	2.5	45274	52419	62	69	334	35.0	35.9	22.5	6.0	0.6	70000
66083	SPRING HILL	29524	2615	10.2	21.8	44.0	17.1	6.9	66993	80540	90	94	2247	1.2	4.9	58.0	29.7	6.1	149730
66085	STILWELL	44411	2172	3.0	9.7	39.6	26.4	21.5	96356	117322	98	99	2051	0.3	1.5	18.7	57.5	21.9	243129
66086	TONGANOXIE	24172	2906	16.2	24.1	43.7	12.7	3.3	58725	67946	83	89	2394	5.7	13.8	53.3	24.7	2.5	136856
66087	TROY	18659	945	28.4	35.8	30.0	4.3	1.6	38761	44361	42	43	754	32.1	38.6	22.8	6.2	0.3	70333
66088	VALLEY FALLS	20908	990	23.8	32.9	35.3	4.9	3.1	45065	51204	61	68	778	19.9	27.4	43.3	7.6	1.8	93333
66090	WATHENA	17348	1371	33.4	37.0	24.2	4.5	0.9	36088	41279	32	28	1042	38.4	34.2	21.5	5.3	0.7	63059
66091	WELDA	16306	141	34.8	36.2	24.1	2.8	2.1	35197	39437	28	22	120	40.8	20.0	28.3	10.8	0.0	65000
66092	WELLSVILLE	23319	1420	19.3	26.4	42.0	9.2	3.0	52907	60998	77	84	1193	10.9	20.0	48.1	18.6	2.4	112277
66093	WESTPHALIA	15292	240	35.4	34.2	27.5	2.1	0.8	35899	40160	31	27	202	36.1	21.8	29.7	12.4	0.0	73846
66094	WHITE CLOUD	19355	226	28.3	36.7	27.0	5.3	2.7	37168	41649	36	33	155	39.4	31.6	22.6	6.5	0.0	64500
66095	WILLIAMSBURG	20496	375	26.9	31.2	31.2	7.2	3.5	43267	50087	57	62	302	24.2	26.5	25.8	20.9	2.7	89048
66097	WINCHESTER	18765	434	22.6	34.1	37.3	4.2	1.8	46600	52687	65	74	363	26.7	22.9	38.0	9.9	2.5	90536
66101	KANSAS CITY	12482	5131	51.8	29.8	14.6	2.5	1.3	23640	28060	4	1	2450	79.8	15.3	4.7	0.2	0.0	31504
66102	KANSAS CITY	15499	10044	37.4	33.3	23.1	4.8	1.4	32862	38135	20	9	5698	51.3	38.5	9.5	0.7	0.1	49200
66103	KANSAS CITY	18648	6433	37.4	35.2	22.7	3.5	1.1	32709	38169	20	9	2226	35.8	54.1	8.2	1.6	0.3	57321
66104	KANSAS CITY	18250	10104	33.1	32.1	26.5	6.4	1.9	36709	43070	34	32	6984	43.1	44.3	11.7	0.8	0.1	54933
66105	KANSAS CITY	13584	934	40.9	26.8	25.7	4.1	2.6	30234	34955	13	3	585	80.2	16.1	1.9	0.5	1.4	26393
66106	KANSAS CITY	19086	8735	24.3	33.0	33.9	7.4	1.4	43772	51880	58	64	5937	21.9	46.2	30.2	1.3	0.4	70600
66109	KANSAS CITY	26111	5835	12.5	23.4	42.5	17.5	4.1	63538	75220	87	93	5036	3.9	27.5	54.7	12.6	1.4	107184
66111	KANSAS CITY	21294	3652	19.5	34.2	36.3	8.8	1.2	46926	56336	66	75	2693	30.8	33.6	28.5	6.5	0.6	73398
66112	KANSAS CITY	23985	5008	24.7	33.4	31.8	7.6	2.5	43613	51408	58	63	2734	7.6	44.7	44.1	3.4	0.2	87529
66113	EDWARDSVILLE	18815	618	28.0	33.0	33.7	4.1	1.3	35544	44569	30	25	566	86.4	9.0	3.5	0.0	1.1	23444
66118	KANSAS CITY	112500	1	0.0	0.0	0.0	100.0	0.0	112500	112500	99	99	1	0.0	0.0	0.0	100.0	0.0	187500
66202	MISSION	33236	8778	18.4	31.5	36.7	9.2	4.2	50075	59899	72	81	4589	0.8	3.3	76.8	18.5	0.6	132026
66203	SHAWNEE	28848	8800	16.5	28.0	39.8	12.5	3.2	54356	66106	79	86	5686	1.5	5.9	77.4	14.9	0.3	135325
66204	OVERLAND PARK	28456	8686	13.9	33.5	40.6	9.1	2.9	51671	61674	75	83	4859	0.7	5.6	82.6	10.6	0.4	122474
66205	MISSION	41202	6093	10.9	23.9	36.4	16.4	12.3	67073	84125	90	94	5120	0.9	4.1	57.3	31.5	6.3	149546
66206	LEAWOOD	48782	4144	6.7	17.3	32.5	23.2	20.3	87774	109448	97	98	3724	0.7	0.5	12.1	68.3	18.5	252151
66207	OVERLAND PARK	45353	5510	8.1	18.7	34.3	21.8	17.2	81619	102467	95	97	4858	0.3	0.3	30.0	56.9	12.5	203464
66208	PRAIRIE VILLAGE	52478	9210	8.7	19.5	39.2	14.8	17.9	73098	90662	92	96	8300	0.3	2.2	51.5	30.1	16.0	168812
66209	LEAWOOD	59565	7757	6.0	10.1	23.5	22.7	37.6	120665	145015	99	100	6484	0.6	0.2	2.0	64.5	32.8	335899
66210	OVERLAND PARK	40636	7893	6.5	18.1	41.5	21.6	12.2	77542	93232	94	96	4868	0.3	0.9	25.7	72.8	0.4	211197
66211	LEAWOOD	82805	1672	5.1	12.4	26.6	19.7	36.1	111140	135098	99	99	1427	0.0	0.4	12.1	36.5	51.0	413551
66212	OVERLAND PARK	32883	15164	14.6	27.6	37.9	14.0	5.9	58425	70267	83	89	9136	0.8	4.2	59.7	34.1	1.2	155530
66213	OVERLAND PARK	46377	11590	5.5	11.9	29.0	27.9	25.8	104539	126762	98	99	8580	0.8	0.3	5.3	81.8	11.9	278607
66214	OVERLAND PARK	35186	5566	14.3	29.1	34.7	15.0	7.1	58038	71437	83	88	2959	0.4	2.8	43.5	53.2	0.1	178857
66215	LENEXA	35675	10936	10.0	24.1	36.7	18.5	10.7	68422	82620	91	95	7411	0.6	1.8	45.2	51.5	1.0	177815
66216	SHAWNEE	36817	9073	8.1	17.9	37.7	21.4	14.9	79006	98469	95	97	7756	0.5	3.6	43.6	46.0	6.3	178297
66217	SHAWNEE	47945	1827	6.7	15.7	34.4	21.0	22.2	86775	104962	97	98	1322	1.5	1.0	16.3	65.1	16.1	260000
66218	SHAWNEE	35377	1668	4.9	9.9	43.5	29.6	12.2	89988	110107	97	98	1575	1.7	0.2	24.0	69.7	4.5	202054
66219	LENEXA	37112	3780	6.0	21.9	36.1	25.0	11.0	79214	97757	95	97	1977	0.0	0.0	12.3	87.1	0.6	216484
	KANSAS	25137		23.6	29.0	32.2	10.1	5.1	47540	57348				21.4	24.4	35.0	16.7	2.5	97470
	UNITED STATES	25866		24.7	27.1	30.8	10.9	6.5	48124	56710				10.9	15.0	33.7	30.1	10.4	145905

ZIP CODE #	POST OFFICE NAME	FINANCIAL SERVICES: Auto Loan	Home Loan	Invest-ments	Retire-ment Plans	THE HOME: Home Improvements: Home Repair	Lawn & Garden	Furnishings: Comput-ers & Hard-ware	Major Appli-ances	TV, Radio, Sound Equip-ment	Furni-ture	ENTERTAINMENT: Dine out/ Carry out	Sports Equip-ment	Fees & Tickets	Toys & Games	Travel	Cable TV	PERSONAL: Apparel & Services	Auto Repairs	Health Insur-ance	Pets & Supplies
66002	ATCHISON	71	59	47	58	63	71	61	66	66	60	79	77	58	79	62	68	74	66	74	81
66006	BALDWIN CITY	110	114	107	114	115	121	108	111	107	107	132	129	110	136	109	106	128	108	110	128
66007	BASEHOR	108	109	96	106	112	116	99	105	100	99	123	125	100	128	102	100	119	102	107	129
66008	BENDENA	83	74	56	70	78	84	68	76	73	68	88	90	67	90	71	75	84	74	82	98
66010	BLUE MOUND	114	80	42	75	93	104	79	98	91	78	107	117	67	105	82	95	97	96	116	136
66012	BONNER SPRINGS	98	101	94	101	101	105	96	98	94	96	117	115	97	119	96	93	114	96	96	113
66013	BUCYRUS	121	151	161	152	148	146	134	133	124	134	156	155	144	166	137	120	156	128	119	147
66014	CENTERVILLE	86	67	44	61	75	85	64	77	72	63	85	90	57	84	67	77	79	75	90	105
66015	COLONY	75	53	28	50	62	69	52	64	60	52	70	78	45	69	54	63	64	63	77	90
66016	CUMMINGS	87	77	59	73	81	87	71	79	76	71	92	94	70	94	73	78	88	77	86	102
66017	DENTON	67	50	33	48	55	66	56	61	62	53	73	69	50	69	55	66	67	61	73	74
66018	DE SOTO	121	136	138	138	132	130	128	126	119	128	150	150	130	153	126	113	148	125	112	139
66020	EASTON	96	90	74	87	94	99	83	90	86	83	105	107	83	108	85	87	101	87	94	113
66021	EDGERTON	97	111	114	113	108	107	103	103	96	104	122	121	106	125	103	92	120	101	91	113
66023	EFFINGHAM	83	62	38	59	71	78	60	72	68	60	80	87	54	80	62	71	74	71	84	98
66025	EUDORA	90	90	83	91	90	92	86	89	84	87	105	106	84	105	85	81	101	89	85	104
66026	FONTANA	114	84	48	79	95	106	82	98	92	81	109	118	72	108	84	96	100	97	115	135
66027	FORT LEAVENWORTH	101	64	61	73	59	69	95	82	97	89	121	109	82	108	79	88	116	97	76	93
66030	GARDNER	108	112	104	113	110	111	106	108	102	108	128	126	106	127	104	98	125	106	100	122
66032	GARNETT	78	61	42	58	67	77	63	71	70	61	83	82	57	81	64	74	77	71	84	90
66033	GREELEY	96	71	44	68	81	89	70	84	79	69	93	101	62	91	72	82	86	83	97	113
66035	HIGHLAND	68	51	32	49	56	66	55	62	62	53	73	70	49	69	55	66	67	62	74	76
66039	KINCAID	77	54	28	51	63	70	53	66	61	52	72	79	45	70	55	64	65	65	78	91
66040	LA CYGNE	96	71	42	67	81	89	69	83	78	68	92	100	61	91	71	81	85	82	97	113
66041	LANCASTER	83	70	50	66	76	82	66	75	71	66	86	89	63	87	68	73	81	73	83	98
66042	LANE	88	84	83	85	87	92	83	87	84	83	104	103	82	102	84	83	99	87	89	103
66043	LANSING	101	110	116	112	109	112	104	105	100	105	125	122	107	125	105	97	123	104	98	117
66044	LAWRENCE	64	50	58	54	50	56	70	60	69	64	86	77	62	81	62	64	82	67	57	68
66045	LAWRENCE	31	19	24	22	19	23	37	27	36	31	45	38	30	40	30	32	42	33	25	31
66046	LAWRENCE	73	68	76	72	67	71	77	72	75	75	94	88	74	90	72	70	91	76	66	80
66047	LAWRENCE	105	93	110	101	92	99	110	102	108	107	136	126	105	129	103	101	132	110	95	114
66048	LEAVENWORTH	79	86	95	87	86	89	86	85	84	85	105	99	88	108	86	82	103	85	81	93
66049	LAWRENCE	117	118	130	125	114	116	125	117	119	124	150	143	123	147	118	111	147	122	104	130
66050	LECOMPTON	99	99	88	96	102	106	91	96	91	90	112	114	92	117	93	92	109	93	98	118
66052	LINWOOD	103	98	82	95	102	108	90	98	93	90	114	116	90	117	93	94	109	95	102	122
66053	LOUISBURG	104	117	119	118	116	117	109	110	104	109	130	128	112	134	110	101	128	107	102	123
66054	MC LOUTH	95	86	69	84	90	97	82	89	86	82	105	104	81	107	84	88	100	87	95	110
66056	MOUND CITY	87	62	34	58	71	80	60	74	69	60	82	89	52	80	63	73	75	73	89	103
66058	MUSCOTAH	85	59	31	56	69	77	58	72	67	58	79	87	50	77	61	71	72	71	86	101
66060	NORTONVILLE	106	77	43	73	88	98	75	91	86	74	101	110	66	99	78	89	93	90	107	126
66061	OLATHE	105	113	123	118	110	111	111	108	106	113	134	128	113	134	109	100	132	109	97	119
66062	OLATHE	129	143	145	149	137	136	133	131	124	137	157	154	137	157	130	116	155	129	114	144
66064	OSAWATOMIE	76	65	55	63	69	77	69	72	73	66	89	84	65	88	68	75	83	72	80	86
66066	OSKALOOSA	95	77	53	74	85	93	74	86	80	73	96	103	68	97	76	83	90	84	96	114
66067	OTTAWA	76	68	57	67	70	78	69	73	72	67	88	84	67	88	69	73	83	72	78	86
66070	OZAWKIE	113	100	76	95	106	113	93	103	98	93	120	122	91	122	95	101	114	100	111	132
66071	PAOLA	105	102	92	101	105	112	99	104	100	98	123	121	98	125	100	101	118	102	106	122
66072	PARKER	77	66	51	65	69	78	67	72	71	66	86	83	64	86	67	73	81	71	78	86
66073	PERRY	100	95	79	91	99	104	87	94	90	87	110	112	86	113	89	91	105	92	99	118
66075	PLEASANTON	72	53	32	50	60	69	55	64	62	53	73	74	48	70	56	66	67	63	76	84
66076	POMONA	78	70	53	66	73	79	64	71	68	64	83	85	63	85	66	70	79	69	77	92
66078	PRINCETON	90	81	65	78	85	91	76	83	80	76	97	99	75	99	78	81	93	81	89	106
66079	RANTOUL	90	82	66	78	86	92	76	83	80	76	98	99	75	99	78	82	93	82	89	106
66080	RICHMOND	84	74	60	72	78	84	71	78	74	70	91	93	68	91	72	76	86	76	83	98
66083	SPRING HILL	115	131	133	133	127	125	122	121	113	123	143	142	125	146	120	108	141	119	106	133
66085	STILWELL	174	213	225	218	206	205	189	186	173	192	219	216	203	228	191	166	220	179	164	205
66086	TONGANOXIE	94	99	93	98	99	102	93	95	91	92	113	111	94	116	93	90	109	93	92	109
66087	TROY	77	61	42	59	66	75	62	69	68	61	81	81	57	80	62	70	75	68	78	87
66088	VALLEY FALLS	89	72	52	70	77	88	75	81	81	72	97	93	69	95	74	84	90	81	92	99
66090	WATHENA	70	60	44	58	62	68	58	64	62	59	75	75	54	72	58	62	71	64	68	79
66091	WELDA	74	52	27	49	60	67	51	63	59	50	69	76	43	67	53	62	63	62	75	88
66092	WELLSVILLE	91	87	75	86	89	96	84	89	86	83	106	103	84	107	85	87	101	87	91	104
66093	WESTPHALIA	73	51	27	48	59	67	50	62	58	50	68	75	43	67	52	61	62	61	74	87
66094	WHITE CLOUD	84	59	31	55	68	76	58	72	67	57	78	86	50	77	60	70	71	71	85	99
66095	WILLIAMSBURG	83	71	54	70	74	83	71	77	76	70	92	88	68	91	71	77	86	76	83	92
66097	WINCHESTER	92	64	34	61	75	84	64	78	73	63	86	94	54	84	66	77	78	77	93	109
66101	KANSAS CITY	46	40	44	38	39	44	45	45	49	46	60	50	44	57	44	49	59	47	47	50
66102	KANSAS CITY	59	55	60	54	54	59	60	59	62	60	77	67	59	76	58	61	76	61	59	64
66103	KANSAS CITY	55	48	57	51	48	52	59	55	59	57	74	67	56	71	55	56	72	59	52	60
66104	KANSAS CITY	65	62	68	59	62	70	65	65	69	65	86	73	66	85	65	71	83	66	70	74
66105	KANSAS CITY	68	60	50	56	58	61	61	66	63	67	80	70	56	70	58	61	79	67	62	69
66106	KANSAS CITY	72	71	73	70	71	77	73	73	75	72	93	84	73	94	73	75	90	74	74	82
66109	KANSAS CITY	93	111	120	110	109	110	102	101	97	102	122	118	108	128	104	95	121	99	94	111
66111	KANSAS CITY	79	79	74	78	79	84	76	79	76	76	94	91	76	95	76	75	91	78	78	90
66112	KANSAS CITY	76	77	88	78	76	82	81	78	81	79	101	92	82	102	80	79	99	81	77	87
66113	EDWARDSVILLE	76	69	54	66	69	73	66	71	67	68	82	81	62	78	65	66	79	70	70	84
66118	KANSAS CITY	146	182	193	182	178	176	162	161	150	161	189	188	172	201	166	146	188	156	145	179
66202	MISSION	87	87	105	91	86	91	96	90	93	94	117	109	95	116	92	89	115	94	84	99
66203	SHAWNEE	88	93	104	94	92	97	94	92	92	93	115	108	95	116	94	90	113	93	87	101
66204	OVERLAND PARK	83	84	98	88	83	87	89	85	86	88	109	101	88	107	86	82	106	88	79	94
66205	MISSION	116	133	162	136	131	136	130	127	124	130	157	149	135	160	131	121	155	127	117	138
66206	LEAWOOD	149	176	201	176	176	185	165	165	157	165	198	188	174	199	170	156	195	162	158	180
66207	OVERLAND PARK	141	169	196	166	168	179	155	157	148	156	186	175	165	189	162	149	184	152	152	171
66208	PRAIRIE VILLAGE	155	179	215	182	177	185	171	169	163	172	206	197	179	208	175	160	203	168	159	185
66209	LEAWOOD	216	262	297	269	255	261	238	233	220	240	279	270	257	288	242	214	280	227	211	257
66210	OVERLAND PARK	131	146	157	153	141	141	138	135	129	141	164	159	143	165	136	123	162	134	119	148
66211	LEAWOOD	239	311	401	308	304	324	274	272	255	279	323	307	307	337	289	256	326	262	252	296
66212	OVERLAND PARK	96	105	123	107	103	109	106	103	102	105	129	120	108	130	106	100	127	104	97	113
66213	OVERLAND PARK	177	195	214	206	186	187	185	179	173	190	220	211	192	221	181	164	218	178	156	197
66214	OVERLAND PARK	104	110	129	115	108	112	112	108	107	112	135	128	113	135	110	103	133	110	99	119
66215	LENEXA	118	129	146	134	126	130	128	124	121	127	153	147	131	154	126	117	151	125	113	137
66216	SHAWNEE	137	159	170	163	154	155	147	144	137	149	174	170	155	178	147	132	173	142	129	160
66217	SHAWNEE	162	179	196	189	173	177	171	165	160	174	204	195	179	203	168	152	202	165	147	184
66218	SHAWNEE	143	165	164	172	158	154	149	147	136	153	173	172	155	175	146	128	172	143	126	161
66219	LENEXA	127	136	157	145	130	131	133	128	126	137	161	152	137	161	130	120	159	129	112	141
	KANSAS	92	87	84	87	89	95	89	91	90	88	111	106	87	110	88	89	107	91	92	105
	UNITED STATES	100	100	100	100	100	100	100	100	100	100	100	100	100	100	100	100	100	100	100	100

POPULATION CHANGE

ZIP CODE		COUNTY FIPS CODE	POPULATION			2000-2004 ANNUAL RATE		HOUSEHOLDS					FAMILIES		
#	POST OFFICE NAME		2000	2004	2009	% Rate	State Centile	2000	2004	2009	% Annual Rate 2000-2004	2004 Average HH Size	2000	2004	% Annual Rate 2000-2004
66220	LENEXA	091	1623	3130	4504	16.7	100	579	1137	1653	17.2	2.75	503	968	16.7
66221	OVERLAND PARK	091	6295	9445	12223	10.0	100	1819	2732	3542	10.0	3.46	1720	2570	9.9
66223	OVERLAND PARK	091	12862	16993	20741	6.8	99	4111	5485	6737	7.0	3.10	3566	4704	6.7
66224	OVERLAND PARK	091	6175	8808	11132	8.7	100	1979	2839	3604	8.9	3.10	1691	2414	8.7
66226	SHAWNEE	091	6798	9601	12201	8.5	99	2225	3172	4053	8.7	3.03	1975	2794	8.5
66227	LENEXA	091	1515	1774	2045	3.8	98	548	654	764	4.3	2.71	464	545	3.9
66401	ALMA	197	2171	2160	2203	-0.1	42	848	854	881	0.2	2.47	616	614	-0.1
66402	AUBURN	177	2665	2859	2978	1.7	87	927	1007	1062	2.0	2.84	766	827	1.8
66403	AXTELL	117	640	635	629	-0.2	39	244	244	243	0.0	2.54	185	183	-0.3
66404	BAILEYVILLE	131	611	638	641	1.0	78	201	213	216	1.4	3.00	160	168	1.2
66406	BEATTIE	117	645	643	638	-0.1	46	250	251	251	0.1	2.53	174	173	-0.1
66407	BELVUE	149	386	435	477	2.9	95	128	144	158	2.8	3.02	98	109	2.5
66408	BERN	131	465	446	430	-1.0	7	171	165	161	-0.8	2.70	139	134	-0.9
66409	BERRYTON	177	2994	3157	3270	1.3	82	1070	1142	1197	1.5	2.76	904	959	1.4
66411	BLUE RAPIDS	117	1397	1390	1381	-0.1	42	553	554	555	0.0	2.44	381	378	-0.2
66412	BREMEN	117	439	453	457	0.7	73	158	165	167	1.0	2.75	122	127	1.0
66413	BURLINGAME	139	1900	1970	2060	0.9	76	778	818	864	1.2	2.37	535	558	1.0
66414	CARBONDALE	139	3116	3192	3330	0.6	69	1179	1223	1288	0.9	2.61	883	909	0.7
66415	CENTRALIA	131	736	721	704	-0.5	25	296	291	285	-0.4	2.37	194	189	-0.6
66416	CIRCLEVILLE	085	462	465	475	0.2	55	181	184	190	0.4	2.53	139	140	0.4
66417	CORNING	131	680	652	630	-1.0	7	235	227	221	-0.8	2.84	177	170	-0.9
66418	DELIA	085	661	716	761	1.9	90	218	237	253	2.0	3.02	176	190	1.8
66419	DENISON	085	511	585	641	3.2	96	180	209	232	3.6	2.78	142	164	3.5
66422	EMMETT	149	501	561	612	2.7	94	181	202	221	2.6	2.78	140	155	2.4
66423	ESKRIDGE	197	772	769	784	-0.1	44	290	291	300	0.1	2.45	204	203	-0.1
66424	EVEREST	013	624	620	619	-0.2	41	249	249	251	0.0	2.49	181	180	-0.1
66425	FAIRVIEW	013	578	609	625	1.2	82	239	257	267	1.7	2.37	177	188	1.4
66427	FRANKFORT	117	1411	1370	1345	-0.7	15	566	554	548	-0.5	2.38	388	377	-0.7
66428	GOFF	131	552	542	529	-0.4	27	189	186	182	-0.4	2.91	141	137	-0.7
66429	GRANTVILLE	087	535	573	617	1.6	87	198	215	233	2.0	2.67	155	168	1.9
66431	HARVEYVILLE	197	1169	1153	1174	-0.3	33	444	441	452	-0.2	2.61	349	345	-0.3
66432	HAVENSVILLE	149	478	466	481	-0.6	18	185	183	190	-0.3	2.55	142	140	-0.3
66434	HIAWATHA	013	5193	5193	5214	0.0	50	2147	2175	2210	0.3	2.32	1428	1432	0.1
66436	HOLTON	085	5344	5444	5643	0.4	66	2133	2197	2302	0.7	2.37	1444	1474	0.5
66438	HOME	117	322	320	317	-0.2	41	118	118	118	0.0	2.69	82	81	-0.3
66439	HORTON	013	2930	2874	2866	-0.5	27	1150	1136	1143	-0.3	2.48	764	747	-0.5
66440	HOYT	085	2025	2063	2120	0.4	66	712	734	763	0.7	2.81	584	598	0.6
66441	JUNCTION CITY	061	21910	21478	21017	-0.5	26	8709	8648	8570	-0.2	2.45	5986	5899	-0.3
66442	FORT RILEY	061	11514	11107	10974	-0.8	11	2202	2113	2101	-1.0	3.57	2125	2036	-1.0
66449	LEONARDVILLE	161	995	1006	1022	0.3	60	368	377	389	0.6	2.56	273	277	0.3
66451	LYNDON	139	2446	2554	2681	1.0	78	946	994	1051	1.2	2.55	720	750	1.0
66502	MANHATTAN	161	39828	40789	41873	0.6	68	15873	16573	17362	1.0	2.26	7612	7877	0.8
66503	MANHATTAN	161	10785	11058	11316	0.6	69	4150	4338	4533	1.1	2.47	2878	2983	0.9
66506	MANHATTAN	161	2258	2261	2263	0.0	51	11	13	14	4.0	1.54	3	3	0.0
66507	MAPLE HILL	197	930	1030	1106	2.4	94	348	391	426	2.8	2.63	273	304	2.6
66508	MARYSVILLE	117	4106	4025	3968	-0.5	26	1755	1741	1733	-0.2	2.24	1111	1092	-0.4
66509	MAYETTA	085	2134	2241	2341	1.2	81	725	768	808	1.4	2.92	578	607	1.2
66510	MELVERN	139	909	966	1023	1.4	85	352	379	406	1.8	2.54	261	278	1.5
66512	MERIDEN	087	3109	3314	3564	1.5	86	1151	1238	1343	1.7	2.68	918	982	1.6
66514	MILFORD	061	1581	1579	1552	0.0	47	574	581	580	0.3	2.71	466	470	0.2
66515	MORRILL	013	468	497	512	1.4	84	171	185	193	1.9	2.69	126	135	1.6
66516	NETAWAKA	085	382	392	403	0.6	70	142	148	154	1.0	2.65	112	116	0.8
66517	OGDEN	161	1780	1797	1823	0.2	58	697	718	745	0.7	2.49	484	494	0.5
66518	OKETO	117	282	287	288	0.4	64	120	124	125	0.8	2.31	92	94	0.5
66520	OLSBURG	149	582	579	601	-0.1	42	235	237	249	0.2	2.44	181	182	0.1
66521	ONAGA	149	1488	1513	1581	0.4	63	594	612	647	0.7	2.37	389	397	0.5
66522	ONEIDA	131	223	237	240	1.4	85	78	84	86	1.8	2.82	62	66	1.5
66523	OSAGE CITY	139	3992	4089	4244	0.6	69	1584	1633	1708	0.7	2.44	1084	1108	0.5
66524	OVERBROOK	045	2313	2414	2534	1.0	78	856	909	967	1.4	2.57	651	685	1.2
66526	PAXICO	197	1287	1391	1475	1.9	89	466	511	549	2.2	2.72	351	382	2.0
66527	POWHATTAN	013	367	362	362	-0.3	33	135	136	138	0.2	2.66	102	102	0.0
66528	QUENEMO	139	588	621	655	1.3	83	211	222	235	1.2	2.80	167	174	1.0
66531	RILEY	161	1416	1468	1513	0.9	76	483	510	535	1.3	2.73	369	387	1.1
66532	ROBINSON	013	724	722	725	-0.1	46	278	281	286	0.3	2.53	202	202	0.0
66533	ROSSVILLE	177	1561	1602	1628	0.6	70	576	598	615	0.9	2.65	440	452	0.6
66534	SABETHA	131	3572	3496	3415	-0.5	23	1290	1271	1249	-0.4	2.47	887	865	-0.6
66535	SAINT GEORGE	149	2202	2301	2425	1.0	79	855	902	960	1.3	2.55	611	638	1.0
66536	SAINT MARYS	149	2999	3132	3293	1.0	79	973	1022	1082	1.2	2.95	679	707	1.0
66537	SCRANTON	139	1028	1072	1126	1.0	78	383	404	428	1.3	2.65	276	289	1.1
66538	SENECA	131	3362	3287	3206	-0.5	21	1308	1291	1267	-0.3	2.46	865	844	-0.6
66539	SILVER LAKE	177	2690	2808	2881	1.0	78	984	1043	1084	1.4	2.66	772	810	1.1
66540	SOLDIER	085	525	533	546	0.4	63	187	191	198	0.5	2.79	144	146	0.3
66541	SUMMERFIELD	117	308	306	303	-0.2	41	104	104	104	0.0	2.87	79	78	-0.3
66542	TECUMSEH	177	2985	3001	3024	0.1	54	1068	1093	1117	0.6	2.75	913	929	0.4
66543	VASSAR	139	766	816	866	1.5	85	308	331	354	1.7	2.47	244	260	1.5
66544	VERMILLION	117	438	425	417	-0.7	14	185	182	180	-0.4	2.32	139	135	-0.7
66546	WAKARUSA	177	1047	1030	1033	-0.4	30	401	400	406	-0.1	2.57	318	314	-0.3
66547	WAMEGO	149	6511	6817	7201	1.1	80	2413	2551	2717	1.3	2.65	1796	1886	1.2
66548	WATERVILLE	117	1004	1008	1005	0.1	53	416	418	419	0.1	2.41	282	281	-0.1
66549	WESTMORELAND	149	1539	1585	1663	0.7	72	598	622	658	0.9	2.48	443	458	0.8
66550	WETMORE	131	625	619	605	-0.2	37	233	230	226	-0.3	2.69	172	168	-0.6
66552	WHITING	085	438	451	466	0.7	72	188	197	205	1.1	2.28	139	144	0.8
66554	RANDOLPH	161	662	674	688	0.4	65	273	282	293	0.8	2.33	201	206	0.6
66603	TOPEKA	177	2038	2134	2216	1.1	80	917	982	1037	1.6	2.07	397	415	1.1
66604	TOPEKA	177	23014	22687	22812	-0.3	32	10206	10215	10407	0.0	2.17	5783	5694	-0.4
66605	TOPEKA	177	19102	19019	19195	-0.1	43	7321	7401	7571	0.3	2.54	5255	5259	0.0
66606	TOPEKA	177	12217	12628	13066	0.8	73	5664	5947	6235	1.2	2.03	2882	2959	0.6
66607	TOPEKA	177	9938	9823	9886	-0.3	36	3298	3263	3303	-0.3	2.71	2172	2116	-0.6
66608	TOPEKA	177	5735	5512	5504	-0.9	9	2402	2342	2370	-0.6	2.20	1414	1357	-1.0
66609	TOPEKA	177	6396	6932	7280	1.9	91	2723	2973	3154	2.1	2.32	1735	1896	2.1
66610	TOPEKA	177	6496	6938	7207	1.6	86	2275	2466	2596	1.9	2.70	1870	2010	1.7
66611	TOPEKA	177	9580	9225	9206	-0.9	9	4520	4410	4455	-0.6	2.06	2479	2376	-1.0
66612	TOPEKA	177	2943	3044	3124	0.8	74	1610	1695	1766	1.2	1.74	599	614	0.6
66614	TOPEKA	177	31640	32924	33956	0.9	77	13166	13833	14418	1.2	2.29	8386	8754	1.0
66615	TOPEKA	177	1537	1755	1894	3.2	96	524	616	678	3.9	2.55	413	484	3.8
	KANSAS					0.7					1.0	2.49			0.8
	UNITED STATES					1.2					1.3	2.58			1.1

# ZIP CODE	POST OFFICE NAME	RACE (%) White 2000	White 2004	Black 2000	Black 2004	Asian/Pacific 2000	Asian/Pacific 2004	% Hispanic Origin 2000	% Hispanic Origin 2004	2004 AGE DISTRIBUTION (%) 0-4	5-9	10-14	15-19	20-24	25-44	45-64	65-84	85+	18+	MEDIAN AGE 2004	% 2004 Males	% 2004 Females
66220	LENEXA	95.4	94.7	2.0	2.2	1.4	1.7	2.0	2.8	5.7	7.3	7.3	5.5	3.9	21.8	39.8	8.3	0.4	76.2	44.1	49.9	50.1
66221	OVERLAND PARK	94.5	93.6	1.9	2.0	2.4	3.0	1.3	1.7	9.2	11.2	11.5	8.8	3.5	28.1	24.2	3.2	0.3	61.8	34.9	50.6	49.4
66223	OVERLAND PARK	92.7	91.4	1.9	2.0	3.3	4.2	2.4	3.0	11.2	11.0	9.3	6.5	4.4	33.6	20.9	2.9	0.2	64.4	32.7	49.8	50.3
66224	OVERLAND PARK	92.2	91.2	2.9	3.0	3.0	3.7	1.8	2.3	11.3	10.9	9.1	6.5	4.0	30.6	22.8	4.7	0.3	64.0	34.0	48.9	51.1
66226	SHAWNEE	94.4	93.4	1.8	2.0	1.6	2.0	2.9	3.6	13.0	11.2	8.1	4.7	3.2	40.1	17.1	2.5	0.2	64.6	32.1	50.0	50.0
66227	LENEXA	97.2	96.8	0.4	0.4	0.4	0.5	1.7	2.2	5.7	6.5	7.4	6.5	5.3	26.0	34.0	7.6	0.9	76.3	41.1	51.1	48.9
66401	ALMA	97.2	96.8	0.3	0.3	0.1	0.1	2.3	2.9	6.2	6.3	7.2	6.8	6.0	23.3	27.2	14.2	2.8	75.9	41.3	50.8	49.2
66402	AUBURN	96.1	95.5	0.5	0.5	0.5	0.6	2.7	3.4	6.3	6.9	8.8	8.3	6.5	24.9	28.8	8.8	0.9	73.0	37.5	48.2	51.8
66403	AXTELL	98.3	98.1	0.0	0.0	0.2	0.2	0.8	0.9	6.1	6.5	7.6	6.8	6.6	21.3	25.8	16.7	2.7	74.8	41.8	49.3	50.7
66404	BAILEYVILLE	99.0	98.9	0.2	0.2	0.0	0.2	0.8	0.9	8.2	8.2	9.3	7.7	5.8	23.7	22.9	12.4	2.0	69.6	37.1	53.0	47.0
66406	BEATTIE	97.8	97.7	0.2	0.2	0.2	0.2	1.4	1.7	5.8	5.8	7.5	7.2	6.5	24.1	26.8	14.5	2.0	76.1	41.0	52.1	47.9
66407	BELVUE	97.4	97.7	0.0	0.0	0.0	0.0	1.6	1.6	9.4	9.7	10.8	6.9	5.3	25.5	21.6	9.4	1.4	65.5	32.3	51.3	48.7
66408	BERN	99.1	98.9	0.0	0.0	0.2	0.2	0.9	1.1	8.1	8.3	10.1	7.2	6.1	20.9	24.9	12.3	2.2	69.3	38.3	52.5	47.5
66409	BERRYTON	96.2	95.6	1.5	1.6	0.4	0.4	2.7	3.5	5.4	6.4	7.8	7.1	5.0	24.2	33.1	10.5	0.6	75.9	42.0	51.4	48.6
66411	BLUE RAPIDS	98.2	97.9	0.3	0.3	0.1	0.1	0.6	0.8	5.9	5.7	6.8	7.1	6.8	21.4	25.0	17.5	3.8	76.8	42.5	49.9	50.1
66412	BREMEN	97.0	97.1	0.2	0.2	0.0	0.0	0.5	0.4	3.8	4.6	6.4	8.8	6.2	23.6	26.5	18.5	1.6	78.2	43.4	52.3	47.7
66413	BURLINGAME	98.1	97.9	0.3	0.3	0.0	0.0	0.8	1.0	5.6	6.5	7.4	6.0	4.7	23.6	27.8	15.1	3.3	76.1	42.6	48.5	51.5
66414	CARBONDALE	97.5	97.3	0.3	0.3	0.2	0.2	2.3	2.8	6.7	6.8	8.7	8.1	6.7	26.2	25.8	10.4	0.6	72.6	37.8	48.8	51.2
66415	CENTRALIA	97.8	97.9	0.1	0.1	0.3	0.3	2.0	2.4	6.4	6.4	7.9	7.2	6.2	19.6	22.9	15.5	7.9	74.6	42.3	50.5	49.5
66416	CIRCLEVILLE	92.0	91.8	0.4	0.4	0.2	0.4	1.5	1.7	7.7	7.5	7.1	6.5	5.4	24.5	28.4	11.2	1.7	73.8	39.1	52.5	47.5
66417	CORNING	98.1	97.7	0.6	0.6	0.4	0.5	0.4	0.6	8.3	7.8	7.8	6.8	6.1	22.1	22.6	15.2	3.4	72.1	39.3	51.2	48.8
66418	DELIA	71.1	70.8	0.5	0.4	0.2	0.3	1.5	1.7	8.7	8.9	9.8	8.2	5.3	24.4	24.0	9.8	0.8	67.5	34.3	50.7	49.3
66419	DENISON	96.3	96.2	0.4	0.5	0.0	0.0	1.0	1.0	7.5	7.2	7.4	6.2	6.2	25.0	27.0	12.5	1.2	73.7	38.5	51.5	48.6
66422	EMMETT	92.8	92.7	0.2	0.2	0.0	0.2	1.4	1.8	9.5	9.6	10.7	7.1	5.4	25.5	21.8	9.3	1.3	65.6	32.3	51.5	48.5
66423	ESKRIDGE	97.9	97.9	0.8	0.8	0.3	0.3	1.0	1.2	5.6	5.9	6.4	6.2	5.7	23.8	28.1	15.7	2.6	78.5	43.0	48.8	51.2
66424	EVEREST	94.1	94.0	1.8	1.8	0.2	0.2	2.1	2.1	6.3	6.5	7.9	6.0	6.0	26.0	26.9	12.1	2.4	75.7	39.3	51.5	48.6
66425	FAIRVIEW	90.8	91.3	1.4	1.3	0.0	0.0	1.4	1.3	5.8	5.8	7.6	6.9	5.9	22.7	28.4	14.9	2.1	76.5	42.0	48.9	51.1
66427	FRANKFORT	98.5	98.5	0.5	0.5	0.1	0.1	0.6	0.6	4.1	5.0	6.7	8.0	5.8	19.6	25.9	19.7	5.3	79.1	45.5	49.9	50.2
66428	GOFF	97.6	97.6	0.7	0.7	0.2	0.2	0.5	0.6	8.3	8.7	9.4	7.0	4.4	25.5	21.0	13.7	2.0	69.2	36.3	52.0	48.0
66429	GRANTVILLE	95.7	95.3	0.2	0.2	0.4	0.5	2.1	2.3	5.2	6.1	7.2	6.5	7.2	25.1	30.7	11.2	0.9	77.3	41.4	51.0	49.0
66431	HARVEYVILLE	97.7	97.2	0.2	0.3	0.3	0.4	1.1	1.3	6.4	6.9	7.3	6.2	4.9	24.1	29.8	13.0	1.3	75.5	41.7	51.3	48.7
66432	HAVENSVILLE	96.7	96.6	0.2	0.2	0.2	0.2	1.1	1.3	6.7	7.5	6.9	6.9	5.2	23.4	27.9	14.2	1.5	75.1	40.7	54.1	45.9
66434	HIAWATHA	90.4	90.1	2.2	2.3	0.1	0.1	2.4	2.5	6.4	6.2	6.3	6.8	6.6	22.3	25.5	15.5	4.4	77.0	41.5	48.1	51.9
66436	HOLTON	93.8	93.5	0.8	0.9	0.2	0.2	1.7	2.0	6.7	6.6	6.5	6.5	6.7	24.1	24.0	15.0	4.0	75.9	40.3	47.5	52.5
66438	HOME	97.8	97.8	0.3	0.3	0.0	0.0	1.2	1.6	5.3	5.6	7.8	7.5	6.6	23.8	27.2	14.4	1.9	76.3	41.1	52.5	47.5
66439	HORTON	81.2	80.7	0.9	0.9	0.5	0.5	2.6	2.7	7.3	7.2	8.1	6.9	6.4	22.3	22.4	15.5	3.9	73.1	38.3	48.1	51.9
66440	HOYT	91.1	90.4	0.1	0.1	0.2	0.3	2.0	2.3	7.0	7.3	8.4	8.0	5.9	26.9	25.8	9.8	0.9	72.3	37.0	51.1	48.9
66441	JUNCTION CITY	62.3	60.2	23.7	24.0	4.0	4.8	7.7	9.1	8.6	7.4	7.1	7.2	8.8	28.9	21.0	9.7	1.4	72.9	31.6	48.7	51.4
66442	FORT RILEY	62.9	60.4	22.2	22.9	2.5	3.0	12.9	15.3	12.6	9.4	7.0	11.2	18.8	38.2	2.3	0.5	0.1	68.1	22.6	62.3	37.7
66449	LEONARDVILLE	97.7	97.4	0.1	0.1	0.2	0.2	1.7	2.1	5.0	5.5	7.4	7.1	4.8	21.9	27.0	17.2	4.3	77.2	44.0	49.9	50.1
66451	LYNDON	97.7	97.3	0.0	0.0	0.3	0.4	0.9	1.1	5.7	6.2	7.1	7.2	5.8	24.6	27.9	13.5	2.0	76.4	41.1	51.2	48.8
66502	MANHATTAN	87.4	85.8	4.8	5.1	3.6	4.5	3.7	4.6	4.8	4.2	4.8	13.6	21.2	28.8	14.5	6.8	1.2	82.9	25.6	53.1	46.9
66503	MANHATTAN	89.8	88.3	3.5	3.7	3.6	4.4	2.5	3.1	5.8	6.0	6.6	8.6	8.0	27.9	26.7	8.6	1.9	76.6	35.9	50.0	50.0
66506	MANHATTAN	89.7	88.3	5.6	6.0	1.7	2.3	3.5	4.4	0.0	0.0	0.0	83.6	14.6	1.7	0.2	0.0	0.0	99.9	18.0	34.5	65.5
66507	MAPLE HILL	96.0	95.6	1.1	1.1	0.3	0.4	2.0	2.3	7.9	7.6	7.1	6.6	5.7	25.7	25.4	12.3	1.7	73.3	38.3	50.9	49.1
66508	MARYSVILLE	98.2	97.9	0.2	0.2	0.4	0.5	0.7	0.8	5.2	5.4	5.9	7.1	5.9	23.2	25.8	17.0	4.6	78.7	43.4	48.2	51.8
66509	MAYETTA	83.2	82.6	0.3	0.3	0.1	0.2	1.2	1.4	7.7	8.0	9.2	7.9	5.4	25.5	25.4	10.3	0.8	70.1	36.2	50.7	49.4
66510	MELVERN	97.8	97.6	0.0	0.0	0.1	0.1	1.1	1.4	6.8	6.5	6.2	7.5	6.2	26.9	25.0	12.5	2.4	75.2	39.6	50.0	50.0
66512	MERIDEN	97.1	96.9	0.4	0.4	0.1	0.2	1.4	1.7	6.8	7.1	7.3	7.4	5.9	27.7	27.6	9.4	0.8	74.4	38.2	51.1	48.9
66514	MILFORD	84.2	82.5	5.5	5.7	2.5	3.0	5.7	6.8	6.3	6.5	7.5	7.5	6.7	26.4	28.9	9.6	0.6	75.4	38.0	51.0	49.0
66515	MORRILL	97.4	97.4	1.5	1.6	0.0	0.0	0.9	0.6	5.4	5.6	7.2	6.6	5.4	22.9	29.0	15.5	2.2	77.5	42.9	48.7	51.3
66516	NETAWAKA	92.4	92.4	0.0	0.0	0.5	0.8	1.1	1.0	7.7	7.9	7.7	6.9	6.1	23.7	28.8	9.4	1.8	73.0	38.6	52.3	47.7
66517	OGDEN	77.5	75.1	11.4	12.1	2.7	3.3	7.0	8.5	10.4	8.6	7.9	7.5	10.1	34.4	15.4	5.2	0.6	69.0	27.6	50.3	49.7
66518	OKETO	96.8	96.9	0.4	0.4	0.0	0.0	0.7	0.4	3.8	4.5	6.3	8.7	5.9	24.0	26.8	18.5	1.4	78.8	43.5	52.6	47.4
66520	OLSBURG	97.8	97.6	0.7	0.7	0.0	0.0	1.6	1.9	5.5	6.6	7.1	5.2	5.0	22.1	32.6	14.2	1.7	77.9	43.9	52.0	48.0
66521	ONAGA	97.2	96.9	0.3	0.3	0.3	0.3	1.8	2.2	6.6	7.0	7.5	5.6	5.4	22.4	24.3	16.5	4.6	75.2	41.5	50.9	49.1
66522	ONEIDA	99.1	99.2	0.0	0.0	0.0	0.0	0.9	1.3	8.4	8.4	9.3	7.6	5.9	24.5	21.9	12.2	1.7	68.8	36.1	52.7	47.3
66523	OSAGE CITY	96.8	96.5	0.3	0.3	0.4	0.4	2.0	2.5	7.2	7.1	7.4	6.6	5.3	23.5	23.7	15.0	4.0	73.7	40.3	48.5	51.5
66524	OVERBROOK	97.7	97.4	0.2	0.2	0.1	0.2	1.2	1.5	6.1	6.3	6.7	6.7	5.2	23.9	27.8	13.8	3.5	76.6	41.9	48.9	51.1
66526	PAXICO	97.3	97.1	0.4	0.4	0.2	0.1	1.8	2.2	7.5	7.6	8.3	7.9	5.6	25.7	25.1	10.9	1.4	71.6	37.5	50.8	49.3
66527	POWHATTAN	48.0	47.0	0.3	0.3	0.0	0.0	5.2	5.5	8.6	6.4	9.1	9.9	9.1	21.6	21.0	12.4	1.9	69.6	33.6	49.5	50.6
66528	QUENEMO	94.7	94.4	0.2	0.2	1.0	1.3	1.2	1.5	7.9	8.2	8.1	8.1	5.8	24.5	25.8	10.6	1.1	71.0	36.2	50.7	49.3
66531	RILEY	91.0	90.5	3.7	3.7	0.8	0.9	3.1	3.7	5.7	6.9	10.6	13.0	4.6	29.7	20.3	7.6	1.6	68.3	30.9	51.6	48.4
66532	ROBINSON	95.3	95.3	0.3	0.3	0.1	0.1	1.1	1.1	5.4	6.2	7.9	8.7	4.9	22.9	28.3	14.7	1.1	75.1	40.8	52.4	47.7
66533	ROSSVILLE	96.1	95.4	0.1	0.1	0.4	0.4	2.7	3.4	7.2	7.7	8.3	7.1	5.7	26.0	25.2	10.7	1.9	72.1	37.1	50.6	49.4
66534	SABETHA	98.0	97.7	0.8	0.9	0.2	0.2	0.5	0.6	7.3	7.1	6.5	6.3	5.5	22.0	21.4	17.3	6.6	74.9	41.5	47.9	52.1
66535	SAINT GEORGE	95.2	94.7	1.1	1.2	0.5	0.7	2.0	2.4	7.0	6.9	7.3	7.1	6.9	30.5	24.9	8.8	0.7	74.5	34.9	49.0	51.0
66536	SAINT MARYS	95.6	95.2	0.7	0.7	0.6	0.7	4.1	4.9	10.4	9.4	9.0	9.0	5.7	23.2	20.0	10.7	2.5	65.4	31.3	49.2	50.8
66537	SCRANTON	94.8	94.3	0.6	0.6	0.6	0.8	1.6	2.0	7.8	8.2	8.4	6.7	5.9	27.2	23.7	10.7	1.4	71.3	36.2	49.2	50.8
66538	SENECA	98.9	98.8	0.3	0.3	0.1	0.1	0.7	0.8	6.9	6.9	7.5	7.2	6.4	21.4	21.8	17.4	4.5	73.9	40.9	49.0	51.0
66539	SILVER LAKE	96.7	96.2	0.3	0.3	0.3	0.4	1.6	2.1	6.2	7.2	8.3	7.6	5.1	26.5	27.9	10.2	1.3	73.1	38.7	51.3	48.8
66540	SOLDIER	90.1	89.9	0.4	0.4	0.2	0.4	1.5	1.5	7.7	7.9	7.3	6.8	5.4	24.8	27.8	10.9	1.5	73.2	38.4	52.2	47.8
66541	SUMMERFIELD	98.1	98.0	0.0	0.0	0.0	0.0	1.0	0.7	6.5	6.5	7.5	6.5	6.5	21.6	25.2	17.0	2.6	74.5	41.5	49.7	50.3
66542	TECUMSEH	94.9	94.2	1.6	1.8	0.2	0.3	3.0	3.8	5.0	5.9	7.0	7.4	5.4	20.4	34.4	13.9	0.8	77.6	44.4	49.7	50.3
66543	VASSAR	97.8	97.7	0.0	0.0	0.3	0.4	1.0	1.4	5.6	5.9	6.5	6.6	5.6	23.0	31.5	13.7	1.5	77.9	43.0	50.0	50.0
66544	VERMILLION	98.6	98.8	0.7	0.7	0.0	0.0	1.1	1.2	4.0	5.9	8.0	8.9	4.9	20.5	28.5	16.5	2.8	75.8	43.8	52.7	47.3
66546	WAKARUSA	93.5	92.7	2.4	2.5	0.4	0.5	2.2	2.8	6.5	6.8	8.7	8.0	5.4	28.4	27.6	8.1	0.6	72.3	37.4	50.6	49.4
66547	WAMEGO	96.8	96.5	0.6	0.6	0.2	0.3	1.8	2.2	7.4	7.3	7.7	8.0	6.7	27.4	23.7	9.8	2.1	72.5	35.6	49.1	50.9
66548	WATERVILLE	98.0	97.8	0.1	0.1	0.2	0.2	1.0	1.2	6.5	6.2	7.2	7.4	5.8	21.1	24.7	16.8	4.4	75.4	42.3	49.2	50.8
66549	WESTMORELAND	97.8	97.5	0.1	0.1	0.1	0.1	1.8	2.2	6.8	7.1	6.9	6.0	5.0	23.7	26.8	14.7	3.1	75.3	41.5	50.0	50.0
66550	WETMORE	97.4	97.1	0.8	0.8	0.2	0.3	0.8	0.8	8.4	8.7	10.3	7.1	3.9	25.9	20.7	13.1	1.9	67.9	35.4	52.5	47.5
66552	WHITING	95.9	95.8	0.9	0.9	0.2	0.2	0.5	0.7	4.9	5.8	7.8	6.2	4.7	25.3	27.3	16.2	2.0	77.6	42.5	50.6	49.5
66554	RANDOLPH	97.4	97.0	0.3	0.3	0.3	0.3	1.7	2.1	5.3	5.8	6.4	6.1	4.9	22.9	29.4	16.0	3.3	78.3	44.1	50.6	49.4
66603	TOPEKA	64.1	61.1	17.1	18.3	0.5	0.7	16.9	19.5	8.6	6.9	6.5	7.8	10.4	30.5	21.5	6.8	1.0	74.1	31.0	54.2	45.8
66604	TOPEKA	83.2	81.8	9.6	10.0	0.9	1.1	5.9	7.3	6.7	6.2	6.2	6.4	7.9	27.6	23.4	13.0	2.7	77.4	36.8	46.9	53.1
66605	TOPEKA	69.1	66.9	20.3	21.0	0.7	0.8	9.9	12.1	7.7	7.6	8.1	7.3	6.6	25.1	25.3	11.1	1.4	72.1	36.2	47.4	52.6
66606	TOPEKA	85.5	83.6	7.5	8.2	0.8	1.0	5.8	7.5	6.5	5.9	5.6	5.8	6.8	28.1	23.9	13.2	4.2	78.6	39.0	47.0	53.0
66607	TOPEKA	51.6	49.2	26.9	26.8	0.3	0.4	25.0	28.7	8.2	7.6	7.4	7.7	8.8	29.2	19.9	10.0	1.3	72.3	32.1	51.1	48.9
66608	TOPEKA	87.3	86.1	5.0	5.4	0.4	0.5	5.4	6.7	7.1	6.8	6.4	9.3	6.5	26.9	23.5	11.9	1.5	73.8	35.9	51.1	48.9
66609	TOPEKA	84.3	82.5	9.0	9.7	1.2	1.3	6.6	8.2	6.6	6.4	6.6	6.4	8.3	28.0	25.7	11.2	0.9	76.7	36.3	48.5	51.5
66610	TOPEKA	91.4	90.2	3.8	4.2	1.5	1.9	3.1	3.9	5.7	6.9	7.8	7.4	4.6	23.5	32.1	10.1	2.1	74.5	41.6	48.6	51.4
66611	TOPEKA	84.2	82.5	8.6	9.3	1.6	1.9	4.6	5.8	6.4	5.5	5.3	5.5	7.3	27.1	22.7	16.2	4.1	79.7	39.5	46.7	53.3
66612	TOPEKA	56.0	53.5	30.6	31.6	1.1	1.3	10.8	12.9	7.6	6.2	5.3	6.3	10.6	30.0	22.6	9.6	1.6	78.0	34.1	51.1	48.9
66614	TOPEKA	88.2	86.7	5.6	5.9	2.1	2.6	4.0	5.0	6.2	6.2	6.5	6.1	6.4	27.3	26.2	13.0	2.0	77.3	39.1	47.5	52.6
66615	TOPEKA	89.0	87.8	6.3	6.6	1.2	1.6	3.1	3.9	6.3	6.3	6.3	6.3	6.1	31.1	26.1	9.8	1.8	77.2	38.3	44.9	55.1
	KANSAS	86.1	84.9	5.7	5.8	1.8	2.2	7.0	8.1	7.1	7.0	7.2	7.5	7.6	27.3	23.4	10.9	2.0	74.4	35.6	49.5	50.5
	UNITED STATES	75.1	73.6	12.3	12.5	3.8	4.2	12.5	14.1	6.9	6.7	7.2	7.0	7.3	28.6	23.8	10.8	1.7	75.1	36.0	49.1	50.9

ZIP CODE #	POST OFFICE NAME	2004 Per Capita Income	2004 HH Income Base	2004 HOUSEHOLD INCOME DISTRIBUTION (%) Less than $25,000	$25,000 to $49,999	$50,000 to $99,999	$100,000 to $149,999	$150,000 or More	MEDIAN HOUSEHOLD INCOME 2004	2009	2004 National Centile	2004 State Centile	2004 Home Value Base	2004 HOME VALUE DISTRIBUTION (%) Less than $50,000	$50,000 to $89,999	$90,000 to $174,999	$175,000 to $399,999	$400,000 or More	2004 Median Home Value
66220	LENEXA	57375	1137	2.3	6.4	25.8	30.3	35.2	125501	145491	100	100	1092	0.0	0.3	14.8	56.8	28.1	291007
66221	OVERLAND PARK	54203	2732	1.4	4.5	18.6	26.5	49.0	147532	172581	100	100	2694	0.7	0.1	2.2	50.0	47.0	390323
66223	OVERLAND PARK	39693	5485	2.6	8.4	36.4	31.3	21.3	102502	125866	98	99	5037	0.3	0.0	15.3	76.8	7.5	231954
66224	OVERLAND PARK	45705	2839	4.9	12.4	23.6	25.1	34.0	117485	144709	99	100	2426	0.6	0.0	7.1	51.4	40.9	357663
66226	SHAWNEE	35053	3172	2.4	9.0	47.0	29.8	11.8	89776	110755	97	98	3109	0.4	0.7	21.0	74.7	3.3	200883
66227	LENEXA	36280	654	8.4	18.2	43.3	20.2	9.9	75630	89307	93	96	627	0.5	0.3	44.7	48.2	6.4	179948
66401	ALMA	21275	854	17.7	36.9	38.6	5.2	1.6	47049	52983	66	76	711	22.6	35.4	31.5	10.4	0.0	81667
66402	AUBURN	24552	1007	11.4	28.9	41.9	11.7	6.1	56702	68274	81	88	916	3.2	26.2	47.9	21.3	1.4	110769
66403	AXTELL	16775	244	34.4	36.5	24.6	2.9	1.6	34711	40809	26	18	205	53.7	23.9	17.6	4.9	0.0	46250
66404	BAILEYVILLE	15634	213	31.0	33.8	31.0	2.8	1.4	37728	42544	38	38	173	29.5	31.8	21.4	12.7	4.6	72813
66406	BEATTIE	18256	251	32.7	31.5	30.3	3.6	2.0	37695	43726	38	38	205	59.0	18.5	17.1	5.4	0.0	44394
66407	BELVUE	18189	144	22.9	38.2	29.2	6.3	3.5	43795	50323	58	64	120	27.5	26.7	35.8	8.3	1.7	82857
66408	BERN	18738	165	25.5	40.6	27.3	4.2	2.4	41034	46456	50	54	135	40.7	23.0	17.0	15.6	3.7	62273
66409	BERRYTON	28024	1142	11.6	19.3	42.4	21.5	5.3	68361	81598	90	95	1060	10.7	9.5	53.0	25.0	1.8	134738
66411	BLUE RAPIDS	19950	554	28.9	37.0	24.9	5.8	3.4	37729	45377	38	38	415	58.1	28.7	12.1	0.7	0.5	39214
66412	BREMEN	15988	165	29.1	40.6	23.0	5.5	1.8	35181	41616	28	21	136	33.8	33.1	23.5	8.1	1.5	66842
66413	BURLINGAME	20587	818	25.8	33.9	32.8	7.0	0.6	40357	47072	47	51	636	29.7	33.2	31.1	5.5	0.5	76324
66414	CARBONDALE	18891	1223	25.5	30.7	36.8	6.9	0.1	43711	50863	58	64	998	17.2	33.9	37.9	10.6	0.4	88791
66415	CENTRALIA	17574	291	43.3	34.0	17.5	2.1	3.1	28026	33360	9	1	222	41.0	35.1	19.8	3.6	0.5	60400
66416	CIRCLEVILLE	22439	184	25.5	31.5	32.1	8.2	2.7	45833	52325	63	72	156	18.6	28.9	31.4	20.5	0.6	94444
66417	CORNING	14052	227	30.0	41.0	28.2	0.9	0.0	36376	41623	33	30	190	34.7	24.7	31.1	8.4	1.1	76316
66418	DELIA	26986	237	18.6	34.6	34.6	7.6	4.6	46755	55425	66	75	203	24.1	30.1	33.5	10.8	1.5	85526
66419	DENISON	19124	209	17.7	39.2	37.8	3.8	1.4	45865	53578	64	72	176	18.8	19.3	40.3	20.5	1.1	103378
66422	EMMETT	21282	202	21.8	39.1	28.2	6.4	4.5	43818	50616	58	64	169	29.0	28.4	33.1	8.3	1.2	79643
66423	ESKRIDGE	18569	291	27.5	32.3	34.7	5.2	0.3	44027	50192	59	65	241	30.7	46.9	19.1	3.3	0.0	64875
66424	EVEREST	17297	249	32.9	33.3	29.7	2.8	1.2	35204	40623	28	22	204	40.2	25.0	26.0	7.8	1.0	62857
66425	FAIRVIEW	21058	257	26.5	33.5	34.6	4.7	0.8	41927	47216	53	58	214	41.6	24.8	25.7	7.0	0.9	66364
66427	FRANKFORT	18171	554	30.7	39.5	23.8	3.1	2.9	34799	41042	27	19	453	54.1	24.5	16.8	3.8	0.9	45698
66428	GOFF	16240	186	28.0	35.0	30.7	4.3	2.2	40340	45372	47	51	157	44.6	28.0	16.6	10.2	0.6	56538
66429	GRANTVILLE	26985	215	11.2	23.3	49.8	9.3	6.5	55674	64518	80	87	180	6.7	36.1	48.9	8.3	0.0	99286
66431	HARVEYVILLE	21659	441	22.5	31.1	37.0	5.9	3.6	47089	52973	66	76	374	20.1	24.3	35.6	20.1	0.0	100417
66432	HAVENSVILLE	19869	183	24.0	34.4	35.0	4.9	1.6	44176	51071	59	65	153	34.6	20.9	34.6	8.5	1.3	76429
66434	HIAWATHA	19384	2175	32.8	30.6	29.6	5.9	1.0	39542	45363	44	47	1565	27.6	36.4	32.1	3.8	0.1	74371
66436	HOLTON	21151	2197	25.2	34.5	31.5	7.4	1.5	41417	48419	51	56	1605	19.3	30.0	38.4	11.5	0.8	90943
66438	HOME	17551	118	32.2	30.5	31.4	3.4	2.5	37817	44304	39	39	96	55.2	18.8	19.8	6.3	0.0	46154
66439	HORTON	15045	1136	42.2	34.5	19.8	2.6	0.9	30647	35820	14	4	831	52.8	28.5	15.9	2.7	0.1	46781
66440	HOYT	21737	734	18.4	28.5	43.3	8.5	1.4	51906	60698	75	84	641	12.5	27.8	48.7	11.1	0.0	101674
66441	JUNCTION CITY	20557	8648	31.9	33.8	25.7	5.7	3.0	36102	43105	32	28	5147	22.6	40.2	31.5	5.3	0.4	77015
66442	FORT RILEY	12561	2113	26.1	46.7	22.2	4.0	1.0	35530	40557	30	24	148	11.5	32.4	40.5	15.5	0.0	100806
66449	LEONARDVILLE	21696	377	20.7	39.8	28.9	5.6	5.0	41989	50726	53	58	299	31.4	28.8	26.4	9.0	4.4	76167
66451	LYNDON	20623	994	20.7	33.3	37.9	6.3	1.7	46542	52897	65	74	840	22.6	35.8	28.8	11.6	1.2	81744
66502	MANHATTAN	19830	16573	39.6	26.5	24.1	7.7	2.2	33332	42080	22	11	7137	15.2	24.7	48.6	10.7	0.8	101936
66503	MANHATTAN	31676	4338	12.2	25.0	37.5	16.1	9.2	63638	77862	88	93	3056	4.2	8.7	52.5	31.2	3.5	147917
66506	MANHATTAN	13853	13	30.8	30.8	23.1	15.4	0.0	37321	40000	37	35	0	0.0	0.0	0.0	0.0	0.0	0
66507	MAPLE HILL	22114	391	18.4	29.2	42.2	8.4	1.8	52092	58341	76	84	341	13.8	21.1	45.5	19.4	0.3	108259
66508	MARYSVILLE	23234	1741	30.7	32.4	26.0	7.9	3.1	39312	46663	44	46	1310	33.5	27.5	31.4	6.6	1.1	74486
66509	MAYETTA	23018	768	17.1	33.5	40.5	6.1	2.9	49572	57942	71	79	663	21.4	24.0	41.5	12.5	0.6	96224
66510	MELVERN	22400	379	22.4	30.3	37.2	5.8	4.2	48155	55113	69	78	310	24.5	25.8	36.5	12.9	0.3	89615
66512	MERIDEN	23018	1238	16.8	24.6	47.1	9.7	1.8	56219	63642	81	87	1106	13.1	16.8	50.5	18.4	1.1	114407
66514	MILFORD	23573	581	14.3	34.1	35.1	12.4	4.1	51599	62084	75	83	479	12.7	10.9	63.5	12.9	0.0	120145
66515	MORRILL	19071	185	25.4	31.9	37.3	4.9	0.5	43525	48014	57	63	155	41.3	24.5	26.5	7.1	0.7	69286
66516	NETAWAKA	19855	148	22.3	30.4	38.5	7.4	1.4	45932	56286	64	72	123	21.1	27.6	30.1	21.1	0.0	93000
66517	OGDEN	17658	718	33.3	32.5	27.3	7.0	0.0	36832	45919	35	32	373	31.6	28.2	40.0	0.3	0.0	79483
66518	OKETO	18991	124	29.0	39.5	24.2	5.7	1.6	35488	40976	29	24	102	37.3	30.4	22.6	8.8	1.0	65000
66520	OLSBURG	21761	237	20.7	35.4	35.4	7.2	1.3	46240	53518	64	73	200	24.0	32.0	24.5	16.0	3.5	79286
66521	ONAGA	18770	612	31.4	36.3	26.6	4.7	1.0	37546	43773	38	37	472	41.7	30.3	22.5	4.2	1.3	59070
66522	ONEIDA	16393	84	31.0	32.1	34.5	2.4	0.0	37357	40000	37	35	68	27.9	33.8	22.1	11.8	4.4	72857
66523	OSAGE CITY	20367	1633	29.2	35.5	27.5	5.8	2.1	38864	45633	42	44	1211	18.7	32.2	42.2	6.9	0.0	88678
66524	OVERBROOK	24306	909	21.3	25.3	41.3	9.7	2.4	53169	61022	77	85	800	13.5	21.1	47.0	15.9	2.5	109107
66526	PAXICO	19688	511	22.7	30.5	40.3	5.1	1.4	47919	53672	68	78	440	23.6	30.0	34.8	10.7	0.9	84667
66527	POWHATTAN	14360	136	31.6	46.3	19.9	2.2	0.0	33911	40000	24	14	103	45.6	25.2	19.4	9.7	0.0	57500
66528	QUENEMO	15274	222	29.7	36.9	29.3	4.1	0.0	35780	41747	31	26	179	50.8	17.3	19.6	8.9	3.4	48750
66531	RILEY	18439	510	24.9	33.5	33.7	5.1	2.8	43700	52866	58	63	392	15.6	50.5	19.1	11.5	3.3	76226
66532	ROBINSON	16198	281	37.4	32.0	25.6	4.3	0.7	32310	37082	19	7	225	36.4	38.2	20.9	4.4	0.0	67250
66533	ROSSVILLE	26689	598	14.4	31.1	40.6	9.9	4.0	53485	63003	78	85	489	9.8	29.7	50.3	10.2	0.0	103152
66534	SABETHA	23774	1271	27.9	33.4	27.6	6.5	4.6	42698	48845	55	60	977	26.6	36.4	29.1	7.5	0.4	72640
66535	SAINT GEORGE	21993	902	23.4	37.9	27.7	8.2	2.8	42260	48818	54	59	746	31.2	18.1	37.8	10.5	2.4	91429
66536	SAINT MARYS	18289	1022	23.5	33.9	32.0	8.4	2.3	45114	52009	61	68	816	11.0	30.3	52.2	5.5	1.0	98068
66537	SCRANTON	18916	404	22.3	39.4	30.7	6.2	1.5	42949	50470	56	61	331	38.1	32.3	23.3	5.7	0.6	64808
66538	SENECA	20922	1291	30.4	37.5	26.4	3.5	2.3	38013	43323	39	41	1009	20.9	34.1	36.0	7.9	1.1	83442
66539	SILVER LAKE	26029	1043	13.1	26.8	44.2	11.6	4.3	59307	69294	84	89	870	4.9	17.5	60.7	16.7	0.2	118562
66540	SOLDIER	21214	191	25.1	32.5	31.4	7.9	3.1	45412	52750	62	70	162	19.1	29.0	31.5	19.8	0.6	93000
66541	SUMMERFIELD	14827	104	33.7	37.5	24.0	2.9	1.9	35000	40754	28	21	87	55.2	23.0	16.1	5.8	0.0	45000
66542	TECUMSEH	28458	1093	9.6	20.0	44.8	20.4	5.1	68633	82054	91	95	1018	6.8	14.4	60.9	17.8	0.1	122979
66543	VASSAR	23300	331	14.8	30.5	46.2	7.3	1.2	53281	61252	77	85	299	12.0	31.8	37.1	16.7	2.3	96607
66544	VERMILLION	20419	182	25.3	35.7	33.5	2.2	3.3	38443	44643	41	42	150	38.0	18.7	32.0	8.0	3.3	81667
66546	WAKARUSA	30058	400	13.3	29.0	36.0	16.8	5.0	58971	70994	84	89	319	18.8	18.5	42.3	19.1	1.3	108578
66547	WAMEGO	21223	2551	22.1	28.3	38.2	9.5	1.9	49602	57761	71	80	1971	12.4	24.1	46.5	16.3	0.8	102823
66548	WATERVILLE	22229	418	31.6	31.6	28.2	4.8	3.8	37416	44374	37	36	345	44.4	36.8	14.8	3.2	0.9	56094
66549	WESTMORELAND	20534	622	26.9	34.7	30.4	6.4	1.6	40903	48313	49	54	512	28.9	29.1	31.5	9.8	0.8	77400
66550	WETMORE	18474	230	28.3	32.6	31.7	4.8	2.6	41649	47171	52	57	194	47.9	29.4	11.9	10.8	0.0	52105
66552	WHITING	20433	197	29.4	38.6	24.4	4.6	3.1	40642	46505	48	53	168	27.4	17.9	35.7	17.9	1.2	96667
66554	RANDOLPH	26462	282	19.2	30.9	35.8	9.2	5.0	50000	62008	72	80	231	22.1	26.0	32.9	15.6	3.5	94091
66603	TOPEKA	13703	982	57.7	28.1	11.4	1.6	1.1	20728	25185	2	0	284	58.1	34.5	5.3	2.1	0.0	43429
66604	TOPEKA	27001	10215	26.6	30.9	30.7	7.9	3.9	42901	52123	56	61	6320	15.7	46.5	33.1	3.9	0.8	78764
66605	TOPEKA	20750	7401	26.3	32.1	30.8	8.4	2.4	43326	51752	57	62	5256	28.4	30.3	37.3	4.1	0.0	73481
66606	TOPEKA	24772	5947	29.7	32.9	27.4	6.9	3.2	39166	47239	43	45	3363	19.5	52.0	22.0	5.7	0.7	70033
66607	TOPEKA	14291	3263	41.4	36.5	17.3	3.3	1.7	30447	36266	13	4	1823	66.9	25.1	6.9	1.1	0.0	38895
66608	TOPEKA	17858	2342	38.2	32.8	26.3	2.2	0.5	32543	39213	19	8	1580	62.2	31.5	5.8	0.5	0.0	39926
66609	TOPEKA	24547	2973	20.7	32.7	34.2	10.2	2.1	46731	56597	66	75	2186	39.1	22.1	33.5	5.2	0.0	67529
66610	TOPEKA	36249	2466	6.4	16.1	43.7	20.4	13.5	77685	93049	94	96	2233	1.8	10.9	46.9	35.5	4.9	157184
66611	TOPEKA	27810	4410	23.2	30.8	32.5	10.1	3.5	46637	55904	65	74	2695	11.6	48.5	32.2	7.4	0.3	78386
66612	TOPEKA	17356	1695	61.1	25.0	12.0	0.7	1.2	18783	22801	1	0	428	67.1	21.0	7.7	4.2	0.0	37361
66614	TOPEKA	30116	13833	16.1	27.4	36.7	14.3	5.6	56943	67038	82	88	9518	2.9	24.3	53.6	17.7	1.6	117133
66615	TOPEKA	27983	616	10.2	22.1	41.2	22.7	3.7	67060	79826	90	94	541	4.1	10.7	58.4	24.4	2.4	128006
	KANSAS	25137		23.6	29.0	32.2	10.1	5.1	47540	57348				21.4	24.4	35.0	16.7	2.5	97470
	UNITED STATES	25866		24.7	27.1	30.8	10.9	6.5	48124	56710				10.9	15.0	33.7	30.1	10.4	145905

ZIP CODE #	POST OFFICE NAME	FINANCIAL SERVICES: Auto Loan	FINANCIAL SERVICES: Home Loan	FINANCIAL SERVICES: Invest-ments	FINANCIAL SERVICES: Retire-ment Plans	THE HOME: Home Improvements: Home Repair	THE HOME: Home Improvements: Lawn & Garden	THE HOME: Furnishings: Comput-ers & Hard-ware	THE HOME: Furnishings: Major Appli-ances	THE HOME: Furnishings: TV, Radio, Sound Equip-ment	THE HOME: Furnishings: Furni-ture	ENTERTAINMENT: Dine out/ Carry out	ENTERTAINMENT: Sports Equip-ment	ENTERTAINMENT: Fees & Tickets	ENTERTAINMENT: Toys & Games	ENTERTAINMENT: Travel	ENTERTAINMENT: Cable TV	PERSONAL: Apparel & Services	PERSONAL: Auto Repairs	PERSONAL: Health Insur-ance	PERSONAL: Pets & Supplies
66220	LENEXA	207	255	280	261	249	254	227	223	209	230	266	257	248	274	233	204	266	216	203	246
66221	OVERLAND PARK	247	308	334	317	297	300	271	264	247	275	314	305	298	326	276	239	317	255	235	292
66223	OVERLAND PARK	174	200	195	208	190	185	180	177	164	186	209	207	186	210	176	154	207	173	151	194
66224	OVERLAND PARK	196	231	236	240	222	218	206	203	188	212	240	236	219	244	205	178	239	197	176	223
66226	SHAWNEE	149	172	170	178	165	160	155	153	142	159	180	179	160	183	152	133	178	149	132	168
66227	LENEXA	128	159	169	159	156	154	142	141	131	141	165	165	151	176	145	127	165	136	126	156
66401	ALMA	93	69	40	65	78	87	67	81	76	66	89	97	59	89	69	79	82	79	94	111
66402	AUBURN	94	110	113	111	107	105	101	100	94	101	119	118	104	123	101	90	118	98	89	111
66403	AXTELL	77	54	28	51	63	71	53	66	62	53	72	80	46	71	55	65	66	65	79	92
66404	BAILEYVILLE	85	59	31	56	69	77	58	72	67	58	79	87	50	77	61	71	72	71	86	101
66406	BEATTIE	84	59	31	55	68	76	58	72	67	57	78	86	49	77	60	70	71	71	85	100
66407	BELVUE	86	73	57	73	77	87	75	80	80	74	97	92	72	96	74	81	90	79	87	95
66408	BERN	92	64	33	60	75	83	63	78	73	62	85	94	54	84	66	76	78	77	93	109
66409	BERRYTON	106	122	122	121	121	122	110	112	105	109	130	131	114	137	112	103	129	108	104	128
66411	BLUE RAPIDS	81	60	38	58	67	79	65	73	73	62	86	83	58	82	65	77	79	73	88	91
66412	BREMEN	79	55	29	52	65	72	55	68	63	54	74	82	47	73	57	66	67	67	81	94
66413	BURLINGAME	79	63	44	61	68	79	66	72	72	63	86	83	60	83	66	75	79	71	83	89
66414	CARBONDALE	71	73	69	73	74	76	70	71	68	69	85	83	70	87	70	67	82	70	69	82
66415	CENTRALIA	69	51	33	49	57	67	56	63	63	53	74	71	49	70	56	66	67	62	75	77
66416	CIRCLEVILLE	103	72	37	68	83	93	71	87	82	70	96	105	60	94	73	86	87	86	104	122
66417	CORNING	71	50	27	48	58	66	50	61	58	49	68	73	43	66	52	61	62	61	73	84
66418	DELIA	131	116	89	110	123	132	107	119	114	107	139	142	105	142	111	117	132	116	129	154
66419	DENISON	85	75	57	72	80	86	71	78	75	70	91	93	69	93	72	77	86	76	85	100
66422	EMMETT	93	79	62	79	83	93	80	86	85	79	103	99	77	103	80	87	97	85	94	103
66423	ESKRIDGE	76	56	37	54	62	74	62	69	70	59	82	78	55	77	62	74	75	69	82	84
66424	EVEREST	78	54	28	51	63	71	54	66	62	53	73	80	46	71	56	65	66	66	79	93
66425	FAIRVIEW	89	63	34	59	73	82	63	77	72	62	85	92	54	83	65	76	77	76	91	105
66427	FRANKFORT	73	54	33	51	60	70	58	65	65	55	76	75	51	73	58	69	70	65	78	82
66428	GOFF	86	60	31	56	70	78	59	73	68	58	80	88	50	78	61	71	73	72	87	102
66429	GRANTVILLE	124	95	60	91	106	116	93	110	102	92	122	132	82	120	95	105	113	108	124	147
66431	HARVEYVILLE	101	72	39	68	83	93	71	87	81	70	95	105	61	94	74	85	87	86	103	120
66432	HAVENSVILLE	92	64	33	60	74	83	63	78	73	62	85	94	54	84	65	76	78	77	93	109
66434	HIAWATHA	71	58	45	56	63	72	61	67	66	59	79	77	56	77	61	69	74	66	76	81
66436	HOLTON	80	66	51	65	71	80	69	75	74	67	89	87	64	87	69	76	83	74	83	91
66438	HOME	86	60	31	56	70	78	59	73	68	58	80	88	50	78	61	71	73	72	87	102
66439	HORTON	61	46	29	44	50	60	50	55	56	47	66	63	44	62	49	59	60	55	66	68
66440	HOYT	98	87	66	83	92	99	81	89	86	81	104	106	79	106	83	88	99	87	97	115
66441	JUNCTION CITY	72	67	69	68	68	73	72	71	73	70	90	85	70	88	70	71	87	73	71	81
66442	FORT RILEY	70	45	41	50	42	49	65	57	66	60	82	75	55	74	54	61	79	67	54	66
66449	LEONARDVILLE	102	72	38	68	83	93	71	87	81	70	95	105	61	93	73	85	87	86	103	121
66451	LYNDON	90	71	46	67	78	86	68	79	75	68	89	95	62	89	70	77	83	78	90	106
66502	MANHATTAN	65	52	61	56	52	57	71	61	69	65	86	78	64	81	63	64	83	68	57	69
66503	MANHATTAN	104	118	136	121	118	122	115	113	109	114	137	132	118	139	116	106	135	113	106	124
66506	MANHATTAN	72	44	56	50	43	52	85	62	83	72	103	87	69	93	68	73	97	76	58	71
66507	MAPLE HILL	105	74	38	70	86	96	73	90	84	72	98	108	62	96	75	88	90	89	107	125
66508	MARYSVILLE	89	65	40	62	73	85	69	79	78	66	92	91	61	88	69	82	84	79	95	100
66509	MAYETTA	108	96	73	91	101	109	89	98	94	89	114	117	87	117	91	96	109	96	106	127
66510	MELVERN	91	81	62	77	86	92	75	83	80	75	97	99	74	99	77	82	92	81	90	107
66512	MERIDEN	94	90	78	88	92	96	85	90	85	85	105	107	84	107	85	85	102	88	90	109
66514	MILFORD	103	91	70	87	96	103	84	94	90	84	109	111	83	111	87	92	104	91	101	121
66515	MORRILL	93	65	34	61	75	84	64	79	74	63	86	95	55	85	66	77	79	78	94	110
66516	NETAWAKA	84	74	56	70	78	85	69	77	74	69	90	91	67	91	71	76	85	75	84	99
66517	OGDEN	57	60	68	62	60	62	64	61	62	62	78	74	64	80	63	59	76	63	57	66
66518	OKETO	80	56	29	52	65	72	55	68	63	54	74	82	47	73	57	66	68	67	81	94
66520	OLSBURG	96	67	35	63	78	88	66	82	76	66	90	99	57	88	69	80	82	81	98	114
66521	ONAGA	76	56	34	54	63	73	59	68	66	57	78	78	52	75	59	70	72	67	80	86
66522	ONEIDA	84	58	31	55	68	76	58	71	66	57	78	86	49	76	60	70	71	70	85	99
66523	OSAGE CITY	85	64	40	61	72	81	65	75	73	63	86	88	58	84	66	76	79	74	88	98
66524	OVERBROOK	97	87	71	84	91	101	86	93	91	84	109	107	83	109	87	93	103	91	101	112
66526	PAXICO	96	69	38	65	79	88	67	82	77	67	90	99	59	89	70	80	83	81	97	113
66527	POWHATTAN	62	46	31	45	51	61	51	56	57	49	68	63	46	64	51	61	62	56	68	68
66528	QUENEMO	68	62	48	60	62	66	59	63	60	61	74	73	56	70	58	59	71	63	63	75
66531	RILEY	92	64	34	61	74	83	64	78	73	63	86	95	55	84	66	77	79	78	93	109
66532	ROBINSON	73	51	28	49	59	67	52	63	60	51	70	75	45	68	53	63	64	62	75	85
66533	ROSSVILLE	121	96	64	91	106	116	91	107	101	91	121	128	85	121	95	104	113	104	121	143
66534	SABETHA	102	75	47	72	84	99	82	92	92	78	108	105	72	103	81	97	98	91	110	115
66535	SAINT GEORGE	91	80	60	77	82	87	77	84	79	78	97	97	72	92	76	78	92	83	85	102
66536	SAINT MARYS	92	70	45	68	78	88	71	82	79	70	94	96	64	92	72	81	87	81	94	106
66537	SCRANTON	79	67	52	67	70	79	68	73	73	67	88	84	66	87	68	74	83	72	79	87
66538	SENECA	87	64	40	61	71	84	69	78	78	66	91	89	61	87	69	82	83	78	93	98
66539	SILVER LAKE	106	103	88	99	106	112	94	101	96	94	118	120	95	122	97	97	114	98	105	126
66540	SOLDIER	106	76	41	72	87	97	74	91	85	73	100	109	64	98	77	89	91	89	107	126
66541	SUMMERFIELD	77	54	28	51	63	70	53	66	61	53	72	79	45	70	55	64	66	65	78	92
66542	TECUMSEH	101	124	134	124	122	122	112	112	105	112	132	130	119	141	115	102	132	108	101	123
66543	VASSAR	92	82	63	78	86	93	76	84	80	76	98	100	74	99	78	82	93	82	90	108
66544	VERMILLION	85	60	32	57	69	78	60	73	69	59	80	88	51	79	62	72	73	72	87	101
66546	WAKARUSA	119	113	94	109	117	123	104	113	107	105	132	134	104	135	107	108	127	110	117	140
66547	WAMEGO	80	81	81	81	82	86	80	81	79	79	97	95	80	99	80	77	94	80	79	92
66548	WATERVILLE	89	66	41	63	73	86	71	80	80	68	94	91	63	89	71	84	86	80	96	100
66549	WESTMORELAND	93	65	34	61	76	85	64	79	74	63	87	96	55	85	67	77	79	78	94	110
66550	WETMORE	90	63	33	59	73	82	62	77	71	61	84	92	53	82	64	75	76	76	91	107
66552	WHITING	84	59	31	56	69	77	58	72	67	58	79	87	50	77	61	70	72	71	86	100
66554	RANDOLPH	100	88	68	85	95	101	83	94	87	82	105	111	78	106	85	89	99	91	101	120
66603	TOPEKA	36	31	36	32	31	35	38	36	39	36	49	43	36	47	36	39	47	38	36	39
66604	TOPEKA	77	82	97	83	81	86	85	82	83	83	105	96	86	106	85	82	103	84	79	89
66605	TOPEKA	71	73	77	72	73	79	74	74	75	73	93	85	75	96	75	76	91	74	75	82
66606	TOPEKA	70	69	76	70	70	75	73	72	73	71	91	85	72	91	72	72	88	73	71	81
66607	TOPEKA	55	48	46	46	48	54	53	53	56	52	69	61	51	67	52	57	66	55	56	60
66608	TOPEKA	56	55	54	53	55	61	55	56	57	54	70	63	56	72	56	58	68	56	58	63
66609	TOPEKA	79	83	85	83	82	84	82	81	79	81	99	96	82	100	81	77	97	82	76	92
66610	TOPEKA	133	160	173	164	156	157	145	143	134	147	170	166	154	175	147	130	169	139	129	157
66611	TOPEKA	75	81	96	84	81	84	83	81	80	82	100	95	84	101	83	77	98	82	76	88
66612	TOPEKA	38	33	41	34	33	37	41	38	42	39	53	45	39	51	39	42	51	41	39	42
66614	TOPEKA	93	101	117	105	99	103	102	98	98	101	123	117	104	124	101	94	121	100	90	108
66615	TOPEKA	104	121	123	124	117	115	110	109	101	112	128	128	114	131	109	96	127	106	96	120
	KANSAS	92	87	84	87	89	95	89	91	90	88	111	106	87	110	88	89	107	91	92	105
	UNITED STATES	100	100	100	100	100	100	100	100	100	100	100	100	100	100	100	100	100	100	100	100

KANSAS

POPULATION CHANGE

A 66616-66938

ZIP CODE			POPULATION			2000-2004 ANNUAL RATE		HOUSEHOLDS					FAMILIES		
#	POST OFFICE NAME	COUNTY FIPS CODE	2000	2004	2009	% Rate	State Centile	2000	2004	2009	% Annual Rate 2000-2004	2004 Average HH Size	2000	2004	% Annual Rate 2000-2004
66616	TOPEKA	177	6307	6210	6241	-0.4	32	2576	2574	2619	0.0	2.41	1651	1629	-0.3
66617	TOPEKA	177	8176	8213	8351	0.1	54	3006	3066	3158	0.5	2.68	2483	2519	0.3
66618	TOPEKA	177	7777	8110	8333	1.0	78	2704	2881	3007	1.5	2.79	2272	2407	1.4
66619	TOPEKA	177	3350	3346	3365	0.0	47	1122	1138	1160	0.3	2.94	888	893	0.1
66701	FORT SCOTT	011	12062	11939	11978	-0.2	36	4873	4863	4916	-0.1	2.39	3199	3159	-0.3
66710	ALTOONA	205	889	882	874	-0.2	38	361	363	363	0.1	2.43	256	254	-0.2
66711	ARCADIA	037	732	788	824	1.8	88	291	314	330	1.8	2.50	204	217	1.5
66712	ARMA	037	2201	2226	2260	0.3	61	934	950	970	0.4	2.28	586	588	0.1
66713	BAXTER SPRINGS	021	6073	6041	6032	-0.1	42	2370	2367	2374	0.0	2.51	1642	1627	-0.2
66714	BENEDICT	205	858	843	830	-0.4	28	350	347	345	-0.2	2.43	259	255	-0.4
66716	BRONSON	011	801	861	896	1.7	88	321	350	367	2.1	2.45	216	233	1.8
66717	BUFFALO	205	414	409	404	-0.3	34	162	162	161	0.0	2.52	113	112	-0.2
66720	CHANUTE	133	10947	10731	10598	-0.5	26	4463	4404	4372	-0.3	2.35	2970	2901	-0.6
66724	CHEROKEE	037	1076	1080	1089	0.1	53	435	440	447	0.3	2.45	293	293	0.0
66725	COLUMBUS	021	6065	5973	5938	-0.4	32	2442	2421	2420	-0.2	2.41	1663	1636	-0.4
66728	CRESTLINE	021	50	49	49	-0.5	26	20	20	20	0.0	2.45	15	15	0.0
66732	ELSMORE	001	289	294	288	0.4	64	113	117	116	0.8	2.47	80	82	0.6
66733	ERIE	133	2326	2416	2451	0.9	77	922	968	990	1.2	2.43	665	691	0.9
66734	FARLINGTON	037	342	346	349	0.3	61	145	148	150	0.5	2.33	103	104	0.2
66735	FRANKLIN	037	398	418	432	1.2	81	168	178	185	1.4	2.35	114	120	1.2
66736	FREDONIA	205	4116	3995	3922	-0.7	15	1723	1683	1661	-0.6	2.30	1141	1105	-0.8
66738	FULTON	011	448	537	593	4.4	99	164	198	221	4.5	2.70	119	142	4.3
66739	GALENA	021	5845	6051	6165	0.8	75	2261	2369	2434	1.1	2.51	1608	1669	0.9
66740	GALESBURG	133	961	960	956	0.0	47	362	364	365	0.1	2.64	289	289	0.0
66743	GIRARD	037	4335	4341	4391	0.0	51	1656	1671	1701	0.2	2.48	1184	1184	0.0
66746	HEPLER	037	272	274	277	0.2	56	101	103	104	0.5	2.66	72	72	0.0
66748	HUMBOLDT	001	2792	2655	2528	-1.2	3	1138	1097	1058	-0.9	2.38	788	750	-1.2
66749	IOLA	001	8662	8257	7887	-1.1	4	3495	3372	3260	-0.8	2.37	2286	2184	-1.1
66751	LA HARPE	001	1032	1137	1158	2.3	93	386	430	443	2.6	2.64	285	315	2.4
66753	MC CUNE	037	1187	1240	1275	1.0	79	451	475	492	1.2	2.61	340	355	1.0
66754	MAPLETON	011	346	414	457	4.3	98	143	173	193	4.6	2.39	101	122	4.5
66755	MORAN	001	1181	1202	1177	0.4	65	474	490	486	0.8	2.41	335	342	0.5
66756	MULBERRY	037	1026	1075	1109	1.1	80	415	439	455	1.3	2.45	282	295	1.1
66757	NEODESHA	205	3657	3688	3688	0.2	58	1453	1476	1485	0.4	2.42	964	969	0.1
66758	NEOSHO FALLS	207	244	239	234	-0.5	24	108	108	107	0.0	2.21	76	75	-0.3
66759	NEW ALBANY	205	398	393	388	-0.3	33	154	154	153	0.0	2.53	116	115	-0.2
66761	PIQUA	207	315	308	301	-0.5	21	123	123	122	0.0	2.50	90	89	-0.3
66762	PITTSBURG	037	23972	24112	24491	0.1	55	9772	9887	10102	0.3	2.29	5557	5557	0.0
66763	FRONTENAC	037	3004	3146	3245	1.1	80	1234	1304	1354	1.3	2.31	785	820	1.0
66767	PRESCOTT	107	534	534	539	0.0	50	210	212	217	0.2	2.33	145	145	0.0
66769	REDFIELD	011	985	1020	1042	0.8	75	369	387	399	1.1	2.60	273	283	0.9
66770	RIVERTON	021	1021	1011	1007	-0.2	37	399	399	400	0.0	2.53	309	307	-0.2
66771	SAINT PAUL	133	927	954	963	0.7	72	314	326	332	0.9	2.78	221	227	0.6
66772	SAVONBURG	001	287	292	286	0.4	64	112	116	115	0.8	2.47	80	81	0.3
66773	SCAMMON	021	1095	1095	1092	0.0	50	425	427	428	0.1	2.56	305	304	-0.1
66775	STARK	133	240	241	241	0.1	53	93	95	95	0.5	2.54	74	74	0.0
66776	THAYER	133	1389	1404	1407	0.3	59	510	519	522	0.4	2.71	407	412	0.3
66777	TORONTO	207	698	684	671	-0.5	25	319	319	318	0.0	1.97	187	184	-0.4
66778	TREECE	021	149	149	148	0.0	50	59	60	60	0.4	2.48	45	45	0.0
66779	UNIONTOWN	011	755	770	780	0.5	66	297	307	314	0.8	2.48	221	226	0.5
66780	WALNUT	037	568	588	600	0.8	75	228	238	245	1.0	2.47	168	175	1.0
66781	WEIR	021	1415	1356	1345	-1.0	7	559	538	537	-0.9	2.52	392	374	-1.1
66783	YATES CENTER	207	2521	2469	2417	-0.5	24	1088	1078	1067	-0.2	2.23	697	684	-0.4
66801	EMPORIA	111	30234	30282	30489	0.0	51	11532	11618	11768	0.2	2.47	7016	6987	-0.1
66830	ADMIRE	111	462	480	492	0.9	77	173	183	189	1.3	2.62	128	134	1.1
66833	ALLEN	111	516	541	556	1.1	80	207	220	229	1.4	2.46	152	160	1.2
66834	ALTA VISTA	197	683	690	705	0.2	59	284	291	300	0.6	2.37	204	207	0.3
66835	AMERICUS	111	1351	1330	1329	-0.4	31	512	512	516	0.0	2.60	394	391	-0.2
66838	BURDICK	127	190	204	213	1.7	88	80	87	92	2.0	2.33	64	65	1.9
66839	BURLINGTON	031	4278	4378	4533	0.6	68	1678	1730	1804	0.7	2.46	1139	1165	0.5
66840	BURNS	017	899	990	1054	2.3	93	332	370	396	2.6	2.68	263	292	2.5
66842	CASSODAY	015	299	314	331	1.2	81	122	129	137	1.3	2.43	99	104	1.2
66843	CEDAR POINT	017	184	183	182	-0.1	41	81	82	82	0.3	2.23	55	55	0.0
66845	COTTONWOOD FALLS	017	1251	1262	1265	0.2	58	503	514	519	0.5	2.24	312	315	0.2
66846	COUNCIL GROVE	127	3632	3674	3724	0.3	61	1519	1551	1586	0.5	2.32	1035	1048	0.3
66849	DWIGHT	127	471	457	459	-0.7	14	203	199	202	-0.5	2.30	144	140	-0.7
66850	ELMDALE	017	131	129	128	-0.4	32	59	59	59	0.0	2.19	41	41	0.0
66851	FLORENCE	115	846	847	854	0.0	51	324	325	328	0.1	2.44	237	236	-0.1
66852	GRIDLEY	031	668	673	691	0.2	57	275	279	289	0.3	2.41	199	200	0.1
66853	HAMILTON	073	548	534	532	-0.6	18	232	228	228	-0.4	2.34	172	168	-0.6
66854	HARTFORD	111	997	1012	1023	0.4	62	385	397	405	0.7	2.47	272	276	0.3
66856	LEBO	031	1827	1884	1960	0.7	72	713	739	773	0.9	2.55	541	557	0.7
66857	LE ROY	031	874	938	998	1.7	88	362	392	421	1.9	2.39	274	295	1.8
66858	LINCOLNVILLE	115	533	541	547	0.4	62	198	201	203	0.4	2.69	138	139	0.2
66859	LOST SPRINGS	115	195	214	225	2.2	92	79	88	92	2.6	2.43	60	66	2.3
66860	MADISON	073	1363	1338	1334	-0.4	27	550	545	547	-0.2	2.35	366	360	-0.4
66861	MARION	115	3437	3452	3474	0.1	53	1399	1409	1423	0.2	2.37	973	972	0.0
66862	MATFIELD GREEN	017	155	155	154	0.0	50	73	74	75	0.3	2.09	49	49	0.0
66864	NEOSHO RAPIDS	111	606	697	753	3.4	97	234	272	297	3.6	2.55	183	211	3.4
66865	OLPE	111	1120	1144	1159	0.5	67	411	426	436	0.9	2.69	317	326	0.7
66866	PEABODY	115	1973	1955	1970	-0.2	38	747	744	753	-0.1	2.48	541	534	-0.3
66868	READING	111	697	704	714	0.2	59	260	267	273	0.6	2.64	200	203	0.3
66869	STRONG CITY	017	1141	1119	1109	-0.5	26	460	459	460	-0.1	2.44	314	310	-0.3
66870	VIRGIL	073	382	376	375	-0.4	31	156	155	156	-0.2	2.43	113	111	-0.4
66871	WAVERLY	031	1283	1314	1362	0.6	68	494	510	532	0.8	2.49	348	356	0.5
66872	WHITE CITY	127	1010	1000	1007	-0.2	37	420	421	429	0.1	2.38	302	300	-0.2
66873	WILSEY	127	337	359	374	1.5	85	134	144	152	1.7	2.49	100	107	1.6
66901	CONCORDIA	029	7179	6968	6724	-0.7	15	2880	2823	2746	-0.5	2.27	1835	1780	-0.7
66930	AGENDA	157	175	189	195	1.8	89	76	83	86	2.1	2.28	54	59	2.1
66932	ATHOL	183	134	131	128	-0.5	21	60	59	58	-0.4	2.19	42	41	-0.6
66933	BARNES	201	317	310	304	-0.5	22	138	137	136	-0.2	2.26	103	101	-0.5
66935	BELLEVILLE	157	3325	3257	3213	-0.5	24	1471	1458	1453	-0.2	2.14	914	895	-0.5
66936	BURR OAK	089	516	493	468	-1.1	5	235	229	221	-0.6	2.15	145	139	-1.0
66937	CLIFTON	201	994	989	979	-0.1	42	409	413	414	0.2	2.39	292	293	0.1
66938	CLYDE	029	1091	1057	1017	-0.7	13	463	453	441	-0.5	2.27	311	302	-0.7
	KANSAS					0.7					1.0	2.49			0.8
	UNITED STATES					1.2					1.3	2.58			1.1

105-A

ZIP CODE #	POST OFFICE NAME	RACE (%) White 2000	White 2004	Black 2000	Black 2004	Asian/Pacific 2000	Asian/Pacific 2004	% Hispanic Origin 2000	% Hispanic Origin 2004	2004 AGE DISTRIBUTION (%) 0-4	5-9	10-14	15-19	20-24	25-44	45-64	65-84	85+	18+	MEDIAN AGE 2004	% 2004 Males	% 2004 Females
66616	TOPEKA	79.4	76.7	1.9	2.1	0.3	0.3	24.9	29.1	7.7	7.2	6.9	6.0	6.5	27.6	22.7	13.5	2.0	74.7	36.4	49.8	50.2
66617	TOPEKA	96.3	95.7	0.6	0.6	0.3	0.3	3.0	3.7	6.3	6.9	7.4	6.8	5.5	24.4	30.2	11.9	0.7	75.3	40.9	50.2	49.8
66618	TOPEKA	95.9	95.3	1.0	1.1	0.4	0.5	2.5	3.1	5.9	6.8	7.4	7.7	5.3	24.6	31.2	10.4	0.7	75.0	40.3	50.4	49.7
66619	TOPEKA	85.8	84.3	7.1	7.6	0.8	1.0	5.2	6.5	9.4	8.3	9.2	9.5	10.2	30.6	18.5	4.1	0.2	66.7	27.1	49.3	50.7
66701	FORT SCOTT	93.3	92.7	3.8	4.0	0.5	0.5	1.4	1.7	6.8	6.1	6.9	6.8	8.4	23.9	23.3	14.5	3.4	76.5	38.2	47.8	52.2
66710	ALTOONA	97.9	98.0	0.1	0.1	0.0	0.0	0.7	0.7	6.1	6.2	7.1	7.7	6.4	22.7	24.9	16.8	2.0	75.6	41.1	49.4	50.6
66711	ARCADIA	96.6	96.3	0.6	0.6	0.1	0.1	0.8	1.0	6.4	6.1	6.9	7.2	7.7	24.8	25.9	12.6	2.5	76.0	39.1	50.4	49.6
66712	ARMA	97.5	97.4	0.5	0.5	0.1	0.1	0.8	1.0	6.8	6.4	5.9	5.8	6.0	24.4	25.0	15.6	4.1	77.3	41.4	47.7	52.3
66713	BAXTER SPRINGS	88.8	88.7	0.9	0.9	0.4	0.4	1.3	1.3	7.1	7.1	7.3	6.6	6.5	26.7	22.9	13.2	2.6	74.3	37.2	48.6	51.4
66714	BENEDICT	97.9	97.6	0.1	0.1	0.0	0.0	0.7	1.0	5.2	5.6	6.5	6.5	6.1	22.2	30.3	15.9	1.8	78.8	43.6	50.4	49.6
66716	BRONSON	96.5	96.4	0.9	1.1	0.3	0.2	0.9	0.9	4.0	4.4	8.6	7.0	6.7	22.7	28.1	16.1	2.4	79.0	42.5	50.3	49.7
66717	BUFFALO	97.6	97.8	0.0	0.0	0.0	0.0	0.2	0.5	5.9	5.9	7.3	7.6	5.9	20.5	29.6	15.9	1.5	76.0	42.9	49.9	50.1
66720	CHANUTE	93.7	93.5	1.3	1.3	0.4	0.5	3.5	3.6	6.5	6.2	6.7	7.8	7.3	24.1	23.5	14.9	3.0	76.5	38.6	47.6	52.4
66724	CHEROKEE	95.7	95.6	0.2	0.2	0.2	0.2	0.7	0.7	6.1	6.2	6.9	7.6	6.0	25.3	26.2	13.1	2.6	76.3	39.6	49.7	50.3
66725	COLUMBUS	94.6	94.6	0.4	0.4	0.4	0.4	1.4	1.4	6.9	6.8	7.0	6.8	6.0	24.7	24.7	14.0	3.0	75.0	39.1	47.6	52.4
66728	CRESTLINE	92.0	93.9	2.0	2.0	0.0	0.0	0.0	0.0	4.1	8.2	8.2	6.1	6.1	30.6	26.5	10.2	0.0	79.6	36.9	55.1	44.9
66732	ELSMORE	96.9	96.6	0.4	0.3	0.4	0.7	0.7	0.7	4.4	4.8	7.1	7.1	6.5	22.1	26.5	18.0	3.4	79.3	43.9	50.3	49.7
66733	ERIE	97.4	97.4	0.1	0.1	0.1	0.1	1.7	1.7	5.1	5.6	7.5	7.0	6.1	23.3	27.7	15.0	2.7	77.2	41.9	49.7	50.3
66734	FARLINGTON	98.0	98.3	0.0	0.0	0.3	0.3	0.3	0.6	7.2	6.9	6.7	6.1	4.9	24.9	26.0	15.3	2.0	75.7	41.0	51.5	48.6
66735	FRANKLIN	96.0	95.7	1.3	1.4	0.0	0.0	1.0	1.0	5.5	5.7	6.0	6.9	6.9	25.8	27.5	12.9	2.6	78.5	40.5	50.7	49.3
66736	FREDONIA	96.5	96.0	0.5	0.6	0.5	0.7	1.9	2.3	5.8	5.9	6.5	6.6	5.7	22.1	25.3	18.0	4.1	77.7	43.0	48.4	51.6
66738	FULTON	96.9	96.3	0.2	0.2	0.5	0.7	0.5	0.6	5.2	5.6	8.4	7.5	6.3	23.5	28.9	12.7	2.1	76.0	41.1	50.8	49.2
66739	GALENA	91.1	90.9	0.7	0.7	0.1	0.1	1.6	1.6	7.0	6.7	7.2	6.8	6.5	26.5	24.9	12.6	1.7	75.0	37.7	48.8	51.2
66740	GALESBURG	96.7	96.7	0.2	0.2	0.1	0.1	2.0	2.1	6.6	6.6	6.8	7.0	6.9	24.0	28.7	12.1	1.6	75.8	39.9	52.0	48.0
66743	GIRARD	97.3	97.1	0.7	0.8	0.2	0.2	0.7	0.9	6.2	6.1	6.8	7.0	6.1	26.0	24.7	13.5	3.7	76.5	39.6	49.1	50.9
66746	HEPLER	98.2	98.2	0.0	0.0	0.4	0.4	0.4	0.4	7.3	7.3	6.2	6.2	4.7	25.2	25.9	15.3	1.8	74.8	40.9	52.2	47.8
66748	HUMBOLDT	94.1	93.3	1.3	1.4	0.1	0.2	4.3	5.2	5.4	5.4	6.1	6.9	6.6	22.9	27.2	16.4	3.2	79.1	42.6	50.1	49.9
66749	IOLA	94.5	94.0	2.1	2.3	0.3	0.3	1.6	2.0	6.9	6.1	6.6	7.7	8.3	23.4	24.4	13.5	3.2	76.3	37.8	48.4	51.6
66751	LA HARPE	95.7	95.3	0.5	0.5	0.4	0.5	0.8	0.8	5.6	5.7	7.9	8.4	8.3	25.4	24.9	12.7	1.1	75.6	38.0	50.8	49.2
66753	MC CUNE	97.6	97.6	0.0	0.0	0.1	0.1	1.0	1.2	5.8	6.0	6.5	6.5	6.7	25.5	29.1	11.6	2.3	77.8	40.6	51.4	48.6
66754	MAPLETON	96.5	96.1	0.3	0.2	0.6	0.7	0.6	0.7	4.8	5.3	8.5	7.3	6.3	23.4	29.0	13.5	1.9	76.6	41.6	50.7	49.3
66755	MORAN	97.0	96.4	0.5	0.5	0.4	0.6	0.5	0.7	4.5	5.0	7.2	7.2	6.4	21.4	27.0	18.1	3.2	78.8	44.0	50.6	49.4
66756	MULBERRY	95.9	95.8	1.3	1.3	0.0	0.0	0.9	1.1	5.5	5.8	6.1	6.9	6.7	26.1	27.3	13.1	2.6	78.7	40.3	50.7	49.3
66757	NEODESHA	96.6	96.1	0.3	0.3	0.2	0.3	2.0	2.5	6.3	6.5	8.1	7.5	6.6	23.8	24.1	13.6	3.7	74.6	38.7	48.2	51.8
66758	NEOSHO FALLS	96.3	96.2	0.8	0.8	0.0	0.0	0.8	0.8	8.4	8.4	5.9	6.3	4.2	23.0	25.9	15.9	2.1	73.6	41.0	52.7	47.3
66759	NEW ALBANY	96.5	96.4	1.0	1.0	0.3	0.3	1.5	1.5	4.3	5.1	6.6	6.6	5.6	20.6	31.3	18.3	1.5	79.6	45.7	50.4	49.6
66761	PIQUA	98.4	98.4	0.3	0.3	0.0	0.0	0.6	0.0	4.6	4.9	4.9	7.1	6.2	24.0	28.9	17.2	2.3	81.5	44.0	53.3	46.8
66762	PITTSBURG	91.0	89.8	2.6	2.8	1.8	2.3	3.3	4.1	6.8	5.9	5.7	8.5	13.0	26.7	20.1	10.8	2.5	78.3	30.5	48.9	51.1
66763	FRONTENAC	97.5	97.2	0.2	0.2	0.1	0.1	0.9	1.1	6.7	6.5	6.5	5.8	5.9	25.6	22.8	14.8	5.4	76.7	39.8	46.0	54.0
66767	PRESCOTT	98.3	98.3	0.9	0.9	0.2	0.2	1.3	1.7	4.7	4.9	6.0	5.8	5.4	20.0	27.9	17.6	7.7	80.7	47.1	51.3	48.7
66769	REDFIELD	97.1	96.9	0.6	0.7	0.2	0.3	1.0	1.2	5.9	6.3	7.8	7.0	6.4	24.0	26.7	13.5	2.5	75.7	40.1	50.9	49.1
66770	RIVERTON	93.0	92.9	1.1	1.2	0.3	0.3	1.1	1.1	6.3	6.8	6.8	5.9	6.1	25.4	29.8	11.5	1.3	76.4	39.1	50.8	49.2
66771	SAINT PAUL	97.5	97.5	0.1	0.1	0.4	0.4	1.9	1.9	6.1	6.2	7.8	6.9	6.7	26.2	22.3	13.9	3.9	75.0	39.4	48.5	51.5
66772	SAVONBURG	96.9	96.6	0.4	0.3	0.4	0.7	0.7	0.7	4.5	4.8	7.2	7.2	6.5	22.3	27.1	17.5	3.1	79.1	43.7	50.0	50.0
66773	SCAMMON	95.2	95.1	0.3	0.3	0.2	0.2	0.6	0.7	6.4	6.7	7.4	6.7	5.8	26.3	26.9	12.0	2.0	75.3	39.0	49.5	50.5
66775	STARK	97.9	98.8	0.0	0.0	0.0	0.0	0.8	0.8	5.8	6.6	6.6	5.8	5.0	21.2	32.8	14.5	1.7	76.8	44.3	53.5	46.5
66776	THAYER	96.3	96.1	0.0	0.0	0.1	0.1	2.5	2.6	6.8	6.6	7.9	7.9	7.1	25.9	24.2	12.3	1.3	73.8	36.7	51.9	48.2
66777	TORONTO	94.3	94.2	2.6	2.6	0.1	0.2	2.0	2.1	3.2	3.4	4.5	5.7	5.3	20.3	32.5	22.2	2.9	84.9	50.5	53.5	46.5
66778	TREECE	91.3	91.3	1.3	1.3	0.0	0.0	0.0	0.0	6.0	6.0	8.7	7.4	5.4	28.9	25.5	11.4	0.7	74.5	38.1	52.4	47.7
66779	UNIONTOWN	97.1	96.9	0.4	0.4	0.1	0.3	1.2	1.4	5.8	6.2	7.5	6.5	6.1	24.3	27.5	13.4	2.6	76.2	40.6	52.0	48.1
66780	WALNUT	98.1	98.0	0.2	0.2	0.2	0.3	0.5	0.3	6.6	7.0	6.8	6.5	4.9	25.3	26.4	14.5	2.0	75.5	40.7	51.5	48.5
66781	WEIR	97.0	97.0	0.2	0.2	0.1	0.2	0.8	0.7	8.7	8.0	7.5	6.3	5.8	27.8	23.2	11.5	1.3	72.0	36.4	51.1	48.9
66783	YATES CENTER	97.6	97.6	0.4	0.4	0.0	0.0	1.4	1.3	5.2	5.1	5.2	7.1	6.7	21.4	25.8	18.7	4.9	80.2	44.5	47.5	52.5
66801	EMPORIA	80.6	77.7	2.6	2.7	2.4	2.9	19.5	23.0	7.2	6.4	6.5	9.1	13.6	26.3	20.1	8.7	2.2	75.8	29.6	49.3	50.7
66830	ADMIRE	97.2	96.9	0.4	0.4	0.4	0.4	1.7	2.3	6.5	6.9	7.7	6.5	6.9	25.4	26.9	12.1	1.3	74.8	39.4	51.7	48.3
66833	ALLEN	97.3	96.7	0.4	0.6	0.4	0.6	1.7	2.2	6.7	6.8	8.0	6.3	6.8	25.5	26.3	12.4	1.3	74.7	39.5	51.9	48.1
66834	ALTA VISTA	97.5	97.4	0.3	0.3	0.3	0.4	2.8	3.3	4.5	4.8	5.5	7.0	5.8	23.3	30.7	15.9	2.5	81.0	44.4	52.9	47.1
66835	AMERICUS	96.7	95.9	0.3	0.3	0.2	0.3	1.9	2.6	6.8	7.0	7.7	7.1	6.2	24.5	29.3	10.0	1.5	74.2	39.0	48.4	51.7
66838	BURDICK	97.4	97.6	0.0	0.0	0.0	0.0	1.1	1.0	5.9	6.9	8.3	5.4	3.9	21.6	27.0	18.1	2.9	75.0	43.7	52.0	48.0
66839	BURLINGTON	96.3	95.8	0.3	0.3	0.6	0.7	1.7	2.1	6.4	6.4	6.7	7.2	6.6	25.3	26.6	11.7	3.2	75.6	39.9	48.7	51.3
66840	BURNS	97.8	97.7	0.3	0.4	0.1	0.1	1.5	1.6	7.5	7.8	7.5	6.1	4.4	22.9	26.9	15.2	1.8	73.5	41.1	52.5	47.5
66842	CASSODAY	96.7	96.5	0.3	0.3	0.3	0.3	2.3	2.9	8.3	8.9	9.6	6.1	4.5	22.3	25.2	13.7	1.6	69.4	38.5	52.9	47.1
66843	CEDAR POINT	97.8	97.8	0.0	0.0	0.0	0.0	1.1	1.1	6.6	6.6	6.0	5.5	4.9	22.4	30.6	14.8	2.7	77.1	43.8	53.0	47.0
66845	COTTONWOOD FALLS	95.6	95.6	1.8	1.9	0.2	0.2	2.0	2.1	5.9	5.9	6.7	6.4	5.2	26.6	22.6	16.3	4.5	77.7	40.9	49.0	51.0
66846	COUNCIL GROVE	98.1	98.0	0.3	0.3	0.2	0.2	2.2	2.3	5.8	6.0	6.9	7.0	5.8	20.9	26.5	16.6	4.5	76.7	43.3	48.9	51.1
66849	DWIGHT	95.8	95.4	0.2	0.2	0.4	0.4	4.0	4.2	5.5	6.1	6.1	7.4	5.3	23.2	30.0	14.0	2.4	77.5	43.0	51.0	49.0
66850	ELMDALE	97.7	97.7	0.0	0.0	0.0	0.0	1.5	1.6	5.4	6.2	6.2	6.2	5.4	22.5	30.2	15.5	2.3	77.5	43.6	51.9	48.1
66851	FLORENCE	95.6	95.2	0.6	0.6	0.2	0.2	3.2	3.9	5.1	5.4	7.1	5.8	4.7	21.4	28.1	19.1	3.3	78.2	45.4	47.0	53.0
66852	GRIDLEY	97.2	97.0	0.6	0.6	0.2	0.2	1.2	1.3	4.6	5.7	8.0	7.0	5.4	23.2	28.1	15.8	2.4	77.3	42.6	50.7	49.3
66853	HAMILTON	97.1	96.8	0.6	0.6	0.2	0.2	1.3	1.5	6.0	6.4	6.9	6.2	5.2	23.2	26.6	16.5	3.0	76.6	42.0	51.7	48.3
66854	HARTFORD	98.2	98.0	0.2	0.3	0.2	0.3	1.6	2.0	5.8	6.2	7.8	7.3	5.5	25.0	27.8	12.9	1.7	75.6	41.1	51.3	48.7
66856	LEBO	97.6	97.0	0.1	0.1	0.2	0.3	2.2	2.7	5.8	6.4	7.8	7.5	5.4	25.6	27.3	12.0	2.1	75.2	39.8	50.6	49.4
66857	LE ROY	98.2	97.8	0.1	0.2	0.0	0.0	0.7	0.9	6.2	6.3	7.1	5.8	5.0	23.7	28.7	14.9	2.4	76.8	42.6	51.5	48.5
66858	LINCOLNVILLE	95.9	95.8	0.9	0.9	0.2	0.2	2.6	3.0	8.3	8.3	6.5	5.9	5.6	22.7	25.9	14.2	2.6	73.6	40.4	50.1	49.9
66859	LOST SPRINGS	96.9	96.3	0.0	0.0	0.0	0.0	3.6	3.7	6.1	6.5	6.5	6.1	6.1	22.4	28.0	15.4	2.8	77.1	42.7	49.5	50.5
66860	MADISON	96.9	96.9	0.2	0.2	0.1	0.2	1.3	1.2	5.4	5.8	7.0	6.8	5.2	22.4	27.3	16.0	4.0	76.8	43.1	49.8	50.2
66861	MARION	97.4	97.2	0.2	0.1	0.1	0.2	1.3	1.6	6.1	6.6	7.0	6.2	4.9	21.1	25.6	17.8	4.9	75.9	43.7	48.6	51.5
66862	MATFIELD GREEN	97.4	97.4	0.0	0.0	0.0	0.0	1.3	1.3	6.5	6.5	6.5	5.2	3.9	21.3	32.9	14.2	3.2	76.8	45.2	53.6	46.5
66864	NEOSHO RAPIDS	97.2	96.6	0.3	0.4	0.0	0.1	3.8	4.7	5.0	5.7	7.6	7.6	5.3	23.2	30.4	13.8	1.3	76.2	42.2	51.7	48.4
66865	OLPE	98.4	98.2	0.2	0.2	0.3	0.4	1.9	2.5	6.9	7.0	8.4	8.0	6.5	26.1	24.2	11.1	1.8	72.6	37.9	52.2	47.8
66866	PEABODY	96.5	96.2	1.2	1.3	0.1	0.1	2.5	3.0	5.2	5.7	7.9	6.9	5.6	21.9	27.6	15.8	3.5	77.1	42.8	49.9	50.1
66868	READING	97.3	96.7	0.3	0.3	0.1	0.1	2.2	3.0	5.3	5.8	7.2	7.4	6.7	24.6	30.1	11.5	1.4	77.1	41.1	51.6	48.4
66869	STRONG CITY	97.9	97.8	0.6	0.6	0.2	0.2	1.6	1.7	6.3	6.3	6.5	7.1	6.4	23.5	28.4	13.5	2.1	76.8	41.0	52.8	47.2
66870	VIRGIL	97.1	97.1	0.3	0.3	0.3	0.3	1.1	1.3	5.3	5.6	6.1	5.9	5.1	22.1	27.1	20.5	2.4	79.0	45.0	51.6	48.4
66871	WAVERLY	97.7	97.5	0.4	0.4	0.2	0.2	1.0	1.2	6.5	6.8	7.2	5.9	5.9	23.6	26.3	13.9	3.7	75.2	41.0	48.4	51.6
66872	WHITE CITY	96.3	96.3	0.6	0.6	0.3	0.3	2.3	2.4	5.9	5.9	6.7	7.1	6.1	23.1	26.5	16.1	2.6	77.3	41.8	49.9	50.1
66873	WILSEY	97.3	97.2	0.3	0.3	0.3	0.3	1.2	1.1	5.9	6.7	8.6	5.6	3.9	21.5	27.3	17.8	2.8	74.7	43.6	50.7	49.3
66901	CONCORDIA	98.0	97.9	0.5	0.5	0.3	0.4	0.7	0.8	5.6	5.4	5.8	8.2	8.0	22.2	22.7	17.1	5.0	79.6	40.8	46.9	53.1
66930	AGENDA	98.9	99.5	0.0	0.0	0.0	0.0	1.7	1.6	3.7	4.8	4.2	6.9	5.3	19.1	30.7	21.7	3.7	82.5	48.8	50.8	49.2
66932	ATHOL	98.5	99.2	0.0	0.0	0.0	0.0	1.5	0.8	4.6	5.3	6.1	6.1	4.6	20.6	29.0	20.6	3.1	79.4	46.8	50.4	49.6
66933	BARNES	99.1	98.7	0.0	0.0	0.3	0.7	0.3	0.3	7.1	7.1	7.1	5.8	3.6	21.9	24.8	19.0	3.6	74.8	43.5	51.9	48.1
66935	BELLEVILLE	98.2	98.2	0.3	0.3	0.3	0.3	1.0	1.0	4.2	4.4	5.4	5.8	5.3	19.1	26.9	22.4	6.5	82.3	48.8	46.7	53.3
66936	BURR OAK	97.5	97.4	0.0	0.0	0.0	0.0	0.6	0.8	5.9	5.9	5.5	5.1	5.3	21.5	28.4	18.9	3.7	79.1	45.6	48.7	51.3
66937	CLIFTON	98.4	98.3	0.1	0.1	0.1	0.1	0.8	0.9	6.4	7.3	7.2	6.6	4.3	23.3	26.3	15.9	2.9	75.2	41.3	51.8	48.2
66938	CLYDE	99.5	99.4	0.0	0.0	0.0	0.0	0.5	0.6	4.9	4.9	6.0	6.5	6.4	21.4	24.4	19.9	5.6	79.3	44.9	48.1	51.9
	KANSAS	86.1	84.9	5.7	5.8	1.8	2.2	7.0	8.1	7.1	7.0	7.2	7.5	7.6	27.3	23.4	10.9	2.0	74.4	35.6	49.5	50.5
	UNITED STATES	75.1	73.6	12.3	12.5	3.8	4.2	12.5	14.1	6.9	6.7	7.2	7.0	7.3	28.6	23.8	10.8	1.7	75.1	36.0	49.1	50.9

ZIP CODE #	POST OFFICE NAME	2004 Per Capita Income	2004 HH Income Base	2004 HOUSEHOLD INCOME DISTRIBUTION (%) Less than $25,000	$25,000 to $49,999	$50,000 to $99,999	$100,000 to $149,999	$150,000 or More	MEDIAN HOUSEHOLD INCOME 2004	2009	2004 National Centile	2004 State Centile	2004 Home Value Base	2004 HOME VALUE DISTRIBUTION (%) Less than $50,000	$50,000 to $89,999	$90,000 to $174,999	$175,000 to $399,999	$400,000 or More	2004 Median Home Value
66616	TOPEKA	18441	2574	30.2	36.0	30.4	2.9	0.5	37914	45553	39	40	1850	38.9	56.6	4.0	0.2	0.4	55467
66617	TOPEKA	29918	3066	8.5	19.8	52.3	13.9	5.5	66926	79842	90	94	2829	5.9	18.1	63.4	12.2	0.5	114788
66618	TOPEKA	28140	2881	8.5	18.1	55.3	13.1	5.0	67217	80161	90	94	2703	3.7	14.5	64.9	16.1	0.8	121692
66619	TOPEKA	21860	1138	14.6	34.8	39.5	8.9	2.2	50503	61019	73	82	554	23.3	37.2	30.3	8.8	0.4	75658
66701	FORT SCOTT	20258	4863	34.3	33.9	25.1	4.0	2.7	35223	41138	28	22	3420	41.0	34.5	19.9	4.3	0.4	61079
66710	ALTOONA	17869	363	36.4	36.4	20.9	3.9	2.5	32459	37771	19	7	293	58.4	20.1	18.8	2.7	0.0	39821
66711	ARCADIA	21930	314	37.3	28.3	25.5	5.7	3.2	34407	42892	25	17	255	46.7	22.0	15.7	15.7	0.0	57727
66712	ARMA	18071	950	37.8	34.4	22.3	4.5	1.0	32168	38891	18	7	686	39.8	35.7	19.8	4.7	0.0	60303
66713	BAXTER SPRINGS	16357	2367	37.4	34.4	24.3	2.4	1.4	32677	37688	20	8	1784	40.5	31.2	23.7	4.1	0.5	63033
66714	BENEDICT	19289	347	33.4	30.8	28.2	4.9	2.6	36324	42096	33	30	296	44.9	27.4	24.0	3.7	0.0	57143
66716	BRONSON	15818	350	37.4	40.3	17.7	3.1	1.4	31622	37411	17	6	302	50.3	28.5	14.2	3.3	3.6	49667
66717	BUFFALO	17052	162	37.7	28.4	28.4	4.3	1.2	33606	38743	23	13	145	60.7	21.4	15.9	2.1	0.0	37083
66720	CHANUTE	20329	4404	34.1	34.1	23.4	5.3	3.3	35642	41232	30	25	3168	45.3	31.2	19.1	4.0	0.5	54421
66724	CHEROKEE	17279	440	28.6	45.0	21.6	3.6	1.1	35763	42616	31	26	345	58.6	24.4	14.2	2.9	0.0	40484
66725	COLUMBUS	17990	2421	37.5	30.2	25.7	4.9	1.8	34494	40597	26	17	1843	42.7	30.8	22.0	4.5	0.0	57079
66728	CRESTLINE	21072	20	25.0	30.0	40.0	5.0	0.0	47309	50000	67	77	17	29.4	23.5	47.1	0.0	0.0	85000
66732	ELSMORE	17832	117	35.9	35.0	24.8	3.4	0.9	34680	40886	26	18	96	44.8	26.0	20.8	5.2	3.1	57143
66733	ERIE	18970	968	29.8	37.5	26.1	5.6	1.0	37804	43705	39	38	754	42.4	30.2	23.2	4.1	0.0	56628
66734	FARLINGTON	20225	148	29.1	29.7	36.5	2.7	2.0	44384	51381	60	66	124	40.3	30.7	24.2	4.8	0.0	65714
66735	FRANKLIN	18695	178	34.3	35.4	24.7	5.1	0.6	33932	41146	24	15	145	54.5	25.5	13.8	4.1	2.1	44091
66736	FREDONIA	17838	1683	36.0	36.2	21.9	4.7	1.2	33455	39098	22	12	1300	49.5	27.9	18.9	3.4	0.3	50700
66738	FULTON	18275	198	37.9	24.8	30.8	3.5	3.0	37404	45871	37	36	172	48.8	27.9	15.1	5.8	2.3	52500
66739	GALENA	16156	2369	36.8	34.4	23.5	4.0	1.3	34184	39690	25	16	1785	47.6	28.9	21.1	2.4	0.1	52214
66740	GALESBURG	20769	364	25.0	39.6	25.3	7.7	2.5	40193	47042	47	51	310	43.6	25.8	25.2	5.5	0.0	62917
66743	GIRARD	20679	1671	27.8	34.4	28.3	6.1	3.4	40638	48016	48	53	1293	36.0	31.8	23.1	9.0	0.1	70396
66746	HEPLER	17611	103	29.1	30.1	35.9	2.9	1.9	43820	51265	58	64	87	37.9	33.3	24.1	4.6	0.0	66250
66748	HUMBOLDT	20016	1097	33.1	34.8	27.4	2.8	1.8	37002	42190	35	33	852	54.9	27.0	16.1	1.9	0.1	46866
66749	IOLA	18299	3372	35.5	35.1	23.0	4.7	1.6	35211	39907	28	22	2378	47.3	30.0	18.2	3.9	0.6	52433
66751	LA HARPE	17246	430	34.2	32.1	26.1	5.8	1.9	36247	41624	33	29	349	45.3	27.5	23.2	3.7	0.3	55000
66753	MC CUNE	19089	475	29.1	36.4	28.8	4.0	1.7	37493	44342	37	37	395	45.1	27.1	17.0	10.1	0.8	56500
66754	MAPLETON	19887	173	39.9	26.6	27.2	3.5	2.9	32583	39086	20	8	150	50.7	28.0	13.3	5.3	2.7	49375
66755	MORAN	18289	490	34.1	35.7	25.3	3.5	1.4	35574	40310	30	25	402	44.0	25.6	23.4	4.5	2.5	57742
66756	MULBERRY	17686	439	33.9	35.5	24.8	5.2	0.5	34091	41143	24	15	358	53.9	25.7	14.3	3.9	2.2	45172
66757	NEODESHA	16224	1476	38.5	32.9	24.7	3.3	0.7	33458	38636	22	12	1088	53.8	28.8	16.0	1.1	0.4	47853
66758	NEOSHO FALLS	14978	108	46.3	32.4	18.5	2.8	0.0	26598	29704	7	1	89	51.7	20.2	20.2	4.5	3.4	48125
66759	NEW ALBANY	19904	154	27.9	33.1	29.2	5.8	3.9	40499	45859	48	53	133	41.4	21.8	28.6	7.5	0.8	62500
66761	PIQUA	15991	123	36.6	31.7	29.3	0.8	1.6	31526	36210	16	5	104	32.7	44.2	19.2	3.9	0.0	65263
66762	PITTSBURG	19356	9887	40.7	26.4	23.9	6.0	3.0	32421	39681	19	7	5723	33.2	29.8	27.1	8.7	1.1	68954
66763	FRONTENAC	21572	1304	31.0	33.4	29.7	3.7	2.2	39007	47211	43	45	982	29.9	33.8	32.0	4.3	0.0	74526
66767	PRESCOTT	17862	212	41.0	19.8	34.9	4.3	0.0	35655	40996	30	25	179	38.0	24.6	27.4	10.1	0.0	74643
66769	REDFIELD	18338	387	28.4	34.9	30.5	4.7	1.6	39205	46380	43	46	326	43.3	30.1	21.2	4.3	1.2	58800
66770	RIVERTON	19954	399	24.6	34.6	33.1	5.8	2.0	44677	50320	60	67	341	27.6	32.0	36.7	3.8	0.0	77500
66771	SAINT PAUL	17993	326	29.5	34.1	29.8	4.9	1.8	38989	44132	43	45	266	42.9	31.2	22.9	2.6	0.4	56333
66772	SAVONBURG	17889	116	35.3	35.3	25.0	3.5	0.9	35000	41115	28	21	95	44.2	25.3	22.1	5.3	3.2	57857
66773	SCAMMON	16465	427	37.0	34.2	21.6	5.9	1.4	34317	40765	25	16	359	54.0	25.4	17.0	3.6	0.0	46184
66775	STARK	17635	95	30.5	40.0	22.1	7.4	0.0	35955	41936	31	27	80	35.0	38.8	25.0	1.3	0.0	70000
66776	THAYER	17913	519	25.4	35.5	31.0	7.7	0.4	40387	46838	47	52	438	39.5	24.7	31.5	3.7	0.7	71111
66777	TORONTO	17578	319	44.5	38.6	12.2	4.1	0.6	26981	30000	7	1	273	54.6	22.0	18.7	4.8	0.0	42647
66778	TREECE	14941	60	43.3	33.3	20.0	1.7	1.7	28118	31809	9	2	52	40.4	30.8	26.9	1.9	0.0	63333
66779	UNIONTOWN	19432	307	29.3	33.9	29.6	5.5	1.6	39263	46458	44	46	256	42.6	29.7	22.7	4.3	0.8	59048
66780	WALNUT	18977	238	28.2	32.4	36.1	2.1	1.3	42853	49802	56	60	199	39.2	29.7	25.6	5.5	0.0	65000
66781	WEIR	18460	538	32.0	35.5	26.6	5.6	0.4	36618	42777	34	31	454	48.9	25.1	21.8	4.2	0.0	51613
66783	YATES CENTER	17124	1078	43.6	31.8	19.4	3.9	1.3	28327	32732	9	2	835	50.8	29.0	15.7	3.7	0.8	49188
66801	EMPORIA	18667	11618	33.6	30.6	27.4	6.7	1.8	36787	44078	35	32	6747	27.6	29.7	34.6	7.7	0.4	80864
66830	ADMIRE	20077	183	21.9	35.0	32.8	8.7	1.6	44722	52365	60	67	152	34.9	31.6	26.3	5.9	1.3	67273
66833	ALLEN	21407	220	21.8	35.5	33.2	8.2	1.4	44499	51865	60	66	182	35.7	33.0	23.6	6.0	1.7	64615
66834	ALTA VISTA	20171	291	26.1	39.5	27.5	3.1	3.8	39656	45367	45	48	234	38.9	36.3	23.9	0.9	0.0	65625
66835	AMERICUS	19525	512	21.1	33.2	39.3	5.1	1.4	46951	54001	66	75	423	26.2	37.1	25.3	11.4	0.0	77232
66838	BURDICK	21773	87	29.9	41.4	19.5	5.8	3.5	35636	40426	30	25	74	51.4	20.3	21.6	6.8	0.0	48333
66839	BURLINGTON	22185	1730	26.2	30.0	31.5	9.8	2.5	44862	52799	61	67	1336	23.9	37.1	30.6	8.0	0.5	78267
66840	BURNS	18779	370	24.9	36.0	34.1	4.1	1.1	39825	47123	45	48	301	36.2	28.6	26.3	7.3	1.7	69318
66842	CASSODAY	25713	129	17.8	32.6	41.1	6.2	2.3	49742	59622	71	80	106	29.3	30.2	30.2	8.5	1.9	78750
66843	CEDAR POINT	24490	82	28.1	31.7	30.5	7.3	2.4	40000	47373	46	50	65	30.8	21.5	36.9	9.2	1.5	82500
66845	COTTONWOOD FALLS	19186	514	34.6	36.8	23.4	3.9	1.4	34865	40506	27	19	375	44.5	30.1	20.8	4.0	0.5	56406
66846	COUNCIL GROVE	24197	1551	33.5	32.1	24.4	5.9	4.1	36451	42643	33	30	1157	36.1	29.2	27.1	7.0	0.6	67012
66849	DWIGHT	18912	199	34.2	35.7	24.1	4.0	2.0	36124	41537	32	28	162	49.4	29.0	14.8	6.8	0.0	50556
66850	ELMDALE	26802	59	23.7	28.8	32.2	11.9	3.4	47371	54561	67	77	49	28.6	14.3	40.8	16.3	0.0	105357
66851	FLORENCE	17523	325	36.0	35.4	23.1	2.8	2.8	33807	38689	23	14	247	63.2	19.8	10.9	5.3	0.8	41216
66852	GRIDLEY	26299	279	28.3	33.3	29.4	5.7	3.2	41182	48240	50	55	227	54.6	21.6	15.9	6.6	1.3	46912
66853	HAMILTON	18563	228	32.9	38.2	21.5	5.7	1.8	35000	41147	28	21	185	67.0	16.2	13.5	2.2	1.1	35735
66854	HARTFORD	19646	397	25.7	35.5	32.5	4.3	2.0	41755	49121	52	57	333	37.2	24.9	31.5	5.1	1.2	73095
66856	LEBO	21240	739	23.6	30.3	36.4	8.1	1.6	46634	54990	65	74	615	21.3	30.9	40.8	5.7	1.3	87787
66857	LE ROY	23015	392	24.5	35.0	32.4	5.4	2.8	43437	50788	57	62	329	31.3	33.1	25.8	9.7	0.0	73571
66858	LINCOLNVILLE	16289	201	34.8	34.8	24.9	5.0	0.5	38013	43628	39	41	169	55.0	18.9	20.7	5.3	0.0	46136
66859	LOST SPRINGS	21599	88	37.5	28.4	26.1	5.7	2.3	36147	40000	32	29	75	58.7	14.7	21.3	5.3	0.0	44583
66860	MADISON	20129	545	33.0	34.7	24.0	5.7	2.6	37318	43798	37	35	415	50.6	25.8	19.0	3.6	1.0	49324
66861	MARION	20034	1409	30.5	30.8	31.3	6.0	1.4	38255	44040	40	41	1144	30.1	35.0	27.6	7.3	0.1	72222
66862	MATFIELD GREEN	23051	74	31.1	33.8	29.7	5.4	0.0	37659	43367	38	38	57	35.1	29.8	28.1	5.3	1.8	69000
66864	NEOSHO RAPIDS	21900	272	19.5	34.6	35.7	7.7	2.6	46957	55162	66	76	237	26.6	20.3	42.6	9.7	0.8	93750
66865	OLPE	18601	426	18.1	38.7	39.2	4.0	0.0	46146	53674	64	73	362	20.7	27.9	43.1	7.7	0.6	92083
66866	PEABODY	18914	744	28.5	37.2	27.7	4.6	2.0	37893	43976	39	39	588	34.7	35.4	24.7	4.4	0.9	63571
66868	READING	20423	267	22.1	33.7	33.3	8.6	2.3	43757	50549	58	64	229	24.5	26.6	38.4	10.0	0.4	88077
66869	STRONG CITY	21329	459	30.5	29.9	30.1	8.1	1.5	40607	47466	48	53	349	49.3	16.3	27.2	6.6	0.6	51923
66870	VIRGIL	16996	155	34.2	38.7	21.3	4.5	1.3	35220	41012	28	22	127	66.9	15.0	11.8	5.5	0.8	35313
66871	WAVERLY	20081	510	29.2	31.0	31.0	5.7	3.1	40452	47857	48	52	425	35.1	28.7	28.2	6.4	1.7	71029
66872	WHITE CITY	19598	421	26.6	38.0	31.1	3.3	1.0	41880	47767	53	57	329	44.1	34.7	15.5	4.6	1.2	56964
66873	WILSEY	20777	144	29.9	40.3	21.5	5.6	2.8	35570	41027	30	25	122	49.2	22.1	21.3	7.4	0.0	51667
66901	CONCORDIA	22330	2823	33.7	32.4	25.8	4.3	3.8	36353	42454	33	30	2028	41.1	38.3	18.9	1.7	0.0	59474
66930	AGENDA	19096	83	28.9	44.6	21.7	2.4	2.4	37311	42339	37	34	69	73.9	13.0	10.1	2.9	0.0	28214
66932	ATHOL	18332	59	37.3	32.2	28.8	1.7	0.0	32954	41545	21	9	49	55.1	26.5	16.3	2.0	0.0	46429
66933	BARNES	20043	137	32.1	43.1	17.5	3.7	3.7	33195	37306	21	10	110	56.4	11.8	24.6	1.8	5.5	39000
66935	BELLEVILLE	21533	1458	37.0	35.4	20.0	4.9	2.7	33344	38626	22	11	1114	49.0	27.7	19.9	2.8	0.6	50973
66936	BURR OAK	17039	229	40.2	41.1	15.3	1.8	1.8	30288	33831	13	3	186	72.0	16.1	9.7	2.2	0.0	25385
66937	CLIFTON	19403	413	38.0	33.9	20.3	4.4	3.4	33380	38470	22	11	329	61.7	21.6	12.5	3.3	0.9	40375
66938	CLYDE	22090	453	29.4	39.1	25.4	4.2	2.0	36642	42322	34	31	368	50.3	35.9	11.1	2.7	0.0	49730
	KANSAS	25137		23.6	29.0	32.2	10.1	5.1	47540	57348				21.4	24.4	35.0	16.7	2.5	97470
	UNITED STATES	25866		24.7	27.1	30.8	10.9	6.5	48124	56710				10.9	15.0	33.7	30.1	10.4	145905

ZIP CODE #	POST OFFICE NAME	FINANCIAL SERVICES: Auto Loan	FINANCIAL SERVICES: Home Loan	FINANCIAL SERVICES: Invest-ments	FINANCIAL SERVICES: Retire-ment Plans	THE HOME: Home Improvements: Home Repair	THE HOME: Home Improvements: Lawn & Garden	THE HOME: Furnishings: Comput-ers & Hard-ware	THE HOME: Furnishings: Major Appli-ances	THE HOME: Furnishings: TV, Radio, Sound Equip-ment	THE HOME: Furnishings: Furni-ture	ENTERTAINMENT: Dine out/ Carry out	ENTERTAINMENT: Sports Equip-ment	ENTERTAINMENT: Fees & Tickets	ENTERTAINMENT: Toys & Games	ENTERTAINMENT: Travel	ENTERTAINMENT: Cable TV	PERSONAL: Apparel & Services	PERSONAL: Auto Repairs	PERSONAL: Health Insur-ance	PERSONAL: Pets & Supplies
66616	TOPEKA	58	62	65	59	62	69	62	61	63	59	79	68	65	85	63	65	76	60	65	67
66617	TOPEKA	107	125	129	123	123	125	114	115	109	114	136	134	119	143	116	106	135	112	107	129
66618	TOPEKA	103	125	133	125	123	123	113	113	106	113	133	132	120	141	116	103	133	109	102	125
66619	TOPEKA	93	97	91	97	95	96	92	93	88	93	111	110	91	111	90	85	108	92	86	106
66701	FORT SCOTT	76	64	51	62	68	77	66	71	71	64	86	82	62	84	66	73	80	71	80	86
66710	ALTOONA	81	55	26	49	63	71	53	66	63	54	74	79	45	71	54	68	68	66	81	93
66711	ARCADIA	89	67	43	64	73	88	74	81	82	70	97	92	65	92	73	87	88	81	97	99
66712	ARMA	67	50	33	48	55	66	56	61	62	53	73	69	49	69	55	66	67	61	74	75
66713	BAXTER SPRINGS	66	56	41	53	59	66	54	60	59	54	71	70	52	72	55	61	67	59	67	76
66714	BENEDICT	85	59	31	56	69	77	58	72	67	58	79	87	50	77	61	71	72	71	86	101
66716	BRONSON	66	51	34	47	58	65	49	59	55	48	65	69	43	64	52	59	61	58	70	81
66717	BUFFALO	78	54	28	51	63	71	54	66	62	53	73	80	46	71	56	65	66	65	79	92
66720	CHANUTE	71	65	56	62	68	77	66	69	70	64	85	78	64	87	67	73	80	68	77	82
66724	CHEROKEE	57	59	58	56	60	67	58	59	61	56	75	66	60	80	60	63	72	58	64	67
66725	COLUMBUS	71	55	38	53	60	70	58	64	64	56	76	73	53	74	58	67	70	64	75	79
66728	CRESTLINE	83	74	56	70	78	83	68	75	72	68	88	90	67	90	70	74	84	73	82	97
66732	ELSMORE	80	56	29	53	65	73	55	68	64	55	75	82	47	73	57	67	68	67	81	95
66733	ERIE	78	58	36	55	65	75	61	70	68	59	81	81	54	78	61	72	74	69	83	89
66734	FARLINGTON	85	60	32	56	69	78	59	73	68	58	80	87	51	78	61	72	73	72	87	101
66735	FRANKLIN	82	55	26	48	62	72	54	67	65	55	76	79	46	72	55	69	69	66	82	94
66736	FREDONIA	69	51	32	49	57	66	55	62	62	52	72	71	48	69	55	65	66	62	74	78
66738	FULTON	88	63	35	60	73	81	62	76	71	61	84	91	54	82	64	75	76	75	90	104
66739	GALENA	72	53	31	48	59	66	51	61	59	52	70	72	46	68	52	63	65	60	72	83
66740	GALESBURG	95	72	45	69	81	90	70	83	78	69	93	99	63	92	72	81	86	81	96	112
66743	GIRARD	76	73	66	69	76	83	70	74	74	69	90	86	71	93	72	76	86	73	81	89
66746	HEPLER	85	59	31	56	69	77	58	72	67	58	79	87	50	77	61	71	72	71	86	101
66748	HUMBOLDT	71	64	55	61	68	77	64	69	69	62	83	79	62	84	66	72	79	68	78	83
66749	IOLA	69	57	44	56	61	69	59	64	64	57	77	73	56	76	59	66	71	63	71	77
66751	LA HARPE	74	64	47	61	68	74	60	67	64	60	77	80	58	79	61	66	73	65	73	87
66753	MC CUNE	87	66	40	62	74	82	63	76	71	63	84	91	57	84	66	74	78	74	87	103
66754	MAPLETON	85	61	34	57	70	79	59	73	68	59	80	88	51	79	62	72	73	72	87	101
66755	MORAN	80	56	29	53	65	73	55	68	64	55	75	82	47	73	57	67	68	67	81	95
66756	MULBERRY	81	55	25	47	62	71	53	66	64	54	75	79	45	71	54	68	68	65	81	93
66757	NEODESHA	63	51	38	50	55	62	53	58	58	52	69	66	50	68	53	59	64	57	65	70
66758	NEOSHO FALLS	60	42	22	40	49	55	41	51	48	41	56	62	35	55	43	50	51	50	61	71
66759	NEW ALBANY	91	64	33	60	74	83	63	78	73	62	85	94	54	83	65	76	78	77	93	108
66761	PIQUA	72	51	26	48	59	66	50	62	58	49	68	74	43	66	52	60	62	61	74	86
66762	PITTSBURG	63	57	62	58	57	63	65	62	66	62	82	75	62	80	63	64	79	65	62	71
66763	FRONTENAC	80	64	46	63	69	80	69	74	75	66	89	84	63	86	68	78	83	74	85	89
66767	PRESCOTT	69	51	34	49	56	67	57	63	64	54	75	70	50	71	56	67	68	63	75	76
66769	REDFIELD	84	62	38	59	71	79	61	73	68	60	81	87	54	80	63	71	75	72	85	100
66770	RIVERTON	81	72	55	68	76	82	67	74	71	67	86	88	65	88	69	73	82	72	80	95
66771	SAINT PAUL	81	67	50	66	71	80	68	74	73	67	89	86	65	88	68	75	83	73	82	91
66772	SAVONBURG	80	56	29	53	65	73	55	69	64	55	75	83	47	74	58	67	68	68	82	96
66773	SCAMMON	68	54	37	51	58	67	56	62	62	54	74	71	52	71	56	65	68	62	73	76
66775	STARK	81	57	30	53	66	74	56	69	64	55	75	83	48	74	58	67	69	68	82	96
66776	THAYER	79	68	51	65	73	78	64	71	68	63	82	85	62	84	66	70	78	69	78	93
66777	TORONTO	57	43	28	41	47	56	47	52	53	45	63	59	42	59	47	56	57	52	63	63
66778	TREECE	70	47	21	40	53	61	45	56	55	46	64	67	38	60	46	59	58	56	70	80
66779	UNIONTOWN	88	61	32	58	71	80	60	75	70	60	82	90	51	80	63	73	74	74	89	104
66780	WALNUT	85	59	31	56	69	77	58	72	67	58	79	87	50	77	61	71	72	71	86	101
66781	WEIR	73	63	49	62	66	74	63	68	67	62	81	78	61	81	63	68	76	67	74	82
66783	YATES CENTER	64	47	30	45	52	62	51	57	57	49	67	65	45	64	51	61	62	57	69	71
66801	EMPORIA	67	59	59	60	60	66	67	65	68	64	84	78	63	83	64	67	81	68	66	75
66830	ADMIRE	95	67	35	63	78	87	66	81	76	65	89	98	56	87	68	79	81	80	97	113
66833	ALLEN	95	66	35	63	77	87	66	81	76	65	89	98	56	87	68	79	81	80	97	113
66834	ALTA VISTA	87	60	32	57	70	79	60	74	69	59	81	89	51	79	62	72	74	73	88	103
66835	AMERICUS	82	72	55	69	76	82	67	74	71	67	86	88	65	88	69	73	82	72	81	96
66838	BURDICK	92	64	34	61	75	84	64	79	73	63	86	95	54	84	66	77	78	77	94	109
66839	BURLINGTON	83	77	69	76	79	85	76	81	78	76	95	94	74	93	76	78	91	80	83	95
66840	BURNS	91	63	33	60	74	83	63	78	72	62	85	93	54	83	65	76	77	76	92	108
66842	CASSODAY	113	79	41	75	92	103	78	97	90	77	106	116	67	103	81	94	96	95	115	134
66843	CEDAR POINT	99	69	36	65	80	90	68	84	79	67	92	102	58	90	71	82	84	83	100	117
66845	COTTONWOOD FALLS	73	54	34	52	60	71	58	66	66	56	77	75	52	73	58	69	70	66	79	82
66846	COUNCIL GROVE	93	72	48	69	78	91	75	84	83	73	99	97	68	96	75	87	91	84	98	105
66849	DWIGHT	79	55	29	52	64	72	54	67	62	54	73	81	46	72	56	66	67	66	80	93
66850	ELMDALE	106	74	39	70	86	97	73	90	84	72	99	109	62	97	76	88	90	89	108	126
66851	FLORENCE	71	53	34	51	58	69	58	64	65	55	76	73	51	72	57	69	70	64	77	79
66852	GRIDLEY	111	83	50	79	94	104	81	97	90	80	107	117	71	106	83	94	99	95	113	132
66853	HAMILTON	79	55	29	52	64	72	54	67	62	53	73	81	46	72	56	65	67	66	80	93
66854	HARTFORD	76	67	54	66	69	77	67	71	71	66	86	82	65	86	67	71	81	70	76	85
66856	LEBO	95	71	42	67	80	89	69	83	77	68	91	99	61	90	71	80	84	81	96	113
66857	LE ROY	100	70	36	66	81	91	69	85	79	68	93	102	59	91	71	83	85	84	101	118
66858	LINCOLNVILLE	79	55	29	52	65	72	55	68	63	54	74	82	47	72	57	66	67	67	81	94
66859	LOST SPRINGS	95	66	35	63	77	87	66	81	76	65	89	98	56	87	68	79	81	80	97	113
66860	MADISON	80	59	37	56	66	77	63	72	71	61	84	82	56	80	63	75	77	71	86	90
66861	MARION	82	59	35	57	67	78	62	72	71	60	83	84	54	80	63	74	76	72	87	94
66862	MATFIELD GREEN	87	61	32	58	71	80	60	74	69	60	81	90	51	80	62	73	74	73	89	104
66864	NEOSHO RAPIDS	90	79	60	75	84	90	74	82	78	74	95	98	72	97	76	80	90	80	89	106
66865	OLPE	80	71	54	68	75	81	66	73	70	66	85	87	65	87	68	72	81	71	79	94
66866	PEABODY	86	61	33	58	70	78	60	73	68	59	80	88	51	79	62	72	74	72	87	102
66868	READING	96	69	38	65	79	89	68	83	77	67	91	99	59	90	70	81	83	81	97	114
66869	STRONG CITY	87	68	45	66	74	83	68	78	75	67	90	91	63	89	69	77	83	77	88	99
66870	VIRGIL	73	53	31	49	61	68	52	63	59	51	69	75	45	68	54	62	64	62	75	87
66871	WAVERLY	92	64	33	60	75	83	63	78	73	62	85	94	54	84	65	76	78	77	93	109
66872	WHITE CITY	83	60	34	56	69	77	58	71	67	58	78	85	50	77	61	70	72	70	85	99
66873	WILSEY	93	66	35	62	76	85	65	80	74	64	87	96	55	85	67	78	80	78	95	111
66901	CONCORDIA	82	67	51	65	72	83	71	77	77	68	92	88	65	89	71	80	85	77	88	93
66930	AGENDA	79	55	29	52	64	72	54	67	63	54	73	81	46	72	56	66	67	66	80	93
66932	ATHOL	73	51	27	48	59	66	50	62	58	50	68	75	43	67	52	61	62	61	74	86
66933	BARNES	82	57	30	54	67	75	57	70	65	56	76	84	48	75	59	68	70	69	83	97
66935	BELLEVILLE	78	57	36	55	64	75	62	70	70	59	82	80	54	78	62	73	75	70	84	88
66936	BURR OAK	59	44	29	43	49	58	49	54	55	47	65	61	44	61	49	58	59	54	65	65
66937	CLIFTON	84	59	31	55	68	76	58	72	67	57	78	86	50	77	60	70	71	71	85	100
66938	CLYDE	84	62	39	59	69	81	67	76	75	64	89	86	59	84	67	80	81	75	91	95
	KANSAS	92	87	84	87	89	95	89	91	90	88	111	106	87	110	88	89	107	91	92	105
	UNITED STATES	100	100	100	100	100	100	100	100	100	100	100	100	100	100	100	100	100	100	100	100

POPULATION CHANGE

ZIP CODE		COUNTY FIPS CODE	POPULATION			2000-2004 ANNUAL RATE		HOUSEHOLDS					FAMILIES		
#	POST OFFICE NAME		2000	2004	2009	% Rate	State Centile	2000	2004	2009	% Annual Rate 2000-2004	2004 Average HH Size	2000	2004	% Annual Rate 2000-2004
66939	COURTLAND	157	450	446	442	-0.2	38	195	194	194	-0.1	2.30	142	140	-0.3
66940	CUBA	157	364	387	397	1.5	85	164	177	183	1.8	2.19	117	125	1.6
66941	ESBON	089	316	300	284	-1.2	2	143	138	133	-0.8	2.17	94	90	-1.0
66942	FORMOSO	089	220	212	201	-0.9	10	104	102	99	-0.5	2.08	76	74	-0.6
66943	GREENLEAF	201	540	528	517	-0.5	21	240	238	236	-0.2	2.16	150	148	-0.3
66944	HADDAM	201	271	264	258	-0.6	18	116	114	112	-0.4	2.25	79	76	-0.9
66945	HANOVER	201	1171	1130	1102	-0.8	11	465	455	449	-0.5	2.42	310	300	-0.8
66946	HOLLENBERG	201	134	139	140	0.9	76	59	62	64	1.2	2.24	44	46	1.1
66948	JAMESTOWN	029	479	456	436	-1.2	3	176	168	161	-1.1	2.57	126	119	-1.3
66949	JEWELL	089	645	615	582	-1.1	4	294	285	274	-0.7	2.16	181	174	-0.9
66951	KENSINGTON	183	619	607	596	-0.5	26	264	261	258	-0.3	2.28	185	182	-0.4
66952	LEBANON	183	448	429	418	-1.0	6	206	200	196	-0.7	2.15	150	144	-1.0
66953	LINN	201	719	689	670	-1.0	7	275	266	261	-0.8	2.37	189	181	-1.0
66955	MAHASKA	201	161	156	153	-0.7	13	53	52	51	-0.5	2.90	36	35	-0.7
66956	MANKATO	089	1732	1642	1554	-1.3	2	759	731	704	-0.9	2.18	487	465	-1.1
66958	MORROWVILLE	201	409	398	390	-0.6	17	170	167	165	-0.4	2.32	115	112	-0.6
66959	MUNDEN	157	242	232	226	-1.0	7	97	94	93	-0.7	2.47	69	66	-1.0
66960	NARKA	157	174	166	163	-1.1	5	82	80	78	-0.6	2.08	58	56	-0.8
66961	NORWAY	157	300	298	295	-0.2	40	112	112	112	0.0	2.66	81	81	0.0
66962	PALMER	201	306	293	285	-1.0	6	117	113	111	-0.8	2.37	82	78	-1.2
66963	RANDALL	089	172	162	153	-1.4	1	74	71	68	-1.0	2.28	53	51	-0.9
66964	REPUBLIC	157	264	258	254	-0.5	20	128	126	125	-0.4	2.05	89	86	-0.8
66966	SCANDIA	157	541	530	522	-0.5	25	232	229	227	-0.3	2.31	161	158	-0.4
66967	SMITH CENTER	183	2531	2488	2446	-0.4	29	1097	1085	1073	-0.3	2.22	717	703	-0.5
66968	WASHINGTON	201	1828	1828	1810	0.0	50	782	791	793	0.3	2.24	493	494	0.1
66970	WEBBER	089	190	183	174	-0.9	9	86	85	82	-0.3	2.15	62	61	-0.4
67001	ANDALE	173	1321	1363	1391	0.7	73	407	429	444	1.3	3.18	332	347	1.1
67002	ANDOVER	015	9220	10528	11604	3.2	96	3163	3667	4085	3.5	2.82	2499	2869	3.3
67003	ANTHONY	077	2834	2751	2673	-0.7	15	1227	1198	1172	-0.6	2.25	783	757	-0.8
67004	ARGONIA	191	969	964	971	-0.1	42	368	368	373	0.0	2.62	257	254	-0.3
67005	ARKANSAS CITY	035	16264	16484	16850	0.3	62	6522	6690	6914	0.6	2.39	4416	4500	0.4
67008	ATLANTA	035	606	606	620	0.0	50	237	239	247	0.2	2.54	180	180	0.0
67009	ATTICA	077	1000	973	947	-0.6	17	404	398	390	-0.4	2.22	262	255	-0.6
67010	AUGUSTA	015	13023	13612	14424	1.1	79	4926	5194	5549	1.3	2.59	3648	3828	1.1
67013	BELLE PLAINE	191	3173	3224	3276	0.4	63	1183	1220	1253	0.7	2.64	899	921	0.6
67016	BENTLEY	173	392	393	395	0.1	52	148	151	154	0.5	2.60	119	120	0.2
67017	BENTON	015	2120	2309	2479	2.0	92	754	833	904	2.4	2.77	610	668	2.2
67018	BLUFF CITY	077	180	172	166	-1.1	5	79	77	75	-0.6	2.23	56	54	-0.9
67019	BURDEN	035	1052	1016	1019	-0.8	11	389	379	383	-0.6	2.68	293	283	-0.8
67020	BURRTON	079	1536	1553	1591	0.3	60	592	606	629	0.6	2.56	439	446	0.4
67021	BYERS	151	131	127	126	-0.7	14	54	53	53	-0.4	2.40	40	39	-0.6
67022	CALDWELL	191	1849	1813	1820	-0.5	26	797	789	799	-0.2	2.23	504	494	-0.5
67023	CAMBRIDGE	035	264	253	254	-1.0	7	105	101	102	-0.9	2.50	78	75	-0.9
67024	CEDAR VALE	019	1224	1233	1255	0.2	56	485	491	503	0.3	2.36	340	342	0.1
67025	CHENEY	173	3002	3283	3457	2.1	92	1066	1187	1267	2.6	2.71	810	890	2.2
67026	CLEARWATER	173	4347	4558	4711	1.1	80	1528	1631	1708	1.6	2.76	1245	1317	1.3
67028	COATS	151	184	179	178	-0.7	17	75	74	74	-0.3	2.42	55	54	-0.4
67029	COLDWATER	033	1131	1107	1093	-0.5	23	510	510	510	0.0	2.11	302	297	-0.4
67030	COLWICH	173	2263	2343	2397	0.8	75	665	702	728	1.3	3.27	574	601	1.1
67031	CONWAY SPRINGS	191	2254	2306	2349	0.5	67	753	779	802	0.8	2.89	554	568	0.6
67035	CUNNINGHAM	095	584	599	615	0.6	70	236	245	255	0.9	2.29	172	177	0.7
67036	DANVILLE	077	164	158	153	-0.9	10	74	72	71	-0.6	2.19	55	53	-0.9
67037	DERBY	173	22842	23781	24521	1.0	77	7967	8496	8906	1.5	2.78	6428	6792	1.3
67038	DEXTER	035	628	626	631	-0.1	45	216	216	220	0.0	2.74	161	160	-0.2
67039	DOUGLASS	015	3582	3742	3963	1.0	79	1279	1348	1439	1.2	2.73	998	1042	1.0
67042	EL DORADO	015	16975	17016	17611	0.1	52	6437	6531	6843	0.3	2.39	4265	4263	0.0
67045	EUREKA	073	3911	3958	3993	0.3	61	1660	1690	1716	0.4	2.26	1043	1053	0.2
67047	FALL RIVER	073	580	578	575	-0.1	45	270	273	273	0.3	2.12	187	187	0.0
67049	FREEPORT	077	52	50	49	-0.9	9	20	19	19	-1.2	2.63	15	14	-1.6
67050	GARDEN PLAIN	173	1772	1823	1857	0.7	72	575	603	622	1.1	3.01	450	467	0.9
67051	GEUDA SPRINGS	191	492	486	489	-0.3	34	196	197	200	0.2	2.47	157	157	0.0
67052	GODDARD	173	5842	6794	7451	3.6	97	1881	2229	2477	4.1	2.99	1567	1837	3.8
67053	GOESSEL	115	766	765	765	0.0	47	274	276	277	0.2	2.61	218	217	-0.1
67054	GREENSBURG	097	1843	1768	1707	-1.0	7	823	801	784	-0.6	2.19	526	508	-0.8
67055	GREENWICH	173	23	26	27	2.9	95	11	13	14	4.0	1.92	9	10	2.5
67056	HALSTEAD	079	2718	2722	2789	0.0	51	1057	1069	1105	0.3	2.53	776	777	0.0
67057	HARDTNER	007	275	266	261	-0.8	12	125	123	122	-0.4	2.16	77	75	-0.6
67058	HARPER	077	2162	2128	2079	-0.4	31	908	902	888	-0.2	2.34	593	585	-0.3
67059	HAVILAND	097	1145	1147	1131	0.0	51	422	427	424	0.3	2.47	309	310	0.1
67060	HAYSVILLE	173	11521	12319	12823	1.6	86	4112	4498	4756	2.1	2.71	3210	3468	1.8
67061	HAZELTON	007	199	199	197	0.0	50	75	76	76	0.3	2.53	54	55	0.4
67062	HESSTON	079	4044	4147	4260	0.6	69	1399	1459	1519	1.0	2.56	1050	1085	0.8
67063	HILLSBORO	115	3856	3871	3892	0.1	53	1427	1439	1452	0.2	2.39	1000	999	0.0
67065	ISABEL	151	249	270	280	1.9	91	95	105	110	2.4	2.57	72	79	2.2
67066	IUKA	151	374	400	414	1.6	86	147	159	167	1.9	2.52	113	121	1.6
67067	KECHI	173	1215	1290	1337	1.4	84	411	443	465	1.8	2.90	343	366	1.5
67068	KINGMAN	095	6433	6548	6721	0.4	65	2487	2558	2651	0.7	2.51	1758	1793	0.5
67070	KIOWA	007	1164	1145	1132	-0.4	30	505	503	502	-0.1	2.24	337	332	-0.4
67071	LAKE CITY	007	97	104	107	1.7	87	41	44	46	1.7	2.36	30	32	1.5
67072	LATHAM	015	297	293	303	-0.3	33	121	121	127	0.0	2.42	90	90	0.0
67073	LEHIGH	115	335	337	338	0.1	55	117	118	119	0.2	2.86	103	103	0.0
67074	LEON	015	1893	1899	1971	0.1	52	676	688	723	0.4	2.65	515	518	0.1
67101	MAIZE	173	2621	2890	3057	2.3	93	892	1003	1076	2.8	2.88	736	820	2.6
67102	MAPLE CITY	035	52	52	53	0.0	50	21	21	22	0.0	2.48	17	17	0.0
67103	MAYFIELD	191	271	268	270	-0.3	36	103	103	105	0.0	2.60	83	82	-0.3
67104	MEDICINE LODGE	007	2796	2727	2687	-0.6	18	1172	1161	1157	-0.2	2.32	787	772	-0.5
67105	MILAN	191	237	238	240	0.1	53	86	87	89	0.3	2.72	70	71	0.3
67106	MILTON	191	451	456	461	0.3	60	152	155	158	0.5	2.94	124	126	0.4
67107	MOUNDRIDGE	113	2777	2850	2924	0.6	70	1039	1078	1116	0.9	2.49	755	776	0.7
67108	MOUNT HOPE	173	1581	1584	1604	0.0	51	546	555	569	0.4	2.77	414	416	0.1
67109	MULLINVILLE	097	408	391	378	-1.0	7	166	161	158	-0.7	2.43	123	119	-0.8
67110	MULVANE	191	7641	7838	7983	0.6	70	2783	2913	3009	1.1	2.67	2166	2246	0.9
67111	MURDOCK	095	203	207	212	0.5	66	80	82	85	0.6	2.52	65	66	0.4
67112	NASHVILLE	095	178	171	173	-0.9	8	75	73	75	-0.6	2.34	58	56	-0.8
67114	NEWTON	079	20558	21109	21855	0.6	71	8036	8336	8718	0.9	2.46	5587	5745	0.7
	KANSAS					0.7					1.0	2.49			0.8
	UNITED STATES					1.2					1.3	2.58			1.1

ZIP CODE #	POST OFFICE NAME	RACE (%) White 2000	White 2004	Black 2000	Black 2004	Asian/Pacific 2000	Asian/Pacific 2004	% Hispanic Origin 2000	% Hispanic Origin 2004	2004 AGE DISTRIBUTION (%) 0-4	5-9	10-14	15-19	20-24	25-44	45-64	65-84	85+	18+	MEDIAN AGE 2004	% 2004 Males	% 2004 Females
66939	COURTLAND	98.7	98.7	0.7	0.7	0.0	0.0	1.3	1.4	5.8	7.0	8.1	7.2	4.7	20.0	27.4	16.8	3.1	74.4	43.3	49.6	50.5
66940	CUBA	99.2	99.0	0.0	0.0	0.0	0.0	1.1	1.3	4.1	4.7	4.4	6.7	5.2	19.6	31.3	20.9	3.1	82.4	48.3	52.2	47.8
66941	ESBON	98.4	98.3	0.0	0.0	0.0	0.0	0.6	0.7	5.3	5.3	6.3	5.7	5.0	20.3	29.0	19.7	3.3	79.0	46.2	50.0	50.0
66942	FORMOSO	99.1	99.1	0.0	0.0	0.0	0.5	0.5	0.5	4.3	5.2	5.2	4.3	3.8	18.4	32.1	24.5	2.4	82.6	51.0	51.9	48.1
66943	GREENLEAF	99.4	99.4	0.0	0.0	0.0	0.2	0.9	1.1	4.2	4.6	7.0	7.2	5.5	22.4	27.5	17.6	4.2	79.6	44.6	51.5	48.5
66944	HADDAM	97.8	98.1	0.0	0.0	0.0	0.0	0.4	0.0	6.8	6.8	6.8	5.7	4.6	21.2	25.4	18.2	4.6	75.4	43.7	53.8	46.2
66945	HANOVER	99.0	98.9	0.3	0.4	0.0	0.1	0.3	0.4	6.0	6.4	6.5	6.6	5.6	20.8	24.9	18.9	4.4	76.8	43.6	52.1	47.9
66946	HOLLENBERG	99.3	100.0	0.0	0.0	0.0	0.0	1.5	1.4	7.9	7.2	5.8	5.8	4.3	21.6	28.1	18.0	1.4	74.8	43.1	54.0	46.0
66948	JAMESTOWN	98.3	97.8	0.0	0.0	0.2	0.2	0.2	0.4	5.7	6.1	7.0	6.8	5.5	23.0	23.7	17.8	4.4	76.5	42.1	50.9	49.1
66949	JEWELL	99.7	99.8	0.0	0.0	0.0	0.0	1.1	1.3	5.7	5.9	6.0	6.7	5.2	19.2	27.0	20.0	4.4	78.1	45.9	47.3	52.7
66951	KENSINGTON	98.2	98.4	0.3	0.3	0.0	0.0	0.8	1.0	4.8	5.1	6.1	6.4	5.1	19.6	28.3	20.4	4.1	79.7	46.8	49.8	50.3
66952	LEBANON	98.7	98.4	0.2	0.2	0.0	0.0	1.1	1.2	4.7	5.1	6.1	5.4	4.2	21.7	29.1	21.2	2.6	80.7	46.9	50.8	49.2
66953	LINN	99.3	99.3	0.1	0.2	0.0	0.0	0.7	0.7	4.8	6.4	6.4	5.1	4.4	19.9	23.8	21.2	8.1	78.7	47.4	49.4	50.7
66955	MAHASKA	98.1	98.1	0.0	0.0	0.0	0.0	0.0	0.0	7.1	7.1	7.1	6.4	4.5	19.9	25.0	18.6	4.5	75.0	43.6	53.2	46.8
66956	MANKATO	98.8	98.6	0.0	0.0	0.1	0.2	0.7	0.8	4.0	4.5	6.2	6.3	5.2	18.2	28.9	21.4	5.5	81.1	48.6	50.4	49.6
66958	MORROWVILLE	98.0	98.2	0.0	0.0	0.0	0.0	0.2	0.5	6.8	6.8	6.8	6.0	4.5	21.4	25.1	18.1	4.5	75.6	43.5	53.0	47.0
66959	MUNDEN	98.8	99.1	0.0	0.0	0.0	0.0	0.4	0.4	6.5	6.5	6.0	6.0	4.3	24.1	28.0	15.5	3.0	77.2	43.2	55.2	44.8
66960	NARKA	98.9	98.8	0.0	0.0	0.0	0.0	0.0	0.0	7.2	7.2	6.6	6.0	4.8	22.3	25.9	16.9	3.0	75.3	42.1	54.8	45.2
66961	NORWAY	98.7	98.3	0.7	0.7	0.0	0.0	1.3	1.3	6.0	6.7	7.7	7.1	4.7	19.5	28.5	16.8	3.0	75.5	43.9	50.3	49.7
66962	PALMER	99.4	99.3	0.0	0.0	0.0	0.0	0.7	0.7	5.1	6.5	6.8	5.5	3.8	20.1	23.6	21.5	7.2	77.1	46.7	49.2	50.9
66963	RANDALL	99.4	99.4	0.0	0.0	0.0	0.0	0.6	0.6	4.3	5.6	7.4	6.2	4.9	19.1	30.3	19.1	3.1	78.4	46.3	52.5	47.5
66964	REPUBLIC	99.2	99.2	0.0	0.0	0.0	0.0	0.8	0.8	4.3	4.7	6.6	7.4	4.7	20.5	30.6	18.6	2.7	79.8	46.1	50.0	50.0
66966	SCANDIA	99.3	99.3	0.2	0.2	0.0	0.0	0.6	0.8	4.3	4.9	6.4	7.4	4.9	20.0	30.9	18.5	2.6	79.8	46.1	50.4	49.6
66967	SMITH CENTER	99.1	99.0	0.0	0.0	0.2	0.2	0.6	0.6	4.3	4.6	6.1	6.3	5.2	19.9	24.6	22.3	6.7	80.5	47.5	47.5	52.5
66968	WASHINGTON	99.1	98.9	0.1	0.1	0.0	0.0	0.8	1.0	6.0	5.7	5.6	5.7	5.4	21.0	25.9	19.5	5.1	78.7	45.4	49.4	50.6
66970	WEBBER	99.0	98.9	0.0	0.0	0.0	0.6	0.5	0.6	3.8	4.9	4.9	4.9	3.8	18.6	32.2	24.6	2.2	83.1	51.0	52.5	47.5
67001	ANDALE	98.7	98.4	0.2	0.2	0.0	0.0	1.7	2.3	9.8	9.7	10.5	8.7	6.0	25.3	19.8	9.1	1.1	64.6	30.0	52.2	47.8
67002	ANDOVER	95.1	94.5	0.6	0.7	1.0	1.2	2.1	2.6	7.8	8.0	8.7	8.0	5.7	27.0	24.8	8.1	2.0	70.0	35.6	48.9	51.1
67003	ANTHONY	96.2	95.9	0.3	0.3	0.2	0.2	1.3	1.6	6.8	6.5	6.6	6.8	6.4	20.3	22.9	19.2	4.5	75.9	42.2	48.5	51.5
67004	ARGONIA	96.8	96.7	0.2	0.2	0.1	0.1	1.6	1.8	5.8	6.3	8.2	9.3	6.3	20.5	25.2	15.5	2.8	73.7	39.7	50.4	49.6
67005	ARKANSAS CITY	89.1	88.3	3.4	3.5	0.6	0.7	3.9	4.7	6.8	6.3	7.0	7.4	7.5	24.0	24.8	13.6	2.5	75.9	38.2	48.1	51.9
67008	ATLANTA	95.4	94.9	0.2	0.2	0.2	0.2	1.2	1.7	6.4	6.6	8.8	7.1	6.4	23.4	26.9	12.7	1.7	73.9	39.2	50.5	49.5
67009	ATTICA	98.1	98.1	0.3	0.3	0.2	0.2	0.6	0.7	4.2	4.6	5.7	6.1	5.9	19.8	26.6	19.3	7.8	81.8	47.8	47.2	52.8
67010	AUGUSTA	96.0	95.5	0.3	0.3	0.4	0.5	2.4	2.9	6.8	7.0	7.8	7.6	6.8	26.6	24.6	10.8	2.1	73.6	36.9	49.2	50.8
67013	BELLE PLAINE	94.0	93.5	0.1	0.1	0.2	0.3	2.1	2.5	6.1	7.2	9.4	8.0	5.4	26.1	25.6	11.3	1.0	72.2	37.8	50.5	49.5
67016	BENTLEY	93.9	92.6	0.0	0.0	0.0	0.0	5.1	6.6	6.9	7.4	9.4	8.9	6.4	27.7	24.7	7.9	0.8	71.0	35.6	51.9	48.1
67017	BENTON	96.5	96.0	1.0	1.2	0.5	0.7	1.3	1.6	6.8	7.3	8.2	7.3	5.3	25.9	28.2	9.8	1.2	73.1	38.7	51.2	48.8
67018	BLUFF CITY	98.3	98.3	0.0	0.0	0.0	0.0	1.1	0.6	5.2	5.8	6.4	5.2	4.1	20.9	30.8	19.8	1.7	79.1	46.5	50.6	49.4
67019	BURDEN	94.8	94.3	0.2	0.2	0.1	0.1	1.1	1.5	6.4	6.4	8.3	7.0	6.7	23.0	26.1	14.0	2.2	74.6	39.6	49.4	50.6
67020	BURRTON	95.0	94.4	0.7	0.8	0.1	0.1	3.9	4.8	7.3	7.5	7.3	7.0	7.4	26.0	25.1	11.1	1.2	73.6	35.8	49.8	50.2
67021	BYERS	95.4	95.3	0.0	0.0	0.8	0.8	3.8	3.2	6.3	7.1	7.1	6.3	6.3	23.6	26.8	15.0	1.6	74.8	40.3	50.4	49.6
67022	CALDWELL	96.6	96.4	0.1	0.1	0.3	0.4	1.1	1.3	5.3	5.6	6.2	6.4	5.9	20.5	26.7	18.5	5.0	78.8	45.1	48.2	51.9
67023	CAMBRIDGE	94.3	93.7	0.4	0.4	0.0	0.0	1.1	1.6	6.7	6.7	6.7	7.1	6.7	23.7	25.7	14.2	2.4	75.1	39.5	48.2	51.8
67024	CEDAR VALE	93.8	93.8	0.3	0.2	0.0	0.0	1.5	1.5	5.2	5.4	7.0	7.1	5.4	18.6	24.7	21.7	5.0	77.6	46.2	49.7	50.3
67025	CHENEY	97.3	96.9	0.1	0.1	0.0	0.1	1.6	2.1	7.1	7.6	9.6	8.6	5.6	26.3	23.2	9.6	2.4	69.9	36.4	50.4	49.6
67026	CLEARWATER	96.7	96.2	0.2	0.3	0.4	0.6	1.2	1.6	7.1	8.1	9.4	8.4	4.9	25.2	25.7	9.6	1.6	70.0	37.1	50.0	50.0
67028	COATS	95.1	95.5	0.0	0.0	0.5	0.6	3.3	3.4	6.7	7.3	6.7	6.2	6.2	24.0	26.8	14.0	2.2	75.4	40.2	50.3	49.7
67029	COLDWATER	98.2	98.1	0.1	0.1	0.4	0.4	1.8	1.8	5.5	5.8	6.4	5.7	4.5	19.2	26.6	21.3	5.1	78.3	47.1	47.0	53.0
67030	COLWICH	98.1	97.7	0.0	0.0	0.4	0.5	1.0	1.3	9.4	9.6	11.2	8.4	5.2	25.4	20.7	8.6	1.6	64.6	32.0	51.0	49.0
67031	CONWAY SPRINGS	97.2	96.8	0.2	0.2	0.1	0.2	1.5	1.8	9.6	9.0	8.8	7.9	5.7	22.9	21.6	11.6	2.8	67.1	34.0	48.3	51.7
67035	CUNNINGHAM	98.6	98.7	0.3	0.3	0.2	0.2	1.0	1.3	4.8	5.3	8.2	6.7	4.2	19.5	28.6	18.0	4.7	76.8	45.7	49.6	50.4
67036	DANVILLE	98.8	98.7	0.0	0.0	0.6	0.6	0.0	0.0	6.3	6.3	6.3	7.0	6.3	20.9	28.5	16.5	1.9	76.6	43.2	51.3	48.7
67037	DERBY	94.2	93.1	1.3	1.5	1.1	1.5	2.8	3.7	6.8	7.8	9.8	8.6	5.1	27.2	25.6	8.3	0.9	69.8	35.8	48.8	51.2
67038	DEXTER	92.2	91.5	0.3	0.3	0.0	0.0	0.8	1.0	5.8	8.8	8.0	7.2	2.9	24.6	24.6	13.3	5.0	73.0	39.8	49.0	51.0
67039	DOUGLASS	96.8	96.6	0.2	0.2	0.3	0.4	1.3	1.6	7.2	7.6	8.2	8.0	6.8	25.9	24.8	10.2	1.4	72.0	36.5	50.2	49.8
67042	EL DORADO	92.3	91.6	3.6	3.9	0.3	0.4	3.0	3.6	7.1	6.3	6.2	6.8	8.3	28.0	22.7	12.4	2.4	76.9	35.9	51.6	48.4
67045	EUREKA	96.4	96.3	0.1	0.1	0.1	0.1	2.2	2.3	6.1	5.9	6.1	6.5	6.3	21.4	24.0	18.8	4.9	77.8	43.4	47.5	52.5
67047	FALL RIVER	97.1	97.2	0.0	0.0	0.0	0.0	0.9	0.9	4.5	4.5	4.5	5.7	5.0	19.0	29.4	25.4	1.9	83.0	49.1	50.7	49.3
67049	FREEPORT	98.1	100.0	0.0	0.0	0.0	0.0	0.0	0.0	4.0	6.0	4.0	8.0	6.0	20.0	34.0	16.0	2.0	86.0	45.6	46.0	54.0
67050	GARDEN PLAIN	97.2	96.7	0.3	0.4	0.2	0.3	1.6	2.1	8.5	8.9	10.8	8.2	5.7	25.2	22.3	9.6	0.9	66.4	34.3	51.1	48.9
67051	GEUDA SPRINGS	95.1	94.7	0.8	0.8	0.4	0.4	2.0	2.7	6.6	6.8	7.8	6.0	6.0	23.7	29.0	12.6	1.7	74.9	40.7	51.2	48.8
67052	GODDARD	95.4	94.6	0.8	1.0	0.4	0.5	1.7	2.2	7.1	7.6	10.1	9.4	6.7	25.5	24.9	7.8	1.0	68.7	34.5	50.3	49.7
67053	GOESSEL	97.3	96.6	0.1	0.1	0.7	0.9	1.2	1.4	4.4	5.1	8.0	7.3	5.5	20.3	27.3	16.5	5.6	77.8	44.7	47.7	52.3
67054	GREENSBURG	97.1	97.0	0.0	0.0	0.1	0.1	1.6	1.7	5.3	5.7	6.7	5.9	5.0	20.4	26.9	19.9	4.3	78.5	45.7	48.4	51.6
67055	GREENWICH	91.3	92.3	4.4	3.9	4.4	3.9	0.0	3.9	7.7	7.7	7.7	7.7	7.7	30.8	23.1	0.0	7.7	76.9	32.5	46.2	53.9
67056	HALSTEAD	96.8	96.4	0.3	0.3	0.4	0.4	2.1	2.7	6.4	6.5	6.7	7.7	7.2	23.8	25.7	13.9	2.2	75.4	39.5	48.5	51.5
67057	HARDTNER	97.1	97.0	0.4	0.4	0.0	0.0	2.6	2.6	5.6	5.6	4.9	6.4	4.5	18.8	29.0	21.4	3.8	79.3	47.6	48.9	51.1
67058	HARPER	97.9	97.7	0.1	0.1	0.1	0.1	1.0	1.3	5.3	5.6	7.0	7.4	6.1	21.2	26.7	17.0	3.8	77.1	43.2	49.0	51.0
67059	HAVILAND	95.9	95.6	0.6	0.6	0.4	0.4	4.3	4.7	6.7	6.5	6.9	7.1	8.5	24.0	24.9	13.3	2.2	76.1	37.3	49.8	50.2
67060	HAYSVILLE	94.1	93.0	0.5	0.6	0.6	0.8	3.1	4.2	7.1	7.5	8.7	8.1	6.1	26.8	24.5	10.4	0.9	71.6	36.2	49.9	50.1
67061	HAZELTON	94.5	94.5	0.5	0.5	0.0	0.0	4.0	4.0	5.5	6.0	8.0	7.5	5.0	19.1	28.1	17.6	3.0	74.9	44.1	48.7	51.3
67062	HESSTON	95.1	94.4	1.3	1.4	0.7	0.9	2.7	3.4	5.7	6.0	7.1	11.0	7.8	22.7	21.2	13.8	4.8	76.8	37.2	48.7	51.3
67063	HILLSBORO	97.4	97.1	0.5	0.5	0.3	0.3	1.6	2.0	5.3	5.5	6.3	7.6	9.6	23.5	21.7	15.4	5.3	79.2	39.6	48.6	51.4
67065	ISABEL	97.6	97.4	0.4	0.4	0.0	0.0	0.8	1.1	5.2	5.6	6.7	6.7	5.2	19.3	30.4	19.3	1.9	78.2	46.0	48.9	51.1
67066	IUKA	98.4	98.8	0.0	0.0	0.0	0.0	1.3	1.3	6.3	7.0	7.8	6.3	5.3	21.3	28.8	16.0	1.5	74.8	42.7	51.3	48.8
67067	KECHI	87.8	85.4	6.4	7.4	2.3	3.0	2.6	3.5	9.1	9.3	8.1	6.8	5.0	27.3	27.3	6.4	0.7	69.2	35.6	49.6	50.4
67068	KINGMAN	97.6	97.3	0.2	0.2	0.3	0.4	1.5	1.8	6.6	6.6	7.5	7.4	5.6	22.5	24.2	16.3	3.5	74.4	41.0	49.0	51.1
67070	KIOWA	95.8	95.6	0.3	0.4	0.1	0.1	3.3	3.5	5.4	5.9	6.5	6.7	4.8	18.9	28.8	19.5	3.6	77.7	46.1	48.5	51.5
67071	LAKE CITY	96.9	98.1	0.0	0.0	0.0	0.0	2.1	1.0	4.8	4.8	5.8	6.7	5.8	18.3	31.7	19.2	2.9	78.9	47.2	47.1	52.9
67072	LATHAM	96.0	95.2	0.7	0.7	0.0	0.0	2.4	3.4	6.8	7.2	7.9	8.2	6.5	25.9	24.2	12.3	1.0	74.1	37.4	48.8	51.2
67073	LEHIGH	97.0	97.3	0.9	1.2	0.0	0.0	2.4	2.7	6.5	8.0	8.3	6.2	4.2	25.5	27.6	12.8	0.9	72.1	40.5	50.2	49.9
67074	LEON	94.2	93.5	2.0	2.2	0.2	0.2	2.6	3.4	6.1	6.6	7.6	7.7	6.3	27.0	27.0	10.9	0.9	75.0	38.5	52.3	47.7
67101	MAIZE	94.8	93.9	0.7	0.9	0.7	1.0	2.2	2.9	7.2	7.4	8.7	7.6	6.7	26.1	26.5	9.1	0.7	72.1	36.2	49.9	50.1
67102	MAPLE CITY	96.2	96.2	0.0	0.0	0.0	0.0	1.9	0.0	7.7	7.7	5.8	5.8	3.9	25.0	28.9	13.5	1.9	78.9	41.3	50.0	50.0
67103	MAYFIELD	96.7	96.6	0.4	0.4	0.4	0.4	1.9	1.9	7.5	7.8	9.7	7.1	4.5	23.5	26.5	12.3	1.1	70.5	39.1	50.0	50.0
67104	MEDICINE LODGE	97.8	97.7	0.4	0.4	0.1	0.1	1.6	1.7	5.2	5.9	6.9	7.6	5.2	22.9	26.6	17.1	2.7	77.3	42.8	48.7	51.3
67105	MILAN	97.1	96.2	0.0	0.0	0.4	0.4	2.1	2.5	8.0	7.6	8.8	8.0	7.1	22.3	26.5	10.5	1.3	70.6	36.4	50.0	50.0
67106	MILTON	96.9	96.5	0.0	0.0	0.2	0.2	2.2	2.9	8.1	8.1	9.0	9.2	7.0	22.6	25.2	9.9	0.9	68.6	34.8	50.2	49.8
67107	MOUNDRIDGE	97.7	97.4	0.4	0.4	0.1	0.2	1.5	1.8	6.3	5.9	7.0	7.0	5.5	22.1	24.4	16.6	5.4	76.1	42.5	48.2	51.8
67108	MOUNT HOPE	97.1	96.5	0.3	0.3	0.2	0.3	2.5	3.2	6.6	7.6	9.1	8.2	4.7	25.6	23.6	11.7	2.9	71.4	37.8	48.9	51.1
67109	MULLINVILLE	98.0	98.0	0.0	0.0	0.5	0.5	2.0	1.8	5.9	6.4	7.4	6.4	5.1	23.0	28.9	15.4	1.5	76.0	41.8	53.2	46.8
67110	MULVANE	96.0	95.5	0.2	0.2	0.3	0.4	2.5	3.2	6.8	7.2	8.6	8.2	6.9	26.5	24.7	9.8	1.3	72.2	35.6	49.1	50.9
67111	MURDOCK	97.5	98.1	0.0	0.0	0.0	0.0	0.5	0.0	6.3	7.3	8.7	7.7	5.8	23.7	26.6	12.1	1.9	73.0	39.8	54.6	45.4
67112	NASHVILLE	98.3	98.3	0.0	0.0	0.0	0.0	1.7	1.8	5.9	6.4	7.0	8.2	5.9	20.5	28.1	15.8	2.3	74.9	42.3	52.1	48.0
67114	NEWTON	88.3	86.6	2.0	2.1	0.6	0.8	11.1	13.4	7.1	6.9	7.3	6.9	6.3	25.9	24.1	12.8	2.8	74.2	37.9	48.8	51.2
	KANSAS	86.1	84.9	5.7	5.8	1.8	2.2	7.0	8.1	7.1	7.0	7.2	7.5	7.6	27.3	23.4	10.9	2.0	74.4	35.6	49.5	50.5
	UNITED STATES	75.1	73.6	12.3	12.5	3.8	4.2	12.5	14.1	6.9	6.7	7.2	7.0	7.3	28.6	23.8	10.8	1.7	75.1	36.0	49.1	50.9

#	POST OFFICE NAME	2004 Per Capita Income	2004 HH Income Base	2004 HOUSEHOLD INCOME DISTRIBUTION (%) Less than $25,000	$25,000 to $49,999	$50,000 to $99,999	$100,000 to $149,999	$150,000 or More	MEDIAN HOUSEHOLD INCOME 2004	2009	2004 National Centile	2004 State Centile	2004 Home Value Base	2004 HOME VALUE DISTRIBUTION (%) Less than $50,000	$50,000 to $89,999	$90,000 to $174,999	$175,000 to $399,999	$400,000 or More	2004 Median Home Value
66939	COURTLAND	18309	194	36.1	33.0	24.7	4.6	1.6	35448	39493	29	24	155	51.6	25.2	15.5	6.5	1.3	48214
66940	CUBA	20323	177	28.3	44.6	21.5	2.8	2.8	37647	42978	38	37	148	75.0	11.5	10.1	3.4	0.0	27143
66941	ESBON	18839	138	34.8	40.6	18.8	3.6	2.2	33277	37513	22	11	113	62.0	20.4	15.9	1.8	0.0	32500
66942	FORMOSO	22283	102	37.3	41.2	13.7	3.9	3.9	33314	37867	22	11	85	67.1	15.3	7.1	7.1	3.5	27917
66943	GREENLEAF	18581	238	35.3	42.0	16.4	4.2	2.1	31712	35784	17	6	197	64.0	18.3	16.2	0.5	1.0	40833
66944	HADDAM	16585	114	42.1	35.1	17.5	5.3	0.0	29417	33427	11	2	93	64.5	18.3	16.1	1.1	0.0	28750
66945	HANOVER	17490	455	33.0	35.6	26.2	4.0	1.3	35657	40102	30	26	370	48.4	27.3	20.0	3.2	1.1	51463
66946	HOLLENBERG	20306	62	27.4	35.5	33.9	3.2	0.0	36247	40729	33	29	51	35.3	37.3	23.5	3.9	0.0	71000
66948	JAMESTOWN	24856	168	23.2	40.5	23.8	4.2	8.3	35624	42357	30	25	141	55.3	33.3	11.4	0.0	0.0	44643
66949	JEWELL	19839	285	38.3	38.3	19.3	1.8	2.5	33539	38160	23	12	216	70.8	19.0	9.7	0.5	0.0	31000
66951	KENSINGTON	17888	261	36.0	30.7	29.1	3.5	0.8	34526	40377	26	17	215	56.3	25.1	14.9	1.9	1.9	45781
66952	LEBANON	17492	200	36.5	36.0	25.0	2.5	0.0	32152	37918	18	6	164	55.5	22.6	17.1	4.3	0.6	40000
66953	LINN	20486	266	31.2	42.9	18.8	4.1	3.0	33479	38364	22	12	212	57.6	23.6	17.9	0.9	0.0	45294
66955	MAHASKA	12608	52	42.3	34.6	17.3	5.8	0.0	28846	30741	10	2	42	61.9	19.1	16.7	2.4	0.0	30000
66956	MANKATO	20697	731	33.0	35.8	23.8	5.2	2.2	35439	39901	29	23	563	60.6	26.3	10.5	1.8	0.9	39931
66958	MORROWVILLE	16238	167	42.5	35.3	16.2	4.8	1.2	29037	33251	10	2	136	64.7	17.7	15.4	2.2	0.0	29375
66959	MUNDEN	21749	94	34.0	35.1	21.3	1.1	8.5	35864	39532	31	26	79	54.4	24.1	10.1	11.4	0.0	41250
66960	NARKA	25696	80	33.8	36.3	21.3	1.3	7.5	35958	40000	31	27	67	55.2	23.9	10.5	10.5	0.0	39167
66961	NORWAY	15738	112	36.6	32.1	26.8	3.6	0.9	35000	40919	28	21	90	54.4	24.4	15.6	5.6	0.0	45000
66962	PALMER	18174	113	31.9	41.6	20.4	3.5	2.7	33592	39062	23	13	90	56.7	25.6	17.8	0.0	0.0	45714
66963	RANDALL	20486	71	26.8	40.9	25.4	5.6	1.4	38787	42316	42	43	59	49.2	23.7	22.0	3.4	1.7	50833
66964	REPUBLIC	22747	126	31.8	32.5	26.2	7.9	1.6	37707	41954	38	38	102	48.0	24.5	22.6	4.9	0.0	52857
66966	SCANDIA	19868	229	32.8	33.2	25.3	7.9	0.9	36737	42123	34	32	185	48.1	24.3	20.5	6.5	0.5	52692
66967	SMITH CENTER	17729	1085	39.6	32.4	22.3	5.2	0.5	31135	36567	15	5	826	48.4	32.0	17.1	1.8	0.7	51884
66968	WASHINGTON	18038	791	33.1	39.6	23.6	2.8	0.9	34849	39824	27	19	609	51.4	33.0	14.0	1.5	0.2	49096
66970	WEBBER	21347	85	37.7	40.0	14.1	3.5	4.7	33251	37670	22	11	71	63.4	16.9	8.5	7.0	4.2	30500
67001	ANDALE	23043	429	9.6	28.0	44.5	13.5	4.4	61542	71814	86	92	370	7.6	20.8	56.0	15.4	0.3	116860
67002	ANDOVER	28990	3667	14.7	20.9	39.0	16.5	8.9	65142	77387	89	93	3137	13.4	15.8	45.9	22.9	1.9	122091
67003	ANTHONY	17499	1198	43.8	28.2	22.0	4.4	1.5	29775	35000	12	3	868	41.6	38.3	17.5	2.5	0.1	55105
67004	ARGONIA	19037	368	26.6	37.5	26.6	6.5	2.7	40000	46543	46	50	288	44.1	21.9	24.7	8.0	1.4	61765
67005	ARKANSAS CITY	19921	6690	34.1	30.8	27.3	5.4	2.4	36776	43853	35	32	4775	40.7	33.5	22.0	3.7	0.2	58598
67008	ATLANTA	21452	239	26.4	29.3	33.9	7.5	2.9	44081	52170	59	65	198	40.4	22.2	28.8	6.6	2.0	68182
67009	ATTICA	20177	398	34.4	35.4	24.6	3.0	2.5	36597	42550	34	31	306	53.6	25.2	16.7	3.9	0.7	46857
67010	AUGUSTA	24259	5194	20.0	25.8	38.9	12.2	3.1	53886	64880	78	86	4063	17.8	28.4	43.8	9.3	0.8	94844
67013	BELLE PLAINE	23813	1220	19.9	26.7	38.9	12.1	2.4	52510	61619	76	84	1008	19.4	31.6	41.8	7.1	0.1	88438
67016	BENTLEY	21436	151	15.9	32.5	42.4	8.6	0.7	51075	59256	74	83	128	25.8	55.5	16.4	2.3	0.0	70000
67017	BENTON	27514	833	13.5	27.1	41.7	9.7	8.0	60595	71112	85	90	725	12.8	25.1	43.7	14.5	3.9	102229
67018	BLUFF CITY	21664	77	36.4	29.9	24.7	5.2	3.9	36909	42343	35	32	62	35.5	24.2	32.3	6.5	1.6	70000
67019	BURDEN	18092	379	31.4	30.6	30.1	5.8	2.1	39218	46717	43	46	307	46.9	22.5	23.8	4.9	2.0	55278
67020	BURRTON	20176	606	22.8	33.5	36.3	5.9	1.5	44632	53229	60	67	467	30.6	36.6	26.6	6.2	0.0	70439
67021	BYERS	21508	53	28.3	35.9	22.6	7.6	5.7	39295	45759	44	46	43	58.1	20.9	14.0	7.0	0.0	43000
67022	CALDWELL	21149	789	36.1	31.3	25.6	4.9	2.0	35932	42356	31	27	616	50.3	27.9	18.7	2.8	0.3	49692
67023	CAMBRIDGE	19138	101	31.7	30.7	29.7	5.9	2.0	38057	45000	39	41	81	53.1	19.8	22.2	2.5	2.5	47727
67024	CEDAR VALE	21451	491	36.5	36.5	20.2	4.3	2.7	35216	40061	28	22	405	60.3	21.5	12.6	4.7	1.0	40349
67025	CHENEY	23052	1187	16.0	28.1	42.6	10.6	2.6	54160	63829	79	86	1005	18.2	38.0	32.3	11.0	0.4	84213
67026	CLEARWATER	25129	1631	13.4	23.5	43.2	15.9	4.0	62094	73351	86	92	1395	8.7	27.6	52.0	11.1	0.6	107412
67028	COATS	21194	74	29.7	39.2	21.6	5.4	4.1	37315	42847	37	34	60	58.3	21.7	13.3	6.7	0.0	40000
67029	COLDWATER	20137	510	36.5	34.3	22.8	2.9	3.5	33575	39235	23	13	380	64.7	23.2	10.8	1.3	0.0	40345
67030	COLWICH	23661	702	12.0	25.9	36.9	18.4	6.8	62766	75887	87	93	624	4.7	24.4	48.1	19.9	3.0	116123
67031	CONWAY SPRINGS	18031	779	22.7	33.4	35.4	6.8	1.7	45538	52750	63	71	630	28.6	34.1	27.9	8.4	1.0	75139
67035	CUNNINGHAM	20272	245	21.6	43.7	28.6	5.7	0.4	39874	45741	46	49	201	44.3	30.9	20.4	3.0	1.5	56389
67036	DANVILLE	25603	72	25.0	27.8	34.7	9.7	2.8	45000	52667	61	68	58	17.2	31.0	39.7	12.1	0.0	91667
67037	DERBY	28493	8496	10.4	20.4	44.2	19.0	6.1	68124	80768	90	95	7090	4.4	23.2	56.6	15.4	0.5	118207
67038	DEXTER	19599	216	31.0	36.1	27.3	1.9	3.7	40736	47658	49	54	167	43.7	31.7	16.2	6.6	1.8	57500
67039	DOUGLASS	23858	1348	15.7	28.9	39.5	12.0	4.0	55737	65615	80	87	1104	19.2	31.6	37.1	11.6	0.5	88875
67042	EL DORADO	21668	6531	28.8	31.1	29.8	6.9	3.4	41070	50055	50	54	4530	25.6	42.4	25.3	6.4	0.4	72707
67045	EUREKA	18321	1690	37.8	34.6	21.8	4.1	1.8	32010	37458	18	6	1238	57.0	21.4	17.5	3.5	0.7	45323
67047	FALL RIVER	19552	273	35.9	36.6	22.0	3.3	2.2	35776	41135	31	26	227	52.4	19.4	15.4	11.0	1.8	48281
67049	FREEPORT	18700	19	26.3	26.3	42.1	5.3	0.0	47368	54641	67	77	15	20.0	33.3	33.3	13.3	0.0	85000
67050	GARDEN PLAIN	25833	603	17.4	21.4	40.6	14.1	6.5	61497	73532	86	92	523	8.6	26.8	47.4	16.4	0.8	107314
67051	GEUDA SPRINGS	23906	197	18.3	30.5	40.1	10.2	1.0	50774	59099	73	82	165	27.3	24.9	40.0	7.9	0.0	87500
67052	GODDARD	23805	2229	13.9	25.2	39.8	15.8	5.4	61192	72792	86	91	1926	13.3	19.1	47.7	17.8	2.2	114776
67053	GOESSEL	18795	276	22.8	35.1	36.2	4.0	1.8	45190	51571	62	69	238	13.5	33.6	41.6	11.3	0.0	93043
67054	GREENSBURG	21341	801	36.5	29.3	27.0	5.4	1.9	34442	41188	26	17	581	43.9	39.2	15.0	1.7	0.2	56455
67055	GREENWICH	57791	13	0.0	7.7	38.5	30.8	23.1	102999	114833	98	99	11	0.0	0.0	45.5	54.6	0.0	181250
67056	HALSTEAD	23914	1069	20.1	30.4	38.0	8.0	3.6	49487	58806	71	79	815	17.4	34.0	42.0	6.5	0.1	88446
67057	HARDTNER	21919	123	33.3	35.0	22.8	5.7	3.3	35194	40889	28	21	99	53.5	29.3	15.2	2.0	0.0	45625
67058	HARPER	21456	902	29.6	35.5	27.7	4.2	3.0	38776	45914	42	43	681	42.4	30.7	22.9	3.8	0.2	57357
67059	HAVILAND	18479	427	29.5	36.1	28.1	4.7	1.6	37391	44151	37	36	332	56.6	29.5	11.1	1.8	0.9	44359
67060	HAYSVILLE	23987	4498	13.7	27.9	43.2	12.5	2.8	56984	66833	82	88	3761	15.0	46.8	34.4	3.5	0.2	80680
67061	HAZELTON	16707	76	31.6	38.2	27.6	1.3	1.3	35000	40000	28	21	63	71.4	14.3	11.1	3.2	0.0	26500
67062	HESSTON	22619	1459	18.1	31.7	35.8	12.9	1.6	50206	58475	72	81	1066	11.1	21.5	57.4	9.9	0.2	110040
67063	HILLSBORO	18829	1439	27.3	37.7	28.8	4.5	1.7	40064	46243	46	50	1092	23.9	32.8	37.4	5.2	0.7	79886
67065	ISABEL	20241	105	27.6	37.1	24.8	5.7	4.8	40274	46311	47	51	85	42.4	23.5	24.7	4.7	4.7	66429
67066	IUKA	20359	159	19.5	38.4	35.2	6.3	0.6	43338	49006	57	62	133	34.6	29.3	33.8	0.8	1.5	75313
67067	KECHI	32125	443	8.4	18.5	43.3	19.9	9.9	71298	84052	92	95	409	3.2	10.5	65.3	19.6	1.5	135362
67068	KINGMAN	22506	2558	26.2	31.8	31.0	7.6	3.4	44009	51565	59	65	1980	29.3	31.1	29.4	9.1	1.1	74793
67070	KIOWA	20119	503	32.2	35.6	25.1	4.4	2.8	35529	40218	30	24	408	60.8	22.8	13.5	2.7	0.3	35667
67071	LAKE CITY	22130	44	34.1	34.1	22.7	4.6	4.6	36518	43194	34	30	35	42.9	22.9	22.9	5.7	5.7	65000
67072	LATHAM	22687	121	23.1	28.9	38.0	8.3	1.7	47792	55294	68	77	100	33.0	30.0	24.0	11.0	2.0	71111
67073	LEHIGH	18643	118	17.8	39.0	37.3	5.1	0.9	44608	52386	60	66	107	28.0	17.8	43.9	5.6	4.7	100521
67074	LEON	21717	688	22.0	27.8	38.7	8.9	2.8	50264	60200	72	81	586	28.8	26.1	30.4	13.1	1.5	80938
67101	MAIZE	30054	1003	9.6	23.3	43.8	15.9	7.5	66379	80101	89	94	873	13.9	28.2	38.5	19.0	0.5	101178
67102	MAPLE CITY	20144	21	23.8	33.3	38.1	4.8	0.0	46113	50000	64	73	17	29.4	35.3	23.5	11.8	0.0	75000
67103	MAYFIELD	21779	103	18.5	36.9	32.0	9.7	2.9	47065	53398	66	76	86	20.9	23.3	41.9	14.0	0.0	98333
67104	MEDICINE LODGE	19593	1161	28.3	39.4	24.9	6.2	1.2	39271	44400	44	46	884	57.1	23.5	16.9	1.8	0.7	43077
67105	MILAN	22709	87	17.2	26.4	41.4	10.3	4.6	53647	62767	78	85	74	25.7	16.2	36.5	18.9	2.7	106818
67106	MILTON	21353	155	14.8	25.8	46.5	9.7	3.2	55449	63724	80	86	133	26.3	16.5	37.6	18.1	1.5	105114
67107	MOUNDRIDGE	21714	1078	18.7	36.7	33.6	8.9	2.0	46847	53521	66	75	793	16.3	25.2	48.3	9.8	0.4	100497
67108	MOUNT HOPE	22730	555	19.3	30.6	37.3	9.4	3.4	50060	58785	72	80	465	20.2	38.1	35.9	5.6	0.2	83125
67109	MULLINVILLE	22311	161	20.5	33.5	36.0	7.5	2.5	45861	53905	63	72	125	43.2	32.0	18.4	4.8	1.6	57083
67110	MULVANE	24662	2913	15.9	25.1	41.3	15.2	2.5	57321	68131	82	88	2364	9.1	32.0	51.9	6.6	0.5	98249
67111	MURDOCK	23557	82	19.5	25.6	40.2	12.2	2.4	53121	61341	77	85	70	14.3	30.0	44.3	10.0	1.4	95714
67112	NASHVILLE	19220	73	30.1	41.1	23.3	4.1	1.4	36113	42747	32	28	60	61.7	18.3	13.3	3.3	3.3	34167
67114	NEWTON	22115	8336	23.1	32.4	34.4	8.0	2.1	45617	52912	63	71	6046	21.1	37.6	33.5	7.5	0.3	80964
	KANSAS	25137		23.6	29.0	32.2	10.1	5.1	47540	57348				21.4	24.4	35.0	16.7	2.5	97470
	UNITED STATES	25866		24.7	27.1	30.8	10.9	6.5	48124	56710				10.9	15.0	33.7	30.1	10.4	145905

ZIP CODE #	POST OFFICE NAME	FINANCIAL SERVICES: Auto Loan	Home Loan	Invest-ments	Retire-ment Plans	THE HOME: Home Improvements: Home Repair	Lawn & Garden	Furnishings: Comput-ers & Hard-ware	Major Appli-ances	TV, Radio, Sound Equip-ment	Furni-ture	ENTERTAINMENT: Dine out/ Carry out	Sports Equip-ment	Fees & Tickets	Toys & Games	Travel	Cable TV	PERSONAL: Apparel & Services	Auto Repairs	Health Insur-ance	Pets & Supplies
66939	COURTLAND	76	53	28	50	62	69	53	65	61	52	71	78	45	70	54	64	65	64	77	90
66940	CUBA	80	56	29	53	65	73	55	69	64	55	75	83	47	73	58	67	68	68	82	95
66941	ESBON	69	51	30	48	57	66	53	62	60	51	71	71	47	68	54	64	65	61	74	79
66942	FORMOSO	84	59	31	55	68	76	58	71	67	57	78	86	49	77	60	70	71	70	85	100
66943	GREENLEAF	67	49	31	47	55	65	53	60	60	51	71	68	47	67	53	64	65	60	72	75
66944	HADDAM	68	47	25	45	55	62	47	58	54	46	63	70	40	62	49	57	58	57	69	81
66945	HANOVER	77	54	28	51	63	70	53	66	61	52	72	79	45	70	55	64	65	65	78	91
66946	HOLLENBERG	82	58	30	54	67	75	57	70	65	56	77	85	48	75	59	69	70	69	84	98
66948	JAMESTOWN	119	83	43	78	97	108	82	101	94	81	111	122	70	108	85	99	101	100	120	141
66949	JEWELL	70	52	33	50	58	68	57	64	64	54	75	72	50	71	57	68	69	63	76	79
66951	KENSINGTON	74	52	27	49	60	68	51	63	59	51	69	76	44	68	53	62	63	62	75	88
66952	LEBANON	68	47	25	45	55	62	47	58	54	46	63	70	40	62	49	57	58	57	69	81
66953	LINN	82	61	39	59	68	80	67	74	75	63	88	85	59	83	66	79	80	74	89	92
66955	MAHASKA	66	46	24	44	54	60	46	56	53	45	62	68	39	60	47	55	56	56	67	79
66956	MANKATO	76	56	35	54	63	73	60	68	68	58	80	78	53	76	60	71	73	68	82	86
66958	MORROWVILLE	68	48	25	45	56	62	47	58	54	47	64	70	40	62	49	57	58	57	69	81
66959	MUNDEN	97	68	35	64	79	88	67	83	77	66	91	100	57	89	69	81	83	82	99	115
66960	NARKA	97	67	35	64	78	88	67	82	77	66	90	99	57	88	69	80	82	81	98	115
66961	NORWAY	76	53	28	50	62	69	52	65	60	52	71	78	45	69	54	63	64	64	77	90
66962	PALMER	73	54	34	52	60	71	58	66	66	56	77	75	52	74	58	69	71	66	79	82
66963	RANDALL	84	59	31	56	69	77	58	72	67	58	79	87	50	77	61	71	72	71	86	100
66964	REPUBLIC	84	59	31	56	69	77	58	72	67	57	79	87	50	77	60	70	72	71	86	100
66966	SCANDIA	83	58	30	55	68	76	57	71	66	57	78	86	49	76	60	69	71	70	84	99
66967	SMITH CENTER	65	48	31	46	54	63	53	59	59	50	70	67	47	66	52	63	64	59	71	73
66968	WASHINGTON	68	50	31	48	55	65	54	61	61	52	71	69	48	68	54	64	65	61	73	76
66970	WEBBER	83	58	30	55	68	76	57	71	66	57	77	85	49	76	59	69	71	70	84	99
67001	ANDALE	114	106	86	102	111	118	98	107	102	98	124	127	97	128	101	104	119	104	113	135
67002	ANDOVER	113	131	135	135	127	125	120	119	111	122	140	139	124	144	119	106	139	116	105	131
67003	ANTHONY	64	48	31	46	53	63	53	59	59	50	70	66	47	66	52	63	64	58	70	71
67004	ARGONIA	81	63	43	60	68	80	66	74	74	64	87	84	60	84	66	77	80	73	86	91
67005	ARKANSAS CITY	72	64	55	62	67	74	66	69	69	64	84	80	63	84	66	71	80	69	74	82
67008	ATLANTA	86	74	57	73	78	87	73	79	78	72	94	92	71	95	74	79	89	78	86	97
67009	ATTICA	77	57	35	54	63	74	61	69	69	58	81	79	53	77	61	72	74	69	83	88
67010	AUGUSTA	91	90	84	89	92	97	88	91	89	87	109	107	88	111	89	89	105	90	92	106
67013	BELLE PLAINE	101	90	68	85	95	102	83	92	88	83	107	110	81	109	85	90	102	90	100	119
67016	BENTLEY	89	80	61	76	84	90	74	82	78	74	95	97	72	97	76	80	90	79	88	105
67017	BENTON	101	121	126	121	120	119	109	110	102	109	128	128	115	136	111	100	127	106	100	123
67018	BLUFF CITY	88	61	32	58	71	80	60	75	70	60	82	90	52	80	63	73	74	74	89	104
67019	BURDEN	77	64	49	64	68	77	66	71	70	64	85	82	62	84	65	71	79	70	78	86
67020	BURRTON	83	69	52	68	74	82	69	76	74	68	90	88	66	89	70	76	84	74	83	93
67021	BYERS	93	65	34	62	76	85	64	80	74	64	87	96	55	85	67	78	79	78	95	111
67022	CALDWELL	79	58	37	56	65	76	63	71	71	60	83	81	56	79	63	75	76	71	85	89
67023	CAMBRIDGE	75	63	49	63	67	75	65	70	69	64	84	80	63	83	65	70	79	69	76	82
67024	CEDAR VALE	86	64	40	61	71	83	68	77	77	66	91	88	61	86	68	81	83	77	92	97
67025	CHENEY	99	91	74	88	96	101	84	92	88	84	107	109	83	110	87	89	102	89	97	116
67026	CLEARWATER	104	104	93	102	105	109	97	101	96	97	119	120	97	122	98	95	115	99	100	121
67028	COATS	93	65	34	61	75	84	64	79	74	63	86	95	55	85	66	77	79	78	94	110
67029	COLDWATER	71	52	33	50	58	69	57	64	64	54	75	73	50	71	57	67	69	64	77	80
67030	COLWICH	108	120	121	122	117	116	113	113	106	114	134	133	115	136	112	101	132	111	100	124
67031	CONWAY SPRINGS	82	71	55	70	74	83	71	76	75	70	92	88	68	91	71	77	86	75	83	92
67035	CUNNINGHAM	86	60	31	57	70	78	59	73	68	58	80	88	51	78	61	72	73	72	87	102
67036	DANVILLE	102	71	37	67	83	93	70	87	81	69	95	104	60	93	73	85	86	85	103	121
67037	DERBY	110	121	123	123	119	121	114	114	109	115	136	133	117	139	114	105	134	112	106	127
67038	DEXTER	86	72	56	72	76	86	74	80	79	73	96	91	71	95	74	81	90	79	87	95
67039	DOUGLASS	104	91	70	88	96	105	88	96	93	87	113	112	85	114	89	95	107	94	104	119
67042	EL DORADO	79	72	64	70	75	84	73	77	77	71	94	88	71	94	74	79	89	76	83	90
67045	EUREKA	67	53	38	50	58	67	56	62	62	54	73	70	51	71	56	65	67	61	72	76
67047	FALL RIVER	71	55	36	50	62	69	52	63	59	51	70	74	46	69	55	63	65	62	74	86
67049	FREEPORT	89	62	33	59	72	81	61	76	71	61	83	92	52	81	64	74	76	75	90	106
67050	GARDEN PLAIN	115	117	105	114	120	124	107	113	107	106	132	134	108	137	109	107	128	110	114	137
67051	GEUDA SPRINGS	94	84	64	80	89	95	78	86	83	78	100	103	76	102	80	85	96	84	93	111
67052	GODDARD	100	111	111	112	108	108	104	104	98	104	123	122	105	125	103	93	121	102	93	115
67053	GOESSEL	90	63	33	60	73	82	62	77	72	62	84	93	53	82	65	75	77	76	92	107
67054	GREENSBURG	79	58	35	55	65	76	61	70	69	59	81	81	54	78	62	73	74	70	84	90
67055	GREENWICH	155	161	186	168	162	170	164	163	159	163	199	192	165	194	164	154	193	165	156	179
67056	HALSTEAD	97	81	60	79	86	96	82	89	87	80	106	103	77	105	82	89	99	88	98	109
67057	HARDTNER	76	57	38	55	63	75	64	70	71	60	84	78	57	79	63	75	77	70	84	85
67058	HARPER	88	63	35	60	72	82	64	77	73	63	86	90	56	83	66	77	79	76	91	102
67059	HAVILAND	84	59	31	56	69	77	58	72	67	58	79	87	50	77	60	70	72	71	86	100
67060	HAYSVILLE	99	94	79	91	97	103	89	95	91	88	112	112	88	114	90	92	107	93	99	116
67061	HAZELTON	77	54	28	51	63	70	53	66	61	53	72	79	45	70	55	64	66	65	78	92
67062	HESSTON	83	90	92	89	89	92	86	86	83	86	104	100	88	106	86	82	102	85	82	96
67063	HILLSBORO	74	60	44	57	65	75	62	69	68	60	81	78	57	79	63	72	75	68	80	84
67065	ISABEL	94	66	34	62	77	86	65	80	75	64	88	97	55	86	67	79	80	79	96	112
67066	IUKA	93	65	34	61	75	84	64	79	74	63	86	95	55	85	66	77	79	78	94	110
67067	KECHI	134	150	146	157	143	139	137	135	125	142	159	158	140	159	133	117	157	132	115	148
67068	KINGMAN	91	77	58	73	82	92	75	84	81	74	98	98	71	98	77	84	92	83	94	105
67070	KIOWA	77	56	33	53	63	73	59	68	67	57	78	79	51	75	59	70	72	68	82	88
67071	LAKE CITY	93	66	36	62	76	86	66	80	76	65	89	96	57	87	68	80	81	79	96	109
67072	LATHAM	88	78	60	74	83	89	73	80	77	72	94	95	71	96	75	79	89	78	87	103
67073	LEHIGH	96	67	35	64	78	88	66	82	77	66	90	99	57	88	69	80	82	81	98	114
67074	LEON	94	83	64	79	88	95	77	85	82	77	100	102	76	102	79	84	95	83	93	110
67101	MAIZE	116	136	141	137	133	131	125	125	117	126	147	147	130	152	125	112	146	122	110	137
67102	MAPLE CITY	90	63	33	60	73	82	62	77	72	61	84	93	53	82	65	75	77	76	92	107
67103	MAYFIELD	93	79	57	75	85	92	74	84	80	74	96	100	71	98	76	82	91	82	92	109
67104	MEDICINE LODGE	75	59	41	56	66	74	59	68	65	57	78	80	54	79	61	69	72	67	79	89
67105	MILAN	101	88	65	83	93	100	81	91	87	81	105	109	79	107	84	89	100	89	100	118
67106	MILTON	100	89	68	85	94	101	83	92	88	83	107	109	81	109	85	90	101	89	99	118
67107	MOUNDRIDGE	86	74	56	72	78	88	75	81	80	73	96	93	71	95	75	83	90	80	90	98
67108	MOUNT HOPE	101	86	66	85	91	101	86	93	91	85	111	108	83	111	86	93	104	91	101	114
67109	MULLINVILLE	98	68	36	65	80	89	68	84	78	67	91	101	58	90	70	82	83	82	100	116
67110	MULVANE	100	95	82	93	97	102	92	96	93	91	114	113	89	114	91	92	109	95	97	114
67111	MURDOCK	95	85	65	81	90	96	78	87	83	78	101	104	77	103	81	85	96	85	94	112
67112	NASHVILLE	81	57	30	54	66	74	56	69	65	55	76	84	48	74	58	68	69	68	83	97
67114	NEWTON	83	74	64	73	78	85	75	80	79	73	96	93	72	96	76	80	91	79	85	95
	KANSAS	92	87	84	87	89	95	89	91	90	88	111	106	87	110	88	89	107	91	92	105
	UNITED STATES	100	100	100	100	100	100	100	100	100	100	100	100	100	100	100	100	100	100	100	100

POPULATION CHANGE

#	POST OFFICE NAME	COUNTY FIPS CODE	POPULATION			2000-2004 ANNUAL RATE		HOUSEHOLDS					FAMILIES		
			2000	2004	2009	% Rate	State Centile	2000	2004	2009	% Annual Rate 2000-2004	2004 Average HH Size	2000	2004	% Annual Rate 2000-2004
67117	NORTH NEWTON	079	1511	1522	1545	0.2	56	601	618	639	0.7	1.88	342	347	0.3
67118	NORWICH	095	823	837	855	0.4	64	303	310	318	0.5	2.60	224	227	0.3
67119	OXFORD	191	1653	1658	1677	0.1	52	643	653	667	0.4	2.47	470	474	0.2
67120	PECK	191	1306	1408	1478	1.8	89	451	494	525	2.2	2.84	363	395	2.0
67122	PIEDMONT	073	294	290	287	-0.3	33	122	121	121	-0.2	2.40	88	87	-0.3
67123	POTWIN	015	703	703	730	0.0	50	275	278	292	0.3	2.53	194	194	0.0
67124	PRATT	151	7979	7953	7968	-0.1	45	3309	3334	3376	0.2	2.29	2148	2142	-0.1
67127	PROTECTION	033	734	722	715	-0.4	30	312	312	313	0.0	2.19	204	202	-0.2
67131	ROCK	035	353	357	362	0.3	61	134	137	140	0.5	2.61	105	106	0.2
67132	ROSALIA	015	445	439	455	-0.3	33	165	165	173	0.0	2.66	123	122	-0.2
67133	ROSE HILL	015	5899	6385	6849	1.9	90	1876	2060	2233	2.2	3.08	1590	1734	2.1
67134	SAWYER	151	432	423	422	-0.5	24	153	152	153	-0.2	2.78	113	111	-0.4
67135	SEDGWICK	079	3154	3346	3493	1.4	84	1111	1199	1269	1.8	2.72	898	960	1.6
67137	SEVERY	073	830	825	826	-0.1	41	348	350	354	0.1	2.36	257	256	-0.1
67138	SHARON	007	427	419	414	-0.4	27	178	177	176	-0.1	2.35	121	119	-0.4
67140	SOUTH HAVEN	191	870	864	870	-0.2	40	321	322	328	0.1	2.68	237	236	-0.1
67142	SPIVEY	095	242	239	243	-0.3	34	104	104	107	0.0	2.28	77	77	0.0
67143	SUN CITY	007	166	180	186	1.9	91	68	75	79	2.3	2.40	51	56	2.2
67144	TOWANDA	015	2948	3096	3267	1.2	81	1034	1099	1170	1.4	2.82	860	906	1.2
67146	UDALL	035	1809	1928	2010	1.5	86	668	721	760	1.8	2.67	522	559	1.6
67147	VALLEY CENTER	173	7948	8161	8310	0.6	71	2824	2960	3058	1.1	2.74	2228	2309	0.8
67149	VIOLA	173	970	1003	1024	0.8	74	313	328	338	1.1	3.03	261	271	0.9
67150	WALDRON	077	144	138	133	-1.0	7	61	59	58	-0.8	2.34	43	42	-0.6
67151	WALTON	079	583	634	672	2.0	91	217	238	254	2.2	2.66	176	192	2.1
67152	WELLINGTON	191	10246	10446	10672	0.5	66	3991	4098	4223	0.6	2.50	2772	2822	0.4
67154	WHITEWATER	015	1501	1513	1572	0.2	57	492	498	521	0.3	2.91	389	390	0.1
67155	WILMORE	033	102	100	99	-0.5	26	50	50	50	0.0	2.00	35	35	0.0
67156	WINFIELD	035	15159	15414	15690	0.4	63	5709	5870	6039	0.7	2.41	3813	3881	0.4
67159	ZENDA	095	210	202	204	-0.9	9	88	86	88	-0.5	2.35	68	66	-0.7
67202	WICHITA	173	2136	2192	2241	0.6	70	399	463	510	3.6	1.95	86	90	1.1
67203	WICHITA	173	28912	28711	29246	-0.2	40	13234	13378	13815	0.3	2.11	7107	7031	-0.3
67204	WICHITA	173	20351	20017	20172	-0.4	30	7950	7958	8127	0.0	2.51	5493	5423	-0.3
67205	WICHITA	173	8296	10737	12313	6.3	99	2700	3566	4157	6.8	3.01	2306	3025	6.6
67206	WICHITA	173	13570	14080	14539	0.9	76	5709	6021	6307	1.3	2.30	3743	3923	1.1
67207	WICHITA	173	23362	24113	25004	0.8	73	10369	10763	11244	0.9	2.23	5958	6038	0.3
67208	WICHITA	173	18790	18276	18334	-0.7	17	7832	7730	7849	-0.3	2.32	4555	4410	-0.8
67209	WICHITA	173	12581	13610	14318	1.9	90	4642	5108	5443	2.3	2.64	3466	3789	2.1
67210	WICHITA	173	11981	12648	13110	1.3	83	3921	4198	4401	1.6	2.90	2973	3156	1.4
67211	WICHITA	173	20940	20507	20657	-0.5	24	9175	9125	9298	-0.1	2.23	4971	4822	-0.7
67212	WICHITA	173	46052	47306	48546	0.6	71	17864	18741	19521	1.1	2.51	12564	13055	0.9
67213	WICHITA	173	21483	20729	20784	-0.8	11	9043	8906	9061	-0.4	2.26	5073	4883	-0.9
67214	WICHITA	173	18004	16894	16815	-1.5	0	6846	6508	6555	-1.2	2.51	4041	3758	-1.7
67215	WICHITA	173	4772	5201	5483	2.1	92	1599	1774	1895	2.5	2.93	1325	1448	2.1
67216	WICHITA	173	24092	23706	23953	-0.4	30	9204	9236	9465	0.1	2.56	6330	6254	-0.3
67217	WICHITA	173	29472	30272	31193	0.6	71	11537	12118	12683	1.2	2.49	8006	8250	0.7
67218	WICHITA	173	22929	22911	23278	0.0	47	10416	10566	10863	0.3	2.15	5563	5502	-0.3
67219	WICHITA	173	10520	10552	10676	0.1	52	3712	3808	3914	0.6	2.76	2777	2816	0.3
67220	WICHITA	173	11532	12417	13043	1.8	89	4302	4678	4962	2.0	2.65	3043	3276	1.8
67221	MCCONNELL AFB	173	540	565	581	1.1	79	11	12	13	2.1	2.58	11	12	2.1
67223	WICHITA	173	494	535	560	1.9	90	145	160	170	2.3	3.33	132	145	2.2
67226	WICHITA	173	15694	17076	18009	2.0	91	6191	6860	7339	2.4	2.43	4155	4563	2.2
67227	WICHITA	173	273	293	306	1.7	88	90	99	105	2.3	2.96	76	82	1.8
67228	WICHITA	173	377	420	447	2.6	94	120	137	148	3.2	2.93	96	108	2.8
67230	WICHITA	173	5890	6669	7202	3.0	95	2007	2320	2544	3.5	2.86	1755	2009	3.2
67232	WICHITA	173	126	125	126	-0.2	38	53	53	54	0.0	2.36	41	41	0.0
67235	WICHITA	173	5889	6975	7671	4.1	98	1859	2252	2515	4.6	3.09	1654	1990	4.5
67301	INDEPENDENCE	125	13583	13086	12581	-0.9	10	5561	5412	5253	-0.6	2.35	3721	3586	-0.9
67330	ALTAMONT	099	1351	1329	1307	-0.4	30	524	521	518	-0.1	2.51	384	379	-0.3
67332	BARTLETT	099	403	400	395	-0.2	39	146	146	146	0.0	2.74	115	115	0.0
67333	CANEY	125	3346	3272	3162	-0.5	22	1330	1313	1280	-0.3	2.47	952	931	-0.5
67335	CHERRYVALE	125	3328	3254	3151	-0.5	21	1344	1326	1296	-0.3	2.42	914	894	-0.5
67336	CHETOPA	021	1819	1811	1791	-0.1	43	779	784	784	0.2	2.26	509	507	-0.1
67337	COFFEYVILLE	125	15213	14693	14175	-0.8	11	6330	6174	6008	-0.6	2.30	4129	3994	-0.8
67341	DENNIS	099	487	477	468	-0.5	24	196	195	194	-0.1	2.45	149	147	-0.3
67342	EDNA	099	798	794	784	-0.1	42	336	338	338	0.1	2.35	235	234	-0.1
67344	ELK CITY	125	882	857	828	-0.7	16	356	351	342	-0.3	2.44	256	250	-0.6
67345	ELK FALLS	049	196	188	180	-1.0	7	90	87	84	-0.8	2.16	63	60	-1.1
67346	GRENOLA	049	380	368	355	-0.8	13	166	162	158	-0.6	2.27	114	110	-0.8
67347	HAVANA	125	269	266	259	-0.3	36	115	115	114	0.0	2.31	88	88	0.0
67349	HOWARD	049	1122	1101	1067	-0.4	27	487	481	468	-0.3	2.18	315	308	-0.5
67351	LIBERTY	125	430	481	497	2.7	94	175	199	209	3.1	2.42	135	153	3.0
67352	LONGTON	049	594	590	574	-0.2	40	241	241	236	0.0	2.45	164	162	-0.3
67353	MOLINE	049	654	628	603	-1.0	8	295	285	276	-0.8	2.08	180	172	-1.1
67354	MOUND VALLEY	099	806	812	808	0.2	56	316	322	324	0.4	2.52	235	238	0.3
67355	NIOTAZE	019	277	287	297	0.8	75	109	114	119	1.1	2.52	76	79	0.9
67356	OSWEGO	099	3229	3189	3145	-0.3	34	1236	1231	1223	-0.1	2.37	848	836	-0.3
67357	PARSONS	099	13696	13448	13241	-0.4	27	5571	5525	5494	-0.2	2.34	3561	3497	-0.4
67360	PERU	019	740	759	781	0.6	70	314	325	337	0.8	2.31	216	222	0.7
67361	SEDAN	019	2088	2111	2153	0.3	60	872	885	905	0.4	2.30	589	592	0.1
67401	SALINA	169	49699	50421	51417	0.3	62	19993	20448	21005	0.5	2.40	13078	13250	0.3
67410	ABILENE	041	10055	10203	10350	0.3	62	4161	4270	4382	0.6	2.35	2816	2864	0.4
67416	ASSARIA	169	1134	1199	1244	1.3	83	398	423	442	1.4	2.76	324	342	1.3
67417	AURORA	029	169	161	154	-1.1	4	64	62	60	-0.7	2.60	50	49	-0.5
67418	BARNARD	105	270	264	261	-0.5	21	123	122	122	-0.2	2.16	90	89	-0.3
67420	BELOIT	123	5082	4975	4868	-0.5	23	2028	2010	1992	-0.2	2.30	1309	1285	-0.4
67422	BENNINGTON	143	1087	1164	1231	1.6	87	406	437	465	1.8	2.66	307	328	1.6
67423	BEVERLY	105	436	437	436	0.1	51	168	170	171	0.3	2.57	126	127	0.2
67425	BROOKVILLE	169	508	522	533	0.6	71	201	210	217	1.0	2.46	147	152	0.8
67427	BUSHTON	159	494	527	537	1.5	86	198	214	220	1.9	2.46	141	152	1.8
67428	CANTON	113	1557	1591	1633	0.5	67	577	595	616	0.7	2.59	455	467	0.6
67430	CAWKER CITY	123	578	571	560	-0.3	34	283	285	284	0.2	2.00	188	188	0.0
67431	CHAPMAN	041	2177	2228	2263	0.6	68	853	887	913	0.9	2.45	632	653	0.8
67432	CLAY CENTER	027	6165	6113	6073	-0.2	38	2593	2597	2600	0.0	2.30	1744	1731	-0.2
67436	DELPHOS	143	740	731	749	-0.3	34	304	303	311	-0.1	2.41	220	217	-0.3
67437	DOWNS	141	1235	1177	1125	-1.1	4	552	533	516	-0.8	2.11	331	316	-1.1
	KANSAS					0.7					1.0	2.49			0.8
	UNITED STATES					1.2					1.3	2.58			1.1

ZIP CODE #	POST OFFICE NAME	RACE (%) White 2000	White 2004	Black 2000	Black 2004	Asian/Pacific 2000	Asian/Pacific 2004	% Hispanic Origin 2000	% Hispanic Origin 2004	2004 AGE DISTRIBUTION (%) 0-4	5-9	10-14	15-19	20-24	25-44	45-64	65-84	85+	18+	MEDIAN AGE 2004	% 2004 Males	% 2004 Females
67117	NORTH NEWTON	94.2	93.4	1.9	2.1	0.7	0.7	2.7	3.4	3.1	2.6	3.1	7.6	13.9	17.0	19.3	24.5	9.1	89.4	48.1	44.5	55.5
67118	NORWICH	95.5	95.2	0.1	0.1	0.1	0.1	1.3	1.7	6.3	6.5	8.0	7.2	6.0	22.6	24.6	15.4	3.5	74.3	41.4	48.9	51.1
67119	OXFORD	95.7	95.2	0.3	0.3	0.4	0.6	1.8	2.2	4.7	5.0	7.0	7.5	7.2	23.6	26.5	14.7	3.7	77.9	41.8	48.1	51.9
67120	PECK	95.3	94.8	0.2	0.3	0.2	0.2	1.7	2.1	5.7	7.0	8.8	8.2	5.3	25.9	29.4	9.0	0.6	73.5	39.2	51.1	48.9
67122	PIEDMONT	95.6	95.5	0.0	0.0	0.0	0.0	1.7	1.7	5.5	5.5	5.9	5.9	5.2	22.8	31.0	16.2	2.1	79.0	44.5	50.7	49.3
67123	POTWIN	95.6	95.5	0.0	0.0	0.1	0.1	1.4	1.7	7.8	7.8	6.8	6.7	5.8	26.0	26.2	11.4	1.4	73.3	38.3	52.2	47.8
67124	PRATT	94.9	94.7	1.2	1.2	0.6	0.6	3.3	3.5	5.9	5.6	6.2	8.1	8.0	21.9	25.0	15.6	3.8	77.9	41.0	48.4	51.7
67127	PROTECTION	97.4	97.4	0.0	0.0	0.1	0.1	2.0	2.1	5.7	6.0	5.7	5.7	4.3	18.7	28.4	19.7	6.0	78.7	48.0	51.4	48.6
67131	ROCK	95.8	95.2	0.3	0.3	0.3	0.6	1.1	1.7	5.0	5.9	8.4	6.7	5.9	23.0	30.0	13.5	1.7	76.5	42.3	51.3	48.7
67132	ROSALIA	96.0	95.4	0.7	0.7	0.0	0.0	2.5	3.0	6.6	7.1	7.7	8.2	6.2	26.0	25.3	11.9	1.1	73.1	38.0	49.2	50.8
67133	ROSE HILL	96.2	95.9	0.6	0.6	0.5	0.6	1.8	2.2	7.3	8.4	10.0	9.0	5.7	28.1	24.7	6.1	0.8	68.1	35.0	50.3	49.7
67134	SAWYER	95.6	95.3	0.2	0.2	0.7	0.7	3.2	3.3	6.6	6.9	6.9	6.2	6.2	23.9	27.4	14.2	1.9	75.7	40.6	50.4	49.7
67135	SEDGWICK	95.5	94.9	0.2	0.2	0.2	0.2	2.9	3.7	6.8	7.1	8.1	7.8	6.3	25.9	25.9	10.5	1.6	72.7	37.7	49.7	50.3
67137	SEVERY	96.0	95.9	0.0	0.0	0.0	0.0	1.3	1.5	5.6	5.9	6.2	6.3	5.1	23.4	30.1	15.8	1.7	78.4	43.3	50.7	49.3
67138	SHARON	97.2	96.9	0.5	0.5	0.2	0.2	1.2	1.0	6.7	6.7	7.6	7.4	5.3	22.2	25.8	16.0	2.4	74.5	40.9	49.2	50.8
67140	SOUTH HAVEN	95.4	95.0	0.1	0.1	0.1	0.1	1.7	2.2	6.5	7.3	9.1	6.9	5.0	23.5	27.7	12.3	1.7	72.7	38.5	50.0	50.0
67142	SPIVEY	97.9	97.9	0.4	0.4	0.0	0.0	1.7	1.7	5.4	6.3	7.5	8.0	3.8	21.3	29.7	16.3	1.7	75.7	43.6	52.7	47.3
67143	SUN CITY	97.0	96.7	0.6	0.6	0.0	0.0	1.2	1.1	5.0	5.0	6.1	6.7	5.0	18.9	31.1	20.0	2.2	80.0	47.1	47.8	52.2
67144	TOWANDA	97.0	96.7	0.3	0.3	0.3	0.4	0.9	1.1	7.3	7.5	8.1	8.0	7.0	25.9	26.5	9.2	0.6	72.3	36.5	50.2	49.8
67146	UDALL	96.2	95.9	0.4	0.4	0.1	0.2	1.9	2.5	7.6	8.0	8.3	7.0	6.4	25.9	26.7	8.9	1.3	71.9	35.6	49.6	50.4
67147	VALLEY CENTER	96.2	95.6	0.6	0.7	0.3	0.4	1.9	2.5	7.4	7.5	8.2	7.8	6.5	26.0	25.5	10.1	1.0	72.0	36.3	49.7	50.4
67149	VIOLA	96.4	96.0	0.3	0.3	0.1	0.2	1.7	2.1	7.4	8.1	9.3	9.5	6.1	24.4	26.3	8.2	0.8	69.0	35.9	50.5	49.6
67150	WALDRON	97.9	98.6	0.0	0.0	0.0	0.0	1.4	0.7	5.1	6.5	6.5	5.1	3.6	21.0	30.4	19.6	2.2	77.5	46.4	50.0	50.0
67151	WALTON	97.4	97.3	0.5	0.5	0.0	0.0	2.1	2.4	7.4	8.2	8.5	8.2	5.5	25.4	26.8	9.0	1.0	70.7	36.7	53.6	46.4
67152	WELLINGTON	93.0	92.1	1.5	1.6	0.4	0.4	6.4	7.7	7.4	6.9	7.4	7.4	6.9	24.2	24.1	13.3	2.5	73.8	37.5	48.9	51.1
67154	WHITEWATER	97.3	97.1	0.1	0.1	0.2	0.3	1.3	1.6	6.0	8.5	8.2	7.8	4.5	22.9	24.6	13.1	4.5	71.9	39.7	50.2	49.8
67155	WILMORE	99.0	99.0	0.0	0.0	0.0	0.0	0.0	0.0	7.0	7.0	7.0	6.0	4.0	22.0	32.0	13.0	2.0	73.0	43.1	52.0	48.0
67156	WINFIELD	89.6	88.3	2.7	2.9	3.1	3.8	4.0	4.8	6.4	6.3	7.0	8.0	8.3	25.6	22.9	12.7	2.9	75.8	37.0	49.9	50.1
67159	ZENDA	98.6	98.5	0.0	0.0	0.0	0.0	1.4	2.0	5.5	6.4	7.4	7.9	5.5	20.3	28.7	15.8	2.5	75.3	42.7	52.5	47.5
67202	WICHITA	62.6	58.7	28.5	31.1	1.5	1.8	9.7	11.8	1.8	1.5	1.3	5.6	14.2	51.8	21.2	2.4	0.2	93.5	34.9	77.0	23.0
67203	WICHITA	79.6	76.8	4.4	4.7	1.2	1.4	17.5	20.6	7.5	6.8	6.1	5.6	7.6	29.4	22.3	12.1	2.6	76.3	35.4	48.8	51.2
67204	WICHITA	78.7	76.0	3.6	3.8	2.0	2.3	21.9	25.0	7.0	6.9	7.0	6.5	6.7	25.0	24.9	14.3	1.7	75.1	38.4	50.0	50.0
67205	WICHITA	93.6	92.2	0.8	1.0	2.6	3.4	2.6	3.5	9.0	9.7	9.7	7.1	4.3	30.9	23.7	5.3	0.3	66.7	34.2	50.9	49.1
67206	WICHITA	88.4	86.7	4.1	4.4	4.3	5.4	2.6	3.4	5.4	5.9	7.2	7.1	6.5	22.6	27.6	15.3	2.5	77.0	41.8	48.3	51.7
67207	WICHITA	74.0	69.7	11.5	12.7	8.1	10.4	5.2	6.5	7.8	7.0	6.3	6.0	8.5	32.4	22.0	8.8	1.1	75.5	33.0	49.1	50.9
67208	WICHITA	58.1	55.2	30.7	32.4	5.3	6.1	4.0	5.0	7.6	7.3	7.5	7.6	10.5	28.2	20.8	8.9	1.7	73.2	31.2	48.8	51.2
67209	WICHITA	89.0	86.8	2.4	2.7	2.9	3.7	5.2	6.7	9.2	8.4	7.4	6.6	6.1	31.5	21.3	8.4	1.1	70.9	33.1	49.8	50.2
67210	WICHITA	61.7	57.4	10.6	11.5	11.3	12.9	17.9	20.7	12.0	10.0	9.0	7.5	10.6	32.3	14.3	4.0	0.4	64.9	25.5	51.8	48.2
67211	WICHITA	75.2	71.4	8.4	9.3	3.6	4.3	13.4	16.5	8.1	7.0	6.8	6.7	8.0	30.5	21.5	9.5	1.9	74.1	33.5	49.8	50.2
67212	WICHITA	89.9	87.8	2.4	2.8	2.4	3.1	4.9	6.3	7.5	7.5	7.8	6.9	6.8	28.3	24.4	9.6	1.2	72.8	35.4	49.0	51.0
67213	WICHITA	81.3	78.2	5.4	6.0	1.7	2.1	11.8	14.9	8.3	7.1	6.5	6.3	8.3	30.3	20.0	10.4	2.9	74.7	33.2	49.5	50.6
67214	WICHITA	25.2	23.4	53.9	53.8	4.5	5.0	19.2	21.6	9.2	8.4	8.7	8.3	8.2	27.7	18.9	9.3	1.4	68.9	30.1	49.4	50.6
67215	WICHITA	92.0	90.0	1.2	1.5	3.3	4.0	4.0	5.5	8.8	8.9	9.3	7.1	6.1	30.2	23.2	6.2	0.3	68.4	33.0	49.8	50.2
67216	WICHITA	75.6	72.1	7.7	8.5	6.6	7.9	7.8	9.8	9.2	8.4	8.1	6.8	7.3	29.2	21.0	9.2	0.8	70.2	31.7	49.3	50.7
67217	WICHITA	84.0	81.3	4.3	4.8	3.5	4.3	6.3	8.2	8.5	7.9	7.5	6.7	6.9	28.6	22.4	10.8	0.7	72.0	33.4	49.2	50.8
67218	WICHITA	74.6	71.0	11.1	12.1	3.8	4.7	11.1	13.5	8.2	6.9	6.1	5.8	7.7	30.5	20.2	11.8	2.8	75.4	34.3	48.5	51.5
67219	WICHITA	58.2	57.7	32.6	32.0	0.9	1.0	8.2	9.7	8.8	8.9	9.4	8.3	6.9	27.8	20.9	8.4	0.5	67.8	30.7	48.7	51.4
67220	WICHITA	60.3	58.5	28.7	29.0	6.1	7.3	3.5	4.3	8.1	7.8	7.5	7.2	9.0	29.3	22.6	7.9	0.7	72.5	32.6	49.2	50.8
67221	MCCONNELL AFB	73.7	69.9	15.4	17.2	2.4	3.2	7.2	9.2	13.6	11.0	8.5	7.6	20.2	35.8	3.0	0.4	0.0	64.3	22.3	56.3	43.7
67223	WICHITA	96.8	96.1	0.6	0.6	0.8	1.1	1.8	2.4	8.2	8.4	10.7	9.4	5.4	25.4	25.8	6.2	0.6	67.1	34.0	51.4	48.6
67226	WICHITA	83.3	80.2	6.8	7.8	6.2	7.8	3.1	4.1	7.5	7.5	7.1	6.2	6.5	29.8	24.4	8.1	3.0	74.1	35.5	48.2	51.8
67227	WICHITA	98.2	97.6	0.0	0.0	0.0	0.0	1.5	1.7	5.5	6.8	9.9	9.9	4.4	24.2	31.4	7.2	0.7	71.3	39.4	51.5	48.5
67228	WICHITA	89.7	87.4	3.5	4.1	4.2	5.5	2.4	2.9	9.3	9.8	9.1	6.7	5.0	28.1	22.6	6.7	2.9	67.1	34.8	49.1	51.0
67230	WICHITA	92.6	91.2	1.7	2.0	3.2	4.0	1.3	1.7	5.8	7.0	8.7	7.4	5.1	20.4	33.5	10.9	1.3	73.8	42.4	49.5	50.6
67232	WICHITA	92.1	90.4	0.8	1.6	2.4	3.2	2.4	4.0	6.4	7.2	7.2	7.2	6.4	25.6	31.2	8.8	0.0	74.4	37.9	52.0	48.0
67235	WICHITA	93.9	92.4	1.0	1.2	1.7	2.3	3.1	4.1	7.9	8.4	9.6	8.6	5.8	26.7	26.3	6.3	0.4	68.3	35.9	49.1	50.9
67301	INDEPENDENCE	88.8	87.7	5.9	6.3	0.5	0.7	3.3	4.1	6.5	6.3	7.2	7.0	7.3	24.5	24.7	14.0	2.7	76.0	38.8	48.9	51.1
67330	ALTAMONT	95.6	95.5	0.0	0.0	0.2	0.2	0.7	0.8	6.2	6.4	8.7	8.0	5.6	24.6	23.6	13.4	3.5	73.2	38.6	47.8	52.2
67332	BARTLETT	93.6	93.3	0.0	0.0	0.5	0.8	1.0	1.3	4.5	6.0	9.0	9.5	3.5	26.5	28.0	11.0	2.0	74.0	40.5	51.5	48.5
67333	CANEY	90.6	89.9	0.2	0.2	0.1	0.1	2.1	2.6	6.4	6.5	7.9	7.1	6.0	24.7	25.0	13.9	2.5	74.7	39.2	47.9	52.1
67335	CHERRYVALE	94.6	94.0	0.2	0.3	0.1	0.1	2.4	2.9	6.5	6.4	7.2	6.9	6.5	24.7	25.2	14.0	2.6	75.7	39.3	48.6	51.4
67336	CHETOPA	90.6	90.2	1.7	1.8	0.0	0.0	0.9	1.1	5.3	5.6	6.9	5.8	5.6	22.3	27.2	17.8	3.6	78.7	44.0	48.9	51.1
67337	COFFEYVILLE	79.5	78.4	9.1	9.3	0.6	0.8	3.3	4.0	6.0	6.0	6.6	6.9	7.4	22.7	24.9	16.0	3.6	77.4	40.7	48.0	52.1
67341	DENNIS	99.0	98.7	0.0	0.0	0.0	0.0	1.6	1.9	5.9	5.5	6.5	5.9	3.6	28.3	29.4	14.1	1.1	78.4	41.9	53.0	47.0
67342	EDNA	89.6	89.3	0.1	0.1	0.1	0.1	0.5	0.5	4.7	5.2	8.6	8.1	5.3	22.8	25.9	15.4	4.2	76.5	42.4	47.1	52.9
67344	ELK CITY	94.9	94.4	0.0	0.0	0.1	0.1	1.8	2.1	5.4	5.7	6.9	6.9	5.7	20.2	30.6	16.0	2.7	77.5	44.5	50.3	49.7
67345	ELK FALLS	96.4	96.8	0.0	0.0	0.0	0.0	2.0	2.1	4.3	4.8	5.3	6.4	5.3	18.1	34.0	19.2	2.7	81.4	48.2	50.0	50.0
67346	GRENOLA	95.3	94.8	0.0	0.0	0.3	0.3	2.4	2.5	4.4	4.9	5.2	4.6	4.9	20.9	31.8	20.4	3.0	82.1	48.3	49.5	50.5
67347	HAVANA	91.5	91.0	0.7	0.8	0.0	0.0	0.0	0.4	3.4	4.1	6.4	6.8	5.6	21.4	35.3	14.3	2.6	81.6	46.7	52.6	47.4
67349	HOWARD	95.0	94.8	0.5	0.5	0.5	0.5	1.9	2.0	4.2	4.5	7.0	6.8	5.1	19.3	26.3	20.4	6.5	79.5	47.6	46.7	53.3
67351	LIBERTY	94.0	93.6	1.2	1.3	0.0	0.0	2.3	2.7	4.2	5.4	7.3	6.4	5.2	21.2	32.6	16.2	1.5	79.4	45.2	51.8	48.2
67352	LONGTON	94.8	94.8	0.0	0.0	0.2	0.2	2.0	2.0	5.3	5.3	7.8	8.6	7.3	20.0	25.9	16.8	3.1	76.3	41.9	49.0	51.0
67353	MOLINE	94.8	94.6	0.3	0.3	0.0	0.0	2.8	2.9	4.3	4.1	4.1	5.4	5.4	18.2	24.7	25.8	8.0	83.9	53.0	47.0	53.0
67354	MOUND VALLEY	93.4	92.9	0.0	0.0	0.1	0.1	1.9	2.2	7.9	7.0	6.7	6.5	7.1	26.2	24.8	12.2	1.6	74.6	37.0	48.5	51.5
67355	NIOTAZE	91.7	92.0	0.4	0.4	0.0	0.0	1.4	1.7	3.8	4.2	7.3	7.0	6.3	23.3	27.9	17.8	2.4	80.5	43.9	49.1	50.9
67356	OSWEGO	92.9	92.3	2.2	2.4	0.2	0.2	1.8	2.2	6.1	5.9	6.7	8.2	9.0	23.9	24.8	12.8	2.6	76.7	37.6	52.0	48.0
67357	PARSONS	87.0	86.1	7.0	7.3	0.5	0.6	4.2	5.1	6.7	6.3	6.9	7.4	7.7	25.1	23.8	13.0	3.2	76.0	37.9	48.8	51.2
67360	PERU	93.2	93.2	0.3	0.3	0.0	0.0	0.8	0.8	4.0	4.2	7.1	7.1	5.8	20.3	27.3	20.7	3.6	80.5	46.2	48.2	51.8
67361	SEDAN	94.2	94.0	0.3	0.4	0.2	0.2	1.4	1.5	5.3	5.3	6.6	7.1	6.3	19.1	25.3	19.9	5.3	78.6	45.3	47.5	52.5
67401	SALINA	88.6	87.1	3.3	3.4	1.9	2.3	6.3	7.6	7.0	6.7	7.2	7.0	7.6	27.1	23.6	11.8	2.0	75.0	36.3	49.2	50.8
67410	ABILENE	96.3	95.9	0.7	0.8	0.3	0.4	2.3	2.7	6.1	6.3	6.9	6.7	5.7	24.3	26.0	15.1	3.0	76.3	41.2	48.7	51.3
67416	ASSARIA	96.4	95.9	0.3	0.3	0.3	0.3	2.0	2.5	7.6	7.8	8.4	8.2	5.8	25.5	25.9	9.9	0.8	71.1	36.6	51.0	49.0
67417	AURORA	99.4	99.4	0.0	0.0	0.0	0.0	0.6	0.6	5.0	6.2	6.8	6.8	5.0	22.4	28.6	17.4	1.9	77.6	43.8	54.7	45.3
67418	BARNARD	99.3	99.6	0.0	0.0	0.0	0.0	0.4	0.4	4.2	4.2	5.7	6.4	6.1	19.7	31.1	20.5	2.3	81.8	47.1	50.0	50.0
67420	BELOIT	97.4	97.2	0.6	0.7	0.3	0.4	1.0	1.2	5.5	5.5	6.5	8.6	6.5	22.1	25.6	14.9	4.9	78.0	41.7	49.6	50.4
67422	BENNINGTON	98.2	97.9	0.2	0.2	0.4	0.4	0.8	1.1	6.2	7.0	8.7	6.6	4.6	25.7	28.3	11.5	1.4	73.8	40.0	51.3	48.7
67423	BEVERLY	97.5	97.7	0.0	0.0	0.2	0.2	1.6	1.6	6.4	7.3	8.9	5.0	4.8	22.0	30.2	13.5	1.8	74.1	42.0	49.7	50.3
67425	BROOKVILLE	98.4	98.3	0.0	0.0	0.0	0.0	2.4	2.7	5.6	6.3	8.1	7.7	4.6	25.2	29.5	11.5	1.2	74.7	40.5	53.8	46.2
67427	BUSHTON	98.0	97.5	0.2	0.2	0.2	0.4	1.6	2.1	3.4	4.4	8.0	9.3	4.0	20.9	30.6	17.5	2.1	77.8	45.1	49.7	50.3
67428	CANTON	98.1	97.8	0.1	0.1	0.5	0.6	1.0	1.1	6.2	6.5	7.7	7.0	6.2	25.2	25.8	12.8	2.7	75.2	39.1	49.4	50.6
67430	CAWKER CITY	97.6	97.4	0.4	0.4	0.4	0.5	0.7	0.9	4.9	5.1	5.4	6.7	5.8	19.4	27.9	22.1	2.8	80.9	46.9	50.4	49.6
67431	CHAPMAN	95.6	95.1	0.4	0.4	0.4	0.5	2.2	2.7	5.5	5.8	6.8	7.4	5.9	24.6	27.3	13.2	3.6	77.0	41.4	49.1	50.9
67432	CLAY CENTER	97.8	97.7	0.6	0.6	0.2	0.2	0.8	0.8	5.3	5.6	6.7	6.7	5.9	22.0	25.8	17.5	4.3	78.2	43.2	49.7	50.3
67436	DELPHOS	98.8	98.6	0.0	0.0	0.0	0.0	1.2	1.4	5.6	5.9	7.5	7.1	5.3	23.4	28.0	14.8	2.3	76.5	42.4	52.0	48.0
67437	DOWNS	98.9	98.8	0.0	0.0	0.2	0.3	0.4	0.5	4.8	4.6	5.4	7.7	6.5	18.7	25.9	20.2	6.3	80.4	46.6	48.9	51.2
	KANSAS	86.1	84.9	5.7	5.8	1.8	2.2	7.0	8.1	7.1	7.0	7.2	7.5	7.6	27.3	23.4	10.9	2.0	74.4	35.6	49.5	50.5
	UNITED STATES	75.1	73.6	12.3	12.5	3.8	4.2	12.5	14.1	6.9	6.7	7.2	7.0	7.3	28.6	23.8	10.8	1.7	75.1	36.0	49.1	50.9

ZIP CODE #	POST OFFICE NAME	2004 Per Capita Income	2004 HH Income Base	2004 Household Income Distribution (%): Less than $25,000	$25,000 to $49,999	$50,000 to $99,999	$100,000 to $149,999	$150,000 or More	Median Household Income: 2004	2009	2004 National Centile	2004 State Centile	2004 Home Value Base	2004 Home Value Distribution (%): Less than $50,000	$50,000 to $89,999	$90,000 to $174,999	$175,000 to $399,999	$400,000 or More	2004 Median Home Value
67117	NORTH NEWTON	25886	618	33.0	22.3	32.2	8.7	3.7	44006	52003	59	65	415	5.1	25.1	58.8	10.4	0.7	108977
67118	NORWICH	20538	310	21.9	34.5	31.9	9.7	1.9	41989	48004	53	58	257	29.2	24.5	38.9	7.4	0.0	84063
67119	OXFORD	21873	653	24.5	31.6	34.5	8.0	1.5	45266	51981	62	69	503	29.8	29.4	34.6	5.6	0.6	79468
67120	PECK	24367	494	13.2	23.9	44.9	16.4	1.6	60802	70069	85	90	443	12.9	23.7	49.2	13.5	0.7	107060
67122	PIEDMONT	20754	121	29.8	28.1	34.7	5.0	2.5	38822	44603	42	43	100	50.0	19.0	19.0	9.0	3.0	50000
67123	POTWIN	25968	278	19.8	32.7	32.4	10.8	4.3	48016	58523	68	78	232	37.9	39.7	12.1	9.1	1.3	62727
67124	PRATT	21699	3334	31.0	31.3	28.6	6.4	2.7	40358	46684	47	52	2418	30.5	33.9	27.1	8.2	0.4	70841
67127	PROTECTION	23117	312	34.9	39.1	20.8	1.3	3.9	33701	39238	23	14	235	67.7	14.0	15.3	3.0	0.0	34750
67131	ROCK	20058	137	23.4	28.5	38.7	8.8	0.7	48094	54523	69	78	118	25.4	30.5	28.0	11.9	4.2	83000
67132	ROSALIA	20410	165	23.6	29.7	37.0	8.5	1.2	46818	56344	66	75	137	37.2	29.2	22.6	9.5	1.5	66250
67133	ROSE HILL	25363	2060	9.1	18.0	47.5	21.1	4.3	71820	84727	92	95	1815	5.8	13.9	66.6	13.1	0.7	115692
67134	SAWYER	18396	152	27.6	37.5	23.7	6.6	4.6	39063	43266	43	45	124	54.8	22.6	14.5	6.5	1.6	44000
67135	SEDGWICK	22407	1199	15.8	29.1	42.2	10.4	2.5	54160	63437	79	86	996	19.0	36.6	33.0	10.0	1.4	83605
67137	SEVERY	21503	350	27.7	30.9	33.1	4.6	3.7	39564	45477	45	48	289	50.2	15.9	21.5	10.4	2.1	49667
67138	SHARON	18652	177	36.2	33.3	23.7	5.7	1.1	35933	41930	31	27	141	66.0	20.6	12.1	1.4	0.0	35250
67140	SOUTH HAVEN	17380	322	28.3	34.5	32.0	4.4	0.9	41232	47763	51	55	261	42.9	30.3	22.6	3.5	0.8	58409
67142	SPIVEY	21957	104	22.1	42.3	25.0	10.6	0.0	38364	44221	41	42	85	38.8	27.1	24.7	9.4	0.0	60714
67143	SUN CITY	21945	75	30.7	36.0	21.3	5.3	6.7	38358	45570	41	42	60	45.0	21.7	20.0	6.7	6.7	63333
67144	TOWANDA	24223	1099	13.3	29.7	39.2	14.7	3.1	57602	66579	82	88	954	20.9	38.1	25.2	13.9	2.0	76460
67146	UDALL	23374	721	18.7	31.8	35.8	11.9	1.8	49636	58014	71	80	619	20.5	32.0	36.5	10.5	0.5	86961
67147	VALLEY CENTER	26959	2960	10.3	25.5	45.2	14.1	4.9	60994	72736	85	91	2487	10.1	27.3	47.3	13.6	1.8	106825
67149	VIOLA	22641	328	12.8	22.9	45.4	15.6	3.4	60625	70820	85	90	286	12.2	25.2	45.5	16.8	0.4	110256
67150	WALDRON	20850	59	37.3	32.2	22.0	5.1	3.4	35433	43628	29	23	48	35.4	25.0	29.2	8.3	2.1	70000
67151	WALTON	21005	238	13.5	35.3	41.6	9.2	0.4	50653	58957	73	82	205	21.0	36.6	28.8	13.7	0.0	82619
67152	WELLINGTON	21328	4098	27.5	31.9	31.6	7.3	1.8	42301	49093	54	59	2948	28.3	38.2	28.2	4.8	0.5	73740
67154	WHITEWATER	23110	498	15.7	32.1	37.4	10.0	4.8	52801	62033	77	84	420	14.1	25.7	52.6	6.4	1.2	96935
67155	WILMORE	22340	50	28.0	36.0	34.0	0.0	2.0	37317	43618	37	35	36	61.1	19.4	13.9	5.6	0.0	43333
67156	WINFIELD	22832	5870	29.2	30.1	31.2	6.7	2.8	41758	49312	52	57	4199	27.6	34.6	29.4	7.9	0.6	74395
67159	ZENDA	19090	86	29.1	40.7	23.3	3.5	3.5	36962	42687	35	33	70	55.7	20.0	17.1	4.3	2.9	44286
67202	WICHITA	14624	463	53.1	28.7	12.7	5.4	0.0	23157	29421	3	1	28	75.0	17.9	0.0	7.1	0.0	41250
67203	WICHITA	22941	13378	27.0	35.9	29.4	6.0	1.6	39855	48086	45	49	7547	18.1	50.5	29.7	1.5	0.2	75162
67204	WICHITA	23011	7958	25.0	27.8	34.3	9.6	3.3	47238	56380	67	77	5780	19.9	41.3	31.5	6.9	0.4	78864
67205	WICHITA	35316	3566	5.2	12.0	43.9	25.5	13.4	85222	104184	96	98	3222	4.7	5.3	48.3	36.7	5.1	164478
67206	WICHITA	51000	6021	15.5	17.5	32.1	14.9	20.0	73680	89114	93	96	4369	3.0	4.6	48.3	34.1	10.1	163435
67207	WICHITA	27470	10763	19.7	30.5	36.3	9.9	3.7	49885	59078	72	80	5829	9.0	30.3	54.6	5.2	1.0	101909
67208	WICHITA	25336	7730	31.9	27.2	28.2	8.3	4.4	40495	48430	48	52	4474	20.4	33.8	36.7	7.3	1.7	83345
67209	WICHITA	26966	5108	10.9	23.3	47.3	14.7	3.9	63164	74274	87	93	4118	6.5	20.8	68.0	4.5	0.3	110201
67210	WICHITA	17908	4198	26.4	31.8	32.1	7.7	2.1	42642	50811	55	60	1878	43.2	17.8	36.5	2.3	0.1	62778
67211	WICHITA	19507	9125	33.7	37.2	23.2	4.6	1.3	33502	39905	22	12	4752	40.7	52.8	5.8	0.7	0.0	55092
67212	WICHITA	27285	18741	13.5	26.3	42.1	14.1	4.0	60502	70533	85	90	13792	4.3	22.5	65.9	7.0	0.4	111598
67213	WICHITA	17511	8906	35.8	35.7	24.5	3.0	1.1	33201	39226	22	10	4692	49.5	47.1	2.8	0.5	0.0	50265
67214	WICHITA	13932	6508	49.9	29.0	17.2	2.9	1.0	25066	30369	5	1	2848	69.0	25.7	4.8	0.5	0.0	38179
67215	WICHITA	25646	1774	5.3	18.8	55.3	16.7	4.0	67540	80736	90	94	1676	12.1	17.7	64.7	5.0	0.5	104569
67216	WICHITA	19640	9236	25.0	34.4	33.3	6.1	1.3	43497	52264	57	62	6501	47.2	40.6	11.3	0.8	0.2	52319
67217	WICHITA	21089	12118	21.3	35.6	34.6	7.4	1.1	45397	54048	62	70	8781	27.9	56.6	14.8	0.6	0.1	64961
67218	WICHITA	22051	10566	31.2	34.7	26.7	5.5	2.0	36706	44454	34	31	5794	21.8	56.8	18.1	3.2	0.2	67290
67219	WICHITA	17701	3808	28.7	32.5	31.4	5.5	1.8	41322	50193	51	56	2664	45.4	41.2	12.6	0.8	0.0	53631
67220	WICHITA	25145	4678	17.8	22.9	41.7	14.1	3.5	59630	69357	84	90	3311	4.1	20.0	70.7	4.9	0.4	111005
67221	MCCONNELL AFB	3475	12	8.3	66.7	25.0	0.0	0.0	37981	42330	39	40	0	0.0	0.0	0.0	0.0	0.0	0
67223	WICHITA	33181	160	5.6	15.0	38.1	24.4	16.9	86936	103997	97	98	153	3.3	8.5	45.1	38.6	4.6	160417
67226	WICHITA	40111	6860	11.6	19.4	37.5	19.1	12.4	72401	85501	92	96	4556	1.6	9.0	47.1	38.5	3.7	158627
67227	WICHITA	24022	99	12.1	23.2	42.4	20.2	2.0	62412	74331	87	92	94	7.5	21.3	55.3	14.9	1.1	111905
67228	WICHITA	39227	137	7.3	16.1	37.2	20.4	19.0	83021	104045	96	97	121	2.5	6.6	43.0	40.5	7.4	171528
67230	WICHITA	47826	2320	5.2	9.1	28.5	28.6	28.7	110402	135490	99	99	2236	1.3	1.0	29.9	53.4	14.4	212195
67232	WICHITA	32442	53	9.4	32.1	37.7	13.2	7.6	58827	69960	83	89	43	11.6	9.3	48.8	27.9	2.3	131250
67235	WICHITA	37702	2252	3.8	10.0	41.3	25.8	19.1	93264	112360	97	98	2153	2.7	2.5	44.5	47.0	3.3	175615
67301	INDEPENDENCE	20010	5412	33.5	32.6	26.2	5.3	2.3	37143	42643	36	33	3819	36.1	33.4	24.4	5.8	0.2	65860
67330	ALTAMONT	17593	521	29.2	35.3	30.3	4.8	0.4	38015	43989	39	41	407	36.4	41.3	17.4	3.7	1.2	62255
67332	BARTLETT	15911	146	27.4	40.4	29.5	2.7	0.0	36018	41009	32	28	122	30.3	27.1	27.9	8.2	6.6	81000
67333	CANEY	20383	1313	31.3	33.1	27.4	6.2	2.0	37925	43818	39	40	994	43.0	30.1	23.3	3.2	0.4	57071
67335	CHERRYVALE	18756	1326	37.9	33.3	23.9	3.3	1.6	35032	40740	28	21	1032	54.2	30.3	11.3	3.9	0.3	46532
67336	CHETOPA	16039	784	42.2	37.8	17.6	2.0	0.4	30000	34578	12	3	581	67.5	22.6	9.1	0.9	0.0	38906
67337	COFFEYVILLE	19089	6174	38.0	32.8	22.6	4.9	1.8	33544	39034	23	13	4359	48.6	27.6	19.7	3.5	0.5	51658
67341	DENNIS	20516	195	31.3	24.1	36.9	6.2	1.5	42879	49008	56	61	171	24.6	30.4	36.3	6.4	2.3	84688
67342	EDNA	20488	338	32.3	29.3	35.8	1.8	0.9	39135	45304	43	45	276	44.9	27.9	23.9	2.9	0.4	57368
67344	ELK CITY	19824	351	39.3	28.8	23.9	4.0	4.0	33055	38898	21	10	293	57.7	23.2	14.3	2.1	2.7	39167
67345	ELK FALLS	19478	87	35.6	33.3	26.4	4.6	0.0	34526	40000	26	17	71	32.4	31.0	29.6	0.0	7.0	73125
67346	GRENOLA	20919	162	34.6	23.5	36.4	4.9	0.6	35000	41560	28	21	135	50.4	22.2	14.1	9.6	3.7	49583
67347	HAVANA	18107	115	34.8	30.4	29.6	5.2	0.0	37444	42716	37	36	98	48.0	22.5	19.4	9.2	1.0	53333
67349	HOWARD	19453	481	36.0	37.2	22.3	2.9	1.7	32666	38753	20	8	363	62.8	22.0	12.7	1.1	1.4	34635
67351	LIBERTY	25414	199	21.1	31.2	36.2	8.0	3.5	47074	54835	66	76	170	28.2	23.5	36.5	8.8	2.9	86250
67352	LONGTON	13875	241	45.2	35.7	14.9	3.7	0.4	27267	30890	8	1	181	60.8	22.1	11.6	2.8	2.8	39250
67353	MOLINE	23606	285	40.4	31.9	17.2	6.7	3.9	30477	38529	13	4	239	71.6	17.6	8.4	2.1	0.4	24415
67354	MOUND VALLEY	15114	322	43.5	32.9	19.9	2.5	1.2	30558	36661	14	4	264	52.7	25.4	16.7	4.6	0.8	46667
67355	NIOTAZE	14753	114	35.1	37.7	23.7	3.5	0.0	33673	37669	23	14	97	63.9	25.8	7.2	1.0	2.1	27500
67356	OSWEGO	17062	1231	33.8	33.3	29.2	3.5	0.2	37066	42647	36	33	952	48.7	26.7	20.3	4.0	0.3	51739
67357	PARSONS	19276	5525	34.3	33.9	24.7	5.1	2.0	34663	39504	26	18	3777	50.1	26.0	19.3	4.2	0.4	49901
67360	PERU	17198	325	39.4	35.1	19.1	4.9	1.5	31120	35887	15	4	271	63.1	21.0	10.3	3.0	2.6	35577
67361	SEDAN	19714	885	38.1	35.7	18.8	4.3	3.2	31554	36325	16	5	676	57.7	20.6	18.2	2.7	0.9	42973
67401	SALINA	22909	20448	25.4	33.9	30.7	6.9	3.1	42272	49595	54	59	14091	12.8	29.3	42.5	14.3	1.1	100121
67410	ABILENE	21395	4270	26.5	33.9	32.1	5.8	1.7	42089	48293	53	58	3256	18.7	35.4	34.8	10.7	0.5	85507
67416	ASSARIA	23181	423	15.1	34.5	39.0	8.0	3.3	50216	58504	72	81	362	19.1	22.4	43.1	14.1	1.4	106818
67417	AURORA	17141	62	30.7	37.1	25.8	4.8	1.6	37376	42385	37	36	50	30.0	42.0	22.0	6.0	0.0	68000
67418	BARNARD	19624	122	31.2	45.9	18.9	3.3	0.8	35000	40889	28	21	96	58.3	17.7	20.8	2.1	1.0	40000
67420	BELOIT	21706	2010	27.0	36.4	27.4	5.7	3.5	39857	46719	45	49	1559	32.7	30.5	27.5	8.5	0.8	71960
67422	BENNINGTON	20725	437	19.7	31.8	39.4	6.4	2.8	48881	55604	70	79	375	21.9	25.6	34.1	17.3	1.1	92794
67423	BEVERLY	16886	170	32.9	37.7	22.9	4.1	2.4	35249	40155	28	23	139	41.7	36.0	18.7	2.2	1.4	55750
67425	BROOKVILLE	24599	210	20.5	33.3	33.3	8.6	4.3	45509	52181	63	71	178	27.0	27.5	27.5	18.0	0.0	84667
67427	BUSHTON	21730	214	28.5	31.3	32.2	6.1	1.9	40969	45377	50	54	180	62.2	21.1	12.2	4.4	0.0	38846
67428	CANTON	19702	595	21.5	37.5	33.8	4.7	2.5	43505	49648	57	62	490	25.5	24.9	39.8	8.4	1.4	89429
67430	CAWKER CITY	24923	285	38.3	30.5	22.8	4.9	3.5	32694	37580	20	9	215	49.3	33.5	13.5	1.9	1.9	50882
67431	CHAPMAN	21049	887	21.3	33.9	35.5	8.5	0.8	45628	51772	63	72	691	21.1	36.0	35.6	6.5	0.7	82016
67432	CLAY CENTER	21070	2597	31.7	31.5	29.4	6.1	1.2	37686	44268	38	38	1938	38.8	28.0	27.1	6.0	0.1	64692
67436	DELPHOS	20825	303	23.4	42.2	25.7	5.9	2.6	39915	46078	46	49	256	48.8	23.1	19.9	7.8	0.4	51500
67437	DOWNS	18121	533	41.8	33.8	19.5	3.8	1.1	29563	33535	11	2	433	62.4	23.1	12.7	1.4	0.5	39257
	KANSAS	25137		23.6	29.0	32.2	10.1	5.1	47540	57348				21.4	24.4	35.0	16.7	2.5	97470
	UNITED STATES	25866		24.7	27.1	30.8	10.9	6.5	48124	56710				10.9	15.0	33.7	30.1	10.4	145905

ZIP CODE #	POST OFFICE NAME	FINANCIAL SERVICES				THE HOME						ENTERTAINMENT						PERSONAL			
						Home Improvements		Furnishings													
		Auto Loan	Home Loan	Investments	Retirement Plans	Home Repair	Lawn & Garden	Computers & Hardware	Major Appliances	TV, Radio, Sound Equipment	Furniture	Dine out/ Carry out	Sports Equipment	Fees & Tickets	Toys & Games	Travel	Cable TV	Apparel & Services	Auto Repairs	Health Insurance	Pets & Supplies
67117	NORTH NEWTON	90	68	45	65	74	89	75	82	84	71	99	92	67	93	74	89	90	82	99	99
67118	NORWICH	98	68	36	65	80	89	68	84	78	67	91	101	58	89	70	82	83	82	99	116
67119	OXFORD	86	74	57	73	77	86	74	80	79	73	95	92	71	95	74	80	90	78	86	96
67120	PECK	111	99	75	94	105	112	91	101	97	91	118	121	90	121	94	100	112	99	110	131
67122	PIEDMONT	90	63	33	59	73	82	62	77	72	61	84	92	53	82	64	75	76	76	91	107
67123	POTWIN	104	87	67	86	92	104	89	96	95	88	115	110	85	114	89	97	108	95	105	115
67124	PRATT	79	66	52	64	71	80	68	74	73	66	88	85	64	86	69	76	82	73	83	90
67127	PROTECTION	85	63	40	60	70	83	69	77	77	66	91	87	61	86	68	82	83	77	92	95
67131	ROCK	84	75	57	71	79	84	69	76	73	69	89	91	68	91	71	75	85	74	83	99
67132	ROSALIA	87	77	58	73	82	88	71	79	76	71	92	95	70	94	74	78	88	77	86	103
67133	ROSE HILL	112	124	119	127	121	120	112	113	105	115	133	133	116	136	112	101	131	110	102	128
67134	SAWYER	93	65	34	61	75	84	64	79	74	63	86	95	55	85	66	77	79	78	94	110
67135	SEDGWICK	98	88	68	84	93	99	81	90	86	81	104	108	79	107	84	88	99	88	97	116
67137	SEVERY	91	64	34	61	75	84	63	78	73	63	85	94	54	84	66	76	78	77	93	109
67138	SHARON	80	56	29	52	65	72	55	68	63	54	74	82	47	73	57	66	68	67	81	94
67140	SOUTH HAVEN	83	60	34	57	69	77	59	71	67	58	79	86	51	78	61	70	72	70	84	98
67142	SPIVEY	91	63	33	60	74	83	63	77	72	62	85	93	53	83	65	76	77	76	92	108
67143	SUN CITY	95	67	35	63	78	87	66	81	76	65	89	98	56	87	68	79	81	80	97	113
67144	TOWANDA	109	97	74	92	103	110	90	100	96	90	116	119	88	119	93	98	110	97	108	129
67146	UDALL	100	89	68	85	94	101	82	91	88	82	106	109	81	109	85	90	101	89	99	118
67147	VALLEY CENTER	106	110	104	109	111	115	104	107	102	104	127	125	105	130	105	101	123	105	104	124
67149	VIOLA	102	103	93	101	105	109	95	100	95	95	117	118	96	121	97	94	113	97	100	121
67150	WALDRON	88	62	32	58	72	80	61	75	70	60	82	91	52	81	63	74	75	74	90	105
67151	WALTON	82	83	76	83	83	84	79	82	77	80	96	97	78	96	78	74	93	81	77	94
67152	WELLINGTON	81	74	62	71	77	85	73	78	77	72	94	89	72	95	74	79	89	76	84	92
67154	WHITEWATER	118	90	56	86	102	112	87	104	97	86	115	125	78	114	90	101	107	103	120	141
67155	WILMORE	81	56	30	53	66	74	56	69	64	55	75	83	48	74	58	67	69	68	82	96
67156	WINFIELD	84	78	71	76	81	89	78	82	81	76	99	95	77	101	79	83	95	81	88	97
67159	ZENDA	81	57	30	54	66	74	56	69	64	55	76	83	48	74	58	68	69	68	82	96
67202	WICHITA	40	35	49	36	35	41	44	40	46	42	57	47	43	56	43	47	55	44	44	45
67203	WICHITA	66	66	72	66	66	71	69	68	69	68	86	79	69	87	69	68	84	69	67	75
67204	WICHITA	79	82	86	79	82	87	80	81	81	80	101	92	82	102	81	81	99	81	81	91
67205	WICHITA	149	171	170	176	165	164	153	153	142	157	180	178	161	184	153	136	178	148	135	171
67206	WICHITA	156	173	204	178	171	179	171	167	164	171	206	195	176	206	172	159	203	168	156	183
67207	WICHITA	86	83	92	87	82	87	89	86	87	88	109	103	87	106	85	83	106	89	80	96
67208	WICHITA	78	78	93	79	77	84	86	81	85	83	107	96	86	107	84	83	104	84	78	89
67209	WICHITA	100	108	109	110	106	108	102	102	98	103	123	119	104	124	102	95	121	101	95	114
67210	WICHITA	78	68	67	70	66	70	75	73	75	76	95	88	71	91	70	71	93	77	68	82
67211	WICHITA	58	57	63	57	57	62	62	60	63	60	78	70	62	80	61	63	76	61	60	65
67212	WICHITA	94	102	110	105	99	101	99	97	95	100	119	114	101	120	98	91	117	97	89	106
67213	WICHITA	53	52	58	53	53	57	57	55	57	55	71	64	56	72	56	57	69	56	55	60
67214	WICHITA	47	41	44	39	41	46	46	46	50	46	61	51	45	58	45	50	59	47	48	51
67215	WICHITA	110	120	112	123	115	112	109	109	101	113	128	128	111	127	106	95	126	107	95	121
67216	WICHITA	73	69	64	68	70	76	70	72	72	70	89	83	69	88	70	72	85	72	73	83
67217	WICHITA	77	74	68	72	75	80	73	75	74	73	92	88	72	93	73	74	88	75	77	87
67218	WICHITA	63	64	72	64	63	68	68	65	68	66	85	77	68	86	67	67	83	67	64	72
67219	WICHITA	70	67	66	65	66	72	68	69	70	69	87	78	67	85	67	70	84	69	70	79
67220	WICHITA	91	98	103	101	94	96	98	94	92	97	117	112	98	117	95	87	115	95	84	103
67221	MCCONNELL AFB	71	45	43	51	41	49	67	58	68	62	85	77	57	76	55	62	81	68	53	66
67223	WICHITA	147	178	190	183	173	173	160	157	147	162	187	184	172	193	162	142	187	153	140	174
67226	WICHITA	138	141	158	149	139	144	143	140	137	145	173	166	143	168	140	131	169	143	129	154
67227	WICHITA	92	115	122	115	113	111	102	102	95	102	119	120	109	127	105	92	119	98	91	113
67228	WICHITA	160	166	192	174	168	176	170	169	164	169	206	199	170	201	169	159	200	171	162	185
67230	WICHITA	176	221	259	223	215	223	197	194	182	200	231	222	216	239	203	179	232	188	178	213
67232	WICHITA	123	109	83	104	115	124	101	112	107	101	130	133	99	133	104	110	124	109	121	144
67235	WICHITA	158	174	192	180	172	178	168	166	159	168	200	194	173	199	168	154	197	165	156	184
67301	INDEPENDENCE	74	62	50	60	66	74	64	69	69	62	83	81	60	82	64	71	78	69	77	85
67330	ALTAMONT	79	57	32	54	65	73	56	68	63	55	75	82	48	74	58	66	68	67	80	94
67332	BARTLETT	79	55	29	52	64	72	54	67	63	54	73	81	46	72	56	66	67	66	80	94
67333	CANEY	80	68	51	67	72	80	68	74	73	67	88	86	65	88	68	74	83	73	81	90
67335	CHERRYVALE	72	60	45	59	64	72	62	67	66	60	80	76	58	79	62	68	75	66	74	80
67336	CHETOPA	59	45	30	43	49	58	49	54	54	46	64	61	44	61	48	57	59	53	63	65
67337	COFFEYVILLE	69	57	47	55	61	69	60	65	64	58	78	75	56	76	60	66	73	65	72	79
67341	DENNIS	80	72	55	68	76	81	66	73	70	66	85	87	65	87	68	72	81	71	79	95
67342	EDNA	87	61	32	57	71	79	60	74	69	59	81	90	51	80	62	73	74	73	88	103
67344	ELK CITY	88	61	30	54	69	79	60	73	71	60	83	87	52	79	61	76	76	73	90	101
67345	ELK FALLS	75	53	28	50	61	69	53	65	61	52	71	77	45	70	55	64	65	64	77	89
67346	GRENOLA	86	60	31	57	70	78	59	73	68	59	80	88	51	79	61	72	73	72	87	102
67347	HAVANA	75	53	28	50	61	69	53	64	61	52	71	77	45	69	54	64	65	63	77	88
67349	HOWARD	71	53	33	50	58	69	57	64	64	55	76	73	51	72	57	68	69	64	77	80
67351	LIBERTY	98	88	67	83	93	99	81	90	86	81	105	107	79	107	83	88	99	87	97	116
67352	LONGTON	56	41	26	40	46	54	45	51	51	43	60	57	40	57	45	54	54	50	60	63
67353	MOLINE	82	61	40	59	67	80	67	75	76	64	89	84	60	84	67	80	81	74	89	91
67354	MOUND VALLEY	61	51	38	50	54	60	51	56	55	51	66	65	49	66	51	56	62	55	62	68
67355	NIOTAZE	60	45	30	43	49	59	50	55	56	47	66	61	44	62	49	59	60	55	66	66
67356	OSWEGO	66	53	38	51	57	66	55	61	61	53	72	69	51	70	55	63	67	60	70	74
67357	PARSONS	67	61	56	60	64	71	62	65	65	61	80	76	61	81	63	67	76	65	70	78
67360	PERU	64	48	32	46	53	63	54	59	60	51	71	66	48	67	53	63	64	59	71	71
67361	SEDAN	75	56	36	54	62	73	61	68	69	58	81	77	54	76	61	72	74	68	81	83
67401	SALINA	76	78	81	78	79	83	79	79	78	77	97	92	79	98	79	77	94	79	77	89
67410	ABILENE	84	64	43	62	71	81	67	76	74	65	87	89	60	85	67	76	81	75	87	97
67416	ASSARIA	102	93	73	89	98	104	86	95	90	86	110	113	84	112	88	92	105	92	101	121
67417	AURORA	81	56	29	53	66	73	56	69	64	55	75	83	47	74	58	67	68	68	82	96
67418	BARNARD	77	54	28	51	63	70	53	66	61	52	72	79	45	70	55	64	65	65	78	91
67420	BELOIT	88	65	42	63	74	82	66	78	74	65	88	92	59	86	68	77	81	77	90	103
67422	BENNINGTON	100	70	36	66	81	91	69	85	79	68	93	103	59	91	71	83	85	84	101	119
67423	BEVERLY	79	55	29	52	64	72	54	67	62	54	73	81	46	72	56	65	67	66	80	93
67425	BROOKVILLE	98	85	64	80	91	99	80	90	86	79	104	106	77	105	82	89	98	87	99	116
67427	BUSHTON	97	68	35	64	79	88	67	83	77	66	90	100	57	88	69	81	82	81	98	115
67428	CANTON	83	74	56	70	78	83	68	75	72	68	88	90	67	90	70	74	84	73	82	97
67430	CAWKER CITY	81	61	40	58	66	79	67	74	75	64	88	83	60	83	66	79	81	74	88	89
67431	CHAPMAN	75	71	68	70	75	81	71	75	73	70	90	88	70	91	73	74	86	75	79	89
67432	CLAY CENTER	73	64	55	62	68	77	66	71	71	64	85	81	63	86	67	73	80	70	79	84
67436	DELPHOS	90	64	35	61	74	83	63	77	72	62	85	93	55	83	65	75	78	76	91	107
67437	DOWNS	63	47	31	45	52	62	52	57	58	49	68	64	46	65	51	61	62	57	69	69
	KANSAS	92	87	84	87	89	95	89	91	90	88	111	106	87	110	88	89	107	91	92	105
	UNITED STATES	100	100	100	100	100	100	100	100	100	100	100	100	100	100	100	100	100	100	100	100

KANSAS
A 67438-67621

POPULATION CHANGE

# POST OFFICE NAME	COUNTY FIPS CODE	POPULATION 2000	2004	2009	2000-2004 ANNUAL RATE % Rate	State Centile	HOUSEHOLDS 2000	2004	2009	% Annual Rate 2000-2004	2004 Average HH Size	FAMILIES 2000	2004	% Annual Rate 2000-2004
67438 DURHAM	115	309	306	306	-0.2	37	126	125	125	-0.2	2.45	89	88	-0.3
67439 ELLSWORTH	053	3612	3613	3629	0.0	50	1238	1251	1272	0.3	2.28	811	813	0.1
67441 ENTERPRISE	041	1123	1086	1085	-0.8	12	413	405	408	-0.5	2.58	302	294	-0.6
67442 FALUN	169	260	265	270	0.5	66	107	110	113	0.7	2.40	82	84	0.6
67443 GALVA	113	1539	1622	1687	1.2	82	548	583	612	1.5	2.78	455	481	1.3
67444 GENESEO	159	525	556	565	1.4	83	242	260	266	1.7	2.13	171	182	1.5
67445 GLASCO	029	664	641	617	-0.8	11	287	279	271	-0.7	2.19	191	184	-0.9
67446 GLEN ELDER	123	626	616	602	-0.4	30	262	263	261	0.1	2.34	175	174	-0.1
67447 GREEN	027	323	321	319	-0.2	41	121	122	123	0.2	2.63	96	97	0.2
67448 GYPSUM	169	1337	1454	1534	2.0	91	499	546	580	2.1	2.66	390	423	1.9
67449 HERINGTON	127	3289	3287	3312	0.0	47	1410	1424	1448	0.2	2.25	879	877	-0.1
67450 HOLYROOD	053	603	608	613	0.2	57	269	274	278	0.4	2.22	191	193	0.3
67451 HOPE	041	1068	1053	1055	-0.3	32	443	442	447	-0.1	2.38	327	324	-0.2
67452 HUNTER	123	132	125	120	-1.3	1	65	63	61	-0.7	1.98	45	43	-1.1
67454 KANOPOLIS	053	663	666	669	0.1	54	295	302	308	0.6	2.21	189	192	0.4
67455 LINCOLN	105	1906	1897	1889	-0.1	43	834	837	840	0.1	2.18	532	529	-0.1
67456 LINDSBORG	113	4452	4535	4629	0.4	66	1663	1712	1765	0.7	2.32	1107	1129	0.5
67457 LITTLE RIVER	159	845	811	785	-1.0	8	307	296	288	-0.9	2.57	222	212	-1.1
67458 LONGFORD	027	286	285	283	-0.1	45	119	120	120	0.2	2.38	92	92	0.0
67459 LORRAINE	053	268	271	273	0.3	60	95	97	98	0.5	2.79	67	68	0.4
67460 MCPHERSON	113	16015	16266	16624	0.4	63	6159	6314	6511	0.6	2.46	4291	4362	0.4
67464 MARQUETTE	113	1016	1049	1078	0.8	73	412	430	446	1.0	2.34	283	293	0.8
67466 MILTONVALE	029	724	698	672	-0.9	10	309	300	291	-0.7	2.27	196	188	-1.0
67467 MINNEAPOLIS	143	3321	3357	3451	0.3	59	1327	1352	1398	0.4	2.34	897	905	0.2
67468 MORGANVILLE	027	399	396	394	-0.2	39	146	147	148	0.2	2.69	116	116	0.0
67470 NEW CAMBRIA	169	520	515	520	-0.2	37	204	204	208	0.0	2.51	158	158	0.0
67473 OSBORNE	141	2077	1993	1908	-1.0	7	881	855	827	-0.7	2.27	546	525	-0.9
67474 PORTIS	141	221	219	212	-0.2	38	98	98	96	0.0	2.11	62	62	0.0
67475 RAMONA	115	189	206	216	2.1	92	76	84	88	2.4	2.45	58	63	2.0
67476 ROXBURY	113	25	28	29	2.7	94	11	12	13	2.1	2.33	9	10	2.5
67478 SIMPSON	123	168	180	183	1.6	87	67	73	75	2.0	2.45	44	47	1.6
67480 SOLOMON	041	1618	1671	1709	0.8	73	620	645	665	0.9	2.57	470	485	0.7
67481 SYLVAN GROVE	105	966	969	970	0.1	52	404	411	416	0.4	2.36	291	294	0.2
67482 TALMAGE	041	12	12	13	0.0	50	4	4	4	0.0	3.00	3	3	0.0
67483 TAMPA	115	364	366	369	0.1	54	136	138	140	0.3	2.65	98	99	0.2
67484 TESCOTT	143	851	940	1012	2.4	93	326	361	390	2.4	2.60	243	266	2.2
67485 TIPTON	123	382	363	349	-1.2	3	161	156	152	-0.7	2.33	112	107	-1.1
67487 WAKEFIELD	027	1263	1258	1251	-0.1	44	480	485	487	0.2	2.53	353	354	0.1
67490 WILSON	053	1020	1017	1020	-0.1	46	426	429	435	0.2	2.23	274	273	-0.1
67491 WINDOM	113	401	406	412	0.3	62	158	161	165	0.4	2.52	124	126	0.4
67492 WOODBINE	041	328	330	331	0.1	55	127	130	132	0.6	2.54	92	93	0.3
67501 HUTCHINSON	155	27947	27788	27708	-0.1	41	10649	10682	10710	0.1	2.37	6673	6623	-0.2
67502 HUTCHINSON	155	23241	23115	23056	-0.1	41	9486	9556	9611	0.2	2.36	6755	6749	0.0
67505 SOUTH HUTCHINSON	155	2606	2547	2517	-0.5	20	1172	1160	1154	-0.2	2.07	703	685	-0.6
67510 ABBYVILLE	155	442	432	427	-0.5	20	167	165	164	-0.3	2.62	128	125	-0.6
67511 ALBERT	009	283	288	284	0.4	64	114	118	118	0.8	2.44	83	86	0.8
67512 ALDEN	159	276	323	343	3.8	98	112	132	141	3.9	2.45	86	100	3.6
67513 ALEXANDER	165	139	135	132	-0.7	16	60	59	58	-0.4	2.29	40	38	-1.2
67514 ARLINGTON	155	808	800	796	-0.2	37	333	332	331	-0.1	2.41	235	232	-0.3
67516 BAZINE	135	441	432	429	-0.5	25	212	212	213	0.0	2.04	140	139	-0.7
67518 BEELER	135	70	69	69	-0.3	32	29	29	29	0.0	2.31	19	19	0.0
67519 BELPRE	047	223	217	211	-0.6	17	94	92	89	-0.5	2.36	69	67	-0.7
67520 BISON	165	319	316	312	-0.2	38	129	129	129	0.0	2.45	85	84	-0.3
67521 BROWNELL	135	142	139	138	-0.5	23	60	60	60	0.0	2.32	40	39	-0.6
67522 BUHLER	155	2014	1980	1963	-0.4	29	712	709	709	-0.1	2.69	573	568	-0.2
67523 BURDETT	145	338	331	323	-0.5	24	142	141	139	-0.2	2.35	104	102	-0.5
67524 CHASE	159	699	667	644	-1.1	5	273	262	254	-1.0	2.55	196	186	-1.2
67525 CLAFLIN	009	1322	1354	1343	0.6	68	507	526	529	0.9	2.57	366	376	0.6
67526 ELLINWOOD	009	2754	2694	2612	-0.5	22	1126	1117	1097	-0.2	2.36	764	750	-0.4
67529 GARFIELD	145	332	325	317	-0.5	23	132	131	129	-0.2	2.48	98	96	-0.5
67530 GREAT BEND	009	19379	18723	18080	-0.8	11	7828	7650	7467	-0.5	2.37	5104	4942	-0.8
67543 HAVEN	155	2159	2201	2218	0.5	66	823	847	860	0.7	2.60	619	632	0.5
67544 HOISINGTON	009	3689	3602	3493	-0.6	19	1536	1519	1491	-0.3	2.31	1004	983	-0.5
67545 HUDSON	185	311	302	296	-0.7	15	135	132	130	-0.5	2.29	94	92	-0.5
67546 INMAN	113	2467	2475	2521	0.1	53	904	913	936	0.2	2.62	691	693	0.1
67547 KINSLEY	047	2012	1934	1867	-0.9	9	899	873	849	-0.7	2.15	540	519	-0.9
67548 LA CROSSE	165	1475	1471	1460	-0.1	46	629	635	638	0.2	2.18	408	408	0.0
67550 LARNED	145	6301	6175	6041	-0.5	26	2357	2323	2282	-0.3	2.27	1506	1471	-0.6
67552 LEWIS	047	770	754	734	-0.5	24	287	282	275	-0.4	2.67	213	208	-0.6
67553 LIEBENTHAL	165	211	205	200	-0.7	16	89	87	86	-0.5	2.36	59	57	-0.8
67554 LYONS	159	4955	4776	4636	-0.9	10	1968	1899	1847	-0.8	2.46	1371	1312	-1.0
67556 MC CRACKEN	165	304	295	289	-0.7	15	145	142	140	-0.5	2.08	96	93	-0.7
67557 MACKSVILLE	185	770	759	749	-0.3	32	288	285	284	-0.3	2.66	209	205	-0.5
67559 NEKOMA	165	65	63	62	-0.7	14	31	30	30	-0.8	2.10	20	20	0.0
67560 NESS CITY	135	1977	1968	1968	-0.1	43	873	888	898	0.4	2.16	556	560	0.2
67561 NICKERSON	155	1664	1706	1723	0.6	69	630	655	667	0.9	2.60	487	503	0.8
67563 OFFERLE	047	338	340	334	0.1	55	133	134	133	0.2	2.54	102	103	0.2
67564 OLMITZ	009	266	263	256	-0.3	36	107	107	106	0.0	2.46	80	80	0.0
67565 OTIS	165	591	582	573	-0.4	32	257	256	255	-0.1	2.27	169	167	-0.3
67566 PARTRIDGE	155	689	724	741	1.2	82	234	248	255	1.4	2.92	187	197	1.2
67567 PAWNEE ROCK	009	544	555	548	0.5	67	189	196	197	0.9	2.83	138	142	0.7
67568 PLEVNA	155	287	276	271	-0.9	9	129	126	124	-0.6	2.19	98	94	-1.0
67570 PRETTY PRAIRIE	155	1094	1175	1214	1.7	88	438	475	494	1.9	2.47	331	356	1.7
67572 RANSOM	135	479	473	470	-0.3	33	199	199	199	0.0	2.31	130	129	-0.2
67573 RAYMOND	159	207	241	256	3.6	97	88	103	110	3.8	2.34	67	78	3.6
67574 ROZEL	145	262	257	250	-0.5	27	108	107	105	-0.2	2.40	79	78	-0.3
67575 RUSH CENTER	165	447	434	426	-0.7	15	208	205	203	-0.3	2.12	137	134	-0.5
67576 SAINT JOHN	185	2197	2161	2128	-0.4	30	920	912	906	-0.2	2.34	590	579	-0.4
67578 STAFFORD	185	1496	1465	1441	-0.5	24	661	653	647	-0.3	2.17	398	389	-0.5
67579 STERLING	155	3086	3017	2957	-0.5	21	991	970	952	-0.5	2.36	674	653	-0.7
67581 SYLVIA	155	513	506	501	-0.3	33	205	204	203	-0.1	2.48	144	141	-0.5
67583 TURON	155	1189	1219	1233	0.6	69	492	509	519	0.8	2.39	353	363	0.5
67584 UTICA	135	345	341	339	-0.3	36	143	143	143	0.0	2.30	93	92	-0.3
67601 HAYS	051	23250	23181	23108	-0.1	46	9448	9567	9657	0.3	2.31	5572	5579	0.0
67621 AGRA	147	599	590	583	-0.4	32	241	238	237	-0.3	2.48	180	176	-0.5
KANSAS					0.7					1.0	2.49			0.8
UNITED STATES					1.2					1.3	2.58			1.1

ZIP CODE #	POST OFFICE NAME	RACE (%) White 2000	White 2004	Black 2000	Black 2004	Asian/Pacific 2000	Asian/Pacific 2004	% Hispanic Origin 2000	% Hispanic Origin 2004	2004 AGE DISTRIBUTION (%) 0-4	5-9	10-14	15-19	20-24	25-44	45-64	65-84	85+	18+	MEDIAN AGE 2004	% 2004 Males	% 2004 Females
67438	DURHAM	96.4	95.8	0.0	0.0	0.0	0.0	3.9	4.6	8.2	8.5	9.8	5.9	5.6	23.5	22.6	14.1	2.0	69.6	35.8	54.6	45.4
67439	ELLSWORTH	90.2	90.0	6.2	6.4	0.4	0.4	3.6	3.7	4.3	4.5	5.4	6.3	7.4	28.4	25.4	14.3	4.1	82.1	41.2	56.6	43.4
67441	ENTERPRISE	96.8	96.6	0.2	0.2	0.1	0.1	1.4	1.8	5.6	6.2	7.4	7.3	5.5	24.5	25.2	15.1	3.2	75.8	40.9	48.1	51.9
67442	FALUN	97.3	97.4	0.0	0.0	0.4	0.4	5.0	6.0	6.8	7.2	6.8	7.2	6.4	24.9	30.6	9.8	0.4	74.7	40.3	50.2	49.8
67443	GALVA	97.8	97.4	0.1	0.1	0.5	0.6	0.8	1.1	7.2	7.6	7.8	6.8	6.2	26.1	26.7	11.0	0.7	73.2	37.4	50.7	49.3
67444	GENESEO	98.1	97.8	0.0	0.0	0.2	0.2	1.7	2.2	3.4	4.3	7.6	8.6	4.1	21.2	30.8	17.6	2.3	78.8	45.4	50.4	49.6
67445	GLASCO	98.8	98.6	0.0	0.0	0.2	0.2	0.2	0.2	4.1	4.7	5.9	6.2	4.5	19.5	28.1	20.6	6.4	81.0	48.4	50.4	49.6
67446	GLEN ELDER	97.8	97.4	0.3	0.3	0.3	0.5	0.6	1.0	4.7	5.0	5.7	6.7	5.7	20.0	27.6	21.8	2.9	80.4	46.5	50.3	49.7
67447	GREEN	97.8	97.8	0.6	0.6	0.0	0.0	0.9	0.9	5.0	5.9	7.8	7.2	5.3	23.4	29.3	14.6	1.6	77.3	42.0	50.8	49.2
67448	GYPSUM	97.5	97.3	0.4	0.4	0.4	0.4	1.1	1.2	5.6	6.1	7.8	6.9	4.8	23.1	30.3	13.6	1.9	76.2	42.3	51.3	48.7
67449	HERINGTON	95.8	95.4	0.9	0.9	0.5	0.6	3.7	4.5	5.6	5.7	7.3	6.3	5.8	22.9	23.7	18.5	4.2	77.3	42.5	48.4	51.6
67450	HOLYROOD	98.0	98.0	0.5	0.5	0.0	0.0	1.8	2.1	4.3	5.4	7.9	8.9	4.8	22.0	27.1	17.1	2.5	75.3	43.1	49.7	50.3
67451	HOPE	98.1	98.0	0.3	0.3	0.3	0.4	0.6	0.8	4.3	4.9	7.8	6.7	5.7	22.1	29.5	16.2	2.7	78.8	44.1	52.2	47.8
67452	HUNTER	99.2	99.2	0.0	0.0	0.0	0.0	0.0	0.0	4.0	4.8	8.8	8.0	4.0	20.8	28.8	18.4	2.4	77.6	44.8	50.4	49.6
67454	KANOPOLIS	96.1	96.0	0.3	0.3	0.2	0.2	10.4	10.8	3.0	5.0	6.6	7.1	6.5	21.0	29.7	18.5	2.7	79.7	45.5	50.0	50.0
67455	LINCOLN	98.0	98.0	0.2	0.2	0.2	0.2	1.1	1.1	5.8	5.8	5.6	5.9	5.3	20.2	25.6	19.6	6.2	79.0	45.9	47.6	52.4
67456	LINDSBORG	97.2	96.9	0.9	0.9	0.3	0.4	1.8	2.2	5.1	5.0	6.1	9.7	11.8	20.7	23.6	13.9	4.2	79.4	38.2	49.3	50.7
67457	LITTLE RIVER	97.3	96.9	0.0	0.0	0.0	0.0	1.8	2.3	6.8	7.4	8.4	5.4	5.6	24.3	22.2	14.9	5.1	74.2	39.9	47.7	52.3
67458	LONGFORD	98.3	98.3	0.4	0.4	0.0	0.0	0.7	0.7	6.3	6.7	7.0	5.3	4.9	24.2	29.5	14.0	2.1	76.5	42.3	55.1	44.9
67459	LORRAINE	98.1	98.2	0.4	0.4	0.0	0.0	1.9	1.9	4.1	5.5	7.8	8.9	4.4	22.5	27.3	17.3	2.2	76.0	43.2	49.8	50.2
67460	MCPHERSON	95.4	94.9	1.2	1.2	0.5	0.6	2.6	3.2	6.5	6.1	7.1	8.0	8.7	24.3	24.0	12.7	2.5	75.8	37.1	48.9	51.1
67464	MARQUETTE	98.8	98.7	0.0	0.0	0.1	0.1	0.8	0.9	5.0	5.4	6.4	6.0	5.4	23.6	28.6	15.7	3.8	79.0	43.8	50.4	49.6
67466	MILTONVALE	98.5	98.4	0.1	0.1	0.1	0.1	1.0	1.3	3.7	4.3	7.0	8.2	7.3	20.5	24.9	17.9	6.2	79.2	44.3	50.1	49.9
67467	MINNEAPOLIS	97.4	97.1	0.8	0.9	0.1	0.1	1.4	1.7	5.6	5.6	6.4	6.6	6.1	23.5	26.1	15.3	4.8	78.0	42.7	49.1	50.9
67468	MORGANVILLE	97.7	98.0	0.5	0.5	0.0	0.0	1.0	1.0	5.1	6.3	7.8	7.3	5.3	23.0	28.5	14.9	1.8	76.3	41.8	50.8	49.2
67470	NEW CAMBRIA	93.5	93.2	2.5	2.3	0.6	0.6	2.9	3.5	5.8	6.4	7.4	7.4	5.1	24.5	30.5	11.8	1.2	75.5	41.5	51.7	48.4
67473	OSBORNE	98.2	98.0	0.1	0.1	0.2	0.3	0.2	0.3	4.8	5.3	7.4	6.9	5.3	20.4	25.8	18.9	5.2	77.9	45.0	48.5	51.5
67474	PORTIS	97.7	97.7	0.5	0.5	0.0	0.5	0.0	0.0	5.0	5.0	6.9	5.9	4.6	20.6	26.5	19.6	5.9	79.5	46.3	46.6	53.4
67475	RAMONA	96.8	96.6	0.0	0.0	0.0	0.0	3.2	3.9	6.3	6.8	6.3	6.3	5.8	22.8	27.2	16.0	2.4	76.7	42.4	50.0	50.0
67476	ROXBURY	100.0	100.0	0.0	0.0	0.0	0.0	0.0	0.0	7.1	7.1	7.1	7.1	7.1	25.0	32.1	7.1	0.0	78.6	37.5	50.0	50.0
67478	SIMPSON	98.2	97.8	0.0	0.6	0.6	0.6	0.6	1.1	5.0	5.0	6.7	6.7	7.2	23.9	27.2	15.0	3.3	78.9	41.9	52.8	47.2
67480	SOLOMON	98.2	97.9	0.1	0.1	0.1	0.2	1.7	2.3	6.5	7.4	8.8	7.7	5.2	25.8	25.5	11.7	1.5	71.6	39.1	50.7	49.3
67481	SYLVAN GROVE	99.0	98.9	0.0	0.0	0.0	0.0	0.9	0.9	3.9	4.6	6.2	7.4	5.5	20.4	31.4	18.0	2.6	80.6	46.0	51.6	48.4
67482	TALMAGE	100.0	100.0	0.0	0.0	0.0	0.0	0.0	0.0	0.0	0.0	0.0	0.0	0.0	25.0	75.0	0.0	0.0	100.0	50.0	50.0	50.0
67483	TAMPA	96.4	95.9	0.0	0.0	0.0	0.0	3.6	4.6	7.9	8.5	7.7	6.0	5.7	23.2	23.8	15.0	2.2	72.4	37.9	53.0	47.0
67484	TESCOTT	96.4	96.1	0.4	0.4	0.2	0.2	1.7	2.0	6.4	6.5	6.8	7.5	5.3	24.7	28.8	11.9	2.1	75.5	40.7	51.9	48.1
67485	TIPTON	99.0	99.2	0.0	0.0	0.0	0.0	0.5	0.6	4.1	5.0	7.7	7.7	4.4	21.5	28.7	17.9	3.0	78.2	44.8	51.2	48.8
67487	WAKEFIELD	97.1	97.0	0.7	0.7	0.1	0.1	1.1	1.0	6.5	6.5	7.5	7.5	5.8	26.2	25.9	11.4	2.8	74.5	39.1	51.2	48.8
67490	WILSON	98.9	99.0	0.0	0.0	0.0	0.0	1.1	1.2	4.9	5.0	6.8	7.7	5.0	19.1	26.1	19.2	6.3	78.0	46.0	47.6	52.4
67491	WINDOM	98.0	97.8	0.3	0.3	0.3	0.3	0.5	0.3	5.7	6.2	7.1	7.4	4.9	22.7	33.0	11.6	1.5	76.4	42.4	51.7	48.3
67492	WOODBINE	97.9	97.9	0.0	0.0	0.3	0.3	0.9	0.9	6.1	6.4	7.3	7.3	4.2	23.6	29.4	14.6	1.2	75.5	42.0	51.2	48.8
67501	HUTCHINSON	85.8	84.3	5.4	5.6	0.5	0.6	9.6	11.6	7.1	6.5	6.5	7.1	9.5	29.1	22.5	10.3	1.5	76.3	34.1	53.1	46.9
67502	HUTCHINSON	95.5	94.8	1.3	1.4	0.7	0.8	2.8	3.5	5.7	6.1	6.2	6.5	5.5	22.6	27.5	16.4	3.6	78.0	43.3	47.6	52.4
67505	SOUTH HUTCHINSON	93.7	92.6	0.9	0.9	0.2	0.3	5.2	6.4	6.8	6.0	5.0	5.0	5.5	22.9	23.2	18.2	7.4	79.2	44.1	46.1	53.9
67510	ABBYVILLE	98.4	98.4	0.0	0.0	0.0	0.0	0.5	0.5	7.4	7.2	6.3	4.6	4.4	22.0	31.9	14.6	1.6	76.4	43.8	52.1	47.9
67511	ALBERT	98.2	98.6	0.0	0.0	0.0	0.0	1.1	1.4	5.6	6.3	9.7	8.3	4.5	22.6	29.2	12.9	1.0	72.2	40.7	50.0	50.0
67512	ALDEN	97.5	96.9	0.0	0.0	0.4	0.3	2.5	3.1	6.5	7.1	7.1	5.6	5.6	25.1	25.7	15.2	2.2	75.5	41.5	52.6	47.4
67513	ALEXANDER	99.3	99.3	0.0	0.0	0.0	0.0	0.0	0.7	3.7	4.4	6.7	5.2	3.7	20.7	30.4	22.2	3.0	80.7	47.9	54.1	45.9
67514	ARLINGTON	97.3	97.1	0.6	0.6	0.0	0.0	1.4	1.8	6.0	6.9	8.0	6.3	4.8	22.5	25.6	16.8	3.3	75.3	42.5	50.5	49.5
67516	BAZINE	98.0	97.7	0.0	0.0	0.0	0.0	1.6	1.6	3.7	4.4	6.5	5.6	4.6	21.8	31.0	20.1	2.3	82.2	47.0	52.6	47.5
67518	BEELER	98.6	100.0	0.0	0.0	0.0	0.0	0.0	0.0	5.8	5.8	5.8	5.8	5.8	20.3	27.5	18.8	4.4	76.8	45.4	47.8	52.2
67519	BELPRE	85.7	83.4	0.5	0.5	0.0	0.0	18.8	22.1	7.4	6.9	7.8	6.5	5.5	26.3	24.0	13.4	2.3	74.2	38.2	49.3	50.7
67520	BISON	97.8	98.1	0.9	1.0	0.0	0.0	0.9	1.0	6.7	6.3	6.3	7.0	5.7	20.6	27.5	17.1	2.9	76.9	42.9	49.1	51.0
67521	BROWNELL	97.9	98.6	0.0	0.0	0.0	0.0	1.4	1.4	3.6	5.0	6.5	5.8	4.3	23.0	30.2	19.4	2.2	80.6	46.1	52.5	47.5
67522	BUHLER	98.2	98.0	0.2	0.2	0.1	0.1	1.5	1.9	6.5	6.9	7.5	8.0	5.7	23.7	25.3	12.8	3.6	73.5	40.1	48.0	52.0
67523	BURDETT	97.3	97.6	0.3	0.3	0.0	0.0	1.8	2.1	7.0	6.7	6.3	6.0	6.0	22.1	27.5	16.6	1.8	76.4	42.3	49.9	50.2
67524	CHASE	96.0	95.4	0.0	0.0	0.0	0.0	5.0	6.2	8.0	7.8	8.3	7.2	5.7	22.5	24.9	13.8	2.0	71.7	38.3	48.1	51.9
67525	CLAFLIN	98.8	98.7	0.2	0.2	0.4	0.4	1.1	1.5	5.9	6.6	8.9	7.5	5.8	22.6	24.7	15.3	2.6	73.1	40.8	50.2	49.9
67526	ELLINWOOD	97.1	96.9	0.2	0.2	0.0	0.0	1.7	2.2	6.2	6.2	6.9	7.8	6.2	21.9	25.2	15.9	3.7	75.6	41.9	47.6	52.5
67529	GARFIELD	97.6	97.5	0.3	0.3	0.0	0.0	1.5	2.2	6.8	6.8	6.8	6.8	5.5	22.5	27.4	15.4	2.2	75.7	41.8	50.5	49.5
67530	GREAT BEND	91.2	89.8	1.4	1.5	0.3	0.4	11.2	13.4	6.7	6.6	7.1	7.8	7.3	23.7	23.9	14.4	2.8	75.5	38.5	48.5	51.5
67543	HAVEN	97.6	97.2	0.2	0.2	0.2	0.3	1.1	1.4	7.0	7.4	8.0	7.2	6.2	24.6	25.4	12.4	1.6	73.1	37.6	50.4	49.6
67544	HOISINGTON	95.9	95.2	1.0	1.1	0.1	0.1	3.0	4.0	6.0	6.0	6.9	6.7	6.0	22.7	25.9	16.2	3.5	76.9	41.9	47.9	52.1
67545	HUDSON	98.1	98.0	0.0	0.0	0.0	0.0	1.6	1.7	5.6	6.3	7.0	7.6	4.6	22.5	28.5	15.9	2.0	76.2	43.0	52.3	47.7
67546	INMAN	98.4	98.2	0.1	0.1	0.0	0.0	0.9	1.2	5.5	6.2	8.2	8.1	4.9	22.6	24.0	15.1	5.5	74.8	41.4	49.5	50.5
67547	KINSLEY	95.0	94.1	0.4	0.4	0.5	0.5	6.9	8.3	5.7	5.5	6.0	6.3	6.3	21.6	24.6	19.9	4.3	79.1	44.1	49.2	50.8
67548	LA CROSSE	98.3	98.3	0.3	0.3	0.1	0.1	1.3	1.4	5.4	5.3	5.9	5.9	5.7	20.9	25.2	19.2	6.4	79.6	45.6	47.3	52.7
67550	LARNED	90.0	89.1	5.7	6.0	0.6	0.8	4.5	5.5	5.5	5.7	6.0	8.4	6.2	24.2	25.7	14.6	3.7	77.2	41.1	53.6	46.4
67552	LEWIS	87.5	85.5	0.3	0.3	0.1	0.1	16.1	18.8	7.0	7.0	7.3	6.8	5.6	25.7	24.8	13.3	2.5	74.7	38.7	50.0	50.0
67553	LIEBENTHAL	99.1	99.0	0.0	0.0	0.0	0.0	0.5	0.5	3.4	4.4	6.8	5.9	3.9	20.0	30.7	22.0	2.9	82.0	47.9	53.7	46.3
67554	LYONS	92.6	91.7	1.7	1.7	0.4	0.4	9.6	11.7	6.6	6.5	7.3	7.4	5.8	22.8	23.9	16.5	3.3	74.8	40.7	48.5	51.5
67556	MC CRACKEN	99.3	99.0	0.0	0.0	0.0	0.0	0.3	0.3	3.7	4.4	6.8	6.1	4.1	20.0	30.5	21.7	2.7	81.0	47.5	53.2	46.8
67557	MACKSVILLE	89.5	88.9	0.1	0.1	0.1	0.1	13.1	13.6	6.7	6.9	7.5	7.3	5.5	24.6	25.2	14.1	2.2	74.4	40.0	50.7	49.3
67559	NEKOMA	98.5	100.0	0.0	0.0	0.0	0.0	0.0	0.0	3.2	3.2	7.9	6.4	4.8	20.6	27.0	23.8	3.2	85.7	48.1	54.0	46.0
67560	NESS CITY	97.9	97.9	0.1	0.1	0.1	0.1	1.9	2.0	6.0	6.0	5.8	5.4	5.1	21.6	26.2	18.5	5.4	78.2	45.0	49.9	50.2
67561	NICKERSON	96.8	96.4	0.4	0.4	0.1	0.1	2.4	3.0	7.4	7.4	6.9	7.0	6.2	25.7	26.7	11.4	1.3	73.6	38.5	50.4	49.6
67563	OFFERLE	95.9	95.0	0.0	0.0	0.6	0.6	4.1	5.0	6.2	6.8	7.4	6.8	5.3	22.4	29.7	13.2	2.4	75.3	41.7	53.8	46.2
67564	OLMITZ	96.6	97.0	0.8	0.8	0.0	0.0	1.1	1.1	5.7	5.3	8.0	8.8	4.2	24.3	28.1	14.5	1.1	74.9	41.6	53.2	46.8
67565	OTIS	98.1	97.9	0.7	0.7	0.2	0.2	1.2	1.2	5.7	5.8	6.2	6.5	5.2	21.3	27.8	18.7	2.8	78.2	44.5	49.7	50.3
67566	PARTRIDGE	95.5	95.0	0.7	0.8	0.2	0.3	1.2	1.5	8.4	8.6	8.4	7.0	6.1	23.5	23.9	12.7	1.4	70.3	35.7	50.0	50.0
67567	PAWNEE ROCK	98.5	98.4	0.0	0.0	0.0	0.0	1.3	1.6	5.8	6.1	9.0	8.3	4.5	22.9	29.7	12.8	0.9	72.8	40.9	50.1	49.9
67568	PLEVNA	99.0	98.9	0.0	0.0	0.0	0.0	0.0	0.0	7.3	7.3	5.8	4.4	4.4	21.4	32.6	15.6	1.5	76.8	44.7	51.8	48.2
67570	PRETTY PRAIRIE	97.9	97.6	0.1	0.1	0.3	0.3	1.5	1.9	4.9	6.2	8.6	7.1	5.2	23.1	28.5	14.2	2.2	75.7	41.8	53.5	46.6
67572	RANSOM	99.0	98.9	0.0	0.0	0.0	0.0	0.6	0.4	5.3	5.7	7.0	5.7	5.1	20.7	26.2	19.7	4.7	77.6	45.4	50.1	49.9
67573	RAYMOND	97.1	96.7	0.0	0.0	0.5	0.4	2.4	3.3	6.6	7.5	7.1	5.8	5.4	23.2	26.1	15.8	2.5	75.5	41.5	51.5	48.6
67574	ROZEL	97.3	96.9	0.4	0.4	0.0	0.0	1.9	2.3	7.0	7.0	6.2	6.2	6.2	22.2	26.5	16.7	2.0	75.1	41.9	49.0	51.0
67575	RUSH CENTER	98.7	98.6	0.0	0.0	0.2	0.2	1.1	1.2	3.7	4.6	6.5	5.5	4.4	22.4	25.8	24.4	2.8	81.6	46.8	49.1	50.9
67576	SAINT JOHN	95.4	95.2	0.2	0.2	0.2	0.2	4.9	5.1	6.1	6.2	7.3	7.4	5.6	23.0	25.0	15.9	3.5	75.4	41.5	49.5	50.5
67578	STAFFORD	96.5	96.4	0.1	0.1	0.0	0.0	3.1	3.1	5.2	5.5	6.7	7.1	5.6	18.9	25.9	19.9	5.3	77.8	45.7	47.7	52.4
67579	STERLING	95.7	95.1	1.3	1.5	0.6	0.8	1.8	2.2	5.8	5.1	5.9	11.5	17.6	22.0	19.2	10.7	2.1	80.2	27.5	47.1	52.9
67581	SYLVIA	97.9	97.4	0.0	0.0	0.4	0.6	1.0	1.4	4.9	5.5	8.3	7.1	4.9	21.9	28.7	15.4	3.2	76.9	43.3	52.0	48.0
67583	TURON	96.1	95.7	0.2	0.2	0.1	0.1	3.3	3.9	6.2	6.5	7.1	6.6	5.9	21.6	27.4	16.2	2.4	76.0	42.3	50.5	49.5
67584	UTICA	99.1	99.4	0.0	0.0	0.0	0.0	0.3	0.0	5.6	5.6	7.0	5.9	5.3	21.1	25.2	19.4	5.0	77.4	44.7	49.3	50.7
67601	HAYS	95.6	94.9	0.8	0.8	1.0	1.2	2.6	3.2	5.8	5.3	5.9	10.1	12.5	26.6	20.9	11.0	2.1	78.9	31.1	48.9	51.1
67621	AGRA	98.8	99.0	0.0	0.0	0.0	0.0	0.3	0.3	6.4	7.1	7.1	6.4	4.8	23.2	29.7	12.9	2.4	75.3	41.4	51.0	49.0
	KANSAS	86.1	84.9	5.7	5.8	1.8	2.2	7.0	8.1	7.1	7.0	7.2	7.5	7.6	27.3	23.4	10.9	2.0	74.4	35.6	49.5	50.5
	UNITED STATES	75.1	73.6	12.3	12.5	3.8	4.2	12.5	14.1	6.9	6.7	7.2	7.0	7.3	28.6	23.8	10.8	1.7	75.1	36.0	49.1	50.9

ZIP CODE #	POST OFFICE NAME	2004 Per Capita Income	2004 HH Income Base	2004 Household Income Distribution (%): Less than $25,000	$25,000 to $49,999	$50,000 to $99,999	$100,000 to $149,999	$150,000 or More	Median Household Income: 2004	2009	2004 National Centile	2004 State Centile	2004 Home Value Base	2004 Home Value Distribution (%): Less than $50,000	$50,000 to $89,999	$90,000 to $174,999	$175,000 to $399,999	$400,000 or More	2004 Median Home Value
67438	DURHAM	21633	125	32.0	31.2	25.6	2.4	8.8	38822	44687	42	43	105	41.9	19.1	32.4	6.7	0.0	70833
67439	ELLSWORTH	19454	1251	29.9	30.9	31.7	6.7	0.7	41154	47974	50	55	951	39.6	33.4	22.6	4.3	0.0	60338
67441	ENTERPRISE	19942	405	24.9	38.0	28.4	4.9	3.7	42178	48616	53	58	327	32.1	33.0	27.5	6.1	1.2	65435
67442	FALUN	21859	110	25.5	35.5	30.9	7.3	0.9	40000	47401	46	50	93	19.4	33.3	35.5	11.8	0.0	87222
67443	GALVA	19488	583	18.4	38.6	33.6	7.0	2.4	45530	51583	63	71	489	16.2	22.1	46.8	13.3	1.6	106057
67444	GENESEO	25236	260	28.1	31.5	31.2	6.9	2.3	41343	46666	51	56	218	56.9	20.6	15.6	6.9	0.0	41176
67445	GLASCO	17741	279	34.8	37.6	24.4	3.2	0.0	33434	37621	22	12	230	68.7	19.1	8.3	3.9	0.0	36563
67446	GLEN ELDER	21246	263	38.0	30.4	24.0	4.9	2.7	32847	37751	20	9	200	50.0	32.5	14.5	2.0	1.0	50000
67447	GREEN	16761	122	23.8	40.2	32.8	3.3	0.0	41647	47322	52	57	99	41.4	21.2	30.3	7.1	0.0	61250
67448	GYPSUM	21890	546	20.3	35.2	33.9	7.5	3.1	46298	52793	65	73	459	21.4	24.6	38.8	12.9	2.4	95606
67449	HERINGTON	20359	1424	36.5	35.5	21.3	4.9	1.9	34469	39663	26	17	1032	47.0	32.6	16.8	3.0	0.7	52952
67450	HOLYROOD	20458	274	28.8	34.7	30.3	5.8	0.4	40362	46200	47	52	221	54.8	27.2	14.9	2.7	0.5	44474
67451	HOPE	21805	442	26.0	40.3	27.4	5.0	1.4	38921	44743	42	44	369	33.3	29.0	30.4	6.8	0.5	75345
67452	HUNTER	24245	63	28.6	30.2	34.9	6.4	0.0	42367	48669	54	59	52	42.3	19.2	30.8	5.8	1.9	62500
67454	KANOPOLIS	19727	302	29.1	41.1	24.2	5.0	0.7	36167	41747	32	29	256	55.5	27.3	14.1	3.1	0.0	40667
67455	LINCOLN	19674	837	35.5	33.3	24.5	5.5	1.2	35317	40262	29	23	652	50.0	33.9	13.2	2.8	0.2	50000
67456	LINDSBORG	22804	1712	24.0	33.8	31.4	7.8	3.0	45570	51453	63	71	1284	14.8	27.2	44.6	12.3	1.1	101199
67457	LITTLE RIVER	17471	296	30.1	34.8	28.7	5.7	0.7	38405	43301	41	42	244	48.0	25.4	22.1	4.5	0.0	54545
67458	LONGFORD	19491	120	33.3	40.8	13.3	10.8	1.7	34041	39478	24	15	98	39.8	26.5	20.4	13.3	0.0	57143
67459	LORRAINE	16304	97	28.9	35.1	28.9	6.2	1.0	40239	45640	47	51	78	55.1	26.9	14.1	3.9	0.0	44286
67460	MCPHERSON	23709	6314	22.7	30.8	36.0	7.7	2.8	47103	53507	66	77	4549	13.2	25.1	49.2	11.7	0.8	103284
67464	MARQUETTE	23989	430	25.6	30.7	31.6	6.5	5.6	44551	50552	60	66	357	35.9	29.4	24.4	7.8	2.5	68750
67466	MILTONVALE	18826	300	35.7	38.0	18.3	6.0	2.0	31310	37210	16	5	227	61.2	21.2	14.5	3.1	0.0	35750
67467	MINNEAPOLIS	21056	1352	25.2	35.7	31.7	4.8	2.7	41491	47853	51	56	1080	30.5	31.8	29.7	7.5	0.6	74388
67468	MORGANVILLE	16378	147	25.9	40.1	30.6	3.4	0.0	40503	47910	48	53	120	41.7	21.7	30.0	6.7	0.0	59091
67470	NEW CAMBRIA	32986	204	18.6	21.1	34.8	15.7	9.8	63351	74094	87	93	173	12.1	13.3	31.2	39.3	4.1	154464
67473	OSBORNE	21602	855	32.9	37.8	21.4	5.6	2.3	33724	39151	23	14	656	56.3	29.1	11.4	2.4	0.8	43971
67474	PORTIS	25550	98	28.6	43.9	18.4	6.1	3.1	34148	40000	25	15	78	59.0	25.6	12.8	2.6	0.0	38750
67475	RAMONA	21557	84	36.9	28.6	26.2	6.0	2.4	36554	41564	34	30	71	57.8	15.5	21.1	5.6	0.0	45000
67476	ROXBURY	24286	12	16.7	25.0	50.0	8.3	0.0	60000	63023	84	90	10	30.0	10.0	60.0	0.0	0.0	100000
67478	SIMPSON	19561	73	31.5	35.6	26.0	1.4	5.5	40364	46376	47	52	52	51.9	19.2	21.2	7.7	0.0	48000
67480	SOLOMON	21171	645	22.0	28.5	41.4	7.0	1.1	49537	55361	71	79	524	20.2	27.5	38.7	12.0	1.5	92000
67481	SYLVAN GROVE	16909	411	34.3	37.5	24.6	2.9	0.7	33248	37730	22	10	335	53.4	26.9	16.1	3.3	0.3	47051
67482	TALMAGE	24792	4	0.0	0.0	100.0	0.0	0.0	75000	75000	93	96	0	0.0	0.0	0.0	0.0	0.0	0
67483	TAMPA	19773	138	33.3	29.7	26.8	2.9	7.3	38980	45000	43	45	116	45.7	18.1	30.2	6.0	0.0	58333
67484	TESCOTT	18958	361	28.5	26.6	38.5	3.6	2.8	46042	51596	64	73	303	35.0	34.7	22.8	7.6	0.0	59100
67485	TIPTON	20297	156	30.8	30.8	32.1	5.8	0.6	39440	45000	44	47	127	41.7	19.7	30.7	6.3	1.6	62500
67487	WAKEFIELD	21455	485	22.3	35.7	31.8	8.3	2.1	44641	51099	60	67	393	19.3	37.4	38.7	4.6	0.0	84111
67490	WILSON	21750	429	28.9	30.1	31.9	7.9	1.2	42129	48727	53	58	349	50.1	33.2	14.3	2.3	0.0	49886
67491	WINDOM	26011	161	13.7	31.1	44.1	8.1	3.1	53728	60655	78	85	136	17.7	25.7	37.5	17.7	1.5	101250
67492	WOODBINE	18861	130	23.1	40.0	30.0	3.9	3.1	40730	47105	49	53	108	28.7	28.7	31.5	11.1	0.0	82727
67501	HUTCHINSON	17250	10682	36.0	35.6	22.9	4.3	1.3	33545	38994	23	13	6852	43.0	39.3	16.1	1.4	0.2	54898
67502	HUTCHINSON	29303	9556	18.7	29.9	35.2	9.8	6.5	51304	61293	74	83	7452	6.0	26.3	51.9	14.1	1.6	110015
67505	SOUTH HUTCHINSON	20865	1160	37.9	30.7	24.9	4.3	2.2	34573	41361	26	18	728	28.3	36.4	31.2	3.9	0.3	76782
67510	ABBYVILLE	18675	165	23.0	33.9	37.0	6.1	0.0	44243	51050	59	66	136	39.7	29.4	27.9	2.9	0.0	55833
67511	ALBERT	19688	118	20.3	40.7	33.9	5.1	0.0	45000	50877	61	68	97	48.5	32.0	19.6	0.0	0.0	51667
67512	ALDEN	19794	132	28.0	35.6	31.8	3.0	1.5	41551	47854	51	56	110	55.5	23.6	18.2	2.7	0.0	44545
67513	ALEXANDER	19330	59	37.3	30.5	25.4	6.8	0.0	34293	38200	25	16	49	77.6	16.3	6.1	0.0	0.0	23500
67514	ARLINGTON	17761	332	30.1	39.5	26.5	3.0	0.9	35308	41023	29	23	267	46.8	32.6	14.6	4.1	1.9	53696
67516	BAZINE	23756	212	29.7	35.4	24.5	8.5	1.9	38530	45953	41	43	171	56.1	26.9	12.9	4.1	0.0	43824
67518	BEELER	19229	29	34.5	34.5	24.1	6.9	0.0	36125	41132	32	28	23	60.9	30.4	8.7	0.0	0.0	37500
67519	BELPRE	21200	92	34.8	37.0	22.8	2.2	3.3	34356	38267	25	16	74	56.8	25.7	14.9	0.0	2.7	42857
67520	BISON	19878	129	34.9	34.1	24.0	4.7	2.3	34279	39739	25	16	99	63.6	19.2	15.2	2.0	0.0	42059
67521	BROWNELL	20896	60	28.3	35.0	25.0	10.0	1.7	38878	45000	42	44	48	58.3	25.0	12.5	4.2	0.0	42000
67522	BUHLER	24133	709	15.8	32.3	37.9	9.2	4.8	51451	61307	75	83	597	18.8	35.5	36.9	8.7	0.2	85278
67523	BURDETT	23035	141	20.6	36.9	30.5	9.9	2.1	44236	51644	59	65	114	54.4	28.1	11.4	5.3	0.9	46667
67524	CHASE	17338	262	29.0	38.9	27.5	3.8	0.8	37827	43775	39	39	218	75.2	19.7	4.1	0.9	0.0	31667
67525	CLAFLIN	18712	526	28.1	37.3	28.0	4.0	2.7	35958	41774	31	27	434	33.2	35.7	26.0	4.8	0.2	65714
67526	ELLINWOOD	19676	1117	32.9	33.3	25.7	5.5	2.7	35224	41489	28	22	870	41.3	34.1	20.1	4.3	0.2	56847
67529	GARFIELD	21678	131	20.6	39.7	27.5	9.9	2.3	42903	50316	56	61	106	50.9	31.1	13.2	4.7	0.0	49286
67530	GREAT BEND	20802	7650	33.9	32.4	25.2	5.9	2.7	37644	43599	38	37	5377	31.4	34.3	29.2	4.6	0.5	69945
67543	HAVEN	20430	847	21.4	34.2	35.3	7.2	1.9	45137	52888	62	69	667	19.9	33.1	39.9	7.1	0.0	86204
67544	HOISINGTON	18458	1519	34.6	35.4	23.5	5.9	0.7	33820	39310	23	14	1167	49.8	29.4	20.1	0.8	0.0	50227
67545	HUDSON	18106	132	31.1	40.9	23.5	3.0	1.5	35000	39054	28	21	108	44.4	27.8	24.1	1.9	1.9	62000
67546	INMAN	19994	913	21.6	34.7	34.4	7.6	1.8	46093	52291	64	73	761	10.5	26.3	52.8	9.9	0.5	104387
67547	KINSLEY	21424	873	36.7	34.4	21.9	4.1	3.0	33009	38737	21	9	658	56.4	29.9	11.7	1.2	0.8	45059
67548	LA CROSSE	21776	635	33.1	34.0	26.0	3.9	3.0	35974	42352	31	28	488	58.0	23.4	16.6	2.1	0.0	45185
67550	LARNED	21891	2323	27.9	33.3	28.5	6.5	3.8	40449	48044	48	52	1700	37.1	36.5	22.1	3.8	0.4	61808
67552	LEWIS	19464	282	32.3	37.2	24.5	2.8	3.2	35906	42165	31	27	227	55.1	27.8	13.7	0.4	3.1	44524
67553	LIEBENTHAL	17679	87	40.2	26.4	25.3	8.1	0.0	32332	38642	19	7	73	75.3	13.7	5.5	5.5	0.0	25833
67554	LYONS	19772	1899	28.7	33.3	28.7	7.5	1.9	40058	46257	46	50	1430	43.6	33.6	18.9	3.4	0.6	55028
67556	MC CRACKEN	20015	142	38.7	27.5	26.1	7.8	0.0	33623	37714	23	13	118	76.3	14.4	5.9	3.4	0.0	25000
67557	MACKSVILLE	18155	285	29.1	28.8	34.7	7.0	0.4	41773	48096	52	57	224	49.1	25.9	19.6	4.9	0.5	51333
67559	NEKOMA	20516	30	33.3	33.3	26.7	6.7	0.0	37333	40000	37	35	25	68.0	20.0	12.0	0.0	0.0	33750
67560	NESS CITY	22502	888	30.4	34.1	27.6	6.0	1.9	37476	43946	37	36	678	46.8	31.0	19.6	2.5	0.2	53607
67561	NICKERSON	18657	655	23.7	39.1	30.2	5.3	1.7	38933	46868	43	44	525	33.9	40.0	21.7	4.4	0.0	61471
67563	OFFERLE	24178	134	15.7	44.0	29.9	7.5	3.0	45807	52839	63	72	112	41.1	39.3	13.4	0.9	5.4	60769
67564	OLMITZ	18597	107	29.0	33.6	28.0	9.4	0.0	37875	43622	39	39	89	49.4	34.8	15.7	0.0	0.0	50625
67565	OTIS	22109	256	34.4	34.4	24.2	4.7	2.3	34756	41063	27	19	202	61.9	20.8	14.9	2.5	0.0	41429
67566	PARTRIDGE	15291	248	28.2	40.3	26.6	4.0	0.8	38540	45610	41	43	206	34.5	29.1	30.1	5.3	1.0	74286
67567	PAWNEE ROCK	17070	196	20.9	40.3	33.7	4.1	1.0	45182	51693	62	69	162	47.5	30.9	21.0	0.6	0.0	52667
67568	PLEVNA	22563	126	23.0	32.5	38.1	6.4	0.0	45000	54531	61	68	104	39.4	29.8	28.9	1.9	0.0	55500
67570	PRETTY PRAIRIE	22025	475	25.5	32.6	34.5	5.5	1.9	42584	50194	55	60	390	28.7	34.9	30.3	5.6	0.5	73830
67572	RANSOM	19413	199	31.7	34.2	25.6	6.0	2.5	37606	42984	38	37	160	53.8	28.8	13.8	3.1	0.6	45714
67573	RAYMOND	20733	103	28.2	35.0	32.0	2.9	1.9	41279	47538	51	56	86	57.0	23.3	17.4	2.3	0.0	44000
67574	ROZEL	22564	107	20.6	36.5	30.8	10.3	1.9	44647	52159	60	67	87	55.2	27.6	11.5	5.8	0.0	45909
67575	RUSH CENTER	27410	205	30.7	35.6	25.4	4.9	3.4	37171	43453	36	34	171	53.2	27.5	14.0	4.1	1.2	45417
67576	SAINT JOHN	21947	912	30.7	35.6	28.2	3.5	2.0	36593	41767	34	31	698	50.4	28.9	17.3	2.9	0.4	49688
67578	STAFFORD	18621	653	35.7	40.0	19.1	3.8	1.4	32442	37310	19	7	505	66.1	23.6	8.3	1.6	0.4	33472
67579	STERLING	18256	970	29.1	35.5	29.3	4.4	1.8	39647	45523	45	48	712	36.9	28.2	27.5	6.6	0.7	69216
67581	SYLVIA	17828	204	33.8	36.3	24.5	3.9	1.5	35271	39398	29	23	165	57.0	25.5	15.2	2.4	0.0	42813
67583	TURON	17110	509	32.2	39.5	24.2	3.5	0.6	35244	40316	28	23	420	51.0	23.1	22.1	3.3	0.5	48919
67584	UTICA	19186	143	33.6	32.9	26.6	5.6	1.4	36700	42047	34	31	115	53.9	28.7	13.9	2.6	0.9	45500
67601	HAYS	23771	9567	31.9	29.3	27.4	6.9	4.5	39491	48039	44	47	5825	11.5	21.6	51.9	13.7	1.3	108146
67621	AGRA	20245	238	32.8	32.8	26.9	2.9	4.6	34182	39849	25	15	190	50.0	20.0	25.3	2.6	2.1	50000
	KANSAS	25137		23.6	29.0	32.2	10.1	5.1	47540	57348				21.4	24.4	35.0	16.7	2.5	97470
	UNITED STATES	25866		24.7	27.1	30.8	10.9	6.5	48124	56710				10.9	15.0	33.7	30.1	10.4	145905

ZIP CODE #	POST OFFICE NAME	FINANCIAL SERVICES: Auto Loan	FINANCIAL SERVICES: Home Loan	FINANCIAL SERVICES: Investments	FINANCIAL SERVICES: Retirement Plans	THE HOME: Home Improvements: Home Repair	THE HOME: Home Improvements: Lawn & Garden	THE HOME: Furnishings: Computers & Hardware	THE HOME: Furnishings: Major Appliances	THE HOME: Furnishings: TV, Radio, Sound Equipment	THE HOME: Furnishings: Furniture	ENTERTAINMENT: Dine out/ Carry out	ENTERTAINMENT: Sports Equipment	ENTERTAINMENT: Fees & Tickets	ENTERTAINMENT: Toys & Games	ENTERTAINMENT: Travel	ENTERTAINMENT: Cable TV	PERSONAL: Apparel & Services	PERSONAL: Auto Repairs	PERSONAL: Health Insurance	PERSONAL: Pets & Supplies
67438	DURHAM	96	67	35	63	78	87	66	82	76	65	89	98	56	88	69	80	81	81	97	114
67439	ELLSWORTH	79	59	38	56	65	77	63	71	71	61	84	81	56	80	63	75	77	71	85	88
67441	ENTERPRISE	94	66	34	62	77	86	65	80	75	64	88	97	55	86	67	79	80	79	96	112
67442	FALUN	82	70	55	70	74	83	71	77	76	70	92	88	68	91	71	77	86	75	83	92
67443	GALVA	87	77	59	73	82	88	71	79	76	71	92	94	70	94	74	78	88	77	86	102
67444	GENESEO	97	69	38	64	80	89	67	83	77	67	91	99	58	89	70	81	83	82	99	115
67445	GLASCO	71	50	26	47	58	65	49	61	56	48	66	73	42	65	51	59	60	60	72	84
67446	GLEN ELDER	81	61	39	58	67	79	66	74	75	63	88	83	59	83	66	79	80	74	88	90
67447	GREEN	80	56	29	53	65	73	55	68	63	54	74	82	47	73	57	67	68	67	81	95
67448	GYPSUM	99	78	52	75	87	95	75	88	83	75	98	106	69	98	78	85	92	86	100	118
67449	HERINGTON	75	58	39	56	63	74	62	69	68	59	81	78	55	78	62	72	74	68	80	85
67450	HOLYROOD	82	57	30	54	67	75	57	70	65	56	76	84	48	75	59	68	70	69	83	97
67451	HOPE	94	66	34	62	76	86	65	80	75	64	88	97	55	86	67	78	80	79	95	112
67452	HUNTER	87	61	32	57	71	79	60	74	69	59	81	89	51	80	62	73	74	73	88	103
67454	KANOPOLIS	71	53	35	51	59	70	58	64	65	55	77	73	52	73	58	69	70	64	77	79
67455	LINCOLN	72	53	34	51	59	69	57	65	65	55	76	73	51	72	57	68	69	64	77	80
67456	LINDSBORG	89	74	56	71	80	89	74	82	80	72	97	96	69	97	75	83	90	81	93	103
67457	LITTLE RIVER	83	58	30	54	67	75	57	70	66	56	77	85	49	75	59	69	70	69	84	98
67458	LONGFORD	84	58	31	55	68	76	58	71	67	57	78	86	49	77	60	70	71	70	85	99
67459	LORRAINE	82	58	30	54	67	75	57	70	65	56	77	85	49	75	59	69	70	69	84	98
67460	MCPHERSON	91	82	69	80	86	93	81	86	84	80	103	101	79	104	82	85	98	85	91	104
67464	MARQUETTE	101	74	43	69	85	94	72	87	82	71	96	105	63	95	75	86	89	86	103	120
67466	MILTONVALE	70	53	34	51	58	69	57	64	64	55	76	72	51	72	57	68	69	64	76	78
67467	MINNEAPOLIS	86	65	40	61	72	82	65	76	73	63	86	90	58	84	66	76	79	75	89	100
67468	MORGANVILLE	80	56	29	53	65	73	55	68	63	54	74	82	47	73	57	67	68	67	81	95
67470	NEW CAMBRIA	113	128	128	127	128	130	118	120	113	117	141	140	122	147	120	112	138	116	114	135
67473	OSBORNE	81	60	39	58	67	79	66	73	74	63	87	83	58	82	65	78	79	73	88	90
67474	PORTIS	90	67	44	65	74	88	74	82	83	71	98	92	66	92	74	88	89	82	98	99
67475	RAMONA	96	67	35	63	78	87	66	82	76	65	89	98	56	87	68	80	81	80	97	114
67476	ROXBURY	91	81	62	77	85	92	75	83	79	75	96	99	73	99	77	81	92	81	90	107
67478	SIMPSON	87	61	32	57	71	79	60	74	69	59	81	89	51	79	62	73	74	73	88	103
67480	SOLOMON	89	77	57	73	82	88	72	81	77	71	93	96	69	94	74	79	87	79	88	105
67481	SYLVAN GROVE	72	50	26	48	59	66	50	62	57	49	67	74	42	66	52	60	61	61	73	86
67482	TALMAGE	135	94	49	89	109	123	93	115	107	92	125	138	79	123	96	112	114	113	137	160
67483	TAMPA	95	66	35	63	77	86	65	81	75	65	88	98	56	87	68	79	81	80	96	113
67484	TESCOTT	89	62	33	59	73	81	62	76	71	61	83	92	53	82	64	74	76	75	91	106
67485	TIPTON	85	60	31	56	70	78	59	73	68	58	80	88	50	78	61	71	73	72	87	101
67487	WAKEFIELD	79	76	80	78	78	83	77	79	77	76	95	94	75	93	77	75	91	80	79	91
67490	WILSON	82	61	38	58	67	79	66	74	74	63	87	84	58	83	66	78	79	74	88	92
67491	WINDOM	101	96	80	93	100	105	88	96	91	88	111	113	88	114	91	92	107	93	100	119
67492	WOODBINE	87	60	32	57	70	79	60	74	69	59	81	89	51	79	62	72	74	73	88	103
67501	HUTCHINSON	58	55	55	54	56	61	58	58	60	56	74	68	57	75	58	61	71	59	61	66
67502	HUTCHINSON	95	103	108	101	103	110	99	100	97	98	121	115	101	122	101	97	118	99	99	112
67505	SOUTH HUTCHINSON	63	57	58	57	58	66	61	61	64	59	79	70	60	78	61	65	75	62	66	71
67510	ABBYVILLE	87	62	35	59	71	80	62	75	70	61	83	89	54	81	64	73	76	74	88	102
67511	ALBERT	87	61	32	57	71	79	60	74	69	59	81	89	51	79	62	72	74	73	88	103
67512	ALDEN	88	61	32	58	71	80	60	75	70	60	82	90	52	80	63	73	74	74	89	104
67513	ALEXANDER	71	54	35	51	59	70	59	65	67	56	78	73	53	74	59	70	71	65	78	79
67514	ARLINGTON	77	54	29	51	63	70	54	66	62	53	72	79	46	71	55	65	66	65	78	91
67516	BAZINE	88	61	32	58	71	80	60	75	70	60	82	90	52	80	63	73	74	74	89	104
67518	BEELER	81	56	30	53	66	74	56	69	64	55	75	83	48	74	58	67	69	68	82	96
67519	BELPRE	91	63	33	60	74	82	62	77	72	62	84	93	53	83	65	75	77	76	92	107
67520	BISON	76	64	50	64	68	77	67	71	71	65	86	81	63	85	66	72	80	70	78	84
67521	BROWNELL	88	61	32	58	71	80	60	75	70	60	82	90	52	80	63	73	74	74	89	104
67522	BUHLER	116	86	50	81	98	108	83	101	94	82	111	121	74	110	86	98	103	99	117	138
67523	BURDETT	98	68	36	65	80	89	67	83	78	67	91	101	58	89	70	82	83	82	99	116
67524	CHASE	80	56	29	53	65	73	55	68	63	54	74	82	47	73	57	67	68	67	81	95
67525	CLAFLIN	87	61	32	57	71	79	60	74	69	59	81	89	51	80	62	73	74	73	88	103
67526	ELLINWOOD	83	59	32	56	67	76	59	71	68	58	80	85	51	78	61	71	73	71	85	97
67529	GARFIELD	97	68	36	64	79	89	67	83	77	66	91	100	57	89	70	81	83	82	99	116
67530	GREAT BEND	78	65	51	63	69	77	67	73	72	66	87	84	63	85	67	74	82	73	81	88
67543	HAVEN	95	68	38	64	78	87	67	81	76	66	90	98	58	88	69	80	82	80	96	112
67544	HOISINGTON	70	54	37	53	59	69	57	64	63	55	75	73	52	73	57	66	69	63	74	79
67545	HUDSON	75	52	27	49	61	68	52	64	60	51	70	77	44	68	54	62	64	63	76	89
67546	INMAN	79	73	63	72	76	84	73	77	76	71	92	88	71	91	74	78	87	76	83	90
67547	KINSLEY	76	57	36	54	63	74	62	69	70	59	82	78	55	78	62	73	75	69	83	85
67548	LA CROSSE	77	61	43	60	66	77	66	71	72	63	86	81	60	82	65	75	79	71	82	85
67550	LARNED	85	66	48	64	72	84	71	78	78	68	93	89	64	89	71	82	85	78	91	96
67552	LEWIS	94	66	34	62	77	86	65	80	75	64	88	97	55	86	67	79	80	79	96	112
67553	LIEBENTHAL	67	51	33	49	55	66	56	62	63	53	74	69	50	70	55	66	67	61	74	74
67554	LYONS	77	64	52	64	69	77	66	72	71	65	85	83	62	83	66	72	80	72	79	87
67556	MC CRACKEN	67	50	33	48	55	66	56	61	63	53	74	69	50	69	55	66	67	61	74	74
67557	MACKSVILLE	66	68	77	71	69	72	69	69	67	69	84	81	69	82	69	65	81	70	67	76
67559	NEKOMA	70	52	34	50	57	69	58	64	65	55	76	71	52	72	57	68	70	64	76	77
67560	NESS CITY	85	61	35	58	69	80	63	74	72	61	85	87	55	81	64	76	77	74	89	98
67561	NICKERSON	75	64	51	64	68	76	66	71	70	65	85	81	64	84	66	71	80	70	77	83
67563	OFFERLE	111	77	41	73	90	101	77	95	88	76	103	114	65	101	79	93	94	93	113	132
67564	OLMITZ	83	58	30	55	67	75	57	71	66	56	77	85	49	76	59	69	70	70	84	98
67565	OTIS	79	65	48	64	69	79	68	74	74	66	89	84	64	86	68	76	82	73	83	88
67566	PARTRIDGE	81	56	30	53	66	74	56	69	64	55	75	83	48	74	58	67	69	68	82	96
67567	PAWNEE ROCK	87	61	32	58	71	80	60	75	69	60	81	90	51	80	63	73	74	74	89	104
67568	PLEVNA	89	62	33	59	73	81	62	76	71	61	83	92	53	82	64	75	76	75	91	106
67570	PRETTY PRAIRIE	97	70	40	67	81	89	69	83	78	68	92	100	60	91	71	81	85	82	98	114
67572	RANSOM	82	57	30	54	67	75	56	70	65	56	76	84	48	75	58	68	69	69	83	97
67573	RAYMOND	88	61	32	58	71	80	61	75	70	60	82	90	52	80	63	73	75	74	89	104
67574	ROZEL	98	68	36	65	80	89	68	84	78	67	91	101	58	90	70	82	83	82	100	116
67575	RUSH CENTER	94	70	46	68	77	92	78	86	87	74	103	96	69	97	77	92	94	86	103	103
67576	SAINT JOHN	83	65	48	63	71	82	69	76	76	67	90	87	63	86	69	79	83	76	88	93
67578	STAFFORD	67	50	32	48	55	65	54	61	61	52	72	69	48	68	54	64	65	60	73	75
67579	STERLING	79	58	35	55	65	75	60	70	68	59	80	82	53	78	61	72	74	70	83	91
67581	SYLVIA	80	56	29	53	65	73	55	68	64	55	75	82	47	73	57	67	68	67	81	95
67583	TURON	70	51	30	48	57	66	53	62	60	51	71	72	46	68	54	63	65	61	74	81
67584	UTICA	81	56	30	53	66	74	56	69	64	55	75	83	48	74	58	67	69	68	82	96
67601	HAYS	78	74	82	76	74	80	81	78	80	78	100	94	78	98	78	78	97	81	76	89
67621	AGRA	91	63	33	60	74	83	63	77	72	62	85	93	53	83	65	76	77	76	92	108
	KANSAS	92	87	84	87	89	95	89	91	90	88	111	106	87	110	88	89	107	91	92	105
	UNITED STATES	100	100	100	100	100	100	100	100	100	100	100	100	100	100	100	100	100	100	100	100

KANSAS

POPULATION CHANGE

A 67622-67867

#	POST OFFICE NAME	COUNTY FIPS CODE	POPULATION 2000	POPULATION 2004	POPULATION 2009	% Rate	State Centile	HOUSEHOLDS 2000	HOUSEHOLDS 2004	HOUSEHOLDS 2009	% Annual Rate 2000-2004	2004 Average HH Size	FAMILIES 2000	FAMILIES 2004	% Annual Rate 2000-2004
67622	ALMENA	137	614	613	606	0.0	46	254	256	253	0.2	1.32	174	110	-10.2
67623	ALTON	141	311	306	295	-0.4	30	142	141	138	-0.2	2.17	93	92	-0.3
67625	BOGUE	065	361	351	342	-0.7	16	153	150	149	-0.5	2.34	108	105	-0.7
67626	BUNKER HILL	167	255	242	231	-1.2	2	118	114	110	-0.8	2.12	78	75	-0.9
67627	CATHARINE	051	59	57	57	-0.8	11	22	22	22	0.0	2.59	16	16	0.0
67628	CEDAR	183	66	65	64	-0.4	32	23	23	23	0.0	2.78	16	16	0.0
67629	CLAYTON	137	66	63	60	-1.1	5	27	26	25	-0.9	2.42	19	18	-1.3
67631	COLLYER	195	428	412	396	-0.9	9	182	179	176	-0.4	2.30	133	130	-0.5
67632	DAMAR	163	219	214	207	-0.5	20	90	89	87	-0.3	2.40	61	60	-0.4
67634	DORRANCE	167	319	302	290	-1.3	1	140	135	131	-0.9	2.24	93	88	-1.3
67635	DRESDEN	039	122	115	109	-1.4	1	50	48	46	-1.0	2.40	35	33	-1.4
67637	ELLIS	051	2382	2374	2366	-0.1	45	989	1004	1015	0.4	2.30	681	685	0.1
67638	GAYLORD	183	738	725	712	-0.4	28	303	300	297	-0.2	2.37	212	209	-0.3
67639	GLADE	147	298	289	284	-0.7	14	121	118	116	-0.6	2.44	90	87	-0.8
67640	GORHAM	167	503	487	471	-0.8	13	210	206	201	-0.5	2.36	148	144	-0.6
67642	HILL CITY	065	2112	2059	2011	-0.6	18	907	902	899	-0.1	2.21	596	588	-0.3
67643	JENNINGS	039	258	243	230	-1.4	1	124	119	115	-1.0	2.04	86	82	-1.1
67644	KIRWIN	147	342	332	325	-0.7	15	135	131	129	-0.7	2.53	101	98	-0.7
67645	LENORA	137	716	682	656	-1.1	3	306	295	286	-0.9	2.28	215	205	-1.1
67646	LOGAN	147	710	689	677	-0.7	15	287	282	279	-0.4	2.29	199	194	-0.6
67647	LONG ISLAND	147	244	236	231	-0.8	12	103	101	100	-0.5	2.34	76	74	-0.6
67648	LUCAS	167	526	514	499	-0.5	20	219	217	212	-0.2	2.20	146	143	-0.5
67649	LURAY	167	178	169	162	-1.2	2	90	87	84	-0.8	1.93	57	55	-0.8
67650	MORLAND	065	458	434	420	-1.3	2	195	188	185	-0.9	2.31	138	133	-0.9
67651	NATOMA	141	590	580	560	-0.4	29	258	257	250	-0.1	2.26	170	168	-0.3
67653	NORCATUR	039	275	259	245	-1.4	1	124	119	115	-1.0	2.18	86	82	-1.1
67654	NORTON	137	4557	4459	4343	-0.5	22	1679	1651	1616	-0.4	2.40	1064	1036	-0.6
67656	OGALLAH	195	401	385	370	-1.0	8	159	156	153	-0.5	2.47	117	114	-0.6
67657	PALCO	163	344	337	327	-0.5	25	156	155	152	-0.2	2.17	107	105	-0.4
67658	PARADISE	167	169	161	155	-1.1	4	75	73	71	-0.6	2.21	48	47	-0.5
67659	PENOKEE	065	15	15	14	0.0	50	8	8	8	0.0	1.75	6	5	-4.2
67660	PFEIFER	051	25	25	25	0.0	50	9	9	9	0.0	2.78	6	6	0.0
67661	PHILLIPSBURG	147	3504	3502	3484	0.0	47	1483	1498	1505	0.2	2.27	983	984	0.0
67663	PLAINVILLE	163	2860	2782	2694	-0.7	17	1187	1171	1150	-0.3	2.34	787	768	-0.6
67664	PRAIRIE VIEW	147	304	294	288	-0.8	12	126	124	122	-0.4	2.37	94	91	-0.6
67665	RUSSELL	167	5262	5119	4954	-0.7	17	2281	2238	2186	-0.5	2.21	1406	1364	-0.7
67669	STOCKTON	163	2014	1947	1884	-0.8	12	820	800	779	-0.6	2.24	529	511	-0.6
67671	VICTORIA	051	1704	1645	1616	-0.8	11	688	677	675	-0.4	2.30	470	458	-0.6
67672	WA KEENEY	195	2490	2412	2325	-0.8	13	1071	1059	1042	-0.3	2.17	686	673	-0.5
67673	WALDO	167	200	190	182	-1.2	2	93	90	87	-0.8	2.11	59	57	-0.8
67675	WOODSTON	163	275	263	252	-1.0	6	120	116	113	-0.8	2.27	80	77	-0.9
67701	COLBY	193	7056	6948	6833	-0.4	32	2774	2774	2768	0.0	2.40	1789	1772	-0.2
67730	ATWOOD	153	1976	1914	1847	-0.8	13	840	829	815	-0.3	2.24	539	527	-0.5
67731	BIRD CITY	023	771	746	731	-0.8	12	352	343	339	-0.6	2.17	223	215	-0.9
67732	BREWSTER	193	400	422	429	1.3	83	159	171	176	1.7	2.47	121	129	1.5
67733	EDSON	181	258	257	258	-0.1	44	96	97	98	0.2	2.65	77	77	0.0
67734	GEM	193	132	124	120	-1.5	0	52	50	49	-0.9	2.48	38	36	-1.3
67735	GOODLAND	181	6013	6063	6125	0.2	58	2468	2519	2576	0.5	2.35	1567	1584	0.3
67736	GOVE	063	321	314	309	-0.5	22	126	125	124	-0.2	2.51	88	86	-0.5
67737	GRAINFIELD	063	430	419	412	-0.6	18	183	181	180	-0.3	2.31	123	120	-0.6
67738	GRINNELL	063	565	550	541	-0.6	17	244	241	239	-0.3	2.28	163	159	-0.6
67739	HERNDON	153	363	346	331	-1.1	4	164	160	157	-0.6	2.16	117	113	-0.8
67740	HOXIE	179	2197	2171	2150	-0.3	35	872	875	877	0.1	2.43	624	621	-0.1
67741	KANORADO	181	464	456	458	-0.4	28	184	184	187	0.0	2.48	131	130	-0.2
67743	LEVANT	193	150	159	161	1.4	84	58	63	65	2.0	2.52	44	47	1.6
67744	LUDELL	153	136	130	124	-1.1	5	54	53	52	-0.4	2.45	38	37	-0.6
67745	MC DONALD	153	491	467	447	-1.2	3	211	205	201	-0.7	2.28	154	148	-0.9
67748	OAKLEY	109	2509	2493	2486	-0.2	41	1027	1033	1036	0.1	2.36	698	696	-0.1
67749	OBERLIN	039	2680	2594	2487	-0.8	13	1143	1120	1088	-0.5	2.21	738	716	-0.7
67751	PARK	063	315	310	306	-0.4	30	135	135	135	0.0	2.30	103	102	-0.2
67752	QUINTER	063	1437	1433	1422	-0.1	46	557	561	562	0.2	2.46	385	385	0.0
67753	REXFORD	193	325	306	295	-1.4	1	145	139	136	-1.0	2.20	107	101	-1.4
67756	SAINT FRANCIS	023	2394	2391	2380	0.0	47	1008	1016	1019	0.2	2.30	697	695	-0.1
67757	SELDEN	179	753	737	724	-0.5	23	305	303	301	-0.2	2.43	209	207	-0.2
67758	SHARON SPRINGS	199	1096	1083	1075	-0.3	35	439	440	441	0.1	2.40	294	291	-0.2
67761	WALLACE	199	260	259	257	-0.1	44	102	103	104	0.2	2.51	79	80	0.3
67762	WESKAN	199	393	391	389	-0.1	42	133	134	135	0.2	2.92	104	104	0.0
67764	WINONA	109	679	671	667	-0.3	35	264	264	265	0.0	2.53	194	193	-0.1
67801	DODGE CITY	057	29198	30333	31726	0.9	77	9627	9903	10239	0.7	2.99	6946	7092	0.5
67831	ASHLAND	025	1183	1181	1189	0.0	46	504	504	509	0.0	2.30	341	338	-0.2
67834	BUCKLIN	057	900	878	896	-0.6	19	348	339	343	-0.6	2.47	240	230	-1.0
67835	CIMARRON	055	2780	2921	3116	1.2	82	1012	1069	1144	1.3	2.71	764	803	1.2
67837	COPELAND	069	544	643	732	4.0	98	189	225	258	4.2	2.86	146	173	4.1
67838	DEERFIELD	093	1274	1351	1436	1.4	84	408	435	465	1.5	3.11	337	357	1.4
67839	DIGHTON	101	1738	1699	1658	-0.5	21	750	742	733	-0.3	2.26	494	484	-0.5
67840	ENGLEWOOD	025	171	171	172	0.0	50	73	73	74	0.0	2.30	49	48	-0.5
67841	ENSIGN	069	340	371	405	2.1	92	125	137	150	2.2	2.71	102	111	2.0
67842	FORD	057	457	510	552	2.6	94	168	187	201	2.6	2.72	132	146	2.4
67844	FOWLER	119	866	871	876	0.1	55	352	354	354	0.1	2.37	247	246	-0.1
67846	GARDEN CITY	055	37415	37751	38141	0.2	58	11988	12112	12243	0.2	3.07	8935	8963	0.1
67849	HANSTON	083	576	597	622	0.9	76	209	219	230	1.1	2.73	161	168	1.0
67850	HEALY	101	417	407	397	-0.6	19	160	158	156	-0.3	2.56	119	117	-0.4
67851	HOLCOMB	055	2652	2672	2694	0.2	57	794	806	816	0.4	3.32	680	689	0.3
67853	INGALLS	069	906	916	961	0.3	60	303	308	324	0.4	2.97	240	243	0.3
67854	JETMORE	083	1509	1534	1583	0.4	63	587	601	625	0.6	2.49	420	427	0.4
67855	JOHNSON	187	2094	2128	2171	0.4	63	739	758	781	0.6	2.73	544	554	0.4
67857	KENDALL	075	101	101	102	0.0	50	38	38	38	0.0	2.61	25	25	0.0
67859	KISMET	175	1684	1816	1951	1.8	89	533	569	606	1.6	3.19	432	458	1.4
67860	LAKIN	093	3296	3418	3594	0.9	76	1147	1197	1267	1.0	2.82	874	907	0.9
67861	LEOTI	203	2387	2347	2313	-0.4	29	915	915	915	0.0	2.54	681	676	-0.2
67862	MANTER	187	312	310	313	-0.2	41	119	120	122	0.2	2.58	94	94	0.0
67863	MARIENTHAL	171	503	480	465	-1.1	5	176	171	168	-0.7	2.81	145	140	-0.8
67864	MEADE	119	2157	2155	2160	0.0	47	828	827	826	0.0	2.51	588	582	-0.2
67865	MINNEOLA	025	1228	1258	1285	0.6	69	476	488	498	0.6	2.53	345	351	0.4
67867	MONTEZUMA	069	1589	1680	1803	1.3	83	514	545	588	1.4	2.88	382	403	1.3
	KANSAS					0.7					1.0	2.49			0.8
	UNITED STATES					1.2					1.3	2.58			1.1

ZIP CODE #	POST OFFICE NAME	RACE (%) White 2000	White 2004	Black 2000	Black 2004	Asian/Pacific 2000	Asian/Pacific 2004	% Hispanic Origin 2000	% Hispanic Origin 2004	2004 AGE DISTRIBUTION (%) 0-4	5-9	10-14	15-19	20-24	25-44	45-64	65-84	85+	18+	MEDIAN AGE 2004	% 2004 Males	% 2004 Females
67622	ALMENA	79.5	78.3	15.5	15.8	0.7	1.0	4.7	5.7	3.6	3.8	4.2	4.2	11.4	43.1	19.6	8.3	1.8	85.6	35.7	73.1	26.9
67623	ALTON	99.4	99.0	0.0	0.0	0.3	0.3	0.6	1.0	4.9	5.6	7.2	6.5	4.9	23.2	26.1	17.7	3.9	77.8	43.7	51.6	48.4
67625	BOGUE	92.0	91.5	6.7	6.8	0.0	0.0	0.8	0.9	4.3	4.6	7.4	7.7	5.1	25.6	21.4	20.2	3.7	78.1	42.9	52.7	47.3
67626	BUNKER HILL	99.2	99.2	0.0	0.0	0.4	0.4	1.2	1.2	4.6	4.6	4.6	5.8	5.0	22.3	32.2	17.8	3.3	82.6	47.0	50.4	49.6
67627	CATHARINE	100.0	100.0	0.0	0.0	0.0	0.0	0.0	0.0	7.0	7.0	7.0	5.3	5.3	28.1	24.6	15.8	0.0	79.0	41.1	54.4	45.6
67628	CEDAR	98.5	98.5	0.0	0.0	0.0	0.0	0.0	0.0	4.6	4.6	6.2	6.2	6.2	21.5	26.2	20.0	4.6	80.0	45.6	52.3	47.7
67629	CLAYTON	98.5	100.0	0.0	0.0	0.0	0.0	0.0	0.0	4.8	6.4	7.9	6.4	4.8	25.4	27.0	14.3	3.2	81.0	41.5	50.8	49.2
67631	COLLYER	98.4	98.1	0.2	0.2	0.0	0.0	1.4	1.7	6.1	6.6	6.8	5.6	5.3	21.6	29.1	17.0	1.9	77.2	43.8	52.7	47.3
67632	DAMAR	98.2	98.1	0.9	0.9	0.0	0.0	0.9	1.4	7.0	7.5	7.5	6.1	5.1	23.8	23.4	16.8	2.8	73.8	41.1	50.0	50.0
67634	DORRANCE	99.1	99.0	0.0	0.0	0.3	0.3	0.9	1.3	4.3	4.6	4.6	6.0	5.0	21.2	33.1	18.2	3.0	83.4	47.6	51.3	48.7
67635	DRESDEN	98.4	98.3	0.8	0.9	0.0	0.0	0.8	0.9	4.4	5.2	6.1	7.0	4.4	20.0	33.0	17.4	2.6	79.1	46.1	55.7	44.4
67637	ELLIS	98.6	98.5	0.0	0.0	0.0	0.0	1.6	1.9	5.5	5.6	6.7	6.2	5.8	26.4	24.8	15.4	3.7	78.3	41.1	48.2	51.9
67638	GAYLORD	98.2	98.2	0.3	0.3	0.0	0.0	0.8	0.7	4.7	5.0	6.1	6.5	5.1	19.9	28.3	20.3	4.3	80.0	46.7	50.1	49.9
67639	GLADE	98.0	97.9	0.3	0.4	0.0	0.0	0.7	0.7	5.9	6.6	7.6	6.9	4.5	22.8	26.6	16.6	2.4	75.8	42.7	53.3	46.7
67640	GORHAM	98.8	98.8	0.0	0.0	0.2	0.2	0.4	0.6	6.2	6.4	5.8	6.2	6.2	22.8	27.9	16.6	2.1	78.0	42.5	49.7	50.3
67642	HILL CITY	94.9	94.8	3.1	3.2	0.4	0.4	1.0	0.9	4.3	4.7	5.9	6.2	5.8	20.1	27.3	21.6	4.2	81.0	46.9	47.3	52.7
67643	JENNINGS	98.5	97.9	0.4	0.4	0.4	0.4	1.2	1.2	4.5	4.9	6.6	6.6	4.5	21.4	30.5	18.5	2.5	79.0	45.6	54.3	45.7
67644	KIRWIN	98.0	97.9	0.3	0.3	0.0	0.0	0.6	0.6	6.0	6.6	7.8	6.6	4.5	23.5	26.2	16.6	2.1	75.9	42.5	53.9	46.1
67645	LENORA	98.3	98.2	0.7	0.7	0.1	0.2	0.7	0.9	6.0	6.2	7.2	5.4	5.0	24.5	28.2	14.8	2.8	77.3	42.3	51.3	48.7
67646	LOGAN	99.4	99.3	0.1	0.2	0.1	0.2	0.1	0.2	5.2	6.0	6.2	6.5	5.4	18.9	28.9	16.8	6.1	78.1	46.0	47.3	52.7
67647	LONG ISLAND	98.8	98.7	0.4	0.4	0.0	0.0	0.8	0.9	5.9	5.9	5.5	5.1	5.1	22.5	28.0	18.6	3.4	79.7	45.0	52.1	47.9
67648	LUCAS	98.1	98.1	1.1	1.2	0.0	0.0	0.4	0.4	3.7	4.5	6.4	5.8	4.1	16.9	30.7	20.0	7.8	81.3	50.8	47.5	52.5
67649	LURAY	96.6	96.5	0.0	0.0	0.0	0.0	1.1	1.2	4.7	5.3	5.9	4.1	4.7	18.9	25.4	25.4	5.3	81.1	49.4	47.9	52.1
67650	MORLAND	97.4	97.2	1.1	1.2	0.2	0.2	0.2	0.2	6.0	6.2	7.1	5.3	4.6	22.1	27.7	18.4	2.5	77.4	44.1	52.1	47.9
67651	NATOMA	99.3	99.5	0.0	0.0	0.2	0.2	0.7	0.7	5.2	5.5	7.1	6.4	4.8	22.9	26.6	17.6	4.0	78.3	43.9	51.7	48.3
67653	NORCATUR	98.2	98.1	0.4	0.4	0.4	0.4	1.1	1.2	4.6	5.0	6.2	7.0	5.0	21.6	30.1	17.4	3.1	79.5	45.3	54.1	46.0
67654	NORTON	94.3	93.8	3.1	3.2	0.5	0.6	2.3	2.8	5.0	5.1	6.2	6.5	7.0	25.3	24.9	15.4	4.5	79.1	41.7	53.6	46.4
67656	OGALLAH	98.8	99.0	0.0	0.0	0.0	0.0	0.8	1.0	6.0	6.5	7.3	6.0	5.7	21.3	28.6	16.9	1.8	76.9	43.4	51.2	48.8
67657	PALCO	98.3	97.9	0.9	0.9	0.0	0.0	1.2	1.2	7.1	7.1	7.4	5.9	4.8	24.0	23.4	17.2	3.0	74.8	41.4	48.7	51.3
67658	PARADISE	97.0	96.9	0.0	0.0	0.0	0.0	1.2	1.2	5.0	5.0	5.6	4.4	5.0	19.3	25.5	25.5	5.0	81.4	49.0	47.2	52.8
67659	PENOKEE	93.3	93.3	6.7	6.7	0.0	0.0	0.0	0.0	0.0	0.0	13.3	6.7	6.7	13.3	26.7	33.3	0.0	86.7	47.5	46.7	53.3
67660	PFEIFER	100.0	100.0	0.0	0.0	0.0	0.0	0.0	0.0	4.0	4.0	8.0	8.0	4.0	32.0	32.0	8.0	0.0	84.0	38.8	52.0	48.0
67661	PHILLIPSBURG	97.9	97.9	0.3	0.3	0.7	0.7	0.8	0.9	5.4	5.6	6.5	6.8	5.8	22.2	25.2	17.5	5.0	77.9	43.4	48.4	51.6
67663	PLAINVILLE	98.3	98.2	0.5	0.5	0.2	0.2	0.5	0.5	6.4	6.3	6.9	6.9	5.9	23.4	22.5	17.8	3.9	76.0	41.0	48.5	51.5
67664	PRAIRIE VIEW	98.7	99.0	0.3	0.3	0.0	0.0	0.7	0.7	6.1	6.1	5.4	5.4	4.8	22.1	27.9	18.7	3.4	79.3	45.0	50.7	49.3
67665	RUSSELL	97.4	97.1	0.6	0.6	0.4	0.6	1.0	1.2	5.6	5.3	6.2	6.2	5.9	22.2	25.0	19.6	4.0	78.9	44.0	48.4	51.6
67669	STOCKTON	95.0	94.5	2.2	2.4	0.3	0.3	1.8	2.3	5.1	5.6	6.6	7.1	5.5	24.9	24.4	16.4	4.3	77.7	42.1	51.8	48.2
67671	VICTORIA	99.4	99.3	0.0	0.0	0.1	0.1	0.7	0.9	5.9	5.8	5.7	5.9	5.8	24.6	24.4	18.0	4.0	79.0	42.5	49.5	50.5
67672	WA KEENEY	97.5	97.2	0.2	0.2	0.7	0.8	0.7	0.8	5.1	5.1	5.7	7.1	6.3	19.7	25.9	19.7	5.6	79.2	45.7	46.3	53.7
67673	WALDO	96.5	96.3	0.0	0.0	0.0	0.0	1.5	1.1	5.3	4.7	5.8	4.2	4.7	18.4	24.7	26.8	5.3	81.6	49.6	47.4	52.6
67675	WOODSTON	98.6	98.1	0.4	0.4	0.4	0.8	1.5	1.5	4.6	7.2	8.4	6.8	3.8	24.0	32.7	11.0	1.5	75.3	42.4	55.1	44.9
67701	COLBY	97.0	96.7	0.5	0.5	0.3	0.4	1.9	2.3	7.1	6.5	6.9	7.0	9.8	25.3	22.9	12.3	2.3	76.3	34.6	48.0	52.0
67730	ATWOOD	98.5	98.5	0.3	0.3	0.1	0.1	0.5	0.6	4.9	5.4	6.1	6.2	4.8	18.6	27.3	21.3	5.4	79.0	47.6	48.9	51.1
67731	BIRD CITY	97.9	97.9	0.1	0.1	0.0	0.0	3.5	3.5	4.8	5.6	7.9	5.6	3.9	20.2	26.0	21.9	4.0	77.8	46.3	50.4	49.6
67732	BREWSTER	97.0	96.9	0.0	0.0	0.0	0.0	2.5	3.1	6.6	7.6	8.5	6.9	5.2	23.7	27.3	12.6	1.7	72.8	40.1	50.7	49.3
67733	EDSON	96.1	96.1	0.4	0.4	0.0	0.0	3.9	3.9	6.2	7.8	8.6	7.4	3.9	26.5	25.7	12.8	1.2	72.4	38.5	52.1	47.9
67734	GEM	98.5	98.4	0.0	0.0	0.0	0.0	1.5	1.6	7.3	7.3	8.1	6.5	6.5	25.0	27.4	11.3	0.8	72.6	37.5	54.0	46.0
67735	GOODLAND	93.8	93.6	0.4	0.4	0.3	0.3	8.3	8.6	6.5	6.2	6.5	7.2	8.6	24.2	23.7	14.4	2.7	77.3	37.5	51.2	48.9
67736	GOVE	98.1	98.1	0.0	0.0	0.0	0.0	1.3	1.3	6.4	6.7	7.6	6.4	5.1	21.0	27.4	17.5	1.9	75.5	42.8	50.0	50.0
67737	GRAINFIELD	98.6	98.8	0.0	0.0	0.0	0.0	1.6	1.7	5.7	6.2	7.9	6.2	4.5	19.8	28.4	18.6	2.6	76.1	44.7	50.1	49.9
67738	GRINNELL	98.8	98.9	0.0	0.0	0.0	0.0	1.6	1.5	5.6	6.2	8.2	6.0	4.4	20.2	27.8	19.1	2.6	76.2	44.6	50.0	50.0
67739	HERNDON	98.6	98.3	0.3	0.3	0.3	0.3	1.9	2.0	3.8	6.4	7.8	7.8	3.8	18.2	30.4	19.9	2.0	76.0	46.3	52.9	47.1
67740	HOXIE	98.7	98.7	0.2	0.2	0.1	0.1	1.2	1.3	4.9	6.1	8.1	7.5	4.2	21.7	27.0	17.5	3.0	76.1	43.4	49.8	50.3
67741	KANORADO	92.9	92.5	0.0	0.0	0.9	0.9	12.7	13.4	4.0	5.0	9.0	7.0	5.3	23.9	28.7	15.1	2.0	77.2	42.4	52.6	47.4
67743	LEVANT	97.3	96.9	0.0	0.0	0.0	0.0	2.7	2.5	6.3	8.2	8.2	6.3	5.0	22.6	28.9	12.6	1.9	73.0	41.3	52.2	47.8
67744	LUDELL	98.5	98.5	0.0	0.0	0.0	0.8	2.2	2.3	3.9	6.9	8.5	8.5	3.1	17.7	29.2	20.0	2.3	73.9	45.8	51.5	48.5
67745	MC DONALD	98.4	98.1	0.6	0.6	0.2	0.2	1.0	1.1	4.3	6.0	6.9	7.5	4.7	19.3	30.8	18.4	2.1	77.7	45.8	52.9	47.1
67748	OAKLEY	96.7	96.6	0.5	0.5	0.2	0.2	1.6	1.6	6.0	5.7	6.7	7.2	6.3	21.6	25.6	17.6	3.5	77.1	42.6	48.3	51.7
67749	OBERLIN	97.8	97.5	0.5	0.6	0.2	0.3	1.0	1.2	4.7	5.0	6.5	7.2	5.3	19.5	25.6	20.9	5.4	78.9	46.2	48.6	51.4
67751	PARK	97.5	97.7	0.0	0.0	0.0	0.0	0.6	0.7	7.4	7.4	6.5	7.4	6.8	22.3	26.5	14.5	1.3	73.9	40.0	50.3	49.7
67752	QUINTER	97.5	97.4	0.1	0.1	0.2	0.2	1.1	1.2	6.2	6.8	7.3	6.1	5.4	19.2	24.6	18.6	5.7	75.6	44.3	48.0	52.0
67753	REXFORD	98.5	98.7	0.0	0.0	0.0	0.0	0.9	1.0	7.5	7.8	8.2	7.2	6.5	24.2	24.5	13.1	1.0	72.6	36.3	52.6	47.4
67756	SAINT FRANCIS	97.9	97.9	0.1	0.1	0.5	0.5	2.3	2.4	4.8	5.4	7.1	6.7	5.4	20.9	26.1	19.3	4.4	78.6	44.9	50.1	49.9
67757	SELDEN	98.5	98.5	0.1	0.1	0.5	0.5	2.0	2.0	6.1	6.4	6.8	7.1	4.9	24.2	25.8	16.6	2.3	76.1	41.8	52.7	47.4
67758	SHARON SPRINGS	95.5	95.4	0.4	0.4	0.3	0.3	4.3	4.5	5.6	6.3	7.9	6.5	5.7	22.7	24.5	17.2	3.6	76.0	42.2	49.0	51.0
67761	WALLACE	93.1	93.1	1.2	1.2	0.0	0.0	5.4	5.8	6.6	8.9	9.7	10.0	2.3	23.6	25.9	11.6	1.5	68.0	38.0	52.9	47.1
67762	WESKAN	93.1	93.1	1.0	1.0	0.0	0.0	5.6	5.9	6.7	9.0	9.5	10.0	2.6	23.5	26.1	11.5	1.3	68.0	37.8	51.9	48.1
67764	WINONA	97.2	97.2	0.7	0.8	0.4	0.5	1.8	1.9	8.9	6.3	7.0	8.1	6.0	24.6	22.7	14.9	1.6	72.7	37.6	50.8	49.2
67801	DODGE CITY	72.5	69.5	1.8	1.7	2.4	2.8	41.2	46.2	9.9	8.6	8.2	7.8	8.5	29.0	18.0	8.3	1.6	68.8	29.3	51.8	48.2
67831	ASHLAND	94.6	94.4	0.2	0.2	0.1	0.1	4.3	4.5	6.9	7.2	7.0	5.8	4.8	21.0	26.8	16.7	3.9	75.0	43.1	50.0	50.0
67834	BUCKLIN	95.7	94.8	0.3	0.3	0.3	0.5	3.3	4.4	6.6	6.5	6.2	7.0	6.7	22.8	25.5	14.6	4.2	75.7	41.0	49.5	50.5
67835	CIMARRON	92.6	91.3	0.3	0.3	0.2	0.3	9.8	11.8	7.8	7.8	9.2	7.5	6.5	27.4	24.3	8.1	1.5	70.3	33.8	49.5	50.5
67837	COPELAND	91.5	90.4	0.0	0.0	0.0	0.0	9.0	10.7	8.2	8.1	8.9	9.3	6.4	28.3	21.8	8.2	0.8	68.6	31.9	53.3	46.7
67838	DEERFIELD	76.7	73.5	0.2	0.2	0.5	0.6	30.8	35.2	10.1	10.1	9.8	7.3	5.7	26.9	21.0	8.6	0.7	65.4	31.0	52.7	47.3
67839	DIGHTON	97.6	97.6	0.0	0.0	0.2	0.2	1.5	1.5	5.4	5.7	6.9	6.3	5.7	23.1	26.4	16.7	4.0	77.5	43.1	50.6	49.4
67840	ENGLEWOOD	94.2	94.2	0.0	0.0	0.0	0.0	4.1	4.7	7.0	7.6	7.0	5.9	4.7	21.1	26.3	16.4	4.1	74.3	42.7	49.1	50.9
67841	ENSIGN	91.2	90.0	0.0	0.0	0.3	0.3	12.1	14.0	8.9	8.4	8.4	7.0	5.9	28.8	24.5	7.3	0.8	69.5	32.7	51.5	48.5
67842	FORD	95.8	94.9	0.4	0.4	0.0	0.0	6.1	8.0	7.3	7.1	7.3	6.1	5.9	27.1	25.1	12.8	1.6	74.7	38.1	51.0	49.0
67844	FOWLER	94.8	94.7	0.2	0.2	0.0	0.0	6.9	7.2	6.3	6.7	7.5	6.3	4.8	24.1	22.7	16.9	4.7	75.0	40.9	48.8	51.2
67846	GARDEN CITY	67.8	64.6	1.3	1.3	3.2	3.6	45.2	50.1	10.8	9.3	8.8	7.7	8.4	29.9	17.9	6.2	0.9	66.6	28.2	51.1	48.9
67849	HANSTON	97.4	97.2	1.2	1.3	0.0	0.0	2.1	2.2	4.2	5.5	7.9	8.0	5.7	21.4	29.5	14.7	3.0	77.7	43.4	51.6	48.4
67850	HEALY	98.1	98.0	0.0	0.0	0.0	0.0	1.2	1.2	6.1	6.6	7.6	6.1	5.9	22.9	27.5	14.5	2.7	75.4	41.5	49.6	50.4
67851	HOLCOMB	83.5	80.7	0.8	0.9	0.3	0.3	21.3	25.6	9.4	9.4	10.9	9.9	7.9	28.9	19.8	3.6	0.3	64.2	27.2	50.1	49.9
67853	INGALLS	91.3	89.9	0.1	0.1	0.0	0.0	10.3	12.2	7.9	8.2	10.2	8.4	6.2	28.8	22.1	7.8	0.6	67.8	32.1	52.3	47.7
67854	JETMORE	97.3	97.3	0.8	0.8	0.0	0.0	2.9	3.0	5.6	6.9	9.4	7.6	5.0	23.5	23.0	15.4	3.6	72.4	40.5	48.6	51.4
67855	JOHNSON	83.6	83.2	0.7	0.7	0.2	0.2	25.1	25.8	8.6	8.3	7.9	6.5	5.9	28.9	21.1	11.2	1.6	70.8	34.1	51.6	48.5
67857	KENDALL	89.1	87.1	1.0	1.0	1.0	1.0	12.9	12.9	6.9	6.9	9.9	6.9	5.0	23.8	21.8	15.8	3.0	70.3	37.9	51.5	48.5
67859	KISMET	77.7	74.3	0.5	0.5	0.1	0.1	37.7	44.2	9.6	8.7	8.8	8.3	8.8	28.0	21.3	6.3	0.3	68.0	29.5	52.1	47.9
67860	LAKIN	81.9	79.3	0.7	0.7	0.4	0.4	24.7	28.8	8.6	8.4	9.0	8.3	7.1	25.8	21.2	9.9	1.7	68.3	32.9	50.9	49.2
67861	LEOTI	85.8	85.3	0.1	0.1	0.1	0.1	19.2	19.8	8.5	8.8	7.4	5.5	5.5	25.5	23.3	12.8	2.7	71.7	36.6	51.2	48.8
67862	MANTER	89.7	89.7	0.0	0.0	0.0	0.0	14.4	14.8	6.8	6.8	8.1	7.4	6.5	25.5	25.8	12.3	1.0	74.5	37.1	50.3	49.7
67863	MARIENTHAL	95.6	95.2	0.0	0.0	0.0	0.0	4.2	5.0	7.3	7.7	8.8	7.3	5.8	24.4	28.1	9.8	0.8	71.3	37.5	52.5	47.5
67864	MEADE	94.2	94.0	0.6	0.6	0.4	0.4	5.4	5.6	6.9	6.8	8.2	6.6	5.8	23.0	23.1	16.1	3.7	73.8	39.7	49.1	50.9
67865	MINNEOLA	97.2	97.0	0.3	0.3	0.1	0.1	4.1	4.5	6.0	6.4	8.0	6.4	5.7	22.1	25.1	16.9	3.2	75.0	41.7	49.1	50.9
67867	MONTEZUMA	93.1	91.7	0.1	0.1	0.1	0.2	9.1	11.0	8.6	7.1	7.4	7.0	7.6	23.9	19.8	13.2	5.5	72.3	35.5	47.6	52.4
	KANSAS	86.1	84.9	5.7	5.8	1.8	2.2	7.0	8.1	7.1	7.0	7.2	7.5	7.6	27.3	23.4	10.9	2.0	74.4	35.6	49.5	50.5
	UNITED STATES	75.1	73.6	12.3	12.5	3.8	4.2	12.5	14.1	6.9	6.7	7.2	7.0	7.3	28.6	23.8	10.8	1.7	75.1	36.0	49.1	50.9

#	POST OFFICE NAME	2004 Per Capita Income	2004 HH Income Base	2004 HOUSEHOLD INCOME DISTRIBUTION (%) Less than $25,000	$25,000 to $49,999	$50,000 to $99,999	$100,000 to $149,999	$150,000 or More	MEDIAN HOUSEHOLD INCOME 2004	2009	2004 National Centile	2004 State Centile	2004 Home Value Base	2004 HOME VALUE DISTRIBUTION (%) Less than $50,000	$50,000 to $89,999	$90,000 to $174,999	$175,000 to $399,999	$400,000 or More	2004 Median Home Value
67622	ALMENA	23596	256	34.0	42.2	17.2	2.3	4.3	33265	37548	22	11	209	56.0	23.9	19.6	0.5	0.0	45968
67623	ALTON	17613	141	38.3	37.6	19.9	2.8	1.4	31542	35439	16	5	111	53.2	26.1	10.8	6.3	3.6	46818
67625	BOGUE	21900	150	36.0	40.0	14.7	2.7	6.7	33238	38322	22	10	123	48.0	28.5	21.1	1.6	0.8	52500
67626	BUNKER HILL	29274	114	29.0	28.1	29.0	6.1	7.9	40000	47389	46	50	92	64.1	29.4	6.5	0.0	0.0	35625
67627	CATHARINE	16184	22	27.3	45.5	22.7	4.6	0.0	35000	45000	28	21	18	33.3	22.2	44.4	0.0	0.0	80000
67628	CEDAR	14692	23	39.1	30.4	26.1	4.4	0.0	31099	47380	15	4	19	57.9	26.3	15.8	0.0	0.0	45000
67629	CLAYTON	17065	26	26.9	38.5	34.6	0.0	0.0	37321	46127	37	35	21	57.1	23.8	19.1	0.0	0.0	42500
67631	COLLYER	17292	179	37.4	29.6	29.1	3.9	0.0	32701	38899	20	9	145	47.6	25.5	21.4	4.1	1.4	53500
67632	DAMAR	18881	89	33.7	39.3	22.5	2.3	2.3	34040	39640	24	15	72	66.7	22.2	8.3	2.8	0.0	35000
67634	DORRANCE	27832	135	28.9	28.9	28.2	5.9	8.2	39686	48404	45	48	109	65.1	28.4	6.4	0.0	0.0	35250
67635	DRESDEN	17246	48	35.4	39.6	22.9	2.1	0.0	31784	37308	17	6	38	55.3	21.1	15.8	7.9	0.0	45000
67637	ELLIS	20888	1004	31.4	35.1	26.4	5.8	1.4	37189	45320	36	34	767	35.6	33.8	25.6	5.0	0.1	66214
67638	GAYLORD	17303	300	36.0	30.0	30.0	3.3	0.7	34715	40161	26	18	247	56.7	25.5	14.6	1.6	1.6	45976
67639	GLADE	18273	118	30.5	38.1	26.3	3.4	1.7	38380	44554	41	42	99	58.6	18.2	18.2	5.1	0.0	39643
67640	GORHAM	21109	206	25.7	39.8	22.3	10.2	1.9	41124	48537	50	55	168	35.7	30.4	25.6	7.1	1.2	70667
67642	HILL CITY	22242	902	33.2	35.8	23.4	5.4	2.2	35487	41112	29	24	686	46.4	36.4	16.3	0.9	0.0	53086
67643	JENNINGS	20241	119	34.5	36.1	26.1	3.4	0.0	32487	37319	19	8	95	56.8	23.2	14.7	4.2	1.1	43500
67644	KIRWIN	17673	131	30.5	39.7	24.4	3.8	1.5	37958	44420	39	40	110	59.1	16.4	19.1	5.5	0.0	38571
67645	LENORA	18087	295	28.1	38.0	30.5	2.7	0.7	37899	42989	39	40	239	51.9	26.4	17.2	4.2	0.4	47500
67646	LOGAN	17596	282	31.9	37.2	25.9	5.0	0.0	36164	41483	32	29	230	57.4	25.2	13.9	2.6	0.9	44333
67647	LONG ISLAND	18735	101	28.7	36.6	29.7	4.0	1.0	37869	42961	39	39	83	39.8	30.1	30.1	0.0	0.0	65833
67648	LUCAS	19559	217	33.6	36.9	21.7	6.9	0.9	36371	42600	33	30	180	61.1	18.9	19.4	0.6	0.0	34231
67649	LURAY	19968	87	42.5	36.8	17.2	3.5	0.0	29584	35624	11	3	71	71.8	12.7	12.7	1.4	1.4	26071
67650	MORLAND	22855	188	34.0	29.8	25.5	5.9	4.8	38187	44090	40	41	158	52.5	29.1	16.5	1.9	0.0	46667
67651	NATOMA	16931	257	39.3	37.4	19.5	3.1	0.8	31047	35520	15	4	202	54.0	25.7	11.9	5.5	3.0	46000
67653	NORCATUR	18990	119	34.5	36.1	26.1	3.4	0.0	32487	37319	19	8	95	56.8	23.2	14.7	4.2	1.1	43500
67654	NORTON	18045	1651	34.7	35.5	23.0	4.4	2.5	34204	39194	25	16	1248	39.5	33.1	24.7	2.3	0.4	64057
67656	OGALLAH	16492	156	37.8	28.2	28.2	5.8	0.0	32544	38483	19	8	126	49.2	27.0	18.3	4.8	0.8	51111
67657	PALCO	21160	155	32.3	39.4	23.2	2.6	2.6	35165	40000	28	21	125	67.2	20.8	8.8	3.2	0.0	35682
67658	PARADISE	18231	73	38.4	39.7	16.4	5.5	0.0	31365	38606	16	5	59	66.1	15.3	15.3	1.7	1.7	28500
67659	PENOKEE	20392	8	37.5	25.0	37.5	0.0	0.0	40000	45000	46	50	6	33.3	33.3	33.3	0.0	0.0	60000
67660	PFEIFER	14800	9	22.2	55.6	22.2	0.0	0.0	37278	42288	36	34	7	14.3	28.6	57.1	0.0	0.0	92500
67661	PHILLIPSBURG	21994	1498	29.5	32.1	31.8	2.9	3.7	41241	47553	51	55	1153	36.5	33.3	27.2	2.1	0.9	68988
67663	PLAINVILLE	17833	1171	32.5	41.1	22.3	2.5	1.6	33890	38566	24	14	889	48.5	33.1	15.4	2.4	0.7	51071
67664	PRAIRIE VIEW	18397	124	29.0	35.5	29.8	4.8	0.8	38001	43351	39	40	102	40.2	30.4	29.4	0.0	0.0	64286
67665	RUSSELL	20163	2238	39.4	28.7	22.2	7.7	2.0	33207	40751	22	10	1642	42.6	36.4	17.4	3.6	0.1	56402
67669	STOCKTON	19811	800	33.5	36.4	25.5	3.0	1.6	35196	39553	28	21	608	51.6	27.3	16.8	3.0	1.3	48077
67671	VICTORIA	19350	677	31.8	34.7	27.6	4.6	1.3	36299	43572	33	29	547	27.2	28.2	40.8	3.8	0.0	82805
67672	WA KEENEY	20809	1059	35.0	31.9	26.3	4.7	2.1	35756	42872	31	26	839	42.8	29.7	24.7	2.7	0.1	59167
67673	WALDO	18259	90	41.1	38.9	16.7	3.3	0.0	30000	34526	12	3	73	71.2	12.3	13.7	1.4	1.4	26071
67675	WOODSTON	16663	116	37.1	31.9	27.6	3.5	0.0	33159	35835	21	10	94	41.5	36.2	16.0	1.1	5.3	60000
67701	COLBY	23509	2774	26.3	31.4	28.9	9.6	3.9	43625	52058	58	63	1942	15.5	29.2	44.3	10.1	0.9	95123
67730	ATWOOD	19726	829	34.3	33.4	25.1	5.4	1.8	35871	42732	31	26	625	47.5	28.3	22.1	2.1	0.0	52583
67731	BIRD CITY	21932	343	37.6	31.2	22.5	3.5	5.3	31741	35678	17	6	271	45.4	28.0	17.3	5.5	3.7	58333
67732	BREWSTER	25350	171	24.6	36.3	28.7	7.0	3.5	40677	48911	48	53	140	39.3	23.6	31.4	5.0	0.7	65000
67733	EDSON	22313	97	16.5	32.0	40.2	8.3	3.1	50931	58820	74	82	78	19.2	32.1	33.3	12.8	2.6	88571
67734	GEM	23278	50	22.0	30.0	36.0	10.0	2.0	48207	63110	69	78	40	42.5	20.0	27.5	10.0	0.0	60000
67735	GOODLAND	20295	2519	30.0	33.0	29.3	5.8	2.0	37462	44021	37	36	1795	23.7	37.4	30.4	7.9	0.6	77860
67736	GOVE	19865	125	29.6	32.8	28.8	6.4	2.4	38470	45764	41	42	102	50.0	27.5	16.7	5.9	0.0	50000
67737	GRAINFIELD	24234	181	28.7	32.6	29.3	6.6	2.8	39351	47096	44	47	150	54.0	26.0	16.0	4.0	0.0	46471
67738	GRINNELL	24403	241	28.6	32.8	29.9	6.2	2.5	39833	47580	45	48	200	53.5	27.0	15.5	4.0	0.0	47083
67739	HERNDON	23452	160	35.6	30.6	23.8	7.5	2.5	35000	41446	28	21	131	58.0	16.0	20.6	5.3	0.0	40455
67740	HOXIE	20631	875	29.6	36.2	24.9	5.9	3.3	37971	43425	39	40	719	35.3	30.2	29.1	4.2	1.3	72887
67741	KANORADO	13023	184	40.2	41.3	17.4	1.1	0.0	29156	33147	11	2	143	41.3	47.6	11.2	0.0	0.0	61522
67743	LEVANT	20613	63	25.4	38.1	27.0	7.9	1.6	39433	49311	44	47	52	40.4	25.0	30.8	3.9	0.0	60000
67744	LUDELL	18154	53	37.7	30.2	22.6	7.6	1.9	34289	40000	25	16	43	58.1	16.3	20.9	4.7	0.0	41250
67745	MC DONALD	22480	205	30.2	29.3	30.7	8.3	1.5	41287	48292	51	56	165	55.2	20.6	22.4	1.8	0.0	43462
67748	OAKLEY	20700	1033	30.4	33.4	26.1	8.2	1.8	37104	44604	36	33	777	36.7	34.6	24.2	4.5	0.0	66186
67749	OBERLIN	18705	1120	35.4	39.3	20.5	4.0	0.9	33497	37729	22	12	859	43.4	30.9	24.3	0.9	0.5	57244
67751	PARK	20218	135	30.4	34.1	28.2	5.2	2.2	36694	43971	34	31	107	43.0	28.0	22.4	6.5	0.0	70385
67752	QUINTER	19765	561	29.4	36.4	27.6	5.2	1.4	37599	44188	38	37	450	32.2	35.1	27.6	4.9	0.2	72444
67753	REXFORD	26303	139	20.1	28.8	38.9	9.4	2.9	50827	60000	74	82	111	40.5	17.1	32.4	8.1	1.8	67000
67756	SAINT FRANCIS	21093	1016	30.7	42.0	19.9	5.5	1.9	34640	39273	26	18	780	38.5	27.3	27.4	5.8	1.0	64167
67757	SELDEN	16352	303	33.3	41.9	21.5	2.0	1.3	34892	38889	27	19	250	50.8	22.8	22.4	3.6	0.4	49500
67758	SHARON SPRINGS	20489	440	31.1	35.5	23.4	6.4	3.6	39420	46268	44	47	358	48.0	31.0	19.6	1.1	0.3	51628
67761	WALLACE	23238	103	34.0	31.1	19.4	9.7	5.8	37356	46545	37	35	79	44.3	30.4	20.3	3.8	1.3	55000
67762	WESKAN	20071	134	33.6	31.3	19.4	9.7	6.0	36998	46443	35	33	103	45.6	31.1	19.4	2.9	1.0	53750
67764	WINONA	23189	264	24.6	38.3	25.8	6.1	5.3	39259	47170	44	46	206	49.5	20.9	25.2	4.4	0.0	51111
67801	DODGE CITY	18340	9903	26.0	32.7	30.7	7.3	3.4	43132	50367	56	61	6539	27.8	32.3	34.3	5.3	0.4	77861
67831	ASHLAND	22468	504	29.6	34.1	26.0	5.4	5.0	38917	46624	42	44	402	52.2	29.4	14.9	3.5	0.0	48043
67834	BUCKLIN	21181	339	24.5	35.7	31.3	5.0	3.5	45492	52115	63	70	278	29.5	45.7	18.7	6.1	0.0	67813
67835	CIMARRON	23123	1069	20.6	34.1	32.7	8.1	4.5	46682	54731	65	75	841	25.2	25.6	40.4	8.0	0.8	89156
67837	COPELAND	21317	225	20.9	35.6	32.4	6.2	4.9	43618	51292	58	63	177	28.3	26.6	40.1	5.1	0.0	83462
67838	DEERFIELD	17597	435	23.5	35.4	31.0	6.7	3.5	43498	50079	57	62	344	48.0	19.8	23.0	9.0	0.3	58750
67839	DIGHTON	22906	742	27.6	34.8	28.3	6.3	3.0	39904	46528	46	49	583	43.6	35.2	18.4	2.7	0.2	56148
67840	ENGLEWOOD	22472	73	30.1	34.3	24.7	5.5	5.5	38356	46856	41	42	58	53.5	31.0	12.1	3.5	0.0	47143
67841	ENSIGN	23292	137	24.1	35.8	31.4	4.4	4.4	42786	50513	55	60	110	37.3	25.5	30.9	6.4	0.0	74545
67842	FORD	19730	187	20.3	36.9	33.7	7.0	2.1	45157	52417	62	69	153	37.9	21.6	26.1	12.4	2.0	73571
67844	FOWLER	22489	354	24.0	42.7	25.7	4.8	2.8	39454	45213	44	47	282	40.4	29.4	24.5	5.3	0.4	63077
67846	GARDEN CITY	18541	12112	25.2	33.0	31.2	7.0	3.7	43654	50918	58	63	8099	23.6	24.7	40.8	10.2	0.8	92004
67849	HANSTON	17735	219	25.6	37.4	30.6	4.1	2.3	42438	49024	54	59	182	44.5	24.2	28.6	2.2	0.6	60625
67850	HEALY	20537	158	22.8	36.7	30.4	5.7	4.4	43901	50399	58	64	124	31.5	42.7	24.2	1.6	0.0	66923
67851	HOLCOMB	18042	806	17.1	28.7	44.3	6.6	3.4	52700	62710	76	84	662	9.7	31.6	50.2	7.7	0.9	96105
67853	INGALLS	20462	308	18.5	38.3	28.9	9.4	4.9	44744	52436	61	67	229	28.8	28.8	32.8	9.6	0.0	78600
67854	JETMORE	18890	601	29.6	36.4	25.3	6.2	2.5	38253	43566	40	41	460	40.4	32.6	22.0	3.9	1.1	60556
67855	JOHNSON	22001	758	24.8	31.3	31.7	6.7	5.5	45357	54080	62	70	525	31.8	29.7	31.6	6.9	0.0	76163
67857	KENDALL	19770	38	26.3	36.8	26.3	7.9	2.6	40000	47368	46	50	31	25.8	35.5	35.5	3.2	0.0	78333
67859	KISMET	16646	569	22.9	36.0	30.2	8.6	2.3	44521	52535	60	66	419	44.6	34.4	16.0	5.0	0.0	53879
67860	LAKIN	19359	1197	23.1	34.0	31.3	8.7	2.9	45404	52081	62	70	940	29.4	26.1	37.1	7.0	0.4	82609
67861	LEOTI	20065	915	29.1	33.6	27.0	7.0	3.4	39554	47314	45	48	705	41.1	27.9	27.4	3.1	0.4	61630
67862	MANTER	25926	120	19.2	27.5	37.5	7.5	8.3	51814	60000	75	83	80	25.0	26.3	40.0	8.8	0.0	87500
67863	MARIENTHAL	27479	171	18.7	26.3	35.1	11.7	8.2	56155	67816	81	87	122	25.4	27.9	39.3	5.7	1.6	85000
67864	MEADE	19836	827	27.2	34.6	27.7	9.2	1.3	40186	46900	47	51	620	38.4	34.0	21.9	3.7	1.9	61522
67865	MINNEOLA	20420	488	28.7	31.8	29.9	5.3	4.3	40833	48777	49	54	388	38.7	26.8	25.8	7.2	1.6	70833
67867	MONTEZUMA	22574	545	20.4	36.5	30.8	5.7	6.6	44913	52759	61	68	407	26.5	28.5	38.6	6.4	0.0	83167
	KANSAS	25137		23.6	29.0	32.2	10.1	5.1	47540	57348				21.4	24.4	35.0	16.7	2.5	97470
	UNITED STATES	25866		24.7	27.1	30.8	10.9	6.5	48124	56710				10.9	15.0	33.7	30.1	10.4	145905

ZIP CODE #	POST OFFICE NAME	FINANCIAL SERVICES: Auto Loan	FINANCIAL SERVICES: Home Loan	FINANCIAL SERVICES: Invest-ments	FINANCIAL SERVICES: Retire-ment Plans	THE HOME: Home Improvements: Home Repair	THE HOME: Home Improvements: Lawn & Garden	THE HOME: Furnishings: Comput-ers & Hard-ware	THE HOME: Furnishings: Major Appli-ances	THE HOME: Furnishings: TV, Radio, Sound Equip-ment	THE HOME: Furnishings: Furni-ture	ENTERTAINMENT: Dine out/ Carry out	ENTERTAINMENT: Sports Equip-ment	ENTERTAINMENT: Fees & Tickets	ENTERTAINMENT: Toys & Games	ENTERTAINMENT: Travel	ENTERTAINMENT: Cable TV	PERSONAL: Apparel & Services	PERSONAL: Auto Repairs	PERSONAL: Health Insur-ance	PERSONAL: Pets & Supplies
67622	ALMENA	6	5	2	4	5	6	4	6	5	4	6	7	4	6	5	5	6	5	7	8
67623	ALTON	69	48	25	46	56	63	48	59	55	47	64	71	41	63	49	58	59	58	70	82
67625	BOGUE	93	65	34	61	75	84	64	79	74	63	86	95	55	85	66	77	79	78	94	110
67626	BUNKER HILL	112	78	41	74	91	102	78	96	89	77	105	116	66	103	80	94	96	95	114	134
67627	CATHARINE	76	53	28	50	62	69	52	65	60	52	71	78	45	69	54	63	64	64	77	90
67628	CEDAR	74	51	27	49	60	67	51	63	59	50	69	76	43	67	53	61	63	62	75	88
67629	CLAYTON	75	52	27	49	61	68	52	64	59	51	70	77	44	68	54	62	64	63	76	89
67631	COLLYER	72	50	26	47	59	66	50	61	57	49	67	74	42	66	52	60	61	61	73	86
67632	DAMAR	82	57	30	54	67	75	57	70	65	56	77	84	48	75	59	68	70	69	83	98
67634	DORRANCE	113	79	41	74	92	103	78	96	90	77	105	116	66	103	81	94	96	95	114	134
67635	DRESDEN	75	52	27	49	61	68	52	64	59	51	70	77	44	68	53	62	64	63	76	89
67637	ELLIS	79	62	43	60	67	77	65	72	71	63	85	82	59	82	65	74	78	71	83	88
67638	GAYLORD	74	52	27	49	61	68	51	63	59	51	69	77	44	68	53	62	63	63	76	88
67639	GLADE	80	56	30	53	66	73	56	69	64	55	75	83	48	74	58	67	69	68	82	95
67640	GORHAM	90	63	33	60	73	82	62	77	72	62	84	93	53	82	65	75	77	76	92	107
67642	HILL CITY	82	61	39	58	67	80	66	74	74	63	87	84	58	83	66	78	80	74	89	91
67643	JENNINGS	75	52	27	49	61	68	52	64	59	51	70	77	44	68	53	62	64	63	76	89
67644	KIRWIN	81	57	30	53	66	74	56	69	64	55	76	83	48	74	58	68	69	68	82	96
67645	LENORA	73	51	27	48	60	67	51	63	58	50	68	75	43	67	52	61	62	62	74	87
67646	LOGAN	74	52	27	49	60	67	51	63	59	50	69	76	44	68	53	62	63	62	75	88
67647	LONG ISLAND	79	55	29	52	64	72	55	68	63	54	74	81	47	72	57	66	67	67	80	94
67648	LUCAS	80	56	29	53	65	73	55	68	63	54	74	82	47	73	57	66	68	67	81	95
67649	LURAY	63	47	31	45	52	62	52	57	58	49	68	64	46	64	51	61	62	57	69	70
67650	MORLAND	95	67	35	63	78	87	66	81	76	65	89	98	56	87	68	80	81	80	97	113
67651	NATOMA	69	48	25	46	56	63	48	59	55	47	64	71	41	63	49	58	59	58	70	82
67653	NORCATUR	75	52	27	49	61	68	52	64	59	51	70	77	44	68	53	62	64	63	76	89
67654	NORTON	70	53	34	50	58	69	58	64	65	55	76	72	51	72	57	68	69	64	77	78
67656	OGALLAH	74	51	27	49	60	67	51	63	59	50	69	76	43	67	53	61	63	62	75	87
67657	PALCO	83	58	30	55	68	76	57	71	66	57	78	86	49	76	60	69	71	70	85	99
67658	PARADISE	66	49	31	47	54	64	53	60	60	51	71	68	47	67	53	63	64	60	72	74
67659	PENOKEE	67	48	27	45	55	62	49	58	55	47	65	69	42	63	50	58	59	58	69	78
67660	PFEIFER	74	52	27	49	61	68	51	63	59	51	69	76	44	68	53	62	63	63	76	88
67661	PHILLIPSBURG	78	66	52	63	70	81	68	74	74	66	88	84	64	86	69	77	82	73	85	89
67663	PLAINVILLE	65	55	47	54	58	65	57	62	60	56	73	72	53	70	57	61	68	62	68	74
67664	PRAIRIE VIEW	79	55	29	52	64	72	54	67	63	54	74	81	46	72	56	66	67	66	80	94
67665	RUSSELL	73	55	36	53	60	72	60	67	68	57	80	75	53	75	60	71	73	67	80	81
67669	STOCKTON	75	56	35	53	62	73	60	68	68	58	80	77	53	76	60	72	73	68	81	85
67671	VICTORIA	79	56	32	54	64	74	58	69	66	56	77	81	50	75	59	69	71	68	82	92
67672	WA KEENEY	71	59	45	56	63	74	62	67	68	60	81	76	57	78	62	71	75	67	78	81
67673	WALDO	62	47	31	45	51	61	52	57	58	49	68	64	46	64	51	61	62	57	68	69
67675	WOODSTON	68	48	25	45	56	62	47	58	54	47	64	70	40	62	49	57	58	57	69	81
67701	COLBY	81	81	79	81	82	86	81	82	81	80	100	97	80	102	81	79	97	82	81	94
67730	ATWOOD	74	55	34	52	61	72	59	67	66	56	78	76	52	74	59	70	71	66	80	84
67731	BIRD CITY	77	58	38	56	63	76	64	70	72	61	84	79	57	80	63	76	77	70	84	85
67732	BREWSTER	113	79	41	75	92	103	78	97	90	77	105	116	67	103	81	94	96	95	115	134
67733	EDSON	107	75	39	71	87	97	74	91	85	73	100	110	63	98	77	89	91	90	109	127
67734	GEM	104	73	38	69	85	95	72	89	83	71	97	107	61	95	75	87	89	88	106	124
67735	GOODLAND	75	62	48	61	66	75	66	70	70	63	85	81	61	82	65	72	79	70	78	84
67736	GOVE	90	63	33	60	73	82	62	77	72	62	84	93	53	82	65	75	77	76	92	107
67737	GRAINFIELD	102	71	37	67	83	92	70	87	81	69	95	104	60	93	73	85	86	85	103	121
67738	GRINNELL	101	70	37	66	82	92	69	86	80	69	94	104	59	92	72	84	86	85	102	120
67739	HERNDON	92	64	34	61	75	84	63	78	73	63	86	94	54	84	66	77	78	77	93	109
67740	HOXIE	91	64	33	60	74	83	63	78	73	62	85	94	54	83	65	76	78	77	93	109
67741	KANORADO	61	41	18	35	46	53	39	49	47	40	56	59	33	53	40	51	51	49	61	70
67743	LEVANT	94	66	34	62	77	86	65	80	75	64	88	97	55	86	67	78	80	79	96	112
67744	LUDELL	81	56	29	53	66	73	56	69	64	55	75	83	47	74	58	67	68	68	82	96
67745	MC DONALD	93	65	34	61	75	84	64	79	74	63	86	95	55	85	66	77	79	78	94	110
67748	OAKLEY	89	62	33	59	72	81	61	76	71	61	83	92	52	81	64	74	76	75	90	106
67749	OBERLIN	71	52	31	49	58	68	54	63	62	53	72	73	48	70	55	65	66	63	75	81
67751	PARK	84	59	31	55	68	77	58	72	67	57	78	86	49	77	60	70	71	71	85	100
67752	QUINTER	82	60	38	58	67	79	65	73	73	62	86	84	57	82	65	77	78	73	88	92
67753	REXFORD	105	73	38	69	85	95	72	89	83	71	98	108	62	96	75	87	89	88	106	124
67756	SAINT FRANCIS	81	60	38	57	67	78	65	73	73	62	86	83	57	81	65	77	78	73	87	91
67757	SELDEN	72	50	26	47	59	66	50	61	57	49	67	74	42	66	51	60	61	60	73	85
67758	SHARON SPRINGS	87	64	39	61	73	81	63	76	71	62	84	91	55	82	65	74	77	75	88	103
67761	WALLACE	79	82	95	86	83	87	84	83	81	83	102	98	84	99	84	78	99	84	80	91
67762	WESKAN	79	82	95	86	83	87	84	84	81	84	102	98	84	99	84	79	99	84	80	91
67764	WINONA	106	74	39	70	87	97	73	91	85	73	99	109	63	97	76	89	90	89	108	126
67801	DODGE CITY	80	75	72	74	74	78	77	79	78	80	98	90	75	95	75	75	96	80	75	87
67831	ASHLAND	94	66	34	62	77	86	65	80	75	64	88	97	55	86	67	79	80	79	96	112
67834	BUCKLIN	96	67	35	64	78	88	66	82	77	66	90	99	57	88	69	80	82	81	98	114
67835	CIMARRON	104	86	62	83	92	99	83	95	89	83	107	113	76	105	84	90	100	94	102	122
67837	COPELAND	110	77	40	73	90	100	76	94	88	75	103	113	65	101	79	92	94	93	112	131
67838	DEERFIELD	87	79	61	76	79	84	75	81	77	77	94	94	71	89	74	76	91	81	81	97
67839	DIGHTON	91	65	37	62	74	85	67	79	76	65	89	94	58	86	68	80	81	78	95	106
67840	ENGLEWOOD	94	66	34	62	77	86	65	80	75	64	88	97	56	86	67	79	80	79	96	112
67841	ENSIGN	106	87	60	83	92	99	84	95	89	85	108	112	77	103	84	90	102	94	102	120
67842	FORD	97	68	35	64	79	88	67	83	77	66	91	100	57	89	69	81	83	82	99	115
67844	FOWLER	98	68	36	65	80	89	68	84	78	67	91	101	58	89	70	82	83	82	99	116
67846	GARDEN CITY	82	77	75	77	76	79	80	81	81	83	102	94	78	100	77	77	101	83	76	89
67849	HANSTON	88	61	32	58	71	80	60	75	69	60	82	90	51	80	63	73	74	74	89	104
67850	HEALY	94	66	36	63	76	86	67	81	76	65	90	96	57	87	69	80	82	80	96	110
67851	HOLCOMB	86	90	86	91	88	89	86	87	82	87	103	103	85	103	84	78	101	86	79	98
67853	INGALLS	109	77	42	73	89	100	76	94	87	75	103	113	65	100	79	91	94	92	111	130
67854	JETMORE	80	58	36	56	65	76	62	71	70	60	83	82	54	79	62	74	75	71	85	91
67855	JOHNSON	99	80	57	78	86	97	81	90	88	80	106	104	76	104	81	90	98	89	100	111
67857	KENDALL	93	65	34	62	76	85	64	80	74	64	87	96	55	85	67	78	79	78	95	111
67859	KISMET	85	77	60	74	77	81	74	79	74	76	92	91	69	87	72	73	88	79	78	93
67860	LAKIN	92	73	49	70	79	87	72	82	78	72	94	97	66	92	73	80	88	81	91	105
67861	LEOTI	89	64	36	60	73	83	65	78	75	64	88	92	57	85	67	78	80	77	93	103
67862	MANTER	121	85	44	80	99	110	84	103	96	83	113	125	71	111	87	101	103	102	123	144
67863	MARIENTHAL	140	97	51	92	114	127	96	119	111	95	130	143	82	127	100	116	119	117	142	166
67864	MEADE	91	64	33	60	74	83	63	78	72	62	85	94	54	83	65	76	77	77	92	108
67865	MINNEOLA	94	66	34	62	77	86	65	80	75	64	88	97	55	86	67	78	80	79	96	112
67867	MONTEZUMA	111	83	52	79	92	107	88	100	99	85	116	115	78	111	88	104	106	99	118	126
	KANSAS	92	87	84	87	89	95	89	91	90	88	111	106	87	110	88	89	107	91	92	105
	UNITED STATES	100	100	100	100	100	100	100	100	100	100	100	100	100	100	100	100	100	100	100	100

KANSAS

POPULATION CHANGE

A 67868-67954

ZIP CODE		COUNTY FIPS CODE	POPULATION			2000-2004 ANNUAL RATE		HOUSEHOLDS					FAMILIES		
#	POST OFFICE NAME		2000	2004	2009	% Rate	State Centile	2000	2004	2009	% Annual Rate 2000-2004	2004 Average HH Size	2000	2004	% Annual Rate 2000-2004
67868	PIERCEVILLE	055	175	173	173	-0.3	36	59	59	59	0.0	2.93	48	47	-0.5
67869	PLAINS	119	1608	1628	1642	0.3	62	548	551	551	0.1	2.95	417	416	-0.1
67870	SATANTA	175	2171	2264	2387	1.0	78	722	751	790	0.9	2.97	562	582	0.8
67871	SCOTT CITY	171	4761	4676	4575	-0.4	28	1921	1914	1900	-0.1	2.40	1333	1317	-0.3
67876	SPEARVILLE	057	1246	1222	1248	-0.5	26	462	452	458	-0.5	2.67	347	337	-0.7
67877	SUBLETTE	081	2493	2581	2710	0.8	75	874	908	955	0.9	2.84	688	710	0.7
67878	SYRACUSE	075	2569	2589	2609	0.2	57	1016	1019	1021	0.1	2.50	691	687	-0.1
67879	TRIBUNE	071	1534	1499	1470	-0.5	20	602	599	598	-0.1	2.46	414	408	-0.3
67880	ULYSSES	067	7909	7968	8060	0.2	57	2742	2801	2872	0.5	2.82	2099	2130	0.4
67882	WRIGHT	057	452	443	454	-0.5	26	169	165	168	-0.6	2.67	128	124	-0.7
67901	LIBERAL	175	20469	21248	22371	0.9	76	6771	6990	7304	0.8	2.98	4976	5098	0.6
67950	ELKHART	129	2561	2589	2660	0.3	60	959	978	1013	0.5	2.59	698	707	0.3
67951	HUGOTON	189	4609	4655	4739	0.2	58	1692	1710	1742	0.3	2.69	1221	1224	0.1
67952	MOSCOW	189	854	870	890	0.4	66	296	304	311	0.6	2.86	236	241	0.5
67953	RICHFIELD	129	218	226	235	0.9	76	93	97	102	1.0	2.33	71	73	0.7
67954	ROLLA	129	717	742	772	0.8	74	254	265	278	1.0	2.80	193	200	0.8
	KANSAS					0.7					1.0	2.49			0.8
	UNITED STATES					1.2					1.3	2.58			1.1

#	POST OFFICE NAME	White 2000	White 2004	Black 2000	Black 2004	Asian/Pacific 2000	Asian/Pacific 2004	% Hispanic Origin 2000	% Hispanic Origin 2004	0-4	5-9	10-14	15-19	20-24	25-44	45-64	65-84	85+	18+	MEDIAN AGE 2004	% 2004 Males	% 2004 Females
67868	PIERCEVILLE	83.4	79.8	0.6	0.6	0.6	0.6	20.0	24.9	9.8	11.0	9.8	7.5	6.9	28.9	19.1	6.4	0.6	64.2	28.5	49.7	50.3
67869	PLAINS	85.0	84.5	0.2	0.2	0.1	0.1	20.4	21.1	11.1	10.5	8.7	6.4	5.2	28.1	18.4	10.3	1.3	65.7	30.8	51.9	48.1
67870	SATANTA	83.0	80.4	0.4	0.4	0.6	0.7	28.7	33.4	9.3	9.1	8.6	7.3	5.6	28.6	21.0	8.8	1.7	68.0	31.9	50.9	49.1
67871	SCOTT CITY	95.4	94.6	0.1	0.1	0.1	0.2	6.5	7.9	6.1	6.4	7.4	7.4	5.5	24.1	26.7	13.2	3.2	75.3	40.8	48.7	51.3
67876	SPEARVILLE	97.8	97.5	0.1	0.1	0.0	0.0	5.4	7.0	5.6	6.1	8.4	7.4	6.1	25.1	25.5	13.8	2.1	74.9	39.9	51.5	48.5
67877	SUBLETTE	86.9	85.0	0.1	0.1	0.6	0.7	18.9	22.2	9.7	8.5	8.4	7.3	7.5	26.0	23.0	8.8	0.8	68.7	31.6	51.5	48.5
67878	SYRACUSE	81.4	80.8	0.5	0.5	0.5	0.5	20.9	21.6	7.2	7.3	7.5	6.9	5.6	25.2	23.0	14.5	2.9	73.5	38.1	50.0	50.0
67879	TRIBUNE	93.1	92.9	0.2	0.2	0.2	0.2	11.5	11.9	7.0	7.1	8.7	7.1	4.9	25.7	22.7	14.2	2.6	72.3	39.6	49.9	50.1
67880	ULYSSES	77.0	76.4	0.2	0.2	0.4	0.4	34.7	35.6	8.9	8.7	8.2	8.0	7.7	27.1	21.9	8.5	1.1	69.4	31.8	50.4	49.6
67882	WRIGHT	93.6	92.1	0.7	0.7	0.4	0.5	11.7	14.7	6.3	6.3	7.7	7.0	6.6	26.0	26.2	12.6	1.4	75.2	38.5	51.7	48.3
67901	LIBERAL	64.1	60.9	4.1	4.0	3.2	3.7	42.9	47.4	9.8	8.8	8.4	7.7	8.6	29.8	18.2	7.3	1.4	68.6	29.1	51.2	48.8
67950	ELKHART	89.0	88.8	0.1	0.1	1.1	1.1	13.7	14.1	8.5	7.7	7.0	7.5	7.2	24.3	23.4	12.6	1.9	72.3	35.7	48.3	51.7
67951	HUGOTON	82.4	81.9	1.0	1.0	0.3	0.3	22.1	22.9	8.6	8.1	8.2	7.2	7.1	26.4	21.4	10.8	2.2	70.6	33.7	49.3	50.7
67952	MOSCOW	86.2	85.5	0.7	0.7	0.2	0.2	19.6	20.1	9.0	8.6	8.3	6.6	5.5	27.5	23.7	9.8	1.2	69.9	34.2	50.5	49.5
67953	RICHFIELD	86.7	86.3	0.5	0.4	0.9	0.9	15.1	15.9	8.9	8.9	10.6	5.3	4.9	24.8	23.5	12.0	1.3	68.1	35.4	48.7	51.3
67954	ROLLA	86.8	86.3	0.4	0.4	0.8	0.8	15.3	15.9	8.5	8.9	9.4	5.7	5.0	24.9	24.1	12.1	1.4	69.7	36.4	49.7	50.3
	KANSAS	86.1	84.9	5.7	5.8	1.8	2.2	7.0	8.1	7.1	7.0	7.2	7.5	7.6	27.3	23.4	10.9	2.0	74.4	35.6	49.5	50.5
	UNITED STATES	75.1	73.6	12.3	12.5	3.8	4.2	12.5	14.1	6.9	6.7	7.2	7.0	7.3	28.6	23.8	10.8	1.7	75.1	36.0	49.1	50.9

ZIP CODE		2004 Per Capita Income	2004 HH Income Base	2004 HOUSEHOLD INCOME DISTRIBUTION (%)					MEDIAN HOUSEHOLD INCOME				2004 Home Value Base	2004 HOME VALUE DISTRIBUTION (%)					2004 Median Home Value
#	POST OFFICE NAME			Less than $25,000	$25,000 to $49,999	$50,000 to $99,999	$100,000 to $149,999	$150,000 or More	2004	2009	2004 National Centile	2004 State Centile		Less than $50,000	$50,000 to $89,999	$90,000 to $174,999	$175,000 to $399,999	$400,000 or More	
67868	PIERCEVILLE	18437	59	10.2	50.9	32.2	5.1	1.7	45795	52585	63	72	47	29.8	27.7	21.3	21.3	0.0	78750
67869	PLAINS	18998	551	26.0	29.8	32.9	8.0	3.5	44096	53015	59	65	424	26.4	35.4	32.1	5.4	0.7	74857
67870	SATANTA	19131	751	24.4	35.3	30.6	6.7	3.1	41947	49229	53	58	576	37.3	30.4	24.7	7.5	0.2	65610
67871	SCOTT CITY	25637	1914	26.8	26.4	32.5	8.8	5.5	46673	59504	65	74	1480	23.6	31.4	37.7	5.1	2.2	82128
67876	SPEARVILLE	21489	452	21.2	32.3	34.7	8.9	2.9	47003	54638	66	76	367	18.5	34.6	32.2	13.9	0.8	86974
67877	SUBLETTE	23400	908	18.7	35.5	31.7	9.0	5.1	46426	56159	65	74	715	28.5	25.2	35.4	10.4	0.6	84700
67878	SYRACUSE	19302	1019	31.3	34.9	24.5	6.5	2.8	36850	43050	35	32	774	31.0	37.9	26.2	4.8	0.1	70349
67879	TRIBUNE	25828	599	28.1	30.4	27.2	7.5	6.8	40225	52434	47	51	471	37.8	29.9	25.1	6.8	0.4	67571
67880	ULYSSES	20553	2801	19.9	33.8	34.0	9.3	3.0	46371	55839	65	73	2194	29.1	27.9	31.2	11.7	0.0	83018
67882	WRIGHT	21286	165	20.6	35.8	34.6	6.7	2.4	45558	53028	63	71	119	18.5	31.1	41.2	9.2	0.0	90556
67901	LIBERAL	18018	6990	27.6	31.9	29.3	8.2	3.0	42361	49581	54	59	4590	27.0	33.3	30.7	7.9	1.1	78013
67950	ELKHART	21685	978	23.8	34.3	30.5	7.5	4.0	42861	51098	56	60	749	26.3	36.3	31.6	5.6	0.1	78269
67951	HUGOTON	21471	1710	21.8	29.4	38.0	7.5	3.3	48716	56677	70	79	1333	24.9	30.5	33.2	10.3	1.1	84549
67952	MOSCOW	24691	304	19.7	31.6	34.5	5.3	8.9	48791	57257	70	79	238	27.3	25.6	27.3	16.8	2.9	85333
67953	RICHFIELD	22076	97	29.9	30.9	34.0	3.1	2.1	41238	48208	51	55	70	32.9	32.9	30.0	4.3	0.0	71667
67954	ROLLA	18365	265	29.8	29.4	34.3	3.4	3.0	41679	49352	52	57	190	32.6	33.2	29.5	4.7	0.0	71176
	KANSAS	25137		23.6	29.0	32.2	10.1	5.1	47540	57348				21.4	24.4	35.0	16.7	2.5	97470
	UNITED STATES	25866		24.7	27.1	30.8	10.9	6.5	48124	56710				10.9	15.0	33.7	30.1	10.4	145905

ZIP CODE		FINANCIAL SERVICES				THE HOME						ENTERTAINMENT						PERSONAL			
						Home Improvements		Furnishings													
#	POST OFFICE NAME	Auto Loan	Home Loan	Invest-ments	Retire-ment Plans	Home Repair	Lawn & Garden	Comput-ers & Hard-ware	Major Appli-ances	TV, Radio, Sound Equip-ment	Furni-ture	Dine out/ Carry out	Sports Equip-ment	Fees & Tickets	Toys & Games	Travel	Cable TV	Apparel & Services	Auto Repairs	Health Insur-ance	Pets & Supplies
67868	PIERCEVILLE	75	83	83	84	80	79	79	78	74	80	93	93	79	94	77	70	92	78	69	86
67869	PLAINS	91	74	53	72	79	89	75	83	81	74	98	96	70	96	75	83	91	82	92	103
67870	SATANTA	90	78	61	77	81	89	78	84	82	78	100	96	75	97	78	82	94	83	88	99
67871	SCOTT CITY	99	83	65	81	90	99	83	92	88	81	106	109	77	106	84	90	100	91	101	116
67876	SPEARVILLE	104	73	38	69	85	95	72	89	83	71	97	107	61	95	75	87	89	88	106	124
67877	SUBLETTE	116	88	54	84	97	107	86	101	95	86	113	121	76	109	88	98	105	100	114	135
67878	SYRACUSE	83	63	39	60	70	78	63	73	70	62	83	86	56	82	64	72	77	72	84	96
67879	TRIBUNE	116	81	42	76	94	106	80	99	92	79	108	119	68	106	83	97	98	97	118	138
67880	ULYSSES	92	82	64	79	85	91	79	86	82	80	100	101	75	98	79	82	95	85	90	105
67882	WRIGHT	98	74	48	71	82	90	74	86	81	74	97	103	65	96	75	83	91	86	96	114
67901	LIBERAL	78	72	70	72	72	75	76	77	77	77	96	89	74	94	73	73	94	79	73	84
67950	ELKHART	95	73	48	71	81	91	74	85	82	73	98	100	67	96	75	84	90	84	97	109
67951	HUGOTON	96	78	54	75	83	92	77	87	83	77	100	101	71	98	78	85	94	86	95	109
67952	MOSCOW	128	89	47	84	104	116	88	109	102	87	119	131	75	117	91	107	109	107	130	152
67953	RICHFIELD	93	65	34	61	76	85	64	79	74	63	87	96	55	85	67	78	79	78	95	111
67954	ROLLA	93	65	34	61	76	85	64	79	74	63	87	96	55	85	67	78	79	78	94	110
	KANSAS	92	87	84	87	89	95	89	91	90	88	111	106	87	110	88	89	107	91	92	105
	UNITED STATES	100	100	100	100	100	100	100	100	100	100	100	100	100	100	100	100	100	100	100	100

POPULATION CHANGE

#	POST OFFICE NAME	COUNTY FIPS CODE	POPULATION			2000-2004 ANNUAL RATE		HOUSEHOLDS					FAMILIES		
			2000	2004	2009	% Rate	State Centile	2000	2004	2009	% Annual Rate 2000-2004	2004 Average HH Size	2000	2004	% Annual Rate 2000-2004
40003	BAGDAD	211	1733	1838	2016	1.4	83	641	691	768	1.8	2.66	518	546	1.3
40004	BARDSTOWN	179	23748	25714	28131	1.9	89	8931	9916	11107	2.5	2.55	6411	6912	1.8
40006	BEDFORD	223	4170	4505	4941	1.8	88	1592	1755	1963	2.3	2.54	1167	1252	1.7
40007	BETHLEHEM	103	312	317	329	0.4	55	119	123	129	0.8	2.58	89	89	0.0
40008	BLOOMFIELD	179	3216	3404	3707	1.4	82	1226	1321	1466	1.8	2.57	925	969	1.1
40009	BRADFORDSVILLE	155	1213	1134	1092	-1.6	1	478	457	450	-1.1	2.48	344	317	-1.9
40010	BUCKNER	185	294	360	436	4.9	99	92	115	141	5.4	3.13	79	97	5.0
40011	CAMPBELLSBURG	103	2572	2635	2757	0.6	64	985	1025	1089	0.9	2.57	750	761	0.3
40012	CHAPLIN	179	486	492	516	0.3	53	198	204	218	0.7	2.41	151	152	0.2
40013	COXS CREEK	179	4670	5359	6061	3.3	96	1612	1904	2206	4.0	2.70	1311	1517	3.5
40014	CRESTWOOD	185	15252	17897	21198	3.8	98	5221	6240	7515	4.3	2.86	4436	5211	3.9
40019	EMINENCE	103	3479	3468	3617	-0.1	35	1406	1424	1506	0.3	2.43	977	953	-0.6
40022	FINCHVILLE	211	673	786	899	3.7	98	255	318	381	5.3	1.93	209	255	4.8
40023	FISHERVILLE	111	2214	2723	3236	5.0	99	778	975	1176	5.5	2.74	654	802	4.9
40025	GLENVIEW	111	204	192	191	-1.4	2	79	76	76	-0.9	2.53	58	53	-2.1
40026	GOSHEN	185	4595	5526	6637	4.4	99	1495	1832	2237	4.9	3.02	1299	1567	4.5
40031	LA GRANGE	185	18040	20002	22697	2.5	93	5254	6081	7202	3.5	2.68	4065	4601	3.0
40033	LEBANON	155	11919	11781	11616	-0.3	28	4290	4337	4373	0.3	2.48	3041	2984	-0.4
40036	LOCKPORT	103	364	388	414	1.5	85	146	158	171	1.9	2.46	111	118	1.5
40037	LORETTO	155	2814	2833	2817	0.2	48	1004	1047	1072	1.0	2.58	741	750	0.3
40040	MACKVILLE	229	1512	1544	1571	0.5	61	571	597	621	1.1	2.59	435	443	0.4
40045	MILTON	223	3045	3372	3751	2.4	93	1210	1368	1550	2.9	2.46	878	965	2.3
40046	MOUNT EDEN	215	1224	1543	1995	5.6	100	469	602	788	6.1	2.56	362	449	5.2
40047	MOUNT WASHINGTON	029	12991	14807	16865	3.1	96	4697	5508	6445	3.8	2.67	3775	4340	3.3
40050	NEW CASTLE	103	1808	1897	2003	1.1	79	717	769	825	1.7	2.39	500	520	0.9
40051	NEW HAVEN	179	4276	4535	4890	1.4	83	1564	1714	1898	2.2	2.61	1165	1241	1.5
40052	NEW HOPE	179	343	336	349	-0.5	20	130	131	141	0.2	2.47	100	98	-0.5
40055	PENDLETON	223	1755	2012	2274	3.3	96	636	743	855	3.7	2.71	503	573	3.1
40056	PEWEE VALLEY	185	3142	3389	3841	1.8	88	1100	1217	1409	2.4	2.71	875	941	1.7
40057	PLEASUREVILLE	103	3144	3367	3619	1.6	86	1202	1309	1427	2.0	2.57	899	954	1.4
40059	PROSPECT	185	11321	12974	14485	3.3	96	4132	4751	5339	3.3	2.71	3430	3863	2.8
40060	RAYWICK	155	851	1005	1079	4.0	98	326	398	440	4.8	2.53	237	283	4.3
40061	SAINT CATHARINE	229	52	54	55	0.9	73	14	15	16	1.6	3.07	11	12	2.1
40062	SAINT FRANCIS	155	21	25	27	4.2	98	10	12	14	4.4	2.08	7	9	6.1
40065	SHELBYVILLE	211	21570	23935	26967	2.5	93	8156	9185	10493	2.8	2.55	5933	6494	2.2
40067	SIMPSONVILLE	211	4587	5280	6022	3.4	97	1324	1579	1855	4.2	2.87	1054	1229	3.7
40068	SMITHFIELD	103	1638	1793	1944	2.2	91	600	668	735	2.6	2.68	473	514	2.0
40069	SPRINGFIELD	229	6597	6634	6718	0.1	46	2490	2575	2671	0.8	2.47	1772	1777	0.1
40070	SULPHUR	103	598	671	734	2.8	94	232	266	296	3.3	2.52	185	207	2.7
40071	TAYLORSVILLE	215	10751	13267	16928	5.1	100	3859	4843	6268	5.5	2.71	3091	3796	5.0
40075	TURNERS STATION	103	986	995	1033	0.2	49	377	386	406	0.6	2.58	290	290	0.0
40076	WADDY	211	2575	2704	2974	1.2	79	947	1012	1128	1.6	2.65	761	795	1.0
40077	WESTPORT	185	581	572	647	-0.4	23	235	237	273	0.2	2.41	177	173	-0.5
40078	WILLISBURG	229	2465	2597	2688	1.2	80	930	1004	1062	1.8	2.52	711	749	1.2
40104	BATTLETOWN	163	1090	1011	1015	-1.8	1	424	406	419	-1.0	2.49	321	299	-1.7
40107	BOSTON	179	2353	2571	2815	2.1	90	879	982	1099	2.6	2.61	663	720	2.0
40108	BRANDENBURG	163	8621	9020	9387	1.1	78	3261	3513	3748	1.8	2.54	2474	2594	1.1
40109	BROOKS	029	2981	2977	3209	0.0	39	1125	1164	1293	0.8	2.56	840	844	0.1
40111	CLOVERPORT	027	2908	2982	3111	0.6	64	1134	1191	1270	1.2	2.48	826	842	0.5
40115	CUSTER	027	1016	1092	1169	1.7	87	381	417	455	2.2	2.62	298	318	1.5
40117	EKRON	163	3557	3904	4161	2.2	91	1283	1441	1568	2.8	2.71	1009	1108	2.2
40118	FAIRDALE	111	9300	9075	9104	-0.6	17	3606	3579	3642	-0.2	2.54	2649	2540	-1.0
40119	FALLS OF ROUGH	027	2447	2536	2634	0.8	72	1020	1086	1153	1.5	2.33	767	796	0.9
40121	FORT KNOX	093	12456	11982	11956	-0.9	8	2776	2709	2762	-0.6	3.42	2607	2527	-0.7
40140	GARFIELD	027	1005	1071	1141	1.5	85	373	405	439	2.0	2.64	288	305	1.4
40142	GUSTON	163	1834	1898	1986	0.8	71	659	700	749	1.4	2.71	534	556	1.0
40143	HARDINSBURG	027	3815	3941	4124	0.8	70	1500	1589	1702	1.4	2.35	1039	1066	0.6
40144	HARNED	027	1665	1743	1840	1.1	78	651	697	751	1.6	2.47	459	477	0.9
40145	HUDSON	027	136	153	168	2.8	95	45	51	57	3.0	3.00	35	39	2.6
40146	IRVINGTON	027	2478	2562	2685	0.8	70	1003	1058	1130	1.3	2.42	721	738	0.6
40150	LEBANON JUNCTION	029	4458	4914	5439	2.3	92	1655	1864	2110	2.8	2.64	1255	1376	2.2
40152	MC DANIELS	027	69	73	77	1.3	82	25	27	29	1.8	2.70	18	19	1.3
40155	MULDRAUGH	163	1303	1272	1290	-0.6	17	520	515	531	-0.2	2.47	320	304	-1.2
40157	PAYNEVILLE	163	1553	1607	1692	0.8	71	567	605	653	1.5	2.66	431	448	0.9
40160	RADCLIFF	093	23678	23621	23890	-0.1	36	9101	9301	9603	0.5	2.52	6319	6263	-0.2
40161	RHODELIA	163	141	164	180	3.6	97	53	63	71	4.2	2.60	41	47	3.3
40162	RINEYVILLE	093	2740	2995	3145	2.1	91	960	1071	1146	2.6	2.80	782	854	2.1
40164	SE REE	027	318	338	360	1.5	84	130	141	153	1.9	2.40	93	98	1.2
40165	SHEPHERDSVILLE	029	27781	30328	33595	2.1	90	10103	11330	12881	2.7	2.67	8077	8865	2.2
40170	STEPHENSPORT	027	220	223	231	0.3	54	96	99	105	0.7	2.19	68	69	0.3
40171	UNION STAR	027	646	666	697	0.7	68	228	241	257	1.3	2.76	170	175	0.7
40175	VINE GROVE	163	11160	11665	12086	1.1	77	4049	4325	4572	1.6	2.69	3110	3246	1.0
40176	WEBSTER	027	599	674	731	2.8	95	210	242	268	3.4	2.79	160	179	2.7
40177	WEST POINT	093	1852	1795	1833	-0.7	11	715	715	748	0.0	2.50	502	487	-0.7
40178	WESTVIEW	027	266	281	298	1.3	81	117	126	137	1.8	2.23	83	87	1.1
40202	LOUISVILLE	111	4875	4807	4843	-0.3	25	2475	2450	2494	-0.2	1.68	780	711	-2.2
40203	LOUISVILLE	111	20238	19957	20118	-0.3	25	9038	8965	9137	-0.2	2.01	3869	3619	-1.6
40204	LOUISVILLE	111	15606	15231	15300	-0.6	17	7857	7769	7900	-0.3	1.90	3259	2990	-2.0
40205	LOUISVILLE	111	23798	23307	23459	-0.5	19	10814	10722	10936	-0.2	2.08	5928	5564	-1.5
40206	LOUISVILLE	111	19679	19663	19978	0.0	39	9463	9652	9970	0.5	1.90	4381	4152	-1.3
40207	LOUISVILLE	111	30164	30197	30616	0.0	42	13968	14161	14542	0.3	2.10	7960	7665	-0.9
40208	LOUISVILLE	111	12936	12597	12663	-0.6	14	5978	5877	5973	-0.4	2.02	2559	2339	-2.1
40209	LOUISVILLE	111	486	465	478	-1.0	6	212	204	211	-0.9	2.22	124	113	-2.2
40210	LOUISVILLE	111	16378	15608	15579	-1.1	5	6436	6209	6273	-0.8	2.50	4185	3872	-1.8
40211	LOUISVILLE	111	23773	23161	23257	-0.6	15	9153	9010	9145	-0.4	2.57	6079	5737	-1.4
40212	LOUISVILLE	111	19916	19354	19401	-0.7	13	7245	7132	7236	-0.4	2.71	5036	4764	-1.3
40213	LOUISVILLE	111	18157	18157	18461	0.0	41	7716	7838	8080	0.4	2.27	4833	4679	-0.8
40214	LOUISVILLE	111	45008	46054	47192	0.5	63	18800	19471	20195	0.8	2.35	12072	11988	-0.2
40215	LOUISVILLE	111	24915	24757	25005	-0.2	32	10305	10337	10550	0.1	2.37	6332	6045	-1.1
40216	LOUISVILLE	111	40044	39431	39735	-0.4	24	16775	16769	17130	0.0	2.33	11092	10626	-1.0
40217	LOUISVILLE	111	12844	12442	12469	-0.8	11	5841	5720	5798	-0.5	2.14	3170	2934	-1.8
40218	LOUISVILLE	111	30652	31365	32141	0.5	63	13404	13906	14428	0.9	2.23	7887	7793	-0.3
40219	LOUISVILLE	111	34838	34617	35309	-0.2	32	13935	14097	14581	0.3	2.43	9688	9422	-0.7
40220	LOUISVILLE	111	32638	33722	34896	0.8	70	14106	14762	15477	1.1	2.24	8591	8606	0.0
40222	LOUISVILLE	111	20429	21076	21696	0.7	69	9248	9665	10069	1.0	2.11	5525	5478	-0.2
	KENTUCKY					0.7					1.2	2.42			0.5
	UNITED STATES					1.2					1.3	2.58			1.1

ZIP CODE #	POST OFFICE NAME	RACE (%) White 2000	White 2004	Black 2000	Black 2004	Asian/Pacific 2000	Asian/Pacific 2004	% Hispanic Origin 2000	% Hispanic Origin 2004	2004 AGE DISTRIBUTION (%) 0-4	5-9	10-14	15-19	20-24	25-44	45-64	65-84	85+	18+	MEDIAN AGE 2004	% 2004 Males	% 2004 Females
40003	BAGDAD	96.7	96.1	1.6	1.7	0.1	0.1	1.9	2.4	6.0	7.0	8.1	7.0	5.0	28.6	26.6	10.5	1.3	74.4	38.6	51.9	48.1
40004	BARDSTOWN	90.3	89.7	7.8	8.0	0.7	0.9	1.1	1.4	7.9	7.5	7.6	7.1	7.4	29.3	23.2	9.0	1.2	72.8	34.4	48.6	51.4
40006	BEDFORD	97.8	97.4	0.3	0.3	0.1	0.2	1.3	1.7	6.7	6.9	7.8	7.0	6.0	29.5	24.7	9.9	1.6	74.3	36.5	49.4	50.6
40007	BETHLEHEM	97.8	97.5	0.3	0.3	0.3	0.6	1.3	1.6	6.6	6.3	6.9	7.3	6.6	29.7	27.8	7.9	1.0	76.3	36.6	50.2	49.8
40008	BLOOMFIELD	94.8	94.3	3.9	4.0	0.1	0.2	1.6	2.0	6.8	6.9	6.8	6.2	6.3	27.8	25.9	11.8	1.5	75.8	38.3	49.7	50.4
40009	BRADFORDSVILLE	97.9	97.8	0.3	0.4	0.0	0.0	1.2	1.2	6.4	6.1	6.9	7.0	7.3	29.5	24.5	11.1	1.3	76.7	37.1	50.1	49.9
40010	BUCKNER	96.9	96.9	1.7	1.7	0.3	0.6	0.7	1.1	6.1	7.2	8.9	7.2	5.0	26.4	31.1	7.5	0.6	73.1	40.0	49.7	50.3
40011	CAMPBELLSBURG	95.9	95.3	1.6	1.6	0.9	1.1	1.7	2.2	6.9	7.4	7.8	6.0	5.3	27.4	26.9	10.8	1.4	74.0	37.6	50.3	49.7
40012	CHAPLIN	98.6	98.8	0.4	0.4	0.0	0.0	1.2	1.6	6.1	6.5	6.3	5.9	5.5	28.1	26.0	14.0	1.6	77.4	40.4	50.6	49.4
40013	COXS CREEK	97.2	96.9	1.8	1.8	0.2	0.3	0.9	1.2	6.9	7.1	7.6	6.5	5.7	28.1	26.1	10.5	1.4	74.3	37.8	49.6	50.4
40014	CRESTWOOD	96.6	96.1	1.6	1.8	0.4	0.5	1.1	1.4	6.9	7.7	8.9	7.3	5.2	27.9	29.0	6.6	0.7	71.8	37.6	49.6	50.5
40019	EMINENCE	87.4	86.2	8.2	8.6	0.3	0.4	3.7	4.8	7.3	7.0	6.8	6.5	6.7	27.6	25.5	11.3	1.4	75.0	37.1	49.2	50.8
40022	FINCHVILLE	85.6	84.6	12.9	13.4	0.5	0.5	1.3	1.8	5.2	5.6	6.1	4.7	4.7	38.6	27.2	7.1	0.8	80.2	38.7	41.2	58.8
40023	FISHERVILLE	95.9	95.5	2.2	2.3	0.6	0.7	1.3	1.7	6.2	7.2	7.2	5.8	4.3	27.1	31.9	9.5	0.8	75.7	41.0	50.2	49.8
40025	GLENVIEW	93.1	91.7	3.9	4.7	2.0	2.6	1.0	1.0	2.6	3.7	5.2	5.2	3.7	15.1	41.7	21.4	1.6	85.4	52.7	47.4	52.6
40026	GOSHEN	97.1	96.7	0.7	0.8	0.5	0.6	0.9	1.1	7.3	8.4	9.8	8.3	4.9	26.2	30.0	4.8	0.4	69.2	37.3	49.6	50.5
40031	LA GRANGE	89.3	88.7	8.2	8.4	0.3	0.4	1.6	2.1	5.8	6.1	6.4	6.0	6.8	34.2	26.5	7.3	0.8	78.0	37.2	57.9	42.1
40033	LEBANON	84.5	84.2	13.6	13.9	0.6	0.6	0.8	0.8	6.6	6.5	7.0	6.2	7.1	30.6	23.6	10.6	1.8	76.2	36.2	51.7	48.3
40036	LOCKPORT	97.8	97.9	0.3	0.3	0.3	0.3	1.9	2.3	7.5	7.5	7.2	6.2	5.7	28.1	26.0	10.8	1.0	74.0	37.4	51.0	49.0
40037	LORETTO	97.8	97.7	0.6	0.6	0.1	0.1	1.1	1.1	7.8	7.6	7.2	6.8	6.5	28.6	22.8	9.9	2.8	73.2	35.2	48.5	51.5
40040	MACKVILLE	98.6	98.4	0.5	0.6	0.0	0.0	0.9	1.2	6.1	6.2	6.7	6.1	6.4	28.7	26.6	12.0	1.4	77.4	39.2	49.6	50.4
40045	MILTON	98.2	98.0	0.2	0.2	0.1	0.1	1.2	1.6	6.6	6.8	6.7	6.1	5.5	29.6	26.4	10.9	1.3	76.1	37.7	49.3	50.7
40046	MOUNT EDEN	98.5	98.3	0.4	0.4	0.1	0.1	0.9	1.2	6.7	7.1	8.3	6.4	6.0	32.2	25.0	7.8	0.6	74.0	36.4	52.0	48.0
40047	MOUNT WASHINGTON	98.4	98.2	0.3	0.3	0.2	0.3	0.6	0.7	7.6	7.9	7.8	5.9	5.5	32.2	24.0	8.1	1.0	72.9	35.6	49.0	51.0
40050	NEW CASTLE	93.2	92.3	4.5	4.7	0.1	0.1	2.1	2.7	6.5	6.3	6.5	5.6	5.9	26.4	26.3	14.0	2.5	77.3	40.2	47.4	52.6
40051	NEW HAVEN	98.2	98.0	0.5	0.5	0.2	0.2	0.8	1.1	7.1	7.1	7.4	7.1	6.6	28.3	25.4	10.1	0.9	74.2	36.4	51.8	48.2
40052	NEW HOPE	98.5	98.5	0.0	0.0	0.3	0.3	0.9	1.2	6.3	6.3	7.7	7.7	7.4	28.0	25.9	9.8	0.9	75.0	36.5	53.9	46.1
40055	PENDLETON	96.5	96.0	1.2	1.3	0.2	0.3	1.5	1.8	6.8	7.1	7.5	6.5	5.5	29.8	27.0	9.2	0.8	74.5	37.8	50.8	49.3
40056	PEWEE VALLEY	95.1	94.5	3.1	3.4	0.5	0.7	1.3	1.7	7.1	7.2	7.3	6.4	5.8	26.4	27.7	10.0	2.1	74.5	38.9	48.1	51.9
40057	PLEASUREVILLE	96.3	95.7	1.0	1.0	0.2	0.2	2.9	3.7	6.9	7.1	7.3	6.3	5.6	28.7	25.3	11.5	1.4	75.0	37.8	51.1	48.9
40059	PROSPECT	91.9	90.2	4.7	5.5	1.9	2.5	1.0	1.3	6.3	7.9	8.4	6.6	3.8	21.1	34.6	10.4	1.0	73.1	42.9	49.7	50.3
40060	RAYWICK	98.9	99.0	0.2	0.2	0.4	0.3	0.7	0.7	7.2	6.6	6.1	6.1	8.4	29.9	25.6	9.6	0.8	76.7	35.5	51.4	48.6
40061	SAINT CATHARINE	86.5	87.0	9.6	11.1	0.0	0.0	1.9	3.7	7.4	7.4	7.4	7.4	7.4	27.8	20.4	13.0	1.9	77.8	35.0	48.2	51.9
40062	SAINT FRANCIS	100.0	100.0	0.0	0.0	0.0	0.0	0.0	0.0	8.0	8.0	8.0	8.0	8.0	32.0	28.0	0.0	0.0	76.0	31.3	52.0	48.0
40065	SHELBYVILLE	84.9	83.9	9.6	9.5	0.6	0.8	5.7	7.2	7.3	7.1	6.8	6.0	6.4	29.9	24.6	10.2	1.7	75.3	36.4	49.3	50.7
40067	SIMPSONVILLE	81.6	80.4	14.5	14.8	0.5	0.6	3.3	4.3	6.5	6.4	6.4	8.5	7.0	31.7	25.5	7.5	0.6	75.5	36.1	46.4	53.6
40068	SMITHFIELD	96.0	95.7	2.2	2.3	0.2	0.3	1.2	1.5	6.7	6.9	6.9	6.5	6.0	28.4	29.0	8.7	1.0	75.6	38.5	51.2	48.8
40069	SPRINGFIELD	85.6	84.7	12.0	12.4	0.4	0.5	2.0	2.6	6.0	6.2	7.3	6.7	6.4	26.8	24.0	13.8	2.8	76.7	38.9	47.8	52.2
40070	SULPHUR	95.2	94.2	1.3	1.3	0.3	0.3	2.7	3.4	6.6	6.4	6.7	6.3	6.4	29.5	27.0	10.4	0.8	76.3	38.0	51.0	49.0
40071	TAYLORSVILLE	97.4	97.2	1.3	1.3	0.1	0.2	1.1	1.4	7.2	7.4	7.4	6.0	5.6	31.3	25.8	8.3	1.0	74.2	36.8	50.2	49.8
40075	TURNERS STATION	97.7	97.4	0.8	0.8	0.5	0.5	1.0	1.1	5.7	6.7	7.8	5.3	5.7	28.2	27.6	11.5	1.3	76.3	39.1	51.6	48.4
40076	WADDY	97.2	96.8	1.0	1.0	0.0	0.0	1.5	1.9	6.5	6.8	6.9	6.3	5.6	30.4	27.4	9.2	0.9	75.8	38.0	50.6	49.5
40077	WESTPORT	97.1	96.5	0.9	0.9	0.3	0.5	0.3	0.5	5.1	6.3	7.7	6.5	4.7	26.1	33.7	8.9	1.1	76.4	41.7	50.5	49.5
40078	WILLISBURG	98.0	97.8	0.9	0.9	0.2	0.2	1.2	1.4	5.9	6.3	6.8	8.7	5.8	28.6	26.0	10.9	1.0	74.9	37.3	53.3	46.7
40104	BATTLETOWN	97.6	97.1	0.4	0.4	0.3	0.5	0.5	0.5	6.1	6.2	6.8	6.7	6.4	27.3	27.9	11.5	1.0	76.7	39.4	50.2	49.9
40107	BOSTON	98.9	98.8	0.2	0.2	0.1	0.1	0.6	0.7	6.3	6.5	7.9	7.5	6.7	30.4	24.9	9.0	0.8	74.7	36.3	51.2	48.9
40108	BRANDENBURG	96.6	96.1	1.7	1.8	0.2	0.3	0.7	1.0	6.9	6.9	7.4	6.8	6.8	28.1	25.6	10.5	1.0	74.6	36.9	48.7	51.3
40109	BROOKS	97.5	97.1	0.6	0.7	0.2	0.2	0.8	1.1	6.8	6.9	7.0	6.5	6.0	30.4	28.4	7.7	0.3	75.3	37.0	50.0	50.0
40111	CLOVERPORT	97.7	97.6	1.1	1.2	0.0	0.0	0.9	1.1	7.1	7.2	6.5	5.8	6.2	25.8	27.2	13.2	1.0	75.6	38.8	50.7	49.3
40115	CUSTER	97.3	97.1	0.3	0.4	0.2	0.2	0.7	0.9	6.2	6.3	6.7	7.3	7.1	26.4	27.7	11.2	1.1	76.2	38.2	51.0	49.0
40117	EKRON	94.4	93.8	3.0	3.2	0.4	0.5	1.0	1.3	7.3	7.4	7.9	7.2	6.7	29.4	25.3	8.4	0.6	73.0	35.5	50.5	49.5
40118	FAIRDALE	97.1	96.5	0.9	1.0	0.3	0.4	1.2	1.7	7.5	7.1	7.2	6.7	6.9	29.9	23.3	10.7	0.8	74.3	34.8	48.9	51.1
40119	FALLS OF ROUGH	98.9	98.8	0.3	0.3	0.1	0.1	0.2	0.2	5.1	5.5	6.6	6.4	5.6	25.0	29.3	15.3	1.3	78.9	42.4	52.6	47.4
40121	FORT KNOX	66.3	63.7	23.0	23.4	2.1	2.6	10.3	13.1	12.5	10.3	7.8	10.9	20.9	34.7	2.8	0.2	0.0	66.0	22.1	61.5	38.5
40140	GARFIELD	96.6	96.4	2.1	2.2	0.1	0.1	0.4	0.7	6.4	6.6	7.7	7.0	6.1	26.5	27.7	11.0	1.0	75.2	38.6	49.8	50.2
40142	GUSTON	95.9	95.4	2.2	2.4	0.4	0.6	0.4	0.6	7.4	7.4	7.8	7.0	6.7	29.7	24.4	8.8	0.8	73.0	35.2	50.5	49.5
40143	HARDINSBURG	93.6	93.3	5.2	5.4	0.2	0.2	0.9	1.2	6.1	6.1	6.2	6.4	7.0	26.1	26.7	12.9	2.5	77.9	39.9	48.1	51.9
40144	HARNED	95.7	95.5	2.9	3.1	0.1	0.1	0.8	0.9	6.0	6.1	6.1	6.4	6.6	25.0	28.1	13.4	2.3	77.9	40.8	47.3	52.7
40145	HUDSON	98.5	98.7	0.0	0.0	0.0	0.0	0.7	1.3	6.5	6.5	7.2	7.2	6.5	22.9	30.1	11.8	1.3	75.2	39.7	51.0	49.0
40146	IRVINGTON	90.1	89.7	8.5	8.7	0.2	0.3	0.8	0.9	6.6	7.5	7.5	6.4	6.0	26.4	23.8	14.2	1.5	74.2	38.0	48.4	51.6
40150	LEBANON JUNCTION	98.2	98.0	0.3	0.4	0.2	0.3	0.6	0.7	5.3	7.3	7.8	7.3	5.7	28.5	27.5	10.0	0.6	75.1	38.1	50.7	49.3
40152	MC DANIELS	98.6	100.0	0.0	0.0	0.0	0.0	0.0	1.4	5.5	5.5	5.5	5.5	5.5	21.9	30.1	19.2	1.4	83.6	45.4	46.6	53.4
40155	MULDRAUGH	82.4	80.6	10.0	10.2	1.1	1.4	7.0	9.0	9.2	7.8	7.6	7.0	8.5	34.3	19.7	5.4	0.6	71.2	29.7	50.9	49.1
40157	PAYNEVILLE	97.6	97.1	0.5	0.6	0.1	0.2	0.6	0.9	7.7	7.5	6.9	7.1	7.1	27.8	25.1	9.7	1.1	73.7	36.1	51.8	48.2
40160	RADCLIFF	66.0	63.5	23.1	23.7	3.7	4.6	5.2	6.6	7.8	7.1	7.7	7.7	8.0	30.0	22.6	8.4	0.7	72.6	33.3	49.2	50.8
40161	RHODELIA	97.2	97.6	0.7	0.6	0.0	0.0	0.7	1.2	7.9	7.9	6.7	7.3	7.9	28.1	24.4	9.2	0.6	72.6	35.0	53.7	46.3
40162	RINEYVILLE	93.1	92.0	2.9	3.1	1.0	1.3	1.6	2.2	6.5	6.9	7.7	7.3	6.5	28.4	27.6	8.5	0.7	74.4	37.5	50.0	50.1
40164	SE REE	98.7	98.5	0.3	0.3	0.0	0.0	0.9	1.2	6.2	6.2	6.2	5.6	5.0	23.7	28.7	16.9	1.5	77.8	42.8	48.5	51.5
40165	SHEPHERDSVILLE	97.9	97.7	0.5	0.5	0.3	0.4	0.6	0.8	7.4	7.4	7.3	6.3	6.1	30.8	26.1	8.1	0.6	74.1	35.7	50.1	49.9
40170	STEPHENSPORT	98.2	98.2	0.9	0.9	0.0	0.0	0.0	0.0	6.3	6.7	7.2	6.7	5.8	26.0	27.4	12.6	1.4	75.3	39.2	52.5	47.5
40171	UNION STAR	98.1	97.9	0.2	0.2	0.0	0.0	1.2	1.5	6.0	6.0	6.5	5.9	6.3	26.4	29.4	12.2	1.4	78.1	40.7	50.6	49.4
40175	VINE GROVE	89.0	88.1	6.2	6.3	1.6	2.0	2.0	2.7	6.5	6.8	7.6	7.7	6.6	28.9	26.0	9.0	0.8	74.3	36.7	50.2	49.8
40176	WEBSTER	97.7	97.3	0.5	0.6	0.0	0.0	0.8	1.2	7.7	7.3	6.7	7.0	7.1	27.7	25.5	9.8	1.2	74.0	36.3	52.4	47.6
40177	WEST POINT	97.2	96.9	1.3	1.4	0.2	0.2	1.1	1.4	6.5	6.6	7.5	6.8	7.5	30.0	24.6	9.9	0.6	75.5	35.5	51.0	49.0
40178	WESTVIEW	98.9	98.6	0.4	0.4	0.0	0.0	0.8	1.1	6.1	6.4	6.1	5.3	5.0	23.5	29.2	17.1	1.4	77.9	43.3	48.8	51.3
40202	LOUISVILLE	27.2	25.3	67.7	69.2	2.5	2.9	1.9	2.1	8.2	7.1	5.7	5.3	7.8	29.4	22.4	12.1	2.0	76.2	35.3	50.8	49.2
40203	LOUISVILLE	35.3	33.0	61.3	63.4	0.4	0.4	1.5	1.8	8.7	7.5	6.8	6.7	8.6	28.3	19.6	10.6	3.4	73.3	33.3	46.9	53.1
40204	LOUISVILLE	85.6	84.2	11.5	12.5	0.8	1.0	1.2	1.5	5.1	4.4	4.5	5.0	7.9	35.8	24.3	10.8	2.1	83.0	37.0	48.4	51.6
40205	LOUISVILLE	96.0	95.3	1.8	2.0	1.0	1.2	0.9	1.1	4.5	4.6	4.9	6.3	6.8	27.8	28.3	13.8	3.2	82.8	41.8	46.9	53.1
40206	LOUISVILLE	86.5	84.8	9.6	10.6	1.8	2.2	1.9	2.4	4.6	4.5	4.5	5.0	8.1	34.1	25.2	11.3	2.7	83.5	38.3	47.4	52.6
40207	LOUISVILLE	94.6	93.7	2.3	2.6	1.9	2.4	1.1	1.4	5.4	5.5	5.7	5.4	5.6	26.9	26.3	15.8	3.4	80.1	42.0	46.7	53.4
40208	LOUISVILLE	60.8	57.8	32.8	34.8	2.2	2.8	2.4	3.1	6.3	5.3	5.6	7.9	14.0	32.5	20.9	6.8	0.9	79.7	31.0	51.2	48.8
40209	LOUISVILLE	88.7	86.0	7.0	8.0	2.3	3.2	2.3	2.6	5.8	6.2	6.7	7.1	6.2	29.9	23.0	13.8	1.3	78.1	38.0	50.3	49.7
40210	LOUISVILLE	9.5	8.6	88.7	89.6	0.1	0.1	0.8	0.9	7.5	7.8	8.9	7.9	6.5	24.6	23.6	11.8	1.3	71.0	35.1	46.1	53.9
40211	LOUISVILLE	3.1	2.9	95.1	95.3	0.1	0.1	0.7	0.8	7.3	7.9	9.3	8.0	6.2	24.5	22.1	12.8	1.9	70.5	35.3	45.3	54.7
40212	LOUISVILLE	43.5	41.6	54.4	56.3	0.1	0.1	0.7	0.8	7.7	8.0	9.3	8.1	6.9	25.8	23.3	9.8	1.1	70.1	33.7	47.0	53.0
40213	LOUISVILLE	80.6	78.6	16.2	17.7	0.9	1.1	1.9	2.4	6.2	6.2	6.4	6.4	6.8	28.0	23.9	14.0	2.2	77.3	38.2	48.1	51.9
40214	LOUISVILLE	84.8	83.2	7.8	8.3	4.1	4.9	3.6	4.3	6.9	6.5	6.5	6.3	6.7	29.7	24.1	11.7	1.6	76.4	36.5	48.8	51.3
40215	LOUISVILLE	69.7	67.8	26.0	27.3	0.9	1.2	2.2	2.8	8.8	8.0	7.7	6.9	7.6	28.3	21.5	9.5	1.6	71.4	33.0	46.7	53.4
40216	LOUISVILLE	75.8	73.7	21.8	23.7	0.5	0.6	1.2	1.6	6.1	6.1	6.4	6.0	6.2	26.5	25.7	15.2	1.8	77.8	40.4	47.4	52.6
40217	LOUISVILLE	90.0	88.9	6.7	7.3	1.3	1.6	1.3	1.6	5.7	5.4	5.3	5.7	7.9	30.8	23.9	13.0	2.5	80.5	38.3	48.4	51.6
40218	LOUISVILLE	57.1	55.7	37.6	38.2	1.7	2.1	3.3	4.0	6.8	6.8	6.9	6.5	7.1	29.2	22.1	12.5	2.0	75.6	36.1	46.8	53.2
40219	LOUISVILLE	81.5	80.2	14.6	15.1	1.1	1.3	2.8	3.7	7.0	6.6	6.6	6.2	6.6	28.8	24.1	12.8	1.5	76.2	37.3	48.1	51.9
40220	LOUISVILLE	86.2	84.3	9.5	10.6	1.7	2.2	2.0	2.5	5.9	5.8	5.9	5.4	6.1	28.9	24.7	14.6	2.6	79.1	39.8	47.1	52.9
40222	LOUISVILLE	89.2	87.6	5.9	6.4	2.8	3.5	1.8	2.3	5.3	5.3	5.3	5.1	5.6	26.4	27.3	16.1	3.6	81.1	42.8	47.1	53.0
	KENTUCKY	90.1	89.5	7.3	7.4	0.8	1.0	1.5	1.9	6.6	6.6	6.8	6.6	7.0	28.9	24.8	11.1	1.5	76.3	36.8	49.1	50.9
	UNITED STATES	75.1	73.6	12.3	12.5	3.8	4.2	12.5	14.1	6.9	6.7	7.2	7.0	7.3	28.6	23.8	10.8	1.7	75.1	36.0	49.1	50.9

INCOME

#	POST OFFICE NAME	2004 Per Capita Income	2004 HH Income Base	2004 Household Income Distribution (%): Less than $25,000	$25,000 to $49,999	$50,000 to $99,999	$100,000 to $149,999	$150,000 or More	Median Household Income: 2004	2009	2004 National Centile	2004 State Centile	2004 Home Value Base	2004 Home Value Distribution (%): Less than $50,000	$50,000 to $89,999	$90,000 to $174,999	$175,000 to $399,999	$400,000 or More	2004 Median Home Value
40003	BAGDAD	22877	691	17.7	35.9	33.4	11.1	1.9	46732	57218	66	86	578	7.1	23.9	37.7	26.1	5.2	118132
40004	BARDSTOWN	23018	9916	26.2	29.8	31.7	8.4	3.9	45143	53557	62	84	7094	8.5	29.7	41.2	18.9	1.7	106877
40006	BEDFORD	19525	1755	29.1	32.7	28.8	8.0	1.5	39718	47423	45	72	1430	26.7	24.6	36.7	11.2	0.8	87955
40007	BETHLEHEM	23843	123	26.8	22.8	31.7	12.2	6.5	50289	60367	72	89	98	36.7	10.2	39.8	13.3	0.0	95000
40008	BLOOMFIELD	19369	1321	29.2	30.1	31.4	7.3	1.9	42230	50914	54	79	1082	17.3	28.6	37.2	16.0	1.0	95625
40009	BRADFORDSVILLE	19709	457	46.6	24.1	20.8	4.4	4.2	27146	33427	7	35	366	45.4	25.4	24.0	4.6	0.6	57727
40010	BUCKNER	38851	115	6.1	13.0	37.4	23.5	20.0	89920	109168	97	99	102	2.9	2.0	18.6	56.9	19.6	238636
40011	CAMPBELLSBURG	20419	1025	28.4	27.4	33.5	8.3	2.4	44784	53585	61	83	848	18.4	30.4	36.9	10.5	3.8	92041
40012	CHAPLIN	21769	204	25.0	31.4	36.8	4.9	2.0	41941	50666	53	78	170	21.8	28.8	30.0	18.8	0.6	89375
40013	COXS CREEK	22757	1904	19.5	26.5	39.2	11.2	3.5	52744	63780	77	91	1693	11.2	18.0	41.5	25.2	4.2	121518
40014	CRESTWOOD	33675	6240	7.9	17.3	39.8	22.8	12.3	79293	99240	95	99	5498	1.5	4.6	30.4	55.2	8.3	209553
40019	EMINENCE	19620	1424	34.1	29.4	26.8	7.0	2.8	37891	47919	39	68	989	12.9	35.1	38.9	11.8	1.2	92143
40022	FINCHVILLE	36692	318	17.0	15.1	34.9	21.7	11.3	75634	88135	93	98	278	2.9	4.7	27.7	50.4	14.4	220833
40023	FISHERVILLE	33504	975	11.3	20.4	36.2	19.5	12.6	76351	91994	94	98	894	5.2	4.7	27.3	51.1	11.7	214236
40025	GLENVIEW	71146	76	6.6	14.5	21.1	14.5	43.4	125000	158940	99	100	71	0.0	1.4	21.1	33.8	43.7	350000
40026	GOSHEN	37272	1832	4.4	13.5	39.3	25.1	17.7	89107	108806	97	99	1718	0.8	0.7	37.7	50.8	10.0	191577
40031	LA GRANGE	25477	6081	16.3	23.3	36.1	16.0	8.4	62735	78294	87	96	5091	7.2	11.1	38.7	38.4	4.7	156727
40033	LEBANON	17915	4337	37.2	31.2	24.3	4.0	3.3	33165	40071	21	54	3222	16.8	36.3	36.2	9.1	1.6	87263
40036	LOCKPORT	26308	158	23.4	22.8	40.5	10.1	3.2	52550	62934	76	91	129	29.5	20.2	31.8	15.5	3.1	90714
40037	LORETTO	17306	1047	29.1	34.2	30.8	5.4	0.5	38782	46704	42	71	886	24.3	33.1	31.7	10.2	0.8	82353
40040	MACKVILLE	19113	597	27.6	35.2	28.5	6.4	2.4	39938	47796	46	73	495	23.8	32.9	31.5	9.3	2.4	78971
40045	MILTON	20995	1368	26.8	28.3	36.8	5.8	2.3	45800	53883	63	85	1134	22.5	31.9	34.0	10.6	1.1	83902
40046	MOUNT EDEN	23482	602	20.1	23.9	42.0	12.1	1.8	53381	63987	77	92	513	16.2	9.0	51.7	22.4	0.8	124877
40047	MOUNT WASHINGTON	23249	5508	17.0	28.2	41.0	10.6	3.3	53577	62455	78	93	4669	3.0	9.8	59.7	25.9	1.5	137035
40050	NEW CASTLE	19816	769	35.9	21.9	31.9	7.5	2.9	38463	50166	41	70	573	17.3	29.5	37.0	13.1	3.1	94405
40051	NEW HAVEN	19281	1714	30.1	30.1	32.2	5.3	2.5	40953	49174	49	76	1407	18.3	30.8	37.2	13.0	0.8	91298
40052	NEW HOPE	18865	131	32.1	29.8	28.2	7.6	2.3	35454	43400	29	62	110	21.8	28.2	30.9	17.3	1.8	90000
40055	PENDLETON	23608	743	17.8	34.7	29.7	13.9	3.9	47610	59114	67	87	645	17.5	16.0	40.2	21.6	4.8	121806
40056	PEWEE VALLEY	32210	1217	13.6	19.5	37.5	18.2	11.2	69820	86467	91	98	1112	3.2	4.2	49.3	33.1	10.3	161496
40057	PLEASUREVILLE	21998	1309	25.4	27.9	35.4	8.3	3.0	46441	56100	65	85	1052	22.0	26.2	34.8	13.6	3.4	92533
40059	PROSPECT	58100	4751	5.7	10.9	24.5	21.5	37.4	119707	146150	99	100	4403	0.7	2.8	9.5	50.8	36.3	318052
40060	RAYWICK	19506	398	23.9	34.7	34.7	5.3	1.5	45000	52239	61	83	329	27.4	25.2	40.7	6.7	0.0	86731
40061	SAINT CATHARINE	12082	15	33.3	33.3	33.3	0.0	0.0	36064	60000	32	63	13	0.0	23.1	53.9	23.1	0.0	115625
40062	SAINT FRANCIS	21800	12	25.0	41.7	25.0	8.3	0.0	40000	45000	46	73	10	30.0	40.0	30.0	0.0	0.0	70000
40065	SHELBYVILLE	23895	9185	22.6	25.1	36.8	11.5	4.0	52082	64085	76	90	6336	2.5	16.6	47.1	29.1	4.8	141808
40067	SIMPSONVILLE	29400	1579	14.3	20.0	38.1	17.5	10.2	70345	84388	91	98	1284	1.3	8.6	37.3	34.6	18.2	185417
40068	SMITHFIELD	24976	668	18.3	31.7	33.1	11.5	5.4	50000	61189	72	89	579	18.8	20.9	39.0	17.6	3.6	109531
40069	SPRINGFIELD	20419	2575	33.9	28.9	27.2	5.8	4.2	38021	45656	39	69	2010	14.8	33.3	36.7	12.2	3.1	92203
40070	SULPHUR	25441	266	18.8	25.9	37.2	13.9	4.1	53592	64294	78	93	232	12.5	25.9	34.1	22.4	5.2	118269
40071	TAYLORSVILLE	25413	4843	18.7	23.5	41.5	12.4	3.9	57941	68227	83	94	4064	11.3	11.2	40.6	34.3	2.7	145196
40075	TURNERS STATION	21005	386	25.1	23.3	40.9	8.8	1.8	50974	60697	74	90	329	27.7	23.4	28.3	13.7	7.0	88750
40076	WADDY	22324	1012	16.5	28.6	42.9	9.9	2.2	52764	63825	77	91	880	6.4	23.9	38.8	28.1	3.0	122685
40077	WESTPORT	30143	237	13.9	24.5	38.8	15.6	7.2	63687	79384	88	96	207	6.3	10.1	33.3	44.4	5.8	175521
40078	WILLISBURG	18321	1004	32.8	36.1	26.2	3.0	2.0	37182	44254	36	66	855	26.1	33.7	26.9	11.9	1.4	77653
40104	BATTLETOWN	19177	406	29.1	33.5	27.8	8.6	1.0	37113	44037	36	66	351	30.5	31.9	25.1	11.1	1.4	78429
40107	BOSTON	18908	982	25.5	37.6	28.2	6.8	1.9	41525	49224	51	77	839	19.8	27.8	38.0	12.4	2.0	94767
40108	BRANDENBURG	22142	3513	24.9	28.6	34.4	9.2	2.9	46883	54917	66	86	2814	16.5	27.0	39.9	15.6	1.0	101247
40109	BROOKS	21717	1164	14.5	36.3	38.8	9.5	0.9	48878	58515	70	88	1045	37.6	12.6	35.6	13.5	0.7	89342
40111	CLOVERPORT	18803	1191	38.0	28.0	25.6	5.5	2.9	33821	40735	24	56	951	39.8	29.2	26.1	4.9	0.0	63456
40115	CUSTER	18405	417	30.2	30.9	33.1	4.6	1.2	40877	48223	49	76	358	29.1	31.0	27.7	11.5	0.8	74828
40117	EKRON	18594	1441	25.4	33.3	33.9	5.6	1.7	43315	51455	57	82	1246	20.7	32.3	38.0	8.7	0.3	85978
40118	FAIRDALE	20231	3579	27.2	31.0	33.8	6.6	1.4	42124	54515	53	79	2837	27.5	31.8	35.9	4.8	0.1	81619
40119	FALLS OF ROUGH	18985	1086	33.2	34.5	27.4	3.2	1.7	34350	40923	25	58	948	30.3	31.2	29.2	8.4	0.8	72830
40121	FORT KNOX	12948	2709	18.7	49.0	27.9	3.0	1.4	37789	42928	38	68	78	42.3	9.0	23.1	23.1	2.6	88571
40140	GARFIELD	18089	405	24.7	36.1	33.6	4.0	1.7	40876	47858	49	75	351	22.2	30.5	34.8	9.7	2.9	87121
40142	GUSTON	22013	700	23.3	25.4	38.7	9.9	2.7	50852	60658	74	90	602	20.3	27.2	39.7	12.1	0.7	94286
40143	HARDINSBURG	20261	1589	38.7	28.9	24.8	3.8	3.8	35101	41521	28	61	1211	25.9	38.3	26.7	7.3	1.9	75348
40144	HARNED	19743	697	37.5	29.0	26.3	4.0	3.3	37276	44338	36	67	551	24.9	34.5	27.4	10.3	2.9	77857
40145	HUDSON	13876	51	37.3	29.4	29.4	3.9	0.0	33639	40757	23	56	44	45.5	29.6	22.7	2.3	0.0	60000
40146	IRVINGTON	18212	1058	37.2	31.6	25.1	4.1	2.0	34160	40000	25	57	824	32.2	32.8	26.5	6.3	2.3	72535
40150	LEBANON JUNCTION	20036	1864	24.5	29.9	35.7	8.2	1.7	44889	52914	61	83	1528	11.9	27.2	44.4	16.1	0.5	103867
40152	MC DANIELS	13767	27	37.0	33.3	29.6	0.0	0.0	30706	35717	14	46	23	39.1	30.4	30.4	0.0	0.0	72500
40155	MULDRAUGH	16604	515	30.3	41.6	23.9	3.7	0.6	34591	42654	26	59	215	51.2	33.5	10.7	4.7	0.0	48438
40157	PAYNEVILLE	17871	605	29.3	33.1	30.1	6.1	1.5	34624	41517	26	59	524	33.0	35.7	19.9	11.1	0.4	68723
40160	RADCLIFF	20229	9301	27.6	31.6	32.4	6.6	1.8	42051	50719	53	79	5742	19.1	24.3	51.6	4.6	0.4	95488
40161	RHODELIA	17725	63	31.8	33.3	27.0	4.8	3.2	32225	37824	18	50	55	32.7	36.4	20.0	10.9	0.0	65625
40162	RINEYVILLE	23469	1071	20.1	26.8	39.2	10.6	3.3	53014	63144	77	92	929	18.7	16.5	50.9	12.3	1.6	109331
40164	SE REE	17925	141	37.6	33.3	27.0	1.4	0.7	30162	36199	13	44	120	35.0	33.3	28.3	3.3	0.0	74167
40165	SHEPHERDSVILLE	22301	11330	19.8	27.8	38.7	10.7	3.0	51755	60908	75	90	9258	13.1	14.0	48.4	23.4	1.1	126987
40170	STEPHENSPORT	21295	99	40.4	27.3	25.3	3.0	4.0	31994	37873	18	49	81	33.3	19.8	39.5	7.4	0.0	83750
40171	UNION STAR	14916	241	37.8	33.6	25.3	1.7	1.7	33178	38383	21	54	209	41.6	20.6	23.4	8.1	6.2	68846
40175	VINE GROVE	21115	4325	20.1	35.0	34.9	8.2	1.9	45793	54846	63	85	3588	13.7	29.2	47.3	8.9	0.9	98854
40176	WEBSTER	16098	242	33.5	33.5	27.7	3.3	2.1	32395	38015	19	51	210	37.6	30.0	18.6	11.4	2.4	64500
40177	WEST POINT	16791	715	31.9	35.4	28.7	3.2	0.8	34691	41716	26	59	484	32.0	35.1	26.0	6.4	0.4	69500
40178	WESTVIEW	19413	126	37.3	33.3	27.0	1.6	0.8	30353	35917	13	45	107	35.5	32.7	28.0	3.7	0.0	72500
40202	LOUISVILLE	13235	2450	73.3	13.7	10.1	1.8	1.1	10386	13745	1	1	112	30.4	34.8	25.0	9.8	0.0	66667
40203	LOUISVILLE	12744	8965	63.5	22.1	12.0	1.8	0.7	16572	21173	1	3	1775	37.2	37.6	19.6	5.6	0.0	63195
40204	LOUISVILLE	31160	7769	30.6	33.6	22.3	7.9	5.5	38421	49168	41	70	3595	8.8	29.0	35.4	20.6	6.3	111928
40205	LOUISVILLE	39502	10722	15.6	24.3	33.1	15.8	11.1	61690	80223	86	95	7891	1.0	6.9	45.7	41.7	4.7	169106
40206	LOUISVILLE	35003	9652	26.7	34.6	22.4	7.8	8.6	40260	49627	47	74	4838	3.4	19.4	45.1	23.1	9.0	125556
40207	LOUISVILLE	46314	14161	15.8	21.9	32.9	14.9	14.6	64111	81958	88	97	10045	0.5	4.1	41.0	42.8	11.6	184139
40208	LOUISVILLE	18875	5877	44.3	30.1	19.2	4.7	1.8	28224	36154	9	38	2051	17.2	48.3	23.9	9.4	1.3	76660
40209	LOUISVILLE	16072	204	41.2	38.7	16.7	2.0	1.5	28550	34080	10	39	116	13.8	62.9	23.3	0.0	0.0	76471
40210	LOUISVILLE	15677	6209	48.3	27.6	19.1	3.3	1.7	26141	32877	6	31	3533	36.9	48.9	13.7	0.3	0.3	59420
40211	LOUISVILLE	15066	9010	49.3	27.9	17.1	3.9	1.9	25429	31636	5	28	5212	27.5	53.6	17.9	0.8	0.3	64581
40212	LOUISVILLE	13727	7132	46.4	28.4	20.4	3.4	1.4	27281	34273	8	35	4145	34.9	50.2	14.7	0.1	0.0	58999
40213	LOUISVILLE	24470	7838	28.1	33.9	27.3	6.5	4.2	38455	48931	41	70	5062	10.0	36.3	42.5	9.9	1.3	93316
40214	LOUISVILLE	23060	19471	29.0	30.8	28.8	8.8	2.6	40974	51978	50	76	11806	7.6	27.9	53.0	10.8	0.8	105056
40215	LOUISVILLE	15105	10337	45.7	30.1	20.9	2.5	0.8	28111	35900	9	38	5416	12.7	64.4	22.3	0.6	0.0	74093
40216	LOUISVILLE	21747	16769	28.1	31.7	31.3	7.0	1.9	40947	51361	49	76	11968	5.9	29.8	61.3	2.8	0.2	100139
40217	LOUISVILLE	23471	5720	30.2	31.0	29.6	7.3	1.9	39549	50138	44	72	3722	6.8	31.3	56.8	4.3	1.0	99409
40218	LOUISVILLE	22836	13906	30.0	31.5	29.7	6.5	2.2	40046	50243	46	73	7510	6.4	30.1	56.1	7.0	0.4	104430
40219	LOUISVILLE	21823	14097	26.1	30.4	33.9	7.9	1.7	44061	55601	59	82	9380	4.8	20.6	71.1	3.5	0.1	108331
40220	LOUISVILLE	31331	14762	17.4	25.8	37.4	14.2	5.3	56085	71128	81	93	9887	1.0	5.7	71.9	20.7	0.7	141480
40222	LOUISVILLE	42034	9665	17.4	22.5	30.8	14.6	14.6	62032	79745	86	96	6207	1.5	4.2	33.9	49.3	11.2	196412
	KENTUCKY	22472		31.8	28.3	28.2	7.8	3.9	39962	49361				22.2	24.9	36.4	14.3	2.1	94344
	UNITED STATES	25866		24.7	27.1	30.8	10.9	6.5	48124	56710				10.9	15.0	33.7	30.1	10.4	145905

ZIP CODE #	POST OFFICE NAME	FINANCIAL SERVICES: Auto Loan	FINANCIAL SERVICES: Home Loan	FINANCIAL SERVICES: Invest-ments	FINANCIAL SERVICES: Retire-ment Plans	THE HOME: Home Improvements: Home Repair	THE HOME: Home Improvements: Lawn & Garden	THE HOME: Furnishings: Comput-ers & Hard-ware	THE HOME: Furnishings: Major Appli-ances	THE HOME: Furnishings: TV, Radio, Sound Equip-ment	THE HOME: Furnishings: Furni-ture	ENTERTAINMENT: Dine out/ Carry out	ENTERTAINMENT: Sports Equip-ment	ENTERTAINMENT: Fees & Tickets	ENTERTAINMENT: Toys & Games	ENTERTAINMENT: Travel	ENTERTAINMENT: Cable TV	PERSONAL: Apparel & Services	PERSONAL: Auto Repairs	PERSONAL: Health Insur-ance	PERSONAL: Pets & Supplies
40003	BAGDAD	98	86	65	82	92	98	80	89	85	80	104	106	78	106	82	88	98	87	97	115
40004	BARDSTOWN	92	81	66	78	85	93	80	86	84	79	103	101	77	104	81	86	97	85	93	106
40006	BEDFORD	84	67	45	63	71	79	66	74	72	66	87	86	60	83	66	74	81	73	83	94
40007	BETHLEHEM	98	88	67	83	93	99	81	90	86	81	105	107	79	107	83	88	99	87	97	116
40008	BLOOMFIELD	92	64	33	56	72	82	62	75	73	62	86	90	54	82	63	78	79	74	91	106
40009	BRADFORDSVILLE	92	62	28	53	70	80	59	74	72	61	84	89	51	80	61	77	77	74	92	106
40010	BUCKNER	160	200	217	206	193	195	176	171	160	178	204	198	193	212	179	155	206	165	152	190
40011	CAMPBELLSBURG	86	70	50	67	75	84	69	77	76	69	91	90	65	90	70	78	85	76	86	98
40012	CHAPLIN	99	66	30	57	75	86	64	80	77	65	91	95	54	86	65	83	82	79	98	113
40013	COXS CREEK	101	89	68	85	95	102	83	92	88	83	107	110	81	109	85	90	102	90	100	119
40014	CRESTWOOD	130	153	159	155	149	150	139	138	130	140	163	161	146	169	140	125	162	134	124	153
40019	EMINENCE	76	64	48	63	67	76	65	70	69	64	84	80	61	83	64	71	78	69	77	85
40022	FINCHVILLE	110	137	146	137	135	133	122	122	113	122	142	143	130	152	125	110	142	118	109	135
40023	FISHERVILLE	123	149	159	151	146	146	134	133	124	135	157	155	142	164	136	120	156	129	120	147
40025	GLENVIEW	217	293	402	287	286	308	255	253	238	261	301	284	290	316	272	240	305	243	235	275
40026	GOSHEN	156	183	184	190	175	172	164	161	150	169	190	188	172	193	162	141	189	156	139	177
40031	LA GRANGE	106	108	100	108	109	115	103	106	102	102	126	123	104	128	103	101	122	104	105	122
40033	LEBANON	78	60	40	56	65	74	60	68	67	60	80	80	55	78	60	70	75	68	79	89
40036	LOCKPORT	117	84	45	74	93	106	80	97	94	81	111	116	71	107	82	100	102	96	117	135
40037	LORETTO	85	58	27	50	65	75	55	69	67	57	78	83	47	74	56	72	71	68	85	98
40040	MACKVILLE	79	70	54	67	74	80	65	72	69	65	84	86	64	86	67	71	80	70	78	93
40045	MILTON	87	71	48	66	77	84	67	77	74	67	88	91	63	88	68	77	83	75	86	102
40046	MOUNT EDEN	96	86	65	82	91	97	79	88	84	79	102	105	78	105	82	86	97	86	95	113
40047	MOUNT WASHINGTON	91	91	83	91	92	97	87	90	87	87	107	105	87	109	87	86	103	88	89	105
40050	NEW CASTLE	78	61	41	58	66	77	64	71	71	62	84	81	58	81	64	75	78	70	83	88
40051	NEW HAVEN	92	66	35	58	73	83	63	76	74	64	87	91	56	84	64	78	80	75	92	106
40052	NEW HOPE	88	60	29	52	68	78	58	72	69	59	82	86	50	78	59	74	74	71	88	101
40055	PENDLETON	98	94	80	91	96	100	88	94	89	89	109	110	86	109	89	88	105	92	94	113
40056	PEWEE VALLEY	120	137	144	137	134	137	128	128	121	129	152	148	132	153	129	117	150	126	117	140
40057	PLEASUREVILLE	95	76	51	71	82	91	74	84	81	74	98	98	69	97	75	85	91	82	95	108
40059	PROSPECT	200	259	318	261	252	263	227	223	209	231	265	255	254	277	236	207	268	215	203	245
40060	RAYWICK	93	62	29	54	70	81	60	75	72	61	85	90	51	80	61	78	77	74	92	106
40061	SAINT CATHARINE	61	54	41	52	58	62	50	56	53	50	65	66	49	66	52	55	62	54	60	72
40062	SAINT FRANCIS	86	57	26	49	65	75	55	69	67	56	78	83	47	74	56	72	71	68	85	98
40065	SHELBYVILLE	88	88	83	87	89	95	86	88	87	85	107	103	86	109	86	87	103	87	89	103
40067	SIMPSONVILLE	124	147	155	148	143	144	135	134	125	135	158	156	141	163	136	121	157	131	120	147
40068	SMITHFIELD	106	96	75	92	101	108	89	98	94	89	114	116	88	117	91	96	109	95	105	125
40069	SPRINGFIELD	86	68	45	64	74	83	67	76	75	66	89	89	62	87	68	78	83	75	88	98
40070	SULPHUR	103	92	70	87	97	104	85	94	90	85	109	112	83	112	87	92	104	91	102	121
40071	TAYLORSVILLE	101	105	95	104	105	108	97	101	95	97	118	118	98	120	98	94	115	98	98	117
40075	TURNERS STATION	87	77	58	73	81	88	71	79	76	71	92	94	70	94	73	78	88	77	86	102
40076	WADDY	94	86	68	82	90	96	79	87	83	79	101	103	78	104	81	85	97	84	92	110
40077	WESTPORT	95	117	124	117	115	114	105	104	97	104	122	122	111	130	107	94	122	101	94	116
40078	WILLISBURG	88	59	27	51	67	77	57	71	69	58	81	85	48	76	58	74	73	70	88	101
40104	BATTLETOWN	90	60	27	52	68	79	58	73	70	59	82	87	49	78	59	76	75	72	90	103
40107	BOSTON	80	70	53	67	74	80	65	72	69	65	84	86	64	86	67	71	80	70	79	94
40108	BRANDENBURG	94	78	53	72	83	91	73	84	81	74	97	99	69	96	75	83	91	82	94	109
40109	BROOKS	89	80	62	76	82	88	75	82	78	76	95	96	72	94	76	78	91	80	85	101
40111	CLOVERPORT	88	59	27	51	67	77	57	71	69	58	81	85	48	76	58	74	73	71	88	101
40115	CUSTER	91	61	28	52	69	79	59	73	71	60	83	88	50	79	60	76	76	73	90	104
40117	EKRON	86	69	46	64	73	80	66	75	72	67	87	89	61	83	66	74	81	74	83	98
40118	FAIRDALE	77	73	62	70	73	79	71	74	73	71	89	85	69	89	71	73	86	74	76	87
40119	FALLS OF ROUGH	77	58	37	52	66	74	55	67	63	55	75	79	49	73	58	68	69	66	80	93
40121	FORT KNOX	75	48	46	55	44	52	71	61	72	66	90	81	61	81	58	66	86	72	57	70
40140	GARFIELD	79	67	47	62	71	78	62	70	68	62	82	84	59	82	64	70	77	69	78	93
40142	GUSTON	100	83	57	77	89	97	77	88	85	78	102	105	73	102	79	88	96	86	99	117
40143	HARDINSBURG	92	62	28	53	70	80	59	74	72	61	84	89	51	80	60	77	77	74	92	106
40144	HARNED	92	62	28	53	70	81	60	75	72	61	85	89	51	80	61	78	77	74	92	106
40145	HUDSON	78	52	24	45	59	68	51	63	61	52	72	76	43	68	52	66	65	63	78	90
40146	IRVINGTON	81	57	30	50	64	72	55	67	64	55	76	80	48	73	56	69	70	66	80	93
40150	LEBANON JUNCTION	85	74	56	71	78	85	70	78	75	70	90	92	67	91	71	77	86	76	84	99
40152	MC DANIELS	63	50	34	45	56	63	47	56	53	46	63	66	42	62	50	56	58	55	67	77
40155	MULDRAUGH	62	56	50	54	56	60	57	59	59	57	73	68	55	70	56	58	70	60	59	68
40157	PAYNEVILLE	89	60	27	52	68	78	58	72	70	59	82	86	49	77	59	75	74	72	89	103
40160	RADCLIFF	73	74	71	74	73	76	73	73	72	73	89	86	72	88	72	70	87	74	70	83
40161	RHODELIA	87	58	26	50	66	76	56	70	68	57	80	84	48	75	57	73	72	70	87	100
40162	RINEYVILLE	101	96	81	93	100	105	89	96	91	89	112	113	88	114	91	92	107	93	99	119
40164	SE REE	74	57	38	51	64	72	54	65	61	53	72	76	48	71	57	65	67	64	77	89
40165	SHEPHERDSVILLE	93	85	69	82	89	95	80	87	84	80	102	103	79	103	82	85	97	85	92	108
40170	STEPHENSPORT	89	60	27	51	68	78	58	72	69	59	82	86	49	77	59	75	74	71	89	102
40171	UNION STAR	78	52	24	45	59	68	50	63	61	51	71	75	43	67	51	65	65	62	77	89
40175	VINE GROVE	85	83	72	81	84	88	79	83	79	79	98	97	77	97	79	79	94	82	83	98
40176	WEBSTER	84	57	26	49	64	74	55	68	66	56	77	82	46	73	55	71	70	68	84	97
40177	WEST POINT	74	55	33	50	61	68	53	63	61	53	72	75	48	71	54	64	67	62	74	85
40178	WESTVIEW	74	58	39	52	65	73	54	65	61	54	73	77	48	72	58	66	68	64	77	90
40202	LOUISVILLE	30	26	36	26	26	30	31	29	34	31	42	34	31	41	31	34	41	32	31	33
40203	LOUISVILLE	34	29	38	28	28	33	35	33	38	35	47	39	34	45	34	38	46	36	35	37
40204	LOUISVILLE	79	75	107	80	73	81	87	80	88	86	110	97	87	111	84	86	108	85	77	89
40205	LOUISVILLE	108	124	154	127	122	127	122	118	117	122	148	139	127	151	123	115	146	119	110	129
40206	LOUISVILLE	91	94	117	98	93	99	101	96	99	99	124	115	102	124	100	96	122	100	91	105
40207	LOUISVILLE	128	143	173	146	141	149	141	138	136	141	171	160	146	172	142	133	169	139	130	151
40208	LOUISVILLE	53	45	54	47	44	50	58	52	59	54	73	64	54	70	53	56	70	57	51	58
40209	LOUISVILLE	49	46	49	44	46	52	50	49	53	49	65	56	50	66	50	54	63	50	52	54
40210	LOUISVILLE	55	49	55	46	48	57	53	53	58	54	72	58	53	68	53	61	69	54	59	61
40211	LOUISVILLE	56	47	51	43	47	57	51	53	58	53	71	57	51	65	51	61	68	54	60	61
40212	LOUISVILLE	51	47	51	44	46	53	51	50	55	51	68	56	51	65	50	56	65	52	54	57
40213	LOUISVILLE	75	75	81	73	75	83	79	77	81	76	100	89	80	102	79	82	97	78	80	86
40214	LOUISVILLE	74	75	78	74	75	81	77	76	77	75	96	88	77	98	76	77	93	77	76	84
40215	LOUISVILLE	48	46	53	44	46	52	50	48	52	49	65	55	50	66	50	54	63	50	51	54
40216	LOUISVILLE	67	71	77	68	71	78	71	70	72	70	90	80	74	94	72	74	88	70	72	78
40217	LOUISVILLE	66	69	77	67	69	76	71	69	72	69	90	79	73	94	72	73	88	70	71	76
40218	LOUISVILLE	68	67	80	68	66	73	72	70	73	72	92	81	73	91	72	73	90	72	70	78
40219	LOUISVILLE	72	74	77	72	74	80	75	75	75	73	94	86	76	96	75	76	91	75	75	84
40220	LOUISVILLE	93	102	116	104	101	105	102	99	99	101	124	116	105	126	102	96	122	100	94	109
40222	LOUISVILLE	123	129	152	134	127	135	130	127	126	132	159	148	133	156	130	123	157	129	120	140
	KENTUCKY	86	74	63	71	77	85	74	80	79	74	96	94	71	95	74	81	91	80	86	98
	UNITED STATES	100	100	100	100	100	100	100	100	100	100	100	100	100	100	100	100	100	100	100	100

#	POST OFFICE NAME	COUNTY FIPS CODE	POPULATION 2000	2004	2009	% Rate	State Centile	HOUSEHOLDS 2000	2004	2009	% Annual Rate 2000-2004	2004 Average HH Size	FAMILIES 2000	2004	% Annual Rate 2000-2004
40223	LOUISVILLE	111	23045	24040	24823	1.0	75	9276	9827	10288	1.4	2.38	6206	6302	0.4
40228	LOUISVILLE	111	12665	12719	12961	0.1	45	4898	4982	5140	0.4	2.55	3570	3508	-0.4
40229	LOUISVILLE	111	29071	32014	34637	2.3	92	10229	11520	12712	2.8	2.74	8099	8899	2.2
40241	LOUISVILLE	111	22465	24818	26426	2.4	93	8742	9874	10699	2.9	2.51	6341	6885	2.0
40242	LOUISVILLE	111	11049	11061	11165	0.0	42	4597	4677	4787	0.4	2.33	3020	2944	-0.6
40243	LOUISVILLE	111	8920	9318	9658	1.0	77	3645	3885	4091	1.5	2.40	2686	2766	0.7
40245	LOUISVILLE	111	16153	19754	22107	4.9	99	5659	6976	7881	5.1	2.83	4690	5667	4.6
40258	LOUISVILLE	111	23991	25023	25883	1.0	75	9462	10039	10531	1.4	2.49	6864	7032	0.6
40272	LOUISVILLE	111	34255	35437	36467	0.8	71	12737	13386	13968	1.2	2.63	9692	9868	0.4
40291	LOUISVILLE	111	27556	29894	31543	1.9	90	10618	11711	12529	2.3	2.55	7997	8577	1.7
40292	LOUISVILLE	111	794	793	794	0.0	39	0	0	0	0.0	0.00	0	0	0.0
40299	LOUISVILLE	111	30488	32719	34399	1.7	87	11818	12848	13684	2.0	2.53	8697	9157	1.2
40311	CARLISLE	181	6973	7009	7061	0.1	46	2781	2846	2914	0.6	2.43	2000	1988	-0.1
40312	CLAY CITY	197	5996	6154	6259	0.6	65	2237	2369	2478	1.4	2.59	1710	1766	0.8
40313	CLEARFIELD	205	2586	2639	2650	0.5	61	1095	1140	1167	1.0	2.29	719	720	0.0
40316	DENNISTON	165	213	225	236	1.3	81	77	84	90	2.1	2.58	57	61	1.6
40322	FRENCHBURG	165	4036	4195	4372	0.9	73	1535	1640	1753	1.6	2.45	1142	1188	0.9
40324	GEORGETOWN	209	28158	30942	33952	2.2	92	10310	11578	12949	2.8	2.55	7552	8254	2.1
40328	GRAVEL SWITCH	155	1805	1784	1766	-0.3	28	694	702	710	0.3	2.52	524	515	-0.4
40330	HARRODSBURG	167	19175	19529	19866	0.4	59	7791	8098	8377	0.9	2.39	5554	5606	0.2
40336	IRVINE	065	13683	13866	13947	0.3	53	5424	5659	5803	1.0	2.43	3956	4010	0.3
40337	JEFFERSONVILLE	173	5006	5367	5609	1.7	86	1861	2047	2181	2.3	2.61	1447	1555	1.7
40342	LAWRENCEBURG	005	18767	20033	21369	1.6	85	7191	7812	8455	2.0	2.55	5423	5743	1.4
40346	MEANS	165	738	767	798	0.9	73	281	300	321	1.6	2.53	219	229	1.1
40347	MIDWAY	239	2353	2439	2537	0.9	72	911	971	1035	1.5	2.37	607	625	0.7
40350	MOOREFIELD	181	378	379	378	0.1	43	140	142	144	0.3	2.67	108	107	-0.2
40351	MOREHEAD	205	19995	19948	19871	-0.1	36	7020	7141	7244	0.4	2.36	4637	4556	-0.4
40353	MOUNT STERLING	173	17334	17898	18445	0.8	70	6958	7362	7734	1.3	2.38	4922	5048	0.6
40355	NEW LIBERTY	187	2175	2289	2427	1.2	80	843	899	965	1.5	2.55	630	654	0.9
40356	NICHOLASVILLE	113	30592	34149	38702	2.6	94	11293	12866	14852	3.1	2.63	8673	9642	2.5
40358	OLYMPIA	011	583	627	662	1.7	88	224	248	267	2.4	2.53	173	187	1.9
40359	OWENTON	187	7006	7312	7731	1.0	76	2748	2921	3139	1.5	2.47	1983	2047	0.8
40360	OWINGSVILLE	011	6497	6637	6866	0.5	61	2572	2687	2836	1.0	2.43	1857	1885	0.4
40361	PARIS	017	18191	18511	18824	0.4	58	7244	7536	7815	0.9	2.43	5117	5164	0.2
40370	SADIEVILLE	209	3434	3718	4027	1.9	89	1259	1396	1540	2.5	2.66	1009	1093	1.9
40371	SALT LICK	011	2512	2897	3183	3.4	97	1025	1211	1359	4.0	2.39	728	835	3.3
40372	SALVISA	167	2030	2076	2108	0.5	63	780	814	841	1.0	2.55	599	609	0.4
40374	SHARPSBURG	011	1624	1616	1652	-0.1	33	680	692	723	0.4	2.34	482	476	-0.3
40376	SLADE	197	492	493	503	0.1	43	194	202	212	1.0	2.44	145	147	0.3
40379	STAMPING GROUND	209	3026	3179	3442	1.2	79	1130	1215	1340	1.7	2.62	885	924	1.0
40380	STANTON	197	6769	6883	7057	0.4	56	2621	2744	2891	1.1	2.47	1935	1973	0.5
40383	VERSAILLES	239	20723	21560	22509	0.9	73	7914	8420	8979	1.5	2.54	6026	6250	0.9
40385	WACO	151	2337	2345	2398	0.1	44	888	911	948	0.6	2.57	696	695	0.0
40387	WELLINGTON	165	1685	1771	1859	1.2	80	690	745	802	1.8	2.32	517	544	1.2
40390	WILMORE	113	7263	7590	8187	1.0	77	2128	2270	2525	1.5	2.69	1613	1677	0.9
40391	WINCHESTER	049	32781	34783	37394	1.4	84	12872	13986	15386	2.0	2.46	9430	9965	1.3
40402	ANNVILLE	109	2389	2492	2572	1.0	75	901	964	1017	1.6	2.55	686	716	1.0
40403	BEREA	151	20410	21404	22330	1.1	78	7818	8416	8969	1.8	2.44	5671	5902	0.9
40404	BEREA	151	426	452	470	1.4	84	2	3	3	10.0	2.67	1	1	0.0
40409	BRODHEAD	203	3234	3321	3429	0.6	65	1286	1355	1436	1.2	2.42	951	973	0.5
40419	CRAB ORCHARD	137	5063	5442	5862	1.7	87	1909	2099	2311	2.3	2.57	1398	1493	1.6
40422	DANVILLE	021	22924	23337	23752	0.4	58	8702	9056	9411	0.9	2.30	5947	5997	0.2
40437	HUSTONVILLE	137	3949	4124	4389	1.0	77	1574	1685	1835	1.6	2.45	1162	1211	1.0
40440	JUNCTION CITY	021	2596	2656	2684	0.5	63	984	1032	1065	1.1	2.57	727	738	0.4
40442	KINGS MOUNTAIN	045	1260	1264	1307	0.1	44	522	539	572	0.8	2.34	379	380	0.1
40444	LANCASTER	079	12211	12849	13309	1.2	80	4748	5063	5291	1.5	2.52	3582	3725	0.9
40447	MC KEE	109	8513	8707	8919	0.5	63	3397	3566	3738	1.2	2.42	2499	2551	0.5
40456	MOUNT VERNON	203	11475	11810	12247	0.7	67	4586	4850	5164	1.3	2.39	3306	3398	0.7
40460	ORLANDO	203	232	233	238	0.1	45	93	97	101	1.0	2.40	69	70	0.3
40461	PAINT LICK	079	2130	2217	2297	1.0	74	822	873	917	1.4	2.54	658	682	0.9
40464	PARKSVILLE	021	900	890	883	-0.3	28	350	355	360	0.3	2.51	271	268	-0.3
40468	PERRYVILLE	021	1614	1543	1523	-1.1	6	661	646	650	-0.5	2.39	493	466	-1.3
40472	RAVENNA	065	1729	1643	1613	-1.2	4	720	704	704	-0.5	2.32	503	477	-1.2
40475	RICHMOND	151	48231	50756	53065	1.2	80	18636	20167	21576	1.9	2.31	11967	12515	1.1
40481	SANDGAP	109	406	403	406	-0.2	31	159	163	168	0.6	2.45	113	112	-0.2
40484	STANFORD	137	11290	12065	13068	1.6	85	4451	4872	5406	2.2	2.43	3226	3433	1.5
40486	TYNER	109	2083	2105	2127	0.3	51	814	846	875	0.9	2.48	630	639	0.3
40489	WAYNESBURG	137	4118	4406	4786	1.6	86	1607	1770	1971	2.3	2.48	1190	1275	1.6
40502	LEXINGTON	067	27779	27388	28262	-0.3	25	13423	13459	14135	0.1	2.02	6806	6409	-1.4
40503	LEXINGTON	067	26980	28509	30234	1.3	81	11259	12150	13156	1.8	2.28	7094	7423	1.1
40504	LEXINGTON	067	24189	24989	26198	0.8	70	10882	11508	12328	1.3	2.11	5728	5670	-0.2
40505	LEXINGTON	067	26433	26539	27547	0.1	45	11113	11432	12125	0.7	2.31	7129	7037	-0.3
40507	LEXINGTON	067	2256	2248	2323	-0.1	34	1175	1204	1282	0.6	1.55	268	247	-1.9
40508	LEXINGTON	067	25931	25918	26728	0.0	39	9099	9294	9862	0.5	2.06	3535	3343	-1.3
40509	LEXINGTON	067	20366	23990	26594	3.9	98	8897	10631	11965	4.3	2.24	5346	6141	3.3
40510	LEXINGTON	067	1111	1534	1843	7.9	100	297	436	539	9.5	2.77	218	309	8.6
40511	LEXINGTON	067	18311	18670	19379	0.5	60	6596	6846	7302	0.9	2.32	4235	4197	-0.2
40513	LEXINGTON	067	8418	9488	10288	2.9	95	3187	3699	4107	3.6	2.56	2375	2667	2.8
40514	LEXINGTON	067	11313	11984	12535	1.4	83	3911	4262	4563	2.0	2.81	3286	3499	1.5
40515	LEXINGTON	067	29782	32615	35036	2.2	91	11541	12952	14207	2.8	2.50	7875	8499	1.8
40516	LEXINGTON	067	2628	2848	3042	1.9	89	979	1088	1189	2.5	2.59	737	794	1.8
40517	LEXINGTON	067	36337	37011	38473	0.4	59	16412	17195	18273	1.1	2.14	8705	8544	-0.4
40601	FRANKFORT	073	48730	49180	49618	0.2	50	20301	20973	21526	0.8	2.26	13131	13076	-0.1
40701	CORBIN	235	28372	29374	30297	0.8	71	11242	11928	12574	1.4	2.41	8023	8267	0.7
40729	EAST BERNSTADT	125	5037	4897	4921	-0.7	13	1953	1958	2014	0.1	2.50	1490	1452	-0.6
40734	GRAY	121	2429	2425	2447	0.0	38	887	908	940	0.6	2.67	695	695	0.0
40737	KEAVY	125	1322	1458	1547	2.3	92	491	556	602	3.0	2.62	395	437	2.4
40740	LILY	125	2668	2784	2893	1.0	76	1005	1075	1141	1.6	2.57	753	782	0.9
40741	LONDON	125	19448	20086	20713	0.8	70	7557	8008	8442	1.4	2.44	5575	5761	0.8
40744	LONDON	125	16658	17719	18530	1.5	84	6370	6970	7456	2.1	2.54	4953	5284	1.5
40754	NEVISDALE	235	175	169	169	-0.8	9	61	60	61	-0.4	2.82	43	41	-1.1
40759	ROCKHOLDS	235	2347	2725	2960	3.6	97	858	1021	1133	4.2	2.65	671	773	3.4
40763	SILER	235	765	730	727	-1.1	5	317	313	319	-0.3	2.33	232	222	-1.0
40769	WILLIAMSBURG	235	17899	18114	18501	0.3	52	6800	7047	7351	0.8	2.44	4771	4787	0.1
40771	WOODBINE	121	464	457	459	-0.4	24	185	187	192	0.3	2.32	135	133	-0.4
	KENTUCKY					0.7					1.2	2.42			0.5
	UNITED STATES					1.2					1.3	2.58			1.1

ZIP CODE		RACE (%)						% Hispanic Origin		2004 AGE DISTRIBUTION (%)										MEDIAN AGE		
#	POST OFFICE NAME	White		Black		Asian/Pacific															%	%
		2000	2004	2000	2004	2000	2004	2000	2004	0-4	5-9	10-14	15-19	20-24	25-44	45-64	65-84	85+	18+	2004	2004 Males	2004 Females
40223	LOUISVILLE	88.0	86.1	7.3	8.2	2.5	3.2	2.2	2.8	5.7	6.4	7.2	6.3	5.6	25.6	29.2	11.7	2.2	76.5	40.8	47.5	52.5
40228	LOUISVILLE	88.0	87.1	8.9	9.2	0.9	1.1	2.0	2.5	6.7	6.6	7.0	6.4	6.4	29.8	25.6	10.5	1.0	75.8	37.2	49.1	50.9
40229	LOUISVILLE	94.1	93.3	3.2	3.5	0.7	0.8	1.2	1.6	7.9	7.6	7.8	6.4	6.7	33.9	22.5	6.9	0.5	72.9	33.5	50.0	50.0
40241	LOUISVILLE	85.4	83.5	9.1	9.7	3.4	4.4	1.6	2.1	7.6	7.7	7.2	6.0	5.2	29.3	26.3	9.4	1.3	73.7	37.5	48.4	51.6
40242	LOUISVILLE	89.7	88.2	6.1	6.7	1.8	2.3	2.1	2.6	6.0	6.1	5.9	6.0	6.3	27.3	27.0	14.4	1.1	78.2	40.2	48.2	51.8
40243	LOUISVILLE	91.5	90.1	5.8	6.6	1.1	1.4	1.7	2.3	5.7	6.4	7.2	6.1	4.9	25.2	29.6	13.4	1.5	76.9	41.8	48.1	51.9
40245	LOUISVILLE	86.4	84.9	9.2	9.9	2.1	2.7	2.8	3.5	8.6	9.0	8.0	5.9	4.7	30.6	27.5	5.3	0.3	70.6	36.0	49.0	51.0
40258	LOUISVILLE	94.1	93.3	4.1	4.7	0.4	0.6	0.8	1.0	6.6	6.5	6.6	6.4	6.7	29.1	24.7	12.6	0.8	76.5	37.4	48.7	51.3
40272	LOUISVILLE	95.4	94.7	2.2	2.5	0.4	0.6	0.9	1.3	7.1	6.9	7.1	6.5	6.6	28.1	24.2	12.6	1.0	74.9	36.9	48.4	51.6
40291	LOUISVILLE	89.8	88.9	6.6	6.9	1.4	1.7	1.7	2.1	6.7	6.9	6.9	6.0	6.1	30.3	26.7	9.8	0.7	75.9	37.1	48.9	51.1
40292	LOUISVILLE	56.1	52.7	36.5	38.8	2.9	3.5	2.8	3.4	0.3	0.5	0.3	68.2	26.0	4.0	0.5	0.3	0.0	98.6	18.6	47.8	52.2
40299	LOUISVILLE	90.4	89.0	6.3	6.9	1.1	1.5	1.8	2.2	7.3	7.5	7.0	5.7	5.0	30.6	25.7	10.1	1.2	74.8	37.8	48.6	51.4
40311	CARLISLE	98.0	97.9	1.0	1.1	0.1	0.1	0.7	0.7	6.2	6.5	6.5	5.7	5.7	28.1	25.6	13.5	2.3	77.4	39.4	48.7	51.3
40312	CLAY CITY	97.9	97.7	1.0	1.1	0.1	0.1	0.7	0.9	7.0	7.4	7.2	7.2	7.0	30.0	24.3	9.2	0.7	73.9	35.0	50.6	49.4
40313	CLEARFIELD	96.8	96.9	0.9	0.9	0.5	0.5	1.6	1.6	6.8	6.7	6.3	5.3	7.0	32.3	23.3	11.1	1.2	77.3	35.3	49.7	50.3
40316	DENNISTON	96.2	96.4	2.4	2.2	0.0	0.0	1.9	2.2	5.3	5.3	5.3	8.0	8.0	28.0	28.4	10.7	0.9	79.1	38.8	51.6	48.4
40322	FRENCHBURG	97.8	97.7	1.4	1.4	0.0	0.1	1.1	1.3	6.0	6.2	6.5	7.3	6.9	27.2	26.1	12.2	1.7	77.0	37.8	49.7	50.3
40324	GEORGETOWN	91.0	90.4	6.1	6.2	0.6	0.7	1.8	2.3	7.7	7.4	7.1	7.5	8.5	31.6	21.6	7.7	1.1	74.2	32.7	48.8	51.2
40328	GRAVEL SWITCH	98.1	97.9	0.8	0.8	0.2	0.2	0.6	0.7	6.1	6.3	7.1	6.3	6.3	28.9	25.8	11.8	1.5	76.6	38.6	51.0	49.1
40330	HARRODSBURG	93.6	93.1	4.0	4.1	0.5	0.7	1.4	1.8	6.3	6.6	7.2	5.7	5.4	28.0	25.9	13.1	1.9	76.4	39.2	48.7	51.3
40336	IRVINE	99.1	99.1	0.1	0.1	0.0	0.0	0.5	0.5	6.3	6.4	7.1	6.0	6.4	29.3	25.1	11.8	1.6	76.5	37.6	48.8	51.2
40337	JEFFERSONVILLE	98.3	98.0	0.3	0.3	0.1	0.1	0.9	1.3	7.8	7.8	7.3	6.8	5.5	31.5	23.9	8.6	0.8	72.7	34.6	51.5	48.5
40342	LAWRENCEBURG	96.5	96.3	2.4	2.5	0.1	0.2	0.8	1.0	7.5	7.7	7.7	5.9	5.1	31.3	24.0	9.4	1.4	73.4	36.2	49.0	51.0
40346	MEANS	99.2	99.1	0.3	0.4	0.0	0.0	0.7	0.8	6.4	6.8	7.3	6.9	6.1	29.5	26.2	10.0	0.8	75.1	36.1	52.4	47.6
40347	MIDWAY	90.2	89.2	6.0	6.3	0.3	0.4	4.8	6.2	6.7	6.0	5.4	5.5	7.9	31.6	25.1	10.6	1.4	79.3	36.5	47.0	53.0
40350	MOOREFIELD	99.2	99.5	0.3	0.3	0.0	0.0	0.8	0.5	6.9	6.9	7.1	6.3	7.7	30.3	24.8	9.2	0.8	75.2	35.8	51.7	48.3
40351	MOREHEAD	95.9	95.9	1.6	1.6	1.0	1.0	1.0	1.0	5.6	5.3	5.7	9.4	13.6	28.5	20.9	9.8	1.2	80.4	30.5	48.6	51.4
40353	MOUNT STERLING	94.1	93.7	4.4	4.6	0.2	0.2	1.2	1.5	6.8	6.7	6.7	5.8	6.1	29.0	25.3	11.8	1.9	76.3	37.5	48.2	51.9
40355	NEW LIBERTY	94.9	94.5	3.0	3.0	0.2	0.3	1.2	1.5	6.9	7.0	7.0	6.3	6.0	28.9	25.6	11.5	0.9	75.4	37.5	51.1	48.9
40356	NICHOLASVILLE	94.3	93.9	3.4	3.5	0.4	0.5	1.3	1.6	7.6	7.4	7.5	6.7	6.7	30.4	24.2	8.5	1.0	73.4	34.6	49.0	51.0
40358	OLYMPIA	98.5	98.1	0.3	0.5	0.0	0.2	0.7	0.6	6.2	6.7	6.5	6.2	6.2	29.4	26.6	10.9	1.3	76.6	37.3	52.3	47.7
40359	OWENTON	97.5	97.3	0.7	0.7	0.3	0.4	0.9	1.2	6.0	6.4	7.3	6.1	5.7	26.5	26.4	13.4	2.3	76.6	39.6	49.5	50.5
40360	OWINGSVILLE	97.4	97.1	1.5	1.6	0.0	0.0	0.9	1.1	6.9	6.9	6.5	5.6	6.0	28.1	24.9	12.5	2.6	76.4	38.4	48.8	51.2
40361	PARIS	90.1	89.4	7.3	7.5	0.1	0.2	2.6	3.3	6.4	6.5	7.0	6.3	5.9	27.7	25.9	12.4	2.0	76.2	38.8	48.7	51.3
40370	SADIEVILLE	97.3	97.0	1.2	1.3	0.2	0.2	0.6	0.7	6.1	6.8	8.0	6.6	5.5	30.4	28.0	7.8	0.8	75.0	37.9	51.4	48.6
40371	SALT LICK	98.8	98.8	0.2	0.1	0.0	0.0	0.2	0.3	6.2	6.4	6.8	6.1	5.5	28.7	27.5	12.2	0.8	76.9	39.0	50.1	49.9
40372	SALVISA	98.6	98.4	0.4	0.4	0.3	0.3	0.2	0.3	6.7	6.9	6.6	5.9	5.1	27.4	29.0	11.1	1.4	76.2	40.3	49.9	50.1
40374	SHARPSBURG	91.6	90.8	6.0	6.3	0.0	0.0	1.6	2.0	6.3	6.4	7.2	5.8	5.3	27.2	25.9	14.1	1.9	76.6	40.1	51.1	49.0
40376	SLADE	99.4	99.6	0.0	0.0	0.0	0.0	0.6	0.6	5.9	6.3	6.5	6.5	6.1	29.4	27.6	10.6	1.2	77.7	38.3	51.3	48.7
40379	STAMPING GROUND	97.2	96.9	1.3	1.4	0.2	0.2	0.9	1.1	7.1	7.4	7.6	6.2	6.0	30.1	25.4	9.0	1.2	74.1	36.5	51.1	48.9
40380	STANTON	99.1	99.0	0.3	0.3	0.0	0.1	0.7	0.9	6.8	6.9	6.9	6.3	6.7	29.7	24.6	10.7	1.5	75.7	36.4	49.9	50.1
40383	VERSAILLES	92.2	91.7	5.4	5.5	0.3	0.4	2.7	3.5	6.2	6.5	7.2	6.8	5.8	28.2	28.2	10.0	1.2	75.9	38.8	48.4	51.7
40385	WACO	98.5	98.3	0.6	0.7	0.0	0.0	0.7	0.9	5.7	6.3	7.7	6.4	5.9	29.6	28.0	9.7	0.8	76.4	38.0	49.2	50.8
40387	WELLINGTON	96.8	96.6	1.7	1.8	0.1	0.1	1.4	1.6	5.8	5.7	6.2	7.9	8.1	28.5	26.7	10.5	0.7	77.6	37.2	52.0	48.1
40390	WILMORE	95.0	94.2	1.8	1.9	1.7	2.3	1.5	1.9	6.7	6.1	6.6	9.7	13.6	30.0	17.0	8.7	1.7	76.7	28.7	50.4	49.6
40391	WINCHESTER	93.6	93.1	4.8	5.0	0.2	0.3	1.2	1.5	6.5	6.5	6.9	6.3	6.2	28.9	25.9	11.4	1.4	76.1	37.8	48.4	51.6
40402	ANNVILLE	98.9	98.8	0.0	0.0	0.0	0.0	0.8	1.0	6.9	7.2	7.8	7.0	6.0	29.7	23.6	10.2	1.6	73.9	35.3	50.2	49.8
40403	BEREA	95.3	94.9	2.4	2.5	0.5	0.6	0.8	1.1	6.8	6.5	6.5	7.6	7.7	30.5	23.4	9.9	1.2	76.7	34.7	48.0	52.0
40404	BEREA	80.3	78.8	13.2	13.7	2.8	3.3	2.8	2.9	2.2	1.3	2.2	42.7	25.0	11.7	6.0	4.9	4.0	92.3	20.3	53.3	46.7
40409	BRODHEAD	99.1	99.0	0.0	0.1	0.2	0.3	0.5	0.7	6.4	6.6	7.3	6.1	5.5	29.3	24.2	13.0	1.8	75.9	38.0	49.3	50.7
40419	CRAB ORCHARD	98.5	98.3	0.6	0.6	0.0	0.0	0.8	1.1	6.7	6.8	7.6	6.8	5.9	28.9	23.7	12.0	1.6	74.8	36.8	49.9	50.1
40422	DANVILLE	85.8	85.2	11.5	11.7	0.7	0.9	1.4	1.8	5.3	5.6	6.4	7.0	8.5	27.1	25.6	12.5	2.0	79.0	38.2	49.7	50.3
40437	HUSTONVILLE	97.8	97.5	0.7	0.7	0.1	0.2	0.9	1.1	6.4	6.5	6.9	6.2	5.9	30.0	25.3	11.6	1.2	76.5	37.6	50.4	49.6
40440	JUNCTION CITY	97.4	97.1	0.9	0.9	0.2	0.3	2.6	3.4	7.3	7.3	8.2	6.0	6.2	29.8	24.0	10.3	0.9	73.2	35.1	48.6	51.4
40442	KINGS MOUNTAIN	98.3	98.1	0.2	0.2	0.0	0.0	1.1	1.3	5.9	6.1	7.2	6.4	5.9	28.2	25.9	13.2	1.3	76.9	39.0	51.3	48.7
40444	LANCASTER	95.2	94.9	3.6	3.7	0.1	0.1	1.5	1.9	6.2	6.4	7.0	6.2	5.5	29.7	25.5	11.8	1.8	76.7	38.7	49.3	50.7
40447	MC KEE	99.2	99.2	0.1	0.1	0.0	0.1	0.6	0.7	6.8	6.8	7.1	6.6	6.8	29.5	24.6	10.7	1.3	75.5	36.2	49.3	50.7
40456	MOUNT VERNON	98.8	98.7	0.2	0.2	0.1	0.1	0.6	0.8	5.9	6.5	6.9	6.2	6.2	30.0	25.1	11.7	1.5	76.6	37.4	50.0	50.1
40460	ORLANDO	97.0	96.6	0.0	0.0	0.0	0.0	0.0	0.4	5.6	6.9	6.9	8.2	4.7	30.5	25.8	11.2	0.4	74.7	38.7	52.4	47.6
40461	PAINT LICK	97.6	97.3	0.7	0.7	0.4	0.5	0.9	1.2	6.3	6.5	6.8	6.1	5.7	30.2	27.2	10.2	1.0	76.5	38.1	50.1	49.9
40464	PARKSVILLE	97.2	97.0	0.8	0.8	0.1	0.2	0.7	0.8	6.0	6.5	8.3	5.1	5.5	29.4	27.2	10.8	1.2	76.2	38.7	51.5	48.5
40468	PERRYVILLE	95.6	95.4	2.6	2.7	0.1	0.1	0.6	0.6	6.7	7.0	6.6	6.1	4.8	27.0	27.9	12.3	1.7	76.0	40.2	48.7	51.3
40472	RAVENNA	98.9	98.9	0.3	0.3	0.0	0.0	0.5	0.6	4.5	5.3	6.4	6.3	5.8	28.4	26.8	14.2	2.2	80.3	40.6	48.0	52.0
40475	RICHMOND	92.0	91.4	5.4	5.5	0.8	1.1	1.0	1.3	6.3	5.7	5.8	9.2	12.3	30.4	20.5	8.6	1.1	79.1	30.7	48.6	51.4
40481	SANDGAP	99.3	99.0	0.3	0.3	0.0	0.0	0.5	0.3	7.9	7.7	6.5	6.5	7.2	28.8	23.8	10.4	1.2	74.4	34.0	50.1	49.9
40484	STANFORD	94.2	93.8	4.3	4.4	0.1	0.2	0.9	1.1	7.1	6.9	7.0	6.3	6.4	29.5	23.9	11.5	1.5	75.2	36.7	48.6	51.4
40486	TYNER	99.3	99.2	0.0	0.0	0.0	0.0	0.2	0.3	6.0	6.1	7.2	6.4	6.4	29.6	24.7	12.2	1.4	76.5	37.4	50.1	49.9
40489	WAYNESBURG	98.6	98.4	0.2	0.2	0.1	0.1	1.0	1.3	6.5	6.5	7.1	6.6	6.2	27.7	24.9	13.5	1.1	75.9	38.0	49.9	50.1
40502	LEXINGTON	92.8	91.7	2.7	2.9	2.4	3.0	2.1	2.7	4.1	4.1	4.9	5.9	9.7	29.6	26.8	12.6	2.3	83.6	38.7	48.3	51.7
40503	LEXINGTON	92.5	91.1	2.6	2.9	3.1	3.9	1.9	2.5	5.1	5.3	5.9	6.6	8.3	28.8	25.8	12.4	1.9	80.4	38.5	48.0	52.0
40504	LEXINGTON	82.8	81.2	11.4	12.0	0.9	1.1	8.9	10.8	6.3	5.4	5.1	6.2	9.9	30.0	21.5	12.9	2.8	80.2	35.7	49.0	51.0
40505	LEXINGTON	78.7	76.8	17.4	18.6	0.6	0.8	3.2	4.2	6.1	6.0	6.2	6.0	6.3	29.3	26.2	12.8	1.2	78.2	38.9	48.3	51.7
40507	LEXINGTON	63.0	61.8	32.1	32.3	1.6	2.2	4.3	5.3	2.5	2.1	2.5	5.5	15.8	37.8	21.2	10.5	2.1	90.8	35.2	57.4	42.6
40508	LEXINGTON	60.1	59.0	31.5	31.2	5.2	6.4	3.3	4.1	3.9	3.6	3.8	19.9	21.3	25.6	15.0	6.0	0.9	86.2	24.4	50.7	49.3
40509	LEXINGTON	81.2	79.5	12.7	13.2	3.1	3.9	2.5	3.2	8.2	7.2	5.6	4.7	6.6	41.0	19.6	6.1	1.1	76.5	32.8	48.5	51.5
40510	LEXINGTON	85.0	84.2	11.9	12.3	1.4	1.6	17.4	21.9	2.7	3.1	4.0	5.0	5.7	32.1	31.4	14.8	1.4	87.6	43.6	57.8	42.2
40511	LEXINGTON	53.4	53.3	40.6	39.7	0.8	1.0	8.1	9.8	5.5	5.5	5.6	5.1	6.3	35.3	25.6	10.2	0.9	80.4	37.2	54.6	45.4
40513	LEXINGTON	91.3	89.6	2.5	2.7	4.8	6.0	1.0	1.3	5.2	6.1	7.9	7.2	6.1	29.0	30.2	7.6	0.7	76.3	38.7	48.6	51.4
40514	LEXINGTON	93.1	91.9	3.1	3.4	2.1	2.7	1.2	1.6	8.5	8.7	8.4	7.3	5.1	32.7	24.6	4.4	0.3	69.7	35.0	48.8	51.2
40515	LEXINGTON	88.8	87.3	5.7	6.0	3.3	4.3	1.6	2.1	7.8	8.0	7.6	6.0	6.2	36.5	22.9	4.4	0.7	72.9	33.0	49.0	51.0
40516	LEXINGTON	87.1	85.6	9.5	10.4	0.6	0.8	2.4	3.0	6.5	6.5	6.8	5.4	5.1	29.4	28.0	10.9	1.4	76.3	39.4	48.6	51.4
40517	LEXINGTON	81.6	80.0	13.1	13.8	2.2	2.7	1.8	2.3	7.1	5.9	5.9	6.1	11.3	38.1	17.8	6.7	1.0	77.7	29.8	47.5	52.5
40601	FRANKFORT	88.2	87.5	9.2	9.4	0.7	0.9	1.2	1.5	6.0	6.0	6.2	6.3	6.9	29.3	26.8	11.2	1.5	78.3	38.3	48.6	51.4
40701	CORBIN	98.3	98.1	0.1	0.1	0.3	0.4	0.6	0.8	7.1	6.9	6.9	6.3	6.3	27.0	25.1	12.6	2.0	75.3	37.7	47.6	52.4
40729	EAST BERNSTADT	96.4	96.1	1.9	2.0	0.1	0.2	0.7	0.9	6.7	6.8	7.3	6.4	6.3	29.3	25.7	10.5	1.1	75.4	36.8	49.7	50.3
40734	GRAY	97.9	97.6	0.5	0.5	0.0	0.0	0.4	0.6	7.5	7.3	7.3	7.0	7.2	28.2	24.5	9.9	1.1	73.6	35.1	51.1	48.9
40737	KEAVY	98.0	97.7	0.1	0.1	0.1	0.1	0.6	0.8	7.5	7.4	7.5	6.3	6.4	30.8	23.1	10.2	0.9	73.8	35.4	48.7	51.3
40740	LILY	98.2	98.0	0.1	0.1	0.1	0.1	0.5	0.6	8.5	7.8	7.2	6.6	7.1	30.3	22.8	8.7	1.0	72.6	33.8	49.3	50.8
40741	LONDON	97.5	97.3	0.8	0.8	0.4	0.5	0.5	0.6	6.5	6.5	6.5	5.8	6.3	29.1	26.1	11.6	1.7	76.9	38.1	49.3	50.7
40744	LONDON	98.0	97.7	0.4	0.4	0.5	0.6	0.6	0.8	7.2	7.1	6.9	6.3	6.4	30.0	25.3	9.9	0.9	75.0	36.2	49.4	50.6
40754	NEVISDALE	98.9	99.4	0.0	0.0	0.0	0.0	0.0	0.0	7.1	7.1	8.3	7.7	5.9	29.0	24.3	10.1	0.6	72.2	36.8	48.5	51.5
40759	ROCKHOLDS	98.8	98.7	0.1	0.2	0.1	0.2	1.0	1.2	6.8	7.4	7.9	6.0	6.2	29.1	24.6	10.8	1.4	74.4	36.1	50.7	49.3
40763	SILER	99.1	99.0	0.0	0.0	0.1	0.1	0.3	0.3	5.9	6.4	7.8	7.3	5.2	27.8	26.3	11.2	2.1	74.5	38.3	51.5	48.5
40769	WILLIAMSBURG	98.1	97.9	0.6	0.7	0.2	0.2	0.6	0.8	6.4	6.5	7.3	7.6	8.7	27.8	23.4	10.7	1.6	75.7	34.7	48.7	51.3
40771	WOODBINE	98.3	98.0	0.0	0.0	0.2	0.2	0.4	0.2	6.8	6.8	6.8	5.9	6.1	25.2	26.9	12.5	3.1	75.9	39.3	47.1	53.0
	KENTUCKY	90.1	89.5	7.3	7.4	0.8	1.0	1.5	1.9	6.6	6.6	6.8	6.6	7.0	28.9	24.8	11.1	1.5	76.3	36.8	49.1	50.9
	UNITED STATES	75.1	73.6	12.3	12.5	3.8	4.2	12.5	14.1	6.9	6.7	7.2	7.0	7.3	28.6	23.8	10.8	1.7	75.1	36.0	49.1	50.9

#	POST OFFICE NAME	2004 Per Capita Income	2004 HH Income Base	2004 Household Income Distribution (%): Less than $25,000	$25,000 to $49,999	$50,000 to $99,999	$100,000 to $149,999	$150,000 or More	Median Household Income: 2004	2009	2004 National Centile	2004 State Centile	2004 Home Value Base	2004 Home Value Distribution (%): Less than $50,000	$50,000 to $89,999	$90,000 to $174,999	$175,000 to $399,999	$400,000 or More	2004 Median Home Value
40223	LOUISVILLE	42254	9827	10.7	22.9	32.7	17.7	16.1	71690	92789	92	98	7060	0.4	3.1	38.6	50.0	7.9	197742
40228	LOUISVILLE	26072	4982	16.2	27.5	39.6	13.5	3.2	56227	71500	81	93	3739	1.6	8.9	72.8	15.4	1.4	132130
40229	LOUISVILLE	22598	11520	15.2	30.4	42.5	9.8	2.2	52867	64348	77	92	9226	3.9	19.5	67.3	9.0	0.4	108506
40241	LOUISVILLE	41894	9874	9.2	18.1	35.6	21.0	16.2	79159	101065	95	99	7590	0.2	1.9	35.9	54.8	7.2	196884
40242	LOUISVILLE	34736	4677	14.7	21.7	38.0	16.4	9.2	64448	81816	88	97	3454	0.8	7.0	50.4	41.1	0.6	161084
40243	LOUISVILLE	41623	3885	11.7	21.4	35.0	19.6	12.4	72308	93322	92	98	3193	0.5	4.5	46.4	47.1	1.5	172585
40245	LOUISVILLE	46419	6976	6.3	13.1	33.0	22.7	24.9	95238	120373	98	100	6210	0.4	3.1	25.6	51.6	19.3	257753
40258	LOUISVILLE	21881	10039	20.9	31.7	37.8	8.0	1.6	47882	60388	68	87	8124	8.3	24.4	63.7	3.5	0.1	102592
40272	LOUISVILLE	22394	13386	20.1	31.4	36.5	9.5	2.6	48626	61161	70	88	10811	12.2	26.7	50.5	10.3	0.3	99344
40291	LOUISVILLE	29803	11711	11.5	23.5	42.3	17.6	5.2	64103	81067	88	97	9476	3.3	8.3	62.1	25.0	1.3	138041
40292	LOUISVILLE	9913	0	0.0	0.0	0.0	0.0	0.0	0	0	0	0	0	0.0	0.0	0.0	0.0	0.0	0
40299	LOUISVILLE	30625	12848	12.2	21.2	41.2	19.3	6.1	67184	85770	90	97	10581	0.4	5.8	59.5	32.5	1.9	149776
40311	CARLISLE	19283	2846	37.4	31.4	23.4	5.1	2.7	33613	40079	23	56	2186	29.9	35.2	28.2	5.4	1.2	72333
40312	CLAY CITY	13302	2369	46.8	30.3	20.4	2.1	0.5	26747	31588	7	34	1896	44.9	30.5	22.5	2.1	0.0	56644
40313	CLEARFIELD	16464	1140	45.6	27.4	22.6	2.6	1.8	27776	33765	8	37	811	40.6	28.2	22.8	8.0	0.4	62071
40316	DENNISTON	12898	84	45.2	35.7	16.7	1.2	1.2	27642	32667	8	36	71	38.0	40.9	19.7	1.4	0.0	61875
40322	FRENCHBURG	14016	1640	49.3	30.7	16.6	2.4	1.0	25415	29702	5	28	1304	42.9	31.4	22.2	3.2	0.4	55706
40324	GEORGETOWN	27281	11578	19.4	23.9	36.4	14.0	6.4	57126	70592	82	94	8267	9.8	14.3	49.4	22.6	4.0	129711
40328	GRAVEL SWITCH	17530	702	38.2	28.2	26.4	5.4	1.9	34159	41631	25	57	581	36.3	26.0	27.9	8.8	1.0	71618
40330	HARRODSBURG	21421	8098	29.3	30.2	32.1	6.2	2.3	40593	49606	48	75	6131	11.4	28.3	43.8	14.2	2.4	100852
40336	IRVINE	15036	5659	47.1	29.9	18.3	3.4	1.3	26519	31382	6	32	4328	46.9	28.6	18.6	5.9	0.0	53585
40337	JEFFERSONVILLE	15352	2047	35.6	33.8	26.1	3.7	0.8	33301	40416	22	54	1703	38.3	29.4	26.3	5.2	0.8	65977
40342	LAWRENCEBURG	22286	7812	18.9	29.4	42.0	7.5	2.2	50979	57999	74	90	6286	8.9	18.6	53.9	17.3	1.4	114804
40346	MEANS	13825	300	48.0	29.0	18.3	3.3	1.3	26268	30668	6	31	245	42.9	32.2	22.5	2.5	0.0	57292
40347	MIDWAY	29336	971	24.2	19.2	37.0	13.7	6.0	58262	72997	83	95	680	10.6	15.3	43.2	23.2	7.7	130822
40350	MOOREFIELD	20510	142	33.1	34.5	26.8	4.2	1.4	36794	43301	35	65	120	35.0	31.7	29.2	4.2	0.0	70000
40351	MOREHEAD	17931	7141	38.8	30.0	22.8	5.9	2.6	32545	40095	19	51	5072	30.2	27.6	30.1	11.0	1.3	79050
40353	MOUNT STERLING	22366	7362	31.7	28.2	29.7	6.8	3.6	39025	49645	43	71	5283	14.9	30.5	37.8	15.4	1.4	98171
40355	NEW LIBERTY	18617	899	28.1	32.3	33.0	6.6	0.0	42713	51221	55	80	739	30.6	19.5	32.5	12.9	4.6	89904
40356	NICHOLASVILLE	23982	12866	21.3	30.6	32.3	11.2	4.7	48164	60206	69	87	9055	10.2	19.7	45.4	21.3	3.5	115706
40358	OLYMPIA	18480	248	32.7	34.3	27.4	4.4	1.2	35205	42458	28	61	213	39.4	26.3	31.9	2.4	0.0	58333
40359	OWENTON	19257	2921	32.9	29.3	29.0	6.3	2.4	37238	45786	36	67	2297	23.8	31.0	33.0	10.1	2.0	84132
40360	OWINGSVILLE	18667	2687	41.1	28.7	22.7	5.3	2.3	32037	39381	18	50	2129	33.4	33.4	25.5	7.1	0.7	68494
40361	PARIS	22737	7536	30.9	27.8	29.5	8.1	3.7	41113	51750	50	77	5250	11.3	29.1	42.3	13.0	4.3	101330
40370	SADIEVILLE	23917	1396	21.2	23.7	37.8	12.4	4.9	54832	67028	79	93	1205	18.1	20.8	38.4	20.8	1.8	110099
40371	SALT LICK	19815	1211	43.9	31.6	18.9	2.6	3.0	28476	34286	10	39	1007	43.4	28.0	19.8	8.4	0.4	56456
40372	SALVISA	24628	814	16.2	30.5	40.7	9.7	3.0	52797	62959	77	92	702	9.0	20.1	48.9	20.5	1.6	112148
40374	SHARPSBURG	20170	692	47.4	29.5	17.2	3.0	2.9	26038	30976	6	30	548	42.9	26.1	20.6	8.6	1.8	62979
40376	SLADE	19024	202	36.6	28.7	25.7	5.5	3.5	35768	43658	31	62	173	46.8	26.0	19.7	6.4	1.2	56111
40379	STAMPING GROUND	22574	1215	24.8	28.6	30.0	13.1	3.5	46321	58464	65	85	977	22.0	20.7	38.4	17.8	1.1	103892
40380	STANTON	18344	2744	39.7	30.7	22.2	4.4	3.1	31745	38447	17	48	2045	34.7	29.6	28.8	5.6	1.3	72199
40383	VERSAILLES	28828	8420	16.1	24.7	37.9	14.4	7.0	60269	75798	85	95	6581	3.3	9.8	51.6	30.0	5.4	145097
40385	WACO	16627	911	34.1	31.2	28.7	5.7	0.3	35526	43808	30	62	770	24.6	29.9	35.1	10.4	0.1	82444
40387	WELLINGTON	14010	745	45.6	35.6	16.5	1.3	0.9	27543	32310	8	36	631	39.6	38.5	19.8	2.1	0.0	59225
40390	WILMORE	19470	2270	30.5	26.8	30.8	7.7	4.2	39669	50264	45	72	1334	5.5	16.9	45.4	29.1	3.2	141259
40391	WINCHESTER	23073	13986	26.2	27.4	34.6	8.7	3.1	46416	56365	65	85	9874	15.6	22.2	42.6	17.5	2.1	108799
40402	ANNVILLE	14233	964	49.3	32.0	15.2	2.4	1.2	25361	29295	5	28	814	43.0	29.7	22.6	4.6	0.1	59194
40403	BEREA	18973	8416	31.2	33.2	27.5	6.4	1.7	38235	46511	40	69	6063	21.9	26.9	41.7	9.2	0.4	91430
40404	BEREA	7981	3	0.0	0.0	100.0	0.0	0.0	67500	81250	90	98	0	0.0	0.0	0.0	0.0	0.0	0
40409	BRODHEAD	15777	1355	46.6	26.5	22.8	3.0	1.1	27659	33501	8	36	1064	43.3	29.0	20.5	7.2	0.0	60000
40419	CRAB ORCHARD	15065	2099	43.1	30.3	21.4	3.4	1.8	30616	35910	14	46	1709	34.6	34.5	26.8	3.8	0.4	69890
40422	DANVILLE	23376	9056	31.2	27.1	29.1	7.8	4.8	41529	51683	51	78	6322	12.5	25.5	42.9	16.3	2.9	105697
40437	HUSTONVILLE	16500	1685	44.9	27.3	21.8	4.3	1.7	29085	35086	10	41	1384	37.8	29.8	27.0	4.8	0.7	68387
40440	JUNCTION CITY	17443	1032	36.9	31.2	27.0	3.5	1.4	34358	41610	25	58	735	28.6	41.6	25.7	4.1	0.0	71897
40442	KINGS MOUNTAIN	16179	539	49.7	33.0	14.1	1.3	1.9	25151	29267	5	27	445	53.3	28.8	12.6	4.7	0.7	47929
40444	LANCASTER	21621	5063	28.4	29.3	33.8	5.6	3.1	41729	50819	52	78	3973	11.7	28.8	44.6	14.0	0.9	102476
40447	MC KEE	12038	3566	54.2	31.8	12.3	1.2	0.6	22086	25032	3	19	2837	49.5	27.5	20.6	2.4	0.0	50615
40456	MOUNT VERNON	14532	4850	47.0	30.9	18.0	2.9	1.2	26733	32022	7	33	3882	48.4	27.0	20.1	4.0	0.4	51778
40460	ORLANDO	11231	97	52.6	36.1	11.3	0.0	0.0	23401	27602	3	22	85	58.8	30.6	10.6	0.0	0.0	44231
40461	PAINT LICK	20446	873	28.9	28.2	33.2	6.6	3.1	44224	53559	59	83	727	21.2	23.9	40.2	14.4	0.3	95917
40464	PARKSVILLE	19405	355	32.1	27.3	32.4	5.9	2.3	42338	52027	54	80	302	28.8	25.8	34.1	10.6	0.7	84400
40468	PERRYVILLE	23641	646	26.2	26.0	36.7	6.7	4.5	47380	59741	67	86	529	8.3	27.4	41.8	20.6	1.9	101618
40472	RAVENNA	16119	704	43.3	29.0	24.3	2.3	1.1	29347	34250	11	42	533	46.2	35.5	15.6	2.8	0.0	52697
40475	RICHMOND	22398	20167	33.2	27.8	28.8	6.9	3.3	38360	47554	41	70	11507	15.8	22.1	44.0	17.2	0.9	110279
40481	SANDGAP	9296	163	63.8	27.0	8.6	0.6	0.0	16260	19191	1	2	109	50.5	22.9	24.8	1.8	0.0	49643
40484	STANFORD	17595	4872	38.4	28.9	26.3	4.8	1.7	33645	40187	23	56	3626	24.3	34.7	33.1	7.1	0.8	82163
40486	TYNER	12018	846	55.8	31.7	11.5	0.5	0.6	21830	24900	3	18	699	41.2	35.6	22.0	1.1	0.0	56276
40489	WAYNESBURG	15652	1770	41.9	36.6	17.3	3.1	1.1	30103	35497	12	44	1471	45.6	26.8	20.5	6.2	1.0	58291
40502	LEXINGTON	44151	13459	24.0	23.9	26.0	12.0	14.2	52576	72035	76	91	7543	0.9	7.4	30.5	47.7	13.7	207249
40503	LEXINGTON	31298	12150	18.2	25.2	35.2	15.1	6.3	56999	74688	82	94	8800	1.0	9.3	68.0	21.1	0.6	133866
40504	LEXINGTON	21541	11508	33.6	33.7	24.8	6.3	1.7	35096	45597	28	61	5064	4.3	19.6	64.8	10.6	0.7	109387
40505	LEXINGTON	23306	11432	29.4	31.6	30.1	6.5	2.4	40256	52021	47	73	7221	7.7	36.6	52.0	3.3	0.5	93351
40507	LEXINGTON	20596	1204	58.0	22.3	13.7	3.2	2.8	20165	25781	2	12	280	18.6	17.1	31.1	25.0	8.2	128125
40508	LEXINGTON	14530	9294	57.6	23.6	13.7	3.0	2.0	20860	25932	2	14	2517	31.4	33.1	18.6	14.5	2.5	67902
40509	LEXINGTON	35433	10631	17.5	24.5	33.7	14.7	9.6	59156	76879	84	95	6209	3.0	9.3	47.5	32.9	7.3	147239
40510	LEXINGTON	24595	436	14.9	17.4	44.3	13.1	10.3	66378	82358	89	97	344	6.1	9.0	17.2	55.2	12.5	223718
40511	LEXINGTON	24717	6846	26.5	26.4	31.1	10.8	5.1	46434	60587	65	85	4085	16.9	27.9	38.0	13.7	3.6	98288
40513	LEXINGTON	43807	3699	9.7	10.8	34.2	23.1	22.1	91689	117193	97	100	3203	2.3	0.7	19.5	67.5	10.1	237258
40514	LEXINGTON	32913	4262	4.8	12.7	49.4	23.8	9.2	79612	101200	95	99	4000	0.4	0.7	64.1	34.6	0.3	155984
40515	LEXINGTON	35794	12952	12.0	22.1	37.4	17.1	11.5	66110	85961	89	97	9250	1.2	10.0	46.4	35.6	6.9	155748
40516	LEXINGTON	38114	1088	15.1	22.6	35.4	15.0	12.0	63332	82315	87	96	808	2.0	4.5	45.8	31.2	16.6	170361
40517	LEXINGTON	23277	17195	27.4	32.9	31.1	6.8	1.8	41070	49749	50	76	6983	2.3	20.1	72.3	5.1	0.2	109151
40601	FRANKFORT	26809	20973	24.3	27.6	32.8	11.2	4.1	47888	60428	68	87	14073	12.0	21.1	48.8	16.4	1.7	109065
40701	CORBIN	17679	11928	43.8	28.9	20.0	4.4	2.8	28641	34965	10	40	8875	34.3	29.5	28.7	5.8	1.7	72981
40729	EAST BERNSTADT	14269	1958	49.1	32.6	14.4	2.8	1.1	25515	30122	5	29	1600	47.3	32.9	15.4	4.3	0.2	53793
40734	GRAY	12300	908	52.2	26.0	18.1	2.5	1.2	23332	28071	3	22	730	44.1	23.2	25.2	6.7	0.8	57544
40737	KEAVY	16808	556	37.6	40.5	15.1	4.0	2.9	30340	36764	13	45	458	36.2	26.2	33.2	3.3	1.1	73333
40740	LILY	16560	1075	44.0	30.1	20.9	2.7	2.2	29265	35318	11	42	846	42.4	34.5	18.1	4.7	0.2	59275
40741	LONDON	17127	8008	40.1	31.4	21.7	4.7	2.2	31452	37254	16	48	6074	29.9	29.5	29.6	9.9	1.3	76796
40744	LONDON	19521	6970	36.9	31.7	22.5	5.4	3.6	34338	41635	25	58	5595	26.4	27.3	36.0	9.4	0.9	85497
40754	NEVISDALE	10361	60	51.7	28.3	18.3	1.7	0.0	23578	27325	4	23	46	60.9	26.1	13.0	0.0	0.0	43750
40759	ROCKHOLDS	12970	1021	48.6	31.4	17.1	1.0	1.9	25640	30029	5	29	819	50.8	25.2	20.0	3.3	0.7	49097
40763	SILER	9793	313	71.6	18.2	9.0	1.3	0.0	16507	19075	1	3	246	72.4	25.6	2.0	0.0	0.0	31304
40769	WILLIAMSBURG	13630	7047	52.7	28.4	15.1	2.3	1.6	23085	27287	3	21	5033	52.4	29.2	15.6	2.5	0.3	47560
40771	WOODBINE	14668	187	49.2	33.7	15.0	0.5	1.6	25371	29276	5	28	145	57.2	26.2	13.8	2.1	0.7	44474
	KENTUCKY	22472		31.8	28.3	28.2	7.8	3.9	39962	49361				22.2	24.9	36.4	14.3	2.1	94344
	UNITED STATES	25866		24.7	27.1	30.8	10.9	6.5	48124	56710				10.9	15.0	33.7	30.1	10.4	145905

ZIP CODE		FINANCIAL SERVICES				THE HOME						ENTERTAINMENT						PERSONAL			
						Home Improvements		Furnishings													
#	POST OFFICE NAME	Auto Loan	Home Loan	Invest-ments	Retire-ment Plans	Home Repair	Lawn & Garden	Comput-ers & Hard-ware	Major Appli-ances	TV, Radio, Sound Equip-ment	Furni-ture	Dine out/ Carry out	Sports Equip-ment	Fees & Tickets	Toys & Games	Travel	Cable TV	Apparel & Services	Auto Repairs	Health Insur-ance	Pets & Supplies
40223	LOUISVILLE	138	155	170	159	152	158	147	145	140	148	176	169	154	179	148	136	174	143	135	161
40228	LOUISVILLE	92	98	102	99	96	100	95	95	92	95	116	111	97	116	95	89	113	94	89	105
40229	LOUISVILLE	87	93	92	92	91	94	89	89	86	88	108	105	90	110	89	84	105	88	84	100
40241	LOUISVILLE	144	162	173	167	158	162	152	150	142	154	180	173	158	179	152	137	178	148	137	166
40242	LOUISVILLE	109	117	136	121	115	121	117	115	113	118	143	134	120	142	117	110	141	116	107	126
40243	LOUISVILLE	131	152	166	152	151	157	142	142	136	142	171	163	150	176	145	134	169	139	134	157
40245	LOUISVILLE	177	214	226	221	207	207	191	187	174	194	221	217	205	228	192	167	222	181	165	206
40258	LOUISVILLE	77	78	74	74	79	85	75	77	77	74	95	89	76	98	76	78	92	76	81	90
40272	LOUISVILLE	81	86	86	83	86	91	83	84	83	82	103	96	84	106	84	83	100	83	84	95
40291	LOUISVILLE	102	116	123	117	114	115	110	109	104	110	131	127	113	134	110	100	129	107	99	120
40292	LOUISVILLE	0	0	0	0	0	0	0	0	0	0	0	0	0	0	0	0	0	0	0	0
40299	LOUISVILLE	103	120	129	122	117	118	112	111	106	112	133	130	117	137	113	102	132	109	101	121
40311	CARLISLE	85	59	31	53	66	77	59	71	69	59	82	84	51	78	60	74	75	70	86	97
40312	CLAY CITY	65	44	20	38	49	57	42	53	51	43	60	63	36	56	43	55	54	52	65	75
40313	CLEARFIELD	66	50	31	46	54	60	49	57	55	50	65	67	44	62	49	57	61	57	64	75
40316	DENNISTON	58	44	28	40	50	56	42	51	48	42	57	60	37	56	44	51	53	50	61	70
40322	FRENCHBURG	65	44	20	38	50	57	42	53	51	43	60	63	36	57	43	55	54	52	65	75
40324	GEORGETOWN	104	102	97	102	103	109	101	103	100	100	124	121	100	124	100	99	120	102	102	118
40328	GRAVEL SWITCH	81	57	30	51	64	73	55	67	64	56	76	80	48	73	56	69	70	66	81	94
40330	HARRODSBURG	79	70	57	67	73	81	69	74	74	68	89	86	67	90	70	76	84	73	81	91
40336	IRVINE	68	46	22	40	52	60	45	56	54	45	63	66	38	60	46	58	57	55	68	78
40337	JEFFERSONVILLE	75	51	23	44	57	66	49	61	59	50	69	73	42	65	50	63	63	60	75	87
40342	LAWRENCEBURG	89	80	64	77	84	91	76	83	80	76	98	98	74	99	78	82	93	81	89	104
40346	MEANS	66	44	20	38	50	58	43	53	51	43	60	64	36	57	43	55	55	53	66	76
40347	MIDWAY	104	100	98	102	102	111	101	104	102	100	126	120	100	127	101	102	121	103	105	119
40350	MOOREFIELD	103	69	31	60	78	90	67	83	80	68	94	100	57	89	68	87	86	82	103	118
40351	MOREHEAD	74	59	46	56	62	69	61	66	66	61	80	78	56	77	60	67	75	67	72	83
40353	MOUNT STERLING	86	71	54	68	76	85	72	78	78	71	94	91	68	93	72	80	88	78	87	97
40355	NEW LIBERTY	82	64	40	58	70	77	60	71	68	61	81	84	55	80	62	71	76	69	82	96
40356	NICHOLASVILLE	90	91	90	91	91	95	90	90	89	89	110	106	90	111	89	87	107	90	87	103
40358	OLYMPIA	88	59	27	51	67	77	57	71	69	58	81	85	48	76	58	74	73	70	88	101
40359	OWENTON	82	61	37	55	68	78	61	72	70	60	83	83	54	79	63	75	76	71	86	95
40360	OWINGSVILLE	84	57	28	51	64	75	57	69	67	57	79	82	49	75	57	72	72	68	85	95
40361	PARIS	86	74	61	72	77	87	75	80	80	74	98	92	73	97	75	82	92	79	87	97
40370	SADIEVILLE	106	89	62	83	95	103	83	94	90	83	109	112	79	109	85	93	102	92	105	124
40371	SALT LICK	89	60	27	52	68	78	58	72	70	59	82	86	49	77	59	75	74	71	89	102
40372	SALVISA	98	91	73	87	95	101	84	92	87	84	107	109	83	110	86	89	102	89	97	116
40374	SHARPSBURG	88	60	28	52	67	77	57	72	69	59	81	86	49	77	58	74	74	71	88	101
40376	SLADE	87	59	27	51	66	76	56	71	68	58	80	84	48	76	57	73	73	70	87	100
40379	STAMPING GROUND	106	78	44	70	86	96	74	89	85	76	102	106	66	98	75	90	94	88	104	122
40380	STANTON	86	58	26	50	65	75	55	69	67	57	79	83	47	74	56	72	71	69	86	99
40383	VERSAILLES	102	112	111	112	110	112	105	106	101	105	126	124	107	129	105	98	124	104	99	119
40385	WACO	76	55	32	50	61	69	54	64	62	55	74	76	48	71	55	66	68	63	76	86
40387	WELLINGTON	58	43	26	38	48	55	41	50	47	41	55	58	36	54	43	50	51	49	59	69
40390	WILMORE	85	76	80	81	76	83	83	82	83	83	104	97	80	99	80	80	100	85	80	93
40391	WINCHESTER	87	79	68	77	82	89	78	83	81	77	99	96	76	99	78	82	95	82	87	99
40402	ANNVILLE	68	46	21	40	52	60	44	55	53	45	63	66	38	59	45	58	57	55	68	79
40403	BEREA	77	61	44	58	66	74	62	69	69	62	82	81	58	81	62	71	77	69	78	87
40404	BEREA	93	73	96	83	73	81	102	89	101	95	127	115	93	118	91	92	123	101	83	100
40409	BRODHEAD	72	48	22	42	55	63	47	58	56	48	66	70	40	62	47	61	60	58	72	83
40419	CRAB ORCHARD	73	49	23	42	55	64	47	59	57	48	67	70	40	63	48	61	61	58	72	83
40422	DANVILLE	84	74	64	72	78	86	76	80	80	74	97	92	73	96	76	82	92	80	87	96
40437	HUSTONVILLE	76	51	23	44	58	66	49	61	59	50	70	73	42	66	50	64	63	61	76	87
40440	JUNCTION CITY	78	58	35	53	63	72	58	67	66	58	78	79	52	75	58	69	72	66	78	88
40442	KINGS MOUNTAIN	71	48	22	41	54	62	46	58	56	47	65	69	39	62	47	60	59	57	71	82
40444	LANCASTER	88	75	56	71	79	88	72	80	78	72	94	94	69	94	74	81	89	79	89	102
40447	MC KEE	53	37	19	32	41	47	36	44	43	37	51	52	31	48	37	46	46	44	53	61
40456	MOUNT VERNON	66	44	20	38	50	57	42	53	51	43	60	64	36	57	43	55	55	53	65	75
40460	ORLANDO	51	34	15	29	39	44	33	41	40	33	47	49	28	44	33	43	42	41	51	58
40461	PAINT LICK	87	70	48	66	76	84	68	77	74	68	89	91	64	89	69	77	84	75	86	100
40464	PARKSVILLE	87	64	35	57	71	80	61	73	70	61	84	87	54	81	62	75	77	72	87	101
40468	PERRYVILLE	101	73	41	69	83	93	71	86	81	70	95	104	62	94	74	85	87	85	102	119
40472	RAVENNA	61	49	35	44	53	60	48	55	54	48	65	64	45	66	49	58	61	54	64	71
40475	RICHMOND	80	69	71	71	70	76	77	76	78	75	97	92	73	94	74	76	93	79	76	89
40481	SANDGAP	31	28	30	27	27	31	32	31	34	31	42	36	31	41	31	34	40	32	32	34
40484	STANFORD	76	55	32	50	61	70	55	65	63	55	75	76	49	72	55	67	69	64	77	86
40486	TYNER	56	38	17	32	43	49	36	45	44	37	51	54	31	49	37	47	47	45	56	64
40489	WAYNESBURG	73	49	22	42	55	64	47	59	57	48	67	71	40	63	48	61	61	59	73	84
40502	LEXINGTON	116	123	158	128	121	128	131	123	126	128	159	148	132	160	129	122	157	127	114	135
40503	LEXINGTON	95	104	118	104	102	108	105	101	102	103	127	118	107	130	105	100	125	102	96	111
40504	LEXINGTON	61	59	72	62	59	64	67	63	66	65	83	76	66	82	65	64	81	66	60	69
40505	LEXINGTON	71	75	80	74	75	80	76	75	76	74	95	87	78	98	76	76	93	75	75	83
40507	LEXINGTON	46	36	52	39	36	42	53	44	54	48	67	56	48	64	48	52	64	51	45	50
40508	LEXINGTON	46	35	42	36	35	41	49	43	51	45	63	52	44	58	44	49	60	47	44	49
40509	LEXINGTON	115	113	121	121	109	112	116	113	111	118	141	134	115	135	111	104	137	115	101	125
40510	LEXINGTON	100	117	129	111	115	125	110	110	109	109	136	123	116	141	114	111	134	108	111	120
40511	LEXINGTON	87	83	87	81	82	91	85	85	88	85	109	97	85	108	85	89	106	86	88	98
40513	LEXINGTON	148	184	200	190	178	180	162	158	148	165	188	183	179	196	165	143	190	153	141	175
40514	LEXINGTON	131	150	146	156	143	139	135	134	124	140	157	157	140	159	132	116	156	130	114	147
40515	LEXINGTON	129	134	140	142	129	130	131	127	123	135	157	151	132	153	126	116	154	128	112	141
40516	LEXINGTON	138	152	154	152	150	152	142	143	136	143	170	168	145	172	143	131	167	141	133	161
40517	LEXINGTON	70	63	74	68	62	66	73	68	72	72	91	84	70	87	68	67	88	73	63	76
40601	FRANKFORT	85	89	91	88	89	94	86	87	86	86	106	102	87	108	87	85	104	87	86	99
40701	CORBIN	75	54	32	49	60	69	55	64	63	55	75	75	48	71	55	67	69	64	77	86
40729	EAST BERNSTADT	67	45	20	39	51	59	43	54	52	44	62	65	37	58	44	56	56	54	67	77
40734	GRAY	62	41	19	36	47	54	40	50	48	41	57	60	34	54	41	52	51	49	62	71
40737	KEAVY	81	57	29	50	63	72	55	67	64	56	76	79	48	72	55	68	70	66	80	92
40740	LILY	80	54	26	47	61	70	52	65	63	53	74	77	45	70	53	67	67	64	79	91
40741	LONDON	74	54	32	49	60	68	54	63	62	54	73	74	48	70	54	65	67	63	75	84
40744	LONDON	87	66	40	60	71	80	64	74	72	65	86	88	58	82	64	75	80	73	85	99
40754	NEVISDALE	55	37	17	32	42	48	36	44	43	36	50	53	30	48	36	46	46	44	55	63
40759	ROCKHOLDS	65	43	20	37	49	57	42	52	51	43	59	63	36	56	43	54	54	52	64	74
40763	SILER	43	29	13	25	33	38	28	35	34	28	39	41	24	37	28	36	36	34	43	49
40769	WILLIAMSBURG	59	42	27	38	46	53	43	50	50	43	59	59	38	56	43	52	55	50	59	67
40771	WOODBINE	65	44	20	38	49	57	42	53	51	43	60	63	36	56	43	55	54	52	65	75
	KENTUCKY	86	74	63	71	77	85	74	80	79	74	96	94	71	95	74	81	91	80	86	98
	UNITED STATES	100	100	100	100	100	100	100	100	100	100	100	100	100	100	100	100	100	100	100	100

POPULATION CHANGE

ZIP CODE # / POST OFFICE NAME	COUNTY FIPS CODE	POPULATION 2000	2004	2009	2000-2004 ANNUAL RATE % Rate	State Centile	HOUSEHOLDS 2000	2004	2009	% Annual Rate 2000-2004	2004 Average HH Size	FAMILIES 2000	2004	% Annual Rate 2000-2004
40801 AGES BROOKSIDE	095	175	168	161	-1.0	7	67	67	66	0.0	2.51	49	47	-1.0
40806 BAXTER	095	2931	2831	2716	-0.8	10	1177	1168	1154	-0.2	2.41	826	795	-0.9
40807 BENHAM	095	62	59	56	-1.2	5	25	25	24	0.0	2.36	16	15	-1.5
40808 BIG LAUREL	095	244	234	224	-1.0	7	93	92	91	-0.3	2.53	72	70	-0.7
40810 BLEDSOE	095	1322	1309	1269	-0.2	29	512	524	524	0.6	2.49	394	394	0.0
40813 CALVIN	013	1349	1325	1310	-0.4	22	409	415	420	0.3	2.58	318	315	-0.2
40815 CAWOOD	095	1306	1272	1224	-0.6	14	504	507	503	0.1	2.51	364	355	-0.6
40818 COALGOOD	095	362	355	343	-0.5	21	148	150	149	0.3	2.37	109	107	-0.4
40819 COLDIRON	095	798	792	767	-0.2	31	326	332	332	0.4	2.39	243	241	-0.2
40820 CRANKS	095	562	550	530	-0.5	18	219	222	221	0.3	2.48	160	157	-0.4
40823 CUMBERLAND	095	6019	5858	5668	-0.6	14	2519	2526	2512	0.1	2.29	1741	1689	-0.7
40824 DAYHOIT	095	53	48	45	-2.3	0	18	17	16	-1.3	2.82	13	12	-1.9
40826 EOLIA	133	620	615	613	-0.2	30	236	242	244	0.6	2.54	186	187	0.1
40828 EVARTS	095	5360	5049	4796	-1.4	2	2066	2014	1976	-0.6	2.51	1503	1423	-1.3
40829 GRAYS KNOB	095	68	66	63	-0.7	12	22	22	22	0.0	3.00	17	17	0.0
40831 HARLAN	095	8262	7955	7632	-0.9	8	3355	3330	3293	-0.2	2.31	2313	2221	-1.0
40843 HOLMES MILL	095	155	147	140	-1.2	3	53	52	51	-0.5	2.83	39	37	-1.2
40845 HULEN	013	1840	1818	1800	-0.3	27	683	697	709	0.5	2.61	523	520	-0.1
40847 KENVIR	095	91	90	87	-0.3	28	30	31	31	0.8	2.90	22	22	0.0
40855 LYNCH	095	74	71	68	-1.0	7	26	26	26	0.0	2.73	20	20	0.0
40858 MOZELLE	131	2518	2465	2408	-0.5	19	993	1011	1024	0.4	2.44	750	743	-0.2
40862 PARTRIDGE	133	518	501	495	-0.8	10	188	188	188	0.0	2.66	147	144	-0.5
40863 PATHFORK	095	583	571	551	-0.5	19	227	229	228	0.2	2.49	170	167	-0.4
40865 PUTNEY	095	561	526	499	-1.5	1	226	219	215	-0.7	2.40	167	158	-1.3
40868 STINNETT	131	344	336	329	-0.6	18	142	144	146	0.3	2.33	105	104	-0.2
40870 TOTZ	095	590	559	532	-1.3	3	239	235	232	-0.4	2.38	181	173	-1.1
40873 WALLINS CREEK	095	3365	3238	3103	-0.9	8	1354	1344	1330	-0.2	2.41	973	938	-0.9
40902 ARJAY	013	1493	1453	1430	-0.6	14	586	591	600	0.2	2.46	422	413	-0.5
40903 ARTEMUS	121	463	460	462	-0.2	32	180	185	191	0.7	2.49	130	129	-0.2
40906 BARBOURVILLE	121	9159	9136	9218	-0.1	36	3601	3681	3811	0.5	2.37	2510	2486	-0.2
40913 BEVERLY	013	44	42	41	-1.1	6	18	18	18	0.0	2.33	13	12	-1.9
40914 BIG CREEK	051	3906	3967	4056	0.4	55	1451	1537	1629	1.4	2.58	1126	1165	0.8
40915 BIMBLE	121	1077	1116	1141	0.8	72	406	433	454	1.5	2.57	321	334	0.9
40921 BRYANTS STORE	121	943	945	949	0.1	43	390	402	415	0.7	2.35	281	282	0.1
40923 CANNON	121	2811	2888	2941	0.6	66	1035	1095	1147	1.3	2.64	823	852	0.8
40927 CLOSPLINT	095	599	567	539	-1.3	3	230	226	222	-0.4	2.51	169	161	-1.1
40930 DEWITT	121	194	193	194	-0.1	33	77	79	82	0.6	2.43	56	56	0.0
40935 FLAT LICK	121	2260	2264	2274	0.0	42	872	900	928	0.8	2.51	656	660	0.1
40940 FRAKES	013	1265	1233	1216	-0.6	16	520	524	533	0.2	2.34	384	377	-0.4
40943 GIRDLER	121	239	246	250	0.7	67	95	101	105	1.5	2.44	76	79	0.9
40946 GREEN ROAD	121	398	409	417	0.6	66	142	150	158	1.3	2.73	114	118	0.8
40949 HEIDRICK	121	2063	2144	2196	0.9	73	788	843	888	1.6	2.54	580	604	1.0
40953 HINKLE	121	236	237	238	0.1	45	90	93	96	0.8	2.55	66	67	0.4
40958 KETTLE ISLAND	013	523	510	502	-0.6	16	199	202	204	0.4	2.52	151	149	-0.3
40962 MANCHESTER	051	15905	16174	16284	0.4	57	5487	5716	5946	1.0	2.48	4063	4119	0.3
40964 MARY ALICE	095	114	111	106	-0.6	14	41	41	41	0.0	2.71	32	31	-0.7
40965 MIDDLESBORO	013	14056	13971	13883	-0.1	32	5857	5988	6109	0.5	2.30	3986	3946	-0.2
40972 ONEIDA	051	2714	2708	2710	-0.1	37	919	944	973	0.6	2.56	701	702	0.0
40977 PINEVILLE	013	9119	9126	9085	0.0	42	3586	3701	3787	0.8	2.38	2612	2619	0.1
40979 ROARK	131	372	362	353	-0.6	14	142	144	146	0.3	2.51	111	110	-0.2
40982 SCALF	121	1278	1286	1294	0.2	47	495	515	534	0.9	2.50	359	363	0.3
40983 SEXTONS CREEK	051	1916	1937	1951	0.3	52	653	681	707	1.0	2.75	516	527	0.5
40988 STONEY FORK	013	706	685	671	-0.7	12	280	282	285	0.2	2.43	210	206	-0.5
40995 TROSPER	121	1123	1094	1094	-0.6	15	450	453	467	0.2	2.42	325	318	-0.5
40997 WALKER	121	110	110	110	0.0	41	41	42	44	0.6	2.60	30	30	0.0
40999 WOOLLUM	121	289	297	303	0.6	66	100	106	111	1.4	2.80	80	83	0.9
41001 ALEXANDRIA	037	16790	17954	18655	1.6	86	5889	6479	6909	2.3	2.77	4704	5050	1.7
41002 AUGUSTA	023	2507	2415	2467	-0.9	8	985	975	1021	-0.2	2.43	701	673	-1.0
41003 BERRY	097	2475	2857	3194	3.4	97	896	1058	1206	4.0	2.70	704	810	3.4
41004 BROOKSVILLE	023	3919	4211	4479	1.7	87	1534	1681	1824	2.2	2.50	1120	1193	1.5
41005 BURLINGTON	015	15154	17413	20587	3.3	97	5232	6156	7433	3.9	2.79	4107	4696	3.2
41006 BUTLER	191	4230	4411	4711	1.0	75	1470	1558	1688	1.4	2.79	1170	1212	0.8
41007 CALIFORNIA	037	3122	3087	3120	-0.3	28	1052	1062	1097	0.2	2.88	853	841	-0.3
41008 CARROLLTON	041	7583	7573	7607	0.0	39	3023	3077	3139	0.4	2.39	2047	2015	-0.4
41010 CORINTH	081	2875	3129	3439	2.0	90	1065	1176	1310	2.4	2.66	822	886	1.8
41011 COVINGTON	117	26728	26017	25887	-0.6	14	12210	12222	12397	0.0	2.06	6010	5647	-1.5
41014 COVINGTON	117	8002	7519	7351	-1.5	2	3324	3212	3199	-0.8	2.33	1914	1743	-2.2
41015 LATONIA	117	22457	22743	22894	0.3	53	8635	8932	9133	0.8	2.52	5980	5961	-0.1
41016 COVINGTON	117	5657	5460	5393	-0.9	9	2235	2218	2231	-0.2	2.45	1438	1356	-1.4
41017 FT MITCHELL	117	39202	39353	39343	0.1	45	14941	15403	15683	0.7	2.53	10598	10567	-0.1
41018 ERLANGER	117	26492	26620	26838	0.1	45	10250	10602	10890	0.8	2.49	7088	7034	-0.2
41030 CRITTENDEN	081	6355	6801	7540	1.6	86	2216	2414	2720	2.0	2.81	1717	1824	1.4
41031 CYNTHIANA	097	14539	15014	15765	0.8	70	5752	6057	6479	1.2	2.44	4074	4156	0.5
41033 DE MOSSVILLE	191	1515	1672	1836	2.4	93	516	580	647	2.8	2.84	421	463	2.3
41034 DOVER	161	994	1070	1100	1.8	88	373	414	437	2.5	2.58	283	305	1.8
41035 DRY RIDGE	081	8475	9803	11212	3.5	97	3073	3622	4212	3.9	2.69	2398	2758	3.4
41039 EWING	069	2548	2836	3026	2.6	94	940	1068	1157	3.1	2.65	721	798	2.4
41040 FALMOUTH	191	7204	7679	8301	1.5	85	2673	2881	3147	1.8	2.64	1966	2062	1.1
41041 FLEMINGSBURG	069	7106	7121	7203	0.1	43	2828	2885	2958	0.5	2.44	2041	2020	-0.2
41042 FLORENCE	015	39822	46642	55604	3.8	98	15614	18694	22741	4.3	2.48	10734	12444	3.5
41043 FOSTER	023	1956	2101	2239	1.7	87	749	823	894	2.2	2.55	564	602	1.6
41044 GERMANTOWN	023	349	381	407	2.1	90	138	153	167	2.5	2.49	105	113	1.7
41045 GHENT	041	1331	1356	1371	0.4	59	450	468	481	0.9	2.87	338	343	0.4
41046 GLENCOE	187	1299	1445	1566	2.5	93	463	522	572	2.9	2.77	357	392	2.2
41048 HEBRON	015	8132	10308	12817	5.7	100	2645	3410	4312	6.2	3.02	2278	2890	5.8
41049 HILLSBORO	069	2045	2110	2159	0.7	69	775	814	844	1.2	2.58	582	595	0.5
41051 INDEPENDENCE	117	17185	19652	20995	3.2	96	5861	6855	7441	3.8	2.86	4794	5464	3.1
41052 JONESVILLE	081	287	322	362	2.7	94	91	105	120	3.4	3.05	72	80	2.4
41055 MAYSLICK	161	1483	1569	1596	1.3	82	561	605	628	1.8	2.59	419	438	1.1
41056 MAYSVILLE	161	14299	13976	13725	-0.5	18	5905	5897	5910	0.0	2.31	3990	3850	-0.8
41059 MELBOURNE	037	2211	2186	2186	-0.3	28	770	777	793	0.2	2.78	613	603	-0.4
41063 MORNING VIEW	117	3821	3805	3788	-0.1	34	1329	1359	1377	0.5	2.78	1051	1043	-0.2
41064 MOUNT OLIVET	201	2269	2340	2426	0.7	68	868	909	956	1.1	2.50	624	634	0.4
41071 NEWPORT	037	22153	21882	21979	-0.3	27	9344	9496	9786	0.4	2.21	5577	5414	-0.7
41073 BELLEVUE	037	6488	6170	6098	-1.2	4	2754	2686	2719	-0.6	2.30	1660	1547	-1.7
KENTUCKY					0.7					1.2	2.42			0.5
UNITED STATES					1.2					1.3	2.58			1.1

ZIP CODE #	POST OFFICE NAME	RACE (%) White 2000	White 2004	Black 2000	Black 2004	Asian/Pacific 2000	Asian/Pacific 2004	% Hispanic Origin 2000	% Hispanic Origin 2004	2004 AGE DISTRIBUTION (%) 0-4	5-9	10-14	15-19	20-24	25-44	45-64	65-84	85+	18+	MEDIAN AGE 2004	% 2004 Males	% 2004 Females
40801	AGES BROOKSIDE	93.7	94.1	5.1	5.4	0.0	0.0	1.1	1.8	8.3	8.3	7.7	7.1	6.0	25.0	26.2	10.7	0.6	71.4	36.3	47.0	53.0
40806	BAXTER	94.9	94.4	1.7	1.7	1.0	1.3	0.5	0.6	6.0	6.0	6.7	6.3	7.2	27.2	27.8	11.7	1.2	77.6	38.8	48.4	51.6
40807	BENHAM	75.8	74.6	22.6	23.7	0.0	0.0	0.0	0.0	5.1	5.1	6.8	6.8	6.8	20.3	32.2	15.3	1.7	83.1	44.4	45.8	54.2
40808	BIG LAUREL	98.8	98.7	0.0	0.0	0.0	0.0	0.0	0.0	6.8	7.3	7.3	8.1	6.8	25.6	23.5	13.3	1.3	73.9	36.8	49.2	50.9
40810	BLEDSOE	99.4	99.2	0.0	0.0	0.0	0.0	0.4	0.6	6.0	7.4	7.4	6.8	6.9	27.7	26.6	10.2	0.9	74.5	36.5	49.7	50.3
40813	CALVIN	95.1	94.9	3.9	4.1	0.2	0.3	0.2	0.4	6.9	6.3	5.2	5.8	7.7	33.2	22.9	9.3	2.6	78.3	35.5	55.1	44.9
40815	CAWOOD	99.2	99.1	0.1	0.1	0.0	0.0	0.5	0.7	6.4	6.8	8.0	6.4	5.7	28.9	26.2	10.5	1.1	74.8	36.5	49.8	50.2
40818	COALGOOD	99.7	100.0	0.0	0.0	0.0	0.0	0.8	1.1	7.0	7.0	7.3	6.2	5.1	29.0	26.5	11.0	0.9	74.4	36.3	48.5	51.6
40819	COLDIRON	98.4	98.1	0.0	0.0	0.0	0.0	0.5	0.5	7.3	7.7	7.6	5.8	5.2	27.7	26.5	10.5	1.8	73.9	37.5	48.2	51.8
40820	CRANKS	97.5	97.3	0.4	0.4	0.2	0.2	0.2	0.6	5.3	5.8	8.2	7.8	6.9	28.2	27.5	9.3	1.1	76.0	37.2	49.1	50.9
40823	CUMBERLAND	92.0	91.7	6.7	6.9	0.0	0.0	0.7	0.9	6.0	6.1	6.6	6.3	6.3	23.7	28.2	14.5	2.4	77.7	41.4	47.4	52.6
40824	DAYHOIT	100.0	100.0	0.0	0.0	0.0	0.0	0.0	0.0	6.3	6.3	4.2	4.2	8.3	31.3	29.2	8.3	2.1	83.3	37.5	47.9	52.1
40826	EOLIA	99.8	99.8	0.0	0.0	0.0	0.0	0.3	0.5	5.7	6.0	7.0	6.5	8.0	30.4	26.7	8.8	1.0	77.6	37.2	53.3	46.7
40828	EVARTS	96.6	96.5	2.2	2.2	0.1	0.1	0.8	1.0	6.4	6.8	7.7	7.2	7.0	27.3	26.2	10.3	1.2	74.7	37.0	48.9	51.1
40829	GRAYS KNOB	95.6	95.5	0.0	0.0	0.0	0.0	0.0	0.0	6.1	6.1	6.1	6.1	6.1	25.8	31.8	12.1	0.0	81.8	41.0	51.5	48.5
40831	HARLAN	94.2	93.7	3.1	3.2	0.8	1.0	0.6	0.7	5.7	5.8	6.3	6.2	6.3	24.6	27.7	15.0	2.4	78.5	41.6	46.8	53.2
40843	HOLMES MILL	98.1	98.0	0.7	0.7	0.0	0.0	0.0	0.7	4.8	7.5	7.5	7.5	8.2	27.2	25.2	11.6	0.7	75.5	35.8	49.7	50.3
40845	HULEN	99.1	99.1	0.1	0.1	0.1	0.1	0.7	0.8	5.6	6.3	6.8	6.8	5.5	30.2	26.2	11.4	1.3	77.4	38.2	51.1	49.0
40847	KENVIR	96.7	97.8	0.0	0.0	0.0	0.0	0.0	0.0	4.4	5.6	8.9	8.9	7.8	26.7	26.7	10.0	1.1	74.4	36.7	50.0	50.0
40855	LYNCH	96.0	95.8	2.7	2.8	0.0	0.0	0.0	0.0	7.0	7.0	5.6	8.5	8.5	25.4	28.2	9.9	0.0	76.1	35.6	45.1	54.9
40858	MOZELLE	99.3	99.2	0.1	0.1	0.0	0.0	0.6	0.9	6.1	6.3	6.6	6.7	6.6	29.5	27.3	10.1	0.8	77.0	37.7	49.9	50.1
40862	PARTRIDGE	99.0	98.8	0.0	0.0	0.0	0.0	0.8	1.0	5.8	6.2	7.6	6.0	6.2	27.0	28.7	11.8	0.8	76.5	38.8	50.3	49.7
40863	PATHFORK	98.5	98.1	0.3	0.4	0.7	0.9	1.4	1.8	5.4	6.0	7.0	6.1	6.8	27.7	28.4	11.6	1.1	77.6	38.8	51.1	48.9
40865	PUTNEY	99.1	99.1	0.0	0.0	0.0	0.0	0.9	1.0	5.3	5.7	6.3	6.7	7.8	25.3	32.3	9.1	1.5	78.7	39.7	50.2	49.8
40868	STINNETT	99.4	99.4	0.0	0.0	0.0	0.0	0.9	1.2	6.3	6.3	6.6	6.6	6.6	28.9	27.4	10.7	0.9	76.8	38.2	49.7	50.3
40870	TOTZ	98.6	98.6	0.0	0.0	0.2	0.2	1.7	2.0	4.5	4.8	5.6	7.5	6.3	24.5	35.6	9.3	2.0	80.5	42.9	47.2	52.8
40873	WALLINS CREEK	98.2	98.0	0.1	0.1	0.0	0.0	0.8	1.0	6.2	6.4	7.4	6.5	6.0	28.0	27.4	11.0	1.3	76.1	38.4	48.8	51.2
40902	ARJAY	99.1	99.0	0.4	0.4	0.0	0.0	0.6	0.8	6.5	6.7	7.6	6.0	6.4	29.0	26.9	10.0	0.8	75.5	36.7	49.1	50.9
40903	ARTEMUS	96.1	95.9	2.8	2.8	0.2	0.2	0.2	0.2	7.0	7.0	7.2	5.9	5.9	29.8	22.8	13.3	1.3	75.0	36.9	49.4	50.7
40906	BARBOURVILLE	96.3	96.1	2.0	2.1	0.1	0.2	0.8	1.0	7.0	6.8	7.2	6.7	7.8	27.4	22.9	12.1	2.0	75.4	35.7	48.7	51.3
40913	BEVERLY	100.0	100.0	0.0	0.0	0.0	0.0	0.0	0.0	4.8	4.8	7.1	4.8	7.1	28.6	31.0	11.9	0.0	83.3	41.3	52.4	47.6
40914	BIG CREEK	99.4	99.3	0.0	0.0	0.0	0.0	0.7	0.9	5.8	6.7	8.2	7.2	7.4	31.3	23.8	8.9	0.9	74.7	35.3	50.1	49.9
40915	BIMBLE	98.5	98.5	0.1	0.1	0.2	0.3	0.7	0.7	7.4	7.4	7.6	6.5	6.6	31.1	24.3	8.2	0.9	73.7	35.2	49.1	50.9
40921	BRYANTS STORE	99.2	99.2	0.2	0.2	0.1	0.1	0.0	0.0	6.7	6.8	6.6	5.9	5.5	28.2	27.3	12.2	1.0	76.5	37.9	51.5	48.5
40923	CANNON	99.5	99.4	0.1	0.1	0.0	0.0	0.4	0.6	7.7	7.7	8.1	6.7	6.3	28.2	26.0	8.6	0.8	72.5	35.0	50.1	49.9
40927	CLOSPLINT	98.0	97.7	0.8	0.9	0.2	0.2	0.3	0.5	4.9	7.6	7.2	7.6	7.9	27.3	25.8	10.8	0.9	75.8	35.6	50.3	49.7
40930	DEWITT	99.0	99.0	0.0	0.0	0.0	0.0	0.5	0.5	8.8	7.3	7.3	5.7	5.7	31.6	24.4	8.3	1.0	72.5	34.8	50.3	49.7
40935	FLAT LICK	98.4	98.2	0.8	0.8	0.0	0.0	0.8	0.9	7.4	7.4	7.1	7.1	6.3	27.2	26.4	10.1	1.1	73.6	36.1	48.9	51.1
40940	FRAKES	99.5	99.5	0.0	0.0	0.1	0.1	0.8	1.1	4.5	4.7	6.0	6.2	6.2	29.5	28.4	13.1	1.4	80.3	40.7	51.0	49.0
40943	GIRDLER	99.2	98.8	0.0	0.4	0.0	0.0	0.0	0.4	8.5	6.9	7.7	6.9	6.5	27.2	26.0	9.4	0.8	72.8	35.3	51.2	48.8
40946	GREEN ROAD	99.3	99.0	0.3	0.2	0.0	0.0	0.0	0.0	7.1	6.9	7.6	6.9	6.6	27.6	26.9	9.5	1.0	74.6	36.5	49.1	50.9
40949	HEIDRICK	97.4	97.2	1.2	1.3	0.2	0.3	0.4	0.5	7.1	7.1	7.4	6.7	6.6	29.6	24.8	9.6	1.1	74.3	35.8	48.3	51.7
40953	HINKLE	97.9	97.9	1.3	1.3	0.0	0.0	0.9	1.3	7.2	7.2	7.2	6.3	6.3	26.2	26.6	11.4	1.7	74.3	38.0	47.7	52.3
40958	KETTLE ISLAND	99.4	99.0	0.0	0.0	0.2	0.2	0.4	0.8	6.3	6.3	6.3	6.9	7.3	27.8	26.3	11.0	2.0	77.1	38.2	48.4	51.6
40962	MANCHESTER	91.5	91.1	7.0	7.2	0.2	0.2	1.7	2.2	5.5	5.9	6.6	6.0	6.7	33.9	24.6	9.7	1.1	78.2	36.4	55.2	44.8
40964	MARY ALICE	96.5	94.6	0.9	0.9	0.0	0.0	0.0	0.0	6.3	6.3	7.2	6.3	7.2	28.8	25.2	11.7	0.9	74.8	37.2	50.5	49.6
40965	MIDDLESBORO	94.1	93.7	3.8	3.8	0.7	0.9	0.8	0.9	6.4	6.3	6.6	6.7	6.4	27.1	25.1	13.6	1.8	76.7	38.6	46.6	53.4
40972	ONEIDA	96.7	96.5	2.1	2.1	0.2	0.2	0.9	1.2	5.1	6.1	10.5	12.3	5.3	27.3	22.9	9.0	1.5	69.9	33.4	50.8	49.2
40977	PINEVILLE	97.1	96.8	1.4	1.5	0.1	0.2	0.6	0.8	5.8	5.9	6.5	6.4	6.3	28.6	26.6	12.2	1.6	77.8	38.8	48.7	51.3
40979	ROARK	99.2	99.5	0.3	0.3	0.0	0.0	0.3	0.6	6.1	6.4	6.6	6.6	6.1	28.2	29.0	10.8	0.3	76.5	38.5	51.7	48.3
40982	SCALF	99.4	99.1	0.0	0.0	0.0	0.0	0.5	0.8	7.5	8.8	8.2	6.9	5.7	29.5	23.2	9.0	1.2	71.5	32.7	50.4	49.6
40983	SEXTONS CREEK	98.9	98.6	0.5	0.5	0.1	0.2	0.4	0.6	7.0	7.0	7.3	6.3	6.4	30.1	23.5	10.6	1.8	74.8	36.1	49.7	50.3
40988	STONEY FORK	99.6	99.4	0.1	0.2	0.0	0.0	0.6	0.7	6.1	6.3	6.3	6.7	7.2	27.7	27.0	11.1	1.6	77.2	38.3	49.2	50.8
40995	TROSPER	99.2	99.2	0.1	0.1	0.1	0.1	0.9	1.2	5.0	5.4	8.0	7.0	6.3	28.3	27.5	11.5	1.0	77.5	38.9	50.7	49.3
40997	WALKER	99.1	99.1	0.0	0.0	0.0	0.0	0.0	0.9	8.2	8.2	7.3	6.4	5.5	30.9	22.7	9.1	1.8	70.0	34.4	48.2	51.8
40999	WOOLLUM	99.0	99.0	0.4	0.3	0.0	0.0	0.0	0.0	7.1	7.1	7.4	7.1	6.7	27.6	26.3	9.8	1.0	74.4	36.4	49.2	50.8
41001	ALEXANDRIA	98.9	98.7	0.1	0.1	0.3	0.4	0.5	0.7	7.6	7.6	7.7	7.1	6.1	29.9	24.4	8.8	0.8	72.7	35.8	49.5	50.5
41002	AUGUSTA	98.1	97.9	0.8	0.9	0.1	0.2	0.6	0.8	6.7	6.6	6.4	6.3	5.9	27.3	25.1	14.1	1.7	76.5	38.8	49.9	50.1
41003	BERRY	97.6	97.1	0.3	0.4	0.1	0.1	1.4	2.0	6.9	6.8	7.1	6.9	6.7	30.5	25.3	9.0	0.8	75.0	36.2	51.1	48.9
41004	BROOKSVILLE	98.5	98.4	0.5	0.5	0.1	0.1	0.5	0.7	6.8	6.8	7.1	6.5	6.3	28.9	24.7	11.5	1.5	75.4	37.2	49.8	50.3
41005	BURLINGTON	95.6	95.0	1.5	1.5	1.0	1.2	1.5	2.0	8.8	8.3	8.1	6.9	6.6	33.3	21.9	5.7	0.4	70.5	32.4	51.0	49.0
41006	BUTLER	98.9	98.7	0.1	0.1	0.2	0.3	0.4	0.5	7.3	7.4	8.8	7.2	6.1	30.0	23.4	8.8	1.1	72.0	34.9	49.3	50.7
41007	CALIFORNIA	98.9	98.7	0.2	0.2	0.3	0.4	0.6	0.8	7.3	7.6	8.6	7.8	4.7	29.6	23.9	9.7	0.7	71.0	36.4	48.7	51.3
41008	CARROLLTON	94.8	94.8	1.9	2.0	0.3	0.3	3.5	3.5	6.5	6.4	6.8	6.2	6.8	29.2	25.0	11.6	1.6	76.5	37.1	50.0	50.1
41010	CORINTH	98.1	98.0	0.6	0.6	0.2	0.3	0.7	0.8	7.5	7.2	7.5	7.0	6.6	29.0	24.9	9.4	1.0	73.6	35.6	51.2	48.8
41011	COVINGTON	85.4	84.7	12.0	12.3	0.5	0.6	1.4	1.8	6.2	5.7	5.8	5.8	7.2	31.0	23.9	12.2	2.3	78.9	37.2	50.2	49.8
41014	COVINGTON	89.7	89.1	7.3	7.7	0.3	0.3	1.0	1.2	7.1	6.8	7.0	6.8	8.0	31.8	22.3	9.4	1.0	75.2	33.8	48.7	51.3
41015	LATONIA	94.6	93.9	3.2	3.6	0.5	0.6	1.0	1.2	8.3	7.5	7.3	6.6	6.4	29.4	22.2	10.5	1.7	72.9	35.1	47.9	52.1
41016	COVINGTON	98.2	98.0	0.5	0.5	0.2	0.3	0.7	0.9	7.0	7.0	7.5	8.0	7.2	29.8	21.3	10.7	1.4	73.5	34.7	49.3	50.7
41017	FT MITCHELL	97.0	96.4	0.9	1.0	1.1	1.4	0.9	1.2	6.9	7.0	7.3	6.7	6.6	28.7	26.0	9.5	1.2	74.8	36.2	48.6	51.4
41018	ERLANGER	94.7	94.0	3.0	3.2	0.6	0.9	1.7	2.2	8.1	7.5	7.2	6.5	7.0	32.4	21.0	9.1	1.2	73.4	33.6	48.9	51.1
41030	CRITTENDEN	98.2	97.9	0.4	0.4	0.3	0.3	1.0	1.3	8.3	8.5	8.3	7.3	7.6	32.4	21.1	6.0	0.6	70.5	31.1	49.5	50.5
41031	CYNTHIANA	95.1	94.7	3.1	3.2	0.2	0.2	1.1	1.4	6.4	6.4	6.8	6.1	6.1	27.9	25.9	12.3	2.2	76.7	38.6	48.4	51.6
41033	DE MOSSVILLE	98.4	98.2	0.9	1.0	0.2	0.2	0.6	0.8	6.8	6.9	8.1	7.1	6.4	32.1	23.2	8.6	0.8	73.6	34.8	53.4	46.7
41034	DOVER	96.2	95.7	1.8	2.0	0.5	0.6	0.9	1.2	6.1	6.7	7.6	6.0	4.6	29.4	27.0	11.4	1.2	75.9	39.4	50.8	49.3
41035	DRY RIDGE	98.4	98.2	0.2	0.2	0.3	0.4	1.0	1.3	8.2	7.9	7.8	7.1	7.1	30.6	22.7	7.7	0.9	71.7	33.2	49.6	50.5
41039	EWING	98.1	97.9	0.8	0.9	0.1	0.1	0.6	0.7	6.1	7.7	8.5	6.3	5.5	30.1	24.9	9.6	1.3	73.6	35.6	50.9	49.1
41040	FALMOUTH	98.0	97.9	0.7	0.7	0.0	0.0	0.9	1.2	6.8	6.8	7.7	7.3	6.8	29.3	23.9	10.2	1.2	74.1	35.9	50.3	49.7
41041	FLEMINGSBURG	96.1	95.8	2.4	2.5	0.2	0.3	0.9	1.1	6.8	6.8	6.8	6.1	6.2	26.7	25.5	13.1	2.0	76.0	38.3	48.1	51.9
41042	FLORENCE	93.7	92.9	2.1	2.1	1.6	2.0	2.8	3.5	7.9	7.4	7.2	6.3	7.3	32.3	22.2	8.4	1.1	73.7	33.7	48.4	51.6
41043	FOSTER	99.4	99.3	0.1	0.1	0.1	0.1	0.3	0.3	6.2	6.4	7.4	7.2	6.5	28.7	25.6	11.0	1.1	75.6	37.5	50.6	49.4
41044	GERMANTOWN	97.1	97.4	2.0	2.1	0.0	0.0	0.0	0.0	6.3	6.3	7.6	7.4	6.3	31.0	23.4	10.5	1.3	75.1	36.3	51.7	48.3
41045	GHENT	94.0	93.9	3.4	3.4	0.0	0.0	2.6	2.7	8.0	7.6	7.7	7.1	6.9	29.1	24.5	8.1	1.0	72.3	35.0	51.1	48.9
41046	GLENCOE	97.9	97.6	0.7	0.7	0.2	0.2	1.3	1.7	7.8	7.9	8.1	6.8	6.4	30.2	23.3	8.4	1.0	72.1	34.0	51.4	48.6
41048	HEBRON	96.3	95.7	1.5	1.6	0.9	1.0	1.2	1.5	9.4	9.2	8.6	6.8	5.8	32.5	21.6	5.8	0.4	68.4	32.7	49.6	50.4
41049	HILLSBORO	98.6	98.4	0.2	0.2	0.2	0.2	0.8	1.0	7.3	6.8	7.1	6.4	6.9	28.3	25.6	10.6	1.1	75.0	36.3	49.9	50.1
41051	INDEPENDENCE	97.6	97.3	0.7	0.7	0.4	0.5	1.0	1.4	8.6	8.0	7.7	7.1	6.8	32.5	21.4	7.3	0.6	71.3	33.0	50.5	49.5
41052	JONESVILLE	97.9	97.5	0.0	0.0	0.4	0.3	1.4	1.9	7.5	7.1	6.8	6.5	6.5	28.6	26.4	9.6	0.9	74.8	36.9	50.6	49.4
41055	MAYSLICK	94.6	94.1	3.4	3.7	0.1	0.1	1.8	2.3	7.1	7.0	6.5	6.0	5.2	29.0	26.6	11.2	1.4	75.6	38.5	50.9	49.1
41056	MAYSVILLE	90.1	89.5	7.9	8.2	0.4	0.5	0.9	1.1	6.2	6.2	6.5	6.3	6.0	27.0	26.2	13.6	2.1	77.3	39.5	48.2	51.8
41059	MELBOURNE	99.2	99.0	0.1	0.1	0.3	0.4	0.4	0.4	6.0	6.3	7.8	7.7	6.4	27.3	26.8	10.6	1.2	75.3	38.5	49.9	50.1
41063	MORNING VIEW	98.7	98.6	0.4	0.5	0.0	0.0	0.3	0.5	6.3	6.7	8.7	7.6	6.0	29.1	26.3	8.6	0.8	73.5	36.7	51.5	48.5
41064	MOUNT OLIVET	98.6	98.6	0.0	0.0	0.0	0.0	0.9	0.9	5.6	5.9	7.2	5.9	5.0	26.4	26.9	14.7	2.4	77.8	41.3	48.8	51.2
41071	NEWPORT	92.4	91.8	4.7	5.0	0.6	0.8	1.5	1.9	7.7	6.7	6.7	7.5	8.5	30.3	21.1	9.8	1.7	74.7	33.5	48.1	51.9
41073	BELLEVUE	98.4	98.2	0.2	0.2	0.4	0.5	0.9	1.2	7.1	6.6	6.8	6.8	7.5	30.5	22.0	11.1	1.8	75.7	35.1	48.1	51.9
	KENTUCKY	90.1	89.5	7.3	7.4	0.8	1.0	1.5	1.9	6.6	6.6	6.8	6.6	7.0	28.9	24.8	11.1	1.5	76.3	36.8	49.1	50.9
	UNITED STATES	75.1	73.6	12.3	12.5	3.8	4.2	12.5	14.1	6.9	6.7	7.2	7.0	7.3	28.6	23.8	10.8	1.7	75.1	36.0	49.1	50.9

INCOME

#	POST OFFICE NAME	2004 Per Capita Income	2004 HH Income Base	2004 HOUSEHOLD INCOME DISTRIBUTION (%) Less than $25,000	$25,000 to $49,999	$50,000 to $99,999	$100,000 to $149,999	$150,000 or More	MEDIAN HOUSEHOLD INCOME 2004	2009	2004 National Centile	2004 State Centile	2004 Home Value Base	2004 HOME VALUE DISTRIBUTION (%) Less than $50,000	$50,000 to $89,999	$90,000 to $174,999	$175,000 to $399,999	$400,000 or More	2004 Median Home Value
40801	AGES BROOKSIDE	11256	67	62.7	22.4	13.4	0.0	1.5	16278	20000	1	3	46	50.0	37.0	13.0	0.0	0.0	50000
40806	BAXTER	16266	1168	45.9	26.5	22.1	3.4	2.1	27621	33353	8	36	837	39.8	34.1	21.9	4.2	0.1	58382
40807	BENHAM	11186	25	60.0	20.0	20.0	0.0	0.0	16048	25000	1	2	17	64.7	35.3	0.0	0.0	0.0	38750
40808	BIG LAUREL	12113	92	54.4	20.7	25.0	0.0	0.0	19472	21870	2	10	71	66.2	31.0	0.0	2.8	0.0	36786
40810	BLEDSOE	10879	524	59.4	24.1	16.6	0.0	0.0	19714	22993	2	10	418	62.9	29.0	7.7	0.5	0.0	38043
40813	CALVIN	8647	415	67.7	24.6	7.7	0.0	0.0	16563	18686	1	3	255	56.1	27.1	12.9	2.0	2.0	42955
40815	CAWOOD	9374	507	65.9	24.5	8.3	1.4	0.0	16889	19369	1	4	391	61.4	26.9	9.7	2.1	0.0	41442
40818	COALGOOD	11100	150	62.0	24.0	12.0	2.0	0.0	18652	22252	1	7	117	65.8	23.1	8.6	2.6	0.0	42292
40819	COLDIRON	11413	332	63.0	22.9	11.1	2.4	0.6	18118	21666	1	6	263	54.0	27.8	14.1	4.2	0.0	39250
40820	CRANKS	7585	222	72.1	23.0	4.1	0.9	0.0	12207	14206	1	1	172	67.4	19.2	12.2	1.2	0.0	32667
40823	CUMBERLAND	14850	2526	54.8	27.0	14.8	1.9	1.6	21271	25540	2	16	1876	57.9	32.7	8.9	0.2	0.2	43943
40824	DAYHOIT	9613	17	47.1	41.2	11.8	0.0	0.0	26058	25000	6	30	13	61.5	23.1	15.4	0.0	0.0	45000
40826	EOLIA	9714	242	66.5	20.3	11.2	0.8	1.2	16619	19565	1	3	192	68.8	25.5	5.7	0.0	0.0	41429
40828	EVARTS	13855	2014	61.9	23.8	11.6	0.7	2.0	17638	20777	1	5	1613	61.8	30.4	7.7	0.1	0.0	38313
40829	GRAYS KNOB	9318	22	50.0	36.4	13.6	0.0	0.0	25000	25000	5	26	17	70.6	23.5	5.9	0.0	0.0	41250
40831	HARLAN	16679	3330	50.6	26.6	16.8	3.8	2.2	24459	29813	4	25	2250	45.6	30.8	17.0	6.4	0.1	53798
40843	HOLMES MILL	10561	52	57.7	32.7	7.7	0.0	1.9	20840	25418	2	14	42	61.9	28.6	9.5	0.0	0.0	40000
40845	HULEN	16696	697	61.0	22.1	10.6	3.0	3.3	20174	23413	2	12	567	53.1	31.4	14.3	1.2	0.0	46875
40847	KENVIR	6038	31	71.0	22.6	6.5	0.0	0.0	10640	10458	1	1	24	70.8	16.7	12.5	0.0	0.0	32500
40855	LYNCH	9331	26	61.5	23.1	15.4	0.0	0.0	17225	17225	1	4	18	44.4	44.4	11.1	0.0	0.0	55000
40858	MOZELLE	11304	1011	60.8	21.2	16.2	1.8	0.0	17493	21130	1	5	823	67.9	23.9	8.0	0.1	0.0	34493
40862	PARTRIDGE	11333	188	52.7	28.7	17.0	1.6	0.0	22516	27967	3	21	164	57.9	30.5	11.0	0.6	0.0	41333
40863	PATHFORK	10306	229	61.6	24.0	10.9	3.5	0.0	17636	20496	1	5	187	66.8	28.3	4.8	0.0	0.0	39891
40865	PUTNEY	16396	219	44.8	29.2	19.2	4.1	2.7	30118	35514	13	44	167	48.5	32.3	19.2	0.0	0.0	55000
40868	STINNETT	10329	144	66.7	21.5	11.1	0.7	0.0	15889	17701	1	2	118	69.5	22.9	6.8	0.9	0.0	35000
40870	TOTZ	21344	235	44.7	31.5	19.6	1.3	3.0	26974	31542	7	34	206	55.8	27.2	12.6	4.4	0.0	47333
40873	WALLINS CREEK	13409	1344	58.9	25.5	12.8	1.9	1.0	20100	23403	2	11	1063	54.9	31.1	11.7	2.1	0.2	45354
40902	ARJAY	9272	591	71.1	17.8	10.3	0.9	0.0	15989	18160	1	2	458	73.8	19.2	5.9	1.1	0.0	24519
40903	ARTEMUS	12785	185	56.2	24.9	13.0	6.0	0.0	21400	25426	2	17	136	49.3	20.6	20.6	8.8	0.7	51111
40906	BARBOURVILLE	13068	3681	57.7	24.1	13.6	3.7	1.0	19133	23006	2	8	2479	44.2	25.9	21.7	8.0	0.3	57526
40913	BEVERLY	9005	18	72.2	22.2	5.6	0.0	0.0	16330	17981	1	3	15	73.3	20.0	6.7	0.0	0.0	21250
40914	BIG CREEK	9714	1537	67.3	17.9	13.3	1.0	0.5	15978	18156	1	2	1260	67.1	24.5	7.1	0.8	0.4	36543
40915	BIMBLE	14005	433	43.0	36.3	15.2	4.9	0.7	29404	35170	11	43	370	31.9	26.5	31.6	8.9	1.1	79737
40921	BRYANTS STORE	11583	402	55.0	34.3	8.0	1.5	1.2	21562	25192	2	17	321	64.2	20.9	12.5	2.5	0.0	41415
40923	CANNON	11308	1095	59.2	23.4	15.7	1.4	0.4	19425	22882	2	9	875	54.7	31.0	13.1	1.1	0.0	46856
40927	CLOSPLINT	14616	226	56.6	32.3	7.5	0.0	3.5	21502	25421	2	17	184	61.4	27.7	10.9	0.0	0.0	39737
40930	DEWITT	9199	79	59.5	34.2	6.3	0.0	0.0	20253	23083	2	12	61	77.1	18.0	4.9	0.0	0.0	24583
40935	FLAT LICK	10128	900	60.2	29.4	8.8	1.6	0.0	19036	22219	2	8	716	64.4	19.0	12.4	4.2	0.0	29878
40940	FRAKES	13472	524	58.0	27.3	12.6	0.6	1.5	19656	23080	2	10	431	62.2	26.0	11.1	0.7	0.0	34821
40943	GIRDLER	11494	101	60.4	21.8	15.8	2.0	0.0	19688	23408	2	10	82	48.8	32.9	17.1	1.2	0.0	51250
40946	GREEN ROAD	13386	150	58.7	20.7	17.3	2.7	0.7	20980	25000	2	15	123	45.5	35.0	18.7	0.8	0.0	54231
40949	HEIDRICK	12258	843	54.8	28.7	11.6	3.7	1.2	21377	25815	2	16	631	34.4	34.9	24.1	6.2	0.5	67727
40953	HINKLE	11103	93	54.8	33.3	9.7	2.2	0.0	21575	25730	2	18	74	47.3	24.3	20.3	8.1	0.0	60000
40958	KETTLE ISLAND	13024	202	49.0	26.7	20.8	2.5	1.0	25417	28791	5	28	168	67.3	25.0	4.8	3.0	0.0	38333
40962	MANCHESTER	12528	5716	59.2	20.5	16.3	2.6	1.4	18965	22676	2	8	4276	55.4	23.1	18.6	2.7	0.2	44615
40964	MARY ALICE	10946	41	48.8	36.6	12.2	2.4	0.0	25723	28616	5	29	32	65.6	28.1	6.3	0.0	0.0	43750
40965	MIDDLESBORO	15069	5988	53.4	27.9	14.5	2.8	1.5	22743	26644	3	21	3989	41.2	32.7	20.9	4.7	0.5	59550
40972	ONEIDA	9866	944	61.9	24.5	12.5	1.2	0.0	18495	21216	1	7	751	62.6	27.8	9.3	0.3	0.0	38827
40977	PINEVILLE	13872	3701	54.5	24.9	16.7	2.1	1.9	21988	25744	3	18	2759	53.2	29.0	14.3	3.2	0.4	46830
40979	ROARK	11514	144	57.6	24.3	16.7	1.4	0.0	20346	24355	2	13	116	67.2	21.6	11.2	0.0	0.0	36500
40982	SCALF	7610	515	75.5	18.3	5.1	1.2	0.0	12346	14555	1	1	414	78.5	12.6	8.9	0.0	0.0	26857
40983	SEXTONS CREEK	9939	681	60.9	22.6	14.7	1.8	0.0	18425	21222	1	7	557	56.0	31.2	11.7	0.5	0.5	43909
40988	STONEY FORK	12085	282	56.4	25.2	16.3	1.4	0.7	20928	23809	2	14	232	66.4	26.3	5.2	2.2	0.0	35385
40995	TROSPER	11819	453	53.4	30.9	13.3	2.4	0.0	21161	24664	2	15	357	75.1	21.3	3.6	0.0	0.0	35268
40997	WALKER	8598	42	57.1	35.7	7.1	0.0	0.0	21062	21733	2	15	33	75.8	18.2	6.1	0.0	0.0	25833
40999	WOOLLUM	10682	106	59.4	20.8	17.0	2.8	0.0	20683	25209	2	13	87	46.0	34.5	18.4	1.2	0.0	53889
41001	ALEXANDRIA	25348	6479	12.6	24.4	44.8	14.0	4.2	62236	75237	86	96	5623	7.7	8.6	56.1	25.1	2.5	134540
41002	AUGUSTA	18121	975	30.4	34.1	31.5	3.3	0.8	38582	44955	41	71	732	25.7	32.2	30.5	11.1	0.6	80000
41003	BERRY	18284	1058	25.6	34.5	31.3	7.7	1.0	41334	50000	51	77	881	24.5	30.9	33.3	10.0	1.4	82910
41004	BROOKSVILLE	19486	1681	30.1	32.1	29.9	6.8	1.1	39812	46310	45	73	1348	27.5	30.8	32.1	8.6	1.1	76351
41005	BURLINGTON	27897	6156	11.8	19.1	47.9	15.4	5.8	67100	79890	90	97	4857	2.5	7.3	50.0	36.8	3.5	156319
41006	BUTLER	19589	1558	21.3	30.8	37.6	8.3	2.1	48236	55398	69	88	1254	16.4	21.8	40.4	21.5	0.0	108234
41007	CALIFORNIA	23696	1062	15.6	26.8	39.3	12.2	6.1	57606	69278	82	94	929	12.4	15.6	41.9	27.7	2.5	122559
41008	CARROLLTON	20373	3077	32.6	24.2	35.7	5.9	1.6	42487	51903	55	80	2142	18.4	25.7	41.5	13.0	1.5	97159
41010	CORINTH	19054	1176	27.6	35.1	29.3	5.4	2.6	37812	45064	39	68	977	25.0	29.2	31.8	13.0	1.0	84296
41011	COVINGTON	26725	12222	31.5	29.2	25.6	8.9	4.8	39743	49591	45	72	5642	11.7	20.7	44.7	20.5	2.5	119432
41014	COVINGTON	19759	3212	33.4	33.0	27.1	5.0	1.4	34172	43025	25	57	1680	22.0	54.1	21.1	2.8	0.0	70602
41015	LATONIA	22736	8932	27.1	27.5	31.2	10.2	3.9	44978	56153	61	83	6330	6.1	34.6	40.0	18.0	1.4	100592
41016	COVINGTON	19818	2218	26.7	33.1	32.7	6.3	1.2	40412	49881	48	74	1450	12.1	46.2	39.9	1.5	0.3	84521
41017	FT MITCHELL	37287	15403	11.0	22.1	37.6	17.2	12.1	68804	84536	91	98	11592	2.1	4.6	50.6	35.3	7.5	162226
41018	ERLANGER	24780	10602	17.1	32.1	38.7	8.7	3.3	50510	61443	73	89	7454	8.3	15.4	66.7	9.3	0.3	111337
41030	CRITTENDEN	21915	2414	16.9	32.0	39.2	8.8	3.1	50730	60789	73	90	1813	25.9	17.1	40.7	14.7	1.7	102071
41031	CYNTHIANA	21906	6057	26.5	32.1	30.7	8.3	2.4	42388	51302	54	80	4431	10.2	30.4	41.5	15.6	2.3	103223
41033	DE MOSSVILLE	17436	580	18.8	36.0	40.3	4.7	0.2	45688	52508	63	84	494	23.5	37.3	33.6	5.5	0.2	76522
41034	DOVER	21096	414	26.8	35.8	28.7	3.9	4.8	40000	48253	46	73	343	28.3	25.4	36.2	7.9	2.3	86324
41035	DRY RIDGE	21034	3622	20.6	32.6	36.0	8.3	2.5	47125	56063	66	86	2879	24.6	15.2	40.2	19.0	1.0	105528
41039	EWING	15954	1068	39.0	27.0	29.0	4.0	0.9	34703	40418	26	60	884	33.8	29.5	25.5	8.7	2.5	75667
41040	FALMOUTH	19838	2881	32.7	30.3	30.0	5.0	2.0	40985	47337	50	76	2197	15.8	32.6	41.4	9.4	0.9	91365
41041	FLEMINGSBURG	18687	2885	38.9	29.7	23.7	5.0	2.7	34012	40405	24	57	2230	27.1	32.9	28.6	10.0	1.4	75833
41042	FLORENCE	26791	18694	17.8	24.9	40.0	12.4	4.9	56384	68353	81	93	12810	9.4	9.4	54.9	25.2	1.1	130849
41043	FOSTER	20024	823	25.0	35.6	28.7	9.1	1.6	40396	47681	47	74	687	21.7	26.9	31.9	18.2	1.3	92375
41044	GERMANTOWN	20801	153	26.8	34.0	30.1	6.5	2.6	42135	50784	53	79	128	36.7	19.5	30.5	5.5	7.8	72500
41045	GHENT	20406	468	22.0	27.4	40.4	7.5	2.8	50650	59852	73	90	369	20.1	31.4	31.7	11.9	4.9	88590
41046	GLENCOE	18249	522	27.6	31.2	31.2	8.4	1.5	41735	50289	52	78	436	18.4	26.2	38.1	14.5	3.0	97273
41048	HEBRON	33799	3410	8.6	15.3	43.0	17.7	15.4	79552	97821	95	99	3001	1.5	6.2	48.3	35.2	8.8	165432
41049	HILLSBORO	14536	814	40.4	37.1	17.0	4.3	1.2	29576	35609	11	43	670	40.8	35.8	20.9	1.6	0.9	57294
41051	INDEPENDENCE	24307	6855	12.7	24.0	46.9	13.1	3.3	60659	73997	85	95	5643	5.0	13.3	59.5	21.3	1.0	132927
41052	JONESVILLE	16463	105	21.0	33.3	38.1	7.6	0.0	45456	53706	62	84	88	18.2	15.9	43.2	22.7	0.0	112500
41055	MAYSLICK	19221	605	37.0	30.6	23.1	5.5	3.8	32525	38608	19	51	477	20.3	28.1	30.2	19.5	1.9	92273
41056	MAYSVILLE	20751	5897	36.6	28.8	24.9	6.6	3.1	34808	43494	27	60	4074	23.4	31.6	32.1	11.4	1.5	84368
41059	MELBOURNE	25260	777	15.8	22.8	40.0	15.4	5.9	62862	76426	87	96	613	9.3	12.2	46.7	28.6	3.3	125791
41063	MORNING VIEW	22373	1359	19.5	25.3	40.6	11.6	3.0	53301	64457	77	92	1167	9.3	17.4	51.3	19.7	2.2	129167
41064	MOUNT OLIVET	16154	909	38.5	30.4	26.7	3.9	0.6	34377	40737	25	59	738	36.6	30.4	26.7	6.4	0.0	71273
41071	NEWPORT	22326	9496	31.4	31.9	27.0	6.5	3.2	37768	46723	38	68	4841	14.5	35.1	39.8	9.9	0.7	90447
41073	BELLEVUE	22981	2686	26.8	28.9	36.2	6.8	1.3	43857	54324	58	82	1782	6.5	50.3	40.2	2.9	0.1	85236
	KENTUCKY	22472		31.8	28.3	28.2	7.8	3.9	39962	49361				22.2	24.9	36.4	14.3	2.1	94344
	UNITED STATES	25866		24.7	27.1	30.8	10.9	6.5	48124	56710				10.9	15.0	33.7	30.1	10.4	145905

ZIP CODE		FINANCIAL SERVICES				THE HOME						ENTERTAINMENT						PERSONAL			
						Home Improvements		Furnishings													
#	POST OFFICE NAME	Auto Loan	Home Loan	Invest-ments	Retire-ment Plans	Home Repair	Lawn & Garden	Comput-ers & Hard-ware	Major Appli-ances	TV, Radio, Sound Equip-ment	Furni-ture	Dine out/ Carry out	Sports Equip-ment	Fees & Tickets	Toys & Games	Travel	Cable TV	Apparel & Services	Auto Repairs	Health Insur-ance	Pets & Supplies
40801	AGES BROOKSIDE	46	34	23	33	37	45	38	42	42	36	50	47	34	47	37	45	46	42	50	50
40806	BAXTER	64	51	37	49	55	63	52	58	57	51	69	66	48	67	52	60	64	57	66	72
40807	BENHAM	43	32	21	31	35	42	35	39	40	34	47	44	32	44	35	42	43	39	47	47
40808	BIG LAUREL	58	39	18	33	44	50	37	47	45	38	53	56	32	50	38	49	48	46	58	66
40810	BLEDSOE	51	34	16	30	39	45	33	41	40	34	47	49	28	44	34	43	43	41	51	59
40813	CALVIN	40	27	12	23	30	35	26	32	31	26	36	38	22	34	26	33	33	32	40	46
40815	CAWOOD	41	29	19	25	32	37	29	35	35	30	41	40	26	38	29	38	38	35	42	46
40818	COALGOOD	49	33	15	29	38	43	32	40	39	33	45	48	27	43	33	42	41	40	49	57
40819	COLDIRON	51	34	16	30	39	45	33	41	40	34	47	50	28	44	34	43	43	41	51	59
40820	CRANKS	33	23	14	20	25	30	23	28	28	24	33	32	21	31	23	30	30	28	34	38
40823	CUMBERLAND	55	41	29	39	45	54	45	50	51	44	61	56	41	57	45	54	56	50	60	61
40824	DAYHOIT	51	34	16	30	39	45	33	41	40	34	47	49	28	44	34	43	43	41	51	59
40826	EOLIA	46	31	14	27	35	41	30	38	36	31	43	45	26	40	31	39	39	37	46	53
40828	EVARTS	57	43	31	40	46	55	45	51	52	45	61	58	41	57	45	55	57	51	61	64
40829	GRAYS KNOB	53	35	16	30	40	46	34	43	41	35	48	51	29	46	35	44	44	42	52	60
40831	HARLAN	66	48	31	44	53	62	51	58	58	50	68	66	45	65	51	62	63	58	69	74
40843	HOLMES MILL	40	42	49	44	42	44	43	43	41	43	52	50	43	51	43	40	50	43	41	47
40845	HULEN	82	55	25	47	62	72	53	66	64	54	75	79	45	71	54	69	68	66	82	94
40847	KENVIR	33	22	10	19	25	29	21	27	26	22	30	32	18	29	22	28	27	26	33	38
40855	LYNCH	41	31	20	30	34	41	34	38	38	32	45	42	30	43	34	41	41	38	45	45
40858	MOZELLE	52	35	16	30	39	45	34	42	40	34	48	50	29	45	34	44	43	42	52	60
40862	PARTRIDGE	57	38	17	33	43	50	37	46	44	37	52	55	31	49	37	48	47	46	57	65
40863	PATHFORK	48	32	15	28	37	42	31	39	38	32	44	47	27	42	32	41	40	39	48	56
40865	PUTNEY	74	50	22	43	56	65	48	60	58	49	68	72	41	64	49	62	62	59	74	85
40868	STINNETT	45	30	14	26	34	40	29	37	35	30	42	44	25	39	30	38	38	36	45	52
40870	TOTZ	96	64	29	55	73	83	62	77	75	63	88	92	53	83	63	80	80	76	95	110
40873	WALLINS CREEK	61	41	18	35	46	53	39	49	47	40	56	59	33	53	40	51	51	49	61	70
40902	ARJAY	43	29	13	25	33	37	28	35	33	28	39	41	24	37	28	36	36	34	43	49
40903	ARTEMUS	55	39	22	36	44	51	41	48	47	40	56	55	36	53	41	50	51	47	58	62
40906	BARBOURVILLE	54	38	23	35	43	50	40	46	46	39	55	54	35	52	40	49	50	46	56	62
40913	BEVERLY	40	26	12	23	30	35	26	32	31	26	36	38	22	34	26	33	33	32	39	45
40914	BIG CREEK	45	31	17	27	35	40	31	38	37	32	44	44	27	41	31	40	40	37	46	52
40915	BIMBLE	68	45	21	39	51	59	44	55	53	45	62	65	37	59	45	57	56	54	67	78
40921	BRYANTS STORE	51	34	16	30	39	45	33	41	40	34	47	50	28	44	34	43	43	41	51	59
40923	CANNON	56	38	17	32	43	49	36	45	44	37	51	54	31	49	37	47	47	45	56	64
40927	CLOSPLINT	50	52	60	54	52	55	53	52	51	52	64	61	53	62	52	49	62	53	50	57
40930	DEWITT	42	28	13	24	32	37	27	34	33	28	39	41	23	36	28	35	35	34	42	48
40935	FLAT LICK	48	32	15	28	36	42	31	39	37	32	44	46	26	41	31	40	40	38	48	55
40940	FRAKES	59	40	18	34	45	52	38	48	46	39	54	57	33	51	39	50	49	48	59	68
40943	GIRDLER	53	35	16	30	40	46	34	43	41	35	48	51	29	46	35	44	44	42	53	60
40946	GREEN ROAD	69	46	21	40	52	60	44	56	54	45	63	66	38	59	45	58	57	55	68	79
40949	HEIDRICK	59	39	18	34	44	51	38	47	46	39	54	57	32	51	39	49	49	47	58	67
40953	HINKLE	53	36	16	31	40	47	34	43	42	35	49	51	29	46	35	45	44	43	53	61
40958	KETTLE ISLAND	62	41	19	36	47	54	40	50	48	41	57	60	34	54	41	52	52	50	62	71
40962	MANCHESTER	54	37	19	32	41	48	36	44	43	37	51	52	31	48	37	47	47	44	54	61
40964	MARY ALICE	56	37	17	32	42	49	36	45	44	37	51	54	31	48	37	47	46	45	56	64
40965	MIDDLESBORO	59	43	27	39	47	55	45	51	52	44	61	60	40	58	45	55	56	52	61	67
40972	ONEIDA	47	32	14	27	36	41	30	38	37	31	43	46	26	41	31	40	39	38	47	54
40977	PINEVILLE	62	42	20	36	47	54	41	50	49	41	58	60	35	54	42	53	52	50	62	70
40979	ROARK	55	37	17	31	41	48	35	44	43	36	50	53	30	47	36	46	45	44	54	63
40982	SCALF	36	24	11	21	27	31	23	29	28	24	33	35	20	31	24	30	30	29	36	41
40983	SEXTONS CREEK	51	34	16	30	39	45	33	42	40	34	47	50	28	45	34	43	43	41	51	59
40988	STONEY FORK	55	37	17	32	42	48	36	45	43	36	51	53	30	48	36	46	46	44	55	63
40995	TROSPER	54	36	16	31	41	47	35	43	42	35	49	52	30	47	35	45	45	43	54	62
40997	WALKER	42	28	13	24	32	37	27	34	33	28	39	41	23	36	28	35	35	34	42	48
40999	WOOLLUM	56	38	17	33	43	49	36	46	44	37	52	54	31	49	37	47	47	45	56	65
41001	ALEXANDRIA	102	105	99	104	106	110	98	101	97	98	120	119	99	123	99	96	117	99	99	119
41002	AUGUSTA	76	58	37	54	63	71	58	66	65	58	77	77	53	75	58	67	72	65	76	86
41003	BERRY	86	64	39	59	70	80	63	74	72	64	86	87	57	83	64	75	79	73	86	97
41004	BROOKSVILLE	87	64	37	58	71	79	61	73	70	62	84	87	55	81	63	74	77	73	86	100
41005	BURLINGTON	113	122	119	125	118	117	113	113	106	116	134	133	115	135	111	101	132	111	101	127
41006	BUTLER	87	76	59	74	80	88	74	80	78	73	95	94	71	95	75	80	90	79	87	100
41007	CALIFORNIA	110	98	74	93	103	111	90	100	96	90	117	119	89	119	93	98	111	98	109	129
41008	CARROLLTON	78	65	50	63	69	78	66	72	72	65	86	83	63	85	67	74	81	71	80	88
41010	CORINTH	90	67	39	60	74	83	64	76	73	64	87	91	57	85	65	77	80	75	89	104
41011	COVINGTON	74	74	91	74	73	80	79	76	81	78	101	89	80	101	79	81	98	79	77	84
41014	COVINGTON	60	62	68	61	62	67	66	63	66	63	82	74	66	85	65	66	80	64	64	69
41015	LATONIA	78	80	85	79	80	86	81	80	81	80	101	93	82	104	81	81	98	80	81	90
41016	COVINGTON	65	66	68	64	66	73	68	67	70	66	87	77	69	90	68	71	84	67	70	75
41017	FT MITCHELL	127	144	160	148	141	143	137	134	129	138	163	158	142	167	137	125	162	133	122	148
41018	ERLANGER	86	88	92	89	87	91	89	88	87	88	109	103	89	109	87	84	106	88	83	98
41030	CRITTENDEN	98	89	70	86	90	95	85	91	86	87	106	106	81	101	84	85	102	91	91	109
41031	CYNTHIANA	85	73	56	69	77	85	72	78	77	71	94	92	69	94	73	80	88	77	87	98
41033	DE MOSSVILLE	93	63	29	55	71	82	61	76	73	62	86	90	52	81	62	78	78	75	93	107
41034	DOVER	90	76	54	71	81	88	71	80	77	71	93	96	68	94	73	80	88	78	89	106
41035	DRY RIDGE	90	80	62	77	82	88	78	84	80	79	98	97	73	94	77	80	94	83	86	101
41039	EWING	80	53	24	46	60	69	51	64	62	52	73	77	44	69	52	67	66	64	79	91
41040	FALMOUTH	89	70	47	65	75	83	69	78	76	69	91	91	63	88	69	79	85	78	87	100
41041	FLEMINGSBURG	82	59	32	53	65	74	58	69	67	58	79	81	51	76	58	71	73	68	82	94
41042	FLORENCE	95	97	99	101	95	98	96	95	92	97	116	112	96	115	94	89	113	95	88	106
41043	FOSTER	92	66	36	60	75	84	64	77	74	64	87	93	56	85	65	78	80	76	92	107
41044	GERMANTOWN	82	75	59	72	75	79	72	77	73	74	90	89	68	85	71	72	86	77	76	91
41045	GHENT	94	85	65	81	87	93	79	87	82	80	101	102	76	100	80	83	96	85	90	108
41046	GLENCOE	81	72	55	69	74	79	68	75	71	70	87	87	65	84	68	71	83	74	77	92
41048	HEBRON	146	164	159	169	158	156	148	147	137	152	174	172	153	175	146	130	171	143	130	164
41049	HILLSBORO	71	47	21	41	54	62	46	57	55	47	65	68	39	61	47	59	59	57	71	81
41051	INDEPENDENCE	98	108	107	110	105	104	100	100	95	102	119	118	102	121	99	90	117	99	90	112
41052	JONESVILLE	80	72	56	69	74	79	68	74	70	69	86	87	65	85	68	71	82	73	77	92
41055	MAYSLICK	91	64	33	58	73	82	62	76	72	62	85	91	54	82	64	76	78	75	91	106
41056	MAYSVILLE	79	62	45	59	67	77	64	71	71	63	85	82	59	83	64	74	79	71	82	89
41059	MELBOURNE	106	105	91	102	108	113	96	103	97	96	120	122	97	124	99	98	116	100	105	126
41063	MORNING VIEW	100	89	68	85	94	101	82	91	87	82	106	109	81	109	85	90	101	89	99	118
41064	MOUNT OLIVET	77	51	23	44	58	67	50	62	60	51	70	74	42	66	50	65	64	61	76	88
41071	NEWPORT	66	67	79	67	67	72	72	69	72	70	90	81	72	92	71	72	88	71	69	76
41073	BELLEVUE	69	73	82	73	73	77	76	73	75	73	93	86	77	96	75	73	91	74	71	80
	KENTUCKY	86	74	63	71	77	85	74	80	79	74	96	94	71	95	74	81	91	80	86	98
	UNITED STATES	100	100	100	100	100	100	100	100	100	100	100	100	100	100	100	100	100	100	100	100

POPULATION CHANGE

ZIP CODE		COUNTY FIPS CODE	POPULATION			2000-2004 ANNUAL RATE		HOUSEHOLDS					FAMILIES		
#	POST OFFICE NAME		2000	2004	2009	% Rate	State Centile	2000	2004	2009	% Annual Rate 2000-2004	2004 Average HH Size	2000	2004	% Annual Rate 2000-2004
41074	DAYTON	037	5922	5634	5568	-1.2	4	2179	2123	2148	-0.6	2.63	1505	1414	-1.5
41075	FORT THOMAS	037	16574	16473	16521	-0.1	32	6772	6882	7058	0.4	2.35	4317	4206	-0.6
41076	NEWPORT	037	14587	15538	16137	1.5	84	5644	6199	6613	2.2	2.38	3661	3866	1.3
41080	PETERSBURG	015	1902	1913	2142	0.1	47	644	663	757	0.7	2.89	528	531	0.1
41083	SANDERS	041	756	769	779	0.4	57	275	286	295	0.9	2.60	198	200	0.2
41085	SILVER GROVE	037	1137	1216	1255	1.6	86	459	503	532	2.2	2.42	305	321	1.2
41086	SPARTA	077	1615	1738	1836	1.7	88	577	631	676	2.1	2.72	423	450	1.5
41091	UNION	015	11758	14351	17487	4.8	99	3821	4755	5899	5.3	3.02	3256	3986	4.9
41092	VERONA	015	2860	3004	3301	1.2	79	993	1064	1190	1.6	2.82	802	840	1.1
41093	WALLINGFORD	069	1766	1828	1873	0.8	71	692	732	762	1.3	2.49	523	539	0.7
41094	WALTON	015	8065	8741	9948	1.9	89	2862	3172	3678	2.5	2.75	2240	2404	1.7
41095	WARSAW	077	4071	4251	4417	1.0	76	1568	1671	1762	1.5	2.49	1127	1164	0.8
41097	WILLIAMSTOWN	081	6411	6933	7644	1.9	89	2431	2675	2997	2.3	2.55	1768	1890	1.6
41098	WORTHVILLE	041	772	835	866	1.9	89	287	317	335	2.4	2.63	208	224	1.8
41101	ASHLAND	019	20218	19128	18302	-1.3	3	8721	8408	8201	-0.9	2.23	5587	5182	-1.8
41102	ASHLAND	019	20406	20336	19890	-0.1	34	7754	7873	7861	0.4	2.38	5839	5750	-0.4
41121	ARGILLITE	089	1138	1156	1161	0.4	55	425	443	457	1.0	2.61	335	341	0.4
41124	BLAINE	127	1064	1073	1090	0.2	49	404	419	436	0.9	2.56	314	318	0.3
41129	CATLETTSBURG	019	9156	9137	8944	-0.1	37	3566	3645	3647	0.5	2.47	2722	2710	-0.1
41132	DENTON	043	549	545	548	-0.2	31	200	203	210	0.4	2.68	158	157	-0.2
41135	EMERSON	135	516	526	536	0.5	59	196	205	214	1.1	2.57	153	156	0.5
41137	FIREBRICK	135	252	255	259	0.3	52	102	106	110	0.9	2.41	82	83	0.3
41139	FLATWOODS	089	8203	8561	8762	1.0	76	3339	3588	3776	1.7	2.36	2483	2597	1.1
41141	GARRISON	135	3618	3709	3788	0.6	64	1362	1433	1501	1.2	2.59	1052	1079	0.6
41143	GRAYSON	043	13077	13355	13699	0.5	61	4922	5175	5455	1.2	2.46	3721	3810	0.6
41144	GREENUP	089	12231	12080	12028	-0.3	27	4664	4730	4834	0.3	2.51	3599	3567	-0.2
41146	HITCHINS	043	607	600	604	-0.3	28	227	230	238	0.3	2.61	178	177	-0.1
41149	ISONVILLE	063	946	956	966	0.3	51	351	365	378	0.9	2.62	266	270	0.4
41159	MARTHA	127	700	705	716	0.2	48	242	250	261	0.8	2.82	191	193	0.3
41164	OLIVE HILL	043	11644	11874	12120	0.5	60	4605	4823	5048	1.1	2.46	3381	3447	0.5
41166	QUINCY	135	864	875	888	0.3	53	308	320	333	0.9	2.73	248	252	0.4
41168	RUSH	019	3121	3204	3219	0.6	65	1152	1212	1247	1.2	2.60	912	937	0.6
41169	RUSSELL	089	5661	5612	5597	-0.2	30	2305	2347	2403	0.4	2.35	1705	1691	-0.2
41171	SANDY HOOK	063	5384	5443	5504	0.3	52	2135	2224	2312	1.0	2.42	1546	1564	0.3
41174	SOUTH PORTSMOUTH	089	759	758	756	0.0	39	304	311	317	0.5	2.32	225	223	-0.2
41175	SOUTH SHORE	089	5169	5152	5141	-0.1	34	2070	2113	2161	0.5	2.43	1540	1534	-0.1
41179	VANCEBURG	135	5549	5554	5632	0.0	42	2145	2200	2287	0.6	2.43	1536	1530	-0.1
41180	WEBBVILLE	127	1673	1689	1718	0.2	50	646	672	701	0.9	2.51	475	481	0.3
41183	WORTHINGTON	089	1701	1657	1643	-0.6	15	676	676	687	0.0	2.42	524	511	-0.6
41189	TOLLESBORO	135	3295	3372	3442	0.6	63	1311	1377	1439	1.2	2.45	980	1002	0.5
41201	ADAMS	127	1135	1162	1190	0.6	63	434	457	479	1.2	2.54	331	339	0.6
41204	BOONS CAMP	115	663	649	645	-0.5	19	257	259	265	0.2	2.51	196	193	-0.4
41214	DEBORD	159	771	759	764	-0.4	23	284	287	296	0.3	2.64	218	215	-0.3
41216	EAST POINT	071	2059	2095	2111	0.4	58	784	820	842	1.1	2.55	630	646	0.6
41219	FLATGAP	115	1943	1941	1940	0.0	39	748	768	787	0.6	2.53	581	583	0.1
41222	HAGERHILL	115	2482	2484	2496	0.0	42	938	964	994	0.7	2.54	711	714	0.1
41224	INEZ	159	4854	4800	4786	-0.3	28	1837	1876	1922	0.5	2.52	1390	1383	-0.1
41226	KEATON	115	380	384	385	0.3	51	138	143	147	0.8	2.69	111	112	0.2
41230	LOUISA	127	8755	9005	9263	0.7	67	3390	3573	3756	1.2	2.48	2504	2568	0.6
41231	LOVELY	159	617	621	621	0.2	47	238	249	256	1.1	2.49	182	186	0.5
41232	LOWMANSVILLE	127	2166	2255	2330	1.0	74	805	857	905	1.5	2.63	638	665	1.0
41234	MEALLY	115	622	606	602	-0.6	15	233	234	239	0.1	2.59	178	175	-0.4
41238	OIL SPRINGS	115	1216	1232	1240	0.3	53	486	508	525	1.1	2.43	381	389	0.5
41240	PAINTSVILLE	115	7505	7492	7527	0.0	38	2971	3040	3133	0.5	2.34	2115	2098	-0.2
41250	PILGRIM	159	985	986	985	0.0	42	377	392	403	0.9	2.52	292	297	0.4
41254	RIVER	115	517	522	524	0.2	50	185	193	199	1.0	2.70	149	152	0.5
41255	SITKA	115	285	283	282	-0.2	31	113	115	117	0.4	2.46	84	84	0.0
41256	STAFFORDSVILLE	115	1653	1793	1869	1.9	90	642	713	761	2.5	2.51	499	540	1.9
41257	STAMBAUGH	115	225	214	212	-1.2	4	86	84	85	-0.6	2.55	70	67	-1.0
41260	THELMA	115	2375	2328	2323	-0.5	20	933	940	963	0.2	2.39	720	708	-0.4
41262	TOMAHAWK	159	1733	1805	1839	1.0	74	639	687	719	1.7	2.62	499	524	1.2
41263	TUTOR KEY	115	435	427	421	-0.4	21	166	168	172	0.3	2.54	135	134	-0.2
41265	VAN LEAR	071	3213	3256	3283	0.3	53	1248	1302	1340	1.0	2.50	959	978	0.5
41267	WARFIELD	159	2926	2921	2913	0.0	38	1153	1190	1221	0.8	2.44	845	848	0.1
41271	WILLIAMSPORT	115	77	75	75	-0.6	14	31	31	32	0.0	2.32	24	23	-1.0
41274	WITTENSVILLE	115	987	1009	1024	0.5	62	384	402	419	1.1	2.51	294	300	0.5
41301	CAMPTON	237	5655	5690	5739	0.2	47	2266	2343	2422	0.8	2.36	1586	1590	0.1
41311	BEATTYVILLE	129	7597	7675	7807	0.2	51	2852	2971	3118	1.0	2.34	2027	2051	0.3
41314	BOONEVILLE	189	4236	4194	4157	-0.2	29	1649	1671	1691	0.3	2.45	1205	1187	-0.4
41317	CLAYHOLE	025	1117	1115	1123	0.0	38	424	433	447	0.5	2.58	320	318	-0.2
41332	HAZEL GREEN	175	1783	1752	1764	-0.4	22	728	735	759	0.2	2.38	554	545	-0.4
41338	ISLAND CITY	189	387	378	371	-0.6	18	151	151	152	0.0	2.50	115	112	-0.6
41339	JACKSON	025	12515	12735	12985	0.4	58	4806	5040	5291	1.1	2.46	3501	3568	0.5
41342	LEE CITY	237	297	276	272	-1.7	1	121	115	115	-1.2	2.40	85	78	-2.0
41348	LOST CREEK	025	962	964	971	0.1	43	362	371	384	0.6	2.59	273	273	0.0
41351	MISTLETOE	189	92	91	90	-0.3	28	29	29	30	0.0	3.14	22	22	0.0
41360	PINE RIDGE	237	503	537	554	1.6	85	175	192	203	2.2	2.74	125	133	1.5
41364	RICETOWN	189	442	436	430	-0.3	26	170	172	174	0.3	2.53	129	128	-0.2
41365	ROGERS	237	555	601	627	1.9	89	218	242	257	2.5	2.48	157	169	1.8
41366	ROUSSEAU	025	193	201	207	1.0	74	79	85	90	1.7	2.36	58	61	1.2
41367	ROWDY	193	388	378	374	-0.6	15	151	152	156	0.2	2.49	113	111	-0.4
41385	VANCLEVE	025	555	555	560	0.0	41	212	220	229	0.9	2.40	162	164	0.3
41386	VINCENT	189	329	319	313	-0.7	12	130	130	131	0.0	2.45	95	92	-0.8
41390	WHICK	025	16	17	17	1.4	84	7	7	8	0.0	2.43	6	6	0.0
41397	ZOE	129	124	125	127	0.2	49	50	52	55	0.9	2.40	37	37	0.0
41419	EDNA	153	243	244	247	0.1	45	94	97	102	0.7	2.52	68	69	0.3
41422	ELSIE	153	77	77	78	0.0	41	32	33	35	0.7	2.33	23	23	0.0
41425	EZEL	175	1126	1157	1190	0.6	66	428	451	476	1.2	2.50	324	333	0.7
41464	ROYALTON	153	380	390	401	0.6	65	137	145	153	1.3	2.69	107	110	0.7
41465	SALYERSVILLE	153	11979	12182	12476	0.4	57	4516	4742	5014	1.2	2.53	3465	3551	0.6
41472	WEST LIBERTY	175	11615	12018	12418	0.8	71	3836	4098	4359	1.6	2.49	2873	2992	1.0
41501	PIKEVILLE	195	25268	26013	26640	0.7	68	10374	11014	11652	1.4	2.30	7298	7539	0.8
41503	SOUTH WILLIAMSON	195	743	711	705	-1.0	6	308	302	308	-0.5	2.18	207	195	-1.4
41512	ASHCAMP	195	507	524	535	0.8	70	177	190	201	1.7	2.72	137	143	1.0
41513	BELCHER	195	567	577	582	0.4	58	230	243	254	1.3	2.37	177	182	0.7
	KENTUCKY					0.7					1.2	2.42			0.5
	UNITED STATES					1.2					1.3	2.58			1.1

ZIP CODE #	POST OFFICE NAME	RACE (%) White 2000	White 2004	Black 2000	Black 2004	Asian/Pacific 2000	Asian/Pacific 2004	% Hispanic Origin 2000	% Hispanic Origin 2004	2004 AGE DISTRIBUTION (%) 0-4	5-9	10-14	15-19	20-24	25-44	45-64	65-84	85+	18+	MEDIAN AGE 2004	% 2004 Males	% 2004 Females
41074	DAYTON	98.4	98.3	0.5	0.5	0.2	0.2	0.6	0.7	8.3	7.6	7.5	7.4	8.1	29.3	21.1	9.8	1.0	72.4	32.4	49.1	50.9
41075	FORT THOMAS	97.5	97.2	0.7	0.7	0.7	0.8	0.7	0.9	5.8	5.9	6.8	6.9	6.3	27.4	25.1	13.3	2.5	77.3	39.1	47.7	52.3
41076	NEWPORT	96.9	96.5	1.2	1.2	1.0	1.2	0.6	0.8	5.8	5.6	5.5	6.8	7.6	28.2	24.4	14.2	1.9	79.9	38.2	47.0	53.0
41080	PETERSBURG	98.4	98.3	0.3	0.3	0.0	0.0	0.8	0.9	6.3	7.0	8.4	7.9	5.9	29.2	27.4	7.2	0.7	73.5	36.8	52.1	47.9
41083	SANDERS	97.2	97.1	1.5	1.4	0.1	0.1	2.1	2.2	8.3	7.9	7.2	6.5	6.4	29.5	25.0	8.6	0.7	72.4	35.8	52.3	47.7
41085	SILVER GROVE	98.4	98.0	0.3	0.3	0.1	0.1	2.4	3.1	8.3	7.7	7.4	6.7	6.3	32.1	19.2	11.5	0.7	72.5	33.6	53.5	46.5
41086	SPARTA	96.5	96.3	1.9	1.9	0.2	0.3	1.1	1.4	7.5	7.6	8.3	6.9	5.9	29.1	23.8	9.6	1.3	72.4	35.4	50.6	49.4
41091	UNION	96.6	95.9	0.5	0.5	1.8	2.4	0.9	1.2	8.0	8.6	8.8	7.2	5.5	29.0	26.5	6.1	0.3	70.1	35.9	50.0	50.1
41092	VERONA	98.2	98.0	0.2	0.3	0.3	0.4	1.0	1.3	6.3	7.5	8.7	6.9	5.4	29.4	27.1	8.1	0.7	73.4	37.1	50.3	49.7
41093	WALLINGFORD	99.4	99.4	0.0	0.0	0.0	0.0	0.6	0.8	6.6	6.7	6.8	5.7	6.2	28.9	27.6	10.1	1.3	76.0	37.9	51.5	48.5
41094	WALTON	97.5	97.0	0.7	0.8	0.6	0.7	1.0	1.3	7.4	7.6	7.7	7.2	6.9	29.1	25.5	8.0	0.7	72.7	35.3	50.0	50.0
41095	WARSAW	96.2	95.8	2.0	2.0	0.3	0.3	1.0	1.3	7.4	7.5	8.0	6.4	5.8	28.7	24.4	10.1	1.7	73.3	36.3	49.6	50.4
41097	WILLIAMSTOWN	98.3	98.0	0.1	0.1	0.5	0.6	1.1	1.4	7.7	7.3	6.9	6.5	6.2	29.0	23.2	11.3	1.9	74.0	36.2	49.1	50.9
41098	WORTHVILLE	98.5	98.4	0.3	0.2	0.0	0.0	2.7	2.9	6.7	6.7	7.4	6.2	7.8	28.9	25.2	10.5	0.6	75.6	36.9	51.1	48.9
41101	ASHLAND	95.7	95.4	2.2	2.2	0.6	0.7	0.7	0.8	5.9	5.6	6.4	6.0	6.0	25.1	25.8	16.9	2.5	78.6	41.6	46.0	54.0
41102	ASHLAND	95.0	94.7	3.7	3.8	0.3	0.4	2.0	2.5	5.0	5.2	5.6	5.5	6.0	28.8	28.7	14.0	1.3	81.0	41.3	51.9	48.1
41121	ARGILLITE	98.8	98.9	0.4	0.4	0.0	0.0	0.7	0.7	6.8	6.8	7.4	5.6	5.9	27.8	28.3	10.6	0.9	75.7	38.2	50.4	49.7
41124	BLAINE	98.7	98.6	0.0	0.0	0.0	0.0	0.2	0.3	5.8	6.1	9.0	6.1	7.1	27.4	25.7	11.7	1.2	75.3	36.0	50.6	49.4
41129	CATLETTSBURG	98.7	98.5	0.6	0.6	0.1	0.1	0.2	0.3	5.4	5.6	6.0	6.0	6.0	27.8	29.1	12.9	1.2	79.3	40.7	49.6	50.4
41132	DENTON	99.1	98.7	0.0	0.0	0.0	0.2	0.9	1.1	7.5	7.3	7.5	6.6	6.1	30.1	23.9	9.9	1.1	73.4	35.6	51.0	49.0
41135	EMERSON	99.4	99.4	0.0	0.0	0.0	0.0	0.4	0.6	5.3	7.2	6.8	6.5	5.3	31.2	24.1	11.8	1.7	77.0	36.8	50.0	50.0
41137	FIREBRICK	99.6	99.6	0.0	0.0	0.0	0.0	0.0	0.4	6.3	6.7	9.0	6.3	6.3	27.5	25.9	10.6	1.6	73.7	36.4	50.6	49.4
41139	FLATWOODS	98.5	98.4	0.3	0.3	0.3	0.3	0.5	0.5	5.4	5.6	6.1	6.2	6.0	26.0	27.7	15.2	1.7	79.0	41.4	47.0	53.0
41141	GARRISON	98.9	98.9	0.3	0.3	0.0	0.1	0.2	0.3	7.2	7.1	7.6	7.1	6.7	29.2	24.1	10.0	1.2	73.9	35.4	48.8	51.2
41143	GRAYSON	98.9	98.7	0.2	0.2	0.2	0.2	0.6	0.7	6.4	6.4	6.7	6.7	7.7	28.1	24.7	11.4	1.8	77.0	36.6	49.0	51.0
41144	GREENUP	97.8	97.8	1.1	1.1	0.2	0.2	0.6	0.7	6.3	6.5	6.8	6.0	6.0	28.0	26.9	12.3	1.2	76.8	38.7	49.5	50.5
41146	HITCHINS	99.5	99.3	0.0	0.0	0.2	0.2	0.5	0.7	7.7	7.7	7.7	6.2	5.8	30.2	23.7	10.3	0.8	73.0	35.4	50.8	49.2
41149	ISONVILLE	99.4	99.4	0.1	0.1	0.0	0.0	0.5	0.5	7.5	7.1	7.2	7.1	6.7	26.9	25.0	11.1	1.4	73.7	35.3	50.4	49.6
41159	MARTHA	98.9	98.9	0.0	0.0	0.0	0.0	0.1	0.1	5.5	6.1	9.1	6.1	7.0	27.7	25.5	11.8	1.3	75.3	36.0	50.8	49.2
41164	OLIVE HILL	99.1	99.1	0.1	0.1	0.0	0.0	0.6	0.8	6.4	6.5	7.0	6.0	6.4	28.5	26.0	12.1	1.2	76.6	38.0	49.5	50.5
41166	QUINCY	99.4	99.3	0.0	0.0	0.1	0.1	0.2	0.3	6.5	6.7	8.6	6.5	6.4	27.7	25.7	10.7	1.1	74.2	36.1	50.9	49.1
41168	RUSH	98.3	98.2	0.7	0.7	0.2	0.3	0.4	0.5	6.1	6.5	7.0	7.6	5.9	30.1	26.3	9.7	0.9	75.4	37.2	50.4	49.6
41169	RUSSELL	97.7	97.6	0.7	0.7	0.9	0.9	0.6	0.6	5.4	5.7	6.1	6.0	5.5	25.3	29.0	15.6	1.5	79.2	42.4	47.4	52.6
41171	SANDY HOOK	99.0	99.0	0.0	0.0	0.0	0.0	0.6	0.6	6.3	6.5	6.9	6.3	6.3	26.9	26.6	12.1	2.1	76.5	38.6	49.1	50.9
41174	SOUTH PORTSMOUTH	98.0	98.0	0.1	0.1	0.0	0.0	0.0	0.0	6.1	6.3	6.6	5.8	5.7	26.4	24.8	15.0	3.3	77.3	40.2	47.2	52.8
41175	SOUTH SHORE	98.5	98.5	0.1	0.1	0.2	0.2	0.3	0.3	6.1	6.3	6.9	5.8	6.1	26.5	26.5	14.4	1.5	77.2	39.5	47.9	52.2
41179	VANCEBURG	99.0	98.9	0.3	0.3	0.0	0.0	0.4	0.6	6.4	6.6	6.6	5.8	6.3	29.1	25.4	12.1	1.8	77.0	38.2	50.3	49.7
41180	WEBBVILLE	97.9	97.6	0.0	0.0	0.1	0.1	0.7	0.8	6.4	6.6	7.1	5.9	6.5	28.4	26.5	11.1	1.6	76.4	38.4	52.2	47.8
41183	WORTHINGTON	98.7	98.8	0.1	0.1	0.0	0.0	0.8	0.8	4.4	5.0	7.1	6.1	6.4	24.5	29.2	15.7	1.8	79.9	42.9	47.0	53.1
41189	TOLLESBORO	98.5	98.3	0.2	0.2	0.0	0.0	0.8	1.0	6.1	6.2	6.6	5.8	6.1	30.1	26.3	11.5	1.4	77.6	38.2	51.0	49.0
41201	ADAMS	99.2	99.1	0.0	0.0	0.0	0.0	0.0	0.1	6.3	6.7	7.1	5.8	6.5	27.5	28.8	10.6	0.8	76.4	38.0	51.8	48.2
41204	BOONS CAMP	98.9	98.8	0.2	0.2	0.0	0.0	0.8	0.9	6.5	6.6	8.0	7.2	6.3	27.3	26.8	10.0	1.2	74.4	37.2	49.5	50.5
41214	DEBORD	99.4	99.2	0.0	0.0	0.1	0.1	0.5	0.5	6.9	7.1	7.4	6.9	6.1	28.3	26.9	9.5	1.1	74.2	36.7	50.7	49.3
41216	EAST POINT	98.7	98.5	0.3	0.3	0.4	0.4	0.6	0.7	6.7	6.5	6.1	6.5	6.2	29.0	28.6	9.4	1.1	76.9	38.6	48.5	51.6
41219	FLATGAP	99.1	99.1	0.2	0.2	0.1	0.1	0.5	0.5	6.0	6.2	6.5	6.3	6.7	27.4	26.9	12.1	1.9	77.5	38.8	51.2	48.8
41222	HAGERHILL	98.2	98.2	0.3	0.3	0.2	0.2	0.9	0.9	6.1	6.3	7.2	6.3	6.2	29.1	28.5	9.5	1.0	76.5	38.0	48.7	51.3
41224	INEZ	99.4	99.4	0.0	0.0	0.1	0.1	0.6	0.6	6.6	6.8	7.2	6.7	6.4	28.5	26.6	9.9	1.2	75.0	37.4	49.6	50.4
41226	KEATON	99.5	99.5	0.0	0.0	0.0	0.0	0.8	0.8	7.3	7.3	7.8	6.8	6.3	29.2	22.1	11.5	1.8	73.4	35.2	51.0	49.0
41230	LOUISA	99.0	98.9	0.2	0.2	0.1	0.1	0.5	0.6	5.7	5.9	6.9	6.4	6.5	28.1	26.5	12.4	1.6	77.5	38.6	48.4	51.6
41231	LOVELY	99.2	99.4	0.2	0.2	0.0	0.0	0.7	0.6	6.0	7.4	8.2	7.1	7.3	29.8	25.0	8.9	0.5	73.9	35.2	51.2	48.8
41232	LOWMANSVILLE	99.7	99.7	0.1	0.0	0.1	0.1	0.2	0.3	6.5	6.5	7.2	6.8	6.9	29.2	27.0	9.5	0.5	75.2	36.4	51.0	49.1
41234	MEALLY	99.4	99.3	0.0	0.0	0.2	0.2	0.2	0.2	6.4	6.3	5.9	6.3	6.9	27.9	28.4	10.9	1.0	78.1	39.2	47.5	52.5
41238	OIL SPRINGS	99.3	99.4	0.2	0.2	0.0	0.0	0.9	0.9	6.5	6.5	6.0	5.7	5.6	29.5	28.3	10.6	1.4	77.8	39.0	49.8	50.2
41240	PAINTSVILLE	98.4	98.4	0.3	0.4	0.4	0.4	0.6	0.6	5.6	5.7	6.1	6.2	6.2	27.2	26.9	14.0	2.2	78.7	40.1	47.0	53.0
41250	PILGRIM	99.4	99.4	0.0	0.0	0.1	0.1	0.6	0.7	5.7	7.3	8.3	7.2	7.1	29.6	25.7	8.6	0.5	73.9	35.7	51.6	48.4
41254	RIVER	99.0	99.2	0.0	0.0	0.0	0.0	1.2	1.2	6.7	7.9	10.2	6.3	6.7	29.9	24.1	7.7	0.6	71.1	33.5	49.6	50.4
41255	SITKA	99.0	98.6	0.4	0.4	0.7	0.7	0.7	0.7	6.0	6.0	7.1	7.8	6.7	27.9	26.5	11.0	1.1	76.7	37.2	49.1	50.9
41256	STAFFORDSVILLE	98.8	98.8	0.0	0.0	0.7	0.7	0.4	0.3	6.3	6.5	6.8	5.9	6.4	27.9	29.6	9.8	0.8	76.9	38.7	48.5	51.5
41257	STAMBAUGH	100.0	100.0	0.0	0.0	0.0	0.0	0.4	0.5	5.1	4.2	6.5	7.0	5.1	30.4	29.0	12.2	0.5	79.9	39.8	49.5	50.5
41260	THELMA	98.2	98.1	0.8	0.8	0.1	0.1	0.6	0.6	6.5	6.3	5.8	5.7	7.2	27.9	27.2	11.9	1.6	78.3	38.8	48.6	51.4
41262	TOMAHAWK	99.1	99.2	0.0	0.0	0.2	0.2	1.0	1.1	7.3	7.8	9.1	6.4	6.9	29.3	24.2	8.3	0.8	71.4	33.6	50.8	49.3
41263	TUTOR KEY	99.8	100.0	0.0	0.0	0.0	0.0	0.7	0.7	5.9	5.4	6.8	6.1	5.9	28.8	30.0	10.3	0.9	78.2	39.5	50.1	49.9
41265	VAN LEAR	98.9	98.8	0.1	0.1	0.5	0.6	0.8	0.9	5.9	6.5	6.7	6.2	6.2	29.9	27.2	10.4	0.9	77.3	38.2	49.2	50.8
41267	WARFIELD	98.9	98.9	0.1	0.1	0.2	0.2	0.4	0.4	8.3	7.3	7.3	6.4	8.4	27.6	24.7	9.0	0.9	73.3	34.0	49.0	51.0
41271	WILLIAMSPORT	98.7	97.3	1.3	1.3	0.0	0.0	0.0	1.3	8.0	5.3	5.3	6.7	8.0	29.3	28.0	9.3	0.0	80.0	36.5	49.3	50.7
41274	WITTENSVILLE	98.8	98.7	0.1	0.1	0.6	0.6	0.3	0.3	6.1	6.5	6.6	6.4	6.7	28.5	27.9	10.4	0.8	76.6	37.9	48.3	51.7
41301	CAMPTON	99.1	99.1	0.3	0.3	0.1	0.1	0.6	0.6	6.5	7.0	7.0	6.3	6.2	28.0	25.7	11.4	1.9	75.5	37.8	49.5	50.5
41311	BEATTYVILLE	95.0	95.0	3.9	3.9	0.1	0.1	0.4	0.4	5.2	5.4	6.2	6.8	7.1	29.6	25.1	12.8	1.8	79.2	38.6	52.4	47.6
41314	BOONEVILLE	99.2	99.2	0.1	0.1	0.1	0.1	0.8	0.9	5.5	6.1	6.7	7.1	6.7	26.2	26.4	13.5	1.9	77.3	39.4	50.2	49.8
41317	CLAYHOLE	99.1	99.2	0.1	0.1	0.0	0.0	1.9	2.3	6.2	6.7	7.4	7.4	7.2	29.5	24.5	10.3	0.8	75.1	36.7	50.6	49.4
41332	HAZEL GREEN	99.4	99.3	0.1	0.1	0.0	0.0	0.5	0.6	6.2	6.4	6.7	6.4	6.7	27.7	26.3	12.0	1.5	76.9	38.0	50.3	49.7
41338	ISLAND CITY	99.2	98.9	0.3	0.3	0.3	0.3	1.0	1.1	5.8	6.1	6.4	5.3	6.4	25.7	30.4	11.9	2.1	78.0	40.8	50.3	49.7
41339	JACKSON	98.7	98.5	0.4	0.4	0.4	0.5	0.5	0.7	5.7	6.3	7.0	6.7	6.5	28.7	26.7	11.0	1.4	76.9	37.7	49.4	50.6
41342	LEE CITY	99.3	99.3	0.0	0.0	0.3	0.4	0.0	0.0	4.7	5.4	7.3	8.0	6.9	27.5	27.2	11.6	1.5	78.3	39.1	52.9	47.1
41348	LOST CREEK	99.1	99.0	0.3	0.3	0.0	0.0	0.7	1.0	7.1	7.2	8.1	7.0	7.1	28.9	23.8	10.2	0.8	73.3	35.6	49.7	50.3
41351	MISTLETOE	98.9	100.0	0.0	0.0	0.0	0.0	0.0	0.0	5.5	5.5	7.7	7.7	5.5	27.5	27.5	12.1	1.1	75.8	40.3	56.0	44.0
41360	PINE RIDGE	98.8	98.9	0.6	0.6	0.0	0.0	0.4	0.4	7.1	7.5	7.6	6.9	6.9	29.6	24.4	9.1	0.9	73.4	35.4	51.8	48.2
41364	RICETOWN	99.3	99.5	0.0	0.0	0.0	0.0	0.5	0.2	6.0	6.4	7.8	7.1	5.5	26.2	26.6	12.8	1.6	75.2	38.7	52.8	47.3
41365	ROGERS	98.9	99.0	0.2	0.2	0.2	0.2	0.4	0.3	7.7	7.3	8.0	6.5	6.7	30.5	23.5	8.8	1.2	73.2	35.4	51.8	48.3
41366	ROUSSEAU	99.5	99.5	0.0	0.0	0.0	0.0	0.0	0.5	4.5	6.5	8.0	4.5	6.5	28.4	30.9	10.0	1.0	78.1	39.6	49.8	50.3
41367	ROWDY	99.2	99.2	0.0	0.0	0.0	0.0	0.5	0.5	7.1	6.6	6.6	5.3	6.1	31.5	26.5	9.3	1.1	76.5	35.7	50.8	49.2
41385	VANCLEVE	97.7	97.5	1.1	1.1	0.5	0.7	0.4	0.4	5.8	5.8	7.0	6.7	8.3	29.4	25.8	10.5	0.9	76.9	36.8	50.6	49.4
41386	VINCENT	98.8	98.8	0.0	0.0	0.0	0.0	0.9	0.9	5.0	5.0	5.3	5.3	7.2	25.4	31.4	13.5	1.9	81.8	42.9	52.7	47.3
41390	WHICK	100.0	100.0	0.0	0.0	0.0	0.0	0.0	0.0	5.9	11.8	11.8	5.9	5.9	47.1	11.8	0.0	0.0	70.6	28.8	58.8	41.2
41397	ZOE	97.6	97.6	1.6	1.6	0.0	0.0	0.0	0.0	5.6	5.6	6.4	6.4	6.4	28.8	26.4	13.6	0.8	77.6	39.7	51.2	48.8
41419	EDNA	100.0	100.0	0.0	0.0	0.0	0.0	0.8	1.2	6.2	6.6	7.4	7.4	6.6	29.9	24.2	10.7	1.2	75.4	35.9	53.3	46.7
41422	ELSIE	100.0	100.0	0.0	0.0	0.0	0.0	0.0	1.3	6.5	6.5	6.5	6.5	7.8	29.9	24.7	10.4	1.3	74.0	35.5	52.0	48.1
41425	EZEL	98.3	98.0	0.4	0.4	0.5	0.7	0.4	0.5	5.9	6.5	6.8	7.6	6.0	27.8	26.5	11.4	1.5	75.1	37.1	51.5	48.5
41464	ROYALTON	99.2	99.0	0.0	0.0	0.0	0.0	0.5	0.5	7.7	7.4	8.0	6.9	7.7	27.7	25.4	8.5	0.8	72.8	34.6	50.8	49.2
41465	SALYERSVILLE	99.3	99.2	0.2	0.2	0.1	0.1	0.4	0.5	7.1	7.0	6.9	6.6	6.9	29.8	24.5	10.0	1.2	75.1	36.0	49.5	50.5
41472	WEST LIBERTY	93.8	93.5	5.2	5.3	0.2	0.2	0.7	0.8	5.3	5.6	6.2	5.8	8.2	33.2	24.0	10.1	1.6	79.4	36.6	56.4	43.6
41501	PIKEVILLE	97.7	97.4	0.7	0.8	0.7	0.9	0.8	0.9	6.3	6.1	6.3	6.2	6.8	29.3	26.4	11.4	1.3	77.8	38.0	48.7	51.3
41503	SOUTH WILLIAMSON	93.5	92.4	0.5	0.6	4.4	5.5	0.3	0.3	4.8	5.1	4.8	5.1	4.1	21.0	30.8	21.7	2.8	82.1	47.5	45.2	54.9
41512	ASHCAMP	98.2	98.1	0.6	0.6	0.2	0.2	0.8	0.8	5.2	6.1	6.9	7.6	5.0	30.2	28.6	9.5	1.0	76.7	38.6	51.5	48.5
41513	BELCHER	99.1	99.1	0.0	0.0	0.0	0.0	0.4	0.4	4.9	5.4	6.8	5.0	5.7	26.7	31.0	14.0	0.5	80.2	42.0	49.1	51.0
	KENTUCKY	90.1	89.5	7.3	7.4	0.8	1.0	1.5	1.9	6.6	6.6	6.8	6.6	7.0	28.9	24.8	11.1	1.5	76.3	36.8	49.1	50.9
	UNITED STATES	75.1	73.6	12.3	12.5	3.8	4.2	12.5	14.1	6.9	6.7	7.2	7.0	7.3	28.6	23.8	10.8	1.7	75.1	36.0	49.1	50.9

ZIP CODE #	POST OFFICE NAME	2004 Per Capita Income	2004 HH Income Base	2004 HOUSEHOLD INCOME DISTRIBUTION (%) Less than $25,000	$25,000 to $49,999	$50,000 to $99,999	$100,000 to $149,999	$150,000 or More	MEDIAN HOUSEHOLD INCOME 2004	2009	2004 National Centile	2004 State Centile	2004 Home Value Base	2004 HOME VALUE DISTRIBUTION (%) Less than $50,000	$50,000 to $89,999	$90,000 to $174,999	$175,000 to $399,999	$400,000 or More	2004 Median Home Value
41074	DAYTON	19337	2123	32.7	35.6	24.3	4.6	2.9	37244	45343	36	67	1260	17.3	52.8	23.7	4.2	2.0	72619
41075	FORT THOMAS	32142	6882	19.8	24.0	35.4	12.1	8.7	56908	69892	82	94	4780	2.7	7.8	56.3	28.6	4.7	146396
41076	NEWPORT	27010	6199	17.3	26.3	39.1	12.8	4.5	55787	68422	80	93	4699	1.7	25.1	49.1	21.7	2.5	118326
41080	PETERSBURG	27001	663	13.7	22.6	38.9	16.7	8.0	61792	73898	86	96	578	10.4	18.5	34.6	33.4	3.1	133333
41083	SANDERS	19384	286	25.9	32.2	33.2	6.3	2.5	41157	49837	50	77	236	38.1	32.2	20.3	5.9	3.4	62727
41085	SILVER GROVE	18077	503	29.4	33.8	32.6	3.6	0.6	37911	45922	39	68	331	35.7	25.7	34.1	3.9	0.6	76250
41086	SPARTA	18886	631	29.6	29.3	30.4	7.8	2.9	40598	49115	48	75	509	19.3	26.1	38.1	14.5	2.0	95732
41091	UNION	35901	4755	7.6	15.8	38.5	22.7	15.4	83476	102764	96	99	4441	4.1	4.1	25.5	54.9	11.4	212301
41092	VERONA	26815	1064	16.0	27.8	36.3	11.7	8.3	56807	68014	81	94	942	13.2	20.6	34.7	24.0	7.5	122817
41093	WALLINGFORD	15638	732	40.4	28.7	25.6	4.5	0.8	31323	36888	16	47	611	40.6	35.4	21.6	1.3	1.2	58712
41094	WALTON	27222	3172	16.2	23.4	39.5	13.2	7.6	59820	71936	84	95	2545	16.8	9.9	40.2	28.3	4.8	129840
41095	WARSAW	21424	1671	29.6	28.7	31.6	7.6	2.5	42567	50898	55	80	1287	18.5	24.9	41.0	13.4	2.3	97308
41097	WILLIAMSTOWN	19891	2675	29.1	30.4	31.4	6.8	2.2	40428	47094	48	74	2051	19.7	24.5	41.1	14.0	0.8	97484
41098	WORTHVILLE	17713	317	28.1	34.1	32.5	4.1	1.3	36730	44583	34	65	260	49.6	28.5	17.7	3.1	1.2	50400
41101	ASHLAND	22916	8408	37.1	28.4	23.4	6.8	4.3	35000	44473	28	61	5312	23.6	37.5	27.5	9.7	1.7	77129
41102	ASHLAND	23923	7873	27.3	29.2	30.8	8.7	4.0	43185	53246	56	81	6381	21.9	35.6	33.1	8.3	1.1	83694
41121	ARGILLITE	15877	443	30.9	38.2	25.5	5.4	0.0	34637	43934	26	59	371	49.9	16.2	29.4	4.6	0.0	50263
41124	BLAINE	11076	419	64.2	21.5	10.3	2.9	1.2	17222	20683	1	4	334	53.9	30.8	14.1	0.6	0.6	43500
41129	CATLETTSBURG	21450	3645	30.8	26.0	32.7	7.9	2.5	41808	52018	52	78	2978	31.0	32.3	29.4	6.2	1.2	74075
41132	DENTON	14414	203	41.4	34.0	20.7	2.5	1.5	31034	36772	15	47	164	50.6	30.5	14.6	4.3	0.0	49375
41135	EMERSON	11342	205	55.6	29.3	12.2	2.9	0.0	21409	25307	2	17	171	69.6	18.7	8.8	1.8	1.2	34028
41137	FIREBRICK	16461	106	42.5	30.2	24.5	1.9	0.9	29354	34291	11	42	88	55.7	18.2	23.9	1.1	1.1	45000
41139	FLATWOODS	21419	3588	33.2	30.9	26.5	6.6	2.8	36468	45685	33	64	2761	24.1	46.7	25.0	4.1	0.2	70456
41141	GARRISON	13578	1433	49.4	26.9	20.1	3.4	0.1	25339	29533	5	27	1179	51.2	31.7	14.4	2.5	0.1	49132
41143	GRAYSON	17426	5175	37.9	31.1	24.8	4.6	1.7	33026	39453	21	53	4120	37.7	31.5	26.0	3.9	0.8	62667
41144	GREENUP	17046	4730	37.4	30.2	25.7	5.8	0.9	34365	42590	25	58	3909	41.4	28.3	24.9	5.1	0.3	60496
41146	HITCHINS	13953	230	40.4	33.5	25.2	0.9	0.0	32631	38821	20	52	186	53.8	28.0	12.9	5.4	0.0	46667
41149	ISONVILLE	11461	365	60.0	21.6	14.0	4.4	0.0	19183	23391	2	9	299	52.8	35.8	8.0	3.3	0.0	47344
41159	MARTHA	9734	250	64.4	22.4	9.2	3.2	0.8	17409	20637	1	5	198	52.5	30.8	15.7	0.5	0.5	45833
41164	OLIVE HILL	15306	4823	46.3	29.0	20.9	2.7	1.1	27163	32232	7	35	3965	51.3	29.1	14.7	4.6	0.3	48773
41166	QUINCY	18314	320	40.9	30.6	24.7	1.9	1.9	30296	35524	13	45	267	55.4	18.7	24.0	1.1	0.8	45167
41168	RUSH	18860	1212	33.4	23.4	35.3	6.4	1.4	42578	51635	55	80	1018	35.5	32.4	20.9	10.8	0.4	67358
41169	RUSSELL	28318	2347	24.7	26.8	33.2	10.4	4.9	48249	59276	69	88	1843	20.3	31.6	37.5	9.0	1.6	87730
41171	SANDY HOOK	15239	2224	49.7	26.6	17.5	5.1	1.2	25184	31505	5	27	1797	47.8	30.2	17.1	4.6	0.3	53240
41174	SOUTH PORTSMOUTH	17461	311	45.3	22.2	26.1	4.8	1.6	29468	35706	11	43	248	41.5	33.5	20.2	4.8	0.0	54773
41175	SOUTH SHORE	17021	2113	40.0	28.7	25.9	4.2	1.2	33181	41335	21	54	1654	34.4	34.5	26.4	4.4	0.4	66000
41179	VANCEBURG	12345	2200	54.9	28.4	13.7	2.2	0.8	21771	25442	3	18	1729	56.1	24.5	14.2	4.5	0.8	45205
41180	WEBBVILLE	13152	672	46.7	31.9	18.6	2.1	0.7	26758	32215	7	34	553	54.3	26.9	14.8	2.2	1.8	46210
41183	WORTHINGTON	23457	676	33.7	31.2	26.5	6.5	2.1	38199	46805	40	69	573	31.1	48.7	19.4	0.9	0.0	65211
41189	TOLLESBORO	17307	1377	40.9	31.6	22.0	3.8	1.7	31244	38117	16	47	1146	47.6	26.5	22.3	3.1	0.4	54912
41201	ADAMS	13174	457	55.6	22.8	17.9	2.0	1.8	20081	24921	2	11	377	59.4	16.2	14.3	7.4	2.7	37500
41204	BOONS CAMP	12950	259	47.1	31.3	20.9	0.8	0.0	26510	30995	6	32	215	54.0	35.4	10.7	0.0	0.0	47167
41214	DEBORD	14764	287	50.5	22.7	19.5	4.9	2.4	24613	29332	4	25	236	43.2	26.7	15.7	10.6	3.8	61000
41216	EAST POINT	21896	820	32.4	28.3	29.0	6.3	3.9	37578	49132	38	68	690	29.1	24.8	33.2	12.2	0.7	85781
41219	FLATGAP	15344	768	46.2	35.8	14.1	2.6	1.3	26738	31589	7	33	641	45.7	32.5	18.6	3.3	0.0	53274
41222	HAGERHILL	15074	964	48.7	26.7	18.8	3.8	2.1	26094	31889	6	30	760	40.5	28.4	25.7	4.9	0.5	62222
41224	INEZ	14402	1876	54.0	24.5	17.7	2.5	1.3	22277	26270	3	20	1506	48.2	23.7	20.8	6.5	0.8	52813
41226	KEATON	14652	143	40.6	44.8	12.6	0.7	1.4	28318	33338	9	38	120	42.5	30.8	24.2	2.5	0.0	56923
41230	LOUISA	16427	3573	47.0	27.3	18.9	4.9	2.0	26750	32727	7	34	2705	45.7	31.0	19.7	3.0	0.6	54915
41231	LOVELY	10414	249	61.0	23.7	14.5	0.8	0.0	19251	22541	2	9	202	48.0	29.7	20.3	2.0	0.0	52500
41232	LOWMANSVILLE	12503	857	50.4	25.8	21.1	2.7	0.0	24645	29278	4	25	709	48.1	28.6	19.0	1.1	3.1	52872
41234	MEALLY	15530	234	37.6	31.6	25.2	5.6	0.0	31567	38362	17	48	191	46.6	34.6	13.6	5.2	0.0	52955
41238	OIL SPRINGS	16532	508	42.5	33.9	17.5	4.5	1.6	29325	34633	11	42	429	41.7	34.7	18.7	4.2	0.7	60729
41240	PAINTSVILLE	18116	3040	46.0	25.1	21.7	4.1	3.1	27954	34095	9	37	2169	37.3	28.2	27.7	6.1	0.7	72318
41250	PILGRIM	12511	392	59.4	25.0	14.3	0.8	0.5	19409	22834	2	9	322	45.7	29.8	22.7	1.9	0.0	55833
41254	RIVER	9709	193	60.1	27.5	9.3	3.1	0.0	17810	20764	1	6	160	65.0	26.3	6.9	1.9	0.0	40000
41255	SITKA	14632	115	54.8	20.9	17.4	4.4	2.6	19757	25559	2	10	91	50.6	23.1	23.1	3.3	0.0	49444
41256	STAFFORDSVILLE	23450	713	37.6	35.2	17.0	4.8	5.5	32771	40758	20	52	576	41.0	30.2	17.0	10.1	1.7	61961
41257	STAMBAUGH	18663	84	46.4	28.6	14.3	4.8	6.0	28617	36370	10	40	71	42.3	33.8	15.5	8.5	0.0	60455
41260	THELMA	17642	940	38.0	30.3	25.5	4.6	1.6	30940	37511	15	46	727	42.1	31.8	23.4	2.5	0.3	57372
41262	TOMAHAWK	11944	687	55.6	28.1	10.9	4.1	1.3	21246	24333	2	15	560	52.0	27.3	10.4	7.9	2.5	47105
41263	TUTOR KEY	14876	168	47.0	25.0	23.8	2.4	1.8	27080	32617	7	34	141	46.1	23.4	27.0	3.6	0.0	63571
41265	VAN LEAR	16369	1302	44.2	28.5	20.7	5.7	0.9	28370	34807	9	39	1066	46.1	30.5	20.0	3.1	0.4	55316
41267	WARFIELD	10983	1190	61.3	22.3	14.5	1.8	0.1	18356	22009	1	6	786	48.1	23.4	26.5	2.0	0.0	53488
41271	WILLIAMSPORT	14813	31	45.2	29.0	22.6	3.2	0.0	27265	30000	8	35	24	50.0	29.2	20.8	0.0	0.0	50000
41274	WITTENSVILLE	17886	402	47.0	27.9	18.2	4.0	3.0	26738	32231	7	33	318	44.0	30.2	18.9	6.3	0.6	57600
41301	CAMPTON	13211	2343	54.2	28.4	14.2	1.9	1.3	22088	25906	3	19	1767	55.7	23.7	15.6	3.7	1.3	44683
41311	BEATTYVILLE	16592	2971	54.8	25.7	13.7	3.8	2.1	21611	26173	2	18	2227	52.8	27.2	18.1	1.5	0.4	47010
41314	BOONEVILLE	13432	1671	63.1	19.8	14.0	2.0	1.1	17261	20141	1	5	1254	58.0	30.8	9.7	1.2	0.4	42908
41317	CLAYHOLE	13838	433	55.7	18.5	22.2	2.8	0.9	20902	25762	2	14	349	61.9	24.9	10.0	3.2	0.0	35962
41332	HAZEL GREEN	14938	735	47.8	33.7	15.7	1.6	1.2	25911	30169	6	30	593	50.8	32.0	14.5	1.9	0.8	49022
41338	ISLAND CITY	8861	151	66.2	25.8	8.0	0.0	0.0	17181	18422	1	4	122	73.8	20.5	5.7	0.0	0.0	35769
41339	JACKSON	13393	5040	53.9	26.7	15.5	2.9	1.0	22108	26555	3	19	3923	58.6	22.2	16.1	2.4	0.7	38472
41342	LEE CITY	9993	115	60.9	30.4	8.7	0.0	0.0	20153	23134	2	12	92	64.1	18.5	17.4	0.0	0.0	35625
41348	LOST CREEK	15027	371	56.6	19.4	21.3	1.4	1.4	21375	25146	2	16	299	60.9	19.4	16.4	3.3	0.0	35694
41351	MISTLETOE	8316	29	69.0	20.7	3.5	6.9	0.0	16552	18481	1	3	24	50.0	37.5	12.5	0.0	0.0	50000
41360	PINE RIDGE	10300	192	58.9	24.0	15.1	1.6	0.5	18737	21967	1	7	162	52.5	22.2	23.5	1.2	0.6	47778
41364	RICETOWN	9967	172	69.8	20.9	2.9	5.8	0.6	16118	18617	1	2	142	47.2	42.3	9.2	1.4	0.0	51667
41365	ROGERS	10284	242	63.2	21.5	14.9	0.4	0.0	17001	20084	1	4	207	45.4	26.1	28.0	0.5	0.0	56786
41366	ROUSSEAU	12439	85	54.1	29.4	11.8	3.5	1.2	21325	25000	2	16	69	75.4	15.9	8.7	0.0	0.0	35357
41367	ROWDY	13573	152	49.3	27.6	19.1	4.0	0.0	25257	29046	5	27	123	45.5	36.6	15.5	2.4	0.0	55000
41385	VANCLEVE	13059	220	54.6	30.5	12.3	0.9	1.8	21471	26111	2	17	167	58.1	25.8	15.6	0.6	0.0	44600
41386	VINCENT	9109	130	63.1	28.5	8.5	0.0	0.0	18636	21144	1	7	105	68.6	23.8	7.6	0.0	0.0	24643
41390	WHICK	5294	7	100.0	0.0	0.0	0.0	0.0	12071	15000	1	1	6	100.0	0.0	0.0	0.0	0.0	12500
41397	ZOE	15181	52	57.7	28.9	11.5	0.0	1.9	20000	22247	2	11	42	61.9	23.8	7.1	7.1	0.0	40000
41419	EDNA	11916	97	55.7	26.8	15.5	2.1	0.0	20354	25000	2	13	80	45.0	26.3	21.3	7.5	0.0	55714
41422	ELSIE	12854	33	51.5	27.3	18.2	3.0	0.0	23584	26114	4	23	27	44.4	25.9	22.2	7.4	0.0	57500
41425	EZEL	20832	451	43.9	28.6	21.1	5.1	1.3	28150	34169	9	38	377	38.2	37.9	17.0	6.4	0.5	63047
41464	ROYALTON	10598	145	56.6	25.5	16.6	1.4	0.0	19382	22271	2	9	120	72.5	17.5	7.5	2.5	0.0	34615
41465	SALYERSVILLE	13251	4742	53.3	27.0	15.4	3.1	1.2	22295	27500	3	20	3825	54.1	25.7	16.6	3.5	0.1	45693
41472	WEST LIBERTY	16445	4098	49.1	29.4	16.1	3.2	2.2	25465	30173	5	28	3225	44.4	29.9	19.3	6.1	0.3	55085
41501	PIKEVILLE	20250	11014	43.7	25.6	22.4	4.6	3.7	29170	37067	11	41	8046	40.0	23.9	25.6	8.7	1.7	67039
41503	SOUTH WILLIAMSON	30189	302	30.8	25.5	27.5	9.6	6.6	42137	57634	53	79	248	6.1	52.4	35.5	6.1	0.0	81250
41512	ASHCAMP	10842	190	54.2	30.0	13.2	2.6	0.0	22635	26707	3	21	158	54.4	31.7	12.7	1.3	0.0	45333
41513	BELCHER	16333	243	40.3	32.1	20.6	7.0	0.0	31183	38445	15	47	210	41.9	35.2	16.2	3.8	2.9	58500
	KENTUCKY	22472		31.8	28.3	28.2	7.8	3.9	39962	49361				22.2	24.9	36.4	14.3	2.1	94344
	UNITED STATES	25866		24.7	27.1	30.8	10.9	6.5	48124	56710				10.9	15.0	33.7	30.1	10.4	145905

ZIP CODE #	POST OFFICE NAME	FINANCIAL SERVICES: Auto Loan	Home Loan	Invest-ments	Retire-ment Plans	THE HOME: Home Improvements: Home Repair	Lawn & Garden	Furnishings: Comput-ers & Hard-ware	Major Appli-ances	TV, Radio, Sound Equip-ment	Furni-ture	ENTERTAINMENT: Dine out/ Carry out	Sports Equip-ment	Fees & Tickets	Toys & Games	Travel	Cable TV	PERSONAL: Apparel & Services	Auto Repairs	Health Insur-ance	Pets & Supplies
41074	DAYTON	70	68	69	67	69	76	72	71	74	69	91	82	71	93	71	74	88	72	74	79
41075	FORT THOMAS	98	112	132	113	111	116	110	107	105	109	133	125	114	136	111	104	131	107	101	117
41076	NEWPORT	86	96	110	96	95	101	94	92	92	93	115	107	98	120	96	92	114	92	90	102
41080	PETERSBURG	124	112	87	107	118	126	103	114	109	103	133	135	102	136	106	111	126	111	122	146
41083	SANDERS	84	73	53	69	74	80	69	76	72	71	89	89	64	84	69	73	84	76	79	94
41085	SILVER GROVE	68	58	45	58	61	69	60	64	63	59	77	73	57	76	59	64	72	63	69	75
41086	SPARTA	86	73	51	68	75	81	69	77	73	71	89	90	64	84	69	74	85	77	81	96
41091	UNION	152	174	172	178	169	168	156	156	145	159	183	182	163	188	156	139	182	151	139	175
41092	VERONA	115	112	96	109	114	119	104	111	105	105	129	130	103	130	105	105	125	108	111	134
41093	WALLINGFORD	73	49	22	42	56	64	47	59	57	48	67	71	40	63	48	62	61	59	73	84
41094	WALTON	111	109	98	108	111	117	104	109	105	104	129	126	104	130	105	104	124	107	109	127
41095	WARSAW	93	73	47	67	78	86	70	81	77	72	93	95	64	88	70	80	87	80	90	105
41097	WILLIAMSTOWN	87	69	45	63	75	83	66	76	73	66	88	90	61	86	67	77	82	75	87	101
41098	WORTHVILLE	88	59	27	51	67	77	57	71	69	58	80	85	48	76	58	74	73	70	88	101
41101	ASHLAND	74	67	65	64	69	79	71	73	75	69	92	82	69	90	71	78	87	74	81	84
41102	ASHLAND	85	80	71	77	83	91	78	83	81	77	99	95	77	100	80	83	95	82	89	98
41121	ARGILLITE	78	52	24	45	59	68	50	63	61	51	71	75	43	68	51	66	65	62	78	90
41124	BLAINE	53	36	16	31	41	47	35	43	42	35	49	52	29	46	35	45	44	43	53	61
41129	CATLETTSBURG	86	72	53	68	77	86	70	78	77	70	92	91	67	92	71	80	87	77	88	99
41132	DENTON	73	49	23	42	55	64	47	59	57	48	67	70	40	63	48	61	61	58	72	83
41135	EMERSON	55	37	17	32	42	48	35	44	43	36	50	53	30	47	36	46	46	44	55	63
41137	FIREBRICK	75	50	23	43	57	65	48	60	58	49	68	72	41	65	49	63	62	60	74	86
41139	FLATWOODS	78	66	52	64	70	81	69	74	74	67	89	84	65	87	69	77	83	73	84	88
41141	GARRISON	66	44	20	38	50	58	43	53	52	44	61	64	36	57	43	56	55	53	66	76
41143	GRAYSON	78	56	31	51	62	71	55	66	64	56	76	78	49	72	56	68	70	65	78	89
41144	GREENUP	78	55	30	49	61	70	54	65	63	54	75	77	47	71	55	67	68	64	78	89
41146	HITCHINS	69	46	21	40	52	60	44	55	53	45	63	66	38	59	45	58	57	55	68	79
41149	ISONVILLE	57	38	17	33	43	49	37	46	44	37	52	55	31	49	37	47	47	45	56	65
41159	MARTHA	52	35	16	30	39	45	33	42	40	34	47	50	28	45	34	43	43	41	51	59
41164	OLIVE HILL	70	47	22	41	53	62	46	57	55	47	65	68	40	62	47	60	59	57	70	80
41166	QUINCY	94	63	29	54	72	82	61	76	74	62	86	91	52	82	62	79	78	75	94	108
41168	RUSH	84	68	46	63	71	78	65	74	70	67	85	87	60	81	65	72	80	73	80	94
41169	RUSSELL	98	93	84	89	95	107	92	97	96	90	118	109	91	118	94	99	112	95	104	112
41171	SANDY HOOK	70	47	21	40	53	61	45	56	54	46	64	67	38	60	46	59	58	56	69	80
41174	SOUTH PORTSMOUTH	78	52	24	45	59	68	50	63	61	51	71	75	43	67	51	65	65	62	77	89
41175	SOUTH SHORE	73	51	28	47	57	67	53	62	62	52	72	72	46	68	53	66	66	62	76	82
41179	VANCEBURG	56	38	18	33	43	49	37	46	44	38	52	54	32	49	38	48	47	45	56	64
41180	WEBBVILLE	62	42	19	36	47	54	40	50	49	41	57	60	34	54	41	52	52	50	62	71
41183	WORTHINGTON	91	73	53	71	78	90	78	84	84	75	101	95	72	98	77	88	93	83	96	100
41189	TOLLESBORO	80	53	24	46	61	70	52	65	62	53	73	77	44	69	52	67	66	64	79	92
41201	ADAMS	63	42	19	36	48	55	41	51	49	42	58	61	35	55	41	53	52	50	63	72
41204	BOONS CAMP	61	41	19	35	46	53	39	49	48	40	56	59	34	53	40	51	51	49	61	70
41214	DEBORD	68	48	27	44	54	63	50	58	58	49	68	68	44	64	50	62	62	58	71	76
41216	EAST POINT	97	76	48	69	82	91	71	83	80	72	96	99	66	94	73	84	89	82	96	112
41219	FLATGAP	73	49	22	42	55	64	47	59	57	48	67	71	40	63	48	61	61	58	73	84
41222	HAGERHILL	70	48	24	43	54	63	48	58	57	48	67	68	41	63	48	61	61	58	71	79
41224	INEZ	67	46	22	40	51	60	45	55	54	45	63	65	39	60	46	58	57	55	68	76
41226	KEATON	74	50	22	43	56	65	48	60	58	49	68	72	41	64	49	62	62	59	74	85
41230	LOUISA	73	51	28	45	57	66	52	61	61	52	72	72	45	67	52	65	65	61	75	83
41231	LOVELY	49	33	15	28	37	43	32	40	38	32	45	47	27	42	32	41	41	39	49	56
41232	LOWMANSVILLE	62	41	19	36	47	54	40	50	48	41	57	60	34	54	41	52	51	49	62	71
41234	MEALLY	75	51	23	44	57	66	49	61	59	50	69	73	42	66	50	64	63	61	75	87
41238	OIL SPRINGS	75	51	23	44	57	66	49	61	59	50	69	73	42	65	50	63	63	60	75	87
41240	PAINTSVILLE	74	53	31	49	59	70	56	65	65	55	76	74	49	72	56	69	69	64	78	83
41250	PILGRIM	59	40	18	34	45	52	38	48	46	39	54	57	33	51	39	50	49	47	59	68
41254	RIVER	49	33	15	29	38	43	32	40	39	33	45	48	27	43	32	42	41	40	49	57
41255	SITKA	68	45	21	39	51	59	44	55	53	45	62	65	37	59	45	57	56	54	68	78
41256	STAFFORDSVILLE	111	74	34	64	84	97	72	90	87	73	102	107	61	96	73	93	92	89	111	127
41257	STAMBAUGH	90	60	27	52	68	78	58	72	70	59	82	86	49	77	59	75	75	72	89	103
41260	THELMA	79	54	26	48	61	70	53	65	63	53	74	78	45	70	54	67	67	64	79	91
41262	TOMAHAWK	59	40	18	34	45	52	38	48	46	39	54	57	32	51	39	50	49	47	59	68
41263	TUTOR KEY	71	48	22	41	54	62	46	58	56	47	65	69	39	62	47	60	59	57	71	82
41265	VAN LEAR	71	53	36	49	58	65	52	61	59	53	71	73	47	67	53	62	65	61	71	81
41267	WARFIELD	45	33	23	30	36	41	35	39	40	35	47	46	31	45	35	42	44	40	46	51
41271	WILLIAMSPORT	66	44	20	38	50	57	42	53	51	43	60	63	36	57	43	55	55	52	65	75
41274	WITTENSVILLE	81	56	29	50	63	73	56	68	66	56	78	79	49	74	57	71	71	67	83	92
41301	CAMPTON	55	39	23	35	43	50	40	46	46	40	55	55	35	52	40	49	51	47	56	63
41311	BEATTYVILLE	74	51	25	44	57	66	50	61	59	50	70	72	43	66	51	64	64	61	75	85
41314	BOONEVILLE	56	40	27	36	44	52	42	49	49	42	58	56	38	54	42	53	54	49	59	63
41317	CLAYHOLE	67	45	20	39	51	59	43	54	52	44	61	65	37	58	44	56	56	54	67	77
41332	HAZEL GREEN	67	45	20	39	51	59	43	54	52	44	61	65	37	58	44	56	56	54	67	77
41338	ISLAND CITY	42	28	13	24	32	36	27	34	33	28	38	40	23	36	27	35	35	33	42	48
41339	JACKSON	61	42	20	36	47	54	41	50	49	41	57	60	35	54	41	52	52	50	62	70
41342	LEE CITY	45	30	14	26	34	39	29	37	35	30	41	44	25	39	30	38	38	36	45	52
41348	LOST CREEK	73	49	22	42	56	64	47	59	57	48	67	71	40	64	48	62	61	59	73	84
41351	MISTLETOE	49	33	15	28	37	43	32	40	38	32	45	47	27	43	32	41	41	39	49	56
41360	PINE RIDGE	53	36	16	31	40	46	34	43	41	35	49	51	29	46	35	45	44	43	53	61
41364	RICETOWN	48	32	14	27	36	42	31	38	37	31	44	46	26	41	31	40	40	38	47	55
41365	ROGERS	48	32	15	28	36	42	31	39	37	32	44	46	26	41	31	40	40	38	48	55
41366	ROUSSEAU	55	37	17	32	42	48	36	45	43	36	51	53	30	48	36	47	46	44	55	64
41367	ROWDY	64	43	19	37	48	56	41	51	50	42	58	61	35	55	42	53	53	51	63	73
41385	VANCLEVE	60	40	18	34	45	52	39	48	46	39	55	58	33	52	39	50	50	48	59	68
41386	VINCENT	42	28	13	24	32	37	27	34	33	28	39	41	23	36	28	35	35	34	42	48
41390	WHICK	24	16	7	14	18	21	16	20	19	16	22	23	13	21	16	20	20	19	24	28
41397	ZOE	69	46	21	40	52	60	44	56	54	45	63	66	38	59	45	58	57	55	68	79
41419	EDNA	56	38	17	33	43	49	36	46	44	37	52	55	31	49	37	47	47	45	56	65
41422	ELSIE	56	38	17	33	43	49	36	46	44	37	52	55	31	49	37	47	47	45	56	65
41425	EZEL	99	67	30	57	75	87	64	80	78	65	91	96	55	86	65	83	83	79	99	114
41464	ROYALTON	54	36	16	31	41	47	35	43	42	35	49	52	30	46	35	45	45	43	53	62
41465	SALYERSVILLE	63	42	20	37	48	55	41	51	50	42	58	61	35	55	42	53	53	51	63	72
41472	WEST LIBERTY	73	50	24	44	56	65	49	60	59	50	69	71	42	65	50	63	63	60	74	83
41501	PIKEVILLE	80	61	42	56	66	75	61	70	69	61	82	82	55	79	62	72	76	70	81	91
41503	SOUTH WILLIAMSON	89	102	112	97	101	111	97	97	96	95	120	108	102	125	101	99	118	95	99	106
41512	ASHCAMP	55	37	17	32	42	48	36	45	43	37	51	54	30	48	36	47	46	44	55	64
41513	BELCHER	73	49	22	42	55	64	47	59	57	48	67	71	40	63	48	61	61	58	73	84
	KENTUCKY	86	74	63	71	77	85	74	80	79	74	96	94	71	95	74	81	91	80	86	98
	UNITED STATES	100	100	100	100	100	100	100	100	100	100	100	100	100	100	100	100	100	100	100	100

POPULATION CHANGE

ZIP CODE		POPULATION			2000-2004 ANNUAL RATE		HOUSEHOLDS					FAMILIES		
#	POST OFFICE NAME	COUNTY FIPS CODE	2000	2004	2009	% Rate	State Centile	2000	2004	2009	% Annual Rate 2000-2004	2004 Average HH Size	2000	2004	% Annual Rate 2000-2004
41514	BELFRY	195	4196	4265	4347	0.4	56	1697	1781	1875	1.1	2.39	1281	1305	0.4
41519	CANADA	195	439	437	436	-0.1	33	175	180	186	0.7	2.43	140	140	0.0
41522	ELKHORN CITY	195	6255	6132	6111	-0.5	20	2518	2557	2637	0.4	2.34	1880	1855	-0.3
41524	FEDSCREEK	195	235	230	230	-0.5	19	96	98	101	0.5	2.35	66	65	-0.4
41527	FOREST HILLS	195	72	72	73	0.0	41	30	31	32	0.8	2.32	24	24	0.0
41528	FREEBURN	195	1600	1521	1509	-1.2	4	650	642	662	-0.3	2.37	486	468	-0.9
41531	HARDY	195	884	883	885	0.0	39	353	362	374	0.6	2.43	255	254	-0.1
41535	HUDDY	195	507	489	486	-0.9	9	203	202	206	-0.1	2.42	150	145	-0.8
41537	JENKINS	195	5949	5944	5970	0.0	39	2398	2477	2544	0.8	2.38	1776	1784	0.1
41539	KIMPER	195	2512	2800	3029	2.6	94	958	1111	1247	3.6	2.52	744	840	2.9
41540	LICK CREEK	195	207	200	198	-0.8	10	83	83	85	0.0	2.41	65	64	-0.4
41543	MC ANDREWS	195	397	367	362	-1.8	0	169	161	163	-1.1	2.28	121	111	-2.0
41544	MC CARR	195	854	824	820	-0.8	9	337	338	349	0.1	2.44	255	249	-0.6
41546	MC VEIGH	195	184	188	190	0.5	62	73	77	80	1.3	2.44	53	54	0.4
41548	MOUTHCARD	195	647	625	621	-0.8	10	268	268	276	0.0	2.33	210	205	-0.6
41553	PHELPS	195	2694	2603	2586	-0.8	10	1050	1054	1084	0.1	2.37	795	776	-0.6
41554	PHYLLIS	195	1206	1143	1135	-1.3	3	485	477	491	-0.4	2.40	369	353	-1.0
41555	PINSONFORK	195	510	520	525	0.5	60	193	202	210	1.1	2.57	141	144	0.5
41557	RACCOON	195	1957	1910	1905	-0.6	17	772	782	809	0.3	2.44	588	581	-0.3
41558	RANSOM	195	1182	1157	1152	-0.5	19	456	465	481	0.5	2.49	364	364	0.0
41559	REGINA	195	653	651	653	-0.1	35	252	261	270	0.8	2.49	199	201	0.2
41560	ROBINSON CREEK	195	273	281	289	0.7	67	109	116	123	1.5	2.42	88	91	0.8
41562	SHELBIANA	195	2150	2081	2068	-0.8	11	826	829	852	0.1	2.51	625	611	-0.5
41563	SHELBY GAP	195	565	594	610	1.2	80	234	254	270	2.0	2.34	181	192	1.4
41564	SIDNEY	195	1758	1733	1726	-0.3	24	675	689	709	0.5	2.52	533	531	-0.1
41566	STEELE	195	1114	1082	1077	-0.7	13	435	439	454	0.2	2.46	323	317	-0.4
41567	STONE	195	1220	1148	1135	-1.4	2	478	462	471	-0.8	2.48	346	325	-1.5
41568	STOPOVER	195	1105	1069	1062	-0.8	10	453	457	470	0.2	2.34	329	322	-0.5
41571	VARNEY	195	698	686	684	-0.4	22	275	280	289	0.4	2.45	207	205	-0.2
41572	VIRGIE	195	2978	3196	3321	1.7	87	1163	1290	1385	2.5	2.48	906	981	1.9
41601	ALLEN	071	761	743	736	-0.6	17	332	335	337	0.2	2.21	236	231	-0.5
41602	AUXIER	071	2389	2352	2334	-0.4	23	1017	1035	1045	0.4	2.26	735	726	-0.3
41603	BANNER	071	1993	2091	2146	1.1	79	755	817	852	1.9	2.56	580	612	1.3
41604	BEAVER	071	780	758	748	-0.7	13	301	302	302	0.1	2.51	224	218	-0.6
41605	BETSY LAYNE	071	1048	1025	1015	-0.5	18	425	429	431	0.2	2.39	303	296	-0.6
41606	BEVINSVILLE	071	2885	2763	2712	-1.0	7	925	905	898	-0.5	2.50	684	651	-1.2
41607	BLUE RIVER	071	29	29	29	0.0	41	12	13	13	1.9	2.23	10	10	0.0
41615	DANA	071	71	81	86	3.2	96	27	32	34	4.1	2.53	21	24	3.2
41616	DAVID	071	8	8	8	0.0	41	3	3	3	0.0	2.67	2	2	0.0
41622	EASTERN	071	621	598	588	-0.9	8	253	252	253	-0.1	2.37	190	185	-0.6
41630	GARRETT	071	1597	1545	1523	-0.8	10	660	662	665	0.1	2.33	481	468	-0.5
41631	GRETHEL	071	1386	1344	1327	-0.7	12	568	573	577	0.2	2.35	408	400	-0.5
41632	GUNLOCK	153	654	669	686	0.5	63	246	259	273	1.2	2.58	194	200	0.7
41635	HAROLD	071	3298	3309	3317	0.1	44	1329	1382	1411	0.9	2.39	982	994	0.3
41636	HI HAT	071	719	701	693	-0.6	16	307	312	315	0.4	2.22	226	223	-0.3
41640	HUEYSVILLE	071	238	231	228	-0.7	12	89	90	90	0.3	2.57	68	66	-0.7
41642	IVEL	071	1721	1683	1666	-0.5	18	680	689	694	0.3	2.44	490	481	-0.4
41643	LACKEY	071	81	77	76	-1.2	4	35	35	34	0.0	2.20	25	24	-1.0
41645	LANGLEY	071	1145	1124	1115	-0.4	22	462	468	472	0.3	2.40	346	343	-0.2
41647	MC DOWELL	071	1432	1413	1403	-0.3	26	565	577	584	0.5	2.44	420	417	-0.2
41649	MARTIN	071	3210	3212	3219	0.0	41	1318	1368	1398	0.9	2.33	904	908	0.1
41650	MELVIN	071	485	466	458	-0.9	8	194	192	191	-0.2	2.27	144	138	-1.0
41653	PRESTONSBURG	071	10526	10712	10801	0.4	58	4277	4509	4634	1.3	2.27	2999	3065	0.5
41655	PRINTER	071	169	161	158	-1.1	5	63	62	62	-0.4	2.60	46	44	-1.0
41660	TEABERRY	071	1928	1901	1889	-0.3	25	743	761	770	0.6	2.49	567	567	0.0
41666	WAYLAND	071	954	908	888	-1.2	5	387	382	380	-0.3	2.38	277	265	-1.0
41701	HAZARD	193	14301	14442	14581	0.2	50	5664	5904	6160	1.0	2.40	4048	4100	0.3
41712	ARY	193	490	478	474	-0.6	16	184	185	189	0.1	2.58	133	129	-0.7
41714	BEAR BRANCH	131	349	338	329	-0.8	11	145	145	146	0.0	2.33	111	108	-0.6
41719	BONNYMAN	193	558	599	619	1.7	87	223	248	266	2.5	2.33	164	178	2.0
41721	BUCKHORN	193	907	890	883	-0.4	21	331	336	345	0.4	2.53	260	258	-0.2
41722	BULAN	119	2855	2806	2787	-0.4	22	1111	1130	1160	0.4	2.48	825	816	-0.3
41723	BUSY	193	1881	1878	1879	0.0	38	682	705	730	0.8	2.66	543	549	0.3
41725	CARRIE	119	15	15	15	0.0	41	4	4	4	0.0	3.75	3	3	0.0
41727	CHAVIES	193	309	295	293	-1.1	6	123	123	127	0.0	2.40	99	97	-0.5
41729	COMBS	193	285	302	311	1.4	83	112	124	132	2.4	2.28	82	88	1.7
41731	CORNETTSVILLE	193	2016	1968	1948	-0.6	17	797	805	817	0.2	2.44	605	596	-0.4
41735	DELPHIA	193	292	276	271	-1.3	2	115	112	115	-0.6	2.46	89	85	-1.1
41736	DICE	193	438	427	423	-0.6	16	176	177	181	0.1	2.41	127	123	-0.8
41740	EMMALENA	119	2485	2481	2480	0.0	38	983	1021	1059	0.9	2.43	736	744	0.3
41743	FISTY	193	6	6	6	0.0	41	2	2	2	0.0	3.00	1	1	0.0
41745	GAYS CREEK	193	129	127	127	-0.4	23	48	49	50	0.5	2.49	38	38	0.0
41746	HAPPY	193	610	607	604	-0.1	33	227	233	240	0.6	2.61	173	173	0.0
41749	HYDEN	131	4788	4666	4551	-0.6	15	1856	1870	1884	0.2	2.45	1387	1361	-0.4
41754	KRYPTON	193	611	674	708	2.3	92	220	253	275	3.3	2.66	175	197	2.8
41759	SASSAFRAS	119	1081	1060	1057	-0.5	21	414	419	432	0.3	2.53	315	312	-0.2
41760	SCUDDY	193	849	841	836	-0.2	29	306	313	322	0.5	2.69	230	229	-0.1
41763	SLEMP	193	358	339	333	-1.3	3	145	142	145	-0.5	2.39	113	108	-1.1
41764	SMILAX	131	737	716	698	-0.7	13	299	303	307	0.3	2.36	227	224	-0.3
41772	VEST	119	90	90	90	0.0	41	35	36	38	0.7	2.50	26	27	0.9
41773	VICCO	193	1143	1134	1129	-0.2	30	464	471	486	0.6	2.41	344	344	0.0
41774	VIPER	193	2986	2958	2940	-0.2	29	1174	1207	1242	0.7	2.45	921	925	0.1
41775	WENDOVER	131	269	265	260	-0.4	24	113	115	117	0.4	2.13	82	82	0.0
41776	WOOTON	131	2375	2338	2289	-0.4	23	942	966	982	0.6	2.41	704	704	0.0
41777	YEADDISS	131	459	453	444	-0.3	26	181	186	189	0.6	2.44	136	136	0.0
41804	BLACKEY	133	400	403	404	0.2	48	163	170	173	1.0	2.37	114	116	0.4
41812	DEANE	133	479	475	474	-0.2	30	189	195	198	0.7	2.44	147	148	0.2
41815	ERMINE	133	539	532	529	-0.3	26	225	230	233	0.5	2.31	167	166	-0.1
41817	GARNER	119	1519	1484	1477	-0.6	18	476	478	492	0.1	2.67	352	344	-0.5
41819	GORDON	133	522	521	520	-0.1	37	207	213	216	0.7	2.45	164	165	0.1
41821	HALLIE	133	557	540	534	-0.7	11	220	221	222	0.1	2.44	157	153	-0.6
41822	HINDMAN	119	2855	2868	2883	0.1	45	1135	1178	1225	0.9	2.31	808	814	0.2
41824	ISOM	133	194	192	191	-0.2	29	80	82	83	0.6	2.34	62	62	0.0
41825	JACKHORN	133	366	359	357	-0.5	21	139	141	142	0.3	2.55	100	99	-0.2
41826	JEREMIAH	133	865	840	830	-0.7	12	366	369	371	0.2	2.28	268	263	-0.4
	KENTUCKY					0.7					1.2	2.42			0.5
	UNITED STATES					1.2					1.3	2.58			1.1

#	ZIP CODE POST OFFICE NAME	RACE (%) White 2000	White 2004	Black 2000	Black 2004	Asian/Pacific 2000	Asian/Pacific 2004	% Hispanic Origin 2000	% Hispanic Origin 2004	2004 AGE DISTRIBUTION (%) 0-4	5-9	10-14	15-19	20-24	25-44	45-64	65-84	85+	18+	MEDIAN AGE 2004	% 2004 Males	% 2004 Females
41514	BELFRY	97.0	96.6	0.9	0.9	1.0	1.2	0.4	0.5	6.3	6.4	6.5	5.7	5.7	28.8	27.6	12.1	1.0	77.3	39.0	48.0	52.0
41519	CANADA	99.8	99.8	0.0	0.0	0.0	0.0	0.5	0.7	6.2	6.2	7.3	6.9	5.7	29.3	25.6	11.4	1.4	76.2	37.9	48.3	51.7
41522	ELKHORN CITY	99.1	99.1	0.3	0.3	0.1	0.1	0.6	0.8	4.9	5.8	6.4	6.7	5.9	27.3	28.4	13.4	1.3	78.7	40.4	49.3	50.7
41524	FEDSCREEK	97.5	97.8	0.0	0.0	0.4	0.4	1.7	2.2	7.0	5.7	4.8	7.8	3.9	31.3	29.6	9.1	0.9	77.4	38.8	50.4	49.6
41527	FOREST HILLS	94.4	94.4	1.4	1.4	1.4	2.8	0.0	0.0	5.6	5.6	5.6	5.6	5.6	27.8	30.6	12.5	1.4	83.3	41.0	45.8	54.2
41528	FREEBURN	98.9	98.7	0.4	0.5	0.1	0.2	1.0	1.3	6.4	7.2	6.3	6.5	6.6	30.0	27.0	9.5	0.6	76.0	35.9	50.0	50.0
41531	HARDY	97.7	97.5	1.2	1.3	0.3	0.5	0.2	0.5	5.7	6.3	7.0	5.3	5.1	28.8	28.7	12.0	1.1	77.5	40.1	47.5	52.6
41535	HUDDY	99.0	99.2	0.4	0.4	0.0	0.0	0.2	0.4	6.1	6.5	7.4	6.1	5.7	26.8	28.0	11.7	1.6	75.9	38.8	50.5	49.5
41537	JENKINS	98.6	98.6	0.6	0.6	0.2	0.3	0.5	0.6	6.0	5.6	6.3	6.4	6.4	26.7	28.1	13.1	1.6	78.1	40.5	48.9	51.1
41539	KIMPER	99.2	99.2	0.0	0.0	0.2	0.3	0.6	0.9	6.3	6.4	6.8	6.1	6.4	31.2	26.8	9.1	1.0	76.8	36.9	49.9	50.1
41540	LICK CREEK	99.5	100.0	0.0	0.0	0.0	0.0	1.0	1.0	6.0	6.5	6.5	6.0	5.5	30.0	29.5	9.0	1.0	77.5	38.2	52.0	48.0
41543	MC ANDREWS	98.7	98.6	0.5	0.5	0.0	0.0	0.0	0.0	7.9	8.2	6.5	5.2	5.2	25.1	29.4	10.9	1.6	73.8	38.7	48.2	51.8
41544	MC CARR	98.0	97.7	0.4	0.4	0.4	0.4	1.3	1.6	5.5	6.1	7.2	6.0	5.8	28.0	29.3	10.9	1.3	77.6	39.3	48.1	51.9
41546	MC VEIGH	96.2	95.7	2.2	2.7	0.0	0.0	0.0	0.0	6.4	7.5	6.9	5.3	6.9	26.6	27.7	11.7	1.1	75.5	37.5	50.0	50.0
41548	MOUTHCARD	99.7	99.7	0.0	0.0	0.0	0.0	0.6	0.8	5.9	6.2	6.2	6.2	5.3	30.1	30.1	9.1	0.8	77.8	38.6	51.2	48.8
41553	PHELPS	99.0	98.9	0.2	0.2	0.1	0.1	0.6	0.9	5.7	6.2	6.3	5.2	5.5	27.4	28.7	13.5	1.5	78.7	40.4	50.1	49.9
41554	PHYLLIS	98.4	98.3	0.3	0.3	0.5	0.4	0.8	0.9	5.9	5.9	6.4	5.6	6.4	28.4	29.6	11.3	0.7	78.5	39.2	50.4	49.6
41555	PINSONFORK	96.5	96.4	2.4	2.3	0.0	0.0	0.0	0.0	6.5	6.9	7.1	5.6	6.5	26.4	28.5	11.4	1.2	76.2	37.9	50.0	50.0
41557	RACCOON	99.0	98.8	0.1	0.1	0.3	0.3	0.6	0.7	6.2	5.8	6.1	5.6	6.0	29.6	30.4	9.3	0.9	78.5	38.9	48.5	51.5
41558	RANSOM	98.1	97.8	0.1	0.1	0.5	0.5	1.4	1.9	5.9	7.0	7.2	6.5	6.9	29.8	26.7	8.7	1.3	75.8	36.7	49.8	50.2
41559	REGINA	99.1	98.9	0.0	0.0	0.0	0.0	0.6	0.9	5.8	6.1	7.1	5.4	5.8	29.2	28.4	11.5	0.6	77.7	39.2	49.9	50.1
41560	ROBINSON CREEK	98.9	98.9	0.0	0.0	0.7	0.7	0.7	0.7	6.8	6.8	6.4	5.3	6.8	31.0	26.0	10.0	1.1	76.5	37.0	49.5	50.5
41562	SHELBIANA	99.5	99.5	0.1	0.1	0.1	0.1	0.3	0.5	6.4	6.5	6.4	6.3	6.5	29.5	27.1	10.4	0.9	76.9	37.4	50.4	49.6
41563	SHELBY GAP	98.4	98.2	0.0	0.0	0.4	0.3	0.9	1.2	4.9	5.9	6.9	6.1	5.1	29.8	30.5	9.9	1.0	78.6	39.8	50.5	49.5
41564	SIDNEY	99.7	99.6	0.1	0.1	0.0	0.0	0.5	0.6	6.1	6.3	7.0	6.4	6.0	29.4	26.4	11.3	1.2	76.7	38.0	49.1	50.9
41566	STEELE	98.7	98.7	0.0	0.0	0.3	0.3	1.1	1.1	6.3	6.4	6.4	7.9	5.0	31.9	26.7	8.8	0.7	76.1	37.1	51.3	48.7
41567	STONE	98.9	98.8	0.4	0.4	0.0	0.0	0.2	0.3	7.1	7.5	7.1	5.7	5.5	26.1	27.9	11.5	1.7	74.9	38.4	49.5	50.5
41568	STOPOVER	98.9	99.0	0.0	0.0	0.1	0.1	0.5	0.7	6.4	7.5	7.3	6.3	7.1	29.5	26.7	9.0	0.4	75.1	34.7	51.0	49.0
41571	VARNEY	99.3	99.0	0.1	0.2	0.1	0.2	0.3	0.3	4.8	5.0	6.3	5.4	7.1	28.9	31.1	9.9	1.6	80.9	39.7	49.9	50.2
41572	VIRGIE	99.8	99.7	0.0	0.0	0.1	0.3	0.7	1.0	5.5	5.8	6.6	5.8	6.5	29.7	28.3	10.8	1.0	78.7	39.0	49.6	50.4
41601	ALLEN	98.8	98.8	0.5	0.5	0.0	0.0	0.1	0.3	5.7	5.8	6.3	5.7	5.4	29.2	27.6	12.5	1.9	78.9	39.8	45.0	55.1
41602	AUXIER	98.6	98.3	0.1	0.1	0.3	0.5	0.6	0.9	6.8	6.7	5.9	5.1	5.6	29.5	27.3	11.9	1.4	77.4	38.9	46.3	53.7
41603	BANNER	98.5	98.3	0.7	0.7	0.3	0.4	0.7	0.8	6.7	7.1	8.3	6.9	6.5	30.7	24.8	8.1	0.9	73.1	35.0	50.7	49.3
41604	BEAVER	98.9	98.7	0.3	0.3	0.0	0.0	0.9	1.3	5.9	7.4	9.5	6.2	5.5	27.0	26.4	10.7	1.3	72.8	36.8	47.5	52.5
41605	BETSY LAYNE	97.7	97.6	0.5	0.5	0.5	0.6	0.3	0.4	5.4	5.7	6.4	6.1	5.3	28.8	28.3	13.1	1.1	78.7	40.3	49.1	50.9
41606	BEVINSVILLE	86.5	85.6	12.6	13.3	0.0	0.1	0.8	1.0	5.1	5.0	5.9	6.0	10.6	33.7	23.5	9.2	1.0	80.2	34.3	57.8	42.2
41607	BLUE RIVER	96.6	100.0	0.0	0.0	0.0	0.0	0.0	0.0	6.9	6.9	6.9	6.9	6.9	27.6	27.6	10.3	0.0	79.3	36.3	48.3	51.7
41615	DANA	98.6	98.8	0.0	0.0	0.0	1.2	0.0	1.2	6.2	7.4	11.1	6.2	6.2	30.9	24.7	7.4	0.0	69.1	34.6	53.1	46.9
41616	DAVID	100.0	100.0	0.0	0.0	0.0	0.0	0.0	0.0	0.0	0.0	0.0	0.0	25.0	75.0	0.0	0.0	0.0	100.0	30.0	50.0	50.0
41622	EASTERN	99.5	99.5	0.2	0.2	0.0	0.0	0.2	0.2	3.5	5.7	7.0	6.2	6.2	35.0	25.1	10.5	0.8	79.6	37.8	49.5	50.5
41630	GARRETT	98.9	98.8	0.0	0.0	0.6	0.7	0.5	0.7	4.9	5.3	6.3	5.5	6.5	28.0	29.6	12.4	1.5	80.1	40.9	50.2	49.8
41631	GRETHEL	97.8	97.5	0.1	0.1	1.4	1.6	0.1	0.2	6.0	6.3	6.4	5.4	6.3	26.4	28.7	13.2	1.4	78.1	40.6	49.1	50.9
41632	GUNLOCK	99.1	99.1	0.0	0.0	0.0	0.0	0.3	0.3	7.8	7.3	7.8	7.3	7.9	28.4	24.4	8.2	0.9	72.7	34.0	49.8	50.2
41635	HAROLD	99.3	99.2	0.3	0.3	0.1	0.2	0.5	0.5	6.9	6.7	6.5	7.4	6.9	30.0	26.3	8.7	0.8	75.4	36.2	50.4	49.7
41636	HI HAT	99.3	99.1	0.0	0.0	0.1	0.1	0.1	0.1	5.6	5.6	5.4	5.7	6.1	27.7	29.4	13.0	1.6	79.6	40.8	47.7	52.4
41640	HUEYSVILLE	99.2	99.1	0.0	0.0	0.4	0.4	0.8	0.4	4.3	4.8	6.9	5.6	7.4	27.7	28.6	13.0	1.7	80.5	40.9	48.9	51.1
41642	IVEL	98.0	97.7	1.2	1.3	0.2	0.3	0.5	0.7	7.2	7.2	6.7	5.7	6.2	31.7	24.5	9.8	1.0	75.5	36.3	49.4	50.6
41643	LACKEY	100.0	100.0	0.0	0.0	0.0	0.0	0.0	1.3	5.2	7.8	9.1	7.8	3.9	28.6	24.7	11.7	1.3	75.3	35.6	50.7	49.4
41645	LANGLEY	99.4	99.3	0.0	0.0	0.4	0.4	0.6	0.7	6.7	6.9	6.6	6.1	7.2	30.1	24.9	10.2	1.3	76.2	36.2	47.5	52.5
41647	MC DOWELL	99.0	98.9	0.0	0.0	0.1	0.1	0.4	0.5	6.5	7.4	6.6	5.7	6.4	27.5	28.0	10.7	1.2	75.6	37.2	48.4	51.6
41649	MARTIN	98.8	98.6	0.1	0.1	0.7	0.8	0.4	0.5	5.8	6.0	6.3	6.0	6.3	28.0	27.0	12.8	1.8	78.2	39.2	47.2	52.8
41650	MELVIN	94.2	94.0	5.0	5.2	0.0	0.0	0.6	1.1	5.8	6.2	7.5	6.2	7.9	29.0	25.5	10.5	1.3	76.2	36.2	51.5	48.5
41653	PRESTONSBURG	98.0	97.7	0.8	0.9	0.3	0.4	0.8	1.0	5.6	5.6	5.9	6.4	6.6	28.7	26.8	12.7	1.9	79.1	39.5	48.7	51.3
41655	PRINTER	98.8	99.4	0.0	0.0	0.0	0.0	0.0	0.0	8.1	5.6	8.1	8.1	8.7	28.6	23.0	9.3	0.6	72.1	33.3	50.3	49.7
41660	TEABERRY	99.5	99.4	0.1	0.1	0.0	0.0	1.0	1.3	7.0	6.2	7.1	7.5	7.7	29.0	27.4	7.4	0.7	74.7	35.7	49.1	50.9
41666	WAYLAND	99.3	99.1	0.0	0.0	0.2	0.3	0.5	0.6	4.6	7.1	8.8	6.8	4.2	28.5	26.1	12.2	1.7	75.2	38.7	50.6	49.5
41701	HAZARD	95.5	95.5	3.2	3.2	0.7	0.7	0.6	0.6	5.9	6.2	6.7	5.9	6.6	29.2	26.5	11.4	1.5	77.7	38.1	48.2	51.8
41712	ARY	99.8	100.0	0.0	0.0	0.0	0.0	0.0	0.0	5.7	6.1	6.5	6.3	7.3	28.7	28.2	10.0	1.3	78.2	38.2	51.3	48.7
41714	BEAR BRANCH	98.9	98.8	0.0	0.0	0.0	0.0	0.0	0.0	7.7	7.7	6.5	5.6	6.5	30.2	24.6	10.1	1.2	74.6	35.2	49.1	50.9
41719	BONNYMAN	97.0	97.2	0.4	0.3	2.3	2.3	0.2	0.2	5.8	5.8	7.0	5.7	6.0	32.2	27.2	9.4	0.8	78.0	37.9	49.9	50.1
41721	BUCKHORN	99.0	98.9	0.4	0.5	0.4	0.5	0.2	0.2	4.4	5.3	9.2	9.9	5.7	27.6	25.5	11.5	0.9	73.5	37.5	51.5	48.5
41722	BULAN	98.6	98.6	0.6	0.6	0.2	0.2	0.5	0.5	6.4	6.3	6.9	5.8	6.1	29.6	27.4	10.3	1.1	76.9	37.9	50.5	49.5
41723	BUSY	99.4	99.3	0.0	0.0	0.2	0.2	0.4	0.4	6.8	6.8	6.7	6.5	7.3	29.5	26.8	8.9	0.9	75.9	36.4	49.8	50.2
41725	CARRIE	100.0	100.0	0.0	0.0	0.0	0.0	0.0	0.0	6.7	6.7	13.3	0.0	6.7	33.3	33.3	0.0	0.0	73.3	38.8	60.0	40.0
41727	CHAVIES	99.7	99.7	0.0	0.0	0.0	0.0	0.0	0.0	6.4	6.1	5.1	5.8	5.1	31.9	28.5	10.5	0.7	78.3	38.1	50.5	49.5
41729	COMBS	95.4	95.4	0.7	0.7	3.9	4.0	0.0	0.0	5.3	5.6	7.0	6.0	5.3	31.5	27.8	10.6	1.0	78.5	39.0	49.7	50.3
41731	CORNETTSVILLE	99.2	99.2	0.1	0.1	0.1	0.1	0.6	0.6	5.0	5.8	6.6	6.8	5.8	29.3	27.4	11.7	1.6	78.2	39.3	49.3	50.7
41735	DELPHIA	99.0	98.9	0.7	0.7	0.0	0.0	0.0	0.4	5.4	5.4	7.3	6.5	5.8	33.0	25.4	9.8	1.5	77.2	37.6	50.4	49.6
41736	DICE	99.8	100.0	0.0	0.0	0.0	0.0	0.0	0.0	5.4	6.1	6.6	6.3	7.5	28.6	28.1	10.1	1.4	78.5	38.2	51.1	49.0
41739	EMMALENA	98.7	98.7	0.4	0.5	0.0	0.0	0.4	0.4	6.5	6.6	7.0	6.1	6.5	29.2	27.5	9.3	1.4	76.3	37.8	51.5	48.5
41743	FISTY	100.0	100.0	0.0	0.0	0.0	0.0	0.0	0.0	0.0	0.0	0.0	0.0	33.3	66.7	0.0	0.0	0.0	100.0	27.5	50.0	50.0
41745	GAYS CREEK	99.2	100.0	0.0	0.0	0.0	0.0	0.0	0.0	3.9	5.5	10.2	9.5	5.5	28.4	25.2	11.0	0.8	74.0	37.1	51.2	48.8
41746	HAPPY	99.2	99.0	0.2	0.2	0.2	0.2	0.0	0.0	6.1	6.3	6.4	5.8	6.9	28.5	28.3	10.5	1.2	77.8	39.0	48.4	51.6
41749	HYDEN	99.1	98.9	0.1	0.1	0.2	0.2	0.5	0.7	6.0	6.1	6.7	6.2	6.3	29.2	26.2	11.7	1.7	77.3	38.4	48.3	51.7
41754	KRYPTON	99.0	99.1	0.0	0.0	0.2	0.2	0.3	0.5	5.3	6.4	8.6	6.8	6.4	33.7	23.6	8.8	0.5	75.4	35.9	50.5	49.6
41759	SASSAFRAS	96.1	95.9	3.1	3.1	0.1	0.1	0.7	0.8	5.3	5.9	7.3	7.3	5.9	28.3	28.7	10.1	1.3	77.3	38.5	51.0	49.0
41760	SCUDDY	99.8	99.8	0.1	0.1	0.0	0.0	0.5	0.5	6.9	6.7	6.9	7.0	7.4	29.6	25.5	9.3	0.8	75.5	35.2	48.6	51.4
41763	SLEMP	99.2	99.1	0.6	0.6	0.0	0.0	0.0	0.3	5.6	5.3	7.1	6.5	5.6	32.7	26.3	9.4	1.5	77.6	37.7	49.9	50.2
41764	SMILAX	99.2	99.2	0.0	0.0	0.1	0.1	0.8	1.1	5.2	5.9	6.8	6.0	7.4	29.5	28.4	9.8	1.1	78.5	38.5	50.0	50.0
41772	VEST	98.9	98.9	0.0	0.0	0.0	0.0	0.0	0.0	6.7	6.7	6.7	6.7	6.7	30.0	26.7	8.9	1.1	75.6	37.1	51.1	48.9
41773	VICCO	99.2	99.2	0.4	0.4	0.0	0.0	0.4	0.4	6.3	6.3	6.6	6.5	6.8	29.2	26.9	10.4	1.1	77.0	37.3	48.9	51.1
41774	VIPER	99.5	99.5	0.0	0.0	0.1	0.1	0.6	0.6	4.4	5.7	6.6	6.1	6.1	30.2	30.4	9.6	1.0	79.5	39.7	48.6	51.5
41775	WENDOVER	98.9	98.9	0.0	0.0	0.4	0.4	0.7	1.1	5.3	5.3	6.8	6.0	6.4	26.0	25.3	15.5	3.4	78.5	41.5	48.3	51.7
41776	WOOTON	99.2	99.1	0.0	0.0	0.1	0.2	0.7	1.0	6.2	5.8	6.4	6.0	7.0	30.0	27.0	10.7	0.9	77.8	37.8	49.8	50.2
41777	YEADDISS	99.1	99.1	0.0	0.0	0.2	0.4	0.9	1.1	4.9	5.7	7.3	7.1	6.4	30.7	27.8	9.5	0.7	77.7	38.0	48.8	51.2
41804	BLACKEY	99.8	99.8	0.0	0.0	0.0	0.0	0.5	0.5	4.5	5.0	6.0	5.5	7.0	25.6	32.0	13.2	1.5	81.1	43.1	48.9	51.1
41812	DEANE	99.4	99.2	0.2	0.2	0.0	0.0	0.4	0.4	5.3	5.5	7.0	6.1	6.3	29.5	28.4	11.0	1.1	79.0	39.5	49.9	50.1
41815	ERMINE	99.6	99.6	0.0	0.0	0.0	0.2	0.4	0.4	5.8	6.2	6.8	5.6	6.0	30.1	28.0	10.5	0.9	77.8	38.2	49.8	50.2
41817	GARNER	98.2	98.2	0.4	0.4	0.7	0.7	0.4	0.5	5.9	6.0	6.5	8.1	10.6	25.7	25.9	10.2	1.2	78.1	35.9	48.6	51.4
41819	GORDON	100.0	100.0	0.0	0.0	0.0	0.0	0.0	0.0	5.2	6.5	7.7	7.7	8.8	30.3	24.4	7.9	1.5	76.0	35.2	50.7	49.3
41821	HALLIE	100.0	100.0	0.0	0.0	0.0	0.0	0.0	0.0	5.6	5.4	5.9	6.9	6.9	29.8	29.1	8.9	1.7	78.9	39.3	49.4	50.6
41822	HINDMAN	98.4	98.4	0.1	0.1	0.1	0.1	1.1	1.2	6.1	6.0	6.5	6.6	7.3	27.5	25.5	12.6	2.1	77.6	38.6	47.8	52.2
41824	ISOM	99.5	99.5	0.0	0.0	0.0	0.0	0.0	0.5	5.2	5.7	6.8	6.3	6.3	29.7	28.1	10.9	1.0	78.7	39.0	50.5	49.5
41825	JACKHORN	98.9	98.9	0.3	0.3	0.0	0.0	0.0	0.3	7.0	7.0	7.0	5.6	7.2	26.2	26.7	11.7	1.7	75.8	37.9	48.8	51.3
41826	JEREMIAH	99.2	99.2	0.1	0.1	0.0	0.0	0.1	0.1	3.7	4.2	6.3	7.0	6.9	27.1	30.7	12.4	1.7	81.4	42.4	48.9	51.1
	KENTUCKY	90.1	89.5	7.3	7.4	0.8	1.0	1.5	1.9	6.6	6.6	6.8	6.6	7.0	28.9	24.8	11.1	1.5	76.3	36.8	49.1	50.9
	UNITED STATES	75.1	73.6	12.3	12.5	3.8	4.2	12.5	14.1	6.9	6.7	7.2	7.0	7.3	28.6	23.8	10.8	1.7	75.1	36.0	49.1	50.9

ZIP CODE #	POST OFFICE NAME	2004 Per Capita Income	2004 HH Income Base	2004 Household Income Distribution (%) Less than $25,000	$25,000 to $49,999	$50,000 to $99,999	$100,000 to $149,999	$150,000 or More	Median Household Income 2004	2009	2004 National Centile	2004 State Centile	2004 Home Value Base	2004 Home Value Distribution (%) Less than $50,000	$50,000 to $89,999	$90,000 to $174,999	$175,000 to $399,999	$400,000 or More	2004 Median Home Value
41514	BELFRY	18614	1781	39.8	29.4	23.3	4.2	3.4	33001	41321	21	53	1399	31.9	28.8	34.4	3.6	1.4	77478
41519	CANADA	13057	180	50.0	28.3	19.4	2.2	0.0	25000	28580	5	26	150	42.0	30.0	27.3	0.7	0.0	58571
41522	ELKHORN CITY	17012	2557	49.0	28.5	18.0	2.8	1.8	25585	30843	5	29	2067	48.5	34.9	13.4	2.7	0.5	51235
41524	FEDSCREEK	9797	98	61.2	36.7	2.0	0.0	0.0	18753	21991	1	8	81	55.6	30.9	13.6	0.0	0.0	47188
41527	FOREST HILLS	29757	31	22.6	32.3	29.0	6.5	9.7	47313	50000	67	86	25	24.0	20.0	44.0	12.0	0.0	102500
41528	FREEBURN	12761	642	56.5	25.1	15.1	1.6	1.7	21390	25144	2	17	512	61.3	28.3	10.2	0.2	0.0	40492
41531	HARDY	17759	362	40.1	24.3	28.5	3.3	3.9	32087	39674	18	50	283	42.4	25.4	31.5	0.4	0.4	61667
41535	HUDDY	17342	202	42.1	24.8	27.7	4.0	1.5	35909	45000	31	63	170	37.7	31.2	28.2	2.9	0.0	75000
41537	JENKINS	14873	2477	48.2	28.2	19.0	3.6	1.0	26200	32014	6	31	1940	49.7	28.2	20.3	1.8	0.0	50273
41539	KIMPER	15910	1111	38.7	31.9	23.7	5.0	0.8	31976	39817	18	49	915	47.0	30.8	18.7	3.5	0.0	54231
41540	LICK CREEK	15107	83	41.0	36.1	19.3	3.6	0.0	30939	36917	15	46	68	44.1	33.8	19.1	2.9	0.0	55000
41543	MC ANDREWS	14347	161	54.0	24.2	19.3	1.9	0.6	22260	28234	3	19	130	42.3	38.5	13.9	2.3	3.1	55000
41544	MC CARR	15865	338	51.5	16.6	26.0	5.0	0.9	23803	29291	4	23	265	41.5	30.2	20.0	8.3	0.0	62619
41546	MC VEIGH	13253	77	48.1	35.1	15.6	1.3	0.0	25922	30000	6	30	62	56.5	30.7	12.9	0.0	0.0	44286
41548	MOUTHCARD	15464	268	41.8	36.2	18.7	3.4	0.0	30204	36522	13	44	221	43.9	35.3	16.7	4.1	0.0	54655
41553	PHELPS	13821	1054	54.2	27.6	16.4	0.5	1.3	22310	26255	3	20	863	52.0	32.0	14.5	0.7	0.8	48517
41554	PHYLLIS	11142	477	61.6	22.4	14.3	1.5	0.2	18887	21882	1	8	388	56.2	24.2	19.6	0.0	0.0	46883
41555	PINSONFORK	12752	202	47.5	34.2	16.3	2.0	0.0	26140	31284	6	31	163	55.2	31.3	13.5	0.0	0.0	45526
41557	RACCOON	16659	782	36.5	34.1	25.3	2.8	1.3	32969	40559	21	53	645	29.2	39.8	23.4	7.0	0.6	72778
41558	RANSOM	13199	465	52.0	23.9	22.4	1.5	0.2	23740	28219	4	23	396	52.3	33.6	11.9	2.3	0.0	48000
41559	REGINA	14277	261	43.7	32.2	19.5	4.6	0.0	28238	33822	9	38	221	45.3	34.8	16.3	2.3	1.4	55250
41560	ROBINSON CREEK	16983	116	36.2	31.9	25.9	4.3	1.7	33610	40320	23	56	99	40.4	24.2	28.3	7.1	0.0	65000
41562	SHELBIANA	15476	829	49.9	25.2	19.1	2.5	3.3	25028	30224	5	26	682	53.1	28.2	15.0	3.4	0.4	46866
41563	SHELBY GAP	12448	254	56.3	29.5	12.2	2.0	0.0	21313	25614	2	16	212	56.6	32.1	11.3	0.0	0.0	43636
41564	SIDNEY	12967	689	49.1	29.8	18.4	2.6	0.2	25442	30248	5	28	572	43.4	30.6	25.4	0.7	0.0	56909
41566	STEELE	12069	439	52.4	34.4	11.4	0.5	1.4	23203	26957	3	22	365	54.3	32.3	10.7	2.7	0.0	47075
41567	STONE	14865	462	47.8	24.7	23.2	3.3	1.1	27102	33809	7	34	379	39.8	35.4	20.1	2.9	1.9	59390
41568	STOPOVER	10705	457	59.5	30.0	10.3	0.2	0.0	20046	23285	2	11	377	66.1	16.2	17.8	0.0	0.0	40692
41571	VARNEY	15395	280	38.9	37.9	18.9	4.3	0.0	32821	40371	20	52	229	51.5	26.6	21.8	0.0	0.0	48704
41572	VIRGIE	18873	1290	41.2	25.7	26.4	4.2	2.6	31788	40255	17	49	1058	47.6	34.8	16.9	0.1	0.6	52841
41601	ALLEN	17708	335	32.2	41.5	22.1	3.6	0.6	33037	39916	21	53	279	44.8	33.7	19.4	1.8	0.4	54028
41602	AUXIER	17019	1035	47.7	22.7	23.2	4.7	1.6	26458	32813	6	32	774	41.5	34.5	18.7	5.3	0.0	58354
41603	BANNER	11097	817	57.2	26.8	14.8	1.0	0.2	20298	24448	2	12	651	48.7	31.2	17.2	2.5	0.5	50955
41604	BEAVER	10591	302	55.0	31.8	11.9	1.3	0.0	20267	24657	2	12	234	58.6	29.9	9.4	2.1	0.0	39167
41605	BETSY LAYNE	24127	429	31.5	36.1	21.5	4.7	6.3	39075	48409	43	71	348	39.4	29.3	20.1	11.2	0.0	61875
41606	BEVINSVILLE	12932	905	61.4	25.1	9.0	2.2	2.3	17235	20558	1	5	737	70.2	22.8	5.7	1.4	0.0	36127
41607	BLUE RIVER	24828	13	30.8	23.1	38.5	0.0	7.7	42330	47338	54	79	11	18.2	27.3	45.5	9.1	0.0	95000
41615	DANA	10997	32	59.4	28.1	12.5	0.0	0.0	20000	28131	2	11	26	42.3	38.5	19.2	0.0	0.0	53333
41616	DAVID	1875	3	100.0	0.0	0.0	0.0	0.0	5000	5000	0	0	0	0.0	0.0	0.0	0.0	0.0	0
41622	EASTERN	14221	252	50.8	29.8	14.3	5.2	0.0	24519	29564	4	25	205	46.3	41.5	11.7	0.5	0.0	52586
41630	GARRETT	13794	662	57.3	21.9	15.1	5.3	0.5	20599	24594	2	13	526	55.1	27.8	16.2	1.0	0.0	41563
41631	GRETHEL	16579	573	53.9	22.2	14.3	6.5	3.1	22772	27285	3	21	442	54.1	33.0	11.8	1.1	0.0	44545
41632	GUNLOCK	12651	259	54.8	32.4	10.8	1.2	0.8	21156	26852	2	15	210	67.6	22.4	6.2	3.8	0.0	34762
41635	HAROLD	14764	1382	55.5	22.7	19.0	2.1	0.7	20000	24970	2	11	1089	51.5	26.6	16.1	5.7	0.1	48443
41636	HI HAT	13465	312	64.4	17.6	14.1	2.9	1.0	16860	20830	1	3	246	58.5	25.6	13.0	2.9	0.0	37273
41640	HUEYSVILLE	14804	90	53.3	18.9	18.9	8.9	0.0	22278	28879	3	20	74	52.7	29.7	16.2	1.4	0.0	47143
41642	IVEL	16515	689	44.7	29.2	20.8	2.5	2.9	29774	36707	12	43	529	37.8	28.7	22.1	10.6	0.8	67558
41643	LACKEY	14541	35	57.1	22.9	17.1	2.9	0.0	20702	26471	2	13	28	67.9	28.6	3.6	0.0	0.0	41667
41645	LANGLEY	13070	468	52.6	27.1	16.5	3.9	0.0	22911	27594	3	21	352	51.7	37.2	11.1	0.0	0.0	48909
41647	MC DOWELL	15310	577	54.3	26.3	15.6	1.7	2.1	22393	27426	3	20	460	61.7	25.7	11.1	1.5	0.0	37692
41649	MARTIN	13680	1368	51.3	29.2	16.3	2.4	0.8	23842	29185	4	23	1013	47.2	36.6	13.5	2.6	0.1	52591
41650	MELVIN	13313	192	58.9	28.1	10.4	1.6	1.0	18281	22077	1	6	154	65.6	25.3	7.1	2.0	0.0	37692
41653	PRESTONSBURG	17808	4509	46.7	26.7	20.0	3.9	2.7	26642	32307	7	33	3320	38.0	29.5	23.6	8.8	0.1	61468
41655	PRINTER	8524	62	71.0	17.7	11.3	0.0	0.0	15680	18842	1	2	47	72.3	14.9	6.4	6.4	0.0	36250
41660	TEABERRY	11988	761	62.8	20.9	11.2	3.6	1.6	17062	20532	1	4	620	72.9	16.6	8.6	0.3	1.6	35185
41666	WAYLAND	13301	382	57.1	23.0	14.9	4.5	0.5	20767	25140	2	13	300	63.7	27.7	8.7	0.0	0.0	42807
41701	HAZARD	15952	5904	47.9	26.9	19.6	3.5	2.2	26362	32233	6	32	4242	44.4	29.7	20.8	4.2	0.9	56695
41712	ARY	13755	185	47.0	31.9	13.5	6.0	1.6	26636	31883	7	33	149	61.1	22.2	15.4	1.3	0.0	41750
41714	BEAR BRANCH	10025	145	64.1	25.5	10.3	0.0	0.0	18059	21130	1	6	116	85.3	12.9	1.7	0.0	0.0	31000
41719	BONNYMAN	18557	248	40.3	28.2	22.6	7.7	1.2	32876	40441	21	53	203	54.2	26.6	11.8	5.9	1.5	46458
41721	BUCKHORN	13444	336	56.6	25.3	9.8	6.6	1.8	20913	25411	2	14	272	63.6	23.2	13.2	0.0	0.0	40750
41722	BULAN	13577	1130	47.8	27.2	22.0	2.8	0.2	26285	31182	6	31	922	58.2	25.3	14.1	1.7	0.7	42165
41723	BUSY	11610	705	54.8	27.1	16.3	1.3	0.6	21626	26187	2	18	563	63.2	25.4	8.0	3.4	0.0	39583
41725	CARRIE	3000	4	100.0	0.0	0.0	0.0	0.0	12500	5000	1	1	0	0.0	0.0	0.0	0.0	0.0	0
41727	CHAVIES	17845	123	33.3	35.0	26.8	4.9	0.0	36760	43396	35	65	102	50.0	23.5	21.6	2.9	2.0	50000
41729	COMBS	20765	124	33.9	29.0	25.0	11.3	0.8	37081	45000	36	66	102	48.0	34.3	7.8	7.8	2.0	52222
41731	CORNETTSVILLE	13722	805	51.8	29.7	14.9	2.5	1.1	23868	28393	4	23	665	58.5	28.7	11.9	0.9	0.0	38839
41735	DELPHIA	12013	112	52.7	32.1	13.4	1.8	0.0	23116	26223	3	22	87	59.8	26.4	13.8	0.0	0.0	41500
41736	DICE	14725	177	47.5	32.2	13.0	5.7	1.7	26319	31880	6	32	143	62.2	21.7	14.7	1.4	0.0	40789
41740	EMMALENA	13664	1021	51.6	26.8	18.9	2.4	0.3	23872	28522	4	24	840	58.8	27.4	12.0	1.8	0.0	42449
41743	FISTY	0	0	0.0	0.0	0.0	0.0	0.0	0	0	0	0	0	0.0	0.0	0.0	0.0	0.0	0
41745	GAYS CREEK	13439	49	59.2	22.5	10.2	8.2	0.0	19383	25000	2	9	40	65.0	22.5	12.5	0.0	0.0	38333
41746	HAPPY	10077	233	67.8	15.9	12.9	2.6	0.9	15214	17291	1	1	187	63.1	19.8	14.4	2.7	0.0	40200
41749	HYDEN	12759	1870	56.0	25.0	15.1	2.7	1.1	20898	24914	2	14	1504	61.0	21.8	15.4	1.3	0.6	40934
41754	KRYPTON	13625	253	45.9	39.5	10.7	1.6	2.4	27899	33539	8	37	207	49.8	36.7	7.7	5.8	0.0	50161
41759	SASSAFRAS	18202	419	42.7	31.5	17.9	6.9	1.0	28988	35193	10	41	346	50.6	30.9	17.3	1.2	0.0	49355
41760	SCUDDY	9489	313	62.6	23.3	13.1	1.0	0.0	17284	20349	1	5	248	53.2	25.8	17.7	2.8	0.4	44667
41763	SLEMP	12477	142	52.1	31.7	12.7	2.8	0.7	23444	26846	3	23	111	60.4	26.1	13.5	0.0	0.0	40417
41764	SMILAX	13162	303	50.5	29.7	18.2	1.3	0.3	24697	29129	4	25	247	69.2	23.5	5.3	2.0	0.0	31750
41772	VEST	12952	36	52.8	25.0	19.4	2.8	0.0	23113	28142	3	22	30	66.7	23.3	10.0	0.0	0.0	40000
41773	VICCO	12663	471	59.5	22.3	14.7	3.0	0.6	18638	22421	1	7	378	53.4	26.7	17.2	2.1	0.5	46486
41774	VIPER	17450	1207	44.2	30.5	20.6	2.6	2.1	28405	34376	9	39	1000	46.8	32.4	18.7	1.8	0.3	52689
41775	WENDOVER	14576	115	54.8	27.8	14.8	1.7	0.9	22882	25978	3	21	93	57.0	28.0	11.8	0.0	3.2	45000
41776	WOOTON	12612	966	56.4	24.1	17.0	2.1	0.4	21236	24866	2	15	776	65.6	25.9	7.7	0.6	0.1	35000
41777	YEADDISS	14568	186	45.7	29.0	21.0	2.7	1.6	27452	32490	8	35	155	81.9	12.9	5.2	0.0	0.0	26406
41804	BLACKEY	12361	170	48.8	34.7	15.9	0.6	0.0	25725	30746	5	29	140	69.3	22.9	7.9	0.0	0.0	37667
41812	DEANE	10999	195	66.2	16.9	14.9	2.1	0.0	17054	19494	1	4	155	52.3	36.8	11.0	0.0	0.0	47308
41815	ERMINE	15692	230	44.8	28.7	22.2	4.4	0.0	27055	32675	7	34	190	39.5	39.0	19.0	2.6	0.0	58696
41817	GARNER	12107	478	55.0	23.6	17.6	2.9	0.8	22185	26400	3	19	378	48.9	29.4	14.3	7.4	0.0	51143
41819	GORDON	9566	213	64.8	28.6	6.6	0.0	0.0	18329	21297	1	6	169	71.6	18.3	10.1	0.0	0.0	26583
41821	HALLIE	14348	221	45.7	28.5	23.5	2.3	0.0	30609	37645	14	46	196	67.9	27.6	4.6	0.0	0.0	30000
41822	HINDMAN	16663	1178	49.0	24.3	20.1	4.9	1.7	25777	32211	6	30	875	45.3	26.1	21.8	5.9	0.9	55533
41824	ISOM	12143	82	59.8	20.7	17.1	2.4	0.0	20000	20785	2	11	65	47.7	40.0	12.3	0.0	0.0	51250
41825	JACKHORN	11748	141	48.2	31.2	20.6	0.0	0.0	25757	30797	5	30	109	67.0	30.3	2.8	0.0	0.0	35357
41826	JEREMIAH	15814	369	41.5	33.6	22.0	1.9	1.1	29413	36348	11	43	307	41.4	37.5	20.5	0.7	0.0	61250
	KENTUCKY	22472		31.8	28.3	28.2	7.8	3.9	39962	49361				22.2	24.9	36.4	14.3	2.1	94344
	UNITED STATES	25866		24.7	27.1	30.8	10.9	6.5	48124	56710				10.9	15.0	33.7	30.1	10.4	145905

ZIP CODE #	POST OFFICE NAME	FINANCIAL SERVICES: Auto Loan	FINANCIAL SERVICES: Home Loan	FINANCIAL SERVICES: Invest-ments	FINANCIAL SERVICES: Retire-ment Plans	THE HOME: Home Improvements: Home Repair	THE HOME: Home Improvements: Lawn & Garden	THE HOME: Furnishings: Comput-ers & Hard-ware	THE HOME: Furnishings: Major Appli-ances	THE HOME: Furnishings: TV, Radio, Sound Equip-ment	THE HOME: Furnishings: Furni-ture	ENTERTAINMENT: Dine out/ Carry out	ENTERTAINMENT: Sports Equip-ment	ENTERTAINMENT: Fees & Tickets	ENTERTAINMENT: Toys & Games	ENTERTAINMENT: Travel	ENTERTAINMENT: Cable TV	PERSONAL: Apparel & Services	PERSONAL: Auto Repairs	PERSONAL: Health Insur-ance	PERSONAL: Pets & Supplies
41514	BELFRY	84	56	25	48	64	73	54	68	65	55	77	81	46	73	55	71	70	67	84	96
41519	CANADA	60	40	18	34	45	52	39	48	47	39	55	58	33	52	39	50	50	48	59	69
41522	ELKHORN CITY	73	50	25	44	57	66	50	61	59	50	70	72	43	66	51	64	63	60	74	84
41524	FEDSCREEK	43	29	13	25	33	38	28	35	34	29	40	42	24	37	28	36	36	35	43	50
41527	FOREST HILLS	130	87	39	75	99	114	84	105	102	86	119	126	72	113	86	109	108	104	130	149
41528	FREEBURN	57	38	17	33	43	50	37	46	44	37	52	55	31	49	37	48	47	46	57	65
41531	HARDY	81	54	25	47	62	71	53	66	64	54	75	78	45	71	54	68	68	65	81	93
41535	HUDDY	69	51	32	48	56	67	56	62	63	53	74	70	49	70	55	67	68	62	75	77
41537	JENKINS	63	44	24	40	49	58	45	53	53	45	62	62	39	58	45	56	56	53	65	71
41539	KIMPER	76	51	23	44	57	66	49	61	59	50	69	73	42	65	50	63	63	60	75	87
41540	LICK CREEK	69	46	21	40	52	60	44	55	53	45	63	66	38	59	45	58	57	55	68	79
41543	MC ANDREWS	61	41	19	36	47	54	40	50	48	41	56	59	34	53	41	52	51	49	61	71
41544	MC CARR	73	49	22	42	55	64	47	59	57	48	67	70	40	63	48	61	61	58	73	84
41546	MC VEIGH	61	41	18	35	46	53	39	49	48	40	56	59	33	53	40	51	51	49	61	70
41548	MOUTHCARD	68	45	21	39	52	59	44	55	53	45	62	66	37	59	45	57	57	54	68	78
41553	PHELPS	62	42	19	36	47	54	40	50	49	41	57	60	34	54	41	52	52	50	62	72
41554	PHYLLIS	50	34	15	29	38	44	32	41	39	33	46	49	28	44	33	42	42	40	50	58
41555	PINSONFORK	62	41	19	36	47	54	40	50	48	41	57	60	34	54	41	52	51	49	62	71
41557	RACCOON	77	51	23	44	58	67	50	62	60	50	70	74	42	66	50	64	64	61	76	88
41558	RANSOM	62	41	19	36	47	54	40	50	48	41	57	60	34	54	41	52	51	49	62	71
41559	REGINA	67	45	20	39	51	59	43	54	52	44	61	65	37	58	44	56	56	54	67	77
41560	ROBINSON CREEK	77	52	24	45	59	68	50	63	60	51	71	75	43	67	51	65	64	62	77	89
41562	SHELBIANA	73	49	22	42	55	64	47	59	57	48	67	71	40	63	48	61	61	59	73	84
41563	SHELBY GAP	55	37	17	32	42	48	35	44	43	36	50	53	30	47	36	46	46	44	55	63
41564	SIDNEY	61	41	19	35	47	54	40	50	48	40	56	59	34	53	40	52	51	49	61	70
41566	STEELE	56	38	17	32	42	49	36	45	44	37	51	54	31	48	37	47	47	45	56	64
41567	STONE	66	46	24	41	51	60	47	56	55	46	64	65	41	61	47	59	59	55	68	74
41568	STOPOVER	47	32	14	27	36	41	30	38	37	31	43	46	26	41	31	40	39	38	47	54
41571	VARNEY	71	48	22	41	54	62	46	57	55	47	65	69	39	61	47	60	59	57	71	82
41572	VIRGIE	88	59	27	51	67	77	57	71	69	58	81	85	48	76	58	74	73	70	88	101
41601	ALLEN	73	49	23	43	56	64	48	60	58	49	68	71	41	64	49	62	62	59	73	84
41602	AUXIER	73	49	22	42	55	63	47	59	57	48	67	70	40	63	48	61	61	58	72	83
41603	BANNER	49	38	24	35	41	45	37	43	41	38	49	50	33	46	37	42	46	42	47	56
41604	BEAVER	50	34	15	29	38	44	32	40	39	33	46	48	28	43	33	42	42	40	50	57
41605	BETSY LAYNE	97	71	43	66	78	93	75	86	86	73	101	98	66	96	75	92	92	86	104	109
41606	BEVINSVILLE	57	41	25	38	46	54	44	50	50	43	59	57	39	56	44	53	54	50	61	64
41607	BLUE RIVER	89	79	60	75	83	89	73	81	78	73	94	96	72	96	75	80	90	79	88	104
41615	DANA	44	40	32	39	40	43	39	41	39	40	48	48	36	45	38	38	46	41	41	49
41616	DAVID	9	7	4	6	7	8	6	7	7	6	9	9	6	8	6	8	8	7	9	10
41622	EASTERN	63	43	19	37	48	55	41	51	50	42	58	61	35	55	42	53	53	51	63	73
41630	GARRETT	56	40	22	36	44	52	41	48	48	40	56	56	36	53	41	51	51	48	59	63
41631	GRETHEL	61	47	37	43	49	60	52	56	59	51	70	62	47	64	51	62	64	57	67	67
41632	GUNLOCK	62	41	19	36	47	54	40	50	48	41	56	59	34	53	40	52	51	49	61	71
41635	HAROLD	67	45	20	38	50	58	43	54	52	44	61	64	37	58	44	56	55	53	66	76
41636	HI HAT	57	38	17	33	43	49	37	46	44	37	52	55	31	49	37	47	47	45	56	65
41640	HUEYSVILLE	64	47	28	44	51	61	50	57	57	48	67	64	44	63	50	60	61	56	68	71
41642	IVEL	75	51	24	44	57	66	50	61	59	50	70	73	42	66	50	64	63	61	75	86
41643	LACKEY	59	40	19	35	45	52	39	49	47	40	55	58	34	52	40	51	50	48	60	68
41645	LANGLEY	51	39	27	36	42	49	41	46	47	40	56	53	37	53	41	49	51	46	54	57
41647	MC DOWELL	69	47	24	40	52	61	46	56	55	47	65	67	40	61	46	59	59	56	69	79
41649	MARTIN	54	39	25	36	43	51	41	47	47	41	56	55	37	53	41	50	52	47	56	61
41650	MELVIN	54	38	20	34	42	50	39	46	45	38	53	54	34	50	39	49	49	46	56	61
41653	PRESTONSBURG	72	53	31	48	58	67	53	62	60	53	71	72	47	68	53	64	66	61	73	82
41655	PRINTER	42	28	13	24	32	36	27	34	33	27	38	40	23	36	27	35	35	33	42	48
41660	TEABERRY	56	38	17	32	43	49	36	45	44	37	51	54	31	49	37	47	47	45	56	65
41666	WAYLAND	57	39	20	35	44	52	40	48	47	39	55	56	34	52	40	50	50	47	58	65
41701	HAZARD	66	48	30	44	52	61	50	57	57	49	68	66	44	64	50	60	62	57	68	74
41712	ARY	67	45	20	39	51	58	43	54	52	44	61	65	37	58	44	56	56	54	67	77
41714	BEAR BRANCH	44	29	13	25	33	38	28	36	34	29	40	42	24	38	29	37	37	35	44	51
41719	BONNYMAN	73	56	37	53	60	70	58	65	65	57	77	75	52	73	58	68	71	65	75	81
41721	BUCKHORN	65	43	20	37	49	56	42	52	50	43	59	62	36	56	42	54	54	52	64	74
41722	BULAN	63	43	19	37	48	55	41	51	50	42	58	61	35	55	42	53	53	51	63	73
41723	BUSY	58	39	18	34	44	51	38	47	45	38	53	56	32	50	38	49	48	47	58	67
41725	CARRIE	21	14	6	12	16	19	14	17	17	14	19	21	12	18	14	18	18	17	21	24
41727	CHAVIES	81	54	24	47	61	70	52	65	63	53	74	78	44	70	53	68	67	64	80	92
41729	COMBS	79	59	39	57	65	78	66	72	74	62	87	81	59	82	65	78	79	72	86	87
41731	CORNETTSVILLE	60	42	22	37	47	55	42	51	50	42	58	59	37	55	43	53	53	50	62	68
41735	DELPHIA	56	37	17	32	42	49	36	45	43	37	51	54	31	48	37	47	46	45	56	64
41736	DICE	67	45	20	39	51	58	43	54	52	44	61	65	37	58	44	56	56	54	67	77
41740	EMMALENA	62	42	19	36	47	55	40	50	49	41	57	60	34	54	41	52	52	50	62	72
41743	FISTY	0	0	0	0	0	0	0	0	0	0	0	0	0	0	0	0	0	0	0	0
41745	GAYS CREEK	63	42	19	37	48	55	41	51	49	42	58	61	35	55	42	53	53	51	63	73
41746	HAPPY	49	33	15	29	37	43	32	40	39	33	45	48	27	43	32	42	41	40	49	57
41749	HYDEN	59	40	18	34	45	52	38	48	46	39	54	57	32	51	39	50	49	47	59	68
41754	KRYPTON	67	47	24	41	52	59	45	55	53	46	63	65	39	59	46	56	57	55	66	76
41759	SASSAFRAS	87	58	26	50	66	76	56	70	68	57	79	84	48	75	57	73	72	69	86	100
41760	SCUDDY	48	32	15	28	36	42	31	39	37	32	44	46	26	42	32	40	40	38	48	55
41763	SLEMP	56	38	17	32	43	49	36	45	44	37	51	54	31	49	37	47	47	45	56	64
41764	SMILAX	59	39	18	34	44	51	38	47	46	39	54	57	32	51	38	49	49	47	58	67
41772	VEST	61	41	18	35	46	53	39	49	48	40	56	59	34	53	40	51	51	49	61	70
41773	VICCO	56	38	19	34	43	50	38	46	45	38	53	55	32	50	38	48	48	46	57	64
41774	VIPER	81	54	24	47	61	70	52	65	63	53	74	78	44	70	53	68	67	64	80	92
41775	WENDOVER	60	40	18	34	45	52	39	48	47	39	55	58	33	52	39	50	50	48	59	69
41776	WOOTON	57	38	17	33	43	50	37	46	45	38	52	55	31	50	38	48	48	46	57	66
41777	YEADDISS	67	45	20	39	51	58	43	54	52	44	61	65	37	58	44	56	56	53	67	77
41804	BLACKEY	55	37	17	32	42	48	36	45	43	36	51	53	30	48	36	46	46	44	55	63
41812	DEANE	50	34	15	29	38	44	33	41	39	33	46	49	28	44	33	42	42	40	50	58
41815	ERMINE	68	46	21	39	52	60	44	55	53	45	63	66	38	59	45	57	57	55	68	78
41817	GARNER	60	41	20	36	46	54	41	50	49	41	57	59	35	54	42	52	52	50	61	69
41819	GORDON	44	30	13	25	33	38	28	36	34	29	40	43	24	38	29	37	37	35	44	51
41821	HALLIE	66	44	20	38	50	58	43	53	51	43	60	64	36	57	43	55	55	53	66	76
41822	HINDMAN	66	48	29	45	53	63	52	58	59	50	69	66	46	65	51	62	63	58	70	73
41824	ISOM	54	36	16	31	41	47	35	43	42	35	49	52	29	46	35	45	45	43	53	61
41825	JACKHORN	56	38	17	33	43	49	36	46	44	37	52	54	31	49	37	47	47	45	56	65
41826	JEREMIAH	68	45	21	39	51	59	44	55	53	45	62	65	37	59	45	57	56	54	68	78
	KENTUCKY	86	74	63	71	77	85	74	80	79	74	96	94	71	95	74	81	91	80	86	98
	UNITED STATES	100	100	100	100	100	100	100	100	100	100	100	100	100	100	100	100	100	100	100	100

POPULATION CHANGE

#	POST OFFICE NAME	COUNTY FIPS CODE	POPULATION			2000-2004 ANNUAL RATE		HOUSEHOLDS					FAMILIES		
			2000	2004	2009	% Rate	State Centile	2000	2004	2009	% Annual Rate 2000-2004	2004 Average HH Size	2000	2004	% Annual Rate 2000-2004
41828	KITE	119	979	1071	1125	2.1	91	349	394	428	2.9	2.72	281	310	2.3
41831	LEBURN	119	1165	1172	1176	0.1	47	454	473	491	1.0	2.48	319	322	0.2
41832	LETCHER	133	464	447	441	-0.9	8	185	185	185	0.0	2.42	141	138	-0.5
41833	LINEFORK	133	298	300	301	0.2	48	112	117	119	1.0	2.56	87	89	0.5
41834	LITTCARR	119	475	473	473	-0.1	34	208	215	224	0.8	2.20	149	149	0.0
41835	MC ROBERTS	133	405	395	392	-0.6	16	159	160	161	0.2	2.47	121	119	-0.4
41836	MALLIE	119	883	874	873	-0.2	29	340	347	359	0.5	2.09	254	252	-0.2
41837	MAYKING	133	735	732	731	-0.1	34	257	263	265	0.5	2.78	208	208	0.0
41838	MILLSTONE	133	691	689	689	-0.1	35	280	288	292	0.7	2.39	209	209	0.0
41839	MOUSIE	119	1278	1270	1270	-0.2	32	487	502	519	0.7	2.48	349	349	0.0
41840	NEON	133	2058	2045	2042	-0.2	32	830	850	859	0.6	2.41	617	615	-0.1
41843	PINE TOP	119	1043	1058	1066	0.3	54	420	441	460	1.2	2.40	319	326	0.5
41844	PIPPA PASSES	119	350	366	376	1.1	77	101	112	120	2.5	2.88	80	86	1.7
41845	PREMIUM	133	354	353	354	-0.1	35	156	161	164	0.8	2.19	107	107	0.0
41847	REDFOX	119	932	914	910	-0.5	21	367	372	384	0.3	2.46	276	273	-0.3
41849	SECO	133	149	147	146	-0.3	26	67	68	68	0.4	2.16	48	48	0.0
41855	THORNTON	133	787	811	823	0.7	68	305	324	333	1.4	2.50	232	241	0.9
41858	WHITESBURG	133	9422	9397	9406	-0.1	36	3763	3873	3924	0.7	2.38	2759	2763	0.0
41859	DEMA	119	319	350	368	2.2	91	119	135	147	3.0	2.59	96	106	2.4
41861	RAVEN	119	118	119	121	0.2	49	44	46	48	1.1	2.48	33	34	0.7
41862	TOPMOST	119	1069	1036	1029	-0.7	11	396	395	405	-0.1	2.62	312	304	-0.6
42001	PADUCAH	145	28274	28149	27961	-0.1	34	12269	12446	12569	0.3	2.22	7928	7743	-0.6
42003	PADUCAH	145	30104	29241	28692	-0.7	13	12672	12568	12545	-0.2	2.26	8369	8009	-1.0
42020	ALMO	035	1936	1973	1998	0.5	59	763	792	815	0.9	2.48	557	559	0.1
42021	ARLINGTON	039	1769	1691	1654	-1.1	6	741	723	719	-0.6	2.34	519	491	-1.3
42023	BARDWELL	039	1998	2080	2124	1.0	74	877	927	960	1.3	2.24	598	612	0.6
42024	BARLOW	007	1368	1519	1633	2.5	93	588	662	722	2.8	2.29	397	432	2.0
42025	BENTON	157	18903	19068	19309	0.2	49	7718	7942	8180	0.7	2.36	5597	5597	0.0
42027	BOAZ	083	2069	2071	2052	0.0	42	827	847	853	0.6	2.41	618	615	-0.1
42028	BURNA	139	846	844	838	-0.1	36	343	346	347	0.2	2.43	239	234	-0.5
42029	CALVERT CITY	157	5422	5484	5558	0.3	52	2183	2258	2330	0.8	2.34	1549	1550	0.0
42031	CLINTON	105	4059	4004	3955	-0.3	26	1688	1702	1715	0.2	2.27	1169	1140	-0.6
42032	COLUMBUS	105	333	336	332	0.2	49	137	141	142	0.7	2.38	95	95	0.0
42035	CUNNINGHAM	039	1784	1816	1825	0.4	58	659	686	700	1.0	2.55	507	515	0.4
42036	DEXTER	035	1254	1164	1136	-1.7	1	473	447	444	-1.3	2.60	355	326	-2.0
42038	EDDYVILLE	143	5251	5343	5435	0.4	58	1753	1822	1890	0.9	2.21	1229	1239	0.2
42039	FANCY FARM	083	1453	1440	1420	-0.2	30	569	574	575	0.2	2.51	432	425	-0.4
42040	FARMINGTON	083	1154	1145	1136	-0.2	31	466	470	473	0.2	2.41	349	342	-0.5
42041	FULTON	075	5697	5527	5292	-0.7	12	2436	2405	2344	-0.3	2.27	1631	1560	-1.0
42044	GILBERTSVILLE	157	3157	3200	3252	0.3	54	1384	1425	1469	0.7	2.22	1007	1010	0.1
42045	GRAND RIVERS	139	2418	2436	2418	0.2	48	1020	1046	1055	0.6	2.32	743	741	-0.1
42047	HAMPTON	139	284	268	259	-1.4	2	110	106	103	-0.9	2.53	76	71	-1.6
42048	HARDIN	157	2410	2686	2848	2.6	94	1021	1163	1255	3.1	2.31	755	834	2.4
42049	HAZEL	035	1765	1900	1967	1.8	88	728	801	843	2.3	2.37	512	542	1.4
42050	HICKMAN	075	3385	3218	3042	-1.2	4	1344	1305	1257	-0.7	2.32	904	847	-1.5
42051	HICKORY	083	2767	2773	2755	0.1	43	1061	1083	1092	0.5	2.52	796	790	-0.2
42053	KEVIL	007	4661	4738	4794	0.4	56	1868	1933	1987	0.8	2.45	1436	1446	0.2
42054	KIRKSEY	035	1262	1421	1506	2.8	95	434	505	547	3.6	2.61	332	375	2.9
42055	KUTTAWA	143	2566	2622	2680	0.5	62	1043	1087	1129	1.0	2.25	737	745	0.3
42056	LA CENTER	007	2304	2269	2310	-0.4	24	917	917	948	0.0	2.37	645	626	-0.7
42058	LEDBETTER	139	2321	2288	2247	-0.3	24	920	928	929	0.2	2.46	680	668	-0.4
42064	MARION	055	8824	8633	8394	-0.5	18	3599	3580	3539	-0.1	2.37	2535	2445	-0.9
42066	MAYFIELD	083	22920	22642	22359	-0.3	27	9272	9278	9273	0.0	2.37	6383	6180	-0.8
42069	MELBER	083	969	1138	1222	3.9	98	370	444	485	4.4	2.49	276	322	3.7
42071	MURRAY	035	26641	26687	26796	0.0	42	10894	11143	11377	0.5	2.14	6425	6296	-0.5
42076	NEW CONCORD	035	1037	995	978	-1.0	7	460	451	451	-0.5	2.21	329	311	-1.3
42078	SALEM	139	1770	1809	1816	0.5	62	740	768	782	0.9	2.25	511	513	0.1
42079	SEDALIA	083	1268	1287	1284	0.4	54	482	497	502	0.7	2.59	364	365	0.1
42081	SMITHLAND	139	2055	1960	1902	-1.1	5	820	794	783	-0.8	2.41	606	571	-1.2
42082	SYMSONIA	083	1844	1764	1717	-1.0	6	785	767	759	-0.5	2.30	571	543	-1.2
42083	TILINE	139	270	278	279	0.7	68	109	114	116	1.1	2.44	84	85	0.3
42085	WATER VALLEY	083	635	614	599	-0.8	10	267	262	258	-0.4	2.34	196	187	-1.1
42086	WEST PADUCAH	145	3728	4115	4292	2.4	93	1475	1669	1774	3.0	2.46	1120	1228	2.2
42087	WICKLIFFE	007	2552	2594	2672	0.4	56	1031	1065	1114	0.8	2.38	735	738	0.1
42088	WINGO	083	2613	2618	2594	0.0	42	1020	1037	1041	0.4	2.52	795	788	-0.2
42101	BOWLING GREEN	227	47918	49493	51925	0.8	70	17513	18481	19797	1.3	2.41	10920	11060	0.3
42103	BOWLING GREEN	227	16248	17088	18137	1.2	80	6694	7164	7736	1.6	2.35	4508	4694	1.0
42104	BOWLING GREEN	227	20742	22707	24553	2.2	91	8341	9276	10184	2.5	2.41	5763	6179	1.7
42120	ADOLPHUS	003	2208	2254	2282	0.5	61	820	847	866	0.8	2.66	618	622	0.2
42122	ALVATON	227	2858	2934	3068	0.6	65	1065	1118	1190	1.2	2.62	871	894	0.6
42123	AUSTIN	009	733	712	711	-0.7	13	293	290	294	-0.2	2.46	218	210	-0.9
42124	BEAUMONT	169	130	137	142	1.2	81	51	55	58	1.8	2.49	40	41	0.6
42127	CAVE CITY	009	5255	5294	5342	0.2	48	2147	2212	2271	0.7	2.39	1531	1527	-0.1
42129	EDMONTON	169	6336	6567	6810	0.9	72	2552	2700	2856	1.3	2.39	1805	1852	0.6
42130	EIGHTY EIGHT	009	110	110	110	0.0	41	49	50	51	0.5	2.20	39	39	0.0
42131	ETOILE	009	94	91	90	-0.8	11	40	39	40	-0.6	2.33	30	29	-0.8
42133	FOUNTAIN RUN	171	1410	1407	1410	-0.1	37	599	608	617	0.4	2.31	431	424	-0.4
42134	FRANKLIN	213	15846	16213	16551	0.5	63	6227	6484	6711	1.0	2.46	4486	4539	0.3
42140	GAMALIEL	171	1262	1288	1300	0.5	61	505	523	534	0.8	2.46	365	367	0.1
42141	GLASGOW	009	27565	28216	28831	0.6	63	11154	11655	12113	1.0	2.37	7872	7981	0.3
42151	HESTAND	171	305	336	354	2.3	92	111	124	133	2.6	2.55	78	84	1.8
42153	HOLLAND	003	415	431	441	0.9	73	166	176	182	1.4	2.45	125	128	0.6
42154	KNOB LICK	169	814	839	869	0.7	68	329	346	364	1.2	2.42	244	249	0.5
42156	LUCAS	009	316	317	320	0.1	44	125	128	131	0.6	2.48	94	94	0.0
42157	MOUNT HERMON	171	417	412	411	-0.3	27	162	164	166	0.3	2.51	122	120	-0.4
42159	OAKLAND	227	1495	1617	1735	1.9	89	577	635	691	2.3	2.54	449	480	1.6
42160	PARK CITY	009	2391	2496	2575	1.0	76	950	1012	1063	1.5	2.47	700	726	0.9
42163	ROCKY HILL	061	154	180	199	3.7	98	68	82	92	4.5	2.20	52	61	3.8
42164	SCOTTSVILLE	003	14581	15060	15467	0.8	70	5687	5968	6201	1.1	2.49	4187	4276	0.5
42166	SUMMER SHADE	169	2259	2304	2357	0.5	60	912	950	989	1.0	2.43	671	680	0.3
42167	TOMPKINSVILLE	171	8863	8909	8983	0.1	46	3575	3653	3735	0.5	2.41	2541	2518	-0.2
42170	WOODBURN	213	1383	1402	1437	0.3	54	504	521	543	0.8	2.65	393	395	0.1
42171	SMITHS GROVE	227	5623	5869	6129	1.0	76	2117	2253	2395	1.5	2.60	1636	1695	0.8
42202	ADAIRVILLE	141	2332	2418	2467	0.9	72	938	992	1025	1.3	2.43	674	691	0.6
42204	ALLENSVILLE	219	669	681	685	0.4	58	255	265	271	0.9	2.55	193	196	0.4
	KENTUCKY					0.7					1.2	2.42			0.5
	UNITED STATES					1.2					1.3	2.58			1.1

POPULATION COMPOSITION

KENTUCKY

41828-42204 B

# ZIP CODE	POST OFFICE NAME	RACE (%) White 2000	White 2004	Black 2000	Black 2004	Asian/Pacific 2000	Asian/Pacific 2004	% Hispanic Origin 2000	% Hispanic Origin 2004	2004 AGE DISTRIBUTION (%) 0-4	5-9	10-14	15-19	20-24	25-44	45-64	65-84	85+	18+	MEDIAN AGE 2004	% 2004 Males	% 2004 Females
41828	KITE	99.5	99.4	0.1	0.1	0.0	0.0	0.3	0.4	6.7	7.8	7.4	6.1	7.1	29.5	24.7	9.7	1.0	74.0	35.5	51.2	48.8
41831	LEBURN	98.6	98.7	0.0	0.0	0.3	0.3	1.1	1.0	5.6	5.9	6.7	5.5	6.1	30.0	28.2	10.5	1.5	78.4	39.2	50.5	49.5
41832	LETCHER	98.9	99.1	0.0	0.0	0.0	0.0	0.4	0.2	4.0	5.4	7.2	8.1	6.5	26.4	27.5	13.4	1.6	78.1	40.9	49.4	50.6
41833	LINEFORK	100.0	100.0	0.0	0.0	0.0	0.0	0.0	0.0	5.7	6.3	7.3	7.3	7.7	30.3	25.7	8.7	1.0	76.0	35.7	50.7	49.3
41834	LITTCARR	99.2	98.9	0.2	0.2	0.0	0.0	0.4	0.6	5.9	5.7	5.3	5.3	5.9	29.6	26.6	14.4	1.3	79.9	40.6	49.7	50.3
41835	MC ROBERTS	93.6	93.4	5.7	6.1	0.0	0.0	1.0	1.0	6.1	6.1	7.1	6.6	7.1	25.3	27.6	12.9	1.3	77.2	40.1	51.1	48.9
41836	MALLIE	98.9	99.0	0.5	0.5	0.2	0.2	0.7	0.7	6.0	5.7	6.1	10.3	14.3	25.3	23.9	7.6	0.9	78.7	31.8	48.5	51.5
41837	MAYKING	99.9	99.6	0.0	0.0	0.0	0.0	0.5	0.6	7.1	7.4	7.1	5.6	6.7	29.0	27.7	8.3	1.1	75.0	36.2	50.6	49.5
41838	MILLSTONE	99.0	98.8	0.3	0.3	0.0	0.0	0.7	1.0	6.2	6.4	6.5	7.0	6.4	27.4	26.3	12.5	1.3	76.3	38.1	51.2	48.8
41839	MOUSIE	98.6	98.6	0.2	0.2	0.3	0.3	0.6	0.6	5.8	6.1	7.2	5.3	5.9	28.7	29.1	10.7	1.3	77.4	39.6	50.1	49.9
41840	NEON	97.0	96.8	2.2	2.3	0.1	0.2	0.7	1.0	5.6	6.6	6.7	6.1	6.4	26.8	28.4	12.0	1.5	77.5	39.1	49.5	50.5
41843	PINE TOP	99.5	99.4	0.2	0.2	0.1	0.1	0.5	0.5	6.3	6.2	6.9	6.4	7.4	29.1	27.7	8.8	1.1	76.8	37.2	48.1	51.9
41844	PIPPA PASSES	99.1	99.2	0.3	0.3	0.3	0.3	0.6	0.3	6.3	6.6	6.8	8.7	11.5	27.1	23.8	8.2	1.1	76.5	33.2	50.6	49.5
41845	PREMIUM	99.7	99.7	0.0	0.0	0.0	0.0	0.3	0.6	4.3	4.8	6.0	5.4	6.8	26.9	31.4	13.0	1.4	81.6	42.7	49.0	51.0
41847	REDFOX	93.0	92.7	6.3	6.6	0.0	0.0	0.9	1.0	5.4	5.6	6.8	7.3	6.8	26.5	28.1	11.7	1.9	77.8	40.3	49.8	50.2
41849	SECO	98.7	98.6	0.7	0.7	0.0	0.0	0.7	1.4	6.8	6.8	6.8	5.4	6.1	27.2	25.9	13.6	1.4	76.2	38.8	50.3	49.7
41855	THORNTON	99.1	99.0	0.1	0.3	0.4	0.5	0.3	0.4	6.0	6.3	6.8	6.8	6.2	28.6	28.2	9.9	1.2	76.8	37.7	49.1	50.9
41858	WHITESBURG	98.8	98.6	0.2	0.2	0.6	0.7	0.5	0.6	5.7	5.9	6.4	5.9	6.1	28.5	28.0	12.1	1.5	78.5	39.7	48.9	51.1
41859	DEMA	99.4	99.7	0.0	0.0	0.0	0.0	0.3	0.3	6.9	7.4	7.4	6.0	7.1	29.7	24.9	9.4	1.1	74.3	35.6	50.9	49.1
41861	RAVEN	98.3	98.3	0.0	0.0	0.9	0.8	0.0	0.0	6.7	6.7	6.7	5.0	6.7	28.6	26.1	12.6	0.8	74.8	38.1	47.9	52.1
41862	TOPMOST	99.0	98.9	0.0	0.0	0.1	0.1	0.3	0.3	5.9	5.9	5.9	7.1	8.0	26.7	28.3	11.2	1.1	78.1	38.4	51.8	48.2
42001	PADUCAH	83.3	82.7	14.3	14.5	0.7	0.9	1.2	1.5	5.7	6.0	6.9	6.0	5.4	25.4	27.4	14.5	2.6	77.6	41.4	47.2	52.9
42003	PADUCAH	87.6	86.8	9.8	10.3	0.5	0.6	1.1	1.4	6.2	6.2	6.5	5.9	6.0	27.1	26.6	13.2	2.3	77.5	40.0	47.6	52.4
42020	ALMO	97.3	96.9	0.9	0.9	0.4	0.5	1.9	2.3	6.7	6.7	6.7	6.3	6.7	29.4	25.1	10.9	1.5	76.0	36.8	49.1	50.9
42021	ARLINGTON	97.4	97.4	2.0	2.0	0.1	0.1	0.8	0.8	7.3	6.9	6.2	5.6	6.3	26.4	24.4	15.1	1.8	76.4	39.5	49.9	50.2
42023	BARDWELL	97.2	97.1	1.3	1.4	0.1	0.1	1.4	1.4	5.3	5.4	6.1	6.0	6.0	25.0	26.7	16.9	2.6	79.6	42.0	48.8	51.3
42024	BARLOW	94.4	94.1	3.7	3.8	0.0	0.0	0.7	0.9	6.8	7.0	6.9	5.4	4.8	27.7	27.3	12.1	2.1	76.0	39.1	50.7	49.3
42025	BENTON	98.5	98.3	0.2	0.2	0.2	0.2	0.8	1.0	5.1	5.4	6.3	5.8	5.6	26.7	27.1	15.8	2.3	79.8	41.9	49.1	50.9
42027	BOAZ	97.3	97.0	1.1	1.2	0.1	0.1	1.0	1.3	6.5	6.5	6.1	6.0	5.8	30.1	27.6	10.3	1.2	77.5	38.4	50.5	49.5
42028	BURNA	98.5	98.5	0.2	0.2	0.0	0.0	0.5	0.5	5.3	5.6	6.5	6.3	5.1	26.0	27.6	15.3	2.4	78.6	41.9	50.0	50.0
42029	CALVERT CITY	98.7	98.5	0.0	0.0	0.2	0.3	0.8	1.0	5.4	5.7	6.4	5.8	5.7	25.5	27.1	15.4	3.1	79.0	42.0	48.5	51.5
42031	CLINTON	87.7	87.4	10.5	10.8	0.1	0.1	1.0	1.1	5.5	5.6	6.2	6.0	5.2	26.3	26.0	15.7	3.3	78.9	42.0	47.1	52.9
42032	COLUMBUS	84.1	84.8	12.9	12.2	0.0	0.0	2.1	2.4	7.4	7.1	6.9	5.4	6.0	26.2	25.9	13.7	1.5	75.0	39.0	51.2	48.8
42035	CUNNINGHAM	98.0	97.9	0.2	0.2	0.0	0.0	0.5	0.6	5.8	6.0	7.0	6.7	7.2	26.5	24.6	13.0	3.1	77.1	38.6	47.6	52.4
42036	DEXTER	98.3	98.0	0.2	0.3	0.2	0.3	1.2	1.6	6.0	6.4	7.4	7.0	6.2	28.9	26.1	10.7	1.3	75.8	37.6	49.7	50.3
42038	EDDYVILLE	89.6	89.1	9.0	9.3	0.2	0.3	0.9	1.2	3.5	3.7	4.3	4.1	6.4	36.0	26.9	13.9	1.3	86.1	40.9	61.8	38.2
42039	FANCY FARM	96.5	96.4	2.1	2.0	0.0	0.1	0.8	1.1	7.9	7.5	7.2	6.9	6.7	27.8	23.1	11.5	1.4	73.1	35.6	50.4	49.6
42040	FARMINGTON	97.8	97.3	1.0	1.2	0.2	0.3	1.0	1.3	5.9	6.3	6.8	6.2	5.8	28.5	26.6	12.1	1.8	77.4	38.9	50.1	49.9
42041	FULTON	82.5	82.0	15.5	15.6	0.4	0.5	0.9	1.1	6.6	6.6	6.0	6.1	6.4	24.0	25.8	15.7	2.9	77.1	41.1	46.5	53.5
42044	GILBERTSVILLE	98.4	98.2	0.0	0.0	0.1	0.1	0.7	0.9	4.2	4.6	5.7	5.2	4.3	23.3	32.2	18.7	2.0	82.4	46.8	50.0	50.0
42045	GRAND RIVERS	98.0	98.0	0.0	0.0	0.0	0.0	0.5	0.5	5.1	5.7	6.0	5.4	4.7	27.7	29.9	14.5	1.0	79.9	42.1	50.4	49.6
42047	HAMPTON	97.9	97.8	0.4	0.4	0.0	0.0	0.4	0.8	4.9	5.2	6.7	6.3	4.9	27.2	27.6	14.6	2.6	78.7	42.0	50.8	49.3
42048	HARDIN	99.0	98.9	0.0	0.0	0.1	0.1	0.8	1.0	5.7	5.7	6.0	5.9	5.0	25.5	28.3	16.2	1.7	79.0	42.6	49.9	50.1
42049	HAZEL	97.7	97.4	1.6	1.8	0.1	0.2	0.6	0.8	5.8	5.8	6.6	6.1	5.2	28.3	26.8	13.4	2.0	78.0	40.8	48.5	51.5
42050	HICKMAN	71.6	70.7	27.5	28.4	0.0	0.0	0.4	0.5	6.1	6.1	6.9	7.2	7.7	26.7	25.0	12.5	1.7	76.4	37.4	49.6	50.4
42051	HICKORY	97.1	96.4	0.8	0.9	0.1	0.2	1.4	2.0	6.7	6.7	6.9	6.2	6.1	28.4	25.3	12.1	1.6	76.1	37.9	49.9	50.1
42053	KEVIL	97.6	97.2	1.2	1.4	0.2	0.3	0.7	1.0	6.6	6.7	6.8	6.3	5.0	29.6	26.4	11.3	1.3	75.9	38.5	50.2	49.8
42054	KIRKSEY	96.6	96.1	2.3	2.5	0.2	0.2	2.1	2.7	5.4	5.6	5.6	5.9	6.3	31.2	27.9	10.8	1.3	80.2	38.7	52.9	47.1
42055	KUTTAWA	96.4	96.2	2.1	2.2	0.2	0.2	0.4	0.4	4.4	4.8	5.3	4.2	3.9	22.7	31.8	18.5	4.4	83.0	47.8	48.0	52.0
42056	LA CENTER	92.8	92.6	5.6	5.7	0.2	0.3	0.6	0.8	6.0	6.0	6.3	6.3	5.5	25.1	25.2	16.2	3.5	77.7	41.6	47.6	52.4
42058	LEDBETTER	99.0	99.0	0.3	0.3	0.1	0.1	0.9	0.9	6.3	6.3	6.3	5.9	6.5	30.8	28.2	8.6	1.1	77.7	37.4	50.5	49.5
42064	MARION	98.2	98.0	0.7	0.7	0.1	0.1	0.5	0.7	5.6	5.7	6.5	6.3	5.9	25.3	27.6	14.7	2.4	78.3	41.4	48.5	51.5
42066	MAYFIELD	89.8	89.0	6.6	6.7	0.3	0.3	3.2	4.0	6.8	6.5	6.4	6.3	6.4	25.9	24.8	14.2	2.8	76.5	39.1	48.6	51.4
42069	MELBER	96.5	95.9	1.4	1.6	0.1	0.2	2.0	2.6	6.5	6.8	7.0	6.1	6.0	26.8	27.3	11.4	2.1	75.7	38.9	49.7	50.4
42071	MURRAY	92.3	91.5	4.3	4.4	1.7	2.2	1.4	1.8	4.7	4.6	4.8	10.1	13.2	24.7	22.1	13.3	2.5	83.0	34.3	48.1	51.9
42076	NEW CONCORD	98.4	98.3	0.2	0.2	0.3	0.4	0.5	0.5	4.4	4.7	5.7	5.0	4.2	22.0	33.7	18.7	1.5	81.9	47.6	47.6	52.4
42078	SALEM	98.8	98.8	0.2	0.2	0.1	0.1	0.6	0.6	5.0	5.3	6.0	5.5	5.3	23.8	27.9	17.8	3.5	80.2	44.4	47.6	52.4
42079	SEDALIA	98.0	97.5	0.8	0.9	0.2	0.2	1.3	1.7	5.8	6.2	7.8	7.3	5.8	27.8	25.9	12.0	1.5	75.7	38.4	50.0	50.0
42081	SMITHLAND	98.4	98.3	0.1	0.1	0.0	0.0	1.3	1.3	5.2	5.8	7.0	5.6	4.7	27.8	27.9	13.7	2.3	78.6	41.1	48.7	51.3
42082	SYMSONIA	99.0	98.9	0.1	0.1	0.1	0.1	0.4	0.6	5.2	5.6	6.5	5.8	4.8	26.6	29.4	14.0	2.2	79.1	42.3	50.1	49.9
42083	TILINE	97.8	97.5	0.0	0.0	0.0	0.0	0.7	0.7	5.4	7.2	7.9	6.1	4.0	29.1	28.8	10.8	0.7	75.9	39.6	49.6	50.4
42085	WATER VALLEY	96.5	95.9	1.9	2.0	0.2	0.3	1.1	1.6	7.0	6.8	5.9	5.9	5.9	26.1	27.0	13.7	1.8	76.9	39.9	50.5	49.5
42086	WEST PADUCAH	96.0	95.4	2.5	2.7	0.4	0.5	0.6	0.8	6.1	6.3	6.2	6.1	5.3	28.9	28.2	11.5	1.4	77.6	39.7	49.5	50.5
42087	WICKLIFFE	96.2	95.9	1.3	1.4	0.4	0.5	0.8	1.0	5.2	5.4	5.7	5.5	5.9	27.3	29.9	13.6	1.5	80.5	41.7	51.5	48.5
42088	WINGO	97.2	96.6	1.5	1.8	0.1	0.2	1.0	1.3	6.9	7.5	7.1	6.4	5.8	26.6	26.8	11.4	1.6	74.1	38.3	49.2	50.8
42101	BOWLING GREEN	82.1	80.7	12.2	12.5	1.5	1.9	3.8	4.8	6.3	5.9	5.9	10.3	14.8	28.2	19.5	8.0	1.2	78.5	29.1	49.5	50.5
42103	BOWLING GREEN	93.0	92.3	3.8	3.9	1.3	1.6	1.9	2.5	6.0	6.2	6.6	6.1	6.4	27.6	27.7	11.8	1.7	77.6	39.2	49.6	50.4
42104	BOWLING GREEN	91.7	90.7	4.9	5.1	1.7	2.2	1.3	1.7	7.4	6.9	6.4	5.8	7.1	31.3	23.3	10.5	1.5	76.0	35.0	48.1	51.9
42120	ADOLPHUS	97.8	97.3	0.1	0.1	0.1	0.1	1.2	1.6	7.1	7.0	7.8	7.3	7.1	29.0	23.8	9.8	1.0	73.6	34.8	50.2	49.8
42122	ALVATON	96.3	95.7	2.1	2.3	0.4	0.6	1.0	1.4	5.9	6.5	7.6	6.5	6.0	29.9	30.0	6.8	0.7	76.0	38.4	49.7	50.3
42123	AUSTIN	98.8	98.5	0.1	0.1	0.0	0.0	0.6	1.0	5.8	6.0	7.7	5.9	6.0	28.0	27.1	12.1	1.4	76.8	39.7	50.4	49.6
42124	BEAUMONT	99.2	99.3	0.0	0.0	0.0	0.0	0.0	0.7	5.8	5.8	7.3	6.6	6.6	28.5	26.3	11.0	2.2	76.6	38.8	48.2	51.8
42127	CAVE CITY	93.6	93.1	5.1	5.4	0.5	0.6	0.7	0.9	6.0	6.2	6.8	6.1	5.6	26.8	27.5	13.3	1.7	77.3	40.5	49.4	50.6
42129	EDMONTON	97.6	97.4	1.4	1.4	0.1	0.1	0.4	0.6	6.6	6.6	6.9	6.2	5.9	27.3	24.5	14.0	2.0	76.1	38.5	48.4	51.6
42130	EIGHTY EIGHT	98.2	99.1	0.9	0.9	0.0	0.0	0.0	0.0	6.4	6.4	6.4	5.5	7.3	28.2	25.5	13.6	0.9	77.3	38.6	52.7	47.3
42131	ETOILE	98.9	98.9	0.0	0.0	0.0	0.0	0.0	0.0	6.6	6.6	8.8	6.6	5.5	25.3	27.5	12.1	1.1	71.4	37.9	51.7	48.4
42133	FOUNTAIN RUN	97.0	96.9	1.0	1.0	0.1	0.1	2.1	2.2	5.8	6.1	7.3	5.9	6.0	27.2	26.5	13.2	2.0	77.3	39.4	49.4	50.6
42134	FRANKLIN	87.6	87.1	10.4	10.6	0.6	0.8	0.9	1.2	7.5	7.4	7.0	6.2	6.0	28.8	24.0	11.3	1.8	74.2	36.5	48.7	51.3
42140	GAMALIEL	97.2	97.2	0.4	0.4	0.0	0.0	1.9	1.9	6.5	6.7	7.4	6.1	5.3	28.1	26.2	12.2	1.6	75.8	38.4	49.8	50.2
42141	GLASGOW	93.7	93.3	4.5	4.6	0.5	0.6	1.0	1.3	6.5	6.4	6.6	5.9	6.3	27.4	25.3	13.4	2.3	76.9	39.1	47.9	52.1
42151	HESTAND	93.4	93.5	3.6	3.6	0.0	0.0	2.6	2.4	7.1	6.9	6.9	5.4	6.3	25.3	22.3	16.4	3.6	75.6	39.3	47.0	53.0
42153	HOLLAND	97.6	97.2	0.5	0.5	0.2	0.5	0.7	0.9	5.8	6.0	6.5	6.7	7.4	24.4	27.4	13.9	1.9	77.5	40.1	51.5	48.5
42154	KNOB LICK	95.5	95.2	3.7	3.8	0.1	0.1	0.5	0.5	6.9	7.0	7.5	6.6	5.7	28.6	24.2	12.2	1.3	74.6	37.1	50.2	49.8
42156	LUCAS	99.1	98.7	0.0	0.0	0.0	0.0	0.3	0.6	6.0	6.0	7.6	6.0	6.3	27.1	27.8	12.0	1.3	76.7	39.3	50.5	49.5
42157	MOUNT HERMON	98.6	98.8	1.0	1.0	0.0	0.0	0.5	0.2	7.0	7.3	6.6	4.9	5.6	29.9	24.5	13.1	1.2	76.2	38.6	51.7	48.3
42159	OAKLAND	88.5	87.9	10.1	10.5	0.1	0.1	1.1	1.5	6.6	6.9	7.1	6.1	4.8	29.1	26.2	11.7	1.6	75.5	38.6	49.9	50.1
42160	PARK CITY	96.3	96.1	2.7	2.8	0.1	0.2	0.5	0.7	7.1	6.9	6.8	6.3	6.1	28.7	24.8	11.9	1.3	75.4	37.3	50.1	49.9
42163	ROCKY HILL	98.1	97.8	0.7	1.1	0.0	0.0	0.0	0.6	6.7	6.7	6.7	5.6	5.6	26.7	26.7	14.4	1.1	76.1	40.3	51.7	48.3
42164	SCOTTSVILLE	97.6	97.4	1.3	1.3	0.1	0.2	0.8	1.0	6.8	6.8	7.1	6.3	6.4	28.1	24.4	12.5	1.7	75.5	37.3	49.3	50.7
42166	SUMMER SHADE	98.2	98.1	1.0	1.0	0.0	0.0	0.9	1.1	5.5	5.9	7.1	5.6	5.7	28.8	27.0	13.0	1.4	77.9	40.2	50.2	49.8
42167	TOMPKINSVILLE	95.2	95.2	3.3	3.3	0.1	0.0	1.3	1.3	6.5	6.4	6.5	5.6	6.4	27.2	25.5	13.9	2.0	77.2	39.1	48.9	51.1
42170	WOODBURN	94.0	93.6	4.6	4.8	0.5	0.6	0.7	1.0	6.9	7.1	6.7	5.7	5.4	28.5	26.7	11.3	1.8	75.5	39.0	50.8	49.2
42171	SMITHS GROVE	94.7	94.3	3.8	4.0	0.1	0.1	0.8	1.1	7.0	7.0	7.0	6.3	6.1	29.3	25.3	10.9	1.2	75.1	36.8	49.3	50.7
42202	ADAIRVILLE	88.1	88.1	10.0	10.0	0.0	0.0	2.4	2.4	6.5	6.7	7.2	5.9	6.0	28.7	25.0	12.3	1.7	76.2	37.9	49.6	50.4
42204	ALLENSVILLE	82.8	83.0	14.8	14.7	0.2	0.2	1.9	1.9	8.7	8.4	8.4	6.9	6.2	27.3	21.3	11.2	1.8	70.3	34.3	49.3	50.7
	KENTUCKY	90.1	89.5	7.3	7.4	0.8	1.0	1.5	1.9	6.6	6.6	6.8	6.6	7.0	28.9	24.8	11.1	1.5	76.3	36.8	49.1	50.9
	UNITED STATES	75.1	73.6	12.3	12.5	3.8	4.2	12.5	14.1	6.9	6.7	7.2	7.0	7.3	28.6	23.8	10.8	1.7	75.1	36.0	49.1	50.9

ZIP CODE #	POST OFFICE NAME	2004 Per Capita Income	2004 HH Income Base	2004 HOUSEHOLD INCOME DISTRIBUTION (%) Less than $25,000	$25,000 to $49,999	$50,000 to $99,999	$100,000 to $149,999	$150,000 or More	MEDIAN HOUSEHOLD INCOME 2004	2009	2004 National Centile	2004 State Centile	2004 Home Value Base	2004 HOME VALUE DISTRIBUTION (%) Less than $50,000	$50,000 to $89,999	$90,000 to $174,999	$175,000 to $399,999	$400,000 or More	2004 Median Home Value
41828	KITE	11215	394	55.3	28.2	12.4	4.1	0.0	21682	25307	2	18	324	67.0	24.1	9.0	0.0	0.0	40351
41831	LEBURN	15107	473	51.0	28.1	15.0	3.4	2.5	24134	29240	4	24	382	59.2	24.9	12.3	3.7	0.0	39318
41832	LETCHER	15134	185	41.1	34.6	22.2	1.1	1.1	29826	37101	12	43	155	40.7	38.1	20.0	1.3	0.0	60750
41833	LINEFORK	10695	117	60.7	20.5	18.0	0.9	0.0	19025	22030	2	8	94	71.3	14.9	11.7	2.1	0.0	28824
41834	LITTCARR	16588	215	55.4	18.6	17.7	6.5	1.9	21010	26118	2	15	174	46.0	32.8	18.4	1.2	1.7	53684
41835	MC ROBERTS	12168	160	60.6	26.3	7.5	5.0	0.6	21314	24273	2	16	143	60.8	32.2	7.0	0.0	0.0	39750
41836	MALLIE	16634	347	52.2	25.9	15.0	4.3	2.6	23171	27951	3	22	259	52.1	26.6	16.6	3.5	1.2	48103
41837	MAYKING	15605	263	45.6	20.5	25.5	4.9	3.4	27526	33711	8	36	208	63.9	20.7	10.6	3.4	1.4	41944
41838	MILLSTONE	11748	288	62.2	22.2	14.2	1.0	0.4	18911	22233	1	8	226	59.3	31.4	6.6	0.4	2.2	40000
41839	MOUSIE	11865	502	55.8	24.5	17.5	2.2	0.0	20516	24459	2	13	397	59.7	25.4	10.8	4.0	0.0	35167
41840	NEON	12877	850	54.9	24.8	17.8	2.1	0.4	22420	26279	3	20	704	65.2	29.6	4.7	0.1	0.4	37593
41843	PINE TOP	11693	441	58.3	26.1	11.8	3.9	0.0	19370	23018	2	9	350	59.7	28.6	9.4	1.7	0.6	44333
41844	PIPPA PASSES	11307	112	55.4	27.7	12.5	4.5	0.0	21458	26692	2	17	90	64.4	24.4	11.1	0.0	0.0	41333
41845	PREMIUM	12820	161	54.0	29.8	14.9	1.2	0.0	22062	25486	3	19	131	71.0	22.1	6.9	0.0	0.0	34821
41847	REDFOX	12669	372	49.7	32.3	13.7	4.3	0.0	25131	29228	5	26	299	60.9	22.1	16.4	0.7	0.0	37155
41849	SECO	13121	68	61.8	23.5	14.7	0.0	0.0	18641	22251	1	7	52	59.6	30.8	5.8	0.0	3.9	38750
41855	THORNTON	12678	324	59.0	25.3	9.9	3.4	2.5	20804	23829	2	13	273	61.5	26.7	8.4	2.9	0.4	41711
41858	WHITESBURG	16427	3873	51.0	23.8	19.7	3.6	1.9	24336	29866	4	24	3042	51.8	28.8	15.5	3.0	1.0	47932
41859	DEMA	11727	135	56.3	28.2	11.9	3.7	0.0	21256	26104	2	16	111	67.6	23.4	9.0	0.0	0.0	40714
41861	RAVEN	12139	46	58.7	21.7	15.2	4.4	0.0	20830	25000	2	14	37	59.5	27.0	8.1	5.4	0.0	41250
41862	TOPMOST	12416	395	50.1	23.8	26.1	0.0	0.0	24920	29903	5	25	319	63.3	28.5	8.2	0.0	0.0	37404
42001	PADUCAH	29101	12446	28.3	25.3	30.4	9.5	6.6	45457	59429	62	84	8654	16.6	24.2	38.8	17.7	2.8	106870
42003	PADUCAH	20497	12568	36.9	28.9	25.2	6.8	2.2	34556	43143	26	59	8441	31.0	24.5	33.5	10.6	0.5	80582
42020	ALMO	19896	792	31.9	35.0	26.4	4.4	2.3	36900	45517	35	65	639	29.0	33.0	29.7	7.5	0.8	74205
42021	ARLINGTON	19329	723	35.8	32.1	24.8	5.4	1.9	34834	40604	27	60	582	47.8	27.7	19.2	4.5	0.9	52031
42023	BARDWELL	20300	927	38.8	38.3	15.6	4.8	2.5	30467	34666	13	45	737	44.6	34.9	16.3	3.7	0.5	55130
42024	BARLOW	19842	662	33.5	36.6	24.0	4.4	1.5	34234	42453	25	58	543	42.0	28.4	19.9	7.6	2.2	58365
42025	BENTON	21472	7942	28.4	29.4	32.7	7.3	2.2	42004	52051	53	79	6502	18.9	28.4	38.1	13.5	1.1	93446
42027	BOAZ	22246	847	27.9	28.1	32.0	8.4	3.7	44609	54977	60	83	722	24.8	27.4	34.6	12.5	0.7	85152
42028	BURNA	17201	346	36.4	32.7	26.6	3.5	0.9	33274	40096	22	54	293	44.4	30.4	18.8	4.8	1.7	55323
42029	CALVERT CITY	24564	2258	25.4	29.2	33.0	9.3	3.2	44100	56238	59	82	1770	25.4	32.4	32.2	10.1	0.0	80417
42031	CLINTON	20303	1702	38.2	29.3	25.1	4.7	2.8	35304	41872	29	61	1369	43.4	34.6	16.6	4.3	1.1	57542
42032	COLUMBUS	18536	141	33.3	38.3	19.9	8.5	0.0	35620	42462	30	62	121	58.7	18.2	15.7	2.5	5.0	41250
42035	CUNNINGHAM	18420	686	25.1	43.2	22.3	7.3	2.2	37148	44471	36	66	592	29.9	35.5	28.0	6.6	0.0	74324
42036	DEXTER	18457	447	36.7	30.7	26.0	3.6	3.1	34739	42370	26	60	378	37.6	33.6	15.9	10.3	2.7	62973
42038	EDDYVILLE	18028	1822	34.4	29.4	28.1	6.9	1.3	36153	45105	32	63	1438	21.2	29.1	33.0	15.3	1.4	89658
42039	FANCY FARM	18671	574	32.8	31.7	28.8	4.9	1.9	38452	46692	41	70	472	30.7	30.7	30.7	7.2	0.6	76765
42040	FARMINGTON	21165	470	27.0	30.6	33.0	7.2	2.1	41293	50831	51	77	401	25.9	33.2	33.7	6.0	1.3	80641
42041	FULTON	20097	2405	38.8	27.6	26.0	4.5	3.2	32846	41213	20	53	1726	42.9	30.2	21.7	4.8	0.4	56989
42044	GILBERTSVILLE	26769	1425	25.5	27.6	32.5	9.8	4.6	46981	59385	66	86	1224	12.9	21.3	40.0	24.0	1.7	117901
42045	GRAND RIVERS	20652	1046	28.8	33.5	29.9	6.2	1.6	36634	45749	34	64	881	35.2	28.6	26.8	7.2	2.3	68851
42047	HAMPTON	16469	106	36.8	33.0	25.5	2.8	1.9	32793	38058	20	52	90	44.4	27.8	21.1	4.4	2.2	56250
42048	HARDIN	17126	1163	42.3	29.3	23.4	4.0	1.0	28882	35093	10	40	941	27.1	25.6	32.7	13.8	0.7	85678
42049	HAZEL	20863	801	31.2	35.7	26.0	4.6	2.5	34963	43198	27	60	669	25.4	30.0	29.9	13.2	1.5	82981
42050	HICKMAN	14323	1305	49.7	33.3	14.8	1.6	0.7	25222	29526	5	27	861	53.1	32.8	10.9	2.9	0.4	48185
42051	HICKORY	21084	1083	31.7	31.0	26.4	8.4	2.5	39444	47817	44	72	921	28.3	34.1	28.6	8.6	0.4	73750
42053	KEVIL	22301	1933	23.4	30.5	35.5	7.8	2.8	45413	56783	62	84	1631	24.5	33.7	29.4	10.7	1.7	81656
42054	KIRKSEY	20099	505	20.8	37.4	32.5	5.7	3.6	42959	52267	56	81	440	28.0	22.1	36.8	11.1	2.1	90000
42055	KUTTAWA	21793	1087	31.3	28.9	28.6	8.6	2.7	40355	49188	47	74	932	26.9	31.7	26.0	13.5	1.9	79344
42056	LA CENTER	19961	917	33.0	27.8	30.0	7.7	1.4	38423	47475	41	70	724	39.2	30.4	22.9	7.3	0.1	67429
42058	LEDBETTER	20772	928	25.7	33.2	31.6	7.0	2.6	42825	51578	55	81	784	18.9	53.7	21.9	4.6	0.9	75042
42064	MARION	18081	3580	37.7	30.4	25.7	4.6	1.7	33319	40365	22	55	2851	41.0	31.9	21.7	5.2	0.2	57596
42066	MAYFIELD	19981	9278	39.2	28.1	23.9	6.5	2.4	33433	41166	22	55	6637	28.2	34.8	30.1	6.4	0.6	75036
42069	MELBER	20893	444	28.4	34.2	24.3	11.7	1.4	40812	48929	49	75	382	21.7	36.4	25.9	15.5	0.5	81389
42071	MURRAY	21417	11143	36.3	30.0	23.9	7.1	2.8	34105	41922	24	57	7098	18.0	26.1	41.7	12.6	1.7	97160
42076	NEW CONCORD	16546	451	41.2	39.0	14.6	4.9	0.2	28037	33272	9	37	385	47.5	22.9	17.7	10.4	1.6	52436
42078	SALEM	19678	768	34.1	32.0	27.7	4.3	1.8	34623	42241	26	59	648	45.1	33.5	16.5	4.6	0.3	54156
42079	SEDALIA	19740	497	31.8	26.8	33.2	4.6	3.6	38505	46929	41	70	427	35.4	27.6	25.5	7.3	4.2	70179
42081	SMITHLAND	22829	794	34.1	31.9	27.0	4.9	2.1	34902	43977	27	60	674	32.8	38.0	19.4	5.6	4.2	70976
42082	SYMSONIA	22246	767	32.7	30.8	24.4	8.7	3.4	40402	48637	48	74	656	27.3	30.8	31.4	10.5	0.0	80862
42083	TILINE	19187	114	30.7	25.4	33.3	10.5	0.0	35000	46580	28	61	104	25.0	31.7	29.8	9.6	3.9	77778
42085	WATER VALLEY	16478	262	42.0	29.8	24.8	2.7	0.8	32347	40207	19	51	218	36.2	35.8	20.2	7.8	0.0	56818
42086	WEST PADUCAH	21052	1669	24.3	32.9	32.1	9.9	0.9	43195	53562	56	81	1419	29.3	24.8	31.6	12.7	1.6	81901
42087	WICKLIFFE	28557	1065	32.8	26.8	30.4	5.8	4.2	39143	48858	43	72	893	38.3	31.1	17.7	10.9	2.0	63952
42088	WINGO	22420	1037	28.9	28.2	32.5	6.9	3.6	43507	53462	57	82	876	32.0	36.9	26.1	4.2	0.8	70957
42101	BOWLING GREEN	18694	18481	37.5	30.1	25.0	4.9	2.6	33133	42095	21	53	10536	22.2	26.5	42.9	7.2	1.3	91466
42103	BOWLING GREEN	31873	7164	20.9	23.7	34.4	12.8	8.3	55466	69934	80	93	5311	9.4	6.3	44.7	34.3	5.3	153277
42104	BOWLING GREEN	28875	9276	20.9	26.9	33.7	13.6	4.9	52191	65578	76	91	6470	4.7	8.5	54.0	30.4	2.5	144167
42120	ADOLPHUS	14857	847	31.9	39.0	26.9	1.8	0.5	34846	41265	27	60	702	38.3	33.3	22.4	5.6	0.4	61081
42122	ALVATON	29805	1118	14.5	26.3	40.3	14.0	4.9	57715	71485	82	94	995	8.5	14.4	54.5	20.1	2.5	121097
42123	AUSTIN	22197	290	29.0	35.2	25.5	4.5	5.9	38889	47216	42	71	240	21.7	33.8	40.4	3.3	0.8	85667
42124	BEAUMONT	14317	55	45.5	30.9	20.0	3.6	0.0	29062	40000	10	41	47	42.6	40.4	17.0	0.0	0.0	55000
42127	CAVE CITY	19820	2212	39.2	29.9	22.9	4.6	3.4	32601	38993	20	52	1689	27.1	34.3	31.9	5.1	1.7	76051
42129	EDMONTON	15829	2700	46.4	30.2	19.0	2.7	1.7	27158	32738	7	35	2140	44.4	29.3	19.1	6.9	0.3	57532
42130	EIGHTY EIGHT	19230	50	28.0	38.0	32.0	2.0	0.0	37799	45757	39	68	42	26.2	35.7	31.0	7.1	0.0	76000
42131	ETOILE	23294	39	30.8	35.9	25.6	2.6	5.1	37321	47372	37	67	32	25.0	34.4	34.4	6.3	0.0	82500
42133	FOUNTAIN RUN	20602	608	40.1	32.4	21.4	2.5	3.6	31531	38369	16	48	497	35.6	31.8	24.6	7.7	0.4	64875
42134	FRANKLIN	20153	6484	27.8	32.3	32.1	6.2	1.6	41083	48565	50	76	4899	14.3	30.1	40.7	13.4	1.6	96141
42140	GAMALIEL	14906	523	46.1	32.9	17.8	1.7	1.5	26672	32016	7	33	426	33.6	46.5	14.8	5.2	0.0	63934
42141	GLASGOW	21279	11655	33.6	30.7	27.8	5.1	2.8	37136	45038	36	66	8427	17.5	31.2	38.8	10.8	1.8	91541
42151	HESTAND	12565	124	51.6	28.2	16.9	3.2	0.0	24194	29272	4	24	88	29.6	29.6	29.6	6.8	4.6	80000
42153	HOLLAND	16387	176	36.9	35.2	22.7	4.6	0.6	32529	38642	19	51	147	30.6	28.6	27.2	12.2	1.4	76563
42154	KNOB LICK	17845	346	39.0	28.9	25.1	4.9	2.0	32017	38800	18	50	278	31.3	30.2	33.5	4.7	0.4	72941
42156	LUCAS	21222	128	28.9	35.9	26.6	4.7	3.9	38179	45323	40	69	106	17.9	37.7	39.6	2.8	1.9	85385
42157	MOUNT HERMON	13368	164	45.7	33.5	17.1	2.4	1.2	28337	35000	9	38	134	37.3	24.6	24.6	10.5	3.0	65000
42159	OAKLAND	25386	635	22.1	24.6	37.6	10.2	5.5	53420	66375	78	92	549	8.4	28.6	44.1	15.7	3.3	102131
42160	PARK CITY	17079	1012	36.1	32.8	25.1	4.6	1.4	32453	38326	19	51	808	26.0	35.0	30.6	7.1	1.4	75758
42163	ROCKY HILL	20801	82	35.4	26.8	26.8	6.1	4.9	31993	36696	18	49	70	25.7	27.1	37.1	10.0	0.0	85000
42164	SCOTTSVILLE	17706	5968	35.1	30.9	27.9	3.9	2.2	35674	42084	30	62	4757	26.6	31.5	30.5	10.4	1.0	79047
42166	SUMMER SHADE	16318	950	42.3	30.6	22.2	4.0	0.8	29124	34882	11	41	804	33.3	33.8	26.2	6.1	0.5	68056
42167	TOMPKINSVILLE	18591	3653	49.1	28.7	17.3	2.1	2.9	25501	30603	5	29	2803	39.0	26.1	27.9	5.9	1.1	67679
42170	WOODBURN	24494	521	19.6	30.5	35.3	10.2	4.4	49918	60899	72	88	453	16.1	14.4	44.2	23.4	2.0	118134
42171	SMITHS GROVE	19025	2253	29.6	32.2	30.0	6.1	2.2	38543	47083	41	71	1931	21.0	27.7	39.7	10.2	1.5	91932
42202	ADAIRVILLE	19797	992	28.8	32.7	31.9	4.6	2.0	40260	47237	47	74	782	30.1	30.4	25.2	9.7	4.6	77143
42204	ALLENSVILLE	20225	265	29.1	31.7	32.1	4.5	2.6	41801	48312	52	78	207	30.4	25.1	29.5	8.2	6.8	84250
	KENTUCKY	22472		31.8	28.3	28.2	7.8	3.9	39962	49361				22.2	24.9	36.4	14.3	2.1	94344
	UNITED STATES	25866		24.7	27.1	30.8	10.9	6.5	48124	56710				10.9	15.0	33.7	30.1	10.4	145905

SPENDING POTENTIAL INDICES KENTUCKY
41828-42204 D

ZIP CODE #	POST OFFICE NAME	FINANCIAL SERVICES: Auto Loan	Home Loan	Invest-ments	Retire-ment Plans	THE HOME: Home Improvements: Home Repair	Lawn & Garden	Furnishings: Comput-ers & Hard-ware	Major Appli-ances	TV, Radio, Sound Equip-ment	Furni-ture	ENTERTAINMENT: Dine out/ Carry out	Sports Equip-ment	Fees & Tickets	Toys & Games	Travel	Cable TV	PERSONAL: Apparel & Services	Auto Repairs	Health Insur-ance	Pets & Supplies
41828	KITE	57	38	17	33	44	50	37	46	45	38	53	55	32	50	38	48	48	46	57	66
41831	LEBURN	70	47	21	41	53	62	46	57	55	46	65	68	39	61	46	59	59	56	70	81
41832	LETCHER	64	45	25	41	50	59	47	55	54	46	64	64	41	60	47	58	58	55	67	72
41833	LINEFORK	52	35	16	30	39	45	33	42	40	34	47	50	28	45	34	43	43	41	51	59
41834	LITTCARR	59	44	29	42	48	58	49	54	55	46	65	60	44	61	48	58	59	54	65	65
41835	MC ROBERTS	57	38	17	33	43	49	37	46	44	37	52	55	31	49	37	48	47	45	56	65
41836	MALLIE	64	46	27	42	51	60	48	56	56	47	65	64	42	62	48	59	60	56	68	72
41837	MAYKING	82	55	25	47	62	71	53	66	64	54	75	79	45	71	54	69	68	65	81	94
41838	MILLSTONE	53	35	16	31	40	46	34	43	41	35	48	51	29	46	35	44	44	42	53	61
41839	MOUSIE	56	37	17	32	42	49	36	45	43	37	51	54	31	48	37	47	46	44	55	64
41840	NEON	56	39	20	34	43	51	39	47	46	39	54	55	33	51	39	49	49	46	57	64
41843	PINE TOP	53	35	16	31	40	46	34	43	41	35	48	51	29	46	35	44	44	42	53	61
41844	PIPPA PASSES	60	41	20	36	46	54	41	50	49	41	57	59	35	54	41	52	52	49	61	68
41845	PREMIUM	53	35	16	31	40	46	34	43	41	35	48	51	29	46	35	44	44	42	53	61
41847	REDFOX	59	39	18	34	44	51	38	47	46	39	54	57	32	51	39	49	49	47	58	67
41849	SECO	53	36	16	31	41	47	35	43	42	35	49	52	29	46	35	45	44	43	53	61
41855	THORNTON	60	40	18	35	45	52	39	48	47	39	55	58	33	52	39	50	50	48	60	69
41858	WHITESBURG	72	49	24	43	55	64	49	60	58	49	68	70	42	64	49	62	62	59	73	82
41859	DEMA	57	38	17	33	43	50	37	46	45	38	52	55	31	50	38	48	48	46	57	66
41861	RAVEN	57	38	17	33	43	50	37	46	45	38	52	55	31	49	38	48	48	46	57	66
41862	TOPMOST	61	41	19	35	47	54	40	50	48	40	56	59	34	53	40	52	51	49	61	70
42001	PADUCAH	91	92	94	89	93	101	91	93	92	90	114	106	92	114	92	94	110	92	96	105
42003	PADUCAH	71	63	57	60	65	72	64	67	68	63	82	78	61	81	64	70	79	67	73	81
42020	ALMO	86	64	41	58	70	78	63	73	72	63	86	88	57	83	64	75	80	73	85	99
42021	ARLINGTON	85	57	26	49	65	74	55	69	66	56	78	82	47	74	56	72	71	68	85	98
42023	BARDWELL	80	56	31	51	63	74	58	68	68	57	80	79	51	75	58	72	72	68	83	90
42024	BARLOW	71	60	47	60	63	72	62	66	66	61	80	76	59	79	62	67	75	65	72	78
42025	BENTON	83	70	52	66	75	83	67	75	73	67	88	88	64	88	69	75	83	74	84	96
42027	BOAZ	89	76	54	71	81	88	70	80	76	70	92	95	67	93	72	79	87	78	88	104
42028	BURNA	78	53	25	47	61	69	51	64	61	52	72	77	44	69	53	65	65	63	78	90
42029	CALVERT CITY	93	80	61	78	85	94	79	86	84	78	102	100	76	102	80	86	96	84	94	107
42031	CLINTON	83	60	35	55	66	76	60	70	69	60	81	83	53	78	60	72	75	69	83	94
42032	COLUMBUS	83	56	25	48	63	73	54	67	65	55	76	80	46	72	55	70	69	67	83	95
42035	CUNNINGHAM	90	60	28	52	68	79	58	73	70	59	82	87	50	78	59	75	75	72	89	103
42036	DEXTER	90	61	27	52	69	79	58	73	71	60	83	87	50	78	59	76	75	72	90	104
42038	EDDYVILLE	61	48	32	45	53	61	49	56	55	47	65	64	44	62	50	58	59	55	66	71
42039	FANCY FARM	85	61	32	54	68	77	58	71	68	59	81	84	51	77	59	73	74	70	85	99
42040	FARMINGTON	87	68	44	64	74	83	66	76	74	66	89	89	61	87	67	77	82	75	87	99
42041	FULTON	76	58	41	53	63	72	60	67	67	59	81	78	54	78	60	71	75	67	78	86
42044	GILBERTSVILLE	100	80	55	73	89	100	76	90	85	75	101	105	69	100	80	90	94	88	105	121
42045	GRAND RIVERS	87	63	34	56	70	79	60	72	70	61	83	86	53	80	61	74	76	71	86	100
42047	HAMPTON	77	53	26	48	60	69	51	64	60	51	71	77	44	68	53	64	65	63	77	90
42048	HARDIN	68	52	33	47	57	65	50	59	57	50	68	70	45	66	52	60	63	59	70	79
42049	HAZEL	83	64	43	62	70	79	65	73	72	64	86	85	60	84	65	75	80	72	83	93
42050	HICKMAN	57	41	28	37	45	53	43	49	50	43	60	56	39	55	43	54	55	50	60	64
42051	HICKORY	98	69	36	61	77	88	66	81	78	67	92	97	58	88	68	83	84	80	97	113
42053	KEVIL	91	76	53	71	81	89	71	81	77	71	93	96	67	94	73	80	88	79	90	107
42054	KIRKSEY	87	78	59	74	82	88	72	79	76	72	93	95	70	95	74	78	88	77	86	103
42055	KUTTAWA	81	69	55	65	75	85	66	76	72	67	87	84	63	82	70	76	82	74	87	94
42056	LA CENTER	80	62	41	59	68	78	64	72	71	62	84	83	58	82	64	74	77	71	84	91
42058	LEDBETTER	83	73	55	69	77	83	67	75	72	67	87	89	66	89	69	74	83	73	81	97
42064	MARION	77	55	30	49	61	70	55	65	64	54	75	76	48	71	55	68	68	64	79	88
42066	MAYFIELD	80	61	42	57	67	76	63	71	70	62	84	82	57	81	63	74	78	70	82	90
42069	MELBER	95	67	36	63	78	87	66	81	76	65	89	98	57	88	68	80	82	80	96	113
42071	MURRAY	73	60	57	60	62	70	69	68	71	66	87	82	64	85	66	70	83	71	71	82
42076	NEW CONCORD	69	46	21	40	52	60	44	56	54	45	63	66	38	59	45	58	57	55	68	79
42078	SALEM	81	56	29	50	63	74	57	68	67	57	79	80	49	74	57	72	72	68	83	92
42079	SEDALIA	89	68	42	63	75	83	65	77	73	65	87	92	59	86	67	77	81	75	89	104
42081	SMITHLAND	104	71	34	62	80	92	68	85	81	69	96	102	58	91	70	87	87	84	104	120
42082	SYMSONIA	93	66	34	58	74	84	63	77	74	64	88	92	55	84	64	79	81	76	93	108
42083	TILINE	88	59	27	51	67	77	57	71	69	58	81	85	48	76	58	74	73	70	88	101
42085	WATER VALLEY	73	49	22	42	55	63	47	59	57	48	67	70	40	63	48	61	61	58	72	83
42086	WEST PADUCAH	88	71	48	66	76	84	67	77	74	68	89	91	63	88	68	77	83	75	86	102
42087	WICKLIFFE	117	92	60	86	99	111	90	102	100	90	119	120	83	117	91	104	111	101	117	133
42088	WINGO	94	78	55	73	84	92	73	83	80	74	97	100	70	97	75	83	91	82	93	110
42101	BOWLING GREEN	70	59	56	59	60	67	66	65	68	64	84	79	62	81	63	67	80	68	68	78
42103	BOWLING GREEN	104	113	118	113	114	119	106	108	103	107	129	126	110	131	109	103	127	107	105	123
42104	BOWLING GREEN	100	102	104	105	101	104	100	100	97	101	122	117	101	121	99	94	119	100	94	113
42120	ADOLPHUS	74	50	23	43	56	65	48	60	58	49	68	72	41	64	49	63	62	60	74	85
42122	ALVATON	116	118	106	116	120	124	108	113	107	108	132	134	109	137	110	107	129	110	113	137
42123	AUSTIN	103	69	31	59	78	90	66	83	80	68	94	99	56	89	67	86	85	82	102	118
42124	BEAUMONT	67	45	20	39	51	59	43	54	52	44	62	65	37	58	44	56	56	54	67	77
42127	CAVE CITY	87	61	31	53	68	78	58	72	69	59	82	86	51	78	60	74	75	71	87	101
42129	EDMONTON	70	48	23	42	54	62	47	58	56	47	66	68	40	62	48	60	60	57	71	80
42130	EIGHTY EIGHT	68	60	46	57	64	68	56	62	59	56	72	74	55	74	57	61	68	60	67	80
42131	ETOILE	102	69	31	59	78	89	66	83	80	67	94	99	56	89	67	86	85	82	102	117
42133	FOUNTAIN RUN	90	60	27	52	68	78	58	73	70	59	82	87	49	78	59	75	75	72	89	103
42134	FRANKLIN	82	67	49	64	72	80	66	73	72	66	87	86	62	86	67	74	81	72	82	93
42140	GAMALIEL	69	46	21	40	52	60	45	56	54	46	63	67	38	60	45	58	58	55	69	79
42141	GLASGOW	83	67	49	63	71	80	67	74	74	66	89	87	63	87	68	77	83	74	84	94
42151	HESTAND	61	41	18	35	46	53	39	49	47	40	56	59	33	53	40	51	51	49	61	70
42153	HOLLAND	76	51	23	44	57	66	49	61	59	50	69	73	42	65	50	63	63	60	75	87
42154	KNOB LICK	78	54	27	48	61	71	54	65	64	54	75	77	47	71	55	69	68	65	80	89
42156	LUCAS	99	66	30	57	75	86	64	80	77	65	91	96	54	86	65	83	82	79	99	114
42157	MOUNT HERMON	63	42	19	37	48	55	41	51	49	42	58	61	35	55	42	53	53	51	63	73
42159	OAKLAND	104	92	70	88	97	104	85	94	90	85	110	113	84	112	88	93	105	92	102	122
42160	PARK CITY	79	53	24	46	60	69	51	64	62	52	73	77	44	69	52	67	66	63	79	91
42163	ROCKY HILL	86	58	26	50	65	75	56	70	67	57	79	83	47	74	57	72	72	69	86	99
42164	SCOTTSVILLE	77	58	36	53	64	71	57	66	64	57	77	78	51	74	57	67	71	65	77	88
42166	SUMMER SHADE	74	50	23	43	57	65	48	60	58	49	68	72	41	65	49	62	62	60	74	85
42167	TOMPKINSVILLE	83	56	27	49	64	74	56	68	66	56	78	81	48	74	56	71	71	68	84	95
42170	WOODBURN	104	92	71	88	97	105	87	96	92	87	112	113	85	114	89	95	107	93	104	121
42171	SMITHS GROVE	84	68	46	63	73	80	64	74	71	65	85	87	60	83	65	73	80	73	82	97
42202	ADAIRVILLE	83	65	42	60	71	79	61	72	69	62	83	86	57	82	63	72	77	70	82	97
42204	ALLENSVILLE	93	67	37	62	76	85	65	79	75	65	88	94	57	86	67	79	81	77	93	109
	KENTUCKY	86	74	63	71	77	85	74	80	79	74	96	94	71	95	74	81	91	80	86	98
	UNITED STATES	100	100	100	100	100	100	100	100	100	100	100	100	100	100	100	100	100	100	100	100

ZIP CODE		COUNTY FIPS CODE	POPULATION			2000-2004 ANNUAL RATE		HOUSEHOLDS					FAMILIES		
#	POST OFFICE NAME		2000	2004	2009	% Rate	State Centile	2000	2004	2009	% Annual Rate 2000-2004	2004 Average HH Size	2000	2004	% Annual Rate 2000-2004
42206	AUBURN	141	4752	4844	4874	0.5	59	1742	1806	1838	0.9	2.64	1335	1351	0.3
42207	BEE SPRING	061	1347	1326	1349	-0.4	23	556	563	587	0.3	2.36	415	409	-0.3
42210	BROWNSVILLE	061	3732	3814	3919	0.5	62	1490	1562	1645	1.1	2.38	1080	1099	0.4
42211	CADIZ	221	11757	12049	12327	0.6	64	4889	5109	5312	1.0	2.34	3511	3562	0.3
42214	CENTER	169	807	821	840	0.4	58	299	309	322	0.8	2.65	228	230	0.2
42215	CERULEAN	047	1319	1307	1304	-0.2	30	510	517	524	0.3	2.51	405	401	-0.2
42217	CROFTON	047	3661	3580	3537	-0.5	18	1410	1411	1414	0.0	2.50	1077	1046	-0.7
42220	ELKTON	219	6191	6235	6235	0.2	48	2416	2475	2512	0.6	2.48	1810	1805	-0.1
42232	GRACEY	047	635	659	668	0.9	72	242	257	264	1.4	2.56	191	197	0.7
42234	GUTHRIE	219	2457	2395	2358	-0.6	16	891	880	877	-0.3	2.70	618	591	-1.1
42236	HERNDON	047	817	854	868	1.1	77	305	325	334	1.5	2.63	231	239	0.8
42240	HOPKINSVILLE	047	40353	39784	39638	-0.3	25	15956	16070	16222	0.2	2.40	11057	10756	-0.7
42252	JETSON	031	288	294	301	0.5	61	110	115	120	1.1	2.56	84	86	0.6
42254	LA FAYETTE	047	279	287	289	0.7	67	112	117	119	1.0	2.45	84	85	0.3
42256	LEWISBURG	141	4755	4741	4753	-0.1	35	1956	1991	2024	0.4	2.38	1402	1385	-0.3
42257	LINDSEYVILLE	061	17	17	17	0.0	41	8	8	8	0.0	2.13	6	6	0.0
42259	MAMMOTH CAVE	061	1095	1145	1190	1.1	77	422	452	481	1.6	2.42	315	329	1.0
42261	MORGANTOWN	031	10217	10477	10753	0.6	64	3963	4152	4339	1.1	2.47	2884	2938	0.4
42262	OAK GROVE	047	7827	8607	8998	2.3	92	2808	3116	3277	2.5	2.76	2026	2174	1.7
42265	OLMSTEAD	141	1026	1088	1120	1.4	83	388	421	439	1.9	2.56	288	304	1.3
42266	PEMBROKE	047	2297	2258	2241	-0.4	22	809	808	809	0.0	2.71	605	584	-0.8
42273	ROCHESTER	031	533	599	645	2.8	95	213	244	266	3.3	2.45	158	175	2.4
42274	ROCKFIELD	227	1742	1981	2171	3.1	95	636	741	827	3.7	2.66	488	552	2.9
42275	ROUNDHILL	031	929	955	982	0.7	66	355	374	392	1.2	2.55	265	272	0.6
42276	RUSSELLVILLE	141	15029	14866	14795	-0.3	28	6000	6059	6111	0.2	2.42	4264	4175	-0.5
42280	SHARON GROVE	219	662	650	641	-0.4	22	259	258	258	-0.1	2.52	196	190	-0.7
42285	SWEEDEN	061	577	566	575	-0.5	21	238	239	249	0.1	2.37	182	179	-0.4
42286	TRENTON	219	1492	1521	1533	0.5	59	563	581	592	0.7	2.61	414	415	0.1
42287	WELCHS CREEK	031	484	493	504	0.4	59	197	205	213	0.9	2.40	152	155	0.5
42301	OWENSBORO	059	40535	42162	43953	0.9	73	16358	17406	18537	1.5	2.35	10877	11162	0.6
42303	OWENSBORO	059	35700	36678	38104	0.6	66	14260	14912	15790	1.1	2.37	9552	9680	0.3
42320	BEAVER DAM	183	7168	7370	7606	0.7	67	2814	2948	3100	1.1	2.47	2071	2114	0.5
42321	BEECH CREEK	177	269	252	244	-1.5	1	109	106	105	-0.7	2.38	82	77	-1.5
42323	BEECHMONT	177	1103	1046	1015	-1.2	3	439	429	427	-0.5	2.44	340	325	-1.1
42324	BELTON	177	1266	1280	1283	0.3	52	494	519	536	1.2	2.47	375	384	0.6
42325	BREMEN	177	2388	2561	2625	1.7	86	948	1040	1092	2.2	2.46	732	784	1.6
42326	BROWDER	177	285	274	268	-0.9	8	122	121	122	-0.2	2.26	87	83	-1.1
42327	CALHOUN	149	4259	4369	4473	0.6	64	1674	1752	1830	1.1	2.43	1241	1264	0.4
42328	CENTERTOWN	183	1666	1643	1664	-0.3	25	633	639	661	0.2	2.57	499	493	-0.3
42330	CENTRAL CITY	177	9778	9744	9678	-0.1	34	3574	3628	3680	0.4	2.42	2556	2521	-0.3
42333	CROMWELL	183	757	768	781	0.3	54	275	286	297	0.9	2.67	213	216	0.3
42337	DRAKESBORO	177	2174	2081	2027	-1.0	7	866	853	851	-0.4	2.44	641	614	-1.0
42338	DUNDEE	183	284	324	350	3.2	96	114	133	147	3.7	2.44	86	96	2.6
42339	DUNMOR	177	825	866	884	1.2	79	321	349	367	2.0	2.48	245	259	1.3
42343	FORDSVILLE	183	2282	2354	2417	0.7	68	906	957	1004	1.3	2.39	634	649	0.6
42344	GRAHAM	177	1021	965	935	-1.3	2	402	391	389	-0.7	2.47	301	284	-1.4
42345	GREENVILLE	177	11213	11033	10903	-0.4	23	4477	4521	4577	0.2	2.31	3265	3204	-0.4
42347	HARTFORD	183	5491	5579	5722	0.4	55	2174	2254	2360	0.9	2.40	1550	1560	0.2
42348	HAWESVILLE	091	4491	4599	4672	0.6	64	1680	1769	1845	1.2	2.59	1287	1322	0.6
42349	HORSE BRANCH	183	1779	1854	1921	1.0	75	679	730	775	1.7	2.53	508	531	1.1
42350	ISLAND	149	1395	1399	1410	0.1	44	588	607	627	0.8	2.30	421	422	0.1
42351	LEWISPORT	091	3975	3998	4058	0.1	47	1527	1574	1638	0.7	2.50	1159	1166	0.1
42352	LIVERMORE	149	2338	2350	2382	0.1	46	930	954	987	0.6	2.46	658	654	-0.1
42354	MC HENRY	183	330	400	447	4.6	99	123	152	173	5.1	2.63	97	118	4.7
42355	MACEO	059	2031	2149	2245	1.3	82	756	819	874	1.9	2.62	598	631	1.3
42361	OLATON	183	718	749	779	1.0	75	273	292	310	1.6	2.57	202	210	0.9
42366	PHILPOT	059	6182	6197	6347	0.1	43	2114	2176	2278	0.7	2.82	1763	1776	0.2
42367	POWDERLY	177	935	897	875	-1.0	7	378	372	371	-0.4	2.41	257	243	-1.3
42368	REYNOLDS STATION	091	981	994	1004	0.3	53	359	373	386	0.9	2.66	275	279	0.3
42369	ROCKPORT	183	572	561	568	-0.5	21	220	221	229	0.1	2.54	174	171	-0.4
42371	RUMSEY	149	634	630	634	-0.2	32	262	267	274	0.5	2.36	180	177	-0.4
42372	SACRAMENTO	149	1926	2005	2050	1.0	74	772	822	860	1.5	2.44	568	589	0.9
42376	UTICA	059	5323	5300	5430	-0.1	34	1944	1983	2076	0.5	2.67	1561	1555	-0.1
42378	WHITESVILLE	183	2908	3076	3210	1.3	82	1042	1132	1209	2.0	2.71	821	869	1.4
42404	CLAY	233	2734	2776	2785	0.4	55	1103	1143	1166	0.8	2.43	803	807	0.1
42406	CORYDON	101	3370	3304	3294	-0.5	21	1253	1260	1284	0.1	2.62	988	969	-0.5
42408	DAWSON SPRINGS	107	7030	6889	6796	-0.5	20	2780	2782	2800	0.0	2.41	2027	1968	-0.7
42409	DIXON	233	2328	2376	2385	0.5	61	917	955	974	1.0	2.41	689	699	0.3
42410	EARLINGTON	107	1984	1995	1996	0.1	46	826	850	869	0.7	2.35	555	550	-0.2
42411	FREDONIA	033	1496	1471	1442	-0.4	22	610	614	614	0.2	2.39	470	462	-0.4
42413	HANSON	107	2394	2531	2588	1.3	82	882	956	1000	1.9	2.64	720	764	1.4
42420	HENDERSON	101	36626	36998	37421	0.2	51	15065	15548	16055	0.8	2.33	10149	10132	0.0
42431	MADISONVILLE	107	27486	27112	26865	-0.3	26	11404	11508	11649	0.2	2.30	7802	7612	-0.6
42436	MANITOU	107	1083	1114	1124	0.7	67	411	433	446	1.2	2.57	344	355	0.7
42437	MORGANFIELD	225	8579	8386	8182	-0.5	18	2848	2840	2823	-0.1	2.49	2006	1938	-0.8
42441	NEBO	107	1473	1397	1361	-1.2	3	573	557	555	-0.7	2.51	443	419	-1.3
42442	NORTONVILLE	107	3138	3198	3216	0.5	59	1231	1283	1317	1.0	2.49	927	939	0.3
42445	PRINCETON	033	11424	11335	11180	-0.2	31	4737	4791	4813	0.3	2.31	3274	3207	-0.5
42450	PROVIDENCE	233	4427	4147	4008	-1.5	1	1803	1718	1685	-1.1	2.37	1286	1189	-1.8
42451	REED	101	914	954	975	1.0	76	340	363	379	1.6	2.63	274	285	0.9
42452	ROBARDS	101	2254	2240	2238	-0.2	32	823	839	856	0.5	2.67	655	650	-0.2
42453	SAINT CHARLES	107	478	507	520	1.4	84	190	207	217	2.0	2.45	153	163	1.5
42455	SEBREE	233	3512	3558	3553	0.3	53	1310	1347	1362	0.7	2.56	948	947	0.0
42456	SLAUGHTERS	233	1597	1642	1654	0.7	67	619	651	668	1.2	2.51	487	500	0.6
42458	SPOTTSVILLE	101	929	975	999	1.1	79	348	374	392	1.7	2.61	284	298	1.1
42459	STURGIS	225	4895	4795	4667	-0.5	20	1998	1999	1986	0.0	2.38	1440	1401	-0.6
42461	UNIONTOWN	225	1646	1599	1550	-0.7	13	676	675	671	0.0	2.37	487	472	-0.7
42462	WAVERLY	225	1697	1718	1709	0.3	53	626	652	665	1.0	2.58	498	506	0.4
42464	WHITE PLAINS	107	1934	2027	2066	1.1	78	722	773	803	1.6	2.62	571	596	1.0
42501	SOMERSET	199	16225	16352	16628	0.2	48	6818	7026	7287	0.7	2.26	4578	4586	0.0
42503	SOMERSET	199	19106	19823	20223	0.9	72	7503	7977	8303	1.5	2.40	5543	5719	0.7
42516	BETHELRIDGE	045	180	217	241	4.5	99	80	99	112	5.1	2.19	58	70	4.5
42518	BRONSTON	231	2979	3224	3373	1.9	89	1201	1338	1429	2.6	2.38	892	963	1.8
42519	BURNSIDE	199	3383	3569	3682	1.3	81	1403	1520	1600	1.9	2.34	989	1035	1.1
42528	DUNNVILLE	045	1538	1566	1586	0.4	59	596	621	641	1.0	2.52	421	424	0.2
	KENTUCKY					0.7					1.2	2.42			0.5
	UNITED STATES					1.2					1.3	2.58			1.1

117-A

ZIP CODE #	POST OFFICE NAME	RACE (%) White 2000	White 2004	Black 2000	Black 2004	Asian/Pacific 2000	Asian/Pacific 2004	% Hispanic Origin 2000	% Hispanic Origin 2004	2004 AGE DISTRIBUTION (%) 0-4	5-9	10-14	15-19	20-24	25-44	45-64	65-84	85+	18+	MEDIAN AGE 2004	% 2004 Males	% 2004 Females
42206	AUBURN	96.0	95.9	2.9	2.9	0.1	0.1	0.5	0.5	7.6	7.6	7.9	6.3	6.2	29.6	22.8	10.1	1.8	72.6	35.5	48.7	51.3
42207	BEE SPRING	99.3	99.2	0.0	0.0	0.2	0.2	0.7	1.0	5.5	5.7	6.0	5.0	4.9	27.2	29.3	15.1	1.4	79.8	41.9	51.3	48.7
42210	BROWNSVILLE	98.5	98.4	0.2	0.2	0.1	0.1	0.5	0.7	6.5	6.4	6.5	5.9	6.3	26.9	25.3	13.7	2.4	76.9	38.8	47.9	52.2
42211	CADIZ	88.9	88.4	9.2	9.5	0.3	0.4	0.9	1.2	5.8	6.0	6.6	5.6	4.8	25.7	27.7	16.1	1.7	78.2	42.0	49.6	50.4
42214	CENTER	97.7	97.6	1.1	1.1	0.0	0.0	1.0	1.2	7.4	7.6	6.9	5.7	6.3	27.0	25.8	11.9	1.2	74.5	36.8	50.1	49.9
42215	CERULEAN	87.6	87.3	11.1	11.3	0.3	0.4	0.7	0.8	6.6	6.9	7.4	6.1	5.4	28.3	26.6	11.8	0.9	75.1	38.7	49.3	50.7
42217	CROFTON	94.2	93.7	4.3	4.6	0.2	0.2	0.4	0.6	6.7	6.8	6.7	6.0	5.5	28.7	26.4	12.0	1.2	75.7	38.3	49.7	50.3
42220	ELKTON	93.4	93.2	5.1	5.3	0.1	0.1	1.6	1.6	7.0	6.7	6.9	6.1	6.0	28.1	25.0	12.4	1.8	75.7	37.7	49.2	50.8
42232	GRACEY	91.8	91.2	6.3	6.5	0.5	0.6	0.9	1.2	6.1	6.5	6.7	4.9	5.3	27.6	28.7	13.4	0.9	77.7	40.9	50.4	49.6
42234	GUTHRIE	76.3	76.0	21.0	21.3	0.3	0.3	2.1	2.1	8.9	8.1	8.4	6.8	6.9	26.4	21.5	11.5	1.6	70.5	33.8	49.0	51.0
42236	HERNDON	92.3	91.6	5.1	5.5	0.5	0.6	1.7	2.3	8.4	8.2	7.6	5.6	6.6	28.8	23.8	10.2	0.8	72.5	35.8	50.6	49.4
42240	HOPKINSVILLE	70.7	70.2	26.5	26.6	0.7	0.9	1.5	1.9	7.4	7.2	7.4	6.5	6.3	27.6	23.2	12.5	2.0	74.1	36.2	47.8	52.2
42252	JETSON	98.6	98.0	0.4	0.3	0.0	0.0	0.7	1.0	7.1	7.1	6.5	7.5	7.5	31.3	23.5	8.8	0.7	74.8	34.6	51.4	48.6
42254	LA FAYETTE	92.1	90.9	5.4	5.6	0.4	0.7	2.2	2.4	9.1	8.0	7.7	5.6	6.6	28.6	23.7	10.1	0.7	71.8	35.7	50.2	49.8
42256	LEWISBURG	98.5	98.4	0.3	0.3	0.2	0.2	0.6	0.6	6.4	6.4	6.6	6.3	5.8	27.7	26.8	12.6	1.5	76.9	39.1	50.2	49.8
42257	LINDSEYVILLE	100.0	100.0	0.0	0.0	0.0	0.0	0.0	0.0	5.9	5.9	11.8	11.8	5.9	35.3	23.5	0.0	0.0	76.5	31.3	58.8	41.2
42259	MAMMOTH CAVE	95.7	95.6	3.4	3.3	0.1	0.1	0.9	1.1	3.8	4.1	5.5	8.1	8.1	23.8	29.6	16.0	1.1	81.8	42.7	51.5	48.5
42261	MORGANTOWN	97.8	97.5	0.6	0.6	0.2	0.2	1.2	1.5	6.5	6.4	6.7	6.8	6.7	28.9	24.8	11.6	1.6	76.2	37.2	49.7	50.3
42262	OAK GROVE	64.6	62.6	23.9	24.4	1.9	2.3	8.7	10.5	15.5	9.1	6.7	5.9	15.9	38.1	6.8	1.8	0.2	66.2	24.1	52.6	47.4
42265	OLMSTEAD	92.3	92.3	6.0	6.0	0.2	0.2	1.3	1.3	7.4	7.2	6.6	5.9	5.7	26.8	25.4	12.8	2.3	75.4	38.3	49.1	50.9
42266	PEMBROKE	82.1	81.0	14.4	14.9	0.7	0.8	1.8	2.2	8.9	8.0	6.9	6.2	6.4	26.0	23.4	11.9	2.3	72.6	34.8	49.9	50.1
42273	ROCHESTER	97.9	97.8	0.0	0.0	0.2	0.2	0.0	0.0	4.5	4.8	6.7	6.3	5.8	24.9	29.4	15.5	2.0	80.0	42.4	49.8	50.3
42274	ROCKFIELD	96.6	96.4	1.7	1.6	0.3	0.3	0.6	0.9	6.2	6.5	7.0	6.6	7.0	29.7	28.9	7.5	0.7	76.4	37.0	50.2	49.8
42275	ROUNDHILL	99.3	99.3	0.1	0.1	0.0	0.0	0.3	0.4	6.8	6.5	6.5	7.4	6.9	29.1	24.5	11.4	0.8	75.9	36.3	51.6	48.4
42276	RUSSELLVILLE	87.3	87.2	10.7	10.8	0.3	0.3	1.2	1.2	7.0	6.9	6.9	6.2	6.5	27.5	25.1	12.1	1.9	75.5	37.8	48.0	52.0
42280	SHARON GROVE	97.9	97.5	0.0	0.0	0.2	0.2	2.0	2.2	8.6	7.7	7.2	6.5	6.6	31.2	22.0	9.4	0.8	72.6	34.0	50.8	49.2
42285	SWEEDEN	99.5	99.5	0.0	0.0	0.0	0.0	0.4	0.4	5.8	5.7	6.4	6.4	6.0	28.5	26.7	13.3	1.4	77.9	38.8	49.8	50.2
42286	TRENTON	91.4	91.3	6.3	6.3	0.4	0.4	1.2	1.2	8.2	8.0	7.3	5.9	5.4	26.8	24.5	12.1	1.8	72.9	36.7	49.4	50.6
42287	WELCHS CREEK	98.8	98.6	0.2	0.2	0.0	0.0	0.4	0.6	7.3	6.9	6.5	7.1	7.5	30.2	24.5	9.3	0.6	75.1	35.1	50.9	49.1
42301	OWENSBORO	91.3	90.9	6.6	6.7	0.4	0.5	1.0	1.2	6.6	6.4	6.7	6.9	7.3	26.1	24.7	13.3	1.9	76.2	37.7	47.5	52.6
42303	OWENSBORO	94.2	93.7	3.5	3.6	0.7	0.8	1.1	1.4	7.0	6.8	6.7	6.6	6.8	27.5	24.3	12.2	2.1	75.4	37.4	48.2	51.8
42320	BEAVER DAM	96.1	95.6	1.6	1.6	0.3	0.4	1.6	2.1	6.1	6.1	6.4	6.7	6.4	27.2	25.5	13.5	2.1	77.4	39.0	48.6	51.5
42321	BEECH CREEK	99.6	99.6	0.0	0.0	0.0	0.0	0.4	0.0	6.0	7.1	6.4	7.1	6.4	28.6	27.0	10.7	0.8	75.8	37.7	50.8	49.2
42323	BEECHMONT	98.8	98.8	0.3	0.3	0.0	0.0	0.3	0.4	7.9	7.3	6.3	6.7	5.8	27.7	26.4	10.8	1.1	74.5	36.9	49.5	50.5
42324	BELTON	98.2	98.1	0.3	0.4	0.2	0.2	1.4	1.7	6.4	6.4	5.8	6.1	5.6	27.2	27.2	13.5	1.8	77.7	39.9	50.6	49.5
42325	BREMEN	99.4	99.3	0.0	0.0	0.1	0.1	0.5	0.7	5.8	6.1	7.2	6.2	5.7	28.9	27.0	11.8	1.4	77.2	38.8	49.8	50.2
42326	BROWDER	98.3	98.2	0.7	0.7	0.7	0.7	0.7	0.7	7.3	6.9	6.2	5.5	5.5	25.9	26.6	14.6	1.5	75.9	40.2	49.3	50.7
42327	CALHOUN	99.0	98.9	0.2	0.2	0.1	0.1	0.7	0.9	5.9	6.0	6.3	6.7	6.1	27.4	26.9	13.1	1.8	77.9	39.8	49.1	51.0
42328	CENTERTOWN	99.0	98.8	0.1	0.1	0.0	0.0	0.9	1.2	6.8	7.1	7.4	6.5	6.0	28.4	24.5	12.1	1.2	74.7	36.0	51.1	48.9
42330	CENTRAL CITY	91.5	91.0	7.3	7.6	0.2	0.2	0.6	0.8	5.4	5.7	6.3	5.8	6.6	30.4	25.1	12.8	1.9	79.3	38.6	52.6	47.4
42333	CROMWELL	97.9	97.5	0.4	0.4	0.3	0.3	1.6	2.1	6.3	6.4	7.0	7.0	7.0	28.7	25.5	10.9	1.2	76.0	36.9	50.0	50.0
42337	DRAKESBORO	91.3	90.7	7.0	7.4	0.1	0.1	1.2	1.5	8.0	7.8	7.4	6.3	5.8	27.4	24.5	11.4	1.5	72.9	36.3	48.2	51.9
42338	DUNDEE	97.5	97.5	0.4	0.3	0.4	0.3	1.4	1.9	6.2	6.5	6.8	6.8	6.8	26.2	27.5	12.0	1.2	76.9	39.5	50.6	49.4
42339	DUNMOR	98.1	97.9	0.4	0.5	0.0	0.0	1.5	1.6	6.0	6.0	5.5	6.0	5.7	27.0	28.1	13.6	2.1	78.8	40.7	50.8	49.2
42343	FORDSVILLE	99.5	99.5	0.1	0.1	0.1	0.1	0.5	0.7	6.4	6.4	7.1	6.2	6.0	26.7	25.3	13.6	2.3	75.9	39.4	49.9	50.1
42344	GRAHAM	99.2	99.2	0.5	0.5	0.0	0.1	0.2	0.2	7.5	7.1	6.1	5.3	5.8	27.7	25.0	13.4	2.3	76.0	38.3	48.0	52.0
42345	GREENVILLE	93.6	93.4	5.1	5.2	0.1	0.2	0.8	1.0	5.7	5.8	5.4	6.5	6.1	25.4	27.4	14.9	2.9	79.3	41.7	48.1	51.9
42347	HARTFORD	97.6	97.4	0.8	0.8	0.2	0.3	0.9	1.2	6.5	6.4	6.4	6.3	6.4	26.4	25.7	12.9	3.0	76.8	39.2	48.7	51.3
42348	HAWESVILLE	98.4	98.4	0.6	0.6	0.1	0.1	0.6	0.5	7.4	7.4	7.9	6.8	5.5	29.1	24.9	10.3	0.8	73.2	36.4	50.2	49.8
42349	HORSE BRANCH	98.7	98.5	0.3	0.3	0.3	0.4	0.5	0.6	5.8	5.9	6.3	6.1	6.6	27.8	28.3	12.1	1.1	78.4	39.2	50.3	49.7
42350	ISLAND	99.3	99.3	0.1	0.1	0.0	0.0	0.5	0.6	7.1	7.0	6.2	5.7	5.3	27.2	28.0	11.9	1.7	76.3	39.4	48.9	51.1
42351	LEWISPORT	97.5	97.6	1.2	1.2	0.3	0.3	1.1	1.1	7.4	7.2	7.1	6.2	6.5	28.5	26.1	9.5	1.5	74.6	35.9	49.2	50.9
42352	LIVERMORE	98.6	98.3	0.0	0.0	0.0	0.0	1.4	1.7	7.3	7.0	6.8	6.3	6.7	26.1	26.2	12.1	1.5	75.4	37.9	48.9	51.2
42354	MC HENRY	98.8	98.5	0.0	0.0	0.3	0.5	0.3	0.3	6.5	7.5	7.5	8.0	6.3	32.0	22.3	9.5	0.5	74.0	34.0	50.0	50.0
42355	MACEO	98.8	98.7	0.3	0.4	0.3	0.3	0.6	0.7	6.7	6.8	7.5	7.2	6.4	28.8	26.9	8.8	0.9	74.6	36.9	51.7	48.3
42361	OLATON	98.5	98.3	0.1	0.1	0.6	0.7	0.6	0.9	5.7	6.1	7.3	5.9	6.4	27.2	27.6	12.4	1.2	77.3	39.2	50.6	49.4
42366	PHILPOT	99.1	98.9	0.1	0.1	0.2	0.2	0.6	0.8	6.9	7.1	7.8	7.3	6.4	28.4	26.2	9.0	0.9	73.6	36.6	50.5	49.5
42367	POWDERLY	96.5	96.1	2.8	2.9	0.0	0.0	0.6	1.1	6.9	6.8	6.2	5.4	6.8	27.4	26.4	12.8	1.2	76.9	38.4	49.5	50.5
42368	REYNOLDS STATION	98.9	98.9	0.3	0.3	0.0	0.0	0.4	0.5	7.3	7.0	7.3	6.7	5.9	27.8	27.0	10.1	0.8	74.0	36.5	50.7	49.3
42369	ROCKPORT	99.3	99.5	0.0	0.0	0.0	0.0	0.0	0.0	7.1	7.1	5.4	5.5	5.0	25.9	29.1	13.7	1.3	77.2	39.1	49.2	50.8
42371	RUMSEY	98.9	98.9	0.3	0.3	0.0	0.0	0.3	0.3	6.0	6.2	6.0	5.6	4.9	26.4	26.2	16.2	2.5	78.4	41.7	49.2	50.8
42372	SACRAMENTO	97.1	97.0	1.3	1.3	0.1	0.1	0.6	0.8	6.7	7.0	6.8	4.8	5.0	28.4	26.6	12.8	1.9	76.5	38.5	51.0	49.0
42376	UTICA	98.3	98.1	0.7	0.7	0.2	0.2	0.2	0.4	6.4	6.6	7.5	7.1	5.9	28.8	26.9	10.0	0.9	75.0	37.6	49.9	50.1
42378	WHITESVILLE	99.2	99.2	0.2	0.2	0.1	0.1	0.3	0.5	7.8	7.6	7.9	7.4	7.0	28.1	22.4	10.9	1.0	72.2	34.7	49.2	50.8
42404	CLAY	97.9	97.7	1.2	1.3	0.3	0.4	0.4	0.4	5.4	5.8	6.8	5.7	5.9	28.4	27.0	13.6	1.6	78.5	40.0	51.0	49.0
42406	CORYDON	94.8	94.5	4.1	4.3	0.1	0.1	0.6	0.8	6.3	7.2	7.4	6.4	6.3	29.2	26.4	10.1	0.9	75.2	37.7	49.6	50.4
42408	DAWSON SPRINGS	98.2	98.0	0.7	0.8	0.1	0.2	0.3	0.4	5.9	6.0	6.6	6.1	5.7	26.5	26.7	14.5	2.2	77.8	40.2	48.7	51.3
42409	DIXON	96.0	95.8	2.8	2.8	0.0	0.0	0.5	0.7	5.1	5.4	6.8	6.9	6.4	28.9	28.0	11.2	1.5	78.3	39.1	50.7	49.3
42410	EARLINGTON	84.2	83.3	14.7	15.5	0.2	0.2	0.8	0.8	6.7	6.4	7.1	6.3	7.1	25.1	26.6	12.4	2.4	76.0	38.9	46.4	53.6
42411	FREDONIA	98.1	98.0	1.0	1.0	0.1	0.1	0.6	0.8	5.7	6.0	6.4	5.4	5.4	26.7	28.3	15.0	1.1	78.7	41.2	49.8	50.2
42413	HANSON	98.2	97.9	0.5	0.6	0.4	0.5	0.7	0.8	5.9	6.3	7.7	6.6	5.4	28.6	29.5	9.4	0.8	75.9	38.9	49.8	50.2
42420	HENDERSON	89.9	89.4	8.2	8.4	0.4	0.5	1.0	1.3	6.5	6.3	6.7	6.3	6.7	28.1	25.7	12.1	1.7	76.7	38.1	48.3	51.7
42431	MADISONVILLE	88.8	88.2	8.9	9.2	0.5	0.6	1.2	1.5	6.1	6.1	6.5	6.2	6.1	26.6	26.4	13.6	2.4	77.5	39.8	47.2	52.8
42436	MANITOU	98.1	97.8	0.6	0.6	0.6	0.6	0.6	0.6	5.8	6.4	7.5	5.9	5.9	29.4	30.2	8.3	0.7	76.8	38.7	50.5	49.6
42437	MORGANFIELD	78.4	77.6	18.7	19.1	0.2	0.2	2.2	2.7	6.1	6.1	6.3	13.7	10.4	23.2	22.4	10.0	1.6	74.7	31.5	52.3	47.7
42441	NEBO	98.3	98.1	0.6	0.6	0.2	0.3	0.3	0.5	5.5	6.0	7.3	7.0	6.2	26.9	30.2	9.8	1.0	76.9	39.8	50.6	49.4
42442	NORTONVILLE	97.4	97.1	1.5	1.5	0.0	0.1	0.6	0.8	6.6	6.8	6.9	6.3	5.9	28.6	26.3	11.3	1.3	75.8	37.6	49.6	50.4
42445	PRINCETON	93.0	92.7	5.6	5.7	0.2	0.2	0.6	0.8	5.5	5.7	6.3	5.8	5.4	25.0	27.6	16.0	2.7	78.8	42.3	48.3	51.7
42450	PROVIDENCE	86.0	84.8	12.5	13.4	0.1	0.1	0.8	1.0	6.4	6.3	6.8	6.2	6.5	26.0	25.6	14.0	2.2	76.9	38.9	47.6	52.4
42451	REED	98.3	98.0	0.7	0.6	0.6	0.7	1.1	1.4	6.2	6.5	6.9	7.1	6.0	28.0	30.2	8.3	0.8	76.1	38.7	50.6	49.4
42452	ROBARDS	98.3	98.1	0.4	0.5	0.1	0.2	0.5	0.6	6.1	6.7	7.5	6.2	5.8	28.5	28.8	9.6	0.9	75.9	38.6	50.5	49.5
42453	SAINT CHARLES	99.0	98.6	0.4	0.4	0.2	0.2	0.2	0.4	6.7	6.7	6.3	5.3	5.9	27.2	27.4	13.6	0.8	76.9	39.7	50.3	49.7
42455	SEBREE	96.6	96.0	0.3	0.3	0.1	0.1	5.6	7.1	7.1	6.9	6.9	5.8	6.8	27.8	23.9	12.5	2.4	75.7	37.0	49.5	50.5
42456	SLAUGHTERS	98.8	98.6	0.4	0.4	0.2	0.2	0.8	1.0	6.3	6.3	6.6	6.4	6.1	27.3	27.6	12.2	1.2	76.6	39.2	49.5	50.6
42458	SPOTTSVILLE	98.3	98.1	0.8	0.7	0.3	0.4	1.0	1.2	6.3	6.6	7.0	6.8	5.9	28.1	30.6	8.0	0.9	76.0	38.9	50.9	49.1
42459	STURGIS	93.1	92.7	5.5	5.8	0.1	0.1	0.9	1.1	5.9	6.0	6.3	6.3	6.5	25.8	27.5	13.7	2.0	78.0	40.3	48.1	51.9
42461	UNIONTOWN	94.7	94.4	4.7	4.9	0.1	0.1	0.2	0.3	6.9	6.8	6.7	7.1	6.5	28.3	25.0	11.3	1.3	75.6	36.6	49.4	50.6
42462	WAVERLY	95.2	94.8	4.2	4.4	0.1	0.1	0.8	1.1	6.5	6.4	6.5	6.7	6.6	29.2	26.5	10.3	1.2	76.4	37.7	49.8	50.2
42464	WHITE PLAINS	97.9	97.8	1.1	1.2	0.2	0.2	1.0	1.3	5.7	7.2	6.9	7.1	6.3	28.4	27.3	9.8	1.3	75.8	37.2	49.2	50.8
42501	SOMERSET	96.3	96.1	2.0	2.0	0.4	0.5	0.8	1.0	6.1	5.9	6.2	6.0	6.4	25.8	24.6	16.1	3.0	78.3	40.6	46.4	53.6
42503	SOMERSET	97.3	96.9	1.1	1.2	0.7	0.9	0.8	1.0	5.9	6.2	6.6	5.9	5.7	29.0	26.4	13.0	1.3	77.6	39.4	49.7	50.3
42516	BETHELRIDGE	98.3	98.2	0.6	0.5	0.0	0.0	1.7	1.8	6.0	6.0	6.0	6.5	6.0	28.6	27.2	12.0	1.8	77.9	39.2	48.4	51.6
42518	BRONSTON	98.4	98.2	0.5	0.5	0.2	0.2	0.5	0.7	5.9	6.3	6.6	7.0	4.8	27.7	27.6	13.1	1.1	76.4	39.0	50.8	49.2
42519	BURNSIDE	98.1	97.9	0.2	0.2	0.0	0.0	0.7	1.0	5.4	6.4	6.6	6.1	5.9	27.2	28.1	13.4	0.9	77.4	40.1	51.5	48.5
42528	DUNNVILLE	99.2	99.2	0.1	0.1	0.1	0.1	0.8	1.0	7.2	7.0	7.2	6.1	5.9	28.0	24.9	12.1	1.5	74.8	37.1	49.7	50.3
	KENTUCKY	90.1	89.5	7.3	7.4	0.8	1.0	1.5	1.9	6.6	6.6	6.8	6.6	7.0	28.9	24.8	11.1	1.5	76.3	36.8	49.1	50.9
	UNITED STATES	75.1	73.6	12.3	12.5	3.8	4.2	12.5	14.1	6.9	6.7	7.2	7.0	7.3	28.6	23.8	10.8	1.7	75.1	36.0	49.1	50.9

#	POST OFFICE NAME	2004 Per Capita Income	2004 HH Income Base	2004 Household Income Distribution (%): Less than $25,000	$25,000 to $49,999	$50,000 to $99,999	$100,000 to $149,999	$150,000 or More	Median Household Income: 2004	2009	2004 National Centile	2004 State Centile	2004 Home Value Base	2004 Home Value Distribution (%): Less than $50,000	$50,000 to $89,999	$90,000 to $174,999	$175,000 to $399,999	$400,000 or More	2004 Median Home Value
42206	AUBURN	17863	1806	31.6	30.1	33.1	4.2	1.1	40739	48001	49	75	1479	24.9	32.4	32.1	10.2	0.4	82430
42207	BEE SPRING	16204	563	45.5	32.9	19.0	2.0	0.7	28861	34110	10	40	494	36.2	38.7	23.1	2.0	0.0	63833
42210	BROWNSVILLE	19392	1562	51.5	25.7	18.0	2.2	2.5	24055	28607	4	24	1220	38.2	35.3	19.3	6.5	0.7	59600
42211	CADIZ	20830	5109	31.9	31.8	28.4	5.3	2.7	38348	45701	41	69	4178	21.5	32.5	30.9	13.4	1.7	85383
42214	CENTER	17881	309	51.1	23.0	16.5	3.2	6.2	23993	29295	4	24	253	41.5	26.9	30.0	1.6	0.0	61667
42215	CERULEAN	19344	517	26.7	29.4	37.3	5.4	1.2	43693	52074	58	82	430	29.3	27.0	31.2	10.2	2.3	83077
42217	CROFTON	17855	1411	30.8	35.2	28.2	4.9	0.9	36677	44050	34	65	1146	37.9	30.1	26.0	4.3	1.8	62073
42220	ELKTON	17964	2475	37.7	32.4	24.8	3.2	2.0	33518	40332	22	55	2001	33.5	33.6	26.8	5.4	0.7	66554
42232	GRACEY	23639	257	19.5	31.9	33.5	10.9	4.3	48807	58733	70	88	224	9.8	22.8	47.8	15.6	4.0	112500
42234	GUTHRIE	15904	880	37.5	32.6	24.9	4.0	1.0	34180	39525	25	57	586	40.3	29.7	23.2	4.8	2.1	60526
42236	HERNDON	21638	325	23.7	31.4	33.2	8.0	3.7	44236	53663	59	83	253	18.2	36.4	34.4	8.7	2.4	85000
42240	HOPKINSVILLE	19735	16070	34.7	29.2	27.4	6.3	2.4	36608	43965	34	64	10526	22.1	34.6	34.2	7.7	1.4	82368
42252	JETSON	16251	115	36.5	35.7	22.6	2.6	2.6	33593	40000	23	55	96	40.6	32.3	21.9	4.2	1.0	63333
42254	LA FAYETTE	21518	117	23.9	32.5	33.3	6.8	3.4	42782	52179	55	81	89	20.2	40.5	33.7	5.6	0.0	78929
42256	LEWISBURG	18746	1991	37.0	33.1	23.9	4.0	2.0	33424	40258	22	55	1646	37.2	30.4	23.0	8.6	0.9	65873
42257	LINDSEYVILLE	12353	8	50.0	37.5	12.5	0.0	0.0	25000	40000	5	26	7	14.3	28.6	57.1	0.0	0.0	106250
42259	MAMMOTH CAVE	13570	452	44.3	35.4	17.9	2.4	0.0	29082	34299	10	41	390	36.7	31.3	30.5	1.5	0.0	61707
42261	MORGANTOWN	17273	4152	37.5	32.7	25.5	2.9	1.3	33316	39107	22	54	3295	38.2	33.4	23.3	4.7	0.4	65111
42262	OAK GROVE	16242	3116	26.4	46.3	22.1	3.7	1.5	36316	41359	33	63	1357	14.5	67.9	14.4	2.4	0.7	75483
42265	OLMSTEAD	21002	421	23.3	29.2	37.1	8.1	2.4	47483	56126	67	87	350	20.3	33.1	29.1	14.0	3.4	85000
42266	PEMBROKE	17526	808	33.2	36.5	21.9	5.0	3.5	36825	43427	35	65	576	17.2	37.0	28.8	11.8	5.2	84146
42273	ROCHESTER	24670	244	33.6	31.6	23.0	9.4	2.5	37934	43308	39	69	211	37.4	26.5	26.5	9.5	0.0	62955
42274	ROCKFIELD	19032	741	26.6	27.3	40.4	3.6	2.2	47419	56600	67	87	628	20.5	23.4	36.2	15.8	4.1	97451
42275	ROUNDHILL	13574	374	45.5	32.1	19.8	1.1	1.6	27836	33105	8	37	307	38.8	37.1	19.9	3.3	1.0	58625
42276	RUSSELLVILLE	19791	6059	33.4	31.3	27.6	5.2	2.5	36949	43823	35	66	4634	23.0	36.8	29.2	9.9	1.1	80022
42280	SHARON GROVE	15309	258	33.3	36.8	26.7	3.1	0.0	31583	37021	17	48	215	31.6	38.1	19.5	9.3	1.4	62500
42285	SWEEDEN	19731	239	33.1	35.2	24.7	3.4	3.8	36322	43432	33	63	202	31.7	31.2	28.2	8.9	0.0	67692
42286	TRENTON	23357	581	36.5	25.1	27.4	6.4	4.7	36513	43008	34	64	461	21.5	26.5	31.0	18.7	2.4	92969
42287	WELCHS CREEK	17711	205	37.1	35.6	23.4	2.0	2.0	34114	40477	24	57	173	40.5	32.4	24.3	2.3	0.6	63000
42301	OWENSBORO	22508	17406	29.9	29.9	31.8	5.8	2.8	40570	49001	48	75	11745	13.1	37.6	40.6	8.0	0.8	89379
42303	OWENSBORO	23578	14912	29.4	28.0	30.2	8.5	3.9	42655	52372	55	80	10407	14.6	35.0	34.8	14.1	1.5	90426
42320	BEAVER DAM	18321	2948	39.2	31.2	22.7	5.0	1.9	32492	38958	19	51	2269	38.1	33.4	24.4	3.8	0.3	64362
42321	BEECH CREEK	17633	106	27.4	46.2	22.6	1.9	1.9	36295	44600	33	63	86	36.1	36.1	23.3	4.7	0.0	65000
42323	BEECHMONT	17047	429	34.0	33.8	27.0	4.0	1.2	35976	43886	31	63	356	33.2	34.6	27.0	5.3	0.0	65000
42324	BELTON	16076	519	37.6	32.4	25.1	4.8	0.2	31659	38767	17	48	470	34.5	38.3	22.8	4.5	0.0	65000
42325	BREMEN	17390	1040	34.9	35.1	24.7	4.4	0.9	34306	41387	25	58	890	34.7	38.0	19.8	7.1	0.5	64359
42326	BROWDER	18038	121	29.8	33.9	33.9	2.5	0.0	36682	42830	34	65	111	47.8	25.2	26.1	0.9	0.0	51923
42327	CALHOUN	20759	1752	32.3	33.5	28.1	2.7	3.4	37820	45227	39	68	1434	35.6	31.6	23.6	7.4	1.7	68230
42328	CENTERTOWN	17054	639	29.0	36.3	31.0	2.7	1.1	41141	48457	50	77	533	46.9	31.9	19.1	2.1	0.0	52357
42330	CENTRAL CITY	17013	3628	40.5	30.3	23.0	4.7	1.5	31265	37569	16	47	2893	41.4	30.9	22.5	4.9	0.2	59483
42333	CROMWELL	15682	286	32.9	37.8	23.8	4.6	1.1	36622	43808	34	64	241	45.2	32.4	16.6	5.8	0.0	56389
42337	DRAKESBORO	14902	853	47.8	27.9	20.3	2.6	1.4	26121	30557	6	31	714	57.1	27.6	14.0	1.3	0.0	43014
42338	DUNDEE	17360	133	33.8	29.3	33.1	2.3	1.5	33576	40983	23	55	120	35.0	31.7	30.0	3.3	0.0	67273
42339	DUNMOR	16220	349	39.0	31.2	23.8	5.7	0.3	31132	39413	15	47	317	32.5	38.8	23.7	5.1	0.0	68654
42343	FORDSVILLE	18741	957	43.3	28.3	23.9	2.3	2.2	30216	36002	13	44	785	49.4	26.6	21.5	2.4	0.0	50789
42344	GRAHAM	13786	391	40.9	41.7	15.6	1.0	0.8	29092	33160	10	41	313	64.2	27.2	6.1	2.2	0.3	38354
42345	GREENVILLE	21386	4521	37.3	28.1	25.3	6.0	3.3	34275	41487	25	58	3628	29.2	35.5	27.2	7.1	1.1	70268
42347	HARTFORD	19267	2254	35.3	31.4	26.4	4.0	2.9	33616	40594	23	56	1734	34.1	34.6	25.4	5.4	0.5	66875
42348	HAWESVILLE	19755	1769	26.6	31.2	33.4	7.3	1.5	42983	50640	56	81	1498	32.8	26.0	29.5	11.1	0.5	78548
42349	HORSE BRANCH	14070	730	45.3	30.0	20.6	3.7	0.4	28377	33779	9	39	620	46.1	34.4	13.6	5.7	0.3	54211
42350	ISLAND	17551	607	37.2	33.9	24.9	3.1	0.8	31687	37689	17	48	520	50.0	29.4	16.7	2.5	1.4	50000
42351	LEWISPORT	20694	1574	25.7	30.8	34.3	7.3	1.9	45167	53141	62	84	1288	29.3	31.0	30.8	8.9	0.2	74578
42352	LIVERMORE	18961	954	40.8	29.6	22.1	5.8	1.8	30790	36287	14	46	716	39.4	33.5	23.6	2.7	0.8	62041
42354	MC HENRY	15139	152	42.1	33.6	20.4	2.6	1.3	30395	35221	13	45	126	58.7	33.3	7.1	0.8	0.0	44500
42355	MACEO	20633	819	21.5	31.3	37.9	6.8	2.6	46677	57270	65	86	720	38.3	27.2	26.3	7.6	0.6	69167
42361	OLATON	15685	292	37.0	33.9	25.0	3.1	1.0	32646	38956	20	52	251	37.1	30.7	23.1	8.4	0.8	65250
42366	PHILPOT	24243	2176	15.6	23.9	44.7	12.5	3.3	59742	70167	84	95	1979	11.1	24.5	45.3	16.7	2.5	111020
42367	POWDERLY	12606	372	48.7	35.8	13.7	1.6	0.3	25466	29483	5	28	287	59.6	32.8	6.6	1.1	0.0	38438
42368	REYNOLDS STATION	20570	373	29.0	32.2	30.3	5.6	3.0	41655	49777	52	78	318	43.4	23.9	28.0	4.7	0.0	65500
42369	ROCKPORT	21159	221	35.8	32.6	24.9	4.5	2.3	35362	42467	29	61	190	42.1	30.0	21.6	6.3	0.0	60000
42371	RUMSEY	18812	267	41.2	32.6	21.4	2.3	2.6	30467	35942	13	45	209	40.7	32.5	20.6	6.2	0.0	59750
42372	SACRAMENTO	17929	822	36.1	32.7	25.8	3.2	2.2	33716	40564	23	56	686	40.4	34.0	20.1	5.5	0.0	59706
42376	UTICA	24600	1983	19.6	30.0	36.6	10.8	3.1	50320	60311	72	89	1728	19.7	35.6	30.8	11.8	2.1	85598
42378	WHITESVILLE	20094	1132	26.8	31.1	34.5	5.7	1.9	41712	50720	52	78	962	26.0	33.6	33.1	7.3	0.1	80316
42404	CLAY	18417	1143	31.2	32.9	30.1	4.6	1.1	35815	44327	31	62	941	52.3	27.7	15.8	3.2	1.0	48648
42406	CORYDON	20817	1260	22.5	26.8	40.5	8.9	1.4	50451	61319	73	89	1053	28.6	34.8	29.4	7.2	0.0	73761
42408	DAWSON SPRINGS	16617	2782	42.2	33.0	20.6	2.9	1.3	29270	34479	11	42	2167	52.8	31.2	14.2	1.3	0.6	47759
42409	DIXON	20639	955	30.9	28.0	32.4	6.7	2.1	40458	48712	48	74	787	37.7	28.7	27.6	5.0	1.0	63431
42410	EARLINGTON	13986	850	49.8	28.2	19.5	2.4	0.1	25134	29766	5	27	609	58.5	31.4	9.0	1.2	0.0	43720
42411	FREDONIA	19573	614	32.7	34.9	24.3	5.2	2.9	37394	44845	37	67	523	37.3	28.5	27.5	6.5	0.2	62361
42413	HANSON	26753	956	20.9	29.5	35.9	9.3	4.4	49591	60735	71	88	838	23.8	30.6	34.3	10.4	1.1	82800
42420	HENDERSON	22989	15548	31.3	28.4	29.8	6.8	3.7	40582	49854	48	75	10224	23.7	31.9	33.8	9.7	1.0	84296
42431	MADISONVILLE	23800	11508	33.7	30.4	25.9	6.3	3.8	37308	45594	37	67	8294	32.2	34.2	26.6	6.3	0.7	69034
42436	MANITOU	26619	433	17.3	35.3	30.7	9.7	6.9	47729	59436	68	87	382	23.3	30.6	30.1	13.1	2.9	82857
42437	MORGANFIELD	22017	2840	28.4	26.7	34.2	7.0	3.8	43889	54000	58	82	2204	30.2	30.4	33.4	5.4	0.7	75858
42441	NEBO	18776	557	30.2	38.1	26.0	2.3	3.4	36915	44590	35	66	466	39.9	28.8	23.6	6.2	1.5	62444
42442	NORTONVILLE	15283	1283	38.4	35.3	22.8	3.0	0.6	32162	37932	18	50	1046	49.6	31.7	16.9	1.4	0.3	50367
42445	PRINCETON	19707	4791	38.8	29.9	24.4	4.7	2.2	32559	39557	19	52	3710	35.5	30.2	27.1	6.7	0.5	65163
42450	PROVIDENCE	17529	1718	39.5	31.2	22.6	5.0	1.7	31750	37291	17	49	1254	62.6	22.5	14.0	0.6	0.3	40186
42451	REED	21422	363	19.0	35.5	35.8	7.7	1.9	46297	57172	65	85	315	38.7	31.8	27.3	1.6	0.6	61190
42452	ROBARDS	23405	839	17.0	29.3	41.4	10.3	2.0	53028	63428	77	92	719	16.6	35.1	33.9	13.9	0.6	88663
42453	SAINT CHARLES	15231	207	43.0	34.8	18.8	2.4	1.0	28884	33300	10	40	186	55.4	26.3	16.7	0.5	1.1	43333
42455	SEBREE	18379	1347	29.2	33.3	31.3	5.2	1.0	38918	47742	42	71	1072	36.9	38.7	20.9	3.0	0.6	62577
42456	SLAUGHTERS	22616	651	23.7	27.8	39.2	6.8	2.6	48610	58035	69	88	567	32.5	33.0	26.6	5.8	2.1	72065
42458	SPOTTSVILLE	23176	374	22.5	27.3	37.2	9.6	3.5	50244	61657	72	89	329	34.7	30.7	32.5	1.2	0.9	67955
42459	STURGIS	22330	1999	32.5	31.0	27.6	5.9	3.0	38159	46474	40	69	1583	37.9	34.2	23.3	3.9	0.7	59527
42461	UNIONTOWN	19444	675	32.2	36.6	24.9	4.9	1.5	36401	44290	33	64	562	52.0	26.9	15.8	5.3	0.0	48281
42462	WAVERLY	19865	652	22.4	27.0	44.2	6.1	0.3	50317	60482	72	89	553	32.4	36.0	23.7	7.8	0.2	66917
42464	WHITE PLAINS	15754	773	36.4	34.0	23.7	4.0	1.9	31918	38010	18	49	641	47.4	28.1	17.5	5.8	1.3	52230
42501	SOMERSET	17241	7026	43.6	32.0	18.9	3.6	1.9	28647	34116	10	40	4767	28.3	37.5	28.6	4.8	0.8	72805
42503	SOMERSET	20700	7977	34.0	31.6	25.2	6.1	3.1	36171	43850	32	63	6182	20.8	24.4	41.7	11.4	1.7	96652
42516	BETHELRIDGE	24681	99	46.5	30.3	15.2	3.0	5.1	26731	31703	7	33	84	47.6	39.3	9.5	3.6	0.0	52857
42518	BRONSTON	22841	1338	37.0	32.9	20.3	6.3	3.6	32211	39766	18	50	1101	29.4	33.7	29.4	7.5	0.0	73281
42519	BURNSIDE	14181	1520	49.9	35.1	11.0	2.1	1.9	25056	29417	5	26	1226	51.8	32.3	12.6	3.0	0.2	48440
42528	DUNNVILLE	13324	621	47.7	33.8	14.7	2.7	1.1	26102	31113	6	31	518	51.5	21.6	22.6	4.3	0.0	48222
	KENTUCKY	22472		31.8	28.3	28.2	7.8	3.9	39962	49361				22.2	24.9	36.4	14.3	2.1	94344
	UNITED STATES	25866		24.7	27.1	30.8	10.9	6.5	48124	56710				10.9	15.0	33.7	30.1	10.4	145905

ZIP CODE #	POST OFFICE NAME	FINANCIAL SERVICES: Auto Loan	Home Loan	Invest-ments	Retire-ment Plans	THE HOME: Home Improvements: Home Repair	Lawn & Garden	Furnishings: Comput-ers & Hard-ware	Major Appli-ances	TV, Radio, Sound Equip-ment	Furni-ture	ENTERTAINMENT: Dine out/ Carry out	Sports Equip-ment	Fees & Tickets	Toys & Games	Travel	Cable TV	PERSONAL: Apparel & Services	Auto Repairs	Health Insur-ance	Pets & Supplies
42206	AUBURN	79	64	45	61	69	76	62	70	68	62	82	82	59	81	63	71	77	69	79	90
42207	BEE SPRING	66	50	32	45	57	64	48	58	55	47	65	68	42	63	50	58	60	57	69	80
42210	BROWNSVILLE	87	60	29	52	67	76	58	71	68	59	81	85	50	76	58	73	74	70	86	99
42211	CADIZ	83	64	42	59	70	80	63	73	71	63	84	85	57	81	64	75	78	72	86	96
42214	CENTER	88	60	29	52	67	78	59	72	70	59	82	85	50	78	59	75	75	71	88	100
42215	CERULEAN	78	65	49	64	69	77	66	71	70	65	85	82	62	84	66	72	80	70	78	87
42217	CROFTON	83	57	28	50	64	74	56	68	66	56	78	81	48	74	56	70	71	67	83	95
42220	ELKTON	84	57	26	49	64	74	55	68	66	56	77	82	46	73	56	71	70	68	84	97
42232	GRACEY	97	86	66	82	91	98	80	89	85	80	103	106	78	105	82	87	98	86	96	114
42234	GUTHRIE	80	55	26	48	62	71	53	66	63	54	74	78	45	71	54	67	67	65	80	92
42236	HERNDON	89	77	59	76	80	90	77	83	82	76	99	96	74	99	77	83	93	82	90	100
42240	HOPKINSVILLE	71	64	61	62	66	73	66	68	69	65	85	79	64	83	65	70	81	68	73	80
42252	JETSON	78	52	24	45	59	68	51	63	61	52	72	76	43	68	51	66	65	63	78	90
42254	LA FAYETTE	82	70	55	70	73	83	72	77	77	71	93	88	69	92	72	78	87	76	84	91
42256	LEWISBURG	84	56	26	49	64	73	54	68	66	55	77	81	46	73	55	71	70	67	84	96
42257	LINDSEYVILLE	49	33	15	29	38	43	32	40	39	33	45	48	27	43	32	42	41	40	49	57
42259	MAMMOTH CAVE	56	44	30	40	50	56	42	50	47	41	56	59	37	55	44	50	52	49	59	69
42261	MORGANTOWN	78	55	28	49	61	70	53	65	63	54	74	77	47	71	54	67	68	64	78	89
42262	OAK GROVE	72	47	44	53	44	51	68	59	69	63	86	78	58	77	57	63	82	69	56	68
42265	OLMSTEAD	91	74	50	69	80	88	70	80	77	70	92	96	65	92	72	80	86	79	91	107
42266	PEMBROKE	88	61	32	55	68	78	60	73	71	61	83	86	52	79	61	75	76	72	88	100
42273	ROCHESTER	114	76	35	66	87	100	74	92	89	75	104	110	63	99	75	96	95	91	114	131
42274	ROCKFIELD	82	72	54	68	76	82	67	74	71	67	87	88	65	88	69	73	82	72	81	96
42275	ROUNDHILL	65	44	20	38	50	57	42	53	51	43	60	63	36	56	43	55	54	52	65	75
42276	RUSSELLVILLE	84	62	39	57	69	78	61	72	70	61	83	85	55	81	62	74	77	71	84	96
42280	SHARON GROVE	73	49	22	42	55	63	47	59	57	48	67	70	40	63	48	61	60	58	72	83
42285	SWEEDEN	88	59	27	51	67	77	57	71	69	58	81	85	48	76	58	74	73	70	88	101
42286	TRENTON	100	84	60	79	89	98	80	90	87	80	105	106	77	105	82	90	99	88	100	115
42287	WELCHS CREEK	80	54	24	46	61	70	52	65	63	53	73	77	44	69	53	67	67	64	80	92
42301	OWENSBORO	75	74	77	73	75	81	75	75	76	74	95	87	75	95	75	77	92	76	77	86
42303	OWENSBORO	81	79	76	78	80	87	80	81	81	78	100	94	79	100	80	82	96	81	84	93
42320	BEAVER DAM	82	58	31	51	65	74	56	69	66	57	78	81	49	75	57	71	72	68	83	95
42321	BEECH CREEK	79	53	24	46	60	69	51	64	62	52	72	76	43	68	52	66	66	63	79	91
42323	BEECHMONT	78	52	24	45	59	68	51	63	61	52	72	76	43	68	51	66	65	63	78	90
42324	BELTON	75	50	23	43	57	65	48	60	58	49	68	72	41	65	49	63	62	60	74	86
42325	BREMEN	81	54	24	47	61	70	52	65	63	53	74	78	44	70	53	68	67	65	80	93
42326	BROWDER	77	52	23	44	58	67	50	62	60	51	70	74	42	67	51	65	64	62	77	88
42327	CALHOUN	85	68	46	65	74	82	67	76	73	67	88	90	61	86	68	76	82	75	86	98
42328	CENTERTOWN	82	55	25	48	63	72	53	67	64	54	76	80	45	71	54	69	69	66	82	95
42330	CENTRAL CITY	75	55	32	49	60	70	55	64	63	54	75	75	48	71	55	67	68	64	77	85
42333	CROMWELL	79	53	24	46	60	69	51	64	62	52	72	76	43	68	52	66	66	63	79	91
42337	DRAKESBORO	68	46	21	40	52	60	44	55	53	45	63	66	38	59	45	58	57	55	68	79
42338	DUNDEE	80	53	24	46	60	70	51	64	62	52	73	77	44	69	52	67	66	64	79	91
42339	DUNMOR	76	51	23	44	57	66	49	61	59	50	69	73	42	66	50	64	63	61	75	87
42343	FORDSVILLE	84	58	28	51	65	74	56	69	66	57	78	82	48	74	57	71	72	68	83	96
42344	GRAHAM	64	43	19	37	49	56	41	52	50	42	59	62	35	55	42	54	53	51	64	74
42345	GREENVILLE	86	66	42	60	72	82	66	76	74	65	88	88	59	85	66	79	81	75	89	99
42347	HARTFORD	80	60	37	56	66	76	61	70	69	60	82	81	55	79	61	73	75	69	83	91
42348	HAWESVILLE	87	70	47	65	75	82	67	76	73	68	88	90	62	86	68	75	83	75	85	100
42349	HORSE BRANCH	67	45	20	39	51	59	43	54	52	44	61	65	37	58	44	56	56	54	67	77
42350	ISLAND	76	51	23	44	58	67	49	62	59	50	70	74	42	66	50	64	63	61	76	87
42351	LEWISPORT	83	73	56	70	77	84	70	76	74	69	90	90	68	90	71	75	85	74	82	96
42352	LIVERMORE	86	60	31	53	67	76	58	71	68	59	80	84	50	76	59	72	74	70	85	98
42354	MC HENRY	75	50	23	43	57	66	48	61	59	49	69	72	41	65	49	63	62	60	75	86
42355	MACEO	87	77	59	74	81	87	72	79	76	72	92	94	70	93	74	77	88	77	85	101
42361	OLATON	76	51	23	44	57	66	49	61	59	50	69	73	42	66	50	64	63	61	75	87
42366	PHILPOT	106	101	84	97	105	110	92	100	95	92	117	119	92	120	95	97	112	97	104	125
42367	POWDERLY	57	38	17	33	43	50	37	46	45	38	52	55	31	50	38	48	48	46	57	66
42368	REYNOLDS STATION	99	72	39	64	79	89	69	83	80	70	95	98	60	89	70	84	87	82	97	113
42369	ROCKPORT	101	68	31	58	77	88	65	82	79	67	93	98	56	88	66	85	84	81	101	116
42371	RUMSEY	78	55	30	50	61	72	57	67	66	56	78	77	49	73	57	70	71	66	81	88
42372	SACRAMENTO	82	55	25	48	62	72	53	67	64	54	75	80	45	71	54	69	69	66	82	95
42376	UTICA	106	94	71	89	99	106	87	96	92	87	112	115	85	114	89	94	106	94	104	124
42378	WHITESVILLE	87	75	57	73	78	86	74	80	78	74	95	93	70	93	74	79	90	79	86	97
42404	CLAY	80	59	34	53	65	73	56	67	65	57	77	80	50	75	57	68	71	66	79	92
42406	CORYDON	91	76	54	71	81	88	71	80	77	71	93	96	68	94	73	80	88	79	90	106
42408	DAWSON SPRINGS	70	50	29	45	55	65	52	60	60	51	71	70	45	67	52	64	65	60	72	79
42409	DIXON	89	67	40	60	74	83	64	76	73	64	87	90	58	85	65	77	80	74	89	104
42410	EARLINGTON	54	40	25	38	44	52	44	49	49	42	58	55	39	55	43	52	53	49	58	60
42411	FREDONIA	88	59	27	51	67	77	57	71	69	58	81	85	49	76	58	74	73	71	88	101
42413	HANSON	113	101	77	96	107	114	93	103	99	93	120	123	91	123	96	102	115	101	112	133
42420	HENDERSON	80	73	67	72	75	82	75	77	78	73	95	90	73	95	75	78	91	77	81	91
42431	MADISONVILLE	85	75	62	72	79	88	75	80	80	74	97	93	72	96	75	82	91	79	89	98
42436	MANITOU	109	98	75	93	103	111	90	100	96	90	117	119	89	119	93	98	111	97	108	129
42437	MORGANFIELD	94	82	65	79	86	96	81	88	86	80	104	101	78	104	82	89	99	86	96	107
42441	NEBO	87	60	30	53	68	77	58	71	69	59	81	85	50	77	59	74	74	70	86	100
42442	NORTONVILLE	72	48	22	41	54	63	46	58	56	47	66	69	39	62	47	60	60	57	71	82
42445	PRINCETON	76	59	39	54	64	74	60	68	67	58	80	78	54	77	60	71	74	67	80	87
42450	PROVIDENCE	73	52	33	47	57	66	53	62	62	53	74	73	47	70	53	65	68	62	73	83
42451	REED	90	80	61	76	85	91	74	82	79	74	96	98	73	98	76	81	91	80	89	106
42452	ROBARDS	95	88	78	87	92	98	85	91	87	85	107	107	84	108	86	88	103	89	95	111
42453	SAINT CHARLES	70	47	21	41	53	61	45	57	55	46	64	68	39	61	46	59	58	56	70	81
42455	SEBREE	83	62	38	57	68	77	61	71	69	61	83	84	55	80	62	73	76	70	83	95
42456	SLAUGHTERS	92	81	61	76	86	92	75	83	80	75	97	99	73	99	77	82	92	81	91	108
42458	SPOTTSVILLE	96	86	66	82	91	98	80	88	85	80	103	105	78	105	82	87	98	86	95	114
42459	STURGIS	85	71	52	67	76	85	71	78	77	69	93	90	67	92	71	81	87	77	88	97
42461	UNIONTOWN	86	58	27	50	66	76	56	70	68	57	79	84	48	75	57	73	72	69	86	99
42462	WAVERLY	83	73	55	69	78	84	68	76	73	68	88	90	66	90	70	75	84	74	82	98
42464	WHITE PLAINS	77	52	24	45	59	68	50	63	61	51	71	75	43	68	51	65	65	62	77	89
42501	SOMERSET	64	50	38	47	54	62	52	58	58	51	69	66	48	67	52	61	64	58	67	72
42503	SOMERSET	86	67	43	62	73	82	66	75	73	65	87	89	60	85	66	76	81	74	87	99
42516	BETHELRIDGE	102	68	31	59	77	89	66	82	79	67	93	98	56	88	67	86	85	81	101	117
42518	BRONSTON	100	70	37	61	79	91	67	83	79	68	94	99	58	90	69	85	86	82	101	117
42519	BURNSIDE	60	43	24	38	48	55	41	50	48	41	57	60	36	55	43	52	52	50	61	71
42528	DUNNVILLE	63	42	19	37	48	55	41	51	49	42	58	61	35	55	42	53	53	51	63	73
	KENTUCKY	86	74	63	71	77	85	74	80	79	74	96	94	71	95	74	81	91	80	86	98
	UNITED STATES	100	100	100	100	100	100	100	100	100	100	100	100	100	100	100	100	100	100	100	100

POPULATION CHANGE

#	POST OFFICE NAME	COUNTY FIPS CODE	POPULATION			2000-2004 ANNUAL RATE		HOUSEHOLDS					FAMILIES		
			2000	2004	2009	% Rate	State Centile	2000	2004	2009	% Annual Rate 2000-2004	2004 Average HH Size	2000	2004	% Annual Rate 2000-2004
42533	FERGUSON	199	911	837	823	-2.0	0	377	357	359	-1.3	2.34	266	243	-2.1
42539	LIBERTY	045	9938	10095	10260	0.4	55	4059	4226	4387	1.0	2.35	2840	2868	0.2
42541	MIDDLEBURG	045	488	501	511	0.6	65	187	197	204	1.2	2.54	133	136	0.5
42544	NANCY	199	4742	4733	4774	0.0	38	1948	1992	2050	0.5	2.38	1440	1429	-0.2
42553	SCIENCE HILL	199	4417	4461	4535	0.2	50	1716	1772	1835	0.8	2.50	1303	1307	0.1
42565	WINDSOR	045	490	496	502	0.3	53	196	203	210	0.8	2.34	141	142	0.2
42566	YOSEMITE	045	395	418	439	1.3	82	155	167	179	1.8	2.50	114	119	1.0
42567	EUBANK	199	5455	5366	5411	-0.4	23	2134	2156	2221	0.2	2.48	1621	1593	-0.4
42602	ALBANY	053	8517	8610	8688	0.3	52	3621	3756	3868	0.9	2.28	2471	2480	0.1
42603	ALPHA	231	3482	3537	3652	0.4	55	1331	1387	1467	1.0	2.52	1020	1039	0.4
42629	JAMESTOWN	207	4686	4614	4588	-0.4	24	1976	1995	2014	0.2	2.25	1366	1333	-0.6
42633	MONTICELLO	231	16191	16972	17907	1.1	78	6489	6973	7536	1.7	2.41	4711	4919	1.0
42634	PARKERS LAKE	147	1591	1607	1618	0.2	51	582	609	629	1.1	2.54	433	441	0.4
42635	PINE KNOT	147	4280	4353	4392	0.4	57	1606	1680	1730	1.1	2.43	1139	1157	0.4
42638	REVELO	147	211	210	210	-0.1	33	81	82	84	0.3	2.56	57	56	-0.4
42642	RUSSELL SPRINGS	207	12457	12628	12719	0.3	54	5328	5534	5665	0.9	2.27	3696	3718	0.1
42647	STEARNS	147	4230	4223	4222	0.0	38	1645	1693	1729	0.7	2.48	1230	1233	0.1
42649	STRUNK	147	1992	2076	2122	1.0	75	745	794	826	1.5	2.61	566	588	0.9
42653	WHITLEY CITY	147	4774	4765	4770	0.0	38	1860	1920	1970	0.8	2.44	1330	1335	0.1
42701	ELIZABETHTOWN	093	40246	42094	43406	1.1	77	15814	16906	17779	1.6	2.44	11341	11774	0.9
42711	BAKERTON	057	206	197	192	-1.1	6	95	93	92	-0.5	2.12	69	65	-1.4
42712	BIG CLIFTY	085	1684	1769	1822	1.2	79	654	703	739	1.7	2.52	495	519	1.1
42713	BONNIEVILLE	099	1664	1807	1923	2.0	90	658	724	780	2.3	2.49	481	514	1.6
42715	BREEDING	001	295	296	295	0.1	44	115	118	120	0.6	2.51	85	84	-0.3
42716	BUFFALO	123	1253	1257	1284	0.1	44	485	495	514	0.5	2.54	377	376	-0.1
42717	BURKESVILLE	057	7342	7327	7271	-0.1	37	3047	3105	3142	0.4	2.32	2087	2058	-0.3
42718	CAMPBELLSVILLE	217	22633	22469	22194	-0.2	31	9164	9289	9357	0.3	2.35	6498	6391	-0.4
42721	CANEYVILLE	085	3733	3769	3817	0.2	50	1499	1551	1602	0.8	2.43	1088	1094	0.1
42722	CANMER	099	588	621	651	1.3	81	226	241	256	1.5	2.58	169	176	1.0
42724	CECILIA	093	3648	3782	3879	0.9	72	1371	1455	1524	1.4	2.60	1082	1122	0.9
42726	CLARKSON	085	4425	4515	4587	0.5	60	1818	1901	1971	1.1	2.37	1359	1383	0.4
42728	COLUMBIA	001	13754	13850	13961	0.2	48	5377	5534	5682	0.7	2.37	3778	3768	-0.1
42729	CUB RUN	099	1257	1331	1395	1.4	83	481	516	549	1.7	2.54	351	367	1.1
42731	DUBRE	169	325	336	344	0.8	70	130	137	143	1.2	2.45	96	98	0.5
42732	EASTVIEW	093	1818	1870	1906	0.7	67	687	723	752	1.2	2.59	521	533	0.5
42733	ELK HORN	217	1494	1541	1552	0.7	68	541	570	586	1.2	2.70	412	422	0.6
42735	FAIRPLAY	001	355	369	376	0.9	73	156	166	173	1.5	2.22	116	120	0.8
42740	GLENDALE	093	1687	1773	1832	1.2	80	619	665	700	1.7	2.66	496	520	1.1
42741	GLENS FORK	001	680	658	653	-0.8	10	276	276	280	0.0	2.38	192	185	-0.9
42742	GRADYVILLE	001	357	401	425	2.8	94	135	155	168	3.3	2.59	107	120	2.7
42743	GREENSBURG	087	9257	9211	9121	-0.1	33	3831	3882	3911	0.3	2.33	2724	2678	-0.4
42746	HARDYVILLE	099	1789	1846	1907	0.7	69	661	691	723	1.1	2.67	494	503	0.4
42748	HODGENVILLE	123	7914	8298	8679	1.1	78	3158	3371	3584	1.6	2.40	2255	2339	0.9
42749	HORSE CAVE	099	5590	5526	5636	-0.3	28	2242	2259	2341	0.2	2.37	1559	1519	-0.6
42753	KNIFLEY	001	738	743	744	0.2	48	292	300	305	0.6	2.48	225	225	0.0
42754	LEITCHFIELD	085	15177	15525	15894	0.5	63	6028	6296	6568	1.0	2.42	4306	4365	0.3
42757	MAGNOLIA	099	3323	3564	3755	1.7	86	1280	1392	1485	2.0	2.56	970	1027	1.4
42762	MILLWOOD	085	527	531	535	0.2	48	189	194	199	0.6	2.74	140	140	0.0
42764	MOUNT SHERMAN	087	818	827	838	0.3	52	334	344	354	0.7	2.40	251	251	0.0
42765	MUNFORDVILLE	099	5059	5346	5623	1.3	81	1931	2075	2214	1.7	2.55	1329	1382	0.9
42776	SONORA	093	2286	2426	2530	1.4	84	800	863	917	1.8	2.72	614	646	1.2
42782	SUMMERSVILLE	087	909	907	898	-0.1	37	338	343	346	0.4	2.64	262	260	-0.2
42784	UPTON	099	2843	2889	2976	0.4	56	1086	1123	1176	0.8	2.57	812	819	0.2
42788	WHITE MILLS	093	337	382	408	3.0	95	117	135	146	3.4	2.83	93	105	2.9
45275	CINCINNATI	015	360	382	430	1.4	84	157	173	202	2.3	1.98	100	106	1.4
	KENTUCKY					0.7					1.2	2.42			0.5
	UNITED STATES					1.2					1.3	2.58			1.1

#	ZIP CODE POST OFFICE NAME	RACE (%) White 2000	White 2004	Black 2000	Black 2004	Asian/Pacific 2000	Asian/Pacific 2004	% Hispanic Origin 2000	% Hispanic Origin 2004	2004 AGE DISTRIBUTION (%) 0-4	5-9	10-14	15-19	20-24	25-44	45-64	65-84	85+	18+	MEDIAN AGE 2004	% 2004 Males	% 2004 Females
42533	FERGUSON	95.8	95.5	2.2	2.3	0.4	0.5	1.0	1.4	5.5	5.5	7.8	7.1	7.5	28.9	24.7	12.0	1.1	76.7	37.0	49.0	51.0
42539	LIBERTY	98.3	98.1	0.4	0.4	0.1	0.2	1.3	1.7	6.4	6.5	6.6	6.4	5.9	26.3	25.8	14.1	2.1	76.7	39.4	48.7	51.3
42541	MIDDLEBURG	98.6	98.4	0.0	0.0	0.0	0.0	1.2	1.6	7.0	7.2	7.2	5.8	4.4	28.9	25.0	13.4	1.2	75.3	38.0	48.9	51.1
42544	NANCY	99.0	98.8	0.1	0.1	0.2	0.3	0.7	1.0	5.7	5.8	6.1	5.6	5.4	26.7	29.4	13.8	1.5	79.1	41.5	49.8	50.2
42553	SCIENCE HILL	98.9	98.7	0.3	0.3	0.1	0.1	0.7	0.9	5.7	5.9	6.6	6.7	6.3	28.2	27.5	12.0	1.1	77.6	39.0	50.3	49.7
42565	WINDSOR	97.1	97.0	1.2	1.4	0.2	0.2	1.2	1.8	7.5	7.7	7.7	7.9	6.7	26.2	24.2	11.1	1.2	72.4	34.7	50.4	49.6
42566	YOSEMITE	98.2	98.1	0.3	0.2	0.0	0.0	1.5	1.9	6.0	6.2	6.7	6.7	6.2	29.0	26.3	11.5	1.4	77.3	38.2	51.0	49.0
42567	EUBANK	98.8	98.6	0.2	0.2	0.1	0.2	1.3	1.7	5.9	6.0	6.5	6.4	6.5	28.6	26.1	12.7	1.3	77.5	38.7	50.7	49.3
42602	ALBANY	99.1	99.0	0.1	0.1	0.2	0.2	1.2	1.6	6.5	6.3	6.1	5.3	5.5	27.6	26.8	14.0	1.8	77.9	40.2	48.5	51.5
42603	ALPHA	99.0	98.9	0.5	0.5	0.0	0.0	1.3	1.7	6.8	6.9	7.1	7.5	6.6	28.4	24.2	11.1	1.3	74.1	36.2	50.9	49.1
42629	JAMESTOWN	97.5	97.5	1.5	1.5	0.2	0.2	0.8	0.8	5.7	6.0	6.2	5.7	5.3	25.8	27.0	15.8	2.6	78.6	41.9	49.1	50.9
42633	MONTICELLO	96.5	96.2	1.7	1.8	0.1	0.1	1.5	1.9	6.9	6.7	6.8	6.4	6.3	28.0	25.1	12.4	1.6	75.7	37.4	49.4	50.6
42634	PARKERS LAKE	98.4	98.1	0.1	0.1	0.0	0.0	0.4	0.6	6.9	7.6	8.7	6.8	5.9	28.1	25.6	9.8	0.8	72.3	35.5	51.2	48.9
42635	PINE KNOT	96.1	95.7	2.1	2.2	0.1	0.1	1.0	1.3	7.2	6.7	7.1	9.8	6.6	27.4	23.1	10.4	1.5	72.6	33.9	49.9	50.1
42638	REVELO	98.6	98.6	0.0	0.0	0.0	0.0	0.5	0.5	4.8	5.7	10.0	8.1	6.2	26.7	24.3	12.4	1.9	73.8	38.1	49.5	50.5
42642	RUSSELL SPRINGS	98.6	98.6	0.2	0.2	0.1	0.1	0.8	0.9	5.5	5.7	6.3	5.9	5.6	26.7	27.8	14.8	1.6	78.8	41.1	48.5	51.5
42647	STEARNS	98.5	98.4	0.2	0.2	0.0	0.0	0.5	0.6	6.3	6.3	7.3	6.8	6.5	28.2	26.4	11.3	1.0	75.9	37.5	49.4	50.6
42649	STRUNK	98.9	98.8	0.1	0.1	0.1	0.1	0.6	0.7	7.8	7.7	9.1	7.0	6.3	28.7	22.9	9.5	1.1	71.1	33.8	49.1	50.9
42653	WHITLEY CITY	98.8	98.7	0.2	0.2	0.0	0.0	0.5	0.6	6.3	6.6	7.8	7.2	6.4	28.9	25.8	10.0	1.0	74.8	35.9	48.9	51.1
42701	ELIZABETHTOWN	89.7	88.4	6.6	7.0	1.6	2.1	1.6	2.1	6.7	6.7	6.9	6.7	6.5	28.9	25.4	10.7	1.5	75.4	37.3	48.7	51.3
42711	BAKERTON	97.1	97.0	1.9	2.0	0.5	0.5	0.5	0.5	5.6	6.1	6.6	5.6	5.6	25.9	27.4	15.7	1.5	78.2	42.1	47.2	52.8
42712	BIG CLIFTY	98.9	98.7	0.1	0.1	0.1	0.2	0.7	0.9	6.7	6.8	6.9	5.9	5.8	30.1	26.4	10.0	1.2	75.9	37.1	51.7	48.3
42713	BONNIEVILLE	96.6	96.4	2.3	2.4	0.1	0.1	0.4	0.5	6.6	6.8	7.7	6.8	5.9	27.3	25.4	12.1	1.4	74.8	37.8	49.1	50.9
42715	BREEDING	96.6	96.3	1.0	1.4	0.3	0.3	0.7	0.3	6.4	6.4	7.1	5.7	7.4	24.7	28.0	12.8	1.4	76.0	39.4	50.0	50.0
42716	BUFFALO	97.4	97.1	1.4	1.5	0.6	0.6	0.6	0.9	5.8	6.4	6.6	6.8	5.8	27.2	27.8	12.4	1.3	77.2	39.9	49.9	50.1
42717	BURKESVILLE	95.4	95.4	3.3	3.3	0.1	0.1	0.7	0.7	5.8	5.9	6.4	6.0	5.7	25.7	26.2	16.0	2.3	78.1	41.5	48.5	51.5
42718	CAMPBELLSVILLE	93.5	93.2	5.2	5.3	0.2	0.3	0.8	1.1	6.0	6.1	6.3	6.7	7.3	26.0	25.9	13.9	1.9	78.1	39.6	48.4	51.6
42721	CANEYVILLE	99.1	99.1	0.1	0.1	0.0	0.0	0.4	0.6	6.0	6.3	7.4	6.4	6.1	27.0	26.8	12.8	1.3	76.4	38.5	49.7	50.3
42722	CANMER	91.3	91.1	6.6	6.8	0.0	0.0	1.2	1.1	6.8	6.6	6.4	6.8	6.1	27.1	26.6	12.2	1.5	76.0	39.4	50.2	49.8
42724	CECILIA	98.5	98.3	0.4	0.4	0.2	0.2	0.7	1.0	6.0	6.2	7.0	6.6	6.2	27.9	28.3	10.9	0.9	76.8	39.3	50.4	49.6
42726	CLARKSON	98.7	98.5	0.1	0.1	0.3	0.3	1.0	1.2	6.2	6.1	6.3	5.6	5.8	26.7	28.5	13.6	1.2	77.9	40.6	50.7	49.4
42728	COLUMBIA	95.6	95.3	2.9	3.0	0.3	0.4	0.8	1.0	6.2	6.0	6.3	6.7	7.8	27.5	24.3	13.2	2.0	78.0	37.8	48.4	51.6
42729	CUB RUN	97.9	97.8	1.1	1.1	0.1	0.1	0.9	1.2	6.8	6.7	7.5	8.0	7.2	24.6	25.6	12.6	1.0	74.2	36.9	51.2	48.8
42731	DUBRE	96.9	96.4	0.6	0.9	0.3	0.3	0.3	0.6	6.0	6.3	7.4	6.0	5.7	27.1	26.5	13.7	1.5	76.8	39.4	50.6	49.4
42732	EASTVIEW	98.6	98.4	0.3	0.3	0.5	0.6	0.6	0.7	6.3	6.2	6.4	6.7	6.5	28.1	26.7	11.9	1.2	77.0	38.9	50.8	49.2
42733	ELK HORN	98.8	98.7	0.3	0.3	0.0	0.0	0.7	0.9	7.0	6.9	7.5	7.4	6.8	26.4	25.2	11.8	1.0	74.0	36.6	51.4	48.6
42735	FAIRPLAY	96.6	96.5	2.5	2.7	0.0	0.0	0.3	0.5	5.4	5.4	5.2	6.0	5.7	27.6	30.1	13.0	1.6	80.2	41.6	50.7	49.3
42740	GLENDALE	96.4	96.0	1.4	1.5	0.7	0.9	1.1	1.4	6.7	6.8	7.1	7.1	6.1	27.5	27.2	10.4	1.2	75.0	38.5	49.9	50.1
42741	GLENS FORK	97.8	97.4	1.0	1.1	0.2	0.2	1.0	1.7	6.5	5.8	5.2	5.5	5.6	26.6	30.2	13.8	1.7	79.8	42.3	50.3	49.7
42742	GRADYVILLE	98.3	98.5	0.8	0.8	0.0	0.0	1.4	1.8	7.7	7.2	6.2	6.5	7.5	27.7	23.7	12.7	0.8	74.3	35.1	49.1	50.9
42743	GREENSBURG	96.0	95.9	2.8	2.9	0.1	0.1	1.0	1.0	5.3	5.4	6.2	6.0	5.8	26.2	27.2	15.4	2.5	79.3	41.9	49.3	50.8
42746	HARDYVILLE	94.3	93.9	4.3	4.5	0.4	0.5	1.6	2.0	6.3	6.4	7.3	7.2	7.0	28.8	25.0	10.4	1.5	75.6	37.1	50.1	50.0
42748	HODGENVILLE	93.0	92.7	5.1	5.2	0.2	0.2	1.2	1.5	6.4	6.4	6.5	6.2	6.0	26.8	25.9	13.6	2.3	77.0	39.8	48.3	51.7
42749	HORSE CAVE	87.7	87.0	11.0	11.6	0.1	0.2	0.7	0.9	6.5	6.5	6.4	5.6	6.0	28.5	25.4	13.1	2.1	77.1	38.9	49.6	50.4
42753	KNIFLEY	98.2	98.1	0.7	0.7	0.1	0.1	1.0	1.2	7.4	7.3	8.3	8.6	7.1	27.2	22.8	10.2	1.1	71.7	34.2	51.7	48.3
42754	LEITCHFIELD	97.9	97.7	0.7	0.8	0.1	0.2	0.8	1.0	6.6	6.6	7.0	6.2	6.5	27.8	24.9	12.7	1.6	76.1	37.7	49.5	50.5
42757	MAGNOLIA	97.9	97.8	0.6	0.6	0.2	0.2	1.1	1.5	6.7	7.1	7.6	6.1	5.7	27.8	25.3	12.5	1.2	74.8	37.8	50.2	49.8
42762	MILLWOOD	97.9	97.6	0.2	0.2	0.2	0.2	0.8	0.9	5.5	5.8	7.2	6.6	6.8	26.4	28.6	12.1	1.1	77.6	39.0	49.0	51.0
42764	MOUNT SHERMAN	97.2	97.1	1.5	1.5	0.4	0.5	0.6	0.7	5.9	6.2	5.9	6.5	5.9	27.1	27.9	13.1	1.5	77.9	40.2	50.1	49.9
42765	MUNFORDVILLE	93.4	92.9	5.6	5.9	0.1	0.1	0.8	1.1	7.1	7.0	7.1	6.6	6.5	26.0	24.7	13.5	1.6	74.9	37.9	49.3	50.7
42776	SONORA	96.2	95.7	1.8	1.9	0.5	0.6	0.7	1.0	7.9	7.8	7.1	9.1	6.2	25.8	24.3	10.4	1.5	70.7	35.5	49.7	50.3
42782	SUMMERSVILLE	96.9	96.9	2.0	2.0	0.0	0.0	0.9	0.9	6.3	6.7	7.9	5.8	6.0	28.1	25.4	12.1	1.7	75.4	37.8	51.1	49.0
42784	UPTON	96.7	96.4	1.4	1.5	0.1	0.2	0.6	0.9	6.6	6.8	7.6	6.9	6.5	27.3	26.0	10.8	1.5	74.8	37.0	50.4	49.6
42788	WHITE MILLS	98.5	98.4	0.0	0.0	0.0	0.0	1.8	2.4	6.0	7.1	8.6	7.9	5.0	27.5	24.9	11.8	1.3	73.0	38.7	52.9	47.1
45275	CINCINNATI	98.3	98.2	0.6	0.5	0.6	0.5	0.6	0.5	7.1	6.8	5.5	3.9	4.2	26.7	22.8	18.9	4.2	78.5	41.5	43.5	56.5
	KENTUCKY	90.1	89.5	7.3	7.4	0.8	1.0	1.5	1.9	6.6	6.6	6.8	6.6	7.0	28.9	24.8	11.1	1.5	76.3	36.8	49.1	50.9
	UNITED STATES	75.1	73.6	12.3	12.5	3.8	4.2	12.5	14.1	6.9	6.7	7.2	7.0	7.3	28.6	23.8	10.8	1.7	75.1	36.0	49.1	50.9

C   42533-45275

#	POST OFFICE NAME	2004 Per Capita Income	2004 HH Income Base	Less than $25,000	$25,000 to $49,999	$50,000 to $99,999	$100,000 to $149,999	$150,000 or More	2004	2009	2004 National Centile	2004 State Centile	2004 Home Value Base	Less than $50,000	$50,000 to $89,999	$90,000 to $174,999	$175,000 to $399,999	$400,000 or More	2004 Median Home Value
42533	FERGUSON	21397	357	34.5	31.7	23.8	3.9	6.2	35570	42948	30	62	234	33.8	35.9	24.4	4.3	1.7	66500
42539	LIBERTY	15195	4226	51.1	28.2	15.9	2.7	2.2	24295	28381	4	24	3391	45.9	31.6	18.4	4.0	0.2	56399
42541	MIDDLEBURG	13999	197	47.2	28.9	20.8	2.0	1.0	27104	32343	7	35	163	51.5	26.4	20.9	1.2	0.0	48958
42544	NANCY	18961	1992	43.7	35.4	16.2	3.4	1.3	28509	33325	10	39	1657	36.6	29.4	26.0	7.4	0.6	70299
42553	SCIENCE HILL	17457	1772	39.7	30.5	23.5	4.7	1.5	31441	37955	16	47	1461	33.5	34.6	24.0	6.4	1.4	69025
42565	WINDSOR	11950	203	62.6	21.7	12.3	3.0	0.5	18325	21361	1	6	164	57.9	20.1	17.1	4.9	0.0	41875
42566	YOSEMITE	18978	167	43.1	37.1	15.0	2.4	2.4	28975	34294	10	40	139	50.4	36.7	8.6	3.6	0.7	49643
42567	EUBANK	16298	2156	43.6	28.9	22.2	4.4	1.0	29574	35342	11	43	1815	40.4	28.7	22.6	7.0	1.3	63323
42602	ALBANY	16447	3756	53.1	27.8	15.0	2.2	1.9	22429	27109	3	20	2950	48.9	30.8	14.0	5.5	0.9	51368
42603	ALPHA	14604	1387	47.5	30.2	17.6	2.5	2.2	26360	31792	6	32	1164	55.3	26.7	12.3	4.9	0.8	45194
42629	JAMESTOWN	15280	1995	49.7	29.4	15.9	4.2	0.8	25170	29298	5	27	1586	35.8	28.7	24.2	10.6	0.8	68595
42633	MONTICELLO	15674	6973	51.5	29.0	14.4	2.6	2.5	23846	28281	4	23	5323	47.2	28.2	17.6	6.6	0.5	53076
42634	PARKERS LAKE	12925	609	61.3	28.6	7.2	0.5	2.5	19779	22041	2	10	496	70.8	22.4	5.0	1.2	0.6	30667
42635	PINE KNOT	10911	1680	60.4	26.0	12.1	1.1	0.4	19639	21759	2	10	1255	52.8	29.6	16.7	0.4	0.6	47240
42638	REVELO	10113	82	59.8	28.1	12.2	0.0	0.0	19084	22212	2	8	66	59.1	33.3	7.6	0.0	0.0	26000
42642	RUSSELL SPRINGS	16483	5534	48.7	32.6	13.1	3.8	1.8	25602	30016	5	29	4447	37.4	33.5	22.5	5.4	1.3	63099
42647	STEARNS	11523	1693	55.9	30.1	12.1	1.1	0.8	21928	24496	3	18	1347	54.2	32.3	11.2	1.8	0.5	45252
42649	STRUNK	10996	794	59.2	27.6	11.1	0.4	1.8	20211	22524	2	12	644	66.0	22.1	10.1	1.9	0.0	40463
42653	WHITLEY CITY	12348	1920	55.4	30.6	11.6	1.6	0.9	22237	24886	3	19	1451	48.7	36.9	11.4	2.8	0.2	51101
42701	ELIZABETHTOWN	24126	16906	24.8	29.4	33.9	8.3	3.7	45618	54676	63	84	12417	10.7	22.8	46.3	17.0	3.2	111995
42711	BAKERTON	17089	93	44.1	36.6	14.0	2.2	3.2	27503	31475	8	36	79	27.9	40.5	27.9	2.5	1.3	70556
42712	BIG CLIFTY	16566	703	33.9	38.3	22.2	5.0	0.7	33567	40241	23	55	597	30.5	29.7	31.2	7.0	1.7	76351
42713	BONNIEVILLE	15979	724	43.1	29.7	21.8	3.9	1.5	29205	34507	11	42	595	42.9	25.4	23.5	7.9	0.3	64592
42715	BREEDING	17207	118	45.8	29.7	14.4	5.1	5.1	26548	33329	6	33	96	56.3	21.9	17.7	3.1	1.0	42500
42716	BUFFALO	19642	495	30.5	36.2	25.9	5.3	2.2	36505	44787	34	64	420	21.0	33.3	33.6	11.4	0.7	86000
42717	BURKESVILLE	15302	3105	49.9	31.4	14.6	3.0	1.1	25062	29793	5	26	2438	42.3	32.0	20.8	3.9	1.0	59692
42718	CAMPBELLSVILLE	19226	9289	38.4	32.3	22.1	4.5	2.7	32838	39077	20	53	6960	19.6	35.5	36.7	7.3	0.9	85534
42721	CANEYVILLE	16983	1551	43.3	32.0	18.9	3.6	2.2	28307	33022	9	38	1257	35.9	33.7	21.9	6.8	1.8	69914
42722	CANMER	14202	241	46.5	24.1	25.7	3.7	0.0	28103	33194	9	38	201	32.8	33.3	25.4	8.5	0.0	72813
42724	CECILIA	19782	1455	21.8	37.3	32.7	6.9	1.3	43305	51837	57	81	1258	23.9	25.3	34.2	13.8	2.8	91282
42726	CLARKSON	17379	1901	35.0	36.7	22.9	4.1	1.4	32159	38473	18	50	1635	33.5	30.4	30.1	5.6	0.4	70048
42728	COLUMBIA	19458	5534	45.1	28.4	18.9	3.7	3.9	27796	34668	8	37	4322	33.3	32.7	26.9	6.0	1.0	68661
42729	CUB RUN	13233	516	42.4	40.5	15.1	1.6	0.4	30000	34924	12	44	447	30.0	36.0	27.5	6.5	0.0	71310
42731	DUBRE	12277	137	53.3	31.4	13.1	2.2	0.0	23155	27550	3	22	116	53.5	29.3	13.8	3.5	0.0	46667
42732	EASTVIEW	17947	723	27.0	36.8	30.7	4.4	1.1	39865	47563	45	73	611	29.3	28.8	31.3	9.8	0.8	78375
42733	ELK HORN	13197	570	50.4	32.6	15.3	0.7	1.1	24764	29515	4	25	479	36.3	35.9	22.8	3.1	1.9	59776
42735	FAIRPLAY	17096	166	44.6	33.7	16.9	2.4	2.4	27581	32324	8	36	143	29.4	32.9	37.1	0.7	0.0	71667
42740	GLENDALE	21076	665	20.5	26.9	42.6	8.9	1.2	52212	62140	76	91	565	12.4	19.1	48.3	19.5	0.7	110819
42741	GLENS FORK	18766	276	46.7	28.3	13.8	6.9	4.4	26401	33541	6	32	235	42.6	32.8	20.9	3.0	0.9	59211
42742	GRADYVILLE	17657	155	43.2	34.2	20.0	0.7	1.9	30318	38218	13	45	132	36.4	23.5	28.8	11.4	0.0	73000
42743	GREENSBURG	19016	3882	45.0	29.1	19.4	4.0	2.6	28339	34296	9	39	3028	32.6	36.8	25.0	5.3	0.3	67178
42746	HARDYVILLE	13519	691	41.7	32.3	22.6	3.5	0.0	30803	36245	14	46	572	37.8	31.5	23.8	7.0	0.0	67600
42748	HODGENVILLE	19896	3371	32.4	31.3	26.9	7.1	2.3	39257	46510	44	72	2606	22.8	28.0	36.1	11.2	2.0	89038
42749	HORSE CAVE	19193	2259	43.8	27.7	22.6	4.1	1.8	29744	35237	12	43	1682	27.7	40.1	27.4	4.5	0.5	71358
42753	KNIFLEY	14424	300	44.7	28.0	24.3	2.0	1.0	27997	33326	9	37	257	45.9	34.6	17.9	0.8	0.8	54200
42754	LEITCHFIELD	18315	6296	38.2	31.9	23.5	4.5	2.0	31947	37904	18	49	4791	28.5	34.3	30.7	6.1	0.4	76174
42757	MAGNOLIA	18296	1392	35.1	31.9	26.0	4.0	3.0	34299	41421	25	58	1175	28.3	31.1	28.1	10.6	2.0	77376
42762	MILLWOOD	19011	194	33.0	26.3	31.4	5.7	3.6	41158	51344	50	77	157	46.5	19.8	23.6	10.2	0.0	56111
42764	MOUNT SHERMAN	30666	344	32.6	32.3	24.1	5.2	5.8	37529	46822	38	67	289	30.5	32.2	27.3	9.7	0.4	74318
42765	MUNFORDVILLE	16640	2075	44.0	31.0	18.9	2.9	3.2	29334	35000	11	42	1616	29.0	38.6	23.8	7.1	1.7	72765
42776	SONORA	15767	863	36.2	29.0	28.9	5.0	1.0	33315	40041	22	54	715	27.0	34.3	25.9	10.1	2.8	77836
42782	SUMMERSVILLE	14686	343	38.8	38.8	17.2	5.0	0.3	29922	36077	12	44	288	51.0	24.0	22.2	2.8	0.0	49375
42784	UPTON	15609	1123	37.3	36.3	21.3	3.6	1.5	31674	37507	17	48	952	34.6	34.1	22.1	7.5	1.8	68667
42788	WHITE MILLS	20833	135	23.0	23.7	37.8	13.3	2.2	52583	63363	76	91	118	30.5	27.1	28.0	14.4	0.0	80000
45275	CINCINNATI	25560	173	17.3	39.3	33.5	7.5	2.3	44164	56988	59	83	153	62.8	12.4	22.2	2.6	0.0	38036
	KENTUCKY	22472		31.8	28.3	28.2	7.8	3.9	39962	49361				22.2	24.9	36.4	14.3	2.1	94344
	UNITED STATES	25866		24.7	27.1	30.8	10.9	6.5	48124	56710				10.9	15.0	33.7	30.1	10.4	145905

ZIP CODE		FINANCIAL SERVICES				THE HOME							ENTERTAINMENT						PERSONAL			
						Home Improvements		Furnishings														
#	POST OFFICE NAME	Auto Loan	Home Loan	Invest-ments	Retire-ment Plans	Home Repair	Lawn & Garden	Comput-ers & Hard-ware	Major Appli-ances	TV, Radio, Sound Equip-ment	Furni-ture	Dine out/ Carry out	Sports Equip-ment	Fees & Tickets	Toys & Games	Travel	Cable TV	Apparel & Services	Auto Repairs	Health Insur-ance	Pets & Supplies
42533	FERGUSON	79	64	47	63	68	79	68	74	74	66	89	83	63	86	67	76	82	73	83	88
42539	LIBERTY	65	45	22	40	50	59	45	54	53	45	62	64	38	59	45	57	57	54	66	74
42541	MIDDLEBURG	67	45	20	39	51	59	43	54	52	44	61	65	37	58	44	56	56	54	67	77
42544	NANCY	84	57	27	49	65	74	55	69	66	56	78	82	47	73	56	71	71	68	84	97
42553	SCIENCE HILL	81	56	27	48	63	72	54	66	64	55	75	79	46	71	54	69	69	66	81	93
42565	WINDSOR	53	35	16	31	40	46	34	43	41	35	48	51	29	46	35	44	44	42	53	61
42566	YOSEMITE	89	60	27	52	68	78	58	72	70	59	82	86	49	77	59	75	74	72	89	103
42567	EUBANK	76	51	23	44	58	67	49	62	59	50	70	74	42	66	50	64	63	61	76	87
42602	ALBANY	68	47	25	41	53	61	47	56	55	47	65	67	40	62	47	59	60	56	68	78
42603	ALPHA	69	47	21	40	53	61	45	56	54	46	64	67	38	60	46	58	58	56	69	80
42629	JAMESTOWN	63	43	22	38	49	57	43	52	51	43	60	62	37	57	44	55	55	52	64	72
42633	MONTICELLO	70	48	23	42	54	62	47	58	56	47	66	68	40	62	47	60	60	57	71	81
42634	PARKERS LAKE	62	42	19	36	47	54	40	50	49	41	57	60	34	54	41	52	52	50	62	71
42635	PINE KNOT	50	34	15	29	38	44	32	41	39	33	46	48	28	43	33	42	42	40	50	58
42638	REVELO	49	33	15	28	37	43	32	39	38	32	45	47	27	42	32	41	41	39	49	56
42642	RUSSELL SPRINGS	69	48	24	42	54	62	46	57	55	47	65	68	40	61	47	59	59	56	70	80
42647	STEARNS	54	36	16	31	41	47	35	43	42	35	49	52	30	47	35	45	45	43	54	62
42649	STRUNK	54	36	16	31	41	47	35	44	42	36	50	52	30	47	36	45	45	43	54	62
42653	WHITLEY CITY	57	38	17	33	43	50	37	46	44	37	52	55	31	49	37	48	47	46	57	65
42701	ELIZABETHTOWN	88	84	77	82	86	92	82	85	84	81	103	100	81	104	83	84	99	85	88	101
42711	BAKERTON	68	46	21	39	52	60	44	55	53	45	62	66	37	59	45	57	57	55	68	78
42712	BIG CLIFTY	77	53	27	47	60	68	51	63	61	52	72	75	44	69	52	65	66	62	77	89
42713	BONNIEVILLE	75	50	23	44	57	66	49	61	58	49	69	72	41	65	49	63	63	60	75	86
42715	BREEDING	81	54	25	47	62	71	53	66	63	54	74	78	45	70	53	68	68	65	81	93
42716	BUFFALO	83	69	48	64	74	81	65	74	71	65	85	88	61	85	66	73	80	72	82	97
42717	BURKESVILLE	64	45	26	39	49	57	45	53	53	45	62	63	39	59	45	56	57	53	64	73
42718	CAMPBELLSVILLE	75	60	44	56	64	72	60	67	66	59	80	79	56	78	60	69	75	67	76	86
42721	CANEYVILLE	78	52	24	45	59	68	50	63	61	51	71	75	43	67	51	65	65	62	77	89
42722	CANMER	69	46	21	40	52	60	45	56	54	45	63	67	38	60	45	58	57	55	69	79
42724	CECILIA	87	71	48	66	76	84	66	76	73	67	88	91	63	88	68	76	82	74	86	101
42726	CLARKSON	74	54	30	48	60	68	51	62	60	52	71	74	45	68	53	64	65	61	75	86
42728	COLUMBIA	84	58	33	53	65	76	60	71	70	60	82	84	52	78	60	74	75	71	85	95
42729	CUB RUN	61	43	23	38	49	56	42	51	49	42	58	61	36	55	43	53	53	51	62	72
42731	DUBRE	57	38	17	33	43	50	37	46	44	37	52	55	31	49	37	48	47	45	56	65
42732	EASTVIEW	80	63	40	58	68	76	59	69	66	60	79	82	55	79	61	69	74	68	79	93
42733	ELK HORN	67	45	20	39	51	59	43	54	52	44	62	65	37	58	44	56	56	54	67	77
42735	FAIRPLAY	72	48	22	41	54	62	46	58	56	47	66	69	39	62	47	60	60	57	71	82
42740	GLENDALE	91	79	59	75	84	91	74	82	79	74	96	98	72	97	76	81	91	80	90	107
42741	GLENS FORK	84	56	26	49	64	74	54	68	66	55	77	81	46	73	55	71	70	67	84	97
42742	GRADYVILLE	86	58	26	50	65	75	56	70	67	57	79	83	47	74	57	72	72	69	86	99
42743	GREENSBURG	80	56	30	50	63	73	56	67	66	56	78	79	49	74	57	70	71	67	81	91
42746	HARDYVILLE	68	46	21	39	52	59	44	55	53	45	62	66	37	59	45	57	57	54	68	78
42748	HODGENVILLE	82	64	42	59	70	79	62	72	70	62	83	85	57	81	64	73	77	71	84	94
42749	HORSE CAVE	82	57	30	51	64	75	58	69	68	58	80	81	50	76	59	73	73	69	85	94
42753	KNIFLEY	67	45	20	39	51	59	43	54	52	44	62	65	37	58	44	57	56	54	67	77
42754	LEITCHFIELD	81	57	31	51	64	73	55	67	65	56	77	80	49	74	57	70	70	67	81	93
42757	MAGNOLIA	88	59	28	52	67	77	57	71	69	58	81	85	49	77	58	74	73	71	87	101
42762	MILLWOOD	98	66	30	57	74	86	63	79	76	65	90	95	54	85	64	82	82	78	98	112
42764	MOUNT SHERMAN	131	97	56	87	107	120	92	111	106	93	127	132	83	123	94	113	117	109	130	152
42765	MUNFORDVILLE	76	54	30	49	60	69	54	64	62	54	75	74	47	70	54	66	67	63	77	87
42776	SONORA	81	55	26	48	62	71	53	66	64	54	75	78	46	71	54	68	68	65	80	92
42782	SUMMERSVILLE	73	49	22	42	55	64	47	59	57	48	67	71	40	63	48	61	61	59	73	84
42784	UPTON	73	51	27	46	57	65	50	60	59	51	69	72	44	66	51	62	64	60	73	83
42788	WHITE MILLS	94	84	64	80	89	95	78	86	83	78	100	103	76	102	80	85	95	84	93	111
45275	CINCINNATI	86	78	61	75	78	83	75	80	76	77	93	92	71	88	74	74	90	80	79	95
	KENTUCKY	86	74	63	71	77	85	74	80	79	74	96	94	71	95	74	81	91	80	86	98
	UNITED STATES	100	100	100	100	100	100	100	100	100	100	100	100	100	100	100	100	100	100	100	100

LOUISIANA

POPULATION CHANGE

A 70001-70422

#	POST OFFICE NAME	COUNTY FIPS CODE	POPULATION 2000	2004	2009	2000-2004 ANNUAL RATE % Rate	State Centile	HOUSEHOLDS 2000	2004	2009	% Annual Rate 2000-2004	2004 Average HH Size	FAMILIES 2000	2004	% Annual Rate 2000-2004
70001	METAIRIE	051	39403	38915	38880	-0.3	17	18402	18357	18561	-0.1	2.11	10033	10059	0.1
70002	METAIRIE	051	19423	19881	20233	0.6	53	8865	9203	9498	0.9	2.16	5047	5209	0.8
70003	METAIRIE	051	43344	43638	44075	0.2	35	16711	17156	17622	0.6	2.53	12091	12345	0.5
70005	METAIRIE	051	25427	25584	25887	0.1	34	12100	12379	12721	0.5	2.06	6761	6887	0.4
70006	METAIRIE	051	16656	16885	17174	0.3	43	7027	7224	7449	0.7	2.32	4641	4787	0.7
70030	DES ALLEMANDS	089	4274	4454	4693	1.0	70	1543	1620	1718	1.2	2.75	1225	1285	1.1
70031	AMA	089	1309	1319	1360	0.2	37	455	463	481	0.4	2.85	356	361	0.3
70032	ARABI	087	8093	7866	7794	-0.7	9	3474	3442	3472	-0.2	2.18	2246	2222	-0.3
70036	BARATARIA	051	1333	1421	1466	1.5	82	500	543	570	2.0	2.62	368	399	1.9
70037	BELLE CHASSE	075	12129	14248	16152	3.9	99	4129	4914	5646	4.2	2.83	3299	3914	4.1
70039	BOUTTE	089	2389	2378	2464	-0.1	22	820	821	855	0.0	2.89	624	623	0.0
70040	BRAITHWAITE	075	3282	3415	3590	0.9	69	1014	1075	1153	1.4	2.84	787	833	1.4
70041	BURAS	075	7206	6976	7244	-0.8	7	2461	2417	2549	-0.4	2.88	1859	1823	-0.5
70043	CHALMETTE	087	32084	31713	31584	-0.3	18	12327	12412	12588	0.2	2.54	8827	8879	0.1
70047	DESTREHAN	089	12674	13917	15046	2.2	91	4114	4542	4938	2.4	3.02	3431	3787	2.4
70049	EDGARD	095	2737	2952	3161	1.8	86	885	971	1055	2.2	3.04	717	785	2.2
70051	GARYVILLE	095	2095	2018	2083	-0.9	5	687	675	708	-0.4	2.98	540	529	-0.5
70052	GRAMERCY	093	3118	3203	3257	0.6	57	1110	1160	1202	1.0	2.76	855	893	1.0
70053	GRETNA	051	17414	17527	17657	0.2	34	6956	7106	7271	0.5	2.36	4281	4368	0.5
70056	GRETNA	051	40264	41352	42134	0.6	57	14567	15156	15651	0.9	2.71	10784	11189	0.9
70057	HAHNVILLE	089	3514	3497	3616	-0.1	22	1214	1220	1273	0.1	2.79	924	927	0.1
70058	HARVEY	051	41797	42886	43891	0.6	56	13617	14029	14488	0.7	3.02	10792	11173	0.8
70062	KENNER	051	18945	18392	18272	-0.7	8	6737	6633	6683	-0.4	2.74	4808	4720	-0.4
70065	KENNER	051	53584	53997	54574	0.2	37	19607	20120	20663	0.6	2.66	14199	14542	0.6
70067	LAFITTE	051	4787	4821	4851	0.2	35	1642	1674	1708	0.5	2.88	1295	1319	0.4
70068	LA PLACE	095	30446	32732	35167	1.7	85	10058	10944	11903	2.0	2.95	8047	8756	2.0
70070	LULING	089	11533	11904	12484	0.8	63	3905	4062	4288	0.9	2.90	3226	3355	0.9
70071	LUTCHER	093	3905	3844	3844	-0.4	15	1303	1302	1324	0.0	2.87	1029	1028	0.0
70072	MARRERO	051	56668	56919	57247	0.1	32	18957	19379	19809	0.5	2.91	15028	15346	0.5
70075	MERAUX	087	8025	8449	8622	1.2	76	2935	3155	3283	1.7	2.68	2180	2338	1.7
70076	MOUNT AIRY	095	683	662	684	-0.7	7	226	223	234	-0.3	2.97	180	177	-0.4
70079	NORCO	089	3706	3705	3843	0.0	27	1364	1373	1433	0.2	2.70	1013	1016	0.1
70080	PARADIS	089	1422	1458	1518	0.6	54	499	515	539	0.8	2.83	382	392	0.6
70081	PILOTTOWN	075	4	4	4	0.0	29	1	1	1	0.0	1.00	1	0	-100.0
70083	PORT SULPHUR	075	4155	4025	4196	-0.8	7	1424	1400	1483	-0.4	2.86	1058	1036	-0.5
70084	RESERVE	095	7450	7462	7758	0.0	30	2553	2587	2725	0.3	2.88	1917	1936	0.2
70085	SAINT BERNARD	087	7500	7443	7446	-0.2	20	2575	2596	2643	0.2	2.81	1972	1987	0.2
70086	SAINT JAMES	093	2243	2220	2221	-0.2	19	675	680	693	0.2	3.16	551	555	0.2
70087	SAINT ROSE	089	6597	7089	7635	1.7	84	2310	2490	2694	1.8	2.85	1766	1899	1.7
70090	VACHERIE	093	7317	7389	7539	0.2	39	2429	2500	2595	0.7	2.95	1940	1995	0.7
70091	VENICE	075	241	220	226	-2.1	0	91	85	89	-1.6	2.56	67	62	-1.8
70092	VIOLET	087	11266	11443	11535	0.4	45	3712	3822	3916	0.7	2.98	3004	3090	0.7
70094	WESTWEGO	051	34150	34291	34578	0.1	32	11843	12103	12402	0.5	2.82	8954	9163	0.5
70112	NEW ORLEANS	071	6361	6546	6613	0.7	59	2445	2512	2538	0.6	2.42	1300	1346	0.8
70113	NEW ORLEANS	071	10421	10163	10007	-0.6	10	4162	4042	3972	-0.7	2.46	2096	2034	-0.7
70114	NEW ORLEANS	071	28535	28530	28442	0.0	29	10409	10410	10383	0.0	2.68	6727	6735	0.0
70115	NEW ORLEANS	071	40371	38672	37715	-1.0	4	18230	17537	17141	-0.9	2.14	8710	8331	-1.0
70116	NEW ORLEANS	071	16876	16606	16394	-0.4	14	8008	7878	7783	-0.4	2.09	3322	3250	-0.5
70117	NEW ORLEANS	071	51258	50414	49818	-0.4	13	18804	18554	18360	-0.3	2.70	12073	11879	-0.4
70118	NEW ORLEANS	071	37212	36300	35687	-0.6	11	15201	14803	14538	-0.6	2.30	7902	7672	-0.7
70119	NEW ORLEANS	071	49794	48849	48237	-0.5	12	18440	17993	17718	-0.6	2.33	9832	9566	-0.6
70121	NEW ORLEANS	051	12998	12888	12875	-0.2	20	5930	5960	6038	0.1	2.09	3188	3194	0.0
70122	NEW ORLEANS	071	46533	45676	45086	-0.4	12	17819	17463	17227	-0.5	2.55	11946	11670	-0.6
70123	NEW ORLEANS	051	27721	27569	27680	-0.1	21	12149	12350	12622	0.4	2.21	7477	7561	0.3
70124	NEW ORLEANS	071	23000	22964	22827	0.0	27	10753	10765	10723	0.0	2.13	6152	6137	-0.1
70125	NEW ORLEANS	071	23465	23211	22967	-0.3	19	8799	8713	8624	-0.2	2.46	5209	5154	-0.2
70126	NEW ORLEANS	071	40834	39529	38809	-0.8	7	14561	14119	13882	-0.7	2.75	10584	10244	-0.8
70127	NEW ORLEANS	071	30625	31622	32110	0.8	63	11416	11776	11977	0.7	2.65	7960	8205	0.7
70128	NEW ORLEANS	071	21400	22094	22339	0.8	63	6957	7212	7353	0.9	3.02	5464	5636	0.7
70129	NEW ORLEANS	071	14972	15488	15644	0.8	65	4659	4794	4849	0.7	3.20	3649	3763	0.7
70130	NEW ORLEANS	071	14770	14868	14956	0.2	35	7312	7445	7526	0.4	1.92	2676	2659	-0.2
70131	NEW ORLEANS	071	28259	30335	31398	1.7	84	10279	11011	11420	1.6	2.72	7375	7887	1.6
70301	THIBODAUX	057	39579	41362	43206	1.0	73	14304	15175	16111	1.4	2.63	10365	11008	1.4
70339	PIERRE PART	007	5514	5990	6379	2.0	88	2105	2337	2540	2.5	2.56	1586	1760	2.5
70341	BELLE ROSE	007	4371	4362	4462	-0.1	26	1482	1502	1563	0.3	2.90	1147	1164	0.4
70342	BERWICK	101	4254	4166	4113	-0.5	11	1586	1574	1572	-0.2	2.64	1137	1127	-0.2
70343	BOURG	109	4451	4751	5069	1.6	82	1443	1560	1687	1.9	3.04	1236	1335	1.8
70344	CHAUVIN	109	6418	6615	6887	0.7	60	2152	2251	2377	1.1	2.94	1759	1837	1.0
70345	CUT OFF	057	13342	13744	14292	0.7	60	4656	4869	5142	1.1	2.79	3693	3861	1.1
70346	DONALDSONVILLE	005	11404	11765	12758	0.7	62	3905	4095	4511	1.1	2.79	2915	3054	1.1
70353	DULAC	109	1140	1210	1282	1.4	80	347	376	404	1.9	3.22	281	302	1.7
70354	GALLIANO	057	4665	4535	4609	-0.7	9	1695	1671	1723	-0.3	2.71	1304	1284	-0.4
70355	GHEENS	057	348	343	349	-0.3	16	108	108	112	0.0	3.18	86	87	0.3
70356	GIBSON	109	1913	1976	2047	0.8	64	666	700	736	1.2	2.82	521	546	1.1
70357	GOLDEN MEADOW	057	3324	3267	3323	-0.4	13	1207	1197	1231	-0.2	2.73	876	867	-0.2
70358	GRAND ISLE	051	1541	1517	1508	-0.4	15	622	623	629	0.0	2.42	436	436	0.0
70359	GRAY	109	6556	6976	7413	1.5	81	2226	2404	2590	1.8	2.90	1725	1862	1.8
70360	HOUMA	109	21390	22888	24249	1.6	83	7589	8231	8841	1.9	2.71	5702	6197	2.0
70363	HOUMA	109	28567	28916	30022	0.3	42	9187	9403	9889	0.6	3.00	7187	7363	0.6
70364	HOUMA	057	27555	29221	30946	1.4	79	10239	10972	11771	1.6	2.65	7317	7842	1.7
70372	LABADIEVILLE	007	3057	3114	3196	0.4	49	1107	1145	1197	0.8	2.72	847	875	0.8
70374	LOCKPORT	057	10509	10651	10989	0.3	43	3717	3835	4022	0.7	2.77	2900	2984	0.7
70375	MATHEWS	057	549	542	552	-0.3	16	199	200	208	0.1	2.71	159	160	0.2
70377	MONTEGUT	109	4089	4100	4213	0.1	31	1333	1352	1407	0.3	3.03	1067	1080	0.3
70380	MORGAN CITY	099	23270	23231	23268	0.0	27	8781	8929	9067	0.4	2.57	6195	6302	0.4
70390	NAPOLEONVILLE	007	7785	7948	8235	0.5	51	2611	2702	2847	0.8	2.87	2015	2085	0.8
70392	PATTERSON	101	7190	7484	7616	1.0	69	2568	2716	2797	1.3	2.74	1922	2036	1.4
70394	RACELAND	057	13584	13975	14530	0.7	59	4843	5065	5351	1.1	2.74	3774	3940	1.0
70395	SCHRIEVER	109	4718	4880	5076	0.8	65	1588	1663	1752	1.1	2.93	1301	1361	1.1
70397	THERIOT	109	1606	1594	1644	-0.2	20	488	494	517	0.3	3.23	402	407	0.3
70401	HAMMOND	105	16895	17727	18868	1.1	74	6554	7005	7590	1.6	2.40	3963	4237	1.6
70402	HAMMOND	105	1032	1128	1204	2.1	90	0	0	0	0.0	0.00	0	0	0.0
70403	HAMMOND	105	21100	22381	24014	1.4	79	7870	8472	9221	1.8	2.57	5439	5853	1.7
70420	ABITA SPRINGS	103	5397	6102	6895	2.9	96	2000	2287	2613	3.2	2.67	1480	1691	3.2
70422	AMITE	091	15029	15206	15817	0.3	41	5253	5394	5700	0.6	2.71	3843	3944	0.6
	LOUISIANA					0.7					0.9	2.59			1.0
	UNITED STATES					1.2					1.3	2.58			1.1

ZIP CODE #	POST OFFICE NAME	RACE (%) White 2000	White 2004	Black 2000	Black 2004	Asian/Pacific 2000	Asian/Pacific 2004	% Hispanic Origin 2000	% Hispanic Origin 2004	2004 AGE DISTRIBUTION (%) 0-4	5-9	10-14	15-19	20-24	25-44	45-64	65-84	85+	18+	MEDIAN AGE 2004	% 2004 Males	% 2004 Females
70001	METAIRIE	86.4	85.4	7.9	8.1	2.1	2.5	6.7	7.4	5.6	5.3	5.4	5.5	7.3	30.9	25.2	12.8	2.0	80.5	38.5	47.8	52.2
70002	METAIRIE	82.8	80.3	6.0	6.6	5.0	6.1	11.0	12.5	5.0	4.7	5.1	5.8	7.7	27.5	26.7	15.3	2.2	81.8	40.9	48.5	51.5
70003	METAIRIE	83.5	82.3	11.0	11.2	1.8	2.3	7.2	8.2	6.1	6.2	6.5	6.2	5.9	26.5	26.4	14.6	1.6	77.4	40.4	47.6	52.4
70005	METAIRIE	94.8	94.0	0.9	1.0	2.3	2.9	4.4	5.0	4.7	4.9	5.3	5.2	5.2	27.1	27.0	17.6	3.1	81.9	43.5	47.4	52.6
70006	METAIRIE	86.7	84.9	3.0	3.1	5.3	6.6	9.2	10.2	5.6	5.6	5.3	5.2	5.9	27.4	27.9	14.9	2.1	80.3	41.4	47.2	52.8
70030	DES ALLEMANDS	89.3	88.8	8.4	8.6	0.1	0.1	2.2	2.4	7.1	7.3	7.2	6.6	5.9	29.9	25.5	9.7	0.8	74.3	36.7	49.4	50.6
70031	AMA	65.5	63.2	33.8	36.1	0.2	0.2	1.0	1.1	6.1	7.4	6.9	9.4	7.7	27.2	26.3	8.6	0.4	73.0	35.6	50.9	49.1
70032	ARABI	94.8	94.8	2.0	2.0	0.8	0.8	5.0	5.1	4.4	4.5	4.6	5.4	5.6	26.1	23.8	22.5	3.0	83.2	44.6	48.0	52.0
70036	BARATARIA	87.0	85.6	11.1	12.2	0.0	0.0	1.9	2.2	5.6	5.8	6.4	6.0	6.0	25.9	30.2	12.7	1.4	78.5	41.2	49.8	50.3
70037	BELLE CHASSE	87.5	85.5	9.0	10.3	0.8	1.2	2.2	2.3	7.7	7.7	8.1	6.8	6.6	31.4	22.3	8.8	0.6	72.2	34.4	49.4	50.6
70039	BOUTTE	40.1	38.7	57.4	58.7	0.2	0.2	2.6	2.8	9.3	8.6	8.8	7.7	8.5	28.2	21.1	6.9	0.9	68.5	30.4	47.1	52.9
70040	BRAITHWAITE	43.5	40.8	54.4	57.0	0.4	0.4	1.8	1.8	6.7	6.8	7.1	6.4	7.5	29.9	22.9	11.1	1.7	75.8	36.7	51.1	48.9
70041	BURAS	65.1	60.3	22.8	24.7	7.6	9.8	1.1	1.2	7.7	7.8	8.2	7.9	7.7	27.4	24.2	8.4	0.7	71.5	33.2	50.8	49.2
70043	CHALMETTE	93.0	92.7	2.1	2.3	1.8	1.9	4.8	5.0	6.3	6.0	6.2	6.2	7.3	27.6	25.6	13.4	1.5	77.9	38.3	48.3	51.7
70047	DESTREHAN	80.9	79.9	16.6	17.2	0.9	1.1	3.6	4.1	7.5	8.1	8.8	7.9	5.9	28.5	26.0	6.5	1.0	70.5	35.8	48.9	51.1
70049	EDGARD	4.7	4.3	94.8	95.2	0.0	0.0	0.2	0.1	6.9	7.2	8.6	8.3	6.9	25.3	24.5	10.9	1.4	72.2	35.4	46.3	53.7
70051	GARYVILLE	47.2	46.8	51.7	51.8	0.3	0.4	0.8	0.8	7.9	7.6	8.5	9.2	7.6	25.0	24.1	9.0	1.1	70.6	32.7	47.2	52.8
70052	GRAMERCY	63.7	61.6	34.7	36.8	0.1	0.1	0.7	0.8	7.1	7.8	8.2	6.7	6.0	28.9	22.3	12.1	0.8	72.6	36.1	49.2	50.8
70053	GRETNA	54.7	52.6	37.2	38.5	3.2	3.6	6.3	6.8	7.2	6.5	6.4	6.5	8.0	29.2	23.0	11.7	1.5	76.0	35.6	50.2	49.8
70056	GRETNA	59.2	57.1	30.7	31.5	4.3	5.2	8.2	8.9	7.8	7.2	7.2	6.9	8.0	30.2	23.8	8.1	0.7	73.6	33.7	48.1	51.9
70057	HAHNVILLE	39.4	37.1	59.4	61.7	0.1	0.1	1.0	1.1	7.6	7.8	8.3	7.4	7.2	29.5	22.4	8.9	1.1	71.6	33.8	49.2	50.8
70058	HARVEY	39.7	37.8	50.9	51.6	5.6	6.6	5.3	5.7	8.2	8.2	8.7	8.3	7.7	29.6	23.3	5.6	0.5	69.7	31.3	48.1	51.9
70062	KENNER	49.2	47.4	45.5	46.8	1.0	1.2	7.1	7.8	8.0	7.8	8.4	7.5	6.8	27.8	22.0	10.2	1.5	71.2	33.9	46.7	53.3
70065	KENNER	75.3	73.3	14.2	14.8	3.5	4.3	15.6	17.0	6.6	6.6	7.3	6.9	7.4	29.6	26.6	8.2	0.9	75.2	35.6	48.4	51.6
70067	LAFITTE	91.1	89.9	1.8	2.0	1.3	1.5	2.7	3.2	6.5	6.5	6.7	6.9	7.8	27.5	27.5	9.9	0.9	76.2	36.4	51.7	48.3
70068	LA PLACE	60.5	58.7	36.2	37.7	0.7	0.8	3.7	4.1	8.3	8.2	8.4	7.7	7.4	30.0	23.3	6.1	0.6	70.3	32.3	48.9	51.1
70070	LULING	81.4	80.5	16.2	16.8	0.8	0.9	2.5	2.8	7.3	7.4	8.1	7.5	7.1	28.5	24.9	8.4	0.8	72.6	35.1	48.1	51.9
70071	LUTCHER	52.0	50.8	47.7	48.8	0.0	0.0	0.4	0.4	6.4	6.6	7.8	7.1	7.0	25.0	24.9	12.8	2.4	75.0	37.6	47.7	52.3
70072	MARRERO	57.8	56.0	36.3	37.1	2.9	3.5	4.5	5.0	7.4	7.6	8.3	7.5	7.0	28.2	24.2	8.8	1.0	72.0	34.2	47.3	52.7
70075	MERAUX	92.2	92.2	4.1	4.1	1.7	1.7	3.7	3.8	7.0	6.9	7.6	7.2	6.7	29.2	25.0	9.4	0.9	74.1	36.2	47.2	52.8
70076	MOUNT AIRY	44.1	42.3	55.2	57.0	0.0	0.0	0.4	0.5	7.6	7.6	8.2	7.0	7.1	24.3	26.1	11.3	0.9	72.2	36.6	48.9	51.1
70079	NORCO	75.6	74.7	22.4	23.1	0.3	0.3	2.0	2.2	6.2	6.3	7.6	7.2	7.2	27.5	22.5	13.6	1.9	75.6	37.4	48.0	52.0
70080	PARADIS	84.6	83.2	12.8	13.8	0.4	0.5	2.3	2.6	8.6	8.1	7.6	7.1	7.1	30.8	23.3	6.8	0.6	71.5	33.3	50.3	49.7
70081	PILOTTOWN	25.0	25.0	75.0	75.0	0.0	0.0	0.0	0.0	0.0	0.0	0.0	0.0	50.0	50.0	0.0	0.0	0.0	100.0	25.0	100.0	0.0
70083	PORT SULPHUR	47.2	43.0	42.3	45.2	0.8	1.0	1.0	1.0	7.2	7.4	8.1	8.1	7.7	25.8	24.8	10.0	0.9	72.2	35.0	49.2	50.8
70084	RESERVE	45.6	43.8	52.8	54.5	0.4	0.4	1.0	1.1	8.3	8.2	8.3	7.5	7.8	26.4	22.5	9.8	1.3	70.7	32.8	48.1	51.9
70085	SAINT BERNARD	89.3	89.4	7.4	7.2	0.3	0.3	8.6	8.7	7.2	7.0	7.7	7.4	7.4	28.9	23.5	9.8	1.1	73.6	35.4	50.0	50.0
70086	SAINT JAMES	11.4	10.1	88.1	89.3	0.0	0.0	1.2	1.3	7.6	7.7	8.2	10.5	8.0	25.4	21.9	9.4	1.3	69.4	31.3	47.1	52.9
70087	SAINT ROSE	55.5	51.1	41.2	45.4	0.5	0.6	4.5	4.7	7.3	7.8	8.2	7.7	7.2	31.4	22.0	7.9	0.5	71.9	33.5	48.2	51.9
70090	VACHERIE	45.7	44.1	53.9	55.4	0.0	0.0	0.6	0.6	7.3	7.1	7.5	7.7	7.8	27.2	24.5	9.8	1.2	73.6	35.2	48.6	51.5
70091	VENICE	83.0	78.6	6.2	7.3	5.0	6.8	0.8	1.4	9.6	8.2	8.2	7.7	6.8	24.6	25.9	8.6	0.5	68.6	32.5	55.9	44.1
70092	VIOLET	66.9	66.9	30.0	30.0	0.8	0.8	4.5	4.5	7.4	7.4	8.7	7.9	7.2	29.4	24.0	7.4	0.5	71.7	33.3	48.5	51.5
70094	WESTWEGO	56.8	54.7	36.3	37.5	3.7	4.2	4.2	4.6	7.5	7.3	8.3	8.1	7.5	28.0	23.2	9.5	0.7	71.8	33.5	48.0	52.0
70112	NEW ORLEANS	17.6	16.0	78.1	79.0	2.9	3.4	1.3	1.4	11.6	11.0	8.1	5.6	12.1	28.1	16.7	6.0	0.9	65.7	25.8	44.0	56.0
70113	NEW ORLEANS	8.2	7.5	89.7	90.3	0.7	0.8	1.6	1.6	7.3	8.0	8.8	7.7	7.4	25.6	22.8	11.1	1.5	71.2	33.5	46.0	54.0
70114	NEW ORLEANS	22.1	20.9	73.4	74.1	1.2	1.4	4.3	4.6	8.9	8.6	9.0	7.9	8.1	28.4	19.5	8.2	1.5	68.7	30.1	46.1	54.0
70115	NEW ORLEANS	45.6	44.2	51.0	52.1	0.9	1.2	3.2	3.5	5.8	5.5	5.9	6.0	7.8	33.7	22.9	10.5	2.0	79.3	35.0	47.0	53.0
70116	NEW ORLEANS	28.6	28.2	68.8	69.0	0.5	0.6	2.5	2.6	6.3	6.2	6.5	6.0	6.7	29.0	26.0	11.6	1.8	77.4	37.8	50.7	49.3
70117	NEW ORLEANS	9.4	8.6	88.8	89.5	0.2	0.3	2.0	2.0	7.7	7.7	8.7	8.2	7.6	25.8	22.7	10.4	1.3	71.0	33.0	46.7	53.4
70118	NEW ORLEANS	44.9	43.4	51.1	52.0	1.5	1.9	3.2	3.6	5.5	5.3	5.7	9.5	12.4	28.1	21.6	10.3	1.7	80.1	31.9	46.1	53.9
70119	NEW ORLEANS	23.7	22.1	71.5	72.8	0.9	1.1	5.6	5.8	5.9	5.8	6.3	7.1	9.9	32.1	22.4	8.8	1.7	78.0	34.3	52.1	47.9
70121	NEW ORLEANS	74.1	72.9	21.5	22.0	1.5	1.8	4.9	5.5	5.3	5.2	5.3	4.9	6.5	30.1	26.2	13.6	3.0	81.1	40.7	48.3	51.7
70122	NEW ORLEANS	23.0	21.3	73.2	74.5	1.1	1.4	3.2	3.3	6.6	6.8	7.5	7.8	7.8	25.2	24.2	12.2	2.0	74.8	36.1	44.9	55.1
70123	NEW ORLEANS	89.4	88.6	7.4	7.7	1.3	1.6	3.1	3.6	5.3	5.2	5.7	5.3	7.0	29.1	26.3	14.1	2.0	80.5	40.3	48.0	52.0
70124	NEW ORLEANS	95.6	94.9	1.4	1.5	1.2	1.6	3.9	4.6	5.4	5.6	5.7	5.7	5.0	27.2	26.9	15.1	3.4	79.7	42.2	46.7	53.3
70125	NEW ORLEANS	24.7	23.6	72.4	73.0	1.1	1.4	2.6	2.7	7.6	7.5	7.0	10.6	9.0	26.4	19.8	9.6	2.6	73.8	30.6	43.4	56.6
70126	NEW ORLEANS	10.4	9.3	87.0	87.9	0.8	0.9	1.5	1.6	7.3	7.3	8.2	7.7	8.1	26.5	23.6	10.2	1.3	72.6	33.2	45.7	54.3
70127	NEW ORLEANS	11.2	9.8	85.8	86.8	1.0	1.3	1.6	1.6	8.3	8.0	8.3	7.6	8.5	27.5	22.9	7.8	1.2	70.8	31.4	45.1	54.9
70128	NEW ORLEANS	8.5	7.3	86.5	87.3	3.0	3.4	1.7	1.6	7.1	8.0	9.0	8.4	8.3	27.6	25.3	5.6	0.7	70.7	31.4	46.2	53.8
70129	NEW ORLEANS	14.9	13.4	50.6	48.9	32.4	35.7	2.2	2.1	9.1	8.3	9.2	8.7	8.5	27.3	20.9	7.3	0.8	68.0	29.1	47.8	52.3
70130	NEW ORLEANS	46.7	46.1	48.7	48.7	1.3	1.7	4.7	5.2	5.4	5.4	5.6	5.8	8.8	35.0	22.9	9.3	1.7	80.3	34.3	50.5	49.5
70131	NEW ORLEANS	49.6	47.7	41.9	42.8	5.4	6.2	4.1	4.5	7.2	7.4	8.0	6.8	7.0	27.9	23.7	10.6	1.4	73.2	35.7	47.1	52.9
70301	THIBODAUX	76.4	75.2	21.6	22.5	0.6	0.7	1.0	1.1	6.9	6.9	7.3	7.9	8.4	28.9	22.6	9.8	1.3	74.7	34.0	48.2	51.8
70339	PIERRE PART	98.4	98.2	0.8	0.8	0.0	0.0	1.0	1.2	6.6	6.6	7.3	6.9	7.0	29.1	25.1	10.5	0.9	75.3	36.5	49.0	51.0
70341	BELLE ROSE	48.3	45.3	51.0	54.0	0.1	0.1	1.2	1.3	7.2	7.2	8.1	7.4	7.9	27.2	24.1	9.7	1.3	73.1	34.5	48.9	51.1
70342	BERWICK	86.3	85.0	8.5	9.1	0.7	1.0	1.5	1.7	7.8	7.2	8.0	7.5	7.3	28.6	23.4	9.4	0.9	72.4	35.0	48.4	51.6
70343	BOURG	90.2	89.1	2.9	3.3	0.3	0.3	0.6	0.8	6.9	7.5	8.2	7.9	6.7	29.5	25.3	7.4	0.7	72.6	35.3	50.6	49.4
70344	CHAUVIN	92.5	91.3	4.2	4.9	0.4	0.4	0.7	0.8	7.2	7.0	7.4	7.4	7.8	27.8	24.3	10.3	0.8	74.0	35.6	51.1	49.0
70345	CUT OFF	88.3	87.1	3.6	3.7	1.8	2.2	2.5	2.8	7.3	7.1	7.4	6.9	6.8	29.0	23.6	10.7	1.2	73.9	36.2	49.3	50.7
70346	DONALDSONVILLE	35.1	31.7	63.6	67.0	0.1	0.2	1.4	1.4	8.2	7.8	8.1	8.1	8.3	26.2	22.3	9.5	1.6	71.0	32.2	47.0	53.0
70353	DULAC	53.1	49.4	1.1	1.2	0.5	0.7	1.5	1.5	7.8	8.4	8.5	8.8	7.9	25.2	23.4	9.3	0.8	69.9	32.4	51.1	48.9
70354	GALLIANO	91.1	89.9	0.5	0.6	0.7	0.9	1.0	1.2	7.0	7.0	7.5	6.1	6.2	30.0	22.4	12.9	0.9	74.6	36.7	50.4	49.6
70355	GHEENS	94.5	93.9	2.9	3.2	0.3	0.3	1.7	2.0	7.3	7.3	7.9	8.2	7.9	31.5	21.3	8.5	0.3	72.3	33.5	50.2	49.9
70356	GIBSON	48.5	45.3	48.9	51.7	0.4	0.4	1.3	1.3	6.6	6.7	7.8	8.0	6.9	26.3	26.8	10.2	0.7	74.0	36.3	48.3	51.7
70357	GOLDEN MEADOW	89.2	87.8	0.6	0.6	0.3	0.4	1.3	1.5	7.0	7.0	7.7	6.9	6.1	29.6	21.9	12.4	1.4	74.1	36.2	49.8	50.2
70358	GRAND ISLE	96.0	95.6	0.2	0.2	0.2	0.3	1.5	1.7	5.1	5.9	7.3	5.5	5.9	26.3	29.3	13.6	1.2	78.2	40.9	51.1	48.9
70359	GRAY	67.7	66.0	28.7	30.0	0.3	0.4	1.3	1.5	8.8	8.2	8.8	7.6	8.4	30.3	21.3	6.1	0.5	69.6	30.2	48.9	51.1
70360	HOUMA	79.6	78.6	17.0	17.5	0.7	0.9	1.6	1.8	7.1	7.1	7.5	7.0	6.6	28.1	24.9	10.1	1.7	74.0	37.2	48.0	52.0
70363	HOUMA	59.1	56.6	26.5	27.2	1.7	2.0	1.7	1.8	8.4	7.7	8.2	8.1	8.6	28.5	21.7	8.1	0.7	70.8	31.0	49.6	50.4
70364	HOUMA	85.2	84.0	9.6	10.2	0.6	0.7	2.1	2.4	7.7	7.2	7.4	6.9	8.0	30.9	21.7	9.3	1.0	73.6	33.3	49.0	51.0
70372	LABADIEVILLE	69.8	66.9	28.6	31.4	0.1	0.1	1.3	1.3	7.7	7.6	7.9	6.7	6.8	28.3	24.7	9.3	1.2	72.9	35.2	48.5	51.5
70374	LOCKPORT	90.3	89.1	2.8	3.3	0.5	0.6	1.6	1.8	6.8	6.8	7.4	6.9	6.8	29.9	24.5	9.9	1.0	74.9	36.0	50.1	49.9
70375	MATHEWS	93.6	93.0	3.6	4.1	0.2	0.2	1.8	2.0	7.4	7.0	7.8	7.8	7.6	30.4	22.7	9.0	0.4	73.1	34.4	49.6	50.4
70377	MONTEGUT	79.1	77.4	1.6	1.9	0.0	0.0	1.1	1.2	7.7	7.4	8.3	8.4	7.5	29.0	22.5	8.2	1.0	71.5	33.3	51.6	48.4
70380	MORGAN CITY	76.1	74.8	16.7	17.1	3.2	3.8	3.5	3.8	7.3	7.1	7.7	7.0	6.8	28.0	24.3	10.6	1.1	73.5	35.6	49.6	50.4
70390	NAPOLEONVILLE	51.0	48.4	48.2	50.6	0.1	0.1	0.9	0.9	7.2	7.5	7.7	7.3	7.1	27.2	24.1	10.2	1.6	73.1	35.5	48.3	51.7
70392	PATTERSON	62.6	61.3	33.6	34.4	0.5	0.6	2.0	2.3	7.3	8.1	8.7	7.7	7.1	29.1	23.1	8.2	0.9	71.0	33.7	49.1	51.0
70394	RACELAND	78.2	77.3	19.3	19.9	0.3	0.4	1.3	1.4	7.3	7.2	7.3	6.7	6.9	28.0	24.4	10.8	1.4	74.2	36.3	48.7	51.3
70395	SCHRIEVER	80.3	78.2	16.6	18.2	0.5	0.7	1.2	1.4	7.5	7.3	7.6	7.5	7.7	30.0	23.8	8.1	0.7	73.1	33.9	48.5	51.5
70397	THERIOT	76.6	74.8	1.8	1.9	0.1	0.1	2.1	2.3	6.7	6.8	8.8	9.1	7.5	27.6	23.3	9.7	0.4	72.1	33.9	51.8	48.2
70401	HAMMOND	64.8	62.6	32.5	34.4	0.7	0.8	2.0	2.2	7.0	6.6	6.5	9.2	14.4	27.5	20.2	7.9	0.7	76.2	28.4	47.4	52.6
70402	HAMMOND	67.7	65.2	29.9	32.4	0.3	0.3	1.2	1.2	1.1	1.6	1.4	38.7	34.7	9.1	6.9	6.2	0.3	94.7	21.0	40.0	60.0
70403	HAMMOND	65.3	63.8	32.9	34.1	0.6	0.7	1.4	1.5	7.4	7.0	7.4	7.0	8.0	28.8	22.9	9.7	1.8	74.1	33.6	47.3	52.7
70420	ABITA SPRINGS	91.1	90.4	6.1	6.5	0.4	0.6	2.6	3.0	8.6	8.4	7.4	6.2	6.1	30.7	24.3	7.6	0.7	71.8	34.4	47.5	52.5
70422	AMITE	53.9	52.1	44.5	46.2	0.3	0.4	1.1	1.2	7.6	7.5	7.8	7.3	7.4	26.4	24.4	10.5	1.1	72.8	34.8	50.1	49.9
	LOUISIANA	63.9	62.8	32.5	33.2	1.3	1.5	2.4	2.6	7.2	7.0	7.4	7.5	7.9	28.0	23.4	10.3	1.4	74.1	34.6	48.5	51.5
	UNITED STATES	75.1	73.6	12.3	12.5	3.8	4.2	12.5	14.1	6.9	6.7	7.2	7.0	7.3	28.6	23.8	10.8	1.7	75.1	36.0	49.1	50.9

INCOME

ZIP CODE #	POST OFFICE NAME	2004 Per Capita Income	2004 HH Income Base	2004 Household Income Distribution (%): Less than $25,000	$25,000 to $49,999	$50,000 to $99,999	$100,000 to $149,999	$150,000 or More	Median Household Income: 2004	2009	2004 National Centile	2004 State Centile	2004 Home Value Base	2004 Home Value Distribution (%): Less than $50,000	$50,000 to $89,999	$90,000 to $174,999	$175,000 to $399,999	$400,000 or More	2004 Median Home Value
70001	METAIRIE	26577	18357	27.4	32.3	28.8	7.9	3.7	41873	47765	53	80	9798	2.2	7.0	48.9	38.7	3.2	162127
70002	METAIRIE	31478	9203	27.1	28.5	25.5	11.2	7.7	44378	49799	60	86	4861	3.2	5.9	22.6	56.3	12.1	219396
70003	METAIRIE	24361	17156	23.6	28.4	33.5	9.7	4.8	47922	54013	68	91	13438	3.3	8.9	58.3	27.2	2.2	141312
70005	METAIRIE	37153	12379	25.3	27.6	27.3	10.5	9.3	47200	53850	67	90	7861	0.8	4.6	30.1	46.2	18.3	205015
70006	METAIRIE	29115	7224	22.7	29.3	31.3	10.4	6.2	47786	54783	68	91	4411	0.4	1.7	36.8	55.0	6.0	191003
70030	DES ALLEMANDS	19866	1620	31.4	26.9	33.8	5.9	2.0	43084	49533	56	83	1393	21.8	28.5	33.4	15.4	0.9	89526
70031	AMA	20704	463	25.1	27.9	34.6	9.3	3.2	47529	55526	67	90	399	15.0	27.8	47.6	9.5	0.0	95481
70032	ARABI	21537	3442	33.2	32.1	28.4	5.1	1.2	36855	41285	35	65	2718	3.5	33.3	59.5	3.7	0.0	96998
70036	BARATARIA	15843	543	35.0	37.9	20.6	5.0	1.5	31793	37615	17	44	455	20.2	17.1	36.0	26.6	0.0	110625
70037	BELLE CHASSE	21672	4914	21.3	28.9	34.0	11.7	4.1	49828	56185	72	93	3672	15.3	10.1	33.7	37.5	3.4	145734
70039	BOUTTE	14570	821	42.9	28.5	23.9	3.1	1.7	30938	36442	15	40	558	35.5	30.8	25.6	8.1	0.0	70000
70040	BRAITHWAITE	15562	1075	38.2	32.6	19.8	5.9	3.5	34286	39760	25	54	896	42.1	10.6	23.2	19.4	4.7	78000
70041	BURAS	15279	2417	38.7	29.2	25.7	4.3	2.1	35096	40544	28	57	1953	59.3	26.0	11.3	3.0	0.5	37993
70043	CHALMETTE	19880	12412	29.6	31.5	30.6	6.7	1.7	40548	45854	48	77	8510	5.6	19.1	63.6	10.7	0.9	112308
70047	DESTREHAN	26639	4542	14.2	23.9	36.1	16.5	9.3	62505	71080	87	99	3909	5.7	11.4	40.3	37.9	4.6	160158
70049	EDGARD	11912	971	46.0	32.2	15.7	5.6	0.5	27287	31866	8	21	789	53.7	13.3	27.3	5.7	0.0	46895
70051	GARYVILLE	12885	675	40.2	28.3	27.9	3.1	0.6	31987	37273	18	45	484	37.0	33.3	28.5	1.2	0.0	59130
70052	GRAMERCY	16858	1160	32.8	29.3	30.3	6.6	1.0	39470	46131	44	75	950	28.7	25.0	34.6	10.5	1.2	85270
70053	GRETNA	17573	7106	40.3	36.6	17.7	3.8	1.7	30448	34395	13	37	3668	11.8	34.0	42.6	10.4	1.2	93879
70056	GRETNA	21086	15156	24.2	30.9	32.4	9.2	3.3	45858	51634	63	88	9206	0.7	16.8	65.3	14.0	3.3	119396
70057	HAHNVILLE	17486	1220	36.3	27.8	25.4	7.8	2.7	40197	45616	47	76	934	20.7	17.0	47.0	15.3	0.0	106386
70058	HARVEY	17826	14029	29.9	28.0	30.5	8.5	3.1	41942	47428	53	80	9650	4.6	20.6	62.3	11.3	1.2	108914
70062	KENNER	14430	6633	41.2	32.2	21.1	4.8	0.7	30138	33944	13	35	3659	8.6	28.6	53.5	8.6	0.7	99740
70065	KENNER	25605	20120	20.3	29.4	33.6	11.0	5.8	50305	58024	72	94	13130	1.5	12.2	49.4	31.3	5.6	147906
70067	LAFITTE	17701	1674	33.9	25.8	29.0	7.8	3.6	38683	45433	42	73	1421	27.7	20.7	30.2	19.6	1.9	93052
70068	LA PLACE	19107	10944	23.5	27.6	36.7	10.2	2.0	48852	55320	70	92	8684	8.1	24.6	52.5	14.1	0.7	106020
70070	LULING	23866	4062	16.8	22.9	39.6	16.8	3.9	62198	70692	86	99	3441	3.9	11.8	45.8	37.2	1.3	151402
70071	LUTCHER	17210	1302	37.3	24.4	25.6	9.7	3.0	37864	43579	39	70	1026	22.6	24.6	40.7	12.1	0.0	92816
70072	MARRERO	17891	19379	29.0	30.9	31.1	6.3	2.7	41633	47033	52	79	14842	4.7	34.2	50.8	9.1	1.2	97085
70075	MERAUX	20927	3155	24.0	24.7	39.2	10.3	1.8	51072	56138	74	94	2562	9.8	15.6	57.8	16.4	0.4	117019
70076	MOUNT AIRY	14713	223	45.7	16.1	30.9	7.2	0.0	31138	34094	15	41	192	46.9	18.8	28.1	6.3	0.0	60625
70079	NORCO	18271	1373	28.0	30.3	34.6	4.9	2.3	40810	47340	49	78	1118	10.6	26.6	51.5	11.4	0.0	99000
70080	PARADIS	18867	515	27.8	36.9	25.4	8.7	1.2	39097	45451	43	74	401	27.4	33.7	31.7	7.2	0.0	76795
70081	PILOTTOWN	8251	0	0.0	0.0	0.0	0.0	0.0	0	0	0	0	0	0.0	0.0	0.0	0.0	0.0	0
70083	PORT SULPHUR	16254	1400	41.9	27.6	25.4	2.7	2.4	31684	36893	17	44	1179	44.9	33.1	15.5	5.2	1.4	54172
70084	RESERVE	16185	2587	37.2	27.0	29.1	5.0	1.8	36401	42225	33	63	1956	24.0	33.5	33.4	9.2	0.0	79602
70085	SAINT BERNARD	15639	2596	35.3	32.9	24.0	5.7	2.0	32998	38339	21	50	2094	29.9	36.2	22.8	9.4	1.7	70209
70086	SAINT JAMES	12606	680	39.7	29.9	26.2	2.5	1.8	31830	37346	17	44	548	36.7	30.5	22.8	7.3	2.7	67955
70087	SAINT ROSE	16089	2490	28.2	36.2	28.9	5.4	1.2	38235	44053	40	72	1707	10.0	22.1	59.3	7.3	1.3	104392
70090	VACHERIE	17059	2500	36.0	23.0	30.5	8.8	1.6	38125	44736	40	71	2169	24.9	25.4	39.1	10.2	0.4	89656
70091	VENICE	14293	85	44.7	25.9	27.1	2.4	0.0	29430	36745	11	32	78	69.2	19.2	11.5	0.0	0.0	27500
70092	VIOLET	16155	3822	32.9	29.1	30.9	5.4	1.7	37081	41422	36	67	3117	10.3	35.9	44.6	8.4	0.7	93255
70094	WESTWEGO	13908	12103	38.7	35.3	22.1	3.2	0.8	31556	35747	17	43	8257	16.6	54.3	24.3	4.5	0.3	75494
70112	NEW ORLEANS	9532	2512	74.8	14.6	6.7	2.1	1.9	9921	12186	0	1	206	8.7	30.1	35.9	17.0	8.3	106522
70113	NEW ORLEANS	10472	4042	68.2	20.7	8.3	1.7	1.0	14114	16386	1	1	839	15.1	44.5	29.8	9.8	0.8	83292
70114	NEW ORLEANS	13943	10410	48.4	28.9	17.5	3.5	1.7	25975	29932	6	16	4529	13.2	43.1	33.3	9.6	0.9	83985
70115	NEW ORLEANS	26923	17537	42.6	25.5	18.4	6.1	7.4	31342	37272	16	43	7195	6.3	15.7	29.6	31.2	17.3	167586
70116	NEW ORLEANS	20101	7878	51.9	27.6	13.1	3.7	3.7	23693	27829	4	9	2444	12.0	21.4	29.2	19.0	18.3	115818
70117	NEW ORLEANS	11803	18554	55.5	28.4	13.0	1.9	1.2	21555	25159	2	5	8921	22.5	50.6	21.9	4.3	0.8	70494
70118	NEW ORLEANS	27652	14803	41.8	25.4	17.7	6.5	8.6	31227	36418	16	42	6949	5.7	23.6	30.8	25.4	14.5	132975
70119	NEW ORLEANS	14911	17993	51.3	29.4	14.7	3.0	1.6	24119	27798	4	11	6776	10.4	33.5	39.0	15.3	1.8	95489
70121	NEW ORLEANS	23394	5960	34.1	30.5	25.5	7.8	2.2	36632	42604	34	65	3444	4.4	14.1	64.3	16.8	0.3	123084
70122	NEW ORLEANS	19199	17463	37.6	28.7	23.6	6.1	4.0	34669	40681	26	55	11069	3.9	32.4	48.3	12.9	2.4	101277
70123	NEW ORLEANS	31627	12350	20.4	28.4	32.9	11.3	6.9	51036	59366	74	94	7749	2.0	6.5	41.1	43.0	7.5	175868
70124	NEW ORLEANS	43479	10765	18.8	23.9	29.6	13.6	14.0	59439	74835	84	98	7526	0.5	4.1	28.0	53.6	13.8	219488
70125	NEW ORLEANS	16608	8713	53.3	20.3	16.2	6.3	3.9	22133	26339	3	6	3466	10.8	18.9	39.3	27.1	3.9	128702
70126	NEW ORLEANS	16085	14119	36.5	32.5	23.5	5.7	1.8	33774	38641	23	53	8002	7.4	40.3	43.5	8.5	0.3	91922
70127	NEW ORLEANS	16823	11776	37.8	29.1	26.0	5.3	1.8	33918	39207	24	53	5687	2.9	25.2	62.5	8.4	1.0	104745
70128	NEW ORLEANS	19141	7212	25.9	28.5	32.0	10.3	3.3	45607	52869	63	88	4852	1.8	21.6	62.4	12.3	2.0	113095
70129	NEW ORLEANS	14422	4794	39.4	31.8	20.3	6.2	2.3	33700	38621	23	52	2534	9.2	25.7	54.9	8.8	1.3	100440
70130	NEW ORLEANS	30634	7445	42.9	28.4	15.5	5.5	7.8	30391	36014	13	37	1937	6.1	13.0	25.8	33.4	21.7	199381
70131	NEW ORLEANS	26851	11011	22.3	26.5	30.3	11.7	9.3	51394	62679	75	95	7461	3.0	19.9	46.5	25.9	4.8	137455
70301	THIBODAUX	19323	15175	34.4	28.9	27.4	6.1	3.2	37287	41870	36	67	10866	25.9	22.5	36.9	13.6	1.2	92129
70339	PIERRE PART	17733	2337	32.0	28.0	34.9	4.0	1.1	39075	45207	43	73	2007	35.2	23.5	29.3	12.0	0.1	74303
70341	BELLE ROSE	15246	1502	41.8	24.6	23.8	7.9	1.9	33868	38032	24	53	1249	35.5	24.7	25.3	13.7	0.9	75052
70342	BERWICK	16510	1574	36.7	29.5	26.6	6.4	0.8	36121	40809	32	62	1153	36.0	20.7	33.6	8.9	0.8	72556
70343	BOURG	18992	1560	22.1	29.7	38.4	6.5	3.2	48152	53690	69	91	1414	20.8	22.7	37.3	16.6	2.6	98364
70344	CHAUVIN	16136	2251	41.1	29.2	23.3	3.5	2.9	31354	36068	16	43	1927	35.4	31.9	22.1	7.8	2.8	66564
70345	CUT OFF	18055	4869	28.1	31.8	32.3	5.6	2.2	41868	47316	53	79	4084	19.7	29.8	40.5	9.8	0.2	90649
70346	DONALDSONVILLE	15150	4095	44.0	26.0	22.3	5.8	1.9	30272	34170	13	36	2555	32.8	30.8	27.1	9.0	0.3	72250
70353	DULAC	10392	376	52.1	27.1	18.6	1.3	0.8	23704	26828	4	10	291	48.8	25.4	24.7	1.0	0.0	51400
70354	GALLIANO	15321	1671	42.6	31.9	20.3	3.0	2.2	29839	34008	12	34	1383	31.7	36.2	24.7	6.9	0.4	69087
70355	GHEENS	14382	108	31.5	33.3	33.3	0.9	0.9	38227	40000	40	71	92	29.4	39.1	23.9	7.6	0.0	68182
70356	GIBSON	13971	700	50.9	29.6	15.9	1.9	1.9	24379	27401	4	11	574	37.8	25.6	27.7	8.4	0.5	72353
70357	GOLDEN MEADOW	13453	1197	44.9	28.3	23.3	2.8	0.7	28865	32825	10	29	963	38.8	32.1	21.7	6.2	1.1	59348
70358	GRAND ISLE	20770	623	31.1	37.2	23.1	5.8	2.7	37568	43741	38	69	497	29.6	33.4	29.2	5.8	2.0	76413
70359	GRAY	15141	2404	33.7	31.2	27.9	6.1	1.0	35249	40688	28	58	1884	32.5	30.7	28.3	8.0	0.4	73333
70360	HOUMA	27105	8231	26.0	22.5	32.3	11.2	8.0	52016	59100	76	96	6489	12.1	19.4	39.8	24.7	4.0	122661
70363	HOUMA	13795	9403	38.7	31.6	24.1	3.7	2.0	32498	36906	19	48	6698	32.0	33.5	29.0	4.7	0.9	72830
70364	HOUMA	18628	10972	30.6	30.6	31.3	6.1	1.5	40030	45602	46	76	7531	20.5	26.2	46.2	6.6	0.6	93089
70372	LABADIEVILLE	15895	1145	38.9	26.6	28.7	5.4	0.4	35406	39834	29	59	923	29.1	34.6	29.1	7.2	0.0	71543
70374	LOCKPORT	17439	3835	29.8	29.4	33.9	5.8	1.0	41688	46822	52	79	3091	26.1	28.7	35.4	8.1	1.7	83718
70375	MATHEWS	17220	200	32.0	33.0	30.5	2.0	2.5	37379	40774	37	68	169	27.8	38.5	27.2	6.5	0.0	70313
70377	MONTEGUT	12972	1352	37.2	35.1	23.7	3.0	1.1	35772	40936	31	61	1134	34.7	35.3	25.4	4.1	0.4	69204
70380	MORGAN CITY	16592	8929	38.5	30.2	25.2	4.7	1.3	33334	38373	22	50	6540	30.3	26.0	35.7	6.9	1.0	82257
70390	NAPOLEONVILLE	15615	2702	42.9	26.7	22.2	5.0	3.2	30556	34469	14	37	2102	36.9	20.9	30.2	11.7	0.4	73333
70392	PATTERSON	14999	2716	39.9	27.4	26.2	6.0	0.5	32753	36903	20	49	1998	26.6	30.5	34.3	8.3	0.4	81497
70394	RACELAND	18515	5065	34.0	32.0	25.0	5.4	3.8	36987	40999	35	66	4054	23.8	30.0	36.0	9.0	1.3	84933
70395	SCHRIEVER	19312	1663	25.5	31.3	32.3	7.5	3.5	45020	50787	61	87	1414	19.0	27.7	36.6	14.3	2.5	94017
70397	THERIOT	16940	494	43.9	23.3	23.1	4.7	5.1	29814	34913	12	34	437	26.1	29.1	29.5	12.8	2.5	83182
70401	HAMMOND	16868	7005	42.6	29.5	20.2	5.8	1.8	30260	34135	13	36	3788	18.3	23.8	37.7	18.3	2.0	98671
70402	HAMMOND	6596	0	0.0	0.0	0.0	0.0	0.0	0	0	0	0	0	0.0	0.0	0.0	0.0	0.0	0
70403	HAMMOND	17341	8472	40.0	27.0	24.5	6.6	1.9	32393	36813	19	47	5900	23.2	23.5	34.8	16.2	2.4	94987
70420	ABITA SPRINGS	22132	2287	18.7	34.1	34.5	7.8	4.9	47419	56092	67	90	1894	7.6	10.6	52.1	26.9	2.8	138052
70422	AMITE	15015	5394	42.2	30.3	21.5	4.3	1.7	30684	34968	14	38	4180	35.3	24.7	27.7	10.3	2.0	75039
	LOUISIANA	19601		35.3	28.5	25.7	7.1	3.5	36550	42223				22.5	24.5	35.6	15.0	2.4	94005
	UNITED STATES	25866		24.7	27.1	30.8	10.9	6.5	48124	56710				10.9	15.0	33.7	30.1	10.4	145905

ZIP CODE #	POST OFFICE NAME	FINANCIAL SERVICES: Auto Loan	Home Loan	Invest-ments	Retire-ment Plans	THE HOME: Home Improvements: Home Repair	Lawn & Garden	Furnishings: Comput-ers & Hard-ware	Major Appli-ances	TV, Radio, Sound Equip-ment	Furni-ture	ENTERTAINMENT: Dine out/ Carry out	Sports Equip-ment	Fees & Tickets	Toys & Games	Travel	Cable TV	PERSONAL: Apparel & Services	Auto Repairs	Health Insur-ance	Pets & Supplies
70001	METAIRIE	75	78	91	79	77	82	81	78	79	80	100	91	82	99	80	78	97	80	75	86
70002	METAIRIE	88	91	115	93	90	98	97	92	96	95	121	109	99	120	97	95	119	96	90	102
70003	METAIRIE	80	88	99	87	88	94	88	86	86	86	108	99	91	110	89	86	106	86	85	95
70005	METAIRIE	98	108	132	108	107	116	109	106	107	108	135	123	113	137	111	107	133	107	103	116
70006	METAIRIE	87	98	116	98	97	104	97	95	94	96	118	109	101	120	99	93	117	95	91	103
70030	DES ALLEMANDS	97	73	43	65	80	89	69	82	79	70	94	98	62	91	70	83	87	80	96	112
70031	AMA	94	84	64	80	89	95	78	86	83	78	100	103	76	103	80	85	95	84	93	111
70032	ARABI	65	68	69	64	69	77	67	68	68	65	84	76	68	86	69	71	81	67	72	76
70036	BARATARIA	78	52	24	45	59	68	50	63	61	51	72	75	43	68	51	66	65	62	78	90
70037	BELLE CHASSE	94	89	76	88	90	96	87	90	87	86	108	105	85	107	86	87	104	90	91	106
70039	BOUTTE	65	57	49	53	57	63	57	61	61	59	74	69	54	69	56	62	71	61	65	72
70040	BRAITHWAITE	71	60	53	56	62	70	61	65	67	62	81	74	59	77	61	70	77	65	73	80
70041	BURAS	77	59	36	54	63	70	57	66	63	58	76	78	51	72	57	66	71	66	75	87
70043	CHALMETTE	69	71	71	69	72	78	71	71	72	69	88	82	72	91	72	73	85	71	74	80
70047	DESTREHAN	117	128	123	130	124	124	116	117	110	120	138	136	120	139	115	106	136	114	106	132
70049	EDGARD	52	44	47	40	44	53	48	50	54	50	66	53	47	60	48	58	63	51	57	57
70051	GARYVILLE	66	47	31	41	51	60	48	56	57	49	68	65	43	63	48	62	63	57	68	75
70052	GRAMERCY	83	58	34	50	64	74	58	69	69	59	81	81	51	76	58	74	75	69	85	94
70053	GRETNA	55	52	56	50	52	59	57	56	60	56	73	64	56	72	56	61	71	57	59	62
70056	GRETNA	77	83	92	84	81	84	82	80	80	83	100	94	84	101	81	77	99	80	74	88
70057	HAHNVILLE	76	64	53	63	67	76	67	71	72	66	88	80	64	85	66	74	82	71	79	84
70058	HARVEY	74	77	83	77	75	79	77	75	76	77	95	87	78	96	76	75	93	76	72	84
70062	KENNER	53	53	61	51	52	58	55	54	57	55	71	62	56	71	55	58	69	55	55	60
70065	KENNER	92	99	113	101	97	101	98	96	95	99	120	112	100	121	97	92	118	96	89	105
70067	LAFITTE	93	66	36	59	73	83	64	77	74	65	88	91	56	83	65	78	81	76	91	106
70068	LA PLACE	81	85	83	85	84	86	80	82	78	81	98	96	81	98	80	76	95	81	77	93
70070	LULING	97	106	106	105	106	110	98	100	95	98	119	116	101	123	99	95	117	97	97	115
70071	LUTCHER	80	66	53	60	69	78	65	72	72	66	88	82	62	84	66	76	83	71	82	91
70072	MARRERO	72	74	78	72	73	78	73	73	74	74	92	83	74	92	73	74	90	73	73	82
70075	MERAUX	83	82	73	81	81	86	79	82	78	80	97	94	78	95	78	77	93	81	80	93
70076	MOUNT AIRY	82	55	25	48	62	72	53	66	64	54	75	79	45	71	54	69	68	66	82	94
70079	NORCO	69	67	67	63	68	77	67	69	71	67	87	77	68	87	68	74	84	69	75	79
70080	PARADIS	86	77	58	73	77	82	73	79	75	75	92	92	69	87	72	75	88	79	80	96
70081	PILOTTOWN	0	0	0	0	0	0	0	0	0	0	0	0	0	0	0	0	0	0	0	0
70083	PORT SULPHUR	85	60	31	53	67	76	58	70	68	58	80	84	51	77	59	72	73	69	85	98
70084	RESERVE	76	61	47	55	64	73	60	67	68	61	82	78	57	79	61	71	77	67	77	87
70085	SAINT BERNARD	73	62	45	58	65	70	59	66	62	60	76	77	55	73	59	63	72	65	70	83
70086	SAINT JAMES	58	49	52	44	48	59	53	55	60	55	73	59	52	66	52	64	70	56	63	64
70087	SAINT ROSE	66	67	66	66	65	69	64	65	64	66	80	74	65	78	64	63	78	65	63	74
70090	VACHERIE	85	66	47	61	72	81	65	75	73	65	87	88	60	84	66	76	81	74	86	98
70091	VENICE	58	51	42	49	51	56	50	54	53	52	64	61	48	60	50	53	62	54	55	64
70092	VIOLET	79	66	50	62	69	75	64	71	69	65	83	84	60	82	64	70	79	70	77	90
70094	WESTWEGO	55	53	54	51	53	58	54	55	56	54	69	63	54	69	54	57	67	55	57	63
70112	NEW ORLEANS	27	22	31	22	21	26	28	26	30	28	37	30	27	36	26	31	36	28	27	29
70113	NEW ORLEANS	37	30	34	28	30	36	35	35	39	35	47	38	33	43	33	41	45	36	39	40
70114	NEW ORLEANS	52	46	56	45	45	52	52	50	55	52	69	58	51	66	51	56	67	53	53	57
70115	NEW ORLEANS	79	73	101	75	70	80	82	78	86	83	108	91	83	106	80	86	105	82	79	88
70116	NEW ORLEANS	58	49	68	49	48	57	58	56	63	59	78	64	57	75	56	65	76	59	60	63
70117	NEW ORLEANS	46	38	43	35	38	46	43	43	48	44	59	47	42	54	42	51	56	45	49	50
70118	NEW ORLEANS	90	80	103	81	79	91	93	88	98	93	122	103	92	117	90	98	118	93	91	100
70119	NEW ORLEANS	50	44	53	43	43	50	50	49	53	50	66	56	49	63	48	55	64	51	52	55
70121	NEW ORLEANS	65	67	79	66	67	74	70	68	71	69	89	78	72	91	71	72	86	69	70	75
70122	NEW ORLEANS	67	66	76	64	65	73	68	67	71	69	89	75	70	86	69	73	87	68	70	76
70123	NEW ORLEANS	90	101	126	101	99	106	99	97	98	99	124	111	105	128	102	99	122	97	94	106
70124	NEW ORLEANS	118	135	169	138	133	139	133	129	128	133	161	152	139	164	135	125	159	130	120	141
70125	NEW ORLEANS	58	53	63	51	52	59	58	57	62	59	77	65	57	73	57	64	74	59	60	65
70126	NEW ORLEANS	62	58	66	55	56	64	61	60	65	62	81	67	62	78	60	66	78	61	63	69
70127	NEW ORLEANS	61	59	69	56	57	65	61	60	65	63	81	67	63	79	61	67	79	62	63	69
70128	NEW ORLEANS	80	81	90	81	78	83	82	80	82	84	104	93	84	103	81	81	102	81	76	90
70129	NEW ORLEANS	65	58	70	58	58	64	64	64	67	65	83	76	62	80	63	67	81	67	64	74
70130	NEW ORLEANS	80	69	103	75	67	77	86	78	89	85	112	95	84	110	82	88	110	86	77	88
70131	NEW ORLEANS	98	106	121	107	104	110	105	103	102	105	128	119	108	129	105	100	126	103	98	113
70301	THIBODAUX	79	71	63	68	73	79	70	75	74	71	90	87	68	88	71	75	86	75	78	90
70339	PIERRE PART	79	61	39	56	66	73	59	68	65	60	78	80	52	74	59	68	73	68	78	91
70341	BELLE ROSE	80	58	32	52	64	72	55	67	64	56	76	80	49	74	56	68	70	66	79	92
70342	BERWICK	76	59	38	54	63	69	56	65	63	57	75	78	51	73	56	65	70	65	74	87
70343	BOURG	97	80	54	74	86	94	75	86	82	75	99	102	70	99	77	85	93	84	96	114
70344	CHAUVIN	89	60	28	52	68	78	58	72	69	59	82	86	49	77	59	75	74	71	89	102
70345	CUT OFF	87	67	42	63	73	81	66	76	73	66	87	89	59	85	66	76	81	75	87	99
70346	DONALDSONVILLE	68	52	46	47	54	64	55	60	64	56	77	69	52	73	55	67	72	61	70	76
70353	DULAC	60	43	25	39	49	55	42	51	48	42	57	60	36	55	43	52	52	50	61	70
70354	GALLIANO	78	52	24	45	59	68	51	63	61	52	72	76	43	68	51	66	65	63	78	90
70355	GHEENS	86	58	26	50	65	75	56	70	67	57	79	83	47	74	57	72	72	69	86	99
70356	GIBSON	64	48	38	42	50	60	50	56	59	52	71	63	46	64	50	64	66	57	68	72
70357	GOLDEN MEADOW	69	46	21	40	52	60	45	56	54	46	63	67	38	60	46	58	58	55	69	79
70358	GRAND ISLE	85	67	46	60	75	85	63	76	72	63	85	89	56	84	67	76	79	75	90	104
70359	GRAY	72	62	45	59	64	68	59	66	62	61	76	76	55	72	59	62	72	65	68	81
70360	HOUMA	106	107	108	105	107	114	104	106	105	104	130	123	105	130	104	105	126	105	107	122
70363	HOUMA	64	56	49	53	57	63	56	60	60	56	73	70	54	71	56	61	70	60	64	73
70364	HOUMA	74	69	63	67	70	75	68	71	70	68	86	83	67	86	68	70	83	71	73	84
70372	LABADIEVILLE	78	57	31	50	62	70	54	65	63	56	75	77	48	70	55	66	69	65	77	89
70374	LOCKPORT	85	63	38	57	70	78	61	72	70	62	84	86	55	81	62	74	77	71	85	98
70375	MATHEWS	86	60	29	52	67	77	57	71	68	58	80	84	50	77	58	73	73	70	86	99
70377	MONTEGUT	71	52	29	46	56	63	50	59	57	51	68	70	44	64	50	60	63	59	69	81
70380	MORGAN CITY	68	56	44	53	59	67	57	63	62	57	75	72	53	72	57	64	70	62	70	78
70390	NAPOLEONVILLE	78	58	38	51	63	72	57	67	66	58	79	78	52	75	58	70	73	66	79	89
70392	PATTERSON	66	55	43	52	57	63	56	60	60	56	72	69	52	68	55	61	68	60	65	73
70394	RACELAND	89	67	41	60	73	82	64	76	74	65	88	90	58	85	65	78	81	75	89	103
70395	SCHRIEVER	92	80	60	76	85	91	75	83	80	75	97	99	72	97	76	82	92	81	90	107
70397	THERIOT	100	70	36	63	79	90	68	83	79	68	93	100	59	90	69	84	85	82	100	116
70401	HAMMOND	61	50	52	51	50	56	59	57	61	57	75	70	55	71	56	59	72	61	57	67
70402	HAMMOND	0	0	0	0	0	0	0	0	0	0	0	0	0	0	0	0	0	0	0	0
70403	HAMMOND	70	60	52	57	62	69	61	65	65	61	79	76	58	76	61	66	75	65	70	79
70420	ABITA SPRINGS	87	90	83	91	88	89	84	86	81	86	101	102	83	101	83	77	98	85	80	99
70422	AMITE	70	53	36	48	57	65	53	61	61	54	72	70	48	68	53	64	67	61	71	79
	LOUISIANA	77	69	66	67	70	77	70	73	74	70	91	84	68	88	70	75	87	74	77	87
	UNITED STATES	100	100	100	100	100	100	100	100	100	100	100	100	100	100	100	100	100	100	100	100

ZIP CODE		POPULATION			2000-2004 ANNUAL RATE		HOUSEHOLDS					FAMILIES		
# POST OFFICE NAME	COUNTY FIPS CODE	2000	2004	2009	% Rate	State Centile	2000	2004	2009	% Annual Rate 2000-2004	2004 Average HH Size	2000	2004	% Annual Rate 2000-2004
70426 ANGIE	117	6272	6444	6627	0.6	57	1826	1919	2015	1.2	2.74	1373	1441	1.1
70427 BOGALUSA	117	20650	20603	20977	-0.1	26	8265	8341	8600	0.2	2.44	5622	5666	0.2
70431 BUSH	103	4766	5309	5958	2.6	95	1757	1980	2246	2.9	2.68	1398	1575	2.8
70433 COVINGTON	103	24207	26762	29909	2.4	93	8926	9985	11300	2.7	2.60	6546	7334	2.7
70435 COVINGTON	103	11463	12343	13607	1.8	85	4004	4363	4869	2.0	2.79	3187	3472	2.0
70436 FLUKER	105	639	637	666	-0.1	24	223	225	239	0.2	2.83	159	161	0.3
70437 FOLSOM	103	5796	6436	7195	2.5	94	2112	2373	2683	2.8	2.71	1634	1836	2.8
70438 FRANKLINTON	117	16102	17073	17838	1.4	79	6033	6504	6897	1.8	2.58	4409	4754	1.8
70441 GREENSBURG	091	3909	3852	3850	-0.4	15	1492	1501	1529	0.1	2.53	1042	1046	0.1
70442 HUSSER	105	500	536	575	1.7	84	180	195	211	1.9	2.74	134	145	1.9
70443 INDEPENDENCE	105	8333	9104	9966	2.1	89	2964	3270	3620	2.3	2.76	2218	2449	2.4
70444 KENTWOOD	105	9887	10508	11216	1.4	81	3614	3899	4220	1.8	2.67	2620	2830	1.8
70445 LACOMBE	103	9154	9844	10877	1.7	85	3342	3647	4086	2.1	2.66	2508	2735	2.1
70446 LORANGER	105	4862	5253	5662	1.8	86	1696	1853	2020	2.1	2.82	1323	1444	2.1
70447 MADISONVILLE	103	4766	5455	6196	3.2	97	1763	2043	2347	3.5	2.66	1343	1554	3.5
70448 MANDEVILLE	103	20332	23148	26220	3.1	97	7170	8228	9412	3.3	2.77	5627	6477	3.4
70449 MAUREPAS	063	2922	3000	3283	0.6	56	1172	1221	1355	1.0	2.46	843	877	0.9
70450 MOUNT HERMON	117	2242	2246	2272	0.0	30	845	860	883	0.4	2.61	633	643	0.4
70452 PEARL RIVER	103	10986	11605	12757	1.3	77	4014	4306	4796	1.7	2.69	3060	3278	1.6
70453 PINE GROVE	091	491	482	481	-0.4	13	166	166	169	0.0	2.90	126	126	0.0
70454 PONCHATOULA	105	19756	21244	22844	1.7	85	7235	7864	8553	2.0	2.69	5381	5842	2.0
70455 ROBERT	105	1396	1550	1695	2.5	94	515	580	642	2.8	2.67	395	444	2.8
70456 ROSELAND	105	2595	2753	2962	1.4	79	924	997	1090	1.8	2.70	665	717	1.8
70458 SLIDELL	103	32814	35856	40190	2.1	90	12500	13852	15728	2.5	2.56	9206	10178	2.4
70460 SLIDELL	103	20130	22120	24774	2.2	91	7194	8011	9077	2.6	2.75	5500	6122	2.6
70461 SLIDELL	103	23034	25424	28378	2.4	93	7977	8897	10034	2.6	2.85	6316	7031	2.6
70462 SPRINGFIELD	063	4520	5134	5923	3.0	96	1752	2018	2360	3.4	2.54	1318	1515	3.3
70466 TICKFAW	105	7207	7678	8252	1.5	82	2603	2805	3049	1.8	2.72	1916	2061	1.7
70467 VARNADO	117	12	12	11	0.0	29	7	7	7	0.0	1.71	5	3	-11.3
70471 MANDEVILLE	103	17476	19332	21597	2.4	93	6137	6831	7700	2.6	2.80	4641	5167	2.6
70501 LAFAYETTE	055	30723	29902	30507	-0.6	9	11280	11066	11410	-0.5	2.55	7132	6976	-0.5
70503 LAFAYETTE	055	26095	27240	28562	1.0	72	9652	10164	10776	1.2	2.50	6576	6936	1.3
70504 LAFAYETTE	055	287	344	386	4.4	100	111	136	155	4.9	2.47	75	91	4.7
70506 LAFAYETTE	055	36202	37752	39594	1.0	71	15399	16237	17228	1.3	2.29	8954	9412	1.2
70507 LAFAYETTE	055	14303	14369	14821	0.1	32	5265	5351	5579	0.4	2.65	3822	3877	0.3
70508 LAFAYETTE	055	27173	29135	30886	1.7	84	10757	11620	12422	1.8	2.48	7123	7686	1.8
70510 ABBEVILLE	113	24158	24764	25620	0.6	54	8897	9227	9661	0.9	2.64	6385	6617	0.8
70512 ARNAUDVILLE	097	8947	9631	10165	1.8	85	3213	3521	3779	2.2	2.71	2470	2705	2.2
70514 BALDWIN	101	4548	4450	4400	-0.5	11	1484	1477	1479	-0.1	2.89	1124	1115	-0.2
70515 BASILE	001	4004	4056	4162	0.3	42	1195	1230	1288	0.7	2.61	833	856	0.6
70516 BRANCH	001	1308	1365	1409	1.0	71	447	473	494	1.3	2.88	359	379	1.3
70517 BREAUX BRIDGE	099	23931	25190	26522	1.2	76	8430	9002	9629	1.6	2.75	6375	6808	1.6
70518 BROUSSARD	055	10157	10610	11123	1.0	72	3642	3856	4093	1.4	2.73	2725	2879	1.3
70520 CARENCRO	055	15037	15838	16781	1.2	76	5239	5600	6008	1.6	2.80	4058	4339	1.6
70525 CHURCH POINT	001	11773	12026	12344	0.5	52	4226	4379	4557	0.8	2.71	3143	3254	0.8
70526 CROWLEY	001	20915	21251	21781	0.4	46	7540	7743	8027	0.6	2.66	5490	5637	0.6
70528 DELCAMBRE	113	2628	2732	2818	0.9	69	983	1037	1083	1.3	2.63	748	787	1.2
70529 DUSON	055	9260	9880	10448	1.5	82	3336	3603	3852	1.8	2.74	2524	2716	1.7
70531 EGAN	001	990	1040	1078	1.2	75	351	373	390	1.4	2.79	269	284	1.3
70532 ELTON	053	2824	2835	2887	0.1	32	1043	1065	1110	0.5	2.31	775	789	0.4
70533 ERATH	113	7087	7330	7598	0.8	65	2509	2627	2755	1.1	2.75	1904	1990	1.0
70535 EUNICE	001	19125	19673	20223	0.7	59	6992	7299	7613	1.0	2.65	5063	5285	1.0
70537 EVANGELINE	001	708	773	818	2.1	89	264	292	313	2.4	2.64	212	234	2.4
70538 FRANKLIN	101	15043	14463	14186	-0.9	5	5287	5165	5127	-0.6	2.77	3996	3897	-0.6
70542 GUEYDAN	113	3662	3723	3852	0.4	46	1425	1467	1537	0.7	2.49	999	1029	0.7
70543 IOTA	001	3367	3482	3575	0.8	64	1227	1282	1332	1.0	2.71	925	965	1.0
70544 JEANERETTE	045	12093	12194	12417	0.2	38	3997	4083	4209	0.5	2.96	3069	3131	0.5
70546 JENNINGS	053	16393	16598	16894	0.3	42	5899	6036	6216	0.5	2.70	4365	4472	0.6
70548 KAPLAN	113	10925	10791	10959	-0.3	17	4117	4114	4226	0.0	2.58	2934	2925	-0.1
70549 LAKE ARTHUR	053	4155	4206	4260	0.3	42	1604	1650	1696	0.7	2.55	1133	1160	0.6
70552 LOREAUVILLE	045	321	327	336	0.4	49	108	112	117	0.9	2.92	85	88	0.7
70554 MAMOU	039	6533	6859	7183	1.2	75	2451	2605	2765	1.4	2.57	1727	1832	1.4
70555 MAURICE	113	5483	5857	6155	1.6	83	1938	2093	2222	1.8	2.79	1503	1619	1.8
70559 MORSE	001	3071	3023	3051	-0.4	15	1106	1103	1127	-0.1	2.74	844	840	-0.1
70560 NEW IBERIA	045	42790	43637	44625	0.5	50	14810	15284	15823	0.7	2.77	10974	11329	0.8
70563 NEW IBERIA	045	18460	18950	19423	0.6	56	6586	6843	7103	0.9	2.74	5140	5335	0.9
70570 OPELOUSAS	097	44812	45698	46586	0.5	50	16430	17062	17696	0.9	2.62	11622	12068	0.9
70577 PORT BARRE	097	4494	4565	4632	0.4	45	1638	1696	1752	0.8	2.68	1233	1276	0.8
70578 RAYNE	001	14752	14982	15374	0.4	45	5331	5472	5676	0.6	2.71	3911	4010	0.6
70581 ROANOKE	053	883	919	943	0.9	69	302	319	332	1.3	2.88	246	259	1.2
70582 SAINT MARTINVILLE	099	19067	19411	20216	0.4	47	6670	6912	7327	0.8	2.76	5001	5176	0.8
70583 SCOTT	055	11508	11943	12431	0.9	67	4176	4382	4609	1.1	2.72	3108	3254	1.1
70584 SUNSET	097	6026	6141	6234	0.5	49	2288	2376	2452	0.9	2.58	1696	1760	0.9
70586 VILLE PLATTE	039	23043	23707	24595	0.7	59	8410	8768	9222	1.0	2.62	6075	6334	1.0
70589 WASHINGTON	097	3786	3873	3987	0.5	53	1406	1465	1535	1.0	2.61	998	1040	1.0
70591 WELSH	053	5047	5150	5249	0.5	51	1835	1899	1961	0.8	2.66	1370	1416	0.8
70592 YOUNGSVILLE	055	12293	13613	14661	2.4	94	4336	4859	5287	2.7	2.80	3385	3779	2.6
70601 LAKE CHARLES	019	35114	34926	35671	-0.1	21	14221	14294	14765	0.1	2.37	8754	8758	0.0
70605 LAKE CHARLES	019	28541	30281	31860	1.4	79	10988	11793	12562	1.7	2.53	7907	8463	1.6
70607 LAKE CHARLES	019	23045	24719	26233	1.7	84	8808	9587	10309	2.0	2.57	6205	6741	2.0
70609 LAKE CHARLES	019	816	816	816	0.0	29	1	1	1	0.0	1.00	0	0	0.0
70611 LAKE CHARLES	019	16805	18078	19090	1.7	85	5833	6375	6829	2.1	2.83	4794	5234	2.1
70615 LAKE CHARLES	019	12681	12715	12988	0.1	31	4172	4251	4414	0.4	2.65	3004	3057	0.4
70630 BELL CITY	019	1076	990	991	-1.9	1	391	366	372	-1.5	2.70	303	283	-1.6
70631 CAMERON	023	3832	4004	4302	1.0	73	1385	1473	1609	1.5	2.68	1020	1083	1.4
70632 CREOLE	023	746	760	806	0.4	49	269	278	299	0.8	2.73	208	215	0.8
70633 DEQUINCY	019	8916	8982	9235	0.2	35	3050	3094	3221	0.3	2.78	2272	2309	0.4
70634 DERIDDER	011	23261	22897	23084	-0.4	15	8854	8861	9077	0.0	2.53	6503	6492	0.0
70637 DRY CREEK	011	808	840	876	0.9	69	296	312	331	1.3	2.60	218	229	1.2
70639 EVANS	115	467	447	446	-1.0	4	176	172	175	-0.5	2.60	131	126	-0.9
70643 GRAND CHENIER	023	838	851	900	0.4	45	325	335	360	0.7	2.53	242	250	0.7
70645 HACKBERRY	023	1699	1782	1919	1.1	74	626	667	729	1.5	2.67	458	488	1.5
70647 IOWA	019	8159	8414	8701	0.7	61	2899	3037	3186	1.1	2.76	2264	2369	1.1
70648 KINDER	003	8681	8909	9425	0.6	56	2680	2803	3036	1.1	2.76	1998	2087	1.0
70650 LACASSINE	053	11	13	14	4.0	99	6	7	8	3.7	1.86	5	6	4.4
LOUISIANA					0.7					0.9	2.59			1.0
UNITED STATES					1.2					1.3	2.58			1.1

ZIP CODE #	POST OFFICE NAME	RACE (%) White 2000	White 2004	Black 2000	Black 2004	Asian/Pacific 2000	Asian/Pacific 2004	% Hispanic Origin 2000	% Hispanic Origin 2004	2004 AGE DISTRIBUTION (%) 0-4	5-9	10-14	15-19	20-24	25-44	45-64	65-84	85+	18+	MEDIAN AGE 2004	% 2004 Males	% 2004 Females
70426	ANGIE	52.4	50.9	47.0	48.4	0.0	0.1	0.7	0.8	6.2	6.2	6.8	6.7	10.3	33.8	20.6	8.5	0.9	77.3	33.1	57.7	42.3
70427	BOGALUSA	69.2	67.5	29.4	30.9	0.3	0.4	0.8	0.8	7.4	7.4	7.3	6.4	6.2	24.2	25.0	14.2	2.0	74.1	38.0	46.9	53.1
70431	BUSH	97.7	97.4	1.1	1.2	0.1	0.2	1.3	1.5	6.0	6.5	7.4	6.7	6.6	26.1	28.7	11.3	0.9	76.2	39.1	50.0	50.0
70433	COVINGTON	86.3	85.5	11.4	11.8	0.6	0.7	2.3	2.6	7.9	7.9	7.4	6.4	5.9	28.0	25.0	10.2	1.5	72.8	36.5	48.5	51.5
70435	COVINGTON	89.5	89.0	9.0	9.3	0.3	0.3	1.5	1.7	6.5	7.1	7.8	7.0	6.4	26.1	28.1	10.3	0.8	74.4	38.0	49.5	50.5
70436	FLUKER	31.5	28.7	67.3	69.9	0.3	0.5	1.3	1.4	8.0	7.7	8.8	7.7	8.2	24.5	23.1	10.5	1.6	71.0	32.6	48.8	51.2
70437	FOLSOM	85.2	84.2	12.9	13.7	0.2	0.3	2.7	2.9	6.5	7.0	7.7	6.9	6.0	26.0	27.8	11.3	0.8	74.3	38.7	48.7	51.3
70438	FRANKLINTON	71.7	71.0	27.5	28.1	0.1	0.1	0.9	1.1	7.4	7.3	7.2	6.9	6.9	25.5	25.2	12.0	1.7	73.9	37.0	48.6	51.4
70441	GREENSBURG	43.8	42.2	55.1	56.6	0.1	0.1	1.2	1.2	6.9	7.1	7.9	7.0	6.5	24.7	24.8	12.8	2.1	73.9	37.3	48.1	51.9
70442	HUSSER	82.6	81.3	15.6	17.0	0.2	0.2	1.4	1.5	7.8	7.7	8.2	7.1	7.5	26.5	24.3	9.9	1.1	72.2	35.0	50.0	50.0
70443	INDEPENDENCE	71.9	70.7	26.0	27.1	0.2	0.3	2.2	2.4	7.6	7.3	7.6	7.4	7.2	27.6	24.1	10.3	1.1	73.1	34.8	49.2	50.8
70444	KENTWOOD	60.7	59.4	38.4	39.6	0.1	0.2	0.9	1.0	7.6	7.6	8.3	7.6	6.9	25.5	23.7	11.3	1.6	72.0	34.8	48.7	51.3
70445	LACOMBE	71.3	70.3	23.5	24.1	0.5	0.5	2.6	2.9	6.2	6.5	7.1	7.0	6.4	25.8	28.9	11.1	1.2	75.9	39.3	48.8	51.3
70446	LORANGER	90.6	89.6	7.8	8.6	0.1	0.1	1.5	1.8	8.0	8.0	8.2	7.1	6.9	28.1	24.0	8.9	0.7	71.4	33.9	50.0	50.0
70447	MADISONVILLE	92.2	91.2	5.2	5.8	0.6	0.7	2.6	2.9	6.5	7.4	8.4	6.8	4.5	29.0	28.2	8.4	0.9	73.3	38.6	50.3	49.7
70448	MANDEVILLE	93.3	92.6	4.2	4.6	0.7	0.8	2.4	2.7	8.5	8.7	8.6	7.5	5.4	28.9	25.0	6.7	0.7	69.1	35.4	48.6	51.4
70449	MAUREPAS	93.2	92.2	5.4	6.0	0.2	0.3	1.7	1.9	6.7	6.7	6.3	6.1	6.3	26.6	29.5	11.1	0.9	76.9	39.0	50.3	49.7
70450	MOUNT HERMON	76.0	72.3	23.1	26.7	0.1	0.1	0.6	0.6	6.8	6.6	7.4	7.0	6.7	25.4	26.3	12.6	1.3	75.0	38.7	48.7	51.3
70452	PEARL RIVER	91.1	90.4	6.6	6.9	0.3	0.4	1.6	1.8	6.9	7.0	7.4	7.0	6.8	27.9	26.7	9.6	0.8	74.5	36.7	50.3	49.7
70453	PINE GROVE	36.5	34.7	62.5	64.1	0.0	0.0	0.8	1.0	8.5	8.3	8.3	8.1	6.9	25.5	24.5	9.1	0.8	70.1	34.2	49.2	50.8
70454	PONCHATOULA	84.4	83.0	14.2	15.4	0.3	0.4	1.1	1.3	7.4	7.3	7.6	7.4	7.3	27.6	24.7	9.7	1.1	73.1	35.1	48.9	51.1
70455	ROBERT	96.6	96.1	1.7	1.8	0.0	0.0	1.4	1.7	7.7	7.9	7.7	6.9	6.5	28.3	25.4	9.1	0.7	72.7	35.0	49.7	50.3
70456	ROSELAND	46.4	44.8	52.2	53.5	0.3	0.3	1.0	1.0	7.1	6.9	8.4	7.4	7.7	25.4	25.6	10.4	1.2	73.2	35.4	49.7	50.4
70458	SLIDELL	87.7	86.6	8.9	9.4	1.1	1.3	2.7	3.0	6.1	6.2	6.9	6.7	6.4	26.4	27.6	12.3	1.6	76.8	39.5	48.7	51.3
70460	SLIDELL	74.0	72.8	21.9	22.7	0.5	0.7	2.7	3.0	8.0	7.7	7.7	7.1	6.8	29.1	24.7	8.3	0.7	72.2	34.4	49.0	51.0
70461	SLIDELL	86.2	84.4	9.5	10.6	1.8	2.2	3.4	3.8	7.1	7.5	8.4	7.9	6.6	27.5	27.3	7.0	0.7	72.1	36.0	49.5	50.5
70462	SPRINGFIELD	87.5	86.2	11.7	12.9	0.1	0.1	0.7	0.7	6.1	6.4	7.3	6.4	6.0	26.4	29.2	11.3	0.9	76.2	39.1	50.3	49.7
70466	TICKFAW	79.1	77.6	18.2	19.5	0.2	0.3	2.6	2.8	7.5	7.2	8.0	7.5	8.2	29.4	23.2	8.1	0.9	72.8	33.0	48.4	51.6
70467	VARNADO	33.3	25.0	66.7	75.0	0.0	0.0	0.0	0.0	0.0	0.0	0.0	16.7	16.7	66.7	0.0	0.0	0.0	100.0	30.0	100.0	0.0
70471	MANDEVILLE	94.9	94.1	2.5	2.8	1.0	1.3	2.5	2.8	6.9	7.9	9.2	7.8	5.2	25.9	27.7	8.1	1.3	70.8	37.9	48.3	51.7
70501	LAFAYETTE	29.4	26.6	68.7	71.3	0.4	0.5	1.2	1.2	7.2	7.1	7.3	7.4	8.8	27.3	22.3	11.2	1.5	73.9	33.8	48.7	51.3
70503	LAFAYETTE	89.8	88.5	6.3	7.0	2.3	2.8	2.1	2.3	5.7	5.9	7.1	10.0	10.0	24.8	24.2	11.1	1.2	76.8	34.8	48.0	52.0
70504	LAFAYETTE	97.2	96.8	2.1	2.3	0.7	0.9	0.7	0.6	4.4	4.9	5.5	4.9	4.1	16.0	25.6	29.9	4.7	82.3	52.1	48.3	51.7
70506	LAFAYETTE	80.0	78.1	16.1	17.4	1.8	2.2	2.2	2.5	6.6	6.0	6.4	6.9	10.8	31.2	21.2	9.6	1.3	77.4	32.2	47.8	52.2
70507	LAFAYETTE	64.8	61.4	32.7	35.9	0.7	0.9	1.6	1.7	8.1	7.5	7.7	7.6	8.1	29.1	22.7	8.2	1.1	72.2	32.3	47.7	52.3
70508	LAFAYETTE	89.2	87.7	7.7	8.8	1.3	1.6	2.1	2.3	7.4	7.0	6.9	6.9	7.8	31.5	24.2	7.1	1.0	74.5	33.9	48.7	51.3
70510	ABBEVILLE	72.9	71.4	22.3	22.9	3.4	4.1	1.6	1.8	7.7	7.3	7.5	7.2	7.2	26.8	23.0	11.5	1.8	73.1	35.5	48.5	51.5
70512	ARNAUDVILLE	79.5	77.4	19.5	21.4	0.1	0.2	0.8	0.8	7.3	7.1	7.6	7.3	7.2	27.1	24.4	10.7	1.3	73.5	36.1	49.2	50.8
70514	BALDWIN	37.5	35.1	52.7	54.0	0.8	1.1	1.4	1.4	7.9	7.5	8.9	7.4	7.5	28.3	23.1	8.8	0.7	70.9	33.2	51.2	48.8
70515	BASILE	73.0	71.6	26.1	27.5	0.3	0.3	0.9	1.0	6.2	6.0	6.5	7.2	10.3	32.0	20.3	9.6	1.9	77.3	33.8	57.9	42.1
70516	BRANCH	91.9	90.4	7.3	8.7	0.1	0.1	0.5	0.6	7.1	8.4	7.7	7.2	7.5	28.4	23.3	9.3	1.2	72.4	34.4	50.6	49.4
70517	BREAUX BRIDGE	68.7	66.8	28.9	30.4	1.3	1.5	0.7	0.8	8.0	7.9	8.0	7.4	7.4	28.7	22.8	8.8	1.1	71.6	33.2	49.7	50.3
70518	BROUSSARD	80.0	77.9	16.8	18.4	1.5	1.9	1.6	1.8	9.1	8.4	7.4	7.1	7.1	32.2	22.0	6.2	0.6	70.6	32.2	49.6	50.4
70520	CARENCRO	71.1	69.4	27.2	28.7	0.4	0.5	1.2	1.3	7.9	7.9	8.2	8.3	7.2	28.9	22.9	7.8	1.0	70.9	33.2	49.0	51.0
70525	CHURCH POINT	76.5	74.4	22.3	24.4	0.1	0.2	1.3	1.4	7.8	7.6	8.0	8.0	7.6	26.6	22.5	10.4	1.5	71.4	34.3	49.0	51.0
70526	CROWLEY	75.1	74.7	23.7	24.0	0.2	0.3	0.9	1.0	8.3	7.7	7.7	7.2	7.6	25.4	22.2	12.0	1.9	72.0	34.6	48.1	51.9
70528	DELCAMBRE	88.7	87.3	8.5	9.6	0.3	0.4	1.6	1.9	8.5	8.4	7.9	6.7	6.3	29.3	22.6	9.3	1.1	71.1	33.0	49.7	50.3
70529	DUSON	82.4	79.8	15.2	17.4	0.4	0.5	1.8	2.0	8.3	7.6	7.7	7.4	8.4	31.1	21.9	7.1	0.6	71.9	32.2	49.4	50.6
70531	EGAN	97.9	97.6	0.4	0.5	0.2	0.2	0.7	0.9	8.1	7.4	7.1	7.8	7.3	27.0	22.9	11.4	1.1	71.9	34.8	50.1	49.9
70532	ELTON	57.1	54.4	37.1	39.3	0.3	0.4	0.9	1.0	6.8	6.7	7.4	6.7	7.5	32.0	22.1	9.9	0.9	75.0	34.6	55.4	44.6
70533	ERATH	91.0	89.8	6.3	7.0	1.3	1.7	1.0	1.1	7.6	7.5	8.0	7.1	6.9	28.1	23.1	10.0	1.6	72.5	34.7	49.0	51.0
70535	EUNICE	75.0	74.2	23.7	24.4	0.2	0.2	1.1	1.2	8.1	7.4	7.8	7.8	8.0	24.8	23.1	11.7	1.5	72.1	34.4	48.7	51.3
70537	EVANGELINE	98.7	98.5	0.4	0.5	0.1	0.3	0.7	0.8	7.2	7.1	7.6	7.9	7.0	27.8	23.9	10.5	0.9	73.1	35.2	51.1	48.9
70538	FRANKLIN	52.3	50.1	45.3	47.1	0.6	0.7	0.7	0.8	7.9	7.8	8.5	7.7	6.7	25.2	23.8	10.9	1.5	70.9	35.5	47.3	52.7
70542	GUEYDAN	92.9	92.6	6.4	6.7	0.1	0.1	0.9	1.0	6.3	6.3	6.6	7.2	7.0	25.5	23.9	14.8	2.4	76.4	39.6	47.7	52.3
70543	IOTA	93.7	92.6	5.6	6.6	0.1	0.1	0.7	0.8	8.3	8.0	7.7	7.7	6.6	27.9	22.3	10.3	1.3	71.3	34.1	49.9	50.1
70544	JEANERETTE	46.7	44.4	50.6	52.7	0.3	0.4	1.7	1.8	8.1	7.8	8.3	8.4	7.7	24.8	23.1	10.4	1.4	70.7	33.7	47.8	52.2
70546	JENNINGS	78.5	77.6	20.0	20.7	0.3	0.3	1.0	1.2	7.9	7.6	7.9	7.6	7.0	25.8	22.6	12.0	1.6	72.0	35.1	47.9	52.1
70548	KAPLAN	91.2	90.3	7.3	8.1	0.3	0.4	1.1	1.3	6.8	6.8	7.0	6.9	7.3	27.1	22.7	12.9	2.5	75.1	37.0	48.2	51.8
70549	LAKE ARTHUR	90.9	90.0	8.1	8.9	0.1	0.1	0.6	0.6	7.8	7.5	7.3	6.6	7.0	26.5	23.5	12.4	1.4	73.4	36.1	48.4	51.6
70552	LOREAUVILLE	77.3	74.9	22.4	25.1	0.0	0.0	0.6	0.6	9.5	8.0	7.3	7.3	7.0	28.8	21.7	8.9	1.5	71.0	33.3	50.8	49.2
70554	MAMOU	72.0	70.1	26.7	28.5	0.1	0.2	0.9	1.0	8.3	8.1	8.4	7.6	6.8	25.5	21.7	12.0	1.8	70.5	34.5	48.2	51.8
70555	MAURICE	87.8	86.4	10.1	11.2	0.8	1.0	1.5	1.8	7.0	7.0	8.3	7.7	6.8	30.4	22.5	9.2	1.2	72.8	35.2	50.2	49.8
70559	MORSE	94.8	93.9	4.1	5.0	0.0	0.0	0.8	0.9	7.7	7.3	8.4	7.5	7.2	26.6	23.9	10.2	1.1	72.1	34.5	50.4	49.6
70560	NEW IBERIA	60.6	59.1	34.3	35.0	2.7	3.2	1.5	1.7	8.5	8.0	8.0	7.6	7.4	28.0	21.8	9.6	1.3	70.9	32.8	48.5	51.5
70563	NEW IBERIA	83.5	81.1	14.7	16.8	0.7	0.8	1.3	1.5	7.2	7.3	8.0	7.4	6.6	26.9	24.3	10.7	1.7	72.9	36.3	48.2	51.8
70570	OPELOUSAS	43.6	41.7	54.9	56.7	0.3	0.3	0.8	0.9	8.2	7.7	7.7	7.7	7.4	25.3	22.7	11.7	1.8	71.6	34.7	47.2	52.8
70577	PORT BARRE	81.2	79.8	18.1	19.5	0.1	0.1	0.6	0.7	7.5	7.4	8.2	7.6	7.3	26.9	23.3	10.8	1.0	72.3	35.1	50.0	50.0
70578	RAYNE	77.0	75.1	22.1	23.9	0.2	0.2	0.9	1.0	8.0	7.9	7.9	7.5	7.1	27.4	22.6	10.1	1.4	71.5	33.9	47.8	52.2
70581	ROANOKE	87.2	85.6	11.4	12.7	0.1	0.2	0.5	0.7	7.8	8.2	8.9	7.4	6.8	25.2	24.4	9.8	1.5	70.3	35.1	50.1	50.0
70582	SAINT MARTINVILLE	60.2	58.8	38.3	39.3	0.5	0.6	1.0	1.1	7.8	7.6	7.6	7.5	7.2	27.7	23.6	9.7	1.3	72.3	34.5	48.7	51.3
70583	SCOTT	77.8	75.3	20.0	22.4	0.6	0.8	1.4	1.6	8.8	8.2	8.1	7.9	8.1	31.1	21.1	6.2	0.6	70.1	31.0	48.8	51.2
70584	SUNSET	61.2	59.3	37.7	39.5	0.1	0.1	1.1	1.1	8.2	7.8	7.6	7.2	7.3	26.7	24.5	9.7	1.0	72.1	35.4	48.7	51.3
70586	VILLE PLATTE	68.2	66.9	30.9	32.1	0.1	0.2	1.1	1.2	8.4	8.0	8.0	7.4	7.0	26.0	22.3	11.3	1.7	71.2	34.5	49.1	50.9
70589	WASHINGTON	53.4	53.1	45.5	45.8	0.1	0.1	0.9	0.9	8.1	7.9	7.5	6.7	5.8	25.3	22.7	14.1	2.1	72.1	37.1	48.6	51.4
70591	WELSH	81.6	80.3	17.2	18.3	0.1	0.1	0.9	1.0	7.6	7.6	7.9	6.9	6.9	26.0	23.2	11.9	2.0	72.6	35.4	49.1	50.9
70592	YOUNGSVILLE	88.8	87.0	8.7	10.0	1.0	1.3	1.6	1.8	8.9	8.5	8.2	6.9	6.7	33.8	20.9	5.6	0.5	70.0	32.3	49.6	50.4
70601	LAKE CHARLES	36.4	34.2	60.9	63.0	0.7	0.9	1.2	1.2	7.4	6.8	7.2	6.6	7.3	25.7	22.7	13.8	2.5	74.5	36.8	46.6	53.4
70605	LAKE CHARLES	91.5	89.6	5.6	6.9	1.4	1.7	1.6	1.9	6.3	6.4	7.1	7.0	7.0	26.9	25.6	12.1	1.6	76.0	38.0	48.0	52.0
70607	LAKE CHARLES	67.4	64.2	29.6	32.5	1.0	1.1	1.4	1.4	8.7	7.7	7.2	7.1	9.2	30.1	21.1	8.3	0.6	72.2	30.6	48.7	51.3
70609	LAKE CHARLES	61.2	56.3	31.0	34.9	4.5	5.3	2.7	2.8	0.0	0.0	0.0	46.2	48.0	5.4	0.4	0.0	0.0	99.9	20.4	45.8	54.2
70611	LAKE CHARLES	93.2	92.1	4.7	5.4	0.4	0.5	1.4	1.7	7.6	7.6	8.3	7.5	7.5	29.8	24.2	6.8	0.6	71.9	33.4	49.4	50.6
70615	LAKE CHARLES	41.0	40.1	56.5	57.1	0.5	0.6	1.4	1.4	6.9	6.6	7.1	7.5	9.1	29.4	23.9	8.8	0.8	75.0	33.9	52.3	47.7
70630	BELL CITY	98.1	97.7	0.8	1.1	0.1	0.1	1.4	1.5	7.4	7.1	7.5	7.4	7.2	27.6	24.6	10.6	0.8	73.5	35.9	50.3	49.7
70631	CAMERON	87.2	86.0	8.9	9.4	0.6	0.7	3.8	4.3	7.4	7.3	7.4	7.0	6.8	28.6	23.9	10.6	1.0	73.3	35.7	51.4	48.6
70632	CREOLE	95.2	94.6	3.2	3.6	0.3	0.3	1.6	2.0	4.6	5.9	8.4	8.0	7.4	28.6	23.8	11.6	1.7	75.8	38.6	50.8	49.2
70633	DEQUINCY	84.5	83.0	13.9	15.0	0.3	0.4	0.8	0.9	7.4	7.3	7.4	6.8	7.0	28.3	22.8	11.5	1.4	73.8	35.2	50.8	49.2
70634	DERIDDER	80.2	78.8	16.1	17.0	0.9	1.0	1.9	2.1	7.2	7.1	7.8	7.0	6.6	26.5	24.6	11.8	1.5	73.6	36.6	48.9	51.1
70637	DRY CREEK	97.2	96.7	0.6	0.7	0.1	0.1	0.6	0.7	6.8	7.0	7.7	6.9	6.9	25.8	26.2	11.6	1.1	74.2	37.6	51.9	48.1
70639	EVANS	94.9	94.6	0.9	0.9	0.2	0.2	1.5	1.8	9.0	7.8	7.4	6.7	5.6	27.3	22.2	13.2	0.9	71.6	35.2	50.3	49.7
70643	GRAND CHENIER	97.5	96.9	0.8	0.9	1.1	1.3	0.8	1.1	4.4	6.9	8.1	7.3	5.5	27.6	26.8	12.3	1.1	75.9	39.4	49.5	50.5
70645	HACKBERRY	97.5	97.1	0.5	0.5	0.7	0.8	1.1	1.4	6.2	6.5	6.7	7.1	6.7	25.9	29.2	10.7	1.1	76.4	39.0	49.6	50.5
70647	IOWA	85.2	82.9	12.6	14.6	0.3	0.4	1.2	1.3	7.5	7.4	8.3	7.5	7.7	29.2	22.8	8.9	0.8	72.1	33.7	49.6	50.4
70648	KINDER	71.5	69.5	23.8	25.2	0.4	0.5	1.2	1.4	6.5	6.5	7.3	6.5	7.3	32.1	22.2	10.4	1.3	75.7	35.4	55.2	44.8
70650	LACASSINE	100.0	100.0	0.0	0.0	0.0	0.0	0.0	0.0	15.4	15.4	0.0	0.0	0.0	23.1	46.2	0.0	0.0	69.2	44.2	69.2	30.8
	LOUISIANA	63.9	62.8	32.5	33.2	1.3	1.5	2.4	2.6	7.2	7.0	7.4	7.5	7.9	28.0	23.4	10.3	1.4	74.1	34.6	48.5	51.5
	UNITED STATES	75.1	73.6	12.3	12.5	3.8	4.2	12.5	14.1	6.9	6.7	7.2	7.0	7.3	28.6	23.8	10.8	1.7	75.1	36.0	49.1	50.9

ZIP CODE #	POST OFFICE NAME	2004 Per Capita Income	2004 HH Income Base	2004 Household Income Distribution (%) Less than $25,000	$25,000 to $49,999	$50,000 to $99,999	$100,000 to $149,999	$150,000 or More	Median Household Income 2004	2009	2004 National Centile	2004 State Centile	2004 Home Value Base	2004 Home Value Distribution (%) Less than $50,000	$50,000 to $89,999	$90,000 to $174,999	$175,000 to $399,999	$400,000 or More	2004 Median Home Value
70426	ANGIE	12787	1919	44.8	31.1	20.6	2.6	0.9	27534	31230	8	22	1541	47.5	25.4	20.1	6.2	0.8	54695
70427	BOGALUSA	15083	8341	48.3	27.6	18.7	4.1	1.3	26147	29252	6	17	5760	36.8	32.0	23.7	6.5	1.1	62415
70431	BUSH	21490	1980	26.3	28.9	32.7	7.3	4.8	44299	51773	59	85	1711	17.7	14.3	27.4	35.9	4.7	136149
70433	COVINGTON	29050	9985	20.4	25.3	30.4	13.4	10.5	54757	65099	79	97	7925	5.6	7.7	38.6	39.9	8.2	170042
70435	COVINGTON	23100	4363	22.8	30.6	29.4	10.2	7.1	46813	54446	66	89	3727	15.5	11.1	32.4	34.2	6.9	143767
70436	FLUKER	10694	225	59.6	24.4	12.4	2.7	0.9	18447	21650	1	3	174	53.5	20.1	20.1	4.6	1.7	43333
70437	FOLSOM	21870	2373	26.9	28.5	31.0	8.5	5.1	43937	51123	58	85	2037	15.6	11.2	29.9	36.2	7.2	147708
70438	FRANKLINTON	15908	6504	45.9	28.1	20.0	3.9	2.1	27338	31050	8	21	5196	33.5	25.3	29.0	10.1	2.1	75031
70441	GREENSBURG	13381	1501	50.8	26.1	18.7	3.7	0.7	24366	27896	4	11	1213	41.0	22.9	23.4	8.1	4.6	63596
70442	HUSSER	16003	195	36.4	29.2	26.7	6.2	1.5	35601	40980	30	60	159	28.9	25.8	31.5	10.1	3.8	83182
70443	INDEPENDENCE	16034	3270	40.5	28.1	24.2	3.9	3.3	32042	36348	18	45	2678	35.7	24.6	29.6	8.7	1.5	75821
70444	KENTWOOD	14478	3899	45.6	27.6	21.5	4.1	1.3	28342	32509	9	26	3061	37.6	20.3	26.0	12.6	3.5	74583
70445	LACOMBE	21364	3647	29.2	27.2	30.1	10.3	3.2	43275	51138	57	84	3117	14.5	19.6	38.7	25.1	2.2	119993
70446	LORANGER	16633	1853	32.3	31.1	28.6	6.0	2.1	39785	45459	45	76	1563	22.5	24.3	33.5	16.6	3.1	95500
70447	MADISONVILLE	29066	2043	19.5	27.3	29.4	13.7	10.1	54019	63309	78	97	1770	8.0	8.3	31.7	42.4	9.7	181852
70448	MANDEVILLE	33843	8228	13.0	18.0	35.7	22.3	11.1	76500	89245	94	100	7101	2.8	3.2	34.5	54.2	5.3	192448
70449	MAUREPAS	18528	1221	31.2	33.3	29.2	5.2	1.1	36474	40880	33	64	1009	24.8	30.0	33.2	12.0	0.0	82422
70450	MOUNT HERMON	14699	860	40.8	37.4	17.7	2.0	2.1	28258	32357	9	25	713	27.6	31.3	20.8	18.1	2.2	76742
70452	PEARL RIVER	18269	4306	35.7	27.5	26.0	7.9	2.9	36777	43844	35	65	3522	23.8	22.6	36.8	15.1	1.7	94441
70453	PINE GROVE	12911	166	45.2	28.9	20.5	3.0	2.4	28477	30245	10	26	140	37.1	24.3	27.9	10.7	0.0	69000
70454	PONCHATOULA	17731	7864	35.7	28.1	26.6	7.0	2.6	35462	40328	29	59	6269	22.5	21.0	36.6	18.8	1.2	100371
70455	ROBERT	17745	580	31.2	29.8	29.8	7.2	1.9	40271	45400	47	77	501	26.0	20.6	34.7	16.8	2.0	97955
70456	ROSELAND	12671	997	49.2	29.2	17.4	3.5	0.8	25588	29465	5	15	779	50.3	18.1	23.8	5.1	2.7	49667
70458	SLIDELL	25552	13852	20.8	27.7	34.5	11.0	6.0	51399	60737	75	95	10588	4.9	15.6	54.4	22.6	2.5	122050
70460	SLIDELL	21708	8011	26.6	27.8	32.2	9.7	3.7	44948	53456	61	87	6347	9.8	20.9	51.1	16.4	1.9	107744
70461	SLIDELL	24801	8897	19.4	22.1	37.6	13.8	7.2	59688	69263	84	98	7545	10.6	8.9	44.9	33.3	2.2	141819
70462	SPRINGFIELD	18387	2018	35.4	30.2	26.5	5.5	2.3	36050	40962	32	62	1735	27.1	25.4	35.2	12.0	0.4	84408
70466	TICKFAW	16012	2805	37.9	28.9	27.5	4.2	1.6	34370	39741	25	54	2145	32.1	24.7	30.3	12.2	0.8	77897
70467	VARNADO	25000	7	57.1	0.0	42.9	0.0	0.0	22183	22183	3	6	5	40.0	60.0	0.0	0.0	0.0	71667
70471	MANDEVILLE	34943	6831	14.2	18.7	31.0	20.3	15.9	75522	88269	93	100	5423	2.0	3.0	29.7	51.5	13.8	215037
70501	LAFAYETTE	13700	11066	51.6	27.7	16.4	2.8	1.6	23891	27576	4	10	5782	34.5	34.9	24.1	5.4	1.1	66016
70503	LAFAYETTE	32966	10164	23.1	22.9	29.5	12.7	11.8	54580	63497	79	97	7350	1.6	8.1	49.0	32.0	9.4	157572
70504	LAFAYETTE	34900	136	15.4	16.9	38.2	16.2	13.2	72112	82625	92	99	123	3.3	2.4	51.2	41.5	1.6	158654
70506	LAFAYETTE	21680	16237	32.7	29.1	28.0	7.3	2.9	38432	44078	41	72	8801	10.9	22.0	54.0	12.3	0.8	108242
70507	LAFAYETTE	19081	5351	29.3	31.6	29.1	8.0	2.1	40695	46971	49	77	3518	23.6	22.0	44.2	9.6	0.6	94906
70508	LAFAYETTE	29821	11620	19.9	27.1	32.1	13.3	7.6	52994	61739	77	96	7775	11.1	7.9	42.1	33.4	5.6	149062
70510	ABBEVILLE	15535	9227	43.3	28.0	22.0	4.6	2.0	29986	33827	12	35	6712	32.1	28.0	28.1	10.4	1.5	75273
70512	ARNAUDVILLE	15293	3521	39.4	28.1	26.8	4.9	0.9	33613	38013	23	51	2914	30.2	32.9	28.3	8.1	0.4	73658
70514	BALDWIN	12653	1477	46.3	27.4	21.9	3.7	0.7	27556	31629	8	23	1228	47.2	23.5	24.8	4.0	0.5	54789
70515	BASILE	13563	1230	48.9	28.5	16.7	3.4	2.5	25642	29752	5	15	950	49.4	23.3	22.5	4.6	0.2	50845
70516	BRANCH	16673	473	34.7	29.8	27.7	6.1	1.7	37467	42361	37	68	392	33.9	28.6	26.5	10.7	0.3	76774
70517	BREAUX BRIDGE	15542	9002	39.2	29.7	24.7	4.8	1.6	33984	38050	24	54	7062	33.0	29.5	28.4	8.2	0.9	72039
70518	BROUSSARD	21634	3856	27.0	29.1	31.1	9.2	3.7	44510	51090	60	86	3010	25.5	17.2	41.7	13.1	2.5	104607
70520	CARENCRO	17785	5600	33.0	30.5	27.3	6.5	2.6	36636	42837	34	65	4251	25.0	26.1	33.6	13.6	1.7	88217
70525	CHURCH POINT	13432	4379	45.1	29.9	21.2	2.8	1.0	28485	32405	10	27	3268	38.8	33.5	20.8	6.1	0.9	61480
70526	CROWLEY	15983	7743	43.1	29.5	20.1	4.9	2.5	29319	33626	11	32	5155	33.5	34.1	23.7	7.5	1.2	69190
70528	DELCAMBRE	17132	1037	36.1	29.2	27.0	6.6	1.2	35298	40055	29	58	811	36.9	26.0	29.2	7.9	0.0	69364
70529	DUSON	17450	3603	33.7	30.4	27.9	6.4	1.7	38627	44524	42	73	2722	34.8	22.7	33.0	8.8	0.8	77561
70531	EGAN	14543	373	44.0	26.0	25.7	3.2	1.1	30872	35000	14	39	313	42.5	34.8	11.2	8.0	3.5	60543
70532	ELTON	17042	1065	46.5	25.6	20.0	6.1	1.8	28319	32007	9	25	837	47.9	25.6	19.7	6.7	0.1	52536
70533	ERATH	16403	2627	35.9	29.7	26.5	5.9	2.0	35048	40188	28	57	2171	31.7	26.4	31.0	10.6	0.3	78309
70535	EUNICE	14848	7299	46.1	27.6	21.1	3.2	2.1	27576	31522	8	23	5097	37.5	31.0	25.1	6.1	0.4	64972
70537	EVANGELINE	13851	292	48.3	26.0	21.2	3.8	0.7	26409	30138	6	18	257	43.2	33.9	17.1	3.9	2.0	58333
70538	FRANKLIN	14987	5165	44.6	28.8	19.9	4.7	2.0	28733	32579	10	28	3778	30.8	32.6	25.2	10.5	0.9	74006
70542	GUEYDAN	16739	1467	41.1	27.5	24.8	4.7	1.8	32151	37002	18	46	1182	36.2	36.6	21.1	4.9	1.2	61833
70543	IOTA	14505	1282	45.2	27.7	20.5	5.3	1.3	28426	32510	9	26	1041	42.3	33.1	19.2	5.0	0.4	57523
70544	JEANERETTE	14064	4083	44.0	27.5	21.9	4.5	2.1	29807	33657	12	34	3170	39.1	31.4	21.6	6.4	1.5	61583
70546	JENNINGS	14338	6036	43.4	29.2	21.9	4.1	1.4	29761	33493	12	33	4356	30.5	34.3	28.8	5.7	0.7	73236
70548	KAPLAN	15819	4114	41.7	27.0	24.9	5.2	1.3	32433	36810	19	47	3150	39.3	28.0	26.4	5.8	0.6	63349
70549	LAKE ARTHUR	15893	1650	43.6	30.1	19.3	5.2	1.8	30492	34864	13	37	1253	38.4	37.4	18.9	4.2	1.1	60223
70552	LOREAUVILLE	15272	112	39.3	26.8	26.8	5.4	1.8	33608	39600	23	51	93	33.3	30.1	30.1	6.5	0.0	70833
70554	MAMOU	12418	2605	56.4	24.6	15.0	2.5	1.5	20156	23300	2	4	1668	47.2	27.5	20.8	4.0	0.6	53760
70555	MAURICE	18244	2093	32.1	30.0	29.5	5.8	2.7	38555	43863	41	72	1759	29.6	22.4	29.5	16.7	1.8	85519
70559	MORSE	14076	1103	44.5	30.9	18.9	2.9	2.8	28906	32840	10	29	880	53.4	28.8	16.8	1.0	0.0	47248
70560	NEW IBERIA	14775	15284	42.0	29.4	22.2	4.5	1.9	30950	35450	15	40	10342	33.0	29.3	29.1	7.9	0.7	74088
70563	NEW IBERIA	21365	6843	29.1	26.8	30.7	9.1	4.3	44675	50404	60	86	5649	17.4	24.3	39.5	16.6	2.3	100184
70570	OPELOUSAS	13415	17062	51.8	25.9	17.2	3.5	1.7	23415	26902	3	9	11393	36.7	32.0	23.5	6.7	1.1	63575
70577	PORT BARRE	14492	1696	43.1	30.2	20.9	4.3	1.5	30354	35082	13	36	1382	44.9	26.1	24.2	4.1	0.7	57553
70578	RAYNE	15174	5472	44.2	29.4	19.9	3.8	2.6	29129	33300	11	31	3898	37.9	29.1	26.1	6.2	0.6	65530
70581	ROANOKE	15214	319	32.9	34.2	25.7	6.3	0.9	37005	42446	35	66	279	26.2	33.7	38.7	1.4	0.0	79375
70582	SAINT MARTINVILLE	15204	6912	40.8	28.5	25.7	3.6	1.4	32389	36978	19	47	5400	36.5	30.3	25.5	7.2	0.4	64693
70583	SCOTT	16598	4382	32.2	34.2	26.9	5.0	1.7	37425	43806	37	68	3367	45.1	22.6	23.4	8.1	0.8	57489
70584	SUNSET	15789	2376	45.1	25.0	23.1	4.9	1.9	29033	32957	10	30	1754	34.5	25.3	26.7	12.1	1.4	71724
70586	VILLE PLATTE	13808	8768	52.8	23.7	18.6	3.6	1.4	22532	26130	3	7	6086	37.6	33.5	22.2	6.1	0.6	61949
70589	WASHINGTON	14277	1465	52.5	25.7	15.9	4.2	1.7	23355	27383	3	9	1050	34.9	36.9	22.0	5.2	1.1	62887
70591	WELSH	15261	1899	41.3	29.7	23.1	4.2	1.7	31340	35331	16	43	1474	33.5	36.9	25.1	4.4	0.1	68203
70592	YOUNGSVILLE	22816	4859	21.1	30.1	33.1	12.0	3.8	48447	56912	69	91	4085	22.6	14.2	42.3	18.6	2.4	111524
70601	LAKE CHARLES	16640	14294	46.6	29.4	18.0	4.0	2.0	27200	31160	7	20	7560	31.8	43.6	20.8	2.9	0.9	64214
70605	LAKE CHARLES	30093	11793	22.7	25.0	31.0	13.1	8.3	52719	60011	77	96	9193	14.2	19.1	43.4	19.5	3.9	114284
70607	LAKE CHARLES	18535	9587	31.6	33.0	27.2	6.5	1.7	36845	42223	35	65	6059	31.0	34.3	28.9	5.7	0.2	68614
70609	LAKE CHARLES	10302	0	0.0	0.0	0.0	0.0	0.0	0	0	0	0	0	0.0	0.0	0.0	0.0	0.0	0
70611	LAKE CHARLES	23275	6375	22.3	25.7	35.7	11.7	4.6	51769	59586	75	96	5357	23.0	19.8	43.7	12.8	0.8	100049
70615	LAKE CHARLES	15880	4251	41.0	28.4	24.1	5.4	1.2	32417	37364	19	47	2966	48.2	32.1	16.6	2.5	0.6	51767
70630	BELL CITY	17923	366	29.2	31.2	30.1	8.5	1.1	42094	48202	53	81	293	39.9	34.8	18.8	5.5	1.0	57973
70631	CAMERON	16345	1473	41.6	26.5	24.4	4.9	2.6	32274	35705	19	47	1200	44.6	31.8	18.9	3.1	1.7	55242
70632	CREOLE	15234	278	35.6	28.8	31.7	3.6	0.4	34775	41247	27	56	236	40.7	29.2	27.5	1.3	1.3	64783
70633	DEQUINCY	15875	3094	36.2	30.5	26.5	5.0	1.8	34377	39202	25	54	2391	43.2	30.2	21.0	5.4	0.3	56552
70634	DERIDDER	18397	8861	35.0	30.0	25.9	6.8	2.3	36150	40457	32	62	6754	32.3	27.5	30.7	8.7	0.8	75984
70637	DRY CREEK	15447	312	38.1	29.5	26.0	6.1	0.3	32680	36773	20	48	286	43.7	26.9	24.1	2.8	2.5	58571
70639	EVANS	15482	172	39.5	33.7	21.5	2.3	2.9	30559	33504	14	38	147	34.7	25.2	27.2	12.9	0.0	67222
70643	GRAND CHENIER	18455	335	36.1	29.0	28.7	3.0	3.3	32125	37714	18	45	284	40.1	23.6	34.9	1.1	0.4	65385
70645	HACKBERRY	18453	667	31.0	26.8	34.3	7.2	0.6	41988	47303	53	81	571	45.5	25.7	19.4	8.6	0.7	58226
70647	IOWA	16972	3037	33.4	31.4	27.8	5.9	1.5	37658	43147	38	70	2467	41.2	30.5	23.8	4.5	0.1	61134
70648	KINDER	17223	2803	36.4	25.8	29.8	5.9	2.3	36603	40932	34	64	2159	29.9	29.4	32.9	7.3	0.5	77457
70650	LACASSINE	13462	7	71.4	0.0	28.6	0.0	0.0	15855	32500	1	2	6	0.0	66.7	33.3	0.0	0.0	80000
	LOUISIANA	19601		35.3	28.5	25.7	7.1	3.5	36550	42223				22.5	24.5	35.6	15.0	2.4	94005
	UNITED STATES	25866		24.7	27.1	30.8	10.9	6.5	48124	56710				10.9	15.0	33.7	30.1	10.4	145905

ZIP CODE #	POST OFFICE NAME	FINANCIAL SERVICES: Auto Loan	Home Loan	Invest-ments	Retire-ment Plans	THE HOME: Home Improvements: Home Repair	Lawn & Garden	Furnishings: Comput-ers & Hard-ware	Major Appli-ances	TV, Radio, Sound Equip-ment	Furni-ture	ENTERTAINMENT: Dine out/ Carry out	Sports Equip-ment	Fees & Tickets	Toys & Games	Travel	Cable TV	PERSONAL: Apparel & Services	Auto Repairs	Health Insur-ance	Pets & Supplies
70426	ANGIE	69	46	21	40	52	60	44	56	54	45	63	66	38	60	45	58	57	55	69	79
70427	BOGALUSA	60	46	35	41	48	57	48	53	55	48	66	60	44	61	48	59	61	54	63	67
70431	BUSH	88	85	73	82	88	92	78	84	80	78	98	99	78	101	80	81	94	81	87	104
70433	COVINGTON	107	117	121	119	114	116	110	110	105	113	133	127	113	133	109	102	131	108	101	122
70435	COVINGTON	93	99	95	98	100	102	91	94	89	92	110	110	93	112	93	88	108	92	91	109
70436	FLUKER	46	36	35	32	36	44	40	42	46	41	55	46	38	49	39	49	52	43	50	50
70437	FOLSOM	100	81	54	77	88	95	77	89	84	77	101	106	71	99	79	86	94	87	99	117
70438	FRANKLINTON	72	52	31	46	57	66	52	61	61	53	72	72	46	68	53	65	66	61	74	82
70441	GREENSBURG	55	41	34	36	44	52	43	49	51	44	60	55	40	55	43	54	57	49	58	62
70442	HUSSER	70	64	50	61	64	67	61	65	61	63	76	75	57	72	60	61	73	65	65	77
70443	INDEPENDENCE	80	58	32	51	63	72	56	67	65	57	77	79	49	72	56	68	71	66	79	91
70444	KENTWOOD	66	49	34	45	53	61	50	57	57	51	68	66	45	63	50	60	63	57	67	74
70445	LACOMBE	87	81	68	80	83	90	79	84	81	78	99	97	77	99	79	82	94	82	87	99
70446	LORANGER	76	68	52	65	68	72	65	70	66	66	81	81	61	77	64	66	78	70	71	84
70447	MADISONVILLE	102	125	132	126	123	121	112	111	103	112	130	130	119	138	114	100	130	107	99	123
70448	MANDEVILLE	128	151	159	156	146	145	138	135	127	140	161	158	144	165	137	121	160	132	119	148
70449	MAUREPAS	85	58	28	50	65	75	56	69	67	57	78	82	48	74	57	71	72	68	84	97
70450	MOUNT HERMON	72	48	22	42	55	63	47	58	56	48	66	70	40	63	48	61	60	58	72	83
70452	PEARL RIVER	86	67	42	61	72	79	63	74	71	64	85	87	57	81	64	74	79	73	84	98
70453	PINE GROVE	63	52	36	48	54	59	50	56	53	51	65	65	46	61	50	54	61	56	60	71
70454	PONCHATOULA	73	66	56	64	67	73	66	69	68	66	83	80	63	81	65	68	80	69	71	82
70455	ROBERT	75	69	54	66	69	73	66	70	66	68	82	81	62	77	65	65	79	70	70	83
70456	ROSELAND	58	42	30	37	45	53	44	50	51	44	61	57	40	56	43	55	57	50	60	64
70458	SLIDELL	91	95	99	96	95	101	93	94	92	93	114	109	94	115	94	91	111	93	92	105
70460	SLIDELL	85	90	88	91	88	90	85	86	82	86	103	100	87	104	85	80	101	85	80	96
70461	SLIDELL	100	109	109	111	106	108	102	102	96	103	121	119	104	121	101	92	119	101	93	114
70462	SPRINGFIELD	87	59	28	51	67	77	57	71	68	58	80	85	49	76	58	74	73	70	87	101
70466	TICKFAW	71	62	46	59	63	68	59	65	61	61	75	75	56	71	59	61	72	65	67	79
70467	VARNADO	81	54	24	47	61	70	52	65	63	53	74	78	44	70	53	68	67	65	80	93
70471	MANDEVILLE	136	155	164	158	151	153	141	141	133	144	167	164	148	170	142	128	166	138	128	157
70501	LAFAYETTE	50	41	45	39	41	49	47	47	52	47	63	52	45	59	46	54	61	49	52	54
70503	LAFAYETTE	115	127	146	131	124	129	126	121	119	126	151	143	129	152	125	115	149	122	111	133
70504	LAFAYETTE	113	136	153	135	135	142	125	125	118	125	149	142	133	151	130	118	147	122	120	137
70506	LAFAYETTE	69	65	76	68	64	68	72	69	71	72	90	82	70	87	69	68	88	72	64	76
70507	LAFAYETTE	74	72	72	71	70	75	72	72	72	73	89	85	70	87	71	70	87	74	70	82
70508	LAFAYETTE	106	110	115	115	107	108	108	106	102	110	129	126	108	127	105	97	127	107	95	118
70510	ABBEVILLE	66	53	41	50	56	64	54	60	60	54	73	69	51	69	54	63	68	60	68	75
70512	ARNAUDVILLE	75	55	30	49	60	67	53	63	60	54	72	74	46	68	53	64	66	62	73	85
70514	BALDWIN	62	47	34	42	50	57	47	54	54	48	65	62	43	61	47	57	61	54	63	70
70515	BASILE	63	46	32	41	50	59	48	55	56	48	67	63	44	62	48	60	62	55	66	71
70516	BRANCH	88	61	31	56	70	79	60	74	69	59	81	89	51	79	62	73	74	73	89	103
70517	BREAUX BRIDGE	72	57	41	53	60	67	56	63	62	57	75	74	52	72	56	64	70	63	71	82
70518	BROUSSARD	85	88	85	89	85	87	85	85	82	86	103	100	85	102	83	79	101	85	79	95
70520	CARENCRO	75	71	65	70	71	76	70	72	70	71	87	84	68	84	69	70	84	72	72	84
70525	CHURCH POINT	62	47	31	42	50	57	47	54	54	47	64	63	43	61	47	56	59	54	63	70
70526	CROWLEY	68	55	44	51	58	66	57	62	63	57	76	71	53	72	57	66	71	63	71	77
70528	DELCAMBRE	78	62	40	57	65	71	59	68	65	61	78	79	54	74	59	66	73	67	74	87
70529	DUSON	77	66	53	64	67	72	65	70	68	67	83	83	61	79	64	67	80	71	72	86
70531	EGAN	76	51	23	44	58	67	49	62	60	50	70	74	42	66	50	64	64	61	76	88
70532	ELTON	48	37	30	34	39	47	41	44	46	40	55	49	37	51	40	49	51	44	52	53
70533	ERATH	77	60	39	57	65	73	59	68	65	59	78	80	54	76	60	68	73	67	77	89
70535	EUNICE	64	49	37	46	53	61	53	58	59	52	70	66	48	67	52	61	65	58	66	72
70537	EVANGELINE	69	46	21	40	52	60	45	56	54	45	63	67	38	60	45	58	57	55	69	79
70538	FRANKLIN	70	53	37	47	57	65	53	61	61	54	73	72	49	69	54	65	68	61	72	80
70542	GUEYDAN	74	53	29	48	59	69	53	64	62	52	72	75	46	69	54	65	66	63	77	86
70543	IOTA	69	49	27	45	55	64	50	59	58	49	69	69	44	65	51	62	62	59	72	78
70544	JEANERETTE	67	52	42	47	54	64	54	60	62	55	74	67	50	68	54	66	70	60	70	75
70546	JENNINGS	64	49	35	45	53	61	51	57	57	51	68	66	46	65	51	60	64	57	66	73
70548	KAPLAN	71	52	31	49	58	67	53	62	60	52	71	73	47	68	54	63	65	61	73	82
70549	LAKE ARTHUR	72	51	28	46	57	66	51	61	59	51	70	72	45	67	52	63	64	61	74	82
70552	LOREAUVILLE	80	57	31	52	63	72	56	67	65	57	77	79	50	74	57	69	71	66	80	91
70554	MAMOU	51	39	33	35	41	49	42	46	48	42	58	51	39	53	41	51	54	46	54	57
70555	MAURICE	82	73	56	71	75	79	70	76	71	71	88	88	66	84	69	71	84	75	77	92
70559	MORSE	73	49	22	42	55	63	47	59	57	48	67	70	40	63	48	61	60	58	72	83
70560	NEW IBERIA	63	54	47	51	55	62	56	59	60	56	73	68	53	70	55	62	70	60	64	71
70563	NEW IBERIA	91	81	67	79	85	93	80	86	84	79	102	100	77	101	81	86	96	85	93	104
70570	OPELOUSAS	55	44	39	40	46	53	47	50	52	47	63	57	44	59	46	55	60	51	58	61
70577	PORT BARRE	72	49	24	43	56	64	47	59	57	48	67	70	41	63	49	61	61	58	72	83
70578	RAYNE	67	52	39	49	56	64	54	60	61	54	73	70	50	68	54	63	68	61	69	76
70581	ROANOKE	79	56	29	52	64	72	55	68	63	54	74	81	47	72	57	66	68	67	80	94
70582	SAINT MARTINVILLE	71	54	38	49	58	67	54	62	62	55	74	72	49	69	54	65	69	62	73	81
70583	SCOTT	70	64	53	62	64	68	63	66	64	64	79	77	59	75	62	64	76	66	67	78
70584	SUNSET	63	54	47	51	55	61	55	58	59	56	72	67	52	69	54	60	69	59	63	71
70586	VILLE PLATTE	59	45	34	42	48	56	48	53	54	47	65	61	44	61	47	57	60	53	62	66
70589	WASHINGTON	61	46	36	41	48	57	48	54	56	49	67	61	45	62	48	60	62	54	64	68
70591	WELSH	66	51	36	50	56	65	55	60	60	53	71	69	49	68	55	63	66	60	70	74
70592	YOUNGSVILLE	95	98	89	99	96	96	91	93	87	94	110	109	91	107	89	84	107	92	85	106
70601	LAKE CHARLES	56	49	55	47	49	57	55	55	59	55	73	61	54	69	54	61	70	56	59	62
70605	LAKE CHARLES	105	112	119	113	111	116	110	110	106	110	133	128	111	133	110	104	130	110	104	121
70607	LAKE CHARLES	70	66	62	64	65	70	67	68	68	67	84	79	65	82	65	67	81	69	68	78
70609	LAKE CHARLES	0	0	0	0	0	0	0	0	0	0	0	0	0	0	0	0	0	0	0	0
70611	LAKE CHARLES	98	99	90	99	99	101	93	96	91	94	113	113	92	113	92	88	110	95	91	112
70615	LAKE CHARLES	61	54	51	51	54	62	56	58	60	57	73	65	55	69	56	61	70	59	62	67
70630	BELL CITY	91	61	29	53	69	79	59	74	71	60	84	88	51	79	60	76	76	73	90	104
70631	CAMERON	69	60	53	58	64	69	59	65	62	59	76	76	56	74	60	63	72	65	69	80
70632	CREOLE	76	52	27	49	61	68	52	64	60	51	70	77	44	69	53	63	64	63	77	89
70633	DEQUINCY	76	58	38	53	62	71	58	67	65	59	78	77	53	74	58	68	73	66	76	85
70634	DERIDDER	78	62	42	58	66	75	62	70	68	61	82	81	57	79	62	71	76	69	79	89
70637	DRY CREEK	78	52	24	45	59	68	51	63	61	52	72	76	43	68	51	66	65	63	78	90
70639	EVANS	76	51	23	44	57	66	49	61	59	50	69	73	42	66	50	64	63	61	75	87
70643	GRAND CHENIER	80	62	40	56	70	78	59	71	67	58	79	83	52	78	62	71	73	70	84	97
70645	HACKBERRY	79	70	54	67	74	80	65	72	69	65	84	86	64	86	67	71	80	70	78	93
70647	IOWA	76	66	49	63	68	73	64	70	67	64	81	81	60	78	63	67	77	69	73	85
70648	KINDER	74	61	45	57	64	72	61	67	67	61	80	78	57	78	61	69	75	67	75	84
70650	LACASSINE	34	35	41	37	35	37	36	36	35	36	43	42	36	42	36	34	42	36	34	39
	LOUISIANA	77	69	66	67	70	77	70	73	74	70	91	84	68	88	70	75	87	74	77	87
	UNITED STATES	100	100	100	100	100	100	100	100	100	100	100	100	100	100	100	100	100	100	100	100

LOUISIANA
POPULATION CHANGE

A 70652-71018

# POST OFFICE NAME	COUNTY FIPS CODE	POPULATION 2000	2004	2009	2000-2004 ANNUAL RATE % Rate	State Centile	HOUSEHOLDS 2000	2004	2009	% Annual Rate 2000-2004	2004 Average HH Size	FAMILIES 2000	2004	% Annual Rate 2000-2004
70652 LONGVILLE	011	2075	2275	2401	2.2	90	754	841	902	2.6	2.65	601	668	2.5
70653 MERRYVILLE	011	3301	3356	3450	0.4	46	1288	1334	1395	0.8	2.47	951	980	0.7
70654 MITTIE	003	523	551	599	1.2	76	197	210	231	1.5	2.62	148	157	1.4
70655 OBERLIN	003	3261	3466	3775	1.4	81	1220	1324	1474	1.9	2.47	857	927	1.9
70656 PITKIN	115	4347	4294	4413	-0.3	17	1580	1587	1656	0.1	2.71	1224	1220	-0.1
70657 RAGLEY	011	3056	3376	3621	2.4	93	1040	1164	1266	2.7	2.90	857	957	2.6
70658 REEVES	003	1025	1197	1374	3.7	98	388	460	535	4.1	2.60	305	361	4.1
70660 SINGER	011	1648	1813	1915	2.3	92	591	678	737	3.3	2.11	467	533	3.2
70661 STARKS	019	2357	2666	2872	2.9	96	936	1076	1177	3.3	2.48	693	796	3.3
70662 SUGARTOWN	011	503	513	521	0.5	50	182	188	194	0.8	2.73	143	147	0.7
70663 SULPHUR	019	26988	27634	28543	0.6	53	10013	10381	10864	0.9	2.61	7297	7568	0.9
70665 SULPHUR	019	9143	9504	9846	0.9	69	3240	3408	3573	1.2	2.79	2565	2698	1.2
70668 VINTON	019	6449	6263	6354	-0.7	8	2358	2310	2373	-0.5	2.67	1782	1747	-0.5
70669 WESTLAKE	019	10309	10499	10828	0.4	48	3846	3967	4142	0.7	2.65	2914	2996	0.7
70706 DENHAM SPRINGS	063	12937	15923	19114	5.0	100	4353	5426	6596	5.3	2.93	3644	4537	5.3
70710 ADDIS	121	2757	2930	3072	1.4	81	982	1060	1128	1.8	2.76	739	798	1.8
70711 ALBANY	063	3567	3793	4231	1.5	81	1313	1417	1603	1.8	2.66	1037	1117	1.8
70712 ANGOLA	125	5496	5592	5752	0.4	47	169	206	266	4.8	2.89	136	166	4.8
70714 BAKER	033	20551	20053	20105	-0.6	11	7120	7079	7218	-0.1	2.77	5529	5494	-0.2
70715 BATCHELOR	077	1683	1745	1798	0.9	67	614	650	683	1.4	2.68	458	485	1.4
70719 BRUSLY	121	3919	4135	4319	1.3	77	1395	1495	1585	1.6	2.76	1117	1194	1.6
70721 CARVILLE	047	508	512	523	0.2	37	181	185	191	0.5	2.69	126	128	0.4
70722 CLINTON	037	6246	6509	6812	1.0	70	2148	2289	2453	1.5	2.70	1621	1728	1.5
70723 CONVENT	093	1999	2120	2197	1.4	79	613	657	691	1.6	3.10	467	501	1.7
70725 DARROW	005	1151	1218	1335	1.3	78	359	385	427	1.7	3.16	282	302	1.6
70726 DENHAM SPRINGS	063	36154	40083	45735	2.5	94	12932	14544	16837	2.8	2.73	9971	11199	2.8
70729 ERWINVILLE	121	577	630	669	2.1	89	212	234	252	2.4	2.69	163	180	2.4
70730 ETHEL	037	4196	4379	4593	1.0	71	1395	1493	1606	1.6	2.76	1075	1149	1.6
70732 FORDOCHE	077	1364	1383	1407	0.3	44	499	514	532	0.7	2.69	396	407	0.7
70733 FRENCH SETTLEMENT	063	1444	1655	1918	3.3	97	540	627	735	3.6	2.64	422	489	3.5
70734 GEISMAR	005	3416	3570	3891	1.0	73	1169	1236	1363	1.3	2.89	891	940	1.3
70736 GLYNN	077	512	531	546	0.9	67	179	188	197	1.2	2.82	134	141	1.2
70737 GONZALES	005	28342	31210	35003	2.3	92	9990	11138	12653	2.6	2.77	7633	8494	2.6
70739 GREENWELL SPRINGS	033	10923	11300	11561	0.8	65	3803	4022	4190	1.3	2.81	3144	3321	1.3
70740 GROSSE TETE	047	1317	1351	1394	0.6	55	492	513	536	1.0	2.63	372	389	1.1
70744 HOLDEN	063	4589	5203	6000	3.0	96	1586	1823	2131	3.3	2.85	1229	1410	3.2
70748 JACKSON	125	7967	8509	9247	1.6	83	2076	2317	2639	2.6	2.69	1539	1721	2.7
70749 JARREAU	077	1612	1705	1774	1.3	77	680	730	772	1.7	2.33	468	502	1.7
70750 KROTZ SPRINGS	097	883	886	892	0.1	31	365	375	384	0.6	2.36	254	260	0.6
70752 LAKELAND	077	877	900	921	0.6	56	332	345	358	0.9	2.61	257	268	1.0
70753 LETTSWORTH	077	1316	1269	1277	-0.9	5	451	441	451	-0.5	2.88	342	334	-0.6
70754 LIVINGSTON	063	7570	8257	9331	2.1	88	2678	2963	3396	2.4	2.75	2108	2330	2.4
70755 LIVONIA	077	1788	1832	1876	0.6	53	672	699	728	0.9	2.62	523	544	0.9
70756 LOTTIE	077	452	452	458	0.0	29	164	165	169	0.1	2.74	123	124	0.2
70757 MARINGOUIN	047	3325	3266	3323	-0.4	13	1107	1097	1130	-0.2	2.98	849	842	-0.2
70759 MORGANZA	077	1112	1259	1363	3.0	96	424	487	537	3.3	2.59	304	350	3.4
70760 NEW ROADS	077	7352	7337	7480	-0.1	26	2604	2649	2754	0.4	2.67	1848	1880	0.4
70761 NORWOOD	037	1196	1213	1251	0.3	44	435	449	472	0.8	2.70	302	312	0.8
70762 OSCAR	077	1059	1096	1128	0.8	65	390	409	427	1.1	2.68	303	318	1.1
70763 PAULINA	093	3270	3370	3438	0.7	60	1074	1122	1163	1.0	3.00	880	920	1.1
70764 PLAQUEMINE	047	17786	18113	18664	0.4	48	6286	6496	6795	0.8	2.74	4694	4850	0.8
70767 PORT ALLEN	121	14348	14515	14884	0.3	40	5074	5207	5420	0.6	2.68	3716	3809	0.6
70769 PRAIRIEVILLE	005	22674	26622	30827	3.9	98	7844	9318	10917	4.1	2.86	6355	7537	4.1
70770 PRIDE	033	3474	3906	4164	2.8	95	1203	1386	1507	3.4	2.82	992	1142	3.4
70772 ROSEDALE	047	737	763	793	0.8	66	260	272	286	1.1	2.81	194	202	1.0
70773 ROUGON	077	392	409	423	1.0	71	153	162	170	1.4	2.52	112	119	1.4
70774 SAINT AMANT	005	8498	9656	11002	3.1	97	3011	3465	3995	3.4	2.79	2394	2753	3.3
70775 SAINT FRANCISVILLE	125	8306	9851	12446	4.1	99	3021	3630	4651	4.4	2.68	2216	2661	4.4
70776 SAINT GABRIEL	047	5334	5529	5689	0.9	67	843	911	973	1.8	2.78	618	668	1.9
70777 SLAUGHTER	037	3943	4156	4363	1.3	76	1399	1502	1608	1.7	2.77	1124	1205	1.7
70778 SORRENTO	005	1616	1864	2138	3.4	98	585	684	794	3.8	2.72	448	523	3.7
70780 SUNSHINE	047	884	972	1041	2.3	91	308	342	371	2.5	2.84	227	251	2.4
70783 VENTRESS	077	2219	2294	2358	0.8	64	882	928	972	1.2	2.40	635	668	1.2
70785 WALKER	063	15310	16934	19270	2.4	93	5340	5994	6917	2.8	2.81	4221	4730	2.7
70788 WHITE CASTLE	047	4454	4665	4893	1.1	74	1550	1657	1768	1.6	2.82	1201	1281	1.5
70789 WILSON	037	505	512	528	0.3	43	190	196	207	0.7	2.59	131	135	0.7
70791 ZACHARY	033	19733	20303	20755	0.7	59	6750	7064	7337	1.1	2.84	5343	5582	1.0
70792 UNCLE SAM	093	142	149	153	1.1	74	48	51	53	1.4	2.92	36	38	1.3
70801 BATON ROUGE	033	66	55	53	-4.2	0	53	40	37	-6.4	1.38	8	4	-15.1
70802 BATON ROUGE	033	31075	29733	29659	-1.0	3	12064	11650	11783	-0.8	2.39	6649	6457	-0.7
70803 BATON ROUGE	033	3876	3862	3860	-0.1	23	16	16	16	0.0	2.56	3	3	0.1
70805 BATON ROUGE	033	31134	31052	31462	-0.1	24	10896	10944	11210	0.1	2.82	7473	7482	0.0
70806 BATON ROUGE	033	27125	27121	27492	0.0	29	12148	12303	12647	0.3	2.11	6261	6324	0.2
70807 BATON ROUGE	033	19096	18582	18593	-0.6	9	5877	5808	5917	-0.3	2.74	4301	4242	-0.3
70808 BATON ROUGE	033	30207	30945	31962	0.6	53	13577	14248	14997	1.1	2.11	7345	7665	1.0
70809 BATON ROUGE	033	19916	20698	21470	0.9	68	9098	9576	10070	1.2	2.11	4889	5170	1.3
70810 BATON ROUGE	033	30137	32978	34925	2.1	90	11242	12468	13379	2.5	2.64	8062	8957	2.5
70811 BATON ROUGE	033	13487	13436	13600	-0.1	23	4690	4769	4912	0.4	2.78	3589	3646	0.4
70812 BATON ROUGE	033	12178	11568	11494	-1.2	2	3830	3691	3723	-0.9	3.10	3112	3000	-0.9
70813 BATON ROUGE	033	2095	2072	2069	-0.3	19	63	59	59	-1.5	4.88	55	51	-1.8
70814 BATON ROUGE	033	13994	13781	13821	-0.4	15	5047	5006	5078	-0.2	2.74	3800	3769	-0.2
70815 BATON ROUGE	033	28971	29313	29852	0.3	41	11294	11615	12018	0.7	2.49	7826	8033	0.6
70816 BATON ROUGE	033	36428	37983	39320	1.0	71	15642	16567	17400	1.4	2.28	9547	10156	1.5
70817 BATON ROUGE	033	27573	29187	30466	1.4	78	9840	10675	11366	1.9	2.73	7876	8516	1.9
70818 BATON ROUGE	033	9721	10016	10293	0.7	60	3464	3639	3803	1.2	2.75	2858	3004	1.2
70819 BATON ROUGE	033	4879	4646	4614	-1.1	3	1766	1720	1741	-0.6	2.55	1276	1239	-0.7
70820 BATON ROUGE	033	14829	16296	17317	2.2	91	6393	6995	7483	2.1	2.32	2237	2437	2.0
71001 ARCADIA	013	4756	4912	5055	0.8	63	1739	1824	1907	1.1	2.53	1218	1277	1.1
71003 ATHENS	027	1147	1150	1161	0.1	31	469	476	487	0.4	2.42	327	332	0.4
71004 BELCHER	017	632	641	663	0.3	44	227	230	239	0.3	2.77	161	163	0.3
71006 BENTON	015	9600	10723	11776	2.6	95	3513	3978	4425	3.0	2.66	2810	3154	2.8
71007 BETHANY	017	882	1020	1104	3.5	98	341	400	438	3.8	2.55	264	309	3.8
71008 BIENVILLE	013	601	583	581	-0.7	7	247	244	247	-0.3	2.39	167	165	-0.3
71016 CASTOR	013	2371	2370	2387	0.0	27	896	903	919	0.2	2.62	657	661	0.1
71018 COTTON VALLEY	119	2123	2083	2100	-0.5	12	873	870	888	-0.1	2.39	612	608	-0.2
LOUISIANA					0.7					0.9	2.59			1.0
UNITED STATES					1.2					1.3	2.58			1.1

#	POST OFFICE NAME	RACE (%) White 2000	White 2004	Black 2000	Black 2004	Asian/Pacific 2000	Asian/Pacific 2004	% Hispanic Origin 2000	% Hispanic Origin 2004	2004 AGE DISTRIBUTION (%) 0-4	5-9	10-14	15-19	20-24	25-44	45-64	65-84	85+	18+	MEDIAN AGE 2004	% 2004 Males	% 2004 Females
70652	LONGVILLE	95.9	95.0	2.5	3.0	0.3	0.4	0.7	0.8	8.3	7.7	8.1	7.0	7.2	28.2	22.6	10.1	0.9	71.7	33.9	51.6	48.4
70653	MERRYVILLE	90.3	89.2	7.5	8.3	0.0	0.1	1.8	1.9	6.7	6.8	6.7	6.6	6.5	26.0	26.7	12.3	1.7	75.6	38.1	49.1	50.9
70654	MITTIE	97.9	97.3	0.4	0.5	0.0	0.0	1.2	1.5	7.3	7.3	8.2	8.2	6.7	26.0	23.4	11.6	1.5	72.4	36.3	50.1	49.9
70655	OBERLIN	66.9	64.0	31.0	33.6	0.2	0.3	0.8	0.9	7.4	7.2	7.8	6.9	6.7	26.3	24.2	11.6	2.0	73.5	36.3	49.4	50.6
70656	PITKIN	94.5	93.9	1.0	1.2	0.1	0.1	1.1	1.2	7.8	7.6	7.8	6.8	6.6	26.4	24.8	11.2	1.0	72.6	35.4	49.2	50.8
70657	RAGLEY	97.2	96.6	1.5	1.8	0.2	0.3	0.4	0.6	8.2	8.0	8.1	7.1	6.8	28.9	23.4	8.9	0.7	71.4	33.5	50.9	49.1
70658	REEVES	95.8	95.0	2.4	2.8	0.2	0.3	0.3	0.4	7.7	7.6	7.9	6.9	5.9	27.3	24.7	11.0	0.9	72.6	34.7	50.8	49.2
70660	SINGER	85.1	82.9	11.8	13.4	1.4	1.8	1.0	1.2	5.4	5.6	7.0	6.8	8.2	36.2	23.2	7.0	0.7	78.3	34.6	60.1	39.9
70661	STARKS	95.8	94.9	3.0	3.6	0.0	0.0	0.3	0.4	7.4	7.3	6.2	5.8	6.3	25.8	27.5	12.7	1.1	75.7	38.9	50.0	50.0
70662	SUGARTOWN	95.0	94.4	2.6	3.1	0.2	0.2	0.6	0.8	7.4	7.6	9.4	8.4	6.8	27.3	22.6	9.8	0.8	70.4	33.3	52.1	48.0
70663	SULPHUR	92.5	91.6	5.5	6.1	0.4	0.5	1.4	1.6	7.5	7.0	7.0	7.0	7.4	27.9	23.9	10.9	1.4	74.2	35.5	49.0	51.0
70665	SULPHUR	97.6	97.1	0.8	1.0	0.3	0.3	1.2	1.5	8.0	7.7	7.6	7.3	7.2	29.3	24.2	8.1	0.7	72.2	33.9	50.0	50.0
70668	VINTON	83.9	82.1	14.2	15.9	0.2	0.2	1.0	1.1	7.1	7.0	7.6	7.4	7.0	27.3	23.8	11.8	1.0	73.9	36.3	49.4	50.6
70669	WESTLAKE	84.0	83.1	14.2	14.9	0.2	0.2	1.5	1.7	7.2	7.0	7.3	7.1	7.4	27.4	24.4	11.2	1.0	74.2	36.0	49.3	50.8
70706	DENHAM SPRINGS	96.1	96.0	2.8	2.7	0.1	0.2	1.1	1.2	8.7	8.3	8.7	7.4	7.2	32.5	20.8	6.1	0.4	69.7	31.9	49.9	50.1
70710	ADDIS	70.9	68.8	27.6	29.5	0.1	0.1	1.7	1.8	7.3	7.0	8.6	8.7	8.8	30.9	21.2	6.7	0.7	71.9	31.4	49.1	50.9
70711	ALBANY	91.8	91.0	6.5	7.1	0.1	0.1	1.2	1.3	7.8	7.4	8.1	7.8	7.8	29.4	22.8	8.3	0.7	71.9	33.2	49.3	50.8
70712	ANGOLA	29.6	27.1	70.2	72.7	0.1	0.1	1.8	1.9	0.8	0.7	0.9	2.0	9.8	61.0	23.7	1.1	0.0	96.7	37.2	95.0	5.0
70714	BAKER	52.7	48.5	45.7	49.8	0.3	0.3	0.8	0.9	7.5	7.3	7.9	8.1	7.3	27.5	23.5	10.0	0.8	72.1	33.4	47.4	52.6
70715	BATCHELOR	52.1	49.3	46.5	49.2	0.1	0.2	1.9	1.9	8.1	7.5	7.5	7.2	7.4	23.3	23.6	13.2	2.1	72.6	36.5	47.5	52.6
70719	BRUSLY	71.2	69.0	27.1	29.0	0.2	0.2	1.6	1.9	7.3	7.2	8.1	7.9	7.7	29.1	24.1	7.9	0.7	72.7	34.6	48.9	51.1
70721	CARVILLE	16.5	15.2	81.5	82.8	0.8	0.8	3.0	3.1	8.0	7.8	8.8	7.8	8.6	26.2	21.3	10.4	1.2	70.7	31.8	46.3	53.7
70722	CLINTON	51.8	50.1	47.3	48.8	0.1	0.2	1.2	1.3	7.1	7.4	7.6	7.7	6.6	25.7	25.4	10.8	1.6	73.0	36.5	49.3	50.8
70723	CONVENT	23.2	20.7	76.2	78.7	0.0	0.0	0.2	0.2	7.1	7.3	8.5	8.1	7.5	26.4	24.7	9.6	0.9	72.1	33.8	48.2	51.8
70725	DARROW	35.0	30.6	63.3	67.7	0.4	0.4	1.0	0.9	7.8	7.7	8.3	7.7	7.1	29.6	22.7	8.4	0.7	71.5	34.1	49.7	50.3
70726	DENHAM SPRINGS	94.6	94.3	3.8	3.8	0.3	0.4	1.3	1.4	7.6	7.4	7.8	7.3	7.4	30.0	23.4	8.2	1.0	72.7	34.0	49.0	51.0
70729	ERWINVILLE	68.1	66.4	30.7	32.5	0.0	0.0	0.7	0.6	7.3	7.0	6.7	7.5	7.1	28.3	26.7	9.1	0.5	74.6	36.2	49.5	50.5
70730	ETHEL	55.2	53.5	43.5	45.0	0.3	0.4	0.8	0.8	6.7	6.9	7.4	6.6	6.8	26.5	26.2	11.4	1.4	74.8	37.3	51.0	49.0
70732	FORDOCHE	85.4	83.4	13.7	15.6	0.2	0.2	0.7	0.8	6.9	6.9	7.2	6.5	6.6	29.4	24.2	11.3	1.0	74.5	36.5	49.5	50.5
70733	FRENCH SETTLEMENT	99.3	99.3	0.2	0.2	0.0	0.0	1.3	1.5	7.2	7.0	6.9	7.1	7.0	28.4	25.1	10.6	0.7	74.8	36.3	49.4	50.6
70734	GEISMAR	64.4	60.8	33.8	37.3	0.2	0.2	1.8	2.0	9.4	8.5	8.3	8.1	8.3	29.4	21.3	6.2	0.6	69.1	30.1	48.4	51.6
70736	GLYNN	72.1	69.7	25.0	27.1	0.4	0.4	2.0	2.1	6.2	6.2	6.2	6.2	6.6	26.6	28.6	12.1	1.3	77.6	39.6	50.3	49.7
70737	GONZALES	79.7	77.8	17.0	18.5	0.4	0.5	4.0	4.6	8.0	7.8	7.8	6.9	7.2	31.6	22.3	7.6	0.9	72.2	33.3	49.2	50.8
70739	GREENWELL SPRINGS	95.3	94.3	3.3	4.0	0.3	0.3	0.9	1.0	6.8	7.0	7.5	7.1	6.8	29.6	26.7	8.0	0.6	74.4	35.8	49.0	51.0
70740	GROSSE TETE	73.6	71.6	25.5	27.5	0.4	0.4	0.7	0.7	7.4	7.4	7.2	6.1	6.8	27.5	26.1	10.7	0.9	74.5	37.1	49.0	51.0
70744	HOLDEN	93.2	92.2	5.3	6.2	0.1	0.1	1.1	1.3	7.1	7.0	8.3	7.9	7.5	29.6	23.5	8.7	0.6	72.5	34.2	49.4	50.6
70748	JACKSON	50.4	49.2	48.4	49.5	0.3	0.4	0.5	0.5	5.5	5.6	5.9	5.6	8.0	34.1	25.5	8.7	1.1	79.7	36.9	60.3	39.8
70749	JARREAU	89.5	88.2	9.0	10.2	0.3	0.4	0.9	1.1	5.9	6.0	5.2	4.6	5.8	24.5	32.9	13.7	1.5	80.1	43.7	50.3	49.7
70750	KROTZ SPRINGS	99.1	99.0	0.2	0.2	0.0	0.0	0.8	0.9	8.0	7.6	7.5	5.5	6.9	29.8	22.0	11.1	1.7	73.3	33.7	49.8	50.2
70752	LAKELAND	69.9	67.1	27.4	29.9	0.2	0.2	2.1	2.2	6.4	6.4	7.2	7.0	6.4	27.9	26.8	10.7	1.1	75.7	38.1	49.9	50.1
70753	LETTSWORTH	39.7	36.4	58.9	62.0	0.0	0.0	0.6	0.6	7.5	8.3	8.2	7.6	7.1	24.0	25.1	10.8	1.3	71.4	35.8	48.2	51.9
70754	LIVINGSTON	96.8	96.4	2.0	2.2	0.1	0.2	0.7	0.8	7.6	7.5	7.6	7.0	7.1	31.2	23.3	8.2	0.6	73.2	34.0	51.0	49.0
70755	LIVONIA	85.4	83.5	13.9	15.7	0.1	0.1	0.5	0.4	7.5	7.3	7.2	6.7	7.3	28.9	23.8	10.3	1.2	74.1	35.7	50.4	49.6
70756	LOTTIE	60.6	57.7	38.5	41.6	0.0	0.0	0.7	0.7	7.7	7.5	7.5	7.7	8.0	27.9	23.0	9.5	1.1	72.4	34.1	49.3	50.7
70757	MARINGOUIN	39.0	37.2	60.2	61.9	0.4	0.5	0.2	0.3	8.0	7.9	8.5	7.8	7.8	25.9	22.1	10.8	1.3	70.9	33.3	47.6	52.5
70759	MORGANZA	61.3	59.3	38.0	39.8	0.1	0.2	0.5	0.5	6.3	6.4	7.0	6.7	7.6	24.8	25.2	14.2	1.8	76.3	38.6	49.3	50.8
70760	NEW ROADS	37.4	36.1	61.3	62.4	0.5	0.6	0.9	1.0	7.0	7.1	8.0	7.1	7.2	23.7	23.3	13.7	2.8	73.4	37.6	47.0	53.0
70761	NORWOOD	41.1	39.3	58.1	59.9	0.1	0.1	0.5	0.5	7.7	7.4	7.6	7.8	7.8	25.4	25.1	10.4	0.9	72.6	35.2	48.4	51.6
70762	OSCAR	91.0	89.9	8.4	9.6	0.0	0.0	1.1	1.3	6.5	6.7	7.7	7.5	6.4	28.2	27.0	9.1	1.0	74.8	38.0	50.3	49.7
70763	PAULINA	83.5	81.7	15.9	17.5	0.2	0.2	0.8	0.9	7.3	7.4	9.4	7.9	7.1	29.8	23.0	7.3	0.9	71.1	34.1	49.1	51.0
70764	PLAQUEMINE	56.3	54.5	42.6	44.3	0.2	0.3	1.1	1.2	6.9	7.2	7.9	7.2	6.9	27.6	24.0	10.9	1.4	73.6	35.7	48.4	51.7
70767	PORT ALLEN	58.7	57.3	39.5	40.7	0.3	0.3	1.4	1.5	7.2	7.1	7.2	6.9	7.3	29.3	24.1	9.9	1.0	74.5	35.4	49.2	50.8
70769	PRAIRIEVILLE	90.8	89.1	7.1	8.5	0.5	0.6	1.8	2.0	8.8	8.3	8.0	6.9	6.8	33.6	22.2	5.0	0.5	70.7	32.5	49.9	50.1
70770	PRIDE	89.1	87.6	9.5	10.8	0.2	0.3	0.8	1.0	6.7	6.9	7.4	6.9	6.9	28.8	26.6	9.3	0.6	74.8	37.2	48.8	51.2
70772	ROSEDALE	55.2	52.8	43.7	46.0	0.7	0.8	0.1	0.1	7.9	7.9	8.3	7.5	6.6	28.4	21.6	10.6	1.3	71.4	34.7	49.2	50.9
70773	ROUGON	77.6	75.3	19.9	21.8	0.3	0.5	1.5	1.7	6.4	6.1	5.9	5.9	6.9	25.7	29.8	12.0	1.5	78.0	40.1	50.4	49.6
70774	SAINT AMANT	98.2	97.8	0.5	0.6	0.3	0.4	0.9	1.1	8.0	7.8	7.8	7.1	7.0	31.6	23.3	6.9	0.6	72.0	33.9	50.0	50.0
70775	SAINT FRANCISVILLE	57.9	55.0	40.8	43.7	0.3	0.3	0.6	0.7	7.1	7.1	8.4	8.0	7.1	25.3	26.3	9.6	1.3	72.1	35.8	48.4	51.6
70776	SAINT GABRIEL	37.3	36.4	61.8	62.7	0.2	0.3	1.0	1.1	3.4	3.5	3.7	4.7	13.5	45.8	20.6	4.4	0.3	87.4	33.8	60.4	39.6
70777	SLAUGHTER	67.9	65.6	30.9	33.1	0.2	0.3	0.6	0.7	7.2	7.4	8.1	7.5	7.0	28.4	24.9	8.8	0.8	72.7	35.1	50.3	49.7
70778	SORRENTO	80.3	77.6	18.1	20.8	0.3	0.3	2.0	2.3	9.2	8.1	7.5	6.7	6.7	30.0	23.1	8.2	0.4	71.5	33.8	51.8	48.2
70780	SUNSHINE	52.3	49.8	47.0	49.4	0.3	0.3	0.9	0.9	8.4	8.3	8.2	6.3	6.7	27.8	24.2	9.3	0.8	71.3	33.4	48.7	51.3
70783	VENTRESS	76.4	74.5	22.3	24.1	0.1	0.1	2.1	2.2	5.9	6.1	6.5	6.1	6.1	27.0	29.8	11.4	1.2	77.6	40.5	50.4	49.7
70785	WALKER	94.7	94.2	3.8	4.2	0.2	0.2	1.0	1.1	8.6	7.9	8.1	6.9	7.2	31.9	21.7	7.1	0.6	71.0	32.2	50.3	49.7
70788	WHITE CASTLE	42.2	41.0	56.8	57.9	0.2	0.2	1.5	1.6	7.4	7.5	8.4	7.6	7.2	25.7	24.0	10.8	1.4	72.0	35.2	47.4	52.6
70789	WILSON	40.8	39.3	58.4	60.0	0.0	0.0	0.4	0.4	7.2	7.2	8.4	7.6	7.8	25.8	25.0	10.2	0.8	72.3	34.8	47.5	52.5
70791	ZACHARY	67.4	62.8	31.1	35.6	0.4	0.5	0.8	0.9	6.8	7.0	7.8	7.8	7.3	27.2	25.4	9.3	1.3	73.5	35.8	48.5	51.5
70792	UNCLE SAM	62.0	59.1	38.0	40.9	0.0	0.0	0.7	0.0	6.7	7.4	10.7	6.7	6.7	26.9	24.2	9.4	1.3	71.1	36.1	50.3	49.7
70801	BATON ROUGE	50.0	45.5	45.5	47.3	1.5	1.8	1.5	1.8	1.8	1.8	1.8	5.5	12.7	41.8	25.5	9.1	0.0	92.7	35.5	70.9	29.1
70802	BATON ROUGE	17.0	15.3	78.4	79.7	3.0	3.4	1.3	1.3	7.2	6.9	6.9	10.5	11.3	26.5	19.5	9.7	1.5	75.1	29.3	47.8	52.2
70803	BATON ROUGE	81.1	77.8	14.6	17.2	1.7	2.2	3.2	3.5	0.2	0.2	0.1	55.6	37.2	4.8	1.2	0.4	0.1	99.0	19.4	34.3	65.7
70805	BATON ROUGE	10.4	8.7	87.5	89.1	0.9	0.9	1.0	0.9	9.1	8.9	9.4	9.1	8.4	26.9	20.8	6.7	0.6	67.1	28.6	46.3	53.7
70806	BATON ROUGE	52.3	49.6	45.5	48.0	0.9	1.1	1.4	1.5	7.4	6.6	6.0	5.8	8.1	29.7	21.1	12.1	3.2	76.7	34.8	45.6	54.4
70807	BATON ROUGE	3.8	3.1	95.4	96.1	0.1	0.1	0.7	0.7	7.9	7.7	7.6	12.2	9.3	25.2	19.5	9.5	1.1	70.7	28.8	49.9	50.1
70808	BATON ROUGE	80.9	77.9	13.6	15.6	3.7	4.6	2.0	2.3	4.9	5.0	5.1	7.9	12.6	26.4	24.1	11.5	2.5	82.0	34.8	48.6	51.4
70809	BATON ROUGE	85.5	82.7	11.1	13.2	1.9	2.4	2.2	2.4	5.5	5.0	5.2	5.6	9.2	30.7	23.8	12.6	2.5	81.5	36.4	47.1	53.0
70810	BATON ROUGE	63.9	62.2	30.9	31.8	2.8	3.4	3.4	3.5	7.4	7.3	7.5	7.3	8.3	29.2	26.0	6.5	0.5	73.6	33.5	48.4	51.6
70811	BATON ROUGE	29.6	26.4	68.7	71.7	0.8	0.9	0.7	0.7	7.1	7.2	8.3	8.2	7.6	25.3	25.3	9.9	1.1	72.3	34.4	46.7	53.3
70812	BATON ROUGE	8.3	6.9	90.6	91.9	0.2	0.2	0.9	0.9	8.8	9.0	9.7	9.4	8.3	25.3	22.9	6.1	0.5	66.8	28.7	46.3	53.7
70813	BATON ROUGE	0.4	0.3	98.6	98.6	0.1	0.1	0.6	0.7	0.5	0.4	2.5	44.4	44.3	5.3	2.5	0.1	0.0	95.4	20.2	54.3	45.7
70814	BATON ROUGE	34.6	30.2	61.0	65.0	3.0	3.5	1.6	1.6	8.2	8.0	8.4	7.3	7.0	29.8	21.8	8.6	1.0	71.0	33.0	47.5	52.5
70815	BATON ROUGE	67.2	64.0	24.9	27.1	6.1	6.9	1.9	2.0	6.7	6.4	7.0	6.9	7.0	25.6	22.7	15.7	2.0	75.7	37.8	47.0	53.0
70816	BATON ROUGE	78.0	74.9	17.2	19.4	2.7	3.4	3.0	3.3	7.1	6.4	6.6	6.5	9.0	33.3	22.6	7.7	0.9	76.3	32.7	48.3	51.7
70817	BATON ROUGE	90.9	88.8	5.7	7.1	1.9	2.4	1.7	2.0	7.6	8.2	7.9	6.8	5.6	31.7	26.5	5.3	0.4	72.0	35.4	49.3	50.7
70818	BATON ROUGE	95.0	94.0	3.5	4.2	0.3	0.4	0.8	1.0	6.9	7.1	7.3	7.2	6.6	28.7	26.5	9.1	0.6	74.2	36.5	48.5	51.6
70819	BATON ROUGE	81.2	78.3	13.5	15.5	2.1	2.7	3.7	4.1	7.3	7.0	6.4	5.5	6.5	30.2	23.4	11.0	2.6	76.0	36.0	46.1	53.9
70820	BATON ROUGE	67.2	64.4	24.0	25.5	4.9	5.9	4.9	5.4	5.7	4.2	4.6	14.4	34.9	24.2	10.1	1.8	0.1	83.1	23.0	52.0	48.0
71001	ARCADIA	43.4	41.6	55.1	56.8	0.2	0.2	1.4	1.4	7.0	7.0	7.7	6.8	6.9	24.2	22.4	13.7	4.3	74.2	37.9	46.5	53.5
71003	ATHENS	59.5	58.7	39.2	40.0	0.2	0.2	0.7	0.8	5.5	6.1	7.2	7.2	6.6	24.9	26.6	13.9	2.0	76.9	39.6	47.2	52.8
71004	BELCHER	53.2	49.3	42.7	46.0	0.0	0.0	3.6	4.1	6.2	6.4	7.8	7.3	6.9	24.3	25.7	13.7	1.6	74.9	38.8	51.8	48.2
71006	BENTON	80.1	77.5	17.7	19.9	0.4	0.4	1.9	2.2	6.2	6.6	7.0	7.2	5.8	26.6	28.8	11.0	0.9	75.9	39.8	49.1	50.9
71007	BETHANY	73.5	69.7	23.5	27.0	0.3	0.5	1.4	1.4	5.3	5.8	7.1	7.0	5.8	26.5	30.2	11.4	1.1	77.6	40.7	49.4	50.6
71008	BIENVILLE	56.4	55.1	42.9	44.4	0.0	0.0	0.2	0.0	5.5	5.5	6.9	7.2	6.2	23.5	27.8	14.8	2.7	77.4	42.2	49.9	50.1
71016	CASTOR	81.4	80.3	17.3	18.2	0.2	0.2	0.9	1.0	7.3	7.0	7.6	8.1	7.2	25.7	22.9	12.6	1.7	73.3	36.4	50.5	49.5
71018	COTTON VALLEY	69.7	67.5	28.5	30.6	0.1	0.1	1.4	1.4	7.2	6.0	6.1	7.0	7.4	24.5	25.1	14.9	1.8	76.5	39.9	48.6	51.4
	LOUISIANA	63.9	62.8	32.5	33.2	1.3	1.5	2.4	2.6	7.2	7.0	7.4	7.5	7.9	28.0	23.4	10.3	1.4	74.1	34.6	48.5	51.5
	UNITED STATES	75.1	73.6	12.3	12.5	3.8	4.2	12.5	14.1	6.9	6.7	7.2	7.0	7.3	28.6	23.8	10.8	1.7	75.1	36.0	49.1	50.9

ZIP CODE #	POST OFFICE NAME	2004 Per Capita Income	2004 HH Income Base	2004 Household Income Distribution (%) Less than $25,000	$25,000 to $49,999	$50,000 to $99,999	$100,000 to $149,999	$150,000 or More	Median Household Income 2004	2009	2004 National Centile	2004 State Centile	2004 Home Value Base	2004 Home Value Distribution (%) Less than $50,000	$50,000 to $89,999	$90,000 to $174,999	$175,000 to $399,999	$400,000 or More	2004 Median Home Value
70652	LONGVILLE	16412	841	32.5	33.8	28.1	4.8	1.0	35230	41284	28	58	720	48.5	22.4	22.2	5.6	1.4	52157
70653	MERRYVILLE	16778	1334	42.3	29.1	22.5	5.0	1.1	31199	34271	15	41	1084	45.7	24.7	23.9	5.5	0.2	56267
70654	MITTIE	14178	210	50.5	21.4	23.3	3.3	1.4	24607	27489	4	12	188	50.0	22.3	18.6	7.5	1.6	50000
70655	OBERLIN	15134	1324	42.4	30.6	22.3	4.1	0.7	30327	34238	13	36	1013	40.5	31.9	20.3	6.1	1.2	59847
70656	PITKIN	14620	1587	42.7	28.2	23.4	4.2	1.5	30678	33580	14	38	1384	40.5	26.2	26.5	6.3	0.5	60941
70657	RAGLEY	18717	1164	27.2	31.8	31.3	6.3	3.4	41261	47035	51	78	999	39.6	25.2	25.1	9.2	0.8	63769
70658	REEVES	16797	460	39.4	30.4	24.4	3.0	2.8	35681	41216	30	60	379	36.9	33.5	25.3	4.2	0.0	59167
70660	SINGER	16844	678	35.7	36.3	24.5	3.0	0.6	33715	38060	23	52	557	53.5	16.5	22.4	7.5	0.0	43710
70661	STARKS	19025	1076	35.7	32.2	25.6	5.4	1.2	35972	41455	31	61	907	45.2	31.1	21.0	2.1	0.7	55118
70662	SUGARTOWN	15738	188	28.7	38.3	27.1	5.9	0.0	34767	40000	27	56	171	48.5	20.5	28.7	2.3	0.0	52500
70663	SULPHUR	19452	10381	28.9	28.6	32.9	7.2	2.5	42292	48441	54	82	7995	26.7	36.4	30.2	6.4	0.3	76495
70665	SULPHUR	22348	3408	20.4	29.2	35.2	10.8	4.4	50308	58539	72	94	2871	31.1	27.4	32.4	7.8	1.3	79045
70668	VINTON	16917	2310	35.2	32.0	27.8	4.0	1.0	34806	40291	27	56	1798	45.7	28.6	20.5	4.7	0.6	55735
70669	WESTLAKE	19911	3967	29.5	28.4	32.9	6.5	2.7	42134	47862	53	81	3068	25.5	36.9	30.4	6.5	0.7	75607
70706	DENHAM SPRINGS	19921	5426	21.7	28.1	37.8	10.2	2.3	50203	55192	72	93	4816	17.4	16.8	46.3	18.6	1.0	114540
70710	ADDIS	17551	1060	24.9	35.6	31.7	7.2	0.7	41944	47680	53	80	863	38.6	18.0	37.9	5.3	0.2	75568
70711	ALBANY	17582	1417	34.4	29.0	28.4	6.1	2.1	37007	41687	35	66	1126	30.3	27.8	32.2	9.0	0.8	80319
70712	ANGOLA	11166	206	1.5	48.1	50.5	0.0	0.0	50160	60312	72	93	87	57.5	6.9	21.8	13.8	0.0	45938
70714	BAKER	18214	7079	26.6	31.6	32.2	7.9	1.7	43281	50404	57	84	5425	15.0	38.8	35.9	8.7	1.6	86136
70715	BATCHELOR	14516	650	45.1	35.5	14.5	3.4	1.5	27751	32051	8	24	493	32.1	32.9	16.8	13.8	4.5	62949
70719	BRUSLY	21123	1495	24.4	26.0	34.2	12.6	2.7	49506	54949	71	92	1267	20.5	15.8	44.0	17.6	2.1	110203
70721	CARVILLE	14487	185	42.7	30.3	21.1	3.2	2.7	28817	32144	10	28	121	43.0	26.5	26.5	4.1	0.0	62500
70722	CLINTON	18300	2289	37.2	27.0	26.2	7.0	2.7	34100	39476	24	54	1884	29.6	18.8	30.6	17.9	3.1	92586
70723	CONVENT	12206	657	42.3	27.7	27.1	1.5	1.4	29621	34939	11	32	506	56.7	23.3	15.4	4.6	0.0	43818
70725	DARROW	17483	385	29.9	31.2	24.2	8.3	6.5	41810	46989	52	79	312	25.0	28.5	17.3	21.2	8.0	82667
70726	DENHAM SPRINGS	19482	14544	25.2	30.4	34.6	7.9	2.0	44911	50335	61	87	11627	23.0	23.5	40.8	12.2	0.6	95079
70729	ERWINVILLE	17181	234	30.8	36.8	24.8	6.8	0.9	40000	45000	46	76	193	40.4	11.4	41.5	6.7	0.0	78333
70730	ETHEL	18883	1493	37.1	24.7	28.4	7.6	2.2	37697	43438	38	70	1302	30.6	20.7	29.7	17.4	1.6	87377
70732	FORDOCHE	19305	514	27.6	31.9	31.9	6.4	2.1	42073	48291	53	81	432	29.9	23.6	36.3	9.7	0.5	85455
70733	FRENCH SETTLEMENT	18280	627	24.4	36.7	33.3	5.1	0.5	43630	49540	58	84	547	19.7	29.1	38.4	11.5	1.3	92321
70734	GEISMAR	18921	1236	22.0	37.0	29.5	8.8	2.7	44235	51913	59	85	1041	40.6	18.5	26.5	10.2	4.1	69265
70736	GLYNN	19640	188	35.6	28.2	26.1	6.9	3.2	37625	42160	38	69	152	28.3	23.7	30.9	16.5	0.7	86250
70737	GONZALES	19981	11138	23.0	28.9	37.4	8.7	2.1	48121	54241	69	91	8757	18.8	21.9	43.3	15.5	0.6	104085
70739	GREENWELL SPRINGS	23714	4022	14.5	25.6	42.6	14.5	2.9	58455	69366	83	98	3461	5.7	14.7	57.7	20.9	1.0	124085
70740	GROSSE TETE	15791	513	33.1	35.7	26.1	4.9	0.2	33754	40188	23	53	424	39.6	25.2	25.7	9.2	0.2	67000
70744	HOLDEN	16145	1823	35.7	28.9	28.0	5.0	2.4	37021	41832	36	66	1473	30.3	24.1	33.6	10.9	1.1	82412
70748	JACKSON	17943	2317	37.0	24.2	26.5	7.3	4.9	36473	42928	33	63	1829	33.1	22.0	21.7	17.2	6.0	79145
70749	JARREAU	23301	730	26.9	31.0	30.4	8.6	3.2	43198	49777	56	83	598	23.1	21.6	24.8	27.6	3.0	108491
70750	KROTZ SPRINGS	16017	375	42.1	33.1	20.8	3.5	0.5	29230	33212	11	31	272	50.0	31.6	17.3	1.1	0.0	50000
70752	LAKELAND	22131	345	36.8	25.5	27.0	7.3	3.5	35559	40212	30	59	281	24.6	21.4	39.2	14.6	0.4	97188
70753	LETTSWORTH	10041	441	58.3	28.6	10.2	3.0	0.0	19947	23583	2	4	345	51.6	27.0	15.9	5.5	0.0	48333
70754	LIVINGSTON	17262	2963	31.2	29.0	33.4	4.9	1.5	41359	46387	51	79	2536	26.7	29.1	34.0	9.3	0.9	81543
70755	LIVONIA	17899	699	33.1	30.8	29.2	5.7	1.3	37347	43036	37	68	572	31.3	28.7	32.3	7.5	0.2	80172
70756	LOTTIE	17762	165	38.2	26.7	26.1	6.7	2.4	34716	39081	26	55	133	39.9	18.1	25.6	16.5	0.0	77500
70757	MARINGOUIN	13324	1097	44.4	28.4	21.0	5.0	1.2	28860	33284	10	28	852	36.5	30.6	22.5	9.4	0.9	69516
70759	MORGANZA	18104	487	39.6	26.1	26.5	5.5	2.3	34887	39230	27	56	348	24.4	24.7	34.8	15.2	0.9	91667
70760	NEW ROADS	16281	2649	46.4	25.9	20.8	4.8	2.1	27853	31860	8	24	1817	24.4	34.4	26.1	13.2	1.9	79215
70761	NORWOOD	13839	449	47.0	27.8	19.8	3.8	1.6	26626	31288	7	19	351	34.2	19.9	29.9	14.8	1.1	80938
70762	OSCAR	21355	409	23.0	28.6	35.9	10.0	2.4	47570	53731	67	90	341	16.1	17.0	44.0	20.8	2.1	120250
70763	PAULINA	19931	1122	19.4	25.6	38.0	16.1	0.9	53804	61509	78	97	959	23.8	21.2	35.0	19.6	0.4	97132
70764	PLAQUEMINE	16919	6496	39.2	27.5	23.2	7.0	3.1	33703	39677	23	52	4990	29.3	25.1	30.9	13.8	0.9	81577
70767	PORT ALLEN	18025	5207	32.6	30.2	27.3	7.7	2.3	39204	44266	43	74	3949	24.8	31.7	32.9	9.7	0.8	82307
70769	PRAIRIEVILLE	24208	9318	15.6	20.4	45.6	15.0	3.4	63216	71496	87	99	8294	15.0	13.0	43.4	25.4	3.2	131640
70770	PRIDE	22551	1386	16.9	27.1	41.0	12.3	2.7	55554	65566	80	97	1265	12.5	17.6	51.1	16.3	2.5	111340
70772	ROSEDALE	15995	272	36.8	27.2	27.2	8.8	0.0	35000	40765	28	57	220	35.9	17.7	32.7	11.8	1.8	82000
70773	ROUGON	21413	162	33.3	30.3	27.2	6.8	2.5	38934	44566	43	73	131	28.2	23.7	29.8	17.6	0.8	86429
70774	SAINT AMANT	19213	3465	22.7	34.5	33.2	7.8	1.8	43171	49900	56	83	2907	25.8	19.3	39.3	14.5	1.1	97608
70775	SAINT FRANCISVILLE	20306	3630	31.8	25.5	29.3	9.7	3.7	42942	49600	56	83	2802	22.4	19.7	28.9	23.4	5.6	106189
70776	SAINT GABRIEL	14732	911	32.1	27.4	30.5	5.6	4.4	38234	44178	40	71	709	24.5	20.6	28.8	19.5	6.6	95074
70777	SLAUGHTER	20794	1502	29.9	26.1	32.6	9.0	2.4	43974	51253	59	85	1267	27.8	22.3	34.0	14.7	1.2	89758
70778	SORRENTO	17208	684	32.8	28.7	32.2	5.1	1.3	41257	48311	51	78	560	32.1	28.2	34.8	4.3	0.5	72000
70780	SUNSHINE	15725	342	42.7	19.9	29.8	4.7	2.9	31190	35884	15	41	276	29.7	28.6	27.2	8.3	6.2	76364
70783	VENTRESS	22314	928	27.7	28.2	32.3	8.3	3.5	42260	48599	54	82	759	20.7	19.9	30.2	26.8	2.5	112361
70785	WALKER	17771	5994	24.7	35.6	32.1	6.2	1.4	42039	47377	53	81	4981	23.3	21.5	41.6	12.3	1.3	97008
70788	WHITE CASTLE	14274	1657	48.5	24.0	21.0	4.9	1.7	26054	30905	6	16	1190	33.0	27.0	27.8	11.8	0.4	72625
70789	WILSON	15665	196	44.4	27.0	21.9	4.1	2.6	28788	33612	10	28	148	34.5	22.3	29.7	13.5	0.0	78889
70791	ZACHARY	21377	7064	24.9	24.1	33.6	14.3	3.2	51085	60060	74	95	5763	18.1	21.1	39.4	19.6	1.7	104046
70792	UNCLE SAM	18924	51	35.3	13.7	31.4	17.7	2.0	51465	48664	75	95	46	39.1	17.4	37.0	6.5	0.0	70000
70801	BATON ROUGE	10967	40	100.0	0.0	0.0	0.0	0.0	15824	18213	1	2	2	0.0	0.0	0.0	100.0	0.0	275000
70802	BATON ROUGE	11786	11650	60.7	25.7	10.7	2.0	0.8	19212	22574	2	3	4885	48.2	37.0	11.8	2.0	1.1	51317
70803	BATON ROUGE	9390	16	81.3	6.3	0.0	12.5	0.0	10000	12093	0	1	2	0.0	100.0	0.0	0.0	0.0	80000
70805	BATON ROUGE	11412	10944	53.2	27.9	15.6	2.5	0.9	23116	26549	3	8	5448	39.6	47.9	11.9	0.5	0.2	56563
70806	BATON ROUGE	23898	12303	40.5	26.9	21.4	6.8	4.5	32197	38433	18	46	5614	8.0	20.4	47.4	20.7	3.5	120699
70807	BATON ROUGE	12529	5808	55.0	22.5	17.6	3.9	1.1	21989	26402	3	6	3260	35.5	38.0	24.0	1.9	0.6	64130
70808	BATON ROUGE	37314	14248	26.9	21.7	26.3	13.4	11.8	52190	61655	76	96	8310	3.2	6.4	40.3	40.4	9.7	175225
70809	BATON ROUGE	35921	9576	21.3	29.4	29.3	11.4	8.6	49266	59049	71	92	4890	3.8	11.9	42.4	29.2	12.6	145486
70810	BATON ROUGE	33463	12468	17.4	23.4	31.2	15.5	12.6	62543	75923	87	99	8978	1.5	14.6	39.0	32.3	12.6	156581
70811	BATON ROUGE	16413	4769	35.3	29.7	27.7	6.1	1.3	35621	41929	30	60	3622	16.1	41.3	38.9	3.2	0.5	84004
70812	BATON ROUGE	12313	3691	41.6	31.1	22.2	4.7	0.5	30873	35952	14	39	2635	13.4	60.7	24.5	1.3	0.2	73731
70813	BATON ROUGE	9854	59	64.4	8.5	22.0	0.0	5.1	16492	19639	1	2	30	23.3	76.7	0.0	0.0	0.0	64286
70814	BATON ROUGE	19892	5006	22.5	33.2	34.4	7.5	2.4	45827	52976	63	88	3750	2.2	20.8	75.7	1.2	0.1	103790
70815	BATON ROUGE	24989	11615	23.5	30.4	30.0	11.8	4.4	46380	54624	65	89	7842	2.8	15.6	63.7	17.6	0.2	127603
70816	BATON ROUGE	28276	16567	19.0	32.1	32.1	11.6	5.2	48937	58145	70	92	8838	3.8	10.3	65.4	19.1	1.5	133197
70817	BATON ROUGE	32313	10675	9.8	19.0	40.0	22.2	8.9	73188	85082	93	100	8772	1.0	4.6	56.5	35.5	2.5	156616
70818	BATON ROUGE	25233	3639	16.9	25.6	39.0	14.0	4.5	57209	67908	82	98	3159	9.6	15.3	54.4	19.9	0.9	118518
70819	BATON ROUGE	21750	1720	16.5	33.2	38.5	10.3	1.5	50158	60548	72	93	1290	4.5	46.2	48.4	0.9	0.0	89559
70820	BATON ROUGE	16402	6995	54.9	23.2	12.7	6.8	2.5	21788	25436	3	6	1482	1.5	8.2	36.8	48.9	4.7	195385
71001	ARCADIA	14376	1824	47.4	26.4	20.7	4.2	1.4	26565	30078	7	18	1302	44.3	29.1	21.5	5.0	0.1	56549
71003	ATHENS	18074	476	44.8	24.2	23.1	5.9	2.1	28907	32446	10	29	387	44.4	24.6	23.3	7.8	0.0	58600
71004	BELCHER	18229	230	33.0	35.2	23.0	4.8	3.9	36536	42625	34	64	179	50.3	24.0	10.6	10.6	4.5	49643
71006	BENTON	24901	3978	24.9	25.2	32.6	11.5	5.8	49861	55352	72	93	3407	17.5	21.0	32.1	24.5	5.0	112625
71007	BETHANY	22269	400	29.8	24.3	31.5	11.0	3.5	47087	54186	66	90	347	21.6	23.6	36.3	18.2	0.3	96600
71008	BIENVILLE	15435	244	48.0	28.3	19.7	2.9	1.2	26397	29808	6	18	199	49.8	27.1	18.1	4.5	0.5	50313
71016	CASTOR	13234	903	45.9	30.9	20.4	1.8	1.1	27684	31418	8	23	739	55.2	23.6	16.4	4.3	0.5	42596
71018	COTTON VALLEY	17173	870	43.1	28.7	22.1	4.7	1.4	29248	32708	11	31	679	51.0	25.2	20.2	3.2	0.4	48879
	LOUISIANA	19601		35.3	28.5	25.7	7.1	3.5	36550	42223				22.5	24.5	35.6	15.0	2.4	94005
	UNITED STATES	25866		24.7	27.1	30.8	10.9	6.5	48124	56710				10.9	15.0	33.7	30.1	10.4	145905

#	POST OFFICE NAME	FINANCIAL SERVICES: Auto Loan	Home Loan	Investments	Retirement Plans	THE HOME: Home Improvements: Home Repair	Lawn & Garden	Furnishings: Computers & Hardware	Major Appliances	TV, Radio, Sound Equipment	Furniture	ENTERTAINMENT: Dine out/ Carry out	Sports Equipment	Fees & Tickets	Toys & Games	Travel	Cable TV	PERSONAL: Apparel & Services	Auto Repairs	Health Insurance	Pets & Supplies
70652	LONGVILLE	78	58	35	53	63	70	56	66	63	57	76	78	50	71	56	66	70	65	75	88
70653	MERRYVILLE	78	53	26	46	60	69	51	63	61	52	72	76	44	68	52	66	66	63	77	89
70654	MITTIE	70	47	21	40	53	61	45	57	55	46	64	68	39	61	46	59	58	56	70	80
70655	OBERLIN	66	46	25	42	52	60	47	56	55	46	64	66	41	61	48	58	58	56	68	75
70656	PITKIN	74	50	23	43	57	65	48	60	58	49	68	72	41	64	49	62	62	60	74	85
70657	RAGLEY	94	74	48	68	78	86	71	81	78	73	94	96	64	89	71	80	88	81	90	105
70658	REEVES	82	55	25	48	62	72	53	67	64	54	75	79	45	71	54	69	68	66	82	94
70660	SINGER	74	50	22	43	56	65	48	60	58	49	68	71	41	64	49	62	62	59	74	85
70661	STARKS	89	59	27	51	67	78	57	72	69	58	81	86	49	77	58	75	74	71	88	102
70662	SUGARTOWN	81	54	25	47	61	71	52	65	63	53	74	78	44	70	53	68	67	65	81	93
70663	SULPHUR	75	73	66	71	73	79	71	74	72	71	89	85	70	89	71	72	86	73	75	85
70665	SULPHUR	94	93	80	90	93	96	87	91	86	88	107	106	86	105	87	85	104	90	89	107
70668	VINTON	76	57	39	52	61	71	59	67	67	59	80	77	53	76	59	71	74	67	78	85
70669	WESTLAKE	82	73	59	70	76	83	71	77	75	70	91	89	68	91	72	76	86	76	83	95
70706	DENHAM SPRINGS	87	87	79	87	86	87	83	85	81	85	101	100	82	99	82	78	98	85	79	97
70710	ADDIS	77	70	55	68	70	74	67	72	68	69	84	83	63	79	66	67	80	72	71	85
70711	ALBANY	75	68	53	65	68	72	65	70	66	67	81	80	61	77	64	65	78	69	69	83
70712	ANGOLA	0	0	0	0	0	0	0	0	0	0	0	0	0	0	0	0	0	0	0	0
70714	BAKER	72	73	74	71	72	77	71	72	71	71	89	82	72	90	71	72	87	71	72	82
70715	BATCHELOR	70	50	28	45	55	63	49	59	57	49	68	69	43	65	50	60	62	58	70	79
70719	BRUSLY	86	86	77	85	87	91	82	85	81	82	100	99	81	101	82	81	97	84	84	98
70721	CARVILLE	54	49	59	47	47	55	53	52	58	55	72	58	55	71	53	59	71	53	54	59
70722	CLINTON	80	68	56	63	71	80	66	72	73	67	88	83	64	86	67	76	84	72	81	91
70723	CONVENT	54	46	53	43	45	54	51	51	57	53	70	56	51	66	50	60	68	53	57	59
70725	DARROW	104	70	32	60	79	91	67	84	81	69	95	101	57	90	68	88	87	83	104	120
70726	DENHAM SPRINGS	81	78	67	76	78	81	75	78	75	76	92	91	72	90	74	74	89	78	77	91
70729	ERWINVILLE	74	67	53	65	67	71	64	69	65	66	80	79	61	75	63	64	77	68	68	81
70730	ETHEL	92	73	48	67	78	86	70	80	77	71	92	95	64	89	70	79	86	79	89	105
70732	FORDOCHE	97	66	31	57	74	85	64	79	76	65	90	94	54	85	65	82	82	78	97	111
70733	FRENCH SETTLEMENT	91	61	28	52	69	79	59	73	71	60	83	88	50	79	60	76	76	73	90	104
70734	GEISMAR	87	79	61	75	80	85	74	81	77	76	94	94	71	91	74	77	90	80	83	99
70736	GLYNN	104	70	32	60	79	91	67	84	81	69	96	101	57	90	69	88	87	84	104	120
70737	GONZALES	88	78	62	75	80	87	75	81	79	76	96	95	72	95	76	80	92	80	86	100
70739	GREENWELL SPRINGS	93	103	101	102	102	103	94	96	91	94	113	113	97	117	95	89	111	94	90	110
70740	GROSSE TETE	78	52	24	45	59	68	51	63	61	52	72	76	43	68	51	66	65	63	78	90
70744	HOLDEN	80	62	40	57	66	73	60	69	66	61	79	81	54	75	60	68	74	69	77	90
70748	JACKSON	72	69	64	66	69	75	66	69	68	67	84	78	66	82	67	69	81	69	72	82
70749	JARREAU	97	71	41	63	80	91	67	82	78	68	93	97	59	90	70	84	85	81	99	115
70750	KROTZ SPRINGS	71	48	22	41	54	62	46	58	56	47	65	69	39	62	47	60	59	57	71	82
70752	LAKELAND	105	75	40	66	84	95	72	87	84	73	99	104	63	96	73	89	91	86	104	121
70753	LETTSWORTH	48	35	26	31	37	44	37	42	43	38	52	47	33	47	36	47	48	42	50	54
70754	LIVINGSTON	81	66	44	61	69	75	63	71	68	65	82	84	58	78	63	69	78	71	77	91
70755	LIVONIA	86	60	30	53	67	77	58	71	69	59	81	84	50	77	59	74	74	70	86	99
70756	LOTTIE	92	61	28	53	70	80	59	74	71	60	84	88	50	79	60	77	76	73	91	105
70757	MARINGOUIN	65	48	38	42	50	60	51	57	60	52	71	64	47	65	50	64	66	58	68	72
70759	MORGANZA	73	61	49	61	64	73	64	68	68	63	83	77	61	81	63	70	78	67	74	80
70760	NEW ROADS	67	55	49	52	57	67	59	62	65	59	79	69	56	74	58	69	74	63	72	74
70761	NORWOOD	70	47	22	41	53	61	46	57	55	46	65	68	39	61	46	59	59	56	70	80
70762	OSCAR	93	80	59	75	86	93	74	84	80	74	97	100	71	98	77	83	92	82	93	111
70763	PAULINA	102	82	53	75	88	97	77	89	85	77	102	106	71	102	78	89	96	87	101	119
70764	PLAQUEMINE	74	61	48	56	63	72	62	68	68	62	82	77	58	78	61	71	77	68	76	83
70767	PORT ALLEN	72	68	63	65	68	75	68	70	70	68	86	80	67	85	68	71	83	70	73	81
70769	PRAIRIEVILLE	102	107	98	109	105	104	99	101	94	102	118	118	99	117	97	90	116	99	91	114
70770	PRIDE	97	94	79	90	96	101	86	93	88	86	108	110	86	110	88	89	104	90	95	114
70772	ROSEDALE	83	56	28	49	63	73	55	68	66	56	78	80	47	73	56	71	71	67	83	95
70773	ROUGON	102	68	31	59	77	89	66	82	79	67	93	98	56	88	67	86	85	81	101	117
70774	SAINT AMANT	85	77	60	74	78	83	73	79	75	75	92	92	70	89	73	75	88	78	80	96
70775	SAINT FRANCISVILLE	86	77	65	74	80	86	74	81	77	75	94	95	70	92	75	78	90	80	84	100
70776	SAINT GABRIEL	87	75	63	70	78	86	73	79	79	74	97	93	71	97	74	82	92	79	87	101
70777	SLAUGHTER	92	83	63	79	85	91	78	85	81	79	99	99	75	97	78	81	94	83	88	105
70778	SORRENTO	75	67	52	64	69	74	63	69	66	64	80	81	61	79	64	66	77	68	72	86
70780	SUNSHINE	84	56	26	49	64	73	54	68	66	55	77	81	46	73	55	71	70	67	84	97
70783	VENTRESS	90	74	53	69	81	90	70	81	77	69	92	95	65	92	73	81	86	79	92	108
70785	WALKER	79	73	57	70	73	77	69	74	70	71	87	86	66	82	68	69	83	74	73	88
70788	WHITE CASTLE	66	48	39	42	51	61	51	58	60	53	72	65	47	65	51	65	67	58	69	73
70789	WILSON	73	51	30	45	56	65	51	61	60	52	71	71	45	66	51	64	65	61	73	83
70791	ZACHARY	92	90	80	87	92	97	83	89	85	84	104	105	83	105	85	85	100	87	91	108
70792	UNCLE SAM	104	70	32	60	79	91	67	84	81	69	95	101	57	90	68	87	87	83	104	119
70801	BATON ROUGE	21	16	21	18	16	18	23	20	22	21	28	26	21	26	20	21	27	23	18	22
70802	BATON ROUGE	41	32	37	31	32	38	40	38	43	39	53	44	37	48	37	44	51	41	42	44
70803	BATON ROUGE	35	22	27	24	21	26	42	31	41	35	51	43	34	46	33	36	48	37	28	35
70805	BATON ROUGE	44	40	48	37	38	45	44	43	48	45	59	48	44	58	43	49	58	44	46	49
70806	BATON ROUGE	69	67	84	68	66	73	73	70	74	73	93	82	73	91	72	74	91	73	70	78
70807	BATON ROUGE	47	40	46	37	40	48	45	45	50	46	61	49	44	57	44	52	59	46	50	52
70808	BATON ROUGE	106	106	131	110	104	113	119	109	115	115	145	132	117	142	114	111	142	115	103	121
70809	BATON ROUGE	102	104	136	111	102	109	112	106	109	111	137	126	113	136	109	105	135	110	98	117
70810	BATON ROUGE	118	134	151	138	131	134	128	124	120	129	152	146	134	155	128	116	151	124	112	137
70811	BATON ROUGE	64	63	65	60	62	69	63	64	66	64	81	72	64	80	63	67	79	64	67	73
70812	BATON ROUGE	52	49	58	46	47	54	52	51	56	53	70	56	53	69	52	57	68	52	53	58
70813	BATON ROUGE	48	29	37	33	29	35	57	42	55	48	69	58	47	62	46	49	65	51	39	48
70814	BATON ROUGE	73	80	86	80	78	80	78	77	76	78	95	90	80	97	78	74	94	77	72	84
70815	BATON ROUGE	81	89	106	88	88	94	89	87	87	88	110	100	92	111	90	87	108	88	85	95
70816	BATON ROUGE	89	91	105	96	89	92	94	91	90	95	114	108	94	112	91	86	112	93	82	100
70817	BATON ROUGE	122	142	144	145	137	134	128	127	118	131	150	149	134	153	127	112	149	124	111	140
70818	BATON ROUGE	104	102	91	100	104	108	96	101	96	97	119	119	95	119	97	95	115	99	100	120
70819	BATON ROUGE	80	82	84	83	82	87	81	82	80	80	99	95	81	100	81	78	96	81	80	92
70820	BATON ROUGE	54	35	45	38	34	41	61	47	61	54	76	64	52	69	51	55	72	56	45	54
71001	ARCADIA	60	47	36	43	50	58	48	54	55	48	65	61	45	62	49	58	61	54	63	68
71003	ATHENS	82	55	25	48	62	72	53	66	64	54	75	79	45	71	54	69	68	66	82	94
71004	BELCHER	94	64	31	57	73	83	62	78	74	63	86	93	53	83	64	78	79	77	94	109
71006	BENTON	96	98	94	95	98	103	93	96	93	93	115	111	93	115	93	94	112	94	96	112
71007	BETHANY	91	82	63	78	84	89	77	84	79	78	97	98	74	96	77	80	93	82	87	104
71008	BIENVILLE	69	46	22	40	52	61	45	56	54	46	64	67	39	60	46	58	58	55	69	79
71016	CASTOR	65	44	20	38	50	57	42	53	51	43	60	63	36	57	43	55	54	52	65	75
71018	COTTON VALLEY	77	52	23	45	59	67	50	62	60	51	71	75	42	67	51	65	64	62	77	89
	LOUISIANA	77	69	66	67	70	77	70	73	74	70	91	84	68	88	70	75	87	74	77	87
	UNITED STATES	100	100	100	100	100	100	100	100	100	100	100	100	100	100	100	100	100	100	100	100

ZIP CODE # / POST OFFICE NAME	COUNTY FIPS CODE	POPULATION 2000	POPULATION 2004	POPULATION 2009	2000-2004 ANNUAL RATE % Rate	2000-2004 ANNUAL RATE State Centile	HOUSEHOLDS 2000	HOUSEHOLDS 2004	HOUSEHOLDS 2009	% Annual Rate 2000-2004	2004 Average HH Size	FAMILIES 2000	FAMILIES 2004	% Annual Rate 2000-2004
71019 COUSHATTA	081	9653	9795	9994	0.3	44	3419	3490	3582	0.5	2.73	2527	2579	0.5
71023 DOYLINE	119	3549	3552	3574	0.0	29	1412	1425	1449	0.2	2.49	1030	1040	0.2
71024 DUBBERLY	119	1299	1312	1329	0.2	39	516	530	545	0.6	2.44	383	393	0.6
71027 FRIERSON	031	1632	1780	1906	2.1	88	627	695	756	2.5	2.56	467	517	2.4
71028 GIBSLAND	013	2021	1960	1953	-0.7	7	845	833	842	-0.3	2.35	555	547	-0.3
71029 GILLIAM	017	191	178	177	-1.6	1	73	69	69	-1.3	2.58	51	48	-1.4
71030 GLOSTER	031	1100	1231	1336	2.7	95	396	451	497	3.1	2.73	309	351	3.0
71031 GOLDONNA	069	1036	1058	1085	0.5	52	400	414	431	0.8	2.56	296	306	0.8
71032 GRAND CANE	031	1547	1628	1712	1.2	76	627	671	716	1.6	2.43	461	493	1.6
71033 GREENWOOD	017	2947	3184	3327	1.8	86	1149	1253	1321	2.1	2.54	838	913	2.0
71034 HALL SUMMIT	081	264	260	261	-0.4	15	101	100	100	-0.2	2.60	75	74	-0.3
71037 HAUGHTON	015	16175	17307	18643	1.6	83	5775	6253	6810	1.9	2.77	4536	4902	1.8
71038 HAYNESVILLE	027	6729	6717	6737	0.0	27	2295	2320	2360	0.3	2.51	1570	1586	0.2
71039 HEFLIN	119	2083	2078	2091	-0.1	24	792	800	815	0.2	2.60	566	572	0.3
71040 HOMER	027	7239	7296	7347	0.2	37	2814	2873	2930	0.5	2.45	1955	1996	0.5
71043 HOSSTON	017	731	712	711	-0.6	10	276	272	276	-0.3	2.62	196	194	-0.2
71044 IDA	017	805	795	796	-0.3	17	343	345	351	0.1	2.30	244	245	0.1
71045 JAMESTOWN	013	845	843	848	-0.1	24	332	334	340	0.1	2.52	226	227	0.1
71046 KEATCHIE	031	1393	1444	1514	0.9	67	547	575	611	1.2	2.42	407	427	1.1
71047 KEITHVILLE	017	11143	11628	11998	1.0	71	3853	4071	4251	1.3	2.72	2993	3156	1.3
71048 LISBON	027	388	391	392	0.2	37	158	162	165	0.6	2.36	113	116	0.6
71049 LOGANSPORT	031	3780	3807	3920	0.2	35	1478	1509	1574	0.5	2.51	1052	1072	0.4
71051 ELM GROVE	015	2505	2624	2783	1.1	74	927	978	1046	1.3	2.68	693	728	1.2
71052 MANSFIELD	031	11102	11208	11631	0.2	39	4178	4273	4502	0.5	2.55	2900	2962	0.5
71055 MINDEN	119	20056	20380	20741	0.4	46	7890	8131	8388	0.7	2.44	5456	5621	0.7
71060 MOORINGSPORT	017	2740	2875	2957	1.1	74	1069	1137	1183	1.5	2.53	800	851	1.5
71061 OIL CITY	017	1958	1929	1929	-0.4	15	801	802	812	0.0	2.40	531	531	0.0
71063 PELICAN	031	873	878	901	0.1	33	331	337	350	0.4	2.61	229	233	0.4
71064 PLAIN DEALING	015	4226	4185	4369	-0.2	19	1564	1567	1659	0.1	2.51	1073	1070	-0.1
71065 PLEASANT HILL	085	1272	1314	1354	0.8	64	484	505	527	1.0	2.51	349	365	1.1
71067 PRINCETON	015	3096	3255	3459	1.2	75	1160	1233	1325	1.5	2.64	867	920	1.4
71068 RINGGOLD	013	3573	3726	3851	1.0	71	1463	1539	1608	1.2	2.42	974	1024	1.2
71069 RODESSA	017	752	715	711	-1.2	3	305	294	297	-0.9	2.43	210	203	-0.8
71070 SALINE	069	1796	1772	1789	-0.3	16	723	726	745	0.1	2.44	518	520	0.1
71071 SAREPTA	119	3440	3433	3470	-0.1	26	1324	1336	1367	0.2	2.57	954	961	0.2
71072 SHONGALOO	119	1468	1475	1485	0.1	32	573	582	593	0.4	2.51	433	440	0.4
71073 SIBLEY	119	2482	2696	2835	2.0	88	879	968	1031	2.3	2.62	642	706	2.3
71075 SPRINGHILL	119	6656	6535	6564	-0.4	13	2777	2756	2801	-0.2	2.32	1847	1829	-0.2
71078 STONEWALL	031	4058	4402	4701	1.9	87	1507	1661	1800	2.3	2.65	1146	1260	2.3
71079 SUMMERFIELD	027	118	119	119	0.2	38	46	47	48	0.5	2.53	34	35	0.7
71082 VIVIAN	017	5462	5410	5444	-0.2	19	2133	2130	2163	0.0	2.50	1430	1426	-0.1
71101 SHREVEPORT	017	9892	9709	9819	-0.4	12	3974	3956	4052	-0.1	2.22	1907	1872	-0.4
71103 SHREVEPORT	017	10618	9855	9745	-1.7	1	3784	3515	3505	-1.7	2.54	2288	2125	-1.7
71104 SHREVEPORT	017	15199	15153	15247	-0.1	24	6730	6746	6845	0.1	2.16	3418	3422	0.0
71105 SHREVEPORT	017	20027	20211	20514	0.2	39	9334	9463	9682	0.3	2.12	5369	5422	0.2
71106 SHREVEPORT	017	33301	33958	34626	0.5	50	12058	12397	12765	0.7	2.67	8698	8953	0.7
71107 SHREVEPORT	017	30768	31603	32243	0.6	57	10810	11265	11635	1.0	2.71	8084	8419	1.0
71108 SHREVEPORT	017	20901	21368	21849	0.5	52	7518	7685	7898	0.5	2.78	5328	5444	0.5
71109 SHREVEPORT	017	25961	25221	25183	-0.7	8	9376	9197	9276	-0.5	2.71	6422	6294	-0.5
71110 BARKSDALE AFB	015	3459	3419	3532	-0.3	18	718	714	752	-0.1	3.67	708	704	-0.1
71111 BOSSIER CITY	015	31054	33945	36954	2.1	90	11952	13185	14504	2.3	2.53	8208	9075	2.4
71112 BOSSIER CITY	015	27336	27858	29460	0.5	49	10574	10894	11647	0.7	2.53	7518	7756	0.7
71115 SHREVEPORT	017	10433	11371	11964	2.1	88	5025	5617	6017	2.7	1.94	2612	2913	2.6
71118 SHREVEPORT	017	23867	23631	23729	-0.2	19	9608	9638	9798	0.1	2.41	6728	6744	0.1
71119 SHREVEPORT	017	11220	11885	12333	1.4	78	4416	4741	4979	1.7	2.49	3203	3435	1.7
71129 SHREVEPORT	017	12044	12344	12588	0.6	54	4989	5161	5315	0.8	2.39	3256	3377	0.9
71201 MONROE	073	21850	21894	22395	0.1	30	9701	9814	10157	0.3	2.18	5484	5547	0.3
71202 MONROE	073	30634	30533	31071	-0.1	23	9631	9730	10042	0.2	2.99	7246	7284	0.1
71203 MONROE	073	33348	35062	36667	1.2	75	12583	13467	14317	1.6	2.47	8556	9165	1.6
71209 MONROE	073	845	854	865	0.3	40	7	8	9	3.2	2.50	2	3	10.0
71219 BASKIN	041	1118	1313	1429	3.9	99	422	503	556	4.2	2.59	321	382	4.2
71220 BASTROP	067	25814	25942	26091	0.1	33	9494	9705	9935	0.5	2.59	6949	7101	0.5
71222 BERNICE	111	3789	3635	3479	-1.0	4	1474	1433	1393	-0.7	2.47	1029	1000	-0.7
71223 BONITA	067	725	676	663	-1.6	1	275	262	262	-1.1	2.58	186	176	-1.3
71225 CALHOUN	073	4918	5205	5415	1.3	78	1804	1937	2043	1.7	2.68	1455	1558	1.6
71226 CHATHAM	049	1584	1645	1700	0.9	68	636	671	705	1.3	2.45	447	471	1.2
71227 CHOUDRANT	061	3385	3464	3606	0.5	53	1302	1354	1431	0.9	2.56	989	1027	0.9
71229 COLLINSTON	067	1507	1560	1583	0.8	66	480	508	526	1.3	2.86	365	385	1.3
71232 DELHI	083	6543	6542	6596	0.0	29	2416	2451	2509	0.3	2.58	1760	1786	0.4
71234 DOWNSVILLE	111	3736	3813	3772	0.5	51	1473	1531	1543	0.9	2.49	1099	1141	0.9
71235 DUBACH	061	3882	4205	4540	1.9	87	1509	1656	1811	2.2	2.54	1135	1243	2.2
71237 EPPS	123	704	725	744	0.7	59	258	271	284	1.2	2.16	195	204	1.1
71238 EROS	049	2452	2529	2599	0.7	61	903	944	984	1.1	2.68	718	750	1.0
71241 FARMERVILLE	111	9909	9662	9268	-0.6	10	3827	3789	3701	-0.2	2.46	2801	2773	-0.2
71243 FORT NECESSITY	041	268	320	351	4.3	99	107	130	144	4.7	2.46	82	99	4.5
71245 GRAMBLING	061	2645	2673	2784	0.3	40	1146	1179	1249	0.7	2.19	637	653	0.7
71250 JONES	067	334	310	310	-1.4	2	124	119	120	-1.0	2.65	86	82	-1.1
71251 JONESBORO	049	9808	10119	10502	0.7	62	3895	4080	4302	1.1	2.42	2727	2857	1.1
71254 LAKE PROVIDENCE	035	7764	7751	7727	0.0	27	2437	2468	2492	0.3	2.85	1734	1755	0.3
71256 LILLIE	111	437	408	383	-1.6	1	166	157	150	-1.3	2.59	118	111	-1.4
71259 MANGHAM	083	2189	2260	2309	0.8	63	827	867	902	1.1	2.60	618	648	1.1
71260 MARION	111	3398	3226	3055	-1.2	2	1323	1277	1235	-0.8	2.53	953	919	-0.9
71261 MER ROUGE	067	1729	1644	1618	-1.2	3	652	632	633	-0.7	2.57	482	467	-0.7
71263 OAK GROVE	123	8808	8958	9215	0.4	47	3357	3462	3610	0.7	2.52	2436	2509	0.7
71264 OAK RIDGE	067	951	946	943	-0.1	22	367	372	378	0.3	2.54	258	262	0.4
71266 PIONEER	123	2861	2934	3017	0.6	54	865	900	940	0.9	2.80	636	661	0.8
71268 QUITMAN	013	2775	2764	2801	-0.1	23	1040	1052	1082	0.3	2.60	759	766	0.2
71269 RAYVILLE	083	12581	12729	12921	0.3	41	4346	4477	4630	0.7	2.63	3180	3273	0.6
71270 RUSTON	061	31222	32330	33975	0.8	66	10818	11410	12253	1.3	2.38	6580	6932	1.2
71275 SIMSBORO	061	2391	2468	2592	0.8	63	858	901	961	1.2	2.72	634	664	1.1
71276 SONDHEIMER	035	683	663	652	-0.7	8	248	244	243	-0.4	2.33	189	186	-0.4
71277 SPEARSVILLE	111	2036	1983	1897	-0.6	10	760	750	730	-0.3	2.64	553	545	-0.3
71280 STERLINGTON	073	2146	2186	2241	0.4	49	803	828	860	0.7	2.61	612	630	0.7
71282 TALLULAH	065	13547	13936	14531	0.7	59	4395	4587	4860	1.0	2.73	3086	3218	1.0
71286 TRANSYLVANIA	035	981	957	942	-0.6	11	287	283	281	-0.3	2.55	219	216	-0.3
LOUISIANA					0.7					0.9	2.59			1.0
UNITED STATES					1.2					1.3	2.58			1.1

ZIP CODE #	POST OFFICE NAME	RACE (%) White 2000	White 2004	Black 2000	Black 2004	Asian/Pacific 2000	Asian/Pacific 2004	% Hispanic Origin 2000	% Hispanic Origin 2004	2004 AGE DISTRIBUTION (%) 0-4	5-9	10-14	15-19	20-24	25-44	45-64	65-84	85+	18+	MEDIAN AGE 2004	% 2004 Males	% 2004 Females
71019	COUSHATTA	57.6	56.1	41.1	42.6	0.1	0.1	1.0	1.1	7.9	7.5	8.3	7.9	7.2	24.4	23.0	11.9	1.9	71.4	34.8	47.8	52.2
71023	DOYLINE	84.9	83.1	13.1	14.4	0.5	0.7	1.1	1.3	5.9	5.8	5.9	6.6	6.5	25.6	28.9	13.6	1.3	78.6	41.3	49.9	50.1
71024	DUBBERLY	68.9	65.8	28.9	31.7	0.1	0.1	1.5	1.8	6.5	6.7	6.3	5.1	6.4	25.5	28.9	13.0	1.8	77.6	40.0	48.4	51.6
71027	FRIERSON	70.3	68.1	27.7	29.7	0.2	0.2	1.5	1.6	7.0	7.0	6.8	7.3	6.6	27.6	26.3	10.4	1.1	74.9	37.5	50.7	49.3
71028	GIBSLAND	35.7	34.2	63.1	64.5	0.2	0.2	0.5	0.6	5.9	6.1	7.8	6.9	6.7	26.1	23.1	14.8	2.7	76.1	39.2	47.9	52.1
71029	GILLIAM	61.8	57.9	36.7	41.0	0.0	0.0	1.1	0.0	5.1	6.2	8.4	7.9	5.6	25.3	25.8	14.0	1.7	74.7	39.7	50.6	49.4
71030	GLOSTER	62.5	59.8	34.9	37.3	0.1	0.2	2.2	2.3	7.1	7.2	7.1	7.8	7.1	28.4	25.4	9.3	0.8	74.2	35.2	49.6	50.4
71031	GOLDONNA	95.3	94.8	3.4	3.7	0.1	0.1	1.0	1.1	6.9	7.0	6.5	5.3	6.3	25.5	28.4	12.6	1.5	76.6	39.4	50.7	49.3
71032	GRAND CANE	63.2	60.6	35.4	37.8	0.0	0.0	1.0	1.0	6.4	6.6	6.8	6.4	6.1	24.0	28.5	13.4	1.8	76.4	40.8	49.5	50.6
71033	GREENWOOD	73.3	69.2	24.1	27.9	0.5	0.6	1.6	1.7	5.5	6.1	7.4	6.8	5.9	26.5	29.9	10.8	1.1	76.9	40.0	49.0	51.0
71034	HALL SUMMIT	83.7	81.5	15.5	17.3	0.0	0.0	0.8	0.8	6.5	6.5	6.9	5.8	6.9	26.2	23.5	15.8	1.9	76.2	39.7	47.3	52.7
71037	HAUGHTON	83.5	81.9	13.3	14.4	0.6	0.7	2.2	2.5	7.6	7.4	7.9	7.4	6.9	29.1	24.4	8.6	0.7	72.4	35.0	49.3	50.7
71038	HAYNESVILLE	51.8	51.3	47.5	48.0	0.1	0.1	0.7	0.7	5.9	5.9	6.4	6.7	7.0	28.2	23.1	13.7	3.0	77.7	38.3	53.1	46.9
71039	HEFLIN	65.2	62.7	33.4	35.7	0.1	0.1	1.4	1.5	6.5	6.6	7.4	7.4	6.8	24.9	26.1	12.5	1.8	75.1	38.6	49.7	50.3
71040	HOMER	50.4	49.9	48.7	49.2	0.2	0.2	0.8	0.8	6.4	6.3	7.6	7.4	6.3	24.1	24.5	15.0	2.5	75.1	39.2	48.4	51.6
71043	HOSSTON	66.9	62.6	32.2	36.4	0.1	0.1	0.3	0.3	4.6	5.6	8.2	7.9	5.3	23.0	27.3	16.3	1.8	76.4	41.6	49.7	50.3
71044	IDA	65.5	61.3	33.0	37.1	0.0	0.0	0.8	0.9	5.3	5.7	7.3	7.3	6.0	21.0	28.2	16.9	2.4	77.4	43.0	50.1	49.9
71045	JAMESTOWN	73.5	72.4	25.0	26.0	0.2	0.2	1.4	1.5	7.0	6.9	7.0	6.9	6.1	24.0	25.2	14.8	2.3	74.9	39.6	49.0	51.0
71046	KEATCHIE	71.7	69.0	25.9	28.3	0.1	0.1	1.8	2.0	6.4	6.7	7.0	6.9	6.1	27.3	26.9	11.3	1.5	75.5	38.6	50.8	49.2
71047	KEITHVILLE	79.8	76.5	17.6	20.5	0.3	0.4	1.7	2.0	6.5	6.4	7.0	7.0	7.5	29.5	25.8	9.6	0.7	76.0	36.2	52.6	47.5
71048	LISBON	49.0	48.1	50.3	51.4	0.0	0.0	0.8	0.5	6.9	6.9	7.7	7.4	6.9	25.1	24.0	13.0	2.1	73.9	37.2	48.6	51.4
71049	LOGANSPORT	71.1	69.2	27.8	29.6	0.2	0.2	1.3	1.4	7.6	7.5	8.0	7.0	6.2	23.6	24.4	13.9	1.8	72.3	37.2	47.2	52.8
71051	ELM GROVE	73.5	71.0	24.4	26.6	0.7	0.8	1.2	1.3	6.4	6.1	8.0	7.4	6.6	26.5	27.5	10.1	1.3	74.8	38.2	51.1	48.9
71052	MANSFIELD	39.1	37.5	59.4	60.8	0.2	0.2	1.5	1.6	7.4	7.3	8.2	7.6	6.9	24.3	24.0	11.8	2.5	72.4	35.8	46.4	53.6
71055	MINDEN	57.1	56.0	41.3	42.2	0.3	0.3	0.7	0.8	6.9	6.9	7.2	7.1	6.2	25.7	24.2	13.6	2.3	74.6	38.0	47.7	52.3
71060	MOORINGSPORT	85.7	83.5	12.1	14.2	0.1	0.1	1.3	1.5	6.9	6.9	7.5	7.0	6.4	27.2	25.5	11.5	1.2	74.6	37.2	48.8	51.2
71061	OIL CITY	70.2	66.2	28.8	32.5	0.1	0.1	1.3	1.5	7.5	7.1	6.8	7.0	7.1	24.7	23.4	14.6	1.8	74.3	37.6	48.6	51.4
71063	PELICAN	47.3	44.7	51.2	53.9	0.1	0.1	1.6	1.6	5.6	5.7	8.5	8.0	6.6	23.7	25.1	13.7	3.2	75.3	39.1	49.4	50.6
71064	PLAIN DEALING	50.7	48.2	47.9	50.3	0.1	0.1	1.2	1.3	6.4	6.5	6.8	6.7	6.5	26.2	25.7	13.0	2.3	76.1	38.4	50.0	50.0
71065	PLEASANT HILL	71.3	68.6	23.3	25.5	0.1	0.1	2.4	2.7	6.4	6.1	8.0	7.1	7.5	26.1	23.1	13.2	2.6	74.7	37.7	47.0	53.0
71067	PRINCETON	77.7	76.3	19.8	20.8	0.4	0.5	1.6	1.9	7.3	7.3	7.8	7.8	6.5	28.4	23.1	10.9	0.8	72.8	35.4	49.4	50.6
71068	RINGGOLD	59.9	57.9	38.9	40.8	0.1	0.1	0.8	0.8	6.8	6.8	7.2	7.1	6.4	22.2	25.2	15.3	3.1	74.9	40.0	47.9	52.1
71069	RODESSA	69.3	66.0	28.3	31.6	0.0	0.0	0.8	1.0	6.0	6.4	6.7	6.4	5.9	23.8	26.9	15.7	2.2	77.1	41.3	49.9	50.1
71070	SALINE	73.9	72.5	24.7	26.0	0.2	0.2	0.7	0.7	6.0	6.0	7.1	6.8	7.2	24.1	26.5	14.0	2.4	76.9	40.0	50.4	49.6
71071	SAREPTA	73.6	72.2	24.5	25.8	0.1	0.1	1.8	2.1	6.4	6.2	6.4	7.1	7.4	24.9	25.1	14.5	2.0	76.8	39.3	47.6	52.4
71072	SHONGALOO	90.2	89.2	9.2	10.1	0.1	0.2	0.5	0.5	6.4	6.6	6.4	5.2	5.8	26.6	27.7	13.1	2.3	77.3	39.9	52.0	48.0
71073	SIBLEY	63.2	59.5	34.8	38.2	0.1	0.1	0.9	1.0	6.5	6.6	6.6	6.8	7.1	28.1	26.4	10.7	1.2	76.4	37.3	52.1	47.9
71075	SPRINGHILL	70.4	69.6	28.2	28.8	0.3	0.3	0.7	0.7	6.4	6.0	6.6	6.7	6.3	23.3	23.8	18.0	3.0	77.2	41.2	46.4	53.6
71078	STONEWALL	74.5	72.2	22.3	24.3	0.2	0.3	1.9	2.0	6.6	6.7	6.9	7.5	6.2	27.7	27.0	10.3	1.1	75.2	37.9	50.0	50.1
71079	SUMMERFIELD	43.2	42.9	55.9	56.3	0.0	0.0	0.0	0.0	7.6	7.6	7.6	7.6	8.4	23.5	22.7	13.5	1.7	72.3	36.1	47.9	52.1
71082	VIVIAN	71.4	68.6	26.8	29.5	0.3	0.4	0.8	0.8	7.3	7.1	7.9	7.6	6.1	24.0	22.5	14.5	3.0	73.0	37.4	46.7	53.3
71101	SHREVEPORT	24.3	23.4	73.1	73.7	0.4	0.4	2.4	2.5	8.2	7.3	6.7	7.4	7.4	24.6	22.5	12.8	3.1	73.4	35.5	48.7	51.3
71103	SHREVEPORT	8.4	7.4	90.3	91.1	0.3	0.3	0.8	0.8	7.1	6.8	7.4	7.1	6.8	22.1	22.3	16.2	4.3	74.2	39.3	45.6	54.5
71104	SHREVEPORT	68.9	65.9	26.6	29.1	1.3	1.5	2.6	2.9	6.9	5.8	5.5	7.8	10.4	30.9	20.8	9.8	2.1	78.2	32.4	47.4	52.6
71105	SHREVEPORT	88.9	87.4	7.3	8.3	2.0	2.4	2.1	2.3	5.6	5.4	5.8	6.2	7.7	28.5	22.6	15.5	2.8	79.8	38.4	47.0	53.1
71106	SHREVEPORT	51.0	49.8	47.0	47.9	0.9	1.1	1.0	1.1	7.2	7.4	7.9	7.8	6.6	24.3	24.6	11.8	2.4	72.5	36.8	46.9	53.1
71107	SHREVEPORT	46.1	44.9	52.1	53.1	0.2	0.3	1.2	1.3	7.4	7.4	8.0	7.7	7.9	26.2	24.2	10.2	1.1	72.6	34.0	48.9	51.1
71108	SHREVEPORT	29.8	26.8	68.3	71.2	0.4	0.5	1.1	1.1	8.4	8.2	9.2	8.8	7.8	27.6	19.6	9.3	1.2	68.9	30.7	46.5	53.5
71109	SHREVEPORT	9.6	8.5	89.2	90.3	0.2	0.2	0.8	0.8	7.3	7.4	8.5	8.9	8.2	24.2	23.8	10.2	1.5	71.4	32.9	45.9	54.1
71110	BARKSDALE AFB	68.6	66.0	22.7	24.0	2.3	2.7	7.6	8.5	12.5	10.6	8.5	10.6	23.1	31.7	3.0	0.1	0.0	65.1	21.7	57.7	42.4
71111	BOSSIER CITY	70.8	70.0	24.1	24.2	1.7	2.1	3.2	3.6	8.2	7.6	7.8	7.2	7.2	29.4	21.5	9.7	1.3	71.9	33.5	48.0	52.0
71112	BOSSIER CITY	76.0	74.3	18.1	19.0	2.0	2.4	4.0	4.5	7.3	6.9	6.9	6.9	7.4	29.7	22.7	11.1	1.1	74.8	34.9	48.8	51.2
71115	SHREVEPORT	82.6	79.9	13.3	15.2	2.0	2.4	2.2	2.5	5.4	5.1	5.2	7.3	10.5	27.5	22.5	12.7	3.8	80.9	35.8	44.7	55.3
71118	SHREVEPORT	80.4	77.9	16.3	18.2	1.1	1.4	2.0	2.3	6.5	6.1	6.4	6.4	7.2	26.7	24.6	13.7	2.5	77.2	38.2	46.5	53.5
71119	SHREVEPORT	51.2	47.6	47.0	50.3	0.5	0.6	1.1	1.3	5.8	5.8	6.5	6.6	6.8	26.2	28.3	12.9	1.2	77.7	39.8	48.3	51.7
71129	SHREVEPORT	61.9	59.1	35.0	37.5	0.5	0.6	2.3	2.4	7.7	6.9	7.0	7.4	8.6	29.9	23.5	8.5	0.7	74.0	33.3	47.9	52.1
71201	MONROE	67.8	64.8	29.8	32.3	1.4	1.7	1.2	1.3	6.7	6.1	5.9	6.1	8.2	27.3	22.5	14.3	3.0	77.8	37.3	46.1	53.9
71202	MONROE	15.1	13.1	83.8	85.8	0.2	0.3	0.9	0.9	8.9	9.3	10.2	10.4	7.7	25.1	19.6	7.8	1.1	65.0	27.6	47.0	53.1
71203	MONROE	62.6	60.5	35.0	36.8	1.1	1.3	1.1	1.3	7.1	6.9	7.3	8.5	10.2	28.8	20.3	9.7	1.1	74.6	30.9	46.9	53.1
71209	MONROE	49.8	43.8	43.7	49.0	4.4	5.0	1.9	2.0	2.0	1.3	1.4	36.3	37.4	12.5	4.8	4.0	0.4	94.3	21.2	36.1	63.9
71219	BASKIN	87.5	86.0	11.5	12.8	0.2	0.3	0.6	0.7	7.2	6.9	6.6	7.0	6.9	26.1	25.8	11.5	2.0	74.9	37.9	49.6	50.4
71220	BASTROP	55.7	55.4	43.5	43.8	0.2	0.2	0.7	0.7	7.3	7.1	7.7	7.2	7.1	25.9	22.9	12.8	1.9	73.5	35.8	47.7	52.3
71222	BERNICE	57.4	55.5	38.7	40.2	0.3	0.3	4.2	4.7	7.3	6.5	6.7	6.6	6.9	24.0	24.2	15.4	2.4	75.6	38.4	47.1	52.9
71223	BONITA	50.1	47.9	48.1	50.2	0.1	0.2	1.4	1.3	5.8	5.8	6.4	7.5	7.0	23.4	26.3	15.4	2.5	77.7	41.1	50.6	49.4
71225	CALHOUN	92.4	90.8	6.0	7.3	0.2	0.3	1.0	1.2	6.8	6.9	7.7	7.1	6.6	29.8	24.8	9.4	0.9	74.2	36.1	49.6	50.4
71226	CHATHAM	72.1	69.5	26.9	29.4	0.1	0.1	0.6	0.6	7.4	7.2	6.7	6.2	6.4	26.4	26.1	12.2	1.5	75.0	37.8	49.5	50.5
71227	CHOUDRANT	86.4	84.9	12.6	13.9	0.1	0.1	1.0	1.1	6.2	6.4	7.1	7.0	6.6	28.9	26.0	10.5	1.4	76.0	37.2	50.1	49.9
71229	COLLINSTON	63.5	61.2	35.9	38.1	0.2	0.2	1.3	1.5	5.8	5.9	6.6	6.5	7.6	30.0	25.1	11.5	1.0	77.9	36.8	53.4	46.6
71232	DELHI	53.3	51.0	45.4	47.5	0.3	0.3	1.3	1.5	7.7	7.5	7.5	6.7	6.9	25.0	23.0	13.2	2.5	73.3	36.9	46.7	53.4
71234	DOWNSVILLE	92.9	91.8	5.9	6.9	0.1	0.1	0.7	0.8	6.2	6.3	6.5	6.4	5.9	29.0	26.8	11.6	1.3	77.0	38.5	50.4	49.6
71235	DUBACH	80.6	79.2	18.0	19.1	0.2	0.2	0.9	1.1	6.9	6.9	7.0	6.7	6.0	27.0	26.0	11.9	1.5	75.1	38.0	48.9	51.1
71237	EPPS	62.6	61.4	36.4	37.8	0.0	0.0	1.3	1.2	4.8	5.1	6.3	6.9	10.1	32.6	22.5	10.3	1.4	80.0	35.0	59.2	40.8
71238	EROS	87.2	85.1	11.3	13.1	0.2	0.3	1.1	1.3	6.9	6.9	7.3	7.1	6.3	28.3	26.3	9.8	1.1	74.6	36.9	49.8	50.2
71241	FARMERVILLE	68.5	67.1	29.5	30.6	0.4	0.5	1.6	1.8	7.1	6.7	6.8	6.1	6.7	26.1	24.7	13.6	2.2	75.6	38.1	48.7	51.3
71243	FORT NECESSITY	90.7	89.4	8.2	9.4	0.0	0.0	0.8	1.3	6.9	6.9	6.6	6.9	6.9	27.8	25.0	11.9	1.3	75.9	36.9	50.3	49.7
71245	GRAMBLING	5.7	5.2	92.1	92.6	0.3	0.3	1.1	1.1	6.9	6.0	5.8	7.7	15.8	24.4	20.8	11.0	1.7	77.4	29.0	47.3	52.7
71250	JONES	54.2	52.7	43.7	45.7	0.0	0.0	1.5	1.6	6.0	6.0	6.4	7.6	7.3	24.8	25.7	14.0	2.2	77.8	39.8	50.2	49.8
71251	JONESBORO	67.5	66.8	31.3	31.8	0.3	0.4	0.5	0.6	6.5	6.4	6.6	6.7	6.7	25.1	24.7	14.6	2.7	76.5	39.1	47.6	52.4
71254	LAKE PROVIDENCE	25.8	25.3	73.1	73.5	0.4	0.4	1.1	1.1	8.2	8.2	9.3	8.4	8.3	26.1	19.3	10.5	1.8	69.4	30.5	49.3	50.7
71256	LILLIE	53.6	50.7	44.6	47.6	0.0	0.0	1.4	1.2	8.6	8.6	7.8	5.9	6.1	26.7	22.6	12.0	1.7	71.6	34.1	49.3	50.7
71259	MANGHAM	76.1	74.3	23.4	25.1	0.1	0.1	1.0	1.2	6.7	6.7	7.4	6.9	6.9	24.6	26.0	13.3	1.6	74.8	38.5	48.1	51.9
71260	MARION	69.5	67.6	28.2	29.9	0.4	0.5	2.3	2.5	6.7	6.6	6.6	6.7	6.9	25.8	26.9	12.3	1.4	76.0	38.6	49.7	50.3
71261	MER ROUGE	54.6	52.3	44.5	46.8	0.1	0.1	1.0	1.0	7.2	6.9	7.1	7.0	7.3	25.0	24.1	13.6	1.8	74.6	37.5	48.2	51.8
71263	OAK GROVE	86.4	85.5	12.3	13.0	0.2	0.2	1.5	1.7	6.7	6.7	7.2	6.6	6.6	24.5	25.1	14.1	2.6	75.3	39.4	48.3	51.7
71264	OAK RIDGE	60.0	58.1	39.5	41.3	0.1	0.1	0.7	0.9	6.9	6.7	5.8	5.8	7.2	23.8	28.0	13.9	2.0	77.4	40.5	48.9	51.1
71266	PIONEER	63.9	62.4	35.2	36.5	0.1	0.1	1.1	1.2	5.5	5.6	6.9	7.0	9.4	30.3	22.0	11.7	1.7	78.3	35.4	56.1	43.9
71268	QUITMAN	73.4	71.5	25.7	27.4	0.1	0.1	0.6	0.7	6.7	6.5	6.6	6.6	6.8	26.6	24.6	13.4	2.3	76.4	38.2	48.3	51.7
71269	RAYVILLE	61.4	60.0	37.6	38.9	0.1	0.2	1.0	1.0	7.6	7.3	7.3	7.0	7.1	27.2	22.5	12.0	2.1	73.7	35.4	47.6	52.4
71270	RUSTON	56.5	54.4	40.3	41.9	1.7	2.1	1.2	1.3	5.8	5.2	5.8	15.3	16.0	24.2	17.0	9.0	1.7	79.4	26.1	48.6	51.4
71275	SIMSBORO	53.9	50.8	44.7	47.6	0.0	0.0	1.4	1.6	7.4	6.7	6.8	7.5	9.2	27.2	24.0	9.9	1.4	74.8	33.7	49.6	50.5
71276	SONDHEIMER	61.4	61.7	37.5	37.3	0.0	0.0	1.8	1.7	6.9	6.8	5.6	6.6	8.0	31.2	22.9	10.4	1.5	77.1	35.5	57.8	42.2
71277	SPEARSVILLE	67.4	65.0	30.7	32.9	0.1	0.1	2.0	2.2	7.9	7.4	7.3	5.8	6.5	25.8	24.4	13.4	1.6	73.8	37.0	49.2	50.8
71280	STERLINGTON	82.6	79.6	14.9	17.6	0.4	0.5	2.6	2.7	6.5	6.2	6.7	8.3	8.6	25.3	24.8	12.2	1.3	75.4	36.4	47.2	52.8
71282	TALLULAH	37.7	36.2	60.5	61.8	0.2	0.2	2.1	2.3	8.3	8.3	7.9	10.1	8.1	25.5	20.6	9.6	1.7	68.8	30.6	50.9	49.2
71286	TRANSYLVANIA	57.1	57.3	41.9	41.8	0.1	0.1	1.6	1.6	6.3	6.0	5.1	6.5	9.2	35.6	21.0	9.0	1.4	79.2	34.4	62.7	37.3
	LOUISIANA	63.9	62.8	32.5	33.2	1.3	1.5	2.4	2.6	7.2	7.0	7.4	7.5	7.9	28.0	23.4	10.3	1.4	74.1	34.6	48.5	51.5
	UNITED STATES	75.1	73.6	12.3	12.5	3.8	4.2	12.5	14.1	6.9	6.7	7.2	7.0	7.3	28.6	23.8	10.8	1.7	75.1	36.0	49.1	50.9

#	POST OFFICE NAME	2004 Per Capita Income	2004 HH Income Base	2004 Household Income Distribution (%): Less than $25,000	$25,000 to $49,999	$50,000 to $99,999	$100,000 to $149,999	$150,000 or More	Median Household Income: 2004	2009	2004 National Centile	2004 State Centile	2004 Home Value Base	2004 Home Value Distribution (%): Less than $50,000	$50,000 to $89,999	$90,000 to $174,999	$175,000 to $399,999	$400,000 or More	2004 Median Home Value
71019	COUSHATTA	13870	3490	48.5	28.6	18.2	3.0	1.7	25822	29133	6	16	2628	44.9	28.5	21.4	4.3	1.0	56204
71023	DOYLINE	20188	1425	29.3	35.8	27.9	5.3	1.6	37886	43325	39	70	1191	33.8	30.7	23.1	10.1	2.4	69784
71024	DUBBERLY	18509	530	33.2	33.6	25.5	5.7	2.1	36009	41313	32	62	445	37.1	31.9	20.7	8.1	2.3	65645
71027	FRIERSON	17391	695	30.5	32.7	31.4	3.5	2.0	39302	45000	44	75	584	31.3	27.9	28.4	11.0	1.4	72000
71028	GIBSLAND	15267	833	49.7	29.7	16.3	2.9	1.4	25152	28338	5	13	650	56.3	23.2	15.2	3.7	1.5	42807
71029	GILLIAM	14466	69	42.0	36.2	15.9	4.4	1.5	28212	33593	9	25	55	54.6	27.3	10.9	7.3	0.0	43750
71030	GLOSTER	20253	451	26.4	32.4	29.9	8.0	3.3	42807	47916	55	82	377	28.9	22.8	36.1	10.6	1.6	87292
71031	GOLDONNA	16191	414	37.7	36.5	19.1	5.3	1.5	30796	35059	14	38	341	54.0	26.1	16.1	3.8	0.0	44808
71032	GRAND CANE	17410	671	40.7	24.9	28.0	5.2	1.2	32481	36078	19	48	563	38.7	20.6	26.1	12.6	2.0	71667
71033	GREENWOOD	21540	1253	31.4	27.2	27.4	9.8	4.2	43698	50258	58	84	1009	23.4	24.0	32.0	19.8	0.8	96163
71034	HALL SUMMIT	15200	100	38.0	35.0	24.0	3.0	0.0	31281	37859	16	42	82	37.8	23.2	36.6	2.4	0.0	70000
71037	HAUGHTON	19968	6253	22.6	31.1	36.3	7.4	2.6	46827	52602	66	89	5249	28.8	17.4	44.8	8.9	0.3	95732
71038	HAYNESVILLE	15629	2320	46.1	29.3	19.1	3.5	2.1	27763	31840	8	24	1736	47.9	22.5	21.5	7.6	0.6	53162
71039	HEFLIN	15530	800	39.1	31.3	26.5	2.0	1.1	31450	34778	16	43	643	37.2	27.5	23.3	7.3	4.7	65197
71040	HOMER	16415	2873	44.3	31.2	18.0	4.7	1.8	29006	33347	10	30	2051	37.2	27.6	24.0	10.4	0.8	67311
71043	HOSSTON	14967	272	47.1	29.0	17.7	3.7	2.6	26543	30487	6	18	222	59.0	21.6	14.4	3.6	1.4	41667
71044	IDA	14264	345	52.2	29.0	16.5	1.7	0.6	23559	27556	4	9	285	66.7	15.1	15.4	1.1	1.8	39479
71045	JAMESTOWN	14003	334	45.5	31.4	19.8	1.8	1.5	27932	31577	9	24	275	51.6	22.6	16.0	8.0	1.8	48043
71046	KEATCHIE	18979	575	37.4	25.0	29.7	5.9	1.9	36233	41193	32	63	497	34.8	19.3	29.8	13.3	2.8	81458
71047	KEITHVILLE	20501	4071	28.7	24.9	32.7	10.4	3.3	46273	52906	64	88	3410	32.5	24.2	28.9	13.3	1.1	77253
71048	LISBON	14898	162	49.4	24.1	22.2	3.7	0.6	25356	28075	5	14	133	48.9	25.6	19.6	6.0	0.0	51667
71049	LOGANSPORT	14699	1509	44.8	28.8	22.4	3.5	0.5	28877	32924	10	29	1187	40.8	28.6	21.6	7.9	1.1	58975
71051	ELM GROVE	18948	978	33.5	25.1	32.4	6.2	2.8	39080	43852	43	74	803	37.9	18.6	25.7	17.1	0.9	74219
71052	MANSFIELD	13831	4273	50.0	26.2	19.6	3.3	0.9	25026	28409	5	13	2883	43.1	31.6	21.9	3.4	0.1	57335
71055	MINDEN	17277	8131	42.5	29.7	20.0	5.2	2.6	30012	33637	12	35	5695	36.0	31.7	23.7	8.0	0.6	65337
71060	MOORINGSPORT	18833	1137	30.6	30.1	31.7	6.6	1.1	40502	46762	48	77	914	37.6	26.4	29.2	5.9	0.9	63714
71061	OIL CITY	15142	802	49.6	29.8	16.2	1.9	2.5	25264	29063	5	14	565	49.0	25.5	17.7	3.9	3.9	51100
71063	PELICAN	10968	337	55.8	29.1	14.2	0.9	0.0	22090	25457	3	6	261	31.8	47.9	18.8	1.5	0.0	63148
71064	PLAIN DEALING	14038	1567	47.8	28.0	20.2	2.9	1.1	26809	30296	7	19	1249	46.6	27.7	19.9	4.6	1.2	55903
71065	PLEASANT HILL	15549	505	47.7	26.1	19.2	5.0	2.0	27445	29113	8	22	371	49.6	27.2	20.8	1.9	0.5	50319
71067	PRINCETON	18556	1233	26.7	32.4	35.4	4.2	1.2	42425	47571	54	82	1002	37.5	25.8	31.3	5.4	0.0	68980
71068	RINGGOLD	14004	1539	50.6	27.6	18.5	2.7	0.7	24494	27141	4	11	1159	47.2	28.0	17.7	6.1	1.0	52955
71069	RODESSA	14408	294	48.3	32.7	15.7	2.7	0.7	26239	29523	6	17	246	63.0	20.7	14.2	1.2	0.8	40588
71070	SALINE	15924	726	46.0	28.7	19.8	3.4	2.1	28476	31922	10	26	595	55.0	22.2	18.3	4.0	0.5	42976
71071	SAREPTA	14640	1336	42.5	32.4	20.7	3.1	1.4	30485	34002	13	37	1022	42.5	27.9	24.6	4.7	0.4	57778
71072	SHONGALOO	18268	582	24.9	41.6	26.3	6.9	0.3	38127	44056	40	71	497	48.3	30.0	19.7	1.8	0.2	52742
71073	SIBLEY	16905	968	36.5	31.8	26.2	3.8	1.7	34513	38689	26	55	781	40.3	26.5	23.9	5.3	4.0	66026
71075	SPRINGHILL	19043	2756	45.4	31.6	17.9	2.4	2.7	27709	30869	8	23	1894	40.9	34.1	21.4	3.3	0.3	58113
71078	STONEWALL	18103	1661	29.7	31.6	31.3	5.7	1.8	41034	46324	50	78	1400	27.2	23.6	34.4	13.7	1.0	88421
71079	SUMMERFIELD	14074	47	53.2	21.3	23.4	2.1	0.0	22892	25000	3	7	38	50.0	21.1	18.4	10.5	0.0	50000
71082	VIVIAN	16529	2130	43.2	28.0	23.6	3.1	2.2	28892	33130	10	29	1597	52.1	30.2	13.3	3.5	0.9	48562
71101	SHREVEPORT	12077	3956	62.9	24.4	10.9	0.9	0.9	16689	19102	1	2	1187	51.1	36.9	8.3	2.4	1.4	49290
71103	SHREVEPORT	13447	3515	60.8	24.1	11.5	1.7	1.9	18712	21640	1	3	1671	60.7	30.6	5.9	2.3	0.5	42229
71104	SHREVEPORT	22440	6746	35.9	34.0	21.2	5.8	3.1	33737	39978	23	52	3413	16.4	40.1	34.5	7.6	1.4	82946
71105	SHREVEPORT	28997	9463	20.8	32.7	32.0	9.7	4.8	46971	54304	66	89	5749	2.1	18.0	67.4	12.2	0.2	115448
71106	SHREVEPORT	28745	12397	35.9	21.4	20.4	9.9	12.3	39661	46460	45	75	8380	22.7	20.0	21.0	27.9	8.4	115872
71107	SHREVEPORT	16754	11265	40.8	26.0	23.7	6.9	2.6	33252	38519	22	50	7770	29.4	29.3	31.1	8.6	1.6	76041
71108	SHREVEPORT	12702	7685	45.8	33.9	17.5	1.8	1.0	27181	30947	7	20	4767	44.5	44.6	9.5	1.4	0.0	53661
71109	SHREVEPORT	12950	9197	51.7	28.9	15.3	2.9	1.2	23806	27238	4	10	5087	51.7	32.7	13.0	2.0	0.7	48575
71110	BARKSDALE AFB	12975	714	16.5	41.7	33.6	8.1	0.0	45578	49493	63	87	8	0.0	0.0	100.0	0.0	0.0	105000
71111	BOSSIER CITY	21622	13185	32.2	29.0	26.0	8.5	4.3	39484	44923	44	75	7796	13.0	24.1	37.4	22.8	2.7	116987
71112	BOSSIER CITY	20086	10894	25.1	32.2	34.1	7.0	1.6	44395	49379	60	86	7549	15.6	35.6	41.8	6.6	0.4	88903
71115	SHREVEPORT	32515	5617	24.5	30.7	27.4	9.9	7.6	45185	51954	62	87	3019	1.4	17.7	58.4	20.7	1.8	125598
71118	SHREVEPORT	21630	9638	25.3	32.4	31.9	8.7	1.7	43714	50105	58	84	6468	3.3	32.3	57.7	6.1	0.5	100503
71119	SHREVEPORT	26775	4741	18.9	29.9	36.6	9.9	4.7	50974	60106	74	94	3786	16.1	24.0	43.3	14.5	2.1	101283
71129	SHREVEPORT	20557	5161	32.2	29.8	27.3	8.8	1.9	39171	45566	43	74	3062	28.6	20.5	42.6	7.5	0.8	91274
71201	MONROE	30602	9814	34.4	25.4	23.4	8.8	8.0	39283	45546	44	74	5411	9.1	16.0	41.4	26.4	7.2	127370
71202	MONROE	11334	9730	51.8	28.2	16.6	2.6	1.0	23652	27021	4	9	5379	47.0	36.8	13.6	2.3	0.2	52031
71203	MONROE	19322	13467	34.3	28.5	27.2	7.2	2.8	37101	42842	36	67	8173	18.1	27.6	42.3	10.9	1.1	94017
71209	MONROE	7424	8	50.0	50.0	0.0	0.0	0.0	25000	27247	5	13	0	0.0	0.0	0.0	0.0	0.0	0
71219	BASKIN	15343	503	47.5	25.5	21.5	3.6	2.0	26345	30000	6	17	429	41.3	32.6	20.1	6.1	0.0	56466
71220	BASTROP	15269	9705	45.2	26.8	22.3	4.0	1.7	28775	32858	10	28	6750	43.1	29.0	21.1	6.2	0.6	58689
71222	BERNICE	15329	1433	44.5	31.7	18.5	3.8	1.5	28541	31839	10	27	1107	40.5	29.7	22.2	6.7	0.9	62394
71223	BONITA	15678	262	60.7	29.4	6.5	1.2	2.3	18522	21631	1	3	201	60.2	21.4	14.9	2.5	1.0	35417
71225	CALHOUN	21780	1937	25.9	33.6	27.7	9.1	3.8	42758	49431	55	82	1652	26.5	17.3	34.7	18.9	2.7	101382
71226	CHATHAM	16476	671	45.8	30.3	16.8	6.0	1.2	27110	31489	7	20	544	48.9	23.4	21.5	4.0	2.2	51500
71227	CHOUDRANT	18929	1354	27.1	33.9	32.4	4.9	1.8	41902	48581	53	80	1122	37.9	20.6	28.0	10.8	2.8	73387
71229	COLLINSTON	15064	508	37.6	31.3	22.8	5.3	3.0	32486	37405	19	48	419	44.6	27.7	22.0	5.5	0.2	59375
71232	DELHI	14378	2451	46.8	29.1	18.7	4.1	1.4	27243	31025	7	21	1809	42.0	31.2	20.2	6.7	0.0	57348
71234	DOWNSVILLE	17153	1531	31.4	36.3	26.6	5.2	0.6	35375	40650	29	58	1306	38.0	21.8	28.6	11.0	0.7	71143
71235	DUBACH	19117	1656	35.6	26.9	29.0	6.2	2.3	37080	43112	36	67	1369	30.5	25.9	29.1	12.4	2.2	76691
71237	EPPS	15080	271	47.2	31.0	18.5	3.0	0.4	26595	30216	7	19	217	47.9	33.2	15.7	3.2	0.0	51875
71238	EROS	19086	944	32.7	31.7	25.3	8.2	2.1	37995	43593	39	71	832	34.9	22.1	30.5	10.5	2.0	75122
71241	FARMERVILLE	17432	3789	37.7	30.7	25.1	5.0	1.5	32868	36685	21	49	2994	36.0	27.0	28.4	7.4	1.1	70556
71243	FORT NECESSITY	16084	130	40.8	38.5	13.9	3.1	3.9	27404	31811	8	22	109	57.8	18.4	15.6	8.3	0.0	45278
71245	GRAMBLING	16241	1179	53.1	27.1	14.8	3.3	1.8	22926	26825	3	7	469	11.3	40.5	38.0	10.2	0.0	87821
71250	JONES	15430	119	58.0	29.4	9.2	0.8	2.5	20206	21669	2	4	92	57.6	23.9	15.2	2.2	1.1	40000
71251	JONESBORO	17564	4080	41.3	28.5	23.6	5.1	1.5	31215	35653	16	41	3013	37.6	31.5	23.5	6.3	1.1	62539
71254	LAKE PROVIDENCE	10898	2468	57.7	27.9	10.9	1.9	1.5	20549	22901	2	5	1461	54.5	28.0	15.3	1.8	0.4	46478
71256	LILLIE	15366	157	43.3	22.3	29.3	4.5	0.6	29736	31646	12	33	126	50.8	31.0	13.5	3.2	1.6	49333
71259	MANGHAM	17182	867	40.4	29.6	22.4	4.6	3.0	32163	37249	18	46	705	40.4	34.3	19.3	6.0	0.0	59000
71260	MARION	15945	1277	43.4	29.2	21.3	4.9	1.3	29707	32539	12	33	1037	47.1	25.2	21.1	4.7	1.9	54766
71261	MER ROUGE	15148	632	51.3	24.2	19.3	3.0	2.2	24067	27674	4	10	477	52.8	25.0	17.6	3.8	0.8	47545
71263	OAK GROVE	15272	3462	44.5	29.1	20.9	3.8	1.7	28333	31845	9	25	2772	45.6	26.8	21.3	4.6	1.7	54939
71264	OAK RIDGE	16133	372	53.0	22.9	15.3	4.8	4.0	22999	26621	3	8	293	35.2	30.4	21.5	12.6	0.3	73750
71266	PIONEER	11606	900	50.3	30.9	15.6	2.3	0.9	24784	27777	4	12	723	51.9	30.2	15.6	2.2	0.1	48043
71268	QUITMAN	17534	1052	36.6	32.9	22.2	6.2	2.1	34582	39898	26	55	853	39.3	22.9	28.8	7.2	1.9	65727
71269	RAYVILLE	14177	4477	50.0	25.0	19.3	3.6	2.1	25021	29145	5	13	3142	35.1	32.0	23.2	9.3	0.4	66538
71270	RUSTON	17352	11410	45.7	23.4	22.7	5.1	3.1	28217	33010	9	25	6087	22.5	22.4	37.4	15.1	2.6	96105
71275	SIMSBORO	15363	901	34.0	34.9	25.9	4.6	0.8	36597	44123	34	64	700	41.9	24.1	25.9	7.1	1.0	63273
71276	SONDHEIMER	16307	244	34.4	36.9	22.1	6.6	0.0	32838	35652	20	49	192	45.8	42.7	9.9	0.0	1.6	55333
71277	SPEARSVILLE	16255	750	38.0	30.7	25.2	4.0	2.1	32764	35939	20	49	632	41.0	27.1	23.7	6.8	1.4	63488
71280	STERLINGTON	21318	828	31.9	29.0	27.4	5.9	5.8	39734	45874	45	75	647	31.4	30.8	30.8	6.2	0.9	73068
71282	TALLULAH	11786	4587	53.6	29.2	13.9	2.4	0.9	22567	25165	3	7	2909	46.0	31.3	17.7	4.0	1.0	55021
71286	TRANSYLVANIA	13543	283	38.9	40.6	14.8	3.9	1.8	29905	33094	12	34	221	53.9	36.7	9.1	0.0	0.5	47167
	LOUISIANA	19601		35.3	28.5	25.7	7.1	3.5	36550	42223				22.5	24.5	35.6	15.0	2.4	94005
	UNITED STATES	25866		24.7	27.1	30.8	10.9	6.5	48124	56710				10.9	15.0	33.7	30.1	10.4	145905

ZIP CODE #	POST OFFICE NAME	FINANCIAL SERVICES: Auto Loan	FINANCIAL SERVICES: Home Loan	FINANCIAL SERVICES: Invest-ments	FINANCIAL SERVICES: Retire-ment Plans	THE HOME: Home Improvements: Home Repair	THE HOME: Home Improvements: Lawn & Garden	THE HOME: Furnishings: Comput-ers & Hard-ware	THE HOME: Furnishings: Major Appli-ances	THE HOME: Furnishings: TV, Radio, Sound Equip-ment	THE HOME: Furnishings: Furni-ture	ENTERTAINMENT: Dine out/ Carry out	ENTERTAINMENT: Sports Equip-ment	ENTERTAINMENT: Fees & Tickets	ENTERTAINMENT: Toys & Games	ENTERTAINMENT: Travel	ENTERTAINMENT: Cable TV	PERSONAL: Apparel & Services	PERSONAL: Auto Repairs	PERSONAL: Health Insur-ance	PERSONAL: Pets & Supplies
71019	COUSHATTA	67	47	30	41	51	60	48	56	57	49	67	66	42	63	48	61	62	56	68	76
71023	DOYLINE	94	64	29	55	72	83	61	77	74	62	87	91	52	82	62	80	79	76	94	109
71024	DUBBERLY	86	57	26	49	65	75	55	69	67	56	78	83	47	74	56	72	71	68	85	98
71027	FRIERSON	72	64	47	60	65	69	61	66	63	62	77	77	57	73	60	63	73	66	68	81
71028	GIBSLAND	59	44	31	40	47	56	47	52	54	46	64	59	42	59	46	57	59	53	63	66
71029	GILLIAM	70	47	21	41	53	61	45	57	55	46	64	68	39	61	46	59	58	56	70	81
71030	GLOSTER	88	80	62	77	80	85	76	82	77	79	96	95	72	90	75	76	92	82	82	97
71031	GOLDONNA	78	52	24	45	59	68	50	63	61	51	71	75	43	67	51	65	65	62	78	89
71032	GRAND CANE	79	53	24	46	60	69	51	64	62	52	73	77	44	69	52	67	66	64	79	91
71033	GREENWOOD	86	75	58	73	79	87	74	80	78	73	95	93	71	95	74	80	89	78	87	99
71034	HALL SUMMIT	74	50	23	43	56	65	48	60	58	49	68	72	41	64	49	63	62	60	74	85
71037	HAUGHTON	83	83	73	81	83	85	77	81	76	79	95	94	76	93	77	75	92	80	78	95
71038	HAYNESVILLE	61	45	34	40	48	57	48	54	56	48	66	60	44	61	47	59	61	54	65	67
71039	HEFLIN	76	51	23	44	58	66	49	61	59	50	70	73	42	66	50	64	63	61	76	87
71040	HOMER	63	50	42	44	52	61	51	57	58	52	70	64	48	65	52	62	66	57	67	72
71043	HOSSTON	74	49	22	43	56	64	48	60	58	49	68	71	41	64	48	62	61	59	73	85
71044	IDA	62	41	19	36	47	54	40	50	48	41	57	60	34	54	41	52	52	50	62	71
71045	JAMESTOWN	67	45	20	38	50	58	43	54	52	44	61	64	37	58	44	56	55	53	66	76
71046	KEATCHIE	83	62	36	56	67	75	60	71	68	61	81	83	53	76	60	71	75	70	81	95
71047	KEITHVILLE	93	81	60	77	84	90	77	85	80	78	98	99	73	95	77	81	94	84	89	105
71048	LISBON	65	44	20	38	49	57	42	53	51	43	60	63	36	56	43	55	54	52	65	75
71049	LOGANSPORT	66	46	26	40	51	59	46	55	55	47	65	64	40	60	46	59	59	55	67	75
71051	ELM GROVE	83	71	53	67	75	81	68	76	72	69	87	88	63	84	69	73	82	75	81	96
71052	MANSFIELD	58	44	34	39	46	54	46	51	53	46	63	59	42	59	46	56	59	52	60	65
71055	MINDEN	64	55	50	52	57	65	57	61	62	57	75	69	55	73	57	65	72	61	67	73
71060	MOORINGSPORT	77	65	47	62	67	74	65	71	69	65	83	81	59	78	64	70	78	70	76	86
71061	OIL CITY	69	46	21	40	52	60	44	55	53	45	63	66	38	59	45	58	57	55	68	79
71063	PELICAN	43	34	33	30	34	42	37	40	43	38	52	43	35	47	37	47	49	41	47	47
71064	PLAIN DEALING	61	44	31	38	47	56	45	52	54	46	64	60	41	58	45	58	59	53	63	69
71065	PLEASANT HILL	74	50	23	43	57	65	48	60	58	49	68	72	41	64	49	63	62	60	74	85
71067	PRINCETON	78	71	56	68	71	75	68	73	69	70	85	84	64	80	67	68	81	72	72	86
71068	RINGGOLD	59	41	25	36	45	53	41	50	50	42	59	58	37	54	42	53	54	49	60	67
71069	RODESSA	66	44	20	38	50	58	43	53	51	43	60	64	36	57	43	55	55	53	66	76
71070	SALINE	73	49	22	42	56	64	47	59	57	48	67	71	40	63	48	61	61	59	73	84
71071	SAREPTA	67	46	28	40	51	60	47	56	56	48	66	65	41	61	47	60	61	56	68	76
71072	SHONGALOO	87	58	26	50	66	76	56	70	68	57	79	84	48	75	57	73	72	69	86	100
71073	SIBLEY	85	57	26	49	65	75	55	69	67	56	78	82	47	74	56	72	71	68	85	98
71075	SPRINGHILL	69	56	46	52	59	70	59	64	66	58	79	72	56	76	59	70	74	64	75	77
71078	STONEWALL	76	70	54	67	70	74	66	71	67	68	83	82	63	78	65	66	80	71	71	84
71079	SUMMERFIELD	67	45	20	39	51	59	43	54	52	44	61	65	37	58	44	56	56	54	67	77
71082	VIVIAN	71	51	32	46	56	66	53	61	62	53	73	70	47	68	53	66	67	61	74	80
71101	SHREVEPORT	38	32	37	30	31	37	37	36	41	37	50	41	36	47	36	42	48	38	40	41
71103	SHREVEPORT	50	42	47	38	41	50	47	47	53	48	64	52	46	59	46	56	62	49	54	55
71104	SHREVEPORT	66	63	77	65	62	68	72	67	71	70	89	81	70	88	69	69	87	71	65	74
71105	SHREVEPORT	80	85	103	86	84	90	89	85	87	87	109	100	90	110	88	85	107	88	82	93
71106	SHREVEPORT	105	109	126	107	107	118	109	108	110	110	137	122	113	135	109	111	135	108	109	121
71107	SHREVEPORT	68	58	53	54	60	67	59	63	64	60	78	72	57	76	59	66	75	63	69	77
71108	SHREVEPORT	50	44	48	42	44	51	48	48	52	48	64	54	47	62	47	54	62	49	52	56
71109	SHREVEPORT	50	43	49	40	42	50	47	47	52	48	64	52	47	60	46	55	62	49	53	55
71110	BARKSDALE AFB	81	52	49	59	47	56	77	66	78	72	98	88	66	87	63	71	94	78	61	76
71111	BOSSIER CITY	76	76	83	77	75	80	78	77	78	79	98	89	79	96	77	77	96	78	74	86
71112	BOSSIER CITY	70	73	78	73	72	76	73	72	72	72	90	83	73	90	72	71	88	72	69	80
71115	SHREVEPORT	88	88	103	92	87	92	94	90	92	93	115	108	94	113	92	88	113	94	84	100
71118	SHREVEPORT	71	75	84	76	74	78	75	74	73	75	92	86	76	93	75	72	90	74	71	82
71119	SHREVEPORT	89	101	108	100	100	103	95	95	92	95	115	111	98	118	97	91	113	94	90	106
71129	SHREVEPORT	75	68	64	69	68	71	69	71	69	70	87	84	66	83	67	67	83	72	68	83
71201	MONROE	89	91	111	91	90	99	96	93	96	95	120	107	97	119	95	97	118	95	93	103
71202	MONROE	49	42	47	39	41	48	46	46	50	47	62	51	45	59	45	52	60	48	50	54
71203	MONROE	70	64	68	64	64	70	69	68	71	69	88	80	67	85	67	70	85	71	68	78
71209	MONROE	35	21	27	24	21	25	41	30	40	35	50	42	34	45	33	35	47	37	28	35
71219	BASKIN	75	50	23	43	57	66	49	61	59	49	69	73	41	65	49	63	63	60	75	86
71220	BASTROP	65	50	38	46	54	62	52	58	59	52	71	67	48	67	52	62	66	58	67	73
71222	BERNICE	67	48	30	43	53	61	48	57	56	48	66	67	43	64	49	59	61	57	67	77
71223	BONITA	76	51	23	44	58	67	49	62	59	50	70	74	42	66	50	64	63	61	76	87
71225	CALHOUN	93	84	65	81	86	92	79	86	82	81	101	101	76	98	80	82	96	85	89	106
71226	CHATHAM	74	52	28	46	58	66	50	61	59	51	69	73	44	67	51	63	64	60	73	85
71227	CHOUDRANT	80	68	49	64	72	78	63	71	68	64	83	85	61	83	65	70	78	70	78	93
71229	COLLINSTON	77	59	36	54	64	71	56	66	63	57	76	78	51	73	57	66	70	65	76	89
71232	DELHI	64	46	30	41	50	59	48	55	56	48	66	63	43	61	48	60	61	55	67	71
71234	DOWNSVILLE	72	59	41	55	62	67	57	64	61	58	74	75	52	70	57	62	69	63	69	81
71235	DUBACH	83	64	40	59	70	79	62	72	70	62	84	85	57	82	63	74	78	71	84	95
71237	EPPS	66	44	20	38	50	58	43	53	51	43	60	64	36	57	43	55	55	53	66	76
71238	EROS	86	71	48	66	74	81	68	76	73	69	88	90	62	84	68	74	83	76	83	97
71241	FARMERVILLE	71	56	42	50	59	68	56	63	64	57	76	73	52	73	57	67	72	63	73	81
71243	FORT NECESSITY	75	50	23	43	57	65	48	60	58	49	68	72	41	65	49	63	62	60	74	86
71245	GRAMBLING	51	41	48	42	40	47	52	49	54	50	67	58	48	61	48	53	64	53	50	55
71250	JONES	77	52	23	44	58	67	50	62	60	51	70	74	42	67	51	65	64	62	77	88
71251	JONESBORO	71	55	39	51	59	68	56	63	63	56	75	72	51	72	56	67	70	62	73	80
71254	LAKE PROVIDENCE	49	37	33	34	39	47	41	44	47	41	56	49	38	52	40	50	53	45	52	54
71256	LILLIE	75	50	23	43	57	66	49	61	59	50	69	73	41	65	49	63	63	60	75	86
71259	MANGHAM	83	56	27	51	65	74	55	68	65	55	76	82	47	73	56	69	70	68	83	96
71260	MARION	75	51	25	45	58	66	49	61	59	50	69	74	42	66	51	63	63	61	75	87
71261	MER ROUGE	67	48	34	42	51	61	49	57	58	50	69	65	44	64	49	63	64	57	69	75
71263	OAK GROVE	70	48	26	43	54	63	48	58	57	49	67	69	42	64	49	61	61	58	71	80
71264	OAK RIDGE	66	49	41	43	51	62	53	58	62	54	74	65	49	67	52	66	69	59	70	73
71266	PIONEER	62	42	19	36	47	54	40	50	49	41	57	60	34	54	41	52	52	50	62	72
71268	QUITMAN	79	59	36	55	65	74	59	68	67	59	79	80	53	77	59	70	73	67	80	90
71269	RAYVILLE	65	47	32	42	51	60	49	56	57	49	67	64	44	63	49	61	62	56	67	73
71270	RUSTON	63	55	62	55	55	61	64	61	65	62	81	72	61	77	61	64	78	64	62	70
71275	SIMSBORO	68	60	46	57	61	65	57	62	59	58	72	72	54	69	57	59	69	61	64	76
71276	SONDHEIMER	69	50	29	46	55	65	52	60	60	51	71	69	46	67	52	64	64	60	73	78
71277	SPEARSVILLE	81	54	25	47	61	71	52	65	63	53	74	78	44	70	53	68	67	65	81	93
71280	STERLINGTON	92	74	52	71	79	89	74	83	81	74	97	96	69	95	74	83	91	82	92	104
71282	TALLULAH	51	39	34	36	41	49	43	46	49	43	59	52	40	55	42	52	55	47	54	57
71286	TRANSYLVANIA	65	46	25	42	51	60	48	56	55	47	65	65	41	61	48	59	59	55	68	73
	LOUISIANA	77	69	66	67	70	77	70	73	74	70	91	84	68	88	70	75	87	74	77	87
	UNITED STATES	100	100	100	100	100	100	100	100	100	100	100	100	100	100	100	100	100	100	100	100

POPULATION CHANGE

ZIP CODE			POPULATION			2000-2004 ANNUAL RATE		HOUSEHOLDS					FAMILIES		
#	POST OFFICE NAME	COUNTY FIPS CODE	2000	2004	2009	% Rate	State Centile	2000	2004	2009	% Annual Rate 2000-2004	2004 Average HH Size	2000	2004	% Annual Rate 2000-2004
71291	WEST MONROE	073	31453	32444	33661	0.7	61	12479	13018	13681	1.0	2.45	8707	9073	1.0
71292	WEST MONROE	073	20012	20607	21264	0.7	59	7509	7837	8198	1.0	2.63	5669	5924	1.0
71295	WINNSBORO	041	14406	14490	14670	0.1	34	5197	5304	5454	0.5	2.61	3810	3886	0.5
71301	ALEXANDRIA	079	24149	24450	25201	0.3	42	9291	9485	9901	0.5	2.48	5878	5988	0.4
71302	ALEXANDRIA	079	14618	14568	14892	-0.1	23	5532	5620	5848	0.4	2.56	3854	3910	0.3
71303	ALEXANDRIA	079	19132	19708	20455	0.7	60	7105	7463	7896	1.2	2.47	4976	5209	1.1
71316	ACME	029	49	47	46	-1.0	4	21	20	20	-1.1	2.35	16	16	0.0
71322	BUNKIE	009	7548	7650	7934	0.3	43	2679	2750	2892	0.6	2.71	1963	2014	0.6
71323	CENTER POINT	009	911	993	1068	2.1	88	313	349	384	2.6	2.66	247	275	2.6
71325	CHENEYVILLE	079	1405	1415	1450	0.2	35	467	482	504	0.8	2.55	337	347	0.7
71326	CLAYTON	107	1889	1892	1906	0.0	30	707	720	737	0.4	2.63	483	494	0.5
71327	COTTONPORT	009	5475	5589	5758	0.5	51	1407	1469	1555	1.0	2.60	1010	1053	1.0
71328	DEVILLE	079	6848	7548	8106	2.3	92	2449	2744	2994	2.7	2.74	2013	2250	2.7
71331	EFFIE	009	873	867	896	-0.2	21	343	346	363	0.2	2.51	266	267	0.1
71333	EVERGREEN	009	931	934	964	0.1	31	395	404	425	0.5	1.98	268	274	0.5
71334	FERRIDAY	029	9236	9545	9769	0.8	64	3517	3707	3868	1.3	2.50	2448	2581	1.3
71336	GILBERT	041	2007	1929	1914	-0.9	5	767	750	757	-0.5	2.53	569	556	-0.5
71340	HARRISONBURG	025	2618	2663	2751	0.4	47	875	908	961	0.9	2.50	657	681	0.9
71341	HESSMER	009	2959	3084	3249	1.0	70	1107	1173	1256	1.4	2.57	811	859	1.4
71342	JENA	059	6830	7010	7245	0.6	56	2621	2725	2856	0.9	2.49	1832	1903	0.9
71343	JONESVILLE	025	6775	6992	7279	0.7	62	2587	2722	2892	1.2	2.48	1911	2010	1.2
71346	LECOMPTE	079	2910	2928	3002	0.2	34	1071	1099	1147	0.6	2.64	751	769	0.6
71350	MANSURA	009	4092	4193	4361	0.6	54	1524	1584	1675	0.9	2.53	1091	1134	0.9
71351	MARKSVILLE	009	11233	11936	12676	1.4	81	4204	4542	4904	1.8	2.56	2980	3220	1.8
71353	MELVILLE	097	2606	2633	2669	0.2	39	992	1021	1052	0.7	2.58	706	726	0.7
71354	MONTEREY	029	2167	2096	2086	-0.8	6	831	811	818	-0.6	2.40	638	623	-0.6
71355	MOREAUVILLE	009	2828	3134	3399	2.5	94	1144	1286	1417	2.8	2.43	797	895	2.8
71356	MORROW	097	238	240	243	0.2	38	101	104	107	0.7	2.31	69	71	0.7
71357	NEWELLTON	107	3316	3294	3272	-0.2	21	1121	1136	1146	0.3	2.49	795	804	0.3
71358	PALMETTO	097	1004	987	991	-0.4	13	384	384	393	0.0	2.47	282	282	0.0
71360	PINEVILLE	079	38402	39222	40444	0.5	52	14151	14693	15412	0.9	2.49	10028	10408	0.9
71362	PLAUCHEVILLE	009	1982	2052	2140	0.8	66	739	778	825	1.2	2.56	528	556	1.2
71366	SAINT JOSEPH	107	1831	1811	1793	-0.3	19	683	687	692	0.1	2.61	466	468	0.1
71367	SAINT LANDRY	039	1267	1371	1458	1.9	87	469	515	556	2.2	2.66	344	377	2.2
71368	SICILY ISLAND	025	1433	1455	1502	0.4	45	578	596	625	0.7	2.44	413	426	0.7
71369	SIMMESPORT	009	3213	3251	3350	0.3	41	1097	1131	1189	0.7	2.61	782	806	0.7
71371	TROUT	059	2875	2986	3105	0.9	68	1053	1108	1167	1.2	2.48	775	816	1.2
71373	VIDALIA	029	7457	7365	7370	-0.3	17	2675	2683	2730	0.1	2.70	1980	1988	0.1
71375	WATERPROOF	107	971	937	918	-0.8	6	404	398	397	-0.4	2.35	239	234	-0.5
71378	WISNER	041	2577	2489	2472	-0.8	6	945	925	933	-0.5	2.58	678	663	-0.5
71401	AIMWELL	025	44	43	44	-0.5	11	20	20	21	0.0	2.15	16	16	0.0
71403	ANACOCO	115	4217	4191	4226	-0.2	21	1647	1682	1734	0.5	2.49	1238	1251	0.3
71404	ATLANTA	127	2261	2248	2270	-0.1	21	304	288	292	-1.3	3.86	224	212	-1.3
71406	BELMONT	085	292	321	341	2.3	91	112	125	135	2.6	2.56	82	91	2.5
71407	BENTLEY	043	973	1054	1086	1.9	87	353	387	405	2.2	2.72	283	311	2.2
71409	BOYCE	079	6265	6893	7386	2.3	92	2405	2703	2952	2.8	2.51	1777	1990	2.7
71411	CAMPTI	069	3279	3426	3583	1.0	73	1245	1319	1397	1.4	2.60	884	936	1.4
71416	CLOUTIERVILLE	069	1047	1011	1029	-0.8	6	413	405	418	-0.5	2.49	283	278	-0.4
71417	COLFAX	043	5292	5078	4956	-1.0	4	1976	1921	1899	-0.7	2.57	1429	1389	-0.7
71418	COLUMBIA	021	6453	6440	6399	-0.1	26	2532	2568	2593	0.3	2.44	1770	1794	0.3
71419	CONVERSE	085	2066	2164	2271	1.1	74	827	879	937	1.5	2.46	606	643	1.4
71422	DODSON	127	1844	1897	1941	0.7	59	690	716	741	0.9	2.61	514	533	0.9
71423	DRY PRONG	043	4218	4329	4364	0.6	56	1563	1628	1665	1.0	2.65	1208	1256	0.9
71424	ELMER	079	1509	1576	1638	1.0	72	531	565	598	1.5	2.74	413	439	1.5
71425	ENTERPRISE	025	12	12	13	0.0	29	4	4	4	0.0	3.00	3	3	0.0
71426	FISHER	085	272	294	312	1.9	86	111	121	130	2.1	2.43	82	90	2.2
71427	FLATWOODS	079	346	346	352	0.0	29	129	131	136	0.4	2.64	94	96	0.5
71429	FLORIEN	085	3333	3423	3556	0.6	57	1314	1371	1444	1.0	2.50	974	1014	1.0
71430	FOREST HILL	079	2321	2395	2473	0.7	62	837	874	915	1.0	2.74	635	660	0.9
71432	GEORGETOWN	043	1074	1093	1092	0.4	47	432	444	450	0.7	2.46	317	325	0.6
71433	GLENMORA	079	4409	4496	4634	0.5	50	1676	1734	1815	0.8	2.59	1236	1276	0.8
71435	GRAYSON	021	3845	3800	3755	-0.3	18	1323	1326	1330	0.1	2.46	978	979	0.0
71438	HINESTON	115	1005	1003	1024	-0.1	26	380	390	407	0.6	2.53	301	308	0.5
71439	HORNBECK	115	1739	1657	1656	-1.1	3	672	655	668	-0.6	2.53	496	478	-0.9
71441	KELLY	021	600	601	596	0.0	30	225	229	231	0.4	2.62	175	178	0.4
71446	LEESVILLE	115	23929	23881	24296	-0.1	26	9326	9506	9870	0.5	2.46	6408	6469	0.2
71447	LENA	079	1265	1275	1304	0.2	37	491	503	523	0.6	2.53	352	360	0.5
71449	MANY	085	9014	9097	9316	0.2	39	3561	3645	3787	0.6	2.41	2501	2562	0.6
71450	MARTHAVILLE	069	1048	1063	1094	0.3	44	419	431	451	0.7	2.47	302	311	0.7
71454	MONTGOMERY	043	2257	2246	2234	-0.1	22	914	923	931	0.2	2.43	643	647	0.2
71455	MORA	069	279	282	288	0.3	40	102	105	109	0.7	2.69	74	76	0.6
71456	NATCHEZ	069	1168	1151	1175	-0.3	16	483	484	502	0.1	2.38	337	337	0.0
71457	NATCHITOCHES	069	27365	28277	29403	0.8	64	9624	10123	10721	1.2	2.53	6214	6536	1.2
71459	LEESVILLE	115	14283	16328	17933	3.2	97	3461	4175	4759	4.5	3.24	3215	3866	4.4
71461	NEWLLANO	115	2119	1983	1971	-1.6	2	829	797	812	-0.9	2.49	577	547	-1.3
71462	NOBLE	085	1460	1555	1636	1.5	81	566	612	654	1.9	2.50	404	436	1.8
71463	OAKDALE	003	11090	11775	12827	1.4	80	3359	3733	4207	2.5	2.54	2412	2680	2.5
71465	OLLA	059	3070	3093	3179	0.2	37	1188	1210	1255	0.4	2.54	876	893	0.5
71466	OTIS	079	511	514	524	0.1	34	188	193	200	0.6	2.66	144	147	0.5
71467	POLLOCK	043	4795	6350	6294	6.8	100	1790	1800	1803	0.1	2.61	1368	1376	0.1
71468	PROVENCAL	069	487	498	515	0.5	52	206	213	223	0.8	2.34	144	149	0.8
71469	ROBELINE	069	3573	3593	3698	0.1	33	1406	1432	1494	0.4	2.51	1030	1051	0.5
71472	SIEPER	079	398	401	408	0.2	37	151	155	161	0.6	2.59	115	118	0.6
71473	SIKES	127	636	674	701	1.4	78	269	286	300	1.5	2.36	197	209	1.4
71479	TULLOS	127	1916	1943	1985	0.3	44	586	604	628	0.7	2.49	428	441	0.7
71483	WINNFIELD	127	10721	10898	11107	0.4	46	4134	4275	4427	0.8	2.42	2905	3005	0.8
71485	WOODWORTH	079	1655	1818	1942	2.2	91	598	671	729	2.8	2.71	466	522	2.7
71486	ZWOLLE	085	4814	4852	4957	0.2	37	1878	1915	1981	0.5	2.52	1312	1334	0.4
	LOUISIANA					0.7					0.9	2.59			1.0
	UNITED STATES					1.2					1.3	2.58			1.1

POPULATION COMPOSITION

LOUISIANA

71291-71486 B

ZIP CODE #	POST OFFICE NAME	RACE (%) White 2000	White 2004	Black 2000	Black 2004	Asian/Pacific 2000	Asian/Pacific 2004	% Hispanic Origin 2000	% Hispanic Origin 2004	2004 AGE DISTRIBUTION (%) 0-4	5-9	10-14	15-19	20-24	25-44	45-64	65-84	85+	18+	MEDIAN AGE 2004	% 2004 Males	% 2004 Females
71291	WEST MONROE	90.0	88.8	8.3	9.2	0.4	0.5	1.2	1.3	7.2	6.9	7.1	6.7	7.0	29.1	22.5	11.8	1.8	74.9	35.5	47.2	52.9
71292	WEST MONROE	88.3	87.0	10.1	11.2	0.3	0.4	1.5	1.7	7.1	7.1	7.2	7.0	6.8	29.1	24.2	10.7	0.9	74.5	35.7	49.2	50.8
71295	WINNSBORO	64.7	63.5	34.1	35.2	0.3	0.3	0.6	0.6	7.5	7.3	7.4	7.3	6.9	25.7	22.8	13.0	2.3	73.4	36.0	48.4	51.6
71301	ALEXANDRIA	45.9	43.2	51.1	53.4	1.4	1.7	1.2	1.3	7.4	7.2	7.8	7.3	7.7	25.8	22.1	12.2	2.5	73.1	35.4	45.9	54.1
71302	ALEXANDRIA	20.5	19.4	78.1	79.2	0.4	0.5	0.5	0.5	7.2	7.2	7.9	7.4	7.2	24.1	24.8	12.8	1.5	73.0	36.6	46.1	54.0
71303	ALEXANDRIA	69.5	66.8	27.4	29.6	1.4	1.8	1.3	1.4	7.7	7.2	7.4	6.8	6.8	27.4	22.6	12.5	1.8	73.5	35.9	47.3	52.7
71316	ACME	93.9	93.6	4.1	4.3	0.0	0.0	0.0	0.0	6.4	6.4	8.5	8.5	6.4	25.5	21.3	14.9	2.1	78.7	38.1	51.1	48.9
71322	BUNKIE	57.7	55.7	41.0	42.9	0.2	0.3	1.5	1.7	7.9	7.7	8.1	7.4	6.9	25.0	22.4	12.3	2.3	71.8	35.5	47.9	52.1
71323	CENTER POINT	96.5	96.0	2.2	2.5	0.0	0.0	0.6	0.5	5.9	6.0	6.3	4.9	6.6	27.6	27.4	12.9	2.3	78.5	39.6	48.9	51.1
71325	CHENEYVILLE	51.6	48.9	46.6	49.3	0.0	0.0	2.3	2.3	5.9	6.0	6.2	8.5	6.7	27.4	25.4	11.9	2.0	76.3	37.3	49.7	50.3
71326	CLAYTON	43.6	41.8	55.5	57.2	0.0	0.0	0.7	0.8	8.4	8.3	8.4	7.5	6.7	22.8	24.2	12.0	2.0	70.4	35.1	47.7	52.3
71327	COTTONPORT	51.4	49.0	47.3	49.6	0.1	0.1	0.7	0.7	5.8	5.6	5.7	6.2	9.3	38.1	20.5	7.6	1.3	79.3	33.9	60.3	39.7
71328	DEVILLE	97.3	96.9	0.5	0.6	0.2	0.3	0.7	0.8	7.4	7.6	7.7	7.5	6.7	29.7	24.0	8.8	0.7	72.5	35.1	49.6	50.4
71331	EFFIE	97.9	97.6	0.8	0.8	0.2	0.2	0.9	1.0	7.7	8.0	7.3	5.7	5.7	28.0	24.9	11.9	0.9	73.6	37.1	49.7	50.3
71333	EVERGREEN	68.6	66.3	29.9	32.0	0.4	0.5	1.3	1.4	4.5	6.1	6.0	7.2	6.9	31.5	24.1	12.2	1.6	79.3	37.5	56.6	43.4
71334	FERRIDAY	47.9	46.5	50.9	52.2	0.2	0.2	0.9	1.0	8.0	7.3	7.1	6.6	6.7	22.3	25.6	14.5	2.1	73.5	38.9	47.4	52.6
71336	GILBERT	77.3	75.3	21.2	23.1	0.0	0.0	1.2	1.4	6.2	6.3	7.1	7.6	6.3	25.8	25.2	14.0	1.7	75.6	39.0	49.0	51.0
71340	HARRISONBURG	79.9	78.4	18.8	20.2	0.4	0.5	0.7	0.8	5.1	5.1	5.4	6.7	9.2	29.7	25.9	11.9	1.0	80.7	37.1	57.3	42.7
71341	HESSMER	93.9	93.3	4.5	4.9	0.0	0.0	1.3	1.5	7.7	7.3	6.9	6.5	5.9	29.3	22.7	11.7	2.0	74.1	36.1	49.0	51.0
71342	JENA	84.4	83.5	13.8	14.5	0.3	0.3	0.9	1.0	6.5	6.6	7.0	7.4	6.0	24.3	25.5	14.5	2.2	75.1	39.1	47.3	52.7
71343	JONESVILLE	70.1	69.2	28.6	29.4	0.1	0.1	1.4	1.5	6.9	6.9	7.2	6.3	7.0	26.4	24.6	12.8	2.0	75.2	37.5	49.7	50.3
71346	LECOMPTE	55.1	52.9	42.9	44.8	0.2	0.2	2.0	2.2	7.5	7.6	7.1	7.1	7.0	25.5	24.2	12.3	1.9	73.8	36.5	47.4	52.6
71350	MANSURA	60.7	58.2	37.3	39.6	0.1	0.1	0.8	0.7	6.6	6.5	7.3	7.4	6.8	26.1	22.4	13.7	3.3	74.9	37.8	48.2	51.9
71351	MARKSVILLE	67.9	66.9	28.4	29.2	0.2	0.3	0.8	0.9	6.9	6.9	7.7	7.3	6.9	26.7	24.2	11.9	1.5	74.1	36.3	47.2	52.8
71353	MELVILLE	70.6	69.6	28.1	28.9	0.5	0.5	1.2	1.2	8.6	8.2	7.9	6.8	6.5	25.2	23.2	12.3	1.4	71.2	34.8	48.0	52.0
71354	MONTEREY	86.1	85.1	11.2	11.8	0.2	0.2	2.8	3.1	6.8	6.5	6.3	6.6	7.1	28.0	25.3	12.0	1.4	76.3	38.0	53.6	46.4
71355	MOREAUVILLE	80.3	79.0	18.0	19.2	0.1	0.1	1.1	1.2	7.1	7.2	7.4	6.4	6.1	25.0	25.4	13.8	1.8	74.6	38.4	48.8	51.2
71356	MORROW	72.3	70.8	25.6	27.5	0.4	0.4	0.8	0.8	7.9	7.1	7.5	6.7	5.8	25.0	22.9	14.6	2.5	73.3	38.4	47.9	52.1
71357	NEWELLTON	53.3	52.7	45.7	46.2	0.2	0.2	1.8	1.8	5.1	5.8	6.1	7.9	8.0	26.6	25.2	13.0	2.2	78.4	38.1	54.1	45.9
71358	PALMETTO	45.4	44.4	53.1	54.1	0.2	0.2	0.7	0.8	7.1	7.2	7.0	6.7	5.8	25.2	23.0	15.2	2.8	74.3	38.4	50.3	49.8
71360	PINEVILLE	83.9	82.1	13.0	14.3	1.0	1.2	1.3	1.4	6.8	6.5	6.9	6.9	7.7	28.0	24.5	11.4	1.3	75.8	36.4	49.1	50.9
71362	PLAUCHEVILLE	93.2	92.5	5.7	6.2	0.4	0.5	1.1	1.2	7.4	6.9	6.5	6.3	6.2	27.0	23.1	14.2	2.4	75.2	37.9	49.7	50.3
71366	SAINT JOSEPH	35.4	34.5	63.0	63.8	0.2	0.2	0.7	0.7	8.9	7.8	7.3	7.6	7.8	23.9	23.3	11.4	2.0	71.6	35.6	46.3	53.7
71367	SAINT LANDRY	91.5	90.7	6.6	7.4	0.1	0.1	1.3	1.5	7.9	7.4	6.6	6.6	7.0	27.9	24.4	10.9	1.5	74.3	35.9	51.6	48.4
71368	SICILY ISLAND	64.8	62.3	33.7	36.0	0.0	0.0	1.7	2.0	7.3	7.3	8.3	7.3	6.3	23.4	24.5	14.0	1.7	72.8	37.9	47.9	52.1
71369	SIMMESPORT	58.8	56.0	40.2	42.8	0.2	0.2	0.8	0.9	8.2	7.8	7.5	7.4	7.4	27.8	21.7	10.8	1.5	71.9	34.4	43.7	56.3
71371	TROUT	87.4	86.6	11.0	11.6	0.0	0.0	0.6	0.7	6.1	6.1	7.0	10.7	6.6	24.7	24.9	11.7	2.3	73.3	37.1	51.5	48.5
71373	VIDALIA	72.4	71.5	26.2	26.9	0.3	0.4	1.4	1.6	6.6	6.8	7.9	7.5	7.2	25.5	25.1	12.2	1.2	74.2	37.2	49.2	50.8
71375	WATERPROOF	23.2	22.5	76.1	76.7	0.0	0.0	0.8	0.8	6.7	6.6	6.2	8.5	7.7	18.0	29.4	13.6	3.3	75.4	41.9	44.9	55.1
71378	WISNER	60.6	57.1	38.1	41.4	0.0	0.0	1.3	1.5	8.2	7.9	7.5	7.2	6.2	22.9	22.7	15.3	2.3	71.9	37.7	46.6	53.4
71401	AIMWELL	97.7	97.7	2.3	2.3	0.0	0.0	0.0	0.0	4.7	4.7	4.7	7.0	9.3	23.3	32.6	14.0	0.0	86.1	42.5	53.5	46.5
71403	ANACOCO	94.8	94.4	0.6	0.6	0.4	0.5	1.5	1.5	6.6	6.8	7.5	6.4	5.6	26.8	26.3	12.7	1.2	75.0	38.6	49.5	50.5
71404	ATLANTA	49.4	46.0	49.4	52.6	0.2	0.3	0.4	0.3	2.7	3.0	3.3	4.1	11.3	46.5	21.0	7.2	0.9	88.8	35.4	74.9	25.1
71406	BELMONT	83.6	81.6	10.3	11.5	0.0	0.0	1.7	1.9	7.8	7.8	7.8	5.9	6.2	28.4	22.4	11.8	1.9	72.9	35.9	49.8	50.2
71407	BENTLEY	96.5	95.7	0.3	0.5	0.2	0.3	1.4	1.7	7.5	7.8	8.8	7.3	5.9	28.6	23.0	10.1	1.1	71.3	34.3	51.1	48.9
71409	BOYCE	75.1	73.3	21.6	22.8	0.2	0.3	1.3	1.5	7.4	7.7	7.5	7.1	6.7	27.1	25.3	10.4	0.8	73.1	35.9	48.5	51.5
71411	CAMPTI	65.5	64.5	33.6	34.5	0.0	0.0	1.3	1.3	8.5	8.4	9.1	8.0	6.2	26.2	22.3	10.1	1.3	68.9	33.0	48.2	51.8
71416	CLOUTIERVILLE	57.3	55.3	28.8	30.2	0.1	0.1	2.8	3.0	6.4	6.4	6.6	6.8	6.7	25.3	23.8	15.2	2.6	76.3	40.0	49.2	50.8
71417	COLFAX	60.9	56.3	36.9	41.5	0.2	0.2	0.8	0.9	7.2	7.4	7.7	7.0	6.2	25.5	24.5	12.5	2.0	73.3	37.0	48.2	51.9
71418	COLUMBIA	80.8	80.5	17.7	18.0	0.1	0.1	1.6	1.6	6.5	6.8	7.1	6.4	5.8	25.6	25.9	14.2	1.9	75.7	39.3	48.5	51.5
71419	CONVERSE	84.7	83.4	6.9	7.2	0.0	0.0	2.7	3.0	5.1	5.6	7.7	7.4	5.6	23.8	27.6	15.6	1.6	77.0	41.6	50.2	49.8
71422	DODSON	86.0	84.9	12.5	13.3	0.4	0.5	1.4	1.7	6.5	6.5	6.6	7.5	6.6	26.2	27.1	11.5	1.4	75.0	37.7	49.9	50.1
71423	DRY PRONG	95.3	94.5	0.9	1.2	0.4	0.4	1.4	1.5	7.9	7.8	7.7	6.7	6.1	27.7	24.7	10.4	1.1	72.3	35.7	50.2	49.8
71424	ELMER	96.6	96.1	1.5	1.7	0.1	0.1	1.2	1.4	7.6	7.4	7.3	6.4	6.2	28.1	24.5	10.8	1.7	73.7	37.1	48.6	51.4
71425	ENTERPRISE	91.7	100.0	0.0	0.0	0.0	0.0	0.0	0.0	0.0	0.0	16.7	16.7	16.7	8.3	41.7	0.0	0.0	83.3	25.0	75.0	25.0
71426	FISHER	76.1	73.8	20.6	23.1	0.0	0.0	0.7	1.0	6.1	6.1	6.8	7.5	6.8	24.5	27.2	12.9	2.0	76.5	39.7	49.3	50.7
71427	FLATWOODS	74.3	71.1	14.7	17.1	0.3	0.3	0.6	0.3	6.7	6.1	6.9	7.8	7.5	26.9	24.9	12.4	0.9	75.4	38.1	50.0	50.0
71429	FLORIEN	84.5	82.9	13.4	14.8	0.0	0.1	0.8	0.9	5.9	5.8	6.5	7.1	6.2	23.6	27.8	15.3	1.8	77.5	41.5	49.3	50.7
71430	FOREST HILL	85.8	83.8	4.2	4.9	1.9	2.3	10.3	11.5	7.1	7.1	7.1	6.8	6.6	27.8	25.5	10.9	1.2	74.6	36.6	50.2	49.8
71432	GEORGETOWN	99.4	99.2	0.3	0.4	0.0	0.0	0.9	1.0	7.3	7.1	7.0	6.1	6.5	27.1	24.6	12.3	1.9	74.8	37.1	48.2	51.8
71433	GLENMORA	82.9	81.6	13.0	14.0	0.4	0.5	2.3	2.7	7.3	7.0	7.5	7.3	7.1	25.9	23.8	12.5	1.6	73.8	36.4	48.8	51.2
71435	GRAYSON	78.4	77.9	19.8	20.2	0.1	0.1	1.4	1.4	5.5	5.9	6.6	6.6	8.4	32.3	23.0	10.2	1.5	78.3	35.5	55.1	45.0
71438	HINESTON	95.7	95.4	0.2	0.2	0.1	0.1	0.9	0.9	8.1	7.7	6.5	6.0	6.7	27.2	25.0	11.1	1.8	74.0	36.2	49.6	50.5
71439	HORNBECK	93.6	93.1	2.2	2.3	0.5	0.5	1.1	1.2	6.6	6.8	7.2	6.1	6.5	26.7	26.0	12.6	1.6	75.7	37.9	48.9	51.1
71441	KELLY	94.0	93.8	4.5	4.7	0.2	0.2	1.0	1.0	6.8	7.7	8.0	6.3	5.2	30.3	25.1	9.7	1.0	73.5	36.2	52.3	47.8
71446	LEESVILLE	74.7	73.4	17.3	17.7	1.9	2.2	4.3	4.7	8.1	7.2	6.7	6.9	8.7	28.4	23.1	10.0	1.1	74.0	33.2	50.5	49.5
71447	LENA	75.4	73.2	14.1	15.6	0.2	0.2	1.1	1.2	6.5	6.3	7.0	7.5	6.8	26.5	24.6	13.7	1.3	75.7	38.7	50.0	50.0
71449	MANY	72.5	71.2	22.6	23.4	0.3	0.3	1.8	2.0	6.6	6.4	6.6	6.3	6.6	23.7	25.7	15.7	2.3	76.6	40.2	48.8	51.2
71450	MARTHAVILLE	79.2	77.5	15.1	16.2	0.2	0.2	1.8	2.0	7.3	7.2	6.9	6.5	6.3	25.6	25.9	12.9	1.4	74.5	38.0	49.6	50.4
71454	MONTGOMERY	84.1	78.8	13.3	18.3	0.0	0.0	1.2	1.3	6.5	6.9	7.1	6.5	6.1	26.6	25.4	13.5	1.5	75.4	38.5	50.7	49.3
71455	MORA	77.1	74.5	12.9	14.5	0.4	0.4	0.7	1.1	6.4	6.4	7.1	7.5	7.1	25.9	25.2	13.5	1.1	75.9	38.3	49.3	50.7
71456	NATCHEZ	47.9	45.3	43.2	45.4	0.1	0.2	1.8	1.9	6.4	6.3	7.6	7.4	7.7	27.1	25.6	10.5	1.3	75.2	36.9	50.7	49.4
71457	NATCHITOCHES	51.1	49.6	45.5	46.7	0.6	0.8	1.4	1.5	7.2	6.3	6.6	11.7	13.6	24.0	19.6	9.4	1.6	75.9	28.2	47.4	52.6
71459	LEESVILLE	59.7	58.5	26.2	26.3	2.7	3.1	11.8	12.3	14.8	10.0	6.5	7.0	22.8	37.2	1.7	0.1	0.0	66.6	22.6	57.6	42.4
71461	NEWLLANO	48.6	47.7	38.2	37.9	4.1	4.8	8.2	8.5	7.1	7.5	8.6	7.8	7.7	32.1	23.0	6.2	0.2	71.8	31.9	50.5	49.5
71462	NOBLE	64.2	62.1	3.0	3.1	0.1	0.1	5.3	5.9	7.7	7.0	6.3	7.0	6.4	25.3	23.7	14.7	2.1	74.5	38.3	49.8	50.2
71463	OAKDALE	70.6	69.6	26.7	27.3	0.9	1.1	9.2	10.1	6.4	6.3	6.6	6.1	7.3	33.8	21.6	10.7	1.3	77.1	35.3	57.0	43.0
71465	OLLA	94.2	93.5	4.5	4.9	0.2	0.3	0.8	0.9	6.8	6.8	7.7	7.2	7.0	27.2	23.5	12.3	1.5	74.2	36.6	48.6	51.4
71466	OTIS	96.7	96.3	1.2	1.4	0.0	0.0	1.0	1.0	7.6	7.2	7.6	6.8	6.2	29.4	23.9	10.3	1.0	73.5	36.0	49.4	50.6
71467	POLLOCK	97.0	96.4	0.5	0.8	0.2	0.2	1.3	1.5	5.9	5.9	5.9	6.1	8.7	36.6	21.8	8.0	1.1	78.2	34.6	61.1	38.9
71468	PROVENCAL	89.1	88.0	6.6	7.0	0.0	0.0	1.0	1.0	5.8	6.4	6.8	5.8	5.4	24.7	26.9	16.1	2.0	77.3	41.3	48.8	51.2
71469	ROBELINE	84.7	83.5	11.7	12.4	0.1	0.1	1.5	1.7	7.5	7.4	6.7	6.2	6.2	26.5	25.0	12.9	1.5	74.6	37.1	48.9	51.1
71472	SIEPER	96.7	96.3	1.3	1.5	0.0	0.0	1.0	1.0	7.5	7.2	7.5	6.7	6.5	29.4	23.9	10.2	1.0	73.6	36.0	49.6	50.4
71473	SIKES	94.8	94.2	3.5	3.9	0.0	0.0	1.3	1.3	6.5	6.5	5.9	6.1	6.7	27.2	27.2	12.3	1.6	77.2	39.0	50.7	49.3
71479	TULLOS	79.8	78.4	18.5	19.6	0.1	0.1	1.0	1.2	4.6	4.7	5.2	5.4	10.6	36.1	22.1	10.3	1.1	82.6	35.6	61.1	38.9
71483	WINNFIELD	63.1	61.7	35.1	36.4	0.2	0.2	0.8	0.9	7.1	7.0	7.4	7.3	6.7	25.6	24.0	12.6	2.3	74.0	37.0	48.9	51.1
71485	WOODWORTH	87.6	85.5	10.2	12.0	0.1	0.1	2.1	2.3	8.4	7.9	6.8	6.5	7.4	28.9	24.0	9.5	0.7	73.2	34.8	50.5	49.5
71486	ZWOLLE	56.9	54.6	19.0	19.4	0.3	0.3	5.6	6.1	7.8	7.7	7.0	7.2	6.5	24.3	24.2	14.0	1.4	72.8	37.5	49.1	50.9
	LOUISIANA	63.9	62.8	32.5	33.2	1.3	1.5	2.4	2.6	7.2	7.0	7.4	7.5	7.9	28.0	23.4	10.3	1.4	74.1	34.6	48.5	51.5
	UNITED STATES	75.1	73.6	12.3	12.5	3.8	4.2	12.5	14.1	6.9	6.7	7.2	7.0	7.3	28.6	23.8	10.8	1.7	75.1	36.0	49.1	50.9

INCOME

#	POST OFFICE NAME	2004 Per Capita Income	2004 HH Income Base	2004 HOUSEHOLD INCOME DISTRIBUTION (%) Less than $25,000	$25,000 to $49,999	$50,000 to $99,999	$100,000 to $149,999	$150,000 or More	MEDIAN HOUSEHOLD INCOME 2004	2009	2004 National Centile	2004 State Centile	2004 Home Value Base	2004 HOME VALUE DISTRIBUTION (%) Less than $50,000	$50,000 to $89,999	$90,000 to $174,999	$175,000 to $399,999	$400,000 or More	2004 Median Home Value
71291	WEST MONROE	22958	13018	29.3	27.1	30.3	9.8	3.6	43720	50525	58	85	9071	16.0	22.1	42.9	17.3	1.6	105776
71292	WEST MONROE	18359	7837	33.8	33.1	24.9	5.7	2.4	34818	40939	27	56	6168	37.6	28.7	24.0	9.2	0.6	65753
71295	WINNSBORO	14092	5304	49.6	31.9	14.5	2.5	1.6	25232	28026	5	14	3914	48.1	27.4	19.3	5.1	0.2	52452
71301	ALEXANDRIA	17074	9485	47.8	27.6	17.5	4.1	3.1	26314	29732	6	17	5155	25.6	34.3	29.1	8.3	2.7	78602
71302	ALEXANDRIA	13989	5620	49.1	29.0	16.8	4.0	1.1	25514	29002	5	14	3546	33.8	39.5	22.3	3.9	0.7	63085
71303	ALEXANDRIA	25143	7463	30.5	29.4	25.7	7.9	6.7	40018	45988	46	76	4767	9.3	21.7	41.6	24.0	3.4	121405
71316	ACME	17231	20	25.0	40.0	30.0	5.0	0.0	37292	40000	36	68	17	41.2	35.3	11.8	11.8	0.0	65000
71322	BUNKIE	13336	2750	51.0	25.2	18.8	3.6	1.4	23974	26484	4	10	1819	39.5	27.1	27.7	3.9	1.9	62425
71323	CENTER POINT	16321	349	27.5	40.7	26.1	3.4	2.3	35770	42583	31	60	315	46.7	28.6	16.2	8.6	0.0	58750
71325	CHENEYVILLE	13461	482	52.9	25.5	17.2	2.9	1.5	23068	26482	3	8	356	45.8	28.1	16.3	9.8	0.0	56250
71326	CLAYTON	11162	720	63.3	22.2	10.4	2.6	1.4	17486	19708	1	3	536	58.8	26.1	9.9	3.2	2.1	41455
71327	COTTONPORT	13099	1469	48.7	28.7	16.6	4.5	1.5	25634	28489	5	15	1031	33.6	33.1	27.2	6.0	0.2	68150
71328	DEVILLE	18356	2744	28.7	30.3	31.2	7.8	2.0	41024	46951	50	78	2440	24.7	27.2	33.3	14.3	0.5	87552
71331	EFFIE	14866	346	40.8	33.8	21.1	2.3	2.0	29820	34090	12	34	287	45.0	17.4	31.4	5.2	1.1	64474
71333	EVERGREEN	18531	404	45.1	31.9	17.3	4.0	1.7	29059	32087	10	30	291	38.8	34.0	20.6	5.2	1.4	59559
71334	FERRIDAY	12958	3707	56.2	25.2	14.6	2.5	1.6	21178	23864	2	5	2578	51.4	25.9	14.7	7.1	0.9	48796
71336	GILBERT	15008	750	47.2	31.2	17.6	2.3	1.7	26998	29711	7	19	605	50.3	33.4	13.6	2.8	0.0	49786
71340	HARRISONBURG	14309	908	46.8	27.4	20.7	4.1	1.0	27263	31045	8	21	771	46.4	26.5	22.3	4.2	0.7	57051
71341	HESSMER	13220	1173	48.3	32.6	14.9	3.6	0.6	25860	29079	6	16	933	33.2	33.1	28.5	5.1	0.0	66371
71342	JENA	15994	2725	41.8	28.0	24.3	4.9	1.0	31122	34901	15	41	2166	39.4	31.9	22.6	5.5	0.7	61154
71343	JONESVILLE	15105	2722	48.7	31.2	14.2	4.1	1.8	25705	29343	5	15	2243	52.2	25.2	17.4	4.1	1.1	47770
71346	LECOMPTE	16544	1099	46.0	25.1	21.8	4.6	2.5	28543	32353	10	27	767	33.5	29.2	22.6	13.7	1.0	72578
71350	MANSURA	14505	1584	46.5	27.5	21.8	3.0	1.1	27347	30711	8	22	1129	31.2	31.3	32.5	5.1	0.0	73869
71351	MARKSVILLE	14792	4542	49.0	28.0	17.5	3.1	2.5	25536	28281	5	15	3367	34.7	36.0	22.5	5.8	1.1	65144
71353	MELVILLE	12477	1021	50.6	27.6	20.0	1.6	0.2	24530	27798	4	12	753	52.6	27.8	17.0	2.7	0.0	47622
71354	MONTEREY	16107	811	36.0	33.3	25.8	4.7	0.3	33557	38280	23	51	682	45.0	24.9	22.7	7.3	0.0	65333
71355	MOREAUVILLE	16691	1286	42.2	27.5	25.8	3.0	1.6	30810	34593	14	39	1008	35.5	30.3	30.1	3.5	0.7	72791
71356	MORROW	15317	104	50.0	29.8	16.4	2.9	1.0	25000	29704	5	13	78	42.3	39.7	15.4	2.6	0.0	54000
71357	NEWELLTON	16188	1136	46.7	30.6	13.3	5.9	3.5	27337	31073	8	21	835	35.0	26.0	22.4	12.8	3.8	69224
71358	PALMETTO	12946	384	52.9	24.2	19.5	2.9	0.5	22943	26687	3	8	300	44.3	35.3	13.3	7.0	0.0	53953
71360	PINEVILLE	19607	14693	34.1	30.3	25.7	6.9	3.0	36462	42028	33	63	10781	23.6	29.4	36.1	9.8	1.2	86292
71362	PLAUCHEVILLE	15535	778	44.9	26.0	23.4	3.6	2.2	28963	33411	10	30	633	41.6	33.0	20.4	5.1	0.0	58492
71366	SAINT JOSEPH	12126	687	56.2	28.0	11.9	2.5	1.5	20911	23959	2	5	425	60.2	24.5	9.4	3.5	2.4	42232
71367	SAINT LANDRY	15619	515	37.1	30.9	25.1	5.8	1.2	33748	39361	23	53	432	37.5	29.9	21.8	9.5	1.4	69000
71368	SICILY ISLAND	15198	596	57.4	19.6	16.1	4.5	2.4	19901	22162	2	4	470	54.0	24.3	16.2	5.5	0.0	43667
71369	SIMMESPORT	11866	1131	58.0	23.7	13.5	3.4	1.4	20467	23441	2	4	813	47.9	26.9	18.7	6.3	0.3	52778
71371	TROUT	16146	1108	39.5	29.2	24.1	5.3	1.8	31635	35439	17	44	949	47.3	27.3	21.6	3.5	0.3	54048
71373	VIDALIA	14408	2683	43.6	29.5	22.3	2.9	1.7	29983	33816	12	35	2009	29.4	42.7	24.6	2.8	0.6	68402
71375	WATERPROOF	18436	398	66.1	17.3	6.0	6.8	3.8	15000	16940	1	1	239	69.0	23.4	5.0	0.0	2.5	32375
71378	WISNER	14063	925	54.2	27.8	14.0	2.2	2.0	22508	25216	3	7	717	44.6	33.9	17.6	3.9	0.0	55203
71401	AIMWELL	14471	20	50.0	35.0	15.0	0.0	0.0	25000	31091	5	13	18	66.7	22.2	11.1	0.0	0.0	37500
71403	ANACOCO	17693	1682	33.3	33.2	28.1	4.2	1.2	37542	41884	38	69	1467	36.6	26.5	32.4	4.0	0.6	68705
71404	ATLANTA	10687	288	40.3	34.4	20.1	2.8	2.4	29794	33309	12	33	236	53.0	22.9	22.0	2.1	0.0	45625
71406	BELMONT	15550	125	30.4	40.0	25.6	4.0	0.0	35970	40849	31	61	111	60.4	22.5	5.4	11.7	0.0	38438
71407	BENTLEY	16335	387	38.2	24.6	30.8	5.4	1.0	35533	39122	30	59	322	27.0	28.9	33.5	10.6	0.0	77222
71409	BOYCE	18177	2703	36.1	30.2	27.6	4.4	1.6	35882	40552	31	61	2147	33.0	24.5	29.9	11.6	1.1	79957
71411	CAMPTI	12521	1319	49.6	29.0	18.5	2.7	0.2	25212	28890	5	13	996	48.7	26.9	16.6	6.9	0.9	52500
71416	CLOUTIERVILLE	15926	405	46.4	31.6	14.8	4.4	2.7	28688	33287	10	27	309	45.6	29.5	16.8	8.1	0.0	59000
71417	COLFAX	14192	1921	47.6	28.6	18.6	4.0	1.2	26807	30500	7	19	1459	44.6	28.9	19.2	6.2	1.2	56382
71418	COLUMBIA	16282	2568	43.9	28.2	22.1	4.2	1.6	29499	33105	11	32	1946	40.7	30.9	21.8	6.1	0.6	62739
71419	CONVERSE	16084	879	44.9	27.9	21.3	4.9	1.0	29183	32513	11	31	734	45.5	34.5	16.9	3.1	0.0	55238
71422	DODSON	15333	716	39.5	33.0	20.8	5.0	1.7	30908	34115	15	40	582	55.2	22.3	18.2	4.1	0.2	44643
71423	DRY PRONG	18539	1628	33.4	33.3	24.8	6.4	2.2	36883	41529	35	66	1398	33.2	27.0	29.8	9.3	0.6	76436
71424	ELMER	18569	565	34.5	30.8	24.6	6.4	3.7	37468	43070	37	69	495	26.9	28.7	29.1	12.3	3.0	82763
71425	ENTERPRISE	10376	4	50.0	0.0	50.0	0.0	0.0	37500	5000	37	69	4	50.0	0.0	50.0	0.0	0.0	55000
71426	FISHER	17669	121	39.7	32.2	19.0	7.4	1.7	31240	35000	16	42	102	52.0	18.6	24.5	4.9	0.0	47500
71427	FLATWOODS	13461	131	38.9	43.5	13.7	3.1	0.8	29437	34581	11	32	107	43.9	29.9	20.6	5.6	0.0	63125
71429	FLORIEN	19122	1371	39.5	34.6	18.9	4.5	2.6	31242	35435	16	42	1169	39.9	28.0	26.4	5.5	0.3	63315
71430	FOREST HILL	17378	874	34.3	28.5	27.9	7.1	2.2	38506	44206	41	72	704	29.1	34.0	21.9	14.4	0.7	73714
71432	GEORGETOWN	18320	444	40.5	28.8	21.4	7.9	1.4	32949	36661	21	49	357	51.5	21.9	22.7	3.9	0.0	48281
71433	GLENMORA	15002	1734	47.0	27.7	19.6	4.3	1.3	27108	30521	7	20	1380	44.5	28.5	19.4	6.1	1.5	56667
71435	GRAYSON	16132	1326	40.4	30.6	23.1	3.9	2.0	32152	35840	18	46	1092	50.0	24.5	20.0	5.6	0.0	50000
71438	HINESTON	15404	390	39.0	33.3	22.6	3.6	1.5	30000	34021	12	35	357	35.9	30.5	28.6	2.0	3.1	66167
71439	HORNBECK	15465	655	35.7	34.2	27.2	2.6	0.3	35184	39189	28	57	567	43.4	21.7	29.8	4.2	0.9	60429
71441	KELLY	20013	229	35.8	28.8	29.3	3.1	3.1	36224	41976	32	63	196	46.4	24.0	21.9	7.7	0.0	54118
71446	LEESVILLE	16827	9506	37.4	33.9	22.8	4.2	1.7	32129	35474	18	46	6172	34.6	28.3	29.3	6.9	0.8	71453
71447	LENA	14613	503	38.2	41.8	15.7	3.2	1.2	30907	35444	15	39	411	45.3	28.2	20.0	6.6	0.0	60806
71449	MANY	17804	3645	44.7	29.3	19.3	4.3	2.5	28132	31927	9	24	2697	38.2	25.2	25.3	10.2	1.2	68267
71450	MARTHAVILLE	20375	431	39.2	28.3	26.5	3.5	2.6	33226	37973	22	50	366	45.1	23.5	17.5	10.9	3.0	63333
71454	MONTGOMERY	17742	923	42.5	30.1	21.2	3.6	2.6	30603	33586	14	38	758	49.3	28.1	20.7	1.6	0.3	50820
71455	MORA	13598	105	37.1	43.8	15.2	3.8	0.0	30980	34709	15	40	86	47.7	27.9	18.6	5.8	0.0	55000
71456	NATCHEZ	17345	484	46.9	29.8	16.3	3.1	3.9	27398	31523	8	22	370	35.4	23.5	27.8	10.5	2.7	74583
71457	NATCHITOCHES	16390	10123	45.3	27.6	19.1	5.0	2.9	28392	32594	9	26	5975	26.3	25.1	34.6	12.6	1.5	88041
71459	LEESVILLE	12438	4175	25.8	49.0	22.7	1.9	0.7	35595	38780	30	59	129	60.5	18.6	10.9	10.1	0.0	42500
71461	NEWLLANO	18658	797	33.3	31.5	27.4	6.7	1.3	38440	41651	41	72	416	29.6	41.4	27.6	1.4	0.0	66154
71462	NOBLE	15992	612	38.7	33.2	22.7	3.4	2.0	31672	36072	17	44	538	53.5	25.3	16.7	4.3	0.2	45682
71463	OAKDALE	13454	3733	47.9	30.2	16.3	4.0	1.6	26356	30584	6	18	2614	39.6	29.7	25.7	4.5	0.5	62434
71465	OLLA	18381	1210	40.1	32.2	21.3	4.4	2.0	32978	36876	21	50	972	52.2	25.0	16.8	5.9	0.2	47921
71466	OTIS	15965	193	34.7	33.7	26.4	5.2	0.0	35756	40572	31	60	161	37.9	31.1	22.4	8.7	0.0	68125
71467	POLLOCK	15355	1800	35.0	32.2	25.6	5.8	1.3	35167	39424	28	57	1470	38.3	25.9	24.8	10.1	0.8	69412
71468	PROVENCAL	16700	213	37.6	37.6	20.2	2.8	1.9	33343	38126	22	51	181	48.1	24.3	21.0	6.6	0.0	53182
71469	ROBELINE	18992	1432	39.7	31.0	22.9	4.1	2.3	32059	36819	18	45	1174	43.8	24.9	22.7	7.8	0.9	59733
71472	SIEPER	16436	155	34.2	34.2	26.5	5.2	0.0	35979	41161	31	62	129	37.2	31.8	23.3	7.8	0.0	67857
71473	SIKES	17260	286	37.1	33.9	23.1	4.6	1.4	33343	36435	22	51	244	57.4	20.9	11.9	7.0	2.9	41818
71479	TULLOS	14154	604	40.1	34.8	20.7	4.0	0.5	31057	35110	15	40	497	66.4	19.9	10.1	2.2	1.4	35985
71483	WINNFIELD	14508	4275	48.4	29.6	16.8	4.0	1.3	26073	29308	6	16	2998	50.5	25.6	17.4	5.9	0.6	49455
71485	WOODWORTH	21184	671	24.7	30.7	31.0	8.9	4.6	46012	52068	64	88	563	16.0	33.2	29.5	19.4	2.0	91125
71486	ZWOLLE	16928	1915	43.6	29.1	21.2	4.0	2.1	29212	32829	11	31	1544	50.3	24.8	20.0	4.5	0.4	49643
	LOUISIANA	19601		35.3	28.5	25.7	7.1	3.5	36550	42223				22.5	24.5	35.6	15.0	2.4	94005
	UNITED STATES	25866		24.7	27.1	30.8	10.9	6.5	48124	56710				10.9	15.0	33.7	30.1	10.4	145905

SPENDING POTENTIAL INDICES

LOUISIANA
71291-71486 D

#	POST OFFICE NAME	Auto Loan	Home Loan	Invest-ments	Retire-ment Plans	Home Repair	Lawn & Garden	Comput-ers & Hard-ware	Major Appli-ances	TV, Radio, Sound Equip-ment	Furni-ture	Dine out/Carry out	Sports Equip-ment	Fees & Tickets	Toys & Games	Travel	Cable TV	Apparel & Services	Auto Repairs	Health Insur-ance	Pets & Supplies
71291	WEST MONROE	82	80	77	80	80	87	80	81	80	79	99	94	79	98	79	80	96	81	82	93
71292	WEST MONROE	78	66	51	61	69	76	64	71	69	64	84	83	61	82	64	71	79	70	78	89
71295	WINNSBORO	63	47	32	42	50	59	48	55	55	48	66	63	43	62	48	59	61	55	65	71
71301	ALEXANDRIA	59	55	62	53	55	62	59	59	63	59	78	66	59	76	59	65	75	60	63	67
71302	ALEXANDRIA	52	46	48	43	46	54	48	50	53	49	64	55	48	61	48	55	62	50	55	58
71303	ALEXANDRIA	91	87	91	85	87	97	89	91	93	90	114	103	89	111	89	94	110	92	95	104
71316	ACME	69	54	37	49	61	68	51	61	57	50	68	72	45	67	54	61	63	60	72	84
71322	BUNKIE	57	44	37	41	47	55	48	52	54	48	65	59	44	61	47	57	61	53	61	64
71323	CENTER POINT	73	63	47	60	64	69	61	66	63	62	77	77	57	73	60	63	73	66	68	81
71325	CHENEYVILLE	58	43	35	38	46	54	46	51	53	47	64	57	42	58	45	57	59	51	61	64
71326	CLAYTON	46	35	31	31	36	44	38	41	44	39	53	46	36	48	37	48	50	42	49	51
71327	COTTONPORT	40	30	20	29	33	40	33	37	37	32	44	41	30	42	33	40	40	37	44	44
71328	DEVILLE	83	71	51	67	74	80	67	75	71	68	87	88	63	84	68	73	82	74	80	95
71331	EFFIE	70	47	21	41	53	61	45	57	55	46	64	68	39	61	46	59	58	56	70	81
71333	EVERGREEN	61	45	27	42	49	58	48	54	55	46	64	62	42	61	48	58	59	54	65	68
71334	FERRIDAY	52	39	34	35	41	49	42	46	49	43	58	52	39	54	42	52	55	47	55	58
71336	GILBERT	71	48	24	41	54	62	47	58	56	48	66	68	40	62	47	60	60	57	71	81
71340	HARRISONBURG	71	47	21	41	54	62	46	57	55	47	65	68	39	61	46	59	59	57	70	81
71341	HESSMER	60	43	24	39	48	55	43	51	50	43	59	60	38	57	44	53	54	51	61	68
71342	JENA	68	51	34	47	56	64	52	60	59	52	70	69	47	66	53	62	65	60	71	78
71343	JONESVILLE	64	47	34	41	51	59	48	55	56	49	67	63	43	62	48	60	62	56	67	73
71346	LECOMPTE	69	54	46	50	57	67	58	63	65	58	78	70	54	73	57	69	74	63	72	76
71350	MANSURA	56	46	41	43	47	56	50	53	56	49	67	58	47	63	49	59	63	53	61	62
71351	MARKSVILLE	62	48	36	44	52	60	49	56	56	50	67	64	46	64	50	60	63	56	65	71
71353	MELVILLE	55	40	27	35	44	51	41	47	48	41	56	54	37	53	41	51	52	47	57	62
71354	MONTEREY	71	51	29	45	58	66	49	60	57	49	68	71	43	65	51	62	62	60	73	84
71355	MOREAUVILLE	68	51	33	47	56	66	52	61	60	51	71	69	47	67	53	64	65	60	73	78
71356	MORROW	59	43	26	41	48	57	47	53	53	45	62	60	41	59	46	56	57	52	63	66
71357	NEWELLTON	66	52	46	48	55	65	57	61	63	56	76	69	53	72	56	67	72	62	71	74
71358	PALMETTO	49	38	34	35	40	48	43	46	49	43	58	50	40	53	42	52	54	46	54	54
71360	PINEVILLE	75	67	57	65	69	76	68	72	71	67	87	83	65	85	68	72	83	72	76	85
71362	PLAUCHEVILLE	69	49	29	46	55	65	52	60	60	51	70	69	46	67	52	66	64	60	73	77
71366	SAINT JOSEPH	49	38	35	33	38	47	41	44	48	42	58	48	39	52	41	51	54	45	53	53
71367	SAINT LANDRY	72	54	32	50	59	67	53	62	61	53	72	73	48	70	54	64	67	61	73	82
71368	SICILY ISLAND	60	45	36	39	47	56	48	53	56	49	67	59	44	60	47	60	62	54	64	67
71369	SIMMESPORT	55	39	25	34	42	50	39	46	47	40	55	53	35	51	39	50	51	46	56	62
71371	TROUT	78	52	24	45	59	68	50	63	61	51	71	75	43	67	51	65	65	62	77	89
71373	VIDALIA	65	50	35	46	53	62	51	57	57	51	69	66	46	65	51	60	64	57	67	73
71375	WATERPROOF	64	51	53	45	51	63	57	60	66	59	80	64	55	71	56	71	76	61	71	70
71378	WISNER	61	44	34	39	47	56	47	53	55	48	65	60	42	60	46	59	61	53	64	68
71401	AIMWELL	59	39	18	34	44	51	38	47	46	39	54	57	32	51	39	49	49	47	58	67
71403	ANACOCO	80	57	31	51	64	72	55	66	64	55	76	79	48	73	56	68	70	66	80	92
71404	ATLANTA	71	48	22	42	54	62	46	58	55	47	65	69	39	62	47	59	59	57	71	82
71406	BELMONT	75	50	23	43	57	65	48	61	58	49	69	72	41	65	49	63	62	60	75	86
71407	BENTLEY	84	56	25	48	64	73	54	68	65	55	77	81	46	73	55	70	70	67	83	96
71409	BOYCE	72	64	53	60	65	71	62	67	66	63	80	77	59	77	62	67	77	66	71	81
71411	CAMPTI	58	41	24	36	45	52	41	48	48	41	57	58	36	54	41	52	52	48	58	66
71416	CLOUTIERVILLE	75	50	23	43	57	65	48	60	58	49	69	72	41	65	49	63	62	60	74	86
71417	COLFAX	62	46	31	41	49	58	48	54	55	48	65	62	43	60	47	58	60	54	64	69
71418	COLUMBIA	69	51	34	45	55	64	51	59	59	51	70	69	46	66	51	63	65	59	71	79
71419	CONVERSE	71	51	28	45	58	66	49	60	57	49	68	71	42	65	51	61	62	59	73	84
71422	DODSON	76	51	23	44	57	66	49	61	59	50	69	73	42	66	50	64	63	61	75	87
71423	DRY PRONG	81	67	47	63	71	78	65	73	71	66	85	85	61	83	65	72	80	72	80	92
71424	ELMER	90	68	42	63	74	82	66	77	73	67	88	92	59	84	67	76	82	76	88	103
71425	ENTERPRISE	59	39	18	34	44	51	38	47	46	39	54	57	32	51	39	49	49	47	58	67
71426	FISHER	81	54	25	47	61	71	52	65	63	53	74	78	44	70	53	68	67	65	81	93
71427	FLATWOODS	67	45	20	39	51	58	43	54	52	44	61	65	37	58	44	56	56	54	67	77
71429	FLORIEN	87	61	32	54	69	79	59	73	69	59	81	87	51	78	61	74	74	72	88	102
71430	FOREST HILL	79	62	43	60	67	76	63	70	69	62	83	81	58	81	63	72	77	69	80	88
71432	GEORGETOWN	85	57	26	49	64	74	55	69	66	56	78	82	47	73	56	71	71	68	85	97
71433	GLENMORA	68	48	29	42	53	62	49	58	58	49	68	67	43	64	49	62	62	58	70	77
71435	GRAYSON	76	52	27	47	59	68	53	63	62	53	73	74	46	69	53	67	67	63	78	86
71438	HINESTON	74	49	22	43	56	64	48	60	58	49	68	71	41	64	48	62	61	59	73	85
71439	HORNBECK	71	51	27	45	57	64	49	59	57	49	67	71	43	65	50	60	61	58	71	82
71441	KELLY	99	66	30	57	75	86	64	80	77	65	91	96	54	86	65	83	82	79	99	114
71446	LEESVILLE	65	54	47	53	55	61	57	59	60	57	74	70	54	71	56	60	70	61	62	72
71447	LENA	70	47	21	40	53	61	45	56	54	46	64	67	38	60	46	59	58	56	69	80
71449	MANY	72	55	41	50	59	68	56	64	64	56	76	74	51	72	57	68	71	64	75	83
71450	MARTHAVILLE	95	63	29	55	72	83	61	76	74	62	87	91	52	82	62	80	79	76	94	109
71454	MONTGOMERY	81	54	25	48	62	71	53	66	63	53	74	79	45	71	54	68	67	65	81	93
71455	MORA	69	46	21	40	52	60	44	56	54	45	63	66	38	60	45	58	57	55	68	79
71456	NATCHEZ	78	52	24	45	59	68	50	63	61	51	71	75	43	67	51	65	65	62	77	89
71457	NATCHITOCHES	63	53	54	51	54	62	59	60	63	58	78	69	57	75	58	64	74	61	64	70
71459	LEESVILLE	67	43	41	49	39	46	64	55	65	59	81	73	54	72	52	59	77	65	51	62
71461	NEWLLANO	66	66	70	69	64	65	68	66	65	69	82	79	67	80	65	61	80	67	58	73
71462	NOBLE	71	52	31	46	59	67	50	61	58	50	68	72	44	66	52	62	63	60	73	85
71463	OAKDALE	51	38	28	34	40	48	40	45	46	40	55	51	36	51	40	49	51	45	54	58
71465	OLLA	88	59	27	51	67	77	57	71	69	58	81	85	49	76	58	74	73	70	88	101
71466	OTIS	68	62	48	59	62	65	59	63	60	61	74	73	56	69	58	59	71	63	63	75
71467	POLLOCK	77	60	38	55	65	72	58	67	64	59	77	79	52	73	58	66	72	67	76	88
71468	PROVENCAL	74	49	22	42	56	64	48	59	57	48	67	71	40	64	48	62	61	59	73	84
71469	ROBELINE	89	61	29	53	68	78	58	72	70	59	82	86	50	78	59	75	75	71	88	102
71472	SIEPER	68	62	48	59	62	65	59	63	60	60	74	73	56	69	58	59	71	63	63	75
71473	SIKES	74	52	28	46	59	67	50	62	59	50	70	73	43	67	52	63	64	61	75	87
71479	TULLOS	70	48	24	42	55	63	47	58	56	47	65	69	40	62	48	60	60	57	71	82
71483	WINNFIELD	55	42	33	38	45	52	44	49	50	44	60	56	41	57	44	53	56	49	57	62
71485	WOODWORTH	92	76	56	75	81	91	77	84	83	76	100	97	73	99	77	85	94	83	93	103
71486	ZWOLLE	72	55	37	49	60	68	55	63	62	54	74	75	49	72	56	66	69	63	74	85
	LOUISIANA	77	69	66	67	70	77	70	73	74	70	91	84	68	88	70	75	87	74	77	87
	UNITED STATES	100	100	100	100	100	100	100	100	100	100	100	100	100	100	100	100	100	100	100	100

# POST OFFICE NAME	COUNTY FIPS CODE	POPULATION 2000	POPULATION 2004	POPULATION 2009	% Rate	State Centile	HOUSEHOLDS 2000	HOUSEHOLDS 2004	HOUSEHOLDS 2009	% Annual Rate 2000-2004	2004 Average HH Size	FAMILIES 2000	FAMILIES 2004	% Annual Rate 2000-2004
03901 BERWICK	031	6494	7265	7929	2.7	96	2363	2725	3052	3.4	2.65	1759	2028	3.4
03902 CAPE NEDDICK	031	2100	2207	2333	1.2	68	894	966	1046	1.8	2.28	591	639	1.9
03903 ELIOT	031	5957	6200	6516	1.0	61	2308	2478	2674	1.7	2.50	1706	1831	1.7
03904 KITTERY	031	7248	7274	7599	0.1	29	3083	3181	3411	0.7	2.23	1873	1931	0.7
03905 KITTERY POINT	031	2295	2460	2627	1.7	82	995	1100	1208	2.4	2.22	656	721	2.3
03906 NORTH BERWICK	031	4275	4586	4899	1.7	82	1578	1753	1925	2.5	2.58	1170	1299	2.5
03907 OGUNQUIT	031	984	1022	1074	0.9	59	557	596	641	1.6	1.71	287	306	1.5
03908 SOUTH BERWICK	031	6676	7179	7679	1.7	85	2405	2648	2896	2.3	2.70	1849	2035	2.3
03909 YORK	031	10786	11431	12138	1.4	74	4359	4759	5185	2.1	2.36	3106	3387	2.1
04001 ACTON	031	2170	2272	2394	1.1	64	869	938	1016	1.8	2.42	627	676	1.8
04002 ALFRED	031	6651	7110	7577	1.6	80	2500	2764	3028	2.4	2.53	1863	2059	2.4
04003 BAILEY ISLAND	005	440	435	449	-0.3	18	216	218	230	0.2	1.99	127	128	0.2
04005 BIDDEFORD	031	22027	22590	23666	0.6	49	9009	9518	10240	1.3	2.28	5580	5897	1.3
04006 BIDDEFORD POOL	031	162	162	167	0.0	26	69	71	74	0.7	2.21	33	33	0.0
04008 BOWDOINHAM	023	2846	2955	3084	0.9	59	1110	1184	1267	1.5	2.49	814	868	1.5
04009 BRIDGTON	005	4451	4544	4718	0.5	44	1764	1827	1926	0.8	2.45	1191	1231	0.8
04010 BROWNFIELD	017	1463	1582	1713	1.9	87	577	643	717	2.6	2.44	398	445	2.7
04011 BRUNSWICK	005	21262	21594	22593	0.4	40	8186	8488	9070	0.9	2.30	5170	5375	0.9
04015 CASCO	005	3434	3614	3816	1.2	69	1311	1411	1517	1.7	2.53	947	1018	1.7
04016 CENTER LOVELL	017	131	135	142	0.7	52	56	59	64	1.2	2.29	41	43	1.1
04017 CHEBEAGUE ISLAND	005	356	408	449	3.3	99	170	199	222	3.8	2.04	127	148	3.7
04019 CLIFF ISLAND	005	87	87	89	0.0	26	39	39	40	0.0	2.23	31	31	0.0
04020 CORNISH	031	2097	2231	2369	1.5	78	765	844	923	2.3	2.53	531	587	2.4
04021 CUMBERLAND CENTER	005	5710	6236	6706	2.1	92	1966	2180	2379	2.5	2.86	1613	1787	2.4
04022 DENMARK	017	729	760	807	1.0	62	301	324	354	1.8	2.35	206	222	1.8
04024 EAST BALDWIN	005	221	225	233	0.4	42	86	89	94	0.8	2.53	67	70	1.0
04027 LEBANON	031	5058	5330	5640	1.2	70	1814	1968	2135	1.9	2.71	1396	1514	1.9
04029 SEBAGO	005	1635	1654	1706	0.3	36	670	690	724	0.7	2.40	480	494	0.7
04030 EAST WATERBORO	031	1284	1422	1545	2.4	96	478	546	608	3.2	2.60	371	422	3.1
04032 FREEPORT	005	7876	8192	8577	0.9	61	3096	3287	3505	1.4	2.44	2178	2309	1.4
04037 FRYEBURG	017	2814	3040	3287	1.8	86	1156	1288	1434	2.6	2.30	778	868	2.6
04038 GORHAM	005	13968	15102	16132	1.9	86	4810	5329	5817	2.4	2.62	3484	3856	2.4
04039 GRAY	005	6468	6928	7375	1.6	81	2490	2725	2956	2.1	2.53	1789	1954	2.1
04040 HARRISON	005	2605	2671	2777	0.6	48	1024	1071	1133	1.1	2.49	728	761	1.1
04041 HIRAM	017	1777	1870	1996	1.2	69	681	735	804	1.8	2.54	489	528	1.8
04042 HOLLIS CENTER	031	4736	5092	5445	1.7	85	1727	1918	2106	2.5	2.65	1316	1460	2.5
04043 KENNEBUNK	031	10452	11384	12259	2.0	90	4223	4719	5203	2.7	2.38	2893	3238	2.7
04046 KENNEBUNKPORT	031	7161	7926	8626	2.4	95	2932	3308	3676	2.9	2.39	2059	2325	2.9
04047 PARSONSFIELD	031	1584	1632	1706	0.7	51	634	676	727	1.5	2.40	439	468	1.5
04048 LIMERICK	031	3592	3818	4056	1.5	77	1325	1455	1590	2.2	2.60	978	1075	2.3
04049 LIMINGTON	031	645	697	746	1.8	86	222	249	275	2.7	2.73	174	195	2.7
04050 LONG ISLAND	005	202	200	206	-0.2	19	93	94	99	0.3	2.13	61	61	0.0
04051 LOVELL	017	839	902	975	1.7	85	329	364	404	2.4	2.48	237	262	2.4
04055 NAPLES	005	3353	3622	3872	1.8	86	1327	1461	1589	2.3	2.47	952	1045	2.2
04061 NORTH WATERBORO	031	2660	3027	3334	3.1	98	890	1032	1159	3.5	2.93	718	833	3.6
04062 WINDHAM	005	15037	16167	17247	1.7	85	5569	6115	6647	2.2	2.54	4053	4438	2.2
04064 OLD ORCHARD BEACH	031	8829	8997	9362	0.4	43	4284	4498	4804	1.2	1.99	2251	2361	1.1
04066 ORRS ISLAND	005	732	721	745	-0.4	14	343	346	365	0.2	2.08	217	218	0.1
04068 PORTER	017	1448	1564	1692	1.8	86	566	627	696	2.4	2.49	413	458	2.5
04069 POWNAL	005	1503	1563	1637	0.9	61	565	602	645	1.5	2.60	443	472	1.5
04071 RAYMOND	005	4688	5088	5455	2.0	88	1772	1961	2139	2.4	2.59	1367	1510	2.4
04072 SACO	031	18167	18711	19618	0.7	51	7306	7751	8337	1.4	2.38	4973	5268	1.2
04073 SANFORD	031	16112	16512	17379	0.6	48	6426	6769	7306	1.2	2.41	4207	4431	1.2
04074 SCARBOROUGH	005	16683	19078	21035	3.2	98	6321	7364	8258	3.7	2.56	4583	5329	3.6
04076 SHAPLEIGH	031	2372	2489	2628	1.1	67	932	1008	1092	1.9	2.46	688	743	1.8
04079 HARPSWELL	005	4017	3995	4113	-0.1	21	1760	1792	1881	0.4	2.23	1175	1193	0.4
04083 SPRINGVALE	031	4413	5088	5650	3.4	99	1747	2071	2356	4.1	2.43	1169	1384	4.1
04084 STANDISH	005	7754	8138	8551	1.1	67	2682	2883	3095	1.7	2.62	2053	2202	1.7
04085 STEEP FALLS	005	2263	2389	2524	1.3	71	786	854	923	2.0	2.75	616	668	1.9
04086 TOPSHAM	023	9232	9709	10212	1.2	68	3471	3756	4059	1.9	2.55	2498	2705	1.9
04087 WATERBORO	031	1899	2049	2196	1.8	85	692	768	843	2.5	2.66	510	565	2.4
04088 WATERFORD	017	559	575	606	0.7	50	223	237	256	1.4	2.43	162	172	1.4
04090 WELLS	031	9740	10445	11241	1.7	82	4145	4552	5013	2.2	2.29	2779	3074	2.4
04091 WEST BALDWIN	005	850	865	895	0.4	42	318	331	349	1.0	2.61	248	258	0.9
04092 WESTBROOK	005	16248	16344	16944	0.1	32	6910	7096	7493	0.6	2.28	4295	4410	0.6
04093 BUXTON	031	6145	7320	8277	4.2	100	2309	2853	3326	5.1	2.56	1721	2126	5.1
04095 WEST NEWFIELD	031	1239	1433	1591	3.5	99	460	546	621	4.1	2.62	343	407	4.1
04096 YARMOUTH	005	8322	8473	8780	0.4	42	3418	3538	3726	0.8	2.37	2294	2369	0.8
04097 NORTH YARMOUTH	005	3117	3347	3568	1.7	83	1083	1183	1281	2.1	2.83	895	977	2.1
04101 PORTLAND	005	17053	17417	18218	0.5	45	8726	9150	9794	1.1	1.76	2598	2695	0.9
04102 PORTLAND	005	17018	16840	17391	-0.3	18	8076	8160	8587	0.2	2.01	3549	3577	0.2
04103 PORTLAND	005	29177	30996	33287	1.4	76	12444	13396	14599	1.8	2.26	7122	7725	1.9
04105 FALMOUTH	005	10295	10854	11482	1.3	70	3942	4231	4550	1.7	2.51	2833	3018	1.5
04106 SOUTH PORTLAND	005	23387	24103	25244	0.7	52	10090	10603	11305	1.2	2.22	6067	6371	1.2
04107 CAPE ELIZABETH	005	9186	9374	9787	0.5	44	3539	3675	3902	0.9	2.52	2641	2736	0.8
04108 PEAKS ISLAND	005	920	947	987	0.7	50	431	451	478	1.1	2.10	249	260	1.0
04109 PORTLAND	005	5	6	7	4.4	100	3	4	4	7.0	1.50	2	2	0.0
04110 CUMBERLAND FORESIDE	005	1206	1381	1520	3.2	98	464	542	607	3.7	2.53	345	403	3.7
04210 AUBURN	001	23328	23526	24084	0.2	34	9803	10187	10731	0.9	2.22	5938	6179	0.9
04216 ANDOVER	017	789	781	818	-0.2	19	344	353	381	0.6	2.21	238	244	0.6
04217 BETHEL	017	3170	3296	3511	0.9	60	1344	1436	1569	1.6	2.29	895	957	1.6
04219 BRYANT POND	017	1842	1978	2135	1.7	83	741	821	910	2.4	2.40	522	579	2.5
04220 BUCKFIELD	017	1715	1841	1986	1.7	83	664	735	814	2.4	2.50	473	524	2.4
04221 CANTON	017	2060	2159	2296	1.1	65	758	820	898	1.9	2.51	539	584	1.9
04222 DURHAM	001	3322	3664	3921	2.3	94	1202	1362	1497	3.0	2.69	961	1089	3.0
04224 DIXFIELD	017	3034	3125	3296	0.7	51	1209	1279	1384	1.3	2.43	869	920	1.4
04225 DRYDEN	007	70	72	76	0.7	50	26	28	30	1.8	2.57	19	20	1.1
04226 EAST ANDOVER	017	146	144	151	-0.3	16	64	66	71	0.7	2.18	44	45	0.5
04228 EAST LIVERMORE	001	342	354	366	0.8	55	118	126	134	1.6	2.69	86	91	1.3
04231 STONEHAM	017	469	517	566	2.3	94	207	235	264	3.0	2.20	148	168	3.0
04236 GREENE	001	4076	4125	4224	0.3	36	1494	1561	1645	1.0	2.63	1186	1239	1.0
04237 HANOVER	017	251	249	261	-0.2	21	106	108	117	0.4	2.31	73	74	0.1
04238 HEBRON	017	950	1037	1127	2.1	91	350	394	441	2.8	2.63	267	301	2.9
04239 JAY	007	5098	5386	5753	1.3	71	2064	2257	2488	2.1	2.38	1480	1622	2.2
04240 LEWISTON	001	35881	36062	36870	0.1	31	15351	15941	16804	0.9	2.10	8704	9025	0.9
MAINE					0.9					1.5	2.33			1.6
UNITED STATES					1.2					1.3	2.58			1.1

ZIP CODE #	POST OFFICE NAME	RACE (%) White 2000	White 2004	Black 2000	Black 2004	Asian/Pacific 2000	Asian/Pacific 2004	% Hispanic Origin 2000	% Hispanic Origin 2004	2004 AGE DISTRIBUTION (%) 0-4	5-9	10-14	15-19	20-24	25-44	45-64	65-84	85+	18+	MEDIAN AGE 2004	% 2004 Males	% 2004 Females
03901	BERWICK	97.3	96.8	0.4	0.4	1.2	1.5	0.5	0.7	6.5	6.5	8.0	8.3	7.1	28.3	25.7	8.8	0.9	73.9	36.7	48.9	51.1
03902	CAPE NEDDICK	98.9	98.8	0.2	0.2	0.2	0.3	0.8	0.9	4.6	5.3	5.9	5.4	4.0	23.5	35.0	14.9	1.5	80.9	45.7	49.2	50.8
03903	ELIOT	98.4	98.2	0.2	0.3	0.4	0.5	0.5	0.6	5.8	6.4	6.9	6.7	5.3	25.7	30.7	11.0	1.7	76.8	41.7	48.1	51.9
03904	KITTERY	95.2	94.6	2.2	2.4	0.8	1.0	1.8	2.1	6.2	6.1	6.5	6.2	7.0	29.5	24.8	11.7	2.2	77.3	37.9	48.8	51.2
03905	KITTERY POINT	98.3	98.2	0.6	0.7	0.4	0.5	0.6	0.8	4.4	5.1	6.3	5.1	3.5	22.5	33.1	17.5	2.5	81.0	46.7	47.8	52.2
03906	NORTH BERWICK	97.1	96.8	0.6	0.7	0.8	1.0	0.6	0.7	5.9	6.3	7.4	7.3	5.7	27.7	29.0	9.2	1.5	75.6	39.3	49.4	50.6
03907	OGUNQUIT	98.5	98.3	0.5	0.6	0.4	0.6	0.7	0.7	2.0	2.8	2.2	2.4	2.9	16.2	39.1	29.0	3.4	91.4	56.9	52.2	47.9
03908	SOUTH BERWICK	97.6	97.3	0.3	0.3	0.7	0.9	0.7	0.8	7.0	7.4	8.6	7.7	5.7	27.8	26.7	8.0	1.2	72.1	37.4	49.0	51.0
03909	YORK	98.3	98.0	0.3	0.3	0.6	0.7	0.7	0.9	4.7	5.8	7.2	5.6	3.7	22.3	32.5	15.9	2.4	78.7	45.5	47.9	52.1
04001	ACTON	98.4	98.4	0.1	0.1	0.2	0.3	0.9	1.1	5.5	6.0	6.7	6.5	4.8	24.1	30.6	14.6	1.1	77.8	42.9	50.2	49.8
04002	ALFRED	98.5	98.4	0.3	0.3	0.3	0.4	0.3	0.3	5.3	6.1	7.1	6.3	5.0	27.1	30.6	11.7	0.8	77.4	41.1	50.7	49.4
04003	BAILEY ISLAND	98.2	98.2	0.2	0.5	0.5	0.5	1.1	1.4	4.4	4.6	4.6	4.1	4.1	22.3	32.0	21.4	2.5	83.2	48.6	49.2	50.8
04005	BIDDEFORD	96.7	96.4	0.6	0.7	1.0	1.2	0.6	0.8	6.3	6.1	6.5	6.9	7.4	28.8	23.4	12.5	2.3	77.6	37.1	47.5	52.6
04006	BIDDEFORD POOL	98.8	98.2	0.0	0.0	1.2	1.2	0.0	0.0	1.2	2.5	3.1	1.2	20.4	16.1	30.3	23.5	1.9	92.6	49.5	39.5	60.5
04008	BOWDOINHAM	97.8	97.6	0.4	0.4	0.5	0.6	0.6	0.7	5.4	6.4	7.2	7.3	5.9	26.6	30.8	9.1	1.4	76.1	40.2	50.0	50.1
04009	BRIDGTON	97.4	97.2	0.4	0.4	0.3	0.4	0.9	1.0	5.3	5.3	5.6	8.3	5.9	23.9	28.9	14.8	2.0	79.9	42.3	49.6	50.4
04010	BROWNFIELD	98.5	98.6	0.1	0.1	0.2	0.3	0.7	0.7	4.2	5.9	6.8	7.5	4.4	24.7	31.9	12.8	1.9	77.9	43.1	49.2	50.8
04011	BRUNSWICK	94.4	93.7	1.7	1.8	1.7	2.2	1.6	1.9	6.1	5.6	6.5	8.7	9.7	25.2	22.9	13.0	2.5	78.1	36.4	48.3	51.7
04015	CASCO	98.0	97.7	0.3	0.3	0.5	0.7	0.5	0.7	6.0	6.3	7.3	6.5	5.2	29.9	27.0	10.5	1.4	76.2	39.5	49.7	50.3
04016	CENTER LOVELL	98.5	99.3	0.0	0.0	0.0	0.0	0.0	0.7	5.2	5.9	6.7	5.9	5.2	24.4	31.1	14.1	1.5	77.8	43.1	49.6	50.4
04017	CHEBEAGUE ISLAND	98.9	98.3	0.0	0.3	0.6	1.0	0.8	1.2	5.4	6.9	7.6	5.9	3.2	19.1	33.6	15.9	2.5	75.7	46.1	47.6	52.5
04019	CLIFF ISLAND	96.6	96.6	0.0	0.0	1.2	1.2	0.0	0.0	5.8	6.9	5.8	3.5	2.3	20.7	32.2	21.8	1.2	78.2	47.8	50.6	49.4
04020	CORNISH	98.5	98.3	0.2	0.3	0.3	0.4	0.4	0.5	5.4	6.1	7.3	5.9	5.3	25.4	27.8	13.6	3.2	76.9	41.8	48.6	51.4
04021	CUMBERLAND CENTER	98.7	98.4	0.2	0.2	0.4	0.6	0.6	0.8	6.9	8.3	9.4	7.4	3.4	25.1	29.7	8.9	1.1	70.5	40.2	48.4	51.6
04022	DENMARK	97.9	97.9	0.4	0.4	0.6	0.7	1.1	1.3	4.2	6.2	6.6	7.0	3.7	25.9	31.5	13.2	1.8	77.6	43.3	49.0	51.1
04024	EAST BALDWIN	99.1	98.7	0.5	0.4	0.5	0.4	0.9	0.4	6.2	6.7	6.7	5.8	4.9	27.6	28.0	12.4	1.8	76.9	40.6	48.9	51.1
04027	LEBANON	98.5	98.3	0.3	0.4	0.3	0.3	0.6	0.8	5.7	6.3	8.5	8.3	5.9	28.2	27.1	8.8	1.1	74.1	38.0	50.0	50.0
04029	SEBAGO	98.4	98.4	0.4	0.4	0.2	0.2	0.3	0.4	4.2	6.1	7.5	5.7	3.9	25.1	32.4	13.9	1.3	78.7	43.6	49.3	50.7
04030	EAST WATERBORO	98.3	98.0	0.2	0.3	0.5	0.6	0.8	0.9	6.1	6.7	7.9	6.2	5.5	28.4	29.4	9.0	0.8	75.1	39.1	50.4	49.7
04032	FREEPORT	97.2	96.9	0.4	0.5	1.1	1.4	0.7	0.9	5.8	6.7	7.5	6.2	4.7	25.7	30.2	11.3	1.9	76.0	41.4	48.6	51.5
04037	FRYEBURG	98.2	98.1	0.3	0.3	0.4	0.5	1.1	1.3	3.6	5.4	7.1	7.7	4.8	23.9	31.5	13.6	2.5	78.4	43.5	47.8	52.2
04038	GORHAM	97.6	97.2	0.4	0.5	0.7	0.9	0.6	0.7	5.9	6.3	7.5	10.3	8.4	26.7	24.6	8.6	1.7	76.0	35.7	48.4	51.6
04039	GRAY	97.9	97.6	0.4	0.5	0.5	0.6	0.6	0.7	5.7	6.0	6.7	6.7	6.0	31.1	28.1	8.6	1.1	77.1	38.7	50.8	49.3
04040	HARRISON	98.5	98.4	0.7	0.8	0.0	0.0	0.5	0.6	5.7	6.3	6.9	8.5	5.5	23.9	30.3	11.8	1.1	77.7	40.6	51.3	48.7
04041	HIRAM	97.9	97.7	0.1	0.1	0.2	0.3	0.5	0.5	6.4	7.0	7.5	7.0	5.1	25.9	29.0	11.0	1.2	74.8	40.2	49.5	50.5
04042	HOLLIS CENTER	98.8	98.7	0.1	0.1	0.3	0.3	0.5	0.6	6.7	7.2	7.7	6.9	5.8	29.9	27.6	7.4	0.8	74.2	37.4	50.1	49.9
04043	KENNEBUNK	98.1	97.8	0.2	0.2	0.9	1.1	0.5	0.6	5.2	6.0	7.9	7.1	4.4	23.1	29.2	14.3	2.8	76.0	42.9	46.7	53.3
04046	KENNEBUNKPORT	98.4	98.2	0.2	0.2	0.5	0.7	0.6	0.7	5.4	6.2	6.8	5.6	4.1	25.0	32.6	12.8	1.5	77.9	43.2	48.0	52.0
04047	PARSONSFIELD	98.2	98.2	0.1	0.1	0.2	0.3	0.8	1.0	5.7	6.2	6.8	6.7	4.4	26.3	29.0	13.0	1.9	76.4	40.9	49.9	50.1
04048	LIMERICK	98.2	98.1	0.4	0.4	0.1	0.2	0.4	0.5	6.7	7.2	8.2	6.9	5.8	29.2	26.0	9.0	1.1	73.8	36.8	50.2	49.8
04049	LIMINGTON	98.1	97.9	0.5	0.6	0.3	0.4	0.3	0.3	6.3	6.6	7.8	7.3	7.6	28.6	27.3	7.0	1.6	74.9	36.1	49.8	50.2
04050	LONG ISLAND	97.0	96.5	0.0	0.0	1.0	1.5	0.5	0.5	4.5	5.0	9.0	7.0	1.5	21.5	33.0	18.0	0.5	76.5	45.7	49.5	50.5
04051	LOVELL	98.8	98.7	0.1	0.1	0.2	0.2	0.4	0.3	4.4	5.9	7.1	7.1	3.9	24.7	31.5	14.4	1.0	77.7	43.3	51.4	48.6
04055	NAPLES	98.2	98.0	0.2	0.2	0.3	0.4	0.2	0.3	5.0	5.7	7.8	6.3	4.9	26.4	29.0	13.6	1.4	77.6	41.7	51.0	49.0
04061	NORTH WATERBORO	98.6	98.4	0.1	0.1	0.1	0.1	0.8	1.1	10.3	9.6	9.1	6.8	5.6	36.4	17.8	4.2	0.3	66.7	31.0	50.2	49.9
04062	WINDHAM	97.6	97.3	0.5	0.5	0.4	0.5	0.4	0.5	6.3	6.6	6.9	6.1	5.6	31.8	26.9	8.6	1.2	76.4	37.9	50.7	49.3
04064	OLD ORCHARD BEACH	97.5	97.3	0.6	0.6	0.5	0.6	1.0	1.2	4.7	4.7	5.4	5.7	6.0	29.4	28.6	13.9	1.7	81.6	41.8	49.0	51.1
04066	ORRS ISLAND	98.2	97.9	0.1	0.1	1.0	1.3	1.4	1.5	4.6	4.4	3.9	4.6	3.9	21.4	35.0	20.5	1.8	84.3	49.0	49.0	51.0
04068	PORTER	97.0	96.7	0.4	0.4	0.4	0.5	0.7	0.8	5.5	5.8	7.6	6.4	6.5	26.7	27.1	12.9	1.5	76.9	40.2	48.9	51.1
04069	POWNAL	97.9	97.6	0.5	0.5	0.4	0.5	0.7	0.9	5.6	6.5	6.7	6.3	4.5	24.7	35.2	9.7	0.9	77.4	42.6	50.0	50.0
04071	RAYMOND	98.4	98.2	0.4	0.4	0.3	0.4	0.6	0.7	5.7	6.1	7.8	6.9	4.8	29.0	28.7	10.1	1.0	75.9	39.9	49.6	50.4
04072	SACO	97.9	97.6	0.3	0.4	0.6	0.8	0.6	0.7	6.1	6.4	7.1	6.7	5.5	29.6	25.5	11.3	1.9	75.9	38.5	47.9	52.1
04073	SANFORD	95.7	95.0	0.5	0.5	2.1	2.7	1.1	1.3	6.4	6.3	7.6	7.2	7.3	26.4	24.2	12.5	2.1	75.1	37.5	48.4	51.6
04074	SCARBOROUGH	97.4	96.9	0.4	0.5	1.2	1.5	0.5	0.6	6.7	7.2	7.6	5.9	4.3	27.4	27.4	12.1	1.6	74.5	40.5	48.7	51.3
04076	SHAPLEIGH	98.4	98.3	0.2	0.2	0.4	0.5	0.9	1.1	5.1	5.8	6.8	6.4	4.9	26.8	29.7	13.0	1.5	77.9	41.9	50.5	49.5
04079	HARPSWELL	97.9	97.6	0.3	0.3	0.5	0.7	1.3	1.5	4.1	4.6	5.7	4.9	3.9	22.8	35.6	16.6	1.8	82.4	47.3	49.5	50.5
04083	SPRINGVALE	95.7	95.0	0.4	0.4	2.0	2.6	0.5	0.6	6.5	6.3	7.3	7.7	7.8	27.4	23.4	11.4	2.2	74.8	36.3	47.8	52.2
04084	STANDISH	98.1	97.9	0.4	0.5	0.3	0.3	0.5	0.6	6.3	6.4	6.7	9.3	9.6	28.1	25.2	7.7	0.8	76.8	34.3	48.5	51.5
04085	STEEP FALLS	98.2	97.9	0.3	0.3	0.4	0.5	0.3	0.4	6.3	6.7	7.4	6.7	6.3	30.2	27.1	8.1	1.2	75.5	37.2	49.1	50.9
04086	TOPSHAM	95.2	94.6	1.3	1.5	1.4	1.7	1.2	1.5	6.7	6.8	8.2	7.3	5.8	28.7	24.4	9.9	2.2	73.5	37.2	48.6	51.4
04087	WATERBORO	99.0	98.9	0.1	0.1	0.2	0.2	0.4	0.5	7.0	7.4	8.3	6.6	5.4	30.2	26.3	8.0	0.8	73.0	36.8	50.6	49.4
04088	WATERFORD	98.8	98.6	0.0	0.2	0.0	0.2	0.4	0.4	5.2	5.4	6.4	6.1	4.5	24.0	32.7	14.3	1.4	79.0	44.1	49.2	50.8
04090	WELLS	98.2	98.0	0.2	0.3	0.5	0.6	0.6	0.8	4.7	5.4	5.8	5.9	4.2	24.5	33.1	14.8	1.7	80.4	44.8	49.1	50.9
04091	WEST BALDWIN	98.9	98.8	0.4	0.4	0.5	0.5	0.5	0.6	6.2	6.5	6.9	5.6	4.9	27.8	27.6	13.0	1.6	76.9	40.6	49.0	51.0
04092	WESTBROOK	96.7	96.2	0.9	1.0	0.9	1.1	0.9	1.1	6.1	6.0	6.6	6.4	6.1	28.5	25.0	12.8	2.4	77.2	39.1	47.5	52.5
04093	BUXTON	97.9	97.6	0.4	0.5	0.6	0.9	0.5	0.5	6.1	6.7	6.9	6.0	5.3	30.7	28.1	9.2	0.9	76.4	39.0	50.4	49.6
04095	WEST NEWFIELD	97.9	97.8	0.1	0.1	0.1	0.1	0.7	0.8	5.8	6.2	7.2	6.8	5.9	25.3	30.5	11.0	1.3	76.3	40.9	51.7	48.3
04096	YARMOUTH	98.5	98.3	0.4	0.4	0.4	0.5	0.6	0.7	4.7	5.7	7.5	7.0	5.3	22.8	32.0	12.8	2.3	77.7	43.3	48.0	52.0
04097	NORTH YARMOUTH	98.7	98.4	0.1	0.1	0.6	0.8	0.5	0.6	6.9	8.2	9.1	6.7	3.7	27.1	30.0	7.5	0.9	71.4	39.3	48.8	51.2
04101	PORTLAND	87.0	85.2	4.6	5.2	3.6	4.6	2.8	3.4	4.3	3.3	3.9	6.0	13.0	39.0	19.4	8.8	2.3	85.8	33.3	50.8	49.2
04102	PORTLAND	91.6	90.2	2.2	2.4	3.4	4.4	1.4	1.6	4.6	4.2	4.5	5.9	10.0	33.6	24.3	11.0	2.0	83.1	36.7	48.1	51.9
04103	PORTLAND	93.4	92.6	1.8	1.9	2.8	3.4	0.9	1.0	5.7	5.4	6.0	6.3	6.6	30.6	23.9	12.6	2.9	78.8	38.7	46.2	53.8
04105	FALMOUTH	97.8	97.3	0.2	0.3	1.2	1.5	0.5	0.6	6.4	7.8	8.4	5.9	3.2	23.2	29.0	12.7	3.4	73.3	42.5	47.6	52.4
04106	SOUTH PORTLAND	95.8	95.2	0.6	0.7	1.6	2.1	1.1	1.4	5.5	5.6	6.3	6.8	6.3	29.6	25.6	12.3	2.1	78.3	39.2	47.4	52.6
04107	CAPE ELIZABETH	98.0	97.6	0.3	0.4	1.1	1.4	0.5	0.6	4.8	6.3	8.3	7.2	4.0	19.4	33.7	13.7	2.6	75.8	45.0	47.9	52.1
04108	PEAKS ISLAND	97.8	97.6	0.0	0.0	1.0	1.3	0.9	1.1	5.3	4.7	6.2	9.3	4.9	19.5	34.6	14.4	1.2	76.1	45.1	47.5	52.5
04109	PORTLAND	100.0	100.0	0.0	0.0	0.0	0.0	0.0	0.0	0.0	0.0	0.0	0.0	0.0	0.0	100.0	0.0	0.0	100.0	50.0	0.0	100.0
04110	CUMBERLAND FORESIDE	98.9	98.6	0.1	0.1	0.6	0.8	0.9	1.2	5.6	6.9	7.7	6.1	3.3	18.8	33.4	15.9	2.5	75.2	46.0	47.6	52.4
04210	AUBURN	97.1	96.8	0.6	0.7	0.6	0.8	0.7	0.9	5.7	5.5	6.5	6.8	6.9	27.3	24.9	13.1	3.5	78.1	39.7	47.7	52.3
04216	ANDOVER	98.7	98.6	0.3	0.3	0.1	0.1	0.3	0.4	4.1	4.6	6.2	5.6	4.5	23.1	36.0	14.6	1.4	81.7	46.1	50.7	49.3
04217	BETHEL	98.2	98.1	0.2	0.2	0.4	0.5	0.6	0.7	5.1	5.4	6.7	6.2	5.0	25.7	30.0	14.4	1.5	78.8	42.4	49.2	50.8
04219	BRYANT POND	98.6	98.4	0.1	0.1	0.2	0.2	0.5	0.7	5.3	5.1	7.7	6.7	4.5	26.1	29.7	13.7	1.2	77.2	41.6	51.1	48.9
04220	BUCKFIELD	98.5	98.4	0.0	0.0	0.4	0.4	0.4	0.5	6.0	6.7	7.6	6.9	5.1	29.2	28.3	9.1	1.1	75.3	38.7	49.3	50.7
04221	CANTON	98.5	98.4	0.1	0.1	0.3	0.3	0.8	0.9	6.0	6.4	7.0	6.8	5.0	25.8	27.7	13.4	2.1	76.4	41.5	49.2	50.8
04222	DURHAM	99.0	98.9	0.1	0.1	0.3	0.4	0.7	0.8	6.0	6.8	7.3	6.6	4.6	31.1	30.3	6.7	0.6	75.6	39.1	49.9	50.1
04224	DIXFIELD	98.2	98.0	0.0	0.0	0.5	0.6	0.8	0.9	5.6	6.3	7.5	6.9	4.5	25.5	28.7	13.2	1.8	75.4	41.4	49.1	50.9
04225	DRYDEN	97.1	98.6	0.0	0.0	0.0	0.0	0.0	0.0	5.6	6.9	6.9	6.9	2.8	25.0	33.3	12.5	0.0	73.6	42.5	54.2	45.8
04226	EAST ANDOVER	98.6	98.6	0.0	0.0	0.0	0.0	0.0	0.0	4.2	4.9	6.3	5.6	4.2	22.9	35.4	15.3	1.4	80.6	46.1	51.4	48.6
04228	EAST LIVERMORE	97.1	96.9	0.3	0.3	0.3	0.6	0.6	0.6	5.9	6.5	7.6	7.1	6.2	26.6	25.4	12.2	2.5	74.6	38.9	51.7	48.3
04231	STONEHAM	98.5	98.5	0.0	0.2	0.2	0.4	0.4	0.4	4.6	5.8	7.2	6.8	4.1	25.0	31.3	14.3	1.0	78.0	43.0	51.5	48.6
04236	GREENE	98.5	98.3	0.5	0.5	0.3	0.4	0.7	0.9	5.8	6.4	7.4	6.7	5.4	30.1	28.9	8.7	0.8	75.8	39.0	50.0	50.0
04237	HANOVER	99.2	99.2	0.0	0.0	0.0	0.0	0.8	0.8	4.8	4.0	7.2	6.4	4.0	24.9	31.7	16.1	0.8	79.9	44.2	51.8	48.2
04238	HEBRON	97.8	97.7	0.1	0.1	0.5	0.7	0.7	0.9	5.4	5.0	9.6	7.6	6.7	29.2	29.4	6.2	1.0	74.1	38.0	51.0	49.0
04239	JAY	97.9	97.7	0.3	0.3	0.3	0.4	0.5	0.6	5.6	5.9	7.3	7.3	5.4	26.0	27.3	13.9	1.3	76.6	40.5	48.5	51.5
04240	LEWISTON	95.8	95.3	1.1	1.2	0.9	1.1	1.3	1.5	5.7	5.4	5.9	6.9	8.8	26.5	23.3	14.6	2.9	79.7	38.4	47.9	52.1
	MAINE	97.0	96.6	0.5	0.6	0.7	0.9	0.7	0.9	5.5	5.8	6.7	6.9	6.5	26.7	27.5	12.5	2.0	77.9	40.2	48.8	51.2
	UNITED STATES	75.1	73.6	12.3	12.5	3.8	4.2	12.5	14.1	6.9	6.7	7.2	7.0	7.3	28.6	23.8	10.8	1.7	75.1	36.0	49.1	50.9

#	POST OFFICE NAME (ZIP CODE)	2004 Per Capita Income	2004 HH Income Base	2004 HOUSEHOLD INCOME DISTRIBUTION (%) Less than $25,000	$25,000 to $49,999	$50,000 to $99,999	$100,000 to $149,999	$150,000 or More	MEDIAN HOUSEHOLD INCOME 2004	2009	2004 National Centile	2004 State Centile	2004 Home Value Base	2004 HOME VALUE DISTRIBUTION (%) Less than $50,000	$50,000 to $89,999	$90,000 to $174,999	$175,000 to $399,999	$400,000 or More	2004 Median Home Value
03901	BERWICK	21282	2725	23.9	27.3	39.3	6.8	2.6	49038	55080	70	87	2075	4.0	8.1	50.8	36.6	0.5	155616
03902	CAPE NEDDICK	36380	966	13.3	19.9	42.3	14.3	10.3	66055	75185	89	98	832	0.8	0.6	12.1	62.1	24.3	281868
03903	ELIOT	27653	2478	18.4	22.7	39.6	14.7	4.6	58973	66285	84	97	1991	1.5	3.8	21.4	62.8	10.6	223081
03904	KITTERY	24807	3181	21.4	31.3	36.6	8.7	2.0	47004	52747	66	84	1913	6.6	3.9	33.8	50.0	5.7	187056
03905	KITTERY POINT	33683	1100	17.6	22.6	38.8	12.7	8.4	58093	64499	83	96	914	7.0	1.1	17.1	45.1	29.8	268992
03906	NORTH BERWICK	22320	1753	17.9	29.0	44.2	6.9	2.1	51986	58262	75	91	1415	0.8	6.4	50.7	39.7	2.5	161974
03907	OGUNQUIT	42056	596	19.6	26.3	33.6	11.7	8.7	54174	63473	79	93	478	0.0	0.4	7.5	58.8	33.3	317526
03908	SOUTH BERWICK	24430	2648	14.7	23.2	46.5	12.5	3.1	59886	66415	84	97	2080	0.0	5.0	35.2	56.0	3.8	192000
03909	YORK	34972	4759	16.2	24.8	35.5	12.7	10.9	59904	67363	84	97	3985	1.8	0.7	10.5	62.3	24.7	287164
04001	ACTON	22358	938	22.0	36.8	32.3	6.6	2.4	42794	47934	55	71	813	3.0	5.9	39.1	45.1	6.9	180030
04002	ALFRED	22035	2764	21.5	30.3	39.3	6.1	2.8	48550	53417	69	87	2366	4.3	8.5	48.4	37.0	1.8	158959
04003	BAILEY ISLAND	27544	218	27.5	27.5	33.0	7.3	4.6	46428	51422	65	83	172	1.7	0.6	35.5	41.3	20.9	221053
04005	BIDDEFORD	20923	9518	31.7	30.6	29.4	6.5	1.9	39261	44306	44	56	4882	1.1	3.1	49.7	41.8	4.3	169908
04006	BIDDEFORD POOL	34232	71	18.3	25.4	36.6	8.5	11.3	63922	69485	88	98	46	0.0	0.0	4.4	28.3	67.4	546875
04008	BOWDOINHAM	23578	1184	23.2	28.8	35.2	7.7	5.1	48109	53476	69	86	980	3.4	10.7	43.5	37.0	5.4	161691
04009	BRIDGTON	19564	1827	29.3	32.2	31.3	3.9	3.2	39138	44193	43	55	1378	2.1	12.5	53.6	27.8	4.0	138048
04010	BROWNFIELD	19170	643	31.3	34.4	26.8	5.4	2.2	37172	41798	36	46	542	4.6	17.2	47.1	27.5	3.7	138660
04011	BRUNSWICK	23733	8488	26.0	31.4	29.2	9.3	4.1	44301	50348	59	77	5376	15.4	5.3	27.1	44.9	7.3	180142
04015	CASCO	22060	1411	23.2	31.1	34.4	7.5	3.8	46163	51721	64	82	1169	5.3	6.8	46.4	36.8	4.8	158473
04016	CENTER LOVELL	19943	59	33.9	33.9	25.4	5.1	1.7	34425	38627	25	36	49	4.1	12.2	49.0	30.6	4.1	142045
04017	CHEBEAGUE ISLAND	56390	199	12.1	19.6	32.2	13.1	23.1	70825	85762	92	99	179	0.0	2.2	12.3	46.4	39.1	327778
04019	CLIFF ISLAND	23161	39	25.6	53.9	10.3	5.1	5.1	35276	40000	29	39	21	0.0	0.0	14.3	57.1	28.6	225000
04020	CORNISH	18859	844	29.6	29.5	35.7	4.3	1.0	41557	46306	52	66	691	3.9	9.4	54.9	30.7	1.2	143349
04021	CUMBERLAND CENTER	36582	2180	12.5	19.2	35.1	16.0	17.2	73736	84665	93	100	1978	0.6	0.9	11.9	67.2	19.4	264640
04022	DENMARK	23739	324	28.1	29.9	30.3	8.0	3.7	41037	47399	50	65	273	1.5	5.9	48.7	37.0	7.0	158500
04024	EAST BALDWIN	18222	89	30.3	32.6	32.6	3.4	1.1	40370	45917	47	60	76	6.6	13.2	55.3	22.4	2.6	136765
04027	LEBANON	17760	1968	28.0	31.8	33.2	6.1	1.0	43226	48370	57	74	1665	7.6	11.7	50.6	28.7	1.6	144138
04029	SEBAGO	21324	690	21.9	38.6	32.0	5.8	1.7	43277	48476	57	74	582	2.2	8.9	50.3	32.8	5.7	150000
04030	EAST WATERBORO	21079	546	18.1	31.5	41.9	6.6	1.8	50161	53837	72	89	456	3.7	1.8	60.3	33.3	0.9	149684
04032	FREEPORT	30801	3287	22.0	21.5	36.2	10.7	9.6	56932	64071	82	95	2566	5.1	6.3	22.6	49.5	16.6	229403
04037	FRYEBURG	21033	1288	32.5	35.3	26.0	4.0	2.2	37009	41605	35	45	989	4.7	13.5	47.4	31.7	2.8	144602
04038	GORHAM	24890	5329	19.7	25.4	38.1	10.9	6.0	54968	61966	80	94	4213	6.2	3.1	33.9	53.2	3.7	187543
04039	GRAY	25275	2725	13.1	31.0	42.3	9.9	3.8	54044	61465	78	93	2094	4.1	4.9	38.4	50.2	2.5	179795
04040	HARRISON	20164	1071	28.9	31.9	31.0	5.0	3.3	39652	43990	45	57	883	6.1	11.6	47.8	28.3	6.2	142561
04041	HIRAM	18273	735	33.7	33.5	26.7	4.1	2.0	36526	40705	34	43	616	5.4	17.4	54.9	21.8	0.7	125885
04042	HOLLIS CENTER	22361	1918	15.7	26.1	49.0	7.0	2.2	54310	60453	79	93	1605	6.6	6.4	44.5	40.1	2.5	165486
04043	KENNEBUNK	30938	4719	18.0	26.3	35.6	11.3	8.8	55335	62169	80	95	3793	0.0	1.6	24.7	57.5	16.2	229918
04046	KENNEBUNKPORT	33328	3308	15.0	25.2	40.5	11.0	8.3	58290	65227	83	96	2812	1.9	4.7	22.8	47.3	23.4	242045
04047	PARSONSFIELD	18974	676	30.2	41.7	22.0	4.0	2.1	35545	40041	30	39	549	7.3	9.8	55.7	21.1	6.0	135073
04048	LIMERICK	21465	1455	24.2	30.5	36.8	6.2	2.4	45983	50899	64	81	1212	5.0	9.4	52.6	31.2	1.9	144261
04049	LIMINGTON	19920	249	23.7	29.7	38.2	6.0	2.4	47349	52811	67	84	210	7.6	10.0	49.5	32.4	0.5	146023
04050	LONG ISLAND	19900	94	31.9	29.8	36.2	2.1	0.0	40000	45455	46	59	67	0.0	6.0	16.4	41.8	35.8	320833
04051	LOVELL	19895	364	31.3	31.6	30.0	5.0	2.2	37666	42358	38	49	305	6.9	13.4	43.3	29.5	6.9	140625
04055	NAPLES	20123	1461	28.8	32.3	32.2	5.3	1.3	41572	46344	52	67	1211	6.2	5.8	51.2	31.3	5.5	145449
04061	NORTH WATERBORO	18348	1032	14.4	37.8	42.4	4.2	1.2	48410	53406	69	86	917	2.2	2.1	72.9	22.8	0.1	139504
04062	WINDHAM	22887	6115	17.9	30.0	40.1	9.1	2.9	51421	58028	75	91	4894	2.5	3.3	45.2	44.7	4.3	173383
04064	OLD ORCHARD BEACH	24389	4498	29.6	33.0	31.4	4.0	2.1	40515	45330	48	62	2485	10.0	9.3	51.6	27.7	1.5	137062
04066	ORRS ISLAND	27666	346	20.5	32.1	33.5	10.1	3.8	48187	54135	69	86	273	0.7	4.4	38.5	44.3	12.1	187868
04068	PORTER	18227	627	32.2	33.8	29.7	2.6	1.8	36889	41057	35	45	517	6.8	16.6	60.9	14.7	1.0	125827
04069	POWNAL	29522	602	15.8	22.9	40.7	13.3	7.3	60129	66977	84	97	530	2.5	1.3	23.6	58.5	14.2	221622
04071	RAYMOND	28501	1961	12.1	29.6	40.9	8.8	8.6	57973	64424	83	96	1686	0.0	0.1	39.6	49.9	10.4	197656
04072	SACO	23438	7751	25.1	24.9	39.8	7.2	3.0	49978	54918	72	88	5266	5.2	4.9	43.0	42.6	4.3	170365
04073	SANFORD	18986	6769	33.6	30.4	30.2	4.6	1.3	36665	41054	34	44	4285	5.5	9.1	63.5	20.9	1.0	135674
04074	SCARBOROUGH	30944	7364	15.4	24.2	36.3	16.7	7.4	61533	70857	86	98	5862	2.7	1.3	20.0	64.0	12.0	236414
04076	SHAPLEIGH	21923	1008	17.5	39.1	34.3	7.4	1.7	46233	51609	64	82	866	1.5	5.7	49.3	40.2	3.4	163333
04079	HARPSWELL	37031	1792	25.1	34.3	23.9	8.4	8.3	42862	48147	56	72	1441	4.9	3.3	25.5	40.7	25.7	248732
04083	SPRINGVALE	21295	2071	28.1	28.3	33.5	6.8	3.4	43019	49470	56	72	1290	0.5	13.3	58.3	27.7	0.2	135284
04084	STANDISH	23327	2883	16.2	27.8	44.1	7.7	4.2	54296	61417	79	93	2471	7.0	4.7	37.8	46.7	3.8	175856
04085	STEEP FALLS	19729	854	19.9	30.8	42.2	6.1	1.1	49460	55421	71	88	749	3.1	7.6	52.9	35.5	0.9	157500
04086	TOPSHAM	24331	3756	17.8	29.6	40.7	9.1	2.9	51994	58064	75	91	2608	4.0	3.2	43.1	47.4	2.3	174509
04087	WATERBORO	20194	768	21.1	36.2	33.1	6.4	3.3	45361	50422	62	80	637	5.3	3.3	57.8	31.2	2.4	148788
04088	WATERFORD	18645	237	34.2	34.2	26.2	4.6	0.8	34546	38627	26	36	197	6.6	13.2	46.7	28.9	4.6	139145
04090	WELLS	26540	4552	19.9	28.8	37.0	9.9	4.6	51025	57670	74	90	3817	1.9	5.1	23.0	54.9	15.1	223279
04091	WEST BALDWIN	17526	331	30.5	31.4	33.2	3.6	1.2	40532	45338	48	62	282	8.2	13.1	53.6	23.1	2.1	135833
04092	WESTBROOK	22494	7096	27.7	30.1	33.9	6.4	1.9	42080	47579	53	69	4419	5.9	3.0	51.3	38.4	1.4	163955
04093	BUXTON	23152	2853	19.2	30.0	39.5	8.4	2.9	50732	56761	73	90	2417	0.6	8.2	46.3	43.4	1.5	167578
04095	WEST NEWFIELD	18854	546	24.7	35.0	34.8	3.9	1.7	42009	46636	53	69	459	3.3	6.1	59.0	31.2	0.4	142700
04096	YARMOUTH	39522	3538	17.4	19.3	35.4	13.6	14.4	65489	77267	89	98	2614	0.8	1.3	14.1	55.7	28.0	276950
04097	NORTH YARMOUTH	29082	1183	8.5	24.5	41.8	16.1	9.2	66564	77070	89	99	1070	0.6	2.3	22.1	63.6	11.5	232452
04101	PORTLAND	21749	9150	42.6	33.1	19.6	2.9	1.8	30376	34720	13	15	1421	1.1	6.5	41.1	45.5	5.8	177737
04102	PORTLAND	29539	8160	29.8	30.1	28.6	6.8	4.7	40339	47749	47	60	3545	0.5	1.9	37.9	50.0	9.7	191390
04103	PORTLAND	26054	13396	23.0	28.3	36.1	8.8	3.9	48682	55162	70	87	7693	0.7	0.9	41.8	54.1	2.5	185151
04105	FALMOUTH	42468	4231	12.7	20.9	30.9	16.6	18.9	72685	84649	92	99	3514	0.0	0.4	10.5	53.2	35.9	322656
04106	SOUTH PORTLAND	26047	10603	22.6	30.5	36.0	8.0	3.0	47442	54022	67	85	6649	0.5	2.4	52.4	42.2	2.5	168668
04107	CAPE ELIZABETH	45142	3675	11.1	19.1	30.8	17.8	21.2	78872	93747	95	100	3168	0.5	0.4	15.8	55.0	28.3	274945
04108	PEAKS ISLAND	35097	451	26.8	26.2	34.2	10.0	2.9	47359	54522	67	85	320	4.4	1.6	29.7	45.6	18.8	223276
04109	PORTLAND	65833	4	0.0	25.0	25.0	50.0	0.0	112500	137500	99	100	4	0.0	0.0	0.0	25.0	75.0	500000
04110	CUMBERLAND FORESIDE	45483	542	12.6	19.4	32.1	13.1	22.9	70746	85312	92	99	487	0.0	2.3	12.3	46.4	39.0	327703
04210	AUBURN	22264	10187	32.3	30.3	28.7	5.9	2.8	38707	43282	42	53	6107	3.8	13.5	66.9	14.4	1.4	118255
04216	ANDOVER	23537	353	33.1	31.7	25.2	6.0	4.0	39034	44542	43	54	294	14.3	14.6	42.2	23.1	5.8	129545
04217	BETHEL	20651	1436	32.2	33.8	27.4	4.0	2.6	37085	41761	36	46	1083	7.5	9.7	44.4	32.4	6.0	142991
04219	BRYANT POND	20146	821	26.8	39.5	26.9	4.1	2.7	39107	43967	43	55	684	11.6	20.9	40.9	23.1	3.5	120297
04220	BUCKFIELD	20044	735	22.9	40.3	30.2	4.9	1.8	40479	45079	48	61	616	7.8	17.7	56.7	17.2	0.7	121324
04221	CANTON	16910	820	33.3	32.0	30.5	3.3	1.0	38379	42643	41	51	686	15.6	23.0	45.2	14.7	1.5	110891
04222	DURHAM	24220	1362	14.1	26.4	46.8	8.3	4.3	57558	63472	82	95	1203	1.6	8.5	45.0	42.8	2.2	165943
04224	DIXFIELD	17702	1279	32.3	33.5	30.3	3.6	0.4	38960	42902	43	54	1027	11.9	26.8	51.1	9.5	0.7	102915
04225	DRYDEN	15271	28	35.7	32.1	28.6	3.6	0.0	35000	37333	28	37	24	16.7	20.8	50.0	12.5	0.0	104167
04226	EAST ANDOVER	23750	66	33.3	31.8	27.3	4.6	3.0	38629	44095	42	52	55	12.7	14.6	45.5	21.8	5.5	131250
04228	EAST LIVERMORE	20157	126	19.1	48.4	23.8	5.6	3.2	39666	43655	45	57	107	25.2	18.7	53.3	2.8	0.0	98125
04231	STONEHAM	22886	235	31.1	32.3	29.4	5.1	2.1	38014	42860	39	50	198	8.1	15.2	43.9	27.3	5.6	135811
04236	GREENE	22306	1561	14.5	32.0	44.6	6.9	2.1	52053	57530	76	91	1363	2.5	12.6	60.5	23.7	0.7	134337
04237	HANOVER	23870	108	28.7	27.8	37.0	2.8	3.7	40917	45458	49	64	88	6.8	5.7	55.7	25.0	6.8	145238
04238	HEBRON	21319	394	16.8	33.8	40.4	7.6	1.5	49699	54961	71	88	325	3.1	13.5	54.2	27.7	1.5	139904
04239	JAY	19676	2257	32.4	30.8	30.1	5.2	1.5	39151	42949	43	55	1801	9.9	16.5	58.3	13.8	1.6	120752
04240	LEWISTON	20240	15941	40.3	30.0	24.1	3.6	1.9	31487	34921	16	22	7810	6.2	14.3	66.9	12.2	0.5	117371
	MAINE	22411		29.6	30.7	30.0	6.5	3.2	40864	45987				8.5	14.0	43.9	28.6	5.1	138610
	UNITED STATES	25866		24.7	27.1	30.8	10.9	6.5	48124	56710				10.9	15.0	33.7	30.1	10.4	145905

ZIP CODE #	POST OFFICE NAME	FINANCIAL SERVICES: Auto Loan	FINANCIAL SERVICES: Home Loan	FINANCIAL SERVICES: Investments	FINANCIAL SERVICES: Retirement Plans	THE HOME: Home Improvements: Home Repair	THE HOME: Home Improvements: Lawn & Garden	THE HOME: Furnishings: Computers & Hardware	THE HOME: Furnishings: Major Appliances	THE HOME: Furnishings: TV, Radio, Sound Equipment	THE HOME: Furnishings: Furniture	ENTERTAINMENT: Dine out/ Carry out	ENTERTAINMENT: Sports Equipment	ENTERTAINMENT: Fees & Tickets	ENTERTAINMENT: Toys & Games	ENTERTAINMENT: Travel	ENTERTAINMENT: Cable TV	PERSONAL: Apparel & Services	PERSONAL: Auto Repairs	PERSONAL: Health Insurance	PERSONAL: Pets & Supplies
03901	BERWICK	82	83	79	84	82	85	81	82	79	81	98	96	80	98	79	76	95	81	77	92
03902	CAPE NEDDICK	127	120	103	114	127	136	111	123	115	110	140	144	107	142	116	119	134	120	132	155
03903	ELIOT	89	109	117	107	107	109	99	98	94	98	117	114	105	124	102	93	117	95	92	108
03904	KITTERY	74	80	89	81	79	83	81	79	78	79	98	93	82	100	80	76	96	79	75	86
03905	KITTERY POINT	100	117	123	116	116	119	107	108	101	107	127	124	112	130	110	100	126	105	101	120
03906	NORTH BERWICK	92	81	63	78	86	93	77	85	82	77	100	100	75	101	79	84	95	83	91	106
03907	OGUNQUIT	122	96	65	87	108	121	90	109	102	90	121	128	81	120	96	109	113	107	129	149
03908	SOUTH BERWICK	90	102	105	104	99	98	96	95	90	97	113	112	98	116	95	85	112	94	84	104
03909	YORK	120	125	121	121	129	135	115	122	114	114	141	142	115	144	119	116	137	119	124	146
04001	ACTON	89	75	54	69	81	89	70	80	76	69	92	95	66	92	73	80	86	79	91	107
04002	ALFRED	90	78	58	74	82	90	75	82	80	74	97	97	72	97	76	83	91	81	91	104
04003	BAILEY ISLAND	93	73	50	66	82	92	69	83	78	68	92	97	62	91	73	83	86	82	98	113
04005	BIDDEFORD	68	66	66	66	67	72	69	69	69	67	86	80	67	86	68	69	83	69	69	78
04006	BIDDEFORD POOL	131	103	70	93	116	130	97	117	110	96	130	137	87	128	103	117	121	115	138	160
04008	BOWDOINHAM	94	84	65	80	88	95	78	86	82	78	100	102	76	102	80	84	95	84	93	110
04009	BRIDGTON	82	62	39	57	70	79	62	73	70	60	82	85	54	80	64	74	76	72	87	97
04010	BROWNFIELD	80	62	41	56	70	79	59	71	67	58	79	84	52	78	63	71	73	70	84	97
04011	BRUNSWICK	79	81	90	82	81	86	82	81	81	81	101	95	83	101	82	79	99	82	79	91
04015	CASCO	93	77	55	71	84	93	72	84	79	71	95	99	67	95	76	83	89	82	96	112
04016	CENTER LOVELL	77	61	41	55	68	77	57	69	65	57	77	81	51	76	61	69	71	68	82	94
04017	CHEBEAGUE ISLAND	148	179	202	178	178	187	164	165	155	165	196	187	175	198	171	155	194	161	158	180
04019	CLIFF ISLAND	88	69	47	62	77	87	65	78	73	64	87	91	58	86	69	78	81	77	92	107
04020	CORNISH	78	69	53	66	73	79	64	71	68	64	83	85	63	85	66	70	79	69	77	92
04021	CUMBERLAND CENTER	137	170	183	173	166	166	151	149	139	152	176	172	163	184	154	135	176	143	134	165
04022	DENMARK	94	74	50	67	83	94	70	84	79	69	94	99	62	92	74	84	87	83	99	115
04024	EAST BALDWIN	74	66	50	62	69	74	61	67	64	61	78	80	60	80	63	66	75	66	73	87
04027	LEBANON	77	68	52	65	72	78	63	70	67	63	82	84	62	84	65	69	78	68	76	90
04029	SEBAGO	86	69	48	63	77	85	65	77	72	64	86	90	59	85	69	77	80	76	90	104
04030	EAST WATERBORO	88	78	60	74	83	89	72	80	77	72	93	95	71	95	74	79	89	78	87	103
04032	FREEPORT	102	115	124	115	114	118	108	109	104	109	130	126	112	132	110	102	129	107	103	121
04037	FRYEBURG	81	64	45	60	72	80	63	73	70	62	83	86	57	84	65	74	78	72	85	97
04038	GORHAM	95	102	104	103	101	103	98	98	94	98	117	115	99	119	97	91	115	97	92	110
04039	GRAY	93	95	89	95	95	98	91	93	89	91	110	109	90	112	90	87	107	92	89	106
04040	HARRISON	83	67	47	62	74	83	65	75	72	64	85	88	59	85	67	76	80	74	87	99
04041	HIRAM	74	62	47	60	66	74	62	68	67	61	81	79	59	80	63	69	76	67	76	84
04042	HOLLIS CENTER	86	89	84	89	88	89	84	86	81	85	102	102	84	103	84	79	99	85	80	99
04043	KENNEBUNK	101	110	122	112	110	114	106	106	102	107	128	122	109	126	107	99	125	106	101	117
04046	KENNEBUNKPORT	123	114	99	109	119	130	107	118	111	109	136	133	104	130	111	114	130	116	127	143
04047	PARSONSFIELD	77	61	41	55	68	77	57	69	65	57	77	81	51	76	61	69	71	68	81	94
04048	LIMERICK	88	80	65	76	84	90	75	83	78	75	96	98	72	96	77	80	91	81	88	104
04049	LIMINGTON	80	83	78	83	82	83	78	80	76	79	95	95	78	95	77	73	92	79	74	92
04050	LONG ISLAND	72	56	38	51	63	71	53	64	60	53	71	75	47	70	57	64	66	63	76	88
04051	LOVELL	84	65	44	59	74	83	62	74	70	61	83	87	55	82	66	75	77	73	88	102
04055	NAPLES	79	68	57	64	73	80	66	74	70	65	85	87	61	83	68	73	80	73	82	94
04061	NORTH WATERBORO	80	83	75	85	81	82	77	78	74	78	92	91	77	92	75	71	90	76	72	89
04062	WINDHAM	83	90	88	90	89	90	85	85	81	85	102	101	86	104	84	79	100	84	79	97
04064	OLD ORCHARD BEACH	73	66	62	66	67	72	68	70	69	67	85	83	65	84	67	68	82	71	71	83
04066	ORRS ISLAND	98	77	52	69	86	97	72	87	82	72	97	102	65	96	77	87	90	86	103	119
04068	PORTER	71	60	47	60	63	71	62	66	66	61	80	76	59	79	62	67	75	65	72	78
04069	POWNAL	100	124	131	124	121	120	110	110	102	110	129	129	117	137	113	99	128	106	98	122
04071	RAYMOND	111	108	96	105	110	114	102	109	102	103	126	128	99	126	103	101	122	108	108	130
04072	SACO	80	80	79	80	81	85	79	80	79	78	98	95	79	98	79	77	95	80	79	93
04073	SANFORD	72	61	49	58	64	72	61	66	66	61	81	77	59	81	62	69	76	66	74	81
04074	SCARBOROUGH	108	123	130	124	122	124	114	115	108	113	135	135	117	140	115	106	134	112	106	130
04076	SHAPLEIGH	92	72	49	65	81	91	68	82	77	67	91	96	61	90	72	82	85	80	96	111
04079	HARPSWELL	140	109	75	101	123	139	104	125	117	104	139	144	94	134	111	125	129	123	148	168
04083	SPRINGVALE	81	68	52	67	72	82	71	76	76	69	92	86	67	90	70	78	85	75	84	90
04084	STANDISH	89	97	96	98	96	96	91	92	87	92	109	109	92	111	91	83	107	91	84	104
04085	STEEP FALLS	78	83	80	83	81	81	78	79	75	79	94	94	79	95	77	72	92	78	72	89
04086	TOPSHAM	88	92	92	92	93	96	88	90	86	88	107	105	89	109	89	85	104	88	87	103
04087	WATERBORO	86	75	58	72	79	86	72	79	76	71	93	92	70	94	73	78	88	77	85	99
04088	WATERFORD	77	60	41	54	68	76	57	68	64	56	76	80	51	75	61	69	71	67	81	93
04090	WELLS	96	87	70	82	93	100	80	90	85	80	103	106	77	104	84	88	98	88	98	116
04091	WEST BALDWIN	73	65	50	62	69	74	60	67	64	60	78	80	59	80	62	66	74	65	72	86
04092	WESTBROOK	68	73	81	72	72	77	73	72	72	72	90	83	75	93	74	72	89	72	70	79
04093	BUXTON	87	89	81	88	90	92	82	86	82	83	101	102	83	104	83	81	98	84	84	102
04095	WEST NEWFIELD	84	66	45	59	74	83	62	75	70	61	83	87	55	82	66	75	77	74	88	102
04096	YARMOUTH	125	143	163	148	141	144	136	133	128	137	162	156	143	164	137	124	160	132	122	147
04097	NORTH YARMOUTH	112	133	135	136	129	126	119	119	110	121	139	139	125	144	119	105	138	115	104	130
04101	PORTLAND	54	46	59	50	45	50	59	53	59	56	74	66	55	70	54	55	72	59	50	59
04102	PORTLAND	81	77	100	82	77	84	87	82	87	85	109	99	86	108	85	85	106	86	80	92
04103	PORTLAND	78	85	101	87	84	88	86	83	83	85	104	98	88	106	86	81	103	84	78	91
04105	FALMOUTH	141	166	188	169	163	169	155	153	147	156	185	176	165	189	158	144	184	150	143	168
04106	SOUTH PORTLAND	76	83	97	83	82	87	84	81	82	83	103	95	86	105	84	81	101	82	78	89
04107	CAPE ELIZABETH	146	183	219	183	178	185	165	162	154	166	194	187	179	203	170	151	195	158	148	177
04108	PEAKS ISLAND	125	98	67	88	110	124	92	111	105	92	124	130	83	122	99	112	115	110	132	152
04109	PORTLAND	168	131	90	119	148	166	124	149	140	123	166	175	111	164	132	150	154	147	176	204
04110	CUMBERLAND FORESIDE	149	180	202	178	179	188	165	166	156	165	196	187	175	199	171	155	194	161	158	180
04210	AUBURN	70	68	72	68	69	75	71	71	72	69	89	82	70	90	71	72	86	71	72	80
04216	ANDOVER	88	69	47	63	78	88	65	79	74	65	88	92	58	86	70	79	81	78	93	108
04217	BETHEL	79	64	45	59	71	79	60	71	67	60	80	83	55	80	64	71	75	70	82	96
04219	BRYANT POND	82	65	45	59	73	81	61	73	69	60	81	85	55	81	65	73	76	72	86	99
04220	BUCKFIELD	80	72	55	68	76	81	66	73	70	66	85	87	65	87	68	72	81	71	79	95
04221	CANTON	77	56	32	49	63	72	53	65	62	54	74	77	47	71	56	67	68	65	79	91
04222	DURHAM	87	103	108	104	101	100	94	94	88	94	110	110	98	115	95	84	110	91	83	103
04224	DIXFIELD	70	59	43	56	63	70	57	64	61	56	74	75	54	74	58	64	69	62	71	82
04225	DRYDEN	67	52	36	47	59	66	49	59	56	49	66	69	44	65	53	60	61	58	70	81
04226	EAST ANDOVER	88	69	47	62	78	87	65	78	74	64	87	92	58	86	69	79	81	77	93	107
04228	EAST LIVERMORE	88	80	63	77	80	85	77	82	77	79	96	95	72	90	75	76	92	82	81	97
04231	STONEHAM	85	67	46	60	75	85	63	76	71	63	85	89	56	84	67	76	79	75	90	104
04236	GREENE	94	84	64	80	89	95	77	86	82	77	100	102	76	102	80	84	95	84	93	111
04237	HANOVER	93	73	50	66	82	93	69	83	78	68	93	97	62	91	74	83	86	82	98	114
04238	HEBRON	90	80	61	76	85	91	74	82	79	74	96	98	73	98	76	81	91	80	89	106
04239	JAY	75	64	47	61	69	76	62	69	67	61	81	81	59	81	63	69	76	67	77	87
04240	LEWISTON	62	57	59	56	58	65	61	61	64	59	78	71	60	78	61	65	75	63	65	70
	MAINE	80	73	65	71	75	82	72	77	75	71	92	90	70	91	73	76	88	76	81	93
	UNITED STATES	100	100	100	100	100	100	100	100	100	100	100	100	100	100	100	100	100	100	100	100

MAINE

POPULATION CHANGE

04250-04464

ZIP CODE		COUNTY FIPS CODE	POPULATION			2000-2004 ANNUAL RATE		HOUSEHOLDS					FAMILIES		
#	POST OFFICE NAME		2000	2004	2009	% Rate	State Centile	2000	2004	2009	% Annual Rate 2000-2004	2004 Average HH Size	2000	2004	% Annual Rate 2000-2004
04250	LISBON	001	3667	3732	3823	0.4	42	1525	1604	1692	1.2	2.31	1011	1064	1.2
04252	LISBON FALLS	001	5335	5366	5485	0.1	32	2065	2137	2244	0.8	2.51	1464	1515	0.8
04253	LIVERMORE	001	2164	2311	2432	1.6	80	869	958	1037	2.3	2.41	622	685	2.3
04254	LIVERMORE FALLS	001	2808	2843	2920	0.3	37	1170	1217	1283	0.9	2.30	727	756	0.9
04255	GREENWOOD	017	410	482	545	3.9	99	165	200	233	4.6	2.41	115	140	4.7
04256	MECHANIC FALLS	001	3001	3126	3252	1.0	61	1088	1159	1234	1.5	2.67	790	840	1.5
04257	MEXICO	017	2959	3100	3306	1.1	64	1298	1400	1534	1.8	2.21	832	899	1.8
04258	MINOT	001	2239	2429	2576	1.9	88	827	920	1002	2.5	2.63	662	737	2.6
04259	MONMOUTH	011	2729	2774	2805	0.4	41	1025	1074	1110	1.1	2.58	775	813	1.1
04260	NEW GLOUCESTER	005	4838	5198	5540	1.7	83	1774	1953	2123	2.3	2.65	1323	1453	2.2
04261	NEWRY	017	67	66	69	-0.4	14	31	32	34	0.8	2.06	21	22	1.1
04263	LEEDS	001	2001	2085	2163	1.0	62	736	791	844	1.7	2.64	548	589	1.7
04265	NORTH MONMOUTH	011	928	1009	1054	2.0	89	366	409	437	2.7	2.47	269	301	2.7
04266	NORTH TURNER	001	443	454	467	0.6	48	169	178	188	1.2	2.54	126	133	1.3
04267	NORTH WATERFORD	017	1297	1344	1422	0.8	57	529	565	615	1.6	2.38	384	411	1.6
04268	NORWAY	017	4656	4923	5263	1.3	73	1990	2161	2374	2.0	2.23	1269	1381	2.0
04270	OXFORD	017	5506	6037	6590	2.2	93	2066	2329	2611	2.9	2.59	1535	1732	2.9
04274	POLAND	001	4914	5178	5406	1.2	70	1855	2009	2154	1.9	2.57	1443	1562	1.9
04275	ROXBURY	017	505	597	676	4.0	100	215	262	304	4.8	2.27	146	177	4.6
04276	RUMFORD	017	6469	6607	6954	0.5	45	2874	3021	3268	1.2	2.15	1754	1849	1.3
04278	RUMFORD CENTER	017	89	88	92	-0.3	18	31	32	34	0.8	2.75	22	22	0.0
04280	SABATTUS	001	5731	6225	6609	2.0	89	2152	2401	2617	2.6	2.58	1645	1836	2.6
04281	SOUTH PARIS	017	4923	5149	5470	1.1	63	2037	2195	2400	1.8	2.24	1286	1390	1.9
04282	TURNER	001	4527	4801	5030	1.4	74	1597	1736	1864	2.0	2.76	1266	1376	2.0
04284	WAYNE	011	572	578	580	0.3	35	242	252	259	1.0	2.29	172	179	0.9
04285	WELD	007	402	414	436	0.7	50	176	187	203	1.4	2.21	130	139	1.6
04287	BOWDOIN	023	2667	2727	2819	0.5	46	968	1018	1079	1.2	2.67	747	786	1.2
04289	WEST PARIS	017	2092	2176	2304	0.9	61	784	837	911	1.6	2.47	561	600	1.6
04290	PERU	017	1515	1533	1601	0.3	36	585	608	652	0.9	2.52	437	454	0.9
04292	SUMNER	017	635	657	695	0.8	55	245	261	284	1.5	2.52	184	197	1.6
04294	WILTON	007	4069	4270	4544	1.1	67	1645	1777	1944	1.8	2.40	1134	1229	1.9
04330	AUGUSTA	011	24254	24705	25168	0.4	43	10684	11204	11660	1.1	2.14	6195	6527	1.2
04341	COOPERS MILLS	015	7	7	7	0.0	26	4	4	4	0.0	1.75	3	3	0.0
04342	DRESDEN	015	1625	1741	1835	1.6	81	642	706	761	2.3	2.47	455	501	2.3
04344	FARMINGDALE	011	2464	2496	2524	0.3	37	1067	1110	1145	0.9	2.22	679	705	0.9
04345	GARDINER	011	11741	11884	12014	0.3	37	4664	4859	5020	1.0	2.41	3189	3326	1.0
04346	RANDOLPH	011	3179	3180	3206	0.0	27	1335	1379	1423	0.8	2.30	904	933	0.8
04347	HALLOWELL	011	2526	2541	2572	0.1	32	1166	1201	1239	0.7	2.03	625	646	0.8
04348	JEFFERSON	015	2891	2997	3103	0.9	58	1144	1226	1302	1.6	2.44	822	882	1.7
04349	KENTS HILL	011	905	934	949	0.7	52	353	377	392	1.6	2.48	251	268	1.6
04350	LITCHFIELD	011	3104	3213	3274	0.8	56	1183	1262	1315	1.5	2.54	892	952	1.5
04351	MANCHESTER	011	2358	2369	2372	0.1	30	942	970	990	0.7	2.44	706	727	0.7
04352	MOUNT VERNON	011	998	1020	1031	0.5	46	401	423	437	1.3	2.40	297	314	1.3
04353	WHITEFIELD	015	2349	2399	2461	0.5	45	868	916	965	1.3	2.55	637	674	1.3
04354	PALERMO	027	1094	1195	1321	2.1	92	436	492	560	2.9	2.43	323	366	3.0
04355	READFIELD	011	2892	2930	2952	0.3	38	1073	1114	1144	0.9	2.63	826	858	0.9
04357	RICHMOND	023	2870	3257	3564	3.0	98	1123	1314	1477	3.8	2.46	780	913	3.8
04358	SOUTH CHINA	011	3436	3600	3689	1.1	64	1291	1395	1463	1.8	2.58	991	1071	1.8
04360	VIENNA	011	654	677	690	0.8	56	272	290	302	1.5	2.33	202	215	1.5
04363	WINDSOR	011	1629	1667	1686	0.5	46	621	654	675	1.2	2.55	455	479	1.2
04364	WINTHROP	011	6763	6829	6866	0.2	35	2714	2826	2906	1.0	2.35	1895	1974	1.0
04401	BANGOR	019	39932	42183	44194	1.3	71	16964	18482	19949	2.0	2.15	9609	10508	2.1
04406	ABBOT	021	796	813	854	0.5	45	351	372	404	1.4	2.19	251	266	1.4
04408	AURORA	009	172	188	210	2.1	92	71	80	93	2.9	2.35	45	51	3.0
04410	BRADFORD	019	1186	1219	1252	0.7	49	434	458	483	1.3	2.66	323	342	1.4
04411	BRADLEY	019	1140	1148	1166	0.2	33	473	490	512	0.8	2.34	335	349	1.0
04412	BREWER	019	8985	9288	9608	0.8	54	3841	4081	4339	1.4	2.24	2400	2563	1.6
04413	BROOKTON	029	186	177	170	-1.2	2	77	76	76	-0.3	2.33	51	51	0.0
04414	BROWNVILLE	021	1170	1188	1244	0.4	40	522	550	596	1.2	2.16	336	355	1.3
04416	BUCKSPORT	009	5441	5922	6628	2.0	89	2272	2560	2955	2.9	2.30	1523	1720	2.9
04417	BURLINGTON	019	561	563	571	0.1	29	224	233	243	0.9	2.42	160	166	0.9
04418	GREENBUSH	019	1421	1444	1473	0.4	40	522	546	572	1.1	2.64	390	409	1.1
04419	CARMEL	019	3732	3853	3966	0.8	53	1392	1474	1558	1.4	2.61	1088	1151	1.3
04421	CASTINE	009	1337	1389	1478	0.9	59	370	404	458	2.1	2.11	221	242	2.2
04422	CHARLESTON	019	1397	1414	1437	0.3	37	431	451	473	1.1	2.57	335	351	1.1
04423	COSTIGAN	019	539	546	557	0.3	37	198	207	217	1.1	2.64	137	143	Rate
04424	DANFORTH	029	958	976	973	0.4	43	407	429	439	1.3	2.24	281	296	1.2
04426	DOVER FOXCROFT	021	4880	5226	5631	1.6	81	1939	2148	2393	2.4	2.36	1354	1503	2.5
04427	CORINTH	019	2511	2604	2687	0.9	58	959	1022	1083	1.5	2.54	715	764	1.6
04428	EDDINGTON	019	2786	2888	2978	0.9	58	1125	1200	1273	1.5	2.39	808	864	1.6
04429	HOLDEN	009	4262	4422	4658	0.9	58	1722	1840	1993	1.6	2.40	1243	1332	1.6
04430	EAST MILLINOCKET	019	1828	1776	1794	-0.7	5	780	781	813	0.0	2.27	555	558	0.1
04431	EAST ORLAND	009	291	311	344	1.6	80	124	137	157	2.4	2.26	91	101	2.5
04434	ETNA	019	992	986	1002	-0.1	21	385	397	416	0.7	2.48	290	300	0.8
04435	EXETER	019	881	937	981	1.5	78	343	374	402	2.1	2.51	260	285	2.2
04438	FRANKFORT	027	1254	1314	1422	1.1	65	469	509	568	1.9	2.58	350	379	1.9
04441	GREENVILLE	021	1713	1781	1890	0.9	60	777	833	911	1.7	2.11	468	502	1.7
04442	GREENVILLE JUNCTION	021	99	102	108	0.7	51	45	48	53	1.5	2.13	28	30	1.6
04443	GUILFORD	021	2110	2146	2249	0.4	41	870	911	984	1.1	2.36	589	618	1.1
04444	HAMPDEN	019	8210	8614	8948	1.1	67	3187	3436	3667	1.8	2.50	2345	2537	1.9
04448	HOWLAND	019	1547	1534	1555	-0.2	20	635	650	679	0.6	2.29	424	436	0.7
04449	HUDSON	019	1377	1437	1488	1.0	63	502	538	572	1.6	2.67	381	409	1.7
04450	KENDUSKEAG	019	1171	1174	1189	0.1	28	470	488	510	0.9	2.41	330	344	1.0
04451	KINGMAN	003	320	304	303	-1.2	1	136	133	137	-0.5	2.29	103	101	-0.5
04453	LAGRANGE	019	930	943	966	0.3	39	355	371	391	1.0	2.54	239	251	1.2
04454	LAMBERT LAKE	029	55	52	50	-1.3	1	23	23	23	0.0	2.26	15	15	0.0
04455	LEE	019	845	835	847	-0.3	17	298	302	314	0.3	2.74	248	252	0.4
04456	LEVANT	019	2171	2307	2412	1.4	77	784	856	920	2.1	2.70	610	668	2.2
04457	LINCOLN	019	6256	6243	6346	-0.1	23	2502	2569	2685	0.6	2.40	1768	1822	0.7
04459	MATTAWAMKEAG	019	739	731	742	-0.3	18	304	310	325	0.5	2.36	211	217	0.7
04460	MEDWAY	003	1590	1555	1573	-0.5	9	632	642	671	0.4	2.42	470	480	0.5
04461	MILFORD	019	2419	2475	2535	0.5	46	959	1011	1066	1.3	2.45	651	689	1.3
04462	MILLINOCKET	019	5226	5045	5092	-0.8	3	2307	2301	2394	-0.1	2.18	1564	1567	0.1
04463	MILO	021	2861	2996	3190	1.1	64	1218	1315	1444	1.8	2.28	813	879	1.9
04464	MONSON	021	742	760	799	0.6	47	333	354	385	1.5	2.14	206	220	1.6
	MAINE					0.9					1.5	2.33			1.6
	UNITED STATES					1.2					1.3	2.58			1.1

125-A

ZIP CODE #	POST OFFICE NAME	RACE (%) White 2000	White 2004	Black 2000	Black 2004	Asian/Pacific 2000	Asian/Pacific 2004	% Hispanic Origin 2000	% Hispanic Origin 2004	2004 AGE DISTRIBUTION (%) 0-4	5-9	10-14	15-19	20-24	25-44	45-64	65-84	85+	18+	MEDIAN AGE 2004	% 2004 Males	% 2004 Females
04250	LISBON	97.5	97.2	0.7	0.8	0.6	0.7	0.5	0.7	7.2	7.0	7.0	6.4	6.3	29.3	23.7	11.8	1.2	74.9	36.9	49.1	50.9
04252	LISBON FALLS	97.3	97.1	0.6	0.7	0.4	0.6	0.9	1.1	7.0	6.7	7.3	7.0	6.9	30.0	24.0	10.0	1.1	74.8	36.1	49.3	50.8
04253	LIVERMORE	98.9	99.0	0.2	0.2	0.0	0.0	0.3	0.4	5.5	5.9	6.3	6.6	5.0	28.3	28.4	12.6	1.4	78.2	40.9	53.3	46.7
04254	LIVERMORE FALLS	97.3	97.2	0.5	0.6	0.2	0.3	1.1	1.3	6.9	6.8	8.0	7.1	6.5	26.7	23.0	12.8	2.2	73.4	37.0	49.2	50.8
04255	GREENWOOD	97.8	97.5	0.0	0.2	0.2	0.4	0.5	0.4	4.8	5.6	7.3	6.4	4.2	26.4	30.9	13.7	0.8	78.0	42.0	50.4	49.6
04256	MECHANIC FALLS	97.3	96.9	0.5	0.5	0.7	0.8	0.5	0.7	6.4	6.7	8.1	7.4	5.5	29.6	25.4	9.5	1.4	74.3	36.9	49.3	50.7
04257	MEXICO	97.9	97.7	0.2	0.2	1.0	1.2	0.3	0.3	5.2	5.5	7.1	6.7	5.5	24.9	25.8	17.7	1.7	77.7	42.4	49.2	50.8
04258	MINOT	98.2	98.0	0.2	0.3	0.4	0.5	0.4	0.4	6.2	6.7	7.7	7.1	5.2	30.6	27.1	8.6	1.0	74.4	38.5	49.7	50.4
04259	MONMOUTH	98.7	98.5	0.2	0.2	0.2	0.2	0.8	1.1	6.9	7.4	7.8	7.2	5.6	28.3	27.1	9.1	0.8	73.0	38.2	48.4	51.6
04260	NEW GLOUCESTER	98.2	97.9	0.2	0.3	0.5	0.6	0.6	0.7	6.8	7.2	8.0	7.4	5.6	31.1	26.2	7.1	0.7	73.1	37.2	50.3	49.7
04261	NEWRY	98.5	100.0	0.0	0.0	0.0	0.0	0.0	0.0	3.0	4.6	6.1	6.1	3.0	21.2	40.9	15.2	0.0	86.4	48.3	51.5	48.5
04263	LEEDS	99.1	98.9	0.2	0.2	0.1	0.1	0.5	0.7	5.2	6.5	8.4	8.3	5.5	28.8	27.9	8.7	0.9	74.1	37.3	50.6	49.5
04265	NORTH MONMOUTH	97.7	97.4	0.9	0.9	0.2	0.3	0.4	0.6	6.7	7.2	7.2	5.7	5.1	27.6	29.2	10.3	1.0	75.3	40.0	48.5	51.5
04266	NORTH TURNER	92.8	91.9	0.0	0.0	0.2	0.2	7.7	9.3	7.7	7.9	7.5	7.1	6.0	26.9	26.4	9.7	0.9	71.8	37.1	48.9	51.1
04267	NORTH WATERFORD	98.7	98.5	0.1	0.2	0.2	0.2	0.4	0.5	5.2	5.5	6.5	6.1	4.5	24.2	32.4	14.3	1.3	78.9	43.9	49.4	50.6
04268	NORWAY	97.8	97.7	0.3	0.4	0.4	0.5	0.5	0.6	5.4	5.5	6.1	5.9	5.8	23.9	29.5	15.0	3.0	79.1	43.3	47.2	52.8
04270	OXFORD	98.0	97.8	0.3	0.3	0.3	0.4	0.5	0.5	5.9	6.2	6.9	7.1	5.5	27.6	28.3	11.4	1.1	76.3	40.0	49.5	50.5
04274	POLAND	98.5	98.4	0.3	0.4	0.2	0.3	0.3	0.4	5.9	6.0	7.5	6.8	4.2	29.4	29.5	9.8	0.8	76.1	40.0	50.6	49.4
04275	ROXBURY	98.0	98.0	0.2	0.2	0.8	1.0	0.0	0.0	3.7	4.5	7.0	7.2	3.7	27.0	27.8	17.6	1.5	79.2	43.6	51.6	48.4
04276	RUMFORD	98.7	98.5	0.1	0.1	0.3	0.3	0.6	0.8	5.5	5.3	6.4	6.7	6.4	23.4	25.3	18.2	2.9	78.4	42.6	47.9	52.1
04278	RUMFORD CENTER	98.9	100.0	0.0	0.0	0.0	0.0	0.0	0.0	4.6	4.6	6.8	5.7	4.6	22.7	34.1	14.8	2.3	80.7	45.6	51.1	48.9
04280	SABATTUS	98.0	97.8	0.2	0.3	0.4	0.5	0.5	0.5	6.4	6.7	7.3	6.8	5.7	31.0	25.9	9.3	0.8	75.2	37.5	50.3	49.7
04281	SOUTH PARIS	97.9	97.7	0.3	0.3	0.9	1.2	0.4	0.4	5.3	5.5	6.3	6.1	6.1	25.7	25.4	16.6	3.0	79.2	41.6	47.8	52.2
04282	TURNER	97.2	96.9	0.1	0.1	0.3	0.4	2.3	2.6	6.6	7.0	8.0	7.6	6.2	28.4	27.0	8.4	0.8	73.6	37.3	49.6	50.5
04284	WAYNE	98.6	98.4	0.4	0.4	0.2	0.2	0.2	0.2	2.8	5.5	8.0	7.6	2.8	22.7	34.3	14.5	1.9	78.2	45.3	50.5	49.5
04285	WELD	97.8	97.8	0.3	0.2	0.0	0.0	0.5	0.7	5.1	5.8	7.7	6.5	2.2	28.7	30.4	12.6	1.0	76.8	41.7	53.9	46.1
04287	BOWDOIN	97.8	97.5	0.3	0.3	0.4	0.4	0.8	0.8	6.2	6.6	8.0	7.7	6.3	29.7	27.6	7.2	0.8	74.5	38.1	49.9	50.1
04289	WEST PARIS	98.8	98.8	0.1	0.1	0.1	0.1	0.3	0.5	6.4	6.4	6.4	5.9	5.2	25.5	26.7	13.5	4.0	76.9	41.4	48.3	51.8
04290	PERU	99.3	99.2	0.0	0.0	0.1	0.2	0.4	0.5	4.4	6.2	7.8	8.3	5.2	25.5	26.7	14.2	1.7	75.9	41.4	50.0	50.0
04292	SUMNER	98.6	98.6	0.2	0.2	0.0	0.0	0.5	0.3	5.6	5.9	5.5	6.2	5.6	26.0	33.5	9.9	1.7	79.3	42.2	49.2	50.8
04294	WILTON	97.5	97.2	0.4	0.4	0.8	1.0	0.4	0.6	5.6	5.7	7.1	7.4	6.6	24.6	29.0	12.1	1.8	77.1	40.6	48.2	51.8
04330	AUGUSTA	96.7	96.3	0.4	0.5	1.2	1.5	0.8	0.9	5.3	5.4	6.4	6.1	6.3	27.3	27.4	13.7	2.3	79.3	40.8	48.3	51.7
04341	COOPERS MILLS	100.0	100.0	0.0	0.0	0.0	0.0	0.0	0.0	0.0	0.0	0.0	0.0	28.6	71.4	0.0	0.0	0.0	100.0	28.8	57.1	42.9
04342	DRESDEN	97.4	97.1	0.3	0.3	0.5	0.6	0.1	0.1	6.7	7.2	7.9	5.9	4.5	28.9	27.6	10.2	1.2	74.6	38.6	51.1	48.9
04344	FARMINGDALE	97.3	97.0	0.8	0.9	0.6	0.7	0.5	0.6	6.5	6.2	6.1	6.9	6.0	25.1	27.0	14.2	2.1	77.0	40.6	45.8	54.2
04345	GARDINER	97.3	97.1	0.4	0.4	0.3	0.4	0.7	0.8	5.7	5.9	6.8	6.8	6.3	27.9	28.3	10.9	1.6	77.2	39.8	48.9	51.1
04346	RANDOLPH	97.4	97.1	0.4	0.4	0.3	0.4	0.8	1.0	5.6	6.0	7.0	6.5	6.1	26.2	27.7	13.5	1.5	77.3	40.4	50.0	50.0
04347	HALLOWELL	97.3	97.1	0.4	0.4	0.9	1.1	1.1	1.3	4.0	4.2	5.8	7.6	7.3	23.7	32.0	12.8	2.5	80.8	43.3	47.7	52.3
04348	JEFFERSON	98.6	98.5	0.1	0.1	0.2	0.2	0.5	0.5	5.3	5.9	7.1	6.7	5.0	25.9	30.7	12.3	1.2	77.0	41.8	49.5	50.5
04349	KENTS HILL	98.5	98.3	0.0	0.0	0.6	0.8	0.4	0.4	5.5	6.1	6.6	5.3	5.6	25.0	33.7	11.2	1.1	78.7	42.8	50.4	49.6
04350	LITCHFIELD	98.4	98.2	0.1	0.1	0.4	0.5	0.7	0.9	5.6	6.1	7.8	7.1	5.0	27.7	29.8	9.9	0.9	75.8	40.0	49.4	50.6
04351	MANCHESTER	97.8	97.6	0.0	0.0	0.4	0.5	0.4	0.6	5.5	6.2	6.9	6.3	5.1	23.5	31.1	13.5	2.0	77.5	43.1	48.5	51.5
04352	MOUNT VERNON	97.7	97.4	0.2	0.3	0.3	0.5	0.4	0.4	4.5	6.0	7.1	8.2	4.8	25.5	33.7	9.3	0.9	76.1	41.5	50.3	49.7
04353	WHITEFIELD	97.3	97.0	0.2	0.2	0.5	0.6	0.9	1.1	4.9	5.7	8.0	7.0	6.0	27.1	29.6	9.8	1.8	76.4	39.7	49.2	50.9
04354	PALERMO	97.7	97.6	0.4	0.3	0.4	0.3	0.3	0.4	5.7	5.8	6.8	5.9	3.9	26.4	31.5	12.9	1.2	77.9	42.1	50.6	49.4
04355	READFIELD	97.7	97.6	0.1	0.1	0.5	0.6	0.9	1.1	6.0	6.4	8.3	8.2	4.5	24.1	31.9	9.8	0.9	73.6	40.4	50.8	49.3
04357	RICHMOND	98.2	98.1	0.4	0.5	0.3	0.4	0.9	1.1	6.3	6.6	7.6	7.3	6.0	27.4	27.5	10.1	1.3	74.5	38.4	49.1	50.9
04358	SOUTH CHINA	98.0	97.8	0.2	0.2	0.4	0.5	0.6	0.8	5.7	6.1	8.3	7.8	5.9	28.4	28.7	8.4	0.8	75.2	37.8	49.9	50.1
04360	VIENNA	98.3	98.2	0.2	0.3	0.2	0.2	0.5	0.6	4.3	5.3	8.4	6.7	5.3	24.8	34.0	10.3	0.9	77.3	42.2	49.6	50.4
04363	WINDSOR	98.5	98.4	0.3	0.2	0.1	0.1	0.6	0.8	6.7	6.7	7.3	6.8	5.7	29.2	26.8	9.8	1.0	75.1	37.6	48.2	51.8
04364	WINTHROP	98.4	98.3	0.3	0.3	0.4	0.5	0.5	0.6	4.5	5.2	6.7	6.8	5.3	23.9	30.4	14.7	2.5	79.2	43.6	49.7	50.3
04401	BANGOR	95.5	95.2	0.9	0.9	1.1	1.3	0.9	1.1	5.7	5.3	6.2	7.1	8.6	28.8	25.0	11.2	2.0	78.8	37.3	47.7	52.3
04406	ABBOT	97.7	97.8	0.1	0.1	0.1	0.1	0.1	0.1	4.1	4.1	5.7	6.3	3.4	24.5	36.2	15.0	0.9	81.3	46.0	50.7	49.3
04408	AURORA	98.3	98.4	0.0	0.0	0.0	0.0	0.6	1.1	5.9	5.3	7.5	5.9	4.3	28.7	32.5	10.1	0.0	76.6	41.1	51.6	48.4
04410	BRADFORD	97.4	97.4	0.3	0.3	0.0	0.0	0.9	1.1	7.1	7.0	7.6	7.2	6.3	29.5	23.6	10.8	0.9	74.1	36.4	52.1	47.9
04411	BRADLEY	98.5	98.3	0.2	0.2	0.2	0.2	0.7	0.7	5.1	5.6	6.3	5.3	5.7	31.4	27.0	12.4	1.3	79.6	40.3	49.5	50.5
04412	BREWER	97.6	97.4	0.3	0.3	0.6	0.7	0.6	0.8	5.5	5.5	6.7	6.4	6.5	27.5	25.4	14.2	2.5	78.3	40.3	47.9	52.1
04413	BROOKTON	95.2	94.4	0.5	0.6	0.0	0.0	1.1	0.6	3.4	4.0	4.5	6.8	5.7	24.3	33.3	17.0	1.1	83.6	45.8	52.5	47.5
04414	BROWNVILLE	98.1	97.8	0.0	0.0	0.1	0.2	0.9	0.9	4.6	4.9	5.9	5.6	6.0	22.1	30.6	17.4	3.0	81.0	45.6	49.6	50.4
04416	BUCKSPORT	98.1	98.1	0.1	0.1	0.2	0.2	0.8	1.0	5.2	5.8	7.1	7.2	5.8	26.8	27.9	12.5	1.8	77.2	40.3	48.4	51.6
04417	BURLINGTON	99.3	99.1	0.0	0.0	0.2	0.4	0.4	0.5	5.2	5.5	5.7	6.6	7.3	26.8	31.1	11.2	0.7	80.1	41.0	53.1	46.9
04418	GREENBUSH	96.5	96.3	0.7	0.8	0.1	0.1	0.3	0.4	5.8	5.9	8.5	10.3	5.5	31.9	25.6	6.3	0.4	72.9	35.8	50.9	49.1
04419	CARMEL	98.3	98.0	0.2	0.2	0.5	0.7	0.4	0.5	5.7	6.2	8.2	7.1	5.9	28.9	28.9	8.5	0.8	75.6	38.8	49.4	50.6
04421	CASTINE	97.1	96.7	0.7	0.7	0.8	0.9	0.6	0.8	3.2	3.1	3.2	9.9	23.2	22.7	20.2	12.1	2.5	89.6	28.0	63.4	36.6
04422	CHARLESTON	98.3	98.0	0.7	0.8	0.2	0.3	0.2	0.4	4.6	5.4	6.7	8.3	6.8	32.5	28.0	7.2	0.6	78.4	37.6	52.3	47.7
04423	COSTIGAN	97.6	97.3	0.0	0.2	0.4	0.6	0.6	0.7	5.3	5.3	5.7	6.8	7.1	31.5	26.9	10.6	0.7	79.9	38.4	51.1	48.9
04424	DANFORTH	99.4	99.4	0.1	0.1	0.2	0.2	0.0	0.1	4.5	4.8	6.9	7.2	4.9	22.3	29.1	18.3	2.0	78.7	44.6	50.7	49.3
04426	DOVER FOXCROFT	96.9	96.7	0.2	0.2	0.5	0.6	0.9	1.0	4.5	5.0	7.0	7.1	5.9	23.3	30.0	14.2	3.0	78.6	43.2	48.6	51.5
04427	CORINTH	98.2	98.0	0.1	0.1	0.1	0.1	0.8	0.9	6.6	6.8	7.2	6.0	5.8	29.5	26.8	10.2	1.2	75.5	37.7	49.3	50.7
04428	EDDINGTON	97.9	97.9	0.2	0.2	0.3	0.4	0.4	0.4	4.9	5.2	6.4	6.7	5.5	28.2	29.2	12.8	1.1	79.1	41.2	49.7	50.4
04429	HOLDEN	98.2	97.9	0.2	0.2	0.5	0.6	0.3	0.4	5.1	5.5	6.6	7.0	4.5	27.5	32.7	10.2	1.0	78.1	42.1	50.7	49.3
04430	EAST MILLINOCKET	98.3	98.2	0.0	0.0	0.4	0.5	0.3	0.3	4.5	5.4	7.3	6.9	3.8	22.8	27.3	20.0	2.1	78.2	44.7	48.2	51.8
04431	EAST ORLAND	97.9	98.1	0.0	0.0	0.0	0.0	0.0	0.3	5.8	5.5	5.8	7.1	3.9	28.0	33.1	10.6	0.3	77.5	42.0	51.5	48.6
04434	ETNA	99.1	99.0	0.2	0.2	0.3	0.4	0.1	0.1	7.3	7.1	6.1	5.3	6.0	29.2	28.5	9.7	0.8	76.4	38.3	47.9	52.1
04435	EXETER	99.0	99.0	0.0	0.0	0.0	0.0	0.1	0.1	5.7	5.1	7.4	5.3	4.7	29.0	29.7	12.6	0.5	78.2	40.4	51.6	48.5
04438	FRANKFORT	97.6	97.5	0.1	0.1	0.2	0.3	0.4	0.5	6.9	6.7	6.5	6.5	6.2	31.3	26.8	8.5	0.6	75.8	36.7	48.7	51.3
04441	GREENVILLE	98.8	98.7	0.1	0.2	0.2	0.3	0.2	0.3	5.0	5.2	5.5	7.5	5.2	20.6	30.9	16.7	3.4	78.4	45.6	48.4	51.6
04442	GREENVILLE JUNCTION	98.0	98.0	0.0	0.0	0.0	0.0	0.0	0.0	3.9	9.8	2.0	5.9	1.0	23.5	44.1	9.8	0.0	81.4	46.0	52.0	48.0
04443	GUILFORD	97.3	97.0	0.3	0.3	0.5	0.6	0.3	0.5	4.9	5.5	6.2	7.0	5.6	25.0	29.4	14.3	2.1	78.9	42.1	48.8	51.2
04444	HAMPDEN	98.0	97.7	0.4	0.4	0.5	0.7	0.5	0.6	5.3	6.0	7.5	7.2	5.7	26.4	30.8	10.1	1.1	76.6	40.5	48.9	51.2
04448	HOWLAND	98.3	98.2	0.2	0.2	0.1	0.1	0.1	0.1	5.7	5.9	6.7	6.4	5.2	25.4	27.3	15.1	2.5	77.4	41.9	47.0	53.0
04449	HUDSON	97.8	97.6	0.5	0.6	0.2	0.3	0.2	0.3	6.9	6.6	6.9	7.2	6.5	32.4	25.6	7.5	0.4	75.2	36.4	50.7	49.3
04450	KENDUSKEAG	97.0	96.9	0.3	0.3	0.0	0.0	0.3	0.5	5.5	5.7	5.8	5.7	6.6	29.3	30.6	10.6	0.3	79.5	39.7	49.8	50.2
04451	KINGMAN	98.1	98.0	0.6	0.7	0.3	0.3	0.3	0.3	4.0	5.3	7.9	6.6	4.9	26.0	29.9	14.8	0.7	78.0	42.5	50.0	50.0
04453	LAGRANGE	97.5	97.5	0.4	0.4	0.5	0.6	0.2	0.2	5.7	6.0	7.3	7.1	6.4	29.3	26.9	9.9	1.4	76.3	38.7	49.4	50.6
04454	LAMBERT LAKE	94.6	96.2	0.0	0.0	0.0	0.0	0.0	0.0	3.9	3.9	3.9	7.7	7.7	25.0	30.8	17.3	0.0	84.6	43.8	50.0	50.0
04455	LEE	98.8	98.8	0.0	0.0	0.1	0.1	0.1	0.1	5.5	6.0	8.7	8.3	3.4	30.3	22.5	14.1	1.2	73.4	38.8	51.7	48.3
04456	LEVANT	97.5	97.4	0.1	0.2	0.2	0.2	0.7	0.8	6.4	6.9	9.2	7.4	5.2	31.2	25.6	7.6	0.6	72.9	36.6	49.5	50.5
04457	LINCOLN	98.4	98.3	0.1	0.1	0.4	0.5	0.3	0.4	5.3	6.0	7.4	6.6	5.4	25.3	27.4	14.3	2.3	77.2	41.2	48.5	51.5
04459	MATTAWAMKEAG	98.1	98.0	0.0	0.0	0.0	0.0	0.1	0.1	6.4	6.2	7.0	6.7	5.1	24.5	27.6	14.6	1.9	76.7	41.5	48.6	51.4
04460	MEDWAY	99.2	99.2	0.1	0.1	0.1	0.1	0.3	0.3	4.6	5.3	7.0	7.5	6.9	25.0	32.0	11.5	0.5	78.6	41.8	53.1	46.9
04461	MILFORD	96.6	96.4	0.1	0.2	0.5	0.6	0.5	0.6	5.5	5.4	6.0	6.5	6.9	33.4	25.5	10.0	0.8	79.0	37.2	49.7	50.3
04462	MILLINOCKET	98.5	98.4	0.1	0.1	0.4	0.5	0.2	0.2	3.4	4.3	6.2	6.8	4.4	21.5	33.1	17.9	2.5	81.8	46.6	48.5	51.5
04463	MILO	98.5	98.3	0.3	0.3	0.2	0.2	0.2	0.3	5.5	5.7	6.3	7.0	5.6	24.3	27.4	15.9	2.3	78.1	42.2	48.2	51.8
04464	MONSON	98.0	98.0	0.0	0.0	0.0	0.0	0.4	0.4	6.1	6.3	6.6	5.8	4.3	22.6	29.2	16.8	2.2	77.0	44.0	49.9	50.1
	MAINE	97.0	96.6	0.5	0.6	0.7	0.9	0.7	0.9	5.5	5.8	6.7	6.9	6.5	26.7	27.5	12.5	2.0	77.9	40.2	48.8	51.2
	UNITED STATES	75.1	73.6	12.3	12.5	3.8	4.2	12.5	14.1	6.9	6.7	7.2	7.0	7.3	28.6	23.8	10.8	1.7	75.1	36.0	49.1	50.9

ZIP CODE #	POST OFFICE NAME	2004 Per Capita Income	2004 HH Income Base	2004 HOUSEHOLD INCOME DISTRIBUTION (%) Less than $25,000	$25,000 to $49,999	$50,000 to $99,999	$100,000 to $149,999	$150,000 or More	MEDIAN HOUSEHOLD INCOME 2004	2009	2004 National Centile	2004 State Centile	2004 Home Value Base	2004 HOME VALUE DISTRIBUTION (%) Less than $50,000	$50,000 to $89,999	$90,000 to $174,999	$175,000 to $399,999	$400,000 or More	2004 Median Home Value
04250	LISBON	20225	1604	27.1	38.4	29.2	3.2	2.1	39337	44482	44	56	1184	23.4	10.5	54.9	11.0	0.3	108401
04252	LISBON FALLS	19830	2137	23.5	35.8	34.3	5.5	0.9	43826	50504	58	75	1605	12.8	7.8	71.7	7.5	0.1	118763
04253	LIVERMORE	20203	958	26.1	34.8	33.0	4.9	1.3	41930	46409	53	69	834	8.9	25.9	55.8	9.5	0.0	108621
04254	LIVERMORE FALLS	16459	1217	39.8	37.1	18.7	3.0	1.3	30232	31664	13	15	798	23.1	33.5	40.1	3.4	0.0	81875
04255	GREENWOOD	22296	200	30.5	31.5	29.0	6.0	3.0	40000	45160	46	59	169	10.1	17.2	45.6	24.9	2.4	124583
04256	MECHANIC FALLS	16915	1159	30.0	36.1	29.3	3.3	1.4	37896	41622	39	50	897	16.3	17.8	58.1	7.0	0.8	106229
04257	MEXICO	18630	1400	41.7	28.6	24.9	3.4	1.4	30900	33380	15	18	942	22.0	33.0	39.6	5.2	0.2	83733
04258	MINOT	22136	920	16.2	31.7	41.7	7.7	2.6	51168	55842	74	90	828	3.5	13.3	58.9	23.3	1.0	132667
04259	MONMOUTH	19820	1074	22.7	30.2	39.9	5.8	1.5	47474	51704	67	85	879	7.7	13.3	53.0	22.4	3.5	131092
04260	NEW GLOUCESTER	22608	1953	17.6	27.3	42.1	10.9	2.1	54390	61551	79	94	1642	5.7	5.0	40.1	45.8	3.4	173333
04261	NEWRY	25099	32	34.4	31.3	25.0	6.3	3.1	37339	42353	37	48	27	7.4	14.8	48.2	25.9	3.7	135417
04263	LEEDS	18163	791	26.2	36.5	30.5	5.3	1.5	40543	44818	48	63	672	7.0	18.8	57.4	15.6	1.2	122396
04265	NORTH MONMOUTH	19723	409	27.4	26.9	39.1	5.9	0.7	46246	50778	64	83	354	14.4	17.5	53.7	13.8	0.6	113520
04266	NORTH TURNER	28002	178	25.8	29.8	28.7	9.0	6.7	47033	53026	66	84	139	7.2	11.5	59.7	21.6	0.0	123397
04267	NORTH WATERFORD	19278	565	33.3	34.3	26.6	4.4	1.4	35159	39195	28	38	470	6.8	13.4	46.4	28.9	4.5	138636
04268	NORWAY	18808	2161	38.9	32.6	21.9	4.9	1.8	31204	34489	15	20	1493	15.9	14.2	49.8	17.6	2.6	115394
04270	OXFORD	19137	2329	24.4	36.8	31.9	5.5	1.5	42562	47227	55	71	1977	10.1	18.4	47.7	22.6	1.3	124586
04274	POLAND	25430	2009	19.0	30.0	36.5	9.2	5.4	50859	56191	74	90	1758	13.2	13.9	45.6	24.2	3.1	128166
04275	ROXBURY	18543	262	34.7	37.8	21.4	5.7	0.4	32867	36016	21	29	189	20.6	30.2	41.8	6.9	0.5	89167
04276	RUMFORD	18613	3021	40.5	30.9	23.2	4.0	1.5	29534	32209	11	12	1817	7.8	28.9	50.7	12.3	0.3	105719
04278	RUMFORD CENTER	18665	32	34.4	31.3	25.0	6.3	3.1	37339	42353	37	48	27	7.4	14.8	48.2	25.9	3.7	135417
04280	SABATTUS	19611	2401	21.5	32.0	40.3	5.1	1.2	46736	50945	66	83	2020	7.1	27.5	55.3	9.4	0.8	114697
04281	SOUTH PARIS	18746	2195	37.8	31.3	25.7	3.7	1.5	36246	40226	33	42	1501	9.1	15.9	55.0	17.8	2.2	122433
04282	TURNER	26252	1736	19.0	30.3	37.0	6.8	6.9	50527	55475	73	89	1450	6.1	11.9	55.3	24.1	2.7	139399
04284	WAYNE	30316	252	19.1	31.8	32.9	8.3	7.9	49096	53216	70	88	208	1.4	9.1	37.0	42.8	9.6	181250
04285	WELD	17978	187	36.9	36.4	23.0	3.2	0.5	32853	36729	20	29	161	16.2	21.1	48.5	13.0	1.2	105449
04287	BOWDOIN	19915	1018	16.9	37.2	38.8	5.1	2.0	47359	52609	67	85	879	9.4	9.8	45.2	34.5	1.1	142361
04289	WEST PARIS	16308	837	36.9	33.7	25.3	3.4	0.7	33833	37341	24	32	665	9.0	25.1	48.7	15.5	1.7	113194
04290	PERU	18270	608	26.8	34.5	34.2	4.1	0.3	41543	46104	51	66	554	10.7	25.3	46.8	17.0	0.4	110177
04292	SUMNER	20031	261	25.3	33.0	33.3	7.3	1.2	41241	45917	51	65	235	8.5	26.4	51.1	12.8	1.3	110142
04294	WILTON	20111	1777	35.1	29.8	26.2	6.5	2.4	37041	40475	36	46	1376	11.9	27.1	45.5	13.4	2.1	103600
04330	AUGUSTA	21209	11204	35.7	31.4	26.4	4.8	1.7	35452	39442	29	39	6862	7.9	14.8	59.4	16.2	1.8	120108
04341	COOPERS MILLS	0	0	0.0	0.0	0.0	0.0	0.0	0	67500	0	0	4	0.0	0.0	100.0	0.0	0.0	125000
04342	DRESDEN	21463	706	24.7	32.7	35.7	4.8	2.1	45163	49230	62	80	597	7.7	12.9	44.7	29.0	5.7	140530
04344	FARMINGDALE	20877	1110	30.9	31.5	31.4	4.4	1.7	40135	45506	47	59	729	10.3	7.3	62.6	19.1	0.8	128562
04345	GARDINER	21388	4859	27.3	31.0	32.6	6.1	3.0	42335	47405	54	70	3588	6.9	15.6	57.4	19.2	0.9	122522
04346	RANDOLPH	18601	1379	34.3	33.4	27.3	4.2	0.8	37430	41711	37	48	1005	11.8	17.9	58.9	10.9	0.5	111136
04347	HALLOWELL	23117	1201	29.1	32.6	30.0	6.3	1.9	39814	44884	45	58	681	3.2	9.3	56.8	30.3	0.4	140783
04348	JEFFERSON	22627	1226	23.4	33.9	32.7	6.9	3.1	44677	49108	60	78	1042	4.5	10.7	48.0	34.2	2.7	152760
04349	KENTS HILL	20003	377	26.3	34.5	30.5	7.2	1.6	42952	47656	56	72	338	3.3	17.8	48.8	29.6	0.6	136735
04350	LITCHFIELD	20470	1262	19.3	37.7	35.0	5.8	2.1	45190	49968	62	80	1073	10.3	13.2	48.6	27.4	0.5	133910
04351	MANCHESTER	32311	970	12.0	30.1	38.6	10.9	8.5	58108	64270	83	96	839	2.0	9.2	38.9	40.3	9.7	174856
04352	MOUNT VERNON	22375	423	24.8	35.0	30.5	6.9	2.8	43157	47670	56	73	360	8.1	12.2	52.8	23.9	3.1	130859
04353	WHITEFIELD	18412	916	29.5	33.5	29.8	5.6	1.6	41427	45723	51	66	773	8.0	18.4	52.7	19.3	1.7	122784
04354	PALERMO	19579	492	32.9	37.4	23.4	4.3	2.0	37127	41525	36	46	446	7.4	24.0	50.7	17.3	0.7	111667
04355	READFIELD	23351	1114	18.9	30.3	37.7	8.5	4.7	50632	55873	73	89	969	2.7	9.7	49.2	34.3	4.1	148283
04357	RICHMOND	20059	1314	28.2	29.8	35.1	5.4	1.5	40501	45621	48	62	991	7.0	12.4	59.2	20.2	1.2	131185
04358	SOUTH CHINA	21259	1395	19.9	37.9	33.6	6.0	2.7	43601	48843	58	75	1160	5.9	12.1	49.6	31.0	1.6	142758
04360	VIENNA	23529	290	27.9	30.3	31.4	5.9	4.5	43186	47950	56	73	246	8.9	18.7	41.5	26.0	4.9	131618
04363	WINDSOR	19226	654	25.1	36.1	32.4	4.4	2.0	43072	47898	56	73	546	9.7	13.7	55.5	19.6	1.5	125000
04364	WINTHROP	22835	2826	24.1	31.1	33.4	9.3	2.2	45857	51079	63	81	2167	7.7	7.6	53.1	29.2	2.5	143960
04401	BANGOR	22128	18482	35.2	30.3	24.9	6.3	3.3	35229	39925	28	38	9995	11.3	19.1	52.8	16.1	0.8	113451
04406	ABBOT	18870	372	35.0	35.5	24.5	4.0	1.1	34356	37728	25	35	322	10.6	34.5	40.4	13.0	1.6	98421
04408	AURORA	15887	80	38.8	36.3	23.8	1.3	0.0	31943	35954	18	25	68	14.7	26.5	42.7	14.7	1.5	105357
04410	BRADFORD	16035	458	28.4	42.4	24.9	3.9	0.4	38020	42737	39	50	377	17.0	28.4	44.6	9.6	0.5	95645
04411	BRADLEY	21033	490	28.0	35.1	32.0	3.3	1.6	41185	46103	50	65	398	13.3	29.2	51.0	6.0	0.5	98108
04412	BREWER	22822	4081	29.2	31.4	30.5	6.5	2.4	40759	46101	49	64	2486	4.2	15.5	63.5	15.9	1.0	117157
04413	BROOKTON	15141	76	44.7	29.0	23.7	2.6	0.0	30000	31131	12	14	64	37.5	25.0	29.7	7.8	0.0	68000
04414	BROWNVILLE	16630	550	44.6	32.4	20.0	2.0	1.1	29642	31235	12	13	420	19.8	45.0	26.0	8.8	0.5	75400
04416	BUCKSPORT	20763	2560	30.3	31.7	31.1	5.9	1.0	39409	44381	44	56	1875	5.9	16.0	57.6	18.6	2.0	125460
04417	BURLINGTON	17711	233	33.1	36.1	25.8	3.0	2.2	35650	38541	30	40	193	30.6	32.6	28.5	8.3	0.0	67941
04418	GREENBUSH	15980	546	31.0	39.6	25.1	3.9	0.6	34680	37774	26	36	461	29.1	32.5	34.5	2.8	1.1	76702
04419	CARMEL	18744	1474	23.1	34.9	35.6	6.0	0.3	44707	50085	60	79	1243	9.2	21.2	52.7	16.7	0.3	118776
04421	CASTINE	25355	404	18.8	28.5	30.2	15.4	7.2	52599	64932	76	92	298	0.7	3.7	11.4	49.3	34.9	345783
04422	CHARLESTON	17056	451	31.7	35.5	28.6	2.7	1.6	38914	43689	42	54	367	16.4	28.3	48.8	6.0	0.5	95417
04423	COSTIGAN	17349	207	33.3	32.9	28.5	3.9	1.5	36356	40478	33	43	168	27.4	26.2	39.3	7.1	0.0	83333
04424	DANFORTH	13810	429	53.9	28.0	15.9	1.4	0.9	22828	25285	3	3	332	31.3	35.5	25.9	6.3	0.9	68276
04426	DOVER FOXCROFT	16736	2148	40.5	30.5	24.4	3.7	0.9	31648	34532	17	24	1655	14.5	28.6	42.5	13.7	0.7	101766
04427	CORINTH	19092	1022	25.7	38.9	29.7	3.4	2.4	40387	45288	47	61	847	21.0	20.3	50.3	8.0	0.4	101250
04428	EDDINGTON	21092	1200	24.3	35.0	33.0	6.3	1.4	42638	48235	55	71	946	8.5	21.4	57.5	12.1	0.6	111019
04429	HOLDEN	28145	1840	20.9	24.6	37.1	11.5	5.9	54925	62302	80	94	1588	14.8	10.5	42.6	30.0	2.2	136137
04430	EAST MILLINOCKET	21366	781	35.5	25.6	32.8	5.1	1.0	36776	41349	35	44	578	18.5	53.6	25.4	1.9	0.5	73509
04431	EAST ORLAND	22889	137	23.4	34.3	32.9	8.0	1.5	41661	46675	52	67	116	8.6	17.2	44.0	25.0	5.2	126389
04434	ETNA	17175	397	32.5	32.2	31.7	2.3	1.3	36889	41595	35	45	336	22.3	24.1	44.1	9.5	0.0	94286
04435	EXETER	16608	374	32.1	39.0	26.2	1.6	1.1	36212	40141	32	42	334	20.7	34.7	35.9	8.7	0.0	85263
04438	FRANKFORT	16667	509	32.2	35.0	28.7	3.1	1.0	36279	40497	33	43	440	17.3	29.3	43.6	9.8	0.0	94545
04441	GREENVILLE	18703	833	41.8	33.1	20.1	3.4	1.7	31572	33761	17	23	583	6.9	20.2	54.7	17.0	1.2	115392
04442	GREENVILLE JUNCTION	29592	48	31.3	27.1	18.8	18.8	4.2	43128	47715	56	73	34	0.0	44.1	35.3	11.8	8.8	100000
04443	GUILFORD	15113	911	41.8	35.0	20.6	2.1	0.4	30148	32582	13	14	697	13.8	32.0	42.9	9.8	1.6	96020
04444	HAMPDEN	27550	3436	17.0	28.6	38.8	10.1	5.5	53883	60922	78	92	2730	3.6	11.7	58.0	25.6	1.1	127290
04448	HOWLAND	16832	650	39.7	32.6	24.9	2.3	0.5	31486	34713	16	22	472	21.4	37.5	38.6	2.5	0.0	82075
04449	HUDSON	17963	538	27.5	31.6	35.9	3.7	1.3	41906	46917	53	69	458	20.3	20.1	51.8	7.9	0.0	100658
04450	KENDUSKEAG	18569	488	30.7	37.1	26.6	3.7	1.8	37451	41927	37	48	413	25.9	24.5	45.5	4.1	0.0	89500
04451	KINGMAN	13528	133	54.9	31.6	12.0	1.5	0.0	22043	25192	3	2	117	44.4	30.8	20.5	2.6	1.7	56500
04453	LAGRANGE	15864	371	36.1	33.2	26.7	3.0	1.1	34692	37819	26	37	287	28.6	30.3	36.9	3.8	0.4	77500
04454	LAMBERT LAKE	14183	23	47.8	30.4	21.7	0.0	0.0	27332	37362	8	7	19	42.1	26.3	26.3	5.3	0.0	62500
04455	LEE	18447	302	25.8	44.0	26.2	3.0	1.0	37041	41389	36	46	275	22.6	33.5	37.8	6.2	0.0	83654
04456	LEVANT	20716	856	24.9	31.2	37.2	4.3	2.5	45165	50427	62	80	729	10.6	24.3	51.2	13.4	0.6	110928
04457	LINCOLN	16807	2569	38.3	34.0	24.1	2.5	1.1	33922	37780	24	32	2014	17.6	38.2	36.5	7.1	0.6	85304
04459	MATTAWAMKEAG	13101	310	54.2	26.8	18.4	0.0	0.7	22707	22013	3	2	238	33.6	44.5	18.5	3.4	0.0	63704
04460	MEDWAY	17373	642	35.4	27.4	34.3	2.3	0.6	36030	39767	32	42	520	34.6	28.1	34.0	2.9	0.4	68158
04461	MILFORD	20808	1011	26.8	28.6	37.7	5.3	1.6	44384	49651	60	77	819	18.1	23.0	55.3	3.7	0.0	99800
04462	MILLINOCKET	19464	2301	42.8	26.1	25.9	4.4	0.9	31110	33889	15	19	1690	25.6	52.4	21.2	0.9	0.0	67890
04463	MILO	14820	1315	45.3	31.8	21.4	1.2	0.3	28048	30340	9	9	991	28.2	36.8	31.1	3.6	0.3	71667
04464	MONSON	17029	354	44.6	35.9	15.0	2.5	2.0	28204	30889	9	10	260	11.2	37.3	35.8	14.6	1.2	92667
	MAINE	22411		29.6	30.7	30.0	6.5	3.2	40864	45987				8.5	14.0	43.9	28.6	5.1	138610
	UNITED STATES	25866		24.7	27.1	30.8	10.9	6.5	48124	56710				10.9	15.0	33.7	30.1	10.4	145905

ZIP CODE #	POST OFFICE NAME	FINANCIAL SERVICES: Auto Loan	FINANCIAL SERVICES: Home Loan	FINANCIAL SERVICES: Investments	FINANCIAL SERVICES: Retirement Plans	THE HOME: Home Improvements: Home Repair	THE HOME: Home Improvements: Lawn & Garden	THE HOME: Furnishings: Computers & Hardware	THE HOME: Furnishings: Major Appliances	THE HOME: Furnishings: TV, Radio, Sound Equipment	THE HOME: Furnishings: Furniture	ENTERTAINMENT: Dine out/Carry out	ENTERTAINMENT: Sports Equipment	ENTERTAINMENT: Fees & Tickets	ENTERTAINMENT: Toys & Games	ENTERTAINMENT: Travel	ENTERTAINMENT: Cable TV	PERSONAL: Apparel & Services	PERSONAL: Auto Repairs	PERSONAL: Health Insurance	PERSONAL: Pets & Supplies
04250	LISBON	79	61	40	58	66	75	61	70	68	61	82	81	56	80	61	71	76	69	79	89
04252	LISBON FALLS	77	67	54	66	70	78	68	73	72	67	87	83	65	87	68	73	82	71	78	87
04253	LIVERMORE	78	69	53	66	73	79	64	71	68	64	83	85	63	85	66	70	79	69	77	92
04254	LIVERMORE FALLS	60	51	42	49	53	58	51	56	54	51	66	66	48	65	51	55	63	56	59	68
04255	GREENWOOD	91	71	49	64	80	90	67	81	76	67	90	95	60	89	72	81	84	80	96	111
04256	MECHANIC FALLS	72	62	48	61	66	72	61	66	65	60	78	77	59	79	62	66	74	65	72	81
04257	MEXICO	65	53	40	50	57	66	55	60	60	53	72	68	50	71	56	64	67	60	71	75
04258	MINOT	93	83	64	79	87	94	77	85	82	77	100	101	76	101	79	84	95	83	92	109
04259	MONMOUTH	78	74	64	72	76	80	70	75	71	70	87	89	68	88	71	71	84	74	76	91
04260	NEW GLOUCESTER	87	90	84	90	89	91	85	87	83	86	103	103	85	104	84	80	101	86	82	100
04261	NEWRY	88	69	47	62	78	87	65	78	73	64	87	92	58	86	69	79	81	77	92	107
04263	LEEDS	77	68	52	65	72	77	63	70	67	63	82	83	62	83	65	69	77	68	76	90
04265	NORTH MONMOUTH	78	69	53	66	73	79	64	71	68	64	83	85	63	85	66	70	79	69	77	92
04266	NORTH TURNER	114	102	77	97	108	115	94	104	100	94	121	124	92	124	97	102	115	101	113	135
04267	NORTH WATERFORD	78	61	42	55	69	77	58	69	65	57	77	81	51	76	61	70	72	68	82	95
04268	NORWAY	68	53	39	50	58	68	56	62	62	54	74	72	50	71	57	65	68	62	73	79
04270	OXFORD	81	67	50	64	72	80	66	74	71	65	85	85	61	83	67	73	80	73	81	93
04274	POLAND	97	98	87	94	100	104	90	96	90	90	111	112	89	112	92	90	107	94	97	116
04275	ROXBURY	72	56	38	51	63	71	53	64	60	52	71	75	47	70	56	64	66	63	75	87
04276	RUMFORD	60	51	46	50	54	62	55	57	59	53	71	65	52	71	55	61	67	57	65	67
04278	RUMFORD CENTER	86	68	48	62	77	86	65	77	73	64	87	90	59	86	69	78	81	76	91	104
04280	SABATTUS	81	72	56	69	74	80	69	75	71	70	88	87	66	86	69	72	83	74	78	91
04281	SOUTH PARIS	66	56	44	54	60	68	58	62	62	56	75	71	55	75	58	65	70	61	70	74
04282	TURNER	113	105	85	101	109	115	98	106	101	98	124	126	96	126	99	102	118	103	110	133
04284	WAYNE	118	92	63	83	104	117	87	105	99	86	117	123	78	115	93	105	109	103	124	144
04285	WELD	68	53	36	48	60	67	50	60	56	49	67	70	45	66	53	60	62	59	71	82
04287	BOWDOIN	85	76	59	73	79	85	71	78	75	72	91	92	69	91	72	76	87	77	83	98
04289	WEST PARIS	65	55	42	54	58	65	56	60	59	55	72	69	53	71	55	60	67	59	65	72
04290	PERU	76	64	47	59	69	76	59	68	65	59	78	81	56	79	62	68	73	67	77	90
04292	SUMNER	81	72	55	68	76	81	66	74	71	66	86	88	65	88	68	72	82	72	80	95
04294	WILTON	77	62	45	61	66	76	66	71	71	63	85	80	61	83	65	74	79	70	80	85
04330	AUGUSTA	66	62	63	61	63	70	63	65	66	62	81	75	63	81	64	67	78	65	68	76
04341	COOPERS MILLS	0	0	0	0	0	0	0	0	0	0	0	0	0	0	0	0	0	0	0	0
04342	DRESDEN	85	75	57	72	80	86	70	77	74	70	90	92	68	92	72	76	86	75	84	100
04344	FARMINGDALE	74	60	43	58	64	74	63	68	69	61	82	78	58	79	63	71	76	68	78	83
04345	GARDINER	78	73	64	71	75	80	71	75	73	70	90	89	70	91	72	73	86	74	78	91
04346	RANDOLPH	65	58	47	55	60	68	58	62	62	57	75	71	56	74	58	64	71	61	68	74
04347	HALLOWELL	62	68	82	69	67	71	68	67	67	68	84	78	70	86	69	66	83	67	64	74
04348	JEFFERSON	91	76	56	71	83	91	71	82	78	71	94	97	67	94	75	81	88	80	92	109
04349	KENTS HILL	84	66	45	59	74	83	62	75	70	62	83	88	56	82	66	75	77	74	89	102
04350	LITCHFIELD	84	72	54	69	76	83	70	77	74	70	90	90	65	87	71	75	85	77	83	96
04351	MANCHESTER	115	118	110	114	122	127	108	116	108	107	133	135	108	137	112	109	129	112	117	140
04352	MOUNT VERNON	91	72	49	65	81	91	68	81	76	67	91	95	60	89	72	82	84	80	96	111
04353	WHITEFIELD	76	68	52	64	72	77	63	69	67	63	81	83	61	83	64	68	77	68	75	89
04354	PALERMO	81	63	43	57	71	80	60	72	68	59	80	84	53	79	64	72	74	71	85	98
04355	READFIELD	95	88	73	85	94	99	82	91	85	81	103	108	79	105	85	87	99	89	97	115
04357	RICHMOND	75	70	61	68	72	77	67	71	70	67	85	85	67	87	68	70	82	71	74	88
04358	SOUTH CHINA	88	76	57	72	81	89	72	81	78	72	94	95	69	95	74	80	89	79	89	103
04360	VIENNA	93	73	50	66	82	92	69	83	78	68	92	97	62	91	73	83	86	82	98	114
04363	WINDSOR	78	71	55	68	72	77	67	72	69	68	84	84	64	82	67	69	81	71	74	88
04364	WINTHROP	86	75	60	72	81	87	72	81	76	71	92	96	68	93	74	78	88	80	88	103
04401	BANGOR	67	65	75	67	65	69	71	68	70	69	88	81	70	86	69	68	85	71	65	76
04406	ABBOT	70	55	37	50	62	69	52	62	59	51	69	73	46	68	55	63	64	61	74	85
04408	AURORA	63	50	34	45	56	63	47	56	53	46	63	66	42	62	50	57	58	56	67	77
04410	BRADFORD	67	57	44	57	59	67	58	62	62	57	75	71	56	74	58	63	70	61	68	74
04411	BRADLEY	77	65	51	65	69	77	67	72	71	66	87	82	64	86	67	73	81	71	78	85
04412	BREWER	72	71	71	70	73	78	72	74	73	70	90	86	71	91	73	73	87	74	75	85
04413	BROOKTON	60	47	32	42	53	59	44	53	50	44	59	62	40	59	47	53	55	52	63	73
04414	BROWNVILLE	61	48	33	43	54	60	45	54	51	45	60	63	40	60	48	54	56	53	64	74
04416	BUCKSPORT	76	64	48	62	68	76	64	70	69	63	83	81	61	82	65	71	78	69	78	86
04417	BURLINGTON	73	57	39	51	64	72	54	65	61	53	72	76	48	71	57	65	67	64	76	88
04418	GREENBUSH	67	61	48	59	61	65	59	63	59	60	73	72	55	69	58	58	70	62	62	74
04419	CARMEL	73	73	65	72	72	74	70	72	68	71	85	84	68	82	68	65	82	71	67	82
04421	CASTINE	123	97	66	87	109	122	91	110	103	90	122	128	81	121	97	110	114	108	130	150
04422	CHARLESTON	74	63	49	63	66	74	65	69	69	63	83	79	62	82	64	70	78	68	75	82
04423	COSTIGAN	75	61	44	58	66	75	60	68	66	59	79	79	55	78	62	68	73	67	77	87
04424	DANFORTH	53	41	28	37	47	52	39	47	44	39	52	55	35	52	42	47	49	46	55	64
04426	DOVER FOXCROFT	65	52	37	50	57	64	53	59	58	52	69	68	49	68	53	60	64	58	67	74
04427	CORINTH	77	70	55	68	70	74	67	72	68	69	84	83	63	79	66	67	81	72	71	85
04428	EDDINGTON	80	70	54	68	74	81	68	74	72	67	87	86	66	88	69	73	82	72	80	92
04429	HOLDEN	103	98	85	93	103	109	90	99	94	90	115	116	89	117	94	96	110	97	105	124
04430	EAST MILLINOCKET	74	64	51	61	68	77	65	70	71	63	85	80	62	85	66	74	80	69	80	85
04431	EAST ORLAND	88	69	47	62	78	87	65	78	74	64	87	92	58	86	69	79	81	77	93	107
04434	ETNA	68	62	48	60	62	65	59	63	60	61	74	73	56	70	58	59	71	63	63	75
04435	EXETER	78	52	24	45	59	68	51	63	61	52	72	76	43	68	51	66	65	63	78	90
04438	FRANKFORT	67	57	45	57	60	67	59	63	62	58	76	72	57	75	58	63	71	62	68	74
04441	GREENVILLE	67	53	36	48	59	67	50	60	56	49	67	70	45	66	53	60	62	59	71	82
04442	GREENVILLE JUNCTION	107	84	57	75	94	106	79	95	89	78	106	111	71	104	84	95	98	94	112	130
04443	GUILFORD	55	48	38	44	51	58	46	51	51	46	62	59	45	63	48	54	58	51	59	65
04444	HAMPDEN	95	105	109	105	104	107	98	99	94	98	118	117	101	121	99	92	116	97	94	113
04448	HOWLAND	72	50	26	44	56	64	48	59	57	49	67	70	42	64	49	61	61	59	72	83
04449	HUDSON	76	70	54	67	70	74	66	71	67	68	83	82	63	78	65	66	80	71	71	84
04450	KENDUSKEAG	71	65	51	62	65	68	62	66	63	64	77	77	58	73	61	62	74	66	66	79
04451	KINGMAN	56	40	21	35	45	51	38	47	45	38	53	56	33	51	39	48	48	46	57	66
04453	LAGRANGE	67	57	41	54	58	63	54	60	57	56	70	70	51	66	54	57	66	60	63	74
04454	LAMBERT LAKE	54	43	29	38	48	54	40	48	46	40	54	57	36	53	43	49	50	48	57	66
04455	LEE	86	67	46	61	76	85	64	77	72	63	85	90	57	84	68	77	79	75	91	105
04456	LEVANT	89	81	63	78	81	86	77	83	78	79	97	96	73	91	76	77	93	83	82	98
04457	LINCOLN	70	51	30	47	57	66	52	61	60	51	70	70	46	67	53	63	64	60	72	79
04459	MATTAWAMKEAG	58	39	18	34	44	51	38	47	45	38	53	56	32	50	38	49	48	47	58	67
04460	MEDWAY	79	53	25	46	60	69	51	64	62	52	72	76	44	69	52	66	66	63	79	91
04461	MILFORD	80	70	55	69	72	79	70	75	73	70	89	86	67	86	69	73	84	74	78	89
04462	MILLINOCKET	61	58	53	54	60	68	58	60	61	56	75	68	58	77	59	64	71	59	67	70
04463	MILO	60	42	23	38	47	55	43	51	50	42	59	59	37	56	43	53	53	50	62	68
04464	MONSON	62	49	33	44	55	61	46	55	52	45	61	65	41	61	49	55	57	54	65	75
	MAINE	80	73	65	71	75	82	72	77	75	71	92	90	70	91	73	76	88	76	81	93
	UNITED STATES	100	100	100	100	100	100	100	100	100	100	100	100	100	100	100	100	100	100	100	100

MAINE
POPULATION CHANGE

A 04468-04673

ZIP CODE #	POST OFFICE NAME	COUNTY FIPS CODE	POPULATION 2000	2004	2009	% Rate	State Centile	HOUSEHOLDS 2000	2004	2009	% Annual Rate 2000-2004	2004 Average HH Size	FAMILIES 2000	2004	% Annual Rate 2000-2004
04468	OLD TOWN	019	10011	10088	10311	0.2	34	4166	4320	4544	0.9	2.28	2538	2650	1.0
04469	ORONO	019	1633	1633	1633	0.0	26	1	1	1	0.0	1.00	0	0	0.0
04471	ORIENT	003	532	526	523	-0.3	18	213	218	222	0.6	2.40	160	164	0.6
04472	ORLAND	009	1847	1963	2170	1.4	77	757	831	946	2.2	2.36	540	593	2.2
04473	ORONO	019	7484	7495	7603	0.0	28	2701	2796	2933	0.8	2.15	1298	1354	1.0
04474	ORRINGTON	019	3528	3623	3718	0.6	49	1397	1475	1556	1.3	2.45	1044	1105	1.4
04475	PASSADUMKEAG	019	441	437	443	-0.2	20	172	176	183	0.5	2.48	129	132	0.5
04476	PENOBSCOT	009	1355	1493	1676	2.3	93	537	613	713	3.2	2.29	373	427	3.2
04478	ROCKWOOD	025	316	316	317	0.0	26	147	152	158	0.8	2.08	91	94	0.8
04479	SANGERVILLE	021	1082	1104	1160	0.5	44	467	493	534	1.3	2.24	301	318	1.3
04481	SEBEC	021	699	723	765	0.8	55	288	308	335	1.6	2.35	205	220	1.7
04487	SPRINGFIELD	019	882	858	867	-0.7	6	351	354	370	0.2	2.42	252	255	0.3
04488	STETSON	019	858	931	985	1.9	88	334	377	412	2.9	2.47	238	270	3.0
04490	TOPSFIELD	029	244	236	229	-0.8	4	101	102	102	0.2	2.31	65	65	0.0
04491	VANCEBORO	029	147	140	135	-1.1	2	68	67	67	-0.4	2.09	45	45	0.0
04492	WAITE	029	202	194	187	-1.0	2	89	89	88	0.0	2.18	59	58	-0.4
04493	WEST ENFIELD	019	1760	1752	1777	-0.1	22	671	686	714	0.5	2.55	506	519	0.6
04495	WINN	019	287	281	284	-0.5	9	116	117	122	0.2	2.40	91	93	0.5
04496	WINTERPORT	027	3699	3926	4275	1.4	75	1432	1570	1763	2.2	2.49	1070	1177	2.3
04497	WYTOPITLOCK	003	398	365	354	-2.0	0	141	133	132	-1.4	2.74	109	103	-1.3
04530	BATH	023	11572	11627	11973	0.1	30	5003	5165	5458	0.8	2.23	3021	3123	0.8
04535	ALNA	015	729	737	752	0.3	35	290	300	312	0.8	2.45	214	222	0.9
04537	BOOTHBAY	015	1878	1995	2094	1.4	76	767	838	899	2.1	2.38	552	604	2.1
04538	BOOTHBAY HARBOR	015	2693	2724	2794	0.3	36	1269	1324	1394	1.0	2.00	740	774	1.1
04539	BRISTOL	015	1313	1420	1505	1.9	87	555	618	672	2.6	2.29	383	428	2.7
04541	CHAMBERLAIN	015	194	219	237	2.9	97	84	98	108	3.7	2.20	55	65	4.0
04543	DAMARISCOTTA	015	1710	1744	1789	0.5	43	780	820	862	1.2	2.01	459	482	1.2
04544	EAST BOOTHBAY	015	374	393	410	1.2	67	182	198	212	2.0	1.98	117	127	2.0
04547	FRIENDSHIP	013	2113	2184	2299	0.8	54	872	924	995	1.4	2.35	612	650	1.4
04548	GEORGETOWN	023	912	913	933	0.0	28	393	403	423	0.6	2.26	262	269	0.6
04549	ISLE OF SPRINGS	015	6	6	6	0.0	26	2	2	2	0.0	3.00	1	1	0.0
04551	BREMEN	015	677	697	719	0.7	50	287	302	318	1.2	2.30	207	219	1.3
04553	NEWCASTLE	015	2052	2117	2186	0.7	52	877	931	984	1.4	2.24	576	613	1.5
04554	NEW HARBOR	015	643	676	705	1.2	68	328	355	378	1.9	1.90	208	225	1.9
04555	NOBLEBORO	015	1601	1677	1746	1.1	64	664	719	768	1.9	2.33	455	493	1.9
04556	EDGECOMB	015	1099	1200	1277	2.1	91	470	526	573	2.7	2.28	331	371	2.7
04558	PEMAQUID	015	202	221	236	2.1	93	96	108	118	2.8	2.04	62	70	2.9
04562	PHIPPSBURG	023	2062	2129	2214	0.8	53	838	890	950	1.4	2.39	608	646	1.4
04563	CUSHING	013	337	349	368	0.8	57	144	153	165	1.4	2.26	102	108	1.4
04564	ROUND POND	015	292	329	357	2.9	97	140	163	180	3.6	1.99	93	108	3.6
04567	SMALL POINT	023	40	43	45	1.7	85	19	21	23	2.4	2.05	13	15	3.4
04568	SOUTH BRISTOL	015	464	467	475	0.2	32	222	230	239	0.8	2.03	151	156	0.8
04570	SQUIRREL ISLAND	015	3	3	3	0.0	26	2	2	2	0.0	1.50	1	1	0.0
04571	TREVETT	015	329	349	366	1.4	75	132	144	155	2.1	2.42	95	104	2.2
04572	WALDOBORO	015	5076	5255	5442	0.8	56	2045	2175	2308	1.5	2.39	1393	1483	1.5
04573	WALPOLE	015	432	434	443	0.1	30	187	193	202	0.8	2.25	127	131	0.7
04574	WASHINGTON	013	1375	1451	1543	1.3	70	527	575	630	2.1	2.47	368	402	2.1
04576	SOUTHPORT	015	678	694	713	0.6	47	327	345	363	1.3	2.01	215	227	1.3
04578	WISCASSET	015	4348	4609	4831	1.4	74	1790	1953	2099	2.1	2.34	1202	1315	2.1
04579	WOOLWICH	023	2829	2949	3082	1.0	62	1112	1195	1284	1.7	2.47	832	895	1.7
04605	ELLSWORTH	009	12278	13684	15485	2.6	96	5156	5918	6896	3.3	2.27	3417	3930	3.4
04606	ADDISON	029	1209	1187	1155	-0.4	12	489	494	495	0.2	2.38	342	346	0.3
04607	GOULDSBORO	009	1249	1362	1524	2.1	91	528	597	689	2.9	2.23	357	405	3.0
04609	BAR HARBOR	009	5295	5740	6397	1.9	87	2413	2693	3092	2.6	2.06	1294	1447	2.7
04611	BEALS	029	616	596	577	-0.8	4	236	235	234	-0.1	2.48	188	188	0.0
04612	BERNARD	009	177	196	221	2.4	96	82	93	107	3.0	2.11	53	59	2.6
04613	BIRCH HARBOR	009	244	265	297	2.0	89	98	110	127	2.8	2.41	67	76	3.0
04614	BLUE HILL	009	1732	1850	2049	1.6	80	762	838	955	2.3	2.21	489	537	2.2
04615	BLUE HILL FALLS	009	465	496	549	1.5	79	227	250	285	2.3	1.98	141	155	2.3
04616	BROOKLIN	009	1040	1100	1213	1.3	73	458	497	562	1.9	2.21	298	323	1.9
04617	BROOKSVILLE	009	707	752	831	1.5	78	312	341	386	2.1	2.21	211	231	2.2
04619	CALAIS	029	3447	3460	3414	0.1	29	1486	1540	1565	0.8	2.17	905	940	0.9
04622	CHERRYFIELD	029	1206	1169	1132	-0.7	4	519	520	519	0.1	2.20	336	338	0.1
04623	COLUMBIA FALLS	029	936	927	905	-0.2	19	395	403	405	0.5	2.30	262	268	0.5
04624	COREA	009	362	390	430	1.8	85	138	156	180	2.9	2.19	90	102	3.0
04625	CRANBERRY ISLES	009	54	55	59	0.4	43	27	28	32	0.9	1.96	14	15	1.6
04626	CUTLER	029	621	609	592	-0.5	10	237	239	239	0.2	2.49	178	180	0.3
04627	DEER ISLE	009	936	993	1092	1.4	75	388	425	484	2.2	2.19	248	273	2.3
04628	DENNYSVILLE	029	678	667	650	-0.4	13	277	281	283	0.3	2.37	191	194	0.4
04630	EAST MACHIAS	029	1681	1655	1616	-0.4	13	707	716	722	0.3	2.19	490	497	0.3
04631	EASTPORT	029	2058	1962	1890	-1.1	2	920	908	903	-0.3	2.12	565	560	-0.2
04634	FRANKLIN	009	2532	2792	3145	2.3	94	1064	1211	1406	3.1	2.30	713	815	3.2
04635	FRENCHBORO	009	38	40	44	1.2	69	18	19	22	1.3	2.11	11	12	2.1
04640	HANCOCK	009	882	973	1095	2.3	95	389	442	512	3.1	2.19	251	285	3.0
04642	HARBORSIDE	009	139	148	164	1.5	79	68	74	84	2.0	2.00	46	50	2.0
04643	HARRINGTON	029	1064	1036	1005	-0.6	6	436	437	436	0.1	2.36	304	305	0.1
04645	ISLE AU HAUT	013	79	83	88	1.2	67	32	34	36	1.4	2.44	21	22	1.1
04646	ISLESFORD	009	74	75	81	0.3	39	33	35	39	1.4	2.14	17	18	1.4
04648	JONESBORO	029	594	585	570	-0.4	14	257	262	264	0.5	2.23	175	179	0.5
04649	JONESPORT	029	1408	1376	1338	-0.5	8	597	603	605	0.2	2.22	397	402	0.3
04650	LITTLE DEER ISLE	009	241	256	282	1.4	76	106	116	132	2.1	2.21	70	77	2.3
04652	LUBEC	029	1653	1613	1568	-0.6	7	737	738	736	0.0	2.14	424	426	0.1
04653	BASS HARBOR	009	453	501	566	2.4	95	199	225	260	2.9	2.23	127	144	3.0
04654	MACHIAS	029	3619	3509	3406	-0.7	4	1471	1467	1463	-0.1	2.13	861	862	0.0
04655	MACHIASPORT	029	995	977	952	-0.4	12	342	345	347	0.2	2.66	237	239	0.2
04656	MANSET	009	346	368	408	1.5	78	145	159	181	2.2	2.31	92	101	2.2
04657	MEDDYBEMPS	029	234	235	231	0.1	29	97	101	102	1.0	2.31	67	70	1.0
04658	MILBRIDGE	029	1415	1377	1337	-0.6	6	603	605	605	0.1	2.18	395	398	0.2
04660	MOUNT DESERT	009	2552	2809	3161	2.3	93	1080	1218	1405	2.9	2.30	715	807	2.9
04666	PEMBROKE	029	1232	1201	1165	-0.6	7	524	527	526	0.1	2.28	368	371	0.2
04667	PERRY	029	1067	1062	1040	-0.1	22	393	402	405	0.5	2.63	288	295	0.6
04668	PRINCETON	029	1730	1693	1647	-0.5	9	686	695	697	0.3	2.44	473	480	0.4
04669	PROSPECT HARBOR	009	393	426	476	1.9	87	156	176	203	2.9	2.36	106	119	2.8
04671	ROBBINSTON	029	525	520	508	-0.2	20	201	205	205	0.5	2.54	149	152	0.5
04673	SARGENTVILLE	009	53	56	62	1.3	71	26	28	32	1.8	2.00	18	19	1.3
	MAINE					0.9					1.5	2.33			1.6
	UNITED STATES					1.2					1.3	2.58			1.1

ZIP CODE #	POST OFFICE NAME	RACE (%) White 2000	White 2004	Black 2000	Black 2004	Asian/Pacific 2000	Asian/Pacific 2004	% Hispanic Origin 2000	% Hispanic Origin 2004	2004 AGE DISTRIBUTION (%) 0-4	5-9	10-14	15-19	20-24	25-44	45-64	65-84	85+	18+	MEDIAN AGE 2004	% 2004 Males	% 2004 Females
04468	OLD TOWN	90.6	89.5	0.5	0.6	1.6	2.0	0.5	0.6	5.2	5.1	6.0	7.9	10.8	29.1	22.7	11.8	1.5	79.8	34.6	48.2	51.9
04469	ORONO	94.3	93.6	2.3	2.6	1.1	1.4	1.4	1.5	0.0	0.0	0.0	54.0	44.6	1.3	0.1	0.1	0.0	99.8	19.6	52.1	48.0
04471	ORIENT	98.3	98.3	0.4	0.4	0.0	0.0	0.4	0.6	4.9	5.1	7.6	6.7	4.8	25.5	32.5	12.4	0.6	77.6	42.3	51.1	48.9
04472	ORLAND	98.3	98.2	0.0	0.0	0.3	0.3	0.4	0.5	5.3	5.8	6.6	6.1	5.2	26.7	31.0	12.1	1.3	78.5	42.1	49.8	50.2
04473	ORONO	93.4	92.6	1.2	1.3	2.8	3.4	1.2	1.4	3.5	3.0	4.0	12.9	27.2	20.1	17.6	10.1	1.6	86.6	24.9	50.5	49.5
04474	ORRINGTON	99.1	99.0	0.2	0.2	0.2	0.3	0.1	0.1	5.3	6.4	6.6	6.2	4.5	26.8	31.5	11.5	1.1	77.6	41.9	49.9	50.2
04475	PASSADUMKEAG	98.4	98.4	0.0	0.0	0.2	0.2	0.5	0.5	5.0	5.7	8.2	7.6	6.9	25.2	27.5	11.7	2.3	76.4	41.0	49.4	50.6
04476	PENOBSCOT	98.1	97.8	0.2	0.1	0.3	0.5	0.4	0.5	3.9	4.2	5.9	5.2	4.8	22.7	32.3	16.6	4.4	82.7	47.0	50.0	50.0
04478	ROCKWOOD	97.5	97.5	0.0	0.0	0.0	0.0	0.0	0.0	3.2	4.8	5.7	6.0	2.5	25.0	38.0	14.2	0.6	81.0	46.4	52.9	47.2
04479	SANGERVILLE	98.3	98.1	0.5	0.5	0.2	0.2	0.4	0.5	3.9	4.4	5.7	7.0	5.4	23.3	32.0	15.7	2.6	81.7	45.1	50.2	49.8
04481	SEBEC	98.3	98.5	0.0	0.0	0.3	0.3	0.9	0.8	4.3	5.3	6.6	6.1	5.8	22.0	35.3	13.3	1.4	79.9	45.0	50.9	49.1
04487	SPRINGFIELD	96.3	96.0	0.6	0.6	0.1	0.1	0.7	0.7	4.1	4.7	6.5	5.8	5.2	23.9	30.7	17.8	1.3	80.9	44.9	52.0	48.0
04488	STETSON	98.7	98.7	0.2	0.2	0.0	0.0	0.0	0.0	6.2	6.4	6.3	7.0	5.8	28.9	28.8	9.6	1.0	76.9	39.1	50.4	49.6
04490	TOPSFIELD	97.5	97.5	0.0	0.0	0.0	0.0	0.0	0.4	3.8	4.2	4.7	5.1	5.1	20.3	39.8	15.7	1.3	83.9	48.6	51.3	48.7
04491	VANCEBORO	95.2	94.3	0.7	0.7	0.0	0.0	1.4	0.7	3.6	4.3	5.0	6.4	5.7	23.6	32.9	17.1	1.4	82.9	45.8	53.6	46.4
04492	WAITE	96.0	95.9	0.0	0.0	0.0	0.0	1.0	0.5	3.6	4.1	4.6	6.2	5.7	22.7	35.6	16.0	1.6	83.5	46.8	50.5	49.5
04493	WEST ENFIELD	98.8	98.9	0.1	0.1	0.1	0.1	0.4	0.5	6.5	6.9	7.1	6.9	5.3	25.9	28.5	11.8	1.1	75.2	39.6	51.1	48.9
04495	WINN	99.0	98.9	0.0	0.0	0.0	0.0	0.7	0.7	4.6	5.0	6.1	6.8	5.0	21.4	31.0	18.5	1.8	80.1	45.8	50.9	49.1
04496	WINTERPORT	98.1	97.9	0.2	0.2	0.3	0.3	0.4	0.5	5.6	6.1	7.0	7.4	6.6	28.4	28.8	9.1	1.0	76.6	38.8	49.6	50.4
04497	WYTOPITLOCK	98.2	98.1	0.0	0.0	0.8	1.1	0.0	0.0	3.0	5.8	9.0	6.6	4.7	25.8	30.1	14.3	0.8	76.7	42.5	49.9	50.1
04530	BATH	95.6	95.2	1.3	1.5	0.6	0.7	1.5	1.8	6.3	5.6	6.8	6.8	7.4	26.1	27.3	11.8	2.1	77.2	39.3	48.4	51.6
04535	ALNA	99.5	99.6	0.0	0.0	0.1	0.1	0.1	0.1	4.1	5.3	9.0	6.8	3.0	25.1	32.3	12.4	2.2	77.1	43.3	49.3	50.8
04537	BOOTHBAY	98.7	98.7	0.1	0.1	0.2	0.3	0.6	0.7	5.0	5.5	6.6	6.1	5.0	24.7	32.2	13.2	1.7	79.2	43.3	50.0	50.0
04538	BOOTHBAY HARBOR	98.1	97.9	0.2	0.2	0.6	0.8	0.8	0.9	4.2	4.2	4.0	4.6	4.0	21.1	33.3	21.0	3.6	84.5	49.9	46.5	53.5
04539	BRISTOL	99.1	99.0	0.2	0.1	0.4	0.5	0.2	0.1	3.9	4.7	6.3	5.4	4.2	24.1	32.8	17.0	1.8	81.7	46.0	50.7	49.3
04541	CHAMBERLAIN	98.5	98.6	0.0	0.0	0.5	0.9	0.0	0.0	3.2	4.1	6.4	5.9	4.6	21.9	32.9	18.7	2.3	82.2	47.2	52.5	47.5
04543	DAMARISCOTTA	98.9	98.9	0.2	0.2	0.2	0.2	0.5	0.6	3.9	4.4	6.1	5.3	4.2	19.3	26.9	22.6	7.3	81.8	50.3	45.5	54.5
04544	EAST BOOTHBAY	99.7	99.8	0.0	0.0	0.0	0.0	0.3	0.5	3.6	4.1	3.3	3.3	1.5	16.8	43.8	20.4	3.3	86.5	54.0	47.8	52.2
04547	FRIENDSHIP	99.4	99.4	0.0	0.0	0.1	0.1	0.5	0.5	5.3	5.6	5.9	5.7	4.4	26.0	28.9	16.1	2.2	79.6	43.1	50.1	49.9
04548	GEORGETOWN	98.8	98.6	0.1	0.1	0.3	0.4	0.7	0.9	4.8	4.1	6.2	7.6	4.8	23.1	34.7	13.5	1.2	79.6	44.7	48.9	51.2
04549	ISLE OF SPRINGS	100.0	100.0	0.0	0.0	0.0	0.0	0.0	0.0	0.0	0.0	0.0	0.0	33.3	66.7	0.0	0.0	0.0	100.0	27.5	50.0	50.0
04551	BREMEN	98.4	98.1	0.7	0.9	0.3	0.4	0.7	0.7	5.6	5.6	4.5	4.6	5.2	21.4	34.0	16.1	3.2	81.9	47.3	48.5	51.5
04553	NEWCASTLE	98.8	98.7	0.2	0.2	0.3	0.4	0.7	0.8	4.3	4.6	5.6	6.7	5.0	20.6	34.2	16.0	3.1	80.6	46.8	47.0	53.0
04554	NEW HARBOR	99.2	99.3	0.0	0.0	0.5	0.6	0.5	0.6	3.0	3.3	3.6	3.4	2.8	16.0	36.0	27.7	4.4	87.7	55.9	47.9	52.1
04555	NOBLEBORO	98.6	98.5	0.1	0.1	0.4	0.5	0.5	0.5	4.7	7.1	7.6	5.7	4.2	22.6	32.3	14.3	1.5	77.1	43.8	48.0	52.0
04556	EDGECOMB	98.7	98.7	0.0	0.0	0.2	0.3	0.1	0.1	4.9	5.3	6.9	5.6	2.3	22.9	35.6	13.8	2.6	78.8	46.1	48.1	51.9
04558	PEMAQUID	99.0	98.6	0.0	0.0	0.5	0.9	0.0	0.5	3.2	3.6	5.4	4.5	3.6	19.0	34.4	23.5	2.7	85.1	51.2	50.7	49.3
04562	PHIPPSBURG	98.6	98.4	0.3	0.3	0.2	0.3	0.6	0.7	4.7	5.4	5.9	5.6	4.8	23.3	34.8	14.3	1.4	80.7	45.2	51.8	48.2
04563	CUSHING	99.4	99.4	0.0	0.0	0.0	0.3	0.6	0.6	5.7	6.0	6.3	5.2	3.7	26.7	30.1	14.0	2.3	78.8	42.4	50.4	49.6
04564	ROUND POND	98.6	98.8	0.0	0.0	0.7	0.9	0.0	0.3	3.3	4.0	6.4	5.8	4.9	21.9	31.3	20.1	2.4	82.1	47.2	51.1	48.9
04567	SMALL POINT	97.5	100.0	0.0	0.0	0.0	0.0	0.0	0.0	4.7	4.7	4.7	4.7	4.7	20.9	39.5	14.0	2.3	86.1	48.1	48.8	51.2
04568	SOUTH BRISTOL	98.9	98.7	0.0	0.0	0.2	0.4	0.7	0.6	3.2	3.4	4.5	4.3	4.5	16.7	37.5	22.7	3.2	85.9	53.4	48.6	51.4
04570	SQUIRREL ISLAND	100.0	100.0	0.0	0.0	0.0	0.0	0.0	0.0	0.0	0.0	0.0	0.0	66.7	33.3	0.0	0.0	0.0	100.0	23.8	66.7	33.3
04571	TREVETT	99.4	100.0	0.0	0.0	0.0	0.0	0.3	0.3	4.0	4.6	5.2	4.6	4.3	19.5	38.4	17.5	2.0	83.4	49.2	50.7	49.3
04572	WALDOBORO	98.6	98.4	0.2	0.3	0.5	0.6	0.3	0.3	6.1	6.4	6.6	6.6	5.6	24.5	27.7	14.3	2.3	76.6	41.2	49.2	50.9
04573	WALPOLE	99.1	99.1	0.0	0.0	0.2	0.2	0.2	0.5	3.5	3.7	4.4	4.4	4.4	17.1	36.9	22.6	3.2	86.2	53.1	49.1	50.9
04574	WASHINGTON	98.8	98.8	0.0	0.0	0.0	0.0	0.4	0.5	4.9	5.5	7.0	7.1	5.4	26.8	32.7	10.0	0.7	77.8	41.0	51.1	48.9
04576	SOUTHPORT	98.8	98.7	0.0	0.0	0.6	0.7	0.0	0.0	2.7	3.3	3.9	3.9	2.9	12.4	39.9	27.0	4.0	87.6	55.9	49.0	51.0
04578	WISCASSET	98.1	97.9	0.3	0.3	0.4	0.5	0.6	0.7	4.7	5.5	6.9	7.0	5.4	25.3	30.7	12.8	1.7	77.7	42.3	50.0	50.0
04579	WOOLWICH	97.6	97.4	0.4	0.4	0.5	0.6	0.8	1.0	4.9	5.9	6.7	6.9	5.2	26.4	31.9	10.9	1.2	78.2	41.6	51.1	48.9
04605	ELLSWORTH	97.5	97.2	0.2	0.3	0.5	0.6	0.5	0.6	5.2	5.6	7.1	6.5	4.9	27.2	28.9	12.7	2.0	77.8	41.3	48.3	51.7
04606	ADDISON	98.1	98.0	0.6	0.6	0.3	0.4	0.2	0.2	4.2	6.2	5.7	7.3	4.5	25.4	32.6	12.6	1.4	78.6	42.6	49.3	50.7
04607	GOULDSBORO	97.1	96.9	0.5	0.5	0.5	0.6	1.4	1.6	5.1	5.1	6.0	5.9	5.3	25.8	31.5	13.4	2.0	80.0	42.7	51.0	49.1
04609	BAR HARBOR	98.0	97.8	0.2	0.2	0.8	1.0	0.6	0.7	4.2	4.2	6.1	6.4	6.7	26.9	29.0	13.7	2.9	81.9	42.5	46.1	53.9
04611	BEALS	97.6	97.5	1.3	1.3	0.2	0.2	2.1	2.4	4.9	5.5	7.9	6.0	4.7	27.4	26.2	15.6	1.9	77.4	41.0	52.0	48.0
04612	BERNARD	97.7	98.0	0.0	0.0	0.6	0.5	0.0	0.5	5.6	6.1	5.6	5.6	2.6	23.0	34.7	14.8	2.0	79.1	45.9	45.4	54.6
04613	BIRCH HARBOR	97.5	96.6	0.4	0.4	0.4	0.8	1.6	1.9	5.3	5.3	6.0	6.0	4.9	25.3	33.2	12.1	1.9	78.9	42.7	51.3	48.7
04614	BLUE HILL	97.8	97.6	0.4	0.4	0.2	0.2	0.1	0.1	3.8	4.6	6.4	7.5	4.7	21.5	34.5	14.0	3.0	80.5	45.7	47.5	52.5
04615	BLUE HILL FALLS	98.1	97.8	0.4	0.4	0.0	0.0	0.0	0.0	3.0	3.6	5.9	6.1	5.9	17.7	37.1	16.5	4.2	83.9	48.8	48.6	51.4
04616	BROOKLIN	98.4	98.2	0.2	0.2	0.5	0.6	0.8	0.9	3.2	3.6	6.0	6.3	4.9	20.0	37.3	16.5	2.3	83.4	48.6	48.3	51.7
04617	BROOKSVILLE	98.7	98.5	0.0	0.0	0.6	0.8	0.4	0.3	4.3	4.7	4.5	5.1	3.5	19.4	38.3	17.7	2.7	83.5	50.3	50.4	49.6
04619	CALAIS	96.8	96.4	0.4	0.4	0.7	1.0	0.7	0.9	4.9	5.1	6.4	6.4	6.3	24.1	27.1	16.5	3.3	80.0	42.8	47.4	52.6
04622	CHERRYFIELD	97.9	97.7	0.1	0.1	0.4	0.5	0.1	0.1	4.6	5.2	6.5	5.9	5.3	22.1	30.5	16.9	2.9	79.6	45.2	47.4	52.6
04623	COLUMBIA FALLS	98.2	98.1	0.0	0.0	0.2	0.2	0.4	0.4	5.6	5.7	6.9	6.7	5.2	27.9	28.5	12.3	1.2	77.9	39.8	51.0	49.0
04624	COREA	94.2	93.9	1.7	1.8	0.6	0.8	1.9	2.8	2.6	2.8	3.9	4.4	6.7	26.9	30.5	20.0	2.3	88.7	46.9	50.3	49.7
04625	CRANBERRY ISLES	98.2	98.2	0.0	0.0	0.0	0.0	0.0	0.0	1.8	1.8	5.5	5.5	3.6	27.3	29.1	20.0	5.5	90.9	47.1	49.1	50.9
04626	CUTLER	96.5	95.9	1.6	1.8	0.5	0.7	2.1	2.5	10.3	10.0	7.2	3.9	3.1	32.7	21.2	9.9	1.6	69.1	33.8	52.9	47.1
04627	DEER ISLE	98.5	98.6	0.2	0.2	0.2	0.2	0.5	0.6	3.5	4.2	6.7	5.6	3.9	19.7	30.1	20.5	5.6	81.4	48.7	46.8	53.2
04628	DENNYSVILLE	98.4	98.2	0.2	0.2	0.0	0.2	0.3	0.2	5.3	5.9	6.3	5.1	5.6	24.0	31.5	14.7	1.8	79.6	43.7	49.2	50.8
04630	EAST MACHIAS	98.2	98.0	0.1	0.1	0.2	0.2	0.1	0.1	4.6	5.1	6.3	6.3	5.7	28.0	28.7	14.0	1.4	79.9	41.5	51.8	48.2
04631	EASTPORT	78.0	76.2	0.3	0.4	0.2	0.2	0.9	1.0	5.8	5.7	6.1	6.3	6.1	23.3	27.8	16.5	2.6	79.0	42.8	47.5	52.6
04634	FRANKLIN	97.0	96.7	0.2	0.2	0.5	0.7	0.4	0.4	5.6	6.0	6.7	5.8	4.7	27.4	30.6	11.5	1.8	77.9	41.4	50.0	50.0
04635	FRENCHBORO	97.4	97.5	0.0	0.0	0.0	0.0	0.0	0.0	5.0	5.0	5.0	5.0	5.0	30.0	25.0	17.5	2.5	85.0	43.0	52.5	47.5
04640	HANCOCK	99.2	99.3	0.2	0.2	0.1	0.1	0.9	1.1	4.7	4.8	4.6	5.8	4.6	23.2	32.6	17.0	2.7	81.4	46.2	48.1	51.9
04642	HARBORSIDE	98.6	98.0	0.0	0.0	1.4	1.4	0.0	0.7	4.7	4.7	4.1	4.1	3.4	16.9	39.9	18.9	3.4	82.4	51.9	51.4	48.7
04643	HARRINGTON	98.1	98.1	0.0	0.0	0.0	0.0	1.4	1.7	4.9	5.3	6.2	5.2	5.6	25.2	31.3	14.9	1.5	80.0	43.4	48.4	51.6
04645	ISLE AU HAUT	100.0	100.0	0.0	0.0	0.0	0.0	3.8	4.8	6.0	8.4	6.0	7.2	2.4	30.1	26.5	13.3	0.0	75.9	41.5	51.8	48.2
04646	ISLESFORD	98.7	98.7	0.0	0.0	0.0	0.0	0.0	0.0	2.7	2.7	5.3	6.7	2.7	24.0	26.7	25.3	4.0	82.7	48.2	49.3	50.7
04648	JONESBORO	99.3	99.3	0.2	0.2	0.0	0.0	0.3	0.5	5.8	6.0	6.0	5.0	4.3	24.8	29.9	16.1	2.2	79.3	43.9	50.6	49.4
04649	JONESPORT	97.8	97.5	0.3	0.4	0.1	0.2	0.4	0.4	5.7	5.7	6.0	4.7	5.5	25.2	26.5	17.3	3.5	79.8	43.2	48.3	51.7
04650	LITTLE DEER ISLE	98.3	97.7	0.4	0.4	0.4	0.8	0.8	0.8	4.7	4.7	6.6	5.5	3.9	21.9	35.6	14.8	2.3	80.5	46.5	52.0	48.1
04652	LUBEC	97.8	97.6	0.3	0.3	0.2	0.3	0.7	0.9	4.7	5.1	6.3	5.9	5.0	23.3	28.5	18.0	3.3	80.0	44.9	47.4	52.6
04653	BASS HARBOR	98.0	97.8	0.0	0.0	0.4	0.6	0.4	0.6	5.6	6.4	5.8	5.8	2.8	22.2	34.3	15.2	2.0	78.6	45.9	45.9	54.1
04654	MACHIAS	96.7	96.2	0.5	0.5	1.0	1.2	0.6	0.8	4.7	4.7	5.7	8.1	11.8	21.9	25.8	14.1	3.3	81.3	39.3	47.5	52.5
04655	MACHIASPORT	98.2	98.1	0.0	0.1	0.2	0.2	0.1	0.1	4.4	4.9	6.2	6.5	5.8	28.7	28.5	13.6	1.4	80.1	41.3	52.1	47.9
04656	MANSET	99.1	98.9	0.0	0.0	0.0	0.0	0.3	0.5	5.4	6.3	5.7	6.5	4.4	26.9	28.3	14.1	2.5	77.7	41.7	48.4	51.6
04657	MEDDYBEMPS	98.3	98.3	0.4	0.4	0.0	0.4	0.0	0.0	5.5	6.0	6.4	5.5	5.1	24.7	30.6	14.9	1.3	79.2	42.9	50.6	49.4
04658	MILBRIDGE	92.7	91.5	0.0	0.0	0.2	0.2	5.9	7.1	3.9	4.6	5.8	5.4	4.6	24.6	28.0	19.9	3.3	82.6	45.8	49.0	51.1
04660	MOUNT DESERT	98.4	98.2	0.3	0.3	0.3	0.3	0.5	0.6	4.5	5.5	6.8	5.8	3.3	27.1	32.5	13.3	1.3	78.8	43.4	48.9	51.1
04666	PEMBROKE	97.5	97.3	0.1	0.1	0.3	0.4	0.4	0.4	5.4	5.8	6.3	5.3	4.9	24.2	29.8	16.2	2.1	79.4	43.9	48.1	51.9
04667	PERRY	69.3	67.8	0.1	0.1	0.1	0.1	0.5	0.7	6.6	6.5	7.4	8.2	7.3	26.3	25.6	10.9	1.2	74.4	37.1	49.4	50.6
04668	PRINCETON	63.1	62.4	0.1	0.1	0.1	0.1	0.8	0.8	6.5	6.6	9.1	9.0	7.7	26.8	23.5	9.5	1.3	72.5	34.8	50.3	49.7
04669	PROSPECT HARBOR	96.7	97.0	0.5	0.5	0.5	0.5	1.8	1.9	4.9	4.9	5.6	5.6	5.4	25.6	32.4	13.6	1.9	80.8	43.4	51.2	48.8
04671	ROBBINSTON	91.8	91.0	0.0	0.0	0.0	0.2	0.2	0.4	6.0	6.0	6.2	7.1	6.4	25.8	28.5	12.5	1.7	77.3	40.7	50.2	49.8
04673	SARGENTVILLE	100.0	100.0	0.0	0.0	0.0	0.0	0.0	0.0	3.6	3.6	5.4	7.1	3.6	19.6	39.3	16.1	1.8	87.5	50.0	44.6	55.4
	MAINE	97.0	96.6	0.5	0.6	0.7	0.9	0.7	0.9	5.5	5.8	6.7	6.9	6.5	26.7	27.5	12.5	2.0	77.9	40.2	48.8	51.2
	UNITED STATES	75.1	73.6	12.3	12.5	3.8	4.2	12.5	14.1	6.9	6.7	7.2	7.0	7.3	28.6	23.8	10.8	1.7	75.1	36.0	49.1	50.9

#	POST OFFICE NAME	2004 Per Capita Income	2004 HH Income Base	2004 Household Income Distribution (%): Less than $25,000	$25,000 to $49,999	$50,000 to $99,999	$100,000 to $149,999	$150,000 or More	Median Household Income: 2004	2009	2004 National Centile	2004 State Centile	2004 Home Value Base	2004 Home Value Distribution (%): Less than $50,000	$50,000 to $89,999	$90,000 to $174,999	$175,000 to $399,999	$400,000 or More	2004 Median Home Value
04468	OLD TOWN	18334	4320	40.0	29.1	24.2	4.9	1.7	32900	36919	21	29	2642	19.2	24.3	49.4	6.8	0.3	97037
04469	ORONO	10954	0	0.0	0.0	0.0	0.0	0.0	0	0	0	0	0	0.0	0.0	0.0	0.0	0.0	0
04471	ORIENT	15630	218	45.0	31.7	20.6	1.8	0.9	28040	31405	9	8	181	16.6	33.2	37.0	12.7	0.6	90625
04472	ORLAND	22042	831	27.9	30.5	32.3	7.8	1.6	42740	47701	55	71	694	7.9	14.7	49.0	24.8	3.6	132477
04473	ORONO	20726	2796	40.1	24.5	24.1	8.1	3.2	34221	39141	25	34	1250	6.5	11.3	51.0	29.2	2.0	141915
04474	ORRINGTON	22042	1475	19.5	32.3	38.2	9.6	0.5	48227	53438	69	86	1259	4.5	14.2	58.3	22.5	0.6	123742
04475	PASSADUMKEAG	18194	176	33.5	36.4	25.0	2.3	2.8	37677	41585	38	49	145	16.6	37.2	46.2	0.0	0.0	87800
04476	PENOBSCOT	22926	613	22.8	38.2	31.8	4.6	2.6	41501	46827	51	66	533	9.6	15.2	42.2	25.1	7.9	144057
04478	ROCKWOOD	18916	152	43.4	30.9	19.7	5.9	0.0	29475	32341	11	12	121	12.4	21.5	43.8	14.9	7.4	115625
04479	SANGERVILLE	15374	493	42.2	35.5	20.5	1.8	0.0	29925	32369	12	13	368	9.5	28.5	46.2	15.2	0.5	104605
04481	SEBEC	16127	308	37.0	37.3	24.0	1.6	0.0	35481	38149	29	39	262	9.2	24.8	46.6	17.9	1.5	118478
04487	SPRINGFIELD	13910	354	48.0	29.1	20.1	2.0	0.9	26052	28743	6	5	304	41.8	29.9	25.3	2.0	1.0	62273
04488	STETSON	15316	377	36.9	42.7	17.5	1.1	1.9	32911	36858	21	29	319	19.8	27.9	42.0	10.3	0.0	93409
04490	TOPSFIELD	16033	102	39.2	39.2	18.6	2.9	0.0	29501	31485	11	12	85	20.0	31.8	37.7	8.2	2.4	86250
04491	VANCEBORO	16018	67	46.3	29.9	22.4	1.5	0.0	27946	34080	9	8	56	37.5	26.8	26.8	8.9	0.0	66000
04492	WAITE	17822	89	42.7	33.7	21.4	2.3	0.0	29584	33170	11	13	74	31.1	27.0	33.8	8.1	0.0	75000
04493	WEST ENFIELD	18307	686	30.6	31.3	31.1	5.1	1.9	38792	43116	42	53	568	19.2	31.7	39.4	9.5	0.2	88958
04495	WINN	16750	117	39.3	37.6	15.4	6.0	1.7	30529	34474	14	17	96	35.4	33.3	25.0	6.3	0.0	66667
04496	WINTERPORT	21126	1570	28.6	26.2	34.0	9.4	1.8	43924	49152	58	76	1292	15.7	16.6	48.8	17.3	1.6	116189
04497	WYTOPITLOCK	10780	133	55.6	30.8	12.0	1.5	0.0	22498	25597	3	2	114	43.9	33.3	16.7	6.1	0.0	54375
04530	BATH	22662	5165	27.9	32.0	31.7	6.4	2.1	41696	46823	52	68	3019	1.7	7.6	48.5	37.1	5.1	155292
04535	ALNA	20465	300	26.3	28.7	38.0	6.7	0.3	46140	50660	64	81	267	3.0	7.5	43.1	39.0	7.5	168403
04537	BOOTHBAY	22375	838	25.4	35.1	28.3	7.9	3.3	42146	47397	53	70	696	0.6	9.2	39.8	41.2	9.2	176250
04538	BOOTHBAY HARBOR	25208	1324	30.1	31.3	26.5	9.5	2.6	40344	45338	47	60	1024	3.6	6.5	33.2	44.4	12.3	192969
04539	BRISTOL	23506	618	24.1	37.5	29.6	6.3	2.4	41576	46375	52	67	519	3.1	7.1	48.6	30.8	10.4	159418
04541	CHAMBERLAIN	24351	98	24.5	32.7	33.7	6.1	3.1	43911	48920	58	76	81	6.2	4.9	38.3	37.0	13.6	177083
04543	DAMARISCOTTA	28696	820	32.6	27.4	28.9	6.8	4.3	42369	49206	54	70	597	10.2	2.7	27.5	46.9	12.7	209211
04544	EAST BOOTHBAY	35474	198	21.2	22.7	32.3	14.1	9.6	54700	65313	79	94	170	4.1	4.1	20.6	48.8	22.4	265385
04547	FRIENDSHIP	23216	924	23.8	35.2	28.8	8.8	3.5	42549	47887	55	70	767	6.0	10.2	44.9	29.5	9.5	146175
04548	GEORGETOWN	30792	403	18.1	27.5	38.5	9.2	6.7	54025	59309	78	93	331	1.8	7.6	26.3	50.5	13.9	221364
04549	ISLE OF SPRINGS	0	0	0.0	0.0	0.0	0.0	0.0	0	0	0	0	0	0.0	0.0	0.0	0.0	0.0	0
04551	BREMEN	32711	302	27.2	37.1	20.9	8.3	6.6	39730	43508	45	57	269	3.7	6.3	31.2	41.3	17.5	199479
04553	NEWCASTLE	27577	931	24.3	32.2	31.3	8.6	3.7	45036	50075	61	79	736	5.0	2.9	32.5	47.6	12.1	200813
04554	NEW HARBOR	29076	355	27.0	34.1	25.6	7.6	5.6	37322	44810	37	47	308	0.3	2.9	29.9	48.1	18.8	241463
04555	NOBLEBORO	23885	719	24.2	34.6	30.7	6.8	3.6	43305	48512	57	74	610	4.6	6.1	37.7	44.4	7.2	178788
04556	EDGECOMB	28295	526	21.3	31.4	32.7	8.6	6.1	46231	51273	64	82	441	3.4	6.1	32.4	42.4	15.7	193883
04558	PEMAQUID	28869	108	25.9	34.3	27.8	7.4	4.6	40000	46553	46	59	91	3.3	3.3	36.3	41.8	15.4	202273
04562	PHIPPSBURG	25391	890	23.3	26.2	37.4	8.4	4.7	50398	55138	73	89	751	4.9	11.2	32.0	40.0	12.0	181042
04563	CUSHING	23780	153	22.2	34.0	32.7	8.5	2.6	43839	48847	58	76	128	5.5	11.7	40.6	31.3	10.9	150000
04564	ROUND POND	30444	163	23.3	33.1	33.7	6.1	3.7	44655	50000	60	78	135	6.7	3.0	40.7	37.0	12.6	174265
04567	SMALL POINT	30982	21	23.8	19.1	38.1	14.3	4.8	57143	62014	82	95	17	0.0	11.8	23.5	52.9	11.8	237500
04568	SOUTH BRISTOL	32581	230	28.7	29.1	29.6	7.8	4.8	41783	46659	52	68	194	2.6	3.6	28.4	40.7	24.7	222000
04570	SQUIRREL ISLAND	0	0	0.0	0.0	0.0	0.0	0.0	0	0	0	0	0	0.0	0.0	0.0	0.0	0.0	0
04571	TREVETT	23185	144	19.4	38.2	30.6	7.6	4.2	44238	49820	59	77	132	0.0	3.0	19.7	62.1	15.2	246429
04572	WALDOBORO	19556	2175	33.1	32.7	28.2	4.5	1.5	38267	42382	40	51	1790	10.7	9.0	51.0	24.0	5.4	138300
04573	WALPOLE	29531	193	29.0	29.0	29.5	7.8	4.7	41676	46422	52	68	163	1.2	4.3	29.5	39.9	25.2	221250
04574	WASHINGTON	17454	575	27.0	39.7	30.1	2.1	1.2	38597	42646	41	52	490	5.1	13.9	55.3	23.5	2.2	135268
04576	SOUTHPORT	39766	345	20.0	35.4	24.9	9.6	10.1	44583	51335	60	78	300	2.0	0.3	24.0	36.0	37.7	315909
04578	WISCASSET	21586	1953	27.2	34.3	28.7	7.6	2.2	40972	45430	50	64	1528	13.2	6.0	31.9	41.0	7.9	173020
04579	WOOLWICH	24581	1195	19.8	35.4	32.6	8.2	4.0	46179	51648	64	82	1023	2.8	10.2	39.7	40.3	7.0	168693
04605	ELLSWORTH	22493	5918	30.6	33.3	27.2	6.3	2.6	38637	43285	42	52	4407	8.6	11.7	44.7	29.5	5.4	144131
04606	ADDISON	17122	494	44.9	29.6	20.7	1.6	3.2	28007	30788	9	8	414	17.9	24.4	38.4	16.7	2.7	104825
04607	GOULDSBORO	20934	597	29.2	35.5	28.8	4.4	2.2	37857	42601	39	49	494	10.3	18.4	42.7	23.5	5.1	126136
04609	BAR HARBOR	27485	2693	30.4	29.3	27.8	7.9	4.6	40977	46808	50	64	1709	2.3	1.8	27.6	48.9	19.4	225760
04611	BEALS	14862	235	40.0	34.5	23.0	2.6	0.0	32043	36053	18	26	191	13.6	28.8	42.9	11.5	3.1	108500
04612	BERNARD	22810	93	26.9	34.4	29.0	7.5	2.2	40451	44451	48	61	73	4.1	5.5	28.8	46.6	15.1	208929
04613	BIRCH HARBOR	20076	110	25.5	36.4	31.8	4.6	1.8	39369	44075	44	56	91	9.9	19.8	45.1	23.1	2.2	122321
04614	BLUE HILL	20760	838	37.6	27.8	26.5	4.5	3.6	32906	36191	21	29	640	3.1	9.5	27.7	47.5	12.2	204435
04615	BLUE HILL FALLS	26776	250	30.0	32.4	23.2	8.8	5.6	37935	42757	39	50	208	5.3	2.9	17.3	51.9	22.6	247561
04616	BROOKLIN	25660	497	29.0	30.4	28.8	7.0	4.8	40893	45819	49	64	413	4.8	4.6	40.4	32.0	18.2	175543
04617	BROOKSVILLE	26626	341	25.5	39.0	24.3	5.3	5.9	39474	44791	44	57	287	7.3	15.3	27.2	31.0	19.2	175962
04619	CALAIS	18879	1540	47.9	21.1	22.1	6.6	2.3	26418	28896	6	6	1036	10.4	28.9	52.1	8.1	0.5	102985
04622	CHERRYFIELD	14598	520	50.8	30.8	15.2	2.3	1.0	24520	27053	4	4	409	14.2	28.9	44.0	9.8	3.2	101826
04623	COLUMBIA FALLS	16797	403	41.4	30.5	23.3	3.2	1.5	30806	33778	14	18	326	20.9	27.3	37.4	12.0	2.5	93000
04624	COREA	22732	156	33.3	28.2	28.2	5.8	4.5	38637	43652	42	52	131	3.1	11.5	38.2	31.3	16.0	169531
04625	CRANBERRY ISLES	26268	28	28.6	25.0	42.9	3.6	0.0	45000	50000	61	79	24	0.0	4.2	33.3	50.0	12.5	262500
04626	CUTLER	15125	239	36.4	41.8	16.7	5.0	0.0	34121	38015	24	33	167	9.0	24.6	40.7	25.2	0.6	119712
04627	DEER ISLE	20011	425	38.4	29.9	24.0	4.7	3.1	34305	38422	25	35	352	7.4	11.7	36.7	24.7	19.6	158871
04628	DENNYSVILLE	15086	281	42.7	33.5	20.3	3.2	0.4	29157	31550	11	11	236	17.8	26.3	41.1	12.3	2.5	100556
04630	EAST MACHIAS	16763	716	37.6	38.7	21.0	1.8	1.0	31495	34794	16	22	583	13.2	19.6	49.7	15.3	2.2	112224
04631	EASTPORT	15479	908	51.2	28.2	17.7	2.5	0.3	24232	26199	4	4	623	20.9	41.1	30.0	7.2	0.8	77381
04634	FRANKLIN	18280	1211	36.5	36.0	22.6	2.3	2.6	34538	38109	26	36	982	13.1	22.1	43.8	18.2	2.8	113542
04635	FRENCHBORO	18302	19	47.4	26.3	21.1	5.3	0.0	27320	30000	8	7	15	6.7	0.0	33.3	53.3	6.7	206250
04640	HANCOCK	21579	442	30.8	32.8	27.8	6.8	1.8	35832	39833	31	40	367	7.1	12.8	39.8	30.3	10.1	147774
04642	HARBORSIDE	30574	74	24.3	33.8	25.7	9.5	6.8	42847	47865	56	72	63	4.8	7.9	25.4	38.1	23.8	232143
04643	HARRINGTON	14668	437	43.5	33.9	20.1	2.3	0.2	28017	30748	9	8	358	21.5	21.0	44.4	10.9	2.2	102055
04645	ISLE AU HAUT	13042	34	47.1	38.2	11.8	2.9	0.0	26471	30000	6	6	28	0.0	14.3	42.9	14.3	28.6	168750
04646	ISLESFORD	23544	35	31.4	25.7	31.4	5.7	5.7	41143	48651	50	65	31	0.0	6.5	29.0	45.2	19.4	281250
04648	JONESBORO	16869	262	45.4	26.7	22.5	4.2	1.2	27510	30256	8	7	221	14.9	24.9	41.6	13.6	5.0	106090
04649	JONESPORT	15869	603	49.4	29.2	15.6	3.7	2.2	25358	28183	5	5	484	15.3	20.9	44.0	18.4	1.5	110714
04650	LITTLE DEER ISLE	23503	116	36.2	32.8	21.6	5.2	4.3	35914	40924	31	41	97	8.3	15.5	35.1	25.8	15.5	157292
04652	LUBEC	13926	738	54.3	30.1	13.4	1.6	0.5	22426	24647	3	2	574	19.5	31.7	36.8	10.1	1.9	88679
04653	BASS HARBOR	21657	225	27.1	35.1	29.8	6.7	1.3	39747	44503	45	58	177	3.4	6.2	29.9	44.6	15.8	205833
04654	MACHIAS	16578	1467	44.2	30.3	21.3	3.1	1.2	28318	30720	9	10	938	14.4	19.7	51.9	12.7	1.3	111245
04655	MACHIASPORT	13826	345	37.7	38.8	20.6	1.7	1.2	31353	34470	16	21	278	13.7	19.4	48.9	15.5	2.5	111905
04656	MANSET	19986	159	35.2	24.5	34.6	5.0	0.6	38834	45285	42	53	128	3.9	4.7	47.7	32.0	11.7	165000
04657	MEDDYBEMPS	16379	101	37.6	35.6	23.8	3.0	0.0	31620	35748	17	24	87	8.1	20.7	54.0	14.9	2.3	116477
04658	MILBRIDGE	13610	605	52.4	31.1	14.6	1.7	0.3	23671	26021	4	3	487	18.5	22.6	39.4	17.5	2.1	106331
04660	MOUNT DESERT	26690	1218	22.3	29.5	35.6	9.2	3.5	47653	53004	68	86	1004	2.5	5.5	26.4	45.4	20.2	229259
04666	PEMBROKE	14633	527	48.8	28.8	19.7	2.7	0.0	25666	28216	5	5	445	17.1	31.0	41.1	10.3	0.5	93148
04667	PERRY	14433	402	42.8	31.3	20.7	3.5	1.7	30652	33384	14	17	316	19.3	28.8	34.5	15.5	1.9	94286
04668	PRINCETON	14909	695	44.3	30.1	21.9	3.2	0.6	28089	30236	9	9	497	21.9	31.4	38.8	6.8	1.0	86489
04669	PROSPECT HARBOR	20642	176	26.7	34.1	32.4	4.6	2.3	40000	43941	46	59	146	8.9	17.8	43.2	24.7	5.5	130263
04671	ROBBINSTON	16246	205	38.1	33.2	22.9	3.9	2.0	33998	37725	24	32	169	17.2	27.2	34.3	18.3	3.0	102315
04673	SARGENTVILLE	24477	28	25.0	42.9	25.0	3.6	3.6	37327	45000	37	47	23	4.4	21.7	34.8	26.1	13.0	140625
	MAINE	22411		29.6	30.7	30.0	6.5	3.2	40864	45987				8.5	14.0	43.9	28.6	5.1	138610
	UNITED STATES	25866		24.7	27.1	30.8	10.9	6.5	48124	56710				10.9	15.0	33.7	30.1	10.4	145905

#	POST OFFICE NAME	FINANCIAL SERVICES: Auto Loan	FINANCIAL SERVICES: Home Loan	FINANCIAL SERVICES: Invest-ments	FINANCIAL SERVICES: Retire-ment Plans	THE HOME: Home Improvements: Home Repair	THE HOME: Home Improvements: Lawn & Garden	THE HOME: Furnishings: Comput-ers & Hard-ware	THE HOME: Furnishings: Major Appli-ances	THE HOME: Furnishings: TV, Radio, Sound Equip-ment	THE HOME: Furnishings: Furni-ture	ENTERTAINMENT: Dine out/ Carry out	ENTERTAINMENT: Sports Equip-ment	ENTERTAINMENT: Fees & Tickets	ENTERTAINMENT: Toys & Games	ENTERTAINMENT: Travel	ENTERTAINMENT: Cable TV	PERSONAL: Apparel & Services	PERSONAL: Auto Repairs	PERSONAL: Health Insur-ance	PERSONAL: Pets & Supplies
04468	OLD TOWN	59	56	60	56	56	61	60	59	61	59	75	69	59	75	59	59	73	60	58	66
04469	ORONO	0	0	0	0	0	0	0	0	0	0	0	0	0	0	0	0	0	0	0	0
04471	ORIENT	66	49	30	45	56	63	47	57	54	47	63	68	41	62	50	57	58	57	68	79
04472	ORLAND	84	73	54	69	78	85	68	77	73	68	88	91	65	90	70	76	84	75	85	100
04473	ORONO	67	59	74	64	58	63	76	66	73	71	92	84	70	88	69	68	89	73	61	74
04474	ORRINGTON	79	80	73	77	82	86	74	78	75	74	92	92	75	96	76	76	90	76	79	94
04475	PASSADUMKEAG	85	57	26	49	65	74	55	69	66	56	78	82	47	74	56	71	71	68	85	98
04476	PENOBSCOT	98	69	36	65	80	89	68	84	78	67	91	101	58	90	70	82	83	82	100	116
04478	ROCKWOOD	67	52	36	47	59	66	49	59	56	49	66	70	44	65	53	60	61	59	70	81
04479	SANGERVILLE	59	42	24	39	47	56	44	51	51	43	60	59	39	57	44	55	55	51	62	67
04481	SEBEC	68	48	26	45	56	63	47	58	54	47	64	70	41	63	49	57	58	57	69	81
04487	SPRINGFIELD	59	44	27	39	50	56	42	51	48	42	57	60	37	56	44	52	53	50	61	71
04488	STETSON	60	55	43	53	55	58	52	56	53	54	65	65	49	62	52	52	63	56	56	67
04490	TOPSFIELD	63	49	34	45	56	62	47	56	53	46	62	66	42	62	50	56	58	55	66	77
04491	VANCEBORO	57	45	30	40	50	56	42	51	48	42	56	59	38	56	45	51	52	50	60	69
04492	WAITE	66	52	35	47	58	65	49	59	55	48	65	69	44	65	52	59	61	58	69	80
04493	WEST ENFIELD	77	65	48	61	69	75	62	70	66	63	80	81	57	77	63	67	76	69	75	89
04495	WINN	76	51	23	44	57	66	49	61	59	50	69	73	42	66	50	64	63	61	75	87
04496	WINTERPORT	81	73	61	73	76	81	73	77	75	72	91	90	70	91	72	74	87	76	79	91
04497	WYTOPITLOCK	51	39	26	35	44	50	37	45	42	37	50	53	33	49	39	45	46	44	53	62
04530	BATH	69	69	75	69	70	75	71	71	72	70	89	84	71	91	71	72	87	72	71	81
04535	ALNA	91	63	33	60	74	83	63	78	72	62	85	93	54	83	65	76	77	76	92	108
04537	BOOTHBAY	89	70	48	67	77	86	70	80	77	69	92	93	64	90	71	79	85	78	91	102
04538	BOOTHBAY HARBOR	86	67	45	61	74	85	65	77	74	64	87	89	59	85	68	79	81	76	91	102
04539	BRISTOL	95	70	41	64	80	90	67	82	77	67	91	98	59	89	71	81	83	81	98	114
04541	CHAMBERLAIN	92	72	49	65	81	91	68	82	77	67	91	96	61	90	72	82	85	81	97	112
04543	DAMARISCOTTA	88	79	74	80	82	92	83	87	86	81	105	100	79	101	83	87	99	87	93	100
04544	EAST BOOTHBAY	119	94	64	85	105	118	88	106	100	88	118	125	79	117	94	107	110	105	126	146
04547	FRIENDSHIP	93	73	50	66	82	92	69	83	78	68	92	97	61	91	73	83	86	82	98	113
04548	GEORGETOWN	118	93	63	84	104	117	87	105	99	87	117	123	78	116	93	106	109	104	125	144
04549	ISLE OF SPRINGS	0	0	0	0	0	0	0	0	0	0	0	0	0	0	0	0	0	0	0	0
04551	BREMEN	128	100	68	91	113	127	95	114	107	94	127	133	85	125	101	114	118	112	135	156
04553	NEWCASTLE	110	78	43	74	90	102	79	95	90	77	106	113	68	103	81	95	97	94	114	129
04554	NEW HARBOR	94	74	50	66	83	93	69	84	79	69	93	98	62	92	74	84	87	82	99	114
04555	NOBLEBORO	97	73	45	67	83	93	70	85	79	69	94	101	61	92	73	84	86	84	101	117
04556	EDGECOMB	117	82	43	77	95	106	81	100	93	80	109	120	69	107	84	97	99	98	118	138
04558	PEMAQUID	100	78	53	71	88	99	74	89	84	73	99	104	66	98	79	89	92	88	105	122
04562	PHIPPSBURG	100	83	60	77	91	100	78	90	86	78	103	107	73	103	82	90	96	89	103	120
04563	CUSHING	92	72	49	65	81	91	68	82	77	67	91	96	61	90	72	82	85	80	97	112
04564	ROUND POND	104	82	56	74	92	103	77	92	87	76	103	108	69	102	82	93	96	91	109	126
04567	SMALL POINT	108	84	58	76	95	107	80	96	90	79	107	112	71	105	85	96	99	94	113	131
04568	SOUTH BRISTOL	112	88	60	79	99	111	83	100	94	82	111	117	74	110	88	100	103	98	118	137
04570	SQUIRREL ISLAND	0	0	0	0	0	0	0	0	0	0	0	0	0	0	0	0	0	0	0	0
04571	TREVETT	95	75	51	67	84	95	70	85	80	70	95	99	63	93	75	85	88	84	100	116
04572	WALDOBORO	79	62	41	57	67	76	61	70	68	60	81	81	56	79	62	72	75	69	81	90
04573	WALPOLE	113	88	60	80	99	112	83	100	94	83	112	117	74	110	89	101	104	99	119	137
04574	WASHINGTON	78	55	29	52	64	72	54	67	62	54	73	81	47	72	56	65	67	66	80	93
04576	SOUTHPORT	136	106	73	96	120	135	100	121	114	99	135	142	90	133	107	121	125	119	143	165
04578	WISCASSET	79	70	59	68	74	81	68	74	72	68	87	87	66	88	70	73	83	73	79	92
04579	WOOLWICH	97	86	66	82	91	98	80	89	85	80	103	106	78	105	82	87	98	86	96	114
04605	ELLSWORTH	84	68	54	65	75	83	67	76	73	67	88	90	62	87	70	76	83	76	86	99
04606	ADDISON	69	54	37	49	61	69	51	62	58	51	69	72	46	68	55	62	64	61	73	84
04607	GOULDSBORO	80	63	43	57	71	80	59	71	67	59	79	84	53	78	63	72	74	70	84	98
04609	BAR HARBOR	79	80	91	80	81	88	80	81	81	80	101	95	80	101	82	81	98	82	82	94
04611	BEALS	67	47	25	44	55	61	46	57	53	46	63	69	40	61	48	56	57	56	68	80
04612	BERNARD	82	64	44	58	72	81	60	73	68	60	81	85	54	80	64	73	75	72	86	99
04613	BIRCH HARBOR	82	64	44	58	72	81	61	73	69	60	81	86	54	80	65	73	76	72	86	100
04614	BLUE HILL	71	58	48	57	62	72	63	67	67	60	81	76	58	77	62	70	75	67	76	79
04615	BLUE HILL FALLS	72	74	85	78	75	79	76	76	74	76	92	89	76	90	76	72	89	77	73	83
04616	BROOKLIN	93	76	59	71	84	93	73	85	80	73	96	99	67	95	77	84	90	84	97	112
04617	BROOKSVILLE	100	78	53	70	88	99	74	89	83	73	99	104	66	98	79	89	92	87	105	121
04619	CALAIS	67	51	35	49	56	66	56	61	62	53	73	69	50	70	55	65	67	61	72	74
04622	CHERRYFIELD	53	40	26	38	44	52	43	48	48	41	57	54	38	54	43	51	52	48	57	59
04623	COLUMBIA FALLS	60	51	40	51	54	61	53	56	56	52	68	64	50	67	52	57	64	56	61	67
04624	COREA	91	71	48	64	80	90	67	81	76	66	90	94	60	89	71	81	83	79	95	110
04625	CRANBERRY ISLES	88	69	47	62	77	87	65	78	73	64	87	91	58	86	69	78	81	77	92	107
04626	CUTLER	59	50	39	50	53	60	52	55	55	51	67	63	50	66	51	56	63	55	60	65
04627	DEER ISLE	77	60	41	54	68	76	57	68	64	56	76	80	51	75	60	68	71	67	81	93
04628	DENNYSVILLE	63	45	26	41	51	59	45	54	52	45	62	63	39	59	46	56	56	53	65	73
04630	EAST MACHIAS	61	46	30	44	51	60	50	55	56	47	66	63	44	62	50	59	60	55	66	68
04631	EASTPORT	52	40	30	39	43	51	45	48	49	43	59	54	41	56	44	52	54	48	56	57
04634	FRANKLIN	71	56	38	50	63	71	53	64	60	52	71	74	47	70	56	64	66	63	75	87
04635	FRENCHBORO	65	51	35	46	58	65	48	58	55	48	65	68	43	64	52	58	60	57	69	80
04640	HANCOCK	80	63	43	57	71	80	59	72	67	59	80	84	53	79	63	72	74	70	85	98
04642	HARBORSIDE	104	81	55	73	92	103	77	92	87	76	103	108	69	102	82	93	96	91	109	126
04643	HARRINGTON	58	46	32	42	51	58	44	52	49	44	59	61	40	58	46	52	55	51	61	70
04645	ISLE AU HAUT	54	42	29	38	48	54	40	48	45	40	54	56	36	53	43	48	50	47	57	66
04646	ISLESFORD	86	67	46	61	76	85	63	76	72	63	85	89	57	84	67	77	79	75	90	104
04648	JONESBORO	61	46	30	44	50	60	51	56	57	48	67	62	45	63	50	60	61	56	67	67
04649	JONESPORT	57	43	28	41	47	57	48	52	53	45	63	59	43	59	47	56	57	52	63	63
04650	LITTLE DEER ISLE	88	69	47	62	78	87	65	78	74	64	87	92	58	86	69	79	81	77	93	107
04652	LUBEC	49	37	24	35	40	48	40	44	45	38	53	50	36	50	40	47	48	44	53	54
04653	BASS HARBOR	82	64	44	58	72	81	60	73	68	60	81	85	54	80	64	73	75	72	86	100
04654	MACHIAS	58	47	36	46	51	57	50	54	54	48	64	63	45	63	50	55	60	54	61	66
04655	MACHIASPORT	60	45	30	43	49	59	50	55	56	48	66	62	45	62	50	59	60	55	66	67
04656	MANSET	78	62	42	56	69	78	58	70	66	57	78	82	52	77	62	70	72	69	83	96
04657	MEDDYBEMPS	64	50	34	46	57	64	48	57	54	47	64	67	43	63	51	58	59	56	68	78
04658	MILBRIDGE	56	38	18	33	43	49	37	45	44	37	52	54	31	49	37	47	47	45	56	64
04660	MOUNT DESERT	99	84	68	78	91	101	80	91	87	79	104	107	74	104	84	91	98	91	103	120
04666	PEMBROKE	63	42	19	36	48	55	41	51	49	41	58	61	35	54	41	53	52	50	63	72
04667	PERRY	61	49	38	46	54	61	49	56	55	48	65	65	45	64	51	57	61	56	64	73
04668	PRINCETON	61	46	31	41	49	57	47	53	53	47	64	63	42	61	47	56	59	54	62	70
04669	PROSPECT HARBOR	84	66	45	59	74	83	62	74	70	61	83	87	55	82	66	75	77	73	88	102
04671	ROBBINSTON	70	55	37	49	62	69	52	62	58	51	69	73	46	68	55	63	64	61	74	85
04673	SARGENTVILLE	83	65	44	59	73	82	61	74	69	61	82	87	55	81	65	74	77	73	87	101
	MAINE	80	73	65	71	75	82	72	77	75	71	92	90	70	91	73	76	88	76	81	93
	UNITED STATES	100	100	100	100	100	100	100	100	100	100	100	100	100	100	100	100	100	100	100	100

ZIP CODE		COUNTY FIPS CODE	POPULATION			2000-2004 ANNUAL RATE		HOUSEHOLDS					FAMILIES		
#	POST OFFICE NAME		2000	2004	2009	% Rate	State Centile	2000	2004	2009	% Annual Rate 2000-2004	2004 Average HH Size	2000	2004	% Annual Rate 2000-2004
04676	SEDGWICK	009	1109	1185	1313	1.6	80	474	517	587	2.1	2.29	311	340	2.1
04677	SORRENTO	009	289	309	343	1.6	81	127	140	160	2.3	2.21	92	102	2.5
04679	SOUTHWEST HARBOR	009	1601	1693	1864	1.3	73	746	810	917	2.0	2.05	438	477	2.0
04680	STEUBEN	029	988	975	950	-0.3	16	403	408	409	0.3	2.39	277	281	0.3
04681	STONINGTON	009	1692	1786	1966	1.3	71	719	778	879	1.9	2.29	482	523	1.9
04683	SUNSET	009	153	163	181	1.5	79	67	73	84	2.0	2.23	47	52	2.4
04684	SURRY	009	1355	1513	1716	2.6	96	549	629	732	3.3	2.41	403	462	3.3
04685	SWANS ISLAND	009	327	343	377	1.1	66	142	154	173	1.9	2.23	91	99	2.0
04691	WHITING	029	540	521	504	-0.8	3	243	242	242	-0.1	2.15	158	158	0.0
04693	WINTER HARBOR	009	988	1036	1137	1.1	65	402	438	496	2.0	2.37	278	303	2.1
04694	BAILEYVILLE	029	2642	2567	2489	-0.7	5	1102	1107	1107	0.1	2.32	765	771	0.2
04730	HOULTON	003	9605	9669	9698	0.2	33	3880	4035	4129	0.9	2.31	2547	2653	1.0
04732	ASHLAND	003	1870	1800	1769	-0.9	3	792	788	792	-0.1	2.28	515	514	-0.1
04733	BENEDICTA	003	228	228	227	0.0	26	83	86	87	0.8	2.64	59	61	0.8
04734	BLAINE	003	461	456	454	-0.3	18	189	193	195	0.5	2.36	141	144	0.5
04735	BRIDGEWATER	003	635	621	614	-0.5	9	259	261	263	0.2	2.38	180	182	0.3
04736	CARIBOU	003	10108	10242	10315	0.3	38	4195	4387	4506	1.1	2.30	2836	2976	1.1
04737	CLAYTON LAKE	003	1	1	1	0.0	26	1	1	1	0.0	1.00	0	0	0.0
04740	EASTON	003	1239	1219	1209	-0.4	13	513	524	532	0.5	2.32	349	357	0.5
04741	ESTCOURT STATION	003	4	4	4	0.0	26	3	3	3	0.0	1.00	1	1	0.0
04742	FORT FAIRFIELD	003	3751	3803	3829	0.3	39	1592	1673	1723	1.2	2.26	1063	1121	1.3
04743	FORT KENT	003	6018	5940	5890	-0.3	16	2432	2491	2528	0.6	2.28	1585	1628	0.6
04745	FRENCHVILLE	003	1260	1236	1224	-0.5	11	490	501	510	0.5	2.39	366	376	0.6
04746	GRAND ISLE	003	533	522	517	-0.5	10	224	227	230	0.3	2.30	167	170	0.4
04747	ISLAND FALLS	003	1273	1236	1219	-0.7	5	535	539	544	0.2	2.29	375	378	0.2
04750	LIMESTONE	003	2410	2346	2328	-0.6	6	833	847	863	0.4	2.26	557	567	0.4
04751	LIMESTONE	003	227	209	202	-1.9	0	83	77	76	-1.8	1.90	56	52	-1.7
04756	MADAWASKA	003	3730	3682	3659	-0.3	17	1687	1730	1761	0.6	2.07	1059	1088	0.6
04757	MAPLETON	003	2853	2781	2749	-0.6	7	1131	1139	1150	0.2	2.44	842	850	0.2
04758	MARS HILL	003	1480	1446	1430	-0.6	8	614	617	621	0.1	2.28	414	417	0.2
04760	MONTICELLO	003	790	775	767	-0.5	11	325	329	332	0.3	2.36	230	233	0.3
04761	NEW LIMERICK	003	981	973	967	-0.2	21	355	365	370	0.7	2.62	267	275	0.7
04762	NEW SWEDEN	003	652	643	638	-0.3	15	259	262	265	0.3	2.45	183	186	0.4
04763	OAKFIELD	003	1017	997	987	-0.5	10	415	421	425	0.3	2.37	284	288	0.3
04764	OXBOW	003	56	53	52	-1.3	1	29	29	29	0.0	1.83	19	19	0.0
04765	PATTEN	019	1452	1428	1444	-0.4	13	614	625	652	0.4	2.23	420	429	0.5
04766	PERHAM	003	442	445	446	0.2	33	166	172	176	0.8	2.59	117	122	0.6
04768	PORTAGE	003	390	383	380	-0.4	12	183	187	189	0.5	2.04	112	115	0.6
04769	PRESQUE ISLE	003	9598	9650	9678	0.1	31	3999	4151	4253	0.9	2.18	2493	2598	1.0
04772	SAINT AGATHA	003	802	843	862	1.2	68	350	386	407	2.3	2.16	236	261	2.4
04773	SAINT DAVID	003	754	752	749	-0.1	23	288	298	303	0.8	2.52	228	237	0.9
04774	SAINT FRANCIS	003	854	832	821	-0.6	7	376	380	385	0.3	2.19	254	258	0.4
04776	SHERMAN	003	1069	1049	1038	-0.4	11	425	433	438	0.4	2.42	326	333	0.5
04777	STACYVILLE	019	403	392	396	-0.7	6	161	161	167	0.0	2.43	115	115	0.0
04779	SINCLAIR	003	290	286	283	-0.3	15	125	128	130	0.6	2.23	88	90	0.5
04780	SMYRNA MILLS	003	442	432	427	-0.5	8	185	187	190	0.3	2.31	137	139	0.3
04781	WALLAGRASS	003	380	380	379	0.0	26	148	153	156	0.8	2.48	113	117	0.8
04783	STOCKHOLM	003	660	646	639	-0.5	9	292	296	299	0.3	2.18	211	215	0.4
04785	VAN BUREN	003	3005	2961	2937	-0.4	14	1240	1264	1281	0.5	2.18	811	830	0.6
04786	WASHBURN	003	1928	1900	1886	-0.3	14	813	830	842	0.5	2.29	585	598	0.5
04787	WESTFIELD	003	645	636	630	-0.3	15	237	241	244	0.4	2.58	173	177	0.5
04841	ROCKLAND	013	7733	7772	8113	0.1	31	3488	3617	3883	0.9	2.09	1978	2055	0.9
04843	CAMDEN	013	5283	5762	6236	2.1	91	2406	2697	3000	2.7	2.06	1425	1601	2.8
04847	HOPE	013	1279	1404	1525	2.2	93	502	568	633	3.0	2.46	372	421	3.0
04848	ISLESBORO	027	603	657	725	2.0	90	280	310	350	2.4	2.12	177	197	2.6
04849	LINCOLNVILLE	027	3860	4336	4863	2.8	97	1609	1850	2128	3.3	2.34	1107	1275	3.4
04851	MATINICUS	013	51	50	52	-0.5	10	26	26	27	0.0	1.92	14	14	0.0
04852	MONHEGAN	015	75	74	75	-0.3	16	46	48	50	1.0	1.54	21	22	1.1
04853	NORTH HAVEN	013	379	396	420	1.0	63	161	172	187	1.6	2.30	108	116	1.7
04854	OWLS HEAD	013	1922	2032	2164	1.3	73	856	930	1018	2.0	2.17	566	616	2.0
04856	ROCKPORT	013	3200	3401	3632	1.4	77	1364	1484	1623	2.0	2.29	914	996	2.0
04857	WILEYS CORNER	013	313	332	355	1.4	75	128	139	152	2.0	2.39	84	91	1.9
04858	SOUTH THOMASTON	013	1095	1167	1248	1.5	79	461	504	553	2.1	2.32	325	355	2.1
04859	SPRUCE HEAD	013	907	978	1052	1.8	85	373	411	452	2.3	2.38	274	302	2.3
04860	TENANTS HARBOR	013	1357	1440	1537	1.4	75	616	669	732	2.0	2.15	399	433	1.9
04861	THOMASTON	013	3599	3728	3912	0.8	57	1371	1472	1598	1.7	2.24	848	910	1.7
04862	UNION	013	3405	3718	4031	2.1	91	1328	1489	1656	2.7	2.47	969	1088	2.8
04863	VINALHAVEN	013	1235	1311	1399	1.4	75	550	596	650	1.9	2.20	341	370	1.9
04864	WARREN	013	3885	4109	4367	1.3	73	1370	1496	1637	2.1	2.55	986	1077	2.1
04901	WATERVILLE	011	26121	26473	26819	0.3	39	10610	11059	11458	1.0	2.18	6422	6724	1.1
04910	ALBION	011	1917	1982	2017	0.8	54	712	757	786	1.5	2.59	536	570	1.5
04911	ANSON	025	1869	1871	1880	0.0	28	729	751	777	0.7	2.48	498	515	0.8
04912	ATHENS	025	847	831	832	-0.5	11	327	332	343	0.4	2.44	227	232	0.5
04915	BELFAST	027	8425	9290	10312	2.3	94	3564	4054	4640	3.1	2.24	2261	2584	3.2
04917	BELGRADE	011	2264	2351	2399	0.9	59	874	931	968	1.5	2.52	653	696	1.5
04918	BELGRADE LAKES	011	162	176	184	2.0	89	69	77	82	2.6	2.29	50	56	2.7
04920	BINGHAM	025	1458	1446	1454	-0.2	21	588	603	625	0.6	2.37	390	400	0.6
04921	BROOKS	027	2414	2590	2835	1.7	82	954	1055	1189	2.4	2.44	650	720	2.4
04922	BURNHAM	027	1142	1190	1283	1.0	62	442	474	526	1.7	2.51	326	350	1.7
04923	CAMBRIDGE	025	852	856	875	0.1	30	344	358	377	0.9	2.39	256	267	1.0
04924	CANAAN	025	1339	1341	1346	0.0	28	520	538	556	0.8	2.49	381	396	0.9
04925	CARATUNK	025	125	125	125	0.0	26	51	53	55	0.9	2.36	32	33	0.7
04927	CLINTON	011	2616	2608	2608	-0.1	22	982	1012	1036	0.7	2.57	729	751	0.7
04928	CORINNA	019	2262	2306	2357	0.5	43	884	921	965	1.0	2.50	654	683	1.0
04929	DETROIT	025	816	816	818	0.0	26	328	338	349	0.7	2.41	227	234	0.7
04930	DEXTER	019	4278	4125	4158	-0.9	3	1764	1756	1824	-0.1	2.31	1221	1221	0.0
04932	DIXMONT	019	1002	1009	1024	0.2	33	383	401	420	1.1	2.52	293	307	1.1
04936	EUSTIS	007	407	429	457	1.3	70	189	204	224	1.8	2.10	108	118	2.1
04937	FAIRFIELD	025	7173	7144	7194	-0.1	22	2807	2875	2981	0.6	2.41	1925	1977	0.6
04938	FARMINGTON	007	9370	9906	10548	1.3	73	3586	3937	4350	2.2	2.24	2076	2286	2.3
04939	GARLAND	019	986	990	1004	0.1	29	378	390	406	0.7	2.54	270	279	0.8
04941	FREEDOM	027	2026	2106	2266	0.9	60	808	870	966	1.8	2.38	574	619	1.8
04942	HARMONY	021	1307	1314	1333	0.1	31	540	558	584	0.8	2.34	407	421	0.8
04943	HARTLAND	025	1992	2056	2099	0.8	53	780	834	880	1.6	2.39	548	587	1.6
04945	JACKMAN	025	972	924	919	-1.2	1	403	394	403	-0.5	2.25	253	248	-0.5
	MAINE					0.9					1.5	2.33			1.6
	UNITED STATES					1.2					1.3	2.58			1.1

ZIP CODE		RACE (%)						% Hispanic Origin		2004 AGE DISTRIBUTION (%)										MEDIAN AGE		
		White		Black		Asian/Pacific																
#	POST OFFICE NAME	2000	2004	2000	2004	2000	2004	2000	2004	0-4	5-9	10-14	15-19	20-24	25-44	45-64	65-84	85+	18+	2004	% 2004 Males	% 2004 Females
04676	SEDGWICK	96.7	96.5	0.2	0.2	0.4	0.4	1.1	1.4	5.7	5.9	6.8	6.2	5.4	24.1	31.1	13.3	1.7	77.8	42.6	51.0	49.0
04677	SORRENTO	96.2	96.1	0.0	0.0	0.4	0.3	0.7	0.7	2.9	2.6	6.2	6.8	4.5	19.1	35.9	20.7	1.3	84.5	47.9	48.5	51.5
04679	SOUTHWEST HARBOR	98.2	98.2	0.4	0.4	0.2	0.2	0.6	0.7	4.2	4.6	6.0	6.1	5.7	24.2	29.3	17.0	3.0	81.5	44.6	47.8	52.2
04680	STEUBEN	97.0	96.6	0.3	0.3	0.4	0.5	0.6	0.6	5.6	6.1	7.0	5.6	5.7	28.5	27.6	12.4	1.4	78.0	39.3	49.4	50.6
04681	STONINGTON	97.5	97.3	0.1	0.1	0.4	0.5	0.6	0.7	4.8	5.3	6.2	6.3	5.7	24.9	29.4	15.4	2.1	79.6	42.9	48.4	51.6
04683	SUNSET	98.7	99.4	0.0	0.0	0.0	0.0	0.0	0.0	6.1	6.1	6.8	5.5	4.9	23.9	30.7	14.1	1.8	77.3	42.5	50.9	49.1
04684	SURRY	96.8	96.8	0.2	0.1	0.4	0.5	0.4	0.4	5.0	6.4	7.9	5.8	3.8	24.4	33.4	12.0	1.5	77.1	42.8	49.9	50.1
04685	SWANS ISLAND	98.5	98.5	0.3	0.3	0.0	0.0	0.0	0.0	5.5	5.8	5.8	5.8	6.4	24.5	27.7	17.2	1.2	79.3	42.7	52.8	47.2
04691	WHITING	97.0	97.1	0.2	0.2	0.0	0.0	0.7	0.8	3.8	4.4	6.5	5.6	6.0	24.0	31.7	16.3	1.7	81.8	44.8	48.6	51.4
04693	WINTER HARBOR	90.0	89.6	2.0	2.3	0.7	0.9	3.6	4.3	10.4	9.1	7.4	6.0	6.7	29.7	18.4	11.1	1.2	69.5	32.2	48.1	51.9
04694	BAILEYVILLE	98.3	98.2	0.1	0.1	0.1	0.1	0.5	0.6	5.4	5.7	6.7	6.0	5.3	25.1	29.5	14.5	1.8	78.5	42.2	49.4	50.6
04730	HOULTON	95.4	95.0	0.3	0.3	0.4	0.6	0.5	0.6	5.5	5.9	6.9	6.7	5.7	24.6	25.9	15.9	3.0	77.4	41.5	48.0	52.0
04732	ASHLAND	98.9	98.8	0.0	0.0	0.2	0.2	0.2	0.2	4.6	5.0	5.9	6.7	5.3	25.8	30.4	14.6	1.6	80.2	42.8	51.7	48.3
04733	BENEDICTA	100.0	100.0	0.0	0.0	0.0	0.0	0.0	0.0	1.8	4.8	8.8	11.4	4.4	23.3	30.7	13.2	1.8	76.3	42.8	51.3	48.7
04734	BLAINE	97.2	96.9	0.4	0.4	0.0	0.0	0.4	0.4	6.4	6.8	7.7	6.8	4.4	27.4	26.8	12.1	1.8	74.6	39.2	48.9	51.1
04735	BRIDGEWATER	98.1	98.1	0.0	0.0	0.0	0.0	0.6	0.6	4.2	4.8	6.0	6.1	4.8	22.7	31.1	18.0	2.3	81.3	45.7	50.1	49.9
04736	CARIBOU	96.3	95.8	0.4	0.4	1.0	1.2	0.5	0.6	5.4	6.0	6.5	6.2	5.3	25.2	28.3	15.1	2.1	78.2	42.1	49.0	51.0
04737	CLAYTON LAKE	100.0	100.0	0.0	0.0	0.0	0.0	0.0	0.0	0.0	0.0	0.0	0.0	100.0	0.0	0.0	0.0	0.0	100.0	22.5	100.0	0.0
04740	EASTON	97.3	97.1	0.3	0.3	0.4	0.5	0.6	0.8	5.4	5.7	5.9	6.2	6.2	25.4	29.1	14.4	1.6	79.3	41.9	48.5	51.5
04741	ESTCOURT STATION	100.0	100.0	0.0	0.0	0.0	0.0	0.0	0.0	0.0	0.0	0.0	0.0	50.0	50.0	0.0	0.0	0.0	100.0	25.0	50.0	50.0
04742	FORT FAIRFIELD	98.2	98.1	0.3	0.3	0.1	0.1	0.8	1.0	5.4	6.1	6.3	6.6	5.5	24.2	28.9	15.3	1.9	78.3	42.2	47.4	52.6
04743	FORT KENT	97.5	97.2	0.3	0.4	0.7	0.9	0.4	0.5	5.2	5.3	5.8	6.7	6.8	26.4	26.7	14.7	2.4	79.7	41.0	49.3	50.7
04745	FRENCHVILLE	99.2	99.1	0.1	0.1	0.2	0.2	0.4	0.7	4.9	5.5	7.2	6.0	4.6	25.9	29.2	14.6	2.1	78.2	42.8	48.2	51.8
04746	GRAND ISLE	98.9	98.9	0.0	0.0	0.2	0.2	0.4	0.4	3.8	4.6	5.9	6.5	3.5	15.9	41.4	17.8	0.6	80.7	49.6	48.9	51.2
04747	ISLAND FALLS	99.1	99.0	0.0	0.0	0.1	0.1	0.6	0.7	5.0	5.2	6.4	5.6	5.7	23.5	30.7	15.8	2.3	80.1	44.1	48.2	51.8
04750	LIMESTONE	91.2	90.6	4.3	4.6	1.2	1.4	3.7	4.1	4.1	4.7	5.5	14.8	9.9	20.9	25.9	12.0	2.1	77.3	36.5	52.6	47.4
04751	LIMESTONE	86.8	85.2	7.1	7.7	1.8	2.4	5.7	6.2	4.3	4.8	4.3	24.4	13.9	20.6	20.6	6.2	1.0	73.2	24.4	56.9	43.1
04756	MADAWASKA	98.0	97.7	0.1	0.1	0.8	1.0	0.2	0.2	4.2	4.5	5.5	5.4	4.8	21.2	32.2	19.2	3.1	82.3	47.7	46.8	53.2
04757	MAPLETON	97.9	97.7	0.0	0.0	0.1	0.1	0.4	0.5	5.3	6.1	6.5	6.2	5.1	28.3	29.7	11.3	1.5	78.3	41.0	51.3	48.7
04758	MARS HILL	97.5	97.3	0.1	0.1	0.2	0.3	0.4	0.4	5.2	5.0	6.4	7.6	6.2	23.3	23.0	19.3	4.1	78.5	42.6	47.7	52.4
04760	MONTICELLO	93.3	93.0	0.0	0.0	0.5	0.7	0.1	0.1	5.0	5.3	7.1	5.7	5.2	24.7	29.4	16.1	1.6	79.1	43.2	48.5	51.5
04761	NEW LIMERICK	95.8	95.6	0.1	0.1	0.1	0.1	0.6	0.7	5.5	6.9	7.4	9.3	6.4	25.0	29.4	9.8	0.5	74.4	38.6	49.0	51.0
04762	NEW SWEDEN	95.1	94.9	0.2	0.2	0.5	0.6	2.0	2.3	3.1	4.7	8.2	7.9	2.6	24.1	34.4	12.8	2.2	79.0	44.6	50.9	49.1
04763	OAKFIELD	98.2	98.2	0.0	0.0	0.0	0.0	0.7	0.9	4.0	5.0	6.2	6.3	4.9	25.5	28.3	17.8	2.0	80.5	43.8	48.9	51.2
04764	OXBOW	100.0	100.0	0.0	0.0	0.0	0.0	0.0	0.0	3.8	3.8	1.9	0.0	3.8	15.1	50.9	17.0	3.8	90.6	52.7	58.5	41.5
04765	PATTEN	99.1	99.1	0.2	0.2	0.0	0.0	0.0	0.0	4.1	4.8	5.4	6.7	4.8	21.9	32.8	17.5	2.1	81.1	46.3	51.0	49.0
04766	PERHAM	97.3	97.1	0.2	0.2	0.0	0.0	0.0	0.0	3.8	4.5	7.2	7.0	6.7	23.6	30.8	14.2	2.3	80.0	43.1	50.6	49.4
04768	PORTAGE	99.5	99.2	0.0	0.0	0.0	0.0	0.0	0.3	3.7	4.4	5.5	5.2	4.2	24.5	33.2	17.2	2.1	82.5	46.4	51.2	48.8
04769	PRESQUE ISLE	95.2	94.8	0.4	0.4	0.8	1.1	0.7	0.8	5.5	5.2	5.7	6.8	8.9	26.9	24.6	13.9	2.6	80.3	38.7	47.7	52.3
04772	SAINT AGATHA	99.6	99.6	0.0	0.0	0.1	0.1	0.3	0.4	4.6	4.7	4.4	4.9	5.0	20.6	38.7	15.3	1.8	82.9	48.0	50.4	49.6
04773	SAINT DAVID	98.4	98.3	0.4	0.4	0.4	0.5	0.3	0.4	5.5	5.5	7.6	7.2	3.5	27.5	31.9	11.0	0.4	75.9	41.3	51.1	48.9
04774	SAINT FRANCIS	99.7	99.6	0.1	0.1	0.0	0.0	0.0	0.0	2.5	4.3	5.9	6.7	6.1	20.2	34.7	17.7	1.8	82.5	47.3	49.6	50.4
04776	SHERMAN	98.0	98.0	0.3	0.3	0.0	0.0	0.2	0.3	4.5	5.2	6.4	6.6	6.1	22.0	33.3	14.1	1.8	79.9	44.5	50.1	49.9
04777	STACYVILLE	94.3	94.1	0.0	0.0	0.3	0.3	1.7	2.0	7.9	7.4	6.1	6.9	5.6	21.7	27.8	15.1	1.5	74.0	40.9	45.7	54.3
04779	SINCLAIR	99.7	99.7	0.0	0.0	0.0	0.0	0.0	0.0	3.2	3.9	3.9	5.2	3.9	16.8	40.6	21.0	1.8	86.0	52.9	51.4	48.6
04780	SMYRNA MILLS	97.7	97.7	0.0	0.0	0.2	0.2	0.5	0.5	3.7	4.2	7.9	8.1	3.7	24.3	33.3	13.9	0.9	79.2	44.0	49.3	50.7
04781	WALLAGRASS	99.2	99.5	0.0	0.0	0.0	0.0	0.3	0.3	7.6	7.6	7.4	6.6	4.7	27.9	24.7	12.1	1.3	73.4	37.6	50.3	49.7
04783	STOCKHOLM	98.3	98.3	0.0	0.0	0.0	0.0	0.2	0.2	3.9	4.5	5.7	6.4	4.2	20.0	36.4	17.3	1.7	82.2	48.1	51.6	48.5
04785	VAN BUREN	98.3	98.2	0.1	0.2	0.1	0.2	0.7	0.9	4.2	5.1	6.4	4.9	4.5	21.9	31.3	18.4	3.3	81.1	46.8	47.3	52.8
04786	WASHBURN	98.4	98.4	0.2	0.2	0.2	0.2	0.3	0.3	5.4	5.5	5.5	5.6	5.2	24.8	30.3	15.8	1.8	80.2	43.6	49.4	50.6
04787	WESTFIELD	97.5	97.6	0.3	0.3	0.0	0.0	0.2	0.2	5.4	6.0	6.6	6.0	4.9	24.7	30.7	13.4	2.5	78.3	42.7	49.5	50.5
04841	ROCKLAND	97.9	97.7	0.3	0.3	0.6	0.8	0.6	0.7	5.5	5.2	5.7	6.3	6.8	25.6	26.2	15.4	3.3	79.7	41.4	46.3	53.7
04843	CAMDEN	98.3	98.2	0.3	0.3	0.4	0.5	0.9	1.0	4.0	4.3	6.0	6.1	5.1	19.3	32.5	17.9	5.0	81.6	48.3	45.6	54.4
04847	HOPE	98.6	98.4	0.2	0.2	0.2	0.3	0.9	1.1	5.7	6.8	8.3	6.6	3.7	28.2	29.4	10.5	0.8	74.7	40.2	49.3	50.7
04848	ISLESBORO	98.2	98.0	0.2	0.2	0.2	0.2	1.3	1.5	5.0	5.3	5.2	4.1	4.1	20.1	36.2	16.7	3.2	81.9	48.1	49.2	50.8
04849	LINCOLNVILLE	98.5	98.4	0.1	0.1	0.3	0.4	0.7	0.8	5.2	5.9	6.9	4.8	4.1	25.2	33.3	13.2	1.4	78.8	43.7	49.6	50.4
04851	MATINICUS	100.0	100.0	0.0	0.0	0.0	0.0	0.0	0.0	0.0	6.0	8.0	2.0	6.0	22.0	40.0	16.0	0.0	84.0	47.5	54.0	46.0
04852	MONHEGAN	97.3	97.3	0.0	0.0	2.7	2.7	0.0	0.0	1.4	2.7	5.4	2.7	8.1	27.0	37.8	12.2	2.7	89.2	50.0	56.8	43.2
04853	NORTH HAVEN	95.3	95.2	1.1	1.0	0.0	0.0	2.4	2.5	6.1	6.3	6.8	5.3	5.1	29.0	28.5	11.1	1.8	77.8	40.1	51.0	49.0
04854	OWLS HEAD	98.8	98.7	0.1	0.2	0.2	0.3	0.3	0.3	4.4	5.1	5.9	4.8	4.0	22.2	31.9	18.9	2.8	81.8	47.4	48.2	51.8
04856	ROCKPORT	98.7	98.4	0.2	0.2	0.4	0.5	0.8	1.0	4.8	5.7	6.9	5.9	4.5	22.5	32.6	15.1	2.1	78.5	44.8	47.7	52.3
04857	WILEYS CORNER	99.4	99.4	0.0	0.0	0.0	0.0	0.3	0.3	5.4	5.7	5.7	5.7	4.5	20.5	32.8	17.5	2.1	79.5	46.2	51.8	48.2
04858	SOUTH THOMASTON	98.1	98.1	0.4	0.3	0.4	0.3	0.3	0.3	5.2	5.6	5.6	5.4	5.2	25.4	30.3	15.2	2.1	80.3	43.6	48.5	51.5
04859	SPRUCE HEAD	97.9	98.0	0.3	0.3	0.4	0.5	0.4	0.5	5.3	5.4	6.5	7.4	4.9	22.5	29.7	17.0	1.3	78.3	43.7	48.0	52.0
04860	TENANTS HARBOR	99.0	99.0	0.1	0.1	0.4	0.4	0.1	0.1	4.7	5.2	5.7	4.7	3.3	20.6	33.3	19.7	2.9	81.4	48.3	49.9	50.1
04861	THOMASTON	97.8	97.6	0.6	0.7	0.5	0.6	0.4	0.5	4.9	5.0	5.6	5.8	7.4	29.1	26.8	13.3	2.3	80.7	40.3	53.6	46.4
04862	UNION	98.6	98.4	0.2	0.2	0.2	0.2	0.4	0.5	6.0	6.5	6.9	7.0	5.4	26.5	29.2	11.2	1.3	76.0	40.3	49.2	50.8
04863	VINALHAVEN	98.1	98.1	0.0	0.0	0.3	0.4	0.0	0.0	6.8	7.1	6.6	5.0	4.0	26.9	26.9	14.1	2.6	76.4	41.0	48.8	51.2
04864	WARREN	97.6	97.4	0.3	0.3	0.4	0.5	0.7	0.8	5.9	6.2	6.7	6.7	6.4	30.6	27.1	9.3	1.1	76.4	37.8	53.1	47.0
04901	WATERVILLE	96.8	96.4	0.5	0.6	0.8	1.0	1.0	1.1	5.3	5.1	5.8	8.9	10.2	23.5	24.1	14.2	2.8	79.8	38.4	47.2	52.8
04910	ALBION	98.5	98.4	0.1	0.1	0.6	0.8	0.4	0.5	6.0	7.4	7.2	7.0	5.4	28.3	25.3	12.2	1.3	75.3	38.5	49.0	51.0
04911	ANSON	97.8	97.7	0.1	0.1	0.3	0.3	0.3	0.4	5.3	5.6	7.0	7.6	6.5	27.0	27.6	12.2	1.2	76.9	39.7	51.0	49.0
04912	ATHENS	99.1	98.9	0.1	0.1	0.1	0.1	0.7	0.7	5.4	5.9	6.7	6.5	5.7	28.4	28.2	11.8	1.4	77.3	39.6	50.2	49.8
04915	BELFAST	97.3	97.2	0.3	0.3	0.3	0.4	0.8	0.9	5.1	5.4	6.2	6.4	6.3	24.2	28.8	15.0	2.8	79.3	42.5	47.9	52.1
04917	BELGRADE	98.8	98.7	0.1	0.1	0.3	0.4	0.4	0.5	4.9	5.7	7.9	6.7	5.2	27.1	30.7	11.1	0.8	77.0	40.8	48.5	51.6
04918	BELGRADE LAKES	98.2	98.3	0.0	0.0	0.0	0.6	0.6	1.1	5.1	5.7	7.4	6.3	4.0	27.8	30.1	13.1	0.6	77.8	41.8	48.3	51.7
04920	BINGHAM	98.8	98.7	0.0	0.0	0.1	0.1	0.3	0.4	6.4	6.2	6.1	6.9	6.0	26.5	26.1	13.8	2.1	76.9	40.2	50.8	49.2
04921	BROOKS	98.7	98.7	0.1	0.1	0.1	0.1	0.6	0.7	6.1	6.5	7.2	6.9	4.9	27.1	28.9	11.0	1.4	75.4	39.4	50.2	49.9
04922	BURNHAM	96.9	96.7	0.2	0.2	0.1	0.1	0.4	0.6	5.9	6.2	7.8	6.9	6.3	27.0	28.6	10.3	1.0	75.9	38.5	50.3	49.7
04923	CAMBRIDGE	99.1	99.0	0.4	0.4	0.1	0.1	0.2	0.5	4.7	5.4	6.4	6.3	4.9	25.5	32.7	13.3	0.8	79.4	42.9	50.4	49.7
04924	CANAAN	97.9	97.6	0.1	0.2	0.2	0.2	0.2	0.3	5.9	6.6	8.6	6.5	5.7	28.7	29.3	7.9	0.8	75.2	37.6	49.9	50.1
04925	CARATUNK	97.6	96.8	0.0	0.0	0.0	0.0	0.0	0.0	3.2	4.8	5.6	5.6	2.4	25.6	36.8	15.2	0.8	81.6	46.5	52.0	48.0
04927	CLINTON	98.2	98.0	0.1	0.2	0.0	0.1	0.9	1.1	6.6	6.7	7.3	7.1	6.6	28.5	27.2	8.8	1.1	75.1	37.1	50.6	49.4
04928	CORINNA	98.2	98.1	0.4	0.4	0.1	0.1	0.5	0.6	5.9	6.2	6.9	6.0	6.1	26.2	27.2	14.2	1.3	77.5	40.6	50.2	49.8
04929	DETROIT	98.8	98.8	0.3	0.3	0.0	0.0	0.7	0.9	8.0	7.6	6.3	5.4	5.4	29.2	27.0	10.7	0.6	75.0	37.8	50.3	49.8
04930	DEXTER	98.6	98.6	0.3	0.3	0.1	0.1	0.6	0.8	6.0	6.0	5.9	6.1	5.4	24.2	28.7	15.4	2.4	78.3	42.4	48.0	52.1
04932	DIXMONT	98.6	98.4	0.0	0.0	0.5	0.6	0.2	0.2	6.4	6.6	5.9	5.4	6.0	27.5	32.5	8.7	1.1	77.8	40.4	50.3	49.8
04936	EUSTIS	95.3	94.9	0.7	0.9	0.3	0.2	0.0	0.0	4.2	4.2	5.6	9.1	8.2	23.5	29.4	14.7	1.2	81.1	42.3	51.8	48.3
04937	FAIRFIELD	97.9	97.7	0.3	0.4	0.4	0.5	0.3	0.4	5.7	6.0	7.5	8.2	6.5	27.4	26.6	10.7	1.5	75.5	38.1	48.7	51.3
04938	FARMINGTON	97.7	97.5	0.2	0.2	0.7	0.8	0.8	0.9	5.0	4.6	5.6	9.6	14.7	23.3	22.5	12.0	2.6	81.3	33.9	46.0	54.0
04939	GARLAND	97.8	97.6	0.2	0.2	0.5	0.5	0.4	0.7	6.9	6.9	7.6	7.9	6.6	25.9	26.4	11.4	0.6	73.8	38.4	49.8	50.2
04941	FREEDOM	97.6	97.6	0.2	0.2	0.1	0.1	1.3	1.4	6.0	6.6	7.5	6.7	5.6	26.0	30.4	10.2	1.0	76.1	39.6	52.1	47.9
04942	HARMONY	97.9	97.6	0.2	0.2	0.3	0.4	0.2	0.2	5.3	5.9	6.0	5.6	4.6	23.9	32.0	15.7	0.9	78.9	44.0	50.2	49.9
04943	HARTLAND	98.0	97.9	0.2	0.3	0.2	0.2	0.5	0.5	6.2	6.2	6.9	6.9	6.5	26.4	26.5	12.9	1.7	76.8	39.9	49.4	50.6
04945	JACKMAN	98.2	97.9	0.2	0.2	0.1	0.1	1.9	2.3	5.7	5.7	6.2	6.8	5.7	24.1	30.4	13.0	2.3	77.4	42.1	50.4	49.6
	MAINE	97.0	96.6	0.5	0.6	0.7	0.9	0.7	0.9	5.5	5.8	6.7	6.9	6.5	26.7	27.5	12.5	2.0	77.9	40.2	48.8	51.2
	UNITED STATES	75.1	73.6	12.3	12.5	3.8	4.2	12.5	14.1	6.9	6.7	7.2	7.0	7.3	28.6	23.8	10.8	1.7	75.1	36.0	49.1	50.9

#	POST OFFICE NAME	2004 Per Capita Income	2004 HH Income Base	2004 Household Income Distribution (%): Less than $25,000	$25,000 to $49,999	$50,000 to $99,999	$100,000 to $149,999	$150,000 or More	Median Household Income: 2004	2009	2004 National Centile	2004 State Centile	2004 Home Value Base	2004 Home Value Distribution (%): Less than $50,000	$50,000 to $89,999	$90,000 to $174,999	$175,000 to $399,999	$400,000 or More	2004 Median Home Value
04676	SEDGWICK	21957	517	29.6	35.4	27.7	5.2	2.1	38207	43077	40	51	425	11.8	12.5	34.4	30.8	10.6	154261
04677	SORRENTO	27091	140	16.4	38.6	30.0	11.4	3.6	47127	53543	66	84	115	0.0	13.0	37.4	44.4	5.2	174107
04679	SOUTHWEST HARBOR	25589	810	32.8	27.0	26.8	10.0	3.3	40550	45698	48	63	539	2.8	4.6	40.3	41.6	10.8	180482
04680	STEUBEN	13875	408	45.8	34.6	16.4	2.5	0.7	27073	29911	7	7	339	21.2	20.9	45.7	10.6	1.5	102530
04681	STONINGTON	17584	778	36.8	36.0	21.6	4.0	1.7	33334	37450	22	31	617	8.6	14.6	38.1	27.2	11.5	147359
04683	SUNSET	21233	73	31.5	35.6	23.3	5.5	4.1	37981	41152	39	50	61	6.6	11.5	39.3	29.5	13.1	160938
04684	SURRY	22462	629	29.9	32.3	28.6	4.8	4.5	40531	45599	48	62	530	3.8	11.7	43.6	30.4	10.6	151000
04685	SWANS ISLAND	16838	154	44.2	27.9	23.4	4.6	0.0	31353	35221	16	21	125	16.0	1.6	34.4	41.6	6.4	169792
04691	WHITING	15307	242	50.4	28.5	17.4	2.1	1.7	24701	26794	4	4	203	27.1	22.2	31.5	12.8	6.4	91667
04693	WINTER HARBOR	16187	438	39.3	39.7	16.4	3.4	1.1	31271	35124	16	21	226	8.9	17.7	57.5	14.2	1.8	119500
04694	BAILEYVILLE	18194	1107	36.7	33.4	24.3	4.6	1.0	34158	37946	25	34	901	14.2	32.1	45.4	7.9	0.4	95877
04730	HOULTON	15743	4035	43.2	32.2	21.1	2.5	1.0	29327	31809	11	11	2833	17.8	35.3	38.6	7.5	0.9	87044
04732	ASHLAND	18074	788	36.8	34.1	25.3	2.5	1.3	35079	38082	28	38	638	25.2	35.4	32.1	6.9	0.3	80000
04733	BENEDICTA	14018	86	39.5	29.1	31.4	0.0	0.0	31094	34589	15	19	77	23.4	19.5	49.4	7.8	0.0	97857
04734	BLAINE	15328	193	35.8	42.5	19.2	2.1	0.5	31029	34274	15	19	156	25.0	42.3	28.2	4.5	0.0	73889
04735	BRIDGEWATER	18123	261	41.8	33.7	18.8	3.1	2.7	30489	33611	13	17	211	22.8	34.1	39.3	3.3	0.5	79706
04736	CARIBOU	17923	4387	40.3	30.8	23.6	3.5	1.7	31714	34900	17	24	3103	18.7	32.7	39.1	9.0	0.5	88433
04737	CLAYTON LAKE	0	0	0.0	0.0	0.0	0.0	0.0	0	0	0	0	0	0.0	0.0	0.0	0.0	0.0	0
04740	EASTON	17676	524	38.2	33.4	23.1	3.4	1.9	32656	36173	20	27	417	25.2	36.2	31.2	6.5	1.0	72742
04741	ESTCOURT STATION	23499	3	33.3	66.7	0.0	0.0	0.0	26965	31982	7	6	2	0.0	0.0	100.0	0.0	0.0	125000
04742	FORT FAIRFIELD	17265	1673	41.1	32.4	20.7	4.7	1.1	31215	34201	16	20	1195	19.6	36.1	36.1	8.3	0.0	84328
04743	FORT KENT	18432	2491	41.6	30.2	23.2	3.0	2.1	31076	33747	15	19	1748	14.5	30.8	44.5	9.4	0.9	99022
04745	FRENCHVILLE	18826	501	35.3	31.7	29.3	2.8	0.8	35855	39587	31	41	428	9.6	33.2	50.9	5.8	0.5	100000
04746	GRAND ISLE	15716	227	44.9	27.3	26.0	1.8	0.0	30201	32572	13	14	195	25.1	47.7	24.6	2.6	0.0	74200
04747	ISLAND FALLS	16417	539	40.3	34.7	21.5	2.8	0.7	31403	34088	16	22	410	25.4	33.9	33.4	7.1	0.2	77647
04750	LIMESTONE	16837	847	33.8	36.4	24.8	4.6	0.5	36279	40537	33	43	599	28.2	36.1	29.4	6.2	0.2	71563
04751	LIMESTONE	19863	77	24.7	37.7	33.8	3.9	0.0	44530	51310	60	77	54	31.5	31.5	29.6	7.4	0.0	70000
04756	MADAWASKA	20373	1730	37.3	28.2	30.7	2.7	1.1	33316	35920	22	31	1131	8.1	33.0	49.3	8.9	0.7	101141
04757	MAPLETON	19112	1139	28.7	35.7	29.9	4.0	1.8	38840	42756	42	54	953	13.4	30.2	44.0	11.5	0.8	99308
04758	MARS HILL	15275	617	48.3	29.2	20.8	1.1	0.7	26269	28502	6	6	407	24.3	39.3	29.7	5.9	0.7	75139
04760	MONTICELLO	13871	329	50.5	34.4	12.8	0.9	1.5	24763	27490	4	4	267	25.8	37.1	33.0	3.8	0.4	78793
04761	NEW LIMERICK	14302	365	41.1	33.2	22.5	2.7	0.6	31992	35222	18	25	304	25.3	32.6	31.9	9.9	0.3	81111
04762	NEW SWEDEN	15475	262	40.1	34.0	22.5	3.1	0.4	32327	35159	19	27	221	18.6	29.4	43.9	7.7	0.5	92813
04763	OAKFIELD	14301	421	45.1	33.0	20.2	1.2	0.5	27807	30475	8	7	321	28.7	35.5	32.7	3.1	0.0	71000
04764	OXBOW	16132	29	51.7	37.9	6.9	3.5	0.0	24012	28596	4	3	28	17.9	21.4	46.4	14.3	0.0	103571
04765	PATTEN	16363	625	42.4	31.7	23.2	1.6	1.1	30396	33734	13	15	493	24.5	40.4	28.0	6.5	0.6	74623
04766	PERHAM	14439	172	37.8	35.5	23.8	2.9	0.0	31506	35000	16	23	153	13.1	37.3	42.5	5.9	1.3	89688
04768	PORTAGE	19660	187	40.6	30.5	25.7	1.6	1.6	32705	35201	20	28	150	22.0	33.3	35.3	8.7	0.7	84667
04769	PRESQUE ISLE	17967	4151	39.9	34.9	19.9	3.3	2.1	31317	34041	16	21	2561	18.2	29.3	43.1	8.2	1.2	93780
04772	SAINT AGATHA	18212	386	39.1	32.6	23.6	3.9	0.8	33104	36037	21	30	288	6.9	29.5	53.5	10.1	0.0	105208
04773	SAINT DAVID	22415	298	36.9	25.5	32.6	3.0	2.0	34727	37642	26	37	254	7.1	25.6	48.4	17.7	1.2	118293
04774	SAINT FRANCIS	14911	380	52.6	27.1	17.9	1.3	1.1	23438	24728	3	3	292	23.3	44.5	29.1	3.1	0.0	72258
04776	SHERMAN	16110	433	40.9	33.3	21.0	3.0	1.9	30418	33645	13	16	372	18.0	35.2	39.0	7.8	0.0	87143
04777	STACYVILLE	14505	161	46.0	36.0	12.4	4.4	1.2	28461	31874	9	10	131	37.4	29.8	28.2	4.6	0.0	64091
04779	SINCLAIR	18400	128	42.2	27.3	24.2	3.9	2.3	29034	32308	10	11	109	5.5	24.8	55.1	14.7	0.0	115865
04780	SMYRNA MILLS	16766	130	39.0	31.0	27.3	2.1	0.5	33101	36675	21	30	160	28.8	30.6	32.5	6.9	1.3	78462
04781	WALLAGRASS	17291	153	31.4	39.9	22.2	5.2	1.3	34419	37898	25	35	133	7.5	30.8	48.9	12.0	0.8	103125
04783	STOCKHOLM	19427	296	40.9	32.1	22.0	3.4	1.7	30437	33852	13	16	252	12.3	30.2	45.6	11.1	0.8	102551
04785	VAN BUREN	13629	1264	54.1	30.1	12.3	2.9	0.6	21829	22979	3	1	840	29.8	37.7	29.3	3.2	0.0	69596
04786	WASHBURN	16968	830	38.0	35.1	23.5	2.3	1.2	32733	35782	20	28	645	19.8	42.3	33.5	4.0	0.3	79521
04787	WESTFIELD	14004	241	37.8	41.1	18.7	2.1	0.4	30846	33964	14	18	208	26.9	38.0	31.7	3.4	0.0	75455
04841	ROCKLAND	18601	3617	41.8	33.1	20.2	3.5	1.4	31955	35112	18	25	2006	5.3	18.6	51.9	22.0	2.2	123836
04843	CAMDEN	30416	2697	29.0	26.1	27.9	10.3	6.8	43692	50340	58	75	1865	4.5	2.6	20.0	49.5	23.4	241218
04847	HOPE	27918	568	20.8	34.2	35.6	5.6	3.9	46451	51546	65	83	490	2.7	3.9	49.0	38.4	6.1	162727
04848	ISLESBORO	29012	310	25.8	35.2	25.8	8.7	4.5	41667	47384	52	67	257	5.5	7.4	33.1	38.1	16.0	189583
04849	LINCOLNVILLE	23730	1850	26.2	30.3	31.7	8.6	3.2	43862	49446	58	76	1538	6.5	11.5	41.0	34.5	6.5	153704
04851	MATINICUS	18400	26	34.6	34.6	30.8	0.0	0.0	45000	50393	61	79	23	34.8	13.0	26.1	17.4	8.7	95000
04852	MONHEGAN	26182	48	41.7	22.9	31.3	4.2	0.0	30000	35000	12	14	35	0.0	0.0	14.3	57.1	28.6	265625
04853	NORTH HAVEN	20526	172	30.2	32.6	30.2	5.2	1.7	44533	50354	60	78	118	0.0	1.7	27.1	52.5	18.6	232353
04854	OWLS HEAD	25751	930	22.3	35.0	31.1	8.0	3.8	43589	49453	58	74	765	3.4	3.9	36.7	44.7	11.2	188542
04856	ROCKPORT	28710	1484	19.1	27.7	35.4	10.6	7.2	52727	60814	77	92	1215	2.9	1.7	24.0	50.3	21.2	245646
04857	WILEYS CORNER	23483	139	28.1	27.3	33.8	7.9	2.9	45753	50855	63	81	114	3.5	5.3	35.1	46.5	9.7	189583
04858	SOUTH THOMASTON	24482	504	22.6	28.6	38.7	7.3	2.8	48600	52931	69	87	415	1.9	3.9	40.5	43.4	10.4	185473
04859	SPRUCE HEAD	24634	411	25.3	28.2	34.3	7.5	4.6	44689	49787	60	79	349	3.7	7.7	39.5	32.1	16.9	172500
04860	TENANTS HARBOR	26546	669	28.9	29.6	31.1	6.7	3.7	43640	48974	58	75	550	1.3	6.0	38.2	42.2	12.4	191892
04861	THOMASTON	19730	1472	32.1	34.2	26.4	4.6	2.7	36673	41428	34	44	977	2.4	6.0	60.6	29.3	1.7	142173
04862	UNION	18866	1489	24.2	35.7	35.0	4.0	1.0	40652	44898	48	63	1256	5.0	9.9	50.1	32.0	3.0	141829
04863	VINALHAVEN	23663	596	31.0	30.0	28.2	5.9	4.9	37513	41803	37	48	466	1.3	7.1	43.1	37.1	11.4	172131
04864	WARREN	18624	1496	24.1	41.9	28.7	3.3	1.9	39167	43705	43	55	1246	6.3	3.9	63.6	24.3	1.9	135131
04901	WATERVILLE	19666	11059	37.4	30.8	24.9	4.9	2.0	34690	38748	26	36	6818	6.6	16.8	60.1	15.4	1.2	117579
04910	ALBION	17131	757	32.5	33.8	27.7	4.8	1.2	38290	42804	40	51	644	10.3	17.9	55.8	14.0	2.2	116333
04911	ANSON	15495	751	41.3	31.8	22.6	3.3	0.9	31118	33904	15	20	604	18.1	28.8	41.2	11.1	0.8	94318
04912	ATHENS	16860	332	43.4	28.9	24.1	2.4	1.2	28119	30792	9	9	293	33.1	28.3	27.3	8.9	2.4	74773
04915	BELFAST	20208	4054	36.0	29.9	26.9	5.2	2.1	35170	39363	28	38	2859	14.5	17.5	44.4	21.0	2.7	118429
04917	BELGRADE	22583	931	27.6	31.9	30.3	6.6	3.7	42758	47762	55	71	787	3.3	13.0	46.5	28.8	8.4	148707
04918	BELGRADE LAKES	22528	77	31.2	32.5	28.6	3.9	3.9	40446	44073	48	61	63	3.2	11.1	47.6	28.6	9.5	142708
04920	BINGHAM	18195	603	39.5	35.8	21.6	2.3	0.8	30424	33459	13	16	465	15.7	35.7	42.4	5.6	0.7	89058
04921	BROOKS	16729	1055	40.1	30.5	23.5	4.5	1.4	32967	36901	21	30	863	15.2	24.2	45.3	14.3	1.0	105625
04922	BURNHAM	15868	474	38.6	35.4	22.4	3.0	0.6	32699	35734	20	28	395	27.9	23.5	34.4	13.7	0.5	88103
04923	CAMBRIDGE	15317	358	38.3	38.8	19.8	2.8	0.3	31548	34334	16	23	316	17.1	34.5	36.1	10.1	2.2	88148
04924	CANAAN	15869	538	39.0	33.8	22.7	4.1	0.4	31593	35287	17	24	426	15.7	24.9	45.5	13.6	0.2	103869
04925	CARATUNK	16590	53	43.4	32.1	18.9	5.7	0.0	29281	32336	11	11	42	9.5	21.4	47.6	14.3	7.1	115625
04927	CLINTON	16633	1012	36.0	35.4	24.0	2.7	2.0	34275	37262	25	34	819	17.8	14.3	57.5	9.3	1.1	109387
04928	CORINNA	18099	921	37.0	33.8	25.1	2.9	1.2	34944	38379	27	37	759	22.7	28.2	42.0	5.9	1.2	89000
04929	DETROIT	15988	338	37.3	38.2	19.5	4.4	0.6	31977	35324	18	25	274	21.9	31.0	41.6	5.5	0.0	86000
04930	DEXTER	15735	1756	44.1	32.5	19.9	2.7	0.7	28822	32136	10	10	1311	23.3	36.4	31.7	8.5	0.1	78945
04932	DIXMONT	18190	401	30.9	31.9	29.9	6.5	0.8	37320	41889	37	47	359	19.8	17.6	48.8	12.0	2.0	105893
04936	EUSTIS	17370	204	40.7	34.8	22.6	2.0	0.0	30863	34004	14	18	120	5.0	29.2	40.0	24.2	1.7	113750
04937	FAIRFIELD	18749	2875	28.5	34.5	31.1	4.6	1.3	39676	44833	45	57	2121	10.1	21.6	57.4	9.9	1.0	110248
04938	FARMINGTON	16776	3937	41.9	33.7	20.7	2.0	1.7	30372	33218	13	15	2453	11.9	20.8	51.5	14.4	1.5	111563
04939	GARLAND	14422	390	41.8	35.1	20.8	1.8	0.5	30703	33045	14	17	350	31.4	27.4	36.9	4.3	0.0	80313
04941	FREEDOM	17471	870	34.5	35.1	25.9	3.8	0.8	35950	40194	31	41	727	16.0	27.5	42.0	13.8	0.8	100081
04942	HARMONY	14446	558	48.2	33.2	15.8	2.2	0.7	25822	28095	6	5	468	19.0	34.4	36.3	8.6	1.7	86190
04943	HARTLAND	15805	834	39.3	35.9	21.3	3.0	0.5	31259	34018	16	21	648	17.0	36.0	37.7	8.6	0.8	87500
04945	JACKMAN	17843	394	34.3	36.8	23.1	5.8	0.0	33510	36903	22	31	283	13.1	28.6	49.1	7.8	1.4	99038
	MAINE	22411		29.6	30.7	30.0	6.5	3.2	40864	45987				8.5	14.0	43.9	28.6	5.1	138610
	UNITED STATES	25866		24.7	27.1	30.8	10.9	6.5	48124	56710				10.9	15.0	33.7	30.1	10.4	145905

ZIP CODE		FINANCIAL SERVICES				THE HOME						ENTERTAINMENT						PERSONAL			
						Home Improvements		Furnishings													
#	POST OFFICE NAME	Auto Loan	Home Loan	Investments	Retirement Plans	Home Repair	Lawn & Garden	Computers & Hardware	Major Appliances	TV, Radio, Sound Equipment	Furniture	Dine out/ Carry out	Sports Equipment	Fees & Tickets	Toys & Games	Travel	Cable TV	Apparel & Services	Auto Repairs	Health Insurance	Pets & Supplies
04676	SEDGWICK	91	64	33	60	74	83	63	78	72	62	85	94	54	83	65	76	77	77	92	108
04677	SORRENTO	101	80	54	72	90	101	75	90	85	74	101	106	67	99	80	91	93	89	107	124
04679	SOUTHWEST HARBOR	87	67	45	63	74	86	69	79	78	67	92	90	62	88	71	83	84	79	94	101
04680	STEUBEN	56	44	30	40	50	56	42	50	47	41	56	59	37	55	44	50	52	49	59	69
04681	STONINGTON	68	54	37	48	60	68	51	61	57	50	68	71	45	67	54	61	63	60	72	83
04683	SUNSET	80	63	43	57	71	80	59	72	67	59	80	84	53	79	63	72	74	71	85	98
04684	SURRY	92	72	49	65	81	91	68	82	77	67	91	96	61	90	72	82	84	80	96	112
04685	SWANS ISLAND	64	50	34	45	56	63	47	57	53	47	63	66	42	62	50	57	59	56	67	78
04691	WHITING	53	40	26	38	44	52	44	49	50	42	58	55	39	55	44	52	53	49	58	59
04693	WINTER HARBOR	60	51	40	51	53	60	52	56	56	51	67	64	50	67	52	56	63	55	61	66
04694	BAILEYVILLE	69	56	40	50	61	69	54	62	61	54	73	72	50	73	56	65	68	61	73	81
04730	HOULTON	61	46	30	43	50	59	48	55	54	47	64	63	43	61	49	57	59	54	65	69
04732	ASHLAND	67	55	40	52	60	67	54	61	59	53	71	71	50	70	56	62	66	60	70	78
04733	BENEDICTA	63	49	34	45	56	62	47	56	53	46	62	66	42	62	50	56	58	55	66	77
04734	BLAINE	57	48	37	48	50	57	50	53	53	49	64	60	47	63	49	53	60	52	57	62
04735	BRIDGEWATER	70	52	35	50	57	69	58	64	65	55	76	72	51	72	57	68	70	64	76	77
04736	CARIBOU	67	54	37	50	58	66	55	61	61	53	72	70	50	71	55	63	67	61	71	77
04737	CLAYTON LAKE	0	0	0	0	0	0	0	0	0	0	0	0	0	0	0	0	0	0	0	0
04740	EASTON	65	54	41	54	57	65	56	60	60	55	72	69	53	71	55	61	67	59	66	72
04741	ESTCOURT STATION	49	39	26	35	44	49	37	44	41	36	49	52	33	49	39	44	46	43	52	60
04742	FORT FAIRFIELD	63	50	36	48	54	62	52	58	57	50	68	66	48	66	53	60	63	57	67	71
04743	FORT KENT	71	54	36	52	60	69	56	64	63	55	74	74	51	72	57	66	68	63	74	81
04745	FRENCHVILLE	73	65	49	62	69	74	60	67	64	60	78	79	59	79	62	65	74	65	72	86
04746	GRAND ISLE	68	46	21	39	52	59	44	55	53	45	62	66	37	59	45	57	57	54	68	78
04747	ISLAND FALLS	64	50	34	45	56	63	47	57	53	47	63	67	42	63	50	57	59	56	67	78
04750	LIMESTONE	61	52	46	52	55	62	57	59	60	55	73	68	54	71	56	61	68	60	64	68
04751	LIMESTONE	59	61	69	63	61	63	66	63	64	63	79	75	65	81	64	61	78	64	59	68
04756	MADAWASKA	62	58	51	55	61	68	58	61	61	56	75	69	57	77	59	64	71	60	68	73
04757	MAPLETON	78	64	44	60	70	76	60	70	66	60	79	83	56	80	62	68	74	68	78	92
04758	MARS HILL	57	43	28	41	47	56	47	52	53	45	62	58	42	59	47	56	57	52	62	63
04760	MONTICELLO	53	40	26	38	43	52	44	48	49	42	58	54	39	55	43	52	53	48	58	58
04761	NEW LIMERICK	70	48	23	41	54	62	46	57	55	47	65	68	39	61	47	59	59	57	70	81
04762	NEW SWEDEN	69	48	25	45	56	63	47	59	55	47	64	71	40	63	49	57	58	58	70	82
04763	OAKFIELD	59	44	28	40	50	57	42	51	48	42	57	60	37	56	44	52	53	51	61	71
04764	OXBOW	50	39	27	35	44	50	37	45	42	37	50	52	33	49	39	45	46	44	53	61
04765	PATTEN	68	47	24	41	53	61	45	56	54	46	63	67	39	60	46	58	58	55	68	79
04766	PERHAM	60	45	30	43	50	59	50	55	56	48	66	62	45	62	50	59	60	55	66	67
04768	PORTAGE	68	53	36	48	60	68	50	61	57	50	68	71	45	67	54	61	63	60	72	83
04769	PRESQUE ISLE	62	51	41	50	54	62	55	58	59	53	71	67	51	69	54	60	67	59	65	70
04772	SAINT AGATHA	74	50	23	43	56	65	48	60	58	49	68	72	41	64	49	63	62	60	74	85
04773	SAINT DAVID	95	75	52	68	85	95	71	85	80	70	95	99	64	94	76	86	89	84	100	116
04774	SAINT FRANCIS	54	41	27	38	45	53	43	49	48	41	57	55	38	54	43	51	52	48	58	62
04776	SHERMAN	70	50	27	47	58	64	49	60	56	48	66	72	42	65	51	59	60	59	71	83
04777	STACYVILLE	66	45	20	38	50	58	43	54	52	44	61	64	37	58	44	56	55	53	66	76
04779	SINCLAIR	70	55	37	49	62	69	52	62	58	51	69	73	46	68	55	62	64	61	73	85
04780	SMYRNA MILLS	68	51	31	45	57	65	48	59	56	48	66	69	42	64	51	60	61	58	70	81
04781	WALLAGRASS	78	54	28	51	63	71	54	66	62	53	72	80	46	71	56	65	66	65	79	92
04783	STOCKHOLM	74	55	33	51	63	71	53	65	61	52	71	77	46	70	56	64	66	64	77	89
04785	VAN BUREN	51	37	22	35	41	48	39	45	45	38	53	51	35	50	39	48	48	45	54	57
04786	WASHBURN	66	48	29	46	54	63	51	58	57	49	67	68	45	65	51	60	62	58	69	75
04787	WESTFIELD	62	47	30	44	51	58	47	54	53	47	63	63	43	61	47	55	58	53	62	70
04841	ROCKLAND	56	51	49	50	53	60	55	55	57	52	70	63	53	70	54	59	66	56	60	63
04843	CAMDEN	92	92	94	90	95	105	88	94	89	90	110	102	88	103	92	91	105	92	100	107
04847	HOPE	125	87	45	82	101	113	86	106	99	85	116	128	73	114	89	104	106	105	126	148
04848	ISLESBORO	104	82	56	74	92	103	77	93	87	76	103	109	69	102	82	93	96	92	110	127
04849	LINCOLNVILLE	96	73	46	68	83	92	70	84	79	69	94	100	62	93	74	84	87	83	99	116
04851	MATINICUS	60	47	32	42	53	60	44	53	50	44	60	63	40	59	47	54	55	53	63	73
04852	MONHEGAN	68	54	37	48	60	68	51	61	57	50	68	71	45	67	54	61	63	60	72	83
04853	NORTH HAVEN	80	63	43	57	71	80	59	71	67	59	79	84	53	78	63	72	74	70	84	98
04854	OWLS HEAD	96	74	48	68	84	93	71	85	80	70	95	101	63	94	74	84	88	84	100	116
04856	ROCKPORT	92	100	100	98	102	106	91	95	89	91	111	110	94	114	95	90	108	93	95	111
04857	WILEYS CORNER	95	75	51	67	84	94	70	85	80	70	94	99	63	93	75	85	88	83	100	116
04858	SOUTH THOMASTON	94	78	56	72	85	94	73	84	80	73	96	100	68	96	76	84	90	83	96	112
04859	SPRUCE HEAD	105	74	40	70	86	97	73	90	84	72	99	109	63	97	76	88	90	89	107	126
04860	TENANTS HARBOR	97	76	52	69	86	96	72	86	81	71	96	101	64	95	76	87	89	85	102	118
04861	THOMASTON	74	59	42	58	63	74	63	69	69	61	83	78	58	80	63	72	76	68	79	82
04862	UNION	77	65	47	62	70	76	61	69	66	61	80	83	58	81	63	68	75	68	77	91
04863	VINALHAVEN	88	69	47	62	78	88	65	79	74	65	88	92	58	86	70	79	81	77	93	108
04864	WARREN	78	67	52	65	71	78	66	72	70	65	85	84	63	85	66	71	80	70	78	89
04901	WATERVILLE	62	60	63	60	61	67	63	63	64	61	79	73	62	79	63	64	76	64	65	71
04910	ALBION	76	60	38	57	66	73	57	67	63	57	76	80	52	75	59	66	70	66	76	90
04911	ANSON	72	49	23	43	55	63	47	59	56	48	66	70	40	63	48	60	60	58	72	83
04912	ATHENS	78	52	24	45	59	68	50	63	61	51	72	75	43	68	51	66	65	62	78	90
04915	BELFAST	71	61	50	58	64	72	61	67	66	61	80	77	58	78	62	68	75	66	74	81
04917	BELGRADE	95	78	55	71	86	95	73	85	81	72	96	100	67	96	77	85	90	84	98	114
04918	BELGRADE LAKES	87	68	47	62	77	87	65	78	73	64	87	91	58	86	69	78	81	77	92	106
04920	BINGHAM	75	54	31	49	60	70	56	65	64	54	76	75	49	72	56	68	69	64	78	85
04921	BROOKS	64	54	42	54	57	64	56	60	59	55	72	68	54	71	56	60	67	59	65	71
04922	BURNHAM	75	50	23	43	57	66	48	61	59	49	69	72	41	65	49	63	62	60	75	86
04923	CAMBRIDGE	67	47	25	41	53	61	45	56	53	45	63	66	39	60	47	57	57	55	68	78
04924	CANAAN	63	57	45	55	57	61	55	59	55	56	68	68	52	65	54	55	66	58	58	70
04925	CARATUNK	66	52	35	47	59	66	49	59	56	49	66	69	44	65	52	59	61	58	70	81
04927	CLINTON	74	58	36	53	63	70	54	64	61	55	73	76	50	72	56	64	68	63	74	86
04928	CORINNA	85	57	26	50	65	74	55	69	67	56	78	82	47	74	56	72	71	68	85	98
04929	DETROIT	73	49	22	42	55	63	47	59	57	48	67	70	40	63	48	61	60	58	72	83
04930	DEXTER	63	46	28	43	51	59	47	55	54	46	63	63	42	61	47	57	58	54	65	72
04932	DIXMONT	73	65	50	62	69	74	60	67	64	60	78	80	59	80	62	66	74	65	72	86
04936	EUSTIS	62	49	33	44	55	61	46	55	52	45	61	65	41	61	49	55	57	54	65	75
04937	FAIRFIELD	71	63	51	62	66	72	62	66	65	61	80	78	60	80	63	66	75	65	71	81
04938	FARMINGTON	61	49	40	48	52	60	53	57	57	51	69	66	49	66	53	59	65	58	64	69
04939	GARLAND	69	46	21	40	52	60	45	56	54	45	63	67	38	60	45	58	57	55	69	79
04941	FREEDOM	69	55	38	53	60	67	55	62	60	54	72	73	51	71	56	62	67	61	70	79
04942	HARMONY	62	43	22	38	49	56	42	52	49	42	58	61	36	55	43	53	53	51	63	73
04943	HARTLAND	71	49	24	43	55	62	47	58	56	48	66	69	40	62	48	60	60	57	70	81
04945	JACKMAN	69	54	37	49	61	69	51	62	58	51	69	72	46	68	55	62	64	61	73	84
	MAINE	80	73	65	71	75	82	72	77	75	71	92	90	70	91	73	76	88	76	81	93
	UNITED STATES	100	100	100	100	100	100	100	100	100	100	100	100	100	100	100	100	100	100	100	100

MAINE

POPULATION CHANGE

A 04947-04989

ZIP CODE		COUNTY FIPS CODE	POPULATION			2000-2004 ANNUAL RATE		HOUSEHOLDS					FAMILIES		
#	POST OFFICE NAME		2000	2004	2009	% Rate	State Centile	2000	2004	2009	% Annual Rate 2000-2004	2004 Average HH Size	2000	2004	% Annual Rate 2000-2004
04947	KINGFIELD	007	1502	1554	1642	0.8	55	633	671	727	1.4	2.32	415	442	1.5
04949	LIBERTY	027	919	952	1023	0.8	57	360	382	422	1.4	2.48	257	274	1.5
04950	MADISON	025	4308	4251	4260	-0.3	16	1805	1837	1897	0.4	2.25	1208	1233	0.5
04951	MONROE	027	225	246	273	2.1	92	89	100	114	2.8	2.46	60	67	2.6
04952	MORRILL	027	1673	1780	1941	1.5	78	665	732	823	2.3	2.43	479	528	2.3
04953	NEWPORT	019	3097	3159	3239	0.5	44	1310	1373	1446	1.1	2.30	875	922	1.2
04954	NEW PORTLAND	025	427	420	420	-0.4	13	177	180	187	0.4	2.33	123	125	0.4
04955	NEW SHARON	007	1305	1338	1406	0.6	48	523	554	600	1.4	2.42	364	387	1.5
04956	NEW VINEYARD	007	725	761	810	1.2	67	279	301	329	1.8	2.53	198	214	1.9
04957	NORRIDGEWOCK	025	4395	4423	4458	0.2	32	1725	1791	1861	0.9	2.47	1270	1322	1.0
04958	NORTH ANSON	025	2342	2366	2394	0.2	35	965	1001	1041	0.9	2.35	659	685	0.9
04961	NEW PORTLAND	025	536	536	540	0.0	26	235	243	253	0.8	2.20	160	166	0.9
04962	NORTH VASSALBORO	011	1185	1202	1212	0.3	39	447	470	485	1.2	2.56	328	345	1.2
04963	OAKLAND	011	7486	7665	7761	0.6	47	2964	3123	3230	1.2	2.45	2097	2211	1.3
04965	PALMYRA	025	1914	1906	1916	-0.1	22	747	767	795	0.6	2.48	528	544	0.7
04966	PHILLIPS	007	1667	1691	1767	0.3	39	681	711	764	1.0	2.37	465	486	1.0
04967	PITTSFIELD	025	4423	4466	4514	0.2	35	1708	1769	1838	0.8	2.44	1203	1249	0.9
04969	PLYMOUTH	019	1332	1380	1423	0.8	57	504	541	576	1.7	2.54	373	402	1.8
04970	RANGELEY	007	1518	1543	1614	0.4	41	675	706	761	1.1	2.18	450	473	1.2
04971	SAINT ALBANS	025	1715	1870	1968	2.1	91	671	758	824	2.9	2.44	495	560	3.0
04973	SEARSMONT	027	472	531	596	2.8	97	193	224	259	3.6	2.37	129	151	3.8
04974	SEARSPORT	027	2669	2740	2928	0.6	49	1144	1214	1339	1.4	2.26	742	789	1.5
04976	SKOWHEGAN	025	9832	10181	10431	0.8	56	4091	4373	4618	1.6	2.28	2673	2863	1.6
04978	SMITHFIELD	025	704	697	699	-0.2	19	280	288	297	0.7	2.42	215	221	0.7
04979	SOLON	025	1178	1179	1185	0.0	27	512	530	549	0.8	2.20	330	342	0.8
04981	STOCKTON SPRINGS	027	2108	2228	2420	1.3	72	873	951	1064	2.0	2.34	613	670	2.1
04982	STRATTON	007	415	435	462	1.1	65	172	185	202	1.7	2.35	103	112	2.0
04983	STRONG	007	1707	1750	1838	0.6	48	674	708	762	1.2	2.45	458	483	1.3
04984	TEMPLE	007	565	570	594	0.2	34	225	233	250	0.8	2.43	162	168	0.9
04985	WEST FORKS	025	84	82	82	-0.6	7	42	42	43	0.0	1.90	26	26	0.1
04986	THORNDIKE	027	932	967	1041	0.9	58	361	387	428	1.7	2.50	261	280	1.7
04987	TROY	027	963	1009	1091	1.1	64	365	390	432	1.6	2.59	275	294	1.6
04988	UNITY	027	1792	1858	1986	0.9	58	679	731	814	1.8	2.22	399	430	1.8
04989	VASSALBORO	011	4326	4393	4426	0.4	40	1667	1740	1790	1.0	2.51	1222	1276	1.0
	MAINE					0.9					1.5	2.33			1.6
	UNITED STATES					1.2					1.3	2.58			1.1

#	POST OFFICE NAME	White 2000	White 2004	Black 2000	Black 2004	Asian/Pacific 2000	Asian/Pacific 2004	% Hispanic 2000	% Hispanic 2004	0-4	5-9	10-14	15-19	20-24	25-44	45-64	65-84	85+	18+	MEDIAN AGE 2004	% 2004 Males	% 2004 Females
04947	KINGFIELD	98.0	97.8	0.1	0.1	0.4	0.5	0.2	0.3	5.6	6.1	7.9	6.5	5.9	26.1	28.6	11.8	1.5	76.5	40.2	50.3	49.7
04949	LIBERTY	98.8	98.8	0.1	0.1	0.1	0.1	0.4	0.5	8.5	8.1	6.8	5.7	4.6	25.6	28.1	11.0	1.6	72.4	38.8	49.1	51.0
04950	MADISON	98.1	98.0	0.1	0.1	0.2	0.2	0.2	0.3	5.9	5.9	5.7	5.7	4.6	25.2	27.8	16.4	2.9	78.6	43.2	47.5	52.5
04951	MONROE	98.2	98.8	0.0	0.0	0.0	0.0	0.9	0.8	6.1	6.5	7.3	6.5	4.5	27.6	30.1	10.2	1.2	75.6	39.8	50.4	49.6
04952	MORRILL	98.3	98.3	0.0	0.0	0.3	0.3	0.2	0.3	6.1	6.5	7.9	5.7	4.9	27.9	28.2	11.7	1.2	76.0	39.4	49.6	50.4
04953	NEWPORT	98.3	98.1	0.2	0.2	0.4	0.6	0.4	0.5	6.3	6.0	6.5	6.7	6.2	26.5	27.1	13.3	1.5	77.1	40.1	48.7	51.4
04954	NEW PORTLAND	98.4	98.3	0.0	0.0	0.0	0.0	0.5	0.5	5.7	6.0	5.7	5.7	5.2	22.6	34.8	12.9	1.4	79.1	44.5	51.0	49.1
04955	NEW SHARON	98.9	98.9	0.2	0.2	0.3	0.4	0.5	0.5	5.1	5.3	6.1	6.1	6.3	24.6	33.6	11.3	1.6	79.8	43.0	50.3	49.7
04956	NEW VINEYARD	98.1	98.2	0.4	0.4	0.1	0.1	0.3	0.4	6.6	5.5	8.7	9.1	4.7	25.0	30.1	9.5	0.9	73.1	40.2	48.9	51.1
04957	NORRIDGEWOCK	98.3	98.1	0.3	0.3	0.3	0.3	0.4	0.5	6.2	6.5	7.1	6.3	5.8	26.8	29.2	10.9	1.3	76.4	39.9	49.7	50.3
04958	NORTH ANSON	98.9	98.9	0.1	0.1	0.0	0.0	0.3	0.3	5.2	5.5	6.1	6.0	5.9	25.8	29.2	14.7	1.7	79.0	42.1	50.0	50.0
04961	NEW PORTLAND	98.5	98.5	0.0	0.0	0.0	0.0	0.4	0.4	5.0	5.6	5.6	5.4	5.0	23.3	34.5	14.0	1.5	80.2	45.0	50.9	49.1
04962	NORTH VASSALBORO	98.4	98.2	0.1	0.1	0.4	0.6	0.4	0.6	4.2	4.9	7.2	7.8	5.7	24.5	33.4	11.2	1.1	78.7	42.3	50.7	49.3
04963	OAKLAND	98.3	98.1	0.2	0.2	0.5	0.6	0.5	0.6	5.7	5.9	7.3	7.6	6.9	26.8	28.3	10.4	1.2	76.3	39.0	48.9	51.1
04965	PALMYRA	98.5	98.3	0.0	0.0	0.4	0.5	0.3	0.4	6.5	6.5	6.4	6.0	6.0	25.6	28.0	13.8	1.3	76.3	40.5	49.7	50.3
04966	PHILLIPS	99.0	98.9	0.1	0.2	0.1	0.2	0.3	0.3	4.9	5.3	6.5	5.6	4.7	24.3	32.8	14.6	1.4	79.2	44.3	50.0	50.0
04967	PITTSFIELD	96.4	96.5	0.8	0.9	1.2	1.4	0.6	0.8	5.6	5.7	7.6	8.6	7.0	26.3	25.5	11.8	1.9	75.4	38.0	48.3	51.8
04969	PLYMOUTH	97.9	97.8	0.0	0.0	0.1	0.1	0.5	0.7	6.7	7.3	7.8	6.6	6.2	30.3	26.4	8.0	0.8	73.8	36.9	49.2	50.8
04970	RANGELEY	99.1	98.9	0.1	0.1	0.1	0.1	0.3	0.3	4.8	5.4	6.1	5.1	4.3	23.7	33.6	15.6	1.6	80.0	45.4	50.0	50.0
04971	SAINT ALBANS	98.5	98.3	0.1	0.2	0.5	0.7	0.4	0.4	6.1	6.4	6.7	6.2	5.3	27.8	29.1	11.4	1.0	76.9	39.7	50.7	49.3
04973	SEARSMONT	98.5	98.7	0.0	0.0	0.0	0.0	0.6	0.8	6.0	6.4	7.2	5.8	4.5	30.9	28.4	9.4	1.3	76.7	38.6	50.1	49.9
04974	SEARSPORT	98.1	98.0	0.3	0.4	0.0	0.0	0.2	0.2	5.6	6.0	6.3	5.6	5.3	25.0	30.2	14.7	1.4	78.8	42.4	48.1	51.9
04976	SKOWHEGAN	97.8	97.6	0.2	0.3	0.5	0.6	0.7	0.8	5.5	5.8	6.8	6.4	6.4	26.8	26.7	13.2	2.4	78.0	40.2	48.2	51.8
04978	SMITHFIELD	98.4	98.1	0.1	0.1	0.4	0.6	1.0	1.2	5.5	6.2	6.6	6.0	4.3	26.1	29.7	14.5	1.2	77.9	42.6	49.5	50.5
04979	SOLON	98.9	99.0	0.3	0.3	0.1	0.1	0.4	0.5	4.7	5.2	6.0	5.3	6.0	25.3	31.6	14.1	1.8	80.5	43.2	52.3	47.8
04981	STOCKTON SPRINGS	97.3	97.2	0.3	0.3	0.3	0.3	0.6	0.7	4.9	5.9	7.6	6.2	4.4	27.0	30.8	12.0	1.1	77.4	41.6	50.0	50.0
04982	STRATTON	96.1	95.9	0.5	0.7	0.2	0.2	0.0	0.0	4.6	4.8	6.4	8.1	7.4	24.4	29.4	13.6	1.4	79.3	41.7	51.0	49.0
04983	STRONG	98.9	98.9	0.1	0.1	0.1	0.2	1.0	1.1	5.7	6.5	7.1	6.5	5.7	25.7	28.9	12.2	1.8	76.1	40.5	50.3	49.7
04984	TEMPLE	98.9	98.8	0.2	0.2	0.4	0.4	0.5	0.7	5.1	5.3	7.4	6.8	5.6	25.8	30.5	12.3	1.2	77.0	41.8	50.4	49.7
04985	WEST FORKS	97.6	97.6	0.0	0.0	0.0	0.0	1.2	1.2	4.9	4.9	6.1	6.1	4.9	25.6	31.7	14.6	1.2	78.1	43.8	52.4	47.6
04986	THORNDIKE	99.1	99.1	0.1	0.1	0.2	0.3	0.3	0.4	5.5	5.7	7.7	6.8	5.6	28.3	28.7	10.9	0.9	76.8	38.8	50.8	49.2
04987	TROY	97.4	97.3	0.0	0.0	0.3	0.4	0.1	0.1	7.0	7.1	7.7	6.3	5.5	25.0	30.3	10.4	0.6	74.0	39.7	51.2	48.8
04988	UNITY	97.7	97.5	0.3	0.4	0.3	0.4	0.8	1.0	4.5	4.6	6.3	10.8	14.2	22.9	23.6	11.6	1.6	81.3	33.3	50.8	49.2
04989	VASSALBORO	98.6	98.5	0.1	0.2	0.1	0.1	0.6	0.7	6.2	6.6	7.9	7.0	5.5	28.1	27.2	10.5	1.1	74.7	38.8	49.2	50.9
	MAINE	97.0	96.6	0.5	0.6	0.7	0.9	0.7	0.9	5.5	5.8	6.7	6.9	6.5	26.7	27.5	12.5	2.0	77.9	40.2	48.8	51.2
	UNITED STATES	75.1	73.6	12.3	12.5	3.8	4.2	12.5	14.1	6.9	6.7	7.2	7.0	7.3	28.6	23.8	10.8	1.7	75.1	36.0	49.1	50.9

#	POST OFFICE NAME	2004 Per Capita Income	2004 HH Income Base	2004 HOUSEHOLD INCOME DISTRIBUTION (%)					MEDIAN HOUSEHOLD INCOME					2004 Home Value Base	2004 HOME VALUE DISTRIBUTION (%)					2004 Median Home Value
				Less than $25,000	$25,000 to $49,999	$50,000 to $99,999	$100,000 to $149,999	$150,000 or More	2004	2009	2004 National Centile	2004 State Centile			Less than $50,000	$50,000 to $89,999	$90,000 to $174,999	$175,000 to $399,999	$400,000 or More	
04947	KINGFIELD	20641	671	30.3	38.5	23.7	4.2	3.4	35568	40054	30	40	482	6.0	11.6	52.9	24.7	4.8	132880
04949	LIBERTY	19004	382	35.9	29.6	27.2	4.5	2.9	36964	41288	35	45	311	9.7	19.3	57.2	12.5	1.3	113542
04950	MADISON	18960	1837	37.9	33.7	21.1	4.6	2.7	32756	36429	20	28	1352	11.1	27.8	47.6	12.8	0.7	104537
04951	MONROE	16857	100	40.0	30.0	24.0	5.0	1.0	33179	37351	21	30	83	15.7	22.9	43.4	18.1	0.0	107500
04952	MORRILL	17669	732	32.4	36.3	26.1	4.2	1.0	35641	39862	30	40	613	11.8	22.7	49.1	15.3	1.1	109144
04953	NEWPORT	17552	1373	38.8	30.7	27.2	2.3	1.1	32522	36247	19	27	917	18.7	27.3	43.3	9.8	1.0	95068
04954	NEW PORTLAND	16608	180	37.8	35.6	22.8	3.3	0.6	33613	36895	23	32	165	12.7	30.9	41.8	12.7	1.8	100987
04955	NEW SHARON	18210	554	34.7	29.8	30.3	4.0	1.3	36570	41074	34	43	466	15.2	16.1	51.1	17.4	0.2	120455
04956	NEW VINEYARD	16656	301	34.2	39.5	22.3	2.7	1.3	32267	35566	18	26	260	9.2	26.5	53.9	10.4	0.0	109184
04957	NORRIDGEWOCK	19468	1791	32.6	30.4	29.0	5.5	2.4	37852	41677	39	49	1484	12.2	25.1	46.4	14.4	2.0	109604
04958	NORTH ANSON	15232	1001	42.0	34.5	21.4	1.8	0.4	29501	31978	11	12	843	17.3	33.3	36.3	11.4	1.7	89295
04961	NEW PORTLAND	17369	243	38.7	35.8	22.2	2.9	0.4	32316	35748	19	26	218	12.4	29.8	42.7	13.3	1.8	103125
04962	NORTH VASSALBORO	23590	470	18.5	28.3	41.9	8.3	3.0	53000	58481	77	92	407	4.7	11.1	42.3	37.4	4.7	155183
04963	OAKLAND	21695	3123	30.1	30.7	30.2	6.5	2.5	38776	43597	42	53	2342	11.7	15.6	51.1	19.0	2.6	123404
04965	PALMYRA	15427	767	36.8	38.3	21.8	2.9	0.3	34157	37647	25	33	633	22.6	26.5	38.1	11.5	1.3	91571
04966	PHILLIPS	17814	711	34.0	37.8	23.4	3.2	1.6	34088	37608	24	33	589	11.7	21.1	39.7	22.6	4.9	119922
04967	PITTSFIELD	17970	1769	32.2	33.8	27.8	5.4	0.9	36567	41191	34	43	1318	10.0	34.1	45.3	9.2	1.4	97156
04969	PLYMOUTH	18103	541	31.2	35.3	26.1	5.7	1.7	35989	40292	31	41	484	15.5	31.6	46.9	5.8	0.2	93415
04970	RANGELEY	19164	706	34.4	37.0	24.1	2.8	1.7	34249	37728	25	34	577	9.0	21.8	36.9	26.0	6.2	127911
04971	SAINT ALBANS	14848	758	41.7	36.8	18.3	2.6	0.5	30077	32786	12	14	609	22.8	22.2	39.4	14.1	1.5	99242
04973	SEARSMONT	20078	224	29.5	34.8	30.4	4.5	0.9	40242	45116	47	60	188	7.5	20.7	52.1	18.1	1.6	122581
04974	SEARSPORT	21162	1214	34.8	31.4	28.3	3.6	1.8	34062	38293	24	33	924	17.4	23.4	37.0	18.8	3.4	107708
04976	SKOWHEGAN	17575	4373	39.4	32.7	23.0	3.9	1.0	31200	34157	15	20	3013	16.5	24.0	46.3	12.6	0.7	103776
04978	SMITHFIELD	23538	288	30.9	30.6	27.8	5.6	5.2	40000	43649	46	59	249	9.2	16.5	50.6	17.3	6.4	118750
04979	SOLON	17389	530	40.2	37.2	19.8	2.1	0.8	30478	33921	13	16	420	12.4	34.5	41.2	10.2	1.7	95652
04981	STOCKTON SPRINGS	21569	951	25.3	34.5	33.3	5.1	1.8	40712	45828	49	63	822	12.3	21.1	47.1	18.1	1.5	112429
04982	STRATTON	17089	185	37.3	36.2	23.2	2.2	1.1	32144	35889	18	26	117	4.3	22.2	47.0	23.9	2.6	122283
04983	STRONG	16928	708	37.3	31.9	26.1	3.1	1.6	33529	36972	22	31	559	13.2	23.8	46.3	14.3	2.3	106527
04984	TEMPLE	17857	233	33.1	38.6	21.9	4.3	2.2	34369	37317	25	35	199	18.6	18.6	45.7	15.1	2.0	109722
04985	WEST FORKS	20855	42	40.5	31.0	21.4	7.1	0.0	31504	32317	16	23	32	12.5	25.0	46.9	12.5	3.1	107143
04986	THORNDIKE	15723	387	40.3	31.5	24.3	3.4	0.5	30223	34164	13	14	313	17.3	22.7	47.9	10.9	1.3	104167
04987	TROY	14858	390	36.2	38.7	23.1	1.8	0.3	32385	35943	19	27	323	23.5	24.8	40.3	11.5	0.0	92115
04988	UNITY	17316	731	45.1	27.4	20.9	4.9	1.6	28165	30783	9	9	434	20.1	16.1	48.9	13.6	1.4	108043
04989	VASSALBORO	19126	1740	27.1	34.0	32.5	4.8	1.6	41751	46394	52	68	1409	10.4	10.4	57.2	21.8	0.2	126745
	MAINE	22411		29.6	30.7	30.0	6.5	3.2	40864	45987				8.5	14.0	43.9	28.6	5.1	138610
	UNITED STATES	25866		24.7	27.1	30.8	10.9	6.5	48124	56710				10.9	15.0	33.7	30.1	10.4	145905

ZIP CODE		FINANCIAL SERVICES				THE HOME						ENTERTAINMENT						PERSONAL			
						Home Improvements		Furnishings													
#	POST OFFICE NAME	Auto Loan	Home Loan	Invest-ments	Retire-ment Plans	Home Repair	Lawn & Garden	Comput-ers & Hard-ware	Major Appli-ances	TV, Radio, Sound Equip-ment	Furni-ture	Dine out/ Carry out	Sports Equip-ment	Fees & Tickets	Toys & Games	Travel	Cable TV	Apparel & Services	Auto Repairs	Health Insur-ance	Pets & Supplies
04947	KINGFIELD	81	64	43	57	72	80	60	72	68	59	80	85	54	79	64	73	75	71	85	99
04949	LIBERTY	80	63	43	57	71	80	59	71	67	59	80	84	53	79	63	72	74	70	84	98
04950	MADISON	72	57	40	51	63	71	55	64	62	55	74	74	51	74	57	66	69	63	75	85
04951	MONROE	65	55	43	55	58	65	57	60	60	56	73	69	54	72	56	61	68	60	66	71
04952	MORRILL	74	58	37	53	63	70	55	64	61	55	74	76	51	73	56	64	69	63	73	86
04953	NEWPORT	65	53	39	51	56	64	54	59	59	53	71	68	51	69	54	61	66	59	67	72
04954	NEW PORTLAND	66	52	35	47	58	65	49	59	55	48	65	69	43	64	52	59	61	58	69	80
04955	NEW SHARON	71	63	48	59	66	71	58	64	62	58	75	77	57	76	60	63	71	63	70	83
04956	NEW VINEYARD	71	56	38	51	63	71	53	64	60	52	71	74	47	70	56	64	66	63	75	87
04957	NORRIDGEWOCK	79	67	48	63	72	78	63	71	68	62	82	85	60	83	65	70	77	69	79	93
04958	NORTH ANSON	64	46	26	41	52	60	44	54	52	45	61	64	39	59	46	56	56	54	66	76
04961	NEW PORTLAND	65	51	35	46	57	64	48	58	54	48	64	68	43	64	51	58	60	57	68	79
04962	NORTH VASSALBORO	98	83	62	77	91	100	78	90	85	77	102	105	73	102	82	89	96	88	102	119
04963	OAKLAND	87	69	48	66	75	86	70	79	77	68	92	91	64	90	71	81	85	78	91	99
04965	PALMYRA	71	48	23	42	55	63	47	58	56	48	66	69	40	63	48	60	60	58	71	82
04966	PHILLIPS	73	55	35	51	63	71	53	64	60	52	71	76	47	70	56	64	66	63	76	88
04967	PITTSFIELD	71	61	46	59	64	71	60	65	64	59	77	76	57	77	60	65	73	64	71	80
04969	PLYMOUTH	73	67	52	64	67	71	64	68	64	65	79	79	60	75	63	64	76	68	68	81
04970	RANGELEY	71	56	38	50	63	70	52	63	59	52	70	74	47	70	56	63	65	62	75	87
04971	SAINT ALBANS	65	47	27	42	53	60	45	55	52	45	62	65	39	60	47	56	57	54	67	77
04973	SEARSMONT	76	68	52	64	72	77	63	70	67	63	81	83	62	83	65	68	77	68	75	90
04974	SEARSPORT	77	61	43	59	65	75	65	71	70	63	84	80	59	79	64	73	78	71	80	85
04976	SKOWHEGAN	62	54	43	52	56	63	55	59	59	54	71	67	52	70	55	60	67	58	64	70
04978	SMITHFIELD	97	76	52	68	85	96	71	86	81	71	96	101	64	95	76	86	89	85	102	118
04979	SOLON	70	48	24	42	54	63	48	58	57	48	67	69	41	63	48	61	61	58	71	80
04981	STOCKTON SPRINGS	86	68	46	65	75	82	65	76	72	65	86	91	60	86	67	74	80	74	86	101
04982	STRATTON	68	53	36	48	60	68	50	61	57	50	68	71	45	67	54	61	63	60	72	83
04983	STRONG	71	53	32	49	60	68	53	63	60	52	71	74	47	69	55	64	65	62	75	84
04984	TEMPLE	79	55	29	52	64	72	54	67	63	54	73	81	46	72	56	66	67	66	80	94
04985	WEST FORKS	68	54	37	48	60	68	50	61	57	50	68	71	45	67	54	61	63	60	72	83
04986	THORNDIKE	61	52	41	52	55	62	54	57	57	53	69	65	51	68	53	58	65	56	62	68
04987	TROY	61	56	44	54	56	59	53	57	54	55	66	66	50	63	52	53	64	57	57	68
04988	UNITY	64	51	37	50	55	64	55	59	60	53	71	67	51	69	54	62	66	59	68	71
04989	VASSALBORO	77	65	49	63	69	77	65	71	69	64	84	82	61	83	65	71	78	70	78	87
	MAINE	80	73	65	71	75	82	72	77	75	71	92	90	70	91	73	76	88	76	81	93
	UNITED STATES	100	100	100	100	100	100	100	100	100	100	100	100	100	100	100	100	100	100	100	100

MARYLAND
POPULATION CHANGE

A 20601-20772

# POST OFFICE NAME	COUNTY FIPS CODE	POPULATION 2000	2004	2009	2000-2004 ANNUAL RATE % Rate	State Centile	HOUSEHOLDS 2000	2004	2009	% Annual Rate 2000-2004	2004 Average HH Size	FAMILIES 2000	2004	% Annual Rate 2000-2004
20601 WALDORF	017	22586	25446	28867	2.9	88	7757	8835	10146	3.1	2.87	6132	6919	2.9
20602 WALDORF	017	21513	22925	25430	1.5	61	7485	8131	9173	2.0	2.79	5562	5986	1.7
20603 WALDORF	017	20738	24306	28148	3.8	96	6955	8206	9601	4.0	2.96	5492	6426	3.8
20606 ABELL	037	523	532	573	0.4	28	207	214	233	0.8	2.49	157	161	0.6
20607 ACCOKEEK	033	6926	7614	8111	2.3	79	2278	2505	2670	2.3	3.03	1822	1990	2.1
20608 AQUASCO	033	1017	1017	1038	0.0	19	363	364	372	0.1	2.79	277	275	-0.2
20609 AVENUE	037	830	859	930	0.8	44	336	353	388	1.2	2.43	249	260	1.0
20611 BEL ALTON	017	708	702	761	-0.2	13	232	234	256	0.2	3.00	188	188	0.0
20613 BRANDYWINE	033	8442	8835	9320	1.1	49	2954	3108	3294	1.2	2.73	2252	2351	1.0
20615 BROOMES ISLAND	009	401	491	584	4.9	99	161	200	241	5.2	2.45	129	159	5.0
20616 BRYANS ROAD	017	4938	5248	5769	1.4	59	1815	1964	2194	1.9	2.67	1372	1472	1.7
20617 BRYANTOWN	017	585	586	624	0.0	21	208	212	230	0.5	2.75	170	173	0.4
20618 BUSHWOOD	037	902	957	1043	1.4	58	357	384	424	1.7	2.49	260	277	1.5
20619 CALIFORNIA	037	6405	6961	7747	2.0	74	2566	2831	3196	2.3	2.43	1725	1885	2.1
20620 CALLAWAY	037	1632	1763	1940	1.8	69	590	642	713	2.0	2.74	448	484	1.8
20621 CHAPTICO	037	996	1078	1188	1.9	71	380	418	467	2.3	2.58	298	326	2.1
20622 CHARLOTTE HALL	017	3568	3997	4491	2.7	86	1085	1244	1429	3.3	3.04	906	1034	3.2
20623 CHELTENHAM	033	2412	2751	2998	3.1	92	627	721	790	3.3	3.73	547	624	3.2
20624 CLEMENTS	037	715	763	834	1.5	62	251	272	302	1.9	2.80	199	215	1.8
20625 COBB ISLAND	017	822	864	944	1.2	52	346	367	406	1.4	2.35	208	217	1.0
20626 COLTONS POINT	037	497	482	515	-0.7	6	220	216	234	-0.4	2.23	154	150	-0.6
20628 DAMERON	037	326	322	345	-0.3	10	132	132	144	0.0	2.43	89	88	-0.3
20630 DRAYDEN	037	332	385	440	3.6	95	133	156	180	3.8	2.47	95	110	3.5
20632 FAULKNER	017	459	476	518	0.9	45	168	178	197	1.4	2.60	127	134	1.3
20634 GREAT MILLS	037	5271	5945	6699	2.9	88	1914	2177	2480	3.1	2.72	1333	1505	2.9
20636 HOLLYWOOD	037	7680	8126	8865	1.3	56	2788	2983	3293	1.6	2.71	2100	2231	1.4
20637 HUGHESVILLE	017	4674	5313	6046	3.1	91	1491	1732	2010	3.6	2.94	1230	1420	3.4
20639 HUNTINGTOWN	009	12644	14369	16492	3.1	91	4048	4652	5393	3.3	3.08	3474	3974	3.2
20640 INDIAN HEAD	017	7914	8369	9277	1.3	55	2935	3129	3509	1.5	2.67	2103	2224	1.3
20645 ISSUE	017	313	381	449	4.7	99	132	163	195	5.1	2.34	100	122	4.8
20646 LA PLATA	017	15921	17544	19610	2.3	81	5466	6162	7033	2.9	2.73	4224	4724	2.7
20650 LEONARDTOWN	037	11322	13105	14965	3.5	94	3948	4657	5411	4.0	2.71	2956	3453	3.7
20653 LEXINGTON PARK	037	19207	20869	23111	2.0	74	6913	7635	8606	2.4	2.58	4607	5010	2.0
20657 LUSBY	009	18105	19945	22518	2.3	81	6126	6735	7629	2.3	2.96	4753	5187	2.1
20658 MARBURY	017	913	927	994	0.4	27	310	321	349	0.8	2.89	234	240	0.6
20659 MECHANICSVILLE	037	20802	22384	24712	1.7	67	6780	7385	8258	2.0	3.02	5577	6048	1.7
20662 NANJEMOY	017	2867	2961	3262	0.8	42	1004	1056	1183	1.2	2.80	762	793	0.9
20664 NEWBURG	017	2990	3184	3527	1.5	60	1103	1203	1358	2.1	2.64	834	899	1.8
20667 PARK HALL	037	194	182	192	-1.5	1	78	74	79	-1.2	2.32	45	42	-1.6
20670 PATUXENT RIVER	037	2838	2899	3077	0.5	33	841	878	958	1.0	2.66	476	489	0.6
20674 PINEY POINT	037	896	1029	1166	3.3	93	357	418	482	3.8	2.37	249	289	3.6
20675 POMFRET	017	1513	1615	1778	1.6	63	516	561	628	2.0	2.88	443	479	1.9
20676 PORT REPUBLIC	009	3274	3885	4561	4.1	97	1123	1345	1594	4.3	2.89	879	1048	4.2
20677 PORT TOBACCO	017	2330	2332	2534	0.0	20	828	842	929	0.4	2.76	669	676	0.3
20678 PRINCE FREDERICK	009	8587	9499	10741	2.4	83	2917	3284	3770	2.8	2.80	2213	2470	2.6
20680 RIDGE	037	1172	1185	1275	0.3	25	507	520	569	0.6	2.26	341	346	0.3
20684 SAINT INIGOES	037	1022	1056	1144	0.8	42	410	429	472	1.1	2.40	279	289	0.8
20685 SAINT LEONARD	009	5464	6377	7420	3.7	96	1880	2215	2602	3.9	2.88	1493	1749	3.8
20687 SCOTLAND	037	339	349	374	0.7	40	150	156	171	0.9	2.24	84	86	0.6
20688 SOLOMONS	009	1796	1913	2111	1.5	60	799	869	979	2.0	2.02	502	537	1.6
20689 SUNDERLAND	009	978	1069	1202	2.1	78	337	373	425	2.4	2.86	283	312	2.3
20690 TALL TIMBERS	037	519	586	659	2.9	89	222	256	293	3.4	2.16	155	177	3.2
20692 VALLEY LEE	037	526	601	681	3.2	93	202	233	268	3.4	2.55	144	166	3.4
20693 WELCOME	017	863	911	997	1.3	54	307	330	368	1.7	2.76	241	257	1.5
20695 WHITE PLAINS	017	4812	5324	5996	2.4	83	1665	1871	2140	2.8	2.83	1366	1526	2.6
20701 ANNAPOLIS JUNCTION	003	797	798	799	0.0	20	14	15	16	1.6	2.20	10	10	0.0
20705 BELTSVILLE	033	20390	21993	23345	1.8	68	7421	8006	8497	1.8	2.74	5067	5398	1.5
20706 LANHAM	033	39620	40238	41864	0.4	27	13778	13981	14544	0.3	2.86	10167	10244	0.2
20707 LAUREL	033	25917	26446	27555	0.5	32	10818	11052	11520	0.5	2.36	6299	6321	0.1
20708 LAUREL	033	25366	25737	26586	0.3	27	10345	10498	10850	0.4	2.43	6296	6306	0.0
20710 BLADENSBURG	033	7710	8064	8429	1.1	49	3121	3283	3437	1.2	2.45	1735	1781	0.6
20711 LOTHIAN	003	6010	6550	7077	2.1	76	2283	2486	2687	2.0	2.63	1625	1758	1.9
20712 MOUNT RAINIER	033	8740	8682	8872	-0.2	16	3579	3531	3596	-0.3	2.46	1930	1871	-0.7
20714 NORTH BEACH	003	3095	3428	3872	2.4	83	1267	1417	1614	2.7	2.42	841	927	2.3
20715 BOWIE	033	25214	25580	26509	0.3	27	8720	8821	9136	0.3	2.84	6852	6874	0.1
20716 BOWIE	033	19598	21431	23074	2.1	79	7520	8315	9008	2.4	2.53	5017	5459	2.0
20720 BOWIE	033	14713	17033	18707	3.5	94	4801	5619	6205	3.8	2.98	3971	4599	3.5
20721 BOWIE	033	22386	25470	27841	3.1	91	7583	8611	9409	3.0	2.94	5946	6702	2.9
20722 BRENTWOOD	033	5741	5589	5681	-0.6	7	1927	1870	1897	-0.7	2.99	1270	1215	-1.0
20723 LAUREL	027	24193	25279	26589	1.0	49	8648	9084	9586	1.2	2.78	6255	6472	0.8
20724 LAUREL	003	13013	15126	16978	3.6	95	5077	5974	6756	3.9	2.46	3267	3795	3.6
20732 CHESAPEAKE BEACH	009	7497	8367	9526	2.6	85	2642	2989	3440	3.0	2.80	2028	2272	2.7
20733 CHURCHTON	003	3454	3465	3572	0.1	22	1243	1246	1283	0.1	2.78	959	955	-0.1
20735 CLINTON	033	32284	34885	37013	1.8	69	10606	11501	12219	1.9	2.97	8409	9056	1.8
20736 OWINGS	009	7743	8763	10036	3.0	89	2544	2922	3387	3.3	2.99	2118	2416	3.2
20737 RIVERDALE	033	19723	20603	21636	1.0	48	6268	6457	6736	0.7	3.18	4483	4573	0.5
20740 COLLEGE PARK	033	22010	22427	23257	0.4	29	8742	8910	9241	0.5	2.49	4289	4289	0.0
20742 COLLEGE PARK	033	8629	8630	8634	0.0	19	64	63	64	-0.4	2.87	15	17	3.0
20743 CAPITOL HEIGHTS	033	40627	41751	43567	0.6	38	14431	14867	15535	0.7	2.80	10286	10530	0.6
20744 FORT WASHINGTON	033	48523	49746	51787	0.6	36	16944	17415	18156	0.7	2.85	13107	13380	0.5
20745 OXON HILL	033	27930	29824	31814	1.6	63	10612	11398	12200	1.7	2.62	7133	7542	1.3
20746 SUITLAND	033	28575	28596	29466	0.0	20	11266	11297	11649	0.1	2.53	7409	7320	-0.3
20747 DISTRICT HEIGHTS	033	39934	40642	42014	0.4	29	15144	15483	16046	0.5	2.61	10308	10370	0.1
20748 TEMPLE HILLS	033	40038	41613	44030	0.9	46	15703	16294	17219	0.9	2.55	10361	10612	0.6
20751 DEALE	003	2111	2213	2334	1.1	51	797	835	880	1.1	2.65	554	575	0.9
20754 DUNKIRK	009	6603	7052	7829	1.6	63	2165	2336	2618	1.8	3.02	1897	2039	1.7
20755 FORT GEORGE G MEADE	003	9922	11864	13550	4.3	98	2444	3006	3493	5.0	3.48	2315	2834	4.9
20758 FRIENDSHIP	003	1022	1013	1051	-0.2	13	417	413	428	-0.2	2.45	297	292	-0.4
20759 FULTON	027	1976	2037	2119	0.7	41	648	674	704	0.9	3.01	568	588	0.8
20762 ANDREWS AFB	033	7935	7408	7437	-1.6	1	1936	1787	1799	-1.9	3.38	1867	1721	-1.9
20763 SAVAGE	027	2208	2146	2216	-0.7	7	846	830	861	-0.5	2.58	575	557	-0.8
20764 SHADY SIDE	003	3818	3966	4160	0.9	46	1447	1501	1574	0.9	2.64	1047	1077	0.7
20769 GLENN DALE	033	4722	4946	5212	1.1	50	1542	1616	1703	1.1	3.06	1241	1294	1.0
20770 GREENBELT	033	21177	22986	24708	2.0	73	9278	10122	10911	2.1	2.27	4897	5224	1.5
20772 UPPER MARLBORO	033	34497	37315	39790	1.9	70	12214	13178	14037	1.8	2.73	8978	9584	1.6
MARYLAND					1.1					1.1	2.60			1.0
UNITED STATES					1.2					1.3	2.58			1.1

# ZIP CODE	POST OFFICE NAME	RACE (%) White 2000	White 2004	Black 2000	Black 2004	Asian/Pacific 2000	Asian/Pacific 2004	% Hispanic Origin 2000	% Hispanic Origin 2004	2004 AGE DISTRIBUTION (%) 0-4	5-9	10-14	15-19	20-24	25-44	45-64	65-84	85+	18+	MEDIAN AGE 2004	% 2004 Males	% 2004 Females
20601	WALDORF	62.8	59.2	31.0	33.7	2.2	2.6	2.5	3.0	7.2	7.3	8.1	7.3	6.5	32.4	24.8	5.9	0.5	72.7	35.0	48.8	51.2
20602	WALDORF	63.4	59.7	30.6	33.5	1.9	2.2	2.8	3.3	8.5	7.5	7.9	7.4	7.8	31.5	22.1	6.4	0.9	71.5	32.6	47.2	52.8
20603	WALDORF	67.4	63.6	24.4	27.0	3.5	4.0	3.8	4.5	8.3	8.2	8.8	7.4	6.6	34.5	21.5	4.3	0.3	69.8	32.7	47.9	52.1
20606	ABELL	88.9	87.6	9.2	10.3	0.6	0.6	1.3	1.5	4.9	5.1	5.8	6.4	5.1	28.0	24.8	18.1	1.9	80.5	42.0	50.9	49.1
20607	ACCOKEEK	45.0	40.6	45.9	49.2	5.1	5.7	2.2	2.7	6.4	7.0	7.7	6.6	5.4	27.9	29.7	8.4	1.0	74.9	39.6	49.3	50.7
20608	AQUASCO	59.3	54.8	36.9	41.1	0.1	0.1	1.9	2.3	5.4	5.9	7.4	6.8	5.7	25.8	28.2	13.9	1.0	76.8	41.1	48.7	51.3
20609	AVENUE	82.7	80.3	15.5	17.6	0.6	0.7	1.2	1.5	4.9	5.1	5.6	5.8	4.8	26.8	27.0	17.9	2.1	80.8	43.2	50.1	49.9
20611	BEL ALTON	81.8	79.2	14.8	16.8	1.0	1.1	2.4	3.0	5.4	6.3	8.3	7.0	4.6	26.4	31.1	10.3	0.9	74.9	41.0	48.7	51.3
20613	BRANDYWINE	61.7	57.0	33.4	37.5	1.2	1.4	1.7	2.2	5.5	6.0	7.8	9.7	4.8	25.3	28.4	11.4	1.1	73.7	39.9	51.6	48.4
20615	BROOMES ISLAND	76.3	73.1	19.5	21.8	1.0	1.2	2.7	3.7	6.5	7.3	8.2	7.1	4.9	28.9	27.5	8.8	0.8	72.7	38.4	49.1	50.9
20616	BRYANS ROAD	52.0	48.5	43.1	46.0	1.4	1.6	2.2	2.6	7.3	7.6	8.4	6.2	5.3	33.2	22.0	9.1	0.9	72.8	35.4	47.1	52.9
20617	BRYANTOWN	84.6	82.4	13.2	15.0	0.5	0.7	1.5	1.9	5.6	6.1	6.5	6.5	4.4	26.3	30.9	12.3	1.4	77.7	41.6	50.5	49.5
20618	BUSHWOOD	75.6	72.7	22.6	25.3	0.7	0.7	1.2	1.5	5.0	5.1	5.5	5.4	4.8	26.2	28.7	17.1	2.0	81.0	43.6	49.2	50.8
20619	CALIFORNIA	86.2	84.2	9.7	10.9	2.1	2.6	1.6	2.0	7.0	7.0	8.1	7.0	5.9	29.7	25.3	8.7	1.3	73.1	37.0	48.9	51.1
20620	CALLAWAY	86.6	84.3	9.2	10.6	1.8	2.1	2.1	2.7	7.4	7.5	8.4	6.8	6.3	29.2	26.6	7.2	0.6	72.0	36.4	50.7	49.4
20621	CHAPTICO	84.7	82.5	13.1	14.9	0.5	0.7	1.5	1.8	7.5	7.3	7.7	6.6	6.1	32.6	21.2	10.0	0.9	73.6	34.4	50.9	49.1
20622	CHARLOTTE HALL	86.2	84.3	10.8	12.1	0.8	1.0	0.8	1.1	6.6	7.0	8.0	6.6	5.3	27.3	25.7	12.1	1.4	74.1	38.8	52.1	47.9
20623	CHELTENHAM	32.1	28.4	60.8	64.1	3.6	3.7	2.4	2.6	6.0	6.8	9.5	9.0	5.9	31.1	26.1	5.2	0.4	71.5	35.8	49.9	50.1
20624	CLEMENTS	84.2	82.0	13.9	15.6	0.4	0.5	1.4	1.6	7.0	7.3	8.7	7.2	6.0	31.2	21.8	10.1	0.8	72.9	34.7	51.4	48.6
20625	COBB ISLAND	95.3	94.3	2.6	3.0	1.3	1.6	0.4	0.5	6.7	5.9	6.7	5.4	8.5	28.0	22.0	14.8	2.0	76.7	37.6	47.7	52.3
20626	COLTONS POINT	85.1	83.2	13.1	14.9	0.6	0.6	1.2	1.5	5.2	5.4	4.6	4.2	3.7	25.3	25.5	22.8	3.3	82.0	46.1	49.0	51.0
20628	DAMERON	84.4	82.3	12.6	14.3	0.9	0.9	1.2	1.6	7.1	6.8	5.9	5.6	4.7	26.4	28.0	14.0	1.6	77.0	41.1	50.0	50.0
20630	DRAYDEN	88.0	86.2	7.8	8.8	1.5	1.8	1.2	1.6	6.0	6.0	6.2	6.0	5.7	25.2	29.6	13.8	1.6	78.2	41.8	51.2	48.8
20632	FAULKNER	77.6	74.6	17.7	20.0	0.7	0.8	0.9	1.1	6.1	6.1	6.7	6.9	6.1	29.0	28.8	9.5	0.8	76.5	39.0	50.6	49.4
20634	GREAT MILLS	70.3	66.8	22.3	24.6	3.7	4.4	2.9	3.6	8.1	7.7	8.4	7.1	6.7	35.0	21.0	5.5	0.4	71.1	32.3	49.6	50.4
20636	HOLLYWOOD	92.7	91.3	4.7	5.5	1.0	1.2	1.5	1.8	6.4	6.8	7.6	6.8	5.4	28.0	28.4	9.4	1.3	74.8	39.1	49.3	50.7
20637	HUGHESVILLE	78.4	75.8	17.9	20.0	1.6	1.9	1.2	1.5	6.6	6.9	7.3	6.8	5.3	28.8	28.3	9.0	1.0	75.0	38.8	51.7	48.3
20639	HUNTINGTOWN	86.0	84.1	11.3	12.7	1.3	1.5	1.3	1.5	6.6	7.4	9.3	7.3	5.1	26.1	30.1	7.3	0.8	72.0	39.0	49.4	50.6
20640	INDIAN HEAD	67.0	64.0	28.1	30.6	1.3	1.4	1.7	1.9	7.4	7.4	8.0	7.3	6.2	29.4	22.5	10.5	1.3	72.6	35.8	49.7	50.4
20645	ISSUE	86.3	84.0	10.9	12.6	1.3	1.3	1.0	1.3	5.0	5.5	5.5	5.0	3.4	20.7	33.3	20.0	1.6	80.8	48.1	51.7	48.3
20646	LA PLATA	77.1	74.3	19.5	21.9	1.2	1.4	1.4	1.7	5.8	6.4	7.3	6.6	5.7	27.2	28.2	11.0	1.8	76.2	39.8	49.2	50.8
20650	LEONARDTOWN	86.1	84.0	10.4	11.7	1.9	2.4	1.3	1.7	6.5	7.1	7.9	6.5	5.1	27.4	25.9	11.6	2.0	74.5	39.4	49.2	50.8
20653	LEXINGTON PARK	68.1	64.1	24.6	27.4	3.3	3.8	3.2	3.9	8.5	7.7	7.4	9.0	10.5	31.2	19.3	5.8	0.6	72.1	29.6	49.0	51.0
20657	LUSBY	82.0	79.4	14.4	16.3	0.9	1.0	2.3	2.8	8.3	8.1	9.3	7.6	6.4	32.0	19.9	7.4	0.9	69.3	33.1	49.0	51.0
20658	MARBURY	49.2	45.3	45.5	49.0	0.9	1.0	1.5	1.7	5.9	6.2	6.3	6.8	6.5	26.3	29.0	11.9	1.2	77.4	40.8	50.9	49.1
20659	MECHANICSVILLE	88.9	87.3	8.5	9.5	0.6	0.7	1.0	1.3	7.3	7.7	8.7	7.4	5.5	30.7	24.7	7.4	0.6	71.6	35.6	50.3	49.7
20662	NANJEMOY	62.8	58.7	34.9	38.8	0.3	0.3	0.9	1.1	6.5	6.7	7.2	6.1	6.6	28.2	27.5	10.3	1.0	75.8	38.9	50.4	49.7
20664	NEWBURG	75.4	72.7	21.1	23.4	1.0	1.2	0.9	1.2	5.4	5.6	6.8	6.9	5.4	25.6	29.2	13.9	1.3	78.0	41.5	50.6	49.4
20667	PARK HALL	84.5	82.4	10.8	12.1	0.5	0.6	2.6	2.8	6.6	6.0	4.4	8.2	8.8	29.1	25.8	9.9	1.1	79.7	36.2	49.5	50.6
20670	PATUXENT RIVER	70.2	66.5	19.8	21.8	3.5	4.1	6.9	8.4	10.9	10.9	8.2	8.0	17.7	41.6	2.6	0.0	0.0	67.6	23.4	65.3	34.7
20674	PINEY POINT	87.3	85.3	8.0	9.1	2.0	2.3	2.2	2.7	5.4	5.8	5.5	5.3	4.2	27.2	30.9	13.8	1.9	80.1	43.0	53.3	46.7
20675	POMFRET	75.0	71.9	19.1	21.6	2.5	2.7	1.1	1.3	5.6	6.2	7.4	6.1	5.4	26.8	31.7	10.2	0.6	77.0	40.7	49.6	50.4
20676	PORT REPUBLIC	82.5	79.6	14.7	17.1	0.6	0.7	1.7	2.0	6.4	7.1	8.0	7.3	5.3	28.3	27.4	9.0	1.2	73.6	38.4	49.2	50.8
20677	PORT TOBACCO	83.6	81.2	13.0	15.0	0.8	1.0	1.3	1.6	4.9	5.8	7.5	6.8	4.5	26.3	31.7	12.0	0.6	77.3	41.8	49.2	50.8
20678	PRINCE FREDERICK	76.3	73.8	21.4	23.6	0.8	1.0	1.2	1.4	6.4	6.9	7.6	7.0	6.5	28.9	25.3	9.6	1.8	74.8	37.5	48.1	51.9
20680	RIDGE	82.9	80.5	14.9	16.9	0.9	1.1	0.5	0.7	5.7	5.8	5.3	6.0	4.5	24.0	29.5	17.3	1.9	79.4	44.1	50.5	49.5
20684	SAINT INIGOES	82.1	79.5	15.1	17.2	1.5	1.7	1.2	1.4	4.4	5.0	6.6	6.3	5.1	25.2	29.6	16.4	1.5	79.6	43.4	50.8	49.2
20685	SAINT LEONARD	86.2	83.8	10.6	12.3	0.9	1.1	1.9	2.5	6.9	7.2	8.5	7.3	5.8	29.7	26.3	7.7	0.6	72.3	37.1	49.3	50.7
20687	SCOTLAND	90.3	88.8	7.1	8.0	0.6	0.6	0.9	1.2	2.9	4.0	4.6	7.7	6.0	20.3	35.0	17.5	2.0	83.7	47.0	49.3	50.7
20688	SOLOMONS	85.1	83.0	12.4	14.2	0.6	0.7	0.7	0.8	4.0	4.4	5.4	4.8	3.5	21.8	25.4	23.6	7.2	83.0	49.5	47.4	52.6
20689	SUNDERLAND	73.3	70.1	24.6	27.5	0.5	0.7	1.2	1.4	4.8	5.8	7.6	6.9	4.8	26.1	33.1	9.7	1.2	77.3	42.0	48.8	51.2
20690	TALL TIMBERS	86.1	84.1	8.7	9.9	2.3	2.6	2.9	3.6	5.5	6.0	5.6	5.1	3.8	29.2	30.7	12.5	1.7	80.0	42.2	54.3	45.7
20692	VALLEY LEE	87.3	85.2	8.6	9.7	1.7	2.0	1.7	2.2	6.2	6.3	6.3	6.0	5.7	26.5	29.0	12.7	1.5	77.4	40.7	51.6	48.4
20693	WELCOME	79.0	76.3	17.5	19.8	0.6	0.6	0.7	0.8	5.4	5.6	6.5	7.1	5.9	27.6	30.3	11.0	0.7	77.9	40.6	49.2	50.8
20695	WHITE PLAINS	70.5	66.7	25.0	28.1	1.3	1.5	1.8	2.1	7.0	6.9	6.9	6.4	5.8	31.5	26.1	8.5	0.8	75.2	36.7	48.8	51.2
20701	ANNAPOLIS JUNCTION	25.1	22.2	74.7	77.4	0.1	0.1	0.5	0.6	0.3	0.3	0.3	2.9	17.7	63.5	14.3	0.8	0.1	99.0	33.3	76.8	23.2
20705	BELTSVILLE	48.3	43.3	32.9	35.2	11.2	12.5	8.4	10.2	6.7	6.4	6.9	6.2	7.9	33.3	22.8	9.0	0.9	76.4	34.9	49.4	50.6
20706	LANHAM	22.4	19.6	67.6	69.5	5.5	5.8	3.9	4.5	7.0	7.3	7.9	7.3	6.7	29.4	24.9	8.7	0.7	73.2	35.2	47.2	52.8
20707	LAUREL	57.6	53.3	30.3	32.8	6.6	7.5	5.7	6.8	6.5	6.4	6.5	5.6	6.4	35.3	23.8	8.5	1.0	77.2	36.4	48.2	51.9
20708	LAUREL	37.4	34.1	51.6	53.5	5.4	6.0	4.9	5.8	8.3	7.3	7.2	6.1	7.6	36.6	19.8	6.5	0.7	73.7	31.9	47.6	52.4
20710	BLADENSBURG	18.0	16.0	68.6	69.4	2.6	2.6	14.6	16.3	8.2	7.3	8.0	7.4	8.7	31.3	20.1	8.1	0.9	72.2	31.5	48.1	51.9
20711	LOTHIAN	81.1	78.1	16.0	18.6	0.6	0.7	1.1	1.3	6.3	6.5	7.0	7.0	5.7	26.8	27.9	11.9	1.1	76.0	39.8	49.6	50.4
20712	MOUNT RAINIER	20.1	18.2	62.3	62.3	2.3	2.4	18.1	20.5	7.1	6.4	7.3	7.5	9.3	33.9	21.4	6.3	0.8	74.8	32.1	49.0	51.0
20714	NORTH BEACH	90.5	89.0	5.9	6.8	0.8	1.1	1.6	1.9	7.7	7.6	7.9	6.0	6.2	33.6	23.5	7.0	0.6	73.1	34.8	47.8	52.2
20715	BOWIE	79.4	75.4	14.5	17.2	2.6	3.2	3.0	3.9	6.4	6.7	7.2	7.2	5.7	26.9	25.7	13.1	1.0	75.5	39.6	48.2	51.8
20716	BOWIE	53.1	47.5	39.9	44.4	3.1	3.6	2.9	3.6	7.8	7.6	7.5	5.9	5.7	35.8	22.0	6.5	1.2	73.4	35.3	47.1	52.9
20720	BOWIE	46.0	41.3	42.1	45.6	7.7	8.5	2.9	3.5	7.2	7.9	8.7	7.6	6.1	29.3	27.6	5.2	0.4	71.7	36.0	47.8	52.2
20721	BOWIE	10.9	9.4	84.3	85.5	2.2	2.3	1.5	1.6	6.8	7.9	8.5	6.6	4.8	29.3	29.6	5.5	1.1	72.6	37.9	46.4	53.6
20722	BRENTWOOD	26.2	23.2	53.3	54.0	4.3	4.5	18.5	21.1	6.4	6.9	8.1	7.9	6.6	28.2	25.6	9.0	1.3	73.8	35.8	48.2	51.8
20723	LAUREL	71.0	66.9	17.4	19.5	7.3	8.4	4.0	4.9	8.3	8.2	8.4	6.5	6.3	35.6	22.0	4.6	0.3	70.9	33.3	49.2	50.8
20724	LAUREL	56.4	51.3	32.1	35.6	6.6	7.6	4.2	4.8	8.4	7.3	6.0	7.1	6.9	38.3	20.2	5.4	0.4	73.8	33.5	49.2	50.8
20732	CHESAPEAKE BEACH	84.9	83.1	11.9	13.2	0.7	0.9	1.4	1.8	7.2	7.4	8.3	7.2	5.8	30.9	26.2	6.4	0.7	72.5	36.4	49.6	50.4
20733	CHURCHTON	87.6	85.7	10.3	11.8	0.4	0.4	1.4	1.8	6.6	7.3	7.4	6.5	4.8	29.0	28.6	9.1	0.7	74.6	39.2	49.1	50.9
20735	CLINTON	21.2	18.2	73.1	75.7	2.6	2.7	1.9	2.2	6.1	6.7	7.8	6.9	5.2	29.0	28.4	8.7	1.2	74.9	38.5	47.3	52.7
20736	OWINGS	85.5	83.5	11.9	13.5	0.8	1.0	1.1	1.4	6.3	7.0	8.3	7.6	5.4	26.9	30.0	7.8	0.7	73.6	39.1	49.3	50.8
20737	RIVERDALE	30.0	27.7	50.4	50.7	4.2	4.3	23.3	26.4	9.1	8.2	8.3	7.5	8.8	33.0	19.5	5.1	0.6	70.1	29.8	51.0	49.0
20740	COLLEGE PARK	67.8	63.6	15.5	17.1	10.6	12.2	6.3	7.8	4.4	4.2	4.6	5.6	18.8	30.8	19.8	10.6	1.3	84.5	31.8	51.9	48.1
20742	COLLEGE PARK	69.2	64.5	16.8	18.9	10.0	11.7	3.7	4.7	0.0	0.0	0.0	60.3	38.4	0.8	0.2	0.2	0.0	99.4	19.1	53.2	46.8
20743	CAPITOL HEIGHTS	3.4	2.9	94.2	94.6	0.3	0.3	1.0	1.1	7.3	7.9	9.3	7.4	6.5	28.2	23.6	9.3	0.6	70.9	34.1	46.0	54.0
20744	FORT WASHINGTON	14.7	12.8	75.4	76.7	6.5	6.8	2.1	2.4	5.6	6.3	7.4	6.7	5.7	26.8	31.1	9.7	0.7	76.6	39.6	47.4	52.6
20745	OXON HILL	8.3	6.8	84.5	85.8	4.3	4.4	1.9	2.1	7.5	7.7	8.6	7.6	7.6	29.7	23.8	7.0	0.5	71.6	32.6	46.1	53.9
20746	SUITLAND	9.0	7.7	87.0	88.0	1.1	1.2	2.4	2.7	7.8	7.6	8.7	7.5	7.6	30.7	22.4	7.0	0.7	71.4	32.1	45.0	55.0
20747	DISTRICT HEIGHTS	6.9	5.7	89.8	90.8	0.8	0.9	1.3	1.4	7.5	7.6	8.8	7.8	7.3	30.7	23.2	6.6	0.7	71.4	32.9	45.1	54.9
20748	TEMPLE HILLS	10.7	9.0	85.6	87.0	1.1	1.1	1.9	2.2	6.3	6.5	7.7	7.0	6.7	29.2	25.7	10.0	0.9	75.1	36.1	45.8	54.2
20751	DEALE	92.6	91.3	5.3	6.1	0.7	0.8	0.7	0.9	5.4	6.2	7.2	6.0	4.6	28.6	30.8	10.1	1.1	77.4	41.0	50.6	49.4
20754	DUNKIRK	91.9	90.4	5.7	6.6	1.0	1.3	0.7	0.9	5.1	6.3	8.0	7.1	5.0	23.3	34.3	10.3	0.7	76.1	42.4	49.6	50.4
20755	FORT GEORGE G MEADE	62.6	59.3	25.1	26.7	3.2	3.7	9.5	11.4	15.1	12.7	8.4	6.8	15.1	37.5	4.0	0.3	0.1	60.7	22.3	52.5	47.5
20758	FRIENDSHIP	93.1	92.0	4.8	5.6	0.4	0.4	0.4	0.7	4.0	5.0	6.6	5.7	4.0	24.1	33.9	15.2	1.6	80.9	45.3	50.1	50.0
20759	FULTON	85.0	82.1	4.2	4.9	8.5	10.2	1.9	2.4	6.6	8.1	9.0	7.1	3.6	22.1	31.7	10.6	1.3	71.6	41.8	50.4	49.6
20762	ANDREWS AFB	65.3	60.7	22.8	25.3	3.3	3.8	8.7	10.8	14.7	10.8	7.2	5.8	14.2	43.0	4.0	0.2	0.0	64.9	24.0	54.8	45.2
20763	SAVAGE	67.7	63.7	20.2	22.4	5.9	6.8	5.3	6.5	7.9	7.4	8.2	8.4	8.8	34.7	18.2	5.9	0.6	71.5	31.2	50.6	49.4
20764	SHADY SIDE	88.0	86.4	9.0	10.1	0.5	0.6	1.3	1.7	7.8	8.2	7.3	5.3	4.5	31.1	27.5	7.6	0.8	73.4	38.1	51.1	48.9
20769	GLENN DALE	37.6	33.5	53.7	57.1	5.5	5.9	2.2	2.6	7.4	7.5	7.1	6.5	5.4	28.6	29.2	7.7	0.6	74.0	38.3	48.5	51.5
20770	GREENBELT	40.0	36.9	41.2	42.4	12.1	13.2	6.5	7.3	6.6	5.6	5.7	6.1	9.3	37.4	22.0	6.6	0.7	78.6	33.0	47.8	52.2
20772	UPPER MARLBORO	33.1	29.2	62.3	65.8	1.6	1.8	2.0	2.3	6.9	7.1	7.2	6.2	5.5	34.0	25.4	7.1	0.6	74.9	36.4	49.2	50.8
	MARYLAND	64.0	61.8	27.9	28.9	4.0	4.6	4.3	5.1	6.6	6.7	7.3	6.9	6.6	29.1	25.1	10.2	1.5	75.2	37.0	48.3	51.7
	UNITED STATES	75.1	73.6	12.3	12.5	3.8	4.2	12.5	14.1	6.9	6.7	7.2	7.0	7.3	28.6	23.8	10.8	1.7	75.1	36.0	49.1	50.9

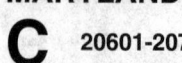

INCOME

ZIP CODE #	POST OFFICE NAME	2004 Per Capita Income	2004 HH Income Base	2004 Household Income Distribution (%): Less than $25,000	$25,000 to $49,999	$50,000 to $99,999	$100,000 to $149,999	$150,000 or More	Median Household Income: 2004	2009	2004 National Centile	2004 State Centile	2004 Home Value Base	2004 Home Value Distribution (%): Less than $50,000	$50,000 to $89,999	$90,000 to $174,999	$175,000 to $399,999	$400,000 or More	2004 Median Home Value
20601	WALDORF	27997	8835	7.0	19.7	45.8	21.8	5.7	72436	81191	92	70	7175	1.7	0.5	14.1	77.9	5.8	232360
20602	WALDORF	23207	8131	17.8	24.3	39.2	15.6	3.2	57729	65607	82	48	5630	0.4	0.6	29.7	68.1	1.2	197859
20603	WALDORF	28607	8206	4.3	18.6	45.7	25.2	6.1	77682	87193	94	77	6366	0.1	0.6	11.3	79.6	8.5	257477
20606	ABELL	31801	214	22.4	17.3	35.1	16.4	8.9	64269	74603	88	60	185	5.4	4.9	18.4	56.2	15.1	223387
20607	ACCOKEEK	32152	2505	6.9	14.8	38.9	27.9	11.5	86122	101106	96	87	2308	0.1	0.9	12.7	72.0	14.3	263934
20608	AQUASCO	30778	364	15.7	14.6	43.1	18.4	8.2	70364	81089	91	68	311	6.4	2.6	24.8	49.8	16.4	221354
20609	AVENUE	30412	353	21.8	18.1	36.8	15.9	7.4	62020	70981	86	55	303	3.3	3.6	25.4	51.8	15.8	214796
20611	BEL ALTON	31211	234	8.1	18.0	37.2	17.5	19.2	75000	88636	93	73	219	0.0	3.7	14.2	52.1	30.1	280172
20613	BRANDYWINE	28585	3108	13.6	17.7	41.1	21.0	6.7	69518	80621	91	67	2757	5.9	2.3	15.1	65.1	11.6	241392
20615	BROOMES ISLAND	30868	200	16.0	22.5	33.5	20.5	7.5	63640	77079	88	59	175	2.3	1.1	10.3	62.9	23.4	275781
20616	BRYANS ROAD	28568	1964	9.7	21.7	46.5	16.5	5.7	65057	75538	89	61	1729	2.0	0.5	22.4	70.6	4.5	204706
20617	BRYANTOWN	32077	212	12.3	13.7	34.9	30.2	9.0	83303	97687	96	85	195	1.5	4.1	7.7	72.3	14.4	283553
20618	BUSHWOOD	27869	384	20.8	18.8	38.8	15.6	6.0	60591	68792	85	52	328	0.6	2.7	32.3	47.3	17.1	206604
20619	CALIFORNIA	30702	2831	12.3	22.1	42.3	16.9	6.5	65815	75148	89	62	2176	2.9	1.7	20.0	67.9	7.5	226873
20620	CALLAWAY	29585	642	12.6	20.6	37.4	20.4	9.0	69914	79450	91	68	521	3.3	1.0	18.4	61.0	16.3	261824
20621	CHAPTICO	26268	418	12.0	24.4	50.5	10.1	3.1	59787	66348	84	50	374	1.9	0.8	21.1	68.2	8.0	213158
20622	CHARLOTTE HALL	27677	1244	10.4	15.6	41.9	22.7	9.5	77109	86300	94	76	1126	0.7	1.2	8.7	71.9	17.5	260476
20623	CHELTENHAM	26644	721	2.5	7.4	43.6	36.2	10.4	95328	110795	98	91	680	0.0	0.0	3.2	87.9	8.8	275789
20624	CLEMENTS	23196	272	17.7	24.3	42.3	13.2	2.6	60000	66661	84	50	239	4.2	1.7	22.2	66.5	5.4	215203
20625	COBB ISLAND	30917	367	10.4	37.3	37.6	10.1	4.6	51421	58580	75	36	317	0.0	0.0	35.3	56.5	8.2	191848
20626	COLTONS POINT	28050	216	27.8	27.3	27.3	13.9	3.7	45376	52061	62	23	180	8.9	6.7	22.8	52.2	9.4	213158
20628	DAMERON	25577	132	25.0	26.5	30.3	14.4	3.8	48783	56180	70	30	106	6.6	0.9	22.6	56.6	13.2	221739
20630	DRAYDEN	31206	156	11.5	20.5	42.3	17.3	8.3	62763	74319	87	56	128	0.8	2.3	16.4	54.7	25.8	313889
20632	FAULKNER	25840	178	17.4	18.0	45.5	13.5	5.6	57408	67726	82	47	138	2.2	0.0	21.7	71.0	5.1	215278
20634	GREAT MILLS	23944	2177	14.5	23.9	46.4	12.1	3.1	60109	66776	84	51	1600	8.4	1.6	38.8	47.8	3.4	177262
20636	HOLLYWOOD	28695	2983	8.2	22.0	46.1	16.6	7.1	68497	77942	91	66	2544	0.6	1.1	20.0	65.5	12.9	232047
20637	HUGHESVILLE	32808	1732	10.1	17.7	29.4	26.6	16.2	87035	98648	97	88	1563	0.4	1.0	12.9	66.7	18.9	296909
20639	HUNTINGTOWN	32994	4652	7.1	13.8	37.2	27.9	14.1	87821	101475	97	88	4356	0.8	0.5	5.3	63.6	29.8	328502
20640	INDIAN HEAD	25325	3129	16.8	28.7	36.0	13.4	5.1	54219	63145	79	42	2456	4.8	11.6	30.5	49.2	3.8	181356
20645	ISSUE	31800	163	12.3	16.0	45.4	22.7	3.7	67665	78780	90	64	139	0.0	0.0	7.9	63.3	28.8	298810
20646	LA PLATA	31018	6162	13.0	19.8	35.8	20.5	10.9	71417	81759	92	68	5090	0.9	0.5	13.7	71.0	14.0	266210
20650	LEONARDTOWN	28484	4657	17.5	20.0	37.1	17.8	7.6	64473	75131	88	61	3879	0.6	1.8	19.0	58.6	19.9	247049
20653	LEXINGTON PARK	24269	7635	19.3	29.2	35.6	12.2	3.7	51237	57691	74	36	4388	6.8	3.0	27.9	55.1	7.2	200870
20657	LUSBY	24719	6735	11.1	24.5	43.6	16.4	4.3	63153	72241	87	57	5774	1.1	0.6	28.8	59.0	10.5	201551
20658	MARBURY	26287	321	14.3	24.0	41.1	15.6	5.0	62094	71793	86	55	274	0.0	4.4	28.8	63.9	2.9	205357
20659	MECHANICSVILLE	24296	7385	11.5	20.3	47.6	16.0	4.5	64380	74296	88	61	6661	0.7	1.0	16.5	74.8	7.0	225379
20662	NANJEMOY	22678	1056	19.2	27.4	36.5	12.1	4.8	53721	61825	78	41	904	9.2	2.3	24.0	51.1	13.4	215287
20664	NEWBURG	25380	1203	17.4	25.2	39.9	13.5	4.1	55401	63884	80	44	961	0.3	4.6	18.4	57.4	19.3	231711
20667	PARK HALL	25410	74	8.1	40.5	37.8	10.8	2.7	51208	57547	74	36	50	20.0	0.0	26.0	52.0	2.0	180556
20670	PATUXENT RIVER	16414	878	28.8	36.8	28.6	4.9	0.9	33741	38347	23	8	16	0.0	0.0	100.0	0.0	0.0	137500
20674	PINEY POINT	32052	418	12.2	18.4	43.8	15.6	10.1	61870	72792	86	54	340	0.6	3.2	16.5	46.8	32.9	329268
20675	POMFRET	34072	561	6.2	11.2	40.1	29.8	12.7	88545	101598	97	88	530	0.2	0.0	3.8	79.6	16.4	277083
20676	PORT REPUBLIC	31988	1345	8.8	16.7	42.2	19.8	12.6	75182	87707	93	73	1197	0.4	0.6	8.9	69.0	21.1	276878
20677	PORT TOBACCO	34531	842	8.6	13.7	39.4	24.1	14.3	83209	96186	96	84	782	0.4	1.4	10.5	62.8	24.9	285443
20678	PRINCE FREDERICK	27450	3284	18.3	21.0	36.5	16.8	7.5	62767	73894	87	57	2548	3.5	1.1	12.8	65.9	16.8	248803
20680	RIDGE	26808	520	29.4	24.0	28.1	13.3	5.2	46300	54575	65	26	424	4.0	0.0	16.8	57.1	22.2	252727
20684	SAINT INIGOES	28460	429	14.2	26.3	36.1	18.4	4.9	57246	67107	82	46	362	4.4	0.6	18.2	50.0	26.8	266393
20685	SAINT LEONARD	28933	2215	10.9	19.5	40.1	21.7	7.9	72238	82081	92	70	1960	1.0	0.4	17.4	61.2	20.1	254909
20687	SCOTLAND	21684	156	33.3	26.3	28.9	9.6	1.9	40000	47810	46	15	112	4.5	0.0	18.8	43.8	33.0	261111
20688	SOLOMONS	36135	869	11.2	26.9	37.9	13.8	10.2	58792	69591	83	49	602	2.2	0.0	16.5	55.3	26.1	300000
20689	SUNDERLAND	32731	373	11.8	12.9	41.0	21.7	12.6	79269	93356	95	80	340	2.1	0.0	4.7	73.8	19.4	304587
20690	TALL TIMBERS	34776	256	13.7	18.0	42.6	14.8	10.9	61684	72954	86	53	203	0.0	3.0	17.7	44.8	34.5	334375
20692	VALLEY LEE	30218	233	12.0	19.7	42.1	17.6	8.6	64002	73677	88	59	188	2.1	2.1	17.6	52.1	26.1	306250
20693	WELCOME	29563	330	10.0	22.7	40.0	17.3	10.0	68006	78309	90	64	286	3.5	1.8	12.9	63.3	18.5	253409
20695	WHITE PLAINS	29352	1871	6.6	18.2	45.2	22.8	7.3	76523	85305	94	75	1733	2.4	0.6	4.9	84.0	8.3	256187
20701	ANNAPOLIS JUNCTION	16797	15	20.0	13.3	46.7	20.0	0.0	61867	77349	86	54	12	25.0	25.0	16.7	33.3	0.0	90000
20705	BELTSVILLE	28270	8006	12.9	21.9	39.0	19.4	6.8	66730	77649	90	63	5017	0.0	1.8	8.6	85.2	4.4	242453
20706	LANHAM	26271	13981	12.2	23.6	40.3	17.5	6.5	64260	75205	88	60	9542	0.7	1.8	14.9	77.1	5.5	225063
20707	LAUREL	30906	11052	13.5	26.0	38.2	16.6	5.7	60088	69492	84	51	6802	1.0	1.3	26.5	67.1	4.1	209633
20708	LAUREL	29216	10498	12.6	28.8	38.0	14.5	6.2	58493	66484	83	49	4333	0.6	0.0	18.3	76.6	4.5	253721
20710	BLADENSBURG	18603	3283	29.2	35.9	28.0	6.0	1.0	38388	42646	41	13	921	0.2	1.5	40.6	56.9	0.8	182165
20711	LOTHIAN	28358	2486	19.6	23.1	32.1	18.1	7.2	58272	70244	83	48	2145	40.4	8.6	5.7	31.3	14.0	98958
20712	MOUNT RAINIER	19696	3531	26.6	37.9	27.5	6.5	1.6	39817	44141	45	15	969	0.4	2.5	45.7	51.2	0.2	176548
20714	NORTH BEACH	29836	1417	10.5	25.8	45.2	14.7	3.9	61690	71012	86	53	1078	0.0	0.6	26.9	65.6	7.0	205308
20715	BOWIE	33137	8821	4.5	13.7	45.8	24.7	11.3	82538	95978	96	84	8143	0.2	0.2	5.2	90.3	4.2	235176
20716	BOWIE	35207	8315	5.2	16.9	44.3	24.3	9.3	80354	93741	95	81	6047	0.3	0.1	10.1	80.0	9.5	234810
20720	BOWIE	35075	5619	4.6	9.7	40.4	29.2	16.2	92828	106378	97	90	5286	0.0	0.2	6.0	79.3	14.5	284729
20721	BOWIE	41084	8611	2.5	7.3	35.4	32.3	22.5	105490	122682	99	95	8037	0.1	0.2	3.0	67.3	29.5	329041
20722	BRENTWOOD	18297	1870	22.1	31.6	35.6	9.0	1.7	47270	52998	67	28	1286	1.6	1.7	56.4	40.1	0.3	162295
20723	LAUREL	32317	9084	6.9	21.6	39.4	21.6	10.7	75330	87167	93	74	6631	4.0	1.4	18.5	63.9	12.2	228152
20724	LAUREL	35024	5974	5.8	18.6	45.5	22.0	8.1	71949	84305	92	69	4179	5.9	2.0	18.0	71.0	3.1	200547
20732	CHESAPEAKE BEACH	29328	2989	8.6	18.4	47.8	19.2	6.0	71877	81585	92	69	2618	1.5	1.9	11.2	77.3	8.1	235544
20733	CHURCHTON	29165	1246	10.0	15.1	45.4	23.9	5.5	75510	86569	93	74	1141	0.0	1.4	22.4	64.9	11.4	222971
20735	CLINTON	28701	11501	8.4	14.5	46.1	22.9	8.1	78050	89101	94	78	10378	0.6	0.7	7.5	88.2	3.0	237798
20736	OWINGS	32202	2922	6.9	14.9	42.3	24.3	11.5	81539	94213	95	82	2688	2.1	0.4	7.3	66.6	23.6	307311
20737	RIVERDALE	19466	6457	17.9	31.4	35.6	12.1	2.9	50564	57737	73	35	3315	0.4	1.1	41.4	56.1	1.2	184155
20740	COLLEGE PARK	27393	8910	19.8	22.3	38.1	14.0	5.9	57746	67000	82	48	5029	0.5	0.9	21.7	73.6	3.2	217211
20742	COLLEGE PARK	16233	63	58.7	14.3	14.3	12.7	0.0	20341	23341	2	1	22	0.0	0.0	13.6	77.3	9.1	269231
20743	CAPITOL HEIGHTS	20791	14867	21.9	28.8	36.2	10.5	2.6	49248	55759	71	32	9472	2.6	2.2	46.5	48.2	0.6	173067
20744	FORT WASHINGTON	34636	17415	6.5	15.1	41.2	25.1	12.0	82335	95379	96	83	14679	0.4	0.5	8.9	80.3	9.9	246478
20745	OXON HILL	22146	11398	20.6	33.3	32.1	11.1	2.9	46506	52266	65	27	5497	0.4	3.4	34.3	59.8	2.1	191637
20746	SUITLAND	23362	11297	18.0	33.7	35.7	10.0	2.6	48564	54655	69	30	4999	0.6	5.1	27.0	65.9	1.4	199175
20747	DISTRICT HEIGHTS	23409	15483	16.3	30.8	39.2	11.4	2.4	52370	60094	76	37	8514	0.7	2.2	27.6	69.0	0.5	197497
20748	TEMPLE HILLS	26786	16294	12.9	29.7	38.7	13.8	4.9	56425	64445	81	45	9999	0.6	3.0	25.2	70.3	0.9	208677
20751	DEALE	29796	835	12.0	16.4	47.9	17.6	6.1	68535	79854	91	66	730	0.7	0.7	17.7	68.2	12.7	227919
20754	DUNKIRK	35581	2336	5.7	11.3	33.2	34.2	15.6	99608	113848	98	93	2235	3.5	1.5	3.5	60.9	30.8	337391
20755	FORT GEORGE G MEADE	15104	3006	13.4	44.1	35.2	6.5	0.9	45935	52261	64	24	82	0.0	0.0	31.7	68.3	0.0	221429
20758	FRIENDSHIP	40136	413	6.1	16.0	40.7	24.0	13.3	80649	100551	95	81	363	0.0	1.7	12.4	56.8	29.2	314205
20759	FULTON	51478	674	4.3	5.8	26.1	26.3	37.5	122522	142090	99	98	637	0.8	0.0	1.3	35.3	62.6	458759
20762	ANDREWS AFB	16432	1787	9.6	41.4	41.1	6.6	1.2	49078	56065	70	31	23	0.0	0.0	47.8	52.2	0.0	176250
20763	SAVAGE	23947	830	15.3	34.0	34.9	12.3	3.5	50616	59780	73	35	342	0.0	0.3	6.7	90.6	2.3	232222
20764	SHADY SIDE	36018	1501	8.1	18.8	47.2	15.9	10.0	73573	81700	93	72	1328	0.0	0.0	30.9	59.3	9.9	197518
20769	GLENN DALE	33004	1616	6.3	10.6	40.6	26.4	16.2	90491	104981	97	89	1340	0.0	0.0	5.8	72.2	21.9	284840
20770	GREENBELT	29551	10122	14.9	32.1	35.2	13.1	4.8	52443	61458	76	37	4757	2.7	16.2	42.4	37.0	1.8	138215
20772	UPPER MARLBORO	33687	13178	6.4	15.5	41.9	26.2	10.0	81134	93108	95	81	11664	1.8	1.6	12.3	75.9	8.4	233440
	MARYLAND	30267		17.9	23.3	34.6	15.0	9.2	59732	70285				2.9	5.4	28.1	49.8	13.8	209514
	UNITED STATES	25866		24.7	27.1	30.8	10.9	6.5	48124	56710				10.9	15.0	33.7	30.1	10.4	145905

#	POST OFFICE NAME	FINANCIAL SERVICES: Auto Loan	Home Loan	Investments	Retirement Plans	THE HOME: Home Improvements: Home Repair	Lawn & Garden	Furnishings: Computers & Hardware	Major Appliances	TV, Radio, Sound Equipment	Furniture	ENTERTAINMENT: Dine out/ Carry out	Sports Equipment	Fees & Tickets	Toys & Games	Travel	Cable TV	PERSONAL: Apparel & Services	Auto Repairs	Health Insurance	Pets & Supplies
20601	WALDORF	112	124	129	129	120	119	117	115	109	120	139	135	120	139	115	103	137	114	101	127
20602	WALDORF	88	96	103	97	93	95	93	91	90	94	113	107	95	115	92	87	112	91	84	101
20603	WALDORF	120	133	134	139	127	125	124	121	114	127	145	143	127	145	120	107	144	120	105	133
20606	ABELL	100	120	133	116	118	123	112	111	108	111	136	127	119	143	115	108	135	109	107	121
20607	ACCOKEEK	130	157	164	159	153	151	141	140	131	142	165	164	149	171	143	126	164	136	125	154
20608	AQUASCO	109	132	146	129	130	132	123	121	117	122	147	140	131	157	126	115	147	118	113	132
20609	AVENUE	107	107	101	101	111	119	100	107	103	99	126	124	100	130	104	106	122	105	113	130
20611	BEL ALTON	121	151	160	151	148	146	135	134	125	134	157	157	143	167	138	121	157	129	120	148
20613	BRANDYWINE	111	122	121	120	121	124	112	114	108	112	135	134	115	140	113	107	133	111	109	131
20615	BROOMES ISLAND	98	122	130	122	120	118	109	109	101	109	127	127	116	135	112	98	127	105	97	120
20616	BRYANS ROAD	102	117	123	117	114	115	110	109	104	110	131	128	114	135	110	100	130	107	98	120
20617	BRYANTOWN	115	143	152	143	140	138	127	127	118	127	148	149	136	158	130	115	148	122	114	140
20618	BUSHWOOD	112	95	73	88	104	115	90	104	98	89	117	121	83	117	95	103	111	102	118	136
20619	CALIFORNIA	107	119	115	121	116	115	108	109	101	110	127	127	111	130	107	97	125	105	98	122
20620	CALLAWAY	105	131	139	131	129	127	117	117	108	116	136	136	124	145	120	105	136	112	104	129
20621	CHAPTICO	93	104	105	105	100	100	98	97	92	99	117	115	100	118	97	88	115	97	86	107
20622	CHARLOTTE HALL	111	137	147	137	135	135	124	123	116	123	145	143	131	154	127	113	145	119	112	136
20623	CHELTENHAM	139	162	162	167	156	152	146	145	134	149	170	169	152	174	144	126	168	140	125	159
20624	CLEMENTS	89	100	102	101	97	96	94	93	89	95	112	110	96	114	93	84	110	93	83	102
20625	COBB ISLAND	123	97	66	87	109	122	91	110	103	90	122	129	81	121	97	110	114	108	130	150
20626	COLTONS POINT	79	92	102	88	91	100	87	87	87	86	108	98	93	113	91	89	106	86	89	95
20628	DAMERON	89	88	82	87	90	97	87	90	88	86	108	103	87	111	87	88	104	88	91	102
20630	DRAYDEN	99	121	134	121	120	123	110	110	103	110	130	126	117	134	114	102	129	107	103	121
20632	FAULKNER	105	99	81	95	102	107	92	99	94	92	116	118	91	118	93	95	111	97	102	123
20634	GREAT MILLS	91	104	103	107	100	97	95	94	88	97	111	111	98	113	93	83	110	92	82	103
20636	HOLLYWOOD	104	124	128	124	122	121	112	112	105	112	132	131	118	139	114	102	131	108	101	125
20637	HUGHESVILLE	128	159	169	159	156	154	142	141	131	141	165	166	151	176	145	128	165	136	127	156
20639	HUNTINGTOWN	137	164	169	166	160	158	147	146	136	148	171	171	155	179	148	131	171	141	130	162
20640	INDIAN HEAD	89	99	106	98	97	101	97	95	94	95	118	110	100	122	97	92	116	94	90	104
20645	ISSUE	94	110	122	104	109	119	104	104	103	103	129	116	110	134	108	106	126	102	106	113
20646	LA PLATA	113	130	142	129	128	132	123	122	118	122	148	142	129	153	125	116	147	120	115	135
20650	LEONARDTOWN	108	120	122	118	120	125	110	113	107	110	133	131	114	137	113	106	131	110	109	129
20653	LEXINGTON PARK	90	91	100	97	88	90	92	89	89	95	113	106	93	110	89	84	111	91	80	99
20657	LUSBY	102	117	117	121	112	110	106	105	98	109	124	123	110	126	105	93	123	103	91	115
20658	MARBURY	96	117	129	114	114	117	108	107	103	107	130	124	115	138	111	102	129	104	100	117
20659	MECHANICSVILLE	99	116	119	117	113	112	106	106	99	107	125	124	110	129	106	95	124	103	94	116
20662	NANJEMOY	80	98	108	95	96	98	91	90	87	90	109	103	97	116	93	85	108	87	83	98
20664	NEWBURG	89	100	105	96	99	105	94	95	93	94	116	108	98	119	96	93	113	93	94	105
20667	PARK HALL	84	92	94	94	89	88	88	87	82	89	104	103	88	105	86	78	102	87	77	95
20670	PATUXENT RIVER	70	45	43	51	41	48	67	57	68	62	84	76	57	76	55	62	81	68	53	65
20674	PINEY POINT	99	116	138	118	114	118	111	109	106	111	133	128	116	136	113	103	132	109	101	119
20675	POMFRET	127	158	168	159	156	153	141	141	131	141	164	165	150	175	144	127	164	136	126	156
20676	PORT REPUBLIC	123	148	155	149	144	144	133	133	124	134	156	154	140	162	135	119	155	129	119	146
20677	PORT TOBACCO	123	151	165	150	149	152	137	137	128	136	161	157	145	168	141	126	160	132	127	150
20678	PRINCE FREDERICK	112	115	111	114	116	121	108	112	107	109	133	132	110	136	110	106	129	110	110	132
20680	RIDGE	93	82	68	80	87	97	82	89	87	81	106	101	79	106	83	90	100	87	97	107
20684	SAINT INIGOES	89	102	111	98	101	109	97	97	96	96	119	109	102	124	100	97	117	95	97	106
20685	SAINT LEONARD	113	131	135	132	127	127	121	120	112	121	142	140	125	145	121	108	140	117	107	132
20687	SCOTLAND	82	65	44	58	73	82	61	73	69	60	82	86	54	81	65	74	76	72	87	100
20688	SOLOMONS	111	108	112	107	112	127	104	112	106	108	133	119	105	118	109	109	126	111	122	126
20689	SUNDERLAND	122	151	160	152	148	146	135	135	125	135	157	158	144	167	138	121	157	130	120	149
20690	TALL TIMBERS	99	113	140	117	112	115	112	109	107	111	134	130	115	138	113	103	133	110	99	118
20692	VALLEY LEE	100	121	135	121	120	122	111	111	104	111	131	128	118	136	114	102	130	108	102	121
20693	WELCOME	103	126	139	123	123	126	116	115	111	115	140	133	124	148	119	110	139	112	107	125
20695	WHITE PLAINS	110	133	140	134	130	129	120	119	112	121	141	139	127	147	122	108	140	116	107	131
20701	ANNAPOLIS JUNCTION	101	91	71	88	92	97	87	93	88	89	109	108	82	104	86	88	104	93	94	112
20705	BELTSVILLE	106	111	128	116	108	112	112	109	107	114	136	128	113	134	110	103	134	111	98	120
20706	LANHAM	100	109	129	110	105	111	108	105	104	109	132	122	111	134	107	102	131	106	96	115
20707	LAUREL	102	101	115	107	98	103	107	102	103	107	131	122	106	127	103	98	128	106	93	113
20708	LAUREL	101	96	111	104	93	98	103	99	100	105	128	118	102	122	98	95	125	103	89	110
20710	BLADENSBURG	65	58	69	61	56	61	65	62	66	67	83	73	64	79	62	63	81	66	58	70
20711	LOTHIAN	116	110	91	107	110	115	104	110	104	107	129	128	100	123	103	102	124	109	108	130
20712	MOUNT RAINIER	66	60	77	63	58	63	70	65	70	69	89	78	68	87	66	67	87	70	61	72
20714	NORTH BEACH	98	108	113	111	106	106	105	103	99	105	125	122	106	126	103	94	123	103	92	113
20715	BOWIE	122	150	168	149	147	152	136	136	128	137	161	155	145	167	140	126	160	132	125	148
20716	BOWIE	126	140	144	146	135	133	131	129	122	134	155	152	134	155	128	115	153	127	113	142
20720	BOWIE	143	173	181	179	166	165	153	150	140	157	178	174	165	183	154	134	178	145	131	165
20721	BOWIE	163	195	210	202	189	190	176	172	161	179	205	200	188	210	177	155	205	167	153	190
20722	BRENTWOOD	74	75	86	73	73	81	75	75	77	78	98	82	78	96	76	78	96	76	75	83
20723	LAUREL	127	137	144	145	131	132	131	127	122	134	155	150	134	154	127	115	154	127	111	141
20724	LAUREL	124	133	132	139	128	127	126	125	118	130	150	147	127	148	122	111	147	124	109	137
20732	CHESAPEAKE BEACH	115	132	130	136	126	123	120	119	110	123	140	139	124	142	118	104	138	116	102	130
20733	CHURCHTON	107	129	134	128	127	127	116	117	109	115	137	136	122	144	119	107	136	113	107	130
20735	CLINTON	112	136	147	137	133	133	124	123	116	124	146	143	131	153	126	113	145	119	111	135
20736	OWINGS	128	155	161	157	151	149	139	139	129	140	163	163	147	171	141	124	162	134	123	153
20737	RIVERDALE	85	83	93	83	80	85	87	85	88	90	112	99	87	111	84	85	111	89	79	93
20740	COLLEGE PARK	90	88	109	91	86	93	103	92	99	98	125	113	100	123	97	94	122	98	86	102
20742	COLLEGE PARK	52	40	48	42	39	46	61	49	59	54	74	64	53	69	52	54	70	56	47	55
20743	CAPITOL HEIGHTS	80	77	87	73	74	85	79	78	84	82	105	86	82	103	79	86	103	80	82	89
20744	FORT WASHINGTON	127	154	176	154	150	153	142	140	134	142	168	163	150	176	145	131	168	137	127	153
20745	OXON HILL	79	76	90	76	74	83	81	78	83	82	105	89	82	102	80	83	102	81	79	88
20746	SUITLAND	83	77	89	78	74	83	82	80	85	85	107	92	83	103	80	84	104	83	79	91
20747	DISTRICT HEIGHTS	84	83	95	83	80	87	86	84	87	88	110	97	87	108	85	86	107	86	81	94
20748	TEMPLE HILLS	93	93	109	93	91	100	96	93	97	98	122	106	98	120	95	96	120	96	92	105
20751	DEALE	101	123	134	121	120	122	113	112	107	112	135	130	120	143	116	105	134	109	103	123
20754	DUNKIRK	140	173	187	175	169	171	154	153	143	155	180	177	166	188	158	139	181	148	139	169
20755	FORT GEORGE G MEADE	84	53	51	61	49	58	79	68	80	74	100	91	68	90	65	73	96	80	63	78
20758	FRIENDSHIP	127	154	173	153	153	159	140	141	132	141	167	159	150	169	146	131	165	137	133	153
20759	FULTON	205	255	277	263	247	249	225	219	204	228	260	253	247	271	229	198	263	211	194	242
20762	ANDREWS AFB	89	57	54	65	52	62	85	73	86	79	107	97	72	96	70	78	103	86	67	83
20763	SAVAGE	91	80	92	89	77	81	90	85	88	92	113	104	87	104	84	82	109	91	76	95
20764	SHADY SIDE	135	143	139	145	140	141	138	138	131	138	164	162	137	164	135	125	161	137	125	153
20769	GLENN DALE	134	161	170	163	158	157	145	145	135	147	170	168	153	176	148	131	169	141	130	159
20770	GREENBELT	93	89	105	95	86	92	98	92	95	98	121	111	96	116	93	90	118	97	84	102
20772	UPPER MARLBORO	129	145	150	148	140	140	135	134	127	137	161	158	139	163	134	121	159	132	119	148
	MARYLAND	108	114	128	115	112	119	113	111	111	114	139	129	116	140	113	109	137	112	106	124
	UNITED STATES	100	100	100	100	100	100	100	100	100	100	100	100	100	100	100	100	100	100	100	100

#	POST OFFICE NAME	COUNTY FIPS CODE	POPULATION			2000-2004 ANNUAL RATE		HOUSEHOLDS					FAMILIES		
			2000	2004	2009	% Rate	State Centile	2000	2004	2009	% Annual Rate 2000-2004	2004 Average HH Size	2000	2004	% Annual Rate 2000-2004
20774	UPPER MARLBORO	033	34211	36637	39196	1.6	65	12457	13319	14258	1.6	2.74	8935	9495	1.4
20776	HARWOOD	003	3146	3317	3581	1.3	54	1131	1191	1285	1.2	2.78	912	953	1.0
20777	HIGHLAND	027	3227	3213	3324	-0.1	17	1049	1055	1096	0.1	3.04	928	927	0.0
20778	WEST RIVER	003	2043	2202	2382	1.8	68	721	774	837	1.7	2.83	591	630	1.5
20779	TRACYS LANDING	003	895	889	923	-0.2	16	356	353	367	-0.2	2.52	245	242	-0.3
20781	HYATTSVILLE	033	12157	12183	12534	0.1	21	4220	4207	4320	-0.1	2.85	2717	2676	-0.4
20782	HYATTSVILLE	033	29381	29355	30452	0.0	18	11022	11022	11450	0.0	2.61	6817	6719	-0.3
20783	HYATTSVILLE	033	45796	49825	53805	2.0	74	14824	15959	17175	1.8	3.09	10068	10733	1.5
20784	HYATTSVILLE	033	24296	24917	26094	0.6	36	8430	8645	9058	0.6	2.87	5922	6023	0.4
20785	HYATTSVILLE	033	39956	40955	42813	0.6	36	13444	13835	14514	0.7	2.95	10265	10482	0.5
20794	JESSUP	027	13938	14358	14852	0.7	41	2785	2944	3128	1.3	2.76	1957	2046	1.1
20812	GLEN ECHO	031	242	230	238	-1.2	3	91	86	88	-1.3	2.67	64	60	-1.5
20814	BETHESDA	031	25539	26400	27919	0.8	43	12238	12624	13310	0.7	2.02	5917	6016	0.4
20815	CHEVY CHASE	031	27420	28794	30684	1.2	51	12266	13024	13925	1.4	2.19	7259	7484	0.7
20816	BETHESDA	031	15431	15446	16222	0.0	20	6193	6190	6483	0.0	2.48	4389	4346	-0.2
20817	BETHESDA	031	33500	34171	35975	0.5	31	12082	12299	12902	0.4	2.76	9585	9684	0.2
20818	CABIN JOHN	031	1253	1280	1335	0.5	33	514	524	544	0.5	2.44	384	387	0.2
20832	OLNEY	031	24027	26158	28548	2.0	75	7972	8598	9320	1.8	3.02	6585	7044	1.6
20833	BROOKEVILLE	031	6331	6751	7207	1.5	61	2045	2170	2305	1.4	3.10	1787	1886	1.3
20837	POOLESVILLE	031	5833	6220	6646	1.5	61	1873	1995	2126	1.5	3.11	1579	1673	1.4
20838	BARNESVILLE	031	207	223	239	1.8	68	67	72	77	1.7	3.07	51	55	1.8
20839	BEALLSVILLE	031	388	427	468	2.3	80	144	159	173	2.4	2.68	110	120	2.1
20841	BOYDS	031	4679	5863	6819	5.5	99	1675	2102	2440	5.5	2.79	1202	1481	5.0
20842	DICKERSON	031	1551	1674	1826	1.8	68	602	651	710	1.9	2.56	460	495	1.7
20850	ROCKVILLE	031	31718	37369	42496	3.9	97	11456	13583	15501	4.1	2.66	8106	9523	3.9
20851	ROCKVILLE	031	13034	13270	13950	0.4	29	4640	4724	4951	0.4	2.79	3212	3227	0.1
20852	ROCKVILLE	031	39158	42617	46524	2.0	75	17750	19334	21081	2.0	2.16	9761	10376	1.5
20853	ROCKVILLE	031	26298	26501	27877	0.2	24	9131	9172	9612	0.1	2.88	7287	7263	-0.1
20854	POTOMAC	031	48164	51020	54849	1.4	56	15618	16450	17603	1.2	3.05	13907	14601	1.2
20855	DERWOOD	031	15320	16255	17598	1.4	58	4987	5358	5849	1.7	3.01	4178	4462	1.6
20860	SANDY SPRING	031	2451	2493	2615	0.4	28	822	830	868	0.2	2.88	630	630	0.0
20861	ASHTON	031	1343	1337	1395	-0.1	16	491	487	506	-0.2	2.64	366	358	-0.5
20862	BRINKLOW	031	374	403	433	1.8	68	121	130	138	1.7	3.08	104	111	1.5
20866	BURTONSVILLE	031	11681	13074	14402	2.7	86	4123	4611	5067	2.7	2.81	2958	3270	2.4
20868	SPENCERVILLE	031	506	541	579	1.6	64	159	169	180	1.5	3.17	132	139	1.2
20871	CLARKSBURG	031	2911	3175	3448	2.1	77	1040	1132	1226	2.0	2.80	844	912	1.8
20872	DAMASCUS	031	11428	12454	13483	2.0	76	3802	4141	4470	2.0	3.00	3089	3341	1.9
20874	GERMANTOWN	031	47052	53481	59606	3.1	91	17842	20156	22331	2.9	2.65	12172	13589	2.6
20876	GERMANTOWN	031	20673	23392	25900	3.0	89	7134	8001	8804	2.7	2.92	5282	5870	2.5
20877	GAITHERSBURG	031	33237	34802	37149	1.1	50	11657	11999	12664	0.7	2.85	7683	7839	0.5
20878	GAITHERSBURG	031	54920	60425	66071	2.3	80	19104	20963	22862	2.2	2.88	14360	15559	1.9
20879	GAITHERSBURG	031	24970	26203	28198	1.1	51	8565	8947	9586	1.0	2.93	6154	6376	0.8
20882	GAITHERSBURG	031	14099	14944	15988	1.4	57	4384	4642	4952	1.4	3.21	3881	4093	1.3
20886	MONTGOMERY VILLAGE	031	28775	31518	34599	2.2	79	10940	11881	12959	2.0	2.64	7346	7888	1.7
20895	KENSINGTON	031	20258	20247	21193	0.0	18	7945	7925	8281	-0.1	2.49	5251	5176	-0.3
20901	SILVER SPRING	031	36457	37076	39035	0.4	28	13400	13519	14147	0.2	2.73	9084	9054	-0.1
20902	SILVER SPRING	031	43643	45601	48635	1.0	49	15364	15901	16848	0.8	2.85	10548	10796	0.6
20903	SILVER SPRING	031	17923	19721	21669	2.3	80	5537	5966	6472	1.8	3.30	4177	4452	1.5
20904	SILVER SPRING	031	48834	52628	57112	1.8	68	18070	19371	20921	1.7	2.70	12747	13533	1.4
20905	SILVER SPRING	031	17076	17756	18919	0.9	47	5440	5642	5989	0.9	3.14	4654	4803	0.7
20906	SILVER SPRING	031	60180	62452	66356	0.9	45	23370	24077	25443	0.7	2.57	14869	15128	0.4
20910	SILVER SPRING	031	36464	36641	38345	0.1	23	16683	16712	17426	0.0	2.16	8135	8000	-0.4
20912	TAKOMA PARK	031	24081	24303	25453	0.2	25	9206	9285	9701	0.2	2.56	5405	5360	-0.2
21001	ABERDEEN	025	19764	20447	21912	0.8	44	7745	8134	8822	1.2	2.50	5392	5586	0.8
21005	ABERDEEN PROVING GRO	025	3225	3684	4104	3.2	92	877	1022	1158	3.7	3.33	782	909	3.6
21009	ABINGDON	025	23406	27218	30977	3.6	96	8699	10299	11873	4.1	2.64	6397	7433	3.6
21010	GUNPOWDER	025	864	823	862	-1.1	3	230	218	229	-1.3	3.77	226	214	-1.3
21012	ARNOLD	003	21012	21484	22495	0.5	33	7491	7643	7998	0.5	2.78	5753	5833	0.3
21013	BALDWIN	005	5324	5432	5644	0.5	31	1815	1863	1945	0.6	2.92	1582	1617	0.5
21014	BEL AIR	025	33643	36686	40360	2.1	77	12461	13616	15085	2.1	2.65	9292	10144	2.1
21015	BEL AIR	025	24172	26435	29171	2.1	79	8448	9249	10257	2.2	2.86	6702	7303	2.0
21017	BELCAMP	025	6148	6923	7678	2.8	88	2331	2657	2981	3.1	2.56	1580	1786	2.9
21028	CHURCHVILLE	025	2487	2818	3148	3.0	90	929	1070	1211	3.4	2.63	767	876	3.2
21029	CLARKSVILLE	027	7892	9023	9936	3.2	93	2379	2682	2930	2.9	3.36	2168	2441	2.8
21030	COCKEYSVILLE	005	22725	24029	25301	1.3	55	10235	10857	11475	1.4	2.20	5351	5532	0.8
21031	HUNT VALLEY	005	62	102	135	12.4	100	1	2	3	17.7	2.50	1	1	0.0
21032	CROWNSVILLE	003	8398	8403	8709	0.0	19	3011	3006	3119	0.0	2.64	2283	2262	-0.2
21034	DARLINGTON	025	3267	3227	3405	-0.3	10	1230	1231	1314	0.0	2.61	941	934	-0.2
21035	DAVIDSONVILLE	003	7653	8018	8525	1.1	50	2559	2680	2850	1.1	2.99	2224	2319	1.0
21036	DAYTON	027	1567	1812	2012	3.6	95	499	585	651	3.8	3.09	448	522	3.7
21037	EDGEWATER	003	16461	17915	19317	2.0	75	6258	6808	7341	2.0	2.62	4466	4807	1.8
21040	EDGEWOOD	025	22350	23726	25915	1.4	58	8008	8560	9432	1.6	2.77	5950	6312	1.4
21042	ELLICOTT CITY	027	35045	36914	39255	1.2	53	11796	12506	13351	1.4	2.94	9991	10537	1.3
21043	ELLICOTT CITY	027	32140	35346	38351	2.3	79	12214	13377	14498	2.2	2.61	8341	9116	2.1
21044	COLUMBIA	027	40285	42624	45461	1.3	56	15990	16949	18121	1.4	2.46	10352	10825	1.1
21045	COLUMBIA	027	36727	38624	41232	1.2	52	13962	14815	15894	1.4	2.58	9758	10207	1.1
21046	COLUMBIA	027	14957	15474	16225	0.8	44	5879	6145	6477	1.1	2.50	3983	4091	0.6
21047	FALLSTON	025	10698	10905	11580	0.5	30	3703	3830	4117	0.8	2.85	3225	3319	0.7
21048	FINKSBURG	013	10211	11029	12201	1.8	69	3572	3887	4329	2.0	2.84	2966	3207	1.9
21050	FOREST HILL	025	14822	16497	18216	2.6	84	5181	5857	6552	2.9	2.79	4132	4625	2.7
21051	FORK	005	523	501	503	-1.0	4	186	178	179	-1.0	2.81	157	150	-1.1
21053	FREELAND	005	2955	3004	3062	0.4	28	1025	1044	1065	0.4	2.87	848	859	0.3
21054	GAMBRILLS	003	9288	10285	11191	2.4	83	3224	3555	3862	2.3	2.88	2539	2789	2.2
21056	GIBSON ISLAND	003	310	325	342	1.1	51	136	142	150	1.0	2.29	101	105	0.9
21057	GLEN ARM	005	4164	4264	4406	0.6	35	1497	1535	1593	0.6	2.55	1141	1156	0.3
21060	GLEN BURNIE	003	27199	27979	29483	0.7	39	10649	10940	11522	0.6	2.53	6998	7124	0.4
21061	GLEN BURNIE	003	47571	48397	51241	0.4	29	18959	19247	20365	0.4	2.50	12360	12365	0.0
21071	GLYNDON	005	351	350	355	-0.1	17	126	126	128	0.0	2.78	97	95	-0.5
21074	HAMPSTEAD	013	13316	14728	16373	2.4	83	4741	5252	5856	2.4	2.80	3715	4081	2.2
21075	ELKRIDGE	027	20512	22926	25184	2.7	85	7641	8464	9270	2.4	2.67	5391	5924	2.2
21076	HANOVER	003	8483	9965	11219	3.9	97	2934	3422	3844	3.7	2.90	2293	2656	3.5
21077	HARMANS	003	263	307	343	3.7	96	103	120	135	3.7	2.56	84	98	3.7
21078	HAVRE DE GRACE	025	15097	15757	17035	1.0	48	5999	6279	6837	1.1	2.48	3987	4167	1.0
21082	HYDES	005	564	575	590	0.5	30	202	206	211	0.5	2.79	171	174	0.4
21084	JARRETTSVILLE	025	6993	7451	8042	1.5	60	2347	2534	2766	1.8	2.94	2014	2162	1.7
	MARYLAND					1.1					1.1	2.60			1.0
	UNITED STATES					1.2					1.3	2.58			1.1

ZIP CODE #	POST OFFICE NAME	RACE (%) White 2000	White 2004	Black 2000	Black 2004	Asian/Pacific 2000	Asian/Pacific 2004	% Hispanic Origin 2000	% Hispanic Origin 2004	2004 AGE DISTRIBUTION (%) 0-4	5-9	10-14	15-19	20-24	25-44	45-64	65-84	85+	18+	MEDIAN AGE 2004	% 2004 Males	% 2004 Females
20774	UPPER MARLBORO	8.1	7.3	88.0	88.6	1.2	1.2	1.4	1.5	6.3	7.0	7.9	6.9	5.7	30.0	27.9	7.4	0.9	74.5	37.3	45.6	54.4
20776	HARWOOD	85.4	82.6	12.5	15.0	0.4	0.5	1.5	2.0	5.1	6.1	7.1	7.1	4.6	23.5	33.3	11.9	1.3	77.4	43.0	49.1	50.9
20777	HIGHLAND	90.1	88.1	2.9	3.5	5.3	6.5	1.3	1.7	6.6	8.3	9.2	7.0	3.5	21.2	32.7	10.6	1.0	71.2	42.0	49.7	50.3
20778	WEST RIVER	85.8	83.4	12.4	14.5	0.5	0.7	1.7	2.0	6.6	7.8	7.4	6.3	4.0	24.5	31.7	10.4	1.4	73.9	41.8	49.4	50.6
20779	TRACYS LANDING	93.0	91.8	4.9	5.7	0.3	0.3	0.5	0.7	3.8	5.0	6.3	5.5	3.8	23.7	33.9	16.2	1.8	81.6	45.9	50.1	49.9
20781	HYATTSVILLE	36.7	33.0	44.9	46.5	3.2	3.3	20.5	23.3	7.7	7.2	7.8	7.7	8.3	31.3	21.9	6.9	1.1	72.7	32.2	49.1	50.9
20782	HYATTSVILLE	26.1	24.4	54.7	53.9	3.9	4.1	18.2	21.1	7.5	6.8	6.7	6.1	7.9	32.7	21.5	9.2	1.7	75.3	33.6	47.9	52.2
20783	HYATTSVILLE	31.0	29.5	39.3	38.9	5.7	5.9	39.2	41.9	7.9	7.0	6.8	6.6	9.1	34.6	19.5	7.6	1.0	74.6	31.6	51.5	48.5
20784	HYATTSVILLE	21.0	19.1	69.3	70.3	2.8	3.0	8.2	9.2	7.5	7.3	8.5	7.7	7.3	29.2	24.2	7.5	0.8	72.1	34.0	48.0	52.0
20785	HYATTSVILLE	10.8	9.3	84.4	85.5	1.1	1.2	2.9	3.3	9.3	9.3	9.4	7.7	7.4	30.2	20.5	5.7	0.5	67.1	29.6	46.0	54.1
20794	JESSUP	50.7	47.7	45.3	47.7	1.8	2.1	1.8	2.3	3.9	4.2	4.7	5.0	9.4	47.1	21.0	4.3	0.4	84.4	35.4	66.1	33.9
20812	GLEN ECHO	94.2	92.6	1.7	2.2	2.5	3.0	1.7	2.2	7.8	8.7	6.5	4.8	3.0	28.7	30.9	8.3	1.3	73.9	41.1	50.0	50.0
20814	BETHESDA	84.5	81.8	3.5	3.9	7.6	8.9	6.2	7.9	5.4	5.5	4.6	4.0	4.9	34.3	24.8	13.1	3.5	82.0	39.7	47.3	52.7
20815	CHEVY CHASE	88.3	86.0	3.7	4.2	4.6	5.6	5.0	6.6	4.7	5.5	6.1	5.3	3.8	22.8	30.1	16.9	4.7	80.3	46.1	45.1	54.9
20816	BETHESDA	92.3	90.5	1.4	1.7	4.1	5.1	4.9	6.5	5.9	7.1	7.7	6.0	3.3	20.7	30.7	15.6	3.0	75.4	44.6	46.7	53.3
20817	BETHESDA	83.9	81.0	2.8	3.2	10.2	12.0	5.1	6.5	5.6	6.9	7.7	6.5	3.7	20.7	31.7	15.5	1.8	75.5	44.4	47.4	52.6
20818	CABIN JOHN	85.5	82.7	3.2	3.7	8.9	10.6	3.3	4.4	4.4	6.6	9.8	7.0	3.0	21.5	38.1	9.2	0.6	74.1	44.0	49.7	50.3
20832	OLNEY	77.9	73.9	9.8	11.3	8.1	9.7	5.3	6.6	7.5	8.3	8.8	7.4	4.9	27.4	28.5	6.4	0.8	70.5	37.1	48.0	52.0
20833	BROOKEVILLE	84.0	81.1	6.6	7.6	6.1	7.3	3.9	5.0	7.1	8.4	9.0	7.0	4.2	25.7	30.8	7.2	0.6	70.9	39.2	49.4	50.6
20837	POOLESVILLE	91.9	90.1	4.5	5.5	1.0	1.2	2.9	3.9	7.0	8.1	9.9	7.7	4.6	27.7	28.8	5.6	0.6	69.5	37.4	49.6	50.4
20838	BARNESVILLE	95.2	94.6	1.9	2.2	0.5	0.9	2.4	3.1	5.4	6.3	7.2	5.8	4.0	21.5	36.3	12.1	1.4	77.1	44.9	48.9	51.1
20839	BEALLSVILLE	84.3	82.0	12.1	13.8	1.0	1.4	2.6	2.8	5.9	7.3	8.2	6.1	3.0	26.5	30.4	11.2	1.4	74.0	41.7	50.4	49.7
20841	BOYDS	77.3	73.6	9.9	11.2	8.8	10.1	5.2	6.7	7.7	7.7	7.3	6.3	5.0	33.0	25.8	6.8	0.5	73.4	36.3	48.8	51.2
20842	DICKERSON	89.2	87.6	7.9	9.0	0.8	0.9	2.1	2.6	5.9	7.1	7.5	6.2	3.7	24.6	31.4	12.1	1.6	75.2	42.5	49.7	50.3
20850	ROCKVILLE	67.5	63.2	9.6	10.1	17.1	19.9	8.2	9.7	6.5	6.8	7.1	6.7	5.3	28.8	26.5	10.4	2.0	75.1	38.8	47.8	52.3
20851	ROCKVILLE	64.6	59.5	8.3	9.0	12.4	13.9	19.5	23.7	6.7	6.4	6.3	6.3	6.7	33.6	23.4	9.8	0.8	76.8	36.4	50.4	49.6
20852	ROCKVILLE	70.5	66.4	6.7	7.3	16.3	18.5	10.4	12.8	5.3	5.2	5.0	4.9	5.5	31.0	24.3	14.7	4.1	81.4	40.8	46.0	54.0
20853	ROCKVILLE	72.7	68.9	7.7	8.4	10.3	11.6	12.8	15.5	5.2	5.9	7.1	6.4	4.8	24.2	29.1	16.3	1.0	77.5	42.9	48.6	51.4
20854	POTOMAC	77.9	74.1	4.5	5.0	14.6	17.4	4.7	6.0	5.7	7.1	8.4	7.3	4.2	20.0	33.6	12.8	1.0	73.9	43.4	48.8	51.2
20855	DERWOOD	68.3	63.7	9.4	10.4	14.9	17.1	8.3	10.2	6.1	7.0	7.9	7.0	5.1	27.0	30.8	8.5	0.6	74.1	39.2	49.3	50.7
20860	SANDY SPRING	77.6	73.6	13.5	15.6	5.2	6.1	4.3	5.6	6.1	7.5	8.5	6.9	3.5	21.5	28.8	13.1	4.1	73.0	42.8	46.9	53.1
20861	ASHTON	83.5	80.3	9.7	11.4	4.0	4.7	3.5	4.6	5.5	7.0	8.5	6.7	3.3	20.3	28.7	15.3	4.9	74.5	44.3	47.1	52.9
20862	BRINKLOW	80.2	76.9	8.6	9.9	7.5	8.9	4.0	5.2	8.2	9.4	9.2	7.0	3.7	27.8	27.5	6.2	1.0	68.7	37.7	49.1	50.9
20866	BURTONSVILLE	45.8	40.6	32.2	35.1	17.0	18.5	5.3	6.3	7.5	7.6	8.3	6.5	6.0	35.1	23.5	5.0	0.7	72.4	34.6	46.8	53.2
20868	SPENCERVILLE	77.9	74.1	12.1	14.1	6.1	7.4	3.0	3.7	5.2	5.9	6.7	6.8	5.0	22.0	33.5	13.9	1.1	77.1	44.0	49.5	50.5
20871	CLARKSBURG	91.9	90.3	4.4	5.1	1.6	2.0	1.8	2.4	5.7	6.7	7.4	6.3	4.4	25.5	32.5	10.6	0.9	76.0	41.9	50.3	49.7
20872	DAMASCUS	89.5	87.1	4.8	5.7	2.2	2.6	4.2	5.6	8.0	8.4	8.9	7.9	6.0	28.5	25.4	6.2	0.6	69.5	35.0	48.6	51.5
20874	GERMANTOWN	64.8	60.2	17.4	19.0	9.8	11.5	9.2	11.2	9.1	8.5	7.6	6.1	6.3	38.5	20.4	3.4	0.2	71.0	32.5	48.5	51.5
20876	GERMANTOWN	59.8	55.3	17.2	18.3	15.4	17.6	9.5	11.4	9.0	8.6	8.6	7.2	6.3	35.5	20.5	4.0	0.3	69.3	32.2	48.9	51.1
20877	GAITHERSBURG	52.2	48.3	17.5	17.9	12.7	13.5	25.8	29.6	7.9	7.4	6.8	6.0	7.0	32.1	21.2	8.7	3.0	74.3	34.4	48.8	51.2
20878	GAITHERSBURG	65.8	61.6	9.0	9.6	18.5	20.9	9.0	10.8	7.3	7.8	8.1	6.9	5.9	31.1	27.3	5.2	0.4	72.3	35.8	49.1	50.9
20879	GAITHERSBURG	59.2	54.2	16.8	18.3	14.0	15.5	12.1	14.7	7.7	7.9	8.1	6.6	6.2	32.9	25.0	5.4	0.4	72.3	34.8	48.4	51.6
20882	GAITHERSBURG	88.1	85.6	5.4	6.4	3.9	4.8	3.0	4.0	7.0	8.3	9.2	7.5	4.4	25.1	30.7	7.1	0.7	70.5	39.2	49.8	50.2
20886	MONTGOMERY VILLAGE	60.6	56.1	17.8	19.4	12.3	13.4	12.6	15.1	7.7	7.4	7.1	6.2	6.6	33.6	24.1	6.6	0.8	74.0	34.7	47.6	52.4
20895	KENSINGTON	81.3	78.0	6.4	7.2	5.3	6.1	9.6	12.2	6.6	6.9	6.6	5.2	4.2	26.4	27.1	14.2	2.9	76.4	41.6	47.5	52.5
20901	SILVER SPRING	51.6	47.7	25.0	25.9	8.7	9.4	17.7	20.7	7.4	7.2	6.9	6.3	6.3	31.1	23.9	9.2	1.7	74.5	36.3	48.5	51.6
20902	SILVER SPRING	54.3	50.0	18.6	19.4	9.5	10.3	23.7	27.3	7.2	7.1	6.9	6.2	6.1	29.6	23.7	11.6	1.8	74.9	37.0	48.6	51.4
20903	SILVER SPRING	33.0	30.4	29.4	28.6	13.6	14.0	35.6	39.8	8.1	7.6	8.0	7.0	8.4	32.4	19.8	7.8	1.0	72.2	31.4	50.2	49.8
20904	SILVER SPRING	40.3	36.0	36.5	38.6	15.4	16.6	8.8	10.0	6.6	6.5	7.0	6.7	7.3	30.6	24.7	9.6	1.1	75.7	35.7	46.6	53.4
20905	SILVER SPRING	61.2	56.9	18.5	20.2	15.6	17.5	4.3	5.2	5.3	6.4	8.2	7.8	5.3	22.8	32.9	10.4	1.0	75.0	41.6	49.3	50.7
20906	SILVER SPRING	52.4	48.3	23.0	24.2	11.7	12.7	17.2	20.1	6.1	6.0	6.3	5.9	6.0	27.9	23.0	14.7	4.0	78.0	39.7	46.0	54.0
20910	SILVER SPRING	50.7	46.9	32.8	34.5	5.8	6.4	13.4	15.6	5.6	5.4	5.5	5.4	7.1	35.2	24.4	8.8	2.6	80.2	36.7	46.9	53.1
20912	TAKOMA PARK	42.6	40.4	35.0	35.2	4.8	5.0	21.6	24.0	7.1	6.6	6.8	6.5	7.8	33.4	23.9	6.7	1.1	75.8	34.8	48.3	51.8
21001	ABERDEEN	70.4	66.6	23.3	26.2	2.1	2.4	2.9	3.4	7.0	6.6	7.2	6.5	7.1	26.1	26.2	12.2	1.2	75.3	38.2	47.9	52.1
21005	ABERDEEN PROVING GRO	50.9	46.3	34.4	37.3	4.3	4.5	11.0	12.7	12.4	11.3	12.1	6.5	11.1	40.6	5.4	0.5	0.1	59.9	23.4	52.9	47.1
21009	ABINGDON	87.9	85.3	7.2	8.6	2.4	2.9	2.2	2.9	9.8	9.3	7.6	5.6	4.9	36.6	20.1	5.7	0.6	69.8	33.4	49.3	50.7
21010	GUNPOWDER	58.1	53.3	30.9	34.0	3.2	3.7	8.5	9.8	14.8	13.6	14.8	7.7	6.6	38.6	3.8	0.1	0.0	50.9	19.4	50.3	49.7
21012	ARNOLD	92.3	90.8	4.1	4.8	1.5	1.9	1.8	2.4	6.5	7.4	7.7	6.9	4.8	27.7	29.3	8.8	0.9	73.9	39.0	48.4	51.6
21013	BALDWIN	97.5	97.0	0.4	0.4	1.2	1.5	1.0	1.4	4.7	6.4	8.3	7.2	4.2	19.7	36.1	12.2	1.3	75.8	44.7	48.9	51.1
21014	BEL AIR	94.1	93.0	2.9	3.4	1.7	2.1	1.2	1.5	6.4	6.8	8.0	7.5	5.9	27.1	26.5	10.4	1.4	73.9	38.3	48.6	51.4
21015	BEL AIR	93.4	92.0	3.4	4.1	1.8	2.2	1.5	1.9	7.5	7.7	8.1	6.8	5.5	28.7	26.0	8.9	0.8	72.4	37.2	48.8	51.2
21017	BELCAMP	79.8	76.4	15.1	17.5	1.6	2.0	3.2	4.0	9.6	9.0	8.1	5.4	5.5	39.4	18.4	3.8	0.8	69.8	32.3	47.4	52.6
21028	CHURCHVILLE	95.5	94.5	2.1	2.6	1.5	1.9	1.5	1.9	4.9	5.8	7.0	6.4	4.7	21.5	33.7	14.6	1.4	78.3	44.8	50.0	50.0
21029	CLARKSVILLE	81.6	77.8	4.8	5.6	11.3	13.8	1.9	2.4	8.8	10.3	10.2	6.6	2.9	27.7	26.1	6.6	0.7	65.9	37.1	50.3	49.7
21030	COCKEYSVILLE	81.1	77.2	7.1	8.7	9.0	10.7	2.9	3.6	4.8	4.9	5.6	6.3	9.3	32.7	24.2	10.6	1.6	81.2	36.1	48.1	51.9
21031	HUNT VALLEY	90.3	87.3	6.5	7.8	3.2	4.9	0.0	1.0	2.0	2.0	2.9	4.9	7.8	15.7	20.6	18.6	25.5	89.2	62.0	47.1	52.9
21032	CROWNSVILLE	89.3	87.6	7.8	8.9	1.1	1.3	1.4	1.8	5.3	5.8	6.6	5.3	4.0	29.1	33.1	9.7	1.0	79.1	41.9	50.6	49.4
21034	DARLINGTON	93.5	92.4	4.7	5.6	0.3	0.3	0.9	1.1	5.1	5.8	7.1	6.6	4.9	25.5	30.1	13.3	1.5	77.6	42.1	51.1	48.9
21035	DAVIDSONVILLE	94.2	93.2	3.2	3.6	1.2	1.5	1.7	2.1	5.6	6.9	7.8	6.5	4.0	22.6	34.8	10.8	1.0	75.4	43.1	50.7	49.4
21036	DAYTON	91.5	89.8	3.3	3.9	3.3	4.0	2.2	2.8	6.8	8.5	9.5	7.2	4.2	22.4	31.7	8.3	1.3	69.8	40.6	50.1	49.9
21037	EDGEWATER	94.0	92.9	3.4	3.9	0.6	0.7	2.6	3.3	6.3	6.6	6.3	5.7	4.6	29.7	28.4	11.1	1.4	77.4	40.3	49.8	50.2
21040	EDGEWOOD	68.9	65.4	25.1	27.7	1.6	1.9	3.2	3.8	8.6	8.2	8.4	7.7	7.9	29.7	22.4	6.7	0.5	70.1	31.9	48.0	52.0
21042	ELLICOTT CITY	82.5	79.2	4.5	5.3	11.2	13.3	1.6	2.0	5.3	7.2	9.1	7.8	4.7	21.7	33.4	9.7	1.1	73.1	41.8	49.3	50.7
21043	ELLICOTT CITY	76.0	72.7	10.0	11.3	10.9	12.5	2.7	3.3	8.3	8.5	8.1	5.9	5.1	34.0	21.7	7.0	1.4	71.1	35.2	48.8	51.2
21044	COLUMBIA	67.0	63.1	20.8	22.6	7.8	9.1	3.8	4.6	6.4	6.6	7.1	6.0	5.5	32.2	26.1	8.3	1.9	75.7	37.4	47.7	52.3
21045	COLUMBIA	61.4	57.2	26.2	28.6	6.9	7.9	5.2	6.1	7.4	7.3	7.2	6.4	6.4	32.4	25.9	6.5	0.7	73.9	35.4	48.5	51.5
21046	COLUMBIA	73.6	69.6	16.2	18.4	6.3	7.4	2.7	3.4	6.9	7.1	7.4	6.8	6.9	33.9	25.9	4.6	0.5	73.9	34.8	48.8	51.2
21047	FALLSTON	97.2	96.6	0.9	1.0	1.1	1.4	0.9	1.2	4.8	5.9	7.5	7.0	4.6	21.1	34.7	13.2	1.3	77.3	44.5	49.7	50.3
21048	FINKSBURG	97.6	97.1	0.8	1.0	0.6	0.7	0.6	0.8	6.2	7.2	8.0	6.7	4.3	25.0	30.6	11.1	1.0	74.4	41.2	50.6	49.4
21050	FOREST HILL	95.7	94.7	2.3	2.7	1.0	1.3	0.9	1.1	6.8	7.3	8.3	7.0	5.2	26.7	27.0	10.1	1.6	72.8	38.8	48.7	51.3
21051	FORK	97.7	97.4	0.8	1.0	0.6	0.6	1.2	1.2	3.2	4.8	8.0	6.2	3.6	19.4	35.1	17.2	2.6	79.0	47.9	51.7	48.3
21053	FREELAND	97.7	97.0	0.5	0.7	0.8	1.0	0.4	0.5	5.4	7.4	8.2	6.5	4.2	24.9	33.1	9.6	0.8	74.6	41.6	49.6	50.4
21054	GAMBRILLS	87.4	85.4	7.8	8.9	2.3	2.7	2.0	2.4	6.8	7.1	7.1	6.1	5.2	31.5	28.4	7.3	0.6	75.1	37.2	49.0	51.1
21056	GIBSON ISLAND	98.4	98.2	0.3	0.3	1.0	0.9	1.0	0.9	4.0	5.2	5.5	4.3	3.4	20.3	34.5	20.6	2.2	82.8	49.7	49.2	50.8
21057	GLEN ARM	89.8	88.1	6.6	7.5	2.3	2.8	1.1	1.3	4.3	5.2	6.4	13.0	3.9	17.1	29.9	16.7	3.6	74.6	45.2	51.6	48.4
21060	GLEN BURNIE	81.9	79.4	13.1	14.8	2.1	2.5	2.1	2.6	6.2	6.1	6.5	6.0	6.3	30.8	24.6	12.2	1.3	77.6	38.1	48.7	51.4
21061	GLEN BURNIE	76.6	73.1	15.6	17.7	4.0	4.8	3.1	3.8	6.9	6.5	6.8	6.5	7.2	32.5	22.3	10.2	1.0	75.8	34.9	48.8	51.2
21071	GLYNDON	93.2	91.4	2.0	2.6	2.9	3.7	0.6	0.9	7.1	8.6	9.1	6.0	3.7	26.3	28.3	9.7	1.1	71.4	39.7	51.4	48.6
21074	HAMPSTEAD	97.8	97.3	0.7	0.8	0.6	0.7	0.8	1.1	7.4	7.8	8.4	6.6	5.0	29.0	25.3	9.4	1.1	72.1	37.3	48.9	51.1
21075	ELKRIDGE	79.5	76.3	10.9	12.5	6.3	7.2	2.3	2.8	9.4	9.1	7.7	6.0	5.2	38.7	18.4	5.1	0.5	69.8	33.4	49.4	50.6
21076	HANOVER	74.9	71.9	17.3	19.0	3.7	4.3	3.1	3.7	6.2	6.8	7.6	6.5	5.1	29.7	28.4	8.8	1.0	75.1	38.8	50.2	49.8
21077	HARMANS	66.5	62.2	24.0	26.7	4.6	5.2	3.4	3.9	6.5	6.8	7.5	6.5	5.2	31.3	29.6	6.2	0.3	75.2	37.4	50.2	49.8
21078	HAVRE DE GRACE	82.3	79.9	13.5	15.0	1.4	1.7	1.8	2.2	6.9	6.9	7.2	6.5	6.1	27.2	25.8	12.1	1.4	75.0	38.7	48.4	51.6
21082	HYDES	98.1	97.7	0.4	0.5	0.5	0.7	1.6	2.1	5.0	6.1	7.7	7.0	4.5	20.0	33.6	14.3	1.9	76.5	44.8	48.5	51.5
21084	JARRETTSVILLE	96.6	95.9	1.9	2.3	0.5	0.6	0.7	0.9	5.2	6.3	8.1	7.7	5.0	24.3	32.5	10.2	0.9	75.4	41.6	50.4	49.6
	MARYLAND	64.0	61.8	27.9	28.9	4.0	4.6	4.3	5.1	6.6	6.7	7.3	6.9	6.6	29.1	25.1	10.2	1.5	75.2	37.0	48.3	51.7
	UNITED STATES	75.1	73.6	12.3	12.5	3.8	4.2	12.5	14.1	6.9	6.7	7.2	7.0	7.3	28.6	23.8	10.8	1.7	75.1	36.0	49.1	50.9

ZIP CODE #	POST OFFICE NAME	2004 Per Capita Income	2004 HH Income Base	2004 HOUSEHOLD INCOME DISTRIBUTION (%) Less than $25,000	$25,000 to $49,999	$50,000 to $99,999	$100,000 to $149,999	$150,000 or More	MEDIAN HOUSEHOLD INCOME 2004	2009	2004 National Centile	2004 State Centile	2004 Home Value Base	2004 HOME VALUE DISTRIBUTION (%) Less than $50,000	$50,000 to $89,999	$90,000 to $174,999	$175,000 to $399,999	$400,000 or More	2004 Median Home Value
20774	UPPER MARLBORO	32751	13319	7.3	17.4	42.4	23.8	9.1	77497	88245	94	77	10800	0.7	1.4	18.2	72.5	7.2	234292
20776	HARWOOD	43527	1191	13.9	14.3	31.3	19.2	21.2	83340	100597	96	85	1075	11.1	3.4	5.5	41.9	38.1	325000
20777	HIGHLAND	53167	1055	2.5	7.2	21.9	25.2	43.2	132916	152792	100	99	1017	0.0	0.0	0.4	31.1	68.5	484152
20778	WEST RIVER	38410	774	15.6	8.5	33.2	21.7	20.9	86352	103554	97	88	710	0.0	0.0	5.5	54.5	40.0	354777
20779	TRACYS LANDING	39127	353	5.4	15.9	43.3	22.1	13.3	79128	98590	95	80	307	0.0	1.3	13.7	55.1	30.0	309559
20781	HYATTSVILLE	20163	4207	20.6	30.3	36.6	10.4	2.1	49099	55562	70	32	2269	0.8	4.6	33.8	60.5	0.4	189232
20782	HYATTSVILLE	23198	11022	19.9	32.2	33.2	10.2	4.5	48094	54034	69	28	5009	1.1	2.0	21.8	69.5	5.7	213562
20783	HYATTSVILLE	19477	15959	19.4	31.7	34.8	10.5	3.7	49033	55046	70	31	7603	1.9	8.9	19.7	67.3	2.3	212222
20784	HYATTSVILLE	22576	8645	14.3	29.0	40.1	13.6	3.0	56166	63988	81	45	5667	0.8	4.1	32.5	61.8	0.9	191570
20785	HYATTSVILLE	19154	13835	22.1	30.1	34.5	10.8	2.5	47659	54071	68	28	7549	0.9	1.3	49.0	47.3	1.5	172762
20794	JESSUP	22810	2944	11.1	18.9	44.0	21.0	5.1	69585	83250	91	67	2236	5.9	4.2	18.4	67.7	3.9	206593
20812	GLEN ECHO	64455	86	0.0	7.0	19.8	26.7	46.5	143134	173859	100	100	76	0.0	0.0	0.0	10.5	89.5	633333
20814	BETHESDA	62749	12624	9.8	14.2	30.7	20.4	24.8	90316	114497	97	89	7308	0.4	0.6	12.0	28.1	59.0	441977
20815	CHEVY CHASE	84532	13024	7.1	11.8	25.6	19.1	36.4	111886	140948	99	96	8578	0.1	0.2	6.4	19.0	74.3	625843
20816	BETHESDA	80158	6190	4.3	6.2	22.3	19.0	48.2	144097	178325	100	100	5383	0.1	0.1	2.4	12.3	85.1	641520
20817	BETHESDA	77210	12299	4.0	6.5	19.7	24.3	45.4	139513	169939	100	99	11081	0.2	0.4	1.3	15.1	83.1	602148
20818	CABIN JOHN	81034	524	5.3	8.6	21.0	21.4	43.7	134318	165405	100	99	477	0.0	0.0	0.4	22.0	77.6	579354
20832	OLNEY	40261	8598	4.3	10.8	32.8	28.2	23.9	102466	125246	98	94	7851	0.5	0.1	7.7	56.8	34.9	349032
20833	BROOKEVILLE	50213	2170	4.4	7.4	27.0	29.0	32.3	117120	141761	99	97	2065	0.1	0.0	2.3	41.0	56.6	432734
20837	POOLESVILLE	36109	1995	5.5	12.7	35.6	26.5	19.7	93378	113829	97	90	1820	0.0	0.2	13.1	52.3	34.5	305667
20838	BARNESVILLE	49128	72	11.1	6.9	18.1	26.4	37.5	122158	148600	99	98	65	0.0	0.0	0.0	30.8	69.2	570313
20839	BEALLSVILLE	45263	159	10.7	14.5	26.4	23.3	25.2	96544	117879	98	92	133	0.8	0.8	6.0	36.1	56.4	431481
20841	BOYDS	37798	2102	7.0	12.4	36.6	28.1	15.9	89583	110331	97	89	1592	0.2	0.6	8.9	57.2	33.2	299153
20842	DICKERSON	49262	651	11.7	13.7	24.1	23.4	27.2	100760	125000	98	94	563	0.9	0.4	4.1	36.6	58.1	452907
20850	ROCKVILLE	44088	13583	9.7	13.6	31.2	21.0	24.5	90394	114737	97	89	10216	1.1	0.5	9.7	42.7	46.0	375854
20851	ROCKVILLE	27927	4724	11.5	20.6	41.0	20.7	6.2	67679	82868	90	64	3162	0.3	0.2	6.2	90.6	2.8	231266
20852	ROCKVILLE	49777	19334	15.2	18.4	30.1	18.0	18.3	74868	93806	93	73	10136	0.4	2.3	14.8	46.0	36.6	300874
20853	ROCKVILLE	40859	9172	5.7	12.9	34.5	26.2	20.7	94360	115615	98	91	8337	0.3	0.3	3.9	69.3	26.3	300227
20854	POTOMAC	78825	16450	3.3	4.4	16.9	20.9	54.5	159749	193374	100	100	15460	0.4	0.3	0.9	11.1	87.3	675316
20855	DERWOOD	40540	5358	6.7	11.3	29.1	26.3	26.7	104114	127468	98	94	4613	0.7	0.0	6.0	56.9	36.4	357819
20860	SANDY SPRING	41682	830	6.1	15.3	28.9	22.2	27.5	99156	128188	98	93	730	0.0	0.0	3.4	48.0	48.6	393243
20861	ASHTON	44055	487	6.4	16.0	29.4	21.2	27.1	96007	125825	98	91	425	0.0	0.0	2.8	46.1	51.1	406081
20862	BRINKLOW	57812	130	4.6	7.7	23.9	26.2	37.7	125000	148309	99	98	122	0.0	0.0	2.5	19.7	77.9	551020
20866	BURTONSVILLE	32334	4611	6.7	17.1	43.6	20.9	11.7	78869	95342	95	80	3329	1.1	0.0	11.7	77.9	9.3	237255
20868	SPENCERVILLE	43838	169	4.7	14.2	33.1	20.1	27.8	95723	126148	98	91	156	0.0	0.0	3.2	56.4	40.4	363415
20871	CLARKSBURG	45031	1132	5.4	9.1	29.1	32.0	24.5	107116	129988	99	95	1030	0.0	0.0	1.8	61.9	36.3	342915
20872	DAMASCUS	30033	4141	9.3	18.2	38.7	23.6	10.2	78459	96939	95	79	3627	0.8	0.4	16.4	64.1	18.2	270614
20874	GERMANTOWN	35015	20156	7.4	19.3	42.6	20.0	10.7	73528	89231	93	72	13907	0.6	0.9	31.6	52.8	14.1	212137
20876	GERMANTOWN	32984	8001	7.6	15.9	38.9	25.7	12.0	81897	102479	96	82	6074	4.0	1.2	17.0	52.7	25.1	272684
20877	GAITHERSBURG	26651	11999	14.7	24.7	35.7	16.8	8.1	60263	74070	85	51	5832	0.7	4.5	18.7	63.1	12.9	255074
20878	GAITHERSBURG	42940	20963	5.9	13.8	32.2	23.7	24.4	96071	118406	98	92	15472	1.1	1.8	8.5	44.9	43.8	365504
20879	GAITHERSBURG	32505	8947	6.4	17.5	41.9	22.8	11.5	78321	94997	95	78	6722	0.9	1.6	22.6	67.1	7.7	227302
20882	GAITHERSBURG	46564	4642	3.4	9.0	29.6	25.4	32.6	113395	139620	99	96	4417	0.2	0.3	3.8	43.4	52.3	413512
20886	MONTGOMERY VILLAGE	34405	11881	8.6	19.5	40.2	19.4	12.2	73856	90058	93	73	8464	0.3	2.3	35.6	52.9	8.9	198284
20895	KENSINGTON	45812	7925	9.0	13.5	30.3	23.6	23.6	93803	117468	98	90	6407	0.3	0.4	5.9	56.0	37.5	343850
20901	SILVER SPRING	32147	13519	11.4	19.8	37.1	19.4	12.3	71561	87299	92	68	9190	0.5	1.8	6.3	84.5	6.8	264515
20902	SILVER SPRING	30599	15901	13.5	20.3	36.7	18.3	11.2	68468	83313	91	65	10991	0.2	1.4	12.5	78.2	7.7	252076
20903	SILVER SPRING	20587	5966	18.9	28.4	32.5	12.9	7.3	52472	62346	76	38	2917	1.5	1.1	9.7	74.4	13.3	264411
20904	SILVER SPRING	33084	19371	10.9	21.5	37.3	17.5	12.9	68130	82699	90	65	11277	0.9	1.0	8.9	67.0	22.2	294415
20905	SILVER SPRING	42115	5642	4.7	10.7	30.5	25.0	29.1	106093	130410	99	95	5205	0.7	0.3	4.0	53.7	41.3	372779
20906	SILVER SPRING	30232	24077	15.4	22.7	37.8	15.0	9.1	61920	75083	86	54	16704	1.1	2.7	16.0	67.6	12.6	241273
20910	SILVER SPRING	35935	16712	15.8	25.3	34.6	14.1	10.3	57841	72237	83	48	6383	0.5	1.8	10.1	61.5	26.1	302652
20912	TAKOMA PARK	28468	9285	19.6	28.3	31.8	11.7	8.6	51807	63648	75	36	4082	0.2	0.8	6.7	69.8	22.5	273472
21001	ABERDEEN	22113	8134	25.3	28.7	34.1	9.2	2.8	45447	51783	62	23	5481	10.2	4.9	48.6	33.9	2.3	149051
21005	ABERDEEN PROVING GRO	14801	1022	12.6	48.7	33.9	4.0	0.8	43120	48511	56	20	100	44.0	26.0	10.0	14.0	6.0	54000
21009	ABINGDON	29543	10299	9.1	21.2	44.8	19.1	5.8	69558	77862	91	67	8408	1.0	0.3	41.5	54.4	2.8	186571
21010	GUNPOWDER	15480	218	4.6	45.9	39.0	10.6	0.0	49783	56785	72	33	8	0.0	0.0	100.0	0.0	0.0	125000
21012	ARNOLD	36360	7643	7.6	16.0	37.1	24.2	15.0	84085	99202	96	86	6695	0.5	0.3	18.0	62.6	18.6	249306
21013	BALDWIN	40970	1863	6.8	14.4	30.3	24.9	23.6	96878	114854	98	93	1757	0.2	0.0	4.2	60.2	35.5	350098
21014	BEL AIR	30960	13616	12.0	20.2	39.5	20.4	7.9	69259	80032	91	66	11208	0.8	0.9	24.1	67.1	7.1	224401
21015	BEL AIR	30431	9249	8.6	21.2	41.8	18.3	10.1	69728	80487	91	67	8075	1.1	1.1	26.9	61.2	9.8	216061
21017	BELCAMP	26044	2657	7.3	24.1	54.7	12.7	1.2	61220	68297	86	53	1930	0.8	1.3	64.8	32.2	0.9	148220
21028	CHURCHVILLE	35201	1070	9.2	20.1	39.8	19.1	11.9	71647	82835	92	69	976	0.6	0.8	13.4	70.7	14.5	256000
21029	CLARKSVILLE	51258	2682	2.1	3.5	23.6	28.6	42.2	134124	155040	100	99	2579	0.3	0.2	0.5	26.4	72.6	490576
21030	COCKEYSVILLE	37921	10857	15.0	32.1	30.2	12.0	10.7	53068	60692	77	39	4770	1.1	0.6	14.5	66.7	17.2	242571
21031	HUNT VALLEY	5276	2	100.0	0.0	0.0	0.0	0.0	12500	16902	1	0	0	0.0	0.0	0.0	0.0	0.0	0
21032	CROWNSVILLE	47139	3006	5.6	16.2	29.6	23.6	25.0	96886	113979	98	93	2696	1.5	1.1	10.8	54.4	32.2	285467
21034	DARLINGTON	25729	1231	17.5	31.9	34.0	11.1	5.5	50589	58072	73	35	1024	4.4	4.9	32.8	44.2	13.7	195876
21035	DAVIDSONVILLE	49824	2680	6.5	11.6	26.5	25.8	29.6	108274	128983	99	96	2527	2.4	1.0	1.4	38.9	56.4	440025
21036	DAYTON	47970	585	4.3	9.2	24.1	32.0	30.4	117121	134979	99	97	547	2.7	0.0	0.6	25.2	71.5	491085
21037	EDGEWATER	37169	6808	8.5	18.8	42.3	19.3	11.1	73313	84682	93	72	5885	0.6	0.2	18.4	60.6	20.2	231702
21040	EDGEWOOD	21196	8560	18.6	27.8	41.9	9.5	2.2	52463	59872	76	38	5834	6.7	9.0	60.0	22.3	2.0	135039
21042	ELLICOTT CITY	43870	12506	5.3	11.4	29.7	25.7	27.9	104949	123619	99	94	11182	0.4	0.3	4.6	53.1	41.6	373282
21043	ELLICOTT CITY	36679	13377	10.2	18.3	35.9	22.2	13.5	77389	93545	94	76	9271	0.6	0.4	9.7	69.8	19.5	273718
21044	COLUMBIA	41004	16949	10.0	17.8	33.5	22.0	16.7	80051	98444	95	80	11324	0.3	3.0	18.1	57.4	21.2	255946
21045	COLUMBIA	34857	14815	9.9	16.3	38.5	23.3	12.0	77492	92245	94	77	10558	0.6	3.2	19.5	73.4	3.4	219316
21046	COLUMBIA	40002	6145	5.5	11.9	45.0	23.3	14.4	83007	101286	96	84	4095	0.3	0.7	19.7	73.5	5.9	244065
21047	FALLSTON	36086	3830	8.0	15.1	35.5	25.5	15.9	86142	102582	96	87	3613	0.2	0.2	5.6	74.5	19.5	283974
21048	FINKSBURG	29516	3887	10.0	18.2	43.2	20.8	7.9	73355	82656	93	72	3588	4.6	1.3	10.1	70.2	13.8	243420
21050	FOREST HILL	33373	5857	9.7	19.2	41.6	20.6	8.9	72808	82717	92	71	4966	1.2	0.2	14.4	70.2	13.9	251247
21051	FORK	31428	178	6.2	23.6	34.8	24.7	10.7	82013	100932	96	82	171	0.0	0.0	2.9	73.7	23.4	285156
21053	FREELAND	29055	1044	11.6	18.3	42.6	20.2	7.3	72152	83297	92	70	944	0.0	0.3	18.0	66.2	15.5	264706
21054	GAMBRILLS	36021	3555	4.8	15.2	40.5	24.5	15.0	83662	97368	96	86	3108	0.3	0.0	18.8	63.9	16.9	230175
21056	GIBSON ISLAND	53346	142	8.5	17.6	28.2	26.1	19.7	89099	106214	97	88	130	1.5	0.0	5.4	40.8	52.3	427273
21057	GLEN ARM	46660	1535	11.2	16.6	31.1	18.8	22.4	84011	103970	96	86	1364	0.4	1.3	7.0	56.2	35.2	339339
21060	GLEN BURNIE	23643	10940	19.1	28.7	39.0	10.8	2.5	51825	60824	75	37	7867	0.7	1.4	56.1	39.3	2.5	166617
21061	GLEN BURNIE	23847	19247	18.7	30.3	37.7	11.0	2.3	50710	57931	73	35	11448	0.6	1.2	46.8	50.8	0.7	176514
21071	GLYNDON	40928	126	4.0	13.5	44.4	20.6	17.5	85118	105350	96	87	113	0.0	0.0	30.1	51.3	18.6	279545
21074	HAMPSTEAD	26413	5252	13.0	21.0	43.0	17.1	6.0	64286	74097	88	60	4578	1.0	0.2	25.8	64.0	9.1	215627
21075	ELKRIDGE	31532	8464	10.1	19.9	41.5	19.7	8.8	71785	84322	92	69	6654	12.7	3.0	20.8	54.5	9.1	210101
21076	HANOVER	31901	3422	7.5	19.3	41.2	22.4	9.6	77260	88561	94	76	3077	12.0	4.1	12.3	68.5	3.2	213187
21077	HARMANS	40165	120	3.3	20.0	41.7	24.2	10.8	82247	94893	96	83	111	12.6	1.8	8.1	75.7	1.8	209559
21078	HAVRE DE GRACE	26400	6279	21.1	27.1	35.4	11.9	4.5	51913	59839	75	37	4220	2.4	3.0	35.7	53.7	5.3	192966
21082	HYDES	37366	206	7.8	17.5	34.5	24.3	16.0	85927	103896	96	87	194	0.0	0.0	3.1	67.5	29.4	329825
21084	JARRETTSVILLE	28837	2534	9.4	19.7	41.7	20.8	8.3	73076	83218	92	71	2354	0.2	0.8	9.5	70.8	18.7	261688
	MARYLAND	30267		17.9	23.3	34.6	15.0	9.2	59732	70285				2.9	5.4	28.1	49.8	13.8	209514
	UNITED STATES	25866		24.7	27.1	30.8	10.9	6.5	48124	56710				10.9	15.0	33.7	30.1	10.4	145905

ZIP CODE		FINANCIAL SERVICES				THE HOME						ENTERTAINMENT						PERSONAL			
						Home Improvements		Furnishings													
#	POST OFFICE NAME	Auto Loan	Home Loan	Investments	Retirement Plans	Home Repair	Lawn & Garden	Computers & Hardware	Major Appliances	TV, Radio, Sound Equipment	Furniture	Dine out/ Carry out	Sports Equipment	Fees & Tickets	Toys & Games	Travel	Cable TV	Apparel & Services	Auto Repairs	Health Insurance	Pets & Supplies
20774	UPPER MARLBORO	124	137	145	141	133	134	130	128	122	132	155	150	133	155	128	117	153	127	114	141
20776	HARWOOD	157	194	210	195	191	192	174	173	162	174	204	201	186	214	179	158	204	167	157	191
20777	HIGHLAND	213	266	289	274	257	259	234	228	213	237	271	264	257	282	238	206	273	220	203	252
20778	WEST RIVER	142	177	190	180	173	172	157	155	145	158	183	181	170	193	161	140	183	150	139	172
20779	TRACYS LANDING	127	153	172	152	152	160	140	141	133	141	167	159	149	169	146	132	165	137	134	153
20781	HYATTSVILLE	76	78	94	79	77	82	82	79	82	82	103	92	83	104	81	80	102	81	75	87
20782	HYATTSVILLE	81	82	104	85	79	85	87	83	86	88	109	98	87	109	85	84	108	87	78	91
20783	HYATTSVILLE	72	78	121	75	74	83	83	78	87	84	111	90	85	117	84	90	111	82	77	86
20784	HYATTSVILLE	86	92	106	92	90	95	92	90	91	93	115	104	95	116	92	90	113	90	85	99
20785	HYATTSVILLE	78	74	85	73	71	80	79	76	82	80	103	87	80	100	77	82	100	79	77	86
20794	JESSUP	103	107	103	111	103	103	101	101	96	105	121	119	101	119	98	90	119	100	90	113
20812	GLEN ECHO	209	281	385	275	274	296	245	243	228	250	288	273	278	304	261	230	293	233	225	263
20814	BETHESDA	161	180	279	189	173	189	185	173	183	188	231	205	198	244	188	183	231	177	162	190
20815	CHEVY CHASE	230	271	410	280	262	284	266	252	258	270	326	295	289	343	273	257	327	254	234	276
20816	BETHESDA	238	326	433	315	317	338	284	282	266	289	335	318	319	358	303	268	340	271	260	304
20817	BETHESDA	252	350	478	336	338	361	305	301	286	310	360	340	343	389	325	289	366	290	275	323
20818	CABIN JOHN	240	323	442	316	315	339	281	279	262	287	331	313	319	349	300	264	336	267	259	303
20832	OLNEY	164	198	212	203	191	191	177	174	162	180	206	201	190	212	178	156	206	169	154	191
20833	BROOKEVILLE	205	256	279	263	248	250	226	220	206	229	262	254	248	272	230	199	264	212	196	244
20837	POOLESVILLE	147	184	198	187	179	179	162	160	149	164	189	186	176	198	166	144	190	154	142	177
20838	BARNESVILLE	184	247	339	243	241	260	216	214	201	221	254	240	245	267	230	203	258	205	198	232
20839	BEALLSVILLE	150	201	238	199	194	198	175	171	161	177	203	196	194	219	181	159	207	165	152	186
20841	BOYDS	144	171	179	175	164	163	153	151	141	157	179	175	161	182	153	134	178	147	133	165
20842	DICKERSON	157	207	254	205	200	208	181	178	168	184	212	204	201	225	189	166	215	172	161	194
20850	ROCKVILLE	148	181	237	181	175	185	171	165	164	172	207	190	184	219	176	164	208	164	153	180
20851	ROCKVILLE	100	115	139	114	111	116	111	109	108	113	137	126	116	142	112	106	136	109	100	118
20852	ROCKVILLE	135	153	224	160	149	158	156	148	152	157	192	176	164	200	158	150	192	152	136	162
20853	ROCKVILLE	144	187	232	180	181	189	168	166	159	170	201	188	182	215	175	159	203	162	152	178
20854	POTOMAC	293	399	538	389	388	414	347	343	323	354	408	387	392	434	369	325	415	329	316	371
20855	DERWOOD	157	197	230	201	190	195	176	172	163	179	207	198	193	218	181	160	209	167	154	189
20860	SANDY SPRING	160	197	218	199	193	199	177	175	164	178	208	200	191	213	182	161	208	169	161	192
20861	ASHTON	154	188	210	188	186	193	170	170	160	171	202	193	183	206	176	158	201	165	159	186
20862	BRINKLOW	236	294	319	303	284	287	259	252	235	262	300	292	284	311	263	228	302	243	224	279
20866	BURTONSVILLE	129	143	145	150	137	135	133	131	123	137	157	153	137	156	130	115	155	129	113	144
20868	SPENCERVILLE	170	224	271	216	219	229	199	199	188	200	236	225	216	250	210	189	237	193	185	214
20871	CLARKSBURG	157	205	241	202	200	204	181	179	168	182	212	206	197	227	188	167	214	173	162	195
20872	DAMASCUS	124	143	146	145	138	137	131	130	122	133	154	152	135	157	130	116	152	127	115	142
20874	GERMANTOWN	133	139	145	147	133	133	136	132	127	140	162	156	136	158	130	119	159	133	115	146
20876	GERMANTOWN	138	150	150	158	143	141	141	138	130	146	166	163	143	165	136	122	164	137	119	152
20877	GAITHERSBURG	99	106	137	108	103	109	108	104	107	110	136	121	111	140	108	106	135	107	97	114
20878	GAITHERSBURG	169	188	212	198	181	184	179	173	168	183	214	204	188	215	177	160	213	173	154	192
20879	GAITHERSBURG	134	146	151	153	140	139	139	136	129	142	164	161	141	164	135	121	162	135	118	149
20882	GAITHERSBURG	200	245	264	251	236	237	217	213	198	221	252	247	234	261	219	191	253	206	188	235
20886	MONTGOMERY VILLAGE	126	135	149	140	130	132	132	129	125	134	159	152	134	158	129	119	156	130	115	141
20895	KENSINGTON	135	181	246	174	175	185	165	161	158	166	198	185	180	217	174	160	201	159	148	173
20901	SILVER SPRING	106	129	178	126	123	132	124	120	122	125	155	138	132	166	128	123	156	121	111	130
20902	SILVER SPRING	110	129	160	124	124	132	123	121	121	125	153	137	129	161	126	121	154	121	113	131
20903	SILVER SPRING	77	86	150	83	82	93	92	86	99	94	126	99	96	137	96	104	127	91	86	94
20904	SILVER SPRING	117	130	161	133	125	131	129	124	124	130	157	146	133	160	128	121	156	126	112	136
20905	SILVER SPRING	171	216	243	218	209	212	191	188	176	193	223	216	208	234	196	172	224	181	167	205
20906	SILVER SPRING	102	110	139	109	108	118	109	108	109	111	138	120	112	139	111	110	136	109	106	118
20910	SILVER SPRING	97	103	163	110	99	108	112	103	112	112	141	124	116	148	112	111	141	108	96	114
20912	TAKOMA PARK	95	99	136	102	95	102	104	99	104	106	132	117	106	135	103	103	131	103	93	109
21001	ABERDEEN	75	77	80	75	77	82	78	77	78	76	97	90	79	99	78	78	95	78	77	87
21005	ABERDEEN PROVING GRO	77	52	50	59	48	56	74	65	75	69	93	85	64	85	62	69	90	75	60	73
21009	ABINGDON	112	120	121	127	115	113	114	112	106	118	135	132	115	133	110	99	133	111	96	123
21010	GUNPOWDER	94	60	57	68	54	65	89	76	90	83	113	102	76	101	73	82	108	90	71	87
21012	ARNOLD	134	161	178	164	156	158	147	144	136	148	172	169	156	178	148	132	172	141	129	159
21013	BALDWIN	156	192	212	196	188	192	172	169	158	174	201	194	187	207	176	155	201	164	154	186
21014	BEL AIR	111	127	136	129	124	126	119	118	113	120	142	137	124	145	119	109	140	116	108	129
21015	BEL AIR	119	138	141	140	133	132	126	125	117	128	148	146	131	152	125	112	147	122	110	137
21017	BELCAMP	96	109	105	114	103	100	98	97	90	102	114	114	101	114	96	84	113	95	82	106
21028	CHURCHVILLE	122	143	153	140	142	147	131	132	126	131	158	152	138	164	135	126	156	129	127	147
21029	CLARKSVILLE	228	282	310	290	272	275	249	244	228	254	290	282	272	299	253	220	291	236	216	269
21030	COCKEYSVILLE	115	116	138	123	113	119	122	116	117	122	149	139	122	144	118	112	146	120	106	129
21031	HUNT VALLEY	16	14	21	15	14	17	18	16	19	17	23	19	17	23	17	19	22	18	18	18
21032	CROWNSVILLE	167	204	227	205	201	205	185	184	173	186	219	213	198	226	191	170	218	179	170	202
21034	DARLINGTON	98	99	91	96	102	107	92	97	93	91	115	114	93	119	94	94	111	94	99	117
21035	DAVIDSONVILLE	191	240	276	240	235	241	214	212	198	215	250	243	232	261	221	195	251	205	194	233
21036	DAYTON	194	244	274	250	236	241	215	210	196	218	249	242	237	259	220	191	252	202	187	232
21037	EDGEWATER	127	152	168	152	149	152	140	139	132	140	166	162	148	172	143	129	165	136	128	153
21040	EDGEWOOD	83	83	87	85	80	84	84	83	82	85	104	97	83	102	81	79	101	84	77	92
21042	ELLICOTT CITY	168	206	233	210	200	205	186	182	173	188	219	210	202	226	190	169	219	177	166	200
21043	ELLICOTT CITY	134	150	158	156	144	145	140	137	130	143	165	161	145	165	138	124	164	136	121	151
21044	COLUMBIA	138	147	171	154	143	149	148	143	141	149	179	169	151	177	145	136	176	145	131	157
21045	COLUMBIA	123	134	151	140	130	134	131	127	124	133	157	150	135	157	129	119	155	128	114	140
21046	COLUMBIA	143	150	158	159	144	145	146	142	137	150	175	168	148	171	141	129	172	143	125	157
21047	FALLSTON	133	163	179	163	161	164	147	147	137	147	173	169	157	179	152	135	172	142	136	161
21048	FINKSBURG	109	135	144	135	133	131	121	120	112	120	140	141	128	150	123	108	140	116	108	133
21050	FOREST HILL	124	148	157	150	145	144	135	134	126	135	158	157	141	164	136	121	157	131	121	148
21051	FORK	113	137	155	136	137	143	126	126	119	126	150	143	134	152	131	118	148	123	121	138
21053	FREELAND	107	133	143	132	130	130	120	119	112	119	141	139	128	150	123	109	141	115	108	131
21054	GAMBRILLS	142	168	173	173	163	160	151	149	139	154	176	174	159	181	151	132	175	145	131	164
21056	GIBSON ISLAND	157	190	214	188	189	198	174	175	164	174	207	197	185	210	181	164	205	170	167	190
21057	GLEN ARM	166	183	207	188	182	190	178	177	170	178	213	206	183	211	180	166	209	176	168	194
21060	GLEN BURNIE	78	87	99	87	85	89	86	84	83	85	105	98	89	108	86	82	104	84	79	92
21061	GLEN BURNIE	82	83	92	86	81	85	86	83	84	86	106	98	86	105	84	81	104	85	78	92
21071	GLYNDON	148	184	195	184	180	178	164	163	152	163	191	191	174	203	167	147	191	157	146	180
21074	HAMPSTEAD	99	117	122	118	114	113	107	106	100	108	126	124	112	131	108	96	125	103	95	116
21075	ELKRIDGE	121	124	128	132	119	120	122	119	115	126	147	141	122	143	117	108	144	120	105	132
21076	HANOVER	134	144	137	147	140	140	133	134	126	137	159	157	135	158	131	120	155	132	121	150
21077	HARMANS	148	166	159	173	158	153	150	149	138	156	175	174	154	175	146	128	173	145	127	164
21078	HAVRE DE GRACE	89	96	101	97	95	99	94	93	91	93	114	107	96	116	94	90	112	92	89	103
21082	HYDES	134	162	182	161	161	169	148	149	140	149	177	169	158	179	154	140	175	145	142	162
21084	JARRETTSVILLE	110	137	145	137	134	132	122	122	113	122	142	142	130	152	125	110	142	117	109	134
	MARYLAND	108	114	128	115	112	119	113	111	111	114	139	129	116	140	113	109	137	112	106	124
	UNITED STATES	100	100	100	100	100	100	100	100	100	100	100	100	100	100	100	100	100	100	100	100

POPULATION CHANGE

MARYLAND
21085-21613

# ZIP CODE POST OFFICE NAME	COUNTY FIPS CODE	POPULATION 2000	2004	2009	2000-2004 ANNUAL RATE % Rate	State Centile	HOUSEHOLDS 2000	2004	2009	% Annual Rate 2000-2004	2004 Average HH Size	FAMILIES 2000	2004	% Annual Rate 2000-2004
21085 JOPPA	025	14579	15476	16805	1.4	58	5593	6023	6619	1.8	2.57	4178	4451	1.5
21087 KINGSVILLE	005	5622	5557	5661	-0.3	11	2002	1983	2026	-0.2	2.80	1643	1617	-0.4
21090 LINTHICUM HEIGHTS	003	9722	9920	10495	0.5	32	3745	3809	4023	0.4	2.59	2759	2784	0.2
21093 LUTHERVILLE TIMONIUM	005	35068	35600	36507	0.4	27	14610	14892	15323	0.5	2.36	10059	10117	0.1
21102 MANCHESTER	013	9369	10126	11118	1.9	70	3183	3464	3829	2.0	2.89	2583	2793	1.9
21104 MARRIOTTSVILLE	027	3809	4344	4883	3.1	92	1189	1360	1534	3.2	3.13	1020	1161	3.1
21108 MILLERSVILLE	003	18941	19716	21146	1.0	47	6392	6606	7061	0.8	2.96	5087	5245	0.7
21111 MONKTON	005	5154	5188	5319	0.2	23	1868	1887	1943	0.2	2.74	1496	1500	0.1
21113 ODENTON	003	21613	26169	29834	4.6	98	8079	9828	11267	4.7	2.66	5877	7039	4.3
21114 CROFTON	003	21378	23299	25162	2.1	76	7969	8601	9248	1.8	2.69	5855	6271	1.6
21117 OWINGS MILLS	005	40422	45665	49585	2.9	89	16598	18779	20438	3.0	2.40	10771	12076	2.7
21120 PARKTON	005	6428	6585	6751	0.6	35	2168	2222	2283	0.6	2.96	1834	1869	0.5
21122 PASADENA	003	57251	59706	63583	1.0	48	20226	21050	22411	0.9	2.83	15876	16361	0.7
21128 PERRY HALL	005	6295	8016	9414	5.9	100	2395	3036	3561	5.7	2.64	1857	2354	5.7
21131 PHOENIX	005	6974	7189	7396	0.7	41	2385	2461	2536	0.7	2.92	2022	2078	0.6
21132 PYLESVILLE	025	2639	2638	2782	0.0	18	898	908	968	0.3	2.90	744	747	0.1
21133 RANDALLSTOWN	005	27139	28616	29870	1.3	54	9914	10447	10922	1.2	2.67	6855	7123	0.9
21136 REISTERSTOWN	005	31527	33721	35560	1.6	64	11621	12410	13097	1.6	2.68	8548	9073	1.4
21140 RIVA	003	3417	3600	3804	1.2	53	1233	1298	1371	1.2	2.77	1008	1053	1.0
21144 SEVERN	003	29892	32451	35064	2.0	73	10179	11004	11871	1.9	2.94	8063	8648	1.7
21146 SEVERNA PARK	003	25033	25712	27021	0.6	37	8731	8974	9440	0.7	2.82	7157	7308	0.5
21152 SPARKS GLENCOE	005	5044	4823	4851	-1.1	4	2148	2035	2041	-1.3	2.37	1377	1293	-1.5
21154 STREET	025	5858	6099	6508	1.0	47	2005	2115	2281	1.3	2.87	1627	1705	1.1
21155 UPPERCO	005	2562	2712	2835	1.4	56	1011	1072	1123	1.4	2.53	776	817	1.2
21156 UPPER FALLS	005	416	425	433	0.5	33	145	148	151	0.5	2.85	110	111	0.2
21157 WESTMINSTER	013	34216	36461	39747	1.5	61	12440	13398	14754	1.8	2.59	8890	9488	1.5
21158 WESTMINSTER	013	18430	19942	22029	1.9	70	6506	7075	7860	2.0	2.79	5107	5498	1.8
21160 WHITEFORD	025	2280	2299	2418	0.2	24	805	823	874	0.5	2.79	638	646	0.3
21161 WHITE HALL	025	5122	5265	5488	0.7	39	1765	1828	1918	0.8	2.86	1438	1479	0.7
21162 WHITE MARSH	005	2824	2886	2968	0.5	33	1084	1107	1139	0.5	2.60	805	816	0.3
21163 WOODSTOCK	005	5216	5926	6463	3.1	91	1829	2112	2324	3.4	2.74	1412	1626	3.4
21201 BALTIMORE	510	14107	13976	13584	-0.2	12	7639	7629	7475	0.0	1.62	2170	2116	-0.6
21202 BALTIMORE	510	23434	22875	22229	-0.6	8	7749	7591	7371	-0.5	1.99	2842	2722	-1.0
21204 TOWSON	005	20157	20723	21332	0.7	39	7109	7317	7580	0.7	2.14	3505	3618	0.8
21205 BALTIMORE	510	18739	17305	16235	-1.9	0	6510	6084	5786	-1.6	2.83	4453	4100	-1.9
21206 BALTIMORE	510	49911	49407	48172	-0.2	11	19781	19715	19391	-0.1	2.49	12523	12381	-0.3
21207 GWYNN OAK	005	49008	48810	48951	-0.1	17	18793	18849	19017	0.1	2.55	12579	12484	-0.2
21208 PIKESVILLE	005	32192	33061	34082	0.6	37	13722	14100	14561	0.6	2.27	8783	8891	0.3
21209 BALTIMORE	005	23050	23872	24206	0.8	44	10351	10752	10949	0.9	2.21	5877	6024	0.6
21210 BALTIMORE	510	11382	11365	11076	0.0	17	5552	5630	5560	0.3	1.90	2509	2487	-0.2
21211 BALTIMORE	510	17311	17130	16565	-0.3	11	8189	8226	8083	0.1	2.06	3882	3832	-0.3
21212 BALTIMORE	510	35740	35258	34651	-0.3	9	13749	13746	13653	0.0	2.34	8421	8291	-0.4
21213 BALTIMORE	510	38264	36645	35026	-1.0	4	13432	12958	12528	-0.8	2.81	9345	8931	-1.1
21214 BALTIMORE	510	20880	20040	19034	-1.0	5	8243	7958	7635	-0.8	2.43	5094	4862	-1.1
21215 BALTIMORE	510	64746	63232	60827	-0.6	8	24613	24274	23654	-0.3	2.57	15652	15310	-0.5
21216 BALTIMORE	510	36750	35100	33319	-1.1	3	13822	13386	12890	-0.8	2.59	8968	8594	-1.0
21217 BALTIMORE	510	42684	39022	36412	-2.1	0	17194	15929	15072	-1.8	2.36	8856	8090	-2.1
21218 BALTIMORE	510	53757	51726	49426	-0.9	5	20437	20007	19372	-0.5	2.32	10184	9761	-1.0
21219 SPARROWS POINT	005	9509	9442	9605	-0.2	15	3607	3576	3640	-0.2	2.60	2581	2537	-0.4
21220 MIDDLE RIVER	005	36498	36999	38039	0.3	26	14165	14365	14786	0.3	2.57	9990	10029	0.1
21221 ESSEX	005	42622	42747	43749	0.1	22	17321	17406	17854	0.1	2.45	11367	11330	-0.1
21222 DUNDALK	005	55261	54746	55643	-0.2	12	22007	21843	22243	-0.2	2.49	15012	14750	-0.4
21223 BALTIMORE	510	30445	28455	26759	-1.6	1	10923	10382	9931	-1.2	2.69	6710	6286	-1.5
21224 BALTIMORE	510	48468	46369	44425	-1.0	4	20027	19346	18748	-0.8	2.36	11592	11031	-1.2
21225 BROOKLYN	003	31148	30850	30763	-0.2	12	11817	11758	11795	-0.1	2.61	8006	7894	-0.3
21226 CURTIS BAY	510	6978	7211	7368	0.8	43	2760	2868	2947	0.9	2.51	1758	1816	0.8
21227 HALETHORPE	005	33333	33439	34245	0.1	22	12852	12893	13222	0.1	2.57	8794	8731	-0.2
21228 CATONSVILLE	005	47390	47604	48381	0.1	23	19233	19395	19782	0.2	2.37	12113	12040	-0.1
21229 BALTIMORE	510	50073	48694	46852	-0.7	7	19545	19234	18751	-0.4	2.48	12342	12018	-0.6
21230 BALTIMORE	510	33117	31791	30235	-1.0	5	13937	13607	13150	-0.6	2.30	7608	7309	-0.9
21231 BALTIMORE	510	15562	14781	13981	-1.2	3	7196	6943	6667	-0.8	2.08	3000	2825	-1.4
21234 PARKVILLE	005	66500	66616	67521	0.0	21	27690	27757	28199	0.1	2.38	17757	17630	-0.2
21236 NOTTINGHAM	005	41324	42154	43427	0.5	31	17304	17788	18417	0.7	2.35	10953	11030	0.2
21237 ROSEDALE	005	25452	26757	28018	1.2	52	10329	10821	11328	1.1	2.44	6743	7002	0.9
21239 BALTIMORE	510	28901	28426	27520	-0.4	8	11847	11716	11448	-0.3	2.40	7308	7172	-0.4
21244 WINDSOR MILL	FIPS	30532	31840	33052	1.0	48	12013	12531	13028	1.0	2.51	7943	8194	0.7
21250 BALTIMORE	005	2418	2418	2418	0.0	19	5	5	5	0.0	1.80	3	3	0.0
21286 TOWSON	005	19179	19592	20227	0.5	33	8524	8654	8943	0.4	2.15	4729	4769	0.2
21401 ANNAPOLIS	003	51608	54121	57575	1.1	51	20929	21960	23386	1.1	2.39	13667	14139	0.8
21402 ANNAPOLIS	003	5261	5333	5443	0.3	26	463	479	509	0.8	3.45	419	433	0.8
21403 ANNAPOLIS	003	28793	29653	31301	0.7	40	12340	12716	13442	0.7	2.30	7430	7539	0.3
21502 CUMBERLAND	001	44707	44463	44224	-0.1	16	17682	17675	17701	0.0	2.28	11246	11119	-0.3
21520 ACCIDENT	023	2032	2220	2355	2.1	78	762	848	916	2.6	2.61	562	620	2.3
21521 BARTON	023	1027	1018	1018	-0.2	13	400	402	406	0.1	2.53	296	294	-0.2
21522 BITTINGER	023	277	287	295	0.8	45	90	94	99	1.0	3.04	67	70	1.0
21523 BLOOMINGTON	023	449	453	462	0.2	25	176	181	187	0.7	2.41	138	141	0.5
21530 FLINTSTONE	001	1550	1530	1514	-0.3	9	567	564	563	-0.1	2.54	434	428	-0.3
21531 FRIENDSVILLE	023	2362	2327	2372	-0.4	9	947	952	988	0.1	2.44	673	669	-0.1
21532 FROSTBURG	001	15391	15406	15404	0.0	20	5791	5838	5870	0.2	2.35	3435	3416	-0.1
21536 GRANTSVILLE	023	3791	4056	4260	1.6	64	1438	1567	1676	2.0	2.53	1073	1159	1.8
21538 KITZMILLER	023	706	684	691	-0.7	6	274	269	275	-0.4	2.54	209	204	-0.6
21539 LONACONING	023	3506	3537	3559	0.2	25	1398	1429	1450	0.5	2.43	975	983	0.2
21540 LUKE	001	80	76	74	-1.2	3	39	37	36	-1.2	1.86	24	22	-2.0
21541 MC HENRY	023	1176	1264	1335	1.7	66	497	544	586	2.2	2.28	343	371	1.9
21545 MOUNT SAVAGE	001	2736	2713	2695	-0.2	13	1064	1067	1069	0.1	2.49	810	805	-0.2
21550 OAKLAND	023	14501	14840	15335	0.6	34	5591	5807	6101	0.9	2.48	3981	4097	0.7
21555 OLDTOWN	001	2024	2065	2081	0.5	31	748	773	786	0.8	2.59	565	578	0.5
21557 RAWLINGS	001	2096	2082	2067	-0.2	16	808	811	811	0.1	2.57	615	611	-0.2
21561 SWANTON	023	2375	2443	2511	0.7	39	929	973	1017	1.1	2.48	683	709	0.9
21562 WESTERNPORT	001	3290	3122	3044	-1.2	2	1320	1265	1242	-1.0	2.38	911	862	-1.3
21601 EASTON	041	19527	20827	22383	1.5	61	8293	8925	9677	1.7	2.27	5287	5632	1.5
21607 BARCLAY	035	416	437	480	1.2	52	153	163	180	1.5	2.68	119	125	1.2
21610 BETTERTON	029	477	491	526	0.7	40	202	212	231	1.1	2.26	152	157	0.8
21612 BOZMAN	041	782	773	810	-0.3	11	369	369	389	0.0	2.09	271	267	-0.4
21613 CAMBRIDGE	019	16649	16573	16714	-0.1	16	7095	7145	7285	0.2	2.24	4482	4456	-0.1
MARYLAND					1.1					1.1	2.60			1.0
UNITED STATES					1.2					1.3	2.58			1.1

ZIP CODE #	POST OFFICE NAME	RACE (%) White 2000	White 2004	Black 2000	Black 2004	Asian/Pacific 2000	Asian/Pacific 2004	% Hispanic Origin 2000	% Hispanic Origin 2004	2004 AGE DISTRIBUTION (%) 0-4	5-9	10-14	15-19	20-24	25-44	45-64	65-84	85+	18+	MEDIAN AGE 2004	% 2004 Males	% 2004 Females
21085	JOPPA	87.8	85.4	8.5	10.1	1.2	1.5	1.8	2.3	5.9	6.0	6.1	6.3	5.5	28.1	28.7	12.5	1.0	78.2	40.6	49.6	50.4
21087	KINGSVILLE	97.2	96.4	0.6	0.8	0.9	1.2	0.9	1.2	4.5	5.9	7.7	6.5	4.4	21.5	32.3	15.8	1.5	77.8	44.8	49.0	51.0
21090	LINTHICUM HEIGHTS	93.9	93.0	1.9	2.1	2.6	3.0	1.2	1.6	4.6	5.2	6.5	6.1	5.0	25.0	28.5	17.5	1.7	79.8	43.7	48.7	51.3
21093	LUTHERVILLE TIMONIUM	89.6	87.3	2.5	3.2	6.4	7.8	1.4	1.8	5.0	5.8	6.7	6.1	4.3	22.3	30.0	17.6	2.1	78.6	44.8	47.3	52.7
21102	MANCHESTER	97.5	97.0	1.0	1.2	0.3	0.3	0.6	0.7	6.1	6.8	7.6	6.8	5.5	26.5	29.9	9.5	1.3	75.2	39.9	49.9	50.1
21104	MARRIOTTSVILLE	92.6	91.3	3.8	4.3	2.3	3.0	1.1	1.4	6.7	8.1	10.4	8.4	4.4	26.8	26.9	7.5	0.9	68.9	37.5	50.9	49.1
21108	MILLERSVILLE	85.7	83.7	8.2	9.0	3.8	4.6	2.0	2.5	6.5	7.3	7.9	7.2	5.5	27.7	29.2	7.8	0.8	73.5	37.8	49.6	50.4
21111	MONKTON	95.5	94.5	2.9	3.6	0.9	1.0	0.7	0.9	5.3	6.5	8.0	6.9	4.4	21.2	35.0	11.5	1.4	75.4	43.7	49.1	50.9
21113	ODENTON	69.8	66.2	22.3	24.7	3.6	4.1	3.7	4.3	9.2	8.5	7.5	5.9	5.7	38.5	19.2	5.2	0.5	71.2	32.9	47.9	52.1
21114	CROFTON	89.9	88.1	5.4	6.3	2.4	2.9	2.5	3.1	8.6	8.6	7.8	6.0	4.9	33.3	24.0	6.1	0.8	71.2	35.4	48.5	51.5
21117	OWINGS MILLS	66.7	61.3	26.3	30.8	3.8	4.3	3.0	3.4	7.1	6.9	6.9	6.4	6.9	34.6	24.1	6.5	0.6	75.0	34.4	48.1	51.9
21120	PARKTON	96.8	96.1	1.2	1.6	0.7	0.8	0.7	0.9	5.7	7.1	8.9	7.0	4.3	23.3	33.1	9.7	0.8	73.5	41.8	49.6	50.4
21122	PASADENA	92.1	90.6	4.9	5.9	1.2	1.4	1.2	1.6	6.6	6.9	7.6	6.8	5.2	30.5	26.5	9.1	0.9	74.6	37.7	49.4	50.6
21128	PERRY HALL	93.6	92.6	2.3	2.7	3.0	3.4	1.4	1.8	5.9	6.0	6.5	6.4	5.1	27.3	26.9	14.6	1.4	77.7	41.0	48.2	51.8
21131	PHOENIX	96.0	95.0	0.9	1.2	2.2	2.7	1.0	1.3	5.4	6.8	8.3	7.1	4.5	18.5	34.8	13.1	1.5	74.8	44.7	48.5	51.5
21132	PYLESVILLE	98.0	97.6	0.5	0.5	0.4	0.5	0.5	0.7	5.6	6.4	7.9	7.2	5.6	26.5	29.8	10.0	1.1	75.6	40.5	49.4	50.6
21133	RANDALLSTOWN	26.9	22.9	68.3	72.0	2.3	2.4	1.6	1.8	6.5	6.7	7.1	6.8	6.5	28.8	25.4	10.3	2.0	75.2	37.5	45.7	54.3
21136	REISTERSTOWN	80.9	77.7	12.7	14.7	3.6	4.2	2.8	3.4	6.7	7.1	7.7	7.1	5.7	29.3	26.3	8.9	1.1	73.8	37.1	48.4	51.6
21140	RIVA	94.5	93.3	3.3	3.9	1.1	1.4	2.1	2.8	6.0	7.1	7.4	6.0	4.0	27.4	32.0	9.4	0.8	75.8	41.0	50.5	49.5
21144	SEVERN	60.9	56.7	30.2	33.1	4.6	5.1	3.5	4.2	8.0	7.9	8.3	6.8	6.5	32.0	24.3	5.9	0.5	71.7	33.9	48.6	51.4
21146	SEVERNA PARK	92.4	91.0	3.9	4.5	2.3	2.8	1.2	1.5	6.0	7.2	7.9	6.9	4.2	23.1	30.6	12.3	1.8	74.1	42.1	48.4	51.6
21152	SPARKS GLENCOE	93.5	92.1	2.0	2.6	3.4	4.1	1.1	1.3	5.9	6.5	6.8	5.7	4.4	26.8	29.6	11.6	2.7	77.1	41.8	47.4	52.6
21154	STREET	95.1	94.1	2.9	3.5	0.4	0.5	1.0	1.4	5.4	6.1	7.6	7.3	5.3	25.4	31.1	10.5	1.3	76.2	41.2	50.7	49.3
21155	UPPERCO	96.2	95.2	1.7	2.2	0.9	1.1	0.9	1.3	5.1	6.1	7.3	6.2	4.0	24.0	32.0	13.9	1.5	77.4	43.6	49.3	50.7
21156	UPPER FALLS	97.4	96.7	1.9	2.4	0.5	0.7	0.7	0.9	4.2	5.7	8.2	5.7	4.0	20.9	30.6	18.6	2.1	77.7	45.7	48.7	51.3
21157	WESTMINSTER	94.5	93.7	3.3	3.7	0.8	1.0	1.1	1.3	5.8	6.2	7.1	7.6	7.3	26.2	26.8	11.4	1.8	76.9	38.9	48.5	51.5
21158	WESTMINSTER	96.2	95.4	1.4	1.6	1.1	1.3	1.0	1.3	7.0	7.5	8.1	6.8	5.3	28.4	25.8	9.2	2.0	73.0	37.6	48.5	51.5
21160	WHITEFORD	98.3	97.8	0.4	0.5	0.2	0.2	0.8	1.1	6.5	6.7	7.9	6.1	6.2	26.3	27.6	11.7	1.0	75.2	39.4	48.9	51.1
21161	WHITE HALL	97.1	96.5	1.4	1.7	0.6	0.7	0.6	0.8	5.6	6.8	8.6	6.9	4.2	25.3	30.6	10.8	1.2	74.3	41.2	50.1	49.9
21162	WHITE MARSH	94.6	93.2	3.5	4.4	0.5	0.6	0.7	0.9	4.7	5.2	6.1	5.8	4.6	24.6	28.7	18.5	1.8	80.5	44.4	49.8	50.2
21163	WOODSTOCK	57.9	57.1	37.0	36.8	3.4	4.2	1.0	1.2	6.4	7.2	7.2	7.1	4.9	26.4	28.9	10.8	1.1	74.5	40.0	49.0	51.0
21201	BALTIMORE	29.0	24.6	63.8	67.9	4.6	4.9	1.8	2.0	4.6	4.5	5.1	5.5	9.5	35.6	21.5	11.9	1.9	82.9	35.2	49.0	51.0
21202	BALTIMORE	19.8	16.5	76.4	79.5	2.3	2.4	1.1	1.2	3.6	3.6	4.1	6.9	12.0	44.1	17.9	7.1	0.9	85.9	33.1	62.7	37.3
21204	TOWSON	88.2	86.0	7.3	8.6	3.0	3.6	1.9	2.4	3.3	3.4	4.1	15.1	16.8	18.5	19.1	15.3	4.6	86.5	33.8	46.9	53.1
21205	BALTIMORE	19.9	19.0	77.2	77.9	0.8	0.7	1.6	1.8	8.1	8.4	9.7	8.6	7.3	25.5	22.0	9.3	1.1	68.4	31.9	45.3	54.7
21206	BALTIMORE	43.0	38.3	53.9	58.5	0.9	0.9	1.3	1.4	7.0	6.8	7.8	7.1	7.5	28.9	23.8	9.8	1.5	74.1	35.4	46.8	53.2
21207	GWYNN OAK	17.0	14.3	79.6	82.2	1.0	1.1	1.5	1.6	6.6	6.8	7.8	7.3	6.6	26.9	25.0	11.4	1.7	74.3	37.1	45.6	54.4
21208	PIKESVILLE	63.5	59.2	32.6	36.3	1.9	2.2	1.6	1.9	5.0	5.3	6.0	6.0	5.2	22.3	27.7	18.8	3.8	79.9	45.2	46.2	53.8
21209	BALTIMORE	82.9	79.0	10.9	13.4	4.3	5.3	1.7	2.1	6.1	5.5	6.1	5.9	6.3	28.1	25.3	14.3	2.5	78.5	39.4	46.6	53.4
21210	BALTIMORE	88.5	85.1	5.1	7.1	4.6	5.6	1.7	2.1	4.1	3.9	4.0	7.8	8.3	24.5	27.7	16.7	3.0	84.8	43.0	46.3	53.7
21211	BALTIMORE	83.9	79.3	10.5	14.0	3.1	3.7	1.8	2.2	5.1	4.8	5.3	5.4	5.9	33.1	24.8	13.0	2.7	81.7	39.3	48.1	52.0
21212	BALTIMORE	56.0	54.2	39.6	40.5	2.3	2.9	1.7	2.1	5.9	6.1	6.4	9.5	8.9	25.8	24.1	11.3	1.8	77.5	36.7	44.7	55.4
21213	BALTIMORE	10.1	8.0	88.0	90.1	0.7	0.7	0.7	0.7	7.0	7.4	8.8	8.5	6.9	25.6	23.8	10.5	1.5	71.8	35.4	44.9	55.1
21214	BALTIMORE	58.4	51.2	37.6	44.4	1.2	1.4	1.7	1.9	6.2	6.1	7.0	6.8	6.4	28.2	25.7	11.2	2.3	76.6	38.9	47.4	52.6
21215	BALTIMORE	16.4	14.3	81.1	83.2	0.5	0.5	1.1	1.1	6.5	6.6	8.0	7.4	6.2	23.3	24.6	15.1	2.3	74.4	39.1	44.4	55.6
21216	BALTIMORE	1.0	0.7	97.5	97.8	0.2	0.2	0.7	0.7	6.2	6.5	8.1	8.2	7.2	24.0	23.9	13.9	2.1	74.5	37.9	44.6	55.4
21217	BALTIMORE	9.0	7.9	88.5	89.5	1.0	1.1	0.9	1.0	7.1	6.8	7.8	8.1	9.8	26.5	22.0	10.3	1.6	73.9	33.2	45.8	54.2
21218	BALTIMORE	24.6	21.5	68.0	70.1	4.8	5.5	1.7	1.9	4.8	4.8	6.0	11.6	13.1	26.4	22.6	9.5	1.2	80.7	31.9	47.8	52.2
21219	SPARROWS POINT	93.6	92.4	5.1	6.0	0.5	0.6	0.7	0.8	4.2	5.0	6.9	6.8	5.3	25.2	29.2	15.5	1.8	79.6	43.1	49.3	50.7
21220	MIDDLE RIVER	83.6	80.7	12.9	15.2	1.0	1.1	1.5	1.9	6.9	6.6	7.3	6.7	6.6	29.2	24.9	10.8	1.1	75.1	36.8	48.7	51.3
21221	ESSEX	76.1	72.5	19.6	22.4	1.3	1.5	2.2	2.6	6.9	6.3	7.0	7.0	7.1	27.6	24.9	11.8	1.4	75.6	37.2	48.2	51.8
21222	DUNDALK	88.8	87.3	8.2	9.1	0.8	1.0	1.4	1.8	5.9	5.9	6.8	6.7	6.2	25.9	25.3	15.5	1.9	77.3	40.4	47.7	52.3
21223	BALTIMORE	25.6	21.9	70.7	74.0	1.5	1.6	1.1	1.2	7.6	7.4	8.2	8.0	7.1	27.2	22.8	10.6	1.2	71.8	34.7	46.8	53.3
21224	BALTIMORE	71.1	67.2	21.6	24.4	1.4	1.6	4.7	5.6	6.1	6.0	6.9	6.5	6.5	29.5	23.0	13.2	2.2	77.0	37.2	47.4	52.6
21225	BROOKLYN	60.0	57.4	36.0	38.1	1.3	1.5	1.8	2.2	7.7	7.6	8.2	7.3	6.8	27.1	22.8	11.2	1.5	72.2	35.3	46.5	53.5
21226	CURTIS BAY	85.5	82.5	10.3	12.6	2.0	2.2	1.6	2.1	8.8	7.7	6.5	5.4	6.0	34.1	22.3	8.3	1.0	73.8	34.8	48.7	51.3
21227	HALETHORPE	82.2	79.8	12.0	13.3	2.9	3.4	2.4	2.8	7.1	6.4	7.0	6.8	7.3	29.8	22.9	11.4	1.3	75.4	36.0	47.9	52.1
21228	CATONSVILLE	73.8	70.4	19.1	21.6	4.6	5.2	2.0	2.4	5.7	5.8	6.3	5.9	5.6	26.0	25.6	14.6	4.5	78.3	41.8	46.6	53.4
21229	BALTIMORE	23.5	20.7	72.8	75.2	1.9	2.1	1.1	1.2	6.8	6.7	7.4	7.1	7.0	27.0	23.6	12.3	2.1	74.7	36.8	44.4	55.6
21230	BALTIMORE	68.5	64.8	27.8	30.9	1.8	2.0	1.5	1.8	6.3	5.9	6.3	5.9	7.2	34.0	22.6	10.5	1.4	78.0	34.9	48.0	52.0
21231	BALTIMORE	50.8	46.8	38.9	41.5	2.2	2.3	9.8	11.5	5.6	5.3	5.9	5.9	8.3	37.1	21.9	8.8	1.2	79.8	34.0	50.1	49.9
21234	PARKVILLE	76.6	73.8	18.0	19.7	3.5	4.3	1.5	1.8	5.7	5.7	6.7	6.6	6.9	28.8	24.6	13.1	1.9	77.9	38.7	47.0	53.0
21236	NOTTINGHAM	87.8	85.2	5.6	6.9	4.6	5.5	1.7	2.2	5.7	5.6	6.2	5.8	6.0	30.3	23.3	13.9	3.2	78.8	39.1	47.1	52.9
21237	ROSEDALE	78.2	73.5	16.0	19.8	3.2	3.8	2.1	2.6	5.9	5.7	6.1	6.0	6.9	30.1	24.0	13.3	2.0	78.7	38.1	47.8	52.2
21239	BALTIMORE	21.6	18.0	74.6	78.1	1.6	1.7	1.2	1.3	6.1	6.3	7.2	7.0	8.1	27.1	25.8	10.8	1.7	76.2	36.9	44.2	55.8
21244	WINDSOR MILL	19.6	16.7	73.0	75.5	3.7	3.9	2.1	2.2	7.8	7.6	7.9	7.2	7.1	32.4	22.0	7.3	0.8	72.1	33.1	46.3	53.7
21250	BALTIMORE	62.1	56.2	19.3	22.5	13.9	15.8	2.3	2.7	0.0	0.0	0.0	51.7	47.3	0.8	0.1	0.1	0.0	99.3	19.8	49.2	50.8
21286	TOWSON	87.4	84.9	6.3	7.5	4.5	5.5	1.6	2.0	4.4	4.6	5.0	6.8	7.4	23.1	24.4	19.9	4.5	83.1	44.1	44.4	55.6
21401	ANNAPOLIS	79.0	77.6	17.2	17.8	1.4	1.7	2.8	3.4	5.7	6.1	6.1	5.8	5.4	27.8	27.7	13.5	1.9	78.6	40.6	48.3	51.7
21402	ANNAPOLIS	83.8	81.1	8.1	9.2	3.2	3.7	7.5	9.3	4.5	4.1	2.8	21.2	48.9	13.8	4.0	0.7	0.1	87.3	21.8	75.6	24.4
21403	ANNAPOLIS	74.6	71.5	20.0	22.2	1.9	2.2	5.1	6.0	6.2	6.1	5.7	4.8	5.2	30.5	28.2	11.8	1.6	79.0	40.0	48.0	52.0
21502	CUMBERLAND	90.8	89.4	7.5	8.5	0.6	0.7	0.9	1.1	5.1	5.1	5.8	5.9	6.3	27.6	25.7	15.8	2.6	80.3	41.1	51.5	48.5
21520	ACCIDENT	98.9	98.8	0.2	0.2	0.2	0.2	0.5	0.6	6.2	6.4	7.3	7.1	6.2	27.0	26.2	12.0	1.7	76.0	39.0	48.6	51.4
21521	BARTON	99.3	99.3	0.3	0.3	0.1	0.1	0.2	0.1	5.6	5.5	5.9	6.4	6.2	24.6	27.2	16.9	1.8	79.1	42.2	49.0	51.0
21522	BITTINGER	98.9	98.6	0.0	0.0	0.4	0.7	0.4	0.4	7.3	7.3	7.7	7.3	5.2	29.3	24.0	10.5	1.4	73.5	37.8	51.2	48.8
21523	BLOOMINGTON	96.9	96.5	2.9	3.5	0.0	0.0	0.7	0.9	5.5	6.0	6.6	8.0	6.4	25.6	26.5	14.1	1.3	76.2	39.9	51.4	48.6
21530	FLINTSTONE	95.4	94.4	4.1	4.8	0.1	0.1	0.4	0.6	5.4	5.8	5.8	11.3	6.1	24.7	25.7	14.0	1.2	74.7	38.5	54.6	45.4
21531	FRIENDSVILLE	99.2	99.0	0.2	0.3	0.2	0.2	0.8	1.1	5.8	5.9	6.8	6.7	5.7	26.1	26.5	14.8	1.8	77.4	40.7	50.2	49.8
21532	FROSTBURG	94.4	93.3	3.4	4.1	0.7	0.9	0.8	1.0	4.3	4.4	4.9	11.4	17.1	21.3	21.1	12.9	2.7	83.6	32.6	47.1	52.9
21536	GRANTSVILLE	99.2	98.9	0.2	0.3	0.2	0.3	0.3	0.4	6.9	6.9	7.2	6.0	5.7	27.8	24.4	12.7	2.5	75.3	38.5	49.0	51.0
21538	KITZMILLER	99.3	99.1	0.1	0.2	0.1	0.2	0.3	0.3	6.9	7.2	8.2	6.3	6.0	27.1	24.0	13.0	1.5	73.7	37.3	48.5	51.5
21539	LONACONING	98.7	98.4	0.4	0.5	0.2	0.2	0.3	0.4	6.1	6.1	6.5	6.1	5.5	25.7	24.5	16.3	3.1	77.3	40.8	48.2	51.8
21540	LUKE	98.8	100.0	0.0	0.0	0.0	0.0	0.0	0.0	4.0	4.0	5.3	6.6	5.3	23.7	23.7	23.7	4.0	85.5	45.8	44.7	55.3
21541	MC HENRY	97.8	97.4	1.0	1.1	0.3	0.4	0.3	0.4	4.7	5.1	5.8	5.2	5.2	27.0	30.1	15.6	1.4	81.8	43.3	52.2	47.8
21545	MOUNT SAVAGE	99.1	98.9	0.4	0.5	0.1	0.1	0.4	0.5	5.4	5.5	6.2	6.9	5.7	24.8	27.2	15.9	2.5	78.7	42.0	47.2	52.8
21550	OAKLAND	98.9	98.7	0.3	0.4	0.3	0.3	0.5	0.6	6.2	6.3	7.2	6.1	6.2	25.6	26.7	13.7	2.1	76.6	39.8	49.0	51.0
21555	OLDTOWN	97.5	97.1	1.4	1.7	0.2	0.2	0.7	0.8	5.5	6.0	6.6	8.2	5.3	26.5	26.6	14.2	1.2	76.1	40.2	51.6	48.4
21557	RAWLINGS	98.1	97.7	0.6	0.7	0.5	0.7	0.5	0.6	6.0	6.5	7.5	5.5	5.1	26.2	25.9	15.9	1.5	76.6	40.5	49.0	51.0
21561	SWANTON	98.3	98.1	1.1	1.3	0.0	0.0	0.3	0.5	5.0	5.3	6.1	6.8	5.7	24.2	29.8	15.6	1.5	79.0	43.0	50.1	49.9
21562	WESTERNPORT	99.2	99.0	0.3	0.4	0.2	0.2	0.3	0.4	5.6	5.4	5.8	5.9	6.0	23.5	23.8	20.8	3.1	79.4	43.4	47.4	52.6
21601	EASTON	78.0	75.4	18.5	20.5	1.4	1.7	2.5	3.0	5.5	5.6	6.2	5.6	5.3	24.3	27.2	16.9	3.4	79.1	43.4	47.0	53.0
21607	BARCLAY	90.4	88.8	6.7	8.0	0.0	0.0	2.9	3.4	7.3	7.8	6.9	5.5	4.8	28.6	26.5	11.4	1.1	74.8	39.0	49.2	50.8
21610	BETTERTON	82.2	79.2	15.7	17.9	0.0	0.0	3.1	4.3	4.1	4.9	6.1	5.3	4.9	21.4	33.4	18.5	1.4	81.7	47.1	48.3	51.7
21612	BOZMAN	95.7	94.6	2.7	3.4	0.3	0.3	0.9	1.2	2.9	2.7	4.3	3.9	3.9	14.2	40.4	26.5	1.3	87.8	54.9	48.9	51.1
21613	CAMBRIDGE	62.7	59.9	35.1	37.5	0.7	0.8	1.2	1.5	5.3	5.5	6.5	6.1	6.1	24.0	27.1	16.7	2.8	78.7	42.6	46.9	53.1
	MARYLAND	64.0	61.8	27.9	28.9	4.0	4.6	4.3	5.1	6.6	6.7	7.3	6.9	6.6	29.1	25.1	10.2	1.5	75.2	37.0	48.3	51.7
	UNITED STATES	75.1	73.6	12.3	12.5	3.8	4.2	12.5	14.1	6.9	6.7	7.2	7.0	7.3	28.6	23.8	10.8	1.7	75.1	36.0	49.1	50.9

ZIP CODE #	POST OFFICE NAME	2004 Per Capita Income	2004 HH Income Base	2004 Household Income Distribution (%): Less than $25,000	$25,000 to $49,999	$50,000 to $99,999	$100,000 to $149,999	$150,000 or More	Median Household Income: 2004	2009	2004 National Centile	2004 State Centile	2004 Home Value Base	2004 Home Value Distribution (%): Less than $50,000	$50,000 to $89,999	$90,000 to $174,999	$175,000 to $399,999	$400,000 or More	2004 Median Home Value
21085	JOPPA	28173	6023	12.5	23.5	44.5	14.1	5.4	62305	71791	87	56	4966	2.0	2.0	33.7	59.1	3.2	189133
21087	KINGSVILLE	38344	1983	12.6	17.4	30.7	21.1	18.3	80281	98717	95	81	1846	0.7	0.9	9.5	63.9	25.1	283429
21090	LINTHICUM HEIGHTS	30399	3809	12.2	22.2	38.6	20.5	6.5	65498	77752	89	62	3301	0.5	0.9	23.0	73.3	2.3	203235
21093	LUTHERVILLE TIMONIUM	47984	14892	10.6	19.6	33.0	17.1	19.8	76533	91837	94	75	12406	0.5	0.2	11.6	67.4	20.4	248456
21102	MANCHESTER	25764	3464	10.7	24.0	44.4	15.8	5.1	63611	73207	88	58	3020	0.7	0.3	18.8	73.6	6.6	220408
21104	MARRIOTTSVILLE	31279	1360	9.7	8.7	44.7	22.9	14.0	82746	96391	96	84	1289	0.7	0.3	5.4	71.1	22.5	273416
21108	MILLERSVILLE	33596	6606	8.6	17.4	35.5	23.1	15.4	80061	92804	95	80	5620	0.6	0.4	20.3	56.1	22.7	249788
21111	MONKTON	46595	1887	5.1	16.9	31.0	20.4	26.6	93749	115354	98	90	1700	0.5	0.3	5.9	44.8	48.5	392837
21113	ODENTON	30684	9828	8.1	17.3	47.8	20.3	6.5	72144	83275	92	70	7568	1.9	1.0	24.8	68.9	3.4	199853
21114	CROFTON	38563	8601	5.4	16.5	38.3	23.4	16.5	83254	99311	96	85	7056	0.2	0.1	26.1	63.3	10.2	238616
21117	OWINGS MILLS	39747	18779	11.7	22.9	37.0	16.1	12.3	67866	80675	90	64	11794	0.2	0.4	36.8	46.3	16.3	202617
21120	PARKTON	34337	2222	9.3	14.1	37.9	22.7	16.0	81485	99180	95	82	2059	0.8	1.5	6.3	65.5	25.9	299798
21122	PASADENA	28825	21050	9.3	20.6	44.8	18.5	6.8	68053	79623	90	65	18498	0.4	0.8	28.3	61.7	8.9	202280
21128	PERRY HALL	32044	3036	7.9	19.7	43.6	21.8	7.0	73584	85134	93	72	2781	0.5	0.4	19.5	72.3	7.3	218794
21131	PHOENIX	53613	2461	5.8	14.8	23.2	23.6	32.7	110978	137743	99	96	2314	0.7	0.1	5.7	40.5	53.0	414170
21132	PYLESVILLE	25509	908	11.3	23.6	43.0	15.4	6.7	64425	75000	88	61	806	2.7	2.0	12.8	66.3	16.3	258029
21133	RANDALLSTOWN	26735	10447	15.3	23.6	39.5	16.7	4.9	62352	73959	87	56	7457	0.2	0.3	48.4	48.7	2.4	176384
21136	REISTERSTOWN	33596	12410	10.6	26.2	36.4	15.9	10.9	63555	75844	87	58	9583	0.3	3.5	35.9	46.7	13.6	193793
21140	RIVA	52284	1298	5.6	12.5	33.7	23.1	25.1	96625	114430	98	92	1223	0.1	1.3	11.8	62.1	24.7	288907
21144	SEVERN	27063	11004	12.8	18.0	41.3	20.3	7.6	69209	80582	91	66	8032	4.0	1.4	14.8	75.9	4.0	221516
21146	SEVERNA PARK	41173	8974	6.8	12.2	32.7	28.3	20.0	96633	112919	98	92	8178	0.2	0.3	4.1	67.6	27.8	304375
21152	SPARKS GLENCOE	52691	2035	9.3	18.3	35.5	17.1	19.8	78625	94543	95	79	1568	0.5	0.5	15.9	53.2	29.9	279150
21154	STREET	24658	2115	14.9	23.2	41.0	15.7	5.3	62183	70772	86	55	1864	3.9	2.0	23.7	57.0	13.4	226102
21155	UPPERCO	37926	1072	11.6	19.0	38.1	18.1	13.3	75826	89011	94	74	954	1.6	1.2	12.6	60.2	24.5	270395
21156	UPPER FALLS	32636	148	18.9	16.2	31.1	23.0	10.8	76387	89419	94	75	131	0.0	0.8	14.5	67.9	16.8	238690
21157	WESTMINSTER	26326	13398	18.4	23.2	38.2	14.9	5.3	57980	65906	83	48	10126	0.4	0.4	20.8	71.3	7.1	222825
21158	WESTMINSTER	26148	7075	12.0	23.6	42.5	16.8	5.1	63238	72598	87	57	5841	0.2	0.8	29.0	63.2	6.8	215512
21160	WHITEFORD	28336	823	13.5	25.5	41.6	9.0	10.5	57636	67038	82	47	708	3.3	2.3	41.1	43.2	10.2	199000
21161	WHITE HALL	28908	1828	11.1	16.0	41.3	24.2	7.4	72948	86373	92	71	1640	0.1	0.5	8.4	72.3	18.7	269461
21162	WHITE MARSH	27053	1107	17.0	20.6	41.2	17.3	3.9	62199	74797	86	56	994	10.3	2.2	20.3	64.4	2.8	206371
21163	WOODSTOCK	36220	2112	10.8	14.8	35.4	22.9	16.2	82450	100771	96	83	1860	1.2	0.7	15.7	54.6	27.8	269274
21201	BALTIMORE	21762	7629	58.6	20.8	14.2	3.4	3.1	18709	20960	1	1	852	11.4	20.0	38.3	20.4	10.0	131903
21202	BALTIMORE	17383	7591	54.8	23.7	15.9	3.5	2.1	21473	23396	2	1	1556	12.7	31.4	40.4	13.6	1.9	95380
21204	TOWSON	42745	7317	21.5	19.6	28.8	11.9	18.3	62089	75189	86	55	4284	0.0	0.7	14.0	53.9	31.4	285098
21205	BALTIMORE	12103	6084	51.6	30.2	13.7	2.8	1.7	23908	26527	4	2	3244	53.5	35.7	9.6	1.1	0.2	47662
21206	BALTIMORE	20005	19715	30.1	30.5	30.9	7.0	1.5	40496	45881	48	16	12096	0.9	16.4	74.5	8.1	0.1	116027
21207	GWYNN OAK	21922	18849	23.5	30.1	34.3	9.6	2.6	46512	52913	65	27	11882	0.8	6.0	75.3	17.4	0.5	134875
21208	PIKESVILLE	42000	14100	16.5	23.0	32.8	14.4	13.3	61830	73085	86	54	10035	0.2	2.1	48.5	38.1	11.1	173362
21209	BALTIMORE	39163	10752	19.1	24.5	30.2	12.8	13.3	57498	68663	82	47	6502	0.6	3.1	36.4	52.0	7.9	192156
21210	BALTIMORE	65574	5630	21.4	18.7	22.2	12.9	24.8	68332	88852	90	65	3363	0.5	4.4	19.5	40.6	35.0	292530
21211	BALTIMORE	25676	8226	30.2	33.2	27.9	5.7	3.0	38058	43466	39	13	4457	8.5	37.7	44.9	7.3	1.7	93130
21212	BALTIMORE	33759	13746	22.8	24.4	28.8	12.4	11.7	53163	63522	77	40	9096	1.3	12.8	38.2	36.7	11.0	168156
21213	BALTIMORE	14245	12958	42.8	30.9	20.9	3.8	1.7	30000	33090	12	3	8393	16.0	50.9	31.6	1.1	0.5	79667
21214	BALTIMORE	25018	7958	21.7	30.0	35.5	9.7	3.2	48307	57049	69	29	5729	0.5	8.1	84.6	6.7	0.2	121088
21215	BALTIMORE	17510	24274	41.5	28.9	21.7	5.5	2.5	31298	34950	16	5	13475	8.0	33.6	50.8	7.0	0.6	98159
21216	BALTIMORE	15024	13386	43.7	29.8	21.2	3.8	1.5	29081	31800	10	3	7662	11.8	48.0	36.9	2.8	0.6	83093
21217	BALTIMORE	15672	15929	54.2	24.8	15.1	3.4	2.6	22258	24764	3	1	5280	28.8	32.9	23.0	13.6	1.8	73403
21218	BALTIMORE	22225	20007	41.4	26.9	21.8	6.0	3.9	31804	35370	17	6	9341	12.6	31.8	42.5	9.5	3.5	95750
21219	SPARROWS POINT	24148	3576	20.8	25.5	38.2	10.8	4.8	53060	62578	77	39	2966	6.8	2.5	44.8	41.4	4.5	166479
21220	MIDDLE RIVER	22216	14365	20.9	32.6	35.6	8.7	2.2	46755	53116	66	27	9723	7.4	6.8	50.4	32.0	3.5	139196
21221	ESSEX	20428	17406	29.7	29.8	30.9	7.9	1.8	40026	45570	46	15	10046	1.3	5.5	64.9	26.4	2.0	138594
21222	DUNDALK	21360	21843	26.1	30.1	34.5	7.4	1.8	44729	51444	60	22	15470	2.9	10.0	75.6	10.9	0.6	118000
21223	BALTIMORE	13408	10382	50.0	29.9	16.2	2.4	1.5	25005	27018	5	2	4803	44.0	38.8	15.9	1.0	0.4	54723
21224	BALTIMORE	19045	19346	38.0	30.1	24.0	5.7	2.2	33198	37433	21	8	12640	9.2	37.0	45.1	8.3	0.6	92995
21225	BROOKLYN	16955	11758	39.8	28.6	24.4	5.4	1.8	32686	37628	20	7	6721	6.3	24.1	52.9	16.5	0.3	114954
21226	CURTIS BAY	22362	2868	26.3	28.2	32.6	9.6	3.3	43247	50549	57	20	2008	7.1	17.8	40.4	33.8	1.0	153451
21227	HALETHORPE	22857	12893	22.4	28.8	36.7	9.5	2.6	48906	56166	70	31	8594	1.2	4.4	70.3	23.6	0.6	144787
21228	CATONSVILLE	31020	19395	16.4	23.4	37.8	15.1	7.3	60519	70344	85	51	13841	0.5	0.8	39.9	55.7	3.1	188685
21229	BALTIMORE	18939	19234	35.0	31.0	26.5	5.7	1.9	35791	39783	31	11	11114	4.2	33.3	55.5	6.7	0.4	98260
21230	BALTIMORE	25913	13607	32.3	25.4	28.0	8.7	5.6	40845	46875	49	16	8023	8.2	30.9	39.5	17.9	3.5	102840
21231	BALTIMORE	24657	6943	40.0	24.1	24.6	6.9	4.4	34546	39074	26	9	2538	10.9	22.8	35.5	27.7	3.1	119733
21234	PARKVILLE	25392	27757	20.1	29.9	35.7	10.8	3.5	50001	57722	72	33	18526	0.3	2.1	63.2	33.5	0.8	149613
21236	NOTTINGHAM	29868	17788	15.3	25.9	40.7	13.4	4.8	57319	66221	82	47	12131	0.4	0.5	52.5	46.2	0.5	169358
21237	ROSEDALE	25310	10821	18.8	27.4	39.6	11.1	3.0	52717	60442	76	39	7248	1.0	1.8	58.1	38.6	0.5	159663
21239	BALTIMORE	23830	11716	24.6	32.5	30.9	8.4	3.6	43520	49715	57	21	7249	1.4	12.5	74.2	11.2	0.8	111664
21244	WINDSOR MILL	23481	12531	18.5	32.3	36.5	9.8	2.9	49296	56001	71	32	6580	0.6	1.5	67.3	29.6	1.1	154117
21250	BALTIMORE	16248	5	100.0	0.0	0.0	0.0	0.0	6250	6250	0	0	5	0.0	0.0	0.0	100.0	0.0	190625
21286	TOWSON	37872	8654	20.2	21.5	31.3	15.9	11.1	59203	70552	84	50	5651	0.3	0.7	33.5	52.4	13.2	216504
21401	ANNAPOLIS	39603	21960	13.1	18.7	34.8	18.7	14.8	73108	85368	92	71	16561	0.8	0.7	15.4	57.4	25.7	260293
21402	ANNAPOLIS	19110	479	2.9	26.3	49.7	13.6	7.5	63533	74434	87	58	124	13.7	0.0	0.0	54.8	31.5	339474
21403	ANNAPOLIS	38677	12716	15.2	20.0	33.6	18.5	12.8	67155	79137	90	63	8218	0.4	0.9	19.8	55.5	23.4	256065
21502	CUMBERLAND	19285	17675	37.9	31.1	24.1	4.7	2.1	33543	36920	23	8	12482	17.1	32.5	40.7	8.5	1.1	90438
21520	ACCIDENT	17632	848	37.7	28.9	25.2	5.9	2.2	34792	37448	27	9	703	10.8	11.4	47.4	24.3	6.1	136630
21521	BARTON	18224	402	35.6	29.4	28.6	5.5	1.0	36124	40000	32	11	313	27.2	30.7	31.0	9.9	1.3	78036
21522	BITTINGER	13893	94	40.4	33.0	19.2	5.3	2.1	30539	32315	14	4	84	9.5	19.1	46.4	21.4	3.6	115789
21523	BLOOMINGTON	20480	181	28.7	27.1	34.8	7.2	2.2	46130	51085	64	25	155	5.8	23.2	51.0	18.1	1.9	117905
21530	FLINTSTONE	19808	564	29.8	43.4	20.4	5.0	1.4	37750	41717	38	13	475	12.4	28.4	41.1	14.7	3.4	105242
21531	FRIENDSVILLE	15859	952	39.7	34.8	20.2	3.7	1.7	30579	33720	14	4	734	18.4	17.7	42.2	17.3	4.4	118864
21532	FROSTBURG	18515	5838	41.7	25.1	26.2	5.5	1.5	31467	34262	16	5	3878	14.4	30.3	40.2	14.3	0.9	96743
21536	GRANTSVILLE	17146	1567	37.1	32.3	24.4	4.5	1.7	32885	35619	21	7	1262	9.5	14.6	53.9	19.3	2.7	126607
21538	KITZMILLER	17082	269	37.6	34.2	23.4	2.2	2.6	30633	34224	14	4	219	33.3	21.0	33.3	12.3	0.0	81364
21539	LONACONING	17105	1429	37.4	32.3	24.9	4.5	0.9	32913	36739	21	7	1071	29.3	36.6	24.8	8.2	1.0	70759
21540	LUKE	15924	37	54.1	29.7	16.2	0.0	0.0	22260	23113	3	2	26	23.1	61.5	15.4	0.0	0.0	67500
21541	MC HENRY	30196	544	25.4	30.5	25.6	8.5	10.1	43804	51652	58	21	458	2.2	9.0	39.3	31.2	18.3	173958
21545	MOUNT SAVAGE	18650	1067	30.8	38.7	24.1	4.3	2.1	36153	40534	32	12	870	24.8	38.2	30.6	4.8	1.6	73810
21550	OAKLAND	17943	5807	37.1	32.4	23.1	4.7	2.7	33560	37092	23	8	4447	9.8	15.3	49.8	20.4	4.7	125789
21555	OLDTOWN	18833	773	24.6	40.2	28.6	5.6	1.0	39852	43836	45	15	661	21.5	28.6	43.3	6.2	0.5	89921
21557	RAWLINGS	18482	811	28.2	34.0	30.3	6.8	0.6	39813	42875	45	14	699	25.6	18.7	41.8	12.5	1.4	100700
21561	SWANTON	23218	973	26.1	28.2	34.9	7.5	3.3	45778	51446	63	24	822	11.1	17.4	35.3	27.0	9.3	134750
21562	WESTERNPORT	15873	1265	43.1	33.1	21.6	1.7	0.6	29542	32580	11	3	948	27.3	42.3	28.1	1.5	0.8	70648
21601	EASTON	33497	8925	26.7	26.7	28.0	9.7	9.0	46476	54936	65	26	6215	2.8	2.9	33.3	39.3	21.7	203805
21607	BARCLAY	20756	163	19.0	29.5	41.7	8.0	1.8	50915	57029	74	36	137	0.7	3.7	41.6	44.5	9.5	185577
21610	BETTERTON	33685	212	17.0	33.5	32.1	8.0	9.4	48682	56200	70	30	178	4.5	4.5	39.3	22.5	29.2	184375
21612	BOZMAN	54011	369	14.1	25.8	30.9	11.7	17.6	65289	83725	89	62	335	0.0	0.6	22.1	38.5	38.8	286905
21613	CAMBRIDGE	21426	7145	37.5	28.4	25.6	5.1	3.4	34058	37752	24	9	4474	7.7	10.7	44.1	28.6	8.9	140868
	MARYLAND	30267		17.9	23.3	34.6	15.0	9.2	59732	70285				2.9	5.4	28.1	49.8	13.8	209514
	UNITED STATES	25866		24.7	27.1	30.8	10.9	6.5	48124	56710				10.9	15.0	33.7	30.1	10.4	145905

#	POST OFFICE NAME	FINANCIAL SERVICES: Auto Loan	Home Loan	Investments	Retirement Plans	THE HOME: Home Improvements: Home Repair	Lawn & Garden	Furnishings: Computers & Hardware	Major Appliances	TV, Radio, Sound Equipment	Furniture	ENTERTAINMENT: Dine out/Carry out	Sports Equipment	Fees & Tickets	Toys & Games	Travel	Cable TV	PERSONAL: Apparel & Services	Auto Repairs	Health Insurance	Pets & Supplies
21085	JOPPA	95	112	119	111	109	111	104	103	98	104	124	120	108	129	105	96	123	101	95	113
21087	KINGSVILLE	138	166	187	164	165	174	153	153	145	153	182	173	162	185	159	145	180	149	147	167
21090	LINTHICUM HEIGHTS	100	119	132	115	118	125	111	111	109	110	136	125	118	141	115	109	134	109	109	121
21093	LUTHERVILLE TIMONIUM	147	173	205	174	170	180	163	161	155	163	196	184	173	200	167	154	194	158	151	176
21102	MANCHESTER	100	118	122	117	117	117	106	107	101	106	126	126	112	134	109	99	125	104	99	121
21104	MARRIOTTSVILLE	134	160	166	164	155	153	143	141	132	146	167	165	152	172	144	126	166	137	124	156
21108	MILLERSVILLE	134	154	166	158	150	152	144	142	135	145	171	166	151	174	144	130	170	140	128	156
21111	MONKTON	167	206	225	209	202	205	184	182	170	186	215	210	199	223	189	166	216	176	165	200
21113	ODENTON	116	131	128	135	125	122	119	118	110	123	139	138	122	140	117	103	138	115	102	129
21114	CROFTON	145	164	167	170	158	156	152	149	140	155	178	175	157	179	149	132	176	147	130	164
21117	OWINGS MILLS	136	140	152	149	135	137	140	135	132	143	169	161	141	165	135	125	166	138	119	150
21120	PARKTON	132	164	176	165	161	160	146	145	135	146	171	169	157	180	150	132	171	140	131	160
21122	PASADENA	109	128	134	129	125	125	118	117	110	119	139	136	123	144	118	106	138	114	105	128
21128	PERRY HALL	115	132	137	134	128	129	122	121	115	124	145	140	127	147	122	110	143	118	109	133
21131	PHOENIX	206	251	276	258	245	249	226	221	208	228	264	256	245	271	230	202	264	215	201	244
21132	PYLESVILLE	96	120	127	120	117	116	107	106	99	106	124	124	113	132	109	96	124	102	95	117
21133	RANDALLSTOWN	98	105	116	107	102	106	103	101	100	104	126	119	106	126	102	97	124	102	94	112
21136	REISTERSTOWN	122	139	149	141	135	137	130	129	123	132	156	150	136	159	131	120	154	127	117	142
21140	RIVA	190	236	254	241	230	230	209	206	192	211	243	240	227	255	213	186	244	199	184	228
21144	SEVERN	111	119	124	121	115	117	114	113	110	116	138	132	117	139	113	106	136	113	103	126
21146	SEVERNA PARK	152	186	204	187	183	186	168	167	157	169	198	193	180	206	173	154	197	162	153	184
21152	SPARKS GLENCOE	166	184	210	190	184	192	179	178	171	179	214	207	185	213	181	166	210	177	169	195
21154	STREET	99	110	107	109	111	112	99	102	96	99	119	120	103	126	102	95	117	99	98	119
21155	UPPERCO	124	150	167	149	149	154	137	137	129	137	162	156	145	166	142	128	161	133	129	150
21156	UPPER FALLS	119	139	154	133	138	149	131	131	129	130	161	146	139	167	136	132	159	128	132	143
21157	WESTMINSTER	92	102	112	103	101	104	100	98	96	99	120	114	103	124	100	94	118	97	92	108
21158	WESTMINSTER	99	113	121	116	111	111	106	105	99	106	125	123	110	128	106	95	123	103	94	115
21160	WHITEFORD	122	116	95	111	120	127	106	115	110	106	134	137	106	138	109	111	129	112	121	145
21161	WHITE HALL	108	134	143	134	131	130	119	119	111	119	139	139	127	148	122	108	139	115	107	132
21162	WHITE MARSH	92	104	111	99	103	113	98	99	98	97	122	111	103	126	102	100	119	97	101	110
21163	WOODSTOCK	131	162	178	162	157	158	145	143	134	146	170	166	155	178	148	131	170	139	128	157
21201	BALTIMORE	50	41	52	42	40	47	52	48	54	51	68	58	49	64	49	53	65	53	49	54
21202	BALTIMORE	49	41	52	41	40	47	50	47	53	49	66	56	48	62	47	53	64	51	49	53
21204	TOWSON	132	135	168	138	133	145	150	138	144	143	181	165	148	179	144	139	177	143	131	151
21205	BALTIMORE	47	42	49	39	41	48	46	46	51	47	63	51	46	61	46	53	61	47	50	52
21206	BALTIMORE	66	66	77	66	65	71	70	68	71	70	89	78	72	90	70	71	87	69	67	75
21207	GWYNN OAK	76	76	86	76	74	81	79	77	80	80	100	88	80	98	78	79	98	79	76	86
21208	PIKESVILLE	129	140	164	141	139	149	138	137	135	138	169	156	142	168	140	133	166	137	133	150
21209	BALTIMORE	113	120	152	125	118	126	124	119	121	124	153	141	127	154	124	119	151	123	113	131
21210	BALTIMORE	168	185	237	188	183	197	185	180	182	186	229	208	193	230	189	181	225	182	174	198
21211	BALTIMORE	69	69	86	70	69	76	75	72	76	74	95	84	76	96	75	76	93	75	72	79
21212	BALTIMORE	109	113	143	115	110	121	118	113	117	118	148	131	121	148	118	117	145	116	110	125
21213	BALTIMORE	56	49	57	46	48	57	54	54	59	55	73	59	54	69	53	62	71	56	59	62
21214	BALTIMORE	80	86	100	86	85	90	88	85	87	86	109	99	90	111	88	86	106	86	83	93
21215	BALTIMORE	62	57	66	54	56	66	61	61	66	62	82	67	62	78	61	68	79	62	66	69
21216	BALTIMORE	55	49	55	46	48	57	52	53	57	54	71	57	53	66	52	60	68	54	58	60
21217	BALTIMORE	52	43	51	41	42	50	51	49	56	51	69	56	49	64	49	57	66	52	54	56
21218	BALTIMORE	73	63	77	63	62	72	76	70	79	74	99	82	73	93	72	79	95	75	73	80
21219	SPARROWS POINT	83	91	93	87	92	98	86	88	87	85	108	100	90	115	89	88	105	86	89	99
21220	MIDDLE RIVER	79	79	82	79	79	85	80	80	81	80	101	93	81	102	80	80	98	80	80	91
21221	ESSEX	70	66	69	66	67	74	70	70	72	69	89	81	70	89	69	72	86	71	72	79
21222	DUNDALK	70	73	79	70	74	81	74	73	76	72	95	83	77	99	75	78	92	73	77	81
21223	BALTIMORE	51	44	48	41	43	51	49	49	54	49	66	54	48	62	48	56	63	50	54	56
21224	BALTIMORE	59	59	69	57	58	66	63	61	65	62	81	69	64	83	63	67	79	62	64	68
21225	BROOKLYN	59	57	64	54	56	64	61	60	65	60	80	68	62	80	61	66	78	61	63	67
21226	CURTIS BAY	78	79	81	79	77	80	81	79	79	80	99	92	80	99	78	77	97	80	75	86
21227	HALETHORPE	77	81	92	79	80	87	83	81	84	81	105	93	85	107	83	85	102	82	82	90
21228	CATONSVILLE	97	108	127	110	107	112	107	105	103	107	130	123	111	132	108	101	128	105	98	114
21229	BALTIMORE	64	61	72	59	59	67	65	63	68	66	85	72	66	84	65	69	83	65	66	71
21230	BALTIMORE	79	76	100	77	75	84	84	80	87	83	109	93	85	111	83	88	106	83	82	89
21231	BALTIMORE	68	62	92	65	60	68	73	68	76	73	96	81	73	95	71	76	94	72	67	76
21234	PARKVILLE	80	86	98	86	84	89	87	84	85	86	107	98	89	108	86	84	105	85	81	92
21236	NOTTINGHAM	96	101	112	104	99	103	101	99	98	102	123	116	103	122	100	94	121	100	92	109
21237	ROSEDALE	85	87	95	89	85	90	89	87	87	89	109	102	89	108	87	84	107	88	82	96
21239	BALTIMORE	77	75	89	73	73	82	80	77	82	80	104	87	81	102	79	83	101	79	79	87
21244	WINDSOR MILL	84	79	89	83	76	83	84	81	84	86	106	95	84	101	81	81	104	85	77	91
21250	BALTIMORE	9	6	7	6	6	7	11	8	11	9	13	11	9	12	9	9	12	10	7	9
21286	TOWSON	108	117	145	119	115	124	120	116	118	118	148	135	123	149	121	116	145	118	112	127
21401	ANNAPOLIS	128	141	169	143	138	146	137	135	133	139	168	155	143	170	139	132	166	135	128	149
21402	ANNAPOLIS	136	98	97	109	91	104	132	116	132	125	166	151	118	151	113	122	160	133	108	132
21403	ANNAPOLIS	115	129	164	132	125	132	129	123	125	129	157	145	134	161	129	122	156	125	114	135
21502	CUMBERLAND	59	57	58	55	58	66	59	60	62	57	76	68	59	77	60	63	72	60	64	68
21520	ACCIDENT	83	59	31	54	67	76	57	71	66	57	78	85	49	76	59	70	71	70	85	98
21521	BARTON	62	65	65	61	66	73	63	64	66	61	81	72	66	87	65	68	78	62	69	72
21522	BITTINGER	80	53	24	46	61	70	52	65	62	53	73	77	44	69	52	67	66	64	80	92
21523	BLOOMINGTON	92	64	31	55	71	82	61	75	73	62	86	90	53	82	62	78	78	75	92	106
21530	FLINTSTONE	96	64	29	56	73	84	62	78	75	63	88	93	53	83	63	81	80	77	96	110
21531	FRIENDSVILLE	66	48	28	44	53	62	50	58	58	49	68	67	44	64	50	61	62	58	70	75
21532	FROSTBURG	61	56	62	57	57	63	64	60	64	61	80	73	62	79	61	63	77	63	61	69
21536	GRANTSVILLE	73	57	38	54	62	70	57	64	63	56	75	75	52	74	57	65	70	63	73	83
21538	KITZMILLER	82	55	25	47	62	71	53	66	64	54	75	79	45	71	54	69	68	65	81	94
21539	LONACONING	55	58	59	55	59	65	57	57	59	55	73	64	60	79	59	61	71	56	62	65
21540	LUKE	48	36	24	35	40	47	40	44	45	38	53	49	36	50	40	47	48	44	53	53
21541	MC HENRY	119	92	61	83	103	117	87	105	99	86	117	123	77	115	92	106	109	103	125	144
21545	MOUNT SAVAGE	67	61	53	58	64	74	63	66	68	61	82	74	62	84	64	71	78	66	75	77
21550	OAKLAND	76	57	35	53	63	72	58	67	66	57	78	77	52	75	59	69	71	66	79	87
21555	OLDTOWN	90	62	31	56	71	81	60	75	71	60	83	90	52	80	62	75	76	74	91	105
21557	RAWLINGS	84	61	35	56	67	77	60	71	69	61	82	84	54	79	61	73	76	70	84	95
21561	SWANTON	103	75	44	67	85	96	72	88	83	72	98	103	63	95	75	89	90	86	105	122
21562	WESTERNPORT	54	50	44	48	52	60	52	54	55	49	67	60	51	68	52	58	63	53	60	62
21601	EASTON	105	109	118	108	110	119	108	109	108	108	135	123	110	133	110	109	131	109	110	121
21607	BARCLAY	89	79	60	75	84	90	73	81	78	73	95	97	72	97	76	80	90	79	88	105
21610	BETTERTON	131	103	70	93	116	130	97	117	110	96	130	137	87	128	103	117	121	115	138	159
21612	BOZMAN	171	160	154	152	170	200	148	169	157	159	195	165	150	162	161	168	182	164	197	193
21613	CAMBRIDGE	67	64	67	61	65	73	66	67	70	65	86	75	66	86	67	72	83	67	73	77
	MARYLAND	108	114	128	115	112	119	113	111	111	114	139	129	116	140	113	109	137	112	106	124
	UNITED STATES	100	100	100	100	100	100	100	100	100	100	100	100	100	100	100	100	100	100	100	100

POPULATION CHANGE

ZIP CODE #	POST OFFICE NAME	COUNTY FIPS CODE	POPULATION 2000	2004	2009	2000-2004 ANNUAL RATE % Rate	State Centile	HOUSEHOLDS 2000	2004	2009	% Annual Rate 2000-2004	2004 Average HH Size	FAMILIES 2000	2004	% Annual Rate 2000-2004
21617	CENTREVILLE	035	6502	7095	7927	2.1	77	2395	2630	2965	2.2	2.60	1773	1930	2.0
21619	CHESTER	035	5331	6034	6891	3.0	90	2200	2525	2914	3.3	2.39	1540	1746	3.0
21620	CHESTERTOWN	029	12185	12894	14031	1.3	56	4826	5195	5766	1.8	2.25	3147	3352	1.5
21622	CHURCH CREEK	019	384	386	393	0.1	23	185	189	195	0.5	2.03	129	130	0.2
21623	CHURCH HILL	035	1523	1571	1698	0.7	42	535	558	614	1.0	2.55	377	389	0.7
21625	CORDOVA	041	2668	2856	3074	1.6	64	937	1012	1098	1.8	2.81	746	798	1.6
21626	CRAPO	019	149	140	139	-1.5	2	56	53	53	-1.3	2.64	38	35	-1.9
21628	CRUMPTON	035	395	464	539	3.9	97	168	199	233	4.1	2.32	124	146	3.9
21629	DENTON	011	8005	8221	8541	0.6	37	3048	3148	3285	0.8	2.49	2177	2227	0.5
21631	EAST NEW MARKET	019	2603	2649	2686	0.4	29	1026	1057	1084	0.7	2.49	756	771	0.5
21632	FEDERALSBURG	011	6255	6452	6731	0.7	42	2453	2541	2660	0.8	2.54	1771	1816	0.6
21634	FISHING CREEK	019	525	503	499	-1.0	4	233	226	227	-0.7	2.16	158	150	-1.2
21635	GALENA	029	1863	2097	2356	2.8	88	754	865	989	3.3	2.40	545	619	3.0
21636	GOLDSBORO	011	1115	1142	1175	0.6	35	400	410	424	0.6	2.75	308	313	0.4
21638	GRASONVILLE	035	3921	4223	4741	1.8	67	1552	1692	1917	2.1	2.49	1143	1237	1.9
21639	GREENSBORO	011	3978	4247	4475	1.6	63	1461	1560	1647	1.6	2.71	1061	1123	1.4
21640	HENDERSON	011	1619	1657	1713	0.6	34	597	611	633	0.6	2.70	450	456	0.3
21643	HURLOCK	019	5218	5634	5881	1.8	69	1964	2141	2257	2.1	2.62	1423	1533	1.8
21644	INGLESIDE	035	117	123	135	1.2	52	46	49	54	1.5	2.51	36	38	1.3
21645	KENNEDYVILLE	029	1238	1415	1598	3.2	93	441	524	610	4.1	2.50	325	382	3.9
21647	MCDANIEL	041	394	391	411	-0.2	14	175	176	187	0.1	2.22	118	117	-0.2
21648	MADISON	019	329	325	328	-0.3	10	125	125	127	0.0	2.54	86	85	-0.3
21649	MARYDEL	011	1626	1675	1744	0.7	41	494	507	529	0.6	3.29	376	383	0.4
21650	MASSEY	029	197	215	238	2.1	78	65	72	81	2.4	2.93	46	51	2.5
21651	MILLINGTON	029	2283	2489	2771	2.1	76	867	959	1082	2.4	2.56	636	697	2.2
21654	OXFORD	041	1400	1404	1473	0.1	22	668	673	712	0.2	2.08	449	445	-0.2
21655	PRESTON	011	4924	5234	5551	1.5	59	1849	1978	2108	1.6	2.65	1435	1523	1.4
21657	QUEEN ANNE	035	873	976	1101	2.7	86	325	364	413	2.7	2.68	247	274	2.5
21658	QUEENSTOWN	035	3735	4127	4650	2.4	82	1407	1563	1773	2.5	2.62	1124	1240	2.3
21659	RHODESDALE	019	1684	1630	1623	-0.8	6	690	677	682	-0.5	2.41	490	474	-0.8
21660	RIDGELY	011	3366	3390	3474	0.2	23	1220	1235	1271	0.3	2.71	901	904	0.1
21661	ROCK HALL	029	2728	3012	3356	2.4	81	1233	1387	1573	2.8	2.17	810	898	2.5
21662	ROYAL OAK	041	366	369	385	0.2	24	162	165	173	0.4	2.24	118	119	0.2
21663	SAINT MICHAELS	041	3658	3779	4011	0.8	42	1694	1770	1895	1.0	2.13	1123	1158	0.7
21665	SHERWOOD	041	224	222	233	-0.2	13	101	102	108	0.2	2.18	68	68	0.0
21666	STEVENSVILLE	035	11478	12818	14532	2.6	85	4112	4613	5260	2.7	2.78	3258	3636	2.6
21667	STILL POND	029	312	387	455	5.2	99	117	147	176	5.5	2.63	86	107	5.2
21668	SUDLERSVILLE	035	1768	1831	1993	0.8	44	666	696	765	1.0	2.58	496	514	0.8
21669	TAYLORS ISLAND	019	220	211	209	-1.0	5	98	95	95	-0.7	2.16	66	63	-1.1
21671	TILGHMAN	041	830	821	860	-0.3	11	357	358	378	0.1	2.29	254	252	-0.2
21672	TODDVILLE	019	434	409	405	-1.4	2	200	190	190	-1.2	2.15	134	126	-1.4
21673	TRAPPE	041	3264	3592	3929	2.3	80	1259	1395	1535	2.4	2.57	979	1072	2.2
21675	WINGATE	019	45	42	42	-1.6	1	22	21	21	-1.1	2.00	15	14	-1.6
21676	WITTMAN	041	247	245	257	-0.2	14	121	122	129	0.2	2.01	81	81	0.0
21677	WOOLFORD	019	308	357	387	3.5	95	129	151	165	3.8	2.36	97	112	3.4
21678	WORTON	029	2174	2478	2803	3.1	92	832	960	1102	3.4	2.57	630	720	3.2
21679	WYE MILLS	041	320	358	395	2.7	86	123	139	155	2.9	2.58	98	110	2.8
21701	FREDERICK	021	32090	35552	40175	2.4	84	12968	14409	16391	2.5	2.37	8017	8848	2.4
21702	FREDERICK	021	30982	34511	39161	2.6	84	11713	13207	15143	2.9	2.56	8107	9038	2.6
21703	FREDERICK	021	26601	30490	35117	3.3	93	9796	11339	13178	3.5	2.66	6866	7852	3.2
21704	FREDERICK	021	4538	5706	6918	5.5	100	1511	1894	2303	5.5	2.97	1246	1547	5.2
21710	ADAMSTOWN	021	2595	3142	3715	4.6	98	938	1153	1377	5.0	2.71	723	881	4.8
21711	BIG POOL	043	1016	1070	1133	1.2	53	380	405	433	1.5	2.64	292	309	1.3
21713	BOONSBORO	043	8206	8487	8883	0.8	44	3055	3185	3361	1.0	2.57	2256	2328	0.7
21716	BRUNSWICK	021	4892	5220	5780	1.5	62	1865	2010	2244	1.8	2.60	1312	1396	1.5
21718	BURKITTSVILLE	021	180	218	257	4.6	98	77	94	112	4.8	2.32	63	76	4.5
21719	CASCADE	043	1600	1596	1657	-0.1	17	590	595	623	0.2	2.67	448	448	0.0
21722	CLEAR SPRING	043	5170	5119	5290	-0.2	12	1865	1865	1945	0.0	2.73	1489	1480	-0.1
21723	COOKSVILLE	027	333	361	386	1.9	71	112	122	131	2.0	2.96	98	107	2.1
21727	EMMITSBURG	021	5652	5976	6474	1.3	55	1534	1675	1880	2.1	2.62	1123	1212	1.8
21733	FAIRPLAY	043	4904	4971	5035	0.3	26	340	368	395	1.9	2.67	277	297	1.7
21737	GLENELG	027	915	1036	1132	3.0	90	278	316	346	3.1	3.25	248	280	2.4
21738	GLENWOOD	027	2310	2475	2628	1.6	65	699	755	806	1.8	3.28	625	671	1.7
21740	HAGERSTOWN	043	56313	58483	61631	0.9	46	22089	23163	24686	1.1	2.34	13930	14467	0.9
21742	HAGERSTOWN	043	23628	25672	27593	2.0	74	9455	10351	11212	2.2	2.43	6615	7160	1.9
21750	HANCOCK	043	3969	3940	4073	-0.2	15	1584	1590	1660	0.1	2.45	1137	1127	-0.2
21754	IJAMSVILLE	021	5590	6286	7179	2.8	87	1788	2034	2345	3.1	3.09	1572	1773	2.9
21755	JEFFERSON	021	6307	6849	7703	2.0	73	2191	2405	2728	2.2	2.82	1778	1938	2.1
21756	KEEDYSVILLE	043	2604	2763	2970	1.4	58	905	964	1042	1.5	2.85	736	778	1.3
21757	KEYMAR	013	2796	2985	3285	1.6	63	981	1056	1171	1.8	2.78	782	836	1.6
21758	KNOXVILLE	021	3813	4127	4531	1.9	71	1364	1489	1646	2.1	2.77	1052	1137	1.9
21765	LISBON	027	70	76	81	2.0	73	29	32	34	2.3	2.38	25	28	2.7
21766	LITTLE ORLEANS	001	649	667	672	0.7	39	251	261	265	0.9	2.56	189	195	0.7
21767	MAUGANSVILLE	043	1057	1021	1048	-0.8	6	465	455	472	-0.5	2.23	299	285	-1.1
21769	MIDDLETOWN	021	9540	10757	12256	2.9	88	3309	3757	4309	3.0	2.86	2697	3040	2.9
21770	MONROVIA	021	5702	5925	6466	0.9	46	1830	1923	2116	1.2	3.08	1626	1701	1.1
21771	MOUNT AIRY	021	25299	29105	33159	3.4	94	8127	9433	10819	3.6	3.08	6905	7957	3.4
21773	MYERSVILLE	021	4842	5278	5909	2.1	76	1672	1829	2058	2.1	2.89	1369	1489	2.0
21774	NEW MARKET	021	8519	10012	11639	3.9	97	2782	3280	3828	4.0	3.05	2320	2719	3.8
21776	NEW WINDSOR	013	6090	6482	7133	1.5	59	2087	2234	2470	1.6	2.90	1688	1793	1.4
21777	POINT OF ROCKS	021	1071	1132	1246	1.3	54	365	389	432	1.5	2.91	283	300	1.4
21778	ROCKY RIDGE	021	891	925	1009	0.9	46	327	343	377	1.1	2.70	264	275	1.0
21779	ROHRERSVILLE	043	937	930	964	-0.2	14	333	332	347	-0.1	2.79	265	262	-0.3
21780	SABILLASVILLE	021	1603	1741	1933	2.0	73	509	563	638	2.4	2.79	411	452	2.3
21782	SHARPSBURG	043	4059	4154	4349	0.6	34	1525	1576	1663	0.8	2.63	1178	1206	0.6
21783	SMITHSBURG	043	9555	10234	11044	1.6	65	3609	3888	4222	1.8	2.62	2743	2922	1.5
21784	SYKESVILLE	013	34900	37768	41628	1.9	71	11612	12654	14053	2.0	2.88	9479	10269	1.9
21787	TANEYTOWN	013	8979	9747	10748	2.0	73	3180	3473	3852	2.1	2.80	2499	2708	1.9
21788	THURMONT	021	10750	11449	12660	1.5	60	4012	4296	4779	1.6	2.65	3062	3247	1.4
21790	TUSCARORA	021	99	111	126	2.7	87	41	46	52	2.7	2.39	32	35	2.1
21791	UNION BRIDGE	021	5310	5452	5908	0.6	37	1850	1912	2084	0.8	2.85	1464	1502	0.6
21793	WALKERSVILLE	021	9420	10266	11487	2.0	76	3131	3457	3908	2.4	2.93	2584	2835	2.2
21794	WEST FRIENDSHIP	027	1876	1993	2126	1.4	59	570	607	648	1.5	3.26	502	533	1.4
21795	WILLIAMSPORT	043	8436	9157	9828	2.0	73	3363	3669	3960	2.1	2.41	2309	2498	1.9
21797	WOODBINE	027	8043	8383	8968	1.0	47	2669	2803	3016	1.2	2.99	2276	2377	1.0
	MARYLAND					1.1					1.1	2.60			1.0
	UNITED STATES					1.2					1.3	2.58			1.1

# ZIP CODE	POST OFFICE NAME	RACE (%) White 2000	White 2004	Black 2000	Black 2004	Asian/Pacific 2000	Asian/Pacific 2004	% Hispanic Origin 2000	% Hispanic Origin 2004	2004 AGE DISTRIBUTION (%) 0-4	5-9	10-14	15-19	20-24	25-44	45-64	65-84	85+	18+	MEDIAN AGE 2004	% 2004 Males	% 2004 Females
21617	CENTREVILLE	84.7	82.1	13.6	15.9	0.4	0.4	0.7	0.9	6.4	7.0	7.5	6.3	4.9	27.8	26.0	11.9	2.3	75.0	39.9	49.2	50.8
21619	CHESTER	90.6	89.0	6.6	7.6	0.9	1.0	1.1	1.4	5.9	6.2	6.6	5.9	4.6	27.7	28.5	13.4	1.1	77.8	41.2	49.5	50.5
21620	CHESTERTOWN	78.2	75.6	19.2	21.4	0.9	1.1	1.5	1.9	4.6	4.9	6.0	8.5	9.1	21.3	25.4	17.1	3.1	80.8	41.9	46.7	53.3
21622	CHURCH CREEK	93.5	92.0	5.0	6.5	0.3	0.3	0.8	0.8	4.2	4.9	6.0	4.9	3.6	23.1	30.6	21.0	1.8	81.9	47.3	49.5	50.5
21623	CHURCH HILL	80.4	77.2	17.2	20.1	0.4	0.5	1.5	2.0	5.0	5.5	6.1	5.8	5.4	33.2	26.5	10.9	1.7	79.6	39.2	52.6	47.4
21625	CORDOVA	87.3	84.7	11.2	13.3	0.3	0.4	1.1	1.4	5.8	6.7	8.0	7.0	4.7	26.1	28.6	11.9	1.2	74.7	40.4	49.3	50.7
21626	CRAPO	94.0	92.9	4.0	5.0	0.0	0.0	0.7	0.0	4.3	5.0	5.7	3.6	4.3	24.3	29.3	21.4	2.1	82.9	46.8	50.0	50.0
21628	CRUMPTON	84.6	81.9	13.7	16.0	0.3	0.4	1.3	1.5	5.8	6.0	7.8	6.0	5.4	30.0	25.9	11.9	1.3	76.5	39.7	48.3	51.7
21629	DENTON	84.4	82.8	13.4	14.6	0.4	0.5	1.1	1.4	5.0	5.5	7.3	6.8	5.7	25.7	27.3	13.9	2.8	77.9	41.4	49.1	50.9
21631	EAST NEW MARKET	88.4	86.0	9.9	11.8	0.7	0.8	1.4	1.9	5.5	5.8	6.3	5.6	5.1	25.6	30.0	14.4	1.8	78.9	42.8	48.7	51.3
21632	FEDERALSBURG	73.3	69.6	23.8	27.0	0.6	0.7	1.3	1.7	6.8	6.7	7.7	7.3	6.2	25.4	25.8	12.6	1.6	74.4	38.1	47.2	52.8
21634	FISHING CREEK	93.5	92.3	5.1	6.4	0.2	0.2	1.5	2.0	4.6	5.0	4.8	7.0	3.6	22.3	29.4	21.3	2.2	81.3	47.4	52.5	47.5
21635	GALENA	90.2	88.3	7.8	9.3	0.3	0.3	2.3	2.9	5.1	5.5	6.5	6.3	4.2	27.3	27.9	15.4	2.1	78.3	42.5	49.8	50.2
21636	GOLDSBORO	90.4	88.6	6.5	7.5	0.6	0.8	2.6	3.4	6.7	7.0	7.9	6.7	5.7	29.2	26.1	9.5	1.1	73.9	37.1	50.3	49.7
21638	GRASONVILLE	79.4	78.0	18.7	19.8	0.3	0.4	1.4	1.7	5.4	5.6	6.1	6.3	4.9	22.1	31.2	16.3	2.0	78.8	44.7	49.1	50.9
21639	GREENSBORO	87.8	85.9	9.0	10.2	0.7	0.8	1.6	2.1	6.2	6.6	8.6	7.5	6.4	29.0	24.3	10.1	1.2	73.6	36.4	48.3	51.7
21640	HENDERSON	86.2	83.7	6.9	7.9	0.4	0.4	8.0	10.1	7.5	7.1	7.5	7.4	7.1	28.7	24.6	9.0	1.2	73.3	35.1	50.9	49.1
21643	HURLOCK	63.6	58.1	33.5	38.6	0.9	1.0	1.7	1.9	6.2	6.5	7.8	7.5	6.3	28.2	25.3	11.2	1.2	74.5	37.8	47.4	52.6
21644	INGLESIDE	90.6	88.6	6.8	8.1	0.0	0.0	2.6	3.3	7.3	7.3	6.5	4.9	4.9	31.7	26.8	9.8	0.8	74.0	39.3	49.6	50.4
21645	KENNEDYVILLE	80.1	77.0	11.2	13.1	0.1	0.1	13.6	15.6	5.4	5.7	5.7	5.9	5.3	26.4	31.6	12.4	1.7	79.8	42.2	54.4	45.7
21647	MCDANIEL	89.1	87.0	10.4	12.5	0.0	0.0	0.8	1.0	4.1	4.6	5.4	4.9	3.6	21.0	30.4	23.3	2.8	82.1	49.3	50.9	49.1
21648	MADISON	93.3	91.7	5.5	6.8	0.3	0.3	1.5	1.9	4.6	4.9	4.9	6.8	3.4	22.2	30.5	20.9	1.9	81.2	47.6	51.4	48.6
21649	MARYDEL	79.1	75.3	5.0	5.5	0.6	0.6	19.9	24.4	7.9	6.3	7.3	9.0	9.2	29.2	22.6	7.5	1.0	73.1	31.8	54.2	45.8
21650	MASSEY	79.2	77.2	16.8	19.1	0.0	0.0	6.1	7.0	5.1	6.5	7.4	7.0	5.1	27.4	26.1	13.0	2.3	76.7	40.1	52.1	47.9
21651	MILLINGTON	83.2	80.6	13.6	15.6	0.4	0.4	4.1	4.8	5.4	6.0	7.6	6.7	5.3	28.9	26.5	12.1	1.5	76.8	39.8	49.7	50.3
21654	OXFORD	91.1	89.4	7.9	9.5	0.2	0.2	0.6	0.8	3.0	3.6	4.8	4.3	2.9	16.2	37.7	23.9	3.6	85.8	55.5	47.7	52.3
21655	PRESTON	82.2	79.5	16.0	18.4	0.6	0.7	0.3	0.3	5.9	6.3	7.3	6.3	5.3	28.5	26.9	12.2	1.3	76.6	39.9	49.7	50.3
21657	QUEEN ANNE	89.5	87.3	9.3	11.2	0.1	0.2	0.8	1.0	6.2	7.3	8.9	6.7	4.4	29.9	25.4	9.9	1.3	73.5	38.4	50.7	49.3
21658	QUEENSTOWN	89.8	88.1	7.7	8.9	0.7	0.8	1.4	1.7	5.9	6.5	6.5	5.6	4.1	23.6	31.5	14.8	1.5	77.5	43.7	50.5	49.5
21659	RHODESDALE	86.0	83.3	12.2	14.5	0.6	0.7	0.8	1.0	5.7	6.0	6.8	6.4	5.2	25.5	29.3	13.6	1.5	77.6	41.8	48.3	51.7
21660	RIDGELY	79.2	76.2	18.1	20.5	0.8	0.9	2.2	2.8	7.4	7.5	8.2	7.2	5.7	28.8	24.0	9.9	1.3	72.6	36.0	48.8	51.2
21661	ROCK HALL	87.9	86.6	10.8	11.8	0.1	0.1	1.1	1.3	4.3	4.7	5.9	5.3	4.2	20.2	32.7	19.9	2.9	82.0	48.6	47.7	52.3
21662	ROYAL OAK	88.3	85.9	11.2	13.6	0.3	0.3	0.6	1.1	3.8	4.6	6.0	4.6	3.5	16.5	37.7	21.1	2.2	82.4	51.5	49.1	51.0
21663	SAINT MICHAELS	85.5	83.9	13.3	14.7	0.2	0.2	0.7	0.9	3.8	4.5	5.6	5.2	3.2	16.3	32.3	26.4	2.7	82.7	52.9	47.0	53.0
21665	SHERWOOD	90.2	88.3	9.4	11.3	0.0	0.0	0.5	0.9	4.1	4.5	5.4	5.0	3.6	19.8	31.5	23.4	2.7	82.4	50.0	50.5	49.6
21666	STEVENSVILLE	94.9	94.0	2.6	3.0	0.9	1.1	0.9	1.1	7.6	7.9	7.9	6.6	4.7	28.2	27.6	8.8	0.7	72.5	38.3	50.0	50.0
21667	STILL POND	80.5	77.3	16.4	18.9	0.3	0.3	3.2	4.1	4.4	4.9	5.2	5.7	4.4	21.5	35.1	16.8	2.1	82.4	47.5	50.7	49.4
21668	SUDLERSVILLE	91.2	89.6	7.3	8.6	0.1	0.1	2.0	2.6	6.9	7.1	6.8	5.8	5.6	27.9	26.5	11.7	1.8	75.6	39.2	50.9	49.2
21669	TAYLORS ISLAND	93.6	92.4	5.0	6.6	0.0	0.0	1.8	1.9	4.7	4.7	4.7	8.1	3.3	22.3	28.9	21.3	1.9	80.1	46.9	53.1	46.9
21671	TILGHMAN	97.8	97.4	0.6	0.7	0.1	0.1	0.2	0.4	3.5	3.9	5.7	4.5	4.8	23.0	31.9	21.0	1.7	84.2	48.2	51.3	48.7
21672	TODDVILLE	94.0	92.7	4.2	5.1	0.2	0.2	0.5	0.2	3.9	4.7	5.9	4.2	4.4	24.0	30.1	21.0	2.0	83.4	47.0	49.9	50.1
21673	TRAPPE	82.6	80.3	14.7	16.6	0.6	0.7	1.4	1.7	5.8	6.4	7.3	5.9	4.7	24.3	29.7	14.2	1.7	76.7	42.2	49.9	50.1
21675	WINGATE	93.3	95.2	4.4	4.8	0.0	0.0	0.0	0.0	4.8	4.8	7.1	4.8	4.8	26.2	26.2	19.1	2.4	83.3	43.8	52.4	47.6
21676	WITTMAN	89.1	86.9	10.5	12.7	0.0	0.0	0.4	1.2	4.1	4.5	5.3	4.9	3.3	20.8	31.4	22.9	2.9	82.5	49.6	49.8	50.2
21677	WOOLFORD	92.5	91.0	6.5	8.1	0.0	0.0	0.7	0.6	4.5	5.0	7.0	4.2	3.1	22.4	32.2	20.5	1.1	81.0	47.3	47.1	52.9
21678	WORTON	80.3	77.3	18.2	20.8	0.1	0.2	1.6	1.9	5.4	6.0	7.5	6.7	5.2	24.3	28.7	14.8	1.5	77.0	41.8	49.4	50.6
21679	WYE MILLS	88.1	85.5	10.3	12.0	0.0	0.6	1.3	2.2	6.4	7.3	8.1	6.7	4.8	27.4	27.1	11.5	0.8	73.7	39.4	49.7	50.3
21701	FREDERICK	84.4	82.7	11.2	12.0	1.7	2.1	2.4	2.9	7.1	7.0	6.6	5.8	6.2	31.5	23.0	10.7	2.1	75.8	36.9	47.2	52.8
21702	FREDERICK	81.2	78.5	10.2	11.3	3.6	4.3	5.0	6.1	7.2	7.0	7.2	6.6	7.0	30.3	24.0	9.3	1.3	74.4	35.8	48.5	51.5
21703	FREDERICK	81.4	78.4	11.4	13.1	3.2	3.7	3.8	4.7	8.7	8.4	8.3	6.8	6.2	34.4	20.8	5.7	0.8	70.4	33.2	49.5	50.5
21704	FREDERICK	88.0	85.6	9.0	10.8	1.1	1.3	1.1	1.4	6.6	7.2	7.5	6.0	4.3	27.6	27.8	11.9	1.2	75.0	40.2	51.4	48.7
21710	ADAMSTOWN	92.9	91.9	4.2	4.7	0.9	1.1	1.6	2.1	7.1	7.5	7.8	6.6	4.3	27.6	25.7	11.1	2.3	73.6	39.7	49.5	50.5
21711	BIG POOL	98.8	98.6	0.0	0.0	0.2	0.3	0.4	0.6	4.6	5.1	7.2	7.4	5.1	27.9	29.5	11.8	1.4	78.4	40.9	50.8	49.3
21713	BOONSBORO	98.5	98.2	0.4	0.5	0.3	0.4	0.6	0.8	5.0	5.5	6.8	6.8	5.4	25.4	28.4	13.6	3.1	78.2	42.3	48.4	51.6
21716	BRUNSWICK	92.1	90.7	5.4	6.3	0.5	0.6	0.9	1.2	6.6	6.4	7.4	7.9	7.1	30.0	23.9	9.6	1.1	74.8	36.5	48.6	51.4
21718	BURKITTSVILLE	97.2	96.3	1.1	1.4	0.6	0.9	1.1	0.9	4.6	5.5	7.8	6.9	4.6	25.7	32.6	11.0	1.4	77.1	41.9	49.5	50.5
21719	CASCADE	92.9	91.3	3.5	4.6	0.6	0.6	1.7	2.1	7.8	8.0	8.0	6.9	5.6	32.9	21.7	8.2	0.9	71.9	33.7	50.5	49.5
21722	CLEAR SPRING	98.5	98.1	0.6	0.9	0.4	0.5	0.3	0.4	6.1	6.6	7.3	6.8	5.1	29.2	27.6	10.3	1.0	75.7	39.0	51.3	48.7
21723	COOKSVILLE	90.1	88.1	5.7	6.9	1.8	2.2	1.5	2.2	7.5	8.9	9.1	8.0	3.9	24.9	31.3	5.8	0.6	69.5	39.2	50.7	49.3
21727	EMMITSBURG	94.1	93.0	3.5	4.1	0.8	0.9	1.3	1.6	4.8	4.5	4.9	13.5	16.4	22.8	18.7	11.0	3.4	82.3	31.0	47.4	52.6
21733	FAIRPLAY	41.5	37.4	58.2	62.2	0.1	0.1	0.5	0.6	1.1	1.3	1.5	2.0	11.1	60.4	19.4	3.2	0.2	95.4	35.8	90.0	10.0
21737	GLENELG	92.4	90.9	4.2	4.8	2.1	2.5	1.9	2.3	7.8	9.6	10.6	6.7	3.8	23.8	28.8	7.9	1.1	67.2	39.0	50.7	49.3
21738	GLENWOOD	92.9	91.5	3.9	4.7	1.4	1.7	1.3	1.7	7.0	8.5	9.6	7.6	4.3	22.9	32.0	7.4	0.7	70.1	40.0	50.7	49.3
21740	HAGERSTOWN	86.2	84.1	10.8	12.4	0.8	1.0	1.5	1.8	6.9	6.4	6.5	6.4	7.8	29.7	22.6	12.0	1.8	76.4	36.2	50.6	49.4
21742	HAGERSTOWN	92.9	91.0	3.5	4.7	1.7	2.0	1.3	1.6	5.9	6.2	6.7	6.2	5.1	25.5	26.7	15.4	2.3	77.1	41.4	48.0	52.0
21750	HANCOCK	97.8	97.3	0.3	0.3	0.2	0.3	0.7	1.0	5.7	6.2	7.2	6.6	5.6	27.4	26.9	12.8	1.6	77.1	39.3	49.9	50.1
21754	IJAMSVILLE	95.5	94.2	1.9	2.6	1.4	1.7	1.1	1.4	7.5	8.7	8.6	7.1	4.4	25.3	30.9	6.9	0.6	70.6	39.5	50.0	50.1
21755	JEFFERSON	95.8	95.0	2.0	2.3	0.7	0.9	1.2	1.6	6.6	7.3	8.2	6.8	4.8	27.9	28.7	8.7	1.1	73.4	39.2	50.0	50.0
21756	KEEDYSVILLE	97.9	97.3	0.7	0.9	0.4	0.5	1.0	1.2	6.4	7.3	7.9	6.4	4.7	28.4	28.6	9.2	0.9	74.1	39.0	51.0	49.0
21757	KEYMAR	96.8	96.3	1.9	2.1	0.3	0.4	1.3	1.6	5.5	6.1	6.9	7.5	5.8	28.1	27.1	11.6	1.5	76.7	40.0	50.5	49.6
21758	KNOXVILLE	94.0	92.8	4.3	5.2	0.4	0.5	0.8	1.0	5.9	6.4	7.3	7.0	5.5	27.0	29.0	10.5	1.4	76.1	39.5	50.7	49.3
21765	LISBON	90.0	88.2	5.7	6.6	1.4	2.6	1.4	1.3	7.9	7.9	9.2	7.9	4.0	23.7	32.9	6.6	0.0	67.1	40.0	50.0	50.0
21766	LITTLE ORLEANS	99.2	99.1	0.3	0.5	0.0	0.0	0.0	0.0	5.7	6.0	6.3	5.7	5.3	27.7	26.8	14.8	1.7	78.4	40.5	51.0	49.0
21767	MAUGANSVILLE	97.6	97.1	0.7	0.8	0.2	0.2	1.3	1.6	5.7	5.8	6.8	6.7	6.1	27.0	23.1	16.7	2.3	77.7	40.0	46.6	53.4
21769	MIDDLETOWN	97.3	96.7	0.9	1.1	0.7	0.8	1.1	1.5	5.4	6.8	8.8	8.2	4.7	25.4	31.2	8.6	1.0	73.7	40.3	49.2	50.8
21770	MONROVIA	96.0	95.2	1.2	1.4	0.9	1.1	2.0	2.6	6.5	7.5	9.7	7.8	4.3	26.3	31.4	6.0	0.5	71.1	39.6	51.1	48.9
21771	MOUNT AIRY	95.6	94.8	2.1	2.5	0.8	1.0	1.3	1.7	7.5	8.3	9.1	7.2	5.0	28.4	26.7	7.2	0.7	70.4	37.1	49.7	50.3
21773	MYERSVILLE	98.0	97.5	0.4	0.5	0.3	0.4	1.3	1.7	6.5	7.5	8.9	6.6	4.9	28.0	27.4	9.3	0.9	72.8	38.7	50.0	50.0
21774	NEW MARKET	94.0	92.8	2.7	3.2	1.3	1.6	2.3	2.9	9.8	9.8	8.8	6.3	4.8	32.6	22.4	5.2	0.4	67.6	34.2	49.7	50.3
21776	NEW WINDSOR	96.0	95.2	2.6	3.2	0.4	0.5	0.8	1.0	6.5	6.9	8.2	7.5	5.7	28.7	26.6	8.6	1.3	73.4	37.7	49.7	50.3
21777	POINT OF ROCKS	92.7	91.3	3.6	4.2	0.9	1.2	0.7	0.9	8.0	8.7	8.8	6.0	3.6	32.8	25.9	5.7	0.6	70.7	36.6	49.5	50.5
21778	ROCKY RIDGE	98.7	98.4	0.1	0.1	0.5	0.4	0.6	0.7	4.9	5.2	6.2	6.4	6.0	26.3	30.5	13.4	1.3	80.1	42.1	49.6	50.4
21779	ROHRERSVILLE	97.7	96.9	0.8	1.1	0.3	0.4	0.8	1.0	5.7	6.3	7.0	6.3	5.0	28.4	30.1	10.0	1.2	76.8	40.1	51.3	48.7
21780	SABILLASVILLE	90.3	88.6	8.6	10.0	0.3	0.5	1.4	1.7	5.7	5.3	6.1	16.0	4.4	25.4	25.3	10.9	1.0	71.2	37.1	55.0	45.0
21782	SHARPSBURG	98.2	97.6	0.4	0.6	0.5	0.7	0.7	0.9	5.2	6.2	7.2	6.0	4.9	28.5	30.3	11.1	0.6	77.6	40.7	50.7	49.3
21783	SMITHSBURG	95.1	93.8	2.2	2.9	0.8	1.0	1.7	2.1	6.9	7.2	7.8	6.7	5.9	28.4	24.9	10.9	1.3	73.7	37.5	49.7	50.3
21784	SYKESVILLE	94.4	93.4	3.2	3.7	1.1	1.4	1.1	1.4	7.2	7.6	8.5	6.9	5.3	27.7	26.7	8.7	1.6	72.4	38.1	49.9	50.1
21787	TANEYTOWN	96.8	96.1	1.4	1.6	0.4	0.5	1.2	1.6	7.4	7.4	8.7	7.6	6.5	28.4	23.5	9.3	1.3	71.7	35.8	49.5	50.5
21788	THURMONT	98.0	97.6	0.6	0.6	0.4	0.5	0.6	0.8	6.9	6.9	7.1	6.4	5.8	29.3	25.5	10.8	1.4	75.2	37.9	49.5	50.5
21790	TUSCARORA	93.9	91.9	3.0	3.6	1.0	0.9	1.0	1.8	7.2	8.1	8.1	6.3	3.6	30.6	26.1	8.1	1.8	71.2	38.3	49.6	50.5
21791	UNION BRIDGE	95.5	94.8	2.9	3.3	0.5	0.6	0.9	1.1	6.3	6.9	8.1	7.0	5.5	26.3	28.0	10.6	1.3	74.3	39.3	50.7	49.3
21793	WALKERSVILLE	93.8	92.8	3.3	3.7	1.0	1.2	1.5	1.9	5.9	7.0	9.2	8.6	6.0	26.2	27.8	8.0	1.4	72.4	37.4	48.4	51.6
21794	WEST FRIENDSHIP	91.0	89.2	4.9	5.9	2.5	2.9	1.7	2.1	7.5	9.1	10.6	6.8	3.4	24.5	28.8	8.4	0.9	67.9	39.5	50.7	49.3
21795	WILLIAMSPORT	97.9	97.4	0.8	1.1	0.6	0.7	0.5	0.6	5.4	5.5	6.3	6.0	5.1	24.2	26.5	16.5	4.5	78.9	43.4	47.0	53.0
21797	WOODBINE	94.6	93.6	3.2	3.7	0.9	1.1	1.4	1.8	6.4	7.5	8.7	7.2	4.7	25.0	30.7	9.0	0.9	72.7	40.4	50.1	49.9
	MARYLAND	64.0	61.8	27.9	28.9	4.0	4.6	4.3	5.1	6.6	6.7	7.3	6.9	6.6	29.1	25.1	10.2	1.5	75.2	37.0	48.3	51.7
	UNITED STATES	75.1	73.6	12.3	12.5	3.8	4.2	12.5	14.1	6.9	6.7	7.2	7.0	7.3	28.6	23.8	10.8	1.7	75.1	36.0	49.1	50.9

ZIP CODE #	POST OFFICE NAME	2004 Per Capita Income	2004 HH Income Base	2004 HOUSEHOLD INCOME DISTRIBUTION (%) Less than $25,000	$25,000 to $49,999	$50,000 to $99,999	$100,000 to $149,999	$150,000 or More	MEDIAN HOUSEHOLD INCOME 2004	2009	2004 National Centile	2004 State Centile	2004 Home Value Base	2004 HOME VALUE DISTRIBUTION (%) Less than $50,000	$50,000 to $89,999	$90,000 to $174,999	$175,000 to $399,999	$400,000 or More	2004 Median Home Value
21617	CENTREVILLE	32170	2630	20.5	18.9	38.5	14.5	7.6	60958	70326	85	52	2059	2.5	3.0	23.2	59.4	12.0	229393
21619	CHESTER	34358	2525	13.2	21.4	41.5	13.4	10.5	64170	75372	88	60	2070	1.9	1.5	24.7	56.4	15.4	214160
21620	CHESTERTOWN	27581	5195	28.1	26.4	30.8	8.9	5.8	45884	52276	64	24	3655	2.2	4.7	38.6	39.5	15.2	187880
21622	CHURCH CREEK	33922	189	30.7	36.0	21.2	5.8	6.4	35509	40615	30	10	161	9.3	18.0	37.9	24.2	10.6	132386
21623	CHURCH HILL	27922	558	16.1	28.7	36.0	13.4	5.7	56543	62901	81	46	444	3.2	6.1	42.3	37.8	10.6	171277
21625	CORDOVA	22901	1012	18.8	24.8	40.5	13.3	2.6	54294	63101	79	43	874	2.1	6.3	28.8	52.1	10.8	211747
21626	CRAPO	28509	53	35.9	37.7	17.0	3.8	5.7	32286	35549	19	6	44	15.9	31.8	43.2	6.8	2.3	92500
21628	CRUMPTON	22862	199	23.1	27.1	40.7	8.0	1.0	49696	56652	71	33	168	20.2	7.7	29.8	38.1	4.2	144643
21629	DENTON	22295	3148	23.3	31.0	33.7	9.4	2.6	45906	50568	64	24	2446	2.8	4.8	43.3	42.3	6.9	172826
21631	EAST NEW MARKET	24115	1057	24.9	30.0	32.8	7.4	4.9	46207	51637	64	25	913	8.4	13.7	42.1	30.6	5.3	137602
21632	FEDERALSBURG	17711	2541	37.2	29.1	26.6	5.4	1.7	35670	38707	30	11	1810	10.1	11.8	49.7	24.3	4.1	135054
21634	FISHING CREEK	34746	226	37.2	36.7	12.0	3.5	10.6	30238	36050	13	4	196	12.8	14.3	32.1	31.1	9.7	143103
21635	GALENA	26206	865	22.9	20.1	42.1	9.8	5.1	55973	62807	81	45	746	1.7	8.3	28.4	52.3	9.3	192769
21636	GOLDSBORO	19225	410	20.2	36.1	35.6	5.4	2.7	46249	51371	64	25	356	12.6	6.2	41.6	34.3	5.3	148305
21638	GRASONVILLE	35012	1692	21.5	16.3	32.8	16.8	12.6	62857	75796	87	57	1366	1.0	4.8	27.6	41.6	25.0	270139
21639	GREENSBORO	18845	1560	25.7	30.9	34.2	7.7	1.5	44303	48872	59	22	1213	1.5	7.5	52.4	35.5	3.1	151930
21640	HENDERSON	17428	611	28.3	34.9	30.9	4.3	1.6	40771	45193	49	16	507	17.8	9.3	44.0	26.6	2.4	126630
21643	HURLOCK	18980	2141	28.4	30.4	33.6	5.5	2.1	43285	48075	57	20	1721	7.8	16.2	52.5	21.3	2.3	123579
21644	INGLESIDE	22195	49	18.4	30.6	40.8	8.2	2.0	50564	60000	73	35	41	0.0	4.9	41.5	43.9	9.8	184375
21645	KENNEDYVILLE	26218	524	21.4	31.1	34.4	6.7	6.5	48272	55322	69	29	413	1.2	7.5	29.5	36.6	25.2	220109
21647	MCDANIEL	27616	176	18.2	33.0	32.4	14.2	2.3	49081	59107	70	32	150	0.0	2.7	37.3	43.3	16.7	227778
21648	MADISON	28408	125	34.4	36.8	15.2	4.8	8.8	31769	38296	17	6	108	11.1	13.0	32.4	32.4	11.1	150000
21649	MARYDEL	13628	507	34.1	29.0	31.4	4.3	1.2	38398	42933	41	14	387	7.8	11.9	50.4	27.4	2.6	135326
21650	MASSEY	19539	72	26.4	25.0	37.5	6.9	4.2	45000	49318	61	23	57	0.0	19.3	38.6	38.6	3.5	146250
21651	MILLINGTON	20648	959	21.6	33.0	37.5	6.3	1.7	44135	50802	59	22	784	12.4	9.6	38.7	36.0	3.4	144369
21654	OXFORD	60950	673	15.5	20.7	26.5	14.6	22.9	71451	100000	92	68	579	0.4	1.9	10.9	31.1	55.8	442949
21655	PRESTON	19975	1978	20.5	35.1	36.5	5.8	2.2	45475	50381	63	24	1694	5.6	10.3	49.2	30.9	4.0	145992
21657	QUEEN ANNE	29426	364	21.2	19.5	37.6	15.4	6.3	56785	66731	81	46	292	2.1	4.1	23.3	62.0	8.6	222222
21658	QUEENSTOWN	39663	1563	13.8	16.1	31.9	21.6	16.6	78415	93145	95	78	1382	0.6	1.2	18.7	45.7	33.9	311200
21659	RHODESDALE	19289	677	25.6	35.6	32.5	6.1	0.3	41735	46497	52	17	579	17.3	22.1	39.6	17.1	4.0	108097
21660	RIDGELY	19549	1235	23.7	34.7	30.3	9.0	2.3	43317	47605	57	20	929	1.7	3.8	44.0	47.7	2.8	175978
21661	ROCK HALL	23501	1387	35.0	33.5	23.3	5.9	2.4	36064	41306	32	11	1113	4.4	6.6	52.6	26.3	10.2	141877
21662	ROYAL OAK	80478	165	19.4	17.0	30.3	7.3	26.1	67585	89082	90	63	141	2.8	3.6	13.5	34.0	46.1	308333
21663	SAINT MICHAELS	45320	1770	21.8	25.0	29.3	10.1	13.8	53220	66574	77	40	1422	1.4	2.7	19.8	42.5	33.6	269231
21665	SHERWOOD	26877	102	20.6	33.3	30.4	12.8	2.9	46995	56211	66	28	87	0.0	3.5	37.9	41.4	17.2	217500
21666	STEVENSVILLE	32149	4613	10.6	15.6	44.7	19.3	9.8	76116	85501	94	74	4196	0.8	1.0	14.4	66.5	17.4	233462
21667	STILL POND	23740	147	19.7	34.0	34.0	6.8	5.4	47859	56013	68	28	124	0.0	8.9	31.5	33.1	26.6	218182
21668	SUDLERSVILLE	20649	696	28.0	26.7	35.6	7.3	2.3	46365	52993	65	26	561	4.8	10.5	43.1	31.4	10.2	148707
21669	TAYLORS ISLAND	34837	95	36.8	36.8	11.6	4.2	10.5	29764	34639	12	3	82	12.2	14.6	31.7	31.7	9.8	143182
21671	TILGHMAN	16348	358	36.6	34.6	26.5	2.2	0.0	35117	40140	28	10	304	2.0	7.9	39.1	33.6	17.4	177273
21672	TODDVILLE	34852	190	36.3	35.8	18.4	3.2	6.3	32439	36193	19	6	159	13.8	31.5	45.9	6.3	2.5	94688
21673	TRAPPE	30955	1395	18.6	27.4	32.0	12.5	9.5	54761	66923	79	43	1102	3.0	4.5	34.4	28.5	29.7	217935
21675	WINGATE	24762	21	38.1	38.1	19.1	0.0	4.8	31091	33586	15	5	18	5.6	33.3	55.6	5.6	0.0	100000
21676	WITTMAN	30473	122	18.0	32.0	33.6	13.9	2.5	50000	57913	72	33	104	0.0	3.9	37.5	42.3	16.4	225000
21677	WOOLFORD	23873	151	21.2	33.1	33.1	9.3	3.3	45325	52016	62	23	130	1.5	7.7	32.3	37.7	20.8	196154
21678	WORTON	25104	960	17.8	32.9	37.5	7.2	4.6	49190	56160	70	32	819	4.0	5.9	44.6	28.8	16.7	157108
21679	WYE MILLS	26340	139	19.4	25.2	40.3	11.5	3.6	53205	62340	77	40	119	1.7	5.9	27.7	60.5	4.2	214773
21701	FREDERICK	31188	14409	17.0	24.6	36.8	14.6	7.0	59155	68572	84	49	9604	0.4	0.9	23.3	65.3	10.0	224801
21702	FREDERICK	28672	13207	15.0	24.4	37.5	16.0	7.1	61051	70938	85	52	8798	0.3	1.1	20.9	66.5	11.3	231785
21703	FREDERICK	28303	11339	12.1	24.0	42.9	14.7	6.3	62570	71483	87	56	8084	1.5	0.3	27.6	63.1	7.6	216122
21704	FREDERICK	34357	1894	10.0	17.7	39.7	21.1	11.5	76924	88463	94	76	1694	1.5	2.0	9.5	59.5	27.6	288284
21710	ADAMSTOWN	31386	1153	15.9	16.9	35.6	22.2	9.5	76548	86252	94	75	961	0.4	0.2	13.9	63.1	22.4	273346
21711	BIG POOL	20061	405	22.0	33.1	36.1	5.7	3.2	46096	50612	64	25	344	5.2	16.6	39.8	36.6	1.7	143023
21713	BOONSBORO	25052	3185	18.7	30.8	36.1	10.9	3.6	50411	56411	73	34	2639	1.6	2.6	42.6	47.8	5.4	181088
21716	BRUNSWICK	23851	2010	21.0	25.9	39.3	10.9	2.9	53024	63052	77	39	1497	0.8	1.0	54.3	42.7	1.2	165663
21718	BURKITTSVILLE	33514	94	12.8	26.6	38.3	12.8	9.6	60000	72406	84	50	82	0.0	0.0	8.5	75.6	15.9	264286
21719	CASCADE	21468	595	25.7	33.1	28.6	6.6	6.1	40344	45551	47	16	419	5.3	4.5	60.6	25.5	4.1	138682
21722	CLEAR SPRING	24028	1865	16.0	26.1	45.3	9.3	3.4	54764	62078	79	43	1604	4.8	4.9	45.8	39.2	5.4	165045
21723	COOKSVILLE	48869	122	3.3	5.7	27.1	32.8	31.2	116088	136025	99	97	114	0.0	0.0	2.6	30.7	66.7	473077
21727	EMMITSBURG	20598	1675	21.1	28.8	38.6	9.3	2.2	50107	58122	72	34	1196	0.5	1.8	37.5	51.0	9.2	192836
21733	FAIRPLAY	17470	368	16.6	28.5	43.5	10.1	1.4	52633	59871	76	38	321	4.1	3.4	48.0	42.7	1.9	166587
21737	GLENELG	39623	316	4.4	10.1	29.4	31.3	24.7	107380	126507	99	96	296	1.4	0.0	0.3	26.0	72.3	507732
21738	GLENWOOD	46560	755	2.3	10.1	26.8	27.0	33.9	117317	135173	99	97	708	0.9	0.0	1.6	28.8	68.8	485256
21740	HAGERSTOWN	19904	23163	33.0	31.8	28.1	5.0	2.1	37403	41468	37	12	13278	4.8	10.0	58.1	25.4	1.6	136871
21742	HAGERSTOWN	28217	10351	19.4	26.9	36.3	11.8	5.7	53162	60465	77	40	7940	2.4	2.7	47.3	42.9	4.7	170995
21750	HANCOCK	17920	1590	30.6	37.0	27.3	4.2	0.9	37459	42113	37	13	1174	9.6	17.5	45.4	25.6	1.9	124103
21754	IJAMSVILLE	39339	2034	6.7	14.4	30.7	27.0	21.1	96874	110099	98	92	1921	0.3	0.0	3.8	59.9	36.1	340687
21755	JEFFERSON	32244	2405	11.9	15.4	39.5	23.6	9.6	77915	88312	94	77	2140	2.6	1.2	9.3	67.2	19.7	289946
21756	KEEDYSVILLE	23579	964	15.3	21.0	48.0	11.3	4.5	60787	68108	85	52	868	2.2	3.9	28.3	60.5	5.1	205488
21757	KEYMAR	24894	1056	16.3	25.4	42.4	10.5	5.4	56925	65290	82	46	858	1.4	2.0	19.1	62.2	15.3	235309
21758	KNOXVILLE	26329	1489	11.8	22.0	42.5	19.5	4.2	64203	73842	88	60	1278	2.4	1.4	22.1	63.3	10.8	225342
21765	LISBON	60104	32	0.0	6.3	28.1	31.3	34.4	119763	138561	99	98	30	0.0	0.0	0.0	26.7	73.3	500000
21766	LITTLE ORLEANS	16389	261	34.1	33.0	28.4	4.6	0.0	36386	40130	33	12	222	9.9	23.0	50.5	14.4	2.3	121429
21767	MAUGANSVILLE	20453	455	29.9	28.1	36.7	5.3	0.0	42516	45543	55	19	275	2.9	3.6	73.8	16.7	2.9	148174
21769	MIDDLETOWN	32389	3757	8.8	18.5	37.7	23.4	11.6	78682	90894	95	79	3340	0.2	0.1	6.1	74.2	19.5	275583
21770	MONROVIA	30814	1923	4.7	16.5	42.5	24.6	11.7	83613	95649	96	85	1854	0.0	0.0	1.9	81.7	16.4	292308
21771	MOUNT AIRY	32914	9433	6.7	14.4	41.4	23.7	13.7	82511	94931	96	84	8635	1.3	0.6	6.4	67.6	24.2	290326
21773	MYERSVILLE	27089	1829	11.0	17.1	48.1	16.5	7.3	67370	78008	90	63	1627	2.1	0.2	16.8	66.7	14.2	266817
21774	NEW MARKET	32725	3280	6.4	13.4	43.9	24.3	12.1	82354	94851	96	83	3034	0.0	0.4	9.1	74.4	16.1	257570
21776	NEW WINDSOR	25422	2234	11.3	21.8	46.4	16.0	4.5	63783	73767	88	59	1880	0.3	1.7	11.7	75.8	10.5	234474
21777	POINT OF ROCKS	29800	389	12.1	11.8	44.2	26.7	5.1	78713	90317	95	79	360	0.0	1.9	10.0	80.0	8.1	231988
21778	ROCKY RIDGE	24621	343	18.1	21.6	42.9	14.3	3.2	60603	70302	85	52	294	3.1	2.0	15.7	62.9	16.3	239394
21779	ROHRERSVILLE	24205	332	16.6	21.1	45.2	12.4	4.8	58683	66489	83	49	291	3.8	2.4	25.4	60.8	7.6	203516
21780	SABILLASVILLE	25696	563	13.7	32.5	36.2	11.9	5.7	53260	62099	77	41	488	3.9	0.0	16.2	62.9	17.0	228058
21782	SHARPSBURG	24088	1576	14.3	30.7	40.8	11.2	3.0	54271	60952	79	43	1375	4.0	6.3	41.5	45.9	2.3	170429
21783	SMITHSBURG	24682	3888	19.1	26.7	38.9	11.0	4.3	53570	60906	78	41	3126	1.3	2.0	42.7	48.1	5.9	180830
21784	SYKESVILLE	30923	12654	10.0	15.4	40.6	24.0	10.0	78166	88721	94	78	11079	0.7	0.4	8.6	76.5	13.9	250166
21787	TANEYTOWN	21953	3473	16.8	28.6	41.7	8.9	4.0	53132	60912	77	40	2636	0.3	1.7	33.4	56.5	8.1	194753
21788	THURMONT	25013	4296	15.4	28.1	42.1	10.4	4.0	55412	64454	80	44	3375	1.2	0.4	21.1	70.1	7.2	215605
21790	TUSCARORA	35159	46	15.2	13.0	37.0	26.1	8.7	77299	88823	94	76	41	0.0	0.0	9.8	80.5	9.8	234722
21791	UNION BRIDGE	26426	1912	13.5	24.4	40.9	15.3	6.0	61762	71823	86	53	1550	0.7	1.4	19.2	64.2	14.5	237857
21793	WALKERSVILLE	26594	3457	9.3	22.7	42.0	19.3	6.7	67705	78372	90	64	3011	0.0	0.3	23.5	71.2	4.9	230514
21794	WEST FRIENDSHIP	37248	607	4.5	10.5	29.3	31.3	24.4	106751	126719	99	95	568	0.0	0.9	1.8	31.9	65.5	486275
21795	WILLIAMSPORT	22250	3669	25.8	28.0	35.5	7.7	3.0	46360	51506	65	26	2818	3.5	5.5	53.1	36.3	1.7	153643
21797	WOODBINE	35539	2803	7.9	13.8	37.9	23.2	17.2	84420	100087	96	86	2559	1.0	0.7	4.8	55.6	37.9	345877
	MARYLAND	30267		17.9	23.3	34.6	15.0	9.2	59732	70285				2.9	5.4	28.1	49.8	13.8	209514
	UNITED STATES	25866		24.7	27.1	30.8	10.9	6.5	48124	56710				10.9	15.0	33.7	30.1	10.4	145905

ZIP CODE		FINANCIAL SERVICES				THE HOME						ENTERTAINMENT						PERSONAL			
						Home Improvements		Furnishings													
#	POST OFFICE NAME	Auto Loan	Home Loan	Invest-ments	Retire-ment Plans	Home Repair	Lawn & Garden	Comput-ers & Hard-ware	Major Appli-ances	TV, Radio, Sound Equip-ment	Furni-ture	Dine out/ Carry out	Sports Equip-ment	Fees & Tickets	Toys & Games	Travel	Cable TV	Apparel & Services	Auto Repairs	Health Insur-ance	Pets & Supplies
21617	CENTREVILLE	110	133	146	133	131	132	122	121	115	122	145	142	129	152	125	113	144	118	111	133
21619	CHESTER	105	127	143	128	125	126	118	116	111	117	140	137	125	147	120	108	139	114	106	128
21620	CHESTERTOWN	101	83	68	81	89	101	88	94	94	85	114	110	82	111	88	97	106	94	105	115
21622	CHURCH CREEK	123	86	46	79	98	113	87	105	101	86	119	123	75	114	88	108	108	104	127	142
21623	CHURCH HILL	95	114	124	111	112	115	105	105	101	105	127	121	112	135	108	100	126	102	98	115
21625	CORDOVA	103	92	70	87	97	104	85	94	90	85	110	112	83	112	87	92	104	92	102	121
21626	CRAPO	142	95	43	82	108	124	92	115	111	93	130	137	78	123	93	119	118	113	141	163
21628	CRUMPTON	100	67	30	58	76	87	65	81	78	66	92	97	55	87	66	84	83	80	100	115
21629	DENTON	82	79	73	75	81	89	76	81	80	76	98	93	76	99	78	82	94	79	86	96
21631	EAST NEW MARKET	93	86	71	82	90	97	80	87	84	80	103	103	80	105	83	86	98	85	94	110
21632	FEDERALSBURG	72	58	44	54	61	69	60	65	66	59	79	76	55	77	59	68	74	65	74	82
21634	FISHING CREEK	123	93	61	89	101	121	103	113	115	97	135	126	91	127	101	121	123	113	135	136
21635	GALENA	101	83	63	79	91	102	83	93	91	81	109	109	78	111	85	95	102	91	106	119
21636	GOLDSBORO	85	76	59	73	79	84	71	78	74	72	91	92	69	90	72	75	87	77	82	97
21638	GRASONVILLE	121	126	127	124	129	141	122	126	122	120	150	142	124	149	125	124	145	124	130	142
21639	GREENSBORO	81	71	55	69	75	82	68	75	72	68	88	87	67	89	69	74	83	73	80	93
21640	HENDERSON	75	68	54	66	69	73	65	70	66	66	81	81	62	78	64	65	78	69	70	84
21643	HURLOCK	82	69	49	65	72	79	66	74	71	66	86	86	62	84	66	73	81	72	81	94
21644	INGLESIDE	89	79	61	75	84	90	73	81	78	73	95	97	72	97	76	80	90	79	88	105
21645	KENNEDYVILLE	111	90	65	85	98	111	88	101	97	87	116	117	81	114	91	101	108	99	115	130
21647	MCDANIEL	93	87	83	82	92	108	80	92	85	86	106	90	81	88	87	91	99	89	107	104
21648	MADISON	120	89	57	85	98	117	97	108	109	92	128	123	86	121	96	115	117	108	130	134
21649	MARYDEL	71	65	51	62	66	69	62	66	63	63	77	77	59	74	61	62	74	66	67	80
21650	MASSEY	75	80	83	76	81	90	79	79	82	76	102	88	83	110	82	85	98	77	85	87
21651	MILLINGTON	89	69	46	64	75	85	68	78	77	68	93	91	63	91	69	81	86	77	91	102
21654	OXFORD	182	186	191	180	193	218	172	187	174	180	218	193	177	195	184	182	208	181	204	210
21655	PRESTON	84	74	57	71	78	85	70	77	75	70	91	91	68	92	72	76	86	75	84	98
21657	QUEEN ANNE	105	122	130	122	121	122	112	113	107	112	134	133	117	140	114	105	132	110	105	127
21658	QUEENSTOWN	134	163	180	162	161	165	149	149	141	149	177	171	159	184	154	139	176	145	139	163
21659	RHODESDALE	77	65	46	61	69	75	60	68	66	61	79	81	58	80	62	68	75	67	76	90
21660	RIDGELY	79	76	68	77	77	81	75	77	75	75	92	90	73	92	74	73	89	76	76	89
21661	ROCK HALL	84	64	43	60	70	83	67	76	75	65	89	86	60	85	68	80	82	76	91	96
21662	ROYAL OAK	231	279	315	277	278	292	256	257	242	257	305	291	273	309	267	241	302	250	246	280
21663	SAINT MICHAELS	147	134	124	128	142	166	128	144	136	134	167	146	127	145	136	144	157	140	166	165
21665	SHERWOOD	90	82	77	78	88	103	76	87	81	81	101	87	76	85	83	87	94	85	102	102
21666	STEVENSVILLE	121	141	146	144	137	136	129	129	120	131	152	150	134	155	129	115	150	126	114	141
21667	STILL POND	106	83	57	75	93	105	78	94	89	78	105	110	70	104	83	95	98	93	111	129
21668	SUDLERSVILLE	84	77	62	73	81	86	71	78	75	71	91	93	70	93	73	76	87	76	83	99
21669	TAYLORS ISLAND	123	93	61	89	101	121	103	113	115	97	135	126	91	127	101	121	123	113	135	136
21671	TILGHMAN	64	50	34	45	56	63	47	57	53	47	63	66	42	62	50	57	59	56	67	77
21672	TODDVILLE	141	95	43	82	107	123	91	114	110	93	129	136	78	122	93	119	118	113	141	162
21673	TRAPPE	126	109	87	106	116	129	107	118	113	106	137	136	102	135	109	116	129	116	129	146
21675	WINGATE	93	62	28	54	71	81	60	75	73	61	85	90	51	81	61	78	78	75	93	107
21676	WITTMAN	93	87	83	82	92	108	80	91	85	86	105	89	81	88	87	91	99	89	107	104
21677	WOOLFORD	102	71	37	67	83	93	70	87	81	70	95	105	60	93	73	85	87	86	104	121
21678	WORTON	103	89	72	85	96	104	85	95	91	84	110	112	81	109	88	94	104	94	105	122
21679	WYE MILLS	109	97	74	92	102	110	89	99	95	89	116	118	88	118	92	97	110	96	107	128
21701	FREDERICK	103	111	120	114	107	110	108	106	104	110	132	124	111	132	107	101	129	106	97	116
21702	FREDERICK	102	108	119	112	105	108	107	104	102	108	130	123	109	128	105	98	128	105	95	115
21703	FREDERICK	109	111	116	119	107	107	110	107	104	113	132	127	110	129	106	97	130	108	93	118
21704	FREDERICK	133	161	177	161	159	164	147	147	138	147	174	168	156	180	151	136	173	142	137	161
21710	ADAMSTOWN	117	128	139	133	126	128	123	122	116	124	147	143	126	145	122	112	144	121	112	134
21711	BIG POOL	91	72	47	66	78	86	68	79	76	68	91	94	63	90	70	79	85	77	90	105
21713	BOONSBORO	96	95	85	91	98	104	89	94	91	88	111	110	89	116	91	92	107	92	98	114
21716	BRUNSWICK	86	87	87	86	88	95	87	88	87	85	108	101	88	112	87	87	105	87	89	99
21718	BURKITTSVILLE	124	111	86	106	117	125	103	114	109	103	132	135	101	135	106	111	126	111	122	146
21719	CASCADE	91	77	59	76	81	91	78	84	83	76	100	97	74	100	78	84	94	83	92	102
21722	CLEAR SPRING	105	94	71	89	99	106	86	96	92	86	112	114	85	114	89	94	106	93	104	124
21723	COOKSVILLE	190	238	258	245	230	232	209	204	190	212	242	236	230	252	213	184	244	196	181	226
21727	EMMITSBURG	81	79	78	78	81	88	81	83	83	79	102	96	80	102	81	83	98	83	85	93
21733	FAIRPLAY	92	86	70	83	90	95	79	87	83	79	101	103	79	104	82	84	97	84	91	109
21737	GLENELG	171	213	231	220	206	207	187	182	170	190	217	211	206	226	191	165	219	176	162	202
21738	GLENWOOD	201	251	272	259	242	245	221	215	201	224	256	249	243	266	225	194	258	207	191	238
21740	HAGERSTOWN	64	64	69	63	64	69	67	65	68	65	84	76	67	85	66	68	82	67	66	74
21742	HAGERSTOWN	95	100	105	100	101	108	97	99	96	96	120	114	99	121	99	96	116	98	98	112
21750	HANCOCK	64	62	56	58	64	70	59	62	62	58	77	71	60	81	61	65	73	61	68	74
21754	IJAMSVILLE	159	198	214	202	192	194	175	172	161	177	204	200	191	213	179	156	205	166	155	191
21755	JEFFERSON	127	146	145	148	142	140	131	132	123	134	155	155	137	160	132	118	153	128	118	147
21756	KEEDYSVILLE	88	108	113	108	107	105	97	97	90	96	113	113	102	120	99	88	113	93	88	108
21757	KEYMAR	113	97	73	93	104	112	91	103	98	91	118	123	88	120	94	100	112	100	112	133
21758	KNOXVILLE	105	111	104	109	112	114	102	106	100	102	124	125	104	128	103	99	121	103	102	124
21765	LISBON	188	234	255	242	227	229	207	201	188	209	239	233	227	249	210	182	241	194	179	223
21766	LITTLE ORLEANS	79	53	24	46	60	69	51	64	62	52	72	76	43	68	52	66	66	63	79	91
21767	MAUGANSVILLE	59	64	67	60	64	72	63	62	65	61	81	69	67	88	65	68	78	61	67	69
21769	MIDDLETOWN	124	147	153	148	145	145	133	133	124	133	156	154	140	164	135	121	155	128	121	148
21770	MONROVIA	124	153	163	154	150	148	137	136	126	137	159	159	146	169	140	123	159	131	121	150
21771	MOUNT AIRY	135	163	173	166	159	157	147	145	136	148	171	170	156	179	148	130	171	141	129	160
21773	MYERSVILLE	117	119	105	118	120	122	108	114	107	110	133	134	110	136	109	105	129	110	111	136
21774	NEW MARKET	142	162	157	168	154	149	146	145	134	151	170	169	151	171	143	125	168	141	123	158
21776	NEW WINDSOR	102	114	113	115	113	114	105	106	100	105	125	124	109	130	106	98	123	103	99	119
21777	POINT OF ROCKS	124	141	135	147	134	129	127	126	116	132	148	147	130	148	123	108	146	122	106	137
21778	ROCKY RIDGE	96	98	91	94	100	105	91	95	92	90	113	112	93	118	93	92	110	93	97	115
21779	ROHRERSVILLE	95	104	100	103	105	107	94	98	92	94	114	115	97	120	97	91	112	94	94	115
21780	SABILLASVILLE	126	101	68	96	111	121	96	111	106	96	126	133	89	127	99	109	118	109	126	149
21782	SHARPSBURG	101	91	70	87	96	102	84	93	89	84	108	110	83	110	86	91	103	90	100	119
21783	SMITHSBURG	98	93	80	91	95	101	89	94	91	89	111	111	87	112	90	90	107	93	96	113
21784	SYKESVILLE	123	142	149	145	138	138	131	130	122	132	154	151	136	158	131	117	153	127	116	143
21787	TANEYTOWN	86	93	91	93	91	93	88	89	85	88	106	104	89	108	87	82	104	87	82	99
21788	THURMONT	97	94	85	93	96	103	92	96	93	91	115	111	91	117	92	93	110	94	97	111
21790	TUSCARORA	120	133	134	139	128	126	123	122	114	127	145	143	126	144	121	108	143	120	107	134
21791	UNION BRIDGE	101	116	117	114	116	118	106	107	103	105	128	125	111	136	109	102	126	104	103	122
21793	WALKERSVILLE	104	124	130	124	121	121	113	112	106	113	133	130	118	139	114	103	132	109	102	123
21794	WEST FRIENDSHIP	161	200	218	207	194	195	176	172	160	179	204	199	194	212	179	155	206	166	153	190
21795	WILLIAMSPORT	76	77	75	74	78	84	75	77	76	73	94	88	76	97	76	77	91	76	80	88
21797	WOODBINE	138	172	184	174	168	167	153	152	141	153	178	177	164	189	156	137	178	146	136	168
	MARYLAND	108	114	128	115	112	119	113	111	111	114	139	129	116	140	113	109	137	112	106	124
	UNITED STATES	100	100	100	100	100	100	100	100	100	100	100	100	100	100	100	100	100	100	100	100

# POST OFFICE NAME	COUNTY FIPS CODE	POPULATION			2000-2004 ANNUAL RATE		HOUSEHOLDS					FAMILIES		
		2000	2004	2009	% Rate	State Centile	2000	2004	2009	% Annual Rate 2000-2004	2004 Average HH Size	2000	2004	% Annual Rate 2000-2004
21798 WOODSBORO	021	2057	2226	2482	1.9	71	701	761	853	2.0	2.93	579	625	1.8
21801 SALISBURY	045	27186	29236	31852	1.7	66	9645	10440	11481	1.9	2.57	6437	6953	1.8
21804 SALISBURY	045	31224	33340	36133	1.6	63	12449	13382	14593	1.7	2.44	7983	8451	1.4
21811 BERLIN	047	19631	22093	24397	2.8	88	8245	9429	10557	3.2	2.32	5939	6712	2.9
21813 BISHOPVILLE	047	2293	2497	2707	2.0	75	884	970	1061	2.2	2.57	678	734	1.9
21814 BIVALVE	045	434	439	461	0.3	25	178	181	191	0.4	2.43	117	117	0.0
21817 CRISFIELD	039	5419	5375	5488	-0.2	14	2301	2309	2385	0.1	2.28	1503	1488	-0.2
21821 DEAL ISLAND	039	1143	1229	1303	1.7	66	485	529	568	2.1	2.32	330	356	1.8
21822 EDEN	045	2637	2948	3239	2.7	86	1023	1163	1295	3.1	2.25	731	820	2.7
21824 EWELL	039	258	286	308	2.5	84	116	131	143	2.9	2.18	79	88	2.6
21826 FRUITLAND	045	3618	3814	4126	1.3	54	1407	1499	1632	1.5	2.54	966	1012	1.1
21829 GIRDLETREE	047	436	425	443	-0.6	8	165	162	170	-0.4	2.62	126	122	-0.8
21830 HEBRON	045	2918	3245	3587	2.5	84	1084	1217	1355	2.8	2.67	847	939	2.5
21835 LINKWOOD	019	410	461	491	2.8	87	174	198	213	3.1	2.30	126	142	2.9
21837 MARDELA SPRINGS	045	3301	3376	3610	0.5	34	1271	1310	1410	0.7	2.57	910	926	0.4
21838 MARION STATION	039	1962	2007	2071	0.5	34	782	809	844	0.8	2.47	560	572	0.5
21840 NANTICOKE	045	408	416	438	0.5	30	187	192	203	0.6	2.17	133	134	0.2
21841 NEWARK	047	768	787	825	0.6	36	304	315	334	0.8	2.48	222	226	0.4
21842 OCEAN CITY	047	10146	10762	11538	1.4	58	5014	5332	5756	1.5	2.02	2719	2858	1.2
21849 PARSONSBURG	045	3024	3115	3328	0.7	41	1137	1179	1267	0.9	2.64	857	878	0.6
21850 PITTSVILLE	045	2437	2659	2905	2.1	77	970	1066	1172	2.3	2.49	700	758	1.9
21851 POCOMOKE CITY	047	7327	7350	7713	0.1	22	2894	2925	3101	0.3	2.48	1988	1980	-0.1
21853 PRINCESS ANNE	039	11888	12297	12737	0.8	44	3049	3190	3364	1.1	2.70	1848	1913	0.8
21856 QUANTICO	045	828	844	890	0.5	30	340	349	370	0.6	2.42	249	252	0.3
21863 SNOW HILL	047	5342	5271	5492	-0.3	9	1981	1974	2087	-0.1	2.48	1432	1410	-0.4
21864 STOCKTON	047	567	557	581	-0.4	8	207	204	215	-0.3	2.73	158	154	-0.6
21865 TYASKIN	045	447	451	472	0.2	25	202	205	216	0.4	2.20	140	139	-0.2
21866 TYLERTON	039	85	94	102	2.4	83	40	45	49	2.8	2.09	27	30	2.5
21869 VIENNA	019	973	947	945	-0.6	7	416	409	413	-0.4	2.31	285	277	-0.7
21871 WESTOVER	039	2177	2239	2305	0.7	39	842	924	997	2.2	1.58	577	579	0.1
21872 WHALEYVILLE	047	517	569	619	2.3	80	222	247	272	2.5	2.30	162	178	2.2
21874 WILLARDS	045	2369	2430	2601	0.6	36	920	949	1022	0.7	2.56	673	686	0.5
21875 DELMAR	045	5123	5518	5993	1.8	67	1918	2079	2271	1.9	2.64	1403	1503	1.6
21901 NORTH EAST	015	12797	13891	15271	2.0	73	4622	5051	5599	2.1	2.73	3474	3769	1.9
21903 PERRYVILLE	015	5407	5727	6208	1.4	56	2059	2199	2406	1.6	2.50	1442	1524	1.3
21904 PORT DEPOSIT	015	6788	7089	7636	1.0	48	2446	2575	2797	1.2	2.74	1853	1933	1.0
21911 RISING SUN	015	8639	9265	10135	1.7	65	3060	3308	3652	1.9	2.76	2381	2559	1.7
21912 WARWICK	015	1028	1103	1212	1.7	66	368	399	443	1.9	2.76	264	283	1.7
21913 CECILTON	015	474	523	580	2.3	81	198	221	247	2.6	2.37	142	156	2.2
21914 CHARLESTOWN	015	644	684	744	1.4	59	255	274	301	1.7	2.49	181	192	1.4
21915 CHESAPEAKE CITY	015	3084	3166	3397	0.6	37	1233	1275	1379	0.8	2.47	934	957	0.6
21917 COLORA	015	2132	2282	2491	1.6	64	712	767	844	1.8	2.95	578	618	1.6
21918 CONOWINGO	015	3875	3982	4295	0.6	38	1319	1365	1484	0.8	2.91	1053	1083	0.7
21919 EARLEVILLE	015	2719	3133	3564	3.4	94	1123	1301	1490	3.5	2.39	818	940	3.3
21921 ELKTON	015	38364	42391	47058	2.4	82	13828	15465	17364	2.7	2.70	10170	11281	2.5
MARYLAND					1.1					1.1	2.60			1.0
UNITED STATES					1.2					1.3	2.58			1.1

#	POST OFFICE NAME	White 2000	White 2004	Black 2000	Black 2004	Asian/Pacific 2000	Asian/Pacific 2004	% Hispanic Origin 2000	% Hispanic Origin 2004	0-4	5-9	10-14	15-19	20-24	25-44	45-64	65-84	85+	18+	MEDIAN AGE 2004	% 2004 Males	% 2004 Females
21798	WOODSBORO	98.2	97.8	0.4	0.5	0.5	0.6	1.0	1.4	6.2	6.8	8.4	7.3	5.2	27.2	27.5	10.4	1.1	73.9	39.5	49.3	50.7
21801	SALISBURY	60.2	57.6	35.7	37.7	1.6	1.8	2.7	3.2	6.7	6.6	6.9	10.1	9.1	24.8	23.3	10.7	1.7	75.8	34.4	46.7	53.3
21804	SALISBURY	76.1	72.5	18.7	21.4	2.6	3.1	2.3	2.8	5.8	6.0	6.4	6.5	8.8	27.8	25.0	12.0	1.8	77.9	37.3	47.7	52.3
21811	BERLIN	84.6	82.7	13.1	14.6	0.7	0.8	1.6	1.9	4.7	5.0	5.6	4.7	4.0	22.1	29.4	22.4	2.1	81.8	47.8	48.5	51.6
21813	BISHOPVILLE	89.8	86.6	8.6	11.4	0.7	0.9	0.7	1.0	5.6	5.9	7.8	6.0	3.3	25.6	31.6	12.9	1.4	76.6	42.6	48.9	51.1
21814	BIVALVE	78.6	74.3	21.0	25.3	0.2	0.2	0.0	0.0	3.4	4.3	7.7	6.4	4.8	21.9	29.4	20.1	2.1	80.6	46.0	49.4	50.6
21817	CRISFIELD	73.3	69.6	23.3	26.4	0.8	1.0	1.4	1.7	6.5	6.5	6.4	6.5	5.3	23.6	25.9	17.0	2.6	76.4	41.9	46.3	53.7
21821	DEAL ISLAND	86.0	83.9	12.6	14.5	0.1	0.1	0.5	0.7	4.1	4.6	5.9	4.7	4.6	21.7	33.0	19.2	2.2	82.7	47.7	48.7	51.3
21822	EDEN	66.3	63.2	31.2	33.9	0.5	0.6	1.2	1.4	5.0	5.3	5.8	11.5	9.4	23.9	26.1	11.6	1.4	80.3	37.0	46.9	53.1
21824	EWELL	93.4	92.0	5.0	6.3	0.0	0.0	0.8	1.1	3.5	4.2	5.2	4.2	4.6	21.0	36.4	18.2	2.8	84.6	49.8	50.0	50.0
21826	FRUITLAND	68.8	65.4	27.5	30.3	1.1	1.3	1.9	2.3	6.6	6.7	7.6	7.0	6.2	26.0	26.2	12.2	1.6	74.8	37.9	46.6	53.4
21829	GIRDLETREE	70.6	64.2	27.8	33.9	0.2	0.5	0.5	0.5	5.2	5.9	7.1	8.0	5.2	25.9	28.2	12.9	1.7	76.2	40.8	47.3	52.7
21830	HEBRON	80.8	76.7	17.2	20.9	0.6	0.7	0.5	0.7	6.8	7.6	8.2	7.2	4.7	30.5	24.7	9.7	0.7	72.9	36.0	48.4	51.6
21835	LINKWOOD	83.7	80.3	15.1	18.4	0.0	0.0	0.7	1.1	6.1	6.3	5.9	5.4	4.6	26.9	29.3	13.7	2.0	78.1	41.8	46.4	53.6
21837	MARDELA SPRINGS	78.6	74.9	19.3	22.4	0.6	0.7	1.4	1.9	5.9	6.2	7.4	6.9	6.4	26.9	27.3	11.8	1.3	76.4	38.7	49.4	50.7
21838	MARION STATION	72.0	68.1	23.9	27.0	0.1	0.2	4.2	5.0	4.9	5.3	5.8	5.0	4.6	23.9	31.0	17.8	1.6	80.7	45.3	48.8	51.2
21840	NANTICOKE	68.6	63.0	30.4	35.8	0.3	0.2	0.7	1.0	2.6	3.1	6.3	3.4	3.6	19.7	31.7	26.7	2.9	85.6	52.5	48.3	51.7
21841	NEWARK	80.7	76.0	16.3	20.8	0.8	0.9	1.6	2.2	5.7	6.2	6.2	5.8	4.8	26.9	29.2	13.1	1.9	77.1	42.1	51.0	49.1
21842	OCEAN CITY	95.4	94.2	2.4	3.1	0.8	1.0	1.3	1.7	3.7	3.9	4.2	3.8	4.2	26.6	28.9	22.9	1.8	86.0	47.4	50.7	49.3
21849	PARSONSBURG	93.0	91.3	4.6	5.8	0.9	1.0	1.0	1.4	6.0	6.2	6.5	7.1	6.1	28.5	29.0	9.5	0.9	76.9	39.0	49.9	50.1
21850	PITTSVILLE	92.2	90.3	4.8	6.0	1.9	2.3	0.8	1.1	7.3	7.5	7.0	5.6	5.2	30.9	25.8	9.8	0.9	74.8	37.0	49.3	50.7
21851	POCOMOKE CITY	60.3	54.8	37.3	42.6	0.5	0.6	1.0	1.1	6.1	6.5	7.7	8.1	6.0	24.2	25.4	13.8	2.2	74.7	39.6	46.7	53.3
21853	PRINCESS ANNE	42.4	38.8	55.5	58.9	0.5	0.5	1.1	1.2	4.5	4.2	4.6	10.4	12.8	32.8	20.2	9.3	1.2	83.9	32.7	56.6	43.4
21856	QUANTICO	62.4	57.0	35.6	40.8	0.2	0.4	0.5	0.6	4.4	4.7	5.6	5.1	3.7	23.5	33.9	17.2	2.0	82.1	46.8	49.5	50.5
21863	SNOW HILL	67.3	62.0	31.3	36.5	0.3	0.3	0.8	0.8	5.0	5.3	6.6	6.4	6.0	26.5	27.1	14.4	2.7	79.0	41.5	49.6	50.4
21864	STOCKTON	68.4	61.9	29.8	36.1	0.5	0.5	0.4	0.2	5.4	6.3	7.2	8.8	5.2	26.4	26.4	12.8	1.6	74.7	39.3	46.1	53.9
21865	TYASKIN	70.0	65.0	28.9	33.7	0.2	0.2	0.2	0.2	3.8	4.4	6.7	5.8	4.2	22.2	32.4	18.6	2.0	81.8	46.9	49.2	50.8
21866	TYLERTON	92.9	91.5	4.7	6.4	0.0	0.0	0.0	1.1	4.3	4.3	5.3	4.3	4.3	21.3	34.0	19.2	3.2	86.2	49.3	51.1	48.9
21869	VIENNA	66.5	61.4	31.6	36.5	0.6	0.7	0.5	0.5	4.4	5.1	7.0	5.6	4.5	23.6	28.9	18.4	2.5	79.6	44.9	47.6	52.4
21871	WESTOVER	54.7	50.4	43.4	47.3	0.3	0.4	1.1	1.3	3.8	4.1	4.2	5.5	8.4	39.6	23.0	10.3	1.1	85.3	37.1	65.6	34.4
21872	WHALEYVILLE	82.6	78.2	15.9	20.0	0.2	0.4	1.2	1.4	5.1	5.8	6.9	5.6	4.2	26.0	30.8	13.7	1.9	78.2	43.0	48.9	51.1
21874	WILLARDS	93.5	92.1	3.8	4.7	1.6	1.9	1.5	2.0	7.1	7.4	7.7	6.1	5.5	29.6	25.8	9.6	1.3	74.1	36.5	49.9	50.1
21875	DELMAR	80.3	76.8	15.4	18.1	1.2	1.4	3.0	3.7	6.7	6.7	7.4	7.2	6.5	27.4	26.0	10.2	1.1	75.0	37.6	48.0	52.0
21901	NORTH EAST	95.7	95.0	1.9	2.2	0.7	0.8	1.2	1.6	6.8	6.8	7.7	7.3	6.5	28.6	26.0	9.4	1.1	74.2	36.6	49.6	50.4
21903	PERRYVILLE	91.0	89.4	6.0	6.9	0.7	0.9	1.9	2.5	6.3	6.6	7.8	6.4	4.9	28.4	26.0	12.5	1.1	75.1	38.9	50.7	49.3
21904	PORT DEPOSIT	93.1	91.8	4.6	5.3	0.6	0.7	1.2	1.5	6.9	6.9	7.7	7.5	5.8	28.7	26.7	9.1	0.7	73.6	37.4	50.1	49.9
21911	RISING SUN	97.7	97.4	0.8	0.9	0.3	0.4	0.8	1.1	6.6	7.2	8.0	7.3	5.8	28.8	24.8	9.9	1.6	73.4	37.1	50.1	49.9
21912	WARWICK	85.8	83.5	11.9	13.7	0.4	0.5	2.0	2.6	6.9	7.1	7.3	6.3	5.2	25.8	27.4	12.9	1.4	75.1	40.4	49.3	50.7
21913	CECILTON	83.3	81.1	14.6	16.4	0.4	0.6	1.9	2.3	7.1	7.3	7.5	6.3	5.4	24.3	27.7	13.2	1.3	74.2	40.6	49.3	50.7
21914	CHARLESTOWN	96.1	95.2	1.9	2.1	0.3	0.4	0.5	0.7	5.1	5.6	7.0	6.9	4.7	29.1	29.2	11.6	0.9	77.9	40.1	51.9	48.1
21915	CHESAPEAKE CITY	95.3	94.5	2.7	3.2	0.3	0.4	1.2	1.5	5.6	6.2	7.2	6.5	4.7	26.6	28.4	13.3	1.5	76.4	41.0	49.3	50.7
21917	COLORA	97.8	97.4	0.8	0.9	0.3	0.4	0.5	0.7	6.9	7.3	7.5	6.9	5.1	29.5	27.1	9.0	0.8	73.5	38.2	50.8	49.2
21918	CONOWINGO	97.5	97.1	0.9	1.2	0.2	0.3	0.4	0.6	6.5	7.4	9.0	6.9	5.6	30.8	25.5	7.8	0.6	72.8	36.6	50.6	49.5
21919	EARLEVILLE	96.2	95.6	2.4	2.7	0.4	0.5	0.8	1.0	4.8	5.2	6.6	5.0	4.0	24.7	32.0	16.3	1.5	80.3	44.9	51.1	48.9
21921	ELKTON	91.3	90.0	5.2	5.9	1.0	1.2	2.0	2.5	7.6	7.4	7.9	6.7	6.4	30.1	24.2	8.9	1.0	72.9	34.9	48.8	51.2
	MARYLAND	64.0	61.8	27.9	28.9	4.0	4.6	4.3	5.1	6.6	6.7	7.3	6.9	6.6	29.1	25.1	10.2	1.5	75.2	37.0	48.3	51.7
	UNITED STATES	75.1	73.6	12.3	12.5	3.8	4.2	12.5	14.1	6.9	6.7	7.2	7.0	7.3	28.6	23.8	10.8	1.7	75.1	36.0	49.1	50.9

# ZIP CODE POST OFFICE NAME	2004 Per Capita Income	2004 HH Income Base	2004 HOUSEHOLD INCOME DISTRIBUTION (%)					MEDIAN HOUSEHOLD INCOME				2004 Home Value Base	2004 HOME VALUE DISTRIBUTION (%)					2004 Median Home Value
			Less than $25,000	$25,000 to $49,999	$50,000 to $99,999	$100,000 to $149,999	$150,000 or More	2004	2009	2004 National Centile	2004 State Centile		Less than $50,000	$50,000 to $89,999	$90,000 to $174,999	$175,000 to $399,999	$400,000 or More	
21798 WOODSBORO	29942	761	14.7	20.2	40.6	13.4	11.0	65637	76433	89	62	654	0.8	0.6	10.7	72.5	15.4	261511
21801 SALISBURY	22960	10440	30.3	26.4	29.2	8.8	5.3	42432	47529	54	18	6764	5.9	8.4	43.8	36.2	5.7	149575
21804 SALISBURY	22553	13382	28.8	30.3	29.6	7.8	3.5	42144	47145	53	18	8703	4.2	10.4	54.4	29.3	1.8	137566
21811 BERLIN	27262	9429	20.8	31.0	34.1	9.0	5.1	48646	55787	70	30	7583	3.7	4.1	39.1	43.7	9.6	182873
21813 BISHOPVILLE	26050	970	22.6	22.4	37.4	11.2	6.4	54082	62350	78	42	845	9.9	4.9	31.2	34.6	19.4	192448
21814 BIVALVE	21307	181	35.4	34.3	22.7	5.0	2.8	37327	40943	37	12	151	14.6	12.6	57.0	15.9	0.0	110938
21817 CRISFIELD	16916	2309	47.1	27.1	18.9	5.1	1.9	26929	29481	7	2	1530	12.6	18.4	53.3	13.7	2.1	110285
21821 DEAL ISLAND	19857	529	32.9	37.2	24.8	4.0	1.1	35608	39198	30	10	458	14.9	21.0	47.4	14.4	2.4	107692
21822 EDEN	26033	1163	24.4	34.7	28.1	9.1	3.7	42454	47648	54	18	979	19.1	12.5	39.3	24.7	4.4	122064
21824 EWELL	21751	131	35.1	35.9	25.2	0.8	3.1	32499	36305	19	7	113	13.3	22.1	52.2	10.6	1.8	103365
21826 FRUITLAND	22000	1499	27.8	34.0	27.3	7.4	3.5	41810	46267	52	17	1054	12.1	13.8	41.3	26.3	6.6	123010
21829 GIRDLETREE	21769	162	28.4	33.3	32.1	1.9	4.3	39382	44316	44	14	133	11.3	13.5	45.1	22.6	7.5	134135
21830 HEBRON	22921	1217	16.4	30.3	42.5	6.8	3.9	52537	59542	76	38	1033	4.9	8.3	53.1	30.1	3.6	141711
21835 LINKWOOD	30599	198	25.3	26.3	32.8	10.6	5.1	48223	52050	69	29	168	14.9	19.1	34.5	25.0	6.6	128947
21837 MARDELA SPRINGS	20060	1310	26.9	30.7	34.4	5.9	2.2	43404	48698	57	21	1083	9.1	17.5	54.1	17.3	2.1	125142
21838 MARION STATION	21044	809	21.5	40.4	29.8	6.3	2.0	44630	49129	60	22	686	14.3	13.4	45.2	23.2	3.9	130372
21840 NANTICOKE	25719	192	21.4	31.3	39.6	7.8	0.0	48187	55691	69	29	164	0.0	4.9	47.6	32.9	14.6	162500
21841 NEWARK	20442	315	30.2	32.1	28.6	4.1	5.1	42729	46830	55	19	269	8.6	7.8	49.4	32.3	1.9	141193
21842 OCEAN CITY	32474	5332	26.2	33.1	27.1	7.6	6.0	41925	46394	53	17	3795	0.9	4.4	33.9	47.4	13.4	203691
21849 PARSONSBURG	21321	1179	21.6	29.7	36.0	10.9	1.8	48826	54546	70	31	984	9.6	12.4	49.6	27.4	1.0	137330
21850 PITTSVILLE	20276	1066	24.8	33.3	34.2	4.9	2.8	42494	47580	55	19	867	11.5	20.5	48.3	16.4	3.2	114807
21851 POCOMOKE CITY	21571	2925	36.9	30.1	23.7	4.9	4.5	33309	37065	22	8	2008	6.8	19.4	48.3	23.7	1.8	122583
21853 PRINCESS ANNE	16307	3190	41.6	29.1	22.0	4.3	3.1	30773	34311	14	5	1958	17.1	14.0	48.3	17.1	3.6	117803
21856 QUANTICO	25445	349	24.9	34.4	26.1	9.2	5.4	41288	47685	51	17	285	8.4	15.1	31.9	35.4	9.1	154605
21863 SNOW HILL	20395	1974	26.8	29.8	34.9	6.5	2.0	43256	48042	57	20	1503	5.9	12.4	51.1	25.1	5.3	136582
21864 STOCKTON	21449	204	29.4	32.4	31.9	2.0	4.4	37086	40285	36	12	165	11.5	13.3	45.5	23.6	6.1	131985
21865 TYASKIN	25473	205	30.7	34.6	23.4	6.8	4.4	38780	43896	42	14	169	12.4	14.2	43.8	24.9	4.7	120313
21866 TYLERTON	16489	45	40.0	33.3	26.7	0.0	0.0	30537	34286	14	4	39	7.7	20.5	59.0	10.3	2.6	108654
21869 VIENNA	18379	409	34.7	32.3	27.6	5.4	0.0	34904	37744	27	9	346	16.2	18.5	42.5	16.5	6.4	115385
21871 WESTOVER	29319	924	33.7	33.4	21.7	5.5	5.7	35447	39950	29	10	777	17.9	17.4	38.6	25.1	1.0	127264
21872 WHALEYVILLE	26012	247	27.1	31.6	27.1	6.9	7.3	42686	47370	55	19	208	18.3	12.5	27.9	27.9	13.5	135294
21874 WILLARDS	19354	949	23.9	36.4	32.5	5.0	2.3	42107	47940	53	18	758	7.9	16.0	61.7	12.7	1.7	123818
21875 DELMAR	21205	2079	24.2	30.5	32.3	9.9	3.1	46629	52301	65	27	1588	6.2	13.4	52.1	25.9	2.3	134091
21901 NORTH EAST	23844	5051	17.5	27.6	38.9	11.6	4.4	54202	62084	79	42	3979	9.1	4.7	35.0	45.6	5.6	177361
21903 PERRYVILLE	22753	2199	19.7	30.1	37.3	10.5	2.4	50161	57083	72	34	1625	3.5	2.8	53.1	38.0	2.6	154030
21904 PORT DEPOSIT	23036	2575	20.5	24.8	41.2	10.2	3.3	53849	61404	78	42	2135	15.2	7.4	31.2	43.7	2.5	166915
21911 RISING SUN	24644	3308	14.8	28.3	38.8	13.5	4.6	55991	63878	81	45	2712	3.5	2.3	37.2	50.9	6.2	185828
21912 WARWICK	22337	399	28.1	27.8	27.6	10.0	6.5	43467	48442	57	21	313	8.6	5.4	33.9	42.2	9.9	179544
21913 CECILTON	24482	221	31.2	27.2	27.2	8.6	5.9	40805	44770	49	16	176	7.4	5.1	37.5	40.3	9.7	175000
21914 CHARLESTOWN	25381	274	14.6	31.0	37.2	13.5	3.7	53523	61096	78	41	233	8.6	4.3	44.6	36.5	6.0	156771
21915 CHESAPEAKE CITY	30451	1275	14.7	22.4	38.2	17.1	7.7	63607	74389	88	58	1092	3.5	1.8	31.2	55.4	8.1	198408
21917 COLORA	24071	767	13.0	24.3	46.3	13.0	3.4	63829	73143	88	59	673	1.9	0.5	41.2	52.2	4.3	183770
21918 CONOWINGO	21441	1365	15.5	27.3	43.5	11.1	2.6	55617	63197	80	44	1193	10.4	4.2	29.1	53.1	3.2	182865
21919 EARLEVILLE	29883	1301	16.5	25.6	42.7	10.5	4.7	54796	63242	79	44	1125	4.0	6.6	42.3	35.9	11.2	167873
21921 ELKTON	24638	15465	17.7	25.5	39.0	12.5	5.3	55772	62800	80	44	11222	3.7	3.6	39.9	47.9	4.8	179809
MARYLAND	30267		17.9	23.3	34.6	15.0	9.2	59732	70285				2.9	5.4	28.1	49.8	13.8	209514
UNITED STATES	25866		24.7	27.1	30.8	10.9	6.5	48124	56710				10.9	15.0	33.7	30.1	10.4	145905

#	POST OFFICE NAME	Auto Loan	Home Loan	Investments	Retirement Plans	Home Repair	Lawn & Garden	Computers & Hardware	Major Appliances	TV, Radio, Sound Equipment	Furniture	Dine out/ Carry out	Sports Equipment	Fees & Tickets	Toys & Games	Travel	Cable TV	Apparel & Services	Auto Repairs	Health Insurance	Pets & Supplies
21798	WOODSBORO	127	133	123	130	136	139	121	128	120	120	147	151	123	154	124	119	144	124	126	153
21801	SALISBURY	84	82	90	82	81	88	86	84	86	85	107	98	86	106	84	86	105	85	83	95
21804	SALISBURY	76	76	84	76	76	82	78	77	78	77	98	90	79	98	78	78	95	78	76	87
21811	BERLIN	100	87	75	83	93	107	83	95	89	86	109	101	80	99	88	94	102	93	109	115
21813	BISHOPVILLE	121	85	45	80	99	111	84	103	96	83	113	124	72	111	87	101	103	102	123	143
21814	BIVALVE	83	63	42	60	69	83	69	76	78	66	91	85	62	86	69	82	83	76	91	92
21817	CRISFIELD	59	48	42	44	50	59	52	55	58	51	69	61	49	66	51	61	65	55	64	65
21821	DEAL ISLAND	87	58	26	50	66	76	56	70	68	57	80	84	48	75	57	73	72	69	87	100
21822	EDEN	95	87	74	83	89	97	82	88	86	83	106	102	81	105	84	88	102	87	93	109
21824	EWELL	89	60	27	52	68	78	58	72	70	59	82	86	49	77	59	75	74	72	89	103
21826	FRUITLAND	83	76	75	75	78	85	76	80	80	77	98	94	75	98	77	81	94	80	83	95
21829	GIRDLETREE	84	77	67	73	82	91	76	82	82	74	99	94	75	104	79	85	94	80	91	99
21830	HEBRON	90	89	82	90	89	93	87	89	85	86	106	104	86	106	85	83	102	88	85	101
21835	LINKWOOD	114	101	77	96	107	114	93	104	99	93	121	123	92	123	96	102	115	101	112	134
21837	MARDELA SPRINGS	81	69	53	68	72	81	71	75	75	69	91	86	68	90	70	76	85	74	82	89
21838	MARION STATION	92	65	36	60	73	85	66	79	77	65	90	92	58	86	67	82	82	78	95	105
21840	NANTICOKE	84	79	76	75	84	98	73	83	77	78	96	81	74	80	79	83	90	81	97	95
21841	NEWARK	91	65	35	61	75	84	64	78	73	63	86	94	55	84	66	76	78	77	93	108
21842	OCEAN CITY	105	81	54	74	92	103	77	93	87	77	103	109	69	101	82	93	96	91	110	127
21849	PARSONSBURG	88	82	66	79	83	88	77	83	79	78	97	97	74	95	77	78	93	82	84	101
21850	PITTSVILLE	81	73	57	70	74	79	69	75	71	70	87	87	66	84	69	71	83	74	76	91
21851	POCOMOKE CITY	80	69	62	67	72	82	73	76	78	72	95	88	70	94	73	80	90	77	84	91
21853	PRINCESS ANNE	67	56	50	55	57	63	60	62	63	60	78	74	56	74	59	63	74	64	65	75
21856	QUANTICO	98	76	52	73	82	97	83	91	92	79	109	102	75	103	82	97	100	91	107	109
21863	SNOW HILL	80	68	53	65	73	82	68	75	74	66	89	86	65	90	70	77	84	74	85	93
21864	STOCKTON	75	82	86	77	83	92	81	80	84	78	104	89	85	112	83	87	100	78	86	88
21865	TYASKIN	90	68	45	65	74	89	75	83	84	71	99	93	67	94	74	89	90	83	99	100
21866	TYLERTON	65	43	20	37	49	57	42	52	51	43	59	63	36	56	43	54	54	52	65	74
21869	VIENNA	79	54	25	47	61	70	52	64	62	53	73	77	45	69	53	67	67	64	79	91
21871	WESTOVER	53	39	24	37	44	51	42	48	47	40	56	55	37	53	42	50	51	47	57	60
21872	WHALEYVILLE	108	76	41	72	88	99	75	92	86	74	101	111	65	99	78	90	92	91	109	128
21874	WILLARDS	78	69	53	67	71	78	68	73	71	68	86	84	65	85	67	71	82	72	77	88
21875	DELMAR	81	77	73	76	79	85	78	80	80	76	98	93	77	99	78	80	94	80	82	93
21901	NORTH EAST	98	93	82	89	95	101	90	95	92	89	113	111	87	112	90	92	108	94	97	114
21903	PERRYVILLE	90	80	64	77	83	91	78	84	82	77	100	98	75	99	79	83	94	83	90	103
21904	PORT DEPOSIT	90	94	91	93	93	95	90	91	87	90	109	107	90	109	89	85	106	91	86	103
21911	RISING SUN	106	97	80	95	101	108	93	100	96	93	117	118	91	118	94	96	112	98	104	122
21912	WARWICK	96	82	64	82	86	97	84	90	90	83	109	103	81	108	84	91	102	89	98	106
21913	CECILTON	91	77	60	77	81	91	79	84	84	78	102	97	76	101	79	85	95	83	92	100
21914	CHARLESTOWN	101	90	69	86	95	102	83	92	89	83	108	110	82	110	86	91	102	90	100	119
21915	CHESAPEAKE CITY	116	105	87	101	111	121	101	110	106	100	129	128	98	131	104	109	123	108	119	137
21917	COLORA	105	107	95	104	109	113	97	103	98	97	121	122	99	125	100	98	117	100	104	125
21918	CONOWINGO	94	93	82	92	92	94	88	91	86	90	108	107	86	105	87	84	104	91	86	105
21919	EARLEVILLE	109	99	86	92	106	117	95	105	101	94	122	120	92	123	99	106	116	103	117	131
21921	ELKTON	97	95	92	96	95	100	94	96	94	94	117	113	93	116	93	92	113	96	93	110
	MARYLAND	108	114	128	115	112	119	113	111	111	114	139	129	116	140	113	109	137	112	106	124
	UNITED STATES	100	100	100	100	100	100	100	100	100	100	100	100	100	100	100	100	100	100	100	100

MASSACHUSETTS — POPULATION CHANGE

A — 01001-01337

# POST OFFICE NAME	COUNTY FIPS CODE	POPULATION 2000	2004	2009	% Rate	State Centile	HOUSEHOLDS 2000	2004	2009	% Annual Rate 2000-2004	2004 Average HH Size	FAMILIES 2000	2004	% Annual Rate 2000-2004
01001 AGAWAM	013	16336	16470	16677	0.2	40	6903	7039	7206	0.5	2.24	4230	4311	0.5
01002 AMHERST	015	32726	33085	33447	0.3	44	9849	10214	10550	0.9	2.41	5039	5228	0.9
01003 AMHERST	015	3990	3981	3979	-0.1	26	28	23	22	-4.5	1.39	5	4	-5.1
01005 BARRE	027	5113	5386	5648	1.2	85	1889	2012	2129	1.5	2.66	1378	1465	1.5
01007 BELCHERTOWN	015	13008	13864	14312	1.5	90	4900	5287	5527	1.8	2.62	3528	3805	1.8
01008 BLANDFORD	013	1176	1179	1178	0.1	33	437	446	451	0.5	2.64	333	340	0.5
01010 BRIMFIELD	013	3373	3499	3564	0.9	74	1262	1327	1368	1.2	2.64	896	942	1.2
01011 CHESTER	013	2171	2153	2138	-0.2	17	851	862	871	0.3	2.48	619	627	0.3
01012 CHESTERFIELD	015	319	326	329	0.5	60	122	128	132	1.1	2.55	89	93	1.0
01013 CHICOPEE	013	22943	22911	23138	0.0	28	9526	9625	9834	0.2	2.33	5773	5848	0.3
01020 CHICOPEE	013	29688	29423	29533	-0.2	16	12776	12878	13103	0.2	2.27	7894	7951	0.2
01022 CHICOPEE	013	2006	2026	2050	0.2	42	811	832	855	0.6	1.94	468	480	0.6
01026 CUMMINGTON	015	1377	1413	1427	0.6	65	532	561	578	1.3	2.31	348	366	1.2
01027 EASTHAMPTON	015	17454	17417	17440	-0.1	26	7393	7533	7678	0.4	2.31	4589	4671	0.4
01028 EAST LONGMEADOW	013	14029	14333	14495	0.5	60	5222	5413	5544	0.9	2.61	3966	4113	0.9
01030 FEEDING HILLS	013	11825	11733	11776	-0.2	19	4363	4394	4472	0.2	2.67	3236	3274	0.3
01031 GILBERTVILLE	027	1648	1671	1715	0.3	48	626	640	662	0.5	2.54	438	446	0.4
01032 GOSHEN	015	268	264	262	-0.4	9	117	118	119	0.2	2.24	79	79	0.0
01033 GRANBY	015	6047	6157	6218	0.4	55	2220	2306	2369	0.9	2.65	1641	1702	0.9
01034 GRANVILLE	013	1967	2016	2039	0.6	63	730	762	783	1.0	2.64	530	553	1.0
01035 HADLEY	015	4798	4922	4993	0.6	64	1896	1984	2047	1.1	2.40	1249	1304	1.0
01036 HAMPDEN	013	5182	5243	5278	0.3	45	1821	1865	1901	0.6	2.77	1466	1501	0.6
01038 HATFIELD	015	2527	2688	2773	1.5	89	1049	1140	1196	2.0	2.36	662	717	1.9
01039 HAYDENVILLE	015	1671	1639	1631	-0.5	6	711	714	723	0.1	2.29	447	447	0.0
01040 HOLYOKE	013	39935	39891	40181	0.0	28	14979	15143	15436	0.3	2.54	9483	9570	0.2
01050 HUNTINGTON	015	2424	2447	2482	0.2	42	901	929	959	0.7	2.63	665	686	0.7
01053 LEEDS	015	1333	1299	1290	-0.6	3	521	518	523	-0.1	2.36	354	351	-0.2
01054 LEVERETT	011	1483	1625	1702	2.2	98	561	627	667	2.7	2.54	399	445	2.6
01056 LUDLOW	013	21230	21732	22103	0.6	61	7666	7980	8232	1.0	2.51	5519	5748	1.0
01057 MONSON	013	8355	8541	8655	0.5	60	3093	3216	3304	0.9	2.60	2208	2296	0.9
01060 NORTHAMPTON	015	15043	14870	14834	-0.3	13	6639	6693	6789	0.2	1.90	2548	2553	0.1
01062 FLORENCE	015	12145	12051	12034	-0.2	19	4713	4770	4848	0.3	2.33	2973	3008	0.3
01063 NORTHAMPTON	015	458	457	456	-0.1	26	7	7	7	0.0	2.57	2	2	0.0
01068 OAKHAM	027	1673	1761	1846	1.2	84	578	613	647	1.4	2.87	467	495	1.4
01069 PALMER	013	10051	10292	10464	0.6	62	4068	4197	4309	0.7	2.42	2666	2754	0.8
01070 PLAINFIELD	015	554	563	566	0.4	52	231	241	248	1.0	2.34	159	165	0.9
01071 RUSSELL	013	1462	1458	1456	-0.1	25	539	547	554	0.4	2.67	425	431	0.3
01072 SHUTESBURY	011	1464	1422	1409	-0.7	2	544	536	540	-0.4	2.64	394	389	-0.3
01073 SOUTHAMPTON	015	5394	5628	5743	1.0	78	1988	2118	2200	1.5	2.66	1558	1658	1.5
01075 SOUTH HADLEY	015	17306	16976	16885	-0.5	6	6620	6621	6700	0.0	2.29	4234	4223	-0.1
01077 SOUTHWICK	013	8828	9194	9376	1.0	77	3318	3508	3627	1.3	2.62	2419	2558	1.3
01080 THREE RIVERS	013	2640	2659	2668	0.2	39	1088	1110	1127	0.5	2.39	714	728	0.5
01081 WALES	013	1681	1794	1856	1.5	91	636	690	723	1.9	2.60	467	507	2.0
01082 WARE	015	10286	10155	10140	-0.3	12	4228	4252	4314	0.1	2.38	2737	2745	0.1
01084 WEST CHESTERFIELD	015	137	140	141	0.5	60	48	50	52	1.0	2.68	35	37	1.3
01085 WESTFIELD	013	40825	41499	41962	0.4	53	15084	15450	15773	0.6	2.53	10239	10518	0.6
01088 WEST HATFIELD	015	643	642	640	0.0	27	304	311	315	0.5	2.06	192	196	0.5
01089 WEST SPRINGFIELD	013	27785	27925	28199	0.1	36	11805	11997	12249	0.4	2.30	7104	7221	0.4
01092 WEST WARREN	027	2636	2672	2743	0.3	47	1050	1075	1113	0.6	2.48	677	691	0.5
01095 WILBRAHAM	013	13352	13652	13824	0.5	60	4853	5030	5157	0.9	2.67	3841	3977	0.8
01096 WILLIAMSBURG	015	2524	2525	2525	0.0	31	990	1015	1034	0.6	2.49	676	691	0.5
01098 WORTHINGTON	015	1212	1221	1221	0.2	39	486	502	512	0.8	2.43	356	367	0.7
01103 SPRINGFIELD	013	2948	2933	3005	-0.1	22	1717	1723	1783	0.1	1.64	620	616	-0.2
01104 SPRINGFIELD	013	22774	23037	23294	0.3	45	9194	9443	9681	0.6	2.40	5621	5745	0.5
01105 SPRINGFIELD	013	12985	13262	13510	0.5	59	5140	5319	5490	0.8	2.32	2608	2685	0.7
01106 LONGMEADOW	013	15882	15761	15761	-0.2	19	5887	5926	5999	0.2	2.59	4500	4526	0.1
01107 SPRINGFIELD	013	10888	10701	10707	-0.4	6	3520	3492	3528	-0.2	3.04	2378	2359	-0.2
01108 SPRINGFIELD	013	25708	26154	26501	0.4	54	9860	10104	10328	0.6	2.58	6051	6181	0.5
01109 SPRINGFIELD	013	30312	30254	30451	-0.1	26	9853	9968	10164	0.3	2.80	6817	6891	0.3
01118 SPRINGFIELD	013	14601	14418	14424	-0.3	12	5835	5838	5914	0.0	2.45	4108	4113	0.0
01119 SPRINGFIELD	013	13348	13286	13336	-0.1	22	4698	4729	4804	0.2	2.53	3273	3298	0.2
01128 SPRINGFIELD	013	2993	2991	2992	0.0	29	1052	1071	1086	0.4	2.75	817	832	0.4
01129 SPRINGFIELD	013	7073	6933	6907	-0.5	5	2803	2792	2820	-0.1	2.46	1945	1940	-0.1
01151 INDIAN ORCHARD	013	8356	8228	8201	-0.4	8	3356	3338	3363	-0.1	2.46	2133	2121	-0.1
01201 PITTSFIELD	003	47704	47343	46925	-0.2	19	20492	20727	20904	0.3	2.22	12375	12512	0.3
01220 ADAMS	003	8809	8984	9171	0.5	56	3992	4130	4282	0.8	2.17	2433	2531	0.9
01222 ASHLEY FALLS	003	783	795	795	0.4	50	284	293	297	0.7	2.71	207	214	0.8
01223 BECKET	003	1175	1149	1128	-0.5	4	450	450	450	0.0	2.53	344	344	0.0
01224 BERKSHIRE	003	273	274	272	0.1	35	105	108	109	0.7	2.53	77	79	0.6
01225 CHESHIRE	003	3437	3443	3417	0.0	32	1380	1413	1430	0.6	2.44	996	1020	0.6
01226 DALTON	003	7024	6902	6801	-0.4	6	2754	2766	2777	0.1	2.45	1888	1896	0.1
01230 GREAT BARRINGTON	003	9807	9661	9529	-0.4	9	3968	3988	4006	0.1	2.24	2462	2476	0.1
01235 HINSDALE	003	2703	2666	2629	-0.3	11	1048	1051	1052	0.1	2.54	749	752	0.1
01236 HOUSATONIC	003	1091	1077	1061	-0.3	12	440	443	444	0.2	2.37	303	305	0.2
01237 LANESBORO	003	2140	2139	2124	0.0	30	841	859	870	0.5	2.48	605	618	0.5
01238 LEE	003	6461	6431	6372	-0.1	22	2619	2661	2685	0.4	2.36	1741	1769	0.4
01240 LENOX	003	5191	5346	5403	0.7	69	2281	2405	2480	1.3	2.10	1337	1410	1.3
01243 MIDDLEFIELD	015	417	420	420	0.2	39	161	166	170	0.7	2.53	118	122	0.8
01245 MONTEREY	003	485	480	475	-0.2	14	211	213	214	0.2	2.07	132	133	0.2
01247 NORTH ADAMS	003	16807	16534	16353	-0.4	7	7139	7161	7209	0.1	2.20	4272	4282	0.1
01253 OTIS	003	1318	1303	1285	-0.3	13	547	555	558	0.3	2.34	373	377	0.3
01254 RICHMOND	003	945	932	919	-0.3	10	384	387	388	0.2	2.40	284	286	0.2
01255 SANDISFIELD	003	831	808	792	-0.7	2	332	331	332	-0.1	2.29	216	215	-0.1
01256 SAVOY	003	750	748	741	-0.1	25	303	310	313	0.5	2.40	214	219	0.5
01257 SHEFFIELD	003	2328	2296	2262	-0.3	10	994	995	996	0.0	2.29	641	642	0.0
01258 SOUTH EGREMONT	003	130	126	123	-0.7	2	64	63	62	-0.4	2.00	37	36	-0.6
01259 SOUTHFIELD	003	710	700	690	-0.3	10	291	292	293	0.1	2.25	206	206	0.0
01262 STOCKBRIDGE	003	1504	1463	1435	-0.7	4	711	702	698	-0.3	1.90	383	377	-0.4
01266 WEST STOCKBRIDGE	003	1964	1957	1939	-0.1	24	782	796	803	0.4	2.34	521	530	0.4
01267 WILLIAMSTOWN	003	8661	8476	8353	-0.5	5	2851	2814	2802	-0.3	2.18	1764	1742	-0.3
01270 WINDSOR	003	817	797	782	-0.6	3	299	297	297	-0.2	2.68	227	225	-0.2
01301 GREENFIELD	011	18283	18283	18388	0.0	30	7987	8138	8327	0.4	2.15	4412	4480	0.4
01330 ASHFIELD	011	1496	1494	1490	0.0	28	611	621	630	0.4	2.40	420	426	0.3
01331 ATHOL	027	13116	13385	13850	0.5	57	5138	5308	5548	0.8	2.47	3461	3564	0.7
01337 BERNARDSTON	011	2680	2825	2907	1.3	86	1030	1105	1155	1.7	2.54	754	808	1.6
MASSACHUSETTS					0.4					0.6	2.48			0.6
UNITED STATES					1.2					1.3	2.58			1.1

ZIP CODE #	POST OFFICE NAME	RACE (%) White 2000	White 2004	Black 2000	Black 2004	Asian/Pacific 2000	Asian/Pacific 2004	% Hispanic Origin 2000	% Hispanic Origin 2004	2004 AGE DISTRIBUTION (%) 0-4	5-9	10-14	15-19	20-24	25-44	45-64	65-84	85+	18+	MEDIAN AGE 2004	% 2004 Males	% 2004 Females
01001	AGAWAM	96.4	95.5	1.1	1.4	1.2	1.5	1.8	2.4	5.3	5.4	5.7	5.3	5.0	26.7	26.6	15.8	4.3	80.4	42.9	46.7	53.3
01002	AMHERST	80.3	77.5	5.1	5.4	8.3	10.0	6.2	7.1	3.1	3.4	4.2	17.7	26.7	19.7	17.4	6.5	1.3	86.1	24.0	48.2	51.9
01003	AMHERST	79.0	75.5	3.7	4.0	12.0	14.6	4.3	5.1	0.1	0.0	0.1	52.7	45.2	1.8	0.2	0.0	0.0	99.6	19.7	50.0	50.0
01005	BARRE	97.6	97.3	0.5	0.6	0.3	0.4	0.8	1.1	6.3	6.8	8.4	7.4	5.6	27.3	26.4	10.0	1.9	73.5	38.2	49.0	51.0
01007	BELCHERTOWN	96.1	95.5	0.8	0.9	1.0	1.3	1.6	1.9	6.6	7.0	7.9	6.7	5.7	29.8	27.5	7.9	1.0	74.1	37.8	48.7	51.3
01008	BLANDFORD	98.7	98.5	0.5	0.6	0.3	0.3	0.3	0.4	5.3	5.9	6.1	6.8	5.5	25.5	34.1	9.8	0.9	78.4	42.1	50.1	49.9
01010	BRIMFIELD	97.7	97.2	0.5	0.6	0.1	0.1	1.3	1.8	6.1	6.7	7.5	7.1	5.2	25.6	30.6	9.9	1.4	75.3	40.8	49.5	50.5
01011	CHESTER	97.9	97.5	0.4	0.5	0.3	0.4	1.2	1.4	5.3	5.9	7.0	6.9	4.9	26.9	31.2	10.9	1.2	77.7	41.7	51.0	49.0
01012	CHESTERFIELD	98.8	98.5	0.0	0.0	0.6	0.6	0.0	0.0	5.8	6.8	7.1	5.8	5.2	26.4	32.8	9.2	0.9	76.7	41.2	50.0	50.0
01013	CHICOPEE	85.2	82.3	2.3	2.7	0.8	0.9	14.9	18.3	6.3	6.1	7.0	6.8	7.1	28.6	22.5	13.2	2.6	76.6	37.1	47.2	52.8
01020	CHICOPEE	94.2	92.6	1.6	1.9	1.1	1.4	3.9	5.4	5.0	5.2	6.2	5.7	6.0	26.3	27.0	16.0	2.5	80.1	42.2	47.9	52.1
01022	CHICOPEE	77.1	72.4	12.3	14.6	1.8	2.2	10.3	13.3	5.2	4.6	4.4	14.8	10.1	25.1	22.0	12.5	1.3	77.3	32.7	50.7	49.3
01026	CUMMINGTON	97.0	96.7	0.4	0.5	0.4	0.4	2.4	2.9	4.2	5.0	6.2	14.7	3.4	27.2	28.5	9.8	1.1	73.0	39.5	50.7	49.3
01027	EASTHAMPTON	95.7	94.8	0.6	0.6	1.6	2.0	2.0	2.4	5.2	5.4	6.1	6.0	6.2	29.5	28.5	11.2	2.0	79.7	40.2	48.3	51.7
01028	EAST LONGMEADOW	97.5	96.9	0.7	1.0	0.9	1.2	0.9	1.3	5.5	6.2	7.2	6.5	4.7	23.3	27.9	15.6	3.2	76.9	43.0	47.6	52.4
01030	FEEDING HILLS	97.1	96.4	0.7	0.9	0.7	0.9	1.9	2.6	5.9	6.2	7.1	6.9	5.8	27.1	29.5	10.2	1.5	76.7	40.2	49.0	51.0
01031	GILBERTVILLE	98.1	97.8	0.6	0.7	0.1	0.2	0.8	1.1	5.5	6.0	8.2	8.5	5.9	25.4	27.9	10.8	1.8	74.8	39.6	49.5	50.5
01032	GOSHEN	98.9	98.9	0.0	0.0	0.4	0.4	1.1	1.1	4.6	4.9	5.7	5.3	4.6	27.7	36.0	10.2	1.1	81.1	43.6	45.5	54.6
01033	GRANBY	96.8	96.2	0.5	0.6	1.0	1.2	1.2	1.5	5.6	6.3	7.6	6.5	5.4	28.2	28.3	11.0	1.3	76.3	39.9	48.8	51.2
01034	GRANVILLE	98.4	98.2	0.4	0.5	0.2	0.3	0.8	1.0	6.2	7.0	7.6	6.8	4.3	26.1	30.6	10.4	0.9	74.4	41.3	52.1	47.9
01035	HADLEY	95.9	95.1	0.8	0.9	1.6	2.0	1.7	2.0	4.5	4.9	5.7	5.8	5.8	26.0	28.7	14.8	3.8	80.9	43.4	47.1	52.9
01036	HAMPDEN	98.3	98.0	0.2	0.2	0.5	0.6	0.6	0.8	5.3	6.1	7.8	7.3	5.0	22.2	31.8	12.5	2.1	76.2	43.0	48.2	51.8
01038	HATFIELD	97.9	97.5	0.2	0.3	0.6	0.8	1.0	1.3	4.6	5.4	6.8	5.3	4.2	23.7	33.1	14.7	2.3	80.0	45.0	48.4	51.6
01039	HAYDENVILLE	97.4	97.0	0.4	0.4	0.7	0.9	1.0	1.2	4.3	4.8	6.6	6.8	5.1	25.8	33.0	11.9	1.8	80.2	43.2	47.4	52.7
01040	HOLYOKE	65.8	61.9	3.7	4.0	0.9	1.1	41.3	45.9	8.0	7.3	8.3	8.1	7.3	25.1	20.6	12.3	3.1	71.6	34.5	47.1	52.9
01050	HUNTINGTON	97.6	97.3	0.4	0.5	0.4	0.4	1.7	2.1	5.7	5.8	7.4	7.8	6.5	27.3	29.6	8.8	1.1	76.3	39.3	49.5	50.6
01053	LEEDS	95.1	94.4	0.3	0.3	0.8	1.0	3.2	3.9	4.5	5.3	7.3	6.5	5.2	22.4	30.6	13.8	4.4	78.7	44.2	43.5	56.5
01054	LEVERETT	95.3	94.7	0.3	0.3	1.4	1.8	1.4	1.8	3.7	4.9	6.6	6.7	4.9	22.7	38.2	10.9	1.5	79.9	45.3	50.3	49.7
01056	LUDLOW	95.8	95.0	2.0	2.3	0.6	0.8	6.5	8.0	5.0	5.2	5.9	6.4	6.8	30.0	25.8	13.2	1.8	80.3	39.8	51.2	48.8
01057	MONSON	97.7	97.2	0.7	0.8	0.3	0.4	1.2	1.6	6.2	6.5	7.0	6.6	5.8	27.7	29.0	9.9	1.3	76.1	39.9	49.2	50.8
01060	NORTHAMPTON	87.7	85.7	2.6	2.9	4.5	5.5	5.9	6.9	3.3	3.0	4.1	10.3	13.8	32.1	22.4	9.0	2.2	86.7	33.5	40.3	59.7
01062	FLORENCE	92.8	91.5	1.6	1.8	1.6	1.9	4.6	5.6	4.8	5.4	5.9	6.1	4.9	25.0	31.5	13.2	3.1	80.0	43.8	48.2	51.8
01063	NORTHAMPTON	79.5	75.9	4.2	4.6	10.9	13.6	4.4	5.0	0.4	0.4	0.4	40.5	49.2	5.7	2.8	0.4	0.0	98.3	20.8	4.8	95.2
01068	OAKHAM	98.3	98.1	0.4	0.4	0.6	0.7	1.0	1.3	5.3	7.9	10.1	8.0	4.3	26.8	30.1	6.8	0.8	71.2	39.2	50.3	49.7
01069	PALMER	96.7	96.0	0.9	1.1	0.7	0.8	1.3	1.7	5.5	5.8	7.3	7.3	6.4	26.8	26.6	12.1	2.3	76.9	39.8	48.8	51.2
01070	PLAINFIELD	98.2	98.1	0.0	0.0	0.2	0.2	0.7	0.9	4.6	8.0	6.9	7.1	2.7	24.7	33.4	11.4	1.2	75.5	43.2	49.2	50.8
01071	RUSSELL	97.5	96.9	0.4	0.6	0.3	0.3	1.5	2.0	6.2	6.5	6.9	7.3	6.3	28.0	28.3	9.7	0.9	76.0	38.8	49.9	50.1
01072	SHUTESBURY	93.7	92.8	1.0	1.1	1.2	1.6	2.2	2.5	4.9	5.8	7.7	8.4	5.5	26.0	35.3	5.8	0.6	75.1	40.8	47.5	52.5
01073	SOUTHAMPTON	98.3	98.0	0.2	0.2	0.6	0.8	0.9	1.1	5.3	6.2	7.7	6.2	5.5	26.4	32.1	9.3	1.4	76.9	40.9	48.4	51.6
01075	SOUTH HADLEY	94.1	92.9	1.2	1.4	2.6	3.2	2.4	2.9	4.4	4.7	5.7	9.9	10.0	23.1	24.9	14.5	2.8	81.6	39.8	41.8	58.2
01077	SOUTHWICK	97.4	96.8	0.5	0.7	0.4	0.5	1.7	2.4	6.4	6.8	7.4	6.6	5.4	28.4	27.5	9.9	1.6	74.8	39.6	50.2	49.8
01080	THREE RIVERS	97.4	96.8	0.3	0.4	0.1	0.2	1.1	1.4	6.0	5.9	7.4	7.0	7.0	28.7	22.6	13.0	2.3	76.3	37.8	46.9	53.1
01081	WALES	97.7	97.3	0.5	0.6	0.2	0.2	0.7	1.0	6.0	6.4	6.5	6.5	5.1	29.5	31.3	8.1	0.7	77.2	39.7	50.1	49.9
01082	WARE	96.6	96.0	0.5	0.6	0.6	0.8	2.0	2.4	6.1	6.0	6.8	7.0	6.7	27.3	25.4	12.3	2.3	76.7	38.9	49.0	51.1
01084	WEST CHESTERFIELD	98.5	99.3	0.0	0.0	0.0	0.0	0.0	0.0	6.4	6.4	7.1	5.7	5.7	27.9	31.4	8.6	0.7	75.7	40.0	50.0	50.0
01085	WESTFIELD	94.6	93.2	0.9	1.1	0.9	1.1	4.9	6.5	5.9	5.9	6.6	8.9	8.5	26.2	24.6	11.3	2.1	77.4	37.0	48.5	51.5
01088	WEST HATFIELD	98.3	98.0	0.2	0.2	0.5	0.6	0.9	1.4	4.7	5.3	5.3	5.0	4.7	25.4	34.9	12.9	1.9	81.9	44.8	50.2	49.8
01089	WEST SPRINGFIELD	90.7	88.4	2.0	2.5	2.0	2.5	5.7	7.7	5.8	5.8	6.7	6.6	6.4	27.4	25.1	13.9	2.3	77.6	39.5	48.7	51.3
01092	WEST WARREN	97.7	97.3	0.4	0.4	0.3	0.3	0.6	0.8	6.1	6.2	7.6	6.9	5.5	27.5	25.3	13.0	2.0	75.9	38.9	49.3	50.8
01095	WILBRAHAM	96.4	95.4	1.2	1.5	1.3	1.7	1.4	1.9	5.5	6.7	7.9	7.2	4.0	21.2	30.5	14.4	2.7	74.9	43.6	48.2	51.8
01096	WILLIAMSBURG	98.7	98.6	0.1	0.1	0.3	0.4	0.6	0.7	4.4	5.3	6.7	6.5	5.0	25.6	34.6	10.4	1.5	79.5	43.0	47.4	52.6
01098	WORTHINGTON	98.4	98.2	0.3	0.3	0.2	0.3	0.9	1.1	4.7	5.5	6.6	6.6	5.5	24.2	35.7	10.1	1.2	79.3	43.4	49.6	50.4
01103	SPRINGFIELD	40.6	36.7	22.3	23.2	3.7	3.6	46.9	50.8	8.0	6.4	5.1	6.0	10.8	32.4	21.9	8.2	1.2	77.6	32.2	47.1	52.9
01104	SPRINGFIELD	63.8	58.6	10.0	10.9	1.1	1.2	33.6	39.3	7.2	7.0	8.0	7.5	7.2	26.6	20.8	13.2	2.6	73.2	35.4	47.2	52.8
01105	SPRINGFIELD	35.1	31.2	23.9	24.1	1.1	1.1	50.1	54.9	9.4	8.3	8.2	8.3	9.2	29.2	18.2	7.6	1.7	69.2	29.2	48.8	51.2
01106	LONGMEADOW	95.0	93.6	0.9	1.1	2.9	3.8	1.4	1.9	6.0	7.0	7.9	7.0	4.5	18.8	30.5	14.8	3.6	74.3	44.3	47.0	53.0
01107	SPRINGFIELD	35.9	33.4	8.8	8.6	0.8	0.9	73.0	75.9	9.4	9.2	10.5	10.4	8.0	25.0	17.9	8.4	1.2	64.4	27.0	47.6	52.4
01108	SPRINGFIELD	61.8	56.5	14.4	15.7	5.4	5.9	23.2	27.9	8.3	7.4	7.9	8.1	8.8	30.3	19.7	8.3	1.4	71.7	31.2	47.9	52.1
01109	SPRINGFIELD	32.0	29.5	49.8	50.6	1.3	1.5	22.7	25.2	7.7	7.9	9.4	11.0	11.0	23.8	19.3	8.6	1.4	69.6	27.6	46.6	53.4
01118	SPRINGFIELD	83.1	79.7	9.2	10.9	2.1	2.5	6.4	8.4	6.6	6.9	6.8	6.0	5.1	26.7	25.2	13.8	2.8	75.9	39.8	46.1	53.9
01119	SPRINGFIELD	70.1	65.4	18.7	21.2	1.4	1.6	11.3	14.1	6.4	6.2	7.4	9.4	11.0	26.1	21.3	10.9	1.4	76.2	32.7	47.6	52.5
01128	SPRINGFIELD	82.5	78.9	11.2	13.3	1.1	1.4	7.2	9.3	6.5	7.0	6.6	6.4	5.4	25.9	27.1	13.2	2.1	75.9	40.3	47.6	52.4
01129	SPRINGFIELD	79.0	75.0	13.6	15.9	1.4	1.6	7.7	9.9	6.1	6.5	6.8	6.4	5.9	27.9	27.7	11.3	1.4	76.5	39.0	47.4	52.6
01151	INDIAN ORCHARD	71.6	66.5	11.9	13.5	0.9	1.0	21.1	25.9	8.3	8.2	8.5	7.2	7.1	30.0	18.9	10.0	1.8	70.4	31.7	47.4	52.6
01201	PITTSFIELD	92.8	91.9	3.5	3.9	1.2	1.4	2.0	2.4	5.9	5.8	6.6	6.4	6.0	25.7	25.4	15.4	3.0	77.8	41.1	47.8	52.2
01220	ADAMS	98.0	97.5	0.4	0.4	0.3	0.4	0.8	1.0	5.4	5.4	6.8	6.2	6.1	24.7	25.9	16.4	3.1	78.6	42.0	47.4	52.6
01222	ASHLEY FALLS	97.2	97.0	1.0	1.1	0.0	0.0	1.5	1.8	7.2	7.8	8.3	6.5	4.4	26.5	27.6	10.3	1.4	72.3	39.8	48.3	51.7
01223	BECKET	98.5	98.4	0.5	0.5	0.2	0.3	0.9	1.1	4.7	5.8	7.8	7.5	4.7	24.4	33.2	10.6	1.4	76.9	42.5	50.8	49.2
01224	BERKSHIRE	98.2	97.5	0.4	0.7	0.7	0.7	0.0	0.4	5.8	6.6	7.3	6.2	5.1	26.6	32.9	9.1	0.4	76.3	41.1	47.8	52.2
01225	CHESHIRE	98.2	97.9	0.4	0.4	0.6	0.8	0.4	0.6	4.9	5.6	6.7	6.7	5.4	25.4	30.8	12.9	1.7	78.9	42.2	49.6	50.4
01226	DALTON	97.8	97.4	0.5	0.6	0.7	0.9	1.0	1.2	5.6	6.2	7.2	7.6	5.9	23.5	27.7	13.9	2.4	76.1	41.4	48.0	52.0
01230	GREAT BARRINGTON	95.5	95.0	1.7	1.9	1.0	1.3	1.8	2.1	4.3	4.8	5.7	8.1	6.1	21.7	30.9	15.1	3.3	80.0	44.4	47.3	52.7
01235	HINSDALE	97.9	97.6	0.4	0.5	0.3	0.5	0.3	0.3	5.1	6.9	7.8	7.4	4.8	28.4	28.9	9.6	1.1	75.5	39.5	51.3	48.7
01236	HOUSATONIC	97.3	96.8	0.9	1.0	0.5	0.7	1.6	1.8	4.6	5.3	6.5	7.1	5.9	23.1	30.7	14.2	2.6	79.1	43.4	47.4	52.7
01237	LANESBORO	97.0	96.5	0.7	0.7	1.2	1.5	0.8	1.0	5.5	6.0	7.1	6.0	5.1	26.1	31.7	11.0	1.4	77.4	41.7	50.4	49.7
01238	LEE	96.8	96.4	0.6	0.7	1.0	1.3	2.3	2.9	4.9	5.2	6.0	6.2	5.7	26.2	28.6	14.9	2.2	79.9	42.4	48.3	51.7
01240	LENOX	96.6	96.1	1.3	1.4	1.1	1.3	1.9	2.3	3.4	4.5	6.8	6.8	4.3	20.3	29.3	18.7	6.0	80.5	47.5	45.8	54.2
01243	MIDDLEFIELD	98.3	98.3	0.2	0.2	0.2	0.2	0.7	1.0	4.8	5.7	6.7	6.4	5.5	24.3	35.5	10.0	1.2	78.8	43.2	49.8	50.2
01245	MONTEREY	96.9	96.3	0.6	0.6	0.6	0.8	1.2	1.7	3.8	4.2	4.4	4.6	5.2	24.6	36.7	15.6	1.0	84.8	46.9	47.5	52.5
01247	NORTH ADAMS	95.5	94.9	1.5	1.7	0.7	0.9	1.8	2.2	5.3	5.3	6.3	8.2	8.8	24.4	23.8	15.0	2.9	79.0	39.5	46.9	53.1
01253	OTIS	96.5	96.1	0.6	0.7	0.9	1.1	0.3	0.3	3.8	5.1	7.1	6.3	4.4	26.2	31.5	14.8	0.8	79.7	43.6	53.0	47.0
01254	RICHMOND	97.0	96.9	1.4	1.5	0.5	0.6	0.4	0.4	3.7	4.6	5.6	7.0	4.4	20.0	37.3	15.0	2.5	81.4	47.6	48.0	52.0
01255	SANDISFIELD	96.9	96.7	0.5	0.5	0.1	0.1	1.0	1.0	4.2	4.7	4.6	5.7	3.6	22.5	36.9	16.5	1.4	82.6	47.6	55.0	45.1
01256	SAVOY	97.5	97.3	0.7	0.8	0.0	0.0	0.7	0.8	5.5	6.4	7.1	5.6	4.4	27.9	31.2	10.6	1.3	77.0	41.0	52.8	47.2
01257	SHEFFIELD	97.4	97.1	1.0	1.1	0.3	0.4	1.3	1.6	4.6	5.4	6.8	5.4	4.8	24.5	31.3	15.2	1.9	79.3	44.1	48.7	51.4
01258	SOUTH EGREMONT	100.0	100.0	0.0	0.0	0.0	0.0	0.0	0.0	6.4	4.8	6.4	0.8	1.6	20.6	43.7	13.5	2.4	82.5	51.3	54.8	45.2
01259	SOUTHFIELD	97.6	97.4	1.6	1.7	0.1	0.1	1.3	1.4	5.3	6.3	6.1	8.7	4.7	25.3	29.9	12.0	1.7	76.3	40.9	52.6	47.4
01262	STOCKBRIDGE	96.4	96.0	1.5	1.6	0.5	0.6	3.5	4.0	3.2	3.6	4.7	4.1	4.4	21.4	34.9	20.2	3.6	85.9	50.5	46.4	53.6
01266	WEST STOCKBRIDGE	98.2	98.1	0.4	0.4	0.7	0.8	0.9	1.0	3.5	4.6	6.0	5.8	4.3	20.3	36.8	16.3	2.4	82.4	48.0	49.2	50.8
01267	WILLIAMSTOWN	91.0	89.7	2.7	2.9	3.2	3.9	2.7	3.2	3.2	3.5	4.7	14.7	17.1	15.5	21.9	14.9	4.6	85.6	35.1	46.6	53.5
01270	WINDSOR	98.9	98.8	0.0	0.0	0.0	0.0	0.1	0.1	5.5	7.2	7.8	6.3	4.4	22.1	36.9	8.7	1.3	75.5	43.3	50.4	49.6
01301	GREENFIELD	93.5	92.6	1.3	1.5	1.1	1.3	3.5	4.2	5.2	5.1	6.3	6.6	6.7	26.9	26.6	13.1	3.6	79.4	40.8	47.3	52.7
01330	ASHFIELD	96.7	96.4	0.6	0.7	0.3	0.5	0.6	0.8	4.7	5.6	6.7	7.0	5.6	23.3	34.3	10.9	1.9	78.9	43.3	49.4	50.6
01331	ATHOL	96.5	95.8	0.6	0.7	0.4	0.6	1.8	2.3	5.9	6.2	7.3	7.5	6.6	25.9	25.3	12.4	2.9	75.7	39.3	48.8	51.2
01337	BERNARDSTON	98.9	98.6	0.2	0.2	0.1	0.1	0.4	0.5	4.2	5.1	6.4	7.3	5.6	23.5	33.8	12.3	2.0	79.3	43.8	49.4	50.6
	MASSACHUSETTS	84.5	82.9	5.4	5.7	3.8	4.5	6.8	7.8	6.2	6.3	6.8	7.0	7.0	28.9	24.5	11.4	2.1	76.8	37.6	48.3	51.7
	UNITED STATES	75.1	73.6	12.3	12.5	3.8	4.2	12.5	14.1	6.9	6.7	7.2	7.0	7.3	28.6	23.8	10.8	1.7	75.1	36.0	49.1	50.9

ZIP CODE #	POST OFFICE NAME	2004 Per Capita Income	2004 HH Income Base	2004 Household Income Distribution (%): Less than $25,000	$25,000 to $49,999	$50,000 to $99,999	$100,000 to $149,999	$150,000 or More	Median Household Income: 2004	2009	2004 National Centile	2004 State Centile	2004 Home Value Base	2004 Home Value Distribution (%): Less than $50,000	$50,000 to $89,999	$90,000 to $174,999	$175,000 to $399,999	$400,000 or More	2004 Median Home Value
01001	AGAWAM	27739	7039	17.0	28.7	38.3	13.1	3.0	53569	64496	78	29	4999	0.7	3.4	43.2	51.3	1.4	178477
01002	AMHERST	27121	10214	25.3	23.7	25.2	15.6	10.3	51558	66283	75	25	5144	0.4	1.1	13.8	70.5	14.3	243710
01003	AMHERST	13005	23	39.1	21.7	34.8	4.4	0.0	35698	40000	30	6	1	0.0	0.0	0.0	100.0	0.0	275000
01005	BARRE	24843	2012	17.8	23.3	40.7	13.6	4.6	57858	70652	83	39	1602	2.3	2.6	32.2	59.9	3.0	197598
01007	BELCHERTOWN	26939	5287	15.9	22.4	41.7	15.4	4.6	61330	73979	86	46	4206	3.1	4.7	20.7	68.5	3.0	200220
01008	BLANDFORD	30602	446	12.6	20.6	47.3	12.6	7.0	61861	74126	86	47	394	0.5	1.5	35.8	54.1	8.1	192910
01010	BRIMFIELD	29804	1327	19.2	23.0	40.0	12.5	5.3	58570	68868	83	40	1177	5.0	2.9	27.9	60.6	3.7	198525
01011	CHESTER	25341	862	18.7	27.8	39.1	10.6	3.8	52764	62847	77	27	746	3.1	6.6	45.8	40.1	4.4	165330
01012	CHESTERFIELD	23472	128	14.8	26.6	47.7	10.9	0.0	57511	64259	82	37	112	0.0	2.7	31.3	62.5	3.6	198684
01013	CHICOPEE	19966	9625	34.0	30.6	27.4	6.6	1.5	37994	44812	39	7	5038	0.8	4.4	69.9	24.8	0.2	145797
01020	CHICOPEE	24415	12878	24.5	32.5	32.0	8.4	2.5	43864	52275	58	14	8825	2.8	5.5	59.8	31.4	0.5	154456
01022	CHICOPEE	23605	832	18.0	36.8	38.9	5.4	0.8	46185	54044	64	17	670	1.3	12.5	77.0	9.1	0.0	116146
01026	CUMMINGTON	27954	561	18.4	30.5	39.2	8.2	3.7	50673	59780	73	23	461	0.2	3.0	29.9	58.1	8.7	202228
01027	EASTHAMPTON	27376	7533	21.4	25.0	36.2	13.6	3.9	52562	62645	76	27	4928	0.2	1.9	45.5	50.5	1.9	178427
01028	EAST LONGMEADOW	36830	5413	13.2	17.4	38.3	19.2	12.0	74378	91389	93	68	4735	0.7	0.3	22.9	68.6	7.6	214466
01030	FEEDING HILLS	27615	4394	15.2	20.6	39.3	19.4	5.6	64211	77763	88	53	3557	0.4	0.7	29.9	67.4	1.6	199264
01031	GILBERTVILLE	27310	640	18.9	23.6	39.7	10.3	7.5	57850	69863	83	39	511	0.4	0.2	27.6	59.5	12.3	215991
01032	GOSHEN	29374	118	12.7	29.7	40.7	12.7	4.2	57131	66933	82	36	103	0.0	3.9	29.1	65.1	1.9	195833
01033	GRANBY	28541	2306	12.8	21.9	43.5	16.8	4.9	62769	74710	87	50	2009	0.0	0.5	34.0	59.5	6.1	192323
01034	GRANVILLE	29856	762	14.8	21.7	41.9	13.0	8.7	62990	74910	87	51	669	0.3	1.8	23.6	67.7	6.6	213889
01035	HADLEY	32501	1984	19.6	18.4	36.7	15.9	9.5	62853	77715	87	51	1546	0.7	0.8	8.5	81.8	8.2	237457
01036	HAMPDEN	33759	1865	13.9	13.8	37.6	24.0	10.8	78063	100095	94	74	1696	1.0	0.5	17.0	73.1	8.4	229655
01038	HATFIELD	30255	1140	19.0	21.5	35.2	19.7	4.7	58654	70949	83	41	918	0.9	1.6	9.7	75.6	12.2	243069
01039	HAYDENVILLE	36184	714	15.8	22.6	34.9	18.1	8.7	62850	78444	87	50	505	0.4	3.0	23.6	64.0	9.1	219628
01040	HOLYOKE	18813	15143	37.7	27.0	25.0	7.4	2.8	35075	41346	28	5	6873	2.6	6.7	61.0	28.2	1.5	148421
01050	HUNTINGTON	24003	929	15.5	25.7	43.2	12.7	2.9	56434	66047	81	35	738	1.2	3.4	45.5	48.1	1.8	174786
01053	LEEDS	28080	518	16.8	27.4	36.5	14.1	5.2	58103	70573	83	39	404	0.0	0.0	20.3	73.8	5.9	218846
01054	LEVERETT	41327	627	10.4	19.3	34.8	19.0	16.6	76927	96336	94	72	530	0.8	1.1	14.3	65.5	18.3	250000
01056	LUDLOW	24590	7980	20.0	25.2	38.7	12.9	3.3	54238	64427	79	31	6234	2.3	1.2	42.0	52.2	2.3	181840
01057	MONSON	27783	3216	15.6	20.8	41.6	16.3	5.8	61601	74513	86	46	2613	1.9	2.3	33.1	57.9	4.8	192838
01060	NORTHAMPTON	32569	6693	26.8	27.6	28.4	9.5	7.8	45952	57391	64	16	2707	0.3	2.9	22.3	59.4	15.1	228339
01062	FLORENCE	31413	4770	18.6	26.4	34.6	13.8	6.7	55184	67149	80	32	3527	0.0	1.3	33.2	60.0	5.5	196320
01063	NORTHAMPTON	12666	7	14.3	28.6	0.0	28.6	28.6	104392	62635	98	92	0	0.0	0.0	0.0	0.0	0.0	0
01068	OAKHAM	29685	613	8.8	18.6	46.7	17.8	8.2	70036	85310	91	63	567	1.1	0.5	16.9	74.6	6.9	234677
01069	PALMER	23147	4197	23.8	26.0	37.4	10.9	2.0	50196	60377	72	22	2846	0.8	4.8	45.4	46.4	2.7	173774
01070	PLAINFIELD	25340	241	24.1	33.6	27.4	8.3	6.6	41694	51086	52	11	205	2.0	3.9	34.6	44.4	15.1	195313
01071	RUSSELL	26330	547	17.0	27.2	41.7	11.9	2.2	53768	64373	78	30	465	3.4	2.8	44.1	47.3	2.4	174513
01072	SHUTESBURY	32628	536	9.9	22.0	41.4	15.9	10.8	70809	83023	92	63	483	0.4	0.8	21.5	67.7	9.5	226261
01073	SOUTHAMPTON	33115	2118	12.0	17.3	45.9	17.9	7.0	73728	84255	93	67	1830	0.4	1.3	18.4	74.2	5.7	221471
01075	SOUTH HADLEY	29048	6621	19.2	26.1	33.3	14.7	6.6	54416	65631	79	31	5009	0.8	1.8	36.5	55.3	5.7	190212
01077	SOUTHWICK	26610	3508	16.2	22.4	42.1	15.3	4.1	62600	75222	87	49	2912	0.0	1.8	31.2	59.6	7.4	204111
01080	THREE RIVERS	20528	1110	21.9	41.1	30.3	5.0	1.8	42423	50497	54	12	739	6.8	10.4	48.9	34.0	0.0	158071
01081	WALES	25745	690	11.6	30.4	43.0	11.5	3.5	56935	66805	82	36	599	5.8	9.0	47.6	35.9	1.7	157593
01082	WARE	22923	4252	26.8	29.6	32.8	8.7	2.1	42701	50690	55	13	2863	1.5	8.9	50.7	37.3	1.6	158735
01084	WEST CHESTERFIELD	21504	50	14.0	26.0	48.0	12.0	0.0	58032	65619	83	39	44	0.0	0.0	31.8	65.9	2.3	203571
01085	WESTFIELD	25670	15450	22.4	24.3	36.0	12.2	5.2	53075	64127	77	28	10596	2.3	3.4	36.7	54.8	2.8	185961
01088	WEST HATFIELD	33326	311	17.4	23.8	37.6	16.7	4.5	59788	69322	84	43	256	1.2	5.9	12.1	77.3	3.5	227907
01089	WEST SPRINGFIELD	25667	11997	26.2	27.3	32.6	9.9	3.9	46457	56307	65	17	7439	2.3	2.3	47.5	45.9	2.0	172213
01092	WEST WARREN	19674	1075	27.9	32.8	29.3	8.8	1.1	38970	47277	43	9	729	1.2	3.6	38.7	53.9	2.6	182154
01095	WILBRAHAM	38561	5030	12.9	16.5	34.0	19.5	17.0	79072	101094	95	76	4507	0.0	0.2	13.5	75.3	11.0	244304
01096	WILLIAMSBURG	26806	1015	15.4	29.2	40.2	11.7	3.6	54499	64476	79	31	847	0.6	2.1	25.5	65.9	5.9	208690
01098	WORTHINGTON	32220	502	15.3	26.9	35.5	14.5	7.8	59429	70244	84	42	448	0.7	2.2	31.9	57.6	7.6	199638
01103	SPRINGFIELD	17090	1723	59.4	24.5	13.8	1.7	0.6	19368	22454	2	1	95	19.0	19.0	41.1	17.9	3.2	104808
01104	SPRINGFIELD	17736	9443	40.8	27.5	24.8	5.7	1.2	31533	36837	16	4	4765	1.5	10.6	81.0	6.8	0.1	116922
01105	SPRINGFIELD	12829	5319	60.5	24.7	11.6	2.0	1.2	18184	21030	1	1	991	9.1	15.6	67.3	6.5	1.5	104934
01106	LONGMEADOW	51315	5926	10.9	13.5	30.2	19.9	25.5	91095	120667	97	86	5301	0.3	0.4	4.7	71.7	22.8	291539
01107	SPRINGFIELD	11565	3492	53.6	22.7	17.7	4.7	1.2	21853	25508	3	2	991	1.2	10.5	66.7	19.7	1.9	134531
01108	SPRINGFIELD	18950	10104	32.7	30.8	26.7	7.1	2.8	37219	43849	36	7	4581	1.2	6.1	73.9	18.4	0.3	131896
01109	SPRINGFIELD	15530	9968	41.4	27.5	24.5	4.8	1.9	31332	36578	16	4	4999	1.8	16.8	75.1	5.5	0.9	112142
01118	SPRINGFIELD	28120	5838	18.3	25.0	38.7	13.4	4.6	56197	67463	81	34	4712	0.8	2.6	73.6	22.8	0.2	143601
01119	SPRINGFIELD	21006	4729	24.0	31.1	33.8	8.3	2.9	45064	53823	61	15	3399	6.6	7.8	73.7	11.8	0.2	128068
01128	SPRINGFIELD	24965	1071	15.6	23.3	39.6	16.3	5.1	60509	72722	85	44	934	0.0	0.4	68.6	30.6	0.3	151330
01129	SPRINGFIELD	26418	2792	16.3	29.4	38.5	13.0	2.8	53456	63884	78	29	2314	0.5	6.8	72.5	19.8	0.4	138815
01151	INDIAN ORCHARD	16710	3338	39.4	30.5	24.1	5.0	1.1	31851	36925	17	4	1512	5.1	11.3	70.6	12.7	0.3	123260
01201	PITTSFIELD	26347	20727	29.2	29.1	28.5	8.7	4.4	41900	50024	53	11	13009	1.7	7.8	60.9	26.7	2.9	139875
01220	ADAMS	22489	4130	34.1	30.1	26.5	7.4	1.9	37445	43882	37	7	2668	5.0	11.1	63.8	19.5	0.7	129645
01222	ASHLEY FALLS	23866	293	22.5	20.5	44.4	6.5	6.1	55530	65367	80	33	256	3.9	2.7	35.6	54.7	3.1	186628
01223	BECKET	27704	450	18.0	25.1	37.3	11.6	8.0	57217	69215	82	36	415	4.1	6.8	43.9	40.7	4.6	165972
01224	BERKSHIRE	26223	108	20.4	22.2	35.2	18.5	3.7	56882	69923	82	35	96	0.0	6.3	34.4	58.3	1.0	195455
01225	CHESHIRE	23777	1413	23.6	26.6	34.2	14.3	1.3	49746	61269	71	21	1228	9.9	5.5	43.4	38.4	2.9	160221
01226	DALTON	29423	2766	18.6	25.3	35.7	13.8	6.7	56429	69318	81	34	2109	3.7	1.9	57.6	34.2	2.6	155276
01230	GREAT BARRINGTON	35890	3988	19.6	24.7	32.2	11.9	11.8	55321	70303	80	33	2873	0.6	1.9	23.5	55.7	18.3	231490
01235	HINSDALE	24227	1051	19.1	30.5	36.5	10.3	3.5	50260	60000	72	22	893	5.4	10.9	44.8	35.8	3.1	152408
01236	HOUSATONIC	30819	443	20.5	26.2	32.7	12.0	8.6	52808	65949	77	27	341	0.6	2.6	30.2	53.4	13.2	194894
01237	LANESBORO	25425	859	20.0	27.1	35.2	13.4	4.3	52175	63352	76	26	732	1.0	4.8	49.9	41.0	3.4	163859
01238	LEE	25649	2661	22.6	28.0	33.8	11.7	3.8	49434	60329	71	20	2004	3.3	2.4	40.1	49.1	5.1	180697
01240	LENOX	29970	2405	23.0	23.7	34.2	13.6	5.6	53003	64778	77	28	1697	2.8	2.3	19.8	61.0	14.1	231885
01243	MIDDLEFIELD	31030	166	15.1	27.1	34.9	15.1	7.8	59165	69763	84	42	148	0.0	2.7	32.4	57.4	7.4	198913
01245	MONTEREY	44975	213	16.4	29.1	31.9	8.9	13.6	55954	72456	81	34	176	0.0	0.0	14.2	58.0	27.8	280769
01247	NORTH ADAMS	20202	7161	38.3	30.7	23.4	5.3	2.3	32809	38195	20	5	4107	8.0	12.4	63.9	15.2	0.5	119346
01253	OTIS	31463	555	19.6	20.2	38.4	12.1	9.7	60419	73900	85	44	475	3.0	4.6	35.6	52.6	4.2	186285
01254	RICHMOND	45906	387	10.6	21.2	31.0	18.6	18.6	76574	105887	94	71	354	2.3	0.3	17.8	61.6	18.1	261957
01255	SANDISFIELD	36529	331	16.6	27.8	36.6	9.7	9.4	55134	67852	80	32	283	0.0	2.1	31.5	49.5	17.0	210106
01256	SAVOY	24026	310	21.0	30.3	37.7	8.1	2.9	48231	56953	69	19	288	9.4	14.2	47.6	26.4	2.4	131548
01257	SHEFFIELD	37535	995	20.7	28.8	28.6	10.2	11.7	50393	63576	73	22	787	1.3	2.5	21.0	64.6	10.7	221494
01258	SOUTH EGREMONT	68647	63	11.1	23.8	36.5	9.5	19.1	61958	83395	86	47	59	0.0	0.0	13.6	44.1	42.4	325000
01259	SOUTHFIELD	35227	292	15.8	27.1	34.9	11.6	10.6	57789	72402	82	38	242	1.7	2.1	31.4	49.6	15.3	203030
01262	STOCKBRIDGE	57698	702	22.5	23.9	28.8	11.7	13.1	54045	70663	78	30	471	0.0	0.2	8.5	58.0	33.3	313736
01266	WEST STOCKBRIDGE	43138	796	16.3	20.9	32.0	14.5	16.3	63765	85627	88	52	689	3.3	2.2	14.5	56.6	23.4	259295
01267	WILLIAMSTOWN	36755	2814	22.9	18.9	27.2	16.2	14.8	63010	83445	87	51	2092	11.4	1.9	25.2	43.6	17.9	204103
01270	WINDSOR	27407	297	15.8	25.9	38.1	12.8	7.4	59764	70559	84	43	279	3.2	7.2	27.6	53.8	8.2	198264
01301	GREENFIELD	22556	8138	33.5	28.4	27.7	7.4	3.0	38314	44342	40	8	4573	1.8	2.6	57.4	35.6	2.6	157300
01330	ASHFIELD	32904	621	15.0	23.4	41.6	14.0	6.1	59006	69720	84	41	508	0.4	2.2	34.5	54.3	8.7	195886
01331	ATHOL	20963	5308	27.2	33.0	29.0	9.4	1.5	41245	50186	51	10	3943	1.9	6.7	60.6	29.4	1.4	146153
01337	BERNARDSTON	27238	1105	15.7	30.1	37.3	10.2	6.8	53452	63450	78	29	961	1.5	4.8	38.5	47.0	8.2	183767
	MASSACHUSETTS	33908		19.9	21.2	32.0	16.1	10.9	61110	77759				0.8	1.2	14.8	55.7	27.5	282585
	UNITED STATES	25866		24.7	27.1	30.8	10.9	6.5	48124	56710				10.9	15.0	33.7	30.1	10.4	145905

SPENDING POTENTIAL INDICES MASSACHUSETTS
01001-01337 D

ZIP CODE #	POST OFFICE NAME	FINANCIAL SERVICES: Auto Loan	Home Loan	Invest-ments	Retire-ment Plans	THE HOME: Home Improvements: Home Repair	Lawn & Garden	Furnishings: Comput-ers & Hard-ware	Major Appli-ances	TV, Radio, Sound Equip-ment	Furni-ture	ENTERTAINMENT: Dine out/ Carry out	Sports Equip-ment	Fees & Tickets	Toys & Games	Travel	Cable TV	PERSONAL: Apparel & Services	Auto Repairs	Health Insur-ance	Pets & Supplies
01001	AGAWAM	82	93	106	92	92	97	90	89	88	89	110	103	94	114	92	88	109	89	86	97
01002	AMHERST	103	97	120	104	96	103	116	104	112	110	140	129	111	136	108	105	136	112	97	115
01003	AMHERST	60	37	46	42	36	44	71	52	69	60	86	73	58	78	57	61	81	64	49	60
01005	BARRE	95	97	90	94	99	105	91	95	93	90	114	110	93	119	93	94	110	92	97	112
01007	BELCHERTOWN	101	108	106	111	105	104	102	102	96	104	122	120	103	121	100	91	119	101	90	112
01008	BLANDFORD	107	129	135	129	128	127	116	116	108	115	136	136	122	144	119	106	135	112	106	131
01010	BRIMFIELD	126	112	86	107	118	127	104	115	110	104	134	137	102	137	107	113	127	112	124	148
01011	CHESTER	102	88	66	83	95	103	82	93	89	82	107	110	78	108	86	92	101	91	104	122
01012	CHESTERFIELD	96	85	65	81	90	97	79	87	84	79	102	104	77	104	81	86	97	85	95	113
01013	CHICOPEE	62	63	69	61	62	69	66	64	68	64	84	74	67	86	66	68	81	65	66	71
01020	CHICOPEE	72	78	85	75	78	86	77	76	79	75	98	86	81	104	79	81	95	76	80	85
01022	CHICOPEE	66	72	80	71	72	77	73	71	72	71	90	82	75	93	73	71	88	71	70	77
01026	CUMMINGTON	92	99	110	100	99	103	96	96	94	95	117	115	98	120	97	92	114	96	92	110
01027	EASTHAMPTON	82	92	101	92	91	94	91	88	88	89	110	104	94	115	91	86	108	88	84	97
01028	EAST LONGMEADOW	124	150	165	147	148	154	138	138	132	137	165	157	147	173	143	131	164	134	131	151
01030	FEEDING HILLS	95	113	125	113	111	113	106	104	100	105	126	122	111	132	108	98	125	103	96	114
01031	GILBERTVILLE	108	100	82	95	105	113	94	102	99	93	121	120	93	125	96	102	115	99	110	128
01032	GOSHEN	84	96	119	100	95	97	95	92	90	94	114	110	98	117	95	87	113	93	84	100
01033	GRANBY	97	118	129	116	116	117	108	107	103	108	129	125	116	138	111	101	129	105	99	117
01034	GRANVILLE	110	122	121	120	124	126	110	115	107	110	133	134	114	139	114	106	130	111	111	134
01035	HADLEY	101	116	137	114	114	123	113	111	111	112	139	127	118	142	116	111	136	111	108	121
01036	HAMPDEN	122	151	163	151	149	149	135	135	126	135	159	157	144	167	139	123	158	131	123	149
01038	HATFIELD	91	105	124	105	103	109	102	100	99	101	124	116	106	128	104	98	122	100	95	109
01039	HAYDENVILLE	106	124	148	128	122	124	120	117	113	119	143	139	124	148	121	110	142	117	106	128
01040	HOLYOKE	61	62	85	61	61	68	67	64	70	67	88	73	67	90	67	72	87	67	66	71
01050	HUNTINGTON	84	95	102	96	94	95	91	90	86	89	108	106	94	113	91	84	107	89	83	100
01053	LEEDS	88	98	117	101	96	99	99	96	95	98	120	115	101	123	99	92	118	97	88	104
01054	LEVERETT	136	156	192	161	153	157	154	149	146	153	185	178	159	189	155	142	183	151	136	163
01056	LUDLOW	82	96	104	93	95	101	90	90	89	89	111	102	96	118	93	90	109	88	89	98
01057	MONSON	97	110	114	109	109	112	104	103	101	102	126	119	108	133	105	100	124	101	99	114
01060	NORTHAMPTON	90	86	112	92	85	91	100	92	98	97	124	113	98	121	96	94	121	98	86	102
01062	FLORENCE	98	113	133	114	111	116	110	107	106	109	133	125	115	138	111	104	132	107	101	117
01063	NORTHAMPTON	129	79	100	89	78	94	153	112	148	129	185	156	125	166	122	130	174	137	104	128
01068	OAKHAM	111	138	146	138	135	133	123	122	114	122	143	143	131	153	126	110	143	118	110	135
01069	PALMER	81	78	72	77	79	86	79	81	81	77	99	93	78	100	78	81	95	80	83	92
01070	PLAINFIELD	107	75	39	71	87	98	74	91	85	73	100	110	63	98	77	89	91	90	109	127
01071	RUSSELL	112	100	76	95	106	113	93	103	98	93	119	122	91	122	95	101	114	100	111	132
01072	SHUTESBURY	112	139	147	139	137	135	124	124	115	124	145	145	132	154	127	112	145	120	111	137
01073	SOUTHAMPTON	114	139	153	140	137	136	127	126	118	126	149	148	134	157	129	115	148	122	113	138
01075	SOUTH HADLEY	91	102	116	101	101	108	101	99	99	99	124	114	105	128	102	98	122	99	96	108
01077	SOUTHWICK	97	107	106	106	105	106	99	100	95	99	119	118	102	123	100	92	117	98	93	113
01080	THREE RIVERS	71	67	60	65	69	77	67	70	71	66	87	79	68	89	68	73	82	68	75	80
01081	WALES	106	96	75	92	101	107	89	98	94	89	114	116	87	116	91	95	109	95	104	125
01082	WARE	75	76	77	74	76	82	77	77	78	75	96	89	78	99	77	78	93	77	77	86
01084	WEST CHESTERFIELD	96	86	65	82	91	97	79	88	84	79	103	105	78	105	82	86	97	86	95	114
01085	WESTFIELD	87	97	108	96	96	100	96	93	93	94	116	109	99	121	96	92	115	93	90	102
01088	WEST HATFIELD	88	101	124	104	99	102	100	96	95	99	119	115	102	122	100	92	118	97	88	105
01089	WEST SPRINGFIELD	79	82	93	82	81	88	84	82	84	83	105	95	86	106	84	84	102	83	82	91
01092	WEST WARREN	66	69	69	65	70	77	67	68	70	65	86	76	70	92	69	72	83	66	73	77
01095	WILBRAHAM	138	158	168	156	158	166	147	149	142	146	177	170	154	182	152	143	174	145	145	165
01096	WILLIAMSBURG	89	99	109	99	99	102	94	94	92	94	115	111	98	119	96	90	113	93	90	107
01098	WORTHINGTON	126	112	85	106	118	127	103	115	110	103	133	136	101	136	106	112	127	111	124	148
01103	SPRINGFIELD	35	32	55	31	30	35	39	36	42	40	54	42	37	55	38	44	54	39	36	39
01104	SPRINGFIELD	55	55	66	53	55	61	59	57	62	58	77	66	59	80	59	64	75	59	61	64
01105	SPRINGFIELD	37	33	55	31	32	37	40	38	45	41	57	43	39	57	39	47	56	41	39	42
01106	LONGMEADOW	173	209	242	207	207	216	194	193	184	194	231	221	205	237	200	182	229	189	182	210
01107	SPRINGFIELD	42	42	73	38	40	46	47	45	52	49	67	50	46	69	47	55	67	47	46	48
01108	SPRINGFIELD	65	63	73	63	62	69	70	67	71	68	88	78	69	88	68	70	86	69	67	73
01109	SPRINGFIELD	59	56	68	53	54	62	60	59	65	61	81	66	61	80	60	66	79	61	61	66
01118	SPRINGFIELD	89	99	113	97	98	105	97	96	97	97	121	110	102	125	99	97	119	95	95	105
01119	SPRINGFIELD	75	79	84	78	78	83	79	78	78	78	97	91	80	98	79	77	95	78	77	87
01128	SPRINGFIELD	89	103	115	100	101	105	98	96	95	98	120	111	103	126	100	95	119	95	92	106
01129	SPRINGFIELD	83	98	107	96	97	100	93	92	90	91	113	106	98	120	95	89	111	90	88	100
01151	INDIAN ORCHARD	55	53	57	51	53	59	58	56	60	55	74	64	58	76	57	61	72	57	59	61
01201	PITTSFIELD	78	81	92	80	81	89	84	82	84	82	105	94	85	106	85	84	102	83	83	90
01220	ADAMS	65	66	69	64	67	75	68	68	70	65	86	77	69	90	69	72	83	68	72	76
01222	ASHLEY FALLS	92	98	95	99	96	96	93	94	89	94	111	111	93	112	92	85	109	93	85	105
01223	BECKET	117	97	70	89	106	116	90	105	99	90	119	124	84	120	95	104	112	103	119	140
01224	BERKSHIRE	86	107	114	107	105	104	96	95	89	95	111	112	102	119	98	86	111	92	85	105
01225	CHESHIRE	81	87	85	84	87	91	80	83	80	80	99	97	83	104	82	80	97	81	82	97
01226	DALTON	93	110	119	107	109	114	103	102	100	101	126	117	109	134	106	101	124	100	99	112
01230	GREAT BARRINGTON	120	119	123	117	123	132	116	121	118	115	146	142	115	147	120	120	141	121	125	144
01235	HINSDALE	95	87	72	84	91	97	83	89	86	82	105	106	81	108	84	87	101	87	94	112
01236	HOUSATONIC	98	107	118	106	108	114	105	105	103	103	128	121	108	131	107	102	126	104	103	116
01237	LANESBORO	84	96	102	95	96	98	89	90	86	88	107	105	93	113	91	85	106	88	86	102
01238	LEE	86	86	90	83	88	95	84	87	86	83	106	101	84	108	86	87	103	87	90	103
01240	LENOX	88	95	104	95	96	102	92	93	89	91	112	107	94	111	94	89	109	92	92	105
01243	MIDDLEFIELD	126	112	85	106	118	127	103	115	110	103	134	137	101	136	107	113	127	112	124	148
01245	MONTEREY	168	132	90	119	148	167	124	150	140	123	166	175	111	164	132	150	155	147	177	204
01247	NORTH ADAMS	62	60	62	58	61	69	63	62	65	60	81	71	63	83	63	67	77	63	67	71
01253	OTIS	125	98	67	89	111	124	93	111	105	92	124	131	83	123	99	112	115	110	132	152
01254	RICHMOND	142	171	193	170	171	179	157	158	149	158	187	179	167	190	164	148	185	154	151	172
01255	SANDISFIELD	148	116	79	105	131	147	109	132	124	108	147	154	98	145	117	132	136	130	156	180
01256	SAVOY	93	82	63	78	87	93	76	85	81	76	98	101	75	101	79	83	94	82	92	109
01257	SHEFFIELD	142	115	84	110	127	140	112	130	123	111	147	153	103	147	116	127	137	128	146	169
01258	SOUTH EGREMONT	233	183	125	165	206	231	172	207	195	171	231	243	154	228	184	208	215	204	245	284
01259	SOUTHFIELD	140	110	75	99	124	139	104	125	117	103	139	146	93	137	110	125	129	123	148	171
01262	STOCKBRIDGE	163	161	177	156	164	182	161	165	167	159	206	190	161	208	166	171	199	167	175	194
01266	WEST STOCKBRIDGE	150	151	145	143	157	171	141	152	145	140	178	173	142	180	148	150	172	149	162	182
01267	WILLIAMSTOWN	139	138	140	136	141	156	141	143	142	137	174	163	139	172	142	143	168	142	148	162
01270	WINDSOR	95	119	126	119	117	115	106	106	98	105	123	124	113	132	108	95	123	102	95	117
01301	GREENFIELD	65	68	78	68	67	73	70	68	70	69	87	80	71	89	70	70	85	69	67	75
01330	ASHFIELD	112	115	119	115	116	122	110	113	110	110	136	135	111	139	112	109	133	112	111	133
01331	ATHOL	73	72	70	69	74	82	71	73	74	69	92	83	73	97	73	77	88	72	78	85
01337	BERNARDSTON	88	107	118	104	105	107	99	98	95	98	119	113	105	126	101	93	118	95	91	107
	MASSACHUSETTS	112	121	148	122	120	127	122	119	121	121	151	138	126	156	123	120	149	120	115	132
	UNITED STATES	100	100	100	100	100	100	100	100	100	100	100	100	100	100	100	100	100	100	100	100

MASSACHUSETTS — POPULATION CHANGE

A 01338-01611

# POST OFFICE NAME	COUNTY FIPS CODE	POPULATION 2000	2004	2009	2000-2004 ANNUAL RATE % Rate	State Centile	HOUSEHOLDS 2000	2004	2009	% Annual Rate 2000-2004	2004 Average HH Size	FAMILIES 2000	2004	% Annual Rate 2000-2004
01338 BUCKLAND	011	99	98	97	-0.2	14	44	44	45	0.0	2.23	32	32	0.0
01339 CHARLEMONT	011	1515	1528	1531	0.2	40	580	595	606	0.6	2.53	397	407	0.6
01340 COLRAIN	011	2177	2152	2142	-0.3	13	822	828	839	0.2	2.60	581	586	0.2
01341 CONWAY	011	1643	1735	1781	1.3	87	636	684	714	1.7	2.53	470	505	1.7
01342 DEERFIELD	011	1388	1378	1376	-0.2	19	539	544	552	0.2	2.53	385	388	0.2
01343 DRURY	003	123	120	118	-0.6	3	50	50	50	0.0	2.40	37	37	0.0
01344 ERVING	011	911	982	1020	1.8	94	380	418	442	2.3	2.35	255	281	2.3
01346 HEATH	011	206	203	202	-0.3	9	78	78	79	0.0	2.60	55	56	0.4
01349 TURNERS FALLS	011	1727	1775	1804	0.7	67	693	721	742	0.9	2.46	441	461	1.1
01350 MONROE BRIDGE	011	78	79	79	0.3	46	36	37	37	0.7	2.14	23	24	1.0
01351 MONTAGUE	011	1984	1962	1960	-0.3	13	804	803	812	0.0	2.44	519	519	0.0
01355 NEW SALEM	011	826	837	841	0.3	47	338	349	356	0.8	2.40	235	243	0.8
01360 NORTHFIELD	011	2953	2978	2982	0.2	40	1159	1178	1193	0.4	2.51	816	830	0.4
01364 ORANGE	011	7552	7501	7488	-0.2	20	3042	3069	3112	0.2	2.43	1978	1996	0.2
01366 PETERSHAM	027	1096	1157	1213	1.3	86	407	437	464	1.7	2.45	278	298	1.7
01367 ROWE	011	565	564	562	0.0	27	231	235	238	0.4	2.40	155	158	0.5
01368 ROYALSTON	027	1216	1266	1319	1.0	77	438	459	483	1.1	2.76	322	336	1.0
01370 SHELBURNE FALLS	011	4622	4636	4655	0.1	34	1837	1870	1907	0.4	2.40	1213	1237	0.5
01373 SOUTH DEERFIELD	011	4506	4492	4487	-0.1	24	1880	1905	1933	0.3	2.35	1231	1250	0.4
01375 SUNDERLAND	011	3777	3779	3786	0.0	31	1633	1671	1706	0.5	2.23	766	783	0.5
01376 TURNERS FALLS	011	6852	6713	6695	-0.5	5	2935	2915	2950	-0.2	2.25	1773	1762	-0.2
01378 WARWICK	011	761	763	762	0.1	33	294	300	304	0.5	2.54	210	215	0.6
01379 WENDELL	011	911	929	937	0.5	56	369	384	393	0.9	2.18	220	228	0.8
01420 FITCHBURG	027	39100	39924	41532	0.5	59	14942	15400	16166	0.7	2.48	9362	9630	0.7
01430 ASHBURNHAM	027	5567	5791	6042	0.9	76	1933	2035	2142	1.2	2.84	1542	1621	1.2
01431 ASHBY	017	2853	2860	2859	0.1	33	983	998	1010	0.4	2.85	787	799	0.4
01432 AYER	017	8043	8286	8379	0.7	69	2982	3054	3125	0.6	2.27	1774	1817	0.6
01436 BALDWINVILLE	027	3188	3378	3551	1.4	88	1116	1196	1271	1.6	2.66	797	852	1.6
01440 GARDNER	027	21355	21431	22013	0.1	34	8507	8602	8913	0.3	2.34	5257	5308	0.2
01450 GROTON	017	9697	10312	10647	1.5	89	3323	3539	3673	1.5	2.89	2610	2780	1.5
01451 HARVARD	027	5160	5435	5702	1.2	85	1786	1899	2009	1.5	2.83	1474	1565	1.4
01452 HUBBARDSTON	027	3909	4234	4507	1.9	96	1308	1424	1525	2.0	2.96	1071	1165	2.0
01453 LEOMINSTER	027	41303	41967	43494	0.4	52	16491	16920	17689	0.6	2.46	10902	11186	0.6
01460 LITTLETON	017	8145	8664	8936	1.5	89	2949	3152	3272	1.6	2.71	2207	2359	1.6
01462 LUNENBURG	027	9365	9775	10200	1.0	78	3523	3716	3913	1.3	2.63	2659	2801	1.2
01463 PEPPERELL	017	10979	11267	11419	0.6	65	3788	3920	4010	0.8	2.87	2971	3074	0.8
01464 SHIRLEY	017	6411	6469	6495	0.2	41	2080	2122	2151	0.5	2.53	1436	1466	0.5
01468 TEMPLETON	027	3103	3318	3515	1.6	92	1100	1191	1274	1.9	2.74	866	936	1.9
01469 TOWNSEND	017	6522	6457	6436	-0.2	14	2207	2211	2227	0.0	2.92	1752	1755	0.0
01473 WESTMINSTER	027	6848	7164	7485	1.1	80	2511	2658	2804	1.4	2.69	1940	2051	1.3
01474 WEST TOWNSEND	017	2676	2720	2736	0.4	52	903	929	943	0.7	2.93	724	743	0.6
01475 WINCHENDON	027	9581	9931	10350	0.9	73	3434	3592	3775	1.1	2.73	2467	2574	1.0
01501 AUBURN	027	15947	16109	16623	0.2	43	6398	6529	6798	0.5	2.44	4422	4506	0.4
01503 BERLIN	027	2403	2584	2739	1.7	94	878	953	1020	2.0	2.70	671	727	1.9
01504 BLACKSTONE	027	8820	9064	9398	0.6	66	3241	3360	3514	0.9	2.69	2360	2441	0.8
01505 BOYLSTON	027	3974	4077	4214	0.6	64	1563	1623	1693	0.9	2.51	1133	1174	0.8
01506 BROOKFIELD	027	3051	3188	3343	1.0	79	1204	1273	1347	1.3	2.50	857	904	1.3
01507 CHARLTON	027	11263	12184	12963	1.9	95	3788	4147	4456	2.2	2.89	3045	3321	2.1
01510 CLINTON	027	13432	13594	13985	0.3	45	5598	5736	5962	0.6	2.35	3402	3477	0.5
01515 EAST BROOKFIELD	027	2091	2155	2232	0.7	70	775	809	847	1.0	2.66	598	623	1.0
01516 DOUGLAS	027	7057	7592	8054	1.7	94	2483	2693	2879	1.9	2.82	1943	2105	1.9
01518 FISKDALE	027	2341	2505	2649	1.6	92	932	1012	1083	2.0	2.47	646	699	1.9
01519 GRAFTON	027	5454	5716	5973	1.1	81	1990	2117	2233	1.5	2.67	1453	1542	1.4
01520 HOLDEN	027	12678	13161	13745	0.9	74	4659	4868	5118	1.0	2.67	3583	3745	1.1
01521 HOLLAND	013	2258	2300	2319	0.4	55	841	870	888	0.8	2.64	622	642	0.6
01522 JEFFERSON	027	2971	3015	3114	0.4	49	1066	1091	1135	0.6	2.76	844	864	0.6
01523 LANCASTER	027	7372	7586	7823	0.7	69	2045	2144	2250	1.1	2.77	1548	1621	1.1
01524 LEICESTER	027	6477	6689	6939	0.8	71	2295	2394	2507	1.0	2.70	1693	1763	1.0
01527 MILLBURY	027	12833	13327	13978	0.9	74	4945	5182	5486	1.1	2.51	3453	3619	1.1
01529 MILLVILLE	027	2724	3042	3291	2.6	99	923	1030	1118	2.6	2.95	720	801	2.5
01531 NEW BRAINTREE	027	1322	1392	1460	1.2	84	488	517	545	1.4	2.69	380	402	1.3
01532 NORTHBOROUGH	027	14013	14303	14829	0.5	57	4906	5055	5286	0.7	2.80	3866	3979	0.7
01534 NORTHBRIDGE	027	4597	4941	5238	1.7	93	1570	1712	1836	2.1	2.74	1207	1308	1.9
01535 NORTH BROOKFIELD	027	4732	4871	5070	0.7	69	1826	1899	1996	0.9	2.53	1248	1295	0.9
01536 NORTH GRAFTON	027	6509	6834	7147	1.2	83	2500	2666	2820	1.5	2.43	1729	1841	1.5
01537 NORTH OXFORD	027	1702	1816	1917	1.5	91	758	816	870	1.8	2.21	496	534	1.8
01540 OXFORD	027	11347	11877	12448	1.1	80	4184	4423	4677	1.3	2.67	3029	3200	1.3
01541 PRINCETON	027	3358	3452	3572	0.7	67	1166	1213	1267	0.9	2.85	960	998	0.9
01542 ROCHDALE	027	2126	2152	2208	0.3	46	700	716	742	0.5	2.78	498	508	0.5
01543 RUTLAND	027	6335	6946	7440	2.2	98	2248	2492	2693	2.5	2.74	1690	1871	2.4
01545 SHREWSBURY	027	31611	33725	35799	1.5	91	12340	13165	14017	1.5	2.55	8673	9253	1.5
01550 SOUTHBRIDGE	027	17214	17202	17656	0.0	29	7077	7138	7389	0.2	2.39	4520	4553	0.2
01560 SOUTH GRAFTON	027	2851	3065	3274	1.7	94	1166	1276	1379	2.1	2.39	748	816	2.1
01562 SPENCER	027	11663	12188	12786	1.0	79	4572	4839	5128	1.3	2.50	3086	3255	1.3
01564 STERLING	027	7272	7567	7883	0.9	76	2579	2716	2858	1.2	2.79	2074	2181	1.2
01566 STURBRIDGE	027	5496	5766	6035	1.1	82	2134	2266	2394	1.4	2.54	1567	1662	1.4
01568 UPTON	027	5562	6181	6671	2.5	99	2014	2230	2409	2.4	2.75	1541	1703	2.4
01569 UXBRIDGE	027	11159	12088	12886	1.9	96	3984	4333	4644	2.0	2.79	3032	3301	2.0
01570 WEBSTER	027	16415	16816	17426	0.6	62	6905	7133	7453	0.8	2.32	4271	4417	0.8
01571 DUDLEY	027	10032	10643	11200	1.4	88	3736	4015	4268	1.7	2.54	2668	2864	1.7
01581 WESTBOROUGH	027	17933	18904	19869	1.3	86	6514	6929	7352	1.5	2.60	4505	4777	1.4
01583 WEST BOYLSTON	027	7488	7686	7998	0.6	65	2415	2513	2658	0.9	2.54	1748	1818	0.9
01585 WEST BROOKFIELD	027	5901	5975	6124	0.3	46	2189	2243	2322	0.6	2.50	1566	1601	0.5
01588 WHITINSVILLE	027	8716	9104	9583	1.0	79	3286	3457	3670	1.2	2.59	2330	2448	1.2
01590 SUTTON	027	8189	8946	9568	2.1	97	2792	3076	3315	2.3	2.91	2268	2496	2.3
01602 WORCESTER	027	21295	21822	22718	0.6	63	8453	8754	9205	0.8	2.40	5518	5708	0.8
01603 WORCESTER	027	19098	19445	20112	0.4	54	7389	7580	7908	0.6	2.48	4448	4557	0.6
01604 WORCESTER	027	31463	32033	33134	0.4	54	13119	13482	14068	0.6	2.32	7665	7850	0.6
01605 WORCESTER	027	27608	28727	30056	0.9	76	10251	10731	11322	1.1	2.45	5996	6296	1.2
01606 WORCESTER	027	19382	19656	20360	0.3	48	8130	8328	8704	0.6	2.33	5142	5264	0.6
01607 WORCESTER	027	9009	9039	9297	0.1	34	3880	3932	4078	0.3	2.29	2219	2239	0.2
01608 WORCESTER	027	3103	3238	3414	1.0	78	1242	1333	1430	1.7	2.34	628	651	0.9
01609 WORCESTER	027	18534	18950	19691	0.5	60	7204	7407	7768	0.7	2.25	3431	3526	0.6
01610 WORCESTER	027	23036	23763	24677	0.7	70	7294	7601	7991	1.0	2.63	4155	4313	0.9
01611 CHERRY VALLEY	027	2229	2311	2407	0.9	73	828	868	912	1.1	2.64	608	636	1.1
MASSACHUSETTS					0.4					0.6	2.48			0.6
UNITED STATES					1.2					1.3	2.58			1.1

#	POST OFFICE NAME	RACE (%) White 2000	White 2004	Black 2000	Black 2004	Asian/Pacific 2000	Asian/Pacific 2004	% Hispanic Origin 2000	% Hispanic Origin 2004	2004 AGE DISTRIBUTION (%) 0-4	5-9	10-14	15-19	20-24	25-44	45-64	65-84	85+	18+	MEDIAN AGE 2004	% 2004 Males	% 2004 Females
01338	BUCKLAND	97.0	95.9	1.0	1.0	1.0	1.0	1.0	1.0	5.1	6.1	7.1	7.1	5.1	25.5	31.6	10.2	2.0	75.5	41.3	53.1	46.9
01339	CHARLEMONT	96.5	96.1	0.3	0.3	0.7	0.8	1.5	1.7	5.0	5.7	6.9	7.1	4.9	24.8	31.4	12.4	1.8	78.0	42.1	49.5	50.5
01340	COLRAIN	98.3	98.0	0.3	0.3	0.3	0.4	0.8	1.1	5.9	7.0	8.2	7.6	4.6	27.2	27.7	10.8	1.0	73.7	39.6	50.6	49.4
01341	CONWAY	98.7	98.3	0.2	0.2	0.6	0.7	0.9	1.3	4.3	5.5	7.3	6.9	4.4	25.8	35.0	9.5	1.3	77.9	42.9	49.5	50.5
01342	DEERFIELD	97.8	97.4	0.4	0.4	0.9	1.1	1.0	1.2	4.8	5.6	8.6	6.3	4.2	25.1	33.2	10.7	1.5	76.5	42.6	48.6	51.4
01343	DRURY	97.6	96.7	0.8	0.8	0.8	0.8	0.0	0.8	4.2	5.0	9.2	8.3	1.7	29.2	29.2	12.5	0.8	76.7	41.3	52.5	47.5
01344	ERVING	97.2	97.0	0.1	0.1	0.2	0.2	0.7	0.8	5.2	5.7	6.5	5.8	5.5	27.9	29.4	12.1	1.8	79.0	41.1	50.2	49.8
01346	HEATH	97.6	97.0	0.0	0.0	0.5	1.0	1.0	1.5	6.4	6.9	7.4	6.9	6.4	25.6	28.6	10.8	1.0	74.4	39.1	51.7	48.3
01349	TURNERS FALLS	95.5	95.1	0.5	0.5	0.9	1.1	1.5	1.8	5.7	5.6	6.7	6.9	6.9	29.7	26.4	10.4	1.8	77.6	38.5	49.1	50.9
01350	MONROE BRIDGE	96.2	96.2	0.0	0.0	0.0	0.0	2.6	2.5	5.1	5.1	6.3	7.6	5.1	25.3	31.7	12.7	1.3	76.0	42.1	48.1	51.9
01351	MONTAGUE	95.6	94.8	0.7	0.8	1.2	1.6	1.4	1.7	5.7	6.0	5.7	5.6	4.7	29.3	31.0	10.5	1.4	79.0	41.3	47.2	52.9
01355	NEW SALEM	95.5	94.9	0.7	0.8	0.7	1.0	0.9	1.1	4.8	5.9	7.3	6.2	3.6	23.7	37.2	10.0	1.4	78.3	44.3	50.2	49.8
01360	NORTHFIELD	98.5	98.4	0.1	0.1	0.2	0.3	0.6	0.6	5.6	5.9	7.1	7.8	6.3	23.2	30.7	11.8	1.8	76.4	41.2	48.2	51.8
01364	ORANGE	96.3	95.7	1.1	1.2	0.5	0.6	1.6	2.0	5.5	5.9	8.5	8.1	6.0	25.8	26.2	12.1	1.9	75.1	38.9	48.3	51.7
01366	PETERSHAM	97.2	96.8	0.6	0.8	0.3	0.4	1.2	1.4	4.8	5.5	6.4	6.1	4.0	23.8	31.4	15.4	2.7	78.6	44.7	51.1	48.9
01367	ROWE	97.0	96.6	0.4	0.4	0.4	0.5	1.8	2.1	5.5	6.2	7.3	7.5	4.4	25.4	30.9	11.5	1.4	76.2	41.0	49.7	50.4
01368	ROYALSTON	98.6	98.3	0.1	0.1	0.6	0.7	1.2	1.4	5.6	7.4	9.6	8.5	3.9	27.5	27.9	8.1	1.7	71.7	39.0	51.7	48.3
01370	SHELBURNE FALLS	97.0	96.6	0.4	0.5	0.5	0.6	1.0	1.1	4.2	4.9	6.4	6.9	6.7	22.8	31.7	13.8	2.7	80.1	43.8	48.6	51.4
01373	SOUTH DEERFIELD	97.3	96.8	0.5	0.6	0.8	0.9	1.6	2.0	4.9	5.2	7.0	6.1	5.1	26.5	31.8	11.6	1.8	79.0	42.4	50.1	49.9
01375	SUNDERLAND	88.8	87.0	2.4	2.6	6.5	7.9	2.4	2.8	4.9	4.7	5.2	5.6	16.9	34.3	20.2	7.2	1.1	82.1	30.5	49.0	51.0
01376	TURNERS FALLS	95.6	95.0	0.8	0.9	0.9	1.1	2.6	3.1	5.6	5.5	6.6	6.9	6.9	24.7	26.9	14.5	2.5	78.3	40.9	48.0	52.0
01378	WARWICK	96.2	95.7	0.1	0.1	0.3	0.4	1.5	1.7	5.9	6.6	6.7	6.2	4.7	26.9	31.5	10.9	0.8	76.8	41.1	50.1	49.9
01379	WENDELL	92.5	91.6	3.4	3.9	0.4	0.5	1.4	1.8	4.2	5.6	7.2	8.3	5.1	28.6	35.3	4.7	1.0	77.3	39.6	50.9	49.1
01420	FITCHBURG	81.9	78.9	3.7	4.0	4.3	5.2	15.0	17.9	6.8	6.6	7.3	7.7	8.9	27.4	21.3	11.6	2.4	75.0	34.6	47.8	52.3
01430	ASHBURNHAM	97.6	97.2	0.2	0.3	0.6	0.8	1.7	2.1	5.9	6.8	8.2	8.2	5.5	26.9	29.4	8.1	0.9	74.0	39.0	50.9	49.1
01431	ASHBY	98.0	97.7	0.3	0.3	0.4	0.5	0.8	1.1	5.6	7.8	8.2	7.8	4.7	28.2	27.9	9.0	0.8	73.4	39.6	50.7	49.3
01432	AYER	83.8	81.5	8.1	9.1	2.9	3.5	8.1	10.0	6.3	5.8	5.6	7.4	6.8	36.2	21.7	8.7	1.7	78.2	36.2	54.7	45.3
01436	BALDWINVILLE	98.0	97.6	0.2	0.3	0.4	0.4	1.9	2.4	6.6	6.6	7.0	7.2	5.8	26.5	24.8	12.8	2.8	75.1	39.4	49.4	50.6
01440	GARDNER	93.3	91.9	2.2	2.6	1.4	1.8	4.0	5.1	6.1	6.0	7.0	6.5	6.4	29.4	23.5	12.5	2.6	76.9	38.3	51.3	48.7
01450	GROTON	97.3	96.8	0.3	0.4	1.0	1.3	1.1	1.4	8.3	9.5	9.8	7.0	3.8	27.0	27.2	6.6	0.8	67.9	37.6	49.5	50.5
01451	HARVARD	95.8	95.0	0.6	0.6	2.1	2.6	1.1	1.4	6.0	7.8	9.2	7.8	3.6	19.0	36.5	9.1	1.0	71.7	43.1	49.1	50.9
01452	HUBBARDSTON	98.4	98.0	0.2	0.2	0.5	0.6	1.3	1.7	7.3	8.1	9.2	7.3	4.9	29.4	26.6	6.5	0.6	70.5	36.9	50.5	49.5
01453	LEOMINSTER	87.1	85.0	3.7	4.1	2.5	3.0	11.0	13.2	7.1	7.0	7.3	6.5	6.2	29.2	23.5	11.3	2.0	74.6	37.2	48.2	51.8
01460	LITTLETON	96.5	95.7	0.3	0.4	1.7	2.2	1.0	1.3	7.9	8.6	8.2	5.6	3.5	28.3	26.1	10.0	1.8	71.6	39.4	47.9	52.1
01462	LUNENBURG	97.0	96.4	0.7	0.8	0.8	1.0	1.2	1.5	5.7	6.5	7.4	6.7	4.7	25.9	30.4	11.2	1.5	76.2	41.4	49.3	50.7
01463	PEPPERELL	97.2	96.6	0.5	0.5	0.7	0.9	1.0	1.3	7.7	8.1	8.9	7.2	5.6	29.2	25.8	6.7	0.8	70.8	36.2	49.2	50.8
01464	SHIRLEY	84.0	81.8	6.7	7.3	2.2	2.6	6.8	8.1	5.7	6.0	6.1	5.6	6.4	35.7	25.2	8.3	0.9	78.9	37.4	57.7	42.3
01468	TEMPLETON	98.3	98.0	0.5	0.5	0.2	0.3	1.0	1.3	6.7	7.1	8.0	6.5	4.7	29.5	27.9	8.9	0.7	73.7	38.5	51.1	49.0
01469	TOWNSEND	97.5	97.0	0.8	0.9	0.2	0.3	1.3	1.6	7.0	7.6	8.5	7.8	6.5	27.9	28.3	5.8	0.7	72.1	36.1	49.6	50.4
01473	WESTMINSTER	97.5	97.0	0.5	0.5	1.1	1.5	1.1	1.4	5.9	6.7	7.6	6.8	5.2	26.4	30.7	9.3	1.4	75.4	40.5	49.7	50.3
01474	WEST TOWNSEND	97.8	97.4	0.6	0.7	0.3	0.3	0.9	1.1	7.0	7.2	7.6	7.5	5.9	27.8	28.4	7.8	0.8	73.7	38.2	49.7	50.3
01475	WINCHENDON	96.0	95.3	0.8	0.9	0.7	0.9	2.0	2.6	7.5	7.4	8.6	7.9	6.1	29.0	23.4	8.8	1.3	71.3	35.5	49.6	50.4
01501	AUBURN	97.5	97.0	0.6	0.7	0.9	1.2	1.1	1.4	5.3	5.8	6.9	6.0	4.8	26.0	27.3	15.1	2.9	78.3	42.2	47.6	52.4
01503	BERLIN	97.6	97.2	0.2	0.2	1.0	1.2	0.5	0.6	6.7	7.7	6.9	6.1	3.8	27.4	29.3	10.7	1.4	74.5	40.9	50.2	49.8
01504	BLACKSTONE	97.4	96.9	0.3	0.4	0.8	1.0	1.0	1.3	6.5	6.8	8.2	7.3	6.3	31.1	23.7	9.0	1.2	73.8	36.2	49.6	50.4
01505	BOYLSTON	96.7	96.0	0.7	0.8	1.4	1.7	0.6	0.8	5.5	6.4	7.3	5.9	4.2	27.4	30.1	11.9	1.2	77.1	41.7	49.4	50.6
01506	BROOKFIELD	98.1	97.7	0.2	0.3	0.3	0.4	0.6	0.8	6.0	6.1	6.9	6.8	6.1	25.7	28.6	12.6	1.4	77.0	41.0	49.5	50.5
01507	CHARLTON	98.1	97.7	0.2	0.3	0.5	0.7	1.0	1.3	7.1	7.7	8.8	6.8	5.2	30.5	25.6	6.8	1.5	71.8	36.9	48.7	51.3
01510	CLINTON	88.2	86.1	2.6	2.9	0.9	1.2	11.6	14.1	6.0	5.9	6.9	6.0	6.3	30.8	23.5	12.2	2.4	77.6	38.2	48.4	51.6
01515	EAST BROOKFIELD	98.5	98.3	0.4	0.5	0.1	0.2	0.8	1.0	6.0	6.5	7.6	6.4	5.0	27.1	27.8	11.8	1.8	76.0	40.4	49.5	50.5
01516	DOUGLAS	97.4	96.8	0.5	0.6	0.7	0.9	1.0	1.2	8.2	8.3	8.3	6.6	5.5	32.4	23.6	6.0	1.3	71.1	35.9	50.0	50.0
01518	FISKDALE	96.3	95.6	0.6	0.8	0.6	0.7	2.3	3.0	6.3	6.6	7.5	7.4	5.5	26.2	26.6	12.0	1.9	74.2	39.1	48.1	51.9
01519	GRAFTON	96.2	95.4	0.6	0.8	1.9	2.4	1.2	1.5	7.5	7.8	7.1	5.7	4.6	29.9	27.2	9.2	1.1	73.8	38.8	48.2	51.8
01520	HOLDEN	97.1	96.5	0.6	0.7	1.1	1.4	1.0	1.3	6.1	6.9	7.5	7.0	4.5	22.5	29.7	13.2	2.6	75.0	42.3	48.0	52.1
01521	HOLLAND	96.9	96.4	0.1	0.1	0.3	0.4	1.4	2.0	5.8	7.4	9.3	6.5	3.9	30.7	27.9	7.7	0.8	73.4	38.5	51.3	48.7
01522	JEFFERSON	98.4	98.0	0.2	0.2	0.6	0.7	0.9	1.2	6.8	7.5	8.8	7.8	5.4	26.4	28.6	8.0	0.7	71.9	38.2	49.8	50.2
01523	LANCASTER	84.5	82.3	10.6	11.9	1.2	1.5	7.5	9.1	5.1	5.6	6.4	6.8	7.6	34.4	24.0	8.4	1.7	79.2	36.7	55.8	44.2
01524	LEICESTER	96.3	95.6	1.1	1.3	0.9	1.1	1.7	2.2	5.7	6.2	7.5	8.4	6.9	26.9	26.6	10.4	1.5	76.3	37.9	48.4	51.6
01527	MILLBURY	97.2	96.6	0.6	0.6	1.1	1.4	1.1	1.3	5.9	6.1	6.8	6.1	5.2	28.3	25.7	13.3	2.7	77.5	40.3	48.5	51.5
01529	MILLVILLE	97.7	97.4	0.8	0.9	0.2	0.2	0.6	0.8	8.1	8.3	9.2	7.3	5.9	32.2	21.3	7.1	0.7	69.6	34.8	49.4	50.6
01531	NEW BRAINTREE	98.3	98.1	0.2	0.3	0.1	0.1	0.5	0.7	6.5	6.5	7.5	8.6	6.4	27.2	27.6	8.5	1.3	74.2	38.1	49.4	50.7
01532	NORTHBOROUGH	93.0	91.4	0.7	0.8	5.1	6.5	1.3	1.6	7.0	8.1	9.0	6.6	3.9	27.4	27.5	9.4	1.1	71.3	39.1	49.1	50.9
01534	NORTHBRIDGE	97.7	97.1	0.3	0.3	0.3	0.5	1.5	2.0	6.9	7.4	7.9	6.5	5.0	27.6	24.4	11.2	3.2	73.6	39.1	47.9	52.1
01535	NORTH BROOKFIELD	97.7	97.2	0.3	0.4	0.2	0.3	1.1	1.4	5.7	6.4	8.4	7.6	6.6	27.6	25.2	10.8	1.7	74.6	37.6	48.9	51.1
01536	NORTH GRAFTON	94.9	94.3	2.1	2.2	1.6	2.0	2.9	3.3	6.5	6.7	6.7	8.7	5.6	29.4	24.5	10.4	1.5	74.5	37.5	48.1	51.9
01537	NORTH OXFORD	96.0	95.2	1.1	1.3	1.2	1.5	2.3	3.0	6.0	6.2	6.5	6.3	5.8	30.7	26.7	10.8	1.1	77.2	38.5	49.7	50.3
01540	OXFORD	96.7	96.1	0.8	1.0	0.8	1.0	1.9	2.5	6.5	6.7	7.4	6.9	6.0	29.3	25.9	10.0	1.4	75.1	37.9	48.4	51.6
01541	PRINCETON	96.8	96.1	0.3	0.4	1.0	1.2	1.5	1.8	5.4	7.0	9.2	7.1	4.3	22.6	35.0	8.4	1.0	73.8	42.1	50.4	49.6
01542	ROCHDALE	96.6	96.0	1.2	1.4	0.9	1.1	1.4	1.7	6.0	6.0	7.3	7.0	6.0	29.0	23.8	11.5	3.5	76.5	37.8	48.1	52.0
01543	RUTLAND	96.6	95.9	1.0	1.2	0.5	0.6	1.3	1.7	7.8	8.5	8.8	7.6	5.0	30.0	24.7	6.8	1.1	69.9	36.1	50.7	49.3
01545	SHREWSBURY	89.1	87.0	1.5	1.7	7.6	9.3	1.6	2.0	7.6	7.8	7.5	5.8	4.3	28.9	25.0	11.1	2.1	73.4	38.8	48.6	51.4
01550	SOUTHBRIDGE	85.2	82.8	1.4	1.6	1.6	1.9	20.2	24.0	6.7	6.3	7.3	6.9	7.1	28.6	22.7	11.8	2.6	75.5	36.4	48.5	51.5
01560	SOUTH GRAFTON	97.8	97.2	0.5	0.6	0.5	0.7	1.1	1.3	7.6	7.1	6.8	6.9	6.2	33.4	20.3	9.9	1.8	73.9	35.2	48.9	51.1
01562	SPENCER	97.9	97.5	0.6	0.7	0.3	0.4	1.3	1.7	6.4	6.2	6.5	6.5	6.8	28.5	26.4	11.1	1.5	76.9	37.9	49.3	50.7
01564	STERLING	98.1	97.7	0.6	0.7	0.4	0.6	0.8	1.0	6.5	7.6	8.3	6.2	4.0	27.5	30.5	8.4	1.1	73.5	40.1	49.6	50.4
01566	STURBRIDGE	97.5	97.0	0.3	0.3	1.5	1.9	0.9	1.1	5.6	6.2	7.2	6.5	4.8	26.2	28.9	12.7	1.8	76.8	41.3	49.5	50.5
01568	UPTON	97.3	96.7	0.5	0.6	1.0	1.3	0.7	1.0	9.5	9.9	8.3	5.4	3.7	28.4	25.5	8.1	1.4	68.8	38.3	48.9	51.1
01569	UXBRIDGE	98.0	97.7	0.2	0.2	0.7	0.9	1.0	1.2	7.9	8.1	8.3	6.7	5.2	31.1	23.1	8.4	1.2	71.4	36.2	49.1	50.9
01570	WEBSTER	94.8	93.8	1.1	1.3	1.0	1.2	4.0	4.9	6.5	6.3	6.4	6.1	5.7	28.6	24.4	13.1	2.9	76.9	38.9	48.3	51.7
01571	DUDLEY	96.8	96.1	0.5	0.6	0.7	0.9	2.0	2.6	5.8	6.1	7.1	8.5	7.9	27.9	24.4	10.7	1.7	76.8	36.8	49.8	50.2
01581	WESTBOROUGH	88.2	85.8	1.4	1.6	8.1	10.0	3.3	4.0	6.9	7.5	8.0	7.3	4.8	28.0	25.2	9.3	3.0	72.6	38.0	49.5	50.5
01583	WEST BOYLSTON	91.6	90.5	5.3	5.9	0.9	1.1	4.8	5.7	4.3	5.0	6.8	6.9	6.7	30.5	25.4	12.0	2.4	80.0	39.4	56.5	43.5
01585	WEST BROOKFIELD	97.8	97.4	0.4	0.4	0.3	0.4	1.1	1.4	5.3	5.6	7.0	7.5	5.9	24.4	26.5	13.4	4.4	77.3	41.7	46.3	53.7
01588	WHITINSVILLE	95.5	94.8	0.8	0.9	0.4	0.5	2.0	2.5	7.5	7.4	7.8	7.1	6.1	28.2	23.3	10.1	2.5	72.7	36.4	47.5	52.5
01590	SUTTON	98.2	97.8	0.3	0.3	0.6	0.8	0.7	0.9	7.5	8.4	8.9	6.2	4.3	28.6	27.6	7.7	0.9	71.1	37.8	49.9	50.1
01602	WORCESTER	87.1	85.0	4.1	4.6	3.1	3.8	5.9	7.3	5.5	5.6	6.4	7.8	7.4	26.2	24.9	13.4	2.7	78.3	39.2	46.7	53.4
01603	WORCESTER	75.1	71.8	6.0	6.5	8.3	9.7	14.8	17.2	6.7	6.3	7.4	7.2	8.5	29.3	20.6	11.7	2.5	75.1	34.8	47.6	52.4
01604	WORCESTER	83.0	80.4	4.8	5.4	5.3	6.5	8.8	10.4	6.4	6.0	6.5	6.1	6.5	32.0	21.1	12.9	2.6	77.3	36.6	48.0	52.0
01605	WORCESTER	74.6	72.0	10.2	10.7	3.2	3.8	20.1	23.1	7.2	6.5	7.1	8.0	9.0	27.5	19.6	11.7	3.4	75.0	33.7	46.6	53.4
01606	WORCESTER	87.0	84.9	4.8	5.3	2.2	2.6	9.0	10.9	6.6	6.3	6.8	6.3	6.1	29.1	23.5	12.6	2.8	76.4	37.9	47.5	52.5
01607	WORCESTER	75.3	71.7	8.6	9.5	5.4	6.5	11.7	14.0	7.5	6.9	7.3	6.5	6.7	32.4	21.0	10.0	1.8	74.4	34.3	48.9	51.1
01608	WORCESTER	40.2	38.2	12.9	13.0	6.0	6.6	58.1	60.4	8.3	9.2	9.0	8.7	10.2	29.5	18.7	5.3	1.1	68.3	28.0	49.1	50.9
01609	WORCESTER	73.0	70.1	7.7	8.1	5.0	5.9	18.1	20.7	5.1	4.5	5.3	11.2	16.3	25.8	19.5	9.8	2.4	81.7	30.2	52.1	47.9
01610	WORCESTER	65.0	61.5	8.7	9.1	7.3	8.2	25.2	28.5	6.7	6.2	6.6	14.0	17.3	26.2	15.6	6.3	1.1	76.3	24.8	49.9	50.1
01611	CHERRY VALLEY	96.2	95.7	1.6	1.8	0.6	0.8	2.2	2.7	6.4	6.7	7.9	7.0	6.4	29.3	24.9	10.4	1.1	74.6	37.2	50.1	49.9
	MASSACHUSETTS	84.5	82.9	5.4	5.7	3.8	4.5	6.8	7.8	6.2	6.3	6.8	7.0	7.0	28.9	24.5	11.4	2.1	76.8	37.6	48.3	51.7
	UNITED STATES	75.1	73.6	12.3	12.5	3.8	4.2	12.5	14.1	6.9	6.7	7.2	7.0	7.3	28.6	23.8	10.8	1.7	75.1	36.0	49.1	50.9

ZIP CODE #	POST OFFICE NAME	2004 Per Capita Income	2004 HH Income Base	2004 Household Income Distribution (%): Less than $25,000	$25,000 to $49,999	$50,000 to $99,999	$100,000 to $149,999	$150,000 or More	Median Household Income: 2004	2009	2004 National Centile	2004 State Centile	2004 Home Value Base	2004 Home Value Distribution (%): Less than $50,000	$50,000 to $89,999	$90,000 to $174,999	$175,000 to $399,999	$400,000 or More	2004 Median Home Value
01338	BUCKLAND	31998	44	13.6	22.7	47.7	13.6	2.3	58257	68047	83	40	39	0.0	2.6	38.5	53.9	5.1	187500
01339	CHARLEMONT	24878	595	21.7	25.9	39.5	8.9	4.0	51709	60788	75	26	492	4.1	3.1	43.5	45.7	3.7	173958
01340	COLRAIN	27569	828	19.6	33.3	37.2	6.6	3.3	47549	56349	67	18	722	4.0	5.8	43.4	42.4	4.4	168750
01341	CONWAY	32327	684	10.7	22.2	39.6	19.3	8.2	67260	81478	90	58	614	0.3	0.5	18.7	66.1	14.3	238298
01342	DEERFIELD	28858	544	17.1	17.3	42.5	16.7	6.4	64051	77371	88	52	441	0.0	3.0	27.2	65.1	4.8	207500
01343	DRURY	23256	50	18.0	34.0	38.0	8.0	2.0	48207	55538	69	19	47	4.3	19.2	55.3	21.3	0.0	126563
01344	ERVING	24265	418	22.7	31.8	34.9	8.1	2.4	45794	53673	63	16	344	2.6	3.8	68.3	25.3	0.0	143571
01346	HEATH	21379	78	20.5	28.2	41.0	9.0	1.3	51045	59162	74	24	68	2.9	5.9	41.2	45.6	4.4	175000
01349	TURNERS FALLS	21437	721	23.4	38.7	27.5	8.6	1.8	41757	48097	52	11	525	4.6	2.3	66.3	25.5	1.3	146094
01350	MONROE BRIDGE	25158	37	24.3	29.7	35.1	8.1	2.7	47333	55778	67	18	29	0.0	0.0	44.8	55.2	0.0	184375
01351	MONTAGUE	26404	803	16.3	25.5	42.5	14.2	1.5	62227	71605	86	49	649	2.8	1.1	30.5	59.0	6.6	196324
01355	NEW SALEM	29054	349	15.5	27.2	45.6	8.0	3.7	55263	64592	80	33	318	0.0	2.8	42.5	51.6	3.1	184146
01360	NORTHFIELD	25539	1178	16.7	25.8	43.7	11.0	2.7	56685	65149	81	35	930	0.0	0.9	41.2	55.6	2.4	188028
01364	ORANGE	20857	3069	28.1	32.7	31.1	6.5	1.5	41146	47592	50	10	2131	4.0	13.5	62.4	19.1	1.0	128153
01366	PETERSHAM	28623	437	17.2	25.6	33.6	17.4	6.2	55957	71430	81	34	370	0.3	1.6	20.0	62.4	15.7	239610
01367	ROWE	26990	235	21.7	28.9	37.0	8.9	3.4	49479	58533	71	20	195	6.2	7.2	44.1	40.0	2.6	161574
01368	ROYALSTON	23308	459	18.3	30.7	36.0	10.0	5.0	50725	61777	73	23	400	2.3	3.8	40.3	47.0	6.8	181356
01370	SHELBURNE FALLS	25522	1870	20.9	27.7	37.4	10.8	3.3	51269	60949	74	24	1382	0.8	2.2	40.7	50.9	5.5	185837
01373	SOUTH DEERFIELD	33067	1905	16.8	22.1	36.0	15.6	9.6	61436	76653	86	46	1490	0.3	0.3	19.1	73.8	6.5	228021
01375	SUNDERLAND	25669	1671	29.2	26.1	30.2	11.3	3.2	44390	54700	60	14	759	2.5	0.0	10.7	77.6	9.2	233957
01376	TURNERS FALLS	21134	2915	38.1	26.2	26.8	6.4	2.5	35683	41364	30	6	1807	2.0	4.0	57.1	34.9	2.1	158622
01378	WARWICK	24302	300	16.0	36.0	33.7	10.3	4.0	48207	57869	69	19	262	1.2	3.8	48.1	46.2	0.8	170349
01379	WENDELL	26109	384	20.3	29.7	37.5	8.9	3.7	50000	60386	72	22	336	4.2	10.4	48.8	36.0	0.6	153365
01420	FITCHBURG	20872	15400	29.9	28.0	30.3	9.8	2.1	42557	51416	55	12	8451	1.3	2.6	47.7	46.5	2.0	172787
01430	ASHBURNHAM	26530	2035	13.2	20.7	43.4	17.7	4.9	65224	79813	89	55	1824	0.4	1.2	27.6	67.4	3.5	208197
01431	ASHBY	26637	998	10.1	23.1	43.8	18.5	4.5	71054	85115	92	64	921	0.4	0.4	20.5	69.7	8.9	230466
01432	AYER	31721	3054	19.1	24.9	31.3	16.4	8.3	57679	75475	82	37	1897	2.5	1.2	12.8	72.1	11.5	247587
01436	BALDWINVILLE	22766	1196	21.2	24.6	35.0	17.4	1.9	54509	67402	79	32	908	1.1	0.3	47.3	48.6	2.8	176961
01440	GARDNER	23389	8602	27.0	29.3	31.5	9.8	2.5	43771	53625	58	14	5175	1.0	2.6	51.7	42.8	1.9	168178
01450	GROTON	43107	3539	7.6	12.3	28.5	28.4	23.1	101996	129259	98	90	3096	0.1	0.1	2.8	40.9	56.2	431639
01451	HARVARD	58255	1899	4.6	8.5	20.9	21.9	44.2	133945	171881	100	98	1729	0.0	0.0	0.8	16.0	83.2	598237
01452	HUBBARDSTON	27290	1424	10.3	16.9	44.8	19.4	8.6	71999	88131	92	65	1308	0.8	1.5	20.8	70.9	6.0	229745
01453	LEOMINSTER	27798	16920	22.3	24.5	34.0	13.8	5.4	52973	65737	77	28	10260	0.9	1.6	26.1	65.7	5.8	214383
01460	LITTLETON	40844	3152	11.1	14.4	30.1	24.6	19.8	89666	116414	97	84	2658	3.2	0.5	2.7	49.1	44.6	378281
01462	LUNENBURG	34011	3716	13.3	21.2	34.0	20.5	11.0	68894	87642	91	61	3286	2.2	0.7	18.4	62.1	16.6	246208
01463	PEPPERELL	32715	3920	10.7	15.8	38.9	21.4	13.1	79074	99894	95	76	3198	3.0	1.6	9.8	66.5	19.2	290015
01464	SHIRLEY	26677	2122	14.4	22.0	36.9	20.2	6.6	65704	82187	89	55	1576	3.3	1.1	20.6	65.5	9.5	234936
01468	TEMPLETON	28684	1191	20.1	20.3	43.4	11.3	4.9	58210	70191	83	39	1056	2.0	2.4	37.6	55.0	3.0	185572
01469	TOWNSEND	27928	2211	11.2	16.5	45.7	19.7	7.0	72990	89101	92	66	1879	1.0	0.6	9.6	82.5	6.3	247483
01473	WESTMINSTER	30530	2658	12.0	20.5	40.2	21.3	5.9	68627	83905	91	60	2357	0.0	0.6	22.1	69.4	7.9	225934
01474	WEST TOWNSEND	29239	929	8.8	17.7	45.8	19.1	8.7	72283	87161	92	66	813	1.0	1.0	19.3	71.8	6.9	230542
01475	WINCHENDON	22387	3592	24.6	23.9	35.7	11.7	4.0	51093	61215	74	24	2715	0.6	3.5	44.4	49.3	2.2	177270
01501	AUBURN	29696	6529	18.5	20.7	36.7	17.3	6.9	60512	75378	85	45	5369	1.7	2.1	22.0	70.1	4.0	214878
01503	BERLIN	37818	953	14.1	15.2	31.5	24.2	15.0	83471	107392	96	80	824	0.0	0.0	3.8	51.7	44.5	376563
01504	BLACKSTONE	25673	3360	15.5	23.8	39.6	17.4	3.7	62610	77216	87	49	2489	0.4	0.6	16.0	75.4	7.7	230217
01505	BOYLSTON	42306	1623	12.0	15.1	32.9	23.8	16.1	82151	107651	96	79	1322	0.5	0.0	11.5	59.9	28.1	282124
01506	BROOKFIELD	24764	1273	19.0	27.1	37.8	12.7	3.4	52867	64448	77	28	1029	5.1	10.0	26.2	55.0	3.7	190982
01507	CHARLTON	28987	4147	12.7	15.7	41.9	23.3	6.5	75724	91317	93	69	3550	0.3	0.5	16.8	74.4	8.1	239305
01510	CLINTON	28473	5736	20.4	25.9	35.7	13.3	4.8	53350	66787	77	29	3301	0.4	0.7	16.9	77.8	4.2	224275
01515	EAST BROOKFIELD	28277	809	14.7	22.0	40.1	17.1	6.2	61235	75639	86	46	700	0.3	0.0	29.6	66.6	3.6	201323
01516	DOUGLAS	27941	2693	11.0	17.2	46.4	20.1	5.2	71212	85922	92	64	2221	0.9	1.3	11.4	80.1	6.5	241576
01518	FISKDALE	31280	1012	21.2	18.9	33.1	17.9	9.0	62189	79224	86	48	725	0.3	1.1	28.8	59.9	9.9	212331
01519	GRAFTON	42250	2117	11.2	15.6	33.1	23.9	16.3	82661	107918	96	79	1746	0.0	0.3	7.0	62.0	30.6	319093
01520	HOLDEN	35882	4868	12.7	14.9	38.3	21.6	12.6	77571	98574	94	73	4434	0.1	0.0	11.4	72.7	15.8	249808
01521	HOLLAND	25940	870	16.2	21.7	44.0	13.5	4.6	60408	70246	85	44	763	0.9	2.8	53.1	39.8	3.4	166059
01522	JEFFERSON	32987	1091	12.5	16.7	31.4	25.1	14.3	81594	104552	95	78	913	0.0	0.3	13.9	70.4	15.3	262064
01523	LANCASTER	29122	2144	15.8	14.6	35.8	20.2	13.7	76123	99477	94	70	1759	0.0	0.3	9.2	69.6	20.9	272989
01524	LEICESTER	25455	2394	18.8	17.8	44.5	14.8	4.1	64515	78503	88	54	1936	0.0	0.0	27.8	69.9	2.3	205804
01527	MILLBURY	29886	5182	18.6	21.4	35.3	18.0	6.6	61903	77598	86	47	3828	0.7	0.7	19.1	73.4	6.1	226437
01529	MILLVILLE	24596	1030	12.8	17.4	47.9	17.3	4.7	65810	80197	89	56	811	0.0	1.7	31.7	63.5	3.1	206056
01531	NEW BRAINTREE	23147	517	18.6	25.3	41.8	11.6	2.7	54306	64501	79	31	394	1.5	0.8	23.1	65.7	8.9	225521
01532	NORTHBOROUGH	42003	5055	7.7	14.1	29.1	25.6	23.3	97804	123572	98	88	4359	0.0	0.1	3.9	57.8	38.3	359565
01534	NORTHBRIDGE	27326	1712	13.4	21.7	38.2	19.6	7.1	66386	82237	89	56	1355	0.2	0.8	8.4	81.3	9.4	249583
01535	NORTH BROOKFIELD	24474	1899	21.8	26.0	36.0	11.6	4.5	51692	63509	75	26	1381	0.4	0.5	32.5	61.6	5.0	198902
01536	NORTH GRAFTON	37175	2666	14.0	19.8	35.4	21.3	9.4	71354	91656	92	64	2061	0.0	0.6	7.9	75.4	16.1	269082
01537	NORTH OXFORD	30847	816	14.8	20.7	42.8	17.9	3.8	60000	73531	84	43	588	0.5	6.5	32.8	56.8	3.4	187195
01540	OXFORD	26643	4423	17.3	19.6	40.0	18.1	5.0	62808	77509	87	50	3564	0.1	1.0	29.3	66.1	3.4	199200
01541	PRINCETON	40965	1213	7.7	9.9	33.5	32.8	16.2	98032	119657	98	88	1111	0.0	0.0	5.4	59.8	34.8	334436
01542	ROCHDALE	26179	716	13.4	21.8	39.3	19.7	5.9	64190	80057	88	53	528	0.0	1.7	29.6	66.3	2.5	198798
01543	RUTLAND	29822	2492	13.7	15.8	41.9	21.3	7.4	75000	90166	93	68	2061	1.0	2.2	14.6	75.5	6.7	236063
01545	SHREWSBURY	40350	13165	13.6	16.5	31.6	22.0	16.2	79081	103777	95	76	9733	0.4	0.7	7.5	63.1	28.3	299114
01550	SOUTHBRIDGE	22459	7138	31.3	28.3	29.4	8.6	2.4	40216	48736	47	9	3373	0.5	2.0	46.1	50.4	1.0	176696
01560	SOUTH GRAFTON	25053	1276	21.2	25.8	38.8	11.8	2.4	51977	62808	75	26	645	1.2	0.6	20.6	66.5	11.0	243898
01562	SPENCER	25378	4839	21.9	24.2	35.0	14.5	4.4	53719	66353	78	29	3253	0.2	0.2	23.9	71.4	4.4	215801
01564	STERLING	37032	2716	9.7	13.8	38.8	19.9	17.8	80746	102719	95	77	2398	0.3	1.4	6.3	60.9	31.1	312186
01566	STURBRIDGE	33472	2266	13.2	20.8	35.1	21.2	9.8	73271	91411	93	67	1925	0.4	2.7	18.0	68.8	10.1	232089
01568	UPTON	45047	2230	12.6	11.5	26.6	23.6	25.7	98377	124857	98	89	1844	0.8	0.0	2.7	52.6	44.0	374541
01569	UXBRIDGE	30975	4333	13.3	18.1	38.2	22.9	7.6	74941	92275	93	68	3483	0.1	0.8	11.7	74.8	12.7	252868
01570	WEBSTER	25439	7133	29.3	25.3	30.4	10.4	4.7	45116	55466	61	15	4154	1.1	1.1	35.7	57.4	4.8	190813
01571	DUDLEY	26365	4015	19.1	24.4	34.7	16.9	4.9	57158	71617	82	36	3002	1.5	0.6	27.7	66.3	3.9	208660
01581	WESTBOROUGH	46550	6929	10.4	14.9	28.9	21.8	24.0	90648	117472	97	85	4648	1.3	0.8	5.3	42.8	49.8	399027
01583	WEST BOYLSTON	30034	2513	16.6	18.7	34.3	21.1	9.4	68591	87288	91	60	2089	0.1	0.5	11.3	70.3	17.9	244855
01585	WEST BROOKFIELD	24399	2243	21.0	26.8	34.6	14.0	3.5	51642	63215	75	25	1752	2.1	2.8	29.2	62.2	3.7	208892
01588	WHITINSVILLE	28581	3457	18.7	25.7	33.1	14.9	7.7	56877	72116	82	35	2035	0.6	0.2	13.0	74.4	11.9	244021
01590	SUTTON	34926	3076	9.7	13.7	35.7	27.4	13.6	87496	107889	97	83	2789	0.3	0.7	9.0	65.6	24.4	289051
01602	WORCESTER	31854	8754	17.0	22.5	36.2	16.8	7.4	59706	75330	84	43	6093	0.2	0.8	26.7	68.1	4.3	209030
01603	WORCESTER	19989	7580	32.0	27.4	30.2	8.1	2.4	40883	50047	49	10	3500	0.5	1.7	53.7	43.0	1.2	168521
01604	WORCESTER	24595	13482	25.4	29.3	31.5	10.2	3.7	44900	55276	61	15	6787	0.5	1.8	40.2	56.4	1.1	185125
01605	WORCESTER	22336	10731	36.5	25.4	22.8	10.0	5.4	36282	44396	33	6	4374	1.2	1.0	35.9	55.8	6.1	196376
01606	WORCESTER	27305	8328	20.2	28.1	35.3	13.0	3.5	51329	62351	74	24	5051	0.9	0.3	39.2	58.7	0.9	185847
01607	WORCESTER	20657	3932	30.2	34.1	27.2	7.0	1.5	38337	46067	41	8	1710	1.4	4.0	53.8	39.1	1.8	163975
01608	WORCESTER	11329	1333	65.0	21.2	10.7	2.3	0.8	16263	18693	1	1	58	29.3	15.5	27.6	15.5	12.1	96000
01609	WORCESTER	24562	7407	39.5	22.9	22.1	9.4	6.1	33915	41948	24	5	2569	1.1	2.6	24.5	56.2	15.6	226718
01610	WORCESTER	14758	7601	42.9	31.4	20.9	3.2	1.7	29470	34855	11	2	1950	1.9	5.4	51.4	40.4	0.9	162787
01611	CHERRY VALLEY	25251	868	15.1	21.4	44.1	16.5	2.9	58297	71276	83	40	642	0.0	0.3	43.3	55.9	0.5	182885
	MASSACHUSETTS	33908		19.9	21.2	32.0	16.1	10.9	61110	77759				0.8	1.2	14.8	55.7	27.5	282585
	UNITED STATES	25866		24.7	27.1	30.8	10.9	6.5	48124	56710				10.9	15.0	33.7	30.1	10.4	145905

ZIP CODE #	POST OFFICE NAME	FINANCIAL SERVICES: Auto Loan	Home Loan	Invest-ments	Retire-ment Plans	THE HOME: Home Improvements: Home Repair	Lawn & Garden	Furnishings: Comput-ers & Hard-ware	Major Appli-ances	TV, Radio, Sound Equip-ment	Furni-ture	ENTERTAINMENT: Dine out/ Carry out	Sports Equip-ment	Fees & Tickets	Toys & Games	Travel	Cable TV	PERSONAL: Apparel & Services	Auto Repairs	Health Insur-ance	Pets & Supplies
01338	BUCKLAND	114	102	77	97	107	115	94	104	100	94	121	124	92	124	97	102	115	101	113	134
01339	CHARLEMONT	94	89	79	88	92	100	87	92	90	86	110	106	87	112	88	91	105	90	95	108
01340	COLRAIN	117	100	74	93	108	118	93	106	101	93	121	125	88	122	97	105	114	104	118	140
01341	CONWAY	106	132	141	132	130	128	118	118	109	118	137	138	126	147	121	106	137	113	105	130
01342	DEERFIELD	94	112	129	114	111	111	105	104	99	105	125	122	110	130	107	96	124	102	93	114
01343	DRURY	89	80	61	76	84	90	74	82	78	74	95	97	72	97	76	80	90	79	88	105
01344	ERVING	76	80	80	75	81	90	78	79	81	76	100	89	82	108	81	84	97	77	85	89
01346	HEATH	94	74	50	67	83	94	70	84	79	69	94	98	62	92	74	84	87	83	99	115
01349	TURNERS FALLS	72	72	74	72	73	79	74	74	75	72	93	85	75	97	74	75	90	74	75	82
01350	MONROE BRIDGE	84	71	56	71	75	84	73	78	78	72	95	89	70	94	73	79	89	77	85	93
01351	MONTAGUE	88	91	101	94	92	97	92	91	90	91	112	108	92	114	92	89	109	92	88	102
01355	NEW SALEM	112	99	76	94	105	113	92	102	98	92	119	121	90	121	95	100	113	99	110	131
01360	NORTHFIELD	82	97	113	97	95	97	92	90	88	92	111	106	97	116	94	86	110	90	83	99
01364	ORANGE	79	68	55	67	72	80	69	74	73	68	89	86	66	88	69	75	84	73	80	89
01366	PETERSHAM	93	108	120	103	107	117	102	102	102	101	127	114	108	132	107	104	125	100	104	111
01367	ROWE	103	87	66	85	92	103	87	95	93	86	113	110	83	112	88	96	106	94	105	117
01368	ROYALSTON	103	92	70	87	97	104	85	94	90	85	109	112	83	112	87	92	104	91	102	121
01370	SHELBURNE FALLS	83	91	98	89	91	96	87	87	86	86	108	101	90	113	89	87	106	86	87	99
01373	SOUTH DEERFIELD	100	121	135	121	119	120	112	111	105	111	132	129	118	139	114	103	132	108	101	122
01375	SUNDERLAND	79	63	82	71	62	69	87	76	86	82	108	98	79	101	78	79	105	86	71	85
01376	TURNERS FALLS	65	65	65	63	66	73	67	67	69	64	85	76	67	88	67	71	82	67	71	75
01378	WARWICK	99	88	67	84	93	100	81	90	87	81	105	108	80	107	84	89	100	88	98	117
01379	WENDELL	84	92	92	94	89	88	88	87	82	88	104	103	88	104	86	77	102	86	76	95
01420	FITCHBURG	69	71	79	70	70	77	75	72	75	72	94	84	75	95	74	75	91	74	73	80
01430	ASHBURNHAM	98	121	129	120	119	118	108	108	101	108	127	126	115	135	111	98	127	104	97	119
01431	ASHBY	99	123	131	123	121	119	110	109	102	109	128	128	117	136	112	99	128	105	98	121
01432	AYER	105	117	131	120	115	117	116	113	111	115	140	134	119	144	115	107	138	113	103	123
01436	BALDWINVILLE	88	90	85	86	91	97	86	88	87	85	108	102	88	113	87	88	105	86	91	103
01440	GARDNER	76	78	82	77	78	84	79	78	80	77	99	91	80	103	79	80	96	79	79	88
01450	GROTON	168	202	217	209	195	195	182	178	166	185	212	207	195	218	183	160	212	173	157	196
01451	HARVARD	219	273	297	282	264	266	241	234	219	244	279	271	265	290	245	212	281	226	208	260
01452	HUBBARDSTON	108	128	134	129	126	124	117	116	109	117	137	137	122	143	118	105	136	113	104	128
01453	LEOMINSTER	91	97	109	98	96	101	98	96	96	97	120	112	100	122	98	95	118	97	92	105
01460	LITTLETON	145	179	196	182	175	175	161	159	149	162	188	186	173	198	164	145	189	154	142	175
01462	LUNENBURG	115	139	149	137	137	140	127	127	122	126	152	146	135	162	131	120	151	123	119	139
01463	PEPPERELL	130	146	147	149	143	144	136	135	127	137	160	158	140	163	135	123	158	132	123	150
01464	SHIRLEY	91	93	85	91	93	97	87	89	87	87	108	104	88	111	88	87	104	87	89	104
01468	TEMPLETON	116	119	108	116	122	126	109	115	109	109	134	136	111	139	112	109	130	112	115	139
01469	TOWNSEND	108	127	135	128	124	124	118	117	110	117	139	138	123	145	119	106	138	114	105	128
01473	WESTMINSTER	117	126	120	123	127	130	114	119	112	114	139	140	118	146	117	112	136	115	116	140
01474	WEST TOWNSEND	115	135	140	136	131	130	124	123	115	124	145	145	128	151	124	110	144	121	109	136
01475	WINCHENDON	90	88	78	85	90	96	84	88	86	83	107	103	84	109	85	87	102	86	91	104
01501	AUBURN	95	109	119	106	108	114	103	103	101	102	126	118	108	131	106	101	124	101	101	114
01503	BERLIN	133	165	176	166	162	160	147	147	137	147	172	172	157	183	151	133	172	142	132	162
01504	BLACKSTONE	95	102	103	103	101	104	99	98	96	99	120	115	101	123	98	93	117	97	93	109
01505	BOYLSTON	143	167	172	166	165	168	150	152	143	150	180	176	159	188	154	142	178	147	143	172
01506	BROOKFIELD	102	86	63	81	91	98	82	92	88	83	107	109	77	105	83	90	101	91	99	118
01507	CHARLTON	118	130	129	132	127	127	122	122	115	123	145	143	124	148	121	110	142	120	110	135
01510	CLINTON	87	93	109	94	92	98	96	93	95	94	119	109	98	122	96	93	116	94	90	101
01515	EAST BROOKFIELD	103	113	113	110	114	118	105	107	103	104	129	125	109	135	108	103	126	105	105	124
01516	DOUGLAS	115	117	108	119	116	120	112	114	109	113	136	133	112	137	111	106	132	112	109	129
01518	FISKDALE	115	108	98	108	112	121	107	112	109	105	134	131	105	135	107	110	128	111	116	133
01519	GRAFTON	155	181	188	186	175	172	165	163	153	168	193	192	172	198	164	145	192	159	143	179
01520	HOLDEN	122	150	169	147	147	152	138	137	131	137	165	157	147	174	142	130	164	133	128	149
01521	HOLLAND	108	97	79	92	102	109	92	102	96	92	117	120	86	116	94	98	111	101	108	128
01522	JEFFERSON	121	145	151	146	142	140	132	131	122	132	154	154	138	162	133	118	153	128	117	145
01523	LANCASTER	120	148	159	147	145	145	134	133	125	133	157	155	142	168	137	122	157	129	121	146
01524	LEICESTER	92	107	114	106	105	107	100	99	95	100	120	115	105	125	101	93	119	98	92	109
01527	MILLBURY	100	114	122	111	112	117	107	107	105	106	131	124	112	137	110	104	129	105	104	119
01529	MILLVILLE	101	111	113	114	107	106	106	104	99	107	125	123	107	126	103	93	123	103	91	114
01531	NEW BRAINTREE	81	96	102	95	95	97	88	88	85	87	106	101	94	114	91	85	105	85	84	97
01532	NORTHBOROUGH	151	189	215	190	184	185	171	168	159	171	200	196	183	212	175	155	201	164	151	184
01534	NORTHBRIDGE	102	120	126	118	118	120	109	110	104	109	131	128	115	138	112	102	130	107	102	123
01535	NORTH BROOKFIELD	84	89	92	88	90	95	88	88	87	86	108	102	90	112	89	87	105	87	88	99
01536	NORTH GRAFTON	123	142	159	145	139	141	135	132	128	135	161	155	140	165	135	124	159	131	121	145
01537	NORTH OXFORD	90	105	112	104	103	104	98	97	93	98	118	114	103	123	99	91	117	96	89	106
01540	OXFORD	93	109	116	108	107	109	102	101	97	101	122	117	107	129	103	95	121	99	94	111
01541	PRINCETON	152	190	203	192	185	184	168	166	155	169	195	194	181	206	172	150	196	160	148	184
01542	ROCHDALE	97	113	121	110	113	118	107	106	105	105	131	121	113	141	110	106	129	103	104	116
01543	RUTLAND	113	130	132	132	125	124	120	118	112	121	141	138	124	145	119	106	140	116	104	129
01545	SHREWSBURY	137	157	174	160	153	157	149	146	141	150	177	171	155	180	149	136	175	145	134	160
01550	SOUTHBRIDGE	71	71	78	70	72	79	76	74	78	73	96	86	76	98	76	78	93	75	76	82
01560	SOUTH GRAFTON	78	83	92	83	83	88	86	83	85	83	106	98	87	111	86	83	104	84	81	90
01562	SPENCER	85	90	96	89	89	95	90	89	90	88	111	103	92	115	90	89	109	89	88	99
01564	STERLING	134	167	177	167	164	161	149	148	138	148	173	173	158	185	152	134	173	143	133	164
01566	STURBRIDGE	118	125	131	125	127	131	119	122	117	118	145	145	121	150	121	116	142	121	119	142
01568	UPTON	169	196	202	199	193	198	178	178	168	178	211	206	189	218	181	165	209	172	166	199
01569	UXBRIDGE	117	133	136	133	130	130	124	123	118	124	148	144	128	154	124	114	146	121	113	136
01570	WEBSTER	80	79	86	78	80	87	84	82	85	81	106	95	84	107	83	86	102	84	84	92
01571	DUDLEY	92	100	103	98	100	105	96	97	95	95	119	112	100	125	98	95	116	95	95	108
01581	WESTBOROUGH	162	191	223	194	185	191	180	176	170	181	214	205	189	221	181	165	214	174	159	192
01583	WEST BOYLSTON	115	123	126	119	124	136	119	121	119	117	147	136	122	150	122	122	143	119	125	135
01585	WEST BROOKFIELD	89	89	84	86	91	100	87	90	89	85	109	102	87	112	89	91	105	88	95	104
01588	WHITINSVILLE	99	106	115	106	106	111	107	105	104	104	130	124	109	135	107	102	128	105	101	116
01590	SUTTON	137	164	170	167	159	157	147	146	136	149	172	170	155	177	148	130	171	141	129	160
01602	WORCESTER	99	114	135	114	112	118	112	109	108	111	136	127	116	141	114	107	134	109	104	119
01603	WORCESTER	68	64	71	64	65	72	71	69	73	68	90	80	70	91	70	73	87	71	72	77
01604	WORCESTER	76	77	90	78	76	82	82	79	82	80	103	93	83	104	81	81	101	81	78	86
01605	WORCESTER	74	72	90	72	71	79	79	76	82	78	102	88	79	102	78	82	100	79	78	85
01606	WORCESTER	82	91	108	90	90	96	90	89	90	90	113	102	94	116	92	90	111	89	86	97
01607	WORCESTER	66	60	64	60	60	66	67	65	69	65	86	76	65	84	65	69	83	68	67	73
01608	WORCESTER	30	30	59	29	28	33	35	32	39	36	51	37	36	54	36	42	51	35	34	36
01609	WORCESTER	74	72	105	74	71	79	84	77	86	82	108	93	83	109	82	85	107	83	76	85
01610	WORCESTER	50	48	70	47	46	52	55	52	59	55	74	61	54	75	54	60	73	55	52	57
01611	CHERRY VALLEY	85	103	114	101	101	103	95	94	91	95	115	109	102	122	98	90	114	92	88	103
	MASSACHUSETTS	112	121	148	122	120	127	122	119	121	121	151	138	126	156	123	120	149	120	115	132
	UNITED STATES	100	100	100	100	100	100	100	100	100	100	100	100	100	100	100	100	100	100	100	100

#	ZIP CODE POST OFFICE NAME	COUNTY FIPS CODE	POPULATION			2000-2004 ANNUAL RATE		HOUSEHOLDS					FAMILIES		
			2000	2004	2009	% Rate	State Centile	2000	2004	2009	% Annual Rate 2000-2004	2004 Average HH Size	2000	2004	% Annual Rate 2000-2004
01612	PAXTON	027	4413	4489	4611	0.4	53	1436	1477	1534	0.7	2.77	1160	1192	0.6
01701	FRAMINGHAM	017	33992	33540	33467	-0.3	11	13958	13932	14044	0.0	2.37	9587	9575	0.0
01702	FRAMINGHAM	017	33165	33464	33692	0.2	41	12305	12389	12521	0.2	2.48	7039	7084	0.2
01718	VILLAGE OF NAGOG WOO	017	420	410	407	-0.6	4	174	170	170	-0.6	2.41	101	99	-0.5
01719	BOXBOROUGH	017	4875	5011	5070	0.7	67	1855	1911	1944	0.7	2.62	1272	1312	0.7
01720	ACTON	017	19864	20250	20536	0.5	56	7307	7491	7647	0.6	2.68	5433	5567	0.6
01721	ASHLAND	017	14716	15334	15656	1.0	77	5737	6005	6170	1.1	2.55	4034	4230	1.1
01730	BEDFORD	017	12477	12498	12564	0.0	32	4584	4630	4697	0.2	2.57	3392	3426	0.2
01731	HANSCOM AFB	017	3036	2961	2945	-0.6	3	850	838	842	-0.3	3.36	821	808	-0.4
01740	BOLTON	027	4192	4382	4576	1.1	80	1439	1518	1599	1.3	2.89	1215	1281	1.3
01741	CARLISLE	017	4684	4704	4697	0.1	35	1606	1629	1640	0.3	2.89	1362	1382	0.3
01742	CONCORD	017	17082	17170	17319	0.1	36	5975	6070	6186	0.4	2.60	4456	4528	0.4
01745	FAYVILLE	027	271	309	339	3.1	100	107	123	136	3.3	2.51	75	86	3.3
01746	HOLLISTON	017	13815	13818	13844	0.0	31	4798	4848	4902	0.2	2.84	3844	3888	0.3
01747	HOPEDALE	027	5738	6105	6434	1.5	89	2168	2345	2501	1.9	2.55	1520	1640	1.8
01748	HOPKINTON	017	13332	13903	14216	1.0	78	4439	4639	4770	1.0	2.96	3620	3784	1.1
01749	HUDSON	017	18173	18300	18425	0.2	37	7013	7145	7267	0.4	2.54	4861	4956	0.5
01752	MARLBOROUGH	017	36210	38154	39318	1.2	86	14484	15395	16003	1.5	2.45	9274	9876	1.5
01754	MAYNARD	017	10373	10214	10196	-0.4	8	4275	4262	4300	-0.1	2.39	2791	2783	-0.1
01756	MENDON	027	5256	5695	6065	1.9	96	1804	1968	2108	2.1	2.89	1442	1570	2.0
01757	MILFORD	027	27107	27542	28417	0.4	52	10540	10793	11223	0.6	2.52	7289	7462	0.6
01760	NATICK	017	31714	32379	33066	0.5	59	12893	13298	13720	0.7	2.39	8421	8680	0.7
01770	SHERBORN	017	4183	4168	4173	-0.1	24	1417	1422	1435	0.1	2.93	1218	1223	0.1
01772	SOUTHBOROUGH	027	8578	9246	9819	1.8	94	2868	3111	3324	1.9	2.96	2368	2568	1.9
01773	LINCOLN	017	5112	5074	5058	-0.2	19	1971	1968	1976	0.0	2.57	1458	1456	0.0
01775	STOW	017	5944	6343	6553	1.5	91	2092	2260	2361	1.8	2.79	1691	1827	1.8
01776	SUDBURY	017	16841	17188	17382	0.5	57	5504	5653	5759	0.6	3.01	4751	4878	0.6
01778	WAYLAND	017	12878	13248	13435	0.7	68	4498	4663	4768	0.9	2.81	3621	3749	0.8
01801	WOBURN	017	37276	37208	37348	0.0	27	15002	15185	15415	0.3	2.43	9656	9768	0.3
01803	BURLINGTON	017	22765	22829	23023	0.1	34	8252	8351	8499	0.3	2.73	6342	6436	0.4
01810	ANDOVER	009	31262	31246	31522	0.0	30	11310	11462	11700	0.3	2.70	8494	8619	0.3
01821	BILLERICA	017	29374	29283	29333	-0.1	24	9941	10056	10190	0.3	2.91	7935	8027	0.3
01824	CHELMSFORD	017	25305	25057	25091	-0.2	15	9338	9348	9451	0.0	2.63	7002	7022	0.1
01826	DRACUT	017	28683	28759	29047	0.1	33	10497	10661	10880	0.4	2.69	7772	7885	0.3
01827	DUNSTABLE	017	2830	3074	3206	2.0	96	922	1017	1072	2.3	3.02	797	879	2.3
01830	HAVERHILL	009	24321	24602	24934	0.3	45	9393	9653	9913	0.6	2.45	5866	6045	0.7
01832	HAVERHILL	009	21105	22170	22908	1.2	83	8366	8878	9261	1.4	2.48	5475	5812	1.4
01833	GEORGETOWN	009	7497	7804	7991	1.0	77	2598	2742	2843	1.3	2.84	2051	2162	1.3
01834	GROVELAND	009	5969	6078	6150	0.4	55	2035	2096	2144	0.7	2.90	1689	1740	0.7
01835	HAVERHILL	009	13416	13754	14170	0.6	64	5172	5386	5616	1.0	2.49	3488	3640	1.0
01840	LAWRENCE	009	4314	4408	4492	0.5	60	1935	1996	2053	0.7	2.14	872	908	1.0
01841	LAWRENCE	009	44583	45234	45814	0.3	48	14191	14483	14778	0.5	3.07	10307	10525	0.5
01843	LAWRENCE	009	23189	24567	25723	1.4	88	8359	8982	9522	1.7	2.71	5740	6155	1.7
01844	METHUEN	009	44130	46313	47946	1.1	82	16650	17682	18493	1.4	2.59	11630	12365	1.5
01845	NORTH ANDOVER	009	27218	28282	29035	0.9	75	9727	10325	10772	1.4	2.56	6905	7329	1.4
01850	LOWELL	017	15741	15684	15699	-0.1	23	5658	5663	5707	0.0	2.74	3803	3810	0.0
01851	LOWELL	017	29263	29235	29328	0.0	29	10031	10029	10107	0.0	2.89	6760	6763	0.1
01852	LOWELL	017	33229	33088	33324	-0.1	22	13071	13192	13431	0.2	2.47	7849	7891	0.1
01854	LOWELL	017	26724	26767	26950	0.0	32	9048	9116	9255	0.2	2.61	5511	5555	0.2
01860	MERRIMAC	009	6147	6258	6336	0.4	54	2237	2302	2354	0.7	2.70	1702	1751	0.7
01862	NORTH BILLERICA	017	9808	9953	10064	0.4	49	3081	3159	3226	0.6	2.78	2378	2444	0.7
01863	NORTH CHELMSFORD	017	8554	8641	8695	0.2	43	3475	3551	3611	0.5	2.43	2307	2361	0.6
01864	NORTH READING	017	13881	13864	13869	0.0	28	4810	4844	4885	0.2	2.84	3766	3790	0.2
01867	READING	017	23711	23368	23333	-0.3	9	8689	8660	8739	-0.1	2.68	6438	6406	-0.1
01876	TEWKSBURY	017	28760	29129	29547	0.3	46	9905	10181	10446	0.7	2.78	7661	7861	0.6
01879	TYNGSBORO	017	11129	11918	12346	1.6	93	3742	4039	4220	1.8	2.95	2956	3191	1.8
01880	WAKEFIELD	017	24874	24521	24509	-0.3	9	9771	9768	9875	0.0	2.49	6618	6618	0.0
01886	WESTFORD	017	20765	21875	22465	1.2	85	6815	7236	7490	1.4	3.01	5811	6170	1.4
01887	WILMINGTON	017	21382	21535	21680	0.2	39	7029	7176	7305	0.5	2.97	5782	5900	0.5
01890	WINCHESTER	017	20820	20715	20801	-0.1	22	7719	7763	7870	0.1	2.62	5724	5758	0.1
01901	LYNN	009	1440	1561	1643	1.9	96	910	1014	1087	2.6	1.47	279	300	1.7
01902	LYNN	009	45741	46315	46926	0.3	46	17378	17684	18046	0.4	2.57	10128	10311	0.4
01904	LYNN	009	17846	17690	17771	-0.2	16	6704	6723	6824	0.1	2.62	4859	4872	0.1
01905	LYNN	009	23974	23683	23744	-0.3	12	8501	8440	8524	-0.2	2.78	5760	5713	-0.2
01906	SAUGUS	009	26095	25862	26003	-0.2	16	9982	10079	10276	0.2	2.54	7144	7213	0.2
01907	SWAMPSCOTT	009	14434	14787	15096	0.6	62	5728	5952	6146	0.9	2.44	3993	4147	0.9
01908	NAHANT	009	3632	3534	3532	-0.6	3	1629	1617	1641	-0.2	2.15	971	963	-0.2
01913	AMESBURY	009	16457	16622	16833	0.2	43	6382	6553	6723	0.6	2.48	4230	4345	0.6
01915	BEVERLY	009	39849	39701	40009	-0.1	23	15744	15932	16265	0.3	2.36	9903	10021	0.3
01921	BOXFORD	009	7846	8314	8602	1.4	88	2550	2733	2856	1.6	3.04	2239	2398	1.6
01922	BYFIELD	009	2829	2928	2998	0.8	72	946	990	1026	1.1	2.96	785	821	1.1
01923	DANVERS	009	25340	25324	25467	0.0	30	9596	9748	9933	0.4	2.49	6589	6691	0.4
01929	ESSEX	009	3192	3203	3227	0.1	34	1272	1294	1320	0.4	2.48	860	876	0.4
01930	GLOUCESTER	009	30275	30555	30946	0.2	42	12593	12922	13258	0.6	2.34	7897	8091	0.6
01938	IPSWICH	009	13070	13297	13485	0.4	54	5316	5485	5626	0.7	2.39	3485	3598	0.8
01940	LYNNFIELD	009	11570	11520	11598	-0.1	22	4194	4251	4338	0.3	2.71	3358	3402	0.3
01944	MANCHESTER	009	5224	5204	5246	-0.1	23	2167	2192	2236	0.3	2.37	1435	1451	0.3
01945	MARBLEHEAD	009	20335	19861	19881	-0.6	4	8524	8437	8545	-0.2	2.34	5669	5613	-0.2
01949	MIDDLETON	009	7377	8345	8949	2.9	100	2126	2476	2707	3.7	2.88	1625	1891	3.6
01950	NEWBURYPORT	009	17102	17275	17539	0.2	43	7477	7666	7879	0.6	2.20	4407	4544	0.7
01951	NEWBURY	009	4026	4006	4022	-0.1	22	1629	1646	1673	0.2	2.41	1068	1076	0.2
01952	SALISBURY	009	7820	8161	8372	1.0	78	3080	3270	3395	1.4	2.48	1989	2108	1.4
01960	PEABODY	009	48094	48814	49728	0.4	49	18570	19235	19887	0.8	2.50	12972	13376	0.7
01966	ROCKPORT	009	7765	7739	7780	-0.1	24	3489	3518	3575	0.2	2.18	2028	2044	0.2
01969	ROWLEY	009	5501	5593	5672	0.4	53	1958	2027	2085	0.8	2.72	1468	1519	0.8
01970	SALEM	009	40444	41466	42506	0.6	64	17507	18208	18898	0.9	2.21	9719	10122	1.0
01982	SOUTH HAMILTON	009	8397	8317	8331	-0.2	16	2714	2716	2749	0.0	2.82	2176	2177	0.0
01983	TOPSFIELD	009	6275	6283	6331	0.0	31	2205	2248	2297	0.5	2.70	1775	1807	0.4
01984	WENHAM	009	4436	4437	4463	0.0	31	1283	1299	1322	0.3	2.67	956	967	0.3
01985	WEST NEWBURY	009	4149	4521	4747	2.0	97	1392	1540	1638	2.4	2.93	1183	1309	2.4
02019	BELLINGHAM	021	15291	15735	16042	0.7	69	5547	5746	5894	0.8	2.74	4274	4429	0.8
02021	CANTON	021	20874	21230	21555	0.4	53	7982	8178	8355	0.6	2.54	5568	5704	0.6
02025	COHASSET	021	7262	7257	7330	0.0	29	2674	2689	2731	0.1	2.67	2015	2027	0.1
02026	DEDHAM	021	23543	23120	23171	-0.4	6	8683	8568	8638	-0.3	2.60	6169	6092	-0.3
02030	DOVER	021	5579	5706	5797	0.5	61	1857	1905	1944	0.6	3.00	1575	1615	0.6
	MASSACHUSETTS					0.4					0.6	2.48			0.6
	UNITED STATES					1.2					1.3	2.58			1.1

ZIP CODE #	POST OFFICE NAME	RACE (%) White 2000	White 2004	Black 2000	Black 2004	Asian/Pacific 2000	Asian/Pacific 2004	% Hispanic Origin 2000	% Hispanic Origin 2004	2004 AGE DISTRIBUTION (%) 0-4	5-9	10-14	15-19	20-24	25-44	45-64	65-84	85+	18+	MEDIAN AGE 2004	% 2004 Males	% 2004 Females
01612	PAXTON	96.7	96.1	0.7	0.8	1.1	1.3	1.5	2.0	4.9	5.8	7.6	9.8	9.6	20.6	27.5	12.7	1.7	77.8	39.3	47.5	52.6
01701	FRAMINGHAM	87.7	85.5	2.6	2.9	6.5	8.0	2.8	3.4	6.2	6.4	5.9	5.2	4.5	29.5	27.6	12.6	2.2	78.2	40.6	48.4	51.6
01702	FRAMINGHAM	71.8	68.9	7.6	8.0	4.1	4.9	19.0	21.7	6.3	6.0	6.1	7.5	8.8	34.5	19.6	9.2	2.0	77.9	34.1	47.2	52.8
01718	VILLAGE OF NAGOG WOO	80.2	76.8	1.7	1.7	14.1	17.3	3.3	4.2	5.1	5.4	7.6	7.6	5.4	31.0	30.7	6.6	0.7	77.1	38.5	49.5	50.5
01719	BOXBOROUGH	88.8	86.5	0.3	0.4	8.5	10.5	1.1	1.3	7.0	8.8	9.1	6.6	4.1	30.2	28.5	5.3	0.4	70.6	37.8	50.5	49.5
01720	ACTON	88.7	86.3	0.7	0.8	8.5	10.6	1.7	2.2	7.1	8.5	8.8	6.7	4.0	27.1	28.7	8.0	1.1	71.1	38.9	49.4	50.6
01721	ASHLAND	91.9	90.6	1.8	2.0	2.5	3.2	2.9	3.5	7.6	8.0	7.0	5.2	4.0	31.0	27.1	9.2	0.9	73.8	38.8	48.2	51.8
01730	BEDFORD	91.3	89.5	1.6	1.8	5.4	6.7	1.8	2.2	6.4	7.2	6.9	5.3	3.6	23.7	27.9	15.8	3.3	75.7	43.4	49.9	50.1
01731	HANSCOM AFB	78.9	76.3	11.1	12.2	2.7	3.4	6.3	7.5	14.3	11.8	10.6	5.3	8.0	44.4	5.0	0.6	0.1	59.5	25.0	51.4	48.6
01740	BOLTON	97.7	97.1	0.2	0.3	1.3	1.8	0.8	1.1	7.5	9.0	8.9	6.5	3.1	26.5	31.3	6.8	0.6	70.4	40.0	50.3	49.7
01741	CARLISLE	93.5	91.9	0.2	0.2	4.9	6.2	1.2	1.5	6.2	8.7	9.7	7.6	3.3	17.3	36.7	9.7	0.8	70.4	43.5	49.2	50.8
01742	CONCORD	91.6	90.2	2.2	2.4	3.0	3.7	2.8	3.3	5.4	6.7	7.7	6.6	4.1	22.4	30.2	14.1	2.8	75.6	43.4	50.0	50.0
01745	FAYVILLE	95.9	95.2	0.4	0.3	1.9	2.6	1.5	1.9	7.4	7.4	7.4	5.8	4.9	24.3	27.2	13.6	1.9	73.8	41.1	47.9	52.1
01746	HOLLISTON	96.7	96.1	0.9	1.0	1.2	1.5	1.4	1.7	7.1	8.5	9.0	6.8	3.9	25.5	29.7	8.8	0.8	71.0	39.6	49.0	51.0
01747	HOPEDALE	97.6	97.1	0.6	0.7	0.7	0.9	1.2	1.5	7.0	7.4	7.2	6.0	4.4	26.7	26.3	12.3	2.7	74.6	40.3	47.8	52.2
01748	HOPKINTON	96.3	95.6	0.7	0.8	1.7	2.1	1.3	1.6	9.2	10.6	9.7	6.2	3.2	28.0	26.3	6.0	0.9	66.1	37.2	49.4	50.6
01749	HUDSON	94.1	93.1	0.9	1.0	1.5	1.9	3.1	3.7	6.5	6.6	6.9	6.0	5.6	30.6	25.6	11.0	1.3	76.2	38.4	49.4	50.6
01752	MARLBOROUGH	87.7	85.6	2.2	2.4	3.8	4.9	6.1	7.2	6.9	6.8	6.6	5.5	5.0	33.9	23.8	9.8	1.8	76.3	37.4	49.3	50.8
01754	MAYNARD	94.8	93.8	0.9	1.1	1.5	2.0	2.8	3.4	6.8	6.9	6.7	5.2	5.0	31.1	26.0	10.4	1.8	76.2	39.2	48.0	52.0
01756	MENDON	98.0	97.6	0.4	0.4	0.6	0.8	1.0	1.3	7.7	8.5	8.7	6.5	4.7	28.7	27.0	7.0	1.2	70.8	38.0	49.5	50.5
01757	MILFORD	93.0	91.7	1.3	1.5	1.8	2.3	4.3	5.4	7.1	7.1	6.9	6.0	5.5	30.3	24.6	10.4	2.2	75.2	37.8	48.6	51.4
01760	NATICK	92.1	90.6	1.6	1.8	3.9	4.8	2.0	2.4	7.0	7.0	6.4	5.2	4.4	30.3	25.1	12.4	2.2	76.1	39.5	47.4	52.6
01770	SHERBORN	96.5	95.7	0.4	0.4	2.4	3.1	1.1	1.4	6.9	9.1	9.8	7.8	3.6	18.2	32.5	10.9	1.3	69.2	42.2	48.3	51.7
01772	SOUTHBOROUGH	94.3	93.1	0.6	0.6	3.7	4.6	1.5	1.9	9.3	10.6	9.5	6.1	3.2	26.8	26.1	7.6	0.9	66.6	37.7	49.9	50.1
01773	LINCOLN	92.0	90.4	1.1	1.2	5.1	6.4	1.0	1.2	6.2	8.1	8.1	6.0	2.9	18.6	32.8	15.4	1.8	73.3	45.0	47.1	52.9
01775	STOW	95.2	94.2	0.5	0.6	2.2	2.7	1.4	1.8	8.2	9.3	7.8	5.6	3.5	26.3	30.0	8.4	1.0	70.7	40.1	50.1	49.9
01776	SUDBURY	94.2	93.0	0.8	0.9	3.8	4.7	1.2	1.5	8.2	9.9	9.6	6.8	3.2	22.1	29.8	9.2	1.3	67.6	40.3	48.9	51.1
01778	WAYLAND	92.2	90.4	0.8	0.9	5.4	6.8	1.2	1.5	6.7	8.3	9.0	6.8	3.4	20.6	30.6	12.9	1.9	71.5	42.6	48.4	51.6
01801	WOBURN	90.6	88.7	1.9	2.1	4.9	6.1	3.1	3.8	5.8	5.7	6.0	5.7	5.6	32.2	23.9	13.3	1.9	79.0	38.7	49.0	51.1
01803	BURLINGTON	86.7	84.3	1.4	1.5	10.7	12.9	1.3	1.5	6.8	6.8	6.5	5.8	4.8	28.6	25.5	13.9	1.3	76.3	39.7	49.2	50.8
01810	ANDOVER	91.6	89.4	0.8	0.9	5.8	7.4	1.8	2.5	6.4	7.5	8.8	7.2	4.7	23.3	29.6	10.7	2.0	72.5	40.8	48.3	51.7
01821	BILLERICA	95.1	94.1	0.8	0.9	2.7	3.4	1.3	1.6	7.0	7.2	7.5	6.3	5.3	31.0	26.3	8.7	0.7	74.4	37.3	49.7	50.3
01824	CHELMSFORD	93.1	91.6	0.8	0.9	4.7	5.9	1.3	1.6	6.5	7.0	7.2	6.3	4.7	26.1	27.5	12.7	2.0	75.3	41.0	48.9	51.1
01826	DRACUT	95.1	94.1	0.8	0.9	2.6	3.3	1.6	2.0	6.7	6.9	7.4	6.2	5.7	31.4	24.1	10.5	1.1	75.1	37.2	49.0	51.0
01827	DUNSTABLE	97.5	97.0	0.1	0.1	1.5	1.9	0.5	0.6	7.8	9.2	9.0	6.4	3.6	27.3	28.7	7.3	0.7	69.8	38.9	48.7	51.3
01830	HAVERHILL	90.0	88.0	2.8	3.2	0.8	1.0	8.9	11.2	6.9	6.5	7.1	6.8	5.9	28.9	23.0	11.7	3.2	75.1	37.9	47.6	52.4
01832	HAVERHILL	86.8	84.0	2.4	2.8	1.8	2.2	11.8	15.0	8.0	7.5	7.3	6.3	6.2	32.3	21.6	9.3	1.5	73.3	35.1	48.2	51.8
01833	GEORGETOWN	98.5	98.2	0.2	0.2	0.4	0.5	0.6	0.9	8.0	8.7	8.2	6.0	4.1	27.2	28.2	8.4	1.2	71.1	38.8	49.7	50.3
01834	GROVELAND	98.4	98.0	0.4	0.4	0.6	0.8	0.5	0.7	7.1	7.9	8.5	7.2	5.1	25.7	27.9	9.7	1.1	72.1	39.1	49.4	50.6
01835	HAVERHILL	93.4	92.0	1.7	2.0	1.7	2.1	3.9	5.2	6.9	7.0	7.2	7.5	6.9	30.7	23.4	9.1	1.3	74.8	36.3	47.0	53.0
01840	LAWRENCE	41.8	37.3	6.5	6.5	1.3	1.4	72.2	77.8	8.3	6.9	6.4	6.7	7.7	27.2	20.5	13.9	2.5	75.1	35.6	49.6	50.4
01841	LAWRENCE	43.6	39.5	5.0	5.0	1.5	1.5	67.7	72.7	9.6	8.8	9.5	9.1	9.6	28.6	16.8	6.4	1.8	66.8	27.3	47.9	52.1
01843	LAWRENCE	59.8	55.1	4.3	4.4	5.5	6.2	41.9	47.0	8.0	7.6	8.3	8.1	8.3	29.1	19.9	9.2	1.5	71.1	31.7	48.0	52.0
01844	METHUEN	89.3	87.0	1.4	1.5	2.4	3.0	9.7	11.9	6.3	6.4	7.2	6.7	6.1	28.5	24.4	12.4	2.4	75.9	38.4	48.1	51.9
01845	NORTH ANDOVER	93.7	92.1	0.7	0.9	4.0	5.1	2.0	2.7	6.8	7.4	7.3	8.3	6.9	25.5	24.8	10.2	2.8	74.6	38.2	48.5	51.6
01850	LOWELL	77.4	74.2	4.6	4.9	6.6	7.9	15.6	18.2	8.2	7.9	8.3	7.7	7.6	31.7	19.7	7.8	1.2	71.0	31.6	49.0	51.0
01851	LOWELL	57.1	52.7	3.8	3.9	31.0	34.9	10.2	11.1	8.1	7.6	8.0	8.1	8.7	32.3	18.9	7.3	1.1	71.4	30.7	49.9	50.1
01852	LOWELL	73.7	70.7	3.9	4.2	10.1	11.6	15.8	18.0	7.0	6.6	7.3	7.3	7.5	31.1	21.4	10.3	1.5	74.7	34.2	49.2	50.8
01854	LOWELL	69.5	66.6	4.8	5.0	14.8	16.7	15.2	16.5	6.6	6.7	7.1	10.0	11.3	28.7	17.6	9.8	2.2	75.5	30.9	49.4	50.7
01860	MERRIMAC	98.3	97.8	0.4	0.5	0.3	0.4	0.9	1.2	7.0	7.8	8.5	7.3	4.9	26.7	26.7	10.0	1.2	71.6	38.9	48.5	51.5
01862	NORTH BILLERICA	93.5	92.4	2.1	2.3	3.0	3.6	2.2	2.7	6.4	6.7	6.9	6.5	6.4	34.1	23.6	8.1	1.4	76.2	36.5	54.0	46.0
01863	NORTH CHELMSFORD	93.1	91.6	0.8	1.0	4.5	5.6	1.1	1.4	6.6	6.6	6.7	6.2	5.6	30.1	26.5	10.4	1.5	76.2	38.8	47.3	52.8
01864	NORTH READING	97.5	96.9	0.4	0.5	1.3	1.7	0.7	0.9	7.4	8.2	8.4	6.0	4.0	27.4	27.4	10.1	1.1	72.0	39.3	49.2	50.8
01867	READING	96.5	95.6	0.4	0.4	2.2	2.9	0.8	1.1	6.9	7.6	7.5	6.3	4.2	26.2	27.2	12.1	2.1	73.9	40.4	48.3	51.7
01876	TEWKSBURY	96.4	95.7	0.7	0.8	1.6	2.1	1.2	1.5	6.8	7.2	7.3	5.8	4.7	30.0	26.3	10.8	1.3	75.0	39.0	49.0	51.0
01879	TYNGSBORO	95.6	94.7	0.5	0.6	2.6	3.3	1.1	1.4	8.7	8.8	8.0	6.6	4.9	31.7	24.4	6.2	0.7	70.1	35.7	49.4	50.6
01880	WAKEFIELD	96.9	96.4	0.5	0.5	1.4	1.8	0.8	1.0	6.3	6.3	6.2	6.0	5.3	29.0	26.4	12.1	2.5	77.3	40.0	47.4	52.6
01886	WESTFORD	93.7	92.1	0.3	0.3	4.8	6.2	1.1	1.3	8.6	9.7	9.3	6.5	3.7	27.9	26.6	6.8	1.0	68.1	37.7	49.8	50.3
01887	WILMINGTON	96.3	95.4	0.4	0.5	2.1	2.6	1.0	1.2	7.9	8.2	7.8	6.1	4.6	30.1	24.2	9.8	1.5	72.3	37.6	49.4	50.6
01890	WINCHESTER	93.1	91.7	0.7	0.8	4.6	5.8	1.0	1.2	7.0	7.9	7.6	5.8	3.7	23.6	27.5	13.5	3.3	73.7	41.9	47.4	52.6
01901	LYNN	57.4	54.5	14.7	14.5	2.2	2.2	26.3	29.0	4.7	4.0	4.1	3.8	4.7	22.1	21.2	29.2	6.2	85.2	50.2	45.1	54.9
01902	LYNN	61.4	57.1	13.3	13.9	7.0	7.8	23.0	27.2	7.5	7.2	7.7	7.7	8.0	29.4	21.1	9.7	1.8	73.0	33.3	48.5	51.5
01904	LYNN	88.1	85.6	3.9	4.4	2.4	2.9	6.2	8.0	6.1	6.2	6.6	6.4	6.2	27.3	26.2	12.7	2.3	77.1	39.6	48.2	51.8
01905	LYNN	65.9	61.6	10.1	10.8	8.9	10.1	18.4	22.1	7.8	7.5	8.6	8.1	7.7	28.5	20.7	9.6	1.5	71.2	32.8	48.8	51.2
01906	SAUGUS	97.3	96.6	0.5	0.5	1.3	1.6	1.0	1.4	5.0	5.3	6.1	5.6	5.1	27.2	27.8	15.6	2.5	80.2	42.5	47.9	52.2
01907	SWAMPSCOTT	97.5	96.9	0.7	0.9	0.7	0.9	1.3	1.7	6.0	6.7	6.9	6.1	4.4	23.8	28.6	13.8	3.7	76.4	42.8	46.3	53.7
01908	NAHANT	97.1	96.5	0.4	0.5	1.1	1.4	1.1	1.4	4.4	4.9	5.3	5.5	3.6	23.5	33.6	15.9	3.5	81.9	46.5	48.1	51.9
01913	AMESBURY	97.2	96.7	0.6	0.8	0.6	0.8	1.0	1.3	6.6	6.7	7.4	7.1	5.8	29.1	25.2	10.2	1.8	74.6	37.9	48.2	51.8
01915	BEVERLY	96.0	95.1	1.0	1.2	1.3	1.7	1.8	2.4	6.1	6.2	6.1	6.9	6.9	27.7	25.1	12.2	2.9	78.1	39.2	47.4	52.6
01921	BOXFORD	97.4	96.7	0.3	0.4	1.3	1.6	0.9	1.2	7.0	8.8	10.3	7.5	3.5	22.0	31.3	8.7	0.9	68.7	40.7	49.9	50.1
01922	BYFIELD	98.3	97.8	0.6	0.7	0.5	0.7	0.7	1.0	7.7	9.1	9.0	6.7	3.7	26.9	28.9	7.4	0.7	70.0	38.6	49.5	50.6
01923	DANVERS	97.7	97.1	0.4	0.5	1.1	1.5	0.9	1.2	5.4	5.8	6.8	6.5	5.8	25.6	27.0	14.3	2.7	77.7	41.7	46.6	53.4
01929	ESSEX	98.5	98.2	0.2	0.2	0.4	0.6	0.9	1.3	5.5	5.7	7.3	7.1	5.8	25.2	30.0	11.8	1.4	77.1	41.3	48.9	51.1
01930	GLOUCESTER	97.0	96.3	0.6	0.8	0.7	1.0	1.5	2.1	5.7	5.9	6.2	5.8	5.6	27.0	28.2	13.4	2.3	78.7	41.5	47.9	52.1
01938	IPSWICH	97.6	97.0	0.4	0.5	0.8	1.1	1.0	1.5	5.6	6.2	6.9	6.0	4.4	24.6	30.7	13.2	2.5	77.3	43.1	47.6	52.4
01940	LYNNFIELD	96.7	95.9	0.4	0.5	2.0	2.5	0.7	0.9	6.2	7.0	7.1	6.1	4.3	21.7	30.0	15.3	2.4	75.8	43.6	49.2	50.8
01944	MANCHESTER	98.9	98.7	0.1	0.1	0.4	0.5	0.8	1.0	4.8	5.5	7.0	7.2	4.5	21.3	32.2	15.2	2.3	78.0	44.8	47.3	52.7
01945	MARBLEHEAD	97.6	97.0	0.4	0.5	1.0	1.3	0.9	1.2	6.2	7.1	7.1	5.6	3.4	24.0	30.7	13.5	2.3	75.9	43.1	47.3	52.7
01949	MIDDLETON	95.6	94.9	1.6	1.7	1.2	1.5	5.8	7.0	6.2	6.8	6.9	6.2	6.2	33.2	24.4	9.1	1.1	76.4	37.5	56.9	43.1
01950	NEWBURYPORT	98.1	97.7	0.4	0.5	0.6	0.8	0.9	1.2	5.4	5.7	6.0	5.8	4.7	27.5	30.7	12.0	2.3	79.1	42.4	46.5	53.5
01951	NEWBURY	98.4	98.0	0.2	0.3	0.4	0.6	1.0	1.4	5.4	6.3	6.6	7.2	4.0	24.7	32.5	11.7	1.7	76.8	43.0	47.8	52.2
01952	SALISBURY	97.5	97.1	0.4	0.5	0.4	0.5	1.2	1.6	6.1	6.2	6.5	6.2	5.4	28.5	28.5	11.2	1.4	77.2	40.2	49.5	50.5
01960	PEABODY	93.9	92.3	1.0	1.2	1.4	1.8	3.4	4.7	5.8	6.0	6.5	5.9	5.1	26.8	26.4	14.9	2.5	77.9	41.5	48.0	52.0
01966	ROCKPORT	97.7	97.3	0.3	0.3	0.5	0.6	1.1	1.4	4.5	5.1	6.2	6.1	4.3	20.7	32.7	16.8	3.8	80.3	46.8	46.3	53.7
01969	ROWLEY	98.4	98.0	0.2	0.3	0.5	0.6	0.9	1.1	6.8	7.7	8.2	6.8	4.4	27.6	28.9	8.0	1.6	72.8	39.6	49.4	50.6
01970	SALEM	85.4	82.7	3.2	3.6	2.0	2.5	11.2	13.8	5.6	5.4	6.0	6.2	7.5	31.8	23.8	11.7	2.1	79.8	37.4	46.4	53.6
01982	SOUTH HAMILTON	94.3	92.8	0.5	0.5	4.2	5.4	1.0	1.3	6.7	7.3	8.3	6.8	5.0	29.4	26.2	9.3	1.2	73.2	37.2	49.0	51.0
01983	TOPSFIELD	97.5	97.0	0.5	0.6	0.8	1.1	1.4	1.9	6.0	7.5	9.0	6.7	4.2	21.9	29.3	13.6	2.0	73.3	42.3	49.2	50.8
01984	WENHAM	97.8	97.2	0.4	0.5	1.4	1.8	0.6	0.9	4.9	5.7	6.4	15.6	15.1	16.6	22.2	11.8	1.8	79.5	31.5	45.1	55.0
01985	WEST NEWBURY	98.5	98.1	0.2	0.2	0.5	0.7	0.7	0.9	7.0	8.6	8.6	6.8	3.8	23.2	32.3	8.5	1.2	71.4	41.1	50.1	49.9
02019	BELLINGHAM	96.9	96.4	0.9	1.1	0.9	1.1	1.2	1.5	7.0	7.2	7.6	6.5	4.7	31.1	25.4	9.5	0.8	74.0	37.8	48.9	51.1
02021	CANTON	92.5	91.1	2.9	3.3	3.0	3.8	1.4	1.7	6.3	6.6	6.8	6.0	4.8	27.0	26.0	13.4	3.2	76.5	40.8	47.3	52.7
02025	COHASSET	98.2	97.9	0.2	0.2	0.8	0.9	0.7	0.8	7.0	8.1	8.4	6.2	3.4	22.2	29.3	13.2	2.2	72.3	42.1	48.5	51.5
02026	DEDHAM	94.4	93.5	1.6	1.8	1.9	2.4	2.4	2.9	6.0	6.3	6.4	5.8	4.9	28.6	25.6	14.0	2.5	77.8	40.6	48.4	51.6
02030	DOVER	95.2	94.1	0.4	0.5	3.6	4.6	1.2	1.5	7.2	9.6	10.0	7.2	3.1	20.5	30.7	10.6	1.1	68.4	41.0	48.7	51.3
	MASSACHUSETTS	84.5	82.9	5.4	5.7	3.8	4.5	6.8	7.8	6.2	6.3	6.8	7.0	7.0	28.9	24.5	11.4	2.1	76.8	37.6	48.3	51.7
	UNITED STATES	75.1	73.6	12.3	12.5	3.8	4.2	12.5	14.1	6.9	6.7	7.2	7.0	7.3	28.6	23.8	10.8	1.7	75.1	36.0	49.1	50.9

ZIP CODE #	POST OFFICE NAME	2004 Per Capita Income	2004 HH Income Base	2004 HOUSEHOLD INCOME DISTRIBUTION (%) Less than $25,000	$25,000 to $49,999	$50,000 to $99,999	$100,000 to $149,999	$150,000 or More	MEDIAN HOUSEHOLD INCOME 2004	2009	2004 National Centile	2004 State Centile	2004 Home Value Base	2004 HOME VALUE DISTRIBUTION (%) Less than $50,000	$50,000 to $89,999	$90,000 to $174,999	$175,000 to $399,999	$400,000 or More	2004 Median Home Value
01612	PAXTON	39572	1477	7.0	15.8	34.3	25.4	17.5	87670	110409	97	83	1404	0.0	0.4	8.5	75.9	15.3	273397
01701	FRAMINGHAM	47901	13932	9.1	16.1	32.7	23.2	18.9	86247	112549	96	82	10448	0.0	0.2	3.2	66.0	30.6	343539
01702	FRAMINGHAM	25190	12389	25.3	25.7	30.0	13.4	5.6	48716	63469	70	19	4644	0.6	1.4	12.4	68.3	17.2	284112
01718	VILLAGE OF NAGOG WOO	51668	170	8.2	12.4	34.1	22.4	22.9	91939	119490	97	86	111	0.0	0.0	4.5	72.1	23.4	297500
01719	BOXBOROUGH	52057	1911	4.8	12.0	28.2	24.3	30.7	109177	144811	99	93	1450	0.0	1.5	12.7	17.5	68.4	529242
01720	ACTON	57330	7491	6.5	11.0	24.8	23.5	34.2	114241	152975	99	94	5828	0.2	0.3	4.4	24.2	70.9	498071
01721	ASHLAND	40436	6005	8.3	16.7	35.0	24.9	15.1	84268	109228	96	81	4764	0.2	0.2	2.5	67.4	29.7	327524
01730	BEDFORD	53340	4630	6.8	10.9	25.4	27.9	29.1	111920	148566	99	94	3836	1.2	0.7	0.8	22.3	75.1	515918
01731	HANSCOM AFB	20246	838	4.3	36.2	43.9	11.2	4.4	57475	69893	82	37	52	11.5	3.9	0.0	28.9	55.8	460000
01740	BOLTON	53705	1518	3.7	9.0	23.1	29.1	35.1	123213	156684	99	96	1424	0.0	0.0	0.6	23.3	76.1	561270
01741	CARLISLE	84071	1629	6.7	7.2	14.1	17.5	54.5	160684	212751	100	99	1532	0.8	0.3	0.1	4.1	94.8	706391
01742	CONCORD	73599	6070	7.0	10.2	22.0	21.5	39.3	123283	166551	99	97	5068	0.4	0.3	0.4	11.3	87.7	686232
01745	FAYVILLE	57036	123	11.4	13.8	22.0	17.1	35.8	105691	150000	99	92	90	0.0	0.0	0.0	32.2	67.8	513514
01746	HOLLISTON	42872	4848	8.4	11.9	31.0	24.1	24.5	97301	124596	98	88	4294	0.0	0.1	3.0	58.1	38.7	368137
01747	HOPEDALE	30471	2345	14.5	16.1	39.9	23.8	5.8	72116	87987	92	66	1858	0.0	0.0	12.2	71.3	16.5	267806
01748	HOPKINTON	55911	4639	6.4	8.9	26.8	23.8	34.2	115222	152072	99	95	4198	0.2	0.2	2.3	36.2	61.1	477667
01749	HUDSON	33892	7145	13.2	17.8	36.5	21.9	10.6	73188	91993	93	67	5085	0.2	0.7	8.0	73.0	18.1	281716
01752	MARLBOROUGH	38136	15395	14.9	19.0	34.6	19.7	11.9	70581	91179	91	63	9931	0.2	2.4	9.6	67.3	20.5	282433
01754	MAYNARD	34358	4262	14.6	17.1	35.7	23.7	9.0	75511	98069	93	69	2999	0.0	0.5	3.8	81.8	14.0	287244
01756	MENDON	35355	1968	10.3	14.2	32.7	26.2	16.7	86256	110597	97	82	1747	0.0	0.0	4.2	52.6	43.3	369079
01757	MILFORD	30073	10793	19.7	21.3	31.9	19.2	7.9	62209	79118	86	48	7307	0.2	0.9	9.0	76.9	13.0	268054
01760	NATICK	49376	13298	11.0	14.1	32.6	23.7	18.7	86602	113700	97	82	9528	0.5	0.2	2.7	53.1	43.5	376752
01770	SHERBORN	83561	1422	5.1	7.7	16.0	18.8	52.5	158370	218136	100	99	1323	0.0	0.0	0.0	5.8	94.2	778915
01772	SOUTHBOROUGH	58685	3111	6.3	10.0	20.4	22.0	41.4	129966	168153	100	98	2757	0.1	0.2	1.2	30.8	67.6	515889
01773	LINCOLN	99656	1968	4.9	6.9	20.9	20.9	46.4	139541	191716	100	98	1755	0.7	0.0	0.0	7.9	91.5	866518
01775	STOW	51495	2260	7.4	7.2	24.1	34.1	27.2	115518	147490	99	95	2005	0.5	0.0	0.4	35.1	64.1	460622
01776	SUDBURY	72567	5653	5.6	6.5	17.2	22.4	48.3	145977	188622	100	99	5278	0.0	0.0	0.3	13.6	86.2	652513
01778	WAYLAND	74816	4663	7.0	8.1	23.4	20.9	40.7	128761	168350	100	98	4343	0.3	0.1	0.4	14.8	84.4	621133
01801	WOBURN	33378	15185	14.6	19.7	37.8	19.1	8.9	67671	86238	90	59	9723	0.4	0.2	2.7	70.5	26.2	336427
01803	BURLINGTON	39472	8351	7.5	14.0	33.4	27.0	18.2	91365	118867	97	86	6798	0.4	1.1	1.6	56.2	40.7	376023
01810	ANDOVER	58090	11462	10.5	10.3	23.9	20.8	34.4	109987	151316	99	93	9106	0.4	0.6	2.6	23.8	72.6	526626
01821	BILLERICA	32253	10056	9.2	15.4	40.0	24.3	11.0	80739	102303	95	77	8628	0.2	0.6	6.2	70.9	22.2	308596
01824	CHELMSFORD	39913	9348	9.3	14.5	31.6	28.0	16.6	90288	116227	97	84	7952	1.7	0.9	3.1	63.9	30.4	340283
01826	DRACUT	30079	10661	12.2	18.9	42.1	19.3	7.5	68544	85050	91	60	8320	0.2	1.6	16.5	71.8	10.0	243721
01827	DUNSTABLE	37851	1017	6.5	9.1	32.7	28.9	22.8	101782	126589	98	90	951	0.5	0.0	1.7	42.8	55.0	421300
01830	HAVERHILL	30831	9653	23.7	19.9	33.4	16.0	7.0	57839	74804	83	38	5722	0.4	1.0	14.9	73.8	9.9	240151
01832	HAVERHILL	27814	8878	19.9	21.4	38.5	15.3	4.9	57624	71870	82	37	5382	0.4	0.8	20.5	70.1	8.3	231197
01833	GEORGETOWN	37052	2742	12.4	9.8	32.2	27.1	18.5	92133	115825	97	87	2393	0.0	0.0	1.3	52.6	46.2	386115
01834	GROVELAND	32384	2096	9.5	14.6	38.4	24.8	12.7	83182	104590	96	80	1853	1.0	0.3	2.2	61.1	35.4	348081
01835	HAVERHILL	31396	5386	12.6	21.2	37.2	21.3	7.8	67344	87337	90	58	3829	0.1	0.5	15.1	74.5	9.8	242917
01840	LAWRENCE	12339	1996	66.5	19.6	11.0	1.6	1.4	13898	17101	1	1	85	0.0	11.8	54.1	18.8	15.3	143403
01841	LAWRENCE	14631	14483	40.3	29.1	22.1	6.6	1.9	31796	39121	17	4	4502	0.9	5.8	45.2	45.8	2.4	171967
01843	LAWRENCE	21340	8982	30.1	27.7	30.1	9.2	2.9	42173	53011	53	11	3915	0.3	2.0	34.0	62.3	1.5	193211
01844	METHUEN	28719	17682	18.9	22.1	35.0	17.2	6.8	60784	77911	85	45	12730	0.6	0.7	14.0	76.5	8.3	241584
01845	NORTH ANDOVER	46812	10325	12.3	14.4	26.6	22.7	24.0	92033	120829	97	87	7596	0.6	0.1	5.8	38.3	55.2	436725
01850	LOWELL	19246	5663	23.7	30.4	35.9	8.3	1.7	46525	55334	65	17	2742	0.3	1.9	44.7	51.8	1.3	178808
01851	LOWELL	22328	10029	21.0	28.2	34.4	12.1	4.4	50641	62695	73	23	4529	1.5	0.8	28.2	66.5	3.0	209082
01852	LOWELL	24950	13192	30.5	24.2	29.7	10.0	5.6	44879	55402	61	15	5838	0.8	1.8	29.8	58.4	9.1	211209
01854	LOWELL	20508	9116	31.1	26.6	28.7	10.3	3.3	42445	52793	54	12	3947	0.4	1.5	28.4	67.0	2.7	206665
01860	MERRIMAC	31704	2302	11.8	21.5	33.8	23.3	9.7	72099	96664	92	66	1972	1.6	3.0	8.6	55.0	31.8	317090
01862	NORTH BILLERICA	29541	3159	8.3	16.7	40.3	25.3	9.4	80137	101525	95	76	2567	1.1	2.4	4.4	72.3	19.8	318691
01863	NORTH CHELMSFORD	37561	3551	12.2	17.5	37.3	21.8	11.3	76043	99023	94	70	2811	0.2	0.9	7.9	79.1	11.9	270566
01864	NORTH READING	40364	4844	6.8	14.4	32.7	25.5	20.6	93025	120513	97	87	4413	0.8	0.3	4.6	43.3	51.1	405345
01867	READING	43397	8660	10.3	12.2	29.9	26.8	20.8	95429	125255	98	88	7297	0.3	0.0	1.8	44.7	53.2	413702
01876	TEWKSBURY	34229	10181	8.8	14.9	37.4	27.8	11.1	83556	106309	96	80	9148	0.5	0.7	3.3	76.6	18.9	305941
01879	TYNGSBORO	34734	4039	10.0	15.1	37.3	24.9	12.8	82447	103979	96	79	3430	0.6	0.6	10.9	60.9	27.1	315467
01880	WAKEFIELD	39510	9768	10.9	17.0	33.8	24.4	14.0	81053	106149	95	78	6939	0.2	0.2	2.2	57.2	40.1	372218
01886	WESTFORD	49072	7236	5.4	8.1	24.9	29.8	31.8	117657	149487	99	95	6674	0.6	0.2	2.1	42.1	55.0	427663
01887	WILMINGTON	32577	7176	8.1	13.0	40.2	28.4	10.4	84578	106162	96	81	6578	0.3	0.2	2.8	66.5	30.3	345462
01890	WINCHESTER	69961	7763	7.4	9.5	23.8	22.9	36.4	118839	157614	99	96	6367	0.1	0.0	1.3	15.5	83.2	641893
01901	LYNN	13004	1014	77.3	14.6	6.4	1.7	0.0	11070	12808	1	0	29	0.0	0.0	51.7	41.4	6.9	173214
01902	LYNN	20241	17684	33.0	28.1	26.7	9.1	3.1	39701	49355	45	9	6578	0.9	1.6	27.0	63.7	6.7	213651
01904	LYNN	30144	6723	14.4	20.2	38.2	21.5	5.7	68546	86513	91	60	5296	0.4	0.5	11.1	82.1	6.0	248749
01905	LYNN	19999	8440	28.6	27.6	30.4	10.1	3.4	44794	55751	61	15	4165	0.3	0.4	24.8	72.2	2.3	212491
01906	SAUGUS	33769	10079	15.1	18.9	37.2	20.3	8.6	68975	89196	91	61	8249	0.5	0.6	3.2	72.3	23.5	313263
01907	SWAMPSCOTT	48620	5952	10.4	15.7	30.2	23.6	20.1	87328	114396	97	83	4561	0.1	1.1	2.7	43.6	52.5	412839
01908	NAHANT	59291	1617	11.3	17.2	33.2	17.3	21.2	81794	109697	96	78	1213	0.0	0.3	1.0	39.2	59.4	449142
01913	AMESBURY	31379	6553	17.5	19.7	35.8	20.5	6.5	65156	83691	89	54	4409	0.3	1.1	13.0	67.5	18.1	273890
01915	BEVERLY	38021	15932	15.9	19.8	34.5	19.2	10.7	67736	88393	90	59	9906	0.4	0.7	3.7	62.5	32.6	341386
01921	BOXFORD	66592	2733	3.2	7.1	19.5	25.0	45.2	139987	183766	100	99	2660	0.0	0.0	3.5	10.5	86.1	615401
01922	BYFIELD	47379	990	6.8	6.3	33.8	29.8	23.3	102970	128989	98	91	861	0.0	0.0	0.4	37.1	62.6	452415
01923	DANVERS	35487	9748	12.6	19.7	35.7	20.0	12.0	72836	95988	92	66	7465	1.1	0.7	4.4	61.4	32.5	349923
01929	ESSEX	44640	1294	17.4	14.8	35.2	18.6	14.1	73419	99656	93	67	860	0.0	0.5	0.9	44.5	54.1	421472
01930	GLOUCESTER	33971	12922	19.6	23.0	35.1	13.8	8.4	57765	74895	82	37	7997	0.0	0.8	7.2	60.8	31.3	315330
01938	IPSWICH	44909	5485	16.0	17.8	30.1	19.7	16.4	74394	102031	93	68	4183	0.2	0.0	3.9	45.6	50.3	401656
01940	LYNNFIELD	54115	4251	7.2	11.3	28.8	23.0	29.7	104658	141253	98	92	4021	0.2	0.0	1.9	26.4	71.6	494493
01944	MANCHESTER	71000	2192	12.9	11.6	26.0	21.2	28.3	98771	136152	98	89	1657	0.7	0.0	0.4	10.4	88.5	676192
01945	MARBLEHEAD	67428	8437	10.9	13.0	26.0	19.9	30.3	100333	139383	98	89	6528	0.1	0.0	1.0	25.4	73.5	530432
01949	MIDDLETON	38274	2476	10.7	12.0	27.7	28.5	21.0	98910	125208	98	89	2164	0.5	0.6	1.1	43.5	54.3	425068
01950	NEWBURYPORT	47507	7666	12.7	18.8	32.7	20.4	15.4	76044	102380	94	70	5050	0.2	0.1	3.8	52.8	43.2	375216
01951	NEWBURY	52578	1646	13.4	17.4	30.3	18.5	20.5	82325	110037	96	79	1315	0.0	0.0	2.4	46.8	50.7	403815
01952	SALISBURY	26483	3270	18.2	24.3	37.3	16.5	3.8	57806	71954	82	38	2327	1.9	1.1	15.5	63.3	18.2	266050
01960	PEABODY	32338	19235	16.6	19.8	34.8	20.1	8.7	66956	86352	90	57	14007	1.5	2.4	3.1	68.8	24.3	319199
01966	ROCKPORT	39210	3518	21.3	17.7	31.8	16.4	12.9	63766	84469	88	52	2484	0.4	0.0	0.7	42.4	56.5	428673
01969	ROWLEY	35283	2027	11.0	14.8	36.3	21.4	16.6	80627	106428	95	77	1715	0.0	0.0	2.2	42.1	55.7	429848
01970	SALEM	31073	18208	21.0	25.1	32.6	15.0	6.3	54046	70993	78	30	9358	0.2	0.5	6.1	77.1	16.3	288212
01982	SOUTH HAMILTON	47119	2716	8.5	12.8	33.4	20.2	25.0	90925	119437	97	85	2278	0.0	0.0	2.6	37.7	59.7	449552
01983	TOPSFIELD	53071	2248	7.9	10.2	22.1	29.0	30.8	116922	155840	99	95	2017	0.0	0.0	0.8	24.9	74.3	521709
01984	WENHAM	54765	1299	13.2	9.2	21.6	23.6	32.4	111591	155725	99	94	1117	0.4	0.4	0.6	24.5	74.1	566088
01985	WEST NEWBURY	46591	1540	7.7	7.8	26.8	26.2	31.6	111477	148508	99	93	1437	0.0	0.0	1.3	31.2	67.6	488908
02019	BELLINGHAM	31209	5746	11.0	15.9	41.1	24.1	8.0	77836	95951	94	74	4858	0.3	0.1	8.5	82.2	8.9	243397
02021	CANTON	46372	8178	12.2	13.8	32.2	23.7	18.2	85897	113066	96	81	6296	0.6	0.0	4.8	47.3	47.4	390446
02025	COHASSET	58545	2689	11.1	11.8	22.0	24.4	30.7	108643	148219	99	93	2349	0.0	0.0	0.8	20.1	79.1	623047
02026	DEDHAM	37604	8568	13.2	16.4	36.0	22.2	12.2	77485	100618	94	73	6850	0.1	0.1	2.9	63.8	33.1	346685
02030	DOVER	95363	1905	2.9	7.1	14.3	16.4	59.2	184363	247589	100	100	1811	0.0	0.0	0.0	3.8	96.2	934610
	MASSACHUSETTS	33908		19.9	21.2	32.0	16.1	10.9	61110	77759				0.8	1.2	14.8	55.7	27.5	282585
	UNITED STATES	25866		24.7	27.1	30.8	10.9	6.5	48124	56710				10.9	15.0	33.7	30.1	10.4	145905

ZIP CODE	FINANCIAL SERVICES				THE HOME						ENTERTAINMENT						PERSONAL			
					Home Improvements		Furnishings													
# POST OFFICE NAME	Auto Loan	Home Loan	Invest-ments	Retire-ment Plans	Home Repair	Lawn & Garden	Comput-ers & Hard-ware	Major Appli-ances	TV, Radio, Sound Equip-ment	Furni-ture	Dine out/ Carry out	Sports Equip-ment	Fees & Tickets	Toys & Games	Travel	Cable TV	Apparel & Services	Auto Repairs	Health Insur-ance	Pets & Supplies
01612 PAXTON	151	184	203	183	182	187	167	167	157	167	197	191	177	203	173	155	196	162	156	183
01701 FRAMINGHAM	142	173	223	174	168	175	165	160	157	165	198	187	175	209	169	155	198	159	146	173
01702 FRAMINGHAM	80	85	125	86	83	91	92	86	93	91	118	101	93	123	92	94	117	90	84	95
01718 VILLAGE OF NAGOG WOO	159	182	225	189	180	184	180	174	171	179	216	208	186	221	181	166	214	176	159	190
01719 BOXBOROUGH	186	209	231	220	202	207	198	191	184	201	235	224	209	236	196	176	234	190	170	212
01720 ACTON	196	250	291	252	242	247	223	218	206	225	261	252	243	275	229	202	263	212	195	238
01721 ASHLAND	133	158	185	163	154	157	149	145	140	149	177	171	157	182	151	135	176	144	131	159
01730 BEDFORD	178	223	268	221	218	225	204	202	192	205	242	233	218	254	211	190	242	198	184	218
01731 HANSCOM AFB	111	73	70	83	67	78	105	91	106	99	133	121	91	120	88	97	128	107	84	104
01740 BOLTON	204	255	277	263	246	248	224	218	204	227	260	253	247	270	228	198	262	211	194	242
01741 CARLISLE	307	397	487	400	386	402	348	342	320	354	406	390	389	425	362	317	411	329	311	375
01742 CONCORD	251	328	416	319	321	340	292	291	275	295	346	329	321	364	308	276	348	282	270	314
01745 FAYVILLE	158	241	323	222	230	240	204	202	192	206	240	228	230	273	220	195	247	194	179	212
01746 HOLLISTON	159	197	215	201	192	193	176	173	162	177	205	201	190	215	180	157	206	168	155	191
01747 HOPEDALE	107	120	127	123	117	118	114	113	107	115	135	132	117	136	113	102	133	111	102	123
01748 HOPKINTON	219	270	296	276	262	266	241	235	222	243	282	272	263	292	245	216	283	228	212	260
01749 HUDSON	112	131	150	133	129	131	125	122	118	124	149	144	130	154	126	115	147	121	112	134
01752 MARLBOROUGH	124	135	159	140	133	137	136	131	131	135	164	155	139	168	135	126	162	132	122	144
01754 MAYNARD	106	124	147	127	122	124	119	116	112	118	141	138	124	147	120	109	140	116	105	127
01756 MENDON	139	164	167	166	158	156	148	147	137	151	173	171	155	179	148	131	172	143	129	161
01757 MILFORD	100	112	125	113	111	115	109	107	106	108	132	126	113	136	110	103	130	107	101	118
01760 NATICK	147	180	237	181	175	184	171	166	164	172	207	193	183	218	176	163	207	165	152	180
01770 SHERBORN	296	399	547	391	389	420	348	345	324	356	410	387	395	431	371	327	416	331	320	374
01772 SOUTHBOROUGH	220	286	342	285	276	284	251	247	231	255	293	282	276	309	259	227	296	238	220	268
01773 LINCOLN	315	419	555	414	408	436	366	362	339	374	430	408	413	452	387	340	436	347	333	394
01775 STOW	189	232	258	240	225	228	209	203	192	211	243	236	227	252	212	185	245	198	181	224
01776 SUDBURY	282	356	421	361	346	357	317	311	292	321	370	357	348	386	326	287	373	301	281	341
01778 WAYLAND	259	344	440	336	335	355	302	300	282	306	356	339	336	376	319	283	360	289	277	325
01801 WOBURN	106	118	138	120	116	121	117	114	113	116	142	134	121	145	118	110	140	115	107	125
01803 BURLINGTON	131	168	212	165	164	169	155	153	146	155	184	178	165	194	161	144	184	152	137	164
01810 ANDOVER	205	249	283	254	242	247	228	223	212	230	269	259	244	278	231	206	268	218	201	244
01821 BILLERICA	123	145	158	146	141	143	135	133	127	135	160	156	141	167	136	123	159	131	121	146
01824 CHELMSFORD	136	164	189	164	161	166	153	151	144	152	181	175	161	188	156	141	180	148	139	165
01826 DRACUT	106	122	134	123	121	123	116	115	111	115	139	135	121	146	117	109	138	113	107	126
01827 DUNSTABLE	151	188	204	194	182	183	166	161	151	168	192	187	182	199	168	146	193	155	143	179
01830 HAVERHILL	100	108	126	109	107	113	111	107	109	108	136	126	113	139	111	107	133	109	104	117
01832 HAVERHILL	93	95	108	96	93	99	100	96	98	98	123	113	100	123	98	96	120	98	92	105
01833 GEORGETOWN	142	163	171	165	161	165	151	151	143	150	179	175	158	185	153	141	177	147	141	168
01834 GROVELAND	122	152	161	152	149	147	135	135	125	135	157	158	144	168	138	122	157	130	121	149
01835 HAVERHILL	106	118	128	121	115	116	115	113	109	115	137	134	117	140	114	104	136	113	101	123
01840 LAWRENCE	30	30	58	27	28	33	34	33	39	37	51	36	34	53	35	43	52	35	34	35
01841 LAWRENCE	53	52	93	48	49	57	59	56	67	63	86	63	59	88	60	71	86	60	58	61
01843 LAWRENCE	72	74	108	71	72	80	79	77	84	81	107	87	80	110	80	87	107	80	77	83
01844 METHUEN	97	110	125	108	108	113	106	104	104	105	130	120	110	136	108	104	129	104	101	115
01845 NORTH ANDOVER	163	187	221	191	184	193	180	176	172	180	217	204	190	222	183	170	215	175	165	193
01850 LOWELL	70	71	79	71	70	75	76	73	76	74	94	87	76	96	75	74	92	75	71	80
01851 LOWELL	86	88	107	90	86	90	92	90	91	93	115	106	92	115	91	88	114	94	83	97
01852 LOWELL	80	80	103	80	78	86	88	84	90	87	113	97	87	113	86	89	111	87	83	92
01854 LOWELL	71	72	101	73	70	76	79	74	81	79	102	88	79	105	78	81	102	78	72	82
01860 MERRIMAC	126	129	117	127	131	135	119	125	118	119	146	148	120	151	121	117	142	121	123	150
01862 NORTH BILLERICA	105	129	140	127	126	127	117	116	110	117	139	135	125	148	120	108	138	113	106	128
01863 NORTH CHELMSFORD	117	134	164	138	132	136	132	128	126	131	158	152	136	161	133	122	156	129	118	140
01864 NORTH READING	148	187	207	186	182	182	166	164	154	166	194	191	178	206	170	150	194	159	146	180
01867 READING	145	184	224	182	178	184	168	165	158	168	199	190	180	211	173	156	200	161	150	178
01876 TEWKSBURY	125	153	167	152	150	150	139	138	131	138	164	161	148	174	142	127	164	134	126	152
01879 TYNGSBORO	142	159	166	165	153	152	149	147	139	152	176	173	153	178	147	131	174	145	128	161
01880 WAKEFIELD	122	151	186	150	148	154	142	139	135	141	169	161	150	179	146	133	169	137	128	150
01886 WESTFORD	194	239	260	246	232	235	214	209	196	216	249	243	233	259	218	190	251	203	187	231
01887 WILMINGTON	126	158	171	157	153	152	140	139	130	141	164	162	149	174	143	126	164	135	124	153
01890 WINCHESTER	228	292	374	288	286	301	266	263	251	268	316	301	289	332	277	249	317	257	242	284
01901 LYNN	23	22	36	21	21	25	26	24	28	26	36	28	26	36	26	30	35	26	26	27
01902 LYNN	63	65	101	64	63	71	73	68	76	72	97	79	73	101	73	78	96	72	68	74
01904 LYNN	101	116	134	114	114	120	112	110	110	111	137	127	118	144	115	109	136	109	106	120
01905 LYNN	70	74	96	73	72	79	78	75	80	77	100	86	80	104	79	81	99	77	75	82
01906 SAUGUS	110	130	146	127	128	134	122	121	119	121	149	139	130	155	126	118	147	119	117	132
01907 SWAMPSCOTT	150	181	227	181	177	186	172	168	164	172	207	195	183	215	176	163	206	167	157	183
01908 NAHANT	165	192	222	190	189	200	184	181	178	182	223	209	192	230	188	177	220	180	175	198
01913 AMESBURY	102	116	130	117	114	118	113	111	109	112	137	130	117	142	114	106	135	110	103	121
01915 BEVERLY	120	132	161	134	130	138	133	128	130	132	163	149	137	167	134	129	161	130	123	141
01921 BOXFORD	267	333	361	343	322	325	293	285	266	297	339	330	322	353	298	258	342	275	254	316
01922 BYFIELD	182	226	240	227	222	219	202	201	187	201	235	235	215	250	206	181	235	194	180	222
01923 DANVERS	117	135	156	135	133	140	130	128	125	129	157	148	135	161	132	123	155	127	121	140
01929 ESSEX	142	167	196	171	164	166	160	156	151	159	190	185	166	197	161	146	188	155	141	171
01930 GLOUCESTER	103	115	133	116	114	119	115	111	111	112	139	131	118	144	115	109	137	112	106	122
01938 IPSWICH	139	165	189	165	163	168	155	153	147	154	186	177	163	192	159	145	184	151	143	167
01940 LYNNFIELD	182	232	280	228	228	238	209	208	197	210	248	238	226	260	219	196	248	202	193	225
01944 MANCHESTER	209	264	325	261	260	273	240	239	227	242	286	272	260	297	251	226	286	233	222	259
01945 MARBLEHEAD	197	247	306	246	242	251	227	224	214	228	270	258	244	283	235	212	270	220	205	242
01949 MIDDLETON	162	197	208	198	193	192	177	176	164	178	207	205	187	216	180	159	206	170	158	194
01950 NEWBURYPORT	139	155	184	158	152	159	152	149	147	152	185	175	157	188	153	144	182	150	140	164
01951 NEWBURY	166	193	223	197	191	194	184	181	174	183	218	214	191	227	186	169	217	179	165	200
01952 SALISBURY	103	92	75	86	99	108	87	97	93	86	112	113	84	115	91	96	106	95	107	124
01960 PEABODY	106	117	135	116	116	124	115	113	114	114	142	130	119	147	117	114	140	113	112	125
01966 ROCKPORT	114	123	144	124	122	130	121	120	120	120	149	141	124	152	123	119	147	121	117	136
01969 ROWLEY	126	156	166	157	154	151	140	139	129	139	163	163	148	173	143	125	162	134	125	154
01970 SALEM	89	96	123	98	94	100	100	95	99	99	124	113	102	127	100	98	122	98	91	105
01982 SOUTH HAMILTON	183	225	249	228	221	226	203	200	188	204	238	230	219	246	208	184	238	194	183	220
01983 TOPSFIELD	183	234	275	229	230	240	210	209	197	211	248	237	227	259	219	197	248	203	195	227
01984 WENHAM	219	282	336	274	277	290	253	253	238	254	300	286	273	314	265	239	300	245	236	272
01985 WEST NEWBURY	180	225	244	232	217	219	198	193	180	201	229	223	217	238	201	174	231	186	171	213
02019 BELLINGHAM	113	134	142	135	131	130	123	122	115	123	145	144	129	152	124	111	144	119	110	135
02021 CANTON	145	185	235	181	180	188	172	168	163	171	205	195	183	218	177	162	205	166	154	181
02025 COHASSET	191	255	321	248	247	258	225	223	211	227	266	254	248	284	237	211	269	216	203	240
02026 DEDHAM	126	150	178	148	148	155	143	141	137	142	173	162	150	179	147	137	171	139	133	153
02030 DOVER	346	465	638	456	454	490	406	402	378	415	478	452	461	503	432	381	485	386	373	437
MASSACHUSETTS	112	121	148	122	120	127	122	119	121	121	151	138	126	156	123	120	149	120	115	132
UNITED STATES	100	100	100	100	100	100	100	100	100	100	100	100	100	100	100	100	100	100	100	100

MASSACHUSETTS

POPULATION CHANGE

A 02032-02364

# ZIP CODE / POST OFFICE NAME	COUNTY FIPS CODE	POPULATION 2000	2004	2009	2000-2004 ANNUAL RATE % Rate	State Centile	HOUSEHOLDS 2000	2004	2009	% Annual Rate 2000-2004	2004 Average HH Size	FAMILIES 2000	2004	% Annual Rate 2000-2004
02032 EAST WALPOLE	021	3593	3680	3742	0.6	62	1323	1356	1382	0.6	2.71	942	966	0.6
02035 FOXBORO	021	16198	16133	16213	-0.1	23	6123	6136	6204	0.1	2.61	4381	4394	0.1
02038 FRANKLIN	021	29510	31062	32093	1.2	84	10138	10654	11014	1.2	2.86	7869	8265	1.2
02043 HINGHAM	023	19875	19743	20208	-0.2	20	7186	7204	7439	0.1	2.70	5477	5484	0.0
02045 HULL	023	11050	11303	11670	0.5	61	4522	4685	4888	0.8	2.41	2821	2918	0.8
02048 MANSFIELD	005	22182	22736	23278	0.6	63	7873	8104	8357	0.7	2.80	5797	5973	0.7
02050 MARSHFIELD	023	24835	25762	27029	0.9	74	9135	9510	10040	1.0	2.70	6746	7024	1.0
02052 MEDFIELD	021	12315	12766	13077	0.9	73	4014	4172	4290	0.9	3.02	3279	3410	0.9
02053 MEDWAY	021	12467	13311	13851	1.6	92	4191	4490	4693	1.6	2.94	3344	3587	1.7
02054 MILLIS	021	7893	7966	8049	0.2	42	3000	3045	3093	0.4	2.60	2161	2194	0.4
02056 NORFOLK	021	10486	10569	10692	0.2	40	2824	2855	2904	0.3	3.08	2417	2444	0.3
02061 NORWELL	023	9747	10380	10935	1.5	90	3245	3495	3718	1.8	2.91	2705	2908	1.7
02062 NORWOOD	021	28587	28240	28347	-0.3	12	11623	11568	11685	-0.1	2.39	7382	7349	-0.1
02066 SCITUATE	023	17359	17234	17659	-0.2	19	6466	6469	6687	0.0	2.64	4777	4776	0.0
02067 SHARON	021	17459	17361	17438	-0.1	21	5954	5948	6004	0.0	2.91	4946	4945	0.0
02071 SOUTH WALPOLE	021	672	712	737	1.4	88	210	225	235	1.6	2.95	183	196	1.6
02072 STOUGHTON	021	27058	27183	27514	0.1	36	10227	10326	10512	0.2	2.59	7248	7335	0.3
02081 WALPOLE	021	18556	19090	19460	0.7	68	6525	6759	6936	0.8	2.69	4845	5020	0.8
02090 WESTWOOD	021	14087	14308	14514	0.4	51	5110	5222	5329	0.5	2.71	3855	3939	0.5
02093 WRENTHAM	021	10521	10999	11304	1.1	80	3393	3584	3713	1.3	2.86	2645	2795	1.3
02108 BOSTON	025	4240	3978	3861	-1.5	0	2524	2387	2330	-1.3	1.47	698	662	-1.2
02109 BOSTON	025	3463	3446	3434	-0.1	22	2022	2048	2063	0.3	1.59	609	617	0.3
02110 BOSTON	025	1579	1523	1494	-0.9	2	961	934	921	-0.7	1.53	338	329	-0.6
02111 BOSTON	025	4692	5147	5366	2.2	98	1737	1967	2083	3.0	2.18	789	895	3.0
02113 BOSTON	025	5836	5983	6036	0.6	64	3715	3871	3945	1.0	1.53	801	841	1.2
02114 BOSTON	025	11039	11106	11177	0.1	37	6394	6466	6534	0.3	1.52	1525	1564	0.6
02115 BOSTON	025	26221	26296	26357	0.1	34	11077	11217	11322	0.3	1.69	2452	2547	0.9
02116 BOSTON	025	18853	18531	18379	-0.4	7	10745	10715	10723	-0.1	1.53	2965	2972	0.1
02118 BOSTON	025	23009	23175	23252	0.2	39	10735	10998	11148	0.6	1.88	3534	3617	0.6
02119 BOSTON	025	23110	22976	22884	-0.1	20	8576	8627	8656	0.1	2.58	5272	5320	0.2
02120 BOSTON	025	13278	13391	13442	0.2	40	5011	5091	5140	0.4	2.44	2133	2188	0.6
02121 BOSTON	025	24934	24038	23560	-0.9	1	8906	8688	8581	-0.6	2.76	6088	5961	-0.5
02122 BOSTON	025	24092	24161	24141	0.1	34	8183	8282	8328	0.3	2.84	5303	5374	0.3
02124 BOSTON	025	51419	50780	50531	-0.3	12	17585	17536	17494	-0.1	2.88	12071	12088	0.0
02125 BOSTON	025	32953	32337	31965	-0.4	6	11312	11198	11139	-0.2	2.83	7043	7004	-0.1
02126 MATTAPAN	025	27900	28116	28175	0.2	39	9392	9595	9699	0.5	2.89	6891	7057	0.6
02127 BOSTON	025	29456	29674	29731	0.2	39	13791	14061	14199	0.5	2.08	6226	6359	0.5
02128 BOSTON	025	38413	37924	37619	-0.3	12	14326	14055	13923	-0.5	2.67	8672	8554	-0.3
02129 CHARLESTOWN	025	15195	15263	15270	0.1	36	7350	7449	7498	0.3	2.03	3219	3273	0.4
02130 JAMAICA PLAIN	025	34579	34258	34128	-0.2	16	13933	13976	14036	0.1	2.31	6539	6619	0.3
02131 ROSLINDALE	025	32379	32071	31862	-0.2	16	12008	11983	11973	-0.1	2.60	7572	7596	0.1
02132 WEST ROXBURY	025	24810	23794	23268	-1.0	1	10461	10133	9973	-0.8	2.28	6210	6037	-0.7
02134 ALLSTON	025	22671	23215	23516	0.6	62	9908	10317	10563	1.0	2.19	2874	2968	0.8
02135 BRIGHTON	025	42626	44049	44711	0.8	71	19606	20510	20983	1.1	2.10	6712	7053	1.2
02136 HYDE PARK	025	27614	26995	26625	-0.5	4	10364	10157	10050	-0.5	2.63	6810	6696	-0.4
02138 CAMBRIDGE	017	34388	34605	35011	0.2	37	13585	13791	14118	0.4	1.87	5268	5326	0.3
02139 CAMBRIDGE	017	35766	36902	37709	0.7	71	14621	15385	15955	1.2	2.08	5823	6068	1.0
02140 CAMBRIDGE	017	17389	17517	17708	0.2	39	8052	8163	8314	0.3	2.11	3667	3713	0.3
02141 CAMBRIDGE	017	12040	12341	12552	0.6	63	5458	5688	5854	1.0	2.13	2439	2536	0.9
02142 CAMBRIDGE	017	1783	1768	1763	-0.2	17	908	905	910	-0.1	1.38	400	330	-4.4
02143 SOMERVILLE	017	25453	25259	25364	-0.2	19	11164	11227	11398	0.1	2.21	4553	4579	0.1
02144 SOMERVILLE	017	23980	23797	23954	-0.2	19	10564	10587	10769	0.1	2.15	4366	4363	0.0
02145 SOMERVILLE	017	26244	26637	27018	0.4	49	9771	9913	10099	0.3	2.67	5728	5809	0.3
02148 MALDEN	017	56417	57477	58262	0.4	55	22983	23550	24036	0.6	2.41	13553	13894	0.6
02149 EVERETT	017	38043	38194	38374	0.1	35	15437	15588	15772	0.2	2.44	9552	9636	0.2
02150 CHELSEA	025	35032	35427	35588	0.3	44	11857	11896	11921	0.1	2.90	7595	7687	0.3
02151 REVERE	025	47296	46945	46696	-0.2	19	19478	19534	19569	0.1	2.39	11875	11953	0.2
02152 WINTHROP	025	18303	17427	16990	-1.2	0	7843	7544	7401	-0.9	2.28	4584	4429	-0.8
02153 MEDFORD	017	1279	1226	1215	-1.0	1	2	2	2	0.0	2.50	1	1	0.0
02155 MEDFORD	017	56159	55536	55677	-0.3	13	22129	22109	22379	0.0	2.41	13525	13511	0.0
02163 BOSTON	025	1245	1330	1379	1.6	92	429	437	444	0.4	2.33	206	210	0.5
02169 QUINCY	021	52188	53320	54474	0.5	60	23819	24462	25127	0.6	2.14	12156	12468	0.6
02170 QUINCY	021	19153	18707	18712	-0.6	4	7888	7748	7799	-0.4	2.34	4379	4304	-0.4
02171 QUINCY	021	17321	18595	19628	1.7	93	7226	7743	8185	1.6	2.31	4011	4291	1.6
02176 MELROSE	017	27263	27004	27109	-0.2	16	11027	11043	11196	0.0	2.42	7132	7142	0.0
02180 STONEHAM	017	22175	21874	21823	-0.3	11	9036	9030	9107	0.0	2.39	5868	5863	0.0
02184 BRAINTREE	021	33721	34684	35423	0.7	67	12558	13004	13387	0.8	2.60	8869	9193	0.9
02186 MILTON	021	26196	25936	26054	-0.2	15	9036	8994	9094	-0.1	2.77	6795	6766	-0.1
02188 WEYMOUTH	021	13595	13977	14334	0.7	67	5549	5762	5959	0.9	2.34	3424	3549	0.9
02189 EAST WEYMOUTH	021	14906	15170	15541	0.4	54	6090	6257	6462	0.6	2.41	3807	3911	0.6
02190 SOUTH WEYMOUTH	021	16797	17035	17443	0.3	48	6843	6989	7207	0.5	2.43	4338	4433	0.5
02191 NORTH WEYMOUTH	021	8696	8832	8985	0.4	51	3548	3625	3708	0.5	2.44	2361	2413	0.5
02199 BOSTON	025	1005	962	939	-1.0	1	732	702	688	-1.0	1.37	186	180	-0.8
02210 BOSTON	025	509	543	558	1.5	91	247	269	280	2.0	1.89	83	92	2.5
02215 BOSTON	025	19254	19658	19974	0.5	59	6611	7018	7318	1.4	1.52	881	959	2.0
02301 BROCKTON	023	61757	64158	67359	0.9	75	22583	23574	24913	1.0	2.66	14583	15200	1.0
02302 BROCKTON	023	32422	32779	33923	0.3	44	11060	11301	11805	0.5	2.86	8163	8324	0.5
02322 AVON	021	4923	4932	5010	0.0	32	1862	1880	1922	0.2	2.62	1321	1333	0.2
02324 BRIDGEWATER	023	23903	25027	26196	1.1	81	7491	7919	8386	1.3	2.71	5565	5868	1.3
02325 BRIDGEWATER	023	1272	1292	1317	0.4	51	27	28	29	0.9	2.57	14	14	0.0
02330 CARVER	023	11150	11694	12272	1.1	82	3979	4192	4426	1.2	2.79	3007	3182	1.3
02332 DUXBURY	023	14263	15021	15775	1.2	85	4952	5258	5565	1.4	2.83	3947	4188	1.4
02333 EAST BRIDGEWATER	023	13048	13604	14167	1.0	78	4373	4609	4846	1.2	2.91	3414	3596	1.2
02338 HALIFAX	023	7433	7588	7831	0.5	59	2738	2810	2918	0.6	2.70	2041	2092	0.5
02339 HANOVER	023	13193	13584	14094	0.7	69	4358	4517	4722	0.9	3.00	3574	3707	0.9
02341 HANSON	023	9555	9896	10325	0.9	73	3141	3285	3456	1.1	3.00	2556	2670	1.0
02343 HOLBROOK	021	10738	10649	10689	-0.2	17	4064	4060	4102	0.0	2.61	2846	2842	0.0
02346 MIDDLEBORO	023	19947	20940	22001	1.2	83	6984	7427	7889	1.5	2.75	5119	5451	1.5
02347 LAKEVILLE	023	9814	10569	11184	1.8	94	3289	3559	3792	1.9	2.90	2657	2874	1.9
02351 ABINGTON	023	14605	15017	15561	0.7	67	5263	5448	5692	0.8	2.72	3746	3878	0.8
02356 NORTH EASTON	005	11523	12079	12487	1.1	81	4028	4283	4482	1.5	2.79	3152	3357	1.5
02357 NORTH EASTON	005	1734	1738	1741	0.1	32	25	27	28	1.8	2.96	9	10	2.5
02359 PEMBROKE	023	16916	18032	19018	1.5	90	5746	6176	6565	1.7	2.90	4553	4893	1.7
02360 PLYMOUTH	023	51684	54795	57842	1.4	88	18418	19660	20933	1.6	2.66	13264	14197	1.6
02364 KINGSTON	023	11780	12226	12710	0.9	74	4248	4434	4641	1.0	2.69	3138	3273	1.0
MASSACHUSETTS					0.4					0.6	2.48			0.6
UNITED STATES					1.2					1.3	2.58			1.1

ZIP CODE #	POST OFFICE NAME	RACE (%) White 2000	White 2004	Black 2000	Black 2004	Asian/Pacific 2000	Asian/Pacific 2004	% Hispanic Origin 2000	% Hispanic Origin 2004	2004 AGE DISTRIBUTION (%) 0-4	5-9	10-14	15-19	20-24	25-44	45-64	65-84	85+	18+	MEDIAN AGE 2004	% 2004 Males	% 2004 Females
02032	EAST WALPOLE	97.9	97.6	0.4	0.4	0.7	0.9	1.5	1.7	6.8	7.2	7.3	6.6	4.7	26.9	26.5	12.5	1.7	74.5	40.3	48.5	51.5
02035	FOXBORO	97.1	96.6	0.8	0.9	1.2	1.5	1.1	1.3	6.7	7.2	7.5	6.8	4.7	27.6	27.0	11.2	1.4	74.1	39.5	49.1	50.9
02038	FRANKLIN	96.0	95.3	1.1	1.2	1.7	2.1	1.1	1.3	9.2	9.5	8.4	6.9	5.2	30.4	22.6	7.0	1.0	69.0	35.4	48.9	51.1
02043	HINGHAM	97.5	97.0	0.4	0.5	0.9	1.1	0.8	1.0	7.2	7.9	7.9	6.6	4.2	22.3	29.3	12.3	2.3	72.5	41.5	47.5	52.5
02045	HULL	97.0	96.4	0.5	0.6	0.9	1.2	1.1	1.4	5.5	5.8	6.3	5.9	5.3	27.2	31.1	11.6	1.3	78.8	41.9	48.2	51.8
02048	MANSFIELD	94.3	93.5	2.2	2.4	2.0	2.4	1.4	1.7	9.4	9.6	8.8	6.0	4.4	33.6	21.8	5.5	0.8	68.2	34.6	49.8	50.2
02050	MARSHFIELD	97.7	97.4	0.5	0.6	0.4	0.5	0.7	0.8	7.5	8.0	7.7	6.4	4.7	27.4	28.2	9.0	1.0	72.7	38.7	48.8	51.2
02052	MEDFIELD	96.8	96.2	0.5	0.6	1.8	2.2	0.9	1.1	8.0	9.7	10.3	7.4	3.9	23.0	28.4	8.4	1.0	66.9	39.0	49.1	50.9
02053	MEDWAY	97.5	97.0	0.6	0.7	1.0	1.3	0.8	1.0	8.3	9.4	9.3	6.7	4.0	29.0	24.2	7.8	1.3	68.2	36.8	48.5	51.5
02054	MILLIS	96.9	96.4	0.7	0.8	1.1	1.4	0.9	1.2	7.7	8.2	7.6	5.6	4.3	29.1	27.4	9.3	0.9	72.9	38.5	48.6	51.4
02056	NORFOLK	89.0	88.0	4.9	5.1	1.2	1.5	4.9	5.5	6.9	8.1	8.1	5.9	4.2	31.9	28.9	5.6	0.5	73.2	38.4	59.0	41.0
02061	NORWELL	97.6	97.1	0.4	0.4	1.2	1.5	0.6	0.8	7.0	8.2	8.4	6.5	3.9	22.7	30.0	11.0	2.3	72.2	41.3	48.7	51.3
02062	NORWOOD	90.5	89.0	2.3	2.5	5.1	6.1	1.7	1.9	5.9	5.8	5.8	5.6	5.1	30.9	23.6	14.3	3.0	79.0	39.6	47.2	52.8
02066	SCITUATE	96.7	96.2	0.5	0.6	0.5	0.6	0.8	1.0	6.8	7.5	7.7	6.2	4.1	23.3	28.7	13.7	2.0	74.0	42.1	47.8	52.2
02067	SHARON	90.0	88.3	3.4	3.8	4.9	6.0	1.1	1.3	6.5	8.0	9.3	7.3	4.3	21.6	31.5	10.1	1.5	71.1	41.3	48.4	51.6
02071	SOUTH WALPOLE	94.1	93.3	2.7	3.1	0.7	0.8	2.4	3.0	7.6	8.0	8.6	7.0	4.6	29.5	26.1	7.9	0.7	70.7	37.3	52.7	47.3
02072	STOUGHTON	88.5	86.9	5.7	6.4	2.2	2.7	1.5	1.9	5.5	5.8	6.5	6.1	5.5	28.1	27.0	13.4	2.2	78.4	40.7	48.0	52.0
02081	WALPOLE	95.0	94.1	1.8	2.0	1.2	1.5	2.1	2.5	6.5	7.3	7.5	6.2	4.4	27.1	26.1	12.3	2.7	74.5	40.2	50.1	49.9
02090	WESTWOOD	96.0	95.2	0.5	0.6	2.5	3.1	0.9	1.2	7.6	8.7	8.3	6.1	3.2	22.0	26.2	14.2	3.9	71.3	41.9	47.9	52.1
02093	WRENTHAM	97.6	97.2	0.6	0.7	0.8	1.0	0.8	1.0	7.2	8.0	8.4	6.5	4.2	26.0	28.4	9.1	2.4	72.2	40.1	49.3	50.7
02108	BOSTON	89.7	87.4	3.8	4.4	4.6	5.8	3.4	4.2	2.9	2.8	1.5	2.6	5.9	41.8	29.5	11.8	1.3	92.0	40.3	53.6	46.4
02109	BOSTON	94.5	93.4	0.7	0.9	3.0	3.7	2.1	2.6	2.4	1.8	1.1	1.4	9.7	46.6	23.0	11.0	3.1	94.1	36.7	47.6	52.4
02110	BOSTON	87.5	84.4	3.4	4.1	6.9	8.7	4.9	6.2	3.6	2.6	1.8	1.6	4.0	28.4	36.2	18.9	2.9	91.3	49.8	48.1	51.9
02111	BOSTON	34.1	30.2	4.2	4.4	58.6	62.1	3.9	4.4	3.0	2.7	3.4	6.3	12.7	34.0	21.5	14.2	2.3	89.0	36.3	53.2	46.8
02113	BOSTON	96.4	95.6	0.4	0.5	1.3	1.6	2.0	2.5	1.9	0.8	0.8	1.1	13.9	51.9	15.0	11.7	3.0	96.2	32.5	45.3	54.7
02114	BOSTON	82.2	79.2	6.6	7.4	7.9	9.6	4.8	5.7	2.8	1.5	1.1	2.2	10.9	48.5	22.7	8.7	1.6	93.4	34.4	52.0	48.0
02115	BOSTON	69.7	64.9	10.2	11.6	12.2	14.5	9.6	11.4	1.8	1.8	1.8	19.0	28.9	29.8	10.6	5.5	0.8	93.7	24.4	50.5	49.5
02116	BOSTON	76.1	72.8	7.1	7.6	13.3	15.7	4.2	4.9	2.5	1.5	1.5	7.8	10.8	42.3	22.4	9.7	1.4	93.6	35.5	51.5	48.5
02118	BOSTON	46.8	42.7	25.7	27.3	12.8	13.9	19.2	21.2	4.1	3.7	4.0	5.1	9.7	43.6	20.8	7.9	1.0	85.7	34.5	56.4	43.6
02119	BOSTON	10.9	10.2	62.9	63.4	0.8	0.8	24.8	26.0	7.4	7.4	8.7	9.0	8.2	29.0	20.9	8.4	1.1	71.1	31.6	46.4	53.6
02120	BOSTON	41.6	37.5	32.1	34.0	9.5	10.3	20.6	22.7	5.2	5.2	5.6	10.4	20.9	29.6	15.9	6.3	1.0	80.8	26.3	52.0	48.0
02121	BOSTON	4.9	4.7	77.6	77.5	0.5	0.5	19.0	19.7	8.8	9.1	10.4	9.1	7.5	28.0	19.1	7.2	0.8	66.1	29.0	44.0	56.0
02122	BOSTON	41.7	39.4	27.9	28.8	13.8	15.0	10.4	11.2	7.4	7.0	7.7	8.1	8.4	31.7	20.0	8.1	1.7	73.0	32.0	48.0	52.0
02124	BOSTON	21.5	19.4	59.7	61.0	5.8	6.4	12.5	13.3	7.7	7.5	8.9	8.4	8.0	30.3	20.9	7.3	0.9	70.7	31.4	46.2	53.8
02125	BOSTON	34.6	31.5	31.3	32.5	11.3	12.7	16.3	17.8	7.1	6.9	8.2	8.6	10.0	32.5	19.0	7.0	0.8	72.7	30.3	48.4	51.6
02126	MATTAPAN	6.6	5.6	83.3	84.4	1.0	1.1	7.2	7.6	7.3	7.4	8.7	8.0	7.3	28.6	23.5	8.3	0.9	71.6	33.3	45.7	54.3
02127	BOSTON	86.8	85.0	3.2	3.6	3.9	4.6	7.6	8.6	5.0	4.9	5.2	5.2	7.2	37.8	21.5	11.3	1.9	81.8	35.8	46.6	53.4
02128	BOSTON	67.7	64.0	3.8	4.0	4.2	4.6	39.0	44.1	7.3	6.6	6.7	6.3	8.0	35.9	18.4	9.2	1.7	75.8	33.2	51.5	48.5
02129	CHARLESTOWN	82.9	80.7	4.8	5.1	5.0	6.0	11.6	13.0	5.6	5.1	5.2	5.0	5.8	41.1	21.1	10.0	1.3	81.2	34.8	45.7	54.4
02130	JAMAICA PLAIN	61.5	57.6	16.0	17.4	4.7	5.3	25.4	28.4	5.1	5.0	5.2	6.4	7.7	39.1	21.8	7.9	1.8	81.1	34.9	47.1	52.9
02131	ROSLINDALE	64.1	60.2	17.7	19.3	2.6	3.0	19.8	22.5	6.8	6.7	6.9	6.8	6.3	31.5	22.1	9.8	3.1	75.4	36.3	46.6	53.4
02132	WEST ROXBURY	89.0	87.0	3.6	4.2	3.9	4.8	3.8	4.7	5.9	5.7	5.0	4.4	4.3	30.0	24.9	16.2	3.6	80.7	41.9	46.2	53.9
02134	ALLSTON	67.1	62.2	5.2	5.9	16.9	19.8	12.4	14.3	2.6	2.1	2.1	6.2	33.9	37.3	10.9	4.2	0.7	91.7	25.8	51.5	48.5
02135	BRIGHTON	76.9	72.9	4.6	5.3	12.0	14.3	7.5	9.0	3.4	2.7	2.8	3.6	19.7	41.7	14.0	9.8	2.3	89.5	29.8	47.7	52.3
02136	HYDE PARK	52.8	48.8	33.8	36.3	1.7	2.0	13.7	15.6	7.3	7.1	7.4	6.9	6.5	29.1	22.5	11.1	2.0	74.0	36.1	46.4	53.6
02138	CAMBRIDGE	76.5	73.3	6.8	7.4	11.5	13.6	5.6	6.4	3.1	2.7	2.7	11.2	19.5	32.4	19.0	8.0	1.5	89.8	30.0	47.6	52.4
02139	CAMBRIDGE	60.3	57.1	16.6	17.1	13.4	15.5	8.8	10.0	4.1	3.4	3.8	8.0	16.1	39.8	17.7	6.2	0.9	86.1	30.3	50.9	49.1
02140	CAMBRIDGE	66.3	64.0	16.0	16.3	11.1	12.8	5.3	5.8	5.3	4.7	4.9	5.6	6.8	39.2	22.9	9.0	1.6	81.7	35.4	46.2	53.8
02141	CAMBRIDGE	70.0	66.8	8.0	8.4	8.6	10.2	11.1	12.9	4.1	3.5	4.1	5.6	10.2	41.5	18.8	10.9	1.5	85.5	33.9	52.1	48.0
02142	CAMBRIDGE	67.1	62.5	3.5	3.7	22.4	26.0	8.0	9.3	5.0	2.0	1.1	7.6	26.2	40.2	11.6	5.7	0.6	91.1	27.1	53.9	46.2
02143	SOMERVILLE	77.9	75.1	5.2	5.7	7.9	9.5	7.0	8.2	4.0	3.2	3.2	4.1	11.1	45.1	17.9	9.6	1.9	87.3	33.4	49.3	50.8
02144	SOMERVILLE	85.1	82.9	5.1	5.5	5.6	6.9	3.7	4.4	3.8	2.9	2.9	5.3	14.6	43.0	17.1	8.9	1.6	88.6	31.9	47.2	52.8
02145	SOMERVILLE	68.6	65.4	9.1	9.6	5.7	6.7	15.3	17.6	6.0	5.5	5.9	6.3	8.7	39.2	19.2	8.0	1.2	79.0	33.0	50.1	49.9
02148	MALDEN	72.2	68.4	8.1	8.8	14.0	16.7	4.8	5.6	5.8	5.4	5.7	5.6	6.5	34.8	22.6	11.7	2.0	79.9	37.0	48.3	51.8
02149	EVERETT	79.7	77.1	6.3	6.9	3.3	4.0	9.5	11.3	6.0	5.7	6.3	5.9	6.8	33.7	21.8	11.7	2.0	78.5	36.6	47.9	52.1
02150	CHELSEA	57.9	54.3	7.3	7.7	4.8	5.2	48.5	52.9	8.2	7.5	7.9	7.2	8.2	32.9	17.4	8.9	1.8	72.2	31.6	50.3	49.7
02151	REVERE	84.4	82.1	2.9	3.3	4.6	5.3	9.5	11.3	5.8	5.6	6.1	6.1	6.3	30.4	23.5	13.7	2.5	78.8	38.6	48.4	51.6
02152	WINTHROP	94.4	93.3	1.7	2.0	1.2	1.5	2.7	3.4	4.9	4.9	5.4	5.5	5.6	30.3	27.1	13.7	2.7	81.7	41.3	46.9	53.1
02153	MEDFORD	77.1	73.6	5.0	5.4	12.7	15.5	4.5	5.2	1.6	1.1	1.1	40.4	28.6	16.7	6.6	3.2	0.7	95.7	21.0	46.2	53.8
02155	MEDFORD	86.4	84.5	6.1	6.7	3.9	4.9	2.6	3.1	4.9	4.7	5.1	6.8	7.4	31.5	22.9	13.9	2.8	82.2	38.3	47.0	53.0
02163	BOSTON	64.9	61.0	7.4	8.1	20.1	22.7	11.0	12.4	6.7	2.9	2.4	3.2	5.2	60.8	12.3	5.7	0.8	86.2	28.6	54.3	45.7
02169	QUINCY	83.0	80.2	3.1	3.3	10.6	12.9	2.5	2.9	5.4	5.1	5.0	4.9	5.9	34.5	22.7	13.6	3.0	81.6	38.5	47.6	52.4
02170	QUINCY	77.1	73.3	1.0	1.1	20.2	23.8	1.6	1.8	4.5	4.3	4.8	5.5	7.3	33.4	24.3	13.8	2.2	83.5	38.9	47.5	52.5
02171	QUINCY	71.0	65.4	2.5	2.5	23.9	29.4	2.1	2.3	4.6	4.4	4.6	5.1	5.7	35.2	26.6	12.1	1.7	83.4	39.8	49.6	50.4
02176	MELROSE	95.1	94.2	1.0	1.1	2.1	2.6	1.1	1.3	6.4	6.5	6.0	5.3	4.5	28.8	26.4	13.1	2.9	77.6	40.7	47.1	52.9
02180	STONEHAM	95.0	94.0	0.9	1.0	2.6	3.2	1.8	2.2	5.6	5.8	6.0	5.5	4.8	27.7	26.1	15.4	3.2	79.0	41.8	47.1	52.9
02184	BRAINTREE	93.9	92.9	1.2	1.3	3.2	3.9	1.2	1.4	6.1	6.3	6.3	5.8	5.1	27.0	25.2	15.3	2.9	77.6	41.0	47.2	52.8
02186	MILTON	85.4	83.9	10.2	11.1	2.1	2.6	1.8	2.0	6.1	6.8	7.4	8.1	6.4	23.0	26.6	12.6	3.0	75.4	40.2	47.4	52.6
02188	WEYMOUTH	94.7	93.8	1.3	1.5	1.9	2.4	0.9	1.0	5.6	5.8	6.2	5.3	4.9	27.6	25.0	15.8	3.8	78.9	41.7	46.4	53.6
02189	EAST WEYMOUTH	94.8	94.1	1.8	2.0	1.3	1.6	1.7	2.0	6.4	6.4	7.0	6.0	5.8	29.9	25.2	11.7	1.7	76.6	38.5	48.0	52.0
02190	SOUTH WEYMOUTH	94.0	93.2	1.8	1.9	1.9	2.3	1.4	1.6	6.7	6.5	6.2	5.8	5.4	30.7	25.3	12.0	1.4	77.0	38.6	48.4	51.6
02191	NORTH WEYMOUTH	97.0	96.6	0.4	0.5	1.2	1.5	1.4	1.6	5.6	5.7	5.7	5.3	4.8	29.4	26.9	14.8	1.8	79.7	41.2	47.4	52.7
02199	BOSTON	85.3	82.4	2.6	3.1	7.9	9.7	2.4	3.1	0.9	0.8	1.0	0.8	2.3	38.5	26.0	24.3	5.3	97.0	50.9	47.2	52.8
02210	BOSTON	90.0	87.9	2.0	2.2	5.1	6.3	2.8	3.3	3.3	2.4	2.8	5.9	11.4	42.2	22.7	8.7	0.7	89.3	35.1	54.7	45.3
02215	BOSTON	74.4	69.8	4.1	4.8	15.3	18.0	7.3	8.9	0.6	0.4	0.3	30.9	36.5	22.6	5.1	3.2	0.5	98.5	22.5	45.6	54.4
02301	BROCKTON	57.4	54.1	18.6	20.2	2.6	3.1	8.7	10.0	7.5	7.0	7.8	8.0	7.5	28.9	21.8	9.7	1.9	72.8	33.8	48.0	52.0
02302	BROCKTON	69.9	67.3	16.0	17.5	1.5	1.8	6.7	7.8	6.7	7.0	8.2	7.3	6.4	28.4	24.1	10.4	1.5	73.5	36.0	48.3	51.7
02322	AVON	89.0	87.2	6.3	7.3	1.1	1.4	2.1	2.6	6.0	6.0	6.9	6.3	6.0	27.2	24.7	15.2	1.9	77.3	39.8	47.3	52.7
02324	BRIDGEWATER	88.4	87.3	4.1	4.5	1.1	1.3	2.7	3.1	6.4	6.4	6.8	7.4	9.4	31.7	23.3	7.6	1.0	76.9	34.9	52.9	47.2
02325	BRIDGEWATER	66.2	63.3	2.4	2.7	1.7	1.9	4.6	5.5	5.4	2.9	3.0	13.5	28.8	30.3	10.5	4.8	0.7	87.5	24.4	46.8	53.2
02330	CARVER	95.8	95.1	1.2	1.4	0.3	0.4	0.8	1.0	6.6	7.1	7.7	6.7	5.6	27.2	25.5	11.8	1.9	74.4	38.3	48.8	51.3
02332	DUXBURY	97.8	97.4	0.6	0.7	0.7	0.8	0.7	0.9	6.7	8.2	8.9	7.0	4.1	21.4	31.2	10.3	2.3	71.6	41.5	48.1	51.9
02333	EAST BRIDGEWATER	96.9	96.4	1.0	1.2	0.5	0.7	0.7	1.0	7.2	7.3	7.8	6.7	5.8	29.4	25.4	9.1	1.4	73.3	37.0	48.9	51.1
02338	HALIFAX	98.1	97.8	0.3	0.4	0.3	0.3	0.6	0.7	6.8	7.1	7.2	6.1	5.0	28.5	26.5	11.4	1.6	75.2	39.1	48.5	51.5
02339	HANOVER	97.7	97.2	0.6	0.6	0.8	1.0	0.7	0.9	7.5	8.3	8.5	7.1	4.8	25.5	27.7	9.3	1.4	71.1	38.7	49.2	50.9
02341	HANSON	96.7	96.3	1.1	1.2	0.4	0.4	0.7	0.8	7.2	7.5	8.0	6.8	5.7	28.1	27.6	8.3	0.9	73.2	37.1	49.2	50.8
02343	HOLBROOK	91.9	90.7	4.0	4.5	1.5	1.9	2.4	2.9	6.0	6.2	6.6	5.9	5.4	29.0	25.1	14.1	1.7	77.5	39.8	48.5	51.5
02346	MIDDLEBORO	96.1	95.6	1.3	1.5	0.5	0.6	0.8	1.0	7.0	7.2	8.0	6.9	5.6	30.1	25.0	8.7	1.6	73.3	36.9	49.3	50.8
02347	LAKEVILLE	97.3	96.8	0.3	0.4	0.6	0.8	1.1	1.3	7.5	8.0	7.7	6.1	4.8	27.4	27.0	9.5	2.0	72.8	39.1	48.4	51.6
02351	ABINGTON	97.5	97.1	0.8	0.9	0.5	0.6	0.7	0.9	6.9	6.9	7.3	6.6	5.9	28.9	25.3	10.4	1.9	74.8	37.7	48.9	51.2
02356	NORTH EASTON	96.0	95.2	1.2	1.4	1.4	1.7	1.1	1.3	7.1	8.0	8.1	6.4	4.6	27.0	28.5	9.0	1.4	72.5	39.0	49.1	50.9
02357	NORTH EASTON	51.6	48.9	0.6	0.6	0.8	1.0	6.5	7.8	0.2	0.1	0.1	40.8	55.8	0.9	1.0	1.0	0.1	99.4	20.8	44.4	55.6
02359	PEMBROKE	97.9	97.5	0.5	0.6	0.5	0.7	0.5	0.7	7.8	8.2	7.8	6.7	4.7	29.2	26.5	8.3	0.9	71.9	37.3	49.6	50.4
02360	PLYMOUTH	94.8	94.2	1.9	2.1	0.6	0.8	1.7	2.0	6.7	7.0	7.3	6.5	5.7	29.8	25.8	9.2	2.0	74.9	37.5	49.6	50.4
02364	KINGSTON	97.0	96.5	1.0	1.1	0.4	0.6	0.8	1.0	8.2	8.0	7.7	5.9	4.1	28.4	24.7	10.6	2.4	72.2	38.3	48.0	52.0
	MASSACHUSETTS	84.5	82.9	5.4	5.7	3.8	4.5	6.8	7.8	6.2	6.3	6.8	7.0	7.0	28.9	24.5	11.4	2.1	76.8	37.6	48.3	51.7
	UNITED STATES	75.1	73.6	12.3	12.5	3.8	4.2	12.5	14.1	6.9	6.7	7.2	7.0	7.3	28.6	23.8	10.8	1.7	75.1	36.0	49.1	50.9

ZIP CODE #	POST OFFICE NAME	2004 Per Capita Income	2004 HH Income Base	2004 Household Income Distribution (%): Less than $25,000	$25,000 to $49,999	$50,000 to $99,999	$100,000 to $149,999	$150,000 or More	Median Household Income: 2004	2009	2004 National Centile	2004 State Centile	2004 Home Value Base	2004 Home Value Distribution (%): Less than $50,000	$50,000 to $89,999	$90,000 to $174,999	$175,000 to $399,999	$400,000 or More	2004 Median Home Value
02032	EAST WALPOLE	38045	1356	8.3	17.4	29.3	27.9	17.1	90737	118040	97	85	1115	0.2	0.0	3.1	65.1	31.6	343075
02035	FOXBORO	42345	6136	11.1	16.0	34.0	20.6	18.2	79720	104378	95	76	4567	1.0	0.6	3.5	64.4	30.5	336619
02038	FRANKLIN	35456	10654	10.2	14.6	34.6	24.9	15.7	85409	108174	96	81	8623	0.2	0.1	4.6	61.0	34.1	341399
02043	HINGHAM	56830	7204	9.1	11.4	27.8	21.9	29.9	103191	136985	98	91	6185	0.2	0.0	2.3	26.0	71.5	553239
02045	HULL	34469	4685	18.1	19.7	37.0	16.7	8.5	63522	80422	87	52	3446	0.0	0.0	9.3	67.7	22.9	277572
02048	MANSFIELD	35254	8104	11.6	15.4	36.6	22.2	14.2	80641	101393	95	77	6122	0.6	0.6	4.7	58.2	35.9	352473
02050	MARSHFIELD	37039	9510	11.9	16.0	35.6	21.6	14.9	80224	101580	95	77	7913	0.3	0.5	4.1	57.2	37.9	348305
02052	MEDFIELD	58802	4172	5.5	9.8	22.6	25.0	37.2	123271	160580	99	97	3561	0.6	0.5	1.2	20.1	77.7	559715
02053	MEDWAY	34929	4490	9.5	13.1	32.6	28.1	16.7	90521	114958	97	85	3812	0.4	0.3	3.4	59.2	36.8	353881
02054	MILLIS	35403	3045	9.4	16.5	39.1	23.3	11.7	77982	101437	94	74	2405	0.3	0.0	1.6	77.6	20.5	309503
02056	NORFOLK	42895	2855	5.8	9.5	31.5	24.9	28.3	104301	132429	98	91	2638	0.2	0.0	2.1	42.3	55.3	424522
02061	NORWELL	49187	3495	7.6	12.3	27.7	23.6	28.8	104206	135914	98	91	3238	0.2	0.3	0.8	30.0	68.8	520154
02062	NORWOOD	35887	11568	14.1	18.3	37.0	19.3	11.3	71715	93034	92	65	6792	0.7	0.1	3.7	66.0	29.5	337167
02066	SCITUATE	44862	6469	10.5	13.9	33.6	22.4	19.7	87325	113037	97	82	5556	0.1	0.1	1.4	40.5	57.9	439408
02067	SHARON	55078	5948	8.4	9.2	26.4	21.8	34.2	112209	150752	99	94	5345	0.2	0.1	2.3	44.9	52.4	414015
02071	SOUTH WALPOLE	35379	225	4.0	10.2	33.8	33.3	18.7	102182	127956	98	90	210	1.0	0.0	1.9	52.9	44.3	385542
02072	STOUGHTON	32452	10326	14.0	19.5	35.6	20.7	10.3	71204	90589	92	64	7824	0.6	0.5	7.7	77.3	13.9	266830
02081	WALPOLE	44275	6759	9.8	14.6	30.1	23.6	22.0	91127	119362	97	86	5821	0.3	0.1	2.0	55.4	42.2	375272
02090	WESTWOOD	56570	5222	9.4	9.3	24.5	24.5	32.3	112612	152888	99	94	4743	0.4	0.2	0.8	19.3	79.4	571588
02093	WRENTHAM	39620	3584	9.0	11.5	33.1	27.9	18.6	93953	119224	98	87	3064	0.3	0.0	2.6	57.8	39.3	360146
02108	BOSTON	113180	2387	15.8	9.6	27.0	14.8	32.8	94202	138386	98	88	805	0.0	0.0	4.5	20.0	75.5	1000001
02109	BOSTON	103791	2048	11.7	15.2	30.3	18.3	24.5	86812	120717	97	82	841	0.0	0.2	5.5	26.9	67.4	554894
02110	BOSTON	104769	934	19.4	10.8	24.5	18.0	27.3	90997	132234	97	85	429	0.0	0.0	2.1	10.0	87.9	748913
02111	BOSTON	22638	1967	44.5	21.6	17.3	9.5	7.1	31030	41583	15	3	342	1.2	0.0	1.5	28.1	69.3	464706
02113	BOSTON	60744	3871	17.1	22.0	33.6	17.5	10.0	62747	84605	87	50	840	0.0	0.6	6.8	43.3	49.3	397531
02114	BOSTON	74385	6466	17.8	16.0	26.7	16.6	23.0	76337	109939	94	70	1722	0.0	0.0	2.2	42.2	55.6	452459
02115	BOSTON	33804	11217	38.9	21.3	20.6	9.7	9.5	36751	48173	35	6	1845	4.2	0.5	2.9	38.0	54.4	440955
02116	BOSTON	95015	10715	19.0	14.4	22.8	16.7	27.1	85324	124743	96	81	3828	0.4	0.1	1.0	18.2	80.2	698718
02118	BOSTON	42942	10998	32.6	18.1	22.1	13.2	14.1	48713	70730	70	19	2741	0.5	0.3	0.5	27.7	71.1	567743
02119	BOSTON	17280	8627	40.8	28.9	21.8	6.1	2.4	30813	36479	14	3	2171	0.4	0.4	17.5	63.1	18.7	250921
02120	BOSTON	18408	5091	40.4	28.8	21.4	6.7	2.7	32682	40044	20	5	767	1.0	0.5	9.4	58.5	30.5	292120
02121	BOSTON	15575	8688	40.1	29.7	22.7	5.1	2.5	30936	36286	15	3	2366	0.9	0.2	11.7	68.3	18.9	285417
02122	BOSTON	21064	8282	24.4	28.8	33.2	9.7	3.9	46832	57634	66	17	3351	0.9	0.6	10.4	73.5	14.5	286043
02124	BOSTON	19586	17536	30.5	27.4	28.0	9.9	4.1	42267	51325	54	12	6624	0.6	0.6	10.6	70.0	18.3	284351
02125	BOSTON	19635	11198	30.8	28.5	27.6	9.4	3.8	41413	50551	51	10	3363	0.4	1.1	12.1	66.6	19.7	276222
02126	MATTAPAN	20679	9595	26.5	28.0	31.2	10.1	4.2	45271	54558	62	16	4151	1.0	0.6	12.1	81.1	5.3	246597
02127	BOSTON	30585	14061	28.0	22.3	30.1	13.3	6.3	49545	64244	71	21	5086	0.8	0.6	8.0	56.6	34.0	334723
02128	BOSTON	18394	14055	33.9	29.8	27.7	6.5	2.1	36899	45559	35	7	4372	0.9	0.7	17.5	65.3	15.7	273289
02129	CHARLESTOWN	55807	7449	22.0	14.6	24.5	19.0	19.9	75721	109604	93	69	2942	0.4	0.0	1.5	37.5	60.6	473821
02130	JAMAICA PLAIN	33981	13976	20.0	21.8	31.7	16.3	10.2	59269	79090	84	42	5498	0.4	0.3	6.6	48.0	44.7	373665
02131	ROSLINDALE	26448	11983	21.6	23.2	34.9	14.5	5.8	55935	70413	81	34	5954	0.4	0.3	6.5	65.6	27.2	312346
02132	WEST ROXBURY	36719	10133	15.0	21.1	35.0	18.4	10.5	67630	86214	90	58	7001	1.8	0.2	4.6	58.8	34.7	349742
02134	ALLSTON	23267	10317	34.0	27.3	26.1	9.3	3.3	37713	47741	38	7	1449	3.1	0.8	14.6	53.7	27.7	306792
02135	BRIGHTON	32129	20510	26.1	20.6	32.2	14.6	6.6	53308	69716	77	28	4987	1.7	0.7	10.2	51.3	36.1	327969
02136	HYDE PARK	23301	10157	25.0	25.3	31.9	14.0	3.7	49636	62089	71	21	5378	0.7	0.8	8.4	81.4	8.7	263367
02138	CAMBRIDGE	53586	13791	17.0	18.5	26.8	16.8	20.9	75981	107116	94	70	4992	0.3	0.5	1.6	21.7	76.0	659131
02139	CAMBRIDGE	37539	15385	21.7	21.8	27.8	16.8	11.8	58813	83515	83	41	4381	0.3	0.6	4.0	36.0	59.0	456782
02140	CAMBRIDGE	47339	8163	18.9	19.1	29.5	15.9	16.6	66748	95852	90	57	3050	0.6	0.0	1.8	31.4	66.2	510309
02141	CAMBRIDGE	33442	5688	27.1	21.3	29.9	13.6	8.1	51575	70431	75	25	1673	0.8	0.5	1.4	44.4	53.0	415278
02142	CAMBRIDGE	63814	905	17.8	22.4	29.8	14.5	15.5	64602	92263	88	54	184	0.5	1.6	0.0	26.1	71.7	551724
02143	SOMERVILLE	33740	11227	21.2	22.5	33.3	15.5	7.5	57803	77025	82	38	3087	0.8	0.8	2.8	52.5	43.1	374492
02144	SOMERVILLE	37860	10587	15.8	19.0	35.9	18.9	10.4	67424	91492	90	58	3425	0.0	0.2	1.1	28.5	70.1	496294
02145	SOMERVILLE	24685	9913	22.8	26.5	33.1	12.0	5.7	50657	65442	73	23	3447	0.6	0.3	4.6	56.0	38.5	356667
02148	MALDEN	27967	23550	20.9	24.1	35.4	14.0	5.7	55220	71292	80	33	11181	1.3	0.4	6.8	76.4	15.0	284419
02149	EVERETT	25015	15588	24.5	26.4	34.0	11.3	3.9	49139	62479	70	20	6947	0.8	0.4	9.5	75.9	13.5	276641
02150	CHELSEA	18119	11896	35.7	27.7	25.4	8.0	3.2	36020	44994	32	6	3724	2.2	2.2	17.1	69.8	8.8	251097
02151	REVERE	25106	19534	28.8	26.2	29.4	10.6	5.0	44368	56417	60	14	9955	0.8	1.3	12.1	72.8	13.0	265020
02152	WINTHROP	35214	7544	15.4	20.6	36.9	18.9	8.1	65391	83577	89	55	4298	0.4	0.3	6.3	65.6	27.5	332964
02153	MEDFORD	7566	0	0.0	0.0	0.0	0.0	0.0	0	0	0	0	0	0.0	0.0	0.0	0.0	0.0	0
02155	MEDFORD	31931	22109	18.2	19.9	34.3	19.7	7.9	64423	83649	88	53	12988	0.3	0.2	2.5	60.1	36.9	354383
02163	BOSTON	27019	437	33.0	29.3	19.7	9.2	8.9	38753	51354	42	8	30	0.0	0.0	3.3	16.7	80.0	666667
02169	QUINCY	32893	24462	20.8	24.8	33.0	14.4	6.9	54417	70116	79	31	11348	1.3	0.5	8.7	72.9	16.7	271797
02170	QUINCY	31012	7748	15.0	22.9	36.7	18.6	6.8	62194	78925	86	48	4136	2.6	0.2	7.1	75.4	14.7	286927
02171	QUINCY	35944	7743	14.1	25.0	34.0	17.0	9.9	62126	80353	86	48	4407	2.8	0.1	9.4	66.7	21.0	289654
02176	MELROSE	40209	11043	14.2	15.4	34.4	22.2	13.7	78280	101894	95	75	7749	0.4	0.1	1.4	52.3	45.8	386996
02180	STONEHAM	35967	9030	14.0	21.5	34.0	20.6	10.0	70625	91049	91	63	6338	0.2	0.1	3.7	60.8	35.3	352640
02184	BRAINTREE	37587	13004	12.0	17.1	36.5	21.4	13.0	77659	100064	94	73	10411	0.3	0.1	3.2	69.7	26.9	326090
02186	MILTON	49959	8994	10.0	12.3	26.8	24.4	26.6	101517	134944	98	89	7682	0.2	0.1	0.9	40.1	58.8	442967
02188	WEYMOUTH	29949	5762	19.9	22.9	33.5	17.6	6.2	60253	76377	85	44	3878	0.5	2.1	6.1	79.1	12.1	278082
02189	EAST WEYMOUTH	28706	6257	17.2	25.1	36.9	15.4	5.4	57775	73653	82	38	4011	0.5	0.6	10.1	79.2	9.6	254595
02190	SOUTH WEYMOUTH	32903	6989	12.6	22.1	37.4	19.9	8.1	66432	84115	89	57	4543	0.0	0.7	7.5	74.3	17.5	296408
02191	NORTH WEYMOUTH	34927	3625	11.9	23.1	35.7	20.8	8.5	69395	88614	91	62	2920	0.3	0.2	9.2	79.4	11.0	254100
02199	BOSTON	120145	702	8.4	25.1	21.5	18.2	26.8	83583	125849	96	80	0	0.0	0.0	0.0	0.0	0.0	0
02210	BOSTON	42269	269	12.6	21.6	36.8	17.5	11.5	70447	94765	91	63	118	0.0	0.0	19.5	55.1	25.4	252778
02215	BOSTON	22836	7018	41.3	25.3	22.4	7.9	3.1	32432	42570	19	5	751	2.0	0.0	14.9	66.4	16.6	242005
02301	BROCKTON	20611	23574	30.1	27.3	29.1	9.7	3.8	42787	52125	55	13	11148	0.5	1.3	25.8	69.7	2.7	207339
02302	BROCKTON	21883	11301	21.0	24.6	38.3	12.3	3.8	53929	65613	78	30	7971	0.5	0.8	34.1	63.7	0.9	189131
02322	AVON	32818	1880	19.5	22.6	32.5	18.0	7.4	59062	76960	84	41	1333	0.0	0.0	10.1	82.8	7.1	245366
02324	BRIDGEWATER	30897	7919	12.5	15.3	40.1	21.7	10.5	78075	93865	94	74	5908	0.1	1.0	8.0	71.7	19.2	290381
02325	BRIDGEWATER	6344	28	14.3	21.4	53.6	10.7	0.0	63053	68488	87	51	6	0.0	0.0	0.0	83.3	16.7	250000
02330	CARVER	25135	4192	18.5	20.7	40.4	15.7	4.6	63204	76210	87	51	3774	0.9	7.2	19.6	67.8	4.6	229673
02332	DUXBURY	52872	5258	7.6	9.0	22.9	29.5	31.0	117885	153328	99	95	4764	0.0	0.0	0.7	23.7	75.6	548453
02333	EAST BRIDGEWATER	29340	4609	11.9	17.4	39.3	22.0	9.4	73751	89712	93	68	3844	0.2	0.5	8.3	78.6	12.4	266832
02338	HALIFAX	29156	2810	13.9	17.4	43.6	18.2	6.8	68601	82404	91	60	2569	1.3	3.6	19.1	66.2	9.9	240750
02339	HANOVER	38887	4517	9.7	10.4	35.4	24.3	20.2	90334	115548	97	84	3979	0.3	0.0	0.5	50.6	48.6	394892
02341	HANSON	29385	3285	9.8	16.0	43.0	21.4	9.8	76691	93445	94	72	2920	0.2	0.0	3.5	79.8	16.5	287236
02343	HOLBROOK	30207	4060	17.9	17.2	39.2	19.1	6.5	65795	82479	89	56	3193	3.6	1.4	11.3	79.1	4.7	230402
02346	MIDDLEBORO	24755	7427	14.2	21.9	45.7	14.9	3.4	62164	75618	86	48	5732	0.8	0.9	10.1	81.1	7.0	242783
02347	LAKEVILLE	32408	3559	9.6	12.2	40.1	26.3	11.8	82409	101868	96	79	3222	0.2	1.0	9.8	70.0	18.9	284880
02351	ABINGTON	29777	5448	14.4	19.5	37.2	20.6	8.3	69306	85689	91	61	4070	0.2	0.4	7.9	78.4	13.1	272848
02356	NORTH EASTON	45501	4283	9.2	12.9	34.2	22.3	21.5	88763	111948	97	84	3697	0.2	0.3	2.5	52.8	44.1	373726
02357	NORTH EASTON	13274	27	22.2	22.2	40.7	0.0	14.8	52426	60000	76	26	13	0.0	0.0	0.0	100.0	0.0	225000
02359	PEMBROKE	34697	6176	11.9	15.7	37.3	22.9	12.1	79011	97959	95	75	5521	0.3	0.1	4.9	70.7	24.1	291209
02360	PLYMOUTH	29534	19660	14.6	20.7	39.2	17.3	8.1	66238	81203	89	56	15487	0.9	1.0	11.1	75.1	11.9	251416
02364	KINGSTON	29354	4434	15.2	21.5	36.7	15.9	10.8	65201	81614	89	54	3535	0.2	0.6	11.7	59.2	28.2	297284
	MASSACHUSETTS	33908		19.9	21.2	32.0	16.1	10.9	61110	77759				0.8	1.2	14.8	55.7	27.5	282585
	UNITED STATES	25866		24.7	27.1	30.8	10.9	6.5	48124	56710				10.9	15.0	33.7	30.1	10.4	145905

#	POST OFFICE NAME	FINANCIAL SERVICES: Auto Loan	FINANCIAL SERVICES: Home Loan	FINANCIAL SERVICES: Invest-ments	FINANCIAL SERVICES: Retire-ment Plans	THE HOME: Home Improvements: Home Repair	THE HOME: Home Improvements: Lawn & Garden	THE HOME: Furnishings: Comput-ers & Hard-ware	THE HOME: Furnishings: Major Appli-ances	THE HOME: Furnishings: TV, Radio, Sound Equip-ment	THE HOME: Furnishings: Furni-ture	ENTERTAINMENT: Dine out/ Carry out	ENTERTAINMENT: Sports Equip-ment	ENTERTAINMENT: Fees & Tickets	ENTERTAINMENT: Toys & Games	ENTERTAINMENT: Travel	ENTERTAINMENT: Cable TV	PERSONAL: Apparel & Services	PERSONAL: Auto Repairs	PERSONAL: Health Insur-ance	PERSONAL: Pets & Supplies
02032	EAST WALPOLE	126	165	201	161	160	163	148	146	139	148	175	170	160	189	154	137	176	143	131	158
02035	FOXBORO	143	167	194	169	164	170	159	155	152	158	191	180	168	198	162	149	190	154	145	171
02038	FRANKLIN	139	158	170	163	153	153	149	146	139	151	176	171	154	179	148	133	174	144	130	160
02043	HINGHAM	185	250	316	240	243	253	222	220	208	223	262	250	243	283	233	209	265	213	200	235
02045	HULL	106	121	146	125	119	122	120	116	115	119	144	139	124	148	120	111	143	117	106	127
02048	MANSFIELD	137	149	160	156	145	145	144	141	135	146	171	166	146	170	141	128	168	140	125	155
02050	MARSHFIELD	131	153	174	155	150	153	144	142	136	144	172	166	151	178	146	133	170	140	130	157
02052	MEDFIELD	234	283	321	292	275	279	260	252	240	261	304	295	279	315	263	232	305	247	226	278
02053	MEDWAY	137	163	176	167	159	158	149	147	139	150	175	173	157	182	150	133	174	144	131	162
02054	MILLIS	119	142	164	146	140	141	134	131	125	133	158	154	140	164	135	121	157	129	118	144
02056	NORFOLK	170	212	228	216	206	206	187	184	172	189	218	214	203	228	191	166	219	178	164	204
02061	NORWELL	190	235	258	240	229	234	209	206	192	211	244	236	228	252	214	188	245	199	187	227
02062	NORWOOD	111	123	158	126	121	129	124	120	121	124	153	140	129	157	126	120	151	121	114	131
02066	SCITUATE	155	185	204	180	184	193	168	170	161	168	202	194	178	210	175	162	200	165	164	189
02067	SHARON	200	261	307	258	253	260	230	227	214	232	270	260	252	287	239	212	273	220	205	247
02071	SOUTH WALPOLE	142	176	187	177	173	171	157	157	146	157	183	184	167	195	161	141	183	151	140	173
02072	STOUGHTON	108	125	145	124	123	129	121	118	117	119	147	137	127	154	123	116	146	118	113	129
02081	WALPOLE	158	192	218	193	189	192	177	175	167	177	210	204	188	220	181	163	209	171	160	192
02090	WESTWOOD	190	245	298	238	240	250	221	220	208	221	262	251	238	277	231	208	262	214	203	237
02093	WRENTHAM	153	188	198	191	183	181	168	166	154	169	195	194	179	205	170	149	195	160	147	183
02108	BOSTON	237	220	392	251	210	236	267	237	273	268	346	292	272	356	259	268	342	257	223	264
02109	BOSTON	218	209	394	241	198	222	247	219	253	252	322	270	258	338	243	251	320	235	204	245
02110	BOSTON	214	205	382	236	195	217	242	215	247	246	315	265	252	329	238	244	312	231	200	240
02111	BOSTON	66	70	100	78	73	72	80	76	74	76	93	97	76	90	79	69	92	82	67	81
02113	BOSTON	118	113	213	130	107	120	134	118	137	136	174	146	139	183	131	136	173	127	111	132
02114	BOSTON	154	148	278	170	140	157	175	155	179	178	228	190	182	239	172	178	226	166	145	173
02115	BOSTON	91	76	131	86	73	85	106	88	108	101	136	113	101	136	98	103	133	100	84	99
02116	BOSTON	204	194	357	221	184	207	231	204	237	234	301	251	239	313	226	235	298	220	193	229
02118	BOSTON	108	104	190	115	100	112	124	111	128	125	163	135	126	169	122	129	162	120	107	124
02119	BOSTON	58	53	76	50	51	60	60	57	66	61	83	64	60	83	59	69	81	60	61	65
02120	BOSTON	61	50	73	54	49	56	68	59	69	65	87	74	64	84	62	67	85	66	57	67
02121	BOSTON	59	52	65	48	49	58	58	56	64	60	80	64	59	78	57	66	78	59	60	64
02122	BOSTON	72	77	121	77	74	83	84	78	87	83	111	93	86	118	86	89	110	83	77	86
02124	BOSTON	74	71	96	69	68	78	78	74	82	79	104	85	79	105	77	84	102	77	76	84
02125	BOSTON	67	67	112	67	64	74	77	71	83	77	104	84	79	110	78	85	104	76	72	79
02126	MATTAPAN	81	77	95	74	75	86	81	80	87	84	109	88	84	109	82	90	107	82	84	91
02127	BOSTON	80	80	114	83	78	87	88	83	90	88	114	98	90	115	88	90	112	87	82	92
02128	BOSTON	56	58	107	56	55	64	67	61	73	68	93	71	68	100	68	77	94	66	63	67
02129	CHARLESTOWN	142	138	247	151	131	148	160	145	167	164	212	174	165	221	159	168	211	155	139	161
02130	JAMAICA PLAIN	98	101	175	106	96	108	114	104	118	115	150	124	118	158	114	119	149	110	100	115
02131	ROSLINDALE	85	94	128	94	91	98	97	93	97	97	122	108	99	127	97	97	122	95	88	101
02132	WEST ROXBURY	107	123	156	123	120	129	122	118	119	121	149	137	127	154	124	118	148	119	113	128
02134	ALLSTON	71	50	69	56	48	57	83	65	81	73	101	87	71	94	70	73	97	76	60	73
02135	BRIGHTON	88	79	134	89	76	86	100	87	102	98	128	108	99	130	95	99	126	95	83	97
02136	HYDE PARK	80	84	103	83	82	89	87	84	87	87	110	96	88	111	87	87	108	86	82	92
02138	CAMBRIDGE	160	160	262	176	154	170	182	164	182	182	231	200	188	238	179	179	228	174	154	183
02139	CAMBRIDGE	109	103	186	117	98	110	123	109	126	124	160	134	127	166	120	124	158	118	102	122
02140	CAMBRIDGE	123	124	224	135	118	133	143	128	147	144	187	155	148	199	143	149	187	137	123	142
02141	CAMBRIDGE	86	87	154	92	83	94	101	91	106	100	134	109	104	142	101	108	134	98	89	101
02142	CAMBRIDGE	156	122	200	140	117	136	181	146	180	168	227	191	168	221	161	169	220	167	136	165
02143	SOMERVILLE	94	90	162	100	86	97	107	95	110	107	140	116	110	146	105	110	139	103	92	106
02144	SOMERVILLE	105	100	182	113	95	107	120	106	123	121	156	131	123	163	117	122	155	115	100	118
02145	SOMERVILLE	77	81	147	83	77	87	92	83	97	92	123	99	95	134	93	100	124	89	82	92
02148	MALDEN	86	92	123	94	90	97	96	92	96	96	121	107	99	125	97	96	120	94	88	101
02149	EVERETT	77	81	108	82	80	87	86	82	87	85	110	96	88	113	87	87	108	85	81	90
02150	CHELSEA	63	62	107	59	59	69	71	67	78	73	100	76	71	104	72	83	100	72	69	73
02151	REVERE	77	81	103	80	79	88	84	81	86	83	108	94	86	110	85	87	106	83	82	90
02152	WINTHROP	102	117	147	118	115	121	116	112	112	115	141	131	120	145	117	111	140	113	106	122
02153	MEDFORD	0	0	0	0	0	0	0	0	0	0	0	0	0	0	0	0	0	0	0	0
02155	MEDFORD	100	112	141	114	110	117	113	109	110	112	138	127	117	142	114	109	137	111	103	119
02163	BOSTON	99	83	109	92	82	91	110	97	108	104	136	123	102	128	100	100	132	109	90	108
02169	QUINCY	92	94	128	99	92	100	102	96	101	101	128	114	104	129	101	100	126	100	92	106
02170	QUINCY	92	104	140	109	103	107	107	102	103	106	129	122	109	132	108	100	128	105	94	111
02171	QUINCY	106	118	163	127	119	122	124	120	117	122	148	147	125	148	125	112	146	125	108	129
02176	MELROSE	120	147	188	145	143	151	140	136	135	139	169	157	148	179	144	135	169	136	127	147
02180	STONEHAM	110	128	151	128	126	132	124	121	119	123	150	141	129	155	126	118	148	121	115	133
02184	BRAINTREE	123	152	182	147	148	156	141	139	136	141	171	159	151	181	146	137	170	137	132	151
02186	MILTON	173	226	277	219	220	229	204	201	193	204	242	230	220	258	213	192	243	196	185	217
02188	WEYMOUTH	92	103	122	104	101	106	102	99	99	102	125	116	106	128	103	98	123	100	94	109
02189	EAST WEYMOUTH	88	99	119	100	98	104	99	96	97	98	121	112	103	125	100	96	120	97	92	105
02190	SOUTH WEYMOUTH	106	116	134	119	113	118	115	112	111	115	140	132	118	142	115	107	138	113	103	123
02191	NORTH WEYMOUTH	108	126	144	123	124	131	121	119	117	119	147	136	127	154	124	117	146	117	114	129
02199	BOSTON	207	198	374	228	188	210	235	208	241	239	306	256	245	321	231	238	304	223	194	232
02210	BOSTON	105	101	190	116	95	107	119	106	122	122	156	130	125	163	117	121	154	113	99	118
02215	BOSTON	67	45	58	51	44	52	77	60	75	67	94	81	65	85	64	67	89	71	56	68
02301	BROCKTON	72	74	87	74	73	79	78	75	79	77	98	88	79	99	78	78	96	78	74	83
02302	BROCKTON	81	89	101	88	87	92	90	87	89	88	111	101	92	114	90	88	109	88	84	95
02322	AVON	111	127	141	123	125	134	121	120	119	120	149	137	128	155	125	120	147	119	118	131
02324	BRIDGEWATER	126	135	142	138	133	136	132	130	127	131	159	154	134	162	131	122	156	130	120	146
02325	BRIDGEWATER	93	73	96	83	73	81	102	89	100	95	126	114	93	118	91	92	122	101	83	100
02330	CARVER	106	99	85	98	101	108	98	102	99	97	121	119	94	119	97	99	116	102	104	119
02332	DUXBURY	195	239	274	243	235	243	216	214	201	218	254	245	234	261	222	197	254	207	197	234
02333	EAST BRIDGEWATER	111	135	146	134	133	133	123	122	116	123	146	142	131	155	126	114	146	119	112	134
02338	HALIFAX	107	122	128	120	121	127	111	115	107	113	134	126	116	133	114	106	131	111	111	125
02339	HANOVER	152	186	204	188	182	184	168	166	156	168	197	193	180	207	172	152	197	161	151	183
02341	HANSON	115	140	150	140	137	137	127	126	119	127	150	148	134	158	130	116	149	123	114	139
02343	HOLBROOK	100	117	134	114	115	122	112	110	109	111	137	126	118	143	115	109	135	109	107	120
02346	MIDDLEBORO	91	103	109	103	102	104	99	98	95	97	118	115	102	123	99	92	117	97	91	108
02347	LAKEVILLE	127	151	157	152	146	146	137	136	129	139	162	158	144	169	138	124	161	132	123	149
02351	ABINGTON	105	124	139	124	122	125	117	115	111	116	140	135	123	147	119	109	139	113	107	126
02356	NORTH EASTON	166	204	221	204	199	202	183	181	171	184	216	209	197	228	188	168	216	175	166	199
02357	NORTH EASTON	91	56	70	63	55	66	108	79	105	91	131	110	88	118	86	92	123	97	73	90
02359	PEMBROKE	131	160	172	160	157	156	145	144	136	145	171	168	154	181	148	132	171	140	130	158
02360	PLYMOUTH	110	120	127	121	119	122	115	115	111	115	139	135	117	142	116	108	136	114	108	129
02364	KINGSTON	108	125	131	126	121	122	115	114	109	117	137	132	120	141	116	105	136	112	103	124
	MASSACHUSETTS	112	121	148	122	120	127	122	119	121	121	151	138	126	156	123	120	149	120	115	132
	UNITED STATES	100	100	100	100	100	100	100	100	100	100	100	100	100	100	100	100	100	100	100	100

MASSACHUSETTS

POPULATION CHANGE

# POST OFFICE NAME	COUNTY FIPS CODE	POPULATION 2000	2004	2009	2000-2004 ANNUAL RATE % Rate	State Centile	HOUSEHOLDS 2000	2004	2009	% Annual Rate 2000-2004	2004 Average HH Size	FAMILIES 2000	2004	% Annual Rate 2000-2004
02367 PLYMPTON	023	2651	2793	2926	1.2	86	857	909	958	1.4	3.07	740	785	1.4
02368 RANDOLPH	021	31014	31162	31626	0.1	36	11326	11442	11677	0.2	2.70	7990	8076	0.3
02370 ROCKLAND	023	17670	17814	18402	0.2	40	6539	6664	6944	0.5	2.64	4584	4671	0.4
02375 SOUTH EASTON	005	9104	9857	10376	1.9	95	3444	3764	4000	2.1	2.62	2425	2664	2.2
02379 WEST BRIDGEWATER	023	6254	6475	6723	0.8	72	2313	2426	2547	1.1	2.62	1689	1768	1.1
02382 WHITMAN	023	13882	14378	15013	0.8	73	4999	5232	5515	1.1	2.74	3604	3773	1.1
02420 LEXINGTON	017	13705	13796	13941	0.2	37	4923	4987	5079	0.3	2.69	3869	3920	0.3
02421 LEXINGTON	017	16645	17166	17566	0.7	70	6183	6453	6677	1.0	2.60	4555	4742	1.0
02445 BROOKLINE	021	21301	21730	22271	0.5	57	9155	9358	9624	0.5	2.27	4739	4864	0.6
02446 BROOKLINE	021	29983	30471	31233	0.4	52	14365	14620	15034	0.4	2.04	5802	5897	0.4
02451 WALTHAM	017	17644	17983	18218	0.5	56	7265	7492	7665	0.7	2.36	4313	4458	0.8
02452 WALTHAM	017	12102	12354	12535	0.5	59	4255	4386	4494	0.7	2.19	2400	2488	0.9
02453 WALTHAM	017	29165	29616	30002	0.4	50	11507	11840	12127	0.7	2.25	5641	5794	0.6
02458 NEWTON	017	14136	14006	14027	-0.2	16	5548	5560	5626	0.1	2.37	3112	3122	0.1
02459 NEWTON CENTER	017	18637	18356	18318	-0.4	8	6707	6662	6706	-0.2	2.67	4900	4869	-0.2
02460 NEWTONVILLE	017	8191	8068	8056	-0.4	8	3374	3355	3380	-0.1	2.40	2045	2035	-0.1
02461 NEWTON HIGHLANDS	017	6543	6471	6484	-0.3	13	2565	2557	2586	-0.1	2.44	1758	1752	-0.1
02462 NEWTON LOWER FALLS	017	1427	1517	1564	1.5	89	520	557	579	1.6	2.61	332	356	1.7
02464 NEWTON UPPER FALLS	017	3169	3147	3149	-0.2	20	1314	1318	1332	0.1	2.33	798	800	0.1
02465 WEST NEWTON	017	11869	11769	11786	-0.2	17	4437	4444	4493	0.0	2.62	3105	3113	0.1
02466 AUBURNDALE	017	7021	7211	7334	0.6	66	2722	2832	2913	0.9	2.31	1723	1794	1.0
02467 CHESTNUT HILL	021	15162	15083	15170	-0.1	22	4967	4939	4991	-0.1	2.39	3247	3226	-0.2
02468 WABAN	017	5341	5425	5469	0.4	51	1858	1910	1946	0.7	2.82	1438	1479	0.7
02472 WATERTOWN	017	32958	32322	32230	-0.5	5	14605	14498	14611	-0.2	2.14	7313	7267	-0.2
02474 ARLINGTON	017	25865	25514	25524	-0.3	11	11665	11670	11804	0.0	2.18	6537	6535	0.0
02476 ARLINGTON	017	16547	16512	16631	-0.1	26	7357	7435	7564	0.3	2.20	4261	4297	0.2
02478 BELMONT	017	24421	24219	24271	-0.2	17	9841	9846	9951	0.0	2.43	6513	6510	0.0
02481 WELLESLEY HILLS	021	14062	13836	13911	-0.4	7	4901	4831	4880	-0.3	2.75	3948	3894	-0.3
02482 WELLESLEY	021	12719	12945	13164	0.4	54	3807	3925	4041	0.7	2.56	2670	2751	0.7
02492 NEEDHAM	021	19995	19977	20103	0.0	29	7232	7271	7360	0.1	2.64	5396	5423	0.1
02493 WESTON	017	11979	11874	11865	-0.2	16	3997	3973	3994	-0.1	2.77	3178	3154	-0.2
02494 NEEDHAM HEIGHTS	021	8844	8983	9142	0.4	51	3352	3413	3487	0.4	2.57	2366	2410	0.4
02532 BUZZARDS BAY	001	12412	13012	13730	1.1	81	5016	5355	5743	1.6	2.28	3228	3443	1.5
02535 CHILMARK	007	1234	1331	1407	1.8	95	542	590	625	2.0	2.26	339	369	2.0
02536 EAST FALMOUTH	001	19377	20378	21586	1.2	84	7757	8290	8906	1.6	2.44	5432	5801	1.6
02537 EAST SANDWICH	001	6238	6885	7488	2.4	98	2304	2579	2840	2.7	2.66	1734	1940	2.7
02538 EAST WAREHAM	023	4851	4772	4871	-0.4	7	1967	1949	2005	-0.2	2.44	1231	1219	-0.2
02539 EDGARTOWN	007	3764	3942	4104	1.1	81	1575	1663	1741	1.3	2.33	953	1005	1.3
02540 FALMOUTH	001	9143	9369	9795	0.6	63	4354	4545	4835	1.0	1.94	2369	2466	1.0
02542 BUZZARDS BAY	001	1581	1510	1555	-1.1	1	504	491	514	-0.6	3.02	416	405	-0.6
02543 WOODS HOLE	001	782	794	824	0.4	50	383	395	417	0.7	1.96	204	210	0.7
02554 NANTUCKET	019	9520	10673	12157	2.7	99	3699	4188	4812	3.0	2.37	2106	2387	3.0
02556 NORTH FALMOUTH	001	3355	3711	4033	2.4	99	1364	1542	1705	2.9	2.33	971	1093	2.8
02559 POCASSET	001	4112	4219	4455	0.6	65	1866	1947	2089	1.0	2.16	1195	1248	1.0
02562 SAGAMORE BEACH	001	2882	3121	3352	1.9	95	1043	1151	1256	2.4	2.58	792	872	2.3
02563 SANDWICH	001	9867	10596	11369	1.7	93	3685	4031	4393	2.1	2.60	2707	2948	2.0
02568 VINEYARD HAVEN	007	9787	10279	10722	1.2	83	4210	4460	4684	1.4	2.28	2447	2591	1.4
02571 WAREHAM	023	10175	10597	11089	1.0	77	4023	4244	4490	1.3	2.45	2651	2788	1.2
02575 WEST TISBURY	007	116	127	135	2.2	98	48	53	57	2.4	2.40	31	35	2.9
02576 WEST WAREHAM	023	3275	3320	3418	0.3	47	1315	1345	1397	0.5	2.42	910	930	0.5
02601 HYANNIS	001	15706	15935	16666	0.3	48	6668	6817	7213	0.5	2.23	3709	3792	0.5
02630 BARNSTABLE	001	1997	2111	2240	1.3	87	861	918	984	1.5	2.29	618	659	1.5
02631 BREWSTER	001	10360	10483	11173	1.5	90	4035	4369	4729	1.9	2.30	2784	3008	1.8
02632 CENTERVILLE	001	11029	11197	11661	0.4	50	4532	4676	4944	0.7	2.30	3087	3177	0.7
02633 CHATHAM	001	4816	4862	5049	0.2	42	2353	2414	2548	0.6	1.94	1388	1421	0.6
02635 COTUIT	001	3294	3426	3615	0.9	76	1412	1484	1584	1.2	2.30	1027	1079	1.2
02638 DENNIS	001	3769	3868	4095	0.6	65	1716	1798	1936	1.1	2.15	1133	1185	1.1
02639 DENNIS PORT	001	3532	3705	3918	1.1	82	1709	1812	1939	1.4	2.01	924	977	1.3
02642 EASTHAM	001	5526	5722	6007	0.8	72	2432	2561	2730	1.2	2.21	1657	1742	1.2
02644 FORESTDALE	001	3824	4018	4250	1.2	83	1258	1337	1431	1.4	3.00	1009	1071	1.4
02645 HARWICH	001	9506	10353	11170	2.0	97	4055	4490	4920	2.4	2.23	2752	3039	2.4
02646 HARWICH PORT	001	1928	1948	2031	0.2	43	993	1017	1073	0.6	1.90	543	550	0.3
02648 MARSTONS MILLS	001	8145	8634	9196	1.4	88	2979	3200	3450	1.7	2.69	2282	2449	1.7
02649 MASHPEE	001	12970	14465	15792	2.6	99	5267	5943	6564	2.9	2.41	3659	4120	2.8
02650 NORTH CHATHAM	001	782	803	835	0.6	66	315	330	351	1.1	2.03	201	211	1.2
02652 NORTH TRURO	001	1206	1260	1326	1.0	79	488	519	556	1.5	2.23	283	300	1.4
02653 ORLEANS	001	6285	6465	6769	0.7	68	3064	3220	3433	1.2	1.96	1758	1842	1.1
02655 OSTERVILLE	001	3842	3881	4024	0.2	43	1749	1787	1874	0.5	2.17	1187	1211	0.5
02657 PROVINCETOWN	001	3431	3476	3604	0.3	47	1837	1899	2005	0.8	1.66	465	479	0.7
02659 SOUTH CHATHAM	001	1027	1033	1067	0.1	37	492	505	529	0.6	2.02	298	305	0.6
02660 SOUTH DENNIS	001	7180	7857	8499	2.1	97	3260	3626	3977	2.5	2.15	2076	2302	2.5
02664 SOUTH YARMOUTH	001	9631	9716	10091	0.2	41	4636	4743	4994	0.5	2.01	2632	2686	0.5
02666 TRURO	001	881	907	949	0.7	69	419	439	467	1.1	2.05	230	241	1.1
02667 WELLFLEET	001	2677	2743	2863	0.6	62	1265	1316	1394	0.9	2.08	706	733	0.9
02668 WEST BARNSTABLE	001	3281	3393	3564	0.8	71	1202	1257	1336	1.1	2.69	914	953	1.0
02670 WEST DENNIS	001	1586	1780	1949	2.8	100	808	926	1030	3.3	1.88	442	505	3.2
02671 WEST HARWICH	001	1112	1171	1240	1.2	84	533	568	609	1.5	2.04	333	354	1.5
02673 WEST YARMOUTH	001	8929	9213	9668	0.7	71	3954	4131	4393	1.0	2.17	2363	2463	1.0
02675 YARMOUTH PORT	001	6916	7184	7580	0.9	75	3197	3380	3618	1.3	2.12	2119	2238	1.3
02702 ASSONET	005	3529	3660	3781	0.9	73	1228	1291	1350	1.2	2.79	1012	1064	1.2
02703 ATTLEBORO	005	41854	43562	45087	1.0	77	15892	16688	17448	1.2	2.56	10845	11403	1.2
02713 CUTTYHUNK	007	86	87	89	0.3	45	46	47	48	0.5	1.85	21	21	0.0
02715 DIGHTON	005	2374	2423	2468	0.5	57	830	859	884	0.8	2.78	666	689	0.8
02717 EAST FREETOWN	005	4998	4965	5015	-0.2	20	1719	1733	1772	0.2	2.83	1390	1400	0.2
02718 EAST TAUNTON	005	6824	7044	7219	0.8	71	2382	2482	2568	1.0	2.84	1864	1941	1.0
02719 FAIRHAVEN	005	16159	16128	16381	-0.1	26	6622	6684	6865	0.2	2.36	4251	4287	0.2
02720 FALL RIVER	005	31684	32217	33040	0.4	53	13298	13733	14273	0.8	2.25	7951	8186	0.7
02721 FALL RIVER	005	25932	26430	27082	0.5	56	10729	11045	11437	0.7	2.37	6719	6904	0.6
02723 FALL RIVER	005	16115	15845	15970	-0.4	7	6773	6744	6879	-0.1	2.31	4154	4128	-0.2
02724 FALL RIVER	005	17624	17450	17639	-0.2	15	7772	7802	7983	0.1	2.22	4598	4604	0.0
02725 SOMERSET	005	2665	2698	2751	0.3	46	942	968	1000	0.6	2.65	709	729	0.7
02726 SOMERSET	005	15552	15569	15743	0.0	31	6035	6123	6268	0.3	2.52	4541	4601	0.3
02738 MARION	023	5117	5278	5465	0.7	70	1995	2079	2172	1.0	2.49	1441	1501	1.0
02739 MATTAPOISETT	023	6268	6285	6435	0.1	33	2532	2563	2648	0.3	2.44	1771	1790	0.3
02740 NEW BEDFORD	005	43489	43417	43993	0.0	27	17823	18020	18477	0.3	2.33	10831	10902	0.2
MASSACHUSETTS					0.4					0.6	2.48			0.6
UNITED STATES					1.2					1.3	2.58			1.1

ZIP CODE #	POST OFFICE NAME	RACE (%) White 2000	White 2004	Black 2000	Black 2004	Asian/Pacific 2000	Asian/Pacific 2004	% Hispanic Origin 2000	% Hispanic Origin 2004	2004 AGE DISTRIBUTION (%) 0-4	5-9	10-14	15-19	20-24	25-44	45-64	65-84	85+	18+	MEDIAN AGE 2004	% 2004 Males	% 2004 Females
02367	PLYMPTON	96.9	96.4	1.0	1.1	0.3	0.4	0.4	0.5	6.1	7.0	8.5	7.0	5.4	26.5	31.6	7.0	0.9	74.0	39.2	48.6	51.5
02368	RANDOLPH	62.9	59.1	20.8	22.3	10.2	12.1	3.3	3.7	6.0	6.1	6.7	6.4	5.8	28.8	26.2	12.0	2.0	77.2	39.2	48.0	52.0
02370	ROCKLAND	94.8	93.8	1.7	2.0	1.1	1.4	1.0	1.3	7.3	7.1	7.1	6.8	6.0	28.8	23.9	11.4	1.7	74.2	37.2	48.0	52.0
02375	SOUTH EASTON	94.6	93.6	2.3	2.6	1.5	1.9	1.3	1.6	6.5	6.9	7.0	5.8	4.9	30.1	28.3	9.6	1.1	75.9	38.9	48.5	51.5
02379	WEST BRIDGEWATER	96.4	95.8	0.9	1.1	0.7	0.9	1.0	1.2	5.9	6.1	6.1	6.0	5.6	26.2	26.6	14.3	3.3	78.2	41.4	48.8	51.2
02382	WHITMAN	97.2	96.7	0.7	0.8	0.4	0.6	0.9	1.1	6.9	6.9	7.5	7.2	6.6	31.1	24.1	8.6	1.2	74.4	35.9	48.9	51.1
02420	LEXINGTON	86.3	83.7	0.9	1.0	11.1	13.4	1.4	1.7	5.1	6.6	8.6	6.9	3.6	18.1	31.2	16.7	3.3	75.0	45.6	47.3	52.7
02421	LEXINGTON	86.0	83.0	1.4	1.5	10.8	13.4	1.4	1.7	5.6	6.8	8.1	6.8	3.9	19.8	30.2	15.3	3.6	74.7	44.4	47.0	53.0
02445	BROOKLINE	82.1	79.0	3.5	3.9	10.6	12.9	3.6	4.2	4.4	4.3	4.8	6.6	8.8	34.7	25.1	9.6	1.8	82.7	35.7	45.5	54.5
02446	BROOKLINE	79.5	76.0	2.4	2.7	14.8	17.7	3.9	4.6	4.3	3.4	3.7	4.9	10.5	41.4	19.7	9.3	2.8	86.0	33.5	45.5	54.5
02451	WALTHAM	82.5	79.8	4.5	4.9	9.4	11.1	5.4	6.4	5.3	5.1	4.9	4.7	5.5	35.6	24.6	12.5	1.8	82.0	38.5	49.1	50.9
02452	WALTHAM	87.3	85.2	3.6	4.0	6.5	7.9	3.8	4.4	4.1	3.6	3.5	12.3	13.3	24.6	23.2	13.1	2.5	86.6	36.2	48.3	51.8
02453	WALTHAM	81.4	78.7	4.7	5.1	6.5	8.0	12.4	14.4	4.5	4.1	4.2	8.4	10.9	37.3	19.3	9.5	1.9	84.7	33.5	50.0	50.0
02458	NEWTON	88.1	85.7	1.6	1.8	7.8	9.7	2.7	3.3	4.6	4.7	5.2	9.9	5.2	33.8	23.4	10.7	2.6	82.1	36.8	46.9	53.1
02459	NEWTON CENTER	87.5	85.2	2.3	2.6	8.0	9.9	2.3	2.8	5.3	6.3	7.2	7.7	5.1	23.1	29.7	13.4	2.3	76.9	42.1	47.4	52.6
02460	NEWTONVILLE	89.6	87.4	1.4	1.6	7.1	8.9	1.9	2.3	5.1	5.5	6.2	6.0	5.0	32.1	26.7	11.0	2.4	79.2	39.4	47.2	52.8
02461	NEWTON HIGHLANDS	85.4	82.5	2.5	2.8	9.3	11.5	3.0	3.5	5.3	6.1	6.4	7.2	5.7	24.9	29.3	12.8	2.3	78.7	41.7	45.2	54.8
02462	NEWTON LOWER FALLS	86.6	84.0	2.3	2.6	9.8	12.1	1.9	2.2	5.1	5.7	7.3	8.2	6.3	21.8	29.7	12.9	3.0	76.2	42.0	45.8	54.3
02464	NEWTON UPPER FALLS	84.2	81.1	2.2	2.4	10.8	13.4	2.2	2.7	6.2	6.4	6.0	5.2	4.7	32.3	26.1	10.2	3.0	78.2	39.2	45.6	54.4
02465	WEST NEWTON	89.9	87.8	1.7	1.9	6.6	8.2	2.7	3.3	6.0	6.5	6.4	5.5	4.4	29.0	27.6	12.3	2.3	77.2	40.6	46.9	53.1
02466	AUBURNDALE	87.5	85.0	2.6	2.9	8.0	9.9	2.9	3.4	6.1	5.7	5.5	6.9	7.4	29.5	24.3	11.8	3.0	79.6	38.2	46.1	54.0
02467	CHESTNUT HILL	85.0	82.1	2.2	2.4	10.0	12.3	2.9	3.4	4.7	5.0	5.5	11.7	16.2	19.1	21.9	12.6	3.4	81.8	34.7	45.4	54.6
02468	WABAN	91.8	90.1	0.8	0.9	5.8	7.2	1.5	1.8	5.1	7.0	8.8	7.3	3.8	17.0	34.6	13.4	3.0	74.3	45.6	47.9	52.1
02472	WATERTOWN	91.4	89.9	1.7	1.9	3.9	4.9	2.7	3.2	4.6	4.1	3.7	4.6	6.5	39.0	21.9	13.0	2.6	85.2	38.0	46.6	53.5
02474	ARLINGTON	90.3	88.4	1.8	2.1	5.4	6.7	1.9	2.3	5.6	5.4	4.9	4.5	4.6	33.8	24.7	14.0	2.5	81.3	40.3	47.0	53.0
02476	ARLINGTON	92.1	90.5	1.5	1.7	4.4	5.5	1.8	2.2	6.2	6.2	5.2	4.5	4.0	30.4	27.0	13.6	2.8	79.5	41.7	46.1	53.9
02478	BELMONT	91.2	89.5	1.1	1.2	5.7	7.1	1.8	2.2	5.6	6.1	6.7	6.1	4.4	27.5	27.2	13.6	2.9	77.6	41.4	46.8	53.2
02481	WELLESLEY HILLS	93.1	91.9	1.1	1.2	4.3	5.2	1.9	2.3	8.0	9.3	8.5	7.5	4.9	19.9	28.4	11.3	2.3	69.9	40.6	47.8	52.2
02482	WELLESLEY	86.6	84.6	2.2	2.4	8.7	10.3	2.7	3.1	5.7	6.3	6.0	13.3	14.2	17.5	22.4	12.5	2.2	79.0	35.1	39.8	60.2
02492	NEEDHAM	95.5	94.6	0.6	0.7	3.0	3.8	1.2	1.4	7.1	8.1	7.6	7.2	4.9	20.9	26.8	13.6	3.9	73.0	41.7	47.7	52.4
02493	WESTON	90.3	88.3	1.2	1.3	6.9	8.5	1.9	2.3	6.5	8.2	8.8	7.8	5.3	17.8	28.9	13.6	3.1	71.8	42.3	47.0	53.0
02494	NEEDHAM HEIGHTS	93.4	92.1	0.9	1.0	4.7	5.8	1.2	1.4	7.1	7.4	6.9	5.9	4.2	24.4	26.3	14.3	3.6	74.7	41.8	47.5	52.5
02532	BUZZARDS BAY	94.5	93.9	1.2	1.4	0.6	0.8	1.1	1.3	5.3	5.3	5.6	7.2	7.8	23.2	27.1	16.3	2.3	80.4	42.1	49.7	50.3
02535	CHILMARK	85.3	85.1	0.3	0.3	0.2	0.3	0.9	1.1	4.5	5.9	5.6	6.1	4.4	23.2	35.5	12.7	2.3	79.9	45.2	48.9	51.1
02536	EAST FALMOUTH	92.3	91.5	2.1	2.4	0.7	0.9	1.5	1.7	5.0	5.6	7.0	6.3	4.5	24.0	29.2	16.8	1.6	78.3	43.6	47.5	52.5
02537	EAST SANDWICH	98.3	98.1	0.2	0.3	0.4	0.5	0.7	0.9	6.0	7.2	8.4	6.6	4.0	22.4	31.6	12.3	1.6	73.8	42.5	48.5	51.5
02538	EAST WAREHAM	85.7	84.2	4.0	4.5	0.6	0.8	1.7	2.1	6.0	6.1	7.3	7.6	6.4	27.2	25.9	12.0	1.5	75.8	38.7	48.4	51.6
02539	EDGARTOWN	93.3	92.6	1.8	2.0	0.6	0.7	1.2	1.4	5.7	5.1	6.7	6.4	4.7	27.2	31.4	11.6	1.1	78.3	41.8	50.8	49.2
02540	FALMOUTH	94.5	93.8	1.5	1.7	1.4	1.7	1.1	1.3	3.1	3.4	4.6	4.6	3.6	18.7	31.3	25.3	5.5	85.7	52.9	45.1	54.9
02542	BUZZARDS BAY	90.9	89.5	3.6	4.0	1.0	1.2	5.4	6.6	15.0	10.5	8.9	5.6	14.2	43.6	1.9	0.2	0.0	62.1	23.5	53.9	46.1
02543	WOODS HOLE	95.0	94.3	1.2	1.3	2.1	2.4	1.2	1.4	3.0	3.2	3.4	4.3	2.8	20.8	34.8	24.6	3.3	87.4	52.8	50.3	49.8
02554	NANTUCKET	87.9	86.6	8.3	9.0	0.7	0.9	2.2	2.6	5.5	5.5	5.2	5.0	5.9	37.7	25.3	8.8	1.2	80.6	37.9	51.4	48.6
02556	NORTH FALMOUTH	96.3	95.9	1.0	1.2	0.7	0.9	0.8	1.0	4.9	5.6	6.3	4.7	3.2	18.5	32.4	20.5	4.0	79.8	49.3	46.9	53.1
02559	POCASSET	96.1	95.6	1.0	1.2	0.6	0.8	0.6	0.7	4.0	4.3	5.1	5.3	4.4	20.2	32.7	21.4	2.8	83.2	49.4	48.1	51.9
02562	SAGAMORE BEACH	94.3	93.5	1.7	1.9	0.8	1.0	1.6	1.9	7.4	7.7	7.2	5.6	4.1	26.2	25.3	13.4	3.2	73.9	39.8	45.9	54.2
02563	SANDWICH	97.8	97.6	0.3	0.3	0.6	0.7	0.6	0.8	6.1	7.2	8.1	6.5	4.0	22.9	28.8	13.8	2.5	74.3	42.3	48.2	51.9
02568	VINEYARD HAVEN	90.2	89.5	2.9	3.2	0.6	0.7	1.0	1.2	5.2	5.5	6.4	6.8	5.3	26.1	30.3	12.4	2.0	78.2	42.0	48.2	51.8
02571	WAREHAM	87.4	85.9	2.9	3.4	0.5	0.6	1.5	1.9	6.3	6.5	7.0	6.7	5.2	26.4	25.7	14.0	2.2	75.9	40.3	47.8	52.2
02575	WEST TISBURY	95.7	95.3	0.9	0.8	0.0	1.6	0.9	0.8	4.7	6.3	7.9	8.7	6.3	22.8	34.7	7.9	0.8	74.0	40.8	47.2	52.8
02576	WEST WAREHAM	87.0	85.5	1.9	2.2	0.5	0.7	1.3	1.5	5.1	5.8	6.9	6.5	4.4	24.8	26.9	17.2	2.4	78.0	42.9	47.7	52.3
02601	HYANNIS	83.2	81.7	6.2	6.7	1.4	1.7	3.1	3.7	5.6	5.3	5.9	6.1	6.6	28.9	24.6	14.3	2.8	79.5	40.0	47.3	52.7
02630	BARNSTABLE	97.8	97.5	0.8	0.9	0.4	0.4	0.4	0.4	3.1	3.8	5.1	5.2	4.2	15.8	36.5	23.6	2.7	84.6	52.5	47.8	52.2
02631	BREWSTER	97.2	96.9	0.8	0.9	0.8	1.0	1.0	1.2	3.4	4.2	6.4	6.6	4.1	18.3	31.1	21.4	4.6	81.5	49.1	46.4	53.6
02632	CENTERVILLE	95.5	94.8	1.4	1.5	0.8	1.0	1.3	1.6	4.6	5.1	6.1	5.3	4.1	22.4	28.5	20.4	3.6	80.7	46.5	47.6	52.4
02633	CHATHAM	95.6	95.2	2.0	2.3	0.3	0.4	1.0	1.2	3.0	3.2	3.5	3.4	3.6	18.1	32.4	27.7	5.1	88.0	55.1	47.9	52.1
02635	COTUIT	97.0	96.6	0.6	0.7	0.2	0.3	0.8	1.0	5.0	5.9	6.4	5.4	3.4	20.9	32.2	18.9	1.9	78.8	46.6	49.4	50.6
02638	DENNIS	97.5	97.2	0.4	0.4	0.6	0.7	1.3	1.6	3.2	3.7	4.3	4.8	3.4	16.0	35.0	26.0	3.7	85.8	54.2	47.7	52.4
02639	DENNIS PORT	90.2	88.9	4.8	5.3	0.4	0.5	2.9	3.4	4.8	4.5	4.9	5.0	5.8	24.8	25.9	21.4	3.0	82.8	45.2	46.5	53.5
02642	EASTHAM	96.3	95.9	1.5	1.6	0.4	0.4	0.8	1.0	3.9	4.0	4.8	4.8	3.7	21.6	32.2	22.7	2.3	84.2	49.4	48.3	51.8
02644	FORESTDALE	96.7	96.3	0.9	1.0	0.6	0.8	1.4	1.6	7.6	8.3	9.5	8.4	5.1	27.6	25.6	7.2	0.8	68.5	36.1	49.8	50.2
02645	HARWICH	95.0	94.6	0.6	0.7	0.4	0.5	1.1	1.3	4.4	4.8	5.9	5.2	3.8	20.8	29.0	21.6	4.6	81.5	48.2	46.4	53.6
02646	HARWICH PORT	97.3	97.0	0.5	0.5	0.1	0.2	0.6	0.7	3.1	3.3	3.9	3.0	2.7	16.5	30.2	31.1	6.2	87.7	57.1	44.4	55.7
02648	MARSTONS MILLS	94.8	94.3	1.4	1.5	0.6	0.8	1.0	1.3	5.9	7.0	8.0	6.8	4.5	24.8	28.9	12.8	1.4	74.3	41.4	49.0	51.0
02649	MASHPEE	90.3	89.4	2.8	3.1	0.6	0.8	1.6	1.9	5.9	6.3	7.6	6.3	4.4	24.5	25.9	17.1	1.9	76.2	42.1	46.8	53.2
02650	NORTH CHATHAM	97.8	97.8	1.2	1.3	0.1	0.1	0.4	0.4	1.3	1.5	2.6	2.4	2.9	12.3	30.5	34.5	12.1	92.5	63.0	42.1	57.9
02652	NORTH TRURO	94.8	94.1	2.7	3.0	0.3	0.6	1.0	1.4	3.3	4.4	6.9	3.9	2.3	27.9	37.7	12.0	1.7	83.3	45.6	46.2	53.8
02653	ORLEANS	97.6	97.3	0.6	0.7	0.5	0.7	0.8	0.9	2.5	2.7	3.8	4.0	3.3	15.0	32.2	31.1	5.5	88.3	57.3	46.9	53.1
02655	OSTERVILLE	96.9	96.5	0.8	0.9	0.5	0.5	1.2	1.4	4.1	4.5	5.4	4.3	2.9	17.4	31.7	25.9	3.9	83.4	53.0	46.5	53.5
02657	PROVINCETOWN	87.6	86.4	7.5	8.3	0.5	0.6	2.2	2.5	1.7	1.8	2.2	3.2	4.6	32.1	36.8	14.5	3.2	92.6	47.1	53.7	46.3
02659	SOUTH CHATHAM	96.5	96.0	1.0	1.2	0.2	0.3	1.4	1.7	3.7	4.2	4.8	4.1	3.8	21.1	32.0	22.2	4.2	85.0	49.9	49.6	50.4
02660	SOUTH DENNIS	96.0	95.6	1.2	1.3	0.2	0.3	1.4	1.6	3.8	4.2	5.1	5.1	3.7	19.6	29.9	24.6	4.0	83.7	50.7	45.9	54.1
02664	SOUTH YARMOUTH	95.3	94.6	1.3	1.5	0.8	1.0	1.5	1.9	4.0	4.1	4.8	4.3	3.6	20.1	25.9	26.7	6.5	84.3	52.0	45.8	54.2
02666	TRURO	95.5	95.0	0.9	1.0	0.6	0.7	1.0	1.3	3.4	4.0	4.5	4.6	3.6	21.0	38.6	17.9	2.4	85.6	49.9	48.4	51.6
02667	WELLFLEET	96.6	96.2	0.9	1.0	0.4	0.5	0.8	1.0	4.1	4.4	4.1	4.6	4.5	20.6	36.8	18.6	2.5	84.6	49.3	47.0	53.0
02668	WEST BARNSTABLE	98.2	97.9	0.4	0.4	0.5	0.6	0.4	0.5	5.8	7.0	8.0	5.9	3.6	21.9	30.4	15.2	2.2	75.2	43.8	48.2	51.8
02670	WEST DENNIS	95.0	94.3	2.6	3.0	0.3	0.4	1.1	1.2	2.9	3.2	4.4	3.2	3.3	22.4	30.0	27.4	3.2	87.5	52.4	45.8	54.2
02671	WEST HARWICH	96.1	95.7	1.6	1.8	0.1	0.1	0.9	1.1	3.7	3.8	4.3	3.8	3.7	18.9	32.0	25.4	4.5	85.6	53.5	47.7	52.3
02673	WEST YARMOUTH	93.1	92.4	2.1	2.3	0.4	0.5	1.8	2.1	5.3	5.4	5.3	5.0	4.4	25.6	26.1	18.9	4.0	81.0	44.3	46.7	53.4
02675	YARMOUTH PORT	98.2	98.0	0.3	0.4	0.4	0.5	0.8	1.0	3.4	4.0	4.9	4.7	3.0	16.8	31.1	27.3	4.8	84.5	53.6	46.7	53.4
02702	ASSONET	97.0	96.6	0.4	0.4	0.8	1.0	0.7	0.9	4.8	5.6	6.6	7.1	6.0	29.2	32.2	7.6	1.0	78.7	40.0	49.6	50.4
02703	ATTLEBORO	91.3	90.0	1.6	1.8	3.3	4.0	4.3	5.1	7.0	6.8	7.1	6.4	5.9	30.7	23.4	10.9	1.9	75.1	37.3	48.7	51.3
02713	CUTTYHUNK	95.4	95.4	0.0	0.0	0.0	0.0	0.0	0.0	5.8	5.8	3.5	3.5	2.3	34.5	33.3	10.3	1.2	81.6	42.2	60.9	39.1
02715	DIGHTON	97.9	97.6	0.4	0.5	0.5	0.6	1.1	1.4	5.7	6.3	7.9	7.0	5.2	28.6	26.7	11.0	1.7	75.7	39.5	49.7	50.3
02717	EAST FREETOWN	95.6	94.9	1.0	1.1	0.6	0.7	0.8	1.0	5.7	6.3	6.8	6.5	5.2	28.9	30.1	9.6	1.0	76.9	39.4	50.4	49.6
02718	EAST TAUNTON	95.2	94.4	1.5	1.7	0.6	0.7	1.4	1.7	7.9	7.8	8.5	7.2	6.3	32.8	22.3	6.6	0.8	71.3	34.4	48.7	51.3
02719	FAIRHAVEN	96.3	95.9	0.6	0.7	0.5	0.6	0.8	1.0	4.7	5.0	6.3	6.3	5.5	25.9	26.9	15.6	3.7	79.9	42.7	47.3	52.7
02720	FALL RIVER	92.9	91.9	2.5	2.8	1.6	2.0	2.6	3.1	6.0	5.8	6.4	6.2	6.7	29.3	22.6	13.5	3.6	77.9	38.0	46.9	53.1
02721	FALL RIVER	90.0	88.6	2.7	3.0	2.3	2.7	4.2	5.0	6.8	6.5	7.6	7.2	7.5	28.3	20.9	12.8	2.5	74.9	35.0	47.4	52.6
02723	FALL RIVER	88.7	87.1	2.7	2.9	4.2	5.1	3.6	4.3	6.6	6.2	7.2	7.1	7.6	28.6	20.6	13.8	2.3	75.7	35.1	47.2	52.9
02724	FALL RIVER	91.8	90.8	2.1	2.3	1.3	1.6	3.2	3.8	6.7	5.8	6.8	6.6	7.2	29.2	22.2	13.2	2.3	76.7	36.6	46.7	53.4
02725	SOMERSET	98.0	97.7	0.2	0.3	0.7	0.9	0.6	0.7	4.6	4.7	5.2	5.7	4.7	24.1	26.2	19.4	5.2	81.7	45.6	44.9	55.2
02726	SOMERSET	98.2	98.0	0.2	0.2	0.5	0.7	0.5	0.6	4.4	4.8	6.1	6.1	5.1	24.7	28.1	17.9	2.8	80.8	44.2	48.0	52.0
02738	MARION	92.2	91.3	1.6	1.8	0.4	0.6	0.6	0.6	5.6	6.5	7.8	6.4	4.0	21.7	29.7	15.4	2.8	75.8	43.6	47.9	52.1
02739	MATTAPOISETT	96.5	96.0	0.6	0.7	0.7	0.9	0.6	0.7	5.1	6.3	7.4	6.0	3.6	23.7	30.5	15.1	2.4	76.9	43.9	47.7	52.4
02740	NEW BEDFORD	72.8	70.6	6.1	6.6	0.8	1.0	10.2	12.0	6.3	5.9	6.7	6.9	7.4	27.1	22.7	13.9	3.0	76.8	37.4	47.1	52.9
	MASSACHUSETTS	84.5	82.9	5.4	5.7	3.8	4.5	6.8	7.8	6.2	6.3	6.8	7.0	7.0	28.9	24.5	11.4	2.1	76.8	37.6	48.3	51.7
	UNITED STATES	75.1	73.6	12.3	12.5	3.8	4.2	12.5	14.1	6.9	6.7	7.2	7.0	7.3	28.6	23.8	10.8	1.7	75.1	36.0	49.1	50.9

#	POST OFFICE NAME	2004 Per Capita Income	2004 HH Income Base	2004 HOUSEHOLD INCOME DISTRIBUTION (%) Less than $25,000	$25,000 to $49,999	$50,000 to $99,999	$100,000 to $149,999	$150,000 or More	MEDIAN HOUSEHOLD INCOME 2004	2009	2004 National Centile	2004 State Centile	2004 Home Value Base	2004 HOME VALUE DISTRIBUTION (%) Less than $50,000	$50,000 to $89,999	$90,000 to $174,999	$175,000 to $399,999	$400,000 or More	2004 Median Home Value
02367	PLYMPTON	29984	909	6.5	14.4	43.1	25.4	10.6	82127	100452	96	78	872	0.0	0.3	3.0	68.7	28.0	322892
02368	RANDOLPH	29533	11442	14.4	19.9	37.6	19.9	8.2	68679	87757	91	61	8422	1.0	0.5	9.4	82.5	6.6	245000
02370	ROCKLAND	29328	6664	15.8	22.5	37.5	17.1	7.1	61463	77535	86	46	4957	0.5	0.7	9.9	85.0	4.0	242841
02375	SOUTH EASTON	37888	3764	9.9	16.3	37.4	22.7	13.7	78789	98538	95	75	2976	1.0	1.0	12.2	54.6	31.3	298239
02379	WEST BRIDGEWATER	30653	2426	15.8	19.7	37.9	20.2	6.3	67700	83317	90	59	2056	1.5	1.6	10.2	73.3	13.5	262143
02382	WHITMAN	28958	5232	13.7	22.4	38.7	18.5	6.8	65022	79673	89	54	3827	0.1	0.7	9.1	85.5	4.6	243251
02420	LEXINGTON	63615	4987	5.5	10.6	22.4	22.6	38.9	123888	163735	99	97	4502	0.3	0.6	0.3	11.8	87.1	648637
02421	LEXINGTON	62964	6453	7.9	10.9	20.4	23.1	37.7	123919	162539	99	97	5219	0.0	0.1	0.5	11.8	87.6	644636
02445	BROOKLINE	69010	9358	12.0	14.2	29.0	18.8	26.0	89285	125616	97	84	4621	0.8	0.3	1.5	27.5	69.9	615706
02446	BROOKLINE	60171	14620	17.5	13.4	26.6	19.6	22.9	83994	122571	96	80	5151	0.3	0.3	2.0	29.3	68.1	537398
02451	WALTHAM	38711	7492	14.5	17.9	33.9	22.0	11.8	73264	97106	93	67	4612	0.7	0.4	2.0	56.8	40.1	366174
02452	WALTHAM	37916	4386	10.9	18.2	36.8	19.4	14.7	76810	100467	94	72	2675	0.0	0.3	2.9	39.9	57.0	430375
02453	WALTHAM	32473	11840	17.9	22.7	32.2	20.3	6.9	62305	83477	87	49	4400	0.4	0.4	2.9	57.0	39.4	371533
02458	NEWTON	57566	5560	12.6	13.6	27.2	17.9	28.7	91999	126858	97	86	3124	1.2	0.4	0.6	23.1	74.8	584538
02459	NEWTON CENTER	68176	6662	8.2	9.4	21.3	20.7	40.4	125863	167780	100	97	5405	0.2	0.5	0.7	10.2	88.4	699538
02460	NEWTONVILLE	62522	3355	8.7	12.4	24.5	23.7	30.7	108472	150425	99	93	2126	0.3	0.5	0.3	13.0	85.8	606557
02461	NEWTON HIGHLANDS	66940	2557	10.3	9.6	21.6	20.2	38.3	118901	160174	99	96	2028	0.5	0.9	0.3	12.8	85.6	637500
02462	NEWTON LOWER FALLS	45950	557	12.9	10.6	32.9	18.1	25.5	88499	119058	97	83	393	0.0	0.0	0.0	7.4	92.6	609742
02464	NEWTON UPPER FALLS	56822	1318	8.5	13.2	31.6	18.4	28.2	93125	126521	97	87	880	1.8	1.5	1.1	21.8	73.8	510125
02465	WEST NEWTON	60503	4444	7.8	11.4	28.3	24.4	28.1	104268	138491	98	91	3404	0.4	0.5	1.4	19.2	78.5	580455
02466	AUBURNDALE	63604	2832	9.3	12.7	23.8	24.7	29.5	107287	143956	99	92	1866	0.4	0.6	0.5	16.4	82.2	616490
02467	CHESTNUT HILL	67810	4939	7.6	12.5	23.1	16.6	40.2	118993	164465	99	96	3793	0.0	0.4	1.6	18.2	79.8	702478
02468	WABAN	88914	1910	7.4	8.1	14.6	16.3	53.5	163276	226555	100	100	1687	0.1	0.5	0.2	2.8	96.3	851019
02472	WATERTOWN	46212	14498	14.1	17.3	33.2	20.2	15.3	76558	102892	94	71	6740	0.3	0.2	1.3	40.2	58.0	433437
02474	ARLINGTON	43001	11670	13.2	16.8	34.6	21.7	13.7	77443	102931	94	72	6514	0.2	0.2	2.4	38.2	59.0	440440
02476	ARLINGTON	51167	7435	13.2	13.2	29.7	23.9	20.0	88308	117088	97	83	4920	0.5	0.1	2.7	34.5	62.3	455556
02478	BELMONT	57911	9846	10.1	11.8	26.9	23.6	27.6	101898	135352	98	90	6277	0.2	0.2	0.1	11.4	88.1	638119
02481	WELLESLEY HILLS	89057	4831	6.0	7.6	17.1	17.2	52.1	156061	211991	100	99	4344	0.1	0.2	1.0	3.1	95.7	940123
02482	WELLESLEY	62330	3925	9.9	8.5	18.1	19.8	43.7	135097	177577	100	98	3071	0.0	0.2	0.4	7.6	91.8	723506
02492	NEEDHAM	67619	7271	8.0	10.5	22.4	22.1	37.0	120156	159969	99	96	6155	0.0	0.0	0.1	11.3	88.6	621647
02493	WESTON	111857	3973	6.2	6.8	13.1	13.0	60.9	192247	256293	100	100	3445	0.7	0.2	0.9	3.3	95.0	1000001
02494	NEEDHAM HEIGHTS	51696	3413	7.6	12.7	28.6	21.5	29.7	102124	138457	98	90	2538	0.4	0.3	0.2	19.1	80.0	553428
02532	BUZZARDS BAY	25766	5355	24.6	26.6	34.3	10.8	3.7	48842	57959	70	20	3963	1.5	0.4	13.9	66.4	17.8	250109
02535	CHILMARK	34475	590	17.0	30.3	29.2	11.0	12.5	52436	65487	76	27	439	0.0	0.0	2.5	5.2	92.3	1000001
02536	EAST FALMOUTH	30982	8290	17.6	26.6	36.9	13.4	5.4	55192	66874	80	32	7016	0.3	0.3	6.6	71.3	21.4	271211
02537	EAST SANDWICH	39244	2579	9.4	17.0	39.5	20.1	14.0	78098	97579	94	74	2311	0.0	0.0	1.1	59.1	39.8	352319
02538	EAST WAREHAM	25242	1949	24.9	32.5	26.8	9.3	6.5	44407	54379	60	14	1465	9.6	5.8	33.9	48.3	2.3	175813
02539	EDGARTOWN	32724	1663	15.0	26.7	37.5	12.2	8.7	56949	70774	82	36	1268	0.0	0.0	1.4	28.2	70.4	539440
02540	FALMOUTH	42553	4545	21.5	24.9	28.2	14.2	11.2	54790	71313	79	32	3201	0.1	0.1	2.6	45.7	51.5	408929
02542	BUZZARDS BAY	16441	491	19.8	37.3	38.7	3.3	1.0	46322	53011	65	17	0	0.0	0.0	0.0	0.0	0.0	0
02543	WOODS HOLE	53156	395	14.4	19.8	30.1	20.8	14.9	70019	94485	91	62	301	0.0	0.0	0.0	15.3	84.7	701471
02554	NANTUCKET	40682	4188	12.2	22.9	31.7	16.8	16.5	69611	95973	91	62	2887	0.4	0.1	0.4	4.2	94.9	932402
02556	NORTH FALMOUTH	43431	1542	13.0	20.3	29.5	22.6	14.6	76654	102331	94	71	1372	0.4	0.2	0.6	43.6	55.3	429796
02559	POCASSET	37044	1947	17.3	23.4	34.5	14.1	10.8	60165	76037	84	44	1608	2.7	0.1	4.7	63.5	29.0	306630
02562	SAGAMORE BEACH	30969	1151	13.6	24.8	36.1	19.0	6.4	62366	78905	87	49	934	0.0	0.1	4.1	68.5	27.3	304933
02563	SANDWICH	34195	4031	14.2	19.2	38.9	18.6	9.1	69219	84264	91	61	3595	0.2	0.3	1.9	71.7	25.9	310114
02568	VINEYARD HAVEN	34565	4460	19.8	27.4	32.2	11.5	9.1	52523	65006	76	27	3249	0.2	0.2	1.9	34.6	63.1	479720
02571	WAREHAM	27348	4244	25.3	26.7	31.6	10.9	5.4	47871	59431	68	18	3081	2.5	2.6	31.7	54.5	8.6	194646
02575	WEST TISBURY	44804	53	9.4	22.6	39.6	15.1	13.2	62618	82963	87	50	40	0.0	0.0	0.0	20.0	80.0	587500
02576	WEST WAREHAM	24803	1345	26.2	23.9	37.4	10.3	2.3	49958	59529	72	21	1163	6.0	11.5	32.1	48.1	2.3	175571
02601	HYANNIS	22285	6817	33.4	27.6	29.3	6.6	3.1	38144	45279	40	8	3814	0.6	0.3	16.4	71.0	11.7	231956
02630	BARNSTABLE	50529	918	12.3	14.9	34.8	19.7	18.3	81239	105501	95	78	824	0.0	0.4	3.5	31.4	64.7	496800
02631	BREWSTER	31609	4369	18.5	25.0	35.8	12.9	7.9	56864	68959	82	35	3681	0.0	0.2	0.4	61.7	37.6	355948
02632	CENTERVILLE	33460	4676	16.6	24.9	36.4	13.6	8.5	58461	71221	83	40	4036	0.3	0.1	5.2	69.2	25.4	293757
02633	CHATHAM	38584	2414	20.6	24.0	31.0	15.4	9.0	55798	72566	80	33	2001	0.4	0.0	1.3	37.3	61.1	465249
02635	COTUIT	36709	1484	12.7	24.1	36.8	15.6	10.7	65357	82736	89	55	1299	0.0	0.0	3.5	55.1	41.4	353734
02638	DENNIS	38011	1798	14.6	23.0	36.2	18.7	7.6	64295	83050	88	53	1560	0.3	0.1	2.8	52.6	44.2	375275
02639	DENNIS PORT	30364	1812	31.1	29.5	25.3	6.4	7.7	39717	46928	45	9	1091	0.4	1.7	19.9	65.4	12.7	237407
02642	EASTHAM	31860	2561	21.7	28.2	34.3	9.3	6.6	50113	61057	72	22	2146	0.0	0.1	1.4	62.7	35.7	346875
02644	FORESTDALE	28200	1337	5.2	21.4	46.9	20.8	5.8	71709	84392	92	65	1215	0.0	0.0	1.7	85.4	12.9	282319
02645	HARWICH	28267	4490	18.8	31.5	34.1	11.1	4.5	49742	59853	71	21	3748	0.2	0.0	3.8	69.2	26.8	299250
02646	HARWICH PORT	31018	1017	32.8	25.7	27.4	8.6	5.5	42134	51957	53	11	789	0.0	0.0	3.6	44.0	52.5	418750
02648	MARSTONS MILLS	30146	3200	13.4	23.8	36.7	16.2	10.0	63482	78593	87	52	2901	0.1	0.1	4.6	71.5	23.7	281822
02649	MASHPEE	31730	5943	14.3	24.2	39.8	14.9	6.9	60641	74932	85	45	4728	1.1	0.7	8.4	66.0	23.8	283219
02650	NORTH CHATHAM	37788	330	18.8	16.1	34.9	18.5	11.8	66561	87647	89	57	288	0.0	0.0	1.0	25.7	73.3	608871
02652	NORTH TRURO	23854	519	24.5	28.9	36.2	6.6	3.9	45363	53780	62	16	421	0.0	0.0	0.2	32.3	67.5	484483
02653	ORLEANS	39699	3220	27.4	21.5	27.4	13.5	10.3	51331	66270	74	25	2504	0.0	0.0	3.5	34.0	62.5	501183
02655	OSTERVILLE	53153	1787	14.8	22.0	31.4	13.4	18.4	66524	87732	89	57	1543	0.0	0.0	0.5	50.0	49.5	397432
02657	PROVINCETOWN	33056	1899	31.3	29.3	26.8	6.6	6.1	39540	49857	44	9	1014	0.0	0.0	0.5	25.8	73.7	567035
02659	SOUTH CHATHAM	31444	505	22.4	31.3	26.3	11.7	8.3	46880	56752	66	18	423	0.0	0.0	0.2	50.1	49.7	398846
02660	SOUTH DENNIS	29249	3626	20.7	29.8	34.1	11.5	4.0	49435	59662	71	20	2965	0.5	0.2	6.9	66.9	25.4	281851
02664	SOUTH YARMOUTH	25980	4743	25.6	33.2	31.5	7.3	2.4	43149	51325	56	13	3559	0.6	0.1	8.0	75.7	15.6	251610
02666	TRURO	32919	439	21.2	23.2	39.4	10.7	5.5	54098	64303	79	30	369	0.0	0.0	1.1	29.5	69.4	491667
02667	WELLFLEET	32034	1316	21.8	27.1	31.5	12.4	7.2	51038	61613	74	24	1041	0.7	1.4	2.6	40.7	54.6	430063
02668	WEST BARNSTABLE	36859	1257	10.8	19.8	37.2	15.2	17.0	75039	93792	93	69	1168	0.7	0.3	2.2	46.2	50.7	403883
02670	WEST DENNIS	36591	926	26.4	31.6	26.4	8.5	7.1	42364	51231	54	12	720	0.0	0.8	7.9	46.1	45.1	367593
02671	WEST HARWICH	36048	568	22.5	30.5	30.1	6.7	10.2	46057	57505	64	16	468	0.0	0.0	2.1	59.4	38.5	315625
02673	WEST YARMOUTH	23827	4131	25.7	32.2	31.0	9.0	2.2	42708	49916	55	13	2956	0.3	0.5	12.7	79.6	6.9	236416
02675	YARMOUTH PORT	40571	3380	14.5	25.3	33.7	15.9	10.6	61968	80228	86	47	3005	0.0	0.1	2.2	66.1	31.6	328247
02702	ASSONET	30709	1291	12.5	12.6	44.5	21.9	8.6	78883	93777	95	75	1173	0.6	0.0	9.8	74.6	15.0	272705
02703	ATTLEBORO	27942	16688	17.3	23.1	40.4	13.7	5.5	59499	71776	84	43	11182	1.1	2.5	13.1	77.4	6.0	241249
02713	CUTTYHUNK	21322	47	38.3	38.3	14.9	8.5	0.0	28722	32248	10	2	19	0.0	0.0	0.0	15.8	84.2	625000
02715	DIGHTON	27307	859	10.0	21.1	45.2	17.2	6.5	68120	80996	90	59	769	0.0	0.0	7.8	84.8	7.4	254776
02717	EAST FREETOWN	28701	1733	11.4	18.2	45.4	20.8	4.2	71344	83086	92	64	1553	0.3	0.0	11.6	76.6	11.5	260463
02718	EAST TAUNTON	25453	2482	13.3	19.3	46.3	16.4	4.7	64208	77166	88	53	2033	0.4	0.0	13.9	78.0	7.6	244902
02719	FAIRHAVEN	25823	6684	25.1	24.4	34.5	12.9	3.1	50465	61380	73	23	5046	0.4	0.5	22.9	69.6	6.7	218438
02720	FALL RIVER	22795	13733	32.7	26.1	30.2	8.0	3.0	40944	49315	49	10	5993	0.8	1.6	17.1	76.3	4.2	223991
02721	FALL RIVER	18008	11045	42.2	26.9	24.7	5.0	1.3	31097	37028	15	3	4306	0.7	0.0	22.3	75.3	1.7	211163
02723	FALL RIVER	17620	6744	44.2	26.5	23.7	4.4	1.2	29544	35863	11	3	2371	0.4	0.6	14.4	83.1	1.5	224013
02724	FALL RIVER	17109	7802	44.5	29.3	21.5	4.1	0.6	29047	34558	10	2	2988	0.2	1.8	20.8	76.5	0.6	215828
02725	SOMERSET	24132	968	19.1	22.5	39.0	15.9	3.5	58602	70644	83	40	820	0.0	0.0	13.9	81.6	4.5	228455
02726	SOMERSET	28372	6123	18.5	20.0	37.8	17.7	6.1	60792	74656	85	45	5158	0.3	0.0	8.1	85.9	5.7	239126
02738	MARION	51759	2079	10.6	20.4	31.6	17.3	20.2	77051	101409	94	72	1693	0.0	0.4	8.9	48.1	42.6	354856
02739	MATTAPOISETT	35948	2563	11.0	22.6	35.3	18.0	13.2	71706	91229	92	65	2104	0.3	0.3	6.6	64.6	28.2	305176
02740	NEW BEDFORD	18464	18020	40.9	28.1	24.1	5.4	1.6	31928	37961	18	4	8370	0.9	2.0	44.1	51.0	1.9	179215
	MASSACHUSETTS	33908		19.9	21.2	32.0	16.1	10.9	61110	77759				0.8	1.2	14.8	55.7	27.5	282585
	UNITED STATES	25866		24.7	27.1	30.8	10.9	6.5	48124	56710				10.9	15.0	33.7	30.1	10.4	145905

#	POST OFFICE NAME	FINANCIAL SERVICES: Auto Loan	FINANCIAL SERVICES: Home Loan	FINANCIAL SERVICES: Invest-ments	FINANCIAL SERVICES: Retire-ment Plans	THE HOME: Home Improvements: Home Repair	THE HOME: Home Improvements: Lawn & Garden	THE HOME: Furnishings: Comput-ers & Hard-ware	THE HOME: Furnishings: Major Appli-ances	THE HOME: Furnishings: TV, Radio, Sound Equip-ment	THE HOME: Furnishings: Furni-ture	ENTERTAINMENT: Dine out/ Carry out	ENTERTAINMENT: Sports Equip-ment	ENTERTAINMENT: Fees & Tickets	ENTERTAINMENT: Toys & Games	ENTERTAINMENT: Travel	ENTERTAINMENT: Cable TV	PERSONAL: Apparel & Services	PERSONAL: Auto Repairs	PERSONAL: Health Insur-ance	PERSONAL: Pets & Supplies
02367	PLYMPTON	120	149	158	149	146	144	133	132	123	132	155	155	141	165	136	119	154	127	118	146
02368	RANDOLPH	102	118	138	118	116	121	114	112	110	114	139	130	119	144	116	109	137	112	106	122
02370	ROCKLAND	104	116	125	115	115	120	111	112	107	111	135	127	114	136	113	106	132	110	107	122
02375	SOUTH EASTON	131	151	172	156	148	149	144	140	135	144	170	165	149	175	144	130	169	139	126	153
02379	WEST BRIDGEWATER	104	125	136	122	122	127	115	115	111	115	139	132	122	146	119	110	138	112	109	125
02382	WHITMAN	106	117	125	118	116	120	114	113	110	112	137	133	116	142	114	107	135	112	106	125
02420	LEXINGTON	199	291	391	272	279	294	249	247	234	252	293	279	280	326	267	237	300	237	222	262
02421	LEXINGTON	199	267	344	257	258	271	238	236	225	240	282	270	260	304	250	225	285	230	215	252
02445	BROOKLINE	200	208	347	227	199	219	228	208	228	231	289	251	239	303	227	226	288	218	194	230
02446	BROOKLINE	158	149	276	172	141	159	179	158	183	181	232	195	185	242	175	180	230	170	147	177
02451	WALTHAM	111	137	193	136	132	140	132	126	128	132	161	147	142	173	136	128	162	127	116	136
02452	WALTHAM	123	135	201	141	131	142	140	132	140	141	176	156	148	184	142	139	175	136	125	145
02453	WALTHAM	99	101	150	107	97	107	112	103	112	111	142	124	114	145	110	110	140	109	98	114
02458	NEWTON	181	197	291	209	191	207	204	193	201	206	254	229	215	262	206	199	252	198	181	212
02459	NEWTON CENTER	218	308	411	294	298	315	266	263	249	270	313	297	299	341	284	251	319	253	240	282
02460	NEWTONVILLE	190	216	295	224	211	223	216	207	208	217	263	245	226	272	218	205	261	209	191	226
02461	NEWTON HIGHLANDS	196	276	363	262	266	280	240	238	225	242	282	269	267	309	255	227	288	229	215	253
02462	NEWTON LOWER FALLS	137	208	279	191	198	207	176	175	165	178	207	197	198	235	189	168	213	167	155	184
02464	NEWTON UPPER FALLS	167	206	262	207	201	208	194	189	184	194	231	222	206	242	199	180	231	188	172	205
02465	WEST NEWTON	190	255	335	247	247	258	229	225	215	230	271	259	250	292	240	215	274	220	203	241
02466	AUBURNDALE	186	255	336	245	246	257	227	224	214	229	269	257	249	294	239	215	273	218	201	238
02467	CHESTNUT HILL	245	316	408	302	310	336	279	283	267	285	335	312	307	349	298	273	336	273	271	306
02468	WABAN	314	397	526	395	390	418	359	356	338	365	426	405	396	440	377	337	428	346	333	388
02472	WATERTOWN	129	134	208	145	129	140	146	135	145	147	184	163	151	191	145	143	182	141	126	149
02474	ARLINGTON	115	133	189	136	129	139	134	127	132	134	166	149	141	174	137	131	165	130	119	139
02476	ARLINGTON	135	171	238	168	164	175	162	156	156	162	197	180	174	212	168	157	198	155	143	167
02478	BELMONT	171	214	296	213	207	220	203	196	195	204	246	227	219	263	210	195	247	195	180	211
02481	WELLESLEY HILLS	298	417	565	400	403	430	361	357	337	367	424	403	407	459	385	341	433	343	327	384
02482	WELLESLEY	230	317	420	302	305	323	279	275	264	282	331	311	310	361	296	266	337	267	251	294
02492	NEEDHAM	230	292	361	290	285	297	264	261	248	266	312	299	287	327	274	245	313	254	239	283
02493	WESTON	400	536	735	525	522	562	471	465	441	481	557	525	532	589	501	444	565	449	431	505
02494	NEEDHAM HEIGHTS	166	212	265	209	207	215	194	191	183	195	230	220	209	244	201	181	231	187	174	206
02532	BUZZARDS BAY	87	83	77	80	85	95	84	87	87	81	106	99	82	106	85	89	101	87	93	101
02535	CHILMARK	132	103	71	93	117	131	98	118	110	97	131	138	87	129	104	118	122	116	139	161
02536	EAST FALMOUTH	109	111	109	108	114	122	104	110	105	105	130	124	105	128	108	106	126	108	114	129
02537	EAST SANDWICH	147	161	160	159	162	169	146	152	142	148	177	173	151	177	151	142	173	148	149	175
02538	EAST WAREHAM	96	85	68	82	89	97	84	91	88	83	107	105	79	105	84	89	101	90	97	110
02539	EDGARTOWN	131	103	70	93	115	130	97	116	109	96	130	136	86	128	103	117	121	115	138	159
02540	FALMOUTH	122	119	128	115	123	139	117	124	121	119	150	133	118	140	122	125	143	124	135	141
02542	BUZZARDS BAY	80	51	49	58	47	55	76	65	77	71	96	87	65	86	62	70	92	77	60	74
02543	WOODS HOLE	180	141	97	128	159	179	133	161	151	132	179	187	119	176	142	161	166	158	190	219
02554	NANTUCKET	156	147	129	144	152	160	137	149	140	139	172	175	133	172	140	141	165	147	154	184
02556	NORTH FALMOUTH	159	144	124	133	154	172	135	152	146	135	176	172	131	174	143	153	167	150	172	191
02559	POCASSET	109	116	118	109	118	130	109	114	112	108	138	129	112	142	115	116	134	112	121	132
02562	SAGAMORE BEACH	111	129	133	130	125	124	119	118	111	119	140	139	123	145	119	107	139	116	105	130
02563	SANDWICH	126	137	136	136	136	141	126	129	122	129	153	147	129	152	128	121	149	127	125	145
02568	VINEYARD HAVEN	127	108	88	101	118	130	103	118	112	102	134	139	95	134	108	117	127	117	133	154
02571	WAREHAM	101	94	81	89	98	107	92	98	96	90	117	113	89	117	94	99	111	97	106	118
02575	WEST TISBURY	182	143	97	129	161	181	135	162	152	133	181	190	120	178	144	163	168	160	192	222
02576	WEST WAREHAM	84	89	95	85	90	100	83	89	84	86	105	93	86	99	87	86	101	86	93	97
02601	HYANNIS	66	65	73	64	65	72	68	68	70	67	86	79	68	86	68	70	84	69	70	77
02630	BARNSTABLE	156	173	186	170	176	191	159	166	156	163	196	180	167	187	168	159	190	162	170	184
02631	BREWSTER	113	104	92	97	111	124	98	110	105	98	127	123	96	125	104	110	121	107	123	135
02632	CENTERVILLE	114	113	111	108	118	132	106	115	110	109	136	123	107	127	112	114	130	113	127	133
02633	CHATHAM	125	105	84	97	115	132	98	115	108	100	130	126	92	121	105	115	122	113	136	147
02635	COTUIT	131	121	105	115	126	137	114	125	118	115	145	142	109	139	118	121	137	124	134	153
02638	DENNIS	130	113	94	105	123	141	105	123	114	109	139	131	101	125	113	122	130	120	144	152
02639	DENNIS PORT	95	81	71	77	86	98	82	89	89	80	107	103	77	105	84	93	101	90	101	112
02642	EASTHAM	120	94	64	85	106	119	89	107	101	88	119	125	79	118	95	107	111	105	127	146
02644	FORESTDALE	118	130	130	132	125	124	123	122	115	125	146	145	124	147	121	109	144	122	107	134
02645	HARWICH	98	90	80	83	96	108	84	95	90	85	110	104	82	105	90	95	104	93	107	116
02646	HARWICH PORT	98	80	60	72	88	100	75	89	84	75	100	102	69	97	80	90	93	88	105	118
02648	MARSTONS MILLS	110	127	131	127	124	124	117	117	110	118	138	136	121	142	118	106	137	115	106	129
02649	MASHPEE	121	107	87	101	115	124	102	114	108	101	130	134	96	131	106	111	124	112	124	146
02650	NORTH CHATHAM	132	123	117	117	130	153	114	130	120	122	150	127	115	125	124	129	140	126	152	148
02652	NORTH TRURO	94	74	50	66	83	93	69	84	79	69	93	98	62	92	74	84	87	82	99	115
02653	ORLEANS	121	110	101	103	117	138	103	118	111	109	136	119	102	117	111	118	127	115	139	137
02655	OSTERVILLE	172	165	160	157	173	202	152	171	160	162	199	170	155	169	165	170	187	166	197	195
02657	PROVINCETOWN	99	78	53	70	87	98	73	88	83	72	98	103	65	97	78	88	91	87	104	120
02659	SOUTH CHATHAM	109	85	58	77	96	108	80	97	91	80	108	113	72	106	86	97	100	95	114	132
02660	SOUTH DENNIS	93	89	87	84	94	106	84	93	88	86	109	99	84	102	89	93	103	91	104	109
02664	SOUTH YARMOUTH	80	72	66	68	76	88	70	78	75	71	91	83	68	83	73	78	85	77	89	92
02666	TRURO	115	90	62	81	102	114	85	103	96	84	114	120	76	113	91	103	106	101	121	140
02667	WELLFLEET	113	89	61	80	100	112	84	101	95	83	112	118	75	111	89	101	104	99	119	138
02668	WEST BARNSTABLE	129	158	169	157	155	156	142	142	133	142	168	165	151	177	146	131	167	137	130	157
02670	WEST DENNIS	116	94	68	85	105	118	88	105	99	89	118	120	81	113	94	105	110	103	124	140
02671	WEST HARWICH	126	99	67	89	111	125	93	112	105	92	125	131	83	123	99	112	116	110	132	153
02673	WEST YARMOUTH	77	73	70	70	76	83	71	76	73	70	90	88	69	90	73	75	86	75	81	92
02675	YARMOUTH PORT	118	124	135	123	126	138	120	124	119	121	149	136	123	142	124	121	144	122	128	137
02702	ASSONET	112	138	148	138	136	135	124	124	116	124	146	145	132	155	127	113	145	119	111	136
02703	ATTLEBORO	98	105	111	105	104	108	103	103	101	102	126	121	104	128	103	98	123	102	97	114
02713	CUTTYHUNK	67	52	36	47	59	66	50	60	56	49	66	70	44	66	53	60	62	59	71	82
02715	DIGHTON	97	118	130	116	116	118	109	108	104	108	131	125	116	139	112	102	130	105	100	118
02717	EAST FREETOWN	105	129	140	127	126	127	117	116	110	116	139	135	125	148	120	108	138	113	106	128
02718	EAST TAUNTON	97	110	116	113	108	107	105	103	98	105	124	122	108	128	104	94	123	102	92	112
02719	FAIRHAVEN	82	87	92	84	88	97	85	86	87	84	108	97	88	111	88	89	104	85	90	97
02720	FALL RIVER	69	69	79	68	69	76	74	71	75	72	94	82	74	94	73	76	91	73	73	79
02721	FALL RIVER	57	54	60	53	54	61	60	58	63	58	78	67	59	78	59	64	75	60	61	64
02723	FALL RIVER	54	51	58	50	51	58	57	55	60	55	75	63	57	75	57	61	72	57	58	61
02724	FALL RIVER	50	48	55	47	48	55	54	51	56	51	69	59	53	70	53	57	67	53	54	57
02725	SOMERSET	84	94	102	89	94	104	91	90	92	89	115	101	96	122	94	95	112	89	95	99
02726	SOMERSET	91	108	119	104	106	114	101	101	99	100	124	114	107	130	105	100	122	99	100	110
02738	MARION	169	205	227	204	204	210	187	187	176	187	221	214	199	227	193	174	219	182	175	205
02739	MATTAPOISETT	117	132	140	128	132	140	123	125	121	122	150	144	128	155	127	122	147	123	125	142
02740	NEW BEDFORD	58	56	63	55	56	63	61	59	63	59	78	68	61	80	61	64	76	60	62	65
	MASSACHUSETTS	112	121	148	122	120	127	122	119	121	121	151	138	126	156	123	120	149	120	115	132
	UNITED STATES	100	100	100	100	100	100	100	100	100	100	100	100	100	100	100	100	100	100	100	100

ZIP CODE		COUNTY FIPS CODE	POPULATION			2000-2004 ANNUAL RATE		HOUSEHOLDS					FAMILIES		
#	POST OFFICE NAME		2000	2004	2009	% Rate	State Centile	2000	2004	2009	% Annual Rate 2000-2004	2004 Average HH Size	2000	2004	% Annual Rate 2000-2004
02743	ACUSHNET	005	10124	10323	10520	0.5	56	3779	3896	4012	0.7	2.65	2826	2914	0.7
02744	NEW BEDFORD	005	11853	11843	12025	0.0	29	4787	4840	4967	0.3	2.44	3086	3106	0.2
02745	NEW BEDFORD	005	23966	24306	24853	0.3	48	9687	9946	10287	0.6	2.40	6539	6711	0.6
02746	NEW BEDFORD	005	14470	14578	14878	0.2	39	5876	5978	6166	0.4	2.41	3650	3706	0.4
02747	NORTH DARTMOUTH	005	19597	19928	20361	0.4	53	6079	6252	6471	0.7	2.70	4687	4835	0.7
02748	SOUTH DARTMOUTH	005	11220	11482	11765	0.5	61	4534	4687	4853	0.8	2.42	3147	3262	0.9
02760	NORTH ATTLEBORO	005	25809	26701	27559	0.8	72	9921	10360	10794	1.0	2.56	6838	7140	1.0
02762	PLAINVILLE	021	7686	7904	8045	0.7	67	3010	3109	3180	0.8	2.52	2041	2109	0.8
02763	ATTLEBORO FALLS	005	1570	1711	1810	2.0	97	542	597	638	2.3	2.87	452	496	2.2
02764	NORTH DIGHTON	005	3702	3911	4058	1.3	87	1337	1430	1499	1.6	2.72	1024	1094	1.6
02766	NORTON	005	17964	18871	19517	1.2	83	5856	6215	6499	1.4	2.77	4459	4728	1.4
02767	RAYNHAM	005	11346	11883	12282	1.1	81	3972	4227	4426	1.5	2.77	3095	3292	1.5
02769	REHOBOTH	005	10004	10678	11144	1.6	92	3465	3748	3958	1.9	2.85	2824	3051	1.8
02770	ROCHESTER	023	4387	4732	5019	1.8	95	1513	1647	1761	2.0	2.87	1243	1352	2.0
02771	SEEKONK	005	13826	13909	14144	0.1	37	5028	5124	5270	0.5	2.71	4006	4074	0.4
02777	SWANSEA	005	15964	15933	16099	-0.1	26	5906	5978	6119	0.3	2.63	4557	4609	0.3
02779	BERKLEY	005	5693	6006	6228	1.3	86	1818	1934	2024	1.5	3.10	1545	1644	1.5
02780	TAUNTON	005	49563	50033	50910	0.2	42	19852	20288	20886	0.5	2.43	12764	13009	0.5
02790	WESTPORT	005	14630	15356	15934	1.2	83	5528	5876	6166	1.5	2.60	4183	4444	1.4
	MASSACHUSETTS					**0.4**					**0.6**	**2.48**			**0.6**
	UNITED STATES					**1.2**					**1.3**	**2.58**			**1.1**

POPULATION COMPOSITION

ZIP CODE		RACE (%)							2004 AGE DISTRIBUTION (%)									MEDIAN AGE			
		White		Black		Asian/Pacific		% Hispanic Origin													% 2004	% 2004
#	POST OFFICE NAME	2000	2004	2000	2004	2000	2004	2000	2004	0-4	5-9	10-14	15-19	20-24	25-44	45-64	65-84	85+	18+	2004	Males	Females
02743	ACUSHNET	97.2	96.8	0.4	0.5	0.2	0.2	0.8	1.0	5.1	5.5	6.8	6.5	5.7	27.1	28.5	13.1	1.7	78.6	41.2	49.1	50.9
02744	NEW BEDFORD	81.1	78.9	3.5	3.8	0.5	0.5	11.4	13.6	7.5	6.8	7.3	7.0	8.0	29.9	19.9	11.6	2.0	74.3	33.3	48.9	51.1
02745	NEW BEDFORD	91.0	89.6	1.9	2.2	0.7	0.8	5.0	6.2	6.1	6.0	6.7	6.4	6.7	28.0	23.4	14.1	2.7	77.4	38.4	47.4	52.6
02746	NEW BEDFORD	75.2	72.8	4.1	4.4	0.6	0.7	17.8	20.3	8.7	7.8	7.9	7.0	8.2	29.2	18.8	10.6	1.9	71.5	31.6	47.7	52.3
02747	NORTH DARTMOUTH	87.7	86.8	1.4	1.5	1.4	1.7	2.0	2.4	4.8	5.0	5.6	11.3	11.0	26.6	23.9	10.3	1.6	81.1	35.4	50.3	49.7
02748	SOUTH DARTMOUTH	96.2	95.6	0.6	0.6	0.9	1.1	0.9	1.0	4.1	4.8	6.3	5.8	4.6	22.4	29.8	18.4	3.9	81.2	46.3	47.8	52.2
02760	NORTH ATTLEBORO	95.9	95.2	1.0	1.1	1.7	2.1	1.3	1.7	7.0	7.3	7.5	6.4	5.5	31.1	25.1	8.8	1.4	74.1	36.9	48.6	51.4
02762	PLAINVILLE	96.8	96.1	0.7	0.8	1.6	2.0	1.0	1.2	6.7	6.8	7.2	6.5	5.7	29.0	25.5	11.4	1.3	75.1	38.3	49.1	50.9
02763	ATTLEBORO FALLS	96.7	96.1	0.5	0.5	2.1	2.6	1.2	1.3	8.1	8.6	9.1	7.1	5.1	27.2	27.1	6.9	0.8	69.7	36.7	48.6	51.4
02764	NORTH DIGHTON	97.7	97.4	0.6	0.7	0.5	0.6	1.0	1.2	5.9	6.4	7.7	6.8	5.1	27.8	27.0	11.4	1.9	75.8	40.1	49.0	51.0
02766	NORTON	92.1	91.4	1.2	1.3	1.0	1.2	1.2	1.4	7.8	7.9	7.7	8.7	9.0	28.2	22.7	6.9	1.2	72.9	34.0	47.7	52.2
02767	RAYNHAM	96.5	95.9	1.0	1.2	0.7	0.9	0.8	1.1	6.7	6.9	7.1	6.6	5.2	27.7	26.5	11.6	1.8	75.1	38.9	47.9	52.2
02769	REHOBOTH	97.7	97.3	0.4	0.4	0.5	0.7	0.5	0.6	5.8	6.6	7.5	6.7	4.7	26.6	31.5	9.6	1.2	75.9	41.1	49.7	50.3
02770	ROCHESTER	96.7	96.3	0.6	0.7	0.4	0.5	0.4	0.5	5.9	7.3	7.8	6.9	4.7	27.9	31.2	7.4	0.9	74.6	39.5	50.6	49.4
02771	SEEKONK	96.5	96.0	0.6	0.6	1.0	1.2	0.8	1.0	5.7	6.3	7.2	6.6	5.3	26.1	29.2	12.2	1.5	76.7	41.0	48.6	51.5
02777	SWANSEA	97.9	97.6	0.4	0.4	0.4	0.5	0.6	0.8	4.7	5.1	6.1	6.4	5.6	26.7	29.2	14.0	2.2	79.8	42.2	49.3	50.7
02779	BERKLEY	96.7	96.2	0.6	0.7	0.4	0.5	1.0	1.2	7.7	8.4	8.9	6.8	4.6	32.8	24.0	6.3	0.6	70.4	35.8	49.4	50.6
02780	TAUNTON	91.2	90.0	2.9	3.3	0.6	0.8	4.3	5.2	7.0	6.7	6.8	6.0	6.2	31.0	23.1	11.3	2.0	75.9	36.9	48.0	52.0
02790	WESTPORT	97.9	97.6	0.2	0.2	0.5	0.7	0.7	0.9	4.6	5.2	6.2	6.1	5.1	27.0	30.5	13.5	1.9	80.0	42.5	48.9	51.1
	MASSACHUSETTS	84.5	82.9	5.4	5.7	3.8	4.5	6.8	7.8	6.2	6.3	6.8	7.0	7.0	28.9	24.5	11.4	2.1	76.8	37.6	48.3	51.7
	UNITED STATES	75.1	73.6	12.3	12.5	3.8	4.2	12.5	14.1	6.9	6.7	7.2	7.0	7.3	28.6	23.8	10.8	1.7	75.1	36.0	49.1	50.9

139-B   Copyright © 2004 ESRI BIS. All rights reserved. Reproduction by any method is prohibited.

#	POST OFFICE NAME	2004 Per Capita Income	2004 HH Income Base	2004 HOUSEHOLD INCOME DISTRIBUTION (%)					MEDIAN HOUSEHOLD INCOME				2004 Home Value Base	2004 HOME VALUE DISTRIBUTION (%)					2004 Median Home Value
				Less than $25,000	$25,000 to $49,999	$50,000 to $99,999	$100,000 to $149,999	$150,000 or More	2004	2009	2004 National Centile	2004 State Centile		Less than $50,000	$50,000 to $89,999	$90,000 to $174,999	$175,000 to $399,999	$400,000 or More	
02743	ACUSHNET	26674	3896	17.5	23.1	42.4	12.5	4.7	59189	70577	84	42	3302	1.8	1.7	17.7	72.6	6.2	225592
02744	NEW BEDFORD	16317	4840	46.0	27.1	21.2	4.7	1.1	27757	32930	8	2	1997	0.3	1.0	38.1	59.5	1.3	185966
02745	NEW BEDFORD	23114	9946	29.2	26.5	32.6	9.0	2.9	43685	52772	58	13	6089	1.4	0.6	27.6	69.5	1.0	197174
02746	NEW BEDFORD	13423	5978	55.2	24.0	17.6	2.5	0.8	21428	25056	2	1	1823	0.1	1.7	41.4	56.3	0.6	182671
02747	NORTH DARTMOUTH	25396	6252	16.6	22.7	39.9	14.7	6.1	61186	74392	86	45	5286	0.4	0.2	11.3	76.9	11.1	247598
02748	SOUTH DARTMOUTH	39175	4687	21.7	21.4	30.6	14.0	12.3	58850	74981	83	41	3790	0.8	0.4	13.2	59.4	26.1	273397
02760	NORTH ATTLEBORO	31813	10360	13.6	21.2	36.6	20.3	8.2	69798	83786	91	62	7421	2.8	1.5	8.2	69.0	18.4	280676
02762	PLAINVILLE	33281	3109	13.8	18.3	38.0	20.3	9.6	69934	88632	91	62	2297	0.4	4.0	11.6	69.7	14.3	267370
02763	ATTLEBORO FALLS	31582	597	8.2	15.9	38.9	28.0	9.1	76663	95350	94	71	507	0.0	0.0	5.3	69.0	25.6	309854
02764	NORTH DIGHTON	28213	1430	12.7	18.8	42.8	18.7	7.0	68261	81182	90	59	1225	0.0	0.2	8.2	82.4	9.1	252032
02766	NORTON	31035	6215	10.8	17.1	40.6	23.2	8.4	77827	92305	94	73	5179	0.2	0.6	7.4	75.0	16.8	280354
02767	RAYNHAM	29730	4227	11.8	17.9	42.0	20.0	8.4	71416	85384	92	65	3585	1.7	3.0	7.5	67.5	20.3	277599
02769	REHOBOTH	33945	3748	10.4	18.8	37.0	21.3	12.5	77699	93725	94	73	3390	0.4	0.1	3.5	66.2	29.8	332411
02770	ROCHESTER	30432	1647	10.2	16.7	39.5	24.1	9.5	76386	92345	94	71	1532	0.0	0.0	5.2	77.7	17.1	281468
02771	SEEKONK	30403	5124	13.4	20.9	41.3	14.0	10.4	66025	80276	89	56	4563	0.0	0.2	7.0	81.8	11.1	264456
02777	SWANSEA	27044	5978	17.1	20.5	40.8	15.6	6.0	61767	75042	86	47	5128	0.4	0.2	13.9	79.8	5.7	230265
02779	BERKLEY	25626	1934	10.1	14.1	48.7	22.9	4.2	75970	87630	94	69	1843	0.0	0.0	9.8	80.5	9.7	274689
02780	TAUNTON	24205	20288	23.8	27.5	34.8	11.0	2.9	48626	58870	70	19	12533	0.4	2.1	18.5	75.7	3.4	230132
02790	WESTPORT	31852	5876	15.5	20.0	38.7	16.6	9.2	65517	80964	89	55	5039	0.4	0.1	9.1	70.1	20.4	271872
	MASSACHUSETTS	33908		19.9	21.2	32.0	16.1	10.9	61110	77759				0.8	1.2	14.8	55.7	27.5	282585
	UNITED STATES	25866		24.7	27.1	30.8	10.9	6.5	48124	56710				10.9	15.0	33.7	30.1	10.4	145905

# POST OFFICE NAME	Auto Loan	Home Loan	Invest-ments	Retire-ment Plans	Home Repair	Lawn & Garden	Comput-ers & Hard-ware	Major Appli-ances	TV, Radio, Sound Equip-ment	Furni-ture	Dine out/ Carry out	Sports Equip-ment	Fees & Tickets	Toys & Games	Travel	Cable TV	Apparel & Services	Auto Repairs	Health Insur-ance	Pets & Supplies
02743 ACUSHNET	97	104	103	100	105	112	98	100	98	96	122	115	101	128	101	99	118	97	102	116
02744 NEW BEDFORD	53	50	57	49	50	57	56	54	59	54	72	62	56	73	55	59	70	56	57	59
02745 NEW BEDFORD	75	75	80	73	76	84	78	77	80	76	100	88	80	103	78	82	96	77	80	85
02746 NEW BEDFORD	44	39	46	38	39	45	45	44	48	44	60	50	44	59	44	49	58	45	46	48
02747 NORTH DARTMOUTH	101	112	118	112	111	115	106	106	103	106	129	124	110	132	108	101	126	105	101	118
02748 SOUTH DARTMOUTH	126	144	155	139	144	155	133	136	131	134	164	150	141	167	139	133	161	132	138	149
02760 NORTH ATTLEBORO	107	122	136	124	120	122	118	115	112	117	141	136	122	146	118	108	140	115	106	126
02762 PLAINVILLE	112	129	141	129	128	132	120	121	115	121	144	138	125	146	123	113	142	119	114	133
02763 ATTLEBORO FALLS	120	144	151	145	141	139	131	130	121	131	153	153	137	161	132	117	152	127	116	144
02764 NORTH DIGHTON	99	119	130	117	117	121	109	109	105	109	131	125	116	139	113	104	130	106	103	120
02766 NORTON	125	137	144	140	135	136	131	130	124	132	156	154	133	157	130	119	153	129	119	144
02767 RAYNHAM	109	130	139	129	127	129	119	118	112	119	141	137	126	148	121	110	140	115	109	130
02769 REHOBOTH	125	156	166	156	153	152	139	139	129	139	162	162	148	172	143	126	162	134	125	153
02770 ROCHESTER	113	141	150	141	139	137	126	125	117	125	147	147	134	156	129	113	146	121	112	139
02771 SEEKONK	106	128	140	126	126	128	118	117	112	117	141	135	125	149	121	110	140	114	109	128
02777 SWANSEA	93	108	115	105	107	112	101	101	99	100	123	116	107	130	104	99	121	99	98	111
02779 BERKLEY	106	128	133	130	125	123	115	114	106	116	134	134	121	140	116	102	133	111	101	126
02780 TAUNTON	80	82	87	81	81	87	84	83	84	82	104	97	84	107	83	83	102	83	81	92
02790 WESTPORT	113	123	126	118	124	132	115	119	115	114	142	136	118	148	119	116	139	116	120	137
MASSACHUSETTS	112	121	148	122	120	127	122	119	121	121	151	138	126	156	123	120	149	120	115	132
UNITED STATES	100	100	100	100	100	100	100	100	100	100	100	100	100	100	100	100	100	100	100	100

MICHIGAN
POPULATION CHANGE

A 48001-48141

ZIP CODE			POPULATION			2000-2004 ANNUAL RATE		HOUSEHOLDS					FAMILIES		
# POST OFFICE NAME		COUNTY FIPS CODE	2000	2004	2009	% Rate	State Centile	2000	2004	2009	% Annual Rate 2000-2004	2004 Average HH Size	2000	2004	% Annual Rate 2000-2004
48001	ALGONAC	147	13446	13521	13910	0.1	27	5321	5480	5750	0.7	2.47	3743	3792	0.3
48002	ALLENTON	147	3198	3330	3464	1.0	63	1062	1130	1198	1.5	2.95	883	931	1.3
48003	ALMONT	087	5616	6244	6746	2.5	95	1956	2219	2443	3.0	2.81	1563	1756	2.8
48005	ARMADA	099	5255	5442	5660	0.8	58	1720	1803	1897	1.1	2.97	1418	1473	0.9
48006	AVOCA	147	3790	4034	4250	1.5	79	1301	1412	1514	2.0	2.85	1080	1161	1.7
48009	BIRMINGHAM	125	19263	18998	19188	-0.3	12	9120	9188	9451	0.2	2.07	5077	4982	-0.4
48014	CAPAC	147	3767	4258	4628	2.9	97	1292	1484	1640	3.3	2.87	1012	1148	3.0
48015	CENTER LINE	099	8531	8650	8990	0.3	36	3821	3913	4109	0.6	2.16	2074	2065	-0.1
48017	CLAWSON	125	12711	12309	12306	-0.8	5	5562	5530	5644	-0.1	2.20	3252	3156	-0.7
48021	EASTPOINTE	099	33473	32927	33850	-0.4	10	13260	13161	13654	-0.2	2.50	8755	8522	-0.6
48022	EMMETT	147	2439	2685	2879	2.3	93	801	899	982	2.8	2.99	667	742	2.5
48023	FAIR HAVEN	147	6966	7529	8019	1.9	87	2677	2920	3142	2.1	2.58	1833	1970	1.7
48025	FRANKLIN	125	14441	14301	14417	-0.2	15	5615	5665	5808	0.2	2.50	4214	4180	-0.2
48026	FRASER	099	15278	15293	15852	0.0	23	6054	6085	6355	0.1	2.48	4118	4057	-0.4
48027	GOODELLS	147	2965	3206	3404	1.9	88	1019	1128	1222	2.4	2.82	830	909	2.2
48028	HARSENS ISLAND	147	1282	1295	1325	0.2	31	592	611	637	0.8	2.12	396	401	0.3
48030	HAZEL PARK	125	19019	18418	18459	-0.8	5	7305	7220	7361	-0.3	2.55	4684	4530	-0.8
48032	JEDDO	147	2090	2173	2259	0.9	62	708	750	792	1.4	2.88	574	602	1.1
48034	SOUTHFIELD	125	31432	32990	34167	1.1	69	15345	16239	17009	1.3	2.02	7648	7837	0.6
48035	CLINTON TOWNSHIP	099	34621	35300	36982	0.5	41	14020	14567	15476	0.9	2.41	9268	9354	0.2
48036	CLINTON TOWNSHIP	099	21573	22332	23529	0.8	58	9156	9610	10254	1.2	2.29	5889	6041	0.6
48038	CLINTON TOWNSHIP	099	39558	43918	47765	2.5	95	17169	19338	21278	2.8	2.26	10417	11432	2.2
48039	MARINE CITY	147	8171	8238	8473	0.2	29	3134	3220	3369	0.6	2.56	2185	2210	0.3
48040	MARYSVILLE	147	9686	9896	10233	0.5	43	4026	4203	4427	1.0	2.35	2742	2812	0.6
48041	MEMPHIS	147	4166	4574	4911	2.2	92	1471	1651	1806	2.8	2.74	1173	1303	2.5
48042	MACOMB	099	16033	19978	23067	5.3	100	5394	6708	7775	5.3	2.97	4608	5704	5.2
48043	MOUNT CLEMENS	099	17351	17131	17636	-0.3	13	7086	7056	7356	-0.1	2.19	3862	3744	-0.7
48044	MACOMB	099	34519	41566	47168	4.5	100	11575	13911	15844	4.4	2.99	9465	11333	4.3
48045	HARRISON TOWNSHIP	099	24382	25590	27017	1.1	69	10692	11299	12024	1.3	2.26	6410	6638	0.8
48047	NEW BALTIMORE	099	31199	35013	38201	2.8	96	11620	13165	14503	3.0	2.64	8433	9405	2.6
48048	NEW HAVEN	099	6700	7338	7843	2.2	92	1940	2192	2399	2.9	2.76	1453	1617	2.6
48049	NORTH STREET	147	5518	5587	5727	0.3	34	1932	2007	2101	0.9	2.77	1592	1638	0.7
48050	NEW HAVEN	099	1707	1786	1867	1.1	67	562	596	630	1.4	2.93	485	509	1.1
48051	NEW BALTIMORE	099	13537	15323	16790	3.0	97	4646	5244	5763	2.9	2.92	3629	4052	2.6
48054	EAST CHINA	147	6929	7275	7604	1.2	70	2557	2747	2929	1.7	2.59	1943	2061	1.4
48059	FORT GRATIOT	147	14611	15036	15607	0.7	50	5679	5953	6284	1.1	2.48	4069	4203	0.8
48060	PORT HURON	147	40933	42311	44278	0.8	56	16261	17106	18212	1.2	2.42	10473	10852	0.8
48062	RICHMOND	099	8257	8718	9174	1.3	74	2978	3194	3407	1.7	2.65	2161	2275	1.2
48063	COLUMBUS	147	4619	4769	4941	0.8	54	1536	1615	1701	1.2	2.95	1270	1322	1.0
48064	CASCO	147	4744	4804	4962	0.3	34	1632	1690	1779	0.8	2.84	1291	1323	0.6
48065	ROMEO	099	10133	10926	11659	1.8	86	3649	3949	4242	1.9	2.74	2791	3002	1.7
48066	ROSEVILLE	099	48619	49591	51832	0.5	41	20271	20962	22180	0.8	2.36	12901	13019	0.2
48067	ROYAL OAK	125	25248	24916	25204	-0.3	12	12195	12383	12800	0.4	2.00	5787	5716	-0.3
48069	PLEASANT RIDGE	125	2610	2554	2555	-0.5	8	1120	1128	1152	0.2	2.26	717	707	-0.3
48070	HUNTINGTON WOODS	125	6140	5954	5951	-0.7	5	2378	2354	2396	-0.2	2.53	1800	1757	-0.6
48071	MADISON HEIGHTS	125	31101	31421	32011	0.2	31	13299	13745	14261	0.8	2.27	8001	8085	0.3
48072	BERKLEY	125	15529	15202	15235	-0.5	8	6678	6701	6847	0.1	2.26	4018	3942	-0.5
48073	ROYAL OAK	125	34816	34213	34473	-0.4	10	16685	16802	17266	0.2	2.01	8660	8485	-0.5
48074	SMITHS CREEK	147	8695	9218	9689	1.4	77	3140	3409	3653	2.0	2.68	2399	2570	1.6
48075	SOUTHFIELD	125	22508	22417	22840	-0.1	19	9289	9332	9621	0.1	2.34	5845	5784	-0.3
48076	SOUTHFIELD	125	28568	28879	29473	0.3	32	10965	11273	11691	0.7	2.51	7483	7564	0.3
48079	SAINT CLAIR	147	12247	12845	13448	1.1	69	4598	4894	5201	1.5	2.62	3448	3627	1.2
48080	SAINT CLAIR SHORES	099	23498	23575	24565	0.1	25	10856	11006	11583	0.3	2.13	6206	6136	-0.3
48081	SAINT CLAIR SHORES	099	22005	21853	22512	-0.2	18	9108	9153	9531	0.1	2.35	4941	4865	-0.4
48082	SAINT CLAIR SHORES	099	17613	17490	18116	-0.2	18	7480	7518	7868	0.1	2.32	4941	4865	-0.4
48083	TROY	125	22318	22411	22697	0.1	27	8999	9171	9429	0.5	2.44	5762	5806	0.2
48084	TROY	125	13767	12858	12820	-1.6	0	6181	5819	5873	-1.4	2.20	3476	3244	-1.6
48085	TROY	125	24310	24078	24408	-0.2	15	7968	8065	8323	0.3	2.98	6900	6936	0.1
48088	WARREN	099	23658	24128	25368	0.5	41	9539	9797	10390	0.6	2.45	6877	7005	0.4
48089	WARREN	099	34313	33826	34792	-0.3	12	12816	12768	13270	-0.1	2.61	8582	8381	-0.6
48091	WARREN	099	32168	32847	34278	0.5	43	12955	13358	14080	0.7	2.46	8197	8274	0.2
48092	WARREN	099	25345	26041	27378	0.6	48	10081	10411	11036	0.8	2.48	7014	7153	0.5
48093	WARREN	099	22896	23432	24477	0.6	44	10208	10614	11232	0.9	2.16	6077	6151	0.3
48094	WASHINGTON	099	12934	14515	15769	2.8	96	4760	5386	5904	3.0	2.69	3659	4099	2.7
48095	WASHINGTON	099	3809	4201	4520	2.3	93	1272	1419	1545	2.6	2.94	1092	1208	2.4
48096	RAY	099	3731	3795	3908	0.4	38	1300	1336	1391	0.6	2.82	1058	1076	0.4
48097	YALE	147	5265	5410	5619	0.6	48	1815	1891	1995	1.0	2.80	1395	1435	0.7
48098	TROY	125	20629	21507	22080	1.0	65	6900	7334	7659	1.5	2.92	5750	6066	1.3
48101	ALLEN PARK	163	29401	28329	27696	-0.9	4	11982	11676	11521	-0.6	2.40	8206	7875	-1.0
48103	ANN ARBOR	161	49122	51989	55674	1.3	76	20913	22409	24315	1.6	2.31	12519	13156	1.2
48104	ANN ARBOR	161	41074	41742	43736	0.4	38	15803	16387	17569	0.9	2.19	5511	5487	-0.1
48105	ANN ARBOR	161	32211	33791	36009	1.1	69	13647	14558	15775	1.5	2.23	7948	8254	0.9
48108	ANN ARBOR	161	24633	27165	29836	2.3	93	10423	11672	13013	2.7	2.28	6029	6588	2.1
48109	ANN ARBOR	161	6076	6202	6334	0.5	42	211	228	254	1.8	4.75	37	44	4.2
48111	BELLEVILLE	163	39271	41543	42513	1.3	75	15782	16947	17504	1.7	2.44	10288	10807	1.2
48114	BRIGHTON	093	19881	21858	24645	2.3	92	6874	7725	8880	2.8	2.82	5659	6295	2.5
48116	BRIGHTON	093	24385	27160	30959	2.6	95	9326	10569	12258	3.0	2.55	6844	7675	2.7
48117	CARLETON	115	9523	9884	10307	0.9	60	3444	3659	3898	1.4	2.70	2644	2780	1.2
48118	CHELSEA	161	11534	11866	12397	0.7	50	4195	4419	4710	1.2	2.53	3072	3166	0.7
48120	DEARBORN	163	7480	8173	8493	2.1	91	2643	2887	3010	2.1	2.83	1466	1560	1.5
48122	MELVINDALE	163	10710	10521	10395	-0.4	10	4443	4443	4419	-0.3	2.36	2690	2603	-0.8
48124	DEARBORN	163	33224	32521	32026	-0.5	8	14192	14037	13940	-0.3	2.31	9016	8777	-0.6
48125	DEARBORN HEIGHTS	163	22681	21934	21482	-0.8	5	8883	8696	8597	-0.5	2.49	6162	5943	-0.9
48126	DEARBORN	163	46683	48090	48517	0.7	52	15724	15979	16057	0.4	2.99	10439	10432	0.0
48127	DEARBORN HEIGHTS	163	35600	35468	35217	-0.1	20	14400	14461	14460	0.1	2.42	9614	9504	-0.3
48128	DEARBORN	163	10371	10170	10017	-0.5	9	4204	4165	4136	-0.2	2.44	2926	2858	-0.6
48130	DEXTER	161	10537	11644	12670	2.4	94	3832	4317	4774	2.8	2.69	3012	3327	2.4
48131	DUNDEE	115	6653	6935	7252	1.0	65	2488	2632	2799	1.3	2.63	1814	1895	1.0
48133	ERIE	115	5264	5540	5886	1.2	72	1927	2076	2253	1.8	2.67	1458	1549	1.4
48134	FLAT ROCK	163	17162	18667	19369	2.0	90	6278	6876	7185	2.2	2.71	4670	5055	1.9
48135	GARDEN CITY	163	30183	29621	29237	-0.4	10	11531	11495	11474	-0.1	2.58	8270	8117	-0.4
48137	GREGORY	093	4466	4769	5216	1.6	82	1588	1731	1927	2.1	2.70	1221	1312	1.7
48138	GROSSE ILE	163	10894	11082	11108	0.4	38	4122	4247	4298	0.7	2.60	3295	3364	0.5
48140	IDA	115	3338	3474	3628	0.9	62	1104	1169	1243	1.4	2.95	932	980	1.2
48141	INKSTER	163	30080	29817	29597	-0.2	16	11155	11190	11210	0.1	2.64	7453	7368	-0.3
	MICHIGAN					0.6					1.0	2.52			0.6
	UNITED STATES					1.2					1.3	2.58			1.1

ZIP CODE #	POST OFFICE NAME	RACE (%) White 2000	White 2004	Black 2000	Black 2004	Asian/Pacific 2000	Asian/Pacific 2004	% Hispanic Origin 2000	% Hispanic Origin 2004	2004 AGE DISTRIBUTION (%) 0-4	5-9	10-14	15-19	20-24	25-44	45-64	65-84	85+	18+	MEDIAN AGE 2004	% 2004 Males	% 2004 Females
48001	ALGONAC	97.8	97.5	0.2	0.2	0.2	0.2	1.0	1.1	5.7	6.1	7.1	6.2	5.6	27.8	28.2	11.7	1.6	77.3	40.0	50.1	49.9
48002	ALLENTON	97.2	96.8	0.9	0.9	0.3	0.4	2.8	3.2	7.4	7.7	7.8	6.9	5.4	30.3	26.6	6.9	0.9	72.7	36.5	51.1	48.9
48003	ALMONT	96.6	96.3	0.2	0.2	0.3	0.4	3.2	3.6	7.0	7.6	8.7	6.8	5.4	30.0	25.3	8.3	0.9	72.4	36.4	49.9	50.1
48005	ARMADA	98.1	97.8	0.1	0.1	0.1	0.2	1.5	1.8	6.5	7.6	8.2	6.9	6.0	28.4	26.8	8.2	1.4	73.2	37.5	50.7	49.3
48006	AVOCA	97.5	97.2	0.5	0.5	0.2	0.3	1.2	1.4	7.1	7.5	8.1	6.7	5.3	29.9	25.9	8.9	0.7	72.9	37.2	51.1	48.9
48009	BIRMINGHAM	96.1	95.4	0.9	1.0	1.5	2.0	1.2	1.4	6.5	6.6	5.9	4.7	3.7	30.3	28.0	12.1	2.1	77.9	40.6	47.9	52.1
48014	CAPAC	93.9	93.3	0.2	0.2	0.3	0.4	9.8	10.9	7.8	7.6	9.0	7.8	7.3	28.5	23.5	7.6	1.0	70.9	33.5	51.1	48.9
48015	CENTER LINE	93.8	93.2	3.1	3.3	1.0	1.3	1.5	1.8	6.2	6.0	6.1	5.1	5.2	26.5	22.9	16.7	5.3	78.7	41.4	44.9	55.1
48017	CLAWSON	96.1	95.4	0.8	0.9	1.3	1.7	1.1	1.3	5.4	5.5	5.9	5.5	5.4	32.7	24.6	13.2	2.0	79.8	39.1	48.5	51.5
48021	EASTPOINTE	92.0	91.1	4.8	5.2	0.9	1.1	1.3	1.5	6.4	6.4	6.9	6.3	5.9	30.0	22.9	12.8	2.3	76.3	37.7	48.8	51.2
48022	EMMETT	98.2	98.0	0.3	0.3	0.4	0.5	1.5	1.7	8.2	8.3	7.9	7.2	5.9	29.8	24.0	7.9	0.8	71.3	35.9	50.8	49.2
48023	FAIR HAVEN	96.9	96.6	0.8	0.9	0.3	0.4	1.3	1.4	7.7	7.5	7.9	6.8	6.1	31.5	23.2	8.5	0.9	72.8	35.2	50.4	49.6
48025	FRANKLIN	92.3	91.1	3.7	4.2	2.2	2.8	1.2	1.4	5.8	6.9	7.5	6.0	3.5	21.4	30.4	16.1	2.3	75.6	44.3	48.7	51.3
48026	FRASER	96.7	96.1	0.9	1.0	0.9	1.3	1.3	1.5	5.6	6.0	7.1	6.6	6.0	27.2	26.1	13.0	2.5	77.2	39.8	46.7	53.4
48027	GOODELLS	95.8	95.6	3.2	3.3	0.1	0.1	1.1	1.2	5.8	6.7	8.7	7.1	5.0	29.5	27.4	8.8	1.0	74.3	38.2	50.9	49.1
48028	HARSENS ISLAND	98.0	97.9	0.2	0.2	0.1	0.1	0.2	0.2	2.9	3.3	4.0	3.9	3.5	17.5	40.6	21.6	2.7	87.3	53.3	51.2	48.8
48030	HAZEL PARK	91.4	90.2	1.9	2.1	1.8	2.4	2.1	2.3	7.2	7.1	7.8	7.2	7.1	32.0	21.0	9.5	1.3	73.6	33.8	49.5	50.5
48032	JEDDO	97.9	97.7	0.1	0.1	0.2	0.2	2.1	2.4	6.4	7.2	8.9	7.9	5.7	30.5	25.4	7.1	0.9	72.3	36.5	51.5	48.5
48034	SOUTHFIELD	38.9	36.0	52.4	54.5	4.2	5.0	1.4	1.5	5.3	5.0	5.3	5.4	7.2	31.0	24.6	12.4	3.9	81.2	38.3	45.6	54.4
48035	CLINTON TOWNSHIP	87.7	86.6	7.1	7.3	2.3	2.9	1.6	1.8	6.6	6.4	6.8	6.1	6.4	30.9	23.8	11.5	1.6	76.6	36.7	48.3	51.7
48036	CLINTON TOWNSHIP	89.4	88.4	6.8	7.2	1.0	1.3	1.5	1.7	6.0	5.9	5.6	5.3	5.7	27.2	26.9	15.3	2.1	79.3	41.1	47.5	52.5
48038	CLINTON TOWNSHIP	95.0	94.2	1.4	1.6	1.6	2.0	2.1	2.3	5.5	5.4	6.1	5.8	7.4	29.7	25.8	12.3	2.1	79.6	38.5	48.0	52.0
48039	MARINE CITY	97.9	97.6	0.1	0.1	0.3	0.3	1.1	1.3	6.4	6.7	7.9	7.8	6.7	28.2	24.2	10.7	1.5	74.4	36.8	48.8	51.3
48040	MARYSVILLE	98.2	97.9	0.2	0.2	0.4	0.6	1.2	1.3	5.8	6.1	6.9	6.4	5.6	26.2	26.1	14.7	2.2	77.4	40.7	48.5	51.5
48041	MEMPHIS	97.4	97.1	0.7	0.8	0.2	0.3	1.6	1.9	7.3	7.8	8.1	6.7	5.0	30.6	24.9	8.8	0.9	72.7	36.9	51.5	48.5
48042	MACOMB	96.7	96.1	0.7	0.7	1.1	1.5	1.4	1.6	8.9	9.5	8.3	5.7	4.0	32.6	22.0	8.5	0.7	69.7	35.7	49.7	50.3
48043	MOUNT CLEMENS	75.9	74.8	19.5	20.2	0.5	0.7	2.3	2.6	6.2	6.1	5.9	6.1	6.3	32.9	24.0	10.6	1.9	78.2	37.2	52.1	47.9
48044	MACOMB	95.8	95.0	0.9	1.1	1.6	2.1	1.5	1.7	9.3	9.2	8.2	6.3	5.4	33.4	21.8	5.9	0.5	69.4	33.4	50.1	49.9
48045	HARRISON TOWNSHIP	94.5	94.0	2.5	2.6	0.6	0.8	1.5	1.7	5.9	5.8	5.8	5.8	6.2	30.5	28.4	10.5	1.1	79.0	39.3	50.1	49.9
48047	NEW BALTIMORE	94.4	94.0	2.4	2.5	0.7	0.9	2.3	2.5	7.9	7.8	7.5	6.1	5.5	33.1	24.0	6.9	1.2	73.0	35.3	49.6	50.4
48048	NEW HAVEN	74.1	72.1	20.6	22.1	0.3	0.4	3.5	3.8	7.3	6.8	6.9	6.0	6.5	37.5	22.4	6.2	0.6	75.4	34.1	58.0	42.0
48049	NORTH STREET	97.8	97.5	0.3	0.3	0.4	0.5	1.3	1.4	6.1	6.6	7.3	6.7	5.5	26.9	30.5	9.5	0.9	75.5	39.5	50.5	49.5
48050	NEW HAVEN	98.0	97.7	0.9	1.0	0.1	0.2	0.4	0.5	6.8	7.3	7.7	6.7	5.5	28.1	27.3	9.9	0.7	73.6	38.4	51.6	48.4
48051	NEW BALTIMORE	93.1	92.3	2.9	3.3	0.9	1.1	2.3	2.6	10.0	9.2	8.6	7.0	6.4	34.6	18.9	4.7	0.5	67.7	31.3	48.9	51.1
48054	EAST CHINA	98.4	98.2	0.3	0.3	0.3	0.3	0.8	0.9	5.0	5.7	7.3	6.5	5.8	24.5	29.8	12.7	2.7	77.8	42.3	49.3	50.7
48059	FORT GRATIOT	95.9	95.4	1.1	1.2	1.1	1.4	1.8	2.0	6.2	6.3	6.9	6.2	6.2	26.6	27.5	12.3	1.9	76.8	39.9	48.0	52.0
48060	PORT HURON	88.2	87.3	6.9	7.3	0.5	0.6	3.9	4.4	7.6	6.9	7.2	6.8	7.4	28.3	22.5	11.3	2.1	74.2	35.4	48.1	51.9
48062	RICHMOND	96.0	95.5	0.5	0.5	0.7	0.9	3.2	3.6	6.4	6.5	7.2	6.4	6.5	28.7	25.4	10.7	2.3	75.8	37.8	49.2	50.8
48063	COLUMBUS	97.0	96.6	0.1	0.1	0.4	0.5	2.3	2.7	7.6	8.6	8.8	7.0	5.4	29.6	25.3	7.3	0.4	70.4	35.6	52.1	47.9
48064	CASCO	96.6	96.3	0.5	0.5	0.3	0.3	0.9	1.1	7.6	7.5	7.9	6.9	6.0	29.4	27.0	7.2	0.7	72.9	35.9	50.5	49.5
48065	ROMEO	95.7	95.3	1.9	2.0	0.5	0.7	2.0	2.2	7.1	7.4	8.2	7.2	5.5	28.5	26.0	9.0	1.2	72.6	36.8	49.7	50.4
48066	ROSEVILLE	93.5	92.5	2.6	2.9	1.7	2.1	1.5	1.7	6.6	6.4	6.5	5.6	6.0	31.4	22.7	12.9	1.9	77.1	37.3	48.4	51.6
48067	ROYAL OAK	95.6	94.9	1.1	1.3	1.1	1.4	1.5	1.7	5.0	4.5	4.8	5.4	6.5	38.2	23.0	10.5	2.1	82.4	37.2	49.5	50.5
48069	PLEASANT RIDGE	96.6	96.1	0.9	1.0	0.9	1.2	1.8	2.0	6.1	6.1	6.5	4.9	3.3	29.0	32.9	9.8	1.6	78.0	41.6	50.0	50.0
48070	HUNTINGTON WOODS	97.0	96.4	0.7	0.8	1.4	1.9	0.9	1.0	7.0	8.3	7.6	6.0	3.4	24.0	31.9	9.5	2.4	73.2	41.4	48.9	51.1
48071	MADISON HEIGHTS	89.6	87.8	1.8	2.0	5.0	6.3	1.6	1.9	6.1	6.0	6.1	5.8	6.1	32.9	22.7	12.6	1.8	78.4	37.5	48.9	51.1
48072	BERKLEY	96.1	95.5	0.7	0.8	1.0	1.4	1.3	1.5	6.6	6.4	6.1	5.9	5.6	34.4	22.5	10.5	1.9	77.3	36.8	48.3	51.7
48073	ROYAL OAK	94.3	93.2	1.8	2.1	2.0	2.6	1.2	1.3	5.2	4.9	4.8	5.3	6.0	33.5	24.6	13.4	2.4	81.9	39.4	48.3	51.8
48074	SMITHS CREEK	96.8	96.4	0.9	1.0	0.2	0.2	1.6	1.8	6.8	6.9	6.9	6.7	6.0	30.8	25.6	9.3	1.0	74.8	36.8	50.5	49.5
48075	SOUTHFIELD	23.7	21.6	71.7	73.5	1.7	2.0	1.1	1.1	5.2	5.6	6.4	6.4	6.3	25.8	28.8	13.0	2.5	78.8	40.8	46.0	54.1
48076	SOUTHFIELD	51.9	48.3	41.8	44.7	2.6	3.2	1.1	1.1	5.6	5.9	6.9	6.6	6.0	26.5	28.1	11.9	2.6	77.4	40.3	46.8	53.2
48079	SAINT CLAIR	97.8	97.5	0.2	0.2	0.6	0.7	1.1	1.3	6.7	6.9	7.7	7.1	6.2	26.2	26.4	11.2	1.6	74.2	38.5	48.6	51.4
48080	SAINT CLAIR SHORES	96.3	95.7	0.8	0.9	1.4	1.8	1.3	1.4	5.1	5.2	5.4	5.0	4.8	26.9	24.5	19.2	4.0	81.3	43.5	46.4	53.6
48081	SAINT CLAIR SHORES	97.7	97.4	0.3	0.4	0.6	0.8	1.0	1.1	4.8	5.3	5.9	5.5	4.7	25.0	27.6	18.1	3.1	80.6	44.3	48.3	51.8
48082	SAINT CLAIR SHORES	96.7	96.3	1.0	1.1	0.5	0.6	1.4	1.5	5.2	5.5	6.1	5.5	4.8	27.2	25.7	17.9	2.2	79.8	42.4	48.2	51.8
48083	TROY	81.4	77.7	2.2	2.3	13.4	16.7	1.8	2.0	7.1	6.9	6.5	5.5	5.6	32.4	23.9	10.2	1.9	76.1	37.0	49.0	51.0
48084	TROY	80.5	76.7	2.4	2.6	14.9	18.3	1.8	2.0	5.4	5.9	6.5	6.5	5.1	32.0	26.2	11.0	1.5	78.0	38.4	50.2	49.8
48085	TROY	84.8	81.3	1.7	1.9	11.4	14.4	1.3	1.5	6.2	7.3	8.4	7.0	5.0	25.3	31.1	9.1	0.8	73.4	39.9	50.1	49.9
48088	WARREN	95.5	94.8	1.0	1.0	1.9	2.4	1.0	1.1	5.3	5.4	5.7	5.5	5.0	25.9	26.1	18.7	2.5	80.3	43.2	48.2	51.8
48089	WARREN	90.8	89.6	2.7	2.9	2.9	3.7	1.7	1.9	8.1	7.6	7.6	6.5	6.6	32.1	19.6	10.4	1.6	72.7	33.7	49.9	50.2
48091	WARREN	88.2	86.6	4.4	4.9	3.5	4.5	1.6	1.8	6.8	6.6	7.0	6.3	6.4	30.0	22.5	12.6	1.7	75.7	36.7	49.8	50.2
48092	WARREN	89.9	88.4	2.6	2.6	4.6	5.8	1.2	1.3	6.1	6.0	6.0	5.5	5.5	28.9	23.8	16.6	1.8	78.7	40.3	49.8	50.2
48093	WARREN	93.5	92.3	2.0	2.3	2.6	3.3	1.1	1.3	4.9	4.9	5.0	4.7	4.5	25.6	23.9	21.8	4.7	82.3	45.2	45.8	54.2
48094	WASHINGTON	97.4	97.0	0.3	0.4	0.6	0.9	2.3	2.6	6.9	7.3	7.2	6.1	5.1	29.0	28.5	9.2	0.7	74.6	38.3	49.9	50.1
48095	WASHINGTON	97.8	97.5	0.1	0.1	0.7	0.9	2.7	3.2	6.7	7.6	8.6	7.1	5.0	26.6	29.0	8.7	0.7	72.2	38.7	50.9	49.1
48096	RAY	97.8	97.4	0.2	0.2	0.4	0.5	1.2	1.5	6.2	6.7	7.3	6.3	4.8	27.3	30.4	9.9	1.1	75.6	40.6	51.1	48.9
48097	YALE	97.3	97.0	0.5	0.6	0.1	0.2	1.9	2.2	8.0	7.7	8.0	7.2	6.5	27.5	23.3	9.4	2.4	71.8	35.2	49.1	50.9
48098	TROY	81.6	77.8	2.3	2.6	14.2	17.7	1.1	1.3	5.1	6.9	8.8	7.7	4.8	21.1	34.9	9.7	1.0	73.7	42.5	49.1	50.9
48101	ALLEN PARK	95.6	94.4	0.7	1.1	0.8	1.1	4.7	5.8	5.4	5.7	6.4	6.0	5.0	26.1	25.7	16.5	3.2	78.8	42.1	47.8	52.2
48103	ANN ARBOR	84.1	81.3	7.2	7.8	5.1	7.0	2.6	2.9	6.3	6.4	6.8	6.0	5.5	31.7	26.6	9.1	1.6	76.5	37.6	48.5	51.5
48104	ANN ARBOR	80.9	77.5	5.4	5.8	9.5	12.2	3.6	4.1	2.9	2.7	2.8	14.4	30.1	25.1	15.2	6.1	0.8	89.6	24.5	50.6	49.4
48105	ANN ARBOR	67.7	63.7	7.7	7.8	20.3	24.2	2.8	3.0	6.7	5.9	5.8	7.0	8.5	34.1	22.3	8.2	1.4	78.2	33.5	49.8	50.2
48108	ANN ARBOR	67.3	65.2	16.3	15.8	10.2	12.8	4.3	4.5	6.9	6.6	6.4	6.3	8.7	35.7	22.2	6.5	0.8	76.4	32.9	49.4	50.6
48109	ANN ARBOR	64.5	59.0	10.1	10.5	20.2	25.0	3.9	4.2	0.5	0.3	0.5	67.2	18.5	9.8	2.1	0.9	0.2	98.1	18.6	50.5	49.5
48111	BELLEVILLE	84.3	79.9	11.2	14.8	1.3	1.7	2.2	2.5	7.1	6.8	7.0	6.6	7.3	33.2	24.2	7.3	0.7	75.3	33.9	50.2	49.8
48114	BRIGHTON	97.5	97.1	0.4	0.4	0.8	1.0	1.0	1.2	6.8	8.1	8.7	7.0	4.6	27.2	29.3	7.8	0.6	71.6	38.6	50.5	49.5
48116	BRIGHTON	96.9	96.5	0.5	0.5	0.8	1.1	1.4	1.5	7.0	7.6	7.8	6.8	5.3	27.9	27.4	8.7	1.4	73.2	38.2	50.0	50.0
48117	CARLETON	95.5	95.1	2.0	2.2	0.3	0.3	1.5	1.7	6.3	6.7	8.1	7.0	6.2	27.8	27.4	9.6	1.0	74.6	37.7	50.4	49.6
48118	CHELSEA	95.7	95.2	1.8	2.0	0.5	0.6	1.5	1.8	4.6	6.4	8.1	8.7	4.8	24.5	28.4	11.0	3.5	75.5	41.0	50.3	49.7
48120	DEARBORN	75.6	70.8	2.9	4.3	3.9	4.9	1.9	2.2	9.5	7.7	7.8	8.3	9.4	24.8	18.3	10.4	3.8	70.0	30.0	53.9	46.1
48122	MELVINDALE	87.4	84.1	5.2	7.2	1.3	1.8	8.9	10.5	6.8	6.6	6.8	6.3	6.3	30.2	24.0	11.4	1.6	76.1	36.7	49.1	51.0
48124	DEARBORN	95.5	94.2	1.0	1.5	1.3	1.7	2.9	3.5	5.8	6.1	6.3	5.6	4.9	27.6	26.1	14.7	2.9	78.3	41.2	48.2	51.8
48125	DEARBORN HEIGHTS	94.3	92.7	1.2	1.8	1.2	1.5	4.0	4.9	6.6	6.6	6.6	5.7	5.3	31.0	23.8	12.9	1.6	76.8	37.8	48.8	51.2
48126	DEARBORN	80.4	76.8	1.4	2.0	1.4	1.8	3.1	3.7	10.4	8.9	8.4	7.3	7.3	28.2	16.7	10.1	2.7	67.8	30.3	50.4	49.6
48127	DEARBORN HEIGHTS	90.0	87.5	2.7	3.8	2.9	3.8	3.0	3.5	6.4	6.3	6.2	5.6	5.2	26.5	23.2	18.0	2.8	77.6	40.9	47.8	52.2
48128	DEARBORN	96.6	95.7	0.4	0.6	0.9	1.2	3.4	4.1	6.4	6.8	7.0	6.2	4.6	27.2	26.6	12.3	3.1	75.9	40.3	48.5	51.5
48130	DEXTER	97.3	96.7	0.4	0.4	0.9	1.2	1.1	1.4	6.5	7.4	8.3	7.3	5.2	26.2	30.2	8.2	0.9	73.0	39.6	50.5	49.5
48131	DUNDEE	97.2	96.8	0.5	0.6	0.3	0.4	1.4	1.6	7.7	7.3	7.4	6.9	7.1	28.9	24.7	8.8	1.3	73.4	34.9	50.3	49.7
48133	ERIE	95.4	94.7	1.0	1.1	0.3	0.5	4.2	4.9	5.7	6.3	7.8	7.4	6.2	27.6	27.5	10.7	0.8	75.5	38.5	50.6	49.4
48134	FLAT ROCK	93.6	91.6	1.7	2.6	1.7	2.3	3.1	3.9	8.1	7.6	7.8	7.3	7.3	30.8	23.5	6.9	0.7	71.8	33.4	49.5	50.5
48135	GARDEN CITY	96.2	95.0	1.1	1.7	0.7	1.0	2.0	2.5	6.2	6.6	7.3	6.3	5.7	30.6	23.7	12.5	1.1	76.0	37.8	49.2	50.8
48137	GREGORY	95.5	94.9	0.6	0.7	0.4	0.6	2.6	3.1	6.3	7.0	7.6	7.0	5.2	28.4	28.9	8.7	1.0	74.5	39.1	50.4	49.7
48138	GROSSE ILE	95.2	93.8	0.4	0.6	2.8	3.7	1.6	1.9	4.6	5.8	7.9	6.9	4.0	21.0	37.0	11.8	1.1	76.9	45.0	49.9	50.1
48140	IDA	98.5	98.4	0.1	0.1	0.3	0.3	1.1	1.2	6.9	7.3	7.9	7.4	6.1	27.1	27.5	8.8	1.0	73.2	37.3	50.9	49.1
48141	INKSTER	25.2	19.8	67.5	72.8	3.4	3.8	1.6	1.6	8.0	7.7	8.9	7.3	6.7	28.9	21.9	9.6	1.1	70.9	32.7	47.8	52.2
	MICHIGAN	80.2	79.2	14.2	14.4	1.8	2.3	3.3	3.6	6.8	6.9	7.4	7.1	6.9	28.1	24.6	10.8	1.6	74.9	36.5	49.1	50.9
	UNITED STATES	75.1	73.6	12.3	12.5	3.8	4.2	12.5	14.1	6.9	6.7	7.2	7.0	7.3	28.6	23.8	10.8	1.7	75.1	36.0	49.1	50.9

#	POST OFFICE NAME	2004 Per Capita Income	2004 HH Income Base	2004 Household Income Distribution (%): Less than $25,000	$25,000 to $49,999	$50,000 to $99,999	$100,000 to $149,999	$150,000 or More	Median Household Income: 2004	2009	2004 National Centile	2004 State Centile	2004 Home Value Base	2004 Home Value Distribution (%): Less than $50,000	$50,000 to $89,999	$90,000 to $174,999	$175,000 to $399,999	$400,000 or More	2004 Median Home Value
48001	ALGONAC	28270	5480	20.3	24.4	37.4	11.5	6.5	54686	61003	79	76	4682	6.6	7.8	38.8	41.5	5.4	168509
48002	ALLENTON	24466	1130	13.4	22.3	41.8	18.1	4.4	65868	73474	89	89	1025	1.5	3.8	35.7	54.7	4.3	204954
48003	ALMONT	26638	2219	12.0	20.4	42.5	20.5	4.6	67235	75022	90	91	1965	10.8	2.5	28.7	50.6	7.4	192270
48005	ARMADA	28174	1803	13.1	16.5	38.5	23.0	8.9	76317	82842	94	95	1643	0.5	3.2	28.2	60.8	7.2	208938
48006	AVOCA	23463	1412	13.1	26.8	42.9	13.2	3.9	57941	64194	83	81	1308	3.8	8.6	37.1	45.2	5.4	176122
48009	BIRMINGHAM	68620	9188	9.8	14.4	32.2	16.1	27.5	87313	103618	97	98	6818	0.1	1.1	13.0	39.5	46.4	372273
48014	CAPAC	21191	1484	21.4	27.8	34.4	12.4	4.0	50584	55521	73	67	1184	1.6	9.0	52.5	35.8	1.0	153571
48015	CENTER LINE	21152	3913	37.8	25.4	27.0	8.4	1.4	35582	40646	30	16	2191	1.6	7.8	80.7	10.0	0.0	128372
48017	CLAWSON	30029	5530	17.3	25.8	39.5	13.1	4.3	56844	66426	82	80	4214	0.7	3.1	58.2	37.7	0.3	165434
48021	EASTPOINTE	23101	13161	21.8	26.8	39.0	10.7	1.8	51297	58286	74	69	11042	2.9	11.5	78.7	6.8	0.2	120962
48022	EMMETT	21114	899	14.6	24.4	47.2	12.4	1.6	59704	65617	84	83	839	4.5	7.0	33.1	52.3	3.0	185114
48023	FAIR HAVEN	24500	2920	19.7	30.0	37.3	9.9	3.0	50201	56187	72	66	2599	38.8	14.9	17.9	23.3	5.2	78178
48025	FRANKLIN	57250	5665	5.9	12.6	28.3	22.9	30.3	105086	123216	99	99	5374	0.1	0.7	6.1	51.8	41.4	364742
48026	FRASER	25555	6085	21.7	25.2	34.3	14.4	4.4	53659	59834	78	74	4427	2.3	6.2	52.9	38.1	0.5	163475
48027	GOODELLS	24231	1128	15.4	27.0	40.8	12.9	3.8	57891	63025	83	81	1032	3.4	4.5	42.5	46.5	3.1	174160
48028	HARSENS ISLAND	37026	611	14.2	23.7	41.6	11.8	8.7	62133	74376	86	86	572	2.8	5.4	37.2	41.3	13.3	189444
48030	HAZEL PARK	19701	7220	27.0	31.8	33.1	6.1	2.1	42264	50448	54	43	5142	6.4	39.5	50.7	3.0	0.4	92745
48032	JEDDO	22494	750	15.1	28.8	38.8	14.1	3.2	58132	62020	83	81	674	7.9	8.5	44.2	36.7	2.8	159565
48034	SOUTHFIELD	34671	16239	20.8	27.1	33.1	11.5	7.4	52010	60229	75	71	6477	2.1	6.2	41.8	47.3	2.6	174884
48035	CLINTON TOWNSHIP	25763	14567	19.3	27.7	37.8	11.8	3.4	52611	59155	76	73	9276	1.8	7.0	63.1	27.6	0.6	149061
48036	CLINTON TOWNSHIP	29065	9610	19.3	30.8	31.8	12.5	5.7	49933	56764	72	66	7552	15.2	16.0	32.0	34.0	2.7	139741
48038	CLINTON TOWNSHIP	31501	19338	18.4	26.3	34.9	14.3	6.1	56304	60980	81	78	12468	7.4	2.0	31.9	57.0	1.7	188632
48039	MARINE CITY	26513	3220	22.6	31.4	32.0	9.1	4.9	46817	52027	66	58	2535	9.9	10.5	47.5	28.7	3.4	140558
48040	MARYSVILLE	25910	4203	22.8	25.7	36.2	11.8	3.5	51467	56026	75	70	3453	7.0	9.1	57.1	25.5	1.5	145105
48041	MEMPHIS	25982	1651	14.4	19.8	43.6	17.6	4.7	65049	71210	89	89	1476	1.0	3.6	32.3	58.0	5.2	196366
48042	MACOMB	31904	6708	6.5	12.5	41.4	29.3	10.4	86071	101879	96	97	6535	0.3	0.3	15.0	79.5	5.0	264462
48043	MOUNT CLEMENS	23423	7056	29.9	28.9	30.6	7.6	3.0	42098	48652	53	43	4143	6.4	19.2	61.0	12.8	0.6	119769
48044	MACOMB	28545	13911	9.0	17.7	41.1	23.7	8.5	77185	87262	94	95	13371	14.2	3.3	10.3	69.4	2.9	222969
48045	HARRISON TOWNSHIP	32088	11299	17.9	26.2	34.6	13.5	7.8	56482	62694	81	79	7725	8.4	3.3	37.2	40.9	10.3	178290
48047	NEW BALTIMORE	30100	13165	13.1	21.2	40.3	18.4	7.2	66610	74043	90	90	10174	1.0	2.4	37.4	54.5	4.8	192240
48048	NEW HAVEN	21780	2192	20.7	26.1	38.4	10.9	3.8	52746	60294	77	73	1763	24.8	26.1	29.7	17.2	2.3	88402
48049	NORTH STREET	24433	2007	12.4	27.4	41.7	15.9	2.6	59632	65772	84	83	1842	2.0	6.8	46.2	44.3	0.7	167203
48050	NEW HAVEN	23962	596	15.6	21.3	41.6	16.8	4.7	66018	74158	89	90	538	0.0	2.8	29.2	59.7	8.4	229891
48051	NEW BALTIMORE	23317	5244	15.7	21.3	42.0	18.1	2.9	64508	73230	88	88	4459	19.7	5.9	17.5	56.4	0.5	187459
48054	EAST CHINA	27410	2747	17.6	23.3	38.7	14.6	5.8	61190	65335	86	85	2335	1.9	2.9	32.2	54.4	8.6	204698
48059	FORT GRATIOT	27892	5953	19.3	27.3	35.9	12.0	5.6	52991	58924	77	74	4922	6.6	13.5	43.0	29.7	7.2	151871
48060	PORT HURON	20052	17106	34.1	30.1	27.5	5.8	2.5	37266	41678	36	24	10530	6.9	25.6	51.2	15.1	1.2	110856
48062	RICHMOND	24440	3194	19.8	25.8	36.1	13.3	5.0	55204	60898	80	77	2428	4.3	4.7	44.4	44.0	2.6	169615
48063	COLUMBUS	24472	1615	11.8	25.6	39.4	18.8	4.4	64049	70653	88	88	1537	13.5	16.7	19.8	45.8	4.2	175083
48064	CASCO	24367	1690	12.8	32.1	34.4	15.2	5.5	55943	60492	81	78	1609	27.6	4.6	26.4	37.7	3.7	150792
48065	ROMEO	29596	3949	17.3	19.5	35.5	17.1	10.6	65571	72857	89	89	3378	10.9	5.0	23.2	47.0	13.8	208866
48066	ROSEVILLE	22735	20962	23.4	31.5	35.5	7.9	1.7	45795	52189	63	55	15422	2.8	16.2	74.6	6.3	0.1	118932
48067	ROYAL OAK	36514	12383	17.0	25.0	36.4	15.3	6.2	58782	69088	83	82	8712	0.6	3.1	48.5	44.7	3.1	172560
48069	PLEASANT RIDGE	47733	1128	7.1	15.2	35.1	22.4	20.2	87756	104988	97	98	1065	0.1	0.9	17.6	56.0	25.5	268594
48070	HUNTINGTON WOODS	51116	2354	8.6	13.7	30.0	22.2	25.6	95685	112134	98	99	2308	0.0	0.4	6.3	68.5	24.8	301188
48071	MADISON HEIGHTS	25002	13745	22.6	30.7	34.2	10.3	2.3	47115	55320	66	59	9380	5.6	10.5	71.4	12.1	0.4	131695
48072	BERKLEY	32243	6701	14.5	22.0	41.7	17.9	4.0	63458	75068	87	87	5672	1.0	3.1	53.2	42.2	0.5	168678
48073	ROYAL OAK	36431	16802	16.5	25.7	35.5	15.4	7.0	58477	68261	83	82	11749	1.3	5.5	37.8	53.5	2.0	183097
48074	SMITHS CREEK	22211	3409	16.2	29.8	42.3	9.5	2.2	52503	59636	76	72	2952	10.1	15.7	48.9	24.1	1.2	124523
48075	SOUTHFIELD	30476	9332	20.2	23.0	34.6	14.4	8.0	58995	68065	84	82	5897	0.6	4.9	44.6	48.0	1.9	174827
48076	SOUTHFIELD	32791	11273	13.9	21.7	35.5	18.7	10.3	68217	79827	90	91	8907	2.2	3.2	31.7	61.4	1.6	197884
48079	SAINT CLAIR	27599	4894	17.5	24.3	37.9	14.2	6.2	60904	65115	85	84	3963	2.5	4.6	42.0	44.5	6.5	177443
48080	SAINT CLAIR SHORES	27856	11006	21.2	31.2	33.3	11.4	3.0	47940	53491	68	61	8438	2.0	8.7	66.4	21.4	1.5	142616
48081	SAINT CLAIR SHORES	29065	9153	17.8	23.1	40.3	13.9	4.9	59323	64780	84	83	8152	0.7	4.2	64.6	27.3	3.3	155033
48082	SAINT CLAIR SHORES	25869	7518	18.5	29.8	38.2	11.3	2.2	51434	57619	75	70	6593	0.6	5.6	73.5	19.0	1.3	145991
48083	TROY	31160	9171	18.0	18.2	38.2	17.8	7.9	66411	78572	89	90	6300	2.8	1.7	29.3	65.2	1.1	200256
48084	TROY	47511	5819	9.3	18.0	35.9	18.9	18.0	78037	94903	94	96	2980	0.2	0.4	13.4	58.3	27.7	314414
48085	TROY	39650	8065	5.5	11.4	34.0	28.7	20.5	98328	114334	98	99	7658	0.7	1.3	8.4	79.6	10.1	265554
48088	WARREN	27584	9797	16.4	25.9	39.3	14.1	4.3	58519	63972	83	82	8618	0.8	3.2	61.5	34.3	0.2	164220
48089	WARREN	19392	12768	24.1	33.5	33.8	7.4	1.3	43768	50141	58	49	9062	5.9	35.3	54.5	4.1	0.3	98549
48091	WARREN	20915	13358	25.8	32.4	32.1	8.0	1.7	42563	48393	55	44	10333	11.8	19.3	61.9	7.0	0.1	113422
48092	WARREN	26272	10411	18.4	26.1	37.5	14.3	3.7	55645	61558	80	77	8267	2.1	3.0	59.6	35.1	0.2	163150
48093	WARREN	28615	10614	20.7	28.6	36.7	10.3	3.7	50504	56233	73	67	8591	1.4	8.4	59.1	30.7	0.4	155903
48094	WASHINGTON	33776	5386	10.1	20.2	36.7	21.2	11.8	74174	81658	93	94	4757	10.8	6.2	17.1	52.7	13.3	244826
48095	WASHINGTON	36668	1419	11.2	9.2	41.1	24.0	14.5	83619	93662	96	97	1281	0.0	0.0	10.2	65.7	24.1	279324
48096	RAY	29056	1336	9.4	14.9	46.6	23.1	6.0	76276	84948	94	95	1215	1.3	1.6	18.7	63.2	15.2	233041
48097	YALE	20671	1891	21.5	29.1	36.7	9.7	3.0	49364	54757	71	65	1551	7.2	14.1	47.5	27.2	3.9	138008
48098	TROY	54477	7334	4.1	12.0	24.0	22.6	37.3	120430	138198	99	100	7103	0.2	0.8	8.3	51.9	38.8	355842
48101	ALLEN PARK	28033	11676	15.6	26.3	39.5	14.3	4.3	57410	64405	82	81	10161	1.7	6.0	70.4	21.5	0.4	143132
48103	ANN ARBOR	37588	22409	14.9	20.9	34.2	18.2	11.9	67918	80103	90	91	15560	4.9	4.7	15.7	61.4	13.3	237359
48104	ANN ARBOR	29106	16387	32.7	23.1	22.7	11.3	10.2	43461	50619	57	47	6618	0.5	5.2	22.7	46.1	25.5	244621
48105	ANN ARBOR	38954	14558	22.3	22.8	28.0	12.8	14.1	56650	65206	81	79	7402	1.4	1.5	20.0	50.8	26.4	282054
48108	ANN ARBOR	35270	11672	18.6	25.7	30.7	14.7	10.3	56054	66789	81	78	6098	5.0	3.8	26.8	46.3	18.1	214775
48109	ANN ARBOR	11535	228	63.2	14.9	18.0	2.2	1.8	16726	19759	1	1	14	0.0	0.0	28.6	64.3	7.1	275000
48111	BELLEVILLE	26421	16947	16.4	27.6	39.0	13.3	3.8	55140	62692	80	76	11902	25.1	10.9	34.3	27.4	2.4	126443
48114	BRIGHTON	36207	7725	9.1	15.7	36.1	23.1	16.0	83206	94951	96	97	7336	5.3	6.8	11.5	59.4	17.1	263919
48116	BRIGHTON	37044	10569	11.4	18.9	34.9	21.6	13.3	75535	84662	93	95	8474	0.7	3.0	21.4	60.3	14.7	245997
48117	CARLETON	27801	3659	14.8	25.0	39.3	14.0	6.9	61351	67842	86	86	3277	18.9	6.7	28.6	41.1	4.7	162765
48118	CHELSEA	32954	4419	13.2	20.5	36.3	19.7	10.3	70562	82584	91	93	3620	0.8	1.9	24.1	62.9	10.4	232532
48120	DEARBORN	22203	2887	34.7	22.7	25.0	10.4	7.2	40708	45203	49	37	1180	5.0	7.0	42.0	38.5	7.5	162632
48122	MELVINDALE	21210	4443	29.0	30.4	32.2	7.0	1.4	42171	47768	53	43	2980	8.5	36.8	53.5	1.0	0.2	93365
48124	DEARBORN	32077	14037	16.9	23.2	37.4	15.0	7.4	61122	67650	85	85	12152	1.2	4.6	61.3	29.2	3.7	152331
48125	DEARBORN HEIGHTS	23376	8696	17.8	31.1	38.8	10.2	2.1	50845	58444	74	68	7378	3.4	24.1	67.9	4.4	0.2	107441
48126	DEARBORN	15647	15979	38.0	29.1	24.0	6.1	2.8	33449	37022	22	11	9861	1.7	9.0	62.5	25.6	1.2	146958
48127	DEARBORN HEIGHTS	27084	14461	18.6	28.2	35.9	12.4	4.9	53097	59894	77	74	12144	3.7	5.0	56.5	32.9	1.8	155978
48128	DEARBORN	34368	4165	11.6	20.1	41.9	16.2	10.2	68788	77684	91	92	4005	0.5	1.5	46.2	50.0	1.8	177365
48130	DEXTER	37545	4317	7.4	18.9	38.0	21.7	14.0	79059	93043	95	96	3672	1.0	2.0	16.5	61.3	19.3	271797
48131	DUNDEE	23347	2632	21.1	24.9	38.2	12.8	3.1	53240	60228	77	74	1984	6.9	14.4	47.6	30.5	0.6	145593
48133	ERIE	24528	2076	18.5	23.5	40.8	13.3	3.9	58476	64675	83	82	1829	8.1	17.2	46.2	28.0	0.6	135335
48134	FLAT ROCK	26395	6876	16.1	24.5	38.5	15.4	5.5	60310	68281	85	84	5435	14.9	12.7	33.7	37.1	1.7	146539
48135	GARDEN CITY	24678	11495	17.4	24.8	42.8	12.1	3.0	56958	64437	82	80	9950	0.7	7.5	81.2	10.4	0.2	133331
48137	GREGORY	28594	1731	11.0	24.3	41.8	16.9	6.0	64731	74660	88	89	1581	2.5	5.9	28.8	58.6	4.2	204156
48138	GROSSE ILE	48312	4247	7.7	13.3	32.8	21.9	24.3	92780	107847	97	98	4000	0.1	1.1	15.1	57.4	26.4	281908
48140	IDA	24259	1169	10.8	23.4	44.7	16.5	4.6	64146	70797	88	88	1059	0.4	4.8	39.5	52.6	2.7	184054
48141	INKSTER	18971	11190	32.9	28.3	29.4	7.2	2.3	39421	44311	44	32	6557	17.8	43.6	36.7	1.5	0.4	80855
	MICHIGAN	25281		23.8	27.4	32.3	10.9	5.5	48729	54505				10.7	16.0	40.3	28.0	5.0	134769
	UNITED STATES	25866		24.7	27.1	30.8	10.9	6.5	48124	56710				10.9	15.0	33.7	30.1	10.4	145905

ZIP CODE		FINANCIAL SERVICES				THE HOME						ENTERTAINMENT						PERSONAL			
						Home Improvements		Furnishings													
#	POST OFFICE NAME	Auto Loan	Home Loan	Investments	Retirement Plans	Home Repair	Lawn & Garden	Computers & Hardware	Major Appliances	TV, Radio, Sound Equipment	Furniture	Dine out/ Carry out	Sports Equipment	Fees & Tickets	Toys & Games	Travel	Cable TV	Apparel & Services	Auto Repairs	Health Insurance	Pets & Supplies
48001	ALGONAC	108	99	82	96	104	112	94	102	98	94	119	119	92	120	96	99	114	100	108	126
48002	ALLENTON	115	103	79	98	109	116	95	105	101	95	123	125	93	125	98	103	117	103	114	136
48003	ALMONT	108	115	108	115	114	116	106	109	102	107	127	128	107	130	106	100	125	106	102	126
48005	ARMADA	111	135	143	136	133	131	122	121	113	122	142	142	129	150	124	109	142	117	108	134
48006	AVOCA	107	95	73	91	101	108	88	98	94	88	114	117	87	116	91	96	108	95	106	126
48009	BIRMINGHAM	177	211	287	215	206	219	203	196	194	205	246	229	217	255	208	192	245	196	182	214
48014	CAPAC	93	85	71	84	88	95	84	89	86	83	105	103	81	106	83	86	100	87	92	106
48015	CENTER LINE	59	60	73	59	60	67	64	62	66	62	83	71	66	86	65	68	80	63	65	68
48017	CLAWSON	85	96	115	98	95	98	96	93	92	94	116	109	99	119	96	90	114	93	86	101
48021	EASTPOINTE	75	83	89	80	83	89	81	80	81	79	101	91	84	106	83	82	99	79	82	88
48022	EMMETT	101	90	69	86	95	102	83	92	88	83	107	110	82	110	86	90	102	90	100	119
48023	FAIR HAVEN	96	94	80	91	94	98	88	93	87	89	108	108	86	107	88	86	105	91	91	110
48025	FRANKLIN	179	227	284	224	224	238	205	204	193	207	244	231	224	253	215	194	244	198	192	222
48026	FRASER	85	92	99	91	92	98	89	90	89	89	111	103	92	114	91	89	108	89	89	101
48027	GOODELLS	101	103	93	100	106	109	94	100	94	94	116	118	96	121	96	94	113	96	100	121
48028	HARSENS ISLAND	133	104	71	94	118	132	98	119	111	98	132	139	88	130	105	119	123	117	140	162
48030	HAZEL PARK	67	68	74	68	69	74	71	70	72	69	89	82	72	91	71	71	86	71	70	77
48032	JEDDO	96	97	86	95	100	104	89	94	89	89	110	112	90	114	91	90	107	91	95	115
48034	SOUTHFIELD	94	96	116	100	94	101	101	97	99	101	125	115	102	123	100	96	122	100	92	107
48035	CLINTON TOWNSHIP	84	90	98	91	89	92	89	88	86	89	109	103	91	110	89	84	107	88	82	97
48036	CLINTON TOWNSHIP	90	94	106	93	94	101	94	94	94	94	118	107	96	117	96	94	115	95	93	104
48038	CLINTON TOWNSHIP	96	105	116	106	104	109	102	101	98	102	124	116	105	124	102	97	122	101	96	112
48039	MARINE CITY	96	96	90	93	98	107	93	97	96	91	118	110	94	123	95	98	113	95	101	112
48040	MARYSVILLE	82	90	96	87	90	97	85	87	84	85	105	98	89	108	88	85	103	85	87	97
48041	MEMPHIS	107	107	95	104	110	114	98	104	99	98	121	123	99	126	100	99	117	101	105	127
48042	MACOMB	134	152	150	155	147	146	137	138	127	141	161	158	142	161	136	122	159	134	123	152
48043	MOUNT CLEMENS	65	67	77	68	67	72	71	69	71	69	88	80	72	91	71	70	86	70	68	75
48044	MACOMB	123	134	126	136	130	129	123	124	115	126	145	144	124	145	121	110	143	121	111	139
48045	HARRISON TOWNSHIP	100	105	115	108	103	106	105	102	100	105	127	121	106	126	103	97	125	104	94	114
48047	NEW BALTIMORE	108	122	129	125	119	119	115	113	109	116	137	134	119	140	114	104	136	112	102	125
48048	NEW HAVEN	100	95	79	93	96	101	91	96	92	92	113	111	88	111	91	91	109	95	96	113
48049	NORTH STREET	98	103	96	100	104	108	94	98	93	93	115	115	96	120	96	93	112	95	97	117
48050	NEW HAVEN	114	101	77	96	107	115	94	104	99	94	121	124	92	123	96	102	115	101	112	134
48051	NEW BALTIMORE	101	106	96	107	103	103	97	99	93	100	117	116	97	114	96	89	114	98	91	112
48054	EAST CHINA	106	105	98	103	108	115	98	105	99	99	123	122	99	123	101	100	118	102	107	125
48059	FORT GRATIOT	98	103	103	102	104	109	98	100	97	98	120	116	100	122	100	97	117	99	99	114
48060	PORT HURON	67	66	71	65	66	72	69	68	70	67	87	79	69	88	68	70	84	69	69	76
48062	RICHMOND	96	94	84	92	96	104	91	95	93	90	114	109	91	116	92	94	109	93	98	110
48063	COLUMBUS	104	111	103	109	110	112	102	105	99	103	123	122	103	124	102	97	120	103	99	121
48064	CASCO	96	108	107	107	107	108	99	100	94	99	117	117	101	121	100	91	116	98	93	113
48065	ROMEO	110	124	128	124	122	124	117	117	111	116	140	137	120	144	118	108	138	115	108	130
48066	ROSEVILLE	71	76	82	75	76	82	75	75	76	74	94	86	78	98	77	76	92	74	75	83
48067	ROYAL OAK	94	103	133	107	101	106	106	101	102	105	129	120	108	131	105	100	127	103	94	111
48069	PLEASANT RIDGE	139	164	193	168	162	167	155	152	147	155	185	178	164	189	158	143	184	151	140	167
48070	HUNTINGTON WOODS	160	208	254	205	204	213	184	183	172	187	217	208	203	228	193	172	219	177	169	199
48071	MADISON HEIGHTS	75	79	90	80	78	84	81	79	80	80	100	92	82	102	81	79	98	80	77	87
48072	BERKLEY	93	107	130	110	105	109	105	102	101	105	127	121	109	130	106	98	125	103	94	112
48073	ROYAL OAK	95	106	128	108	105	110	106	103	103	105	129	121	109	131	107	101	127	104	97	113
48074	SMITHS CREEK	96	85	65	81	90	97	79	87	84	79	102	104	77	104	81	86	97	85	95	113
48075	SOUTHFIELD	96	106	121	107	104	109	104	102	100	104	126	118	107	127	104	98	124	102	96	112
48076	SOUTHFIELD	105	126	153	126	123	128	119	117	114	119	144	136	126	151	122	113	143	116	108	127
48079	SAINT CLAIR	104	105	98	103	107	114	101	104	101	100	125	121	101	127	102	101	120	102	106	121
48080	SAINT CLAIR SHORES	76	85	99	83	84	92	83	82	83	83	104	93	87	107	86	84	102	82	83	90
48081	SAINT CLAIR SHORES	88	103	114	99	102	109	97	97	95	96	119	109	103	123	101	96	117	95	96	106
48082	SAINT CLAIR SHORES	78	89	96	85	89	95	84	85	83	83	104	95	88	108	87	85	102	83	86	93
48083	TROY	101	108	126	111	106	111	109	106	106	109	133	125	111	134	108	103	131	107	99	117
48084	TROY	134	146	211	156	141	151	150	141	147	152	186	167	159	193	151	145	185	144	131	156
48085	TROY	150	193	220	193	187	191	170	168	157	171	198	193	186	211	176	154	200	162	151	183
48088	WARREN	86	101	114	98	99	105	96	95	94	95	117	108	101	123	99	94	116	93	92	103
48089	WARREN	68	69	76	69	69	74	73	71	73	71	90	83	73	92	72	71	88	72	70	78
48091	WARREN	70	70	73	68	70	77	72	71	74	70	91	82	72	93	72	75	88	72	74	80
48092	WARREN	84	96	108	94	95	101	93	92	91	92	114	105	97	118	95	91	112	91	89	100
48093	WARREN	80	91	104	87	90	98	87	87	87	87	109	98	92	112	91	89	107	86	88	95
48094	WASHINGTON	133	138	129	136	138	143	127	132	124	129	155	153	129	155	128	123	151	129	128	154
48095	WASHINGTON	141	175	187	177	172	170	156	155	144	156	182	181	167	193	159	140	182	149	138	171
48096	RAY	107	133	141	133	130	129	118	118	110	118	138	138	126	147	121	107	138	114	106	130
48097	YALE	92	81	62	78	85	93	78	85	83	77	101	100	76	101	79	85	95	83	92	106
48098	TROY	209	261	288	268	253	256	231	225	210	234	268	260	253	279	235	204	270	217	201	249
48101	ALLEN PARK	86	99	112	96	98	106	95	94	94	94	118	107	100	122	98	95	116	93	94	103
48103	ANN ARBOR	115	127	151	131	125	129	125	122	120	126	151	144	129	153	125	117	149	123	112	135
48104	ANN ARBOR	91	85	117	89	82	91	107	91	103	100	130	115	102	128	98	97	126	100	84	101
48105	ANN ARBOR	117	119	158	125	115	124	132	120	128	128	161	146	132	161	127	123	158	126	111	133
48108	ANN ARBOR	110	111	138	119	108	113	119	112	114	118	145	135	119	144	115	109	143	116	102	124
48109	ANN ARBOR	45	28	35	31	27	33	54	39	52	45	65	55	44	59	43	46	61	48	37	45
48111	BELLEVILLE	96	90	88	91	90	95	91	92	91	92	114	109	89	110	89	89	110	93	90	107
48114	BRIGHTON	141	163	166	165	159	160	147	147	137	149	173	170	155	176	148	133	172	143	133	164
48116	BRIGHTON	128	146	156	151	142	143	136	134	127	138	161	157	142	164	136	122	160	132	120	148
48117	CARLETON	112	113	99	110	114	118	104	110	103	105	128	128	104	129	105	103	124	107	108	130
48118	CHELSEA	113	134	147	135	132	134	124	123	117	124	147	144	131	153	127	115	146	121	114	136
48120	DEARBORN	87	84	93	86	84	87	89	88	89	91	112	103	88	110	86	84	111	91	81	95
48122	MELVINDALE	68	67	68	63	67	76	69	69	73	67	90	79	70	92	70	75	86	69	74	78
48124	DEARBORN	94	110	126	107	109	116	105	104	103	104	128	118	110	133	108	103	127	103	102	113
48125	DEARBORN HEIGHTS	76	84	90	80	84	91	82	81	83	80	103	91	86	109	84	84	100	80	84	89
48126	DEARBORN	64	63	70	62	62	67	66	65	67	67	84	73	65	83	65	66	83	67	64	71
48127	DEARBORN HEIGHTS	85	96	107	93	96	103	93	92	92	92	115	104	97	119	95	93	113	91	93	101
48128	DEARBORN	107	126	141	123	125	132	118	118	115	117	144	134	125	150	122	116	142	116	115	129
48130	DEXTER	135	162	173	166	157	156	147	144	135	149	171	169	155	177	147	130	171	140	127	159
48131	DUNDEE	97	84	65	82	88	98	83	90	88	82	107	104	80	107	83	89	100	88	97	110
48133	ERIE	99	95	81	92	97	103	89	95	91	90	112	112	88	113	91	92	108	93	97	115
48134	FLAT ROCK	103	106	101	106	104	107	102	103	99	103	124	120	102	124	100	96	121	102	97	116
48135	GARDEN CITY	82	95	105	93	94	98	90	89	87	89	110	103	95	115	92	87	108	88	85	99
48137	GREGORY	109	121	118	120	122	123	110	113	106	109	132	133	114	138	112	105	130	109	108	131
48138	GROSSE ILE	166	199	217	199	196	204	179	180	169	181	213	204	192	215	185	167	211	175	170	199
48140	IDA	101	111	107	108	111	113	100	103	98	100	121	122	104	128	103	97	119	100	100	121
48141	INKSTER	69	64	75	63	63	71	70	68	73	70	91	77	70	88	69	74	89	70	70	77
	MICHIGAN	91	91	93	89	91	98	90	91	91	90	113	106	90	113	90	91	109	91	92	105
	UNITED STATES	100	100	100	100	100	100	100	100	100	100	100	100	100	100	100	100	100	100	100	100

ZIP CODE			POPULATION			2000-2004 ANNUAL RATE		HOUSEHOLDS					FAMILIES		
#	POST OFFICE NAME	COUNTY FIPS CODE	2000	2004	2009	% Rate	State Centile	2000	2004	2009	% Annual Rate 2000-2004	2004 Average HH Size	2000	2004	% Annual Rate 2000-2004
48144	LAMBERTVILLE	115	9024	9290	9682	0.7	51	3214	3386	3607	1.2	2.74	2593	2711	1.1
48145	LA SALLE	115	3863	3831	3942	-0.2	16	1363	1385	1458	0.4	2.77	1097	1106	0.2
48146	LINCOLN PARK	163	40008	39399	38927	-0.4	11	16204	16130	16077	-0.1	2.43	10575	10344	-0.5
48150	LIVONIA	163	27591	27826	27832	0.2	29	10829	11064	11173	0.5	2.48	7773	7830	0.2
48152	LIVONIA	163	31820	32604	32868	0.6	45	12341	12750	12949	0.8	2.53	8720	8924	0.6
48154	LIVONIA	163	41134	40861	40550	-0.2	18	14919	15019	15055	0.2	2.64	11588	11537	-0.1
48157	LUNA PIER	115	1506	1484	1524	-0.4	11	600	606	637	0.2	2.45	412	410	-0.1
48158	MANCHESTER	161	6983	7348	7780	1.2	72	2616	2818	3041	1.8	2.57	1946	2057	1.3
48159	MAYBEE	115	2592	2667	2769	0.7	50	854	899	954	1.2	2.97	683	712	1.0
48160	MILAN	115	12831	13231	13845	0.7	53	4218	4491	4806	1.5	2.62	3119	3272	1.1
48161	MONROE	115	25104	25993	27193	0.8	58	9678	10222	10906	1.3	2.50	6664	6942	1.0
48162	MONROE	115	29416	29977	31192	0.5	40	11314	11794	12538	1.0	2.47	7829	8049	0.7
48164	NEW BOSTON	163	7644	8006	8150	1.1	67	2608	2759	2832	1.3	2.88	2105	2211	1.2
48165	NEW HUDSON	125	5200	5557	5774	1.6	82	1828	1992	2103	2.0	2.78	1408	1513	1.7
48166	NEWPORT	115	10489	11621	12563	2.4	94	3684	4139	4549	2.8	2.81	2855	3173	2.5
48167	NORTHVILLE	163	36088	38217	39570	1.4	76	14161	15169	15856	1.6	2.41	9997	10603	1.4
48169	PINCKNEY	093	19212	21280	23998	2.4	94	6665	7526	8644	2.9	2.80	5346	5963	2.6
48170	PLYMOUTH	163	40561	41398	41781	0.5	42	16530	17049	17349	0.7	2.36	11082	11320	0.5
48173	ROCKWOOD	163	10240	10818	11119	1.3	74	3965	4245	4405	1.6	2.54	2858	3027	1.4
48174	ROMULUS	163	29823	30588	30906	0.6	46	10988	11403	11626	0.9	2.66	7886	8068	0.5
48176	SALINE	161	17789	19789	21587	2.5	95	6291	7117	7882	3.0	2.75	4856	5411	2.6
48178	SOUTH LYON	125	23710	25665	27488	1.9	88	8939	9865	10719	2.4	2.59	6535	7110	2.0
48179	SOUTH ROCKWOOD	115	2983	3250	3469	2.0	90	1068	1187	1291	2.5	2.74	822	903	2.2
48180	TAYLOR	163	65865	65258	64709	-0.2	15	24774	24813	24816	0.0	2.60	17749	17540	-0.3
48182	TEMPERANCE	115	20631	22128	23635	1.7	84	7475	8237	9012	2.3	2.67	5808	6301	1.9
48183	TRENTON	163	40718	41739	42106	0.6	45	15961	16563	16868	0.9	2.50	11401	11687	0.6
48184	WAYNE	163	19062	19358	19395	0.4	37	7373	7560	7636	0.6	2.51	4845	4908	0.3
48185	WESTLAND	163	48236	50129	50897	0.9	61	22137	23288	23847	1.2	2.13	12137	12413	0.5
48186	WESTLAND	163	38213	39268	39671	0.6	48	14341	14952	15262	1.0	2.61	10072	10382	0.7
48187	CANTON	163	44953	45705	45922	0.4	38	16337	16825	17065	0.7	2.71	12051	12255	0.4
48188	CANTON	163	31413	36501	39158	3.6	99	11153	12995	13977	3.7	2.81	8510	9815	3.4
48189	WHITMORE LAKE	161	14367	15304	16644	1.5	79	5341	5791	6403	1.9	2.57	3906	4152	1.5
48191	WILLIS	161	2775	3040	3287	2.2	92	1001	1123	1239	2.7	2.70	801	886	2.4
48192	WYANDOTTE	163	44683	44248	43873	-0.2	15	18341	18359	18360	0.0	2.38	11820	11633	-0.4
48195	SOUTHGATE	163	30136	29846	29594	-0.2	15	12836	12862	12867	0.1	2.31	8043	7907	-0.4
48197	YPSILANTI	161	54862	58773	63508	1.6	83	21314	23194	25512	2.0	2.31	11265	12164	1.8
48198	YPSILANTI	161	38995	39488	41687	0.3	34	15878	16498	17766	0.9	2.38	9759	9794	0.1
48201	DETROIT	163	15188	15252	15263	0.1	27	7583	7528	7517	-0.2	1.80	2321	2261	-0.6
48202	DETROIT	163	22280	22696	22853	0.4	40	9141	9305	9390	0.4	2.27	4190	4123	-0.4
48203	HIGHLAND PARK	163	45247	43709	42918	-0.8	4	16371	15874	15659	-0.7	2.69	10019	9512	-1.2
48204	DETROIT	163	42562	40552	39473	-1.1	2	15492	14849	14547	-1.0	2.70	10158	9576	-1.4
48205	DETROIT	163	65686	64797	64145	-0.3	12	19529	19081	18844	-0.5	3.38	14897	14380	-0.8
48206	DETROIT	163	33259	31581	30717	-1.2	2	12199	11558	11267	-1.3	2.65	7570	7044	-1.7
48207	DETROIT	163	24826	24702	24656	-0.1	19	11570	11603	11645	0.1	2.00	5012	4889	-0.6
48208	DETROIT	163	11200	10542	10216	-1.4	1	4475	4213	4097	-1.4	2.40	2242	2059	-2.0
48209	DETROIT	163	38880	38273	37791	-0.4	11	11833	11489	11304	-0.7	3.31	8184	7832	-1.0
48210	DETROIT	163	40175	39918	39640	-0.2	18	12919	12683	12564	-0.4	3.13	8743	8450	-0.8
48211	DETROIT	163	10627	9981	9682	-1.5	1	3273	3046	2949	-1.7	2.98	2089	1910	-2.1
48212	HAMTRAMCK	163	46058	45715	45371	-0.2	17	15222	14959	14810	-0.4	2.89	9687	9346	-0.8
48213	DETROIT	163	44741	42850	41847	-1.0	3	14020	13499	13266	-0.9	3.13	10019	9532	-1.2
48214	DETROIT	163	33608	31534	30527	-1.5	0	13307	12588	12249	-1.3	2.35	6785	6235	-2.0
48215	DETROIT	163	18994	17704	17091	-1.6	0	6721	6320	6149	-1.4	2.75	4246	3921	-1.9
48216	DETROIT	163	6709	6546	6439	-0.6	7	2456	2380	2341	-0.7	2.61	1357	1289	-1.2
48217	DETROIT	163	10515	10126	9907	-0.9	3	3973	3860	3808	-0.7	2.62	2642	2526	-1.1
48218	RIVER ROUGE	163	9917	9359	9074	-1.4	1	3640	3446	3356	-1.3	2.71	2503	2335	-1.6
48219	DETROIT	163	59964	58817	58036	-0.5	9	21815	21596	21477	-0.2	2.68	14700	14346	-0.6
48220	FERNDALE	125	24929	23884	23821	-1.0	3	10919	10720	10902	-0.4	2.21	5762	5499	-1.1
48221	DETROIT	163	45886	44100	43077	-0.9	3	16804	16322	16081	-0.7	2.66	11677	11185	-1.0
48223	DETROIT	163	35348	34186	33530	-0.8	5	12125	11795	11641	-0.7	2.88	8466	8108	-1.0
48224	DETROIT	163	55924	55473	54996	-0.2	16	18814	18586	18438	-0.3	2.96	13278	12922	-0.6
48225	HARPER WOODS	163	14223	13890	13662	-0.6	8	6276	6180	6123	-0.4	2.22	3747	3616	-0.8
48226	DETROIT	163	6116	6520	6705	1.5	80	2630	2919	3062	2.5	1.44	612	650	1.4
48227	DETROIT	163	61065	58185	56650	-1.1	2	20740	19997	19659	-0.9	2.89	14783	14060	-1.2
48228	DETROIT	163	65049	64444	63841	-0.2	15	23226	23019	22885	-0.2	2.79	15858	15486	-0.6
48229	ECORSE	163	11229	10644	10339	-1.3	1	4339	4151	4063	-1.0	2.55	2733	2568	-1.5
48230	GROSSE POINTE	163	18116	17888	17696	-0.3	13	7203	7190	7176	0.0	2.49	4864	4771	-0.5
48234	DETROIT	163	46450	45178	44368	-0.7	7	15764	15356	15142	-0.6	2.92	11177	10737	-0.9
48235	DETROIT	163	52704	51884	51265	-0.4	11	19496	19441	19403	-0.1	2.64	13492	13259	-0.4
48236	GROSSE POINTE	163	31611	30752	30216	-0.7	7	12245	12030	11921	-0.4	2.55	9186	8930	-0.7
48237	OAK PARK	125	32410	31625	31717	-0.6	7	12561	12478	12716	-0.2	2.53	8234	8030	-0.6
48238	DETROIT	163	45069	42867	41720	-1.2	2	16409	15683	15355	-1.1	2.70	10839	10186	-1.5
48239	REDFORD	163	37588	36499	35814	-0.7	6	14871	14595	14446	-0.4	2.50	10087	9748	-0.8
48240	REDFORD	163	18906	18342	17991	-0.7	6	7200	7065	6991	-0.4	2.55	4814	4650	-0.8
48301	BLOOMFIELD HILLS	125	14690	14406	14466	-0.5	9	5647	5645	5765	0.0	2.54	4429	4376	-0.3
48302	BLOOMFIELD HILLS	125	16402	16388	16652	0.0	22	6367	6508	6738	0.5	2.48	4725	4773	0.2
48304	BLOOMFIELD HILLS	125	16947	17152	17468	0.3	33	6725	6932	7179	0.7	2.42	5040	5127	0.4
48306	ROCHESTER	125	23168	24437	25355	1.3	73	7724	8305	8755	1.7	2.94	6582	7038	1.6
48307	ROCHESTER	125	37997	40052	41447	1.3	73	15736	16842	17688	1.6	2.35	9984	10531	1.3
48309	ROCHESTER	125	28495	28679	29114	0.2	28	10430	10711	11072	0.6	2.53	7681	7776	0.3
48310	STERLING HEIGHTS	099	41953	42689	44515	0.4	39	14653	15048	15849	0.6	2.82	11140	11284	0.3
48312	STERLING HEIGHTS	099	32153	33060	34632	0.7	49	13016	13494	14269	0.9	2.41	8742	8898	0.4
48313	STERLING HEIGHTS	099	33486	34188	35644	0.5	43	12332	12803	13531	0.9	2.65	9143	9275	0.3
48314	STERLING HEIGHTS	099	16834	19107	20979	3.0	98	6301	7156	7898	3.0	2.65	4360	4924	2.9
48315	UTICA	099	22661	25432	27747	2.8	96	8091	9160	10087	3.0	2.75	6290	7029	2.7
48316	UTICA	099	21197	23528	25729	2.5	95	7764	8759	9709	2.9	2.68	6085	6757	2.5
48317	UTICA	099	25867	25604	26433	-0.2	14	10572	10555	11003	0.0	2.41	6741	6592	-0.5
48320	KEEGO HARBOR	125	4337	4196	4186	-0.8	5	1963	1942	1974	-0.3	2.16	1082	1043	-0.9
48322	WEST BLOOMFIELD	125	30143	32171	33624	1.5	81	11221	12168	12909	1.9	2.60	8307	8834	1.5
48323	WEST BLOOMFIELD	125	18122	18327	18605	0.3	33	6306	6515	6733	0.8	2.79	5203	5328	0.6
48324	WEST BLOOMFIELD	125	17764	18551	19096	1.0	66	6244	6602	6887	1.3	2.79	5021	5264	1.1
48326	AUBURN HILLS	125	18976	19663	20166	0.8	59	8187	8693	9090	1.4	2.21	4706	4865	0.8
48327	WATERFORD	125	21076	21882	22558	0.9	61	8771	9321	9789	1.4	2.33	5504	5728	0.9
48328	WATERFORD	125	25942	26349	26941	0.4	37	10635	10999	11442	0.8	2.26	6273	6357	0.3
48329	WATERFORD	125	26070	26510	27141	0.4	38	9959	10367	10818	1.0	2.54	7341	7526	0.6
48331	FARMINGTON	125	21873	22154	22521	0.3	34	7878	8168	8453	0.9	2.70	6206	6340	0.5
	MICHIGAN					0.6					1.0	2.52			0.6
	UNITED STATES					1.2					1.3	2.58			1.1

ZIP CODE #	POST OFFICE NAME	RACE (%) White 2000	White 2004	Black 2000	Black 2004	Asian/Pacific 2000	Asian/Pacific 2004	% Hispanic Origin 2000	% Hispanic Origin 2004	2004 AGE DISTRIBUTION (%) 0-4	5-9	10-14	15-19	20-24	25-44	45-64	65-84	85+	18+	MEDIAN AGE 2004	% 2004 Males	% 2004 Females
48144	LAMBERTVILLE	97.9	97.6	0.3	0.3	0.6	0.7	1.6	1.8	5.9	6.8	8.0	7.3	5.4	26.6	29.2	9.8	1.0	74.7	39.7	49.6	50.4
48145	LA SALLE	97.9	97.7	0.4	0.4	0.3	0.4	2.4	2.7	4.9	5.9	7.4	7.2	5.6	28.0	29.7	10.7	0.8	77.2	39.9	51.4	48.6
48146	LINCOLN PARK	93.3	91.6	2.1	2.7	0.5	0.7	6.4	7.8	6.9	6.8	7.0	5.9	6.1	31.4	22.9	11.6	1.5	75.8	36.4	49.1	51.0
48150	LIVONIA	96.2	95.0	0.8	1.1	1.3	1.7	1.9	2.3	6.5	6.7	6.8	5.8	4.8	29.5	24.2	13.8	2.1	76.4	39.5	48.6	51.4
48152	LIVONIA	93.7	91.8	1.4	2.1	3.0	4.0	1.8	2.1	5.3	5.9	7.1	6.7	5.2	26.0	28.3	13.7	1.9	77.4	41.5	48.7	51.3
48154	LIVONIA	96.4	95.2	0.7	1.1	1.6	2.1	1.6	1.9	5.2	5.7	7.2	6.6	5.4	23.0	28.0	16.1	2.9	77.8	43.1	48.1	51.9
48157	LUNA PIER	95.5	95.2	0.2	0.2	0.0	0.0	3.0	3.4	7.6	7.9	8.3	6.7	5.3	28.8	26.5	8.1	0.9	71.8	36.6	49.2	50.8
48158	MANCHESTER	97.3	97.0	0.3	0.3	0.2	0.3	2.5	2.9	6.0	6.5	7.6	6.7	5.3	26.0	30.9	9.6	1.4	75.6	40.3	49.9	50.1
48159	MAYBEE	90.9	90.1	7.1	7.8	0.3	0.3	1.2	1.4	6.3	7.0	8.6	7.6	6.0	29.6	25.9	8.2	0.9	73.4	35.9	51.9	48.1
48160	MILAN	87.1	86.8	9.5	9.4	0.6	0.8	3.7	4.1	5.7	6.1	6.9	6.2	6.1	34.1	25.5	8.3	1.0	77.4	36.7	55.2	44.8
48161	MONROE	92.0	91.5	4.2	4.4	0.6	0.7	2.7	3.1	7.6	7.2	7.3	7.0	6.8	28.7	23.2	10.8	1.6	73.7	35.4	49.1	50.9
48162	MONROE	95.0	94.4	2.1	2.3	0.9	1.1	1.9	2.2	6.4	6.4	7.1	6.8	6.5	27.7	24.7	11.9	2.5	75.9	37.7	48.1	51.9
48164	NEW BOSTON	93.5	92.5	4.0	4.5	0.4	0.5	2.3	2.8	6.7	7.2	7.9	6.7	5.1	29.0	28.5	8.0	0.9	73.9	37.9	50.7	49.3
48165	NEW HUDSON	97.6	97.2	0.3	0.4	0.3	0.4	1.8	2.1	7.4	8.0	7.9	6.6	5.6	32.0	25.7	6.1	0.7	72.5	35.8	51.0	49.0
48166	NEWPORT	96.2	95.9	0.9	1.0	0.2	0.3	2.6	2.9	8.6	8.1	8.0	7.0	6.6	31.6	23.5	6.2	0.5	71.1	32.7	50.8	49.2
48167	NORTHVILLE	91.3	89.3	3.0	3.7	3.8	4.9	1.6	1.9	5.4	6.3	7.0	6.1	4.9	26.4	30.9	11.6	1.4	77.3	41.6	47.7	52.3
48169	PINCKNEY	97.3	97.0	0.8	0.9	0.4	0.6	1.0	1.1	6.9	7.5	8.1	6.8	5.2	30.6	27.3	7.1	0.6	73.1	37.3	50.8	49.2
48170	PLYMOUTH	93.6	92.0	2.2	2.8	2.3	3.1	1.5	1.9	5.7	6.2	6.3	5.5	4.7	28.8	28.9	11.9	2.0	78.4	41.0	49.2	50.8
48173	ROCKWOOD	96.3	95.4	0.6	0.8	0.5	0.6	2.3	2.8	6.2	6.3	6.7	6.1	6.3	29.2	29.0	9.6	0.6	77.0	38.5	50.7	49.3
48174	ROMULUS	71.1	66.3	24.0	28.4	1.0	1.2	2.2	2.5	7.6	7.6	8.4	7.1	6.5	30.2	24.4	7.6	0.8	71.9	34.0	48.7	51.3
48176	SALINE	95.4	94.4	0.9	1.0	2.1	2.8	1.4	1.7	6.7	7.9	8.9	7.4	5.2	26.2	28.2	7.9	1.7	71.8	38.2	48.4	51.6
48178	SOUTH LYON	97.0	96.4	0.4	0.5	0.9	1.2	1.4	1.6	7.9	7.9	7.4	5.7	4.9	29.5	24.7	10.6	1.4	73.2	37.9	49.2	50.9
48179	SOUTH ROCKWOOD	97.2	96.9	0.3	0.4	0.1	0.1	1.1	1.3	5.8	7.0	7.3	7.1	6.5	27.9	28.9	8.9	0.6	75.2	38.2	52.1	47.9
48180	TAYLOR	86.1	82.6	8.8	11.5	1.7	2.1	3.2	3.8	7.6	7.2	7.5	6.6	6.9	29.7	23.0	10.4	1.1	73.7	34.7	48.2	51.8
48182	TEMPERANCE	97.5	97.0	0.4	0.5	0.4	0.7	2.1	2.4	6.3	6.8	7.9	7.5	5.7	26.7	27.4	10.6	1.2	74.2	38.7	48.9	51.1
48183	TRENTON	94.5	92.9	1.5	2.2	1.5	2.1	2.8	3.4	6.2	6.4	7.0	6.3	5.9	27.5	27.6	11.7	1.4	76.4	38.9	48.3	51.7
48184	WAYNE	84.5	80.7	11.2	14.4	1.5	1.7	1.9	2.3	7.3	7.0	7.3	6.5	6.6	30.0	23.3	10.5	1.4	74.4	35.6	48.1	51.9
48185	WESTLAND	86.6	82.7	6.2	8.7	4.0	5.0	2.5	3.0	6.1	5.8	5.8	5.3	6.4	32.5	22.1	13.6	2.6	79.3	37.6	47.2	52.8
48186	WESTLAND	87.9	84.9	7.6	9.7	1.4	1.9	2.4	2.8	7.8	7.6	7.4	6.1	6.0	32.0	22.8	9.1	1.1	73.5	34.8	49.2	50.8
48187	CANTON	84.9	80.6	4.0	5.6	8.5	10.8	2.2	2.7	7.6	7.7	7.8	6.5	6.5	30.7	25.7	6.6	0.8	72.8	35.1	49.3	50.7
48188	CANTON	82.5	77.6	5.4	7.5	9.1	11.5	2.5	2.9	10.2	9.6	7.7	5.4	5.7	35.5	21.2	4.4	0.4	69.1	32.8	49.3	50.7
48189	WHITMORE LAKE	95.8	95.4	1.7	1.7	0.6	0.8	1.3	1.5	7.4	7.6	7.5	7.6	5.1	31.7	25.5	6.9	0.7	72.8	36.1	51.3	48.7
48191	WILLIS	91.5	90.8	6.3	6.8	0.3	0.3	0.8	0.9	5.6	6.2	7.7	6.7	5.6	28.1	29.8	9.3	1.1	76.4	39.9	50.3	49.7
48192	WYANDOTTE	94.6	92.9	1.6	2.3	1.3	1.8	2.8	3.4	5.7	5.7	6.4	6.3	6.4	28.2	25.5	13.4	2.4	78.3	39.4	48.3	51.7
48195	SOUTHGATE	93.7	91.9	2.1	3.0	1.7	2.2	4.0	4.8	5.4	5.5	6.2	5.9	6.2	29.0	25.5	14.4	1.9	79.4	39.7	48.1	52.0
48197	YPSILANTI	65.1	62.6	25.1	26.1	4.5	5.7	3.0	3.3	7.1	6.3	5.6	10.2	12.7	34.6	18.0	4.8	0.6	77.8	28.9	50.0	50.0
48198	YPSILANTI	65.1	62.9	29.0	30.4	1.4	1.8	2.4	2.7	8.0	7.4	7.5	6.5	7.9	31.1	22.8	7.9	1.0	73.4	32.8	48.4	51.6
48201	DETROIT	16.1	12.1	75.3	79.3	5.4	5.8	1.9	1.8	6.0	6.0	6.3	5.4	7.5	32.0	23.1	11.6	2.2	78.8	36.1	50.5	49.5
48202	DETROIT	9.2	7.1	84.8	87.1	3.1	3.3	1.1	1.1	6.6	6.3	7.3	6.8	7.8	29.8	23.4	10.1	2.0	76.3	35.2	49.6	50.4
48203	HIGHLAND PARK	9.3	6.9	86.6	89.4	0.3	0.3	0.8	0.8	8.2	8.8	9.5	7.4	6.6	27.0	21.3	9.9	1.3	68.9	32.2	46.9	53.1
48204	DETROIT	1.3	0.9	97.0	97.6	0.1	0.1	0.7	0.7	7.9	8.4	9.4	7.5	6.2	26.2	20.8	11.9	1.8	69.7	33.1	45.5	54.5
48205	DETROIT	10.0	7.3	84.1	87.2	3.6	3.5	0.8	0.8	9.5	10.3	12.6	9.6	7.5	28.3	17.3	4.2	0.7	61.6	25.4	46.8	53.2
48206	DETROIT	1.6	1.1	96.4	97.1	0.3	0.3	0.5	0.5	8.1	8.2	9.2	7.4	6.2	25.8	21.3	11.6	2.4	70.0	33.8	45.5	54.5
48207	DETROIT	7.4	5.4	90.1	92.3	0.5	0.5	0.9	0.9	5.4	5.7	6.7	6.3	6.3	27.3	26.5	13.9	2.0	78.1	39.6	45.7	54.3
48208	DETROIT	9.2	7.0	87.1	89.7	0.2	0.2	2.5	2.3	6.5	6.8	8.3	6.7	5.9	28.4	24.3	11.2	1.9	74.1	36.6	48.5	51.5
48209	DETROIT	52.1	47.9	8.9	10.5	0.6	0.6	58.6	61.9	10.3	9.1	9.0	7.9	9.3	31.5	16.3	6.1	0.7	67.0	27.5	53.0	47.0
48210	DETROIT	37.0	33.7	38.7	40.4	1.1	1.2	29.9	31.8	10.2	9.4	9.4	7.5	8.2	29.8	16.8	7.4	1.3	66.4	28.1	51.0	49.0
48211	DETROIT	15.6	12.4	74.7	77.4	2.0	2.3	1.0	1.0	8.6	8.4	8.9	7.7	7.9	28.5	19.9	8.7	1.4	69.6	31.2	52.5	47.6
48212	HAMTRAMCK	38.3	34.0	43.1	45.3	8.9	10.4	1.3	1.4	8.4	7.9	8.8	7.4	7.3	30.5	19.5	8.4	1.7	70.3	31.6	52.1	47.9
48213	DETROIT	2.1	1.4	96.1	97.0	0.1	0.1	0.6	0.6	8.9	9.6	11.1	8.6	7.2	26.1	19.8	7.8	0.9	65.0	28.5	46.1	53.9
48214	DETROIT	7.5	5.6	90.5	92.6	0.3	0.3	0.7	0.8	6.5	6.6	7.6	6.3	5.7	25.2	23.3	15.6	3.2	75.6	39.2	46.1	53.9
48215	DETROIT	7.0	5.1	90.4	92.5	0.4	0.4	0.9	0.9	8.3	8.5	10.1	8.1	6.8	26.0	23.0	8.4	0.9	68.1	31.3	46.3	53.7
48216	DETROIT	35.3	31.0	38.9	42.4	0.4	0.5	38.3	39.4	7.5	7.2	7.7	7.3	7.5	32.8	21.3	7.7	1.0	73.4	32.9	51.7	48.4
48217	DETROIT	10.3	9.2	85.1	86.0	0.5	0.5	5.6	5.9	6.2	6.5	7.9	7.2	6.0	25.4	22.9	16.1	2.0	75.1	38.6	46.8	53.2
48218	RIVER ROUGE	52.6	47.7	42.0	46.4	0.2	0.3	5.0	5.6	8.4	8.1	9.1	7.8	7.4	27.8	21.2	8.9	1.3	69.7	31.7	47.3	52.7
48219	DETROIT	12.0	9.1	84.8	88.0	0.6	0.6	1.0	0.9	7.2	7.9	9.2	7.6	6.7	28.6	24.6	7.2	1.1	71.0	33.1	46.1	53.9
48220	FERNDALE	81.3	80.1	13.9	14.4	1.2	1.6	1.7	2.0	5.9	5.7	6.0	6.1	7.3	36.4	22.2	8.9	1.6	78.8	34.9	49.2	50.9
48221	DETROIT	3.3	2.4	94.3	95.5	0.3	0.3	0.7	0.7	6.1	6.7	7.9	7.2	6.0	25.8	24.5	14.3	1.5	75.0	37.9	45.1	54.9
48223	DETROIT	12.9	9.4	83.2	87.1	1.1	1.1	1.2	1.1	8.9	9.4	10.3	8.2	6.9	29.2	21.8	5.0	0.5	66.5	29.7	46.4	53.6
48224	DETROIT	17.6	13.5	79.2	83.6	0.7	0.7	1.1	1.0	8.3	8.9	10.3	8.6	6.9	30.4	20.2	5.2	1.3	67.0	30.2	46.4	53.6
48225	HARPER WOODS	85.9	81.9	10.3	13.6	1.7	2.2	1.6	1.9	6.3	6.2	6.3	5.5	4.9	30.2	22.4	14.5	3.6	77.7	39.1	46.8	53.3
48226	DETROIT	22.4	16.6	73.2	79.2	1.4	1.4	2.6	2.5	1.8	1.6	2.0	5.5	10.8	38.7	28.7	9.6	1.3	92.9	39.4	64.0	36.0
48227	DETROIT	2.1	1.4	96.1	97.0	0.1	0.1	0.6	0.6	7.9	8.6	10.0	8.1	6.9	27.7	22.9	7.2	0.7	68.4	31.1	46.0	54.0
48228	DETROIT	23.5	19.6	69.7	73.5	0.6	0.7	3.4	3.5	8.7	9.0	9.9	7.9	6.5	30.1	19.9	7.0	1.0	67.4	30.6	47.0	53.0
48229	ECORSE	52.2	48.4	40.6	43.6	0.2	0.2	8.9	10.0	7.9	7.4	7.8	7.0	7.1	28.2	22.6	10.8	1.2	72.6	34.1	48.6	51.4
48230	GROSSE POINTE	93.9	92.0	2.3	3.3	1.6	2.1	1.7	2.0	6.1	6.9	7.9	7.3	5.5	24.5	29.3	10.8	1.7	74.6	40.2	48.0	52.0
48234	DETROIT	6.1	4.3	91.4	93.5	0.6	0.5	0.6	0.6	8.1	8.8	10.4	8.2	6.7	27.3	21.2	8.2	1.2	67.6	31.0	45.9	54.1
48235	DETROIT	1.7	1.1	96.3	97.1	0.2	0.2	0.6	0.6	6.3	7.1	8.5	7.2	5.8	26.7	25.4	11.7	1.3	73.6	36.6	44.3	55.7
48236	GROSSE POINTE	94.7	93.1	2.4	3.1	2.0	2.6	1.1	1.3	5.8	6.7	7.6	6.8	4.5	21.3	29.3	15.5	2.6	75.6	43.4	48.1	51.9
48237	OAK PARK	46.9	44.3	45.9	47.8	2.2	2.7	1.3	1.4	6.7	7.0	8.2	7.2	6.2	28.7	23.7	10.6	1.8	73.6	35.7	46.7	53.3
48238	DETROIT	1.2	0.9	97.1	97.6	0.1	0.1	0.7	0.7	8.0	8.5	9.4	7.7	6.7	27.0	20.3	11.0	1.4	69.5	32.3	45.8	54.2
48239	REDFORD	81.5	77.5	14.7	18.1	1.2	1.5	2.4	2.8	6.8	7.0	7.2	6.1	5.3	31.1	22.9	11.6	2.0	75.3	37.4	49.0	51.1
48240	REDFORD	93.4	91.4	2.9	4.2	0.7	0.9	1.9	2.3	7.1	7.0	7.2	6.4	6.0	31.6	21.3	10.6	2.9	74.8	36.0	49.1	50.9
48301	BLOOMFIELD HILLS	92.6	91.1	2.1	2.4	4.1	5.2	1.3	1.5	5.4	7.0	8.0	6.7	3.6	18.8	32.2	16.6	1.8	75.1	45.3	49.2	50.8
48302	BLOOMFIELD HILLS	83.8	80.8	6.0	6.5	8.4	10.8	1.3	1.5	4.0	5.0	6.2	6.4	4.5	19.0	34.3	18.5	2.2	80.7	48.0	48.1	51.9
48304	BLOOMFIELD HILLS	87.1	84.4	3.9	4.4	7.5	9.6	1.5	1.7	4.3	5.4	6.8	6.6	4.3	16.6	35.1	18.6	2.4	79.1	48.6	47.6	52.5
48306	ROCHESTER	92.4	90.7	1.9	2.2	4.6	5.8	1.3	1.6	6.5	8.3	9.5	7.9	4.5	23.6	32.0	7.1	0.7	70.3	39.8	49.2	50.8
48307	ROCHESTER	88.0	85.8	2.5	2.8	6.9	8.6	2.4	2.7	7.2	7.3	6.8	6.0	6.0	32.6	24.3	8.2	1.6	75.2	36.2	48.6	51.4
48309	ROCHESTER	88.4	86.0	3.9	4.4	6.0	7.8	2.4	2.7	5.6	6.4	6.8	8.1	6.4	23.9	29.3	11.4	2.3	77.3	40.8	48.1	51.9
48310	STERLING HEIGHTS	86.5	83.9	1.2	1.4	7.7	9.7	1.2	1.4	6.3	6.4	6.7	6.2	6.3	30.4	26.7	9.8	1.3	76.9	37.0	49.6	50.4
48312	STERLING HEIGHTS	92.4	90.9	1.7	1.8	4.1	5.3	1.2	1.4	5.6	5.7	5.9	5.8	5.4	27.4	26.8	14.6	2.8	79.3	41.1	48.2	51.8
48313	STERLING HEIGHTS	94.9	94.0	1.0	1.1	2.2	2.8	1.6	1.8	6.5	6.7	7.0	6.7	6.4	30.3	26.4	8.6	1.6	75.7	36.7	49.1	50.9
48314	STERLING HEIGHTS	89.7	87.3	1.3	1.4	5.5	7.5	1.4	1.5	6.9	7.0	7.7	6.1	5.8	31.3	24.0	9.3	2.1	74.6	36.5	48.8	51.2
48315	UTICA	95.9	94.9	0.7	0.8	1.9	2.6	1.4	1.6	5.8	6.6	7.9	6.7	5.0	24.5	29.0	12.7	1.9	75.4	41.1	48.0	52.0
48316	UTICA	96.5	95.8	0.5	0.6	1.3	1.7	1.2	1.4	6.2	6.5	7.2	6.4	5.8	28.6	28.3	10.3	0.7	76.2	38.8	49.7	50.3
48317	UTICA	92.7	91.4	1.2	1.3	3.1	4.0	2.5	2.8	6.7	6.3	6.6	6.3	7.5	35.6	22.7	7.4	1.0	76.7	34.0	51.0	49.0
48320	KEEGO HARBOR	94.6	93.9	0.8	0.9	1.0	1.3	3.2	3.6	5.7	5.8	6.8	6.0	5.3	35.2	24.7	9.3	1.0	78.0	37.5	51.0	49.0
48322	WEST BLOOMFIELD	80.1	76.3	6.5	7.3	9.9	12.6	1.4	1.6	5.9	6.6	7.3	6.1	4.4	23.7	28.2	14.9	2.7	76.2	42.5	48.3	51.7
48323	WEST BLOOMFIELD	86.7	84.2	4.2	4.8	6.8	8.6	1.3	1.4	5.7	6.9	7.7	6.6	4.5	23.2	32.2	12.1	1.1	75.3	42.3	49.5	50.5
48324	WEST BLOOMFIELD	90.3	88.3	3.7	4.3	4.2	5.4	1.5	1.7	7.8	9.0	8.3	6.1	3.8	27.9	28.5	7.7	0.9	70.9	38.5	50.4	49.6
48326	AUBURN HILLS	77.2	74.4	11.8	12.7	6.5	8.0	4.6	5.2	7.4	6.4	5.5	5.5	8.3	37.9	20.9	7.1	1.1	77.6	33.1	50.5	49.5
48327	WATERFORD	93.2	92.0	2.1	2.4	1.6	2.1	3.8	4.5	8.0	7.5	6.2	5.3	6.4	35.2	22.7	7.8	0.9	75.3	35.0	49.7	50.3
48328	WATERFORD	89.7	88.3	5.2	5.7	1.2	1.5	5.1	5.9	6.8	6.3	5.8	5.5	6.9	35.1	22.6	9.3	1.8	78.1	35.8	50.8	49.2
48329	WATERFORD	95.2	94.4	1.3	1.4	1.1	1.4	2.8	3.2	6.7	6.8	6.7	5.7	5.0	30.9	26.4	10.3	1.5	76.2	38.3	49.3	50.7
48331	FARMINGTON	84.3	81.3	5.1	5.7	8.4	10.7	1.3	1.5	5.9	6.6	7.6	7.1	5.5	24.5	30.9	11.0	1.1	75.3	40.8	48.9	51.1
	MICHIGAN	80.2	79.2	14.2	14.4	1.8	2.3	3.3	3.6	6.8	6.9	7.4	7.1	6.9	28.1	24.6	10.8	1.6	74.9	36.5	49.1	50.9
	UNITED STATES	75.1	73.6	12.3	12.5	3.8	4.2	12.5	14.1	6.9	6.7	7.2	7.0	7.3	28.6	23.8	10.8	1.7	75.1	36.0	49.1	50.9

#	ZIP CODE POST OFFICE NAME	2004 Per Capita Income	2004 HH Income Base	2004 Household Income Distribution (%) Less than $25,000	$25,000 to $49,999	$50,000 to $99,999	$100,000 to $149,999	$150,000 or More	Median Household Income 2004	2009	2004 National Centile	2004 State Centile	2004 Home Value Base	2004 Home Value Distribution (%) Less than $50,000	$50,000 to $89,999	$90,000 to $174,999	$175,000 to $399,999	$400,000 or More	2004 Median Home Value
48144	LAMBERTVILLE	28841	3386	14.4	21.6	41.1	15.2	7.6	65399	73196	89	89	3106	2.8	3.9	44.7	44.9	3.7	172932
48145	LA SALLE	27381	1385	14.8	20.4	42.8	15.7	6.3	67095	75494	90	90	1267	1.4	7.0	43.7	43.2	4.8	171920
48146	LINCOLN PARK	22869	16130	22.5	30.5	36.4	8.6	2.0	47059	54004	66	59	12602	4.5	28.7	64.7	2.1	0.1	101618
48150	LIVONIA	29965	11064	13.9	22.8	41.7	16.2	5.4	63600	72161	88	88	9932	0.3	2.6	55.1	41.6	0.4	168619
48152	LIVONIA	33259	12750	15.0	20.8	34.8	18.2	11.2	67552	76544	90	91	10697	0.4	2.9	34.6	54.6	7.5	204513
48154	LIVONIA	31612	15019	11.1	19.7	39.7	20.4	9.1	73921	82093	93	94	13981	0.6	2.1	25.3	70.9	1.1	206943
48157	LUNA PIER	22533	606	29.2	23.6	37.0	8.1	2.2	45696	51943	63	55	453	4.9	21.4	47.5	23.0	3.3	124564
48158	MANCHESTER	31020	2818	13.3	21.7	39.0	18.2	7.7	65545	77225	89	89	2351	2.3	5.0	27.5	55.4	9.9	217210
48159	MAYBEE	24519	899	11.5	25.1	42.1	16.2	5.1	63761	70875	88	88	809	1.5	7.1	46.9	42.4	2.2	164543
48160	MILAN	26580	4491	15.7	22.3	38.5	17.8	5.7	63207	73027	87	87	3592	4.0	6.6	40.0	45.1	4.4	174184
48161	MONROE	24212	10222	27.8	24.9	31.9	11.2	4.3	47359	53351	67	60	7567	17.9	13.5	41.5	23.4	3.6	127352
48162	MONROE	25190	11794	22.2	25.5	36.4	11.4	4.5	52043	58550	76	71	8407	3.0	6.2	54.4	34.2	2.2	156080
48164	NEW BOSTON	27605	2759	13.6	21.6	37.8	18.7	8.4	67973	76538	90	91	2530	5.6	10.0	32.4	45.9	6.1	181071
48165	NEW HUDSON	30067	1992	11.4	18.4	40.6	20.1	9.4	75041	84994	93	95	1812	17.7	7.1	12.9	58.3	4.1	210291
48166	NEWPORT	24699	4139	13.0	29.4	38.3	14.5	4.8	56666	63639	81	79	3652	26.2	20.4	23.9	27.4	2.1	99922
48167	NORTHVILLE	46499	15169	9.7	17.0	29.8	20.7	22.8	86493	100750	97	98	12266	1.5	4.1	16.0	49.8	28.7	313549
48169	PINCKNEY	31427	7526	8.6	18.3	43.6	20.9	8.6	74606	84437	93	94	6803	0.6	2.0	20.8	64.7	11.8	239883
48170	PLYMOUTH	41559	17049	12.4	20.9	31.3	19.1	16.3	75222	84118	93	95	13544	4.1	4.3	18.9	54.9	17.9	234936
48173	ROCKWOOD	28894	4245	15.5	24.1	38.7	15.6	6.1	61687	68663	86	86	3394	1.9	10.0	54.5	30.8	2.8	148824
48174	ROMULUS	22726	11403	23.8	25.2	35.0	12.2	3.8	50969	57764	74	68	8725	17.1	16.7	48.2	16.9	1.2	112153
48176	SALINE	35053	7117	10.0	15.7	35.9	25.0	13.4	82022	96641	96	97	5987	1.4	2.8	14.7	64.1	17.1	257764
48178	SOUTH LYON	33062	9865	11.8	21.6	35.6	19.6	11.4	71357	82749	92	93	8551	6.3	7.0	21.7	52.3	12.7	221437
48179	SOUTH ROCKWOOD	25089	1187	17.9	26.4	36.2	14.2	5.4	58870	63743	83	82	1039	11.2	8.5	39.4	39.1	1.9	157019
48180	TAYLOR	22299	24813	23.8	29.4	33.4	10.5	2.8	46687	52762	65	58	17540	7.3	20.8	62.7	8.9	0.3	110731
48182	TEMPERANCE	26605	8237	16.3	21.8	40.4	16.7	4.8	63196	69344	87	87	7261	6.7	7.9	41.4	40.8	3.3	165736
48183	TRENTON	28881	16563	17.1	24.2	35.9	16.6	6.2	60177	67300	85	84	13053	5.1	6.5	45.9	41.6	1.0	166312
48184	WAYNE	24228	7560	22.9	26.4	35.6	11.4	3.6	50746	57772	73	68	5111	3.6	16.7	68.4	11.2	0.1	115585
48185	WESTLAND	26934	23288	22.9	29.9	34.2	10.6	2.4	47063	52347	66	59	13057	4.6	8.2	62.0	25.1	0.1	148693
48186	WESTLAND	24164	14952	18.0	26.0	40.0	13.3	2.7	55352	63510	80	77	11573	7.6	11.7	67.3	13.2	0.2	128169
48187	CANTON	32672	16825	11.6	17.0	36.8	23.4	11.1	78104	88655	94	96	12699	3.4	1.3	15.0	72.3	8.0	225812
48188	CANTON	33531	12995	10.3	18.2	34.2	24.5	12.9	80703	93551	95	96	11194	18.3	2.9	14.2	55.0	9.7	216312
48189	WHITMORE LAKE	31081	5791	10.4	21.7	40.6	19.4	7.8	68093	78557	90	91	4940	13.1	10.7	16.6	51.6	8.0	204499
48191	WILLIS	32340	1123	16.1	17.6	35.9	21.6	8.8	72722	82269	92	93	1028	1.8	4.7	32.2	55.3	6.1	199788
48192	WYANDOTTE	25684	18359	22.4	28.4	34.6	10.5	4.1	49088	55229	70	64	13289	4.7	10.1	58.8	25.4	1.0	132707
48195	SOUTHGATE	26056	12862	20.4	29.3	36.4	11.0	2.9	50346	56054	73	67	9464	1.4	9.1	72.6	16.6	0.3	129846
48197	YPSILANTI	26679	23194	25.2	24.9	31.6	13.1	5.2	49843	59061	72	65	11785	8.7	6.4	26.5	56.0	2.5	193317
48198	YPSILANTI	24577	16498	22.1	32.6	32.8	9.2	3.3	45640	53041	63	55	9923	10.3	19.9	58.5	9.0	2.4	112240
48201	DETROIT	13441	7528	68.0	20.8	8.6	1.6	1.1	14322	16721	1	0	286	9.1	23.4	26.9	34.6	5.9	132609
48202	DETROIT	15640	9305	52.6	25.6	15.9	3.9	2.0	23065	26468	3	1	2638	34.5	25.7	25.1	11.5	3.3	69531
48203	HIGHLAND PARK	14614	15874	51.7	23.8	17.1	4.8	2.6	23759	27222	4	1	6853	40.7	34.6	14.5	5.5	4.7	58412
48204	DETROIT	14597	14849	45.1	30.1	19.2	3.9	1.7	28408	33127	9	3	7992	43.7	35.8	19.2	1.2	0.1	56537
48205	DETROIT	13548	19081	37.2	29.3	25.9	5.9	1.7	35380	40182	29	15	12192	21.5	47.6	29.9	0.9	0.2	74896
48206	DETROIT	15497	11558	46.7	28.6	18.3	4.4	2.0	26890	31638	7	2	5100	41.9	29.0	22.4	6.0	0.7	59176
48207	DETROIT	21383	11603	46.9	24.0	21.1	5.8	2.3	27297	31177	8	3	3233	44.9	18.7	23.5	11.5	1.3	58651
48208	DETROIT	12928	4213	58.2	23.9	13.7	3.1	1.2	19851	22726	2	1	1600	54.0	25.3	16.2	4.0	0.6	44622
48209	DETROIT	12462	11489	44.5	29.5	20.1	4.4	1.6	29103	34353	11	4	5290	60.7	31.6	5.8	1.8	0.1	41058
48210	DETROIT	12373	12683	45.4	29.1	20.7	3.5	1.4	27630	33114	8	3	6470	60.0	31.8	7.3	0.9	0.0	42373
48211	DETROIT	11373	3046	50.9	29.5	14.6	4.1	1.0	24416	29112	4	2	1442	66.9	21.4	9.3	2.1	0.4	36978
48212	HAMTRAMCK	13357	14959	44.0	30.4	20.4	3.8	1.5	28914	33520	10	4	7913	37.2	34.6	26.1	1.9	0.1	65213
48213	DETROIT	12213	13499	47.4	29.1	18.2	3.8	1.6	26876	30836	7	2	7004	47.0	37.0	15.0	0.9	0.0	52720
48214	DETROIT	16446	12588	52.1	23.6	16.5	5.1	2.7	23614	27018	4	1	5209	54.2	21.4	12.6	7.9	4.0	45626
48215	DETROIT	15500	6320	48.0	26.7	18.5	4.8	2.0	26612	30614	7	2	2814	50.5	23.7	16.7	7.6	1.5	49421
48216	DETROIT	16438	2380	47.6	25.9	21.2	3.5	1.9	26968	31510	7	3	929	42.8	33.7	18.6	4.8	0.0	57644
48217	DETROIT	19161	3860	41.5	27.6	24.5	4.2	2.2	30993	35393	15	6	2565	41.3	42.9	15.2	0.6	0.1	56782
48218	RIVER ROUGE	15282	3445	39.7	30.9	22.5	5.3	1.6	32012	36212	18	8	2018	42.2	43.6	13.4	0.8	0.0	56031
48219	DETROIT	20047	21596	30.0	27.8	30.2	8.9	3.2	42294	47302	54	43	14329	11.1	35.8	46.2	6.8	0.2	92773
48220	FERNDALE	26580	10720	21.2	29.1	37.0	10.1	2.7	49756	59200	71	65	7026	3.7	15.8	65.6	14.7	0.3	122306
48221	DETROIT	22172	16322	26.6	28.3	28.9	11.1	5.1	44151	49221	59	50	12264	10.4	24.9	46.3	16.9	1.5	107622
48223	DETROIT	18032	11795	32.6	28.1	27.1	8.9	3.3	39859	44969	45	33	7230	20.3	23.9	41.2	14.2	0.3	98330
48224	DETROIT	18748	18586	26.2	29.8	32.0	9.6	2.5	44212	49910	59	50	13080	10.0	33.8	50.5	5.6	0.1	95159
48225	HARPER WOODS	27644	6180	20.2	28.0	38.8	10.3	2.6	51428	58215	75	70	4994	2.1	14.4	68.2	15.1	0.1	126173
48226	DETROIT	25024	2919	44.1	24.4	22.5	5.5	3.6	30781	33678	14	6	66	6.1	54.6	31.8	7.6	0.0	72000
48227	DETROIT	16302	19997	36.5	30.6	24.4	6.3	2.2	34909	39143	27	14	12483	22.1	41.3	34.1	2.3	0.2	77869
48228	DETROIT	15985	23019	35.6	31.8	26.0	5.3	1.3	35384	39927	29	15	14624	16.1	50.6	32.4	0.7	0.2	78566
48229	ECORSE	16052	4151	41.3	30.4	22.5	4.1	1.8	30148	33574	13	5	2553	46.4	39.2	11.8	1.8	0.8	52658
48230	GROSSE POINTE	49433	7190	11.8	16.6	29.0	19.0	23.6	82889	92829	96	97	5427	0.8	2.2	11.5	45.0	40.6	356346
48234	DETROIT	16741	15356	34.3	29.2	27.9	6.5	2.1	36537	40982	34	21	10067	29.7	49.1	20.3	0.8	0.2	66671
48235	DETROIT	21129	19441	28.8	29.0	29.7	8.9	3.7	42927	47716	56	45	14108	12.5	34.3	48.5	4.5	0.2	92860
48236	GROSSE POINTE	49202	12030	10.3	14.1	32.3	21.2	22.2	87582	100210	97	98	11372	0.8	1.9	12.8	52.2	32.4	305788
48237	OAK PARK	24297	12478	23.8	26.4	34.4	11.3	4.1	49884	58542	72	66	8496	1.9	9.5	69.8	18.5	0.3	138756
48238	DETROIT	14491	15683	44.9	27.4	21.8	4.4	1.5	28890	33360	10	4	8069	39.3	37.3	21.6	1.7	0.1	60839
48239	REDFORD	25706	14595	17.0	27.5	41.0	12.1	2.5	54968	62774	80	76	13210	2.7	10.6	75.0	11.4	0.3	128867
48240	REDFORD	23503	7065	15.2	30.8	42.7	9.1	2.2	53166	61222	77	74	6189	1.7	16.5	77.5	4.3	0.1	114263
48301	BLOOMFIELD HILLS	75590	5645	6.3	10.8	23.2	20.0	39.7	121007	139096	99	100	5202	0.0	0.3	2.9	37.9	59.0	455847
48302	BLOOMFIELD HILLS	78957	6508	7.6	12.5	24.2	16.1	39.6	114538	133564	99	100	5803	0.2	1.0	8.7	30.9	59.2	468350
48304	BLOOMFIELD HILLS	74801	6932	6.8	13.8	24.2	18.0	37.2	111898	131657	99	99	6307	0.0	1.5	6.1	46.1	46.4	382716
48306	ROCHESTER	50251	8305	6.9	8.9	23.8	27.6	32.9	117128	135848	99	100	7694	0.1	0.4	5.6	49.8	44.2	376158
48307	ROCHESTER	36656	16842	13.4	21.7	35.7	18.0	11.2	68401	79927	91	92	11973	7.3	2.6	22.0	56.1	12.0	223866
48309	ROCHESTER	41284	10711	11.5	13.4	32.3	21.2	21.7	86553	102308	97	98	9188	2.8	3.6	15.7	62.5	15.4	270999
48310	STERLING HEIGHTS	26424	15048	14.9	21.7	38.7	18.6	6.2	64698	70692	88	89	12486	6.9	1.4	23.8	67.7	0.3	193134
48312	STERLING HEIGHTS	27879	13494	17.8	24.2	38.6	14.5	5.0	59159	64250	84	83	9880	1.2	4.5	35.7	58.2	0.3	183564
48313	STERLING HEIGHTS	28604	12803	15.0	18.5	41.2	19.3	6.0	67555	74689	90	91	9829	0.4	3.3	39.3	56.0	1.1	183921
48314	STERLING HEIGHTS	30510	7156	15.2	20.3	36.9	17.3	10.3	67494	76062	90	91	5674	10.3	2.8	20.1	51.0	15.8	235826
48315	UTICA	34986	9160	15.8	17.2	29.5	21.0	16.5	75416	82256	93	95	8393	6.7	8.2	14.5	50.8	19.8	265987
48316	UTICA	36674	8759	9.0	17.3	36.5	22.1	15.0	80294	88340	95	96	7518	0.4	1.2	19.0	66.1	13.3	232710
48317	UTICA	27915	10555	16.2	27.2	39.8	12.6	4.2	56110	62244	81	78	6205	5.9	3.6	46.7	41.0	2.9	167319
48320	KEEGO HARBOR	39511	1942	14.1	24.8	38.7	11.5	10.9	59569	70693	84	83	1412	5.5	5.5	41.5	40.1	7.4	169883
48322	WEST BLOOMFIELD	50323	12168	9.5	14.7	28.8	20.9	26.2	93987	108959	98	99	9471	0.4	0.3	7.1	67.9	24.4	297088
48323	WEST BLOOMFIELD	54547	6515	7.2	11.5	26.1	21.0	34.2	109758	128368	99	99	6240	0.2	0.4	9.5	46.8	43.1	368813
48324	WEST BLOOMFIELD	50470	6602	5.1	13.1	32.2	23.8	25.9	99304	116312	98	99	6178	0.4	0.7	14.5	49.5	34.9	314417
48326	AUBURN HILLS	31956	8693	16.7	26.7	37.5	13.0	6.1	56877	66095	82	80	4479	13.1	12.7	40.8	28.5	5.1	147618
48327	WATERFORD	32096	9321	15.6	26.8	37.0	15.8	4.8	58640	68720	83	82	6731	0.6	3.4	44.8	46.0	5.1	177220
48328	WATERFORD	28733	10999	18.8	28.6	36.1	11.9	4.6	52541	61558	76	73	7371	3.1	7.8	50.9	32.3	5.8	159940
48329	WATERFORD	35478	10367	9.6	20.5	42.5	18.6	8.8	70811	83193	92	93	9329	0.5	3.2	46.1	43.9	6.3	175339
48331	FARMINGTON	50859	8168	6.2	11.3	28.8	22.8	30.8	105914	124985	99	99	6887	0.3	0.2	5.2	64.2	30.1	333968
	MICHIGAN	25281		23.8	27.4	32.3	10.9	5.5	48729	54505				10.7	16.0	40.3	28.0	5.0	134769
	UNITED STATES	25866		24.7	27.1	30.8	10.9	6.5	48124	56710				10.9	15.0	33.7	30.1	10.4	145905

SPENDING POTENTIAL INDICES

MICHIGAN

48144-48331 D

ZIP CODE #	POST OFFICE NAME	FINANCIAL SERVICES: Auto Loan	Home Loan	Invest-ments	Retire-ment Plans	THE HOME: Home Improvements: Home Repair	Lawn & Garden	Furnishings: Comput-ers & Hard-ware	Major Appli-ances	TV, Radio, Sound Equip-ment	Furni-ture	ENTERTAINMENT: Dine out/ Carry out	Sports Equip-ment	Fees & Tickets	Toys & Games	Travel	Cable TV	PERSONAL: Apparel & Services	Auto Repairs	Health Insur-ance	Pets & Supplies
48144	LAMBERTVILLE	104	125	132	124	124	124	113	113	106	113	133	132	120	141	116	104	133	110	105	126
48145	LA SALLE	113	113	100	110	116	121	103	110	104	103	128	130	105	133	106	105	124	107	112	134
48146	LINCOLN PARK	73	78	84	75	78	85	78	77	79	75	98	87	81	104	79	81	96	76	80	85
48150	LIVONIA	96	114	126	112	112	116	107	106	103	106	129	122	113	135	109	102	127	104	101	116
48152	LIVONIA	109	127	144	127	125	131	121	119	116	120	146	137	127	151	123	115	144	118	113	131
48154	LIVONIA	110	129	144	128	128	135	121	121	116	120	145	137	127	150	124	116	144	118	116	132
48157	LUNA PIER	87	76	59	74	80	88	74	81	79	73	95	94	72	96	75	80	90	79	87	100
48158	MANCHESTER	113	123	117	121	124	127	113	116	110	112	136	136	116	142	115	109	133	113	113	135
48159	MAYBEE	114	105	84	101	110	117	97	106	101	97	124	126	96	127	100	103	118	103	113	135
48160	MILAN	100	111	115	111	111	113	105	105	102	104	127	125	109	133	107	100	125	104	100	119
48161	MONROE	87	85	83	83	85	92	85	87	86	84	107	101	84	106	85	86	103	87	88	100
48162	MONROE	92	87	83	86	89	96	88	90	90	87	110	105	87	111	88	90	106	90	92	105
48164	NEW BOSTON	117	119	108	115	121	126	109	115	110	109	136	135	111	140	112	111	132	112	116	139
48165	NEW HUDSON	115	130	132	132	126	125	122	121	114	123	144	143	124	146	120	108	142	119	107	133
48166	NEWPORT	103	103	93	101	103	107	97	101	96	98	119	118	96	119	97	94	116	100	98	118
48167	NORTHVILLE	151	176	210	179	172	180	166	163	157	167	199	188	176	203	169	155	197	161	151	178
48169	PINCKNEY	121	141	143	143	138	136	127	127	119	129	150	150	133	155	128	114	148	124	114	142
48170	PLYMOUTH	131	152	173	153	149	155	143	142	136	143	171	163	150	174	145	134	170	140	133	156
48173	ROCKWOOD	103	109	106	107	110	114	103	105	101	102	126	123	105	131	104	101	123	103	103	121
48174	ROMULUS	88	87	83	86	87	91	85	87	85	85	106	101	85	106	85	84	103	86	85	100
48176	SALINE	130	151	165	155	146	149	140	137	131	141	166	159	148	170	141	127	165	135	124	151
48178	SOUTH LYON	116	132	142	134	128	130	124	122	117	125	148	142	129	150	124	113	146	120	111	134
48179	SOUTH ROCKWOOD	102	101	90	97	103	108	94	99	95	94	117	117	94	121	96	96	114	97	101	120
48180	TAYLOR	78	81	88	79	81	87	82	81	83	80	103	93	84	106	82	83	100	81	81	90
48182	TEMPERANCE	102	107	101	106	108	112	100	103	98	99	121	120	101	125	101	97	118	101	101	120
48183	TRENTON	97	107	112	105	106	111	103	103	101	102	125	118	106	129	104	100	123	101	100	114
48184	WAYNE	84	86	89	84	86	93	86	86	87	84	108	99	87	111	86	88	105	85	87	97
48185	WESTLAND	78	79	90	81	78	84	82	80	81	82	102	94	83	102	81	80	100	82	77	88
48186	WESTLAND	84	92	99	92	91	95	90	89	88	89	110	104	92	113	90	86	108	88	85	98
48187	CANTON	120	136	146	140	132	134	128	126	120	129	152	147	133	154	128	116	151	125	113	139
48188	CANTON	136	147	141	152	142	141	136	136	128	140	161	159	139	160	133	121	159	134	120	151
48189	WHITMORE LAKE	116	124	119	124	121	122	116	117	110	117	139	137	116	139	115	106	136	116	108	132
48191	WILLIS	115	140	147	140	138	137	125	126	117	125	147	147	133	156	128	114	146	121	114	140
48192	WYANDOTTE	81	87	95	85	87	93	87	86	86	85	108	98	89	111	88	87	105	85	86	94
48195	SOUTHGATE	78	84	96	83	83	90	85	83	85	84	106	96	88	110	86	85	104	84	82	91
48197	YPSILANTI	91	84	95	89	82	87	96	89	93	94	117	108	92	113	90	88	114	94	82	99
48198	YPSILANTI	81	80	87	81	78	84	84	81	83	83	104	96	83	103	82	81	102	83	78	91
48201	DETROIT	32	27	37	28	27	31	35	32	36	34	45	38	33	44	33	36	44	35	33	36
48202	DETROIT	50	41	49	40	40	48	49	47	53	49	66	54	47	61	47	54	63	50	51	54
48203	HIGHLAND PARK	55	48	57	46	47	55	54	53	59	54	72	59	53	68	53	60	70	55	57	60
48204	DETROIT	57	48	52	44	48	58	53	54	59	54	72	58	52	66	52	63	69	55	62	62
48205	DETROIT	62	57	70	55	55	63	62	61	67	64	84	69	64	83	62	69	82	63	63	69
48206	DETROIT	59	49	55	45	48	59	55	56	62	56	75	60	54	69	54	65	72	57	63	64
48207	DETROIT	59	53	69	52	52	61	60	58	65	61	81	66	60	78	59	67	78	61	62	66
48208	DETROIT	44	37	41	34	37	44	42	42	47	42	57	46	40	52	41	50	54	44	49	49
48209	DETROIT	60	51	50	50	50	53	57	58	60	60	75	65	54	72	54	57	75	60	55	62
48210	DETROIT	56	48	49	46	47	53	53	54	57	55	71	60	51	67	51	57	69	56	55	59
48211	DETROIT	49	39	43	36	39	47	45	46	51	46	62	50	43	56	43	53	59	48	52	53
48212	HAMTRAMCK	53	48	54	47	47	54	54	53	57	54	71	60	53	69	52	58	69	55	55	59
48213	DETROIT	54	46	53	43	45	54	51	51	57	53	70	56	51	66	50	60	68	53	57	59
48214	DETROIT	55	47	56	44	47	56	53	53	59	53	72	59	52	67	52	61	69	55	59	60
48215	DETROIT	59	53	63	50	51	60	58	57	63	59	78	63	58	75	57	66	76	59	62	66
48216	DETROIT	62	53	55	50	52	59	60	60	64	61	80	67	57	75	57	65	77	62	63	66
48217	DETROIT	70	65	70	61	64	75	68	68	73	69	91	74	69	86	68	76	88	69	75	78
48218	RIVER ROUGE	57	52	57	50	51	59	58	56	61	57	76	64	57	73	56	62	73	58	59	63
48219	DETROIT	73	71	82	69	69	78	74	73	78	76	97	81	76	96	74	79	95	74	76	83
48220	FERNDALE	77	82	95	84	82	85	85	82	83	83	104	98	86	105	84	80	102	84	78	90
48221	DETROIT	81	81	90	77	79	91	81	81	85	83	106	87	84	102	83	88	103	82	86	92
48223	DETROIT	70	68	81	67	66	74	72	70	75	73	94	80	74	93	71	76	92	72	71	79
48224	DETROIT	75	73	86	72	71	79	77	75	80	78	100	86	79	101	77	81	98	77	75	84
48225	HARPER WOODS	79	87	102	86	87	94	87	86	87	86	109	98	91	112	89	87	106	86	85	93
48226	DETROIT	59	52	81	57	51	59	66	59	68	64	85	72	65	84	63	67	83	65	60	66
48227	DETROIT	65	60	70	57	58	68	64	63	69	66	86	69	66	84	64	71	84	64	67	72
48228	DETROIT	61	56	65	54	55	63	61	60	65	62	81	67	62	80	61	67	79	61	63	68
48229	ECORSE	56	52	57	49	51	58	57	55	60	56	75	63	57	73	56	62	72	57	59	62
48230	GROSSE POINTE	154	190	237	191	186	195	177	173	166	177	210	200	190	219	182	164	210	170	159	188
48234	DETROIT	67	63	73	59	61	70	66	65	71	68	89	72	68	87	66	74	87	67	70	75
48235	DETROIT	77	75	84	71	73	85	76	75	80	78	101	81	79	97	77	83	98	76	81	86
48236	GROSSE POINTE	154	200	251	195	196	206	179	178	169	181	212	202	196	224	188	169	214	173	164	192
48237	OAK PARK	82	85	96	85	83	90	88	85	87	87	109	98	89	109	87	86	107	87	83	94
48238	DETROIT	56	48	54	44	47	56	53	53	58	54	72	58	52	67	52	61	69	54	59	61
48239	REDFORD	83	94	103	92	93	98	91	90	89	89	112	103	95	117	93	89	110	89	88	98
48240	REDFORD	78	88	96	86	87	92	86	85	84	84	105	97	89	109	87	84	103	84	83	92
48301	BLOOMFIELD HILLS	234	313	418	306	305	328	274	272	256	279	323	306	308	340	291	258	327	262	253	295
48302	BLOOMFIELD HILLS	243	313	430	311	305	329	282	277	266	287	336	314	315	352	297	267	339	269	259	302
48304	BLOOMFIELD HILLS	226	297	386	287	291	313	260	262	246	266	310	291	290	324	278	250	312	252	247	284
48306	ROCHESTER	192	235	270	240	229	236	212	207	197	215	250	239	232	259	217	193	251	202	189	229
48307	ROCHESTER	119	126	141	132	123	127	126	122	120	126	151	145	128	151	123	115	149	123	111	135
48309	ROCHESTER	144	167	187	170	164	171	156	155	147	158	186	177	164	186	158	144	184	152	145	169
48310	STERLING HEIGHTS	98	115	126	115	113	115	107	106	102	107	128	124	112	133	109	99	127	104	98	117
48312	STERLING HEIGHTS	88	98	113	98	97	103	96	95	94	96	118	110	100	119	98	93	116	95	91	104
48313	STERLING HEIGHTS	99	116	130	116	113	116	109	107	104	109	131	125	114	135	111	102	130	106	99	118
48314	STERLING HEIGHTS	114	121	126	125	118	120	117	116	111	119	140	136	118	139	115	106	137	115	105	128
48315	UTICA	139	145	142	144	146	158	134	141	133	137	166	154	138	159	138	134	160	137	144	159
48316	UTICA	129	155	170	157	151	153	142	140	132	143	167	162	150	173	144	129	167	137	127	153
48317	UTICA	95	94	101	98	93	97	97	95	95	97	119	113	96	118	94	91	116	97	89	107
48320	KEEGO HARBOR	108	125	152	127	124	128	123	120	118	122	148	141	128	154	124	115	147	120	110	129
48322	WEST BLOOMFIELD	160	214	266	204	208	219	188	188	178	190	223	212	206	238	199	180	225	182	175	202
48323	WEST BLOOMFIELD	194	241	304	241	236	250	219	217	205	222	259	248	239	267	227	203	259	211	202	237
48324	WEST BLOOMFIELD	185	228	256	232	221	226	204	200	188	207	239	231	222	247	208	183	240	194	181	220
48326	AUBURN HILLS	100	94	115	101	92	97	104	98	102	104	129	119	102	125	99	97	126	103	90	110
48327	WATERFORD	100	111	121	113	108	110	109	106	104	108	130	126	111	133	108	99	129	106	96	116
48328	WATERFORD	89	96	110	98	94	99	96	94	93	96	117	110	98	118	96	91	115	95	88	103
48329	WATERFORD	118	140	152	141	137	139	130	129	123	130	154	150	137	161	132	119	153	126	118	141
48331	FARMINGTON	179	224	260	226	217	222	198	196	183	203	232	224	216	241	203	179	233	189	175	214
	MICHIGAN	91	91	93	89	91	98	90	91	91	90	113	106	90	113	90	91	109	91	92	105
	UNITED STATES	100	100	100	100	100	100	100	100	100	100	100	100	100	100	100	100	100	100	100	100

# POST OFFICE NAME	COUNTY FIPS CODE	POPULATION 2000	POPULATION 2004	POPULATION 2009	2000-2004 ANNUAL RATE % Rate	2000-2004 ANNUAL RATE State Centile	HOUSEHOLDS 2000	HOUSEHOLDS 2004	HOUSEHOLDS 2009	% Annual Rate 2000-2004	2004 Average HH Size	FAMILIES 2000	FAMILIES 2004	% Annual Rate 2000-2004
48334 FARMINGTON	125	18012	19216	20578	1.5	80	7589	8191	8909	1.8	2.30	4963	5329	1.7
48335 FARMINGTON	125	23971	25374	26545	1.4	76	11202	11998	12701	1.6	2.09	6014	6246	0.9
48336 FARMINGTON	125	26601	27459	28243	0.8	54	11006	11644	12213	1.3	2.30	6762	7004	0.8
48340 PONTIAC	125	25490	25303	25464	-0.2	17	9933	10033	10254	0.2	2.52	6049	5964	-0.3
48341 PONTIAC	125	19278	18728	18828	-0.7	6	7039	6941	7090	-0.3	2.56	4305	4141	-0.9
48342 PONTIAC	125	21767	22319	22921	0.6	46	7353	7609	7907	0.8	2.88	4976	5057	0.4
48346 CLARKSTON	125	22671	23762	24640	1.1	68	8615	9225	9738	1.6	2.55	6220	6563	1.3
48348 CLARKSTON	125	20317	21158	21673	1.0	63	6841	7256	7555	1.4	2.90	5752	6046	1.2
48350 DAVISBURG	125	7448	8053	8424	1.9	87	2563	2827	3007	2.3	2.84	2010	2191	2.1
48353 HARTLAND	093	4961	6091	7226	5.0	100	1717	2165	2626	5.6	2.80	1434	1788	5.3
48356 HIGHLAND	125	8598	8835	9039	0.6	48	3049	3223	3371	1.3	2.74	2444	2554	1.0
48357 HIGHLAND	125	8476	8829	9079	1.0	63	3029	3224	3374	1.5	2.74	2322	2432	1.1
48359 LAKE ORION	125	8505	9097	9479	1.6	83	3291	3559	3755	1.9	2.53	2137	2261	1.3
48360 LAKE ORION	125	9977	10651	11086	1.6	82	3439	3725	3928	1.9	2.85	2828	3023	1.6
48362 LAKE ORION	125	14206	14595	14924	0.6	48	5271	5514	5728	1.1	2.62	3801	3924	0.8
48363 OAKLAND	125	4102	4297	4423	1.1	68	1496	1596	1670	1.5	2.69	1191	1252	1.2
48367 LEONARD	125	4773	4837	4907	0.3	35	1658	1708	1760	0.7	2.78	1332	1356	0.4
48370 OXFORD	125	1672	1658	1666	-0.2	16	553	561	575	0.3	2.85	453	455	0.1
48371 OXFORD	125	19333	20909	21886	1.9	88	6867	7576	8065	2.3	2.74	5207	5671	2.0
48374 NOVI	125	11819	12786	13353	1.9	88	3499	3800	4004	2.0	3.36	3123	3367	1.8
48375 NOVI	125	20404	20921	21560	0.6	46	7943	8278	8653	1.0	2.50	5253	5372	0.5
48377 NOVI	125	10928	11584	11980	1.4	77	5374	5815	6118	1.9	1.99	2618	2762	1.3
48380 MILFORD	125	6355	7012	7587	2.3	93	2121	2395	2643	2.9	2.88	1810	2025	2.7
48381 MILFORD	125	12886	12966	12969	0.1	24	4679	4780	4894	0.5	2.67	3570	3599	0.2
48382 COMMERCE TOWNSHIP	125	19969	20978	21685	1.2	70	6930	7384	7740	1.5	2.84	5625	5947	1.3
48383 WHITE LAKE	125	12399	12765	13038	0.7	51	4207	4413	4584	1.1	2.88	3399	3526	0.9
48386 WHITE LAKE	125	15784	16363	16775	0.9	59	5871	6226	6500	1.4	2.59	4414	4603	1.0
48390 WALLED LAKE	125	19697	21235	22485	1.8	86	7946	8620	9207	1.9	2.46	5365	5788	1.8
48393 WIXOM	125	15455	16670	17478	1.8	87	6692	7138	7486	1.5	2.33	3727	3966	1.5
48401 APPLEGATE	151	1510	1542	1587	0.5	43	578	600	628	0.9	2.56	429	440	0.6
48412 ATTICA	087	6045	6535	6953	1.9	87	2077	2303	2502	2.5	2.81	1675	1838	2.2
48413 BAD AXE	063	8158	8151	8242	0.0	22	3085	3146	3253	0.5	2.48	2137	2150	0.1
48414 BANCROFT	155	2537	2632	2691	0.9	60	889	940	978	1.3	2.80	716	750	1.1
48415 BIRCH RUN	145	9769	9756	9726	0.0	21	3599	3667	3726	0.4	2.65	2800	2822	0.2
48416 BROWN CITY	151	5419	5685	5963	1.1	69	1884	2012	2149	1.6	2.82	1472	1557	1.3
48417 BURT	145	3146	3153	3150	0.1	24	1071	1096	1117	0.5	2.87	870	882	0.3
48418 BYRON	155	4090	4293	4457	1.2	70	1399	1489	1566	1.5	2.88	1167	1231	1.3
48419 CARSONVILLE	151	2629	2706	2801	0.7	50	999	1048	1103	1.1	2.57	724	752	0.9
48420 CLIO	049	21251	22237	23131	1.1	67	7910	8417	8878	1.5	2.60	5946	6215	1.1
48421 COLUMBIAVILLE	087	6971	7248	7566	0.9	62	2428	2583	2750	1.5	2.80	1968	2076	1.3
48422 CROSWELL	151	6540	6828	7103	1.0	66	2370	2519	2665	1.4	2.70	1779	1869	1.2
48423 DAVISON	049	30986	32445	33828	1.1	67	12737	13438	14141	1.3	2.41	8415	8745	0.9
48426 DECKER	151	1179	1197	1225	0.4	37	426	441	459	0.8	2.71	328	336	0.6
48427 DECKERVILLE	151	3209	3260	3347	0.4	37	1242	1288	1348	0.9	2.45	868	887	0.5
48428 DRYDEN	087	4840	5020	5224	0.9	60	1648	1746	1853	1.4	2.86	1382	1453	1.2
48429 DURAND	155	10009	10051	10154	0.1	27	3732	3827	3938	0.6	2.59	2794	2832	0.3
48430 FENTON	093	32701	36133	39439	2.4	94	12303	13865	15353	2.9	2.58	9131	10117	2.4
48432 FILION	063	900	893	900	-0.2	17	350	356	367	0.4	2.49	267	268	0.1
48433 FLUSHING	049	25110	26405	27645	1.2	71	9702	10314	10914	1.5	2.53	7201	7561	1.2
48435 FOSTORIA	157	1965	1989	2024	0.3	34	672	694	721	0.8	2.86	542	555	0.6
48436 GAINES	049	3529	3565	3629	0.2	31	1183	1210	1245	0.5	2.95	978	991	0.3
48438 GOODRICH	049	6132	6520	6843	1.5	78	2063	2228	2372	1.8	2.90	1723	1847	1.7
48439 GRAND BLANC	049	40171	42493	44727	1.3	75	15874	16927	17995	1.5	2.48	11091	11660	1.2
48441 HARBOR BEACH	063	4539	4506	4551	-0.2	17	1801	1829	1891	0.4	2.44	1269	1271	0.0
48442 HOLLY	125	18972	19479	19889	0.6	47	6818	7133	7407	1.1	2.69	5123	5294	0.8
48444 IMLAY CITY	087	8869	9339	9818	1.2	72	3153	3372	3607	1.6	2.72	2306	2444	1.4
48445 KINDE	063	1440	1447	1471	0.1	27	566	582	606	0.7	2.47	401	407	0.4
48446 LAPEER	087	31031	31784	32913	0.6	45	11087	11632	12307	1.1	2.60	8141	8434	0.8
48449 LENNON	155	3804	3811	3869	0.0	24	1402	1429	1473	0.5	2.66	1076	1083	0.2
48450 LEXINGTON	151	4905	5152	5380	1.2	70	2194	2345	2490	1.6	2.19	1418	1491	1.2
48451 LINDEN	049	12160	12970	13642	1.5	80	4446	4815	5131	1.9	2.68	3443	3674	1.5
48453 MARLETTE	151	5167	5184	5286	0.1	25	1829	1867	1938	0.5	2.67	1347	1357	0.2
48454 MELVIN	151	1276	1330	1380	1.0	65	458	486	514	1.4	2.74	363	382	1.2
48455 METAMORA	087	8235	8501	8843	0.8	54	2915	3084	3275	1.3	2.75	2383	2497	1.1
48456 MINDEN CITY	151	1090	1163	1222	1.5	81	381	416	447	2.1	2.77	284	306	1.8
48457 MONTROSE	049	8796	8879	9036	0.2	30	3004	3074	3170	0.5	2.83	2401	2436	0.3
48458 MOUNT MORRIS	049	25234	25848	26721	0.6	45	9776	10149	10609	0.9	2.54	6757	6910	0.5
48460 NEW LOTHROP	155	2452	2481	2497	0.3	33	891	925	950	0.9	2.66	702	721	0.6
48461 NORTH BRANCH	087	7804	8246	8670	1.3	74	2549	2743	2935	1.7	2.99	2085	2221	1.5
48462 ORTONVILLE	125	12564	12828	13031	0.5	43	4201	4375	4523	1.0	2.90	3504	3615	0.7
48463 OTISVILLE	049	4716	4835	4970	0.6	46	1710	1776	1846	0.9	2.72	1367	1406	0.7
48464 OTTER LAKE	087	2267	2382	2492	1.2	70	793	856	915	1.8	2.73	644	689	1.6
48465 PALMS	151	752	775	800	0.7	52	302	318	335	1.2	2.40	222	230	0.8
48466 PECK	151	1665	1695	1737	0.4	39	600	623	650	0.9	2.68	463	475	0.6
48467 PORT AUSTIN	063	2671	2719	2772	0.4	39	1239	1295	1353	1.1	2.08	788	811	0.7
48468 PORT HOPE	063	1356	1404	1446	0.8	58	570	608	644	1.5	2.30	426	449	1.2
48469 PORT SANILAC	151	1374	1352	1375	-0.4	11	642	646	668	0.2	2.08	411	406	-0.3
48470 RUTH	063	929	926	934	-0.1	20	346	353	364	0.5	2.62	264	266	0.2
48471 SANDUSKY	151	6051	6129	6306	0.3	34	2304	2369	2479	0.7	2.47	1585	1606	0.3
48472 SNOVER	151	2018	2089	2161	0.8	58	700	736	774	1.2	2.82	538	559	0.8
48473 SWARTZ CREEK	049	19622	20492	21263	1.0	66	7565	8026	8441	1.4	2.54	5674	5940	1.1
48475 UBLY	151	2609	2699	2783	0.8	57	1001	1055	1108	1.2	2.54	714	744	1.0
48502 FLINT	049	984	948	946	-0.9	4	222	198	198	-2.7	1.32	46	39	-3.8
48503 FLINT	049	29425	28812	29305	-0.5	8	12575	12441	12779	-0.3	2.27	6934	6696	-0.8
48504 FLINT	049	38391	39550	41060	0.7	52	14086	14621	15318	0.9	2.66	9591	9774	0.5
48505 FLINT	049	35428	34500	35173	-0.6	7	12520	12275	12623	-0.5	2.77	8717	8424	-0.8
48506 FLINT	049	33349	34361	35705	0.7	52	12987	13506	14168	0.9	2.52	8514	8719	0.6
48507 FLINT	049	32298	33031	34342	0.5	44	13868	14291	15000	0.7	2.29	8655	8783	0.4
48509 BURTON	049	10148	10354	10725	0.5	41	3828	3939	4118	0.7	2.62	2855	2906	0.4
48519 BURTON	049	7323	7822	8385	1.6	82	2874	3099	3348	1.8	2.52	1986	2095	1.3
48529 BURTON	049	11240	11411	11923	0.4	37	4442	4528	4760	0.5	2.51	2872	2870	0.0
48532 FLINT	049	19817	20554	21367	0.9	60	8409	8794	9230	1.1	2.30	5288	5454	0.7
48601 SAGINAW	145	48112	46623	46231	-0.7	5	17265	16993	17136	-0.4	2.70	12386	12035	-0.7
48602 SAGINAW	145	33292	33004	32982	-0.2	16	13215	13243	13430	0.1	2.42	8166	8036	-0.4
48603 SAGINAW	145	38379	39559	40270	0.7	53	16585	17511	18201	1.3	2.21	10352	10735	0.7
MICHIGAN					0.6					1.0	2.52			0.6
UNITED STATES					1.2					1.3	2.58			1.1

#	POST OFFICE NAME	RACE (%) White 2000	White 2004	Black 2000	Black 2004	Asian/Pacific 2000	Asian/Pacific 2004	% Hispanic Origin 2000	% Hispanic Origin 2004	2004 AGE DISTRIBUTION (%) 0-4	5-9	10-14	15-19	20-24	25-44	45-64	65-84	85+	18+	MEDIAN AGE 2004	% 2004 Males	% 2004 Females
48334	FARMINGTON	84.0	81.4	7.2	8.1	6.0	7.5	1.5	1.6	5.7	5.9	6.6	5.9	4.5	23.9	26.8	17.2	3.5	77.8	43.5	47.1	52.9
48335	FARMINGTON	77.8	73.6	6.7	7.4	13.4	16.7	1.7	1.9	5.5	5.2	5.3	5.2	6.2	35.7	22.7	11.5	2.6	80.7	36.4	48.4	51.6
48336	FARMINGTON	86.2	83.9	7.2	8.2	3.9	5.0	1.4	1.6	6.4	6.2	6.1	6.1	5.7	29.5	25.0	12.4	2.6	77.2	39.2	48.1	51.9
48340	PONTIAC	56.1	52.8	27.9	29.7	2.7	3.3	16.2	17.7	9.6	8.9	8.5	6.9	7.8	33.3	17.9	6.3	1.0	69.0	29.6	49.1	50.9
48341	PONTIAC	32.2	30.4	60.4	61.7	1.2	1.4	7.5	8.1	7.5	7.5	7.8	7.9	6.8	30.2	21.9	8.9	1.5	72.2	33.5	48.7	51.3
48342	PONTIAC	25.7	23.7	59.9	60.6	3.2	4.0	13.2	14.1	9.0	9.3	9.7	8.1	7.3	28.3	20.5	7.1	0.7	66.9	29.8	48.5	51.5
48346	CLARKSTON	95.5	94.6	0.9	1.0	1.2	1.6	2.9	3.4	7.0	7.2	7.1	6.3	6.0	30.5	26.0	8.9	1.1	74.6	36.8	49.5	50.5
48348	CLARKSTON	96.8	96.2	0.8	0.9	0.9	1.2	1.8	2.1	7.5	8.3	8.8	7.0	4.9	27.8	29.3	6.1	0.5	70.8	37.7	50.0	50.0
48350	DAVISBURG	96.5	96.0	1.2	1.4	0.4	0.6	2.1	2.5	7.6	7.9	8.2	6.4	5.4	29.8	27.8	6.3	0.5	72.1	36.7	49.5	50.6
48353	HARTLAND	98.1	97.8	0.3	0.3	0.3	0.4	1.0	1.2	6.3	7.4	8.0	7.1	4.9	26.7	30.1	8.6	0.9	73.7	39.3	49.7	50.4
48356	HIGHLAND	97.9	97.5	0.2	0.3	0.4	0.6	1.2	1.5	7.2	7.2	7.3	7.2	5.9	29.7	27.8	7.0	0.8	73.7	37.2	50.6	49.4
48357	HIGHLAND	97.1	96.7	0.3	0.4	0.4	0.5	1.2	1.5	7.5	7.6	8.7	7.5	6.3	28.9	26.0	6.8	0.7	71.5	35.3	50.3	49.7
48359	LAKE ORION	93.3	92.2	1.8	2.1	1.3	1.7	4.3	4.9	8.5	8.0	6.8	5.8	7.1	35.8	21.1	5.8	1.1	73.1	33.6	50.1	49.9
48360	LAKE ORION	95.4	94.5	1.7	1.9	1.6	2.1	2.0	2.3	9.8	9.8	8.7	5.9	4.2	33.1	23.2	4.9	0.3	67.7	34.5	50.8	49.2
48362	LAKE ORION	96.7	96.1	0.7	0.8	0.9	1.2	1.9	2.3	7.8	7.8	7.4	6.1	5.3	32.9	25.1	6.5	1.2	73.1	36.1	50.2	49.8
48363	OAKLAND	96.7	96.2	0.9	1.0	1.0	1.3	0.9	1.0	6.1	7.5	8.4	6.5	4.5	24.9	32.0	9.5	0.7	73.8	40.5	50.1	49.9
48367	LEONARD	97.2	96.8	0.9	1.0	0.2	0.3	2.3	2.7	6.7	7.6	8.3	7.3	5.1	28.1	29.0	7.2	0.9	72.3	37.5	51.2	48.9
48370	OXFORD	97.0	96.4	1.4	1.6	0.4	0.6	0.9	1.1	5.7	6.8	7.5	8.6	4.5	25.3	32.3	8.3	1.1	73.6	40.7	51.5	48.6
48371	OXFORD	97.0	96.5	0.5	0.5	0.5	0.6	2.1	2.4	8.2	8.2	7.9	6.7	5.7	31.9	24.3	6.3	0.8	71.3	35.2	49.4	50.6
48374	NOVI	87.9	85.1	1.0	1.2	9.4	11.9	1.5	1.7	8.9	10.8	11.7	7.9	4.1	30.2	23.2	3.1	0.2	62.7	33.1	50.2	49.8
48375	NOVI	85.4	82.0	2.1	2.3	10.4	13.5	1.9	2.2	7.0	7.2	7.4	5.8	5.0	31.9	26.0	8.4	1.4	74.4	37.6	48.6	51.4
48377	NOVI	88.5	86.2	2.7	3.1	5.7	7.4	1.9	2.2	6.7	5.9	4.9	4.5	10.8	37.1	20.4	8.5	1.3	80.1	33.6	49.3	50.8
48380	MILFORD	97.6	97.3	0.5	0.5	0.3	0.4	1.4	1.6	6.4	7.9	8.6	7.1	4.4	27.1	30.0	7.4	1.1	72.5	39.0	50.6	49.4
48381	MILFORD	97.4	96.9	0.4	0.5	0.5	0.6	1.2	1.4	7.3	7.8	8.1	6.9	5.2	28.0	27.3	8.3	1.1	72.4	37.5	48.8	51.2
48382	COMMERCE TOWNSHIP	97.4	96.9	0.4	0.5	0.8	1.0	1.1	1.3	7.8	8.8	8.9	6.5	4.3	29.1	27.6	6.7	0.5	70.2	37.4	50.3	49.7
48383	WHITE LAKE	97.0	96.5	0.5	0.6	0.4	0.6	1.7	2.1	8.0	8.2	8.6	6.8	5.7	31.2	25.2	5.6	0.6	70.7	34.8	49.7	50.3
48386	WHITE LAKE	96.2	95.6	1.0	1.2	0.8	1.0	1.9	2.2	6.4	7.1	7.3	5.9	4.7	28.3	30.2	9.2	0.9	75.3	40.1	50.2	49.8
48390	WALLED LAKE	95.6	94.6	0.6	0.7	2.0	2.7	1.4	1.6	7.4	7.7	7.4	5.4	4.6	32.1	25.4	9.1	1.0	74.1	37.7	49.0	51.0
48393	WIXOM	91.3	90.2	2.3	2.4	2.6	3.3	2.9	3.3	8.6	7.6	7.0	6.2	9.1	37.7	18.4	4.8	0.6	73.1	30.8	51.8	48.2
48401	APPLEGATE	97.7	97.4	0.1	0.1	0.1	0.1	1.7	2.0	6.5	6.9	7.7	6.0	4.7	23.7	27.4	15.6	1.5	74.8	41.2	49.8	50.2
48412	ATTICA	97.5	97.2	0.2	0.3	0.4	0.4	2.3	2.6	6.9	7.4	8.2	6.6	5.1	28.9	26.6	9.6	0.7	73.2	37.6	50.8	49.2
48413	BAD AXE	97.9	97.7	0.2	0.3	0.4	0.5	1.5	1.6	6.2	6.6	6.8	7.2	5.9	25.8	24.9	13.5	3.2	75.9	39.4	48.3	51.7
48414	BANCROFT	97.5	97.2	0.0	0.0	0.1	0.2	1.4	1.6	6.1	6.7	7.8	6.9	6.5	26.6	29.1	9.2	1.1	75.2	38.8	50.2	49.9
48415	BIRCH RUN	96.7	96.1	0.5	0.7	0.3	0.3	2.7	3.3	6.7	7.0	7.5	6.7	5.7	28.6	26.6	10.2	1.0	74.5	37.7	49.4	50.6
48416	BROWN CITY	98.2	98.0	0.2	0.2	0.2	0.3	2.5	2.9	7.9	7.7	8.0	7.7	6.3	27.5	24.2	9.7	1.0	71.7	35.4	50.5	49.5
48417	BURT	93.5	92.3	1.5	1.9	0.3	0.3	4.4	5.3	6.9	7.2	8.6	6.4	6.1	28.0	27.5	8.5	0.8	73.2	36.9	51.2	48.8
48418	BYRON	97.6	97.3	0.2	0.2	0.3	0.4	1.2	1.3	7.8	8.0	8.0	6.5	5.4	29.8	25.5	8.2	0.9	72.2	36.3	50.9	49.1
48419	CARSONVILLE	97.9	97.7	0.1	0.1	0.2	0.2	1.7	2.0	5.9	6.3	6.8	6.1	5.9	24.0	27.3	15.8	1.8	76.7	41.8	49.3	50.7
48420	CLIO	96.0	95.2	1.1	1.5	0.3	0.4	1.9	2.3	6.0	6.2	7.1	6.7	6.6	27.6	28.0	10.6	1.3	76.7	38.5	49.7	50.3
48421	COLUMBIAVILLE	97.4	97.1	0.4	0.5	0.2	0.3	1.8	2.1	6.2	7.0	8.1	7.5	5.9	27.9	28.8	8.1	0.4	73.9	37.6	51.0	49.0
48422	CROSWELL	94.8	94.3	0.1	0.1	0.1	0.1	6.2	6.9	7.4	7.5	8.2	7.1	6.2	27.0	24.8	10.7	1.2	72.4	36.2	50.6	49.4
48423	DAVISON	95.2	94.2	1.5	1.9	0.6	0.8	2.0	2.4	6.2	6.2	7.0	6.9	7.9	27.4	26.3	10.9	1.3	76.6	37.3	47.8	52.2
48426	DECKER	97.0	96.7	0.4	0.5	0.0	0.0	1.9	2.1	6.4	7.6	7.6	7.8	6.8	27.2	23.1	11.3	1.7	73.3	36.1	52.2	47.8
48427	DECKERVILLE	96.3	95.9	0.1	0.1	0.3	0.3	4.4	5.1	5.6	5.8	6.9	6.7	6.1	24.5	26.5	14.9	3.0	77.6	41.4	48.9	51.1
48428	DRYDEN	97.8	97.6	0.1	0.1	0.3	0.3	1.2	1.4	6.8	7.7	8.3	6.6	4.7	28.4	28.7	8.3	0.6	73.0	38.7	51.4	48.7
48429	DURAND	97.2	97.0	0.1	0.1	0.2	0.2	1.8	2.0	7.0	7.3	7.5	6.4	6.0	28.1	25.4	10.4	1.9	74.3	37.4	49.0	51.0
48430	FENTON	97.0	96.4	0.4	0.5	0.7	1.0	1.4	1.7	6.8	7.2	7.5	6.4	5.1	28.4	27.4	9.8	1.4	74.5	38.4	49.3	50.7
48432	FILION	98.2	97.9	0.2	0.2	0.3	0.5	0.4	0.7	5.8	6.3	7.3	6.4	5.9	26.2	26.7	13.2	2.2	76.3	40.7	51.5	48.5
48433	FLUSHING	94.5	93.3	2.5	3.2	0.7	1.0	1.8	2.1	5.3	6.2	7.4	6.9	5.7	24.2	29.0	13.6	1.8	76.6	41.5	47.5	52.5
48435	FOSTORIA	97.9	97.6	0.2	0.2	0.1	0.1	1.2	1.5	7.5	7.6	8.4	7.2	6.6	28.0	25.0	8.6	1.2	72.2	36.0	52.4	47.6
48436	GAINES	96.9	96.4	0.4	0.5	0.3	0.4	1.1	1.4	7.0	7.3	7.6	6.8	6.1	28.4	28.5	7.7	0.7	74.0	37.8	50.7	49.3
48438	GOODRICH	97.8	97.3	0.3	0.5	0.5	0.6	1.0	1.3	6.8	8.0	8.7	6.9	4.4	29.0	28.8	6.9	0.6	71.7	37.8	51.6	48.4
48439	GRAND BLANC	89.5	87.2	5.5	6.9	2.5	3.1	1.8	2.1	6.6	7.0	7.3	6.2	6.0	28.7	26.3	10.5	1.5	75.3	37.8	48.9	51.1
48441	HARBOR BEACH	97.3	96.8	0.0	0.1	0.9	1.1	1.0	1.2	6.0	6.2	7.1	7.2	5.8	22.7	25.7	16.6	2.6	75.6	41.3	50.3	49.7
48442	HOLLY	95.5	94.9	1.7	1.9	0.4	0.6	2.5	2.9	6.8	7.1	7.7	6.8	5.8	30.2	27.0	7.7	1.0	74.1	36.8	50.5	49.5
48444	IMLAY CITY	93.3	92.5	0.4	0.4	0.8	1.0	11.9	13.4	7.4	7.4	8.0	7.1	6.7	28.6	22.8	10.1	1.8	72.8	35.4	49.6	50.4
48445	KINDE	98.2	98.0	0.2	0.2	0.4	0.5	0.4	0.5	6.3	6.1	6.2	6.7	5.7	25.6	25.4	15.8	2.4	76.7	40.7	49.8	50.2
48446	LAPEER	95.1	94.6	1.9	2.1	0.5	0.6	2.3	2.6	6.6	6.8	7.4	6.6	6.7	29.4	25.7	9.5	1.4	75.1	37.0	50.7	49.3
48449	LENNON	96.4	95.8	0.3	0.5	0.2	0.2	3.0	3.5	6.7	7.0	8.7	7.1	5.9	28.5	25.4	9.7	1.1	73.3	36.2	49.6	50.4
48450	LEXINGTON	98.1	97.9	0.1	0.1	0.2	0.3	1.7	2.0	5.3	5.6	6.0	5.3	4.4	23.2	28.9	18.9	2.4	79.7	45.1	48.0	52.0
48451	LINDEN	97.5	97.1	0.2	0.3	0.5	0.6	1.1	1.3	7.6	7.7	7.8	6.3	5.5	29.3	25.9	9.1	0.9	73.0	37.1	49.6	50.4
48453	MARLETTE	96.3	95.9	1.0	1.1	0.2	0.3	2.0	2.3	7.4	7.6	8.1	8.5	6.6	25.3	22.9	11.3	2.4	71.3	35.3	50.1	49.9
48454	MELVIN	97.1	96.6	0.4	0.5	0.2	0.2	1.0	1.3	8.1	8.1	7.9	7.1	5.4	28.1	24.1	10.1	1.2	71.5	36.5	52.1	47.9
48455	METAMORA	97.6	97.3	0.1	0.1	0.4	0.5	1.3	1.6	6.2	7.0	7.8	6.7	5.3	26.8	30.8	8.8	0.6	74.6	39.8	50.6	49.4
48456	MINDEN CITY	98.1	98.1	0.0	0.0	0.1	0.1	1.4	1.6	6.6	7.0	7.9	7.0	5.3	26.4	24.7	13.0	2.2	73.6	38.2	51.6	48.4
48457	MONTROSE	95.8	94.9	1.5	2.0	0.1	0.1	2.2	2.7	6.3	6.9	8.6	7.6	6.2	28.5	25.8	8.9	1.2	73.2	36.3	50.4	49.6
48458	MOUNT MORRIS	75.4	73.8	20.6	21.7	0.3	0.4	2.5	2.7	7.5	7.3	8.0	7.1	7.2	27.3	23.4	11.2	1.1	72.8	34.7	48.3	51.7
48460	NEW LOTHROP	98.1	97.9	0.0	0.0	0.1	0.1	1.1	1.3	5.6	6.0	6.7	7.4	6.5	27.3	28.4	10.8	1.3	77.0	39.4	50.1	49.9
48461	NORTH BRANCH	97.2	96.9	0.1	0.1	0.2	0.2	2.5	3.0	7.9	8.1	8.9	7.9	6.6	27.6	24.4	8.0	0.6	70.2	34.1	50.4	49.7
48462	ORTONVILLE	97.6	97.2	0.4	0.4	0.5	0.7	1.3	1.6	6.8	7.6	8.6	7.1	5.3	29.6	28.8	5.8	0.5	72.4	37.7	50.6	49.4
48463	OTISVILLE	94.7	93.5	2.6	3.4	0.3	0.3	1.3	1.5	6.0	6.5	7.4	6.4	6.3	27.2	30.4	9.4	0.6	76.2	39.7	50.9	49.1
48464	OTTER LAKE	96.8	96.6	0.4	0.5	0.2	0.3	1.8	2.1	6.3	6.7	7.4	6.8	6.2	28.9	27.4	9.8	0.7	75.4	37.8	50.6	49.5
48465	PALMS	97.1	96.9	0.0	0.0	0.1	0.1	2.8	3.1	6.5	7.1	7.2	6.3	5.4	24.4	26.6	14.3	2.2	74.7	40.0	51.5	48.5
48466	PECK	97.0	96.7	0.4	0.4	0.2	0.2	2.4	2.7	7.4	7.4	7.5	6.5	6.0	26.8	24.5	12.9	1.1	73.6	37.4	50.4	49.6
48467	PORT AUSTIN	98.8	98.7	0.1	0.1	0.2	0.3	0.9	1.1	4.3	4.6	4.8	4.6	4.0	19.3	33.0	22.7	2.8	83.2	50.7	50.4	49.7
48468	PORT HOPE	98.6	98.5	0.0	0.1	0.2	0.1	0.7	0.9	4.6	5.0	6.8	6.3	4.8	20.0	29.5	20.7	2.4	79.3	46.7	51.6	48.4
48469	PORT SANILAC	97.2	96.8	0.1	0.1	0.5	0.7	1.3	1.5	5.4	5.5	5.2	5.3	5.3	21.2	28.1	21.3	2.7	80.1	46.3	47.1	52.9
48470	RUTH	98.6	98.5	0.0	0.0	0.3	0.4	0.9	0.9	7.6	8.0	7.9	6.7	5.3	25.8	24.5	12.2	2.1	71.9	37.6	52.2	47.8
48471	SANDUSKY	96.3	95.7	0.5	0.6	1.0	1.3	3.0	3.4	5.9	6.1	7.3	7.0	6.4	26.4	24.8	13.4	2.7	76.2	39.3	48.5	51.5
48472	SNOVER	98.0	97.8	0.1	0.1	0.0	0.0	1.3	1.5	7.4	7.7	7.1	6.9	6.0	28.3	24.5	10.5	1.5	73.5	36.3	50.2	49.8
48473	SWARTZ CREEK	96.4	95.6	1.0	1.3	0.5	0.7	1.7	2.1	5.7	6.2	6.8	6.3	5.5	26.3	29.3	12.6	1.3	77.3	40.9	48.5	51.5
48475	UBLY	98.6	98.5	0.1	0.1	0.1	0.2	0.7	0.7	7.1	7.3	7.5	7.1	5.3	27.5	23.7	12.4	2.1	73.0	37.7	50.1	49.9
48502	FLINT	44.9	38.1	48.9	55.7	0.4	0.4	3.8	3.9	1.3	1.4	1.7	6.7	15.0	53.6	17.4	3.0	0.1	94.9	33.8	78.9	21.1
48503	FLINT	49.0	45.6	45.2	48.3	0.7	0.8	2.7	2.9	8.3	7.9	7.4	6.1	6.6	27.8	23.1	11.2	1.7	72.8	34.7	46.7	53.4
48504	FLINT	29.3	27.1	65.9	68.1	0.4	0.4	2.0	2.1	8.4	8.7	9.7	8.6	7.6	27.2	21.4	7.5	1.1	68.4	30.5	46.5	53.5
48505	FLINT	11.4	9.5	84.3	86.5	0.1	0.1	2.0	2.0	9.3	9.6	10.2	8.2	7.3	25.2	19.6	9.7	0.8	65.9	29.3	46.4	53.6
48506	FLINT	88.2	85.9	5.5	6.9	0.6	0.7	5.4	6.1	8.5	8.0	7.7	6.7	6.8	29.8	22.0	9.4	1.2	71.7	33.5	49.1	50.9
48507	FLINT	81.9	78.7	13.2	15.9	0.9	1.1	3.1	3.4	7.8	7.0	6.9	5.9	6.6	29.6	22.7	11.9	1.6	74.9	35.6	47.2	52.8
48509	BURTON	93.8	92.5	3.0	3.9	0.5	0.6	2.3	2.7	6.1	6.4	7.4	6.8	5.7	27.4	26.7	12.4	1.3	75.9	39.2	48.5	51.5
48519	BURTON	93.2	91.3	2.9	4.0	0.6	0.8	1.9	2.3	6.9	6.9	7.3	6.6	5.9	29.7	23.5	11.4	1.4	74.6	37.1	48.7	51.3
48529	BURTON	89.6	86.8	4.6	6.5	1.0	1.2	2.7	3.2	8.7	8.0	8.3	6.7	7.6	32.2	19.8	7.9	0.9	70.9	31.6	49.2	50.9
48532	FLINT	75.1	70.4	17.6	21.2	3.2	4.0	2.2	2.4	5.7	5.7	6.9	6.7	6.4	26.3	26.1	13.7	2.7	77.6	39.9	46.9	53.1
48601	SAGINAW	30.9	28.7	60.5	62.4	0.2	0.2	11.1	11.6	8.4	8.7	9.6	8.1	7.2	24.5	22.6	9.9	1.1	68.2	31.5	45.9	54.1
48602	SAGINAW	78.5	74.8	11.8	13.9	0.6	0.8	11.3	13.2	7.8	7.2	7.4	6.9	7.6	29.8	21.1	9.9	2.2	73.5	33.7	48.0	52.0
48603	SAGINAW	88.7	86.3	5.4	6.6	2.7	3.3	4.2	5.0	5.1	5.2	5.8	6.0	7.1	23.8	27.3	15.7	4.0	80.4	42.7	46.8	53.2
	MICHIGAN	80.2	79.2	14.2	14.4	1.8	2.3	3.3	3.6	6.8	6.9	7.4	7.1	6.9	28.1	24.6	10.8	1.6	74.9	36.5	49.1	50.9
	UNITED STATES	75.1	73.6	12.3	12.5	3.8	4.2	12.5	14.1	6.9	6.7	7.2	7.0	7.3	28.6	23.8	10.8	1.7	75.1	36.0	49.1	50.9

ZIP CODE #	POST OFFICE NAME	2004 Per Capita Income	2004 HH Income Base	2004 HOUSEHOLD INCOME DISTRIBUTION (%) Less than $25,000	$25,000 to $49,999	$50,000 to $99,999	$100,000 to $149,999	$150,000 or More	MEDIAN HOUSEHOLD INCOME 2004	2009	2004 National Centile	2004 State Centile	2004 Home Value Base	2004 HOME VALUE DISTRIBUTION (%) Less than $50,000	$50,000 to $89,999	$90,000 to $174,999	$175,000 to $399,999	$400,000 or More	2004 Median Home Value
48334	FARMINGTON	39846	8191	13.7	19.3	34.3	18.0	14.8	70720	82323	92	93	6045	0.2	3.3	15.7	68.1	12.8	259365
48335	FARMINGTON	41190	11998	15.7	22.1	34.4	14.0	13.9	63745	75542	88	88	5224	1.4	4.2	8.4	70.0	16.2	286233
48336	FARMINGTON	33618	11644	17.2	23.5	33.8	16.3	9.3	61594	71721	86	86	8452	3.5	4.7	34.4	55.5	2.0	188931
48340	PONTIAC	17993	10033	34.0	32.0	27.2	5.2	1.7	36144	42611	32	20	5223	9.9	39.7	44.4	5.8	0.3	90366
48341	PONTIAC	22160	6941	33.4	26.8	27.9	8.0	4.0	38206	46006	40	27	3938	13.4	29.0	45.4	11.2	1.0	99281
48342	PONTIAC	16026	7609	40.2	27.5	24.3	5.8	2.2	32328	39857	19	9	3950	19.2	48.2	29.4	2.9	0.3	73467
48346	CLARKSTON	35584	9225	10.9	18.0	39.2	20.5	11.4	74477	88231	93	94	7256	4.4	7.0	23.1	56.6	9.0	212109
48348	CLARKSTON	39887	7256	6.5	15.6	32.6	25.0	20.4	91748	108297	97	98	6890	7.2	3.8	13.6	51.2	24.3	275480
48350	DAVISBURG	30854	2827	7.7	20.1	40.0	19.5	12.8	74922	86833	93	94	2587	12.8	5.5	16.4	52.5	12.8	225860
48353	HARTLAND	33956	2165	7.3	16.2	40.6	22.1	13.9	79909	91180	95	96	2062	0.6	8.6	13.9	66.4	10.4	244905
48356	HIGHLAND	31011	3223	10.3	19.0	42.9	17.8	10.1	74897	85867	93	94	2941	0.5	1.9	32.1	55.8	9.7	201558
48357	HIGHLAND	27820	3224	15.7	23.0	37.7	15.8	7.8	61074	72711	85	85	3025	34.6	4.0	17.8	35.4	8.2	151287
48359	LAKE ORION	28961	3559	14.8	22.8	38.7	16.3	7.4	62800	75074	87	87	2725	12.4	4.3	32.6	45.1	5.5	176552
48360	LAKE ORION	40173	3725	7.0	10.4	34.0	28.5	20.2	97590	114694	98	99	3257	0.5	0.4	10.0	69.9	19.2	281761
48362	LAKE ORION	35595	5514	11.8	17.1	36.1	22.3	12.8	77631	91182	94	96	4610	0.7	2.4	25.9	55.2	15.8	223758
48363	OAKLAND	47466	1596	13.5	17.7	27.9	20.5	20.4	83342	100699	96	97	1540	16.8	5.2	9.0	35.8	33.3	293038
48367	LEONARD	34017	1708	11.7	18.2	37.3	19.5	13.4	73914	86532	93	94	1597	12.3	4.5	13.2	48.9	21.2	259149
48370	OXFORD	36908	561	11.8	18.5	31.0	18.7	20.0	80989	96883	95	97	513	0.0	1.8	16.4	54.2	27.7	289773
48371	OXFORD	30264	7576	11.3	20.2	39.7	21.3	7.6	70558	82828	91	92	6529	12.5	8.2	21.8	49.4	8.0	194306
48374	NOVI	47678	3800	4.1	9.7	22.2	25.9	38.2	125689	148100	100	100	3700	17.0	1.2	1.7	39.0	41.2	358920
48375	NOVI	40394	8278	7.5	17.6	37.5	21.8	15.6	80125	96161	95	96	5964	3.1	1.6	27.7	56.9	10.8	225228
48377	NOVI	35399	5815	13.6	31.8	36.1	11.8	6.7	53824	61891	78	75	3087	27.3	6.9	9.4	45.5	10.9	197546
48380	MILFORD	42019	2395	5.0	15.4	35.8	23.3	20.6	88922	103300	97	98	2283	0.4	6.3	20.5	47.2	25.7	270729
48381	MILFORD	32423	4780	13.1	19.6	35.7	20.9	10.8	71658	83315	92	93	4222	9.6	5.6	21.9	49.3	13.6	222140
48382	COMMERCE TOWNSHIP	42093	7384	8.1	14.8	35.9	22.4	18.9	85605	102471	96	97	7064	4.5	1.7	20.4	52.5	20.9	246824
48383	WHITE LAKE	31504	4413	8.4	18.9	38.8	21.5	12.4	76766	90582	94	95	4151	15.3	10.7	17.6	47.8	8.7	201162
48386	WHITE LAKE	32656	6226	11.8	21.4	37.3	18.6	10.9	71460	83279	92	93	5650	8.6	2.6	23.1	56.9	8.9	211434
48390	WALLED LAKE	33510	8620	13.6	20.6	39.6	17.4	8.8	66794	78960	90	90	6910	3.6	1.6	36.0	51.8	7.0	194363
48393	WIXOM	30695	7138	15.8	32.7	31.8	12.9	6.8	51923	61661	75	70	3695	14.7	5.5	13.3	58.9	7.6	218279
48401	APPLEGATE	19811	600	25.5	34.0	33.8	5.0	1.7	44150	49193	59	50	522	9.2	20.5	46.0	21.8	2.5	118956
48412	ATTICA	24452	2303	15.7	27.4	36.7	17.1	3.2	56727	62348	81	79	2122	3.4	7.2	37.7	48.9	2.8	178093
48413	BAD AXE	20479	3146	31.2	30.8	29.0	5.9	3.1	40219	42351	47	35	2506	14.1	29.5	43.3	12.1	1.0	96974
48414	BANCROFT	22069	940	18.7	30.9	37.7	9.5	3.3	50339	55508	73	66	847	6.3	11.9	55.5	25.0	1.3	137118
48415	BIRCH RUN	23008	3667	19.8	28.9	35.8	11.9	3.6	51099	57200	74	69	3153	11.5	15.5	53.2	19.3	0.5	119184
48416	BROWN CITY	18806	2012	23.7	33.7	32.6	7.6	2.4	44635	47843	60	52	1688	7.8	13.0	48.4	27.2	3.7	137808
48417	BURT	19990	1096	24.6	26.4	34.9	11.3	2.8	49002	53766	70	64	1008	10.9	20.7	55.5	12.0	0.9	111250
48418	BYRON	24784	1489	13.2	21.6	46.4	13.5	5.2	62047	68774	86	86	1383	1.6	6.7	46.8	43.0	2.0	167575
48419	CARSONVILLE	17695	1048	34.1	32.5	27.6	4.0	1.8	36947	40041	35	22	900	14.3	26.8	39.9	16.8	2.2	102817
48420	CLIO	24226	8417	20.1	28.1	36.9	11.5	3.4	51438	57608	75	70	6910	4.8	19.3	56.5	18.2	1.2	123564
48421	COLUMBIAVILLE	23863	2583	12.6	30.0	41.2	13.1	3.0	56809	62741	81	80	2337	2.7	7.6	50.6	36.7	2.4	157643
48422	CROSWELL	17650	2519	28.1	33.7	31.4	5.5	1.3	40816	43591	49	38	2113	10.9	19.6	49.4	19.1	1.1	116400
48423	DAVISON	25792	13438	21.7	29.9	32.8	11.3	4.3	48381	53480	69	62	9546	11.5	10.4	51.4	24.8	2.0	136053
48426	DECKER	19228	441	26.1	35.4	30.2	6.6	1.8	41766	44691	52	42	376	13.3	17.0	48.7	18.6	2.4	115123
48427	DECKERVILLE	19993	1288	33.0	33.7	26.1	4.4	2.8	36750	40353	35	22	1052	14.0	23.6	42.3	17.2	3.0	108285
48428	DRYDEN	30061	1746	6.8	19.8	43.9	20.7	8.8	73764	83096	93	94	1615	1.2	5.9	23.5	55.2	14.2	235870
48429	DURAND	21319	3827	23.9	28.9	35.9	8.8	2.6	46846	50938	66	59	3152	12.2	15.4	52.1	19.4	0.9	118740
48430	FENTON	31209	13865	14.4	20.9	37.4	18.4	8.9	65937	75097	89	90	11663	2.3	5.6	31.9	49.0	11.3	200998
48432	FILION	19256	356	26.7	36.0	31.2	4.5	1.7	40783	43627	49	38	310	11.0	31.6	41.9	13.9	1.6	99583
48433	FLUSHING	28615	10314	16.2	24.9	37.3	15.1	6.4	60842	67458	85	84	9045	5.7	7.7	55.3	28.2	3.0	149121
48435	FOSTORIA	21855	694	19.0	32.4	35.5	9.8	3.3	48856	52831	70	63	608	6.7	20.1	47.9	23.4	2.0	134250
48436	GAINES	25717	1210	10.2	22.1	44.5	16.8	6.5	68385	76304	91	92	1137	0.8	8.1	49.9	37.6	3.6	161769
48438	GOODRICH	31528	2228	10.0	16.3	39.6	21.2	12.8	78377	87704	95	96	2106	1.1	1.3	27.4	61.3	8.9	212335
48439	GRAND BLANC	32176	16927	14.3	22.1	38.1	16.9	8.5	64649	71829	88	89	12857	5.0	6.9	45.1	38.4	4.6	165577
48441	HARBOR BEACH	18239	1829	34.7	33.2	26.9	4.1	1.2	35769	37886	31	17	1489	15.3	26.7	39.1	16.5	2.4	98977
48442	HOLLY	27413	7133	14.6	23.9	37.5	16.2	7.7	62758	74434	87	87	6189	13.4	6.3	32.1	42.6	5.6	170759
48444	IMLAY CITY	21325	3372	25.2	27.9	32.1	10.7	4.2	47285	52775	67	60	2527	5.1	9.4	46.1	36.0	3.4	157539
48445	KINDE	17599	582	33.2	35.1	26.8	3.4	1.6	37206	40240	36	24	478	19.7	34.9	31.8	11.5	2.1	84884
48446	LAPEER	23625	11632	19.2	28.0	37.3	11.9	3.7	52573	58327	76	73	9179	7.8	7.3	45.4	36.2	3.3	157725
48449	LENNON	22044	1429	17.9	30.4	41.0	9.0	1.7	51363	57078	74	69	1320	28.9	12.0	41.7	17.1	0.3	103488
48450	LEXINGTON	24534	2345	29.1	35.0	27.6	5.8	2.6	40619	44495	48	37	1969	5.7	15.3	51.3	23.2	4.5	129751
48451	LINDEN	29542	4815	12.2	22.2	40.8	18.3	6.6	66430	75197	89	90	4264	7.5	5.8	34.8	46.3	5.7	179270
48453	MARLETTE	18407	1867	30.0	31.9	30.3	6.1	1.8	40666	43074	48	37	1457	9.2	20.7	50.7	17.2	2.2	116094
48454	MELVIN	20295	486	24.1	31.1	36.2	6.0	2.7	42867	44843	56	45	430	8.8	14.4	47.4	25.8	3.5	134921
48455	METAMORA	31397	3084	14.0	17.8	38.8	19.4	10.0	69960	77253	91	92	2853	6.2	3.9	24.5	51.7	13.6	224301
48456	MINDEN CITY	16463	416	31.3	33.4	29.8	4.1	1.4	37404	40827	37	25	366	14.8	26.0	37.2	17.5	4.6	102000
48457	MONTROSE	21438	3074	20.3	27.0	38.7	11.1	3.0	52333	59582	76	72	2733	11.1	20.5	57.7	10.1	0.6	108146
48458	MOUNT MORRIS	19653	10149	29.5	31.9	29.8	7.0	1.7	40221	45457	47	35	8011	37.2	27.6	30.0	5.0	0.3	68256
48460	NEW LOTHROP	27258	925	18.8	26.7	38.3	11.7	4.5	53670	59322	78	75	797	2.6	10.9	60.2	25.0	1.3	136300
48461	NORTH BRANCH	19893	2743	16.8	31.4	39.3	11.2	1.3	51278	57244	74	69	2354	3.7	12.9	48.6	32.9	1.9	149858
48462	ORTONVILLE	32146	4375	8.3	16.3	38.8	26.1	10.5	81697	96273	95	97	4076	1.7	1.8	20.1	65.5	10.8	238787
48463	OTISVILLE	23302	1776	13.9	30.5	39.9	13.9	1.9	55602	62240	80	77	1624	4.1	20.2	47.6	27.5	0.6	135825
48464	OTTER LAKE	21511	856	18.1	30.0	41.0	8.1	2.8	51177	56358	74	69	756	3.3	9.7	59.4	25.9	1.7	138669
48465	PALMS	19064	318	30.8	33.3	30.5	2.8	2.5	38102	41173	40	27	286	13.3	22.7	41.6	16.4	5.9	110119
48466	PECK	18130	623	28.6	34.4	30.2	5.1	1.8	40872	43630	49	38	517	13.7	20.3	45.8	17.6	2.5	111887
48467	PORT AUSTIN	21620	1295	34.9	32.6	25.6	5.1	1.9	36595	39961	34	21	1120	9.6	25.1	41.0	19.2	5.2	112500
48468	PORT HOPE	21264	608	30.8	35.0	26.5	4.8	3.0	37558	41389	38	25	558	16.5	28.9	38.2	12.9	3.6	95909
48469	PORT SANILAC	20675	646	36.8	31.6	26.5	4.0	1.1	36483	40117	33	21	550	14.2	15.3	49.1	18.7	2.7	119608
48470	RUTH	18064	353	28.9	34.3	30.9	4.3	1.7	37436	40000	37	25	310	13.9	20.0	41.0	21.6	3.6	114151
48471	SANDUSKY	19316	2369	32.0	32.0	29.4	4.8	1.9	39769	42268	45	33	1786	11.7	23.4	49.2	14.1	1.8	108596
48472	SNOVER	19653	736	26.8	34.7	29.9	5.8	2.9	40502	43380	48	36	628	13.1	23.4	48.7	13.2	1.6	104932
48473	SWARTZ CREEK	26296	8026	16.4	26.2	39.0	14.5	3.9	57763	64253	82	81	7093	10.4	7.3	53.9	27.2	1.3	142079
48475	UBLY	18900	1055	28.9	33.9	31.0	4.7	1.4	38707	41535	42	29	901	12.9	28.9	42.2	14.1	2.0	100353
48502	FLINT	14761	198	56.1	35.4	5.6	1.5	1.5	20607	22865	2	1	23	39.1	30.4	30.4	0.0	0.0	58333
48503	FLINT	20537	12441	40.6	26.5	22.8	6.6	3.6	32346	36797	19	9	6835	24.2	39.7	28.7	6.4	1.0	75643
48504	FLINT	17029	14621	38.0	29.3	25.2	6.0	1.6	34203	38269	25	12	9448	36.9	43.6	16.9	2.2	0.4	58967
48505	FLINT	13901	12275	50.2	26.0	18.0	4.2	1.6	24879	28484	4	2	6739	60.1	32.7	6.2	0.7	0.3	43232
48506	FLINT	18386	13506	34.6	30.0	27.0	6.8	1.5	36656	41382	34	22	9674	34.4	31.2	30.1	4.1	0.3	69506
48507	FLINT	22976	14291	27.9	29.9	31.9	7.7	2.6	42542	47515	55	44	9658	19.1	35.2	38.7	6.7	0.3	85523
48509	BURTON	27092	3939	14.4	28.1	41.3	11.6	4.7	56953	63595	82	80	3690	7.6	24.0	55.7	12.2	0.5	108418
48519	BURTON	22495	3099	24.9	27.6	36.3	8.2	3.1	47974	53435	68	61	2441	8.8	30.2	50.6	10.4	0.0	102471
48529	BURTON	18679	4528	30.3	32.6	30.8	5.0	1.4	39326	43560	44	31	2987	25.4	52.2	20.8	1.7	0.0	67422
48532	FLINT	27030	8794	27.8	29.4	29.2	8.3	5.2	43845	48972	58	49	5755	9.7	23.4	43.7	21.1	2.1	115285
48601	SAGINAW	15382	16993	45.7	28.8	18.9	4.7	1.9	27708	31354	8	3	10901	52.2	28.0	17.2	2.5	0.1	48170
48602	SAGINAW	18997	13243	32.4	32.8	27.6	5.8	1.4	36968	41846	35	23	8882	24.2	45.2	27.7	2.7	0.2	69883
48603	SAGINAW	28986	17511	23.2	28.6	30.6	12.0	5.6	47830	52557	68	61	11839	5.3	10.0	55.5	27.0	2.3	142591
	MICHIGAN	25281		23.8	27.4	32.3	10.9	5.5	48729	54505				10.7	16.0	40.3	28.0	5.0	134769
	UNITED STATES	25866		24.7	27.1	30.8	10.9	6.5	48124	56710				10.9	15.0	33.7	30.1	10.4	145905

# ZIP CODE / POST OFFICE NAME	Auto Loan	Home Loan	Investments	Retirement Plans	Home Repair	Lawn & Garden	Computers & Hardware	Major Appliances	TV, Radio, Sound Equipment	Furniture	Dine out/Carry out	Sports Equipment	Fees & Tickets	Toys & Games	Travel	Cable TV	Apparel & Services	Auto Repairs	Health Insurance	Pets & Supplies
	FINANCIAL SERVICES				**THE HOME**						**ENTERTAINMENT**						**PERSONAL**			
48334 FARMINGTON	118	136	165	135	133	143	132	129	128	132	161	148	139	165	135	128	160	129	124	141
48335 FARMINGTON	110	119	172	127	115	123	125	117	122	125	154	140	129	159	125	120	153	121	108	129
48336 FARMINGTON	102	113	133	115	111	116	113	110	109	112	137	129	116	140	113	107	135	111	103	120
48340 PONTIAC	62	59	68	60	57	62	65	62	65	64	82	73	64	81	62	64	80	65	60	69
48341 PONTIAC	78	76	88	75	75	83	81	79	83	81	104	90	82	104	80	84	102	81	80	88
48342 PONTIAC	63	58	67	55	56	64	64	62	68	64	85	70	64	83	63	69	83	64	65	70
48346 CLARKSTON	124	140	149	142	137	139	131	131	124	132	156	153	135	159	131	120	154	129	119	145
48348 CLARKSTON	156	187	196	190	182	184	167	166	155	169	195	192	179	202	169	150	195	160	149	185
48350 DAVISBURG	122	138	137	138	136	137	125	127	118	126	148	148	130	152	127	115	147	123	117	143
48353 HARTLAND	127	152	156	151	150	149	137	138	128	137	161	161	143	169	139	125	160	133	125	153
48356 HIGHLAND	113	135	140	135	133	132	122	122	114	121	143	143	128	151	124	111	142	118	111	137
48357 HIGHLAND	111	116	106	114	115	118	107	111	104	108	130	130	107	130	108	103	127	109	106	129
48359 LAKE ORION	106	114	109	116	111	111	106	107	100	108	126	126	107	127	104	96	124	105	96	120
48360 LAKE ORION	160	186	187	193	178	175	167	165	153	172	195	193	175	198	165	144	193	160	142	181
48362 LAKE ORION	126	146	157	150	142	143	136	133	127	137	160	156	142	164	136	122	159	131	119	147
48363 OAKLAND	179	198	199	198	195	202	181	184	173	184	217	211	188	217	184	170	214	180	173	208
48367 LEONARD	124	155	164	155	152	150	138	137	128	137	161	161	147	171	141	124	160	132	123	152
48370 OXFORD	140	173	185	173	171	169	155	155	144	155	181	181	165	192	159	140	181	149	139	171
48371 OXFORD	118	126	122	127	124	127	119	120	115	119	143	140	121	145	118	111	140	118	113	135
48374 NOVI	223	261	264	272	250	246	234	230	213	241	271	268	246	276	231	201	270	223	198	253
48375 NOVI	134	157	178	163	153	154	148	144	138	149	174	169	155	178	148	132	173	142	128	157
48377 NOVI	105	97	98	100	95	101	100	100	99	102	125	119	97	118	97	95	121	103	95	115
48380 MILFORD	163	198	208	200	193	194	176	175	163	178	206	203	189	214	179	158	206	169	157	195
48381 MILFORD	121	133	132	133	130	132	125	125	119	126	149	147	127	152	124	115	147	124	115	140
48382 COMMERCE TOWNSHIP	160	193	203	197	188	188	173	170	159	175	201	198	185	209	175	154	201	165	152	189
48383 WHITE LAKE	125	147	148	151	142	138	132	131	121	135	154	154	138	159	131	115	153	127	114	144
48386 WHITE LAKE	117	134	134	133	132	132	122	123	116	123	145	144	126	149	123	112	143	120	113	138
48390 WALLED LAKE	108	128	141	129	124	125	119	117	112	120	141	138	125	147	120	108	140	115	105	128
48393 WIXOM	102	97	106	103	94	98	105	100	101	104	128	121	102	123	99	95	125	104	90	112
48401 APPLEGATE	90	66	39	59	75	84	63	77	73	63	87	91	56	84	66	78	80	76	92	106
48412 ATTICA	111	98	75	94	104	112	91	101	97	91	118	120	89	120	94	99	112	98	109	130
48413 BAD AXE	84	69	50	65	74	83	68	76	74	67	89	89	64	89	69	77	84	75	86	97
48414 BANCROFT	99	88	67	84	93	100	81	90	86	81	105	108	80	107	84	89	100	88	98	116
48415 BIRCH RUN	89	89	81	87	91	96	84	88	85	83	105	103	85	108	86	86	101	86	90	104
48416 BROWN CITY	84	74	57	71	78	85	71	77	75	70	91	91	69	92	72	77	86	76	84	98
48417 BURT	92	82	62	78	87	93	76	84	80	76	98	100	74	100	78	82	93	82	91	108
48418 BYRON	106	107	95	104	110	114	98	104	98	97	121	123	99	126	100	99	117	101	105	126
48419 CARSONVILLE	80	60	35	53	67	75	57	69	65	57	78	81	50	75	59	70	72	68	82	95
48420 CLIO	91	93	88	90	94	99	88	91	88	87	109	106	89	112	90	88	106	89	92	107
48421 COLUMBIAVILLE	102	99	84	95	102	107	91	97	93	91	114	115	91	117	93	93	109	95	100	121
48422 CROSWELL	76	65	49	61	69	76	63	70	68	62	83	81	60	83	64	71	78	68	78	88
48423 DAVISON	87	89	93	89	88	94	88	88	87	88	108	103	88	109	87	86	106	88	86	101
48426 DECKER	83	74	57	71	78	84	69	76	73	69	89	91	67	91	71	75	84	74	82	98
48427 DECKERVILLE	76	68	56	64	73	80	65	72	70	64	85	83	64	88	68	74	81	70	80	90
48428 DRYDEN	113	139	146	139	137	135	124	124	115	123	145	145	132	154	127	112	144	120	112	138
48429 DURAND	81	80	73	77	82	87	76	80	77	75	95	93	76	98	78	78	92	78	82	95
48430 FENTON	109	123	130	124	121	124	116	115	111	116	139	135	120	143	117	108	137	114	107	128
48432 FILION	78	68	51	64	72	78	63	71	68	63	82	84	61	83	65	70	78	69	77	91
48433 FLUSHING	97	111	116	109	111	115	103	104	100	102	124	120	108	130	106	100	123	101	101	117
48435 FOSTORIA	100	90	68	85	94	100	83	92	88	84	107	109	81	108	85	89	102	90	98	117
48436 GAINES	102	120	122	119	119	119	108	109	102	107	127	128	113	135	110	100	126	105	101	124
48438 GOODRICH	122	149	154	150	145	142	133	132	123	134	155	155	140	163	134	118	154	128	117	146
48439 GRAND BLANC	109	120	130	122	118	122	115	114	110	115	139	133	119	140	115	107	137	113	106	127
48441 HARBOR BEACH	77	55	32	51	62	72	58	67	66	56	78	78	50	74	58	70	71	67	81	87
48442 HOLLY	104	114	112	114	113	114	106	108	101	107	127	126	108	129	106	98	125	106	99	121
48444 IMLAY CITY	90	80	70	79	84	91	80	85	83	79	101	100	77	100	80	84	96	84	90	103
48445 KINDE	66	61	52	57	64	70	58	63	62	57	75	73	57	78	60	64	71	61	69	78
48446 LAPEER	87	89	85	88	90	94	85	87	85	84	105	102	86	108	86	84	102	86	86	101
48449 LENNON	91	85	70	81	87	93	79	86	82	81	100	101	78	101	81	82	96	84	89	105
48450 LEXINGTON	90	72	50	66	81	90	68	81	76	67	91	95	62	90	72	81	85	79	94	110
48451 LINDEN	111	123	123	122	122	124	112	115	108	114	135	133	116	137	114	106	133	112	108	130
48453 MARLETTE	79	68	53	67	72	79	67	73	71	66	86	85	65	87	68	72	81	71	79	90
48454 MELVIN	89	79	60	75	84	90	73	81	78	73	95	97	72	97	75	80	90	79	88	105
48455 METAMORA	120	134	132	132	135	137	121	125	117	121	146	147	126	153	124	116	143	121	120	145
48456 MINDEN CITY	82	59	34	53	67	76	57	69	66	57	78	82	50	76	59	70	72	68	83	96
48457 MONTROSE	94	88	73	84	92	98	82	89	86	81	105	105	81	108	84	88	100	86	94	111
48458 MOUNT MORRIS	72	70	68	68	71	77	69	71	71	69	87	81	69	86	70	71	84	71	73	82
48460 NEW LOTHROP	117	104	79	99	110	118	96	106	102	96	124	127	94	127	99	105	118	104	115	137
48461 NORTH BRANCH	90	86	75	86	87	91	83	87	83	83	103	102	82	103	83	82	99	86	86	102
48462 ORTONVILLE	124	151	159	152	148	146	135	135	125	135	158	158	143	167	138	121	158	130	120	149
48463 OTISVILLE	98	91	75	87	94	101	85	92	89	85	109	109	84	110	87	90	104	90	97	114
48464 OTTER LAKE	95	84	64	80	89	96	78	87	83	78	101	103	77	103	80	85	96	84	94	112
48465 PALMS	79	61	39	56	69	77	58	70	65	57	77	82	51	77	61	69	72	69	82	95
48466 PECK	79	69	51	65	73	79	64	72	69	64	83	85	62	84	66	71	79	70	78	93
48467 PORT AUSTIN	76	60	42	55	68	76	57	68	64	56	76	80	51	75	60	68	71	67	80	93
48468 PORT HOPE	85	64	40	59	73	82	61	75	70	61	82	88	54	81	65	74	76	73	88	103
48469 PORT SANILAC	73	57	39	52	65	72	54	65	61	54	73	76	48	72	58	65	67	64	77	89
48470 RUTH	81	61	39	59	68	77	61	71	68	61	81	84	55	80	63	71	75	70	82	93
48471 SANDUSKY	79	65	47	63	70	77	64	71	70	64	84	83	61	84	65	72	79	70	79	90
48472 SNOVER	91	78	58	74	83	90	73	82	78	73	95	97	70	96	75	81	90	80	90	106
48473 SWARTZ CREEK	94	99	97	97	100	105	94	96	93	93	115	112	96	118	95	93	112	94	96	111
48475 UBLY	80	63	44	61	68	77	63	71	70	63	84	83	59	82	64	72	78	70	80	90
48502 FLINT	27	21	27	24	21	24	29	26	29	27	36	33	27	34	26	27	35	29	24	29
48503 FLINT	62	61	72	59	60	67	66	63	68	65	85	73	66	84	65	69	83	65	65	71
48504 FLINT	63	59	67	56	58	66	62	62	66	63	82	69	63	81	62	68	80	63	65	70
48505 FLINT	55	46	53	42	45	54	52	52	58	53	71	57	51	66	51	61	68	54	58	60
48506 FLINT	64	63	65	61	63	68	65	65	67	64	83	75	65	84	65	67	80	65	66	73
48507 FLINT	72	72	77	71	72	79	74	73	75	73	94	85	75	95	74	76	91	74	75	83
48509 BURTON	95	106	109	102	106	112	99	101	98	98	122	116	103	128	102	99	120	98	100	114
48519 BURTON	78	81	85	80	81	86	80	80	80	79	99	92	81	101	80	80	96	80	80	90
48529 BURTON	65	65	65	64	65	70	66	66	67	65	83	77	66	83	66	66	80	66	66	74
48532 FLINT	84	87	96	87	87	94	89	88	88	87	110	101	90	112	89	88	108	88	87	97
48601 SAGINAW	58	53	60	50	52	60	56	56	61	58	76	63	57	74	56	63	73	58	61	64
48602 SAGINAW	62	62	68	61	62	67	66	64	67	64	83	74	66	84	65	67	81	65	65	70
48603 SAGINAW	85	90	104	90	90	98	91	90	91	90	113	104	93	115	93	91	111	91	90	100
MICHIGAN	91	91	93	89	91	98	90	91	91	90	113	106	90	113	90	91	109	91	92	105
UNITED STATES	100	100	100	100	100	100	100	100	100	100	100	100	100	100	100	100	100	100	100	100

ZIP CODE #	POST OFFICE NAME	COUNTY FIPS CODE	POPULATION 2000	2004	2009	2000-2004 ANNUAL RATE % Rate	State Centile	HOUSEHOLDS 2000	2004	2009	% Annual Rate 2000-2004	2004 Average HH Size	FAMILIES 2000	2004	% Annual Rate 2000-2004
48604	SAGINAW	145	12225	12477	12621	0.5	42	4464	4652	4795	1.0	2.49	3101	3176	0.6
48607	SAGINAW	145	2528	2384	2345	-1.4	1	1037	979	972	-1.4	2.26	496	456	-2.0
48609	SAGINAW	145	12631	12929	13052	0.6	44	4897	5141	5304	1.2	2.48	3691	3828	0.9
48610	ALGER	051	3558	3772	3946	1.4	77	1513	1647	1763	2.0	2.27	1063	1141	1.7
48611	AUBURN	017	6173	6375	6464	0.8	55	2316	2452	2530	1.4	2.58	1718	1796	1.1
48612	BEAVERTON	051	9221	9735	10458	1.3	74	3709	3999	4385	1.8	2.42	2685	2856	1.5
48613	BENTLEY	017	1191	1237	1263	0.9	61	415	443	461	1.6	2.59	323	340	1.2
48614	BRANT	145	1266	1271	1266	0.1	26	451	464	472	0.7	2.73	353	359	0.4
48615	BRECKENRIDGE	057	3045	3144	3239	0.8	55	1175	1230	1286	1.1	2.55	857	887	0.8
48616	CHESANING	145	7320	7243	7212	-0.3	14	2772	2805	2849	0.3	2.55	2084	2086	0.0
48617	CLARE	035	8664	8865	9250	0.5	44	3315	3447	3662	0.9	2.52	2275	2339	0.7
48618	COLEMAN	111	5466	5517	5642	0.2	30	2080	2143	2229	0.7	2.57	1542	1568	0.4
48619	COMINS	135	707	713	752	0.2	29	295	302	324	0.6	2.36	215	218	0.3
48620	EDENVILLE	111	50	49	50	-0.5	9	22	22	23	0.0	2.23	17	17	0.0
48621	FAIRVIEW	135	1400	1476	1592	1.3	73	554	593	649	1.6	2.42	388	410	1.3
48622	FARWELL	035	6185	6355	6642	0.6	48	2404	2516	2676	1.1	2.48	1765	1827	0.8
48623	FREELAND	145	11663	12538	13025	1.7	85	3772	4170	4431	2.4	2.68	2989	3269	2.1
48624	GLADWIN	051	16056	16919	18067	1.2	73	6523	7037	7689	1.8	2.36	4703	5013	1.5
48625	HARRISON	035	13584	14081	14583	0.9	59	5595	5928	6259	1.4	2.34	3858	4026	1.0
48626	HEMLOCK	145	6312	6309	6312	0.0	22	2274	2316	2360	0.4	2.72	1804	1820	0.2
48628	HOPE	111	1851	1879	1934	0.4	36	741	774	815	1.0	2.42	559	574	0.6
48629	HOUGHTON LAKE	143	8364	8841	9443	1.3	75	3663	3937	4273	1.7	2.21	2494	2646	1.4
48631	KAWKAWLIN	017	4647	4659	4655	0.1	25	1695	1741	1769	0.6	2.64	1308	1327	0.3
48632	LAKE	035	5502	5623	5834	0.5	43	2346	2448	2586	1.0	2.29	1642	1686	0.6
48634	LINWOOD	017	4695	4714	4722	0.1	27	1755	1808	1843	0.7	2.57	1373	1397	0.4
48635	LUPTON	129	1724	1722	1733	0.0	21	747	765	784	0.6	2.24	526	531	0.2
48636	LUZERNE	135	827	880	954	1.5	78	347	375	412	1.8	2.35	235	250	1.5
48637	MERRILL	145	3442	3500	3539	0.4	38	1277	1325	1366	0.9	2.63	996	1023	0.6
48640	MIDLAND	111	32584	32761	33324	0.1	27	12524	12818	13253	0.6	2.47	8658	8727	0.2
48642	MIDLAND	111	31967	33300	34484	1.0	64	12286	13020	13707	1.4	2.53	8780	9207	1.1
48647	MIO	135	4846	5047	5416	1.0	63	1954	2058	2237	1.2	2.44	1356	1410	0.9
48649	OAKLEY	145	2083	2058	2044	-0.3	13	767	775	785	0.2	2.65	578	578	0.0
48650	PINCONNING	017	7585	7583	7582	0.0	22	2922	2996	3049	0.6	2.52	2148	2172	0.3
48651	PRUDENVILLE	143	4862	5052	5310	0.9	61	2202	2315	2465	1.2	2.18	1509	1562	0.8
48652	RHODES	051	1523	1671	1801	2.2	92	571	641	705	2.8	2.60	426	472	2.4
48653	ROSCOMMON	143	10284	10744	11305	1.0	66	4352	4642	4974	1.5	2.28	3041	3193	1.0
48654	ROSE CITY	129	2789	2857	2915	0.6	45	1066	1116	1160	1.1	2.45	752	778	0.8
48655	SAINT CHARLES	145	6266	6310	6318	0.2	28	2344	2408	2458	0.6	2.61	1813	1844	0.4
48656	SAINT HELEN	143	4373	4534	4762	0.9	59	1990	2093	2229	1.2	2.16	1307	1353	0.8
48657	SANFORD	111	7684	8014	8287	1.0	65	3024	3225	3395	1.5	2.48	2278	2394	1.2
48658	STANDISH	011	5946	5996	6092	0.2	29	2081	2143	2226	0.7	2.49	1436	1458	0.4
48659	STERLING	011	3147	3240	3345	0.7	51	1172	1231	1298	1.2	2.56	853	885	0.9
48661	WEST BRANCH	129	9724	9797	9879	0.2	29	3939	4055	4160	0.7	2.38	2756	2801	0.4
48662	WHEELER	057	1484	1555	1610	1.1	68	546	586	619	1.7	2.64	429	456	1.5
48701	AKRON	157	1610	1564	1554	-0.7	6	629	624	632	-0.2	2.47	461	451	-0.5
48703	AU GRES	011	3407	3471	3551	0.4	40	1526	1592	1667	1.0	2.17	1039	1068	0.7
48705	BARTON CITY	001	642	727	820	3.0	97	292	336	386	3.4	2.15	200	226	2.9
48706	BAY CITY	017	40921	41037	41096	0.1	25	16683	17119	17427	0.6	2.37	11413	11534	0.3
48708	BAY CITY	017	28910	28224	27900	-0.6	8	11771	11700	11724	-0.1	2.37	7373	7198	-0.6
48710	UNIVERSITY CENTER	017	7	8	8	3.2	98	1	1	1	0.0	3.00	1	1	0.0
48720	BAY PORT	063	1328	1372	1407	0.8	55	544	574	601	1.3	2.37	378	393	0.9
48721	BLACK RIVER	001	454	459	486	0.3	32	189	194	208	0.6	2.37	137	139	0.3
48722	BRIDGEPORT	145	3200	3127	3102	-0.5	8	1247	1249	1266	0.0	2.49	924	915	-0.2
48723	CARO	157	12929	12970	13027	0.1	25	4796	4901	5014	0.5	2.49	3330	3358	0.2
48725	CASEVILLE	063	2735	2945	3090	1.8	86	1300	1433	1535	2.3	2.04	833	901	1.9
48726	CASS CITY	157	6158	6152	6194	0.0	22	2386	2427	2487	0.4	2.49	1702	1711	0.1
48727	CLIFFORD	087	1276	1368	1441	1.7	84	458	505	544	2.3	2.71	345	376	2.1
48728	CURRAN	001	561	668	773	4.2	99	285	345	406	4.6	1.93	190	227	4.3
48729	DEFORD	157	1776	1820	1844	0.6	45	633	662	683	1.1	2.73	494	511	0.8
48730	EAST TAWAS	069	5108	5036	5012	-0.3	12	2330	2360	2413	0.3	2.13	1485	1481	-0.1
48731	ELKTON	063	1957	1936	1951	-0.3	14	749	758	781	0.3	2.51	540	540	0.0
48732	ESSEXVILLE	017	11955	11903	11853	-0.1	19	4944	5024	5079	0.4	2.31	3255	3247	-0.1
48733	FAIRGROVE	157	1965	1958	1964	-0.1	20	745	758	775	0.4	2.54	559	562	0.1
48734	FRANKENMUTH	145	7244	7212	7214	-0.1	19	2961	3001	3057	0.3	2.32	2030	2025	-0.1
48735	GAGETOWN	157	819	841	853	0.6	48	305	321	332	1.2	2.57	220	228	0.8
48737	GLENNIE	001	1376	1371	1456	-0.1	20	619	630	682	0.4	2.16	428	430	0.1
48738	GREENBUSH	001	1258	1300	1410	0.8	56	594	619	680	1.0	2.09	405	415	0.6
48739	HALE	069	4563	4520	4495	-0.2	15	1975	2011	2052	0.4	2.24	1369	1373	0.1
48740	HARRISVILLE	001	2526	2653	2867	1.2	70	1075	1152	1272	1.6	2.20	726	767	1.3
48741	KINGSTON	157	2183	2184	2189	0.0	23	788	803	819	0.4	2.67	617	622	0.2
48742	LINCOLN	001	1778	1879	2067	1.3	75	781	852	962	2.1	2.15	534	575	1.8
48743	LONG LAKE	069	60	64	67	1.5	80	31	34	36	2.2	1.88	21	22	1.1
48744	MAYVILLE	157	4592	4702	4786	0.6	45	1634	1709	1775	1.1	2.72	1261	1305	0.8
48745	MIKADO	001	1551	1664	1822	1.7	84	613	666	740	2.0	2.47	455	488	1.7
48746	MILLINGTON	157	9270	9307	9366	0.1	26	3302	3385	3472	0.6	2.74	2632	2672	0.4
48747	MUNGER	017	1580	1572	1567	-0.1	19	549	560	567	0.5	2.63	426	429	0.2
48748	NATIONAL CITY	069	1910	1930	1929	0.3	32	870	901	924	0.8	2.14	610	624	0.5
48749	OMER	011	950	941	951	-0.2	15	385	391	404	0.4	2.40	271	272	0.1
48750	OSCODA	069	9101	9111	9151	0.0	23	3920	4031	4159	0.7	2.25	2577	2608	0.3
48754	OWENDALE	063	1351	1376	1399	0.4	40	496	516	537	0.9	2.54	361	371	0.6
48755	PIGEON	063	3116	3242	3347	0.9	62	1278	1356	1431	1.4	2.34	931	977	1.1
48756	PRESCOTT	129	4584	4711	4791	0.7	49	1905	1993	2059	1.1	2.36	1323	1363	0.7
48757	REESE	157	4005	4057	4091	0.3	34	1547	1604	1650	0.9	2.52	1158	1184	0.5
48759	SEBEWAING	063	3453	3429	3467	-0.2	18	1464	1484	1533	0.3	2.30	981	980	0.0
48760	SILVERWOOD	087	1063	1108	1143	1.0	65	385	411	432	1.6	2.68	305	322	1.3
48761	SOUTH BRANCH	001	1267	1323	1382	1.0	66	588	634	678	1.8	2.08	398	420	1.3
48762	SPRUCE	001	1092	1319	1528	4.5	100	480	591	698	5.0	2.23	337	410	4.7
48763	TAWAS CITY	069	4887	4914	4922	0.1	27	1922	1983	2040	0.7	2.31	1338	1366	0.5
48765	TURNER	011	750	761	773	0.3	36	293	303	314	0.8	2.51	213	218	0.6
48766	TWINING	011	1509	1500	1519	-0.1	18	552	558	576	0.3	2.69	405	405	0.0
48767	UNIONVILLE	157	2308	2309	2315	0.0	23	870	887	907	0.5	2.56	656	661	0.2
48768	VASSAR	157	10311	10334	10380	0.1	24	3698	3784	3875	0.6	2.65	2818	2851	0.3
48770	WHITTEMORE	069	2195	2135	2109	-0.7	7	863	861	873	-0.1	2.48	616	606	-0.4
48801	ALMA	057	12603	12738	12919	0.3	32	4464	4601	4756	0.7	2.42	2987	3032	0.4
48806	ASHLEY	057	1714	1745	1772	0.4	39	641	668	693	1.0	2.57	491	506	0.7
	MICHIGAN					0.6					1.0	2.52			0.6
	UNITED STATES					1.2					1.3	2.58			1.1

ZIP CODE		RACE (%)						% Hispanic Origin		2004 AGE DISTRIBUTION (%)										MEDIAN AGE		
#	POST OFFICE NAME	White		Black		Asian/Pacific																
		2000	2004	2000	2004	2000	2004	2000	2004	0-4	5-9	10-14	15-19	20-24	25-44	45-64	65-84	85+	18+	2004	% 2004 Males	% 2004 Females
48604	SAGINAW	86.0	83.3	7.3	8.8	1.1	1.4	8.0	9.3	6.8	6.4	6.5	9.7	9.9	25.8	21.9	11.3	1.7	76.8	33.5	48.2	51.8
48607	SAGINAW	14.6	12.5	76.9	78.9	0.6	0.6	10.2	10.3	7.7	7.6	8.9	7.7	7.1	23.8	25.0	10.8	1.5	71.3	35.0	49.8	50.3
48609	SAGINAW	97.1	96.5	0.5	0.7	0.5	0.7	2.9	3.5	5.1	5.6	6.7	6.7	5.5	23.5	31.5	13.5	1.9	78.2	43.0	48.4	51.6
48610	ALGER	97.3	97.1	0.1	0.2	0.2	0.3	0.9	1.0	5.0	5.3	6.1	5.8	5.0	21.7	30.1	19.5	1.6	79.8	45.7	50.1	49.9
48611	AUBURN	97.9	97.6	0.3	0.3	0.3	0.4	1.8	2.1	6.4	6.5	7.2	7.0	6.4	27.8	26.2	11.0	1.3	75.4	38.2	50.1	49.9
48612	BEAVERTON	97.8	97.6	0.2	0.2	0.2	0.2	1.3	1.4	5.9	6.0	6.7	6.2	5.7	24.7	28.7	14.8	1.4	77.5	41.7	50.2	49.8
48613	BENTLEY	98.4	98.1	0.2	0.2	0.0	0.0	8.5	9.8	6.1	6.6	8.7	7.5	5.8	28.1	26.5	9.8	1.1	74.0	37.6	50.4	49.6
48614	BRANT	97.6	97.2	0.2	0.2	0.4	0.5	1.5	1.8	6.7	6.9	7.6	7.3	7.0	28.4	26.8	8.7	0.8	74.1	36.2	49.2	50.8
48615	BRECKENRIDGE	96.5	96.2	0.1	0.1	0.1	0.1	3.9	4.5	6.7	6.8	7.8	7.3	7.0	27.7	24.5	10.6	1.7	74.1	36.5	50.2	49.8
48616	CHESANING	97.4	96.8	0.3	0.3	0.2	0.2	3.7	4.5	6.3	6.4	6.9	6.9	6.0	27.0	26.8	11.9	1.9	76.1	39.0	49.4	50.6
48617	CLARE	97.4	97.1	0.3	0.3	0.3	0.3	1.2	1.4	7.5	7.1	7.7	7.2	7.2	24.9	23.5	12.8	2.2	73.5	36.6	48.2	51.8
48618	COLEMAN	97.4	97.2	0.1	0.1	0.2	0.2	1.1	1.3	6.6	6.8	7.6	6.7	6.5	28.3	24.6	11.7	1.3	74.9	37.3	50.4	49.6
48619	COMINS	98.6	98.6	0.1	0.1	0.0	0.0	0.6	0.6	3.8	4.1	5.6	5.1	4.8	17.7	35.6	22.2	1.3	83.3	50.2	50.1	49.9
48620	EDENVILLE	98.0	100.0	0.0	0.0	0.0	0.0	0.0	0.0	4.1	6.1	6.1	4.1	6.1	24.5	32.7	16.3	0.0	83.7	44.4	46.9	53.1
48621	FAIRVIEW	98.1	98.0	0.1	0.1	0.0	0.0	0.4	0.5	5.4	5.7	6.7	6.2	5.8	19.0	28.4	19.0	3.9	78.3	45.9	46.4	53.6
48622	FARWELL	97.1	96.8	0.2	0.3	0.4	0.5	1.6	1.8	5.6	5.8	6.5	6.2	5.6	24.8	28.4	15.6	1.5	78.1	42.0	49.4	50.6
48623	FREELAND	90.8	89.4	6.0	7.0	0.6	0.7	2.6	3.1	6.2	6.6	7.2	6.0	6.1	33.1	25.9	8.0	0.9	76.3	37.0	54.7	45.3
48624	GLADWIN	97.6	97.3	0.1	0.1	0.4	0.5	0.8	0.9	5.4	5.7	6.3	6.1	5.0	21.7	28.2	19.6	2.0	78.6	44.8	49.9	50.1
48625	HARRISON	97.0	96.8	0.5	0.5	0.3	0.4	1.2	1.4	5.7	6.0	6.8	6.2	5.3	23.3	28.1	17.3	1.4	77.7	42.6	50.2	49.8
48626	HEMLOCK	98.0	97.6	0.1	0.1	0.2	0.3	2.0	2.5	6.7	7.1	7.7	6.7	5.8	26.6	27.8	10.5	1.1	74.4	38.6	49.2	50.8
48628	HOPE	98.3	98.1	0.3	0.3	0.1	0.2	0.5	0.6	5.5	6.0	6.8	5.4	4.8	26.0	30.4	14.2	1.0	78.3	42.2	50.2	49.8
48629	HOUGHTON LAKE	97.9	97.7	0.5	0.6	0.2	0.3	0.8	1.0	4.6	5.4	6.1	5.3	4.6	20.2	31.2	20.5	2.2	80.7	47.7	48.8	51.2
48631	KAWKAWLIN	96.7	96.3	0.4	0.4	0.3	0.4	2.0	2.3	6.4	6.6	6.9	6.3	5.7	26.5	28.9	11.1	1.7	76.4	40.0	49.7	50.3
48632	LAKE	97.7	97.5	0.2	0.2	0.2	0.2	1.3	1.5	4.9	5.3	6.0	5.8	4.9	21.6	30.9	19.2	1.4	80.1	46.0	50.5	49.5
48634	LINWOOD	97.3	97.1	0.6	0.6	0.3	0.4	1.7	2.0	6.1	6.3	6.6	6.4	5.6	26.5	29.7	11.5	1.4	77.2	40.4	50.5	49.5
48635	LUPTON	98.4	98.3	0.1	0.1	0.2	0.2	1.3	1.4	4.4	4.5	5.4	5.4	4.7	19.1	32.0	22.8	1.8	81.9	49.6	50.6	49.4
48636	LUZERNE	98.7	98.6	0.0	0.0	0.2	0.2	0.5	0.5	5.3	5.1	5.6	5.7	5.3	18.5	31.5	21.3	1.7	80.6	47.9	49.3	50.7
48637	MERRILL	97.8	97.3	0.1	0.1	0.2	0.2	2.6	3.2	6.1	6.4	7.1	6.8	5.8	27.2	27.5	11.6	1.5	76.3	39.2	49.6	50.4
48640	MIDLAND	94.8	94.1	1.3	1.4	2.0	2.6	1.6	1.8	6.3	6.5	7.4	8.1	7.9	26.0	24.9	11.1	2.0	75.7	37.1	49.2	50.8
48642	MIDLAND	94.9	94.2	1.3	1.4	1.8	2.3	1.8	2.1	6.8	7.1	8.1	7.2	6.1	27.8	24.8	10.4	1.7	73.3	37.1	48.2	51.9
48647	MIO	97.4	97.2	0.1	0.1	0.1	0.1	1.2	1.4	5.6	5.7	7.2	7.2	4.9	21.7	28.9	17.0	1.9	76.9	43.5	49.6	50.4
48649	OAKLEY	97.5	97.0	0.5	0.6	0.3	0.3	2.7	3.4	6.3	6.5	7.5	7.5	6.1	28.0	25.6	11.4	1.2	75.1	37.8	50.1	49.9
48650	PINCONNING	97.1	96.8	0.3	0.3	0.2	0.2	1.9	2.2	5.8	6.3	6.9	6.3	6.2	27.0	28.4	11.5	1.6	77.1	39.8	50.1	49.9
48651	PRUDENVILLE	98.1	97.9	0.1	0.1	0.1	0.2	0.7	0.9	4.5	4.7	5.5	5.1	4.8	18.6	31.5	23.4	2.0	82.3	49.8	49.0	51.0
48652	RHODES	97.8	97.6	0.1	0.1	0.1	0.1	1.2	1.4	5.3	6.0	7.3	6.5	5.0	26.0	29.1	13.8	1.1	77.4	41.3	50.2	49.8
48653	ROSCOMMON	98.1	97.9	0.3	0.3	0.3	0.3	0.9	1.0	4.3	4.6	6.0	5.7	4.7	19.4	31.2	21.8	2.3	81.5	48.4	50.5	49.5
48654	ROSE CITY	97.7	97.6	0.2	0.2	0.1	0.1	1.5	1.7	5.4	5.3	6.6	7.1	5.9	21.2	28.1	17.4	3.1	77.8	44.0	49.3	50.7
48655	SAINT CHARLES	97.0	96.5	0.3	0.4	0.2	0.3	2.7	3.3	6.7	6.9	7.4	6.8	6.1	26.9	26.9	11.2	1.2	74.9	38.5	49.6	50.4
48656	SAINT HELEN	98.3	98.2	0.1	0.1	0.2	0.3	0.7	0.8	4.3	4.5	5.8	5.4	4.3	19.1	30.1	24.4	2.0	82.1	49.9	49.7	50.3
48657	SANFORD	97.9	97.7	0.1	0.1	0.3	0.4	0.8	1.0	6.3	6.7	7.3	5.8	5.3	27.4	29.2	11.3	0.8	76.2	39.7	50.5	49.5
48658	STANDISH	91.7	91.0	5.0	5.4	0.4	0.6	2.2	2.5	5.6	5.6	6.3	6.4	7.5	30.2	24.5	12.2	1.8	78.7	38.2	53.3	46.7
48659	STERLING	98.1	97.9	0.0	0.0	0.2	0.2	1.7	1.9	6.0	6.1	7.2	6.6	6.1	25.3	27.4	13.6	1.9	76.7	40.7	50.8	49.2
48661	WEST BRANCH	97.8	97.4	0.1	0.1	0.7	0.9	0.9	1.0	5.6	6.1	7.2	6.3	5.3	24.1	27.5	15.9	1.9	77.0	41.9	49.4	50.7
48662	WHEELER	96.4	96.0	0.1	0.1	0.1	0.1	4.9	5.7	6.7	7.1	7.8	6.8	5.7	27.7	25.7	11.4	1.1	74.2	37.5	51.6	48.4
48701	AKRON	96.7	96.5	0.2	0.2	0.2	0.2	4.5	5.1	6.4	6.2	6.7	6.1	6.8	26.8	25.5	13.6	1.9	76.7	39.2	49.9	50.1
48703	AU GRES	97.2	96.9	0.1	0.1	0.4	0.5	1.0	1.1	4.7	4.8	5.3	5.2	4.5	19.4	31.8	22.5	1.8	82.1	48.8	50.6	49.4
48705	BARTON CITY	98.8	98.8	0.0	0.0	0.2	0.1	1.1	1.1	3.2	3.4	4.8	4.8	4.1	17.1	35.1	25.3	2.2	84.7	53.0	51.9	48.1
48706	BAY CITY	96.3	95.8	0.7	0.7	0.6	0.8	3.1	3.5	5.8	6.0	6.7	6.1	5.8	26.0	27.2	14.2	2.3	77.8	40.9	48.1	51.9
48708	BAY CITY	90.4	89.5	3.1	3.4	0.5	0.7	6.9	7.9	6.7	6.4	7.0	6.9	7.0	27.7	24.5	11.8	2.1	75.7	37.1	48.7	51.3
48710	UNIVERSITY CENTER	100.0	100.0	0.0	0.0	0.0	0.0	0.0	0.0	0.0	0.0	0.0	0.0	25.0	75.0	0.0	0.0	0.0	100.0	30.0	50.0	50.0
48720	BAY PORT	98.0	98.0	0.3	0.3	0.2	0.3	2.1	2.3	4.8	5.4	6.7	6.5	5.9	24.3	28.7	15.8	1.9	78.6	42.6	51.2	48.8
48721	BLACK RIVER	97.1	97.2	0.0	0.0	0.0	0.0	0.9	0.7	4.6	5.2	6.3	5.2	4.4	19.6	33.8	19.4	1.5	80.6	48.3	51.0	49.0
48722	BRIDGEPORT	88.3	86.1	7.6	9.2	0.4	0.5	5.9	7.0	5.6	5.9	6.0	5.6	5.9	25.8	30.2	13.7	1.4	79.1	41.9	48.8	51.2
48723	CARO	94.6	94.1	1.7	1.8	0.4	0.6	3.1	3.6	5.6	6.0	7.0	6.6	6.3	27.4	26.4	12.4	2.3	77.1	39.2	49.3	50.7
48725	CASEVILLE	98.5	98.4	0.1	0.1	0.2	0.2	1.1	1.4	3.5	3.6	4.5	5.0	4.6	17.8	32.1	25.9	3.1	85.3	52.3	49.6	50.4
48726	CASS CITY	97.5	97.2	0.2	0.3	0.3	0.4	1.5	1.7	6.1	6.3	7.0	7.0	6.5	25.6	25.2	13.9	2.4	76.2	39.6	49.7	50.3
48727	CLIFFORD	96.5	96.3	0.8	0.8	0.3	0.4	2.0	2.2	6.7	6.1	9.2	7.2	5.7	28.9	25.5	9.9	0.9	73.8	37.1	49.9	50.2
48728	CURRAN	99.1	99.1	0.0	0.0	0.0	0.2	1.1	1.1	2.4	2.5	4.0	4.3	3.4	13.8	35.5	31.4	2.5	87.6	57.4	51.1	49.0
48729	DEFORD	97.1	96.9	0.3	0.3	0.1	0.1	1.8	2.0	5.9	6.3	7.8	7.1	7.1	26.2	28.4	10.2	1.0	75.5	38.6	51.2	48.9
48730	EAST TAWAS	97.4	97.3	0.2	0.2	0.5	0.6	1.0	1.1	4.7	5.0	6.5	5.6	5.0	21.0	28.2	20.7	3.3	80.3	46.5	47.5	52.5
48731	ELKTON	97.4	97.1	0.3	0.3	0.4	0.5	3.8	4.3	7.7	7.6	7.4	5.9	6.0	26.1	25.1	12.1	2.0	73.4	37.2	50.2	49.9
48732	ESSEXVILLE	95.3	94.7	1.1	1.2	0.7	0.8	2.5	2.9	5.6	5.9	6.8	6.8	6.5	24.3	27.2	13.8	3.2	77.5	40.9	47.3	52.7
48733	FAIRGROVE	96.5	96.3	0.2	0.2	0.2	0.2	4.5	5.1	5.9	6.3	7.0	5.5	6.6	26.8	27.7	12.0	2.3	77.3	39.7	49.1	50.9
48734	FRANKENMUTH	98.4	98.0	0.3	0.5	0.4	0.5	1.3	1.6	4.7	5.0	6.7	6.7	5.4	19.7	28.1	17.7	6.0	79.0	46.1	46.8	53.2
48735	GAGETOWN	95.1	94.7	0.2	0.2	0.2	0.4	4.3	4.6	5.4	5.8	7.3	7.6	6.0	26.2	26.8	13.2	1.9	76.0	40.3	51.1	48.9
48737	GLENNIE	97.8	97.7	0.1	0.1	0.2	0.2	0.8	0.9	4.1	4.5	4.9	4.4	4.2	16.6	33.6	25.9	2.0	83.6	53.3	51.4	48.7
48738	GREENBUSH	97.8	97.6	0.4	0.4	0.4	0.5	0.3	0.4	4.2	4.6	4.5	4.2	3.4	17.0	31.8	28.1	2.3	83.8	53.8	50.6	49.4
48739	HALE	97.4	97.3	0.1	0.1	0.2	0.2	0.8	0.8	4.4	4.5	6.2	6.0	4.3	18.3	30.6	23.6	2.2	80.9	49.5	51.0	49.0
48740	HARRISVILLE	97.4	97.2	0.5	0.6	0.2	0.3	0.6	0.6	4.7	4.9	5.4	5.0	4.9	19.2	31.2	21.6	3.2	81.9	49.0	49.4	50.6
48741	KINGSTON	95.8	95.4	1.0	1.0	0.2	0.3	1.6	1.8	7.0	7.1	7.9	7.4	6.1	27.5	24.9	11.1	1.1	73.4	36.9	50.4	49.6
48742	LINCOLN	98.3	98.1	0.1	0.1	0.1	0.1	0.6	0.7	4.3	4.6	5.3	5.1	4.3	19.0	29.8	23.8	3.8	82.6	50.5	49.4	50.6
48743	LONG LAKE	98.3	100.0	0.0	0.0	0.0	0.0	0.0	0.0	3.1	3.1	3.1	3.1	3.1	14.1	37.5	29.7	3.1	90.6	59.2	50.0	50.0
48744	MAYVILLE	97.5	97.2	0.2	0.2	0.1	0.2	1.5	1.8	6.8	7.0	7.7	6.8	6.3	27.0	26.6	10.4	1.5	74.2	37.5	50.5	49.5
48745	MIKADO	97.4	96.9	0.0	0.0	0.2	0.3	1.1	1.2	5.8	6.1	7.0	5.6	4.8	22.8	30.0	16.1	1.9	76.9	43.7	52.0	48.0
48746	MILLINGTON	97.6	97.3	0.3	0.3	0.2	0.2	1.3	1.5	6.2	6.6	7.7	6.9	6.1	27.7	27.9	10.0	0.9	75.4	38.0	49.7	50.3
48747	MUNGER	97.2	97.0	0.1	0.1	0.3	0.3	9.1	10.4	6.0	6.6	7.3	6.7	5.7	24.8	29.4	12.0	1.7	75.9	40.6	51.0	49.0
48748	NATIONAL CITY	97.8	97.8	0.1	0.1	0.4	0.4	0.7	0.6	3.2	3.6	5.5	5.7	4.5	17.9	34.2	23.9	1.7	84.2	50.9	50.3	49.7
48749	OMER	97.0	96.9	0.0	0.0	0.1	0.1	1.1	1.2	5.3	5.4	6.3	6.3	6.2	24.7	28.5	15.9	1.5	79.2	42.6	49.5	50.5
48750	OSCODA	95.6	95.5	0.8	0.8	0.8	0.8	1.3	1.3	5.4	5.6	6.8	6.6	4.9	22.2	28.4	18.7	1.3	77.9	44.0	49.7	50.3
48754	OWENDALE	97.6	97.2	0.7	0.7	0.2	0.4	3.9	4.4	6.5	7.1	8.1	6.5	6.2	26.0	25.4	12.7	1.7	74.4	38.3	52.0	48.0
48755	PIGEON	97.2	96.9	0.5	0.5	0.4	0.6	2.1	2.3	4.0	4.4	6.4	5.7	4.8	19.8	29.2	22.6	3.0	81.2	48.3	49.9	50.1
48756	PRESCOTT	96.5	96.3	0.2	0.2	0.1	0.1	1.5	1.7	5.1	5.4	6.4	6.1	5.4	22.0	28.9	19.0	1.7	79.3	44.7	49.9	50.1
48757	REESE	97.8	97.5	0.1	0.1	0.6	0.7	2.3	2.7	6.1	6.3	7.0	6.6	6.8	25.9	27.5	12.3	1.6	76.6	39.4	49.8	50.2
48759	SEBEWAING	98.6	98.4	0.1	0.1	0.1	0.2	3.1	3.5	5.9	5.6	6.0	6.9	6.3	24.6	26.5	15.3	2.9	78.2	41.6	48.2	51.9
48760	SILVERWOOD	94.5	94.2	2.5	2.6	0.3	0.4	0.9	1.2	6.8	6.9	7.5	7.2	6.0	27.0	26.5	11.1	1.1	74.1	37.7	50.4	49.6
48761	SOUTH BRANCH	99.1	99.0	0.0	0.0	0.2	0.2	1.3	1.3	4.5	4.6	4.8	4.2	3.9	17.4	33.1	25.2	2.3	83.0	52.9	49.8	50.2
48762	SPRUCE	99.0	99.0	0.0	0.0	0.1	0.1	0.6	0.5	2.8	3.0	4.4	4.3	3.8	17.0	33.0	29.1	2.7	87.0	55.7	51.1	48.9
48763	TAWAS CITY	97.7	97.7	0.4	0.4	0.6	0.6	0.8	0.9	4.4	4.8	6.2	6.5	5.2	21.4	27.8	19.6	4.0	80.3	45.9	48.6	51.4
48765	TURNER	97.9	97.8	0.1	0.1	0.3	0.3	1.2	1.3	5.0	6.6	6.7	6.0	5.3	22.3	29.2	17.4	1.6	77.7	43.7	51.1	48.9
48766	TWINING	96.2	95.9	0.2	0.2	0.1	0.1	0.9	0.9	6.3	7.1	7.7	7.3	6.3	23.8	28.2	11.9	1.2	74.1	39.5	51.1	48.9
48767	UNIONVILLE	96.8	96.4	0.0	0.0	0.4	0.6	3.0	3.3	6.0	6.2	6.8	7.4	6.1	26.8	25.9	12.7	2.2	76.2	39.1	50.5	49.5
48768	VASSAR	94.5	93.9	2.7	2.8	0.5	0.6	2.4	2.7	6.5	6.9	7.9	9.2	6.3	27.0	25.1	10.0	1.2	72.2	35.8	50.8	49.2
48770	WHITTEMORE	98.1	98.1	0.2	0.2	0.1	0.1	1.0	0.9	5.6	5.9	7.0	6.0	5.5	23.2	29.3	15.8	1.7	77.8	42.9	49.6	50.4
48801	ALMA	94.4	93.6	0.4	0.5	0.7	0.9	5.6	6.5	5.9	5.8	6.1	10.2	11.0	23.0	21.7	12.1	4.1	78.1	35.3	46.3	53.7
48806	ASHLEY	98.1	97.9	0.2	0.2	0.2	0.2	1.6	1.8	6.5	6.4	6.4	6.2	5.9	27.5	26.4	12.6	2.4	77.2	39.5	50.8	49.2
	MICHIGAN	80.2	79.2	14.2	14.4	1.8	2.3	3.3	3.6	6.8	6.9	7.4	7.1	6.9	28.1	24.6	10.8	1.6	74.9	36.5	49.1	50.9
	UNITED STATES	75.1	73.6	12.3	12.5	3.8	4.2	12.5	14.1	6.9	6.7	7.2	7.0	7.3	28.6	23.8	10.8	1.7	75.1	36.0	49.1	50.9

ZIP CODE #	POST OFFICE NAME	2004 Per Capita Income	2004 HH Income Base	2004 Household Income Distribution (%) Less than $25,000	$25,000 to $49,999	$50,000 to $99,999	$100,000 to $149,999	$150,000 or More	Median Household Income 2004	2009	2004 National Centile	2004 State Centile	2004 Home Value Base	2004 Home Value Distribution (%) Less than $50,000	$50,000 to $89,999	$90,000 to $174,999	$175,000 to $399,999	$400,000 or More	2004 Median Home Value
48604	SAGINAW	20569	4652	26.2	30.9	33.9	6.9	2.1	43673	49491	58	48	3579	15.1	39.2	39.6	5.5	0.6	86544
48607	SAGINAW	10965	979	69.6	17.8	9.0	3.2	0.5	14192	16589	1	0	356	78.1	14.3	6.5	1.1	0.0	31714
48609	SAGINAW	28183	5141	17.4	27.5	36.8	12.3	6.0	54520	61363	79	75	4651	8.5	15.0	53.9	20.1	2.5	121102
48610	ALGER	18008	1647	37.8	33.3	23.3	4.5	1.1	32551	35310	19	9	1449	22.2	28.4	36.0	12.1	1.3	89241
48611	AUBURN	23985	2452	18.8	26.8	39.4	12.1	2.9	54154	60506	79	75	2024	8.1	14.1	57.1	19.6	1.1	119689
48612	BEAVERTON	18937	3999	33.1	32.8	26.5	5.8	1.9	36025	38964	32	19	3340	19.0	23.8	39.0	17.5	0.8	102083
48613	BENTLEY	18438	443	30.3	32.7	27.5	7.2	2.3	38876	42481	42	29	402	21.1	31.3	35.1	11.9	0.5	86875
48614	BRANT	20102	464	23.7	32.3	33.8	8.0	2.2	44557	49504	60	51	409	12.0	22.7	48.7	14.2	2.4	108886
48615	BRECKENRIDGE	20004	1230	23.9	36.8	30.9	6.8	1.7	42299	47351	54	44	1011	17.4	30.7	43.5	8.0	0.4	91681
48616	CHESANING	22715	2805	25.1	29.6	32.6	10.2	2.5	45451	49941	62	54	2349	7.6	19.6	53.5	18.4	0.9	112114
48617	CLARE	18850	3447	34.8	32.8	24.9	5.1	2.5	35720	38510	30	17	2442	15.2	25.5	42.3	15.7	1.4	100537
48618	COLEMAN	19426	2143	27.6	31.6	32.6	6.4	1.8	41280	47263	51	40	1823	20.5	30.8	39.3	8.8	0.6	88345
48619	COMINS	21879	302	31.1	37.1	24.2	4.6	3.0	36219	39203	32	20	273	16.9	24.2	36.6	17.2	5.1	99800
48620	EDENVILLE	22627	22	22.7	40.9	31.8	4.6	0.0	42313	46120	54	44	19	10.5	26.3	57.9	5.3	0.0	105357
48621	FAIRVIEW	16937	593	40.0	35.1	20.1	3.4	1.5	30545	32497	14	6	471	14.4	34.8	38.0	11.0	1.7	90625
48622	FARWELL	19045	2516	32.6	35.3	24.5	5.4	2.2	35955	39706	31	18	2192	18.0	26.3	42.0	12.9	0.8	98129
48623	FREELAND	24904	4170	16.9	21.0	40.2	16.7	5.2	62173	70238	86	86	3659	7.7	11.2	46.3	32.6	2.2	144859
48624	GLADWIN	18976	7037	35.0	34.7	23.4	4.9	2.1	34722	37152	26	14	5961	17.5	23.3	40.1	17.5	1.6	103720
48625	HARRISON	17140	5928	41.9	33.1	19.7	3.5	1.8	29904	32064	12	5	4914	29.9	29.6	29.8	10.1	0.6	76156
48626	HEMLOCK	22234	2316	20.2	28.8	37.5	9.8	3.6	50706	57565	73	67	2039	9.9	16.9	48.4	23.0	1.9	119370
48628	HOPE	24260	774	23.1	33.5	31.0	9.3	3.1	45167	50466	62	53	704	15.1	23.0	43.2	17.1	1.7	105417
48629	HOUGHTON LAKE	19821	3937	35.2	36.9	22.2	3.8	1.9	32621	35748	20	10	3359	15.2	29.3	36.5	17.1	2.0	95686
48631	KAWKAWLIN	22097	1741	18.5	34.6	32.6	11.0	3.3	47466	53138	67	60	1587	17.6	18.3	44.0	19.2	0.9	111711
48632	LAKE	19513	2448	34.5	38.1	21.2	4.3	2.0	32273	35476	19	9	2163	24.3	26.6	35.0	13.2	0.9	88596
48634	LINWOOD	22680	1808	19.3	32.2	35.2	10.7	2.7	48725	54336	70	63	1658	7.6	23.5	49.7	18.0	1.2	111831
48635	LUPTON	18867	765	38.2	35.8	20.9	3.1	2.0	31697	35069	17	7	699	17.9	28.5	36.1	16.5	1.1	96375
48636	LUZERNE	17834	375	37.3	36.0	23.2	2.9	0.5	32607	33775	20	10	314	21.7	30.6	34.4	12.1	1.3	85625
48637	MERRILL	22565	1325	22.2	32.5	34.3	8.4	2.6	46604	51889	65	57	1184	10.8	27.5	44.8	16.2	0.8	104952
48640	MIDLAND	29693	12818	23.9	24.7	29.6	12.4	9.4	51659	59912	75	70	9833	6.4	20.9	42.1	26.3	4.2	123917
48642	MIDLAND	28051	13020	21.4	25.2	31.1	13.7	8.7	54021	62524	78	75	10037	9.1	16.1	47.7	23.8	3.4	124354
48647	MIO	16233	2058	40.8	34.8	20.3	3.4	0.7	30335	32067	13	5	1699	17.6	37.8	31.1	12.5	1.0	82179
48649	OAKLEY	19912	775	24.1	33.4	33.0	8.0	1.4	44388	49299	60	51	674	15.9	24.5	44.2	15.1	0.3	103797
48650	PINCONNING	20185	2996	29.3	29.3	32.0	7.5	1.8	41025	44811	50	39	2628	12.5	32.4	45.2	9.6	0.3	95720
48651	PRUDENVILLE	20300	2315	40.7	29.9	23.5	3.9	1.9	30437	32387	13	5	1898	9.9	31.7	37.6	19.9	1.0	98333
48652	RHODES	18172	641	31.2	33.1	27.3	6.9	1.6	37275	40829	36	24	582	19.6	25.4	40.2	14.1	0.7	96170
48653	ROSCOMMON	20242	4642	30.7	35.9	26.4	4.9	2.1	36720	39596	34	22	4036	12.1	27.9	40.8	15.6	3.6	103609
48654	ROSE CITY	17608	1116	35.3	34.6	23.8	4.6	1.8	34167	37207	25	12	903	15.7	31.9	37.4	13.6	1.3	94135
48655	SAINT CHARLES	22184	2408	23.3	30.4	34.0	9.3	3.0	46668	51941	65	58	2054	7.1	26.1	48.7	17.0	1.1	109809
48656	SAINT HELEN	18620	2093	42.8	35.3	17.0	2.6	2.4	29621	31241	11	4	1736	27.8	36.4	27.1	8.3	0.4	71852
48657	SANFORD	22830	3225	22.8	33.0	31.1	9.7	3.4	45302	51895	62	54	2813	15.9	24.1	40.7	17.5	1.7	105361
48658	STANDISH	17557	2143	37.9	28.6	26.0	6.2	1.2	34208	37076	25	12	1672	18.4	31.2	41.1	7.7	1.7	90515
48659	STERLING	17587	1231	34.0	30.8	29.0	4.8	1.5	37486	41080	37	25	1056	20.9	29.8	38.5	9.3	1.4	89036
48661	WEST BRANCH	19506	4055	32.1	34.3	26.9	4.9	1.9	37140	39859	36	23	3322	11.4	26.9	44.3	15.9	1.5	106362
48662	WHEELER	17773	586	25.8	38.2	29.4	4.8	1.9	39885	43508	46	34	514	21.8	27.2	41.3	8.0	1.8	91136
48701	AKRON	19651	624	28.7	34.0	29.7	5.5	2.2	40458	43565	48	36	524	17.0	38.4	34.4	9.9	0.4	84286
48703	AU GRES	22187	1592	36.1	31.9	23.8	5.5	2.7	35785	39360	31	17	1322	9.7	23.0	40.3	23.2	3.8	114951
48705	BARTON CITY	19694	336	38.4	35.1	21.1	3.6	1.8	31820	33801	17	8	306	13.1	31.4	37.3	15.4	2.9	98095
48706	BAY CITY	23743	17119	27.1	29.0	30.6	9.6	3.7	43799	48822	58	49	13867	13.4	24.6	43.1	17.3	1.6	105608
48708	BAY CITY	19221	11700	35.4	30.4	26.0	6.3	2.0	35283	39294	29	15	8106	12.7	42.2	37.7	6.6	0.8	85822
48710	UNIVERSITY CENTER	0	0	0.0	0.0	0.0	0.0	0.0	0	0	0	0	0	0.0	0.0	0.0	0.0	0.0	0
48720	BAY PORT	19011	574	29.4	36.8	28.6	4.0	1.2	39524	43468	44	32	490	20.2	27.6	39.2	11.6	1.4	94231
48721	BLACK RIVER	22901	194	26.3	38.7	23.7	7.7	3.6	38753	44064	42	29	173	9.3	19.7	39.9	26.0	5.2	123828
48722	BRIDGEPORT	23237	1249	23.1	30.0	33.3	11.4	2.2	47225	53530	67	59	1111	9.9	27.0	52.4	10.0	0.7	104989
48723	CARO	19645	4901	28.6	33.1	29.4	7.3	1.6	39976	43476	46	34	3906	13.8	22.8	46.8	15.9	0.8	108501
48725	CASEVILLE	22419	1433	34.7	36.7	22.3	4.1	2.3	34283	37087	25	13	1206	15.5	20.9	39.5	20.7	3.4	110045
48726	CASS CITY	18799	2427	29.8	35.1	27.2	6.8	1.2	38667	42775	42	29	1966	13.9	24.6	45.9	15.0	0.6	106586
48727	CLIFFORD	19114	505	25.5	28.9	37.0	7.1	1.4	44889	48411	61	53	434	10.4	21.9	44.0	18.7	5.1	119531
48728	CURRAN	21253	345	38.6	36.2	20.3	3.2	1.7	31864	33804	17	8	319	12.2	27.6	37.6	18.8	3.8	104167
48729	DEFORD	18650	662	25.1	33.7	34.0	6.0	1.2	43625	47417	58	48	565	14.9	23.5	44.8	15.0	1.8	104755
48730	EAST TAWAS	19050	2360	37.1	35.7	22.3	3.9	1.1	32981	35014	21	10	1831	7.1	34.1	40.1	15.8	2.9	100930
48731	ELKTON	17811	758	33.0	33.3	29.6	3.3	0.9	36029	38852	32	19	608	17.1	33.7	37.5	10.2	1.5	89167
48732	ESSEXVILLE	24625	5024	30.2	28.8	28.3	9.0	3.7	39182	43381	43	30	3637	11.2	17.1	49.6	20.4	1.7	118298
48733	FAIRGROVE	20625	758	26.0	35.1	30.2	6.2	2.5	41952	45792	53	42	652	12.1	35.3	41.7	10.1	0.8	92576
48734	FRANKENMUTH	31948	3001	20.1	25.3	33.4	13.3	7.9	56922	61232	82	80	2222	0.8	3.9	44.6	46.7	4.0	176130
48735	GAGETOWN	18325	321	28.4	35.2	29.3	6.2	0.9	39370	42984	44	32	274	24.1	27.7	37.6	10.2	0.4	87368
48737	GLENNIE	18222	630	38.9	40.5	17.6	1.9	1.1	30668	33058	14	6	562	18.0	32.6	40.6	7.5	1.4	89375
48738	GREENBUSH	22246	619	27.5	41.7	25.2	4.4	1.3	37170	41399	36	24	555	8.8	19.6	39.6	29.6	2.3	124335
48739	HALE	18643	2011	38.2	35.3	20.6	3.5	2.4	31815	35137	17	7	1772	17.8	24.7	39.1	17.3	1.1	102950
48740	HARRISVILLE	19904	1152	36.2	36.4	20.8	4.3	2.3	33526	36412	22	11	930	10.8	25.5	41.4	17.7	4.6	110778
48741	KINGSTON	18838	803	27.2	31.5	32.6	7.5	1.3	42353	45453	54	44	689	9.9	19.6	49.6	19.2	1.7	116487
48742	LINCOLN	21300	852	36.0	34.9	23.2	3.6	2.2	32988	35601	21	10	728	11.8	25.8	40.8	18.0	3.6	106920
48743	LONG LAKE	20117	34	38.2	35.3	20.6	5.9	0.0	31070	35000	15	6	31	19.4	32.3	32.3	16.1	0.0	88333
48744	MAYVILLE	20082	1709	23.8	31.7	33.7	9.0	1.8	45454	48956	62	54	1465	10.2	17.4	47.9	23.2	1.3	124541
48745	MIKADO	18419	666	34.1	36.6	24.3	3.2	1.8	34353	36855	25	13	577	15.4	34.3	40.0	8.8	1.4	90313
48746	MILLINGTON	21907	3385	17.2	31.5	38.3	10.6	2.5	51080	54924	74	69	3001	9.2	15.2	55.5	19.5	0.6	121586
48747	MUNGER	21859	560	20.0	29.1	37.5	10.0	3.4	50743	56589	73	67	519	7.3	24.7	55.5	9.4	3.1	111630
48748	NATIONAL CITY	22570	901	31.6	39.3	22.5	4.4	2.1	35133	37479	28	15	848	11.6	28.2	39.5	19.5	1.3	108036
48749	OMER	20797	391	34.3	31.5	25.8	5.6	2.8	36040	40000	32	19	342	19.9	33.9	35.4	9.7	1.2	86829
48750	OSCODA	19632	4031	35.3	34.6	24.3	3.9	1.9	34826	37004	27	14	3058	13.2	36.3	36.6	12.9	1.0	90711
48754	OWENDALE	18959	516	25.2	37.8	31.2	4.5	1.4	39526	43622	44	32	444	18.5	30.9	35.6	14.0	1.1	90612
48755	PIGEON	24901	1356	23.3	34.7	30.8	6.9	4.4	43593	48788	58	48	1149	7.8	25.9	38.6	20.2	7.5	112925
48756	PRESCOTT	14995	1993	46.2	32.2	18.0	2.8	0.9	26905	29320	7	3	1640	31.6	30.7	27.9	8.8	0.9	73333
48757	REESE	23124	1604	22.8	29.6	35.6	9.7	2.4	47789	51390	68	61	1365	16.0	14.4	48.7	20.5	0.4	120506
48759	SEBEWAING	19804	1484	30.1	36.1	27.2	5.3	1.4	37866	41305	39	26	1189	13.9	38.1	38.4	9.2	0.5	88503
48760	SILVERWOOD	21307	411	22.1	32.4	33.6	9.3	2.7	45894	50196	64	55	363	6.9	16.8	47.9	25.9	2.5	139951
48761	SOUTH BRANCH	19178	634	41.3	36.8	17.0	3.6	1.3	29600	32130	11	4	578	17.0	38.1	32.9	11.8	0.4	84727
48762	SPRUCE	21323	591	32.3	36.6	24.0	4.7	2.4	37154	38977	36	23	546	6.2	21.8	40.7	26.2	5.1	121429
48763	TAWAS CITY	19303	1983	30.0	37.8	25.3	5.1	1.9	37623	40744	38	26	1686	8.8	32.4	41.1	15.6	2.0	100307
48765	TURNER	17364	303	36.0	31.4	26.7	4.6	1.3	36700	39382	34	22	260	21.5	28.9	33.1	13.5	3.1	89474
48766	TWINING	15773	558	38.4	30.3	26.7	3.2	1.4	34501	37343	26	13	483	24.6	34.8	31.9	7.9	0.8	77286
48767	UNIONVILLE	20356	887	21.0	39.7	30.6	7.3	1.5	43229	47006	57	47	769	13.3	31.1	43.6	11.2	0.9	97131
48768	VASSAR	20339	3784	21.5	33.7	35.3	7.2	2.3	46079	50888	64	56	3202	11.4	22.8	50.4	15.1	0.3	110526
48770	WHITTEMORE	17024	861	36.2	33.1	25.2	3.7	1.7	34772	37153	27	14	727	17.2	36.2	33.6	11.4	1.7	86397
48801	ALMA	20597	4601	32.6	31.0	27.1	7.2	2.0	37847	40427	39	26	3213	14.4	32.5	39.6	12.9	0.6	93783
48806	ASHLEY	20291	668	22.9	37.0	31.6	6.4	2.1	43686	47658	58	49	572	16.4	27.5	42.5	12.2	1.4	98974
	MICHIGAN	25281		23.8	27.4	32.3	10.9	5.5	48729	54505				10.7	16.0	40.3	28.0	5.0	134769
	UNITED STATES	25866		24.7	27.1	30.8	10.9	6.5	48124	56710				10.9	15.0	33.7	30.1	10.4	145905

ZIP CODE		FINANCIAL SERVICES				THE HOME						ENTERTAINMENT						PERSONAL			
						Home Improvements		Furnishings													
#	POST OFFICE NAME	Auto Loan	Home Loan	Investments	Retirement Plans	Home Repair	Lawn & Garden	Computers & Hardware	Major Appliances	TV, Radio, Sound Equipment	Furniture	Dine out/ Carry out	Sports Equipment	Fees & Tickets	Toys & Games	Travel	Cable TV	Apparel & Services	Auto Repairs	Health Insurance	Pets & Supplies
48604	SAGINAW	70	74	79	72	74	81	74	73	75	72	93	84	76	97	75	76	90	73	75	82
48607	SAGINAW	35	28	33	26	28	34	33	33	37	33	45	36	32	42	32	39	43	35	38	38
48609	SAGINAW	97	107	107	104	107	110	99	101	96	99	120	117	102	125	101	96	118	98	97	115
48610	ALGER	71	54	34	48	61	69	51	62	59	51	69	73	45	68	54	63	64	61	74	86
48611	AUBURN	85	94	94	91	94	97	87	89	85	86	106	104	90	111	89	85	104	86	87	103
48612	BEAVERTON	78	61	40	56	67	76	59	69	66	58	78	81	53	77	61	70	73	68	81	92
48613	BENTLEY	79	69	52	66	74	79	64	72	69	64	83	85	62	85	66	71	79	70	78	93
48614	BRANT	98	73	42	65	80	90	69	82	79	70	94	98	62	92	71	84	87	81	97	113
48615	BRECKENRIDGE	77	71	60	68	74	81	69	73	73	68	89	85	68	91	70	74	84	72	79	89
48616	CHESANING	87	82	71	79	85	93	79	84	82	78	101	97	79	102	81	84	96	82	90	101
48617	CLARE	78	62	44	60	68	76	63	71	69	62	83	83	58	81	64	72	77	70	81	90
48618	COLEMAN	82	69	49	64	74	81	65	73	71	65	86	87	62	86	66	74	81	72	83	96
48619	COMINS	88	69	47	62	77	87	65	78	73	64	87	91	58	86	69	78	81	77	92	107
48620	EDENVILLE	81	72	55	68	76	81	66	74	71	66	86	88	65	88	68	72	82	72	80	95
48621	FAIRVIEW	73	54	32	48	61	69	51	63	59	51	70	74	45	68	54	64	65	62	75	87
48622	FARWELL	80	61	40	56	68	78	61	71	69	60	82	82	55	79	63	73	75	70	84	93
48623	FREELAND	87	100	101	100	99	99	91	92	86	91	108	107	95	113	92	84	107	89	85	103
48624	GLADWIN	75	60	43	55	66	75	58	67	65	58	77	77	53	74	61	69	72	66	79	87
48625	HARRISON	68	53	35	48	59	67	51	61	57	50	68	71	45	67	54	61	63	60	72	82
48626	HEMLOCK	90	87	77	85	89	95	83	88	85	83	104	102	83	106	84	85	100	86	89	104
48628	HOPE	95	83	62	78	88	95	77	87	83	77	100	103	74	100	80	85	95	85	95	112
48629	HOUGHTON LAKE	75	58	38	53	65	74	56	67	63	55	75	78	49	73	59	67	69	66	79	90
48631	KAWKAWLIN	85	86	79	82	86	91	81	84	82	81	101	97	82	103	82	82	98	83	85	98
48632	LAKE	76	58	38	53	66	74	56	67	64	56	76	79	50	74	59	69	70	67	80	91
48634	LINWOOD	90	84	70	80	88	94	78	86	82	78	100	101	77	102	81	83	96	84	91	107
48635	LUPTON	72	56	38	51	63	71	53	64	60	53	71	75	47	70	57	64	66	63	76	88
48636	LUZERNE	71	56	38	50	63	70	52	63	59	52	70	74	47	70	56	63	65	62	75	86
48637	MERRILL	85	88	83	85	89	94	82	85	82	81	102	100	84	106	84	83	99	83	86	101
48640	MIDLAND	104	107	112	107	107	113	106	106	104	105	130	124	107	130	106	102	127	106	103	120
48642	MIDLAND	98	105	111	106	104	109	101	101	99	101	124	117	104	125	102	97	121	100	97	114
48647	MIO	69	52	34	47	59	67	50	60	57	49	67	71	44	66	52	61	62	59	72	83
48649	OAKLEY	82	71	57	70	75	83	72	77	76	71	92	88	69	92	72	78	87	76	83	92
48650	PINCONNING	79	71	57	68	74	81	68	74	72	67	88	86	67	90	70	74	83	72	80	91
48651	PRUDENVILLE	73	60	45	55	66	75	56	67	62	57	75	75	52	71	60	67	70	65	79	87
48652	RHODES	78	65	46	60	71	78	61	71	67	60	80	83	56	80	64	70	75	69	80	94
48653	ROSCOMMON	76	62	46	57	69	77	60	69	66	59	79	81	54	78	63	70	73	69	80	92
48654	ROSE CITY	73	57	38	52	63	72	56	66	63	55	75	76	50	73	58	67	69	65	78	87
48655	SAINT CHARLES	90	81	65	78	85	93	77	84	82	77	100	99	76	102	79	84	95	82	91	105
48656	SAINT HELEN	68	54	37	48	60	68	51	61	57	50	68	71	45	67	54	61	63	60	72	83
48657	SANFORD	91	81	62	77	85	92	75	83	79	75	97	99	73	98	77	81	92	81	90	107
48658	STANDISH	75	58	38	55	64	73	59	67	66	58	79	78	54	76	60	70	73	67	79	86
48659	STERLING	80	58	34	53	64	74	57	68	66	58	79	80	51	75	58	70	72	67	81	91
48661	WEST BRANCH	78	61	43	57	67	75	60	70	67	59	80	82	55	79	62	70	74	69	80	91
48662	WHEELER	75	66	51	63	70	76	62	69	66	62	81	81	61	82	64	68	76	67	74	87
48701	AKRON	74	66	55	61	70	78	64	70	70	63	85	81	63	88	66	74	81	69	79	87
48703	AU GRES	81	63	42	57	70	80	62	72	70	60	82	84	55	80	64	74	76	72	86	96
48705	BARTON CITY	72	56	39	51	64	71	53	64	60	53	71	75	48	71	57	64	66	63	76	88
48706	BAY CITY	78	81	80	77	82	88	78	80	80	77	98	91	80	102	80	81	95	79	83	91
48708	BAY CITY	60	63	70	62	63	68	65	63	65	63	81	73	66	84	65	65	79	64	64	70
48710	UNIVERSITY CENTER	0	0	0	0	0	0	0	0	0	0	0	0	0	0	0	0	0	0	0	0
48720	BAY PORT	78	59	37	56	66	73	58	68	65	58	77	81	52	76	60	68	71	67	79	90
48721	BLACK RIVER	92	72	49	65	81	91	68	82	77	67	91	96	61	90	72	82	85	81	97	112
48722	BRIDGEPORT	75	86	91	83	86	90	81	81	80	80	100	93	86	107	84	81	99	79	80	90
48723	CARO	79	67	52	63	71	79	66	73	72	65	87	85	63	86	67	75	82	72	82	91
48725	CASEVILLE	78	61	42	55	69	77	58	69	65	57	77	81	52	76	62	69	72	68	82	94
48726	CASS CITY	74	62	47	58	67	75	62	68	68	61	82	79	59	82	63	72	77	67	78	85
48727	CLIFFORD	84	73	55	69	78	84	68	76	73	68	88	90	66	90	70	75	83	74	83	99
48728	CURRAN	68	55	40	50	62	70	52	62	58	52	69	71	47	67	56	62	65	61	73	82
48729	DEFORD	87	69	45	64	74	83	66	76	73	66	88	90	61	87	67	76	82	74	86	100
48730	EAST TAWAS	63	52	45	51	56	64	54	59	59	53	71	68	51	69	55	61	66	59	67	73
48731	ELKTON	65	63	58	60	65	71	61	63	64	59	78	73	62	82	63	66	75	62	68	76
48732	ESSEXVILLE	81	81	79	79	82	90	80	82	82	79	101	93	81	102	81	83	97	81	85	93
48733	FAIRGROVE	82	71	56	66	76	85	69	76	76	68	91	89	67	94	71	79	86	75	87	97
48734	FRANKENMUTH	99	113	125	112	112	118	107	108	104	107	130	123	112	132	110	103	128	106	104	118
48735	GAGETOWN	64	66	66	63	68	75	65	66	67	63	83	74	67	89	67	70	80	64	71	75
48737	GLENNIE	67	52	36	47	59	66	49	60	56	49	66	70	44	65	53	60	62	59	70	81
48738	GREENBUSH	79	62	42	56	70	78	58	70	66	58	78	83	52	77	62	71	73	69	83	96
48739	HALE	71	55	37	50	62	70	52	63	59	52	70	74	47	69	56	63	65	62	75	86
48740	HARRISVILLE	75	59	40	53	66	75	56	67	64	56	75	78	50	74	60	68	70	66	80	91
48741	KINGSTON	81	70	53	67	74	81	67	74	72	67	87	87	65	87	68	74	82	73	81	94
48742	LINCOLN	74	60	45	56	65	77	61	69	68	60	81	75	56	74	63	72	74	68	82	84
48743	LONG LAKE	64	50	34	45	57	64	47	57	54	47	64	67	42	63	51	57	59	56	68	78
48744	MAYVILLE	87	77	59	74	81	88	73	80	78	73	94	94	71	95	74	79	89	78	87	101
48745	MIKADO	77	60	41	55	68	77	58	69	65	57	77	80	52	76	61	70	72	68	82	93
48746	MILLINGTON	92	87	73	83	90	96	81	87	84	81	103	102	81	106	83	85	99	85	91	107
48747	MUNGER	83	88	86	85	89	93	82	85	81	81	101	99	84	106	84	82	99	82	84	99
48748	NATIONAL CITY	81	65	45	59	72	81	61	73	68	61	81	85	55	81	65	73	76	71	85	99
48749	OMER	82	62	41	59	68	80	66	74	74	64	88	84	59	84	66	78	80	74	88	92
48750	OSCODA	73	58	42	54	64	73	57	66	64	56	76	76	52	75	59	67	70	65	77	86
48754	OWENDALE	70	69	63	65	71	78	66	69	69	65	85	80	67	90	68	71	82	67	75	83
48755	PIGEON	94	78	61	74	84	98	78	87	85	78	102	96	73	95	80	89	95	86	102	107
48756	PRESCOTT	60	47	32	42	53	60	44	53	50	44	60	63	40	59	47	54	55	53	63	73
48757	REESE	91	82	65	79	86	93	78	85	82	78	100	100	76	101	80	84	95	83	91	106
48759	SEBEWAING	66	62	57	61	64	71	63	65	65	61	80	75	62	80	63	67	76	65	70	76
48760	SILVERWOOD	95	79	56	73	86	95	73	85	81	73	97	101	69	97	77	85	91	84	97	114
48761	SOUTH BRANCH	68	53	36	48	60	67	50	60	57	50	67	71	45	66	53	61	62	59	71	83
48762	SPRUCE	78	65	49	59	71	81	60	72	67	61	81	80	56	76	65	72	75	70	84	93
48763	TAWAS CITY	74	60	44	57	64	73	61	67	66	59	79	78	56	78	61	69	74	67	77	84
48765	TURNER	79	56	31	49	63	72	54	66	63	54	74	78	47	72	56	68	68	65	80	92
48766	TWINING	78	53	26	47	60	70	52	64	62	53	73	76	45	69	53	67	67	64	79	90
48767	UNIONVILLE	80	72	59	68	76	84	69	76	75	68	91	88	68	94	72	77	86	74	84	94
48768	VASSAR	80	78	70	75	80	86	74	78	76	74	94	91	75	97	76	77	90	77	81	94
48770	WHITTEMORE	77	54	29	47	61	70	52	64	61	52	72	76	45	69	54	66	66	63	78	90
48801	ALMA	78	69	63	68	72	80	73	75	76	71	93	88	70	92	72	77	88	76	80	89
48806	ASHLEY	85	71	52	68	76	84	69	77	75	69	91	90	66	90	70	77	85	76	85	97
	MICHIGAN	91	91	93	89	91	98	90	91	91	90	113	106	90	113	90	91	109	91	92	105
	UNITED STATES	100	100	100	100	100	100	100	100	100	100	100	100	100	100	100	100	100	100	100	100

MICHIGAN

POPULATION CHANGE

A 48807-49029

#	POST OFFICE NAME	COUNTY FIPS CODE	POPULATION 2000	2004	2009	% Rate	State Centile	HOUSEHOLDS 2000	2004	2009	% Annual Rate 2000-2004	2004 Average HH Size	FAMILIES 2000	2004	% Annual Rate 2000-2004
48807	BANNISTER	057	986	995	1001	0.2	30	378	390	401	0.7	2.55	288	293	0.4
48808	BATH	037	3730	4540	5383	4.7	100	1363	1694	2049	5.3	2.67	1054	1297	5.0
48809	BELDING	067	11231	11770	12414	1.1	68	4021	4284	4592	1.5	2.68	2905	3055	1.2
48811	CARSON CITY	117	4944	4961	5057	0.1	25	1219	1245	1298	0.5	2.82	897	905	0.2
48813	CHARLOTTE	045	19937	20591	21499	0.8	55	7431	7829	8346	1.2	2.57	5466	5713	1.1
48815	CLARKSVILLE	067	2138	2232	2347	1.0	66	770	819	877	1.5	2.72	584	613	1.2
48817	CORUNNA	155	6673	6700	6761	0.1	27	2536	2610	2690	0.7	2.47	1846	1879	0.4
48818	CRYSTAL	117	2588	2656	2758	0.6	46	1021	1070	1133	1.1	2.47	715	738	0.8
48819	DANSVILLE	065	2290	2410	2475	1.2	72	792	852	892	1.7	2.82	649	689	1.4
48820	DEWITT	037	14377	16158	18402	2.8	96	5129	5875	6823	3.3	2.74	4088	4636	3.0
48821	DIMONDALE	045	5700	6013	6328	1.3	74	2167	2338	2512	1.8	2.49	1585	1693	1.6
48822	EAGLE	037	2450	2622	2914	1.6	83	887	972	1104	2.2	2.69	732	795	2.0
48823	EAST LANSING	065	47828	48682	49834	0.4	39	18988	19663	20486	0.8	2.23	7893	7994	0.3
48824	EAST LANSING	065	2688	2688	2688	0.0	23	15	14	14	-1.6	2.57	1	0	-100.0
48825	EAST LANSING	065	8022	8009	8007	0.0	21	395	398	404	0.2	2.11	191	187	-0.5
48827	EATON RAPIDS	045	15657	16130	16704	0.7	52	5661	5917	6234	1.1	2.71	4327	4479	0.8
48829	EDMORE	117	3481	3542	3667	0.4	39	1311	1355	1426	0.8	2.59	965	987	0.5
48831	ELSIE	037	3314	3531	3828	1.5	79	1240	1350	1494	2.0	2.61	925	993	1.7
48832	ELWELL	057	1598	1644	1680	0.7	50	593	623	649	1.2	2.62	453	471	0.9
48834	FENWICK	117	3353	3455	3587	0.7	52	963	1017	1081	1.3	2.95	763	798	1.1
48835	FOWLER	037	4054	4334	4813	1.6	82	1408	1542	1749	2.2	2.81	1107	1198	1.9
48836	FOWLERVILLE	093	11589	13058	14843	2.9	97	3999	4604	5335	3.4	2.82	3103	3534	3.1
48837	GRAND LEDGE	045	17768	18803	20056	1.3	76	6821	7355	7998	1.8	2.55	5014	5369	1.6
48838	GREENVILLE	117	16721	17150	17782	0.6	46	6458	6740	7101	1.0	2.51	4527	4664	0.7
48840	HASLETT	065	12009	12315	12565	0.6	46	5315	5520	5702	0.9	2.22	3060	3117	0.4
48841	HENDERSON	155	927	928	932	0.0	23	313	320	327	0.5	2.90	252	256	0.4
48842	HOLT	065	17818	18299	18580	0.6	48	6900	7208	7439	1.0	2.51	4897	5039	0.7
48843	HOWELL	093	32526	38235	44541	3.9	99	11760	14077	16701	4.3	2.67	8754	10440	4.2
48845	HUBBARDSTON	067	1042	1047	1091	0.1	27	350	359	382	0.6	2.65	273	276	0.3
48846	IONIA	067	19738	20189	20924	0.5	44	5497	5751	6124	1.1	2.61	3864	3991	0.8
48847	ITHACA	057	6581	6546	6600	-0.1	19	2479	2513	2580	0.3	2.53	1799	1801	0.0
48848	LAINGSBURG	155	8270	8460	8855	0.5	44	2906	3037	3239	1.0	2.78	2336	2419	0.8
48849	LAKE ODESSA	067	6012	6134	6374	0.5	41	2207	2286	2413	0.8	2.68	1655	1693	0.5
48850	LAKEVIEW	117	4700	4929	5173	1.1	69	1715	1828	1952	1.5	2.66	1274	1342	1.2
48851	LYONS	067	2225	2276	2369	0.5	44	827	864	916	1.0	2.63	606	626	0.8
48854	MASON	065	17220	17651	17904	0.6	45	6397	6717	6951	1.2	2.56	4741	4892	0.7
48855	HOWELL	093	11926	13534	15463	3.0	98	3934	4575	5334	3.6	2.95	3275	3771	3.4
48856	MIDDLETON	057	732	741	752	0.3	34	268	276	285	0.7	2.66	204	207	0.3
48857	MORRICE	155	2497	2520	2542	0.2	30	863	887	910	0.7	2.83	692	704	0.4
48858	MOUNT PLEASANT	073	44714	49254	54877	2.3	93	15468	17685	20444	3.2	2.45	7799	8776	2.8
48860	MUIR	067	1352	1409	1480	1.0	65	498	529	567	1.4	2.65	371	389	1.1
48861	MULLIKEN	045	1788	1855	1931	0.9	60	631	669	711	1.4	2.75	506	530	1.1
48864	OKEMOS	065	20293	20240	20423	-0.1	20	8033	8158	8376	0.4	2.44	5125	5136	0.1
48865	ORLEANS	067	1700	1836	1966	1.8	87	626	692	755	2.4	2.65	476	519	2.1
48866	OVID	037	4478	4863	5333	2.0	89	1614	1786	1995	2.4	2.67	1217	1331	2.1
48867	OWOSSO	155	28592	29039	29521	0.4	37	11238	11635	12042	0.8	2.47	7779	7937	0.5
48871	PERRINTON	057	2365	2438	2496	0.7	53	856	899	938	1.2	2.66	661	688	1.0
48872	PERRY	155	7486	7714	7899	0.7	52	2670	2799	2914	1.1	2.75	2093	2175	0.9
48873	PEWAMO	067	2010	2089	2215	0.9	61	667	707	764	1.4	2.95	521	546	1.1
48875	PORTLAND	067	9145	9776	10457	1.6	82	3285	3581	3898	2.1	2.73	2528	2725	1.8
48876	POTTERVILLE	045	3655	3772	3916	0.7	54	1345	1415	1498	1.2	2.66	1019	1062	1.0
48877	RIVERDALE	057	2123	2213	2292	1.0	65	746	794	838	1.5	2.74	587	619	1.3
48878	ROSEBUSH	073	1561	1569	1689	0.1	27	556	569	626	0.6	2.75	405	409	0.2
48879	SAINT JOHNS	037	17706	18812	20785	1.4	78	6392	6942	7844	2.0	2.64	4777	5134	1.7
48880	SAINT LOUIS	057	9812	9827	9929	0.0	24	2654	2706	2794	0.5	2.48	1862	1874	0.2
48881	SARANAC	067	4984	5228	5506	1.1	69	1868	2003	2151	1.7	2.47	1390	1473	1.4
48883	SHEPHERD	073	6842	7250	7844	1.4	76	2492	2686	2962	1.8	2.69	1866	2003	1.7
48884	SHERIDAN	117	4082	4078	4184	0.0	22	1521	1553	1626	0.5	2.44	1142	1151	0.2
48885	SIDNEY	117	876	944	1005	1.8	86	330	365	396	2.4	2.58	259	281	1.9
48886	SIX LAKES	117	2337	2420	2516	0.8	58	900	944	995	1.1	2.56	668	692	0.8
48888	STANTON	117	6853	7155	7502	1.0	66	2532	2696	2877	1.5	2.61	1864	1959	1.2
48889	SUMNER	057	1430	1450	1473	0.3	36	515	534	553	0.9	2.68	402	412	0.6
48890	SUNFIELD	067	2072	2136	2221	0.7	53	732	771	818	1.2	2.75	586	611	1.0
48891	VESTABURG	117	3450	3571	3732	0.8	57	1261	1332	1417	1.3	2.67	968	1012	1.1
48892	WEBBERVILLE	065	4154	4308	4450	0.9	60	1504	1591	1670	1.3	2.70	1159	1211	1.0
48893	WEIDMAN	073	4585	4964	5500	1.9	88	1779	1975	2241	2.5	2.51	1314	1442	2.2
48895	WILLIAMSTON	065	10775	11142	11354	0.8	57	4001	4194	4340	1.1	2.65	3021	3122	0.8
48897	WOODLAND	015	1614	1704	1815	1.3	74	598	645	699	1.8	2.64	451	480	1.5
48906	LANSING	037	26651	27229	28271	0.5	43	10496	10961	11622	1.0	2.47	6639	6813	0.6
48910	LANSING	065	35105	34967	35400	-0.1	20	15488	15732	16215	0.4	2.20	8335	8262	-0.2
48911	LANSING	065	41121	42472	43646	0.8	55	16279	17100	17874	1.2	2.46	10702	11032	0.7
48912	LANSING	065	18318	17879	17840	-0.6	7	7975	7952	8079	-0.1	2.23	4009	3866	-0.9
48915	LANSING	065	10256	10209	10286	-0.1	19	4060	4116	4223	0.3	2.47	2387	2372	-0.2
48917	LANSING	045	31408	32057	33254	0.5	42	13694	14344	15208	1.1	2.21	8355	8553	0.6
48933	LANSING	065	2227	2109	2091	-1.3	1	1368	1313	1322	-1.0	1.58	324	296	-2.1
49001	KALAMAZOO	077	22670	22567	23124	-0.1	19	9433	9517	9911	0.2	2.30	5121	5055	-0.3
49002	PORTAGE	077	17997	18503	19159	0.7	49	7641	8058	8522	1.3	2.27	4763	4906	0.7
49004	KALAMAZOO	077	15511	15838	16357	0.5	43	6033	6230	6530	0.8	2.51	4335	4443	0.6
49006	KALAMAZOO	077	22443	24162	25640	1.8	86	9550	10548	11443	2.4	2.13	3824	4111	1.7
49007	KALAMAZOO	077	12417	12295	12520	-0.2	15	4811	4840	5016	0.1	2.39	2215	2159	-0.6
49008	KALAMAZOO	077	21494	21051	21263	-0.5	8	7194	7136	7376	-0.2	2.08	3615	3515	-0.7
49009	KALAMAZOO	077	32574	35266	37256	1.9	88	13313	14699	15816	2.4	2.36	8435	9167	2.0
49010	ALLEGAN	005	16506	17681	19027	1.6	83	6155	6700	7329	2.0	2.58	4476	4827	1.8
49011	ATHENS	025	2345	2381	2404	0.4	37	882	912	936	0.8	2.61	680	694	0.5
49012	AUGUSTA	077	2966	2997	3066	0.2	31	1165	1196	1243	0.6	2.49	845	857	0.3
49013	BANGOR	159	5672	5903	6149	0.9	62	2009	2114	2230	1.2	2.74	1470	1528	0.9
49014	BATTLE CREEK	025	22816	22984	23190	0.2	28	8572	8758	8954	0.5	2.51	5820	5864	0.2
49015	BATTLE CREEK	025	34784	34811	34972	0.0	23	14184	14410	14674	0.4	2.35	9101	9104	0.0
49017	BATTLE CREEK	025	35640	35923	36328	0.2	29	14513	14837	15211	0.5	2.39	9327	9364	0.1
49021	BELLEVUE	045	6333	6512	6770	0.7	49	2357	2482	2633	1.2	2.61	1834	1910	1.0
49022	BENTON HARBOR	021	35317	35051	35094	-0.2	17	13427	13571	13830	0.3	2.53	8915	8874	-0.1
49024	PORTAGE	077	28125	29336	30568	1.0	65	10987	11657	12347	1.4	2.50	7712	8094	1.1
49026	BLOOMINGDALE	159	2264	2288	2346	0.3	32	801	820	852	0.6	2.69	601	608	0.3
49028	BRONSON	023	6852	6876	7046	0.1	25	2442	2479	2573	0.4	2.73	1765	1768	0.0
49029	BURLINGTON	025	1668	1725	1750	0.8	57	620	654	675	1.3	2.64	480	500	1.1
	MICHIGAN					0.6					1.0	2.52			0.6
	UNITED STATES					1.2					1.3	2.58			1.1

#	POST OFFICE NAME	White 2000	White 2004	Black 2000	Black 2004	Asian/Pacific 2000	Asian/Pacific 2004	% Hispanic Origin 2000	% Hispanic Origin 2004	0-4	5-9	10-14	15-19	20-24	25-44	45-64	65-84	85+	18+	MEDIAN AGE 2004	% 2004 Males	% 2004 Females
48807	BANNISTER	97.6	97.3	0.2	0.2	0.1	0.1	2.0	2.4	7.2	7.3	7.8	6.2	5.7	29.3	23.9	10.8	1.7	73.8	36.8	51.3	48.7
48808	BATH	96.0	95.7	0.6	0.6	0.5	0.6	2.2	2.5	6.6	7.3	8.1	6.4	5.2	29.2	28.2	8.3	0.8	74.0	38.1	49.3	50.8
48809	BELDING	96.7	96.2	0.5	0.5	0.4	0.4	2.6	3.0	8.0	7.7	8.1	7.5	6.9	28.8	22.2	9.2	1.5	71.2	34.0	49.6	50.4
48811	CARSON CITY	79.6	78.1	15.8	16.9	0.3	0.4	3.5	4.0	4.9	5.1	6.4	6.2	8.8	38.5	20.8	8.3	1.0	79.8	34.8	63.3	36.7
48813	CHARLOTTE	96.6	96.2	0.6	0.6	0.4	0.5	2.8	3.2	6.7	6.8	7.2	7.0	6.5	27.8	26.4	10.1	1.6	75.0	37.4	49.3	50.7
48815	CLARKSVILLE	98.1	97.8	0.2	0.2	0.1	0.1	1.5	1.9	6.6	7.1	7.6	6.8	5.8	27.1	27.0	10.3	1.6	74.5	37.9	50.6	49.4
48817	CORUNNA	97.1	96.9	0.5	0.5	0.2	0.3	1.8	2.0	5.9	6.1	6.6	6.3	6.7	27.4	27.1	12.1	1.8	77.7	39.4	49.9	50.1
48818	CRYSTAL	97.5	97.3	0.2	0.2	0.2	0.3	1.2	1.4	6.2	6.4	6.9	6.7	6.2	25.1	28.1	13.3	1.2	76.5	39.4	49.8	50.2
48819	DANSVILLE	97.3	97.0	0.3	0.3	0.4	0.5	1.8	2.0	7.1	7.4	7.4	6.7	5.5	29.1	27.8	8.1	1.0	73.7	37.9	50.0	50.0
48820	DEWITT	95.7	95.2	0.8	0.9	0.8	1.0	2.4	2.7	6.8	7.5	8.6	7.2	5.7	26.5	28.5	8.3	0.9	72.3	37.8	49.8	50.2
48821	DIMONDALE	92.6	91.5	3.7	4.2	0.7	0.9	3.3	3.8	4.8	5.6	6.7	6.7	5.9	22.3	32.1	13.1	2.8	78.6	43.7	48.0	52.0
48822	EAGLE	98.0	97.8	0.3	0.3	0.4	0.5	1.8	2.1	6.3	7.1	7.9	6.9	5.2	24.3	31.3	10.3	0.7	74.1	40.9	50.8	49.2
48823	EAST LANSING	82.8	81.1	6.3	6.3	7.4	8.9	2.9	3.3	3.7	3.6	4.1	12.5	26.5	23.2	17.3	7.4	1.8	86.0	24.9	48.3	51.7
48824	EAST LANSING	80.0	77.1	11.4	12.2	5.4	7.1	2.2	2.6	0.0	0.0	0.0	70.8	28.4	0.9	0.0	0.0	0.0	99.7	18.5	43.0	57.0
48825	EAST LANSING	78.7	75.4	8.8	9.4	9.9	12.5	2.5	2.8	0.9	0.7	0.6	61.5	26.6	8.2	1.3	0.3	0.1	97.3	18.9	47.6	52.4
48827	EATON RAPIDS	96.3	95.9	0.4	0.5	0.4	0.4	2.6	3.0	7.2	7.3	7.4	6.4	6.4	27.6	26.4	8.6	1.1	72.7	36.8	49.5	50.5
48829	EDMORE	96.6	96.2	0.3	0.3	0.1	0.2	3.1	3.5	7.0	7.2	8.0	6.6	6.4	26.7	23.1	11.1	1.9	73.2	36.9	49.3	50.7
48831	ELSIE	98.2	98.0	0.1	0.1	0.2	0.2	1.8	2.2	7.0	7.0	8.0	6.3	6.4	26.4	25.8	11.2	1.9	74.1	37.7	50.5	49.5
48832	ELWELL	97.8	97.5	0.2	0.2	0.1	0.1	2.3	2.6	6.6	6.8	7.9	7.6	6.3	28.2	24.3	11.5	0.9	73.8	36.7	49.9	50.1
48834	FENWICK	90.4	89.5	6.4	7.1	0.3	0.4	3.2	3.6	6.4	6.5	6.6	6.5	6.7	32.4	25.9	8.4	0.8	76.4	36.9	57.3	42.7
48835	FOWLER	99.2	99.1	0.0	0.0	0.2	0.2	0.9	1.1	8.7	8.7	8.4	6.9	5.9	27.5	21.7	10.8	1.5	70.0	34.7	50.7	49.3
48836	FOWLERVILLE	97.0	96.7	0.2	0.2	0.4	0.5	1.1	1.3	7.7	7.8	8.7	7.5	6.0	30.3	23.2	7.6	1.2	70.8	35.1	50.4	49.6
48837	GRAND LEDGE	96.6	96.2	0.6	0.7	0.6	0.7	2.2	2.5	6.0	6.4	7.3	7.1	6.3	25.9	29.1	10.4	1.4	75.8	39.5	48.7	51.3
48838	GREENVILLE	96.7	96.3	0.4	0.5	0.4	0.5	2.6	3.0	6.8	6.8	7.5	6.8	6.5	28.3	24.4	10.9	2.1	74.4	37.7	49.6	50.4
48840	HASLETT	93.1	91.9	2.1	2.3	2.2	2.9	2.5	2.9	5.3	5.3	7.7	7.6	6.5	29.2	27.3	9.4	1.7	76.6	37.7	46.9	53.1
48841	HENDERSON	98.3	98.2	0.1	0.1	0.1	0.1	1.3	1.6	5.8	6.5	8.0	7.0	5.6	26.4	27.5	12.0	1.3	75.4	39.9	50.2	49.8
48842	HOLT	93.1	92.0	2.3	2.6	1.1	1.6	3.4	4.0	6.4	6.7	7.7	7.4	6.8	27.4	27.4	8.8	1.6	74.4	37.2	47.8	52.2
48843	HOWELL	96.8	96.4	0.4	0.4	0.8	1.0	1.5	1.7	7.9	7.9	7.7	6.5	5.9	30.7	24.4	7.9	1.1	72.4	35.6	50.2	49.8
48845	HUBBARDSTON	93.2	92.7	4.4	4.8	0.3	0.3	2.1	2.2	7.2	7.4	7.7	6.7	6.3	29.1	26.2	8.8	0.7	73.7	35.5	54.8	45.2
48846	IONIA	81.4	79.9	13.2	14.1	0.5	0.6	4.1	4.5	5.7	5.6	5.8	7.5	14.4	32.2	20.0	7.5	1.4	79.4	30.7	61.0	39.0
48847	ITHACA	96.4	95.9	0.2	0.3	0.3	0.4	4.1	4.7	6.9	7.0	7.2	6.8	6.7	26.7	24.8	11.7	2.2	74.4	36.9	48.3	51.7
48848	LAINGSBURG	97.5	97.2	0.4	0.4	0.1	0.2	1.5	1.7	6.5	7.2	8.1	6.9	5.4	28.2	28.9	7.9	1.0	73.7	38.3	50.6	49.4
48849	LAKE ODESSA	96.2	95.7	0.2	0.2	0.4	0.5	3.7	4.3	7.6	7.6	7.8	7.3	6.6	27.9	23.8	9.9	1.4	72.4	35.5	49.1	50.9
48850	LAKEVIEW	96.9	96.6	0.2	0.2	0.2	0.3	2.2	2.4	7.0	7.0	7.8	7.0	6.4	26.2	23.6	13.1	2.0	73.8	37.3	49.3	50.7
48851	LYONS	96.8	96.5	0.2	0.2	0.1	0.1	2.2	2.5	6.3	6.8	7.9	7.2	6.0	28.3	26.9	9.5	1.1	74.6	37.1	51.2	48.8
48854	MASON	95.0	94.4	1.7	1.8	0.7	0.9	2.6	3.0	5.7	6.0	7.2	7.4	6.5	27.6	28.3	10.1	1.3	76.4	38.8	49.7	50.3
48855	HOWELL	97.8	97.5	0.1	0.1	0.4	0.5	1.0	1.4	7.4	7.9	8.3	6.9	5.2	29.6	26.6	7.5	0.7	71.9	36.9	51.2	48.8
48856	MIDDLETON	97.0	96.8	0.1	0.1	0.0	0.1	2.1	2.3	7.0	8.0	8.9	7.0	5.7	27.7	23.4	11.5	0.9	71.0	36.1	49.3	50.7
48857	MORRICE	97.1	96.8	0.3	0.3	0.2	0.4	1.6	1.9	7.8	8.0	7.9	6.2	5.6	31.1	24.4	8.1	0.9	72.5	35.4	51.1	48.9
48858	MOUNT PLEASANT	89.7	88.8	2.6	2.7	1.9	2.5	2.4	2.7	4.9	4.5	5.2	18.2	19.0	23.4	16.6	7.0	1.3	82.2	24.5	46.6	53.4
48860	MUIR	96.8	96.5	0.1	0.1	0.2	0.2	1.7	2.0	7.2	7.5	8.5	7.7	6.8	29.9	23.3	8.0	1.1	72.0	33.8	50.8	49.2
48861	MULLIKEN	96.9	96.5	0.4	0.4	0.1	0.2	2.0	2.4	6.3	6.6	7.5	7.0	6.7	27.0	28.0	9.5	1.4	75.1	38.1	51.1	49.0
48864	OKEMOS	84.3	81.3	4.1	4.3	8.7	11.2	2.2	2.5	5.1	5.6	7.3	7.6	9.2	26.4	28.9	8.4	1.5	77.3	36.6	48.4	51.6
48865	ORLEANS	98.0	97.7	0.1	0.1	0.2	0.2	1.7	2.0	7.4	7.4	7.7	7.6	6.5	30.0	24.4	8.4	0.7	72.9	34.5	51.4	48.6
48866	OVID	97.3	97.2	0.2	0.2	0.2	0.2	2.8	3.0	7.8	7.5	7.5	6.5	6.4	28.0	24.0	10.4	2.0	73.3	36.4	48.9	51.1
48867	OWOSSO	97.3	97.0	0.2	0.2	0.4	0.6	2.3	2.7	6.9	6.8	7.3	6.9	6.5	27.2	24.7	12.0	1.7	74.9	37.3	48.5	51.5
48871	PERRINTON	97.1	96.8	0.2	0.2	0.0	0.0	2.3	2.7	6.0	6.7	7.8	6.4	5.4	27.3	26.9	11.8	1.9	75.6	39.5	50.4	49.6
48872	PERRY	97.6	97.3	0.2	0.2	0.4	0.5	1.0	1.2	7.7	7.8	8.3	7.2	6.1	29.0	25.2	7.9	0.8	71.8	35.2	48.3	51.7
48873	PEWAMO	98.7	98.5	0.0	0.0	0.1	0.1	1.0	1.2	8.9	9.3	8.2	6.6	6.0	27.9	20.7	10.2	1.2	68.6	33.5	49.6	50.4
48875	PORTLAND	97.9	97.6	0.3	0.3	0.2	0.3	1.4	1.7	7.7	7.8	8.1	7.2	6.2	28.3	24.9	8.8	1.0	72.0	35.1	49.2	50.8
48876	POTTERVILLE	96.2	95.8	0.4	0.4	0.2	0.3	3.7	4.3	7.0	7.0	7.6	7.7	6.6	27.9	27.4	8.0	0.9	73.7	36.1	48.8	51.3
48877	RIVERDALE	97.4	97.1	0.2	0.3	0.1	0.1	2.3	2.7	7.9	7.1	7.5	7.4	6.3	28.7	24.6	9.9	0.8	72.6	36.2	51.0	49.0
48878	ROSEBUSH	95.2	95.1	0.6	0.6	0.4	0.5	1.3	1.3	7.4	7.5	8.0	7.0	6.3	28.9	24.0	9.8	1.2	73.0	35.8	48.1	51.9
48879	SAINT JOHNS	97.0	96.7	0.4	0.4	0.5	0.6	2.5	2.8	7.0	7.0	7.6	7.0	6.6	27.2	24.9	10.4	2.2	73.8	37.1	49.7	50.3
48880	SAINT LOUIS	79.1	77.7	15.1	16.1	0.4	0.5	5.2	5.8	4.4	4.5	5.1	5.9	8.8	39.3	21.7	9.1	1.3	82.9	35.5	64.9	35.1
48881	SARANAC	95.5	94.9	2.0	2.2	0.3	0.3	1.9	2.3	7.0	7.0	7.3	6.8	6.6	30.1	24.9	9.1	1.2	74.3	36.5	51.9	48.1
48883	SHEPHERD	95.4	95.1	0.4	0.5	0.3	0.3	2.2	2.5	6.8	7.0	8.2	7.7	6.7	29.2	24.9	8.8	0.9	73.3	35.5	49.5	50.5
48884	SHERIDAN	93.6	92.9	3.8	4.3	0.3	0.4	1.9	2.3	6.4	6.4	6.8	6.9	6.9	30.6	25.2	9.9	0.9	76.2	36.7	53.7	46.4
48885	SIDNEY	98.0	97.9	0.3	0.3	0.1	0.1	1.1	1.3	5.5	6.0	7.9	7.4	6.6	27.3	27.3	10.7	0.7	76.0	38.4	50.2	49.8
48886	SIX LAKES	96.3	96.1	0.4	0.5	0.1	0.2	1.6	1.9	7.2	7.3	8.0	6.6	6.9	25.3	25.0	13.3	1.3	73.2	37.3	49.5	50.5
48888	STANTON	97.2	96.9	0.2	0.2	0.3	0.5	2.4	2.7	6.4	6.7	7.9	7.0	6.4	27.0	25.7	11.6	1.4	74.5	37.6	49.8	50.2
48889	SUMNER	98.0	97.9	0.2	0.2	0.0	0.0	2.0	2.3	7.7	6.6	7.1	7.5	6.3	27.0	25.0	11.6	1.2	73.5	37.4	50.1	49.9
48890	SUNFIELD	97.4	97.1	0.3	0.3	0.2	0.2	2.0	2.3	7.1	7.5	8.1	7.2	6.0	27.5	25.6	9.6	1.4	73.1	36.8	49.3	50.7
48891	VESTABURG	97.9	97.7	0.3	0.3	0.2	0.3	1.7	1.9	6.9	6.9	8.4	7.5	6.4	27.4	24.8	10.9	1.0	72.8	36.3	50.8	49.2
48892	WEBBERVILLE	96.9	96.6	0.5	0.5	0.4	0.5	1.5	1.7	7.1	7.4	8.2	7.0	6.2	30.7	24.5	7.8	1.1	72.9	35.4	49.5	50.5
48893	WEIDMAN	96.2	96.0	0.4	0.5	0.2	0.2	1.4	1.6	6.8	6.8	7.2	6.1	5.2	27.3	26.2	13.2	1.1	75.3	39.1	50.1	49.9
48895	WILLIAMSTON	97.3	96.8	0.4	0.4	0.6	0.8	1.7	2.0	6.4	7.2	8.5	7.1	5.1	25.6	29.6	9.5	1.1	73.5	39.0	48.9	51.1
48897	WOODLAND	97.5	97.2	0.1	0.1	0.3	0.4	2.5	2.9	6.6	6.9	7.6	7.1	5.7	27.4	26.1	11.3	1.4	74.5	38.2	51.3	48.7
48906	LANSING	73.0	71.3	12.8	13.1	3.2	4.0	12.5	13.6	8.0	7.4	7.7	6.9	6.7	29.8	22.7	9.6	1.1	72.7	33.9	49.8	50.2
48910	LANSING	76.3	73.6	13.7	14.9	1.9	2.5	7.9	9.0	7.5	6.7	6.3	6.3	8.6	33.2	21.2	8.7	1.5	75.9	33.0	48.0	52.1
48911	LANSING	61.7	59.6	27.0	27.8	3.3	4.1	7.6	8.4	8.6	8.0	8.0	7.3	7.5	29.7	22.1	8.0	0.9	70.9	32.0	46.7	53.3
48912	LANSING	72.8	70.6	13.4	13.9	2.2	3.6	11.0	12.2	6.8	6.4	6.8	6.5	8.4	33.8	21.4	8.6	1.3	76.2	32.9	48.9	51.1
48915	LANSING	47.5	45.2	40.0	41.1	1.7	2.1	11.2	12.3	8.5	8.0	7.8	7.2	7.6	30.8	21.2	7.9	1.1	71.3	31.5	48.9	51.2
48917	LANSING	83.7	82.1	8.9	9.4	2.6	3.4	4.9	5.5	5.8	5.6	6.0	6.1	8.1	28.0	26.6	11.9	2.0	79.0	37.9	47.0	53.0
48933	LANSING	54.2	51.2	30.8	31.7	5.5	6.9	9.2	10.2	5.0	4.0	4.1	6.3	12.0	39.2	20.3	8.0	1.1	84.2	30.9	53.0	47.0
49001	KALAMAZOO	72.8	70.6	16.9	18.0	1.0	1.3	7.4	8.2	7.9	7.2	6.9	6.7	8.8	32.9	19.6	8.0	2.1	74.3	32.0	48.4	51.6
49002	PORTAGE	92.4	91.1	3.2	3.6	1.5	2.0	2.1	2.5	6.4	6.4	6.4	6.2	6.5	29.8	24.7	12.0	1.7	77.0	37.2	48.6	51.4
49004	KALAMAZOO	87.6	86.6	8.1	8.6	0.8	1.0	2.2	2.5	7.5	7.4	7.4	6.6	5.3	26.8	24.9	12.3	1.8	73.4	37.6	47.8	52.2
49006	KALAMAZOO	80.5	78.4	11.6	12.4	4.0	4.9	2.6	2.9	4.8	4.1	4.1	11.0	25.4	24.5	14.8	9.0	2.2	84.7	25.3	48.2	51.8
49007	KALAMAZOO	43.4	42.0	48.9	49.7	0.8	1.0	4.6	5.0	7.1	7.5	7.3	8.6	15.8	28.2	17.4	6.8	1.4	74.0	26.9	49.1	50.9
49008	KALAMAZOO	84.7	82.8	8.7	9.4	3.5	4.3	2.1	2.4	4.1	3.8	3.4	25.2	14.0	21.5	16.8	9.6	1.7	86.6	24.8	48.0	52.0
49009	KALAMAZOO	89.5	88.1	5.8	6.3	2.1	2.7	1.9	2.2	6.2	6.4	6.7	6.7	4.7	26.4	26.0	10.7	2.3	76.9	36.6	47.8	52.2
49010	ALLEGAN	94.5	94.0	2.3	2.4	0.4	0.5	2.4	2.8	6.8	6.8	7.1	7.2	6.5	27.6	25.8	10.8	1.4	74.7	37.4	49.9	50.1
49011	ATHENS	97.1	96.7	0.2	0.2	0.3	0.3	1.5	1.9	6.4	7.0	7.7	6.3	6.3	27.6	24.7	12.9	1.5	75.7	38.1	49.7	50.3
49012	AUGUSTA	96.6	96.1	0.5	0.6	0.4	0.4	1.4	1.6	5.5	6.6	8.1	6.9	3.9	25.3	31.2	11.3	1.3	75.2	41.7	49.6	50.4
49013	BANGOR	82.0	80.4	8.4	8.9	0.1	0.2	10.9	12.3	7.6	7.2	7.8	7.7	7.2	25.5	24.6	11.0	1.4	72.4	35.5	49.6	50.4
49014	BATTLE CREEK	85.9	84.8	8.7	9.2	0.9	1.2	4.0	4.5	6.4	6.5	7.4	7.5	6.9	28.7	25.2	10.1	1.3	75.2	36.2	50.4	49.6
49015	BATTLE CREEK	84.7	82.9	7.7	8.3	2.9	3.7	4.1	4.6	6.7	6.5	7.0	6.7	6.3	27.5	24.4	12.3	2.0	75.6	37.3	48.7	51.3
49017	BATTLE CREEK	75.4	74.0	19.8	20.8	0.5	0.6	2.5	2.8	6.7	6.8	7.5	6.7	6.3	26.2	25.5	12.4	1.9	74.8	37.9	47.7	52.3
49021	BELLEVUE	97.2	96.9	0.5	0.5	0.3	0.4	1.7	2.1	5.8	6.3	7.1	6.7	6.0	26.4	28.9	11.6	1.2	76.6	40.0	50.3	49.7
49022	BENTON HARBOR	40.1	38.9	56.6	57.8	0.3	0.3	2.8	2.8	8.7	8.4	8.7	7.5	6.6	25.5	22.4	10.7	1.5	69.4	33.1	47.2	52.8
49024	PORTAGE	89.9	88.4	4.0	4.3	3.3	4.3	1.8	2.1	7.1	7.2	7.8	7.5	6.4	27.2	25.8	9.8	1.3	73.2	36.2	47.6	52.4
49026	BLOOMINGDALE	92.9	92.2	2.4	2.6	0.3	0.4	4.7	5.4	6.6	7.0	7.8	6.8	6.2	26.1	25.9	11.8	1.9	74.2	38.8	50.1	49.9
49028	BRONSON	93.8	93.1	0.3	0.3	0.1	0.2	6.5	7.3	6.9	6.9	7.5	7.3	7.1	26.5	23.1	11.0	1.8	74.2	35.8	50.8	49.2
49029	BURLINGTON	97.9	97.6	0.1	0.1	0.3	0.4	1.0	1.1	5.0	5.6	7.4	7.0	6.3	27.7	28.6	11.5	1.3	77.6	40.2	50.1	49.9
	MICHIGAN	80.2	79.2	14.2	14.4	1.8	2.3	3.3	3.6	6.8	6.9	7.4	7.1	6.9	28.1	24.6	10.8	1.6	74.9	36.5	49.1	50.9
	UNITED STATES	75.1	73.6	12.3	12.5	3.8	4.2	12.5	14.1	6.9	6.7	7.2	7.0	7.3	28.6	23.8	10.8	1.7	75.1	36.0	49.1	50.9

#	POST OFFICE NAME	2004 Per Capita Income	2004 HH Income Base	2004 Household Income Distribution (%): Less than $25,000	$25,000 to $49,999	$50,000 to $99,999	$100,000 to $149,999	$150,000 or More	Median Household Income: 2004	2009	2004 National Centile	2004 State Centile	2004 Home Value Base	2004 Home Value Distribution (%): Less than $50,000	$50,000 to $89,999	$90,000 to $174,999	$175,000 to $399,999	$400,000 or More	2004 Median Home Value
48807	BANNISTER	21124	390	26.9	36.2	28.2	5.4	3.3	40315	43582	47	35	327	15.3	25.1	41.9	15.9	1.8	103750
48808	BATH	28769	1694	13.2	21.3	45.3	14.8	5.5	63681	69943	88	88	1499	4.3	6.9	48.4	37.4	3.0	156696
48809	BELDING	19384	4284	26.7	31.1	33.4	6.4	2.4	43580	47182	57	47	3374	7.5	16.6	54.1	20.3	1.4	117070
48811	CARSON CITY	16109	1245	30.7	32.0	30.5	5.5	1.4	38820	41511	42	29	976	12.7	31.1	42.9	12.7	0.6	96630
48813	CHARLOTTE	22838	7829	18.8	30.2	38.5	10.2	2.3	50759	55945	73	68	6346	7.4	14.4	54.5	22.3	1.4	125338
48815	CLARKSVILLE	23153	819	21.9	29.7	34.4	9.5	4.5	48870	52172	70	63	724	3.7	11.3	45.0	36.3	3.6	155990
48817	CORUNNA	21053	2610	28.1	29.4	32.4	8.3	1.8	42934	46384	56	46	2103	5.6	20.2	55.9	17.2	1.1	117217
48818	CRYSTAL	19240	1070	30.1	37.7	25.4	4.9	2.0	37305	40899	37	24	910	16.9	27.0	37.7	14.0	4.4	97237
48819	DANSVILLE	24655	852	14.4	23.8	43.1	14.8	3.9	61048	68106	85	85	784	3.2	9.3	53.1	32.1	2.3	151718
48820	DEWITT	29566	5875	11.0	19.8	41.7	19.5	8.0	71430	77744	92	93	5002	0.8	4.0	40.8	50.0	4.4	183346
48821	DIMONDALE	26974	2338	17.8	26.8	37.4	13.9	4.2	56574	60129	81	79	2073	19.8	7.2	38.6	32.6	1.7	143806
48822	EAGLE	33627	972	8.2	21.5	45.4	17.9	7.0	69648	77280	91	92	917	0.6	5.7	38.7	50.4	4.7	184012
48823	EAST LANSING	25711	19663	38.1	23.8	22.0	8.7	7.4	36034	39994	32	19	8415	5.0	6.3	39.9	43.5	5.3	173022
48824	EAST LANSING	12616	14	100.0	0.0	0.0	0.0	0.0	15000	15599	1	0	0	0.0	0.0	0.0	0.0	0.0	0
48825	EAST LANSING	12913	398	53.5	24.4	16.3	5.8	0.0	23265	25000	3	1	66	0.0	9.1	60.6	30.3	0.0	145652
48827	EATON RAPIDS	23494	5917	16.4	26.2	43.2	11.6	2.6	56281	62257	81	78	5034	3.5	14.3	53.5	28.1	0.6	138097
48829	EDMORE	16636	1355	36.0	32.0	27.0	3.8	1.1	35069	37141	28	14	1088	17.4	29.6	44.7	7.4	0.9	93300
48831	ELSIE	19617	1350	24.2	34.0	35.3	4.8	1.7	44323	50177	59	50	1099	8.7	22.6	50.1	16.8	1.7	112331
48832	ELWELL	19655	623	24.1	30.3	37.7	7.1	0.8	46663	50156	65	58	539	23.2	22.3	38.0	16.0	0.6	100126
48834	FENWICK	16593	1017	24.9	33.6	34.4	5.9	1.2	43381	46797	57	47	888	18.4	22.2	43.8	14.2	1.5	103727
48835	FOWLER	22526	1542	16.7	26.8	43.3	11.5	1.6	56146	61194	81	78	1344	2.8	8.3	52.3	34.5	2.2	150139
48836	FOWLERVILLE	24989	4604	13.9	23.9	43.4	14.1	4.7	61145	69101	85	85	3875	8.9	3.6	30.4	54.1	3.0	187257
48837	GRAND LEDGE	27877	7355	15.0	23.9	41.2	14.6	5.3	61730	67093	86	86	6060	5.9	6.9	48.9	35.6	2.7	156110
48838	GREENVILLE	19743	6740	27.1	35.1	29.4	6.6	1.9	40725	44240	49	37	5294	12.4	20.4	48.8	17.1	1.3	112317
48840	HASLETT	30775	5520	25.6	23.7	30.9	11.8	8.0	50908	56531	74	68	3262	1.9	6.7	46.0	41.6	3.8	166232
48841	HENDERSON	20375	320	20.0	32.2	35.9	8.8	3.1	48345	53023	69	62	286	7.3	17.8	47.6	25.5	1.8	124510
48842	HOLT	26984	7208	17.1	29.8	34.9	13.8	4.4	52889	60673	77	73	5458	13.8	8.3	51.6	24.9	1.4	132239
48843	HOWELL	30110	14077	11.3	21.1	40.4	19.5	7.7	69795	79734	91	92	11325	5.6	3.0	19.1	61.2	11.1	231985
48845	HUBBARDSTON	18524	359	22.8	34.5	35.4	6.1	1.1	44419	49085	60	51	311	14.5	19.6	45.7	19.6	0.6	110417
48846	IONIA	18059	5751	26.5	30.1	35.6	5.8	2.1	44965	49234	61	53	4424	15.9	23.6	44.0	15.1	1.5	103558
48847	ITHACA	19820	2513	28.5	31.9	31.4	6.7	1.5	41358	44603	51	41	2031	15.1	29.6	44.0	10.6	0.7	94865
48848	LAINGSBURG	27829	3037	15.5	25.6	40.0	12.1	6.8	59722	63850	84	83	2750	5.9	6.5	46.0	37.1	4.6	158983
48849	LAKE ODESSA	21967	2286	23.0	32.4	33.1	8.9	2.7	44634	48130	60	52	1923	10.9	14.5	48.7	22.7	3.2	122278
48850	LAKEVIEW	18259	1828	27.3	34.3	32.3	4.7	1.4	40721	44071	49	37	1511	12.8	26.6	42.5	16.9	1.2	99846
48851	LYONS	21389	864	20.6	30.0	39.1	8.6	1.7	49416	52097	71	65	750	8.5	23.1	48.4	19.2	0.8	113462
48854	MASON	25732	6717	15.1	28.9	38.1	13.9	4.1	55931	63257	81	77	5493	9.6	7.4	48.6	32.3	2.2	151801
48855	HOWELL	28779	4575	10.8	18.3	42.0	20.7	8.3	73370	80996	93	94	4227	2.5	2.9	21.4	64.9	8.3	226519
48856	MIDDLETON	21153	276	23.6	35.5	32.6	6.2	2.2	41530	44852	51	41	234	12.8	29.1	44.0	12.4	1.7	100610
48857	MORRICE	21717	887	14.0	32.7	41.5	7.8	4.1	52292	57671	76	71	791	5.7	15.7	54.4	22.1	2.2	132825
48858	MOUNT PLEASANT	18660	17685	38.1	29.5	23.2	6.4	2.8	34071	37569	24	12	9269	12.1	17.9	48.5	20.1	1.5	116069
48860	MUIR	18271	529	28.2	32.9	31.6	6.4	1.0	41101	44929	50	39	437	14.4	24.7	44.4	15.3	1.1	102425
48861	MULLIKEN	22741	669	15.0	28.3	42.0	12.1	2.7	55246	60696	80	77	608	4.6	15.6	55.8	21.9	2.1	123415
48864	OKEMOS	38409	8158	18.6	19.0	29.0	16.5	17.0	68827	77447	91	92	5627	1.4	2.4	25.4	59.5	11.3	216140
48865	ORLEANS	19639	692	24.3	35.7	32.4	6.7	1.0	41931	45319	53	42	585	15.2	22.2	44.1	15.9	2.6	109972
48866	OVID	20341	1786	21.4	32.4	37.2	7.2	1.9	45921	51199	64	56	1482	7.1	16.0	53.9	22.0	1.0	121201
48867	OWOSSO	20559	11635	27.3	33.4	30.3	6.8	2.3	41228	45192	51	40	8813	10.0	20.2	52.7	16.0	1.2	112014
48871	PERRINTON	21667	899	20.8	33.7	33.8	8.9	2.8	46080	50165	64	56	783	8.7	21.6	46.9	22.1	0.8	119940
48872	PERRY	23312	2799	16.6	26.2	42.8	10.5	4.0	56555	62196	81	79	2426	11.5	10.4	48.0	27.7	2.5	140714
48873	PEWAMO	19301	707	18.4	34.9	36.6	7.9	2.1	46704	50537	66	58	617	7.1	18.0	52.4	21.1	1.5	123450
48875	PORTLAND	23976	3581	17.2	26.8	41.1	11.3	3.6	55115	59356	80	76	3048	7.4	11.2	50.9	28.8	1.7	138594
48876	POTTERVILLE	23144	1415	17.4	29.8	39.2	10.4	3.3	52192	57346	76	71	1204	20.9	13.8	42.9	21.4	1.0	116304
48877	RIVERDALE	17233	794	26.7	35.9	32.0	4.5	0.9	40849	44532	49	38	681	19.8	29.4	40.4	9.7	0.7	91410
48878	ROSEBUSH	18800	569	27.4	32.0	30.6	7.2	2.8	40614	44224	48	37	488	13.9	23.8	45.7	15.6	1.0	105303
48879	SAINT JOHNS	23498	6942	17.8	29.1	39.9	10.5	2.8	52679	58099	76	73	5690	6.3	8.9	52.0	31.1	1.7	141611
48880	SAINT LOUIS	16834	2706	30.3	33.8	28.6	6.4	1.0	39195	42637	43	31	2123	20.6	34.8	35.5	8.7	0.4	84016
48881	SARANAC	22106	2003	23.2	29.9	37.1	7.3	2.5	47880	51698	68	61	1675	7.7	12.1	54.9	23.3	2.0	132619
48883	SHEPHERD	20425	2686	23.2	31.6	35.4	8.0	1.8	46323	51482	65	57	2239	12.6	23.1	50.1	13.4	0.9	107995
48884	SHERIDAN	18504	1553	29.9	33.6	31.1	4.4	1.0	38877	41677	42	29	1327	19.5	24.0	42.7	13.3	0.5	98564
48885	SIDNEY	19927	365	21.9	34.8	35.3	6.9	1.1	45411	48823	62	54	317	13.6	22.7	48.6	14.8	0.3	107115
48886	SIX LAKES	17380	944	31.6	34.0	30.1	3.6	0.7	37112	39558	36	23	805	16.2	28.7	46.6	8.3	0.3	96587
48888	STANTON	18091	2696	28.3	33.3	32.2	4.9	1.3	39911	41995	46	34	2223	16.8	23.8	45.5	13.2	0.6	102070
48889	SUMNER	18129	534	25.5	36.1	32.2	4.9	1.3	41191	44648	50	40	458	15.3	31.0	42.1	10.3	1.3	96296
48890	SUNFIELD	22771	771	17.5	26.2	41.1	12.5	2.7	54871	60000	80	76	681	5.0	17.5	52.0	23.6	1.9	123856
48891	VESTABURG	17398	1332	27.8	38.1	29.1	3.5	1.4	38547	42095	41	28	1127	20.2	28.6	40.8	9.4	1.0	91667
48892	WEBBERVILLE	22183	1591	18.6	28.4	39.5	11.9	1.6	52474	59397	76	72	1397	16.8	6.8	44.8	29.6	2.0	142269
48893	WEIDMAN	21122	1975	24.1	36.7	30.4	6.6	2.2	42263	47297	54	43	1777	14.5	24.0	42.4	17.6	1.5	108050
48895	WILLIAMSTON	30361	4194	14.6	21.5	36.8	17.1	9.9	66440	75940	89	90	3515	3.5	5.7	41.0	44.3	5.6	174832
48897	WOODLAND	20700	645	25.6	32.3	30.2	8.7	3.3	41985	45563	53	43	546	4.2	14.5	50.6	26.9	3.9	127734
48906	LANSING	21378	10961	30.4	30.3	29.8	6.9	2.7	40539	46210	48	36	7460	20.6	28.9	39.5	10.1	1.0	90634
48910	LANSING	21201	15732	28.4	34.5	31.2	4.8	1.1	39314	44303	44	31	9500	9.3	39.8	48.3	2.4	0.2	90567
48911	LANSING	21774	17100	25.5	31.4	32.5	7.9	2.7	44135	49847	59	50	10432	11.8	27.7	49.2	10.7	0.6	98308
48912	LANSING	21661	7952	32.6	31.3	28.3	5.7	2.2	38202	43247	40	27	4281	17.4	32.6	40.5	9.4	0.2	90045
48915	LANSING	19820	4116	33.2	30.7	26.6	7.2	2.2	37028	42210	36	23	2498	16.8	41.2	36.3	5.5	0.2	82308
48917	LANSING	29566	14344	19.1	28.7	35.8	12.1	4.4	51955	56955	75	70	9125	5.0	9.1	52.4	31.3	2.2	151740
48933	LANSING	18833	1313	57.7	24.5	14.6	2.3	0.9	19243	22067	2	1	150	8.7	36.7	44.0	10.7	0.0	93043
49001	KALAMAZOO	19277	9517	33.9	31.6	28.3	5.1	1.1	36768	41570	35	22	5268	18.4	36.1	42.7	2.5	0.3	84893
49002	PORTAGE	26182	8058	22.9	30.8	32.5	10.0	3.9	46263	51038	64	57	5659	8.8	13.8	55.4	20.0	2.1	119942
49004	KALAMAZOO	22094	6230	20.6	33.7	35.1	7.9	2.8	46716	52895	66	58	5226	9.3	23.7	50.3	15.2	1.5	111099
49006	KALAMAZOO	20538	10548	37.2	30.5	24.6	5.8	2.0	35183	39173	28	15	4454	6.5	14.0	69.3	9.8	0.5	116278
49007	KALAMAZOO	14533	4840	50.6	26.8	19.1	2.1	1.3	24553	28272	4	2	1507	33.5	37.3	24.6	3.1	1.5	65305
49008	KALAMAZOO	26044	7136	29.6	25.7	26.9	10.1	7.8	44127	49146	59	49	4237	4.6	18.9	45.6	27.9	3.1	135718
49009	KALAMAZOO	29275	14699	24.6	25.1	29.4	12.8	8.2	50388	55725	73	67	9998	10.5	9.2	34.7	40.3	5.3	164244
49010	ALLEGAN	20714	6700	22.4	33.0	35.3	7.2	2.2	45577	49155	63	55	5400	12.3	19.7	48.7	17.9	1.4	116311
49011	ATHENS	20897	912	24.6	29.9	34.4	9.5	1.5	46509	50170	65	57	782	14.5	27.2	46.0	12.0	0.3	99701
49012	AUGUSTA	34339	1196	14.9	27.5	36.2	11.6	9.8	60073	67411	84	84	1025	4.9	13.3	42.9	31.1	7.8	152117
49013	BANGOR	16703	2114	33.0	34.7	26.4	4.7	1.2	35869	39411	31	18	1645	21.2	30.8	40.4	7.1	0.6	87750
49014	BATTLE CREEK	21303	8758	28.0	30.9	30.4	7.6	3.2	42093	46216	53	43	6276	22.7	22.6	34.4	19.0	1.3	100416
49015	BATTLE CREEK	22984	14410	26.7	31.4	30.2	8.7	3.1	42860	47261	56	45	9798	13.2	27.2	40.9	16.7	1.9	104804
49017	BATTLE CREEK	21008	14837	29.7	30.4	30.3	7.4	2.1	40468	44936	48	36	10855	18.9	36.1	34.2	10.3	0.5	84148
49021	BELLEVUE	21984	2482	18.5	32.3	38.6	9.1	1.6	49285	53496	71	64	2207	7.2	18.0	50.2	23.2	1.4	124639
49022	BENTON HARBOR	16000	13571	45.2	27.1	21.6	4.5	1.7	29028	32229	10	4	7967	27.3	28.7	36.1	7.3	0.7	81940
49024	PORTAGE	30556	11657	17.6	24.4	35.1	14.4	8.5	58454	65020	83	82	8293	0.8	5.5	53.8	36.3	3.7	159650
49026	BLOOMINGDALE	18436	820	26.3	32.4	32.1	8.2	1.0	43971	47254	59	49	685	11.5	26.1	41.0	20.4	0.9	107262
49028	BRONSON	18258	2479	27.7	33.6	31.9	5.2	1.6	40702	43007	49	37	2013	14.2	30.5	42.3	11.6	1.5	96911
49029	BURLINGTON	21805	654	24.8	29.7	36.2	7.0	2.3	47099	51422	66	59	567	19.1	25.9	38.5	14.8	1.8	98636
	MICHIGAN	25281		23.8	27.4	32.3	10.9	5.5	48729	54505				10.7	16.0	40.3	28.0	5.0	134769
	UNITED STATES	25866		24.7	27.1	30.8	10.9	6.5	48124	56710				10.9	15.0	33.7	30.1	10.4	145905

ZIP CODE #	POST OFFICE NAME	FINANCIAL SERVICES: Auto Loan	Home Loan	Invest-ments	Retire-ment Plans	THE HOME: Home Improvements: Home Repair	Lawn & Garden	Furnishings: Comput-ers & Hard-ware	Major Appli-ances	TV, Radio, Sound Equip-ment	Furni-ture	ENTERTAINMENT: Dine out/ Carry out	Sports Equip-ment	Fees & Tickets	Toys & Games	Travel	Cable TV	PERSONAL: Apparel & Services	Auto Repairs	Health Insur-ance	Pets & Supplies
48807	BANNISTER	100	69	33	60	77	89	66	82	79	67	93	98	57	88	67	85	85	81	100	115
48808	BATH	106	120	121	120	117	117	111	111	104	111	131	130	114	135	111	101	130	109	101	124
48809	BELDING	80	72	61	70	74	81	71	76	75	70	91	89	69	92	71	76	87	75	80	92
48811	CARSON CITY	64	55	43	54	58	65	56	60	59	55	72	69	53	71	55	60	67	59	65	71
48813	CHARLOTTE	89	85	74	82	88	93	81	85	83	80	102	100	80	105	82	84	98	84	89	104
48815	CLARKSVILLE	101	89	68	85	94	102	83	92	88	83	108	109	82	110	86	91	102	90	100	118
48817	CORUNNA	79	73	64	71	76	83	72	76	75	71	92	88	71	93	73	76	87	75	81	91
48818	CRYSTAL	78	64	46	60	69	77	62	71	68	62	82	82	58	81	64	71	76	70	80	91
48819	DANSVILLE	100	105	99	105	105	106	98	101	95	99	119	119	99	121	98	93	116	99	95	117
48820	DEWITT	106	129	137	129	126	126	117	116	109	116	137	136	123	145	119	106	137	113	105	128
48821	DIMONDALE	92	100	106	98	99	106	96	97	95	95	118	111	99	121	98	95	116	96	95	109
48822	EAGLE	118	146	155	147	144	142	131	130	121	130	152	152	139	162	134	117	152	125	117	144
48823	EAST LANSING	83	72	86	77	71	78	93	81	90	86	113	102	86	107	84	83	109	89	75	90
48824	EAST LANSING	22	13	17	15	13	16	26	19	25	22	32	27	21	28	21	22	30	23	18	22
48825	EAST LANSING	47	36	48	41	36	40	52	45	51	48	64	58	47	60	46	47	62	51	41	50
48827	EATON RAPIDS	88	96	96	96	96	98	90	92	88	90	109	108	93	113	91	86	107	90	87	104
48829	EDMORE	73	54	33	52	61	70	56	65	63	55	75	76	50	72	57	66	68	64	77	84
48831	ELSIE	78	71	60	67	75	82	68	73	73	67	89	85	68	92	70	75	84	72	81	91
48832	ELWELL	82	73	56	70	77	83	68	75	73	68	88	89	67	90	70	74	84	74	82	96
48834	FENWICK	83	69	47	64	74	81	64	73	71	65	85	87	61	85	66	73	80	72	82	97
48835	FOWLER	98	90	73	87	93	101	86	92	89	85	109	108	84	111	87	91	104	90	97	113
48836	FOWLERVILLE	101	108	102	108	106	108	100	102	97	101	121	120	102	123	100	94	118	100	96	116
48837	GRAND LEDGE	97	108	112	109	107	109	102	102	97	101	122	120	105	126	102	95	120	100	95	114
48838	GREENVILLE	78	68	54	66	72	79	67	73	71	66	86	86	64	86	68	72	82	72	79	90
48840	HASLETT	91	98	111	100	98	103	98	97	95	97	119	114	99	121	98	94	116	97	93	108
48841	HENDERSON	97	82	59	78	88	96	77	87	84	77	101	103	74	102	79	86	95	85	96	113
48842	HOLT	92	99	106	101	98	101	98	97	94	98	118	115	99	119	97	90	116	97	90	107
48843	HOWELL	111	124	131	127	121	122	117	116	110	118	139	136	121	142	116	106	138	115	104	128
48845	HUBBARDSTON	72	64	49	61	68	73	59	66	63	59	77	78	58	78	61	65	73	64	71	85
48846	IONIA	73	67	58	66	69	74	66	69	68	65	83	82	64	84	66	68	80	69	72	83
48847	ITHACA	81	68	52	65	73	81	67	74	73	66	88	86	64	89	68	75	83	73	83	93
48848	LAINGSBURG	105	121	123	120	119	119	111	111	105	110	131	131	115	137	112	102	130	108	102	125
48849	LAKE ODESSA	93	81	62	79	85	94	79	86	84	78	102	100	77	103	80	86	96	84	93	106
48850	LAKEVIEW	76	67	54	64	71	79	65	71	69	64	84	82	63	85	67	72	80	69	78	88
48851	LYONS	87	78	65	78	81	88	78	82	80	77	98	95	75	98	77	80	93	81	85	97
48854	MASON	91	99	105	99	98	101	95	95	92	95	115	111	97	117	96	90	113	95	90	106
48855	HOWELL	113	137	143	138	133	131	123	122	114	123	143	143	130	151	124	109	143	118	108	135
48856	MIDDLETON	84	80	69	76	83	90	76	81	80	75	98	94	76	102	78	82	93	79	87	99
48857	MORRICE	99	88	67	83	93	100	81	90	86	81	105	107	80	107	84	88	100	88	97	116
48858	MOUNT PLEASANT	68	58	63	61	58	63	72	65	70	67	88	81	66	84	66	66	84	70	62	74
48860	MUIR	76	65	50	64	68	76	66	71	70	65	85	81	63	84	66	71	80	70	77	85
48861	MULLIKEN	99	91	72	87	95	101	83	92	88	83	107	109	82	110	86	89	102	89	98	117
48864	OKEMOS	126	133	160	141	131	136	138	131	132	137	167	158	140	166	135	126	164	135	119	145
48865	ORLEANS	82	72	55	70	76	83	70	76	74	69	90	89	68	91	71	76	85	74	82	94
48866	OVID	83	77	63	73	80	87	73	79	78	73	95	92	73	97	75	80	90	77	85	97
48867	OWOSSO	73	71	68	68	72	78	70	72	73	69	89	84	70	91	71	73	86	72	75	84
48871	PERRINTON	88	82	70	78	86	93	78	83	82	77	100	97	78	104	80	84	96	81	90	103
48872	PERRY	93	96	90	96	96	99	90	93	88	91	110	109	91	111	91	87	107	91	89	107
48873	PEWAMO	91	81	63	78	86	92	76	83	80	76	97	99	74	99	78	82	93	81	90	106
48875	PORTLAND	97	96	85	94	98	103	90	95	91	90	112	112	90	114	91	91	108	93	96	114
48876	POTTERVILLE	91	93	85	92	92	95	87	90	85	88	105	105	86	105	87	83	103	89	86	104
48877	RIVERDALE	76	66	51	64	70	76	63	69	67	63	82	82	62	83	64	69	77	68	75	87
48878	ROSEBUSH	81	71	55	70	74	81	70	76	74	69	90	88	67	90	70	75	85	75	81	92
48879	SAINT JOHNS	89	91	88	89	93	98	87	90	87	86	108	105	88	111	89	87	105	88	90	105
48880	SAINT LOUIS	60	52	40	50	55	61	52	56	55	50	67	64	50	67	52	57	63	55	62	68
48881	SARANAC	89	78	60	75	82	90	75	82	79	74	96	96	73	97	76	81	91	80	89	103
48883	SHEPHERD	83	81	71	79	82	85	76	80	76	77	95	94	75	95	77	76	91	79	79	95
48884	SHERIDAN	76	60	40	57	65	73	59	67	65	59	78	79	55	77	60	68	73	66	76	87
48885	SIDNEY	83	73	56	70	78	83	68	75	72	68	88	90	67	90	70	74	83	73	82	97
48886	SIX LAKES	80	58	32	52	64	73	56	67	65	56	76	80	49	74	57	69	70	66	80	92
48888	STANTON	76	64	49	61	68	75	63	69	68	62	82	82	60	82	64	70	78	68	76	88
48889	SUMNER	77	67	51	65	70	77	66	71	70	65	85	83	63	85	66	71	80	70	77	87
48890	SUNFIELD	97	92	76	88	96	101	84	91	87	84	107	109	84	110	87	88	102	89	96	115
48891	VESTABURG	74	63	48	62	67	74	62	68	66	62	81	79	60	81	63	68	76	67	74	84
48892	WEBBERVILLE	93	87	74	85	89	93	82	88	84	83	103	104	80	103	82	83	99	87	89	107
48893	WEIDMAN	91	71	46	65	78	87	67	79	76	67	90	94	61	89	70	80	84	78	92	107
48895	WILLIAMSTON	105	126	136	127	124	124	116	115	109	115	137	135	122	144	118	105	136	112	104	127
48897	WOODLAND	88	78	59	74	82	88	72	80	77	72	93	95	71	95	74	78	89	78	87	103
48906	LANSING	72	71	76	70	70	76	75	73	76	74	94	86	75	94	74	75	92	75	73	82
48910	LANSING	62	61	70	63	61	65	69	64	68	66	84	77	67	85	66	65	82	67	62	70
48911	LANSING	72	75	85	77	74	77	78	75	75	77	95	89	78	96	76	73	93	76	70	82
48912	LANSING	64	61	72	63	61	66	71	66	70	68	88	80	69	87	68	68	85	70	64	73
48915	LANSING	65	64	75	64	63	68	70	67	71	69	88	79	69	88	68	70	86	69	66	74
48917	LANSING	90	93	105	97	91	95	95	92	91	95	116	109	95	114	93	88	113	94	85	102
48933	LANSING	41	33	44	36	33	38	44	39	44	42	56	49	41	53	41	43	54	44	39	44
49001	KALAMAZOO	60	59	68	60	58	63	65	62	64	63	80	74	64	80	63	62	78	64	60	68
49002	PORTAGE	82	84	89	84	83	87	86	84	84	84	105	100	86	106	84	82	102	85	80	94
49004	KALAMAZOO	74	81	85	80	81	85	79	78	78	78	97	91	81	101	80	77	95	78	76	87
49006	KALAMAZOO	62	49	60	52	48	54	71	58	69	64	86	76	63	81	62	63	82	66	55	65
49007	KALAMAZOO	49	39	48	40	38	44	51	46	53	49	66	56	48	62	47	51	63	50	46	52
49008	KALAMAZOO	86	87	106	90	86	93	97	90	94	93	118	108	96	117	94	91	116	94	85	99
49009	KALAMAZOO	97	95	102	98	94	98	102	97	99	99	124	117	100	123	98	94	121	100	90	109
49010	ALLEGAN	86	74	57	69	78	86	71	78	77	71	93	92	68	94	72	80	88	77	87	100
49011	ATHENS	87	78	59	74	82	88	72	80	76	72	93	95	70	95	74	78	88	78	86	103
49012	AUGUSTA	121	128	123	128	130	136	120	124	119	120	147	144	123	151	122	118	143	121	122	143
49013	BANGOR	75	61	46	57	64	71	61	67	66	61	80	79	57	79	61	68	76	67	74	85
49014	BATTLE CREEK	77	75	76	74	75	81	76	77	77	75	96	90	76	96	76	77	93	77	77	88
49015	BATTLE CREEK	74	76	83	76	76	81	78	76	77	76	96	89	79	98	78	77	94	77	75	85
49017	BATTLE CREEK	68	70	74	68	70	76	71	70	72	69	89	81	72	90	71	72	86	71	71	79
49021	BELLEVUE	92	82	64	78	87	93	76	84	80	76	98	100	75	100	78	82	93	82	90	108
49022	BENTON HARBOR	57	52	57	49	52	58	56	56	59	56	73	64	55	73	55	61	71	57	59	64
49024	PORTAGE	104	112	124	115	110	114	110	107	106	110	133	126	113	134	109	103	131	108	100	120
49026	BLOOMINGDALE	81	69	51	66	73	80	67	74	72	66	87	86	64	87	68	73	82	72	81	93
49028	BRONSON	80	69	54	65	73	80	66	73	71	66	87	86	64	87	68	74	82	72	81	92
49029	BURLINGTON	100	77	48	70	84	94	73	86	83	74	99	102	67	97	75	87	92	84	99	116
	MICHIGAN	91	91	93	89	91	98	90	91	91	90	113	106	90	113	90	91	109	91	92	105
	UNITED STATES	100	100	100	100	100	100	100	100	100	100	100	100	100	100	100	100	100	100	100	100

MICHIGAN

POPULATION CHANGE

A 49030-49248

ZIP CODE # / POST OFFICE NAME	COUNTY FIPS CODE	POPULATION 2000	2004	2009	2000-2004 ANNUAL RATE % Rate	State Centile	HOUSEHOLDS 2000	2004	2009	% Annual Rate 2000-2004	2004 Average HH Size	FAMILIES 2000	2004	% Annual Rate 2000-2004
49030 BURR OAK	149	2682	2694	2728	0.1	27	960	978	1005	0.4	2.75	707	711	0.1
49031 CASSOPOLIS	027	7236	7378	7572	0.5	41	2838	2956	3098	1.0	2.47	1993	2050	0.7
49032 CENTREVILLE	149	3046	3130	3196	0.6	48	918	963	1001	1.1	3.03	682	706	0.8
49033 CERESCO	025	1676	1683	1688	0.1	27	643	660	674	0.6	2.55	516	523	0.3
49034 CLIMAX	077	2467	2488	2547	0.2	29	906	931	970	0.6	2.66	710	721	0.4
49036 COLDWATER	023	24501	25393	26362	0.8	59	8711	9203	9729	1.3	2.44	5949	6205	1.0
49038 COLOMA	021	9919	9690	9612	-0.6	8	3986	3988	4039	0.0	2.41	2776	2733	-0.4
49040 COLON	149	3256	3141	3149	-0.8	4	1298	1274	1298	-0.4	2.46	924	894	-0.8
49042 CONSTANTINE	149	5124	5080	5116	-0.2	16	1899	1921	1966	0.3	2.64	1410	1407	-0.1
49043 COVERT	159	2765	2771	2846	0.1	24	968	979	1018	0.3	2.80	668	667	0.0
49045 DECATUR	159	6493	6741	7033	0.9	61	2258	2369	2506	1.1	2.69	1618	1676	0.8
49046 DELTON	015	7725	8052	8537	1.0	65	2844	3015	3248	1.4	2.66	2152	2256	1.1
49047 DOWAGIAC	027	15281	15531	15911	0.4	38	5794	6009	6281	0.9	2.48	4073	4167	0.5
49048 KALAMAZOO	077	25125	25617	26446	0.5	41	9583	9998	10525	1.0	2.52	6436	6593	0.6
49050 DOWLING	015	1369	1407	1477	0.7	49	536	561	599	1.1	2.50	415	431	0.9
49051 EAST LEROY	025	2018	2154	2231	1.6	82	730	794	835	2.0	2.70	567	609	1.7
49052 FULTON	077	819	886	931	1.9	88	293	323	345	2.3	2.73	237	259	2.1
49053 GALESBURG	077	5507	5671	5856	0.7	51	2047	2142	2250	1.1	2.59	1501	1551	0.8
49055 GOBLES	159	6289	6490	6739	0.7	54	2312	2431	2566	1.2	2.64	1713	1777	0.9
49056 GRAND JUNCTION	159	4293	4371	4540	0.4	39	1527	1574	1656	0.7	2.71	1136	1156	0.4
49057 HARTFORD	159	6665	6845	7090	0.6	48	2307	2409	2533	1.0	2.75	1687	1740	0.7
49058 HASTINGS	015	18278	19331	20652	1.3	75	6850	7375	8018	1.8	2.57	5038	5355	1.5
49060 HICKORY CORNERS	015	1831	1834	1888	0.0	24	715	727	760	0.4	2.50	545	548	0.1
49061 JONES	027	1769	1841	1907	0.9	62	663	704	744	1.4	2.62	484	507	1.1
49064 LAWRENCE	159	3896	3937	4040	0.3	32	1367	1400	1457	0.6	2.75	1025	1035	0.2
49065 LAWTON	159	5873	6162	6435	1.1	69	2049	2196	2334	1.6	2.69	1573	1664	1.3
49066 LEONIDAS	149	786	794	803	0.2	31	252	258	265	0.6	3.07	204	207	0.3
49067 MARCELLUS	027	4670	4851	5025	0.9	61	1735	1839	1942	1.4	2.63	1298	1360	1.1
49068 MARSHALL	025	14974	15440	15683	0.7	53	5907	6187	6377	1.1	2.46	4120	4251	0.7
49070 MARTIN	005	2211	2243	2360	0.3	36	772	801	859	0.9	2.77	594	607	0.5
49071 MATTAWAN	159	8308	8725	9112	1.2	70	2958	3162	3354	1.6	2.75	2358	2496	1.4
49072 MENDON	149	3283	3573	3771	2.0	90	1204	1330	1423	2.4	2.67	910	994	2.1
49073 NASHVILLE	015	5151	5418	5776	1.2	72	1904	2047	2226	1.7	2.63	1440	1530	1.4
49076 OLIVET	045	4323	4496	4665	0.9	62	1373	1460	1551	1.5	2.70	1012	1064	1.2
49078 OTSEGO	005	8640	8640	9035	0.0	23	3209	3268	3475	0.4	2.62	2380	2392	0.1
49079 PAW PAW	159	12548	12924	13376	0.7	52	4783	5013	5269	1.1	2.53	3460	3579	0.8
49080 PLAINWELL	005	15257	15901	16838	1.0	65	5693	6061	6538	1.5	2.59	4281	4500	1.2
49082 QUINCY	023	6873	6952	7154	0.3	33	2433	2494	2600	0.6	2.76	1808	1832	0.3
49083 RICHLAND	077	6574	6594	6768	0.1	25	2508	2550	2657	0.4	2.59	1943	1951	0.1
49085 SAINT JOSEPH	021	23533	23683	23761	0.2	28	9711	9913	10107	0.5	2.31	6363	6418	0.2
49087 SCHOOLCRAFT	077	5799	5868	5978	0.3	33	2055	2116	2192	0.7	2.77	1605	1636	0.5
49088 SCOTTS	077	2820	2965	3100	1.2	71	1029	1100	1169	1.6	2.68	824	872	1.3
49089 SHERWOOD	023	2011	2067	2134	0.7	49	758	793	830	1.1	2.61	574	594	0.8
49090 SOUTH HAVEN	159	15056	15385	15970	0.5	43	5928	6165	6506	0.9	2.43	4010	4115	0.6
49091 STURGIS	149	20948	21373	21815	0.5	41	7793	8040	8307	0.7	2.61	5411	5507	0.4
49092 TEKONSHA	025	2308	2279	2282	-0.3	13	880	886	901	0.2	2.57	643	638	-0.2
49093 THREE RIVERS	149	17769	17810	18031	0.1	24	6970	7112	7315	0.5	2.46	4833	4865	0.2
49094 UNION CITY	023	4226	4297	4411	0.4	38	1621	1676	1747	0.8	2.56	1175	1200	0.5
49095 VANDALIA	027	2281	2341	2415	0.6	46	901	943	991	1.1	2.48	662	684	0.8
49096 VERMONTVILLE	045	3268	3364	3485	0.7	50	1164	1224	1294	1.2	2.74	924	962	1.0
49097 VICKSBURG	077	10146	10127	10329	0.0	21	3775	3820	3954	0.3	2.65	2935	2941	0.1
49098 WATERVLIET	021	6331	6404	6427	0.3	33	2434	2504	2555	0.7	2.50	1694	1717	0.3
49099 WHITE PIGEON	149	5811	5996	6163	0.7	54	2218	2339	2448	1.3	2.56	1612	1678	1.0
49101 BARODA	021	3290	3254	3234	-0.3	13	1253	1261	1275	0.2	2.54	916	909	-0.2
49102 BERRIEN CENTER	021	1620	1636	1636	0.2	31	479	491	499	0.6	2.97	373	378	0.3
49103 BERRIEN SPRINGS	021	12098	12123	12147	0.1	24	4083	4166	4247	0.5	2.61	2959	2977	0.1
49104 BERRIEN SPRINGS	021	58	57	56	-0.4	10	20	19	19	-1.2	1.16	13	5	-20.1
49106 BRIDGMAN	021	4858	4919	4933	0.3	34	1903	1968	2012	0.8	2.40	1354	1380	0.5
49107 BUCHANAN	021	10678	10511	10444	-0.4	11	4177	4191	4239	0.1	2.49	2936	2904	-0.3
49111 EAU CLAIRE	021	3949	4112	4185	1.0	63	1387	1478	1534	1.5	2.57	1050	1107	1.3
49112 EDWARDSBURG	027	9373	9648	9940	0.7	50	3714	3899	4094	1.2	2.47	2692	2792	0.9
49113 GALIEN	021	2207	2177	2163	-0.3	12	839	849	862	0.3	2.55	612	610	-0.1
49116 LAKESIDE	021	214	205	203	-1.0	3	114	112	113	-0.4	1.83	69	67	-0.7
49117 NEW BUFFALO	021	4228	4253	4267	0.1	28	1855	1916	1963	0.8	2.21	1194	1210	0.3
49120 NILES	027	35587	36217	36721	0.4	39	14170	14683	15149	0.8	2.44	9755	9980	0.5
49125 SAWYER	021	2801	2703	2671	-0.8	4	1188	1174	1183	-0.3	2.30	826	804	-0.6
49126 SODUS	021	1164	1152	1145	-0.2	14	475	481	487	0.3	2.23	310	309	-0.1
49127 STEVENSVILLE	021	10090	10160	10205	0.2	28	3990	4097	4192	0.6	2.46	2857	2888	0.3
49128 THREE OAKS	021	4341	4204	4157	-0.8	5	1773	1757	1773	-0.2	2.39	1226	1196	-0.6
49129 UNION PIER	021	808	782	773	-0.8	5	375	372	375	-0.2	2.08	243	236	-0.7
49130 UNION	027	1785	1853	1917	0.9	60	725	772	816	1.5	2.40	541	569	1.2
49201 JACKSON	075	46561	47823	49428	0.6	48	15048	15718	16553	1.0	2.55	10690	11055	0.8
49202 JACKSON	075	20179	20486	21126	0.4	37	8487	8783	9213	0.8	2.24	5098	5152	0.3
49203 JACKSON	075	38557	39108	40401	0.3	36	15205	15695	16461	0.8	2.48	10195	10333	0.3
49220 ADDISON	091	2574	2694	2802	1.1	67	1003	1076	1144	1.7	2.50	735	777	1.3
49221 ADRIAN	091	40323	41575	42950	0.7	53	13938	14716	15561	1.3	2.51	9597	10019	1.0
49224 ALBION	025	14232	13981	13972	-0.4	10	5115	5088	5153	-0.1	2.47	3468	3401	-0.5
49227 ALLEN	059	1367	1414	1478	0.8	57	493	518	550	1.2	2.72	365	379	0.9
49228 BLISSFIELD	091	5547	5541	5611	0.0	21	2131	2178	2252	0.5	2.46	1549	1560	0.2
49229 BRITTON	091	3203	3216	3280	0.1	27	1119	1149	1197	0.6	2.80	904	919	0.4
49230 BROOKLYN	075	9607	9932	10264	0.8	57	3836	4041	4247	1.2	2.44	2806	2913	0.9
49232 CAMDEN	059	2759	2852	2973	0.8	56	943	991	1050	1.2	2.86	720	747	0.9
49233 CEMENT CITY	059	3207	3410	3588	1.5	78	1226	1329	1424	1.9	2.56	965	1034	1.6
49234 CLARKLAKE	075	2789	2940	3074	1.3	73	1073	1152	1225	1.7	2.53	817	866	1.4
49235 CLAYTON	091	2302	2261	2284	-0.4	10	835	840	868	0.1	2.69	646	643	-0.1
49236 CLINTON	091	4833	4977	5127	0.7	51	1833	1925	2021	1.2	2.59	1377	1428	0.9
49237 CONCORD	075	3093	3176	3287	0.6	48	1129	1178	1237	1.0	2.69	863	888	0.7
49238 DEERFIELD	091	1604	1614	1633	0.2	28	544	556	573	0.5	2.86	424	428	0.2
49240 GRASS LAKE	075	7146	7620	8020	1.5	80	2525	2742	2932	2.0	2.71	1992	2136	1.7
49241 HANOVER	075	2528	2738	2914	1.9	88	924	1021	1105	2.4	2.67	730	797	2.1
49242 HILLSDALE	059	15363	15775	16436	0.6	47	5785	6046	6418	1.0	2.45	3853	3973	0.7
49245 HOMER	025	5150	5112	5100	-0.2	17	1892	1912	1939	0.3	2.66	1405	1402	-0.1
49246 HORTON	075	3163	3350	3510	1.4	76	1162	1256	1338	1.9	2.67	951	1018	1.6
49247 HUDSON	091	5947	6150	6384	0.8	57	2235	2364	2503	1.3	2.57	1645	1715	1.0
49248 JASPER	091	847	844	856	-0.1	20	312	317	328	0.4	2.65	246	247	0.1
MICHIGAN					0.6					1.0	2.52			0.6
UNITED STATES					1.2					1.3	2.58			1.1

ZIP CODE #	POST OFFICE NAME	RACE (%) White 2000	White 2004	Black 2000	Black 2004	Asian/Pacific 2000	Asian/Pacific 2004	% Hispanic Origin 2000	% Hispanic Origin 2004	2004 AGE DISTRIBUTION (%) 0-4	5-9	10-14	15-19	20-24	25-44	45-64	65-84	85+	18+	MEDIAN AGE 2004	% 2004 Males	% 2004 Females
49030	BURR OAK	97.7	97.4	0.5	0.5	0.2	0.3	1.6	1.9	6.8	7.0	7.7	7.5	6.6	28.5	23.8	11.0	1.2	74.1	35.9	50.6	49.4
49031	CASSOPOLIS	77.6	76.2	15.8	16.6	1.2	1.6	1.7	1.8	6.6	6.8	7.3	6.2	5.7	25.4	28.0	12.2	1.8	75.4	39.7	49.7	50.3
49032	CENTREVILLE	95.5	95.1	2.2	2.4	0.2	0.3	1.2	1.4	7.4	7.1	7.4	7.3	7.4	28.2	23.1	10.5	1.5	73.5	35.5	50.5	49.5
49033	CERESCO	97.2	96.9	0.5	0.6	0.4	0.5	1.3	1.5	5.1	6.4	7.6	6.1	3.6	24.5	33.1	12.7	1.1	77.0	43.1	50.4	49.6
49034	CLIMAX	97.2	96.9	0.4	0.5	0.5	0.5	1.7	1.9	6.2	6.8	7.6	6.8	5.6	25.5	28.8	11.4	1.4	75.0	39.8	49.5	50.5
49036	COLDWATER	90.9	90.2	4.6	4.9	0.7	0.8	3.2	3.7	5.7	5.5	6.3	6.1	6.6	30.0	25.8	12.2	1.9	78.8	38.9	51.0	49.0
49038	COLOMA	94.6	94.3	2.4	2.6	0.5	0.5	2.7	2.8	6.3	6.4	7.1	6.6	5.9	26.5	27.0	12.8	1.4	76.1	39.5	49.1	50.9
49040	COLON	97.6	97.4	0.4	0.5	0.2	0.3	0.7	0.8	7.0	7.0	7.4	6.9	6.1	26.0	25.3	12.3	2.0	74.3	37.5	49.7	50.3
49042	CONSTANTINE	95.3	94.7	1.2	1.4	0.6	0.8	1.7	2.0	6.9	6.8	7.9	7.3	7.0	28.0	25.1	10.2	1.0	73.9	35.9	50.4	49.6
49043	COVERT	53.5	51.7	32.6	33.4	0.1	0.1	15.4	16.9	8.2	8.1	8.8	7.5	6.7	24.3	23.6	11.5	1.4	70.0	35.2	50.6	49.4
49045	DECATUR	89.2	88.3	3.4	3.6	0.2	0.3	11.4	13.0	7.2	7.2	8.3	7.6	6.7	27.0	23.6	10.9	1.5	72.7	35.2	51.1	48.9
49046	DELTON	97.4	97.2	0.3	0.3	0.2	0.3	1.4	1.5	6.1	6.5	7.4	6.7	5.4	26.7	28.6	11.3	1.2	75.8	39.7	50.3	49.7
49047	DOWAGIAC	85.1	83.9	7.9	8.3	0.4	0.5	5.3	6.1	7.1	6.9	7.3	6.9	6.4	26.0	25.0	12.7	1.8	74.5	37.6	49.3	50.7
49048	KALAMAZOO	79.4	78.0	14.9	15.8	1.0	1.2	2.9	3.3	7.4	7.2	7.8	7.0	6.9	29.2	23.1	9.9	1.4	73.1	34.4	48.4	51.6
49050	DOWLING	98.1	97.9	0.2	0.2	0.1	0.1	1.2	1.3	5.7	6.3	6.3	5.8	5.7	25.8	31.4	12.0	1.0	78.2	41.6	51.2	48.8
49051	EAST LEROY	97.0	96.5	0.6	0.7	0.4	0.5	1.3	1.7	5.9	6.3	6.9	6.4	5.6	25.3	29.9	12.8	0.9	76.4	41.2	49.2	50.8
49052	FULTON	97.4	97.2	0.4	0.3	0.1	0.2	1.0	1.2	6.2	6.7	7.6	7.1	6.2	26.1	28.1	10.8	1.2	74.9	39.0	50.7	49.3
49053	GALESBURG	96.1	95.5	1.0	1.2	0.5	0.6	1.1	1.3	6.7	7.3	7.9	7.0	5.8	26.9	26.8	10.0	1.6	73.7	37.7	49.7	50.3
49055	GOBLES	95.2	94.6	1.0	1.1	0.3	0.3	2.7	3.1	6.6	7.0	7.9	7.9	5.9	26.2	27.1	10.1	1.4	73.6	38.0	50.7	49.3
49056	GRAND JUNCTION	85.5	84.0	4.7	5.1	0.2	0.2	9.7	11.1	7.6	7.7	8.5	7.2	6.7	26.9	24.1	10.3	1.0	71.4	34.9	50.6	49.4
49057	HARTFORD	86.8	85.6	1.0	1.1	0.2	0.3	15.4	17.4	7.7	7.5	8.4	7.5	6.9	27.3	23.9	9.9	1.0	71.9	34.5	50.8	49.3
49058	HASTINGS	97.6	97.3	0.2	0.2	0.3	0.3	1.6	1.8	7.0	7.2	7.6	6.5	6.1	27.1	24.9	11.4	2.1	74.1	37.5	49.2	50.8
49060	HICKORY CORNERS	97.6	97.2	0.1	0.1	0.8	1.0	1.5	1.8	5.2	5.9	7.1	7.4	4.7	24.5	31.4	12.3	1.4	77.2	42.0	49.5	50.5
49061	JONES	95.0	94.4	1.8	1.9	0.6	0.9	1.7	2.0	4.8	5.9	7.4	7.2	5.9	26.5	28.8	12.3	1.1	77.5	40.7	51.2	48.8
49064	LAWRENCE	85.0	83.4	2.8	3.1	0.3	0.4	13.6	15.4	6.9	6.9	8.0	7.6	6.5	26.1	26.2	10.4	1.4	73.4	36.8	49.8	50.2
49065	LAWTON	93.4	92.6	1.0	1.1	0.3	0.5	6.8	7.7	6.8	6.9	7.8	7.5	6.3	25.6	26.6	10.2	2.3	73.7	38.3	49.1	50.9
49066	LEONIDAS	97.6	97.5	0.6	0.8	0.0	0.0	0.5	0.5	8.4	8.3	8.4	8.2	6.2	24.4	24.2	10.2	1.6	69.9	34.5	48.9	51.1
49067	MARCELLUS	96.3	95.9	0.9	1.0	0.3	0.3	1.7	2.0	6.7	6.8	7.1	7.1	6.4	26.9	26.4	11.6	1.0	75.0	37.9	50.6	49.5
49068	MARSHALL	96.5	96.0	0.3	0.3	0.5	0.6	2.6	3.0	6.2	6.4	7.2	6.6	5.9	25.9	26.3	12.9	2.6	76.1	39.8	48.2	51.8
49070	MARTIN	97.1	96.6	0.2	0.2	0.5	0.6	2.2	2.6	7.6	7.5	8.3	7.0	6.3	28.2	24.1	9.9	1.1	72.1	35.5	50.6	49.4
49071	MATTAWAN	94.7	94.0	1.5	1.6	0.6	0.7	2.7	3.1	7.1	7.4	7.9	7.9	6.5	27.1	28.1	7.2	0.8	72.5	36.5	49.7	50.3
49072	MENDON	96.9	96.6	0.8	0.8	0.2	0.2	1.6	1.8	7.3	7.6	8.4	6.6	5.5	26.2	24.5	12.8	1.1	72.4	37.5	50.1	49.9
49073	NASHVILLE	97.5	97.2	0.3	0.3	0.4	0.5	0.7	0.9	6.4	7.1	8.3	6.9	6.2	27.0	26.2	10.7	1.2	73.6	36.9	50.0	50.0
49076	OLIVET	92.4	92.0	4.0	4.1	0.8	1.0	1.7	1.9	7.3	6.6	6.9	8.9	14.4	27.6	21.0	6.5	0.9	75.6	28.3	50.9	49.1
49078	OTSEGO	97.2	96.8	0.4	0.4	0.5	0.6	1.5	1.8	6.6	7.0	7.7	7.1	6.2	27.9	26.1	10.2	1.4	74.1	37.3	50.0	50.0
49079	PAW PAW	94.4	93.8	1.9	2.1	0.3	0.4	3.0	3.4	6.2	6.5	7.4	7.0	6.3	26.9	27.7	10.6	1.5	75.7	38.9	49.7	50.3
49080	PLAINWELL	97.1	96.7	0.4	0.4	0.4	0.5	1.5	1.7	6.6	6.8	7.5	6.7	5.7	27.1	27.6	10.6	1.4	74.7	38.7	49.6	50.4
49082	QUINCY	98.0	97.8	0.3	0.3	0.2	0.3	1.0	1.2	7.9	7.6	7.9	7.6	6.5	26.2	25.0	10.2	1.0	71.7	35.5	50.3	49.7
49083	RICHLAND	95.9	95.2	1.6	1.9	0.8	1.0	1.3	1.6	5.6	6.6	7.5	7.9	4.9	22.7	32.5	11.3	1.0	75.3	42.0	49.2	50.9
49085	SAINT JOSEPH	93.2	92.8	2.8	3.1	2.3	2.3	1.6	1.7	5.2	5.7	6.8	7.0	6.1	24.8	27.7	14.1	2.7	77.9	41.7	49.3	50.7
49087	SCHOOLCRAFT	96.9	96.4	0.5	0.5	0.7	0.9	1.0	1.2	6.1	7.1	8.7	7.6	5.3	26.8	28.6	8.8	1.1	72.9	38.6	49.9	50.1
49088	SCOTTS	97.9	97.6	0.5	0.5	0.4	0.4	1.0	1.1	5.8	6.4	7.4	6.3	5.4	25.6	31.2	11.0	0.9	76.2	41.3	50.3	49.7
49089	SHERWOOD	97.0	96.9	0.3	0.2	0.2	0.2	0.9	1.0	6.3	6.6	7.5	7.0	6.0	27.6	26.1	11.6	1.3	75.3	37.4	51.5	48.5
49090	SOUTH HAVEN	83.6	82.3	10.3	11.0	0.5	0.6	5.8	6.7	6.0	6.3	7.3	7.1	6.2	24.7	27.2	13.2	2.1	75.9	40.1	48.8	51.2
49091	STURGIS	93.7	92.9	0.9	1.0	0.8	1.0	8.5	9.6	8.1	7.4	7.1	6.9	7.7	26.9	22.8	10.8	2.2	73.1	34.6	49.2	50.8
49092	TEKONSHA	97.3	97.1	0.3	0.3	0.1	0.1	0.7	0.8	6.0	6.5	7.2	6.1	5.6	27.5	27.6	12.2	1.4	76.7	39.6	50.2	49.9
49093	THREE RIVERS	89.3	88.4	6.8	7.2	0.6	0.8	2.1	2.4	7.1	6.8	7.3	6.8	6.4	27.4	24.7	11.7	1.8	74.6	37.0	49.3	50.7
49094	UNION CITY	97.1	96.8	0.4	0.4	0.3	0.4	0.9	1.1	6.5	6.5	7.2	7.1	6.8	27.1	25.2	12.2	1.4	75.3	37.5	50.2	49.8
49095	VANDALIA	80.8	79.6	13.6	14.1	1.8	2.3	1.8	2.0	5.6	6.1	7.2	6.8	5.9	25.0	28.7	13.3	1.5	77.0	40.8	51.4	48.6
49096	VERMONTVILLE	97.5	97.2	0.2	0.3	0.3	0.4	1.1	1.3	6.2	6.6	7.5	7.8	6.1	26.6	28.1	10.1	1.1	74.5	38.3	50.9	49.1
49097	VICKSBURG	97.3	97.0	0.4	0.4	0.5	0.6	1.1	1.3	5.7	6.6	8.0	7.6	5.8	25.7	28.9	10.5	1.2	74.8	39.7	49.5	50.5
49098	WATERVLIET	94.7	94.5	1.1	1.2	0.4	0.4	4.9	5.1	7.0	7.2	7.5	6.5	5.6	28.0	24.9	11.7	1.5	74.2	37.3	48.8	51.2
49099	WHITE PIGEON	96.6	96.3	0.2	0.3	0.5	0.7	1.5	1.8	5.5	5.9	7.0	6.6	6.0	26.9	29.2	11.7	1.2	77.3	40.1	49.3	50.7
49101	BARODA	96.2	96.1	0.4	0.5	0.5	0.5	2.6	2.6	6.4	6.8	7.3	6.4	5.4	28.2	26.3	11.5	1.6	75.2	38.9	50.1	49.9
49102	BERRIEN CENTER	87.5	86.7	6.5	7.3	1.1	1.0	7.7	7.6	6.1	6.7	7.5	7.7	5.6	27.6	24.2	11.6	2.9	74.1	37.6	51.4	48.6
49103	BERRIEN SPRINGS	70.9	69.7	14.9	16.2	6.4	6.3	7.9	7.9	5.5	5.4	5.9	8.8	13.0	25.7	23.1	10.7	1.8	78.8	33.4	48.5	51.6
49104	BERRIEN SPRINGS	55.2	54.4	25.9	28.1	8.6	8.8	8.6	7.0	1.8	1.8	1.8	21.1	42.1	15.8	12.3	1.8	1.8	94.7	22.8	45.6	54.4
49106	BRIDGMAN	97.2	97.0	0.7	0.8	0.4	0.5	1.3	1.3	5.3	5.6	7.0	6.3	5.2	25.2	28.7	13.4	3.3	77.9	42.5	49.2	50.8
49107	BUCHANAN	91.7	91.2	5.1	5.5	0.4	0.4	1.7	1.7	6.3	6.4	7.2	6.5	6.6	27.1	26.2	11.9	1.9	76.2	38.4	49.4	50.6
49111	EAU CLAIRE	89.3	88.7	5.4	5.9	0.3	0.3	10.3	10.5	6.1	6.2	7.4	7.0	6.3	27.2	25.4	12.6	1.9	75.8	38.7	50.9	49.1
49112	EDWARDSBURG	96.2	95.7	0.9	1.0	0.4	0.5	1.1	1.3	5.8	6.2	7.5	6.4	5.2	26.9	28.3	12.5	1.3	76.5	40.3	50.5	49.5
49113	GALIEN	96.1	96.0	0.4	0.5	0.4	0.4	1.5	1.5	5.2	5.5	6.8	7.1	6.7	25.8	29.6	12.2	1.2	78.2	40.6	50.5	49.5
49116	LAKESIDE	91.6	90.7	6.5	7.3	0.5	0.5	0.5	0.5	3.4	3.9	4.9	3.9	2.4	20.0	35.1	23.4	2.9	85.4	51.0	50.7	49.3
49117	NEW BUFFALO	95.9	95.7	1.4	1.6	0.5	0.5	2.1	2.1	4.8	5.1	5.3	4.6	4.7	22.0	32.7	19.2	1.8	82.1	47.3	49.8	50.2
49120	NILES	89.7	89.1	6.3	6.8	0.5	0.5	2.5	2.6	6.3	6.4	7.1	6.6	6.4	26.0	26.6	12.8	1.9	76.2	39.1	48.7	51.3
49125	SAWYER	96.3	96.1	0.8	0.9	0.3	0.3	2.0	2.0	4.9	5.6	6.5	5.6	4.5	23.3	30.6	16.7	2.3	79.5	44.8	49.6	50.4
49126	SODUS	88.2	87.4	7.3	8.1	0.4	0.4	10.2	10.3	6.2	6.2	6.3	6.3	4.9	26.7	26.7	14.4	2.3	77.3	41.0	51.9	48.1
49127	STEVENSVILLE	95.7	95.4	1.1	1.3	1.2	1.2	1.3	1.3	5.6	6.0	7.2	6.9	5.8	25.1	29.2	12.4	1.8	76.7	41.0	48.7	51.3
49128	THREE OAKS	96.5	96.3	1.2	1.4	0.2	0.2	1.5	1.6	6.0	6.1	6.5	6.4	5.4	25.6	28.4	13.8	1.9	77.5	41.3	49.2	50.8
49129	UNION PIER	90.2	89.3	7.3	8.2	0.3	0.3	1.9	1.9	4.4	4.7	5.9	4.7	2.9	20.5	34.0	20.1	2.8	82.4	48.7	50.5	49.5
49130	UNION	97.2	96.9	0.5	0.6	0.3	0.4	1.1	1.2	4.9	5.7	7.1	6.6	5.0	25.1	32.7	11.8	1.1	78.1	42.4	50.4	49.6
49201	JACKSON	86.7	85.7	10.0	10.6	0.6	0.8	2.1	2.4	5.7	5.8	6.5	6.0	6.5	31.4	26.2	10.4	1.5	78.4	38.5	56.2	43.8
49202	JACKSON	88.3	87.1	6.8	7.4	0.7	0.9	3.2	3.7	8.2	6.9	6.4	6.2	7.6	29.0	20.4	12.3	2.9	74.9	34.8	47.5	52.5
49203	JACKSON	78.9	77.4	15.9	16.9	0.8	1.0	3.0	3.3	7.8	7.6	7.9	7.0	6.3	26.7	23.1	11.8	1.9	72.5	35.6	47.7	52.3
49220	ADDISON	98.0	97.7	0.2	0.2	0.3	0.4	1.4	1.6	6.3	6.8	7.4	5.8	5.2	25.8	29.1	12.3	1.4	75.7	40.1	50.4	49.6
49221	ADRIAN	86.4	85.1	4.9	5.1	0.7	0.9	12.1	13.5	6.6	6.4	6.7	7.3	8.0	28.6	23.5	10.7	2.1	76.2	35.3	50.6	49.4
49224	ALBION	71.7	70.2	23.3	24.5	0.5	0.6	3.7	4.1	6.6	6.5	7.3	9.6	10.8	24.1	21.9	11.6	1.6	75.0	32.8	47.9	52.1
49227	ALLEN	97.7	97.5	0.3	0.3	0.2	0.2	0.8	0.9	6.9	7.1	7.5	7.1	5.9	26.3	26.7	10.9	1.6	74.1	37.8	51.2	48.8
49228	BLISSFIELD	95.6	95.0	0.2	0.2	0.1	0.1	7.0	8.2	5.7	6.1	7.5	7.5	6.8	27.1	25.3	12.0	2.2	76.0	38.2	49.4	50.6
49229	BRITTON	97.2	96.8	0.3	0.3	0.3	0.3	2.9	3.4	6.2	6.9	8.7	7.4	5.5	28.1	26.7	9.5	1.2	73.6	37.6	49.6	50.4
49230	BROOKLYN	97.6	97.3	0.2	0.3	0.3	0.4	1.2	1.4	4.7	5.8	6.9	6.4	4.9	24.7	30.9	14.1	1.6	78.4	43.0	50.2	49.8
49232	CAMDEN	98.0	97.9	0.0	0.1	0.1	0.2	0.7	0.8	8.4	8.3	8.1	7.2	6.5	25.1	25.4	10.1	1.0	70.5	34.4	50.4	49.6
49233	CEMENT CITY	97.9	97.7	0.3	0.4	0.3	0.4	1.2	1.4	5.5	6.3	7.0	6.5	4.8	25.0	31.0	12.6	1.3	77.0	41.7	50.7	49.3
49234	CLARKLAKE	97.9	97.6	0.2	0.2	0.2	0.3	1.2	1.4	4.9	6.0	7.6	6.7	4.6	25.1	30.9	12.8	1.5	77.0	42.3	50.7	49.4
49235	CLAYTON	97.4	97.0	0.3	0.4	0.1	0.1	3.4	4.0	5.8	6.6	8.1	7.1	5.8	26.5	28.5	10.8	0.7	75.1	38.8	51.4	48.6
49236	CLINTON	98.2	98.0	0.2	0.2	0.2	0.2	1.6	1.8	6.1	6.7	7.3	6.9	5.3	27.6	28.1	10.9	1.1	75.6	39.2	49.3	50.7
49237	CONCORD	98.0	97.7	0.2	0.2	0.4	0.4	0.9	1.1	7.1	7.5	7.8	7.1	5.5	26.7	27.0	10.1	1.1	73.0	37.6	49.4	50.6
49238	DEERFIELD	96.6	96.1	0.4	0.5	0.2	0.3	3.8	4.5	8.1	7.9	7.3	7.1	6.3	27.6	23.9	10.7	1.2	72.5	35.8	49.1	50.9
49240	GRASS LAKE	97.1	96.9	1.6	1.6	0.1	0.2	1.0	1.2	6.5	7.1	7.5	6.3	4.8	29.0	28.2	9.5	1.1	74.9	38.8	50.9	49.1
49241	HANOVER	98.2	98.0	0.2	0.3	0.0	0.0	1.0	1.1	6.3	6.9	7.9	7.6	5.4	28.8	25.5	10.4	1.1	73.5	37.6	50.7	49.3
49242	HILLSDALE	97.1	96.7	0.6	0.6	0.6	0.7	1.3	1.5	6.5	6.2	6.6	8.5	9.6	25.3	23.5	11.9	1.9	76.6	35.3	48.9	51.1
49245	HOMER	97.6	97.4	0.2	0.2	0.0	0.0	1.5	1.7	6.9	6.9	7.9	7.6	7.0	27.4	25.1	9.8	1.4	73.4	36.2	49.6	50.4
49246	HORTON	98.2	98.0	0.2	0.2	0.4	0.5	0.9	1.0	5.3	6.3	8.0	7.0	5.0	25.5	31.0	11.1	0.9	75.9	41.1	51.3	48.8
49247	HUDSON	97.2	96.9	0.2	0.2	0.4	0.5	2.0	2.3	6.2	6.3	7.5	7.6	6.4	27.0	25.8	11.9	1.4	75.3	37.8	49.9	50.2
49248	JASPER	97.4	97.3	0.4	0.4	0.1	0.1	3.3	3.7	6.0	6.3	7.2	7.8	7.0	24.9	28.4	10.9	1.4	75.7	39.4	51.3	48.7
	MICHIGAN	80.2	79.2	14.2	14.4	1.8	2.3	3.3	3.6	6.8	6.9	7.4	7.1	6.9	28.1	24.6	10.8	1.6	74.9	36.5	49.1	50.9
	UNITED STATES	75.1	73.6	12.3	12.5	3.8	4.2	12.5	14.1	6.9	6.7	7.2	7.0	7.3	28.6	23.8	10.8	1.7	75.1	36.0	49.1	50.9

INCOME

ZIP CODE #	POST OFFICE NAME	2004 Per Capita Income	2004 HH Income Base	2004 HOUSEHOLD INCOME DISTRIBUTION (%) Less than $25,000	$25,000 to $49,999	$50,000 to $99,999	$100,000 to $149,999	$150,000 or More	MEDIAN HOUSEHOLD INCOME 2004	2009	2004 National Centile	2004 State Centile	2004 Home Value Base	2004 HOME VALUE DISTRIBUTION (%) Less than $50,000	$50,000 to $89,999	$90,000 to $174,999	$175,000 to $399,999	$400,000 or More	2004 Median Home Value
49030	BURR OAK	19282	978	22.1	33.8	35.7	6.7	1.7	44485	48010	60	51	818	15.5	26.9	41.0	14.7	2.0	99254
49031	CASSOPOLIS	22146	2956	29.3	29.4	30.8	7.1	3.4	42296	45933	54	44	2343	13.7	23.3	40.8	15.6	6.7	108713
49032	CENTREVILLE	17213	963	27.4	34.1	29.4	7.0	2.2	41040	44487	50	39	784	11.4	25.9	47.3	14.4	1.0	106065
49033	CERESCO	25294	660	17.7	30.0	36.4	12.6	3.3	52014	56761	76	71	623	4.3	11.1	51.4	30.0	3.2	148018
49034	CLIMAX	22950	931	17.8	28.4	42.4	8.1	3.3	52345	59214	76	72	810	13.2	15.6	51.1	18.2	2.0	117188
49036	COLDWATER	20431	9203	25.6	33.6	31.6	7.0	2.2	42104	45377	53	43	7212	13.6	23.6	42.1	18.3	2.4	107985
49038	COLOMA	21626	3988	26.6	32.7	31.3	6.6	2.9	42835	48325	56	45	3205	11.7	23.8	47.7	14.3	2.5	108834
49040	COLON	18855	1274	29.9	34.5	30.1	4.3	1.2	36256	38967	33	20	1050	15.3	30.8	41.8	10.7	1.4	96833
49042	CONSTANTINE	19787	1921	24.0	31.7	36.7	6.1	1.5	45530	49069	63	54	1579	15.3	19.5	52.1	11.9	1.1	107281
49043	COVERT	13351	979	47.1	26.2	21.9	4.1	0.8	26680	29801	7	2	735	31.6	30.8	29.0	7.2	1.5	73364
49045	DECATUR	18595	2369	28.1	34.5	29.9	5.5	2.0	39842	43335	45	33	1861	16.8	27.6	38.5	15.6	1.5	97667
49046	DELTON	21459	3015	20.9	33.2	33.8	9.3	2.8	46743	51125	66	58	2574	5.2	15.9	49.9	27.9	1.1	127033
49047	DOWAGIAC	20119	6009	28.8	33.0	29.5	6.3	2.5	41292	45429	51	40	4571	11.6	29.2	42.0	14.7	2.5	101393
49048	KALAMAZOO	21263	9998	26.3	32.5	31.0	7.5	2.7	43377	49020	57	47	6985	14.9	31.2	41.6	11.6	0.7	94855
49050	DOWLING	25094	561	18.0	31.7	38.3	10.5	1.4	50255	55300	72	66	508	3.9	12.0	59.7	24.4	0.0	133636
49051	EAST LEROY	21933	794	21.0	27.6	40.2	7.6	3.7	51064	54153	74	68	731	13.7	20.1	40.5	22.0	3.7	117841
49052	FULTON	22124	323	21.4	25.7	39.6	10.2	3.1	52490	58153	76	72	289	9.7	22.2	44.6	22.2	1.4	118351
49053	GALESBURG	25067	2142	20.7	27.7	36.0	10.7	4.9	51368	57821	74	69	1802	16.2	14.2	45.8	21.4	2.5	123630
49055	GOBLES	21147	2431	23.9	32.9	33.7	6.8	2.8	44875	48655	61	52	2020	11.0	21.6	48.4	17.2	1.8	114795
49056	GRAND JUNCTION	16401	1574	31.2	35.3	27.1	4.8	1.6	36832	40706	35	22	1280	22.3	31.4	35.2	10.6	0.5	85340
49057	HARTFORD	16777	2409	32.1	33.5	28.7	4.2	1.5	38370	41918	41	28	1812	21.3	33.4	37.7	7.0	0.6	84267
49058	HASTINGS	22800	7375	20.5	31.7	35.3	9.0	3.5	48116	52530	69	62	6030	4.8	14.0	56.6	21.9	2.7	127658
49060	HICKORY CORNERS	42925	727	13.6	20.8	38.1	15.3	12.2	68279	75320	90	92	637	0.8	12.1	42.5	30.3	14.3	167230
49061	JONES	22694	704	25.4	25.3	38.9	6.5	3.8	49345	53031	71	64	591	13.4	18.1	45.2	18.8	4.6	114063
49064	LAWRENCE	17917	1400	29.4	31.0	31.6	6.0	1.9	40764	44433	49	38	1157	13.7	25.8	45.4	14.0	1.2	100812
49065	LAWTON	21705	2196	19.9	30.8	35.4	11.1	2.8	49407	53424	71	65	1835	8.0	15.9	43.2	31.8	1.1	136184
49066	LEONIDAS	16722	258	24.8	33.3	32.6	7.4	1.9	40700	42762	49	37	226	15.0	28.8	45.1	9.7	1.3	101667
49067	MARCELLUS	20353	1839	24.5	32.9	33.4	6.5	2.7	44295	48102	59	50	1539	9.4	26.1	45.7	17.5	1.4	109973
49068	MARSHALL	23969	6187	22.2	29.9	33.9	10.4	3.7	47970	52087	68	61	4827	7.3	15.9	48.7	26.7	1.4	128568
49070	MARTIN	19421	801	22.2	33.2	34.3	8.6	1.6	45738	49433	63	55	673	13.7	15.2	50.4	19.2	1.6	121509
49071	MATTAWAN	25168	3162	14.1	24.8	44.4	12.2	4.4	60058	65161	84	84	2872	15.0	9.9	43.7	28.2	3.2	139307
49072	MENDON	19370	1330	21.0	34.4	36.8	6.8	1.0	46098	49578	64	57	1153	10.7	23.8	51.3	13.9	0.4	106758
49073	NASHVILLE	19597	2047	23.1	33.4	34.8	6.9	1.8	43641	47988	58	48	1713	10.6	21.7	46.9	18.2	2.6	111719
49076	OLIVET	19336	1460	22.3	29.7	39.5	7.2	1.3	48263	53856	69	62	1072	5.9	21.6	52.7	18.0	1.8	116422
49078	OTSEGO	21215	3268	19.7	33.5	37.5	7.4	1.8	47441	51655	67	60	2680	10.2	17.2	56.0	15.5	1.2	118679
49079	PAW PAW	22743	5013	21.9	29.0	37.3	9.6	2.2	48972	52636	70	63	4018	7.7	15.4	53.2	22.0	1.7	123882
49080	PLAINWELL	23439	6061	20.2	29.8	35.0	11.0	4.1	50073	54994	72	66	5108	12.1	11.5	47.4	27.5	1.6	135545
49082	QUINCY	18763	2494	22.0	35.8	33.8	6.9	1.4	44473	48141	60	51	2070	9.7	24.4	44.6	18.9	2.3	110196
49083	RICHLAND	36029	2550	13.3	23.7	37.3	15.9	9.8	64949	73933	88	89	2202	2.8	1.8	43.6	35.7	16.1	179904
49085	SAINT JOSEPH	30559	9913	22.2	24.9	32.9	11.8	8.2	52984	58114	77	73	7548	3.1	6.1	51.6	33.9	5.2	156216
49087	SCHOOLCRAFT	28092	2116	16.3	20.0	39.6	16.7	7.4	63687	71715	88	88	1807	2.3	6.8	45.5	40.8	4.7	166367
49088	SCOTTS	24239	1100	13.2	29.4	39.6	15.3	2.6	56035	63065	81	78	1018	3.4	10.7	49.8	34.3	1.8	149843
49089	SHERWOOD	17729	793	23.8	41.9	29.0	4.3	1.0	39153	43590	43	30	653	16.4	34.3	38.1	10.1	1.1	89250
49090	SOUTH HAVEN	21160	6165	28.9	33.3	27.3	7.6	2.8	40711	44780	49	37	4902	14.3	18.1	42.1	20.1	5.5	117857
49091	STURGIS	20061	8040	25.8	33.0	32.4	6.3	2.5	42742	46448	55	45	5753	9.1	25.5	47.7	15.9	1.8	107793
49092	TEKONSHA	20852	886	23.1	31.9	34.9	8.6	1.5	45892	50121	64	55	745	13.8	23.5	44.6	16.4	1.7	103952
49093	THREE RIVERS	21902	7112	26.5	32.7	30.9	7.0	3.0	43029	46846	56	46	5522	12.2	26.2	44.5	15.6	1.6	104893
49094	UNION CITY	19675	1676	28.5	33.2	30.7	6.3	1.3	41962	45429	53	42	1346	16.1	30.0	42.1	11.1	0.7	95300
49095	VANDALIA	22429	943	24.6	28.5	37.4	6.9	2.6	46805	50340	66	58	758	12.0	19.1	39.2	26.1	3.6	123165
49096	VERMONTVILLE	20876	1224	19.3	30.2	38.2	11.2	1.1	50430	54933	73	67	1092	7.0	19.3	52.8	20.0	1.0	118249
49097	VICKSBURG	25126	3820	15.7	27.5	39.6	13.7	3.6	56412	63299	81	78	3314	4.2	14.3	47.7	31.2	2.7	145241
49098	WATERVLIET	22035	2504	28.4	30.1	32.7	6.2	2.5	42485	47193	55	44	2019	15.6	26.0	44.3	11.8	2.3	100278
49099	WHITE PIGEON	23155	2339	22.9	30.3	35.4	6.9	4.6	47727	51817	68	60	1975	12.4	24.7	39.8	18.2	5.0	108838
49101	BARODA	24157	1261	21.7	29.3	36.2	7.9	4.9	49026	53173	70	64	1084	24.1	7.5	43.9	21.1	3.4	121543
49102	BERRIEN CENTER	16756	491	25.5	32.0	32.6	8.6	1.4	44608	46866	60	52	414	22.5	22.5	34.5	20.1	0.5	104661
49103	BERRIEN SPRINGS	21259	4166	30.0	25.8	31.5	8.4	4.2	42912	46895	56	45	2676	6.0	10.5	48.8	31.2	3.5	147550
49104	BERRIEN SPRINGS	35788	19	21.1	26.3	31.6	5.3	15.8	52140	54641	76	71	9	0.0	0.0	44.4	55.6	0.0	187500
49106	BRIDGMAN	26573	1968	21.3	24.9	36.2	12.4	5.2	52944	59646	77	73	1658	8.3	13.3	43.9	27.8	6.7	139356
49107	BUCHANAN	20640	4191	25.8	34.5	30.6	6.7	2.5	41814	46891	52	42	3293	11.5	27.3	43.3	16.2	1.7	107704
49111	EAU CLAIRE	19266	1478	27.2	31.8	32.9	5.9	2.2	42744	46419	55	45	1251	15.3	22.1	42.5	18.2	2.0	110012
49112	EDWARDSBURG	24560	3899	21.6	32.6	33.6	8.1	4.1	45481	49483	63	54	3391	16.1	15.5	44.3	20.7	3.5	118542
49113	GALIEN	20611	849	22.7	35.1	31.8	9.0	1.4	43620	48884	58	48	716	8.4	29.6	45.7	14.3	2.1	105814
49116	LAKESIDE	41691	112	17.0	27.7	29.5	15.2	10.7	57188	68100	82	81	98	4.1	3.1	32.7	40.8	19.4	214706
49117	NEW BUFFALO	33234	1916	25.0	26.9	30.1	9.7	8.5	48094	54905	69	62	1572	3.4	10.5	41.7	28.7	15.8	160500
49120	NILES	20889	14683	28.1	32.5	30.9	6.3	2.2	41237	45984	51	40	11409	11.5	31.4	42.8	12.7	1.6	98291
49125	SAWYER	31749	1174	18.5	32.7	35.6	8.0	5.2	49025	55400	70	64	1011	9.1	9.5	39.2	28.7	13.6	156130
49126	SODUS	21738	481	31.0	32.6	27.7	5.8	2.9	39368	44053	44	32	411	31.1	19.2	36.0	13.1	0.5	89423
49127	STEVENSVILLE	31212	4097	18.5	25.0	35.4	12.1	9.0	57051	62568	82	80	3241	10.6	4.6	48.8	29.6	6.4	154341
49128	THREE OAKS	23295	1757	26.4	29.5	33.2	7.6	3.4	44563	49964	60	52	1448	10.7	16.5	44.9	21.8	6.2	120977
49129	UNION PIER	35907	372	20.4	25.0	31.7	12.6	10.2	56450	63870	81	79	328	3.7	6.4	37.2	35.1	17.7	184000
49130	UNION	26532	772	15.5	31.2	40.2	9.7	3.4	52464	57336	76	72	671	6.3	13.1	38.9	35.5	6.3	149432
49201	JACKSON	22809	15718	23.9	27.3	34.5	9.9	4.5	48762	53485	70	63	12373	12.0	14.1	45.1	26.1	2.7	129735
49202	JACKSON	19220	8783	33.1	35.8	26.7	3.4	1.0	36018	39905	32	19	5530	16.7	43.2	36.0	3.9	0.1	80317
49203	JACKSON	22508	15695	27.2	29.3	32.3	7.9	3.3	43914	48471	58	49	11186	14.1	26.5	43.6	14.9	0.9	103020
49220	ADDISON	22848	1076	22.9	32.2	31.0	10.0	3.9	45383	50503	62	54	898	7.6	16.9	37.0	31.9	6.7	147449
49221	ADRIAN	21115	14716	24.1	31.2	33.6	8.0	3.2	45925	50508	64	56	10720	11.7	16.2	49.4	21.3	1.4	118720
49224	ALBION	17526	5088	34.7	31.5	27.5	4.8	1.6	36621	40151	34	21	3413	16.3	40.9	34.0	8.3	0.5	82099
49227	ALLEN	20374	518	20.1	32.8	39.0	6.6	1.5	48312	52349	69	62	441	8.6	22.9	48.3	18.6	1.6	115091
49228	BLISSFIELD	22476	2178	24.9	28.9	34.2	9.8	2.2	46558	49894	65	57	1785	10.9	13.2	52.3	21.9	1.6	130201
49229	BRITTON	24063	1149	13.8	25.1	43.1	14.7	3.3	59859	64760	84	84	1011	2.2	8.0	50.1	37.0	2.8	156385
49230	BROOKLYN	26317	4041	18.3	28.1	37.0	11.6	5.1	53426	58106	78	74	3550	5.3	8.8	40.5	38.4	7.0	165929
49232	CAMDEN	19149	991	26.4	35.8	28.9	6.4	2.5	41532	45000	51	41	848	14.3	19.6	34.7	29.4	2.1	119231
49233	CEMENT CITY	24835	1329	19.9	30.9	33.0	13.0	3.2	49142	53172	70	64	1224	6.2	12.4	40.0	38.6	2.8	156206
49234	CLARKLAKE	35296	1152	15.0	25.1	39.6	11.5	8.9	59403	63593	84	83	1022	4.1	11.0	32.6	37.3	15.1	181522
49235	CLAYTON	21541	840	21.4	29.4	38.9	8.6	1.7	49371	53862	71	65	729	9.1	16.9	46.1	26.3	1.7	128676
49236	CLINTON	26174	1925	15.0	23.4	44.2	13.6	3.8	59031	65034	84	82	1670	9.2	6.8	40.8	38.3	4.9	164444
49237	CONCORD	21968	1178	20.2	27.6	39.0	10.6	2.6	52060	55481	76	71	991	9.2	15.7	47.1	26.3	1.6	129554
49238	DEERFIELD	20900	556	19.1	28.1	38.9	11.5	2.5	52330	56406	76	72	469	2.6	9.2	60.3	25.6	2.4	140469
49240	GRASS LAKE	27466	2742	13.4	21.8	43.8	13.9	7.1	62587	68998	87	86	2417	4.4	5.2	36.5	48.0	6.0	185916
49241	HANOVER	20517	1021	22.3	32.9	34.6	7.4	2.8	45914	50498	64	55	890	21.0	13.6	41.4	22.0	2.0	116992
49242	HILLSDALE	20421	6046	28.4	33.1	29.6	6.6	2.2	41282	44334	51	40	4379	11.9	25.6	41.8	19.1	1.6	108328
49245	HOMER	19367	1912	26.7	31.8	33.4	5.3	2.8	42641	46480	55	45	1570	22.9	30.4	33.5	11.3	2.0	85714
49246	HORTON	27175	1256	12.9	28.9	37.1	15.0	6.1	59667	63747	84	83	1151	3.0	6.1	45.3	40.8	4.9	166097
49247	HUDSON	20661	2364	23.6	32.9	34.9	6.9	1.7	45169	49790	62	53	1928	11.4	23.5	47.6	15.6	1.9	108565
49248	JASPER	22454	317	17.7	34.4	37.9	7.6	2.5	48712	53989	70	63	277	9.8	20.2	51.3	17.7	1.1	118990
	MICHIGAN	25281		23.8	27.4	32.3	10.9	5.5	48729	54505				10.7	16.0	40.3	28.0	5.0	134769
	UNITED STATES	25866		24.7	27.1	30.8	10.9	6.5	48124	56710				10.9	15.0	33.7	30.1	10.4	145905

ZIP CODE		FINANCIAL SERVICES				THE HOME						ENTERTAINMENT						PERSONAL			
						Home Improvements		Furnishings													
#	POST OFFICE NAME	Auto Loan	Home Loan	Invest-ments	Retire-ment Plans	Home Repair	Lawn & Garden	Comput-ers & Hard-ware	Major Appli-ances	TV, Radio, Sound Equip-ment	Furni-ture	Dine out/ Carry out	Sports Equip-ment	Fees & Tickets	Toys & Games	Travel	Cable TV	Apparel & Services	Auto Repairs	Health Insur-ance	Pets & Supplies
49030	BURR OAK	83	75	62	73	79	85	71	77	74	71	91	92	70	92	73	75	86	76	82	97
49031	CASSOPOLIS	89	74	56	70	80	88	72	81	78	72	95	95	68	95	74	81	89	79	90	104
49032	CENTREVILLE	90	73	50	68	79	86	69	79	76	69	91	94	65	91	70	79	85	77	89	105
49033	CERESCO	98	93	80	89	97	103	87	93	90	86	110	110	87	113	89	92	106	91	98	116
49034	CLIMAX	97	88	69	84	92	99	81	89	86	81	104	106	80	107	84	87	99	87	96	114
49036	COLDWATER	77	66	53	63	71	78	66	72	70	65	85	84	62	85	67	72	80	71	79	90
49038	COLOMA	79	72	62	70	75	83	71	76	74	70	91	88	70	92	72	76	87	74	81	91
49040	COLON	79	62	40	57	68	76	59	69	67	59	80	82	54	78	61	70	74	68	80	92
49042	CONSTANTINE	88	71	48	66	76	84	68	77	75	68	90	91	64	89	69	78	84	76	87	101
49043	COVERT	70	47	21	41	53	61	45	57	55	46	64	68	39	61	46	59	59	56	70	81
49045	DECATUR	83	68	50	63	74	83	66	75	73	65	88	88	62	88	68	77	82	74	86	98
49046	DELTON	91	81	63	77	86	93	75	84	80	75	97	100	73	99	78	82	92	82	91	108
49047	DOWAGIAC	76	70	60	66	73	80	68	73	72	67	88	84	67	90	70	74	84	71	79	89
49048	KALAMAZOO	75	73	77	74	73	79	76	75	77	75	96	88	76	96	75	76	93	76	74	85
49050	DOWLING	100	90	71	86	95	101	83	92	88	83	107	109	82	110	86	90	102	89	98	117
49051	EAST LEROY	77	91	97	88	90	93	84	84	81	83	101	97	89	107	86	81	100	82	80	93
49052	FULTON	97	86	66	82	91	98	80	89	85	80	103	106	78	105	82	87	98	86	96	114
49053	GALESBURG	99	96	83	93	98	103	90	95	91	90	112	112	89	114	91	92	108	93	97	115
49055	GOBLES	87	80	65	76	84	90	75	81	79	74	96	95	74	99	77	81	92	79	88	102
49056	GRAND JUNCTION	82	57	29	50	64	73	55	68	65	56	77	81	48	73	56	70	71	67	82	94
49057	HARTFORD	76	62	45	59	67	75	61	68	67	61	81	80	58	81	62	70	76	67	77	87
49058	HASTINGS	90	84	72	81	87	94	80	85	83	79	102	101	79	104	82	84	97	84	90	105
49060	HICKORY CORNERS	155	163	155	158	168	174	148	158	147	148	181	184	150	188	154	149	177	153	158	189
49061	JONES	102	81	52	74	88	97	76	88	85	76	102	105	71	101	78	89	95	86	101	118
49064	LAWRENCE	82	67	47	64	73	80	65	74	71	64	85	87	61	85	66	73	80	72	83	95
49065	LAWTON	94	84	67	82	88	95	80	87	84	80	102	102	78	103	81	85	97	85	92	108
49066	LEONIDAS	82	73	56	70	77	83	68	75	72	68	87	89	66	89	70	74	83	73	81	97
49067	MARCELLUS	85	75	57	72	79	86	71	78	76	71	92	92	69	93	73	77	87	76	85	99
49068	MARSHALL	83	86	85	84	87	92	82	85	83	82	102	99	84	105	84	83	99	83	85	98
49070	MARTIN	87	77	59	73	81	87	71	79	76	71	92	94	70	94	73	78	88	77	85	102
49071	MATTAWAN	98	107	104	108	105	105	100	101	94	101	119	118	101	120	99	91	117	99	91	113
49072	MENDON	86	72	52	68	77	84	67	76	73	68	89	91	65	89	69	76	83	75	85	100
49073	NASHVILLE	82	73	56	70	76	82	69	76	73	69	89	89	67	89	70	74	84	74	81	94
49076	OLIVET	84	72	65	72	75	81	76	78	78	74	96	95	72	95	74	77	92	79	80	96
49078	OTSEGO	86	78	63	75	82	89	75	81	79	74	96	94	74	98	76	81	91	79	87	100
49079	PAW PAW	87	82	71	80	85	91	80	84	82	79	100	99	78	102	80	82	96	83	87	101
49080	PLAINWELL	92	88	77	86	91	96	83	89	85	83	104	104	83	106	85	85	100	87	91	107
49082	QUINCY	84	71	53	68	76	84	68	76	74	68	89	90	65	89	70	76	84	75	85	98
49083	RICHLAND	122	149	159	151	146	146	134	133	124	135	157	155	143	164	137	121	157	129	120	147
49085	SAINT JOSEPH	93	107	121	107	106	111	102	101	99	102	124	117	107	129	104	98	123	100	97	112
49087	SCHOOLCRAFT	107	121	122	120	120	121	110	112	105	110	132	131	115	138	112	103	130	109	104	127
49088	SCOTTS	93	98	92	96	100	103	90	94	89	90	110	111	92	115	92	89	108	91	93	112
49089	SHERWOOD	75	65	48	62	69	75	61	68	65	61	79	81	59	80	62	67	75	66	74	88
49090	SOUTH HAVEN	83	70	53	66	75	83	69	76	74	68	90	88	65	89	70	77	85	75	85	96
49091	STURGIS	80	72	62	70	75	81	72	76	75	71	92	89	70	91	72	76	87	76	81	91
49092	TEKONSHA	86	76	58	73	81	87	71	78	75	71	91	93	69	93	73	77	87	76	85	101
49093	THREE RIVERS	86	73	58	69	77	85	73	78	78	72	95	93	69	94	73	80	90	78	86	98
49094	UNION CITY	82	68	48	65	72	81	67	74	72	66	87	87	63	87	67	75	82	73	83	94
49095	VANDALIA	95	75	49	69	82	91	71	83	79	71	95	99	65	94	73	84	88	82	96	112
49096	VERMONTVILLE	92	82	62	78	86	93	75	84	80	75	97	100	74	100	78	82	93	81	91	108
49097	VICKSBURG	100	96	84	93	99	105	91	96	93	90	114	114	90	117	92	93	110	94	99	117
49098	WATERVLIET	89	75	55	72	80	90	74	82	80	73	96	95	70	95	75	83	90	81	92	103
49099	WHITE PIGEON	99	82	57	77	88	96	77	87	84	77	101	104	73	102	79	87	95	85	98	116
49101	BARODA	98	89	70	85	93	98	83	91	86	84	106	107	81	106	84	88	101	89	95	114
49102	BERRIEN CENTER	81	74	58	71	76	80	70	76	72	71	88	88	67	86	70	72	84	75	77	92
49103	BERRIEN SPRINGS	78	82	91	84	81	85	84	82	81	82	102	98	84	103	83	79	100	83	77	91
49104	BERRIEN SPRINGS	116	92	120	104	91	101	128	112	126	120	159	144	117	148	115	116	154	127	104	125
49106	BRIDGMAN	105	92	69	87	98	106	85	96	91	85	111	114	83	112	88	94	105	93	105	125
49107	BUCHANAN	77	71	62	70	74	80	71	75	73	70	89	87	69	90	71	74	85	74	78	89
49111	EAU CLAIRE	82	70	53	67	74	81	68	75	72	68	88	88	65	87	69	74	83	74	81	94
49112	EDWARDSBURG	99	84	61	80	90	98	80	89	86	80	104	106	76	105	81	89	98	87	99	115
49113	GALIEN	80	74	61	72	77	83	71	76	75	71	91	89	70	92	72	76	87	75	81	92
49116	LAKESIDE	129	102	69	92	114	128	96	115	108	95	128	135	86	127	102	116	119	114	136	158
49117	NEW BUFFALO	117	100	80	94	109	119	96	109	104	95	125	129	90	126	100	108	118	108	121	141
49120	NILES	74	71	67	69	73	80	70	73	73	69	89	84	70	92	71	74	86	72	76	85
49125	SAWYER	120	98	71	92	107	120	94	109	104	93	125	127	87	124	98	109	116	107	124	142
49126	SODUS	88	64	38	59	71	81	64	75	73	64	87	88	57	84	64	77	80	74	88	100
49127	STEVENSVILLE	105	115	118	114	114	118	109	110	106	109	133	129	112	137	110	104	130	109	105	124
49128	THREE OAKS	86	76	62	74	80	89	75	81	80	74	97	93	73	97	76	82	91	80	88	98
49129	UNION PIER	127	100	68	91	113	126	94	114	107	94	127	133	85	125	101	114	118	112	134	155
49130	UNION	107	88	59	81	94	103	82	94	90	82	109	112	77	109	84	94	102	92	106	125
49201	JACKSON	91	89	84	87	91	97	87	90	88	86	109	105	87	110	88	89	105	89	92	106
49202	JACKSON	59	56	60	56	57	62	61	60	63	59	78	70	60	78	60	63	75	61	61	67
49203	JACKSON	75	77	84	75	77	84	78	78	80	77	99	89	80	101	79	80	96	78	79	87
49220	ADDISON	92	81	62	77	86	93	75	84	80	75	97	100	74	99	78	82	92	82	91	108
49221	ADRIAN	78	77	77	76	78	83	76	78	77	76	95	91	76	96	77	77	92	78	78	90
49224	ALBION	67	58	54	56	60	68	60	63	65	60	79	73	59	79	60	67	75	63	69	76
49227	ALLEN	90	78	58	74	83	90	73	82	78	73	94	97	70	96	75	81	89	80	90	106
49228	BLISSFIELD	91	77	58	73	82	91	74	82	80	74	97	97	71	97	75	83	91	81	92	105
49229	BRITTON	105	98	80	94	102	108	90	98	94	90	114	116	90	118	93	95	110	95	103	124
49230	BROOKLYN	96	93	84	89	97	104	87	94	90	86	110	109	86	113	90	92	105	92	99	115
49232	CAMDEN	88	76	56	73	80	88	73	80	78	73	95	94	70	95	74	80	89	79	88	101
49233	CEMENT CITY	95	95	85	92	98	102	87	93	88	87	108	110	88	111	89	88	104	90	94	113
49234	CLARKLAKE	131	134	124	130	137	145	123	130	123	123	153	152	125	156	127	125	148	127	133	156
49235	CLAYTON	93	83	63	78	87	94	76	85	81	76	99	101	75	101	79	83	94	82	92	109
49236	CLINTON	98	100	92	98	101	107	94	98	94	93	116	114	95	120	95	94	112	95	98	115
49237	CONCORD	93	83	64	80	87	94	79	86	84	79	102	101	77	103	80	85	96	84	93	107
49238	DEERFIELD	93	86	71	82	90	97	80	87	84	80	103	103	80	105	83	86	98	85	94	110
49240	GRASS LAKE	108	116	109	113	117	120	105	109	103	105	128	129	108	133	107	102	125	106	107	129
49241	HANOVER	86	79	63	76	83	88	73	80	76	73	93	95	72	96	75	78	89	78	85	102
49242	HILLSDALE	80	68	57	67	72	80	69	74	74	68	90	87	66	89	69	75	85	74	80	91
49245	HOMER	88	69	45	64	75	84	66	77	74	67	89	91	61	88	68	78	83	75	88	102
49246	HORTON	95	115	122	114	113	113	104	104	97	103	122	121	110	130	106	95	122	100	95	115
49247	HUDSON	81	74	62	71	78	85	72	77	76	71	92	89	71	95	73	78	88	75	83	94
49248	JASPER	96	85	65	81	90	96	79	87	83	79	102	104	77	104	81	86	97	85	94	112
	MICHIGAN	91	91	93	89	91	98	90	91	91	90	113	106	90	113	90	91	109	91	92	105
	UNITED STATES	100	100	100	100	100	100	100	100	100	100	100	100	100	100	100	100	100	100	100	100

ZIP CODE		COUNTY FIPS CODE	POPULATION			2000-2004 ANNUAL RATE		HOUSEHOLDS			% Annual Rate 2000-2004	2004 Average HH Size	FAMILIES		% Annual Rate 2000-2004
#	POST OFFICE NAME		2000	2004	2009	% Rate	State Centile	2000	2004	2009			2000	2004	
49249	JEROME	059	3079	3245	3414	1.2	73	1181	1273	1366	1.8	2.54	916	976	1.5
49250	JONESVILLE	059	5842	6133	6439	1.2	70	2172	2323	2484	1.6	2.50	1605	1694	1.3
49251	LESLIE	065	6057	6168	6217	0.4	40	2172	2257	2316	0.9	2.72	1655	1695	0.6
49252	LITCHFIELD	059	2614	2707	2842	0.8	58	984	1035	1104	1.2	2.52	699	724	0.8
49253	MANITOU BEACH	091	2847	2862	2920	0.1	27	1152	1184	1233	0.7	2.41	811	819	0.2
49254	MICHIGAN CENTER	075	3418	3417	3487	0.0	22	1385	1407	1457	0.4	2.42	968	968	0.0
49255	MONTGOMERY	023	2013	2159	2282	1.7	84	654	709	759	1.9	3.02	488	523	1.6
49256	MORENCI	091	4312	4230	4268	-0.5	9	1577	1580	1626	0.0	2.64	1195	1182	-0.3
49259	MUNITH	075	2921	3028	3149	0.9	59	1043	1099	1161	1.2	2.65	809	842	1.0
49262	NORTH ADAMS	059	1415	1458	1516	0.7	52	539	566	599	1.2	2.57	409	424	0.9
49264	ONONDAGA	065	1956	2046	2102	1.1	67	666	711	744	1.6	2.85	529	558	1.3
49265	ONSTED	091	4576	4962	5248	1.9	89	1688	1873	2023	2.5	2.65	1346	1476	2.2
49266	OSSEO	059	3083	3206	3352	0.9	62	1158	1232	1313	1.5	2.59	867	910	1.2
49267	OTTAWA LAKE	115	4062	4109	4247	0.3	33	1464	1510	1592	0.7	2.71	1137	1161	0.5
49268	PALMYRA	091	1443	1404	1416	-0.6	7	482	478	493	-0.2	2.70	374	367	-0.4
49269	PARMA	075	6291	6626	6917	1.2	72	2228	2380	2517	1.6	2.76	1772	1871	1.3
49270	PETERSBURG	115	5801	5919	6135	0.5	41	1982	2062	2180	0.9	2.85	1606	1658	0.8
49271	PITTSFORD	059	2265	2436	2603	1.7	85	798	877	956	2.3	2.77	633	689	2.0
49272	PLEASANT LAKE	075	2091	2173	2254	0.9	61	796	842	887	1.3	2.57	612	638	1.0
49274	READING	059	3295	3417	3579	0.9	60	1218	1285	1367	1.3	2.64	901	938	1.0
49275	RIDGEWAY	091	30	29	30	-0.8	4	8	8	8	0.0	3.63	6	6	0.0
49276	RIGA	091	1038	1029	1044	-0.2	16	361	364	377	0.2	2.75	288	288	0.0
49277	RIVES JUNCTION	075	3481	3745	3955	1.7	85	1188	1301	1395	2.2	2.86	981	1063	1.9
49279	SAND CREEK	091	1143	1142	1159	0.0	22	397	405	419	0.5	2.81	305	307	0.2
49283	SPRING ARBOR	075	3467	3560	3655	0.6	47	1092	1145	1199	1.1	2.44	735	758	0.7
49284	SPRINGPORT	075	3383	3449	3526	0.5	41	1275	1322	1370	0.9	2.61	959	982	0.6
49285	STOCKBRIDGE	065	5299	5651	5868	1.5	80	1862	2027	2144	2.0	2.75	1441	1547	1.7
49286	TECUMSEH	091	14312	14872	15368	0.9	61	5506	5855	6181	1.5	2.52	4002	4202	1.2
49287	TIPTON	091	2054	2122	2184	0.8	55	754	794	834	1.2	2.67	602	627	1.0
49288	WALDRON	059	1456	1454	1499	0.0	21	531	541	568	0.4	2.67	385	386	0.1
49301	ADA	081	11191	12024	12742	1.7	85	3658	3974	4246	2.0	3.02	3159	3401	1.8
49302	ALTO	081	7617	8026	8397	1.2	73	2485	2646	2793	1.5	3.02	2115	2232	1.3
49303	BAILEY	121	770	787	805	0.5	44	260	271	282	1.0	2.87	205	212	0.8
49304	BALDWIN	085	4410	4926	5530	2.6	95	1775	2050	2378	3.5	2.12	1058	1202	3.1
49305	BARRYTON	107	2505	2539	2634	0.3	35	1016	1049	1111	0.8	2.41	737	748	0.4
49306	BELMONT	081	7914	8825	9540	2.6	95	2761	3112	3391	2.9	2.83	2217	2468	2.6
49307	BIG RAPIDS	107	18534	18773	19446	0.3	34	6289	6530	6964	0.9	2.37	3536	3598	0.4
49309	BITELY	123	2063	2128	2245	0.7	53	853	895	958	1.1	2.35	600	621	0.8
49310	BLANCHARD	073	2834	3026	3274	1.6	82	1048	1147	1270	2.2	2.62	791	859	2.0
49315	BYRON CENTER	081	15031	16136	17188	1.7	84	5285	5789	6248	2.2	2.78	4070	4394	1.8
49316	CALEDONIA	081	13242	14437	15489	2.1	90	4604	5083	5512	2.4	2.84	3715	4084	2.3
49318	CASNOVIA	121	1416	1454	1494	0.6	48	473	495	516	1.1	2.87	375	387	0.7
49319	CEDAR SPRINGS	081	12832	14153	15195	2.3	93	4492	5018	5440	2.6	2.80	3473	3835	2.4
49321	COMSTOCK PARK	081	16058	16720	17472	1.0	63	6281	6600	6953	1.2	2.53	4013	4128	0.7
49322	CORAL	117	1104	1152	1203	1.0	66	399	422	448	1.3	2.73	307	321	1.1
49323	DORR	005	7781	8522	9260	2.2	92	2513	2813	3114	2.7	3.03	2101	2334	2.5
49325	FREEPORT	015	1819	1988	2152	2.1	91	593	659	725	2.5	3.02	488	538	2.3
49326	GOWEN	081	2754	2813	2912	0.5	43	1017	1054	1105	0.8	2.61	778	796	0.5
49327	GRANT	123	8168	8855	9518	1.9	89	2738	3010	3278	2.3	2.92	2095	2279	2.0
49328	HOPKINS	005	3728	4026	4363	1.8	87	1243	1366	1504	2.3	2.92	985	1071	2.0
49329	HOWARD CITY	117	6844	7717	8418	2.9	97	2427	2780	3080	3.3	2.77	1850	2096	3.0
49330	KENT CITY	081	4832	5019	5220	0.9	61	1565	1650	1735	1.3	3.02	1275	1331	1.0
49331	LOWELL	081	14906	15976	16900	1.6	84	5083	5512	5890	1.9	2.83	3935	4216	1.6
49332	MECOSTA	107	2944	3141	3325	1.5	81	1274	1393	1509	2.1	2.25	920	989	1.7
49333	MIDDLEVILLE	015	9464	10318	11191	2.1	90	3320	3682	4059	2.5	2.80	2638	2899	2.2
49336	MORLEY	107	3917	4047	4233	0.8	55	1353	1421	1516	1.2	2.84	1019	1056	0.8
49337	NEWAYGO	123	11953	12375	13019	0.8	58	4634	4878	5207	1.2	2.52	3397	3531	0.9
49338	PARIS	123	2271	2422	2571	1.5	80	855	928	1002	2.0	2.61	596	636	1.5
49339	PIERSON	117	2221	2313	2412	1.0	63	775	823	873	1.4	2.81	601	631	1.2
49340	REMUS	107	2898	3104	3339	1.6	83	1066	1169	1286	2.2	2.65	785	849	1.9
49341	ROCKFORD	081	29256	31626	33632	1.9	87	9910	10810	11587	2.1	2.92	8091	8744	1.8
49342	RODNEY	107	1509	1600	1686	1.4	77	597	645	694	1.8	2.48	429	455	1.4
49343	SAND LAKE	081	5854	6237	6634	1.5	79	2092	2265	2439	1.9	2.74	1620	1736	1.6
49344	SHELBYVILLE	005	3096	3225	3416	1.0	64	1197	1270	1367	1.4	2.53	907	951	1.1
49345	SPARTA	081	12461	13128	13807	1.2	72	4495	4790	5086	1.5	2.72	3419	3610	1.3
49346	STANWOOD	107	4932	5381	5767	2.1	91	1999	2245	2467	2.8	2.39	1527	1682	2.3
49347	TRUFANT	117	1325	1339	1376	0.3	32	517	533	558	0.7	2.51	386	393	0.4
49348	WAYLAND	005	11523	12402	13356	1.7	85	4095	4483	4908	2.2	2.73	3140	3398	1.9
49349	WHITE CLOUD	123	8127	8617	9155	1.4	77	2983	3213	3465	1.8	2.62	2150	2286	1.5
49401	ALLENDALE	139	12405	14385	16081	3.6	99	3135	3821	4434	4.8	2.97	2115	2542	4.4
49402	BRANCH	105	1260	1307	1378	0.9	60	583	618	664	1.4	2.07	401	418	1.0
49403	CONKLIN	139	2775	2814	2955	0.3	36	902	937	1004	0.9	2.83	733	755	0.7
49404	COOPERSVILLE	139	7854	8265	8828	1.2	72	2669	2864	3111	1.7	2.85	2071	2201	1.4
49405	CUSTER	105	1520	1535	1582	0.2	31	568	582	609	0.6	2.60	401	405	0.2
49408	FENNVILLE	005	9081	9547	10191	1.2	71	3368	3617	3933	1.7	2.59	2371	2497	1.2
49410	FOUNTAIN	105	1728	1876	1995	2.0	89	706	791	861	2.7	2.23	493	544	2.3
49411	FREE SOIL	105	1598	1681	1768	1.2	72	588	628	670	1.6	2.64	433	456	1.2
49412	FREMONT	123	11390	11550	12067	0.3	36	4204	4329	4588	0.7	2.61	3047	3092	0.4
49415	FRUITPORT	121	5799	5919	6075	0.5	42	2067	2143	2232	0.9	2.74	1626	1667	0.6
49417	GRAND HAVEN	139	27726	28898	30882	1.0	65	10646	11300	12277	1.4	2.51	7593	7993	1.2
49418	GRANDVILLE	081	25484	27307	29156	1.6	84	9205	9926	10681	1.8	2.72	6816	7264	1.5
49419	HAMILTON	005	6478	7178	7852	2.4	94	2165	2434	2703	2.8	2.95	1812	2020	2.6
49420	HART	127	6661	6948	7330	1.0	65	2252	2375	2543	1.3	2.73	1636	1704	1.0
49421	HESPERIA	127	5979	6245	6582	1.0	66	2252	2394	2562	1.5	2.60	1653	1735	1.2
49423	HOLLAND	005	46883	49063	52366	1.1	67	16284	17358	18871	1.5	2.65	11240	11787	1.1
49424	HOLLAND	139	40304	43960	47964	2.1	90	13924	15478	17171	2.5	2.79	10758	11837	2.3
49425	HOLTON	121	3662	3778	3904	0.7	54	1268	1330	1394	1.1	2.84	970	1005	0.8
49426	HUDSONVILLE	139	27069	28911	31212	1.6	82	8717	9486	10410	2.0	3.03	7239	7832	1.9
49428	JENISON	139	25030	26713	29086	1.5	81	8592	9346	10354	2.0	2.82	6748	7247	1.7
49431	LUDINGTON	105	16771	17326	18036	0.8	55	6927	7265	7676	1.1	2.35	4623	4782	0.8
49435	MARNE	139	3412	3434	3606	0.2	28	1096	1124	1203	0.6	2.90	882	897	0.4
49436	MEARS	127	1647	1753	1864	1.5	79	654	711	770	2.0	2.43	499	536	1.7
49437	MONTAGUE	121	6686	7030	7340	1.2	71	2575	2755	2921	1.6	2.53	1882	1992	1.4
49440	MUSKEGON	121	1037	1108	1174	1.6	82	391	440	488	2.8	1.97	146	157	1.7
49441	MUSKEGON	121	35075	36079	37303	0.7	50	14552	15241	16005	1.1	2.34	9497	9781	0.7
	MICHIGAN					0.6					1.0	2.52			0.6
	UNITED STATES					1.2					1.3	2.58			1.1

#	POST OFFICE NAME	RACE (%) White 2000	White 2004	Black 2000	Black 2004	Asian/Pacific 2000	Asian/Pacific 2004	% Hispanic Origin 2000	% Hispanic Origin 2004	2004 AGE DISTRIBUTION (%) 0-4	5-9	10-14	15-19	20-24	25-44	45-64	65-84	85+	18+	MEDIAN AGE 2004	% 2004 Males	% 2004 Females
49249	JEROME	98.0	97.8	0.3	0.3	0.2	0.2	1.2	1.4	5.0	5.6	7.2	6.4	4.6	24.2	31.6	14.2	1.3	78.0	43.3	50.7	49.3
49250	JONESVILLE	97.0	96.6	1.0	1.1	0.5	0.6	1.4	1.6	6.4	6.7	7.5	8.5	6.6	25.2	25.1	11.4	2.5	74.6	37.2	49.2	50.8
49251	LESLIE	96.6	96.1	0.4	0.5	0.4	0.5	2.5	2.9	7.1	7.2	8.0	7.2	6.1	29.0	26.5	8.1	0.9	73.2	36.2	49.9	50.1
49252	LITCHFIELD	97.8	97.5	0.3	0.3	0.2	0.2	1.7	2.0	7.0	7.1	7.0	6.7	6.0	25.6	25.5	13.2	2.1	75.0	38.3	49.5	50.5
49253	MANITOU BEACH	98.1	97.9	0.2	0.2	0.3	0.3	1.6	2.0	5.1	5.6	7.1	6.3	5.0	25.0	32.0	12.8	1.2	78.3	42.5	50.8	49.2
49254	MICHIGAN CENTER	97.5	97.1	0.4	0.5	0.4	0.5	1.6	1.9	5.5	6.1	7.0	5.7	5.1	27.6	27.9	13.5	1.6	78.0	41.1	50.9	49.1
49255	MONTGOMERY	97.1	97.0	0.7	0.7	0.1	0.1	0.6	0.6	9.9	9.3	9.6	8.0	6.9	25.6	19.7	10.1	1.0	65.7	30.6	51.9	48.1
49256	MORENCI	96.9	96.6	0.2	0.3	0.2	0.3	3.4	4.0	6.9	6.9	7.9	6.8	6.7	26.3	25.0	11.1	2.3	74.3	37.0	50.4	49.6
49259	MUNITH	97.2	96.8	0.6	0.6	0.2	0.2	1.8	2.1	6.7	7.0	7.5	6.9	5.5	28.7	25.1	10.7	2.0	74.4	37.8	49.9	50.1
49262	NORTH ADAMS	98.4	98.3	0.3	0.3	0.2	0.3	1.3	1.5	6.9	7.2	7.2	6.5	5.8	26.6	25.5	13.0	1.4	74.7	38.4	50.5	49.5
49264	ONONDAGA	95.9	95.3	0.4	0.3	0.2	0.2	2.6	3.1	6.9	7.4	8.3	7.4	5.9	28.6	26.9	7.7	0.9	72.6	36.8	50.1	50.0
49265	ONSTED	97.2	96.8	0.2	0.2	0.3	0.4	2.0	2.4	5.8	6.7	7.9	6.6	4.9	26.0	30.3	11.0	0.8	75.4	40.1	49.2	50.8
49266	OSSEO	97.9	97.8	0.3	0.3	0.3	0.3	0.7	0.8	6.5	6.6	7.0	6.8	6.3	27.5	26.1	12.0	1.2	75.6	38.0	50.5	49.5
49267	OTTAWA LAKE	95.8	95.4	2.1	2.3	0.2	0.2	2.1	2.5	5.7	6.1	7.1	7.0	5.9	25.5	30.3	11.4	1.0	76.7	40.8	50.3	49.7
49268	PALMYRA	87.7	86.0	0.6	0.6	0.2	0.2	12.8	14.7	6.5	6.5	7.6	8.5	6.1	27.6	24.1	11.7	1.6	74.2	37.0	51.8	48.2
49269	PARMA	97.1	96.7	0.6	0.7	0.4	0.5	1.6	1.8	6.5	7.7	8.5	7.3	5.2	27.5	26.9	9.3	1.0	72.2	37.8	50.7	49.3
49270	PETERSBURG	97.9	97.7	0.2	0.2	0.1	0.1	2.1	2.4	6.5	6.9	7.9	7.1	6.2	28.4	27.3	8.8	0.9	74.2	37.3	51.4	48.6
49271	PITTSFORD	97.9	97.7	0.1	0.1	0.1	0.1	0.9	1.0	6.7	6.8	7.2	7.6	6.4	25.5	26.5	12.0	1.4	74.7	38.0	50.0	50.0
49272	PLEASANT LAKE	97.5	97.2	0.3	0.3	0.1	0.1	1.8	2.1	5.9	6.8	7.5	6.7	5.3	28.4	28.3	10.5	0.7	75.6	38.8	51.2	48.8
49274	READING	98.1	98.0	0.2	0.2	0.2	0.2	1.1	1.2	6.7	7.0	8.1	7.6	5.7	26.8	24.9	11.8	1.4	73.0	37.5	50.8	49.2
49275	RIDGEWAY	96.7	100.0	0.0	0.0	0.0	0.0	0.0	3.5	6.9	6.9	6.9	6.9	6.9	27.6	37.9	0.0	0.0	79.3	36.3	44.8	55.2
49276	RIGA	96.2	95.6	0.2	0.2	0.2	0.2	4.6	5.4	6.4	7.0	7.3	7.3	5.6	25.5	28.4	11.2	1.4	74.7	39.5	51.5	48.5
49277	RIVES JUNCTION	97.6	97.2	0.2	0.2	0.1	0.2	1.5	1.8	6.5	7.1	8.1	7.0	5.6	26.8	28.4	9.7	0.9	74.0	38.7	50.4	49.6
49279	SAND CREEK	97.1	96.7	0.3	0.3	0.1	0.2	3.2	3.9	5.8	6.0	7.7	7.9	6.8	25.1	28.1	11.1	1.4	75.7	39.1	51.1	48.9
49283	SPRING ARBOR	96.2	95.5	1.3	1.5	1.0	1.4	1.6	1.9	4.7	5.1	6.0	12.4	14.8	20.3	19.5	12.4	4.8	80.1	33.3	45.1	54.9
49284	SPRINGPORT	97.1	96.7	0.4	0.5	0.2	0.3	1.1	1.4	6.2	6.6	8.6	6.7	5.7	26.9	26.8	11.2	1.2	74.4	38.3	50.9	49.1
49285	STOCKBRIDGE	97.2	96.8	0.3	0.4	0.2	0.3	1.8	2.2	6.9	7.0	7.5	6.9	6.1	28.4	26.4	9.3	1.5	74.0	37.4	50.0	50.0
49286	TECUMSEH	96.3	95.8	0.3	0.3	0.6	0.8	3.9	4.5	6.6	6.8	7.1	7.0	5.9	27.1	26.8	11.3	1.6	75.0	38.2	48.7	51.3
49287	TIPTON	97.7	97.3	0.2	0.2	0.2	0.3	1.6	1.9	5.9	6.7	7.9	6.6	5.0	28.0	29.7	9.1	1.0	75.3	39.8	50.9	49.2
49288	WALDRON	98.2	97.9	0.2	0.2	0.1	0.1	1.0	1.0	7.0	7.3	8.1	7.3	6.2	26.1	25.2	11.6	1.3	72.6	36.4	49.9	50.1
49301	ADA	96.0	95.1	0.6	0.7	1.9	2.5	1.1	1.4	6.8	8.2	9.2	7.9	4.8	22.4	32.0	8.2	0.7	70.8	40.1	50.3	49.7
49302	ALTO	97.6	97.2	0.3	0.3	0.8	1.0	1.2	1.5	7.1	7.9	9.5	7.5	5.4	27.3	27.8	6.9	0.6	70.5	36.9	50.5	49.6
49303	BAILEY	94.4	93.5	0.3	0.4	0.0	0.1	5.7	6.7	6.6	7.8	9.7	7.6	6.1	29.9	22.7	8.8	0.9	70.9	34.5	52.6	47.4
49304	BALDWIN	74.6	73.7	20.3	20.9	0.2	0.3	2.2	2.4	4.5	4.4	4.8	11.6	4.7	19.0	28.9	19.7	2.6	81.1	45.8	54.7	45.3
49305	BARRYTON	97.2	97.0	0.7	0.8	0.1	0.1	1.1	1.2	5.6	5.6	6.5	6.8	5.4	22.5	28.7	17.5	1.5	78.0	43.3	49.4	50.6
49306	BELMONT	97.1	96.6	0.6	0.7	0.7	0.9	1.5	1.8	7.6	8.4	8.6	7.4	5.3	26.6	26.2	9.0	0.9	70.5	37.1	50.4	49.6
49307	BIG RAPIDS	88.5	87.3	6.8	7.3	1.7	2.2	1.5	1.7	5.5	4.9	5.2	16.6	18.4	22.1	17.3	8.4	1.5	81.0	24.8	51.0	49.0
49309	BITELY	89.4	88.9	5.9	6.2	0.2	0.2	2.8	3.1	6.7	7.0	7.5	6.4	5.9	23.6	27.1	14.8	1.1	74.7	40.1	51.6	48.4
49310	BLANCHARD	96.2	95.7	0.8	0.9	0.4	0.4	1.7	1.9	6.8	7.4	8.2	6.7	5.0	27.8	26.2	10.9	1.0	73.1	36.8	51.3	48.7
49315	BYRON CENTER	97.3	96.7	0.5	0.6	0.8	1.0	1.3	1.6	7.2	7.4	8.2	7.1	5.9	27.7	24.2	11.3	1.1	72.7	36.6	50.0	50.0
49316	CALEDONIA	95.8	95.1	1.1	1.3	1.3	1.7	1.5	1.8	7.6	7.9	8.4	7.3	6.0	26.7	25.5	9.8	0.8	71.4	36.5	49.6	50.4
49318	CASNOVIA	95.3	94.4	0.1	0.1	0.1	0.2	5.7	6.7	6.9	7.3	8.9	7.3	6.4	30.3	23.5	8.5	0.9	72.4	35.0	52.1	47.9
49319	CEDAR SPRINGS	96.9	96.3	0.2	0.3	0.4	0.5	2.1	2.6	7.8	7.8	8.4	7.4	6.5	29.8	23.5	8.0	1.0	71.3	34.7	49.8	50.2
49321	COMSTOCK PARK	90.6	89.2	2.7	3.0	1.5	1.9	5.6	6.6	8.1	7.1	7.0	6.7	10.6	32.2	20.2	7.4	0.6	74.0	29.9	50.5	49.5
49322	CORAL	97.6	97.2	0.2	0.2	0.3	0.4	0.6	0.8	6.5	7.8	9.8	7.6	6.1	26.6	24.1	10.6	1.0	71.2	35.5	50.9	49.1
49323	DORR	97.0	96.6	0.4	0.5	0.2	0.3	1.9	2.3	8.5	8.3	8.9	8.0	7.0	31.0	22.0	5.7	0.6	69.0	32.4	50.3	49.7
49325	FREEPORT	97.3	97.0	0.4	0.5	0.2	0.3	1.3	1.5	7.6	8.0	8.7	7.2	5.8	29.1	25.1	7.8	0.8	71.2	35.7	50.5	49.6
49326	GOWEN	97.3	96.8	0.8	1.0	0.3	0.4	1.3	1.6	5.9	6.3	7.5	7.0	6.0	28.5	28.3	9.7	0.9	75.7	38.4	51.6	48.5
49327	GRANT	93.8	93.2	0.4	0.4	0.2	0.2	8.5	9.5	7.9	8.0	8.9	8.0	6.6	28.1	22.8	8.8	1.1	70.2	34.0	50.6	49.4
49328	HOPKINS	94.3	93.5	0.4	0.4	0.4	0.6	4.0	4.8	7.8	8.0	8.7	7.8	6.6	28.2	23.8	8.1	1.0	70.5	34.7	51.7	48.3
49329	HOWARD CITY	96.5	96.1	0.3	0.4	0.3	0.4	1.7	2.0	8.0	8.1	8.5	7.3	6.2	29.2	23.0	8.8	0.9	70.7	34.4	49.8	50.2
49330	KENT CITY	96.6	96.0	0.2	0.2	0.2	0.2	5.1	6.2	7.7	7.8	8.6	7.9	6.8	29.8	23.5	7.2	0.9	70.8	33.7	50.0	50.1
49331	LOWELL	96.8	96.3	0.7	0.7	0.6	0.7	2.1	2.5	7.2	7.6	8.9	7.5	5.8	28.5	25.0	8.1	1.5	71.4	36.0	49.9	50.1
49332	MECOSTA	93.4	92.8	2.2	2.4	0.2	0.3	1.4	1.5	5.9	6.1	6.7	5.6	4.7	22.0	27.0	20.4	1.5	77.7	44.2	50.5	49.5
49333	MIDDLEVILLE	97.0	96.6	0.2	0.3	0.4	0.6	1.4	1.6	8.0	8.0	8.2	7.4	6.2	29.1	24.3	7.9	0.8	71.2	34.8	49.9	50.1
49336	MORLEY	96.3	96.0	0.4	0.4	0.2	0.3	0.9	1.2	8.0	8.0	8.3	7.0	6.3	27.8	23.4	10.3	0.9	71.4	34.4	49.9	50.1
49337	NEWAYGO	96.0	95.5	0.3	0.3	0.2	0.3	3.7	4.3	6.8	7.0	7.7	7.1	5.8	25.2	26.4	12.6	1.4	73.9	38.7	50.6	49.5
49338	PARIS	97.2	96.9	0.8	0.9	0.2	0.2	0.8	0.9	6.3	6.7	7.8	6.2	6.0	28.0	25.9	12.2	1.1	75.4	38.0	50.6	49.4
49339	PIERSON	96.9	96.5	0.1	0.1	0.4	0.5	1.1	1.3	7.3	7.9	8.5	6.9	5.9	28.2	25.4	9.3	0.6	72.0	36.1	50.4	49.6
49340	REMUS	94.6	94.0	1.9	2.0	0.1	0.2	1.4	1.7	6.2	6.5	7.1	6.4	5.2	24.1	27.8	15.3	1.4	76.2	41.2	49.9	50.1
49341	ROCKFORD	97.4	97.0	0.4	0.5	0.5	0.7	1.2	1.5	8.2	8.7	9.1	7.4	5.6	27.8	25.6	7.1	0.7	69.4	35.6	49.9	50.1
49342	RODNEY	97.2	96.8	0.3	0.3	0.5	0.7	0.5	0.4	5.3	5.5	5.8	5.8	5.7	22.5	29.9	18.3	1.4	79.9	44.7	51.3	48.7
49343	SAND LAKE	96.6	96.1	0.4	0.4	0.3	0.3	2.3	2.8	7.1	7.3	8.6	7.8	6.2	28.1	25.5	8.8	0.7	71.8	36.2	50.7	49.3
49344	SHELBYVILLE	96.9	96.7	0.3	0.3	0.2	0.3	2.2	2.6	6.3	6.6	7.3	6.5	5.2	26.7	28.4	11.8	1.1	75.6	40.0	51.7	48.3
49345	SPARTA	96.5	95.9	0.4	0.4	0.4	0.5	3.1	3.7	7.4	7.6	8.2	7.5	6.6	29.0	23.5	8.9	1.3	71.9	35.0	49.1	50.9
49346	STANWOOD	97.0	96.6	0.7	0.8	0.4	0.5	1.1	1.3	6.1	6.2	6.3	5.7	4.5	22.3	27.5	19.9	1.6	77.8	44.2	49.7	50.3
49347	TRUFANT	97.5	97.2	0.2	0.2	0.4	0.5	1.1	1.3	6.4	6.9	7.7	6.5	5.5	27.4	25.8	12.6	1.3	75.0	37.9	51.5	48.5
49348	WAYLAND	96.9	96.6	0.4	0.4	0.2	0.3	1.8	2.1	8.4	8.0	7.9	7.3	6.5	30.0	22.5	8.3	1.2	71.1	34.2	49.6	50.5
49349	WHITE CLOUD	93.2	92.6	2.6	2.8	0.3	0.3	2.7	3.0	6.7	6.8	8.1	8.3	6.8	25.7	25.3	11.3	1.1	73.3	37.1	51.0	49.0
49401	ALLENDALE	93.7	92.9	2.7	2.8	0.9	1.2	2.8	3.4	6.9	5.8	5.3	20.1	23.5	22.7	11.1	4.0	0.6	79.4	22.5	46.9	53.1
49402	BRANCH	96.0	95.5	1.6	1.8	0.2	0.4	2.1	2.5	4.4	4.7	5.9	5.6	4.6	24.1	31.4	17.8	1.6	81.6	45.5	51.4	48.6
49403	CONKLIN	94.2	93.3	0.5	0.5	0.2	0.3	6.6	7.8	6.9	7.0	9.0	8.0	6.3	29.3	23.3	8.5	1.8	72.0	35.5	51.0	49.0
49404	COOPERSVILLE	97.0	96.5	0.2	0.2	0.4	0.5	2.6	3.1	7.2	7.3	8.2	7.8	6.8	29.1	23.6	8.9	1.2	72.4	34.8	50.0	50.0
49405	CUSTER	96.8	96.4	0.3	0.3	0.3	0.3	2.5	2.9	5.0	5.2	6.7	6.4	5.3	25.2	29.1	15.5	1.6	79.0	42.6	50.5	49.5
49408	FENNVILLE	87.3	86.1	1.3	1.4	0.4	0.5	17.4	19.4	7.4	7.5	7.6	6.6	5.8	26.5	26.8	10.4	1.4	73.3	37.6	51.0	49.0
49410	FOUNTAIN	93.6	92.9	3.1	3.4	0.4	0.4	1.6	1.9	4.4	4.9	6.2	5.4	4.9	27.1	30.8	14.6	1.8	81.4	43.3	53.4	46.6
49411	FREE SOIL	95.0	94.5	1.5	1.7	0.3	0.3	1.4	1.6	5.0	5.7	7.0	6.7	4.8	25.6	30.9	13.1	1.3	78.4	42.2	52.4	47.7
49412	FREMONT	96.3	95.9	0.5	0.6	0.6	0.8	2.2	2.5	6.8	6.9	8.2	7.4	6.5	23.7	24.6	13.6	2.3	73.0	38.2	48.1	51.9
49415	FRUITPORT	97.3	96.8	0.4	0.5	0.3	0.5	1.7	2.0	6.2	6.6	7.7	7.0	5.9	27.7	27.8	10.1	1.2	75.0	38.6	50.1	49.9
49417	GRAND HAVEN	96.4	95.9	0.3	0.3	0.7	1.0	2.1	2.5	6.6	6.7	7.2	6.9	6.2	28.0	25.9	10.7	1.8	75.0	37.7	49.1	50.9
49418	GRANDVILLE	95.0	94.1	1.4	1.6	1.5	1.9	2.8	3.4	7.6	7.4	7.9	7.5	8.0	28.1	22.4	9.8	1.4	72.4	33.4	49.0	51.0
49419	HAMILTON	96.6	96.0	0.2	0.2	0.7	0.9	3.2	3.8	8.9	8.5	8.6	7.4	6.5	31.2	21.8	6.4	0.7	69.2	32.4	50.8	49.2
49420	HART	87.3	85.9	0.4	0.4	0.2	0.2	16.3	18.5	7.4	7.0	7.7	7.5	6.8	26.3	22.5	12.3	2.6	72.8	35.9	50.4	49.6
49421	HESPERIA	94.1	93.5	1.1	1.2	0.3	0.4	3.4	3.9	6.8	6.9	8.3	7.9	6.7	25.3	25.7	11.4	1.0	73.1	37.2	51.0	49.0
49423	HOLLAND	82.2	80.3	2.0	2.0	2.9	3.7	18.0	19.9	7.7	7.2	7.1	8.4	10.8	26.9	19.4	10.0	2.6	74.0	31.4	48.2	51.8
49424	HOLLAND	84.1	81.5	1.6	1.7	6.0	7.5	12.8	14.5	9.4	8.7	8.0	6.6	6.5	32.0	21.1	6.9	0.7	69.7	31.7	50.3	49.7
49425	HOLTON	96.0	95.5	0.4	0.5	0.3	0.4	1.9	2.3	6.5	6.7	8.0	7.8	7.0	27.6	26.5	9.0	0.8	73.9	36.6	51.8	48.2
49426	HUDSONVILLE	97.6	97.1	0.4	0.4	0.7	0.9	1.4	1.7	8.9	8.7	8.9	7.7	7.2	28.1	21.3	8.0	1.1	68.6	32.0	49.3	50.7
49428	JENISON	96.9	96.3	0.6	0.6	1.0	1.3	1.8	2.1	6.5	6.9	7.9	7.6	9.0	25.4	24.2	10.3	2.2	74.4	35.6	48.2	51.8
49431	LUDINGTON	96.0	95.6	0.6	0.6	0.3	0.4	3.3	3.8	5.6	5.9	7.1	6.8	5.7	23.8	27.5	14.9	2.7	77.2	41.7	48.5	51.5
49435	MARNE	97.3	96.9	0.4	0.4	0.2	0.3	1.9	2.3	6.8	7.2	8.3	7.1	5.9	27.0	24.9	10.6	2.3	73.2	38.1	49.9	50.1
49436	MEARS	89.6	88.4	0.3	0.3	0.2	0.2	12.3	14.0	5.3	5.8	6.7	6.5	7.0	22.5	31.6	13.8	0.9	77.8	42.4	51.8	48.2
49437	MONTAGUE	96.4	96.0	0.6	0.7	0.3	0.4	3.1	3.6	5.9	6.2	7.1	7.2	6.7	24.9	27.4	13.3	1.3	76.4	39.9	49.3	50.7
49440	MUSKEGON	51.8	47.6	41.5	45.5	0.1	0.1	5.7	6.3	6.3	6.1	5.9	7.6	9.0	32.2	17.9	11.3	3.7	77.5	33.1	54.3	45.7
49441	MUSKEGON	88.2	87.0	7.1	7.8	0.7	0.9	3.5	4.0	6.1	6.2	7.0	6.3	6.2	25.6	25.4	14.5	2.6	76.8	39.8	48.3	51.7
	MICHIGAN	80.2	79.2	14.2	14.4	1.8	2.3	3.3	3.6	6.8	6.9	7.4	7.1	6.9	28.1	24.6	10.8	1.6	74.9	36.5	49.1	50.9
	UNITED STATES	75.1	73.6	12.3	12.5	3.8	4.2	12.5	14.1	6.9	6.7	7.2	7.0	7.3	28.6	23.8	10.8	1.7	75.1	36.0	49.1	50.9

ZIP CODE #	POST OFFICE NAME	2004 Per Capita Income	2004 HH Income Base	2004 Household Income Distribution (%): Less than $25,000	$25,000 to $49,999	$50,000 to $99,999	$100,000 to $149,999	$150,000 or More	Median Household Income: 2004	2009	2004 National Centile	2004 State Centile	2004 Home Value Base	2004 Home Value Distribution (%): Less than $50,000	$50,000 to $89,999	$90,000 to $174,999	$175,000 to $399,999	$400,000 or More	2004 Median Home Value
49249	JEROME	24867	1273	19.2	29.8	36.5	10.1	4.6	50822	55863	74	68	1178	10.3	12.7	34.5	39.9	2.7	157600
49250	JONESVILLE	20568	2323	24.6	34.9	31.5	6.9	2.1	42954	46164	56	46	1927	16.6	24.3	43.5	14.5	1.0	100873
49251	LESLIE	23583	2257	17.6	28.6	39.3	11.2	3.5	54098	60911	79	75	1922	6.4	16.7	53.9	21.5	1.5	124747
49252	LITCHFIELD	19533	1035	27.9	29.0	34.8	6.8	1.6	43662	46194	58	48	829	14.1	27.6	44.3	13.6	0.4	98155
49253	MANITOU BEACH	25416	1184	22.9	29.1	30.3	12.7	5.0	47332	53041	67	60	1028	3.4	14.3	37.7	37.6	7.1	163636
49254	MICHIGAN CENTER	22481	1407	20.6	30.6	38.5	9.1	1.2	47910	52172	68	61	1166	5.1	19.7	57.8	16.8	0.6	116540
49255	MONTGOMERY	15745	709	28.6	34.0	30.6	4.4	2.4	41793	45312	52	42	595	18.2	22.5	39.2	16.6	3.5	103953
49256	MORENCI	19585	1580	22.5	33.7	36.3	5.5	2.0	45090	49363	61	53	1257	8.3	25.8	52.2	12.0	1.8	105984
49259	MUNITH	23782	1099	15.5	28.6	42.7	10.2	3.1	54172	59962	79	75	994	21.2	8.6	38.0	30.3	1.9	126404
49262	NORTH ADAMS	20955	566	23.5	35.9	33.2	5.1	2.3	43951	47789	58	49	487	10.5	29.0	43.3	15.4	1.9	100781
49264	ONONDAGA	19653	711	20.0	31.7	37.1	9.6	1.7	48639	54319	70	63	625	9.4	18.4	48.2	23.5	0.5	124656
49265	ONSTED	28567	1873	14.7	24.2	37.6	15.3	8.1	63088	66834	87	87	1662	1.0	5.4	37.2	48.5	7.9	188049
49266	OSSEO	19798	1232	23.7	33.3	34.9	7.5	0.7	43986	47344	59	49	1062	14.7	22.8	43.2	17.2	2.1	110714
49267	OTTAWA LAKE	24463	1510	15.7	25.6	39.7	15.0	4.0	58383	64898	83	81	1326	2.3	7.8	46.3	37.3	6.3	164976
49268	PALMYRA	20198	478	16.5	35.4	36.0	11.5	0.6	47243	51578	67	59	409	5.4	15.9	55.0	22.5	1.2	134007
49269	PARMA	22423	2380	16.9	29.0	39.6	11.2	3.2	54315	58065	79	75	2120	15.2	12.3	43.2	27.2	2.1	137332
49270	PETERSBURG	26137	2062	15.1	22.7	41.1	15.8	5.3	62722	68956	87	87	1765	1.9	6.2	45.7	43.1	3.1	168995
49271	PITTSFORD	19193	877	22.2	33.8	34.6	7.8	1.7	45203	49001	62	53	770	14.7	24.3	42.0	16.2	2.9	105851
49272	PLEASANT LAKE	24028	842	14.9	30.5	42.5	8.7	3.4	55225	59593	80	77	757	5.3	10.2	48.1	33.6	2.9	154663
49274	READING	19163	1285	25.8	35.6	31.4	5.3	1.9	41107	44509	50	39	1088	15.1	27.7	40.6	14.8	1.8	98977
49275	RIDGEWAY	21121	8	0.0	25.0	50.0	25.0	0.0	75000	75000	93	95	7	0.0	0.0	71.4	28.6	0.0	137500
49276	RIGA	24864	364	15.9	26.1	39.3	13.5	5.2	57750	62608	82	81	329	2.1	7.6	48.0	38.3	4.0	164375
49277	RIVES JUNCTION	21979	1301	17.3	25.1	42.5	11.7	3.4	56785	61486	81	79	1193	6.0	16.1	50.8	25.8	1.3	138261
49279	SAND CREEK	19713	405	18.0	35.1	38.0	7.4	1.5	48002	52541	68	61	352	9.9	18.2	48.6	20.5	2.8	121212
49283	SPRING ARBOR	20071	1145	27.0	27.0	32.1	12.1	1.8	46665	49099	65	58	773	19.8	9.8	36.7	31.6	2.1	143594
49284	SPRINGPORT	20567	1322	21.3	33.9	35.6	7.2	2.0	45939	50000	64	56	1114	9.1	26.4	41.2	21.4	2.0	111938
49285	STOCKBRIDGE	24443	2027	18.5	29.3	36.5	12.2	3.6	52223	58902	76	71	1665	4.1	8.5	48.1	37.1	2.2	159788
49286	TECUMSEH	26747	5855	17.6	26.2	38.8	13.0	4.4	55170	60437	80	77	4632	2.3	6.8	54.2	35.5	1.2	157735
49287	TIPTON	27419	794	13.1	22.7	46.1	12.3	5.8	61690	67831	86	86	730	6.4	4.4	35.1	49.5	4.7	184036
49288	WALDRON	17212	541	30.7	34.6	29.4	4.4	0.9	39737	42475	45	33	446	18.4	30.0	34.1	16.1	1.4	91591
49301	ADA	43052	3974	7.9	17.1	31.1	19.5	24.4	88757	103343	97	98	3827	1.0	0.9	24.6	53.0	20.6	252920
49302	ALTO	29510	2646	8.5	19.6	44.4	16.0	11.4	70605	78519	91	93	2482	1.3	3.4	27.3	59.7	8.4	211959
49303	BAILEY	19491	271	23.3	34.7	31.7	7.8	2.6	45099	49034	61	53	232	9.5	22.8	51.7	15.1	0.9	108491
49304	BALDWIN	15925	2050	49.9	31.7	14.5	2.6	1.3	25073	27270	5	2	1612	36.9	28.4	25.3	7.6	1.8	67323
49305	BARRYTON	16911	1049	35.7	38.5	21.7	2.9	1.2	33323	37064	22	11	915	26.1	29.1	31.8	12.4	0.7	80686
49306	BELMONT	28419	3112	12.4	22.3	41.5	15.6	8.2	66900	74172	90	90	3011	15.9	6.8	32.2	40.0	5.0	165868
49307	BIG RAPIDS	18006	6530	41.2	27.3	22.7	6.2	2.6	31781	33514	17	7	3762	11.4	22.3	47.2	17.6	1.6	110498
49309	BITELY	16314	895	39.2	35.6	22.0	2.1	1.0	31711	35407	17	7	767	25.8	28.6	35.6	9.4	0.7	84846
49310	BLANCHARD	19525	1147	25.5	37.6	28.7	6.3	2.0	41179	46138	50	39	1005	17.5	23.8	42.3	14.6	1.8	100997
49315	BYRON CENTER	30014	5789	13.4	25.7	40.7	13.2	7.1	60654	66011	85	84	4825	5.0	3.9	44.6	41.7	4.9	170177
49316	CALEDONIA	27981	5083	13.9	20.6	42.2	14.0	9.3	64479	71513	88	88	4521	8.2	6.9	34.9	43.2	6.8	175033
49318	CASNOVIA	21622	495	21.8	28.9	33.9	11.1	4.2	49395	53474	71	65	428	4.9	16.6	59.1	19.2	0.2	118432
49319	CEDAR SPRINGS	21558	5018	18.5	29.0	40.4	9.7	2.4	51797	57252	75	70	4384	10.8	14.9	49.0	24.0	1.2	126062
49321	COMSTOCK PARK	23930	6600	18.9	32.2	36.0	9.8	3.1	49016	53132	70	64	3867	8.2	7.6	58.8	24.1	1.3	140436
49322	CORAL	18088	422	22.5	40.3	30.8	4.5	1.9	41556	45000	52	41	364	9.1	27.2	45.6	16.5	1.7	105769
49323	DORR	21931	2813	12.0	25.8	47.2	13.2	1.9	61260	65951	86	85	2642	4.9	9.3	52.6	30.7	2.6	146234
49325	FREEPORT	21545	659	15.2	29.0	44.3	8.2	3.3	54621	59632	79	76	605	4.6	9.4	48.3	34.7	3.0	150493
49326	GOWEN	21437	1054	20.2	26.2	43.9	8.1	1.6	52957	57625	77	73	966	14.0	15.9	45.0	24.4	0.6	117733
49327	GRANT	18369	3010	26.2	31.6	34.8	6.1	1.4	43612	46444	58	48	2578	12.5	20.7	46.3	19.1	1.4	115116
49328	HOPKINS	20345	1366	21.2	28.9	37.4	9.4	3.2	49926	52948	72	66	1188	7.2	15.1	54.6	21.2	2.0	127488
49329	HOWARD CITY	18180	2780	22.7	34.0	36.8	5.8	0.7	45160	48675	62	53	2395	12.5	19.7	48.9	17.8	1.0	113623
49330	KENT CITY	20025	1650	19.5	29.8	38.2	10.0	2.6	50600	55379	73	67	1442	12.4	12.7	54.6	18.3	2.0	118652
49331	LOWELL	22947	5512	18.4	24.0	40.9	12.7	3.9	57032	62287	82	80	4760	10.8	6.7	43.9	34.1	4.5	146036
49332	MECOSTA	21742	1393	30.4	35.5	27.5	4.2	2.4	37365	41634	37	25	1189	16.8	23.0	38.6	20.5	1.0	105887
49333	MIDDLEVILLE	23686	3682	13.8	28.1	43.3	11.0	3.9	56452	61525	81	79	3262	7.7	7.1	46.9	34.6	3.8	150829
49336	MORLEY	16529	1421	28.8	37.0	28.1	4.9	1.3	38568	42245	41	28	1197	22.0	25.0	36.3	15.8	1.0	94345
49337	NEWAYGO	20612	4878	26.2	33.9	31.8	5.8	2.2	42016	45687	53	43	4183	14.9	21.0	42.6	20.6	0.9	111434
49338	PARIS	16879	928	33.7	35.1	25.0	4.3	1.8	36345	39374	33	20	796	14.8	26.1	43.7	14.6	0.8	101724
49339	PIERSON	21515	823	17.1	31.4	39.0	9.2	3.3	50990	54732	74	68	737	5.0	17.8	49.4	24.7	3.1	131700
49340	REMUS	18890	1169	29.9	33.7	28.7	5.1	2.5	39193	43569	43	30	1007	17.1	25.5	36.0	20.0	1.5	102557
49341	ROCKFORD	28709	10810	13.8	19.1	41.3	17.5	8.3	68135	76296	90	91	9651	4.6	3.7	40.3	45.8	5.7	178421
49342	RODNEY	20527	645	26.8	37.8	27.6	5.4	2.3	38113	42192	40	27	561	14.4	22.3	40.5	21.4	1.4	112340
49343	SAND LAKE	20731	2265	20.2	29.4	40.9	8.3	1.2	50296	54085	72	66	2073	11.7	15.4	50.6	21.3	1.1	122933
49344	SHELBYVILLE	24634	1270	16.9	33.7	37.1	9.1	3.2	49466	53211	71	65	1102	10.4	8.6	43.4	31.6	6.0	150536
49345	SPARTA	21358	4790	18.5	31.3	37.9	9.9	2.4	50126	55563	72	66	4078	12.8	13.8	49.6	21.3	2.4	121446
49346	STANWOOD	25631	2245	23.4	30.7	33.0	8.5	4.5	46093	51350	64	56	1971	10.4	17.2	40.9	29.7	1.8	128183
49347	TRUFANT	19411	533	23.6	39.2	30.2	4.9	2.1	40523	43340	48	36	470	7.5	24.3	53.8	13.4	1.1	109250
49348	WAYLAND	22074	4483	16.4	32.3	38.7	9.3	3.3	51050	54994	74	68	3797	14.1	9.7	47.5	25.2	3.6	133565
49349	WHITE CLOUD	15869	3213	35.7	33.9	25.8	3.6	0.9	35815	38631	31	18	2560	23.9	27.0	39.3	9.3	0.5	88814
49401	ALLENDALE	18537	3821	18.9	29.9	38.0	9.8	3.5	51100	55870	74	69	2738	14.9	7.0	47.1	29.1	1.9	148984
49402	BRANCH	19691	618	38.2	34.0	22.5	3.9	1.5	32459	35785	19	9	531	23.2	28.4	35.2	11.7	1.5	87167
49403	CONKLIN	21287	937	16.4	30.7	39.9	10.0	2.9	52273	56933	76	71	845	4.9	8.4	52.4	31.4	3.0	146117
49404	COOPERSVILLE	22637	2864	19.7	24.4	41.9	10.0	4.0	54557	60266	79	76	2445	14.3	6.9	50.6	24.3	3.9	140585
49405	CUSTER	16569	582	35.4	33.7	25.3	4.6	1.0	35600	39130	30	17	491	19.1	27.9	38.7	12.4	1.8	94265
49408	FENNVILLE	23372	3617	21.9	30.6	36.1	7.7	3.6	47883	51733	68	61	3072	12.4	13.6	42.9	25.3	5.9	132798
49410	FOUNTAIN	20015	791	35.3	31.5	26.2	4.4	2.7	34654	38597	26	13	692	22.1	25.3	37.7	13.4	1.5	94091
49411	FREE SOIL	18035	628	30.3	32.5	30.6	5.3	1.4	40758	45680	49	38	561	16.2	25.1	41.7	14.1	2.9	101297
49412	FREMONT	20710	4329	28.6	32.0	30.6	5.9	2.8	40932	43259	49	39	3448	11.4	22.6	47.4	17.6	1.0	112261
49415	FRUITPORT	23401	2143	18.1	30.8	36.9	10.3	4.0	51177	54952	74	69	1911	4.5	16.3	53.9	22.6	2.8	128538
49417	GRAND HAVEN	26104	11300	17.0	27.7	38.7	12.0	4.6	54712	60154	79	76	9104	8.9	7.0	45.9	33.9	4.2	152406
49418	GRANDVILLE	25846	9926	15.2	27.5	37.9	14.4	5.1	56920	62533	82	80	7474	3.4	5.1	53.0	35.7	2.8	160543
49419	HAMILTON	22551	2434	11.9	28.4	46.4	9.7	3.6	58113	63271	83	81	2224	7.9	8.7	41.1	39.4	2.9	163660
49420	HART	15174	2375	36.2	33.2	26.0	3.2	1.4	34349	36597	25	13	1846	18.5	30.7	37.9	10.9	1.9	90940
49421	HESPERIA	16752	2394	34.0	34.0	27.0	3.6	1.4	36055	39170	32	19	2046	21.4	26.3	40.4	10.8	1.2	93019
49423	HOLLAND	23355	17358	19.8	31.2	35.5	9.0	4.5	49138	53380	70	64	12509	4.7	9.9	54.8	26.7	3.9	140116
49424	HOLLAND	26660	15478	13.1	26.4	41.0	13.3	6.1	59079	64731	84	83	12368	9.7	4.7	44.2	35.3	6.1	162094
49425	HOLTON	17928	1330	24.3	34.9	32.6	5.9	2.3	43064	47468	56	46	1123	20.8	25.0	40.4	12.8	1.0	95220
49426	HUDSONVILLE	24272	9486	11.5	22.0	46.6	15.1	4.8	63284	69756	87	87	8372	5.0	4.3	44.6	43.3	2.8	169988
49428	JENISON	24702	9346	15.0	22.6	43.3	14.7	4.4	61279	66080	86	85	7849	1.4	4.5	60.9	31.0	2.2	158956
49431	LUDINGTON	20724	7265	34.3	29.7	27.3	6.2	2.5	37034	40468	36	23	5379	10.4	26.0	41.8	19.4	2.4	107400
49435	MARNE	24216	1124	14.9	21.7	45.5	13.3	4.7	61212	66240	86	85	1029	1.5	5.9	52.0	35.7	5.0	161817
49436	MEARS	22214	711	26.4	34.9	30.2	5.5	3.0	40403	44044	48	36	600	12.0	20.3	37.5	23.7	6.5	121084
49437	MONTAGUE	21990	2755	24.5	30.5	34.8	7.6	2.6	45770	49389	63	55	2322	6.8	23.3	50.3	17.0	2.7	113406
49440	MUSKEGON	14646	440	54.6	26.6	16.1	2.7	0.0	22513	27965	3	1	98	58.2	23.5	17.4	1.0	0.0	47143
49441	MUSKEGON	22520	15241	27.5	32.8	29.6	6.6	3.5	41226	45497	50	40	11459	10.7	25.8	45.9	15.4	2.3	105587
	MICHIGAN	25281		23.8	27.4	32.3	10.9	5.5	48729	54505				10.7	16.0	40.3	28.0	5.0	134769
	UNITED STATES	25866		24.7	27.1	30.8	10.9	6.5	48124	56710				10.9	15.0	33.7	30.1	10.4	145905

ZIP CODE #	POST OFFICE NAME	FINANCIAL SERVICES: Auto Loan	FINANCIAL SERVICES: Home Loan	FINANCIAL SERVICES: Invest-ments	FINANCIAL SERVICES: Retire-ment Plans	THE HOME: Home Improvements: Home Repair	THE HOME: Home Improvements: Lawn & Garden	THE HOME: Furnishings: Comput-ers & Hard-ware	THE HOME: Furnishings: Major Appli-ances	THE HOME: Furnishings: TV, Radio, Sound Equip-ment	THE HOME: Furnishings: Furni-ture	ENTERTAINMENT: Dine out/Carry out	ENTERTAINMENT: Sports Equip-ment	ENTERTAINMENT: Fees & Tickets	ENTERTAINMENT: Toys & Games	ENTERTAINMENT: Travel	ENTERTAINMENT: Cable TV	PERSONAL: Apparel & Services	PERSONAL: Auto Repairs	PERSONAL: Health Insur-ance	PERSONAL: Pets & Supplies
49249	JEROME	108	86	58	78	94	104	81	95	90	81	108	112	74	106	84	95	100	93	109	128
49250	JONESVILLE	86	72	52	69	77	85	69	77	75	69	90	91	66	91	70	77	85	76	86	100
49251	LESLIE	100	90	72	88	94	102	87	94	91	86	111	110	85	112	88	92	105	92	100	115
49252	LITCHFIELD	87	67	41	61	73	81	63	75	72	64	86	89	58	84	65	75	79	73	87	101
49253	MANITOU BEACH	102	84	60	78	92	102	79	91	87	78	104	108	73	104	83	91	97	90	104	122
49254	MICHIGAN CENTER	77	78	74	75	79	86	75	77	77	74	95	89	76	98	77	78	91	76	81	90
49255	MONTGOMERY	81	62	40	58	68	77	62	71	69	62	83	83	56	81	62	73	77	70	82	92
49256	MORENCI	82	72	55	70	76	83	70	76	74	69	90	89	68	90	71	76	85	74	82	94
49259	MUNITH	100	94	77	90	96	101	87	94	89	88	110	110	86	110	88	89	105	92	96	115
49262	NORTH ADAMS	86	77	59	73	81	87	71	79	76	71	92	94	70	94	73	77	87	77	85	102
49264	ONONDAGA	88	82	66	78	85	90	75	82	78	75	95	97	75	98	77	80	91	80	87	104
49265	ONSTED	113	112	99	108	116	122	103	111	104	102	128	130	102	132	106	106	123	108	114	136
49266	OSSEO	82	73	56	70	77	83	68	75	72	68	88	90	66	89	70	74	83	73	81	97
49267	OTTAWA LAKE	102	98	82	94	101	106	89	97	92	89	113	115	89	116	92	93	108	94	100	121
49268	PALMYRA	89	81	63	77	85	91	75	82	79	75	96	98	74	98	77	81	92	80	89	105
49269	PARMA	94	92	79	89	94	98	85	91	86	85	106	107	85	108	86	86	102	88	92	110
49270	PETERSBURG	111	112	100	109	115	119	102	108	103	102	126	128	104	131	105	103	123	105	109	132
49271	PITTSFORD	85	76	58	72	80	86	70	78	74	70	91	93	69	93	72	76	86	76	84	100
49272	PLEASANT LAKE	84	94	96	92	94	97	87	88	85	86	105	103	91	111	89	84	104	86	85	101
49274	READING	83	69	50	65	75	83	66	75	72	66	87	88	62	87	68	75	81	74	85	97
49275	RIDGEWAY	123	109	83	104	115	124	101	112	107	101	130	133	99	133	104	110	124	109	121	144
49276	RIGA	109	100	80	96	105	112	92	101	97	92	118	120	91	121	95	99	113	98	108	129
49277	RIVES JUNCTION	90	97	92	95	98	100	88	91	86	88	106	108	91	112	90	85	104	88	89	108
49279	SAND CREEK	89	79	60	75	84	90	73	81	78	73	95	97	72	97	75	80	90	79	88	105
49283	SPRING ARBOR	75	75	82	74	74	81	75	75	76	75	95	87	75	95	76	77	93	77	76	86
49284	SPRINGPORT	86	77	59	73	81	87	71	78	75	71	91	93	69	93	73	77	87	76	85	101
49285	STOCKBRIDGE	106	95	75	92	99	108	91	99	96	90	117	115	89	118	92	98	111	96	106	122
49286	TECUMSEH	93	100	101	98	100	105	95	96	94	94	116	113	97	121	97	93	114	95	95	110
49287	TIPTON	112	107	90	103	111	117	98	107	102	98	125	126	99	128	101	103	120	104	111	133
49288	WALDRON	73	63	49	62	66	73	62	67	66	61	80	78	60	80	62	67	75	66	73	82
49301	ADA	171	213	231	219	207	208	188	184	172	190	218	213	206	228	192	166	220	177	164	204
49302	ALTO	117	145	155	146	142	141	129	128	119	129	150	149	138	159	132	115	150	123	114	141
49303	BAILEY	90	80	61	76	85	91	74	82	79	74	96	98	73	98	76	81	91	80	89	106
49304	BALDWIN	59	46	32	42	52	58	44	53	49	43	58	61	39	58	46	53	54	52	62	72
49305	BARRYTON	71	54	34	48	60	68	51	62	58	51	69	73	45	68	54	63	64	61	74	85
49306	BELMONT	114	125	123	124	123	127	114	117	109	117	137	133	117	136	115	107	134	114	111	131
49307	BIG RAPIDS	65	55	57	56	56	62	67	62	67	63	83	76	62	80	62	65	79	66	62	72
49309	BITELY	65	51	35	46	58	65	48	58	55	48	65	68	43	64	51	58	60	57	69	79
49310	BLANCHARD	82	71	55	69	75	82	68	75	73	68	88	88	66	89	70	74	83	73	82	94
49315	BYRON CENTER	124	123	111	120	126	132	114	121	115	114	142	143	115	146	117	116	137	118	123	147
49316	CALEDONIA	112	123	119	122	122	123	112	115	108	113	135	135	115	139	114	106	132	112	108	132
49318	CASNOVIA	101	89	68	85	95	101	83	92	88	83	107	109	81	109	85	90	102	89	99	118
49319	CEDAR SPRINGS	94	87	70	84	90	96	82	88	85	82	104	104	80	105	83	86	99	86	93	110
49321	COMSTOCK PARK	88	85	88	88	84	87	86	86	85	87	106	102	85	104	84	81	104	87	80	98
49322	CORAL	79	69	53	66	73	79	65	72	70	65	85	85	64	86	67	71	80	70	78	91
49323	DORR	101	100	87	99	100	103	92	97	91	93	113	114	92	115	92	90	110	94	94	116
49325	FREEPORT	102	94	76	90	99	105	87	95	90	87	110	113	86	113	89	92	106	92	100	120
49326	GOWEN	93	79	56	74	84	92	73	83	80	74	96	99	71	97	76	82	91	81	92	109
49327	GRANT	85	74	57	72	77	85	72	78	77	72	93	91	70	94	73	78	88	77	85	96
49328	HOPKINS	95	85	65	81	90	96	79	87	83	79	101	104	77	104	81	86	96	85	94	112
49329	HOWARD CITY	80	71	55	68	74	80	68	74	71	68	87	87	65	86	68	72	82	72	78	92
49330	KENT CITY	97	87	67	83	90	96	81	89	85	82	104	105	79	103	82	86	99	87	94	112
49331	LOWELL	92	100	100	100	100	101	93	95	89	93	112	112	95	115	94	87	110	93	89	108
49332	MECOSTA	82	65	46	60	72	82	62	74	70	63	84	83	57	79	65	74	78	72	87	96
49333	MIDDLEVILLE	98	97	87	96	100	105	91	96	92	91	113	113	92	116	93	92	109	94	97	115
49336	MORLEY	79	65	44	60	68	75	62	70	67	63	81	82	57	78	62	69	76	69	77	90
49337	NEWAYGO	87	70	49	66	75	83	68	77	75	69	90	90	64	88	69	77	84	76	86	99
49338	PARIS	71	58	43	56	63	71	58	65	63	57	76	75	54	75	59	66	71	64	73	82
49339	PIERSON	99	84	61	78	91	99	78	90	85	78	102	106	74	103	82	89	97	88	101	118
49340	REMUS	81	68	53	64	73	84	65	75	71	66	86	83	62	81	68	75	80	73	86	94
49341	ROCKFORD	116	132	132	134	129	129	121	121	113	122	143	142	125	146	121	109	141	118	109	135
49342	RODNEY	85	69	48	63	76	85	65	76	72	64	86	90	59	85	68	76	80	75	89	103
49343	SAND LAKE	94	80	58	75	85	92	74	84	80	74	97	100	72	98	76	83	92	82	93	110
49344	SHELBYVILLE	101	88	65	82	94	102	81	92	88	81	106	109	78	108	85	91	100	90	102	120
49345	SPARTA	88	83	72	81	86	92	80	85	82	79	100	99	78	101	81	82	96	83	88	102
49346	STANWOOD	95	86	75	82	90	103	82	91	86	84	106	97	81	97	85	90	100	89	102	107
49347	TRUFANT	77	67	52	65	71	78	66	71	70	65	84	83	63	85	66	71	80	70	77	88
49348	WAYLAND	96	86	68	83	89	96	82	89	85	82	104	104	79	104	83	86	99	88	94	110
49349	WHITE CLOUD	73	53	31	48	60	68	53	63	61	52	72	73	46	69	54	65	66	62	75	85
49401	ALLENDALE	86	78	79	81	77	80	90	83	87	86	109	102	84	104	83	80	105	88	76	93
49402	BRANCH	70	55	37	49	62	69	52	62	58	51	69	73	46	68	55	62	64	61	73	85
49403	CONKLIN	99	88	67	84	93	100	82	90	87	82	105	107	80	107	84	89	100	88	98	116
49404	COOPERSVILLE	98	96	83	94	97	100	90	95	90	91	111	112	88	111	90	89	107	93	94	113
49405	CUSTER	73	57	38	52	64	72	55	65	62	54	73	77	49	72	58	65	68	64	77	88
49408	FENNVILLE	100	85	61	80	90	98	81	90	87	81	105	106	76	103	82	89	99	89	99	115
49410	FOUNTAIN	77	61	41	55	68	77	57	69	65	57	77	81	51	76	61	69	71	68	82	94
49411	FREE SOIL	81	64	43	57	72	80	60	72	68	59	80	84	54	79	64	72	75	71	85	99
49412	FREMONT	89	71	49	68	77	88	72	81	79	70	94	94	66	93	73	82	88	80	93	102
49415	FRUITPORT	103	92	70	87	97	104	85	94	90	85	110	112	83	112	87	92	104	92	102	121
49417	GRAND HAVEN	92	98	98	99	97	101	94	95	92	94	115	110	96	116	94	90	112	94	90	105
49418	GRANDVILLE	98	107	109	109	105	106	102	101	97	102	122	120	104	124	101	93	119	100	93	113
49419	HAMILTON	98	99	90	98	99	101	93	96	92	94	114	115	93	115	93	89	111	95	92	113
49420	HART	67	54	40	52	58	66	56	61	61	55	73	71	52	72	56	63	69	61	69	76
49421	HESPERIA	76	57	34	51	63	71	55	66	63	55	75	77	49	73	57	67	69	65	77	88
49423	HOLLAND	93	88	84	89	89	95	90	91	90	89	112	108	88	111	88	89	108	92	90	106
49424	HOLLAND	109	114	108	116	113	114	107	109	103	108	128	128	107	129	106	99	125	107	102	125
49425	HOLTON	82	71	53	68	76	82	67	75	72	67	87	89	65	88	69	74	82	73	82	96
49426	HUDSONVILLE	105	113	109	115	111	112	106	106	101	107	126	125	107	128	105	97	124	105	98	120
49428	JENISON	94	106	114	108	104	105	101	100	96	101	120	118	104	123	101	92	119	99	91	110
49431	LUDINGTON	73	65	61	63	69	76	66	70	70	65	85	81	64	86	67	72	81	70	77	85
49435	MARNE	105	109	100	107	111	115	99	104	99	99	122	123	101	127	102	99	119	101	104	126
49436	MEARS	92	72	49	65	81	91	68	82	77	67	91	96	61	90	73	82	85	81	97	112
49437	MONTAGUE	88	76	58	71	81	90	74	82	80	73	96	94	70	96	76	83	91	80	91	102
49440	MUSKEGON	38	34	52	36	34	40	42	38	44	41	56	45	42	55	42	45	54	42	41	43
49441	MUSKEGON	70	74	80	72	74	81	74	74	75	73	93	85	76	96	75	76	90	74	75	82
	MICHIGAN	91	91	93	89	91	98	90	91	91	90	113	106	90	113	90	91	109	91	92	105
	UNITED STATES	100	100	100	100	100	100	100	100	100	100	100	100	100	100	100	100	100	100	100	100

MICHIGAN

POPULATION CHANGE

A 49442-49710

#	POST OFFICE NAME	COUNTY FIPS CODE	POPULATION			2000-2004 ANNUAL RATE		HOUSEHOLDS					FAMILIES		
			2000	2004	2009	% Rate	State Centile	2000	2004	2009	% Annual Rate 2000-2004	2004 Average HH Size	2000	2004	% Annual Rate 2000-2004
49442	MUSKEGON	121	45622	46283	47507	0.3	36	15750	16208	16890	0.7	2.60	10458	10606	0.3
49444	MUSKEGON	121	26992	26954	27457	0.0	21	10232	10342	10671	0.3	2.55	7082	7057	-0.1
49445	MUSKEGON	121	20807	21470	22076	0.7	54	7702	8067	8411	1.1	2.64	5926	6137	0.8
49446	NEW ERA	127	2250	2317	2457	0.7	51	799	839	904	1.2	2.73	623	646	0.9
49448	NUNICA	139	3325	3393	3551	0.5	42	1216	1265	1347	0.9	2.67	942	970	0.7
49449	PENTWATER	127	2789	2889	3042	0.8	58	1192	1255	1342	1.2	2.27	852	886	0.9
49450	PULLMAN	005	3498	3735	4002	1.6	82	1093	1172	1267	1.7	3.15	828	876	1.3
49451	RAVENNA	121	5727	6052	6314	1.3	75	1949	2094	2218	1.7	2.87	1572	1672	1.5
49452	ROTHBURY	127	1944	2094	2243	1.8	86	694	762	830	2.2	2.73	533	579	2.0
49453	SAUGATUCK	005	3051	3204	3405	1.2	70	1435	1531	1653	1.5	2.05	801	834	1.0
49454	SCOTTVILLE	105	4501	4528	4655	0.1	28	1701	1738	1813	0.5	2.55	1255	1265	0.2
49455	SHELBY	127	5388	5667	5993	1.2	71	1934	2074	2231	1.7	2.70	1443	1530	1.4
49456	SPRING LAKE	139	17725	18888	20332	1.5	79	7085	7727	8480	2.1	2.41	4899	5263	1.7
49457	TWIN LAKE	121	9024	9804	10372	2.0	89	3282	3630	3899	2.4	2.69	2499	2731	2.1
49459	WALKERVILLE	127	1460	1512	1598	0.8	58	507	540	584	1.5	2.60	375	393	1.1
49460	WEST OLIVE	139	8652	9062	9655	1.1	68	2778	2958	3201	1.5	2.96	2290	2420	1.3
49461	WHITEHALL	121	8403	8614	8846	0.6	46	3164	3299	3441	1.0	2.55	2302	2368	0.7
49464	ZEELAND	139	22761	25680	28509	2.9	97	7520	8613	9702	3.2	2.95	5841	6617	3.0
49503	GRAND RAPIDS	081	37896	38262	39799	0.2	31	14799	14961	15696	0.3	2.41	7115	6999	-0.4
49504	GRAND RAPIDS	081	39786	39980	41169	0.1	25	15266	15436	16069	0.3	2.54	9500	9389	-0.3
49505	GRAND RAPIDS	081	31754	32039	33158	0.2	30	12740	13002	13595	0.5	2.37	7891	7863	-0.1
49506	GRAND RAPIDS	081	36245	35679	36485	-0.4	11	12314	12272	12705	-0.1	2.60	8183	7983	-0.6
49507	GRAND RAPIDS	081	39788	40091	41559	0.2	29	12731	12829	13351	0.2	3.09	9043	8962	-0.2
49508	GRAND RAPIDS	081	38048	40913	43848	1.7	85	14538	15797	17093	2.0	2.56	9922	10634	1.6
49509	GRAND RAPIDS	081	53453	56077	59291	1.1	69	20920	22243	23753	1.5	2.51	13458	13983	0.9
49512	GRAND RAPIDS	081	11895	13545	14832	3.1	98	5800	6584	7223	3.0	2.04	2818	3172	2.8
49525	GRAND RAPIDS	081	27019	28658	30314	1.4	77	9913	10608	11319	1.6	2.63	7133	7541	1.3
49544	GRAND RAPIDS	081	28605	30226	32015	1.3	75	11117	11894	12724	1.6	2.51	7274	7655	1.2
49546	GRAND RAPIDS	081	30709	32987	34966	1.7	85	11581	12543	13401	1.9	2.55	8140	8655	1.5
49548	GRAND RAPIDS	081	32084	31681	32561	-0.3	13	12490	12376	12800	-0.2	2.54	8200	7972	-0.7
49601	CADILLAC	165	20245	20959	22267	0.8	58	7987	8423	9105	1.3	2.45	5565	5792	1.0
49612	ALDEN	009	1037	1147	1291	2.4	94	440	500	576	3.1	2.29	310	346	2.6
49613	ARCADIA	101	759	850	951	2.7	96	345	392	446	3.1	2.16	246	276	2.7
49614	BEAR LAKE	101	2637	2840	3098	1.8	86	1062	1163	1289	2.2	2.41	748	808	1.8
49615	BELLAIRE	009	4188	4646	5350	2.5	95	1696	1922	2262	3.0	2.34	1219	1363	2.7
49616	BENZONIA	019	2194	2402	2714	2.2	91	870	973	1122	2.7	2.39	585	645	2.3
49617	BEULAH	019	3222	3623	4156	2.8	96	1299	1487	1737	3.2	2.40	915	1033	2.9
49618	BOON	165	596	653	708	2.2	92	222	247	271	2.5	2.64	168	184	2.2
49619	BRETHREN	101	1062	1120	1209	1.3	73	414	444	487	1.7	2.50	302	320	1.4
49620	BUCKLEY	055	1987	2287	2555	3.4	98	700	820	930	3.8	2.78	531	616	3.6
49621	CEDAR	089	2643	2845	3100	1.8	86	1039	1148	1280	2.4	2.47	768	838	2.1
49622	CENTRAL LAKE	009	2629	2790	3143	1.4	77	1065	1156	1328	2.0	2.38	770	825	1.6
49623	CHASE	085	1325	1449	1617	2.1	91	490	544	617	2.5	2.66	346	380	2.2
49625	COPEMISH	101	1184	1284	1406	1.9	89	451	500	557	2.5	2.57	325	355	2.1
49629	ELK RAPIDS	009	2235	2341	2597	1.1	68	1005	1074	1213	1.6	2.17	689	725	1.2
49630	EMPIRE	089	1314	1366	1460	0.9	62	596	630	687	1.3	2.16	399	415	0.9
49631	EVART	133	6289	6525	6769	0.9	60	2450	2588	2735	1.3	2.48	1765	1840	1.0
49632	FALMOUTH	113	1187	1252	1349	1.3	73	456	492	541	1.8	2.53	350	373	1.5
49633	FIFE LAKE	079	3454	3953	4438	3.2	98	1353	1596	1839	4.0	2.43	987	1150	3.7
49635	FRANKFORT	019	3799	3981	4393	1.1	68	1637	1760	1987	1.7	2.19	1090	1150	1.3
49636	GLEN ARBOR	089	329	334	353	0.4	37	154	159	172	0.8	2.10	101	103	0.5
49637	GRAWN	055	3336	3555	3839	1.5	79	1223	1329	1462	2.0	2.65	883	949	1.7
49638	HARRIETTA	165	910	1042	1156	3.2	98	352	411	463	3.7	2.54	247	284	3.3
49639	HERSEY	133	2639	2752	2862	1.0	65	995	1061	1126	1.5	2.58	716	752	1.2
49640	HONOR	019	1341	1434	1602	1.6	82	599	654	745	2.1	2.17	436	469	1.7
49642	IDLEWILD	085	1222	1331	1482	2.0	90	515	568	643	2.3	2.33	351	383	2.1
49643	INTERLOCHEN	019	5061	5638	6301	2.6	95	2002	2274	2587	3.0	2.48	1462	1642	2.8
49644	IRONS	085	1799	1931	2133	1.7	84	838	919	1034	2.2	2.10	552	596	1.8
49645	KALEVA	101	1588	1693	1838	1.5	80	655	711	785	2.0	2.37	460	493	1.6
49646	KALKASKA	079	8331	8629	9200	0.8	58	3251	3452	3770	1.4	2.45	2278	2384	1.1
49648	KEWADIN	009	1886	2152	2496	3.2	98	782	914	1082	3.7	2.34	586	677	3.5
49649	KINGSLEY	055	5870	6607	7345	2.8	96	1927	2200	2486	3.2	2.95	1497	1695	3.0
49650	LAKE ANN	019	2378	2775	3242	3.7	99	894	1064	1265	4.2	2.61	675	792	3.8
49651	LAKE CITY	113	7488	7979	8673	1.5	79	2993	3253	3604	2.0	2.42	2151	2306	1.7
49653	LAKE LEELANAU	089	2137	2228	2385	1.0	65	819	876	959	1.6	2.50	607	641	1.3
49654	LELAND	089	559	587	630	1.2	70	258	279	307	1.9	2.03	186	198	1.5
49655	LEROY	133	3031	3120	3232	0.7	50	1134	1193	1261	1.2	2.61	854	888	0.9
49656	LUTHER	085	1840	1970	2173	1.6	83	776	849	955	2.1	2.31	533	576	1.8
49657	MC BAIN	113	3628	3957	4338	2.1	90	1230	1368	1529	2.5	2.84	960	1058	2.3
49659	MANCELONA	009	6473	7326	8414	3.0	97	2446	2815	3285	3.4	2.59	1793	2036	3.0
49660	MANISTEE	101	14332	15166	16378	1.3	76	5722	6175	6802	1.8	2.31	3795	4036	1.5
49663	MANTON	165	5252	5619	6054	1.6	83	1922	2085	2278	1.9	2.68	1421	1520	1.6
49664	MAPLE CITY	089	2145	2276	2459	1.4	77	837	907	1002	1.9	2.49	630	676	1.7
49665	MARION	133	4378	4687	4946	1.6	83	1686	1844	1984	2.1	2.53	1219	1315	1.8
49667	MERRITT	113	714	736	783	0.7	53	262	275	298	1.2	2.67	195	203	1.0
49668	MESICK	165	3501	3938	4329	2.8	96	1334	1528	1707	3.3	2.57	981	1107	2.9
49670	NORTHPORT	089	2175	2347	2558	1.8	87	923	1016	1130	2.3	2.23	651	706	1.9
49675	ONEKAMA	101	1217	1287	1384	1.3	75	486	530	586	2.1	2.15	327	351	1.7
49676	RAPID CITY	009	3546	3898	4348	2.3	92	1444	1628	1856	2.9	2.39	1064	1184	2.6
49677	REED CITY	133	5835	5801	5931	-0.1	18	2245	2274	2372	0.3	2.48	1571	1569	0.0
49679	SEARS	133	1235	1304	1366	1.3	74	470	506	540	1.8	2.52	341	362	1.4
49680	SOUTH BOARDMAN	079	1699	1976	2235	3.6	99	601	715	827	4.2	2.76	465	546	3.9
49682	SUTTONS BAY	089	4350	4820	5335	2.4	94	1627	1841	2081	3.0	2.59	1246	1393	2.7
49683	THOMPSONVILLE	019	1758	1988	2263	2.9	97	718	828	959	3.4	2.39	520	592	3.1
49684	TRAVERSE CITY	055	33676	36239	39566	1.7	85	13142	14499	16187	2.3	2.45	8971	9722	1.9
49686	TRAVERSE CITY	055	29282	31240	33912	1.5	80	12062	13125	14533	2.0	2.32	7886	8453	1.7
49688	TUSTIN	133	2394	2443	2546	0.5	42	892	929	987	1.0	2.61	680	701	0.7
49689	WELLSTON	101	1707	1852	2024	1.9	89	708	780	866	2.3	2.31	517	562	2.0
49690	WILLIAMSBURG	055	6453	6787	7291	1.2	71	2461	2637	2886	1.6	2.54	1829	1940	1.4
49701	MACKINAW CITY	047	928	1016	1111	2.2	91	434	487	543	2.8	2.08	283	313	2.4
49705	AFTON	031	660	762	841	3.4	99	223	266	302	4.2	2.80	169	200	4.0
49706	ALANSON	047	4610	4916	5308	1.5	80	1838	2002	2204	2.0	2.45	1341	1441	1.7
49707	ALPENA	007	24511	24139	23717	-0.4	11	10202	10295	10309	0.2	2.30	6716	6657	-0.2
49709	ATLANTA	119	3358	3464	3643	0.7	53	1491	1579	1702	1.4	2.18	1038	1084	1.0
49710	BARBEAU	033	345	350	363	0.3	36	161	167	176	0.9	2.10	121	123	0.4
	MICHIGAN					0.6					1.0	2.52			0.6
	UNITED STATES					1.2					1.3	2.58			1.1

ZIP CODE #	POST OFFICE NAME	RACE (%) White 2000	White 2004	Black 2000	Black 2004	Asian/Pacific 2000	Asian/Pacific 2004	% Hispanic Origin 2000	% Hispanic Origin 2004	2004 AGE DISTRIBUTION (%) 0-4	5-9	10-14	15-19	20-24	25-44	45-64	65-84	85+	18+	MEDIAN AGE 2004	% 2004 Males	% 2004 Females
49442	MUSKEGON	70.5	67.9	22.9	25.1	0.4	0.5	5.5	6.1	7.9	7.4	7.7	7.1	8.0	30.7	20.2	9.4	1.8	72.9	32.6	51.1	48.9
49444	MUSKEGON	59.4	58.9	36.4	36.7	0.5	0.6	3.2	3.5	7.9	7.8	8.2	7.2	6.6	27.1	23.1	10.6	1.4	71.4	34.6	48.3	51.7
49445	MUSKEGON	94.6	93.7	2.4	2.9	0.4	0.6	1.8	2.2	5.8	6.4	8.2	7.6	6.1	25.2	27.7	11.5	1.6	74.7	39.3	49.3	50.7
49446	NEW ERA	93.7	93.1	0.4	0.4	0.4	0.5	8.5	9.4	6.3	7.0	7.4	7.4	5.9	25.0	26.9	12.6	1.5	74.3	39.3	50.5	49.5
49448	NUNICA	96.7	96.4	0.7	0.7	0.2	0.2	1.8	2.2	6.5	7.2	8.6	7.0	4.9	30.0	25.9	9.1	1.0	73.2	37.3	51.7	48.3
49449	PENTWATER	96.0	95.5	0.2	0.2	0.4	0.5	4.1	4.9	4.3	5.0	6.0	6.2	5.0	19.0	32.3	19.9	2.3	80.4	48.1	50.0	50.0
49450	PULLMAN	75.1	72.9	6.6	6.9	0.3	0.4	22.6	25.3	9.3	8.9	10.1	8.0	7.7	29.9	18.3	7.1	0.6	66.6	28.7	51.5	48.5
49451	RAVENNA	96.5	96.0	0.4	0.5	0.1	0.1	2.6	3.1	6.7	7.4	8.9	8.2	5.8	29.8	22.9	9.3	1.1	71.8	35.2	49.9	50.1
49452	ROTHBURY	92.0	91.3	0.1	0.1	0.4	0.5	8.7	9.7	7.3	7.4	8.9	7.8	7.4	28.0	24.1	8.6	0.5	71.4	34.8	51.7	48.3
49453	SAUGATUCK	95.9	95.4	0.9	0.9	0.5	0.6	4.1	4.8	4.9	5.5	5.6	5.2	5.2	23.9	33.4	14.1	2.1	80.6	44.8	49.0	51.0
49454	SCOTTVILLE	95.7	95.3	0.5	0.5	0.3	0.4	3.6	4.1	6.1	6.4	7.4	7.2	6.4	24.9	26.1	13.3	2.3	75.6	39.8	49.5	50.5
49455	SHELBY	87.7	86.5	0.3	0.4	0.2	0.3	15.8	17.6	6.9	6.8	7.5	7.1	6.8	25.0	26.1	12.3	1.5	74.2	37.9	50.2	49.9
49456	SPRING LAKE	97.0	96.6	0.5	0.6	0.6	0.7	1.6	1.9	6.4	6.5	7.0	6.3	5.6	26.8	27.0	12.2	2.3	76.2	39.7	48.5	51.5
49457	TWIN LAKE	92.7	91.8	2.9	3.3	0.2	0.2	2.6	3.0	7.0	7.3	8.0	7.0	6.5	29.3	26.0	8.1	0.8	73.3	35.5	50.8	49.2
49459	WALKERVILLE	84.6	82.7	1.2	1.2	0.1	0.1	19.5	22.3	7.8	8.0	8.7	9.1	6.8	26.1	22.6	9.9	1.1	69.4	33.0	51.6	48.4
49460	WEST OLIVE	91.6	90.5	1.3	1.4	0.9	1.2	9.0	10.4	8.1	8.1	8.3	7.8	6.3	30.0	23.8	7.1	0.5	70.4	33.9	52.6	47.4
49461	WHITEHALL	96.7	96.2	0.8	1.0	0.3	0.4	1.5	1.9	6.2	6.6	7.5	7.1	6.1	25.1	28.4	11.2	2.0	74.9	39.8	48.7	51.3
49464	ZEELAND	92.7	91.2	0.8	0.9	2.1	2.8	5.3	6.3	8.9	8.4	8.5	7.2	6.9	30.8	19.4	8.4	1.7	69.7	31.7	48.9	51.1
49503	GRAND RAPIDS	61.9	58.5	21.1	22.7	1.3	1.6	20.9	23.3	8.3	6.9	6.3	6.9	11.7	34.8	17.2	6.7	1.3	74.9	29.5	52.3	47.7
49504	GRAND RAPIDS	84.5	82.6	3.1	3.3	1.1	1.4	13.2	15.2	8.3	7.4	7.2	6.6	7.5	30.7	19.7	10.3	2.3	73.2	33.0	49.8	50.2
49505	GRAND RAPIDS	83.7	81.3	9.9	11.4	1.5	1.9	4.0	4.6	7.9	7.3	6.9	6.3	6.7	30.3	20.1	12.1	2.5	73.9	34.4	48.3	51.7
49506	GRAND RAPIDS	74.9	73.3	20.0	21.0	1.2	1.5	3.7	4.1	7.1	6.9	7.1	10.5	10.5	25.4	20.9	8.9	2.9	74.8	31.8	46.9	53.1
49507	GRAND RAPIDS	40.8	38.7	42.2	42.8	1.4	1.7	22.8	24.9	10.2	9.3	9.3	8.4	8.5	31.1	17.1	5.4	0.9	66.1	27.8	49.6	50.5
49508	GRAND RAPIDS	77.2	74.6	13.2	14.1	5.1	6.3	4.0	4.5	7.5	7.2	7.7	7.2	7.8	29.5	22.6	9.1	1.5	73.1	33.6	47.4	52.6
49509	GRAND RAPIDS	84.1	81.7	5.0	5.5	2.8	3.5	9.9	11.6	7.9	7.2	7.0	7.0	8.5	32.8	20.0	8.6	1.1	73.8	32.0	49.1	50.9
49512	GRAND RAPIDS	75.0	72.0	12.7	13.5	7.4	9.3	4.1	4.7	7.9	6.1	5.0	5.2	11.4	38.8	18.1	6.6	0.9	78.3	30.6	50.3	49.7
49525	GRAND RAPIDS	94.3	93.3	2.0	2.2	1.3	1.7	1.8	2.2	6.3	6.6	8.1	9.1	8.1	25.7	26.2	9.0	1.0	74.0	35.7	48.7	51.3
49544	GRAND RAPIDS	95.2	94.4	1.2	1.4	0.9	1.1	2.5	3.0	7.1	6.8	7.3	7.2	8.2	30.5	22.5	9.1	1.4	74.5	33.8	49.8	50.2
49546	GRAND RAPIDS	88.6	86.6	5.0	5.7	3.7	4.7	1.9	2.2	6.6	6.8	7.7	7.0	6.5	22.8	26.4	12.6	3.7	74.5	39.9	47.2	52.8
49548	GRAND RAPIDS	83.9	81.5	5.8	6.5	3.2	4.0	7.8	9.2	8.6	7.9	7.4	7.0	7.6	32.8	19.8	7.8	1.0	71.7	32.0	49.3	50.7
49601	CADILLAC	97.3	97.0	0.2	0.2	0.6	0.7	0.9	1.0	6.4	6.4	7.1	7.0	6.8	26.1	25.4	12.7	2.0	75.7	38.6	49.0	51.0
49612	ALDEN	96.8	96.6	0.1	0.1	0.6	0.8	0.9	1.0	5.2	5.4	6.1	5.8	5.1	25.6	31.2	14.1	1.4	79.7	43.1	51.0	49.0
49613	ARCADIA	98.8	98.6	0.1	0.1	0.1	0.1	1.5	1.9	5.3	5.7	6.2	4.9	3.5	21.3	29.4	21.8	1.9	79.4	47.3	49.1	50.9
49614	BEAR LAKE	97.0	96.7	0.0	0.0	0.6	0.7	3.3	3.7	5.2	6.6	7.0	5.4	4.2	24.2	28.0	17.2	2.3	77.7	43.3	50.3	49.8
49615	BELLAIRE	97.4	97.2	0.1	0.1	0.3	0.4	1.0	1.1	5.6	5.8	6.1	5.6	4.7	23.0	29.1	17.5	2.7	78.7	44.5	49.0	51.0
49616	BENZONIA	94.4	94.0	0.6	0.7	0.2	0.2	2.5	2.8	6.0	5.9	6.5	5.7	5.0	24.3	28.1	16.0	2.4	77.8	42.9	49.3	50.7
49617	BEULAH	96.3	96.1	0.2	0.2	0.2	0.3	1.3	1.4	5.5	5.6	5.9	5.1	4.6	23.4	29.4	18.9	1.7	79.9	45.0	50.2	49.8
49618	BOON	98.0	97.9	0.2	0.2	0.2	0.2	0.7	0.8	6.4	6.9	7.5	6.6	6.3	25.9	26.0	12.9	1.5	75.0	39.1	51.3	48.7
49619	BRETHREN	97.4	97.1	0.3	0.4	0.1	0.2	1.7	2.0	5.3	5.8	6.3	5.7	4.8	21.8	31.9	16.7	1.7	79.3	45.2	50.1	49.9
49620	BUCKLEY	96.8	96.6	0.3	0.3	0.1	0.2	2.0	2.3	7.5	7.6	7.5	7.0	6.3	27.1	26.1	9.9	1.2	73.0	36.7	50.3	49.7
49621	CEDAR	97.4	97.1	0.3	0.3	0.5	0.6	1.3	1.4	5.2	5.9	7.3	7.2	5.0	23.6	31.0	13.3	1.6	77.0	42.5	50.4	49.6
49622	CENTRAL LAKE	97.8	97.7	0.2	0.2	0.0	0.1	0.5	0.6	5.2	5.4	6.3	6.0	5.1	23.8	29.6	16.8	2.0	79.5	44.0	50.0	50.0
49623	CHASE	85.3	84.3	11.3	12.0	0.2	0.2	1.4	1.6	6.6	6.8	7.5	7.0	6.4	24.0	27.1	13.5	1.3	74.6	39.3	49.7	50.3
49625	COPEMISH	96.3	96.0	0.3	0.4	0.0	0.0	2.1	2.4	6.7	6.9	7.1	6.9	6.5	26.3	27.7	11.1	0.9	75.2	38.2	53.0	47.0
49629	ELK RAPIDS	97.3	97.1	0.2	0.2	0.3	0.3	2.0	2.3	4.0	4.8	6.5	6.8	4.9	20.1	31.2	20.0	1.8	79.9	46.9	50.2	49.9
49630	EMPIRE	98.6	98.4	0.1	0.1	0.3	0.4	0.5	0.5	3.7	4.4	5.6	5.9	4.4	17.4	35.7	20.3	2.6	82.7	49.8	49.3	50.7
49631	EVART	97.0	96.7	0.5	0.5	0.3	0.4	1.1	1.2	6.1	6.2	7.1	7.9	6.4	23.2	26.6	15.0	1.5	75.9	40.2	49.2	50.9
49632	FALMOUTH	97.8	97.7	0.3	0.3	0.2	0.2	1.2	1.4	7.0	6.9	8.2	8.6	5.5	26.0	24.3	12.7	1.0	72.7	38.3	50.5	49.5
49633	FIFE LAKE	95.5	95.1	1.4	1.6	0.1	0.1	0.8	0.9	6.1	6.3	7.2	6.7	5.9	28.0	26.9	12.2	0.8	76.1	39.0	52.0	48.0
49635	FRANKFORT	97.0	96.8	0.2	0.2	0.3	0.3	1.5	1.7	4.7	4.9	5.8	5.2	4.8	20.2	28.7	21.7	4.0	81.2	48.1	48.1	52.0
49636	GLEN ARBOR	99.4	99.4	0.0	0.0	0.3	0.3	0.6	0.6	2.4	3.0	3.6	3.9	3.0	9.3	37.7	32.6	4.5	88.6	59.4	48.2	51.8
49637	GRAWN	95.7	95.4	0.2	0.1	0.4	0.5	1.4	1.6	6.3	6.6	7.9	7.2	7.0	29.9	25.2	8.9	0.9	74.8	36.5	49.6	50.4
49638	HARRIETTA	97.6	97.6	0.0	0.0	0.0	0.0	1.0	1.3	6.0	6.3	6.2	6.1	5.6	23.5	28.6	16.7	1.0	77.7	42.6	51.2	48.9
49639	HERSEY	97.8	97.6	0.2	0.2	0.3	0.3	0.9	1.0	6.9	6.8	7.4	7.2	6.6	26.1	25.7	12.0	1.3	74.5	37.2	49.4	50.6
49640	HONOR	96.1	95.8	0.4	0.4	0.1	0.1	1.0	1.2	5.6	5.7	5.7	5.2	4.3	23.2	31.8	17.2	1.5	79.7	45.3	50.4	49.6
49642	IDLEWILD	82.7	81.6	13.8	14.5	0.3	0.2	1.6	1.7	6.0	6.4	7.1	6.7	5.9	22.3	28.1	16.0	1.5	76.3	41.8	50.0	50.0
49643	INTERLOCHEN	96.8	96.6	0.1	0.1	0.2	0.3	1.0	1.2	6.7	6.8	7.0	6.8	5.7	29.9	26.2	9.9	1.0	75.4	37.8	50.1	50.0
49644	IRONS	96.4	96.1	0.5	0.5	0.2	0.2	1.2	1.4	4.9	4.6	4.0	4.4	4.1	17.4	33.8	25.3	1.5	83.8	52.8	51.0	49.0
49645	KALEVA	96.6	96.4	0.3	0.2	0.1	0.1	2.5	3.0	6.3	6.6	6.4	6.6	5.6	23.5	29.5	13.6	2.1	76.9	41.6	49.6	50.4
49646	KALKASKA	97.5	97.2	0.3	0.3	0.3	0.5	0.8	0.9	7.0	6.8	6.8	6.2	6.1	27.1	25.4	13.0	1.6	75.6	38.4	49.6	50.4
49648	KEWADIN	96.9	96.6	0.4	0.4	0.1	0.1	1.9	2.2	3.5	4.0	5.8	5.8	4.6	18.9	32.9	22.9	1.7	82.7	49.4	51.0	49.0
49649	KINGSLEY	96.4	96.1	0.8	0.9	0.2	0.3	1.3	1.5	8.4	8.3	8.2	7.3	6.5	30.8	22.1	7.7	0.7	70.1	33.1	50.8	49.2
49650	LAKE ANN	97.4	97.2	0.3	0.3	0.1	0.1	1.2	1.4	7.8	7.8	7.5	6.5	5.9	31.4	23.9	8.5	0.8	72.9	35.8	49.8	50.2
49651	LAKE CITY	97.5	97.2	0.1	0.1	0.3	0.3	1.1	1.3	6.3	6.4	7.0	6.6	5.8	24.9	26.7	14.7	1.7	76.0	40.4	50.0	50.0
49653	LAKE LEELANAU	92.8	92.3	0.7	0.7	0.4	0.5	3.8	4.3	4.9	5.5	7.1	6.1	4.4	21.8	31.0	17.4	1.9	78.4	45.1	50.5	49.5
49654	LELAND	95.0	94.2	0.0	0.0	0.5	0.7	5.0	5.8	3.1	3.6	5.3	4.8	4.6	16.5	34.2	25.0	2.9	84.5	53.4	48.9	51.1
49655	LEROY	98.0	97.8	0.2	0.2	0.2	0.3	0.8	0.9	6.0	6.3	7.3	7.1	6.6	26.2	26.2	13.2	1.2	76.0	39.4	49.1	50.9
49656	LUTHER	95.2	94.9	0.7	0.7	0.2	0.2	1.5	1.7	5.6	5.8	6.5	6.0	5.2	23.0	29.0	17.4	1.5	78.0	43.6	50.4	49.6
49657	MC BAIN	97.6	97.4	0.3	0.4	0.3	0.3	1.3	1.5	7.3	7.4	8.4	7.5	6.5	26.7	22.9	11.7	1.6	72.3	36.3	50.2	49.8
49659	MANCELONA	96.8	96.6	0.2	0.2	0.2	0.2	1.2	1.4	7.5	7.4	7.4	6.4	5.6	25.5	25.4	13.6	1.3	73.8	38.2	50.5	49.5
49660	MANISTEE	92.8	92.2	2.5	2.6	0.5	0.6	2.2	2.4	5.0	5.3	6.1	6.4	6.1	25.1	27.7	15.5	2.8	79.7	42.4	50.8	49.2
49663	MANTON	97.5	97.2	0.2	0.3	0.3	0.4	1.1	1.3	6.4	6.6	8.2	7.3	6.5	26.6	26.1	11.0	1.4	74.0	37.8	50.1	49.9
49664	MAPLE CITY	97.9	97.6	0.1	0.1	0.3	0.4	1.0	1.1	5.3	6.2	8.9	7.5	3.6	25.1	29.6	11.9	1.9	74.4	41.4	49.9	50.1
49665	MARION	98.0	97.8	0.3	0.3	0.1	0.1	1.3	1.5	6.2	6.5	7.8	7.3	6.0	25.7	25.1	14.2	1.2	75.0	39.1	50.5	49.5
49667	MERRITT	97.6	97.3	0.1	0.1	0.1	0.3	0.7	0.8	6.1	6.1	8.0	8.4	5.0	25.3	26.5	13.7	0.8	74.6	39.8	51.2	48.8
49668	MESICK	97.2	97.0	0.1	0.2	0.2	0.2	1.0	1.1	6.9	7.2	7.6	7.1	5.9	26.0	25.7	12.5	1.2	73.9	38.2	52.3	47.7
49670	NORTHPORT	93.2	92.6	0.3	0.3	0.1	0.1	6.9	7.8	3.1	3.9	6.0	5.7	4.1	16.1	34.7	23.4	3.2	83.3	51.2	49.7	50.3
49675	ONEKAMA	92.1	90.8	0.1	0.1	0.0	0.1	10.8	12.4	5.3	5.7	6.1	5.4	4.7	21.5	28.4	19.8	3.2	79.3	46.1	50.7	49.3
49676	RAPID CITY	97.4	97.2	0.1	0.1	0.3	0.4	1.2	1.4	5.3	5.5	6.2	5.8	4.9	24.2	31.3	15.3	1.5	79.2	43.9	51.0	49.0
49677	REED CITY	96.9	96.6	0.6	0.7	0.2	0.3	1.0	1.2	6.5	6.6	7.2	7.4	7.1	25.6	25.4	12.3	1.9	74.9	37.3	48.4	51.6
49679	SEARS	97.7	97.6	0.3	0.3	0.2	0.2	0.6	0.5	6.2	6.4	7.6	6.5	6.1	22.9	27.8	15.4	1.2	75.8	41.1	52.7	47.3
49680	SOUTH BOARDMAN	97.7	97.4	0.2	0.3	0.2	0.3	0.9	1.1	7.6	7.8	9.2	7.5	6.1	28.3	23.7	9.1	0.8	70.7	34.6	50.5	49.5
49682	SUTTONS BAY	82.9	82.9	0.1	0.1	0.1	0.2	5.8	6.4	5.8	6.5	8.1	7.3	5.3	21.4	30.4	13.9	1.4	74.9	42.0	50.5	49.5
49683	THOMPSONVILLE	96.6	96.4	0.1	0.1	0.1	0.1	1.8	2.0	6.1	6.8	7.6	5.9	5.0	27.7	27.7	12.4	0.8	75.9	39.2	50.8	49.3
49684	TRAVERSE CITY	96.5	96.1	0.3	0.4	0.6	0.7	1.6	1.8	6.2	6.3	7.2	6.8	6.9	27.3	26.5	10.8	1.9	75.9	38.2	48.2	51.8
49686	TRAVERSE CITY	96.8	96.4	0.3	0.3	0.6	0.7	1.6	1.8	5.4	5.7	6.8	6.7	6.1	25.7	27.7	13.8	2.2	78.1	41.0	48.3	51.7
49688	TUSTIN	98.1	98.0	0.1	0.1	0.3	0.4	0.7	0.7	6.5	6.6	7.4	7.7	6.3	26.9	26.0	11.4	1.2	74.4	37.5	51.7	48.3
49689	WELLSTON	94.7	94.3	1.9	2.1	0.2	0.2	0.8	0.9	5.3	5.7	6.3	6.4	5.5	24.4	29.9	15.2	1.4	78.7	42.9	53.5	46.5
49690	WILLIAMSBURG	97.1	96.8	0.3	0.3	0.5	0.6	1.8	2.0	5.0	6.1	7.5	6.6	4.6	24.7	31.3	12.4	1.8	76.6	42.5	49.6	50.5
49701	MACKINAW CITY	92.9	92.5	0.3	0.4	0.0	0.1	0.3	0.4	5.6	5.5	5.4	4.4	4.3	23.0	32.9	16.4	2.4	80.5	46.0	48.6	51.4
49705	AFTON	96.5	96.5	0.6	0.5	0.0	0.0	0.3	0.3	6.7	6.7	7.0	6.0	5.3	24.8	28.4	14.3	0.9	75.3	40.9	51.2	48.8
49706	ALANSON	94.7	94.5	0.3	0.3	0.2	0.3	0.7	0.7	6.7	6.9	7.3	6.0	4.9	28.2	28.0	10.7	1.2	75.3	38.5	50.6	49.4
49707	ALPENA	98.2	97.9	0.3	0.3	0.4	0.5	0.6	0.6	5.6	5.7	6.2	6.7	6.6	23.9	27.1	15.6	2.6	78.5	42.0	48.3	51.7
49709	ATLANTA	98.0	97.8	0.4	0.5	0.2	0.2	0.5	0.6	4.5	4.7	5.2	5.4	5.1	18.8	31.9	22.4	2.0	82.1	49.2	48.9	51.1
49710	BARBEAU	83.2	82.6	0.6	0.9	0.3	0.3	0.6	0.9	5.7	5.7	6.3	5.4	4.3	24.6	30.9	16.0	1.1	78.9	43.8	51.4	48.6
	MICHIGAN	80.2	79.2	14.2	14.4	1.8	2.3	3.3	3.6	6.8	6.9	7.4	7.1	6.9	28.1	24.6	10.8	1.6	74.9	36.5	49.1	50.9
	UNITED STATES	75.1	73.6	12.3	12.5	3.8	4.2	12.5	14.1	6.9	6.7	7.2	7.0	7.3	28.6	23.8	10.8	1.7	75.1	36.0	49.1	50.9

ZIP CODE #	POST OFFICE NAME	2004 Per Capita Income	2004 HH Income Base	2004 Household Income Distribution (%) Less than $25,000	$25,000 to $49,999	$50,000 to $99,999	$100,000 to $149,999	$150,000 or More	Median Household Income 2004	2009	2004 National Centile	2004 State Centile	2004 Home Value Base	2004 Home Value Distribution (%) Less than $50,000	$50,000 to $89,999	$90,000 to $174,999	$175,000 to $399,999	$400,000 or More	2004 Median Home Value
49442	MUSKEGON	15797	16208	37.5	32.3	25.4	3.8	1.1	33511	36886	22	11	11043	26.9	37.2	32.6	3.2	0.1	74705
49444	MUSKEGON	18780	10342	35.7	29.6	27.2	5.2	2.4	36147	39526	32	20	7543	28.4	23.0	38.6	8.3	1.7	86733
49445	MUSKEGON	23968	8067	17.1	29.1	39.1	11.0	3.8	53005	57284	77	74	7130	6.7	15.0	55.5	19.8	3.1	122346
49446	NEW ERA	19033	839	24.1	32.7	34.6	6.7	2.0	44939	47365	61	53	729	15.1	27.4	39.9	15.5	2.1	103987
49448	NUNICA	21368	1265	21.0	32.2	36.1	7.6	3.2	47161	51621	66	59	1098	8.2	12.0	49.4	25.0	5.5	138087
49449	PENTWATER	24818	1255	24.1	29.7	34.3	8.9	3.0	46172	51570	64	57	1097	7.5	12.9	44.6	27.6	7.5	133965
49450	PULLMAN	13670	1172	32.9	34.8	27.7	3.6	1.0	35959	38918	31	19	874	24.6	26.5	35.8	12.1	0.9	88734
49451	RAVENNA	18971	2094	23.3	33.4	34.6	6.7	2.0	45576	49247	63	54	1823	7.6	18.6	54.6	18.1	1.2	119025
49452	ROTHBURY	17321	762	29.9	36.0	28.5	3.2	2.5	38545	41526	41	28	659	23.5	26.4	37.0	12.3	0.8	90109
49453	SAUGATUCK	34283	1531	21.3	31.7	30.8	9.6	6.7	47386	52135	67	60	1190	6.6	3.8	31.3	43.3	15.0	195122
49454	SCOTTVILLE	18539	1738	30.5	32.6	29.3	6.2	1.4	40350	43235	47	36	1432	14.3	26.4	42.3	14.9	2.1	102000
49455	SHELBY	19158	2074	28.9	33.8	29.3	5.1	2.9	39594	42277	45	33	1707	16.3	31.1	36.4	13.7	2.6	93321
49456	SPRING LAKE	31183	7727	16.8	30.1	32.9	11.0	9.3	53265	58040	77	74	6098	8.9	6.8	40.9	34.9	8.6	162373
49457	TWIN LAKE	19225	3630	24.0	29.9	37.7	7.4	1.0	47194	51277	67	59	3205	16.4	22.0	46.5	14.4	0.7	106228
49459	WALKERVILLE	15040	540	39.1	33.5	24.1	2.8	0.6	32189	35000	18	8	441	27.4	28.6	32.0	11.1	0.9	83537
49460	WEST OLIVE	25099	2958	10.0	24.0	48.2	11.8	6.1	63066	69873	87	87	2736	10.2	9.9	31.0	40.7	8.3	172866
49461	WHITEHALL	23911	3299	20.9	26.8	37.9	9.7	4.7	51785	55276	75	70	2728	6.9	16.5	52.6	21.6	2.4	122998
49464	ZEELAND	22193	8613	15.2	26.7	43.6	11.0	3.7	56057	61498	81	78	7433	6.1	10.3	47.9	33.7	2.1	157163
49503	GRAND RAPIDS	18264	14961	38.0	32.8	22.5	4.4	2.3	33349	37435	22	11	6409	13.5	33.7	38.7	11.5	2.5	93220
49504	GRAND RAPIDS	20750	15436	26.6	32.1	32.3	6.6	2.4	43068	48955	56	46	9882	7.3	26.7	56.5	9.3	0.3	106376
49505	GRAND RAPIDS	21961	13002	23.7	33.5	33.4	7.1	2.4	44212	49462	59	50	8624	2.6	18.6	67.8	10.3	0.7	114299
49506	GRAND RAPIDS	29551	12272	20.5	24.2	32.3	11.5	11.6	55798	61401	80	77	9018	3.3	14.2	42.4	32.3	7.9	154795
49507	GRAND RAPIDS	15693	12829	31.5	29.9	30.4	6.3	2.0	39778	44769	45	33	8175	12.2	37.4	47.1	3.1	0.2	90480
49508	GRAND RAPIDS	25381	15797	19.4	27.8	36.2	11.9	4.8	52415	57747	76	72	10070	1.7	5.4	67.4	24.7	0.9	149437
49509	GRAND RAPIDS	21819	22243	21.3	33.2	36.2	6.9	2.4	46419	51385	65	57	14035	7.0	17.0	65.8	9.9	0.3	111456
49512	GRAND RAPIDS	28773	6584	23.9	33.5	29.5	8.6	4.6	44261	47321	59	50	2293	8.9	4.6	47.8	37.2	1.5	158999
49525	GRAND RAPIDS	26645	10608	17.9	26.4	36.6	12.5	6.7	54820	61343	79	76	8248	3.0	5.1	56.2	30.9	4.9	153912
49544	GRAND RAPIDS	24099	11894	20.3	29.1	37.1	10.0	3.4	50493	53754	73	67	8195	8.8	7.7	53.5	28.2	1.9	144341
49546	GRAND RAPIDS	34537	12543	19.1	23.0	28.7	14.6	14.6	61142	65223	85	85	8916	0.5	2.3	33.4	51.6	12.3	209038
49548	GRAND RAPIDS	19467	12376	22.1	36.6	35.6	4.7	1.1	43629	49047	58	48	9264	28.4	21.2	48.1	2.3	0.1	90444
49601	CADILLAC	20903	8423	29.6	33.6	27.0	7.1	2.7	39475	42131	44	32	6473	16.2	25.6	37.9	17.7	2.6	100688
49612	ALDEN	22958	500	25.6	34.2	32.6	5.4	2.2	43028	46755	56	46	433	10.2	20.3	43.7	20.3	5.5	118167
49613	ARCADIA	24055	392	28.8	36.2	26.0	5.6	3.3	37827	41628	39	26	344	8.1	24.7	39.0	23.6	4.7	117544
49614	BEAR LAKE	19957	1163	30.0	35.3	28.3	4.5	1.9	38732	42120	42	29	1015	12.9	20.1	41.2	22.0	3.8	115554
49615	BELLAIRE	24328	1922	25.5	32.1	31.7	6.9	3.8	43063	46954	56	46	1651	4.2	14.5	45.3	26.2	9.8	144480
49616	BENZONIA	17775	973	33.7	37.2	23.6	3.9	1.5	35338	38353	29	15	780	12.4	20.8	41.8	19.5	5.5	113908
49617	BEULAH	21287	1487	27.1	35.6	29.1	5.3	2.9	40068	43248	46	34	1277	7.7	17.2	38.2	27.7	9.2	138587
49618	BOON	17727	247	30.8	34.8	27.5	4.9	2.0	38192	42205	40	27	217	19.8	27.7	37.3	13.8	1.4	93438
49619	BRETHREN	18975	444	27.3	36.3	29.3	5.2	2.0	39204	42525	43	31	398	16.1	23.9	38.9	19.1	2.0	100000
49620	BUCKLEY	17217	820	22.6	41.5	31.1	3.3	1.6	41308	45342	51	41	698	14.9	18.9	45.6	19.3	1.3	116189
49621	CEDAR	24652	1148	18.5	32.0	37.0	8.7	3.8	49670	54027	71	65	994	1.5	6.5	39.9	39.6	12.4	179950
49622	CENTRAL LAKE	22857	1156	25.3	33.6	32.1	6.8	2.3	43531	47140	57	47	973	6.5	21.6	40.8	22.5	8.6	126082
49623	CHASE	16113	544	35.1	32.4	26.3	4.8	1.5	36654	39427	34	21	464	22.0	33.0	35.6	8.6	0.9	82333
49625	COPEMISH	15860	500	30.0	42.2	24.2	3.4	0.2	35413	39047	29	16	426	20.4	30.1	33.6	15.3	0.7	89394
49629	ELK RAPIDS	26517	1074	27.6	30.8	29.1	8.0	4.6	40085	43767	46	34	861	4.5	7.0	34.7	36.5	17.3	189254
49630	EMPIRE	29562	630	18.9	36.8	31.9	8.1	4.3	44884	51535	61	52	535	0.8	6.5	32.9	36.8	23.0	203125
49631	EVART	17515	2588	34.1	36.1	24.1	3.7	2.0	35555	38190	30	16	2023	19.1	30.6	37.3	11.4	1.6	90419
49632	FALMOUTH	18398	492	28.7	40.2	25.0	4.1	2.0	37838	40542	39	26	422	16.4	33.9	37.7	10.2	1.9	89714
49633	FIFE LAKE	20041	1596	27.4	37.4	28.2	4.6	2.4	40032	43280	46	34	1404	15.0	28.4	41.2	13.5	2.0	102083
49635	FRANKFORT	22685	1760	31.4	32.8	27.4	5.2	3.2	37457	40817	37	25	1408	7.6	15.7	42.8	26.8	7.2	137054
49636	GLEN ARBOR	36035	159	18.9	27.7	33.3	12.6	7.6	53242	63799	77	74	146	0.0	2.1	11.0	32.9	54.1	454545
49637	GRAWN	18026	1329	20.8	39.1	34.8	5.0	0.2	44580	49503	60	52	1114	11.0	24.2	48.7	15.5	0.6	107427
49638	HARRIETTA	15265	411	33.8	39.7	24.1	2.4	0.0	34104	37700	24	12	349	24.6	35.5	33.8	5.7	0.3	78030
49639	HERSEY	17670	1061	28.8	36.5	29.0	4.0	1.7	40310	43022	47	35	884	14.9	30.9	41.5	11.1	1.6	95606
49640	HONOR	22909	654	24.8	38.1	29.5	5.1	2.6	40206	42913	47	35	565	5.1	13.5	45.8	31.2	4.4	144590
49642	IDLEWILD	17424	568	39.3	31.5	23.4	4.4	1.4	33126	35190	21	11	482	26.4	33.8	30.7	8.3	0.8	75581
49643	INTERLOCHEN	21639	2274	19.3	38.0	35.1	4.8	2.8	45453	49061	62	54	1987	7.8	13.7	50.9	23.7	3.9	132599
49644	IRONS	17523	919	40.8	37.5	17.4	2.8	1.4	30246	32327	13	5	799	24.8	27.0	33.7	13.3	1.3	85469
49645	KALEVA	19086	711	29.3	35.7	29.4	4.2	1.4	39195	41786	43	31	594	17.5	30.8	34.9	15.3	1.5	92000
49646	KALKASKA	18321	3452	29.9	36.3	27.9	4.7	1.2	38062	40966	39	27	2798	15.5	23.1	49.8	10.7	1.0	102671
49648	KEWADIN	26922	914	21.0	34.1	31.7	8.5	4.6	46043	51388	64	56	815	4.4	7.6	35.1	29.5	23.4	187772
49649	KINGSLEY	18563	2200	19.3	35.0	37.0	6.5	2.3	46423	50870	65	57	1880	12.9	12.0	51.6	21.8	1.8	128159
49650	LAKE ANN	21433	1064	18.3	35.2	36.8	7.0	2.7	47465	50727	67	60	973	5.1	8.1	57.3	27.8	1.8	145272
49651	LAKE CITY	18801	3253	31.5	37.8	24.9	3.8	2.0	36282	39080	33	20	2689	16.9	28.6	38.6	14.5	1.3	97319
49653	LAKE LEELANAU	26594	876	17.6	34.0	35.4	7.9	5.1	48724	55087	70	63	747	2.5	4.0	30.3	41.9	21.3	226899
49654	LELAND	41473	279	11.1	29.0	36.6	15.4	7.9	59786	69085	84	84	248	1.2	2.0	14.9	47.2	34.7	317391
49655	LEROY	18100	1193	29.3	35.3	29.7	4.7	1.0	38352	42099	41	28	1079	19.6	29.0	38.7	10.8	2.0	91845
49656	LUTHER	17419	849	39.3	33.3	21.6	4.2	1.5	31839	34130	17	8	736	34.4	25.1	30.2	8.8	1.5	72800
49657	MC BAIN	17739	1368	24.6	37.3	30.9	4.8	2.6	41392	44006	51	41	1171	10.4	28.4	45.0	13.9	2.3	105550
49659	MANCELONA	17024	2815	32.6	36.3	26.4	3.2	1.5	36285	38773	33	20	2334	19.2	30.2	37.4	12.0	1.2	90800
49660	MANISTEE	19794	6175	33.0	32.5	27.9	4.1	2.5	37385	40193	37	25	4693	10.6	35.0	37.1	15.8	1.5	95590
49663	MANTON	16867	2085	30.6	36.5	26.6	4.7	1.7	37009	39971	35	23	1753	19.2	28.5	39.5	12.4	0.5	93432
49664	MAPLE CITY	25789	907	20.0	32.8	33.9	9.4	4.1	47632	51908	67	60	790	3.7	7.1	33.9	39.9	15.4	188291
49665	MARION	17056	1844	34.9	34.9	25.3	2.9	2.1	34283	37658	25	13	1525	21.8	33.4	32.9	10.8	1.2	84142
49667	MERRITT	17400	275	32.4	38.6	23.6	3.6	1.8	36641	39411	34	21	231	19.9	27.7	38.1	12.6	1.7	92750
49668	MESICK	16732	1528	32.3	37.3	25.7	3.3	1.4	36525	40461	34	21	1327	22.4	27.4	37.6	11.4	1.2	90260
49670	NORTHPORT	28959	1016	21.2	31.1	32.9	8.7	6.2	48222	52943	69	62	858	3.9	6.6	25.2	39.6	24.7	230342
49675	ONEKAMA	24395	530	31.1	27.9	29.3	7.0	4.7	39588	41895	45	33	441	9.1	17.7	39.9	21.5	11.8	124457
49676	RAPID CITY	24356	1628	23.0	35.6	30.4	7.1	3.9	44347	48032	60	51	1431	7.1	17.5	37.7	25.8	11.9	140558
49677	REED CITY	18514	2274	30.8	33.3	29.4	5.2	1.4	38535	40515	41	28	1795	15.6	32.2	42.4	8.7	1.1	92883
49679	SEARS	16552	506	35.2	34.8	25.7	3.0	1.4	34836	37329	27	14	436	21.3	28.7	39.0	9.9	1.2	90000
49680	SOUTH BOARDMAN	16549	715	26.0	41.1	26.9	5.3	0.7	39275	41978	44	31	622	14.6	30.9	42.1	11.4	1.0	96087
49682	SUTTONS BAY	27117	1841	19.3	25.7	38.4	10.1	6.6	54305	58950	79	75	1554	3.9	3.7	29.1	42.7	20.7	220207
49683	THOMPSONVILLE	18110	828	28.6	40.3	27.2	2.9	1.0	38632	41589	42	29	728	16.1	24.6	41.5	16.8	1.1	105252
49684	TRAVERSE CITY	25625	14499	20.7	31.4	34.0	8.6	5.3	48231	52374	69	62	11026	6.2	7.3	43.6	36.9	6.0	163126
49686	TRAVERSE CITY	28617	13125	22.3	32.3	29.8	8.9	6.7	45946	50535	64	56	10134	6.5	9.3	41.1	33.4	9.7	162736
49688	TUSTIN	18147	929	27.9	35.4	29.9	5.2	1.6	39953	42381	46	34	792	19.8	28.4	37.3	12.4	2.2	92456
49689	WELLSTON	20818	780	32.2	36.8	25.4	3.7	1.9	35741	39530	31	17	663	25.5	28.2	36.2	8.6	1.5	84302
49690	WILLIAMSBURG	26650	2637	16.3	30.6	34.5	12.0	6.6	52491	58304	76	72	2298	1.4	4.9	37.8	44.7	11.2	186770
49701	MACKINAW CITY	25729	487	28.5	34.1	29.6	4.9	2.9	40305	44611	47	35	405	5.4	19.0	40.5	27.4	7.7	133446
49705	AFTON	15513	266	31.6	40.6	21.8	3.8	2.3	35801	38430	31	18	228	13.2	29.4	43.0	11.4	3.1	100000
49706	ALANSON	21431	2002	24.5	38.2	29.3	5.6	2.4	41752	46840	52	41	1674	9.7	16.9	48.8	22.0	2.6	118168
49707	ALPENA	20271	10269	34.0	31.3	28.5	4.3	1.8	37182	40152	36	24	7908	9.7	30.7	45.3	13.3	1.0	99512
49709	ATLANTA	19620	1579	36.2	37.6	21.3	2.9	2.0	32408	34800	19	9	1347	18.2	27.8	39.4	13.4	1.3	95000
49710	BARBEAU	21788	167	28.1	37.1	29.9	4.2	0.6	40168	45291	47	35	152	9.2	29.6	42.8	17.8	0.7	105000
	MICHIGAN	25281		23.8	27.4	32.3	10.9	5.5	48729	54505				10.7	16.0	40.3	28.0	5.0	134769
	UNITED STATES	25866		24.7	27.1	30.8	10.9	6.5	48124	56710				10.9	15.0	33.7	30.1	10.4	145905

ZIP CODE #	POST OFFICE NAME	FINANCIAL SERVICES: Auto Loan	FINANCIAL SERVICES: Home Loan	FINANCIAL SERVICES: Invest-ments	FINANCIAL SERVICES: Retire-ment Plans	THE HOME: Home Improvements: Home Repair	THE HOME: Home Improvements: Lawn & Garden	THE HOME: Furnishings: Comput-ers & Hard-ware	THE HOME: Furnishings: Major Appli-ances	THE HOME: Furnishings: TV, Radio, Sound Equip-ment	THE HOME: Furnishings: Furni-ture	ENTERTAINMENT: Dine out/ Carry out	ENTERTAINMENT: Sports Equip-ment	ENTERTAINMENT: Fees & Tickets	ENTERTAINMENT: Toys & Games	ENTERTAINMENT: Travel	ENTERTAINMENT: Cable TV	PERSONAL: Apparel & Services	PERSONAL: Auto Repairs	PERSONAL: Health Insur-ance	PERSONAL: Pets & Supplies
49442	MUSKEGON	60	55	54	54	55	61	58	58	59	57	73	68	56	73	57	59	71	59	60	67
49444	MUSKEGON	69	63	62	61	64	71	65	67	69	65	84	76	64	82	65	70	81	67	70	77
49445	MUSKEGON	89	95	93	92	96	100	88	91	87	87	109	106	91	113	90	88	106	88	91	106
49446	NEW ERA	85	73	54	68	78	85	68	77	73	68	89	91	65	89	71	76	84	76	85	100
49448	NUNICA	87	84	71	81	87	92	77	83	79	77	97	99	77	100	79	80	93	81	86	104
49449	PENTWATER	95	75	52	69	84	94	72	85	81	72	96	100	65	95	76	86	89	84	99	114
49450	PULLMAN	76	58	34	52	62	69	55	65	62	56	74	77	49	71	56	65	69	64	74	87
49451	RAVENNA	87	76	58	73	80	87	73	80	77	72	94	94	71	95	74	79	89	78	86	100
49452	ROTHBURY	79	63	43	60	67	76	63	70	69	63	83	82	58	80	63	71	77	69	79	89
49453	SAUGATUCK	114	95	71	91	101	114	95	105	103	93	124	121	89	122	96	106	116	104	117	130
49454	SCOTTVILLE	79	64	45	62	70	77	62	71	68	62	81	84	58	81	64	70	76	69	79	92
49455	SHELBY	86	69	49	65	75	84	68	77	75	68	90	90	63	88	69	78	84	76	87	99
49456	SPRING LAKE	108	110	107	109	112	118	106	109	105	105	130	127	106	132	107	105	126	108	109	126
49457	TWIN LAKE	83	74	56	70	77	83	69	76	73	69	89	90	67	89	70	74	84	74	81	96
49459	WALKERVILLE	65	53	38	50	57	64	52	59	57	51	68	68	48	67	53	59	64	58	67	75
49460	WEST OLIVE	110	116	108	115	115	117	106	110	103	108	129	129	108	130	107	101	126	108	104	127
49461	WHITEHALL	102	84	58	79	91	100	81	91	88	80	105	108	76	105	83	91	99	90	103	119
49464	ZEELAND	98	97	88	96	97	101	92	95	91	92	113	112	91	113	92	90	109	94	94	112
49503	GRAND RAPIDS	58	52	63	55	52	56	63	58	63	61	79	70	60	77	59	60	77	63	56	64
49504	GRAND RAPIDS	71	72	79	72	72	78	76	74	76	73	94	86	76	95	75	75	91	75	74	81
49505	GRAND RAPIDS	69	73	82	73	72	77	76	73	75	74	93	87	77	96	75	73	91	75	71	80
49506	GRAND RAPIDS	108	118	140	121	116	122	118	114	113	117	143	134	122	144	118	111	141	115	107	126
49507	GRAND RAPIDS	66	64	72	64	63	67	69	67	69	69	87	78	68	86	67	68	86	69	64	74
49508	GRAND RAPIDS	90	93	102	97	91	94	94	92	91	95	114	110	95	113	92	86	112	94	84	102
49509	GRAND RAPIDS	75	77	82	79	76	79	79	77	77	78	96	92	79	97	77	74	94	78	72	85
49512	GRAND RAPIDS	84	80	91	87	77	81	86	82	83	87	105	98	84	101	81	78	103	85	74	91
49525	GRAND RAPIDS	95	108	115	109	106	108	102	101	97	102	122	118	106	126	103	94	121	99	93	112
49544	GRAND RAPIDS	86	86	88	88	86	89	87	86	85	87	106	103	86	106	85	82	104	87	81	98
49546	GRAND RAPIDS	121	131	149	136	129	135	129	126	124	130	156	146	133	155	128	120	154	127	118	139
49548	GRAND RAPIDS	73	69	63	68	70	74	69	71	70	69	87	84	67	86	68	69	83	72	71	83
49601	CADILLAC	79	70	59	68	73	81	70	75	73	69	89	87	67	89	70	75	85	74	81	91
49612	ALDEN	88	71	50	65	79	88	67	79	75	66	89	93	61	88	71	79	83	78	92	107
49613	ARCADIA	88	69	47	62	78	88	65	79	74	65	88	92	58	86	70	79	81	77	93	108
49614	BEAR LAKE	83	63	41	58	72	81	61	73	69	60	81	86	54	80	64	73	75	72	87	100
49615	BELLAIRE	98	77	53	70	87	97	73	87	82	72	97	102	66	96	77	87	91	86	103	119
49616	BENZONIA	65	58	54	57	62	68	58	63	61	57	74	73	55	72	59	62	70	63	67	76
49617	BEULAH	84	69	51	65	75	84	67	77	73	66	88	89	62	87	69	77	82	76	87	99
49618	BOON	78	64	45	59	70	78	60	70	66	59	79	82	55	79	63	70	74	69	80	94
49619	BRETHREN	83	62	39	57	71	80	60	73	68	59	80	86	52	79	63	72	74	71	86	100
49620	BUCKLEY	77	66	50	64	69	76	64	70	68	64	83	82	62	83	65	70	78	69	77	87
49621	CEDAR	91	90	80	86	94	99	82	90	84	82	103	105	81	106	86	86	99	87	93	111
49622	CENTRAL LAKE	91	75	53	69	82	91	70	82	77	70	93	96	65	93	74	81	87	80	94	110
49623	CHASE	77	55	30	49	62	71	53	65	62	53	73	77	46	70	55	67	67	64	79	91
49625	COPEMISH	75	52	26	45	59	67	50	62	59	51	70	74	43	67	51	64	64	61	76	87
49629	ELK RAPIDS	100	76	48	69	86	97	72	88	82	72	97	103	64	96	76	87	90	86	104	121
49630	EMPIRE	108	86	60	78	96	107	81	96	91	80	108	113	74	107	86	96	101	95	112	130
49631	EVART	73	58	39	52	64	72	55	65	62	55	74	76	50	74	58	67	69	64	77	88
49632	FALMOUTH	78	62	44	57	69	78	60	70	67	59	79	82	54	78	63	70	74	69	82	93
49633	FIFE LAKE	80	66	48	63	71	80	64	73	70	64	84	84	60	84	66	73	79	71	82	93
49635	FRANKFORT	84	64	44	60	72	83	65	75	73	63	87	87	58	84	67	78	80	75	90	98
49636	GLEN ARBOR	128	101	69	91	113	127	95	114	107	94	127	134	85	126	101	115	118	113	135	156
49637	GRAWN	77	69	53	66	70	75	65	71	67	66	82	83	61	79	65	67	79	71	73	87
49638	HARRIETTA	66	51	35	46	58	65	49	58	55	48	65	68	43	64	52	59	61	58	69	80
49639	HERSEY	80	60	36	54	66	75	58	68	66	58	79	81	52	76	59	70	73	67	80	92
49640	HONOR	85	66	45	60	75	84	63	76	71	62	84	88	56	83	67	76	78	74	89	103
49642	IDLEWILD	71	53	33	47	60	68	51	62	58	50	69	72	45	67	53	62	64	61	74	85
49643	INTERLOCHEN	85	76	59	73	80	86	71	79	75	71	92	93	69	93	73	77	87	77	84	100
49644	IRONS	62	49	33	44	55	62	46	56	52	46	62	65	41	61	49	56	58	55	66	76
49645	KALEVA	76	57	36	54	64	74	59	68	66	57	78	78	52	75	60	70	72	68	81	89
49646	KALKASKA	73	60	44	57	65	73	59	67	65	59	78	77	55	77	61	68	73	66	76	85
49648	KEWADIN	107	84	57	76	95	106	79	96	90	79	106	112	71	105	85	96	99	94	113	131
49649	KINGSLEY	88	78	60	75	82	87	74	81	77	74	94	95	71	93	75	78	90	80	85	101
49650	LAKE ANN	84	82	74	81	83	86	78	81	77	78	96	97	77	97	78	76	93	80	80	97
49651	LAKE CITY	79	60	38	54	68	76	57	69	65	57	77	81	51	76	60	70	72	68	82	95
49653	LAKE LEELANAU	114	89	59	81	100	112	85	101	96	84	113	119	76	112	90	102	105	100	120	138
49654	LELAND	146	115	78	104	129	145	108	130	123	107	145	153	97	143	115	131	135	128	154	178
49655	LEROY	79	64	45	59	71	78	60	71	67	60	80	83	56	80	63	70	75	69	81	95
49656	LUTHER	70	53	34	48	60	68	50	61	58	50	68	72	45	67	53	62	63	60	73	84
49657	MC BAIN	84	69	47	65	75	82	66	75	72	65	86	90	61	86	68	74	81	74	85	99
49659	MANCELONA	77	58	36	53	64	73	56	66	64	56	76	78	50	74	58	67	70	65	78	90
49660	MANISTEE	69	63	55	60	66	74	63	67	67	61	82	77	62	83	65	70	77	67	74	80
49663	MANTON	74	63	46	59	67	73	59	67	64	59	78	79	57	78	61	66	73	65	74	86
49664	MAPLE CITY	105	90	67	84	97	105	84	95	91	84	109	113	80	111	87	94	103	93	106	125
49665	MARION	76	56	33	51	63	71	55	65	63	55	74	77	49	72	56	66	68	64	77	88
49667	MERRITT	79	62	42	56	70	78	58	70	66	58	78	82	52	77	62	71	73	69	83	96
49668	MESICK	75	57	36	52	63	71	54	65	62	54	74	76	49	72	56	65	68	64	76	88
49670	NORTHPORT	112	88	60	79	99	111	83	100	94	82	111	117	74	109	88	100	103	98	118	136
49675	ONEKAMA	94	73	50	67	82	93	70	84	80	69	94	98	63	93	74	85	87	83	99	113
49676	RAPID CITY	100	77	50	71	87	97	73	88	83	73	98	104	65	97	77	88	91	87	104	121
49677	REED CITY	73	62	48	58	65	73	62	67	67	61	81	79	59	80	62	69	76	67	75	84
49679	SEARS	75	54	31	48	61	70	52	64	61	52	72	75	45	69	54	65	66	63	77	89
49680	SOUTH BOARDMAN	73	66	51	63	68	72	61	67	64	62	78	79	59	78	62	65	75	66	70	84
49682	SUTTONS BAY	109	98	83	95	105	115	95	104	99	94	121	121	91	120	98	102	114	102	113	129
49683	THOMPSONVILLE	70	59	44	57	63	69	58	64	62	58	75	75	54	73	59	63	70	64	70	81
49684	TRAVERSE CITY	87	95	100	95	93	96	90	91	87	91	109	106	92	111	91	85	107	90	85	102
49686	TRAVERSE CITY	94	97	101	97	97	104	95	97	94	95	117	111	95	116	96	93	113	96	95	109
49688	TUSTIN	77	65	48	62	69	77	63	70	68	62	82	82	60	82	64	70	77	69	78	89
49689	WELLSTON	82	65	44	58	73	82	61	73	69	60	82	86	55	81	65	74	76	72	87	101
49690	WILLIAMSBURG	98	101	99	100	104	108	94	99	93	94	115	116	95	118	97	93	112	97	99	117
49701	MACKINAW CITY	91	71	49	64	80	90	67	81	76	67	90	95	60	89	72	81	84	80	96	111
49705	AFTON	74	58	40	52	65	74	55	66	62	54	73	77	49	73	58	66	68	65	78	90
49706	ALANSON	85	72	55	69	78	84	69	79	74	69	89	93	64	89	71	76	84	78	86	101
49707	ALPENA	71	63	54	60	66	74	63	68	68	62	82	78	61	82	65	70	77	67	75	82
49709	ATLANTA	73	57	39	51	64	72	54	65	61	53	72	76	48	71	57	65	67	64	77	89
49710	BARBEAU	77	61	42	55	68	77	57	69	65	57	77	81	51	76	61	69	71	68	81	94
	MICHIGAN	91	91	93	89	91	98	90	91	91	90	113	106	90	113	90	91	109	91	92	105
	UNITED STATES	100	100	100	100	100	100	100	100	100	100	100	100	100	100	100	100	100	100	100	100

POPULATION CHANGE

ZIP CODE		COUNTY FIPS CODE	POPULATION			2000-2004 ANNUAL RATE		HOUSEHOLDS					FAMILIES		
#	POST OFFICE NAME		2000	2004	2009	% Rate	State Centile	2000	2004	2009	% Annual Rate 2000-2004	2004 Average HH Size	2000	2004	% Annual Rate 2000-2004
49712	BOYNE CITY	029	7779	8426	9163	1.9	88	3151	3471	3839	2.3	2.42	2170	2363	2.0
49713	BOYNE FALLS	029	2075	2271	2473	2.2	91	795	894	994	2.8	2.52	589	652	2.4
49715	BRIMLEY	033	2491	2700	2877	1.9	89	977	1088	1186	2.6	2.48	707	774	2.2
49716	BRUTUS	031	835	859	910	0.7	50	331	346	372	1.1	2.48	240	247	0.7
49718	CARP LAKE	047	723	767	831	1.4	77	317	343	379	1.9	2.23	216	230	1.5
49719	CEDARVILLE	097	1692	1835	2077	1.9	89	750	833	965	2.5	2.20	529	579	2.2
49720	CHARLEVOIX	029	9694	10189	10886	1.2	71	3972	4260	4637	1.7	2.36	2757	2914	1.3
49721	CHEBOYGAN	031	15430	15945	16654	0.8	56	6326	6707	7170	1.4	2.33	4344	4539	1.0
49724	DAFTER	033	1040	1029	1056	-0.3	14	383	388	407	0.3	2.65	285	284	-0.1
49725	DE TOUR VILLAGE	033	865	898	935	0.9	60	403	428	456	1.4	2.10	260	271	1.0
49726	DRUMMOND ISLAND	033	984	993	1017	0.2	30	463	478	500	0.8	2.08	304	308	0.3
49727	EAST JORDAN	009	7503	7990	8742	1.5	79	2778	3004	3344	1.9	2.62	2053	2192	1.6
49728	ECKERMAN	033	255	252	259	-0.3	13	104	106	112	0.5	2.38	71	71	0.0
49729	ELLSWORTH	009	1564	1670	1867	1.6	82	603	658	751	2.1	2.50	463	500	1.8
49730	ELMIRA	009	2142	2452	2806	3.2	98	772	906	1060	3.8	2.70	596	691	3.5
49733	FREDERIC	039	1607	1764	1897	2.2	92	645	728	801	2.9	2.39	471	525	2.6
49735	GAYLORD	137	18696	20232	22216	1.9	88	7302	7959	8932	2.4	2.52	5194	5680	2.1
49736	GOETZVILLE	033	643	745	822	3.5	99	302	358	403	4.1	2.08	209	244	3.7
49738	GRAYLING	039	10575	10928	11327	0.8	56	4145	4384	4645	1.3	2.39	2926	3055	1.0
49740	HARBOR SPRINGS	047	7135	7674	8300	1.7	85	2964	3262	3605	2.3	2.29	2025	2192	1.9
49743	HAWKS	141	982	1025	1058	1.0	66	381	410	435	1.7	2.48	271	287	1.4
49744	HERRON	007	988	969	949	-0.5	9	366	367	368	0.1	2.62	287	285	-0.2
49746	HILLMAN	119	4005	4261	4532	1.5	78	1629	1774	1931	2.0	2.34	1124	1210	1.8
49747	HUBBARD LAKE	007	1739	1802	1868	0.8	59	702	751	802	1.6	2.39	524	551	1.2
49749	INDIAN RIVER	031	4276	4516	4755	1.3	74	1868	2015	2167	1.8	2.23	1305	1386	1.4
49751	JOHANNESBURG	137	2079	2167	2324	1.0	65	869	925	1012	1.5	2.34	646	678	1.1
49752	KINROSS	033	406	419	436	0.7	54	157	166	177	1.3	2.52	114	119	1.0
49753	LACHINE	007	1996	2020	2006	0.3	33	785	813	826	0.8	2.47	592	607	0.6
49755	LEVERING	047	1975	2180	2392	2.4	93	783	884	989	2.9	2.45	552	614	2.5
49756	LEWISTON	135	4241	4620	5020	2.0	90	1932	2150	2383	2.6	2.15	1291	1416	2.2
49757	MACKINAC ISLAND	097	523	554	619	1.4	76	252	274	313	2.0	2.02	144	152	1.3
49759	MILLERSBURG	141	1775	1830	1881	0.7	53	761	808	855	1.4	2.24	539	564	1.1
49760	MORAN	097	374	436	512	3.7	99	165	197	236	4.3	2.21	117	137	3.8
49762	NAUBINWAY	097	1437	1610	1853	2.7	96	634	731	865	3.4	2.18	430	489	3.1
49765	ONAWAY	141	4155	4331	4508	1.0	65	1701	1813	1931	1.5	2.35	1158	1219	1.2
49766	OSSINEKE	007	2568	2531	2485	-0.3	12	1021	1033	1038	0.3	2.43	752	751	0.0
49768	PARADISE	033	586	580	595	-0.2	14	284	290	305	0.5	2.00	194	195	0.1
49769	PELLSTON	047	1715	1822	1957	1.4	78	558	603	659	1.8	2.97	425	454	1.6
49770	PETOSKEY	047	15568	16705	18091	1.7	84	6220	6822	7548	2.2	2.38	4068	4404	1.9
49774	PICKFORD	033	1723	1881	2042	2.1	91	659	736	815	2.6	2.56	487	537	2.3
49775	POINTE AUX PINS	097	71	75	84	1.3	74	42	45	52	1.6	1.67	17	18	1.4
49776	POSEN	141	2178	2291	2366	1.2	72	895	977	1041	2.1	2.33	632	678	1.7
49777	PRESQUE ISLE	141	1036	1048	1060	0.3	33	484	500	518	0.8	2.09	358	364	0.4
49779	ROGERS CITY	141	5185	5180	5260	0.0	22	2243	2306	2408	0.7	2.19	1481	1498	0.3
49780	RUDYARD	033	2377	2494	2617	1.1	69	930	998	1070	1.7	2.49	691	730	1.3
49781	SAINT IGNACE	097	5965	6608	7561	2.4	94	2415	2742	3216	3.0	2.36	1616	1809	2.7
49782	BEAVER ISLAND	029	551	588	632	1.5	81	258	282	309	2.1	2.09	155	166	1.6
49783	SAULT SAINTE MARIE	033	21744	22215	23120	0.5	43	7800	8162	8726	1.1	2.30	4859	5001	0.7
49788	KINCHELOE	033	5322	5496	5653	0.8	55	930	1010	1085	2.0	2.95	720	771	1.6
49792	TOWER	031	84	89	94	1.4	76	41	44	48	1.7	2.02	30	32	1.5
49795	VANDERBILT	137	1920	2122	2346	2.4	94	731	826	934	2.9	2.54	522	582	2.6
49799	WOLVERINE	031	2438	2627	2799	1.8	86	931	1027	1119	2.3	2.55	674	733	2.2
49801	IRON MOUNTAIN	043	12548	12460	12367	-0.2	17	5208	5266	5318	0.3	2.32	3409	3396	-0.1
49802	KINGSFORD	043	6626	6439	6326	-0.7	6	2792	2769	2772	-0.2	2.25	1796	1751	-0.6
49806	AU TRAIN	003	396	391	401	-0.3	13	175	178	187	0.4	2.12	117	117	0.0
49807	BARK RIVER	041	3308	3412	3465	0.7	53	1266	1343	1397	1.4	2.54	951	993	1.0
49812	CARNEY	109	1330	1327	1327	-0.1	21	547	558	570	0.5	2.30	381	383	0.1
49814	CHAMPION	103	1969	1915	1889	-0.7	7	788	787	798	0.0	2.43	593	585	-0.3
49815	CHANNING	043	529	543	547	0.6	47	219	231	238	1.3	2.35	154	160	0.9
49816	CHATHAM	003	377	387	403	0.6	47	151	160	171	1.4	2.42	105	110	1.1
49817	COOKS	153	500	517	531	0.8	57	186	197	206	1.4	2.62	138	144	1.0
49818	CORNELL	041	789	775	769	-0.4	10	311	314	320	0.2	2.46	240	239	-0.1
49820	CURTIS	097	981	1040	1162	1.4	77	433	474	545	2.2	2.14	293	316	1.8
49821	DAGGETT	109	1272	1246	1234	-0.5	9	512	513	518	0.1	2.36	355	350	-0.3
49822	DEERTON	003	310	307	315	-0.2	15	146	149	157	0.5	2.05	103	104	0.2
49825	EBEN JUNCTION	003	172	171	175	-0.1	18	71	73	77	0.7	2.33	50	50	0.0
49826	RUMELY	003	371	368	377	-0.2	16	154	157	166	0.5	2.33	108	109	0.2
49827	ENGADINE	097	297	328	375	2.4	93	121	138	161	3.1	2.33	82	92	2.7
49829	ESCANABA	041	17987	17904	17906	-0.1	19	7561	7687	7856	0.4	2.27	4722	4730	0.0
49831	FELCH	043	124	127	128	0.6	45	57	60	62	1.2	2.10	41	43	1.1
49833	LITTLE LAKE	103	294	290	286	-0.3	12	120	121	123	0.2	2.40	83	83	0.0
49834	FOSTER CITY	043	619	639	645	0.8	54	256	271	279	1.4	2.36	180	187	0.9
49835	GARDEN	041	914	931	934	0.4	40	392	411	424	1.1	2.27	275	283	0.7
49836	GERMFASK	153	491	491	499	0.0	23	198	202	210	0.5	2.32	150	151	0.2
49837	GLADSTONE	041	10023	10159	10202	0.3	35	3979	4129	4244	0.9	2.45	2845	2908	0.5
49838	GOULD CITY	097	340	361	403	1.4	78	163	178	205	2.1	1.99	110	118	1.7
49839	GRAND MARAIS	003	476	478	486	0.1	27	241	250	262	0.9	1.46	169	134	-5.3
49840	GULLIVER	153	874	882	898	0.2	30	357	370	385	0.9	2.38	271	278	0.6
49841	GWINN	103	5577	5148	5000	-1.9	0	2280	2189	2196	-1.0	2.35	1630	1546	-1.2
49847	HERMANSVILLE	109	1020	1085	1120	1.5	78	433	474	500	2.2	2.20	294	316	1.7
49848	INGALLS	109	203	213	217	1.1	69	76	82	85	1.8	2.57	48	51	1.4
49849	ISHPEMING	103	12159	12117	12046	-0.1	20	4981	5089	5202	0.5	2.33	3337	3367	0.2
49853	MC MILLAN	095	1233	1270	1300	0.7	52	524	557	584	1.5	2.23	394	413	1.1
49854	MANISTIQUE	153	6915	7027	7191	0.4	38	2828	2933	3065	0.9	2.28	1912	1956	0.5
49855	MARQUETTE	103	31862	32419	32623	0.4	39	12317	12950	13445	1.2	2.22	7187	7423	0.8
49858	MENOMINEE	109	12890	12650	12559	-0.4	10	5604	5618	5689	0.1	2.23	3571	3523	-0.3
49861	MICHIGAMME	103	1284	1280	1267	-0.1	20	600	618	630	0.7	2.06	415	423	0.5
49862	MUNISING	003	4668	4833	5056	0.8	58	1912	2024	2170	1.4	2.23	1260	1316	1.0
49866	NEGAUNEE	103	8250	8194	8141	-0.2	18	3368	3423	3490	0.4	2.35	2277	2285	0.1
49868	NEWBERRY	095	5772	5817	5891	0.2	29	1947	2006	2080	0.7	2.39	1339	1359	0.4
49870	NORWAY	043	3361	3324	3289	-0.3	13	1430	1439	1448	0.2	2.30	948	936	-0.3
49873	PERRONVILLE	109	143	158	166	2.4	93	62	71	76	3.2	2.21	43	48	2.6
49874	POWERS	109	1260	1312	1342	1.0	63	429	460	482	1.7	2.71	306	324	1.4
49876	QUINNESEC	043	1182	1202	1205	0.4	38	434	452	462	1.0	2.63	355	365	0.7
49878	RAPID RIVER	041	4378	4424	4464	0.3	32	1861	1935	2003	0.9	2.23	1320	1350	0.5
	MICHIGAN					0.6					1.0	2.52			0.6
	UNITED STATES					1.2					1.3	2.58			1.1

ZIP CODE #	POST OFFICE NAME	RACE (%) White 2000	White 2004	Black 2000	Black 2004	Asian/Pacific 2000	Asian/Pacific 2004	% Hispanic Origin 2000	% Hispanic Origin 2004	2004 AGE DISTRIBUTION (%) 0-4	5-9	10-14	15-19	20-24	25-44	45-64	65-84	85+	18+	MEDIAN AGE 2004	% 2004 Males	% 2004 Females
49712	BOYNE CITY	97.5	97.3	0.1	0.1	0.2	0.3	0.7	0.8	6.5	6.5	7.3	6.7	5.8	25.1	27.9	12.9	1.3	75.3	40.2	49.9	50.1
49713	BOYNE FALLS	97.5	97.4	0.1	0.1	0.2	0.2	0.6	0.6	6.9	7.1	7.5	6.9	4.8	28.1	25.6	12.2	1.0	74.0	38.3	50.6	49.4
49715	BRIMLEY	59.8	59.1	0.1	0.1	0.2	0.3	0.8	0.9	8.0	7.7	7.3	7.0	6.5	28.5	23.6	10.7	0.8	72.7	34.9	49.6	50.4
49716	BRUTUS	92.7	92.4	0.2	0.2	0.4	0.4	0.5	0.5	6.9	6.9	6.5	5.6	4.9	26.4	27.5	13.6	1.8	76.5	40.1	50.3	49.7
49718	CARP LAKE	93.4	93.0	0.7	0.8	0.0	0.1	0.8	0.8	5.9	5.1	7.0	5.7	4.4	24.5	33.3	12.9	1.2	78.2	43.1	51.0	49.0
49719	CEDARVILLE	92.3	92.0	0.1	0.1	0.3	0.4	0.7	0.8	4.1	4.6	5.7	5.9	3.9	20.6	32.3	20.8	2.1	81.9	48.9	50.3	49.7
49720	CHARLEVOIX	95.6	95.2	0.3	0.3	0.5	0.6	1.3	1.5	5.9	6.5	7.0	6.4	5.0	24.5	29.1	13.6	2.1	76.3	41.6	48.9	51.1
49721	CHEBOYGAN	93.8	93.4	0.2	0.3	0.3	0.3	0.8	0.9	5.9	6.2	6.4	6.0	5.3	23.9	28.0	16.1	2.2	77.6	42.4	49.3	50.7
49724	DAFTER	84.5	84.0	0.5	0.7	0.3	0.4	0.9	1.1	6.6	6.4	6.4	6.4	6.4	27.0	27.8	12.0	1.0	76.7	40.0	51.8	48.2
49725	DE TOUR VILLAGE	88.4	88.3	0.0	0.0	0.2	0.2	1.6	1.7	4.1	3.9	3.7	4.6	4.1	17.5	34.3	25.5	2.3	85.4	53.4	50.1	49.9
49726	DRUMMOND ISLAND	89.1	88.9	0.2	0.2	0.1	0.1	0.6	0.6	4.2	4.3	4.3	4.5	3.7	19.4	35.4	22.1	2.0	84.3	51.6	51.6	48.4
49727	EAST JORDAN	95.4	95.1	0.2	0.2	0.3	0.3	1.3	1.5	7.5	7.4	7.4	6.5	5.7	26.2	24.8	12.7	2.0	73.7	38.2	49.8	50.2
49728	ECKERMAN	94.1	94.1	0.0	0.0	0.0	0.0	0.4	0.4	2.4	3.2	5.2	4.8	3.2	18.3	37.3	23.8	2.0	86.1	52.9	52.8	47.2
49729	ELLSWORTH	97.5	97.3	0.3	0.2	0.3	0.3	1.4	1.6	6.9	7.0	7.4	7.1	4.9	24.4	27.5	13.3	1.6	74.0	40.2	50.4	49.6
49730	ELMIRA	96.8	96.5	0.2	0.2	0.4	0.5	0.8	1.0	6.9	7.2	7.6	6.4	5.1	27.4	26.1	12.5	0.9	74.0	38.8	50.7	49.3
49733	FREDERIC	97.5	97.3	0.1	0.1	0.2	0.2	0.9	1.0	4.7	5.2	6.8	7.2	4.8	22.8	30.6	16.7	1.3	78.3	44.1	51.7	48.3
49735	GAYLORD	97.4	97.1	0.2	0.2	0.4	0.5	0.8	1.0	6.3	6.8	8.0	7.0	5.5	26.9	25.8	12.2	1.5	74.2	38.5	49.4	50.6
49736	GOETZVILLE	91.6	91.4	0.2	0.1	0.2	0.1	1.1	1.3	5.1	5.0	4.6	4.7	5.1	19.5	34.9	18.9	2.3	82.6	48.0	50.3	49.7
49738	GRAYLING	95.8	95.4	2.0	2.1	0.3	0.4	1.0	1.1	5.7	5.7	6.7	6.9	5.9	24.4	27.6	15.4	1.8	77.6	41.6	51.3	48.7
49740	HARBOR SPRINGS	93.9	93.5	0.9	1.0	0.4	0.6	0.9	1.1	5.2	5.6	6.4	5.8	4.0	24.5	31.8	15.1	1.7	79.1	44.1	50.5	49.5
49743	HAWKS	98.5	98.4	0.2	0.3	0.1	0.1	0.3	0.2	4.8	5.3	6.1	5.8	5.6	22.0	30.8	17.7	2.2	80.3	45.4	51.0	49.0
49744	HERRON	98.6	98.5	0.3	0.3	0.0	0.1	0.6	0.8	5.8	6.1	7.2	7.2	6.1	24.1	28.1	14.1	1.3	76.0	41.1	50.7	49.3
49746	HILLMAN	98.7	98.6	0.1	0.1	0.1	0.2	0.7	0.7	4.8	5.1	5.8	5.7	5.7	20.8	29.3	19.8	3.0	80.8	46.4	49.5	50.5
49747	HUBBARD LAKE	98.6	98.5	0.1	0.1	0.1	0.1	0.5	0.6	4.7	5.2	6.4	5.7	4.7	20.6	30.6	19.9	2.0	80.1	46.6	50.8	49.2
49749	INDIAN RIVER	96.5	96.2	0.4	0.4	0.1	0.2	1.2	1.4	5.5	5.5	5.5	4.9	4.5	21.5	30.1	20.7	2.1	80.3	46.9	50.1	49.9
49751	JOHANNESBURG	98.6	98.4	0.2	0.2	0.1	0.1	0.1	0.2	5.3	5.7	6.5	5.4	4.6	23.7	30.1	17.3	1.4	79.1	44.1	51.1	48.9
49752	KINROSS	81.8	80.9	0.0	0.0	0.5	0.5	1.0	1.4	5.7	6.0	6.4	6.2	6.2	23.6	29.4	15.0	1.4	78.0	42.4	50.8	49.2
49753	LACHINE	98.4	98.2	0.3	0.3	0.1	0.2	0.9	1.0	5.0	5.3	7.1	6.5	5.5	24.1	29.7	15.4	1.6	78.7	42.9	49.7	50.4
49755	LEVERING	93.9	93.6	0.6	0.6	0.2	0.2	0.8	0.8	6.7	6.5	7.2	5.9	4.8	24.7	30.4	12.7	1.2	75.4	41.2	50.6	49.5
49756	LEWISTON	98.3	98.2	0.2	0.2	0.1	0.1	0.9	1.0	4.3	4.4	5.5	5.2	4.4	18.6	30.9	24.5	2.2	82.6	50.5	49.6	50.4
49757	MACKINAC ISLAND	75.7	75.5	0.0	0.0	0.4	0.5	0.6	0.5	3.6	3.8	6.1	6.5	7.0	27.3	32.5	12.3	0.9	82.7	42.6	51.6	48.4
49759	MILLERSBURG	98.2	98.1	0.2	0.2	0.2	0.2	0.6	0.8	4.8	4.9	5.0	5.1	4.4	20.2	31.0	22.3	2.4	82.0	49.2	49.7	50.3
49760	MORAN	73.5	73.2	0.3	0.2	0.3	0.2	1.1	1.2	4.6	5.7	7.3	6.9	5.3	25.5	28.9	14.2	1.6	78.0	42.3	50.2	49.8
49762	NAUBINWAY	84.0	83.5	0.1	0.1	0.1	0.2	1.3	1.6	4.0	4.3	5.2	5.5	4.5	20.4	32.6	21.4	2.1	82.9	49.0	50.3	49.7
49765	ONAWAY	96.8	96.5	0.3	0.3	0.3	0.3	0.8	1.0	5.7	5.7	6.1	7.2	6.3	22.6	28.0	16.3	2.1	77.8	42.6	49.8	50.2
49766	OSSINEKE	98.4	98.3	0.2	0.2	0.2	0.2	0.5	0.6	5.6	5.7	6.1	6.6	5.9	24.5	30.5	13.4	1.7	78.5	42.2	50.7	49.4
49768	PARADISE	94.0	94.1	0.0	0.0	0.0	0.0	0.5	0.5	2.8	3.1	4.8	4.8	3.1	18.5	36.7	24.0	2.2	86.2	53.2	52.2	47.8
49769	PELLSTON	90.5	90.1	1.2	1.2	0.3	0.3	0.9	1.0	8.0	8.1	8.5	6.9	5.6	28.9	24.0	9.0	1.1	70.8	35.2	51.3	48.7
49770	PETOSKEY	95.3	95.0	0.2	0.2	0.6	0.8	1.0	1.1	6.1	6.2	7.0	7.2	7.1	25.5	26.4	11.9	2.7	76.2	39.0	48.1	51.9
49774	PICKFORD	87.9	87.7	0.5	0.5	0.2	0.3	1.0	1.2	5.8	6.1	6.3	5.4	4.9	23.5	30.9	15.4	1.6	78.5	43.7	50.8	49.2
49775	POINTE AUX PINS	100.0	100.0	0.0	0.0	0.0	0.0	0.0	0.0	1.3	1.3	1.3	1.3	0.0	4.0	65.3	24.0	1.3	94.7	59.8	49.3	50.7
49776	POSEN	98.5	98.4	0.5	0.6	0.1	0.0	0.4	0.5	5.3	5.5	5.9	6.3	6.1	22.2	30.2	16.3	2.2	79.7	44.1	51.1	48.9
49777	PRESQUE ISLE	98.7	98.4	0.3	0.3	0.3	0.3	0.4	0.5	3.3	3.8	5.0	4.0	3.6	15.9	33.4	28.9	2.0	85.5	53.9	51.7	48.3
49779	ROGERS CITY	98.3	98.1	0.2	0.2	0.2	0.3	0.4	0.5	4.7	4.9	5.7	5.6	5.8	21.5	28.0	20.5	3.3	81.1	46.2	48.6	51.4
49780	RUDYARD	90.1	89.7	0.2	0.2	0.4	0.5	1.1	1.2	6.4	6.6	7.1	6.5	6.3	24.5	28.7	12.5	1.4	75.6	40.7	50.2	49.8
49781	SAINT IGNACE	73.9	73.2	0.3	0.3	0.4	0.5	0.8	0.8	5.2	6.1	7.2	7.0	5.6	25.2	27.1	14.2	2.4	77.2	41.2	49.9	50.1
49782	BEAVER ISLAND	98.4	98.1	0.0	0.0	0.0	0.0	0.2	0.2	4.3	4.6	4.8	6.3	4.1	15.7	36.4	22.6	1.4	82.5	50.4	49.3	50.7
49783	SAULT SAINTE MARIE	75.9	75.1	5.0	5.2	0.6	0.7	1.6	1.7	5.1	5.1	5.4	7.5	10.5	30.9	22.7	10.9	2.0	80.8	35.4	54.0	46.0
49788	KINCHELOE	61.6	59.9	19.2	20.4	0.6	0.8	2.9	3.2	6.2	5.4	4.9	5.0	8.4	47.7	19.2	3.1	0.2	80.5	33.7	72.0	28.0
49792	TOWER	96.4	95.5	0.0	0.0	0.0	1.1	0.0	0.0	4.5	4.5	7.9	7.9	5.6	22.5	31.5	13.5	2.3	76.4	43.2	51.7	48.3
49795	VANDERBILT	97.1	96.9	0.2	0.2	0.2	0.2	0.8	0.9	6.8	6.8	7.0	5.7	6.0	28.2	24.7	13.7	1.1	76.1	38.6	49.8	50.2
49799	WOLVERINE	96.5	96.3	0.0	0.1	0.0	0.1	0.7	0.8	7.2	7.1	7.0	6.1	5.3	26.7	26.2	13.1	1.3	74.6	38.9	50.6	49.5
49801	IRON MOUNTAIN	97.9	97.6	0.1	0.2	0.6	0.8	0.9	1.0	5.4	6.0	7.5	6.7	5.7	23.8	26.8	15.2	2.9	76.7	41.8	49.7	50.3
49802	KINGSFORD	97.9	97.7	0.2	0.2	0.4	0.5	0.5	0.6	6.0	6.0	7.1	6.8	6.2	24.7	25.0	14.5	3.7	75.8	40.9	48.6	51.4
49806	AU TRAIN	93.4	93.4	0.0	0.0	0.0	0.3	0.8	1.0	5.1	5.4	5.9	5.4	4.9	22.5	31.2	16.9	2.8	80.1	45.5	49.1	50.9
49807	BARK RIVER	96.2	96.1	0.1	0.2	0.2	0.3	0.3	0.4	5.6	5.9	6.5	6.4	6.2	25.9	30.1	12.3	1.2	78.2	41.1	51.3	48.7
49812	CARNEY	89.2	89.4	0.1	0.1	0.1	0.1	1.1	1.1	6.3	6.4	6.8	6.4	5.4	24.6	26.8	14.7	2.7	76.3	41.3	50.6	49.4
49814	CHAMPION	98.7	98.7	0.1	0.1	0.1	0.1	0.3	0.3	5.2	5.5	6.3	6.1	6.4	23.3	32.3	13.6	1.3	79.4	43.1	51.7	48.3
49815	CHANNING	97.7	97.2	0.0	0.0	0.2	0.2	0.8	1.1	5.7	6.1	6.6	6.5	5.9	22.3	29.8	15.7	1.5	77.7	42.9	50.6	49.4
49816	CHATHAM	95.8	95.9	0.3	0.3	0.0	0.0	0.8	0.5	4.9	5.2	5.4	5.4	4.9	20.7	35.4	16.0	2.1	81.1	46.7	50.1	49.9
49817	COOKS	91.0	90.9	0.2	0.2	0.4	0.4	0.4	0.6	4.3	4.8	6.0	5.0	4.6	20.5	33.9	19.3	1.6	81.6	47.6	51.3	48.7
49818	CORNELL	96.5	96.5	0.0	0.0	0.1	0.1	0.5	0.5	5.2	5.8	6.6	6.6	5.7	25.3	32.1	11.9	0.9	78.5	42.1	52.5	47.5
49820	CURTIS	89.3	89.1	0.2	0.2	0.1	0.1	1.4	1.5	4.1	4.5	5.2	4.3	3.7	21.4	32.7	22.6	1.4	83.1	49.8	49.9	50.1
49821	DAGGETT	94.1	94.1	0.2	0.2	0.2	0.2	0.6	0.6	6.2	6.5	6.7	6.2	5.6	22.6	28.5	15.3	2.5	76.3	42.5	51.5	48.5
49822	DEERTON	94.8	95.1	0.0	0.0	0.0	0.0	0.3	0.3	4.6	4.9	4.9	5.5	5.2	21.2	36.5	15.3	2.0	81.8	46.7	51.1	48.9
49825	EBEN JUNCTION	94.8	95.3	0.0	0.0	0.0	0.0	0.6	0.6	4.1	5.3	4.7	5.9	5.3	19.9	38.0	15.2	1.8	82.5	47.4	50.9	49.1
49826	RUMELY	94.9	95.1	0.0	0.0	0.0	0.0	0.5	0.5	4.4	4.9	4.6	5.4	5.4	20.7	37.8	15.0	1.9	82.9	47.2	50.5	49.5
49827	ENGADINE	86.2	85.7	0.0	0.0	0.0	0.3	1.7	1.8	4.3	4.6	5.2	5.2	4.6	22.3	32.0	20.1	1.8	82.6	47.7	50.9	49.1
49829	ESCANABA	96.0	95.9	0.1	0.1	0.4	0.4	0.6	0.6	5.7	5.7	6.4	7.0	6.8	24.7	25.4	14.8	3.5	78.1	40.7	48.1	51.9
49831	FELCH	98.4	97.6	0.0	0.0	0.0	0.8	0.0	0.0	5.5	6.3	7.1	7.1	5.5	23.6	29.9	13.4	1.6	76.4	41.8	51.2	48.8
49833	LITTLE LAKE	97.3	97.6	0.3	0.3	0.0	0.0	0.0	0.0	3.8	3.8	5.2	5.9	5.9	23.5	34.8	15.2	2.1	83.5	46.3	49.0	51.0
49834	FOSTER CITY	98.2	97.8	0.0	0.0	0.2	0.2	0.7	0.8	5.3	5.8	6.9	6.6	5.6	23.3	30.4	14.4	1.7	77.8	42.8	50.4	49.6
49835	GARDEN	90.3	90.2	0.1	0.1	0.2	0.2	0.4	0.4	4.6	4.7	5.3	4.7	4.0	20.5	31.8	22.2	2.2	82.5	49.2	51.6	48.4
49836	GERMFASK	89.8	89.6	0.2	0.2	0.0	0.0	0.2	0.2	7.3	7.1	5.5	4.1	4.9	23.4	28.9	16.3	2.4	77.2	43.2	50.1	49.9
49837	GLADSTONE	96.5	96.5	0.1	0.1	0.4	0.4	0.4	0.4	5.8	6.1	6.8	6.9	6.4	23.6	28.9	13.7	1.9	76.9	41.5	49.2	50.8
49838	GOULD CITY	88.2	88.1	0.3	0.3	0.0	0.0	0.9	1.4	3.6	3.9	5.0	4.2	3.3	19.1	34.9	24.4	1.7	84.5	52.4	48.2	51.8
49839	GRAND MARAIS	79.8	78.2	14.5	15.7	0.2	0.2	1.3	1.3	2.5	2.9	4.0	4.8	5.9	30.5	32.2	15.3	1.9	87.2	44.6	61.9	38.1
49840	GULLIVER	89.1	88.8	0.2	0.2	0.0	0.0	1.4	1.5	4.9	5.1	6.7	6.5	4.0	24.8	30.5	16.3	1.3	78.8	43.8	52.3	47.7
49841	GWINN	94.3	94.4	0.6	0.6	0.6	0.6	1.2	1.2	6.6	6.1	6.3	6.1	6.4	26.7	29.8	11.2	1.0	77.4	39.6	50.3	49.7
49847	HERMANSVILLE	95.9	95.9	0.1	0.1	0.1	0.1	0.7	0.7	6.3	6.5	6.5	6.0	5.4	24.0	27.1	15.2	3.1	77.0	42.0	50.1	49.9
49848	INGALLS	97.5	97.7	0.0	0.0	0.5	0.5	0.0	0.0	4.2	5.2	5.6	6.6	6.1	22.5	31.0	16.0	2.8	80.8	44.9	49.3	50.7
49849	ISHPEMING	97.8	97.8	0.1	0.1	0.2	0.2	0.6	0.6	5.7	5.8	6.3	6.5	6.8	24.8	27.5	14.1	2.6	78.4	40.9	48.4	51.7
49853	MC MILLAN	93.3	93.2	0.2	0.2	0.3	0.3	0.3	0.2	4.6	5.1	5.3	5.0	4.6	19.5	35.1	19.4	1.4	81.4	48.6	50.8	49.2
49854	MANISTIQUE	88.2	87.7	2.0	2.2	0.5	0.7	1.0	1.1	5.7	5.9	6.5	5.9	5.6	24.6	27.0	16.3	2.6	78.2	42.1	49.9	50.1
49855	MARQUETTE	93.3	93.2	2.5	2.5	0.8	0.8	0.8	0.8	4.4	4.4	5.0	9.5	12.6	26.5	25.1	10.6	1.9	82.6	35.6	50.8	49.2
49858	MENOMINEE	97.8	97.8	0.1	0.1	0.3	0.3	0.9	0.9	5.8	5.7	6.2	6.6	6.9	24.0	27.9	14.6	2.4	78.4	41.6	49.1	50.9
49861	MICHIGAMME	96.0	95.9	0.1	0.1	0.2	0.2	0.5	0.4	3.8	4.9	5.2	4.6	3.4	22.2	37.3	17.0	1.5	83.2	47.8	51.7	48.3
49862	MUNISING	89.7	89.1	3.2	3.4	0.6	0.7	1.0	1.0	5.0	5.3	6.1	6.2	5.7	25.7	27.6	15.8	2.7	79.6	42.5	51.2	48.8
49866	NEGAUNEE	97.1	97.0	0.2	0.2	0.3	0.3	0.4	0.5	5.3	5.4	6.4	6.3	6.7	26.1	27.9	13.1	2.9	79.1	41.3	49.1	50.9
49868	NEWBERRY	80.6	80.2	9.1	9.5	0.4	0.4	2.1	2.1	5.2	5.3	5.8	6.2	8.1	30.9	23.7	12.6	2.3	79.9	37.6	56.7	43.3
49870	NORWAY	97.7	97.5	0.0	0.0	0.2	0.3	0.6	0.7	6.4	6.4	7.3	6.8	6.1	26.1	24.0	14.1	2.9	75.4	39.1	49.2	50.8
49873	PERRONVILLE	94.4	94.9	0.0	0.0	0.0	0.0	0.0	0.6	7.0	7.0	7.0	6.3	5.7	26.0	26.6	12.7	1.9	74.7	39.5	50.6	49.4
49874	POWERS	97.4	97.3	0.0	0.0	0.0	0.0	0.6	0.6	6.2	6.2	6.2	6.0	5.6	24.9	25.8	15.6	3.4	77.6	41.8	50.5	49.5
49876	QUINNESEC	98.5	98.3	0.0	0.0	0.3	0.4	0.3	0.3	4.7	6.2	7.3	9.5	4.2	27.3	30.3	9.3	1.2	75.1	40.3	50.3	49.8
49878	RAPID RIVER	93.0	92.9	1.6	1.7	0.3	0.3	0.4	0.5	4.5	5.0	6.1	5.5	5.0	23.6	31.9	16.7	1.7	80.9	45.2	52.6	47.5
	MICHIGAN	80.2	79.2	14.2	14.4	1.8	2.3	3.3	3.6	6.8	6.9	7.4	7.1	6.9	28.1	24.6	10.8	1.6	74.9	36.5	49.1	50.9
	UNITED STATES	75.1	73.6	12.3	12.5	3.8	4.2	12.5	14.1	6.9	6.7	7.2	7.0	7.3	28.6	23.8	10.8	1.7	75.1	36.0	49.1	50.9

INCOME

ZIP CODE #	POST OFFICE NAME	2004 Per Capita Income	2004 HH Income Base	2004 Household Income Distribution (%) Less than $25,000	$25,000 to $49,999	$50,000 to $99,999	$100,000 to $149,999	$150,000 or More	Median Household Income 2004	2009	2004 National Centile	2004 State Centile	2004 Home Value Base	2004 Home Value Distribution (%) Less than $50,000	$50,000 to $89,999	$90,000 to $174,999	$175,000 to $399,999	$400,000 or More	2004 Median Home Value
49712	BOYNE CITY	23336	3471	24.4	34.6	31.1	6.5	3.4	42762	46918	55	45	2858	9.1	14.6	44.1	23.6	8.7	134435
49713	BOYNE FALLS	21696	894	25.2	33.6	31.9	6.6	2.8	43671	47928	58	48	762	13.1	18.2	43.2	21.4	4.1	118802
49715	BRIMLEY	19941	1088	27.8	34.5	31.0	5.2	1.6	41280	43737	51	40	882	16.6	26.2	46.0	10.2	1.0	99697
49716	BRUTUS	22536	346	21.4	40.2	30.6	4.1	3.8	41564	46352	52	41	308	10.7	18.2	43.5	18.8	8.8	118033
49718	CARP LAKE	23327	343	30.0	33.2	27.7	5.3	3.8	39871	43880	46	34	293	14.3	24.6	35.5	21.8	3.8	107813
49719	CEDARVILLE	23359	833	29.5	33.7	27.3	7.0	2.5	38396	41234	41	28	709	5.5	15.2	40.9	31.9	6.5	148438
49720	CHARLEVOIX	25295	4260	23.5	32.2	31.2	8.9	4.2	44424	48710	60	51	3438	7.2	12.4	42.1	29.2	9.2	148675
49721	CHEBOYGAN	20723	6707	33.8	35.0	23.3	4.6	3.3	35532	37889	30	16	5336	11.5	23.2	43.1	18.8	3.5	110380
49724	DAFTER	18734	388	27.8	34.3	32.2	4.4	1.3	41961	45501	53	42	340	14.4	30.9	41.2	12.1	1.5	96957
49725	DE TOUR VILLAGE	23733	428	34.8	30.6	26.6	4.9	3.0	39332	42361	44	31	387	13.2	17.3	37.5	26.9	5.2	127744
49726	DRUMMOND ISLAND	24138	478	34.1	30.8	27.8	3.6	3.8	38340	41428	41	27	402	13.9	24.1	32.8	24.9	4.2	109896
49727	EAST JORDAN	19383	3004	26.4	35.0	30.8	5.4	2.4	41982	45519	53	42	2476	10.9	19.3	42.0	21.2	6.6	119077
49728	ECKERMAN	17324	106	36.8	34.0	23.6	3.8	1.9	33151	37041	21	11	92	17.4	23.9	41.3	13.0	4.4	100000
49729	ELLSWORTH	21059	658	20.5	35.9	35.9	5.8	2.0	45930	50305	64	56	566	12.9	15.6	40.3	22.6	8.7	131034
49730	ELMIRA	19528	906	23.4	35.5	32.6	6.0	2.5	43525	47392	57	47	793	12.0	21.2	48.3	16.8	1.8	111719
49733	FREDERIC	19628	728	27.6	38.9	26.2	5.6	1.7	37820	41517	39	26	628	19.1	23.6	39.0	16.9	1.4	99583
49735	GAYLORD	23160	7959	23.3	32.8	32.5	8.1	3.3	44854	48964	61	52	6482	7.6	13.1	50.6	26.2	2.5	132339
49736	GOETZVILLE	23066	358	33.0	36.6	24.9	3.9	1.7	36966	40918	35	23	330	14.2	26.7	45.5	11.5	2.1	103636
49738	GRAYLING	19197	4384	30.4	38.5	24.1	4.7	2.4	35663	37846	30	17	3508	12.3	29.6	43.6	12.9	1.7	99437
49740	HARBOR SPRINGS	28497	3262	22.1	29.6	31.7	9.9	6.7	48132	54581	69	62	2791	5.8	6.1	31.7	40.0	16.4	194833
49743	HAWKS	16210	410	32.7	40.2	23.4	2.7	1.0	35000	37749	28	14	365	17.5	32.6	38.9	9.6	1.4	89833
49744	HERRON	18672	367	27.8	36.8	28.9	4.1	2.5	40446	44516	48	36	341	11.7	27.3	44.0	15.5	1.5	102754
49746	HILLMAN	17354	1774	37.7	35.2	22.5	3.2	1.5	32215	34652	18	8	1483	19.0	28.7	34.3	16.1	1.9	92991
49747	HUBBARD LAKE	21324	751	30.2	35.4	26.6	5.2	2.5	39937	41647	46	34	678	10.6	21.5	43.8	20.9	3.1	116593
49749	INDIAN RIVER	22411	2015	28.8	35.9	26.7	4.8	3.9	38830	42715	42	29	1733	9.1	17.2	39.0	26.8	7.9	130515
49751	JOHANNESBURG	22883	925	22.5	38.6	29.0	7.1	2.8	41394	45289	51	41	849	9.0	16.6	49.6	20.9	4.0	123828
49752	KINROSS	17954	166	34.3	33.7	26.5	3.6	1.8	37341	40202	37	25	142	21.1	26.1	40.1	11.3	1.4	93636
49753	LACHINE	18653	813	29.9	35.3	28.4	4.7	1.7	37618	42131	38	26	750	14.0	29.7	39.7	15.3	1.2	97121
49755	LEVERING	20749	884	28.6	35.5	27.6	5.0	3.3	39564	43151	45	33	763	13.0	21.4	40.1	22.0	3.5	114931
49756	LEWISTON	19472	2150	36.7	38.5	18.7	3.8	2.3	31941	34614	18	8	1868	12.0	31.0	38.1	17.1	1.9	99704
49757	MACKINAC ISLAND	33061	274	19.3	40.5	27.7	5.1	7.3	40322	43822	47	35	175	1.7	7.4	30.9	29.7	30.3	218333
49759	MILLERSBURG	20009	808	32.1	41.2	21.2	3.7	1.9	35227	38055	28	15	707	16.8	23.6	39.9	16.7	3.0	102431
49760	MORAN	20353	197	32.0	35.0	27.9	3.6	1.5	36801	39300	35	22	165	14.6	23.0	44.2	17.0	1.2	109583
49762	NAUBINWAY	18270	731	38.7	33.9	22.6	4.0	0.8	32906	35179	21	10	626	18.5	25.7	39.6	14.1	2.1	98372
49765	ONAWAY	17201	1813	38.7	37.7	19.9	2.3	1.5	31150	33652	15	6	1434	24.8	28.5	33.3	11.7	1.7	84778
49766	OSSINEKE	19786	1033	30.8	31.9	29.5	4.8	3.0	38331	41953	41	27	880	10.9	29.7	42.8	15.5	1.1	101250
49768	PARADISE	20554	290	39.0	34.5	22.4	2.8	1.4	31890	35829	18	8	253	17.0	23.3	44.7	12.3	2.8	101603
49769	PELLSTON	16805	603	24.9	39.6	28.9	4.3	2.3	39856	43899	45	33	519	14.1	26.2	42.8	14.8	2.1	105032
49770	PETOSKEY	24561	6822	26.5	30.8	29.3	9.3	4.1	43385	47392	57	47	4916	5.9	8.8	41.1	36.5	7.7	162919
49774	PICKFORD	18230	736	30.4	36.4	28.3	3.8	1.1	38879	42515	42	30	666	12.5	29.0	44.4	12.5	1.7	101339
49775	POINTE AUX PINS	40467	45	17.8	33.3	33.3	0.0	15.6	48658	54580	70	63	43	9.3	23.3	16.3	25.6	25.6	212500
49776	POSEN	19678	977	31.0	35.0	27.9	4.5	1.5	37064	39817	36	23	871	14.5	26.6	44.9	13.3	0.7	98908
49777	PRESQUE ISLE	26156	500	25.4	36.8	29.4	5.8	2.6	39520	43052	44	32	477	4.2	14.1	40.9	36.9	4.0	149755
49779	ROGERS CITY	19110	2306	37.8	36.0	21.2	3.7	1.3	33305	34931	22	11	1798	18.0	35.4	36.7	9.0	0.9	85811
49780	RUDYARD	18799	998	30.8	34.0	29.7	4.2	1.4	40161	42273	47	35	864	18.9	28.7	42.0	9.8	0.6	93088
49781	SAINT IGNACE	19356	2742	30.8	36.0	27.8	3.7	1.7	37449	40254	37	25	2101	12.0	21.2	47.5	17.6	1.8	110996
49782	BEAVER ISLAND	26982	282	28.4	42.6	19.2	5.7	4.3	35476	40071	29	16	257	3.9	11.7	36.6	37.4	10.5	167361
49783	SAULT SAINTE MARIE	18051	8162	36.5	30.8	26.8	4.5	1.5	35943	38362	31	18	5638	19.4	31.1	35.9	12.9	0.7	89379
49788	KINCHELOE	13682	1010	30.4	36.5	29.0	3.6	0.5	38258	41622	40	27	541	25.9	25.0	46.6	2.4	0.2	89224
49792	TOWER	16348	44	36.4	45.5	18.2	0.0	0.0	30000	33852	12	5	37	32.4	29.7	29.7	8.1	0.0	75000
49795	VANDERBILT	18522	826	30.4	38.3	27.0	3.0	1.3	36623	40776	34	21	656	9.8	29.9	46.0	12.5	1.8	105114
49799	WOLVERINE	16468	1027	33.6	38.3	23.9	2.5	1.8	34359	36794	25	13	866	17.8	25.9	42.2	12.4	1.9	100164
49801	IRON MOUNTAIN	21906	5266	32.7	31.6	26.3	6.9	2.5	37910	40917	39	26	4195	21.2	32.3	29.9	14.9	1.7	85351
49802	KINGSFORD	19875	2769	33.7	32.9	27.0	4.9	1.5	35809	39696	31	18	2067	17.6	50.8	23.4	6.8	1.5	73693
49806	AU TRAIN	22867	178	28.7	33.2	30.3	6.2	1.7	42629	47004	55	44	148	12.2	28.4	41.9	15.5	2.0	104630
49807	BARK RIVER	21276	1343	22.9	34.8	33.7	6.9	1.8	44431	48877	60	51	1154	14.4	27.8	40.6	15.3	1.8	98108
49812	CARNEY	18148	558	35.1	33.9	26.2	3.8	1.1	34098	37089	24	12	461	24.7	30.4	33.8	9.1	2.0	83088
49814	CHAMPION	19793	787	25.7	36.6	32.0	4.8	0.9	41915	46606	53	42	723	26.6	33.1	33.2	6.0	1.2	77500
49815	CHANNING	18996	231	32.9	34.2	27.3	4.3	1.3	36747	41533	34	22	211	24.2	31.3	35.6	9.0	0.0	82813
49816	CHATHAM	17997	160	31.3	38.8	24.4	4.4	1.3	36231	40201	32	20	142	17.6	30.3	40.9	11.3	0.0	92727
49817	COOKS	20597	197	31.0	32.5	28.4	5.1	3.1	39303	43386	44	31	181	17.1	23.8	37.0	20.4	1.7	106696
49818	CORNELL	20094	314	25.5	34.4	32.5	7.0	0.6	43039	47453	56	46	294	13.6	32.0	42.2	11.9	0.3	96500
49820	CURTIS	19642	474	38.0	35.9	20.5	4.2	1.5	32702	35494	20	10	410	20.7	22.2	40.2	14.2	2.7	98529
49821	DAGGETT	17943	513	34.5	34.3	26.9	2.9	1.4	35721	39106	30	17	422	22.3	30.6	36.0	9.0	2.1	86250
49822	DEERTON	24151	149	25.5	37.6	28.9	5.4	2.7	41204	45183	50	40	129	10.9	30.2	39.5	17.1	2.3	101786
49825	EBEN JUNCTION	20958	73	26.0	37.0	28.8	5.5	2.7	41119	43369	50	39	63	9.5	30.2	44.4	15.9	0.0	102679
49826	RUMELY	21260	157	25.5	38.2	28.0	5.7	2.6	41113	45685	50	39	136	10.3	29.4	41.9	16.2	2.2	102885
49827	ENGADINE	17052	138	39.1	33.3	23.2	3.6	0.7	32999	35550	21	10	119	21.9	22.7	42.0	11.8	1.7	98125
49829	ESCANABA	20250	7687	35.8	29.1	28.0	5.0	2.1	35453	38565	29	16	5393	13.6	32.2	41.4	12.0	0.8	95421
49831	FELCH	22293	60	28.3	33.3	31.7	5.0	1.7	40888	41549	49	38	55	18.2	25.5	43.6	12.7	0.0	101250
49833	LITTLE LAKE	15877	121	43.8	31.4	21.5	1.7	1.7	29048	31412	10	4	104	27.9	28.9	38.5	4.8	0.0	82222
49834	FOSTER CITY	19148	271	32.5	33.6	27.7	4.8	1.5	37634	41589	38	26	247	23.5	29.6	36.0	10.5	0.4	85588
49835	GARDEN	20616	411	34.8	33.3	24.8	4.9	2.2	35977	40410	31	19	382	22.3	28.5	28.0	19.1	2.1	88500
49836	GERMFASK	18512	202	38.6	30.2	26.2	3.5	1.5	35000	38632	28	14	182	30.2	29.7	29.7	9.9	0.6	73000
49837	GLADSTONE	20921	4129	27.2	29.6	32.7	9.3	1.2	43087	46525	56	46	3512	14.0	32.5	36.5	15.6	1.4	94980
49838	GOULD CITY	21480	178	38.2	36.5	19.7	4.5	1.1	32306	35145	19	9	153	18.3	23.5	38.6	16.3	3.3	98929
49839	GRAND MARAIS	30561	250	28.0	39.6	25.6	4.0	2.8	36252	40397	33	20	232	14.2	29.3	34.9	16.8	4.7	100806
49840	GULLIVER	21894	370	26.0	37.8	26.0	7.0	3.2	39392	44161	44	32	339	16.5	24.2	38.4	17.1	3.8	103009
49841	GWINN	19141	2189	29.6	33.7	31.6	3.8	1.3	37286	41604	36	24	1451	24.6	30.8	37.5	7.1	0.0	83291
49847	HERMANSVILLE	19712	474	36.5	31.2	26.8	4.6	0.8	35400	37454	29	16	386	28.0	29.0	34.2	8.0	0.8	78333
49848	INGALLS	15662	82	35.4	36.6	24.4	3.7	0.0	33403	37314	22	11	67	19.4	35.8	38.8	6.0	0.0	85000
49849	ISHPEMING	19481	5089	30.8	33.4	30.5	4.6	0.8	39130	43036	43	30	3931	24.6	41.8	29.3	4.2	0.2	71213
49853	MC MILLAN	19122	557	32.5	37.3	25.1	3.6	1.4	34945	37318	27	14	490	19.6	17.8	43.9	16.3	2.5	108989
49854	MANISTIQUE	19241	2933	39.1	30.8	24.0	4.2	1.9	32517	35468	19	9	2307	27.0	31.0	28.6	12.2	1.3	79519
49855	MARQUETTE	22002	12950	33.6	28.7	28.1	6.3	3.4	38442	41473	41	28	7987	6.0	22.7	53.0	16.8	1.5	112822
49858	MENOMINEE	19793	5618	34.3	32.4	28.2	3.5	1.5	35873	38021	31	18	4196	26.1	34.6	31.4	7.6	0.3	75854
49861	MICHIGAMME	24636	618	29.1	33.0	30.3	4.9	2.8	39301	44034	44	31	549	27.5	24.4	31.7	11.8	4.6	86250
49862	MUNISING	20521	2024	31.1	32.7	29.8	4.7	1.6	39369	42053	44	32	1578	15.5	33.0	37.6	11.6	2.3	92300
49866	NEGAUNEE	20298	3423	28.2	34.3	31.2	4.9	1.3	40461	44390	48	36	2703	18.3	35.6	37.9	7.8	0.4	84952
49868	NEWBERRY	17145	2006	35.3	36.5	23.7	3.2	1.2	34075	35807	24	12	1560	26.7	32.0	35.7	5.3	0.3	78230
49870	NORWAY	20982	1439	33.4	34.1	25.2	4.9	2.4	35629	39398	30	17	1110	24.2	40.5	26.3	8.4	0.5	71442
49873	PERRONVILLE	20047	71	35.2	31.0	29.6	4.2	0.0	35440	40000	29	16	58	25.9	25.9	37.9	10.3	0.0	86667
49874	POWERS	15793	460	35.2	34.8	25.2	3.9	0.9	33875	36644	24	12	384	27.1	30.2	35.2	6.3	1.3	80345
49876	QUINNESEC	18607	452	21.5	38.3	33.0	6.6	0.7	44860	48805	61	52	422	11.6	53.8	30.3	3.3	1.0	81096
49878	RAPID RIVER	23352	1935	29.5	33.9	28.6	5.7	2.4	39275	44631	44	31	1719	15.7	27.9	36.6	18.2	1.7	102425
	MICHIGAN	25281		23.8	27.4	32.3	10.9	5.5	48729	54505				10.7	16.0	40.3	28.0	5.0	134769
	UNITED STATES	25866		24.7	27.1	30.8	10.9	6.5	48124	56710				10.9	15.0	33.7	30.1	10.4	145905

ZIP CODE #	POST OFFICE NAME	FINANCIAL SERVICES Auto Loan	Home Loan	Invest-ments	Retire-ment Plans	THE HOME Home Improvements Home Repair	Lawn & Garden	Furnishings Comput-ers & Hard-ware	Major Appli-ances	TV, Radio, Sound Equip-ment	Furni-ture	ENTERTAINMENT Dine out/ Carry out	Sports Equip-ment	Fees & Tickets	Toys & Games	Travel	Cable TV	PERSONAL Apparel & Services	Auto Repairs	Health Insur-ance	Pets & Supplies
49712	BOYNE CITY	93	76	55	71	82	92	74	84	81	73	97	98	69	96	76	85	91	83	96	108
49713	BOYNE FALLS	89	73	54	69	80	90	72	82	78	71	94	95	66	93	74	82	88	80	93	105
49715	BRIMLEY	82	66	46	61	73	82	63	74	71	63	84	86	58	83	66	75	78	73	86	98
49716	BRUTUS	91	76	57	72	82	91	73	83	80	73	96	97	68	95	76	83	90	82	93	107
49718	CARP LAKE	88	69	47	63	78	88	65	79	74	65	88	92	58	87	70	79	81	78	93	108
49719	CEDARVILLE	87	68	47	62	77	87	65	78	73	64	87	91	58	85	69	78	80	77	92	106
49720	CHARLEVOIX	101	80	55	74	88	99	78	90	86	77	102	105	70	100	80	90	95	89	104	119
49721	CHEBOYGAN	80	63	45	59	69	79	64	72	71	62	84	84	58	82	65	74	78	72	84	92
49724	DAFTER	80	66	49	63	71	80	65	73	71	64	86	85	61	85	67	74	80	72	82	92
49725	DE TOUR VILLAGE	84	66	45	60	75	84	62	75	71	62	84	88	56	83	67	76	78	74	89	103
49726	DRUMMOND ISLAND	85	67	45	60	75	84	63	76	71	62	84	89	56	83	67	76	78	75	90	104
49727	EAST JORDAN	83	70	51	67	75	82	67	75	73	67	88	88	64	88	69	75	82	74	83	96
49728	ECKERMAN	70	55	37	49	62	69	52	62	58	51	69	73	46	68	55	62	64	61	74	85
49729	ELLSWORTH	88	73	52	67	79	87	68	79	75	68	90	93	63	90	71	78	84	77	90	105
49730	ELMIRA	87	73	53	68	79	87	68	78	74	68	89	92	64	90	71	78	84	77	88	103
49733	FREDERIC	78	63	46	58	70	78	60	71	67	59	80	83	54	78	63	71	74	70	82	95
49735	GAYLORD	92	80	64	76	85	94	78	86	83	77	100	100	73	100	80	86	95	85	95	109
49736	GOETZVILLE	81	64	44	58	72	81	60	73	68	60	81	85	54	80	64	73	75	71	86	99
49738	GRAYLING	77	60	41	56	67	76	60	70	67	59	80	81	54	78	62	71	74	69	82	91
49740	HARBOR SPRINGS	114	88	56	81	99	110	84	100	94	83	112	119	75	111	88	100	104	99	117	137
49743	HAWKS	70	51	31	47	58	66	51	61	58	50	69	71	45	67	53	62	63	60	73	82
49744	HERRON	83	67	45	63	73	80	63	74	70	63	83	88	58	83	65	72	78	72	84	98
49746	HILLMAN	69	54	37	49	61	69	51	62	58	51	69	72	46	68	55	62	64	61	73	85
49747	HUBBARD LAKE	87	68	45	63	76	85	65	77	72	65	86	90	59	84	68	76	80	76	91	103
49749	INDIAN RIVER	86	65	42	60	74	83	63	76	72	62	85	89	56	83	66	76	78	75	90	103
49751	JOHANNESBURG	91	71	49	64	80	90	67	81	76	67	90	95	60	89	72	81	84	80	96	111
49752	KINROSS	77	60	41	54	68	76	57	68	64	56	76	80	51	75	61	69	71	67	81	94
49753	LACHINE	80	60	37	55	69	77	58	70	66	57	78	83	51	77	61	70	72	69	83	97
49755	LEVERING	84	68	49	64	75	84	66	76	73	65	87	88	61	86	69	76	81	75	87	99
49756	LEWISTON	71	56	38	50	63	70	52	63	59	52	70	74	47	69	56	63	65	62	75	86
49757	MACKINAC ISLAND	113	89	61	80	100	112	84	101	95	83	112	118	75	111	89	101	105	99	119	138
49759	MILLERSBURG	76	59	40	54	67	75	57	68	64	56	76	79	51	75	60	68	70	67	80	92
49760	MORAN	75	61	43	56	67	74	58	68	64	58	76	79	53	74	60	67	71	67	77	89
49762	NAUBINWAY	68	53	36	48	60	67	50	60	57	50	67	71	45	66	53	61	63	60	71	83
49765	ONAWAY	69	52	32	47	58	67	52	61	59	51	70	71	46	67	53	63	64	60	73	81
49766	OSSINEKE	75	66	54	64	71	78	64	71	68	64	83	82	62	84	66	71	79	69	78	88
49768	PARADISE	70	55	37	49	62	69	52	62	58	51	69	73	46	68	55	62	64	61	73	85
49769	PELLSTON	79	67	52	66	71	79	68	73	72	67	88	84	65	87	68	74	82	72	80	89
49770	PETOSKEY	84	86	87	85	88	92	82	85	82	82	101	101	83	104	84	82	98	84	85	101
49774	PICKFORD	80	62	41	56	70	78	58	71	66	58	78	83	52	77	62	71	73	70	84	97
49775	POINTE AUX PINS	114	90	61	81	101	114	85	102	96	84	113	119	76	112	90	102	105	100	120	139
49776	POSEN	77	57	36	54	64	75	60	69	68	58	80	79	53	76	61	72	73	68	82	88
49777	PRESQUE ISLE	93	72	48	65	81	92	69	83	78	68	93	97	61	91	73	83	86	82	98	113
49779	ROGERS CITY	70	52	34	49	58	68	56	63	63	53	74	72	49	70	56	66	68	63	75	79
49780	RUDYARD	82	60	36	56	69	78	59	72	67	58	79	85	51	78	62	71	73	71	85	98
49781	SAINT IGNACE	74	61	45	57	65	74	61	68	66	60	79	79	56	77	62	69	74	68	77	86
49782	BEAVER ISLAND	95	75	51	68	84	95	71	85	80	70	95	100	63	93	75	85	88	84	101	116
49783	SAULT SAINTE MARIE	59	54	54	54	55	60	58	58	59	56	73	69	56	72	57	58	70	59	58	67
49788	KINCHELOE	41	41	44	42	41	43	43	42	43	42	53	51	42	54	42	41	51	43	41	47
49792	TOWER	62	42	19	36	47	54	40	50	49	41	57	60	34	54	41	52	52	50	62	71
49795	VANDERBILT	80	63	43	57	71	79	59	71	67	59	79	84	53	78	63	72	74	70	84	98
49799	WOLVERINE	71	54	36	50	61	70	54	63	61	52	72	73	48	70	56	64	66	62	75	84
49801	IRON MOUNTAIN	73	72	70	69	75	83	70	74	72	69	89	82	71	90	72	74	85	72	79	85
49802	KINGSFORD	63	62	60	61	64	71	63	64	65	61	80	73	63	81	64	66	76	64	69	73
49806	AU TRAIN	84	66	45	59	74	83	62	75	70	61	83	87	55	82	66	75	77	73	88	102
49807	BARK RIVER	84	77	63	72	81	88	72	79	76	71	92	92	70	94	74	78	88	77	85	99
49812	CARNEY	70	55	38	51	61	69	54	63	61	53	72	73	49	71	56	64	67	62	74	83
49814	CHAMPION	75	68	55	64	72	78	63	71	67	63	82	83	61	83	66	70	78	69	78	91
49815	CHANNING	76	59	40	54	67	75	56	67	63	55	75	79	50	74	60	68	70	66	80	92
49816	CHATHAM	74	58	39	52	65	73	55	66	62	54	73	77	49	72	58	66	68	65	78	90
49817	COOKS	92	72	49	65	81	91	68	82	77	67	91	96	61	90	72	82	85	80	97	112
49818	CORNELL	82	68	49	63	74	82	64	74	70	63	84	87	60	84	67	73	79	72	84	98
49820	CURTIS	72	56	38	51	63	71	53	64	60	53	71	75	48	70	57	64	66	63	76	88
49821	DAGGETT	72	55	37	51	62	71	55	64	62	53	73	74	49	71	57	66	67	63	76	85
49822	DEERTON	84	66	45	60	74	84	62	75	70	62	83	88	56	82	66	75	78	74	89	103
49825	EBEN JUNCTION	83	65	44	59	73	82	61	74	69	61	82	87	55	81	65	74	77	73	87	101
49826	RUMELY	84	66	45	60	74	84	62	75	71	62	84	88	56	82	66	75	78	74	89	103
49827	ENGADINE	68	53	36	48	60	67	50	60	57	50	67	71	45	66	53	61	62	59	71	83
49829	ESCANABA	62	64	70	63	65	71	65	65	66	63	81	74	66	83	66	67	79	65	67	73
49831	FELCH	78	64	46	59	71	78	60	70	66	60	79	83	56	80	63	70	75	69	80	94
49833	LITTLE LAKE	65	51	35	46	57	64	48	58	54	47	64	67	43	63	51	58	60	57	68	79
49834	FOSTER CITY	77	60	41	54	68	76	57	68	64	56	76	80	51	75	60	68	71	67	81	93
49835	GARDEN	79	62	42	56	70	79	59	71	66	58	79	83	52	78	62	71	73	70	83	97
49836	GERMFASK	74	58	40	52	65	73	55	66	62	54	73	77	49	72	58	66	68	65	78	90
49837	GLADSTONE	76	71	62	69	73	80	71	74	73	69	89	85	69	90	71	75	85	73	79	86
49838	GOULD CITY	73	57	39	52	65	72	54	65	61	54	72	76	48	72	58	65	67	64	77	89
49839	GRAND MARAIS	90	70	48	63	79	89	66	80	75	66	89	93	59	88	71	80	83	79	94	109
49840	GULLIVER	88	69	47	63	78	88	65	79	74	65	88	92	58	87	70	79	82	78	93	108
49841	GWINN	72	60	49	58	64	71	60	66	64	60	78	78	56	76	60	66	73	66	72	84
49847	HERMANSVILLE	74	57	39	52	64	73	56	66	63	55	75	76	50	73	59	68	69	65	78	88
49848	INGALLS	76	51	23	44	58	66	49	62	59	50	70	73	42	66	50	64	63	61	76	87
49849	ISHPEMING	65	64	60	61	66	72	63	65	65	61	80	74	63	82	64	67	76	64	69	76
49853	MC MILLAN	74	56	35	51	64	72	54	65	61	53	72	77	47	71	57	65	67	64	77	89
49854	MANISTIQUE	74	57	38	53	63	73	58	67	65	56	77	76	52	74	59	69	71	66	79	85
49855	MARQUETTE	69	69	80	71	68	73	75	71	73	73	92	85	74	91	73	71	90	74	68	79
49858	MENOMINEE	65	60	54	58	63	69	60	63	63	59	77	73	59	80	61	65	74	62	68	75
49861	MICHIGAMME	86	68	46	61	76	86	64	77	72	63	86	90	57	85	68	77	80	76	91	105
49862	MUNISING	77	62	44	58	68	77	61	70	68	60	80	81	56	79	63	71	75	69	81	91
49866	NEGAUNEE	63	70	74	67	71	76	67	67	67	66	84	75	70	88	69	69	81	66	70	74
49868	NEWBERRY	59	44	28	42	49	58	47	54	53	45	63	61	42	60	47	56	57	53	64	67
49870	NORWAY	63	67	70	64	68	76	67	66	69	64	86	74	70	92	69	72	83	65	71	74
49873	PERRONVILLE	75	59	40	53	66	75	56	67	63	55	75	78	50	74	59	67	69	66	79	92
49874	POWERS	70	57	41	54	62	70	57	64	62	56	75	74	53	73	58	65	69	63	73	81
49876	QUINNESEC	79	70	53	67	74	80	65	72	69	65	84	86	64	86	67	71	80	70	78	93
49878	RAPID RIVER	89	70	48	63	79	89	66	80	75	66	89	93	59	88	70	80	82	78	94	109
	MICHIGAN	91	91	93	89	91	98	90	91	91	90	113	106	90	113	90	91	109	91	92	105
	UNITED STATES	100	100	100	100	100	100	100	100	100	100	100	100	100	100	100	100	100	100	100	100

ZIP CODE		POPULATION			2000-2004 ANNUAL RATE		HOUSEHOLDS					FAMILIES		
# POST OFFICE NAME	COUNTY FIPS CODE	2000	2004	2009	% Rate	State Centile	2000	2004	2009	% Annual Rate 2000-2004	2004 Average HH Size	2000	2004	% Annual Rate 2000-2004
49879 REPUBLIC	103	980	971	963	-0.2	15	433	441	451	0.4	2.19	303	306	0.2
49880 ROCK	041	1253	1179	1157	-1.4	1	522	505	508	-0.8	2.33	373	355	-1.2
49881 SAGOLA	043	357	367	369	0.7	49	147	155	159	1.3	2.37	103	108	1.1
49883 SENEY	153	184	182	184	-0.3	13	58	59	61	0.4	2.86	43	43	0.0
49884 SHINGLETON	003	878	944	1000	1.7	85	212	242	267	3.2	3.46	161	180	2.7
49885 SKANDIA	103	2489	2470	2461	-0.2	17	983	1004	1030	0.5	2.45	728	736	0.3
49886 SPALDING	109	371	405	422	2.1	91	136	152	161	2.7	2.61	95	104	2.2
49887 STEPHENSON	109	2569	2597	2610	0.3	32	1109	1152	1184	0.9	2.20	739	753	0.4
49891 TRENARY	003	684	717	750	1.1	68	307	333	358	1.9	2.08	213	228	1.6
49892 VULCAN	043	2277	2327	2340	0.5	43	915	955	978	1.0	2.41	638	655	0.6
49893 WALLACE	109	2115	2144	2163	0.3	35	851	887	914	1.0	2.41	624	641	0.6
49894 WELLS	041	732	693	682	-1.3	1	308	300	302	-0.6	2.30	216	206	-1.1
49895 WETMORE	003	959	979	1003	0.5	43	167	177	187	1.4	3.75	123	128	0.9
49896 WILSON	109	1583	1670	1715	1.3	74	545	593	623	2.0	2.81	397	425	1.6
49905 ATLANTIC MINE	061	3776	3753	3713	-0.1	18	1379	1391	1394	0.2	2.61	900	894	-0.2
49908 BARAGA	013	1915	1841	1757	-0.9	3	790	764	731	-0.8	1.85	498	473	-1.2
49910 BERGLAND	131	550	528	509	-1.0	3	258	255	252	-0.3	2.07	168	163	-0.7
49911 BESSEMER	053	3314	3211	3087	-0.7	5	1501	1485	1456	-0.3	2.13	894	866	-0.8
49912 BRUCE CROSSING	131	1059	1063	1043	0.1	26	459	473	477	0.7	2.22	299	303	0.3
49913 CALUMET	083	8677	8490	8356	-0.5	8	3534	3511	3502	-0.2	2.32	2125	2074	-0.6
49916 CHASSELL	061	3345	3317	3278	-0.2	16	1349	1353	1352	0.1	2.38	892	879	-0.3
49919 COVINGTON	013	232	221	208	-1.1	2	90	88	84	-0.5	2.42	63	61	-0.8
49920 CRYSTAL FALLS	071	4883	4958	5051	0.4	37	2152	2228	2313	0.8	2.13	1360	1384	0.4
49921 DODGEVILLE	061	487	479	472	-0.4	10	180	180	180	0.0	2.66	109	107	-0.4
49925 EWEN	131	716	697	675	-0.6	7	318	317	315	-0.1	2.19	203	199	-0.5
49927 GAASTRA	071	354	347	348	-0.5	9	134	133	135	-0.2	2.50	92	90	-0.5
49930 HANCOCK	061	7714	7610	7504	-0.3	12	3118	3130	3128	0.1	2.29	1807	1781	-0.3
49931 HOUGHTON	061	8157	8268	8282	0.3	35	2571	2630	2655	0.5	2.35	1181	1183	0.0
49935 IRON RIVER	071	7960	8062	8210	0.3	34	3479	3583	3709	0.7	2.15	2174	2201	0.3
49938 IRONWOOD	053	8801	8344	7959	-1.3	1	3932	3794	3683	-0.8	2.15	2374	2247	-1.3
49945 LAKE LINDEN	061	3470	3373	3304	-0.7	6	1451	1437	1427	-0.2	2.30	982	959	-0.6
49946 LANSE	013	4044	3848	3628	-1.2	2	1659	1610	1547	-0.7	2.31	1094	1046	-1.1
49947 MARENISCO	053	1046	1179	1236	2.9	97	260	319	351	4.9	2.76	184	223	4.6
49948 MASS CITY	131	781	753	726	-0.9	4	345	340	334	-0.3	2.21	227	220	-0.7
49950 MOHAWK	083	1317	1346	1369	0.5	43	606	631	651	1.0	1.98	371	380	0.6
49952 NISULA	061	92	89	87	-0.8	5	40	39	39	-0.6	2.28	25	24	-1.0
49953 ONTONAGON	131	4337	4150	3993	-1.0	3	1903	1864	1835	-0.5	2.14	1216	1171	-0.9
49958 PELKIE	013	2169	2082	1991	-1.0	3	601	588	571	-0.5	3.16	403	387	-1.0
49962 SKANEE	013	334	317	299	-1.2	2	163	159	153	-0.6	1.99	114	109	-1.1
49965 TOIVOLA	061	407	396	389	-0.6	7	176	175	174	-0.1	2.13	114	111	-0.6
49967 TROUT CREEK	061	655	648	635	-0.3	14	319	323	323	0.3	1.98	202	201	-0.1
49968 WAKEFIELD	053	2737	2607	2492	-1.1	2	1180	1153	1127	-0.5	2.15	743	706	-1.2
49969 WATERSMEET	053	1472	1485	1465	0.2	30	552	579	584	1.1	1.92	386	398	0.7
49970 WATTON	013	337	321	303	-1.1	2	148	144	139	-0.6	2.15	104	100	-0.9
MICHIGAN					0.6					1.0	2.52			0.6
UNITED STATES					1.2					1.3	2.58			1.1

#	POST OFFICE NAME	White 2000	White 2004	Black 2000	Black 2004	Asian/Pacific 2000	Asian/Pacific 2004	% Hispanic Origin 2000	% Hispanic Origin 2004	0-4	5-9	10-14	15-19	20-24	25-44	45-64	65-84	85+	18+	MEDIAN AGE 2004	% 2004 Males	% 2004 Females
49879	REPUBLIC	97.4	97.4	0.0	0.0	0.0	0.0	0.1	0.1	3.6	3.9	6.0	5.1	4.8	18.7	31.7	23.5	2.7	83.2	49.7	51.3	48.7
49880	ROCK	96.7	96.7	0.1	0.1	0.5	0.4	0.4	0.5	4.4	4.8	5.9	6.6	5.8	24.1	33.2	13.7	1.5	81.1	44.1	50.9	49.1
49881	SAGOLA	97.8	97.6	0.0	0.0	0.0	0.3	0.8	0.8	6.0	6.0	6.5	6.3	6.0	22.1	30.0	15.5	1.6	77.4	43.0	50.4	49.6
49883	SENEY	93.5	92.9	0.5	0.6	0.0	0.0	0.0	0.0	9.9	6.6	5.0	3.3	3.9	22.5	27.5	18.1	3.3	76.4	44.1	50.6	49.5
49884	SHINGLETON	84.6	84.2	7.5	7.5	0.3	0.4	1.1	1.3	4.9	5.3	5.7	6.4	5.8	27.3	29.2	13.6	1.8	80.0	41.8	55.6	44.4
49885	SKANDIA	95.7	95.6	0.2	0.2	0.2	0.2	0.8	0.8	5.8	5.9	6.6	6.4	5.3	25.6	32.0	11.5	1.1	77.7	41.6	51.7	48.3
49886	SPALDING	95.4	95.3	0.0	0.3	0.0	0.3	0.5	0.5	6.4	6.9	6.9	6.2	5.7	25.4	26.9	13.3	2.2	75.6	40.2	50.9	49.1
49887	STEPHENSON	95.7	95.8	0.1	0.1	0.3	0.3	0.4	0.4	5.3	5.6	6.2	6.1	5.5	22.2	29.8	16.2	3.1	78.8	44.4	49.9	50.1
49891	TRENARY	93.4	93.3	3.2	3.2	0.0	0.0	1.2	1.3	5.0	5.4	5.7	5.2	4.9	22.7	33.5	15.5	2.1	80.9	45.5	52.3	47.7
49892	VULCAN	98.6	98.5	0.1	0.1	0.2	0.2	0.4	0.3	4.9	5.5	7.1	6.8	5.6	24.8	29.5	13.3	2.6	78.3	42.5	50.5	49.6
49893	WALLACE	98.5	98.6	0.1	0.1	0.2	0.2	0.5	0.5	5.4	6.1	6.9	6.6	5.7	24.4	29.1	14.5	1.5	77.4	42.2	51.1	48.9
49894	WELLS	95.9	95.8	0.0	0.0	0.4	0.4	0.7	0.6	6.1	6.4	7.2	6.1	5.2	26.0	26.0	15.3	1.9	76.6	40.5	50.5	49.5
49895	WETMORE	71.7	69.9	24.1	25.8	0.2	0.2	1.3	1.5	3.1	3.5	4.3	4.8	8.4	41.6	24.2	9.2	1.0	86.7	36.9	67.2	32.8
49896	WILSON	88.8	89.3	0.1	0.1	0.1	0.1	1.0	1.1	6.7	7.0	7.3	6.5	5.7	26.7	26.7	12.3	1.4	74.9	39.0	51.6	48.4
49905	ATLANTIC MINE	96.0	95.7	1.9	2.0	0.5	0.7	0.5	0.5	6.8	6.5	7.5	7.4	6.7	25.5	24.4	13.2	1.9	74.1	37.5	52.8	47.2
49908	BARAGA	61.1	59.8	15.5	16.3	0.5	0.7	1.4	1.4	5.3	5.4	5.9	6.3	7.9	36.7	21.7	8.8	2.2	79.9	35.5	60.2	39.8
49910	BERGLAND	98.2	98.1	0.0	0.0	0.4	0.4	0.2	0.2	2.5	3.8	4.6	5.7	3.6	19.3	36.7	21.2	2.7	86.0	50.8	51.5	48.5
49911	BESSEMER	97.1	97.0	0.2	0.2	0.4	0.5	0.6	0.8	4.6	4.8	6.1	6.8	5.9	22.6	27.4	17.8	4.0	80.4	44.5	50.0	50.0
49912	BRUCE CROSSING	97.4	97.1	0.1	0.1	0.3	0.3	0.8	0.9	3.8	4.1	5.8	5.8	5.1	21.8	31.2	19.2	3.2	82.1	47.4	52.4	47.6
49913	CALUMET	97.9	97.7	0.5	0.5	0.2	0.3	0.8	0.9	6.3	6.3	6.9	7.3	6.4	22.9	25.3	15.4	3.3	75.9	40.6	50.5	49.5
49916	CHASSELL	94.7	94.1	1.8	1.9	1.5	1.9	0.6	0.7	5.5	5.7	6.9	7.3	8.1	25.2	26.1	13.5	1.8	77.3	38.3	53.5	46.5
49919	COVINGTON	94.4	94.1	0.4	0.5	0.0	0.0	0.9	1.4	5.4	5.9	6.3	5.9	5.0	21.3	32.1	15.4	2.7	78.3	45.1	52.5	47.5
49920	CRYSTAL FALLS	97.9	97.8	0.2	0.2	0.2	0.2	0.8	0.9	4.0	4.4	5.3	5.7	5.0	18.7	31.3	20.6	5.0	82.7	49.2	49.4	50.6
49921	DODGEVILLE	94.9	94.0	0.2	0.2	3.3	4.2	0.8	1.0	6.1	5.9	7.9	8.8	11.7	28.2	22.8	8.4	0.4	75.2	30.7	54.1	45.9
49925	EWEN	96.8	96.6	0.0	0.0	0.4	0.6	0.7	0.9	4.0	4.3	5.6	5.6	5.2	20.7	32.7	19.4	2.6	82.6	48.1	50.7	49.4
49927	GAASTRA	96.6	96.5	1.1	1.2	0.0	0.0	0.6	0.9	5.2	4.6	4.6	6.9	6.3	20.5	27.7	21.3	2.9	81.0	46.0	49.9	50.1
49930	HANCOCK	97.1	96.8	0.5	0.5	0.7	0.9	0.7	0.9	5.6	5.3	5.8	6.6	9.9	24.9	23.7	13.8	4.5	79.7	38.5	50.3	49.7
49931	HOUGHTON	90.5	88.8	1.6	1.7	5.9	7.4	0.8	0.9	3.5	3.3	4.2	19.7	29.4	18.6	13.3	6.5	1.6	86.1	23.3	58.7	41.3
49935	IRON RIVER	95.3	94.9	1.7	1.8	0.2	0.3	0.5	0.6	4.5	4.8	5.9	6.5	5.4	22.5	27.0	19.5	3.9	80.4	45.3	49.6	50.4
49938	IRONWOOD	97.6	97.4	0.1	0.1	0.2	0.3	0.9	1.0	5.4	5.2	5.8	6.6	6.0	22.4	26.0	18.3	4.3	79.7	44.0	47.8	52.2
49945	LAKE LINDEN	98.2	98.1	0.2	0.2	0.2	0.3	0.6	0.7	6.4	6.5	6.1	5.6	5.3	21.5	28.3	17.2	3.1	77.4	44.0	50.6	49.4
49946	LANSE	83.8	83.4	0.2	0.2	0.2	0.3	0.7	0.7	5.6	5.9	7.0	5.9	4.9	24.6	27.3	15.5	3.3	77.8	42.0	48.1	51.9
49947	MARENISCO	79.2	80.6	16.1	14.7	0.2	0.3	2.0	2.1	2.4	2.8	3.4	4.8	8.9	28.2	27.7	18.1	3.8	89.0	44.7	61.7	38.3
49948	MASS CITY	97.2	96.7	0.0	0.0	0.1	0.1	1.0	1.3	5.7	5.8	5.1	4.9	4.8	22.3	32.3	16.5	2.7	81.0	45.9	53.0	47.0
49950	MOHAWK	95.4	95.3	3.3	3.4	0.1	0.1	0.7	0.8	4.4	4.6	5.4	10.6	4.8	19.5	30.7	17.4	2.8	78.2	45.5	52.8	47.3
49952	NISULA	95.7	95.5	0.0	0.0	1.1	1.1	0.0	0.0	4.5	4.5	4.5	5.6	5.6	21.4	36.0	15.7	2.3	83.2	47.5	57.3	42.7
49953	ONTONAGON	97.2	96.9	0.0	0.0	0.1	0.2	0.7	0.9	4.5	4.8	5.4	5.8	4.4	20.4	31.4	19.8	3.5	81.4	48.0	49.9	50.1
49958	PELKIE	81.2	80.4	6.4	6.7	0.5	0.6	1.0	1.1	5.2	5.5	6.0	6.1	6.5	27.8	27.6	12.8	2.5	79.6	40.2	56.0	44.0
49962	SKANEE	89.2	88.6	0.0	0.0	0.3	0.3	0.3	0.0	4.7	3.2	6.3	5.7	2.8	20.8	37.9	16.1	2.5	82.0	49.1	52.7	47.3
49965	TOIVOLA	92.6	92.2	3.2	3.5	0.3	0.3	0.5	0.5	4.8	5.3	5.3	6.3	7.3	25.3	30.3	13.9	1.5	80.8	41.9	56.3	43.7
49967	TROUT CREEK	96.6	96.1	0.0	0.0	0.9	1.2	0.6	0.8	4.0	4.3	5.6	5.3	5.1	20.8	32.4	19.1	3.4	82.4	48.1	54.0	46.0
49968	WAKEFIELD	97.9	97.7	0.0	0.0	0.2	0.2	0.3	0.3	3.7	3.8	4.5	5.3	5.6	22.0	28.5	21.6	5.0	84.8	48.2	49.5	50.5
49969	WATERSMEET	71.7	71.6	8.2	8.4	0.2	0.2	1.6	1.8	4.1	4.8	5.6	10.0	10.9	25.7	23.7	14.1	1.1	81.0	36.0	60.7	39.3
49970	WATTON	94.7	94.4	0.3	0.3	0.0	0.0	1.2	1.3	5.3	5.9	6.5	5.9	5.0	21.8	31.5	15.3	2.8	78.5	44.7	52.3	47.7
	MICHIGAN	80.2	79.2	14.2	14.4	1.8	2.3	3.3	3.6	6.8	6.9	7.4	7.1	6.9	28.1	24.6	10.8	1.6	74.9	36.5	49.1	50.9
	UNITED STATES	75.1	73.6	12.3	12.5	3.8	4.2	12.5	14.1	6.9	6.7	7.2	7.0	7.3	28.6	23.8	10.8	1.7	75.1	36.0	49.1	50.9

MICHIGAN   INCOME

C   49879-49970

#	POST OFFICE NAME	2004 Per Capita Income	2004 HH Income Base	2004 HOUSEHOLD INCOME DISTRIBUTION (%) Less than $25,000	$25,000 to $49,999	$50,000 to $99,999	$100,000 to $149,999	$150,000 or More	MEDIAN HOUSEHOLD INCOME 2004	2009	2004 National Centile	2004 State Centile	2004 Home Value Base	2004 HOME VALUE DISTRIBUTION (%) Less than $50,000	$50,000 to $89,999	$90,000 to $174,999	$175,000 to $399,999	$400,000 or More	2004 Median Home Value
49879	REPUBLIC	17953	441	40.1	34.5	22.5	1.4	1.6	30461	34723	13	6	392	40.6	37.2	17.9	3.8	0.5	60926
49880	ROCK	19686	505	31.9	34.5	28.1	4.2	1.4	38993	44158	43	30	455	22.6	36.3	34.5	5.5	1.1	81000
49881	SAGOLA	18877	155	32.3	33.6	27.7	4.5	1.9	37328	41613	37	24	142	24.7	31.7	34.5	9.2	0.0	81818
49883	SENEY	14077	59	44.1	28.8	23.7	3.4	0.0	31707	35755	17	7	55	30.9	29.1	27.3	10.9	1.8	75000
49884	SHINGLETON	13929	242	26.5	35.5	32.2	4.6	1.2	40790	42810	49	38	211	18.5	32.2	37.4	10.9	1.0	89167
49885	SKANDIA	20715	1004	25.6	32.2	34.1	5.6	2.6	42635	45827	55	44	880	17.1	24.9	43.1	14.6	0.5	101333
49886	SPALDING	16749	152	34.9	33.6	26.3	4.6	0.7	35399	38102	29	16	125	26.4	28.8	36.0	8.0	0.8	81875
49887	STEPHENSON	18949	1152	34.4	34.7	26.7	3.0	1.1	35720	38907	30	17	961	20.1	31.0	38.9	8.7	1.3	88671
49891	TRENARY	19245	333	33.3	38.4	23.4	4.5	0.3	34366	38218	25	13	302	22.9	30.1	37.4	9.6	0.0	86250
49892	VULCAN	19484	955	31.3	33.3	27.5	6.1	1.8	39172	41171	43	30	841	22.1	27.9	35.0	13.6	1.4	89884
49893	WALLACE	20450	887	25.9	34.7	33.3	5.0	1.1	40891	43623	49	39	784	16.2	25.4	42.5	15.1	0.9	104741
49894	WELLS	19051	300	36.0	29.7	27.3	5.7	1.1	37212	41667	36	24	242	15.3	46.3	31.0	7.4	0.0	81765
49895	WETMORE	12650	177	27.1	36.7	29.9	5.1	1.1	40735	44723	49	38	162	22.2	21.0	37.0	19.1	0.6	102174
49896	WILSON	15329	593	32.0	36.3	27.2	3.7	0.8	35135	38505	28	15	497	22.7	28.8	37.6	9.3	1.6	87917
49905	ATLANTIC MINE	16595	1391	33.4	34.3	26.3	4.5	1.5	35982	39871	31	19	1109	37.5	26.9	24.0	10.4	1.3	63493
49908	BARAGA	19714	764	39.0	35.5	20.6	4.1	0.8	33534	36219	23	12	513	25.0	35.9	33.3	5.3	0.6	79043
49910	BERGLAND	18701	255	37.3	39.2	19.6	2.8	1.2	29730	33113	12	5	209	42.1	26.3	20.6	10.1	1.0	60938
49911	BESSEMER	20357	1485	41.0	34.0	20.3	2.9	1.8	30394	32720	13	5	1121	50.8	29.4	16.0	3.8	0.2	49472
49912	BRUCE CROSSING	16965	473	41.4	33.4	20.7	3.4	1.1	30735	32328	14	6	393	37.4	33.8	21.4	6.6	0.8	63125
49913	CALUMET	16671	3511	43.7	32.6	18.1	3.7	1.9	28366	31128	9	3	2758	44.7	32.7	17.1	4.9	0.7	55194
49916	CHASSELL	19031	1353	37.2	30.2	24.7	5.9	2.0	35351	37534	29	15	1055	23.0	33.2	28.5	12.7	2.6	82957
49919	COVINGTON	20845	88	25.0	35.2	34.1	5.7	0.0	43191	45000	56	47	81	27.2	30.9	32.1	9.9	0.0	74167
49920	CRYSTAL FALLS	18280	2228	38.3	34.5	23.2	3.4	0.6	32539	34661	19	9	1876	30.0	32.0	28.4	8.6	1.1	72787
49921	DODGEVILLE	15855	180	43.3	23.3	24.4	6.7	2.2	31509	32981	16	7	123	22.0	39.8	23.6	14.6	0.0	75417
49925	EWEN	17360	317	43.9	31.9	19.6	3.5	1.3	29130	30820	11	4	254	41.7	33.1	20.9	3.5	0.8	61667
49927	GAASTRA	15363	133	42.1	33.8	21.1	2.3	0.8	31774	33634	17	7	113	47.8	23.0	20.4	8.0	0.9	52778
49930	HANCOCK	17862	3130	38.6	33.9	21.7	4.2	1.6	31785	34123	17	7	2068	27.3	35.6	28.4	7.6	1.0	72807
49931	HOUGHTON	15305	2630	48.9	23.7	21.0	5.5	1.0	25953	27232	6	2	1184	11.9	30.2	43.2	13.8	0.8	105061
49935	IRON RIVER	18454	3583	42.1	32.5	21.3	2.9	1.3	30210	32270	13	5	2820	38.1	33.1	21.0	6.8	1.1	60540
49938	IRONWOOD	17181	3794	45.5	30.7	18.7	3.6	1.5	27698	29425	8	3	2763	47.3	29.9	17.9	4.7	0.3	52980
49945	LAKE LINDEN	18498	1437	34.6	33.4	26.5	4.1	1.4	34697	38101	26	13	1158	33.0	30.7	22.4	11.6	2.3	69355
49946	LANSE	18511	1610	34.2	32.3	28.3	4.4	0.9	36462	39318	33	21	1253	22.7	33.3	35.3	7.8	1.0	83578
49947	MARENISCO	15548	319	27.0	40.1	28.2	3.1	1.6	39194	44440	43	30	295	28.1	21.4	20.3	24.1	6.1	91364
49948	MASS CITY	19809	340	30.9	37.1	28.2	2.7	1.2	35959	39732	31	19	304	46.7	32.9	15.8	4.0	0.7	53226
49950	MOHAWK	20985	631	35.0	38.0	20.3	3.8	2.9	32749	35420	20	10	565	36.8	26.9	21.1	10.8	4.4	63723
49952	NISULA	16044	39	41.0	35.9	20.5	2.6	0.0	29265	32308	11	4	33	36.4	33.3	30.3	0.0	0.0	63750
49953	ONTONAGON	19747	1864	37.5	32.9	23.4	4.1	2.0	32927	34894	21	10	1497	44.2	34.9	16.4	4.3	0.3	56119
49958	PELKIE	14454	588	31.0	35.5	27.0	5.1	1.4	38428	41382	41	28	512	28.3	32.0	31.3	7.6	0.8	73846
49962	SKANEE	20162	159	42.1	28.3	26.4	1.9	1.3	32032	34070	18	8	147	17.7	27.2	43.5	11.6	0.0	100481
49965	TOIVOLA	17439	175	38.3	35.4	22.3	3.4	0.6	31599	34589	17	7	148	31.1	33.1	29.1	6.1	0.7	70833
49967	TROUT CREEK	18853	323	40.6	36.2	19.5	3.1	0.6	30942	34105	15	6	270	40.0	33.7	21.5	4.4	0.4	59310
49968	WAKEFIELD	18091	1153	43.6	32.9	19.2	2.8	1.6	28342	30028	9	3	940	57.2	26.9	13.7	2.0	0.1	44646
49969	WATERSMEET	23234	579	30.7	37.1	21.8	5.9	4.5	35915	39556	31	18	479	28.2	25.5	22.1	17.5	6.7	83966
49970	WATTON	23659	144	25.0	33.3	34.7	5.6	1.4	44383	45753	60	51	132	25.8	31.8	31.8	9.1	1.5	74444
	MICHIGAN	25281		23.8	27.4	32.3	10.9	5.5	48729	54505				10.7	16.0	40.3	28.0	5.0	134769
	UNITED STATES	25866		24.7	27.1	30.8	10.9	6.5	48124	56710				10.9	15.0	33.7	30.1	10.4	145905

#	POST OFFICE NAME	FINANCIAL SERVICES				THE HOME						ENTERTAINMENT						PERSONAL			
						Home Improvements		Furnishings													
		Auto Loan	Home Loan	Invest-ments	Retire-ment Plans	Home Repair	Lawn & Garden	Comput-ers & Hard-ware	Major Appli-ances	TV, Radio, Sound Equip-ment	Furni-ture	Dine out/ Carry out	Sports Equip-ment	Fees & Tickets	Toys & Games	Travel	Cable TV	Apparel & Services	Auto Repairs	Health Insur-ance	Pets & Supplies
49879	REPUBLIC	67	52	36	47	59	66	49	60	56	49	66	70	44	65	53	60	62	59	70	81
49880	ROCK	78	61	42	55	69	77	58	69	65	57	77	81	52	76	61	70	72	68	82	95
49881	SAGOLA	76	59	41	54	67	75	56	68	63	56	75	79	50	74	60	68	70	67	80	92
49883	SENEY	69	54	37	49	61	68	51	61	58	51	68	72	46	68	54	62	64	60	73	84
49884	SHINGLETON	79	69	51	64	74	80	64	72	69	64	83	85	61	84	66	71	78	70	80	94
49885	SKANDIA	90	65	37	61	75	84	64	78	73	63	86	93	55	84	66	77	79	77	92	108
49886	SPALDING	73	59	41	54	65	73	56	66	63	55	75	77	51	74	59	67	69	65	77	88
49887	STEPHENSON	74	54	31	48	60	69	53	63	61	53	72	74	46	69	54	66	66	63	77	86
49891	TRENARY	69	54	37	49	61	68	51	61	57	50	68	72	45	67	54	61	63	60	72	84
49892	VULCAN	75	63	48	58	69	78	61	70	67	60	81	80	57	81	64	71	75	69	81	90
49893	WALLACE	82	69	49	64	74	80	64	73	70	64	84	87	61	85	66	72	79	71	81	96
49894	WELLS	62	60	56	58	62	69	60	62	63	59	78	70	61	81	61	65	74	61	67	71
49895	WETMORE	81	63	43	57	71	80	60	72	68	59	80	84	53	79	64	72	75	71	85	99
49896	WILSON	71	59	42	54	65	71	55	64	61	55	73	76	51	73	58	64	68	63	73	86
49905	ATLANTIC MINE	69	56	42	54	61	70	58	64	64	56	76	73	54	76	59	67	71	63	73	79
49908	BARAGA	65	50	35	49	54	64	55	60	60	52	72	67	50	68	54	63	66	59	70	72
49910	BERGLAND	66	52	35	46	58	65	49	59	55	48	65	69	43	64	52	59	61	58	69	80
49911	BESSEMER	69	54	39	52	59	69	59	64	65	56	77	72	54	75	59	68	71	64	75	77
49912	BRUCE CROSSING	64	50	34	45	57	64	47	57	54	47	64	67	42	63	50	57	59	56	67	78
49913	CALUMET	61	50	38	47	53	62	52	57	58	50	69	65	48	66	53	60	64	57	67	70
49916	CHASSELL	77	57	38	54	64	73	60	68	67	58	79	81	53	77	61	69	73	68	79	90
49919	COVINGTON	87	68	46	61	77	86	64	77	73	64	86	91	57	85	68	78	80	76	91	106
49920	CRYSTAL FALLS	66	51	34	47	56	65	51	59	57	50	68	68	45	66	53	61	63	59	70	77
49921	DODGEVILLE	55	57	66	59	57	59	61	59	59	59	75	71	61	76	60	57	73	60	55	63
49925	EWEN	65	51	35	46	57	64	48	58	54	47	64	67	43	63	51	58	60	57	68	79
49927	GAASTRA	65	51	34	46	57	65	49	58	56	48	66	68	44	64	52	59	61	58	69	78
49930	HANCOCK	61	52	50	52	54	62	58	59	61	56	75	68	54	72	57	62	70	60	64	69
49931	HOUGHTON	53	40	47	43	40	45	61	49	59	54	74	65	53	69	52	54	70	56	46	56
49935	IRON RIVER	66	50	34	47	56	65	53	60	60	51	70	68	47	67	54	63	64	60	72	76
49938	IRONWOOD	58	47	38	45	50	58	50	54	55	48	66	62	46	63	50	57	61	54	62	65
49945	LAKE LINDEN	70	54	37	51	60	70	56	64	63	54	74	73	51	72	57	67	69	63	75	81
49946	LANSE	67	57	45	53	61	70	57	63	63	55	75	72	54	75	59	66	70	62	73	78
49947	MARENISCO	78	61	41	55	68	77	57	69	65	57	77	81	51	76	61	69	71	68	82	95
49948	MASS CITY	67	60	50	55	64	72	57	64	62	56	75	73	55	77	60	66	71	63	73	81
49950	MOHAWK	72	55	37	51	62	71	55	64	62	54	73	74	49	71	57	66	68	64	76	84
49952	NISULA	62	49	33	44	55	62	46	55	52	45	62	65	41	61	49	56	57	54	65	76
49953	ONTONAGON	70	54	37	51	59	69	57	64	63	54	75	72	51	72	57	67	69	63	76	80
49958	PELKIE	77	61	43	57	68	77	60	69	67	59	79	81	54	78	62	70	74	69	81	91
49962	SKANEE	68	53	36	48	60	68	50	61	57	50	68	71	45	67	54	61	63	60	72	83
49965	TOIVOLA	64	50	34	45	56	63	47	57	54	47	63	67	42	63	50	57	59	56	67	78
49967	TROUT CREEK	64	50	34	45	56	63	47	57	53	47	63	66	42	62	50	57	59	56	67	78
49968	WAKEFIELD	64	48	32	46	53	63	53	58	59	50	70	66	47	66	53	62	64	58	70	72
49969	WATERSMEET	87	69	47	62	77	87	65	78	73	64	87	91	58	86	69	78	81	77	92	107
49970	WATTON	88	69	47	62	77	87	65	78	73	64	87	91	58	86	69	78	81	77	92	107
	MICHIGAN	91	91	93	89	91	98	90	91	91	90	113	106	90	113	90	91	109	91	92	105
	UNITED STATES	100	100	100	100	100	100	100	100	100	100	100	100	100	100	100	100	100	100	100	100

POPULATION CHANGE

# POST OFFICE NAME	COUNTY FIPS CODE	POPULATION 2000	2004	2009	2000-2004 ANNUAL RATE % Rate	State Centile	HOUSEHOLDS 2000	2004	2009	% Annual Rate 2000-2004	2004 Average HH Size	FAMILIES 2000	2004	% Annual Rate 2000-2004
55001 AFTON	163	2851	2912	3133	0.5	43	999	1042	1142	1.0	2.79	837	857	0.6
55003 BAYPORT	163	2871	2872	2943	0.0	28	659	673	719	0.5	2.15	422	413	-0.5
55005 BETHEL	003	3380	3920	4427	3.6	93	1090	1297	1495	4.2	3.02	909	1057	3.6
55006 BRAHAM	065	2700	2976	3433	2.3	83	1042	1169	1371	2.7	2.54	741	807	2.0
55007 BROOK PARK	115	2267	2353	2533	0.9	56	838	885	966	1.3	2.66	633	653	0.7
55008 CAMBRIDGE	059	12366	13780	16268	2.6	85	4574	5188	6242	3.0	2.58	3264	3609	2.4
55009 CANNON FALLS	049	7868	8469	9088	1.8	74	2954	3232	3517	2.1	2.59	2160	2303	1.5
55011 CEDAR	003	9299	10196	11165	2.2	81	3006	3370	3761	2.7	3.03	2501	2749	2.3
55012 CENTER CITY	025	1806	2050	2442	3.0	90	557	645	781	3.5	3.11	429	487	3.0
55013 CHISAGO CITY	025	4796	5660	6875	4.0	94	1754	2093	2573	4.3	2.64	1290	1514	3.8
55014 CIRCLE PINES	003	25131	27013	29369	1.7	73	7996	8761	9717	2.2	2.94	6391	6859	1.7
55016 COTTAGE GROVE	163	30117	32482	35728	1.8	75	9768	10767	12067	2.3	3.01	8307	9013	1.9
55017 DALBO	059	725	787	914	2.0	77	259	288	341	2.5	2.73	194	210	1.9
55018 DENNISON	049	969	1026	1095	1.4	66	341	366	396	1.7	2.80	278	293	1.2
55019 DUNDAS	131	914	1068	1255	3.7	94	345	405	479	3.8	2.64	256	297	3.6
55020 ELKO	139	2110	2663	3502	5.6	99	669	856	1139	6.0	3.11	572	721	5.6
55021 FARIBAULT	131	27265	29947	33954	2.2	82	9772	10872	12502	2.5	2.58	6778	7334	1.9
55024 FARMINGTON	037	21290	25353	29291	4.2	95	7035	8440	9830	4.4	2.99	5635	6662	4.0
55025 FOREST LAKE	003	18626	20356	22567	2.1	80	6810	7607	8586	2.6	2.66	5080	5534	2.0
55026 FRONTENAC	049	492	507	529	0.7	50	206	214	226	0.9	2.35	158	161	0.4
55027 GOODHUE	049	2595	2564	2668	-0.3	17	924	926	975	0.1	2.77	724	710	-0.5
55030 GRASSTON	065	268	276	294	0.7	49	99	104	112	1.2	2.65	77	79	0.6
55031 HAMPTON	037	1734	1837	1986	1.4	66	572	615	673	1.7	2.98	455	479	1.2
55032 HARRIS	025	3191	3699	4460	3.5	93	1101	1296	1582	3.9	2.85	855	985	3.4
55033 HASTINGS	037	25674	27323	29730	1.5	68	9094	9791	10780	1.8	2.72	6805	7153	1.2
55036 HENRIETTE	115	101	107	117	1.4	66	37	40	44	1.9	2.67	28	30	1.6
55037 HINCKLEY	115	3707	3952	4299	1.5	69	1439	1555	1717	1.8	2.52	978	1027	1.2
55038 HUGO	163	12507	15706	18496	5.5	98	4103	5251	6288	6.0	2.99	3398	4263	5.5
55040 ISANTI	059	9599	12059	15063	5.5	98	3252	4172	5304	6.0	2.88	2546	3191	5.5
55041 LAKE CITY	157	7026	7332	7721	1.0	59	2813	2974	3175	1.3	2.42	1974	2033	0.7
55042 LAKE ELMO	163	7518	8648	9762	3.4	91	2542	2975	3414	3.8	2.89	2100	2410	3.3
55043 LAKELAND	163	3771	3841	4097	0.4	42	1406	1467	1595	1.0	2.62	1056	1071	0.3
55044 LAKEVILLE	037	35069	40231	45783	3.3	91	11044	12672	14487	3.3	3.17	9401	10670	3.0
55045 LINDSTROM	025	5299	5920	6993	2.6	86	2024	2287	2737	2.9	2.51	1505	1660	2.3
55046 LONSDALE	131	2845	3362	3965	4.0	94	1005	1209	1445	4.4	2.76	765	901	3.9
55047 MARINE ON SAINT CROI	163	2628	2734	2940	0.9	57	970	1033	1133	1.5	2.64	764	794	0.9
55049 MEDFORD	147	2020	2151	2284	1.5	69	753	817	880	1.9	2.61	573	606	1.3
55051 MORA	065	9784	10375	11254	1.4	66	3850	4142	4556	1.7	2.48	2710	2838	1.1
55052 MORRISTOWN	131	1938	2125	2411	2.2	81	720	800	918	2.5	2.63	541	587	1.9
55053 NERSTRAND	131	956	1056	1201	2.4	83	316	351	403	2.5	3.00	261	286	2.2
55054 NEW MARKET	139	317	424	572	7.1	100	127	172	235	7.4	2.47	109	145	7.0
55055 NEWPORT	163	3707	3704	3949	0.0	26	1414	1443	1570	0.5	2.55	966	952	-0.3
55056 NORTH BRANCH	025	10910	13345	16493	4.9	97	3820	4731	5912	5.2	2.82	2969	3598	4.6
55057 NORTHFIELD	131	22064	24192	27077	2.2	81	6533	7408	8576	3.0	2.63	4572	5041	2.3
55060 OWATONNA	147	27101	28554	30252	1.2	64	10359	11051	11854	1.5	2.54	7239	7523	0.9
55063 PINE CITY	115	9184	10104	11193	2.3	82	3514	3925	4416	2.6	2.53	2465	2677	2.0
55065 RANDOLPH	037	915	966	1045	1.3	65	310	332	364	1.6	2.90	247	259	1.1
55066 RED WING	049	18285	18826	19789	0.7	49	7310	7632	8133	1.0	2.38	4783	4840	0.3
55067 ROCK CREEK	115	550	594	651	1.8	76	187	206	230	2.3	2.88	145	157	1.9
55068 ROSEMOUNT	037	20690	23200	25908	2.7	87	6693	7572	8532	3.0	3.06	5560	6185	2.5
55069 RUSH CITY	025	4199	4599	5345	2.2	80	1476	1651	1962	2.7	2.60	1065	1159	2.0
55070 SAINT FRANCIS	003	5080	6352	7438	5.4	98	1700	2183	2611	6.1	2.91	1347	1685	5.4
55071 SAINT PAUL PARK	163	5300	5330	5661	0.1	32	1922	1973	2134	0.6	2.67	1420	1415	-0.1
55072 SANDSTONE	115	4703	5053	5440	1.7	73	1469	1606	1785	2.1	2.47	1003	1065	1.4
55073 SCANDIA	163	3137	3312	3600	1.3	65	1080	1165	1288	1.8	2.84	920	976	1.4
55074 SHAFER	025	939	1153	1428	5.0	98	335	416	520	5.2	2.77	257	313	4.8
55075 SOUTH SAINT PAUL	037	20173	20450	22027	0.3	39	8124	8315	9047	0.6	2.45	5240	5185	-0.3
55076 INVER GROVE HEIGHTS	037	18509	19936	21922	1.8	75	7027	7718	8608	2.2	2.57	5136	5481	1.5
55077 INVER GROVE HEIGHTS	037	11395	12521	13899	2.2	82	4286	4747	5310	2.4	2.61	2858	3074	1.7
55079 STACY	025	7372	8177	9374	2.5	85	2509	2840	3311	3.0	2.87	2024	2244	2.5
55080 STANCHFIELD	059	2441	2748	3255	2.8	88	890	1019	1226	3.2	2.69	678	758	2.7
55082 STILLWATER	163	30923	32838	35787	1.4	67	11233	12145	13476	1.9	2.63	8448	8951	1.4
55084 TAYLORS FALLS	025	1429	1715	2102	4.4	96	527	638	790	4.6	2.69	386	457	4.1
55087 WARSAW	131	292	318	361	2.0	79	96	106	121	2.4	2.98	77	83	1.8
55088 WEBSTER	131	1723	1874	2165	2.0	78	583	642	748	2.3	2.91	490	533	2.0
55089 WELCH	049	1876	1929	2044	0.7	48	638	668	717	1.1	2.88	507	520	0.6
55092 WYOMING	003	9544	10372	11677	2.0	78	3260	3601	4110	2.4	2.87	2641	2856	1.9
55101 SAINT PAUL	123	22166	23153	23919	1.0	60	8490	8869	9211	1.0	2.51	4198	4172	-0.2
55102 SAINT PAUL	123	18299	18648	19082	0.5	42	8735	8986	9292	0.7	1.95	3305	3251	-0.4
55103 SAINT PAUL	123	13238	14341	15131	1.9	77	4435	4736	4982	1.6	2.99	2605	2694	0.8
55104 SAINT PAUL	123	48381	48556	49232	0.1	30	18007	18261	18697	0.3	2.47	9287	8986	-0.8
55105 SAINT PAUL	123	26543	26822	27388	0.3	36	11141	11437	11834	0.6	2.16	5780	5649	-0.5
55106 SAINT PAUL	123	54318	53986	54317	-0.1	22	18547	18325	18453	-0.3	2.91	11865	11331	-1.1
55107 SAINT PAUL	123	16133	16728	17385	0.9	55	5564	5746	5983	0.8	2.86	3477	3459	-0.1
55108 SAINT PAUL	123	16397	16164	16248	-0.3	15	6770	6727	6830	-0.2	2.14	3434	3261	-1.2
55109 SAINT PAUL	123	29116	29134	29439	0.0	28	11365	11580	11852	0.4	2.47	7645	7541	-0.3
55110 SAINT PAUL	123	39985	41851	43594	1.1	60	15047	16004	16854	1.5	2.59	11006	11408	0.9
55112 SAINT PAUL	123	44721	45004	45684	0.2	33	17049	17464	17967	0.6	2.43	11551	11457	-0.2
55113 SAINT PAUL	123	37605	37438	37784	-0.1	24	16277	16501	16867	0.3	2.17	9644	9399	-0.6
55114 SAINT PAUL	123	1309	1376	1418	1.2	62	713	759	790	1.5	1.75	249	249	0.0
55115 SAINT PAUL	163	9248	9908	10826	1.6	72	3140	3424	3802	2.1	2.88	2500	2659	1.5
55116 SAINT PAUL	123	22871	23163	23655	0.3	37	10990	11287	11658	0.6	2.00	5409	5298	-0.5
55117 SAINT PAUL	123	40890	41502	42251	0.4	39	16401	16822	17272	0.6	2.45	9675	9543	-0.3
55118 SAINT PAUL	037	27005	27882	29991	0.8	51	11544	12018	13049	1.0	2.29	7144	7218	0.2
55119 SAINT PAUL	123	37840	38596	39361	0.5	43	15202	15654	16110	0.7	2.43	9670	9666	0.0
55120 SAINT PAUL	037	4722	4845	5187	0.6	47	1732	1795	1941	0.8	2.68	1225	1234	0.2
55121 SAINT PAUL	037	7451	8711	9919	3.7	94	3139	3722	4287	4.1	2.34	1780	2024	3.1
55122 SAINT PAUL	037	29454	32572	36137	2.4	84	11752	13145	14723	2.7	2.47	7699	8333	1.9
55123 SAINT PAUL	037	26701	28825	31707	1.8	76	8900	9592	10582	1.8	3.00	6968	7382	1.4
55124 SAINT PAUL	037	45485	48440	53125	1.5	69	16330	17693	19667	1.9	2.72	12390	13041	1.2
55125 SAINT PAUL	163	40093	46344	52548	3.5	92	14469	16949	19484	3.8	2.71	10893	12536	3.4
55126 SAINT PAUL	123	25940	26504	27135	0.5	44	10129	10522	10914	0.9	2.50	7171	7260	0.3
55127 SAINT PAUL	123	17030	17892	18512	1.2	62	6445	6885	7209	1.6	2.58	4686	4914	1.1
55128 SAINT PAUL	163	27392	28953	31440	1.3	65	10548	11378	12578	1.8	2.54	7305	7606	1.0
55129 SAINT PAUL	163	6380	8526	10357	7.1	100	2211	3021	3737	7.6	2.82	1775	2381	7.2
MINNESOTA					1.4					1.6	2.50			1.0
UNITED STATES					1.2					1.3	2.58			1.1

ZIP CODE		RACE (%)						% Hispanic Origin		2004 AGE DISTRIBUTION (%)										MEDIAN AGE		
#	POST OFFICE NAME	White 2000	White 2004	Black 2000	Black 2004	Asian/Pacific 2000	Asian/Pacific 2004	2000	2004	0-4	5-9	10-14	15-19	20-24	25-44	45-64	65-84	85+	18+	2004	% 2004 Males	% 2004 Females
55001	AFTON	96.7	96.1	0.3	0.3	1.0	1.2	1.0	1.2	4.8	6.8	8.2	7.1	4.7	21.2	37.8	8.5	0.9	75.6	43.6	49.7	50.3
55003	BAYPORT	70.5	67.8	19.8	22.6	0.7	0.8	3.5	3.7	2.4	2.6	3.6	3.7	14.7	44.2	19.2	8.0	1.7	89.5	34.8	74.2	25.8
55005	BETHEL	96.9	96.5	0.2	0.3	0.3	0.4	0.9	1.1	8.4	8.1	8.9	8.6	6.4	33.5	22.2	3.7	0.3	69.4	31.9	52.2	47.8
55006	BRAHAM	97.4	97.1	0.2	0.3	0.2	0.3	0.6	0.6	7.2	6.9	7.3	7.4	7.2	28.5	23.9	10.1	1.6	74.1	35.4	51.0	49.0
55007	BROOK PARK	97.2	96.9	0.4	0.5	0.2	0.2	0.7	0.8	6.1	6.6	8.0	7.7	6.5	26.3	26.7	11.3	0.9	74.4	38.6	51.2	48.8
55008	CAMBRIDGE	97.4	97.0	0.3	0.4	0.5	0.7	0.8	0.9	6.6	6.7	6.9	7.8	7.4	26.1	23.8	11.5	3.3	74.6	38.0	48.5	51.5
55009	CANNON FALLS	98.4	98.1	0.1	0.2	0.5	0.5	0.9	1.1	6.2	6.6	8.1	7.6	6.4	27.4	25.5	10.4	1.8	74.1	37.8	50.4	49.6
55011	CEDAR	97.6	97.2	0.2	0.3	0.4	0.5	0.9	1.1	7.5	7.9	8.9	8.2	6.0	32.0	25.1	4.2	0.3	70.7	35.0	51.7	48.3
55012	CENTER CITY	97.8	97.5	0.4	0.5	0.4	0.5	1.0	1.3	7.5	7.4	8.2	7.8	5.4	28.4	25.2	9.0	1.1	71.5	36.3	52.2	47.9
55013	CHISAGO CITY	97.6	97.1	0.4	0.6	0.4	0.5	1.1	1.3	7.0	7.1	7.5	7.0	5.7	26.1	25.8	10.3	3.6	74.0	39.0	49.4	50.7
55014	CIRCLE PINES	94.0	92.9	1.9	2.4	1.4	1.7	1.6	1.9	7.8	8.4	9.0	7.7	6.4	34.5	21.4	4.5	0.3	69.7	33.5	52.7	47.3
55016	COTTAGE GROVE	93.5	92.1	2.4	3.1	1.5	1.8	2.6	3.1	8.7	8.6	9.0	7.5	6.0	32.3	22.3	5.3	0.2	68.9	32.6	49.5	50.5
55017	DALBO	98.6	98.5	0.0	0.0	0.6	0.6	0.6	0.6	5.8	6.5	7.2	7.4	6.0	26.9	28.5	9.9	1.8	75.9	39.9	49.9	50.1
55018	DENNISON	97.4	97.0	0.1	0.1	0.4	0.5	0.5	0.8	6.7	7.1	7.4	7.6	5.7	25.4	30.0	9.0	1.1	73.5	39.5	52.2	47.8
55019	DUNDAS	97.5	96.9	0.7	0.8	0.6	0.8	1.5	1.7	5.4	6.0	8.8	8.7	6.7	27.3	27.7	8.7	0.7	74.1	37.4	51.1	48.9
55020	ELKO	98.5	98.2	0.1	0.2	0.3	0.3	0.9	1.1	8.0	8.6	9.4	7.4	4.9	30.4	25.7	5.4	0.4	69.4	35.7	52.2	47.8
55021	FARIBAULT	92.0	90.6	2.1	2.5	1.5	1.8	7.1	8.5	6.7	6.6	7.2	7.8	7.1	28.7	23.1	10.7	2.1	74.6	35.9	51.6	48.4
55024	FARMINGTON	95.2	94.2	0.7	1.0	1.9	2.4	1.6	2.1	11.4	10.3	8.6	6.7	5.6	37.2	15.7	3.7	0.7	65.5	30.7	50.6	49.4
55025	FOREST LAKE	97.5	97.2	0.3	0.4	0.6	0.6	0.9	1.1	6.8	7.1	7.7	7.1	6.1	28.2	27.4	8.3	1.3	73.9	37.6	50.0	50.1
55026	FRONTENAC	98.4	98.0	0.2	0.4	0.4	0.6	0.6	0.6	5.9	7.3	6.7	6.3	3.2	25.6	31.8	11.4	1.8	75.5	42.3	48.9	51.1
55027	GOODHUE	97.7	97.2	0.0	0.0	0.4	0.5	1.5	1.9	6.5	6.8	7.9	7.5	6.6	26.7	26.3	10.7	1.1	74.1	37.4	52.5	47.5
55030	GRASSTON	98.1	98.2	0.0	0.4	0.0	0.0	0.8	0.7	6.2	6.5	6.9	6.9	7.3	26.1	27.9	11.6	0.7	76.1	38.6	52.9	47.1
55031	HAMPTON	98.3	97.9	0.1	0.2	0.3	0.3	1.0	1.3	6.6	7.1	8.3	8.3	6.0	28.4	25.4	9.0	0.8	72.2	36.8	51.3	48.7
55032	HARRIS	98.3	98.0	0.3	0.4	0.2	0.3	1.0	1.2	6.3	7.7	8.5	7.9	4.9	29.6	25.3	9.2	0.6	72.2	37.1	52.1	47.9
55033	HASTINGS	97.3	96.9	0.4	0.5	0.6	0.7	1.1	1.4	6.7	6.7	7.6	7.2	6.9	28.8	25.4	9.2	1.5	74.5	36.4	50.3	49.8
55036	HENRIETTE	98.0	97.2	0.0	0.9	0.0	0.0	0.0	0.0	6.5	6.5	5.6	5.6	5.6	27.1	27.1	15.9	0.0	76.6	41.6	51.4	48.6
55037	HINCKLEY	91.3	90.7	0.4	0.6	0.6	0.7	1.3	1.6	6.2	6.7	8.1	8.3	6.1	25.4	26.0	11.9	1.4	73.5	37.9	49.9	50.1
55038	HUGO	96.9	96.4	0.2	0.3	1.3	1.5	1.3	1.6	9.3	9.3	9.0	6.9	5.6	33.0	22.5	4.0	0.4	68.0	33.2	50.7	49.3
55040	ISANTI	97.8	97.5	0.3	0.4	0.3	0.4	0.8	1.0	7.7	7.9	8.2	7.8	7.4	30.3	23.5	6.6	0.7	71.2	33.5	51.4	48.6
55041	LAKE CITY	97.4	97.0	0.5	0.6	1.0	1.2	1.7	2.0	5.2	5.9	6.8	6.9	5.4	24.6	27.3	15.0	2.9	77.6	41.6	49.1	50.9
55042	LAKE ELMO	95.9	95.3	0.4	0.5	1.7	2.0	1.3	1.6	7.0	7.9	8.2	7.1	5.3	25.8	30.3	7.8	0.5	72.1	38.9	50.5	49.5
55043	LAKELAND	97.2	96.9	0.1	0.1	0.5	0.6	1.3	1.5	5.8	6.1	7.6	7.2	5.1	27.4	31.9	8.2	0.8	75.8	40.1	49.8	50.2
55044	LAKEVILLE	95.0	94.2	1.1	1.3	1.6	1.9	1.9	2.3	9.8	10.1	10.0	7.6	4.8	32.9	21.1	3.5	0.2	65.0	32.5	50.6	49.4
55045	LINDSTROM	97.9	97.6	0.5	0.7	0.3	0.4	1.2	1.4	6.5	7.0	7.9	7.8	5.4	26.4	25.7	11.4	1.9	73.3	38.3	50.8	49.2
55046	LONSDALE	98.7	98.4	0.1	0.2	0.2	0.2	0.7	0.8	7.8	7.3	8.6	7.9	6.4	29.7	22.5	8.5	1.3	70.9	34.4	52.0	48.0
55047	MARINE ON SAINT CROI	98.1	97.8	0.3	0.3	0.4	0.5	0.9	1.1	5.2	6.1	7.5	6.8	4.4	21.7	35.8	11.0	1.4	76.6	44.1	50.7	49.3
55049	MEDFORD	95.5	94.6	0.1	0.1	0.5	0.6	4.7	5.8	8.1	7.8	7.7	6.5	6.9	30.6	22.7	8.7	1.0	72.1	33.9	50.9	49.1
55051	MORA	97.2	96.9	0.2	0.3	0.4	0.5	1.0	1.2	6.3	6.5	7.0	7.1	6.7	24.1	26.2	14.1	2.2	75.7	39.9	50.0	50.0
55052	MORRISTOWN	98.7	98.5	0.1	0.1	0.0	0.1	4.4	5.3	6.2	7.3	9.5	6.9	5.5	27.4	24.4	11.4	1.4	73.1	37.2	50.5	49.5
55053	NERSTRAND	98.9	98.8	0.1	0.2	0.4	0.4	0.7	1.0	7.7	8.0	9.0	7.9	5.4	27.9	24.5	8.8	0.9	70.2	36.3	50.9	49.2
55054	NEW MARKET	98.1	98.1	0.3	0.2	0.3	0.2	1.0	1.2	8.3	9.0	9.4	7.1	4.5	30.7	25.5	5.0	0.7	68.6	35.3	52.4	47.6
55055	NEWPORT	91.8	90.4	1.7	2.2	1.6	1.8	4.3	5.1	7.7	7.2	7.3	6.6	7.6	29.8	24.1	8.1	1.7	73.6	34.5	48.4	51.6
55056	NORTH BRANCH	97.4	97.0	0.2	0.2	0.9	1.1	1.2	1.5	8.9	8.4	8.7	7.0	6.5	32.0	20.7	6.9	1.1	69.5	32.5	50.0	50.0
55057	NORTHFIELD	93.9	92.8	0.7	1.0	2.0	2.4	4.7	5.6	5.4	5.6	6.3	14.5	16.7	21.3	20.3	8.1	1.8	78.5	26.7	48.6	51.4
55060	OWATONNA	94.7	93.8	1.3	1.6	1.0	1.2	3.9	4.6	7.1	6.9	7.7	7.5	6.9	27.4	23.7	10.8	2.0	73.5	36.2	49.3	50.8
55063	PINE CITY	97.9	97.6	0.2	0.3	0.2	0.3	0.9	1.1	6.0	6.1	7.3	7.1	6.3	25.9	25.0	14.2	2.2	76.1	39.9	50.7	49.3
55065	RANDOLPH	98.5	98.1	0.1	0.1	0.2	0.3	0.9	1.0	6.5	7.3	8.2	8.3	5.9	28.0	26.0	9.1	0.8	72.4	37.2	51.4	48.7
55066	RED WING	95.1	94.4	1.2	1.5	0.8	0.9	1.2	1.5	6.0	6.1	6.6	7.2	7.1	25.5	25.7	12.9	2.8	76.6	39.3	48.7	51.3
55067	ROCK CREEK	98.4	98.2	0.0	0.0	0.6	0.7	0.6	0.7	7.1	7.4	8.6	6.9	5.4	27.4	26.1	10.1	1.0	72.6	37.8	52.0	48.0
55068	ROSEMOUNT	92.9	91.7	2.0	2.5	2.2	2.6	1.8	2.2	9.2	9.4	9.6	8.2	5.5	33.0	20.6	4.3	0.3	66.5	31.9	49.9	50.1
55069	RUSH CITY	94.1	93.2	2.4	3.0	0.9	1.0	1.8	2.0	6.5	6.5	7.2	6.9	6.8	29.6	23.9	10.8	1.9	75.5	36.6	53.0	47.0
55070	SAINT FRANCIS	95.8	95.0	0.2	0.3	1.3	1.5	1.0	1.3	11.0	9.4	8.3	7.7	7.1	36.3	16.3	3.7	0.3	66.5	28.6	49.6	50.4
55071	SAINT PAUL PARK	94.1	92.8	2.2	2.9	1.1	1.3	2.7	3.2	7.3	7.2	8.2	7.4	6.8	29.3	23.8	9.3	0.8	72.8	35.9	49.8	50.2
55072	SANDSTONE	85.7	84.2	5.1	6.4	0.7	0.8	5.7	6.7	5.1	5.3	6.5	6.9	6.8	31.7	23.8	11.2	2.9	78.4	37.8	57.9	42.1
55073	SCANDIA	97.7	97.5	0.2	0.3	0.8	1.0	0.7	0.8	5.4	6.9	8.1	8.2	5.0	24.6	33.9	7.3	0.7	74.3	40.6	51.5	48.5
55074	SHAFER	96.3	95.7	0.1	0.1	2.8	3.2	1.0	1.0	6.9	7.4	8.9	8.0	6.6	27.9	24.9	8.1	1.3	71.3	36.0	50.3	49.7
55075	SOUTH SAINT PAUL	92.8	91.5	1.3	1.6	0.8	1.0	6.3	7.6	7.3	6.7	6.6	6.5	7.4	30.7	22.5	10.6	1.7	75.3	35.8	48.8	51.2
55076	INVER GROVE HEIGHTS	92.4	91.1	1.8	2.2	1.4	1.7	4.8	5.6	7.1	7.0	7.2	7.1	6.4	30.5	25.8	8.0	0.8	74.2	35.9	48.6	51.4
55077	INVER GROVE HEIGHTS	90.6	89.1	2.6	3.2	3.1	3.6	3.6	4.3	7.3	7.5	7.6	7.0	7.5	34.0	21.5	6.5	1.1	73.1	32.7	50.7	49.4
55079	STACY	97.6	97.2	0.3	0.4	0.3	0.4	1.3	1.5	8.1	8.3	8.4	7.2	5.7	32.8	24.4	4.8	0.5	70.6	34.8	52.1	47.9
55080	STANCHFIELD	98.0	97.7	0.2	0.2	0.3	0.3	1.1	1.4	6.2	6.5	7.4	7.1	5.9	27.4	27.6	11.0	1.0	75.3	39.4	51.8	48.2
55082	STILLWATER	96.7	96.1	0.8	1.0	0.9	1.1	1.2	1.4	6.1	7.1	8.3	7.4	5.4	25.7	29.8	8.8	1.4	73.6	39.7	50.0	50.0
55084	TAYLORS FALLS	95.5	94.6	0.1	0.1	3.4	4.1	0.8	0.9	6.8	6.8	8.5	8.2	6.7	28.1	24.5	9.0	1.5	72.2	36.2	50.0	50.0
55087	WARSAW	99.7	99.7	0.0	0.0	0.0	0.0	1.0	1.3	6.3	7.2	7.9	6.9	5.4	26.7	27.4	11.0	1.3	74.5	38.9	50.3	49.7
55088	WEBSTER	98.6	98.4	0.1	0.2	0.2	0.3	0.8	1.0	7.5	8.2	8.9	7.6	4.8	27.7	27.1	7.7	0.5	70.0	37.3	52.1	47.9
55089	WELCH	94.7	94.5	0.5	0.6	0.2	0.2	0.9	1.1	6.2	6.8	7.2	7.4	6.3	25.4	30.4	9.3	1.0	74.7	39.7	51.3	48.7
55092	WYOMING	97.6	97.2	0.2	0.3	0.7	0.8	0.8	1.0	7.9	8.0	8.4	7.3	5.9	31.2	24.8	6.0	0.7	71.2	35.5	50.8	49.2
55101	SAINT PAUL	47.7	42.2	15.3	18.1	25.7	28.2	10.6	11.7	9.2	8.1	9.3	8.7	9.2	30.6	17.5	6.5	1.0	68.3	28.3	51.2	48.8
55102	SAINT PAUL	78.0	74.2	10.9	13.1	3.9	4.5	6.2	7.4	4.9	4.6	5.5	5.8	7.8	36.3	23.2	9.9	2.0	81.5	36.1	49.0	51.0
55103	SAINT PAUL	38.3	33.9	21.2	23.3	29.3	31.4	9.1	10.0	9.0	8.9	10.2	9.8	9.3	28.1	17.3	6.3	1.3	65.8	26.8	49.8	50.2
55104	SAINT PAUL	62.9	58.9	20.3	23.4	9.8	10.5	4.2	4.7	6.8	6.0	7.0	10.3	12.0	31.3	19.4	6.0	1.3	75.8	29.3	48.3	51.7
55105	SAINT PAUL	93.0	91.2	1.8	2.5	2.4	3.2	2.0	2.6	5.2	5.0	5.4	9.2	10.9	30.5	24.3	7.8	1.6	80.7	34.3	45.6	54.4
55106	SAINT PAUL	58.3	52.6	10.7	12.7	19.9	22.8	10.4	11.5	9.7	8.5	9.2	8.5	8.4	29.0	17.9	7.4	1.4	67.5	28.9	49.5	50.5
55107	SAINT PAUL	58.5	53.1	6.7	8.0	8.1	9.8	32.6	36.1	9.0	8.5	9.4	7.8	7.6	29.1	18.5	7.5	2.6	68.2	30.4	49.3	50.7
55108	SAINT PAUL	80.9	77.4	5.1	6.4	10.4	12.4	3.1	3.6	6.0	4.5	4.4	8.5	12.5	33.6	18.2	8.3	4.0	82.0	31.8	47.0	53.0
55109	SAINT PAUL	90.7	88.3	2.9	3.9	3.4	4.3	2.1	2.6	6.4	6.4	7.3	6.6	6.2	27.8	24.7	12.3	2.4	75.6	38.4	48.2	51.8
55110	SAINT PAUL	95.7	94.8	0.9	1.2	1.5	1.9	1.6	1.9	6.4	6.7	7.4	7.2	6.5	27.3	26.1	11.0	1.5	75.0	38.1	48.7	51.4
55112	SAINT PAUL	90.1	87.7	2.6	3.5	3.9	5.0	1.9	2.4	6.0	6.0	6.3	7.4	8.5	27.7	25.5	10.9	1.7	78.2	36.3	48.4	51.6
55113	SAINT PAUL	89.4	86.7	2.7	3.6	5.1	6.5	1.9	2.3	4.8	4.6	5.3	6.1	7.0	26.9	25.3	16.5	3.6	82.0	41.7	46.6	53.4
55114	SAINT PAUL	74.3	69.4	11.8	14.5	7.8	9.4	5.0	5.8	5.7	4.9	4.4	5.2	7.6	39.9	23.8	6.3	2.2	82.1	34.7	48.8	51.2
55115	SAINT PAUL	96.7	96.0	0.8	1.0	0.8	0.9	1.1	1.4	6.6	8.2	10.0	8.3	5.2	24.0	28.7	8.0	1.0	69.6	38.4	49.3	50.7
55116	SAINT PAUL	87.3	84.6	4.5	5.7	3.5	4.4	4.9	5.7	5.6	5.4	5.4	5.5	6.7	29.9	24.1	13.4	4.1	80.4	39.4	45.8	54.2
55117	SAINT PAUL	70.1	65.7	10.0	12.3	13.0	14.7	5.1	5.9	7.9	7.2	7.6	7.4	7.8	30.1	21.3	9.0	1.7	72.8	32.7	48.3	51.7
55118	SAINT PAUL	89.9	88.4	2.2	2.6	1.7	2.0	7.7	9.0	5.7	5.8	6.2	6.0	5.9	24.5	26.7	16.0	3.3	78.6	42.2	46.9	53.1
55119	SAINT PAUL	78.9	74.8	9.0	11.2	6.3	7.7	4.3	5.0	7.9	7.2	7.0	6.4	7.2	30.8	21.9	10.1	1.5	74.0	34.5	48.9	51.1
55120	SAINT PAUL	94.0	92.8	1.5	1.9	2.8	3.4	1.4	1.7	6.1	7.3	8.9	7.2	5.2	24.1	29.6	10.4	1.1	72.6	40.0	47.5	52.6
55121	SAINT PAUL	84.8	81.8	4.3	5.4	6.5	7.8	3.5	4.3	7.5	6.8	6.7	5.9	7.8	39.8	19.3	5.7	0.5	75.7	31.7	50.0	50.0
55122	SAINT PAUL	86.8	84.5	3.5	4.3	6.4	7.5	2.3	2.7	7.1	7.1	7.3	6.8	6.7	34.4	24.9	5.4	0.3	74.2	34.3	48.6	51.4
55123	SAINT PAUL	90.3	88.5	3.1	3.8	4.0	4.8	1.9	2.3	9.1	10.1	9.7	7.4	5.2	33.0	22.6	2.8	0.2	66.0	32.9	49.6	50.4
55124	SAINT PAUL	91.8	90.1	1.9	2.4	3.4	4.1	2.0	2.5	7.2	7.3	7.9	7.6	6.5	30.1	27.1	5.6	0.7	72.7	35.4	48.8	51.2
55125	SAINT PAUL	89.8	88.0	2.7	3.4	5.1	5.9	2.2	2.6	9.4	9.4	8.2	6.0	5.1	33.6	21.9	5.6	0.8	68.8	34.0	48.2	51.8
55126	SAINT PAUL	93.3	91.5	1.0	1.4	3.7	4.8	1.3	1.7	5.4	6.2	7.6	7.3	5.4	25.9	31.5	9.9	0.8	76.0	40.6	48.3	51.7
55127	SAINT PAUL	92.5	90.5	1.1	1.4	4.4	5.7	1.4	1.8	5.8	6.8	7.8	7.1	6.0	25.1	31.4	9.3	0.7	75.0	40.2	48.0	52.0
55128	SAINT PAUL	92.2	90.7	2.2	2.9	2.4	2.9	2.8	3.4	7.8	7.7	8.1	6.8	6.1	32.4	22.5	7.7	0.9	71.8	34.8	48.2	51.8
55129	SAINT PAUL	91.6	90.0	1.6	2.1	4.8	5.6	2.0	2.4	9.6	9.8	8.1	6.2	4.6	32.6	24.3	4.7	0.2	68.1	34.7	49.5	50.6
	MINNESOTA	89.5	88.0	3.5	4.2	2.9	3.4	2.9	3.4	6.8	6.8	7.2	7.3	7.4	28.6	23.9	10.1	1.9	74.9	36.1	49.6	50.5
	UNITED STATES	75.1	73.6	12.3	12.5	3.8	4.2	12.5	14.1	6.9	6.7	7.2	7.0	7.3	28.6	23.8	10.8	1.7	75.1	36.0	49.1	50.9

#	ZIP CODE / POST OFFICE NAME	2004 Per Capita Income	2004 HH Income Base	2004 HOUSEHOLD INCOME DISTRIBUTION (%) Less than $25,000	$25,000 to $49,999	$50,000 to $99,999	$100,000 to $149,999	$150,000 or More	MEDIAN HOUSEHOLD INCOME 2004	2009	2004 National Centile	2004 State Centile	2004 Home Value Base	2004 HOME VALUE DISTRIBUTION (%) Less than $50,000	$50,000 to $89,999	$90,000 to $174,999	$175,000 to $399,999	$400,000 or More	2004 Median Home Value
55001	AFTON	46513	1042	4.7	10.4	27.5	31.9	25.6	108279	138565	99	99	1006	0.8	0.2	3.0	55.6	40.5	357895
55003	BAYPORT	24759	673	15.0	22.7	38.9	17.7	5.7	63471	80764	87	86	541	0.0	0.7	40.9	50.7	7.8	189583
55005	BETHEL	25148	1297	7.3	23.1	49.2	14.7	5.6	66706	78783	90	89	1251	9.2	3.0	26.3	58.6	3.0	190914
55006	BRAHAM	22114	1169	23.4	31.0	32.9	10.0	2.7	46666	55944	65	56	923	9.8	12.5	52.2	24.2	1.4	132832
55007	BROOK PARK	20065	885	23.5	31.3	35.9	7.2	2.0	46222	54218	64	55	801	12.2	18.7	39.7	27.1	2.3	130440
55008	CAMBRIDGE	25462	5188	19.4	26.2	37.9	11.6	4.9	54633	64225	79	76	3891	2.9	6.9	44.2	43.1	2.9	167893
55009	CANNON FALLS	29993	3232	17.1	22.8	37.9	15.0	7.2	61304	76516	86	83	2725	7.0	4.6	26.4	51.7	10.4	200458
55011	CEDAR	25521	3370	6.5	20.9	49.8	18.0	4.8	68645	81264	91	90	3315	5.8	3.5	27.8	59.1	3.8	197271
55012	CENTER CITY	22353	645	13.5	25.0	43.3	14.6	3.7	61674	72875	86	84	578	3.3	4.3	27.2	56.6	8.7	211852
55013	CHISAGO CITY	29146	2093	15.7	21.7	40.2	15.5	6.9	62816	75597	87	85	1720	3.1	2.3	27.7	54.2	12.6	219403
55014	CIRCLE PINES	28664	8761	7.6	17.8	45.0	21.0	8.5	75098	89244	93	93	8069	5.6	1.5	31.9	57.0	4.0	192451
55016	COTTAGE GROVE	28936	10767	5.5	16.6	47.2	23.5	7.2	77724	95084	94	94	9978	0.6	0.8	28.9	67.1	2.7	197486
55017	DALBO	21593	288	19.4	24.0	45.5	8.0	3.1	53434	64180	78	73	259	5.8	6.6	46.7	36.7	4.3	159539
55018	DENNISON	31167	366	8.5	24.3	41.0	18.9	7.4	67479	84279	90	89	336	1.2	3.6	18.8	57.1	19.4	240000
55019	DUNDAS	32550	405	10.9	21.7	42.2	16.8	8.4	68029	85149	90	89	347	2.0	3.8	28.0	52.7	13.5	221250
55020	ELKO	34754	856	4.6	11.2	43.8	24.7	15.8	86055	106277	96	96	823	0.2	0.2	8.1	61.0	30.4	321981
55021	FARIBAULT	23517	10872	19.1	28.3	38.6	11.0	3.1	52169	62047	76	71	8551	6.9	7.1	45.0	36.7	4.3	159994
55024	FARMINGTON	27676	8440	5.9	15.6	52.7	20.4	5.3	75385	90761	93	93	7717	5.5	1.9	15.0	73.7	3.9	217213
55025	FOREST LAKE	30787	7607	11.2	19.6	42.7	18.6	7.9	69115	85860	91	90	6375	3.0	1.0	23.5	62.5	10.1	221995
55026	FRONTENAC	32419	214	11.2	27.6	42.1	14.0	5.1	61714	76195	86	84	197	2.5	5.6	29.4	47.7	14.7	201923
55027	GOODHUE	24585	926	13.0	27.7	44.0	11.1	4.3	57236	68001	82	79	803	4.2	6.6	34.9	42.8	11.5	187321
55030	GRASSTON	20525	104	20.2	37.5	30.8	8.7	2.9	44207	51948	59	46	95	11.6	11.6	47.4	28.4	1.1	138281
55031	HAMPTON	28356	615	9.1	20.0	43.7	18.9	8.3	70654	87799	91	91	550	2.0	0.9	21.8	58.4	16.9	234685
55032	HARRIS	25546	1296	12.2	23.7	45.4	13.6	5.2	63303	76680	87	86	1208	1.2	2.8	36.8	52.7	6.4	195833
55033	HASTINGS	28861	9791	11.2	21.7	41.5	19.2	6.4	68445	84959	91	90	8083	4.4	1.6	27.6	58.8	7.6	202368
55036	HENRIETTE	21051	40	17.5	35.0	37.5	7.5	2.5	48190	56155	69	60	37	8.1	13.5	48.7	27.0	2.7	139583
55037	HINCKLEY	19948	1555	30.7	30.4	29.8	6.8	2.3	40744	48831	49	30	1235	9.9	22.2	44.1	21.5	2.4	120359
55038	HUGO	32417	5251	5.8	13.1	48.7	21.3	11.1	79286	96476	95	94	4996	1.8	0.8	15.8	66.4	15.2	232273
55040	ISANTI	24064	4172	12.3	25.8	45.6	13.0	3.3	60032	69207	84	82	3745	4.0	3.7	47.9	41.0	3.4	167658
55041	LAKE CITY	25728	2974	19.9	29.5	37.3	9.1	4.1	50401	60437	73	67	2442	8.2	7.1	46.0	34.2	4.6	152549
55042	LAKE ELMO	42896	2975	7.7	16.4	29.0	25.1	21.8	93590	123802	98	98	2857	17.6	1.8	8.2	42.3	30.2	299058
55043	LAKELAND	37439	1467	8.8	12.7	43.6	26.3	8.7	82093	102734	96	95	1372	1.0	1.3	27.3	60.9	9.6	210714
55044	LAKEVILLE	34579	12672	5.3	9.8	39.8	28.6	16.5	92419	120180	97	98	11631	4.0	0.5	7.2	70.3	18.0	266927
55045	LINDSTROM	27326	2287	14.7	24.4	41.9	13.9	5.2	61149	73179	85	83	1970	5.3	2.4	34.0	50.1	8.2	195918
55046	LONSDALE	26576	1209	14.6	19.9	44.3	16.3	4.8	62985	75783	87	85	1095	1.5	3.7	35.6	50.3	9.0	192996
55047	MARINE ON SAINT CROI	40817	1033	9.5	12.1	35.0	26.8	16.6	88687	117197	97	97	946	0.3	0.3	10.8	61.8	26.7	310931
55049	MEDFORD	24456	817	15.5	27.2	44.6	9.6	3.2	55773	64375	80	78	718	8.8	11.7	38.7	35.2	5.6	153571
55051	MORA	22802	4142	26.2	32.4	31.4	6.8	3.2	43287	50491	57	41	3382	11.9	15.5	44.7	26.1	1.8	132033
55052	MORRISTOWN	23660	800	19.0	28.4	38.5	11.4	2.8	52510	61707	76	71	697	11.3	11.9	40.2	30.9	5.7	139773
55053	NERSTRAND	23440	351	12.0	27.6	43.0	13.1	4.3	60709	71330	85	82	313	1.6	3.2	28.1	52.4	14.7	219898
55054	NEW MARKET	45437	172	4.7	9.9	43.0	25.0	17.4	88659	109052	97	97	165	0.6	0.0	10.9	58.2	30.3	322619
55055	NEWPORT	30832	1443	14.9	29.0	39.0	13.6	3.5	55398	71385	80	77	1015	0.0	7.0	49.4	38.5	5.1	164461
55056	NORTH BRANCH	26301	4731	14.1	23.6	43.1	12.4	6.8	61181	72439	86	83	4053	8.1	2.3	34.6	51.6	3.4	184706
55057	NORTHFIELD	26523	7408	14.4	23.0	38.6	16.8	7.3	62857	77227	87	85	5521	3.8	1.0	27.1	59.8	8.3	213329
55060	OWATONNA	25208	11051	17.7	28.0	38.9	11.7	3.8	53627	62986	78	74	8707	3.5	6.3	53.1	34.0	3.1	153054
55063	PINE CITY	22299	3925	25.5	30.8	32.8	8.0	2.9	44988	52936	61	49	3231	8.7	13.8	47.6	27.2	2.7	134976
55065	RANDOLPH	29033	332	9.0	19.9	43.7	19.3	8.1	70325	87624	91	91	297	1.7	1.0	20.9	59.3	17.2	240254
55066	RED WING	27090	7632	20.0	25.9	38.3	10.3	5.5	53613	65574	78	74	5675	4.9	7.8	45.0	38.0	4.4	161194
55067	ROCK CREEK	22343	206	21.8	26.7	39.8	9.2	2.4	50939	61100	74	68	187	4.8	9.6	50.8	32.1	2.7	146071
55068	ROSEMOUNT	28146	7572	6.8	14.3	48.9	22.3	7.8	77759	95043	94	94	6867	2.5	0.6	22.5	70.5	3.9	209523
55069	RUSH CITY	22542	1651	20.8	29.4	36.0	10.6	3.2	49780	61258	71	65	1353	5.8	8.0	46.9	35.6	3.8	154931
55070	SAINT FRANCIS	23449	2183	11.0	26.3	46.9	13.4	2.5	60608	70592	85	82	1914	3.8	13.5	34.3	46.9	1.4	171596
55071	SAINT PAUL PARK	26441	1973	8.9	27.3	43.3	16.9	3.7	62827	79234	87	85	1629	6.2	2.8	58.0	31.3	1.7	156010
55072	SANDSTONE	20596	1606	27.0	29.0	33.4	8.0	2.6	45178	53624	62	51	1244	14.0	24.0	40.1	20.2	1.8	111475
55073	SCANDIA	34397	1165	7.4	15.0	39.3	27.4	10.9	83297	106616	96	96	1115	0.6	0.3	13.1	69.4	16.6	265000
55074	SHAFER	25645	416	14.7	24.0	40.1	15.6	5.5	61605	73081	86	83	366	3.6	4.1	31.4	50.0	10.9	205797
55075	SOUTH SAINT PAUL	27007	8315	16.7	27.8	39.5	13.2	3.0	55511	71202	80	77	5992	1.1	2.9	59.6	35.8	0.6	159230
55076	INVER GROVE HEIGHTS	31051	7718	9.8	20.7	40.6	22.3	6.6	70383	87545	91	91	6790	6.4	2.1	32.3	54.7	4.5	189539
55077	INVER GROVE HEIGHTS	34569	4747	7.9	24.0	37.2	19.4	11.5	71521	89694	92	91	3034	12.4	3.3	13.7	47.8	22.8	258835
55079	STACY	27490	2840	8.7	24.1	43.6	18.1	5.4	65672	77822	89	88	2685	8.5	1.4	30.0	57.7	2.4	195520
55080	STANCHFIELD	24887	1019	14.4	27.4	41.3	13.3	3.6	57715	68475	82	80	934	2.6	8.5	39.0	46.0	4.0	175000
55082	STILLWATER	39678	12145	10.7	15.7	34.1	24.1	15.5	82169	106329	96	95	10182	0.6	0.6	15.7	58.9	24.2	261168
55084	TAYLORS FALLS	23573	638	18.3	28.4	38.2	11.4	3.6	53144	63364	77	73	543	5.0	4.6	41.1	43.7	5.7	173732
55087	WARSAW	26479	106	11.3	21.7	45.3	16.0	5.7	66446	80709	89	88	97	2.1	5.2	30.9	49.5	12.4	201389
55088	WEBSTER	31127	642	7.3	17.0	45.3	20.7	9.7	75652	90599	93	93	611	1.0	1.2	12.4	63.0	22.4	289953
55089	WELCH	31869	668	9.9	22.2	40.3	17.5	10.2	67826	84440	90	89	579	3.8	4.0	21.4	55.6	15.2	230529
55092	WYOMING	26688	3601	10.4	19.4	46.0	19.7	4.4	68113	81121	90	89	3354	6.3	3.5	27.0	57.5	5.7	200649
55101	SAINT PAUL	20340	8869	33.6	29.8	26.8	7.4	2.5	37888	49671	39	18	3111	3.7	20.7	59.7	15.1	0.8	119846
55102	SAINT PAUL	30700	8986	25.4	30.4	28.9	10.2	5.2	44335	58397	60	46	4151	2.5	12.2	56.5	21.0	7.7	137712
55103	SAINT PAUL	15272	4736	35.5	29.9	25.7	7.4	1.5	36409	47174	33	12	2017	3.8	26.5	56.5	12.4	0.7	113315
55104	SAINT PAUL	25134	18261	25.1	27.4	30.1	12.1	5.3	47333	62828	67	58	10119	1.2	9.9	51.8	32.2	4.8	148432
55105	SAINT PAUL	42970	11437	12.9	22.2	31.9	18.1	14.8	69380	97735	91	90	7661	0.3	1.4	21.5	61.8	15.0	240067
55106	SAINT PAUL	18665	18325	24.3	32.3	32.1	9.1	2.2	44143	56905	59	45	11365	0.9	13.5	72.0	13.2	0.4	129144
55107	SAINT PAUL	20023	5746	24.2	27.3	37.5	8.6	2.5	48499	62991	69	62	3374	1.3	13.0	70.0	14.7	1.0	122708
55108	SAINT PAUL	31063	6727	21.7	27.0	29.1	13.4	8.8	51633	69426	75	70	3150	0.4	1.9	34.3	57.9	5.6	198400
55109	SAINT PAUL	29828	11580	15.7	21.8	39.2	17.0	6.2	62923	81179	87	85	8815	2.0	1.4	46.6	48.1	1.9	175027
55110	SAINT PAUL	34518	16004	11.0	20.0	39.4	19.9	9.8	70632	91690	91	91	13141	0.2	0.9	33.8	57.0	8.1	197401
55112	SAINT PAUL	34559	17464	12.9	23.9	35.1	17.2	10.9	65876	86337	89	88	12807	8.1	2.1	28.1	56.7	4.9	192080
55113	SAINT PAUL	36090	16501	14.5	24.3	34.3	17.0	9.9	62989	83321	87	85	11664	1.0	3.4	29.6	62.0	4.0	196960
55114	SAINT PAUL	26284	759	38.7	27.3	24.4	5.7	4.0	34931	43579	27	8	259	0.0	7.3	56.0	36.7	0.0	158413
55115	SAINT PAUL	39551	3424	8.2	15.7	36.0	22.4	17.8	83554	106889	96	96	3065	0.3	0.6	16.8	60.8	21.6	265571
55116	SAINT PAUL	39887	11287	21.1	23.1	30.6	14.5	10.6	56243	75497	81	78	6455	0.5	3.0	26.7	60.3	9.5	209825
55117	SAINT PAUL	24524	16822	23.4	29.1	33.0	10.5	4.1	47506	60137	67	59	10438	4.8	11.7	49.9	31.8	1.9	144873
55118	SAINT PAUL	37751	12018	17.9	23.5	32.0	15.6	11.1	61665	78822	86	84	8492	0.3	1.3	32.3	54.4	11.8	206391
55119	SAINT PAUL	28044	15654	18.2	27.0	35.6	13.7	5.5	55217	72172	80	77	11142	4.9	5.1	52.7	35.8	1.5	154921
55120	SAINT PAUL	44142	1795	6.6	12.9	36.7	24.0	19.8	89042	117691	97	97	1538	0.0	0.0	16.6	59.6	23.8	267045
55121	SAINT PAUL	33135	3722	10.4	23.8	40.3	18.6	7.0	63520	79969	87	86	1811	0.0	3.0	17.8	72.4	6.8	219607
55122	SAINT PAUL	37253	13145	6.6	19.7	41.9	20.7	11.1	74287	92071	93	92	10034	0.4	1.1	29.1	59.9	9.5	209379
55123	SAINT PAUL	38434	9592	4.2	12.4	35.2	29.0	19.1	96780	124638	98	98	7957	0.2	1.1	12.8	71.1	14.7	267736
55124	SAINT PAUL	36792	17693	6.4	17.6	38.7	25.1	12.3	80878	101536	95	95	15354	4.1	1.8	20.0	64.4	9.7	218541
55125	SAINT PAUL	40905	16949	3.8	14.3	39.1	26.1	16.7	88712	114529	97	97	14651	0.4	0.4	19.3	66.6	13.3	244490
55126	SAINT PAUL	41923	10522	8.7	16.3	34.3	23.2	17.7	84501	114938	96	96	9376	3.2	1.6	25.2	61.9	8.2	216123
55127	SAINT PAUL	56726	6885	6.4	18.2	29.4	22.0	24.0	90940	126991	97	97	6094	4.1	1.8	25.5	42.4	26.1	227456
55128	SAINT PAUL	29903	11378	12.1	22.7	39.8	20.5	4.9	66431	82630	89	88	9208	5.3	1.7	33.4	57.1	2.6	190616
55129	SAINT PAUL	46194	3021	3.7	10.8	27.2	31.3	27.0	110133	141981	99	100	2751	0.0	0.2	11.6	54.7	33.5	331184
	MINNESOTA	29624		18.6	25.2	34.9	14.0	7.4	56724	71660				6.6	9.7	36.5	40.5	6.8	168676
	UNITED STATES	25866		24.7	27.1	30.8	10.9	6.5	48124	56710				10.9	15.0	33.7	30.1	10.4	145905

ZIP CODE	FINANCIAL SERVICES				THE HOME						ENTERTAINMENT						PERSONAL			
					Home Improvements		Furnishings													
# POST OFFICE NAME	Auto Loan	Home Loan	Invest-ments	Retire-ment Plans	Home Repair	Lawn & Garden	Comput-ers & Hard-ware	Major Appli-ances	TV, Radio, Sound Equip-ment	Furni-ture	Dine out/ Carry out	Sports Equip-ment	Fees & Tickets	Toys & Games	Travel	Cable TV	Apparel & Services	Auto Repairs	Health Insur-ance	Pets & Supplies
55001 AFTON	170	212	228	216	206	206	188	184	172	189	218	214	204	229	191	167	219	178	164	204
55003 BAYPORT	103	115	130	116	114	119	112	111	108	112	136	130	116	137	113	105	133	111	105	122
55005 BETHEL	107	119	118	123	115	112	111	110	103	113	130	129	113	131	108	96	128	108	95	120
55006 BRAHAM	89	77	59	75	81	89	76	82	80	75	98	96	73	98	76	82	92	80	89	101
55007 BROOK PARK	87	74	55	70	80	87	69	79	75	69	90	93	66	91	72	78	85	77	88	104
55008 CAMBRIDGE	94	94	94	95	96	101	94	96	93	93	115	112	93	116	94	92	111	95	95	109
55009 CANNON FALLS	115	114	102	113	116	123	108	114	109	107	134	132	109	138	110	109	129	111	115	133
55011 CEDAR	107	121	122	124	117	115	112	111	104	114	132	131	115	134	111	99	130	109	98	122
55012 CENTER CITY	97	109	109	109	108	108	100	101	95	100	119	119	103	123	101	92	117	99	93	114
55013 CHISAGO CITY	111	116	109	117	116	120	111	113	108	110	134	131	111	135	110	106	130	111	110	128
55014 CIRCLE PINES	121	137	135	141	132	130	126	125	117	128	148	146	129	150	124	111	146	122	110	137
55016 COTTAGE GROVE	120	140	141	142	134	132	126	125	117	129	148	146	132	152	126	112	147	122	110	137
55017 DALBO	95	84	64	80	89	95	78	86	83	78	100	103	76	103	80	85	95	84	93	111
55018 DENNISON	114	141	149	141	138	137	126	125	117	125	147	147	134	156	129	113	146	121	113	139
55019 DUNDAS	123	126	117	126	127	135	120	124	120	119	148	144	121	151	121	119	143	121	124	142
55020 ELKO	150	175	174	180	168	164	157	156	145	161	183	183	164	187	156	137	182	151	135	171
55021 FARIBAULT	87	85	79	84	86	92	83	86	84	82	104	101	83	105	84	84	100	85	87	100
55024 FARMINGTON	119	130	124	134	126	125	120	120	113	123	142	140	123	143	118	107	139	117	107	133
55025 FOREST LAKE	114	125	128	127	123	124	117	118	112	118	141	138	121	144	117	108	139	116	108	132
55026 FRONTENAC	122	108	83	103	114	123	101	112	108	101	131	133	99	133	104	110	124	109	121	143
55027 GOODHUE	106	99	80	95	103	109	91	99	95	91	116	118	90	119	94	96	111	96	105	125
55030 GRASSTON	87	78	59	74	82	88	72	80	76	72	93	95	70	95	74	78	88	77	86	103
55031 HAMPTON	110	137	145	137	134	132	122	121	113	121	142	142	130	151	125	110	142	117	109	134
55032 HARRIS	108	109	98	107	110	113	101	106	100	101	124	125	101	127	102	99	120	103	104	126
55033 HASTINGS	108	119	126	120	118	121	114	114	109	114	137	133	117	140	114	106	135	113	106	127
55036 HENRIETTE	96	75	51	68	84	95	71	85	80	70	95	100	63	94	75	85	88	84	101	116
55037 HINCKLEY	79	67	56	65	72	79	67	74	72	66	87	88	63	87	69	73	82	74	80	93
55038 HUGO	136	155	154	160	149	145	141	140	130	145	165	164	146	167	139	122	164	137	121	153
55040 ISANTI	97	106	106	108	103	103	101	100	95	101	119	119	101	121	99	90	117	99	89	111
55041 LAKE CITY	99	84	64	82	89	100	85	92	90	83	109	106	81	109	85	93	103	90	101	112
55042 LAKE ELMO	171	199	204	202	194	197	178	178	166	181	210	206	190	215	180	162	209	173	162	200
55043 LAKELAND	129	157	165	157	154	152	141	141	131	141	165	165	149	174	144	127	165	137	126	155
55044 LAKEVILLE	157	173	168	180	167	166	159	158	148	163	187	185	163	188	156	140	185	155	140	175
55045 LINDSTROM	104	102	89	100	103	109	97	101	97	96	120	119	96	120	97	97	115	100	103	120
55046 LONSDALE	103	114	113	114	111	111	106	106	100	106	126	126	108	129	105	96	124	105	96	119
55047 MARINE ON SAINT CROI	139	171	187	170	169	172	154	155	145	154	182	178	164	189	159	142	181	150	143	170
55049 MEDFORD	103	91	70	87	97	104	84	94	90	84	109	112	83	111	87	92	104	91	101	121
55051 MORA	93	76	54	72	82	92	75	84	81	74	98	98	69	96	76	84	91	83	95	108
55052 MORRISTOWN	98	86	68	84	90	99	84	91	89	83	108	106	82	109	85	91	102	89	98	112
55053 NERSTRAND	100	107	104	108	105	106	101	102	96	101	121	121	101	123	100	93	118	101	94	116
55054 NEW MARKET	161	182	175	190	173	167	164	162	150	171	191	190	169	191	159	139	189	158	138	177
55055 NEWPORT	103	114	125	115	112	115	114	111	110	112	138	132	116	142	113	105	136	112	102	121
55056 NORTH BRANCH	105	114	111	117	111	112	107	107	101	109	127	125	109	128	105	97	125	105	97	119
55057 NORTHFIELD	107	107	122	113	106	110	114	109	110	113	139	131	113	137	110	105	136	113	100	121
55060 OWATONNA	93	93	88	92	94	99	90	93	90	89	111	109	90	113	91	89	108	92	92	108
55063 PINE CITY	93	75	55	70	81	91	74	84	82	73	98	98	68	97	76	85	92	83	96	109
55065 RANDOLPH	110	135	144	136	133	132	122	121	113	121	142	142	129	150	124	110	142	117	109	134
55066 RED WING	97	90	81	88	93	102	90	94	94	88	114	109	88	115	91	95	109	93	100	111
55067 ROCK CREEK	103	92	70	87	97	104	85	94	90	85	110	112	83	112	87	92	104	92	102	121
55068 ROSEMOUNT	123	134	129	137	130	129	125	125	117	127	148	146	126	149	122	111	145	122	111	138
55069 RUSH CITY	96	81	63	79	87	96	81	89	87	80	105	102	77	104	82	89	98	87	97	109
55070 SAINT FRANCIS	96	107	105	110	103	101	100	99	92	102	117	116	101	117	97	87	115	97	85	108
55071 SAINT PAUL PARK	94	110	116	109	107	107	102	101	97	102	122	118	106	127	103	94	121	99	92	111
55072 SANDSTONE	95	71	45	66	80	92	72	84	82	70	97	98	64	93	74	87	89	84	101	110
55073 SCANDIA	128	157	167	158	154	153	141	140	131	141	164	164	149	173	144	127	164	135	126	155
55074 SHAFER	108	101	86	103	102	110	99	103	100	100	124	119	98	123	98	99	118	101	104	119
55075 SOUTH SAINT PAUL	86	94	106	95	93	97	95	92	93	93	116	109	97	120	95	90	114	93	88	101
55076 INVER GROVE HEIGHTS	111	123	126	127	119	119	116	114	109	118	138	134	119	139	114	104	136	113	102	126
55077 INVER GROVE HEIGHTS	128	132	141	138	128	131	131	128	125	133	159	152	132	156	127	119	156	130	116	143
55079 STACY	111	123	122	126	119	117	115	114	107	117	136	135	117	137	113	101	134	113	100	126
55080 STANCHFIELD	108	94	70	89	101	109	88	98	94	87	114	117	84	116	91	97	108	96	108	128
55082 STILLWATER	142	163	177	166	160	164	153	151	145	152	182	176	160	187	154	141	180	148	140	167
55084 TAYLORS FALLS	97	86	71	86	90	100	87	92	91	86	111	106	85	111	87	92	105	91	98	108
55087 WARSAW	108	124	124	123	124	125	112	114	107	111	133	134	117	141	115	105	132	110	107	131
55088 WEBSTER	118	146	156	147	144	142	131	130	121	130	152	153	139	162	134	117	152	126	117	144
55089 WELCH	126	141	140	140	141	144	130	133	126	129	156	154	134	162	133	125	153	129	128	150
55092 WYOMING	111	118	109	119	117	118	108	111	105	110	131	130	110	133	108	102	128	108	105	128
55101 SAINT PAUL	70	64	83	66	62	69	74	69	76	73	95	83	73	93	71	74	93	74	68	77
55102 SAINT PAUL	80	78	111	84	76	83	90	82	90	88	113	100	90	115	87	88	111	87	78	91
55103 SAINT PAUL	59	59	76	61	59	63	66	63	65	64	82	76	65	81	65	64	80	66	60	68
55104 SAINT PAUL	85	82	107	86	80	87	93	87	93	92	117	105	92	116	90	90	114	92	82	96
55105 SAINT PAUL	127	135	183	143	131	139	142	134	138	142	175	161	145	178	141	134	173	138	123	147
55106 SAINT PAUL	72	73	82	73	72	77	78	75	78	76	97	88	78	99	77	76	95	77	73	82
55107 SAINT PAUL	77	78	87	79	77	80	83	80	81	82	102	95	82	103	80	78	101	83	74	87
55108 SAINT PAUL	94	92	117	98	91	98	104	97	102	101	128	118	102	126	100	97	125	103	91	107
55109 SAINT PAUL	101	109	115	109	108	112	106	106	103	105	129	123	108	132	106	101	126	105	101	117
55110 SAINT PAUL	119	136	150	138	134	137	129	128	123	130	155	149	134	158	130	119	153	126	117	140
55112 SAINT PAUL	118	127	141	129	124	129	125	123	120	125	152	144	128	153	124	117	149	123	114	136
55113 SAINT PAUL	105	115	138	117	114	121	115	113	112	114	141	131	118	142	116	110	138	114	108	123
55114 SAINT PAUL	64	52	67	59	52	57	71	62	69	66	87	79	65	82	64	64	85	70	58	70
55115 SAINT PAUL	156	185	190	189	178	176	166	164	152	169	193	191	175	199	166	145	193	159	144	180
55116 SAINT PAUL	102	111	148	114	109	117	116	111	114	115	144	131	119	148	116	113	142	114	105	121
55117 SAINT PAUL	80	81	97	84	80	85	87	83	85	86	107	99	87	107	85	83	105	86	78	91
55118 SAINT PAUL	114	123	144	125	122	130	125	122	121	123	153	141	128	153	125	119	150	123	117	133
55119 SAINT PAUL	92	96	108	97	95	101	98	96	96	97	121	112	99	122	97	95	118	97	92	106
55120 SAINT PAUL	155	189	213	195	183	186	172	167	159	173	201	195	185	208	174	154	202	164	150	184
55121 SAINT PAUL	111	104	118	113	100	105	113	108	109	115	139	130	110	132	106	102	136	113	96	120
55122 SAINT PAUL	128	136	149	143	131	133	134	130	127	136	161	154	136	159	130	120	159	131	115	144
55123 SAINT PAUL	163	183	184	191	175	172	168	166	155	173	197	194	174	198	165	146	195	162	143	182
55124 SAINT PAUL	140	154	162	161	149	150	146	143	136	149	173	168	150	173	143	130	171	142	127	158
55125 SAINT PAUL	158	170	176	179	163	163	162	159	152	167	193	188	165	190	158	143	190	159	139	175
55126 SAINT PAUL	141	161	178	166	158	162	152	149	143	153	180	174	159	182	153	138	179	148	136	165
55127 SAINT PAUL	189	230	263	232	226	230	212	208	198	212	250	243	226	262	216	193	249	204	189	229
55128 SAINT PAUL	107	115	117	119	111	111	110	109	104	113	131	128	112	131	108	98	129	108	96	120
55129 SAINT PAUL	177	213	223	221	205	204	189	185	172	194	219	215	203	225	190	165	220	179	162	204
MINNESOTA	107	106	108	107	107	113	106	107	105	105	131	126	105	131	105	104	127	107	105	123
UNITED STATES	100	100	100	100	100	100	100	100	100	100	100	100	100	100	100	100	100	100	100	100

ZIP CODE		COUNTY FIPS CODE	POPULATION			2000-2004 ANNUAL RATE		HOUSEHOLDS					FAMILIES		
#	POST OFFICE NAME		2000	2004	2009	% Rate	State Centile	2000	2004	2009	% Annual Rate 2000-2004	2004 Average HH Size	2000	2004	% Annual Rate 2000-2004
55150	MENDOTA	037	203	243	279	4.3	96	80	97	113	4.6	2.48	46	54	3.8
55301	ALBERTVILLE	171	3987	5443	7257	7.6	100	1390	1959	2670	8.4	2.77	1137	1577	8.0
55302	ANNANDALE	171	6579	7496	9159	3.1	91	2569	2980	3706	3.6	2.49	1823	2063	3.0
55303	ANOKA	003	41090	42821	45913	1.0	58	14546	15451	16887	1.4	2.72	10738	11164	0.9
55304	ANDOVER	003	39300	45789	51882	3.7	93	12247	14522	16724	4.1	3.15	10623	12407	3.7
55305	HOPKINS	053	18763	20242	21515	1.8	75	8654	9453	10115	2.1	2.12	5028	5192	0.8
55306	BURNSVILLE	037	15500	16708	18425	1.8	75	5975	6559	7325	2.2	2.54	4087	4311	1.3
55307	ARLINGTON	143	2964	3049	3151	0.7	49	1154	1207	1263	1.1	2.47	786	798	0.4
55308	BECKER	141	6124	7678	9932	5.5	98	1980	2514	3290	5.8	3.05	1646	2053	5.3
55309	BIG LAKE	141	12248	15414	19984	5.6	99	4034	5159	6776	6.0	2.98	3214	4026	5.4
55310	BIRD ISLAND	129	1667	1649	1646	-0.3	18	675	680	689	0.2	2.37	442	431	-0.6
55311	OSSEO	053	20714	25468	29011	5.0	98	6890	8614	9901	5.4	2.95	5767	7105	5.0
55312	BROWNTON	085	1664	1726	1803	0.9	55	628	661	701	1.2	2.60	459	470	0.6
55313	BUFFALO	171	18272	22543	28598	5.1	98	6373	8032	10388	5.6	2.76	4838	5937	4.9
55314	BUFFALO LAKE	129	1385	1383	1385	0.0	26	540	548	556	0.4	2.41	387	383	-0.2
55315	CARVER	019	2242	2526	3025	2.9	89	767	879	1065	3.3	2.87	617	694	2.8
55316	CHAMPLIN	053	22193	23679	24961	1.5	69	7425	7979	8461	1.7	2.97	5923	6232	1.2
55317	CHANHASSEN	019	16157	19217	23659	4.2	95	5577	6681	8276	4.3	2.88	4337	5103	3.9
55318	CHASKA	019	19491	24157	30319	5.2	98	6819	8466	10672	5.2	2.82	5077	6156	4.6
55319	CLEAR LAKE	141	4919	5904	7486	4.4	96	1676	2039	2619	4.7	2.88	1388	1659	4.3
55320	CLEARWATER	145	3878	4361	5118	2.8	88	1322	1520	1822	3.3	2.87	1036	1164	2.8
55321	COKATO	171	4972	5453	6529	2.2	81	1626	1793	2172	2.3	2.98	1184	1273	1.7
55322	COLOGNE	019	2887	3244	3880	2.8	88	994	1134	1370	3.2	2.85	771	860	2.6
55324	DARWIN	093	1128	1177	1267	1.0	59	452	480	525	1.4	2.45	357	371	0.9
55325	DASSEL	093	4058	4309	4643	1.4	67	1517	1634	1786	1.8	2.60	1113	1167	1.1
55327	DAYTON	053	3843	3878	3963	0.2	34	1232	1259	1298	0.5	3.08	1036	1039	0.1
55328	DELANO	171	7186	8306	10199	3.5	92	2433	2852	3553	3.8	2.89	1905	2187	3.3
55329	EDEN VALLEY	093	1982	2119	2291	1.6	71	739	806	887	2.1	2.62	540	574	1.5
55330	ELK RIVER	141	26669	32073	40442	4.4	96	8961	10915	13948	4.8	2.91	7153	8526	4.2
55331	EXCELSIOR	053	18683	19678	21325	1.2	63	6821	7188	7789	1.2	2.72	5199	5413	1.0
55332	FAIRFAX	129	2130	2119	2118	-0.1	22	843	849	859	0.2	2.42	570	557	-0.5
55333	FRANKLIN	129	757	772	786	0.5	42	295	303	311	0.6	2.45	186	185	-0.1
55334	GAYLORD	143	3030	3050	3115	0.2	33	1161	1186	1226	0.5	2.50	804	799	-0.2
55335	GIBBON	143	1971	1977	2027	0.1	30	734	747	776	0.4	2.55	521	516	-0.2
55336	GLENCOE	085	8403	8491	8729	0.3	36	3139	3209	3344	0.5	2.60	2267	2257	-0.1
55337	BURNSVILLE	037	44665	47758	52320	1.6	71	17691	19252	21370	2.0	2.46	11526	12056	1.1
55338	GREEN ISLE	143	800	870	928	2.0	78	293	322	347	2.3	2.70	233	251	1.8
55339	HAMBURG	019	929	993	1144	1.6	70	333	362	422	2.0	2.73	263	279	1.4
55340	HAMEL	053	5316	5678	5958	1.6	70	1711	1843	1945	1.8	3.08	1437	1519	1.3
55341	HANOVER	171	1296	1515	1818	3.7	94	422	500	607	4.1	3.03	361	424	3.9
55342	HECTOR	129	1895	1882	1880	-0.2	21	802	808	816	0.2	2.33	540	528	-0.5
55343	HOPKINS	053	24282	24697	25476	0.4	41	11550	11896	12350	0.7	2.04	5673	5516	-0.7
55344	EDEN PRAIRIE	053	10397	11678	12776	2.8	88	4771	5399	5938	3.0	2.14	2528	2746	2.0
55345	MINNETONKA	053	22679	23100	23891	0.4	42	8485	8775	9166	0.8	2.60	6476	6521	0.2
55346	EDEN PRAIRIE	053	18673	19277	19926	0.8	51	6632	6930	7219	1.0	2.78	5154	5266	0.5
55347	EDEN PRAIRIE	053	25831	28463	30521	2.3	83	9054	9980	10714	2.3	2.85	6897	7410	1.7
55349	HOWARD LAKE	171	3752	4200	5092	2.7	87	1377	1561	1919	3.0	2.69	1010	1118	2.4
55350	HUTCHINSON	085	17247	18148	19082	1.2	63	6788	7258	7751	1.6	2.47	4621	4819	1.0
55352	JORDAN	139	6890	7961	10016	3.5	92	2314	2718	3473	3.9	2.89	1791	2055	3.3
55353	KIMBALL	145	3045	3211	3458	1.3	65	1075	1155	1266	1.7	2.77	822	859	1.0
55354	LESTER PRAIRIE	085	2188	2204	2250	0.2	33	802	819	847	0.5	2.69	609	608	0.0
55355	LITCHFIELD	093	9566	10013	10685	1.1	60	3728	3963	4296	1.5	2.44	2530	2617	0.8
55356	LONG LAKE	053	5334	5349	5472	0.1	30	1907	1930	1988	0.3	2.75	1475	1462	-0.2
55357	LORETTO	053	2382	2629	2806	2.4	83	768	853	915	2.5	3.08	627	682	2.0
55358	MAPLE LAKE	171	4889	5497	6679	2.8	88	1786	2040	2519	3.2	2.69	1322	1474	2.6
55359	MAPLE PLAIN	053	6211	6467	6695	1.0	57	2172	2290	2392	1.3	2.79	1716	1767	0.7
55360	MAYER	019	1528	1726	2068	2.9	89	530	608	738	3.3	2.83	420	472	2.8
55362	MONTICELLO	171	13748	16770	21236	4.8	97	4842	6008	7729	5.2	2.77	3652	4418	4.6
55363	MONTROSE	171	2141	2408	2926	2.8	88	799	917	1135	3.3	2.61	582	651	2.7
55364	MOUND	053	14740	15177	15727	0.7	49	5876	6102	6367	0.9	2.48	4082	4114	0.2
55366	NEW AUBURN	143	318	331	343	1.0	57	114	120	125	1.2	2.76	89	91	0.5
55367	NEW GERMANY	019	950	1055	1254	2.5	85	348	393	472	2.9	2.68	277	306	2.4
55368	NORWOOD	019	2254	2427	2841	1.8	75	827	902	1066	2.1	2.68	633	675	1.5
55369	OSSEO	053	33093	35090	37164	1.4	66	12044	12937	13819	1.7	2.70	9085	9476	1.0
55370	PLATO	085	749	748	766	0.0	26	290	295	307	0.4	2.54	222	221	-0.1
55371	PRINCETON	095	12054	13699	16231	3.1	90	4427	5116	6150	3.5	2.65	3279	3712	3.0
55372	PRIOR LAKE	139	23080	28030	36216	4.7	96	7960	9813	12835	5.1	2.86	6416	7761	4.6
55373	ROCKFORD	053	4659	5450	6571	3.8	94	1712	2032	2485	4.1	2.68	1279	1480	3.5
55374	ROGERS	053	7925	9444	10528	4.2	95	2539	3078	3467	4.6	3.06	2145	2556	4.2
55375	SAINT BONIFACIUS	053	1878	2330	2641	5.2	98	682	856	978	5.5	2.72	546	671	5.0
55376	SAINT MICHAEL	171	8767	11649	15356	6.9	100	2812	3816	5122	7.5	3.04	2264	3018	7.0
55378	SAVAGE	139	20104	26395	35393	6.6	100	6473	8471	11389	6.5	3.12	5425	7051	6.4
55379	SHAKOPEE	139	23983	31329	42118	6.5	99	8656	11553	15812	7.0	2.67	6261	8141	6.4
55381	SILVER LAKE	085	1890	1894	1929	0.1	30	720	734	759	0.5	2.58	526	524	-0.1
55382	SOUTH HAVEN	145	3776	4225	4881	2.7	87	1345	1531	1799	3.1	2.76	1061	1180	2.5
55384	SPRING PARK	053	1590	1523	1536	-1.0	2	872	841	855	-0.9	1.60	395	357	-2.4
55385	STEWART	085	1273	1296	1345	0.4	41	500	518	547	0.8	2.50	344	346	0.1
55386	VICTORIA	019	2948	3865	4969	6.6	99	1015	1357	1768	7.1	2.79	825	1084	6.6
55387	WACONIA	019	9035	10444	12596	3.5	92	3170	3719	4553	3.8	2.67	2362	2707	3.3
55388	WATERTOWN	019	4420	4983	5947	2.9	89	1557	1789	2170	3.3	2.70	1177	1319	2.7
55389	WATKINS	093	2403	2443	2572	0.4	41	852	882	943	0.8	2.69	631	636	0.2
55390	WAVERLY	171	2439	2729	3306	2.7	87	853	972	1197	3.1	2.77	642	714	2.5
55391	WAYZATA	053	15220	15203	15569	0.0	26	5969	6038	6235	0.3	2.47	4041	3958	-0.5
55395	WINSTED	085	2825	3013	3182	1.5	69	1061	1155	1241	2.0	2.54	750	794	1.4
55396	WINTHROP	143	2537	2500	2548	-0.4	15	1023	1021	1053	-0.1	2.37	695	674	-0.7
55397	YOUNG AMERICA	019	2486	2645	3074	1.5	68	868	937	1099	1.8	2.82	636	670	1.2
55398	ZIMMERMAN	141	10274	12545	15985	4.8	97	3432	4261	5501	5.2	2.94	2762	3358	4.7
55401	MINNEAPOLIS	053	3531	4211	4904	4.2	96	2557	3017	3513	4.0	1.24	474	525	2.4
55402	MINNEAPOLIS	053	176	167	168	-1.2	1	154	148	150	-0.9	1.12	16	14	-3.1
55403	MINNEAPOLIS	053	15317	16151	17012	1.3	65	10375	11152	11862	1.7	1.39	1864	1797	-0.9
55404	MINNEAPOLIS	053	27634	27818	28341	0.2	33	11439	11429	11651	0.0	2.10	3726	3472	-1.7
55405	MINNEAPOLIS	053	15426	15637	16156	0.3	39	6906	7010	7275	0.4	2.10	2608	2504	-1.0
55406	MINNEAPOLIS	053	32513	33318	34453	0.6	46	14871	15375	16012	0.8	2.15	7471	7307	-0.5
55407	MINNEAPOLIS	053	36073	36200	36998	0.1	30	13463	13443	13742	0.0	2.65	7374	6997	-1.2
55408	MINNEAPOLIS	053	31437	31489	32215	0.0	29	14808	14803	15171	0.0	2.10	4759	4449	-1.6
	MINNESOTA					1.4					1.6	2.50			1.0
	UNITED STATES					1.2					1.3	2.58			1.1

ZIP CODE #	POST OFFICE NAME	RACE (%) White 2000	White 2004	Black 2000	Black 2004	Asian/Pacific 2000	Asian/Pacific 2004	% Hispanic Origin 2000	% Hispanic Origin 2004	2004 AGE DISTRIBUTION (%) 0-4	5-9	10-14	15-19	20-24	25-44	45-64	65-84	85+	18+	MEDIAN AGE 2004	% 2004 Males	% 2004 Females
55150	MENDOTA	94.6	93.8	1.0	0.8	1.5	1.7	1.5	2.1	3.3	3.7	4.5	5.8	4.9	16.1	27.2	30.0	4.5	84.4	52.8	45.7	54.3
55301	ALBERTVILLE	98.6	98.4	0.1	0.2	0.4	0.5	0.8	1.0	12.2	10.7	9.0	6.1	5.0	39.5	13.3	3.9	0.4	64.1	29.9	50.5	49.6
55302	ANNANDALE	98.3	98.1	0.3	0.3	0.2	0.2	0.8	1.0	6.6	6.7	7.8	7.0	6.1	26.1	24.8	12.9	2.1	74.5	38.3	50.3	49.7
55303	ANOKA	95.3	94.5	1.3	1.6	0.9	1.1	1.5	1.8	7.9	7.7	7.9	7.0	7.0	31.9	23.4	6.3	1.0	72.2	33.8	50.9	49.1
55304	ANDOVER	96.6	95.9	0.5	0.7	1.0	1.2	1.1	1.3	8.9	9.2	9.8	7.4	5.0	32.8	23.1	3.6	0.3	67.3	33.2	51.2	48.8
55305	HOPKINS	93.4	91.3	2.2	3.1	2.4	3.2	1.4	1.8	4.4	4.9	5.8	5.8	5.1	27.9	28.8	14.3	3.0	80.8	42.4	46.9	53.1
55306	BURNSVILLE	89.6	87.4	2.9	3.8	3.5	4.2	2.6	3.3	7.5	7.2	7.5	6.9	7.6	33.8	24.0	5.3	0.3	73.4	32.9	50.0	50.1
55307	ARLINGTON	96.4	95.6	0.2	0.2	0.4	0.4	4.4	5.4	7.0	7.3	7.4	7.5	5.6	27.1	21.3	13.7	3.2	73.5	36.8	49.5	50.5
55308	BECKER	98.1	97.8	0.2	0.3	0.3	0.4	0.7	0.9	10.5	9.4	9.0	7.3	6.9	34.7	17.1	4.8	0.3	66.5	29.3	50.7	49.3
55309	BIG LAKE	97.5	97.1	0.2	0.2	0.4	0.5	1.3	1.6	9.8	9.2	8.6	7.0	6.3	34.2	19.7	4.7	0.5	68.0	31.1	50.4	49.6
55310	BIRD ISLAND	97.4	96.9	0.0	0.0	0.3	0.4	2.9	3.5	5.6	6.1	7.2	8.0	5.8	22.7	24.8	16.8	3.1	75.5	41.7	51.6	48.5
55311	OSSEO	94.7	93.0	1.1	1.7	2.7	3.6	0.9	1.3	8.7	9.7	9.4	7.1	3.8	34.4	23.8	3.0	0.1	67.4	34.6	49.4	50.6
55312	BROWNTON	96.0	95.2	0.2	0.2	0.6	0.7	3.4	4.2	6.4	6.4	7.1	7.1	6.0	26.5	26.8	11.8	2.0	75.4	38.9	49.9	50.1
55313	BUFFALO	97.3	96.9	0.4	0.5	0.6	0.7	1.0	1.3	8.1	7.8	7.9	7.3	7.1	29.2	23.2	8.0	1.5	71.6	34.4	49.9	50.1
55314	BUFFALO LAKE	95.5	94.7	0.0	0.0	0.4	0.4	5.3	6.4	6.4	6.4	6.9	6.1	5.9	24.5	22.9	16.2	4.7	76.7	40.8	49.9	50.1
55315	CARVER	98.1	97.7	0.1	0.1	0.3	0.4	1.1	1.4	7.1	7.3	7.9	8.2	6.6	32.0	24.4	6.1	0.4	72.6	35.6	51.7	48.3
55316	CHAMPLIN	95.0	93.6	1.4	2.0	1.7	2.2	1.1	1.5	8.6	8.7	9.5	7.6	6.2	33.9	21.5	3.8	0.3	68.5	32.6	50.1	49.9
55317	CHANHASSEN	94.3	93.3	0.8	1.0	3.3	3.9	2.3	2.7	9.6	10.2	9.6	6.3	3.9	32.7	23.0	4.3	0.4	66.4	34.5	49.9	50.1
55318	CHASKA	94.2	93.3	0.9	1.1	1.6	1.9	5.3	6.1	9.4	9.1	8.7	7.4	6.3	32.7	20.7	4.8	0.9	68.2	32.4	50.1	49.9
55319	CLEAR LAKE	98.4	98.1	0.3	0.4	0.2	0.3	0.6	0.7	8.0	7.8	8.2	7.2	5.3	29.7	25.2	8.1	0.6	71.3	36.2	51.8	48.2
55320	CLEARWATER	98.5	98.3	0.1	0.2	0.3	0.3	0.6	0.7	8.0	8.2	8.2	7.3	6.0	28.5	25.4	7.7	0.7	71.0	35.9	51.0	49.1
55321	COKATO	97.4	97.0	0.2	0.2	0.3	0.4	1.9	2.3	9.0	8.6	9.0	9.4	6.5	23.8	20.2	10.7	2.8	66.9	33.2	50.1	49.9
55322	COLOGNE	98.1	97.7	0.0	0.1	1.0	1.2	0.9	1.2	8.2	8.4	8.2	6.5	5.4	33.1	21.6	7.7	1.1	71.0	34.8	52.2	47.8
55324	DARWIN	98.1	97.6	0.1	0.2	0.1	0.2	1.2	1.3	5.1	5.6	6.8	7.3	5.2	22.8	31.6	14.1	1.5	77.8	43.4	51.2	48.9
55325	DASSEL	98.1	97.8	0.1	0.1	0.6	0.7	1.1	1.4	7.1	7.1	7.3	6.9	5.9	24.3	26.3	12.6	2.5	74.1	39.3	51.1	48.9
55327	DAYTON	96.0	95.0	0.6	0.9	0.7	0.9	2.2	2.8	7.7	7.9	8.5	7.4	5.9	30.0	26.7	5.5	0.4	71.3	35.9	50.3	49.7
55328	DELANO	98.2	97.9	0.3	0.3	0.5	0.6	0.9	1.0	8.2	7.7	8.4	7.3	5.9	30.2	24.4	6.8	1.2	71.0	35.5	49.8	50.2
55329	EDEN VALLEY	98.6	98.3	0.3	0.4	0.5	0.6	1.1	1.3	7.0	6.9	7.5	7.8	7.3	25.8	23.3	12.6	1.9	73.9	36.0	50.9	49.1
55330	ELK RIVER	97.3	96.8	0.4	0.5	0.6	0.7	1.3	1.5	8.6	8.3	8.5	7.3	7.0	31.9	21.7	5.9	0.9	69.9	32.4	50.6	49.4
55331	EXCELSIOR	97.2	96.5	0.5	0.6	1.1	1.4	1.3	1.6	7.1	8.4	9.4	6.8	4.4	25.3	29.5	8.4	0.8	70.6	39.4	49.7	50.3
55332	FAIRFAX	94.3	93.3	0.1	0.1	0.1	0.1	5.6	6.8	7.1	6.9	7.0	6.7	5.7	23.2	22.5	16.5	4.3	74.7	40.7	48.8	51.3
55333	FRANKLIN	95.6	95.1	0.0	0.0	0.1	0.3	2.0	2.6	6.5	6.9	7.6	7.1	4.7	21.6	25.0	17.1	3.5	74.1	42.0	50.1	49.9
55334	GAYLORD	90.8	89.1	0.2	0.2	0.6	0.7	13.2	15.8	6.4	6.7	7.3	7.1	5.8	25.1	23.1	15.4	3.3	75.3	38.9	50.7	49.3
55335	GIBBON	97.3	96.8	0.1	0.1	0.4	0.5	1.9	2.4	7.0	7.0	7.5	7.0	5.7	23.8	23.9	15.5	2.6	73.8	39.7	52.2	47.9
55336	GLENCOE	94.6	93.7	0.2	0.2	0.6	0.7	9.4	11.5	7.4	7.3	7.6	7.0	5.5	27.8	23.0	12.0	2.5	73.2	37.0	50.0	50.0
55337	BURNSVILLE	86.8	84.4	4.5	5.6	4.4	5.2	3.0	3.6	7.0	6.5	6.7	6.5	8.0	32.5	23.5	8.2	1.0	75.7	33.8	48.9	51.1
55338	GREEN ISLE	98.5	98.2	0.1	0.2	0.3	0.3	1.3	1.6	6.6	7.1	8.6	6.7	6.0	27.6	25.8	10.2	1.5	73.5	38.1	52.4	47.6
55339	HAMBURG	98.3	98.0	0.1	0.1	0.9	0.9	1.4	1.7	7.2	7.4	7.7	7.4	6.1	31.1	23.2	8.9	1.2	73.3	36.1	51.5	48.5
55340	HAMEL	96.8	95.9	0.3	0.4	1.7	2.2	0.8	1.0	7.3	9.2	9.4	8.4	4.1	28.6	26.8	5.8	0.4	68.4	36.5	51.1	48.9
55341	HANOVER	98.7	98.4	0.1	0.1	0.4	0.5	0.5	0.6	10.0	10.0	9.1	6.9	5.4	32.3	21.7	4.3	0.4	66.6	33.0	50.1	49.9
55342	HECTOR	96.4	95.8	0.0	0.0	0.2	0.2	4.0	4.8	6.0	6.2	7.1	6.9	6.0	25.0	24.7	14.8	3.4	76.5	40.4	48.5	51.5
55343	HOPKINS	85.6	82.2	4.2	5.7	5.1	6.2	4.4	5.4	5.3	4.9	5.2	5.2	8.0	33.9	22.9	11.2	3.4	81.3	36.8	47.3	52.7
55344	EDEN PRAIRIE	84.0	80.5	5.0	6.6	6.8	8.1	3.3	4.2	6.5	5.8	6.0	5.9	8.8	37.7	20.7	7.3	1.3	78.1	32.6	49.1	50.9
55345	MINNETONKA	95.6	94.5	0.9	1.2	1.9	2.4	1.1	1.5	5.7	6.8	7.8	7.1	4.2	23.4	31.8	11.7	1.5	74.7	42.2	49.0	51.0
55346	EDEN PRAIRIE	92.0	89.8	2.1	3.0	4.0	5.0	1.1	1.4	7.6	8.3	9.0	7.8	5.0	28.7	28.1	5.1	0.4	69.8	36.5	48.7	51.3
55347	EDEN PRAIRIE	92.4	90.3	1.3	1.8	4.7	5.9	1.2	1.5	8.2	9.1	9.5	7.0	4.6	31.7	25.5	4.2	0.2	68.6	35.2	49.3	50.7
55349	HOWARD LAKE	97.9	97.6	0.4	0.5	0.4	0.5	1.0	1.1	7.9	8.1	8.6	7.5	5.9	27.3	23.4	10.0	1.4	70.7	34.9	50.1	49.9
55350	HUTCHINSON	96.8	96.3	0.3	0.4	0.8	0.9	1.8	2.2	7.3	7.1	7.1	7.5	7.5	28.0	23.2	10.4	2.0	73.6	35.5	49.4	50.6
55352	JORDAN	95.6	94.9	0.6	0.7	0.4	0.4	4.0	4.9	8.3	8.1	8.7	7.7	7.1	29.6	22.7	6.8	1.1	70.1	32.9	51.0	49.0
55353	KIMBALL	98.5	98.3	0.2	0.3	0.4	0.5	0.6	0.7	7.4	7.8	8.2	7.2	5.8	28.4	23.9	10.3	1.2	72.1	36.0	51.9	48.2
55354	LESTER PRAIRIE	97.5	97.0	0.1	0.1	0.1	0.1	4.2	5.2	7.6	7.7	8.0	7.7	5.8	28.5	22.2	11.3	1.3	72.0	35.6	50.7	49.3
55355	LITCHFIELD	95.8	95.1	0.3	0.4	0.3	0.4	3.9	4.7	6.6	6.2	7.0	7.0	6.3	25.2	24.8	13.4	3.6	75.9	39.2	49.7	50.3
55356	LONG LAKE	97.4	96.6	0.6	0.9	0.8	1.0	0.9	1.2	5.6	6.9	8.7	8.1	4.2	24.2	32.1	9.1	1.1	73.1	41.0	49.9	50.1
55357	LORETTO	97.4	96.8	0.4	0.7	0.9	1.2	0.8	1.0	8.8	9.5	9.1	7.3	4.8	31.0	23.6	5.6	0.4	67.9	34.8	50.9	49.1
55358	MAPLE LAKE	98.9	98.7	0.2	0.2	0.2	0.3	0.6	0.7	6.8	6.8	7.6	8.1	6.9	27.7	24.7	10.2	1.4	73.8	37.4	51.3	48.7
55359	MAPLE PLAIN	97.8	97.1	0.2	0.3	0.9	1.2	0.8	1.1	6.4	7.4	8.5	7.4	5.3	25.6	29.5	8.3	1.6	72.7	39.8	49.9	50.1
55360	MAYER	98.2	98.0	0.4	0.5	0.5	0.5	0.5	0.6	6.6	7.0	8.1	6.4	6.0	28.7	26.3	9.5	1.5	74.3	37.5	51.3	48.7
55362	MONTICELLO	97.4	97.0	0.3	0.3	0.5	0.6	1.6	2.0	9.1	8.6	8.4	7.3	7.3	31.9	19.9	6.5	1.0	69.4	31.8	49.3	50.7
55363	MONTROSE	98.4	98.0	0.3	0.4	0.1	0.2	0.7	0.9	6.8	7.2	7.8	7.4	6.2	32.4	23.7	7.4	1.0	73.2	34.6	52.2	47.8
55364	MOUND	96.7	95.8	0.5	0.8	1.3	1.7	0.8	1.1	6.1	6.9	7.3	6.3	4.8	29.0	30.3	8.4	1.0	75.8	39.9	51.5	48.5
55366	NEW AUBURN	94.3	93.4	0.0	0.0	0.0	0.0	7.6	9.1	10.0	8.2	7.3	7.9	6.7	26.6	22.4	9.7	1.5	70.1	33.2	50.5	49.6
55367	NEW GERMANY	98.3	98.0	0.4	0.6	0.5	0.6	0.3	0.5	6.5	6.8	7.8	6.1	6.0	28.6	27.0	9.9	1.4	75.3	38.0	52.2	47.8
55368	NORWOOD	98.1	97.8	0.1	0.2	0.8	1.0	1.7	2.1	6.7	6.8	7.6	7.7	7.0	29.7	23.2	9.9	1.4	74.3	36.0	50.5	49.5
55369	OSSEO	94.8	93.3	1.0	1.5	2.3	2.9	1.2	1.6	6.4	6.9	7.9	7.7	6.3	31.0	27.3	5.9	0.6	73.9	36.0	49.4	50.6
55370	PLATO	98.5	98.3	0.1	0.1	0.5	0.5	1.3	1.6	7.1	7.4	6.7	6.6	4.8	28.2	28.1	9.9	1.3	74.9	38.5	50.9	49.1
55371	PRINCETON	98.0	97.7	0.2	0.2	0.3	0.4	1.0	1.1	7.1	7.1	7.6	7.3	6.6	28.7	24.0	9.6	2.1	73.8	36.3	49.4	50.6
55372	PRIOR LAKE	95.7	95.1	0.7	0.9	1.0	1.1	1.0	1.3	8.6	8.8	8.3	6.8	5.1	32.8	24.4	4.7	0.4	69.8	35.1	50.4	49.6
55373	ROCKFORD	97.7	97.3	0.3	0.5	0.6	0.6	1.1	1.3	9.3	8.7	8.8	7.6	6.7	32.8	21.1	4.5	0.4	68.5	31.7	49.8	50.2
55374	ROGERS	97.5	96.9	0.3	0.5	0.7	0.9	0.9	1.1	10.3	10.2	8.9	6.2	4.9	33.4	21.2	4.7	0.4	66.8	33.3	50.1	49.9
55375	SAINT BONIFACIUS	97.0	96.3	0.2	0.2	0.9	1.2	1.8	2.3	10.5	9.5	6.9	5.2	5.0	37.4	19.4	5.5	0.7	70.0	32.7	51.7	48.3
55376	SAINT MICHAEL	98.5	98.2	0.1	0.1	0.4	0.5	0.9	1.1	10.5	9.8	9.0	6.7	5.4	35.7	16.9	5.4	0.6	66.3	31.3	50.4	49.6
55378	SAVAGE	90.6	89.1	1.6	1.9	5.5	6.5	1.6	2.0	12.0	11.7	9.7	6.0	4.0	37.8	16.3	2.4	0.1	62.7	31.5	50.6	49.4
55379	SHAKOPEE	90.9	89.6	1.2	1.4	2.3	2.7	5.8	6.6	9.0	8.2	7.3	5.7	6.3	37.5	19.1	6.0	0.8	71.9	32.3	49.9	50.1
55381	SILVER LAKE	98.8	98.8	0.3	0.3	0.2	0.2	0.4	0.5	6.3	6.4	7.1	7.1	6.0	28.3	24.9	11.9	1.9	75.7	37.5	50.9	49.1
55382	SOUTH HAVEN	98.7	98.5	0.3	0.3	0.2	0.2	0.7	0.9	7.1	7.4	8.3	7.2	6.0	26.5	26.3	10.3	0.8	72.8	37.5	51.8	48.2
55384	SPRING PARK	96.5	95.5	1.2	1.7	0.8	1.0	0.9	1.1	3.7	3.6	3.5	3.2	4.7	26.9	25.2	15.8	13.4	87.5	48.1	47.3	52.7
55385	STEWART	97.7	97.4	0.2	0.2	0.3	0.3	2.2	2.7	6.0	6.0	6.9	7.1	6.6	27.8	25.2	12.5	2.0	76.7	38.6	52.8	47.2
55386	VICTORIA	98.1	97.8	0.2	0.3	0.8	0.9	0.8	1.0	8.8	9.1	8.3	6.6	5.1	30.1	24.4	7.1	0.5	69.5	36.1	50.1	49.9
55387	WACONIA	97.1	96.6	0.3	0.4	0.9	1.1	1.2	1.5	8.5	8.2	7.7	7.3	8.1	29.8	20.2	8.1	2.0	71.4	33.1	48.0	52.0
55388	WATERTOWN	98.1	97.8	0.3	0.4	0.5	0.6	1.2	1.5	7.3	7.1	7.7	7.3	6.8	28.1	23.7	9.7	2.2	73.1	36.3	49.1	51.0
55389	WATKINS	99.3	99.2	0.2	0.3	0.1	0.1	0.3	0.4	6.6	7.0	7.4	7.8	6.0	26.2	24.5	12.0	2.7	74.0	38.0	51.4	48.6
55390	WAVERLY	98.0	97.6	0.3	0.4	0.2	0.3	1.6	2.0	7.4	7.4	7.4	7.3	6.2	30.9	24.1	8.4	0.9	72.9	35.3	52.4	47.6
55391	WAYZATA	96.6	95.7	0.4	0.6	1.5	1.9	1.2	1.5	5.4	6.3	7.1	6.4	4.2	24.2	31.9	12.2	2.4	76.8	42.9	48.7	51.4
55395	WINSTED	98.5	98.3	0.1	0.2	0.3	0.5	0.9	1.0	7.5	7.3	7.6	6.7	6.6	28.5	22.0	10.9	3.0	73.2	35.8	49.0	51.0
55396	WINTHROP	95.9	95.3	0.1	0.1	0.1	0.1	4.1	5.0	6.3	6.4	6.6	6.9	5.7	24.2	24.7	15.5	3.7	75.7	41.1	50.3	49.7
55397	YOUNG AMERICA	98.0	97.7	0.3	0.3	0.4	0.5	2.5	3.0	6.9	6.5	7.4	8.1	8.4	28.3	22.9	9.7	1.8	74.4	34.7	49.1	50.9
55398	ZIMMERMAN	98.1	97.8	0.2	0.2	0.3	0.4	0.8	1.0	9.0	8.6	8.7	7.7	6.6	33.4	20.7	5.0	0.4	68.8	32.1	50.8	49.2
55401	MINNEAPOLIS	75.5	72.9	15.3	17.0	4.4	4.9	2.5	3.1	1.8	1.1	0.8	1.7	8.8	50.5	24.1	9.9	1.3	95.8	36.9	56.2	43.8
55402	MINNEAPOLIS	75.0	69.5	17.1	21.6	6.3	7.2	2.8	3.6	1.2	0.6	0.6	1.2	8.4	49.1	29.9	8.4	0.6	97.6	40.4	65.3	34.7
55403	MINNEAPOLIS	80.0	74.8	10.1	13.6	3.4	4.1	5.4	6.8	2.0	1.5	1.3	3.1	13.6	46.3	20.7	9.5	2.0	94.1	34.5	55.0	45.0
55404	MINNEAPOLIS	43.2	37.8	28.3	33.3	4.5	4.8	15.2	16.5	7.1	5.6	5.4	7.8	15.6	35.5	15.1	5.4	2.6	78.8	28.5	53.8	46.2
55405	MINNEAPOLIS	67.7	63.9	16.2	19.1	9.5	9.9	4.5	5.1	6.2	5.6	5.3	5.5	10.7	39.4	21.4	5.3	0.6	79.9	32.2	52.7	47.3
55406	MINNEAPOLIS	78.2	73.7	8.8	11.6	2.8	3.3	5.8	7.1	5.7	5.4	5.7	6.0	6.9	32.6	26.6	9.0	2.2	79.7	38.2	48.2	51.8
55407	MINNEAPOLIS	51.8	46.3	22.0	26.2	5.3	5.7	18.0	19.8	8.2	7.4	7.7	7.7	8.5	34.7	19.3	5.2	1.4	72.1	31.1	50.2	49.8
55408	MINNEAPOLIS	62.4	57.7	16.5	19.6	5.6	6.1	15.7	17.3	6.2	4.9	4.9	5.5	12.8	44.7	15.4	4.3	1.3	81.1	29.8	52.1	47.9
	MINNESOTA	89.5	88.0	3.5	4.2	2.9	3.4	2.9	3.4	6.8	6.8	7.2	7.3	7.4	28.6	23.9	10.1	1.9	74.9	36.1	49.6	50.5
	UNITED STATES	75.1	73.6	12.3	12.5	3.8	4.2	12.5	14.1	6.9	6.7	7.2	7.0	7.3	28.6	23.8	10.8	1.7	75.1	36.0	49.1	50.9

ZIP CODE #	POST OFFICE NAME	2004 Per Capita Income	2004 HH Income Base	2004 Household Income Distribution (%) Less than $25,000	$25,000 to $49,999	$50,000 to $99,999	$100,000 to $149,999	$150,000 or More	Median Household Income 2004	2009	2004 National Centile	2004 State Centile	2004 Home Value Base	2004 Home Value Distribution (%) Less than $50,000	$50,000 to $89,999	$90,000 to $174,999	$175,000 to $399,999	$400,000 or More	2004 Median Home Value
55150	MENDOTA	40443	97	10.3	17.5	36.1	19.6	16.5	75661	92390	93	93	61	1.6	0.0	23.0	45.9	29.5	270833
55301	ALBERTVILLE	29784	1959	6.9	20.5	46.0	21.2	5.4	73135	86232	92	92	1762	0.5	0.6	19.2	77.1	2.6	216420
55302	ANNANDALE	29245	2980	18.4	24.4	39.0	12.6	5.6	56942	69383	82	79	2533	8.8	7.4	31.9	44.0	7.8	179947
55303	ANOKA	28675	15451	12.3	20.0	44.6	17.1	6.0	66269	78786	89	88	11990	1.2	1.0	29.5	63.9	4.5	199742
55304	ANDOVER	30987	14522	4.6	10.7	47.5	27.1	10.2	83930	102699	96	96	13902	1.9	1.1	15.8	72.6	8.6	227416
55305	HOPKINS	56254	9453	10.8	20.8	30.6	17.8	20.0	77557	105901	94	94	6269	0.2	3.2	16.7	57.6	22.4	254626
55306	BURNSVILLE	35870	6559	7.5	20.4	41.3	20.0	10.8	73406	89944	93	92	4795	12.4	3.0	16.8	59.8	8.1	217747
55307	ARLINGTON	23318	1207	22.9	30.2	36.0	7.0	3.9	47290	55465	67	58	913	6.8	18.4	50.1	21.1	3.6	120142
55308	BECKER	25862	2514	6.2	22.4	51.4	14.8	5.3	65895	77441	89	88	2192	1.9	2.2	25.1	65.4	5.4	208563
55309	BIG LAKE	24644	5159	9.2	21.4	50.1	15.7	3.6	64635	76183	88	87	4630	2.9	3.0	26.9	60.9	6.4	201998
55310	BIRD ISLAND	23564	680	23.5	32.2	33.8	7.8	2.7	45218	51986	62	51	564	22.7	28.2	37.4	7.6	4.1	88684
55311	OSSEO	43701	8614	2.4	7.8	34.1	31.5	24.2	106251	140079	99	99	8401	0.2	0.4	10.9	65.6	22.9	281035
55312	BROWNTON	23294	661	19.7	29.5	37.8	9.1	3.9	50717	59309	73	68	573	4.7	18.9	48.9	22.2	5.4	131958
55313	BUFFALO	28813	8032	13.2	21.8	41.4	16.4	7.2	65098	78913	89	87	6518	5.4	2.8	28.5	55.1	8.2	201060
55314	BUFFALO LAKE	21693	548	20.1	33.9	37.6	7.1	1.3	47220	53839	67	58	462	14.9	25.1	37.9	18.2	3.9	106731
55315	CARVER	30496	879	5.2	15.2	49.7	21.7	8.1	77661	96435	94	94	786	1.5	1.2	16.7	64.9	15.8	244030
55316	CHAMPLIN	30701	7979	5.2	14.2	47.6	25.9	7.1	79941	102683	95	95	7282	0.2	0.4	30.7	64.4	4.4	193530
55317	CHANHASSEN	47150	6681	4.6	12.5	31.4	27.6	23.9	101750	135099	98	99	6156	0.0	0.1	12.1	59.8	28.0	290856
55318	CHASKA	33375	8466	10.6	18.7	38.1	21.6	11.1	75829	97843	94	93	6760	11.9	1.5	15.9	56.5	14.3	226012
55319	CLEAR LAKE	29066	2039	8.1	19.2	47.9	18.8	6.0	71527	83555	92	92	1912	0.6	2.0	26.2	64.0	7.2	214682
55320	CLEARWATER	24963	1520	13.4	24.7	42.5	13.8	5.7	60370	72305	85	82	1358	1.8	7.1	42.0	44.1	5.0	173295
55321	COKATO	21609	1793	19.1	27.2	38.0	11.8	3.9	53696	65410	78	74	1406	5.0	7.5	39.7	43.2	4.6	170441
55322	COLOGNE	28375	1134	9.4	17.3	49.3	18.2	5.8	72208	88829	92	92	1013	1.2	1.0	26.4	59.1	12.3	216900
55324	DARWIN	27388	480	16.3	27.1	37.7	14.8	4.2	56554	68539	81	79	440	4.1	10.7	34.3	44.3	6.6	177381
55325	DASSEL	24126	1634	17.5	27.3	39.2	13.2	2.9	54738	66620	79	76	1369	4.5	10.3	40.0	41.0	4.2	163374
55327	DAYTON	38826	1259	7.2	13.8	36.8	27.2	15.1	86509	118429	97	96	1223	8.1	1.6	21.0	58.1	11.2	212879
55328	DELANO	30254	2852	9.9	21.9	41.4	18.5	8.2	68180	82953	90	90	2450	1.1	1.2	24.9	58.3	14.5	224147
55329	EDEN VALLEY	18764	806	30.0	28.8	33.3	5.6	2.4	43050	51591	56	40	676	10.8	18.9	44.1	23.2	3.0	117730
55330	ELK RIVER	26231	10915	12.0	19.2	45.3	18.0	5.6	67383	79542	90	89	9445	3.1	1.3	23.7	66.3	5.6	212476
55331	EXCELSIOR	60200	7188	7.4	11.7	26.6	21.3	33.1	107661	152564	99	99	6288	0.2	0.2	5.9	46.8	46.9	382691
55332	FAIRFAX	22484	849	28.9	35.2	27.6	5.3	3.1	40707	47829	49	29	681	22.3	35.4	32.6	6.2	3.5	80948
55333	FRANKLIN	19598	303	21.5	40.3	31.0	6.3	1.0	41324	48688	51	32	238	31.1	33.6	25.2	6.7	3.4	67500
55334	GAYLORD	20845	1186	27.5	31.2	32.4	6.6	2.4	45162	51648	62	51	941	5.8	23.3	49.2	17.9	3.8	117357
55335	GIBBON	20756	747	25.3	32.7	32.4	6.6	3.1	43642	50949	58	44	625	12.6	31.8	35.0	14.2	6.2	97188
55336	GLENCOE	24443	3209	17.9	26.4	42.9	9.8	3.1	55022	63752	80	77	2732	7.3	8.3	50.0	31.2	3.3	143878
55337	BURNSVILLE	33829	19252	11.5	23.8	37.3	17.8	9.6	66538	82712	89	89	12565	2.2	3.3	20.4	70.1	4.0	213633
55338	GREEN ISLE	26051	322	16.2	24.2	44.7	9.6	5.3	60731	68896	85	83	292	4.1	5.8	33.2	47.6	9.3	190152
55339	HAMBURG	26770	362	12.7	19.3	48.1	15.5	4.4	63342	79910	87	86	324	0.0	2.5	40.7	49.7	7.1	187791
55340	HAMEL	46199	1843	4.0	11.7	35.1	27.3	21.9	98323	129994	98	98	1738	4.3	1.8	7.5	62.0	24.4	280443
55341	HANOVER	34303	500	4.6	10.8	44.4	28.8	11.4	87295	110848	97	96	476	0.0	0.0	13.7	75.2	11.1	253226
55342	HECTOR	23443	808	26.6	33.9	30.2	6.3	3.0	41204	48670	50	32	678	21.1	27.0	38.9	9.1	3.8	92549
55343	HOPKINS	38454	11896	15.6	30.3	33.0	13.1	8.0	53854	72524	78	75	5909	1.1	4.5	35.9	49.9	8.7	189447
55344	EDEN PRAIRIE	44260	5399	10.7	20.2	37.6	18.6	12.9	73475	99384	93	92	2603	1.3	0.8	27.1	52.7	18.2	227129
55345	MINNETONKA	51577	8775	7.1	13.7	29.9	26.8	22.5	98530	132881	98	99	7738	0.1	0.0	7.4	75.0	17.5	266159
55346	EDEN PRAIRIE	45395	6930	5.5	10.9	32.1	28.5	23.0	101785	134119	98	99	6103	0.0	0.1	12.8	74.3	12.7	260917
55347	EDEN PRAIRIE	59659	9980	4.1	9.3	28.1	25.3	33.3	113065	155029	99	100	9184	0.2	0.0	12.4	52.8	34.6	316202
55349	HOWARD LAKE	22817	1561	18.0	27.0	40.6	11.0	3.5	53735	65383	78	75	1302	6.0	7.1	35.6	44.3	7.1	178214
55350	HUTCHINSON	25489	7258	18.3	28.0	39.7	10.4	3.6	53069	62371	77	72	5339	5.1	5.5	46.7	38.5	4.2	159996
55352	JORDAN	26421	2718	11.7	20.1	46.9	15.2	6.0	65512	79667	89	87	2315	7.7	6.2	22.0	50.6	13.5	212852
55353	KIMBALL	23106	1155	17.5	29.1	39.2	10.5	3.7	53135	64119	77	72	1010	5.0	12.7	44.3	35.6	2.5	148299
55354	LESTER PRAIRIE	23180	819	18.2	27.7	40.9	10.7	2.4	53481	62217	78	73	705	4.7	6.8	53.3	32.6	2.6	146706
55355	LITCHFIELD	24963	3963	23.2	30.2	32.8	9.1	4.7	46532	56460	65	55	3115	8.1	13.2	51.5	23.9	3.3	129901
55356	LONG LAKE	68828	1930	6.8	15.6	29.4	20.5	27.7	95968	137170	98	98	1678	0.2	0.5	14.0	46.6	38.7	297452
55357	LORETTO	40572	853	5.5	14.3	32.8	26.7	20.6	95209	127148	98	98	779	3.7	2.2	8.5	55.5	30.2	300962
55358	MAPLE LAKE	27808	2040	13.2	23.9	42.6	15.0	5.4	62988	77228	87	85	1766	2.2	3.5	37.3	49.5	7.6	189603
55359	MAPLE PLAIN	42877	2290	7.6	16.4	33.0	24.0	19.0	86550	120583	97	96	2007	0.1	0.5	13.9	54.9	30.6	275847
55360	MAYER	28981	608	12.5	21.6	42.3	16.3	7.4	64516	82215	88	87	535	2.8	1.7	28.8	52.2	14.6	220263
55362	MONTICELLO	24522	6008	13.0	26.0	41.9	16.2	2.9	59820	70614	84	81	4855	8.3	2.4	27.0	57.3	4.9	194064
55363	MONTROSE	26449	917	16.1	23.7	44.8	12.2	3.2	60926	70622	85	83	782	12.4	7.3	31.1	39.5	9.7	173171
55364	MOUND	49632	6102	9.3	15.8	35.8	21.6	17.6	83024	113288	96	95	5140	0.5	2.5	23.7	44.9	28.4	247893
55366	NEW AUBURN	21104	120	21.7	32.5	33.3	8.3	4.2	47330	55838	67	58	105	11.4	19.1	43.8	21.9	3.8	119643
55367	NEW GERMANY	29889	393	12.7	23.2	43.0	14.5	6.6	62114	78647	86	84	341	2.1	2.1	30.8	49.0	16.1	215678
55368	NORWOOD	26996	902	14.0	20.8	45.3	15.9	4.0	63568	81212	88	86	750	1.9	1.6	41.3	46.8	8.4	185598
55369	OSSEO	35687	12937	5.4	15.4	42.5	26.6	10.1	81935	106970	96	95	11241	0.9	0.3	32.1	64.4	2.2	196139
55370	PLATO	28511	295	17.3	18.6	47.1	13.6	3.4	62837	75118	87	85	269	2.2	6.3	35.7	49.4	6.3	187917
55371	PRINCETON	25183	5116	17.2	25.5	40.7	12.4	4.1	56517	67211	81	78	4417	5.4	5.0	44.4	41.8	3.4	166303
55372	PRIOR LAKE	39293	9813	6.4	12.0	39.0	26.1	16.6	89164	111658	97	97	8808	0.3	0.8	10.1	65.3	23.5	277101
55373	ROCKFORD	29264	2032	9.5	26.2	39.3	17.7	7.4	65681	78944	89	88	1686	19.3	12.0	12.6	45.2	10.9	188859
55374	ROGERS	34842	3078	4.5	9.9	42.7	31.6	11.3	90603	118617	97	97	2945	1.7	0.7	8.5	78.7	10.3	261828
55375	SAINT BONIFACIUS	30537	856	10.6	14.4	47.1	20.0	7.9	76729	98683	94	93	751	0.0	0.0	23.2	74.4	2.4	219289
55376	SAINT MICHAEL	29618	3816	8.3	16.3	43.5	22.0	9.9	78071	94441	94	94	3395	0.1	0.4	19.9	71.3	8.4	222865
55378	SAVAGE	33767	8471	4.6	10.8	42.8	30.7	11.2	88755	112512	97	97	7787	0.3	0.2	8.5	79.9	11.1	249160
55379	SHAKOPEE	31488	11553	9.1	20.8	44.0	19.3	6.8	70389	84891	91	91	9401	3.4	1.8	21.4	67.5	6.0	213783
55381	SILVER LAKE	22726	734	21.0	26.4	39.4	11.2	2.0	51741	61632	75	70	605	3.5	9.1	54.7	28.8	4.0	140650
55382	SOUTH HAVEN	25163	1531	14.4	27.1	39.6	14.1	4.8	58755	71874	83	81	1435	4.7	9.0	35.5	44.2	6.6	176651
55384	SPRING PARK	60414	841	21.9	27.1	24.9	11.9	14.3	51204	73999	74	69	416	0.5	1.9	16.6	38.2	42.8	345455
55385	STEWART	22705	518	18.9	32.2	38.2	8.5	2.1	49166	57854	70	64	448	11.6	19.0	43.3	21.0	5.1	122857
55386	VICTORIA	44240	1357	6.0	12.4	35.9	28.5	17.2	93055	124867	97	98	1242	0.2	0.2	8.3	65.9	25.4	278974
55387	WACONIA	35556	3719	12.1	18.5	37.5	19.8	12.2	74980	96875	93	93	3119	1.0	0.4	18.8	65.5	14.3	235368
55388	WATERTOWN	27194	1789	16.7	22.8	37.8	17.5	5.3	62636	81707	87	84	1468	9.5	2.6	31.3	45.2	11.5	192014
55389	WATKINS	21209	882	23.4	26.9	35.5	12.0	2.3	49774	59348	71	65	739	10.4	16.1	45.9	24.1	3.5	124352
55390	WAVERLY	24979	972	16.4	24.8	41.9	12.5	4.5	60126	69881	84	82	848	17.7	6.5	27.4	40.8	7.7	171176
55391	WAYZATA	87041	6038	8.1	14.4	24.5	18.5	34.6	106150	156037	99	99	4964	0.3	0.6	9.5	42.8	46.8	378455
55395	WINSTED	24805	1155	18.1	29.5	39.7	8.9	3.7	51665	61422	75	70	905	2.5	6.2	52.3	34.9	4.1	154442
55396	WINTHROP	22359	1021	25.9	31.7	33.6	5.8	3.0	43253	50529	57	41	841	11.2	20.2	45.9	16.1	6.7	114411
55397	YOUNG AMERICA	23709	937	15.8	25.9	40.5	14.5	3.3	58966	76862	84	81	712	3.0	1.3	48.6	42.1	5.1	171241
55398	ZIMMERMAN	26127	4261	7.7	22.3	49.8	15.2	5.0	65395	76930	89	87	4035	2.6	1.7	31.1	58.5	6.2	200959
55401	MINNEAPOLIS	64621	3017	23.2	20.7	32.0	14.8	9.3	57867	86201	83	80	865	0.2	11.1	39.0	38.4	11.3	174178
55402	MINNEAPOLIS	58760	148	24.3	27.0	29.1	12.8	6.8	49243	72466	71	64	62	0.0	17.7	66.1	16.1	0.0	130000
55403	MINNEAPOLIS	53534	11152	32.1	28.6	21.5	7.2	10.6	38980	55089	43	22	2350	0.8	4.1	26.8	35.7	32.6	256140
55404	MINNEAPOLIS	16205	11429	49.5	30.1	15.3	4.1	1.1	25308	32338	5	1	1346	7.4	20.2	49.7	20.0	2.7	126508
55405	MINNEAPOLIS	39959	7010	20.6	28.1	26.9	13.4	11.0	51573	74201	75	69	2948	2.8	8.1	20.8	42.2	26.1	235363
55406	MINNEAPOLIS	29689	15375	19.4	29.8	34.5	12.3	4.1	50665	67408	73	67	11065	0.3	8.1	62.4	27.5	1.6	147321
55407	MINNEAPOLIS	21863	13443	23.1	30.7	32.9	10.8	2.5	46443	62024	65	55	8102	2.6	13.2	63.3	20.4	0.5	134614
55408	MINNEAPOLIS	30326	14803	24.9	33.8	26.9	9.0	5.4	42182	57087	53	36	3873	4.1	7.0	33.8	42.7	12.5	190130
	MINNESOTA	29624		18.6	25.2	34.9	14.0	7.4	56724	71660				6.6	9.7	36.5	40.5	6.8	168676
	UNITED STATES	25866		24.7	27.1	30.8	10.9	6.5	48124	56710				10.9	15.0	33.7	30.1	10.4	145905

ZIP CODE #	POST OFFICE NAME	FINANCIAL SERVICES: Auto Loan	Home Loan	Invest-ments	Retire-ment Plans	THE HOME: Home Improvements: Home Repair	Lawn & Garden	Furnishings: Comput-ers & Hard-ware	Major Appli-ances	TV, Radio, Sound Equip-ment	Furni-ture	ENTERTAINMENT: Dine out/Carry out	Sports Equip-ment	Fees & Tickets	Toys & Games	Travel	Cable TV	PERSONAL: Apparel & Services	Auto Repairs	Health Insur-ance	Pets & Supplies
55150	MENDOTA	153	143	137	136	152	179	132	151	140	142	174	148	134	145	144	150	163	146	177	172
55301	ALBERTVILLE	118	134	129	139	128	123	121	120	111	125	141	140	124	141	118	103	139	116	102	131
55302	ANNANDALE	120	102	75	95	109	119	96	109	103	96	124	128	89	122	99	107	117	108	121	142
55303	ANOKA	106	120	128	123	117	117	114	112	107	114	136	132	117	138	113	103	134	111	101	123
55304	ANDOVER	136	157	156	161	151	148	142	141	131	145	166	165	147	169	141	124	164	137	123	156
55305	HOPKINS	155	175	213	179	171	180	172	166	166	171	209	194	180	214	174	164	207	167	157	183
55306	BURNSVILLE	130	130	142	139	124	128	133	128	127	136	161	153	133	156	127	119	158	131	113	142
55307	ARLINGTON	96	77	52	73	83	94	77	86	84	75	100	101	71	99	78	88	93	85	99	110
55308	BECKER	113	128	123	134	122	117	115	114	106	120	134	134	119	135	112	98	133	111	97	125
55309	BIG LAKE	105	115	111	119	111	109	107	106	100	110	126	125	108	126	104	94	124	105	93	117
55310	BIRD ISLAND	94	69	43	66	77	90	75	84	84	71	99	96	66	94	74	89	90	84	101	105
55311	OSSEO	179	209	209	216	200	196	188	186	172	193	219	217	196	223	186	163	218	181	161	204
55312	BROWNTON	96	83	64	81	88	97	82	89	87	81	105	103	79	106	82	88	99	87	96	109
55313	BUFFALO	111	124	127	127	121	121	116	115	109	117	137	135	119	140	115	104	135	113	104	128
55314	BUFFALO LAKE	88	70	48	68	76	85	71	79	77	69	92	93	65	91	71	79	86	78	89	100
55315	CARVER	123	142	140	147	136	132	128	127	117	131	149	148	132	151	126	110	147	123	109	139
55316	CHAMPLIN	129	144	142	150	138	135	133	131	123	137	156	155	136	156	130	115	154	129	113	144
55317	CHANHASSEN	193	220	215	229	210	204	198	196	181	206	230	229	205	232	194	169	228	190	167	214
55318	CHASKA	136	146	144	151	140	139	138	136	129	142	164	161	139	162	134	122	161	135	120	151
55319	CLEAR LAKE	111	136	141	137	132	130	121	121	112	122	141	141	128	149	123	108	141	117	107	133
55320	CLEARWATER	104	105	97	105	105	110	101	104	100	101	124	121	101	125	101	98	120	102	101	119
55321	COKATO	100	89	72	88	93	102	89	95	93	88	113	110	86	113	89	93	107	93	100	113
55322	COLOGNE	111	127	129	129	124	122	118	117	110	119	138	138	121	142	117	104	137	115	103	129
55324	DARWIN	108	96	73	91	101	109	89	98	94	89	114	117	87	117	91	96	109	96	106	127
55325	DASSEL	96	90	76	88	93	100	86	92	89	85	109	107	85	111	87	90	104	90	96	111
55327	DAYTON	159	190	198	192	186	183	173	172	160	173	202	202	181	212	174	154	201	167	153	190
55328	DELANO	123	137	135	139	134	134	126	127	119	128	150	148	130	153	126	115	147	124	115	141
55329	EDEN VALLEY	77	66	51	65	69	78	67	72	71	66	86	82	64	85	67	72	81	71	78	86
55330	ELK RIVER	108	120	119	123	116	115	111	110	104	113	131	129	114	133	109	99	129	108	98	122
55331	EXCELSIOR	214	263	296	270	256	260	238	232	219	240	278	270	257	288	242	213	279	226	209	256
55332	FAIRFAX	86	72	59	71	77	86	75	81	80	73	96	94	70	93	75	82	90	81	90	98
55333	FRANKLIN	76	65	50	64	68	77	67	71	71	65	86	81	64	85	66	72	80	70	77	84
55334	GAYLORD	85	69	51	68	74	84	71	78	76	70	92	90	66	91	71	78	86	77	86	96
55335	GIBBON	89	68	45	65	75	86	71	80	79	68	93	93	63	90	71	82	86	80	94	102
55336	GLENCOE	100	89	71	87	92	101	87	93	91	87	111	109	85	112	87	92	105	92	99	113
55337	BURNSVILLE	115	120	134	126	117	120	121	117	116	122	147	140	122	146	118	111	144	120	106	130
55338	GREEN ISLE	113	100	76	95	106	114	93	103	99	93	120	123	91	122	96	101	114	100	111	133
55339	HAMBURG	117	104	80	99	110	118	97	107	103	97	125	128	95	127	99	105	119	104	116	138
55340	HAMEL	192	231	240	237	224	221	206	204	189	210	240	238	220	248	207	181	239	197	179	224
55341	HANOVER	149	169	162	176	160	155	152	151	139	158	177	176	156	177	148	129	175	147	128	165
55342	HECTOR	89	71	51	70	77	87	73	81	79	71	95	94	68	94	73	81	88	80	90	101
55343	HOPKINS	108	106	129	112	103	110	115	109	112	115	142	130	114	139	111	108	139	114	101	121
55344	EDEN PRAIRIE	134	127	150	138	123	130	139	132	135	140	171	160	136	164	132	127	167	139	119	147
55345	MINNETONKA	179	212	231	214	209	215	193	194	182	195	229	222	205	234	198	179	227	188	181	214
55346	EDEN PRAIRIE	174	199	208	207	192	190	184	180	170	188	216	211	192	218	181	161	214	177	157	198
55347	EDEN PRAIRIE	232	277	286	287	267	264	247	243	226	253	287	283	264	294	247	215	287	235	212	268
55349	HOWARD LAKE	93	87	74	86	89	95	85	89	87	84	106	104	83	107	85	86	102	88	91	106
55350	HUTCHINSON	95	89	78	88	92	98	87	92	89	87	110	107	85	110	87	89	105	91	94	109
55352	JORDAN	111	117	110	118	115	117	110	112	105	111	132	130	110	132	109	102	129	110	104	126
55353	KIMBALL	101	90	71	87	94	102	86	94	91	86	110	110	84	112	87	92	105	92	100	117
55354	LESTER PRAIRIE	98	85	66	83	89	99	84	91	89	83	109	106	81	109	85	91	102	89	99	111
55355	LITCHFIELD	98	83	63	80	89	99	82	91	89	81	107	105	79	108	84	92	101	89	101	113
55356	LONG LAKE	251	302	337	309	294	297	275	270	255	278	323	315	294	333	278	246	323	264	241	297
55357	LORETTO	169	202	207	206	196	192	181	180	167	184	211	211	190	220	182	160	210	174	158	198
55358	MAPLE LAKE	111	109	97	107	112	119	103	109	104	102	128	127	102	131	105	105	123	107	112	130
55359	MAPLE PLAIN	160	193	202	194	188	186	174	173	162	175	204	203	184	214	176	156	203	168	154	191
55360	MAYER	128	120	97	116	125	131	110	120	114	111	140	142	109	143	113	115	134	117	125	151
55362	MONTICELLO	97	102	101	104	100	101	98	98	94	99	118	115	99	118	96	90	115	97	90	109
55363	MONTROSE	103	103	93	102	104	107	97	100	96	97	119	119	96	120	97	94	115	99	98	119
55364	MOUND	162	194	212	197	189	190	178	175	166	179	210	205	189	218	180	161	209	171	157	192
55366	NEW AUBURN	94	83	62	79	88	94	77	85	82	77	99	102	75	101	79	84	94	83	93	110
55367	NEW GERMANY	129	114	87	109	121	130	106	117	112	106	137	140	104	139	109	115	130	114	127	151
55368	NORWOOD	111	104	86	101	108	115	98	106	102	98	124	124	97	127	100	103	119	103	111	129
55369	OSSEO	132	152	158	156	147	146	140	139	130	142	165	163	145	168	139	124	163	136	122	152
55370	PLATO	116	103	79	98	109	117	95	106	101	95	123	126	93	126	98	104	117	103	114	136
55371	PRINCETON	104	95	77	93	98	105	91	98	94	91	115	115	89	116	92	95	110	96	102	119
55372	PRIOR LAKE	154	181	183	186	175	171	163	162	150	167	190	189	171	195	162	142	189	157	140	177
55373	ROCKFORD	114	121	112	120	118	119	112	114	107	114	134	134	112	134	111	103	131	113	105	130
55374	ROGERS	150	173	170	179	166	160	156	154	143	161	181	181	161	184	153	134	180	150	132	169
55375	SAINT BONIFACIUS	119	135	130	141	128	124	122	120	111	126	142	141	125	142	118	104	140	117	102	132
55376	SAINT MICHAEL	128	144	141	149	138	134	132	131	121	136	154	153	135	155	129	114	152	128	112	143
55378	SAVAGE	150	168	164	175	160	156	154	152	141	159	180	178	158	180	150	132	178	148	130	166
55379	SHAKOPEE	121	130	129	135	125	125	123	122	116	126	146	143	125	146	120	109	144	121	108	134
55381	SILVER LAKE	93	80	62	78	85	93	79	86	84	78	102	100	76	102	80	85	96	84	93	105
55382	SOUTH HAVEN	110	99	79	95	104	111	93	102	97	93	118	121	90	120	95	99	113	100	108	129
55384	SPRING PARK	136	149	187	150	147	160	151	146	149	150	188	169	156	190	154	149	185	149	144	160
55385	STEWART	91	77	58	75	82	91	76	83	81	75	98	97	73	98	77	83	92	82	91	103
55386	VICTORIA	174	204	206	212	195	192	183	180	167	188	212	209	193	216	181	157	211	174	155	197
55387	WACONIA	142	152	143	157	148	149	141	142	134	144	168	165	144	169	139	128	164	139	129	159
55388	WATERTOWN	104	114	112	114	113	115	106	108	102	106	128	126	109	131	107	100	125	105	101	121
55389	WATKINS	93	77	56	73	82	93	77	85	83	75	100	98	72	99	78	87	93	83	96	106
55390	WAVERLY	106	97	82	97	101	110	96	101	99	95	121	117	94	122	96	100	115	99	106	120
55391	WAYZATA	280	341	405	347	333	345	314	307	294	316	372	355	338	384	321	288	372	301	282	337
55395	WINSTED	100	87	67	85	91	101	87	93	92	85	111	108	83	111	87	93	105	91	101	113
55396	WINTHROP	85	71	54	68	77	86	71	79	77	70	93	92	67	94	73	80	87	78	89	99
55397	YOUNG AMERICA	105	91	72	90	95	106	91	98	96	90	117	113	88	117	91	97	110	96	105	118
55398	ZIMMERMAN	109	121	117	124	116	114	112	111	104	115	132	131	113	132	109	98	130	109	97	123
55401	MINNEAPOLIS	90	86	161	99	81	91	102	90	104	103	132	111	106	139	100	103	131	96	84	100
55402	MINNEAPOLIS	86	77	131	88	74	83	96	85	97	95	123	106	96	125	92	94	121	93	79	95
55403	MINNEAPOLIS	102	90	126	99	89	99	113	101	112	108	142	125	109	137	106	107	138	111	97	113
55404	MINNEAPOLIS	48	39	53	42	38	43	52	46	53	49	66	58	48	63	48	50	64	52	45	52
55405	MINNEAPOLIS	114	111	157	117	108	119	126	117	126	125	159	141	127	159	122	123	156	124	111	129
55406	MINNEAPOLIS	83	89	108	92	89	93	93	89	90	91	113	106	94	114	92	87	111	91	83	97
55407	MINNEAPOLIS	77	77	91	79	76	81	84	80	83	82	104	96	83	105	82	80	102	83	76	87
55408	MINNEAPOLIS	83	74	119	82	71	80	93	82	95	91	119	103	91	119	88	91	117	91	78	92
	MINNESOTA	107	106	108	107	107	113	106	107	105	105	131	126	105	131	105	104	127	107	105	123
	UNITED STATES	100	100	100	100	100	100	100	100	100	100	100	100	100	100	100	100	100	100	100	100

#	POST OFFICE NAME	COUNTY FIPS CODE	POPULATION			2000-2004 ANNUAL RATE		HOUSEHOLDS					FAMILIES		
			2000	2004	2009	% Rate	State Centile	2000	2004	2009	% Annual Rate 2000-2004	2004 Average HH Size	2000	2004	% Annual Rate 2000-2004
55409	MINNEAPOLIS	053	22014	21936	22368	-0.1	24	8917	8962	9210	0.1	2.36	4820	4618	-1.0
55410	MINNEAPOLIS	053	18668	18809	19344	0.2	33	8808	8970	9298	0.4	2.09	4809	4677	-0.7
55411	MINNEAPOLIS	053	31695	32597	33668	0.7	48	9342	9482	9748	0.4	3.38	6453	6321	-0.5
55412	MINNEAPOLIS	053	24918	26094	27200	1.1	60	8794	9106	9458	0.8	2.86	5504	5464	-0.2
55413	MINNEAPOLIS	053	12197	12147	12429	-0.1	24	5678	5689	5849	0.1	2.09	2370	2233	-1.4
55414	MINNEAPOLIS	053	24154	25370	26625	1.2	62	9265	9770	10311	1.3	2.17	2607	2521	-0.8
55415	MINNEAPOLIS	053	2066	2054	2078	-0.1	22	545	535	545	-0.4	2.36	83	75	-2.4
55416	MINNEAPOLIS	053	26787	27152	27966	0.3	39	13636	14023	14572	0.7	1.91	6084	5900	-0.7
55417	MINNEAPOLIS	053	24992	24335	24646	-0.6	7	10721	10522	10735	-0.4	2.23	6145	5751	-1.6
55418	MINNEAPOLIS	053	30906	30745	31346	-0.1	22	13564	13607	13962	0.1	2.23	7195	6860	-1.1
55419	MINNEAPOLIS	053	17207	17363	17823	0.2	34	7437	7592	7856	0.5	2.25	4428	4324	-0.6
55420	MINNEAPOLIS	053	21417	21143	21579	-0.3	16	9191	9193	9464	0.0	2.27	5617	5376	-1.0
55421	MINNEAPOLIS	003	25181	25332	26674	0.1	32	11200	11503	12321	0.6	2.19	6362	6222	-0.5
55422	MINNEAPOLIS	053	27691	28134	29044	0.4	40	11666	11997	12504	0.7	2.27	7194	7067	-0.4
55423	MINNEAPOLIS	053	34538	35588	36996	0.7	50	15111	15674	16389	0.9	2.24	8755	8663	-0.3
55424	MINNEAPOLIS	053	9936	9703	9841	-0.6	8	3727	3657	3727	-0.5	2.65	2775	2647	-1.1
55425	MINNEAPOLIS	053	8925	8996	9262	0.2	34	3918	3988	4136	0.4	2.23	2084	2013	-0.8
55426	MINNEAPOLIS	053	25688	26536	27654	0.8	51	11505	12047	12673	1.1	2.13	6311	6246	-0.2
55427	MINNEAPOLIS	053	23554	24172	24980	0.6	47	9919	10291	10723	0.9	2.30	6331	6338	0.0
55428	MINNEAPOLIS	053	29305	29099	29744	-0.2	20	11858	11888	12242	0.1	2.37	7468	7164	-1.0
55429	MINNEAPOLIS	053	25715	25608	26197	-0.1	24	10328	10346	10641	0.0	2.45	6450	6217	-0.9
55430	MINNEAPOLIS	053	21313	20851	21138	-0.5	10	8130	7991	8140	-0.4	2.57	5191	4900	-1.4
55431	MINNEAPOLIS	053	18542	18584	19075	0.1	30	7874	8016	8314	0.4	2.28	5117	5018	-0.5
55432	MINNEAPOLIS	003	30530	30691	32458	0.1	32	12498	12870	13887	0.7	2.37	8163	8064	-0.3
55433	MINNEAPOLIS	003	34958	36581	39418	1.1	60	13141	14059	15454	1.6	2.59	9376	9689	0.8
55434	MINNEAPOLIS	003	27586	28540	30488	0.8	53	10117	10761	11749	1.5	2.64	7493	7698	0.6
55435	MINNEAPOLIS	053	11324	10946	11138	-0.8	3	6402	6263	6427	-0.5	1.71	2518	2304	-2.1
55436	MINNEAPOLIS	053	13095	13103	13436	0.0	28	5605	5675	5860	0.3	2.31	3693	3596	-0.6
55437	MINNEAPOLIS	053	18711	18664	19096	-0.1	25	8026	8097	8355	0.2	2.26	5201	5045	-0.7
55438	MINNEAPOLIS	053	17563	17488	17875	-0.1	24	7387	7456	7692	0.2	2.31	4747	4598	-0.8
55439	MINNEAPOLIS	053	8884	9096	9429	0.6	45	3521	3642	3799	0.8	2.49	2670	2689	0.2
55441	MINNEAPOLIS	053	17904	18040	18502	0.2	33	7223	7370	7620	0.5	2.38	4667	4569	-0.5
55442	MINNEAPOLIS	053	13017	13918	14656	1.6	71	4741	5112	5417	1.8	2.72	3675	3866	1.2
55443	MINNEAPOLIS	053	26398	28734	30666	2.0	78	9405	10267	10992	2.1	2.79	6851	7305	1.5
55444	MINNEAPOLIS	053	15392	15908	16624	0.8	52	5048	5247	5508	0.9	3.03	4008	4070	0.4
55445	MINNEAPOLIS	053	8919	9274	9674	0.9	57	3261	3378	3522	0.8	2.74	2334	2341	0.1
55446	MINNEAPOLIS	053	12990	15790	17775	4.7	97	4656	5657	6369	4.7	2.79	3469	4151	4.3
55447	MINNEAPOLIS	053	22340	22792	23499	0.5	43	8355	8593	8918	0.7	2.54	5934	5930	0.0
55448	MINNEAPOLIS	003	27207	28875	31358	1.4	67	9632	10465	11592	2.0	2.74	7351	7757	1.3
55449	MINNEAPOLIS	003	11887	15039	17783	5.7	99	3968	5155	6258	6.4	2.91	3235	4112	5.8
55454	MINNEAPOLIS	053	7545	8113	8550	1.7	73	2838	2979	3116	1.2	2.12	1097	1075	-0.5
55455	MINNEAPOLIS	053	1110	1116	1124	0.1	32	23	20	21	-3.2	5.40	2	1	-15.1
55602	BRIMSON	137	249	250	253	0.1	31	129	133	137	0.7	1.88	85	85	0.0
55603	FINLAND	075	767	856	988	2.6	86	308	350	412	3.1	2.42	213	235	2.3
55604	GRAND MARAIS	031	3292	3656	4197	2.5	85	1502	1705	2000	3.0	2.11	910	998	2.2
55605	GRAND PORTAGE	031	615	689	795	2.7	87	268	307	363	3.3	2.24	159	176	2.4
55606	HOVLAND	031	156	175	202	2.7	87	77	88	104	3.2	1.99	46	51	2.5
55607	ISABELLA	075	254	284	328	2.7	86	115	131	155	3.1	2.16	78	87	2.6
55612	LUTSEN	031	447	491	561	2.2	82	204	228	266	2.7	2.15	131	142	1.9
55613	SCHROEDER	031	187	205	235	2.2	81	84	94	110	2.7	2.18	54	59	2.1
55614	SILVER BAY	075	2526	2869	3344	3.0	90	1035	1196	1420	3.5	2.32	707	794	2.8
55615	TOFTE	031	226	248	283	2.2	81	102	114	133	2.7	2.18	66	71	1.7
55616	TWO HARBORS	075	7203	7938	9078	2.3	83	3011	3375	3928	2.7	2.30	2033	2215	2.0
55702	ALBORN	137	412	404	405	-0.5	11	159	159	162	0.0	2.48	118	114	-0.8
55703	ANGORA	137	723	723	730	0.0	27	286	293	302	0.6	2.44	203	201	-0.2
55704	ASKOV	115	1015	1080	1175	1.5	68	404	438	485	1.9	2.47	275	290	1.3
55705	AURORA	137	3627	3596	3627	-0.2	19	1528	1546	1586	0.3	2.27	1016	993	-0.5
55706	BABBITT	137	2106	2209	2285	1.1	61	922	987	1039	1.6	2.20	665	689	0.8
55707	BARNUM	017	3190	3362	3619	1.2	64	1212	1305	1430	1.8	2.57	897	943	1.2
55709	BOVEY	061	6370	6525	6883	0.6	45	2586	2698	2902	1.0	2.41	1826	1856	0.4
55710	BRITT	137	1389	1381	1401	-0.1	22	534	544	564	0.4	2.53	423	420	-0.2
55711	BROOKSTON	137	588	653	696	2.5	85	201	228	247	3.0	2.83	155	171	2.3
55712	BRUNO	115	310	338	371	2.1	79	124	138	154	2.6	2.45	84	91	1.9
55717	CANYON	137	285	311	328	2.1	80	123	138	148	2.7	2.25	91	99	2.0
55718	CARLTON	017	2993	3252	3540	2.0	78	1096	1216	1350	2.5	2.61	825	894	1.9
55719	CHISHOLM	137	7133	7104	7177	-0.1	24	3059	3094	3176	0.3	2.23	1887	1835	-0.7
55720	CLOQUET	017	15255	15897	16920	1.0	58	6157	6516	7050	1.3	2.41	4118	4224	0.6
55721	COHASSET	061	3072	3412	3734	2.5	85	1149	1306	1460	3.1	2.60	885	982	2.5
55723	COOK	137	2558	2618	2678	0.6	45	1089	1144	1194	1.2	2.24	751	763	0.4
55724	COTTON	137	745	809	851	2.0	77	300	332	356	2.4	2.41	217	234	1.8
55725	CRANE LAKE	137	105	102	102	-0.7	5	50	49	50	-0.5	2.06	35	33	-1.4
55726	CROMWELL	017	847	986	1112	3.6	93	353	420	483	4.2	2.31	255	296	3.6
55731	ELY	137	6050	6211	6409	0.6	47	2715	2837	2979	1.0	2.08	1601	1611	0.2
55732	EMBARRASS	137	1514	1490	1505	-0.4	13	610	615	633	0.2	2.42	437	428	-0.5
55733	ESKO	017	4155	4616	5083	2.5	85	1458	1646	1841	2.9	2.80	1181	1308	2.4
55734	EVELETH	137	6461	6361	6405	-0.4	13	2785	2786	2854	0.0	2.21	1756	1699	-0.8
55735	FINLAYSON	001	2205	2278	2504	0.8	51	896	945	1059	1.3	2.39	609	624	0.6
55736	FLOODWOOD	137	1480	1472	1484	-0.1	22	614	622	637	0.3	2.32	383	371	-0.8
55738	FORBES	137	588	612	628	1.0	57	216	230	240	1.5	2.66	171	177	0.8
55741	GILBERT	137	4092	4084	4136	-0.1	25	1800	1835	1892	0.5	2.22	1151	1130	-0.4
55742	GOODLAND	061	452	469	495	0.9	55	189	200	215	1.3	2.35	137	141	0.7
55744	GRAND RAPIDS	061	19954	20968	22316	1.2	62	8128	8733	9499	1.7	2.34	5546	5796	1.0
55746	HIBBING	137	18261	18260	18528	0.0	27	7887	8039	8302	0.5	2.22	4945	4870	-0.4
55748	HILL CITY	001	1114	1321	1606	4.1	95	452	547	678	4.6	2.41	300	352	3.8
55749	HOLYOKE	017	267	272	287	0.4	42	121	126	135	1.0	2.16	84	84	0.0
55750	HOYT LAKES	137	2082	2037	2042	-0.5	10	916	919	939	0.1	2.22	649	631	-0.7
55751	IRON	137	1655	1731	1791	1.1	60	655	703	743	1.7	2.44	490	509	0.9
55752	JACOBSON	001	469	533	638	3.1	90	191	222	270	3.6	2.40	130	147	2.9
55756	KERRICK	115	511	556	610	2.0	78	216	240	268	2.5	2.32	147	159	1.9
55757	KETTLE RIVER	017	879	913	976	0.9	56	366	389	424	1.4	2.34	253	260	0.6
55760	MCGREGOR	001	2954	3309	3932	2.7	87	1327	1516	1833	3.2	2.18	882	979	2.5
55763	MAKINEN	137	667	681	696	0.5	43	271	283	294	1.0	2.40	183	185	0.3
55765	MEADOWLANDS	137	827	809	812	-0.5	9	333	332	340	-0.1	2.38	241	234	-0.7
55766	MELRUDE	137	102	116	124	3.1	90	40	46	51	3.3	2.48	29	32	2.3
55767	MOOSE LAKE	017	3611	3754	3948	0.9	57	1096	1178	1283	1.7	2.28	693	719	0.9
	MINNESOTA					1.4					1.6	2.50			1.0
	UNITED STATES					1.2					1.3	2.58			1.1

ZIP CODE # POST OFFICE NAME	RACE (%) White 2000	White 2004	Black 2000	Black 2004	Asian/Pacific 2000	Asian/Pacific 2004	% Hispanic Origin 2000	% Hispanic Origin 2004	2004 AGE DISTRIBUTION (%) 0-4	5-9	10-14	15-19	20-24	25-44	45-64	65-84	85+	18+	MEDIAN AGE 2004	% 2004 Males	% 2004 Females
55409 MINNEAPOLIS	73.3	69.4	16.1	19.0	2.6	3.0	6.3	7.1	6.5	6.0	6.4	5.9	6.4	34.9	23.0	7.9	2.9	77.4	36.1	48.0	52.0
55410 MINNEAPOLIS	93.6	92.0	1.5	2.0	2.3	2.8	1.6	2.1	6.3	5.9	5.1	4.7	4.5	34.9	27.4	9.5	1.8	79.8	39.3	47.0	53.0
55411 MINNEAPOLIS	18.8	14.8	55.9	60.8	15.1	14.9	5.1	5.1	10.6	11.4	12.2	10.6	7.8	25.7	16.3	4.6	0.8	59.0	23.4	47.7	52.3
55412 MINNEAPOLIS	48.9	42.3	31.1	36.9	11.2	12.0	3.6	3.9	8.6	8.7	9.6	8.5	7.2	30.3	19.7	6.2	1.2	67.8	30.6	48.1	51.9
55413 MINNEAPOLIS	77.4	72.5	7.0	9.3	4.1	4.8	9.1	11.1	5.2	4.7	5.3	5.5	8.5	37.2	21.7	9.2	2.7	81.8	35.2	51.5	48.5
55414 MINNEAPOLIS	78.6	73.4	5.5	7.8	10.2	12.3	3.5	4.3	2.8	2.0	2.0	17.5	36.2	24.8	10.4	3.7	0.7	91.9	23.5	52.6	47.4
55415 MINNEAPOLIS	54.7	47.1	33.6	40.7	3.3	3.8	5.3	5.8	1.7	1.3	2.0	6.2	12.3	41.9	23.7	7.8	3.2	92.2	37.4	64.7	35.4
55416 MINNEAPOLIS	91.9	89.4	3.1	4.4	2.8	3.6	1.6	2.1	5.3	5.0	4.6	4.2	6.3	36.9	24.0	10.5	3.1	82.3	37.6	47.8	52.2
55417 MINNEAPOLIS	85.5	82.2	6.7	8.8	2.4	2.9	3.6	4.3	6.4	6.0	5.6	5.4	5.6	32.8	24.6	11.3	2.4	78.8	38.5	50.0	50.1
55418 MINNEAPOLIS	83.4	79.9	5.2	6.9	3.6	4.4	5.4	6.6	5.9	5.6	5.6	5.5	6.5	32.2	23.5	12.5	2.6	79.6	38.2	49.2	50.8
55419 MINNEAPOLIS	86.5	83.9	6.9	8.5	2.5	3.0	2.8	3.3	6.7	6.5	5.9	5.0	5.5	32.0	25.8	9.9	2.7	77.9	38.6	47.2	52.8
55420 MINNEAPOLIS	84.4	80.7	4.1	5.4	7.2	8.7	3.3	4.2	5.8	5.7	5.7	5.4	6.1	30.6	24.0	15.0	1.8	79.6	39.4	49.1	50.9
55421 MINNEAPOLIS	86.9	84.6	3.8	4.9	3.7	4.5	3.1	3.7	5.7	5.4	5.6	5.4	6.6	29.8	23.5	15.0	2.9	80.2	39.4	47.9	52.1
55422 MINNEAPOLIS	89.8	86.8	4.7	6.5	2.4	3.0	1.9	2.5	6.2	6.2	5.8	5.3	4.7	29.5	24.7	14.2	3.5	78.5	40.7	48.3	51.7
55423 MINNEAPOLIS	81.3	77.0	6.7	8.8	5.3	6.5	6.3	7.6	6.1	5.6	5.4	5.6	6.8	32.0	23.0	12.9	2.6	79.6	37.9	49.3	50.8
55424 MINNEAPOLIS	96.6	95.6	0.6	0.8	1.7	2.1	1.3	1.7	7.5	8.5	8.6	6.6	3.6	23.4	28.0	12.0	1.9	70.9	40.7	48.1	51.9
55425 MINNEAPOLIS	77.7	73.6	9.1	11.4	6.0	7.1	7.6	8.7	6.1	5.2	5.4	5.6	8.0	33.0	23.3	11.9	1.7	80.1	36.6	50.8	49.2
55426 MINNEAPOLIS	87.1	84.0	5.1	6.8	3.6	4.3	3.9	4.8	5.6	5.2	5.2	5.2	6.9	33.1	22.6	13.3	2.9	80.8	38.0	47.8	52.2
55427 MINNEAPOLIS	89.4	86.6	4.1	5.5	3.6	4.4	2.0	2.6	5.9	5.8	5.8	5.4	5.4	29.9	25.9	14.1	1.8	78.9	40.1	48.1	51.9
55428 MINNEAPOLIS	81.2	76.8	9.0	11.8	4.3	5.2	4.2	5.2	6.6	6.3	6.4	6.1	6.8	29.4	21.9	12.6	3.8	77.0	37.5	47.8	52.2
55429 MINNEAPOLIS	69.9	64.1	15.7	19.5	8.4	9.8	3.4	4.0	6.9	6.6	7.1	6.8	7.3	31.2	20.7	12.1	1.5	75.4	34.8	48.8	51.2
55430 MINNEAPOLIS	65.9	59.5	17.1	21.5	10.1	11.6	3.7	4.2	7.5	7.1	7.5	6.9	7.5	30.6	20.4	10.4	2.0	73.8	33.6	49.1	50.9
55431 MINNEAPOLIS	91.3	88.9	2.7	3.8	3.7	4.5	1.7	2.2	5.2	5.5	5.7	5.0	4.6	27.6	26.9	17.0	2.5	80.5	42.8	48.2	51.9
55432 MINNEAPOLIS	89.2	87.2	2.9	3.7	3.0	3.6	2.7	3.3	6.4	6.1	6.3	6.0	7.1	30.1	25.0	11.9	1.1	77.8	36.9	48.9	51.1
55433 MINNEAPOLIS	92.5	91.1	2.5	3.2	1.7	2.0	1.7	2.1	7.7	7.5	7.6	6.8	7.4	31.3	22.8	8.1	0.8	73.2	33.5	48.4	51.6
55434 MINNEAPOLIS	94.1	93.0	0.7	0.9	2.2	2.7	1.6	2.0	7.0	6.9	7.1	7.0	6.9	32.3	25.2	7.2	0.3	74.6	34.5	49.6	50.4
55435 MINNEAPOLIS	90.4	87.9	2.4	3.4	5.3	6.5	1.2	1.6	3.3	3.6	4.0	3.5	5.0	19.6	23.7	27.4	10.1	86.9	53.8	40.3	59.7
55436 MINNEAPOLIS	95.8	94.5	0.8	1.1	2.1	2.7	1.1	1.5	4.7	5.8	7.2	6.6	4.3	19.1	30.7	18.6	3.1	77.8	46.4	46.6	53.4
55437 MINNEAPOLIS	91.0	88.7	2.2	3.0	4.3	5.3	2.2	2.7	4.7	4.9	5.8	5.7	5.3	24.7	29.3	17.2	2.5	81.1	44.2	47.1	52.9
55438 MINNEAPOLIS	91.6	89.4	1.9	2.5	4.6	5.8	1.0	1.3	4.6	5.1	5.9	6.1	6.3	25.5	32.9	11.4	2.2	80.6	42.6	46.6	53.4
55439 MINNEAPOLIS	94.6	93.0	1.1	1.6	2.9	3.8	1.0	1.3	4.7	6.1	7.4	6.7	4.2	17.3	33.2	18.8	1.7	77.5	47.2	47.9	52.1
55441 MINNEAPOLIS	90.3	87.7	3.1	4.2	3.6	4.4	2.0	2.6	5.5	5.7	6.5	7.0	7.4	29.9	28.6	8.7	0.6	77.9	37.3	49.5	50.5
55442 MINNEAPOLIS	92.7	90.6	1.7	2.4	3.9	4.9	1.3	1.6	7.2	7.9	7.6	6.7	4.7	28.8	28.7	7.8	0.7	72.9	38.2	48.6	51.4
55443 MINNEAPOLIS	71.8	66.3	14.9	18.2	8.7	10.5	2.7	3.0	8.5	8.2	7.9	6.8	7.2	32.3	22.9	5.9	0.4	71.1	32.7	49.5	50.5
55444 MINNEAPOLIS	76.9	71.7	8.1	10.4	11.8	14.1	1.6	1.9	7.6	7.8	8.4	7.4	6.8	31.4	25.5	4.8	0.3	71.6	33.8	50.0	50.0
55445 MINNEAPOLIS	77.0	71.5	9.6	12.6	9.5	11.6	1.6	1.9	8.7	8.1	6.9	6.2	6.2	35.4	23.6	4.7	0.2	72.5	33.7	48.8	51.2
55446 MINNEAPOLIS	91.2	88.8	1.7	2.4	5.4	6.8	1.7	2.2	8.4	9.1	9.3	6.9	4.5	32.8	23.9	4.9	0.3	68.7	34.3	48.5	51.6
55447 MINNEAPOLIS	91.6	89.5	3.6	4.6	3.0	3.7	1.5	1.9	6.6	7.4	7.6	6.3	5.5	30.1	26.9	9.0	0.7	74.4	37.4	49.6	50.4
55448 MINNEAPOLIS	94.2	93.0	1.8	2.3	1.5	1.9	1.3	1.6	7.4	7.7	8.3	7.3	6.4	31.7	24.5	6.3	0.5	72.0	34.4	48.9	51.1
55449 MINNEAPOLIS	91.3	89.7	1.4	1.9	3.6	4.4	2.1	2.4	9.4	8.9	8.0	6.8	6.7	33.4	22.6	4.0	0.2	69.4	32.0	50.1	49.9
55454 MINNEAPOLIS	42.1	36.0	32.2	37.3	15.8	16.6	5.7	6.1	7.7	3.8	3.8	16.5	23.0	26.6	12.5	5.6	0.6	82.0	24.0	51.2	48.8
55455 MINNEAPOLIS	87.4	84.1	3.3	4.7	4.8	6.0	2.8	3.7	0.1	0.1	0.1	68.9	27.9	2.5	0.3	0.2	0.0	99.2	18.6	53.6	46.4
55602 BRIMSON	98.0	98.0	0.0	0.0	0.0	0.0	0.0	0.0	4.0	4.0	5.2	6.8	3.2	23.2	37.2	15.6	0.8	82.4	46.7	54.4	45.6
55603 FINLAND	97.9	97.7	0.3	0.2	0.3	0.2	0.5	0.7	5.5	5.8	6.8	7.4	5.6	23.0	31.4	13.8	0.7	77.7	42.5	51.6	48.4
55604 GRAND MARAIS	91.6	91.2	0.2	0.2	0.4	0.4	0.7	0.8	4.3	4.8	5.5	5.2	4.7	22.6	34.1	15.7	3.2	82.0	46.5	49.7	50.3
55605 GRAND PORTAGE	69.4	68.7	0.7	0.9	0.3	0.4	1.6	1.7	5.7	6.5	6.8	4.6	4.2	23.8	36.0	11.2	1.2	78.1	43.9	51.8	48.2
55606 HOVLAND	69.2	68.0	0.6	1.1	0.6	0.6	1.3	1.1	5.7	6.9	6.9	4.6	4.0	22.9	37.1	10.9	1.1	77.1	44.4	51.4	48.6
55607 ISABELLA	97.6	98.2	0.0	0.0	0.4	0.4	0.4	0.4	3.2	3.9	4.9	6.0	4.6	19.4	41.2	16.2	0.7	85.2	48.1	52.1	47.9
55612 LUTSEN	97.3	97.0	0.5	0.6	0.2	0.4	0.0	0.2	3.1	4.9	6.5	4.9	3.3	22.0	39.9	14.7	0.8	82.7	47.5	51.3	48.7
55613 SCHROEDER	97.3	96.6	0.5	0.5	0.5	0.5	0.0	0.0	2.9	4.9	6.3	4.9	2.9	22.4	40.0	14.6	1.0	83.4	47.5	51.7	48.3
55614 SILVER BAY	97.6	97.3	0.2	0.2	0.2	0.2	0.6	0.7	5.2	5.3	6.9	6.6	4.9	20.2	25.1	24.1	1.8	78.0	45.6	51.5	48.5
55615 TOFTE	97.4	96.4	0.4	0.8	0.4	0.4	0.0	0.0	3.2	4.8	6.5	4.8	3.2	22.6	39.5	14.5	0.8	82.3	47.2	51.6	48.4
55616 TWO HARBORS	98.2	98.0	0.1	0.1	0.2	0.2	0.6	0.7	5.6	5.6	6.2	6.4	6.1	23.0	29.3	14.9	3.0	78.6	43.2	49.2	50.8
55702 ALBORN	93.9	93.6	0.0	0.0	0.5	0.5	1.2	1.5	5.5	5.9	7.9	6.9	5.7	22.0	30.5	14.6	1.0	76.7	41.8	50.7	49.3
55703 ANGORA	96.5	96.4	0.0	0.0	0.3	0.3	0.7	0.7	4.7	5.3	6.1	6.8	4.3	24.6	34.0	12.2	2.1	79.7	44.1	51.9	48.1
55704 ASKOV	96.5	96.1	0.3	0.4	0.2	0.3	0.7	0.7	5.9	6.1	7.7	7.9	6.0	22.8	26.2	15.7	1.8	75.4	41.0	50.4	49.6
55705 AURORA	98.2	98.1	0.0	0.0	0.3	0.4	0.4	0.5	4.7	5.6	5.7	6.5	4.9	21.8	30.9	17.1	2.8	80.1	45.5	50.4	49.6
55706 BABBITT	98.8	98.7	0.1	0.1	0.1	0.1	0.1	0.1	3.8	4.2	6.0	6.0	4.8	18.2	27.5	27.1	2.4	82.3	49.4	49.6	50.4
55707 BARNUM	97.4	97.1	0.2	0.2	0.3	0.3	0.8	0.9	5.7	6.0	6.8	7.1	6.4	24.8	29.5	12.4	1.3	77.0	41.1	51.3	48.7
55709 BOVEY	97.4	97.1	0.1	0.1	0.2	0.2	0.7	0.8	5.5	5.4	6.8	6.7	6.6	24.8	29.3	13.2	1.8	78.1	41.4	50.5	49.5
55710 BRITT	97.2	96.9	0.1	0.1	0.5	0.6	0.9	1.1	4.3	5.1	7.2	6.7	5.2	22.7	36.1	11.6	1.2	79.2	44.3	51.5	48.5
55711 BROOKSTON	74.0	73.1	0.2	0.3	0.0	0.0	0.9	0.8	8.4	8.4	7.8	8.0	5.5	28.0	22.5	10.3	1.1	70.3	35.1	51.9	48.1
55712 BRUNO	97.1	97.0	0.7	0.6	0.3	0.3	0.0	0.3	3.9	4.1	5.3	5.9	5.3	20.7	33.7	19.5	1.5	83.1	47.6	53.0	47.0
55717 CANYON	99.0	99.0	0.0	0.0	0.0	0.0	0.4	0.3	3.2	3.5	6.1	6.4	3.9	21.2	41.8	12.9	1.0	83.6	47.6	52.4	47.6
55718 CARLTON	94.8	94.3	0.2	0.3	0.2	0.2	0.6	0.8	5.7	5.9	7.0	7.2	6.3	25.6	28.9	11.6	1.9	76.7	40.6	50.2	49.8
55719 CHISHOLM	97.7	97.5	0.1	0.1	0.3	0.4	0.6	0.7	5.4	5.1	6.1	6.5	6.6	24.0	27.6	15.3	3.7	79.3	42.4	49.5	50.5
55720 CLOQUET	87.6	87.0	0.2	0.2	0.4	0.4	0.7	0.8	6.5	6.5	7.3	7.0	7.0	25.7	24.8	13.0	2.2	75.3	38.3	48.5	51.5
55721 COHASSET	96.0	95.7	0.2	0.2	0.2	0.2	0.5	0.7	5.8	6.4	6.5	6.8	5.6	22.8	32.9	11.8	1.3	77.1	42.3	49.8	50.2
55723 COOK	96.5	96.3	0.1	0.1	0.2	0.2	0.4	0.4	3.6	4.5	5.6	6.4	4.4	21.0	36.3	15.9	2.3	81.9	47.5	52.1	47.9
55724 COTTON	98.7	98.5	0.0	0.1	0.0	0.0	0.4	0.5	4.0	4.5	7.2	6.8	3.5	23.0	37.5	11.7	2.0	80.1	45.5	51.2	48.8
55725 CRANE LAKE	82.9	83.3	0.0	0.0	1.0	1.0	0.0	0.0	2.9	3.9	3.9	4.9	3.9	18.6	46.1	15.7	0.0	86.3	50.9	52.9	47.1
55726 CROMWELL	96.8	96.6	0.0	0.0	0.1	0.2	0.5	0.6	5.8	6.2	6.4	6.6	5.5	22.1	28.6	16.3	2.5	77.5	43.2	51.2	48.8
55731 ELY	97.1	96.7	0.6	0.7	0.2	0.2	0.7	0.9	3.5	4.0	5.3	8.2	7.1	20.7	30.6	17.1	3.6	83.7	45.7	51.2	48.8
55732 EMBARRASS	98.0	97.9	0.1	0.1	0.1	0.1	0.3	0.4	4.9	5.6	6.4	6.0	5.5	22.1	33.8	14.5	1.3	79.3	44.7	52.8	47.3
55733 ESKO	97.9	97.5	0.2	0.3	0.6	0.7	0.4	0.5	6.2	6.8	8.5	7.5	5.4	26.8	28.6	9.6	0.7	73.7	39.4	50.2	49.8
55734 EVELETH	97.0	96.9	0.1	0.2	0.4	0.5	0.3	0.4	4.7	5.5	6.5	6.5	5.2	24.0	29.6	14.4	3.6	79.3	43.5	48.9	51.1
55735 FINLAYSON	97.1	96.8	0.4	0.4	0.5	0.5	1.0	1.2	5.4	6.3	6.7	6.6	4.7	23.8	30.4	15.0	1.3	77.5	43.0	52.3	47.7
55736 FLOODWOOD	97.6	97.6	0.1	0.1	0.3	0.3	0.7	0.8	6.1	6.3	6.8	7.0	6.1	23.0	26.6	16.0	2.1	76.6	41.8	50.8	49.3
55738 FORBES	94.6	94.0	0.5	0.7	0.3	0.5	1.7	2.0	3.6	6.7	7.0	9.5	4.4	25.7	33.0	9.3	0.8	76.0	41.3	52.5	47.6
55741 GILBERT	98.3	98.1	0.1	0.1	0.3	0.4	0.2	0.3	4.6	5.0	6.4	6.9	5.0	24.5	29.4	15.9	2.3	79.7	43.7	50.9	49.1
55742 GOODLAND	97.8	97.9	0.0	0.0	0.0	0.0	0.7	0.6	5.5	5.1	6.8	6.6	6.0	23.5	30.1	15.6	0.9	78.5	43.1	52.9	47.1
55744 GRAND RAPIDS	97.0	96.6	0.2	0.2	0.4	0.5	0.6	0.7	5.2	5.5	6.4	7.2	6.7	23.0	29.1	14.3	2.7	78.5	42.4	49.3	50.7
55746 HIBBING	97.3	97.0	0.5	0.6	0.3	0.3	0.7	0.8	5.2	5.3	6.3	7.0	7.0	23.4	27.1	15.4	3.4	79.0	42.1	48.6	51.4
55748 HILL CITY	97.4	97.2	0.2	0.2	0.0	0.0	1.1	1.3	5.3	5.4	7.3	7.9	6.3	23.5	27.7	15.0	1.7	77.1	41.4	49.9	50.1
55749 HOLYOKE	95.9	95.6	0.4	0.4	0.8	0.7	0.0	0.0	6.3	6.6	6.3	6.6	5.2	25.0	33.5	9.6	1.1	76.5	41.9	53.3	46.7
55750 HOYT LAKES	99.1	99.0	0.3	0.3	0.1	0.1	0.2	0.3	4.2	4.5	5.5	5.7	5.9	20.8	29.8	22.0	1.7	82.5	47.2	49.5	50.5
55751 IRON	96.9	96.7	0.2	0.4	0.2	0.3	1.0	1.0	5.1	5.7	7.1	8.1	4.7	24.5	32.5	11.6	0.7	76.6	41.7	54.1	45.9
55752 JACOBSON	97.0	97.0	0.2	0.2	0.2	0.2	0.4	0.6	3.2	3.2	3.9	5.3	3.9	19.7	34.7	24.4	1.7	86.3	52.1	52.0	48.0
55756 KERRICK	97.3	96.6	0.6	0.7	0.2	0.4	0.4	0.4	3.6	4.1	5.4	5.9	5.4	20.5	34.4	19.1	1.6	83.1	47.7	52.9	47.1
55757 KETTLE RIVER	98.8	98.7	0.0	0.0	0.2	0.2	0.8	1.0	5.7	5.8	6.7	6.7	6.4	23.3	29.8	14.5	1.2	77.8	42.2	52.4	47.7
55760 MCGREGOR	92.7	92.4	0.3	0.3	0.2	0.2	0.5	0.6	4.0	4.2	6.0	5.6	4.8	19.0	31.6	23.0	1.8	82.4	49.4	50.7	49.4
55763 MAKINEN	98.2	98.4	0.0	0.0	0.0	0.0	0.2	0.3	4.1	4.3	6.0	7.5	3.1	23.5	35.8	14.2	1.5	80.6	45.7	53.3	46.7
55765 MEADOWLANDS	96.9	96.7	0.0	0.0	0.1	0.1	0.7	0.7	5.1	6.4	7.5	6.2	4.0	24.9	30.9	13.4	1.7	76.9	42.6	52.7	47.3
55766 MELRUDE	99.0	99.1	0.0	0.0	0.0	0.0	0.0	0.0	4.3	5.2	7.8	6.9	2.6	24.1	36.2	9.5	3.5	78.5	44.5	50.0	50.0
55767 MOOSE LAKE	86.9	84.7	7.2	9.0	0.5	0.6	2.4	2.7	5.1	4.8	4.9	5.5	8.8	32.9	21.3	13.3	3.3	82.2	37.8	60.0	40.0
MINNESOTA	89.5	88.0	3.5	4.2	2.9	3.4	2.9	3.4	6.8	6.8	7.2	7.3	7.4	28.6	23.9	10.1	1.9	74.9	36.1	49.6	50.5
UNITED STATES	75.1	73.6	12.3	12.5	3.8	4.2	12.5	14.1	6.9	6.7	7.2	7.0	7.3	28.6	23.8	10.8	1.7	75.1	36.0	49.1	50.9

ZIP CODE #	POST OFFICE NAME	2004 Per Capita Income	2004 HH Income Base	2004 HOUSEHOLD INCOME DISTRIBUTION (%) Less than $25,000	$25,000 to $49,999	$50,000 to $99,999	$100,000 to $149,999	$150,000 or More	MEDIAN HOUSEHOLD INCOME 2004	2009	2004 National Centile	2004 State Centile	2004 Home Value Base	2004 HOME VALUE DISTRIBUTION (%) Less than $50,000	$50,000 to $89,999	$90,000 to $174,999	$175,000 to $399,999	$400,000 or More	2004 Median Home Value
55409	MINNEAPOLIS	37997	8962	12.4	21.7	33.7	19.6	12.7	70375	97723	91	91	6345	0.9	4.5	35.6	48.3	10.7	196256
55410	MINNEAPOLIS	51179	8970	8.3	17.1	34.2	24.7	15.8	83105	119758	96	95	6927	0.1	0.4	12.2	73.6	13.7	248011
55411	MINNEAPOLIS	13695	9482	36.8	31.7	23.9	5.2	2.4	34155	43357	25	6	4864	3.3	24.6	60.9	10.4	0.9	111116
55412	MINNEAPOLIS	20401	9106	21.7	30.9	34.5	10.1	2.8	47395	62063	67	58	7140	1.7	21.2	66.4	10.2	0.6	114441
55413	MINNEAPOLIS	26141	5689	32.3	27.2	28.7	7.8	4.0	41559	55107	52	33	2638	0.8	9.0	57.7	29.4	3.2	148836
55414	MINNEAPOLIS	22664	9770	39.0	26.6	22.4	7.0	5.0	33821	43937	24	6	2270	1.4	4.9	38.9	47.9	6.8	184419
55415	MINNEAPOLIS	17060	535	40.4	27.1	21.9	7.3	3.4	32891	42981	21	4	182	0.6	15.4	60.4	23.6	0.0	139394
55416	MINNEAPOLIS	55343	14023	11.2	21.9	33.1	20.2	13.7	71351	101678	92	91	8567	0.4	3.7	24.5	55.8	15.7	225356
55417	MINNEAPOLIS	36359	10522	11.7	24.0	38.0	19.0	7.4	64690	87653	88	87	9009	0.4	3.4	46.9	48.3	1.1	174123
55418	MINNEAPOLIS	27967	13607	19.4	29.2	34.4	13.2	3.8	51048	67401	74	68	9730	1.6	6.9	55.4	35.8	0.4	154468
55419	MINNEAPOLIS	46841	7592	9.9	17.6	33.5	22.3	16.8	80535	113304	95	95	5773	0.1	1.3	18.7	67.8	12.2	226261
55420	MINNEAPOLIS	30107	9193	15.0	27.4	39.4	14.5	3.7	57100	75042	82	79	6553	3.0	1.1	43.3	51.9	0.7	177527
55421	MINNEAPOLIS	26524	11503	21.5	32.6	33.3	9.6	3.0	46196	56121	64	54	7293	3.5	5.3	59.9	30.2	1.1	148906
55422	MINNEAPOLIS	35192	11997	12.3	24.4	37.5	17.4	8.3	64400	85216	88	87	9619	0.4	3.0	49.8	44.0	2.8	171015
55423	MINNEAPOLIS	31658	15674	16.8	28.0	35.7	14.7	4.7	55546	74959	80	77	10913	0.8	0.8	44.0	54.0	0.4	179326
55424	MINNEAPOLIS	64017	3657	6.3	9.9	25.5	23.0	35.4	115462	161422	99	100	3317	0.1	0.3	4.6	49.4	45.6	373894
55425	MINNEAPOLIS	30664	3988	15.9	29.6	37.8	12.3	4.4	53406	69327	78	73	1996	0.7	4.5	35.2	57.0	2.7	187901
55426	MINNEAPOLIS	33803	12047	16.1	26.9	36.4	14.6	5.9	56590	75127	81	79	7637	0.4	3.5	44.1	50.1	1.9	177529
55427	MINNEAPOLIS	36111	10291	11.6	23.1	38.1	18.4	8.8	66760	88528	90	89	7514	0.4	2.5	29.3	66.5	1.5	193816
55428	MINNEAPOLIS	26964	11888	18.4	27.5	35.4	15.5	3.3	53578	70632	78	74	7606	1.3	2.1	54.7	41.5	0.5	166761
55429	MINNEAPOLIS	25585	10346	17.1	29.3	37.1	13.9	2.6	53144	69965	77	73	6642	0.0	2.6	73.7	23.0	0.7	151441
55430	MINNEAPOLIS	22780	7991	19.3	30.9	35.9	12.1	1.8	49742	65885	71	65	5891	0.9	5.7	77.9	15.0	0.6	137870
55431	MINNEAPOLIS	37810	8016	13.2	20.2	36.8	20.5	9.3	70063	93308	91	91	6255	0.2	0.4	20.3	76.6	2.5	210630
55432	MINNEAPOLIS	28395	12870	14.3	27.5	40.2	13.4	4.6	57613	69168	82	80	8744	5.8	2.9	45.0	45.3	1.1	170208
55433	MINNEAPOLIS	27060	14059	13.1	25.2	42.3	15.2	4.3	61572	74180	86	83	10462	2.5	1.2	47.9	47.2	1.3	172881
55434	MINNEAPOLIS	26948	10761	8.2	25.1	47.9	15.7	3.2	64197	76766	88	87	9492	12.4	5.4	45.7	36.3	0.2	156765
55435	MINNEAPOLIS	48911	6263	23.0	25.3	27.7	11.5	12.6	52151	72801	76	71	3505	1.4	5.7	36.2	39.7	17.1	199948
55436	MINNEAPOLIS	65998	5675	8.6	15.4	26.8	20.6	28.6	97679	142258	98	98	4596	0.2	0.8	11.9	51.2	36.0	332063
55437	MINNEAPOLIS	43951	8097	10.5	19.9	34.6	20.1	14.8	74112	102737	93	92	6242	0.3	1.5	17.0	70.8	10.4	229540
55438	MINNEAPOLIS	51296	7456	6.5	17.5	33.0	21.6	21.5	86610	122689	97	96	6017	0.2	0.7	27.5	54.3	17.4	246966
55439	MINNEAPOLIS	69463	3642	5.6	11.4	24.4	24.1	34.6	114731	162529	99	100	3284	0.0	0.1	5.1	47.7	47.2	387240
55441	MINNEAPOLIS	45051	7370	8.5	20.4	31.6	20.8	18.7	79594	113511	95	95	4962	1.3	0.8	16.3	66.6	15.1	247344
55442	MINNEAPOLIS	52119	5112	4.3	12.6	28.3	27.0	27.8	105614	139998	99	99	4496	0.4	3.7	11.3	66.4	18.2	282492
55443	MINNEAPOLIS	30708	10267	9.7	19.9	38.6	23.9	7.9	74963	98032	93	92	7651	0.4	1.9	29.8	63.3	4.6	202591
55444	MINNEAPOLIS	28877	5247	3.5	19.0	46.0	24.3	7.3	77812	100571	94	94	4868	0.3	3.0	42.5	52.5	1.8	179514
55445	MINNEAPOLIS	31842	3378	5.9	18.6	44.9	21.5	9.2	76757	98850	94	93	3084	0.3	8.3	38.2	53.0	0.3	180187
55446	MINNEAPOLIS	51398	5657	4.0	8.5	27.0	29.1	31.5	113522	152410	99	100	4870	0.2	0.1	12.1	53.3	34.3	337449
55447	MINNEAPOLIS	46545	8593	5.9	14.0	34.8	23.3	22.0	91434	125480	97	98	7121	0.4	0.2	18.6	67.1	13.7	246095
55448	MINNEAPOLIS	29418	10465	7.8	19.1	48.3	18.9	6.0	69158	82431	91	90	9137	0.5	1.1	40.9	56.7	1.0	186433
55449	MINNEAPOLIS	31286	5155	7.8	15.8	44.6	21.6	10.2	77158	92108	94	94	4758	11.3	3.3	16.5	63.3	5.5	214161
55454	MINNEAPOLIS	14054	2979	63.0	20.0	11.3	4.6	1.1	17331	21923	1	1	422	0.0	13.3	64.2	22.5	0.0	144231
55455	MINNEAPOLIS	12059	20	75.0	15.0	5.0	5.0	0.0	15938	18958	1	0	2	0.0	0.0	100.0	0.0	0.0	112500
55602	BRIMSON	25905	133	31.6	29.3	33.1	4.5	1.5	40378	49083	47	28	127	29.9	32.3	30.7	7.1	0.0	74091
55603	FINLAND	20818	350	24.9	33.1	33.4	5.7	2.9	43844	50837	58	44	309	13.9	25.2	36.6	21.0	3.2	107188
55604	GRAND MARAIS	27683	1705	25.9	31.2	31.7	7.6	3.6	43540	53029	57	43	1370	7.5	10.3	43.8	31.8	6.7	150617
55605	GRAND PORTAGE	23458	307	30.0	26.4	31.9	8.8	2.9	42374	53022	54	37	256	16.0	20.7	30.5	22.7	10.2	114865
55606	HOVLAND	26535	88	29.6	27.3	30.7	9.1	3.4	42370	52192	54	37	73	16.4	20.6	30.1	21.9	11.0	114773
55607	ISABELLA	26133	131	22.1	29.0	38.2	7.6	3.1	48656	56137	70	63	120	7.5	15.8	39.2	27.5	10.0	148077
55612	LUTSEN	32526	228	18.9	36.0	28.1	11.0	6.1	45377	57665	62	52	196	5.1	7.1	30.1	44.4	13.3	200000
55613	SCHROEDER	32078	94	19.2	36.2	28.7	10.6	5.3	45000	57117	61	50	81	2.5	6.2	29.6	46.9	14.8	214583
55614	SILVER BAY	20649	1196	23.4	34.9	34.2	6.9	0.6	42785	50051	55	39	1027	18.1	44.7	28.0	8.0	1.3	74500
55615	TOFTE	31996	114	18.4	36.0	29.0	10.5	6.1	45761	57575	63	53	98	4.1	8.2	29.6	43.9	14.3	200000
55616	TWO HARBORS	24993	3375	23.9	27.8	36.5	9.5	2.3	48533	56873	69	62	2732	7.7	20.9	48.9	20.0	2.5	117863
55702	ALBORN	20261	159	21.4	31.5	38.4	8.2	0.6	46676	54557	65	56	144	21.5	22.2	34.0	22.2	0.0	99000
55703	ANGORA	21252	293	26.6	30.0	34.8	5.8	2.7	43343	53802	57	42	262	17.6	29.8	42.8	9.2	0.8	93684
55704	ASKOV	24798	438	29.2	32.0	30.1	6.6	2.1	37929	45832	39	18	370	12.2	21.9	42.2	23.2	0.5	114925
55705	AURORA	23564	1546	27.2	30.3	32.7	7.6	2.3	43421	52589	57	42	1321	28.2	41.2	27.2	3.0	0.5	68245
55706	BABBITT	24479	987	24.6	37.9	29.1	5.6	2.8	40353	49961	47	27	903	23.9	42.8	23.7	6.5	3.1	68682
55707	BARNUM	22354	1305	21.5	30.0	37.3	9.7	1.5	48659	57455	70	63	1176	12.9	16.1	45.4	24.4	1.2	123858
55709	BOVEY	21371	2698	27.9	30.6	32.5	7.3	1.7	42855	51404	56	39	2249	17.4	27.0	41.0	13.6	1.2	98615
55710	BRITT	25157	544	16.4	27.6	39.2	13.8	3.1	55908	68906	81	78	515	11.7	16.3	48.2	20.6	3.3	126847
55711	BROOKSTON	18455	228	26.3	25.9	37.3	10.5	0.0	47379	56328	67	58	185	11.9	16.2	53.0	18.4	0.5	119551
55712	BRUNO	22928	138	28.3	26.1	33.3	10.1	2.2	45652	54545	63	53	130	15.4	15.4	41.5	25.4	2.3	126316
55717	CANYON	36042	138	15.2	33.3	36.2	8.7	6.5	51305	62171	74	69	133	7.5	14.3	39.1	36.1	3.0	145833
55718	CARLTON	23131	1216	19.0	31.3	36.4	11.6	1.8	49766	58676	71	65	1056	8.9	16.6	45.7	28.2	0.6	133742
55719	CHISHOLM	20848	3094	31.7	31.6	29.9	5.6	1.2	37287	45352	36	15	2524	30.6	35.5	26.7	6.9	0.4	68876
55720	CLOQUET	22029	6516	27.9	27.0	33.4	9.9	1.8	45353	53455	62	51	5078	8.3	20.6	51.0	19.7	0.5	118687
55721	COHASSET	22419	1306	23.1	25.0	40.4	10.0	1.7	51414	61690	75	69	1159	11.0	13.1	40.9	29.4	5.6	135171
55723	COOK	23729	1144	26.5	28.7	35.6	5.8	3.5	45766	55094	63	53	1010	14.6	25.8	36.5	17.8	5.3	105945
55724	COTTON	27404	332	19.9	32.2	36.8	7.2	3.9	48348	58307	69	61	316	14.6	22.8	38.9	22.2	1.6	111979
55725	CRANE LAKE	32540	49	18.4	26.5	38.8	10.2	6.1	55841	75000	81	78	45	2.2	6.7	28.9	40.0	22.2	235000
55726	CROMWELL	21680	420	30.5	31.9	30.0	6.0	1.7	40639	49090	48	29	373	16.1	22.0	43.7	18.0	0.3	113564
55731	ELY	23411	2837	32.4	32.2	26.5	5.6	3.3	37254	46368	36	15	2229	12.0	33.6	34.9	15.3	4.3	97406
55732	EMBARRASS	22807	615	21.3	32.7	36.4	7.8	1.8	46564	56441	65	55	592	22.3	37.3	33.5	6.4	0.5	78226
55733	ESKO	24959	1646	14.3	22.8	44.6	15.3	3.0	61802	72980	86	84	1576	3.5	9.4	52.8	32.6	1.8	147990
55734	EVELETH	22618	2786	30.4	29.8	31.6	6.9	1.3	39822	48250	45	25	2264	20.2	37.0	33.8	8.5	0.5	79551
55735	FINLAYSON	21342	945	30.3	29.1	32.0	6.2	2.4	40433	49422	48	28	830	14.7	16.4	48.1	18.9	1.9	121538
55736	FLOODWOOD	19832	622	38.1	29.7	24.8	4.5	2.9	36161	44272	32	11	530	26.2	31.1	34.3	8.3	0.0	79231
55738	FORBES	19060	230	25.2	27.4	42.2	4.4	0.9	48090	56908	68	60	213	28.6	31.0	36.2	4.2	0.0	79706
55741	GILBERT	22495	1835	29.1	29.4	33.9	5.8	1.8	43384	52160	57	42	1539	26.5	39.1	28.2	5.7	0.6	70607
55742	GOODLAND	20099	200	29.5	29.0	37.5	3.0	1.0	42929	51274	56	40	186	13.4	28.0	46.8	11.8	0.0	102703
55744	GRAND RAPIDS	23126	8733	25.7	29.9	33.0	8.7	2.8	44826	53160	61	49	6866	9.0	17.7	45.4	24.8	3.1	126400
55746	HIBBING	22836	8039	31.3	28.5	30.5	7.5	2.3	40726	49971	49	30	6163	20.0	35.5	39.4	4.7	0.4	84023
55748	HILL CITY	19931	547	33.5	30.7	27.1	5.7	3.1	37834	45947	39	18	418	27.5	23.7	31.6	15.6	1.7	87368
55749	HOLYOKE	26700	126	21.4	29.4	38.1	7.9	3.2	49310	59573	71	64	118	10.2	17.8	47.5	21.2	3.4	120000
55750	HOYT LAKES	23592	919	23.3	32.9	33.8	9.4	0.7	45644	54972	63	53	851	37.0	54.3	7.6	1.1	0.0	55188
55751	IRON	23866	703	18.2	26.2	44.5	9.8	1.3	53524	64312	78	74	673	22.4	27.0	42.9	7.4	0.2	90700
55752	JACOBSON	21013	222	32.0	30.6	27.5	7.2	2.7	36776	46160	35	14	204	15.2	17.2	38.7	25.5	3.4	123913
55756	KERRICK	24399	240	27.9	26.3	32.5	10.4	2.9	46060	55554	64	54	226	15.0	16.8	40.3	25.2	2.7	125000
55757	KETTLE RIVER	21324	389	26.5	33.9	33.2	4.6	1.8	42082	49124	53	35	336	18.2	17.6	43.5	19.9	0.9	113182
55760	MCGREGOR	21813	1516	36.7	32.1	23.9	4.6	2.6	33397	40782	22	5	1301	15.5	20.8	36.1	24.4	3.2	117745
55763	MAKINEN	20481	283	27.6	29.7	36.0	5.3	1.4	44411	53410	60	47	271	27.3	32.1	34.3	6.3	0.0	76600
55765	MEADOWLANDS	20113	332	31.3	30.7	29.5	6.3	2.1	39743	48730	45	25	296	24.7	31.4	38.2	5.7	0.0	79167
55766	MELRUDE	22047	46	19.6	30.4	43.5	6.5	0.0	50000	63856	72	66	44	18.2	27.3	43.2	11.4	0.0	100000
55767	MOOSE LAKE	19303	1178	30.1	30.5	31.5	5.5	2.4	40587	48902	48	29	857	8.8	18.9	53.0	18.2	1.2	119410
	MINNESOTA	29624		18.6	25.2	34.9	14.0	7.4	56724	71660				6.6	9.7	36.5	40.5	6.8	168676
	UNITED STATES	25866		24.7	27.1	30.8	10.9	6.5	48124	56710				10.9	15.0	33.7	30.1	10.4	145905

ZIP CODE #	POST OFFICE NAME	FINANCIAL SERVICES: Auto Loan	FINANCIAL SERVICES: Home Loan	FINANCIAL SERVICES: Invest-ments	FINANCIAL SERVICES: Retire-ment Plans	THE HOME: Home Improvements: Home Repair	THE HOME: Home Improvements: Lawn & Garden	THE HOME: Furnishings: Comput-ers & Hard-ware	THE HOME: Furnishings: Major Appli-ances	THE HOME: Furnishings: TV, Radio, Sound Equip-ment	THE HOME: Furnishings: Furni-ture	ENTERTAINMENT: Dine out/ Carry out	ENTERTAINMENT: Sports Equip-ment	ENTERTAINMENT: Fees & Tickets	ENTERTAINMENT: Toys & Games	ENTERTAINMENT: Travel	ENTERTAINMENT: Cable TV	PERSONAL: Apparel & Services	PERSONAL: Auto Repairs	PERSONAL: Health Insur-ance	PERSONAL: Pets & Supplies
55409	MINNEAPOLIS	120	131	160	136	128	133	133	127	128	132	161	151	136	164	132	124	159	129	117	140
55410	MINNEAPOLIS	135	159	200	163	156	160	155	150	147	154	186	178	161	192	156	143	184	151	136	163
55411	MINNEAPOLIS	63	57	70	55	55	64	63	61	68	65	85	69	64	84	62	70	83	64	64	70
55412	MINNEAPOLIS	76	78	92	80	78	82	84	80	83	82	104	96	84	106	83	80	102	83	77	88
55413	MINNEAPOLIS	74	69	85	73	68	73	82	75	80	78	100	92	79	99	77	76	98	80	70	82
55414	MINNEAPOLIS	74	52	72	59	51	59	85	67	83	76	105	90	74	97	72	75	100	79	62	76
55415	MINNEAPOLIS	60	54	86	59	53	60	66	60	68	65	86	72	66	86	64	68	84	65	59	67
55416	MINNEAPOLIS	139	146	196	155	142	151	154	146	150	154	190	175	157	192	152	146	187	151	134	160
55417	MINNEAPOLIS	106	119	146	123	117	121	120	116	115	119	145	138	123	148	120	111	143	118	106	126
55418	MINNEAPOLIS	81	87	102	88	86	91	90	87	88	88	111	102	91	113	90	87	108	89	84	95
55419	MINNEAPOLIS	138	156	190	161	153	159	154	148	147	154	185	176	160	189	154	142	184	150	136	163
55420	MINNEAPOLIS	90	98	115	99	96	102	98	96	96	98	121	111	101	123	99	94	119	97	91	105
55421	MINNEAPOLIS	76	82	94	82	81	86	83	81	82	82	102	94	85	104	83	81	100	82	78	89
55422	MINNEAPOLIS	105	118	136	119	117	123	117	114	113	115	142	133	120	145	118	111	140	114	109	125
55423	MINNEAPOLIS	93	99	116	100	98	103	103	99	101	101	126	117	104	128	102	98	124	101	94	108
55424	MINNEAPOLIS	209	271	341	268	265	277	243	240	227	245	287	274	267	302	254	226	289	233	220	260
55425	MINNEAPOLIS	92	95	112	99	94	99	99	96	96	99	121	113	100	120	97	93	119	98	90	105
55426	MINNEAPOLIS	99	101	121	105	99	105	106	102	103	106	131	120	106	129	104	100	128	105	95	112
55427	MINNEAPOLIS	110	123	143	125	121	126	121	118	116	121	146	138	125	149	121	113	144	118	110	129
55428	MINNEAPOLIS	85	91	107	92	89	94	93	90	91	92	115	105	95	116	92	89	113	91	85	99
55429	MINNEAPOLIS	83	89	102	90	87	91	91	87	88	89	111	103	92	113	90	86	109	89	82	96
55430	MINNEAPOLIS	78	82	92	83	81	86	84	82	83	83	104	96	86	107	84	81	102	83	79	89
55431	MINNEAPOLIS	113	129	147	129	127	134	124	123	120	124	151	141	130	154	126	118	149	122	117	134
55432	MINNEAPOLIS	94	96	99	96	95	101	96	96	95	95	118	111	96	118	95	93	115	96	93	107
55433	MINNEAPOLIS	96	104	111	108	101	102	102	100	96	103	122	118	103	123	100	92	120	100	89	109
55434	MINNEAPOLIS	100	108	109	108	105	107	102	102	98	103	123	120	104	124	102	95	121	102	94	114
55435	MINNEAPOLIS	114	115	145	115	116	131	118	119	120	120	150	130	120	144	121	122	145	120	125	130
55436	MINNEAPOLIS	187	234	299	229	228	245	216	213	207	217	261	242	234	272	226	209	261	210	202	231
55437	MINNEAPOLIS	128	150	180	150	148	156	144	141	138	143	174	163	151	179	147	137	172	140	134	154
55438	MINNEAPOLIS	158	182	206	186	178	182	173	170	163	173	206	199	180	210	174	158	204	168	154	186
55439	MINNEAPOLIS	226	270	324	258	270	296	240	250	234	248	294	269	260	291	257	241	290	241	252	274
55441	MINNEAPOLIS	147	164	186	171	159	163	159	153	149	160	189	181	165	191	157	143	188	154	137	170
55442	MINNEAPOLIS	189	224	244	231	217	220	205	201	190	208	241	233	218	246	206	184	240	197	180	221
55443	MINNEAPOLIS	119	129	135	134	124	124	125	122	117	127	149	145	127	149	122	111	147	122	107	134
55444	MINNEAPOLIS	122	139	138	143	134	131	127	126	118	130	149	149	131	151	125	111	148	124	110	139
55445	MINNEAPOLIS	121	137	139	140	132	130	127	126	118	129	149	148	130	152	125	112	148	124	110	138
55446	MINNEAPOLIS	200	227	232	237	218	215	209	205	193	215	245	239	217	247	205	182	243	201	178	225
55447	MINNEAPOLIS	163	182	201	190	177	182	174	170	164	176	208	199	182	208	173	157	206	169	153	188
55448	MINNEAPOLIS	112	126	127	129	122	121	117	116	110	119	139	136	121	141	116	104	137	114	103	128
55449	MINNEAPOLIS	132	146	139	151	140	136	133	132	123	138	156	155	135	155	129	115	153	129	114	146
55454	MINNEAPOLIS	36	32	60	33	31	36	45	37	47	42	59	46	43	62	42	47	59	42	37	41
55455	MINNEAPOLIS	36	22	27	25	21	26	42	31	41	36	51	43	34	46	34	36	48	38	29	35
55602	BRIMSON	83	65	44	58	73	82	61	74	69	61	82	86	55	81	65	74	76	72	87	101
55603	FINLAND	84	68	49	62	76	85	64	76	72	64	85	89	58	85	68	76	80	75	89	102
55604	GRAND MARAIS	99	77	52	70	86	98	75	89	85	74	101	103	67	98	79	91	93	88	105	117
55605	GRAND PORTAGE	89	70	48	63	79	89	66	80	75	65	89	93	59	87	70	80	82	78	94	109
55606	HOVLAND	90	70	48	63	79	89	66	80	75	66	89	93	59	88	71	80	83	79	94	109
55607	ISABELLA	96	75	51	68	85	95	71	85	80	70	95	100	63	94	76	86	88	84	101	117
55612	LUTSEN	119	93	64	84	105	118	88	106	99	87	118	124	79	116	94	106	110	104	125	145
55613	SCHROEDER	119	93	63	84	105	118	88	106	99	87	118	124	78	116	94	106	109	104	125	145
55614	SILVER BAY	77	64	49	61	69	78	64	72	70	63	84	82	60	83	66	73	78	71	82	89
55615	TOFTE	118	93	63	84	104	117	87	105	99	87	117	123	78	116	93	106	109	104	124	144
55616	TWO HARBORS	90	79	65	75	84	95	77	86	83	76	100	98	73	99	80	87	94	84	96	106
55702	ALBORN	86	67	46	61	76	85	64	77	72	63	85	90	57	84	68	77	79	75	91	105
55703	ANGORA	83	69	53	64	76	85	67	77	74	66	89	89	63	91	71	78	84	76	89	100
55704	ASKOV	110	77	41	73	90	101	76	94	88	75	103	113	65	101	79	92	94	93	112	131
55705	AURORA	85	74	59	69	78	87	72	79	78	71	94	91	69	93	73	81	88	78	89	98
55706	BABBITT	75	78	78	73	80	88	74	78	76	73	93	88	75	96	77	79	90	76	82	90
55707	BARNUM	93	79	59	76	84	93	76	85	82	75	99	100	73	99	78	84	93	83	93	108
55709	BOVEY	79	70	58	67	74	83	70	75	74	68	89	87	67	89	71	77	84	74	83	92
55710	BRITT	88	98	96	96	99	101	89	92	87	88	107	108	91	113	92	86	105	90	90	107
55711	BROOKSTON	83	70	53	68	74	84	70	77	76	69	91	89	66	90	71	78	85	76	85	94
55712	BRUNO	95	75	51	67	84	95	70	85	80	70	94	99	63	93	75	85	88	84	100	116
55717	CANYON	137	109	75	98	122	136	102	122	115	101	137	144	92	135	109	123	127	120	144	167
55718	CARLTON	95	84	67	82	88	97	82	89	87	81	106	104	80	106	83	88	100	87	96	109
55719	CHISHOLM	65	64	63	62	66	73	65	66	67	63	83	75	65	85	66	69	79	65	71	75
55720	CLOQUET	79	73	63	70	75	84	73	76	77	71	93	87	72	95	74	79	89	75	83	90
55721	COHASSET	96	81	58	77	87	95	76	86	82	76	99	103	73	100	79	85	94	84	96	113
55723	COOK	85	72	56	67	79	88	70	79	77	68	92	92	66	94	73	81	86	78	91	102
55724	COTTON	112	88	60	80	98	111	84	100	95	83	113	116	76	111	89	101	105	99	118	134
55725	CRANE LAKE	115	90	61	81	101	114	85	102	96	84	114	120	76	112	90	102	106	101	121	140
55726	CROMWELL	85	67	46	61	75	85	63	76	72	63	85	89	57	84	67	76	79	75	90	104
55731	ELY	79	65	51	61	71	81	66	74	72	64	86	83	61	83	68	76	80	73	86	92
55732	EMBARRASS	87	72	54	69	78	88	74	81	80	72	96	93	69	94	75	84	89	80	93	100
55733	ESKO	90	112	120	111	109	109	100	100	94	100	118	117	107	126	103	92	118	97	90	110
55734	EVELETH	76	67	56	64	71	81	68	73	74	66	89	83	66	89	70	77	83	72	83	88
55735	FINLAYSON	87	68	46	61	77	86	64	77	73	64	86	91	58	85	69	78	80	76	92	106
55736	FLOODWOOD	77	58	38	55	64	75	61	69	68	58	81	79	54	77	62	72	74	69	82	88
55738	FORBES	81	72	55	69	76	82	67	74	71	67	86	88	65	88	69	73	82	72	80	96
55741	GILBERT	76	66	54	63	71	80	67	72	72	65	87	83	65	89	68	76	82	71	82	88
55742	GOODLAND	78	64	46	59	71	78	60	70	67	60	80	83	56	80	63	70	75	69	81	94
55744	GRAND RAPIDS	83	74	63	71	78	87	74	79	78	72	95	92	71	95	75	81	90	79	87	96
55746	HIBBING	77	68	58	66	72	81	70	74	74	68	90	84	67	90	70	77	85	73	82	88
55748	HILL CITY	79	60	39	57	66	78	63	72	71	61	84	82	56	80	64	75	77	71	86	90
55749	HOLYOKE	92	82	63	78	87	93	76	84	81	76	98	100	74	100	78	83	93	82	91	109
55750	HOYT LAKES	66	77	86	73	76	83	73	73	73	72	91	82	77	94	76	74	89	72	74	80
55751	IRON	87	85	75	82	88	93	79	84	81	79	100	100	80	103	81	82	96	82	87	104
55752	JACOBSON	86	67	46	61	76	85	63	76	72	63	85	89	57	84	67	77	79	75	90	104
55756	KERRICK	96	75	52	68	85	95	71	85	80	70	95	100	64	94	76	86	88	84	101	117
55757	KETTLE RIVER	90	63	34	60	74	82	62	77	72	62	84	93	53	83	65	75	77	76	92	107
55760	MCGREGOR	81	63	43	57	71	80	60	72	68	59	80	84	53	79	64	72	74	71	85	98
55763	MAKINEN	83	66	46	60	74	82	62	74	70	62	83	87	56	82	66	74	77	73	87	101
55765	MEADOWLANDS	80	60	38	57	66	78	64	72	72	61	84	82	57	81	64	75	77	71	86	90
55766	MELRUDE	94	73	50	66	83	93	69	83	78	69	93	98	62	92	74	84	86	82	99	114
55767	MOOSE LAKE	57	44	30	42	48	56	47	52	52	45	62	59	43	59	47	55	57	52	61	64
	MINNESOTA	107	106	108	107	107	113	106	107	105	105	131	126	105	131	105	104	127	107	105	123
	UNITED STATES	100	100	100	100	100	100	100	100	100	100	100	100	100	100	100	100	100	100	100	100

MINNESOTA
POPULATION CHANGE
A 55768-55992

#	POST OFFICE NAME	COUNTY FIPS CODE	POPULATION 2000	2004	2009	2000-2004 ANNUAL RATE % Rate	State Centile	HOUSEHOLDS 2000	2004	2009	% Annual Rate 2000-2004	2004 Average HH Size	FAMILIES 2000	2004	% Annual Rate 2000-2004
55768	MOUNTAIN IRON	137	2535	2591	2659	0.5	44	1115	1159	1210	0.9	2.22	713	714	0.0
55769	NASHWAUK	061	3397	3458	3649	0.4	41	1466	1521	1636	0.9	2.27	946	951	0.1
55771	ORR	137	1750	1805	1848	0.7	50	744	782	814	1.2	2.31	497	506	0.4
55775	PENGILLY	061	1263	1276	1335	0.2	35	541	557	595	0.7	2.29	384	384	0.0
55779	SAGINAW	137	3571	3747	3866	1.1	61	1244	1341	1413	1.8	2.68	964	1015	1.2
55780	SAWYER	017	89	106	120	4.2	95	24	29	33	4.6	3.66	17	20	3.9
55781	SIDE LAKE	137	434	445	456	0.6	46	182	190	198	1.0	2.29	138	141	0.5
55783	STURGEON LAKE	115	2530	2665	2884	1.2	63	1020	1100	1214	1.8	2.38	704	738	1.1
55784	SWAN RIVER	061	315	332	353	1.2	64	117	126	136	1.8	2.63	85	89	1.1
55785	SWATARA	001	245	289	346	4.0	94	91	109	133	4.3	2.65	65	77	4.1
55787	TAMARACK	001	577	647	758	2.7	87	254	290	345	3.2	2.21	168	186	2.4
55790	TOWER	137	2429	2428	2455	0.0	26	1085	1107	1140	0.5	2.18	722	710	-0.4
55792	VIRGINIA	137	10903	10914	11067	0.0	29	5054	5162	5329	0.5	2.02	2784	2706	-0.7
55793	WARBA	061	506	524	552	0.8	54	211	223	240	1.3	2.35	156	161	0.8
55795	WILLOW RIVER	115	1295	1332	1424	0.7	49	523	548	597	1.1	2.38	367	375	0.5
55797	WRENSHALL	017	1244	1372	1503	2.3	83	448	508	571	3.0	2.54	319	351	2.3
55798	WRIGHT	017	651	702	757	1.8	75	241	267	294	2.4	2.52	170	182	1.6
55801	DULUTH	137	40	52	60	6.4	99	14	19	22	7.5	2.74	11	14	5.8
55802	DULUTH	137	2484	2414	2417	-0.7	6	1408	1382	1407	-0.4	1.49	372	348	-1.6
55803	DULUTH	137	16265	16991	17513	1.0	60	6085	6475	6789	1.5	2.60	4586	4759	0.9
55804	DULUTH	137	14397	14511	14748	0.2	34	5531	5673	5860	0.6	2.51	3964	3947	-0.1
55805	DULUTH	137	10593	11003	11403	0.9	56	5138	5342	5590	0.9	2.02	1923	1920	0.0
55806	DULUTH	137	9786	9729	9819	-0.1	22	4425	4471	4581	0.2	2.14	2230	2141	-1.0
55807	DULUTH	137	10284	10292	10454	0.0	29	4443	4523	4669	0.4	2.23	2660	2599	-0.5
55808	DULUTH	137	5818	5898	5989	0.3	39	2445	2523	2602	0.7	2.32	1539	1527	-0.2
55810	DULUTH	137	8548	8460	8558	-0.2	18	3312	3341	3436	0.2	2.48	2335	2335	-0.4
55811	DULUTH	137	24801	25779	26405	0.9	56	9002	9416	9828	1.1	2.38	6036	6117	0.3
55812	DULUTH	137	10994	10919	11010	-0.2	21	3808	3848	3955	0.3	2.25	1856	1778	-1.0
55901	ROCHESTER	109	41806	49246	57714	3.9	94	16285	19238	22720	4.0	2.50	10524	12232	3.6
55902	ROCHESTER	109	18602	20037	22390	1.8	75	7483	8164	9249	2.1	2.39	4839	5099	1.2
55904	ROCHESTER	109	23704	25401	28281	1.6	72	9061	9918	11244	2.2	2.49	5929	6255	1.3
55906	ROCHESTER	109	16581	18083	20388	2.1	79	6460	7153	8184	2.4	2.46	4414	4719	1.6
55909	ADAMS	099	1275	1288	1333	0.2	35	480	485	505	0.2	2.56	353	348	-0.3
55910	ALTURA	169	2949	2937	3011	-0.1	24	1057	1076	1125	0.4	2.73	814	810	-0.1
55912	AUSTIN	099	26741	27563	28572	0.7	50	11177	11617	12139	0.9	2.31	7067	7119	0.2
55917	BLOOMING PRAIRIE	039	3378	3470	3645	0.6	47	1249	1307	1393	1.1	2.58	907	925	0.5
55918	BROWNSDALE	099	1333	1324	1348	-0.2	21	524	527	542	0.1	2.51	382	374	-0.5
55919	BROWNSVILLE	055	1150	1192	1239	0.9	54	450	476	503	1.3	2.50	334	345	0.8
55920	BYRON	109	6081	6396	7015	1.2	62	2118	2277	2538	1.7	2.81	1746	1836	1.2
55921	CALEDONIA	055	5232	5416	5618	0.8	53	2005	2114	2232	1.3	2.49	1338	1369	0.5
55922	CANTON	045	1362	1413	1488	0.9	55	440	460	489	1.1	3.06	326	333	0.5
55923	CHATFIELD	045	4768	4943	5302	0.9	54	1783	1890	2061	1.4	2.55	1301	1339	0.7
55924	CLAREMONT	039	1252	1301	1418	0.9	56	458	482	532	1.2	2.68	349	360	0.7
55925	DAKOTA	169	714	739	764	0.8	53	260	276	291	1.4	2.64	202	209	0.8
55926	DEXTER	099	622	640	659	0.7	49	230	239	248	0.9	2.54	175	177	0.3
55927	DODGE CENTER	039	3556	3966	4512	2.6	86	1273	1443	1667	3.0	2.70	968	1074	2.5
55929	DOVER	109	945	1029	1158	2.0	78	342	383	440	2.7	2.69	261	284	2.0
55932	ELGIN	157	1985	2029	2137	0.5	44	710	738	790	0.9	2.75	531	539	0.4
55933	ELKTON	099	518	502	508	-0.7	4	175	172	175	-0.4	2.80	128	122	-1.1
55934	EYOTA	109	2877	2973	3251	0.8	52	1059	1123	1250	1.4	2.65	828	855	0.8
55935	FOUNTAIN	045	648	743	824	3.3	91	248	289	325	3.7	2.56	191	218	3.2
55936	GRAND MEADOW	099	1703	1726	1763	0.3	39	647	666	688	0.7	2.53	445	443	-0.1
55939	HARMONY	045	2349	2466	2612	1.2	61	875	928	996	1.4	2.59	598	616	0.7
55940	HAYFIELD	039	2458	2635	2930	1.7	72	882	960	1086	2.0	2.66	653	693	1.4
55941	HOKAH	055	1307	1356	1408	0.9	55	508	537	568	1.3	2.53	385	399	0.8
55943	HOUSTON	055	3541	3543	3633	0.0	28	1355	1376	1435	0.4	2.53	985	976	-0.2
55944	KASSON	039	5737	6500	7458	3.0	89	2128	2453	2857	3.4	2.65	1550	1741	2.8
55945	KELLOGG	157	1188	1207	1260	0.4	40	427	440	467	0.7	2.74	316	318	0.2
55946	KENYON	049	3458	3645	3890	1.3	64	1298	1374	1478	1.4	2.61	945	976	0.8
55947	LA CRESCENT	055	7483	7768	8096	0.9	56	2841	2993	3165	1.2	2.56	2087	2147	0.7
55949	LANESBORO	045	1397	1413	1467	0.3	36	616	633	667	0.6	2.23	392	391	-0.1
55951	LE ROY	099	1475	1512	1554	0.6	46	608	629	652	0.8	2.40	413	414	0.1
55952	LEWISTON	169	2210	2437	2623	2.3	83	773	869	954	2.8	2.76	596	654	2.2
55953	LYLE	099	1177	1199	1237	0.4	42	432	444	462	0.7	2.70	325	324	-0.1
55954	MABEL	045	1559	1579	1641	0.3	37	637	656	691	0.7	2.31	417	416	-0.1
55955	MANTORVILLE	039	1723	2094	2487	4.7	97	570	695	829	4.8	3.01	476	570	4.3
55956	MAZEPPA	157	1871	2015	2160	1.8	75	696	760	827	2.1	2.65	516	551	1.6
55957	MILLVILLE	157	616	627	652	0.4	41	213	220	232	0.8	2.85	154	156	0.3
55959	MINNESOTA CITY	169	1087	1095	1113	-0.3	17	413	418	435	0.3	2.62	321	318	-0.2
55960	ORONOCO	109	3142	3460	3881	2.3	82	1162	1314	1502	2.9	2.63	886	972	2.2
55961	OSTRANDER	045	586	597	622	0.4	42	233	239	253	0.6	2.50	178	179	0.1
55962	PETERSON	045	992	1019	1067	0.6	47	348	364	388	1.1	2.75	262	269	0.6
55963	PINE ISLAND	049	4376	5008	5602	3.2	91	1563	1825	2074	3.7	2.69	1205	1374	3.1
55964	PLAINVIEW	157	3780	3980	4239	1.2	63	1355	1455	1576	1.7	2.65	980	1027	1.1
55965	PRESTON	045	1709	1737	1806	0.4	40	695	719	760	0.8	2.31	483	486	0.2
55967	RACINE	099	1096	1169	1229	1.5	69	382	413	438	1.9	2.83	298	315	1.3
55968	READS LANDING	157	83	84	86	0.3	37	37	38	40	0.6	2.21	29	29	0.0
55969	ROLLINGSTONE	169	1080	1054	1067	-0.6	8	404	404	419	0.0	2.61	314	307	-0.5
55970	ROSE CREEK	099	1265	1270	1297	0.1	31	453	460	474	0.4	2.75	349	346	-0.2
55971	RUSHFORD	169	2885	3060	3258	1.4	67	1146	1242	1347	1.9	2.37	787	827	1.2
55972	SAINT CHARLES	169	4660	4711	4814	0.3	36	1663	1712	1781	0.7	2.72	1227	1228	0.0
55973	SARGEANT	099	392	403	415	0.7	48	126	131	136	0.9	2.92	96	97	0.2
55974	SPRING GROVE	055	2286	2395	2500	1.1	61	936	1000	1063	1.6	2.34	650	676	0.9
55975	SPRING VALLEY	045	4622	4828	5099	1.0	60	1805	1909	2044	1.3	2.50	1269	1305	0.7
55976	STEWARTVILLE	109	6902	7251	7953	1.2	62	2550	2751	3077	1.8	2.58	1857	1934	1.0
55977	TAOPI	099	376	422	455	2.8	88	128	146	159	3.1	2.89	108	120	2.5
55979	UTICA	169	570	655	718	3.3	91	186	219	245	3.9	2.93	146	167	3.2
55981	WABASHA	157	4146	4379	4652	1.3	65	1677	1800	1942	1.7	2.33	1121	1167	1.0
55982	WALTHAM	099	612	615	624	0.2	32	214	216	220	0.2	2.83	175	174	-0.1
55983	WANAMINGO	049	1458	1521	1602	1.0	58	552	582	620	1.3	2.58	393	404	0.7
55985	WEST CONCORD	039	2090	2195	2416	1.2	62	794	846	943	1.5	2.58	599	623	0.9
55987	WINONA	169	35868	36690	37774	0.5	44	13693	14277	15006	1.0	2.31	7847	7877	0.1
55990	WYKOFF	045	945	987	1042	1.0	60	385	409	439	1.4	2.41	281	291	0.8
55991	ZUMBRO FALLS	157	1856	1953	2070	1.2	63	710	761	820	1.7	2.52	529	554	1.1
55992	ZUMBROTA	049	4408	4707	5028	1.6	70	1708	1847	1997	1.9	2.52	1213	1278	1.2
	MINNESOTA					1.4					1.6	2.50			1.0
	UNITED STATES					1.2					1.3	2.58			1.1

ZIP CODE #	POST OFFICE NAME	RACE (%) White 2000	White 2004	Black 2000	Black 2004	Asian/Pacific 2000	Asian/Pacific 2004	% Hispanic Origin 2000	% Hispanic Origin 2004	2004 AGE DISTRIBUTION (%) 0-4	5-9	10-14	15-19	20-24	25-44	45-64	65-84	85+	18+	MEDIAN AGE 2004	% 2004 Males	% 2004 Females
55768	MOUNTAIN IRON	98.3	98.1	0.0	0.1	0.1	0.2	0.4	0.5	5.4	5.2	6.1	7.2	7.1	23.2	29.2	14.5	1.9	78.8	41.9	49.2	50.8
55769	NASHWAUK	97.9	97.7	0.2	0.2	0.2	0.2	0.3	0.4	4.9	5.1	6.9	6.6	5.6	24.2	28.7	15.6	2.5	78.9	42.8	50.1	49.9
55771	ORR	76.9	76.2	0.0	0.0	0.6	0.7	0.9	1.0	5.3	5.7	6.3	6.0	5.2	22.4	31.2	16.6	1.2	79.0	44.3	52.4	47.7
55775	PENGILLY	97.5	97.4	0.2	0.2	0.1	0.1	0.2	0.2	4.9	5.4	5.8	5.3	5.1	20.0	32.9	18.0	2.6	80.6	47.0	49.2	50.8
55779	SAGINAW	95.4	94.9	0.5	0.5	0.3	0.4	1.2	1.5	5.8	6.2	7.0	6.8	6.1	28.2	30.6	8.5	0.9	76.7	40.1	53.0	47.0
55780	SAWYER	65.2	65.1	0.0	0.0	0.0	0.0	1.1	1.9	7.6	7.6	8.5	7.6	5.7	25.5	24.5	12.3	0.9	70.8	36.4	51.9	48.1
55781	SIDE LAKE	97.7	97.5	0.0	0.2	0.0	0.0	0.7	0.5	4.3	4.3	6.3	8.3	2.5	22.5	36.2	14.2	1.6	79.6	45.9	53.0	47.0
55783	STURGEON LAKE	96.1	95.6	1.1	1.4	0.2	0.2	0.8	1.0	5.1	5.3	5.9	6.3	5.9	23.8	30.2	16.1	1.4	79.9	43.5	52.2	47.8
55784	SWAN RIVER	97.5	97.6	0.0	0.0	0.0	0.0	0.6	0.6	5.7	5.7	6.3	6.6	5.4	23.8	29.2	16.0	1.2	78.0	43.0	53.3	46.7
55785	SWATARA	97.1	97.2	0.4	0.4	0.0	0.0	1.2	1.0	5.2	5.2	7.3	8.3	5.5	22.5	30.5	14.5	1.0	76.8	42.4	50.9	49.1
55787	TAMARACK	92.7	92.3	0.2	0.3	0.2	0.2	0.4	0.6	4.2	4.5	6.2	5.7	4.8	18.9	30.6	23.0	2.2	81.6	49.0	50.1	49.9
55790	TOWER	93.3	93.3	0.2	0.2	0.5	0.6	0.8	1.0	3.6	4.2	5.1	5.2	4.3	20.1	37.9	17.8	1.8	83.6	48.9	51.9	48.2
55792	VIRGINIA	95.6	95.3	0.4	0.5	0.5	0.6	0.8	0.9	4.7	4.7	5.2	6.4	6.9	23.3	28.4	15.9	4.6	81.8	44.2	47.7	52.3
55793	WARBA	98.0	97.9	0.2	0.2	0.0	0.0	0.8	1.0	5.5	4.6	7.3	7.1	6.7	23.3	31.1	13.7	0.8	78.4	42.6	52.3	47.7
55795	WILLOW RIVER	96.0	95.6	1.2	1.4	0.2	0.2	1.1	1.4	5.7	6.2	6.5	6.5	5.8	25.2	28.8	14.2	1.1	77.6	41.2	51.5	48.5
55797	WRENSHALL	95.8	95.5	0.2	0.2	0.3	0.3	0.4	0.4	5.5	5.8	6.4	7.8	5.9	25.8	27.7	11.3	3.9	77.3	41.2	51.2	48.8
55798	WRIGHT	97.5	97.3	0.2	0.1	0.2	0.1	0.6	0.9	6.6	6.7	6.4	5.7	5.3	21.8	25.6	18.1	3.9	76.4	43.4	50.4	49.6
55801	DULUTH	97.5	100.0	0.0	0.0	0.0	0.0	0.0	0.0	5.8	7.7	7.7	7.7	3.9	30.8	28.9	7.7	0.0	76.9	38.0	53.9	46.2
55802	DULUTH	91.8	91.2	1.7	2.0	1.1	1.2	1.2	1.5	1.9	1.7	2.6	2.9	5.5	19.6	31.5	24.9	9.7	92.4	55.1	44.1	55.9
55803	DULUTH	97.4	97.0	0.3	0.4	0.7	0.9	0.5	0.7	5.5	6.5	7.7	7.0	5.3	25.7	30.0	10.9	1.4	75.5	40.7	50.5	49.5
55804	DULUTH	97.1	96.7	0.3	0.4	0.7	0.9	0.7	0.8	5.9	6.4	7.0	7.0	5.4	23.9	29.5	12.2	2.8	76.1	41.6	48.0	52.0
55805	DULUTH	84.0	82.1	4.4	5.4	2.0	2.4	1.7	1.9	6.7	4.8	5.2	5.9	18.8	30.3	18.2	7.7	2.3	80.5	28.8	49.6	50.4
55806	DULUTH	86.2	84.9	3.1	3.8	1.1	1.4	1.4	1.7	7.3	5.8	6.4	7.9	10.3	30.6	22.0	8.1	1.8	76.2	32.2	49.2	50.8
55807	DULUTH	94.1	93.6	0.8	1.0	0.7	0.8	0.8	0.9	6.0	5.8	6.7	6.4	7.1	27.8	24.4	13.1	2.8	77.8	38.2	48.1	51.9
55808	DULUTH	95.4	95.0	0.3	0.3	0.3	0.4	0.7	0.8	7.0	6.5	7.0	7.3	7.2	27.4	22.8	12.6	2.2	75.1	36.6	49.1	50.9
55810	DULUTH	97.2	96.9	0.1	0.1	0.3	0.4	0.5	0.7	5.5	6.2	7.0	7.1	5.4	25.8	27.3	13.4	2.2	76.7	40.6	48.6	51.4
55811	DULUTH	95.1	94.3	1.5	2.0	0.9	1.1	1.1	1.3	4.5	5.0	5.8	8.7	9.6	24.3	25.2	13.5	3.3	81.0	39.5	49.2	50.8
55812	DULUTH	94.2	93.4	0.9	1.1	1.8	2.2	1.1	1.2	3.7	3.5	4.2	18.5	22.8	20.3	17.9	7.0	2.1	85.6	24.4	49.2	50.8
55901	ROCHESTER	88.4	86.4	2.7	3.3	6.0	7.1	2.4	2.9	7.9	7.5	7.2	6.7	7.2	31.9	20.9	8.6	2.2	73.1	34.1	48.1	51.9
55902	ROCHESTER	91.9	90.3	1.7	2.1	4.1	4.9	2.6	3.1	6.6	6.9	7.4	6.8	5.8	28.1	26.1	10.7	1.6	74.5	38.2	48.9	51.1
55904	ROCHESTER	85.1	82.6	5.8	7.2	4.8	5.5	4.1	4.7	7.4	6.8	6.7	7.1	8.3	31.4	23.3	8.0	1.0	75.0	34.1	50.4	49.6
55906	ROCHESTER	90.4	88.9	2.5	3.0	4.8	5.6	1.8	2.1	6.3	6.4	7.6	7.2	6.0	26.1	27.5	11.4	1.5	74.9	39.2	49.4	50.6
55909	ADAMS	99.2	99.0	0.1	0.2	0.2	0.3	0.6	0.7	6.4	6.8	8.8	7.2	5.0	24.1	22.4	15.5	4.0	73.5	39.7	51.0	49.0
55910	ALTURA	99.0	98.9	0.2	0.3	0.3	0.3	0.4	0.5	7.2	7.6	8.0	7.3	6.5	25.7	25.8	10.7	1.3	72.8	37.5	53.1	46.9
55912	AUSTIN	93.1	91.8	0.8	0.9	2.1	2.5	5.7	6.7	6.5	6.1	6.4	6.3	6.9	24.4	23.2	16.3	3.9	77.2	40.2	48.9	51.1
55917	BLOOMING PRAIRIE	96.7	96.1	0.2	0.2	0.5	0.6	3.9	4.8	6.7	6.7	7.4	6.9	6.1	25.8	22.5	14.8	3.1	74.4	38.5	49.0	51.0
55918	BROWNSDALE	96.0	95.4	0.2	0.2	0.0	0.0	3.8	4.6	5.6	5.6	7.1	7.5	7.9	23.2	26.0	15.2	2.0	77.3	40.4	51.3	48.7
55919	BROWNSVILLE	99.1	98.9	0.2	0.2	0.2	0.3	0.5	0.6	6.2	6.9	8.2	7.1	6.7	25.9	28.4	9.4	1.1	74.1	38.6	52.2	47.8
55920	BYRON	98.1	97.6	0.3	0.3	0.6	0.8	0.7	0.9	7.4	7.4	8.9	8.0	7.1	28.4	25.3	6.9	0.6	71.3	34.3	49.7	50.3
55921	CALEDONIA	98.6	98.3	0.3	0.4	0.2	0.2	0.7	0.9	6.0	6.1	7.5	7.7	6.7	23.5	24.8	14.5	3.4	75.2	39.8	49.2	50.9
55922	CANTON	98.8	98.6	0.1	0.1	0.1	0.1	1.1	1.5	9.8	9.4	8.8	7.9	6.7	22.2	22.7	11.3	1.3	67.0	31.8	50.6	49.4
55923	CHATFIELD	98.5	98.3	0.5	0.6	0.2	0.2	0.7	0.8	6.3	6.8	7.4	6.4	6.2	26.5	23.6	13.5	3.3	75.4	39.1	49.6	50.4
55924	CLAREMONT	93.1	91.7	0.0	0.0	0.1	0.1	7.5	9.2	7.8	7.8	7.8	6.8	6.2	29.1	22.4	10.9	1.2	72.3	35.5	52.5	47.5
55925	DAKOTA	98.7	98.7	0.0	0.0	0.1	0.1	1.0	1.2	5.8	6.6	7.9	7.0	5.4	25.7	29.6	11.0	1.0	74.8	40.5	52.4	47.6
55926	DEXTER	97.6	97.3	0.3	0.3	0.5	0.5	0.6	0.8	8.0	8.3	8.8	6.6	5.2	27.2	22.7	12.0	1.4	70.2	37.1	48.0	52.0
55927	DODGE CENTER	94.6	93.6	0.2	0.3	0.4	0.5	4.6	5.8	7.7	7.5	7.7	7.6	6.8	28.4	22.4	9.8	2.0	72.3	34.7	49.6	50.4
55929	DOVER	98.1	97.9	0.3	0.3	0.2	0.2	1.2	1.6	5.9	6.6	8.7	8.9	6.5	25.6	26.7	9.9	1.2	72.4	37.0	52.2	47.8
55932	ELGIN	98.7	98.5	0.1	0.1	0.2	0.3	0.8	1.0	7.3	8.1	9.5	7.4	6.7	28.0	23.3	8.4	1.2	70.3	34.6	51.8	48.2
55933	ELKTON	99.2	99.0	0.0	0.0	0.4	0.4	0.8	0.8	6.2	6.4	8.4	6.6	5.8	23.7	22.5	16.1	4.4	74.9	40.5	50.4	49.6
55934	EYOTA	98.1	97.7	0.2	0.3	0.4	0.6	0.7	1.0	7.0	7.4	8.4	7.9	6.6	28.2	24.9	8.5	1.2	72.1	35.3	49.8	50.2
55935	FOUNTAIN	99.1	99.1	0.2	0.1	0.2	0.1	0.5	0.5	7.3	6.9	6.1	6.1	6.6	26.4	27.7	11.7	1.4	76.2	38.5	52.5	47.5
55936	GRAND MEADOW	98.9	98.8	0.0	0.0	0.2	0.2	0.5	0.6	6.8	6.8	7.2	7.3	6.6	26.1	23.4	12.8	3.0	74.6	38.0	49.8	50.2
55939	HARMONY	99.2	99.0	0.1	0.1	0.1	0.2	0.5	0.6	6.3	6.7	8.4	7.3	6.1	21.3	23.5	16.3	4.1	73.3	40.8	50.0	50.0
55940	HAYFIELD	97.9	97.5	0.2	0.3	0.7	0.8	1.8	2.1	6.5	7.2	7.6	8.0	6.9	24.4	23.9	11.6	3.9	73.2	38.4	49.4	50.6
55941	HOKAH	98.8	98.6	0.2	0.3	0.2	0.3	0.4	0.3	5.8	6.6	8.3	7.2	6.3	26.5	29.4	9.0	1.0	74.9	39.0	51.3	48.8
55943	HOUSTON	98.7	98.6	0.3	0.4	0.2	0.3	0.6	0.6	5.3	6.3	7.5	6.6	5.7	26.0	27.9	12.3	2.3	76.5	40.4	50.5	49.5
55944	KASSON	97.6	97.0	0.3	0.4	0.6	0.7	2.0	2.5	8.3	7.7	8.4	6.6	7.4	28.1	22.3	9.5	1.7	71.3	34.8	48.7	51.4
55945	KELLOGG	98.7	98.5	0.0	0.0	0.3	0.4	1.1	1.2	5.2	6.0	7.7	7.5	5.6	24.0	29.5	13.1	1.4	76.3	41.3	51.5	48.6
55946	KENYON	97.3	96.8	0.1	0.1	0.8	0.9	1.8	2.2	7.1	7.0	7.1	6.9	6.4	27.2	23.8	11.9	2.7	74.2	37.9	51.0	49.0
55947	LA CRESCENT	98.0	97.6	0.4	0.5	0.7	0.8	0.7	0.8	6.4	6.6	7.7	7.6	6.2	24.9	26.4	12.2	2.0	74.2	39.7	49.3	50.8
55949	LANESBORO	99.1	99.1	0.1	0.1	0.2	0.2	0.2	0.2	5.1	5.7	6.2	6.0	5.8	23.1	28.4	16.6	3.1	79.0	43.7	50.0	50.0
55951	LE ROY	99.3	99.1	0.1	0.1	0.1	0.2	0.6	0.9	5.5	6.0	8.3	7.7	6.4	25.1	24.5	13.4	3.1	75.3	39.8	51.3	48.7
55952	LEWISTON	98.7	98.6	0.3	0.5	0.1	0.2	1.1	1.4	8.6	8.3	8.1	7.5	6.5	27.1	22.0	10.1	1.9	70.2	34.8	50.6	49.5
55953	LYLE	99.4	99.3	0.0	0.0	0.2	0.2	0.3	0.3	6.0	6.2	7.9	7.6	7.9	24.4	26.1	12.3	1.6	75.4	39.1	52.4	47.6
55954	MABEL	99.0	98.9	0.0	0.0	0.1	0.1	0.4	0.4	4.8	6.8	7.8	6.5	5.6	19.9	25.3	19.0	4.5	76.0	44.1	47.8	52.2
55955	MANTORVILLE	98.4	98.1	0.0	0.0	0.2	0.2	0.8	0.9	9.5	9.5	9.9	7.7	6.5	28.6	21.9	5.4	1.0	66.3	32.2	49.8	50.2
55956	MAZEPPA	98.3	98.1	0.4	0.6	0.2	0.2	0.4	0.5	5.8	6.9	8.5	7.5	5.3	27.5	26.6	10.1	1.7	74.0	38.5	50.8	49.2
55957	MILLVILLE	98.1	97.9	0.0	0.0	0.2	0.2	1.5	1.8	6.7	8.9	9.7	8.0	6.9	28.1	21.5	9.3	1.0	68.9	34.2	52.8	47.2
55959	MINNESOTA CITY	97.4	96.9	0.5	0.6	1.1	1.2	0.6	0.8	6.4	6.9	7.0	6.9	6.3	28.0	28.3	9.1	1.1	75.6	37.5	51.2	48.8
55960	ORONOCO	95.6	94.7	1.2	1.6	1.5	1.8	1.7	2.0	6.7	7.3	8.1	7.4	5.3	28.1	28.3	8.1	0.7	73.2	38.0	51.5	48.5
55961	OSTRANDER	99.3	99.2	0.2	0.2	0.3	0.3	0.5	0.7	7.4	7.5	7.2	5.9	5.2	23.6	24.8	16.3	2.2	74.4	39.6	52.1	47.9
55962	PETERSON	99.0	98.8	0.0	0.0	0.2	0.3	0.4	0.5	5.6	5.8	6.9	7.1	5.9	24.0	28.2	14.2	2.5	76.9	41.8	51.2	48.8
55963	PINE ISLAND	98.1	97.7	0.2	0.3	0.4	0.5	0.6	0.8	6.4	6.8	7.6	7.4	6.6	25.8	27.2	10.2	2.1	74.4	39.2	49.7	50.3
55964	PLAINVIEW	97.1	96.5	0.0	0.0	0.1	0.1	4.6	5.7	7.8	7.3	7.4	7.6	7.8	28.0	20.1	10.8	3.1	72.7	34.2	49.0	51.0
55965	PRESTON	98.9	98.7	0.1	0.1	0.2	0.2	0.6	0.7	5.5	6.3	7.3	7.0	6.3	22.3	24.2	16.8	4.2	75.9	41.5	51.0	49.1
55967	RACINE	98.5	98.4	0.3	0.3	0.1	0.1	0.4	0.4	6.4	7.1	9.7	7.3	5.9	27.9	25.4	9.0	1.4	72.1	37.5	49.3	50.7
55968	READS LANDING	98.8	100.0	0.0	0.0	0.0	0.0	1.2	1.2	4.8	6.0	8.3	9.5	4.8	25.0	29.8	11.9	0.0	72.6	40.6	50.0	50.0
55969	ROLLINGSTONE	98.8	98.8	0.2	0.2	0.3	0.3	0.5	0.6	6.7	7.1	7.5	6.6	6.2	26.6	26.3	11.9	1.2	74.6	38.9	52.2	47.8
55970	ROSE CREEK	97.6	97.2	0.1	0.2	0.3	0.5	2.2	2.6	5.6	6.1	7.6	6.5	6.7	24.0	27.4	14.1	2.1	76.9	41.0	51.0	49.0
55971	RUSHFORD	99.0	98.8	0.2	0.2	0.2	0.4	0.2	0.2	5.8	6.0	7.0	6.8	5.6	23.8	25.4	15.1	4.6	76.7	41.5	47.8	52.2
55972	SAINT CHARLES	93.7	92.8	0.7	0.8	2.7	3.1	3.8	4.4	8.5	8.1	8.3	8.0	7.0	26.2	21.2	10.8	2.1	70.0	33.3	49.5	50.5
55973	SARGEANT	97.5	97.5	0.3	0.3	0.3	0.3	0.5	0.7	7.9	8.4	8.9	6.5	5.2	26.6	22.8	12.2	1.5	70.0	37.2	47.6	52.4
55974	SPRING GROVE	99.0	98.8	0.2	0.3	0.3	0.3	0.7	0.9	5.1	5.6	7.4	6.9	5.8	23.3	27.5	14.2	4.1	77.2	42.1	50.8	49.2
55975	SPRING VALLEY	99.0	98.8	0.2	0.2	0.1	0.1	0.5	0.5	5.7	6.1	7.6	7.1	6.6	24.9	25.3	13.8	2.8	76.1	39.4	49.2	50.9
55976	STEWARTVILLE	97.6	97.1	0.6	0.8	0.5	0.6	0.9	1.2	7.8	7.4	7.7	7.8	7.0	27.8	22.5	9.5	2.4	72.1	34.6	48.3	51.7
55977	TAOPI	99.2	99.3	0.3	0.2	0.0	0.0	0.0	0.0	7.4	8.3	10.4	9.0	3.8	26.5	23.5	10.4	0.7	67.8	35.9	53.6	46.5
55979	UTICA	98.3	97.9	0.5	0.6	0.2	0.3	1.6	1.8	9.5	9.0	8.6	7.5	6.0	27.2	20.6	10.1	1.7	67.9	33.3	49.8	50.2
55981	WABASHA	98.4	98.3	0.4	0.6	0.1	0.2	0.4	0.4	5.1	5.3	6.4	6.6	5.6	21.9	28.5	16.9	3.9	78.9	44.5	48.8	51.2
55982	WALTHAM	97.9	97.6	0.3	0.5	0.2	0.2	2.1	2.6	5.7	6.7	9.8	8.0	5.7	25.0	24.2	13.5	1.5	72.4	38.9	52.4	47.6
55983	WANAMINGO	98.6	98.4	0.1	0.1	0.4	0.5	0.3	0.5	7.7	7.3	6.6	7.4	5.9	27.0	23.0	12.8	2.5	73.4	37.6	51.2	48.9
55985	WEST CONCORD	96.7	96.1	0.1	0.1	0.2	0.3	3.2	4.0	7.1	7.1	7.7	7.3	6.8	26.9	23.4	11.9	1.8	73.3	36.6	49.9	50.1
55987	WINONA	95.4	94.4	0.9	1.2	2.2	2.7	1.2	1.5	5.1	5.1	5.6	10.3	13.2	25.4	21.9	10.8	2.6	80.8	32.4	48.1	51.9
55990	WYKOFF	98.5	98.3	0.3	0.4	0.1	0.1	0.5	0.7	4.9	5.2	6.2	6.4	5.8	25.6	28.7	14.7	2.6	79.8	42.4	50.8	49.2
55991	ZUMBRO FALLS	98.3	97.9	0.4	0.5	0.4	0.6	0.6	0.7	5.8	6.5	7.9	7.6	5.7	29.7	27.6	8.6	0.7	74.8	38.2	51.4	48.6
55992	ZUMBROTA	97.1	96.6	0.6	0.8	0.6	0.7	1.0	1.2	6.5	6.7	7.7	7.5	6.7	25.3	24.4	12.5	2.8	74.4	38.9	49.4	50.6
	MINNESOTA	89.5	88.0	3.5	4.2	2.9	3.4	2.9	3.4	6.8	6.8	7.2	7.3	7.4	28.6	23.9	10.1	1.9	74.9	36.1	49.6	50.5
	UNITED STATES	75.1	73.6	12.3	12.5	3.8	4.2	12.5	14.1	6.9	6.7	7.2	7.0	7.3	28.6	23.8	10.8	1.7	75.1	36.0	49.1	50.9

#	POST OFFICE NAME	2004 Per Capita Income	2004 HH Income Base	2004 HOUSEHOLD INCOME DISTRIBUTION (%) Less than $25,000	$25,000 to $49,999	$50,000 to $99,999	$100,000 to $149,999	$150,000 or More	MEDIAN HOUSEHOLD INCOME 2004	2009	2004 National Centile	2004 State Centile	2004 Home Value Base	2004 HOME VALUE DISTRIBUTION (%) Less than $50,000	$50,000 to $89,999	$90,000 to $174,999	$175,000 to $399,999	$400,000 or More	2004 Median Home Value
55768	MOUNTAIN IRON	21605	1159	31.4	29.2	32.0	5.9	1.6	38828	48110	42	21	856	19.0	32.9	38.3	9.7	0.0	87344
55769	NASHWAUK	19546	1521	33.2	33.5	27.4	5.4	0.5	36733	44513	34	13	1260	28.8	33.1	29.4	8.3	0.4	72299
55771	ORR	21375	782	31.1	32.4	27.9	5.8	2.9	39770	49221	45	25	654	18.7	29.1	31.4	15.1	5.8	92727
55775	PENGILLY	29168	557	25.0	23.5	36.8	9.5	5.2	51520	61359	75	69	514	10.3	28.2	38.7	21.2	1.6	109375
55779	SAGINAW	24570	1341	15.2	25.2	42.8	12.5	4.3	59344	72415	84	81	1269	7.8	15.0	45.1	31.1	1.0	139418
55780	SAWYER	12025	29	37.9	27.6	27.6	6.9	0.0	33610	38629	23	5	23	8.7	17.4	47.8	26.1	0.0	122500
55781	SIDE LAKE	26527	190	16.8	33.2	39.5	7.4	3.2	50000	59405	72	66	183	8.2	24.0	38.8	26.2	2.7	120982
55783	STURGEON LAKE	22588	1100	28.6	29.2	31.3	7.9	3.1	43483	51909	57	43	993	15.9	19.4	40.1	22.6	2.0	118563
55784	SWAN RIVER	17888	126	29.4	28.6	36.5	4.0	1.6	43775	52281	58	44	120	12.5	24.2	49.2	14.2	0.0	109783
55785	SWATARA	18117	109	32.1	33.9	24.8	4.6	4.6	35963	44605	31	11	96	22.9	20.8	41.7	13.5	1.0	100000
55787	TAMARACK	21116	290	35.9	32.1	24.5	4.5	3.1	34053	40375	24	6	250	15.6	21.2	36.4	24.8	2.0	117241
55790	TOWER	26505	1107	25.5	25.8	36.7	8.8	3.3	48605	60950	69	62	977	12.7	24.1	28.6	24.7	10.0	118295
55792	VIRGINIA	22386	5162	35.9	28.8	27.7	6.0	1.6	36638	45008	34	13	3373	17.9	42.8	33.3	5.4	0.5	77868
55793	WARBA	20192	223	28.3	30.5	35.9	4.0	1.4	42678	50328	55	38	204	15.2	27.5	47.1	10.3	0.0	100000
55795	WILLOW RIVER	21755	548	28.8	30.5	31.8	6.2	2.7	42447	50599	54	37	485	16.7	21.0	40.8	19.8	1.7	112862
55797	WRENSHALL	23310	508	21.3	30.5	38.2	8.3	1.8	48330	57719	69	61	448	9.8	18.1	45.8	24.3	2.0	125000
55798	WRIGHT	18967	267	28.1	34.8	30.0	5.2	1.9	38973	46750	43	22	228	14.5	20.6	46.5	18.4	0.0	118939
55801	DULUTH	23122	19	21.1	26.3	36.8	15.8	0.0	54641	60000	79	76	18	0.0	16.7	33.3	50.0	0.0	175000
55802	DULUTH	23974	1382	55.6	16.0	20.3	5.5	2.5	19639	22260	2	1	385	0.3	4.4	30.9	61.8	2.6	197024
55803	DULUTH	28971	6475	14.9	25.0	38.3	15.4	6.4	61857	76968	86	84	6011	4.5	12.1	51.6	29.5	2.3	139129
55804	DULUTH	30668	5673	17.1	25.2	36.3	14.4	7.1	57873	71940	83	80	5122	1.9	13.6	57.5	23.9	3.1	130781
55805	DULUTH	17668	5342	47.3	31.2	16.9	3.0	1.5	26406	32712	6	1	1944	12.3	48.9	33.5	4.5	0.8	79498
55806	DULUTH	17618	4471	44.6	30.3	20.6	3.4	1.1	28681	35959	10	2	2157	13.2	44.3	36.5	5.9	0.1	83214
55807	DULUTH	21359	4523	30.9	36.0	26.4	5.1	1.6	37517	46564	38	16	3158	9.7	46.2	40.1	3.7	0.4	85327
55808	DULUTH	20041	2523	30.2	34.6	28.8	5.1	1.2	38074	46778	40	19	1906	25.0	29.0	43.8	2.3	0.0	84718
55810	DULUTH	23977	3341	21.6	29.5	35.3	10.8	2.8	49091	59558	70	64	3020	12.7	20.7	51.6	13.9	1.1	111132
55811	DULUTH	25246	9416	21.1	25.4	37.3	12.0	4.3	52956	64868	77	72	7586	4.2	11.9	59.0	22.9	2.0	128568
55812	DULUTH	28101	3848	27.9	28.1	25.5	10.0	8.5	44308	54576	59	46	2095	0.7	12.4	56.0	27.1	3.8	136107
55901	ROCHESTER	30734	19238	14.7	23.3	37.1	17.2	7.8	63880	82502	88	86	14011	1.6	7.5	58.8	30.2	1.9	150665
55902	ROCHESTER	44953	8164	13.2	19.4	29.6	17.1	20.7	75112	104920	93	93	6095	3.1	4.8	34.7	45.2	12.3	194099
55904	ROCHESTER	25631	9918	18.9	27.1	39.2	9.9	5.0	53563	67639	78	74	7283	8.0	15.2	58.3	17.8	0.7	119573
55906	ROCHESTER	34453	7153	16.0	23.7	32.9	14.8	12.6	62676	83464	87	84	5695	6.6	10.2	42.5	36.0	4.8	153094
55909	ADAMS	19605	485	26.0	34.6	30.9	5.8	2.7	41322	48824	51	32	402	11.2	22.9	42.0	18.9	5.0	113406
55910	ALTURA	23195	1076	19.3	31.0	36.4	9.3	3.9	49722	58599	71	65	916	5.6	10.0	40.7	34.2	9.5	157099
55912	AUSTIN	25705	11617	28.8	31.1	28.8	7.3	4.0	40866	50108	49	30	8858	11.5	28.7	44.0	14.4	1.3	101523
55917	BLOOMING PRAIRIE	22861	1307	19.7	30.3	39.6	8.2	2.3	50026	58840	72	66	1111	5.1	16.0	51.8	23.9	3.2	130048
55918	BROWNSDALE	20567	527	27.3	28.3	34.5	9.5	0.4	45596	54524	63	52	439	15.5	17.5	49.7	14.8	2.5	109559
55919	BROWNSVILLE	22713	476	22.3	29.6	37.4	6.3	4.4	48147	57438	69	60	419	12.7	26.3	35.6	21.2	4.3	109073
55920	BYRON	29294	2277	10.3	21.4	44.9	17.7	5.6	68410	85381	91	90	1991	2.9	5.1	51.7	36.8	3.5	159526
55921	CALEDONIA	20710	2114	28.1	31.2	32.0	5.4	3.3	42097	50517	53	36	1690	12.8	31.2	39.8	14.0	2.3	96871
55922	CANTON	14814	460	35.4	31.5	23.9	6.1	3.0	35552	41181	30	9	390	22.1	18.7	38.0	17.4	3.9	106034
55923	CHATFIELD	25325	1890	19.5	27.5	39.7	9.6	3.7	52652	63864	76	71	1552	5.9	9.7	51.4	27.5	5.5	142520
55924	CLAREMONT	21793	482	21.0	28.6	38.4	8.7	3.3	50307	58446	72	67	403	9.9	13.7	43.4	28.8	4.2	134423
55925	DAKOTA	25586	276	17.0	28.6	38.0	10.1	6.2	53818	65735	78	75	255	8.2	12.6	36.9	31.8	10.6	153804
55926	DEXTER	24482	239	25.9	27.6	34.7	6.7	5.0	45691	54102	63	53	199	12.6	16.1	41.2	22.6	7.5	124632
55927	DODGE CENTER	21727	1443	18.9	29.3	40.2	9.2	2.5	51447	60795	75	69	1227	8.6	14.5	52.2	23.6	1.2	128125
55929	DOVER	23726	383	18.3	29.2	40.5	8.4	3.7	51644	63358	75	70	315	5.1	11.4	40.0	35.6	7.9	156696
55932	ELGIN	24686	738	15.7	26.4	43.4	10.7	3.8	55722	65707	80	78	623	5.3	11.1	44.5	33.7	5.5	146811
55933	ELKTON	20744	172	25.0	32.0	33.1	7.0	2.9	43189	51242	56	41	139	10.1	22.3	42.5	19.4	5.8	116848
55934	EYOTA	26558	1123	13.5	26.2	41.1	13.6	5.6	60038	76703	84	82	951	5.3	13.1	50.6	27.6	3.5	137054
55935	FOUNTAIN	23532	289	16.3	30.8	38.8	12.5	1.7	52355	61866	76	71	252	4.4	16.7	36.1	32.5	10.3	156250
55936	GRAND MEADOW	26781	666	20.7	28.1	37.4	9.5	4.4	50906	61730	74	68	542	6.1	19.9	44.3	23.1	6.6	122368
55939	HARMONY	17998	928	32.3	32.4	27.8	5.3	2.2	37976	45072	39	18	755	12.9	24.5	42.5	17.0	3.2	107880
55940	HAYFIELD	22363	960	17.1	29.7	39.8	11.2	2.3	52076	63313	76	70	804	8.3	11.6	47.0	28.2	4.9	137815
55941	HOKAH	25106	537	17.9	26.1	42.8	9.3	3.9	55216	66094	80	77	473	7.4	16.7	47.4	25.6	3.0	129792
55943	HOUSTON	21022	1376	24.1	33.2	33.5	6.3	3.0	44599	52311	60	48	1166	11.6	19.7	39.8	22.9	6.0	118140
55944	KASSON	24050	2453	16.0	26.7	42.3	11.7	3.3	58095	67451	83	80	2091	9.3	8.7	44.5	34.7	2.7	149539
55945	KELLOGG	24842	440	17.5	32.1	35.7	10.2	4.6	50417	60128	73	67	388	7.7	15.0	37.1	33.3	7.0	147826
55946	KENYON	23757	1374	17.0	28.5	41.7	9.6	3.3	53302	64035	77	73	1153	5.7	9.8	43.0	33.2	8.2	154307
55947	LA CRESCENT	26621	2993	16.3	27.2	39.3	12.9	4.3	56211	67779	81	78	2412	6.3	9.3	55.4	25.9	3.2	135623
55949	LANESBORO	21558	633	30.8	30.7	30.0	6.5	2.1	40320	48275	47	27	480	8.5	20.2	44.6	21.3	5.4	123547
55951	LE ROY	23626	629	21.3	36.9	33.7	5.1	3.0	43050	51674	56	40	523	16.4	27.0	40.3	12.6	3.6	96635
55952	LEWISTON	22183	869	19.5	28.9	40.6	7.4	3.7	50981	60423	74	68	743	10.1	10.1	43.1	30.7	6.1	141272
55953	LYLE	20724	444	20.1	35.1	33.3	7.7	3.8	45670	55271	63	53	360	10.6	16.1	51.9	16.4	5.0	117857
55954	MABEL	18840	656	33.2	38.6	22.3	4.3	1.7	34209	40910	25	7	553	17.9	32.0	38.0	9.2	2.9	90143
55955	MANTORVILLE	27567	695	10.7	18.9	42.2	17.8	10.5	70050	82979	91	90	638	3.0	3.5	33.5	49.1	11.0	202551
55956	MAZEPPA	24284	760	18.6	27.6	39.2	10.5	4.1	53132	64091	77	72	675	12.3	9.8	38.5	34.1	5.3	148307
55957	MILLVILLE	20653	220	19.1	35.5	37.7	5.9	1.8	45413	53008	62	52	182	5.0	9.9	41.8	31.9	11.5	151923
55959	MINNESOTA CITY	26401	418	15.8	25.4	40.7	13.9	4.3	58602	70093	83	81	378	14.6	10.1	38.6	35.7	1.1	143137
55960	ORONOCO	35441	1314	11.6	21.3	37.8	17.1	12.2	66489	88755	89	88	1211	16.1	7.4	26.1	43.1	7.3	176114
55961	OSTRANDER	24437	239	25.5	26.8	36.8	6.3	4.6	47133	53776	66	57	204	14.7	17.2	38.2	25.0	4.9	124074
55962	PETERSON	18973	364	22.5	35.2	32.7	6.6	3.0	44355	51344	60	47	297	10.1	14.5	36.4	29.6	9.4	146591
55963	PINE ISLAND	26265	1825	16.1	23.6	39.4	14.4	6.6	61260	76186	86	83	1608	8.8	7.3	38.7	40.5	4.6	163382
55964	PLAINVIEW	21563	1455	20.8	30.5	37.5	8.7	2.5	48491	57628	69	62	1206	10.3	12.2	51.5	24.3	1.7	130230
55965	PRESTON	23255	719	27.4	28.0	35.1	7.1	2.5	45274	52587	62	51	576	8.9	20.0	44.8	21.7	4.7	122500
55967	RACINE	23815	413	11.6	27.4	45.0	13.6	2.4	59141	71776	84	81	363	3.0	5.8	48.8	36.9	5.5	154779
55968	READS LANDING	28980	38	13.2	34.2	39.5	7.9	5.3	52962	63172	77	72	32	0.0	12.5	50.0	31.3	6.3	143750
55969	ROLLINGSTONE	25286	404	20.3	24.8	40.1	11.1	3.7	53489	64368	78	74	359	5.3	7.8	47.6	34.8	4.5	153611
55970	ROSE CREEK	26337	460	17.2	27.4	39.8	12.0	3.7	54501	66969	79	75	399	5.8	17.8	46.4	25.6	4.5	128074
55971	RUSHFORD	20752	1242	26.9	30.8	35.1	6.0	1.3	44935	52369	61	49	991	8.3	21.6	46.2	21.1	2.8	117770
55972	SAINT CHARLES	22286	1712	19.7	29.0	37.9	9.5	3.8	51157	61923	74	69	1325	7.4	9.1	46.6	32.9	4.0	143167
55973	SARGEANT	21385	131	26.7	27.5	33.6	6.9	5.3	45380	55395	62	52	109	11.9	15.6	43.1	22.0	7.3	123214
55974	SPRING GROVE	21976	1000	30.2	35.8	26.2	4.7	3.1	39465	46456	44	24	833	15.3	34.8	28.5	19.2	2.3	89919
55975	SPRING VALLEY	21016	1909	24.9	32.5	33.9	6.3	2.4	43590	50697	58	43	1545	10.6	18.7	45.0	21.8	4.0	124567
55976	STEWARTVILLE	24702	2751	17.8	26.4	39.6	12.8	3.4	55100	70114	80	77	2204	14.6	8.9	52.5	22.7	1.4	126529
55977	TAOPI	21023	146	19.9	31.5	36.3	8.2	4.1	48789	58273	70	63	132	9.1	15.2	30.3	33.3	12.1	153571
55979	UTICA	21666	219	19.2	29.2	38.8	8.2	4.6	50977	60529	74	68	186	12.4	9.1	36.0	33.9	8.6	146591
55981	WABASHA	26021	1800	25.2	30.9	31.4	7.9	4.6	45000	53840	61	50	1461	7.0	18.6	43.1	28.3	3.1	127679
55982	WALTHAM	24626	216	20.4	33.8	35.7	4.6	5.6	47456	55691	67	58	194	8.3	12.9	50.0	25.8	3.1	132258
55983	WANAMINGO	22855	582	22.9	27.0	36.8	10.0	3.4	50107	60600	72	66	495	8.7	8.9	48.5	29.3	4.7	144242
55985	WEST CONCORD	23148	846	21.6	25.8	39.5	10.3	2.8	52229	62047	76	71	732	4.2	18.0	46.6	26.5	4.6	134951
55987	WINONA	23041	14277	27.6	29.8	31.0	8.1	3.5	42865	51858	56	39	9859	7.1	12.1	51.4	27.1	2.3	134176
55990	WYKOFF	23579	409	23.2	37.2	30.3	4.9	4.4	42755	49903	55	39	351	12.8	23.1	39.6	19.1	5.4	114509
55991	ZUMBRO FALLS	27146	761	18.3	23.4	38.4	13.9	6.0	58763	72985	83	81	668	8.7	12.3	29.6	41.8	7.6	172674
55992	ZUMBROTA	29332	1847	16.9	27.1	38.1	11.5	6.4	56568	69556	81	79	1476	6.0	4.5	44.0	39.8	5.7	165483
	MINNESOTA	29624		18.6	25.2	34.9	14.0	7.4	56724	71660				6.6	9.7	36.5	40.5	6.8	168676
	UNITED STATES	25866		24.7	27.1	30.8	10.9	6.5	48124	56710				10.9	15.0	33.7	30.1	10.4	145905

ZIP CODE #	POST OFFICE NAME	FINANCIAL SERVICES: Auto Loan	FINANCIAL SERVICES: Home Loan	FINANCIAL SERVICES: Invest-ments	FINANCIAL SERVICES: Retire-ment Plans	THE HOME: Home Improvements: Home Repair	THE HOME: Home Improvements: Lawn & Garden	THE HOME: Furnishings: Comput-ers & Hard-ware	THE HOME: Furnishings: Major Appli-ances	THE HOME: Furnishings: TV, Radio, Sound Equip-ment	THE HOME: Furnishings: Furni-ture	ENTERTAINMENT: Dine out/ Carry out	ENTERTAINMENT: Sports Equip-ment	ENTERTAINMENT: Fees & Tickets	ENTERTAINMENT: Toys & Games	ENTERTAINMENT: Travel	ENTERTAINMENT: Cable TV	PERSONAL: Apparel & Services	PERSONAL: Auto Repairs	PERSONAL: Health Insur-ance	PERSONAL: Pets & Supplies
55768	MOUNTAIN IRON	70	66	59	64	68	76	67	70	69	64	84	79	65	84	67	71	80	69	75	80
55769	NASHWAUK	74	55	35	52	61	72	58	66	65	56	77	76	51	74	59	69	71	66	79	84
55771	ORR	84	66	45	59	74	83	62	75	70	61	83	87	55	82	66	75	77	73	88	102
55775	PENGILLY	86	98	107	93	98	107	93	94	93	92	116	105	98	120	97	96	113	92	96	103
55779	SAGINAW	99	101	92	99	102	105	93	97	92	93	114	115	94	117	94	91	111	95	96	116
55780	SAWYER	69	58	45	58	61	69	60	64	64	59	77	73	57	77	60	65	72	63	70	76
55781	SIDE LAKE	104	82	56	74	92	104	77	93	87	76	103	109	69	102	82	93	96	92	110	127
55783	STURGEON LAKE	90	72	51	67	79	89	70	81	77	69	92	94	64	91	73	81	86	80	93	106
55784	SWAN RIVER	79	64	44	58	71	79	60	71	67	59	79	83	54	79	63	71	74	70	82	96
55785	SWATARA	81	64	44	58	72	81	60	73	68	60	81	85	54	80	64	73	75	71	86	99
55787	TAMARACK	80	62	43	56	70	79	59	71	67	58	79	83	53	78	63	71	73	70	84	97
55790	TOWER	98	77	52	70	86	97	73	87	82	72	98	103	65	97	77	88	91	86	103	119
55792	VIRGINIA	63	61	64	60	63	70	64	64	66	62	82	74	64	83	65	67	78	65	68	73
55793	WARBA	78	66	48	62	71	78	61	70	67	61	80	83	58	81	64	70	76	69	79	93
55795	WILLOW RIVER	85	69	50	66	76	85	68	78	75	67	90	90	63	89	70	78	84	76	88	100
55797	WRENSHALL	96	83	64	81	87	97	82	89	87	81	106	103	79	106	83	89	100	87	96	108
55798	WRIGHT	82	64	44	58	73	82	61	73	69	60	82	86	54	80	65	73	76	72	87	100
55801	DULUTH	107	84	57	76	95	107	79	96	90	79	106	112	71	105	85	96	99	94	113	131
55802	DULUTH	49	47	65	48	47	53	54	51	56	53	70	59	54	70	54	57	68	54	53	56
55803	DULUTH	100	118	125	116	117	119	107	108	103	107	128	126	113	135	110	101	127	105	102	121
55804	DULUTH	104	117	124	115	117	121	109	111	106	109	133	129	114	139	112	106	131	109	107	126
55805	DULUTH	48	42	54	45	41	46	53	48	53	50	66	59	50	64	49	50	64	52	46	53
55806	DULUTH	50	48	58	50	48	52	55	51	55	53	68	62	54	68	53	53	67	54	50	56
55807	DULUTH	62	66	76	65	66	71	68	66	68	66	85	76	70	88	68	68	83	67	66	72
55808	DULUTH	69	63	56	62	65	71	65	67	67	63	82	77	62	80	64	67	78	67	71	78
55810	DULUTH	82	89	91	87	89	93	84	86	83	84	103	99	87	106	86	83	101	84	84	96
55811	DULUTH	88	92	96	91	92	98	91	91	91	89	112	106	92	114	92	90	109	91	91	103
55812	DULUTH	96	97	118	101	96	103	105	100	102	103	128	119	104	125	102	98	125	104	94	110
55901	ROCHESTER	107	113	125	118	109	112	113	109	108	114	136	129	114	135	110	103	134	111	98	120
55902	ROCHESTER	145	163	184	167	160	166	157	154	150	158	189	179	164	190	158	146	187	153	144	169
55904	ROCHESTER	88	93	101	96	92	94	94	91	90	93	113	109	94	114	92	86	111	92	84	101
55906	ROCHESTER	116	128	140	130	125	129	124	122	119	124	149	143	127	151	124	115	147	122	113	135
55909	ADAMS	85	62	39	60	69	82	67	76	76	64	89	87	59	85	67	80	81	76	91	95
55910	ALTURA	106	87	60	82	95	103	82	94	89	82	107	113	77	108	85	92	101	92	106	125
55912	AUSTIN	84	82	82	80	84	93	83	84	86	81	106	97	84	109	84	88	102	84	89	96
55917	BLOOMING PRAIRIE	96	81	60	78	87	96	79	88	86	78	103	102	76	103	81	88	97	86	98	111
55918	BROWNSDALE	82	70	53	68	74	82	69	76	74	69	90	88	67	90	70	76	84	74	82	93
55919	BROWNSVILLE	94	79	57	75	85	92	74	84	80	74	97	100	71	98	76	83	91	82	93	110
55920	BYRON	112	131	133	133	127	124	119	118	111	121	140	139	124	144	119	105	139	116	104	130
55921	CALEDONIA	85	67	46	65	73	83	69	77	76	68	91	89	63	88	69	79	84	77	88	96
55922	CANTON	82	57	30	54	67	75	57	70	65	56	76	84	48	75	59	68	70	69	83	97
55923	CHATFIELD	103	88	69	85	94	104	87	96	94	86	113	112	83	112	89	97	106	95	106	119
55924	CLAREMONT	93	80	62	78	85	93	79	86	84	78	102	100	76	102	80	85	96	84	93	105
55925	DAKOTA	109	97	74	92	103	110	90	99	95	90	116	118	88	118	92	98	110	97	108	128
55926	DEXTER	115	81	42	76	94	105	80	98	92	79	108	119	68	105	83	96	98	97	117	137
55927	DODGE CENTER	89	82	70	82	85	93	82	86	84	80	103	99	80	103	82	85	98	84	89	100
55929	DOVER	110	84	53	80	95	104	81	97	91	81	108	116	73	107	84	94	100	95	111	131
55932	ELGIN	99	101	94	101	101	102	96	99	93	97	116	117	95	117	95	90	113	98	93	114
55933	ELKTON	91	77	59	75	82	94	81	87	87	77	103	98	75	100	80	90	96	86	98	103
55934	EYOTA	101	106	101	106	106	107	100	102	96	100	120	121	100	122	100	93	117	101	96	118
55935	FOUNTAIN	97	86	65	81	91	98	80	88	85	80	103	105	78	105	82	87	98	86	96	114
55936	GRAND MEADOW	101	98	88	98	100	108	96	100	97	94	119	115	95	121	96	97	114	97	101	115
55939	HARMONY	80	58	34	55	66	76	61	71	69	59	81	83	53	78	62	73	74	70	85	92
55940	HAYFIELD	90	86	74	85	88	95	83	87	85	82	104	101	82	106	84	86	100	85	90	103
55941	HOKAH	95	94	83	92	95	98	88	92	88	88	109	110	87	110	88	86	105	91	90	110
55943	HOUSTON	84	73	56	71	77	85	72	78	77	71	92	92	69	92	73	78	87	77	86	97
55944	KASSON	90	99	96	98	97	97	91	92	87	92	109	108	93	110	91	84	107	91	85	104
55945	KELLOGG	121	88	51	83	101	112	86	104	97	85	115	125	76	114	89	102	106	102	122	143
55946	KENYON	93	89	78	89	91	98	87	91	88	86	108	105	86	109	87	88	103	89	93	106
55947	LA CRESCENT	104	100	87	99	103	107	94	101	95	95	117	120	92	118	95	94	112	99	101	122
55949	LANESBORO	81	59	36	56	66	77	63	72	71	61	84	83	55	80	63	75	76	72	86	92
55951	LE ROY	90	76	59	75	81	90	77	83	82	76	99	96	73	98	77	83	93	82	91	101
55952	LEWISTON	98	84	63	82	89	98	83	90	88	82	107	105	79	107	83	90	100	89	99	112
55953	LYLE	94	73	48	71	80	90	73	84	81	72	97	98	67	95	74	83	89	83	95	108
55954	MABEL	75	54	33	52	61	71	57	66	65	55	77	77	50	73	58	69	70	66	79	85
55955	MANTORVILLE	118	135	131	140	128	124	121	120	111	126	141	141	125	142	119	104	140	117	102	132
55956	MAZEPPA	92	95	89	95	96	101	90	93	90	89	111	108	92	114	91	89	107	91	92	106
55957	MILLVILLE	106	74	39	70	87	97	74	91	85	73	99	109	63	97	76	89	91	89	108	126
55959	MINNESOTA CITY	110	98	75	93	103	111	92	101	97	91	118	120	90	120	94	100	112	99	109	129
55960	ORONOCO	128	147	147	146	145	145	133	135	126	134	158	158	138	163	135	122	156	131	124	152
55961	OSTRANDER	110	77	40	73	90	101	76	94	88	75	103	114	65	101	79	92	94	93	112	131
55962	PETERSON	93	67	38	63	77	86	66	80	75	65	89	96	57	88	68	79	81	79	95	110
55963	PINE ISLAND	101	110	105	108	111	113	100	103	97	99	120	122	103	126	102	96	118	100	100	121
55964	PLAINVIEW	92	77	59	76	81	91	79	85	84	77	101	98	75	100	78	85	95	84	93	102
55965	PRESTON	95	68	40	65	77	89	71	83	80	69	94	97	62	91	72	85	86	82	99	109
55967	RACINE	85	104	115	102	102	104	96	95	92	95	115	110	102	123	99	90	115	93	88	104
55968	READS LANDING	116	81	42	76	94	106	80	99	92	79	108	119	68	106	83	97	98	97	118	138
55969	ROLLINGSTONE	106	94	72	89	99	107	87	96	92	87	112	115	85	115	90	95	107	94	104	124
55970	ROSE CREEK	117	101	76	96	108	117	96	106	102	95	124	126	92	125	98	105	117	104	117	137
55971	RUSHFORD	70	70	67	67	72	79	68	71	71	67	87	80	69	90	70	73	84	70	76	82
55972	SAINT CHARLES	91	86	75	86	87	93	85	88	86	85	106	102	83	106	84	85	101	87	89	102
55973	SARGEANT	115	81	42	76	94	105	80	98	92	79	108	119	68	105	83	96	98	97	117	137
55974	SPRING GROVE	94	66	34	62	76	86	65	80	75	64	88	97	55	86	67	78	80	79	95	112
55975	SPRING VALLEY	85	68	50	66	74	83	70	78	76	68	91	92	64	90	71	79	85	78	88	98
55976	STEWARTVILLE	92	95	89	94	95	99	91	93	90	91	111	108	91	112	91	88	108	92	90	106
55977	TAOPI	108	78	45	74	90	100	77	93	87	76	102	112	67	101	79	91	94	92	109	128
55979	UTICA	103	84	63	84	90	101	86	94	93	85	112	109	81	110	86	94	104	93	104	115
55981	WABASHA	106	77	45	73	87	100	80	94	91	78	107	109	70	103	81	96	97	93	112	123
55982	WALTHAM	113	99	73	94	105	113	92	103	98	92	119	123	89	121	95	101	113	100	112	134
55983	WANAMINGO	101	79	52	76	89	97	76	90	84	76	100	108	69	100	79	87	93	88	102	121
55985	WEST CONCORD	94	83	66	81	87	95	81	87	85	80	103	102	79	104	82	86	98	85	94	107
55987	WINONA	79	75	76	75	76	82	80	78	80	77	99	93	78	100	78	79	96	79	79	90
55990	WYKOFF	103	72	38	68	84	94	71	88	82	70	96	106	61	94	74	86	87	87	105	122
55991	ZUMBRO FALLS	104	104	91	101	107	111	95	101	96	95	118	120	96	122	97	96	114	98	103	124
55992	ZUMBROTA	112	103	87	102	107	117	103	108	106	100	129	124	100	129	103	108	123	106	115	127
	MINNESOTA	107	106	108	107	107	113	106	107	105	105	131	126	105	131	105	104	127	107	105	123
	UNITED STATES	100	100	100	100	100	100	100	100	100	100	100	100	100	100	100	100	100	100	100	100

# POST OFFICE NAME	COUNTY FIPS CODE	POPULATION			2000-2004 ANNUAL RATE		HOUSEHOLDS					FAMILIES		
		2000	2004	2009	% Rate	State Centile	2000	2004	2009	% Annual Rate 2000-2004	2004 Average HH Size	2000	2004	% Annual Rate 2000-2004
56001 MANKATO	013	39338	42143	45883	1.6	72	14851	16300	18193	2.2	2.34	8006	8446	1.3
56003 MANKATO	103	12777	13914	15368	2.0	79	5095	5656	6356	2.5	2.46	3468	3742	1.8
56007 ALBERT LEA	047	22038	22218	22418	0.2	34	9154	9350	9561	0.5	2.32	5875	5816	-0.2
56009 ALDEN	047	1577	1609	1628	0.5	43	625	649	666	0.9	2.48	463	469	0.3
56010 AMBOY	013	1380	1396	1479	0.3	36	563	577	620	0.6	2.39	414	414	0.0
56011 BELLE PLAINE	139	5779	7077	9033	4.9	97	2048	2572	3355	5.5	2.68	1485	1814	4.8
56013 BLUE EARTH	043	4903	4829	4742	-0.4	14	2031	2032	2026	0.0	2.28	1310	1270	-0.7
56014 BRICELYN	043	885	868	852	-0.5	11	373	371	368	-0.1	2.34	246	237	-0.9
56016 CLARKS GROVE	047	933	982	1016	1.2	63	361	389	409	1.8	2.43	272	286	1.2
56017 CLEVELAND	079	1464	1533	1651	1.1	60	549	585	641	1.5	2.62	411	429	1.0
56019 COMFREY	033	826	808	810	-0.5	9	341	338	344	-0.2	2.38	260	252	-0.7
56020 CONGER	047	253	253	253	0.0	27	107	109	111	0.4	2.32	79	79	0.0
56021 COURTLAND	103	1253	1328	1444	1.4	66	423	458	507	1.9	2.90	338	360	1.5
56022 DARFUR	165	310	304	300	-0.5	11	138	137	137	-0.2	2.22	105	102	-0.7
56023 DELAVAN	043	628	623	614	-0.2	19	261	263	263	0.2	2.37	194	191	-0.4
56024 EAGLE LAKE	013	2320	2536	2799	2.1	80	838	935	1052	2.6	2.71	621	676	2.0
56025 EASTON	043	610	618	614	0.3	37	225	233	235	0.8	2.65	172	174	0.3
56026 ELLENDALE	147	1404	1433	1485	0.5	43	539	559	588	0.9	2.56	399	403	0.2
56027 ELMORE	043	993	963	940	-0.7	5	405	398	394	-0.4	2.21	268	256	-1.1
56028 ELYSIAN	079	1295	1392	1520	1.7	73	512	560	622	2.1	2.48	368	392	1.5
56029 EMMONS	047	578	574	573	-0.2	21	238	241	246	0.3	2.38	181	179	-0.3
56030 ESSIG	015	205	214	221	1.0	59	70	75	79	1.6	2.85	52	54	0.9
56031 FAIRMONT	091	13336	13300	13241	-0.1	25	5620	5685	5733	0.3	2.28	3686	3617	-0.4
56032 FREEBORN	047	632	630	629	-0.1	24	252	255	259	0.3	2.47	189	186	-0.4
56033 FROST	043	379	371	363	-0.5	10	172	171	170	-0.1	2.17	117	113	-0.8
56034 GARDEN CITY	013	467	528	593	2.9	89	186	214	245	3.4	2.46	141	158	2.7
56035 GENEVA	047	523	514	512	-0.4	13	209	209	212	0.0	2.44	153	149	-0.6
56036 GLENVILLE	047	1547	1544	1547	-0.1	25	646	657	669	0.4	2.35	454	449	-0.3
56037 GOOD THUNDER	013	970	1021	1105	1.2	63	355	378	415	1.5	2.70	266	277	1.0
56039 GRANADA	091	822	804	794	-0.5	9	325	324	325	-0.1	2.48	224	217	-0.7
56041 HANSKA	015	1108	1095	1103	-0.3	17	433	435	446	0.1	2.52	320	314	-0.4
56042 HARTLAND	047	586	593	596	0.3	37	246	254	260	0.8	2.33	181	181	0.0
56043 HAYWARD	047	687	681	680	-0.2	19	272	274	277	0.2	2.45	205	202	-0.4
56044 HENDERSON	143	2094	2255	2386	1.8	75	731	796	853	2.0	2.82	524	557	1.5
56045 HOLLANDALE	047	2251	2220	2215	-0.3	15	850	853	864	0.1	2.60	660	648	-0.4
56046 HOPE	147	59	61	63	0.8	52	23	24	26	1.0	2.54	18	19	1.3
56047 HUNTLEY	043	68	66	65	-0.7	5	30	30	30	0.0	2.20	23	22	-1.0
56048 JANESVILLE	161	3735	3904	4106	1.1	60	1353	1438	1537	1.4	2.62	1005	1043	0.9
56050 KASOTA	079	2164	2245	2406	0.9	55	837	887	968	1.4	2.53	645	670	0.9
56051 KIESTER	043	798	779	763	-0.6	8	352	347	344	-0.3	2.24	247	237	-1.0
56052 KILKENNY	079	687	732	804	1.5	69	270	291	324	1.8	2.52	203	215	1.4
56054 LAFAYETTE	103	1750	1892	2076	1.9	76	629	695	779	2.4	2.67	484	524	1.9
56055 LAKE CRYSTAL	013	3590	3751	4039	1.0	60	1373	1455	1593	1.4	2.54	980	1012	0.8
56057 LE CENTER	079	3520	3742	4061	1.5	67	1303	1405	1547	1.8	2.60	919	964	1.1
56058 LE SUEUR	079	6042	6676	7403	2.4	84	2328	2614	2944	2.8	2.52	1646	1795	2.1
56060 LEWISVILLE	165	561	551	544	-0.4	12	222	221	219	-0.1	2.49	158	153	-0.8
56062 MADELIA	165	3120	3116	3113	0.0	26	1193	1204	1213	0.2	2.51	789	773	-0.5
56063 MADISON LAKE	013	2618	2856	3148	2.1	79	996	1105	1238	2.5	2.58	745	809	2.0
56065 MAPLETON	013	2430	2509	2695	0.8	51	908	956	1049	1.2	2.56	674	694	0.7
56068 MINNESOTA LAKE	043	922	891	872	-0.8	3	380	374	372	-0.4	2.38	261	250	-1.0
56069 MONTGOMERY	079	4028	4248	4607	1.3	65	1537	1641	1802	1.6	2.58	1023	1060	0.8
56071 NEW PRAGUE	079	9325	11064	13552	4.1	95	3209	3874	4822	4.5	2.82	2473	2916	4.0
56072 NEW RICHLAND	161	2301	2290	2366	-0.1	22	891	901	946	0.3	2.47	632	624	-0.3
56073 NEW ULM	015	16317	16581	16926	0.4	40	6462	6689	6949	0.8	2.35	4340	4361	0.1
56074 NICOLLET	103	1695	1752	1881	0.8	52	635	671	734	1.3	2.61	476	492	0.8
56075 NORTHROP	091	13	13	13	0.0	27	4	4	4	0.0	3.25	3	3	0.0
56078 PEMBERTON	013	984	982	1042	-0.1	25	347	353	381	0.4	2.74	261	259	-0.2
56080 SAINT CLAIR	013	1090	1163	1267	1.5	69	386	419	464	2.0	2.78	295	314	1.5
56081 SAINT JAMES	165	6693	6631	6572	-0.2	18	2599	2589	2582	-0.1	2.53	1760	1706	-0.7
56082 SAINT PETER	103	11650	12289	13204	1.3	65	3635	3931	4356	1.9	2.49	2361	2472	1.1
56083 SANBORN	127	967	898	885	-1.7	0	368	348	348	-1.3	2.58	273	252	-1.9
56085 SLEEPY EYE	015	5815	5913	6041	0.4	41	2251	2320	2404	0.7	2.49	1540	1546	0.1
56087 SPRINGFIELD	015	2896	2924	2970	0.2	35	1140	1165	1200	0.5	2.40	737	730	-0.2
56088 TRUMAN	091	1983	1954	1934	-0.4	15	780	781	784	0.0	2.36	527	512	-0.7
56089 TWIN LAKES	047	868	855	852	-0.4	15	356	358	362	0.1	2.39	271	266	-0.4
56090 VERNON CENTER	013	915	928	984	0.3	39	339	348	375	0.6	2.67	265	267	0.2
56091 WALDORF	161	589	577	593	-0.5	11	232	232	242	0.0	2.49	180	176	-0.5
56093 WASECA	161	12908	13425	14079	0.9	57	4589	4855	5172	1.3	2.52	3181	3274	0.7
56096 WATERVILLE	079	2841	3024	3282	1.5	68	1126	1214	1336	1.8	2.42	796	837	1.2
56097 WELLS	043	3889	3832	3763	-0.4	15	1536	1529	1520	-0.1	2.44	1056	1024	-0.7
56098 WINNEBAGO	043	2330	2284	2240	-0.5	11	973	965	955	-0.2	2.29	651	627	-0.9
56101 WINDOM	033	5979	6009	6021	0.1	32	2487	2535	2573	0.5	2.29	1656	1639	-0.2
56110 ADRIAN	105	1925	1927	1954	0.0	29	714	722	741	0.3	2.60	503	496	-0.3
56111 ALPHA	063	666	663	663	-0.1	22	261	264	267	0.3	2.51	207	205	-0.2
56113 ARCO	081	413	400	394	-0.8	4	171	168	167	-0.4	2.33	132	127	-0.9
56114 AVOCA	101	476	437	418	-2.0	0	204	191	185	-1.5	2.29	148	134	-2.3
56115 BALATON	083	1333	1313	1326	-0.4	14	539	540	552	0.0	2.43	393	383	-0.6
56116 BEAVER CREEK	133	641	627	625	-0.5	9	247	246	249	-0.1	2.55	200	196	-0.5
56117 BIGELOW	105	494	505	521	0.5	44	179	185	192	0.8	2.73	139	141	0.3
56118 BINGHAM LAKE	033	444	450	453	0.3	39	165	168	170	0.4	2.56	132	131	-0.2
56119 BREWSTER	105	917	975	1022	1.5	67	345	372	394	1.8	2.62	259	273	1.3
56120 BUTTERFIELD	165	861	852	843	-0.3	18	331	333	333	0.1	2.56	233	228	-0.5
56121 CEYLON	091	803	786	775	-0.5	10	334	333	334	-0.1	2.36	236	229	-0.7
56122 CHANDLER	101	593	572	558	-0.8	3	218	213	211	-0.5	2.69	167	160	-1.0
56123 CURRIE	101	760	829	859	2.1	79	331	368	388	2.5	2.25	253	274	1.9
56125 DOVRAY	101	48	45	43	-1.5	0	19	18	18	-1.3	2.50	14	13	-1.7
56127 DUNNELL	091	414	405	400	-0.5	10	174	174	174	0.0	2.33	120	116	-0.8
56128 EDGERTON	117	2172	2153	2145	-0.2	19	864	873	883	0.2	2.40	626	617	-0.3
56129 ELLSWORTH	105	764	759	770	-0.2	21	308	309	315	0.1	2.32	199	193	-0.7
56131 FULDA	101	2355	2291	2263	-0.7	6	923	905	902	-0.5	2.44	629	597	-1.2
56132 GARVIN	083	488	548	586	2.8	88	199	228	247	3.3	2.40	156	174	2.6
56134 HARDWICK	133	434	422	420	-0.7	6	170	168	171	-0.3	2.51	124	120	-0.8
56136 HENDRICKS	081	1259	1240	1231	-0.4	14	509	507	507	-0.1	2.27	330	319	-0.8
56137 HERON LAKE	063	1229	1219	1219	-0.2	19	456	458	465	0.1	2.55	308	301	-0.5
56138 HILLS	133	1016	997	995	-0.4	12	378	377	382	-0.1	2.53	277	268	-0.8
MINNESOTA					1.4					1.6	2.50			1.0
UNITED STATES					1.2					1.3	2.58			1.1

#	POST OFFICE NAME	RACE (%) White 2000	White 2004	Black 2000	Black 2004	Asian/Pacific 2000	Asian/Pacific 2004	% Hispanic Origin 2000	% Hispanic Origin 2004	2004 AGE DISTRIBUTION (%) 0-4	5-9	10-14	15-19	20-24	25-44	45-64	65-84	85+	18+	MEDIAN AGE 2004	% 2004 Males	% 2004 Females
56001	MANKATO	93.5	92.4	1.6	2.0	2.5	3.0	2.0	2.4	5.1	4.5	4.8	11.3	20.1	24.0	18.9	9.2	2.1	82.5	27.6	49.4	50.6
56003	MANKATO	96.6	96.0	0.6	0.8	1.3	1.7	1.5	1.8	7.0	6.6	6.8	6.9	8.2	30.4	24.2	8.9	1.0	75.5	34.1	49.2	50.8
56007	ALBERT LEA	93.7	92.7	0.3	0.4	0.7	0.9	8.4	9.9	6.1	5.8	6.2	6.5	6.5	23.8	25.2	16.3	3.7	77.9	41.5	48.3	51.7
56009	ALDEN	98.2	97.9	0.1	0.1	0.4	0.6	2.0	2.4	6.3	6.3	6.7	6.5	5.7	25.5	25.4	15.2	2.5	76.8	40.7	51.3	48.7
56010	AMBOY	99.0	98.9	0.1	0.1	0.1	0.1	0.9	1.1	4.8	5.2	7.1	7.5	6.0	23.8	27.6	14.7	3.4	78.3	42.4	51.2	48.9
56011	BELLE PLAINE	97.5	97.2	0.1	0.2	0.6	0.7	1.1	1.5	7.5	7.3	8.0	7.6	6.9	28.6	21.3	10.6	2.2	72.4	35.7	50.3	49.7
56013	BLUE EARTH	97.0	96.4	0.2	0.3	0.4	0.5	3.8	4.6	5.1	5.6	6.5	6.7	6.0	20.8	26.5	16.9	5.9	78.5	44.5	48.0	52.0
56014	BRICELYN	97.9	97.7	0.6	0.7	0.1	0.1	2.8	3.5	5.1	6.0	6.5	6.9	5.7	20.3	27.5	19.0	3.1	77.9	44.8	51.4	48.6
56016	CLARKS GROVE	98.7	98.5	0.2	0.3	0.3	0.4	2.8	3.5	5.2	6.2	7.2	8.3	5.0	24.1	25.7	15.8	2.6	75.6	41.4	51.4	48.6
56017	CLEVELAND	97.8	97.3	0.1	0.1	1.2	1.5	1.2	1.5	6.1	6.5	7.4	7.2	6.4	24.5	29.9	10.4	1.5	75.5	39.5	51.9	48.1
56019	COMFREY	98.1	97.9	0.0	0.0	0.9	1.0	1.1	1.2	5.9	6.7	7.4	7.1	5.5	23.6	26.4	15.4	2.1	75.0	40.7	51.6	48.4
56020	CONGER	98.4	98.8	0.0	0.0	0.0	0.0	2.0	2.0	4.0	4.4	6.7	6.7	6.3	24.1	31.2	14.6	2.0	80.2	43.8	49.4	50.6
56021	COURTLAND	98.4	98.1	0.0	0.0	0.4	0.5	1.6	2.0	7.2	7.6	8.4	7.8	6.3	25.8	28.2	7.6	1.2	71.9	36.7	51.4	48.6
56022	DARFUR	96.1	95.7	0.0	0.0	0.3	0.7	2.6	3.6	5.9	5.9	6.6	6.6	5.6	22.0	28.0	17.1	2.3	77.0	43.6	53.6	46.4
56023	DELAVAN	98.6	98.4	0.2	0.3	0.2	0.2	1.4	1.8	4.5	5.8	6.9	5.8	5.0	22.5	31.3	16.4	1.9	79.1	44.8	52.7	47.4
56024	EAGLE LAKE	97.4	96.9	0.5	0.7	0.6	0.7	1.2	1.4	8.4	8.1	7.7	7.2	7.2	31.2	23.3	6.2	0.7	71.5	32.6	50.6	49.5
56025	EASTON	97.7	97.4	0.5	0.5	0.2	0.2	1.2	1.3	3.7	6.6	7.9	7.4	4.7	22.0	30.9	15.9	0.8	76.5	43.6	51.8	48.2
56026	ELLENDALE	99.1	98.9	0.0	0.0	0.3	0.4	1.1	1.5	5.6	5.8	7.2	7.9	6.1	25.1	27.7	12.0	2.7	76.6	40.5	51.7	48.3
56027	ELMORE	93.6	92.6	1.4	1.7	0.9	1.0	3.9	4.8	5.7	6.4	5.9	12.5	4.6	18.0	26.8	16.6	3.5	72.5	42.2	51.8	48.2
56028	ELYSIAN	99.1	98.9	0.0	0.0	0.2	0.2	0.8	1.0	6.2	6.5	6.5	5.3	5.8	25.5	29.5	13.2	1.5	77.5	41.5	50.4	49.6
56029	EMMONS	97.8	97.0	0.4	0.5	0.2	0.2	2.4	3.3	5.1	5.6	6.6	5.9	5.8	23.9	28.9	16.2	2.1	79.1	43.2	49.7	50.4
56030	ESSIG	99.5	99.1	0.0	0.0	0.5	0.5	0.5	0.5	6.5	7.5	7.5	7.5	5.6	22.4	27.6	13.6	1.9	72.9	40.6	52.8	47.2
56031	FAIRMONT	96.2	95.5	0.4	0.5	0.6	0.7	2.6	3.2	5.7	5.7	6.8	7.0	6.5	22.5	26.6	15.6	3.7	77.3	42.2	48.6	51.4
56032	FREEBORN	98.9	98.7	0.0	0.0	0.3	0.3	0.5	0.6	6.0	6.7	7.8	6.4	5.2	26.0	26.0	14.9	1.0	75.7	39.2	51.1	48.9
56033	FROST	97.1	96.2	0.0	0.0	0.5	0.5	3.7	4.6	6.2	5.9	7.3	7.0	6.7	24.5	27.0	12.9	2.4	76.3	40.4	53.6	46.4
56034	GARDEN CITY	98.1	97.5	0.2	0.2	0.2	0.4	1.5	2.1	5.1	5.7	7.0	6.3	6.3	24.8	30.7	12.7	1.5	77.8	42.2	50.6	49.4
56035	GENEVA	98.5	98.4	0.0	0.0	0.2	0.2	2.7	3.5	6.8	6.8	7.2	6.8	6.4	25.3	26.9	11.9	2.0	74.3	39.1	50.2	49.8
56036	GLENVILLE	98.7	98.5	0.0	0.0	0.4	0.5	1.0	1.2	5.9	6.3	6.7	5.6	5.6	25.3	28.1	14.7	1.9	77.7	41.4	52.1	47.9
56037	GOOD THUNDER	98.1	97.9	0.1	0.1	0.4	0.5	0.6	0.8	8.4	7.0	9.8	7.2	6.5	27.6	21.6	11.0	1.1	69.6	34.4	50.6	49.4
56039	GRANADA	98.1	97.5	0.0	0.0	0.0	0.1	2.1	2.5	6.0	6.5	7.3	5.9	6.2	23.3	29.9	13.2	1.9	76.6	41.8	51.5	48.5
56041	HANSKA	99.0	98.9	0.2	0.2	0.2	0.2	1.0	1.1	6.9	6.9	6.8	5.9	6.2	28.4	24.8	12.4	1.8	76.0	37.8	52.2	47.9
56042	HARTLAND	98.3	97.8	0.0	0.0	0.0	0.0	1.4	1.7	5.1	5.6	6.8	6.4	5.9	25.8	27.7	15.4	1.5	78.6	42.0	52.3	47.7
56043	HAYWARD	98.1	97.8	0.0	0.0	0.0	0.0	1.8	2.4	6.6	6.8	6.0	6.5	4.9	23.9	30.1	13.7	1.6	76.2	42.1	51.3	48.8
56044	HENDERSON	97.6	97.3	0.0	0.0	0.4	0.4	3.2	3.9	6.9	7.3	8.6	7.7	6.0	27.7	24.7	9.9	1.2	72.5	36.3	51.6	48.4
56045	HOLLANDALE	97.8	97.3	0.0	0.1	0.2	0.2	2.8	3.5	5.6	6.9	7.3	7.3	5.5	26.0	26.2	13.7	1.6	75.5	40.2	51.5	48.5
56046	HOPE	98.3	100.0	0.0	0.0	0.0	0.0	0.0	1.6	6.6	4.9	8.2	6.6	4.9	26.2	29.5	13.1	0.0	77.1	40.5	50.8	49.2
56047	HUNTLEY	97.1	95.5	0.0	0.0	0.0	0.0	5.9	7.6	4.6	6.1	7.6	6.1	6.1	21.2	30.3	15.2	3.0	78.8	44.2	53.0	47.0
56048	JANESVILLE	97.3	96.8	0.9	1.2	0.3	0.3	1.3	1.5	7.5	7.5	7.0	6.0	6.2	29.1	24.1	10.6	2.0	74.0	36.2	51.7	48.3
56050	KASOTA	98.2	98.0	0.2	0.3	0.2	0.2	1.0	1.2	5.5	6.0	7.8	6.7	5.3	26.3	32.1	9.8	0.6	76.9	40.5	52.3	47.8
56051	KIESTER	98.8	98.5	0.3	0.3	0.1	0.1	1.5	1.8	5.5	5.9	6.8	5.8	4.5	23.0	26.1	19.6	2.8	78.3	44.1	51.7	48.3
56052	KILKENNY	98.5	98.4	0.0	0.0	0.3	0.3	1.3	1.5	5.7	6.7	6.8	7.0	5.1	26.0	29.5	11.9	1.4	76.4	40.7	52.6	47.4
56054	LAFAYETTE	99.1	99.1	0.0	0.0	0.1	0.2	0.7	0.9	7.0	7.2	8.0	7.2	5.6	26.1	25.1	11.5	2.3	72.9	38.5	51.6	48.4
56055	LAKE CRYSTAL	98.2	97.9	0.3	0.4	0.3	0.4	0.8	0.9	7.2	7.1	6.8	6.2	6.5	27.0	24.1	12.3	2.9	74.8	37.8	50.6	49.4
56057	LE CENTER	95.5	94.6	0.0	0.0	0.4	0.4	6.5	8.2	6.8	6.8	7.4	7.5	6.9	27.1	22.3	12.2	3.0	74.5	36.9	49.4	50.6
56058	LE SUEUR	94.5	93.8	0.2	0.2	0.3	0.3	6.6	7.6	6.0	6.8	7.6	7.8	6.1	26.0	24.8	12.1	2.8	74.3	38.8	49.6	50.4
56060	LEWISVILLE	94.7	93.5	0.7	0.9	0.2	0.2	5.0	6.0	7.8	8.0	7.8	6.5	4.5	21.6	25.1	16.9	1.8	72.6	40.7	50.3	49.7
56062	MADELIA	88.6	86.8	0.5	0.7	0.4	0.5	16.0	18.7	7.0	6.9	7.6	6.9	6.8	23.9	22.3	14.5	4.0	73.8	38.3	48.5	51.5
56063	MADISON LAKE	98.4	98.1	0.2	0.3	0.5	0.7	1.1	1.3	6.1	6.5	6.9	6.4	5.6	26.7	29.2	11.6	1.0	76.6	40.0	50.9	49.1
56065	MAPLETON	97.9	97.7	0.0	0.0	0.4	0.4	2.3	2.8	7.6	6.5	6.8	7.5	5.8	24.8	23.4	13.8	3.9	74.6	38.8	50.2	49.8
56068	MINNESOTA LAKE	99.5	99.6	0.0	0.0	0.0	0.0	0.7	0.7	4.6	5.4	6.4	7.4	6.3	25.1	26.7	15.3	2.8	78.9	41.9	51.6	48.4
56069	MONTGOMERY	95.0	93.9	0.2	0.3	0.3	0.4	7.3	8.9	7.5	7.5	7.9	7.5	6.2	27.9	22.6	11.0	1.9	72.4	35.5	51.0	49.0
56071	NEW PRAGUE	98.6	98.3	0.1	0.1	0.3	0.4	0.7	1.0	7.9	8.5	9.3	7.7	5.3	27.9	21.7	9.7	2.1	69.0	35.6	49.2	50.8
56072	NEW RICHLAND	99.0	98.8	0.0	0.0	0.2	0.3	1.1	1.4	6.2	6.5	7.6	6.7	5.2	23.7	24.4	15.7	4.0	75.4	41.0	50.3	49.7
56073	NEW ULM	98.3	98.0	0.1	0.1	0.5	0.6	1.2	1.4	5.3	5.3	6.3	8.1	8.9	25.4	25.8	12.9	2.1	78.4	38.6	49.8	50.2
56074	NICOLLET	98.7	98.5	0.1	0.1	0.4	0.5	0.6	0.7	5.8	6.8	7.8	7.4	6.1	27.6	26.7	10.3	1.6	74.9	38.3	51.7	48.3
56075	NORTHROP	100.0	100.0	0.0	0.0	0.0	0.0	0.0	0.0	0.0	0.0	15.4	0.0	0.0	38.5	46.2	0.0	0.0	84.6	43.8	84.6	15.4
56078	PEMBERTON	98.6	98.4	0.0	0.0	0.2	0.3	1.9	2.3	6.8	7.0	6.9	6.2	5.8	25.8	26.3	12.4	2.8	75.4	39.0	52.2	47.8
56080	SAINT CLAIR	99.6	99.5	0.2	0.3	0.0	0.0	0.6	0.8	7.3	7.3	7.9	7.5	7.0	28.7	24.1	8.6	1.6	72.8	35.7	50.9	49.1
56081	SAINT JAMES	87.3	85.4	0.3	0.4	0.5	0.6	17.3	20.2	8.0	7.7	7.0	6.5	7.4	22.8	23.2	14.6	2.9	73.4	37.3	48.7	51.3
56082	SAINT PETER	94.9	94.0	1.4	1.7	1.4	1.6	2.6	3.1	4.9	5.0	5.8	13.5	16.6	22.6	19.8	9.6	2.2	80.5	28.6	50.0	50.0
56083	SANBORN	98.7	98.7	0.0	0.0	0.2	0.3	0.6	0.7	5.6	5.8	6.8	6.5	6.5	23.1	27.4	15.9	2.6	77.7	41.8	51.9	48.1
56085	SLEEPY EYE	96.0	95.3	0.2	0.2	0.3	0.3	4.9	5.9	6.6	6.5	7.1	7.6	6.2	24.4	24.2	13.3	4.1	74.5	39.9	49.9	50.1
56087	SPRINGFIELD	98.5	98.2	0.0	0.0	0.5	0.6	1.7	2.1	6.0	6.1	7.2	7.3	5.8	21.3	22.9	17.5	5.9	75.8	42.4	48.1	51.9
56088	TRUMAN	99.0	99.0	0.2	0.2	0.1	0.1	0.7	0.9	5.1	5.5	7.1	6.2	5.8	19.5	27.0	17.7	6.1	78.1	45.5	48.1	51.9
56089	TWIN LAKES	98.9	98.7	0.1	0.1	0.1	0.1	1.4	1.9	4.7	5.0	6.6	6.8	6.3	22.9	31.7	14.6	1.4	79.7	43.6	51.0	49.0
56090	VERNON CENTER	99.6	99.6	0.0	0.0	0.1	0.1	0.8	1.0	6.6	7.0	7.4	6.4	6.0	24.6	25.8	14.1	2.2	75.0	39.5	51.6	48.4
56091	WALDORF	99.2	99.1	0.0	0.0	0.2	0.2	1.2	1.6	6.6	6.6	6.4	5.7	5.6	24.6	28.1	14.9	1.6	76.8	41.3	52.7	47.3
56093	WASECA	92.9	91.7	3.1	3.9	0.6	0.7	3.8	4.5	6.9	6.8	6.6	6.8	7.0	30.2	23.4	10.3	2.1	75.6	36.2	52.8	47.2
56096	WATERVILLE	98.0	97.8	0.1	0.1	0.3	0.3	0.4	0.5	5.8	6.0	6.5	6.1	5.5	25.2	27.4	14.8	2.8	77.7	41.7	49.7	50.3
56097	WELLS	97.0	96.4	0.1	0.1	0.5	0.6	4.0	4.8	6.7	6.9	6.5	6.6	6.0	21.5	25.0	16.9	3.9	75.7	41.8	49.3	50.7
56098	WINNEBAGO	97.0	96.5	0.0	0.0	0.5	0.6	4.8	5.8	5.0	5.1	5.9	6.4	6.3	21.3	26.9	18.6	4.4	79.9	44.9	50.0	50.0
56101	WINDOM	97.6	97.5	0.3	0.3	0.6	0.6	1.5	1.5	5.4	5.8	6.8	6.9	5.9	22.5	27.1	15.9	3.7	77.8	42.7	48.7	51.3
56110	ADRIAN	97.0	96.4	0.2	0.2	0.4	0.5	2.4	3.0	6.3	6.8	8.3	6.5	5.9	23.9	23.6	14.5	4.3	74.5	39.7	49.9	50.1
56111	ALPHA	99.4	99.4	0.0	0.0	0.5	0.5	0.6	0.5	5.7	6.0	6.8	6.2	3.8	27.0	26.4	16.4	1.7	77.8	42.0	51.7	48.3
56113	ARCO	98.8	98.8	0.0	0.0	0.0	0.0	0.7	0.8	5.5	6.5	6.5	5.3	5.5	23.3	27.5	17.3	2.8	78.0	43.2	52.3	47.8
56114	AVOCA	99.0	99.1	0.0	0.0	0.0	0.0	0.0	0.0	5.3	6.6	8.5	6.9	3.2	24.7	29.3	14.2	1.4	74.4	42.0	53.6	46.5
56115	BALATON	98.7	98.6	0.1	0.1	0.2	0.2	0.8	1.1	7.2	7.0	7.5	7.5	6.1	24.8	23.9	13.0	3.0	73.4	37.7	49.8	50.2
56116	BEAVER CREEK	99.1	99.2	0.0	0.0	0.2	0.2	0.3	0.2	6.9	6.9	6.4	6.2	6.7	24.7	28.6	12.1	1.6	76.2	40.2	51.2	48.8
56117	BIGELOW	97.8	97.2	0.0	0.0	0.4	0.4	2.0	2.6	7.5	7.9	7.5	6.7	5.5	27.1	23.2	13.1	1.4	72.5	37.7	52.1	47.9
56118	BINGHAM LAKE	95.5	95.6	0.9	1.1	1.4	1.3	2.0	2.0	6.0	8.0	10.9	9.1	5.8	25.3	23.3	10.7	0.9	68.9	36.0	51.8	48.2
56119	BREWSTER	97.5	97.1	0.1	0.2	0.3	0.3	1.9	2.2	7.7	7.6	7.1	6.4	6.0	26.0	25.9	11.6	2.0	73.6	38.2	51.4	48.6
56120	BUTTERFIELD	88.4	86.3	0.0	0.0	5.8	6.8	12.1	14.3	8.0	7.3	6.9	7.8	7.5	23.1	25.0	12.4	2.0	73.2	37.1	51.8	48.2
56121	CEYLON	98.6	98.4	0.0	0.0	0.5	0.5	1.1	1.4	5.2	5.6	6.6	6.2	6.0	22.8	29.3	15.9	2.4	78.8	43.5	52.3	47.7
56122	CHANDLER	98.5	98.4	0.0	0.0	0.0	0.0	6.6	6.8	6.1	6.8	9.1	6.8	6.3	22.2	27.3	12.1	3.3	73.6	40.0	53.7	46.3
56123	CURRIE	99.1	99.2	0.1	0.1	0.0	0.0	0.5	0.5	4.5	5.0	5.9	5.7	4.8	21.5	31.7	19.5	1.5	81.3	46.8	51.6	48.4
56125	DOVRAY	100.0	100.0	0.0	0.0	0.0	0.0	0.0	0.0	6.7	6.7	6.7	4.4	4.4	20.0	31.1	17.8	2.2	80.0	45.5	53.3	46.7
56127	DUNNELL	98.3	98.0	0.0	0.0	0.5	0.5	1.5	1.7	5.2	5.4	6.2	6.2	6.2	23.2	28.6	16.5	2.5	79.5	43.6	53.1	46.9
56128	EDGERTON	98.5	98.4	0.1	0.1	0.4	0.5	0.9	1.0	5.3	5.7	7.2	6.6	5.7	20.3	25.6	18.6	5.0	76.9	44.5	49.9	50.1
56129	ELLSWORTH	98.6	98.3	0.1	0.1	0.0	0.0	0.8	0.9	6.2	5.9	6.5	5.9	5.8	22.4	23.5	18.6	5.3	77.3	42.8	48.8	51.3
56131	FULDA	97.5	97.3	0.1	0.1	0.2	0.2	2.1	2.3	5.6	6.5	7.4	7.4	5.2	21.5	24.9	17.2	4.3	75.3	42.8	48.8	51.2
56132	GARVIN	98.6	98.4	0.0	0.0	0.2	0.4	1.4	1.5	5.5	5.7	6.6	5.8	5.8	24.5	30.1	15.0	1.1	78.7	42.6	52.4	47.6
56134	HARDWICK	96.8	96.9	0.0	0.0	0.2	0.2	0.9	1.0	6.4	7.1	8.5	7.6	5.9	22.5	28.7	11.9	1.4	73.0	39.4	52.4	47.6
56136	HENDRICKS	99.3	99.4	0.1	0.1	0.3	0.3	0.2	0.2	5.1	5.2	6.3	6.4	5.0	19.4	21.5	23.5	7.7	78.3	47.0	47.7	52.3
56137	HERON LAKE	95.2	95.1	0.0	0.0	0.3	0.3	7.1	7.2	6.2	6.3	7.2	7.5	6.4	22.5	23.5	15.2	5.3	75.2	40.6	50.9	49.1
56138	HILLS	98.3	98.4	0.2	0.2	0.3	0.3	1.1	1.0	6.0	6.4	7.8	6.3	5.4	25.3	24.5	13.3	4.9	75.3	40.0	49.0	51.1
	MINNESOTA	89.5	88.0	3.5	4.2	2.9	3.4	2.9	3.4	6.8	6.8	7.2	7.3	7.4	28.6	23.9	10.1	1.9	74.9	36.1	49.6	50.5
	UNITED STATES	75.1	73.6	12.3	12.5	3.8	4.2	12.5	14.1	6.9	6.7	7.2	7.0	7.3	28.6	23.8	10.8	1.7	75.1	36.0	49.1	50.9

#	POST OFFICE NAME	2004 Per Capita Income	2004 HH Income Base	2004 Household Income Distribution (%): Less than $25,000	$25,000 to $49,999	$50,000 to $99,999	$100,000 to $149,999	$150,000 or More	Median Household Income: 2004	2009	2004 National Centile	2004 State Centile	2004 Home Value Base	2004 Home Value Distribution (%): Less than $50,000	$50,000 to $89,999	$90,000 to $174,999	$175,000 to $399,999	$400,000 or More	2004 Median Home Value
56001	MANKATO	24144	16300	26.7	30.8	29.6	8.5	4.5	43097	52181	56	41	10034	10.5	10.0	46.9	30.1	2.5	141259
56003	MANKATO	30769	5656	15.6	27.1	37.0	13.0	7.2	58040	70557	83	80	4314	5.1	5.3	42.9	43.3	3.4	168683
56007	ALBERT LEA	22384	9350	29.3	32.2	29.1	6.7	2.8	40439	47958	48	28	7038	13.2	25.8	43.1	16.4	1.7	104354
56009	ALDEN	21717	649	20.8	33.7	36.2	6.8	2.5	46948	53802	66	57	565	11.7	26.9	45.5	13.3	2.7	106495
56010	AMBOY	22203	577	25.1	30.9	35.0	6.1	3.0	43955	52070	58	44	490	11.0	26.5	42.9	16.3	3.3	105313
56011	BELLE PLAINE	25037	2572	15.8	21.7	43.6	16.1	2.9	63903	78813	88	87	2007	5.4	1.4	28.3	58.2	6.7	201462
56013	BLUE EARTH	21747	2032	27.4	35.5	29.6	5.1	2.5	40986	48508	50	31	1580	15.9	32.6	41.1	9.8	0.6	92162
56014	BRICELYN	19873	371	31.0	35.3	27.2	4.9	1.6	37619	43808	38	16	315	40.3	26.0	20.6	9.5	3.5	60217
56016	CLARKS GROVE	23424	389	18.8	34.2	37.5	6.9	2.6	47864	55129	68	60	338	12.4	18.3	43.8	21.6	3.9	116667
56017	CLEVELAND	25664	585	14.0	27.4	44.6	11.3	2.7	57147	67213	82	79	521	1.5	10.9	51.3	32.1	4.2	147809
56019	COMFREY	23570	338	25.2	35.5	29.9	5.9	3.6	43050	50793	56	40	281	15.7	24.2	36.7	20.3	3.2	105250
56020	CONGER	31198	109	15.6	31.2	36.7	11.0	5.5	53973	61880	78	75	97	13.4	16.5	32.0	29.9	8.3	137500
56021	COURTLAND	27211	458	13.3	21.6	46.7	13.3	5.0	62128	74871	86	84	408	3.9	11.0	38.7	41.4	4.9	164583
56022	DARFUR	25663	137	16.1	36.5	39.4	5.8	2.2	48507	54440	69	62	115	24.4	23.5	36.5	11.3	4.4	93571
56023	DELAVAN	23312	263	22.1	34.2	34.2	6.8	2.7	44851	51405	61	49	223	30.5	22.9	29.2	13.0	4.5	84231
56024	EAGLE LAKE	22579	935	16.0	28.2	44.5	8.5	2.8	54691	64102	79	76	806	17.5	7.2	42.4	30.9	2.0	145455
56025	EASTON	19682	233	26.2	34.8	28.8	7.7	2.6	39492	45483	44	24	198	18.2	26.3	39.4	8.6	7.6	98462
56026	ELLENDALE	22674	559	22.4	27.7	39.5	7.3	3.0	49908	58464	72	65	496	5.2	18.6	46.8	25.0	4.4	128676
56027	ELMORE	22513	398	33.4	36.2	23.4	4.8	2.3	33940	40000	24	6	334	53.9	27.3	13.8	4.2	0.9	46829
56028	ELYSIAN	25001	560	19.1	28.2	41.4	7.7	3.6	52178	61808	76	71	495	7.3	13.3	35.8	35.8	7.9	163068
56029	EMMONS	21635	241	25.3	31.5	32.8	8.7	1.7	44531	51185	60	47	206	8.7	34.5	37.4	15.1	4.4	99333
56030	ESSIG	26237	75	14.7	25.3	41.3	12.0	6.7	58032	72494	83	80	64	6.3	9.4	39.1	42.2	3.1	165625
56031	FAIRMONT	23603	5685	29.7	29.4	31.6	5.2	4.1	40363	48981	47	27	4341	13.8	30.3	40.3	14.1	1.4	100428
56032	FREEBORN	23382	255	19.2	33.7	36.9	6.3	3.9	47766	54758	68	59	220	16.8	22.3	44.1	10.9	5.9	109028
56033	FROST	21796	171	30.4	38.0	22.2	7.0	2.3	38608	45000	41	21	141	35.5	27.0	26.2	9.2	2.1	67222
56034	GARDEN CITY	26545	214	16.8	23.4	44.9	12.2	2.8	57075	68018	82	79	190	6.3	10.5	45.8	34.2	3.2	148148
56035	GENEVA	21522	209	25.8	28.7	33.5	10.1	1.9	44799	53707	61	48	184	6.0	21.7	51.1	19.0	2.2	118056
56036	GLENVILLE	20619	657	21.3	37.9	34.9	5.5	0.5	42916	49821	56	40	558	13.8	28.5	42.7	12.0	3.1	97679
56037	GOOD THUNDER	17659	378	23.3	33.9	38.4	3.7	0.8	45571	53360	63	52	330	4.6	21.8	53.6	17.3	2.7	119048
56039	GRANADA	19290	324	24.4	42.6	29.0	2.5	1.5	40978	47990	50	31	268	30.2	31.3	24.6	10.5	3.4	67083
56041	HANSKA	22609	435	19.1	31.3	39.1	7.4	3.2	49758	58150	71	65	372	14.5	21.8	34.4	22.6	6.7	114024
56042	HARTLAND	23991	254	19.7	35.0	36.6	6.7	2.0	46503	53138	65	55	217	12.0	20.3	47.0	14.8	6.0	119551
56043	HAYWARD	23339	274	17.2	31.0	40.9	8.8	2.2	51574	58786	75	70	232	10.8	12.9	33.6	33.2	9.5	143519
56044	HENDERSON	21599	796	18.5	26.6	42.5	9.4	3.0	53691	62326	78	74	683	6.4	16.4	41.9	30.2	5.1	140264
56045	HOLLANDALE	21586	853	20.4	33.1	36.9	7.3	2.3	46859	54127	66	56	737	9.5	18.1	43.0	25.8	3.7	123365
56046	HOPE	22869	24	20.8	25.0	41.7	12.5	0.0	52860	66506	77	72	23	0.0	8.7	43.5	43.5	4.4	170833
56047	HUNTLEY	26119	30	23.3	23.3	43.3	10.0	0.0	52915	60000	77	72	25	28.0	24.0	32.0	16.0	0.0	85000
56048	JANESVILLE	22391	1438	19.9	28.7	39.4	9.6	2.5	51059	59568	74	68	1251	7.8	13.7	52.4	23.9	2.3	131156
56050	KASOTA	30351	887	13.2	23.9	41.3	13.9	7.8	60301	74034	85	82	794	6.1	11.8	33.0	42.4	6.7	172727
56051	KIESTER	19459	347	31.4	36.3	27.4	3.8	1.2	37795	42987	39	18	287	43.6	29.3	18.1	4.5	4.5	58043
56052	KILKENNY	25759	291	18.6	27.5	41.6	9.3	3.1	53379	63440	77	73	268	6.7	7.1	31.0	48.9	6.3	186290
56054	LAFAYETTE	22268	695	18.7	29.6	38.9	10.4	2.5	50975	60045	74	68	597	8.2	16.4	41.9	27.3	6.2	131926
56055	LAKE CRYSTAL	21723	1455	19.2	32.2	39.3	7.6	1.7	48885	57725	70	63	1221	9.7	16.5	50.3	20.8	2.8	121670
56057	LE CENTER	24139	1405	23.7	26.3	37.5	9.4	3.1	50029	59653	72	66	1151	4.6	11.9	51.4	29.5	2.7	142336
56058	LE SUEUR	26823	2614	19.6	27.1	38.1	10.6	4.6	53053	62322	77	72	2137	7.2	10.3	42.8	36.5	3.3	149229
56060	LEWISVILLE	20706	221	24.0	42.5	27.2	4.5	1.8	37574	44077	38	16	190	25.8	22.1	33.2	15.3	3.7	98000
56062	MADELIA	19817	1204	26.5	34.7	30.2	6.5	2.2	41317	48307	51	32	880	13.4	31.8	40.8	11.6	2.4	95000
56063	MADISON LAKE	32283	1105	11.6	23.1	43.8	12.9	8.6	63453	78480	87	86	989	4.5	6.7	29.7	49.8	9.4	195568
56065	MAPLETON	23175	956	20.7	30.8	37.0	8.5	3.0	48493	57383	69	62	791	4.3	17.1	54.5	20.1	4.1	126500
56068	MINNESOTA LAKE	22477	374	22.2	35.8	31.8	8.6	1.6	42091	49571	53	36	309	23.0	29.5	35.6	10.7	1.3	87000
56069	MONTGOMERY	21280	1641	25.1	27.5	36.8	8.2	2.3	46864	56087	66	56	1366	6.0	10.6	49.1	31.3	3.0	143000
56071	NEW PRAGUE	25768	3874	15.4	21.6	42.3	15.8	5.0	62985	77686	87	85	3379	0.7	4.5	28.3	55.1	11.4	215103
56072	NEW RICHLAND	22051	901	19.8	34.5	37.0	6.4	2.3	46753	54668	66	56	750	8.8	22.0	45.1	22.1	2.0	118701
56073	NEW ULM	26134	6689	22.9	28.6	35.7	8.8	4.0	48432	56902	69	61	5407	9.7	12.9	52.2	23.0	2.2	128562
56074	NICOLLET	24368	671	18.6	27.1	42.0	9.2	3.0	53327	63492	77	73	591	6.6	9.1	45.0	33.0	6.3	152641
56075	NORTHROP	0	0	0.0	0.0	0.0	0.0	0.0	0	55000	0	0	0	0.0	0.0	0.0	0.0	0.0	0
56078	PEMBERTON	21000	353	18.7	32.6	37.1	7.7	4.0	48969	56450	70	63	305	7.5	14.4	45.3	25.3	7.5	136685
56080	SAINT CLAIR	24077	419	14.3	29.6	41.1	10.5	4.5	54800	65842	79	76	369	4.9	7.1	52.3	33.3	2.4	147943
56081	SAINT JAMES	19223	2589	26.5	36.2	30.8	5.1	1.5	39725	46358	45	24	1982	20.2	28.0	38.3	11.3	2.2	92448
56082	SAINT PETER	22580	3931	20.8	29.1	35.8	10.8	3.5	50048	61030	72	66	2937	7.9	6.5	48.9	34.0	2.7	152137
56083	SANBORN	22674	348	21.6	35.6	36.2	4.0	2.6	44353	51631	60	47	293	40.3	25.6	23.2	9.6	1.4	60263
56085	SLEEPY EYE	23121	2320	23.7	31.8	36.2	5.3	3.1	45328	52985	62	51	1909	8.7	17.4	48.5	22.3	3.0	122809
56087	SPRINGFIELD	20581	1165	28.9	35.3	27.9	5.3	2.6	40709	48746	49	29	949	21.7	30.5	41.5	5.2	1.2	87192
56088	TRUMAN	22068	781	24.1	34.8	31.5	7.3	2.3	42760	51425	55	39	602	16.1	37.0	33.2	9.1	4.5	86885
56089	TWIN LAKES	26355	358	17.6	31.0	38.6	9.8	3.1	51205	60567	74	69	328	7.9	20.1	37.8	29.3	4.9	133523
56090	VERNON CENTER	21693	348	19.5	32.2	36.8	7.2	4.3	48118	56519	69	60	296	10.8	18.2	51.4	15.5	4.1	115217
56091	WALDORF	20320	232	22.0	33.2	37.1	6.5	1.3	46341	52835	65	55	202	11.4	19.3	46.0	18.3	5.0	125625
56093	WASECA	23039	4855	20.1	29.9	37.6	8.5	3.9	49989	58911	72	66	3923	4.6	13.9	55.1	23.8	2.6	131384
56096	WATERVILLE	23493	1214	23.8	28.8	35.5	9.3	2.6	47754	56593	68	59	1012	6.9	9.7	49.2	30.1	4.1	140723
56097	WELLS	19624	1529	32.2	31.4	28.1	6.3	2.0	36594	42727	34	13	1238	24.2	31.9	31.4	10.1	2.3	81648
56098	WINNEBAGO	21139	965	27.5	36.6	28.8	5.2	2.0	40033	46680	46	26	771	34.4	33.3	23.4	7.4	1.6	65952
56101	WINDOM	20798	2535	29.9	34.1	28.2	4.9	2.9	37665	44948	38	17	1994	17.6	25.7	43.9	10.9	1.9	99236
56110	ADRIAN	18787	722	28.4	33.2	29.6	6.7	2.1	41564	49064	52	33	617	21.2	32.4	34.9	10.4	1.1	84767
56111	ALPHA	21865	264	14.8	34.9	43.9	3.4	3.0	50176	56310	72	67	221	19.9	27.6	31.2	14.5	6.8	93929
56113	ARCO	21965	168	29.8	32.7	32.7	3.6	1.2	40368	45224	47	28	144	22.9	20.1	38.9	16.7	1.4	107000
56114	AVOCA	20962	191	22.0	39.3	33.0	4.2	1.6	41961	47519	53	35	161	32.9	16.8	30.4	13.7	6.2	91250
56115	BALATON	21372	540	24.1	37.0	33.2	5.2	0.6	42273	49845	54	36	452	27.0	31.2	29.2	12.0	0.7	77667
56116	BEAVER CREEK	20732	246	22.0	32.9	38.2	4.5	2.4	45000	51798	61	50	208	13.9	21.2	38.5	21.2	5.3	118103
56117	BIGELOW	17618	185	28.7	34.1	31.4	4.3	1.6	41126	47171	50	31	155	22.6	32.9	26.5	16.1	1.9	83929
56118	BINGHAM LAKE	19195	168	27.4	39.3	27.4	3.6	2.4	39094	45407	43	22	139	28.8	39.6	20.1	8.6	2.9	67727
56119	BREWSTER	19279	372	26.1	30.4	34.4	8.6	0.5	44810	52982	61	48	321	28.4	27.1	32.7	10.6	1.3	80789
56120	BUTTERFIELD	17048	333	32.4	34.8	28.8	3.0	0.9	36384	41075	33	12	277	40.4	30.7	17.0	7.2	4.7	59138
56121	CEYLON	21335	333	27.6	40.5	25.5	3.9	2.4	38321	45387	40	20	282	39.7	26.2	20.2	9.2	4.6	60500
56122	CHANDLER	18860	213	28.2	37.6	25.8	6.1	2.4	40306	45807	47	27	172	22.1	27.9	37.8	11.1	1.2	90000
56123	CURRIE	26979	368	22.3	39.1	25.8	9.2	3.5	43351	50155	57	42	317	23.0	21.1	31.2	22.4	2.2	104934
56125	DOVRAY	18389	18	22.2	44.4	27.8	5.6	0.0	40000	45000	46	26	15	40.0	20.0	26.7	13.3	0.0	75000
56127	DUNNELL	19200	174	28.2	42.5	26.4	2.3	0.6	37617	43628	38	16	149	48.3	27.5	17.5	2.7	4.0	51389
56128	EDGERTON	19645	873	29.8	36.9	27.0	4.6	1.7	38312	45045	40	19	743	22.9	24.8	38.9	11.4	2.0	93977
56129	ELLSWORTH	18717	309	35.0	32.0	26.2	5.5	1.3	33332	39072	22	5	264	55.3	22.0	14.4	4.9	3.4	47813
56131	FULDA	18618	905	32.2	34.4	26.6	4.8	2.1	37239	43544	36	14	746	26.1	33.2	27.8	9.8	3.1	78036
56132	GARVIN	24236	228	20.6	37.7	29.8	9.2	2.6	46183	52998	64	54	191	25.7	16.8	33.0	21.5	3.1	106944
56134	HARDWICK	17821	168	25.0	42.9	26.8	4.8	0.6	41549	47474	51	33	142	34.5	21.1	27.5	14.8	2.1	80000
56136	HENDRICKS	18322	507	37.1	34.5	22.5	3.8	2.2	33803	38105	23	6	411	32.4	30.9	26.0	10.2	0.5	68690
56137	HERON LAKE	18389	458	28.0	38.0	26.2	5.5	2.4	39064	45489	43	22	377	40.9	29.7	21.5	5.0	2.9	60676
56138	HILLS	18833	377	23.9	35.0	35.8	4.2	1.1	43367	49119	57	42	327	13.5	31.5	42.5	11.3	1.2	94714
	MINNESOTA	29624		18.6	25.2	34.9	14.0	7.4	56724	71660				6.6	9.7	36.5	40.5	6.8	168676
	UNITED STATES	25866		24.7	27.1	30.8	10.9	6.5	48124	56710				10.9	15.0	33.7	30.1	10.4	145905

SPENDING POTENTIAL INDICES — MINNESOTA — 56001-56138 D

ZIP CODE #	POST OFFICE NAME	FINANCIAL SERVICES: Auto Loan	Home Loan	Invest-ments	Retire-ment Plans	THE HOME: Home Improvements: Home Repair	Lawn & Garden	Furnishings: Comput-ers & Hard-ware	Major Appli-ances	TV, Radio, Sound Equip-ment	Furni-ture	ENTERTAINMENT: Dine out/ Carry out	Sports Equip-ment	Fees & Tickets	Toys & Games	Travel	Cable TV	PERSONAL: Apparel & Services	Auto Repairs	Health Insur-ance	Pets & Supplies
56001	MANKATO	82	77	85	79	76	82	87	81	86	84	107	99	84	105	83	82	104	86	78	92
56003	MANKATO	105	112	116	115	110	112	108	108	104	109	131	127	110	132	107	100	128	107	100	121
56007	ALBERT LEA	75	71	69	69	73	80	72	74	75	71	92	86	72	93	73	76	88	74	78	86
56009	ALDEN	97	68	36	64	79	89	67	83	77	66	91	100	57	89	70	81	83	82	99	116
56010	AMBOY	96	67	35	64	79	88	67	82	77	66	90	99	57	88	69	80	82	81	98	114
56011	BELLE PLAINE	104	95	78	94	98	107	93	99	97	92	118	114	91	119	93	98	112	97	104	118
56013	BLUE EARTH	81	64	46	62	70	81	67	74	74	65	88	85	62	86	68	77	82	74	86	92
56014	BRICELYN	78	57	35	55	64	75	61	70	69	59	81	80	54	77	61	73	74	69	83	88
56016	CLARKS GROVE	87	82	74	81	85	91	79	84	81	79	99	99	78	100	80	81	95	83	87	102
56017	CLEVELAND	97	98	93	93	101	107	91	97	93	91	114	113	92	118	95	95	111	95	101	117
56019	COMFREY	102	71	37	67	83	93	70	87	81	69	95	104	60	93	73	85	86	85	103	121
56020	CONGER	117	103	77	98	109	117	95	106	102	95	123	126	93	126	98	104	117	103	115	137
56021	COURTLAND	102	127	135	127	125	123	114	113	105	113	132	133	121	141	116	102	132	109	101	125
56022	DARFUR	103	72	38	68	84	94	71	88	82	70	96	106	61	94	74	86	88	87	105	122
56023	DELAVAN	100	70	36	66	81	91	69	85	79	68	93	103	59	91	71	83	85	84	101	119
56024	EAGLE LAKE	87	93	90	94	91	91	88	89	84	89	105	105	88	106	87	80	103	88	80	100
56025	EASTON	94	66	34	62	77	86	65	81	75	64	88	97	56	86	68	79	80	79	96	112
56026	ELLENDALE	93	83	63	79	88	94	77	85	81	77	99	101	75	101	79	83	94	83	92	110
56027	ELMORE	86	63	40	61	70	83	68	77	77	65	91	88	60	86	68	81	83	77	92	97
56028	ELYSIAN	105	83	57	75	93	104	78	94	88	77	105	110	70	103	83	94	97	92	111	128
56029	EMMONS	93	65	34	62	76	85	64	79	74	64	87	96	55	85	67	78	79	78	95	111
56030	ESSIG	111	108	96	103	112	120	101	108	105	100	128	126	102	132	104	107	123	105	114	132
56031	FAIRMONT	80	72	69	71	75	84	74	78	78	73	95	90	72	96	75	80	91	78	84	92
56032	FREEBORN	105	73	38	69	85	95	72	89	83	71	97	107	62	95	75	87	89	88	106	124
56033	FROST	86	60	31	56	70	78	59	73	68	58	80	88	50	78	61	71	73	72	87	102
56034	GARDEN CITY	105	93	71	88	98	106	86	96	92	86	111	114	84	114	89	94	106	93	104	123
56035	GENEVA	95	67	35	63	78	87	66	81	76	65	89	98	56	87	68	80	81	80	97	113
56036	GLENVILLE	80	63	44	62	69	78	64	72	70	63	84	84	59	83	65	72	78	71	81	91
56037	GOOD THUNDER	75	63	49	63	67	75	65	70	69	64	84	80	62	83	65	70	78	69	76	83
56039	GRANADA	87	60	32	57	70	79	60	74	69	59	81	89	51	79	62	72	74	73	88	103
56041	HANSKA	94	79	56	75	85	92	74	84	80	74	97	101	71	98	76	83	91	82	93	111
56042	HARTLAND	90	80	60	76	84	90	74	82	78	74	95	97	72	97	76	80	90	80	89	106
56043	HAYWARD	93	82	61	78	87	93	76	84	81	76	98	101	74	100	78	83	93	82	92	109
56044	HENDERSON	97	84	65	82	89	97	82	89	87	81	106	104	79	106	83	89	100	87	97	110
56045	HOLLANDALE	102	71	37	67	83	93	70	87	81	69	95	104	60	93	73	85	86	85	103	121
56046	HOPE	93	83	63	79	88	94	77	85	81	77	99	101	75	101	79	83	94	83	92	110
56047	HUNTLEY	104	73	38	69	85	95	72	89	83	71	97	107	61	95	74	87	88	87	106	123
56048	JANESVILLE	95	81	61	79	86	95	80	87	85	79	103	102	76	103	81	87	97	86	95	108
56050	KASOTA	117	113	96	108	117	124	103	112	106	103	130	133	103	134	107	108	125	109	117	140
56051	KIESTER	79	55	29	52	64	72	55	67	63	54	74	81	47	72	57	66	67	66	80	94
56052	KILKENNY	104	92	70	88	98	105	85	95	91	85	110	113	84	113	88	93	105	92	103	122
56054	LAFAYETTE	96	84	65	82	91	97	79	90	84	79	101	107	75	102	82	85	95	88	97	115
56055	LAKE CRYSTAL	83	78	68	76	81	88	76	81	78	75	96	94	75	98	77	79	92	79	85	97
56057	LE CENTER	101	85	65	83	91	101	85	93	91	84	111	108	81	110	86	94	104	92	102	114
56058	LE SUEUR	103	96	81	95	99	108	93	99	96	92	118	115	92	119	94	97	112	97	103	118
56060	LEWISVILLE	93	65	34	62	76	85	64	80	74	64	87	96	55	85	67	78	79	79	95	111
56062	MADELIA	82	64	45	63	70	80	67	75	74	65	88	86	61	86	67	76	81	74	85	92
56063	MADISON LAKE	131	119	98	114	125	133	112	123	116	112	142	145	108	143	115	118	136	121	129	154
56065	MAPLETON	101	78	52	76	86	97	79	90	87	77	104	105	72	102	80	89	96	89	102	115
56068	MINNESOTA LAKE	97	68	35	64	79	88	67	83	77	66	90	100	57	88	69	81	82	81	98	115
56069	MONTGOMERY	86	74	58	73	78	87	75	80	79	74	96	93	72	96	75	81	90	79	87	97
56071	NEW PRAGUE	107	106	96	105	107	113	102	106	102	101	126	123	102	129	102	102	122	104	106	123
56072	NEW RICHLAND	91	73	51	71	79	88	73	82	79	72	95	96	68	94	74	82	89	81	92	104
56073	NEW ULM	88	90	89	88	91	98	88	90	88	87	109	104	89	112	89	89	106	89	91	103
56074	NICOLLET	95	92	84	93	94	96	89	93	88	89	109	111	87	109	89	86	105	93	91	110
56075	NORTHROP	0	0	0	0	0	0	0	0	0	0	0	0	0	0	0	0	0	0	0	0
56078	PEMBERTON	105	73	38	69	85	95	72	89	83	71	97	108	62	96	75	87	89	88	106	124
56080	SAINT CLAIR	93	103	104	105	100	99	97	96	91	98	115	114	98	116	96	86	113	96	85	106
56081	SAINT JAMES	78	64	49	64	69	77	66	72	70	65	85	84	61	84	66	72	79	71	79	89
56082	SAINT PETER	92	81	77	82	83	93	88	89	90	85	111	105	84	108	86	90	105	91	93	103
56083	SANBORN	106	74	39	70	86	96	73	90	84	72	99	109	62	97	76	88	90	89	107	126
56085	SLEEPY EYE	96	76	52	73	83	93	77	87	84	75	100	102	70	98	78	87	93	86	99	111
56087	SPRINGFIELD	87	63	37	60	71	82	65	76	73	63	86	90	56	83	66	77	79	76	90	101
56088	TRUMAN	90	66	40	63	73	86	70	80	79	67	93	92	62	89	70	83	85	80	96	102
56089	TWIN LAKES	102	89	66	85	95	102	83	92	88	83	107	110	80	109	85	91	102	90	101	120
56090	VERNON CENTER	105	73	39	69	85	95	72	89	83	71	98	107	62	96	75	87	89	88	106	124
56091	WALDORF	91	64	33	60	74	83	63	78	73	62	85	94	54	84	65	76	78	77	93	109
56093	WASECA	93	85	71	82	88	94	82	88	85	82	104	104	80	105	83	86	100	87	92	108
56096	WATERVILLE	97	75	49	71	83	93	75	86	83	73	99	101	68	97	76	87	91	85	100	113
56097	WELLS	80	59	37	57	66	78	64	72	72	61	85	82	56	81	64	76	77	72	86	90
56098	WINNEBAGO	83	60	37	58	68	79	64	74	73	62	85	85	56	82	65	77	78	73	88	94
56101	WINDOM	78	62	46	60	68	77	64	72	70	62	83	84	58	82	65	72	77	71	82	91
56110	ADRIAN	80	64	46	63	70	78	66	73	71	65	86	85	61	85	66	73	80	72	82	91
56111	ALPHA	99	69	36	66	81	91	69	85	79	68	93	102	58	91	71	83	84	84	101	118
56113	ARCO	93	65	35	62	76	85	65	80	74	64	87	96	55	86	67	78	80	79	95	111
56114	AVOCA	87	61	32	57	71	79	60	74	69	59	81	89	51	79	62	72	74	73	88	103
56115	BALATON	79	69	58	66	75	83	69	75	74	67	90	87	67	94	71	78	85	74	85	93
56116	BEAVER CREEK	96	67	35	63	78	87	66	82	76	65	89	98	56	87	68	80	81	80	97	114
56117	BIGELOW	87	61	32	57	71	79	60	74	69	59	81	89	51	79	62	73	74	73	88	103
56118	BINGHAM LAKE	89	63	35	60	73	82	63	76	72	62	84	92	54	83	65	75	77	75	91	105
56119	BREWSTER	82	66	48	65	71	80	68	75	73	66	88	87	63	87	68	75	82	74	83	92
56120	BUTTERFIELD	68	58	45	58	61	69	60	64	63	59	77	73	57	76	59	64	72	63	69	75
56121	CEYLON	71	69	64	65	72	80	68	71	72	66	88	81	68	93	70	75	84	70	79	84
56122	CHANDLER	92	64	33	60	75	83	63	78	73	62	85	94	54	84	66	76	78	77	93	109
56123	CURRIE	104	80	52	73	91	102	76	92	86	75	102	109	68	101	81	92	95	91	109	127
56125	DOVRAY	83	58	30	55	68	76	57	71	66	57	78	85	49	76	59	69	71	70	84	99
56127	DUNNELL	58	62	65	59	63	70	61	61	64	59	79	68	65	85	64	66	76	60	66	68
56128	EDGERTON	81	59	35	56	66	77	62	72	70	60	82	83	54	79	62	74	75	71	86	93
56129	ELLSWORTH	71	54	35	51	59	70	59	65	66	56	78	73	53	74	59	70	71	65	78	79
56131	FULDA	71	62	57	62	66	71	63	68	65	62	79	81	59	77	63	65	75	68	72	83
56132	GARVIN	103	75	44	70	86	97	73	89	83	72	98	106	63	96	76	88	90	88	106	123
56134	HARDWICK	81	57	30	53	66	74	56	69	64	55	75	83	48	74	58	68	69	68	82	96
56136	HENDRICKS	65	55	47	54	58	66	59	62	62	57	75	71	55	71	58	64	70	62	69	72
56137	HERON LAKE	79	58	36	56	65	76	63	71	71	60	83	81	55	79	63	75	76	71	85	89
56138	HILLS	88	61	32	58	71	80	60	75	70	60	82	90	52	80	63	73	74	74	89	104
	MINNESOTA	107	106	108	107	107	113	106	107	105	105	131	126	105	131	105	104	127	107	105	123
	UNITED STATES	100	100	100	100	100	100	100	100	100	100	100	100	100	100	100	100	100	100	100	100

#	POST OFFICE NAME	COUNTY FIPS CODE	POPULATION 2000	POPULATION 2004	POPULATION 2009	2000-2004 ANNUAL RATE % Rate	2000-2004 ANNUAL RATE State Centile	HOUSEHOLDS 2000	HOUSEHOLDS 2004	HOUSEHOLDS 2009	% Annual Rate 2000-2004	2004 Average HH Size	FAMILIES 2000	FAMILIES 2004	% Annual Rate 2000-2004
56139	HOLLAND	117	643	634	630	-0.3	15	259	260	263	0.1	2.44	202	199	-0.4
56141	IONA	101	404	447	467	2.4	84	154	175	185	3.1	2.55	107	118	2.3
56142	IVANHOE	081	1438	1407	1393	-0.5	10	594	593	593	0.0	2.28	387	374	-0.8
56143	JACKSON	063	4933	4913	4914	-0.1	24	2066	2091	2125	0.3	2.26	1328	1303	-0.5
56144	JASPER	133	1212	1232	1241	0.4	41	506	524	537	0.8	2.35	351	354	0.2
56145	JEFFERS	033	763	744	739	-0.6	7	327	325	328	-0.1	2.29	227	219	-0.8
56146	KANARANZI	133	286	283	282	-0.3	18	95	96	97	0.3	2.94	69	67	-0.7
56147	KENNETH	133	542	528	527	-0.6	7	191	190	192	-0.1	2.78	140	136	-0.7
56149	LAKE BENTON	081	1319	1311	1308	-0.1	22	563	570	573	0.3	2.29	376	370	-0.4
56150	LAKEFIELD	063	3185	3231	3257	0.3	39	1277	1315	1345	0.7	2.39	881	882	0.0
56151	LAKE WILSON	101	1019	986	964	-0.8	4	409	404	400	-0.3	2.44	308	295	-1.0
56152	LAMBERTON	127	1550	1514	1504	-0.6	8	648	644	651	-0.2	2.24	418	404	-0.8
56153	LEOTA	105	92	91	92	-0.3	18	27	27	27	0.0	3.37	21	21	0.0
56155	LISMORE	105	469	464	470	-0.3	18	185	185	189	0.0	2.51	142	139	-0.5
56156	LUVERNE	133	5633	5793	5912	0.7	48	2328	2422	2505	0.9	2.32	1573	1597	0.4
56157	LYND	083	814	842	872	0.8	53	296	310	325	1.1	2.72	229	235	0.6
56158	MAGNOLIA	133	538	532	532	-0.3	18	194	195	198	0.1	2.72	142	138	-0.7
56159	MOUNTAIN LAKE	033	2872	2934	2964	0.5	43	1041	1069	1088	0.6	2.62	714	712	-0.1
56160	ODIN	165	414	401	393	-0.8	4	175	171	170	-0.5	2.35	128	123	-0.9
56161	OKABENA	063	587	578	577	-0.4	14	222	222	225	0.0	2.60	175	172	-0.4
56162	ORMSBY	091	344	334	329	-0.7	5	142	140	140	-0.3	2.39	107	104	-0.7
56164	PIPESTONE	117	5958	5950	5940	0.0	26	2464	2500	2534	0.3	2.31	1576	1548	-0.4
56165	READING	105	429	424	430	-0.3	17	153	153	156	0.0	2.77	126	124	-0.4
56166	REVERE	127	342	335	333	-0.5	10	132	131	133	-0.2	2.49	99	96	-0.7
56167	ROUND LAKE	063	951	997	1032	1.1	61	408	434	454	1.5	2.30	307	319	0.9
56168	RUSHMORE	105	1087	1038	1045	-1.1	2	405	391	396	-0.8	2.65	306	290	-1.3
56169	RUSSELL	083	752	741	753	-0.4	15	288	289	298	0.1	2.56	216	211	-0.6
56170	RUTHTON	117	791	768	761	-0.7	5	314	311	313	-0.2	2.47	240	232	-0.8
56171	SHERBURN	091	1898	1906	1903	0.1	31	791	808	817	0.5	2.34	525	519	-0.3
56172	SLAYTON	101	2958	2867	2813	-0.7	4	1257	1234	1225	-0.4	2.26	817	778	-1.1
56173	STEEN	133	474	467	466	-0.4	15	172	172	175	0.0	2.66	125	122	-0.6
56174	STORDEN	033	416	406	403	-0.6	8	185	184	185	-0.1	2.21	134	130	-0.7
56175	TRACY	083	3228	3327	3430	0.7	50	1286	1334	1387	0.9	2.42	813	820	0.2
56176	TRIMONT	091	1191	1183	1175	-0.2	21	487	491	495	0.2	2.33	329	322	-0.5
56178	TYLER	081	1806	1835	1852	0.4	40	745	770	788	0.8	2.32	508	511	0.1
56180	WALNUT GROVE	127	1051	1068	1075	0.4	40	450	462	470	0.6	2.31	310	309	-0.1
56181	WELCOME	091	1073	1048	1035	-0.6	8	439	438	439	-0.1	2.39	305	296	-0.7
56183	WESTBROOK	033	1379	1340	1332	-0.7	6	591	583	587	-0.3	2.23	395	378	-1.0
56185	WILMONT	105	766	756	766	-0.3	15	286	286	291	0.0	2.64	219	214	-0.5
56186	WOODSTOCK	117	408	392	384	-0.9	2	159	156	156	-0.5	2.51	120	115	-1.0
56187	WORTHINGTON	105	12427	12803	13177	0.7	50	4736	4883	5037	0.7	2.56	3149	3153	0.0
56201	WILLMAR	067	22320	22529	22756	0.2	35	8681	8861	9067	0.5	2.46	5582	5523	-0.3
56207	ALBERTA	149	292	291	299	-0.1	24	105	106	111	0.2	2.75	89	89	0.0
56208	APPLETON	151	3599	3606	3628	0.1	30	1027	1042	1065	0.3	2.12	603	588	-0.6
56209	ATWATER	067	2345	2304	2307	-0.4	13	924	928	945	0.1	2.46	650	636	-0.5
56210	BARRY	011	112	115	116	0.6	47	41	43	44	1.1	2.58	28	28	0.0
56211	BEARDSLEY	011	438	433	432	-0.3	17	183	184	186	0.1	2.35	123	120	-0.6
56212	BELLINGHAM	073	623	601	588	-0.8	3	250	245	244	-0.5	2.45	183	175	-1.1
56214	BELVIEW	127	794	799	800	0.2	33	295	302	307	0.6	2.58	214	214	0.0
56215	BENSON	151	4981	4938	4948	-0.2	19	2023	2032	2061	0.1	2.36	1338	1301	-0.7
56216	BLOMKEST	067	842	817	814	-0.7	5	282	276	278	-0.5	2.96	233	224	-0.9
56218	BOYD	073	611	594	583	-0.7	6	243	239	237	-0.4	2.49	167	160	-1.0
56219	BROWNS VALLEY	155	1002	979	940	-0.5	9	404	399	387	-0.3	2.36	262	250	-1.1
56220	CANBY	173	2991	2892	2808	-0.8	4	1226	1199	1175	-0.5	2.29	757	714	-1.4
56221	CHOKIO	149	790	784	804	-0.2	20	294	296	310	0.2	2.34	208	204	-0.5
56222	CLARA CITY	023	1961	1910	1884	-0.6	7	782	765	758	-0.5	2.37	537	511	-1.2
56223	CLARKFIELD	173	1639	1643	1621	0.1	30	627	638	636	0.4	2.41	424	419	-0.3
56224	CLEMENTS	127	468	462	460	-0.3	16	178	180	182	0.3	2.57	134	132	-0.4
56225	CLINTON	011	733	725	724	-0.3	18	285	285	288	0.0	2.41	188	183	-0.6
56226	CLONTARF	151	233	226	224	-0.7	5	86	84	84	-0.6	2.68	69	66	-1.0
56227	CORRELL	011	327	318	317	-0.7	6	133	131	133	-0.4	2.43	101	98	-0.7
56228	COSMOS	093	1092	1192	1297	2.1	80	425	474	525	2.6	2.43	306	332	1.9
56229	COTTONWOOD	083	1601	1776	1903	2.5	85	603	679	738	2.8	2.58	436	476	2.1
56230	DANUBE	129	960	983	996	0.6	45	363	376	386	0.8	2.61	284	289	0.4
56231	DANVERS	151	512	594	643	3.6	93	192	226	249	3.9	2.63	143	166	3.6
56232	DAWSON	073	2342	2330	2311	-0.1	22	980	992	999	0.3	2.27	635	624	-0.4
56235	DONNELLY	149	476	475	489	-0.1	25	204	208	218	0.5	2.28	142	141	-0.2
56236	DUMONT	155	646	615	585	-1.2	1	240	231	223	-0.9	2.66	181	172	-1.2
56237	ECHO	173	694	739	751	1.5	69	283	305	314	1.8	2.42	203	213	1.1
56239	GHENT	083	561	556	566	-0.2	19	205	206	213	0.1	2.69	160	158	-0.3
56240	GRACEVILLE	011	941	977	999	0.9	56	362	380	393	1.2	2.44	236	241	0.5
56241	GRANITE FALLS	173	4297	4151	4046	-0.8	3	1806	1770	1746	-0.5	2.29	1159	1096	-1.3
56243	GROVE CITY	093	1708	1830	1978	1.6	72	651	709	777	2.0	2.57	468	496	1.4
56244	HANCOCK	149	1233	1246	1282	0.3	36	461	474	496	0.7	2.54	317	317	0.0
56245	HANLEY FALLS	173	708	694	677	-0.5	11	258	255	250	-0.3	2.72	192	185	-0.9
56248	HERMAN	051	849	895	938	1.3	64	356	382	406	1.7	2.30	236	246	1.0
56249	HOLLOWAY	151	408	487	534	4.3	96	154	187	208	4.7	2.60	114	134	3.9
56251	KANDIYOHI	067	1018	1003	1002	-0.4	15	396	398	405	0.1	2.51	308	303	-0.4
56252	KERKHOVEN	151	1123	1102	1097	-0.4	12	435	432	436	-0.2	2.55	303	293	-0.8
56253	LAKE LILLIAN	067	1190	1144	1138	-0.9	2	474	466	472	-0.4	2.45	331	317	-1.0
56255	LUCAN	127	538	534	532	-0.2	20	202	203	206	0.1	2.63	149	147	-0.3
56256	MADISON	073	3715	3671	3629	-0.3	17	1506	1510	1510	0.1	2.34	1008	981	-0.6
56257	MARIETTA	073	776	749	733	-0.8	3	337	331	328	-0.4	2.26	232	221	-1.1
56258	MARSHALL	083	14558	14817	15263	0.4	41	5525	5710	5970	0.8	2.42	3400	3392	-0.1
56260	MAYNARD	023	971	1061	1107	2.1	80	321	361	383	2.8	2.75	247	270	2.1
56262	MILAN	023	747	716	701	-1.0	2	319	312	308	-0.5	2.29	211	200	-1.3
56263	MILROY	127	807	806	807	0.0	26	303	307	312	0.3	2.63	224	222	-0.2
56264	MINNEOTA	083	2553	2550	2583	0.0	26	987	1000	1027	0.3	2.45	691	680	-0.4
56265	MONTEVIDEO	023	7825	7794	7769	-0.1	24	3264	3303	3328	0.3	2.32	2172	2134	-0.4
56266	MORGAN	127	2162	2217	2258	0.6	46	842	878	909	1.0	2.48	598	608	0.4
56267	MORRIS	149	7262	7542	7875	0.9	56	2687	2856	3051	1.5	2.35	1611	1653	0.6
56270	MORTON	129	1218	1350	1430	2.5	84	471	532	572	2.9	2.53	326	356	2.1
56271	MURDOCK	151	933	911	906	-0.6	8	370	368	371	-0.1	2.48	262	253	-0.8
56273	NEW LONDON	067	5080	5227	5314	0.7	49	1884	1979	2047	1.2	2.59	1435	1472	0.6
56274	NORCROSS	051	242	239	243	-0.3	16	107	107	110	0.0	2.22	75	73	-0.6
	MINNESOTA					1.4					1.6	2.50			1.0
	UNITED STATES					1.2					1.3	2.58			1.1

ZIP CODE #	POST OFFICE NAME	RACE (%) White 2000	White 2004	Black 2000	Black 2004	Asian/Pacific 2000	Asian/Pacific 2004	% Hispanic Origin 2000	% Hispanic Origin 2004	2004 AGE DISTRIBUTION (%) 0-4	5-9	10-14	15-19	20-24	25-44	45-64	65-84	85+	18+	MEDIAN AGE 2004	% 2004 Males	% 2004 Females
56139	HOLLAND	98.9	98.9	0.0	0.0	0.0	0.0	0.3	0.5	5.7	6.2	8.5	6.9	5.5	23.2	26.5	15.8	1.7	75.4	41.2	52.4	47.6
56141	IONA	97.8	98.0	0.0	0.0	0.5	0.5	1.5	1.6	5.2	7.8	9.8	9.0	4.0	24.2	24.6	13.0	2.5	70.7	39.1	49.2	50.8
56142	IVANHOE	99.4	99.4	0.0	0.0	0.0	0.0	0.4	0.4	4.6	5.5	6.6	6.0	5.8	22.6	25.2	18.6	5.1	78.9	44.0	49.1	50.9
56143	JACKSON	95.4	95.2	0.2	0.2	2.9	3.0	1.4	1.5	5.4	5.3	6.3	7.2	7.0	23.5	25.3	15.7	4.3	78.7	41.7	50.6	49.4
56144	JASPER	98.2	98.2	0.2	0.2	0.2	0.2	0.7	0.7	6.2	6.5	7.5	6.4	5.0	24.6	24.9	16.2	2.8	75.8	41.3	48.2	51.8
56145	JEFFERS	98.6	98.5	0.3	0.3	0.3	0.3	1.2	1.1	4.7	5.1	5.9	5.8	5.5	23.3	29.2	17.6	3.0	80.9	44.8	50.7	49.3
56146	KANARANZI	94.1	94.0	1.1	1.1	1.8	1.8	1.8	1.8	7.1	7.1	7.8	6.7	6.0	25.8	26.5	11.3	1.8	73.1	37.6	51.9	48.1
56147	KENNETH	96.7	96.6	0.0	0.0	0.6	0.6	1.1	1.3	6.6	7.0	8.5	7.6	5.9	23.1	27.3	12.3	1.7	72.9	38.9	51.3	48.7
56149	LAKE BENTON	98.3	98.3	0.1	0.1	0.2	0.2	0.8	0.8	6.2	6.2	6.8	6.2	5.3	22.4	24.7	18.9	3.4	76.6	42.9	50.0	50.0
56150	LAKEFIELD	99.2	99.1	0.0	0.0	0.2	0.2	0.9	0.9	5.1	5.7	6.9	6.5	5.9	22.6	26.6	17.1	3.7	78.2	43.2	49.4	50.6
56151	LAKE WILSON	98.1	98.1	0.1	0.1	0.3	0.3	1.6	1.6	6.3	6.8	7.5	6.7	6.2	23.0	28.3	13.3	1.9	75.0	40.6	53.0	47.0
56152	LAMBERTON	99.4	99.3	0.0	0.0	0.1	0.1	0.6	0.5	5.2	5.0	6.5	5.6	5.4	20.9	23.3	20.5	7.5	78.9	46.0	49.1	50.9
56153	LEOTA	98.9	98.9	0.0	0.0	1.1	1.1	0.0	0.0	4.4	6.6	6.6	6.6	4.4	18.7	29.7	20.9	2.2	75.8	46.0	51.7	48.4
56155	LISMORE	97.7	97.4	0.0	0.0	1.1	1.3	1.7	2.2	6.7	7.1	8.8	7.5	5.6	22.8	26.5	12.7	2.2	72.4	39.2	50.2	49.8
56156	LUVERNE	97.5	97.4	0.7	0.7	0.6	0.6	1.4	1.4	6.0	5.8	7.1	6.7	6.2	22.0	23.4	18.4	4.4	76.7	42.2	48.1	51.9
56157	LYND	96.6	96.0	0.3	0.4	0.4	0.5	3.3	4.3	6.7	6.9	8.2	7.6	7.2	26.7	27.0	8.8	1.0	73.6	36.1	51.7	48.3
56158	MAGNOLIA	94.4	94.0	0.9	0.9	1.7	1.9	1.7	1.9	7.0	7.1	8.1	7.0	5.8	25.6	26.3	11.1	2.1	72.9	37.6	51.5	48.5
56159	MOUNTAIN LAKE	87.1	87.0	0.6	0.6	5.4	5.6	4.8	4.8	7.3	8.1	8.0	6.5	5.4	22.7	19.1	17.0	5.8	72.5	39.0	49.3	50.8
56160	ODIN	97.3	97.0	0.0	0.0	1.2	1.5	0.2	0.5	4.5	5.2	6.5	5.7	6.0	18.7	33.7	16.5	3.2	80.3	46.7	50.1	49.9
56161	OKABENA	98.8	98.8	0.2	0.2	0.0	0.0	2.9	2.9	6.2	6.8	7.4	6.9	5.9	22.5	27.9	14.4	2.1	75.3	40.5	49.8	50.2
56162	ORMSBY	98.3	97.9	0.0	0.0	0.9	0.9	0.3	0.6	5.1	5.4	6.9	6.0	6.0	19.5	32.9	15.9	2.4	79.0	45.6	50.0	50.0
56164	PIPESTONE	95.5	95.4	0.3	0.3	0.6	0.6	0.9	0.9	6.2	6.1	7.0	6.9	6.5	23.9	22.6	16.5	4.2	76.3	40.4	47.9	52.2
56165	READING	97.2	96.5	0.2	0.5	0.5	0.7	0.9	1.4	8.3	8.0	7.1	6.6	5.7	25.7	25.9	11.8	0.9	73.1	39.1	48.1	51.9
56166	REVERE	99.1	98.8	0.3	0.3	0.6	0.6	0.9	0.9	4.5	5.4	7.2	6.9	5.4	25.1	28.1	15.8	1.8	77.0	42.6	51.0	49.0
56167	ROUND LAKE	98.4	98.0	0.0	0.0	0.1	0.1	1.5	1.8	5.0	6.2	7.8	7.1	5.6	24.0	29.3	13.5	1.4	75.9	41.5	50.6	49.5
56168	RUSHMORE	97.7	97.3	0.0	0.0	0.4	0.5	1.9	2.4	6.8	7.0	7.6	6.5	5.6	24.7	26.9	13.1	1.8	74.4	40.1	50.8	49.2
56169	RUSSELL	97.2	96.8	0.1	0.1	0.7	0.9	2.4	2.8	6.8	6.6	7.6	7.3	4.7	26.3	26.7	12.4	1.6	74.6	39.5	51.2	48.9
56170	RUTHTON	98.6	98.6	0.3	0.3	0.1	0.1	0.3	0.3	7.7	7.8	7.6	7.3	5.5	25.3	24.7	12.5	1.7	72.3	37.9	51.3	48.7
56171	SHERBURN	99.0	98.9	0.0	0.0	0.2	0.3	0.8	0.9	6.0	6.2	7.6	6.9	5.4	22.4	27.1	15.8	2.7	76.1	41.8	49.2	50.8
56172	SLAYTON	99.0	99.0	0.1	0.1	0.3	0.3	0.5	0.5	5.3	5.7	6.6	6.2	5.0	21.7	25.3	19.9	4.4	78.3	44.7	47.4	52.6
56173	STEEN	96.0	96.2	0.6	0.6	1.1	1.1	1.3	1.5	6.4	6.9	7.9	6.6	5.8	25.7	25.5	12.0	3.2	74.1	38.3	50.3	49.7
56174	STORDEN	98.3	98.5	0.0	0.0	0.0	0.0	1.9	2.0	5.9	6.2	6.2	5.9	5.4	23.4	28.8	15.5	2.7	78.8	43.1	51.7	48.3
56175	TRACY	90.9	89.6	0.3	0.3	5.8	6.8	2.1	2.4	6.6	6.4	7.0	6.9	6.5	21.5	23.7	16.7	4.7	75.7	41.2	47.8	52.2
56176	TRIMONT	98.5	98.3	0.3	0.4	0.1	0.2	0.3	0.3	4.8	5.5	7.0	6.3	5.7	19.7	28.2	17.2	5.6	78.4	45.6	47.4	52.6
56178	TYLER	98.3	98.3	0.1	0.1	0.3	0.3	1.8	1.8	6.9	6.6	6.2	5.6	5.5	23.2	23.8	18.2	4.2	76.6	42.4	49.5	50.5
56180	WALNUT GROVE	98.3	98.4	0.4	0.4	1.0	0.9	0.1	0.1	5.7	5.6	6.2	5.7	5.2	22.5	26.9	18.6	3.7	78.8	44.4	48.9	51.1
56181	WELCOME	98.9	98.7	0.0	0.0	0.2	0.2	0.9	1.1	6.3	6.5	6.7	7.7	4.9	22.4	28.4	14.9	2.2	75.9	41.8	51.4	48.6
56183	WESTBROOK	98.7	98.7	0.1	0.1	0.2	0.2	0.6	0.7	5.5	6.0	5.4	4.9	4.3	17.4	27.5	21.9	7.2	79.6	49.8	48.0	52.0
56185	WILMONT	99.2	99.1	0.0	0.0	0.3	0.3	0.4	0.5	6.4	7.5	8.2	6.6	5.2	23.5	26.6	13.8	2.3	73.7	40.3	52.4	47.6
56186	WOODSTOCK	98.0	98.0	0.0	0.0	0.7	0.8	0.3	0.5	5.9	6.4	6.6	6.4	6.4	23.7	29.6	13.3	1.8	77.0	41.5	50.8	49.2
56187	WORTHINGTON	78.8	75.6	1.7	2.1	6.5	7.6	17.6	20.3	7.6	7.0	6.5	6.5	7.7	25.7	22.4	13.3	3.3	74.9	36.5	50.0	50.1
56201	WILLMAR	89.8	88.1	0.8	1.0	0.6	0.7	13.5	16.0	7.1	6.4	7.1	7.4	9.4	25.5	22.8	11.5	2.9	75.3	34.8	48.5	51.5
56207	ALBERTA	97.3	97.3	0.0	0.0	0.0	0.0	1.0	1.4	6.5	7.2	7.6	7.6	5.8	23.7	27.5	13.4	0.7	74.6	40.3	51.9	48.1
56208	APPLETON	73.8	73.0	8.6	9.0	9.4	9.7	4.3	4.4	3.1	3.6	4.3	3.9	8.0	37.1	24.6	11.4	3.9	86.5	39.6	67.4	32.6
56209	ATWATER	98.3	98.0	0.1	0.1	0.3	0.3	1.3	1.6	5.4	5.7	7.3	6.4	6.5	24.9	28.3	13.2	2.4	77.2	41.4	50.5	49.5
56210	BARRY	99.1	99.1	0.0	0.0	0.9	0.9	0.0	0.0	5.2	5.2	7.0	7.8	6.1	20.0	25.2	20.0	3.5	77.4	44.1	48.7	51.3
56211	BEARDSLEY	99.5	99.3	0.0	0.0	0.5	0.5	0.7	0.5	5.5	5.8	5.8	7.4	5.1	21.5	28.4	17.6	3.0	78.8	44.4	51.3	48.7
56212	BELLINGHAM	99.7	99.5	0.2	0.2	0.2	0.2	0.3	0.3	5.3	5.8	8.5	6.8	5.3	23.1	25.1	17.8	2.2	76.4	41.9	54.6	45.4
56214	BELVIEW	98.7	98.8	0.0	0.0	0.6	0.6	0.5	0.5	6.4	6.5	6.9	7.5	6.3	23.7	24.4	14.8	3.6	75.1	40.8	52.9	47.1
56215	BENSON	98.4	98.3	0.2	0.2	0.2	0.2	1.5	1.5	6.5	6.5	6.7	6.4	6.6	23.7	23.6	15.9	4.1	75.9	40.4	48.9	51.2
56216	BLOMKEST	97.5	97.2	0.1	0.1	1.2	1.4	2.5	3.1	8.3	8.3	8.9	6.9	6.1	25.8	25.1	9.2	1.4	70.1	35.9	53.6	46.4
56218	BOYD	98.9	98.7	0.0	0.0	0.7	0.8	0.0	0.0	4.9	7.1	8.1	7.4	6.1	22.6	30.0	12.3	1.7	75.3	42.0	49.3	50.7
56219	BROWNS VALLEY	87.8	87.4	0.0	0.0	0.4	0.5	1.4	1.6	6.7	5.4	6.4	7.0	6.5	18.0	22.7	21.9	5.4	77.4	45.0	48.8	51.2
56220	CANBY	98.6	98.3	0.1	0.2	0.1	0.1	0.9	1.1	5.3	5.1	6.6	7.1	7.3	20.4	23.7	19.4	5.1	78.9	43.7	49.1	50.9
56221	CHOKIO	99.2	99.2	0.0	0.0	0.1	0.1	0.3	0.1	5.9	5.6	5.4	5.4	6.0	18.4	22.5	22.5	8.6	79.2	47.6	45.2	54.9
56222	CLARA CITY	98.2	98.2	0.3	0.3	0.2	0.2	1.8	1.8	6.1	6.7	6.7	6.0	5.0	21.8	24.2	18.1	5.4	76.7	43.3	49.4	50.6
56223	CLARKFIELD	98.5	98.3	0.1	0.1	0.2	0.3	1.0	1.3	6.2	6.1	6.8	6.3	6.0	21.8	23.2	17.9	5.7	76.6	42.7	49.8	50.2
56224	CLEMENTS	99.2	98.7	0.0	0.0	0.4	0.4	1.3	1.3	6.5	6.5	7.6	7.6	4.6	24.9	27.7	13.9	0.9	74.2	40.3	53.0	47.0
56225	CLINTON	98.2	98.2	0.0	0.0	0.8	0.8	0.0	0.0	6.2	6.5	6.8	6.6	6.1	22.9	22.5	16.7	5.8	75.5	41.6	49.2	50.8
56226	CLONTARF	99.6	100.0	0.0	0.0	0.0	0.0	1.7	1.8	7.1	7.1	8.4	7.1	4.9	24.8	26.1	14.2	0.4	73.0	39.7	54.0	46.0
56227	CORRELL	99.1	99.1	0.0	0.0	0.3	0.3	0.0	0.0	4.4	5.7	7.2	6.0	3.8	23.3	28.6	19.2	1.9	78.6	44.8	53.5	46.5
56228	COSMOS	98.4	98.2	0.0	0.0	0.8	0.9	0.5	0.6	6.3	6.7	6.4	6.4	5.1	26.4	25.2	14.8	2.8	76.1	40.5	50.1	49.9
56229	COTTONWOOD	97.4	97.0	0.1	0.1	0.5	0.6	1.3	1.5	7.8	8.1	8.2	6.6	5.9	26.1	23.5	11.4	2.4	71.6	36.0	52.5	47.5
56230	DANUBE	96.8	96.3	0.0	0.0	0.3	0.3	5.2	6.3	6.5	7.0	7.4	6.9	6.2	23.7	27.6	12.3	2.3	74.7	38.7	52.7	47.3
56231	DANVERS	99.0	99.2	0.0	0.0	0.0	0.0	1.0	0.8	6.2	6.4	7.9	7.4	6.2	23.6	28.6	12.3	1.4	75.3	40.7	53.2	46.8
56232	DAWSON	98.5	98.3	0.2	0.3	0.3	0.4	0.4	0.5	5.8	5.8	6.1	6.8	5.8	20.1	26.6	18.0	5.1	77.9	44.7	48.2	51.8
56235	DONNELLY	98.5	98.3	0.0	0.0	0.2	0.2	0.4	0.6	4.8	4.8	5.1	8.0	5.9	23.0	29.1	17.7	1.7	80.6	44.2	51.0	49.1
56236	DUMONT	99.1	98.9	0.2	0.2	0.2	0.2	0.9	1.3	6.3	6.3	7.6	7.8	5.7	22.4	25.2	16.9	1.6	75.1	41.2	53.2	46.8
56237	ECHO	97.7	97.4	0.0	0.0	0.1	0.1	1.0	1.1	6.2	6.5	7.2	6.8	5.3	24.8	26.1	14.6	2.6	76.1	41.1	51.0	49.0
56239	GHENT	97.5	97.3	0.5	0.5	0.2	0.2	0.5	0.7	8.5	8.1	7.4	6.5	7.4	25.9	25.0	10.1	1.3	72.3	34.6	52.0	48.0
56240	GRACEVILLE	99.2	99.2	0.0	0.0	0.5	0.5	0.1	0.1	5.7	5.9	7.4	6.9	5.6	19.3	24.1	20.0	5.1	76.5	44.4	48.4	51.6
56241	GRANITE FALLS	91.3	90.9	0.1	0.1	0.2	0.2	2.0	2.1	6.1	5.9	6.8	7.0	6.5	22.9	25.6	15.0	4.2	76.8	41.8	47.9	52.1
56243	GROVE CITY	98.2	97.8	0.1	0.1	0.6	0.8	1.3	1.6	6.4	6.5	8.0	6.9	6.5	25.6	25.8	12.6	1.6	74.6	38.8	51.5	48.5
56244	HANCOCK	98.5	98.5	0.1	0.1	0.2	0.2	0.4	0.5	6.7	6.6	6.7	6.3	7.1	25.7	26.9	11.8	2.3	76.0	38.0	52.8	47.2
56245	HANLEY FALLS	92.4	91.2	0.3	0.3	0.1	0.1	9.9	11.8	8.7	7.9	6.9	6.5	6.6	27.4	22.8	11.8	1.4	72.3	35.7	53.6	46.4
56248	HERMAN	98.6	98.4	0.1	0.2	0.4	0.5	0.5	0.6	5.7	5.5	5.8	7.2	6.5	21.2	26.5	17.7	4.0	78.6	43.8	48.7	51.3
56249	HOLLOWAY	97.3	96.9	0.0	0.0	1.0	1.0	2.5	2.7	4.1	9.0	8.2	6.4	4.5	24.4	27.3	15.2	0.8	73.5	41.3	52.6	47.4
56251	KANDIYOHI	97.7	97.2	0.5	0.7	0.5	0.7	1.3	1.5	5.8	6.8	7.9	7.7	6.2	25.9	27.1	11.6	1.1	74.9	37.7	50.2	49.9
56252	KERKHOVEN	95.7	95.6	0.2	0.2	0.0	0.0	4.2	4.3	7.6	7.4	7.7	7.1	5.5	25.1	22.2	14.2	3.1	73.0	38.3	49.4	50.6
56253	LAKE LILLIAN	97.8	97.6	0.2	0.2	0.2	0.2	2.4	2.9	6.0	6.4	8.2	6.8	5.0	25.0	27.7	12.9	2.0	75.1	40.6	52.6	47.4
56255	LUCAN	98.5	98.7	0.0	0.0	0.4	0.4	0.7	0.8	6.0	6.6	7.5	6.6	6.6	25.1	26.4	13.3	2.1	75.7	39.4	51.9	48.1
56256	MADISON	98.8	98.6	0.2	0.3	0.3	0.4	0.2	0.3	4.6	5.4	6.5	7.2	5.5	19.0	27.0	18.9	5.9	78.8	46.0	49.1	50.9
56257	MARIETTA	99.4	99.2	0.1	0.1	0.4	0.4	0.3	0.1	5.6	6.1	6.5	6.4	5.2	20.8	30.3	16.6	2.4	77.8	44.5	54.1	45.9
56258	MARSHALL	92.1	90.5	2.5	3.1	1.5	1.8	5.4	6.5	6.5	6.0	6.9	10.1	13.0	25.7	20.2	9.3	2.3	76.3	30.6	48.4	51.6
56260	MAYNARD	98.5	98.4	0.0	0.0	0.2	0.2	1.0	1.0	4.9	5.8	6.6	6.1	6.1	22.9	28.0	13.8	5.8	78.3	43.5	50.1	50.0
56262	MILAN	95.7	95.7	0.0	0.0	0.4	0.4	3.5	3.6	6.0	6.3	6.7	5.9	6.0	22.2	29.1	14.8	3.1	77.4	43.1	53.1	46.9
56263	MILROY	98.4	98.4	0.1	0.1	0.4	0.5	0.6	0.7	6.8	7.2	7.9	7.2	6.5	25.6	24.3	12.8	1.7	73.6	37.6	52.6	47.4
56264	MINNEOTA	97.8	97.5	0.2	0.2	0.2	0.2	2.4	2.9	6.8	6.8	7.3	6.3	6.2	23.7	23.8	14.5	4.5	75.3	40.0	49.6	50.4
56265	MONTEVIDEO	97.4	97.3	0.2	0.2	0.4	0.4	1.6	1.7	6.0	6.2	7.2	7.0	6.5	23.6	25.4	15.1	3.1	76.1	40.7	48.9	51.1
56266	MORGAN	93.7	93.8	0.1	0.1	0.1	0.1	1.4	1.4	6.8	6.8	7.1	7.2	5.7	23.9	23.8	15.2	3.5	74.6	40.1	50.3	49.7
56267	MORRIS	95.2	94.4	1.2	1.6	1.1	1.4	1.1	1.3	5.3	5.0	5.2	12.3	14.1	22.6	20.6	12.3	2.6	81.0	30.5	48.1	52.0
56270	MORTON	83.3	83.8	0.2	0.2	0.3	0.3	4.8	5.9	7.5	8.0	8.2	7.0	5.9	25.8	25.0	11.0	1.7	71.9	36.3	51.9	48.2
56271	MURDOCK	97.2	97.3	0.2	0.2	0.0	0.0	3.0	3.1	7.2	7.5	8.2	6.5	5.7	25.1	24.4	12.6	2.7	73.0	38.8	52.5	47.5
56273	NEW LONDON	98.9	98.6	0.1	0.1	0.2	0.2	0.7	0.8	5.8	6.3	7.4	6.9	5.7	25.4	27.6	12.7	2.2	76.1	40.2	50.3	49.7
56274	NORCROSS	99.2	99.2	0.0	0.0	0.4	0.4	0.0	0.0	5.0	5.9	6.3	6.3	5.0	22.2	31.0	15.9	2.5	78.7	44.7	50.2	49.8
	MINNESOTA	89.5	88.0	3.5	4.2	2.9	3.4	2.9	3.4	6.8	6.8	7.2	7.3	7.4	28.6	23.9	10.1	1.9	74.9	36.1	49.6	50.5
	UNITED STATES	75.1	73.6	12.3	12.5	3.8	4.2	12.5	14.1	6.9	6.7	7.2	7.0	7.3	28.6	23.8	10.8	1.7	75.1	36.0	49.1	50.9

#	POST OFFICE NAME	2004 Per Capita Income	2004 HH Income Base	2004 Household Income Distribution (%): Less than $25,000	$25,000 to $49,999	$50,000 to $99,999	$100,000 to $149,999	$150,000 or More	Median Household Income: 2004	2009	2004 National Centile	2004 State Centile	2004 Home Value Base	2004 Home Value Distribution (%): Less than $50,000	$50,000 to $89,999	$90,000 to $174,999	$175,000 to $399,999	$400,000 or More	2004 Median Home Value
56139	HOLLAND	20130	260	30.4	33.9	28.1	5.8	1.9	38547	44825	41	20	217	24.4	26.7	27.2	18.4	3.2	88077
56141	IONA	16301	175	34.3	30.3	30.9	2.9	1.7	35200	38773	28	8	146	30.1	24.0	28.8	12.3	4.8	85000
56142	IVANHOE	18504	593	33.9	35.8	25.5	4.1	0.8	35331	39792	29	9	478	31.0	32.9	25.9	9.4	0.8	72222
56143	JACKSON	22643	2091	27.1	34.7	29.5	6.4	2.3	41655	47817	52	33	1629	13.0	30.6	40.6	13.4	2.5	97857
56144	JASPER	20274	524	30.9	36.3	27.3	2.9	2.7	38587	44507	41	20	432	37.0	31.0	24.8	5.6	1.6	61818
56145	JEFFERS	23422	325	29.9	37.2	23.7	3.7	5.5	37657	45000	38	17	270	44.4	22.2	14.8	15.2	3.3	57143
56146	KANARANZI	19361	96	22.9	36.5	33.3	5.2	2.1	44203	50411	59	46	80	12.5	23.8	36.3	21.3	6.3	113333
56147	KENNETH	16359	190	25.8	41.1	28.4	4.2	0.5	41329	47770	51	32	161	32.9	21.1	29.8	14.3	1.9	82778
56149	LAKE BENTON	17298	570	31.9	41.6	23.7	2.6	0.2	35000	39712	28	8	452	32.7	31.0	26.1	9.1	1.1	68444
56150	LAKEFIELD	18867	1315	27.9	36.7	29.7	4.7	0.9	39446	45522	44	24	1076	24.6	28.1	34.9	9.8	2.7	86282
56151	LAKE WILSON	28801	404	31.7	38.9	23.0	2.7	3.7	35860	41148	31	10	356	36.0	25.0	23.9	14.3	0.8	71818
56152	LAMBERTON	19976	644	34.8	30.9	28.1	4.8	1.4	36184	42990	32	11	515	41.9	28.5	21.9	6.0	1.6	58830
56153	LEOTA	12255	27	29.6	48.2	18.5	3.7	0.0	35712	42288	30	10	23	30.4	17.4	26.1	21.7	4.4	95000
56155	LISMORE	18270	185	32.4	33.0	28.7	3.8	2.2	38404	45226	41	20	156	32.1	20.5	30.8	14.7	1.9	85000
56156	LUVERNE	22484	2422	27.7	30.5	31.5	7.4	3.0	43386	50729	57	42	1885	8.3	28.1	48.5	13.4	1.6	108689
56157	LYND	24210	310	17.4	28.1	38.1	10.0	6.5	53401	64377	78	73	269	7.8	16.4	42.0	30.5	3.4	138782
56158	MAGNOLIA	20573	195	24.1	34.9	34.4	4.1	2.6	44400	50000	60	47	163	16.0	23.3	35.0	19.6	6.1	109914
56159	MOUNTAIN LAKE	16045	1069	34.6	39.5	21.1	3.5	1.3	34541	40092	26	7	867	33.3	36.7	24.1	5.4	0.5	66765
56160	ODIN	22649	171	23.4	35.7	30.4	8.8	1.8	45134	52220	62	50	147	28.6	16.3	29.9	19.7	5.4	98333
56161	OKABENA	17677	222	22.1	44.6	28.4	3.6	1.4	39532	45346	44	24	188	28.2	23.9	31.4	10.1	6.4	85556
56162	ORMSBY	23929	140	20.7	35.7	32.1	9.3	2.1	46122	53723	64	54	119	20.2	18.5	33.6	19.3	8.4	110156
56164	PIPESTONE	20435	2500	32.3	34.2	26.1	5.1	2.3	36499	43216	34	12	1891	23.6	34.3	32.3	8.6	1.1	78008
56165	READING	18870	153	19.0	43.1	32.0	4.6	1.3	43363	50357	57	42	129	17.8	22.5	40.3	15.5	3.9	109375
56166	REVERE	18629	131	28.2	35.9	27.5	8.4	0.0	36589	44688	34	13	109	23.9	29.4	31.2	13.8	1.8	85625
56167	ROUND LAKE	22452	434	22.4	37.8	32.5	5.5	1.8	43473	49716	57	43	358	20.7	21.5	34.9	16.2	6.7	102315
56168	RUSHMORE	18492	391	27.6	36.8	26.9	6.7	2.1	40078	46712	46	26	332	19.9	34.0	26.8	16.9	2.4	85517
56169	RUSSELL	19042	289	22.8	36.7	33.9	5.5	1.0	42769	50000	55	39	246	15.9	22.8	37.4	23.2	0.8	103378
56170	RUTHTON	18618	311	34.4	36.7	23.8	4.5	0.6	34405	40333	25	7	266	27.8	27.8	22.6	18.8	3.0	80000
56171	SHERBURN	20705	808	30.8	34.8	26.9	5.5	2.1	36998	44935	35	14	643	22.7	28.0	31.6	14.0	3.7	89082
56172	SLAYTON	22188	1234	27.2	34.8	31.2	5.2	1.7	42308	49103	54	36	1016	25.0	28.2	37.1	8.5	1.3	85676
56173	STEEN	19848	172	23.8	35.5	34.9	4.7	1.2	43628	50181	58	43	146	13.0	27.4	39.0	16.4	4.1	103846
56174	STORDEN	27718	184	29.4	31.5	29.9	6.5	2.7	38167	45285	40	19	154	44.8	20.8	14.3	16.2	3.9	57273
56175	TRACY	19717	1334	29.6	35.4	26.8	6.6	1.6	39803	48204	45	25	1052	31.5	31.1	27.3	9.1	1.1	76000
56176	TRIMONT	24698	491	29.5	34.6	28.7	3.9	3.3	40554	48350	48	28	411	32.4	26.5	27.5	9.0	4.6	75400
56178	TYLER	20101	770	31.4	37.0	24.3	5.1	2.2	36667	41625	34	13	616	21.3	37.7	31.2	8.0	2.0	79815
56180	WALNUT GROVE	19620	462	34.4	32.7	26.2	5.2	1.5	35558	42186	30	9	391	43.2	27.9	20.0	7.9	1.0	57794
56181	WELCOME	21064	438	26.5	36.1	30.4	4.1	3.0	41232	49702	51	32	365	22.5	36.4	29.6	9.3	2.2	76200
56183	WESTBROOK	20717	583	36.9	34.0	20.6	5.7	2.9	35054	41179	28	8	493	43.4	26.8	17.9	9.9	2.0	61061
56185	WILMONT	17475	286	28.3	41.6	23.1	4.9	2.1	36901	43505	35	14	240	25.8	24.6	24.2	19.2	6.3	89167
56186	WOODSTOCK	18474	156	33.3	33.3	27.6	3.2	2.6	39216	42730	43	23	128	31.3	19.5	23.4	21.1	4.7	88000
56187	WORTHINGTON	21899	4883	28.9	30.3	29.6	7.1	4.2	42616	50602	55	38	3450	14.6	28.4	42.1	14.2	0.8	99313
56201	WILLMAR	24598	8861	26.6	29.4	30.4	9.2	4.4	43969	53839	59	45	6017	5.6	13.0	55.3	23.2	2.9	124632
56207	ALBERTA	19871	106	17.0	35.9	39.6	5.7	1.9	47363	54525	67	58	89	11.2	34.8	32.6	19.1	2.3	97000
56208	APPLETON	17660	1042	38.1	29.8	25.0	5.8	1.4	35655	41502	30	10	797	31.0	33.6	26.9	7.2	1.4	73311
56209	ATWATER	24840	928	22.3	29.2	38.0	7.1	3.3	48707	59009	70	63	767	9.5	20.5	46.8	17.5	5.7	115804
56210	BARRY	15627	43	37.2	34.9	23.3	2.3	2.3	34062	36518	24	6	36	33.3	27.8	27.8	11.1	0.0	70000
56211	BEARDSLEY	19002	184	37.0	33.2	22.3	4.4	3.3	33037	35817	21	4	156	54.5	18.0	14.7	11.5	1.3	45882
56212	BELLINGHAM	18297	245	33.9	34.3	25.3	4.1	2.5	34159	39190	25	6	207	40.1	15.5	25.6	17.4	1.5	72500
56214	BELVIEW	20430	302	20.2	37.4	34.4	6.3	1.7	45000	51806	61	50	251	23.1	22.7	33.1	16.3	4.8	99545
56215	BENSON	20957	2032	25.6	35.1	32.3	5.3	1.7	40095	47220	46	26	1590	12.3	30.4	45.2	10.3	1.8	97143
56216	BLOMKEST	22223	276	18.1	34.8	34.8	7.3	5.1	47632	56930	67	59	233	12.5	20.6	42.1	19.3	5.6	113603
56218	BOYD	23657	239	25.5	34.7	26.4	8.8	4.6	41374	50179	51	33	200	40.0	25.5	21.5	9.0	4.0	68750
56219	BROWNS VALLEY	19460	399	39.9	31.1	21.3	3.0	4.8	32468	40291	19	3	309	64.1	15.9	12.0	7.4	0.7	36375
56220	CANBY	19398	1199	36.0	31.4	26.3	4.4	1.9	35844	42207	31	10	930	29.0	28.4	32.6	9.1	0.9	76087
56221	CHOKIO	20777	296	28.0	30.7	34.8	6.1	0.3	41849	49765	52	34	243	26.8	35.0	30.5	7.0	0.8	76875
56222	CLARA CITY	20032	765	24.7	39.2	28.8	5.0	2.4	39967	47401	46	25	623	14.3	32.7	38.7	12.2	2.1	93364
56223	CLARKFIELD	19367	638	28.8	33.2	30.9	4.9	2.2	40241	48026	47	27	513	29.6	32.0	25.2	11.5	1.8	72031
56224	CLEMENTS	20795	180	23.3	34.4	33.3	6.1	2.8	42357	50000	54	37	152	27.0	18.4	34.2	13.2	7.2	101190
56225	CLINTON	19781	285	29.8	37.5	25.6	5.3	1.8	37307	42939	37	15	232	46.6	24.6	23.3	4.3	1.3	56154
56226	CLONTARF	26308	84	17.9	33.3	36.9	7.1	4.8	49079	54902	70	63	73	15.1	24.7	41.1	16.4	2.7	106250
56227	CORRELL	16916	131	32.1	41.2	22.9	3.8	0.0	35661	39157	30	10	116	38.8	21.6	24.1	11.2	4.3	68571
56228	COSMOS	20967	474	23.6	33.1	35.4	5.9	1.9	44203	53275	59	46	411	12.2	23.6	39.7	18.3	6.3	107276
56229	COTTONWOOD	24290	679	21.7	30.0	36.1	7.8	4.4	48578	57927	69	62	565	11.2	22.0	47.8	17.2	2.0	116833
56230	DANUBE	26360	376	17.6	33.2	33.5	10.1	5.6	49360	57512	71	64	321	17.1	29.6	38.0	12.8	2.5	94200
56231	DANVERS	21412	226	19.5	34.1	35.8	8.0	2.7	48007	54421	68	60	194	21.1	23.7	34.0	18.0	3.1	99091
56232	DAWSON	23461	992	30.9	31.3	27.6	6.9	3.4	38971	47917	43	21	795	23.5	27.3	35.9	10.8	2.5	88673
56235	DONNELLY	26188	208	24.0	26.4	38.9	7.7	2.9	49501	58334	71	64	187	18.2	32.1	36.4	11.8	1.6	89706
56236	DUMONT	19506	231	28.1	37.2	26.4	3.0	5.2	39320	47339	44	23	197	37.6	19.8	24.9	17.3	0.5	77308
56237	ECHO	21060	305	27.9	36.1	27.9	5.3	3.0	41075	47860	50	31	260	31.5	23.1	33.5	8.9	3.1	80769
56239	GHENT	20993	206	19.9	30.6	38.4	9.2	1.9	49540	57128	71	64	175	13.1	20.0	47.4	17.1	2.3	112500
56240	GRACEVILLE	16091	380	36.3	38.4	21.1	2.6	1.6	33262	37324	22	4	315	33.7	32.1	27.0	5.7	1.6	69423
56241	GRANITE FALLS	22454	1770	30.1	30.6	30.3	6.1	2.9	39127	47131	43	23	1372	15.1	29.1	43.3	11.3	1.2	99302
56243	GROVE CITY	20760	709	24.3	33.2	33.4	7.1	2.1	43638	51511	58	44	592	12.3	20.8	41.1	21.8	4.1	117548
56244	HANCOCK	23802	474	21.7	37.3	28.9	9.3	2.7	43312	50764	57	42	390	33.1	28.2	26.2	8.7	3.9	73077
56245	HANLEY FALLS	17484	255	25.1	38.4	31.0	5.1	0.4	41797	48359	52	34	215	25.6	21.4	30.7	18.6	3.7	97222
56248	HERMAN	20238	382	31.2	30.6	31.4	5.5	1.3	37573	45000	38	16	327	34.9	32.4	25.1	6.1	1.5	67115
56249	HOLLOWAY	19366	187	25.1	36.9	30.5	4.3	3.2	42039	48767	53	35	159	24.5	26.4	25.8	18.2	5.0	88750
56251	KANDIYOHI	25715	398	16.6	29.2	44.0	7.0	3.3	54559	65023	79	76	343	2.9	12.5	51.3	28.6	4.7	138542
56252	KERKHOVEN	20173	432	28.5	33.8	30.6	4.2	3.0	40714	47182	49	30	345	19.7	29.0	37.1	11.9	2.3	91800
56253	LAKE LILLIAN	21368	466	23.6	35.6	32.0	5.6	3.2	42893	51486	56	40	402	15.2	15.9	44.3	19.2	5.5	124545
56255	LUCAN	19207	203	22.7	39.9	30.5	4.9	2.0	41829	49602	52	34	163	20.9	29.5	36.2	12.9	0.6	89545
56256	MADISON	20305	1510	32.3	33.3	27.2	5.4	1.9	37086	44414	36	14	1210	31.7	30.5	26.7	9.2	1.9	71948
56257	MARIETTA	20091	331	34.4	33.8	25.4	4.2	2.1	34383	39409	25	7	282	43.6	19.2	19.5	16.0	1.8	61667
56258	MARSHALL	23699	5710	27.8	25.9	33.8	8.9	3.6	46212	54673	64	55	3559	4.6	13.5	53.2	26.8	1.9	133454
56260	MAYNARD	18006	361	25.2	34.4	33.5	5.0	1.9	43422	50380	57	43	311	20.6	17.4	39.6	17.7	4.8	109226
56262	MILAN	21367	312	28.9	30.5	33.7	5.8	1.3	42533	48324	55	38	262	34.4	28.6	24.8	10.7	1.5	66500
56263	MILROY	20046	307	22.5	38.1	30.9	5.9	2.6	42656	50914	55	38	251	22.3	29.1	34.7	12.8	1.2	88056
56264	MINNEOTA	20441	1000	26.2	30.6	35.5	6.2	1.5	45126	52254	62	50	823	16.5	27.8	41.9	12.6	1.1	98304
56265	MONTEVIDEO	22015	3303	30.2	30.1	30.6	7.3	1.8	40761	48576	49	30	2538	13.8	29.3	41.3	14.0	1.8	100541
56266	MORGAN	22105	878	25.6	29.3	33.8	7.5	3.8	44754	53838	61	48	747	22.2	26.8	35.3	11.7	4.0	91364
56267	MORRIS	22717	2856	32.1	26.8	29.9	7.0	4.1	42519	51335	55	38	1902	8.0	26.4	42.3	21.1	2.1	112575
56270	MORTON	21361	532	21.2	32.0	37.8	6.4	2.6	46493	54263	65	55	448	27.2	26.3	31.9	11.4	3.1	84483
56271	MURDOCK	21489	368	27.2	36.4	28.0	4.6	3.8	41306	47880	51	32	310	21.0	28.1	32.3	12.3	6.5	91304
56273	NEW LONDON	26478	1979	18.7	28.9	38.3	9.5	4.7	52404	64159	76	71	1739	9.6	8.1	41.4	35.5	5.4	149580
56274	NORCROSS	22429	107	31.8	29.0	29.9	7.5	1.9	39317	48244	44	23	91	27.5	23.1	37.4	9.9	2.2	89167
	MINNESOTA	29624		18.6	25.2	34.9	14.0	7.4	56724	71660				6.6	9.7	36.5	40.5	6.8	168676
	UNITED STATES	25866		24.7	27.1	30.8	10.9	6.5	48124	56710				10.9	15.0	33.7	30.1	10.4	145905

ZIP CODE #	POST OFFICE NAME	FINANCIAL SERVICES: Auto Loan	FINANCIAL SERVICES: Home Loan	FINANCIAL SERVICES: Invest-ments	FINANCIAL SERVICES: Retire-ment Plans	THE HOME: Home Improvements: Home Repair	THE HOME: Home Improvements: Lawn & Garden	THE HOME: Furnishings: Comput-ers & Hard-ware	THE HOME: Furnishings: Major Appli-ances	THE HOME: Furnishings: TV, Radio, Sound Equip-ment	THE HOME: Furnishings: Furni-ture	ENTERTAINMENT: Dine out/ Carry out	ENTERTAINMENT: Sports Equip-ment	ENTERTAINMENT: Fees & Tickets	ENTERTAINMENT: Toys & Games	ENTERTAINMENT: Travel	ENTERTAINMENT: Cable TV	PERSONAL: Apparel & Services	PERSONAL: Auto Repairs	PERSONAL: Health Insur-ance	PERSONAL: Pets & Supplies
56139	HOLLAND	89	62	32	59	72	81	61	76	71	61	83	91	52	81	64	74	75	75	90	105
56141	IONA	75	53	28	50	61	69	52	64	60	51	70	77	44	69	54	63	64	63	77	89
56142	IVANHOE	73	53	32	50	59	69	56	64	63	54	74	75	49	71	56	66	68	64	77	83
56143	JACKSON	77	69	62	68	73	80	71	75	75	69	91	88	68	91	72	76	86	75	81	90
56144	JASPER	69	66	68	67	68	72	67	69	67	66	82	82	65	80	67	66	79	69	70	80
56145	JEFFERS	97	68	35	64	79	88	67	83	77	66	90	100	57	89	69	81	82	82	99	115
56146	KANARANZI	103	72	38	68	84	94	71	88	82	70	96	106	61	94	74	86	88	87	105	122
56147	KENNETH	82	57	30	54	67	75	57	70	65	56	77	85	48	75	59	69	70	69	84	98
56149	LAKE BENTON	61	51	42	50	54	62	54	58	58	53	70	66	51	67	54	60	65	58	65	68
56150	LAKEFIELD	77	57	35	55	63	73	60	68	67	58	79	79	53	76	60	70	72	68	81	87
56151	LAKE WILSON	127	89	46	84	103	116	88	108	101	87	119	131	75	116	91	106	108	107	129	151
56152	LAMBERTON	77	56	34	54	63	73	59	68	67	57	79	79	52	76	60	71	72	68	82	88
56153	LEOTA	75	52	27	49	61	68	52	64	59	51	70	77	44	68	53	62	63	63	76	89
56155	LISMORE	83	58	30	55	67	76	57	71	66	56	77	85	49	76	59	69	70	70	84	98
56156	LUVERNE	77	70	67	69	73	82	72	76	76	70	92	88	70	91	73	78	88	76	83	90
56157	LYND	96	96	90	97	96	99	94	95	91	94	114	112	92	114	92	88	110	95	90	108
56158	MAGNOLIA	101	71	37	67	82	92	70	86	81	69	94	104	60	93	73	85	86	85	103	120
56159	MOUNTAIN LAKE	71	52	32	50	58	68	55	64	63	53	74	73	49	71	56	66	67	63	76	81
56160	ODIN	96	67	35	63	78	87	66	82	76	66	90	99	57	88	69	80	82	81	97	114
56161	OKABENA	83	58	30	55	68	76	57	71	66	57	78	86	49	76	60	69	71	70	85	99
56162	ORMSBY	103	72	38	68	84	94	71	88	82	70	96	106	61	94	74	86	88	87	105	123
56164	PIPESTONE	78	60	43	58	66	76	64	71	70	61	83	82	57	80	64	73	77	71	82	88
56165	READING	95	66	35	62	77	86	65	81	75	64	88	97	56	86	68	79	80	80	96	112
56166	REVERE	85	59	31	56	69	77	58	72	67	58	79	87	50	77	60	71	72	71	86	100
56167	ROUND LAKE	93	65	34	62	76	85	64	80	74	64	87	96	55	85	67	78	79	78	95	111
56168	RUSHMORE	89	62	32	59	72	81	61	76	71	61	83	91	52	81	64	74	75	75	90	105
56169	RUSSELL	88	62	33	59	72	80	61	75	70	60	82	90	53	81	63	73	75	74	89	104
56170	RUTHTON	83	58	30	55	68	76	57	71	66	57	78	86	49	76	59	69	71	70	84	99
56171	SHERBURN	82	60	37	57	67	78	64	73	72	61	85	84	56	81	64	76	77	72	87	92
56172	SLAYTON	84	63	41	59	69	82	67	76	75	64	89	86	59	85	67	80	81	75	90	95
56173	STEEN	96	67	35	63	78	88	66	82	76	66	90	99	57	88	69	80	82	81	98	114
56174	STORDEN	111	77	40	73	90	101	76	94	88	75	103	114	65	101	79	92	94	93	112	131
56175	TRACY	80	60	38	57	66	78	64	72	71	61	84	82	56	80	64	75	77	72	86	90
56176	TRIMONT	98	72	44	69	80	94	77	88	87	74	102	101	68	97	77	91	93	87	105	111
56178	TYLER	75	59	42	58	64	75	64	69	70	61	83	78	58	80	63	72	77	69	80	83
56180	WALNUT GROVE	76	56	35	53	62	73	60	68	67	57	79	78	53	76	60	71	72	67	81	86
56181	WELCOME	72	69	63	65	72	80	68	71	72	66	88	81	68	93	70	75	84	70	79	84
56183	WESTBROOK	80	58	34	55	65	76	61	70	69	59	81	82	53	78	61	73	74	70	84	91
56185	WILMONT	84	58	31	55	68	76	58	71	66	57	78	86	49	76	60	70	71	70	85	99
56186	WOODSTOCK	84	59	31	55	68	76	58	72	67	57	78	86	49	77	60	70	71	71	85	100
56187	WORTHINGTON	81	77	76	76	78	86	79	80	81	78	100	93	78	99	79	81	96	81	83	92
56201	WILLMAR	87	83	85	84	83	90	87	87	88	86	109	102	85	108	86	86	105	88	86	98
56207	ALBERTA	99	69	36	65	80	90	68	84	78	67	92	101	58	90	71	82	84	83	100	117
56208	APPLETON	57	42	27	40	46	55	46	51	51	44	60	58	40	57	46	54	55	51	61	63
56209	ATWATER	101	81	58	78	88	99	81	91	88	80	106	106	75	105	82	92	99	90	103	116
56210	BARRY	68	52	33	48	58	67	53	61	60	51	70	70	47	68	54	63	65	61	73	79
56211	BEARDSLEY	81	56	30	53	66	74	56	69	64	55	75	83	48	74	58	67	69	68	82	96
56212	BELLINGHAM	81	57	30	54	66	74	56	69	65	55	76	83	48	74	58	68	69	68	82	96
56214	BELVIEW	96	67	35	63	78	88	66	82	76	66	90	99	57	88	69	80	82	81	98	114
56215	BENSON	82	64	43	62	70	80	66	74	73	64	87	86	60	85	67	76	80	74	86	94
56216	BLOMKEST	119	83	44	79	97	109	82	101	95	81	111	122	70	109	85	99	101	100	121	141
56218	BOYD	106	74	39	70	87	97	73	91	85	72	99	109	63	97	76	89	90	89	108	126
56219	BROWNS VALLEY	76	58	38	55	64	75	62	69	69	59	81	78	55	78	62	73	75	69	83	86
56220	CANBY	76	55	34	53	62	73	59	68	67	57	79	78	52	75	60	71	72	67	81	86
56221	CHOKIO	84	62	40	60	69	82	68	76	76	65	90	86	60	85	68	81	82	76	91	94
56222	CLARA CITY	82	60	36	57	67	78	63	73	71	61	84	84	55	81	64	75	77	72	87	94
56223	CLARKFIELD	80	59	36	56	66	77	62	72	71	60	83	82	55	79	63	74	76	71	86	91
56224	CLEMENTS	97	67	35	64	79	88	67	82	77	66	90	99	57	88	69	81	82	81	98	115
56225	CLINTON	80	60	38	57	66	78	65	72	73	62	85	82	57	81	64	77	78	72	87	89
56226	CLONTARF	113	101	77	96	107	114	93	103	99	93	120	123	91	123	96	101	114	101	112	133
56227	CORRELL	74	52	27	49	60	68	51	63	59	51	69	76	44	68	53	62	63	62	75	88
56228	COSMOS	81	70	54	69	73	82	70	75	74	69	90	87	67	90	70	76	85	74	82	91
56229	COTTONWOOD	103	83	59	81	89	100	84	94	91	83	109	109	78	108	84	93	102	92	104	117
56230	DANUBE	125	87	46	82	101	114	86	106	99	85	116	128	73	114	89	104	106	105	127	148
56231	DANVERS	101	72	40	68	83	93	71	86	81	70	95	104	61	94	73	84	87	85	102	119
56232	DAWSON	91	66	41	64	74	87	71	81	80	68	94	93	62	90	71	85	86	81	97	103
56235	DONNELLY	108	76	40	71	88	99	75	92	86	74	101	111	64	99	77	90	92	91	110	128
56236	DUMONT	88	69	47	62	78	87	65	79	74	65	87	92	58	86	69	79	81	77	93	107
56237	ECHO	92	64	34	61	75	84	64	79	73	63	86	95	54	84	66	77	78	78	94	110
56239	GHENT	89	75	58	75	79	89	77	83	82	76	99	95	73	98	77	83	93	81	90	99
56240	GRACEVILLE	65	49	31	46	54	64	53	59	59	50	70	67	47	66	53	62	64	59	71	74
56241	GRANITE FALLS	88	64	39	61	72	84	68	78	77	65	90	90	59	86	68	81	82	78	93	100
56243	GROVE CITY	84	73	56	71	76	85	72	78	77	71	93	90	70	93	73	78	88	77	85	95
56244	HANCOCK	111	78	41	73	91	101	77	95	88	76	104	114	65	102	80	93	95	94	113	132
56245	HANLEY FALLS	78	62	44	61	67	76	63	71	69	62	83	82	59	82	64	71	77	70	79	88
56248	HERMAN	78	57	36	55	64	75	62	70	70	59	82	80	54	78	62	73	75	70	84	88
56249	HOLLOWAY	91	64	33	60	74	83	63	78	72	62	85	94	54	83	65	76	78	77	93	108
56251	KANDIYOHI	89	97	97	94	97	101	90	93	89	89	111	108	93	116	92	89	108	90	91	107
56252	KERKHOVEN	93	65	34	61	76	85	64	79	74	63	87	96	55	85	67	78	79	78	95	111
56253	LAKE LILLIAN	91	69	44	63	78	88	66	80	75	65	88	94	58	87	69	79	82	79	95	110
56255	LUCAN	91	64	33	60	74	83	63	78	73	62	85	94	54	84	65	76	78	77	93	109
56256	MADISON	82	60	36	57	67	78	63	73	71	61	84	84	55	80	63	75	76	72	87	94
56257	MARIETTA	82	57	30	54	67	75	57	70	65	56	77	85	48	75	59	69	70	69	84	98
56258	MARSHALL	87	78	75	79	79	86	85	83	86	82	106	100	81	104	82	84	101	85	84	96
56260	MAYNARD	91	64	33	60	74	83	63	78	73	62	85	94	54	83	65	76	78	77	93	108
56262	MILAN	89	62	32	59	72	81	61	76	70	60	83	91	52	81	63	74	75	75	90	105
56263	MILROY	93	68	40	65	78	86	67	81	75	66	89	97	59	87	69	78	82	80	93	110
56264	MINNEOTA	89	64	37	61	73	83	65	77	74	64	87	91	57	85	66	78	80	76	92	103
56265	MONTEVIDEO	83	65	45	63	71	82	69	76	76	66	90	87	62	88	69	79	83	75	88	94
56266	MORGAN	86	73	59	72	77	86	75	81	80	73	96	94	70	93	75	81	90	81	89	98
56267	MORRIS	85	69	64	70	73	82	78	80	82	75	100	96	72	97	76	82	95	83	86	96
56270	MORTON	83	74	62	74	77	84	75	79	77	74	95	91	72	94	74	77	90	78	82	92
56271	MURDOCK	96	67	35	63	78	88	66	82	76	66	90	99	57	88	69	80	82	81	98	114
56273	NEW LONDON	122	89	53	83	103	115	87	106	99	86	117	126	76	115	91	104	107	104	125	146
56274	NORCROSS	90	63	33	60	74	82	62	77	72	62	84	93	53	83	65	75	77	76	92	107
	MINNESOTA	107	106	108	107	107	113	106	107	105	105	131	126	105	131	105	104	127	107	105	123
	UNITED STATES	100	100	100	100	100	100	100	100	100	100	100	100	100	100	100	100	100	100	100	100

POPULATION CHANGE

#	POST OFFICE NAME	COUNTY FIPS CODE	POPULATION 2000	POPULATION 2004	POPULATION 2009	2000-2004 ANNUAL RATE % Rate	2000-2004 ANNUAL RATE State Centile	HOUSEHOLDS 2000	HOUSEHOLDS 2004	HOUSEHOLDS 2009	% Annual Rate 2000-2004	2004 Average HH Size	FAMILIES 2000	FAMILIES 2004	% Annual Rate 2000-2004
56276	ODESSA	011	364	354	352	-0.7	6	151	149	150	-0.3	2.38	113	109	-0.8
56277	OLIVIA	129	3669	3619	3619	-0.3	15	1459	1463	1484	0.1	2.40	954	928	-0.7
56278	ORTONVILLE	011	2886	2887	2895	0.0	28	1218	1231	1247	0.3	2.28	818	804	-0.4
56279	PENNOCK	067	1343	1363	1376	0.4	39	464	480	493	0.8	2.84	369	374	0.3
56280	PORTER	173	391	374	361	-1.0	2	160	155	151	-0.7	2.41	118	111	-1.4
56281	PRINSBURG	067	643	643	644	0.0	27	249	254	259	0.5	2.53	197	196	-0.1
56282	RAYMOND	067	1701	1674	1669	-0.4	13	605	604	610	0.0	2.77	465	454	-0.6
56283	REDWOOD FALLS	127	7020	7125	7173	0.4	39	2835	2926	2993	0.8	2.33	1813	1812	0.0
56284	RENVILLE	129	2173	2188	2202	0.2	33	807	820	834	0.4	2.57	569	565	-0.2
56285	SACRED HEART	129	1506	1520	1534	0.2	35	590	600	611	0.4	2.53	419	414	-0.3
56287	SEAFORTH	127	191	192	192	0.1	32	74	76	77	0.6	2.46	54	54	0.0
56288	SPICER	067	3958	4071	4145	0.7	48	1660	1746	1810	1.2	2.33	1169	1198	0.6
56289	SUNBURG	067	592	581	580	-0.4	12	243	244	247	0.1	2.38	181	177	-0.5
56291	TAUNTON	083	330	356	376	1.8	75	114	126	135	2.4	2.71	85	91	1.6
56292	VESTA	127	506	513	516	0.3	39	191	197	201	0.7	2.60	142	143	0.2
56293	WABASSO	127	1045	1046	1047	0.0	29	389	396	402	0.4	2.54	270	268	-0.2
56294	WANDA	127	293	285	283	-0.7	6	112	111	112	-0.2	2.57	90	88	-0.5
56295	WATSON	023	392	373	365	-1.2	1	154	150	148	-0.6	2.49	109	103	-1.3
56296	WHEATON	155	2265	2148	2038	-1.2	1	982	945	909	-0.9	2.20	616	574	-1.7
56297	WOOD LAKE	173	890	901	893	0.3	37	358	365	366	0.5	2.47	255	253	-0.2
56301	SAINT CLOUD	145	29887	32370	35398	1.9	77	10234	11354	12727	2.5	2.61	5865	6327	1.8
56303	SAINT CLOUD	145	24027	25498	27863	1.4	67	9749	10521	11731	1.8	2.35	5925	6190	1.0
56304	SAINT CLOUD	141	15185	16719	19604	2.3	82	5984	6743	8103	2.9	2.28	3110	3361	1.8
56307	ALBANY	145	4254	4577	4981	1.7	74	1475	1623	1805	2.3	2.75	1076	1147	1.5
56308	ALEXANDRIA	041	21696	23474	25866	1.9	76	8911	9826	11038	2.3	2.34	5860	6275	1.6
56309	ASHBY	051	1107	1132	1170	0.5	44	427	442	462	0.8	2.50	318	322	0.3
56310	AVON	145	5412	5748	6204	1.4	67	1888	2057	2275	2.0	2.62	1516	1617	1.5
56311	BARRETT	051	768	761	774	-0.2	18	284	285	294	0.1	2.49	207	203	-0.5
56312	BELGRADE	145	2674	2663	2785	-0.1	24	981	999	1065	0.4	2.60	688	678	-0.3
56313	BOCK	095	106	115	130	1.9	77	46	51	58	2.5	2.24	37	40	1.9
56314	BOWLUS	097	1034	1062	1134	0.6	47	360	378	411	1.2	2.81	266	273	0.6
56315	BRANDON	041	1444	1547	1699	1.6	72	571	624	697	2.1	2.47	426	453	1.5
56316	BROOTEN	145	1063	1098	1174	0.8	51	422	446	486	1.3	2.46	290	296	0.5
56318	BURTRUM	153	1361	1468	1567	1.8	75	502	548	592	2.1	2.68	351	373	1.4
56319	CARLOS	041	1246	1379	1538	2.4	84	487	551	627	3.0	2.49	357	393	2.3
56320	COLD SPRING	145	7302	7808	8477	1.6	71	2560	2800	3103	2.1	2.75	1984	2115	2.1
56323	CYRUS	121	951	1043	1196	2.2	81	362	404	470	2.6	2.58	264	288	2.1
56324	DALTON	111	1100	1139	1214	0.8	53	447	470	507	1.2	2.42	338	347	0.6
56326	EVANSVILLE	041	1520	1631	1788	1.7	72	597	652	729	2.1	2.39	401	428	1.6
56327	FARWELL	121	832	886	982	1.5	69	317	344	389	1.9	2.58	235	249	1.4
56328	FLENSBURG	097	32	38	44	4.1	95	11	13	16	4.0	2.92	9	10	2.5
56329	FOLEY	009	6860	7592	8652	2.4	84	2336	2648	3087	3.0	2.79	1781	1967	2.4
56330	FORESTON	095	1122	1213	1372	1.9	76	400	441	507	2.3	2.75	312	337	1.8
56331	FREEPORT	145	2082	2209	2408	1.4	67	691	756	844	2.1	2.91	557	594	1.5
56332	GARFIELD	041	1197	1275	1394	1.5	69	440	476	530	1.9	2.68	338	358	1.4
56333	GILMAN	009	207	214	235	0.8	52	82	87	98	1.4	2.46	67	70	1.0
56334	GLENWOOD	121	6550	7181	8208	2.2	81	2683	3002	3503	2.7	2.32	1777	1933	2.0
56336	GREY EAGLE	153	2487	2577	2666	0.8	54	937	986	1035	1.2	2.60	683	702	0.7
56338	HILLMAN	097	1616	1767	1937	2.1	80	631	705	789	2.6	2.51	468	509	2.0
56339	HOFFMAN	051	1025	1031	1055	0.1	32	404	412	427	0.5	2.34	266	263	-0.3
56340	HOLDINGFORD	145	2343	2641	2944	2.9	89	818	945	1077	3.5	2.77	631	711	2.9
56341	HOLMES CITY	041	83	88	96	1.4	66	32	35	39	2.1	2.51	26	27	0.9
56342	ISLE	065	2182	2516	2938	3.4	92	959	1116	1319	3.6	2.25	632	718	3.1
56343	KENSINGTON	041	722	752	813	1.0	58	298	317	349	1.5	2.37	225	234	0.9
56345	LITTLE FALLS	097	14800	15351	16291	0.9	55	5638	5966	6459	1.3	2.50	3885	3999	0.7
56347	LONG PRAIRIE	153	6946	7471	7928	1.7	73	2606	2856	3083	2.2	2.56	1822	1935	1.4
56349	LOWRY	121	523	583	671	2.6	86	199	226	265	3.0	2.58	154	171	2.5
56350	MC GRATH	001	326	369	441	3.0	89	146	168	204	3.4	2.20	96	108	2.8
56352	MELROSE	145	5673	5871	6280	0.8	53	2032	2140	2329	1.2	2.71	1496	1531	0.6
56353	MILACA	095	7220	8303	9678	3.3	91	2704	3175	3775	3.9	2.55	1905	2178	3.2
56354	MILTONA	041	1040	1178	1331	3.0	89	418	485	560	3.6	2.43	315	356	2.9
56355	NELSON	041	512	557	616	2.0	78	192	214	241	2.6	2.58	149	162	1.4
56357	OAK PARK	009	188	201	226	1.6	71	63	69	79	2.2	2.91	51	54	1.4
56358	OGILVIE	065	2561	2845	3166	2.5	85	923	1036	1166	2.8	2.75	688	755	2.2
56359	ONAMIA	095	3761	4214	4842	2.7	87	1405	1602	1876	3.1	2.53	958	1060	2.4
56360	OSAKIS	041	2896	3138	3426	1.9	77	1157	1280	1425	2.4	2.38	788	841	1.5
56361	PARKERS PRAIRIE	111	2670	2764	2947	0.8	53	1028	1079	1167	1.2	2.47	723	738	0.5
56362	PAYNESVILLE	145	5827	6049	6464	0.9	56	2176	2308	2519	1.4	2.58	1596	1645	0.7
56363	PEASE	095	163	199	239	4.8	97	62	77	94	5.2	2.58	49	60	4.9
56364	PIERZ	097	5121	5505	5963	1.7	73	1788	1962	2167	2.2	2.75	1325	1418	1.6
56367	RICE	009	5578	6330	7299	3.0	90	1903	2213	2605	3.6	2.86	1515	1717	3.0
56368	RICHMOND	145	4058	4165	4443	0.6	47	1502	1577	1717	1.2	2.63	1169	1196	0.5
56373	ROYALTON	097	2685	2909	3175	1.9	77	943	1041	1157	2.4	2.79	735	797	1.9
56374	SAINT JOSEPH	145	9602	10310	11091	1.7	73	2225	2517	2837	2.9	2.98	1644	1808	2.3
56375	SAINT STEPHEN	145	898	963	1046	1.7	72	302	332	369	2.3	2.90	246	264	1.7
56377	SARTELL	145	11412	12957	14588	3.0	90	4026	4686	5400	3.6	2.73	3024	3431	3.0
56378	SAUK CENTRE	145	6422	6564	6965	0.5	44	2441	2554	2768	1.1	2.53	1701	1720	0.3
56379	SAUK RAPIDS	009	13703	15546	17983	3.0	90	5142	5964	7047	3.6	2.56	3555	3994	2.8
56381	STARBUCK	121	2228	2571	3016	3.4	92	908	1069	1279	3.9	2.32	607	692	3.1
56382	SWANVILLE	097	1725	1813	1947	1.2	62	621	661	721	1.5	2.74	473	492	0.9
56384	UPSALA	097	178	213	243	4.3	96	86	105	121	4.8	2.03	59	69	3.8
56385	VILLARD	121	806	984	1188	4.8	97	286	357	441	5.4	2.75	218	266	4.8
56386	WAHKON	095	833	902	1020	1.9	76	366	403	463	2.3	2.24	241	257	1.5
56387	WAITE PARK	145	5990	6407	6973	1.6	71	2765	3036	3381	2.2	2.09	1438	1497	1.0
56389	WEST UNION	153	88	90	92	0.5	44	32	33	35	0.7	2.73	27	27	0.0
56401	BRAINERD	035	27799	29444	33672	1.8	75	11014	12061	13794	2.2	2.41	7258	7703	1.4
56425	BAXTER	035	5561	6409	7456	3.4	92	1922	2252	2663	3.8	2.82	1519	1743	3.3
56431	AITKIN	001	7860	9139	11035	3.6	93	3424	4050	4982	4.0	2.21	2272	2605	3.3
56433	AKELEY	057	1402	1516	1691	1.9	76	589	643	726	2.1	2.35	422	450	1.4
56434	ALDRICH	159	33	33	33	0.0	27	17	17	18	0.0	1.94	12	12	0.0
56435	BACKUS	021	2860	2864	2937	0.0	29	1121	1141	1188	0.4	2.43	801	793	-0.2
56437	BERTHA	153	1226	1223	1250	-0.1	25	449	454	470	0.3	2.69	325	320	-0.4
56438	BROWERVILLE	153	2051	2141	2223	1.0	59	769	817	861	1.4	2.59	545	563	0.8
56440	CLARISSA	153	1451	1453	1483	0.0	29	538	547	567	0.4	2.50	356	352	-0.3
56441	CROSBY	035	6362	7009	7985	2.3	83	2669	2980	3445	2.6	2.31	1741	1884	1.9
	MINNESOTA					1.4					1.6	2.50			1.0
	UNITED STATES					1.2					1.3	2.58			1.1

#	POST OFFICE NAME	RACE (%) White 2000	White 2004	Black 2000	Black 2004	Asian/Pacific 2000	Asian/Pacific 2004	% Hispanic Origin 2000	% Hispanic Origin 2004	2004 AGE DISTRIBUTION (%) 0-4	5-9	10-14	15-19	20-24	25-44	45-64	65-84	85+	18+	MEDIAN AGE 2004	% 2004 Males	% 2004 Females
56276	ODESSA	99.2	99.2	0.0	0.0	0.3	0.3	0.3	0.3	4.5	5.7	6.8	5.9	3.7	23.5	28.5	19.8	1.7	78.8	45.0	53.4	46.6
56277	OLIVIA	96.8	96.2	0.1	0.2	0.2	0.2	5.8	6.9	5.9	6.5	7.8	6.9	5.9	23.2	24.7	15.3	3.8	75.0	41.0	49.6	50.4
56278	ORTONVILLE	97.9	97.8	0.4	0.4	0.3	0.4	0.5	0.5	4.5	4.9	6.7	7.7	6.1	18.0	27.1	20.7	4.4	79.2	46.4	47.1	52.9
56279	PENNOCK	95.5	94.8	0.2	0.2	0.3	0.4	4.2	5.1	6.4	6.8	8.4	7.4	6.3	26.3	26.7	10.3	1.3	73.8	37.8	51.9	48.1
56280	PORTER	99.2	99.2	0.3	0.3	0.0	0.0	0.0	0.0	7.2	7.2	7.2	5.9	5.6	25.7	28.3	11.2	1.6	74.6	39.5	52.1	47.9
56281	PRINSBURG	98.8	98.6	0.2	0.2	0.3	0.3	0.8	0.8	6.5	6.4	6.8	7.6	5.8	25.0	24.3	15.4	2.2	75.6	40.0	50.9	49.1
56282	RAYMOND	96.7	96.2	0.5	0.6	0.1	0.1	3.9	4.8	7.2	7.7	8.5	7.7	5.6	26.9	23.3	11.1	2.0	71.6	36.1	51.1	48.9
56283	REDWOOD FALLS	92.7	92.7	0.2	0.2	0.5	0.5	1.7	1.8	6.3	6.5	7.1	6.9	6.3	24.0	25.3	13.7	3.9	75.5	40.2	49.4	50.6
56284	RENVILLE	94.2	93.2	0.1	0.1	0.2	0.4	7.0	8.2	6.6	7.5	7.5	7.2	5.5	22.8	22.9	15.7	4.3	73.5	39.7	49.5	50.5
56285	SACRED HEART	97.5	97.2	0.1	0.1	0.2	0.3	4.1	4.9	5.1	6.8	7.1	8.2	5.3	23.8	25.9	15.8	1.9	75.3	41.2	51.3	48.8
56287	SEAFORTH	99.0	99.0	0.0	0.0	0.5	0.5	1.1	0.5	6.3	6.3	6.8	7.8	6.3	22.9	25.5	14.6	3.7	75.5	41.3	53.1	46.9
56288	SPICER	98.7	98.5	0.1	0.2	0.2	0.2	1.0	1.2	5.2	5.8	7.2	6.9	6.2	24.1	29.4	13.6	1.7	77.5	41.7	49.9	50.1
56289	SUNBURG	99.0	99.0	0.3	0.3	0.2	0.2	0.3	0.3	4.8	5.0	6.9	7.2	6.5	26.0	28.2	13.6	1.7	78.7	41.3	53.5	46.5
56291	TAUNTON	97.0	96.4	0.0	0.0	0.3	0.6	1.8	2.0	7.6	8.2	9.6	6.5	5.6	24.7	24.4	10.7	2.8	70.2	36.2	52.8	47.2
56292	VESTA	98.8	98.8	0.2	0.2	0.2	0.2	0.4	0.4	8.8	8.6	8.6	7.0	6.6	26.1	19.3	13.5	1.6	70.0	34.9	52.8	47.2
56293	WABASSO	99.1	99.1	0.0	0.0	0.1	0.1	0.4	0.5	6.8	6.6	7.4	7.8	6.1	22.8	22.3	15.4	4.9	73.2	39.3	49.5	50.5
56294	WANDA	99.0	99.0	0.0	0.0	0.3	0.4	1.4	1.4	5.3	4.6	10.2	9.5	5.3	23.2	30.2	10.9	1.1	73.0	40.1	53.7	46.3
56295	WATSON	98.0	97.6	0.0	0.0	0.8	0.8	1.3	1.3	5.9	6.7	8.0	6.7	5.9	23.1	28.7	13.7	1.3	74.5	41.0	51.7	48.3
56296	WHEATON	99.2	99.1	0.0	0.0	0.4	0.4	1.2	1.5	5.2	5.6	6.3	6.6	5.9	19.8	23.4	21.0	6.2	78.4	45.5	48.0	52.1
56297	WOOD LAKE	96.1	95.6	0.0	0.0	0.1	0.1	3.6	4.2	6.6	6.7	7.0	7.0	5.7	26.5	24.5	13.5	2.6	75.7	40.0	51.9	48.1
56301	SAINT CLOUD	92.9	91.6	1.8	2.2	3.3	3.9	1.5	1.8	5.6	5.4	5.9	12.4	18.5	26.7	18.3	6.4	0.8	79.4	26.3	50.1	49.9
56303	SAINT CLOUD	93.7	92.6	1.4	1.8	2.6	3.2	1.2	1.4	6.3	6.3	6.9	8.3	7.9	29.8	23.4	10.0	1.1	75.9	34.9	49.7	50.3
56304	SAINT CLOUD	89.8	87.9	3.7	4.8	2.8	3.3	1.5	1.8	5.8	5.1	5.1	7.2	16.9	29.1	18.7	8.9	3.3	80.8	29.9	51.3	48.7
56307	ALBANY	98.8	98.7	0.1	0.2	0.1	0.2	0.6	0.7	8.0	7.5	7.4	7.7	7.0	26.5	21.4	11.3	3.3	72.0	35.3	50.2	49.8
56308	ALEXANDRIA	98.4	98.1	0.2	0.3	0.5	0.6	0.7	0.8	5.6	5.5	6.2	6.9	8.0	23.8	25.4	15.3	3.3	78.9	40.7	49.2	50.8
56309	ASHBY	98.4	98.2	0.1	0.1	0.0	0.0	0.3	0.4	4.3	4.8	6.8	7.1	5.7	21.3	29.4	18.0	2.6	79.4	45.0	50.4	49.7
56310	AVON	98.7	98.5	0.1	0.1	0.4	0.5	1.2	1.4	7.1	7.2	7.2	9.4	8.5	26.6	24.4	8.9	0.9	74.1	35.1	53.5	46.5
56311	BARRETT	98.4	98.2	0.7	0.9	0.1	0.1	0.4	0.5	5.4	5.7	6.6	6.3	5.5	22.2	26.2	17.2	5.0	78.5	43.9	51.3	48.8
56312	BELGRADE	99.3	99.2	0.1	0.1	0.1	0.1	0.6	0.7	5.9	7.0	7.9	8.1	4.8	25.8	22.6	14.3	3.6	73.6	39.1	51.5	48.5
56313	BOCK	98.1	99.1	0.0	0.0	0.0	0.0	0.9	0.9	6.1	7.0	7.8	8.7	6.1	28.7	25.2	9.6	0.9	73.0	38.4	53.0	47.0
56314	BOWLUS	99.4	99.3	0.1	0.1	0.2	0.2	0.4	0.5	7.6	7.2	7.2	7.1	6.9	29.2	23.0	10.5	1.5	73.7	35.6	53.9	46.1
56315	BRANDON	98.6	98.5	0.0	0.0	0.7	0.8	0.4	0.5	5.4	5.4	8.0	6.7	5.6	23.6	30.5	13.3	1.6	76.7	42.1	51.2	48.8
56316	BROOTEN	99.0	98.8	0.1	0.1	0.1	0.1	1.6	1.9	7.0	7.2	8.0	7.2	6.1	23.9	25.1	13.2	2.3	72.5	38.1	51.5	48.5
56318	BURTRUM	99.2	99.1	0.1	0.1	0.2	0.2	0.6	0.7	6.6	6.9	7.6	6.3	6.4	25.1	27.6	12.1	1.4	75.1	38.4	52.9	47.1
56319	CARLOS	99.0	98.8	0.2	0.2	0.3	0.4	0.6	0.6	5.4	5.9	6.8	6.7	5.7	26.6	27.2	14.4	1.3	77.5	40.5	52.5	47.5
56320	COLD SPRING	97.9	97.4	0.4	0.5	0.2	0.2	2.1	2.4	7.4	7.6	8.1	7.2	5.8	27.2	23.4	11.3	2.0	72.2	37.1	50.4	49.6
56323	CYRUS	98.4	98.1	0.6	0.8	0.2	0.2	0.2	0.4	4.7	6.1	8.9	8.1	5.1	23.1	28.8	13.6	1.6	74.6	40.8	51.0	49.0
56324	DALTON	99.1	99.0	0.2	0.3	0.3	0.4	0.4	0.4	5.1	5.3	6.7	7.2	5.3	21.7	33.1	13.8	1.9	78.2	44.2	52.3	47.7
56326	EVANSVILLE	99.3	99.3	0.0	0.0	0.2	0.2	0.1	0.1	5.9	5.8	6.5	6.4	6.7	22.8	25.7	15.8	4.4	77.3	42.1	50.3	49.7
56327	FARWELL	98.6	98.3	0.2	0.2	0.4	0.5	0.4	0.5	5.6	6.0	7.3	6.2	5.4	24.3	29.6	13.9	1.7	77.3	41.8	51.0	49.0
56328	FLENSBURG	100.0	100.0	0.0	0.0	0.0	0.0	0.0	0.0	5.3	5.3	10.5	10.5	5.3	23.7	23.7	15.8	0.0	73.7	37.5	52.6	47.4
56329	FOLEY	98.2	97.8	0.5	0.6	0.3	0.3	0.4	0.5	7.6	7.3	7.5	7.6	7.7	27.6	22.4	10.2	2.1	73.1	34.8	51.9	48.1
56330	FORESTON	98.8	98.6	0.1	0.2	0.1	0.2	1.4	1.8	7.7	7.7	8.0	8.6	6.0	29.3	22.8	9.3	0.7	71.2	34.7	52.8	47.2
56331	FREEPORT	99.5	99.3	0.1	0.2	0.1	0.1	0.2	0.4	6.8	6.8	8.3	8.9	6.0	27.4	23.5	10.4	1.9	72.2	35.5	52.4	47.6
56332	GARFIELD	98.5	98.4	0.0	0.0	0.3	0.4	0.3	0.4	6.4	6.6	8.2	6.4	5.9	26.4	27.0	12.2	1.0	74.9	39.3	50.3	49.7
56333	GILMAN	99.0	99.1	0.0	0.0	0.0	0.5	0.0	0.5	8.9	8.4	7.5	7.5	7.0	28.0	22.4	8.9	1.4	70.6	34.0	52.8	47.2
56334	GLENWOOD	98.9	98.8	0.2	0.2	0.1	0.1	0.6	0.7	5.0	5.3	6.8	7.1	5.4	21.6	26.3	18.2	4.4	78.2	44.2	49.2	50.8
56336	GREY EAGLE	99.0	98.8	0.1	0.2	0.2	0.3	0.2	0.3	5.2	6.1	8.6	7.2	5.4	24.0	27.2	14.9	1.5	75.5	41.3	51.7	48.4
56338	HILLMAN	97.5	97.3	0.1	0.1	0.2	0.2	0.8	1.0	6.9	6.4	6.5	6.8	6.2	25.8	26.7	13.6	1.1	75.9	39.8	52.6	47.4
56339	HOFFMAN	98.5	98.4	0.4	0.6	0.1	0.1	0.3	0.2	5.6	5.5	6.0	6.4	6.1	21.5	23.5	18.9	6.4	79.0	44.1	47.9	52.1
56340	HOLDINGFORD	99.2	99.1	0.0	0.0	0.2	0.3	0.2	0.3	7.1	7.2	8.3	7.8	7.2	26.6	23.4	11.1	1.5	72.5	36.0	51.9	48.1
56341	HOLMES CITY	98.8	100.0	0.0	0.0	0.0	0.0	0.0	0.0	6.8	6.8	8.0	5.7	4.6	23.9	28.4	13.6	2.3	75.0	41.4	53.4	46.6
56342	ISLE	93.5	93.6	0.2	0.2	0.3	0.3	1.1	1.3	6.1	6.1	5.9	5.3	5.1	21.7	28.9	19.0	2.0	78.5	44.9	50.4	49.6
56343	KENSINGTON	98.5	98.3	0.1	0.1	0.4	0.5	0.6	0.7	4.9	5.5	6.7	5.9	5.5	23.0	31.8	15.4	1.5	79.4	44.2	51.1	48.9
56345	LITTLE FALLS	98.0	97.7	0.3	0.4	0.4	0.4	0.7	0.9	6.6	6.4	7.4	7.7	6.8	24.7	23.9	13.7	3.0	74.6	38.8	49.1	50.9
56347	LONG PRAIRIE	96.1	95.7	0.1	0.1	0.4	0.5	4.5	5.1	6.6	6.0	7.5	7.4	6.9	23.1	25.0	14.3	3.3	75.5	39.8	49.8	50.2
56349	LOWRY	98.5	98.3	0.0	0.0	0.2	0.3	0.4	0.3	4.8	7.0	8.2	9.8	4.6	22.8	28.6	13.0	1.0	74.1	40.3	53.3	46.7
56350	MC GRATH	97.2	96.8	0.3	0.3	0.3	0.5	1.2	1.9	5.7	6.0	7.1	5.7	5.2	20.9	31.4	16.3	1.9	78.1	44.7	52.9	47.2
56352	MELROSE	97.6	97.1	0.3	0.3	0.3	0.4	6.6	8.0	7.6	7.6	7.7	7.2	6.2	26.7	21.1	13.4	2.6	72.4	36.2	50.7	49.3
56353	MILACA	97.7	97.4	0.3	0.4	0.2	0.3	0.8	0.9	6.4	6.6	7.8	7.7	5.9	26.2	23.8	12.8	2.8	74.3	38.6	49.5	50.5
56354	MILTONA	98.9	98.9	0.0	0.0	0.3	0.3	0.7	0.9	5.7	5.8	7.4	5.9	4.4	25.0	28.9	16.0	1.0	77.3	42.5	52.8	47.2
56355	NELSON	98.6	98.6	0.0	0.2	0.0	0.0	1.0	0.9	5.0	7.0	8.1	6.5	6.5	27.5	28.2	10.4	0.9	75.4	38.9	52.4	47.6
56357	OAK PARK	97.9	97.5	0.0	0.0	0.0	0.5	1.1	1.5	8.0	7.5	6.5	7.5	6.5	26.4	27.9	9.5	0.5	73.1	36.7	50.8	49.3
56358	OGILVIE	97.5	97.5	0.1	0.1	0.8	0.9	0.7	0.9	6.2	6.6	9.1	7.9	6.4	28.1	24.9	10.1	0.8	73.2	35.7	52.0	48.0
56359	ONAMIA	79.0	78.4	0.5	0.5	0.1	0.2	1.1	1.3	6.5	6.5	7.0	8.7	5.9	22.6	25.4	15.1	2.3	74.1	39.9	49.8	50.2
56360	OSAKIS	98.1	97.9	0.1	0.2	0.4	0.5	0.8	0.9	6.6	6.5	6.7	5.5	5.4	22.9	24.4	17.4	4.7	76.6	42.5	49.8	50.3
56361	PARKERS PRAIRIE	98.9	98.7	0.0	0.0	0.1	0.1	0.5	0.6	5.2	5.1	6.6	7.6	5.9	22.1	27.4	16.8	3.4	78.2	43.3	50.5	49.5
56362	PAYNESVILLE	98.8	98.5	0.1	0.2	0.3	0.4	0.9	1.1	6.6	6.5	7.1	7.1	5.9	25.2	24.6	14.1	2.9	75.3	39.5	50.7	49.4
56363	PEASE	96.9	96.5	1.2	1.5	0.6	0.5	0.6	0.5	6.5	7.5	9.1	7.0	6.0	28.1	23.6	11.1	1.0	71.9	37.1	51.8	48.2
56364	PIERZ	99.2	99.1	0.0	0.0	0.0	0.0	0.4	0.4	7.5	7.4	7.5	7.3	6.5	27.1	22.2	11.8	2.6	73.1	35.5	51.5	48.5
56367	RICE	98.8	98.6	0.1	0.1	0.2	0.3	0.6	0.8	7.7	7.4	8.3	7.8	6.2	30.0	24.8	7.1	0.6	71.7	34.7	51.7	48.3
56368	RICHMOND	98.7	98.4	0.2	0.2	0.3	0.3	0.8	0.9	6.3	6.7	7.3	6.8	5.6	28.5	24.6	13.0	1.4	75.3	38.5	51.8	48.2
56373	ROYALTON	99.0	98.9	0.0	0.0	0.3	0.5	0.5	0.7	8.0	7.7	8.5	8.2	6.5	29.0	23.6	7.7	0.9	70.6	33.5	52.3	47.7
56374	SAINT JOSEPH	97.2	96.6	0.7	0.8	1.1	1.3	1.0	1.2	5.0	4.9	5.8	17.1	20.3	21.0	17.7	7.3	0.9	80.2	24.3	48.0	52.0
56375	SAINT STEPHEN	99.2	99.2	0.0	0.0	0.2	0.3	0.5	0.5	6.7	7.3	9.4	7.1	6.2	31.9	24.5	6.4	0.6	72.3	35.5	52.5	47.5
56377	SARTELL	97.6	97.1	0.4	0.5	1.2	1.4	0.7	0.9	9.2	8.4	7.9	7.4	7.6	32.2	19.3	6.2	1.7	70.0	31.6	49.0	51.0
56378	SAUK CENTRE	98.7	98.5	0.2	0.3	0.2	0.3	0.7	0.9	6.6	6.6	7.5	8.7	5.8	24.5	22.5	15.0	2.8	73.4	38.2	48.8	51.2
56379	SAUK RAPIDS	97.5	97.0	0.5	0.6	0.7	0.9	0.9	1.1	7.3	7.0	7.5	7.5	7.6	31.0	21.9	8.5	1.8	73.6	33.7	48.7	51.3
56381	STARBUCK	98.9	98.8	0.2	0.2	0.0	0.0	0.5	0.5	5.3	5.7	6.8	7.3	5.1	20.7	26.4	17.5	5.3	76.9	44.4	48.8	51.2
56382	SWANVILLE	98.5	98.4	0.0	0.0	0.7	0.8	1.0	1.1	8.1	8.2	8.7	7.2	6.1	23.4	24.9	11.7	1.7	70.5	36.8	51.2	48.8
56384	UPSALA	98.9	98.6	0.0	0.0	0.0	0.5	0.6	0.5	6.6	7.0	8.9	7.5	6.1	24.9	23.9	13.2	1.9	71.8	37.7	52.1	47.9
56385	VILLARD	99.1	99.1	0.0	0.0	0.3	0.3	0.6	0.7	6.3	6.3	7.2	7.8	7.1	22.6	28.2	12.9	1.6	75.4	40.0	51.3	48.7
56386	WAHKON	95.2	95.2	0.1	0.2	0.0	0.1	1.1	1.3	5.0	5.2	5.0	4.9	4.8	21.3	30.7	21.5	1.7	81.4	47.2	51.2	48.8
56387	WAITE PARK	93.1	91.7	0.7	0.9	3.3	4.1	1.9	2.3	6.7	4.9	4.7	6.3	13.6	32.5	16.5	12.6	2.2	80.4	30.0	48.5	51.5
56389	WEST UNION	100.0	100.0	0.0	0.0	0.0	0.0	0.0	0.0	6.7	7.8	6.7	7.8	6.7	23.3	27.8	11.1	2.2	72.2	40.0	50.0	50.0
56401	BRAINERD	96.8	96.4	0.4	0.5	0.4	0.4	0.8	1.0	6.8	6.3	7.0	7.5	7.9	25.9	23.6	12.6	2.4	75.7	37.0	49.0	51.0
56425	BAXTER	98.5	98.2	0.1	0.1	0.5	0.6	0.6	0.8	7.0	7.3	8.5	7.8	6.7	25.6	24.6	10.7	1.7	72.0	36.7	48.2	51.8
56431	AITKIN	97.5	97.3	0.2	0.3	0.3	0.3	0.5	0.6	4.9	4.8	5.5	5.1	5.0	18.9	29.5	22.3	3.9	81.6	49.0	49.6	50.4
56433	AKELEY	97.2	97.0	0.1	0.2	0.2	0.2	0.7	0.8	5.1	5.9	6.2	6.1	4.0	21.5	32.3	17.4	1.6	78.9	45.8	51.5	48.6
56434	ALDRICH	97.0	100.0	0.0	0.0	0.0	0.0	0.0	0.0	9.1	6.1	6.1	6.1	6.1	24.2	24.2	18.2	0.0	78.8	38.8	48.5	51.5
56435	BACKUS	97.6	97.2	0.1	0.1	0.4	0.4	0.2	0.3	4.3	5.0	6.5	6.6	4.0	18.6	30.6	20.7	3.8	80.0	48.2	50.1	49.9
56437	BERTHA	98.9	98.8	0.0	0.0	0.1	0.1	0.3	0.4	6.3	6.2	7.2	7.0	7.4	21.8	26.7	15.0	2.5	76.0	40.7	47.7	52.3
56438	BROWERVILLE	97.2	96.9	0.0	0.0	0.3	0.4	1.3	1.5	6.5	6.7	8.0	7.6	6.7	23.0	25.0	14.7	1.9	73.8	39.2	50.7	49.3
56440	CLARISSA	98.4	97.9	0.2	0.4	0.3	0.3	0.6	0.8	5.2	5.6	7.0	7.0	6.5	20.7	25.9	16.7	5.4	77.2	43.4	50.0	50.0
56441	CROSBY	98.2	97.9	0.2	0.2	0.2	0.3	0.6	0.7	6.0	6.1	6.3	6.1	5.8	22.4	26.9	17.5	2.9	77.9	43.2	48.8	51.2
	MINNESOTA	89.5	88.0	3.5	4.2	2.9	3.4	2.9	3.4	6.8	6.8	7.2	7.3	7.4	28.6	23.9	10.1	1.9	74.9	36.1	49.6	50.5
	UNITED STATES	75.1	73.6	12.3	12.5	3.8	4.2	12.5	14.1	6.9	6.7	7.2	7.0	7.3	28.6	23.8	10.8	1.7	75.1	36.0	49.1	50.9

#	POST OFFICE NAME	2004 Per Capita Income	2004 HH Income Base	2004 HOUSEHOLD INCOME DISTRIBUTION (%) Less than $25,000	$25,000 to $49,999	$50,000 to $99,999	$100,000 to $149,999	$150,000 or More	MEDIAN HOUSEHOLD INCOME 2004	2009	2004 National Centile	2004 State Centile	2004 Home Value Base	2004 HOME VALUE DISTRIBUTION (%) Less than $50,000	$50,000 to $89,999	$90,000 to $174,999	$175,000 to $399,999	$400,000 or More	2004 Median Home Value
56276	ODESSA	17043	149	32.9	39.6	22.8	4.7	0.0	35219	38495	28	9	133	39.9	20.3	23.3	12.0	4.5	68125
56277	OLIVIA	21173	1463	26.8	34.2	28.9	7.3	2.8	41392	48500	51	33	1153	16.2	26.3	42.2	12.1	3.2	99202
56278	ORTONVILLE	20358	1231	34.3	37.9	21.9	3.8	2.0	34587	39677	26	7	991	27.6	37.2	26.5	7.0	1.7	69805
56279	PENNOCK	21935	480	17.3	29.6	39.2	10.6	3.3	52103	63981	76	70	427	9.4	12.7	41.0	31.6	5.4	144703
56280	PORTER	20686	155	25.2	34.8	32.9	6.5	0.7	42338	50238	54	36	130	20.0	26.2	30.0	20.0	3.9	97143
56281	PRINSBURG	24696	254	21.3	34.3	31.1	7.1	6.3	45797	55327	63	53	233	6.4	30.5	46.8	13.3	3.0	102035
56282	RAYMOND	19863	604	23.5	34.4	33.3	5.3	3.5	45413	52843	62	52	497	11.1	23.9	45.3	16.3	3.4	112500
56283	REDWOOD FALLS	26284	2926	22.4	30.9	34.5	8.4	3.9	47067	57256	66	57	2255	14.6	22.0	47.2	15.1	1.2	108006
56284	RENVILLE	20056	820	22.6	33.9	35.0	7.2	1.3	44563	51680	60	47	655	20.0	33.1	35.9	8.7	2.3	86694
56285	SACRED HEART	20898	600	19.5	36.8	36.8	5.0	1.8	45519	51742	63	52	491	25.7	32.2	31.0	10.0	1.2	80833
56287	SEAFORTH	21331	76	19.7	38.2	32.9	6.6	2.6	45000	51386	61	50	63	23.8	22.2	31.8	17.5	4.8	98333
56288	SPICER	30272	1746	19.1	27.6	36.3	11.5	5.6	53986	67813	78	75	1443	4.4	7.6	40.4	38.3	9.4	168704
56289	SUNBURG	21579	244	27.1	34.4	32.0	4.9	1.6	41791	49802	52	34	214	13.6	15.4	46.7	21.0	3.3	125000
56291	TAUNTON	20726	126	21.4	28.6	41.3	5.6	3.2	50000	55659	72	66	105	14.3	27.6	34.3	19.1	4.8	108929
56292	VESTA	20103	197	25.4	35.0	29.4	6.6	3.6	42344	51330	54	37	166	34.3	30.7	25.3	8.4	1.2	70769
56293	WABASSO	22753	396	27.3	34.1	30.6	4.8	3.3	41818	50194	52	34	328	36.9	21.7	32.6	7.3	1.5	75263
56294	WANDA	19458	111	25.2	36.9	28.8	6.3	2.7	40970	47345	50	31	94	28.7	23.4	31.9	10.6	5.3	86667
56295	WATSON	22277	150	22.7	30.7	38.0	6.7	2.0	47571	54195	67	59	126	31.8	19.8	26.2	19.1	3.2	86000
56296	WHEATON	21508	945	34.8	32.4	22.3	7.1	3.4	36615	44819	34	13	751	39.2	25.6	28.5	5.9	0.9	64556
56297	WOOD LAKE	20362	365	27.1	35.1	31.0	4.9	1.9	42594	49784	55	38	308	28.9	29.9	25.7	12.3	3.3	73125
56301	SAINT CLOUD	26245	11354	24.4	27.6	30.0	10.9	7.1	47977	59509	68	60	6983	4.3	7.3	48.9	35.8	3.7	154882
56303	SAINT CLOUD	25464	10521	21.8	31.2	31.6	11.3	4.0	47180	59169	67	57	7144	1.6	10.5	71.1	15.8	1.1	125806
56304	SAINT CLOUD	24266	6743	26.5	31.2	30.2	7.6	4.6	43345	52246	57	42	3415	7.6	10.0	50.6	29.0	2.8	139969
56307	ALBANY	21312	1623	27.9	29.1	30.4	8.2	4.4	44423	53928	60	47	1298	6.7	12.1	53.4	24.1	3.7	134736
56308	ALEXANDRIA	25236	9826	27.4	28.3	31.9	8.5	4.0	44821	54418	61	48	7316	5.3	8.0	46.5	36.2	4.0	152250
56309	ASHBY	22264	442	25.3	34.8	30.3	5.2	4.3	41095	49084	50	31	379	17.4	21.1	41.2	16.9	3.4	109318
56310	AVON	26493	2057	14.7	25.3	40.6	13.3	6.1	60167	74333	84	82	1873	2.9	6.3	47.6	38.7	4.5	164339
56311	BARRETT	20208	285	26.7	30.5	34.0	6.3	2.5	43142	50000	56	41	240	23.3	19.2	35.4	16.7	5.4	103049
56312	BELGRADE	19315	999	33.6	31.4	26.7	6.1	2.1	37567	45827	38	16	834	19.8	26.0	33.3	16.9	4.0	98974
56313	BOCK	23423	51	23.5	27.5	41.2	5.9	2.0	49088	60000	70	63	49	6.1	10.2	53.1	30.6	0.0	144792
56314	BOWLUS	19962	378	26.2	27.3	36.8	7.9	1.9	46631	53843	65	56	331	5.4	22.4	44.4	23.3	4.5	123843
56315	BRANDON	23787	624	25.5	31.1	31.6	9.0	2.9	44874	53932	61	49	541	10.0	15.3	43.4	30.5	0.7	128373
56316	BROOTEN	23315	446	27.4	33.6	29.8	5.6	3.6	42075	50444	53	35	382	22.5	25.1	34.6	15.7	2.1	95294
56318	BURTRUM	20336	548	26.8	32.7	30.3	8.0	2.2	43004	50890	56	40	476	13.9	19.5	40.8	23.1	2.7	115341
56319	CARLOS	27757	551	19.8	29.2	36.5	10.3	4.2	50666	61342	73	67	500	9.8	13.4	36.4	35.2	5.2	150510
56320	COLD SPRING	25772	2800	15.8	26.4	40.8	11.9	5.1	58184	70477	83	80	2435	4.4	6.0	48.1	38.3	3.2	158584
56323	CYRUS	22417	404	25.7	35.9	29.0	5.0	4.5	42243	49802	54	36	338	17.2	24.9	34.0	18.6	5.3	104902
56324	DALTON	24753	470	18.9	35.3	34.0	7.9	3.8	46639	56215	65	56	426	12.2	14.3	43.4	27.5	2.6	130804
56326	EVANSVILLE	19671	652	34.1	29.3	27.8	7.2	1.7	39859	48068	45	25	523	16.6	19.7	38.6	22.9	2.1	111738
56327	FARWELL	22433	344	25.3	33.7	29.9	6.1	4.9	43791	52195	58	44	300	13.3	14.7	38.3	30.3	3.3	134375
56328	FLENSBURG	14934	13	30.8	38.5	23.1	7.7	0.0	37321	45000	37	15	11	0.0	18.2	63.6	18.2	0.0	129167
56329	FOLEY	21649	2648	21.5	26.6	38.8	9.3	3.8	51349	60266	74	69	2298	8.5	13.6	46.8	28.1	3.0	140427
56330	FORESTON	21369	441	18.6	34.7	37.0	7.5	2.3	47646	56459	68	59	398	6.0	10.3	47.2	34.7	1.8	148182
56331	FREEPORT	21161	756	22.5	30.0	32.4	10.1	5.0	48458	57948	69	61	671	6.9	13.3	45.6	28.5	5.8	139833
56332	GARFIELD	19154	476	22.1	33.4	37.6	5.9	1.1	45960	55361	64	54	434	12.0	9.2	48.2	28.3	2.3	140873
56333	GILMAN	23597	87	26.4	25.3	39.1	5.8	3.5	48009	55841	68	60	79	11.4	8.9	35.4	38.0	6.3	162500
56334	GLENWOOD	27392	3002	27.2	32.8	29.2	6.0	4.8	41602	50365	52	33	2397	9.2	20.5	44.4	22.8	3.1	119299
56336	GREY EAGLE	23784	986	24.8	32.1	30.5	8.3	4.4	44108	52449	59	45	905	11.5	17.4	39.2	29.7	2.2	128708
56338	HILLMAN	20222	705	28.9	32.2	29.8	6.7	2.4	40313	48384	47	27	659	10.9	14.1	42.9	29.1	2.9	135302
56339	HOFFMAN	19882	412	34.7	29.6	27.2	6.6	1.9	37476	46154	37	16	322	20.8	32.6	30.4	13.7	2.5	85217
56340	HOLDINGFORD	21472	945	21.6	32.9	34.1	7.9	3.5	47075	56243	66	57	853	6.0	17.2	48.7	26.4	1.8	137416
56341	HOLMES CITY	23357	35	22.9	31.4	34.3	8.6	2.9	46148	58531	64	54	32	0.0	12.5	40.6	43.8	3.1	168750
56342	ISLE	22426	1116	30.1	31.5	28.8	6.6	3.1	40123	48131	47	26	972	11.0	19.3	42.2	25.4	2.1	124219
56343	KENSINGTON	23701	317	22.7	31.9	33.1	8.5	3.8	47046	56898	66	57	282	12.8	10.6	34.4	39.7	2.5	157258
56345	LITTLE FALLS	21060	5966	28.2	30.1	31.3	7.6	2.7	42731	51117	55	38	4576	8.3	20.1	50.5	19.8	1.4	119966
56347	LONG PRAIRIE	18567	2856	31.6	33.5	27.8	4.9	2.1	37841	45271	39	18	2295	13.1	23.4	44.7	17.4	1.4	107482
56349	LOWRY	20001	226	22.6	35.4	34.1	5.3	2.7	42068	49148	53	35	194	7.7	12.9	46.4	28.4	4.6	132500
56350	MC GRATH	23566	168	33.9	32.7	23.2	5.4	4.8	34613	43385	26	7	151	15.2	17.9	45.0	19.9	2.0	121875
56352	MELROSE	20026	2140	26.0	31.6	32.5	6.4	3.6	44065	52589	59	45	1799	10.5	19.3	46.2	21.7	2.3	116885
56353	MILACA	20237	3175	29.0	30.9	30.8	6.4	2.9	42366	50333	54	37	2625	7.9	14.1	49.6	26.5	1.9	133636
56354	MILTONA	22349	485	25.8	31.6	33.0	7.0	2.7	45289	53698	62	51	425	5.4	10.6	42.4	37.7	4.0	154360
56355	NELSON	21208	214	19.6	33.2	37.4	7.9	1.9	46881	55414	66	57	189	7.9	7.4	52.4	27.0	5.3	143092
56357	OAK PARK	21296	69	15.9	26.1	42.0	11.6	4.4	54374	65397	79	75	65	9.2	20.0	38.5	29.2	3.1	139063
56358	OGILVIE	20792	1036	23.0	32.1	35.2	7.2	2.5	46603	53862	65	56	880	15.1	20.7	40.9	21.8	1.5	116260
56359	ONAMIA	19493	1602	34.4	28.9	25.8	7.9	2.9	37075	45274	36	14	1231	11.9	17.4	41.9	25.5	3.3	123320
56360	OSAKIS	20067	1280	33.2	30.5	28.3	6.3	1.8	38723	46434	42	21	1036	11.1	21.6	44.2	20.7	2.4	113431
56361	PARKERS PRAIRIE	19620	1079	33.6	31.9	26.8	4.6	3.1	36346	43262	33	12	919	17.3	23.6	40.4	17.3	1.4	103327
56362	PAYNESVILLE	22593	2308	22.9	28.9	35.3	9.5	3.5	48650	59134	70	62	1944	5.7	16.6	50.1	23.3	4.3	124815
56363	PEASE	22434	77	18.2	37.7	32.5	7.8	3.9	45448	52593	62	52	71	5.6	7.0	57.8	28.2	1.4	140625
56364	PIERZ	18501	1962	30.1	30.2	31.2	6.2	2.4	41827	49447	52	34	1651	8.1	15.9	43.4	28.9	3.6	135837
56367	RICE	23806	2213	13.9	26.4	46.1	9.4	4.2	56512	65353	81	78	2042	10.9	8.6	44.5	32.7	3.4	147321
56368	RICHMOND	22961	1577	17.8	28.7	40.3	10.5	2.7	52507	63530	76	71	1412	3.7	8.0	53.8	31.3	3.2	147863
56373	ROYALTON	21489	1041	19.7	31.1	37.2	8.5	3.6	49198	58712	71	64	874	5.7	15.5	46.9	29.4	2.5	139234
56374	SAINT JOSEPH	19570	2517	15.7	29.5	39.1	11.3	4.5	54529	66153	79	75	2141	3.6	4.9	56.5	32.7	2.2	153680
56375	SAINT STEPHEN	29783	332	7.5	21.4	46.1	16.3	8.7	67537	85677	90	89	309	1.9	4.5	53.4	34.6	5.5	161623
56377	SARTELL	31217	4686	14.5	21.8	42.5	14.5	6.7	63318	76033	87	86	3775	9.3	4.9	43.1	39.1	3.7	165938
56378	SAUK CENTRE	22051	2554	25.5	30.8	33.7	7.2	2.9	44135	54251	59	45	2049	7.9	25.2	43.8	21.3	1.8	116593
56379	SAUK RAPIDS	24590	5964	17.5	26.7	41.5	11.1	3.3	54711	63489	79	76	4389	4.1	7.5	58.2	28.1	2.1	147500
56381	STARBUCK	20177	1069	32.3	31.3	28.7	6.3	1.4	38963	46151	43	21	870	12.5	25.5	42.3	16.2	3.5	109200
56382	SWANVILLE	18087	661	26.9	31.5	34.5	5.3	1.8	43748	50540	58	44	573	10.7	18.5	49.9	19.0	1.9	115650
56384	UPSALA	25540	105	27.6	32.4	31.4	5.7	2.9	41143	48834	50	32	88	8.0	20.5	39.8	28.4	3.4	133333
56385	VILLARD	17881	357	29.4	37.5	23.8	5.0	4.2	39357	46688	44	24	309	12.9	22.7	46.9	15.5	1.9	112269
56386	WAHKON	22648	403	29.5	31.5	28.3	7.7	3.0	40097	48305	46	26	349	10.9	16.1	40.7	28.7	3.7	134375
56387	WAITE PARK	22888	3036	26.6	37.7	29.8	3.5	2.4	39210	46432	43	23	1262	4.4	17.1	54.0	23.7	0.7	130429
56389	WEST UNION	21634	33	21.2	30.3	33.3	12.1	3.0	48642	58080	70	62	31	3.2	12.9	41.9	38.7	3.2	146875
56401	BRAINERD	22566	12061	29.1	29.8	30.6	7.3	3.2	41993	50647	53	35	8718	9.8	15.6	42.5	27.3	4.8	132481
56425	BAXTER	22793	2252	13.1	28.4	44.8	9.9	3.9	57591	69012	82	80	1991	2.4	3.2	51.4	42.0	1.1	164146
56431	AITKIN	23730	4050	32.2	30.5	27.8	6.2	3.3	38175	47281	40	19	3280	8.3	16.1	42.5	29.9	3.2	135147
56433	AKELEY	20501	643	30.3	34.4	27.8	6.2	1.2	37778	46118	38	17	561	19.8	16.4	31.2	28.5	4.1	125223
56434	ALDRICH	19867	17	29.4	41.2	29.4	0.0	0.0	36079	42288	32	11	14	21.4	42.9	35.7	0.0	0.0	70000
56435	BACKUS	19386	1141	31.2	35.1	26.2	5.5	1.9	37635	45704	38	17	1017	10.3	18.2	38.5	29.5	3.4	133546
56437	BERTHA	15342	454	39.9	31.5	20.5	7.7	0.4	33374	39758	22	5	348	24.7	34.5	27.0	13.2	0.6	77143
56438	BROWERVILLE	18200	817	34.5	27.3	29.4	7.3	1.5	37952	45150	39	18	648	10.8	30.4	46.0	12.2	0.6	99500
56440	CLARISSA	20974	547	34.9	36.0	19.4	4.8	4.9	35723	43931	30	10	444	21.0	29.7	38.7	9.5	1.1	89211
56441	CROSBY	21600	2980	33.1	31.6	27.3	5.8	2.3	37782	46143	38	17	2461	11.2	24.2	36.5	23.7	4.4	114819
	MINNESOTA	29624		18.6	25.2	34.9	14.0	7.4	56724	71660				6.6	9.7	36.5	40.5	6.8	168676
	UNITED STATES	25866		24.7	27.1	30.8	10.9	6.5	48124	56710				10.9	15.0	33.7	30.1	10.4	145905

# ZIP CODE	POST OFFICE NAME	FINANCIAL SERVICES: Auto Loan	FINANCIAL SERVICES: Home Loan	FINANCIAL SERVICES: Investments	FINANCIAL SERVICES: Retirement Plans	THE HOME: Home Improvements: Home Repair	THE HOME: Home Improvements: Lawn & Garden	THE HOME: Furnishings: Computers & Hardware	THE HOME: Furnishings: Major Appliances	THE HOME: Furnishings: TV, Radio, Sound Equipment	THE HOME: Furnishings: Furniture	ENTERTAINMENT: Dine out/ Carry out	ENTERTAINMENT: Sports Equipment	ENTERTAINMENT: Fees & Tickets	ENTERTAINMENT: Toys & Games	ENTERTAINMENT: Travel	ENTERTAINMENT: Cable TV	PERSONAL: Apparel & Services	PERSONAL: Auto Repairs	PERSONAL: Health Insurance	PERSONAL: Pets & Supplies
56276	ODESSA	73	51	27	48	60	67	51	62	58	50	68	75	43	67	52	61	62	62	74	87
56277	OLIVIA	90	66	39	63	75	84	66	78	74	65	88	93	58	86	67	77	81	77	91	105
56278	ORTONVILLE	77	58	38	55	64	75	62	70	70	59	82	79	55	78	62	74	75	69	83	87
56279	PENNOCK	92	92	84	91	92	95	87	91	86	88	107	108	85	107	87	84	103	90	88	107
56280	PORTER	90	63	33	60	73	82	62	77	72	62	84	93	53	82	65	75	77	76	92	107
56281	PRINSBURG	113	79	41	75	92	103	78	96	90	77	105	116	67	103	81	94	96	95	115	134
56282	RAYMOND	97	71	42	68	81	89	70	84	79	69	93	101	61	91	72	81	86	83	97	114
56283	REDWOOD FALLS	97	83	69	82	88	98	85	92	90	83	109	107	80	106	85	92	102	92	100	111
56284	RENVILLE	88	64	39	61	72	84	68	78	77	66	91	90	60	87	69	82	83	78	94	100
56285	SACRED HEART	84	70	52	66	77	85	69	78	76	67	91	91	65	93	71	79	85	77	89	100
56287	SEAFORTH	96	67	35	63	78	87	66	82	76	65	89	99	56	88	69	80	81	81	97	114
56288	SPICER	121	94	61	88	105	116	90	106	100	89	119	127	81	119	94	105	111	105	123	144
56289	SUNBURG	92	65	36	61	76	85	64	79	74	63	87	95	55	85	67	78	79	78	94	110
56291	TAUNTON	103	72	38	68	84	94	71	88	82	70	96	106	61	94	74	86	88	87	105	122
56292	VESTA	95	66	35	62	77	86	65	81	75	65	88	97	56	87	68	79	80	80	96	112
56293	WABASSO	98	72	45	69	80	94	77	88	87	74	103	100	68	98	78	92	94	87	105	110
56294	WANDA	90	63	33	60	74	82	62	77	72	62	84	93	53	83	65	75	77	76	92	107
56295	WATSON	100	70	37	66	82	91	69	85	80	68	93	103	59	92	72	84	85	84	102	119
56296	WHEATON	74	63	53	62	67	75	65	70	69	64	83	82	61	80	65	70	78	70	78	85
56297	WOOD LAKE	89	64	37	61	73	82	64	77	72	63	85	92	56	84	66	76	78	76	90	104
56301	SAINT CLOUD	100	95	104	100	92	97	107	98	103	104	130	120	103	126	100	97	126	104	90	109
56303	SAINT CLOUD	82	84	94	86	83	88	87	84	85	86	107	100	88	108	86	83	105	86	80	93
56304	SAINT CLOUD	77	73	86	77	72	78	85	78	83	81	104	96	82	102	80	79	102	83	74	87
56307	ALBANY	94	80	60	77	85	94	79	87	85	78	102	101	75	102	80	87	96	85	96	107
56308	ALEXANDRIA	94	79	62	77	85	95	80	88	86	78	103	102	75	102	81	88	97	87	97	109
56309	ASHBY	98	72	45	69	82	91	72	86	80	71	95	103	63	93	74	84	88	85	100	116
56310	AVON	100	110	109	111	108	109	103	104	98	104	123	122	105	126	103	94	121	102	95	116
56311	BARRETT	93	65	34	62	76	85	65	80	74	64	87	96	55	85	67	78	80	79	95	111
56312	BELGRADE	87	63	38	61	72	82	65	77	74	64	87	90	57	84	66	78	80	76	91	101
56313	BOCK	84	75	57	71	79	85	69	77	74	69	90	92	68	92	72	76	85	75	83	99
56314	BOWLUS	92	78	56	74	84	91	73	83	79	73	95	99	70	96	75	81	90	81	92	109
56315	BRANDON	106	75	40	70	87	97	74	91	85	73	99	109	63	97	76	89	91	89	108	126
56316	BROOTEN	92	75	55	75	81	91	77	85	83	76	100	98	72	99	77	85	93	83	93	103
56318	BURTRUM	94	72	46	66	81	91	68	83	78	68	92	98	60	90	72	82	85	82	98	114
56319	CARLOS	114	96	70	90	104	114	90	103	98	89	117	121	85	118	94	102	111	100	115	136
56320	COLD SPRING	107	102	89	101	104	111	99	104	100	98	123	121	97	124	99	100	118	102	105	122
56323	CYRUS	105	73	38	69	85	95	72	89	83	71	98	108	62	96	75	87	89	88	106	124
56324	DALTON	104	77	49	74	88	98	76	91	86	76	102	109	67	100	79	89	94	90	106	124
56326	EVANSVILLE	80	60	38	57	67	77	63	72	70	60	83	83	55	80	63	74	76	71	85	92
56327	FARWELL	104	74	40	69	85	96	72	89	83	71	97	107	62	96	75	87	89	88	106	123
56328	FLENSBURG	79	55	29	52	64	72	54	67	63	54	74	81	46	72	56	66	67	66	80	94
56329	FOLEY	97	85	65	82	90	98	82	89	87	81	105	105	79	106	83	89	100	87	97	112
56330	FORESTON	94	84	64	80	89	95	77	86	82	77	100	102	76	102	80	84	95	84	93	111
56331	FREEPORT	109	80	46	76	91	101	78	94	88	77	104	113	68	103	81	92	96	92	110	129
56332	GARFIELD	84	71	52	67	77	84	66	76	72	66	87	90	63	88	69	75	82	74	85	100
56333	GILMAN	93	83	63	79	87	94	76	85	81	77	99	101	75	101	79	83	94	83	92	109
56334	GLENWOOD	104	85	66	82	93	103	86	96	93	84	111	112	79	109	87	96	104	95	108	121
56336	GREY EAGLE	106	82	54	75	93	104	78	94	88	77	104	111	70	103	82	94	97	92	111	128
56338	HILLMAN	86	68	47	63	76	84	64	76	72	64	86	90	59	85	68	76	80	75	88	103
56339	HOFFMAN	79	59	38	56	65	77	63	71	71	60	83	81	56	79	63	75	76	71	85	89
56340	HOLDINGFORD	97	81	59	78	87	96	79	88	85	78	103	103	75	103	80	88	96	86	97	111
56341	HOLMES CITY	105	75	41	70	87	97	73	90	84	72	99	108	63	97	76	89	90	89	107	125
56342	ISLE	85	64	41	60	72	83	65	76	73	63	87	88	57	84	67	78	80	75	91	100
56343	KENSINGTON	97	74	48	67	84	94	70	85	80	70	95	101	62	93	75	85	88	84	101	117
56345	LITTLE FALLS	80	74	62	72	77	84	73	77	76	71	92	90	71	92	73	77	87	76	83	92
56347	LONG PRAIRIE	77	63	46	61	68	77	64	70	69	62	83	81	60	82	64	72	77	69	80	88
56349	LOWRY	93	65	34	62	76	85	64	80	74	64	87	96	55	85	67	78	79	78	95	111
56350	MC GRATH	88	69	47	62	78	87	65	78	73	64	87	92	58	86	69	79	81	77	92	107
56352	MELROSE	87	72	57	72	78	86	73	81	78	72	94	95	68	92	74	79	88	80	88	101
56353	MILACA	84	69	50	66	74	84	69	77	76	68	90	89	65	89	70	79	84	75	87	96
56354	MILTONA	92	72	49	65	81	91	68	82	77	67	91	96	61	90	73	82	85	81	97	112
56355	NELSON	87	79	61	75	83	89	73	80	77	73	93	95	71	96	75	78	89	78	86	103
56357	OAK PARK	99	88	67	84	93	100	82	91	87	82	106	108	80	108	84	89	100	88	98	117
56358	OGILVIE	97	79	54	73	83	91	75	85	81	76	98	100	69	94	76	83	92	84	94	110
56359	ONAMIA	84	65	44	60	73	83	64	75	72	63	85	87	57	83	67	77	79	74	89	99
56360	OSAKIS	82	62	39	58	70	79	62	73	70	61	83	85	55	81	64	74	76	72	86	96
56361	PARKERS PRAIRIE	82	62	41	59	69	80	64	73	72	62	85	85	57	82	65	76	78	73	87	94
56362	PAYNESVILLE	96	77	54	72	84	95	77	87	85	75	101	101	70	99	79	89	94	86	101	111
56363	PEASE	93	83	63	79	87	94	76	85	81	76	99	101	75	101	79	83	94	82	92	109
56364	PIERZ	86	67	43	63	74	83	66	77	74	65	88	90	60	86	68	77	81	76	89	100
56367	RICE	100	102	94	102	101	103	96	99	94	97	117	117	96	118	96	91	114	97	93	115
56368	RICHMOND	98	82	62	78	88	98	80	90	86	79	104	104	75	103	82	89	98	88	100	114
56373	ROYALTON	96	83	63	80	87	95	81	88	85	80	104	103	77	104	81	87	98	87	95	110
56374	SAINT JOSEPH	86	98	110	100	97	98	95	93	90	94	113	111	98	118	95	87	112	93	85	103
56375	SAINT STEPHEN	121	132	132	135	128	126	126	125	118	127	149	148	126	150	123	111	147	124	109	137
56377	SARTELL	120	131	134	135	127	127	125	124	117	127	148	146	126	148	122	111	145	123	110	136
56378	SAUK CENTRE	85	75	67	74	79	88	77	82	80	75	98	95	73	97	77	82	92	81	89	98
56379	SAUK RAPIDS	91	89	91	92	88	92	91	90	89	91	111	107	90	110	88	86	108	91	85	102
56381	STARBUCK	79	58	37	56	65	76	63	71	70	60	83	81	55	79	63	74	76	71	85	89
56382	SWANVILLE	87	65	39	61	74	81	63	75	71	62	84	91	56	83	65	74	77	74	88	103
56384	UPSALA	94	65	34	62	76	85	65	80	74	64	87	96	55	86	67	78	80	79	95	111
56385	VILLARD	89	63	34	59	73	81	62	76	71	61	83	91	53	81	64	74	76	75	90	105
56386	WAHKON	86	67	45	61	75	85	64	76	72	63	86	89	57	84	68	77	79	75	90	103
56387	WAITE PARK	68	63	72	68	61	66	69	66	68	70	86	80	68	82	66	65	84	70	62	74
56389	WEST UNION	107	75	39	70	87	97	74	91	85	73	99	110	63	98	76	89	91	90	108	127
56401	BRAINERD	82	75	70	74	78	84	76	79	78	74	96	93	73	96	76	79	92	80	83	95
56425	BAXTER	88	100	104	101	98	97	94	93	87	94	110	110	96	113	93	84	109	92	83	102
56431	AITKIN	89	68	45	63	76	87	68	79	77	66	91	92	61	88	71	82	84	79	95	104
56433	AKELEY	82	64	43	58	72	81	60	73	68	60	81	85	54	80	64	73	75	72	86	100
56434	ALDRICH	60	51	40	51	54	61	53	56	56	52	68	64	50	67	52	57	64	55	61	67
56435	BACKUS	82	63	41	57	71	80	60	72	68	59	80	85	53	79	63	72	74	71	85	99
56437	BERTHA	69	51	32	48	56	66	55	62	61	52	72	71	48	69	55	65	66	61	74	78
56438	BROWERVILLE	80	59	37	56	66	77	62	71	70	60	82	82	55	79	62	74	75	71	85	91
56440	CLARISSA	88	67	44	63	73	86	71	80	80	68	94	91	63	90	71	84	86	79	95	99
56441	CROSBY	83	63	42	60	70	81	66	75	74	64	87	85	59	84	67	78	80	74	89	95
	MINNESOTA	107	106	108	107	107	113	106	107	105	105	131	126	105	131	105	104	127	107	105	123
	UNITED STATES	100	100	100	100	100	100	100	100	100	100	100	100	100	100	100	100	100	100	100	100

MINNESOTA

POPULATION CHANGE

A 56442-56587

ZIP CODE		POPULATION			2000-2004 ANNUAL RATE		HOUSEHOLDS					FAMILIES		
#	POST OFFICE NAME	COUNTY FIPS CODE	2000	2004	2009	% Rate	State Centile	2000	2004	2009	% Annual Rate 2000-2004	2004 Average HH Size	2000	2004	% Annual Rate 2000-2004
56442	CROSSLAKE	035	1972	2233	2576	3.0	89	938	1080	1264	3.4	2.07	660	740	2.7
56443	CUSHING	097	1912	1976	2071	0.8	52	771	812	866	1.2	2.43	569	585	0.7
56444	DEERWOOD	035	2727	3058	3513	2.7	87	1143	1296	1507	3.0	2.34	846	935	2.4
56446	EAGLE BEND	153	1543	1518	1547	-0.4	13	614	612	632	-0.1	2.48	433	420	-0.7
56447	EMILY	035	933	1023	1162	2.2	81	402	448	517	2.6	2.28	276	299	1.9
56448	FIFTY LAKES	035	384	429	491	2.6	86	187	212	246	3.0	2.02	128	141	2.3
56449	FORT RIPLEY	035	1042	1078	1173	0.8	53	364	384	425	1.3	2.81	289	298	0.7
56450	GARRISON	035	608	723	857	4.2	95	286	348	419	4.7	2.08	197	231	3.8
56452	HACKENSACK	021	1826	2019	2175	2.4	84	848	953	1042	2.8	2.10	608	666	2.2
56453	HEWITT	153	1143	1157	1191	0.3	37	424	435	454	0.6	2.65	323	324	0.1
56455	IRONTON	035	147	157	176	1.6	70	61	66	74	1.9	2.38	45	47	1.0
56456	JENKINS	035	216	233	262	1.8	75	89	98	112	2.3	2.38	64	69	1.8
56458	LAKE GEORGE	057	214	232	260	1.9	77	85	94	106	2.4	2.47	64	69	1.8
56461	LAPORTE	057	2714	2907	3231	1.6	72	1019	1106	1246	2.0	2.63	793	845	1.5
56464	MENAHGA	159	3695	3778	3929	0.5	44	1414	1471	1556	0.9	2.48	973	984	0.3
56465	MERRIFIELD	035	734	937	1161	5.9	99	276	355	443	6.1	2.64	206	258	5.4
56466	MOTLEY	097	1605	1665	1756	0.9	55	680	719	774	1.3	2.30	479	492	0.6
56467	NEVIS	057	2124	2321	2606	2.1	80	919	1016	1156	2.4	2.28	680	735	1.9
56468	NISSWA	035	4210	4885	5646	3.6	93	1767	2086	2446	4.0	2.34	1296	1493	3.4
56469	PALISADE	001	1401	1563	1853	2.6	86	583	662	798	3.0	2.36	435	483	2.5
56470	PARK RAPIDS	057	9475	10501	11854	2.5	84	3953	4456	5114	2.9	2.32	2684	2942	2.2
56472	PEQUOT LAKES	035	5525	7082	8712	6.0	99	2365	3075	3838	6.4	2.30	1622	2036	5.5
56473	PILLAGER	021	3104	3198	3321	0.7	50	1161	1220	1288	1.2	2.61	889	914	0.7
56474	PINE RIVER	021	3684	3941	4201	1.6	71	1495	1609	1731	1.7	2.43	996	1038	1.0
56475	RANDALL	097	1386	1484	1601	1.6	71	501	548	601	2.1	2.71	376	401	1.5
56477	SEBEKA	159	2752	2790	2867	0.3	39	1080	1117	1167	0.8	2.48	769	773	0.1
56479	STAPLES	021	6566	6743	6998	0.6	47	2538	2639	2776	0.9	2.52	1687	1713	0.4
56481	VERNDALE	159	2120	2138	2187	0.2	34	817	840	875	0.7	2.53	601	602	0.0
56482	WADENA	159	6849	6878	7045	0.1	31	2723	2775	2883	0.5	2.41	1743	1719	-0.3
56484	WALKER	021	3678	3771	3897	0.6	46	1456	1506	1574	0.8	2.35	1010	1016	0.1
56501	DETROIT LAKES	005	15560	16884	18450	1.9	77	6412	7051	7823	2.3	2.35	4212	4519	1.7
56510	ADA	107	2296	2277	2267	-0.2	19	989	991	993	0.1	2.27	608	589	-0.7
56511	AUDUBON	005	1548	1604	1706	0.8	54	609	647	704	1.4	2.42	448	463	0.8
56514	BARNESVILLE	027	3412	3655	3946	1.6	72	1317	1440	1583	2.1	2.48	951	1013	1.5
56515	BATTLE LAKE	111	2837	2976	3192	1.1	61	1193	1271	1384	1.5	2.27	872	907	0.9
56516	BEJOU	087	289	288	300	-0.1	24	109	110	117	0.2	2.62	84	84	0.0
56517	BELTRAMI	119	422	417	421	-0.3	17	169	170	175	0.1	2.45	124	122	-0.4
56518	BLUFFTON	111	426	437	463	0.6	46	151	157	169	0.9	2.77	119	122	0.6
56519	BORUP	107	267	251	245	-1.4	0	105	100	99	-1.1	2.51	80	74	-1.8
56520	BRECKENRIDGE	167	4524	4569	4622	0.2	35	1774	1817	1864	0.6	2.44	1178	1171	-0.1
56521	CALLAWAY	005	1058	1036	1092	-0.5	10	369	369	397	0.0	2.81	285	279	-0.5
56522	CAMPBELL	167	781	778	783	-0.1	24	283	285	290	0.2	2.71	217	214	-0.3
56523	CLIMAX	119	676	671	676	-0.2	20	262	265	272	0.3	2.53	189	186	-0.4
56524	CLITHERALL	111	688	710	755	0.7	51	284	298	321	1.1	2.38	211	216	0.6
56525	COMSTOCK	027	123	125	131	0.4	40	47	48	52	0.5	2.60	40	40	0.0
56527	DEER CREEK	111	892	922	982	0.8	52	334	349	376	1.0	2.64	252	257	0.5
56528	DENT	111	1607	1724	1873	1.7	72	652	712	785	2.1	2.42	487	520	1.6
56529	DILWORTH	027	3018	3290	3586	2.1	79	1166	1296	1439	2.5	2.48	779	838	1.7
56531	ELBOW LAKE	051	2178	2228	2292	0.5	44	898	928	966	0.8	2.37	597	599	0.1
56533	ELIZABETH	111	443	456	484	0.7	49	159	166	178	1.0	2.74	122	124	0.4
56534	ERHARD	111	1186	1243	1334	1.1	61	483	514	558	1.5	2.42	360	374	0.9
56535	ERSKINE	119	1099	1264	1375	3.4	91	417	492	547	4.0	2.41	261	298	3.2
56536	FELTON	027	421	433	459	0.7	48	165	173	186	1.1	2.46	120	123	0.6
56537	FERGUS FALLS	111	18900	19841	21346	1.2	61	7589	8074	8814	1.5	2.36	4870	5018	0.7
56540	FERTILE	119	1865	1868	1886	0.0	29	765	775	792	0.3	2.32	506	498	-0.4
56542	FOSSTON	119	2497	2499	2523	0.0	29	1044	1059	1085	0.3	2.26	651	639	-0.4
56543	FOXHOME	167	245	243	244	-0.2	19	95	96	97	0.3	2.51	72	71	-0.3
56544	FRAZEE	005	4203	4512	4897	1.7	73	1558	1708	1889	2.2	2.57	1128	1201	1.5
56545	GARY	107	491	512	523	1.0	58	192	203	210	1.3	2.52	140	145	0.8
56546	GEORGETOWN	027	437	449	475	0.6	47	166	174	187	1.1	2.57	130	134	0.7
56547	GLYNDON	027	2467	2678	2914	2.0	77	841	926	1022	2.3	2.89	672	726	1.8
56548	HALSTAD	107	849	829	819	-0.6	8	334	329	327	-0.4	2.42	226	217	-1.0
56549	HAWLEY	027	3417	3601	3855	1.2	64	1258	1344	1461	1.6	2.64	940	979	1.0
56550	HENDRUM	107	433	424	420	-0.5	10	166	165	165	-0.1	2.56	119	116	-0.6
56551	HENNING	111	2252	2342	2500	0.9	57	946	998	1079	1.3	2.27	634	650	0.6
56552	HITTERDAL	027	482	494	522	0.6	46	183	189	202	0.8	2.61	149	151	0.3
56553	KENT	167	176	174	174	-0.3	17	65	65	67	0.0	2.68	52	51	-0.5
56554	LAKE PARK	005	2979	3145	3391	1.3	65	1231	1323	1453	1.7	2.37	878	917	1.0
56556	MCINTOSH	119	1030	1135	1206	2.3	83	411	470	514	3.2	2.10	269	299	2.5
56557	MAHNOMEN	087	2842	3027	3243	1.5	69	1145	1248	1365	2.1	2.38	759	803	1.3
56560	MOORHEAD	027	32245	33869	36272	1.2	62	12723	13617	14859	1.6	2.37	7961	8242	0.8
56562	MOORHEAD	027	1607	1614	1629	0.1	31	2	2	2	0.0	2.50	1	1	0.0
56563	MOORHEAD	027	1429	1480	1540	0.8	54	0	0	0	0.0	0.00	0	0	0.0
56565	NASHUA	167	142	141	141	-0.2	20	57	57	58	0.0	2.46	44	43	-0.5
56566	NAYTAHWAUSH	087	1072	1099	1149	0.6	46	322	333	352	0.8	3.25	246	249	0.3
56567	NEW YORK MILLS	111	3184	3317	3543	1.0	58	1202	1273	1381	1.4	2.53	847	870	0.6
56568	NIELSVILLE	119	260	255	257	-0.5	11	102	102	105	0.0	2.50	68	66	-0.7
56569	OGEMA	005	1150	1183	1262	0.7	49	401	419	454	1.0	2.82	284	288	0.3
56570	OSAGE	005	1026	1070	1143	1.0	58	402	429	468	1.5	2.49	302	314	0.9
56571	OTTERTAIL	111	1842	2147	2437	3.7	93	758	904	1044	4.2	2.35	566	659	3.6
56572	PELICAN RAPIDS	111	5397	5915	6498	2.2	80	2058	2263	2504	2.3	2.57	1466	1568	1.6
56573	PERHAM	111	5612	6114	6697	2.0	79	2210	2443	2712	2.4	2.46	1497	1608	1.7
56574	PERLEY	107	280	274	272	-0.5	10	111	111	111	0.0	2.47	81	78	-0.9
56575	PONSFORD	005	889	927	989	1.0	58	323	344	374	1.5	2.69	242	252	1.0
56576	RICHVILLE	111	912	1065	1211	3.7	93	391	464	536	4.1	2.29	289	335	3.5
56577	RICHWOOD	005	556	569	605	0.6	45	206	216	234	1.1	2.63	164	168	0.6
56578	ROCHERT	005	846	882	943	1.0	58	333	354	385	1.5	2.49	253	262	0.8
56579	ROTHSAY	167	1024	1050	1089	0.6	46	391	406	427	0.9	2.59	291	295	0.3
56580	SABIN	027	1299	1400	1518	1.8	75	478	524	578	2.2	2.67	389	420	1.8
56581	SHELLY	107	439	429	424	-0.5	9	179	176	176	-0.4	2.34	121	116	-1.0
56583	TINTAH	155	240	227	216	-1.3	1	95	92	88	-0.8	2.47	73	69	-1.3
56584	TWIN VALLEY	107	2000	2023	2034	0.3	36	785	804	815	0.6	2.38	523	521	-0.1
56585	ULEN	027	907	909	954	0.1	30	340	346	370	0.4	2.42	226	222	-0.4
56586	UNDERWOOD	111	1777	1845	1970	0.9	56	720	759	821	1.3	2.43	533	548	0.7
56587	VERGAS	111	1324	1524	1719	3.4	92	551	644	736	3.7	2.37	417	477	3.2
	MINNESOTA					1.4					1.6	2.50			1.0
	UNITED STATES					1.2					1.3	2.58			1.1

# POST OFFICE NAME	2004 Per Capita Income	2004 HH Income Base	2004 HOUSEHOLD INCOME DISTRIBUTION (%)					MEDIAN HOUSEHOLD INCOME				2004 Home Value Base	2004 HOME VALUE DISTRIBUTION (%)					2004 Median Home Value
			Less than $25,000	$25,000 to $49,999	$50,000 to $99,999	$100,000 to $149,999	$150,000 or More	2004	2009	2004 National Centile	2004 State Centile		Less than $50,000	$50,000 to $89,999	$90,000 to $174,999	$175,000 to $399,999	$400,000 or More	
56442 CROSSLAKE	35898	1080	19.2	31.8	32.3	10.3	6.5	49223	63844	71	64	1021	2.9	7.3	23.6	42.5	23.7	236581
56443 CUSHING	23247	812	27.3	31.4	30.8	6.8	3.7	41864	50000	52	34	742	9.8	18.6	42.5	26.0	3.1	121617
56444 DEERWOOD	28770	1296	22.3	27.9	35.0	11.3	3.5	49746	61777	71	65	1153	7.5	7.9	31.6	46.1	6.9	182717
56446 EAGLE BEND	19356	612	32.7	37.9	22.1	4.7	2.6	35291	42598	29	9	495	23.2	32.1	31.5	11.3	1.8	81452
56447 EMILY	23668	448	28.1	35.0	26.1	5.8	4.9	40613	49567	48	29	414	3.6	13.5	40.6	35.3	7.0	156818
56448 FIFTY LAKES	28145	212	25.9	36.8	25.5	6.6	5.2	40837	50000	49	30	196	3.6	10.2	36.7	41.3	8.2	173750
56449 FORT RIPLEY	20572	384	22.7	30.5	38.0	6.5	2.3	47626	57306	67	59	364	8.0	13.7	41.8	34.1	2.5	147826
56450 GARRISON	25039	348	31.9	30.8	26.7	6.6	4.0	37884	46369	39	18	298	12.8	13.4	43.0	27.2	3.7	133824
56452 HACKENSACK	24330	953	24.6	37.7	28.1	7.6	2.1	40185	50161	47	27	862	5.5	11.8	33.9	41.0	7.9	171622
56453 HEWITT	15567	435	34.3	39.5	20.7	4.1	1.4	35179	40902	28	8	387	20.9	26.9	39.5	10.9	1.8	92576
56455 IRONTON	22174	66	21.2	34.9	34.9	7.6	1.5	45899	54435	64	53	62	8.1	22.6	53.2	16.1	0.0	116667
56456 JENKINS	21876	98	25.5	33.7	29.6	7.1	4.1	42867	52628	56	39	86	14.0	9.3	40.7	27.9	8.1	137500
56458 LAKE GEORGE	22925	94	25.5	36.2	25.5	7.5	5.3	40634	50839	48	29	87	9.2	13.8	42.5	31.0	3.5	144318
56461 LAPORTE	21569	1106	24.5	33.4	30.9	8.4	2.8	45000	53466	61	50	985	13.8	17.9	38.0	26.9	3.5	126689
56464 MENAHGA	18876	1471	35.9	33.2	24.0	3.9	2.9	35301	42121	29	9	1219	19.9	21.8	42.3	14.7	1.3	103547
56465 MERRIFIELD	23884	355	20.9	29.3	35.5	9.9	4.5	49847	62022	72	65	332	2.7	10.8	40.4	38.0	8.1	166667
56466 MOTLEY	19749	719	33.5	31.7	28.0	5.2	1.7	37411	45358	37	16	574	15.5	22.1	39.2	20.6	2.6	112376
56467 NEVIS	25274	1016	24.8	35.4	28.9	7.8	3.1	41994	50663	53	35	907	9.0	14.3	36.2	34.8	5.6	152237
56468 NISSWA	32136	2086	18.7	24.6	36.3	12.5	7.8	56254	70633	81	78	1897	2.9	6.9	31.3	40.4	18.6	207210
56469 PALISADE	21048	662	31.0	34.0	26.9	5.6	2.6	37746	46737	38	17	618	11.0	21.2	44.3	20.9	2.6	116898
56470 PARK RAPIDS	23203	4456	32.0	30.6	25.9	7.8	3.7	38975	47650	43	22	3396	10.7	18.0	40.2	26.5	4.6	129308
56472 PEQUOT LAKES	26612	3075	27.0	30.1	29.9	7.9	5.0	44175	54442	59	45	2563	5.0	9.2	34.3	37.5	13.9	179563
56473 PILLAGER	22802	1220	20.9	31.5	35.7	8.9	3.0	48194	58441	69	61	1101	12.7	14.1	39.5	26.6	7.1	136472
56474 PINE RIVER	18327	1609	34.5	31.6	28.0	4.0	1.9	36581	43528	34	13	1274	10.4	25.4	42.4	19.4	2.5	112024
56475 RANDALL	19979	548	24.6	33.2	33.8	5.8	2.6	44005	51562	59	45	488	13.1	23.8	42.6	19.3	1.2	112188
56477 SEBEKA	18126	1117	33.7	34.3	25.9	4.6	1.6	36670	42844	34	13	943	22.1	25.5	34.9	16.7	1.0	94123
56479 STAPLES	18212	2639	33.8	32.7	26.2	5.0	2.4	36350	43685	33	12	2021	21.6	25.3	38.9	12.8	1.3	94960
56481 VERNDALE	17050	840	33.5	35.7	25.6	4.3	1.0	36174	42298	32	11	717	19.1	29.9	35.2	14.9	1.0	91923
56482 WADENA	18318	2775	38.2	30.0	24.7	4.4	2.7	35392	41744	29	9	2040	18.9	31.7	36.3	12.6	0.5	89277
56484 WALKER	23714	1506	28.5	26.8	32.2	8.8	3.7	44395	55254	60	47	1208	6.9	9.7	37.0	33.1	13.3	163056
56501 DETROIT LAKES	23198	7051	30.0	30.1	27.9	8.2	3.7	40896	50221	49	30	5527	11.2	19.3	41.6	23.5	4.5	125017
56510 ADA	20198	991	33.4	33.7	24.3	6.5	2.1	36287	42687	33	11	765	30.1	30.1	33.5	5.8	0.7	77328
56511 AUDUBON	22411	647	26.0	30.9	33.5	5.9	3.7	44345	53746	60	46	555	11.4	17.1	42.5	26.1	2.9	127425
56514 BARNESVILLE	23402	1440	21.5	31.5	37.0	5.6	4.4	47493	57388	67	58	1209	13.2	21.5	50.6	14.0	0.7	106862
56515 BATTLE LAKE	27390	1271	29.0	30.8	29.3	7.1	3.9	40702	50345	49	29	1119	8.4	14.1	44.1	28.6	4.8	134608
56516 BEJOU	16316	110	30.0	41.8	21.8	6.4	0.0	35787	41587	31	10	90	18.9	14.4	30.0	22.2	14.4	127778
56517 BELTRAMI	22991	170	27.1	35.3	27.1	7.7	2.9	37674	45824	38	17	148	39.2	27.7	25.0	6.8	1.4	66000
56518 BLUFFTON	19922	157	21.0	36.9	30.6	7.6	3.8	44764	54675	61	48	143	9.8	18.2	51.1	20.3	0.7	129018
56519 BORUP	19008	100	23.0	37.0	33.0	7.0	0.0	45000	50787	61	50	84	20.2	23.8	44.1	7.1	4.8	98333
56520 BRECKENRIDGE	20865	1817	27.0	29.8	33.9	7.2	2.2	43988	51807	59	45	1378	17.7	27.2	40.6	13.6	0.9	95932
56521 CALLAWAY	16399	369	32.3	31.7	28.7	5.7	1.6	38238	45816	40	19	334	21.9	30.5	28.7	14.7	4.2	87037
56522 CAMPBELL	19626	285	20.0	37.5	33.7	6.3	2.5	45100	51744	61	50	268	31.0	21.6	36.6	9.7	1.1	84615
56523 CLIMAX	21541	265	23.4	32.5	32.8	8.7	2.6	45140	52553	62	50	223	30.0	29.6	31.4	7.2	1.8	77500
56524 CLITHERALL	20977	298	31.2	32.6	28.2	5.4	2.7	38191	45456	40	19	253	17.8	16.2	40.3	22.9	2.8	118403
56525 COMSTOCK	22217	48	14.6	29.2	47.9	8.3	0.0	54460	61708	79	75	45	11.1	24.4	44.4	15.6	4.4	117188
56527 DEER CREEK	16290	349	31.2	36.7	27.5	3.2	1.4	36850	43578	35	14	298	17.5	25.8	37.6	16.8	2.4	104070
56528 DENT	24342	712	26.3	33.7	29.2	7.0	3.8	41997	51513	53	35	672	10.1	17.1	39.9	30.4	2.5	136080
56529 DILWORTH	18211	1296	33.0	30.5	29.0	6.6	0.9	40183	48788	47	26	939	14.1	30.8	43.7	11.5	0.0	94663
56531 ELBOW LAKE	20591	928	31.5	34.4	25.4	6.1	2.6	37800	45970	39	18	733	22.9	32.5	35.9	7.6	1.1	82685
56533 ELIZABETH	20994	166	19.9	33.7	38.0	7.8	0.6	47828	55440	68	60	150	16.7	20.0	40.0	21.3	2.0	116667
56534 ERHARD	25887	514	23.4	32.1	32.5	7.4	4.7	44825	53415	61	48	465	15.5	18.9	35.7	26.2	3.7	125636
56535 ERSKINE	21076	492	34.4	35.8	21.5	4.9	3.5	34870	42810	27	8	375	45.6	28.0	19.7	5.6	1.1	55690
56536 FELTON	26978	173	21.4	27.8	34.7	12.1	4.1	50612	61036	73	67	142	17.6	21.1	45.8	14.1	1.4	107576
56537 FERGUS FALLS	24441	8074	29.1	30.0	28.7	8.3	3.9	41487	50836	51	33	5872	9.4	21.9	46.5	20.7	1.6	117003
56540 FERTILE	19532	775	35.6	35.2	22.3	4.7	2.2	33351	40266	22	5	616	34.4	33.3	23.9	7.1	1.3	66500
56542 FOSSTON	19629	1059	38.7	28.9	23.6	6.0	2.8	33137	40618	21	4	768	36.1	30.7	30.2	2.6	0.4	68209
56543 FOXHOME	20820	96	19.8	36.5	35.4	6.3	2.1	45639	52257	63	53	90	32.2	21.1	36.7	8.9	1.1	82500
56544 FRAZEE	20673	1708	29.3	31.4	30.1	5.3	3.9	40460	49519	48	28	1367	17.0	19.1	38.5	21.8	3.6	115592
56545 GARY	18260	203	29.1	35.0	30.1	4.4	1.5	40476	46308	48	28	176	33.5	30.7	26.7	7.4	1.7	70833
56546 GEORGETOWN	26312	174	17.2	27.0	38.5	13.2	4.0	54763	64737	79	76	154	9.7	22.7	48.1	18.2	1.3	114394
56547 GLYNDON	22536	926	16.9	27.7	43.1	9.0	3.5	54549	65073	79	76	812	16.0	18.2	49.0	16.1	0.6	112755
56548 HALSTAD	20429	329	30.7	34.4	25.2	6.7	3.0	38762	46335	42	21	257	33.1	28.8	31.1	4.7	2.3	71563
56549 HAWLEY	21313	1344	22.8	29.0	36.6	8.9	2.7	48281	59494	69	61	1066	16.4	24.4	45.6	12.5	1.1	102488
56550 HENDRUM	20084	165	22.4	38.8	30.3	7.3	1.2	42500	49247	55	38	141	32.6	27.7	30.5	7.1	2.1	73571
56551 HENNING	19863	998	37.4	30.5	25.8	4.1	1.9	33847	40743	24	6	822	14.4	24.8	38.6	18.5	3.8	108621
56552 HITTERDAL	22072	189	20.6	31.2	38.6	5.8	3.7	48420	59432	69	61	174	22.4	23.0	40.8	12.1	1.7	97273
56553 KENT	22755	65	20.0	38.5	27.7	7.7	6.2	44308	53860	59	46	60	21.7	16.7	43.3	16.7	1.7	105769
56554 LAKE PARK	24696	1323	25.1	30.0	32.4	8.2	4.3	45935	56352	64	54	1122	11.1	17.0	34.9	32.4	4.6	138073
56556 MCINTOSH	26160	470	30.6	34.9	26.4	4.3	3.8	37435	45964	37	16	354	39.0	35.3	22.3	3.4	0.0	58667
56557 MAHNOMEN	16981	1248	36.9	34.1	24.2	4.1	0.7	33236	38390	22	4	996	24.3	29.6	33.3	9.2	3.5	84179
56560 MOORHEAD	23907	13617	28.6	27.7	30.9	9.1	3.7	43206	53424	56	41	9155	6.2	22.2	56.7	14.5	0.4	112244
56562 MOORHEAD	10633	0	0.0	0.0	0.0	0.0	0.0	0	0	0	0	2	0.0	0.0	100.0	0.0	0.0	112500
56563 MOORHEAD	6679	0	0.0	0.0	0.0	0.0	0.0	0	0	0	0	0	0.0	0.0	0.0	0.0	0.0	0
56565 NASHUA	21525	57	21.1	36.8	35.1	5.3	1.8	44303	52079	59	46	54	33.3	20.4	38.9	7.4	0.0	80000
56566 NAYTAHWAUSH	12525	333	40.5	31.2	23.4	3.0	1.8	31162	35977	15	2	249	22.5	30.9	31.7	12.9	2.0	86136
56567 NEW YORK MILLS	18940	1273	30.9	34.2	28.4	4.3	2.3	39502	47063	44	24	981	13.2	22.3	43.0	18.5	3.1	116574
56568 NIELSVILLE	17772	102	30.4	38.2	24.5	5.9	1.0	34194	40373	25	7	86	47.7	26.7	17.4	5.8	2.3	53333
56569 OGEMA	14737	419	40.3	29.6	23.2	6.2	0.7	33315	39709	22	5	320	28.8	28.4	29.1	10.6	3.1	80800
56570 OSAGE	19185	429	24.9	39.9	29.1	4.7	1.4	40293	47846	47	27	385	11.2	18.2	41.8	25.7	3.1	130357
56571 OTTERTAIL	25439	904	24.9	35.0	29.4	5.9	4.9	42466	51918	54	38	812	10.8	13.3	42.0	26.6	7.3	138702
56572 PELICAN RAPIDS	20366	2263	29.5	31.6	29.4	7.1	2.4	40607	49525	48	29	1800	11.1	20.3	38.9	26.1	3.5	122396
56573 PERHAM	21663	2443	29.0	31.8	29.5	6.2	3.6	40656	49925	48	29	1875	9.2	19.7	43.8	24.3	3.1	122460
56574 PERLEY	20818	111	20.7	39.6	31.5	7.2	0.9	43079	50211	56	41	96	32.3	26.0	33.3	7.3	1.0	77500
56575 PONSFORD	15640	344	39.0	32.6	23.3	3.8	1.5	33017	39469	21	4	291	18.6	24.4	38.5	17.5	1.0	103533
56576 RICHVILLE	26648	464	25.2	33.8	29.7	7.1	4.1	42340	52022	54	36	424	11.3	15.6	40.8	27.6	4.7	135455
56577 RICHWOOD	25480	216	22.7	31.0	27.3	11.6	7.4	47610	59141	67	59	204	11.3	11.8	34.3	32.4	10.3	147619
56578 ROCHERT	19909	354	25.1	35.9	33.1	4.5	1.4	42919	51255	56	40	330	15.2	17.0	49.1	17.3	1.5	116154
56579 ROTHSAY	20556	406	23.7	36.0	31.8	6.2	2.5	43489	50499	57	43	357	21.9	26.6	32.5	17.7	1.4	92619
56580 SABIN	25888	524	15.1	24.1	45.0	12.2	3.6	60296	73148	85	82	465	7.7	14.6	55.9	20.7	1.1	124881
56581 SHELLY	21139	176	32.4	34.1	25.0	6.3	2.3	37346	46386	37	15	137	33.6	29.2	30.7	4.4	2.2	70556
56583 TINTAH	19371	92	29.4	33.7	27.2	7.6	2.2	40000	45751	46	26	83	28.9	26.5	25.3	16.9	2.4	79000
56584 TWIN VALLEY	17964	804	36.0	32.3	26.5	3.4	1.9	35362	41307	29	9	659	41.4	29.0	23.4	4.9	1.4	59113
56585 ULEN	19985	346	28.3	34.7	27.8	7.5	1.7	41997	50968	53	35	264	32.6	29.2	34.9	3.4	0.0	78571
56586 UNDERWOOD	24563	759	24.6	30.4	33.3	7.9	3.7	44806	55042	61	48	659	12.9	17.8	41.1	25.6	2.6	122235
56587 VERGAS	26819	644	21.1	34.9	32.1	7.8	4.0	45218	55313	62	51	577	10.2	16.1	41.9	29.6	2.1	132167
MINNESOTA	29624		18.6	25.2	34.9	14.0	7.4	56724	71660				6.6	9.7	36.5	40.5	6.8	168676
UNITED STATES	25866		24.7	27.1	30.8	10.9	6.5	48124	56710				10.9	15.0	33.7	30.1	10.4	145905

ZIP CODE #	POST OFFICE NAME	RACE (%) White 2000	White 2004	Black 2000	Black 2004	Asian/Pacific 2000	Asian/Pacific 2004	% Hispanic Origin 2000	% Hispanic Origin 2004	2004 AGE DISTRIBUTION (%) 0-4	5-9	10-14	15-19	20-24	25-44	45-64	65-84	85+	18+	MEDIAN AGE 2004	% 2004 Males	% 2004 Females
56442	CROSSLAKE	99.2	98.9	0.3	0.4	0.2	0.2	0.5	0.8	3.6	4.0	4.6	3.2	3.1	16.7	33.3	29.0	2.4	85.7	55.4	51.1	49.0
56443	CUSHING	98.2	98.0	0.4	0.5	0.1	0.2	0.8	1.0	4.6	6.3	6.5	7.3	5.8	22.4	29.9	16.4	1.0	77.6	43.3	52.5	47.5
56444	DEERWOOD	98.4	98.1	0.3	0.4	0.1	0.1	0.6	0.7	5.0	5.4	6.4	5.8	4.4	18.8	32.1	19.6	2.5	79.4	47.5	49.9	50.1
56446	EAGLE BEND	99.0	98.9	0.1	0.1	0.2	0.2	1.0	1.3	6.4	5.9	6.5	7.1	7.6	22.2	27.3	14.7	2.4	77.1	41.3	51.3	48.7
56447	EMILY	98.1	97.9	0.3	0.4	0.3	0.4	0.8	1.0	4.4	4.9	5.6	4.7	4.2	18.3	30.2	26.0	1.8	82.2	51.0	51.9	48.1
56448	FIFTY LAKES	98.2	97.9	0.3	0.5	0.3	0.2	0.8	0.7	4.2	4.7	5.1	4.2	3.7	17.3	30.1	28.7	2.1	83.2	53.3	52.7	47.3
56449	FORT RIPLEY	98.4	98.1	0.1	0.1	0.3	0.3	0.7	0.8	5.6	5.7	7.9	7.6	6.7	26.0	27.4	12.4	0.8	76.2	39.7	52.0	48.0
56450	GARRISON	74.2	74.3	0.0	0.1	0.2	0.3	0.7	0.7	6.5	6.5	7.2	6.5	4.8	23.0	27.8	16.6	1.1	75.4	42.1	50.5	49.5
56452	HACKENSACK	96.4	96.1	0.1	0.1	0.2	0.3	0.3	0.4	3.7	4.0	4.7	4.2	3.6	15.3	35.5	26.9	2.2	84.9	55.0	51.2	48.8
56453	HEWITT	98.7	98.5	0.1	0.1	0.2	0.2	0.6	0.7	7.0	7.3	9.3	8.1	7.3	23.4	25.7	10.8	1.1	71.7	35.7	51.8	48.2
56455	IRONTON	98.0	97.5	0.0	0.6	0.7	0.6	0.7	1.3	5.7	5.7	7.0	6.4	6.4	24.2	30.6	12.7	1.3	77.7	41.1	51.6	48.4
56456	JENKINS	99.1	98.7	0.0	0.0	0.5	0.4	0.5	0.4	6.0	6.0	5.6	5.2	5.2	23.2	29.2	18.5	1.3	79.0	44.4	50.2	49.8
56458	LAKE GEORGE	96.7	96.1	0.0	0.4	0.5	0.4	0.9	0.9	4.3	4.7	4.7	4.7	4.3	19.8	34.5	21.6	1.3	83.2	49.5	50.9	49.1
56461	LAPORTE	93.5	93.1	0.2	0.2	0.3	0.3	0.6	0.7	5.6	6.3	7.2	8.1	6.3	24.0	29.3	12.2	1.0	75.7	40.4	51.4	48.6
56464	MENAHGA	97.9	97.7	0.2	0.2	0.1	0.2	0.5	0.6	6.6	6.8	7.5	6.9	5.5	21.8	24.5	17.7	2.9	74.8	41.5	50.1	49.9
56465	MERRIFIELD	98.8	98.8	0.1	0.2	0.0	0.0	0.4	0.5	5.3	5.9	6.4	5.6	4.8	23.6	30.8	16.5	1.1	78.9	44.1	51.4	48.6
56466	MOTLEY	98.3	98.1	0.1	0.1	0.2	0.2	1.3	1.6	7.0	6.9	6.6	5.6	5.5	23.0	25.7	17.7	2.1	76.3	41.7	49.0	51.1
56467	NEVIS	97.7	97.5	0.3	0.3	0.1	0.1	0.6	0.7	3.8	4.9	5.8	6.1	4.2	19.5	32.7	21.2	1.8	81.8	48.8	50.3	49.7
56468	NISSWA	98.8	98.7	0.2	0.3	0.2	0.2	0.6	0.7	4.6	5.2	6.2	5.4	4.0	22.6	32.6	18.1	1.4	80.4	46.3	51.9	48.1
56469	PALISADE	98.1	98.0	0.4	0.5	0.1	0.1	0.4	0.5	4.5	5.1	6.7	5.3	4.9	20.7	31.4	20.3	1.3	80.6	46.9	52.2	47.8
56470	PARK RAPIDS	97.0	96.7	0.2	0.2	0.3	0.4	0.8	0.9	5.9	5.6	6.0	6.2	6.1	20.5	27.3	19.3	3.1	78.8	44.7	48.9	51.1
56472	PEQUOT LAKES	98.7	98.5	0.3	0.3	0.2	0.3	0.5	0.6	5.3	5.6	6.4	5.8	4.7	22.1	29.0	19.3	1.9	79.0	45.1	48.9	51.1
56473	PILLAGER	98.2	97.8	0.0	0.1	0.5	0.6	0.7	0.8	5.5	6.3	8.9	7.2	5.2	26.2	28.2	11.8	0.7	74.6	39.9	51.3	48.7
56474	PINE RIVER	97.8	97.4	0.3	0.3	0.2	0.3	0.7	0.8	5.4	6.0	7.7	8.3	6.0	22.3	26.8	14.7	2.8	75.4	41.2	49.3	50.7
56475	RANDALL	98.0	97.7	0.4	0.5	0.3	0.4	0.2	0.3	6.2	6.9	7.5	8.0	6.5	25.5	26.2	12.0	1.4	74.3	38.6	51.5	48.5
56477	SEBEKA	98.0	97.7	0.4	0.5	0.3	0.4	1.2	1.4	6.7	7.1	7.2	6.3	5.9	23.6	26.7	14.6	1.9	74.7	40.3	51.2	48.8
56479	STAPLES	97.5	97.1	0.2	0.2	0.4	0.5	1.2	1.5	6.5	6.6	7.5	7.3	8.1	24.0	24.7	13.2	2.3	75.2	38.2	50.1	49.9
56481	VERNDALE	97.6	97.1	0.2	0.3	0.3	0.4	1.2	1.4	7.2	7.3	7.4	7.1	6.6	23.4	26.2	13.3	1.5	73.9	38.6	50.8	49.2
56482	WADENA	98.0	97.7	0.7	0.9	0.2	0.2	0.6	0.7	6.5	6.1	7.0	7.1	7.0	22.8	24.1	15.9	3.5	76.2	40.3	49.8	50.2
56484	WALKER	82.7	80.7	0.2	0.3	0.2	0.3	1.1	1.2	4.4	5.5	6.7	6.3	4.1	21.1	29.9	19.1	2.8	78.8	46.3	50.7	49.3
56501	DETROIT LAKES	90.7	90.2	0.3	0.3	0.4	0.5	0.9	1.0	6.1	6.1	6.8	7.3	6.1	23.3	26.8	14.7	2.8	76.3	41.2	49.1	50.9
56510	ADA	96.2	96.1	0.1	0.1	0.5	0.5	2.8	2.9	6.3	6.5	7.4	6.5	5.0	23.4	23.5	17.9	3.6	75.5	41.9	48.5	51.5
56511	AUDUBON	95.9	95.5	0.0	0.0	0.1	0.1	0.8	0.9	6.6	6.6	6.2	5.9	5.0	24.1	29.9	13.7	2.1	76.4	41.9	52.1	47.9
56514	BARNESVILLE	99.2	99.1	0.1	0.1	0.2	0.2	0.6	0.8	6.7	6.8	7.2	8.0	5.1	25.0	25.8	12.7	2.7	74.0	39.0	50.9	49.1
56515	BATTLE LAKE	98.7	98.3	0.2	0.3	0.4	0.5	0.6	0.8	4.4	4.6	5.7	5.7	4.8	17.6	31.4	22.4	3.6	81.8	49.7	50.0	50.0
56516	BEJOU	82.0	80.9	0.0	0.0	0.0	0.4	0.4	0.7	8.0	7.6	8.3	6.6	5.2	23.6	25.7	13.2	1.7	71.9	38.0	51.0	49.0
56517	BELTRAMI	97.4	97.1	0.0	0.0	0.0	0.0	2.4	2.9	5.0	5.8	7.4	6.7	6.2	22.3	29.3	14.6	2.6	77.5	42.7	50.6	49.4
56518	BLUFFTON	98.8	98.9	0.0	0.0	0.0	0.0	0.2	0.2	6.9	6.9	7.1	7.3	5.5	24.7	28.6	11.4	1.6	74.1	39.7	53.6	46.5
56519	BORUP	94.8	94.4	0.8	0.8	0.4	0.4	1.9	2.0	6.0	5.2	8.4	7.6	6.4	22.7	26.7	16.3	0.8	75.3	40.9	53.8	46.2
56520	BRECKENRIDGE	97.7	97.7	0.1	0.1	0.2	0.2	1.7	1.8	6.3	6.1	8.1	7.6	6.8	24.6	23.8	12.9	3.8	74.4	38.8	47.7	52.3
56521	CALLAWAY	70.2	68.3	0.1	0.1	0.3	0.3	0.9	1.0	7.3	7.5	8.2	8.4	6.6	23.4	25.6	12.0	1.1	71.6	36.5	50.5	49.5
56522	CAMPBELL	97.7	97.6	0.3	0.3	0.0	0.0	1.3	1.3	6.4	5.3	9.1	8.2	4.2	26.2	26.4	12.5	1.7	72.9	39.8	51.7	48.3
56523	CLIMAX	97.2	96.6	0.3	0.5	0.0	0.0	3.1	3.7	5.5	6.3	8.4	6.4	5.7	24.3	27.7	13.6	2.2	75.7	40.7	51.0	49.0
56524	CLITHERALL	98.8	98.7	0.0	0.0	0.2	0.1	0.3	0.4	4.9	5.5	6.6	6.6	5.1	20.7	31.8	16.9	1.8	78.9	45.3	52.7	47.3
56525	COMSTOCK	97.6	96.8	0.0	0.0	0.0	0.8	0.8	0.0	4.0	7.2	6.4	7.2	3.2	25.6	28.8	16.0	1.6	77.6	42.8	54.4	45.6
56527	DEER CREEK	98.2	97.9	0.1	0.1	0.0	0.0	0.7	0.9	7.3	7.7	7.7	7.1	6.2	22.8	26.3	13.6	1.5	72.9	38.8	52.1	47.9
56528	DENT	99.1	99.1	0.1	0.1	0.0	0.0	0.4	0.5	4.9	5.2	6.2	6.2	4.2	20.1	32.6	19.6	1.1	79.7	47.0	52.3	47.7
56529	DILWORTH	91.9	90.6	0.0	0.0	0.2	0.3	7.5	9.1	8.1	8.0	8.8	7.3	7.1	27.3	21.3	9.6	2.4	70.6	33.7	48.2	51.8
56531	ELBOW LAKE	97.9	97.6	0.1	0.0	0.3	0.4	0.9	1.0	5.8	5.8	7.0	7.0	5.8	23.1	24.0	17.8	3.9	77.3	42.1	48.2	51.8
56533	ELIZABETH	98.4	98.3	0.0	0.0	0.5	0.4	0.5	0.7	5.7	7.7	8.1	7.7	5.3	25.0	26.8	13.2	0.7	73.7	39.3	52.2	47.8
56534	ERHARD	97.6	97.2	0.2	0.2	0.8	0.9	0.6	0.8	6.0	5.9	7.2	7.0	4.8	24.1	29.8	13.8	1.5	76.3	41.8	52.5	47.6
56535	ERSKINE	95.5	95.2	0.1	0.1	0.0	0.1	0.3	0.4	6.9	6.8	6.6	5.6	5.5	18.9	25.0	18.2	6.6	75.9	44.8	49.0	51.0
56536	FELTON	97.2	96.8	0.2	0.2	0.2	0.5	1.4	1.6	7.2	7.6	8.1	7.9	5.5	23.6	26.6	11.6	2.1	71.8	38.8	50.6	49.4
56537	FERGUS FALLS	97.5	97.2	0.5	0.7	0.5	0.6	0.7	0.9	5.9	6.0	6.7	7.4	7.0	23.6	24.7	14.8	4.0	77.3	40.6	48.5	51.6
56540	FERTILE	97.6	97.4	0.0	0.0	0.2	0.3	1.0	1.2	5.9	5.4	6.2	5.8	4.9	21.3	24.0	20.2	6.4	78.8	45.5	48.6	51.4
56542	FOSSTON	96.2	95.9	0.3	0.4	0.5	0.6	0.6	0.8	6.2	5.8	6.3	6.7	7.0	21.0	23.7	18.6	4.7	77.1	42.5	48.0	52.0
56543	FOXHOME	97.6	97.1	0.4	0.4	0.0	0.0	1.2	1.2	6.6	5.4	9.1	8.6	4.1	26.8	25.9	11.9	1.7	72.4	39.3	50.6	49.4
56544	FRAZEE	96.0	95.5	0.3	0.3	0.7	0.8	0.6	0.8	6.1	6.1	6.9	7.6	6.8	23.3	26.8	13.6	2.9	76.2	40.7	49.8	50.2
56545	GARY	95.9	95.9	0.0	0.0	0.0	0.0	1.4	1.6	6.5	6.5	6.8	6.8	6.5	25.2	26.0	14.3	1.6	75.8	39.7	52.3	47.7
56546	GEORGETOWN	97.7	97.6	0.2	0.5	0.5	0.5	2.1	2.2	5.1	7.6	8.2	8.0	4.2	26.5	28.3	10.5	1.6	73.1	39.3	51.9	48.1
56547	GLYNDON	96.8	96.2	0.1	0.2	0.2	0.2	4.1	5.0	8.5	8.6	8.6	7.7	6.2	27.0	24.7	8.0	0.8	69.3	34.4	51.3	48.7
56548	HALSTAD	94.4	94.0	0.1	0.1	0.6	0.6	6.7	6.9	5.9	6.0	7.1	7.4	5.3	20.6	25.3	18.1	4.2	75.4	43.4	48.9	51.2
56549	HAWLEY	98.6	98.3	0.1	0.1	0.2	0.3	0.6	0.7	6.4	6.6	8.4	8.5	5.8	24.6	24.6	12.3	2.8	73.0	38.0	50.7	49.3
56550	HENDRUM	95.2	94.8	0.0	0.0	0.2	0.5	2.8	2.8	6.1	6.8	7.6	8.3	6.6	25.5	28.5	9.2	1.4	73.6	40.0	50.5	49.5
56551	HENNING	98.6	98.3	0.0	0.1	0.6	0.7	0.5	0.6	5.2	5.0	5.7	5.6	6.0	18.3	28.0	21.3	5.0	80.6	48.0	49.1	50.9
56552	HITTERDAL	98.3	98.4	0.0	0.0	0.2	0.4	0.6	0.6	5.7	6.9	9.9	9.7	4.7	24.9	26.5	10.9	0.8	70.9	37.9	53.0	47.0
56553	KENT	98.3	98.9	0.0	0.0	0.0	0.0	2.3	1.7	6.3	6.9	8.6	9.2	6.3	20.1	31.0	10.3	1.2	71.3	39.1	51.7	48.3
56554	LAKE PARK	97.7	97.4	0.2	0.2	0.2	0.3	0.5	0.6	5.9	5.9	6.3	5.7	5.2	22.3	30.7	16.3	1.8	78.3	44.2	52.2	47.8
56556	MCINTOSH	98.3	98.1	0.0	0.0	0.2	0.3	1.3	1.5	5.1	5.2	5.6	5.3	5.2	17.4	25.1	22.6	8.6	80.7	50.4	48.3	51.7
56557	MAHNOMEN	71.5	70.6	0.1	0.1	0.1	0.1	1.0	1.1	6.6	6.6	7.6	6.4	5.8	22.0	25.2	15.7	4.1	74.8	41.2	50.0	50.0
56560	MOORHEAD	92.9	91.9	0.6	0.8	1.1	1.4	4.2	5.0	6.3	6.3	6.9	9.3	10.9	25.6	21.6	11.0	2.3	76.3	33.2	48.3	51.7
56562	MOORHEAD	94.2	92.9	2.0	2.5	2.4	2.9	1.4	1.7	1.1	1.0	0.8	48.6	39.5	4.3	2.5	1.9	0.3	96.6	19.8	37.1	63.0
56563	MOORHEAD	86.0	84.3	1.5	1.9	2.0	2.5	6.2	7.3	2.6	3.0	2.6	40.3	34.1	11.4	4.2	1.6	0.3	90.3	20.2	41.2	58.8
56565	NASHUA	97.2	97.2	0.0	0.0	0.0	0.0	1.4	1.4	6.4	5.0	11.4	8.5	3.6	26.2	27.0	10.6	1.4	70.9	38.9	51.1	48.9
56566	NAYTAHWAUSH	25.0	24.2	0.4	0.6	0.0	0.0	1.0	1.0	9.3	8.6	9.8	8.8	8.6	21.8	22.6	9.8	0.6	66.5	29.2	50.3	49.7
56567	NEW YORK MILLS	98.4	98.2	0.1	0.2	0.2	0.2	0.8	0.9	6.2	6.3	7.4	6.8	6.2	23.4	24.2	15.8	3.7	75.9	40.7	49.9	50.1
56568	NIELSVILLE	96.5	96.1	0.0	0.0	0.0	0.0	3.5	4.3	4.3	5.1	7.5	6.3	5.9	20.8	28.6	17.3	4.3	78.8	45.1	50.2	49.8
56569	OGEMA	46.4	44.2	0.0	0.0	0.1	0.1	1.5	1.5	8.8	8.5	8.7	9.0	7.2	22.7	23.7	10.7	0.9	68.6	32.2	51.7	48.4
56570	OSAGE	97.3	97.0	0.0	0.0	0.5	0.6	0.2	0.4	7.4	7.0	6.3	6.7	5.3	23.6	27.7	14.9	1.1	75.3	40.9	52.8	47.2
56571	OTTERTAIL	99.0	98.8	0.1	0.1	0.3	0.4	0.5	0.6	4.5	5.0	5.8	6.1	4.9	20.2	31.9	20.3	1.4	80.8	47.2	52.1	47.9
56572	PELICAN RAPIDS	87.6	85.8	0.3	0.4	1.7	2.0	10.9	12.7	6.1	6.0	7.2	7.3	6.2	22.4	26.1	15.5	3.3	75.9	41.6	51.1	48.9
56573	PERHAM	97.8	97.5	0.3	0.3	0.3	0.4	1.4	1.7	6.2	6.3	7.6	7.4	6.3	23.3	25.3	14.4	3.2	75.0	40.5	50.4	49.6
56574	PERLEY	95.4	94.9	0.0	0.0	0.4	0.4	2.1	2.2	6.2	6.9	7.3	8.0	6.6	25.9	29.2	8.8	1.1	74.1	40.2	51.1	48.9
56575	PONSFORD	61.4	60.2	0.0	0.0	0.2	0.3	0.8	1.0	7.7	7.7	7.7	8.5	5.8	21.0	25.6	14.9	1.2	71.6	38.5	51.7	48.3
56576	RICHVILLE	98.9	98.7	0.1	0.1	0.3	0.4	0.4	0.6	4.5	5.1	6.0	6.6	4.8	21.1	31.6	19.2	1.1	80.2	46.2	52.9	47.1
56577	RICHWOOD	89.9	89.6	0.4	0.4	0.4	0.4	0.5	0.5	5.3	5.5	8.1	8.6	4.8	23.2	32.0	11.8	0.9	75.6	41.5	52.0	48.0
56578	ROCHERT	97.0	96.9	0.0	0.0	0.1	0.1	0.2	0.3	6.0	6.2	6.6	7.0	7.0	24.3	31.3	10.8	0.8	77.1	40.2	53.1	46.9
56579	ROTHSAY	97.7	97.4	0.2	0.2	0.4	0.5	0.9	0.9	7.1	7.0	7.7	6.8	4.8	25.9	26.5	12.8	1.5	73.7	39.4	51.3	48.7
56580	SABIN	97.3	96.9	0.2	0.3	0.3	0.4	1.2	1.5	6.4	7.2	7.9	8.2	5.3	28.4	27.5	8.4	0.6	73.2	36.5	52.4	47.6
56581	SHELLY	94.3	94.2	0.0	0.0	0.7	0.7	6.8	7.0	6.1	5.8	7.2	6.8	5.6	20.8	25.6	18.0	4.2	76.0	43.5	49.0	51.1
56583	TINTAH	99.2	99.1	0.0	0.0	0.4	0.4	0.4	0.4	5.7	6.6	7.5	7.9	5.7	19.8	26.0	18.9	1.8	74.9	42.7	52.0	48.0
56584	TWIN VALLEY	94.6	94.5	0.2	0.2	0.1	0.1	2.2	2.2	6.6	5.8	6.1	6.4	6.5	20.7	23.7	18.8	5.4	77.6	43.5	49.8	50.2
56585	ULEN	98.8	98.9	0.1	0.1	0.1	0.1	0.4	0.6	5.3	5.5	7.3	7.2	5.6	21.3	23.8	16.7	7.4	76.9	43.5	49.3	50.7
56586	UNDERWOOD	98.6	98.3	0.2	0.2	0.4	0.5	0.7	0.8	5.4	5.5	5.8	5.9	5.2	21.2	32.3	16.6	2.3	79.9	45.8	52.2	47.8
56587	VERGAS	98.2	98.0	0.1	0.1	0.2	0.3	0.6	0.6	4.9	5.4	5.5	6.4	6.0	21.3	32.4	17.3	0.9	79.9	45.3	52.4	47.6
	MINNESOTA	89.5	88.0	3.5	4.2	2.9	3.4	2.9	3.4	6.8	6.8	7.2	7.3	7.4	28.6	23.9	10.1	1.9	74.9	36.1	49.6	50.5
	UNITED STATES	75.1	73.6	12.3	12.5	3.8	4.2	12.5	14.1	6.9	6.7	7.2	7.0	7.3	28.6	23.8	10.8	1.7	75.1	36.0	49.1	50.9

ZIP CODE #	POST OFFICE NAME	FINANCIAL SERVICES: Auto Loan	Home Loan	Investments	Retirement Plans	THE HOME: Home Improvements: Home Repair	Lawn & Garden	Furnishings: Computers & Hardware	Major Appliances	TV, Radio, Sound Equipment	Furniture	ENTERTAINMENT: Dine out/ Carry out	Sports Equipment	Fees & Tickets	Toys & Games	Travel	Cable TV	PERSONAL: Apparel & Services	Auto Repairs	Health Insurance	Pets & Supplies
56442	CROSSLAKE	126	99	67	89	111	125	93	112	105	92	125	131	83	123	99	113	116	110	133	153
56443	CUSHING	97	75	49	68	84	95	71	86	80	70	95	101	63	94	75	86	88	85	101	118
56444	DEERWOOD	117	88	55	81	100	113	85	103	97	84	114	122	75	112	89	103	105	101	122	141
56446	EAGLE BEND	77	61	42	58	66	77	64	71	71	62	84	81	58	81	64	74	77	70	83	87
56447	EMILY	92	72	49	65	81	91	68	82	77	67	91	96	61	90	72	82	85	80	97	112
56448	FIFTY LAKES	97	76	52	68	85	96	71	86	81	71	96	101	64	95	76	86	89	85	102	118
56449	FORT RIPLEY	95	80	59	75	87	95	75	86	81	74	98	101	71	99	78	85	92	84	96	113
56450	GARRISON	88	69	47	62	78	88	65	79	74	65	88	92	58	86	70	79	81	77	93	108
56452	HACKENSACK	87	68	47	62	77	86	64	78	73	64	86	91	58	85	69	78	80	76	92	106
56453	HEWITT	75	52	27	49	61	68	52	64	59	51	70	77	44	68	53	62	63	63	76	89
56455	IRONTON	85	74	56	71	79	85	70	77	74	69	90	92	68	91	71	76	85	75	84	99
56456	JENKINS	88	69	47	62	78	88	65	79	74	65	87	92	58	86	70	79	81	77	93	107
56458	LAKE GEORGE	96	75	51	68	85	95	71	86	80	70	95	100	63	94	76	86	88	84	101	117
56461	LAPORTE	98	75	47	70	84	93	72	86	81	71	96	102	64	95	75	85	89	84	100	117
56464	MENAHGA	81	60	37	56	68	78	61	71	69	59	81	83	54	79	63	73	75	71	85	94
56465	MERRIFIELD	105	85	60	78	95	105	80	94	89	80	106	111	74	106	85	94	99	93	109	127
56466	MOTLEY	74	61	45	58	65	73	60	67	65	59	79	78	56	78	61	68	73	66	75	85
56467	NEVIS	98	77	52	69	86	97	72	87	82	72	97	102	65	96	77	87	90	86	103	119
56468	NISSWA	127	100	69	91	113	126	95	113	107	94	127	133	85	125	101	114	118	112	133	155
56469	PALISADE	85	66	43	60	74	83	62	75	71	62	84	89	55	82	66	75	78	74	89	103
56470	PARK RAPIDS	89	69	50	64	77	88	70	80	79	68	93	93	63	91	72	83	86	80	95	105
56472	PEQUOT LAKES	104	79	52	73	89	102	78	92	88	76	104	107	69	102	82	94	96	91	110	123
56473	PILLAGER	99	79	56	74	88	98	77	89	85	76	102	104	70	101	80	90	95	88	103	117
56474	PINE RIVER	77	56	33	53	63	73	58	68	65	56	77	79	50	74	59	69	70	67	81	89
56475	RANDALL	89	72	51	69	78	87	71	80	78	70	93	94	66	92	72	80	87	79	90	102
56477	SEBEKA	78	56	33	53	64	73	58	68	66	56	77	80	50	75	59	69	71	68	81	90
56479	STAPLES	71	60	49	58	64	72	62	67	67	60	81	77	59	81	62	69	76	66	75	81
56481	VERNDALE	73	56	37	54	62	70	56	65	62	56	74	76	51	73	57	65	69	64	74	84
56482	WADENA	66	57	53	55	60	69	60	63	65	58	78	73	57	77	61	67	74	64	71	77
56484	WALKER	96	74	50	68	83	95	74	86	83	72	98	99	66	95	77	88	91	85	102	113
56501	DETROIT LAKES	90	69	50	66	77	88	72	81	80	70	95	95	65	93	73	84	88	81	95	105
56510	ADA	76	56	36	54	62	74	61	69	69	58	81	78	54	77	61	73	74	68	82	85
56511	AUDUBON	93	73	50	66	82	92	69	83	78	68	92	97	61	91	73	83	86	82	98	113
56514	BARNESVILLE	101	75	46	73	85	95	76	89	85	75	100	105	68	99	77	88	93	88	103	117
56515	BATTLE LAKE	105	85	62	78	94	105	80	95	90	80	107	111	73	105	85	95	100	94	110	128
56516	BEJOU	77	54	28	51	63	70	53	66	61	53	72	79	46	71	55	64	66	65	78	92
56517	BELTRAMI	95	70	43	67	79	91	73	85	83	71	98	99	65	94	74	87	89	84	101	110
56518	BLUFFTON	89	79	60	75	83	89	73	81	77	73	94	96	71	96	75	79	89	79	87	104
56519	BORUP	86	60	32	57	70	79	60	74	69	59	80	89	51	79	62	72	73	73	88	103
56520	BRECKENRIDGE	81	67	52	66	71	80	70	75	75	68	90	88	65	89	70	76	84	75	84	91
56521	CALLAWAY	85	58	29	53	67	76	57	71	67	57	78	85	48	76	58	71	71	70	85	99
56522	CAMPBELL	96	67	35	64	78	88	66	82	77	66	90	99	57	88	69	80	82	81	98	114
56523	CLIMAX	93	68	41	65	76	88	71	82	80	69	94	96	62	91	72	84	86	82	98	107
56524	CLITHERALL	80	68	55	64	74	81	65	74	70	65	85	87	60	83	68	73	80	74	84	96
56525	COMSTOCK	105	73	38	69	85	95	72	89	83	71	98	108	62	96	75	87	89	88	106	124
56527	DEER CREEK	70	57	40	55	61	69	57	64	62	56	75	74	53	74	58	64	69	63	72	80
56528	DENT	100	78	53	71	88	99	74	89	84	73	99	104	66	98	79	89	92	88	105	122
56529	DILWORTH	61	59	67	60	59	64	65	63	65	63	81	74	64	80	64	64	79	65	62	69
56531	ELBOW LAKE	83	60	37	58	68	79	64	74	73	62	85	85	56	82	65	77	78	73	88	94
56533	ELIZABETH	104	73	38	69	85	95	72	89	83	71	97	107	61	95	75	87	89	88	106	124
56534	ERHARD	112	80	44	75	92	104	78	96	90	77	105	115	67	104	81	95	96	95	114	134
56535	ERSKINE	85	64	42	61	71	84	69	77	78	66	92	88	62	87	69	82	84	77	93	96
56536	FELTON	116	86	55	83	98	109	85	102	95	85	113	122	76	111	88	99	105	101	117	137
56537	FERGUS FALLS	88	77	69	76	82	90	81	85	85	78	103	99	77	102	81	86	97	85	92	102
56540	FERTILE	78	57	35	54	64	74	60	69	68	58	80	80	52	76	61	71	73	69	82	89
56542	FOSSTON	73	55	35	53	60	72	60	67	68	57	79	75	53	75	60	71	72	67	80	82
56543	FOXHOME	95	66	35	63	77	86	65	81	75	65	88	97	56	87	68	79	81	80	96	113
56544	FRAZEE	90	70	46	65	77	88	70	80	78	68	92	93	63	90	71	82	85	79	94	105
56545	GARY	83	58	30	55	68	76	57	71	66	57	78	86	49	76	60	69	71	70	84	99
56546	GEORGETOWN	123	86	45	81	100	112	85	105	97	84	114	126	72	112	88	102	104	103	125	146
56547	GLYNDON	98	95	84	94	97	100	90	95	90	91	112	113	89	112	90	88	108	94	93	114
56548	HALSTAD	81	61	40	58	67	80	67	74	76	64	89	83	60	84	67	80	81	74	89	90
56549	HAWLEY	93	72	47	68	79	91	75	84	83	72	99	97	67	95	75	87	91	83	99	106
56550	HENDRUM	92	65	35	61	75	84	65	79	74	64	87	94	56	85	67	78	80	78	94	108
56551	HENNING	76	59	39	54	65	75	59	68	66	57	78	79	53	76	61	71	72	68	81	89
56552	HITTERDAL	102	75	44	71	85	95	73	88	82	72	97	106	65	97	76	86	90	86	103	120
56553	KENT	110	77	40	73	90	100	76	94	88	75	103	113	65	101	79	92	94	93	112	131
56554	LAKE PARK	98	77	53	72	86	96	75	88	84	74	100	103	68	99	78	88	93	87	102	116
56556	MCINTOSH	97	72	46	69	80	95	79	88	89	75	104	100	70	99	78	93	95	88	105	109
56557	MAHNOMEN	67	50	34	48	56	65	53	60	60	52	71	69	48	68	54	63	65	60	71	76
56560	MOORHEAD	78	78	89	81	77	82	84	80	82	82	103	96	83	102	82	79	100	83	76	89
56562	MOORHEAD	0	0	0	0	0	0	0	0	0	0	0	0	0	0	0	0	0	0	0	0
56563	MOORHEAD	0	0	0	0	0	0	0	0	0	0	0	0	0	0	0	0	0	0	0	0
56565	NASHUA	96	67	35	63	78	87	66	82	76	65	89	99	56	88	69	80	81	81	97	114
56566	NAYTAHWAUSH	63	53	48	49	56	63	53	58	59	53	71	67	51	71	55	62	68	58	65	74
56567	NEW YORK MILLS	80	63	43	59	69	79	63	72	70	61	83	83	57	81	65	74	77	71	84	93
56568	NIELSVILLE	72	54	36	52	59	71	60	66	67	57	79	74	53	74	59	71	72	66	79	79
56569	OGEMA	70	51	31	48	57	67	55	62	62	53	73	71	48	69	55	65	66	62	75	79
56570	OSAGE	82	63	41	57	71	80	60	73	68	59	81	85	53	79	64	73	75	71	86	100
56571	OTTERTAIL	102	80	55	72	90	101	75	91	85	75	101	106	67	100	80	91	94	89	107	124
56572	PELICAN RAPIDS	84	68	52	64	73	83	70	77	76	68	92	90	64	90	71	79	86	77	87	98
56573	PERHAM	87	71	52	67	76	86	71	80	78	70	93	92	65	91	72	81	86	79	90	100
56574	PERLEY	93	65	34	61	76	85	64	79	74	63	87	96	55	85	67	78	79	78	94	110
56575	PONSFORD	72	56	36	51	63	71	53	64	60	52	71	75	47	70	56	64	66	63	76	88
56576	RICHVILLE	104	81	55	73	91	103	77	92	87	76	103	108	68	101	82	93	95	91	109	126
56577	RICHWOOD	122	85	45	79	99	111	84	103	97	83	113	124	71	111	87	102	103	102	123	144
56578	ROCHERT	87	64	38	60	74	82	62	76	71	62	84	90	54	82	65	75	77	75	89	104
56579	ROTHSAY	92	68	42	66	77	86	69	80	77	68	91	95	61	90	70	80	84	79	93	106
56580	SABIN	109	98	80	97	102	107	94	103	97	95	118	123	89	117	95	96	113	102	105	127
56581	SHELLY	81	61	40	59	67	80	68	74	76	64	89	83	60	84	67	80	81	74	89	90
56583	TINTAH	87	60	32	57	70	79	60	74	69	59	81	89	51	79	62	72	73	73	88	103
56584	TWIN VALLEY	69	56	43	55	60	68	59	64	63	57	76	74	54	73	59	65	70	64	73	78
56585	ULEN	69	70	78	72	71	75	71	71	69	71	86	84	71	84	71	67	84	72	70	80
56586	UNDERWOOD	101	79	54	72	89	100	75	90	85	74	100	106	67	99	80	91	93	89	107	123
56587	VERGAS	108	84	58	76	95	107	80	96	90	79	107	112	71	105	85	96	99	94	113	131
	MINNESOTA	107	106	108	107	107	113	106	107	105	105	131	126	105	131	105	104	127	107	105	123
	UNITED STATES	100	100	100	100	100	100	100	100	100	100	100	100	100	100	100	100	100	100	100	100

MINNESOTA

POPULATION CHANGE

A 56588-56763

#	POST OFFICE NAME	COUNTY FIPS CODE	POPULATION 2000	POPULATION 2004	POPULATION 2009	2000-2004 ANNUAL RATE % Rate	2000-2004 ANNUAL RATE State Centile	HOUSEHOLDS 2000	HOUSEHOLDS 2004	HOUSEHOLDS 2009	% Annual Rate 2000-2004	2004 Average HH Size	FAMILIES 2000	FAMILIES 2004	% Annual Rate 2000-2004
56588	VINING	111	474	489	520	0.7	51	197	206	222	1.1	2.37	147	150	0.5
56589	WAUBUN	087	1020	1037	1080	0.4	41	406	417	441	0.6	2.49	287	290	0.2
56590	WENDELL	051	415	421	430	0.3	39	168	172	178	0.6	2.38	125	125	0.0
56592	WINGER	119	382	384	390	0.1	32	161	164	169	0.4	2.34	113	113	0.0
56593	WOLF LAKE	005	464	475	503	0.6	45	159	167	180	1.2	2.84	115	118	0.6
56594	WOLVERTON	167	801	805	811	0.1	32	307	313	320	0.5	2.57	237	237	0.0
56601	BEMIDJI	007	29773	32054	35004	1.8	74	11068	12142	13511	2.2	2.50	7339	7825	1.5
56621	BAGLEY	029	4115	4266	4422	0.9	54	1585	1685	1788	1.5	2.47	1088	1123	0.8
56623	BAUDETTE	077	3359	3466	3599	0.7	51	1417	1496	1591	1.3	2.29	930	952	0.6
56626	BENA	021	467	461	472	-0.3	16	172	171	177	-0.1	2.70	127	123	-0.8
56627	BIG FALLS	071	462	437	419	-1.3	1	229	222	219	-0.7	1.97	152	142	-1.6
56628	BIGFORK	061	1630	1815	1995	2.6	85	708	805	904	3.1	2.19	496	547	2.3
56629	BIRCHDALE	071	41	41	41	0.0	27	21	22	22	1.1	1.86	15	15	0.0
56630	BLACKDUCK	061	1470	1498	1585	0.4	42	603	628	677	1.0	2.30	411	413	0.1
56633	CASS LAKE	021	3524	3509	3628	-0.1	24	1230	1229	1283	0.0	2.85	882	861	-0.6
56634	CLEARBROOK	029	1226	1297	1352	1.3	65	511	550	585	1.8	2.24	321	335	1.0
56636	DEER RIVER	061	4338	4569	4887	1.2	63	1590	1709	1866	1.7	2.64	1135	1188	1.1
56637	TALMOON	061	207	251	287	4.6	96	77	95	110	5.1	2.63	54	65	4.5
56639	EFFIE	061	384	382	398	-0.1	22	162	165	177	0.4	2.13	110	109	-0.2
56641	FEDERAL DAM	021	348	344	352	-0.3	17	136	136	142	0.0	2.50	89	87	-0.5
56644	GONVICK	029	907	879	885	-0.7	4	386	380	389	-0.4	2.31	256	247	-0.8
56646	GULLY	119	482	474	478	-0.4	13	202	203	208	0.1	2.33	142	139	-0.5
56647	HINES	007	1242	1283	1374	0.8	51	458	483	526	1.3	2.64	342	350	0.6
56649	INTERNATIONAL FALLS	071	10565	10303	10015	-0.6	7	4500	4504	4496	0.0	2.24	2907	2821	-0.7
56650	KELLIHER	007	1163	1165	1241	0.0	29	448	457	496	0.5	2.51	313	310	-0.2
56651	LENGBY	119	508	506	511	-0.1	24	207	210	215	0.3	2.40	148	146	-0.3
56652	LEONARD	029	1032	1009	1017	-0.5	9	403	401	411	-0.1	2.50	291	284	-0.6
56653	LITTLEFORK	071	1635	1581	1531	-0.8	4	628	624	619	-0.2	2.46	442	427	-0.8
56654	LOMAN	071	101	102	100	0.2	35	44	46	46	1.1	2.22	31	31	0.0
56655	LONGVILLE	021	1496	1606	1708	1.7	73	696	763	825	2.2	2.10	477	510	1.6
56657	MARCELL	061	258	294	325	3.1	91	121	140	158	3.5	2.09	92	104	2.9
56659	MAX	061	161	163	170	0.3	37	67	69	73	0.7	2.36	49	49	0.0
56660	MIZPAH	071	290	280	271	-0.8	3	113	111	110	-0.4	2.41	73	70	-1.0
56661	NORTHOME	071	918	913	917	-0.1	22	359	365	375	0.4	2.43	245	243	-0.2
56662	OUTING	021	555	612	656	2.3	83	277	311	339	2.8	1.97	181	197	2.0
56663	PENNINGTON	007	200	220	243	2.3	82	79	87	97	2.3	2.53	60	64	1.5
56666	PONEMAH	007	1029	1100	1197	1.6	70	247	267	294	1.9	4.09	207	220	1.4
56667	PUPOSKY	007	982	1011	1079	0.7	49	393	413	448	1.2	2.45	287	293	0.5
56668	RANIER	071	88	88	86	0.0	27	29	30	30	0.8	2.90	21	21	0.0
56669	KABETOGAMA	071	309	315	318	0.5	42	144	151	155	1.1	2.09	101	102	0.2
56670	REDBY	007	2105	2251	2449	1.6	71	521	563	620	1.8	3.97	437	464	1.4
56671	REDLAKE	007	1881	2001	2170	1.5	68	540	583	641	1.8	3.40	427	451	1.3
56672	REMER	021	1931	2040	2158	1.3	65	836	901	969	1.8	2.23	552	577	1.1
56673	ROOSEVELT	135	1328	1345	1380	0.3	37	490	506	530	0.8	2.66	373	378	0.3
56676	SHEVLIN	029	928	911	918	-0.4	12	357	357	366	0.0	2.53	267	261	-0.5
56678	SOLWAY	007	1464	1561	1706	1.5	69	547	594	660	2.0	2.63	414	439	1.4
56680	SPRING LAKE	061	203	241	273	4.1	95	93	112	129	4.5	2.15	66	77	3.7
56681	SQUAW LAKE	061	252	255	266	0.3	37	96	99	104	0.7	2.58	70	70	0.0
56682	SWIFT	135	940	951	973	0.3	36	303	312	325	0.7	3.04	243	246	0.3
56683	TENSTRIKE	007	195	206	222	1.3	65	83	89	98	1.7	2.30	60	63	1.2
56684	TRAIL	119	273	268	270	-0.4	12	113	113	117	0.0	2.37	79	78	-0.3
56685	WASKISH	007	116	116	123	0.0	27	61	62	67	0.4	1.81	38	37	-0.6
56686	WILLIAMS	077	969	979	1009	0.2	35	402	416	439	0.8	2.35	281	283	0.2
56688	WIRT	061	90	94	99	1.0	60	34	36	39	1.4	2.61	25	26	0.9
56701	THIEF RIVER FALLS	113	11982	12388	12840	0.8	52	4894	5148	5429	1.2	2.32	3082	3138	0.4
56710	ALVARADO	089	526	527	521	0.0	29	197	199	199	0.2	2.65	146	143	-0.5
56711	ANGLE INLET	077	118	120	124	0.4	41	53	55	58	0.9	2.18	36	37	0.7
56713	ARGYLE	089	927	914	897	-0.3	15	353	354	354	0.1	2.56	252	246	-0.6
56714	BADGER	135	1177	1186	1210	0.2	33	471	483	502	0.6	2.46	348	348	0.0
56715	BROOKS	125	266	263	266	-0.3	17	109	110	114	0.2	2.39	70	69	-0.3
56716	CROOKSTON	119	10027	10103	10264	0.2	33	3676	3776	3910	0.6	2.40	2299	2279	-0.1
56720	DONALDSON	069	89	85	82	-1.1	2	37	36	35	-0.6	2.36	26	24	-1.9
56721	EAST GRAND FORKS	119	7685	7790	7933	0.3	39	2992	3085	3196	0.7	2.50	1984	1992	0.1
56722	EUCLID	119	1333	1309	1319	-0.4	12	492	490	501	-0.1	2.67	383	373	-0.6
56723	FISHER	119	1578	1584	1601	0.1	31	547	558	574	0.5	2.84	444	445	0.1
56724	GATZKE	089	141	138	135	-0.5	10	62	62	62	0.0	2.23	43	41	-1.1
56725	GOODRIDGE	113	798	758	759	-1.2	1	308	297	302	-0.9	2.55	228	216	-1.3
56726	GREENBUSH	135	1032	1061	1095	0.7	48	416	437	460	1.2	2.32	279	284	0.4
56727	GRYGLA	089	1083	1064	1060	-0.4	12	448	450	457	0.1	2.35	306	299	-0.5
56728	HALLOCK	069	1554	1517	1485	-0.6	8	618	611	606	-0.3	2.35	406	390	-0.9
56729	HALMA	069	172	171	168	-0.1	22	72	73	73	0.3	2.34	54	53	-0.4
56732	KARLSTAD	069	1349	1328	1303	-0.4	13	543	543	540	0.0	2.33	361	351	-0.7
56733	KENNEDY	069	555	531	515	-1.0	2	227	220	216	-0.7	2.41	158	149	-1.4
56734	LAKE BRONSON	069	518	513	505	-0.2	18	238	238	237	0.0	2.16	147	142	-0.8
56735	LANCASTER	069	794	788	775	-0.2	20	328	329	328	0.1	2.40	221	215	-0.7
56736	MENTOR	119	1302	1356	1402	1.0	58	535	568	597	1.4	2.39	399	413	0.8
56737	MIDDLE RIVER	089	857	835	816	-0.6	7	374	372	370	-0.1	2.24	243	235	-0.8
56738	NEWFOLDEN	089	1518	1488	1458	-0.5	11	603	604	604	0.0	2.46	446	436	-0.5
56740	NOYES	069	64	62	61	-0.7	4	23	23	22	0.0	2.70	17	16	-1.4
56741	OAK ISLAND	077	31	31	32	0.0	27	16	17	18	1.4	1.82	11	11	0.0
56742	OKLEE	125	580	572	580	-0.3	15	268	271	281	0.3	2.11	174	170	-0.6
56744	OSLO	089	512	485	469	-1.3	1	215	208	205	-0.8	2.33	149	139	-1.6
56748	PLUMMER	125	784	782	796	-0.1	25	326	334	348	0.6	2.34	214	213	-0.1
56750	RED LAKE FALLS	125	2695	2761	2837	0.6	45	1029	1077	1131	1.1	2.41	677	686	0.3
56751	ROSEAU	135	6120	6343	6582	0.9	54	2393	2512	2646	1.2	2.48	1671	1708	0.5
56754	SAINT HILAIRE	113	881	839	840	-1.1	2	345	334	341	-0.8	2.49	260	248	-1.1
56755	SAINT VINCENT	069	188	183	178	-0.6	6	79	78	77	-0.3	2.35	57	55	-0.8
56756	SALOL	135	577	582	594	0.2	34	208	213	221	0.6	2.73	159	160	0.2
56757	STEPHEN	089	1179	1140	1112	-0.8	4	471	462	459	-0.5	2.47	315	300	-1.1
56758	STRANDQUIST	089	858	834	813	-0.7	6	336	333	331	-0.2	2.50	234	225	-0.9
56759	STRATHCONA	135	756	763	783	0.2	35	298	307	321	0.7	2.44	211	212	0.1
56760	VIKING	089	512	500	492	-0.6	8	214	214	214	0.0	2.33	161	157	-0.6
56761	WANNASKA	135	737	747	766	0.3	39	280	288	300	0.7	2.59	206	207	0.1
56762	WARREN	089	2471	2432	2395	-0.4	13	1010	1009	1007	0.0	2.30	672	652	-0.7
56763	WARROAD	135	4042	4100	4200	0.3	39	1476	1526	1590	0.8	2.64	1050	1059	0.2
	MINNESOTA					1.4					1.6	2.50			1.0
	UNITED STATES					1.2					1.3	2.58			1.1

# ZIP CODE	POST OFFICE NAME	RACE (%) White 2000	White 2004	Black 2000	Black 2004	Asian/Pacific 2000	Asian/Pacific 2004	% Hispanic Origin 2000	% Hispanic Origin 2004	2004 AGE DISTRIBUTION (%) 0-4	5-9	10-14	15-19	20-24	25-44	45-64	65-84	85+	18+	MEDIAN AGE 2004	% 2004 Males	% 2004 Females
56588	VINING	98.7	98.6	0.0	0.0	0.0	0.2	0.4	0.6	4.9	5.5	6.3	6.3	5.1	20.9	31.1	17.8	2.0	78.9	45.6	52.8	47.2
56589	WAUBUN	74.0	72.7	0.0	0.0	0.1	0.1	0.8	0.9	7.1	7.6	8.0	5.9	5.8	22.0	26.8	14.6	2.2	73.5	40.6	53.1	46.9
56590	WENDELL	98.3	98.1	0.0	0.0	0.0	0.0	0.2	0.2	4.0	4.5	6.9	6.9	5.5	21.1	29.2	19.0	2.9	80.1	45.6	49.9	50.1
56592	WINGER	96.6	96.1	0.0	0.0	0.0	0.0	0.8	0.8	6.3	6.5	7.0	6.8	5.7	22.7	28.1	14.8	2.1	75.8	41.4	52.1	47.9
56593	WOLF LAKE	94.4	94.1	0.0	0.0	0.9	1.1	0.4	0.6	7.2	7.4	7.8	8.0	6.3	23.0	26.5	12.8	1.1	72.8	38.4	52.6	47.4
56594	WOLVERTON	98.0	98.1	0.3	0.3	0.3	0.3	1.0	0.9	7.3	6.8	7.8	6.6	5.1	27.0	25.2	12.8	1.4	73.8	39.6	50.4	49.6
56601	BEMIDJI	87.0	86.4	0.4	0.5	0.8	0.9	0.9	1.1	6.7	6.4	6.8	8.7	10.9	25.7	22.9	10.3	1.8	75.8	32.8	49.4	50.6
56621	BAGLEY	83.7	83.3	0.3	0.4	0.3	0.4	0.9	1.0	6.8	6.8	6.6	7.1	7.3	23.4	25.3	14.0	2.7	75.6	39.1	49.2	50.8
56623	BAUDETTE	96.7	96.4	0.3	0.4	0.2	0.3	0.7	0.8	4.4	5.4	7.7	6.9	5.4	22.9	29.6	14.9	2.9	77.7	43.3	49.8	50.2
56626	BENA	46.0	42.7	0.0	0.0	0.4	0.4	1.3	1.3	7.6	7.4	7.8	6.9	5.6	24.7	24.7	14.1	1.1	73.3	37.9	49.7	50.3
56627	BIG FALLS	97.0	96.8	0.0	0.0	0.2	0.2	0.0	0.0	4.1	4.1	4.6	5.3	5.3	20.4	34.8	19.9	1.6	84.0	48.8	53.6	46.5
56628	BIGFORK	97.2	97.0	0.3	0.4	0.1	0.2	0.4	0.4	3.6	4.3	6.2	6.0	4.7	19.7	32.5	20.3	2.6	81.7	48.3	51.4	48.6
56629	BIRCHDALE	97.6	97.6	0.0	0.0	0.0	0.0	0.0	0.0	4.9	4.9	7.3	7.3	4.9	24.4	26.8	19.5	0.0	82.9	42.5	56.1	43.9
56630	BLACKDUCK	94.4	94.1	0.4	0.5	0.2	0.2	0.5	0.7	4.9	5.6	7.4	7.7	5.2	23.6	25.4	16.2	3.9	77.2	42.2	47.4	52.6
56633	CASS LAKE	38.8	36.8	0.0	0.0	0.1	0.1	1.8	2.0	8.8	8.2	9.7	8.8	7.2	23.9	22.6	9.4	1.3	67.2	31.9	48.2	51.8
56634	CLEARBROOK	93.2	93.2	0.1	0.1	0.2	0.2	0.8	0.8	5.1	5.3	6.9	7.3	5.9	21.0	24.2	18.0	6.3	77.8	43.8	49.5	50.5
56636	DEER RIVER	77.0	76.7	0.1	0.1	0.2	0.3	1.0	1.0	7.6	7.2	7.4	7.7	6.1	21.8	26.9	13.3	1.9	72.8	39.0	50.2	49.8
56637	TALMOON	98.6	98.4	0.5	0.4	0.0	0.0	0.0	0.4	4.0	4.4	6.8	5.6	5.2	20.3	31.1	20.7	2.0	81.7	47.3	50.6	49.4
56639	EFFIE	95.6	95.0	0.0	0.0	0.5	0.5	0.8	0.8	3.9	4.7	5.5	5.2	4.5	20.7	30.6	19.9	5.0	81.9	48.8	52.9	47.1
56641	FEDERAL DAM	77.0	74.4	0.0	0.0	0.3	0.3	0.9	0.9	4.7	5.5	6.7	7.3	4.4	20.1	32.0	17.7	1.7	77.9	45.9	50.3	49.7
56644	GONVICK	92.2	91.8	0.0	0.0	0.0	0.0	1.3	1.6	4.7	4.8	5.8	6.5	6.1	22.5	29.4	17.8	2.5	80.9	44.7	52.8	47.2
56646	GULLY	96.9	96.4	0.0	0.0	0.4	0.6	1.0	1.1	5.3	5.9	7.4	5.9	6.1	22.8	28.9	15.2	2.5	78.3	42.7	54.2	45.8
56647	HINES	96.7	96.5	0.2	0.2	0.1	0.1	0.9	1.1	5.1	6.3	8.0	8.5	4.6	24.0	28.0	14.0	1.6	74.9	40.9	51.4	48.6
56649	INTERNATIONAL FALLS	96.1	95.8	0.3	0.3	0.3	0.3	0.6	0.7	5.6	5.9	6.9	6.3	5.9	23.8	27.6	15.5	2.6	77.6	42.1	49.1	50.9
56650	KELLIHER	88.2	87.5	0.3	0.3	0.1	0.1	0.5	0.4	6.4	6.9	8.0	8.1	5.4	20.4	27.0	15.5	2.4	73.6	41.1	52.2	47.8
56651	LENGBY	97.6	97.2	0.2	0.4	0.2	0.2	0.8	0.8	6.7	6.5	5.9	6.3	5.5	21.3	28.7	16.8	2.2	76.9	43.2	49.4	50.6
56652	LEONARD	98.2	98.0	0.2	0.2	0.3	0.3	0.4	0.5	6.3	6.5	7.1	7.3	4.9	24.1	27.4	14.0	2.4	75.5	40.9	53.9	46.1
56653	LITTLEFORK	96.7	96.5	0.1	0.1	0.0	0.0	0.7	0.9	4.9	5.9	7.7	6.6	5.1	23.0	30.1	14.2	2.7	77.0	43.1	50.8	49.2
56654	LOMAN	98.0	98.0	0.0	0.0	0.0	0.0	0.0	0.0	4.9	4.9	5.9	6.9	4.9	22.6	31.4	16.7	2.0	78.4	45.0	52.9	47.1
56655	LONGVILLE	88.2	87.7	0.1	0.1	0.2	0.3	0.4	0.4	3.3	3.7	4.7	4.6	3.6	15.2	35.3	27.5	2.1	85.5	54.7	51.5	48.5
56657	MARCELL	96.5	96.6	0.4	0.3	0.0	0.0	0.4	0.7	4.8	4.8	5.8	6.8	4.8	19.7	34.0	17.7	1.7	80.6	47.0	51.0	49.0
56659	MAX	56.5	55.2	0.6	0.6	0.0	0.0	1.2	1.2	9.2	8.0	7.4	8.0	5.5	20.3	25.8	14.1	1.8	69.9	37.5	52.8	47.2
56660	MIZPAH	95.2	95.0	0.0	0.0	0.3	0.4	0.7	0.7	5.7	6.4	6.8	6.4	5.0	20.4	27.9	17.9	3.6	76.8	44.5	51.1	48.9
56661	NORTHOME	95.0	94.6	0.0	0.0	0.3	0.4	0.8	1.0	5.3	6.6	7.1	7.1	4.4	19.1	29.8	17.9	2.9	76.2	45.3	51.6	48.4
56662	OUTING	97.3	96.9	0.0	0.0	0.4	0.3	0.5	0.7	3.6	4.1	5.6	5.1	4.4	16.8	33.8	24.5	2.1	83.8	52.1	51.3	48.7
56663	PENNINGTON	49.5	48.2	0.0	0.0	0.0	0.0	1.0	0.9	7.7	7.7	10.5	8.6	5.5	23.6	27.3	8.2	0.9	68.6	35.0	50.5	49.6
56666	PONEMAH	2.6	2.5	0.2	0.3	0.1	0.1	1.7	1.6	14.8	12.5	12.3	11.2	9.3	23.0	12.9	3.9	0.2	53.0	19.7	48.8	51.2
56667	PUPOSKY	94.3	93.9	0.0	0.0	0.4	0.4	0.7	0.8	4.7	5.4	7.0	7.7	5.9	22.7	30.8	14.1	1.7	77.9	42.8	51.3	48.7
56668	RANIER	97.7	96.6	0.0	0.0	0.0	1.1	0.0	0.0	4.6	4.6	5.7	4.6	4.6	19.3	39.8	15.9	1.1	80.7	48.8	50.0	50.0
56669	KABETOGAMA	76.4	75.6	0.0	0.0	0.0	0.0	0.7	1.0	5.1	5.7	6.7	6.4	5.1	22.5	32.7	14.6	1.3	78.4	44.2	52.7	47.3
56670	REDBY	2.6	2.5	0.2	0.3	0.1	0.1	1.7	1.6	14.5	12.5	12.3	11.2	9.3	23.1	12.9	3.9	0.2	53.2	19.8	48.6	51.4
56671	REDLAKE	3.0	2.9	0.3	0.4	0.0	0.0	1.5	1.6	11.5	10.4	10.9	11.2	8.3	25.2	16.9	5.2	0.4	60.2	23.6	48.4	51.6
56672	REMER	94.1	93.5	0.1	0.1	0.4	0.4	0.6	0.7	3.8	5.0	6.9	6.7	4.3	18.7	33.3	19.3	2.0	79.6	48.3	51.4	48.6
56673	ROOSEVELT	98.2	98.1	0.2	0.2	0.1	0.1	0.3	0.4	6.7	7.2	8.2	8.4	5.8	26.0	27.0	9.8	1.0	72.3	37.9	52.5	47.5
56676	SHEVLIN	96.4	96.2	0.0	0.0	0.1	0.1	0.3	0.4	5.7	6.2	7.4	7.0	6.8	24.4	28.4	12.7	1.4	75.9	40.6	50.9	49.1
56678	SOLWAY	96.0	95.8	0.1	0.1	0.4	0.5	0.7	0.7	6.3	6.7	7.6	8.4	7.1	26.3	27.2	9.4	0.9	74.1	37.1	52.2	47.8
56680	SPRING LAKE	90.6	90.9	0.5	0.4	0.0	0.0	0.0	0.4	4.6	5.4	7.1	6.2	5.4	20.3	29.9	19.5	1.7	78.8	45.7	50.6	49.4
56681	SQUAW LAKE	53.6	52.2	0.4	0.8	0.0	0.0	1.6	2.0	8.6	8.2	7.5	7.8	5.9	19.2	24.3	16.1	2.4	71.0	37.9	52.6	47.5
56682	SWIFT	97.2	97.0	0.2	0.2	0.3	0.4	0.2	0.2	8.0	7.8	8.4	9.7	7.5	26.0	24.6	7.4	0.7	69.9	34.2	52.4	47.6
56683	TENSTRIKE	95.4	95.6	0.5	0.5	0.0	0.0	1.0	1.0	5.3	5.8	5.3	7.8	6.3	24.3	30.6	13.6	1.0	77.7	42.4	53.4	46.6
56684	TRAIL	97.1	96.3	0.0	0.0	0.4	0.8	1.1	1.5	5.2	6.0	7.1	5.6	6.0	22.4	30.2	15.3	2.2	78.0	43.3	54.5	45.5
56685	WASKISH	96.6	95.7	0.9	0.9	0.0	0.0	0.0	0.0	5.2	5.2	6.9	6.9	5.2	18.1	27.6	20.7	4.3	78.5	46.7	51.7	48.3
56686	WILLIAMS	98.5	98.3	0.2	0.3	0.2	0.3	0.5	0.5	4.2	6.5	8.2	6.2	3.9	23.9	31.7	14.1	1.3	76.4	43.3	52.3	47.7
56688	WIRT	95.6	95.7	0.0	0.0	0.0	0.0	0.0	0.0	3.2	5.3	6.4	7.5	3.2	19.2	35.1	19.2	1.1	79.8	48.6	52.1	47.9
56701	THIEF RIVER FALLS	96.8	96.4	0.2	0.3	0.7	0.8	1.4	1.7	6.3	5.7	6.2	6.9	8.1	25.5	25.1	13.1	3.3	78.0	38.6	49.1	50.9
56710	ALVARADO	94.7	93.6	0.0	0.0	0.0	0.0	7.4	9.1	7.2	6.5	7.0	7.6	7.2	26.9	23.3	12.9	1.3	73.8	37.4	49.0	51.0
56711	ANGLE INLET	99.2	100.0	0.0	0.0	0.0	0.0	0.0	0.8	3.3	5.8	6.7	5.0	3.3	24.2	35.8	14.2	1.7	79.2	45.8	52.5	47.5
56713	ARGYLE	95.3	94.5	0.1	0.1	0.1	0.1	5.1	6.1	6.0	6.4	7.4	7.4	5.1	23.3	25.9	16.5	1.9	74.6	41.5	50.1	49.9
56714	BADGER	99.1	98.9	0.3	0.3	0.1	0.1	0.5	0.7	8.0	7.7	6.9	7.4	5.7	28.8	23.4	10.4	1.7	72.8	36.6	52.5	47.6
56715	BROOKS	99.3	99.6	0.0	0.0	0.0	0.0	0.0	0.0	4.9	4.9	6.5	7.6	7.2	20.9	26.2	19.0	2.7	79.1	43.6	51.0	49.1
56716	CROOKSTON	92.4	91.3	0.5	0.6	0.5	0.6	7.5	9.0	6.0	5.9	6.4	8.5	11.7	22.8	21.9	12.9	4.0	77.5	36.4	48.9	51.2
56720	DONALDSON	98.9	98.8	0.0	0.0	0.0	0.0	3.4	4.7	5.9	5.9	8.2	5.9	4.7	18.8	34.1	14.1	2.4	74.1	45.4	54.1	45.9
56721	EAST GRAND FORKS	91.3	90.0	0.5	0.6	0.3	0.4	7.3	8.8	7.1	6.6	7.7	8.1	9.8	25.8	23.2	10.3	1.5	73.8	34.2	49.8	50.2
56722	EUCLID	97.5	97.1	0.2	0.2	0.0	0.0	1.7	2.1	5.8	6.4	7.7	8.1	5.7	25.5	26.1	13.5	1.2	75.0	39.1	53.1	46.9
56723	FISHER	96.8	96.1	0.3	0.4	0.1	0.1	3.0	3.8	6.3	7.0	9.1	7.8	6.1	25.8	27.6	9.7	0.6	72.5	37.3	51.3	48.7
56724	GATZKE	98.6	97.8	0.0	0.0	0.7	0.7	0.0	0.0	5.8	5.8	6.5	6.5	5.1	23.2	29.0	14.5	3.6	77.5	43.0	52.2	47.8
56725	GOODRIDGE	98.8	98.6	0.1	0.1	0.5	0.7	0.4	0.3	7.1	7.0	6.5	6.7	6.3	24.1	28.4	12.7	1.2	74.9	39.7	52.4	47.6
56726	GREENBUSH	98.8	98.8	0.2	0.3	0.2	0.2	0.2	0.2	7.6	7.5	6.7	5.5	4.0	26.9	22.6	15.0	4.3	75.1	39.8	50.4	49.6
56727	GRYGLA	96.2	95.8	0.1	0.1	0.6	0.6	0.1	0.3	5.6	5.9	6.7	6.7	5.0	21.8	28.8	16.3	3.4	77.8	43.9	52.6	47.4
56728	HALLOCK	97.6	97.2	0.1	0.1	0.3	0.3	1.7	2.1	6.3	6.4	6.6	7.1	5.0	19.6	25.7	17.4	5.9	75.8	44.3	48.0	52.0
56729	HALMA	97.7	97.7	0.0	0.0	0.6	0.6	0.6	1.2	5.9	6.4	8.2	5.9	4.7	22.8	28.7	15.8	1.8	75.4	41.8	53.2	46.8
56732	KARLSTAD	97.9	97.7	0.0	0.0	0.2	0.2	0.7	0.7	6.5	6.9	6.6	5.7	4.5	21.5	26.4	16.9	5.0	76.7	43.3	48.6	51.4
56733	KENNEDY	98.7	98.5	0.0	0.0	0.2	0.2	3.1	4.0	5.8	6.2	7.5	6.6	4.7	21.7	29.9	14.7	2.8	76.3	43.3	51.0	49.0
56734	LAKE BRONSON	98.5	98.3	1.0	1.2	0.0	0.0	0.4	0.4	6.2	6.0	6.2	6.2	4.7	20.5	26.9	20.7	2.5	77.6	45.1	53.4	46.6
56735	LANCASTER	98.6	98.4	0.1	0.3	0.4	0.5	0.8	0.9	6.6	6.9	6.7	7.1	4.7	22.2	27.2	16.1	2.5	75.4	42.5	51.8	48.2
56736	MENTOR	98.2	97.9	0.1	0.1	0.2	0.2	0.5	0.8	5.6	6.0	6.3	6.6	4.9	20.5	32.7	15.5	1.8	78.0	45.1	52.1	47.9
56737	MIDDLE RIVER	98.7	98.6	0.0	0.0	0.2	0.2	0.5	0.6	6.4	6.2	5.5	5.6	5.6	24.6	28.9	15.2	2.0	78.6	42.5	48.7	51.3
56738	NEWFOLDEN	98.7	98.5	0.1	0.1	0.3	0.3	0.6	0.7	6.2	6.3	6.1	6.5	6.5	24.5	28.6	14.1	1.4	77.6	41.0	52.8	47.2
56740	NOYES	98.4	98.4	0.0	0.0	0.0	0.0	0.0	0.0	6.5	6.5	6.5	6.5	4.8	22.6	29.0	14.5	3.2	80.7	43.0	51.6	48.4
56741	OAK ISLAND	100.0	100.0	0.0	0.0	0.0	0.0	0.0	0.0	6.5	6.5	6.5	6.5	3.2	25.8	32.3	12.9	0.0	80.7	42.5	58.1	41.9
56742	OKLEE	99.3	99.1	0.2	0.2	0.0	0.0	0.2	0.2	4.9	5.2	6.1	7.3	7.0	21.2	26.2	19.2	2.8	79.6	43.8	50.7	49.3
56744	OSLO	94.7	93.4	0.2	0.2	0.0	0.2	7.6	9.3	6.8	6.6	7.0	6.0	6.0	24.5	26.8	14.2	2.1	75.9	40.8	53.0	47.0
56748	PLUMMER	98.9	98.9	0.9	0.9	0.0	0.0	0.1	0.1	7.4	7.0	6.7	5.6	6.8	24.3	26.9	12.4	2.9	75.5	39.0	51.8	48.2
56750	RED LAKE FALLS	96.4	96.5	0.0	0.0	0.1	0.1	0.4	0.4	5.9	5.8	6.6	7.1	6.6	23.3	25.9	15.5	3.4	77.0	41.5	50.0	50.1
56751	ROSEAU	98.3	98.1	0.1	0.1	0.6	0.7	0.4	0.5	7.2	7.2	7.7	7.4	5.5	27.3	24.1	11.0	2.6	73.1	37.4	50.5	49.5
56754	SAINT HILAIRE	98.4	98.2	0.2	0.4	0.2	0.4	0.5	0.4	5.7	6.2	7.6	7.0	5.8	24.6	30.6	11.6	0.8	75.7	41.3	52.8	47.2
56755	SAINT VINCENT	97.9	98.4	0.0	0.0	0.5	0.6	0.5	1.1	6.6	7.1	6.6	6.6	5.5	22.4	28.4	14.8	2.2	75.4	42.0	50.8	49.2
56756	SALOL	96.7	96.4	0.0	0.0	1.0	1.2	0.4	0.5	7.6	7.9	9.6	7.2	6.2	31.8	21.7	7.2	0.9	70.3	33.4	51.9	48.1
56757	STEPHEN	94.1	92.8	0.1	0.1	0.1	0.2	7.7	9.4	5.8	6.0	7.0	6.9	6.8	21.4	26.3	17.4	2.4	77.2	42.3	51.1	48.9
56758	STRANDQUIST	99.0	98.9	0.1	0.1	0.0	0.0	0.5	0.6	5.6	6.1	6.8	8.6	5.8	22.8	28.5	14.2	1.6	75.9	40.7	53.4	46.6
56759	STRATHCONA	99.1	98.8	0.1	0.1	0.3	0.3	0.0	0.1	6.8	7.0	6.6	6.0	5.0	25.4	25.2	14.9	3.2	76.0	40.7	53.6	46.4
56760	VIKING	97.7	97.0	0.2	0.2	0.2	0.2	1.6	2.0	6.0	6.8	7.8	6.8	5.6	24.0	28.8	12.8	1.4	75.2	40.6	53.8	46.2
56761	WANNASKA	98.9	98.8	0.1	0.1	0.1	0.1	0.4	0.4	6.3	6.4	7.5	8.0	4.4	28.0	25.6	12.1	1.7	73.9	39.0	55.0	45.0
56762	WARREN	98.1	97.8	0.2	0.2	0.0	0.1	2.3	2.8	5.0	5.3	6.9	6.9	5.8	22.5	25.6	17.4	4.7	78.3	43.5	49.5	50.5
56763	WARROAD	88.6	87.2	0.2	0.2	5.8	7.1	0.6	0.7	7.8	7.7	8.8	8.4	6.9	29.0	22.5	7.3	1.5	70.1	33.7	51.1	48.9
	MINNESOTA	89.5	88.0	3.5	4.2	2.9	3.4	2.9	3.4	6.8	6.8	7.2	7.3	7.4	28.6	23.9	10.1	1.9	74.9	36.1	49.6	50.5
	UNITED STATES	75.1	73.6	12.3	12.5	3.8	4.2	12.5	14.1	6.9	6.7	7.2	7.0	7.3	28.6	23.8	10.8	1.7	75.1	36.0	49.1	50.9

ZIP CODE #	POST OFFICE NAME	2004 Per Capita Income	2004 HH Income Base	2004 HOUSEHOLD INCOME DISTRIBUTION (%) Less than $25,000	$25,000 to $49,999	$50,000 to $99,999	$100,000 to $149,999	$150,000 or More	MEDIAN HOUSEHOLD INCOME 2004	2009	2004 National Centile	2004 State Centile	2004 Home Value Base	2004 HOME VALUE DISTRIBUTION (%) Less than $50,000	$50,000 to $89,999	$90,000 to $174,999	$175,000 to $399,999	$400,000 or More	2004 Median Home Value
56588	VINING	20505	206	31.6	31.1	29.1	5.3	2.9	39078	45000	43	22	175	17.1	18.3	37.1	24.0	3.4	119375
56589	WAUBUN	17365	417	29.3	37.4	29.7	3.1	0.5	38773	43783	42	21	353	17.0	26.6	37.1	16.4	2.8	101096
56590	WENDELL	23789	172	25.0	34.9	30.2	5.2	4.7	41131	50000	50	31	147	18.4	23.1	40.1	15.7	2.7	104167
56592	WINGER	21103	164	34.2	31.7	27.4	4.9	1.8	36368	44656	33	12	139	46.0	24.5	20.9	7.2	1.4	54231
56593	WOLF LAKE	15313	167	34.7	30.5	31.1	3.0	0.6	37349	42737	37	15	142	20.4	24.7	40.1	12.7	2.1	97000
56594	WOLVERTON	19659	313	22.0	36.4	33.6	6.4	1.6	44860	50726	61	49	272	19.1	24.3	39.3	16.5	0.7	97200
56601	BEMIDJI	21561	12142	28.4	31.3	28.6	8.2	3.4	41660	50774	52	34	9063	17.2	18.6	42.0	20.0	2.2	114932
56621	BAGLEY	18925	1685	36.7	27.1	26.8	7.2	2.2	36702	45270	34	13	1367	26.6	22.8	38.8	10.3	1.5	90893
56623	BAUDETTE	21957	1496	28.9	34.4	27.7	5.8	3.2	39070	46935	43	22	1214	19.8	30.6	39.8	7.9	1.9	89306
56626	BENA	15364	171	42.7	22.2	29.2	5.3	0.6	29039	34779	10	2	139	34.5	18.0	33.8	13.0	0.7	85625
56627	BIG FALLS	22462	222	34.7	36.9	21.6	4.1	2.7	35944	44503	31	11	183	43.7	29.5	20.8	5.5	0.6	54107
56628	BIGFORK	23631	805	29.3	32.6	28.8	6.1	3.2	39729	48595	45	24	706	14.5	21.7	39.5	21.7	2.7	113000
56629	BIRCHDALE	22684	22	36.4	27.3	36.4	0.0	0.0	37303	54545	36	15	20	20.0	30.0	45.0	5.0	0.0	90000
56630	BLACKDUCK	17802	628	38.7	32.8	22.6	4.8	1.1	32533	39567	19	3	526	30.8	21.9	35.9	11.0	0.4	84615
56633	CASS LAKE	14048	1229	40.0	29.5	24.7	4.9	0.9	31180	36398	15	3	877	25.4	28.2	30.7	12.3	3.4	84375
56634	CLEARBROOK	17069	550	43.1	26.7	25.8	3.6	0.7	30535	37446	14	2	407	28.5	29.5	28.8	12.3	1.0	80152
56636	DEER RIVER	17426	1709	35.1	32.8	24.5	5.4	2.3	35762	43155	31	10	1418	20.2	27.6	34.1	15.2	3.0	94638
56637	TALMOON	20112	95	33.7	28.4	26.3	7.4	4.2	38626	47882	42	21	83	15.7	20.5	39.8	21.7	2.4	112500
56639	EFFIE	23638	165	26.1	37.6	29.7	4.2	2.4	39297	48646	44	23	137	11.7	27.0	39.4	19.7	2.2	102500
56641	FEDERAL DAM	19559	136	35.3	33.1	22.8	5.9	2.9	34518	41532	26	7	121	9.9	24.0	30.6	28.1	7.4	122656
56644	GONVICK	19891	380	40.0	24.5	28.7	4.0	2.9	35211	42630	28	8	326	26.1	29.8	33.1	9.8	1.2	81364
56646	GULLY	17908	203	37.9	34.5	21.7	3.9	2.0	30932	36863	15	2	168	47.0	28.6	20.2	3.0	1.2	54545
56647	HINES	18475	483	30.0	32.3	29.8	6.2	1.7	40522	48432	48	28	451	22.4	20.4	39.7	15.5	2.0	102993
56649	INTERNATIONAL FALLS	25482	4504	29.5	28.5	32.1	6.7	3.2	42740	51840	55	39	3547	19.3	26.5	41.8	11.6	0.9	96193
56650	KELLIHER	15442	457	44.2	29.8	20.6	4.4	1.1	29022	34355	10	2	388	33.3	23.5	32.0	9.8	1.6	79583
56651	LENGBY	17922	210	34.8	33.8	25.7	4.3	1.4	33745	40478	23	5	176	32.4	29.0	34.7	3.4	0.6	75385
56652	LEONARD	20609	401	32.7	31.2	26.4	7.5	2.2	38157	46427	40	19	366	17.5	29.8	38.8	12.6	1.4	93571
56653	LITTLEFORK	23216	624	26.3	28.5	33.7	9.1	2.4	44313	55166	59	46	554	21.1	25.3	44.4	8.1	1.1	94167
56654	LOMAN	19104	46	34.8	26.1	37.0	2.2	0.0	38604	48201	41	20	42	23.8	31.0	35.7	9.5	0.0	85000
56655	LONGVILLE	25331	763	28.7	35.8	24.9	7.2	3.4	39088	48564	43	22	703	5.4	14.8	30.0	41.1	8.7	174292
56657	MARCELL	26587	140	22.1	34.3	32.1	8.6	2.9	44382	53905	60	47	132	11.4	18.9	40.9	25.0	3.8	125000
56659	MAX	14833	69	49.3	33.3	11.6	2.9	2.9	25429	31350	5	1	59	23.7	30.5	28.8	10.2	6.8	83750
56660	MIZPAH	17256	111	38.7	30.6	23.4	4.5	2.7	32756	40000	20	3	91	39.6	30.8	19.8	8.8	1.1	59500
56661	NORTHOME	16949	365	38.4	31.5	24.7	3.8	1.6	32543	40536	19	3	317	30.6	28.1	32.2	8.5	0.6	77500
56662	OUTING	22231	311	37.0	33.1	21.9	6.1	1.9	33270	40354	22	5	284	12.0	17.3	33.8	31.0	6.0	130435
56663	PENNINGTON	17357	87	34.5	32.2	27.6	5.8	0.0	35366	41385	29	9	76	29.0	11.8	36.8	18.4	4.0	106250
56666	PONEMAH	7856	267	53.9	25.5	17.2	3.0	0.4	22563	26104	3	1	154	29.2	37.7	28.6	4.6	0.0	72500
56667	PUPOSKY	19742	413	29.5	31.0	31.2	6.3	1.9	40844	49364	49	30	369	19.0	24.4	39.6	14.6	2.4	101367
56668	RANIER	24462	30	13.3	30.0	40.0	13.3	3.3	60000	78022	84	81	27	3.7	3.7	51.9	37.0	3.7	147917
56669	KABETOGAMA	23411	151	30.5	35.8	23.8	8.6	1.3	36435	45758	33	12	134	17.9	28.4	38.8	11.9	3.0	95556
56670	REDBY	8094	563	53.3	25.8	17.2	3.2	0.5	22913	25833	3	1	324	29.3	37.0	28.7	4.9	0.0	72727
56671	REDLAKE	12001	583	45.6	28.3	20.1	2.4	3.6	27839	32140	8	2	410	20.0	41.7	34.4	3.9	0.0	80769
56672	REMER	19029	901	36.7	32.9	23.8	5.6	1.1	33027	40259	21	4	826	13.4	22.4	36.2	23.4	4.6	115299
56673	ROOSEVELT	18902	506	22.9	37.2	32.2	5.1	2.6	42347	49332	54	37	474	19.4	25.3	44.7	9.5	1.1	97353
56676	SHEVLIN	21927	357	30.0	31.4	30.5	4.2	3.9	40101	48523	46	26	324	22.5	22.8	40.7	13.0	0.9	97895
56678	SOLWAY	21240	594	22.4	32.2	36.2	6.7	2.5	46782	55201	66	56	554	14.6	23.3	44.0	16.4	1.6	111239
56680	SPRING LAKE	22914	112	35.7	30.4	24.1	6.3	3.6	36299	42788	33	11	96	18.8	21.9	36.5	19.8	3.1	107143
56681	SQUAW LAKE	13403	99	49.5	33.3	11.1	3.0	3.0	25306	30742	5	1	84	23.8	29.8	29.8	9.5	7.1	85000
56682	SWIFT	17410	312	19.2	39.7	33.0	5.1	2.9	43192	49878	56	41	294	16.3	26.9	46.3	10.2	0.3	100000
56683	TENSTRIKE	25288	89	20.2	40.5	31.5	5.6	2.3	43947	52608	58	44	83	14.5	15.7	56.6	12.1	1.2	116875
56684	TRAIL	17718	113	37.2	34.5	22.1	3.5	2.7	31628	36141	17	3	93	46.2	29.0	20.4	3.2	1.1	55833
56685	WASKISH	21716	62	45.2	29.0	19.4	4.8	1.6	27792	34298	8	2	52	34.6	23.1	30.8	9.6	1.9	77500
56686	WILLIAMS	18848	416	29.3	41.8	22.4	5.1	1.4	37240	43329	36	14	384	23.7	26.3	39.3	7.8	2.9	90000
56688	WIRT	16438	36	33.3	36.1	25.0	5.6	0.0	35000	41148	28	8	33	21.2	21.2	48.5	9.1	0.0	104688
56701	THIEF RIVER FALLS	21333	5148	32.1	29.6	30.2	5.1	3.0	39113	47679	43	23	3843	24.6	27.5	37.1	10.4	0.4	87452
56710	ALVARADO	19481	199	23.1	26.1	43.7	7.0	0.0	50405	56467	73	67	169	22.5	27.8	40.8	7.7	1.2	89500
56711	ANGLE INLET	20257	55	40.0	32.7	20.0	5.5	1.8	31326	38621	16	3	50	22.0	26.0	44.0	6.0	2.0	95000
56713	ARGYLE	18989	354	31.9	30.5	28.5	7.1	2.0	41133	46719	50	31	296	31.1	36.5	28.4	3.4	0.7	68387
56714	BADGER	21327	483	25.7	31.5	32.9	7.5	2.5	45183	50887	62	51	410	26.1	21.5	40.7	10.7	1.0	93333
56715	BROOKS	17551	110	37.3	34.6	21.8	5.5	0.9	32948	39205	21	4	87	44.8	27.6	25.3	2.3	0.0	56429
56716	CROOKSTON	21785	3776	27.4	32.3	28.8	7.8	3.8	42370	52010	54	37	2636	29.7	31.0	33.8	5.1	0.5	76681
56720	DONALDSON	22882	36	22.2	38.9	27.8	5.6	5.6	38581	51429	41	20	31	45.2	22.6	32.3	0.0	0.0	62500
56721	EAST GRAND FORKS	20393	3085	30.4	27.9	31.8	7.3	2.5	42135	49616	53	36	2069	10.2	17.9	60.8	11.0	0.1	111944
56722	EUCLID	23541	490	18.8	28.6	38.8	9.8	4.1	51849	61882	75	70	438	17.1	28.3	40.2	14.2	0.2	95556
56723	FISHER	23707	558	13.4	30.7	39.8	12.0	4.1	54818	65825	79	77	482	11.6	23.7	51.2	12.5	1.0	107339
56724	GATZKE	20167	62	30.7	40.3	24.2	3.2	1.6	35884	42346	31	11	52	38.5	21.2	34.6	5.8	0.0	73333
56725	GOODRIDGE	20726	297	30.6	30.3	30.0	5.1	4.0	39228	47487	44	23	251	21.5	26.7	33.5	17.5	0.8	92045
56726	GREENBUSH	23672	437	29.8	33.2	30.4	3.7	3.0	39892	45672	46	25	357	28.9	22.7	41.2	6.7	0.6	87250
56727	GRYGLA	18657	450	34.2	36.7	24.0	3.3	1.8	34311	40540	25	7	379	35.9	22.2	33.5	7.7	0.8	77045
56728	HALLOCK	22441	611	25.0	33.9	32.4	5.9	2.8	43036	50776	56	40	495	32.9	34.1	29.3	3.2	0.4	68846
56729	HALMA	17758	73	31.5	37.0	27.4	2.7	1.4	37981	41743	39	19	66	34.9	30.3	30.3	4.6	0.0	72000
56732	KARLSTAD	16358	543	37.8	33.9	25.2	2.6	0.6	32486	37727	19	3	424	35.9	32.6	30.0	1.7	0.0	65000
56733	KENNEDY	23267	220	21.8	38.6	27.7	6.4	5.5	39736	47353	45	25	189	45.0	24.3	25.4	3.2	2.1	57917
56734	LAKE BRONSON	19299	238	42.9	34.5	20.2	1.3	1.3	29390	34067	11	2	200	59.5	23.0	10.5	5.0	2.0	43871
56735	LANCASTER	19069	329	30.4	35.9	28.3	4.6	0.9	37430	43113	37	15	279	42.3	30.1	22.9	3.9	0.7	57167
56736	MENTOR	24090	568	23.6	33.5	32.8	6.5	3.7	43840	53306	58	44	513	26.9	21.6	34.5	15.4	1.6	92143
56737	MIDDLE RIVER	21194	372	33.6	35.5	24.2	3.5	3.2	36535	43412	34	12	312	35.9	25.0	28.9	9.3	1.0	73889
56738	NEWFOLDEN	17972	604	29.5	35.1	30.8	3.6	1.0	39543	45838	44	24	529	27.4	23.1	37.6	9.8	2.1	89342
56740	NOYES	18068	23	26.1	34.8	30.4	4.4	4.4	38604	54545	41	20	20	30.0	45.0	25.0	0.0	0.0	62500
56741	OAK ISLAND	23672	17	35.3	29.4	29.4	5.9	0.0	37343	40000	37	15	16	12.5	25.0	56.3	6.3	0.0	105000
56742	OKLEE	19827	271	36.5	34.7	22.1	5.5	1.1	33399	40130	22	5	214	44.4	27.1	24.3	3.3	0.9	57059
56744	OSLO	20990	208	33.7	27.4	30.3	7.2	1.4	40294	45565	47	27	176	31.3	31.8	29.6	6.8	0.6	74286
56748	PLUMMER	18543	334	30.8	36.2	27.0	4.8	1.2	37772	43661	38	17	281	30.6	23.5	37.0	8.9	0.0	83235
56750	RED LAKE FALLS	18117	1077	31.9	32.9	29.5	4.2	1.5	39035	44869	43	22	876	29.7	34.3	29.6	5.8	0.7	74125
56751	ROSEAU	21915	2512	20.8	34.6	34.6	7.6	2.4	46417	53007	65	55	2076	21.4	15.9	47.7	14.5	0.5	105769
56754	SAINT HILAIRE	21876	334	24.9	28.4	37.4	5.4	3.9	47111	56895	66	57	304	18.4	27.0	39.1	14.8	0.7	100000
56755	SAINT VINCENT	21025	78	26.9	34.6	32.1	3.9	2.6	40903	48002	49	31	67	28.4	41.8	25.4	4.5	0.0	62778
56756	SALOL	19314	213	16.0	36.2	41.3	6.1	0.5	48370	53789	69	61	195	31.8	14.9	40.5	12.3	0.5	96500
56757	STEPHEN	20114	462	30.1	33.8	27.3	6.3	2.6	38561	45457	41	20	386	32.9	36.0	26.2	4.4	0.5	66563
56758	STRANDQUIST	15911	333	38.1	33.0	24.9	3.9	0.0	32897	38063	21	4	293	42.0	28.7	25.3	4.1	0.0	59038
56759	STRATHCONA	20012	307	31.6	32.9	30.0	4.6	1.0	38419	45100	41	20	271	26.6	20.7	41.0	10.7	1.1	94412
56760	VIKING	21667	214	26.6	34.1	31.3	5.6	2.3	41540	49156	51	33	195	33.3	20.0	37.4	7.2	2.1	85000
56761	WANNASKA	19090	288	23.3	26.0	44.4	5.6	0.7	50243	56488	72	67	271	21.4	21.8	43.9	12.6	0.4	96852
56762	WARREN	22295	1009	26.6	31.3	33.2	7.1	1.8	43572	50992	57	43	809	23.6	32.3	37.5	6.1	0.6	83750
56763	WARROAD	20443	1526	19.1	36.3	35.7	6.0	2.9	46187	52277	64	54	1242	23.8	17.7	46.0	11.6	0.9	103557
	MINNESOTA	29624		18.6	25.2	34.9	14.0	7.4	56724	71660				6.6	9.7	36.5	40.5	6.8	168676
	UNITED STATES	25866		24.7	27.1	30.8	10.9	6.5	48124	56710				10.9	15.0	33.7	30.1	10.4	145905

ZIP CODE #	POST OFFICE NAME	FINANCIAL SERVICES: Auto Loan	FINANCIAL SERVICES: Home Loan	FINANCIAL SERVICES: Invest-ments	FINANCIAL SERVICES: Retire-ment Plans	THE HOME: Home Improvements: Home Repair	THE HOME: Home Improvements: Lawn & Garden	THE HOME: Furnishings: Comput-ers & Hard-ware	THE HOME: Furnishings: Major Appli-ances	THE HOME: Furnishings: TV, Radio, Sound Equip-ment	THE HOME: Furnishings: Furni-ture	ENTERTAINMENT: Dine out/ Carry out	ENTERTAINMENT: Sports Equip-ment	ENTERTAINMENT: Fees & Tickets	ENTERTAINMENT: Toys & Games	ENTERTAINMENT: Travel	ENTERTAINMENT: Cable TV	PERSONAL: Apparel & Services	PERSONAL: Auto Repairs	PERSONAL: Health Insur-ance	PERSONAL: Pets & Supplies
56588	VINING	80	65	49	60	72	81	62	73	69	62	82	86	57	81	66	73	77	72	84	97
56589	WAUBUN	73	53	32	51	60	70	56	65	64	54	75	75	49	72	57	67	68	65	78	84
56590	WENDELL	104	72	38	68	84	95	72	88	82	71	97	107	61	95	74	87	88	87	105	123
56592	WINGER	89	63	35	59	73	82	62	76	71	61	83	91	53	82	64	75	76	75	90	106
56593	WOLF LAKE	79	55	29	52	64	72	54	67	63	54	73	81	46	72	56	66	67	66	80	94
56594	WOLVERTON	87	65	40	63	73	82	65	76	73	64	87	90	58	85	67	76	80	75	88	101
56601	BEMIDJI	81	74	71	74	75	80	78	79	78	76	97	94	74	95	76	77	93	80	79	92
56621	BAGLEY	79	60	38	56	66	76	62	70	69	60	82	81	55	79	62	73	75	70	83	90
56623	BAUDETTE	83	66	47	64	72	81	66	75	73	65	87	87	61	86	68	75	81	74	85	95
56626	BENA	70	55	38	50	62	70	52	63	59	51	70	73	46	69	55	63	65	62	74	86
56627	BIG FALLS	75	59	40	53	66	74	55	67	63	55	74	78	50	73	59	67	69	66	79	91
56628	BIGFORK	86	71	55	66	78	86	68	79	74	67	89	92	62	88	71	78	83	78	90	104
56629	BIRCHDALE	72	56	38	51	63	71	53	64	60	53	71	75	47	70	57	64	66	63	76	87
56630	BLACKDUCK	69	51	33	48	57	67	54	62	61	52	72	70	48	69	55	65	66	61	74	78
56633	CASS LAKE	59	52	50	51	54	59	55	57	58	53	71	67	52	70	55	58	68	58	60	68
56634	CLEARBROOK	63	47	31	45	51	62	52	57	58	49	69	64	46	65	51	62	63	57	69	69
56636	DEER RIVER	77	60	40	56	65	75	60	69	67	59	80	79	54	78	61	71	74	68	81	89
56637	TALMOON	90	71	48	64	79	89	67	80	75	66	89	94	60	88	71	80	83	79	95	110
56639	EFFIE	75	73	77	74	75	80	73	76	73	73	90	89	72	88	74	72	87	76	76	88
56641	FEDERAL DAM	83	65	45	59	74	83	62	74	70	61	83	87	55	82	66	75	77	73	88	102
56644	GONVICK	74	56	37	54	61	73	62	68	69	59	81	76	55	77	61	73	74	68	81	82
56646	GULLY	76	53	28	50	62	69	52	65	60	52	71	78	45	69	54	63	64	64	77	90
56647	HINES	88	61	32	57	71	80	61	75	71	60	83	89	53	81	63	75	76	74	90	103
56649	INTERNATIONAL FALLS	93	75	56	71	81	92	76	85	84	74	100	98	71	99	77	87	94	84	97	107
56650	KELLIHER	68	50	32	44	55	63	48	58	56	49	67	68	43	64	50	60	62	58	69	80
56651	LENGBY	69	52	34	50	57	68	58	64	65	55	76	71	51	72	57	68	69	64	76	77
56652	LEONARD	93	65	35	62	76	85	65	79	75	64	87	95	56	85	67	78	80	78	95	110
56653	LITTLEFORK	100	77	49	72	86	95	73	87	82	73	98	104	66	97	77	86	91	86	101	119
56654	LOMAN	72	56	38	51	63	71	53	64	60	53	71	75	48	70	57	64	66	63	76	88
56655	LONGVILLE	90	71	48	64	80	90	67	81	76	66	90	94	60	89	71	81	83	79	95	110
56657	MARCELL	95	74	51	67	84	94	70	84	79	69	94	99	63	93	75	85	87	83	100	115
56659	MAX	60	46	30	42	52	59	44	53	50	44	59	62	39	58	46	53	55	52	63	73
56660	MIZPAH	69	52	35	50	58	68	56	63	63	53	74	71	50	70	56	66	68	62	75	78
56661	NORTHOME	69	53	35	49	58	68	54	62	61	52	72	71	48	69	55	64	66	61	74	80
56662	OUTING	74	58	40	53	66	74	55	66	62	54	74	77	49	73	59	66	68	65	78	90
56663	PENNINGTON	74	58	40	53	66	74	55	66	62	55	74	78	49	73	59	67	69	65	78	91
56666	PONEMAH	44	35	49	33	34	41	43	41	49	44	60	47	42	58	42	50	59	45	45	47
56667	PUPOSKY	87	61	32	58	71	80	60	75	69	60	81	90	51	80	63	73	74	74	89	104
56668	RANIER	121	95	65	86	107	120	90	108	101	89	120	126	80	119	95	108	112	106	128	148
56669	KABETOGAMA	83	65	44	59	73	82	61	74	69	61	82	86	55	81	65	74	76	73	87	101
56670	REDBY	44	35	49	33	34	41	43	41	49	44	60	47	42	58	42	50	59	45	45	47
56671	REDLAKE	56	51	62	49	49	57	55	54	60	57	75	60	57	74	55	62	73	55	57	62
56672	REMER	72	57	39	51	64	72	54	65	61	53	72	76	48	71	57	65	67	64	76	88
56673	ROOSEVELT	83	70	51	66	75	82	65	74	71	65	85	88	62	86	68	73	80	73	83	98
56676	SHEVLIN	100	71	38	66	82	92	70	86	80	69	94	103	60	92	72	84	86	84	102	119
56678	SOLWAY	91	79	59	74	83	90	74	83	78	74	95	97	70	95	76	81	90	81	90	106
56680	SPRING LAKE	85	65	42	58	73	83	62	75	70	61	83	88	55	82	65	75	77	74	89	103
56681	SQUAW LAKE	59	46	31	41	52	58	43	52	49	43	58	61	39	57	46	52	54	51	62	71
56682	SWIFT	85	75	57	72	80	86	70	77	74	70	90	92	69	92	72	76	86	75	84	100
56683	TENSTRIKE	106	74	39	70	86	96	73	90	84	72	98	109	62	96	76	88	90	89	107	125
56684	TRAIL	76	53	28	50	62	69	52	65	60	52	71	78	45	69	54	63	65	64	77	90
56685	WASKISH	68	53	36	48	60	67	50	60	57	50	67	71	45	66	53	60	62	59	71	82
56686	WILLIAMS	78	57	34	53	66	74	55	68	63	55	75	81	48	73	58	67	69	67	81	94
56688	WIRT	73	57	39	52	64	72	54	65	61	53	72	76	48	71	57	65	67	64	77	89
56701	THIEF RIVER FALLS	75	68	58	67	71	78	69	72	72	67	88	83	67	89	69	73	83	72	78	85
56710	ALVARADO	93	65	34	62	76	85	64	80	74	64	87	96	55	85	67	78	79	78	95	111
56711	ANGLE INLET	75	59	40	53	66	74	55	67	63	55	74	78	50	73	59	67	69	66	79	91
56713	ARGYLE	88	62	32	58	72	80	61	75	70	60	82	91	52	81	63	74	75	74	90	105
56714	BADGER	84	75	57	71	79	85	69	77	73	69	89	91	68	91	71	75	85	74	83	99
56715	BROOKS	68	51	33	49	56	67	56	62	63	53	74	70	50	70	56	67	68	62	74	75
56716	CROOKSTON	76	74	77	74	76	83	77	77	78	75	96	90	76	97	77	78	93	78	80	88
56720	DONALDSON	98	68	36	64	80	89	67	83	78	67	91	100	58	89	70	82	83	82	99	116
56721	EAST GRAND FORKS	70	71	77	72	71	76	73	72	72	71	90	84	73	90	72	71	87	73	71	80
56722	EUCLID	102	83	65	82	91	100	83	94	89	82	107	112	76	105	85	91	100	93	104	120
56723	FISHER	110	93	70	90	102	109	89	101	94	88	113	121	83	114	91	96	107	99	110	131
56724	GATZKE	85	57	26	49	64	74	55	68	66	56	77	82	46	73	56	71	70	68	84	97
56725	GOODRIDGE	93	69	41	65	78	87	67	80	75	66	89	97	59	89	69	79	82	79	94	110
56726	GREENBUSH	88	75	58	74	78	88	77	82	81	75	99	94	73	98	76	83	92	81	89	97
56727	GRYGLA	80	56	29	49	63	72	54	67	64	55	75	79	47	72	55	69	69	66	81	93
56728	HALLOCK	91	66	41	63	74	87	71	81	80	68	94	93	62	90	71	84	86	80	97	103
56729	HALMA	75	53	27	50	61	69	52	64	60	51	70	77	44	69	54	63	64	63	76	89
56732	KARLSTAD	66	48	28	45	54	62	50	58	57	48	67	67	44	64	51	60	61	58	69	75
56733	KENNEDY	102	71	37	67	83	93	70	87	81	69	95	104	60	93	73	85	86	85	103	121
56734	LAKE BRONSON	68	51	33	49	56	66	56	62	62	53	73	69	49	69	55	66	67	62	74	75
56735	LANCASTER	81	57	31	54	66	75	58	70	66	57	78	84	50	76	59	69	71	69	83	96
56736	MENTOR	99	75	48	69	86	96	72	87	82	71	97	103	64	95	76	87	90	86	103	120
56737	MIDDLE RIVER	89	60	27	52	68	78	58	72	70	59	82	87	49	78	59	75	75	72	89	103
56738	NEWFOLDEN	80	56	29	53	65	73	55	68	64	55	75	82	47	73	57	67	68	67	81	95
56740	NOYES	88	62	32	58	72	80	61	75	70	60	82	91	52	81	63	73	75	74	89	105
56741	OAK ISLAND	73	57	39	52	65	73	54	65	61	54	73	76	48	72	58	65	67	64	77	89
56742	OKLEE	68	51	33	49	56	67	56	62	63	53	74	70	50	70	56	66	67	62	74	75
56744	OSLO	89	62	32	58	72	81	61	76	70	60	83	91	52	81	63	74	75	74	90	105
56748	PLUMMER	79	55	29	52	64	72	54	67	62	54	73	81	46	72	56	66	67	66	80	93
56750	RED LAKE FALLS	74	56	37	55	62	71	59	66	65	57	78	77	53	75	59	68	71	66	77	83
56751	ROSEAU	87	76	59	74	80	88	73	80	78	73	94	94	71	95	74	79	89	78	87	100
56754	SAINT HILAIRE	88	78	59	74	82	88	72	80	77	72	93	95	71	95	74	78	88	78	86	103
56755	SAINT VINCENT	89	62	33	59	73	81	62	76	71	61	83	92	53	82	64	74	76	75	91	106
56756	SALOL	84	75	58	72	79	85	70	77	74	70	90	92	68	91	72	75	86	76	83	98
56757	STEPHEN	83	61	37	58	68	80	65	74	74	63	86	86	57	83	65	78	79	74	89	95
56758	STRANDQUIST	72	50	26	48	59	66	50	61	57	49	67	74	42	66	52	60	61	61	73	86
56759	STRATHCONA	84	64	41	62	71	79	64	74	71	63	84	87	58	83	65	73	78	73	85	96
56760	VIKING	89	65	37	61	74	83	64	77	72	63	85	92	56	84	66	76	78	76	91	105
56761	WANNASKA	83	68	47	64	74	81	64	74	70	64	84	88	60	85	66	72	79	72	82	98
56762	WARREN	85	66	45	64	72	83	70	77	77	68	92	88	64	89	70	80	84	77	89	95
56763	WARROAD	86	75	58	74	77	85	75	80	78	74	95	92	71	92	74	78	90	79	84	95
	MINNESOTA	107	106	108	107	107	113	106	107	105	105	131	126	105	131	105	104	127	107	105	123
	UNITED STATES	100	100	100	100	100	100	100	100	100	100	100	100	100	100	100	100	100	100	100	100

POPULATION CHANGE

# POST OFFICE NAME	COUNTY FIPS CODE	POPULATION 2000	2004	2009	2000-2004 ANNUAL RATE % Rate	State Centile	HOUSEHOLDS 2000	2004	2009	% Annual Rate 2000-2004	2004 Average HH Size	FAMILIES 2000	2004	% Annual Rate 2000-2004
38601 ABBEVILLE	071	2289	2261	2322	-0.3	25	880	898	946	0.5	2.52	634	635	0.0
38603 ASHLAND	009	3772	3773	3785	0.0	39	1448	1491	1537	0.7	2.45	1048	1069	0.5
38606 BATESVILLE	107	15002	15516	15976	0.8	71	5441	5768	6072	1.4	2.65	3964	4162	1.2
38610 BLUE MOUNTAIN	139	3277	3355	3423	0.6	64	1203	1266	1322	1.2	2.58	899	937	1.0
38611 BYHALIA	093	14725	15645	16482	1.4	84	5246	5710	6129	2.0	2.74	4010	4327	1.8
38614 CLARKSDALE	027	26323	25103	23822	-1.1	3	9118	8870	8571	-0.7	2.74	6447	6211	-0.9
38617 COAHOMA	027	3015	2910	2767	-0.8	8	959	942	912	-0.4	3.07	677	657	-0.7
38618 COLDWATER	137	10218	10638	11184	1.0	74	3698	3962	4273	1.6	2.68	2827	3003	1.4
38619 COMO	107	4883	4812	4849	-0.3	24	1769	1789	1845	0.3	2.69	1283	1280	-0.1
38620 COURTLAND	107	3721	3970	4113	1.5	86	1185	1301	1381	2.2	2.86	920	1000	2.0
38621 CRENSHAW	107	2318	2272	2269	-0.5	20	804	806	822	0.1	2.82	603	597	-0.2
38625 DUMAS	139	1241	1370	1447	2.4	92	473	535	577	2.9	2.56	354	396	2.7
38626 DUNDEE	143	1386	1578	1885	3.1	94	479	558	685	3.7	2.83	327	380	3.6
38627 ETTA	145	933	1086	1185	3.6	97	354	422	468	4.2	2.57	274	324	4.0
38629 FALKNER	139	1223	1183	1169	-0.8	9	473	471	476	-0.1	2.51	355	350	-0.3
38632 HERNANDO	033	16885	20007	24443	4.1	98	6071	7371	9230	4.7	2.67	4747	5718	4.5
38633 HICKORY FLAT	009	2279	2321	2354	0.4	58	875	908	940	0.9	2.56	662	681	0.7
38635 HOLLY SPRINGS	093	15552	15399	15464	-0.2	29	5158	5249	5386	0.4	2.64	3779	3809	0.2
38637 HORN LAKE	033	15256	17702	21434	3.6	96	5330	6333	7840	4.1	2.80	4070	4777	3.8
38641 LAKE CORMORANT	033	2106	2285	2716	1.9	89	726	807	981	2.5	2.83	553	608	2.3
38642 LAMAR	009	2213	2187	2183	-0.3	26	753	769	787	0.5	2.84	584	591	0.3
38643 LAMBERT	119	3539	3490	3439	-0.3	24	1233	1248	1258	0.3	2.75	850	852	0.1
38645 LYON	027	1026	975	922	-1.2	3	344	337	326	-0.5	2.89	263	254	-0.8
38646 MARKS	119	4272	4155	4071	-0.7	13	1552	1552	1555	0.0	2.63	1086	1075	-0.2
38647 MICHIGAN CITY	009	1246	1246	1250	0.0	39	457	473	488	0.8	2.63	337	345	0.6
38650 MYRTLE	145	3836	4161	4396	1.9	89	1451	1603	1718	2.4	2.59	1112	1218	2.2
38651 NESBIT	033	5671	7005	8736	5.1	99	2084	2646	3383	5.8	2.63	1722	2174	5.6
38652 NEW ALBANY	145	15345	15526	15822	0.3	53	5959	6139	6349	0.7	2.49	4313	4398	0.5
38654 OLIVE BRANCH	033	28509	35704	44706	5.4	99	10101	12916	16519	6.0	2.76	8235	10438	5.7
38655 OXFORD	071	32922	34811	37027	1.3	82	12085	13173	14447	2.1	2.28	6722	7238	1.8
38658 POPE	107	2201	2469	2627	2.7	93	820	941	1022	3.3	2.62	636	722	3.0
38659 POTTS CAMP	093	2454	2656	2765	1.9	88	897	1003	1068	2.7	2.56	661	733	2.5
38661 RED BANKS	093	1907	2093	2200	2.2	91	701	791	848	2.9	2.65	550	616	2.7
38663 RIPLEY	139	11216	11279	11317	0.1	46	4361	4505	4618	0.8	2.44	3130	3201	0.5
38664 ROBINSONVILLE	143	1285	1697	2212	6.8	99	524	724	985	7.9	2.34	321	442	7.8
38665 SARAH	137	2804	2959	3114	1.3	82	1030	1121	1213	2.0	2.59	787	849	1.8
38666 SARDIS	107	7306	7160	7179	-0.5	20	2687	2706	2774	0.2	2.60	1927	1924	0.0
38668 SENATOBIA	137	12698	13289	13960	1.1	79	4244	4572	4940	1.8	2.67	3190	3408	1.6
38670 SLEDGE	119	1545	1580	1607	0.5	63	529	552	574	1.0	2.86	383	395	0.7
38671 SOUTHAVEN	033	27255	32645	40305	4.3	98	10427	12915	16408	5.2	2.52	7643	9394	5.0
38672 SOUTHAVEN	033	1702	2309	3005	7.4	99	573	797	1061	8.1	2.89	489	675	7.9
38673 TAYLOR	071	971	1080	1184	2.5	93	373	430	485	3.4	2.50	243	270	2.5
38674 TIPLERSVILLE	139	982	955	946	-0.7	13	382	381	385	-0.1	2.50	289	285	-0.3
38676 TUNICA	143	6699	7736	9463	3.4	96	2321	2788	3553	4.4	2.74	1585	1881	4.1
38677 UNIVERSITY	071	257	279	296	2.0	89	95	106	115	2.6	2.62	64	70	2.1
38680 WALLS	033	8226	9656	11814	3.8	97	2959	3579	4494	4.6	2.70	2244	2688	4.3
38683 WALNUT	139	4802	4694	4646	-0.5	17	1964	1970	1994	0.1	2.38	1432	1422	-0.2
38685 WATERFORD	093	884	942	972	1.5	85	328	362	383	2.4	2.48	246	270	2.2
38701 GREENVILLE	151	30458	29943	29567	-0.4	21	10933	11014	11091	0.2	2.69	7617	7603	0.0
38703 GREENVILLE	151	19307	19177	19045	-0.2	31	6650	6798	6899	0.5	2.75	4900	4950	0.2
38720 ALLIGATOR	027	334	336	325	0.1	47	138	142	140	0.7	2.37	105	107	0.4
38721 ANGUILLA	125	2403	2350	2281	-0.5	17	758	770	774	0.4	3.05	565	568	0.1
38725 BENOIT	011	1326	1370	1394	0.8	70	458	486	503	1.4	2.79	354	372	1.2
38726 BEULAH	011	157	152	150	-0.8	10	49	48	49	-0.5	2.04	34	34	0.0
38730 BOYLE	011	2001	2047	2067	0.5	63	739	774	794	1.1	2.58	561	583	0.9
38731 CHATHAM	151	167	165	163	-0.3	26	72	73	74	0.3	2.26	54	55	0.4
38732 CLEVELAND	011	20179	20011	19929	-0.2	30	6948	7107	7219	0.5	2.58	4709	4764	0.3
38733 CLEVELAND	011	148	147	146	-0.2	31	4	4	4	0.0	2.50	3	3	0.1
38736 DODDSVILLE	133	1732	1696	1672	-0.5	18	248	248	249	0.0	4.40	184	182	-0.3
38737 DREW	133	8646	8820	8887	0.5	59	1387	1470	1516	1.4	2.86	1013	1062	1.1
38740 DUNCAN	011	852	853	853	0.0	40	280	287	292	0.6	2.78	199	202	0.4
38744 GLEN ALLAN	151	106	105	104	-0.2	29	40	41	41	0.6	2.56	30	31	0.8
38746 GUNNISON	011	1127	1097	1084	-0.6	14	372	373	376	0.1	2.94	262	261	-0.1
38748 HOLLANDALE	151	5986	5926	5851	-0.2	28	1991	2020	2032	0.3	2.93	1507	1517	0.2
38751 INDIANOLA	133	13434	13303	13185	-0.2	29	4379	4410	4439	0.2	2.98	3347	3343	0.0
38753 INVERNESS	133	1847	1828	1817	-0.2	28	638	645	653	0.3	2.78	487	488	0.1
38754 ISOLA	053	1580	1570	1545	-0.2	32	580	587	587	0.3	2.67	419	420	0.1
38756 LELAND	151	6915	6750	6640	-0.6	16	2460	2470	2483	0.1	2.73	1808	1796	-0.2
38759 MERIGOLD	011	1176	1204	1215	0.6	64	470	495	510	1.2	2.41	337	352	1.0
38761 MOORHEAD	133	3145	3066	3020	-0.6	15	844	834	832	-0.3	3.24	655	642	-0.5
38762 MOUND BAYOU	011	3522	3522	3528	0.0	39	1171	1210	1236	0.8	2.90	855	875	0.6
38769 ROSEDALE	011	3499	3496	3491	0.0	37	1123	1153	1171	0.6	2.95	816	829	0.4
38771 RULEVILLE	133	3556	3559	3547	0.0	40	1134	1149	1159	0.3	2.97	861	866	0.1
38773 SHAW	011	4084	4084	4080	0.0	39	1404	1441	1465	0.6	2.80	1054	1071	0.4
38774 SHELBY	011	3099	3092	3085	-0.1	36	978	999	1013	0.5	3.01	718	727	0.3
38778 SUNFLOWER	133	1939	1932	1918	-0.1	35	608	619	626	0.4	3.12	451	456	0.3
38780 WAYSIDE	151	310	323	326	1.0	75	104	112	115	1.8	2.88	88	94	1.6
38801 TUPELO	081	28789	28622	28730	-0.1	33	11117	11275	11479	0.3	2.50	7768	7800	0.1
38804 TUPELO	081	18653	18780	18899	0.2	48	7394	7621	7795	0.7	2.37	5109	5202	0.4
38821 AMORY	095	12687	12345	12046	-0.6	13	5098	5078	5069	-0.1	2.40	3633	3585	-0.3
38824 BALDWYN	117	7350	7504	7611	0.5	61	2825	2944	3031	1.0	2.52	2064	2132	0.8
38826 BELDEN	115	4548	4730	4864	0.9	73	1625	1726	1802	1.4	2.73	1296	1366	1.3
38827 BELMONT	141	2669	2747	2749	0.7	67	1075	1126	1147	1.1	2.44	784	814	0.9
38828 BLUE SPRINGS	145	3220	3315	3408	0.7	67	1230	1296	1354	1.2	2.56	944	985	1.0
38829 BOONEVILLE	117	18286	18631	18881	0.4	59	7015	7318	7548	1.0	2.43	5059	5228	0.8
38833 BURNSVILLE	141	2539	2484	2429	-0.5	18	1021	1020	1018	0.0	2.44	747	740	-0.2
38834 CORINTH	003	27481	27318	27153	-0.1	33	11458	11670	11869	0.4	2.30	7799	7851	0.2
38838 DENNIS	141	1689	1699	1685	0.1	47	666	684	693	0.6	2.48	514	524	0.3
38841 ECRU	115	3683	3786	3906	0.7	65	1419	1482	1549	1.0	2.53	1065	1102	0.8
38843 FULTON	057	11622	11838	12093	0.4	58	4404	4584	4769	1.0	2.41	3199	3294	0.7
38844 GATTMAN	095	313	322	321	0.7	66	132	140	143	1.4	2.29	100	104	0.9
38846 GLEN	003	2523	2607	2642	0.8	70	971	1031	1071	1.4	2.53	742	780	1.2
38847 GOLDEN	057	3522	4103	4487	3.7	97	1376	1641	1829	4.2	2.50	1042	1234	4.1
38848 GREENWOOD SPRINGS	095	886	926	930	1.0	78	352	378	390	1.7	2.44	265	281	1.4
38849 GUNTOWN	081	4488	4646	4716	0.8	72	1676	1770	1823	1.3	2.61	1275	1333	1.1
MISSISSIPPI					0.6					1.2	2.57			0.9
UNITED STATES					1.2					1.3	2.58			1.1

ZIP CODE #	POST OFFICE NAME	RACE (%) White 2000	White 2004	Black 2000	Black 2004	Asian/Pacific 2000	Asian/Pacific 2004	% Hispanic Origin 2000	% Hispanic Origin 2004	2004 AGE DISTRIBUTION (%) 0-4	5-9	10-14	15-19	20-24	25-44	45-64	65-84	85+	18+	MEDIAN AGE 2004	% 2004 Males	% 2004 Females
38601	ABBEVILLE	45.8	44.6	53.3	54.4	0.1	0.1	1.0	1.0	7.0	7.3	7.4	6.2	7.3	30.1	24.2	9.4	1.3	74.6	34.4	48.6	51.4
38603	ASHLAND	64.2	63.4	33.5	34.3	0.1	0.1	1.2	1.2	6.4	6.3	6.7	6.3	6.5	25.2	24.6	15.9	2.2	76.8	39.7	49.1	50.9
38606	BATESVILLE	58.3	56.7	40.4	41.8	0.3	0.3	1.2	1.4	7.8	7.6	7.6	7.3	7.0	27.3	22.8	10.8	1.7	72.4	34.3	48.6	51.4
38610	BLUE MOUNTAIN	71.2	70.6	26.4	26.6	0.2	0.2	2.4	3.0	6.8	6.9	7.1	7.2	8.0	28.1	23.4	10.7	1.8	75.1	34.6	48.2	51.8
38611	BYHALIA	62.5	61.1	35.7	36.9	0.1	0.2	1.9	2.0	7.4	7.3	7.3	6.7	6.4	28.3	25.5	10.3	1.0	74.0	36.6	49.9	50.1
38614	CLARKSDALE	31.0	29.9	67.5	68.3	0.5	0.6	0.9	0.9	8.8	8.4	8.7	8.4	7.5	24.7	21.2	10.5	1.9	69.1	31.9	46.0	54.0
38617	COAHOMA	13.5	11.9	85.1	86.6	0.3	0.3	0.7	0.7	11.3	10.3	10.8	9.2	7.2	24.5	16.8	8.3	1.7	61.3	26.0	46.4	53.6
38618	COLDWATER	64.0	62.8	35.0	36.0	0.1	0.1	0.9	1.0	7.2	7.2	7.3	7.3	6.8	26.7	25.3	10.9	1.4	74.0	36.5	49.1	50.9
38619	COMO	44.4	42.2	54.7	56.8	0.0	0.0	1.0	1.1	7.7	8.4	7.7	6.2	6.3	25.4	24.6	12.4	1.4	72.5	36.3	48.3	51.7
38620	COURTLAND	51.7	49.5	47.1	49.2	0.2	0.2	1.3	1.5	7.8	7.5	7.7	11.9	8.2	27.3	20.7	7.8	1.0	70.3	30.4	49.0	51.0
38621	CRENSHAW	35.5	32.8	63.6	66.3	0.1	0.2	1.0	1.0	7.9	7.9	8.8	8.0	7.9	27.9	21.2	9.2	1.2	70.5	31.7	47.4	52.6
38625	DUMAS	94.0	93.4	5.0	5.5	0.1	0.2	1.0	1.2	6.4	6.5	7.5	6.4	6.4	29.4	24.0	11.7	1.7	75.8	36.9	51.6	48.4
38626	DUNDEE	25.5	22.8	71.9	74.3	0.2	0.3	1.4	1.5	7.7	7.7	9.8	8.5	7.0	26.1	21.6	10.5	1.2	69.6	33.3	48.6	51.4
38627	ETTA	96.3	96.0	3.4	3.6	0.0	0.0	1.0	1.3	6.3	6.3	7.0	6.9	6.4	30.2	24.2	10.5	2.3	76.5	35.1	48.6	51.4
38629	FALKNER	79.8	78.3	18.6	20.0	0.0	0.1	1.4	1.4	6.3	6.3	6.9	6.9	7.7	28.3	24.9	11.2	1.4	76.5	36.4	49.2	50.8
38632	HERNANDO	81.4	80.9	16.8	16.9	0.5	0.7	1.8	2.2	7.0	7.2	7.1	6.3	5.6	28.6	26.2	10.8	1.2	74.7	37.8	50.5	49.6
38633	HICKORY FLAT	88.9	88.7	10.4	10.7	0.0	0.0	0.5	0.6	8.7	8.1	7.2	6.3	6.6	27.1	23.3	11.4	1.4	72.0	34.3	49.1	50.9
38635	HOLLY SPRINGS	32.7	30.8	66.4	68.2	0.1	0.1	0.7	0.7	6.8	6.8	7.1	8.0	10.3	27.7	22.1	9.8	1.3	75.1	32.4	49.8	50.2
38637	HORN LAKE	83.7	82.1	11.7	12.5	0.9	1.1	4.1	4.9	10.0	9.1	8.8	7.1	7.3	35.8	16.9	4.7	0.3	67.7	29.2	49.0	51.0
38641	LAKE CORMORANT	79.4	78.5	16.7	16.9	1.1	1.2	3.6	4.3	7.1	7.2	7.2	6.4	5.6	29.9	25.9	9.9	1.0	74.5	36.8	51.7	48.3
38642	LAMAR	39.0	37.0	60.4	62.3	0.1	0.1	1.1	1.1	9.1	8.6	8.0	6.7	7.2	26.9	22.6	9.9	0.9	70.1	32.9	47.8	52.2
38643	LAMBERT	36.7	34.9	62.1	63.6	0.2	0.3	0.7	0.8	8.9	8.3	9.0	8.1	6.7	25.0	21.6	10.9	1.5	68.7	32.2	47.9	52.1
38645	LYON	20.5	18.0	78.0	80.3	0.0	0.0	2.7	2.6	9.0	8.2	9.2	10.5	6.2	23.4	23.4	9.1	1.0	66.7	29.7	47.6	52.4
38646	MARKS	33.2	32.6	65.8	66.3	0.2	0.3	0.4	0.4	7.3	7.1	8.8	8.1	6.5	25.0	22.0	12.9	2.5	71.7	34.9	46.3	53.7
38647	MICHIGAN CITY	40.2	39.3	58.7	59.5	0.2	0.2	1.3	1.3	8.2	7.9	7.9	6.7	7.2	26.9	21.9	12.0	1.4	72.0	33.5	49.6	50.4
38650	MYRTLE	91.1	89.9	8.0	9.0	0.1	0.1	0.7	0.8	7.7	7.4	7.3	6.7	6.8	29.2	23.1	10.7	1.2	73.6	34.9	48.8	51.2
38651	NESBIT	83.6	82.5	14.8	15.5	0.7	0.8	1.2	1.4	6.1	6.8	7.1	5.9	4.5	26.7	30.4	11.6	1.0	76.1	41.1	49.0	51.0
38652	NEW ALBANY	77.4	76.2	20.5	21.4	0.3	0.4	2.2	2.6	7.7	7.5	7.0	6.1	6.0	28.5	22.8	12.3	2.1	74.0	36.0	48.6	51.4
38654	OLIVE BRANCH	86.4	85.4	11.7	12.3	0.4	0.5	1.4	1.6	8.1	8.0	7.9	6.6	5.3	31.3	23.2	8.9	0.7	71.7	35.2	49.3	50.7
38655	OXFORD	72.4	70.8	24.2	25.2	1.9	2.4	1.2	1.3	5.1	5.1	5.7	13.3	15.2	28.5	17.7	8.1	1.5	80.9	27.8	49.0	51.1
38658	POPE	67.1	64.8	32.1	34.4	0.2	0.2	0.5	0.5	7.3	6.9	7.1	7.3	7.9	27.7	23.6	11.1	1.2	74.5	35.7	50.1	49.9
38659	POTTS CAMP	65.3	62.5	34.0	36.6	0.1	0.1	0.5	0.6	6.0	6.1	7.0	7.6	7.2	29.7	25.0	10.3	1.2	76.4	36.2	50.9	49.1
38661	RED BANKS	60.1	57.6	37.9	40.1	0.2	0.2	1.9	2.1	7.3	7.3	7.2	6.6	6.6	28.5	25.3	10.3	1.1	74.3	35.6	49.3	50.7
38663	RIPLEY	81.2	79.8	16.0	16.9	0.2	0.2	2.6	3.1	6.8	6.6	6.6	6.7	7.0	28.3	22.8	12.7	2.5	76.0	36.6	48.9	51.2
38664	ROBINSONVILLE	34.7	32.5	60.1	61.9	1.3	1.4	4.7	5.1	8.5	7.8	7.9	7.8	8.0	31.2	22.5	5.9	0.4	71.2	30.4	50.6	49.4
38665	SARAH	80.7	79.8	18.2	18.9	0.1	0.1	1.1	1.2	7.8	7.7	7.8	6.7	6.0	30.2	23.2	10.0	0.8	72.6	35.0	49.8	50.2
38666	SARDIS	39.1	37.7	59.9	61.2	0.1	0.2	1.1	1.1	8.3	8.2	8.2	7.2	7.1	26.8	21.3	11.2	1.8	70.9	33.2	47.1	52.9
38668	SENATOBIA	67.5	65.9	31.3	32.7	0.2	0.3	0.9	1.0	6.7	6.8	7.6	9.7	9.6	26.0	22.4	9.7	1.6	74.9	32.7	48.2	51.8
38670	SLEDGE	15.7	14.8	83.8	84.7	0.0	0.0	0.7	0.8	8.9	8.6	10.1	9.0	7.9	27.1	18.7	8.7	1.0	66.8	28.9	44.9	55.1
38671	SOUTHAVEN	90.7	89.7	6.2	6.7	0.8	1.0	2.3	2.7	7.7	7.3	7.4	6.6	6.9	31.9	22.6	8.9	0.7	73.7	33.6	48.8	51.2
38672	SOUTHAVEN	85.0	83.8	13.2	14.0	0.8	1.0	1.2	1.4	6.1	6.8	7.6	6.1	4.4	27.2	30.9	10.3	0.7	75.4	41.0	48.9	51.1
38673	TAYLOR	74.8	73.2	23.9	25.2	0.6	0.8	0.5	0.7	5.8	5.9	6.8	7.5	12.5	29.2	20.8	10.0	1.5	77.7	32.0	50.3	49.7
38674	TIPLERSVILLE	84.7	83.8	14.2	15.1	0.0	0.0	0.7	0.7	5.9	6.2	7.3	6.6	6.9	28.9	24.8	12.0	1.4	76.8	37.2	49.4	50.6
38676	TUNICA	27.4	26.4	70.9	71.6	0.4	0.5	2.3	2.4	8.7	8.0	8.6	8.4	8.1	25.9	21.6	9.3	1.5	69.5	30.9	47.2	52.8
38677	UNIVERSITY	58.8	57.0	38.5	39.8	1.6	1.8	1.6	1.4	6.5	7.2	9.3	8.6	9.7	31.5	21.5	5.4	0.4	72.4	30.1	48.8	51.3
38680	WALLS	86.1	84.7	9.0	9.4	0.8	1.0	4.7	5.8	7.5	7.5	7.5	6.6	6.0	33.1	24.1	7.3	0.6	73.6	34.3	51.1	48.9
38683	WALNUT	93.3	92.8	5.7	6.1	0.0	0.0	0.8	0.9	6.1	6.2	6.9	6.1	6.2	28.6	25.1	13.4	1.5	77.2	38.2	49.0	51.0
38685	WATERFORD	64.0	61.8	35.4	37.5	0.1	0.1	0.6	0.5	5.9	6.3	6.9	7.1	7.2	29.8	25.1	10.6	1.1	76.8	36.4	52.1	47.9
38701	GREENVILLE	35.7	34.9	62.8	63.3	0.8	0.9	0.8	0.9	8.7	8.2	8.3	7.6	8.1	25.7	22.5	9.4	1.6	70.3	32.1	47.2	52.9
38703	GREENVILLE	28.6	26.8	70.0	71.5	0.5	0.6	0.7	0.8	8.4	8.4	8.9	7.6	7.3	25.2	22.2	10.1	2.0	69.6	32.3	46.7	53.3
38720	ALLIGATOR	47.0	42.9	51.2	55.1	0.9	0.9	1.2	1.2	9.5	8.6	7.4	6.3	6.6	26.2	22.9	10.7	1.8	70.8	34.8	47.6	52.4
38721	ANGUILLA	27.2	26.0	71.4	72.3	0.3	0.3	2.0	2.1	8.8	9.3	8.9	8.0	8.0	25.1	22.7	7.9	1.3	67.8	29.9	47.5	52.6
38725	BENOIT	29.3	26.7	68.6	71.0	0.2	0.2	1.8	1.8	8.8	8.4	8.8	9.1	7.5	26.9	19.6	9.8	1.1	68.6	30.1	49.5	50.5
38726	BEULAH	45.9	43.4	52.2	54.6	0.6	0.7	1.3	1.3	3.3	3.3	4.0	8.6	13.8	38.8	20.4	7.2	0.7	85.5	31.9	69.7	30.3
38730	BOYLE	67.3	65.1	31.1	33.0	0.4	0.5	1.3	1.5	6.8	6.8	8.0	6.8	7.9	28.7	25.2	8.7	1.1	74.5	34.4	49.7	50.3
38731	CHATHAM	46.7	42.4	51.5	56.4	0.0	0.0	1.2	1.2	6.1	6.1	8.5	7.9	7.9	23.0	26.1	12.1	2.4	73.9	38.8	48.5	51.5
38732	CLEVELAND	46.3	45.0	51.9	52.8	0.8	0.9	1.3	1.4	6.8	6.6	6.9	9.2	12.0	26.7	21.3	8.9	1.6	75.3	30.6	47.0	53.1
38733	CLEVELAND	76.4	74.8	21.6	23.1	0.7	0.7	0.7	0.7	2.0	1.4	2.0	21.8	40.1	15.0	9.5	7.5	0.7	93.2	22.8	42.2	57.8
38736	DODDSVILLE	32.2	30.0	66.7	68.8	0.2	0.2	1.1	1.2	5.3	5.1	5.3	6.3	13.9	40.7	16.2	6.4	1.1	81.3	30.7	67.3	32.7
38737	DREW	29.2	28.6	69.6	70.3	0.4	0.4	0.9	0.8	4.0	3.9	4.3	7.2	13.8	43.7	17.7	4.7	0.7	84.3	32.3	74.9	25.1
38740	DUNCAN	22.3	20.5	75.4	76.8	0.1	0.1	1.6	1.9	8.3	7.6	8.7	9.0	6.0	23.6	21.0	12.5	3.3	69.1	35.4	47.6	52.4
38744	GLEN ALLAN	47.2	42.9	51.9	55.2	0.0	0.0	0.9	1.0	6.7	5.7	8.6	7.6	7.6	23.8	25.7	11.4	2.9	73.3	38.2	48.6	51.4
38746	GUNNISON	21.7	19.9	76.5	78.3	0.4	0.4	1.1	1.2	8.8	7.4	9.4	10.0	6.4	23.2	22.6	10.9	1.4	67.7	32.2	47.6	52.4
38748	HOLLANDALE	36.2	34.4	62.8	64.5	0.1	0.1	1.0	0.9	8.1	8.0	9.0	9.2	8.1	24.9	21.7	9.8	1.4	69.3	31.9	46.7	53.3
38751	INDIANOLA	28.1	27.6	70.7	71.1	0.5	0.5	1.2	1.2	8.4	8.3	9.3	8.2	8.3	27.1	20.2	8.6	1.6	68.9	30.4	46.0	54.0
38753	INVERNESS	37.3	36.8	61.5	61.9	0.6	0.6	1.6	1.7	7.0	6.9	8.2	8.6	8.6	25.3	23.0	10.7	1.6	73.3	33.7	46.6	53.5
38754	ISOLA	34.2	32.5	63.2	64.5	0.2	0.2	3.4	3.8	8.4	8.0	8.6	7.5	8.6	25.6	22.6	8.9	1.9	70.6	32.0	47.8	52.2
38756	LELAND	37.1	34.8	61.6	63.8	0.1	0.2	1.0	1.1	8.7	8.5	8.5	7.5	8.1	25.9	21.6	9.9	1.5	70.0	31.7	48.1	51.9
38759	MERIGOLD	42.7	41.2	55.8	57.2	0.2	0.2	1.0	0.9	6.6	6.6	7.2	7.1	7.2	26.9	25.5	11.1	1.7	75.3	36.6	47.8	52.2
38761	MOORHEAD	21.8	21.0	77.1	77.9	0.2	0.2	1.6	1.6	8.8	7.9	8.0	14.1	13.3	22.8	18.0	5.8	1.1	70.2	24.2	48.2	51.8
38762	MOUND BAYOU	2.9	2.6	96.1	96.3	0.1	0.2	0.5	0.4	9.0	8.1	8.4	10.3	8.4	24.9	20.8	8.6	1.5	68.4	29.2	44.7	55.3
38769	ROSEDALE	15.8	14.4	82.7	83.9	0.4	0.5	1.1	1.0	8.6	9.2	9.8	9.4	6.9	27.4	18.9	8.3	1.5	66.6	29.3	46.3	53.8
38771	RULEVILLE	21.0	20.2	78.2	79.0	0.4	0.4	1.0	1.0	8.5	8.2	8.4	7.8	8.3	24.0	20.9	10.7	3.3	70.1	31.8	45.7	54.3
38773	SHAW	19.4	18.1	79.5	80.7	0.3	0.3	1.1	1.1	8.1	7.8	8.6	8.9	7.9	26.2	21.9	9.1	1.4	70.1	31.5	48.0	52.0
38774	SHELBY	9.9	9.2	88.5	89.0	0.1	0.1	1.3	1.4	10.0	9.5	9.1	11.1	6.9	24.8	17.1	9.4	2.1	64.0	28.1	45.7	54.3
38778	SUNFLOWER	30.6	29.9	66.2	67.0	0.3	0.3	3.7	3.7	9.3	8.8	9.8	8.1	7.9	28.1	18.2	8.2	1.7	67.4	28.9	49.1	50.9
38780	WAYSIDE	89.0	87.0	10.3	11.8	0.0	0.0	1.0	1.2	6.5	6.5	8.4	9.0	8.4	28.8	22.3	9.3	0.9	73.1	34.9	50.8	49.2
38801	TUPELO	65.0	62.8	32.8	34.5	0.7	0.9	1.3	1.5	8.1	7.8	8.1	7.0	6.6	28.9	22.6	9.4	1.5	71.7	34.1	47.0	53.0
38804	TUPELO	75.6	74.9	22.4	22.8	0.6	0.8	1.4	1.6	6.9	6.9	7.1	6.6	6.3	29.1	23.6	11.4	2.0	75.0	36.6	48.9	51.1
38821	AMORY	80.1	79.5	19.1	19.5	0.1	0.2	0.6	0.7	6.6	6.6	7.4	6.7	6.4	26.2	24.3	13.6	2.3	75.3	37.8	47.1	52.9
38824	BALDWYN	72.5	71.6	26.1	26.9	0.1	0.2	0.8	0.8	7.7	7.1	7.7	6.8	6.6	27.5	23.0	11.7	2.0	73.5	35.6	47.8	52.2
38826	BELDEN	77.9	76.7	21.2	22.2	0.4	0.5	0.7	0.9	7.6	7.8	7.9	6.7	5.7	28.3	26.3	8.7	1.0	72.6	36.6	49.2	50.9
38827	BELMONT	94.0	93.1	0.8	0.8	0.0	0.0	6.4	7.6	7.0	6.9	6.6	5.7	6.3	28.9	24.0	13.2	1.5	76.1	37.2	49.4	50.6
38828	BLUE SPRINGS	91.8	90.5	7.2	8.3	0.1	0.1	0.8	1.0	6.5	6.6	6.9	6.1	6.6	28.7	25.2	12.1	1.4	76.4	37.8	50.1	50.0
38829	BOONEVILLE	87.5	86.7	11.3	11.9	0.2	0.2	0.6	0.8	6.6	6.6	6.7	7.9	7.9	26.8	23.0	12.6	2.0	76.5	35.9	49.0	51.0
38833	BURNSVILLE	98.1	97.9	0.4	0.4	0.1	0.2	1.1	1.2	6.8	6.7	8.3	7.0	6.8	27.2	24.4	11.4	1.3	73.9	36.1	48.8	51.2
38834	CORINTH	85.5	85.1	12.9	13.3	0.3	0.3	1.3	1.4	6.4	6.4	6.5	5.9	6.0	27.3	25.6	13.6	2.2	77.1	39.0	48.5	51.6
38838	DENNIS	95.9	95.6	3.0	3.1	0.0	0.0	1.2	1.5	6.2	6.5	7.1	6.2	6.0	28.0	25.8	12.7	1.5	76.4	38.4	49.2	50.8
38841	ECRU	88.6	87.6	9.4	10.0	0.1	0.1	2.9	3.5	7.7	7.6	7.4	6.8	6.4	29.5	22.2	10.9	1.7	73.3	35.4	49.9	50.1
38843	FULTON	89.4	88.6	9.5	10.2	0.3	0.3	1.2	1.3	6.2	6.1	6.7	7.7	7.9	25.9	23.9	13.6	2.2	77.6	37.2	48.4	51.6
38844	GATTMAN	92.0	91.0	7.4	8.4	0.0	0.0	0.6	0.6	6.2	6.2	6.8	6.5	7.5	28.6	25.2	12.1	0.9	77.0	36.7	50.0	50.0
38846	GLEN	98.7	98.6	0.3	0.4	0.1	0.1	0.6	0.5	7.7	7.4	7.1	6.5	6.3	29.1	25.1	9.7	1.1	73.9	35.7	51.3	48.8
38847	GOLDEN	97.6	97.3	0.4	0.4	0.0	0.0	2.0	2.2	7.0	7.0	7.0	5.9	6.3	29.1	25.1	11.6	1.0	75.4	36.8	50.1	49.9
38848	GREENWOOD SPRINGS	92.2	91.1	7.1	8.0	0.0	0.0	0.5	0.5	6.3	6.3	6.9	6.5	6.9	28.4	25.3	12.1	1.4	76.7	37.5	50.1	49.9
38849	GUNTOWN	89.3	88.2	9.7	10.6	0.2	0.2	0.7	0.8	7.6	7.4	7.8	7.0	6.4	29.2	23.3	9.9	1.6	73.1	35.1	49.9	50.1
	MISSISSIPPI	61.4	60.6	36.3	36.8	0.7	0.8	1.4	1.6	7.3	7.1	7.4	7.4	7.8	27.8	23.0	10.6	1.6	73.9	34.5	48.5	51.5
	UNITED STATES	75.1	73.6	12.3	12.5	3.8	4.2	12.5	14.1	6.9	6.7	7.2	7.0	7.3	28.6	23.8	10.8	1.7	75.1	36.0	49.1	50.9

INCOME

ZIP CODE				2004 HOUSEHOLD INCOME DISTRIBUTION (%)					MEDIAN HOUSEHOLD INCOME					2004 HOME VALUE DISTRIBUTION (%)					
#	POST OFFICE NAME	2004 Per Capita Income	2004 HH Income Base	Less than $25,000	$25,000 to $49,999	$50,000 to $99,999	$100,000 to $149,999	$150,000 or More	2004	2009	2004 National Centile	2004 State Centile	2004 Home Value Base	Less than $50,000	$50,000 to $89,999	$90,000 to $174,999	$175,000 to $399,999	$400,000 or More	2004 Median Home Value
38601	ABBEVILLE	15741	898	42.2	31.3	21.6	3.7	1.2	30358	35745	13	47	738	34.8	28.7	26.8	5.4	4.2	71864
38603	ASHLAND	13698	1491	48.6	31.9	15.4	3.5	0.6	25750	28923	5	19	1245	41.7	36.7	19.0	2.7	0.0	56311
38606	BATESVILLE	16363	5768	41.4	29.9	20.8	5.4	2.5	31305	35627	16	55	4303	40.0	31.1	23.0	5.0	0.9	62090
38610	BLUE MOUNTAIN	16097	1266	37.9	31.3	26.0	3.6	1.2	32624	36292	20	63	992	40.8	33.4	20.6	4.9	0.3	60990
38611	BYHALIA	17480	5710	32.9	31.1	28.5	5.1	2.4	37186	41836	36	81	4706	28.8	31.9	27.6	10.9	0.9	75686
38614	CLARKSDALE	15135	8870	49.0	25.0	18.4	5.1	2.5	25606	29304	5	16	5215	41.9	32.7	18.8	5.6	1.1	58006
38617	COAHOMA	11427	942	58.0	25.2	11.5	3.3	2.1	19665	22125	2	3	561	56.5	26.6	13.0	3.0	0.9	44859
38618	COLDWATER	16927	3962	35.3	29.6	28.0	6.2	0.9	36770	41490	35	79	3196	24.7	37.4	26.9	10.1	1.0	80000
38619	COMO	14035	1789	46.1	27.2	21.0	4.8	0.9	28074	31877	9	32	1424	42.7	33.5	19.4	4.0	0.4	61301
38620	COURTLAND	14578	1301	38.7	33.2	21.8	4.4	1.9	33624	38372	23	67	1099	47.0	30.5	17.7	4.5	0.5	53490
38621	CRENSHAW	11910	806	53.5	29.2	14.0	2.2	1.1	22316	24694	3	7	609	57.0	28.9	12.8	1.3	0.0	42917
38625	DUMAS	16213	535	37.6	30.8	26.4	4.5	0.8	34516	36699	26	71	458	39.3	28.4	26.0	5.5	0.9	64865
38626	DUNDEE	14056	558	45.5	27.4	19.0	6.6	1.4	27327	30512	8	28	376	48.7	25.3	20.7	5.1	0.3	52941
38627	ETTA	16407	422	35.6	32.7	28.2	2.1	1.4	37304	42341	36	81	353	42.2	30.3	14.7	12.2	0.6	58088
38629	FALKNER	17958	471	37.8	34.2	22.3	3.6	2.1	34513	37348	26	71	388	36.1	32.2	26.6	4.9	0.3	65789
38632	HERNANDO	23569	7371	20.0	27.5	38.7	9.8	4.1	52209	58724	76	97	6199	11.3	18.9	41.9	25.3	2.6	123743
38633	HICKORY FLAT	15464	908	40.0	29.9	24.1	5.3	0.8	32490	34523	19	63	738	29.4	40.9	26.8	2.9	0.0	67963
38635	HOLLY SPRINGS	15634	5249	45.5	29.5	18.3	3.9	2.9	27519	31013	8	29	3820	30.7	34.5	26.1	7.3	1.4	71168
38637	HORN LAKE	19627	6333	18.3	41.1	33.0	5.5	2.2	43746	48693	58	91	4503	3.2	47.9	44.6	4.3	0.1	89467
38641	LAKE CORMORANT	19933	807	25.0	32.3	32.5	6.7	3.5	44131	49289	59	92	614	17.1	22.0	41.7	17.6	1.6	109507
38642	LAMAR	15693	769	44.9	36.5	15.3	1.8	1.4	28353	31628	9	35	652	25.8	46.8	23.0	3.1	1.4	70204
38643	LAMBERT	12140	1248	54.6	24.4	16.9	3.0	1.1	21624	24054	2	6	834	62.2	26.1	10.8	0.6	0.2	41707
38645	LYON	19180	337	49.3	25.2	16.3	4.8	4.5	25518	29698	5	16	259	50.2	34.4	8.9	6.2	0.4	49906
38646	MARKS	13845	1552	50.5	28.7	16.6	2.7	1.6	24646	28098	4	12	1019	58.9	27.6	11.7	1.1	0.8	44972
38647	MICHIGAN CITY	12588	473	48.2	34.0	15.0	2.5	0.2	26218	28800	6	21	392	30.1	43.4	22.7	3.3	0.5	64667
38650	MYRTLE	16087	1603	31.8	33.1	30.9	3.7	0.4	36205	40708	32	78	1328	32.5	30.4	30.5	6.6	0.0	70442
38651	NESBIT	25964	2646	17.5	25.2	38.0	14.5	4.7	59703	63989	84	98	2407	11.9	10.0	37.9	38.5	1.8	156815
38652	NEW ALBANY	18685	6139	35.5	31.7	26.8	3.4	2.6	35130	38973	28	74	4611	24.6	36.4	30.2	8.1	0.7	77809
38654	OLIVE BRANCH	25773	12916	12.7	25.3	43.5	13.3	5.2	61705	67582	86	99	11112	3.8	10.0	51.7	32.0	2.5	148794
38655	OXFORD	19719	13173	42.1	25.0	23.5	6.0	3.3	31024	36066	15	53	7432	22.8	20.1	31.3	21.6	4.2	103860
38658	POPE	15378	941	35.9	37.0	22.5	3.6	1.0	32429	37195	19	62	821	43.7	37.3	14.0	4.6	0.4	57687
38659	POTTS CAMP	15393	1003	39.0	33.9	22.7	2.5	1.9	31911	35829	18	59	834	38.3	36.0	22.1	3.4	0.4	63864
38661	RED BANKS	18989	791	33.6	31.7	28.7	3.8	2.2	37569	41604	38	82	655	37.9	31.3	27.0	3.4	0.5	66014
38663	RIPLEY	15857	4505	39.6	34.3	21.3	3.8	1.1	31805	35083	17	58	3429	36.3	31.8	26.1	5.3	0.5	64912
38664	ROBINSONVILLE	18207	724	33.0	35.1	27.5	3.2	1.2	34060	39098	24	69	206	60.2	15.5	16.5	5.8	1.9	42500
38665	SARAH	17436	1121	29.8	40.5	22.2	5.1	2.4	37084	42786	36	81	926	35.3	25.7	28.1	9.4	1.5	76709
38666	SARDIS	14387	2706	48.8	26.9	18.8	3.6	1.9	25812	29143	6	20	1990	50.1	29.0	16.0	4.0	1.0	49911
38668	SENATOBIA	20849	4572	28.9	28.3	32.0	7.3	3.5	41329	46804	51	89	3440	17.2	25.5	40.5	16.3	0.5	100184
38670	SLEDGE	10788	552	54.9	29.5	12.1	1.8	1.6	21945	24441	3	6	368	70.4	19.0	8.7	1.1	0.8	37188
38671	SOUTHAVEN	23871	12915	18.5	30.7	40.0	8.2	2.6	50622	57035	73	96	9331	3.3	28.1	56.6	10.9	1.2	104970
38672	SOUTHAVEN	27366	797	14.2	21.6	39.3	18.3	6.7	68797	75633	91	99	758	5.8	4.1	40.4	46.6	3.2	174573
38673	TAYLOR	17634	430	37.7	27.9	27.7	4.9	1.9	34607	40098	26	72	283	32.5	29.3	23.0	13.4	1.8	72500
38674	TIPLERSVILLE	17229	381	38.3	33.6	23.4	3.4	1.3	33611	36913	23	67	320	38.4	31.9	24.1	4.7	0.9	63438
38676	TUNICA	13396	2788	53.2	24.2	17.4	3.3	1.8	22555	24901	3	8	1557	40.5	33.7	20.2	4.6	1.0	63616
38677	UNIVERSITY	19123	106	34.0	27.4	26.4	11.3	0.9	36981	44540	35	80	79	20.3	17.7	38.0	24.1	0.0	117188
38680	WALLS	21658	3579	21.0	30.2	37.1	8.9	2.8	48887	54375	70	96	2647	11.4	32.3	40.1	14.2	2.1	100592
38683	WALNUT	15476	1970	43.9	32.1	20.3	2.7	1.0	28985	32373	10	39	1618	44.5	29.7	20.1	4.9	0.8	55705
38685	WATERFORD	15034	362	40.3	30.9	24.9	2.8	1.1	31747	35318	17	58	309	38.8	35.9	21.4	3.9	0.0	64079
38701	GREENVILLE	17144	11014	45.3	26.3	19.3	5.4	3.8	28680	33012	10	36	6477	38.2	28.3	22.5	8.6	2.3	65552
38703	GREENVILLE	14768	6798	43.4	28.7	22.6	3.5	1.8	29415	33770	11	42	4307	37.8	45.5	13.5	2.9	0.4	58587
38720	ALLIGATOR	18432	142	45.1	21.1	26.1	4.9	2.8	30753	35000	14	51	117	65.8	20.5	12.8	0.9	0.0	39167
38721	ANGUILLA	11514	770	52.9	24.3	19.1	3.3	0.5	23160	26115	3	8	568	54.4	32.0	13.6	0.0	0.0	47222
38725	BENOIT	13630	486	50.0	25.5	17.5	4.5	2.5	25000	28077	5	13	289	47.8	28.0	17.0	7.3	0.0	52500
38726	BEULAH	14225	48	45.8	37.5	14.6	2.1	0.0	28160	32327	9	33	32	31.3	50.0	12.5	3.1	3.1	58571
38730	BOYLE	19440	774	34.2	32.0	21.5	7.5	4.8	34795	40785	27	72	620	24.2	24.5	36.5	12.9	1.9	91509
38731	CHATHAM	18419	73	49.3	31.5	11.0	4.1	4.1	25223	28139	5	15	56	42.9	19.6	30.4	3.6	3.6	63333
38732	CLEVELAND	16309	7107	42.1	27.1	23.1	5.1	2.6	30801	35411	14	51	4443	30.6	31.9	28.3	8.9	0.4	75028
38733	CLEVELAND	7791	4	0.0	0.0	100.0	0.0	0.0	75000	100000	93	100	3	0.0	0.0	100.0	0.0	0.0	106250
38736	DODDSVILLE	9365	248	42.3	29.4	23.0	3.6	1.6	28799	33532	10	38	182	44.5	31.3	19.8	4.4	0.0	54348
38737	DREW	10165	1470	49.9	27.8	19.5	2.4	0.4	25034	28331	5	14	967	55.2	32.1	9.2	3.1	0.4	47194
38740	DUNCAN	13285	287	53.7	22.0	18.5	3.5	2.4	22379	25689	3	7	203	61.6	26.1	8.4	2.0	2.0	43286
38744	GLEN ALLAN	16080	41	48.8	31.7	12.2	4.9	2.4	25407	27295	5	15	32	43.8	18.8	31.3	6.3	0.0	60000
38746	GUNNISON	11881	373	56.3	23.3	16.4	1.6	2.4	21505	23992	2	5	234	66.7	22.7	7.7	1.3	1.7	34565
38748	HOLLANDALE	13250	2020	48.6	29.0	15.9	3.8	2.8	25757	29873	5	19	1366	50.8	27.4	16.7	3.9	1.2	49481
38751	INDIANOLA	14705	4410	43.3	28.0	20.9	4.5	3.2	29922	34054	12	44	2814	29.5	44.5	20.0	5.9	0.2	65326
38753	INVERNESS	17725	645	40.2	27.6	24.2	5.9	2.2	33196	37754	21	66	461	24.3	36.7	30.6	3.7	4.8	79583
38754	ISOLA	14360	587	47.4	31.7	17.0	2.7	1.2	26335	29433	6	21	408	48.8	33.1	13.5	4.7	0.0	51000
38756	LELAND	14262	2470	43.4	31.7	18.4	5.4	1.1	29011	33181	10	40	1598	36.2	34.4	22.5	5.6	1.3	64702
38759	MERIGOLD	15429	495	49.5	26.7	19.8	3.0	1.0	25221	28752	5	14	358	53.4	31.0	12.6	2.2	0.8	47736
38761	MOORHEAD	10953	834	52.6	25.5	15.5	5.4	1.0	23300	25878	3	9	504	45.2	42.1	11.3	1.4	0.0	52824
38762	MOUND BAYOU	9851	1210	59.2	27.4	11.1	1.8	0.5	20241	22786	2	4	689	53.0	37.9	8.7	0.4	0.0	48202
38769	ROSEDALE	10145	1153	57.0	29.8	9.9	1.6	1.7	20525	22686	2	4	672	55.8	33.6	9.2	1.0	0.3	46100
38771	RULEVILLE	13157	1149	50.0	27.9	18.1	2.4	1.7	25029	28437	5	13	706	53.7	34.6	11.1	0.7	0.0	48700
38773	SHAW	12153	1441	54.1	26.6	14.9	2.7	1.7	22395	25114	3	7	971	52.3	32.3	12.6	2.3	0.5	48308
38774	SHELBY	11311	999	62.7	23.2	10.4	1.7	2.0	17121	19471	1	1	571	62.7	28.6	7.2	0.9	0.7	41854
38778	SUNFLOWER	15920	619	48.6	30.4	14.5	3.4	3.1	25865	30218	6	20	389	45.8	39.9	8.7	5.1	0.5	53438
38780	WAYSIDE	15254	112	36.6	29.5	27.7	3.6	2.7	35752	41147	31	77	90	43.3	33.3	21.1	2.2	0.0	57500
38801	TUPELO	23819	11275	28.9	30.7	28.9	6.9	4.5	41141	46116	50	88	7293	11.3	29.9	43.5	13.7	1.6	100746
38804	TUPELO	22101	7621	31.3	31.7	26.5	6.7	3.9	38203	43018	40	84	5276	17.9	31.2	34.9	12.6	3.5	91298
38821	AMORY	17376	5078	35.7	33.9	24.7	4.1	1.6	34427	37966	25	71	3885	25.8	36.3	30.2	6.8	0.9	75595
38824	BALDWYN	16086	2944	41.3	30.2	24.0	3.6	0.9	31960	35608	18	59	2256	33.5	33.6	27.3	5.6	0.0	67950
38826	BELDEN	27641	1726	22.3	28.1	30.9	9.4	9.2	49669	56458	71	96	1486	15.4	23.0	31.7	25.9	4.0	111517
38827	BELMONT	17672	1126	39.6	31.6	23.2	3.9	1.7	32377	35733	19	62	869	27.5	40.4	25.6	6.1	0.5	72398
38828	BLUE SPRINGS	16655	1296	36.9	30.0	28.9	3.4	0.9	32885	37130	21	65	1094	34.1	36.0	24.9	5.0	0.0	67054
38829	BOONEVILLE	16488	7318	40.5	33.8	19.8	4.5	1.3	30848	34300	14	52	5699	35.7	37.1	21.9	4.7	0.6	62364
38833	BURNSVILLE	15401	1020	47.7	28.5	17.9	4.3	1.6	26490	29235	6	22	769	40.6	40.6	16.1	2.7	0.0	58951
38834	CORINTH	18251	11670	41.2	29.8	22.6	4.6	1.8	31515	35228	16	56	8471	29.0	35.9	25.4	8.5	1.2	71221
38838	DENNIS	16892	684	35.5	34.9	24.4	4.0	1.2	34224	38090	25	70	582	33.0	34.2	27.3	5.5	0.0	64909
38841	ECRU	19806	1482	29.9	35.2	28.7	4.0	2.2	37429	41879	37	82	1199	30.7	38.5	25.9	4.7	0.2	71309
38843	FULTON	18323	4584	36.9	32.3	22.9	5.2	2.8	33927	37617	24	69	3673	29.3	39.7	24.0	6.3	0.7	70882
38844	GATTMAN	18163	140	43.6	29.3	23.6	2.9	0.7	28580	32093	10	36	119	49.6	19.3	19.3	11.8	0.0	51000
38846	GLEN	17088	1031	35.9	34.0	25.0	3.2	1.9	33257	37638	22	66	852	42.7	32.8	19.3	4.8	0.5	57294
38847	GOLDEN	16274	1641	36.2	35.4	23.5	3.8	1.1	34975	38468	27	73	1374	41.1	39.2	16.3	3.4	0.1	57029
38848	GREENWOOD SPRINGS	16313	378	41.8	31.0	23.8	2.7	0.8	29816	32877	12	43	330	45.8	21.5	24.2	7.6	0.9	55600
38849	GUNTOWN	18228	1770	32.6	33.7	27.7	4.8	1.3	35606	40430	30	77	1470	30.7	28.7	31.3	8.8	0.5	75316
	MISSISSIPPI	18480		36.7	30.0	24.5	5.9	2.8	34621	39377				29.7	30.4	28.7	9.7	1.6	75922
	UNITED STATES	25866		24.7	27.1	30.8	10.9	6.5	48124	56710				10.9	15.0	33.7	30.1	10.4	145905

ZIP CODE #	POST OFFICE NAME	FINANCIAL SERVICES: Auto Loan	FINANCIAL SERVICES: Home Loan	FINANCIAL SERVICES: Invest-ments	FINANCIAL SERVICES: Retire-ment Plans	THE HOME: Home Improvements: Home Repair	THE HOME: Home Improvements: Lawn & Garden	THE HOME: Furnishings: Comput-ers & Hard-ware	THE HOME: Furnishings: Major Appli-ances	THE HOME: Furnishings: TV, Radio, Sound Equip-ment	THE HOME: Furnishings: Furni-ture	ENTERTAINMENT: Dine out/ Carry out	ENTERTAINMENT: Sports Equip-ment	ENTERTAINMENT: Fees & Tickets	ENTERTAINMENT: Toys & Games	ENTERTAINMENT: Travel	ENTERTAINMENT: Cable TV	PERSONAL: Apparel & Services	PERSONAL: Auto Repairs	PERSONAL: Health Insur-ance	PERSONAL: Pets & Supplies
38601	ABBEVILLE	70	52	32	47	57	64	50	60	57	51	68	71	45	65	51	60	63	59	69	80
38603	ASHLAND	64	43	19	37	49	56	41	52	50	42	59	62	35	55	42	54	53	51	64	73
38606	BATESVILLE	72	57	42	53	61	69	57	64	63	57	76	75	52	73	58	66	71	64	73	82
38610	BLUE MOUNTAIN	77	54	28	48	60	69	52	64	61	53	72	76	45	69	53	66	66	63	77	88
38611	BYHALIA	86	63	34	56	69	78	60	72	69	60	82	86	53	80	61	74	76	71	86	100
38614	CLARKSDALE	60	53	57	50	53	62	57	58	62	57	76	65	56	72	56	64	73	59	64	67
38617	COAHOMA	50	40	49	37	39	47	47	47	53	48	66	53	45	62	46	56	63	49	52	54
38618	COLDWATER	81	58	34	51	64	73	57	68	66	58	79	80	50	76	57	71	73	67	81	93
38619	COMO	65	47	31	42	52	60	47	56	56	48	66	65	42	62	48	60	61	56	67	75
38620	COURTLAND	73	59	39	55	62	67	56	64	61	58	74	75	51	70	56	62	69	64	70	82
38621	CRENSHAW	59	41	26	36	45	53	42	50	50	43	59	57	37	55	42	54	54	50	60	67
38625	DUMAS	78	52	24	45	59	68	51	63	61	51	72	75	43	68	51	66	65	63	78	90
38626	DUNDEE	56	48	49	47	49	56	56	55	59	53	72	63	53	70	54	60	69	57	59	62
38627	ETTA	79	53	24	46	60	69	51	64	62	52	73	77	44	69	52	67	66	64	79	91
38629	FALKNER	85	57	26	49	64	74	55	69	66	56	78	82	47	73	56	71	71	68	85	97
38632	HERNANDO	99	91	73	88	94	101	86	93	89	87	109	109	84	109	87	90	104	91	97	114
38633	HICKORY FLAT	74	50	23	43	56	65	48	60	58	49	68	72	41	64	49	63	62	60	74	85
38635	HOLLY SPRINGS	67	49	31	43	53	61	49	57	57	50	68	67	44	64	49	61	63	57	68	76
38637	HORN LAKE	78	79	83	83	76	77	80	78	76	81	97	93	79	94	77	71	94	80	69	86
38641	LAKE CORMORANT	86	80	68	79	81	87	78	82	80	78	98	96	76	97	78	79	94	81	83	97
38642	LAMAR	84	56	25	49	64	73	54	68	66	55	77	81	46	73	55	71	70	67	84	96
38643	LAMBERT	55	40	32	35	43	51	43	48	50	44	60	54	39	55	42	54	56	49	58	61
38645	LYON	82	65	69	57	64	79	73	76	85	75	102	82	70	91	71	90	97	78	89	88
38646	MARKS	60	44	34	40	47	56	47	53	55	48	66	59	43	60	47	59	61	53	63	66
38647	MICHIGAN CITY	62	42	19	36	47	55	40	50	49	41	57	60	34	54	41	52	52	50	62	72
38650	MYRTLE	79	53	24	45	60	69	51	64	61	52	72	76	43	68	52	66	65	63	78	90
38651	NESBIT	100	104	94	101	106	109	94	99	94	94	116	118	96	121	97	94	113	96	99	120
38652	NEW ALBANY	77	62	45	58	66	74	62	68	68	61	82	81	57	80	62	71	77	68	77	88
38654	OLIVE BRANCH	99	114	113	117	111	108	103	103	95	105	121	121	107	124	102	91	119	100	90	114
38655	OXFORD	70	62	68	65	63	69	71	68	71	68	88	83	67	85	68	68	84	71	67	78
38658	POPE	76	51	23	44	58	66	49	61	59	50	70	73	42	66	50	64	63	61	76	87
38659	POTTS CAMP	75	50	23	43	57	66	49	61	59	50	69	73	41	65	49	63	63	60	75	86
38661	RED BANKS	95	63	29	55	72	83	61	76	74	62	87	91	52	82	62	79	79	76	94	109
38663	RIPLEY	69	50	31	46	55	63	50	59	57	50	68	69	44	65	50	60	62	58	69	78
38664	ROBINSONVILLE	58	54	65	51	51	59	58	56	62	60	78	63	59	78	57	64	77	58	59	65
38665	SARAH	82	60	34	54	66	75	57	68	66	58	78	82	51	76	58	70	72	67	81	94
38666	SARDIS	64	48	33	44	51	59	49	56	55	49	66	64	44	62	49	58	61	56	65	71
38668	SENATOBIA	96	78	57	73	83	93	77	86	85	77	102	100	72	99	77	88	95	85	97	109
38670	SLEDGE	46	37	36	33	37	45	41	43	47	42	56	47	39	51	40	50	53	44	50	51
38671	SOUTHAVEN	86	87	88	90	85	88	87	86	84	88	105	101	86	104	84	80	103	86	79	96
38672	SOUTHAVEN	103	128	135	128	126	124	114	114	106	114	133	133	121	141	117	103	133	110	102	126
38673	TAYLOR	66	63	59	63	63	67	62	64	62	63	77	75	60	73	62	60	74	65	63	74
38674	TIPLERSVILLE	81	54	25	47	62	71	53	66	63	54	74	78	45	70	53	68	68	65	81	93
38676	TUNICA	55	44	42	40	45	54	49	51	56	49	67	56	46	61	48	59	63	53	61	61
38677	UNIVERSITY	64	74	91	76	73	74	73	70	69	72	87	84	75	89	73	67	86	71	64	77
38680	WALLS	82	88	86	89	86	87	84	84	80	85	101	99	84	102	83	77	99	84	77	94
38683	WALNUT	69	46	21	40	53	61	45	56	54	46	64	67	38	60	46	58	58	56	69	80
38685	WATERFORD	72	48	22	41	54	63	46	58	56	47	66	69	39	62	47	60	60	57	71	82
38701	GREENVILLE	67	60	62	57	61	68	63	65	67	64	83	73	62	79	62	70	80	66	70	75
38703	GREENVILLE	61	53	51	50	53	61	55	57	60	56	74	65	54	72	55	62	70	58	63	68
38720	ALLIGATOR	82	55	25	47	62	72	53	66	64	54	75	79	45	71	54	69	68	66	82	94
38721	ANGUILLA	56	42	36	37	44	53	45	50	53	46	63	55	42	57	45	57	59	51	60	62
38725	BENOIT	59	47	42	41	49	58	49	54	57	50	68	60	46	62	50	61	64	55	64	67
38726	BEULAH	66	44	21	38	50	58	43	53	52	44	61	64	36	57	43	56	55	53	66	75
38730	BOYLE	82	67	48	65	71	81	68	75	74	67	89	86	64	87	68	76	83	74	83	92
38731	CHATHAM	78	52	24	45	59	68	51	63	61	52	72	76	43	68	52	66	65	63	78	90
38732	CLEVELAND	64	58	58	55	58	65	60	62	64	60	78	71	58	75	59	65	75	62	66	73
38733	CLEVELAND	106	122	150	126	120	123	120	116	114	120	144	139	124	148	121	111	143	118	106	127
38736	DODDSVILLE	68	51	31	47	55	63	51	58	57	51	68	68	46	66	51	60	63	58	68	76
38737	DREW	36	27	22	25	29	35	30	32	34	30	41	36	27	37	29	36	38	33	39	40
38740	DUNCAN	56	44	46	39	44	55	50	52	58	51	69	56	48	61	48	62	66	53	61	61
38744	GLEN ALLAN	78	52	24	45	59	68	50	63	60	51	71	75	43	67	51	65	65	62	77	89
38746	GUNNISON	52	41	43	36	41	50	46	48	53	47	64	51	44	57	45	57	61	49	57	56
38748	HOLLANDALE	61	50	42	45	51	59	51	56	57	52	69	63	48	64	51	60	65	56	64	68
38751	INDIANOLA	63	56	58	53	56	65	60	61	65	60	79	68	59	76	59	67	76	62	66	70
38753	INVERNESS	90	63	35	56	70	80	62	75	73	63	86	89	54	83	63	77	79	74	90	103
38754	ISOLA	72	48	23	42	55	63	47	58	56	48	66	70	40	63	48	61	60	58	72	82
38756	LELAND	58	50	47	45	50	58	52	55	57	52	70	61	50	66	52	60	66	55	62	65
38759	MERIGOLD	70	47	21	40	53	61	45	56	54	46	64	67	38	60	46	59	58	56	69	80
38761	MOORHEAD	51	45	51	42	44	51	49	49	54	50	67	54	49	64	48	56	65	50	53	56
38762	MOUND BAYOU	42	34	37	31	34	41	38	39	43	39	52	43	37	48	37	45	50	40	44	46
38769	ROSEDALE	43	34	40	31	34	41	40	40	46	41	56	44	39	51	39	48	54	42	46	47
38771	RULEVILLE	59	48	48	44	48	58	52	55	59	54	72	61	50	67	51	63	69	56	63	66
38773	SHAW	53	41	38	37	42	51	45	48	52	46	62	53	42	56	44	55	58	49	57	58
38774	SHELBY	48	39	49	35	38	46	46	45	52	47	64	51	45	60	44	55	62	48	50	52
38778	SUNFLOWER	77	64	57	59	64	74	66	71	73	68	89	79	63	81	65	76	84	72	79	84
38780	WAYSIDE	70	64	50	61	64	67	61	65	62	63	76	75	58	72	60	61	73	65	65	77
38801	TUPELO	89	84	80	84	84	90	84	86	85	84	105	101	83	104	83	84	102	86	85	101
38804	TUPELO	83	72	63	68	75	84	72	77	77	71	94	90	69	92	72	79	89	77	85	96
38821	AMORY	64	57	48	53	59	67	56	60	60	55	73	69	54	73	57	63	69	60	67	74
38824	BALDWYN	75	51	25	45	57	67	51	62	60	51	71	73	43	67	51	65	64	61	76	85
38826	BELDEN	120	111	90	107	114	121	102	111	105	104	129	130	100	128	103	107	124	108	116	139
38827	BELMONT	81	54	25	47	62	71	52	66	63	53	74	78	45	70	53	68	68	65	81	93
38828	BLUE SPRINGS	77	56	30	49	62	70	53	64	62	54	73	77	47	71	54	66	67	63	77	89
38829	BOONEVILLE	71	52	33	47	57	65	52	61	60	52	71	72	47	68	53	63	66	61	72	81
38833	BURNSVILLE	71	47	21	41	54	62	46	57	55	47	65	68	39	61	46	59	59	57	70	81
38834	CORINTH	69	55	41	51	59	67	56	62	62	55	74	72	52	72	56	64	69	61	71	79
38838	DENNIS	79	53	24	46	60	69	51	64	62	52	72	76	43	68	52	66	66	63	79	91
38841	ECRU	91	66	37	59	73	82	63	76	73	65	87	90	56	83	64	77	80	75	89	104
38843	FULTON	82	58	32	52	65	75	58	69	67	58	79	81	51	76	58	72	73	68	83	94
38844	GATTMAN	78	53	24	45	59	68	51	63	61	52	72	76	43	68	52	66	65	63	78	90
38846	GLEN	81	55	25	47	62	71	53	66	63	54	75	79	45	70	54	68	68	65	81	93
38847	GOLDEN	77	51	23	44	58	67	50	62	60	50	70	74	42	66	50	64	64	61	76	88
38848	GREENWOOD SPRINGS	75	50	23	43	57	66	49	61	59	49	69	73	41	65	49	63	63	60	75	86
38849	GUNTOWN	87	61	31	54	68	78	59	72	70	60	82	86	51	79	60	75	75	71	87	100
	MISSISSIPPI	76	64	54	60	66	74	64	70	70	65	85	81	61	82	64	71	80	70	76	86
	UNITED STATES	100	100	100	100	100	100	100	100	100	100	100	100	100	100	100	100	100	100	100	100

POPULATION CHANGE

ZIP CODE		COUNTY FIPS CODE	POPULATION			2000-2004 ANNUAL RATE		HOUSEHOLDS					FAMILIES		
#	POST OFFICE NAME		2000	2004	2009	% Rate	State Centile	2000	2004	2009	% Annual Rate 2000-2004	2004 Average HH Size	2000	2004	% Annual Rate 2000-2004
38850	HOULKA	017	3308	3416	3503	0.8	69	1214	1282	1340	1.3	2.66	907	949	1.1
38851	HOUSTON	017	9364	9369	9434	0.0	39	3515	3599	3704	0.6	2.57	2570	2607	0.3
38852	IUKA	141	9149	8971	8794	-0.5	20	3875	3896	3903	0.1	2.23	2618	2598	-0.2
38855	MANTACHIE	057	5513	5525	5614	0.1	42	2167	2214	2287	0.5	2.50	1630	1649	0.3
38856	MARIETTA	117	959	987	1003	0.7	67	369	389	402	1.3	2.54	288	301	1.0
38857	MOOREVILLE	081	1265	1270	1267	0.1	45	437	448	454	0.6	2.80	339	345	0.4
38858	NETTLETON	095	7097	7044	6993	-0.2	31	2724	2777	2817	0.5	2.54	2016	2030	0.2
38859	NEW SITE	117	876	857	851	-0.5	18	333	334	338	0.1	2.57	261	259	-0.2
38860	OKOLONA	017	6384	6429	6490	0.2	50	2408	2485	2565	0.7	2.56	1727	1765	0.5
38862	PLANTERSVILLE	081	2899	2958	2980	0.5	61	1075	1121	1147	1.0	2.61	791	815	0.7
38863	PONTOTOC	115	16996	17565	18181	0.8	71	6452	6783	7116	1.2	2.56	4760	4956	1.0
38864	RANDOLPH	115	1181	1362	1489	3.4	95	446	522	577	3.8	2.61	350	406	3.6
38865	RIENZI	003	4314	4458	4522	0.8	71	1679	1781	1848	1.4	2.50	1314	1381	1.2
38866	SALTILLO	081	8665	9099	9299	1.2	80	3389	3660	3810	1.8	2.46	2455	2622	1.6
38868	SHANNON	081	4861	4832	4823	-0.1	33	1843	1879	1906	0.5	2.57	1365	1377	0.2
38870	SMITHVILLE	095	2815	2811	2775	0.0	37	1102	1129	1141	0.6	2.49	806	816	0.3
38871	THAXTON	115	1621	1807	1948	2.6	93	595	671	731	2.9	2.69	479	536	2.7
38873	TISHOMINGO	141	2579	2502	2443	-0.7	11	1065	1055	1050	-0.2	2.37	760	746	-0.4
38876	TREMONT	057	1251	1291	1324	0.7	68	505	531	554	1.2	2.43	377	393	1.0
38878	VARDAMAN	013	3175	3187	3197	0.1	45	1220	1252	1282	0.6	2.54	864	877	0.4
38901	GRENADA	043	18266	17906	17645	-0.5	20	6911	6950	7012	0.1	2.50	4815	4790	-0.1
38912	AVALON	015	870	872	868	0.1	42	358	370	379	0.8	2.36	262	268	0.5
38913	BANNER	013	649	684	703	1.2	82	255	275	290	1.8	2.48	189	202	1.6
38914	BIG CREEK	013	424	408	407	-0.9	7	181	179	184	-0.3	2.26	136	134	-0.4
38915	BRUCE	013	4525	4515	4537	-0.1	36	1844	1884	1938	0.5	2.36	1269	1283	0.3
38916	CALHOUN CITY	013	5283	5228	5228	-0.3	27	2119	2157	2213	0.4	2.36	1508	1518	0.2
38917	CARROLLTON	015	3348	3306	3275	-0.3	25	1229	1243	1261	0.3	2.49	946	950	0.1
38920	CASCILLA	135	2213	2227	2233	0.2	48	807	834	858	0.8	2.67	627	643	0.6
38921	CHARLESTON	135	6863	6852	6861	0.0	37	2470	2541	2616	0.7	2.67	1762	1794	0.4
38922	COFFEEVILLE	161	4028	3928	3841	-0.6	15	1678	1682	1688	0.1	2.33	1169	1156	-0.3
38923	COILA	015	1759	1739	1722	-0.3	26	640	650	660	0.4	2.68	495	499	0.2
38924	CRUGER	051	984	986	977	0.1	42	359	369	375	0.7	2.67	250	255	0.5
38925	DUCK HILL	097	2839	3096	3262	2.1	90	1105	1240	1341	2.8	2.50	821	909	2.4
38927	ENID	135	955	1018	1051	1.5	85	357	391	414	2.2	2.60	273	296	1.9
38929	GORE SPRINGS	043	713	687	669	-0.9	7	262	261	261	-0.1	2.63	202	198	-0.5
38930	GREENWOOD	083	27584	27434	26989	-0.1	34	10139	10302	10345	0.4	2.58	6839	6872	0.1
38940	HOLCOMB	043	2779	2970	3044	1.6	86	1047	1156	1218	2.4	2.57	820	895	2.1
38941	ITTA BENA	083	6534	6289	6103	-0.9	7	1825	1782	1755	-0.6	2.91	1326	1283	-0.8
38943	MC CARLEY	015	1085	1071	1061	-0.3	25	420	425	432	0.3	2.52	315	316	0.1
38944	MINTER CITY	083	895	832	793	-1.7	2	289	275	268	-1.2	3.03	223	211	-1.3
38948	OAKLAND	161	1825	1818	1795	-0.1	35	741	760	771	0.6	2.39	501	509	0.4
38949	PARIS	071	290	278	284	-1.0	5	111	110	115	-0.2	2.53	81	80	-0.3
38950	PHILIPP	135	481	469	466	-0.6	15	182	183	188	0.1	2.56	136	136	0.0
38951	PITTSBORO	013	910	1002	1058	2.3	91	343	389	421	3.0	2.47	251	282	2.8
38952	SCHLATER	083	693	673	661	-0.7	11	253	244	239	-0.9	1.19	181	78	-18.0
38953	SCOBEY	161	323	320	315	-0.2	29	128	131	132	0.6	2.44	88	89	0.3
38954	SIDON	083	2183	2127	2078	-0.6	14	794	794	795	0.0	2.66	601	598	-0.1
38961	TILLATOBA	161	639	634	624	-0.2	31	259	265	268	0.5	2.39	177	179	0.3
38963	TUTWILER	135	4314	4268	4267	-0.3	27	1421	1437	1472	0.3	2.95	1009	1010	0.0
38964	VANCE	119	110	104	100	-1.3	2	42	41	41	-0.6	2.54	31	30	-0.8
38965	WATER VALLEY	161	8331	8402	8419	0.2	51	3278	3380	3460	0.7	2.46	2280	2329	0.5
38967	WINONA	097	7427	7318	7323	-0.4	23	2836	2853	2917	0.1	2.52	2024	2018	-0.1
39038	BELZONI	053	7256	7151	7026	-0.3	24	2381	2398	2404	0.2	2.94	1728	1724	-0.1
39039	BENTON	163	2111	2122	2113	0.1	46	767	784	792	0.5	2.48	575	583	0.3
39040	BENTONIA	163	3544	3602	3612	0.4	57	1270	1318	1339	0.9	2.73	950	976	0.6
39041	BOLTON	049	3548	3537	3503	-0.1	35	1225	1250	1263	0.5	2.82	916	923	0.2
39042	BRANDON	121	29650	32388	35281	2.1	90	10959	12293	13727	2.7	2.61	8381	9351	2.6
39044	BRAXTON	127	3138	3507	3802	2.7	93	1162	1336	1486	3.3	2.62	877	996	3.0
39045	CAMDEN	089	1390	1407	1474	0.3	54	446	462	492	0.8	3.03	342	350	0.6
39046	CANTON	089	22765	23033	24237	0.3	53	7243	7477	8010	0.8	2.99	5533	5646	0.5
39047	BRANDON	121	26398	29071	31805	2.3	92	10119	11451	12845	3.0	2.53	7463	8414	2.7
39051	CARTHAGE	079	18246	18523	18938	0.4	55	6548	6757	7016	0.7	2.63	4817	4923	0.5
39056	CLINTON	049	25148	25417	25373	0.3	52	8888	9206	9372	0.8	2.57	6554	6691	0.5
39057	CONEHATTA	101	2327	2378	2391	0.5	62	812	850	873	1.1	2.80	606	629	0.9
39059	CRYSTAL SPRINGS	029	11873	11807	11821	-0.1	34	4302	4376	4459	0.4	2.63	3185	3212	0.2
39063	DURANT	051	3835	3759	3691	-0.5	20	1378	1374	1374	-0.1	2.66	969	956	-0.3
39066	EDWARDS	049	4418	4604	4651	1.0	75	1483	1577	1621	1.5	2.91	1127	1184	1.2
39067	ETHEL	007	2322	2344	2349	0.2	52	915	941	955	0.7	2.48	674	687	0.5
39069	FAYETTE	063	7274	6949	6772	-1.1	4	2378	2337	2337	-0.4	2.70	1680	1633	-0.7
39071	FLORA	089	4329	4453	4669	0.7	66	1471	1562	1675	1.4	2.85	1152	1205	1.1
39073	FLORENCE	121	17535	18578	19865	1.4	83	6384	6919	7569	1.9	2.67	4955	5343	1.8
39074	FOREST	123	14634	15037	15506	0.6	65	5207	5450	5714	1.1	2.73	3828	3968	0.9
39078	GEORGETOWN	029	936	966	981	0.8	69	352	373	387	1.4	2.59	255	268	1.2
39079	GOODMAN	051	1942	1956	1949	0.2	50	516	532	539	0.7	2.86	373	381	0.5
39082	HARRISVILLE	127	1172	1246	1306	1.5	84	436	476	511	2.1	2.61	322	349	1.9
39083	HAZLEHURST	029	10760	10923	11036	0.4	54	3874	4024	4138	0.9	2.65	2833	2914	0.7
39086	HERMANVILLE	021	2480	2553	2662	0.7	67	893	950	1017	1.5	2.64	634	667	1.2
39088	HOLLY BLUFF	163	156	146	143	-1.6	2	60	57	57	-1.2	2.56	47	45	-1.0
39090	KOSCIUSKO	007	12222	12311	12365	0.2	50	4760	4889	4962	0.6	2.45	3288	3340	0.4
39092	LAKE	123	3031	3219	3370	1.4	84	1101	1189	1263	1.8	2.70	833	890	1.6
39094	LENA	079	3407	3418	3484	0.1	44	1271	1301	1349	0.6	2.63	947	960	0.3
39095	LEXINGTON	051	7789	7811	7760	0.1	43	2766	2833	2872	0.6	2.71	1946	1973	0.3
39096	LORMAN	063	860	1199	1416	8.1	100	316	459	560	9.2	2.61	225	322	8.8
39097	LOUISE	053	1403	1353	1316	-0.9	8	477	470	466	-0.4	2.88	329	322	-0.5
39108	MC COOL	007	1630	1645	1651	0.2	52	660	684	699	0.8	2.40	468	480	0.5
39110	MADISON	089	24054	27440	30415	3.2	95	8323	9728	10997	3.7	2.77	6931	8006	3.5
39111	MAGEE	127	10706	10801	11066	0.2	51	3915	4047	4247	0.8	2.52	2768	2832	0.5
39113	MAYERSVILLE	055	2073	2018	1944	-0.6	14	654	655	649	0.0	2.68	460	456	-0.2
39114	MENDENHALL	127	10356	10522	10797	0.4	56	3731	3880	4072	0.9	2.63	2805	2891	0.7
39116	MIZE	129	3358	3367	3357	0.1	42	1239	1269	1292	0.6	2.65	928	942	0.4
39117	MORTON	123	8572	8704	8937	0.4	55	3099	3213	3359	0.9	2.66	2289	2350	0.6
39119	MOUNT OLIVE	031	2918	2900	2975	-0.2	32	1104	1124	1181	0.4	2.58	785	790	0.2
39120	NATCHEZ	001	34616	33566	32338	-0.7	10	13769	13709	13554	-0.1	2.41	9472	9329	-0.4
39140	NEWHEBRON	077	1569	1604	1640	0.5	62	581	609	637	1.1	2.63	428	445	0.9
39144	PATTISON	021	973	980	1009	0.2	50	349	364	384	1.0	2.69	240	248	0.8
	MISSISSIPPI					0.6					1.2	2.57			0.9
	UNITED STATES					1.2					1.3	2.58			1.1

ZIP CODE #	POST OFFICE NAME	RACE (%) White 2000	White 2004	Black 2000	Black 2004	Asian/Pacific 2000	Asian/Pacific 2004	% Hispanic Origin 2000	% Hispanic Origin 2004	2004 AGE DISTRIBUTION (%) 0-4	5-9	10-14	15-19	20-24	25-44	45-64	65-84	85+	18+	MEDIAN AGE 2004	% 2004 Males	% 2004 Females
38850	HOULKA	72.3	71.4	26.1	26.7	0.0	0.1	2.0	2.4	7.1	7.2	7.9	7.5	6.6	28.2	22.7	11.2	1.7	73.2	35.4	49.8	50.2
38851	HOUSTON	62.9	61.3	34.6	35.7	0.3	0.4	3.3	3.8	7.6	7.3	7.6	7.2	6.7	27.6	22.0	11.9	2.0	73.2	35.4	49.1	50.9
38852	IUKA	95.9	95.4	2.9	3.1	0.2	0.2	0.8	0.9	5.2	5.5	6.3	5.4	5.4	25.9	26.1	17.3	2.9	79.8	42.6	48.1	51.9
38855	MANTACHIE	97.8	97.5	1.2	1.4	0.1	0.1	0.7	0.8	6.4	6.5	8.0	6.4	6.1	30.1	23.5	11.6	1.5	75.1	36.4	49.0	51.0
38856	MARIETTA	97.7	97.4	0.8	0.9	0.0	0.0	1.0	1.2	6.4	6.5	6.6	5.8	6.2	29.5	25.1	12.5	1.5	77.1	37.8	51.6	48.4
38857	MOOREVILLE	96.8	96.5	2.4	2.6	0.2	0.3	1.0	1.3	6.8	6.9	7.2	6.5	6.4	30.6	24.3	10.1	1.2	75.0	36.4	51.7	48.3
38858	NETTLETON	73.4	71.5	25.7	27.5	0.3	0.3	0.8	0.9	7.0	7.0	7.7	6.5	6.8	28.3	24.2	11.0	1.5	74.3	36.0	48.3	51.7
38859	NEW SITE	98.6	98.5	0.3	0.4	0.0	0.0	1.3	1.4	8.1	7.7	6.4	5.6	6.4	28.2	25.7	10.7	1.2	74.7	36.0	53.1	46.9
38860	OKOLONA	44.6	43.2	54.6	55.9	0.1	0.1	0.8	0.8	8.2	7.7	8.3	6.8	6.9	26.3	23.1	11.1	1.8	71.6	34.6	47.3	52.7
38862	PLANTERSVILLE	68.0	65.6	30.4	32.6	0.0	0.0	1.9	2.2	7.2	7.1	8.1	7.1	7.4	29.7	23.2	9.1	1.1	73.3	34.5	49.2	50.8
38863	PONTOTOC	84.2	83.0	14.0	14.9	0.1	0.2	1.8	2.1	7.2	7.1	7.6	7.0	6.6	28.4	23.1	11.3	1.8	74.0	35.9	48.5	51.5
38864	RANDOLPH	94.7	94.2	3.6	3.9	0.1	0.1	1.9	2.3	8.2	7.9	8.1	6.6	6.8	28.6	21.4	11.0	1.4	71.7	33.5	50.4	49.6
38865	RIENZI	90.6	89.9	8.1	8.8	0.1	0.1	1.1	1.2	6.8	6.8	7.0	5.9	6.3	29.0	25.1	11.6	1.4	75.7	36.9	50.6	49.4
38866	SALTILLO	91.5	90.6	6.9	7.4	0.5	0.6	0.9	1.2	7.5	7.3	7.0	6.4	6.0	31.6	23.4	9.5	1.4	74.4	35.4	48.4	51.6
38868	SHANNON	60.2	57.8	38.6	40.8	0.1	0.1	0.8	0.9	7.8	7.6	7.5	6.9	7.2	29.6	23.2	9.3	0.9	73.0	34.3	49.7	50.3
38870	SMITHVILLE	91.0	90.0	8.0	8.9	0.2	0.2	0.7	0.8	6.4	6.4	6.9	6.3	6.5	28.4	25.4	12.1	1.6	76.5	37.9	49.7	50.3
38871	THAXTON	96.8	96.7	2.5	2.6	0.0	0.0	1.0	1.2	6.8	6.8	7.6	7.1	7.4	28.6	24.1	10.7	1.0	74.4	35.7	49.9	50.1
38873	TISHOMINGO	89.3	88.8	9.5	9.9	0.0	0.0	0.7	0.9	6.2	6.2	6.3	5.7	5.5	26.7	26.8	14.9	1.7	77.8	40.7	48.6	51.4
38876	TREMONT	98.6	98.5	0.5	0.5	0.1	0.1	0.5	0.5	6.5	6.4	7.1	6.0	6.7	29.4	24.1	12.3	1.6	76.4	37.0	50.8	49.2
38878	VARDAMAN	71.6	70.9	24.4	25.2	0.1	0.1	6.1	6.2	6.4	6.3	7.1	6.8	6.8	28.2	24.4	12.3	1.7	76.1	36.8	48.9	51.1
38901	GRENADA	55.1	53.8	43.7	44.8	0.4	0.6	0.7	0.8	7.2	7.0	7.7	7.1	6.7	26.9	22.7	12.5	2.3	73.8	36.2	46.5	53.6
38912	AVALON	95.1	95.0	4.7	4.8	0.1	0.1	0.0	0.0	5.2	5.3	4.8	5.2	6.3	26.2	31.7	13.9	1.6	81.9	43.1	50.1	49.9
38913	BANNER	90.1	90.2	8.8	8.8	0.2	0.2	1.1	1.2	6.4	6.1	6.4	6.1	6.7	26.5	25.6	14.3	1.8	77.3	39.2	51.3	48.7
38914	BIG CREEK	80.9	79.7	18.6	19.9	0.0	0.0	0.2	0.0	5.6	5.9	5.9	5.9	6.1	25.5	29.4	13.7	2.0	79.2	41.9	49.0	51.0
38915	BRUCE	67.6	67.3	30.5	30.8	0.1	0.1	1.3	1.3	7.0	6.7	6.9	6.5	6.5	26.0	23.9	14.5	2.1	75.2	37.7	49.1	50.9
38916	CALHOUN CITY	65.8	64.9	33.1	33.9	0.1	0.1	0.9	0.9	6.9	6.4	6.4	6.5	6.6	25.5	24.7	13.5	3.4	76.2	38.6	46.2	53.8
38917	CARROLLTON	68.0	67.7	31.4	31.7	0.3	0.3	0.7	0.7	5.6	6.0	6.9	6.7	7.2	27.4	26.8	11.5	1.9	78.0	38.2	51.5	48.5
38920	CASCILLA	65.2	64.3	34.0	34.9	0.1	0.1	0.9	0.9	7.0	6.9	8.1	7.1	6.8	25.7	26.1	10.9	1.3	73.6	36.5	48.0	52.0
38921	CHARLESTON	37.0	36.2	62.3	63.1	0.2	0.2	1.2	1.2	7.3	7.3	8.8	7.8	6.8	25.7	22.6	11.6	2.1	71.9	34.2	46.6	53.4
38922	COFFEEVILLE	57.2	55.7	42.2	43.7	0.1	0.1	0.7	0.8	5.9	5.6	7.2	6.5	6.1	26.1	26.7	13.8	2.2	77.4	39.9	48.1	51.9
38923	COILA	53.7	53.0	45.5	46.2	0.1	0.1	0.9	0.9	6.4	6.4	6.8	7.0	7.0	24.7	27.1	13.0	1.6	76.3	39.5	49.1	51.0
38924	CRUGER	21.1	20.3	78.2	79.0	0.1	0.1	1.8	1.7	8.4	8.1	8.8	7.0	7.5	23.7	21.7	12.5	2.2	70.4	35.0	47.5	52.5
38925	DUCK HILL	58.2	54.9	41.4	44.6	0.0	0.0	0.4	0.4	7.2	7.4	7.6	6.4	6.2	26.2	25.4	12.2	1.5	74.0	37.2	47.9	52.1
38927	ENID	71.9	70.6	27.4	28.7	0.1	0.1	0.5	0.5	6.2	6.4	8.6	6.9	6.2	26.8	23.8	13.3	2.0	74.6	37.1	51.1	48.9
38929	GORE SPRINGS	54.3	51.1	45.3	48.5	0.0	0.0	0.6	0.7	4.7	5.2	7.9	5.8	5.2	24.5	31.4	13.5	1.8	78.8	42.7	47.7	52.3
38930	GREENWOOD	33.4	32.5	64.8	65.5	0.8	1.0	1.0	1.0	8.3	8.1	8.3	7.9	7.4	26.2	20.9	10.6	2.3	70.4	32.4	45.9	54.1
38940	HOLCOMB	72.3	69.0	26.9	30.1	0.1	0.1	0.4	0.4	6.6	6.9	7.9	7.1	6.2	28.5	24.3	11.3	1.3	74.3	36.2	49.7	50.3
38941	ITTA BENA	14.8	13.2	80.2	81.1	0.3	0.3	6.2	6.9	7.5	7.2	7.6	10.1	15.2	27.4	17.2	6.5	1.1	73.6	26.2	49.5	50.5
38943	MC CARLEY	68.0	67.3	31.2	32.0	0.0	0.0	0.9	0.9	5.0	5.4	6.5	6.2	5.7	27.5	29.7	12.3	1.7	79.4	40.8	49.1	50.9
38944	MINTER CITY	39.6	35.9	58.4	61.7	0.1	0.1	2.2	2.4	8.7	8.8	8.5	7.1	5.8	24.2	25.2	10.7	1.1	70.1	35.4	48.2	51.8
38948	OAKLAND	54.1	53.1	45.2	46.1	0.1	0.1	1.0	1.1	7.0	7.2	7.8	6.2	6.7	24.9	25.3	13.5	1.5	74.2	38.2	50.5	49.5
38949	PARIS	97.2	97.5	1.7	1.8	0.0	0.0	0.7	0.4	7.2	6.8	6.5	5.4	5.8	28.8	25.9	12.6	1.1	76.3	37.5	47.1	52.9
38950	PHILIPP	40.1	38.6	59.3	60.8	0.0	0.0	1.5	1.7	6.4	6.4	7.5	7.7	7.3	21.8	27.1	14.5	1.5	74.8	39.0	48.0	52.0
38951	PITTSBORO	66.6	65.2	32.5	34.1	0.0	0.0	0.9	0.7	6.5	6.5	7.0	6.6	6.4	27.1	23.5	14.0	2.6	76.0	37.8	48.2	51.8
38952	SCHLATER	26.0	23.0	72.9	75.6	0.1	0.2	1.0	1.3	4.0	3.6	3.0	6.1	18.0	48.1	12.9	3.7	0.6	87.1	29.6	77.1	22.9
38953	SCOBEY	70.6	69.1	28.8	30.0	0.3	0.3	0.9	0.9	8.1	7.5	6.9	5.9	7.5	26.3	24.1	12.8	0.9	73.8	36.1	46.9	53.1
38954	SIDON	53.1	51.0	45.6	47.5	0.4	0.4	1.2	1.3	7.9	7.9	7.7	7.8	6.2	27.8	24.5	9.2	1.1	72.0	34.1	49.3	50.7
38961	TILLATOBA	70.4	69.4	28.8	29.8	0.2	0.2	0.9	1.0	8.4	7.4	6.9	5.8	7.6	26.0	23.8	12.8	1.3	73.8	35.9	46.9	53.2
38963	TUTWILER	22.9	21.8	75.6	76.6	0.8	0.8	0.5	0.5	7.5	8.6	9.3	8.7	8.0	25.7	19.8	10.9	1.5	69.4	31.6	46.5	53.5
38964	VANCE	40.9	39.4	57.3	59.6	0.0	0.0	0.0	0.0	13.5	6.7	6.7	8.7	5.8	22.1	23.1	13.5	0.0	67.3	33.3	53.9	46.2
38965	WATER VALLEY	66.9	66.3	32.1	32.7	0.2	0.2	1.0	1.0	6.6	6.7	7.3	6.4	6.8	26.2	25.1	13.1	1.9	75.7	37.7	48.6	51.4
38967	WINONA	49.9	48.6	49.2	50.3	0.4	0.5	0.9	0.9	6.6	6.6	8.0	7.4	7.0	24.6	23.2	14.1	2.6	74.4	37.6	45.7	54.4
39038	BELZONI	26.8	25.9	72.0	72.8	0.3	0.3	1.3	1.4	8.6	8.2	9.3	8.6	8.8	25.7	19.6	9.2	2.0	68.5	29.9	46.9	53.1
39039	BENTON	51.7	50.1	47.2	48.6	0.1	0.2	5.1	5.7	6.3	6.3	7.1	6.9	7.3	29.6	24.1	11.1	1.4	76.2	36.3	53.2	46.8
39040	BENTONIA	62.4	60.4	36.5	38.4	0.1	0.1	0.5	0.5	7.1	7.0	7.3	6.7	7.0	26.7	25.0	11.7	1.6	74.7	36.8	48.8	51.2
39041	BOLTON	33.0	28.8	66.2	70.3	0.0	0.0	0.6	0.6	7.1	7.0	7.2	7.4	7.4	26.0	26.1	10.3	1.6	74.3	36.6	48.2	51.9
39042	BRANDON	81.6	80.8	17.0	17.5	0.5	0.5	1.3	1.5	7.0	6.9	7.1	7.0	7.1	28.4	25.9	9.7	1.1	74.8	36.3	48.7	51.3
39044	BRAXTON	70.1	68.8	28.2	29.2	0.2	0.2	0.7	0.8	7.0	7.1	7.9	7.0	6.6	27.2	26.4	9.8	1.2	73.8	36.0	49.4	50.6
39045	CAMDEN	15.1	12.0	83.7	86.9	0.5	0.5	0.4	0.3	7.8	8.2	10.9	8.5	7.4	22.9	21.7	11.3	1.5	68.1	32.4	48.4	51.6
39046	CANTON	25.2	22.8	73.8	76.2	0.2	0.3	1.1	1.1	8.6	8.7	8.7	8.1	7.8	25.6	21.9	9.3	1.4	69.0	31.4	47.0	53.0
39047	BRANDON	85.2	83.8	12.7	13.6	1.1	1.4	1.0	1.2	7.2	7.2	7.1	6.4	5.9	33.0	25.2	7.4	0.6	74.5	35.5	48.6	51.4
39051	CARTHAGE	56.3	54.6	36.8	37.8	0.2	0.3	2.3	2.6	7.4	7.3	7.1	6.7	7.1	27.4	23.1	11.9	1.9	74.2	35.3	50.2	49.8
39056	CLINTON	73.2	70.0	24.4	27.2	1.4	1.7	0.9	1.0	6.3	6.3	6.9	7.9	9.9	28.0	23.1	9.9	1.6	76.6	34.0	47.3	52.7
39057	CONEHATTA	56.4	56.2	10.8	11.4	0.0	0.0	1.2	1.2	8.8	8.3	8.4	8.0	7.0	27.7	21.2	9.6	1.1	69.6	31.5	48.7	51.4
39059	CRYSTAL SPRINGS	47.7	46.2	51.3	52.8	0.1	0.1	0.9	1.0	7.0	6.7	7.0	8.6	7.6	27.3	23.8	10.7	1.4	74.4	34.7	48.2	51.9
39063	DURANT	31.6	30.3	67.3	68.6	0.2	0.3	0.7	0.7	7.1	7.0	8.4	7.9	8.5	24.2	22.1	12.4	2.5	72.6	33.9	47.5	52.5
39066	EDWARDS	24.8	21.2	74.4	78.0	0.1	0.1	0.9	0.9	8.0	7.9	8.3	7.5	7.6	25.9	24.1	9.5	1.3	71.0	33.5	47.0	53.0
39067	ETHEL	69.9	69.1	28.4	29.2	0.3	0.3	1.4	1.5	6.4	6.6	6.8	7.0	6.4	25.2	26.0	14.0	1.6	75.8	38.5	50.0	50.0
39069	FAYETTE	8.4	8.0	91.2	91.6	0.1	0.1	0.6	0.6	7.6	7.4	7.9	7.9	9.0	28.9	21.8	8.1	1.5	72.5	31.9	50.7	49.3
39071	FLORA	49.5	44.4	49.9	54.8	0.1	0.1	0.4	0.4	8.2	7.8	7.3	6.6	6.9	29.2	24.3	8.8	1.1	72.8	34.3	48.0	52.0
39073	FLORENCE	82.2	80.8	16.7	17.9	0.2	0.2	0.9	1.1	7.2	7.0	7.2	7.1	7.1	28.7	25.3	9.4	1.0	74.3	35.5	49.4	50.7
39074	FOREST	47.6	46.1	47.8	48.6	0.3	0.3	6.1	6.9	8.1	7.8	8.0	7.3	6.9	27.6	22.3	10.5	1.6	71.7	33.8	48.7	51.3
39078	GEORGETOWN	54.2	52.7	44.8	46.2	0.0	0.0	1.0	1.1	7.0	7.4	9.0	6.8	6.2	27.3	23.7	11.6	0.9	72.5	36.1	49.4	50.6
39079	GOODMAN	28.7	27.3	70.4	71.7	0.0	0.0	0.6	0.6	8.1	7.5	7.7	17.4	15.3	21.6	14.5	7.1	0.9	72.8	23.1	50.1	49.9
39082	HARRISVILLE	64.3	63.0	35.1	36.3	0.2	0.2	1.5	1.4	8.3	7.8	7.5	6.2	6.9	27.1	24.0	11.2	1.1	72.6	35.4	50.9	49.1
39083	HAZLEHURST	39.4	38.2	59.1	60.1	0.3	0.3	1.4	1.6	7.0	7.0	7.4	7.4	7.5	25.9	24.1	11.7	1.9	74.3	36.0	48.3	51.7
39086	HERMANVILLE	26.3	24.9	73.2	74.4	0.0	0.0	0.8	0.8	8.3	8.2	8.2	7.8	7.7	24.6	22.6	10.8	1.7	70.8	32.4	47.4	52.6
39088	HOLLY BLUFF	57.7	56.2	41.7	43.8	0.0	0.0	6.4	6.9	7.5	7.5	8.2	8.2	6.2	27.4	24.0	9.6	1.4	72.6	34.5	50.0	50.0
39090	KOSCIUSKO	57.4	56.5	40.8	41.7	0.3	0.3	1.4	1.4	6.5	6.5	7.2	6.8	6.7	24.9	23.5	15.0	2.9	75.8	38.2	47.7	52.3
39092	LAKE	62.6	60.7	36.4	38.2	0.0	0.0	1.3	1.6	7.7	7.5	7.9	7.3	7.0	27.1	23.1	10.9	1.5	72.4	34.4	48.7	51.3
39094	LENA	53.8	52.1	45.4	46.9	0.0	0.1	1.0	1.1	7.1	7.0	7.8	7.1	7.0	26.2	24.4	11.6	1.7	73.7	36.2	49.5	50.5
39095	LEXINGTON	20.6	19.7	78.5	79.3	0.3	0.3	1.2	1.1	7.7	7.9	8.8	8.1	7.9	25.1	21.5	11.1	2.0	70.6	32.9	46.7	53.3
39096	LORMAN	16.9	16.1	83.1	83.9	0.0	0.0	1.3	1.3	6.0	5.9	6.8	9.3	7.5	25.8	23.8	12.8	2.1	75.7	37.2	48.5	51.5
39097	LOUISE	21.0	19.6	78.1	79.4	0.6	0.7	0.6	0.7	7.2	7.1	9.4	8.4	8.2	26.1	21.1	11.0	1.6	71.3	33.3	47.7	52.3
39108	MC COOL	66.0	65.0	32.2	33.2	0.5	0.5	1.7	1.6	6.7	6.8	6.9	6.3	6.3	24.4	24.9	15.6	2.0	75.8	39.5	49.2	50.8
39110	MADISON	87.6	84.7	10.4	12.9	1.3	1.6	0.7	0.9	7.8	8.6	8.6	6.8	4.4	29.4	25.4	7.8	1.4	70.6	37.2	48.3	51.8
39111	MAGEE	68.2	66.8	30.1	31.3	0.2	0.2	1.8	2.1	6.9	7.0	7.4	7.4	6.8	27.0	23.5	12.1	2.0	74.1	35.8	49.0	51.0
39113	MAYERSVILLE	34.9	34.2	64.1	64.8	0.0	0.0	0.4	0.5	6.1	5.9	7.8	8.8	8.8	30.9	20.7	9.9	1.1	75.1	33.6	53.8	46.2
39114	MENDENHALL	61.0	59.5	38.0	39.4	0.1	0.2	0.8	0.9	7.7	7.6	8.1	6.9	6.7	26.8	23.5	11.3	1.6	72.5	35.1	48.3	51.7
39116	MIZE	83.7	83.4	15.8	16.0	0.1	0.1	0.6	0.6	7.0	7.1	8.0	7.3	6.8	28.0	23.4	10.8	1.6	73.4	35.3	49.6	50.4
39117	MORTON	71.0	69.7	24.7	25.2	0.1	0.2	7.9	9.3	6.8	6.6	7.7	6.7	6.5	28.1	24.2	11.4	2.0	74.8	36.3	49.8	50.2
39119	MOUNT OLIVE	50.7	47.4	48.2	51.3	0.2	0.2	0.5	0.5	7.9	7.9	8.2	6.5	6.8	26.5	23.2	11.7	1.5	72.1	35.3	48.3	51.7
39120	NATCHEZ	45.2	43.7	53.6	55.0	0.3	0.3	0.8	0.8	6.8	6.8	7.3	6.8	6.9	23.9	25.6	13.9	2.0	74.9	38.8	46.5	53.5
39140	NEWHEBRON	60.6	58.6	38.9	41.0	0.1	0.1	0.5	0.6	7.4	7.5	8.2	6.4	6.9	26.0	24.0	11.8	1.9	73.2	36.0	47.9	52.1
39144	PATTISON	23.2	22.4	76.2	77.0	0.1	0.1	0.9	0.9	8.8	7.9	7.4	8.2	8.7	26.5	21.6	9.4	1.6	71.4	31.5	49.8	50.2
	MISSISSIPPI	61.4	60.6	36.3	36.8	0.7	0.8	1.4	1.6	7.3	7.1	7.4	7.4	7.8	27.8	23.0	10.6	1.6	73.9	34.5	48.5	51.5
	UNITED STATES	75.1	73.6	12.3	12.5	3.8	4.2	12.5	14.1	6.9	6.7	7.2	7.0	7.3	28.6	23.8	10.8	1.7	75.1	36.0	49.1	50.9

#	POST OFFICE NAME	2004 Per Capita Income	2004 HH Income Base	2004 Household Income Distribution (%): Less than $25,000	$25,000 to $49,999	$50,000 to $99,999	$100,000 to $149,999	$150,000 or More	Median Household Income: 2004	2009	2004 National Centile	2004 State Centile	2004 Home Value Base	2004 Home Value Distribution (%): Less than $50,000	$50,000 to $89,999	$90,000 to $174,999	$175,000 to $399,999	$400,000 or More	2004 Median Home Value
38850	HOULKA	14454	1282	39.2	35.6	21.5	3.2	0.6	31351	35536	16	56	1036	46.1	34.2	15.6	3.5	0.6	53922
38851	HOUSTON	14936	3599	42.8	32.7	20.1	3.6	0.8	29711	32834	12	43	2848	42.6	34.6	18.4	4.3	0.2	55850
38852	IUKA	18795	3896	39.2	35.4	18.6	4.3	2.6	31284	34516	16	55	3070	35.3	37.4	21.3	5.1	0.9	63322
38855	MANTACHIE	16033	2214	37.9	34.3	23.8	2.9	1.2	32629	36265	20	64	1821	33.8	35.8	22.4	7.9	0.2	69817
38856	MARIETTA	15258	389	39.1	34.2	21.1	5.4	0.3	32416	35387	19	62	333	38.1	32.7	24.3	1.8	3.0	62561
38857	MOOREVILLE	17537	448	27.5	37.5	25.7	7.1	2.2	38813	44693	42	85	359	24.8	33.4	32.0	8.4	1.4	76250
38858	NETTLETON	16828	2777	37.4	30.9	26.6	3.5	1.6	33179	37130	21	66	2189	42.4	30.0	22.6	4.3	0.6	60217
38859	NEW SITE	13236	334	40.7	39.2	17.1	3.0	0.0	31020	34751	15	52	305	46.6	32.1	18.7	2.6	0.0	53500
38860	OKOLONA	15568	2485	43.5	30.7	20.4	3.4	1.9	30290	33052	13	46	1872	42.0	34.8	17.1	4.4	1.8	59740
38862	PLANTERSVILLE	16088	1121	33.4	36.2	25.0	4.6	0.8	34201	38935	25	70	874	34.2	34.9	21.9	8.8	0.2	69195
38863	PONTOTOC	17750	6783	36.7	31.8	24.9	4.1	2.4	33641	37312	23	68	5185	27.4	36.6	28.0	6.4	1.6	73294
38864	RANDOLPH	17128	522	30.8	38.3	23.8	6.7	0.4	35349	40674	29	75	441	36.3	42.9	13.6	6.8	0.5	63688
38865	RIENZI	18501	1781	34.6	32.1	26.9	4.8	1.6	36229	40506	32	78	1496	35.4	32.3	22.3	7.7	2.3	65517
38866	SALTILLO	20432	3660	28.0	31.3	32.5	6.6	1.7	40402	46091	48	87	2819	22.4	29.8	37.5	8.4	1.9	87034
38868	SHANNON	17461	1879	32.9	33.3	28.8	4.0	1.0	36874	41667	35	80	1542	36.8	33.7	25.0	4.4	0.2	65689
38870	SMITHVILLE	16218	1129	35.1	35.7	24.5	4.2	0.6	35745	39506	31	77	947	35.2	30.2	26.3	6.6	1.8	67609
38871	THAXTON	18910	671	26.7	33.1	33.1	4.3	2.8	41841	46933	52	89	564	27.0	42.0	24.7	5.0	1.4	68116
38873	TISHOMINGO	17681	1055	41.1	33.2	20.2	3.3	2.2	30467	33456	13	48	897	35.5	37.0	25.4	2.1	0.0	62750
38876	TREMONT	15647	531	36.5	39.4	20.3	3.2	0.6	32343	35891	19	61	432	42.1	30.3	19.7	5.8	2.1	59189
38878	VARDAMAN	16888	1252	44.6	29.0	20.3	4.2	2.0	30051	33988	12	44	997	49.7	32.4	15.4	2.5	0.1	50376
38901	GRENADA	15924	6950	42.1	30.5	21.3	4.3	1.8	30099	33161	12	45	4658	22.3	38.7	28.9	9.3	0.8	78154
38912	AVALON	21752	370	27.0	27.8	36.2	7.3	1.6	47017	53734	66	94	314	29.6	39.8	28.7	1.0	1.0	66957
38913	BANNER	16548	275	39.3	33.5	20.7	5.8	0.7	35078	40381	28	74	233	38.6	35.2	20.2	5.6	0.4	57361
38914	BIG CREEK	19742	179	36.3	31.3	26.3	4.5	1.7	35281	41020	29	75	150	39.3	25.3	31.3	3.3	0.7	63529
38915	BRUCE	17571	1884	43.7	29.9	20.5	3.8	2.1	29767	33234	12	43	1415	42.9	30.6	21.5	3.9	1.1	56526
38916	CALHOUN CITY	16672	2157	45.6	29.3	20.6	3.3	1.3	27707	31228	8	30	1616	43.6	35.3	18.3	2.7	0.2	55389
38917	CARROLLTON	17588	1243	39.6	31.5	21.2	3.9	3.8	31024	35438	15	53	1001	42.1	28.2	17.7	11.0	1.1	58281
38920	CASCILLA	13317	834	43.9	30.8	21.6	3.4	0.4	28058	31150	9	32	689	49.5	38.5	9.1	2.0	0.9	50522
38921	CHARLESTON	12413	2541	51.3	29.2	15.9	2.6	0.9	24098	26383	4	10	1932	59.9	26.7	11.3	1.9	0.2	41724
38922	COFFEEVILLE	16626	1682	44.1	31.8	19.0	3.8	1.4	29212	31944	11	40	1369	49.6	31.7	13.3	4.9	0.5	50417
38923	COILA	16559	650	38.2	35.4	21.5	3.5	1.4	32207	37742	18	60	572	38.6	33.2	22.0	5.6	0.5	59028
38924	CRUGER	13190	369	55.8	27.4	11.4	3.0	2.4	20276	22502	2	4	282	59.2	29.1	8.5	2.8	0.4	41333
38925	DUCK HILL	15512	1240	40.7	33.1	21.2	3.7	1.3	32039	35743	18	60	1024	42.0	35.5	17.2	4.3	1.1	57810
38927	ENID	13206	391	38.9	40.7	17.7	2.1	0.8	28844	32883	10	38	327	45.0	29.1	16.5	9.5	0.0	57857
38929	GORE SPRINGS	14970	261	43.3	30.3	21.5	3.1	1.9	31188	34306	15	54	218	48.6	26.2	20.2	5.1	0.0	51875
38930	GREENWOOD	15626	10302	50.6	25.0	16.8	5.2	2.5	24524	27526	4	11	5598	33.4	36.0	22.7	6.7	1.3	65855
38940	HOLCOMB	15747	1156	35.0	38.4	21.3	4.3	1.0	32683	37022	20	64	954	36.3	31.2	22.0	8.6	1.9	65254
38941	ITTA BENA	12384	1782	53.7	25.7	14.0	3.8	2.9	22549	25354	3	7	1049	44.3	41.8	12.0	1.4	0.5	54161
38943	MC CARLEY	14199	425	44.0	29.2	23.5	2.4	0.9	28990	32521	10	39	374	41.7	31.8	15.2	11.2	0.0	61190
38944	MINTER CITY	14015	275	34.9	36.0	21.5	6.6	1.1	30906	37882	15	52	163	33.7	38.7	23.3	3.7	0.6	67045
38948	OAKLAND	16937	760	45.3	33.0	17.6	2.5	1.6	26798	30572	7	24	611	54.0	25.2	12.6	7.5	0.7	47216
38949	PARIS	18749	110	29.1	33.6	28.2	7.3	1.8	37810	45377	39	83	89	43.8	29.2	18.0	4.5	4.5	59167
38950	PHILIPP	13652	183	50.3	29.0	14.2	4.9	1.6	24754	26497	4	12	145	50.3	31.7	11.7	6.2	0.0	49865
38951	PITTSBORO	20148	389	37.3	34.5	22.4	3.9	2.1	32765	36893	20	65	317	50.2	26.8	18.3	3.8	1.0	49861
38952	SCHLATER	24473	244	45.5	25.0	20.9	6.2	2.5	26528	31315	6	23	143	52.5	28.7	13.3	5.6	0.0	46500
38953	SCOBEY	14721	131	42.8	37.4	14.5	3.1	2.3	27925	31001	9	32	106	41.5	31.1	17.9	5.7	3.8	61250
38954	SIDON	14243	794	45.6	29.7	20.2	3.0	1.5	27662	32078	8	30	559	46.0	29.3	17.2	6.6	0.9	53516
38961	TILLATOBA	15034	265	43.0	37.4	14.3	3.0	2.3	27732	31356	8	30	214	41.6	31.8	17.8	5.1	3.7	61176
38963	TUTWILER	12408	1437	53.3	28.0	13.7	2.9	2.2	22752	24955	3	8	887	61.9	25.9	9.1	2.3	0.8	42008
38964	VANCE	14880	41	46.3	24.4	24.4	2.4	2.4	27295	33630	8	28	30	56.7	23.3	13.3	3.3	3.3	43333
38965	WATER VALLEY	17974	3380	40.1	30.9	22.7	4.8	1.6	31225	34877	16	54	2600	40.1	30.4	21.1	7.1	1.3	61976
38967	WINONA	16524	2853	45.5	30.4	16.6	5.5	2.0	28841	32244	10	38	2061	33.8	40.4	21.2	3.4	1.1	59896
39038	BELZONI	11750	2398	56.0	23.9	16.6	2.0	1.5	21099	23378	2	5	1448	42.6	37.3	18.4	1.4	0.3	57329
39039	BENTON	18321	784	42.1	27.8	21.9	5.9	2.3	30392	34563	13	48	638	44.0	27.7	22.6	5.3	0.3	57451
39040	BENTONIA	15236	1318	35.7	33.2	26.3	4.1	0.6	33417	38351	22	67	1062	42.7	29.9	21.7	5.2	0.6	57156
39041	BOLTON	21558	1250	35.4	24.1	29.6	6.7	4.2	38928	43982	42	86	1027	33.7	31.9	22.6	10.8	1.0	66474
39042	BRANDON	25482	12293	18.1	28.3	37.4	11.8	4.4	53132	60744	77	98	9686	17.2	18.1	45.1	17.8	1.7	116005
39044	BRAXTON	17347	1336	36.2	29.5	25.9	6.1	2.3	35438	39373	29	76	1108	41.6	27.3	25.1	5.4	0.6	60658
39045	CAMDEN	13031	462	40.0	35.7	18.6	3.7	2.0	28706	33965	10	36	377	53.9	20.4	22.8	1.1	1.9	46778
39046	CANTON	15802	7477	40.5	27.0	22.9	6.5	3.2	32315	37967	19	61	4901	37.4	31.4	17.8	10.0	3.5	63843
39047	BRANDON	31069	11451	14.9	24.3	37.4	15.2	8.2	62516	69877	87	99	9474	7.5	14.6	50.5	24.1	3.4	134088
39051	CARTHAGE	15042	6757	42.3	32.1	19.5	4.7	1.5	30217	33586	13	46	5357	41.4	30.5	21.2	5.1	1.8	60415
39056	CLINTON	24623	9206	19.0	28.9	36.7	11.0	4.5	51808	60073	75	97	6867	9.2	22.7	52.1	14.7	1.3	108460
39057	CONEHATTA	14121	850	36.7	34.2	25.7	2.6	0.8	34925	39242	27	73	701	44.9	33.8	15.3	5.9	0.1	55000
39059	CRYSTAL SPRINGS	14334	4376	45.9	28.0	20.5	4.4	1.1	28149	31185	9	33	3332	38.0	33.6	19.8	7.9	0.6	59876
39063	DURANT	13632	1374	52.0	28.4	16.1	1.5	2.0	23624	26991	4	9	973	50.8	31.2	15.3	0.8	1.9	49400
39066	EDWARDS	15574	1577	40.3	29.1	23.7	4.4	2.4	31818	35235	17	58	1185	41.2	31.7	18.0	8.0	1.1	59766
39067	ETHEL	17604	941	43.8	30.8	18.3	4.6	2.6	29348	32906	11	41	778	46.0	30.2	17.7	3.3	2.7	54493
39069	FAYETTE	10382	2337	58.9	25.7	13.2	1.8	0.4	19088	21378	2	2	1824	51.4	36.4	10.5	1.6	0.1	48792
39071	FLORA	20878	1562	29.5	25.7	31.9	9.0	3.9	43504	50922	57	91	1261	21.8	33.2	21.0	21.9	2.1	84104
39073	FLORENCE	21064	6919	24.9	31.0	33.1	8.8	2.3	44246	49899	59	92	5711	28.2	23.6	39.1	8.4	0.8	87857
39074	FOREST	16153	5450	44.4	30.7	19.5	2.4	3.0	28782	32013	10	37	4215	52.2	27.4	15.0	4.5	0.9	47886
39078	GEORGETOWN	16313	373	47.2	29.2	18.2	3.2	2.1	26752	29699	7	24	300	52.7	24.7	18.7	3.3	0.7	46522
39079	GOODMAN	10648	532	57.3	24.1	13.9	3.2	1.5	19103	20584	2	2	301	62.5	26.6	9.0	1.0	1.0	37237
39082	HARRISVILLE	17212	476	34.0	31.3	26.3	8.4	0.0	36092	39548	32	77	422	48.6	24.2	21.6	5.7	0.0	53333
39083	HAZLEHURST	14327	4024	42.6	31.5	20.1	4.6	1.2	29257	32922	11	41	3038	41.0	31.8	19.7	7.2	0.3	61440
39086	HERMANVILLE	15196	950	47.5	29.2	15.8	5.2	2.4	26784	31201	7	24	761	57.0	22.2	14.9	4.9	1.1	43141
39088	HOLLY BLUFF	15497	57	43.9	31.6	21.1	1.8	1.8	30349	34074	13	47	37	40.5	24.3	27.0	8.1	0.0	58750
39090	KOSCIUSKO	14934	4889	48.8	28.0	17.6	4.2	1.4	25718	28503	5	18	3488	41.8	34.5	17.4	5.8	0.6	58107
39092	LAKE	14702	1189	40.9	32.2	22.5	2.2	2.3	29145	33116	11	40	990	50.1	30.3	13.8	5.1	0.7	49927
39094	LENA	14466	1301	45.3	30.1	18.5	5.5	0.6	27779	31042	8	31	1111	49.7	28.4	14.6	4.7	2.6	50467
39095	LEXINGTON	13349	2833	56.4	25.0	13.2	3.7	1.7	20080	22387	2	3	2132	51.8	27.1	16.1	4.1	0.9	48410
39096	LORMAN	12144	459	59.9	20.5	14.2	5.0	0.4	18097	19226	1	2	382	46.3	29.3	14.1	0.8	9.4	55833
39097	LOUISE	10683	470	55.3	28.7	11.9	2.1	1.9	20163	23189	2	4	352	65.6	28.4	6.0	0.0	0.0	30263
39108	MC COOL	19438	684	43.6	33.5	17.5	2.8	2.6	29412	32418	11	42	588	45.8	28.7	18.9	3.6	3.1	54717
39110	MADISON	35185	9728	7.3	17.0	38.4	23.2	14.1	81914	100317	96	100	9124	4.8	4.9	45.5	38.0	6.8	163818
39111	MAGEE	14866	4047	44.7	30.5	19.9	2.6	2.3	28575	31612	10	35	2984	40.8	31.6	20.1	7.0	0.4	63455
39113	MAYERSVILLE	12783	655	55.9	23.7	15.6	2.3	2.6	21513	24170	2	5	448	52.7	20.1	17.6	7.1	2.5	47000
39114	MENDENHALL	15397	3880	40.2	31.8	22.9	3.9	1.2	31953	35733	18	59	3062	39.4	30.8	24.2	4.8	0.8	63669
39116	MIZE	14646	1269	36.4	37.3	23.2	2.4	0.8	34069	38575	24	69	1071	39.7	36.3	20.5	2.0	1.5	63112
39117	MORTON	16166	3213	40.6	31.2	22.7	3.7	1.8	31672	34938	17	57	2513	46.0	34.5	15.9	3.1	0.6	54375
39119	MOUNT OLIVE	16564	1124	45.7	27.5	20.3	3.8	2.7	27885	31103	8	31	889	44.3	33.5	16.9	4.1	1.2	55101
39120	NATCHEZ	18177	13709	45.9	28.5	18.6	3.9	3.2	27776	31514	8	30	9621	32.2	35.0	23.2	7.3	2.4	67784
39140	NEWHEBRON	15660	609	37.8	33.7	23.3	3.6	1.6	31384	35912	16	56	502	43.4	39.6	11.2	4.8	1.0	54024
39144	PATTISON	12478	364	49.7	30.5	14.0	5.8	0.0	25151	29156	5	14	292	54.1	28.8	12.3	3.1	1.7	47778
	MISSISSIPPI	18480		36.7	30.0	24.5	5.9	2.8	34621	39377				29.7	30.4	28.7	9.7	1.6	75922
	UNITED STATES	25866		24.7	27.1	30.8	10.9	6.5	48124	56710				10.9	15.0	33.7	30.1	10.4	145905

ZIP CODE		FINANCIAL SERVICES				THE HOME						ENTERTAINMENT						PERSONAL			
						Home Improvements		Furnishings													
#	POST OFFICE NAME	Auto Loan	Home Loan	Invest-ments	Retire-ment Plans	Home Repair	Lawn & Garden	Comput-ers & Hard-ware	Major Appli-ances	TV, Radio, Sound Equip-ment	Furni-ture	Dine out/ Carry out	Sports Equip-ment	Fees & Tickets	Toys & Games	Travel	Cable TV	Apparel & Services	Auto Repairs	Health Insur-ance	Pets & Supplies
38850	HOULKA	72	48	22	42	55	63	47	59	56	48	66	70	40	63	48	61	60	58	72	83
38851	HOUSTON	71	49	26	43	55	63	48	58	56	48	67	70	41	63	48	60	61	58	70	81
38852	IUKA	76	53	29	48	60	70	54	64	63	53	74	75	47	70	54	67	67	64	78	87
38855	MANTACHIE	75	50	23	44	57	66	49	61	59	50	69	73	41	65	50	63	63	60	75	86
38856	MARIETTA	73	49	22	42	55	64	47	59	57	48	67	70	40	63	48	61	61	58	73	84
38857	MOOREVILLE	92	63	30	55	71	81	60	75	72	62	85	90	52	81	62	78	78	74	92	106
38858	NETTLETON	80	54	24	46	61	70	52	65	63	53	74	78	44	70	53	68	67	64	80	92
38859	NEW SITE	64	43	19	37	49	56	41	52	50	42	59	62	35	55	42	54	53	51	64	73
38860	OKOLONA	71	50	30	44	55	63	50	59	59	51	70	71	44	67	51	63	65	59	71	81
38862	PLANTERSVILLE	77	54	29	48	60	69	53	64	62	54	73	76	46	69	53	65	67	63	76	88
38863	PONTOTOC	82	58	32	53	65	74	58	69	67	58	79	81	51	76	58	71	73	68	82	93
38864	RANDOLPH	84	56	26	49	64	73	54	68	66	55	77	81	46	73	55	71	70	67	84	97
38865	RIENZI	85	60	30	52	67	76	57	70	67	58	80	84	50	76	58	72	73	69	85	98
38866	SALTILLO	82	68	51	66	73	81	67	74	73	67	88	87	64	87	68	74	82	73	82	93
38868	SHANNON	82	58	31	52	64	73	56	68	65	57	77	81	49	73	57	69	71	67	80	93
38870	SMITHVILLE	75	52	25	45	58	66	50	61	59	50	70	73	43	66	50	63	63	61	75	86
38871	THAXTON	85	71	50	66	76	83	66	75	72	66	87	90	63	87	68	75	82	73	84	99
38873	TISHOMINGO	79	53	24	46	60	69	51	64	62	52	72	76	43	68	52	66	66	63	79	91
38876	TREMONT	72	48	22	41	54	63	46	58	56	47	66	69	39	62	47	60	60	57	71	82
38878	VARDAMAN	81	54	25	47	61	71	52	65	63	53	74	78	44	70	53	68	67	65	81	93
38901	GRENADA	67	51	37	46	54	63	52	59	60	52	71	67	48	67	52	63	66	59	69	75
38912	AVALON	83	73	55	69	77	83	67	75	72	67	87	89	66	89	69	74	83	73	81	97
38913	BANNER	77	52	23	45	59	68	50	63	60	51	71	75	43	67	51	65	64	62	77	89
38914	BIG CREEK	84	57	26	49	64	74	55	68	66	56	77	82	46	73	56	71	70	68	84	97
38915	BRUCE	76	52	29	45	58	67	52	62	62	53	73	73	45	68	52	67	67	62	76	86
38916	CALHOUN CITY	71	50	29	44	55	63	50	59	59	50	70	70	44	66	50	62	64	59	71	80
38917	CARROLLTON	80	56	30	51	63	73	57	68	67	57	79	79	50	74	58	72	72	68	83	91
38920	CASCILLA	67	45	20	39	51	58	43	54	52	44	61	65	37	58	44	56	56	54	67	77
38921	CHARLESTON	60	41	22	36	46	54	41	50	49	42	58	59	36	54	41	53	53	50	61	69
38922	COFFEEVILLE	73	49	22	42	55	64	47	59	57	48	67	71	40	63	48	61	61	58	73	84
38923	COILA	83	56	25	48	63	73	54	67	65	55	76	81	46	72	55	70	69	67	83	96
38924	CRUGER	62	43	28	38	47	56	44	52	52	45	62	60	39	57	44	56	57	52	63	70
38925	DUCK HILL	73	49	22	42	55	64	47	59	57	48	67	70	40	63	48	61	61	58	73	84
38927	ENID	65	43	20	37	49	57	42	52	51	43	59	63	36	56	43	54	54	52	64	74
38929	GORE SPRINGS	74	50	23	43	56	65	48	60	58	49	68	72	41	64	49	62	62	59	74	85
38930	GREENWOOD	58	51	57	49	51	59	56	56	60	56	74	63	55	71	55	62	71	57	61	64
38940	HOLCOMB	76	51	23	44	58	67	49	62	59	50	70	74	42	66	50	64	63	61	76	87
38941	ITTA BENA	57	46	44	41	46	55	51	53	58	51	70	59	48	64	49	61	66	54	62	63
38943	MC CARLEY	67	45	20	39	51	59	44	54	53	44	62	65	37	58	44	57	56	54	67	77
38944	MINTER CITY	80	53	24	46	61	70	52	65	62	53	73	77	44	69	52	67	66	64	80	92
38948	OAKLAND	74	52	27	45	59	67	50	62	59	50	69	73	43	66	51	63	63	61	75	87
38949	PARIS	80	64	43	61	71	77	61	71	67	61	80	85	57	81	63	70	75	69	80	95
38950	PHILIPP	66	44	20	38	50	58	43	53	51	43	60	64	36	57	43	55	55	53	66	76
38951	PITTSBORO	96	64	29	55	73	84	62	78	75	63	88	93	53	83	63	81	80	77	96	110
38952	SCHLATER	5	4	3	3	4	4	4	4	4	4	5	5	3	5	4	4	5	4	5	5
38953	SCOBEY	68	45	21	39	51	59	44	55	53	45	62	65	37	59	45	57	56	54	67	78
38954	SIDON	71	48	22	41	54	62	46	58	56	47	66	69	40	62	47	60	60	57	71	81
38961	TILLATOBA	68	45	21	39	51	59	44	55	53	45	62	65	37	59	45	57	56	54	67	78
38963	TUTWILER	57	44	40	38	45	54	48	52	56	49	66	57	45	60	47	60	63	53	61	63
38964	VANCE	71	48	22	41	54	62	46	57	55	47	65	69	39	62	47	60	59	57	71	82
38965	WATER VALLEY	76	57	37	52	62	71	57	66	65	57	77	78	51	75	57	68	72	66	77	87
38967	WINONA	71	51	35	46	55	66	53	61	63	54	74	70	48	69	53	67	69	62	74	80
39038	BELZONI	54	42	36	39	44	53	46	50	52	46	62	55	43	57	45	55	58	50	58	60
39039	BENTON	86	62	33	55	68	77	60	72	69	61	82	85	52	78	60	73	75	71	85	99
39040	BENTONIA	78	53	24	45	59	68	51	63	61	52	72	76	43	68	52	66	65	63	78	90
39041	BOLTON	97	82	66	76	86	97	79	88	87	81	106	101	77	103	81	91	100	87	99	112
39042	BRANDON	94	101	98	99	100	103	94	97	92	95	114	113	96	116	95	90	112	95	92	110
39044	BRAXTON	75	64	47	61	66	71	62	68	64	63	78	79	57	74	61	64	75	67	70	83
39045	CAMDEN	67	49	34	42	52	62	50	58	59	51	70	66	45	64	50	63	65	58	70	76
39046	CANTON	71	63	62	58	64	72	64	67	70	65	85	76	63	83	64	72	82	67	73	80
39047	BRANDON	109	121	127	124	117	118	114	112	107	116	135	132	117	136	113	102	134	111	101	125
39051	CARTHAGE	72	50	27	45	56	65	50	60	59	51	70	71	44	66	51	63	64	60	73	83
39056	CLINTON	93	93	98	95	92	98	95	94	93	95	116	110	95	115	93	90	113	95	89	105
39057	CONEHATTA	74	50	23	43	56	65	48	60	58	49	68	72	41	64	49	63	62	60	74	85
39059	CRYSTAL SPRINGS	64	48	34	44	52	60	49	56	56	50	67	65	44	63	49	59	62	56	65	73
39063	DURANT	60	44	34	40	47	56	48	53	55	48	66	59	43	60	47	59	61	53	63	66
39066	EDWARDS	75	57	44	51	61	70	58	65	67	59	81	76	54	78	58	70	76	66	76	86
39067	ETHEL	82	55	25	48	62	72	53	67	64	54	75	80	45	71	54	69	69	66	82	94
39069	FAYETTE	42	33	34	30	33	41	37	39	43	38	52	42	36	46	36	47	49	40	46	46
39071	FLORA	93	79	62	79	83	94	81	87	86	80	105	99	78	104	81	87	98	85	94	102
39073	FLORENCE	90	81	63	78	83	88	77	83	79	78	97	97	74	94	77	79	93	82	85	101
39074	FOREST	78	56	34	51	62	70	56	66	65	57	77	78	50	74	56	69	71	66	78	89
39078	GEORGETOWN	80	53	24	46	60	69	51	64	62	52	73	77	44	69	52	67	66	64	79	91
39079	GOODMAN	48	37	41	33	37	44	42	43	48	43	59	50	40	56	41	50	56	45	49	53
39082	HARRISVILLE	85	57	26	49	64	74	55	68	66	56	78	82	47	73	56	71	71	68	84	97
39083	HAZLEHURST	66	47	31	42	51	60	49	56	57	49	68	65	43	63	49	61	62	56	68	74
39086	HERMANVILLE	75	51	24	44	57	66	49	61	59	50	70	73	42	66	50	64	64	61	75	86
39088	HOLLY BLUFF	75	50	23	43	57	65	48	60	58	49	68	72	41	65	49	63	62	60	74	86
39090	KOSCIUSKO	59	46	37	43	49	57	49	54	55	48	65	61	45	62	49	57	61	54	62	66
39092	LAKE	72	52	27	46	57	64	50	60	58	51	69	71	43	65	50	61	63	60	71	82
39094	LENA	71	48	22	41	54	62	46	58	56	47	66	69	39	62	47	60	60	57	71	82
39095	LEXINGTON	56	43	40	39	44	54	48	51	55	48	66	56	45	59	47	59	62	52	61	62
39096	LORMAN	47	37	39	33	37	46	42	44	48	43	58	47	40	52	41	52	55	45	52	51
39097	LOUISE	46	36	37	32	36	44	40	42	47	42	56	45	39	50	39	50	54	43	50	49
39108	MC COOL	88	59	27	51	67	77	57	71	69	58	81	85	48	76	58	74	73	70	88	101
39110	MADISON	134	160	166	165	154	153	143	141	131	147	167	165	152	171	143	125	166	137	123	155
39111	MAGEE	65	49	34	45	53	61	50	57	56	50	67	66	45	64	50	59	62	57	65	73
39113	MAYERSVILLE	61	44	30	38	47	56	45	52	54	46	64	60	41	58	45	57	59	53	63	69
39114	MENDENHALL	69	53	36	48	57	65	53	60	60	53	72	70	48	69	53	63	67	60	70	78
39116	MIZE	73	49	22	42	55	64	47	59	57	48	67	71	40	63	48	61	61	59	73	84
39117	MORTON	75	56	38	51	61	69	56	64	63	56	75	77	50	72	56	66	70	64	75	85
39119	MOUNT OLIVE	80	54	24	46	61	70	52	65	63	53	74	78	44	70	53	68	67	64	80	92
39120	NATCHEZ	69	56	47	52	59	68	58	63	65	58	78	72	55	75	58	69	74	64	73	78
39140	NEWHEBRON	68	54	38	52	58	66	55	61	60	54	72	70	51	71	55	62	67	60	68	76
39144	PATTISON	51	40	38	35	40	49	44	47	51	45	61	51	41	55	43	55	58	48	56	56
	MISSISSIPPI	76	64	54	60	66	74	64	70	70	65	85	81	61	82	64	71	80	70	76	86
	UNITED STATES	100	100	100	100	100	100	100	100	100	100	100	100	100	100	100	100	100	100	100	100

# POST OFFICE NAME	COUNTY FIPS CODE	POPULATION 2000	2004	2009	2000-2004 ANNUAL RATE % Rate	State Centile	HOUSEHOLDS 2000	2004	2009	% Annual Rate 2000-2004	2004 Average HH Size	FAMILIES 2000	2004	% Annual Rate 2000-2004
39145 PELAHATCHIE	121	5464	5700	6042	1.0	76	1963	2096	2274	1.6	2.71	1523	1615	1.4
39146 PICKENS	051	3144	3086	3068	-0.4	21	1049	1052	1066	0.1	2.93	777	771	-0.2
39149 PINOLA	127	1785	1848	1910	0.8	72	644	684	724	1.4	2.70	479	503	1.2
39150 PORT GIBSON	021	8744	9121	9582	1.0	76	2577	2761	2986	1.6	2.65	1758	1862	1.4
39152 PULASKI	123	564	615	654	2.1	90	213	237	256	2.5	2.59	154	169	2.2
39153 RALEIGH	129	8870	8904	8891	0.1	45	3335	3429	3501	0.7	2.56	2521	2569	0.4
39154 RAYMOND	049	9873	10290	10434	1.0	75	3085	3314	3432	1.7	2.60	2395	2549	1.5
39156 REDWOOD	149	486	492	490	0.3	54	191	201	206	1.2	2.45	144	149	0.8
39157 RIDGELAND	089	21396	23667	26048	2.4	92	9496	10604	11826	2.6	2.15	5191	5751	2.4
39159 ROLLING FORK	125	4177	4062	3938	-0.7	13	1405	1415	1422	0.2	2.80	1024	1021	-0.1
39160 SALLIS	007	2851	2826	2814	-0.2	30	1004	1020	1029	0.4	2.77	762	768	0.2
39162 SATARTIA	163	544	577	589	1.4	83	187	204	212	2.1	2.83	141	152	1.8
39166 SILVER CITY	053	961	914	884	-1.2	3	323	316	311	-0.5	2.89	219	211	-0.9
39168 TAYLORSVILLE	129	4626	4753	4793	0.6	65	1657	1737	1787	1.1	2.73	1253	1301	0.9
39169 TCHULA	051	3767	3624	3528	-0.9	7	1168	1148	1139	-0.4	3.15	866	844	-0.6
39170 TERRY	049	7008	7059	7029	0.2	50	2507	2588	2628	0.8	2.72	2017	2062	0.5
39175 UTICA	049	5117	5385	5481	1.2	81	1661	1779	1840	1.6	2.96	1252	1328	1.4
39176 VAIDEN	015	2354	2427	2453	0.7	68	921	979	1018	1.5	2.39	648	682	1.2
39177 VALLEY PARK	055	198	189	180	-1.1	4	71	69	68	-0.7	2.74	49	48	-0.5
39179 VAUGHAN	163	1368	1372	1366	0.1	43	441	453	459	0.6	3.03	331	338	0.5
39180 VICKSBURG	149	33322	33173	32895	-0.1	34	12684	12889	13032	0.4	2.54	8848	8906	0.2
39183 VICKSBURG	149	15581	15212	14925	-0.6	16	5801	5804	5818	0.0	2.59	4168	4122	-0.3
39189 WALNUT GROVE	079	1159	1341	1456	3.5	96	462	546	602	4.0	2.44	335	392	3.8
39191 WESSON	029	7714	8041	8216	1.0	75	2599	2785	2902	1.6	2.69	1989	2109	1.4
39192 WEST	007	2172	2197	2195	0.3	53	819	846	860	0.8	2.57	606	620	0.5
39194 YAZOO CITY	163	20508	20638	20664	0.2	48	6466	6560	6638	0.3	2.79	4610	4632	0.1
39201 JACKSON	049	1097	1064	1048	-0.7	10	98	90	88	-2.0	3.34	32	29	-2.3
39202 JACKSON	049	9712	9224	8960	-1.2	3	4081	3887	3804	-1.1	1.97	1610	1483	-1.9
39203 JACKSON	049	9575	9079	8903	-1.2	2	2786	2672	2660	-1.0	2.78	1727	1628	-1.4
39204 JACKSON	049	19542	19017	18688	-0.6	13	7358	7199	7144	-0.5	2.58	4676	4496	-0.9
39206 JACKSON	049	26659	26225	25839	-0.4	21	9909	9812	9761	-0.2	2.61	6563	6391	-0.6
39208 PEARL	121	28451	29422	31378	0.8	71	9488	10248	11386	1.8	2.45	6681	7104	1.5
39209 JACKSON	049	34712	33278	32501	-1.0	5	11550	11257	11174	-0.6	2.94	8440	8133	-0.9
39211 JACKSON	049	24316	25351	25761	1.0	76	10713	11431	11842	1.5	2.18	6670	7008	1.2
39212 JACKSON	049	31613	31919	31881	0.2	52	11473	11751	11911	0.6	2.71	8516	8653	0.4
39213 JACKSON	049	27913	26699	25999	-1.0	5	10002	9795	9722	-0.5	2.68	6938	6718	-0.8
39216 JACKSON	049	3929	3971	3973	0.3	52	1649	1686	1709	0.5	2.04	828	827	0.0
39218 RICHLAND	121	5780	6151	6589	1.5	85	2175	2372	2603	2.1	2.59	1625	1758	1.9
39232 FLOWOOD	121	2753	3851	4817	8.2	100	1304	1806	2282	8.0	2.12	727	997	7.7
39272 BYRAM	049	7417	8419	8911	3.0	94	2744	3208	3476	3.7	2.62	2191	2535	3.5
39301 MERIDIAN	075	27417	26727	26307	-0.6	15	10783	10765	10811	0.0	2.41	7106	6988	-0.4
39305 MERIDIAN	075	19332	19912	20077	0.7	68	7759	8169	8397	1.2	2.33	5337	5561	1.0
39307 MERIDIAN	075	18203	17477	17063	-1.0	6	6762	6572	6507	-0.7	2.43	4541	4359	-1.0
39309 MERIDIAN	075	658	608	585	-1.8	1	13	13	13	0.0	2.54	10	10	0.0
39320 BAILEY	075	1393	1346	1314	-0.8	8	526	519	516	-0.3	2.59	394	384	-0.6
39322 BUCKATUNNA	153	1989	2079	2135	1.1	78	703	753	790	1.6	2.75	549	582	1.4
39323 CHUNKY	101	885	899	898	0.4	56	339	351	357	0.8	2.56	256	263	0.6
39325 COLLINSVILLE	075	4655	5073	5243	2.0	90	1756	1950	2050	2.5	2.60	1375	1512	2.3
39326 DALEVILLE	075	450	532	573	4.0	98	164	198	217	4.5	2.69	127	153	4.5
39327 DECATUR	101	4396	4513	4541	0.6	65	1571	1655	1702	1.2	2.47	1148	1197	1.0
39328 DE KALB	069	5040	5038	5031	0.0	37	1956	2007	2059	0.6	2.47	1388	1409	0.4
39330 ENTERPRISE	023	2723	2617	2597	-0.9	6	1065	1044	1059	-0.5	2.51	763	742	-0.7
39332 HICKORY	101	1732	1736	1722	0.1	42	683	699	708	0.7	2.47	515	522	0.3
39335 LAUDERDALE	075	3173	3188	3167	0.1	46	1250	1293	1315	0.8	2.42	928	948	0.5
39336 LAWRENCE	101	378	379	375	0.1	42	137	141	143	0.7	2.69	102	104	0.5
39337 LITTLE ROCK	101	1525	1503	1478	-0.3	24	609	618	623	0.4	2.43	456	459	0.2
39338 LOUIN	061	2625	2712	2829	0.8	70	983	1044	1118	1.4	2.59	702	739	1.2
39339 LOUISVILLE	159	16713	16681	16605	-0.1	36	6248	6393	6518	0.5	2.53	4492	4551	0.3
39341 MACON	103	6641	6841	7094	0.7	68	2390	2540	2719	1.4	2.63	1687	1776	1.2
39342 MARION	075	1230	1201	1177	-0.6	16	431	430	431	-0.1	2.73	307	304	-0.2
39345 NEWTON	101	7074	6890	6762	-0.6	14	2714	2704	2711	-0.1	2.47	1937	1912	-0.3
39346 NOXAPATER	159	2333	2348	2345	0.2	48	907	936	955	0.7	2.51	665	679	0.5
39347 PACHUTA	023	928	924	934	-0.1	34	358	367	381	0.6	2.52	256	260	0.4
39348 PAULDING	061	513	535	562	1.0	76	184	198	214	1.7	2.70	137	145	1.3
39350 PHILADELPHIA	099	28210	28667	29181	0.4	57	10465	10908	11375	1.0	2.57	7590	7834	0.8
39352 PORTERVILLE	069	1052	1052	1050	0.0	39	388	401	412	0.8	2.62	276	282	0.5
39354 PRESTON	069	2413	2475	2502	0.6	64	933	984	1022	1.3	2.52	685	715	1.0
39355 QUITMAN	023	8042	8150	8202	0.3	54	3108	3235	3340	1.0	2.46	2252	2320	0.7
39356 ROSE HILL	061	1562	1630	1716	1.0	77	614	657	709	1.6	2.48	436	462	1.4
39358 SCOOBA	069	2193	2164	2149	-0.3	25	742	754	769	0.4	2.46	529	532	0.1
39359 SEBASTOPOL	123	233	239	246	0.6	64	107	111	116	0.9	2.15	76	78	0.6
39360 SHUBUTA	023	4376	4235	4188	-0.8	9	1630	1620	1641	-0.1	2.61	1178	1158	-0.4
39361 SHUQUALAK	103	1313	1377	1443	1.1	80	491	533	577	2.0	2.58	360	387	1.7
39362 STATE LINE	041	2848	2967	3017	1.0	75	993	1068	1116	1.7	2.73	759	808	1.5
39363 STONEWALL	023	1849	1931	1966	1.0	77	737	786	819	1.5	2.46	534	564	1.3
39364 TOOMSUBA	075	2703	2582	2508	-1.1	4	983	966	962	-0.4	2.65	755	736	-0.6
39365 UNION	101	3898	3845	3799	-0.3	24	1495	1502	1513	0.1	2.48	1063	1056	-0.2
39366 VOSSBURG	061	1619	1672	1746	0.8	69	555	593	638	1.6	2.82	427	452	1.4
39367 WAYNESBORO	153	15929	16040	16194	0.2	48	5953	6152	6360	0.8	2.58	4383	4488	0.6
39401 HATTIESBURG	035	40948	41787	42716	0.5	61	16185	16861	17572	1.0	2.35	9392	9648	0.6
39402 HATTIESBURG	073	27728	28938	30049	1.0	77	10821	11506	12137	1.5	2.49	7503	7919	1.3
39406 HATTIESBURG	035	4046	4178	4260	0.8	69	490	570	625	3.6	2.00	177	200	2.9
39421 BASSFIELD	065	4151	4108	4041	-0.2	28	1458	1493	1513	0.6	2.73	1098	1115	0.3
39422 BAY SPRINGS	061	6189	6444	6767	1.0	74	2271	2425	2613	1.6	2.59	1657	1753	1.3
39423 BEAUMONT	111	2894	2802	2776	-0.8	10	1065	1057	1065	-0.2	2.65	805	792	-0.4
39425 BROOKLYN	035	953	955	960	0.1	42	356	364	373	0.5	2.62	275	278	0.3
39426 CARRIERE	109	13504	14834	16137	2.2	91	4956	5575	6194	2.8	2.66	3918	4366	2.6
39427 CARSON	065	1341	1312	1286	-0.5	18	515	522	528	0.3	2.51	360	361	0.1
39428 COLLINS	031	11262	11395	11688	0.3	53	4044	4205	4424	0.9	2.65	2994	3083	0.7
39429 COLUMBIA	091	17415	17045	16562	-0.5	18	6359	6347	6283	0.0	2.54	4598	4548	-0.3
39437 ELLISVILLE	067	11963	12003	11934	0.1	44	4136	4241	4297	0.6	2.57	3074	3127	0.4
39439 HEIDELBERG	061	4872	4948	5079	0.4	55	1757	1839	1937	1.1	2.69	1322	1370	0.8
39440 LAUREL	067	20975	20286	19788	-0.8	9	8033	7885	7813	-0.4	2.51	5231	5060	-0.8
39443 LAUREL	067	22193	21570	21129	-0.7	12	8499	8467	8476	-0.1	2.54	6474	6384	-0.3
39451 LEAKESVILLE	041	7268	7161	7053	-0.4	23	1967	1986	2001	0.2	2.54	1458	1459	0.0
MISSISSIPPI					0.6					1.2	2.57			0.9
UNITED STATES					1.2					1.3	2.58			1.1

#	POST OFFICE NAME	RACE (%) White 2000	White 2004	Black 2000	Black 2004	Asian/Pacific 2000	Asian/Pacific 2004	% Hispanic Origin 2000	% Hispanic Origin 2004	2004 AGE DISTRIBUTION (%) 0-4	5-9	10-14	15-19	20-24	25-44	45-64	65-84	85+	18+	MEDIAN AGE 2004	% 2004 Males	% 2004 Females
39145	PELAHATCHIE	78.0	76.9	20.7	21.6	0.2	0.3	2.1	2.4	7.9	7.5	6.8	6.4	7.0	28.4	24.8	10.2	1.0	74.1	35.6	49.8	50.3
39146	PICKENS	14.9	13.6	84.5	85.9	0.2	0.2	1.0	0.9	8.9	8.4	8.9	8.1	7.8	25.9	20.6	10.0	1.5	68.9	31.2	47.7	52.3
39149	PINOLA	47.3	45.7	52.0	53.5	0.1	0.2	0.5	0.5	7.6	7.7	8.6	7.0	7.1	27.1	22.9	10.4	1.6	71.8	34.0	48.2	51.8
39150	PORT GIBSON	12.4	11.9	86.9	87.2	0.2	0.2	0.8	0.8	6.2	6.5	7.0	12.4	16.5	23.0	18.7	7.8	1.8	76.2	25.9	45.9	54.1
39152	PULASKI	73.8	72.2	25.4	26.7	0.0	0.0	2.5	2.9	5.5	5.9	7.8	6.7	6.5	27.8	25.7	12.5	1.6	76.9	38.6	48.6	51.4
39153	RALEIGH	77.8	77.3	21.3	21.8	0.2	0.2	0.6	0.6	7.4	7.1	7.4	7.0	6.5	26.6	23.6	12.7	1.9	73.9	36.4	48.9	51.1
39154	RAYMOND	66.6	62.5	32.5	36.5	0.2	0.3	0.7	0.9	5.5	5.2	5.4	12.3	10.4	25.5	23.4	10.6	1.7	77.4	34.0	51.3	48.7
39156	REDWOOD	85.2	82.9	13.2	15.2	0.6	0.8	0.8	0.6	5.7	6.1	6.3	6.1	5.9	26.4	31.1	11.6	0.8	78.3	41.0	50.0	50.0
39157	RIDGELAND	73.3	70.3	22.4	24.9	2.8	3.3	1.4	1.6	6.9	6.7	6.1	6.7	8.6	36.0	20.7	6.6	1.8	77.0	33.1	46.9	53.1
39159	ROLLING FORK	30.6	29.4	68.1	69.2	0.3	0.3	0.9	0.9	8.6	8.6	8.7	7.6	7.8	23.7	23.2	9.6	2.3	69.3	32.0	47.1	53.0
39160	SALLIS	40.0	39.1	59.4	60.3	0.0	0.0	1.2	1.2	7.5	7.2	7.9	7.5	7.5	26.6	23.0	11.0	1.8	73.0	34.3	48.5	51.5
39162	SATARTIA	80.0	78.0	18.9	20.8	0.0	0.0	0.6	0.7	7.5	7.3	6.6	5.6	6.2	26.3	26.3	12.8	1.4	75.2	38.8	50.1	49.9
39166	SILVER CITY	27.1	25.6	72.1	73.4	0.1	0.1	1.0	1.1	6.1	6.1	9.0	9.7	7.9	23.1	24.0	12.3	1.9	72.8	35.9	48.3	51.8
39168	TAYLORSVILLE	55.9	53.8	43.2	45.3	0.0	0.0	0.6	0.6	6.8	6.8	8.1	7.5	7.7	26.3	23.6	11.9	1.2	73.8	35.8	49.0	51.0
39169	TCHULA	8.0	7.3	91.3	91.8	0.0	0.0	0.4	0.4	10.2	9.1	10.6	9.2	10.0	23.9	18.4	7.6	1.0	64.9	25.7	45.1	54.9
39170	TERRY	63.7	59.9	35.6	39.2	0.2	0.2	0.5	0.6	6.0	6.4	6.8	6.2	6.2	25.8	29.4	12.1	1.2	77.2	40.7	48.7	51.4
39175	UTICA	39.6	35.7	59.2	63.0	0.1	0.1	1.4	1.5	7.1	7.5	7.6	7.6	8.1	25.5	23.6	11.2	1.8	73.6	34.3	49.6	50.4
39176	VAIDEN	44.4	43.5	54.6	55.6	0.1	0.1	0.8	0.8	5.2	6.6	6.8	7.5	7.6	26.4	25.3	12.7	1.9	77.3	37.8	50.2	49.8
39177	VALLEY PARK	50.5	50.3	49.0	49.2	0.0	0.0	0.5	0.5	6.9	7.4	7.9	5.8	4.8	24.3	28.0	13.2	1.6	73.5	40.2	46.0	54.0
39179	VAUGHAN	38.8	36.5	60.6	62.8	0.0	0.0	1.1	1.0	7.6	6.6	8.2	8.2	6.9	25.9	22.3	11.7	2.6	72.3	35.8	49.4	50.6
39180	VICKSBURG	57.0	54.8	41.1	42.9	0.7	0.9	1.2	1.3	7.8	7.4	7.8	6.9	7.1	27.2	24.0	10.2	1.8	72.9	35.0	46.7	53.3
39183	VICKSBURG	49.3	49.0	49.1	49.1	0.4	0.5	0.7	0.8	7.5	7.6	8.2	7.3	7.1	26.1	25.5	9.5	1.2	72.3	34.8	47.6	52.4
39189	WALNUT GROVE	58.7	57.0	33.2	33.9	0.0	0.1	1.3	1.6	7.2	7.2	7.8	7.2	6.6	26.0	25.1	11.3	1.6	73.3	36.3	48.2	51.8
39191	WESSON	69.4	67.5	29.4	31.1	0.1	0.2	0.9	1.0	6.5	6.7	6.8	9.5	9.3	26.2	23.8	10.2	1.1	76.2	33.6	49.3	50.7
39192	WEST	53.9	52.7	44.3	45.3	0.1	0.1	1.5	1.4	7.1	7.4	8.1	7.8	6.1	25.4	22.8	13.4	2.1	72.5	36.1	47.9	52.1
39194	YAZOO CITY	40.8	40.0	57.8	58.4	0.5	0.6	5.2	6.0	7.8	7.5	7.9	7.4	7.3	29.2	21.3	9.7	1.8	72.2	33.3	51.8	48.2
39201	JACKSON	17.0	14.3	81.0	83.5	0.2	0.2	1.0	1.0	1.9	1.6	1.6	10.2	21.0	44.6	15.2	3.6	0.3	91.3	29.8	77.9	22.1
39202	JACKSON	49.2	47.3	48.7	50.3	0.7	0.9	0.9	1.0	5.8	5.1	5.2	9.7	14.5	31.5	19.6	6.6	2.1	80.6	29.9	49.7	50.3
39203	JACKSON	2.3	1.9	96.8	97.0	0.1	0.1	1.2	1.1	7.4	7.0	6.7	11.7	15.0	24.2	18.8	7.8	1.4	75.3	26.7	47.4	52.6
39204	JACKSON	25.3	22.4	72.9	75.6	0.6	0.7	0.7	0.7	9.6	8.5	8.3	7.6	9.5	29.4	17.0	8.3	1.8	69.2	29.1	46.5	53.6
39206	JACKSON	14.5	12.9	83.7	85.1	0.7	0.8	0.7	0.7	7.7	7.2	7.6	7.7	9.3	29.5	22.5	7.0	1.5	73.1	31.1	45.7	54.3
39208	PEARL	75.4	74.3	22.3	23.0	0.7	0.9	1.8	2.1	6.5	6.1	6.0	6.4	8.2	33.1	22.4	10.0	1.3	77.8	35.3	49.3	50.7
39209	JACKSON	10.1	9.6	88.8	89.3	0.1	0.1	0.9	0.9	9.5	9.5	9.9	8.9	8.3	27.4	19.5	6.3	0.8	65.7	27.7	45.8	54.2
39211	JACKSON	80.8	78.2	16.7	18.8	1.5	1.9	1.0	1.1	5.6	5.9	6.0	5.3	5.0	27.9	26.0	15.7	2.6	79.2	40.9	47.0	53.0
39212	JACKSON	43.8	39.6	54.7	58.7	0.5	0.5	0.7	0.8	8.4	8.0	8.4	7.5	7.3	31.1	20.4	8.0	0.9	70.6	31.9	47.5	52.5
39213	JACKSON	2.1	1.9	97.3	97.4	0.2	0.2	0.5	0.5	7.4	7.6	8.2	7.5	7.6	24.9	23.3	11.6	2.0	72.3	34.4	45.3	54.7
39216	JACKSON	61.0	59.1	35.5	36.4	2.6	3.3	0.4	0.5	5.8	5.4	5.4	4.9	6.5	31.6	20.4	15.2	4.9	80.4	38.2	47.3	52.7
39218	RICHLAND	89.6	88.4	7.7	8.4	1.5	1.8	0.9	1.1	8.8	8.0	6.8	6.1	7.0	32.8	21.5	8.3	0.7	72.8	33.0	49.6	50.4
39232	FLOWOOD	82.2	79.1	14.9	17.5	1.3	1.5	1.8	2.2	7.8	6.8	5.8	5.4	7.4	40.5	19.1	6.2	1.1	76.4	32.0	46.6	53.4
39272	BYRAM	83.9	80.8	14.7	17.3	0.6	0.7	0.7	0.9	7.7	7.3	6.8	6.3	6.6	33.2	23.5	8.3	0.5	74.5	34.5	48.0	52.0
39301	MERIDIAN	49.9	48.9	48.8	49.6	0.4	0.4	1.0	1.1	7.8	7.4	7.5	6.8	7.4	27.1	22.4	11.3	2.3	73.2	34.5	46.9	53.1
39305	MERIDIAN	79.9	77.6	17.9	19.8	0.9	1.1	1.5	1.6	6.4	6.3	6.8	6.7	6.8	26.9	24.0	13.1	3.2	76.9	38.0	47.8	52.2
39307	MERIDIAN	46.9	44.6	51.4	53.5	0.5	0.6	1.0	1.1	7.1	6.8	6.9	7.8	7.4	27.0	22.0	12.9	2.1	74.7	35.7	48.3	51.8
39309	MERIDIAN	61.1	56.9	28.7	31.6	2.7	3.1	7.3	8.2	11.4	8.2	6.9	14.0	17.1	36.5	4.8	1.2	0.0	71.2	22.8	56.7	43.3
39320	BAILEY	78.8	76.2	20.2	22.8	0.1	0.1	0.7	0.7	6.2	6.5	7.4	6.6	6.8	27.6	27.3	10.6	1.0	76.1	37.4	48.5	51.5
39322	BUCKATUNNA	57.2	55.5	42.1	43.7	0.0	0.0	0.8	0.8	9.0	8.3	8.1	7.2	7.6	26.9	22.4	9.4	1.1	70.3	32.6	48.0	52.0
39323	CHUNKY	82.9	82.2	13.1	13.8	0.3	0.3	3.6	3.5	6.3	6.6	7.8	6.1	6.6	27.1	25.5	12.7	1.3	75.5	37.9	50.7	49.3
39325	COLLINSVILLE	91.2	90.0	8.0	9.0	0.3	0.4	0.7	0.8	6.9	7.1	7.8	6.8	6.3	28.4	25.1	10.4	1.2	74.0	37.0	49.4	50.6
39326	DALEVILLE	67.8	63.2	31.1	35.7	0.4	0.4	0.4	0.4	5.6	6.2	7.7	6.2	6.2	27.4	27.6	11.8	1.1	76.7	39.3	48.7	51.3
39327	DECATUR	72.1	70.7	26.9	28.3	0.2	0.2	0.8	0.8	7.1	6.5	6.3	10.8	10.1	24.6	21.9	11.5	1.2	77.0	32.4	50.1	49.9
39328	DE KALB	40.1	39.3	58.6	59.4	0.2	0.2	0.8	0.8	7.4	7.1	7.2	6.5	6.9	25.3	23.8	12.9	2.9	74.5	36.8	47.6	52.4
39330	ENTERPRISE	71.9	70.0	27.3	29.2	0.1	0.1	0.6	0.6	6.3	6.6	7.7	6.4	6.4	27.3	24.5	13.0	1.8	75.5	37.9	49.5	50.5
39332	HICKORY	69.8	68.8	28.4	29.4	0.2	0.2	1.4	1.4	7.4	7.3	7.9	6.5	6.1	27.3	23.2	12.2	2.2	73.7	36.7	49.2	50.8
39335	LAUDERDALE	65.8	63.5	32.4	34.6	0.5	0.5	1.1	1.2	6.7	6.5	6.2	6.8	7.7	28.2	26.5	10.5	1.0	76.9	37.0	50.2	49.8
39336	LAWRENCE	53.2	52.0	46.0	47.5	0.0	0.0	0.5	0.5	7.1	7.1	7.1	6.1	6.3	27.4	24.8	12.7	1.3	74.7	36.9	48.6	51.5
39337	LITTLE ROCK	91.7	91.3	7.9	8.3	0.0	0.0	0.5	0.4	6.7	6.7	6.7	5.5	6.5	27.3	25.6	13.6	1.5	76.7	38.2	51.6	48.4
39338	LOUIN	48.0	46.2	51.4	53.0	0.0	0.0	0.6	0.6	7.6	7.4	7.7	7.0	7.0	26.4	23.1	11.8	2.0	73.0	35.7	48.4	51.6
39339	LOUISVILLE	53.7	53.0	44.7	45.4	0.1	0.1	1.2	1.2	6.9	6.8	7.2	7.1	7.3	25.5	23.9	13.0	2.3	74.8	36.7	48.7	51.3
39341	MACON	31.5	30.1	67.3	68.5	0.2	0.2	1.0	1.1	8.0	7.9	8.0	7.7	7.1	26.6	21.7	11.1	2.0	71.5	33.9	47.5	52.5
39342	MARION	50.4	46.3	48.4	52.3	0.4	0.5	1.6	1.8	10.1	9.3	8.5	6.4	7.4	29.5	19.7	7.2	1.8	68.3	29.9	43.6	56.5
39345	NEWTON	48.9	48.1	49.8	50.5	0.3	0.3	0.8	0.8	7.9	7.2	7.4	7.0	6.8	25.9	22.4	12.9	2.7	73.5	35.9	46.9	53.1
39346	NOXAPATER	61.1	60.2	38.2	39.1	0.0	0.0	1.0	1.0	6.6	6.7	7.5	7.2	5.9	24.9	25.9	13.3	2.0	74.8	38.3	49.1	50.9
39347	PACHUTA	50.9	49.2	48.7	50.2	0.0	0.0	0.8	0.8	6.8	6.8	7.5	6.1	6.8	26.5	25.3	12.3	1.8	75.2	38.0	47.4	52.6
39348	PAULDING	31.0	29.5	68.8	70.3	0.0	0.0	0.6	0.6	7.3	7.3	8.2	7.5	7.9	25.8	23.2	11.0	1.9	72.5	34.3	49.0	51.0
39350	PHILADELPHIA	64.8	62.9	19.7	20.2	0.2	0.3	1.2	1.3	8.0	7.7	7.6	6.9	6.8	26.8	22.7	11.7	1.9	72.6	34.9	48.0	52.0
39352	PORTERVILLE	29.3	28.5	69.6	70.3	0.1	0.1	0.9	0.8	7.9	7.8	7.5	6.9	7.0	27.4	22.9	10.7	1.9	72.5	34.3	49.0	51.1
39354	PRESTON	49.3	48.9	43.3	43.9	0.1	0.1	0.6	0.7	6.0	6.1	7.1	6.5	6.8	25.4	25.7	14.1	2.4	77.0	39.7	48.4	51.6
39355	QUITMAN	70.0	69.4	29.3	29.9	0.1	0.1	0.7	0.7	6.6	6.6	7.1	6.4	6.3	25.0	24.8	14.7	2.5	75.7	39.1	48.1	51.9
39356	ROSE HILL	52.4	50.6	47.0	48.8	0.0	0.0	1.4	1.5	6.9	6.8	7.4	5.9	6.5	26.9	24.7	12.5	2.3	75.3	37.9	50.1	49.9
39358	SCOOBA	39.5	38.7	59.6	60.4	0.0	0.0	0.6	0.7	6.3	6.0	6.2	14.6	11.6	23.0	20.5	10.6	1.3	77.5	29.8	50.1	49.9
39359	SEBASTOPOL	89.3	88.3	9.4	10.0	0.0	0.0	1.7	2.1	6.7	6.7	6.7	8.0	7.1	26.4	26.8	10.0	1.7	74.9	36.6	50.6	49.4
39360	SHUBUTA	45.3	43.7	54.0	55.6	0.1	0.1	0.8	0.8	7.6	7.4	7.9	6.9	7.0	25.9	24.3	11.6	1.5	72.9	35.9	47.8	52.2
39361	SHUQUALAK	33.7	32.4	64.5	65.7	0.0	0.0	1.1	1.2	7.9	7.7	8.4	7.3	7.1	26.1	23.8	9.6	2.1	71.5	33.6	49.9	50.1
39362	STATE LINE	52.4	51.1	47.2	48.4	0.0	0.0	0.3	0.3	8.7	8.4	8.3	8.2	7.4	27.0	21.5	9.5	1.1	69.5	31.9	48.8	51.2
39363	STONEWALL	74.7	73.2	24.5	26.0	0.1	0.1	0.7	0.7	8.1	8.0	8.5	6.4	6.2	26.9	23.1	11.3	1.4	71.3	34.7	48.3	51.7
39364	TOOMSUBA	57.2	52.8	41.7	45.9	0.2	0.3	0.6	0.7	6.4	6.5	7.6	7.4	7.5	27.0	26.8	9.6	1.4	75.3	36.1	48.1	51.9
39365	UNION	76.9	76.1	22.0	22.8	0.1	0.1	0.6	0.7	6.8	6.7	7.3	6.4	6.0	24.8	24.0	15.4	2.7	75.1	38.8	48.0	52.0
39366	VOSSBURG	20.8	19.4	79.0	80.3	0.0	0.1	0.3	0.2	7.4	7.4	8.8	7.9	8.9	25.5	23.0	9.9	1.4	71.7	32.5	48.2	51.9
39367	WAYNESBORO	59.7	58.4	39.6	40.8	0.2	0.2	0.7	0.8	7.7	7.6	8.0	7.0	7.4	26.4	23.7	10.8	1.5	72.4	34.6	47.9	52.1
39401	HATTIESBURG	49.4	48.0	48.4	49.4	0.8	1.0	1.4	1.5	7.6	6.6	6.7	7.3	11.6	30.1	19.1	9.2	2.0	75.4	30.0	47.8	52.2
39402	HATTIESBURG	82.8	81.4	14.8	15.8	1.1	1.3	1.2	1.4	7.0	6.7	7.1	6.5	8.4	29.5	23.4	10.2	1.3	75.4	34.5	47.5	52.5
39406	HATTIESBURG	57.3	54.0	39.0	41.4	2.6	3.4	1.6	1.9	2.9	1.1	0.4	35.6	44.8	13.4	1.4	0.4	0.0	95.2	21.1	40.2	59.8
39421	BASSFIELD	46.7	45.2	52.4	53.7	0.3	0.3	0.8	0.8	7.8	7.6	7.6	7.1	8.0	27.2	22.6	10.5	1.7	72.7	33.7	48.6	51.4
39422	BAY SPRINGS	48.5	46.8	50.7	52.3	0.1	0.1	0.6	0.6	7.2	7.2	7.9	6.8	6.9	26.2	23.4	12.2	2.3	73.5	36.2	47.0	53.0
39423	BEAUMONT	61.7	61.4	36.9	37.3	0.0	0.0	0.7	0.7	7.8	7.6	8.3	6.6	7.3	28.1	24.0	9.6	0.8	72.3	34.0	49.1	50.9
39425	BROOKLYN	90.4	89.1	9.0	10.1	0.0	0.0	0.9	1.2	7.3	7.2	6.8	6.0	6.1	28.1	26.6	10.9	1.1	75.0	36.9	49.4	50.6
39426	CARRIERE	94.1	93.4	3.6	3.9	0.2	0.3	1.5	1.8	7.1	7.2	7.2	6.8	6.5	26.9	25.9	11.5	0.9	74.3	37.0	49.4	50.6
39427	CARSON	46.9	45.3	51.9	53.3	0.2	0.2	0.4	0.4	7.2	7.1	7.3	7.0	7.2	24.9	25.2	12.6	1.5	74.2	36.5	48.3	51.7
39428	COLLINS	53.2	51.2	45.8	47.6	0.2	0.2	1.0	1.1	8.0	7.8	8.1	6.9	7.2	26.2	22.2	11.8	1.9	72.0	34.3	48.3	51.7
39429	COLUMBIA	63.0	61.7	35.7	36.8	0.3	0.4	0.6	0.6	6.9	6.9	8.0	7.3	7.0	26.2	22.8	12.6	2.3	73.6	36.0	48.7	51.3
39437	ELLISVILLE	82.7	81.4	16.0	16.9	0.2	0.2	1.1	1.3	6.3	6.4	6.2	8.9	7.9	27.1	23.9	11.8	1.4	77.4	36.0	49.8	50.2
39439	HEIDELBERG	43.4	41.4	54.6	56.4	0.0	0.1	0.6	0.6	7.4	7.3	7.7	7.0	7.4	25.7	24.2	11.7	1.6	73.4	35.2	48.2	51.8
39440	LAUREL	47.7	45.9	47.8	48.8	0.6	0.7	3.8	4.5	7.7	7.2	7.3	6.7	7.2	26.4	21.1	13.8	2.6	73.8	35.2	47.0	53.0
39443	LAUREL	83.3	81.9	15.2	16.2	0.2	0.2	1.1	1.3	7.0	6.9	6.9	6.4	6.6	27.1	25.7	12.2	1.3	75.5	37.4	49.1	50.9
39451	LEAKESVILLE	68.8	68.3	29.7	30.2	0.1	0.1	1.1	1.1	5.6	5.5	5.2	6.2	11.3	35.6	20.5	8.6	1.4	80.7	33.4	62.4	37.6
	MISSISSIPPI	61.4	60.6	36.3	36.8	0.7	0.8	1.4	1.6	7.3	7.1	7.4	7.4	7.8	27.8	23.0	10.6	1.6	73.9	34.5	48.5	51.5
	UNITED STATES	75.1	73.6	12.3	12.5	3.8	4.2	12.5	14.1	6.9	6.7	7.2	7.0	7.3	28.6	23.8	10.8	1.7	75.1	36.0	49.1	50.9

#	POST OFFICE NAME	2004 Per Capita Income	2004 HH Income Base	2004 Household Income Distribution (%): Less than $25,000	$25,000 to $49,999	$50,000 to $99,999	$100,000 to $149,999	$150,000 or More	Median Household Income: 2004	2009	2004 National Centile	2004 State Centile	2004 Home Value Base	2004 Home Value Distribution (%): Less than $50,000	$50,000 to $89,999	$90,000 to $174,999	$175,000 to $399,999	$400,000 or More	2004 Median Home Value
39145	PELAHATCHIE	18803	2096	29.6	32.7	30.9	4.5	2.3	38272	42886	40	85	1681	33.7	32.8	25.6	6.4	1.4	67656
39146	PICKENS	11786	1052	54.1	27.8	13.2	2.8	2.2	22016	25261	3	6	818	55.3	30.4	11.7	1.5	1.1	45784
39149	PINOLA	14326	684	41.4	35.5	17.0	4.5	1.6	29378	33257	11	41	597	58.1	27.6	10.9	2.4	1.0	45890
39150	PORT GIBSON	13890	2761	48.9	26.5	16.9	6.0	1.7	25883	30188	6	20	2114	47.3	31.0	16.1	4.7	1.0	52762
39152	PULASKI	16915	237	33.3	36.3	23.2	7.2	0.0	37673	42188	38	83	197	45.2	30.0	19.8	4.6	0.5	55588
39153	RALEIGH	17120	3429	38.3	29.9	25.3	4.2	2.3	32852	36486	20	65	2905	42.5	26.4	22.9	6.8	1.3	61324
39154	RAYMOND	21299	3314	20.6	28.8	35.2	11.7	3.8	50655	58605	73	97	2738	19.4	22.2	38.5	18.1	1.8	103696
39156	REDWOOD	23971	201	25.4	28.4	30.4	12.4	3.5	45767	51072	63	93	166	33.7	17.5	31.9	14.5	2.4	86000
39157	RIDGELAND	32540	10604	19.3	32.4	30.7	10.0	7.6	48220	56517	69	96	5598	7.8	16.0	41.0	27.4	7.8	130566
39159	ROLLING FORK	14460	1415	49.3	26.4	18.5	3.6	2.3	25462	29316	5	16	913	45.6	32.5	20.0	1.9	0.0	53750
39160	SALLIS	14206	1020	46.6	30.3	19.7	2.5	1.0	26630	30466	7	24	850	61.3	24.0	10.8	3.3	0.6	40000
39162	SATARTIA	14768	204	37.8	33.3	22.6	5.4	1.0	32746	36981	20	64	172	43.6	27.3	24.4	4.7	0.0	59167
39166	SILVER CITY	14296	316	44.9	34.5	15.2	3.5	1.9	26474	30622	6	22	228	37.7	27.6	21.5	12.7	0.4	72414
39168	TAYLORSVILLE	15545	1737	39.0	33.3	21.4	4.2	2.2	32272	36157	18	61	1458	40.7	34.2	18.6	6.4	0.1	60803
39169	TCHULA	8589	1148	69.5	17.9	8.1	2.1	2.4	13137	14975	1	1	629	59.9	30.1	8.1	0.3	1.6	42978
39170	TERRY	25214	2588	26.9	26.1	31.3	10.7	5.0	47158	53704	66	95	2247	17.7	24.9	35.5	19.2	2.7	106658
39175	UTICA	16836	1779	32.6	33.3	24.9	7.3	2.1	36776	42940	35	80	1443	37.1	30.7	17.8	12.1	2.2	63931
39176	VAIDEN	23318	979	51.3	22.2	16.7	5.2	4.7	23954	27360	4	10	771	47.5	29.4	16.6	6.5	0.0	52635
39177	VALLEY PARK	15284	69	46.4	20.3	30.4	1.5	1.5	29070	30000	10	40	47	38.3	23.4	21.3	17.0	0.0	65000
39179	VAUGHAN	14344	453	43.7	28.0	20.1	4.9	3.3	29535	34101	11	42	372	40.1	31.2	22.0	6.7	0.0	63939
39180	VICKSBURG	21325	12889	31.4	28.3	28.6	8.4	3.4	40827	46659	49	88	8953	26.1	29.6	32.6	10.1	1.6	83028
39183	VICKSBURG	18473	5804	36.9	30.3	21.7	8.6	2.6	33875	39016	24	68	3994	35.4	21.9	29.6	11.6	1.5	75502
39189	WALNUT GROVE	17089	546	41.9	32.8	21.3	2.8	1.3	30348	34553	13	47	444	34.9	44.4	19.6	0.9	0.2	60690
39191	WESSON	15584	2785	37.9	30.4	24.8	5.6	1.4	32546	36849	19	63	2331	40.5	29.5	24.1	5.1	0.8	61395
39192	WEST	20696	846	41.1	31.9	16.9	6.3	3.8	30392	34901	13	48	704	47.9	31.8	16.1	2.7	1.6	52000
39194	YAZOO CITY	13441	6560	50.1	25.5	18.6	3.8	2.0	24890	28580	4	13	4162	42.5	32.0	19.7	5.5	0.4	57417
39201	JACKSON	8150	90	70.0	23.3	5.6	1.1	0.0	15000	15648	1	1	19	84.2	15.8	0.0	0.0	0.0	32917
39202	JACKSON	19728	3887	45.7	29.3	16.2	4.2	4.6	27092	31044	7	25	1242	26.3	12.2	40.4	17.2	4.0	112784
39203	JACKSON	9764	2672	64.2	24.0	9.1	2.0	0.7	17646	20428	1	2	1067	68.6	26.6	3.5	0.6	0.8	40724
39204	JACKSON	14876	7199	48.8	29.7	17.2	2.6	1.7	25671	28399	5	17	3383	36.2	50.8	11.8	1.2	0.1	58260
39206	JACKSON	20616	9812	33.2	33.5	23.8	6.2	3.3	36195	41155	32	78	5457	15.3	53.1	27.0	3.5	1.2	74195
39208	PEARL	19014	10248	27.9	31.9	30.9	7.0	2.3	41009	46038	50	88	6857	21.7	42.2	27.8	7.1	1.2	77982
39209	JACKSON	12627	11257	45.9	31.8	18.6	2.6	1.1	27279	30847	8	27	5987	40.9	44.9	11.6	2.2	0.4	55257
39211	JACKSON	45520	11431	15.3	24.4	32.3	12.2	15.9	62557	72462	87	99	8258	1.5	16.4	49.1	25.4	7.6	134131
39212	JACKSON	18854	11751	25.8	34.9	31.9	5.7	1.7	42520	47871	55	90	8664	18.4	53.3	24.9	3.3	0.1	72625
39213	JACKSON	13247	9795	50.9	27.8	16.3	3.6	1.3	24325	27466	4	11	5451	45.6	38.1	14.1	2.1	0.1	53004
39216	JACKSON	23106	1686	40.6	28.4	17.5	6.6	6.8	31169	34424	15	54	881	9.1	27.9	39.8	16.9	6.2	112130
39218	RICHLAND	19821	2372	25.1	32.9	34.1	6.4	1.5	43726	49812	58	91	1865	33.2	26.3	36.6	3.9	0.0	74712
39232	FLOWOOD	26668	1806	22.2	32.2	33.4	10.6	1.6	46714	52838	66	94	977	22.3	18.2	52.3	5.6	1.5	100743
39272	BYRAM	23787	3208	14.4	28.1	45.5	10.2	1.9	56913	64232	82	98	2923	6.8	21.8	60.4	9.8	1.3	106141
39301	MERIDIAN	14537	10765	49.1	28.2	18.0	3.5	1.2	25671	29925	5	17	6694	43.1	32.6	19.3	4.5	0.5	57753
39305	MERIDIAN	27488	8169	25.4	27.8	30.6	10.2	6.0	47503	53476	67	95	5622	13.4	26.9	39.1	16.7	3.9	103494
39307	MERIDIAN	15267	6572	45.9	28.7	20.8	3.3	1.3	27885	31944	8	31	4298	35.8	46.5	14.0	3.4	0.3	59327
39309	MERIDIAN	3571	13	46.2	23.1	30.8	0.0	0.0	27290	37321	8	28	8	0.0	37.5	62.5	0.0	0.0	108333
39320	BAILEY	20407	519	26.2	32.0	29.5	11.4	1.0	43470	50000	57	91	447	23.9	34.9	28.0	12.1	1.1	77431
39322	BUCKATUNNA	12483	753	48.2	31.6	15.8	3.6	0.8	25720	29316	5	19	659	59.8	20.9	13.8	4.7	0.8	37733
39323	CHUNKY	16603	351	36.2	27.1	31.9	4.8	0.0	35559	39089	30	76	299	45.5	25.1	26.8	2.3	0.3	57500
39325	COLLINSVILLE	20080	1950	27.1	27.3	36.0	7.3	2.3	45716	50916	63	93	1686	20.3	29.6	32.4	15.4	2.3	90139
39326	DALEVILLE	20786	198	27.3	26.8	28.3	15.7	2.0	42389	43509	54	90	182	29.7	19.8	29.7	14.8	6.0	90500
39327	DECATUR	16076	1655	41.2	27.4	25.6	4.4	1.5	32576	35125	20	63	1314	36.8	33.8	23.7	5.3	0.5	64677
39328	DE KALB	14665	2007	48.0	31.7	15.6	3.8	0.8	26159	29307	6	21	1568	46.4	35.6	14.9	2.4	0.6	53758
39330	ENTERPRISE	15939	1044	42.5	30.3	21.5	4.8	1.0	29854	33555	12	44	856	46.0	29.3	20.6	4.0	0.1	54789
39332	HICKORY	16132	699	38.8	31.8	24.9	3.9	0.7	31041	34812	15	53	579	47.5	26.1	21.1	4.0	1.4	53816
39335	LAUDERDALE	18871	1293	29.6	35.3	28.0	5.7	1.4	40276	46120	47	87	1049	36.1	39.4	20.0	3.7	0.8	62043
39336	LAWRENCE	13201	141	40.4	36.2	21.3	1.4	0.7	30162	34335	13	46	121	48.8	28.1	19.0	4.1	0.0	51364
39337	LITTLE ROCK	18273	618	37.5	26.5	31.4	3.1	1.5	35193	38597	28	75	566	42.6	30.4	21.4	5.1	0.5	59545
39338	LOUIN	16385	1044	48.0	31.5	16.0	2.6	1.9	25889	28909	6	20	888	53.9	24.0	16.8	4.2	1.1	46392
39339	LOUISVILLE	16892	6393	41.3	30.4	22.1	4.2	2.0	31262	34816	16	55	4815	32.5	36.7	22.3	6.8	1.8	66758
39341	MACON	14232	2540	49.7	28.0	15.5	4.6	2.2	25200	28520	5	14	1882	51.8	26.9	16.1	4.3	1.0	48862
39342	MARION	11819	430	53.0	24.9	20.2	1.2	0.7	23146	25793	3	8	182	34.1	40.1	22.5	3.3	0.0	65000
39345	NEWTON	16016	2704	42.0	31.5	20.9	4.1	1.6	30071	33703	12	45	2036	43.1	33.5	19.6	3.8	0.0	57216
39346	NOXAPATER	15137	936	40.6	34.5	19.9	4.4	0.6	30650	35412	14	50	775	37.3	37.0	21.3	3.9	0.5	63615
39347	PACHUTA	13209	367	51.0	28.9	15.3	3.3	1.6	24243	26883	4	10	299	35.5	39.5	24.8	0.0	0.3	63229
39348	PAULDING	13420	198	48.5	27.8	18.7	3.0	2.0	25758	27316	5	19	169	53.3	21.9	22.5	2.4	0.0	47381
39350	PHILADELPHIA	17035	10908	41.2	30.6	21.6	4.4	2.2	31252	35028	16	54	8453	35.0	37.6	19.6	5.8	2.1	63858
39352	PORTERVILLE	13983	401	44.4	29.7	20.0	6.0	0.0	29233	32226	11	41	353	47.3	30.6	20.4	1.1	0.6	52065
39354	PRESTON	14729	984	47.5	31.8	15.9	2.1	2.7	26628	30071	7	23	826	43.1	32.0	18.8	5.6	0.6	56552
39355	QUITMAN	18456	3235	40.0	30.7	24.1	3.4	1.8	32218	35805	18	60	2619	40.4	34.8	20.0	4.5	0.3	59382
39356	ROSE HILL	14570	657	44.0	34.1	16.7	2.7	2.4	27140	30991	7	26	535	35.3	35.1	27.3	1.3	0.9	66484
39358	SCOOBA	14088	754	45.6	31.3	16.5	6.0	0.7	27164	30952	7	26	571	41.9	33.8	19.8	2.8	1.8	56370
39359	SEBASTOPOL	19811	111	44.1	31.5	19.8	1.8	2.7	28935	31706	10	38	87	59.8	21.8	16.1	2.3	0.0	42273
39360	SHUBUTA	12999	1620	48.8	30.9	15.6	3.5	1.2	25697	28507	5	18	1376	49.2	32.1	14.3	3.5	0.9	51000
39361	SHUQUALAK	17761	533	43.0	26.6	20.6	6.9	2.8	30499	34143	14	49	429	53.6	21.5	17.7	4.0	3.3	46837
39362	STATE LINE	12345	1068	46.2	32.3	18.7	2.3	0.6	26962	30413	7	25	880	53.2	27.8	16.5	1.7	0.8	47083
39363	STONEWALL	16715	786	43.8	27.2	24.2	3.3	1.5	29565	33195	11	42	632	49.4	32.1	15.2	2.5	0.8	50556
39364	TOOMSUBA	16495	966	31.8	37.6	24.7	4.1	1.8	35503	40365	30	76	801	44.4	27.0	15.5	11.5	1.6	55494
39365	UNION	17766	1502	41.7	28.6	23.1	3.4	3.2	30482	33754	13	49	1188	42.3	33.2	21.0	3.2	0.3	59785
39366	VOSSBURG	12488	593	48.9	28.0	18.9	3.2	1.0	25608	27320	5	17	519	55.9	23.9	17.7	1.7	0.8	44917
39367	WAYNESBORO	15343	6152	44.5	32.2	16.5	4.5	2.2	28781	31504	10	37	4939	50.3	27.5	17.1	4.4	0.7	49684
39401	HATTIESBURG	15234	16861	48.2	30.5	16.3	3.6	1.4	25997	29251	6	21	8366	38.5	34.2	21.1	5.8	0.4	63384
39402	HATTIESBURG	28135	11506	25.0	26.7	29.7	10.7	7.9	47861	54546	68	95	8061	13.2	15.8	41.4	24.9	4.7	120763
39406	HATTIESBURG	8978	570	69.0	26.8	4.2	0.0	0.0	13910	15104	1	1	13	38.5	53.9	7.7	0.0	0.0	55000
39421	BASSFIELD	12506	1493	50.6	30.9	14.9	2.6	1.0	24635	27534	4	12	1243	53.8	30.4	14.0	1.4	0.4	47050
39422	BAY SPRINGS	15189	2425	46.4	29.0	19.6	3.6	1.4	27420	30130	8	29	1962	44.1	32.0	16.0	6.6	1.4	56591
39423	BEAUMONT	14511	1057	43.8	37.3	14.9	3.4	0.7	28417	32241	9	35	893	52.0	26.2	17.0	4.6	0.2	47603
39425	BROOKLYN	14471	364	46.4	30.0	16.5	6.9	0.3	27202	30915	7	27	315	42.5	27.9	26.7	1.3	1.6	60714
39426	CARRIERE	18934	5575	31.3	31.0	28.3	6.5	2.9	38766	43259	42	85	4754	21.4	24.0	39.3	13.3	2.0	96290
39427	CARSON	11999	522	51.5	34.1	11.5	1.7	1.2	23623	25606	4	9	422	53.8	30.6	14.0	1.7	0.0	47241
39428	COLLINS	18871	4205	43.8	30.4	18.7	3.5	3.5	28724	32162	10	37	3375	45.2	30.8	20.1	3.4	0.6	57115
39429	COLUMBIA	14947	6347	46.7	28.4	18.8	4.0	2.1	27165	30469	7	26	4877	36.2	32.0	24.7	6.3	0.9	65426
39437	ELLISVILLE	17084	4241	35.4	32.0	25.7	4.6	2.3	34076	38303	24	69	3451	37.8	28.7	24.4	8.1	1.0	63670
39439	HEIDELBERG	12805	1839	46.4	33.6	17.1	2.2	0.7	26915	29978	7	25	1509	46.0	35.5	15.0	1.7	1.9	54384
39440	LAUREL	17905	7885	44.7	29.4	18.1	4.2	3.7	28206	31227	9	34	4887	43.7	30.1	18.3	6.2	1.6	56620
39443	LAUREL	16985	8467	35.0	34.7	23.8	5.0	1.6	33786	37878	23	68	7083	37.8	28.9	26.0	6.4	1.0	65672
39451	LEAKESVILLE	14402	1986	40.8	31.8	22.2	3.9	1.3	31665	34550	17	57	1636	38.0	33.1	23.2	4.7	1.1	62462
	MISSISSIPPI	18480		36.7	30.0	24.5	5.9	2.8	34621	39377				29.7	30.4	28.7	9.7	1.6	75922
	UNITED STATES	25866		24.7	27.1	30.8	10.9	6.5	48124	56710				10.9	15.0	33.7	30.1	10.4	145905

ZIP CODE	FINANCIAL SERVICES				THE HOME						ENTERTAINMENT						PERSONAL			
					Home Improvements		Furnishings													
# POST OFFICE NAME	Auto Loan	Home Loan	Invest-ments	Retire-ment Plans	Home Repair	Lawn & Garden	Comput-ers & Hard-ware	Major Appli-ances	TV, Radio, Sound Equip-ment	Furni-ture	Dine out/ Carry out	Sports Equip-ment	Fees & Tickets	Toys & Games	Travel	Cable TV	Apparel & Services	Auto Repairs	Health Insur-ance	Pets & Supplies
39145 PELAHATCHIE	90	68	41	62	74	82	65	77	74	66	88	91	58	84	66	77	82	76	88	103
39146 PICKENS	55	41	36	36	43	52	45	49	52	46	63	54	42	56	44	56	59	50	58	60
39149 PINOLA	71	50	25	44	55	63	48	59	56	49	67	70	42	63	49	60	61	58	70	81
39150 PORT GIBSON	59	49	50	44	49	58	53	55	60	54	73	61	51	67	52	64	70	56	63	65
39152 PULASKI	83	55	25	48	63	72	53	67	64	54	76	80	45	72	54	69	69	66	82	95
39153 RALEIGH	83	56	25	48	63	73	54	67	65	55	76	80	46	72	55	70	69	67	83	95
39154 RAYMOND	87	89	91	88	90	96	85	88	85	86	106	101	87	106	87	86	103	87	89	102
39156 REDWOOD	84	87	86	87	89	91	82	85	81	82	100	100	83	102	83	80	97	83	83	99
39157 RIDGELAND	100	103	114	108	100	103	105	101	100	105	126	121	105	124	101	94	124	103	91	112
39159 ROLLING FORK	64	49	41	44	51	62	54	58	62	54	74	64	50	67	53	66	69	59	69	71
39160 SALLIS	71	50	28	45	56	64	49	59	57	50	68	71	43	64	50	61	62	59	71	82
39162 SATARTIA	79	53	24	45	60	69	51	64	61	52	72	76	43	68	52	66	65	63	78	90
39166 SILVER CITY	61	48	50	43	48	60	54	57	63	56	76	61	52	67	53	68	72	58	67	67
39168 TAYLORSVILLE	78	53	26	47	60	70	52	64	63	53	73	76	45	69	53	67	67	64	79	90
39169 TCHULA	40	31	35	28	31	38	36	37	41	37	50	41	34	46	35	43	48	38	42	44
39170 TERRY	95	103	105	101	102	107	96	97	94	96	118	111	100	120	98	95	116	95	96	112
39175 UTICA	85	67	47	60	71	81	64	74	73	66	87	85	60	84	66	77	82	73	85	97
39176 VAIDEN	107	72	33	62	81	94	69	87	84	71	98	104	59	93	71	90	89	86	107	123
39177 VALLEY PARK	79	53	24	46	60	69	51	64	61	52	72	76	43	68	52	66	66	63	79	90
39179 VAUGHAN	82	55	25	47	62	71	53	66	64	54	75	79	45	71	54	69	68	65	81	94
39180 VICKSBURG	76	78	79	76	77	82	76	77	77	77	95	89	77	95	76	77	93	77	77	88
39183 VICKSBURG	69	66	69	64	66	72	66	68	69	67	85	77	67	83	66	70	83	68	70	78
39189 WALNUT GROVE	79	53	24	46	60	69	51	64	61	52	72	76	43	68	52	66	66	63	78	90
39191 WESSON	77	56	33	51	61	70	55	65	63	56	75	76	49	71	55	66	69	64	76	87
39192 WEST	101	68	31	58	76	88	65	81	79	66	92	97	55	87	66	85	84	81	100	116
39194 YAZOO CITY	60	49	46	46	50	58	52	55	58	53	70	62	50	66	52	60	66	56	62	66
39201 JACKSON	1	1	1	1	1	1	1	1	1	1	1	1	1	1	1	1	1	1	1	1
39202 JACKSON	57	50	66	53	49	55	60	56	61	59	77	68	58	74	57	60	75	60	55	63
39203 JACKSON	39	32	37	30	32	38	37	37	42	38	51	41	36	47	36	44	49	39	41	43
39204 JACKSON	53	49	57	48	48	53	54	52	57	54	70	61	54	69	53	57	69	54	54	59
39206 JACKSON	74	71	84	70	69	77	76	74	79	77	99	84	77	96	75	79	96	76	74	83
39208 PEARL	70	73	74	73	73	76	72	72	70	71	88	85	72	89	72	69	86	72	69	81
39209 JACKSON	52	46	54	44	45	52	50	50	55	51	68	56	50	66	50	56	66	51	53	58
39211 JACKSON	132	148	175	151	146	154	144	141	138	145	174	164	150	175	146	135	172	142	133	155
39212 JACKSON	68	73	79	74	72	74	74	72	71	73	90	85	75	91	73	69	88	73	67	79
39213 JACKSON	50	44	50	41	43	51	48	48	53	49	65	53	48	61	47	56	63	50	54	56
39216 JACKSON	67	66	85	66	64	72	72	69	75	72	93	79	73	93	72	75	91	72	70	77
39218 RICHLAND	77	76	68	76	75	77	73	75	71	74	89	88	71	86	72	69	86	75	71	86
39232 FLOWOOD	85	77	77	80	76	80	81	81	80	82	101	96	77	95	77	77	97	83	76	93
39272 BYRAM	87	100	99	102	97	95	90	90	84	92	106	106	94	108	90	80	105	88	80	100
39301 MERIDIAN	55	45	41	42	46	53	47	50	52	48	63	58	45	60	47	54	60	51	55	61
39305 MERIDIAN	93	95	98	94	95	101	93	94	92	92	115	110	94	115	93	91	111	94	93	108
39307 MERIDIAN	56	49	48	46	50	57	51	53	56	51	68	60	50	66	51	58	65	54	59	64
39309 MERIDIAN	53	44	36	44	43	47	47	48	48	47	60	57	43	55	44	46	57	50	46	56
39320 BAILEY	85	75	57	72	80	86	70	77	74	70	90	92	68	92	72	76	86	75	84	100
39322 BUCKATUNNA	65	43	20	37	49	57	42	52	50	43	59	63	36	56	43	54	54	52	64	74
39323 CHUNKY	79	54	27	48	61	69	52	65	62	53	73	77	45	69	53	66	67	64	78	90
39325 COLLINSVILLE	87	72	50	68	78	85	68	78	74	68	89	93	64	89	70	76	83	76	87	103
39326 DALEVILLE	90	80	61	76	84	90	74	82	78	74	95	97	72	97	76	80	90	79	88	105
39327 DECATUR	74	52	27	46	58	67	53	63	62	52	72	73	46	68	53	66	66	62	76	84
39328 DE KALB	63	46	31	41	50	58	46	54	54	47	64	62	42	60	46	57	59	53	64	71
39330 ENTERPRISE	73	52	27	46	57	65	50	60	58	51	69	72	44	65	50	62	63	60	72	83
39332 HICKORY	75	50	23	44	57	66	49	61	59	50	69	73	41	65	50	63	63	60	75	86
39335 LAUDERDALE	78	62	42	58	67	73	60	68	66	60	80	81	56	78	61	68	75	67	76	89
39336 LAWRENCE	67	45	20	39	51	58	43	54	52	44	61	65	37	58	44	56	56	53	67	77
39337 LITTLE ROCK	84	56	25	48	63	73	54	68	65	55	77	81	46	72	55	70	70	67	83	96
39338 LOUIN	80	54	24	46	61	70	52	65	62	53	73	77	44	69	53	67	67	64	80	92
39339 LOUISVILLE	73	54	36	50	59	69	56	64	64	55	76	74	50	73	56	68	70	64	75	83
39341 MACON	64	47	31	42	51	59	49	55	56	48	66	65	43	63	48	59	62	56	65	73
39342 MARION	47	41	43	38	40	47	43	44	48	44	59	50	43	58	43	49	57	45	48	53
39345 NEWTON	70	50	30	45	55	64	51	60	59	51	70	70	45	66	51	63	64	59	72	80
39346 NOXAPATER	71	48	22	41	54	62	46	58	56	47	65	69	39	62	47	60	60	57	71	82
39347 PACHUTA	63	42	19	36	48	55	40	51	49	41	57	60	34	54	41	53	52	50	62	72
39348 PAULDING	68	46	21	39	52	60	44	55	53	45	62	66	38	59	45	57	57	55	68	78
39350 PHILADELPHIA	74	56	39	51	60	70	57	65	65	57	78	75	52	74	57	69	72	65	76	84
39352 PORTERVILLE	69	46	21	40	52	60	45	56	54	45	63	67	38	60	45	58	57	55	69	79
39354 PRESTON	70	47	21	40	53	61	45	56	54	46	64	67	38	60	46	59	58	56	69	80
39355 QUITMAN	78	59	38	53	64	73	59	68	67	59	80	80	53	77	60	71	74	68	80	89
39356 ROSE HILL	68	46	21	39	52	59	44	55	53	45	62	66	37	59	45	57	57	54	68	78
39358 SCOOBA	69	46	21	40	53	61	45	56	54	46	63	67	38	60	46	58	58	55	69	80
39359 SEBASTOPOL	80	54	24	46	61	70	52	65	63	53	74	78	44	70	53	67	67	64	80	92
39360 SHUBUTA	64	43	20	37	49	56	41	52	50	42	59	62	35	55	42	54	53	51	64	73
39361 SHUQUALAK	86	58	26	50	66	75	56	70	67	57	79	83	47	75	57	73	72	69	86	99
39362 STATE LINE	64	43	19	37	48	56	41	52	50	42	58	62	35	55	42	54	53	51	64	73
39363 STONEWALL	76	52	26	46	59	67	50	62	60	51	71	74	44	67	51	64	65	62	76	88
39364 TOOMSUBA	71	63	47	59	64	68	60	65	62	61	76	76	56	72	59	62	72	65	67	80
39365 UNION	78	55	31	50	62	72	57	67	67	56	78	78	50	74	57	71	71	67	81	88
39366 VOSSBURG	66	44	20	38	50	58	43	54	52	44	61	64	36	57	44	56	55	53	66	76
39367 WAYNESBORO	71	50	28	44	55	64	50	59	58	50	69	70	43	66	50	62	63	59	72	81
39401 HATTIESBURG	53	43	46	43	43	49	53	50	55	51	68	60	49	63	49	54	65	53	51	58
39402 HATTIESBURG	97	105	112	108	104	107	101	101	97	101	121	118	103	122	101	94	119	100	94	112
39406 HATTIESBURG	26	16	20	18	16	19	31	23	30	26	38	32	25	34	25	26	35	28	21	26
39421 BASSFIELD	64	43	20	37	49	56	42	52	50	42	59	62	35	56	42	54	54	52	64	74
39422 BAY SPRINGS	73	50	24	44	56	65	49	60	59	50	69	71	42	65	50	63	63	60	74	83
39423 BEAUMONT	68	51	30	46	55	62	49	58	56	50	66	68	44	63	49	58	62	58	66	77
39425 BROOKLYN	71	48	22	41	54	62	46	58	56	47	65	69	39	62	47	60	60	57	71	82
39426 CARRIERE	83	71	52	67	74	79	68	75	71	69	87	87	63	83	68	72	82	74	79	93
39427 CARSON	57	38	17	33	43	50	37	46	44	37	52	55	31	49	37	48	47	45	57	65
39428 COLLINS	88	64	41	58	70	81	64	75	74	65	88	88	57	83	65	79	81	75	89	100
39429 COLUMBIA	69	49	29	44	54	63	49	58	57	49	67	68	43	64	49	61	62	58	70	79
39437 ELLISVILLE	78	60	41	55	65	73	59	68	67	60	80	79	54	77	60	70	75	68	79	89
39439 HEIDELBERG	65	43	20	37	49	57	42	52	51	43	59	63	36	56	43	54	54	52	65	74
39440 LAUREL	69	56	50	53	59	69	61	64	68	60	82	73	58	78	61	71	77	65	74	77
39443 LAUREL	75	58	36	53	63	70	55	65	62	56	74	77	50	72	56	65	69	64	75	87
39451 LEAKESVILLE	66	45	23	40	51	59	45	55	53	45	63	64	39	59	46	57	57	54	67	75
MISSISSIPPI	76	64	54	60	66	74	64	70	70	65	85	81	61	82	64	71	80	70	76	86
UNITED STATES	100	100	100	100	100	100	100	100	100	100	100	100	100	100	100	100	100	100	100	100

# POST OFFICE NAME	COUNTY FIPS CODE	POPULATION 2000	2004	2009	2000-2004 ANNUAL RATE % Rate	State Centile	HOUSEHOLDS 2000	2004	2009	% Annual Rate 2000-2004	2004 Average HH Size	FAMILIES 2000	2004	% Annual Rate 2000-2004
39452 LUCEDALE	039	20948	21440	21930	0.6	63	7344	7671	7980	1.0	2.74	5822	6037	0.9
39455 LUMBERTON	073	7998	8014	8296	0.1	42	2938	3020	3191	0.7	2.64	2236	2272	0.4
39456 MC LAIN	041	1261	1285	1281	0.4	59	444	465	475	1.1	2.76	331	343	0.8
39459 MOSELLE	067	3253	3678	3864	2.9	94	1207	1402	1505	3.6	2.60	911	1049	3.4
39461 NEELY	041	1189	1168	1145	-0.4	21	437	442	446	0.3	2.49	337	338	0.1
39462 NEW AUGUSTA	111	1897	1968	1995	0.9	73	686	730	752	1.5	2.66	517	544	1.2
39464 OVETT	067	2079	2096	2084	0.2	50	778	804	817	0.8	2.59	613	628	0.6
39465 PETAL	035	18671	19395	19915	0.9	73	6736	7124	7436	1.3	2.70	5185	5446	1.2
39466 PICAYUNE	109	25205	26475	28218	1.2	80	9515	10234	11143	1.7	2.57	7012	7467	1.5
39470 POPLARVILLE	109	11114	11787	12547	1.4	83	4022	4388	4788	2.1	2.55	3008	3253	1.9
39474 PRENTISS	065	8614	8522	8391	-0.3	27	3249	3304	3348	0.4	2.56	2351	2367	0.2
39475 PURVIS	073	9068	9678	10109	1.5	86	3256	3553	3773	2.1	2.68	2575	2783	1.8
39476 RICHTON	111	7691	7673	7651	-0.1	36	2829	2893	2943	0.5	2.62	2174	2206	0.3
39478 SANDY HOOK	091	1968	1929	1859	-0.5	20	747	755	748	0.3	2.54	546	548	0.1
39479 SEMINARY	031	5616	6081	6419	1.9	88	2133	2362	2552	2.4	2.56	1622	1778	2.2
39480 SOSO	067	2491	2542	2545	0.5	61	979	1024	1047	1.1	2.48	762	789	0.8
39481 STRINGER	061	1478	1549	1634	1.1	79	556	597	646	1.7	2.59	439	468	1.5
39482 SUMRALL	073	6643	6973	7222	1.2	80	2382	2562	2702	1.7	2.71	1869	1990	1.5
39483 FOXWORTH	091	5162	4934	4739	-1.1	5	1887	1850	1818	-0.5	2.67	1457	1417	-0.7
39501 GULFPORT	047	25887	25492	26276	-0.4	22	9487	9512	10023	0.1	2.48	5895	5831	-0.3
39503 GULFPORT	047	36231	39953	43296	2.3	92	12713	14424	16014	3.0	2.69	9739	10934	2.8
39507 GULFPORT	047	19333	19416	20132	0.1	45	8457	8675	9184	0.6	2.18	4931	4927	0.0
39520 BAY SAINT LOUIS	045	17577	18469	20136	1.2	81	6955	7507	8393	1.8	2.42	4576	4866	1.5
39525 DIAMONDHEAD	045	5886	6851	7861	3.6	97	2548	3016	3528	4.1	2.25	1908	2230	3.7
39530 BILOXI	047	14125	13845	14378	-0.5	20	6180	6247	6654	0.3	2.20	3296	3238	-0.4
39531 BILOXI	047	19721	21204	22696	1.7	87	8060	8939	9812	2.5	2.31	4992	5408	1.9
39532 BILOXI	047	25585	27961	30157	2.1	91	9422	10520	11574	2.6	2.65	7236	7987	2.4
39534 BILOXI	047	3666	3540	3551	-0.8	8	343	312	322	-2.2	3.05	330	300	-2.2
39540 DIBERVILLE	047	7642	7920	8317	0.8	72	2843	3025	3250	1.5	2.62	1982	2078	1.1
39553 GAUTIER	059	16062	17234	18313	1.7	87	5824	6429	6995	2.4	2.67	4458	4860	2.1
39556 KILN	045	5888	6761	7709	3.3	95	2114	2492	2910	4.0	2.71	1607	1872	3.7
39560 LONG BEACH	047	19743	20131	21039	0.5	59	7440	7779	8314	1.1	2.56	5367	5539	0.7
39561 MC HENRY	131	1124	1142	1168	0.4	56	410	425	443	0.9	2.27	316	324	0.6
39562 MOSS POINT	059	16720	17291	18026	0.8	71	5818	6155	6554	1.3	2.80	4709	4938	1.1
39563 MOSS POINT	059	15819	15564	15967	-0.4	22	5703	5768	6057	0.3	2.67	4217	4215	0.0
39564 OCEAN SPRINGS	059	31875	33863	35824	1.4	84	12005	13060	14110	2.0	2.58	8807	9485	1.5
39565 OCEAN SPRINGS	059	14660	16902	18594	3.4	95	4905	5780	6480	3.9	2.91	4012	4691	3.8
39567 PASCAGOULA	059	13964	13638	13562	-0.6	16	5378	5361	5596	-0.1	2.31	3418	3351	-0.5
39571 PASS CHRISTIAN	047	14812	15900	16997	1.7	87	5689	6252	6825	2.3	2.52	4063	4418	2.0
39572 PEARLINGTON	045	1782	1896	2080	1.5	85	684	750	845	2.2	2.53	480	519	1.9
39573 PERKINSTON	131	6579	7118	7635	1.9	87	2207	2450	2684	2.5	2.77	1726	1899	2.3
39574 SAUCIER	047	10986	11912	12757	1.9	88	3807	4222	4616	2.5	2.80	3011	3304	2.2
39576 WAVELAND	045	6679	6979	7575	1.0	78	2729	2922	3245	1.6	2.38	1793	1887	1.2
39577 WIGGINS	131	8493	8834	9172	0.9	73	3066	3250	3426	1.4	2.66	2319	2437	1.2
39581 PASCAGOULA	059	12296	12380	12829	0.2	48	4502	4624	4886	0.6	2.65	3321	3365	0.3
39601 BROOKHAVEN	085	23274	23294	23402	0.0	40	8876	9079	9263	0.5	2.50	6347	6429	0.3
39629 BOGUE CHITTO	085	5817	5845	5847	0.1	46	2169	2225	2260	0.6	2.61	1697	1723	0.4
39630 BUDE	037	1155	1069	1030	-1.8	1	482	461	456	-1.0	2.28	307	290	-1.3
39631 CENTREVILLE	157	3820	3888	3928	0.4	58	1408	1481	1535	1.2	2.56	1008	1050	1.0
39633 CROSBY	157	1064	1055	1055	-0.2	30	414	425	436	0.6	2.48	289	294	0.4
39638 GLOSTER	005	3965	3885	3860	-0.5	19	1569	1585	1611	0.2	2.45	1122	1121	0.0
39641 JAYESS	077	4271	4358	4380	0.5	61	1610	1695	1750	1.2	2.57	1249	1303	1.0
39643 KOKOMO	091	1561	1398	1301	-2.6	0	554	510	487	-1.9	2.74	435	397	-2.1
39645 LIBERTY	005	5473	5588	5642	0.5	61	2141	2244	2313	1.1	2.48	1578	1637	0.9
39647 MC CALL CREEK	037	1892	1759	1695	-1.7	2	755	725	718	-1.0	2.41	553	525	-1.2
39648 MCCOMB	113	20903	20710	20594	-0.2	29	8090	8187	8313	0.3	2.47	5531	5535	0.0
39652 MAGNOLIA	113	8502	8640	8711	0.4	57	3148	3289	3399	1.0	2.58	2321	2400	0.8
39653 MEADVILLE	037	1639	1523	1448	-1.7	1	611	584	577	-1.1	2.50	444	419	-1.4
39654 MONTICELLO	077	4297	4286	4334	-0.1	36	1671	1702	1758	0.4	2.46	1185	1193	0.2
39656 OAK VALE	077	344	344	347	0.0	39	133	136	142	0.5	2.53	103	105	0.5
39657 OSYKA	113	1985	2089	2141	1.2	81	713	767	804	1.7	2.67	529	563	1.5
39661 ROXIE	037	3554	4148	4550	3.7	97	1277	1523	1704	4.2	2.72	952	1124	4.0
39662 RUTH	085	904	945	965	1.1	78	349	374	391	1.6	2.53	268	285	1.5
39663 SILVER CREEK	077	3189	3162	3184	-0.2	30	1202	1225	1265	0.5	2.58	896	905	0.2
39664 SMITHDALE	005	2133	2079	2048	-0.6	15	848	851	857	0.1	2.44	650	645	-0.2
39665 SONTAG	077	1723	1751	1782	0.4	57	647	670	696	0.8	2.61	504	516	0.6
39666 SUMMIT	113	8755	8728	8694	-0.1	35	3283	3363	3429	0.6	2.53	2451	2485	0.3
39667 TYLERTOWN	147	12575	12062	11373	-1.0	6	4638	4566	4425	-0.4	2.60	3397	3315	-0.6
39668 UNION CHURCH	063	767	745	727	-0.7	12	307	309	310	0.2	2.41	214	213	-0.1
39669 WOODVILLE	157	6426	6444	6471	0.1	43	2108	2183	2251	0.8	2.52	1476	1514	0.6
39701 COLUMBUS	087	16436	15693	15367	-1.1	4	6085	5922	5876	-0.6	2.49	3959	3807	-0.9
39702 COLUMBUS	087	22100	22303	22346	0.2	52	8106	8349	8482	0.7	2.61	6132	6255	0.5
39705 COLUMBUS	087	14240	14363	14432	0.2	51	5552	5744	5865	0.8	2.43	3923	3994	0.4
39710 COLUMBUS	087	277	278	277	0.1	44	8	8	8	0.0	2.50	7	8	3.2
39730 ABERDEEN	095	12598	12410	12192	-0.4	23	4654	4702	4731	0.2	2.59	3401	3407	0.0
39735 ACKERMAN	019	5348	5289	5281	-0.3	26	2078	2116	2173	0.4	2.46	1482	1493	0.2
39739 BROOKSVILLE	103	4551	4659	4815	0.6	63	1572	1664	1777	1.4	2.79	1166	1223	1.1
39740 CALEDONIA	087	4989	5263	5380	1.3	82	1808	1945	2016	1.7	2.70	1413	1508	1.5
39741 CEDARBLUFF	025	1085	1053	1044	-0.7	11	394	395	402	0.1	2.66	294	291	-0.2
39743 CRAWFORD	087	2381	2387	2407	0.1	42	802	829	854	0.8	2.87	615	628	0.5
39744 EUPORA	155	5563	5678	5951	0.5	61	2089	2164	2306	0.9	2.55	1508	1548	0.6
39745 FRENCH CAMP	019	1656	1724	1770	1.0	74	542	584	618	1.8	2.56	407	435	1.6
39746 HAMILTON	095	3252	3212	3143	-0.3	25	1229	1246	1250	0.3	2.58	926	928	0.1
39747 KILMICHAEL	097	2512	2552	2583	0.4	56	955	996	1032	1.0	2.55	697	721	0.8
39750 MABEN	105	2192	2615	2976	4.2	98	859	1056	1234	5.0	2.46	626	759	4.6
39751 MANTEE	155	2019	2065	2160	0.5	63	788	823	874	1.0	2.51	609	633	0.7
39752 MATHISTON	155	2585	2799	3003	1.9	88	1015	1127	1236	2.5	2.46	746	820	2.3
39755 PHEBA	025	762	803	838	1.2	82	281	304	324	1.9	2.63	205	219	1.6
39756 PRAIRIE	095	528	538	534	0.4	59	188	198	201	1.2	2.72	139	145	1.0
39759 STARKVILLE	105	37766	39547	41986	1.1	79	14563	15757	17289	1.9	2.26	8254	8785	1.5
39762 MISSISSIPPI STATE	105	1643	1723	1829	1.1	79	11	12	14	2.1	2.58	3	4	7.0
39766 STEENS	087	2103	2090	2078	-0.2	32	825	838	845	0.4	2.49	615	618	0.1
39767 STEWART	155	556	568	587	0.5	62	229	239	252	1.0	2.38	169	175	0.7
39769 STURGIS	105	1721	1670	1721	-0.7	11	686	686	726	0.0	2.37	503	495	-0.4
39772 WEIR	019	1558	1603	1633	0.7	66	577	610	638	1.3	2.62	418	437	1.1
MISSISSIPPI					0.6					1.2	2.57			0.9
UNITED STATES					1.2					1.3	2.58			1.1

#	POST OFFICE NAME	RACE (%) White 2000	White 2004	Black 2000	Black 2004	Asian/Pacific 2000	Asian/Pacific 2004	% Hispanic Origin 2000	% Hispanic Origin 2004	2004 AGE DISTRIBUTION (%) 0-4	5-9	10-14	15-19	20-24	25-44	45-64	65-84	85+	18+	MEDIAN AGE 2004	% 2004 Males	% 2004 Females
39452	LUCEDALE	90.2	89.5	8.1	8.5	0.2	0.2	1.5	1.8	8.0	7.8	8.3	7.0	6.8	28.6	22.7	9.8	1.2	71.6	33.7	50.3	49.7
39455	LUMBERTON	80.2	79.9	18.6	18.8	0.1	0.2	1.0	1.2	7.4	7.5	7.9	6.9	6.4	27.3	24.5	10.9	1.2	72.9	35.6	49.1	51.0
39456	MC LAIN	64.3	63.5	35.0	35.8	0.1	0.1	0.7	0.7	8.9	9.6	10.6	6.9	6.4	27.2	20.7	8.4	1.4	66.8	31.0	48.1	51.9
39459	MOSELLE	87.1	84.7	11.4	13.4	0.2	0.2	1.3	1.5	7.3	7.0	6.2	6.4	6.1	28.6	25.6	11.4	1.3	75.8	36.9	50.3	49.7
39461	NEELY	92.7	92.6	6.8	6.9	0.2	0.2	0.4	0.4	7.7	7.5	6.7	6.3	7.8	30.8	22.8	9.6	0.9	74.4	33.3	53.2	46.8
39462	NEW AUGUSTA	73.1	71.6	25.6	26.9	0.1	0.1	1.1	1.1	8.0	7.9	7.6	7.0	7.5	28.0	23.7	9.2	1.1	71.8	33.4	51.0	49.0
39464	OVETT	95.3	94.5	3.0	3.5	0.1	0.1	0.8	1.1	7.3	7.2	6.9	6.8	6.9	28.9	25.0	10.3	0.8	74.6	36.0	50.7	49.3
39465	PETAL	90.9	89.8	7.8	8.6	0.2	0.3	1.1	1.3	7.4	7.3	8.4	7.3	6.9	28.7	23.0	9.9	1.1	72.6	34.9	48.5	51.5
39466	PICAYUNE	81.0	79.9	16.5	17.3	0.4	0.5	1.5	1.7	7.3	7.2	7.4	6.9	6.5	26.9	24.5	12.0	1.3	73.9	36.4	48.2	51.8
39470	POPLARVILLE	86.3	85.1	11.9	12.7	0.3	0.4	1.1	1.3	7.2	7.1	7.2	7.2	7.8	26.3	24.3	11.4	1.5	74.7	35.5	49.2	50.8
39474	PRENTISS	40.4	39.1	58.7	59.8	0.2	0.2	0.8	0.8	7.3	7.2	7.9	7.1	6.7	24.8	24.6	12.4	2.0	73.3	36.4	47.8	52.2
39475	PURVIS	90.7	90.0	8.1	8.5	0.2	0.2	1.1	1.3	8.1	7.6	7.5	6.6	7.0	29.9	22.5	9.6	1.3	72.9	34.3	48.4	51.6
39476	RICHTON	87.6	87.2	11.3	11.7	0.2	0.2	1.0	0.9	8.0	7.6	7.3	6.3	7.2	27.8	23.6	11.1	1.2	73.3	34.6	48.9	51.1
39478	SANDY HOOK	69.7	68.4	28.9	29.9	0.1	0.1	1.6	1.8	5.2	5.9	6.8	7.1	7.5	26.4	26.8	12.9	1.5	77.9	39.2	49.8	50.2
39479	SEMINARY	92.0	90.5	7.0	8.4	0.1	0.1	0.7	0.8	7.1	7.1	7.8	7.2	6.2	28.6	24.0	11.0	1.2	73.7	35.5	49.5	50.5
39480	SOSO	71.6	69.0	27.5	29.9	0.1	0.2	0.6	0.7	6.9	6.9	7.4	6.6	6.7	27.9	24.6	11.5	1.5	74.9	36.7	49.5	50.5
39481	STRINGER	83.0	82.0	15.9	16.7	0.4	0.5	0.8	1.0	6.5	6.5	7.5	6.1	6.5	29.1	24.9	11.8	1.3	75.9	37.1	49.7	50.3
39482	SUMRALL	88.7	87.6	10.3	11.2	0.1	0.1	0.7	0.8	7.3	7.3	8.1	7.6	7.2	29.3	23.5	8.9	1.0	72.7	34.2	49.7	50.4
39483	FOXWORTH	79.1	77.8	20.1	21.1	0.1	0.1	0.6	0.7	7.8	7.6	7.6	6.0	7.6	27.7	24.6	10.0	1.2	73.4	34.4	49.3	50.7
39501	GULFPORT	44.0	41.6	52.2	54.1	1.1	1.3	2.3	2.5	7.9	7.2	6.9	7.8	9.8	27.5	20.9	10.4	1.6	74.0	32.1	49.6	50.4
39503	GULFPORT	75.3	73.6	20.4	21.3	1.5	1.8	2.3	2.6	7.7	7.4	7.7	7.0	7.4	31.5	23.1	7.7	0.5	72.9	33.4	49.9	50.1
39507	GULFPORT	78.0	75.7	18.0	19.5	1.2	1.6	2.9	3.4	5.7	5.5	5.9	6.4	7.3	28.4	24.2	15.2	1.6	79.2	39.0	48.7	51.3
39520	BAY SAINT LOUIS	87.2	85.9	9.0	9.6	1.2	1.5	1.8	2.1	6.0	6.1	7.1	6.5	6.1	26.4	28.1	12.2	1.5	76.6	39.7	50.2	49.8
39525	DIAMONDHEAD	95.3	94.5	1.8	2.0	0.9	1.2	3.0	3.5	4.8	4.9	5.0	4.2	3.1	20.1	32.0	24.3	1.7	82.5	50.6	48.6	51.4
39530	BILOXI	56.8	54.2	29.5	29.6	10.8	12.9	2.6	2.9	6.4	5.8	6.0	6.5	7.8	26.1	23.6	15.3	2.5	78.2	38.8	49.0	51.0
39531	BILOXI	72.0	68.5	19.6	21.6	3.3	4.1	4.3	4.9	8.5	7.2	7.0	6.0	8.6	32.5	18.5	10.5	1.3	74.1	32.1	49.2	50.8
39532	BILOXI	88.2	86.1	5.9	6.7	3.5	4.3	2.1	2.5	6.8	6.8	7.3	6.5	6.5	29.6	25.4	10.3	0.7	75.1	37.2	49.8	50.2
39534	BILOXI	66.9	63.4	19.2	20.6	3.0	3.7	9.0	10.3	6.1	3.6	1.9	30.2	38.6	18.5	1.0	0.0	0.1	87.5	21.1	65.8	34.2
39540	DIBERVILLE	77.7	74.8	11.9	12.7	7.1	8.7	2.6	3.1	7.1	6.8	7.3	7.1	7.4	31.8	23.2	8.7	0.6	74.6	34.2	49.8	50.2
39553	GAUTIER	70.1	67.8	26.0	27.8	1.2	1.4	2.5	3.0	8.4	7.9	7.7	6.9	6.9	29.3	24.1	8.4	0.6	71.9	33.6	49.4	50.6
39556	KILN	97.0	96.6	1.7	1.9	0.2	0.2	1.2	1.5	8.1	7.6	7.9	7.3	6.8	29.4	23.9	8.6	0.5	72.1	34.0	51.0	49.0
39560	LONG BEACH	85.4	83.5	9.7	10.6	2.4	3.1	2.2	2.6	6.7	6.7	7.3	7.6	7.1	28.1	24.8	10.9	1.0	74.6	36.3	48.1	51.9
39561	MC HENRY	89.5	88.4	8.5	9.3	0.4	0.5	2.0	1.9	6.4	6.0	6.3	12.7	12.4	24.8	22.9	8.1	0.4	78.0	30.2	52.2	47.8
39562	MOSS POINT	91.4	90.0	7.1	8.3	0.4	0.4	0.7	0.8	7.0	7.1	7.9	7.0	6.6	29.0	25.3	9.6	0.7	73.8	35.5	50.4	49.6
39563	MOSS POINT	28.4	26.7	70.1	71.8	0.3	0.3	1.0	1.1	6.5	6.9	7.8	7.1	7.0	24.5	26.5	12.2	1.5	74.4	37.5	47.8	52.3
39564	OCEAN SPRINGS	87.8	85.8	6.7	7.6	3.0	3.7	2.3	2.8	6.3	6.4	7.4	7.0	6.5	28.9	25.5	10.8	1.3	75.5	37.7	48.5	51.5
39565	OCEAN SPRINGS	93.8	92.8	3.6	4.1	0.7	0.8	1.4	1.7	7.6	7.6	8.2	7.3	6.6	31.2	23.2	7.8	0.6	71.9	34.0	50.7	49.3
39567	PASCAGOULA	70.6	67.8	26.7	29.0	0.5	0.6	2.4	2.8	6.6	6.1	6.1	7.1	10.3	26.3	22.3	12.9	2.3	77.5	35.7	52.1	47.9
39571	PASS CHRISTIAN	77.8	76.9	17.8	17.9	2.2	2.6	1.6	1.9	6.8	6.7	6.8	6.5	6.0	26.7	26.5	12.7	1.4	75.8	38.7	48.8	51.2
39572	PEARLINGTON	80.0	78.7	17.6	18.6	0.3	0.4	1.5	1.8	5.8	6.1	6.7	6.8	5.6	25.0	30.6	12.4	1.1	77.5	41.1	50.8	49.2
39573	PERKINSTON	90.6	90.0	7.6	7.8	0.3	0.4	1.3	1.5	6.9	6.9	7.3	8.8	8.4	27.2	24.6	9.2	0.6	74.9	34.0	50.7	49.3
39574	SAUCIER	93.7	92.8	4.1	4.6	0.4	0.6	1.3	1.6	8.3	8.0	8.2	7.2	6.7	30.5	23.4	7.2	0.4	71.0	33.4	51.5	48.5
39576	WAVELAND	86.0	84.3	10.9	12.0	1.4	1.8	1.9	2.2	6.1	6.3	7.9	7.2	6.4	25.2	26.4	13.2	1.5	75.3	39.1	47.4	52.6
39577	WIGGINS	74.1	72.9	24.7	25.8	0.1	0.1	1.1	1.3	7.4	7.4	7.9	6.8	6.6	27.2	23.7	11.6	1.5	73.2	35.5	48.5	51.5
39581	PASCAGOULA	62.4	58.7	32.5	35.5	1.5	1.8	5.6	6.4	9.3	8.3	8.2	7.1	8.1	29.0	21.6	7.8	0.6	70.0	30.7	49.3	50.7
39601	BROOKHAVEN	64.5	63.3	34.4	35.5	0.3	0.4	0.7	0.8	7.2	7.3	7.2	6.5	6.7	26.8	23.9	12.3	2.0	74.4	36.5	47.5	52.5
39629	BOGUE CHITTO	83.9	82.3	15.4	16.9	0.1	0.1	0.7	0.8	7.0	6.9	7.0	6.4	7.0	28.2	24.9	11.2	1.4	75.2	36.4	50.3	49.7
39630	BUDE	46.7	47.9	52.6	51.4	0.0	0.1	0.8	1.0	7.5	7.3	7.7	7.8	7.3	24.1	22.4	14.2	1.8	73.0	36.2	46.0	54.0
39631	CENTREVILLE	40.9	39.9	58.8	59.8	0.0	0.0	0.2	0.2	7.1	6.9	7.4	7.3	7.4	23.9	25.0	12.3	2.7	74.3	37.3	47.7	52.3
39633	CROSBY	54.1	53.1	44.6	45.6	0.1	0.1	1.2	1.2	6.5	6.5	6.8	6.5	6.3	25.9	25.7	13.7	2.3	76.4	39.5	49.3	50.7
39638	GLOSTER	49.2	48.7	49.9	50.5	0.0	0.0	0.9	0.9	6.2	6.3	8.0	7.3	6.9	24.3	26.0	13.3	1.8	75.1	38.4	47.4	52.6
39641	JAYESS	78.6	78.8	20.5	20.1	0.2	0.3	0.9	1.0	7.2	7.1	6.8	6.1	6.5	27.4	25.4	12.3	1.2	75.3	36.8	49.6	50.4
39643	KOKOMO	66.9	65.3	32.3	33.7	0.1	0.1	0.4	0.6	7.9	7.7	7.2	6.8	7.2	26.1	24.6	11.4	1.3	73.3	35.3	48.6	51.4
39645	LIBERTY	58.8	57.6	40.1	41.3	0.1	0.1	0.8	0.9	6.1	6.3	7.1	6.6	6.7	25.1	26.4	13.9	1.8	76.5	39.3	49.2	50.8
39647	MC CALL CREEK	82.1	82.6	17.5	16.9	0.0	0.1	0.4	0.5	7.2	6.8	5.5	6.1	6.3	25.2	25.2	15.0	2.6	76.8	39.7	49.2	50.8
39648	MCCOMB	46.4	45.4	52.2	53.2	0.4	0.4	0.8	0.8	8.0	7.8	7.8	6.7	7.3	25.2	22.6	12.4	2.4	72.6	34.9	46.1	54.0
39652	MAGNOLIA	45.0	44.7	54.0	54.3	0.1	0.2	0.8	0.7	7.0	6.9	7.4	7.0	7.6	25.7	25.2	11.8	1.5	74.6	36.4	49.1	50.9
39653	MEADVILLE	72.7	73.3	26.2	25.3	0.2	0.3	0.6	0.7	5.7	5.7	6.5	7.6	7.2	22.9	26.5	15.0	3.0	77.4	40.7	48.5	51.5
39654	MONTICELLO	73.2	71.4	25.6	27.1	0.5	0.6	0.6	0.7	6.9	6.8	7.5	6.7	7.0	26.1	23.5	13.5	1.9	74.8	37.2	47.6	52.4
39656	OAK VALE	59.9	57.9	40.1	41.9	0.0	0.0	0.3	0.6	7.3	7.0	6.7	7.6	7.6	26.2	25.3	11.3	1.2	74.7	35.3	49.4	50.6
39657	OSYKA	55.5	54.3	43.6	44.7	0.1	0.1	0.8	0.7	8.3	7.9	7.4	7.2	7.0	24.4	23.3	12.6	1.9	72.0	35.6	48.2	51.8
39661	ROXIE	46.4	45.6	52.6	53.4	0.1	0.1	0.6	0.5	7.6	7.7	8.0	8.2	7.3	25.9	23.9	10.1	1.2	71.5	34.4	48.7	51.3
39662	RUTH	87.0	87.1	12.6	12.3	0.0	0.0	0.4	0.5	6.9	7.0	7.7	6.8	7.5	28.0	24.3	10.6	1.2	74.3	36.0	50.4	49.6
39663	SILVER CREEK	49.4	47.4	49.8	51.8	0.3	0.3	0.5	0.5	7.1	7.1	8.2	7.5	6.9	26.4	24.2	11.2	1.5	73.1	35.6	48.4	51.6
39664	SMITHDALE	78.2	76.9	[illegible]	21.7	0.1	0.1	0.8	0.8	5.9	6.1	6.5	6.0	6.4	25.6	27.4	14.4	1.8	77.9	40.7	50.3	49.7
39665	SONTAG	54.0	51.7	45.2	47.2	0.3	0.3	1.2	1.3	6.8	6.9	7.7	7.3	7.9	26.5	25.0	10.9	1.3	74.4	35.8	48.0	52.0
39666	SUMMIT	69.1	68.4	30.0	30.6	0.3	0.3	0.7	0.7	6.6	6.7	7.4	6.7	7.4	26.2	25.7	12.2	1.3	75.7	37.3	48.3	51.7
39667	TYLERTOWN	52.4	50.9	46.2	47.5	0.3	0.3	1.3	1.4	7.4	7.3	8.1	7.3	7.1	25.5	23.2	12.2	2.0	72.9	35.2	47.7	52.3
39668	UNION CHURCH	43.2	41.7	55.7	56.9	0.3	0.3	0.8	0.8	5.8	6.0	7.1	7.8	7.9	23.8	24.7	14.6	2.3	76.6	39.5	46.3	53.7
39669	WOODVILLE	25.7	25.1	73.8	74.3	0.0	0.0	0.4	0.4	5.2	5.6	7.3	7.3	9.6	30.6	22.1	10.8	1.6	77.7	35.1	55.3	44.7
39701	COLUMBUS	28.2	27.0	70.2	71.2	0.4	0.5	1.1	1.1	7.7	7.6	8.2	8.6	9.4	26.4	20.7	9.8	1.7	71.9	31.0	45.4	54.6
39702	COLUMBUS	64.3	62.3	34.4	36.2	0.2	0.3	0.7	0.8	7.7	7.7	8.1	7.4	6.7	27.7	22.4	10.4	2.0	72.0	34.9	46.7	53.4
39705	COLUMBUS	70.7	67.4	25.6	28.3	1.5	1.8	1.9	2.2	8.3	6.9	6.4	6.0	9.3	30.6	22.9	8.7	1.1	74.8	33.0	50.7	49.3
39710	COLUMBUS	75.8	73.0	16.3	17.6	2.5	2.9	4.7	5.4	15.1	9.4	6.5	5.0	19.8	40.7	3.2	0.4	0.0	66.9	23.6	55.8	44.2
39730	ABERDEEN	50.1	48.7	49.1	50.4	0.3	0.4	0.5	0.6	7.2	7.1	8.4	7.3	7.3	26.1	22.8	11.7	2.2	72.7	35.2	47.1	52.9
39735	ACKERMAN	69.9	69.4	28.7	29.1	0.2	0.2	1.0	1.0	6.7	6.7	6.9	6.8	6.7	25.2	25.2	13.5	2.3	75.6	38.8	47.9	52.2
39739	BROOKSVILLE	25.1	24.2	73.8	74.6	0.0	0.0	1.3	1.4	8.9	8.7	8.7	7.8	7.9	25.3	21.0	10.1	1.6	69.1	31.1	47.8	52.2
39740	CALEDONIA	85.3	83.6	13.3	14.8	0.3	0.4	1.0	1.2	7.7	7.7	8.1	7.1	6.8	30.0	23.4	8.2	1.0	72.2	34.6	50.0	50.0
39741	CEDARBLUFF	52.6	51.1	46.7	48.2	0.0	0.0	0.8	0.8	7.5	7.2	7.6	7.7	7.6	27.5	23.3	10.5	1.0	73.0	34.8	48.7	51.3
39743	CRAWFORD	15.3	14.3	84.0	84.9	0.1	0.1	0.3	0.4	9.1	8.5	8.6	7.8	7.5	27.5	21.4	8.4	1.2	69.1	31.3	47.2	52.8
39744	EUPORA	71.4	70.0	26.6	27.8	0.1	0.1	2.3	2.8	7.0	6.6	7.1	6.8	7.0	24.4	23.5	14.5	3.2	75.2	38.8	48.4	51.6
39745	FRENCH CAMP	71.6	70.9	26.9	27.7	0.1	0.1	0.9	0.8	6.6	7.3	7.4	11.8	7.2	22.6	22.6	12.5	2.2	70.3	34.1	49.9	50.1
39746	HAMILTON	81.3	79.5	17.7	19.4	0.1	0.1	1.6	1.8	6.2	6.4	7.5	7.2	7.1	29.4	24.0	11.0	1.4	75.7	36.4	49.7	50.3
39747	KILMICHAEL	61.7	60.9	37.6	38.4	0.1	0.1	1.2	1.3	7.0	6.9	6.8	5.9	6.5	24.3	25.6	14.6	2.3	75.8	39.5	49.1	50.9
39750	MABEN	68.8	65.0	30.5	34.2	0.1	0.2	0.6	0.7	8.0	7.7	7.3	6.5	7.0	27.2	23.3	11.6	1.4	73.2	35.0	47.1	52.9
39751	MANTEE	90.5	89.7	8.8	9.4	0.2	0.3	0.8	1.0	6.8	6.8	6.8	5.8	5.7	28.1	24.8	13.6	1.6	76.0	38.7	51.3	48.7
39752	MATHISTON	81.9	81.1	17.1	17.8	0.3	0.3	0.9	1.0	6.9	6.9	7.4	7.0	7.5	26.6	24.5	12.0	1.4	74.9	36.6	48.0	52.0
39755	PHEBA	53.3	51.3	46.1	48.0	0.1	0.1	0.3	0.4	8.0	7.7	7.5	6.7	7.1	27.2	23.3	11.0	1.6	73.0	35.2	49.1	50.9
39756	PRAIRIE	18.9	17.1	80.5	82.2	0.2	0.2	0.4	0.4	8.0	7.6	6.3	7.1	7.3	28.6	25.1	8.6	1.5	73.8	34.6	50.0	50.0
39759	STARKVILLE	57.7	56.0	38.1	39.0	2.8	3.4	1.1	1.3	6.1	5.5	5.9	12.8	17.4	26.5	17.2	7.6	1.1	78.9	26.1	49.7	50.3
39762	MISSISSIPPI STATE	71.7	70.3	24.8	25.2	2.6	3.3	1.0	1.1	2.7	3.1	3.6	24.3	31.8	17.6	10.8	5.5	0.6	87.8	22.6	48.7	51.3
39766	STEENS	74.1	71.6	24.7	27.1	0.2	0.3	0.4	0.4	5.3	6.4	8.3	6.5	5.3	28.4	26.2	12.3	1.4	75.9	38.5	48.1	51.9
39767	STEWART	79.5	78.5	19.1	19.7	0.0	0.0	1.8	1.9	7.0	7.0	7.0	5.8	6.3	26.2	25.0	13.9	1.6	75.2	38.6	50.7	49.3
39769	STURGIS	74.5	73.4	24.6	25.6	0.1	0.1	0.6	0.7	6.0	6.0	6.2	6.7	6.5	30.2	24.8	12.2	1.5	77.7	37.5	52.5	47.5
39772	WEIR	53.8	52.9	45.3	46.0	0.1	0.1	0.5	0.5	7.4	7.3	8.1	7.5	7.3	23.8	23.9	12.6	2.2	72.6	36.5	47.9	52.2
	MISSISSIPPI	61.4	60.6	36.3	36.8	0.7	0.8	1.4	1.6	7.3	7.1	7.4	7.4	7.8	27.8	23.0	10.6	1.6	73.9	34.5	48.5	51.5
	UNITED STATES	75.1	73.6	12.3	12.5	3.8	4.2	12.5	14.1	6.9	6.7	7.2	7.0	7.3	28.6	23.8	10.8	1.7	75.1	36.0	49.1	50.9

#	POST OFFICE NAME	2004 Per Capita Income	2004 HH Income Base	2004 Household Income Distribution (%): Less than $25,000	$25,000 to $49,999	$50,000 to $99,999	$100,000 to $149,999	$150,000 or More	Median Household Income: 2004	2009	2004 National Centile	2004 State Centile	2004 Home Value Base	2004 Home Value Distribution (%): Less than $50,000	$50,000 to $89,999	$90,000 to $174,999	$175,000 to $399,999	$400,000 or More	2004 Median Home Value
39452	LUCEDALE	16643	7671	31.7	32.5	29.2	4.9	1.7	38062	42497	39	84	6448	32.8	30.4	27.3	8.4	1.1	70851
39455	LUMBERTON	14670	3020	43.5	31.7	19.2	3.8	1.7	28617	32611	10	36	2521	36.8	32.4	22.7	6.5	1.7	63273
39456	MC LAIN	13554	465	47.7	33.1	15.9	1.9	1.3	26576	29889	7	23	397	55.7	25.4	15.4	3.0	0.5	43571
39459	MOSELLE	16516	1402	41.8	34.0	16.9	4.9	2.4	28997	32505	10	39	1198	38.8	24.0	29.4	6.8	1.1	65287
39461	NEELY	16431	442	36.0	35.1	23.5	4.5	0.9	34195	37792	25	70	385	38.2	29.6	24.7	5.2	2.3	65345
39462	NEW AUGUSTA	13566	730	45.5	28.4	22.1	4.0	0.1	28266	30852	9	34	586	39.8	37.0	18.1	3.6	1.5	63226
39464	OVETT	14884	804	40.1	34.2	20.5	4.1	1.1	30465	33733	13	48	713	44.2	25.7	18.9	10.8	0.4	58830
39465	PETAL	17431	7124	33.6	29.8	28.6	6.7	1.3	37935	43087	39	84	5752	27.7	29.7	34.9	7.5	0.3	77571
39466	PICAYUNE	17123	10234	39.1	30.2	23.7	4.8	2.3	32106	36169	18	60	7800	27.8	30.6	30.4	10.0	1.2	78182
39470	POPLARVILLE	16941	4388	35.7	33.3	23.8	5.0	2.3	35100	39522	28	74	3555	32.2	28.1	25.8	11.5	2.5	76230
39474	PRENTISS	14596	3304	50.0	26.7	17.7	3.4	2.2	25000	27457	5	13	2671	45.1	33.2	18.8	2.3	0.6	55530
39475	PURVIS	18586	3553	27.0	35.1	29.2	6.4	2.3	40529	46669	48	87	2948	22.7	26.0	39.8	10.4	1.2	91461
39476	RICHTON	15567	2893	39.4	32.9	22.3	3.9	1.4	31776	35050	17	58	2420	42.2	33.1	19.8	4.3	0.6	56460
39478	SANDY HOOK	13501	755	46.9	31.4	18.8	2.4	0.5	27255	30000	7	27	666	52.1	19.8	20.3	7.1	0.8	48478
39479	SEMINARY	15822	2362	40.9	31.8	22.0	3.8	1.5	31271	34220	16	55	2039	40.4	28.9	22.9	7.0	0.8	63576
39480	SOSO	17271	1024	35.0	36.2	22.2	4.7	2.0	33062	37665	21	65	862	38.9	28.7	23.1	8.8	0.6	61875
39481	STRINGER	17192	597	38.0	31.3	22.3	6.5	1.8	34437	38749	26	71	523	40.9	32.3	18.4	6.7	1.7	62212
39482	SUMRALL	18377	2562	34.9	33.4	24.6	3.8	3.4	35000	39857	28	74	2170	28.9	30.2	28.3	9.2	3.5	76395
39483	FOXWORTH	12802	1850	46.0	32.5	18.8	2.0	0.7	27186	30744	7	27	1534	43.7	34.2	15.7	6.2	0.2	56218
39501	GULFPORT	15605	9512	44.8	32.2	17.9	3.5	1.7	27957	30889	9	32	5121	23.6	45.0	26.2	4.2	1.0	72415
39503	GULFPORT	20274	14424	25.3	32.0	32.1	7.5	3.2	43984	48811	59	92	10788	14.9	27.3	41.7	13.7	2.4	97414
39507	GULFPORT	24899	8675	30.7	32.1	25.4	8.6	3.3	38746	42959	42	85	4926	4.3	22.1	52.6	17.6	3.4	117017
39520	BAY SAINT LOUIS	19113	7507	35.4	34.5	23.5	4.3	2.4	34171	38121	25	70	5561	23.7	29.5	36.6	8.9	1.4	85809
39525	DIAMONDHEAD	30671	3016	16.7	27.1	36.6	12.4	7.1	55603	61435	80	98	2746	2.4	8.1	48.2	37.6	3.8	160706
39530	BILOXI	19213	6247	43.9	31.3	18.1	3.8	2.8	28479	31578	10	35	2917	19.5	39.0	27.7	9.8	4.0	79790
39531	BILOXI	20524	8939	30.1	36.1	26.2	5.1	2.6	37490	41692	37	82	3350	6.4	27.2	42.8	19.5	4.2	106205
39532	BILOXI	21907	10520	20.3	32.2	36.6	8.1	2.8	47798	53644	68	95	8610	13.8	22.5	46.4	15.4	1.9	108738
39534	BILOXI	10241	312	22.4	54.5	18.6	3.9	0.6	35414	39163	29	75	9	0.0	22.2	77.8	0.0	0.0	120833
39540	DIBERVILLE	17751	3025	26.0	41.7	27.2	4.0	1.1	38001	43257	39	84	2209	25.0	36.1	33.2	4.1	1.6	81850
39553	GAUTIER	20391	6429	25.7	29.9	33.5	7.8	3.2	45849	51011	63	94	4820	19.9	30.2	39.7	9.5	0.8	89970
39556	KILN	17745	2492	34.0	33.3	25.2	5.2	2.4	36440	40789	33	79	2021	33.8	26.4	25.7	12.6	1.6	71903
39560	LONG BEACH	21813	7779	24.7	31.1	32.8	8.2	3.3	45628	51138	63	93	5424	7.1	24.6	53.5	12.7	2.1	109458
39561	MC HENRY	19387	425	27.5	34.8	30.8	4.5	2.4	40991	47358	50	88	366	28.4	24.9	33.9	9.8	3.0	86129
39562	MOSS POINT	18151	6155	24.9	34.9	31.2	7.2	1.7	41152	46536	50	89	5135	24.3	36.5	30.9	7.6	0.7	79003
39563	MOSS POINT	17716	5768	33.8	33.6	24.8	5.7	2.2	35569	40218	30	76	4265	25.2	46.8	22.2	5.1	0.7	68487
39564	OCEAN SPRINGS	25292	13060	17.6	31.0	35.0	11.5	4.8	51177	56603	74	97	10202	6.4	22.5	50.6	17.6	3.0	115492
39565	OCEAN SPRINGS	17683	5780	21.6	35.4	35.2	6.9	0.9	44830	50373	61	93	5211	21.5	29.3	36.6	11.6	1.0	88988
39567	PASCAGOULA	19602	5361	38.8	29.9	21.9	6.4	3.0	32460	35244	19	62	3168	15.7	40.5	31.1	10.0	2.7	82056
39571	PASS CHRISTIAN	24607	6252	29.2	28.3	28.9	8.4	5.2	43404	47716	57	90	5030	13.4	26.1	36.3	19.2	4.9	105633
39572	PEARLINGTON	15716	750	39.5	35.2	19.9	3.7	1.7	33649	36241	23	68	612	39.5	32.5	23.5	2.9	1.5	62549
39573	PERKINSTON	17092	2450	33.8	29.9	28.7	5.4	2.2	37887	42385	39	83	2103	35.0	21.3	29.3	12.2	2.3	80404
39574	SAUCIER	18674	4222	29.1	33.9	30.2	4.1	2.7	40213	45000	47	87	3588	23.2	30.2	32.0	12.4	2.1	85941
39576	WAVELAND	19649	2922	33.1	34.1	26.8	3.7	2.3	37080	40461	36	81	2096	11.9	27.7	44.4	13.9	2.1	102576
39577	WIGGINS	16314	3250	43.2	26.6	22.2	5.4	2.7	30383	34613	13	47	2547	33.7	26.7	28.0	9.0	2.7	76372
39581	PASCAGOULA	18071	4624	35.4	30.5	25.0	6.7	2.4	36386	39618	33	79	2519	10.3	48.0	34.8	6.7	0.2	83210
39601	BROOKHAVEN	16271	9079	43.0	29.1	20.0	6.2	1.8	29760	33200	12	43	6634	34.4	30.6	26.4	7.7	0.9	68250
39629	BOGUE CHITTO	15961	2225	37.7	34.2	22.1	5.5	0.6	33272	37656	22	66	1914	38.5	30.9	25.2	4.9	0.6	61270
39630	BUDE	12247	461	60.5	24.3	13.0	1.7	0.4	19154	20923	2	3	337	54.3	32.1	13.7	0.0	0.0	45167
39631	CENTREVILLE	13213	1481	51.9	27.6	16.3	2.6	1.6	23458	26216	3	9	1226	46.3	29.1	16.2	7.3	1.1	53600
39633	CROSBY	12380	425	58.8	23.3	13.2	3.3	1.4	19689	22621	2	3	339	58.4	22.1	16.2	0.6	2.7	34914
39638	GLOSTER	14413	1585	49.3	31.1	15.4	2.8	1.3	25415	28237	5	15	1300	48.9	25.5	19.0	5.3	1.3	51111
39641	JAYESS	15029	1695	47.7	24.8	22.8	3.8	0.9	26902	30630	7	25	1462	34.1	32.6	26.5	4.7	2.1	69054
39643	KOKOMO	12764	510	43.9	31.8	22.0	2.4	0.0	28723	32169	10	37	423	46.1	28.1	21.3	4.5	0.0	54024
39645	LIBERTY	17259	2244	45.2	29.8	19.6	3.9	1.5	28127	31414	9	33	1859	40.3	27.4	23.0	7.2	2.2	61306
39647	MC CALL CREEK	18445	725	45.7	27.0	22.8	2.8	1.8	27408	31065	8	29	651	43.2	29.8	19.5	7.5	0.0	58091
39648	MCCOMB	15664	8187	48.8	29.0	16.3	3.4	2.5	25702	28843	5	18	5410	42.5	33.4	19.3	4.2	0.6	56940
39652	MAGNOLIA	14835	3289	47.5	30.6	16.3	3.7	1.9	26538	30299	6	23	2648	41.1	31.7	19.6	6.0	1.7	58020
39653	MEADVILLE	17638	584	36.0	35.3	22.8	4.1	1.9	34800	39567	27	72	481	40.3	32.9	19.5	7.3	0.0	57381
39654	MONTICELLO	19404	1702	37.8	24.9	30.0	4.8	2.5	34896	40000	27	73	1304	32.0	38.7	25.1	3.7	0.5	69716
39656	OAK VALE	16311	136	34.6	31.6	31.6	0.7	1.5	32715	37834	20	64	120	34.2	40.8	18.3	6.7	0.0	61765
39657	OSYKA	14448	767	47.6	29.9	15.1	4.7	2.7	27135	31039	7	26	636	39.0	28.1	20.1	11.6	1.1	64545
39661	ROXIE	13151	1523	49.6	27.2	19.3	2.6	1.3	25227	28257	5	15	1268	53.0	28.8	14.3	3.6	0.4	47397
39662	RUTH	17940	374	32.6	33.7	28.3	4.3	1.1	39674	44828	45	86	323	36.5	23.5	22.0	16.7	1.2	69762
39663	SILVER CREEK	14199	1225	44.2	28.5	23.8	3.3	0.2	28319	32491	9	34	1021	42.6	32.9	17.7	5.6	1.2	57190
39664	SMITHDALE	18610	851	35.3	36.2	23.2	3.6	1.8	31968	35883	18	59	722	40.9	32.8	16.9	7.8	1.7	60000
39665	SONTAG	17431	670	38.1	31.0	22.7	6.7	1.5	35000	40832	28	74	574	49.7	31.0	14.3	5.1	0.0	50345
39666	SUMMIT	19502	3363	40.7	25.8	23.9	5.6	4.1	31522	35905	16	57	2756	31.0	26.5	27.4	12.0	3.1	78308
39667	TYLERTOWN	14467	4566	49.1	27.3	18.5	3.0	2.2	25583	28902	5	16	3627	39.5	28.1	24.9	5.2	2.3	63976
39668	UNION CHURCH	15698	309	43.0	35.3	16.8	1.0	3.9	30695	35648	14	50	288	55.6	37.2	4.9	0.0	2.4	46098
39669	WOODVILLE	14031	2183	54.1	25.6	14.7	2.3	3.3	21518	24462	2	5	1784	54.4	25.7	14.2	3.8	1.9	45938
39701	COLUMBUS	15114	5922	50.9	26.8	15.5	4.4	2.4	24193	27912	4	10	3235	36.5	32.0	21.2	8.2	2.0	63949
39702	COLUMBUS	18013	8349	34.0	31.5	26.7	5.6	2.2	36799	41448	35	80	6357	16.9	40.9	35.7	6.1	0.4	82154
39705	COLUMBUS	26943	5744	26.5	29.4	28.2	9.7	6.3	44669	50028	60	92	3499	15.0	21.9	43.5	16.4	3.2	107288
39710	COLUMBUS	2193	8	12.5	62.5	25.0	0.0	0.0	40000	45000	46	86	0	0.0	0.0	0.0	0.0	0.0	0
39730	ABERDEEN	15062	4702	41.0	32.5	21.6	3.5	1.5	30822	34291	14	51	3463	36.3	30.6	23.7	8.0	1.4	66081
39735	ACKERMAN	16176	2116	42.4	32.7	18.0	4.8	2.0	30568	32987	14	49	1590	33.8	34.0	25.0	6.0	1.3	67117
39739	BROOKSVILLE	13132	1664	50.2	30.4	14.2	3.3	1.9	24792	28036	4	12	1354	52.3	27.0	14.0	4.1	2.5	47737
39740	CALEDONIA	19098	1945	22.9	36.2	32.6	6.4	1.9	42671	49225	55	90	1631	21.8	32.9	33.1	11.5	0.7	86286
39741	CEDARBLUFF	15251	395	42.8	21.3	31.1	4.1	0.8	31703	35558	17	57	328	29.9	50.0	11.6	8.5	0.0	62692
39743	CRAWFORD	12185	829	50.7	28.2	16.2	4.1	0.8	24485	28773	4	11	680	59.7	20.6	11.0	7.8	0.9	40149
39744	EUPORA	15009	2164	43.4	29.1	23.5	3.4	0.7	30101	32704	12	45	1544	36.1	35.8	23.7	3.5	0.9	67069
39745	FRENCH CAMP	13092	584	43.3	36.5	17.0	2.7	0.5	28351	31918	9	34	480	39.8	32.5	20.0	5.0	2.7	61277
39746	HAMILTON	17314	1246	31.0	31.4	32.8	4.3	0.6	37425	41269	37	82	1037	30.0	31.3	28.5	9.3	0.9	73161
39747	KILMICHAEL	15637	996	47.5	32.1	15.5	3.1	1.8	26382	30546	6	22	805	49.6	32.6	16.8	1.1	0.0	50636
39750	MABEN	19814	1056	41.8	32.8	19.5	2.8	3.2	30602	36288	14	50	837	37.9	30.0	25.8	5.4	1.0	66013
39751	MANTEE	18591	823	36.1	35.6	20.2	5.6	2.6	36265	40612	33	79	732	44.0	34.4	15.7	4.8	1.1	55057
39752	MATHISTON	16206	1127	40.6	37.9	17.1	2.3	2.1	30775	34387	14	51	918	43.5	29.9	23.1	3.6	0.0	58696
39755	PHEBA	16372	304	41.5	27.6	25.7	3.3	2.0	30932	36120	15	52	250	33.2	42.0	18.0	6.8	0.0	59767
39756	PRAIRIE	14602	198	38.4	37.9	15.7	4.6	3.5	30162	33658	13	46	156	55.1	32.7	5.1	7.1	0.0	45789
39759	STARKVILLE	18901	15757	46.3	24.2	18.8	8.1	2.6	27891	33045	8	31	7932	26.7	22.3	33.6	14.9	2.6	91876
39762	MISSISSIPPI STATE	2392	12	75.0	8.3	8.3	8.3	0.0	12041	12857	1	0	0	0.0	0.0	0.0	0.0	0.0	0
39766	STEENS	18360	838	26.6	35.4	32.1	5.6	0.2	40000	46229	46	86	709	18.1	33.2	39.9	7.2	1.7	88629
39767	STEWART	17303	239	49.0	31.8	15.9	0.8	2.5	25680	29694	5	18	198	46.0	34.3	17.7	2.0	0.0	58000
39769	STURGIS	17040	686	40.4	30.9	21.0	6.7	1.0	30534	36212	14	49	563	43.5	27.0	22.0	7.5	0.0	59605
39772	WEIR	17988	610	46.1	32.1	15.6	3.3	3.0	27461	30452	8	29	501	41.1	34.7	18.2	5.0	1.0	58241
	MISSISSIPPI	18480		36.7	30.0	24.5	5.9	2.8	34621	39377				29.7	30.4	28.7	9.7	1.6	75922
	UNITED STATES	25866		24.7	27.1	30.8	10.9	6.5	48124	56710				10.9	15.0	33.7	30.1	10.4	145905

ZIP CODE #	POST OFFICE NAME	FINANCIAL SERVICES: Auto Loan	FINANCIAL SERVICES: Home Loan	FINANCIAL SERVICES: Investments	FINANCIAL SERVICES: Retirement Plans	THE HOME: Home Improvements: Home Repair	THE HOME: Home Improvements: Lawn & Garden	THE HOME: Furnishings: Computers & Hardware	THE HOME: Furnishings: Major Appliances	THE HOME: Furnishings: TV, Radio, Sound Equipment	THE HOME: Furnishings: Furniture	ENTERTAINMENT: Dine out/Carry out	ENTERTAINMENT: Sports Equipment	ENTERTAINMENT: Fees & Tickets	ENTERTAINMENT: Toys & Games	ENTERTAINMENT: Travel	ENTERTAINMENT: Cable TV	PERSONAL: Apparel & Services	PERSONAL: Auto Repairs	PERSONAL: Health Insurance	PERSONAL: Pets & Supplies
39452	LUCEDALE	80	61	38	56	67	75	58	69	66	59	79	81	54	77	60	70	74	67	80	93
39455	LUMBERTON	69	50	29	46	55	63	49	58	57	50	67	69	44	64	50	60	62	58	69	78
39456	MC LAIN	71	47	21	41	54	62	46	57	55	46	65	68	39	61	46	59	59	56	70	81
39459	MOSELLE	81	55	26	47	62	71	53	65	63	54	74	78	45	70	54	68	68	65	80	93
39461	NEELY	73	49	22	42	55	63	47	59	57	48	67	70	40	63	48	61	60	58	72	83
39462	NEW AUGUSTA	68	46	22	40	52	59	45	55	53	45	63	66	38	59	45	57	57	55	67	77
39464	OVETT	70	51	28	45	56	63	48	58	56	49	66	69	43	64	49	59	61	57	69	80
39465	PETAL	70	67	60	66	68	73	66	69	67	66	82	79	65	81	66	67	79	68	69	79
39466	PICAYUNE	75	58	38	53	62	70	57	66	64	57	77	77	52	73	58	67	71	65	76	85
39470	POPLARVILLE	74	59	39	56	63	71	58	66	64	58	77	77	53	74	59	66	71	66	74	84
39474	PRENTISS	63	46	32	40	49	58	48	55	56	48	66	62	43	61	47	60	61	55	66	71
39475	PURVIS	78	70	57	70	72	78	69	73	71	69	87	85	67	86	69	72	83	72	76	87
39476	RICHTON	74	53	28	47	58	66	52	62	60	52	71	73	45	67	52	64	65	61	74	84
39478	SANDY HOOK	65	43	20	37	49	57	42	52	51	43	59	63	36	56	43	54	54	52	64	74
39479	SEMINARY	68	56	39	52	59	64	54	61	58	55	70	71	49	67	54	59	66	60	66	77
39480	SOSO	78	55	29	49	62	70	53	65	62	54	74	77	46	71	54	67	68	64	78	90
39481	STRINGER	83	56	27	50	64	73	55	68	65	55	76	82	47	73	56	70	69	67	83	96
39482	SUMRALL	83	69	49	65	73	79	66	74	71	67	86	87	62	84	66	73	81	73	81	94
39483	FOXWORTH	64	43	20	37	49	56	42	52	50	42	59	62	35	56	42	54	54	51	64	74
39501	GULFPORT	56	50	56	48	49	58	55	54	59	55	73	61	54	70	54	61	70	56	59	62
39503	GULFPORT	81	81	76	79	80	83	78	80	77	79	96	93	77	95	77	76	94	80	77	92
39507	GULFPORT	76	73	83	75	73	80	79	77	79	78	99	89	78	95	77	78	96	79	76	85
39520	BAY SAINT LOUIS	72	64	55	60	67	74	62	68	66	62	81	79	59	80	64	69	77	67	75	84
39525	DIAMONDHEAD	105	98	94	93	104	123	91	104	96	98	120	101	92	100	99	103	112	101	121	118
39530	BILOXI	58	51	63	51	51	59	60	57	63	58	77	66	58	74	58	63	75	60	60	64
39531	BILOXI	68	58	67	62	56	63	70	65	71	68	88	80	66	84	65	67	86	71	62	73
39532	BILOXI	83	87	83	85	87	90	81	84	80	82	100	98	82	101	82	80	97	82	82	97
39534	BILOXI	69	44	42	50	40	47	65	56	66	61	82	75	56	74	53	60	79	66	52	64
39540	DIBERVILLE	67	67	63	67	67	70	66	67	65	66	81	78	65	81	65	64	78	67	65	76
39553	GAUTIER	82	78	71	75	78	83	75	78	77	76	95	91	74	94	75	77	92	78	79	93
39556	KILN	77	69	53	66	70	75	66	72	68	67	83	83	61	79	65	68	79	71	73	87
39560	LONG BEACH	78	82	85	83	81	83	80	80	78	80	97	94	81	98	80	75	95	80	75	89
39561	MC HENRY	77	69	53	66	72	77	64	71	68	65	83	84	63	83	66	69	79	69	75	90
39562	MOSS POINT	86	70	47	65	74	82	66	76	73	67	87	89	62	86	67	75	82	74	85	99
39563	MOSS POINT	67	64	66	60	64	73	64	66	68	65	85	72	66	82	65	71	82	66	72	76
39564	OCEAN SPRINGS	88	99	105	99	97	99	94	93	90	94	113	108	97	115	94	87	111	92	86	102
39565	OCEAN SPRINGS	82	75	59	72	75	80	71	76	72	72	89	89	68	86	70	72	85	76	77	92
39567	PASCAGOULA	67	64	65	61	64	72	66	67	69	65	85	76	65	85	66	70	82	67	71	77
39571	PASS CHRISTIAN	96	87	76	83	90	100	84	91	88	86	108	102	81	102	86	90	103	90	98	110
39572	PEARLINGTON	73	51	26	44	57	66	49	60	58	49	68	72	42	65	50	62	62	60	74	85
39573	PERKINSTON	78	69	52	65	71	76	65	71	68	66	83	84	62	81	65	69	79	70	76	90
39574	SAUCIER	83	76	60	73	76	80	73	78	73	75	91	90	69	86	72	72	87	78	77	92
39576	WAVELAND	74	61	48	59	66	74	63	69	68	61	81	81	58	80	63	69	76	69	77	86
39577	WIGGINS	73	56	39	51	60	68	57	64	64	57	77	75	52	74	57	67	72	64	74	83
39581	PASCAGOULA	67	64	65	64	65	71	68	67	69	66	86	78	67	86	67	69	83	68	69	76
39601	BROOKHAVEN	66	53	43	49	56	64	54	59	60	54	72	68	51	69	54	63	68	59	68	75
39629	BOGUE CHITTO	75	55	30	49	60	68	53	63	61	54	72	75	46	69	53	64	66	62	74	86
39630	BUDE	52	35	17	31	40	46	34	43	41	35	48	51	29	46	35	44	44	42	52	60
39631	CENTREVILLE	58	42	30	36	45	53	43	50	51	44	61	57	39	56	43	55	56	50	60	65
39633	CROSBY	58	39	18	33	44	51	37	47	45	38	53	56	32	50	38	49	48	46	58	66
39638	GLOSTER	64	44	24	38	49	57	44	53	52	44	62	62	38	58	44	56	56	53	65	73
39641	JAYESS	72	49	22	42	55	64	47	59	57	48	66	70	40	63	48	61	60	58	72	83
39643	KOKOMO	66	44	20	38	50	58	43	53	51	43	60	64	36	57	43	55	55	53	66	76
39645	LIBERTY	79	54	26	47	61	70	53	65	63	53	74	77	45	70	54	68	67	64	80	91
39647	MC CALL CREEK	84	56	26	49	64	73	55	68	66	55	77	81	47	73	55	71	70	67	84	96
39648	MCCOMB	62	49	41	45	51	59	52	56	58	52	70	64	48	66	51	60	66	57	64	69
39652	MAGNOLIA	70	48	25	42	54	62	47	58	57	48	67	68	41	63	48	61	61	58	71	80
39653	MEADVILLE	79	56	31	51	62	73	58	68	67	57	79	78	50	74	58	71	72	67	82	89
39654	MONTICELLO	83	62	38	58	68	78	63	72	71	62	84	84	56	81	63	74	77	71	85	94
39656	OAK VALE	78	52	24	45	59	68	50	63	61	51	71	75	43	67	51	65	65	62	77	89
39657	OSYKA	69	48	26	44	54	63	49	58	58	49	68	68	43	64	50	62	62	58	71	78
39661	ROXIE	67	45	21	39	51	59	44	54	53	44	62	65	37	58	44	57	56	54	67	77
39662	RUTH	85	57	26	50	65	75	55	69	66	56	78	83	47	74	56	71	71	68	85	98
39663	SILVER CREEK	68	46	23	40	52	60	45	55	54	46	64	66	39	60	46	58	58	55	68	78
39664	SMITHDALE	85	57	27	51	65	75	56	69	66	56	78	83	47	74	57	71	71	69	85	98
39665	SONTAG	86	57	26	50	65	75	55	69	67	56	79	83	47	74	56	72	71	69	85	98
39666	SUMMIT	88	64	37	59	71	81	63	75	73	63	86	89	56	83	65	77	79	75	90	102
39667	TYLERTOWN	70	47	24	41	53	62	47	57	56	47	66	68	40	62	47	60	60	57	70	79
39668	UNION CHURCH	71	48	23	41	54	62	46	57	56	47	65	68	40	62	47	60	60	57	71	81
39669	WOODVILLE	61	46	36	41	49	58	48	55	56	49	67	61	44	62	48	60	62	55	65	69
39701	COLUMBUS	57	48	48	44	49	57	52	54	57	52	70	61	49	65	51	60	66	55	61	64
39702	COLUMBUS	74	64	53	60	67	74	63	69	68	63	83	80	61	82	64	71	79	68	75	86
39705	COLUMBUS	97	95	92	95	94	100	95	95	94	94	117	112	93	115	93	92	113	96	92	109
39710	COLUMBUS	63	40	38	46	37	44	60	52	61	56	76	69	51	68	49	56	73	61	48	59
39730	ABERDEEN	64	50	40	46	53	61	51	57	58	52	69	66	48	67	51	61	65	57	65	72
39735	ACKERMAN	69	51	33	46	56	64	51	59	59	51	70	69	46	67	52	63	65	59	71	78
39739	BROOKSVILLE	69	46	21	40	52	60	45	56	54	46	63	67	38	60	45	58	58	55	69	79
39740	CALEDONIA	84	73	54	69	77	83	68	76	73	68	88	90	66	89	70	75	84	74	83	98
39741	CEDARBLUFF	77	51	23	44	58	67	49	62	60	50	70	74	42	66	50	64	64	61	76	88
39743	CRAWFORD	61	45	29	41	50	56	45	53	51	45	61	63	40	58	45	53	56	52	61	71
39744	EUPORA	69	48	27	43	53	62	49	58	57	49	68	68	42	63	49	62	62	58	71	78
39745	FRENCH CAMP	66	44	20	38	50	58	43	54	52	44	61	64	36	57	44	56	55	53	66	76
39746	HAMILTON	84	56	25	49	64	73	54	68	66	55	77	81	46	73	55	71	70	67	84	96
39747	KILMICHAEL	75	50	23	44	57	66	49	61	59	50	69	73	41	65	49	63	63	60	75	86
39750	MABEN	92	62	28	53	70	81	60	75	72	61	84	89	51	80	61	77	77	74	92	106
39751	MANTEE	88	59	27	51	67	77	57	71	69	58	80	85	48	76	58	74	73	70	87	101
39752	MATHISTON	75	50	23	44	57	66	49	61	59	50	69	73	41	65	50	63	63	60	75	87
39755	PHEBA	81	54	25	47	62	71	53	66	63	54	74	78	45	70	53	68	68	65	81	93
39756	PRAIRIE	75	50	23	43	57	65	48	60	58	49	68	72	41	65	49	63	62	60	74	86
39759	STARKVILLE	65	51	57	54	52	58	68	61	68	63	84	77	61	79	61	64	81	67	59	70
39762	MISSISSIPPI STATE	37	23	29	26	22	27	44	32	43	37	54	45	36	48	35	38	50	40	30	37
39766	STEENS	77	63	44	59	68	74	59	68	65	59	78	81	56	78	61	67	73	66	76	90
39767	STEWART	77	52	23	45	59	68	50	63	60	51	71	75	43	67	51	65	64	62	77	89
39769	STURGIS	76	51	24	45	58	67	50	62	60	51	71	74	43	67	51	65	64	61	76	87
39772	WEIR	89	60	27	51	67	78	57	72	69	59	81	86	49	77	58	75	74	71	89	102
	MISSISSIPPI	76	64	54	60	66	74	64	70	70	65	85	81	61	82	64	71	80	70	76	86
	UNITED STATES	100	100	100	100	100	100	100	100	100	100	100	100	100	100	100	100	100	100	100	100

ZIP CODE		COUNTY FIPS CODE	POPULATION			2000-2004 ANNUAL RATE		HOUSEHOLDS					FAMILIES		
#	POST OFFICE NAME		2000	2004	2009	% Rate	State Centile	2000	2004	2009	% Annual Rate 2000-2004	2004 Average HH Size	2000	2004	% Annual Rate 2000-2004
39773	WEST POINT	025	20402	20534	20684	0.2	48	7568	7828	8097	0.8	2.57	5457	5589	0.6
39776	WOODLAND	017	1910	2048	2135	1.7	86	682	746	794	2.1	2.75	529	573	1.9
	MISSISSIPPI					0.6					1.2	2.57			0.9
	UNITED STATES					1.2					1.3	2.58			1.1

#	POST OFFICE NAME	RACE (%)								2004 AGE DISTRIBUTION (%)										MEDIAN AGE	% 2004 Males	% 2004 Females
		White		Black		Asian/Pacific		% Hispanic Origin														
		2000	2004	2000	2004	2000	2004	2000	2004	0-4	5-9	10-14	15-19	20-24	25-44	45-64	65-84	85+	18+	2004		
39773	WEST POINT	41.6	40.9	57.6	58.2	0.2	0.2	0.9	0.9	7.7	7.4	7.9	7.2	7.8	26.0	23.0	11.1	1.9	72.8	34.0	47.6	52.4
39776	WOODLAND	56.8	54.6	41.2	43.0	0.4	0.4	2.5	2.8	7.5	7.4	8.6	8.1	7.1	27.7	22.7	9.5	1.5	71.6	34.4	50.2	49.8
	MISSISSIPPI	61.4	60.6	36.3	36.8	0.7	0.8	1.4	1.6	7.3	7.1	7.4	7.4	7.8	27.8	23.0	10.6	1.6	73.9	34.5	48.5	51.5
	UNITED STATES	75.1	73.6	12.3	12.5	3.8	4.2	12.5	14.1	6.9	6.7	7.2	7.0	7.3	28.6	23.8	10.8	1.7	75.1	36.0	49.1	50.9

ZIP CODE		2004 Per Capita Income	2004 HH Income Base	2004 HOUSEHOLD INCOME DISTRIBUTION (%)					MEDIAN HOUSEHOLD INCOME				2004 Home Value Base	2004 HOME VALUE DISTRIBUTION (%)					2004 Median Home Value
#	POST OFFICE NAME			Less than $25,000	$25,000 to $49,999	$50,000 to $99,999	$100,000 to $149,999	$150,000 or More	2004	2009	2004 National Centile	2004 State Centile		Less than $50,000	$50,000 to $89,999	$90,000 to $174,999	$175,000 to $399,999	$400,000 or More	
39773	WEST POINT	17069	7828	41.4	28.4	21.7	6.0	2.6	31033	35646	15	53	5605	27.2	40.5	24.5	6.7	1.1	69378
39776	WOODLAND	17179	746	44.9	28.4	21.1	2.7	3.0	30086	31727	12	45	626	48.2	30.8	16.0	4.3	0.6	52391
	MISSISSIPPI	18480		36.7	30.0	24.5	5.9	2.8	34621	39377				29.7	30.4	28.7	9.7	1.6	75922
	UNITED STATES	25866		24.7	27.1	30.8	10.9	6.5	48124	56710				10.9	15.0	33.7	30.1	10.4	145905

#	POST OFFICE NAME	FINANCIAL SERVICES				THE HOME						ENTERTAINMENT						PERSONAL			
						Home Improvements		Furnishings													
		Auto Loan	Home Loan	Invest-ments	Retire-ment Plans	Home Repair	Lawn & Garden	Comput-ers & Hard-ware	Major Appli-ances	TV, Radio, Sound Equip-ment	Furni-ture	Dine out/ Carry out	Sports Equip-ment	Fees & Tickets	Toys & Games	Travel	Cable TV	Apparel & Services	Auto Repairs	Health Insur-ance	Pets & Supplies
39773	WEST POINT	72	57	44	52	60	69	58	64	65	58	78	75	54	75	58	68	73	64	73	82
39776	WOODLAND	84	61	37	55	67	76	59	71	69	60	81	84	53	77	60	72	75	70	84	96
	MISSISSIPPI	76	64	54	60	66	74	64	70	70	65	85	81	61	82	64	71	80	70	76	86
	UNITED STATES	100	100	100	100	100	100	100	100	100	100	100	100	100	100	100	100	100	100	100	100

MISSOURI — POPULATION CHANGE

A 63005-63146

# POST OFFICE NAME	COUNTY FIPS CODE	POPULATION 2000	2004	2009	% Rate	State Centile	HOUSEHOLDS 2000	2004	2009	% Annual Rate 2000-2004	2004 Average HH Size	FAMILIES 2000	2004	% Annual Rate 2000-2004
63005 CHESTERFIELD	189	16359	17370	17854	1.4	77	5407	5788	5991	1.6	2.99	4491	4746	1.3
63010 ARNOLD	099	34224	36085	39063	1.3	74	12584	13412	14688	1.5	2.67	9528	9991	1.1
63011 BALLWIN	189	37746	38725	39384	0.6	56	13829	14257	14576	0.7	2.70	10910	11059	0.3
63012 BARNHART	099	9770	10313	11057	1.3	74	3189	3421	3719	1.7	2.99	2690	2850	1.4
63013 BEAUFORT	071	1606	1784	1944	2.5	89	546	613	676	2.8	2.91	441	489	2.5
63014 BERGER	071	1118	1174	1242	1.2	72	419	445	475	1.4	2.64	319	333	1.0
63015 CATAWISSA	071	1661	1863	2045	2.7	91	596	678	754	3.1	2.74	467	523	2.7
63016 CEDAR HILL	099	7235	7686	8274	1.4	77	2480	2673	2917	1.8	2.83	1942	2058	1.4
63017 CHESTERFIELD	189	42170	42386	42765	0.1	37	16138	16412	16706	0.4	2.48	11746	11668	-0.2
63019 CRYSTAL CITY	099	3876	4063	4329	1.1	71	1567	1662	1795	1.4	2.35	1076	1114	0.8
63020 DE SOTO	099	19772	21045	22705	1.5	78	7240	7807	8533	1.8	2.65	5441	5771	1.4
63021 BALLWIN	189	55634	58176	59757	1.1	70	20449	21437	22114	1.1	2.69	15384	15851	0.7
63023 DITTMER	099	5215	5700	6237	2.1	87	1883	2083	2308	2.4	2.73	1468	1595	2.0
63025 EUREKA	189	11122	12368	13164	2.5	89	3671	4040	4294	2.3	3.00	3067	3329	2.0
63026 FENTON	189	42072	43617	45366	0.9	64	15196	15880	16676	1.0	2.73	11663	11979	0.6
63028 FESTUS	099	22848	24288	26138	1.5	78	8322	8952	9756	1.7	2.65	6199	6538	1.3
63030 FLETCHER	221	211	228	242	1.8	84	73	80	86	2.2	2.85	59	63	1.6
63031 FLORISSANT	189	50526	50549	50818	0.0	33	19281	19439	19679	0.2	2.56	13666	13458	-0.4
63033 FLORISSANT	189	44238	43999	44076	-0.1	27	17291	17263	17380	0.0	2.52	11921	11625	-0.6
63034 FLORISSANT	189	16798	17624	18349	1.1	72	5798	6083	6350	1.1	2.88	4802	4991	0.9
63036 FRENCH VILLAGE	187	685	695	702	0.3	47	280	287	292	0.6	2.42	220	221	0.1
63037 GERALD	071	3154	3484	3824	2.4	88	1204	1341	1486	2.6	2.57	889	972	2.1
63038 GLENCOE	189	6874	7553	7942	2.2	88	2351	2604	2755	2.4	2.89	2012	2200	2.1
63039 GRAY SUMMIT	071	827	790	816	-1.1	5	307	297	311	-0.8	2.66	245	233	-1.2
63040 GROVER	189	6943	7850	8334	2.9	93	2363	2700	2879	3.2	2.91	1874	2110	2.8
63041 GRUBVILLE	071	429	495	552	3.4	95	150	176	198	3.8	2.81	120	138	3.3
63042 HAZELWOOD	189	19578	19490	19513	-0.1	27	8598	8597	8655	0.0	2.26	5040	4915	-0.6
63043 MARYLAND HEIGHTS	189	21814	22103	22284	0.3	45	9289	9435	9551	0.4	2.33	5682	5607	-0.3
63044 BRIDGETON	189	14597	13962	13779	-1.0	5	5793	5558	5511	-1.0	2.42	3966	3716	-1.5
63048 HERCULANEUM	099	2849	3060	3317	1.7	82	1071	1165	1282	2.0	2.54	736	782	1.4
63049 HIGH RIDGE	099	14337	15249	16462	1.5	78	5202	5608	6130	1.8	2.71	3954	4186	1.4
63050 HILLSBORO	099	13925	14611	15711	1.1	72	4885	5218	5693	1.6	2.76	3870	4060	1.1
63051 HOUSE SPRINGS	099	12816	13744	14948	1.7	82	4530	4922	5420	2.0	2.79	3501	3736	1.5
63052 IMPERIAL	099	21292	24476	27495	3.3	95	7335	8513	9669	3.6	2.87	5944	6819	3.3
63055 LABADIE	071	2147	2229	2374	0.9	65	771	810	873	1.2	2.75	609	628	0.7
63056 LESLIE	071	2142	2257	2393	1.2	74	796	848	908	1.5	2.66	615	644	1.1
63060 LONEDELL	071	2678	2986	3288	2.6	90	931	1054	1175	3.0	2.83	734	818	2.6
63068 NEW HAVEN	071	4256	4550	4880	1.6	81	1567	1693	1835	1.8	2.65	1172	1244	1.4
63069 PACIFIC	071	15300	16144	17046	1.3	74	5258	5612	6002	1.5	2.65	3918	4109	1.1
63070 PEVELY	099	5599	5911	6349	1.3	74	2045	2189	2383	1.6	2.69	1552	1631	1.2
63071 RICHWOODS	221	1108	1158	1206	1.0	69	388	412	435	1.4	2.81	290	302	1.0
63072 ROBERTSVILLE	071	3183	3448	3725	1.9	84	1097	1201	1311	2.2	2.86	880	950	1.8
63074 SAINT ANN	189	15164	14951	14924	-0.3	21	6902	6837	6860	-0.2	2.18	3895	3724	-1.1
63077 SAINT CLAIR	071	11097	11709	12499	1.3	74	4207	4485	4839	1.5	2.59	3042	3179	1.0
63080 SULLIVAN	071	11250	11687	12292	0.9	65	4380	4588	4871	1.1	2.51	3102	3184	0.6
63084 UNION	071	14385	15232	16275	1.4	76	5286	5672	6135	1.7	2.65	3866	4074	1.2
63087 VALLES MINES	187	701	710	717	0.3	44	253	259	264	0.6	2.73	198	199	0.1
63088 VALLEY PARK	189	7724	8042	8200	1.0	67	3244	3421	3521	1.3	2.31	1831	1864	0.4
63089 VILLA RIDGE	071	5914	6214	6610	1.2	72	2113	2247	2416	1.5	2.77	1646	1720	1.0
63090 WASHINGTON	071	20283	20971	22119	0.8	63	7656	7992	8517	1.0	2.59	5468	5597	0.6
63091 ROSEBUD	073	1214	1268	1330	1.0	69	485	512	541	1.3	2.41	373	388	0.9
63101 SAINT LOUIS	510	809	754	701	-1.6	1	429	396	367	-1.9	1.89	189	168	-2.7
63102 SAINT LOUIS	510	1270	1242	1197	-0.5	16	654	633	598	-0.8	1.20	66	60	-2.2
63103 SAINT LOUIS	510	4656	4562	4384	-0.5	18	2939	2877	2758	-0.5	1.38	427	388	-2.2
63104 SAINT LOUIS	510	18469	17842	16913	-0.8	9	8021	7775	7400	-0.7	2.22	3857	3641	-1.4
63105 SAINT LOUIS	189	14631	14890	15031	0.4	49	6390	6499	6577	0.4	2.00	3232	3172	-0.4
63106 SAINT LOUIS	510	10645	9795	9110	-1.9	0	4247	3905	3637	-2.0	2.40	2359	2106	-2.6
63107 SAINT LOUIS	510	16356	15085	14006	-1.9	1	5641	5212	4853	-1.8	2.83	3710	3363	-2.3
63108 SAINT LOUIS	510	19622	19650	19079	0.0	33	10168	10314	10040	0.3	1.62	2829	2726	-0.9
63109 SAINT LOUIS	510	29614	28791	27279	-0.7	12	14362	14030	13365	-0.6	2.04	7162	6781	-1.3
63110 SAINT LOUIS	510	20621	19538	18326	-1.3	3	8275	7853	7384	-1.2	2.38	4391	4057	-1.8
63111 SAINT LOUIS	510	21137	20154	18935	-1.1	4	8797	8350	7845	-1.2	2.33	4760	4390	-1.9
63112 SAINT LOUIS	510	23068	21900	20589	-1.2	3	10045	9655	9153	-0.9	2.23	4911	4519	-1.9
63113 SAINT LOUIS	510	16840	15543	14438	-1.9	1	6253	5788	5400	-1.8	2.61	3693	3332	-2.4
63114 SAINT LOUIS	189	38644	37568	37258	-0.7	12	16027	15660	15619	-0.5	2.38	9939	9424	-1.2
63115 SAINT LOUIS	189	25268	23846	22293	-1.4	2	9998	9498	8942	-1.2	2.51	6246	5799	-1.7
63116 SAINT LOUIS	510	47670	46428	44038	-0.6	13	20497	19883	18876	-0.7	2.32	11378	10738	-1.4
63117 SAINT LOUIS	189	9367	9176	9137	-0.4	18	4455	4386	4390	-0.4	2.06	2125	2011	-1.3
63118 SAINT LOUIS	510	30451	28449	26494	-1.6	1	11404	10513	9757	-1.9	2.68	6664	5983	-2.5
63119 SAINT LOUIS	189	34400	33970	33899	-0.3	22	14759	14631	14668	-0.2	2.26	8790	8475	-0.9
63120 SAINT LOUIS	510	13269	12168	11329	-2.0	0	4430	4088	3827	-1.9	2.88	3152	2857	-2.3
63121 SAINT LOUIS	189	28471	27996	27973	-0.4	19	11388	11262	11312	-0.3	2.45	7183	6882	-1.0
63122 SAINT LOUIS	189	38533	38448	38601	-0.1	30	15966	16038	16203	0.1	2.35	10404	10152	-0.6
63123 SAINT LOUIS	189	49835	49305	49154	-0.3	24	22161	22076	22148	-0.1	2.22	13567	13104	-0.8
63124 SAINT LOUIS	189	9815	9571	9510	-0.6	14	4196	4111	4107	-0.5	2.30	2802	2685	-1.0
63125 SAINT LOUIS	189	33150	33532	33779	0.3	43	14194	14466	14671	0.5	2.28	8808	8711	-0.3
63126 SAINT LOUIS	189	15626	15219	15069	-0.6	13	6662	6528	6502	-0.5	2.33	4599	4398	-1.1
63127 SAINT LOUIS	189	4431	4346	4310	-0.5	19	1816	1791	1786	-0.3	2.31	1220	1173	-0.9
63128 SAINT LOUIS	189	29290	30004	30502	0.6	55	11936	12308	12592	0.7	2.40	8351	8409	0.2
63129 SAINT LOUIS	189	51191	52833	53749	0.8	61	19197	19871	20310	0.8	2.64	14141	14413	0.5
63130 SAINT LOUIS	189	34547	34267	34278	-0.2	25	13206	13137	13207	-0.1	2.36	7757	7497	-0.8
63131 SAINT LOUIS	189	15918	15444	15310	-0.7	11	5789	5647	5629	-0.6	2.72	4681	4501	-0.9
63132 SAINT LOUIS	189	14300	14360	14483	0.1	36	6254	6328	6420	0.3	2.25	3825	3764	-0.4
63133 SAINT LOUIS	189	8165	7874	7773	-0.9	9	2748	2680	2670	-0.6	2.89	1958	1867	-1.1
63134 SAINT LOUIS	189	15624	14804	14599	-1.3	3	5857	5569	5518	-1.2	2.64	4008	3725	-1.7
63135 SAINT LOUIS	189	22821	22330	22210	-0.5	17	8578	8402	8380	-0.5	2.63	5906	5637	-1.1
63136 SAINT LOUIS	189	53747	52265	51788	-0.7	12	20067	19597	19521	-0.6	2.65	14064	13392	-1.2
63137 SAINT LOUIS	189	21224	21130	21056	-0.1	28	8298	8262	8260	-0.1	2.46	5573	5417	-0.7
63138 SAINT LOUIS	189	21879	21721	21707	-0.2	26	8561	8512	8536	-0.1	2.54	5812	5636	-0.7
63139 SAINT LOUIS	510	24187	23237	21912	-0.9	6	11670	11283	10700	-0.8	2.01	5539	5195	-1.5
63140 SAINT LOUIS	189	449	385	372	-3.6	0	157	136	132	-3.3	2.82	112	95	-3.8
63141 SAINT LOUIS	189	20032	19925	19910	-0.1	27	7998	8017	8067	0.1	2.37	5535	5416	-0.5
63143 SAINT LOUIS	189	11073	10591	10371	-1.0	5	5634	5424	5351	-0.9	1.95	2479	2290	-1.9
63144 SAINT LOUIS	189	9042	8770	8678	-0.7	10	4636	4519	4498	-0.6	1.94	2151	2007	-1.6
63146 SAINT LOUIS	189	30464	32316	33380	1.4	77	14121	14972	15507	1.4	2.14	7865	8062	0.6
MISSOURI					0.8					0.9	2.46			0.4
UNITED STATES					1.2					1.3	2.58			1.1

POPULATION COMPOSITION
MISSOURI
63005-63146 B

ZIP CODE #	POST OFFICE NAME	RACE (%) White 2000	White 2004	Black 2000	Black 2004	Asian/Pacific 2000	Asian/Pacific 2004	% Hispanic Origin 2000	% Hispanic Origin 2004	2004 AGE DISTRIBUTION (%) 0-4	5-9	10-14	15-19	20-24	25-44	45-64	65-84	85+	18+	MEDIAN AGE 2004	% 2004 Males	% 2004 Females
63005	CHESTERFIELD	93.4	91.8	1.9	2.4	3.5	4.4	1.6	1.8	7.0	8.5	9.6	7.6	5.3	24.3	31.5	5.9	0.4	69.6	38.2	49.9	50.1
63010	ARNOLD	97.9	97.7	0.2	0.2	0.4	0.6	1.1	1.2	7.3	7.2	7.4	6.7	6.4	30.5	24.0	9.6	0.9	73.9	35.8	49.1	50.9
63011	BALLWIN	93.3	91.8	1.7	2.1	3.4	4.3	1.7	1.9	6.6	7.2	7.5	6.7	5.3	25.0	27.7	12.3	1.6	74.3	40.1	48.4	51.6
63012	BARNHART	98.0	97.7	0.3	0.4	0.4	0.5	1.2	1.3	8.0	7.9	8.0	7.7	7.0	30.9	24.2	5.9	0.4	71.1	33.2	50.6	49.4
63013	BEAUFORT	98.9	98.8	0.2	0.2	0.2	0.3	0.8	0.7	6.3	6.7	8.2	7.5	6.2	27.1	27.0	10.1	0.8	74.2	38.3	51.5	48.5
63014	BERGER	98.5	98.3	0.4	0.3	0.2	0.2	0.4	0.3	6.4	6.8	7.3	6.6	4.9	26.4	28.0	12.6	0.9	75.5	40.1	51.3	48.7
63015	CATAWISSA	98.4	98.2	0.2	0.3	0.4	0.4	0.8	1.0	6.1	6.7	8.2	7.5	6.4	28.3	27.4	8.5	0.8	74.3	37.6	50.3	49.7
63016	CEDAR HILL	98.3	98.1	0.1	0.1	0.3	0.3	0.7	0.8	6.8	7.0	8.1	7.6	6.4	28.9	25.8	8.5	0.9	73.3	36.7	49.7	50.4
63017	CHESTERFIELD	91.0	88.9	1.9	2.4	5.8	7.3	1.4	1.6	4.7	5.7	6.7	6.2	4.8	21.2	31.4	15.3	4.1	78.9	45.4	47.3	52.7
63019	CRYSTAL CITY	94.0	93.5	3.6	3.9	0.4	0.5	0.5	0.6	7.2	6.7	6.5	6.4	6.2	25.6	23.6	14.8	3.2	75.9	39.1	47.5	52.5
63020	DE SOTO	97.5	97.3	0.9	1.0	0.2	0.3	0.9	1.0	6.9	6.7	7.0	6.8	6.7	27.4	26.0	10.9	1.7	75.3	37.5	49.4	50.6
63021	BALLWIN	92.5	90.9	1.9	2.3	4.0	5.0	1.5	1.7	7.9	8.3	8.2	6.6	5.5	29.8	25.9	7.2	0.8	71.4	36.3	48.3	51.7
63023	DITTMER	98.5	98.4	0.1	0.1	0.2	0.3	0.6	0.7	6.2	6.5	7.8	7.8	6.1	28.9	27.7	8.2	0.7	74.6	37.7	50.7	49.3
63025	EUREKA	97.7	97.2	0.5	0.6	0.6	0.8	1.1	1.2	8.1	8.3	8.3	7.1	5.5	29.3	25.2	6.9	1.4	70.4	36.0	49.2	50.8
63026	FENTON	97.1	96.6	0.7	0.8	0.8	1.1	1.1	1.3	7.6	7.6	7.7	6.8	6.6	30.3	25.9	6.8	0.8	72.9	35.3	49.6	50.4
63028	FESTUS	95.9	95.5	2.2	2.3	0.6	0.8	0.8	0.9	6.9	6.9	7.4	7.0	6.5	27.7	24.6	11.3	1.8	74.5	37.0	48.8	51.2
63030	FLETCHER	97.6	97.4	0.5	0.4	0.0	0.0	1.4	1.3	8.3	7.9	6.6	6.6	7.9	29.4	23.7	8.8	0.9	72.8	34.7	50.4	49.6
63031	FLORISSANT	85.3	82.6	11.8	14.1	0.8	1.0	1.4	1.6	6.6	6.8	7.5	6.8	6.3	28.5	23.7	11.9	1.8	74.9	37.2	47.6	52.4
63033	FLORISSANT	53.3	49.3	43.8	47.7	0.8	0.9	1.2	1.3	6.3	6.3	7.2	7.0	6.6	26.0	24.9	13.7	2.1	76.0	38.7	46.4	53.6
63034	FLORISSANT	67.0	61.7	29.8	34.6	1.4	1.8	1.0	1.1	5.4	6.3	7.8	7.9	6.1	24.3	31.4	9.7	1.1	75.4	40.7	48.2	51.8
63036	FRENCH VILLAGE	98.3	98.1	0.0	0.0	0.0	0.0	0.4	0.4	5.6	6.2	7.3	6.5	5.0	25.6	29.9	13.0	0.9	76.8	41.3	51.2	48.8
63037	GERALD	99.0	98.9	0.0	0.0	0.2	0.3	0.7	0.7	5.4	5.7	7.1	7.1	6.3	26.5	26.8	13.4	1.8	77.4	40.5	51.5	48.5
63038	GLENCOE	95.4	94.3	1.6	1.9	1.8	2.4	1.5	1.7	7.9	8.8	9.3	7.5	4.8	26.5	28.7	6.1	0.4	68.8	37.3	49.3	50.7
63039	GRAY SUMMIT	96.5	96.0	1.6	1.8	0.4	0.5	0.5	0.5	7.2	7.7	7.2	6.8	5.4	28.4	26.8	9.6	0.8	73.5	37.9	50.5	49.5
63040	GROVER	94.6	93.3	1.2	1.5	3.0	3.8	1.3	1.4	9.8	10.1	9.5	6.4	4.3	32.5	22.2	4.9	0.4	66.4	34.5	48.7	51.3
63041	GRUBVILLE	98.6	98.4	0.2	0.4	0.0	0.0	0.7	0.8	7.1	7.3	8.5	8.5	5.7	27.7	26.1	8.5	0.8	72.1	36.3	51.1	48.9
63042	HAZELWOOD	78.8	75.5	17.3	20.1	1.3	1.6	1.8	2.0	6.1	5.8	6.6	6.6	7.9	31.7	22.5	11.5	1.2	77.6	35.4	48.3	51.7
63043	MARYLAND HEIGHTS	86.6	84.2	5.3	6.2	6.3	7.7	1.8	2.0	6.0	5.8	6.2	6.2	6.9	32.8	24.7	10.5	1.0	78.3	36.9	48.8	51.2
63044	BRIDGETON	87.6	85.3	8.2	9.7	2.2	2.7	2.1	2.3	4.9	5.1	6.2	6.5	6.1	25.2	28.2	15.3	2.5	79.8	42.4	48.0	52.0
63048	HERCULANEUM	95.0	94.6	3.7	4.0	0.3	0.4	0.6	0.6	7.5	7.0	6.6	6.5	6.7	27.4	22.5	12.9	2.9	74.9	37.3	47.3	52.8
63049	HIGH RIDGE	98.1	97.8	0.2	0.3	0.3	0.4	1.1	1.3	7.1	7.2	7.8	6.7	6.4	31.8	25.5	7.0	0.5	73.8	35.4	49.8	50.2
63050	HILLSBORO	98.1	97.9	0.4	0.4	0.2	0.3	1.0	1.1	6.4	6.8	7.7	7.8	6.5	28.6	26.8	8.7	0.7	74.2	36.9	50.6	49.4
63051	HOUSE SPRINGS	97.8	97.6	0.2	0.2	0.2	0.2	1.1	1.2	7.2	7.5	8.3	7.3	6.7	31.2	24.4	7.0	0.5	72.4	34.6	50.0	50.0
63052	IMPERIAL	98.0	97.7	0.2	0.2	0.4	0.5	1.3	1.4	8.2	8.0	8.1	7.2	6.7	32.9	22.8	5.8	0.4	71.3	33.3	50.5	49.5
63055	LABADIE	97.1	96.8	1.2	1.3	0.3	0.4	0.7	0.8	7.5	7.9	7.9	6.5	5.4	28.9	26.7	8.7	0.7	72.9	37.2	50.3	49.7
63056	LESLIE	98.7	98.6	0.1	0.1	0.2	0.3	0.5	0.5	5.8	6.4	7.6	7.2	6.4	26.9	26.9	11.7	1.1	75.9	39.1	51.3	48.7
63060	LONEDELL	97.7	97.6	0.6	0.7	0.2	0.2	0.5	0.5	6.8	7.0	8.4	7.1	5.9	27.3	26.9	10.0	0.6	73.4	37.2	50.1	49.9
63068	NEW HAVEN	98.4	98.3	0.5	0.6	0.1	0.1	0.6	0.7	7.0	7.1	7.5	7.3	5.9	26.6	24.1	12.4	2.2	73.9	37.8	49.8	50.2
63069	PACIFIC	93.0	92.3	4.9	5.3	0.4	0.5	0.9	1.0	6.6	6.8	7.2	6.7	7.3	30.7	25.2	8.5	1.0	75.4	36.5	53.4	46.6
63070	PEVELY	96.7	96.4	1.0	1.1	0.3	0.4	1.1	1.2	7.7	7.3	7.3	7.1	7.4	29.3	24.2	9.0	0.6	73.5	34.5	50.2	49.8
63071	RICHWOODS	98.3	98.1	0.2	0.3	0.1	0.1	0.5	0.6	7.9	7.4	6.9	7.9	7.1	26.6	23.8	11.0	1.4	73.0	35.6	51.0	49.0
63072	ROBERTSVILLE	94.0	93.6	3.6	3.9	0.2	0.2	0.9	1.1	6.8	7.0	8.0	7.5	6.8	28.4	26.8	8.2	0.5	73.4	36.4	51.2	48.8
63074	SAINT ANN	83.0	80.1	11.4	13.5	2.0	2.4	3.8	4.2	6.3	6.0	6.3	6.0	7.0	30.0	23.5	13.2	1.8	77.9	37.9	48.4	51.6
63077	SAINT CLAIR	97.6	97.4	0.8	0.9	0.2	0.2	0.6	0.7	7.2	7.0	7.7	6.8	6.9	28.5	24.3	10.4	1.3	74.1	35.8	49.9	50.2
63080	SULLIVAN	98.4	98.1	0.2	0.2	0.6	0.7	0.9	1.1	7.1	6.9	7.3	6.6	6.6	27.1	23.7	12.7	2.0	74.8	37.1	49.0	51.0
63084	UNION	97.2	97.0	1.1	1.2	0.2	0.2	0.9	1.0	7.1	7.1	7.8	6.9	6.7	29.2	23.9	10.0	1.3	73.8	35.9	49.8	50.2
63087	VALLES MINES	98.2	98.3	0.0	0.0	0.0	0.0	0.4	0.6	6.1	6.5	7.2	6.6	5.5	26.2	29.0	12.1	0.9	76.3	40.3	51.7	48.3
63088	VALLEY PARK	90.2	88.2	3.8	4.7	3.6	4.5	2.2	2.5	9.2	7.9	5.7	4.4	6.4	39.3	17.8	7.9	1.3	74.5	33.1	48.3	51.7
63089	VILLA RIDGE	95.8	95.4	2.0	2.1	0.3	0.4	0.7	0.8	7.2	7.2	7.6	6.9	6.4	29.0	25.8	9.3	0.8	74.0	36.7	50.5	49.5
63090	WASHINGTON	98.1	97.9	0.6	0.6	0.4	0.5	0.6	0.7	7.4	7.2	7.2	6.7	6.7	27.9	23.4	11.4	2.1	74.1	36.8	49.3	50.7
63091	ROSEBUD	98.1	98.0	0.0	0.0	0.5	0.6	0.3	0.2	6.4	6.4	6.5	6.7	6.1	23.9	26.3	14.9	2.9	76.5	41.4	50.0	50.0
63101	SAINT LOUIS	10.1	8.1	88.8	90.7	0.0	0.0	0.6	0.7	8.0	7.2	7.2	6.6	8.8	33.4	22.6	5.8	0.5	73.7	32.7	44.4	55.6
63102	SAINT LOUIS	56.9	51.1	38.1	43.4	2.4	2.9	1.0	1.1	1.4	1.0	0.5	1.5	9.5	50.8	26.1	8.5	0.7	96.9	38.7	70.9	29.1
63103	SAINT LOUIS	44.4	39.2	48.2	52.6	3.6	4.3	3.1	3.3	1.8	1.5	1.5	3.2	22.2	21.6	21.0	21.4	5.9	94.2	43.3	48.8	51.2
63104	SAINT LOUIS	39.8	35.0	56.4	61.1	0.9	1.0	2.0	1.9	8.5	7.7	7.3	6.3	8.0	32.6	21.2	7.2	1.3	72.6	31.9	48.5	51.5
63105	SAINT LOUIS	85.2	82.8	7.3	8.2	5.5	6.9	1.6	1.7	3.8	4.0	5.7	8.5	9.1	31.3	23.4	11.4	2.8	82.3	36.3	49.5	50.5
63106	SAINT LOUIS	4.6	4.0	93.7	94.4	0.1	0.2	0.8	0.8	10.8	10.8	10.5	8.2	7.2	23.8	17.4	9.8	1.6	62.7	27.0	42.7	57.3
63107	SAINT LOUIS	8.4	6.6	90.0	91.8	0.4	0.4	0.6	0.6	7.9	9.0	10.0	8.6	6.9	24.3	20.8	10.7	1.7	67.6	31.3	46.1	53.9
63108	SAINT LOUIS	49.9	46.7	43.3	45.2	4.4	5.7	2.0	2.2	2.9	2.8	3.0	8.3	15.4	29.2	23.4	12.5	2.6	89.6	35.4	48.6	51.4
63109	SAINT LOUIS	93.4	92.1	2.8	3.5	1.3	1.6	2.1	2.3	5.9	5.5	5.3	5.2	6.0	33.3	22.6	13.0	3.1	80.1	38.6	46.6	53.4
63110	SAINT LOUIS	41.1	37.2	54.1	57.9	1.2	1.4	1.8	1.8	7.5	7.8	8.2	9.0	8.9	30.1	19.5	7.5	1.6	71.9	30.5	47.0	53.1
63111	SAINT LOUIS	68.6	63.3	23.7	28.2	2.1	2.6	4.1	4.4	7.6	6.8	7.3	6.6	7.6	29.5	20.6	10.5	3.5	74.3	34.5	48.1	51.9
63112	SAINT LOUIS	17.2	15.8	78.5	79.5	2.1	2.6	0.9	1.0	6.4	6.2	7.5	7.1	9.3	29.3	20.3	12.2	1.9	75.7	32.9	45.8	54.2
63113	SAINT LOUIS	0.9	0.7	97.9	98.1	0.1	0.1	0.6	0.6	6.3	6.8	9.2	8.5	6.6	23.1	22.6	13.8	3.2	72.5	36.9	45.7	54.3
63114	SAINT LOUIS	74.1	70.5	20.9	23.9	1.7	2.1	2.4	2.6	6.9	6.7	7.0	6.7	7.0	29.9	22.9	11.3	1.7	75.4	36.2	48.0	52.0
63115	SAINT LOUIS	0.7	0.6	98.0	98.2	0.1	0.1	0.5	0.5	6.7	7.1	8.8	7.5	6.1	24.0	22.5	15.1	2.2	72.7	37.5	44.4	55.6
63116	SAINT LOUIS	72.8	68.8	17.7	20.5	4.6	5.5	3.6	3.8	7.2	6.7	6.8	6.5	7.3	32.0	21.6	9.9	2.2	75.4	35.0	48.3	51.7
63117	SAINT LOUIS	81.6	79.3	13.6	15.1	2.7	3.4	1.7	1.8	5.0	4.8	5.3	6.1	7.5	33.7	23.3	11.6	2.8	81.3	37.3	46.5	53.5
63118	SAINT LOUIS	38.7	33.2	52.4	57.6	4.0	4.4	3.8	3.7	8.9	8.7	9.6	8.4	8.6	30.0	18.1	6.6	1.2	67.7	28.9	48.0	52.0
63119	SAINT LOUIS	88.9	87.3	7.8	8.8	1.6	2.0	1.3	1.5	5.6	6.1	6.6	6.7	6.2	25.5	25.2	13.5	4.7	78.0	40.8	45.9	54.1
63120	SAINT LOUIS	3.7	3.0	95.1	95.9	0.1	0.1	0.5	0.6	7.6	9.0	10.2	10.9	7.3	23.2	19.8	11.0	1.0	66.1	29.2	45.6	54.4
63121	SAINT LOUIS	17.7	15.3	79.6	82.0	0.7	0.8	1.1	1.0	6.6	6.8	7.8	7.2	8.4	26.3	24.9	10.8	1.4	74.6	35.4	45.2	54.8
63122	SAINT LOUIS	92.4	90.9	5.4	6.5	1.0	1.3	1.1	1.2	6.2	6.7	6.7	6.1	5.0	24.0	27.2	14.5	3.7	76.5	42.0	46.0	54.0
63123	SAINT LOUIS	95.8	95.0	0.8	1.0	1.8	2.2	1.2	1.4	5.3	5.4	5.8	5.7	5.8	27.2	24.0	18.0	2.8	80.0	41.9	47.0	53.0
63124	SAINT LOUIS	94.3	93.2	2.6	3.1	2.2	2.8	1.0	1.1	4.6	5.9	7.0	6.2	4.2	16.8	30.2	20.0	5.3	78.5	48.7	46.7	53.3
63125	SAINT LOUIS	95.7	94.9	1.5	1.9	1.0	1.2	1.9	2.1	5.6	5.5	6.1	6.0	6.5	26.4	24.0	17.3	2.7	79.2	41.0	47.2	52.8
63126	SAINT LOUIS	96.3	95.6	0.8	1.0	1.6	2.1	1.0	1.1	4.7	5.2	6.1	5.6	4.7	23.3	27.2	20.9	2.4	80.6	45.3	47.0	53.0
63127	SAINT LOUIS	96.1	95.3	1.1	1.4	1.4	1.7	1.2	1.3	3.7	4.8	6.4	6.4	4.1	17.2	29.1	20.4	8.0	80.7	49.3	46.8	53.2
63128	SAINT LOUIS	97.6	97.0	0.4	0.5	1.1	1.5	0.9	1.1	4.5	4.9	5.9	6.2	5.8	21.3	29.5	19.0	3.1	80.9	46.0	47.6	52.5
63129	SAINT LOUIS	97.1	96.5	0.6	0.7	1.2	1.6	1.1	1.3	5.8	6.2	7.1	7.0	6.9	26.6	28.6	10.4	1.4	76.6	39.0	48.8	51.2
63130	SAINT LOUIS	50.2	47.0	43.0	45.7	2.6	3.0	1.7	1.8	5.6	5.5	6.0	11.7	11.0	27.2	21.9	9.7	1.4	79.2	32.3	46.5	53.5
63131	SAINT LOUIS	94.4	93.1	0.9	1.2	3.6	4.6	1.0	1.1	5.3	6.6	7.7	7.1	4.3	17.4	32.9	16.7	1.9	75.7	45.9	48.4	51.6
63132	SAINT LOUIS	56.4	54.0	36.6	38.1	4.2	5.1	1.9	2.0	5.7	5.8	6.5	6.1	6.8	25.7	26.1	14.6	2.7	78.2	40.3	46.2	53.8
63133	SAINT LOUIS	10.4	8.8	87.4	89.1	0.3	0.3	0.9	0.8	7.4	7.7	9.5	9.2	8.5	24.3	22.6	9.6	1.2	69.9	32.0	44.5	55.5
63134	SAINT LOUIS	38.7	35.9	57.8	60.5	0.6	0.7	2.2	2.2	7.7	7.6	9.1	7.9	7.6	28.0	21.4	9.6	1.2	70.8	32.3	45.9	54.2
63135	SAINT LOUIS	53.3	48.6	43.7	48.3	0.6	0.7	1.1	1.1	6.8	7.0	8.6	8.1	7.2	26.8	22.7	11.0	1.8	72.4	35.3	46.4	53.7
63136	SAINT LOUIS	17.1	14.6	81.0	83.6	0.4	0.4	0.6	0.6	8.2	8.3	9.1	8.1	7.6	26.6	21.7	9.0	1.5	69.4	31.7	44.3	55.7
63137	SAINT LOUIS	52.1	47.2	45.9	50.8	0.3	0.4	0.9	0.9	6.8	6.9	8.1	7.3	6.9	28.2	21.5	12.3	2.0	73.8	35.8	46.7	53.3
63138	SAINT LOUIS	43.2	38.5	53.9	58.5	0.7	0.8	1.0	1.0	8.9	8.4	7.8	7.2	8.2	29.2	19.5	9.2	1.6	70.5	31.4	46.5	53.5
63139	SAINT LOUIS	88.8	86.4	6.5	8.0	2.1	2.7	1.9	2.1	5.3	4.9	4.8	5.3	7.0	34.4	23.3	12.2	2.7	81.9	38.0	48.6	51.4
63140	SAINT LOUIS	21.2	17.4	76.6	80.3	0.5	0.5	0.7	1.0	9.1	9.1	12.0	8.3	7.0	26.2	19.5	8.1	0.8	64.9	28.5	45.2	54.8
63141	SAINT LOUIS	89.3	86.9	3.2	3.9	5.9	7.3	1.7	1.9	4.9	5.9	6.3	6.2	5.9	21.5	30.2	16.5	2.5	79.2	44.4	48.1	51.9
63143	SAINT LOUIS	77.6	73.9	15.1	17.9	3.7	4.6	2.4	2.5	6.0	5.1	4.9	5.4	9.1	36.2	23.9	8.1	1.2	80.9	35.0	49.7	50.3
63144	SAINT LOUIS	89.4	87.4	4.6	5.5	3.8	4.8	1.8	2.0	5.7	5.4	5.5	5.2	7.5	36.1	21.3	11.1	2.3	80.2	36.0	46.2	53.8
63146	SAINT LOUIS	84.9	82.0	6.1	7.3	6.9	8.5	2.1	2.2	5.0	5.1	5.3	5.2	6.1	29.9	25.9	15.0	2.5	81.2	40.8	47.6	52.4
	MISSOURI	84.9	84.1	11.3	11.5	1.2	1.4	2.1	2.3	6.7	6.6	7.0	7.0	7.3	27.6	24.2	11.7	1.9	75.6	36.8	48.7	51.3
	UNITED STATES	75.1	73.6	12.3	12.5	3.8	4.2	12.5	14.1	6.9	6.7	7.2	7.0	7.3	28.6	23.8	10.8	1.7	75.1	36.0	49.1	50.9

ZIP CODE #	POST OFFICE NAME	2004 Per Capita Income	2004 HH Income Base	2004 Household Income Distribution (%): Less than $25,000	$25,000 to $49,999	$50,000 to $99,999	$100,000 to $149,999	$150,000 or More	Median Household Income: 2004	2009	2004 National Centile	2004 State Centile	2004 Home Value Base	2004 Home Value Distribution (%): Less than $50,000	$50,000 to $89,999	$90,000 to $174,999	$175,000 to $399,999	$400,000 or More	2004 Median Home Value
63005	CHESTERFIELD	65482	5788	4.4	7.1	20.2	21.1	47.3	142520	170425	100	100	5032	1.6	0.5	2.9	34.0	61.1	447811
63010	ARNOLD	23884	13412	14.8	28.3	40.7	13.9	2.4	55900	64307	81	91	10979	10.1	8.8	61.5	19.1	0.4	122401
63011	BALLWIN	41287	14257	9.1	14.0	34.6	24.7	17.6	86213	108502	96	99	12248	0.5	2.0	27.3	64.0	6.2	208190
63012	BARNHART	23260	3421	8.3	24.6	48.5	16.2	2.3	63643	74609	88	95	3175	8.5	8.9	57.9	23.2	1.5	127039
63013	BEAUFORT	21539	613	14.9	30.0	43.6	8.5	3.1	53221	61455	77	89	552	10.1	16.1	34.2	34.1	5.4	145556
63014	BERGER	22387	445	19.3	32.8	36.2	8.5	3.2	48173	55256	69	83	375	14.4	23.5	33.9	23.2	5.1	112061
63015	CATAWISSA	21694	678	18.6	31.0	37.0	12.5	0.9	50500	58605	73	86	578	10.7	22.0	42.6	22.7	2.1	118137
63016	CEDAR HILL	21292	2673	17.3	27.2	44.7	7.7	3.1	53573	62112	78	90	2403	16.4	15.4	45.9	21.5	0.7	117350
63017	CHESTERFIELD	51645	16412	7.5	14.9	28.1	22.7	26.9	98914	123749	98	99	12813	0.6	1.1	9.5	68.9	19.9	281062
63019	CRYSTAL CITY	20982	1662	32.3	25.6	32.9	6.0	3.3	41625	48864	52	71	1207	8.0	26.2	52.9	12.1	0.8	106480
63020	DE SOTO	20550	7807	25.6	31.0	34.4	6.8	2.3	45030	52660	61	78	6208	12.4	26.8	42.7	16.9	1.2	105404
63021	BALLWIN	36478	21437	7.8	17.9	38.4	21.4	14.5	78676	97888	95	98	17985	0.4	2.6	42.6	48.9	5.5	182941
63023	DITTMER	20583	2083	18.7	29.2	41.1	10.0	1.1	51458	60065	75	87	1810	11.5	21.3	44.0	21.7	1.6	115101
63025	EUREKA	33727	4040	6.1	15.3	38.1	25.4	15.2	85245	104763	96	99	3723	3.1	6.0	33.2	42.6	15.1	198412
63026	FENTON	28082	15880	13.3	23.3	39.1	17.7	6.6	63757	76602	88	95	13245	16.6	5.4	41.4	34.6	2.0	143622
63028	FESTUS	22444	8952	22.9	29.8	36.1	8.1	3.1	47561	54930	67	82	6906	12.5	19.0	46.6	20.5	1.3	114985
63030	FLETCHER	16413	80	33.8	36.3	23.8	3.8	2.5	35000	41287	28	44	67	34.3	25.4	26.9	13.4	0.0	73750
63031	FLORISSANT	26018	19439	14.4	27.6	41.4	13.7	2.9	56911	70088	82	92	15564	1.6	38.0	52.9	7.2	0.2	95320
63033	FLORISSANT	26507	17263	15.2	28.8	38.6	13.3	4.1	55423	68461	80	91	12613	1.2	20.4	73.9	4.4	0.1	109659
63034	FLORISSANT	34168	6083	4.7	16.1	41.6	25.5	12.1	82818	103324	96	99	5885	0.5	4.9	53.9	38.4	2.5	161420
63036	FRENCH VILLAGE	19741	287	30.7	33.8	27.2	7.0	1.4	39875	45639	46	66	253	18.6	22.5	38.7	15.4	4.7	103606
63037	GERALD	22861	1341	25.1	28.9	33.1	9.0	4.0	47057	54435	66	82	1106	13.1	23.1	40.8	20.8	2.3	112687
63038	GLENCOE	51256	2604	5.2	10.1	30.0	26.9	27.9	106322	131641	99	100	2420	0.9	2.6	10.2	57.8	28.5	297397
63039	GRAY SUMMIT	26537	297	13.8	23.2	45.8	12.8	4.4	58983	68693	84	93	246	8.5	17.9	27.2	40.2	6.1	162500
63040	GROVER	40091	2700	6.0	10.4	35.9	30.8	16.9	95911	119295	98	99	2409	0.0	3.0	16.4	75.0	5.7	244530
63041	GRUBVILLE	21387	176	15.3	27.3	45.5	9.1	2.8	54403	63547	79	90	151	9.3	20.5	47.0	22.5	0.7	113306
63042	HAZELWOOD	25364	8597	17.4	32.2	38.4	10.6	1.4	50285	62345	72	86	5044	6.6	39.3	51.0	3.2	0.0	92305
63043	MARYLAND HEIGHTS	29847	9435	13.0	25.3	43.3	13.9	4.5	60286	73562	85	93	6512	0.6	6.7	75.6	16.8	0.3	128165
63044	BRIDGETON	27968	5558	16.2	25.7	37.2	16.3	4.6	56812	70830	81	92	4096	4.8	13.0	58.1	23.9	0.2	130622
63048	HERCULANEUM	19790	1165	31.1	27.4	33.7	4.9	2.9	41823	49837	52	72	810	10.1	25.9	46.8	16.1	1.1	106132
63049	HIGH RIDGE	23350	5608	15.7	26.9	42.7	12.2	2.5	55989	64359	81	91	4776	18.0	11.2	52.5	16.4	1.9	113625
63050	HILLSBORO	23128	5218	17.4	28.1	39.9	11.3	3.3	53625	62104	78	90	4321	12.2	12.0	41.2	33.3	1.3	139519
63051	HOUSE SPRINGS	21860	4922	15.8	32.0	40.5	9.2	2.6	51866	60185	75	88	4165	28.6	15.3	39.0	15.7	1.4	99827
63052	IMPERIAL	24346	8513	12.5	24.1	45.1	14.8	3.5	61812	71485	86	94	7303	11.5	7.7	55.6	24.0	1.2	135628
63055	LABADIE	30886	810	13.6	21.2	43.0	13.0	9.3	62803	73192	87	94	686	12.8	10.9	26.5	34.8	14.9	174000
63056	LESLIE	20564	848	18.5	35.5	37.3	7.3	1.4	47467	54512	67	82	751	9.9	20.9	39.8	26.5	2.9	118463
63060	LONEDELL	21681	1054	15.3	30.0	40.9	10.5	3.3	52712	60878	76	89	909	17.1	21.6	33.8	24.0	3.6	105873
63068	NEW HAVEN	22836	1693	18.6	32.2	36.9	9.8	2.6	49259	57463	71	85	1364	9.2	19.7	41.9	25.4	3.7	119502
63069	PACIFIC	27532	5612	19.6	22.3	37.8	12.5	7.8	57048	66482	82	92	4375	11.2	14.8	33.6	30.1	10.3	142077
63070	PEVELY	19095	2189	24.1	30.8	36.4	7.8	1.0	46716	54578	66	81	1717	29.7	21.2	37.2	11.4	0.5	88908
63071	RICHWOODS	17817	412	39.8	31.1	23.1	3.2	2.9	30999	36728	15	24	330	41.2	23.0	27.0	7.6	1.2	66667
63072	ROBERTSVILLE	23581	1201	15.3	29.5	42.8	9.9	2.5	55020	62484	80	90	1055	19.9	17.3	35.6	25.5	1.7	111777
63074	SAINT ANN	22681	6837	27.9	35.0	29.7	6.2	1.3	39277	49335	44	65	3963	3.4	67.3	27.4	1.6	0.4	77635
63077	SAINT CLAIR	21063	4485	25.8	30.5	33.8	8.3	1.7	45411	52599	62	79	3457	17.6	27.7	39.4	14.2	1.2	94866
63080	SULLIVAN	20663	4588	31.0	31.3	29.8	5.2	2.8	40273	46659	47	67	3408	15.8	27.8	38.6	15.9	1.9	97657
63084	UNION	22375	5672	21.0	31.4	36.4	7.8	3.4	48059	55401	68	83	4525	16.0	16.5	43.4	21.7	2.4	116703
63087	VALLES MINES	17741	259	29.7	33.6	27.8	7.3	1.5	40701	46698	49	68	223	20.2	22.0	37.2	16.6	4.0	102616
63088	VALLEY PARK	26463	3421	18.2	27.8	40.0	10.7	3.4	53476	65636	78	89	2246	1.0	9.1	57.0	32.6	0.3	152975
63089	VILLA RIDGE	21970	2247	18.5	29.6	38.0	10.6	3.3	51222	59874	74	87	1868	25.4	12.4	30.1	28.5	3.5	116845
63090	WASHINGTON	25910	7992	17.3	27.4	40.5	10.2	4.6	54099	62682	79	90	6056	4.5	7.8	54.5	30.0	3.2	138636
63091	ROSEBUD	22995	512	23.4	35.4	32.8	6.5	2.0	43424	49581	57	75	440	16.1	16.4	41.4	20.9	5.2	117442
63101	SAINT LOUIS	17064	396	45.7	34.1	19.4	0.0	0.8	27069	33123	7	9	14	0.0	0.0	100.0	0.0	0.0	103125
63102	SAINT LOUIS	33442	633	27.8	28.3	35.7	4.1	4.1	43300	56763	57	75	10	20.0	0.0	60.0	20.0	0.0	112500
63103	SAINT LOUIS	19832	2877	65.9	23.0	9.1	0.9	1.2	16833	19127	1	1	36	80.6	0.0	0.0	19.4	0.0	40833
63104	SAINT LOUIS	23388	7775	38.9	28.0	22.0	6.9	4.2	33879	41022	24	38	2888	11.8	20.2	39.0	25.1	4.0	116732
63105	SAINT LOUIS	59990	6499	11.8	20.5	26.9	16.1	24.8	77722	102675	94	98	3494	0.5	0.5	6.4	34.1	58.5	453047
63106	SAINT LOUIS	9576	3905	72.4	18.2	7.5	1.1	0.8	13031	15776	1	0	615	47.8	23.6	23.7	4.9	0.0	52935
63107	SAINT LOUIS	11374	5212	56.7	28.5	11.2	2.4	1.2	21498	24645	2	1	2277	47.1	39.8	10.1	1.8	1.1	52198
63108	SAINT LOUIS	30439	10314	44.1	22.7	19.0	6.3	7.9	30983	38787	15	23	2631	6.2	17.8	28.9	31.9	15.2	165882
63109	SAINT LOUIS	28582	14030	22.1	32.6	32.3	10.2	3.0	46041	55467	64	80	8352	2.2	20.2	62.7	14.5	0.5	115559
63110	SAINT LOUIS	18141	7853	38.3	31.2	23.3	4.5	2.7	32818	39933	20	32	3183	12.1	37.4	41.9	8.3	0.4	90429
63111	SAINT LOUIS	15148	8350	46.4	30.3	19.3	3.1	0.9	27139	32262	7	9	3651	33.1	49.5	17.0	0.3	0.2	61483
63112	SAINT LOUIS	18875	9655	51.6	24.1	16.2	4.9	3.2	23742	28810	4	3	3432	30.9	28.6	24.3	10.5	5.7	74488
63113	SAINT LOUIS	12434	5788	54.2	27.5	15.3	2.2	0.8	22385	25467	3	2	2841	48.8	36.6	13.5	0.8	0.3	51012
63114	SAINT LOUIS	21592	15660	24.9	35.8	31.2	6.3	1.9	40732	50795	49	69	10189	8.7	68.1	21.7	1.4	0.2	73251
63115	SAINT LOUIS	15600	9498	46.5	30.6	18.1	3.4	1.4	27356	31759	8	10	5286	32.7	53.6	13.2	0.5	0.1	59672
63116	SAINT LOUIS	19181	19883	35.3	33.1	25.3	4.5	1.8	35115	41819	28	45	11302	13.4	51.9	31.0	3.5	0.2	78530
63117	SAINT LOUIS	43227	4386	19.2	22.8	33.3	12.4	12.3	60186	77647	85	93	2425	1.9	11.8	42.7	28.9	14.6	158729
63118	SAINT LOUIS	13943	10513	46.9	31.3	17.2	3.0	1.7	26859	31904	7	8	3915	38.1	35.7	22.1	4.0	0.2	61155
63119	SAINT LOUIS	36575	14631	15.7	23.1	35.6	15.9	9.7	63055	79574	87	95	10987	0.9	7.0	45.6	36.3	10.2	167674
63120	SAINT LOUIS	11727	4088	53.5	28.0	14.2	3.0	1.3	23041	26922	3	2	2252	50.2	43.0	5.3	1.2	0.3	49917
63121	SAINT LOUIS	20399	11262	33.5	31.7	25.6	6.6	2.5	36055	44580	32	51	6411	17.5	55.9	21.9	4.7	0.1	69173
63122	SAINT LOUIS	42065	16038	13.4	20.3	32.4	17.8	16.1	71468	91051	92	97	12800	0.7	4.4	30.7	48.5	15.7	213805
63123	SAINT LOUIS	28256	22076	18.6	32.3	34.7	11.0	3.6	49224	61260	71	85	16087	1.3	13.8	69.3	14.9	0.7	118970
63124	SAINT LOUIS	97639	4111	11.8	10.9	22.0	12.6	42.7	118409	149353	99	100	3279	0.0	1.8	3.4	24.3	70.5	647263
63125	SAINT LOUIS	24081	14466	24.4	33.0	32.7	7.6	2.3	44203	54246	59	76	10300	5.2	27.9	58.9	7.7	0.4	105970
63126	SAINT LOUIS	32175	6528	12.8	25.1	39.6	16.3	6.1	62878	77833	87	94	5596	0.7	3.6	57.7	35.0	3.0	157935
63127	SAINT LOUIS	46876	1791	14.5	20.3	30.4	13.7	21.1	72239	92004	92	97	1403	0.1	5.8	30.5	35.8	27.8	231522
63128	SAINT LOUIS	37673	12308	11.1	22.0	35.8	18.3	12.8	68262	85873	90	97	9565	0.7	5.7	38.0	47.3	8.2	183948
63129	SAINT LOUIS	31607	19871	10.2	21.5	38.5	21.3	8.5	71195	87414	92	97	15641	0.3	5.6	45.9	45.3	3.1	172730
63130	SAINT LOUIS	30736	13137	25.3	25.4	27.3	10.8	11.2	49269	63161	71	85	7997	4.8	30.2	22.6	31.6	10.9	126676
63131	SAINT LOUIS	69165	5647	6.0	9.2	23.8	19.1	41.8	126850	154502	100	100	5412	0.3	1.4	11.4	37.9	49.0	394778
63132	SAINT LOUIS	35261	6328	19.9	25.7	31.2	12.8	10.5	55395	71172	80	91	3862	1.7	22.6	29.1	35.9	10.7	162915
63133	SAINT LOUIS	13184	2680	43.2	32.4	19.4	3.9	1.0	28503	34344	10	14	1612	46.2	49.1	4.5	0.2	0.0	51821
63134	SAINT LOUIS	17767	5569	29.8	35.8	27.7	5.6	1.0	37780	45772	38	60	3441	15.5	74.3	9.5	0.7	0.0	66512
63135	SAINT LOUIS	21294	8402	25.2	31.8	32.5	7.9	2.7	44225	53981	59	76	6101	10.6	56.1	28.7	4.3	0.3	77047
63136	SAINT LOUIS	17861	19597	33.7	33.6	25.4	5.6	1.7	35910	43361	31	50	11928	14.9	65.7	18.6	0.6	0.2	69822
63137	SAINT LOUIS	21115	8262	25.2	34.9	30.9	6.9	2.1	41804	51810	52	72	6104	6.7	74.9	16.7	1.5	0.2	72408
63138	SAINT LOUIS	23270	8512	22.8	34.5	31.4	8.4	2.8	43367	54458	57	75	4436	2.6	37.1	54.7	5.2	0.4	98857
63139	SAINT LOUIS	24549	11283	27.5	34.2	30.5	5.7	2.1	40341	48460	47	68	6765	6.9	46.7	42.7	3.7	0.1	87735
63140	SAINT LOUIS	13051	136	47.1	30.2	16.2	5.9	0.7	27029	34297	7	8	69	34.8	63.8	1.5	0.0	0.0	54565
63141	SAINT LOUIS	61771	8017	8.2	13.6	29.3	20.1	28.9	97402	121736	98	99	6080	0.8	1.2	15.0	43.1	39.9	337994
63143	SAINT LOUIS	22936	5424	35.3	30.8	26.5	5.9	1.5	35493	43986	29	48	2358	6.5	47.2	42.0	4.1	0.2	87418
63144	SAINT LOUIS	39643	4519	16.2	25.1	37.2	13.3	8.2	59778	75961	84	93	3235	0.4	6.0	62.2	25.0	6.5	139460
63146	SAINT LOUIS	36253	14972	14.4	25.3	35.9	15.8	8.6	62404	77511	87	94	9288	1.1	5.0	47.6	44.8	1.6	170608
	MISSOURI	23864		27.0	29.4	30.1	9.0	4.5	44017	52626				15.2	22.7	39.0	19.7	3.4	109184
	UNITED STATES	25866		24.7	27.1	30.8	10.9	6.5	48124	56710				10.9	15.0	33.7	30.1	10.4	145905

ZIP CODE		FINANCIAL SERVICES				THE HOME						ENTERTAINMENT						PERSONAL			
						Home Improvements		Furnishings													
#	POST OFFICE NAME	Auto Loan	Home Loan	Invest-ments	Retire-ment Plans	Home Repair	Lawn & Garden	Comput-ers & Hard-ware	Major Appli-ances	TV, Radio, Sound Equip-ment	Furni-ture	Dine out/ Carry out	Sports Equip-ment	Fees & Tickets	Toys & Games	Travel	Cable TV	Apparel & Services	Auto Repairs	Health Insur-ance	Pets & Supplies
63005	CHESTERFIELD	253	304	385	317	293	305	282	271	265	287	337	315	309	351	288	260	339	266	245	299
63010	ARNOLD	89	98	97	98	96	97	92	92	88	92	110	107	94	112	91	85	108	90	85	103
63011	BALLWIN	145	172	195	174	170	175	161	159	151	161	191	183	170	195	164	148	189	156	148	174
63012	BARNHART	102	105	98	105	103	105	99	101	96	100	120	120	99	120	98	92	117	100	94	116
63013	BEAUFORT	102	89	66	84	94	101	82	92	88	82	107	109	80	109	85	91	101	89	100	119
63014	BERGER	97	82	59	78	89	96	77	87	83	77	100	104	73	101	79	86	94	85	97	115
63015	CATAWISSA	93	86	68	82	90	96	79	87	83	79	101	103	78	104	81	85	97	84	92	110
63016	CEDAR HILL	92	89	77	87	90	94	84	89	84	85	104	105	82	104	84	83	101	87	87	106
63017	CHESTERFIELD	172	201	240	206	197	207	189	186	179	191	226	214	201	230	193	176	225	183	174	204
63019	CRYSTAL CITY	68	68	70	65	69	77	70	70	72	68	89	79	70	90	71	74	85	70	74	78
63020	DE SOTO	87	75	57	71	80	88	73	80	78	72	95	94	70	96	74	81	89	79	89	101
63021	BALLWIN	134	155	164	160	151	150	143	141	133	145	168	165	150	173	143	127	167	138	124	155
63023	DITTMER	90	81	62	77	84	90	75	83	79	76	96	98	73	97	77	80	92	81	88	105
63025	EUREKA	144	165	161	169	158	155	149	148	137	153	174	173	154	177	147	130	172	144	129	164
63026	FENTON	110	119	114	120	117	117	110	112	105	112	131	131	111	132	109	101	129	109	102	126
63028	FESTUS	91	84	73	82	87	94	82	87	85	81	104	101	80	104	83	86	99	86	92	104
63030	FLETCHER	86	60	31	53	67	76	58	71	68	59	81	84	50	76	59	72	74	70	85	98
63031	FLORISSANT	90	99	106	99	98	101	96	95	93	95	116	110	99	120	96	91	114	94	89	104
63033	FLORISSANT	86	99	111	98	97	102	96	94	93	95	117	109	100	121	97	92	115	93	90	103
63034	FLORISSANT	132	158	165	160	154	153	142	142	132	144	167	164	150	172	144	128	166	137	127	155
63036	FRENCH VILLAGE	81	64	43	57	72	80	60	72	68	59	80	84	54	79	64	72	75	71	85	99
63037	GERALD	100	81	54	75	87	96	76	88	84	76	101	104	71	100	78	88	95	86	99	117
63038	GLENCOE	203	243	251	252	233	231	216	212	197	221	251	246	231	256	216	187	251	205	184	233
63039	GRAY SUMMIT	112	101	78	96	106	114	93	103	99	94	120	123	92	123	96	101	114	100	111	132
63040	GROVER	167	189	182	197	180	174	170	169	156	177	198	198	175	199	166	145	196	164	143	185
63041	GRUBVILLE	96	86	65	81	91	97	79	88	84	79	102	105	78	105	82	86	97	86	95	113
63042	HAZELWOOD	78	79	91	82	77	81	83	80	81	83	102	94	83	101	81	78	100	82	74	88
63043	MARYLAND HEIGHTS	93	100	114	103	98	102	100	97	97	100	122	115	103	124	99	94	120	98	90	107
63044	BRIDGETON	88	104	118	102	102	106	99	97	95	98	119	112	104	124	101	94	118	96	92	106
63048	HERCULANEUM	70	70	72	68	71	77	71	71	73	69	90	82	72	92	72	73	87	71	74	80
63049	HIGH RIDGE	89	97	96	98	95	95	91	92	86	92	109	108	92	110	90	83	107	90	83	103
63050	HILLSBORO	98	94	80	91	96	101	88	94	90	88	110	110	87	112	89	90	106	92	95	113
63051	HOUSE SPRINGS	92	90	78	88	90	93	85	89	85	87	105	104	83	103	85	83	102	89	86	104
63052	IMPERIAL	100	109	105	111	106	105	101	101	95	103	120	119	102	120	99	91	118	99	91	113
63055	LABADIE	122	130	123	128	130	133	119	123	116	119	144	145	121	149	121	114	141	120	118	144
63056	LESLIE	93	75	49	69	81	89	70	81	78	71	94	97	66	93	72	81	88	79	92	109
63060	LONEDELL	99	87	66	83	92	99	81	90	86	81	105	107	79	107	83	88	99	87	97	116
63068	NEW HAVEN	95	86	69	83	90	97	82	89	86	81	104	105	80	106	83	87	99	87	95	111
63069	PACIFIC	108	113	105	112	113	117	106	109	104	106	129	127	107	132	106	102	125	106	105	125
63070	PEVELY	81	73	58	70	75	80	70	75	72	71	89	88	67	87	70	73	85	75	78	92
63071	RICHWOODS	94	63	29	54	72	82	61	76	74	62	86	91	52	82	62	79	78	75	94	108
63072	ROBERTSVILLE	108	96	73	92	102	109	89	99	95	89	115	118	87	118	92	97	109	96	107	127
63074	SAINT ANN	66	66	71	66	66	72	70	69	71	68	88	80	70	90	70	70	85	70	69	76
63077	SAINT CLAIR	86	75	58	73	79	87	74	80	78	73	95	93	71	95	74	80	90	78	86	98
63080	SULLIVAN	83	70	54	67	74	82	69	76	75	69	91	89	66	90	70	77	85	75	84	95
63084	UNION	90	85	72	82	87	93	82	87	84	82	103	100	80	104	82	85	99	85	90	103
63087	VALLES MINES	82	65	44	59	73	82	61	73	69	61	82	86	55	81	65	73	76	72	86	100
63088	VALLEY PARK	88	87	93	92	84	86	90	87	86	91	109	104	88	106	86	81	107	89	77	96
63089	VILLA RIDGE	94	88	73	85	91	96	83	89	85	83	104	104	81	104	84	85	100	87	91	109
63090	WASHINGTON	96	98	94	97	100	105	94	97	94	92	116	114	95	120	95	94	112	95	97	114
63091	ROSEBUD	103	72	37	64	81	92	69	85	82	70	97	101	61	93	71	87	88	84	102	119
63101	SAINT LOUIS	47	40	48	43	39	42	46	44	47	47	59	52	45	56	43	45	58	47	41	49
63102	SAINT LOUIS	71	75	98	76	74	82	79	76	80	78	100	87	81	101	80	80	99	78	76	83
63103	SAINT LOUIS	37	30	41	31	30	36	42	36	43	38	53	44	39	51	39	42	51	41	38	40
63104	SAINT LOUIS	71	65	83	66	63	71	75	71	77	74	97	84	74	94	72	77	94	75	70	79
63105	SAINT LOUIS	158	172	281	185	165	181	180	167	179	184	227	199	193	238	182	178	226	172	155	184
63106	SAINT LOUIS	31	26	33	24	25	30	30	30	34	31	42	33	30	40	29	36	41	32	33	34
63107	SAINT LOUIS	46	37	42	34	37	45	43	44	49	44	60	47	41	54	42	52	57	45	50	50
63108	SAINT LOUIS	71	63	101	69	61	70	79	70	81	77	102	86	78	101	75	80	99	76	69	79
63109	SAINT LOUIS	75	81	99	82	80	85	84	81	82	82	103	95	85	105	84	81	101	83	77	88
63110	SAINT LOUIS	59	55	67	55	54	60	62	59	64	61	80	69	62	79	60	63	78	62	59	66
63111	SAINT LOUIS	47	44	50	44	44	49	50	48	52	48	65	56	49	64	49	52	63	50	50	53
63112	SAINT LOUIS	59	49	59	48	48	56	60	57	64	59	79	66	57	73	56	64	76	61	59	64
63113	SAINT LOUIS	47	39	42	35	39	47	43	44	49	44	59	48	42	54	42	52	57	46	51	51
63114	SAINT LOUIS	67	71	79	70	71	77	73	71	73	71	91	82	75	95	73	73	89	71	71	78
63115	SAINT LOUIS	57	47	50	43	47	57	52	54	59	53	71	57	51	65	51	63	68	55	62	62
63116	SAINT LOUIS	59	58	65	58	58	63	64	61	64	61	80	71	63	81	62	64	78	63	61	67
63117	SAINT LOUIS	117	121	159	127	119	128	130	123	127	129	161	147	132	161	128	124	158	128	115	135
63118	SAINT LOUIS	51	46	55	44	45	52	52	50	55	52	69	57	51	67	50	57	67	52	53	56
63119	SAINT LOUIS	110	121	143	123	120	127	120	117	116	119	146	137	124	148	121	114	144	118	112	130
63120	SAINT LOUIS	49	40	44	36	40	48	45	46	51	46	62	50	44	56	44	54	59	47	53	53
63121	SAINT LOUIS	69	65	75	65	63	71	70	68	72	71	91	78	71	88	69	72	88	71	69	77
63122	SAINT LOUIS	126	148	179	148	146	154	141	139	136	141	171	160	149	176	145	135	169	138	132	151
63123	SAINT LOUIS	81	90	102	88	90	97	89	88	88	87	110	100	92	113	91	89	108	87	88	96
63124	SAINT LOUIS	277	352	483	347	344	375	322	315	306	326	386	357	357	402	339	309	389	309	300	343
63125	SAINT LOUIS	74	77	83	75	78	86	77	77	78	76	97	87	79	99	79	80	94	77	80	85
63126	SAINT LOUIS	96	110	125	107	109	118	105	105	104	105	130	118	111	133	109	105	128	103	105	114
63127	SAINT LOUIS	144	170	205	169	168	178	160	159	153	160	192	182	170	197	165	152	191	156	152	173
63128	SAINT LOUIS	119	135	155	136	134	142	130	129	125	130	158	148	136	158	133	124	155	128	124	141
63129	SAINT LOUIS	111	127	141	130	124	126	121	119	114	121	144	139	125	147	121	110	143	118	108	130
63130	SAINT LOUIS	102	104	130	105	102	112	111	105	110	110	138	122	113	137	109	108	135	108	102	116
63131	SAINT LOUIS	234	304	391	300	298	318	269	267	251	273	317	301	299	330	284	252	320	258	249	291
63132	SAINT LOUIS	103	113	135	114	112	120	114	111	111	113	140	128	117	141	115	110	138	112	107	121
63133	SAINT LOUIS	54	46	52	43	45	54	51	51	57	53	70	57	51	65	50	60	67	53	57	59
63134	SAINT LOUIS	63	62	71	59	60	68	65	63	68	65	85	72	67	86	65	69	83	64	65	71
63135	SAINT LOUIS	74	77	88	76	76	83	79	77	80	78	100	88	81	102	79	80	98	77	77	85
63136	SAINT LOUIS	65	61	72	58	59	68	65	63	69	66	86	71	66	84	65	71	84	65	67	72
63137	SAINT LOUIS	69	73	79	71	73	79	74	73	75	72	94	84	76	98	75	76	91	73	74	81
63138	SAINT LOUIS	79	80	92	81	79	84	85	82	84	84	105	96	85	105	83	82	103	84	78	90
63139	SAINT LOUIS	65	67	79	68	66	72	72	68	71	69	89	80	72	91	71	70	87	70	67	75
63140	SAINT LOUIS	50	43	56	40	41	49	50	48	55	51	69	55	50	67	49	57	67	51	51	55
63141	SAINT LOUIS	196	226	289	228	224	241	215	214	208	219	262	242	229	264	223	209	259	212	206	235
63143	SAINT LOUIS	60	54	66	58	54	58	67	61	65	63	82	76	63	79	62	61	80	66	56	67
63144	SAINT LOUIS	98	103	145	109	101	108	110	103	109	110	138	124	114	142	110	107	136	107	97	114
63146	SAINT LOUIS	103	111	133	114	109	116	112	109	108	112	137	127	115	136	112	106	134	110	103	119
	MISSOURI	87	82	79	80	83	90	82	85	85	82	104	99	81	103	82	85	100	85	87	100
	UNITED STATES	100	100	100	100	100	100	100	100	100	100	100	100	100	100	100	100	100	100	100	100

MISSOURI
POPULATION CHANGE

A 63147-63543

# POST OFFICE NAME	COUNTY FIPS CODE	POPULATION 2000	POPULATION 2004	POPULATION 2009	2000-2004 ANNUAL RATE % Rate	2000-2004 ANNUAL RATE State Centile	HOUSEHOLDS 2000	HOUSEHOLDS 2004	HOUSEHOLDS 2009	% Annual Rate 2000-2004	2004 Average HH Size	FAMILIES 2000	FAMILIES 2004	% Annual Rate 2000-2004
63147 SAINT LOUIS	510	13197	12495	11749	-1.3	3	4504	4255	3994	-1.3	2.64	2942	2719	-1.8
63301 SAINT CHARLES	183	46012	48252	54304	1.1	71	18320	19630	22558	1.6	2.33	11726	12154	0.9
63303 SAINT CHARLES	183	41857	44933	51347	1.7	82	16248	17679	20468	2.0	2.53	11154	11762	1.3
63304 SAINT CHARLES	183	40465	46949	55480	3.6	96	13426	15853	19007	4.0	2.94	11258	13093	3.6
63330 ANNADA	163	163	164	165	0.1	38	81	82	84	0.3	2.00	59	59	0.0
63332 AUGUSTA	183	1131	1276	1486	2.9	92	438	501	591	3.2	2.55	336	378	2.8
63333 BELLFLOWER	139	707	706	717	0.0	30	255	257	263	0.2	2.75	189	187	-0.3
63334 BOWLING GREEN	163	7662	7750	7839	0.3	43	2226	2282	2340	0.6	2.51	1530	1535	0.1
63336 CLARKSVILLE	163	1438	1481	1514	0.7	59	590	612	631	0.9	2.42	394	399	0.3
63339 CURRYVILLE	163	1672	1683	1700	0.2	39	566	577	588	0.5	2.80	452	453	0.1
63341 DEFIANCE	183	3381	3762	4355	2.5	89	1167	1319	1547	2.9	2.85	980	1086	2.5
63343 ELSBERRY	113	4432	4634	5075	1.1	69	1627	1702	1866	1.1	2.68	1180	1212	0.6
63344 EOLIA	113	1039	1052	1099	0.3	44	409	416	435	0.4	2.47	291	289	-0.2
63345 FARBER	007	530	519	516	-0.5	18	218	216	217	-0.2	2.40	161	156	-0.7
63347 FOLEY	113	2443	2688	3025	2.3	88	845	935	1057	2.4	2.87	668	727	2.0
63348 FORISTELL	183	4364	5354	6483	4.9	99	1519	1896	2327	5.4	2.82	1261	1548	4.9
63349 HAWK POINT	113	1389	1425	1545	0.6	56	515	529	574	0.6	2.69	387	390	0.2
63350 HIGH HILL	139	654	664	677	0.4	47	271	278	286	0.6	2.33	180	181	0.1
63351 JONESBURG	139	1206	1228	1251	0.4	50	478	491	505	0.6	2.43	314	315	0.1
63352 LADDONIA	007	942	931	926	-0.3	23	374	372	372	-0.1	2.50	266	259	-0.6
63353 LOUISIANA	163	5207	5200	5248	0.0	30	2093	2102	2138	0.1	2.40	1399	1375	-0.4
63357 MARTHASVILLE	219	4618	5147	5919	2.6	90	1648	1871	2184	3.0	2.69	1317	1472	2.7
63359 MIDDLETOWN	139	1616	1726	1812	1.6	80	635	684	724	1.8	2.52	481	507	1.3
63361 MONTGOMERY CITY	139	3848	3857	3919	0.1	34	1575	1592	1630	0.3	2.37	1085	1073	-0.3
63362 MOSCOW MILLS	113	3508	4437	5363	5.7	99	1203	1534	1864	5.9	2.89	940	1179	5.5
63363 NEW FLORENCE	139	1631	1620	1638	-0.2	26	602	602	613	0.0	2.53	437	430	-0.4
63366 O FALLON	183	55408	70077	86564	5.7	99	18775	24003	29968	6.0	2.91	15116	19018	5.6
63367 LAKE SAINT LOUIS	183	10184	11917	14130	3.8	97	3918	4673	5625	4.2	2.55	3072	3599	3.8
63369 OLD MONROE	113	1891	2121	2426	2.7	91	680	767	880	2.9	2.77	517	572	2.4
63373 PORTAGE DES SIOUX	183	685	648	722	-1.3	3	256	246	277	-0.9	2.63	193	181	-1.5
63376 SAINT PETERS	183	66925	74978	87655	2.7	91	22919	26184	31090	3.2	2.85	18322	20593	2.8
63377 SILEX	113	2404	2457	2677	0.5	53	885	885	967	0.5	2.69	664	667	0.1
63379 TROY	113	16463	18482	20997	2.8	92	5849	6603	7536	2.9	2.75	4442	4929	2.5
63381 TRUXTON	219	629	629	693	0.0	32	235	238	264	0.3	2.64	181	180	-0.1
63382 VANDALIA	007	4574	4542	4531	-0.2	26	1404	1401	1406	-0.1	2.22	885	859	-0.7
63383 WARRENTON	219	12870	14505	16960	2.9	92	4850	5504	6496	3.0	2.61	3566	3976	2.6
63384 WELLSVILLE	139	2026	2085	2148	0.7	58	760	787	816	0.8	2.52	520	528	0.4
63385 WENTZVILLE	183	13779	17777	22161	6.2	99	4793	6350	8063	6.8	2.78	3788	4871	6.1
63386 WEST ALTON	183	595	639	725	1.7	82	220	240	276	2.1	2.66	158	168	1.5
63388 WILLIAMSBURG	027	660	754	838	3.2	94	262	302	338	3.4	2.50	190	214	2.8
63389 WINFIELD	113	4543	4943	5581	2.0	86	1622	1771	2007	2.1	2.78	1244	1341	1.8
63390 WRIGHT CITY	219	6889	7962	9323	3.5	96	2580	3014	3562	3.7	2.63	1944	2232	3.3
63401 HANNIBAL	127	21546	21857	22232	0.3	47	8524	8708	8921	0.5	2.40	5674	5663	-0.1
63430 ALEXANDRIA	045	617	628	637	0.4	49	242	250	258	0.8	2.51	179	181	0.3
63431 ANABEL	121	384	386	384	0.1	37	133	135	135	0.4	2.86	103	103	0.0
63432 ARBELA	199	571	573	590	0.1	35	206	204	207	-0.2	2.81	152	148	-0.6
63433 ASHBURN	163	246	246	248	0.0	32	99	100	102	0.2	2.43	68	68	0.0
63434 BETHEL	205	541	525	515	-0.7	11	206	199	196	-0.8	2.64	158	151	-1.1
63435 CANTON	111	3991	4069	4188	0.5	51	1355	1382	1428	0.5	2.49	893	889	-0.1
63436 CENTER	173	1035	1050	1069	0.3	47	411	418	428	0.4	2.40	284	283	-0.1
63437 CLARENCE	205	1570	1680	1734	1.6	81	643	695	722	1.9	2.34	436	460	1.3
63438 DURHAM	111	649	666	687	0.6	56	233	242	251	0.9	2.75	182	186	0.5
63439 EMDEN	205	238	235	234	-0.3	22	78	77	77	-0.3	3.01	59	57	-0.8
63440 EWING	111	1263	1303	1348	0.7	60	508	529	551	1.0	2.44	390	399	0.5
63441 FRANKFORD	163	869	885	900	0.4	50	353	363	372	0.7	2.41	256	258	0.2
63443 HUNNEWELL	205	383	378	375	-0.3	22	157	156	155	-0.2	2.39	106	103	-0.7
63445 KAHOKA	045	4080	4089	4122	0.1	34	1594	1618	1654	0.4	2.45	1083	1073	-0.2
63446 KNOX CITY	103	495	474	459	-1.0	5	220	212	206	-0.9	2.23	148	139	-1.5
63447 LA BELLE	111	1169	1185	1219	0.3	45	463	472	489	0.5	2.39	297	296	-0.1
63448 LA GRANGE	111	1657	1705	1766	0.7	58	696	724	756	0.9	2.35	461	468	0.4
63450 LENTNER	205	138	156	165	2.9	93	54	62	66	3.3	2.44	35	40	3.2
63451 LEONARD	205	252	247	244	-0.5	18	97	95	94	-0.5	2.54	69	66	-1.0
63452 LEWISTOWN	111	870	886	911	0.4	50	343	352	365	0.6	2.46	232	233	0.1
63453 LURAY	045	507	525	537	0.8	64	197	208	216	1.3	2.52	150	156	0.9
63454 MAYWOOD	127	1070	1078	1094	0.2	40	388	395	404	0.4	2.72	307	308	0.1
63456 MONROE CITY	173	4183	4242	4362	0.3	46	1656	1696	1759	0.6	2.45	1137	1139	0.0
63457 MONTICELLO	111	469	481	495	0.6	56	183	190	198	0.9	2.35	140	143	0.5
63458 NEWARK	103	240	230	222	-1.0	5	98	94	92	-1.0	2.45	66	61	-1.8
63459 NEW LONDON	173	4562	4679	4797	0.6	56	1728	1783	1837	0.7	2.62	1315	1333	0.3
63460 NOVELTY	103	481	461	447	-1.0	6	200	194	190	-0.7	2.38	142	135	-1.2
63461 PALMYRA	127	5458	5385	5409	-0.3	21	2088	2074	2099	-0.2	2.48	1489	1452	-0.6
63462 PERRY	173	1311	1335	1363	0.4	50	552	568	584	0.7	2.29	363	364	0.1
63463 PHILADELPHIA	127	624	655	673	1.2	72	222	234	243	1.3	2.78	178	185	0.9
63464 PLEVNA	103	132	126	122	-1.1	4	61	59	57	-0.8	2.14	43	41	-1.1
63466 SAINT PATRICK	045	450	455	461	0.3	43	178	183	188	0.7	2.49	140	142	0.3
63468 SHELBINA	205	2639	2544	2496	-0.9	8	1105	1067	1049	-0.8	2.29	713	672	-1.4
63469 SHELBYVILLE	205	1184	1150	1132	-0.7	11	461	446	438	-0.8	2.37	313	296	-1.3
63471 TAYLOR	127	559	580	594	0.9	65	226	236	244	1.0	2.46	181	187	0.8
63472 WAYLAND	045	1227	1231	1242	0.1	35	516	526	538	0.5	2.34	356	355	-0.1
63473 WILLIAMSTOWN	111	302	306	314	0.3	45	130	132	136	0.4	2.32	91	91	0.0
63474 WYACONDA	045	535	524	526	-0.5	18	239	238	242	-0.1	2.20	172	167	-0.7
63501 KIRKSVILLE	001	20876	21041	21327	0.2	40	8081	8208	8392	0.4	2.22	4148	4073	-0.4
63530 ATLANTA	121	986	1054	1077	1.6	81	364	391	402	1.7	2.70	279	295	1.3
63531 BARING	103	426	441	441	0.8	64	159	166	167	1.0	2.66	113	115	0.4
63532 BEVIER	121	1339	1341	1328	0.0	34	548	554	554	0.3	2.42	377	372	-0.3
63533 BRASHEAR	001	1517	1479	1479	-0.6	14	571	562	567	-0.4	2.62	443	427	-0.9
63534 CALLAO	121	813	804	791	-0.3	24	334	334	333	0.0	2.41	239	234	-0.5
63535 COATSVILLE	197	131	140	147	1.6	81	54	58	61	1.7	2.41	41	43	1.1
63536 DOWNING	197	1012	1031	1059	0.4	50	405	415	429	0.6	2.48	283	284	0.1
63537 EDINA	103	2013	1966	1920	-0.6	15	828	810	793	-0.5	2.32	546	521	-1.1
63538 ELMER	121	293	307	310	1.1	71	130	137	140	1.2	2.24	94	97	0.7
63539 ETHEL	121	320	332	334	0.9	65	143	149	152	1.0	2.23	104	106	0.5
63540 GIBBS	001	415	404	404	-0.6	13	155	152	153	-0.5	2.65	112	108	-0.9
63541 GLENWOOD	197	375	400	421	1.5	79	148	159	168	1.7	2.52	111	117	1.3
63543 GORIN	199	407	410	425	0.2	39	152	151	154	-0.2	2.72	106	103	-0.7
MISSOURI					0.8					0.9	2.46			0.4
UNITED STATES					1.2					1.3	2.58			1.1

Copyright © 2004 ESRI BIS. All rights reserved. Reproduction by any method is prohibited.   165-A

ZIP CODE #	POST OFFICE NAME	RACE (%) White 2000	White 2004	Black 2000	Black 2004	Asian/Pacific 2000	Asian/Pacific 2004	% Hispanic Origin 2000	% Hispanic Origin 2004	2004 AGE DISTRIBUTION (%) 0-4	5-9	10-14	15-19	20-24	25-44	45-64	65-84	85+	18+	MEDIAN AGE 2004	% 2004 Males	% 2004 Females
63147	SAINT LOUIS	9.3	7.4	89.3	91.2	0.1	0.2	0.5	0.5	5.8	6.1	7.9	8.9	8.7	27.2	23.5	10.4	1.6	75.3	34.6	49.0	51.0
63301	SAINT CHARLES	94.0	93.4	3.0	3.2	0.7	0.9	2.1	2.3	5.9	5.8	5.9	7.4	9.1	27.1	24.8	12.2	1.8	78.6	37.2	49.0	51.0
63303	SAINT CHARLES	93.8	93.0	3.2	3.4	1.3	1.6	1.4	1.6	6.7	6.8	7.4	6.6	7.1	30.7	25.2	8.5	0.9	75.0	35.7	49.1	50.9
63304	SAINT CHARLES	95.1	94.5	2.4	2.6	1.0	1.2	1.2	1.4	8.8	8.9	9.0	7.3	5.8	29.9	23.2	6.3	0.8	68.4	34.0	49.0	51.0
63330	ANNADA	95.7	95.7	2.5	3.1	0.0	0.0	0.6	0.6	4.9	6.7	7.3	6.1	3.7	26.2	28.1	15.2	1.8	76.8	42.9	51.2	48.8
63332	AUGUSTA	98.4	98.3	0.3	0.3	0.4	0.4	0.6	0.6	4.8	5.6	7.5	6.2	4.7	25.2	31.0	13.4	1.6	78.2	42.9	50.7	49.3
63333	BELLFLOWER	97.7	97.3	0.3	0.3	0.4	0.6	1.0	1.3	6.4	6.8	8.5	9.6	6.8	25.2	25.6	9.8	1.3	72.4	37.1	53.0	47.0
63334	BOWLING GREEN	82.1	80.8	15.9	17.0	0.2	0.2	1.0	1.1	4.7	4.9	6.0	6.3	9.0	34.6	22.7	9.7	2.1	80.7	36.2	60.9	39.1
63336	CLARKSVILLE	92.0	91.2	5.5	6.1	0.2	0.2	1.5	1.6	5.7	6.4	7.4	6.5	5.0	25.9	26.1	14.5	2.4	76.6	41.0	48.7	51.3
63339	CURRYVILLE	94.0	93.5	4.5	4.9	0.1	0.1	0.3	0.4	7.3	7.6	9.0	7.4	6.4	26.3	23.5	11.6	1.1	71.7	35.7	52.6	47.4
63341	DEFIANCE	97.6	97.2	1.1	1.3	0.3	0.4	0.8	0.9	6.6	8.0	8.6	7.2	4.3	27.8	30.1	6.9	0.7	72.2	39.0	50.4	49.7
63343	ELSBERRY	95.1	94.7	2.1	2.2	0.2	0.3	2.3	2.5	6.9	7.0	8.4	7.9	6.7	25.4	24.7	11.2	1.9	72.4	37.2	48.7	51.3
63344	EOLIA	93.1	92.5	4.8	5.3	0.2	0.3	1.0	1.1	5.9	6.3	7.3	7.0	5.9	24.2	28.0	13.2	2.1	76.1	40.5	49.3	50.7
63345	FARBER	98.9	98.8	0.0	0.0	0.2	0.2	0.0	0.0	4.4	5.0	6.7	4.2	6.4	26.0	30.3	15.2	1.7	81.1	43.3	49.7	50.3
63347	FOLEY	96.8	96.5	0.8	0.9	0.2	0.3	1.0	1.1	6.8	7.0	8.9	8.6	6.8	28.0	25.5	8.0	0.6	71.8	35.6	50.3	49.7
63348	FORISTELL	95.6	95.2	2.9	3.1	0.2	0.2	0.9	1.1	6.6	7.0	8.3	7.8	5.2	27.4	28.3	8.6	0.8	73.0	38.5	50.8	49.3
63349	HAWK POINT	97.8	97.6	0.9	1.0	0.2	0.3	0.3	0.3	7.2	7.2	8.5	8.5	6.3	26.7	24.4	10.0	1.3	72.2	36.2	51.8	48.2
63350	HIGH HILL	95.6	94.9	1.1	1.2	0.9	1.2	1.4	1.5	5.6	5.9	7.2	5.9	6.5	24.9	26.5	13.9	3.8	77.7	41.2	50.0	50.0
63351	JONESBURG	95.5	94.9	1.1	1.1	0.9	1.2	1.3	1.6	5.5	5.9	7.2	5.8	6.5	24.8	26.4	13.9	4.0	77.9	41.2	49.8	50.2
63352	LADDONIA	98.3	98.3	0.5	0.5	0.0	0.0	0.1	0.1	6.0	6.4	8.1	6.6	5.6	25.7	26.6	13.6	1.4	75.3	40.4	50.0	50.1
63353	LOUISIANA	92.0	91.3	4.2	4.6	0.3	0.4	3.6	4.0	6.4	6.3	6.8	6.3	6.1	24.4	24.5	16.1	3.2	76.7	40.9	48.9	51.1
63357	MARTHASVILLE	98.1	97.9	0.6	0.6	0.4	0.4	0.7	0.7	5.9	6.1	7.4	7.0	5.8	27.1	28.2	11.3	1.2	76.2	39.9	51.0	49.0
63359	MIDDLETOWN	98.4	98.4	0.8	0.9	0.1	0.1	0.4	0.5	5.7	6.0	7.1	6.1	5.6	23.5	28.5	15.2	2.1	77.4	42.4	51.6	48.4
63361	MONTGOMERY CITY	95.4	94.9	2.8	3.1	0.1	0.2	0.4	0.5	5.7	5.9	6.4	7.8	6.7	25.7	26.2	13.5	2.2	77.2	39.7	49.3	50.7
63362	MOSCOW MILLS	96.0	95.6	1.5	1.7	0.2	0.2	1.2	1.4	9.1	8.4	8.5	7.5	7.0	30.6	21.7	6.7	0.7	69.4	31.9	50.7	49.3
63363	NEW FLORENCE	96.9	96.5	1.7	1.8	0.1	0.1	1.0	1.1	5.2	5.7	7.0	6.2	5.6	23.6	28.5	13.5	4.7	78.0	42.8	49.3	50.7
63366	O FALLON	95.5	94.9	2.0	2.3	0.7	1.0	1.5	1.6	9.9	9.3	8.4	6.7	5.8	33.5	19.4	6.5	0.5	68.0	32.2	49.2	50.8
63367	LAKE SAINT LOUIS	95.6	95.1	2.1	2.3	0.9	1.1	1.3	1.5	6.2	6.5	7.0	6.6	5.6	26.1	29.3	11.8	0.8	76.1	40.3	49.5	50.6
63369	OLD MONROE	98.6	98.4	0.3	0.4	0.1	0.1	0.9	1.0	7.6	7.8	8.2	6.7	6.7	29.1	23.9	8.9	1.0	72.3	35.1	50.2	49.8
63373	PORTAGE DES SIOUX	98.3	98.2	0.2	0.2	0.2	0.2	1.0	1.1	5.6	6.3	8.0	6.5	5.9	27.2	26.7	12.4	1.5	76.1	39.7	52.6	47.4
63376	SAINT PETERS	95.0	94.3	2.4	2.6	1.0	1.3	1.5	1.6	7.8	7.8	8.4	7.6	6.4	30.5	24.3	6.6	0.7	71.2	34.4	49.0	51.0
63377	SILEX	97.8	97.7	0.9	1.0	0.1	0.2	0.7	0.8	6.6	6.8	7.5	7.5	6.3	25.2	26.2	12.3	1.8	74.6	39.0	51.5	48.5
63379	TROY	95.1	94.7	2.6	2.8	0.2	0.3	1.2	1.4	7.9	7.5	8.3	7.6	6.8	28.8	22.2	9.3	1.6	71.4	34.4	48.9	51.1
63381	TRUXTON	96.7	96.3	0.6	0.6	0.5	0.6	0.3	0.3	5.7	6.4	7.0	7.5	5.9	24.6	29.4	12.2	1.3	76.8	40.6	50.6	49.4
63382	VANDALIA	80.6	79.5	16.8	17.9	0.4	0.4	1.0	1.0	4.6	4.3	4.2	5.3	7.2	39.1	20.5	11.7	3.1	83.7	37.7	33.6	66.4
63383	WARRENTON	96.5	96.2	1.4	1.5	0.3	0.4	1.1	1.2	6.9	7.0	7.5	7.1	6.0	26.8	24.1	13.0	1.5	73.9	37.8	49.0	51.0
63384	WELLSVILLE	94.3	93.8	3.6	3.8	0.1	0.1	0.8	0.9	6.5	6.1	7.9	6.8	6.3	23.9	22.1	15.9	4.5	75.2	40.3	49.1	50.9
63385	WENTZVILLE	90.8	90.8	6.9	6.8	0.4	0.5	1.0	1.2	7.8	7.9	8.5	7.5	6.3	27.9	24.3	8.8	1.2	71.2	35.3	48.9	51.1
63386	WEST ALTON	99.2	99.1	0.0	0.0	0.2	0.2	0.5	0.6	5.0	8.0	7.0	8.0	7.4	26.8	26.5	10.8	0.6	74.2	38.6	54.2	45.9
63388	WILLIAMSBURG	95.0	94.4	1.8	2.1	0.0	0.0	1.8	2.1	5.0	5.8	7.2	7.7	5.6	26.3	26.0	15.4	1.1	77.2	40.3	51.5	48.5
63389	WINFIELD	97.9	97.7	0.4	0.5	0.3	0.3	0.6	0.7	7.5	7.3	8.6	7.9	6.9	28.2	24.4	8.4	0.9	71.8	35.2	49.7	50.3
63390	WRIGHT CITY	94.2	93.9	3.2	3.4	0.1	0.1	2.1	2.2	7.0	6.8	7.1	6.6	6.0	27.4	26.9	11.2	1.0	75.1	38.7	50.6	49.4
63401	HANNIBAL	91.9	91.2	5.6	6.1	0.4	0.5	1.0	1.1	6.8	6.6	7.0	7.5	7.7	25.6	23.6	12.7	2.6	75.3	37.0	47.2	52.8
63430	ALEXANDRIA	99.4	99.0	0.2	0.2	0.2	0.2	0.5	0.5	6.4	6.2	6.9	5.7	5.6	25.6	29.3	13.1	1.3	76.9	41.1	50.8	49.2
63431	ANABEL	97.7	97.7	1.3	1.3	0.0	0.0	1.3	1.3	6.7	6.7	7.0	6.5	5.7	25.4	28.8	11.7	1.6	75.7	39.8	52.3	47.7
63432	ARBELA	99.3	99.1	0.0	0.0	0.2	0.2	1.4	1.6	8.9	8.4	7.3	6.8	5.6	26.0	23.6	12.6	0.9	71.2	36.3	51.8	48.2
63433	ASHBURN	92.3	91.1	6.1	6.5	0.4	0.4	0.4	0.4	5.7	5.7	5.7	6.5	5.7	23.2	29.3	15.5	2.9	78.5	43.3	50.4	49.6
63434	BETHEL	97.6	97.7	1.1	1.1	0.0	0.0	1.1	1.0	6.3	6.1	6.9	7.1	5.9	24.4	30.1	11.4	1.9	76.2	40.6	50.5	49.5
63435	CANTON	95.8	95.3	1.8	2.0	0.5	0.7	1.2	1.3	7.9	7.1	6.4	9.0	12.7	24.8	18.1	11.2	2.9	75.2	29.7	48.2	51.8
63436	CENTER	99.1	99.1	0.1	0.1	0.0	0.0	0.9	1.1	7.4	6.9	6.3	5.9	5.7	24.6	23.0	16.7	3.6	75.7	40.3	51.1	48.9
63437	CLARENCE	98.5	98.5	0.6	0.5	0.1	0.1	0.5	0.5	5.8	6.1	7.5	6.5	5.8	22.3	26.0	16.3	3.8	76.4	42.3	47.3	52.7
63438	DURHAM	99.4	99.4	0.2	0.2	0.0	0.0	0.2	0.3	6.6	6.6	6.6	7.2	6.8	26.7	26.4	12.0	1.1	75.5	38.3	52.9	47.2
63439	EMDEN	97.9	97.9	1.3	1.3	0.0	0.0	0.8	0.9	6.4	6.8	6.8	7.2	6.0	24.7	27.2	12.3	2.6	75.3	39.8	49.4	50.6
63440	EWING	99.2	99.2	0.2	0.2	0.1	0.1	0.2	0.2	6.6	6.8	7.1	6.9	6.1	25.6	26.2	13.1	1.7	75.2	39.3	51.7	48.4
63441	FRANKFORD	96.7	96.4	3.0	3.3	0.0	0.0	0.0	0.0	4.8	5.1	6.9	7.7	6.9	24.5	29.3	13.2	1.7	78.5	40.8	52.5	47.5
63443	HUNNEWELL	97.4	97.1	1.8	2.1	0.0	0.0	0.5	0.5	7.1	6.9	6.1	6.6	5.6	23.0	25.9	15.1	3.7	75.7	41.6	48.9	51.1
63445	KAHOKA	98.6	98.5	0.1	0.1	0.1	0.1	0.9	0.9	6.3	6.5	7.1	6.5	6.0	24.3	25.3	14.3	3.7	75.9	40.2	48.7	51.3
63446	KNOX CITY	98.8	98.7	0.2	0.2	0.2	0.2	1.2	1.3	5.9	5.9	6.3	6.3	5.7	22.8	28.1	16.7	2.3	78.1	43.3	48.7	51.3
63447	LA BELLE	95.2	94.9	3.4	3.6	0.1	0.1	1.0	1.3	6.8	6.8	7.1	6.2	5.8	22.1	23.6	16.4	5.2	76.0	41.3	48.9	51.1
63448	LA GRANGE	90.7	89.9	7.6	8.3	0.0	0.0	0.5	0.4	7.3	7.0	6.2	6.1	5.8	27.1	25.3	12.7	2.4	75.7	38.7	48.8	51.2
63450	LENTNER	98.6	98.7	0.7	0.6	0.0	0.0	0.7	0.6	5.1	5.1	7.1	6.4	5.8	21.2	26.9	18.0	4.5	78.9	44.6	48.1	51.9
63451	LEONARD	98.4	98.0	0.8	0.8	0.0	0.0	0.4	0.4	7.3	7.7	7.7	6.9	6.1	22.3	25.1	14.6	2.4	72.5	38.1	47.0	53.0
63452	LEWISTOWN	98.3	98.3	1.3	1.4	0.0	0.0	0.3	0.3	8.0	8.0	6.4	5.0	5.6	21.9	24.2	18.2	2.7	74.7	41.0	48.4	51.6
63453	LURAY	99.4	99.2	0.2	0.2	0.0	0.0	0.4	0.4	6.5	6.3	6.9	7.4	5.3	28.6	24.6	13.9	0.6	75.8	39.0	54.1	45.9
63454	MAYWOOD	97.7	97.4	1.1	1.2	0.2	0.2	0.4	0.4	7.2	7.2	6.7	6.9	6.0	26.4	26.7	11.8	1.0	74.2	38.4	50.7	49.3
63456	MONROE CITY	93.0	92.3	5.5	6.1	0.1	0.2	0.5	0.6	6.3	6.6	7.2	6.3	6.5	24.2	26.5	13.5	2.8	75.7	40.3	48.6	51.4
63457	MONTICELLO	98.9	98.8	0.2	0.2	0.0	0.0	0.0	0.0	5.6	5.8	7.1	5.8	5.4	25.2	27.9	13.5	3.7	78.0	42.1	52.2	47.8
63458	NEWARK	98.8	99.1	0.0	0.0	0.0	0.0	1.3	1.3	5.7	5.7	6.1	6.1	5.7	23.9	28.3	16.5	2.2	80.0	43.5	48.7	51.3
63459	NEW LONDON	97.0	96.7	1.9	2.1	0.1	0.2	0.4	0.4	6.1	6.7	6.9	6.7	5.7	25.8	28.9	12.0	1.3	76.1	40.3	50.6	49.4
63460	NOVELTY	99.0	98.7	0.0	0.0	0.2	0.2	0.8	1.1	4.8	5.2	6.5	6.1	5.6	22.6	29.3	17.4	2.6	79.6	44.6	50.3	49.7
63461	PALMYRA	97.1	96.8	1.9	2.0	0.2	0.3	0.5	0.6	6.6	6.6	6.8	6.4	6.4	25.8	24.1	13.9	3.4	76.2	39.3	48.4	51.6
63462	PERRY	98.7	98.6	0.5	0.5	0.1	0.1	0.6	0.8	4.0	5.5	6.1	6.4	5.5	23.2	29.1	16.3	4.1	80.6	44.6	47.9	52.1
63463	PHILADELPHIA	99.4	99.2	0.2	0.2	0.0	0.0	0.0	0.0	7.0	6.9	7.3	7.8	7.0	25.3	26.1	11.6	0.9	73.1	37.6	50.7	49.3
63464	PLEVNA	99.2	99.2	0.0	0.0	0.0	0.0	1.5	0.8	4.8	4.8	6.4	6.4	5.6	23.8	28.6	17.5	2.4	79.4	44.2	50.8	49.2
63466	SAINT PATRICK	99.8	99.6	0.0	0.0	0.2	0.2	0.9	0.9	5.9	5.7	5.7	5.5	4.8	25.5	30.1	15.4	1.3	79.3	43.0	50.3	49.7
63468	SHELBINA	97.8	97.6	1.2	1.3	0.0	0.0	0.3	0.3	5.9	6.0	6.9	6.2	6.3	23.0	24.3	16.2	5.2	77.4	42.0	46.5	53.5
63469	SHELBYVILLE	97.5	97.4	0.8	0.8	0.4	0.4	1.2	1.2	5.8	5.7	6.4	10.4	6.0	23.1	26.4	13.9	2.3	74.2	40.1	49.3	50.7
63471	TAYLOR	99.1	99.1	0.0	0.0	0.7	0.7	0.9	1.0	6.9	6.7	6.7	7.4	5.9	25.5	26.7	13.3	0.9	75.0	39.2	51.0	49.0
63472	WAYLAND	98.8	98.8	0.1	0.1	0.1	0.1	0.6	0.6	6.1	6.3	6.9	6.2	6.4	26.0	28.1	12.4	1.6	76.9	40.0	50.9	49.1
63473	WILLIAMSTOWN	97.4	96.7	1.0	1.3	0.0	0.0	1.3	1.6	9.5	8.8	8.8	6.2	4.6	24.5	23.2	12.8	1.6	69.0	36.0	50.3	49.7
63474	WYACONDA	99.3	99.2	0.0	0.0	0.0	0.0	0.2	0.2	6.3	6.9	7.1	5.3	5.3	23.3	29.2	14.5	2.1	76.2	42.4	50.4	49.6
63501	KIRKSVILLE	95.2	94.5	1.4	1.5	1.7	2.2	1.4	1.5	5.1	4.8	5.2	16.2	13.6	24.1	18.8	10.0	2.3	81.6	28.3	46.8	53.2
63530	ATLANTA	99.3	99.2	0.0	0.0	0.0	0.0	0.1	0.2	7.0	7.3	8.8	6.6	6.5	26.5	24.5	11.8	1.0	72.7	35.3	50.5	49.5
63531	BARING	99.5	99.6	0.0	0.0	0.0	0.0	0.2	0.2	7.7	7.9	7.7	6.4	4.5	24.9	24.9	14.1	1.8	72.6	39.2	50.1	49.9
63532	BEVIER	97.5	97.3	0.2	0.2	0.2	0.3	0.5	0.4	6.3	6.6	8.1	5.7	5.4	26.3	24.2	15.1	2.1	75.3	39.4	50.1	49.9
63533	BRASHEAR	99.0	98.9	0.1	0.1	0.1	0.1	0.4	0.3	5.7	7.0	8.6	8.9	2.8	25.6	27.9	12.4	1.2	73.0	39.3	51.5	48.6
63534	CALLAO	97.4	97.4	0.1	0.1	0.0	0.0	0.6	0.6	4.0	4.4	6.2	7.2	6.5	25.1	30.7	13.9	2.0	81.1	42.9	52.1	47.9
63535	COATSVILLE	99.2	99.3	0.0	0.0	0.0	0.0	0.0	0.0	6.4	6.4	7.1	6.4	5.0	23.6	27.1	16.4	1.4	75.7	41.5	53.6	46.4
63536	DOWNING	97.3	97.4	0.1	0.1	0.2	0.2	1.1	1.1	6.6	6.8	8.3	6.3	5.5	25.4	24.4	14.5	2.2	74.3	39.0	49.4	50.6
63537	EDINA	97.8	97.7	0.2	0.2	0.1	0.1	0.5	0.5	6.6	6.6	6.7	5.9	5.2	21.2	23.2	20.0	4.6	76.1	43.4	46.9	53.1
63538	ELMER	98.6	98.7	0.0	0.0	0.0	0.0	0.3	0.3	8.5	7.8	7.5	5.9	6.5	24.1	25.1	13.0	1.6	72.3	35.5	51.8	48.2
63539	ETHEL	98.8	98.8	0.0	0.0	0.0	0.0	0.3	0.3	7.5	7.8	7.5	6.0	6.3	24.4	25.6	13.3	1.5	73.5	36.4	51.2	48.8
63540	GIBBS	98.6	98.5	0.0	0.0	0.0	0.0	0.5	0.5	6.9	6.9	6.7	6.7	4.7	22.8	30.9	12.4	2.0	75.3	41.6	50.3	49.8
63541	GLENWOOD	99.2	99.3	0.0	0.0	0.0	0.0	0.0	0.0	6.0	6.3	7.3	6.8	5.0	23.8	25.8	17.3	2.0	76.0	41.9	50.5	49.5
63543	GORIN	99.0	99.0	0.3	0.5	0.0	0.0	1.2	1.5	9.0	7.8	6.6	6.3	5.9	26.8	23.7	12.7	1.2	72.7	36.9	52.0	48.1
	MISSOURI	84.9	84.1	11.3	11.5	1.2	1.4	2.1	2.3	6.7	6.6	7.0	7.0	7.3	27.6	24.2	11.7	1.9	75.6	36.8	48.7	51.3
	UNITED STATES	75.1	73.6	12.3	12.5	3.8	4.2	12.5	14.1	6.9	6.7	7.2	7.0	7.3	28.6	23.8	10.8	1.7	75.1	36.0	49.1	50.9

#	POST OFFICE NAME	2004 Per Capita Income	2004 HH Income Base	2004 Household Income Distribution (%): Less than $25,000	$25,000 to $49,999	$50,000 to $99,999	$100,000 to $149,999	$150,000 or More	Median Household Income: 2004	2009	2004 National Centile	2004 State Centile	2004 Home Value Base	2004 Home Value Distribution (%): Less than $50,000	$50,000 to $89,999	$90,000 to $174,999	$175,000 to $399,999	$400,000 or More	2004 Median Home Value
63147	SAINT LOUIS	15551	4255	41.6	27.3	25.3	4.7	1.1	31272	35866	16	25	2808	20.9	62.5	15.2	1.0	0.4	68625
63301	SAINT CHARLES	26086	19630	19.1	29.5	35.7	11.7	4.0	51203	61019	74	87	12758	9.4	8.7	56.7	23.4	1.8	128857
63303	SAINT CHARLES	30251	17679	11.2	27.0	38.9	16.3	6.6	61548	71407	86	94	12235	4.6	5.8	43.9	44.2	1.5	166238
63304	SAINT CHARLES	30928	15853	7.4	16.3	45.1	22.1	9.1	76377	88464	94	98	14477	0.9	2.7	41.1	50.0	5.3	183164
63330	ANNADA	29666	82	29.3	30.5	24.4	9.8	6.1	40000	50000	46	67	66	30.3	15.2	30.3	15.2	9.1	104167
63332	AUGUSTA	29056	501	11.6	25.8	39.7	16.8	6.2	62943	76032	87	95	411	1.0	12.4	30.7	42.1	13.9	192014
63333	BELLFLOWER	15496	257	29.2	39.3	28.0	2.7	0.8	36877	41067	35	55	209	38.8	27.8	18.2	15.3	0.0	61786
63334	BOWLING GREEN	16293	2282	35.9	28.1	29.2	5.1	1.6	37813	44153	39	60	1658	24.4	26.1	35.1	13.2	1.3	89278
63336	CLARKSVILLE	19296	612	35.5	31.9	23.5	6.7	2.5	35775	41843	31	49	461	28.2	26.0	32.3	8.2	5.2	83710
63339	CURRYVILLE	14453	577	35.9	31.2	29.1	3.6	0.2	34237	40161	25	40	481	30.8	10.2	42.0	14.1	2.9	110147
63341	DEFIANCE	30674	1319	10.2	19.5	36.6	24.8	9.0	75683	88139	93	98	1211	11.6	4.2	13.9	49.0	21.4	263095
63343	ELSBERRY	18484	1702	28.0	31.7	33.1	6.1	1.2	41092	48402	50	70	1297	21.4	26.1	36.0	15.7	0.8	92902
63344	EOLIA	17981	416	29.1	34.9	30.8	4.8	0.5	39717	45771	45	66	338	21.0	26.3	34.0	16.3	2.4	95625
63345	FARBER	20419	216	25.5	35.2	32.4	5.6	1.4	44667	52199	60	77	175	46.3	26.9	18.3	8.6	0.0	55417
63347	FOLEY	19146	935	19.5	31.2	40.6	7.3	1.4	49556	56924	71	85	778	22.9	18.8	33.4	21.7	3.2	104231
63348	FORISTELL	27947	1896	10.6	22.2	43.7	17.4	6.1	66899	79085	90	96	1726	7.1	7.0	27.1	53.2	5.6	196469
63349	HAWK POINT	17910	529	27.0	34.2	30.8	6.6	1.3	38810	45755	42	64	420	17.4	16.2	38.8	26.0	1.7	117692
63350	HIGH HILL	18488	278	36.7	26.3	32.0	4.7	0.4	37184	42797	36	56	209	27.3	30.6	30.6	10.1	1.4	78846
63351	JONESBURG	17532	491	37.3	26.7	31.0	4.7	0.4	36389	42194	33	53	366	26.8	31.2	31.7	9.6	0.8	79200
63352	LADDONIA	20201	372	23.4	41.1	27.2	6.5	1.9	40314	47931	47	68	289	39.5	28.7	24.6	5.2	2.1	65962
63353	LOUISIANA	19689	2102	32.5	31.0	28.9	5.1	2.4	37823	44451	39	60	1542	29.1	27.3	31.5	10.3	1.9	77684
63357	MARTHASVILLE	26522	1871	15.7	26.2	37.2	15.9	5.1	58852	69997	83	92	1637	5.4	10.5	39.6	39.2	5.3	159569
63359	MIDDLETOWN	16298	684	35.1	33.5	27.6	3.1	0.7	35123	40346	28	45	569	26.4	20.7	33.6	14.9	4.4	93929
63361	MONTGOMERY CITY	18372	1592	34.2	31.1	28.5	5.5	0.7	37579	42634	38	59	1181	16.6	31.5	32.5	17.5	1.9	93409
63362	MOSCOW MILLS	19263	1534	18.3	30.5	41.8	8.3	1.1	50733	58368	73	86	1256	24.3	17.0	30.6	26.4	1.8	111167
63363	NEW FLORENCE	16912	602	36.4	28.7	29.6	4.3	1.0	38023	42971	39	61	503	22.1	23.5	33.0	19.5	2.0	97031
63366	O FALLON	26193	24003	10.0	21.9	46.1	16.6	5.3	65582	78134	89	96	21262	10.7	5.3	37.7	43.9	2.4	165988
63367	LAKE SAINT LOUIS	37120	4673	9.5	20.4	36.7	20.0	13.4	74732	86222	93	98	3851	0.5	5.2	29.9	51.1	13.4	202794
63369	OLD MONROE	21077	767	21.0	25.4	39.4	13.2	1.0	52919	60000	77	89	633	11.5	16.3	47.1	21.6	3.5	118448
63373	PORTAGE DES SIOUX	23615	246	15.0	26.4	45.9	9.8	2.9	57422	67640	82	92	203	2.5	25.1	46.8	23.2	2.5	116223
63376	SAINT PETERS	26780	26184	8.0	21.7	47.3	17.9	5.2	68003	79230	90	96	22636	1.9	4.4	65.1	28.0	0.7	148050
63377	SILEX	18684	885	25.1	32.0	34.7	7.0	1.2	44342	51398	60	77	735	19.5	18.0	30.1	27.6	4.9	122627
63379	TROY	20400	6603	21.3	29.4	37.7	9.5	2.2	49485	56496	71	85	5032	10.5	12.5	45.9	28.0	3.2	132117
63381	TRUXTON	22790	238	25.2	21.0	37.8	11.3	4.6	52655	62277	76	89	208	8.2	17.8	29.8	40.4	3.9	156250
63382	VANDALIA	15921	1401	39.2	34.2	23.1	2.6	1.0	31267	36412	16	25	1003	37.3	34.4	23.3	4.4	0.6	62349
63383	WARRENTON	20524	5504	24.4	34.6	30.9	6.8	3.2	42590	50642	55	74	4530	15.6	13.9	44.6	23.7	2.3	123270
63384	WELLSVILLE	14625	787	37.2	38.4	21.7	1.9	0.8	33470	38548	22	36	570	39.8	26.5	24.6	8.1	1.1	61860
63385	WENTZVILLE	25653	6350	15.1	22.2	43.2	13.9	5.6	60844	71066	85	94	4977	7.3	7.2	37.1	42.0	6.4	170421
63386	WEST ALTON	21352	240	17.5	41.3	29.6	7.5	4.2	42364	50826	54	73	204	17.2	34.8	43.1	4.9	0.0	88261
63388	WILLIAMSBURG	18322	302	28.2	38.1	29.5	2.3	2.0	40875	47659	49	70	257	33.1	28.0	28.8	7.0	3.1	71957
63389	WINFIELD	20215	1771	22.8	26.7	41.1	7.5	2.0	50323	57503	73	86	1464	19.5	16.0	42.8	19.6	2.1	115972
63390	WRIGHT CITY	26055	3014	21.4	28.3	36.2	10.0	4.1	50231	60638	72	86	2390	14.5	14.0	38.2	26.7	6.7	129439
63401	HANNIBAL	20104	8708	33.9	30.9	27.4	5.5	2.3	35659	42600	30	49	5930	27.6	29.4	31.9	10.4	0.7	80569
63430	ALEXANDRIA	19597	250	29.6	35.6	29.6	3.2	2.0	38822	45300	42	64	204	32.8	25.0	31.4	9.3	1.5	73636
63431	ANABEL	15586	135	22.2	46.7	26.7	3.7	0.7	36432	42585	33	53	115	22.6	27.0	34.8	14.8	0.9	91000
63432	ARBELA	15006	204	41.2	38.2	12.8	4.4	3.4	31032	36331	15	24	164	48.2	18.9	23.8	9.2	0.0	53333
63433	ASHBURN	16822	100	48.0	23.0	21.0	6.0	2.0	26093	31695	6	6	81	34.6	30.9	17.3	14.8	2.5	60714
63434	BETHEL	14645	199	35.2	36.7	26.6	1.5	0.0	35381	38276	29	47	154	23.4	26.6	27.3	15.6	7.1	90000
63435	CANTON	19369	1382	37.8	32.0	21.1	4.8	4.3	34699	40000	26	43	968	32.8	27.5	32.8	5.0	2.1	75270
63436	CENTER	16257	418	39.0	34.0	21.8	4.6	0.7	31862	37086	17	27	309	35.0	27.5	21.0	9.1	7.4	75682
63437	CLARENCE	18339	695	38.6	35.7	19.6	4.0	2.2	35121	39498	28	45	525	39.8	27.4	20.0	11.6	1.1	63919
63438	DURHAM	16360	242	27.3	38.0	29.8	3.7	1.2	38623	44445	42	63	206	27.2	27.2	36.9	8.3	0.5	83571
63439	EMDEN	14104	77	32.5	33.8	29.9	3.9	0.0	36909	41372	35	55	60	20.0	28.3	33.3	13.3	5.0	92500
63440	EWING	17590	529	31.2	37.1	26.8	3.8	1.1	35972	41292	31	51	430	28.6	24.7	32.1	13.5	1.2	83636
63441	FRANKFORD	17674	363	33.9	31.7	28.1	6.3	0.0	35150	41676	28	46	298	37.3	20.8	30.9	10.1	1.0	60909
63443	HUNNEWELL	18652	156	37.8	26.3	28.2	6.4	1.3	35897	41445	31	50	118	35.6	12.7	35.6	15.3	0.9	92000
63445	KAHOKA	17848	1618	37.5	33.9	22.3	4.7	1.7	31860	37316	17	27	1227	36.8	31.1	26.2	4.7	1.2	67092
63446	KNOX CITY	14568	212	46.7	35.4	14.6	3.3	0.0	26459	29318	6	7	170	50.0	21.8	14.7	13.5	0.0	50000
63447	LA BELLE	14097	472	46.4	31.8	19.3	2.1	0.4	27223	31834	7	9	348	56.0	22.4	15.8	5.8	0.0	43438
63448	LA GRANGE	17906	724	33.4	38.5	23.8	2.8	1.5	36355	41919	33	53	555	43.2	30.3	21.1	5.2	0.2	57813
63450	LENTNER	17264	62	40.3	32.3	21.0	4.8	1.6	35000	40000	28	44	44	36.4	29.6	18.2	13.6	2.3	75000
63451	LEONARD	17259	95	35.8	41.1	19.0	2.1	2.1	35131	39074	28	45	78	42.3	28.2	19.2	10.3	0.0	58571
63452	LEWISTOWN	16366	352	41.2	29.0	24.7	4.0	1.1	29480	33964	11	17	256	48.1	31.3	15.2	2.7	2.7	52381
63453	LURAY	21414	208	32.2	32.2	26.0	3.4	6.3	36045	43896	32	51	171	39.8	23.4	21.6	12.3	2.9	73462
63454	MAYWOOD	16989	395	24.3	40.5	29.4	4.1	1.8	39930	47257	46	66	340	31.8	16.8	37.4	12.9	1.2	92273
63456	MONROE CITY	17864	1696	30.7	36.8	26.3	5.2	1.1	37064	42773	36	56	1279	21.7	28.0	38.5	9.9	2.0	90523
63457	MONTICELLO	21594	190	24.7	39.5	25.8	4.7	5.3	35955	42016	31	50	174	31.0	20.7	24.7	19.0	4.6	87000
63458	NEWARK	13173	94	47.9	35.1	13.8	3.2	0.0	25846	28579	6	6	75	52.0	21.3	13.3	13.3	0.0	47000
63459	NEW LONDON	19057	1783	24.0	37.8	31.6	5.1	1.6	41556	47248	52	71	1475	22.1	30.7	30.4	14.7	2.1	85060
63460	NOVELTY	13262	194	42.8	43.8	12.4	1.0	0.0	28497	31390	10	14	158	44.9	17.7	19.0	13.3	5.1	58889
63461	PALMYRA	19029	2074	30.7	28.6	33.5	5.9	1.4	41294	49798	51	71	1596	17.5	27.4	38.9	15.3	0.9	95786
63462	PERRY	19521	568	31.5	32.9	30.5	4.1	1.1	38623	45128	42	63	440	28.6	33.4	24.3	9.1	4.6	78889
63463	PHILADELPHIA	15366	234	28.6	38.9	27.8	4.3	0.4	35000	42048	28	44	196	17.9	27.6	37.2	15.3	2.0	102500
63464	PLEVNA	14423	59	42.4	45.8	11.9	0.0	0.0	28565	31082	10	14	48	45.8	16.7	18.8	14.6	4.2	60000
63466	SAINT PATRICK	24812	183	18.0	37.2	38.3	4.4	2.2	47530	52720	67	82	152	26.3	12.5	40.1	17.1	4.0	108333
63468	SHELBINA	20586	1067	39.2	32.3	21.6	5.0	2.0	32022	37171	18	28	802	39.2	32.9	21.6	6.1	0.3	61711
63469	SHELBYVILLE	16226	446	34.8	36.3	25.6	3.4	0.0	33913	38437	24	39	332	36.5	32.8	19.6	7.2	3.9	60294
63471	TAYLOR	23044	236	18.2	38.6	33.5	5.9	3.8	46364	53871	65	80	204	17.2	22.6	40.2	18.1	2.0	102500
63472	WAYLAND	17060	526	39.0	35.9	20.9	2.9	1.3	30861	35187	14	23	425	37.9	31.5	24.7	5.2	0.7	62738
63473	WILLIAMSTOWN	15517	132	50.0	22.0	24.2	1.5	2.3	25000	25742	5	4	106	42.5	24.5	23.6	4.7	4.7	67143
63474	WYACONDA	19133	238	37.8	28.6	29.0	4.6	0.0	33527	38912	22	36	192	39.1	39.6	13.5	5.7	2.1	57241
63501	KIRKSVILLE	19691	8208	44.1	26.7	20.3	5.3	3.6	29761	35798	12	18	4487	20.2	26.0	37.4	13.9	2.5	95746
63530	ATLANTA	15558	391	32.2	37.9	25.3	3.6	1.0	36000	41337	32	51	319	45.1	21.6	25.7	7.2	0.3	58611
63531	BARING	16337	166	36.8	29.5	28.3	3.6	1.8	35308	37094	29	47	136	41.2	27.9	19.9	6.6	4.4	56667
63532	BEVIER	18922	554	35.9	37.9	20.9	3.3	2.0	34254	39263	25	41	452	46.2	26.6	21.5	4.9	0.9	55000
63533	BRASHEAR	18387	562	27.2	34.9	30.6	5.7	1.6	38996	47601	43	64	462	22.1	20.8	39.6	13.0	4.6	100373
63534	CALLAO	17913	334	36.8	34.1	25.8	1.8	1.5	34409	39141	25	41	276	47.8	23.2	22.1	6.2	0.7	54615
63535	COATSVILLE	25897	58	36.2	32.8	24.1	3.5	3.5	33610	37969	23	37	47	36.2	10.6	38.3	10.6	4.3	95000
63536	DOWNING	19122	415	39.8	33.3	20.2	3.1	3.6	32702	36969	20	32	332	39.2	18.7	27.4	11.5	3.3	69500
63537	EDINA	14745	810	40.0	39.6	18.5	1.7	0.1	30572	33904	14	21	597	31.8	27.1	32.0	7.4	1.7	74625
63538	ELMER	16029	137	40.9	39.4	16.1	1.5	2.2	28463	32261	9	13	113	37.2	22.1	31.0	8.9	0.9	76875
63539	ETHEL	16352	149	40.3	40.3	16.1	1.3	2.0	28614	32272	10	15	122	39.3	23.8	27.1	9.0	0.8	72222
63540	GIBBS	15851	152	36.2	32.9	27.0	4.0	0.0	34522	41888	26	42	122	35.3	19.7	29.5	11.5	4.1	78000
63541	GLENWOOD	24969	159	35.9	33.3	24.5	2.5	3.8	34230	38028	25	40	130	34.6	11.5	39.2	10.8	3.9	95556
63543	GORIN	12909	151	48.3	35.1	10.6	4.6	1.3	25828	30667	6	6	121	53.7	20.7	19.0	5.8	0.8	44375
	MISSOURI	23864		27.0	29.4	30.1	9.0	4.5	44017	52626				15.2	22.7	39.0	19.7	3.4	109184
	UNITED STATES	25866		24.7	27.1	30.8	10.9	6.5	48124	56710				10.9	15.0	33.7	30.1	10.4	145905

ZIP CODE #	POST OFFICE NAME	FINANCIAL SERVICES: Auto Loan	FINANCIAL SERVICES: Home Loan	FINANCIAL SERVICES: Investments	FINANCIAL SERVICES: Retirement Plans	THE HOME: Home Improvements: Home Repair	THE HOME: Home Improvements: Lawn & Garden	THE HOME: Furnishings: Computers & Hardware	THE HOME: Furnishings: Major Appliances	THE HOME: Furnishings: TV, Radio, Sound Equipment	THE HOME: Furnishings: Furniture	ENTERTAINMENT: Dine out/Carry out	ENTERTAINMENT: Sports Equipment	ENTERTAINMENT: Fees & Tickets	ENTERTAINMENT: Toys & Games	ENTERTAINMENT: Travel	ENTERTAINMENT: Cable TV	PERSONAL: Apparel & Services	PERSONAL: Auto Repairs	PERSONAL: Health Insurance	PERSONAL: Pets & Supplies
63147	SAINT LOUIS	58	54	61	51	53	62	57	56	61	58	76	61	58	73	57	64	74	57	61	65
63301	SAINT CHARLES	83	89	98	88	88	94	89	87	88	87	109	101	91	112	89	87	107	88	85	97
63303	SAINT CHARLES	107	112	120	116	109	112	111	109	106	111	134	129	111	133	108	101	131	110	99	121
63304	SAINT CHARLES	128	144	145	149	139	136	133	132	123	137	156	154	137	157	131	116	154	129	115	144
63330	ANNADA	101	79	54	71	89	100	74	90	84	74	100	105	67	99	79	90	93	88	106	123
63332	AUGUSTA	95	115	124	112	113	117	105	105	101	104	126	120	112	133	108	100	125	102	100	115
63333	BELLFLOWER	69	60	45	57	64	69	56	62	60	56	73	74	54	74	58	61	69	61	68	81
63334	BOWLING GREEN	64	51	36	49	55	63	53	58	58	51	69	67	49	67	53	60	64	58	67	72
63336	CLARKSVILLE	78	59	38	55	66	76	61	70	68	59	81	80	54	78	62	72	74	69	83	90
63339	CURRYVILLE	74	49	23	43	56	64	48	60	57	49	67	71	41	64	49	62	61	59	73	85
63341	DEFIANCE	118	138	140	136	136	136	125	126	118	125	148	147	130	154	127	116	147	122	116	141
63343	ELSBERRY	83	67	45	63	72	80	65	74	72	65	86	87	61	85	66	74	80	72	83	95
63344	EOLIA	80	58	33	54	66	73	56	68	64	56	76	82	50	75	58	67	70	67	80	94
63345	FARBER	92	62	28	54	70	81	60	75	72	61	85	89	51	80	61	78	77	74	92	106
63347	FOLEY	88	79	62	76	81	86	75	81	77	76	95	95	72	91	75	77	91	80	83	99
63348	FORISTELL	109	124	122	122	122	123	112	114	107	113	133	133	116	138	114	104	132	111	106	129
63349	HAWK POINT	86	64	36	57	70	79	60	72	70	61	83	86	54	80	62	74	76	71	85	100
63350	HIGH HILL	77	57	33	52	63	71	54	65	63	55	75	78	49	73	56	66	69	64	77	90
63351	JONESBURG	77	56	32	50	63	70	54	65	62	54	74	77	48	72	55	66	68	64	77	89
63352	LADDONIA	80	68	53	67	72	80	68	74	73	67	88	86	66	88	68	74	83	73	80	90
63353	LOUISIANA	80	61	39	57	67	77	62	71	70	61	83	82	57	80	63	73	77	70	83	91
63357	MARTHASVILLE	102	111	107	110	111	112	102	105	98	102	123	123	104	127	103	97	120	102	99	121
63359	MIDDLETOWN	76	52	26	47	60	68	51	63	60	51	70	75	43	68	52	64	64	62	76	88
63361	MONTGOMERY CITY	75	55	34	53	62	71	57	66	64	55	76	77	51	73	58	67	69	65	78	86
63362	MOSCOW MILLS	88	79	61	76	81	87	76	82	78	77	96	95	73	93	76	79	92	81	84	99
63363	NEW FLORENCE	76	58	35	53	64	71	55	65	63	56	75	78	50	73	56	66	69	64	76	89
63366	O FALLON	110	119	113	121	115	115	110	111	104	113	131	129	111	130	108	99	128	109	99	123
63367	LAKE SAINT LOUIS	124	147	160	149	144	144	137	135	128	137	161	159	142	167	138	124	160	133	122	149
63369	OLD MONROE	93	82	63	79	86	94	78	85	82	77	100	100	76	101	79	84	95	83	92	108
63373	PORTAGE DES SIOUX	100	89	68	84	94	101	82	91	87	82	106	108	80	108	84	89	101	88	98	117
63376	SAINT PETERS	106	121	123	124	117	115	111	110	103	113	131	129	115	133	110	98	129	108	97	121
63377	SILEX	85	70	48	65	76	83	66	75	72	66	87	90	62	87	67	75	82	73	85	100
63379	TROY	90	78	59	75	81	89	76	83	81	76	98	96	73	96	76	82	92	82	90	102
63381	TRUXTON	97	86	66	82	91	97	80	88	84	80	103	105	78	104	82	86	98	86	95	113
63382	VANDALIA	44	36	28	35	39	45	38	41	42	36	50	47	36	50	38	44	46	41	48	50
63383	WARRENTON	87	75	58	71	79	87	71	80	76	72	93	91	68	90	73	78	87	78	87	99
63384	WELLSVILLE	62	46	28	44	51	60	49	56	55	47	65	64	43	62	49	58	59	55	67	71
63385	WENTZVILLE	101	107	103	105	108	112	100	102	99	99	122	121	102	128	102	98	119	100	101	120
63386	WEST ALTON	91	81	62	77	86	92	75	83	80	75	97	99	73	99	77	82	92	81	90	107
63388	WILLIAMSBURG	82	58	32	55	67	75	58	70	66	57	77	85	50	76	59	69	71	69	83	97
63389	WINFIELD	90	81	62	77	83	89	76	83	79	77	97	97	73	95	77	79	92	82	86	103
63390	WRIGHT CITY	111	95	71	90	101	110	91	102	97	92	118	119	86	116	93	100	111	101	111	129
63401	HANNIBAL	71	66	63	64	67	75	68	69	71	66	87	80	67	88	68	72	83	69	74	81
63430	ALEXANDRIA	87	66	39	59	72	80	62	74	71	63	84	88	56	83	63	75	78	72	86	101
63431	ANABEL	78	58	35	55	66	73	57	68	64	56	75	81	51	75	59	66	70	66	78	92
63432	ARBELA	78	53	25	47	61	69	52	64	61	52	72	77	44	69	53	66	66	64	78	91
63433	ASHBURN	77	52	23	45	58	67	50	62	60	51	71	74	42	67	51	65	64	62	77	88
63434	BETHEL	70	49	26	46	57	64	48	60	56	48	65	72	41	64	50	58	59	59	71	83
63435	CANTON	75	66	65	65	67	76	71	72	75	70	92	84	69	91	70	76	88	74	77	84
63436	CENTER	73	51	25	44	57	65	48	60	58	49	68	71	42	65	50	62	62	59	73	84
63437	CLARENCE	73	54	33	51	60	70	57	65	64	55	75	75	50	72	57	68	69	65	78	84
63438	DURHAM	72	64	49	61	68	73	59	66	63	59	77	78	58	78	61	65	73	64	71	85
63439	EMDEN	74	55	33	52	63	70	54	64	61	53	72	77	48	71	56	63	66	63	75	88
63440	EWING	72	59	41	56	64	70	56	64	61	56	73	77	52	74	58	63	68	63	72	85
63441	FRANKFORD	79	53	24	46	60	69	51	64	62	52	73	77	44	69	52	67	66	64	79	91
63443	HUNNEWELL	72	56	38	54	61	71	60	66	67	57	79	75	54	75	60	70	72	66	78	81
63445	KAHOKA	73	56	36	53	61	71	58	66	65	56	77	76	52	74	58	69	71	65	77	83
63446	KNOX CITY	53	39	26	38	43	52	43	48	49	41	57	54	39	54	43	51	52	48	58	59
63447	LA BELLE	57	42	26	40	46	55	45	51	50	43	59	58	39	57	45	53	54	51	61	64
63448	LA GRANGE	79	53	25	46	60	69	51	64	62	52	73	76	44	69	52	66	66	63	79	91
63450	LENTNER	69	52	34	49	57	68	57	63	64	54	75	71	51	71	56	67	68	63	75	76
63451	LEONARD	80	56	29	53	65	73	55	68	63	54	74	82	47	73	57	66	68	67	81	95
63452	LEWISTOWN	65	49	32	47	54	65	54	60	61	52	72	67	48	68	54	64	65	60	72	72
63453	LURAY	87	77	59	73	81	87	71	79	76	71	92	94	70	94	73	78	87	77	86	102
63454	MAYWOOD	79	63	41	58	68	75	59	69	66	60	79	82	55	79	61	69	74	67	78	92
63456	MONROE CITY	74	59	40	55	64	72	57	65	63	57	76	77	53	75	58	66	70	64	75	86
63457	MONTICELLO	84	75	57	71	79	85	69	77	74	69	89	91	68	91	71	75	85	75	83	99
63458	NEWARK	52	39	25	38	43	51	43	48	48	41	57	54	38	54	43	51	52	48	57	58
63459	NEW LONDON	79	69	52	66	73	80	67	73	71	66	86	85	64	87	68	73	81	71	80	91
63460	NOVELTY	57	40	21	38	46	52	39	49	45	39	53	59	34	52	41	48	48	48	58	68
63461	PALMYRA	78	64	47	61	69	77	63	70	69	63	83	82	60	83	64	71	78	69	79	89
63462	PERRY	73	58	40	55	63	73	60	67	66	58	78	77	55	76	60	69	73	66	78	84
63463	PHILADELPHIA	69	61	46	58	64	69	56	63	60	56	73	75	55	74	58	61	69	61	68	81
63464	PLEVNA	56	39	20	37	45	51	38	48	44	38	52	57	33	51	40	46	47	47	57	66
63466	SAINT PATRICK	99	88	66	83	93	100	81	90	87	81	105	108	79	107	84	89	100	88	98	117
63468	SHELBINA	81	59	35	55	65	77	62	71	72	61	84	82	55	79	62	76	77	71	86	91
63469	SHELBYVILLE	65	51	35	50	56	63	52	59	57	51	68	68	48	67	52	59	63	58	66	74
63471	TAYLOR	91	81	62	77	85	92	75	83	79	75	96	99	73	98	77	81	92	81	90	107
63472	WAYLAND	75	50	23	43	57	66	49	61	59	50	69	73	41	65	49	63	63	60	75	86
63473	WILLIAMSTOWN	67	45	21	39	51	59	44	55	53	45	62	65	38	59	45	57	56	54	67	77
63474	WYACONDA	76	53	28	50	62	69	53	65	61	52	71	78	45	70	55	64	65	64	77	90
63501	KIRKSVILLE	68	56	57	58	58	64	67	64	68	64	84	79	62	81	63	66	80	68	65	75
63530	ATLANTA	68	55	40	54	59	66	56	62	61	56	73	71	53	72	56	63	69	61	68	75
63531	BARING	79	55	29	52	64	72	54	67	62	53	73	81	46	72	56	65	67	66	80	93
63532	BEVIER	82	60	34	54	67	75	57	69	66	58	79	82	52	76	59	70	73	68	81	95
63533	BRASHEAR	80	67	46	63	72	79	63	72	68	62	82	86	59	83	65	70	77	70	80	95
63534	CALLAO	78	56	30	50	62	71	53	65	63	54	74	78	47	71	55	67	68	64	78	90
63535	COATSVILLE	113	79	41	75	92	103	78	96	90	77	105	116	67	103	81	94	96	95	115	134
63536	DOWNING	86	60	32	57	70	78	59	73	68	59	80	88	51	79	62	72	73	72	87	102
63537	EDINA	58	42	26	40	47	56	45	52	51	43	60	59	40	57	45	54	55	51	62	66
63538	ELMER	68	45	21	39	51	59	44	55	53	45	62	65	37	59	44	57	56	54	67	78
63539	ETHEL	68	46	21	40	52	60	44	55	53	45	63	66	38	59	45	58	57	55	68	79
63540	GIBBS	76	54	29	51	62	69	53	65	60	52	71	78	45	70	55	63	65	64	77	90
63541	GLENWOOD	114	79	42	75	92	104	78	97	90	77	106	117	67	104	81	95	97	96	115	135
63543	GORIN	65	44	21	39	50	58	43	54	51	43	60	64	37	57	44	55	55	53	65	76
	MISSOURI	87	82	79	80	83	90	82	85	85	82	104	99	81	103	82	85	100	85	87	100
	UNITED STATES	100	100	100	100	100	100	100	100	100	100	100	100	100	100	100	100	100	100	100	100

MISSOURI

A 63544-63848

POPULATION CHANGE

#	POST OFFICE NAME	COUNTY FIPS CODE	POPULATION			2000-2004 ANNUAL RATE		HOUSEHOLDS					FAMILIES		
			2000	2004	2009	% Rate	State Centile	2000	2004	2009	% Annual Rate 2000-2004	2004 Average HH Size	2000	2004	% Annual Rate 2000-2004
63544	GREEN CASTLE	211	428	518	586	4.6	98	177	212	238	4.3	2.44	128	150	3.8
63545	GREEN CITY	211	1235	1269	1338	0.6	57	549	561	589	0.5	2.26	357	356	-0.1
63546	GREENTOP	001	892	879	889	-0.3	21	363	362	369	-0.1	2.43	272	266	-0.5
63547	HURDLAND	103	571	590	590	0.8	61	223	232	233	0.9	2.54	158	161	0.4
63548	LANCASTER	197	1014	1025	1048	0.3	42	419	424	434	0.3	2.42	278	275	-0.3
63549	LA PLATA	121	2310	2302	2276	-0.1	29	910	906	897	-0.1	2.49	596	576	-0.8
63551	LIVONIA	171	371	372	374	0.1	34	150	151	152	0.2	2.46	113	112	-0.2
63552	MACON	121	7879	7680	7531	-0.6	14	3355	3300	3264	-0.4	2.25	2161	2077	-0.9
63555	MEMPHIS	199	3667	3804	3985	0.9	65	1445	1486	1540	0.7	2.48	970	974	0.1
63556	MILAN	211	3805	3942	4147	0.8	64	1479	1523	1593	0.7	2.49	974	980	0.1
63557	NEW BOSTON	115	196	196	194	0.0	32	80	81	80	0.3	2.42	62	61	-0.4
63558	NEW CAMBRIA	121	728	675	648	-1.8	1	298	279	270	-1.5	2.39	213	196	-1.9
63559	NOVINGER	001	1863	2046	2172	2.2	87	755	838	897	2.5	2.44	551	596	1.9
63560	POLLOCK	211	670	679	699	0.3	45	278	283	291	0.4	2.39	196	195	-0.1
63561	QUEEN CITY	197	1154	1180	1215	0.5	54	486	501	520	0.7	2.25	328	330	0.1
63563	RUTLEDGE	199	338	352	369	1.0	68	99	102	105	0.7	3.45	75	75	0.0
63565	UNIONVILLE	171	3712	3795	3868	0.5	53	1600	1637	1670	0.5	2.28	1047	1046	0.0
63566	WINIGAN	115	250	271	285	1.9	84	106	115	122	1.9	2.36	81	86	1.4
63567	WORTHINGTON	171	468	470	474	0.1	36	198	199	201	0.1	2.36	146	144	-0.3
63601	PARK HILLS	187	15024	15197	15461	0.3	43	5990	6123	6288	0.5	2.45	4108	4109	0.0
63620	ANNAPOLIS	093	1284	1533	1664	4.3	98	512	623	685	4.7	2.41	362	432	4.3
63621	ARCADIA	093	955	934	926	-0.5	16	319	313	312	-0.5	2.74	231	223	-0.8
63622	BELGRADE	221	1128	1165	1206	0.8	61	445	468	492	1.2	2.49	335	346	0.8
63623	BELLEVIEW	093	1007	943	925	-1.5	1	385	364	361	-1.3	2.40	275	255	-1.8
63624	BISMARCK	187	3057	2957	2963	-0.8	9	1185	1156	1169	-0.6	2.53	884	847	-1.0
63625	BLACK	179	703	680	681	-0.8	9	241	237	242	-0.4	2.66	181	176	-0.7
63626	BLACKWELL	221	1382	1430	1479	0.8	63	469	494	519	1.2	2.89	363	376	0.8
63627	BLOOMSDALE	186	2954	3147	3266	1.5	79	1080	1158	1213	1.7	2.71	821	866	1.3
63628	BONNE TERRE	187	12001	12122	12305	0.2	42	4656	4760	4882	0.5	2.52	3442	3454	0.1
63629	BUNKER	179	874	840	841	-0.9	7	360	354	361	-0.4	2.29	255	245	-0.9
63630	CADET	221	3509	3619	3740	0.7	60	1284	1351	1421	1.2	2.67	963	995	0.8
63631	CALEDONIA	221	974	1015	1054	1.0	68	387	408	431	1.3	2.49	292	303	0.9
63633	CENTERVILLE	179	492	479	482	-0.6	13	205	204	209	-0.1	2.23	150	146	-0.6
63636	DES ARC	093	652	627	617	-0.9	7	264	256	256	-0.7	2.45	184	175	-1.2
63637	DOE RUN	187	1614	1625	1635	0.2	39	586	595	604	0.4	2.70	430	427	-0.2
63638	ELLINGTON	179	3386	3585	3748	1.4	76	1379	1481	1572	1.7	2.40	954	1004	1.2
63640	FARMINGTON	187	22910	24065	24844	1.2	72	7932	8473	8869	1.6	2.41	5485	5757	1.2
63645	FREDERICKTOWN	123	10917	11199	11576	0.6	56	4365	4513	4704	0.8	2.43	3086	3128	0.3
63648	IRONDALE	221	1812	1842	1893	0.4	48	673	695	727	0.8	2.61	522	531	0.4
63650	IRONTON	093	4926	4856	4832	-0.3	21	1983	1976	1988	-0.1	2.38	1379	1347	-0.6
63653	LEADWOOD	187	1164	1152	1159	-0.2	25	424	424	430	0.0	2.72	322	315	-0.5
63654	LESTERVILLE	179	682	660	661	-0.8	10	294	289	295	-0.4	2.26	207	200	-0.8
63655	MARQUAND	123	1448	1496	1548	0.8	61	562	586	610	1.0	2.55	416	426	0.6
63656	MIDDLE BROOK	093	539	509	500	-1.3	2	218	209	208	-1.0	2.43	151	141	-1.6
63660	MINERAL POINT	221	4763	4835	4946	0.4	47	1368	1419	1483	0.9	2.78	1057	1079	0.5
63662	PATTON	017	1836	1888	1924	0.7	58	706	732	750	0.9	2.55	536	546	0.4
63664	POTOSI	221	8534	8730	9028	0.5	54	3338	3464	3643	0.9	2.45	2371	2416	0.4
63665	REDFORD	179	403	401	407	-0.1	27	171	173	179	0.3	2.27	118	117	-0.2
63670	SAINTE GENEVIEVE	186	11147	11135	11281	0.0	30	4159	4213	4318	0.3	2.56	3064	3047	-0.1
63673	SAINT MARY	186	1967	1948	1957	-0.2	25	729	728	738	0.0	2.66	548	538	-0.4
63675	VULCAN	093	138	133	131	-0.9	8	65	63	63	-0.7	2.11	45	43	-1.1
63701	CAPE GIRARDEAU	031	31900	31789	32017	-0.1	29	13062	13142	13338	0.1	2.32	8294	8128	-0.5
63703	CAPE GIRARDEAU	031	9965	9979	10122	0.0	33	3725	3752	3839	0.2	2.15	1872	1800	-0.9
63730	ADVANCE	207	2897	2977	3055	0.6	57	1205	1249	1292	0.9	2.35	839	849	0.3
63732	ALTENBURG	157	724	839	912	3.5	96	290	341	375	3.9	2.46	215	248	3.4
63735	BELL CITY	207	858	907	946	1.3	75	348	372	391	1.6	2.44	241	251	1.0
63736	BENTON	201	4131	4075	4060	-0.3	21	1507	1504	1513	-0.1	2.68	1150	1127	-0.5
63739	BURFORDVILLE	031	732	804	844	2.2	87	274	305	323	2.6	2.64	223	244	2.1
63740	CHAFFEE	201	5739	5665	5675	-0.3	22	2300	2288	2311	-0.1	2.45	1601	1558	-0.6
63743	DAISY	031	98	97	97	-0.2	25	32	32	33	0.0	2.97	26	26	0.0
63744	DELTA	031	284	325	349	3.2	94	120	139	151	3.5	2.34	94	107	3.1
63747	FRIEDHEIM	031	454	450	450	-0.2	25	167	168	170	0.1	2.62	134	133	-0.2
63748	FROHNA	157	1179	1288	1372	2.1	87	455	507	549	2.6	2.54	340	371	2.1
63750	GIPSY	017	80	80	81	0.0	32	30	30	31	0.0	2.67	23	23	0.0
63751	GLENALLEN	017	1051	1077	1096	0.6	55	381	392	400	0.7	2.74	302	306	0.3
63755	JACKSON	031	20712	21548	22032	0.9	67	7883	8281	8534	1.2	2.58	5967	6135	0.7
63760	LEOPOLD	017	315	326	333	0.8	63	111	115	119	0.8	2.83	89	91	0.5
63763	MC GEE	223	334	324	320	-0.7	11	130	127	127	-0.6	2.55	90	86	-1.1
63764	MARBLE HILL	017	6028	6190	6304	0.6	56	2286	2360	2415	0.8	2.56	1699	1724	0.3
63766	MILLERSVILLE	031	812	865	893	1.5	79	297	320	333	1.8	2.70	240	254	1.3
63769	OAK RIDGE	031	1461	1579	1647	1.8	84	550	604	636	2.2	2.61	433	466	1.7
63770	OLD APPLETON	157	210	221	229	1.2	73	82	87	91	1.4	2.54	63	66	1.1
63771	ORAN	201	2517	2487	2482	-0.3	23	969	967	974	-0.1	2.57	704	688	-0.5
63775	PERRYVILLE	157	15518	15728	16096	0.3	45	5896	6026	6226	0.5	2.55	4197	4205	0.0
63780	SCOTT CITY	201	6766	6801	6855	0.1	37	2592	2634	2681	0.4	2.57	1913	1907	-0.1
63781	SEDGEWICKVILLE	017	911	942	964	0.8	63	352	368	380	1.1	2.56	270	278	0.7
63782	STURDIVANT	017	238	243	247	0.5	53	88	91	93	0.8	2.67	67	68	0.4
63783	UNIONTOWN	157	286	282	284	-0.3	21	104	104	106	0.0	2.71	79	78	-0.3
63785	WHITEWATER	031	767	878	943	3.2	94	280	325	352	3.6	2.70	220	250	3.1
63787	ZALMA	017	1076	1092	1105	0.4	47	437	448	457	0.6	2.44	333	336	0.2
63801	SIKESTON	201	23148	23662	24126	0.5	53	9062	9334	9592	0.7	2.48	6396	6462	0.2
63821	ARBYRD	069	927	868	843	-1.5	1	389	368	360	-1.3	2.36	263	244	-1.8
63822	BERNIE	207	2684	2716	2777	0.3	44	1144	1172	1211	0.6	2.32	800	800	0.0
63823	BERTRAND	133	1379	1374	1403	-0.1	28	585	594	618	0.4	2.26	405	402	-0.2
63825	BLOOMFIELD	207	4399	4656	4886	1.3	76	1722	1835	1942	1.5	2.44	1258	1317	1.1
63827	BRAGG CITY	155	688	659	632	-1.0	5	266	257	249	-0.8	2.56	191	181	-1.3
63829	CARDWELL	069	1344	1333	1328	-0.2	25	580	582	582	0.1	2.29	378	371	-0.4
63830	CARUTHERSVILLE	155	7675	7453	7204	-0.7	11	2979	2913	2841	-0.5	2.53	1976	1890	-1.0
63833	CATRON	143	227	226	222	-0.1	28	90	91	91	0.3	2.48	69	68	-0.3
63834	CHARLESTON	133	6508	6957	7374	1.6	81	2555	2784	3007	2.0	2.44	1740	1857	1.5
63837	CLARKTON	069	1839	1820	1808	-0.2	25	743	737	735	-0.2	2.47	529	515	-0.6
63841	DEXTER	207	13052	13110	13375	0.1	36	5428	5509	5679	0.4	2.34	3735	3715	-0.1
63845	EAST PRAIRIE	133	5948	5894	6023	-0.2	25	2405	2419	2513	0.1	2.41	1659	1635	-0.3
63846	ESSEX	207	1566	1582	1629	0.2	42	614	628	654	0.5	2.51	455	455	0.0
63848	GIDEON	143	1441	1425	1391	-0.3	24	562	564	558	0.1	2.41	393	386	-0.4
	MISSOURI					0.8					0.9	2.46			0.4
	UNITED STATES					1.2					1.3	2.58			1.1

ZIP CODE #	POST OFFICE NAME	RACE (%) White 2000	White 2004	Black 2000	Black 2004	Asian/Pacific 2000	Asian/Pacific 2004	% Hispanic Origin 2000	% Hispanic Origin 2004	2004 AGE DISTRIBUTION (%) 0-4	5-9	10-14	15-19	20-24	25-44	45-64	65-84	85+	18+	MEDIAN AGE 2004	% 2004 Males	% 2004 Females
63544	GREEN CASTLE	99.3	99.2	0.0	0.0	0.0	0.2	0.2	0.0	8.1	8.3	7.5	5.8	4.3	21.8	25.5	16.4	2.3	72.2	40.0	49.8	50.2
63545	GREEN CITY	98.2	98.0	0.0	0.0	0.6	0.7	4.1	4.5	5.8	5.9	6.5	5.8	5.9	22.3	27.5	17.0	3.2	78.3	43.2	47.0	53.0
63546	GREENTOP	98.8	98.6	0.1	0.1	0.7	0.7	0.3	0.3	5.7	5.8	6.7	5.7	5.6	23.3	30.0	14.6	2.6	78.3	43.3	49.6	50.4
63547	HURDLAND	99.5	99.5	0.0	0.0	0.0	0.0	0.2	0.2	7.8	7.6	7.8	6.3	4.8	24.9	24.9	14.1	1.9	72.7	39.2	49.8	50.2
63548	LANCASTER	99.0	98.9	0.0	0.0	0.2	0.2	0.5	0.6	7.2	7.1	7.1	6.4	6.3	22.9	23.4	16.3	3.1	74.6	39.3	46.1	54.0
63549	LA PLATA	98.7	98.6	0.1	0.1	0.1	0.1	1.1	1.4	7.5	7.1	7.0	5.8	5.6	23.4	22.1	17.2	4.3	74.6	39.8	47.9	52.1
63551	LIVONIA	98.9	99.2	0.0	0.0	0.0	0.0	0.3	0.3	5.9	6.5	7.3	7.0	5.1	23.9	30.1	12.6	1.6	76.3	41.5	51.3	48.7
63552	MACON	94.2	93.6	4.1	4.6	0.3	0.3	0.8	0.9	6.6	6.1	6.0	5.8	6.3	23.4	25.6	15.9	4.3	77.7	42.0	48.6	51.5
63555	MEMPHIS	98.8	98.7	0.1	0.1	0.1	0.1	0.8	0.9	7.2	7.0	7.6	7.0	6.2	22.6	21.2	16.6	4.7	73.6	39.5	47.6	52.4
63556	MILAN	91.9	90.9	0.2	0.2	0.2	0.2	14.4	16.1	7.3	6.8	6.7	6.2	6.2	26.0	23.0	13.8	4.2	75.0	38.1	50.8	49.2
63557	NEW BOSTON	99.5	99.5	0.0	0.0	0.0	0.0	0.5	0.5	8.2	7.7	9.2	5.6	5.1	24.0	25.0	13.8	1.5	71.4	37.5	49.5	50.5
63558	NEW CAMBRIA	98.8	98.7	0.1	0.2	0.0	0.0	0.3	0.3	4.6	5.2	6.8	5.9	5.2	21.6	30.1	18.2	2.4	79.6	45.4	50.2	49.8
63559	NOVINGER	99.0	99.0	0.1	0.1	0.2	0.2	0.9	1.1	6.6	6.8	6.9	6.2	5.7	26.2	27.1	12.8	1.8	75.8	39.5	50.5	49.5
63560	POLLOCK	98.1	97.9	0.2	0.2	0.0	0.0	2.1	2.5	6.6	6.8	6.0	5.0	5.2	24.3	27.1	16.9	2.1	77.5	42.3	49.8	50.2
63561	QUEEN CITY	98.5	98.6	0.0	0.0	0.1	0.1	0.8	0.9	5.8	5.9	5.9	5.6	4.8	22.3	25.8	19.2	4.8	78.7	44.8	48.3	51.7
63563	RUTLEDGE	97.9	97.4	1.5	1.7	0.0	0.0	0.0	0.0	10.5	9.4	9.1	7.4	6.3	27.0	19.0	10.2	1.1	66.8	30.7	54.6	45.5
63565	UNIONVILLE	99.1	99.1	0.1	0.1	0.2	0.2	0.7	0.7	6.9	5.6	6.1	6.3	5.6	22.7	24.0	19.0	3.7	77.6	42.8	48.4	51.7
63566	WINIGAN	99.6	99.6	0.0	0.0	0.0	0.0	0.8	0.4	8.1	8.1	8.9	5.9	4.4	22.1	24.7	15.9	1.9	70.5	39.0	49.1	50.9
63567	WORTHINGTON	99.8	99.8	0.0	0.0	0.0	0.0	0.2	0.4	6.4	7.2	8.5	5.3	3.8	26.0	25.5	15.7	1.5	74.5	40.1	52.6	47.5
63601	PARK HILLS	98.0	97.8	0.3	0.4	0.3	0.4	0.8	0.8	7.4	6.9	7.1	7.0	7.3	28.1	22.5	12.3	1.4	74.6	35.3	48.1	51.9
63620	ANNAPOLIS	94.5	94.4	3.5	3.7	0.0	0.0	0.3	0.2	5.4	5.9	7.2	7.2	5.5	24.1	29.1	14.0	1.5	76.6	41.2	49.7	50.3
63621	ARCADIA	97.6	97.6	0.7	0.8	0.0	0.0	0.4	0.4	5.7	5.7	6.0	5.9	6.0	21.0	26.5	17.8	5.6	78.7	44.8	45.6	54.4
63622	BELGRADE	97.9	97.7	0.4	0.3	0.4	0.5	0.3	0.3	6.6	6.8	6.9	6.7	6.2	26.2	26.7	12.5	1.6	75.6	38.3	50.6	49.4
63623	BELLEVIEW	98.0	98.0	0.6	0.6	0.0	0.0	0.6	0.5	4.7	4.9	5.6	5.8	6.6	24.1	29.4	16.5	2.4	81.2	43.9	50.6	49.4
63624	BISMARCK	98.5	98.4	0.1	0.1	0.1	0.1	1.0	1.1	6.6	6.4	6.9	6.8	6.4	26.8	26.0	12.8	1.3	75.9	38.5	49.7	50.3
63625	BLACK	94.6	94.1	1.6	1.8	0.1	0.3	0.6	0.7	4.9	5.7	6.3	8.7	5.9	23.1	30.0	14.0	1.5	76.6	41.4	53.2	46.8
63626	BLACKWELL	97.3	97.1	0.4	0.4	0.1	0.1	0.6	0.6	7.8	7.4	7.8	7.6	7.9	29.7	22.6	8.7	0.6	72.7	33.5	50.1	49.9
63627	BLOOMSDALE	98.7	98.6	0.1	0.1	0.1	0.1	0.5	0.6	7.1	7.1	7.7	7.1	6.0	28.0	25.1	10.8	1.1	73.7	37.2	50.5	49.5
63628	BONNE TERRE	98.5	98.3	0.2	0.2	0.2	0.2	0.4	0.5	6.1	6.2	6.9	6.8	6.3	25.8	25.8	14.6	1.6	76.8	39.9	49.9	50.1
63629	BUNKER	93.1	92.5	0.7	0.8	0.1	0.2	1.1	1.3	5.6	5.8	6.0	8.2	6.7	25.4	29.1	12.3	1.1	76.8	39.5	52.9	47.1
63630	CADET	97.5	97.2	0.5	0.6	0.1	0.1	0.6	0.7	7.8	7.5	7.9	7.4	7.8	29.7	22.9	8.6	0.6	72.4	33.1	51.0	49.0
63631	CALEDONIA	98.3	98.2	0.1	0.1	0.0	0.0	0.8	0.9	6.4	6.6	6.5	5.6	6.1	26.5	27.7	13.3	1.3	77.1	39.0	49.4	50.6
63633	CENTERVILLE	95.3	95.0	1.2	1.3	0.2	0.2	0.6	0.6	5.0	5.6	6.1	7.1	5.9	23.4	30.1	15.5	1.5	78.3	42.7	51.6	48.4
63636	DES ARC	98.8	98.7	0.2	0.2	0.0	0.0	0.5	0.3	5.4	5.9	7.5	6.9	4.6	25.8	26.8	15.8	1.3	76.9	41.4	49.3	50.7
63637	DOE RUN	98.6	98.4	0.0	0.0	0.3	0.4	1.0	1.1	6.8	7.0	7.3	7.0	6.0	26.5	27.1	11.1	1.1	73.9	38.8	50.8	49.2
63638	ELLINGTON	96.2	95.8	0.2	0.2	0.3	0.3	0.9	1.0	6.5	6.3	6.7	6.1	6.3	23.5	27.1	15.8	1.8	76.7	40.9	49.6	50.4
63640	FARMINGTON	93.1	92.6	4.6	4.9	0.5	0.6	1.0	1.1	5.3	5.4	5.7	6.4	7.2	30.1	24.1	13.2	2.6	79.8	38.7	53.5	46.5
63645	FREDERICKTOWN	98.4	98.2	0.1	0.2	0.3	0.4	0.5	0.6	6.0	6.0	6.8	6.6	6.4	25.4	25.1	15.1	2.6	77.1	40.3	48.1	51.9
63648	IRONDALE	98.0	97.9	0.1	0.1	0.1	0.2	0.7	0.8	6.3	6.6	7.4	6.6	7.1	25.7	26.0	12.8	1.5	75.7	37.9	48.9	51.1
63650	IRONTON	96.1	96.0	2.1	2.1	0.2	0.2	0.8	0.8	6.5	6.5	6.9	6.4	6.6	24.0	26.0	14.6	2.6	76.0	40.0	48.2	51.8
63653	LEADWOOD	97.9	97.9	0.2	0.2	0.0	0.0	1.0	1.0	5.9	8.4	8.3	7.4	5.8	28.6	23.5	10.9	1.2	72.2	34.3	48.2	51.8
63654	LESTERVILLE	97.4	97.1	0.3	0.5	0.0	0.0	0.2	0.3	5.5	5.6	4.9	5.2	5.5	24.1	30.3	17.6	1.5	80.8	44.6	50.5	49.6
63655	MARQUAND	97.4	97.3	0.1	0.1	0.2	0.2	0.8	0.9	6.2	6.6	7.1	6.1	5.7	25.6	27.4	13.9	1.5	76.5	40.3	49.2	50.8
63656	MIDDLE BROOK	97.4	97.5	0.9	0.8	0.0	0.0	0.6	0.8	5.3	5.7	5.7	6.1	7.1	25.9	30.1	12.4	1.8	79.8	41.6	52.9	47.2
63660	MINERAL POINT	88.6	87.6	8.8	9.6	0.2	0.2	0.7	0.7	5.7	5.7	6.2	6.7	8.7	32.7	23.4	9.4	1.5	78.5	35.7	57.9	42.2
63662	PATTON	97.7	97.5	0.4	0.4	0.1	0.1	0.4	0.4	5.8	6.1	7.8	6.9	6.3	25.7	25.6	14.4	1.4	76.0	38.9	49.7	50.3
63664	POTOSI	96.6	96.3	1.5	1.6	0.2	0.3	0.9	1.0	6.6	6.4	6.8	7.2	7.4	26.9	24.5	12.9	1.2	75.7	37.3	49.9	50.1
63665	REDFORD	96.0	95.8	0.5	0.5	0.0	0.3	1.0	1.3	5.7	5.7	6.5	5.7	5.2	22.7	28.2	17.2	3.0	78.3	43.8	49.9	50.1
63670	SAINTE GENEVIEVE	97.8	97.6	1.0	1.1	0.2	0.3	0.8	0.9	6.1	6.5	7.1	6.8	6.3	25.7	25.3	13.7	2.6	76.0	39.9	50.0	50.0
63673	SAINT MARY	97.8	97.7	1.0	1.0	0.1	0.1	0.6	0.7	6.3	7.1	7.8	7.1	6.3	26.2	26.5	11.8	0.9	74.3	38.4	52.6	47.4
63675	VULCAN	98.6	99.3	0.0	0.0	0.0	0.0	0.7	0.0	5.3	6.0	6.8	6.8	4.5	28.6	25.6	15.0	1.5	77.4	41.7	51.1	48.9
63701	CAPE GIRARDEAU	91.6	90.7	5.4	5.9	1.1	1.5	1.0	1.1	5.5	5.5	6.2	7.3	9.6	27.1	24.6	12.1	2.1	79.1	36.7	48.8	51.2
63703	CAPE GIRARDEAU	79.6	77.4	16.8	18.7	0.8	1.0	1.3	1.4	5.7	4.8	5.1	14.3	14.3	23.1	16.5	12.0	4.4	81.0	28.8	44.7	55.3
63730	ADVANCE	98.2	98.0	0.1	0.1	0.1	0.2	0.8	0.9	4.9	5.0	6.2	6.4	6.0	25.7	25.4	17.2	3.2	80.1	42.4	47.2	52.8
63732	ALTENBURG	97.8	97.7	1.0	1.1	0.0	0.0	0.4	0.4	6.0	6.6	6.7	5.5	5.2	27.3	26.1	14.9	1.8	77.6	40.6	51.7	48.3
63735	BELL CITY	93.4	93.1	5.2	5.5	0.0	0.0	0.7	0.9	5.5	7.7	7.9	6.8	5.8	26.8	24.6	13.0	1.8	74.1	37.9	49.5	50.5
63736	BENTON	95.4	94.9	3.6	3.9	0.0	0.0	0.9	1.0	7.0	6.7	7.7	7.0	7.1	27.9	25.5	9.8	1.3	74.4	36.2	50.0	50.0
63739	BURFORDVILLE	98.8	98.6	0.0	0.0	0.0	0.0	0.3	0.3	7.2	7.5	6.2	6.1	5.1	28.1	28.0	10.6	1.2	75.4	38.6	51.4	48.6
63740	CHAFFEE	98.7	98.5	0.1	0.1	0.1	0.1	0.8	0.9	6.5	6.6	7.6	6.7	6.6	26.2	24.2	13.6	2.1	75.2	37.8	48.6	51.4
63743	DAISY	98.0	97.9	1.0	1.0	0.0	0.0	0.0	0.0	6.2	6.2	8.3	6.2	6.2	27.8	25.8	11.3	2.1	75.3	38.9	51.6	48.5
63744	DELTA	97.9	97.9	0.0	0.0	0.0	0.0	0.7	0.6	6.2	6.2	6.5	5.9	4.9	24.6	29.9	14.5	1.5	77.5	42.1	51.4	48.6
63747	FRIEDHEIM	97.8	97.8	0.9	0.9	0.2	0.2	0.4	0.2	5.8	6.2	8.2	6.2	6.0	28.4	25.1	12.0	2.0	76.4	39.1	49.8	50.2
63748	FROHNA	98.3	98.1	0.6	0.7	0.2	0.2	0.3	0.3	5.6	6.4	7.3	5.9	5.8	25.9	26.2	15.1	1.8	76.9	40.4	51.9	48.1
63750	GIPSY	97.5	97.5	1.3	1.3	0.0	0.0	0.0	0.0	6.3	6.3	6.3	7.5	5.0	22.5	28.8	16.3	1.3	73.8	42.5	50.0	50.0
63751	GLENALLEN	97.5	97.3	0.4	0.5	0.2	0.2	0.8	0.8	6.4	6.5	7.2	7.9	5.9	24.8	26.7	13.4	1.3	74.9	39.2	50.2	49.8
63755	JACKSON	97.1	96.8	1.0	1.1	0.4	0.6	0.8	0.9	6.8	7.0	7.6	6.9	6.1	28.7	24.6	10.6	1.5	74.3	36.8	48.7	51.3
63760	LEOPOLD	99.1	99.1	0.0	0.0	0.3	0.3	0.6	0.6	5.2	5.8	7.4	7.4	7.4	23.9	27.6	14.1	1.2	77.0	40.9	48.2	51.8
63763	MC GEE	97.9	97.8	0.0	0.0	0.0	0.0	0.0	0.3	6.8	6.5	6.2	5.9	5.6	21.0	28.4	17.9	1.9	77.5	43.7	49.7	50.3
63764	MARBLE HILL	97.6	97.4	0.1	0.1	0.3	0.4	0.7	0.8	6.3	6.4	7.2	7.0	6.7	25.9	25.4	13.2	1.9	75.7	38.6	49.2	50.8
63766	MILLERSVILLE	99.3	99.3	0.4	0.4	0.0	0.0	0.5	0.6	6.7	7.1	6.9	6.5	4.9	28.1	28.2	10.2	1.5	75.3	39.1	49.9	50.1
63769	OAK RIDGE	97.9	97.7	0.7	0.8	0.0	0.0	0.6	0.6	6.6	6.9	7.4	6.1	5.5	29.2	26.1	10.7	1.6	75.4	38.0	49.8	50.2
63770	OLD APPLETON	98.1	97.3	0.5	0.5	0.5	0.5	0.5	0.5	6.8	7.2	7.2	5.9	5.9	28.1	25.8	11.3	1.8	74.7	38.3	50.7	49.3
63771	ORAN	97.1	96.9	1.4	1.5	0.0	0.0	1.7	1.9	7.3	7.1	7.9	6.8	6.2	27.2	23.5	12.0	2.1	73.4	36.8	49.5	50.5
63775	PERRYVILLE	98.2	97.9	0.1	0.1	0.8	1.0	0.6	0.6	7.0	6.9	7.0	6.6	6.2	27.7	23.6	12.5	2.6	75.1	37.6	49.5	50.6
63780	SCOTT CITY	98.4	98.2	0.3	0.3	0.0	0.1	0.7	0.8	6.4	6.8	7.9	7.1	6.3	28.5	24.8	11.0	1.4	74.4	36.4	49.5	50.5
63781	SEDGEWICKVILLE	98.7	98.5	0.1	0.1	0.3	0.4	0.3	0.4	6.6	6.7	7.2	7.2	6.3	27.2	24.1	13.1	1.7	75.2	37.5	50.9	49.2
63782	STURDIVANT	98.3	98.4	0.0	0.0	0.0	0.0	0.4	0.0	6.2	6.6	7.8	6.6	6.2	28.0	25.9	11.9	0.8	75.3	37.5	51.9	48.2
63783	UNIONTOWN	98.6	98.9	0.0	0.0	0.7	0.7	0.4	0.0	6.7	6.7	6.7	6.4	6.4	27.0	25.5	13.1	1.4	75.9	40.0	53.6	46.5
63785	WHITEWATER	97.9	97.6	0.0	0.0	0.1	0.1	0.5	0.7	5.9	6.4	6.5	6.0	5.1	25.2	29.2	14.5	1.3	77.5	41.4	50.9	49.1
63787	ZALMA	98.1	97.9	0.5	0.5	0.1	0.1	0.2	0.3	6.0	6.3	7.0	6.9	5.7	25.5	28.1	13.3	1.3	76.6	39.9	51.4	48.6
63801	SIKESTON	80.3	78.9	17.6	18.8	0.4	0.5	1.2	1.3	7.3	7.0	7.5	7.0	6.5	26.2	24.3	12.3	2.0	73.9	36.9	47.5	52.5
63821	ARBYRD	98.6	98.5	0.1	0.1	0.0	0.0	1.3	1.5	6.6	6.5	6.6	6.5	5.7	25.2	26.5	14.4	2.2	76.6	40.2	50.6	49.4
63822	BERNIE	96.8	96.7	1.7	1.8	0.0	0.0	0.5	0.5	5.7	5.7	6.2	6.4	6.6	25.4	27.0	15.0	2.0	78.6	41.0	47.2	52.8
63823	BERTRAND	91.9	91.1	7.2	8.0	0.0	0.0	0.3	0.4	5.7	6.1	5.7	4.3	4.2	25.6	30.0	15.8	2.8	79.7	44.0	47.7	52.3
63825	BLOOMFIELD	98.1	97.9	0.5	0.5	0.0	0.0	0.6	0.8	5.4	5.7	7.0	6.5	5.9	26.6	26.3	14.2	2.3	77.6	40.6	49.0	51.0
63827	BRAGG CITY	86.1	84.4	12.2	13.8	0.0	0.0	1.0	1.2	5.6	5.9	7.4	7.4	7.0	25.6	26.1	12.8	2.1	76.5	38.3	49.6	50.4
63829	CARDWELL	98.1	98.1	0.5	0.6	0.0	0.0	1.2	1.2	6.0	5.8	6.1	7.0	6.1	25.7	25.9	14.8	2.8	78.0	40.5	49.1	50.9
63830	CARUTHERSVILLE	69.2	67.0	28.4	30.3	0.5	0.6	1.6	1.8	9.8	8.6	8.7	7.6	7.0	24.6	21.1	11.0	1.6	68.3	31.9	47.4	52.6
63833	CATRON	90.3	89.8	8.8	9.7	0.0	0.0	0.0	0.0	5.8	5.8	7.1	6.2	6.2	25.7	27.4	14.6	1.3	77.0	40.3	51.3	48.7
63834	CHARLESTON	61.0	60.0	37.7	38.5	0.2	0.3	1.0	1.0	7.9	7.6	7.2	7.6	6.3	24.9	23.2	12.9	2.4	72.5	36.6	46.4	53.6
63837	CLARKTON	94.1	93.6	3.2	3.6	0.1	0.2	2.4	2.4	7.3	7.5	8.3	6.7	5.8	27.1	24.0	12.3	1.2	72.9	36.2	48.8	51.2
63841	DEXTER	97.6	97.4	0.4	0.4	0.2	0.2	0.9	1.0	6.2	6.1	6.3	6.1	6.1	25.6	25.8	15.1	2.6	77.7	40.7	47.4	52.6
63845	EAST PRAIRIE	94.6	94.0	3.6	3.9	0.0	0.0	1.1	1.2	7.0	6.6	6.6	6.7	7.1	26.2	24.8	13.2	2.0	75.8	37.5	47.8	52.2
63846	ESSEX	95.0	94.8	3.6	3.8	0.1	0.1	0.6	0.7	6.5	6.7	7.4	6.7	5.8	28.2	24.0	12.9	1.8	75.2	37.7	48.8	51.2
63848	GIDEON	98.1	97.8	0.4	0.4	0.0	0.0	0.9	1.1	6.7	6.3	7.9	7.2	7.5	24.8	21.8	14.5	3.2	74.6	37.9	47.4	52.6
	MISSOURI	84.9	84.1	11.3	11.5	1.2	1.4	2.1	2.3	6.7	6.6	7.0	7.0	7.3	27.6	24.2	11.7	1.9	75.6	36.8	48.7	51.3
	UNITED STATES	75.1	73.6	12.3	12.5	3.8	4.2	12.5	14.1	6.9	6.7	7.2	7.0	7.3	28.6	23.8	10.8	1.7	75.1	36.0	49.1	50.9

ZIP CODE #	POST OFFICE NAME	2004 Per Capita Income	2004 HH Income Base	2004 Household Income Distribution (%): Less than $25,000	$25,000 to $49,999	$50,000 to $99,999	$100,000 to $149,999	$150,000 or More	Median Household Income: 2004	2009	2004 National Centile	2004 State Centile	2004 Home Value Base	2004 Home Value Distribution (%): Less than $50,000	$50,000 to $89,999	$90,000 to $174,999	$175,000 to $399,999	$400,000 or More	2004 Median Home Value
63544	GREEN CASTLE	15499	212	43.4	32.1	20.8	2.8	0.9	30337	35594	13	20	173	47.4	18.5	24.3	9.3	0.6	55000
63545	GREEN CITY	16471	561	43.5	31.4	21.6	2.3	1.3	29495	35339	11	17	423	40.9	28.6	24.1	5.0	1.4	59625
63546	GREENTOP	17283	362	34.3	35.1	26.2	3.6	0.8	36532	42240	34	54	289	26.6	27.3	31.1	10.4	4.5	83611
63547	HURDLAND	16982	232	36.6	29.7	27.6	3.9	2.2	35227	36814	28	46	189	40.7	27.0	20.1	6.9	5.3	57955
63548	LANCASTER	17345	424	40.3	31.4	23.4	3.3	1.7	31990	37778	18	28	305	37.7	34.1	21.0	6.2	1.0	62206
63549	LA PLATA	16564	906	36.9	37.5	20.3	4.1	1.2	32685	38056	20	32	652	36.7	30.7	26.7	5.5	0.5	68000
63551	LIVONIA	15868	151	36.4	42.4	15.9	4.0	1.3	34156	38359	25	40	128	43.0	23.4	28.1	5.5	0.0	57500
63552	MACON	19648	3300	36.8	32.5	23.6	5.0	2.1	33633	38897	23	37	2385	23.4	30.4	34.9	10.6	0.8	85569
63555	MEMPHIS	18406	1486	39.2	33.9	20.0	4.2	2.7	32484	38081	19	30	1115	38.8	28.2	26.6	5.8	0.6	65357
63556	MILAN	14700	1523	44.1	32.3	19.3	3.4	0.9	28744	33440	10	15	1043	38.3	32.4	22.6	6.1	0.6	61505
63557	NEW BOSTON	17024	81	34.6	39.5	21.0	3.7	1.2	33246	38412	22	35	67	34.3	26.9	26.9	10.5	1.5	71250
63558	NEW CAMBRIA	17616	279	32.3	38.0	25.5	3.2	1.1	36826	42043	35	55	230	33.9	26.1	32.6	7.4	0.0	72500
63559	NOVINGER	18791	838	37.0	35.9	20.9	3.3	2.9	33253	40106	22	35	689	43.3	22.6	21.3	10.7	2.0	56739
63560	POLLOCK	17732	283	38.9	31.1	25.4	2.5	2.1	32745	37868	20	32	223	29.2	24.7	31.8	8.5	5.8	79063
63561	QUEEN CITY	17816	501	44.7	32.7	20.0	1.4	1.2	29894	35226	12	19	369	49.9	22.5	22.2	3.5	1.9	50208
63563	RUTLEDGE	10515	102	50.0	25.5	16.7	7.8	0.0	25000	30643	5	4	84	39.3	23.8	26.2	8.3	2.4	63333
63565	UNIONVILLE	16541	1637	45.5	33.4	18.3	1.9	1.0	27639	31715	8	11	1232	36.9	33.8	22.7	5.3	1.4	63115
63566	WINIGAN	17345	115	37.4	36.5	21.7	3.5	0.9	33453	40000	22	36	94	40.4	23.4	25.5	9.6	1.1	63333
63567	WORTHINGTON	15122	199	37.2	45.7	12.6	4.5	0.0	32610	36591	20	31	167	55.7	20.4	17.4	4.8	1.8	46724
63601	PARK HILLS	16807	6123	39.3	32.4	23.2	4.0	1.1	32598	37978	20	31	4076	27.7	40.2	26.0	5.8	0.4	71845
63620	ANNAPOLIS	14135	623	44.6	35.0	17.8	2.1	0.5	28754	33201	10	15	512	40.2	25.2	23.1	10.0	1.6	66750
63621	ARCADIA	15980	313	36.4	28.1	28.4	4.8	2.2	34050	39527	24	39	238	23.1	32.8	38.2	5.5	0.4	80667
63622	BELGRADE	16755	468	35.7	34.0	25.0	4.5	0.9	35249	40821	28	46	388	35.8	27.6	25.8	8.8	2.1	72121
63623	BELLEVIEW	19716	364	40.9	36.0	17.9	3.3	1.9	29363	33991	11	16	306	34.3	22.2	22.6	16.0	4.9	76316
63624	BISMARCK	14750	1156	41.5	34.1	20.9	2.7	0.9	30308	35293	13	20	922	42.5	29.1	21.4	6.0	1.1	57340
63625	BLACK	14248	237	40.5	33.8	22.8	2.1	0.8	30360	35000	13	21	199	39.2	29.2	25.1	4.5	2.0	67500
63626	BLACKWELL	14036	494	34.8	37.7	24.1	2.2	1.2	35711	40763	30	49	410	35.6	30.5	22.0	10.2	1.7	67500
63627	BLOOMSDALE	21096	1158	25.9	28.3	37.3	6.0	2.5	45641	52228	63	79	970	15.4	19.3	39.5	25.6	0.3	115720
63628	BONNE TERRE	19080	4760	30.3	32.5	29.8	5.8	1.6	40730	46658	49	69	3778	19.5	28.7	37.0	13.2	1.6	93492
63629	BUNKER	15274	354	44.9	33.1	18.9	2.0	1.1	28283	32317	9	13	292	40.4	29.5	20.6	6.9	2.7	61739
63630	CADET	13757	1351	41.3	34.6	21.0	2.7	0.4	31468	36369	16	25	1096	43.7	31.3	15.6	7.9	1.5	57263
63631	CALEDONIA	16646	408	36.5	39.7	17.9	5.4	0.5	35097	40538	28	45	346	34.1	25.4	29.2	10.7	0.6	72500
63633	CENTERVILLE	16842	204	42.2	33.3	21.1	2.5	1.0	30000	34464	12	19	167	36.5	28.7	27.5	4.8	2.4	71250
63636	DES ARC	14461	256	45.7	33.6	17.2	3.1	0.4	27540	32041	8	10	211	38.4	33.7	22.8	5.2	0.0	61389
63637	DOE RUN	15560	595	33.5	36.8	25.2	1.9	2.7	35677	41447	30	49	492	43.7	21.1	19.1	13.4	2.6	59394
63638	ELLINGTON	14443	1481	43.8	33.8	19.6	2.4	0.5	29270	33053	11	16	1073	33.8	31.4	28.1	6.4	0.3	65047
63640	FARMINGTON	18950	8473	33.4	32.3	25.9	6.0	2.5	37289	42938	36	57	6140	14.3	27.1	38.1	18.0	2.6	103094
63645	FREDERICKTOWN	15235	4513	43.5	33.7	19.1	3.0	0.8	29398	33575	11	16	3330	30.1	34.4	27.0	7.7	0.8	70283
63648	IRONDALE	15971	695	36.1	32.1	27.5	3.0	1.3	34123	40039	24	40	577	41.6	24.6	26.7	5.7	1.4	61250
63650	IRONTON	17151	1976	44.6	28.7	22.1	3.0	1.6	28383	33018	9	13	1466	31.2	37.7	25.4	5.1	0.6	67439
63653	LEADWOOD	13260	424	42.0	36.6	18.4	2.8	0.2	29526	34830	11	17	329	57.1	33.7	6.7	2.4	0.0	46908
63654	LESTERVILLE	17907	289	42.6	31.8	20.1	4.2	1.4	30137	33851	13	20	233	34.3	29.6	29.2	5.2	1.7	75667
63655	MARQUAND	14799	586	41.1	35.2	19.5	2.7	1.5	30663	35409	14	22	479	30.9	26.3	30.3	12.1	0.4	78793
63656	MIDDLE BROOK	16593	209	39.7	36.8	18.7	3.8	1.0	29610	34707	11	18	174	32.2	23.6	25.3	14.4	4.6	78889
63660	MINERAL POINT	14021	1419	47.2	27.6	19.9	2.9	2.4	27165	32305	7	9	1167	48.8	22.1	21.3	7.8	0.0	51985
63662	PATTON	17389	732	29.1	40.4	24.5	4.2	1.8	37823	42949	39	60	619	25.0	27.3	28.8	18.9	0.0	86282
63664	POTOSI	16912	3464	45.2	28.3	21.8	3.1	1.7	28403	33743	9	13	2494	35.5	32.4	24.9	6.7	0.5	68324
63665	REDFORD	14772	173	48.0	33.0	16.2	2.3	0.6	27020	30320	7	8	137	32.1	31.4	29.9	6.6	0.0	71364
63670	SAINTE GENEVIEVE	21312	4213	23.6	32.5	34.4	7.9	1.6	45009	52050	61	78	3401	12.7	23.8	44.8	16.9	1.8	109366
63673	SAINT MARY	19245	728	20.2	37.8	35.7	3.6	2.8	42609	48831	55	74	624	23.2	18.8	38.3	18.4	1.3	104286
63675	VULCAN	16785	63	46.0	33.3	17.5	3.2	0.0	27287	32959	8	10	52	38.5	34.6	23.1	3.9	0.0	62000
63701	CAPE GIRARDEAU	25427	13142	27.0	29.9	29.5	8.4	5.2	43356	51423	57	75	8555	7.7	16.2	49.0	23.3	3.9	126026
63703	CAPE GIRARDEAU	15437	3752	48.2	32.0	16.2	2.5	1.2	26113	31066	6	7	1848	41.7	30.6	25.0	2.7	0.1	61538
63730	ADVANCE	17281	1249	38.2	32.4	24.2	4.0	1.2	33223	39341	22	35	973	30.6	33.1	29.4	5.8	1.1	74200
63732	ALTENBURG	20918	341	23.8	32.8	35.5	6.5	1.5	45877	51867	64	80	295	24.1	26.8	35.3	13.2	0.7	89038
63735	BELL CITY	15867	372	45.7	29.8	18.3	3.5	2.7	27764	31662	8	11	264	56.8	23.1	15.9	3.4	0.8	42174
63736	BENTON	18305	1504	29.7	32.8	29.2	6.1	2.3	38190	45464	40	62	1240	32.3	23.2	31.1	11.6	1.8	80000
63739	BURFORDVILLE	23552	305	20.7	30.8	39.3	3.9	5.3	48644	58258	70	84	274	15.0	19.3	32.1	24.8	8.8	117949
63740	CHAFFEE	19655	2288	36.8	28.2	28.5	4.8	1.8	34930	41881	27	44	1661	28.8	34.4	29.1	7.1	0.5	71126
63743	DAISY	16635	32	21.9	34.4	37.5	6.3	0.0	46505	55748	65	81	27	18.5	22.2	33.3	22.2	3.7	104167
63744	DELTA	20153	139	31.7	31.7	28.8	6.5	1.4	36653	46165	34	54	116	24.1	27.6	29.3	19.0	0.0	87500
63747	FRIEDHEIM	18611	168	22.6	34.5	36.3	6.0	0.6	45888	52971	64	80	142	23.9	19.7	29.6	21.8	4.9	97500
63748	FROHNA	18333	507	28.6	34.1	31.0	5.7	0.6	41458	46975	51	71	437	23.6	26.1	39.1	8.9	2.3	90750
63750	GIPSY	13302	30	53.3	23.3	20.0	3.3	0.0	23514	29032	4	3	25	36.0	28.0	24.0	12.0	0.0	67500
63751	GLENALLEN	14665	392	39.0	32.1	24.2	3.1	1.5	31789	36291	17	27	327	29.7	29.7	26.9	11.3	2.5	75000
63755	JACKSON	22154	8281	22.3	30.8	35.1	8.0	3.8	47554	56343	67	82	6553	12.1	15.8	46.5	23.3	2.4	122340
63760	LEOPOLD	16944	115	28.7	34.8	30.4	3.5	2.6	39220	45245	43	65	98	25.5	19.4	37.8	15.3	2.0	102500
63763	MC GEE	13566	127	38.6	45.7	14.2	1.6	0.0	30996	34028	15	23	107	45.8	30.8	21.5	1.9	0.0	53462
63764	MARBLE HILL	15506	2360	37.6	34.1	24.2	3.1	1.0	33143	37847	21	34	1815	30.4	29.6	28.9	9.6	1.5	76541
63766	MILLERSVILLE	20342	320	26.6	30.3	33.4	6.6	3.1	43695	52383	58	76	283	12.4	15.2	47.4	22.6	2.5	130793
63769	OAK RIDGE	20185	604	23.7	33.1	34.3	6.6	2.3	45206	53274	62	78	520	18.1	17.7	38.9	21.2	4.2	113514
63770	OLD APPLETON	19635	87	26.4	32.2	34.5	5.8	1.2	44596	51013	60	77	75	17.3	20.0	41.3	16.0	5.3	108036
63771	ORAN	16773	967	36.4	29.3	29.0	3.7	1.7	35037	42082	28	45	750	34.5	36.8	22.1	5.6	0.9	64176
63775	PERRYVILLE	19323	6026	28.4	33.6	31.7	4.3	2.0	40610	46083	48	68	4740	15.2	24.9	45.8	13.4	0.7	103521
63780	SCOTT CITY	19212	2634	28.1	34.0	31.0	4.8	2.1	40000	47924	46	67	2065	24.7	29.4	37.1	8.6	0.2	84877
63781	SEDGEWICKVILLE	16453	368	34.8	34.2	26.6	3.8	0.5	37993	43350	39	61	307	17.6	26.1	45.0	11.4	0.0	101232
63782	STURDIVANT	14228	91	36.3	41.8	19.8	2.2	0.0	34590	37624	26	43	73	38.4	32.9	24.7	4.1	0.0	60714
63783	UNIONTOWN	17132	104	28.9	28.9	37.5	4.8	0.0	45000	49212	61	78	91	13.2	20.9	49.5	9.9	6.6	108854
63785	WHITEWATER	17417	325	31.1	31.7	28.3	7.1	1.9	37359	47548	37	58	272	23.9	26.8	30.2	18.4	0.7	88889
63787	ZALMA	15110	448	42.9	33.3	20.3	2.7	0.9	29503	33894	11	17	370	34.3	30.3	26.2	7.8	1.4	66944
63801	SIKESTON	17994	9334	37.4	29.2	26.3	5.4	1.9	34338	40918	25	41	6085	26.0	26.5	36.6	9.7	1.2	86121
63821	ARBYRD	15143	368	46.5	37.0	11.7	1.4	3.5	27114	32701	7	9	283	64.3	21.6	9.2	5.0	0.0	41900
63822	BERNIE	16085	1172	43.3	34.6	18.5	2.2	1.4	29075	33598	10	16	835	41.1	36.1	18.8	4.1	0.0	57376
63823	BERTRAND	21068	594	40.7	28.6	22.4	4.4	3.9	33184	40316	21	35	462	37.7	31.6	24.2	5.0	1.5	65667
63825	BLOOMFIELD	17007	1835	39.1	34.5	21.5	3.3	1.5	31425	37025	16	25	1413	38.6	27.7	25.5	7.4	0.9	68465
63827	BRAGG CITY	13751	257	48.3	28.8	19.1	3.9	0.0	26103	31461	6	6	196	59.2	27.6	12.2	1.0	0.0	43333
63829	CARDWELL	15636	582	47.8	31.6	16.5	2.2	1.9	26795	32885	7	8	429	64.6	21.5	12.1	1.9	0.0	41319
63830	CARUTHERSVILLE	14475	2913	51.9	26.9	14.7	4.3	2.2	23545	28047	4	3	1680	41.9	32.2	20.4	5.4	0.1	57366
63833	CATRON	17710	91	37.4	33.0	23.1	4.4	2.2	34527	39531	26	42	73	43.8	23.3	28.8	4.1	0.0	61250
63834	CHARLESTON	16341	2784	47.8	28.1	16.6	4.0	3.5	26757	32002	7	8	1709	40.0	30.6	21.2	7.0	1.2	62669
63837	CLARKTON	13171	737	55.0	26.5	14.9	3.1	0.5	22101	25950	3	2	503	60.8	26.2	8.8	4.0	0.2	41866
63841	DEXTER	19042	5509	40.6	30.2	21.5	5.3	2.4	31551	37267	16	26	3924	23.9	33.2	30.2	11.2	1.5	81879
63845	EAST PRAIRIE	13831	2419	49.0	29.2	18.0	3.2	0.6	25461	30057	5	5	1590	46.1	31.5	19.3	2.8	0.4	53758
63846	ESSEX	16815	628	42.0	33.4	19.1	3.3	2.1	30100	34864	12	19	494	52.8	21.1	21.7	4.5	0.0	47778
63848	GIDEON	15907	564	46.3	29.8	18.6	3.6	1.8	27069	31657	7	9	365	58.6	29.6	11.0	0.6	0.3	43824
	MISSOURI	23864		27.0	29.4	30.1	9.0	4.5	44017	52626				15.2	22.7	39.0	19.7	3.4	109184
	UNITED STATES	25866		24.7	27.1	30.8	10.9	6.5	48124	56710				10.9	15.0	33.7	30.1	10.4	145905

ZIP CODE # POST OFFICE NAME	FINANCIAL SERVICES Auto Loan	Home Loan	Investments	Retirement Plans	THE HOME Home Improvements: Home Repair	Lawn & Garden	Furnishings: Computers & Hardware	Major Appliances	TV, Radio, Sound Equipment	Furniture	ENTERTAINMENT Dine out/ Carry out	Sports Equipment	Fees & Tickets	Toys & Games	Travel	Cable TV	PERSONAL Apparel & Services	Auto Repairs	Health Insurance	Pets & Supplies
63544 GREEN CASTLE	71	48	22	41	54	62	46	58	56	47	65	68	40	62	47	60	59	57	71	81
63545 GREEN CITY	62	46	28	43	50	60	49	55	56	47	66	63	43	62	49	59	60	55	67	70
63546 GREENTOP	66	57	44	56	60	67	57	61	60	56	73	71	55	73	57	61	69	60	66	75
63547 HURDLAND	78	54	29	51	63	71	54	67	62	53	73	80	46	71	56	65	66	66	79	92
63548 LANCASTER	70	51	32	49	57	67	55	63	62	53	73	71	49	70	55	66	67	62	75	78
63549 LA PLATA	69	51	31	48	56	66	55	62	62	53	73	70	48	69	54	66	67	61	74	77
63551 LIVONIA	74	49	22	43	56	64	48	60	57	48	67	71	40	64	48	62	61	59	73	84
63552 MACON	72	57	41	54	61	70	59	66	66	58	78	76	54	77	59	69	73	65	76	82
63555 MEMPHIS	78	57	35	54	64	74	60	69	68	58	80	80	53	77	61	72	73	69	83	88
63556 MILAN	56	46	40	45	48	55	51	52	54	49	66	61	47	64	50	55	62	53	57	62
63557 NEW BOSTON	75	52	26	48	60	68	51	63	60	51	70	76	44	68	53	63	64	63	76	89
63558 NEW CAMBRIA	77	53	27	49	62	70	52	65	61	52	72	78	45	70	54	65	65	64	78	91
63559 NOVINGER	76	61	42	58	65	73	61	68	66	60	80	79	56	78	61	69	74	67	76	85
63560 POLLOCK	69	53	36	50	58	68	56	63	63	54	74	71	51	71	56	66	68	62	74	77
63561 QUEEN CITY	67	51	33	49	56	65	54	60	60	52	71	69	48	68	54	63	65	60	71	75
63563 RUTLEDGE	66	46	24	43	53	60	45	56	52	45	61	67	39	60	47	55	56	55	67	78
63565 UNIONVILLE	65	47	28	43	53	62	49	57	56	48	66	65	43	63	49	60	60	56	69	74
63566 WINIGAN	75	52	25	47	59	67	50	63	59	51	70	75	43	67	52	63	63	62	76	88
63567 WORTHINGTON	67	45	20	39	51	59	43	54	52	44	62	65	37	58	44	57	56	54	67	77
63601 PARK HILLS	62	54	47	52	55	63	56	59	60	55	74	68	54	73	56	62	70	59	64	70
63620 ANNAPOLIS	64	43	20	37	49	56	42	52	50	42	59	62	35	56	42	54	54	51	64	74
63621 ARCADIA	73	55	36	52	60	71	60	66	67	57	79	74	53	75	59	71	72	66	79	81
63622 BELGRADE	79	53	24	45	60	69	51	63	61	52	72	76	43	68	52	66	65	63	78	90
63623 BELLEVIEW	86	60	33	55	67	79	62	73	72	61	85	85	54	80	62	77	77	73	89	97
63624 BISMARCK	66	48	28	44	53	60	48	56	55	48	65	66	43	62	48	58	60	55	66	74
63625 BLACK	72	48	22	42	55	63	47	58	56	48	66	70	40	63	47	61	60	58	72	83
63626 BLACKWELL	74	53	29	47	58	66	51	61	59	52	70	73	45	66	52	62	64	61	73	84
63627 BLOOMSDALE	100	77	48	70	84	93	73	85	82	73	98	102	67	97	74	86	91	84	99	116
63628 BONNE TERRE	76	65	53	61	70	78	64	71	69	63	83	82	61	83	66	72	79	70	79	88
63629 BUNKER	66	44	20	38	50	58	43	54	52	44	61	64	36	57	44	56	55	53	66	76
63630 CADET	66	47	25	42	52	59	46	55	53	47	63	65	40	59	46	56	58	55	65	75
63631 CALEDONIA	78	52	24	45	59	68	50	63	61	51	71	75	43	67	51	66	65	62	78	89
63633 CENTERVILLE	70	48	24	42	54	62	47	58	56	47	66	68	41	62	48	60	60	57	71	79
63636 DES ARC	67	45	20	39	51	58	43	54	52	44	61	64	37	58	44	56	56	53	66	77
63637 DOE RUN	79	53	25	46	60	69	51	64	62	52	73	76	44	69	52	66	66	63	79	90
63638 ELLINGTON	64	44	22	39	50	57	43	53	51	43	60	63	37	57	44	54	54	52	64	74
63640 FARMINGTON	71	59	46	56	62	71	60	66	66	59	79	75	57	77	61	68	74	65	74	80
63645 FREDERICKTOWN	64	47	28	43	52	60	47	56	55	47	65	65	42	62	48	58	59	55	67	73
63648 IRONDALE	79	53	24	45	60	69	51	64	61	52	72	76	43	68	52	66	65	63	78	90
63650 IRONTON	68	51	33	48	56	66	54	61	61	53	72	70	49	69	54	65	66	61	73	76
63653 LEADWOOD	68	45	21	39	51	59	44	55	53	45	62	66	37	59	45	57	56	54	68	78
63654 LESTERVILLE	67	49	31	47	54	65	54	60	61	52	72	68	48	68	53	65	65	60	72	74
63655 MARQUAND	71	48	22	41	54	62	46	57	55	47	65	69	39	62	47	60	59	57	71	82
63656 MIDDLE BROOK	75	51	24	44	57	66	50	61	59	50	70	73	42	66	50	64	63	61	75	85
63660 MINERAL POINT	66	44	20	38	50	58	43	54	52	44	61	64	36	57	44	56	55	53	66	76
63662 PATTON	84	56	26	49	64	73	54	68	65	55	77	81	46	73	55	70	70	67	83	96
63664 POTOSI	73	51	27	45	57	66	51	61	60	51	71	72	45	67	52	65	65	61	75	82
63665 REDFORD	63	42	20	37	48	55	41	51	49	42	58	61	35	55	42	53	53	51	63	72
63670 SAINTE GENEVIEVE	85	76	62	73	81	89	74	80	79	73	96	93	72	97	76	81	91	79	88	99
63673 SAINT MARY	87	70	47	65	76	83	66	76	73	66	88	90	62	87	67	76	82	74	86	101
63675 VULCAN	67	45	20	39	51	58	43	54	52	44	61	64	37	58	44	56	56	53	66	77
63701 CAPE GIRARDEAU	83	83	89	84	84	89	86	85	85	84	106	101	86	106	85	83	103	86	82	96
63703 CAPE GIRARDEAU	47	44	51	44	43	48	50	47	51	48	63	56	49	62	48	50	61	50	48	52
63730 ADVANCE	70	50	29	46	56	66	53	61	61	51	71	70	46	67	53	65	65	61	74	79
63732 ALTENBURG	82	73	56	70	78	83	68	75	72	68	88	90	67	89	70	74	83	73	81	97
63735 BELL CITY	73	49	22	42	55	64	47	59	57	48	67	70	40	63	48	61	61	58	73	84
63736 BENTON	83	68	47	64	72	78	65	73	70	66	85	86	60	82	65	72	80	72	80	94
63739 BURFORDVILLE	100	88	66	83	93	100	81	91	87	82	106	108	79	108	84	90	100	89	99	118
63740 CHAFFEE	76	65	50	61	69	77	64	70	70	63	84	81	61	85	65	73	79	69	80	88
63743 DAISY	80	71	54	67	75	80	65	73	69	65	84	86	64	86	67	71	80	71	78	94
63744 DELTA	89	59	27	51	67	77	57	72	69	58	81	86	49	77	58	75	74	71	88	102
63747 FRIEDHEIM	79	70	53	67	74	79	65	72	69	65	84	86	63	85	67	71	79	70	78	93
63748 FROHNA	77	65	47	62	70	76	61	69	66	61	79	82	58	80	63	68	75	67	76	90
63750 GIPSY	67	45	20	39	51	58	43	54	52	44	61	65	37	58	44	56	56	53	67	77
63751 GLENALLEN	75	51	24	44	58	66	49	61	59	50	69	73	42	66	50	63	63	60	75	86
63755 JACKSON	92	79	60	76	84	91	76	84	81	76	99	100	73	98	78	83	93	83	92	107
63760 LEOPOLD	78	68	50	64	72	78	63	70	68	63	82	84	61	83	65	70	77	69	77	92
63763 MC GEE	64	44	22	38	50	57	42	53	51	43	59	63	36	57	43	54	54	52	64	74
63764 MARBLE HILL	70	52	30	47	57	65	51	60	58	51	69	71	45	67	51	62	64	59	71	81
63766 MILLERSVILLE	88	78	60	74	83	89	72	80	77	72	94	96	71	96	75	79	89	78	87	104
63769 OAK RIDGE	84	75	57	71	79	85	69	77	74	69	90	92	68	92	71	76	85	75	83	99
63770 OLD APPLETON	80	71	54	68	75	81	66	73	70	66	85	87	64	87	68	72	81	71	79	94
63771 ORAN	80	55	27	48	62	70	53	65	63	54	74	78	46	70	54	67	68	65	79	91
63775 PERRYVILLE	76	69	57	66	72	79	67	72	71	65	86	83	66	88	68	73	82	70	78	88
63780 SCOTT CITY	79	67	50	65	70	78	67	73	71	66	86	84	63	85	67	73	81	72	80	89
63781 SEDGEWICKVILLE	79	53	24	46	60	69	51	64	62	52	73	77	44	69	52	67	66	63	79	91
63782 STURDIVANT	72	48	22	41	54	62	46	58	56	47	66	69	39	62	47	60	60	57	71	82
63783 UNIONTOWN	74	66	50	63	70	75	61	68	65	61	79	81	60	81	63	67	75	66	73	88
63785 WHITEWATER	89	59	27	51	67	77	57	72	69	58	81	86	49	77	58	74	74	71	88	102
63787 ZALMA	69	46	21	40	53	61	45	56	54	46	64	67	38	60	46	58	58	55	69	80
63801 SIKESTON	69	59	51	56	62	69	60	64	65	60	79	75	58	78	60	67	75	65	71	79
63821 ARBYRD	67	45	20	39	51	59	43	54	52	44	62	65	37	58	44	57	56	54	67	77
63822 BERNIE	66	46	25	42	52	60	47	56	55	47	65	65	41	61	48	59	59	56	68	74
63823 BERTRAND	89	61	29	54	69	79	59	74	70	60	82	88	50	79	60	75	75	73	90	104
63825 BLOOMFIELD	74	52	28	47	58	68	54	63	62	53	73	73	47	69	54	67	67	63	77	83
63827 BRAGG CITY	66	44	20	38	50	58	43	54	52	44	61	64	37	57	44	56	55	53	66	76
63829 CARDWELL	67	45	20	39	51	59	44	55	53	44	62	65	37	58	44	57	56	54	67	77
63830 CARUTHERSVILLE	52	45	49	43	45	52	51	50	54	50	67	58	49	65	50	56	64	52	54	57
63833 CATRON	81	55	26	48	62	72	54	67	65	55	76	79	46	72	55	70	69	66	82	93
63834 CHARLESTON	58	50	51	47	51	59	54	56	59	54	72	63	53	70	54	61	69	57	62	65
63837 CLARKTON	61	41	19	35	46	53	40	50	48	40	56	59	34	53	40	51	51	49	61	70
63841 DEXTER	76	57	37	53	62	72	58	66	66	57	78	78	53	75	59	69	72	66	78	86
63845 EAST PRAIRIE	56	41	26	38	45	53	43	49	50	42	59	57	38	56	43	52	54	49	59	64
63846 ESSEX	79	53	25	46	60	69	52	64	62	52	73	76	44	69	52	67	66	64	79	90
63848 GIDEON	73	49	22	42	55	64	47	59	57	48	67	71	40	63	48	61	61	59	73	84
MISSOURI	87	82	79	80	83	90	82	85	85	82	104	99	81	103	82	85	100	85	87	100
UNITED STATES	100	100	100	100	100	100	100	100	100	100	100	100	100	100	100	100	100	100	100	100

#	POST OFFICE NAME	COUNTY FIPS CODE	POPULATION 2000	2004	2009	2000-2004 ANNUAL RATE % Rate	State Centile	HOUSEHOLDS 2000	2004	2009	% Annual Rate 2000-2004	2004 Average HH Size	FAMILIES 2000	2004	% Annual Rate 2000-2004
63849	GOBLER	155	168	163	158	-0.7	11	66	65	63	-0.4	2.51	48	46	-1.0
63851	HAYTI	155	4531	4332	4154	-1.1	5	1798	1741	1689	-0.8	2.42	1160	1096	-1.3
63852	HOLCOMB	069	1727	1730	1726	0.0	34	685	684	683	0.0	2.52	504	494	-0.5
63855	HORNERSVILLE	069	1601	1603	1603	0.0	33	650	653	654	0.1	2.45	448	440	-0.4
63857	KENNETT	069	13070	13017	12968	-0.1	28	5251	5257	5258	0.0	2.41	3588	3513	-0.5
63862	LILBOURN	143	1764	1704	1645	-0.8	9	699	686	672	-0.4	2.47	487	468	-0.9
63863	MALDEN	069	6537	6415	6350	-0.4	19	2621	2591	2579	-0.3	2.41	1769	1712	-0.8
63866	MARSTON	143	852	828	801	-0.7	12	364	359	353	-0.3	2.30	246	238	-0.8
63867	MATTHEWS	143	1948	1885	1820	-0.8	10	745	729	714	-0.5	2.57	572	551	-0.9
63868	MOREHOUSE	143	1760	1720	1669	-0.5	15	711	703	692	-0.3	2.45	494	478	-0.8
63869	NEW MADRID	143	4268	4064	3904	-1.2	4	1643	1585	1544	-0.8	2.46	1141	1078	-1.3
63870	PARMA	143	1988	1949	1902	-0.5	18	781	778	771	-0.1	2.51	572	559	-0.5
63873	PORTAGEVILLE	143	5262	5116	4949	-0.7	12	2057	2028	1990	-0.3	2.49	1443	1393	-0.8
63876	SENATH	069	2121	2078	2056	-0.5	18	870	855	850	-0.4	2.32	578	556	-0.9
63877	STEELE	155	5503	5524	5428	0.1	36	2170	2203	2190	0.4	2.48	1523	1512	-0.2
63879	WARDELL	155	924	886	850	-1.0	6	365	353	342	-0.8	2.50	263	249	-1.3
63901	POPLAR BLUFF	023	32955	33445	34092	0.4	47	13460	13786	14192	0.6	2.36	8995	9007	0.0
63931	BRIAR	181	657	649	655	-0.3	23	253	253	257	0.0	2.57	176	172	-0.5
63932	BROSELEY	023	2014	1972	1976	-0.5	18	807	800	809	-0.2	2.45	582	565	-0.7
63933	CAMPBELL	069	3995	4290	4464	1.7	82	1625	1780	1871	2.2	2.37	1109	1189	1.7
63934	CLUBB	223	109	103	101	-1.3	3	40	38	38	-1.2	2.68	28	26	-1.7
63935	DONIPHAN	181	8920	9165	9408	0.6	57	3588	3718	3850	0.8	2.42	2502	2540	0.4
63936	DUDLEY	207	971	985	1004	0.3	47	373	381	390	0.5	2.59	283	284	0.1
63937	ELLSINORE	035	1613	1813	1959	2.8	92	650	745	819	3.3	2.40	486	547	2.8
63939	FAIRDEALING	181	680	681	689	0.0	33	285	288	294	0.3	2.36	212	211	-0.1
63940	FISK	023	751	735	736	-0.5	17	323	320	324	-0.2	2.29	228	221	-0.7
63941	FREMONT	035	510	499	502	-0.5	17	199	198	201	-0.1	2.47	139	135	-0.7
63942	GATEWOOD	181	374	379	385	0.3	45	145	148	152	0.5	2.56	113	114	0.2
63943	GRANDIN	035	2668	2754	2827	0.8	61	979	1017	1052	0.9	2.70	741	756	0.5
63944	GREENVILLE	223	1658	1583	1562	-1.1	4	677	650	646	-1.0	2.40	484	456	-1.4
63945	HARVIELL	023	920	943	959	0.6	55	347	360	370	0.9	2.62	264	269	0.4
63950	LODI	223	59	55	54	-1.6	1	22	21	21	-1.1	2.62	16	15	-1.5
63951	LOWNDES	223	135	131	129	-0.7	11	52	51	51	-0.5	2.57	36	35	-0.7
63952	MILL SPRING	223	863	904	935	1.1	71	334	354	370	1.4	2.55	240	249	0.9
63953	NAYLOR	181	1294	1269	1278	-0.5	19	525	517	524	-0.4	2.45	381	369	-0.8
63954	NEELYVILLE	023	1527	1520	1528	-0.1	27	614	618	628	0.2	2.46	413	405	-0.5
63955	OXLY	181	645	644	652	0.0	30	274	276	281	0.2	2.33	196	193	-0.4
63956	PATTERSON	223	1526	1490	1491	-0.6	15	626	614	621	-0.5	2.41	463	446	-0.9
63957	PIEDMONT	223	3965	4536	4951	3.2	94	1684	1964	2176	3.7	2.27	1126	1286	3.2
63960	PUXICO	207	3065	3160	3246	0.7	59	1143	1196	1245	1.1	2.35	806	825	0.6
63961	QULIN	023	1626	1595	1598	-0.5	19	673	667	675	-0.2	2.37	481	466	-0.7
63963	SHOOK	223	280	271	268	-0.8	10	121	118	118	-0.6	2.30	86	82	-1.1
63964	SILVA	223	1001	947	932	-1.3	3	419	397	394	-1.3	2.34	294	273	-1.7
63965	VAN BUREN	035	2621	2566	2586	-0.5	17	1126	1119	1143	-0.2	2.23	745	722	-0.7
63966	WAPPAPELLO	223	2178	2117	2101	-0.7	12	1006	986	988	-0.5	2.15	663	636	-1.0
63967	WILLIAMSVILLE	223	1996	1942	1932	-0.6	13	837	822	826	-0.4	2.35	586	565	-0.9
64001	ALMA	107	690	687	700	-0.1	28	280	281	289	0.1	2.44	206	203	-0.3
64011	BATES CITY	107	3505	3684	3838	1.2	73	1262	1336	1399	1.4	2.76	1009	1054	1.0
64012	BELTON	037	25880	28187	31555	2.0	86	9561	10511	11867	2.3	2.65	7055	7595	1.8
64014	BLUE SPRINGS	095	22956	24255	25254	1.3	75	8191	8733	9161	1.5	2.75	6319	6597	1.0
64015	BLUE SPRINGS	095	28790	29949	30986	0.9	67	10501	11038	11507	1.2	2.71	8114	8368	0.7
64016	BUCKNER	095	4208	4376	4519	0.9	67	1551	1630	1697	1.2	2.68	1198	1234	0.7
64017	CAMDEN	177	471	473	495	0.1	36	181	184	194	0.4	2.55	136	134	-0.4
64018	CAMDEN POINT	165	846	831	871	-0.4	19	313	311	330	-0.2	2.67	253	246	-0.7
64019	CENTERVIEW	101	1982	2093	2191	1.3	74	719	764	803	1.4	2.73	569	593	1.0
64020	CONCORDIA	107	3584	3636	3732	0.3	47	1361	1381	1423	0.3	2.52	955	948	-0.2
64021	CORDER	107	634	595	601	-1.5	2	259	244	248	-1.4	2.44	182	169	-1.7
64022	DOVER	107	340	342	348	0.1	38	132	134	137	0.4	2.39	98	97	-0.2
64024	EXCELSIOR SPRINGS	047	16173	17041	17930	1.2	74	5995	6403	6805	1.6	2.56	4365	4564	1.1
64029	GRAIN VALLEY	095	8190	10163	11506	5.2	99	2975	3748	4267	5.6	2.71	2347	2879	4.9
64030	GRANDVIEW	095	24849	25648	26481	0.8	61	9701	10116	10525	1.0	2.51	6479	6546	0.2
64034	GREENWOOD	095	5744	6518	7120	3.0	93	2014	2312	2551	3.3	2.82	1694	1916	2.9
64035	HARDIN	177	1187	1242	1317	1.1	70	468	493	526	1.2	2.52	347	358	0.7
64036	HENRIETTA	177	468	518	562	2.4	89	130	148	165	3.1	2.93	92	103	2.7
64037	HIGGINSVILLE	107	6060	6367	6664	1.2	72	2302	2430	2557	1.3	2.45	1601	1656	0.8
64040	HOLDEN	101	6157	6593	6971	1.6	81	2306	2476	2625	1.7	2.64	1712	1800	1.2
64048	HOLT	047	3968	4213	4452	1.4	77	1408	1515	1615	1.7	2.77	1173	1244	1.4
64050	INDEPENDENCE	095	23469	23310	23690	-0.2	26	9787	9807	10045	0.1	2.33	6013	5821	-0.8
64052	INDEPENDENCE	095	21100	20810	21065	-0.3	21	9581	9553	9749	-0.1	2.17	5492	5249	-1.1
64053	INDEPENDENCE	095	5594	5368	5407	-1.0	6	2406	2333	2368	-0.7	2.28	1357	1257	-1.8
64054	INDEPENDENCE	095	4196	4044	4073	-0.9	8	1879	1833	1861	-0.6	2.20	1101	1031	-1.5
64055	INDEPENDENCE	095	33208	33925	35082	0.5	53	14455	14927	15564	0.8	2.26	9406	9374	-0.1
64056	INDEPENDENCE	095	14805	15293	15776	0.8	61	5254	5499	5722	1.1	2.77	4118	4215	0.6
64057	INDEPENDENCE	095	11314	11978	12580	1.4	76	4329	4559	4785	1.2	2.57	3095	3185	0.7
64058	INDEPENDENCE	095	6521	6617	6727	0.3	47	2214	2274	2332	0.6	2.89	1831	1848	0.2
64060	KEARNEY	047	9625	10768	11544	2.7	91	3299	3736	4041	3.0	2.86	2715	3026	2.6
64061	KINGSVILLE	101	2747	2954	3136	1.7	82	1031	1116	1191	1.9	2.64	827	878	1.4
64062	LAWSON	177	5967	6305	6695	1.3	75	2089	2231	2390	1.6	2.80	1687	1775	1.2
64063	LEES SUMMIT	095	20227	21649	22878	1.6	81	7807	8325	8802	1.5	2.60	5488	5775	1.2
64064	LEES SUMMIT	095	11921	14064	15512	4.0	97	4417	5269	5858	4.2	2.64	3554	4162	3.8
64067	LEXINGTON	107	5916	5801	5887	-0.5	19	2356	2322	2368	-0.3	2.42	1656	1598	-0.8
64068	LIBERTY	047	33246	34363	35559	0.8	62	12159	12707	13278	1.0	2.59	8945	9155	0.6
64070	LONE JACK	095	2426	2534	2619	1.0	69	880	929	967	1.3	2.73	731	760	0.9
64071	MAYVIEW	107	887	899	919	0.3	45	325	332	340	0.5	2.69	250	251	0.1
64074	NAPOLEON	107	685	694	708	0.3	45	253	259	266	0.6	2.63	200	201	0.1
64075	OAK GROVE	095	9191	10142	10789	2.3	88	3251	3637	3907	2.7	2.76	2555	2794	2.1
64076	ODESSA	107	8658	9176	9603	1.4	76	3247	3465	3643	1.5	2.63	2396	2508	1.1
64077	ORRICK	177	1786	1924	2092	1.8	83	671	730	801	2.0	2.64	519	556	1.6
64078	PECULIAR	037	6891	8004	9243	3.6	96	2380	2783	3233	3.8	2.87	1968	2268	3.4
64079	PLATTE CITY	165	8071	9795	11325	4.7	98	2948	3602	4201	4.8	2.67	2239	2676	4.3
64080	PLEASANT HILL	037	9967	11133	12594	2.6	90	3646	4109	4688	2.9	2.69	2814	3114	2.4
64081	LEES SUMMIT	095	18112	21270	23759	3.9	97	7092	8044	8838	3.0	2.57	4728	5415	3.2
64082	LEES SUMMIT	095	5537	6670	7541	4.5	98	1874	2279	2593	4.7	2.93	1623	1950	4.4
64083	RAYMORE	037	12565	15123	17792	4.5	98	4557	5522	6545	4.6	2.71	3592	4290	4.3
64084	RAYVILLE	177	1495	1479	1549	-0.3	24	552	551	582	0.0	2.68	451	444	-0.4
	MISSOURI					0.8					0.9	2.46			0.4
	UNITED STATES					1.2					1.3	2.58			1.1

ZIP CODE #	POST OFFICE NAME	RACE (%) White 2000	White 2004	Black 2000	Black 2004	Asian/Pacific 2000	Asian/Pacific 2004	% Hispanic Origin 2000	% Hispanic Origin 2004	2004 AGE DISTRIBUTION (%) 0-4	5-9	10-14	15-19	20-24	25-44	45-64	65-84	85+	18+	MEDIAN AGE 2004	% 2004 Males	% 2004 Females
63849	GOBLER	83.9	82.2	13.1	14.7	0.0	0.6	3.0	3.7	4.9	6.1	8.0	8.6	6.1	23.9	28.8	12.3	1.2	76.1	39.8	49.7	50.3
63851	HAYTI	49.8	47.4	48.7	51.0	0.2	0.3	1.1	1.2	8.4	7.9	9.0	7.8	6.6	23.2	20.8	13.4	2.9	69.8	34.4	44.9	55.1
63852	HOLCOMB	96.2	96.1	0.7	0.8	0.1	0.1	3.2	3.3	7.2	7.3	7.5	6.8	5.8	25.8	25.3	12.6	1.7	73.8	38.4	50.3	49.7
63855	HORNERSVILLE	94.3	94.1	3.1	3.2	0.3	0.3	4.3	4.4	5.5	5.7	7.1	6.7	6.4	24.1	28.1	14.3	2.1	77.7	41.4	50.9	49.1
63857	KENNETT	85.5	84.8	11.8	12.5	0.5	0.5	2.3	2.3	7.8	7.1	7.1	6.8	6.3	25.4	23.7	13.3	2.4	73.7	36.8	46.4	53.6
63862	LILBOURN	64.9	62.2	33.6	36.3	0.1	0.1	1.0	1.0	6.3	6.6	9.3	7.7	6.7	24.2	24.2	12.8	2.1	73.1	37.0	47.7	52.4
63863	MALDEN	79.3	78.3	18.2	19.2	0.3	0.3	1.3	1.3	7.2	7.5	7.3	6.4	5.8	24.9	23.8	14.7	2.5	74.1	38.0	46.6	53.4
63866	MARSTON	80.2	78.1	18.8	20.9	0.0	0.0	1.8	1.8	8.0	7.9	7.1	5.4	5.7	25.9	25.5	13.2	1.5	73.8	37.8	49.8	50.2
63867	MATTHEWS	97.6	97.2	0.8	0.9	0.1	0.1	1.3	1.4	7.0	7.1	7.2	5.5	6.3	26.9	27.2	11.6	1.2	75.1	37.5	50.9	49.1
63868	MOREHOUSE	96.8	96.3	1.1	1.2	0.1	0.1	1.8	2.2	6.5	6.3	6.6	5.5	6.1	27.3	25.4	14.7	1.7	77.4	38.8	48.7	51.3
63869	NEW MADRID	71.3	69.5	27.6	29.2	0.2	0.3	0.7	0.7	7.2	7.2	7.6	6.8	6.6	25.4	24.5	12.4	2.2	73.6	36.7	48.0	52.0
63870	PARMA	79.6	78.0	19.1	20.5	0.0	0.0	0.6	0.6	6.1	6.0	7.3	6.4	7.1	26.4	25.5	13.3	1.8	76.8	38.2	48.7	51.3
63873	PORTAGEVILLE	85.6	84.1	12.9	14.4	0.2	0.3	0.7	0.8	6.7	6.0	7.5	6.9	7.3	25.3	24.9	13.4	2.0	75.6	38.3	48.0	52.0
63876	SENATH	92.9	92.8	0.6	0.7	0.1	0.1	9.6	9.6	7.0	6.8	6.0	4.8	5.3	24.7	24.0	17.5	3.9	77.1	41.6	48.6	51.4
63877	STEELE	87.2	85.4	10.9	12.5	0.1	0.1	2.1	2.3	7.4	7.5	7.5	7.2	6.5	25.3	24.0	12.7	2.0	73.2	36.1	48.1	51.9
63879	WARDELL	84.4	82.5	13.9	15.6	0.1	0.1	1.0	1.0	5.6	6.1	7.5	7.5	7.2	25.3	26.1	12.8	2.0	76.3	38.1	49.7	50.3
63901	POPLAR BLUFF	91.4	90.7	5.8	6.3	0.5	0.6	1.1	1.2	6.5	6.4	6.3	6.2	6.4	25.7	25.3	14.8	2.3	77.0	39.5	47.5	52.5
63931	BRIAR	96.2	95.7	0.0	0.0	0.2	0.3	0.6	0.9	6.0	6.5	8.8	6.9	6.2	25.7	25.0	14.0	0.9	74.3	38.4	52.4	47.6
63932	BROSELEY	96.6	96.2	1.5	1.7	0.2	0.2	0.5	0.6	5.9	5.7	6.2	6.3	6.0	25.6	26.0	16.3	2.0	78.3	41.3	49.9	50.1
63933	CAMPBELL	98.4	98.4	0.2	0.1	0.1	0.1	1.1	1.1	6.6	6.4	6.7	5.8	6.3	25.8	24.2	15.5	2.9	76.8	39.7	48.3	51.7
63934	CLUBB	98.2	97.1	0.9	1.0	0.0	0.0	0.9	1.0	5.8	5.8	6.8	6.8	5.8	22.3	25.2	18.5	2.9	75.7	42.5	52.4	47.6
63935	DONIPHAN	97.6	97.4	0.0	0.0	0.3	0.3	1.0	1.1	6.2	6.2	6.8	6.4	5.9	24.3	25.4	16.3	2.5	77.0	40.9	48.2	51.8
63936	DUDLEY	97.6	97.6	0.1	0.1	0.1	0.2	1.0	1.1	6.0	6.1	7.0	6.4	7.5	26.7	25.8	13.4	1.1	77.2	38.3	50.9	49.1
63937	ELLSINORE	97.3	97.1	0.3	0.3	0.2	0.3	0.4	0.4	6.0	6.2	6.8	8.3	6.6	24.6	26.9	13.5	1.1	75.3	39.0	48.8	51.2
63939	FAIRDEALING	97.5	97.4	0.2	0.2	0.2	0.2	0.7	0.7	6.0	5.9	6.3	6.5	6.3	24.4	28.3	15.0	1.3	77.8	41.3	49.1	51.0
63940	FISK	97.9	98.0	0.3	0.3	0.0	0.0	1.3	1.4	6.0	6.3	6.4	5.6	5.7	25.7	26.9	15.5	1.9	77.8	41.5	49.3	50.8
63941	FREMONT	93.3	92.8	0.2	0.2	0.2	0.2	2.8	3.0	5.8	6.2	6.8	5.6	4.8	24.5	29.7	15.2	1.4	77.6	42.6	50.7	49.3
63942	GATEWOOD	98.4	98.4	0.0	0.0	0.0	0.0	1.1	1.3	5.0	5.3	6.6	7.4	6.6	24.0	29.8	13.7	1.6	78.6	41.9	52.0	48.0
63943	GRANDIN	97.8	97.6	0.0	0.0	0.1	0.2	0.5	0.5	7.1	7.0	7.5	7.3	6.3	26.1	24.1	13.3	1.4	74.1	37.6	49.5	50.5
63944	GREENVILLE	97.7	97.5	0.2	0.2	0.2	0.3	0.7	0.7	5.3	5.4	6.1	6.7	6.0	23.0	26.7	18.4	2.4	79.0	43.4	50.7	49.3
63945	HARVIELL	96.3	95.9	0.7	0.7	0.3	0.3	0.8	0.7	6.5	6.7	7.1	6.7	5.7	28.1	27.4	11.0	0.9	75.7	37.8	50.2	49.8
63950	LODI	96.6	98.2	0.0	0.0	0.0	0.0	0.0	0.0	3.6	5.5	7.3	5.5	5.5	20.0	29.1	21.8	1.8	80.0	46.9	49.1	50.9
63951	LOWNDES	97.8	97.7	0.0	0.0	0.0	0.0	0.0	0.0	6.9	6.9	6.9	5.3	6.1	22.1	26.7	17.6	1.5	74.8	42.3	49.6	50.4
63952	MILL SPRING	96.8	96.6	0.0	0.0	0.2	0.4	0.5	0.4	6.4	6.2	6.9	6.9	6.2	23.0	25.7	17.0	1.8	76.1	40.9	49.9	50.1
63953	NAYLOR	94.6	94.2	0.1	0.1	0.3	0.4	1.6	1.8	6.5	6.4	6.3	6.2	6.5	24.4	25.5	16.2	1.9	77.0	40.2	47.8	52.2
63954	NEELYVILLE	87.1	85.9	10.3	11.3	0.3	0.4	0.3	0.3	6.6	6.9	7.9	6.8	6.1	28.6	24.7	11.0	1.4	74.3	36.2	50.6	49.4
63955	OXLY	96.4	96.3	0.0	0.0	0.0	0.2	1.1	1.2	6.4	6.2	6.1	5.4	5.4	25.8	28.1	14.9	1.7	78.1	41.4	50.6	49.4
63956	PATTERSON	97.2	97.1	0.5	0.5	0.0	0.0	0.6	0.7	5.6	5.8	6.5	6.7	5.5	21.9	28.1	17.6	2.4	78.0	43.7	49.3	50.7
63957	PIEDMONT	97.7	97.5	0.2	0.2	0.2	0.3	0.5	0.6	5.4	5.4	6.6	6.3	5.9	22.5	25.2	19.1	3.5	78.6	43.4	48.3	51.7
63960	PUXICO	96.9	96.7	1.7	1.8	0.0	0.1	0.9	0.9	4.8	4.7	6.0	12.2	7.6	23.9	22.5	15.7	2.8	76.9	38.1	51.7	48.3
63961	QULIN	97.7	97.5	0.5	0.6	0.0	0.0	0.6	0.7	5.5	5.8	7.3	6.3	6.0	26.5	24.8	15.9	1.9	77.6	40.3	50.6	49.4
63963	SHOOK	97.9	98.2	0.0	0.0	0.0	0.0	0.7	0.4	5.9	5.9	5.9	5.9	5.9	21.8	29.5	17.7	1.5	78.6	44.1	51.3	48.7
63964	SILVA	97.8	97.5	0.3	0.3	0.1	0.1	0.7	0.8	5.5	5.5	6.6	6.8	5.8	23.3	24.7	18.7	3.2	78.1	42.8	49.6	50.4
63965	VAN BUREN	95.6	95.3	0.2	0.2	0.1	0.1	1.8	2.1	5.7	5.9	6.3	5.8	5.4	23.9	27.9	16.7	2.3	78.5	43.0	49.1	50.9
63966	WAPPAPELLO	97.9	97.8	0.3	0.3	0.1	0.1	0.6	0.6	4.8	4.7	4.9	5.5	5.5	19.4	32.6	21.5	1.2	82.3	48.9	51.1	48.9
63967	WILLIAMSVILLE	98.0	97.8	0.2	0.2	0.1	0.2	0.5	0.5	5.4	5.5	5.8	5.8	6.1	23.3	30.1	16.9	1.1	79.9	43.7	51.0	49.0
64001	ALMA	99.3	99.4	0.0	0.0	0.1	0.2	0.1	0.3	5.7	6.0	7.0	6.0	5.0	24.6	28.0	15.9	2.0	77.4	42.5	49.3	50.7
64011	BATES CITY	96.7	96.3	0.9	0.9	0.2	0.3	1.4	1.6	6.4	6.5	7.6	7.7	6.7	28.2	28.5	8.0	0.6	74.9	37.4	51.9	48.2
64012	BELTON	93.6	93.0	2.5	2.7	0.7	0.9	4.1	4.6	7.8	7.7	7.8	6.9	6.6	29.6	22.8	9.6	1.4	72.5	34.5	48.8	51.2
64014	BLUE SPRINGS	93.4	91.8	2.6	3.4	1.1	1.5	3.0	3.5	7.8	7.5	7.8	7.4	7.2	31.2	23.5	6.5	1.0	72.4	33.2	48.6	51.4
64015	BLUE SPRINGS	93.4	91.8	2.9	3.8	1.0	1.3	2.4	2.8	6.9	7.0	7.7	7.4	7.0	28.5	27.0	7.8	0.8	73.9	35.5	49.2	50.8
64016	BUCKNER	96.7	96.1	0.2	0.3	0.3	0.3	1.4	1.7	6.3	6.8	8.2	7.1	6.6	27.2	26.5	10.4	0.9	74.3	36.9	49.7	50.3
64017	CAMDEN	97.9	97.9	0.4	0.4	0.0	0.0	1.3	1.3	6.1	6.6	7.6	7.4	6.1	28.5	24.3	12.1	1.3	74.8	37.1	50.5	49.5
64018	CAMDEN POINT	98.5	98.4	0.0	0.0	0.0	0.0	0.6	0.6	7.2	7.7	6.1	5.8	5.1	27.9	30.1	9.0	1.1	75.2	39.7	50.7	49.3
64019	CENTERVIEW	96.6	96.2	0.6	0.6	0.5	0.7	1.7	1.8	6.4	6.6	7.4	7.3	6.5	27.7	27.4	10.0	0.8	74.9	38.2	50.7	49.3
64020	CONCORDIA	98.3	98.1	0.6	0.7	0.2	0.3	0.7	0.8	6.0	6.3	7.3	6.7	5.5	24.7	23.2	15.3	4.9	76.1	40.5	47.8	52.2
64021	CORDER	96.5	96.5	1.3	1.3	0.2	0.2	1.0	1.0	5.2	5.6	6.9	6.9	6.4	23.4	28.2	14.8	2.7	78.2	42.1	49.9	50.1
64022	DOVER	92.4	91.5	4.7	5.3	0.3	0.3	1.8	1.8	5.9	5.9	7.0	7.9	5.9	26.0	27.8	12.3	1.5	76.6	39.4	49.7	50.3
64024	EXCELSIOR SPRINGS	94.6	94.2	2.4	2.5	0.4	0.5	1.7	1.8	7.2	6.7	6.8	8.1	7.1	26.4	24.9	11.2	1.7	74.5	36.6	49.4	50.6
64029	GRAIN VALLEY	96.2	95.3	0.9	1.2	0.6	0.8	2.4	2.9	9.3	8.5	7.7	6.4	5.8	35.2	20.4	6.3	0.5	70.6	31.9	50.0	50.0
64030	GRANDVIEW	59.8	54.1	33.6	38.8	1.2	1.4	4.3	4.7	7.2	6.8	7.3	7.3	7.9	29.2	23.5	9.7	1.1	74.3	34.2	48.1	51.9
64034	GREENWOOD	95.8	94.8	1.8	2.4	0.5	0.6	1.9	2.2	9.7	9.2	8.0	5.8	4.6	34.4	21.0	6.7	0.5	69.4	33.8	49.6	50.4
64035	HARDIN	97.7	97.5	0.4	0.5	0.1	0.1	0.7	0.6	6.7	7.1	8.1	7.0	5.7	25.4	25.9	11.9	2.2	73.8	39.0	51.5	48.5
64036	HENRIETTA	91.7	91.1	4.7	5.2	0.0	0.0	2.1	2.3	6.2	6.0	6.2	7.0	8.7	34.6	22.2	8.7	0.6	78.4	33.7	56.8	43.2
64037	HIGGINSVILLE	93.0	92.4	4.1	4.4	0.5	0.6	1.3	1.5	6.3	6.3	6.9	6.7	6.3	25.0	24.5	14.0	3.9	76.2	39.9	47.4	52.6
64040	HOLDEN	96.1	95.7	0.9	1.0	0.3	0.4	1.3	1.5	6.1	6.3	7.8	7.5	6.9	27.1	24.7	12.2	1.6	75.3	38.2	50.1	49.9
64048	HOLT	97.9	97.7	0.5	0.5	0.1	0.1	1.1	1.2	5.7	6.5	8.0	7.1	4.7	26.6	32.0	8.8	0.7	75.2	40.5	50.5	49.5
64050	INDEPENDENCE	91.0	89.2	2.8	3.6	1.2	1.5	3.9	4.6	7.3	6.5	6.6	6.7	7.2	27.7	22.1	13.1	2.8	75.6	36.7	47.3	52.7
64052	INDEPENDENCE	90.8	89.0	2.5	3.2	1.2	1.5	4.5	5.3	6.7	6.2	5.5	5.0	5.6	28.5	25.1	15.3	2.2	78.6	40.4	48.5	51.5
64053	INDEPENDENCE	89.9	87.8	2.7	3.6	1.2	1.5	5.2	6.3	7.4	6.7	6.1	5.4	7.3	30.4	24.3	10.9	1.5	76.7	36.5	51.0	49.0
64054	INDEPENDENCE	91.0	89.3	2.0	2.5	1.9	2.3	3.7	4.6	6.3	6.1	5.9	5.2	5.3	30.6	26.6	12.6	1.5	78.6	39.2	50.7	49.3
64055	INDEPENDENCE	94.0	92.6	2.1	2.6	1.0	1.4	3.0	3.5	5.2	5.2	5.9	6.0	6.2	25.9	26.4	17.2	2.2	80.1	42.0	46.9	53.1
64056	INDEPENDENCE	89.8	87.7	3.9	5.0	1.2	1.6	3.9	4.6	8.4	8.0	8.2	7.9	7.5	28.1	22.1	9.1	0.8	70.4	32.3	48.9	51.1
64057	INDEPENDENCE	93.5	92.2	2.1	2.6	1.1	1.4	3.4	4.1	6.3	6.4	6.8	7.0	7.4	26.4	26.4	10.8	2.6	76.4	38.7	46.8	53.2
64058	INDEPENDENCE	94.7	93.7	0.9	1.2	1.5	1.8	2.3	2.7	6.7	6.8	7.5	7.9	7.1	27.7	27.4	8.2	0.8	73.9	35.9	49.2	50.8
64060	KEARNEY	97.2	96.9	0.6	0.6	0.4	0.5	1.6	1.8	8.4	8.3	8.6	7.6	6.0	30.1	23.4	6.7	1.0	69.6	34.2	49.3	50.8
64061	KINGSVILLE	97.4	97.2	0.5	0.5	0.2	0.1	0.8	1.0	6.0	6.4	6.9	5.8	5.6	28.0	28.7	11.5	1.1	77.1	40.3	50.6	49.4
64062	LAWSON	97.4	97.1	0.5	0.6	0.4	0.5	1.1	1.2	6.8	6.9	8.2	8.0	6.2	26.2	27.0	9.6	1.1	72.8	37.4	50.5	49.5
64063	LEES SUMMIT	93.4	91.6	3.0	4.1	0.8	1.2	2.1	2.5	9.1	8.5	8.1	6.8	6.3	32.8	20.6	7.0	0.9	70.1	32.7	47.4	52.6
64064	LEES SUMMIT	92.3	90.2	4.2	5.6	1.5	2.0	1.8	2.1	6.8	7.4	7.2	6.3	4.7	26.8	31.1	9.0	0.9	74.7	39.9	49.2	50.9
64067	LEXINGTON	92.7	92.0	4.8	5.2	0.4	0.5	1.8	2.1	5.5	5.8	7.2	6.7	6.1	24.8	26.0	15.2	2.7	77.3	40.7	48.0	52.0
64068	LIBERTY	94.2	93.6	2.3	2.4	0.7	0.8	2.6	2.9	6.7	6.7	7.5	7.7	7.8	28.3	24.5	9.3	1.5	74.6	35.5	48.3	51.7
64070	LONE JACK	97.2	96.6	1.2	1.5	0.3	0.3	1.5	1.8	5.7	7.1	8.2	7.3	3.7	27.5	30.6	9.2	0.8	74.5	40.1	50.6	49.4
64071	MAYVIEW	94.5	93.9	3.8	4.2	0.0	0.0	1.0	1.1	5.8	6.5	7.9	7.9	5.7	28.3	25.4	11.0	1.7	73.8	37.8	50.6	49.4
64074	NAPOLEON	96.5	96.0	1.0	1.2	0.2	0.3	0.9	1.2	6.6	6.8	7.1	6.6	4.9	26.8	29.3	10.8	1.2	75.5	40.1	52.2	47.8
64075	OAK GROVE	97.2	96.6	0.2	0.3	0.5	0.7	1.4	1.7	7.3	7.3	8.5	7.6	6.1	28.5	24.6	9.0	1.4	72.1	35.4	49.5	50.5
64076	ODESSA	97.0	96.7	1.1	1.2	0.2	0.3	0.8	0.9	7.0	6.8	8.0	7.2	6.8	28.1	23.4	11.3	1.5	73.8	36.4	49.4	50.6
64077	ORRICK	98.2	98.0	0.2	0.2	0.0	0.1	1.3	1.5	6.2	6.5	7.5	7.3	6.0	27.3	26.2	11.8	1.1	75.3	38.2	50.6	49.4
64078	PECULIAR	96.5	96.1	0.9	1.0	0.6	0.8	1.3	1.4	7.3	7.9	8.4	7.6	5.0	27.5	27.4	8.2	0.7	71.7	36.9	49.9	50.1
64079	PLATTE CITY	94.3	93.8	1.9	2.1	0.7	0.8	2.0	2.2	7.1	7.4	7.6	7.1	6.0	30.6	25.6	7.4	1.3	73.2	36.3	50.3	49.7
64080	PLEASANT HILL	97.6	97.3	0.4	0.4	0.3	0.4	1.3	1.5	7.4	7.6	8.3	6.8	5.7	29.3	23.3	10.1	1.5	72.2	36.0	49.5	50.5
64081	LEES SUMMIT	93.2	90.6	4.0	5.9	1.0	1.5	1.7	2.2	7.6	7.7	7.6	6.3	4.2	26.8	21.5	12.5	5.8	73.0	39.4	46.4	53.6
64082	LEES SUMMIT	95.8	94.6	2.0	2.7	0.9	1.2	1.4	1.7	6.9	7.5	8.3	7.4	4.8	26.6	29.6	8.8	0.3	72.5	39.0	48.7	51.3
64083	RAYMORE	95.3	94.8	1.7	1.9	0.7	0.9	1.8	2.1	7.5	7.6	7.8	6.9	5.3	27.7	23.5	10.7	3.1	72.7	37.3	48.2	51.8
64084	RAYVILLE	97.3	97.0	0.3	0.4	0.2	0.3	0.8	0.9	6.2	6.5	7.2	6.4	5.6	24.3	31.8	11.2	0.9	76.2	41.3	51.0	49.0
	MISSOURI	84.9	84.1	11.3	11.5	1.2	1.4	2.1	2.3	6.7	6.6	7.0	7.0	7.3	27.6	24.2	11.7	1.9	75.6	36.8	48.7	51.3
	UNITED STATES	75.1	73.6	12.3	12.5	3.8	4.2	12.5	14.1	6.9	6.7	7.2	7.0	7.3	28.6	23.8	10.8	1.7	75.1	36.0	49.1	50.9

ZIP CODE #	POST OFFICE NAME	2004 Per Capita Income	2004 HH Income Base	2004 Household Income Distribution (%): Less than $25,000	$25,000 to $49,999	$50,000 to $99,999	$100,000 to $149,999	$150,000 or More	Median Household Income: 2004	2009	2004 National Centile	2004 State Centile	2004 Home Value Base	2004 Home Value Distribution (%): Less than $50,000	$50,000 to $89,999	$90,000 to $174,999	$175,000 to $399,999	$400,000 or More	2004 Median Home Value
63849	GOBLER	15730	65	43.1	30.8	23.1	3.1	0.0	28574	35756	10	14	48	58.3	25.0	14.6	2.1	0.0	45000
63851	HAYTI	13983	1741	58.8	27.4	10.9	1.3	1.7	18962	22048	2	1	950	57.5	33.3	6.3	3.0	0.0	43661
63852	HOLCOMB	15348	684	45.5	32.2	18.7	2.3	1.3	27316	32368	8	10	550	49.8	33.1	13.3	3.3	0.6	50222
63855	HORNERSVILLE	15766	653	43.2	30.8	20.2	3.4	2.5	29578	35708	11	17	492	54.1	29.9	14.0	2.0	0.0	47701
63857	KENNETT	16642	5257	44.7	26.2	22.3	4.9	1.9	29810	35089	12	18	3383	27.8	34.0	31.4	6.4	0.4	77026
63862	LILBOURN	16493	686	45.6	28.0	19.5	5.3	1.6	27463	32757	8	10	509	53.6	37.5	8.3	0.6	0.0	46967
63863	MALDEN	15441	2591	46.6	29.3	20.0	2.9	1.3	27113	32056	7	9	1785	43.0	36.6	17.4	2.9	0.0	55845
63866	MARSTON	18158	359	47.1	27.6	19.5	3.1	2.8	27091	31565	7	9	248	63.7	24.2	10.5	1.2	0.4	38095
63867	MATTHEWS	14338	729	37.0	41.8	18.5	2.5	0.1	32612	38340	20	31	555	42.0	36.2	19.5	2.2	0.2	60263
63868	MOREHOUSE	15635	703	43.2	36.8	16.2	2.8	0.9	29822	35191	12	18	543	66.1	23.9	8.1	1.7	0.2	36188
63869	NEW MADRID	16501	1585	43.4	27.6	22.2	4.7	2.2	28986	34197	10	15	1078	31.9	40.1	23.5	4.3	0.3	66466
63870	PARMA	15528	778	45.9	27.0	22.6	3.0	1.5	27711	32434	8	11	556	59.2	27.9	10.3	2.7	0.0	42154
63873	PORTAGEVILLE	16885	2028	41.3	28.2	24.5	4.0	2.0	32310	38064	19	29	1359	37.6	31.3	25.5	5.4	0.2	65367
63876	SENATH	14962	855	45.7	31.6	19.4	2.8	0.5	27795	33566	8	11	625	42.6	38.1	16.0	3.0	0.3	56549
63877	STEELE	17265	2203	42.3	28.8	21.1	5.7	2.1	31325	37286	16	25	1487	41.6	32.2	21.5	4.1	0.6	59577
63879	WARDELL	14151	353	46.7	29.8	19.3	3.7	0.6	27100	32212	7	9	268	58.2	28.4	11.9	1.5	0.0	43714
63901	POPLAR BLUFF	19314	13786	40.9	30.3	20.9	5.0	2.9	31114	37073	15	24	9442	29.8	29.1	29.8	8.8	2.5	77721
63931	BRIAR	11321	253	56.9	29.3	11.5	1.6	0.8	21807	24225	3	1	202	50.0	24.8	21.8	3.5	0.0	50000
63932	BROSELEY	18017	800	41.5	30.3	21.4	4.4	2.5	30836	37133	14	23	640	40.6	35.6	20.2	3.4	0.2	58696
63933	CAMPBELL	16653	1780	42.4	30.1	24.2	2.3	1.1	29873	35388	12	19	1282	48.4	34.9	13.5	2.3	0.9	51307
63934	CLUBB	9738	38	55.3	36.8	7.9	0.0	0.0	21459	25000	2	1	30	53.3	23.3	20.0	3.3	0.0	48333
63935	DONIPHAN	15150	3718	49.1	30.7	15.7	2.7	1.8	25513	29194	5	5	2865	39.5	27.9	24.7	7.0	0.9	63398
63936	DUDLEY	14872	381	43.8	29.1	22.3	4.5	0.3	27955	32836	9	12	301	33.9	26.6	27.2	10.3	2.0	75833
63937	ELLSINORE	17088	745	42.2	29.4	22.4	4.0	2.0	30311	36412	13	20	609	37.1	25.3	30.4	5.9	1.3	69342
63939	FAIRDEALING	15236	288	45.1	33.7	16.3	2.8	2.1	28148	31827	9	12	240	47.5	27.5	13.8	10.8	0.4	54000
63940	FISK	18961	320	42.2	28.1	23.4	2.5	3.8	32058	37950	18	28	252	42.1	32.9	20.2	3.2	1.6	54878
63941	FREMONT	17215	198	41.9	34.3	16.2	4.0	3.5	30000	36219	12	19	161	28.0	25.5	35.4	9.9	1.2	83125
63942	GATEWOOD	18118	148	43.2	30.4	21.0	4.1	1.4	30726	34208	14	22	126	30.2	34.9	25.4	7.9	1.6	68462
63943	GRANDIN	13283	1017	48.9	31.3	14.6	3.8	1.5	25654	29922	5	5	816	42.3	28.7	21.8	6.3	1.0	58750
63944	GREENVILLE	14727	650	50.0	32.2	13.4	1.5	2.9	25000	28963	5	4	515	56.1	19.0	18.5	3.5	2.9	45000
63945	HARVIELL	16158	360	37.8	28.9	28.9	2.8	1.7	34752	42617	26	44	296	19.3	34.1	33.1	10.8	2.7	87297
63950	LODI	11455	21	52.4	33.3	14.3	0.0	0.0	23551	23551	4	3	17	41.2	23.5	29.4	5.9	0.0	65000
63951	LOWNDES	12967	51	39.2	45.1	13.7	2.0	0.0	30423	33745	13	21	43	44.2	30.2	23.3	2.3	0.0	55000
63952	MILL SPRING	12668	354	47.7	35.6	14.1	1.7	0.9	25949	29784	6	6	276	59.8	21.4	12.7	5.4	0.7	38000
63953	NAYLOR	18987	517	47.8	31.9	15.9	2.3	2.1	26141	30422	6	7	404	60.6	26.5	7.4	5.0	0.5	38000
63954	NEELYVILLE	12960	618	47.7	36.3	13.1	2.1	0.8	26022	30275	6	6	451	58.3	27.1	12.6	1.8	0.2	43182
63955	OXLY	12844	276	51.5	33.7	13.4	1.5	0.0	24224	28102	4	4	230	47.8	26.1	20.9	3.5	1.7	52083
63956	PATTERSON	18437	614	43.7	23.6	26.7	1.8	4.2	30635	35665	14	22	499	34.3	21.2	31.9	10.4	2.2	84022
63957	PIEDMONT	14878	1964	51.5	28.3	15.9	3.4	0.9	24101	28025	4	3	1446	42.5	29.4	23.5	3.9	0.6	57660
63960	PUXICO	14913	1196	45.3	31.9	19.1	2.8	0.8	27707	32557	8	11	919	38.6	30.4	24.7	6.0	0.3	63451
63961	QULIN	15120	667	46.6	30.4	19.0	2.9	1.1	26665	31653	7	7	513	45.0	32.0	19.7	3.3	0.0	55667
63963	SHOOK	16481	118	42.4	39.0	15.3	1.7	1.7	29418	33465	11	17	99	49.5	24.2	20.2	3.0	3.0	50500
63964	SILVA	13306	397	52.4	32.8	12.3	1.0	1.5	23440	26992	3	3	305	53.1	21.0	20.7	4.9	0.3	47791
63965	VAN BUREN	18948	1119	45.8	31.6	16.3	3.6	2.8	27912	33453	8	12	852	31.3	31.3	28.8	7.4	1.2	70182
63966	WAPPAPELLO	18087	986	39.1	36.3	19.8	4.4	0.5	32027	36446	18	28	809	47.1	23.2	25.3	4.3	0.0	53219
63967	WILLIAMSVILLE	20666	822	41.0	28.8	24.3	3.2	2.7	30459	35522	13	21	672	40.2	25.7	25.7	8.2	0.2	62500
64001	ALMA	24919	281	22.4	31.0	38.1	3.9	4.6	46496	54173	65	81	225	16.4	33.3	32.9	15.1	2.2	90278
64011	BATES CITY	22546	1336	18.3	23.2	41.9	14.4	2.3	55436	65525	80	91	1175	26.3	9.2	37.6	24.0	2.9	121875
64012	BELTON	23276	10511	18.5	27.5	40.9	9.9	3.1	52835	61016	77	89	8071	16.5	21.1	46.0	13.1	3.3	108868
64014	BLUE SPRINGS	26833	8733	12.2	23.3	44.5	15.4	4.7	62776	75290	87	94	6629	0.8	8.4	68.0	21.9	0.9	124392
64015	BLUE SPRINGS	29058	11038	11.5	24.3	40.3	15.9	8.0	63338	75877	87	95	8659	3.9	6.1	59.7	27.6	2.7	142472
64016	BUCKNER	22181	1630	18.2	30.0	39.4	10.1	2.4	51618	62461	75	88	1311	7.8	33.6	39.9	16.8	2.0	96837
64017	CAMDEN	20897	184	24.5	32.6	35.9	6.5	0.5	45000	51698	61	78	143	23.1	35.0	33.6	7.7	0.7	81154
64018	CAMDEN POINT	27982	311	9.0	25.1	44.4	17.4	4.2	65122	78616	89	96	277	2.5	8.7	53.1	29.6	6.1	149167
64019	CENTERVIEW	20837	764	20.6	30.9	38.0	8.0	2.6	48774	56314	70	84	651	15.1	16.6	44.1	21.0	3.2	127408
64020	CONCORDIA	20729	1381	28.0	32.1	31.6	6.4	2.0	41686	49818	52	72	1005	11.3	33.5	41.4	12.0	1.7	96959
64021	CORDER	18891	244	32.8	32.8	27.9	4.1	2.5	37304	45000	36	57	180	26.1	36.7	26.7	8.9	1.7	72143
64022	DOVER	20072	134	30.6	30.6	32.1	5.2	1.5	39522	48094	44	65	97	24.7	14.4	38.1	18.6	4.1	106875
64024	EXCELSIOR SPRINGS	22411	6403	23.0	28.4	36.2	9.3	3.1	48618	58103	70	84	4789	10.8	21.5	49.6	17.3	0.9	110152
64029	GRAIN VALLEY	26150	3748	11.5	26.0	45.0	14.2	3.3	61814	73816	86	94	3138	6.1	15.5	52.6	24.7	1.2	135315
64030	GRANDVIEW	22653	10116	21.1	33.3	33.1	10.5	2.1	46081	55656	64	80	6344	4.4	39.0	51.0	5.1	0.5	95024
64034	GREENWOOD	30267	2312	8.1	17.4	45.3	22.1	7.1	76049	87810	94	98	2164	2.9	6.3	52.6	31.7	6.6	156575
64035	HARDIN	20614	493	23.5	32.1	38.5	4.7	1.2	46642	55322	65	81	381	20.5	37.8	32.0	9.5	0.3	78500
64036	HENRIETTA	15804	148	28.4	28.4	37.2	5.4	0.7	45403	52133	62	79	106	25.5	47.2	17.0	10.4	0.0	70588
64037	HIGGINSVILLE	21045	2430	28.4	32.8	30.4	5.0	3.5	40799	48348	49	69	1770	16.4	33.8	34.4	13.3	2.2	89720
64040	HOLDEN	19039	2476	25.7	34.3	32.7	5.5	1.9	41901	50334	53	73	1959	19.2	23.7	37.0	18.3	1.8	105096
64048	HOLT	30195	1515	10.0	22.4	44.5	16.2	6.9	65448	78027	89	96	1364	5.6	8.3	40.5	40.1	5.5	166892
64050	INDEPENDENCE	19153	9807	33.4	33.6	27.2	4.4	1.4	36306	43571	33	53	5676	14.7	55.1	27.2	2.8	0.3	76644
64052	INDEPENDENCE	21447	9553	27.1	38.2	28.5	4.8	1.5	38248	45722	40	62	6372	13.3	57.3	26.2	2.9	0.4	76724
64053	INDEPENDENCE	18239	2333	34.6	41.4	19.5	3.0	1.5	33668	40292	23	37	1335	40.5	54.7	4.6	0.3	0.0	54293
64054	INDEPENDENCE	21897	1833	28.6	38.3	26.7	5.0	1.4	38091	45628	40	61	1104	21.4	47.7	27.6	3.3	0.0	72500
64055	INDEPENDENCE	26084	14927	19.1	33.5	34.8	9.5	3.1	47946	57290	68	83	10880	6.6	21.7	61.1	10.2	0.4	107291
64056	INDEPENDENCE	19917	5499	22.1	28.1	39.0	9.3	1.6	49867	59399	72	85	3855	6.2	31.5	56.4	5.5	0.5	99008
64057	INDEPENDENCE	26641	4559	15.5	27.1	37.0	15.5	4.9	60132	70982	84	93	3307	0.5	13.8	57.4	26.9	1.4	134520
64058	INDEPENDENCE	21463	2274	13.5	29.1	43.0	12.9	1.5	56257	67061	81	91	1899	5.6	30.1	51.3	12.3	0.7	106821
64060	KEARNEY	27449	3736	9.7	20.3	46.1	18.2	5.7	69378	81208	91	97	3063	2.5	3.0	53.1	36.8	4.6	161441
64061	KINGSVILLE	23608	1116	17.7	28.4	39.8	10.2	3.9	52805	62525	77	89	997	13.3	14.2	35.3	34.9	2.2	138490
64062	LAWSON	22770	2231	17.2	26.3	41.5	12.1	2.9	56039	65222	81	91	1890	6.9	14.8	49.1	27.4	1.9	130399
64063	LEES SUMMIT	28388	8325	14.0	23.9	41.6	16.2	4.4	61731	75011	86	94	6016	1.0	11.7	63.9	23.0	0.4	130793
64064	LEES SUMMIT	42601	5269	6.5	16.3	31.6	24.0	21.6	91337	110388	97	99	4673	1.7	1.3	28.4	56.1	12.4	214318
64067	LEXINGTON	21659	2322	28.8	31.9	30.2	6.9	2.3	40707	48569	49	69	1681	22.4	33.1	34.0	8.4	2.2	84352
64068	LIBERTY	28359	12707	14.8	25.6	39.1	13.9	6.7	60745	71229	85	93	9653	5.7	8.1	50.6	32.3	3.2	146622
64070	LONE JACK	27796	929	14.1	19.9	43.8	16.2	6.0	66240	79816	89	96	835	5.8	10.4	33.5	43.1	7.2	175893
64071	MAYVIEW	19498	332	16.6	35.2	41.3	5.7	1.2	46579	56560	65	81	274	29.2	22.6	30.7	11.7	5.8	86875
64074	NAPOLEON	24208	259	16.6	28.2	40.9	11.2	3.1	56028	65317	81	91	216	20.8	21.8	34.3	19.9	3.2	107353
64075	OAK GROVE	23010	3637	18.8	25.9	40.4	11.4	3.5	54989	65886	80	90	2859	4.1	17.2	49.7	26.1	2.9	119380
64076	ODESSA	22375	3465	23.6	33.1	31.2	8.5	3.6	44295	51569	59	77	2677	14.3	19.9	43.6	19.7	2.5	113514
64077	ORRICK	21339	730	20.7	31.0	39.2	8.1	1.1	48638	57263	70	84	598	19.9	28.4	39.3	11.9	0.5	92439
64078	PECULIAR	23869	2783	13.9	23.6	46.0	12.3	4.3	59742	67705	84	93	2419	3.3	7.4	53.8	32.9	2.7	151130
64079	PLATTE CITY	26707	3602	15.1	21.7	41.2	16.6	5.6	62233	74519	86	94	2672	2.4	6.6	50.0	33.8	7.2	157955
64080	PLEASANT HILL	29301	4109	14.3	26.6	41.6	11.3	6.3	58583	67012	83	92	3367	6.1	14.8	41.4	33.9	3.8	142777
64081	LEES SUMMIT	34923	8044	16.8	18.0	35.2	18.1	12.0	68574	85162	91	97	5793	1.2	3.5	44.2	43.9	7.2	177361
64082	LEES SUMMIT	35258	2279	3.6	15.0	43.9	23.5	14.0	82190	97474	96	99	2093	0.3	0.9	28.4	61.8	8.6	204849
64083	RAYMORE	26412	5522	12.2	22.9	45.2	15.8	3.9	63179	75029	87	95	4690	2.9	4.5	56.2	35.5	0.9	154508
64084	RAYVILLE	22201	551	18.0	30.0	38.1	11.3	2.7	51473	60633	75	87	483	14.5	14.5	44.9	25.1	1.0	119401
	MISSOURI	23864		27.0	29.4	30.1	9.0	4.5	44017	52626				15.2	22.7	39.0	19.7	3.4	109184
	UNITED STATES	25866		24.7	27.1	30.8	10.9	6.5	48124	56710				10.9	15.0	33.7	30.1	10.4	145905

ZIP CODE		FINANCIAL SERVICES				THE HOME						ENTERTAINMENT						PERSONAL			
						Home Improvements		Furnishings													
#	POST OFFICE NAME	Auto Loan	Home Loan	Invest-ments	Retire-ment Plans	Home Repair	Lawn & Garden	Comput-ers & Hard-ware	Major Appli-ances	TV, Radio, Sound Equip-ment	Furni-ture	Dine out/ Carry out	Sports Equip-ment	Fees & Tickets	Toys & Games	Travel	Cable TV	Apparel & Services	Auto Repairs	Health Insur-ance	Pets & Supplies
63849	GOBLER	74	50	23	43	56	65	48	60	58	49	68	72	41	64	49	62	62	59	74	85
63851	HAYTI	52	40	37	37	42	50	45	48	51	45	62	53	42	57	44	54	58	49	56	58
63852	HOLCOMB	73	49	22	42	55	64	47	59	57	48	67	70	40	63	48	61	61	58	73	84
63855	HORNERSVILLE	67	48	27	45	54	63	50	58	57	48	67	68	43	64	50	61	61	58	70	77
63857	KENNETT	64	52	42	49	55	63	54	58	59	53	71	67	50	70	54	62	67	58	66	72
63862	LILBOURN	71	51	29	46	56	65	52	61	61	51	71	71	46	68	52	64	65	61	73	80
63863	MALDEN	62	48	34	44	52	59	49	55	55	48	65	64	45	63	49	57	61	55	64	70
63866	MARSTON	79	53	24	46	60	69	51	64	61	52	72	76	43	68	52	66	66	63	78	90
63867	MATTHEWS	65	47	28	44	52	60	47	55	54	47	64	65	42	62	47	57	59	55	65	74
63868	MOREHOUSE	72	48	22	42	55	63	47	58	56	47	66	70	40	62	47	60	60	58	72	83
63869	NEW MADRID	65	52	41	48	55	63	54	59	61	54	73	68	51	69	54	63	68	59	68	73
63870	PARMA	72	49	23	43	55	64	48	59	57	48	67	70	41	64	48	62	61	58	73	83
63873	PORTAGEVILLE	73	54	33	48	59	68	53	63	62	54	73	73	48	70	54	66	68	62	75	84
63876	SENATH	61	43	24	40	48	57	45	52	52	44	61	61	39	58	45	56	56	52	64	68
63877	STEELE	75	54	34	49	59	68	55	63	63	55	75	75	49	72	55	67	70	64	75	85
63879	WARDELL	67	45	20	39	51	58	43	54	52	44	61	64	37	58	44	56	56	53	66	77
63901	POPLAR BLUFF	72	59	48	57	63	71	62	66	67	60	81	77	58	80	62	70	76	66	75	81
63931	BRIAR	55	37	17	32	41	48	35	44	43	36	50	53	30	47	36	46	46	44	54	63
63932	BROSELEY	82	56	26	48	63	72	54	67	65	55	76	80	46	72	55	70	69	66	82	94
63933	CAMPBELL	70	50	27	45	56	64	50	60	58	50	69	70	44	66	50	62	63	59	72	80
63934	CLUBB	47	32	17	29	36	42	33	39	39	33	45	46	28	43	33	41	41	39	48	53
63935	DONIPHAN	66	46	24	41	51	60	47	55	55	46	64	65	40	61	47	58	58	55	68	74
63936	DUDLEY	72	49	23	42	55	63	47	58	56	48	66	70	40	63	48	61	60	58	72	83
63937	ELLSINORE	75	53	28	47	59	67	51	62	60	52	71	74	45	68	52	64	65	61	75	86
63939	FAIRDEALING	68	45	21	39	51	59	44	55	53	45	62	65	37	59	45	57	56	54	67	78
63940	FISK	82	55	25	47	62	72	53	66	64	54	75	79	45	71	54	69	68	66	82	94
63941	FREMONT	75	53	29	50	61	70	54	65	63	53	74	76	47	71	55	66	67	64	78	87
63942	GATEWOOD	87	59	27	50	66	76	56	71	68	58	80	84	48	76	57	73	73	70	87	100
63943	GRANDIN	68	45	20	39	51	59	44	55	53	44	62	65	37	58	44	57	56	54	67	78
63944	GREENVILLE	63	44	23	40	50	58	45	53	52	44	62	63	39	58	45	56	56	53	65	72
63945	HARVIELL	68	59	44	56	62	68	56	62	60	56	73	73	54	73	57	61	69	61	68	79
63950	LODI	56	38	17	33	43	49	36	46	44	37	52	55	31	49	37	47	47	45	56	65
63951	LOWNDES	63	42	19	36	48	55	41	51	49	41	57	61	34	54	41	53	52	50	62	72
63952	MILL SPRING	60	41	20	36	46	53	40	49	47	40	56	58	34	53	40	51	51	49	60	69
63953	NAYLOR	88	59	27	51	67	77	57	71	68	58	80	85	48	76	58	74	73	70	87	101
63954	NEELYVILLE	60	40	19	35	45	52	39	48	47	40	55	58	33	52	40	50	50	48	59	68
63955	OXLY	56	38	17	33	43	49	36	46	44	37	52	54	31	49	37	47	47	45	56	65
63956	PATTERSON	82	56	27	49	63	73	55	67	66	55	77	80	47	73	56	71	70	67	83	94
63957	PIEDMONT	59	42	24	38	47	55	44	51	50	43	59	59	38	56	44	54	54	50	62	66
63960	PUXICO	64	45	24	40	50	58	45	54	53	45	63	63	39	59	46	57	57	54	66	72
63961	QULIN	68	45	21	39	51	59	44	55	53	45	62	65	37	59	45	57	56	54	67	78
63963	SHOOK	70	48	23	42	54	62	46	58	55	47	65	69	40	62	47	60	59	57	71	81
63964	SILVA	54	38	22	35	43	50	40	47	46	39	54	54	35	51	40	49	50	46	57	61
63965	VAN BUREN	73	53	31	50	59	69	56	64	63	54	74	74	49	71	56	67	68	64	77	82
63966	WAPPAPELLO	66	52	35	46	58	65	49	59	55	48	65	69	43	64	52	59	61	58	70	80
63967	WILLIAMSVILLE	85	64	39	57	72	81	61	73	70	61	83	87	54	81	63	74	77	72	87	101
64001	ALMA	110	77	40	73	90	100	76	94	88	75	103	113	65	101	79	92	94	93	112	131
64011	BATES CITY	95	92	77	89	94	98	85	91	86	86	106	107	84	107	86	86	102	89	92	111
64012	BELTON	89	91	87	91	90	94	88	89	86	88	107	104	88	107	87	84	104	89	86	101
64014	BLUE SPRINGS	101	113	117	116	109	109	108	106	101	109	128	126	110	130	106	96	126	105	94	116
64015	BLUE SPRINGS	107	123	127	124	120	121	114	113	107	114	134	132	118	138	114	103	133	111	102	125
64016	BUCKNER	87	86	78	84	88	93	82	86	83	81	103	100	82	106	83	84	99	84	87	101
64017	CAMDEN	86	76	57	72	80	86	70	78	75	70	91	93	69	93	72	77	86	76	85	101
64018	CAMDEN POINT	99	119	124	119	117	117	107	107	100	107	126	126	113	133	109	98	125	104	98	119
64019	CENTERVIEW	90	82	66	79	86	92	76	83	79	76	97	99	75	99	78	81	93	81	88	106
64020	CONCORDIA	85	70	51	68	74	85	72	78	78	70	93	90	67	91	72	80	87	77	88	95
64021	CORDER	76	56	36	54	62	74	61	69	69	58	81	78	54	77	61	72	74	68	82	85
64022	DOVER	82	64	44	63	70	79	65	74	71	64	85	86	60	84	66	73	79	72	83	93
64024	EXCELSIOR SPRINGS	89	81	68	80	84	92	80	85	83	79	101	98	78	102	80	84	96	83	90	101
64029	GRAIN VALLEY	99	114	113	117	109	106	103	102	95	106	120	120	107	122	102	89	119	100	88	112
64030	GRANDVIEW	75	79	87	81	77	80	81	78	78	80	98	93	81	99	79	74	96	80	72	86
64034	GREENWOOD	119	138	137	142	133	129	124	123	114	128	145	144	129	148	123	108	143	120	106	135
64035	HARDIN	74	71	65	67	74	82	70	73	74	68	91	84	70	96	72	77	86	72	81	87
64036	HENRIETTA	91	61	28	53	69	80	59	74	71	60	83	88	50	79	60	77	76	73	91	105
64037	HIGGINSVILLE	82	70	56	68	74	83	72	77	77	70	93	89	68	93	72	79	87	76	85	93
64040	HOLDEN	80	70	54	68	74	81	68	74	72	67	87	86	66	88	68	73	82	72	80	92
64048	HOLT	118	130	126	128	131	133	117	121	114	117	141	143	122	149	120	113	139	117	116	142
64050	INDEPENDENCE	59	60	67	60	61	66	64	62	64	62	80	72	64	82	64	64	78	63	63	68
64052	INDEPENDENCE	61	65	70	63	65	70	66	65	66	64	82	74	67	85	66	66	80	65	66	71
64053	INDEPENDENCE	54	57	61	55	57	63	58	57	60	56	74	65	60	78	59	61	72	57	60	63
64054	INDEPENDENCE	62	67	75	67	67	71	69	67	68	67	85	78	70	89	69	67	83	67	66	73
64055	INDEPENDENCE	80	84	89	83	83	90	83	83	83	82	104	96	85	105	84	83	101	83	83	93
64056	INDEPENDENCE	74	79	88	78	77	81	78	77	77	78	97	89	80	99	78	77	96	77	74	85
64057	INDEPENDENCE	93	104	113	106	102	105	100	99	95	100	119	115	102	120	100	92	117	98	92	108
64058	INDEPENDENCE	89	94	91	95	92	93	89	90	85	90	107	107	89	108	88	82	105	89	82	102
64060	KEARNEY	108	124	126	128	120	118	115	113	106	117	135	133	119	138	113	101	133	111	99	124
64061	KINGSVILLE	100	89	68	85	94	101	82	91	87	82	106	108	81	108	85	89	101	89	98	117
64062	LAWSON	101	92	73	88	97	103	85	93	89	85	109	111	84	112	88	91	104	91	100	119
64063	LEES SUMMIT	100	111	116	115	108	108	108	105	101	108	128	124	110	130	106	96	126	104	93	114
64064	LEES SUMMIT	153	181	189	184	177	178	163	163	152	165	192	188	173	197	165	147	190	157	147	180
64067	LEXINGTON	85	67	49	65	73	84	71	78	78	68	93	90	65	91	71	81	86	78	90	97
64068	LIBERTY	102	113	120	116	111	112	109	107	103	109	130	126	112	133	108	99	128	106	98	118
64070	LONE JACK	101	120	124	120	119	119	108	109	101	107	127	128	114	135	110	99	126	105	100	123
64071	MAYVIEW	85	75	56	71	79	85	69	77	74	69	90	92	67	91	71	76	85	75	84	100
64074	NAPOLEON	103	92	70	88	96	103	86	94	90	86	110	111	83	110	87	91	105	92	100	119
64075	OAK GROVE	92	95	89	95	95	98	90	92	88	90	110	108	91	112	90	86	107	91	89	106
64076	ODESSA	94	81	60	78	85	94	79	86	84	78	102	101	76	102	80	87	96	85	95	108
64077	ORRICK	90	80	61	76	85	91	74	82	79	74	96	98	73	98	76	81	91	80	89	106
64078	PECULIAR	93	108	110	108	105	105	99	99	93	99	117	116	102	121	99	89	115	97	89	110
64079	PLATTE CITY	100	109	110	111	107	108	104	103	99	104	124	121	105	125	102	95	122	102	94	115
64080	PLEASANT HILL	112	118	115	119	118	120	112	114	109	112	136	134	114	139	112	106	133	112	108	130
64081	LEES SUMMIT	127	142	147	142	139	144	129	132	124	134	156	147	135	154	132	122	153	128	125	144
64082	LEES SUMMIT	139	167	171	170	162	159	149	149	138	151	174	174	157	182	150	132	173	144	131	164
64083	RAYMORE	99	113	117	116	110	109	104	104	97	106	123	121	108	124	104	92	121	101	92	114
64084	RAYVILLE	96	85	65	81	90	96	79	87	83	79	101	104	77	104	81	86	96	85	94	112
	MISSOURI	87	82	79	80	83	90	82	85	85	82	104	99	81	103	82	85	100	85	87	100
	UNITED STATES	100	100	100	100	100	100	100	100	100	100	100	100	100	100	100	100	100	100	100	100

POPULATION CHANGE

#	POST OFFICE NAME	COUNTY FIPS CODE	POPULATION			2000-2004 ANNUAL RATE		HOUSEHOLDS					FAMILIES		
			2000	2004	2009	% Rate	State Centile	2000	2004	2009	% Annual Rate 2000-2004	2004 Average HH Size	2000	2004	% Annual Rate 2000-2004
64085	RICHMOND	177	8786	9041	9517	0.7	58	3491	3627	3855	0.9	2.44	2368	2398	0.3
64086	LEES SUMMIT	095	19950	22725	24588	3.1	93	7242	8336	9088	3.4	2.72	5615	6306	2.8
64088	SIBLEY	095	1341	1413	1466	1.2	74	475	507	531	1.6	2.79	388	407	1.1
64089	SMITHVILLE	047	8225	9343	10143	3.0	93	3003	3443	3766	3.3	2.68	2332	2632	2.9
64093	WARRENSBURG	101	24361	24816	25520	0.4	50	8952	9174	9500	0.6	2.41	5275	5246	-0.1
64096	WAVERLY	107	1133	1143	1166	0.2	41	426	432	444	0.3	2.47	297	296	-0.1
64097	WELLINGTON	107	1326	1353	1387	0.5	52	530	546	563	0.7	2.44	366	369	0.2
64098	WESTON	165	2943	2989	3149	0.4	48	1157	1190	1268	0.7	2.50	846	854	0.2
64101	KANSAS CITY	095	335	366	387	2.1	87	14	20	24	8.8	5.30	2	2	0.0
64105	KANSAS CITY	095	2417	2582	2699	1.6	80	1760	1914	2026	2.0	1.26	235	234	-0.1
64106	KANSAS CITY	095	6573	6642	6806	0.3	42	2520	2568	2663	0.4	2.12	1042	1004	-0.9
64108	KANSAS CITY	095	6712	7093	7429	1.3	75	2634	2822	2995	1.6	2.28	1343	1388	0.8
64109	KANSAS CITY	095	12159	11661	11728	-1.0	6	5129	4927	4980	-0.9	2.22	2347	2137	-2.2
64110	KANSAS CITY	095	17240	16738	16877	-0.7	11	6970	6827	6949	-0.5	2.28	3564	3347	-1.5
64111	KANSAS CITY	095	17734	17348	17579	-0.5	16	10301	10142	10340	-0.4	1.65	2665	2452	-1.9
64112	KANSAS CITY	095	8527	8609	8848	0.2	42	5531	5656	5863	0.5	1.51	1334	1262	-1.3
64113	KANSAS CITY	095	11473	11305	11453	-0.4	20	4832	4828	4938	0.0	2.34	3206	3094	-0.8
64114	KANSAS CITY	095	23267	23219	23644	-0.1	30	11825	11982	12325	0.3	1.90	5668	5463	-0.9
64116	KANSAS CITY	047	16434	16520	16923	0.1	37	7797	7888	8126	0.3	2.09	4049	3940	-0.6
64117	KANSAS CITY	047	13571	13658	14086	0.2	39	5644	5768	6015	0.5	2.37	3662	3625	-0.2
64118	KANSAS CITY	047	38432	39143	40438	0.4	50	16484	16956	17657	0.7	2.30	10546	10506	-0.1
64119	KANSAS CITY	047	25613	25719	26428	0.1	36	10120	10293	10683	0.4	2.47	7147	7078	-0.2
64120	KANSAS CITY	095	527	495	496	-1.5	2	234	223	225	-1.1	2.22	124	113	-2.2
64123	KANSAS CITY	095	10826	10669	10817	-0.3	21	3902	3803	3845	-0.6	2.74	2475	2325	-1.5
64124	KANSAS CITY	095	13080	13355	13727	0.5	53	4635	4687	4809	0.3	2.82	2870	2798	-0.6
64125	KANSAS CITY	095	2317	2259	2278	-0.6	14	825	802	810	-0.7	2.80	533	500	-1.5
64126	KANSAS CITY	095	6860	6855	7011	0.0	31	2440	2442	2507	0.0	2.80	1604	1554	-0.7
64127	KANSAS CITY	095	21052	20716	21018	-0.4	20	7818	7696	7838	-0.4	2.63	4782	4532	-1.3
64128	KANSAS CITY	095	14865	14547	14738	-0.5	17	5742	5681	5805	-0.3	2.55	3609	3442	-1.1
64129	KANSAS CITY	095	10246	9855	9930	-0.9	7	4272	4162	4234	-0.6	2.33	2633	2469	-1.5
64130	KANSAS CITY	095	26896	26254	26547	-0.6	14	10327	10222	10436	-0.2	2.54	6788	6485	-1.1
64131	KANSAS CITY	095	23701	23766	24303	0.1	34	10374	10465	10771	0.2	2.21	5838	5668	-0.7
64132	KANSAS CITY	095	16099	15900	16126	-0.3	23	6375	6371	6514	0.0	2.48	4032	3875	-0.9
64133	KANSAS CITY	095	32524	32791	33504	0.2	40	13771	14024	14441	0.4	2.31	8778	8628	-0.4
64134	KANSAS CITY	095	22909	23343	24053	0.4	50	8468	8739	9090	0.7	2.66	6060	6067	0.0
64136	KANSAS CITY	095	1183	1378	1508	3.7	96	444	535	597	4.5	2.28	319	374	3.8
64137	KANSAS CITY	095	10589	10476	10630	-0.3	24	4376	4394	4502	0.1	2.32	2699	2604	-0.8
64138	KANSAS CITY	095	25976	26630	27458	0.6	55	10714	11116	11568	0.9	2.36	7036	7051	0.1
64139	KANSAS CITY	095	987	1130	1225	3.2	94	256	300	330	3.8	3.41	182	207	3.1
64145	KANSAS CITY	095	4532	4923	5220	2.0	85	1910	2121	2280	2.5	2.27	1286	1385	1.8
64146	KANSAS CITY	095	1328	1430	1501	1.8	83	655	720	765	2.3	1.83	382	400	1.1
64147	KANSAS CITY	095	743	741	761	-0.1	29	266	271	284	0.4	2.73	232	234	0.2
64149	KANSAS CITY	095	377	469	542	5.3	99	136	175	204	6.1	2.68	119	152	5.9
64150	RIVERSIDE	165	3109	3090	3233	-0.1	27	1282	1283	1358	0.0	2.25	753	731	-0.7
64151	KANSAS CITY	165	22870	23669	25239	0.8	63	9686	10160	10957	1.1	2.33	6358	6502	0.5
64152	KANSAS CITY	165	22757	24165	25989	1.4	77	8418	9029	9808	1.7	2.65	6246	6596	1.3
64153	KANSAS CITY	165	3579	4218	4769	3.9	97	1448	1723	1966	4.2	2.45	954	1106	3.5
64154	KANSAS CITY	165	4628	5459	6166	4.0	97	2056	2458	2806	4.3	2.14	1147	1328	3.5
64155	KANSAS CITY	047	16823	17801	18797	1.3	76	6094	6514	6935	1.6	2.70	4716	4943	1.1
64156	KANSAS CITY	047	1045	1197	1303	3.3	94	406	471	518	3.6	2.54	292	333	3.1
64157	KANSAS CITY	047	3170	4458	5417	8.4	100	1034	1455	1770	8.4	3.06	886	1224	7.9
64158	KANSAS CITY	047	2433	3074	3503	5.7	99	799	999	1136	5.4	3.08	666	821	5.1
64161	KANSAS CITY	047	427	386	384	-2.4	0	174	160	161	-2.0	2.41	121	108	-2.6
64163	KANSAS CITY	165	635	648	680	0.5	52	325	335	355	0.7	1.93	155	153	-0.3
64164	KANSAS CITY	165	345	365	391	1.3	75	127	136	147	1.6	2.68	87	92	1.3
64165	KANSAS CITY	047	56	64	70	3.2	94	24	28	31	3.7	2.29	21	24	3.2
64166	KANSAS CITY	047	255	293	318	3.3	95	88	102	112	3.5	2.87	77	89	3.5
64167	KANSAS CITY	047	396	441	471	2.6	90	128	144	156	2.8	3.06	111	123	2.4
64401	AGENCY	021	1603	1783	1882	2.5	89	584	656	698	2.8	2.72	472	523	2.4
64402	ALBANY	075	2589	2495	2391	-0.9	8	1115	1076	1031	-0.8	2.24	710	668	-1.4
64421	AMAZONIA	003	1079	1131	1174	1.1	71	428	452	472	1.3	2.50	309	320	0.8
64422	AMITY	063	511	554	581	1.9	84	196	215	227	2.2	2.58	150	161	1.7
64423	BARNARD	147	600	585	588	-0.6	14	238	235	239	-0.3	2.23	179	174	-0.7
64424	BETHANY	081	4280	4118	4067	-0.9	7	1792	1717	1692	-1.0	2.29	1162	1085	-1.6
64426	BLYTHEDALE	081	489	489	488	0.0	32	198	198	198	0.0	2.47	135	132	-0.5
64427	BOLCKOW	003	636	636	645	0.0	32	235	237	242	0.2	2.68	180	178	-0.3
64428	BURLINGTON JUNCTION	147	908	886	892	-0.6	14	376	371	377	-0.3	2.38	262	254	-0.7
64429	CAMERON	049	10359	10661	11005	0.7	58	3019	3142	3290	0.9	2.47	2039	2084	0.5
64430	CLARKSDALE	063	707	768	805	2.0	85	285	313	331	2.2	2.45	219	236	1.8
64431	CLEARMONT	147	445	421	421	-1.3	3	204	196	199	-0.9	2.15	141	132	-1.5
64432	CLYDE	147	211	206	207	-0.6	15	61	60	61	-0.4	3.07	46	44	-1.0
64433	CONCEPTION	147	274	267	268	-0.6	14	48	47	48	-0.5	5.09	36	35	-0.7
64434	CONCEPTION JUNCTION	147	303	296	297	-0.6	15	113	111	114	-0.4	2.37	85	82	-0.8
64436	COSBY	003	858	862	876	0.1	37	332	336	344	0.3	2.55	257	256	-0.1
64437	CRAIG	087	961	910	883	-1.3	3	401	384	375	-1.0	2.37	281	263	-1.6
64438	DARLINGTON	075	235	227	217	-0.8	9	70	67	64	-1.0	3.27	53	50	-1.4
64439	DEARBORN	165	1951	1981	2036	0.4	47	768	791	823	0.7	2.50	559	560	0.0
64440	DE KALB	021	681	655	645	-0.9	7	251	243	241	-0.8	2.68	193	183	-1.2
64441	DENVER	227	174	176	179	0.3	43	76	77	78	0.3	2.29	57	57	0.0
64442	EAGLEVILLE	081	652	658	660	0.2	41	282	285	286	0.3	2.31	202	200	-0.2
64443	EASTON	021	1494	1465	1457	-0.5	19	577	573	576	-0.2	2.56	441	431	-0.5
64444	EDGERTON	165	1232	1333	1441	1.9	84	479	526	575	2.2	2.53	381	409	1.7
64445	ELMO	147	450	437	439	-0.7	11	183	179	182	-0.5	2.43	124	119	-1.0
64446	FAIRFAX	005	1177	1145	1123	-0.7	13	523	514	509	-0.4	2.22	352	339	-0.9
64448	FAUCETT	021	779	802	809	0.7	59	303	316	321	1.0	2.54	233	238	0.5
64449	FILLMORE	003	460	459	467	-0.1	30	190	191	196	0.1	2.40	135	134	-0.2
64451	FOREST CITY	087	415	400	391	-0.9	8	168	163	160	-0.7	2.45	115	109	-1.3
64453	GENTRY	075	241	232	222	-0.9	8	88	85	81	-0.8	2.71	67	64	-1.1
64454	GOWER	049	2268	2340	2433	0.7	60	827	863	906	1.0	2.62	621	637	0.6
64455	GRAHAM	147	492	505	516	0.6	56	207	216	224	1.0	2.34	151	155	0.6
64456	GRANT CITY	227	1370	1369	1379	0.0	31	577	575	578	-0.1	2.30	370	360	-0.6
64457	GUILFORD	147	372	363	365	-0.6	14	130	128	131	-0.4	2.55	98	95	-0.7
64458	HATFIELD	081	207	205	204	-0.2	25	72	71	71	-0.3	2.89	59	58	-0.4
64459	HELENA	003	595	610	626	0.6	55	233	241	249	0.8	2.37	178	181	0.4
64461	HOPKINS	147	806	929	1012	3.4	95	328	383	423	3.7	2.43	223	256	3.3
	MISSOURI					0.8					0.9	2.46			0.4
	UNITED STATES					1.2					1.3	2.58			1.1

ZIP CODE #	POST OFFICE NAME	RACE (%) White 2000	White 2004	Black 2000	Black 2004	Asian/Pacific 2000	Asian/Pacific 2004	% Hispanic Origin 2000	% Hispanic Origin 2004	2004 AGE DISTRIBUTION (%) 0-4	5-9	10-14	15-19	20-24	25-44	45-64	65-84	85+	18+	MEDIAN AGE 2004	% 2004 Males	% 2004 Females
64085	RICHMOND	94.9	94.4	3.0	3.3	0.1	0.2	1.1	1.2	7.0	6.7	7.3	7.0	6.7	25.7	23.7	13.1	2.7	74.7	37.7	48.5	51.5
64086	LEES SUMMIT	93.8	92.3	2.7	3.6	0.9	1.2	2.3	2.8	7.8	7.8	8.3	7.2	6.3	32.4	24.1	5.6	0.5	71.6	34.2	49.6	50.4
64088	SIBLEY	96.6	96.2	0.5	0.6	0.2	0.2	1.7	2.1	6.2	6.7	7.9	7.5	6.0	25.3	28.7	11.0	0.9	74.8	38.8	51.2	48.8
64089	SMITHVILLE	96.8	96.4	0.2	0.3	0.5	0.7	1.7	1.9	7.7	7.5	7.5	6.8	5.7	29.7	24.6	9.2	1.2	72.9	36.6	48.9	51.1
64093	WARRENSBURG	89.3	87.9	5.1	5.6	2.2	2.9	2.2	2.5	5.7	5.2	5.9	12.6	17.4	25.6	17.9	8.2	1.5	79.5	26.8	48.8	51.2
64096	WAVERLY	97.5	97.4	0.6	0.7	0.2	0.2	1.2	1.3	5.2	6.1	7.2	9.5	4.7	22.7	27.0	15.1	2.7	74.2	40.9	50.5	49.5
64097	WELLINGTON	97.7	97.6	0.8	0.8	0.2	0.2	1.3	1.3	6.5	6.7	6.7	5.3	5.3	26.9	27.5	12.7	2.3	76.4	40.4	50.8	49.2
64098	WESTON	97.7	97.6	0.1	0.1	0.2	0.3	0.8	0.9	5.3	5.8	7.8	6.3	6.1	24.1	32.1	10.9	1.8	77.0	41.7	48.8	51.2
64101	KANSAS CITY	64.2	57.7	33.7	40.2	0.6	0.6	0.9	1.1	0.3	0.3	0.0	0.0	12.3	72.4	14.5	0.3	0.0	99.5	33.7	82.0	18.0
64105	KANSAS CITY	71.6	66.8	17.7	21.2	1.9	2.4	8.5	9.5	2.1	1.0	0.7	1.4	14.2	50.2	18.9	9.9	1.7	95.8	34.0	57.9	42.1
64106	KANSAS CITY	33.7	30.7	48.0	49.9	9.7	10.8	7.5	7.8	7.4	6.5	5.7	5.8	10.3	36.2	18.7	7.7	1.8	77.5	31.6	56.9	43.1
64108	KANSAS CITY	44.0	40.6	32.0	34.5	1.2	1.5	39.4	40.5	7.9	6.9	7.1	7.3	9.4	31.9	20.4	7.9	1.2	73.5	31.3	52.5	47.5
64109	KANSAS CITY	24.6	21.8	70.2	72.9	0.7	0.7	4.7	4.9	6.7	5.8	7.1	8.0	8.5	30.3	23.2	9.1	1.3	75.6	35.4	50.0	50.0
64110	KANSAS CITY	40.2	36.6	53.8	56.9	1.6	2.0	3.4	3.6	6.6	6.5	7.0	8.6	11.1	30.8	22.1	6.7	0.7	76.1	31.2	47.4	52.6
64111	KANSAS CITY	73.2	69.3	14.0	16.4	1.7	2.1	15.8	17.5	3.9	3.1	2.9	4.1	11.9	42.5	21.1	8.6	1.9	88.3	34.0	53.7	46.3
64112	KANSAS CITY	86.8	84.2	3.9	4.9	5.9	7.1	3.7	4.3	2.5	2.1	2.1	3.7	12.5	41.1	22.3	11.3	2.5	92.1	34.7	50.3	49.7
64113	KANSAS CITY	95.8	94.7	1.6	2.1	1.0	1.3	1.8	2.1	7.2	7.6	6.3	4.8	3.0	28.9	30.0	10.3	1.8	75.8	41.0	48.7	51.3
64114	KANSAS CITY	88.1	85.4	6.6	8.2	2.2	2.8	3.5	4.1	4.8	4.7	4.2	4.0	4.6	30.1	24.6	17.7	5.3	83.9	43.4	45.7	54.3
64116	KANSAS CITY	86.4	84.5	4.0	4.3	4.2	5.2	6.0	6.7	6.2	5.7	5.5	5.4	8.0	31.5	24.5	11.5	1.7	79.4	36.7	48.3	51.7
64117	KANSAS CITY	88.2	87.2	4.9	5.1	2.1	2.7	5.3	5.9	8.0	7.1	7.0	5.8	7.4	31.2	21.6	10.9	1.1	74.5	34.4	47.2	52.8
64118	KANSAS CITY	90.7	89.4	3.3	3.7	1.8	2.3	4.4	4.9	6.7	6.2	6.2	5.8	7.4	31.0	24.0	11.4	1.2	77.4	36.1	49.0	51.1
64119	KANSAS CITY	93.6	92.7	1.9	2.1	1.4	1.8	3.8	4.3	6.6	6.6	6.7	6.1	6.1	29.2	25.9	11.2	1.5	76.2	37.8	48.1	51.9
64120	KANSAS CITY	80.1	76.8	6.1	7.1	3.8	4.9	11.8	13.3	8.5	6.7	5.5	5.5	7.7	26.5	24.4	12.9	2.4	77.0	37.2	53.1	46.9
64123	KANSAS CITY	65.9	61.3	8.0	9.4	5.5	6.7	30.3	33.3	8.3	7.7	7.9	6.9	7.1	29.7	21.2	9.5	1.7	72.0	33.2	50.5	49.5
64124	KANSAS CITY	49.0	44.0	18.4	21.3	7.2	8.3	30.0	31.6	9.3	8.4	7.8	7.5	8.2	30.9	19.8	7.2	0.9	70.2	30.5	51.6	48.4
64125	KANSAS CITY	79.3	76.1	5.9	7.1	1.7	2.1	17.7	19.8	9.3	8.2	8.1	7.4	7.8	30.1	19.3	8.5	1.2	70.0	31.1	51.0	49.0
64126	KANSAS CITY	53.5	49.7	25.3	26.7	3.9	4.9	22.4	24.4	10.0	10.2	9.4	7.6	7.0	28.4	18.3	8.2	0.9	65.7	29.2	48.9	51.2
64127	KANSAS CITY	24.8	21.7	60.9	63.5	1.4	1.6	15.6	16.1	8.6	8.3	9.1	8.3	7.5	26.8	20.4	9.6	1.4	68.9	31.3	46.9	53.1
64128	KANSAS CITY	6.0	5.0	90.1	91.2	0.3	0.4	2.9	3.0	7.4	7.6	8.5	8.1	7.3	24.8	21.2	13.1	2.0	71.4	34.8	45.6	54.4
64129	KANSAS CITY	60.0	54.8	34.4	39.2	0.6	0.7	4.5	4.9	7.2	6.7	6.9	7.0	9.0	30.1	23.1	9.1	0.9	75.1	33.7	49.4	50.7
64130	KANSAS CITY	3.4	2.7	94.1	95.0	0.2	0.2	1.2	1.2	7.1	7.4	8.9	8.1	6.6	25.0	21.8	13.7	1.5	71.6	35.4	44.9	55.2
64131	KANSAS CITY	53.4	49.3	40.9	44.6	1.8	2.1	3.1	3.4	7.1	6.4	6.1	6.0	7.8	30.1	23.3	11.2	2.1	77.1	36.0	45.8	54.2
64132	KANSAS CITY	17.1	14.9	79.1	81.3	0.5	0.6	1.7	1.8	8.7	8.1	8.9	8.6	8.8	27.6	20.6	7.9	0.8	69.0	29.6	44.8	55.2
64133	KANSAS CITY	82.2	78.5	13.4	16.6	1.0	1.3	2.7	3.1	6.1	5.8	6.0	6.1	6.4	26.4	25.2	15.5	2.6	78.5	40.6	47.6	52.5
64134	KANSAS CITY	47.7	41.6	46.8	52.5	0.9	1.1	3.0	3.1	7.7	7.4	8.5	8.1	7.4	29.0	21.9	9.2	0.7	71.4	32.9	48.1	51.9
64136	KANSAS CITY	92.1	90.1	4.3	5.5	0.7	0.9	2.8	3.4	7.2	7.0	6.0	6.5	5.2	28.1	24.3	11.8	3.9	75.5	39.5	47.8	52.3
64137	KANSAS CITY	67.9	62.2	27.1	32.3	1.3	1.6	3.4	3.8	6.6	6.3	6.4	6.1	8.4	31.0	21.8	12.0	1.4	77.2	34.6	48.2	51.8
64138	KANSAS CITY	68.2	63.1	27.0	31.7	1.2	1.5	2.9	3.2	6.2	5.9	6.7	6.4	7.3	27.5	24.7	13.5	1.7	77.3	38.4	47.1	52.9
64139	KANSAS CITY	87.1	84.9	9.0	10.5	0.7	1.0	2.8	3.3	7.0	6.7	5.8	6.3	5.8	28.5	24.7	11.8	3.5	76.3	39.1	48.0	52.0
64145	KANSAS CITY	87.8	85.3	8.3	10.0	1.5	2.0	3.2	3.7	4.6	4.7	5.1	5.4	4.8	18.4	31.5	21.4	4.1	82.2	50.0	46.8	53.2
64146	KANSAS CITY	84.2	81.1	11.5	13.9	1.1	1.4	3.7	4.3	5.9	5.7	5.6	6.0	5.9	26.6	24.3	15.6	4.3	79.3	40.8	47.1	52.9
64147	KANSAS CITY	30.4	26.9	65.8	69.2	0.4	0.5	3.1	3.2	26.9	15.3	8.0	4.9	15.4	20.2	6.5	2.7	0.3	47.2	15.0	42.5	57.5
64149	KANSAS CITY	94.2	92.1	2.4	4.3	0.8	1.1	1.9	2.4	7.3	8.1	9.0	8.1	4.3	26.7	29.0	7.7	0.0	70.2	37.5	48.4	51.6
64150	RIVERSIDE	84.6	83.1	6.1	6.4	2.5	3.1	7.1	7.8	7.6	6.3	5.6	6.4	8.8	30.3	22.7	10.0	2.5	77.1	34.7	50.5	49.6
64151	KANSAS CITY	90.8	89.7	4.2	4.5	1.9	2.5	2.9	3.3	6.6	6.3	6.6	6.0	6.8	30.9	27.2	8.6	1.0	76.7	37.1	49.0	51.0
64152	KANSAS CITY	91.5	90.5	3.4	3.8	2.0	2.5	3.3	3.7	7.0	7.2	7.5	7.0	6.7	29.2	27.5	7.3	0.6	74.1	36.1	49.6	50.5
64153	KANSAS CITY	89.9	88.6	3.1	3.4	2.3	2.9	3.9	4.5	8.0	7.5	7.2	6.0	6.8	40.6	19.7	3.9	0.4	73.7	32.3	49.4	50.6
64154	KANSAS CITY	86.0	84.5	7.4	7.9	2.4	3.1	3.1	3.5	7.0	5.9	5.3	5.7	7.4	35.5	20.6	9.3	3.4	78.6	34.3	47.4	52.6
64155	KANSAS CITY	93.3	92.3	2.5	2.8	1.4	1.8	3.9	4.4	8.4	8.0	7.5	6.3	6.2	34.2	23.1	5.5	0.8	72.1	33.9	49.2	50.8
64156	KANSAS CITY	94.8	94.2	1.3	1.4	0.4	0.6	2.8	3.3	8.0	6.9	7.4	7.1	6.5	31.0	24.3	8.2	0.6	73.3	35.5	50.0	50.0
64157	KANSAS CITY	95.6	94.8	1.8	2.0	0.5	0.6	2.5	2.8	11.0	9.9	8.9	6.8	5.8	34.6	19.6	3.3	0.2	66.0	31.1	49.2	50.8
64158	KANSAS CITY	91.1	89.9	4.3	4.7	1.9	2.5	3.9	4.3	12.4	11.1	8.4	5.6	4.4	42.0	14.5	1.5	0.0	64.5	30.8	48.9	51.1
64161	KANSAS CITY	96.5	95.9	0.7	0.8	0.2	0.3	0.7	0.8	5.2	5.7	8.6	7.0	6.7	28.8	29.5	7.5	1.0	76.2	36.7	54.2	45.9
64163	KANSAS CITY	90.1	89.5	2.8	3.1	0.8	0.9	3.3	3.7	6.6	6.8	8.0	6.0	4.9	34.3	25.9	7.1	0.3	74.9	36.0	54.3	45.7
64164	KANSAS CITY	92.5	92.1	1.7	1.6	0.6	0.8	2.9	3.0	6.0	7.1	8.5	7.4	4.4	30.4	28.8	6.9	0.6	73.4	37.6	53.2	46.9
64165	KANSAS CITY	98.2	98.4	0.0	0.0	0.0	0.0	0.0	1.6	6.3	6.3	9.4	7.8	3.1	28.1	32.8	6.3	0.0	71.9	39.2	48.4	51.6
64166	KANSAS CITY	97.7	97.3	0.0	0.3	0.4	0.3	1.6	1.4	5.8	6.8	8.2	8.2	3.8	29.7	30.4	7.2	0.0	73.7	38.9	50.9	49.2
64167	KANSAS CITY	96.5	95.9	1.5	1.8	0.5	0.7	2.3	2.7	8.8	8.4	8.4	6.8	5.9	33.8	22.9	4.8	0.2	70.3	33.6	49.4	50.6
64401	AGENCY	98.6	98.4	0.2	0.2	0.3	0.3	1.1	1.2	5.9	5.9	7.9	7.6	4.8	28.5	28.3	10.2	0.9	75.2	38.8	51.3	48.7
64402	ALBANY	98.9	98.7	0.1	0.1	0.2	0.3	0.5	0.6	6.1	6.1	6.2	6.1	5.8	22.2	23.9	19.5	4.3	77.6	43.3	48.7	51.3
64421	AMAZONIA	98.8	98.8	0.3	0.3	0.1	0.1	1.2	1.2	6.5	6.7	7.1	5.8	5.8	26.5	30.2	10.4	1.1	76.1	40.0	53.0	47.0
64422	AMITY	98.4	98.6	0.0	0.0	0.2	0.2	0.6	0.7	6.9	7.8	7.0	4.9	6.1	26.9	24.9	14.3	1.3	74.6	40.5	51.3	48.7
64423	BARNARD	97.7	97.1	0.2	0.2	0.8	1.2	1.0	1.2	6.2	6.3	7.4	6.7	6.7	28.2	23.1	13.5	2.1	76.1	37.4	53.3	46.7
64424	BETHANY	98.8	98.7	0.2	0.2	0.1	0.2	0.8	0.8	6.7	6.2	5.6	5.2	5.7	22.9	23.3	18.7	5.6	78.3	43.2	47.0	53.0
64426	BLYTHEDALE	98.4	98.2	0.2	0.2	0.6	0.6	0.6	0.6	7.0	7.8	7.0	5.5	4.5	23.5	25.8	17.0	2.0	74.6	41.0	52.6	47.4
64427	BOLCKOW	98.7	98.4	0.2	0.2	0.2	0.2	0.8	0.8	7.4	7.2	8.2	6.0	6.9	27.2	25.6	10.4	1.1	73.4	36.2	50.9	49.1
64428	BURLINGTON JUNCTION	99.0	99.0	0.1	0.1	0.1	0.1	0.3	0.3	6.1	6.2	7.3	7.6	6.9	25.1	23.9	14.3	2.6	75.7	38.3	49.1	50.9
64429	CAMERON	87.4	86.5	10.2	10.8	0.3	0.4	1.3	1.4	5.5	5.3	5.2	5.6	8.2	35.1	21.3	11.2	2.6	80.5	37.0	61.0	39.0
64430	CLARKSDALE	98.6	98.4	0.0	0.0	0.1	0.3	0.9	0.9	5.7	6.1	6.5	6.9	6.1	25.1	28.7	13.2	1.7	77.2	41.4	50.8	49.2
64431	CLEARMONT	98.9	98.8	0.0	0.0	0.2	0.2	0.5	0.5	5.9	5.7	5.5	6.9	6.7	21.6	26.6	19.2	1.9	79.1	43.5	47.0	53.0
64432	CLYDE	97.6	97.1	0.0	0.0	1.0	1.0	1.0	1.5	6.3	6.3	6.8	6.8	6.8	28.6	22.3	13.6	2.4	76.7	37.3	51.9	48.1
64433	CONCEPTION	97.8	97.4	0.0	0.0	1.1	1.1	1.1	1.1	6.4	6.4	7.5	6.7	6.7	28.8	22.1	13.5	1.9	75.3	36.7	52.4	47.6
64434	CONCEPTION JUNCTION	97.7	97.3	0.3	0.3	1.0	1.0	1.0	1.4	6.4	6.4	7.4	6.8	6.8	28.0	23.0	13.2	2.0	75.0	37.1	53.0	47.0
64436	COSBY	98.7	98.7	0.1	0.1	0.4	0.5	1.1	1.3	5.0	5.9	8.8	6.3	5.2	27.4	26.2	13.9	1.3	75.8	39.7	51.3	48.7
64437	CRAIG	98.1	97.9	0.1	0.1	0.1	0.1	0.5	0.6	4.6	5.2	6.8	6.3	4.7	22.8	29.2	18.0	2.4	79.5	44.8	51.2	48.8
64438	DARLINGTON	97.9	97.8	0.4	0.4	0.9	0.9	1.7	1.8	5.7	6.2	7.9	7.1	6.2	23.4	24.2	15.9	3.5	74.9	41.0	52.0	48.0
64439	DEARBORN	97.6	97.5	0.3	0.3	0.3	0.4	1.5	1.7	5.9	6.4	7.0	6.2	6.0	26.3	28.2	12.4	1.7	77.0	40.3	50.7	49.3
64440	DE KALB	98.5	98.5	0.0	0.0	0.0	0.2	0.3	0.3	7.5	7.5	7.0	6.6	6.3	28.2	22.8	13.0	1.2	73.7	36.9	50.1	49.9
64441	DENVER	99.4	98.9	0.6	0.6	0.0	0.0	0.0	0.6	4.0	4.6	8.0	6.3	5.7	21.6	29.6	18.8	1.7	79.6	45.0	53.4	46.6
64442	EAGLEVILLE	97.6	97.6	0.2	0.2	0.5	0.5	1.1	1.1	7.0	7.5	6.8	5.6	4.7	23.1	26.4	16.9	2.0	75.2	41.3	52.1	47.9
64443	EASTON	97.3	96.9	0.1	0.1	0.5	0.6	1.5	1.8	5.4	5.8	6.6	6.8	5.6	22.5	30.8	14.9	1.7	78.1	43.2	49.0	51.0
64444	EDGERTON	97.2	97.0	0.0	0.0	0.2	0.2	1.8	2.0	5.6	6.3	7.8	6.1	4.7	27.6	28.8	11.6	1.5	76.4	40.9	51.0	49.0
64445	ELMO	99.3	99.5	0.0	0.0	0.0	0.0	0.2	0.2	6.2	6.2	7.6	7.8	7.1	24.5	22.7	15.1	3.0	75.3	38.0	48.5	51.5
64446	FAIRFAX	99.0	99.0	0.3	0.3	0.0	0.0	0.3	0.4	4.7	5.0	6.6	6.0	6.1	21.7	29.0	17.3	3.6	79.9	44.9	47.3	52.8
64448	FAUCETT	97.8	97.8	0.3	0.3	0.3	0.3	1.5	1.8	4.4	6.4	8.1	7.2	5.7	28.6	27.6	11.2	0.9	76.4	38.9	51.1	48.9
64449	FILLMORE	98.0	97.6	0.2	0.2	0.2	0.4	0.9	1.1	7.8	7.8	7.4	6.1	6.3	27.5	25.1	11.1	0.9	73.0	36.4	52.1	47.9
64451	FOREST CITY	97.6	97.8	0.2	0.3	0.0	0.0	0.2	0.3	6.0	6.3	7.5	5.5	5.0	25.8	26.8	15.0	2.3	76.5	41.3	51.8	48.3
64453	GENTRY	97.9	97.8	0.0	0.0	0.0	0.4	0.4	0.4	7.8	7.8	10.8	8.2	5.6	24.1	20.3	14.2	1.3	68.5	36.0	52.2	47.8
64454	GOWER	99.1	99.0	0.2	0.2	0.0	0.0	0.7	0.7	6.2	6.4	7.2	6.8	6.2	27.6	24.1	12.4	3.2	75.6	38.9	48.0	52.0
64455	GRAHAM	99.0	99.0	0.2	0.2	0.0	0.0	0.0	0.0	5.2	5.4	5.9	5.5	5.2	23.8	27.9	18.0	3.2	79.8	44.4	51.5	48.5
64456	GRANT CITY	99.1	99.1	0.2	0.2	0.1	0.1	0.2	0.2	5.5	5.7	6.4	5.9	6.9	22.1	23.7	18.4	5.3	78.7	43.4	47.6	52.4
64457	GUILFORD	97.6	97.3	0.3	0.3	0.8	1.1	0.8	1.1	6.3	6.3	7.4	6.6	6.6	28.1	23.1	13.5	1.9	76.0	37.4	53.2	46.8
64458	HATFIELD	95.7	95.6	0.0	0.0	0.0	0.0	2.4	2.9	7.3	6.8	6.8	5.4	4.4	22.9	27.8	16.6	2.0	75.6	42.1	51.7	48.3
64459	HELENA	99.3	99.5	0.3	0.3	0.0	0.0	0.8	0.8	6.7	6.9	6.9	5.7	5.4	24.6	26.9	13.6	3.3	75.6	41.0	49.0	51.0
64461	HOPKINS	98.5	98.4	0.1	0.1	0.1	0.2	0.4	0.4	6.7	6.4	6.4	7.0	7.3	24.8	24.2	15.0	2.4	76.2	38.7	51.5	48.6
	MISSOURI	84.9	84.1	11.3	11.5	1.2	1.4	2.1	2.3	6.7	6.6	7.0	7.0	7.3	27.6	24.2	11.7	1.9	75.6	36.8	48.7	51.3
	UNITED STATES	75.1	73.6	12.3	12.5	3.8	4.2	12.5	14.1	6.9	6.7	7.2	7.0	7.3	28.6	23.8	10.8	1.7	75.1	36.0	49.1	50.9

MISSOURI — INCOME

C 64085-64461

#	POST OFFICE NAME	2004 Per Capita Income	2004 HH Income Base	2004 Household Income Distribution (%): Less than $25,000	$25,000 to $49,999	$50,000 to $99,999	$100,000 to $149,999	$150,000 or More	Median Household Income: 2004	2009	2004 National Centile	2004 State Centile	2004 Home Value Base	2004 Home Value Distribution (%): Less than $50,000	$50,000 to $89,999	$90,000 to $174,999	$175,000 to $399,999	$400,000 or More	2004 Median Home Value
64085	RICHMOND	22066	3627	28.8	31.0	29.1	7.9	3.1	40930	48493	49	70	2545	13.2	28.8	43.1	12.8	2.0	101055
64086	LEES SUMMIT	31773	8336	9.6	18.6	44.2	18.8	8.8	70980	83870	92	97	6642	1.0	3.1	62.0	29.6	4.4	155394
64088	SIBLEY	21996	507	15.0	29.8	42.6	10.3	2.4	53903	64831	78	90	430	8.4	25.4	44.0	19.3	3.0	108108
64089	SMITHVILLE	29756	3443	13.1	20.5	44.1	16.6	5.8	65048	77177	89	96	2919	2.2	6.2	46.0	42.4	3.2	166250
64093	WARRENSBURG	19683	9174	34.8	26.9	28.5	7.3	2.6	38069	45100	39	61	4794	10.6	19.3	49.4	19.0	1.8	115610
64096	WAVERLY	20017	432	29.9	29.4	32.6	5.1	3.0	42357	50178	54	73	320	35.6	30.3	26.9	5.3	1.9	66000
64097	WELLINGTON	21364	546	26.7	31.0	33.0	7.3	2.0	43804	52144	58	76	413	14.8	39.7	32.2	11.9	1.5	85595
64098	WESTON	25014	1190	19.6	24.4	42.1	10.7	3.3	55229	66829	80	90	893	3.6	17.7	47.0	26.2	5.5	138681
64101	KANSAS CITY	11074	20	10.0	65.0	25.0	0.0	0.0	43100	54145	56	75	0	0.0	0.0	0.0	0.0	0.0	0
64105	KANSAS CITY	33209	1914	36.9	33.9	21.9	4.5	2.8	34442	43142	26	42	44	13.6	25.0	31.8	29.6	0.0	102778
64106	KANSAS CITY	15580	2568	49.3	30.3	15.6	3.7	1.1	25399	31289	5	5	293	39.9	24.9	29.4	5.1	0.7	71750
64108	KANSAS CITY	20060	2822	38.3	33.2	19.8	5.8	2.8	31397	37596	16	25	1034	41.0	27.0	18.6	12.5	1.0	60130
64109	KANSAS CITY	17741	4927	49.8	25.3	18.0	4.7	2.3	25151	30217	5	5	1877	35.8	28.5	20.3	14.1	1.4	66792
64110	KANSAS CITY	21500	6827	37.8	27.7	24.9	6.2	3.4	34749	41954	26	44	3499	19.0	30.1	40.4	8.6	1.9	91187
64111	KANSAS CITY	26959	10142	38.0	33.5	21.0	4.9	2.6	32291	39339	19	29	2489	6.6	25.4	47.1	18.6	2.4	112299
64112	KANSAS CITY	51768	5656	29.1	26.5	26.6	9.0	8.9	44110	56533	59	76	1656	0.7	8.6	35.0	33.0	22.8	191901
64113	KANSAS CITY	61140	4828	5.5	12.5	31.3	23.9	26.8	100853	120050	98	100	4512	0.5	3.8	21.4	55.5	18.8	230459
64114	KANSAS CITY	32989	11982	19.9	30.5	35.4	10.2	4.2	49715	60447	71	85	7734	3.3	22.3	51.8	20.6	1.9	119742
64116	KANSAS CITY	30015	7888	22.6	37.5	27.0	7.3	5.6	41370	49415	51	71	3641	4.2	24.1	46.5	19.9	5.4	116872
64117	KANSAS CITY	21048	5768	23.9	36.9	31.8	5.8	1.6	42313	49961	54	73	3628	3.9	30.9	61.5	3.4	0.3	97165
64118	KANSAS CITY	27778	16956	15.8	31.8	38.7	10.1	3.6	51728	60784	75	88	10789	5.5	12.6	64.9	16.3	0.8	123658
64119	KANSAS CITY	27681	10293	13.1	29.0	39.9	12.8	5.3	55865	65812	81	91	7935	1.4	18.7	57.8	21.3	0.8	117096
64120	KANSAS CITY	14687	223	40.4	40.4	17.9	1.4	0.0	29383	33878	11	16	127	94.5	3.9	1.6	0.0	0.0	18929
64123	KANSAS CITY	15146	3803	36.4	33.3	24.6	4.7	1.0	34169	41435	25	40	2196	48.5	37.2	12.8	0.9	0.6	51190
64124	KANSAS CITY	12541	4687	45.8	32.3	18.2	2.5	1.2	27224	32600	7	10	2111	50.8	33.9	11.8	3.0	0.5	49575
64125	KANSAS CITY	16041	802	40.2	32.8	21.0	3.1	3.0	30747	36292	14	22	463	75.4	16.0	6.7	1.9	0.0	37637
64126	KANSAS CITY	11657	2442	47.8	31.9	17.8	2.2	0.3	26160	31241	6	7	1333	67.4	28.7	3.2	0.7	0.0	37566
64127	KANSAS CITY	14762	7696	50.9	29.3	15.5	2.4	1.9	24429	29137	4	4	3185	68.2	21.3	9.9	0.4	0.3	38044
64128	KANSAS CITY	14999	5681	50.3	27.3	18.2	2.7	1.6	24749	29549	4	4	3247	54.7	35.8	8.5	0.5	0.6	47516
64129	KANSAS CITY	20160	4162	25.9	38.2	28.8	5.8	1.4	38677	46432	42	63	2535	25.6	46.7	26.5	0.8	0.4	70759
64130	KANSAS CITY	15143	10222	46.4	30.3	18.7	3.4	1.2	27176	32038	7	9	6161	45.7	44.0	9.2	0.7	0.4	52902
64131	KANSAS CITY	24567	10465	25.1	31.7	31.8	8.9	2.5	43509	52190	57	75	5842	8.4	26.1	49.7	15.5	0.4	112546
64132	KANSAS CITY	15188	6371	41.5	34.5	20.4	2.8	1.0	30240	34693	13	20	3102	37.0	47.6	14.6	0.8	0.0	58571
64133	KANSAS CITY	25887	14024	20.3	30.5	36.5	9.5	3.3	49268	58488	71	85	9978	3.5	35.3	51.7	9.2	0.3	98603
64134	KANSAS CITY	19660	8739	22.1	35.8	33.2	7.4	1.5	44753	52725	61	77	6142	7.3	57.3	31.6	3.4	0.4	80667
64136	KANSAS CITY	27917	535	23.0	19.8	35.7	17.0	4.5	59562	70014	84	93	429	2.8	13.3	52.5	31.0	0.5	137702
64137	KANSAS CITY	23567	4394	20.0	33.2	35.6	9.4	1.7	46729	55219	66	81	2497	1.7	38.6	54.1	5.2	0.4	97477
64138	KANSAS CITY	24745	11116	19.3	33.3	35.0	9.8	2.6	47828	57078	68	83	7651	2.7	38.1	52.4	6.4	0.4	96967
64139	KANSAS CITY	19421	300	20.7	21.7	35.3	16.7	5.7	59067	69685	84	93	226	1.8	11.5	51.3	34.1	1.3	144697
64145	KANSAS CITY	35147	2121	15.7	21.1	35.2	18.8	9.2	64566	79186	88	95	1633	1.0	5.8	27.9	52.2	13.1	209567
64146	KANSAS CITY	32958	720	16.7	36.8	31.7	9.9	5.0	47606	58211	67	83	458	2.6	13.5	59.6	22.1	2.2	127740
64147	KANSAS CITY	10875	271	54.2	28.4	15.5	0.4	1.5	22354	28370	3	2	37	24.3	16.2	0.0	27.0	32.4	235000
64149	KANSAS CITY	41941	175	5.7	14.9	44.0	18.3	17.1	78809	101232	95	98	160	0.6	8.1	17.5	53.8	20.0	264286
64150	RIVERSIDE	21068	1283	28.1	35.7	27.6	6.5	2.2	39968	47959	46	66	458	9.6	15.5	49.8	24.2	0.9	119949
64151	KANSAS CITY	34841	10160	11.7	23.1	39.6	17.8	7.8	65612	77336	89	96	6879	1.4	3.9	48.5	42.1	4.1	168305
64152	KANSAS CITY	33109	9029	9.8	20.2	40.8	17.8	11.4	70745	83621	92	97	7056	0.6	3.4	53.4	34.6	8.0	161614
64153	KANSAS CITY	30978	1723	11.7	21.9	44.1	15.3	7.0	64636	76127	88	96	1092	0.6	1.2	51.7	42.9	3.7	171138
64154	KANSAS CITY	31611	2458	15.9	27.5	36.1	15.2	5.2	57425	67343	82	92	1108	2.5	2.4	37.2	49.8	8.0	191731
64155	KANSAS CITY	28148	6514	8.3	21.0	47.8	18.9	4.0	69804	80698	91	97	5576	0.1	4.1	66.0	29.5	0.2	148350
64156	KANSAS CITY	27562	471	15.7	42.7	29.1	7.4	5.1	45697	54606	63	79	420	59.5	10.7	10.0	16.7	3.1	38696
64157	KANSAS CITY	26724	1455	8.0	20.3	46.3	18.6	6.7	68739	81237	91	97	1326	15.7	5.1	36.1	35.1	8.1	162903
64158	KANSAS CITY	28855	999	2.3	9.1	57.4	26.0	5.2	79613	92424	95	99	865	1.2	1.5	36.9	60.5	0.0	186200
64161	KANSAS CITY	23523	160	16.9	28.8	47.5	6.3	0.6	52554	63344	76	88	122	13.1	37.7	38.5	4.9	5.7	89444
64163	KANSAS CITY	26854	335	18.5	36.4	39.4	5.1	0.6	45795	56700	63	79	203	50.3	12.8	23.7	12.8	0.5	49500
64164	KANSAS CITY	27228	136	13.2	23.5	41.2	16.9	5.2	64129	77254	88	95	107	17.8	7.5	33.6	38.3	2.8	155208
64165	KANSAS CITY	37227	28	3.6	17.9	50.0	21.4	7.1	75000	93727	93	98	26	0.0	0.0	30.8	69.2	0.0	212500
64166	KANSAS CITY	30742	102	5.9	14.7	49.0	22.6	7.8	77896	89963	94	98	95	0.0	3.2	29.5	65.3	2.1	209375
64167	KANSAS CITY	26662	144	6.3	16.7	50.7	20.8	5.6	75457	87548	93	98	133	0.0	2.3	45.9	45.1	6.8	178906
64401	AGENCY	24139	656	16.3	30.5	38.9	9.6	4.7	52357	61541	76	88	568	12.0	13.4	48.4	21.5	4.8	128689
64402	ALBANY	21639	1076	38.0	32.1	23.1	3.6	3.2	31186	36559	15	24	784	35.6	30.7	26.2	6.5	1.0	71304
64421	AMAZONIA	23500	452	25.9	28.8	35.6	4.9	4.9	46264	54966	64	80	380	31.3	26.8	27.4	11.6	2.9	79048
64422	AMITY	18047	215	27.9	38.6	27.0	4.7	1.9	35680	39439	30	49	169	23.1	27.2	29.0	18.9	1.8	89643
64423	BARNARD	18759	235	29.4	39.2	26.8	3.8	0.9	37305	42746	37	57	189	36.5	25.9	24.3	11.6	1.6	71500
64424	BETHANY	16748	1717	39.3	34.6	21.2	4.0	0.9	32499	36825	19	30	1227	31.1	31.8	31.5	5.0	0.6	76118
64426	BLYTHEDALE	14226	198	43.4	34.3	19.7	1.5	1.0	28029	31863	9	12	160	47.5	23.8	20.6	7.5	0.6	53636
64427	BOLCKOW	18296	237	27.9	35.4	28.7	5.9	2.1	40580	47200	48	68	197	39.1	30.5	24.4	5.1	1.0	61471
64428	BURLINGTON JUNCTION	18806	371	33.4	34.2	24.0	7.6	0.8	35704	41723	30	49	285	42.8	26.7	19.0	10.5	1.1	59318
64429	CAMERON	17086	3142	30.4	32.3	29.7	5.8	1.8	39593	46665	45	66	2125	12.2	30.3	42.5	13.7	1.2	101099
64430	CLARKSDALE	18580	313	29.1	36.7	27.8	5.8	0.6	38505	43019	41	62	262	17.9	28.6	35.9	15.7	1.9	100000
64431	CLEARMONT	18935	196	40.3	28.1	26.5	3.6	1.5	31993	38409	18	28	143	30.8	31.5	29.4	6.3	2.1	80789
64432	CLYDE	14006	60	31.7	38.3	26.7	3.3	0.0	35882	42725	31	50	48	35.4	29.2	22.9	12.5	0.0	70000
64433	CONCEPTION	9010	47	31.9	36.2	27.7	4.3	0.0	36699	42803	34	54	38	36.8	26.3	23.7	13.2	0.0	70000
64434	CONCEPTION JUNCTION	17773	111	27.9	39.6	27.0	4.5	0.9	38070	43481	39	61	89	39.3	27.0	20.2	12.4	1.1	65000
64436	COSBY	26567	336	19.6	29.2	36.6	8.3	6.3	51675	60741	75	88	287	19.5	18.8	40.1	19.5	2.1	109943
64437	CRAIG	17340	384	40.6	36.2	18.5	2.1	2.6	30489	34549	13	21	305	47.9	23.3	20.3	7.2	1.3	53095
64438	DARLINGTON	14872	67	28.4	38.8	25.4	4.5	3.0	36106	42348	32	52	55	32.7	16.4	32.7	16.4	1.8	92500
64439	DEARBORN	24203	791	19.2	28.7	38.2	10.1	3.8	51617	61509	75	88	631	10.5	20.8	40.3	25.0	3.5	120023
64440	DE KALB	19317	243	20.2	37.0	34.6	6.6	1.7	44869	53818	61	78	203	28.1	31.5	28.6	11.3	0.5	76333
64441	DENVER	16779	77	36.4	41.6	18.2	3.9	0.0	33349	36844	22	36	62	51.6	17.7	22.6	8.1	0.0	48889
64442	EAGLEVILLE	16480	285	38.6	37.2	21.1	2.1	1.1	30900	34758	15	23	229	39.3	27.1	21.4	10.0	2.2	63438
64443	EASTON	22981	573	15.4	32.3	41.5	7.0	3.8	51414	60397	75	87	491	13.2	22.0	41.3	15.7	7.7	121230
64444	EDGERTON	25365	526	16.9	24.1	43.2	11.8	4.0	57053	68281	82	92	458	9.0	17.0	49.3	20.1	4.6	120619
64445	ELMO	17508	179	38.6	34.6	21.2	5.6	0.0	32903	40479	21	33	133	56.4	26.3	11.3	4.5	1.5	46731
64446	FAIRFAX	20933	514	31.1	37.4	25.1	3.3	3.1	35840	41879	31	50	373	42.1	34.6	18.5	4.0	0.8	58939
64448	FAUCETT	23441	316	17.1	28.8	41.8	9.5	2.9	52483	61336	76	88	268	14.6	17.9	37.3	27.6	2.6	121324
64449	FILLMORE	21684	191	26.2	33.0	31.9	4.7	4.2	44437	51023	60	77	158	36.1	29.8	28.5	4.4	1.3	67000
64451	FOREST CITY	20337	163	27.0	42.3	23.3	3.1	4.3	36335	41619	33	53	133	35.3	35.3	16.5	9.0	3.8	64333
64453	GENTRY	16346	85	38.8	29.4	28.2	3.5	0.0	32736	36367	20	32	70	34.3	15.7	31.4	18.6	0.0	90000
64454	GOWER	22828	863	19.4	26.7	39.4	11.6	3.0	52732	61490	77	89	711	8.3	25.7	44.9	18.6	2.5	111161
64455	GRAHAM	18905	216	31.5	36.1	26.4	4.6	1.4	37150	42360	36	56	172	42.4	14.5	22.7	13.4	7.0	73333
64456	GRANT CITY	16267	575	44.2	33.7	18.3	2.6	1.2	28558	32527	10	14	426	61.3	23.9	11.3	3.3	0.2	41111
64457	GUILFORD	16722	128	28.9	39.8	26.6	3.9	0.8	37299	43385	36	57	103	37.9	25.2	23.3	12.6	1.0	69167
64458	HATFIELD	16309	71	26.8	45.1	23.9	2.8	1.4	36057	41204	32	51	58	22.4	31.0	24.1	15.5	6.9	87143
64459	HELENA	22850	241	17.8	37.3	34.0	7.1	3.7	45484	52065	63	79	216	19.0	20.8	31.5	26.9	1.9	111607
64461	HOPKINS	16691	383	36.8	32.1	27.4	2.9	0.8	34373	40483	25	41	298	56.0	23.8	13.1	6.4	0.7	37727
	MISSOURI	23864		27.0	29.4	30.1	9.0	4.5	44017	52626				15.2	22.7	39.0	19.7	3.4	109184
	UNITED STATES	25866		24.7	27.1	30.8	10.9	6.5	48124	56710				10.9	15.0	33.7	30.1	10.4	145905

ZIP CODE #	POST OFFICE NAME	FINANCIAL SERVICES: Auto Loan	Home Loan	Investments	Retirement Plans	THE HOME: Home Improvements: Home Repair	Lawn & Garden	Furnishings: Computers & Hardware	Major Appliances	TV, Radio, Sound Equipment	Furniture	ENTERTAINMENT: Dine out/ Carry out	Sports Equipment	Fees & Tickets	Toys & Games	Travel	Cable TV	PERSONAL: Apparel & Services	Auto Repairs	Health Insurance	Pets & Supplies
64085	RICHMOND	87	70	50	69	76	87	73	80	79	71	95	92	68	93	73	82	88	79	91	98
64086	LEES SUMMIT	120	138	139	141	132	130	126	124	116	129	148	146	130	150	124	110	146	122	109	137
64088	SIBLEY	98	87	67	83	92	99	81	90	86	81	104	107	79	107	83	88	99	87	97	116
64089	SMITHVILLE	109	126	130	127	122	122	116	115	109	117	137	134	120	141	116	105	136	113	104	127
64093	WARRENSBURG	69	61	68	64	61	65	74	67	73	70	91	84	69	88	69	68	88	72	63	76
64096	WAVERLY	85	62	39	60	70	82	67	76	76	64	89	87	59	85	67	80	81	76	91	96
64097	WELLINGTON	83	71	55	70	75	83	71	77	75	70	91	89	68	91	71	77	86	75	83	93
64098	WESTON	93	89	79	88	92	98	87	92	88	86	108	107	85	108	87	88	103	90	94	107
64101	KANSAS CITY	0	0	0	0	0	0	0	0	0	0	0	0	0	0	0	0	0	0	0	0
64105	KANSAS CITY	58	47	64	53	46	51	64	56	63	60	80	72	59	75	58	59	77	63	52	63
64106	KANSAS CITY	46	39	55	40	38	44	48	45	51	48	64	53	47	61	46	50	62	48	45	50
64108	KANSAS CITY	64	56	71	57	54	60	65	62	68	66	85	73	63	82	62	67	83	66	61	69
64109	KANSAS CITY	56	48	56	47	47	55	57	54	60	56	74	63	54	69	54	60	71	58	57	62
64110	KANSAS CITY	68	64	82	65	62	69	72	68	73	72	92	81	72	91	70	72	90	72	66	76
64111	KANSAS CITY	61	52	72	58	51	56	68	60	67	64	84	76	64	81	62	63	82	67	56	67
64112	KANSAS CITY	101	97	158	108	94	103	114	103	114	113	144	126	116	147	111	111	143	110	95	114
64113	KANSAS CITY	182	220	268	223	216	226	205	201	193	206	244	233	220	252	211	190	244	198	186	220
64114	KANSAS CITY	82	90	109	91	89	95	91	88	88	90	111	103	93	113	91	87	109	89	85	96
64116	KANSAS CITY	83	86	100	88	85	90	91	87	88	89	111	103	91	111	89	86	109	89	82	95
64117	KANSAS CITY	67	68	74	68	68	73	71	69	71	69	88	81	71	89	70	70	86	70	69	77
64118	KANSAS CITY	87	92	101	94	89	93	92	90	89	92	112	105	93	112	90	86	110	91	83	99
64119	KANSAS CITY	90	103	112	103	101	105	99	97	94	98	119	113	102	122	100	92	117	96	91	107
64120	KANSAS CITY	52	39	28	38	42	51	44	48	49	42	58	53	39	55	43	52	53	48	57	57
64123	KANSAS CITY	56	54	60	54	53	58	60	57	60	58	75	68	59	75	58	59	73	59	56	62
64124	KANSAS CITY	49	44	47	42	43	48	50	48	52	49	65	55	48	62	48	52	63	50	49	53
64125	KANSAS CITY	61	55	60	54	55	62	64	61	67	61	82	71	62	81	62	67	79	64	63	67
64126	KANSAS CITY	46	39	41	37	39	45	45	44	49	44	60	52	43	58	44	50	57	46	48	51
64127	KANSAS CITY	54	47	54	44	45	53	53	52	58	54	72	59	52	69	52	60	70	54	56	59
64128	KANSAS CITY	55	45	50	41	45	54	51	52	58	52	71	57	50	65	50	61	67	54	59	60
64129	KANSAS CITY	65	63	68	63	63	68	67	66	68	65	84	77	66	85	66	67	82	67	66	74
64130	KANSAS CITY	55	47	53	44	46	56	51	52	57	53	70	57	51	66	51	60	68	53	58	60
64131	KANSAS CITY	73	73	90	75	72	79	78	75	78	78	99	87	79	98	77	78	97	77	73	83
64132	KANSAS CITY	52	47	57	47	46	52	52	50	55	53	69	57	52	67	51	56	67	52	51	57
64133	KANSAS CITY	78	87	97	86	86	91	86	84	84	85	105	97	88	108	86	83	103	84	81	92
64134	KANSAS CITY	69	74	83	75	73	76	75	73	73	74	92	86	77	94	75	71	90	73	69	80
64136	KANSAS CITY	86	105	116	103	103	105	97	96	93	97	117	111	104	125	100	92	117	94	90	105
64137	KANSAS CITY	75	76	87	79	74	79	80	77	78	80	98	91	80	97	78	75	97	79	71	85
64138	KANSAS CITY	77	84	95	85	83	87	84	82	82	83	103	96	87	105	84	80	101	83	78	90
64139	KANSAS CITY	87	105	119	104	103	105	98	97	94	98	118	113	104	125	101	92	117	95	90	106
64145	KANSAS CITY	106	115	133	116	114	122	115	114	113	114	141	132	118	141	116	111	138	114	110	124
64146	KANSAS CITY	81	85	108	86	84	92	90	86	90	89	113	100	92	114	90	90	111	89	85	95
64147	KANSAS CITY	43	32	41	32	30	37	42	39	45	42	57	46	39	53	38	46	55	43	40	44
64149	KANSAS CITY	151	182	187	184	177	173	163	162	150	164	189	189	171	198	164	144	189	156	142	178
64150	RIVERSIDE	68	59	69	64	59	65	72	67	71	69	89	82	68	86	67	67	86	72	64	75
64151	KANSAS CITY	110	118	132	123	116	119	117	115	112	118	141	136	119	141	116	107	139	116	104	127
64152	KANSAS CITY	121	136	143	140	132	132	128	126	120	129	151	148	132	153	127	114	150	125	113	139
64153	KANSAS CITY	110	107	115	115	102	105	111	106	106	113	135	128	109	129	105	98	132	110	93	118
64154	KANSAS CITY	99	91	107	99	88	94	101	96	98	102	125	116	98	117	95	92	121	101	88	107
64155	KANSAS CITY	107	124	122	127	119	115	111	111	103	115	130	129	116	132	110	97	129	107	95	121
64156	KANSAS CITY	108	105	87	103	103	107	98	103	97	101	120	120	95	116	97	94	117	102	99	120
64157	KANSAS CITY	117	133	128	139	126	122	120	119	110	125	139	139	123	140	117	102	138	115	101	130
64158	KANSAS CITY	127	144	138	150	137	132	130	129	119	135	151	151	134	151	126	111	149	125	109	141
64161	KANSAS CITY	89	82	65	79	85	90	76	83	79	76	97	99	75	99	78	80	93	81	87	104
64163	KANSAS CITY	81	76	63	74	76	80	72	77	72	74	90	89	69	86	72	71	86	76	75	90
64164	KANSAS CITY	103	114	111	112	112	114	104	106	99	105	124	124	106	126	105	97	122	104	99	120
64165	KANSAS CITY	110	137	146	138	135	133	123	122	114	122	143	143	130	152	125	110	143	118	109	135
64166	KANSAS CITY	115	143	151	143	140	138	127	127	118	127	148	148	135	158	130	114	148	122	113	140
64167	KANSAS CITY	117	132	127	138	126	121	119	118	109	124	139	138	123	139	116	102	137	115	100	129
64401	AGENCY	105	94	71	89	99	106	86	96	92	86	112	114	85	114	89	94	106	93	104	124
64402	ALBANY	81	60	38	58	67	79	65	73	73	62	86	83	58	82	65	77	79	73	88	91
64421	AMAZONIA	94	84	64	80	89	95	77	86	82	78	100	102	76	102	80	84	95	84	93	111
64422	AMITY	84	59	31	55	68	77	58	72	67	57	78	86	50	77	60	70	71	71	85	100
64423	BARNARD	79	55	29	52	64	72	54	67	63	54	74	81	46	72	56	66	67	66	80	94
64424	BETHANY	62	49	35	47	53	62	52	57	57	50	68	65	47	67	52	60	63	57	67	70
64426	BLYTHEDALE	57	43	28	41	47	56	47	52	53	45	62	58	42	59	47	56	57	52	62	63
64427	BOLCKOW	79	69	52	66	74	79	64	72	69	64	84	86	63	85	66	71	79	70	79	94
64428	BURLINGTON JUNCTION	72	57	40	55	62	72	60	66	66	58	78	75	55	76	60	69	72	65	77	81
64429	CAMERON	69	61	53	60	64	70	64	67	66	62	81	78	60	79	63	67	76	67	71	79
64430	CLARKSDALE	83	58	30	54	67	75	57	70	66	56	77	85	49	75	59	69	70	69	84	98
64431	CLEARMONT	66	49	33	47	54	65	55	60	61	52	72	67	49	68	54	65	66	60	72	73
64432	CLYDE	79	55	29	52	64	72	55	67	63	54	74	81	47	72	57	66	67	66	80	94
64433	CONCEPTION	79	55	29	52	65	72	55	68	63	54	74	82	47	73	57	66	67	67	81	94
64434	CONCEPTION JUNCTION	79	55	29	52	65	72	55	68	63	54	74	82	47	73	57	66	67	67	81	94
64436	COSBY	121	88	50	83	100	112	86	104	97	85	115	125	75	113	89	102	105	102	122	143
64437	CRAIG	68	52	34	48	57	67	54	61	60	52	71	70	48	68	55	64	65	61	73	78
64438	DARLINGTON	89	62	32	58	72	81	61	76	70	60	83	91	52	81	63	74	75	74	90	105
64439	DEARBORN	94	84	68	83	88	96	82	88	86	81	105	103	80	106	83	87	99	86	94	107
64440	DE KALB	83	74	56	70	78	84	68	76	73	68	88	90	67	90	70	75	84	74	82	98
64441	DENVER	69	48	25	46	56	63	48	59	55	47	65	71	41	63	50	58	59	58	70	82
64442	EAGLEVILLE	63	47	29	45	52	61	50	57	57	48	67	65	44	63	50	60	61	57	68	71
64443	EASTON	94	84	64	80	89	95	77	86	82	77	100	102	76	102	80	84	95	84	93	111
64444	EDGERTON	100	93	76	90	98	103	86	94	89	86	109	111	85	112	88	91	105	91	99	118
64445	ELMO	69	52	34	50	57	68	57	63	64	54	75	71	51	71	57	68	69	63	75	76
64446	FAIRFAX	78	57	35	55	64	75	61	70	69	59	81	80	54	78	61	73	74	69	83	88
64448	FAUCETT	95	85	65	81	90	96	78	87	83	78	101	104	77	103	81	85	96	85	94	112
64449	FILLMORE	84	74	57	71	79	84	69	76	73	69	89	91	67	91	71	75	84	74	82	98
64451	FOREST CITY	90	63	33	60	73	82	62	77	72	62	84	93	53	82	65	75	77	76	92	107
64453	GENTRY	80	56	29	53	65	73	55	68	64	55	75	82	47	73	57	67	68	67	81	95
64454	GOWER	98	86	65	82	92	98	80	89	85	80	103	106	78	106	82	87	98	87	96	115
64455	GRAHAM	80	56	29	53	65	73	55	68	64	54	75	82	47	73	57	67	68	67	81	95
64456	GRANT CITY	63	46	29	44	52	61	50	56	56	48	66	65	44	63	50	59	60	56	67	71
64457	GUILFORD	79	55	29	52	65	72	55	68	63	54	74	82	47	73	57	66	67	67	81	94
64458	HATFIELD	85	59	31	56	69	78	59	73	68	58	79	88	50	78	61	71	72	72	87	101
64459	HELENA	89	80	61	76	84	90	74	82	78	74	95	97	72	97	76	80	90	79	88	105
64461	HOPKINS	54	56	57	53	57	64	56	56	58	54	72	62	58	77	57	60	69	55	61	62
	MISSOURI	87	82	79	80	83	90	82	85	85	82	104	99	81	103	82	85	100	85	87	100
	UNITED STATES	100	100	100	100	100	100	100	100	100	100	100	100	100	100	100	100	100	100	100	100

ZIP CODE		COUNTY FIPS CODE	POPULATION			2000-2004 ANNUAL RATE		HOUSEHOLDS					FAMILIES		
#	POST OFFICE NAME		2000	2004	2009	% Rate	State Centile	2000	2004	2009	% Annual Rate 2000-2004	2004 Average HH Size	2000	2004	% Annual Rate 2000-2004
64463	KING CITY	075	1620	1562	1504	-0.9	9	636	611	587	-0.9	2.51	452	427	-1.3
64465	LATHROP	049	3975	4237	4499	1.5	79	1500	1618	1734	1.8	2.59	1143	1209	1.3
64466	MAITLAND	087	535	617	656	3.4	95	222	258	278	3.6	2.39	155	177	3.2
64467	MARTINSVILLE	081	248	251	251	0.3	44	91	92	92	0.3	2.71	68	67	-0.4
64468	MARYVILLE	147	14405	14775	15181	0.6	56	5160	5394	5656	1.1	2.23	2727	2759	0.3
64469	MAYSVILLE	063	2302	2238	2234	-0.7	12	851	828	830	-0.6	2.62	616	588	-1.1
64470	MOUND CITY	087	1950	1919	1898	-0.4	20	868	861	860	-0.2	2.18	546	529	-0.7
64471	NEW HAMPTON	081	597	605	606	0.3	45	243	246	247	0.3	2.31	173	172	-0.1
64473	OREGON	087	1490	1452	1427	-0.6	14	578	566	558	-0.5	2.46	406	389	-1.0
64474	OSBORN	063	749	800	834	1.6	80	297	320	337	1.8	2.50	213	224	1.2
64475	PARNELL	147	423	502	553	4.1	98	180	215	240	4.3	2.33	122	144	4.0
64476	PICKERING	147	477	459	460	-0.9	7	197	193	197	-0.5	2.38	145	140	-0.8
64477	PLATTSBURG	049	3572	3678	3865	0.7	59	1377	1429	1513	0.9	2.52	990	1005	0.4
64479	RAVENWOOD	147	972	945	949	-0.7	12	380	376	384	-0.3	2.50	270	263	-0.6
64480	REA	003	455	454	463	-0.1	30	181	183	188	0.3	2.48	138	137	-0.2
64481	RIDGEWAY	081	867	928	961	1.6	81	353	378	390	1.6	2.45	252	263	1.0
64482	ROCK PORT	005	2345	2308	2281	-0.4	20	1056	1056	1057	0.0	2.14	667	652	-0.5
64483	ROSENDALE	003	679	679	689	0.0	32	250	252	257	0.2	2.69	193	192	-0.1
64484	RUSHVILLE	021	1111	1097	1107	-0.3	22	447	446	454	-0.1	2.46	323	316	-0.5
64485	SAVANNAH	003	7585	7749	7947	0.5	53	2901	2985	3081	0.7	2.52	2053	2071	0.2
64486	SHERIDAN	227	627	637	645	0.4	48	266	270	274	0.4	2.36	183	181	-0.3
64487	SKIDMORE	147	785	737	736	-1.5	2	337	321	325	-1.1	2.30	214	200	-1.6
64489	STANBERRY	075	1852	1785	1711	-0.9	8	707	681	652	-0.9	2.53	500	472	-1.4
64490	STEWARTSVILLE	049	2085	2160	2240	0.8	64	784	821	858	1.1	2.63	600	618	0.7
64491	TARKIO	005	2269	2246	2219	-0.2	25	891	885	879	-0.2	2.26	563	545	-0.8
64492	TRIMBLE	049	1167	1340	1476	3.3	95	459	533	592	3.6	2.51	350	400	3.2
64493	TURNEY	049	390	455	508	3.7	96	155	183	207	4.0	2.49	127	149	3.8
64494	UNION STAR	063	908	890	895	-0.5	18	364	360	365	-0.3	2.47	259	250	-0.8
64496	WATSON	005	193	186	181	-0.9	8	72	70	69	-0.7	2.66	51	49	-0.9
64497	WEATHERBY	063	432	431	435	-0.1	30	166	166	168	0.0	2.60	128	126	-0.4
64498	WESTBORO	005	446	426	415	-1.1	5	180	174	171	-0.8	2.43	144	137	-1.2
64499	WORTH	227	211	214	217	0.3	46	90	91	92	0.3	2.35	67	66	-0.4
64501	SAINT JOSEPH	021	12747	12444	12348	-0.6	15	5275	5167	5156	-0.5	2.28	2943	2797	-1.2
64503	SAINT JOSEPH	021	12287	12164	12121	-0.2	25	4853	4844	4862	0.0	2.48	3350	3268	-0.6
64504	SAINT JOSEPH	021	11576	11325	11209	-0.5	17	4474	4409	4395	-0.3	2.56	3143	3028	-0.9
64505	SAINT JOSEPH	003	12358	12624	12886	0.5	53	4692	4823	4958	0.7	2.57	3363	3389	0.2
64506	SAINT JOSEPH	021	21507	22259	22667	0.8	63	8317	8664	8880	1.0	2.26	5238	5316	0.4
64507	SAINT JOSEPH	021	12693	12613	12658	-0.2	27	4816	4831	4886	0.1	2.44	3039	2981	-0.5
64601	CHILLICOTHE	117	11786	11659	11484	-0.3	24	4651	4626	4589	-0.1	2.32	3014	2932	-0.7
64620	ALTAMONT	061	473	483	500	0.5	53	188	193	202	0.6	2.50	145	147	0.3
64622	BOGARD	033	935	972	1004	0.9	66	351	365	377	0.8	2.66	260	265	0.5
64623	BOSWORTH	033	661	674	690	0.5	51	265	272	280	0.6	2.48	197	199	0.2
64624	BRAYMER	025	1767	1767	1799	0.0	32	694	696	712	0.1	2.46	475	465	-0.5
64625	BRECKENRIDGE	025	627	646	662	0.7	59	259	269	277	0.9	2.40	180	182	0.3
64628	BROOKFIELD	115	6209	6177	6106	-0.1	27	2610	2601	2573	-0.1	2.30	1641	1593	-0.7
64630	BROWNING	115	389	380	375	-0.6	15	163	160	159	-0.4	2.38	108	104	-0.9
64631	BUCKLIN	115	987	943	916	-1.1	5	434	417	406	-0.9	2.26	284	266	-1.5
64632	CAINSVILLE	129	732	815	855	2.6	90	317	355	372	2.7	2.29	214	234	2.1
64633	CARROLLTON	033	5354	5403	5496	0.2	41	2179	2208	2254	0.3	2.36	1438	1423	-0.3
64635	CHULA	117	700	690	677	-0.3	21	267	268	266	0.1	2.56	197	192	-0.6
64636	COFFEY	061	239	250	262	1.1	70	96	101	107	1.2	2.47	65	67	0.7
64637	COWGILL	025	571	591	611	0.8	63	226	236	245	1.0	2.50	168	172	0.6
64638	DAWN	117	349	339	329	-0.7	11	148	145	142	-0.5	2.34	101	96	-1.2
64639	DE WITT	033	453	446	450	-0.4	20	180	178	181	-0.3	2.51	145	141	-0.7
64640	GALLATIN	061	3049	3110	3233	0.5	51	1282	1312	1370	0.6	2.33	877	879	0.1
64641	GALT	079	472	506	512	1.7	81	205	222	226	1.9	2.28	147	155	1.3
64642	GILMAN CITY	081	887	864	854	-0.6	13	367	358	354	-0.6	2.41	259	248	-1.0
64643	HALE	033	694	711	729	0.6	55	282	290	299	0.7	2.45	199	201	0.2
64644	HAMILTON	025	2973	2979	3039	0.1	34	1176	1183	1212	0.1	2.47	819	807	-0.4
64645	HARRIS	211	112	113	116	0.2	41	48	48	49	0.0	2.35	33	33	0.0
64646	HUMPHREYS	211	473	473	484	0.0	32	186	186	189	0.0	2.54	130	127	-0.6
64647	JAMESON	061	350	400	441	3.2	94	147	170	190	3.5	2.34	110	125	3.1
64648	JAMESPORT	061	2205	2209	2252	0.0	34	721	728	750	0.2	3.03	531	525	-0.3
64649	KIDDER	025	1023	1118	1183	2.1	87	387	425	452	2.2	2.63	303	327	1.8
64650	KINGSTON	025	891	912	931	0.6	54	346	358	368	0.8	2.54	252	254	0.2
64651	LACLEDE	115	726	767	779	1.3	75	296	314	319	1.4	2.44	217	226	1.0
64652	LAREDO	079	454	493	498	2.0	85	194	213	217	2.2	2.31	143	154	1.8
64653	LINNEUS	115	885	866	849	-0.5	17	338	332	328	-0.4	2.61	248	239	-0.9
64654	LOCK SPRINGS	061	239	250	264	1.1	70	89	95	98	1.0	2.69	70	72	0.7
64655	LUCERNE	171	200	202	203	0.2	42	85	86	87	0.3	2.35	64	64	0.0
64656	LUDLOW	117	412	401	389	-0.6	13	168	165	161	-0.4	2.43	108	103	-1.1
64657	MC FALL	075	527	508	486	-0.9	8	206	198	189	-0.9	2.47	156	147	-1.4
64658	MARCELINE	041	3367	3265	3191	-0.7	10	1357	1317	1289	-0.7	2.43	903	855	-1.3
64659	MEADVILLE	115	924	903	884	-0.5	15	363	355	348	-0.5	2.54	256	245	-1.0
64660	MENDON	041	530	524	515	-0.3	23	222	222	222	0.0	2.36	158	155	-0.5
64661	MERCER	129	1046	1039	1024	-0.2	26	447	444	440	-0.2	2.34	319	311	-0.6
64664	MOORESVILLE	117	304	289	278	-1.2	4	129	124	121	-0.9	2.33	98	92	-1.5
64667	NEWTOWN	211	392	395	406	0.2	40	152	153	156	0.2	2.58	106	104	-0.5
64668	NORBORNE	033	1643	1676	1715	0.5	51	698	715	735	0.6	2.34	480	482	0.1
64670	PATTONSBURG	061	959	1036	1109	1.8	83	403	438	471	2.0	2.37	283	301	1.5
64671	POLO	025	1889	1971	2060	1.0	68	740	776	814	1.1	2.54	544	560	0.7
64672	POWERSVILLE	171	268	270	272	0.2	40	113	115	116	0.4	2.35	86	85	-0.3
64673	PRINCETON	129	2771	2713	2666	-0.5	17	1169	1148	1130	-0.4	2.31	787	755	-1.0
64674	PURDIN	115	517	506	496	-0.5	17	221	217	214	-0.4	2.33	154	149	-0.8
64676	ROTHVILLE	041	392	387	381	-0.3	22	148	148	148	0.0	2.61	105	103	-0.5
64679	SPICKARD	079	732	745	730	0.4	49	301	308	303	0.5	2.42	208	209	0.1
64681	SUMNER	041	260	257	253	-0.3	23	118	118	118	0.0	2.18	84	82	-0.6
64682	TINA	033	431	440	449	0.5	53	168	173	178	0.7	2.54	127	129	0.4
64683	TRENTON	079	8485	8092	7704	-1.1	4	3601	3453	3306	-1.0	2.24	2331	2177	-1.6
64686	UTICA	117	323	307	295	-1.2	4	122	118	114	-0.8	2.60	92	87	-1.3
64688	WHEELING	117	406	461	482	3.0	93	162	186	197	3.3	2.48	115	128	2.6
64689	WINSTON	061	751	764	790	0.4	48	288	295	308	0.6	2.59	218	220	0.2
64701	HARRISONVILLE	037	13741	14330	15647	1.0	68	5135	5411	5970	1.2	2.58	3716	3837	0.8
64720	ADRIAN	013	2764	2847	2937	0.7	59	1018	1049	1080	0.7	2.65	745	754	0.3
64722	AMORET	013	449	454	464	0.3	43	167	169	172	0.3	2.69	126	126	0.0
	MISSOURI					0.8					0.9	2.46			0.4
	UNITED STATES					1.2					1.3	2.58			1.1

ZIP CODE #	POST OFFICE NAME	RACE (%) White 2000	White 2004	Black 2000	Black 2004	Asian/Pacific 2000	Asian/Pacific 2004	% Hispanic Origin 2000	% Hispanic Origin 2004	2004 AGE DISTRIBUTION (%) 0-4	5-9	10-14	15-19	20-24	25-44	45-64	65-84	85+	18+	MEDIAN AGE 2004	% 2004 Males	% 2004 Females
64463	KING CITY	98.5	98.5	0.2	0.2	0.3	0.3	0.9	1.0	6.9	7.0	8.2	6.9	6.0	24.0	21.7	15.9	3.3	73.8	38.6	48.9	51.2
64465	LATHROP	96.9	96.6	1.3	1.5	0.1	0.1	1.3	1.5	7.0	6.8	7.6	7.3	6.4	27.5	26.3	9.6	1.5	74.1	37.2	49.3	50.7
64466	MAITLAND	99.8	99.8	0.0	0.0	0.0	0.0	0.4	0.3	3.7	4.7	6.7	7.3	7.0	24.0	31.8	12.6	2.3	80.6	43.1	53.3	46.7
64467	MARTINSVILLE	98.0	98.4	0.0	0.0	0.0	0.0	1.6	1.6	6.8	6.8	6.4	6.8	5.6	23.5	25.9	15.9	2.4	75.3	41.0	52.2	47.8
64468	MARYVILLE	95.5	95.0	1.9	2.1	1.2	1.5	0.9	1.0	4.2	4.1	4.7	14.7	18.4	23.6	18.2	9.6	2.6	83.9	27.6	49.7	50.3
64469	MAYSVILLE	98.7	98.6	0.0	0.0	0.2	0.2	0.6	0.7	7.3	7.2	7.7	7.1	5.9	24.0	22.9	14.0	3.8	73.4	39.0	48.5	51.5
64470	MOUND CITY	98.7	98.7	0.1	0.1	0.1	0.1	0.5	0.5	4.9	5.0	6.0	6.0	5.6	22.4	25.7	19.5	4.9	80.3	45.1	48.2	51.8
64471	NEW HAMPTON	99.3	99.2	0.2	0.2	0.2	0.2	1.2	1.2	6.9	6.3	6.0	6.3	5.6	23.6	24.0	15.9	5.5	76.7	42.0	49.8	50.3
64473	OREGON	98.1	98.1	0.1	0.1	0.2	0.2	0.3	0.3	5.8	5.9	7.6	6.8	5.6	26.0	24.2	14.2	4.0	76.2	39.9	49.5	50.5
64474	OSBORN	98.0	98.0	0.5	0.5	0.0	0.0	0.5	0.5	6.6	6.8	7.5	6.9	5.4	28.3	24.9	12.5	1.3	74.9	38.1	47.8	52.3
64475	PARNELL	98.4	98.6	0.0	0.0	0.2	0.2	0.5	0.4	6.6	6.6	6.4	7.0	7.4	25.3	23.9	14.3	2.6	76.3	38.1	52.0	48.0
64476	PICKERING	97.5	97.2	0.8	0.9	0.6	0.7	0.2	0.2	6.3	6.1	5.9	4.4	6.5	27.5	27.0	14.2	2.2	79.5	39.6	51.6	48.4
64477	PLATTSBURG	93.1	92.6	4.6	5.0	0.2	0.2	1.1	1.2	6.6	6.5	6.4	7.9	5.6	25.7	26.5	12.1	2.8	75.3	40.0	49.5	50.5
64479	RAVENWOOD	99.1	99.2	0.1	0.1	0.1	0.1	0.0	0.0	6.8	6.4	6.6	7.8	8.4	27.6	24.7	10.4	1.5	76.0	35.9	51.5	48.5
64480	REA	97.8	97.6	0.9	1.1	0.4	0.7	0.7	0.7	6.0	6.0	5.7	5.7	5.1	26.4	28.2	15.2	1.8	78.4	41.8	52.4	47.6
64481	RIDGEWAY	97.8	97.8	0.0	0.1	0.2	0.2	1.2	1.1	6.5	6.4	6.7	6.5	5.7	23.6	25.9	16.6	2.3	76.3	41.3	51.2	48.8
64482	ROCK PORT	99.0	98.9	0.1	0.1	0.2	0.2	0.7	0.8	4.5	4.7	5.9	5.9	5.3	22.1	28.7	18.6	4.4	81.1	46.2	49.1	50.9
64483	ROSENDALE	98.8	98.8	0.0	0.0	0.0	0.0	0.7	0.7	7.4	7.2	7.8	6.2	7.2	27.5	25.5	10.2	1.0	73.9	35.9	50.5	49.5
64484	RUSHVILLE	98.6	98.5	0.0	0.0	0.2	0.3	0.7	0.7	6.0	6.3	7.1	6.6	6.2	27.4	26.7	12.0	1.6	76.4	39.4	50.6	49.4
64485	SAVANNAH	98.6	98.5	0.2	0.3	0.2	0.3	0.7	0.7	6.3	6.5	7.6	7.0	6.3	25.1	24.3	13.5	3.4	75.4	38.9	47.1	52.9
64486	SHERIDAN	98.7	98.7	0.0	0.0	0.0	0.0	0.5	0.5	7.2	6.9	5.5	6.3	6.0	22.6	24.8	17.9	2.8	76.6	42.1	51.8	48.2
64487	SKIDMORE	99.4	99.3	0.4	0.4	0.0	0.0	0.0	0.0	6.0	6.4	6.9	5.3	5.6	25.9	28.1	14.1	1.8	77.5	41.5	52.2	47.8
64489	STANBERRY	98.4	98.3	0.1	0.1	0.3	0.4	0.2	0.2	6.6	6.8	7.8	6.4	5.8	22.6	23.0	16.8	4.1	74.9	41.0	49.2	50.8
64490	STEWARTSVILLE	97.8	97.7	0.7	0.7	0.1	0.1	0.8	0.9	5.9	6.2	7.1	7.3	6.2	26.3	26.3	12.7	2.0	76.2	39.8	49.9	50.1
64491	TARKIO	93.4	92.8	5.5	5.9	0.2	0.3	0.8	0.9	4.8	5.7	7.9	10.2	6.3	22.4	24.3	14.5	4.0	74.0	39.0	51.4	48.6
64492	TRIMBLE	97.4	97.1	0.5	0.6	0.3	0.5	1.1	1.3	7.1	7.7	6.9	6.6	4.7	25.8	30.3	9.7	1.3	74.3	40.0	51.3	48.7
64493	TURNEY	97.2	96.7	0.3	0.4	0.3	0.2	1.3	1.5	5.9	6.2	6.8	6.6	5.7	23.7	30.6	13.0	1.5	76.5	41.8	51.0	49.0
64494	UNION STAR	97.7	97.6	0.3	0.3	0.1	0.1	1.1	1.2	5.8	5.8	8.9	7.3	4.6	26.7	24.2	14.0	2.6	74.7	39.6	52.3	47.8
64496	WATSON	99.0	98.9	0.5	0.5	0.0	0.0	1.0	1.1	4.3	4.8	5.9	5.9	6.5	25.3	31.2	14.5	1.6	81.2	43.2	52.7	47.3
64497	WEATHERBY	97.7	97.5	0.0	0.0	0.2	0.2	0.7	1.2	7.9	7.9	7.9	5.8	5.6	24.6	26.0	13.2	1.2	72.4	38.2	51.5	48.5
64498	WESTBORO	98.9	99.3	0.0	0.0	0.0	0.0	0.7	0.7	4.5	5.2	6.6	5.9	4.9	23.5	32.2	15.7	1.6	79.8	44.7	50.0	50.0
64499	WORTH	99.1	99.1	0.5	0.5	0.0	0.0	0.0	0.5	4.2	5.1	7.5	6.1	5.6	21.5	29.0	18.7	2.3	79.0	45.0	53.7	46.3
64501	SAINT JOSEPH	85.9	84.7	10.1	11.0	0.3	0.4	3.0	3.4	7.8	6.9	7.2	7.1	8.2	30.7	19.6	10.3	2.3	73.9	33.0	49.4	50.6
64503	SAINT JOSEPH	94.9	94.4	2.2	2.4	0.3	0.4	3.2	3.6	7.3	7.0	7.0	6.8	6.7	27.5	22.9	12.9	2.0	74.6	36.8	47.6	52.4
64504	SAINT JOSEPH	95.9	95.5	1.3	1.5	0.2	0.2	2.6	2.9	6.3	6.3	7.9	7.5	6.4	28.3	24.0	11.9	1.6	74.9	37.2	49.4	50.6
64505	SAINT JOSEPH	95.8	95.4	1.9	2.1	0.3	0.3	1.7	1.9	6.5	6.6	7.5	7.1	6.4	27.7	24.4	11.4	2.3	75.1	37.1	48.0	52.0
64506	SAINT JOSEPH	91.1	90.2	6.1	6.6	1.0	1.2	2.2	2.4	5.2	5.1	5.5	6.3	8.7	28.5	23.7	13.9	3.1	80.9	38.4	51.3	48.7
64507	SAINT JOSEPH	93.1	92.5	4.2	4.4	0.5	0.6	2.3	2.6	6.6	6.0	6.6	8.1	9.0	27.8	21.9	11.8	2.2	77.0	34.8	48.1	51.9
64601	CHILLICOTHE	95.1	94.7	2.9	3.1	0.3	0.4	0.8	0.8	6.3	6.1	6.5	6.1	6.5	24.8	24.7	15.4	3.6	77.4	40.6	45.4	54.6
64620	ALTAMONT	98.9	99.2	0.0	0.0	0.0	0.0	0.6	0.6	6.2	6.0	5.6	5.4	4.4	23.0	30.9	17.2	1.5	78.5	44.7	49.1	50.9
64622	BOGARD	98.9	98.9	0.1	0.1	0.1	0.1	0.5	0.5	6.0	7.4	8.9	6.4	5.4	24.7	25.7	13.8	1.9	73.8	39.5	52.7	47.3
64623	BOSWORTH	99.1	99.1	0.2	0.2	0.2	0.2	0.2	0.2	5.3	5.8	7.4	6.7	5.3	24.0	26.7	16.5	2.2	77.3	42.1	51.2	48.8
64624	BRAYMER	98.6	98.4	0.1	0.1	0.2	0.2	0.5	0.5	6.5	7.0	8.1	6.9	5.9	23.5	23.3	15.1	3.7	73.9	39.3	49.0	51.0
64625	BRECKENRIDGE	97.6	97.5	0.0	0.0	0.3	0.3	1.0	0.9	6.7	7.4	9.4	6.2	4.5	25.5	26.3	12.2	1.7	72.6	38.3	53.1	46.9
64628	BROOKFIELD	97.4	97.2	1.0	1.1	0.2	0.2	0.8	0.8	6.3	6.3	6.6	6.2	6.2	22.2	23.9	18.2	4.1	76.9	42.2	46.8	53.2
64630	BROWNING	98.7	98.4	0.3	0.3	0.0	0.0	0.8	0.8	6.3	6.3	6.6	5.8	6.1	24.5	24.5	17.4	2.6	77.6	40.2	47.6	52.4
64631	BUCKLIN	98.6	98.4	0.1	0.1	0.0	0.0	0.9	1.0	5.2	5.7	6.9	6.3	5.1	24.1	25.2	18.2	3.3	78.3	42.8	48.9	51.1
64632	CAINSVILLE	98.1	98.0	0.1	0.1	0.4	0.4	0.7	0.6	5.9	5.8	6.1	6.4	6.5	22.1	26.4	18.3	2.6	78.2	43.1	50.6	49.5
64633	CARROLLTON	95.7	95.2	2.6	2.8	0.2	0.2	0.9	1.0	7.1	6.6	6.6	6.0	5.9	23.3	23.8	16.4	4.3	76.1	40.7	47.7	52.3
64635	CHULA	99.3	99.1	0.0	0.1	0.1	0.1	0.1	0.1	8.0	7.8	6.8	6.1	6.4	23.5	26.1	13.2	2.2	73.6	38.2	49.7	50.3
64636	COFFEY	97.1	96.8	0.0	0.0	0.4	0.4	2.1	2.4	7.6	7.6	6.8	6.0	5.2	24.0	23.6	16.4	2.8	74.0	39.3	46.8	53.2
64637	COWGILL	98.6	98.5	0.2	0.2	0.0	0.0	0.4	0.3	6.3	6.8	8.6	7.1	5.4	23.2	26.9	14.4	1.4	74.3	39.5	53.8	46.2
64638	DAWN	98.9	99.1	0.0	0.0	0.0	0.0	0.0	0.0	6.2	5.9	6.8	6.5	6.2	23.6	28.3	14.5	2.1	76.7	41.6	50.7	49.3
64639	DE WITT	97.4	96.9	1.8	2.0	0.2	0.2	0.2	0.2	4.7	5.2	6.3	6.5	5.4	25.6	29.6	15.7	1.1	79.8	43.0	52.5	47.5
64640	GALLATIN	99.2	99.1	0.1	0.1	0.1	0.1	0.5	0.6	6.8	6.6	6.9	6.1	5.5	23.4	25.4	15.9	3.5	75.8	41.0	47.6	52.4
64641	GALT	98.3	98.4	0.6	0.6	0.0	0.0	1.1	1.0	8.7	7.5	6.3	5.9	5.9	21.9	26.7	15.0	2.0	73.5	40.6	49.4	50.6
64642	GILMAN CITY	97.4	97.2	0.0	0.0	0.2	0.4	1.2	1.2	6.6	6.4	6.6	5.3	6.8	26.3	24.2	15.7	2.1	77.3	39.1	49.5	50.5
64643	HALE	99.7	99.7	0.0	0.0	0.1	0.1	0.6	0.7	7.7	7.9	7.9	6.3	6.2	25.5	20.5	15.5	2.5	72.6	37.3	48.0	52.0
64644	HAMILTON	98.8	98.7	0.1	0.1	0.1	0.1	0.8	0.9	7.0	7.0	7.4	6.9	5.8	24.2	22.3	16.1	3.4	74.4	39.1	48.3	51.7
64645	HARRIS	98.2	98.2	0.0	0.0	0.0	0.0	1.8	2.7	8.9	8.0	7.1	7.1	5.3	24.8	23.0	14.2	1.8	70.8	36.6	52.2	47.8
64646	HUMPHREYS	98.5	98.3	0.2	0.2	0.2	0.2	1.7	1.9	8.3	7.4	6.6	6.3	5.1	24.5	26.0	14.0	1.9	74.0	39.3	52.0	48.0
64647	JAMESON	98.6	98.8	0.0	0.0	0.9	0.8	0.3	0.0	7.8	7.3	7.5	6.8	6.5	24.5	25.3	13.5	1.0	73.0	37.0	50.8	49.3
64648	JAMESPORT	98.5	98.4	0.1	0.1	0.5	0.5	0.5	0.6	7.7	7.9	8.3	7.6	6.3	23.1	24.2	13.1	1.9	71.5	35.9	49.3	50.7
64649	KIDDER	98.9	98.7	0.3	0.4	0.1	0.3	1.7	1.9	7.4	7.7	7.9	8.0	5.8	24.4	25.9	11.9	1.1	72.1	38.5	50.5	49.5
64650	KINGSTON	98.7	98.6	0.1	0.1	0.1	0.1	0.6	0.7	5.8	7.4	7.6	7.5	6.8	23.8	26.8	13.1	1.4	74.6	39.6	51.0	49.0
64651	LACLEDE	97.8	97.4	1.1	1.2	0.1	0.1	1.2	1.6	5.6	5.9	7.4	5.7	5.5	24.0	27.3	16.3	2.4	77.6	42.0	50.5	49.5
64652	LAREDO	98.5	98.2	0.0	0.0	0.0	0.0	1.3	1.4	5.5	6.1	6.5	6.5	5.5	22.7	30.6	14.4	2.2	77.7	43.4	50.7	49.3
64653	LINNEUS	98.9	98.6	0.3	0.6	0.1	0.1	0.2	0.2	7.3	7.0	6.0	6.6	5.7	24.3	27.3	13.7	2.2	75.9	40.5	49.9	50.1
64654	LOCK SPRINGS	99.6	99.6	0.0	0.0	0.0	0.0	0.0	0.0	10.8	10.8	9.2	7.2	6.4	24.4	21.6	8.4	1.2	64.4	28.9	50.8	49.2
64655	LUCERNE	99.0	99.5	0.0	0.0	0.0	0.0	0.5	0.5	5.9	5.9	5.0	5.9	4.0	22.3	30.2	18.8	2.0	79.2	45.7	51.0	49.0
64656	LUDLOW	98.8	98.5	0.2	0.3	0.2	0.3	0.0	0.0	6.2	6.0	6.7	6.5	6.2	23.7	28.4	13.7	2.5	77.3	41.4	49.1	50.9
64657	MC FALL	97.9	97.6	0.4	0.4	0.8	1.0	1.7	2.0	5.7	6.3	7.5	6.7	5.9	23.2	25.4	15.8	3.5	75.6	41.5	52.4	47.6
64658	MARCELINE	98.3	98.1	0.1	0.1	0.2	0.3	0.6	0.8	5.9	5.9	7.4	7.4	7.1	23.7	24.4	14.8	3.4	75.8	40.1	47.1	52.9
64659	MEADVILLE	99.2	99.2	0.2	0.2	0.1	0.2	0.4	0.6	8.1	7.6	6.9	5.0	5.7	25.7	24.9	13.2	3.0	74.6	39.1	48.8	51.2
64660	MENDON	99.1	98.9	0.2	0.2	0.0	0.2	0.4	0.4	6.5	6.7	6.5	5.5	5.5	22.7	25.8	18.5	2.3	76.9	42.4	49.8	50.2
64661	MERCER	98.8	98.8	0.5	0.5	0.0	0.0	0.2	0.2	5.0	5.4	6.5	5.4	6.4	21.2	28.9	18.8	2.5	79.8	45.1	50.6	49.4
64664	MOORESVILLE	99.7	100.0	0.0	0.0	0.0	0.0	0.3	0.4	5.9	6.9	6.9	5.9	5.2	22.8	31.5	13.2	1.7	77.5	42.2	51.6	48.4
64667	NEWTOWN	98.0	98.0	0.3	0.3	0.0	0.0	2.6	3.0	9.9	8.6	6.8	7.1	5.3	24.1	22.0	14.2	2.0	70.1	36.2	53.2	46.8
64668	NORBORNE	97.2	97.0	1.8	2.0	0.0	0.0	0.7	0.8	6.6	6.7	5.9	6.4	5.6	23.8	26.9	15.5	2.7	76.9	41.4	48.8	51.3
64670	PATTONSBURG	97.6	97.6	0.0	0.0	0.2	0.3	1.7	1.6	7.6	7.2	6.9	6.1	5.7	24.2	24.3	15.9	2.0	74.6	39.3	47.8	52.2
64671	POLO	98.0	97.8	0.3	0.4	0.1	0.2	0.9	0.9	5.4	5.7	7.5	7.0	6.0	23.9	30.1	12.9	1.6	77.0	41.5	49.6	50.4
64672	POWERSVILLE	98.9	99.3	0.0	0.0	0.0	0.0	0.4	0.4	5.6	5.9	4.8	5.9	4.1	22.2	30.7	18.9	1.9	80.0	46.1	51.1	48.9
64673	PRINCETON	98.7	98.6	0.0	0.1	0.1	0.1	0.4	0.4	6.3	6.3	6.2	5.9	5.6	23.3	25.3	17.6	3.7	77.7	42.6	49.2	50.8
64674	PURDIN	98.8	98.8	0.2	0.2	0.0	0.0	0.6	0.8	6.9	6.9	6.9	5.9	5.9	23.9	24.3	16.8	2.4	75.9	39.6	48.2	51.8
64676	ROTHVILLE	99.0	99.2	0.0	0.0	0.0	0.0	0.0	0.3	7.2	6.5	6.5	5.4	5.4	23.0	25.6	18.1	2.3	76.7	42.0	50.4	49.6
64679	SPICKARD	98.4	98.3	0.3	0.3	0.1	0.1	0.6	0.4	6.4	6.3	5.9	5.9	5.9	24.2	28.1	15.4	1.9	77.7	41.8	49.9	50.1
64681	SUMNER	99.2	99.2	0.0	0.0	0.0	0.0	0.0	0.4	7.0	5.8	6.6	5.5	5.5	23.0	26.1	18.3	2.3	77.4	42.5	49.4	50.6
64682	TINA	98.8	98.6	0.0	0.0	0.5	0.5	0.5	0.5	5.2	6.1	7.7	5.9	5.2	25.0	25.7	16.8	2.3	76.8	41.7	50.2	49.8
64683	TRENTON	97.5	97.2	0.4	0.5	0.2	0.3	1.8	2.0	6.2	6.0	6.4	6.6	6.4	22.2	24.7	17.5	4.1	78.1	42.2	47.2	52.9
64686	UTICA	99.4	99.0	0.3	0.3	0.0	0.0	0.3	0.3	5.9	6.5	7.2	5.5	5.5	23.1	30.6	13.7	2.0	76.6	42.1	51.8	48.2
64688	WHEELING	99.8	99.8	0.0	0.0	0.0	0.0	0.3	0.4	7.8	7.6	7.2	6.1	5.9	23.0	25.4	14.5	2.6	73.8	40.7	51.8	48.2
64689	WINSTON	98.9	98.7	0.1	0.1	0.0	0.1	0.4	0.5	6.4	6.5	6.0	6.0	4.7	23.7	29.3	15.8	1.4	77.1	42.7	49.4	50.7
64701	HARRISONVILLE	96.4	96.0	0.8	0.8	0.5	0.6	1.3	1.4	7.4	7.2	7.4	7.0	6.3	27.1	24.0	11.6	2.0	73.5	37.0	48.5	51.5
64720	ADRIAN	98.6	98.3	0.1	0.1	0.1	0.2	1.2	1.3	6.9	6.7	7.6	6.9	6.7	26.2	22.6	14.1	2.5	74.6	37.8	49.4	50.6
64722	AMORET	98.2	98.2	0.0	0.0	0.0	0.0	2.0	2.0	5.5	6.2	6.6	6.6	6.0	25.6	27.5	14.3	1.8	77.8	41.2	51.1	48.9
	MISSOURI	84.9	84.1	11.3	11.5	1.2	1.4	2.1	2.3	6.7	6.6	7.0	7.0	7.3	27.6	24.2	11.7	1.9	75.6	36.8	48.7	51.3
	UNITED STATES	75.1	73.6	12.3	12.5	3.8	4.2	12.5	14.1	6.9	6.7	7.2	7.0	7.3	28.6	23.8	10.8	1.7	75.1	36.0	49.1	50.9

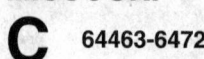

ZIP CODE #	POST OFFICE NAME	2004 Per Capita Income	2004 HH Income Base	2004 HOUSEHOLD INCOME DISTRIBUTION (%) Less than $25,000	$25,000 to $49,999	$50,000 to $99,999	$100,000 to $149,999	$150,000 or More	MEDIAN HOUSEHOLD INCOME 2004	2009	2004 National Centile	2004 State Centile	2004 Home Value Base	2004 HOME VALUE DISTRIBUTION (%) Less than $50,000	$50,000 to $89,999	$90,000 to $174,999	$175,000 to $399,999	$400,000 or More	2004 Median Home Value
64463	KING CITY	16682	611	38.8	35.4	21.0	2.8	2.1	31660	36810	17	26	450	43.3	23.3	26.2	5.8	1.3	60800
64465	LATHROP	23256	1618	22.1	27.4	36.3	11.0	3.2	50410	58798	73	86	1306	9.8	18.1	48.5	20.6	3.1	118555
64466	MAITLAND	17456	258	38.8	33.0	21.7	4.3	2.3	33617	38450	23	37	196	46.9	21.9	18.4	10.7	2.0	54286
64467	MARTINSVILLE	16117	92	27.2	41.3	28.3	3.3	0.0	36181	40778	32	52	75	33.3	32.0	25.3	8.0	1.3	73750
64468	MARYVILLE	19074	5394	36.3	29.5	26.5	5.5	2.2	36125	42073	32	52	2869	11.6	20.7	45.9	20.0	1.8	115671
64469	MAYSVILLE	14994	828	36.7	34.9	24.0	4.2	0.1	34042	39133	24	39	642	33.6	24.0	30.5	10.3	1.6	74688
64470	MOUND CITY	18248	861	43.4	30.1	21.5	3.4	1.6	29174	33859	11	16	626	38.3	28.0	26.7	6.1	1.0	65833
64471	NEW HAMPTON	18150	246	27.2	37.8	31.3	3.3	0.4	36499	41172	34	54	198	35.9	28.8	28.8	6.6	0.0	71818
64473	OREGON	19012	566	27.2	37.8	29.5	3.4	2.1	38347	44145	41	62	457	30.0	36.3	26.5	6.1	1.1	71932
64474	OSBORN	20040	320	24.7	35.9	32.5	4.4	2.5	41356	46081	51	71	247	17.0	33.6	32.4	16.2	0.8	89531
64475	PARNELL	17334	215	36.7	32.6	27.0	2.8	0.9	34520	40699	26	42	168	57.7	23.8	11.3	6.6	0.6	34583
64476	PICKERING	20009	193	24.9	34.7	34.7	3.6	2.1	45113	50167	61	78	157	26.1	17.8	33.1	19.8	3.2	106875
64477	PLATTSBURG	23118	1429	25.2	28.8	32.1	9.4	4.5	46891	54650	66	81	1123	11.4	19.4	44.8	21.0	3.4	116002
64479	RAVENWOOD	21456	376	23.9	38.8	27.4	7.2	2.7	39843	46256	45	66	296	31.8	31.4	26.7	9.5	0.7	70952
64480	REA	20345	183	23.5	34.4	34.4	6.0	1.6	44746	50000	61	77	148	30.4	21.0	34.5	8.8	5.4	87500
64481	RIDGEWAY	14798	378	40.5	38.1	17.7	2.9	0.8	30376	35118	13	21	291	48.5	28.2	14.4	6.5	2.4	51875
64482	ROCK PORT	22458	1056	36.7	30.3	24.5	6.3	2.3	35829	41647	31	50	756	27.8	34.5	29.2	7.4	1.1	74348
64483	ROSENDALE	18020	252	28.2	36.1	28.2	6.0	1.6	40000	45878	46	67	209	39.7	33.0	22.0	4.8	0.5	58958
64484	RUSHVILLE	23381	446	22.9	33.4	34.1	6.5	3.1	44377	53714	60	77	371	27.2	27.0	31.5	11.9	2.4	83261
64485	SAVANNAH	21282	2985	26.8	32.9	29.7	7.2	3.4	42721	49792	55	74	2240	13.0	25.4	46.2	14.2	1.2	103137
64486	SHERIDAN	17272	270	34.8	37.0	22.6	3.7	1.9	34430	38476	25	42	216	48.6	20.8	19.4	6.9	4.2	52308
64487	SKIDMORE	17700	321	33.3	34.9	28.0	3.4	0.3	35350	40884	29	47	253	53.4	20.6	17.8	5.5	2.8	47069
64489	STANBERRY	15987	681	36.9	35.0	23.1	3.7	1.5	34075	39269	24	39	529	40.3	26.5	24.8	7.6	1.0	61528
64490	STEWARTSVILLE	19252	821	26.4	33.7	30.0	7.7	2.2	41842	49053	52	72	655	19.1	27.8	32.2	19.7	1.2	95694
64491	TARKIO	17798	885	37.1	34.1	22.9	4.6	1.2	33197	38695	21	35	626	38.0	35.8	22.7	3.4	0.2	62462
64492	TRIMBLE	32763	533	18.4	27.2	36.2	9.0	9.2	53308	62276	77	89	461	2.4	18.4	42.7	29.1	7.4	138056
64493	TURNEY	23903	183	17.5	33.9	33.3	13.1	2.2	49011	57515	70	84	162	9.3	15.4	38.3	32.7	4.3	140278
64494	UNION STAR	18331	360	31.1	36.1	26.7	4.2	1.9	37665	43302	38	59	290	29.3	28.3	26.2	14.1	2.1	78947
64496	WATSON	17827	70	31.4	31.4	28.6	5.7	2.9	38399	44440	41	62	47	40.4	27.7	29.8	2.1	0.0	63750
64497	WEATHERBY	16837	166	29.5	36.1	28.9	4.8	0.6	36813	41969	35	55	138	31.2	15.2	35.5	15.2	2.9	100000
64498	WESTBORO	21888	174	27.6	36.8	24.7	6.3	4.6	37395	43839	37	58	121	50.4	19.8	23.1	5.0	1.7	49792
64499	WORTH	16484	91	35.2	40.7	19.8	4.4	0.0	34527	35744	26	42	73	48.0	20.6	23.3	8.2	0.0	53000
64501	SAINT JOSEPH	15875	5167	44.8	31.7	20.0	2.2	1.3	28284	33624	9	13	2662	29.8	45.7	20.8	3.5	0.3	66919
64503	SAINT JOSEPH	20478	4844	28.8	31.9	30.5	6.4	2.4	40115	48267	46	67	3524	27.1	36.4	31.2	4.9	0.3	76463
64504	SAINT JOSEPH	18895	4409	31.3	30.5	32.4	4.3	1.5	39260	46822	44	65	3323	36.6	34.7	22.4	5.9	0.4	62760
64505	SAINT JOSEPH	21935	4823	27.0	31.0	30.2	8.6	3.2	42939	50803	56	74	3630	18.7	32.3	35.1	12.6	1.4	88583
64506	SAINT JOSEPH	26895	8664	26.7	26.9	31.4	9.3	5.8	46214	54068	64	80	5665	4.0	12.6	58.2	23.1	2.2	127306
64507	SAINT JOSEPH	19258	4831	30.3	35.4	26.9	5.4	2.0	37370	44527	37	58	3301	19.8	43.3	28.9	6.7	1.2	79432
64601	CHILLICOTHE	20148	4626	34.6	32.1	24.6	5.6	3.2	36801	42802	35	55	3284	27.6	26.7	32.9	11.0	1.8	84427
64620	ALTAMONT	21602	193	22.8	37.3	31.6	6.7	1.6	40615	48917	48	68	162	21.6	20.4	34.0	22.8	1.2	106818
64622	BOGARD	15564	365	38.9	32.1	24.7	3.3	1.1	32762	37496	20	32	295	36.3	19.7	28.1	13.2	2.7	76111
64623	BOSWORTH	18142	272	30.5	33.8	28.7	6.3	0.7	36778	41443	35	55	221	42.5	25.8	18.6	8.1	5.0	59167
64624	BRAYMER	16546	696	37.5	35.6	21.7	4.5	0.7	33062	38353	21	34	527	38.0	31.7	20.7	8.5	1.1	63444
64625	BRECKENRIDGE	16849	269	40.9	27.5	24.2	7.4	0.0	31567	36604	17	26	213	46.0	24.4	16.4	12.2	0.9	57083
64628	BROOKFIELD	18052	2601	38.8	33.6	22.1	4.2	1.4	31817	37048	17	27	1938	39.6	30.4	22.6	7.2	0.2	61765
64630	BROWNING	14223	160	46.3	35.0	16.3	1.9	0.6	27814	33074	8	11	122	60.7	17.2	18.9	3.3	0.0	32857
64631	BUCKLIN	17724	417	41.7	33.6	20.1	2.9	1.7	29603	35156	11	18	324	56.2	23.2	15.7	4.3	0.6	43939
64632	CAINSVILLE	15605	355	40.9	36.6	19.2	2.5	0.9	30185	35000	13	20	275	57.1	26.2	12.0	4.0	0.7	44583
64633	CARROLLTON	18747	2208	36.3	37.8	17.9	4.6	3.4	33602	38514	23	37	1540	34.9	32.9	25.0	6.6	0.7	72288
64635	CHULA	16662	268	38.1	31.3	25.8	2.6	2.2	35915	42012	31	50	212	42.5	20.8	25.5	11.3	0.0	61538
64636	COFFEY	16457	101	41.6	33.7	17.8	4.0	3.0	32750	35450	20	32	81	40.7	32.1	14.8	11.1	1.2	58333
64637	COWGILL	16883	236	35.6	33.9	24.6	4.7	1.3	33529	38364	22	36	192	31.3	20.8	30.7	16.2	1.0	84286
64638	DAWN	21348	145	37.9	30.3	24.8	4.8	2.1	35245	41741	28	46	105	48.6	16.2	21.0	11.4	2.9	52500
64639	DE WITT	18186	178	23.0	41.0	32.0	2.8	1.1	41500	46534	51	71	142	26.8	26.1	31.0	12.7	3.5	80000
64640	GALLATIN	21995	1312	31.9	34.4	26.3	5.1	2.4	35854	41892	31	50	974	26.3	27.9	30.6	14.4	0.8	85233
64641	GALT	16015	222	38.3	39.2	20.7	1.8	0.0	31758	37699	17	27	176	53.4	16.5	18.8	7.4	4.0	47143
64642	GILMAN CITY	15884	358	41.3	33.8	21.2	3.1	0.6	30896	35423	15	23	288	56.3	19.8	17.7	4.5	1.7	45000
64643	HALE	16570	290	33.5	37.6	24.1	4.8	0.0	33906	39613	24	39	234	50.0	27.8	17.1	4.3	0.9	50000
64644	HAMILTON	17522	1183	36.3	34.6	23.2	4.0	2.0	33515	39095	22	36	872	27.4	31.0	27.8	12.4	1.5	79333
64645	HARRIS	15951	48	41.7	33.3	20.8	2.1	2.1	31514	36151	16	26	35	65.7	11.4	14.3	5.7	2.9	34167
64646	HUMPHREYS	16872	186	38.7	35.0	21.0	3.2	2.2	33174	38636	21	35	140	48.6	15.7	27.9	6.4	1.4	52857
64647	JAMESON	24779	170	34.7	39.4	17.7	2.9	5.3	32461	35955	19	30	133	36.1	18.8	31.6	12.0	1.5	83500
64648	JAMESPORT	13713	728	39.3	37.5	16.5	4.8	1.9	31161	35550	15	24	572	32.3	23.3	32.7	10.3	1.4	77500
64649	KIDDER	17743	425	28.9	33.2	32.9	3.5	1.4	40413	45956	48	68	353	19.0	25.2	32.3	21.3	2.3	101500
64650	KINGSTON	17234	358	30.7	36.9	26.3	5.0	1.1	35390	41556	29	47	297	31.3	23.6	24.9	13.5	6.7	78056
64651	LACLEDE	15082	314	42.0	32.5	20.7	4.5	0.3	31373	35589	16	25	249	54.6	11.7	26.1	6.0	1.6	43947
64652	LAREDO	16253	213	33.3	40.9	23.5	2.4	0.0	35990	41526	32	51	170	48.2	22.4	18.2	10.6	0.6	52000
64653	LINNEUS	17293	332	34.0	33.4	25.9	3.9	2.7	36614	41646	34	54	267	40.1	22.9	25.8	9.4	1.9	67941
64654	LOCK SPRINGS	15121	93	36.6	40.9	19.4	3.2	0.0	31080	34091	15	24	76	26.3	18.4	32.9	22.4	0.0	103571
64655	LUCERNE	21151	86	30.2	38.4	23.3	3.5	4.7	36517	41929	34	54	70	27.1	35.7	18.6	17.1	1.4	76667
64656	LUDLOW	20223	165	43.6	26.7	23.6	4.9	1.2	29737	36399	12	18	111	58.6	14.4	20.7	5.4	0.9	40500
64657	MC FALL	23713	198	28.8	36.9	26.3	4.6	3.5	36114	41465	32	52	162	35.2	15.4	30.3	16.1	3.1	88000
64658	MARCELINE	18094	1317	40.0	32.3	22.8	2.7	2.2	32019	36824	18	28	988	41.1	30.1	22.1	6.3	0.5	61977
64659	MEADVILLE	17278	355	28.5	40.6	25.6	3.9	1.4	37662	42609	38	59	294	34.0	33.3	20.4	7.8	4.4	70000
64660	MENDON	17147	222	37.8	37.4	21.6	2.3	0.9	33058	37040	21	34	185	38.9	22.7	24.9	10.8	2.7	65417
64661	MERCER	16184	444	40.1	34.0	21.2	4.3	0.5	30647	35247	14	22	371	60.9	17.8	13.2	6.2	1.9	40357
64664	MOORESVILLE	19236	124	32.3	31.5	29.0	5.7	1.6	37316	43616	37	57	103	54.4	24.3	16.5	3.9	1.0	45500
64667	NEWTOWN	16623	153	41.2	33.3	20.3	2.6	2.6	31255	36738	16	25	112	64.3	10.7	17.9	5.4	1.8	35455
64668	NORBORNE	19498	715	36.2	36.5	19.9	4.3	3.1	34546	39946	26	43	541	34.2	26.1	28.5	9.8	1.5	71731
64670	PATTONSBURG	19527	438	40.0	34.5	18.0	4.1	3.4	32396	36798	19	30	349	38.4	27.8	20.1	12.9	0.9	65952
64671	POLO	21619	776	23.3	32.7	32.0	8.6	3.4	45652	53599	63	79	647	23.5	17.5	33.1	23.7	2.3	105824
64672	POWERSVILLE	20593	115	30.4	38.3	23.5	3.5	4.4	36418	41726	33	53	94	27.7	35.1	16.0	19.2	2.1	76250
64673	PRINCETON	17790	1148	35.9	34.2	24.4	4.3	1.3	34359	39665	25	41	860	43.6	27.7	17.3	7.8	3.6	58871
64674	PURDIN	15517	217	42.4	35.5	18.9	2.8	0.5	30640	36202	14	22	169	54.4	20.7	18.3	5.3	1.2	42500
64676	ROTHVILLE	15478	148	37.8	37.8	22.3	2.0	0.0	33005	37736	21	33	123	37.4	22.0	26.8	10.6	3.3	68125
64679	SPICKARD	16649	308	43.8	32.8	19.5	2.9	1.0	28815	33407	10	15	232	56.0	21.1	16.4	4.3	2.2	43636
64681	SUMNER	18583	118	38.1	38.1	22.0	1.7	0.0	32588	38173	20	31	98	40.8	22.5	23.5	10.2	3.1	62857
64682	TINA	15755	173	33.5	36.4	27.2	2.9	0.0	35143	40000	28	45	139	33.1	24.5	26.6	11.5	4.3	75833
64683	TRENTON	19000	3453	40.1	32.6	20.2	4.6	2.4	31228	36346	16	24	2424	41.4	27.4	22.7	7.7	0.8	62135
64686	UTICA	17126	118	33.1	31.4	30.5	4.2	0.9	36819	43881	35	55	99	57.6	24.2	16.2	2.0	0.0	41667
64688	WHEELING	21573	186	31.2	33.3	23.7	7.5	4.3	42166	48257	53	73	147	38.1	19.1	28.6	14.3	0.0	81250
64689	WINSTON	18642	295	25.8	39.0	28.5	5.8	1.0	37750	43948	38	59	244	26.2	21.7	31.6	19.3	1.2	95556
64701	HARRISONVILLE	22170	5411	19.9	29.0	39.9	8.9	2.4	50859	59061	74	87	4063	9.1	19.1	46.8	23.1	1.9	118141
64720	ADRIAN	18480	1049	28.5	32.5	30.7	6.4	1.9	40514	47171	48	68	798	14.4	35.2	37.2	11.8	1.4	90405
64722	AMORET	19781	169	26.0	32.5	30.2	8.3	3.0	41986	49536	53	73	142	28.9	16.9	29.6	23.2	1.4	97500
	MISSOURI	23864		27.0	29.4	30.1	9.0	4.5	44017	52626				15.2	22.7	39.0	19.7	3.4	109184
	UNITED STATES	25866		24.7	27.1	30.8	10.9	6.5	48124	56710				10.9	15.0	33.7	30.1	10.4	145905

ZIP CODE		FINANCIAL SERVICES				THE HOME						ENTERTAINMENT						PERSONAL			
						Home Improvements		Furnishings													
#	POST OFFICE NAME	Auto Loan	Home Loan	Invest-ments	Retire-ment Plans	Home Repair	Lawn & Garden	Comput-ers & Hard-ware	Major Appli-ances	TV, Radio, Sound Equip-ment	Furni-ture	Dine out/ Carry out	Sports Equip-ment	Fees & Tickets	Toys & Games	Travel	Cable TV	Apparel & Services	Auto Repairs	Health Insur-ance	Pets & Supplies
64463	KING CITY	70	52	32	49	58	68	55	63	62	53	73	72	49	70	55	66	67	63	75	80
64465	LATHROP	94	84	68	82	88	96	82	88	86	81	105	103	80	105	83	87	99	86	94	108
64466	MAITLAND	76	53	28	50	61	69	52	64	60	51	70	78	44	69	54	63	64	63	77	90
64467	MARTINSVILLE	66	58	48	55	63	70	58	63	63	56	76	73	56	79	60	65	71	62	71	78
64468	MARYVILLE	66	56	60	58	57	63	68	63	68	64	84	78	63	81	63	65	81	68	63	74
64469	MAYSVILLE	66	50	31	47	55	63	52	59	58	50	69	68	46	66	52	61	63	59	69	75
64470	MOUND CITY	66	50	32	47	55	65	53	60	59	51	70	68	47	67	53	63	64	59	71	75
64471	NEW HAMPTON	61	58	54	55	61	68	58	61	61	56	75	69	58	79	60	64	71	59	67	72
64473	OREGON	86	60	31	57	70	78	59	73	68	59	80	88	51	79	62	72	73	72	87	102
64474	OSBORN	80	66	50	66	70	79	68	74	73	67	88	85	64	87	68	74	82	73	81	89
64475	PARNELL	52	57	59	53	57	63	56	55	58	54	72	62	59	78	58	60	69	54	59	61
64476	PICKERING	76	68	52	64	72	77	63	70	67	63	81	83	61	83	65	68	77	68	75	90
64477	PLATTSBURG	93	81	63	79	86	94	79	87	83	78	101	102	76	102	80	85	95	85	94	108
64479	RAVENWOOD	86	77	58	73	81	87	71	79	75	71	91	94	69	93	73	77	87	76	85	101
64480	REA	91	64	33	60	74	83	63	78	73	62	85	94	54	83	65	76	78	77	93	108
64481	RIDGEWAY	62	45	27	43	50	59	47	55	54	46	63	63	41	60	48	56	57	54	65	70
64482	ROCK PORT	84	60	35	57	69	79	63	74	71	61	84	86	54	81	64	75	76	73	88	97
64483	ROSENDALE	78	69	52	65	73	79	64	71	68	64	83	85	62	84	66	70	78	69	77	92
64484	RUSHVILLE	94	80	58	76	86	93	75	85	81	75	98	101	72	99	77	83	92	83	94	111
64485	SAVANNAH	86	71	53	70	76	86	74	80	79	72	95	91	69	94	73	81	89	79	89	96
64486	SHERIDAN	74	51	27	49	60	67	51	63	59	50	69	76	43	67	53	61	63	62	75	88
64487	SKIDMORE	73	52	28	49	60	67	51	63	58	50	69	75	44	67	53	61	63	62	74	87
64489	STANBERRY	70	51	30	48	57	66	53	62	60	51	70	72	46	68	54	63	64	61	74	81
64490	STEWARTSVILLE	83	68	48	66	74	81	67	75	72	66	87	89	62	87	68	74	81	74	84	96
64491	TARKIO	68	51	33	49	56	67	56	62	63	53	74	70	50	70	55	66	67	62	74	76
64492	TRIMBLE	140	111	73	106	123	134	106	125	117	105	139	150	96	139	110	120	129	123	141	167
64493	TURNEY	103	79	49	75	88	97	76	90	85	75	101	108	68	100	78	88	93	88	103	122
64494	UNION STAR	82	57	30	54	67	75	57	70	65	56	76	84	48	75	59	68	70	69	83	97
64496	WATSON	86	60	31	57	70	78	59	73	68	58	80	88	50	78	61	71	73	72	87	102
64497	WEATHERBY	72	62	45	59	64	68	59	65	62	60	75	76	55	72	59	62	71	65	68	81
64498	WESTBORO	97	67	35	64	79	88	67	82	77	66	90	99	57	88	69	81	82	81	98	115
64499	WORTH	70	49	26	46	57	64	48	60	56	48	65	72	41	64	50	59	60	59	71	83
64501	SAINT JOSEPH	48	46	52	45	46	51	51	49	53	49	65	57	51	66	50	53	63	50	50	54
64503	SAINT JOSEPH	73	68	63	67	70	78	71	72	74	69	90	83	69	91	71	75	86	72	77	83
64504	SAINT JOSEPH	71	66	58	63	68	76	66	69	70	64	85	79	65	87	67	72	81	68	75	82
64505	SAINT JOSEPH	80	80	78	78	82	88	79	81	80	77	99	93	80	102	80	81	96	80	83	93
64506	SAINT JOSEPH	84	90	104	91	89	95	91	89	89	90	112	104	93	112	92	88	109	90	87	98
64507	SAINT JOSEPH	68	65	63	64	67	73	67	68	69	65	85	78	67	87	67	70	82	68	71	78
64601	CHILLICOTHE	77	61	45	59	67	77	64	71	71	62	84	82	59	83	65	74	78	71	82	89
64620	ALTAMONT	95	70	42	65	80	90	68	83	77	67	91	98	59	90	71	82	84	81	98	114
64622	BOGARD	76	52	26	47	59	68	51	63	61	51	71	75	44	68	52	65	65	62	77	88
64623	BOSWORTH	79	56	31	53	65	73	57	69	65	56	77	81	49	74	59	69	70	68	82	93
64624	BRAYMER	69	51	32	49	57	66	54	61	61	52	71	71	48	68	54	64	65	61	73	78
64625	BRECKENRIDGE	65	49	32	47	54	64	54	60	61	51	72	67	48	68	54	64	65	60	72	72
64628	BROOKFIELD	65	55	43	53	59	67	57	61	61	55	73	70	54	73	57	63	69	60	69	74
64630	BROWNING	56	41	26	40	46	54	45	50	50	43	59	57	39	56	45	53	54	50	60	63
64631	BUCKLIN	68	49	30	47	55	65	52	60	59	50	70	69	46	67	53	63	64	60	72	77
64632	CAINSVILLE	59	44	29	42	49	58	47	53	53	45	63	60	42	60	47	56	57	53	64	66
64633	CARROLLTON	75	55	36	52	61	71	59	66	66	57	78	78	52	75	59	69	72	67	78	85
64635	CHULA	77	54	28	51	63	70	53	66	61	53	72	79	45	70	55	64	66	65	78	92
64636	COFFEY	66	49	32	47	54	65	55	60	61	52	72	67	49	68	54	65	66	60	72	73
64637	COWGILL	75	55	32	52	63	69	53	65	60	53	71	78	47	71	55	63	66	63	76	89
64638	DAWN	84	61	38	59	68	80	66	75	74	63	87	86	58	83	66	78	79	74	89	95
64639	DE WITT	82	58	30	54	67	75	57	70	66	56	77	85	49	75	59	69	70	69	84	98
64640	GALLATIN	86	64	41	61	72	84	68	77	76	65	90	89	60	86	68	81	82	77	92	98
64641	GALT	67	46	22	40	52	60	45	55	54	45	63	65	39	60	46	58	57	55	68	77
64642	GILMAN CITY	63	47	30	45	52	61	51	57	57	49	67	65	45	64	51	60	61	57	68	70
64643	HALE	64	53	41	53	56	64	55	59	59	54	72	68	52	70	55	61	67	59	65	70
64644	HAMILTON	73	55	35	53	61	70	57	65	64	56	76	75	51	73	58	67	69	64	76	83
64645	HARRIS	61	46	30	44	50	60	50	55	56	48	66	62	45	63	50	60	61	55	66	67
64646	HUMPHREYS	73	53	32	51	60	69	56	65	63	54	74	75	49	71	56	67	68	64	77	84
64647	JAMESON	105	74	39	70	86	96	73	90	84	72	98	108	62	96	76	88	90	89	107	125
64648	JAMESPORT	71	53	32	50	59	67	54	63	61	52	72	73	48	70	55	64	66	62	74	82
64649	KIDDER	84	59	31	56	69	77	58	72	67	58	79	87	50	77	60	70	72	71	86	100
64650	KINGSTON	79	56	30	52	65	72	55	68	63	54	74	81	47	73	57	66	68	67	80	94
64651	LACLEDE	69	47	21	40	53	61	45	56	54	46	63	67	38	60	46	58	58	55	69	79
64652	LAREDO	68	48	25	45	55	62	47	58	54	46	63	70	40	62	49	57	58	57	69	81
64653	LINNEUS	82	57	30	54	66	74	56	70	65	56	76	84	48	75	58	68	69	69	83	97
64654	LOCK SPRINGS	74	51	27	49	60	67	51	63	58	50	69	76	43	67	53	61	62	62	75	87
64655	LUCERNE	84	66	45	60	74	84	62	75	71	62	84	88	56	82	66	75	78	74	89	103
64656	LUDLOW	79	60	39	57	65	78	66	73	74	63	87	81	59	82	65	78	79	73	87	88
64657	MC FALL	108	75	39	71	88	98	75	92	86	74	101	111	64	99	77	90	92	91	110	128
64658	MARCELINE	70	58	43	54	62	71	59	64	65	57	77	74	55	76	59	68	72	64	74	80
64659	MEADVILLE	80	56	29	52	65	72	55	68	63	54	74	82	47	73	57	66	68	67	81	94
64660	MENDON	73	51	27	48	60	67	51	62	58	50	68	75	43	67	52	61	62	62	74	87
64661	MERCER	65	50	33	45	57	64	47	57	54	47	64	68	42	63	50	57	59	57	68	79
64664	MOORESVILLE	81	57	30	54	66	74	56	69	64	55	76	83	48	74	58	68	69	68	82	96
64667	NEWTOWN	69	52	34	50	57	68	58	63	65	55	76	71	51	72	57	68	69	63	76	77
64668	NORBORNE	77	56	34	54	63	74	60	69	67	57	79	79	52	76	60	71	72	68	82	88
64670	PATTONSBURG	77	57	35	54	63	74	61	69	69	58	81	79	53	77	61	72	73	69	83	88
64671	POLO	96	73	45	65	81	91	69	83	79	69	93	98	62	91	72	84	87	81	98	113
64672	POWERSVILLE	82	64	44	58	72	81	61	73	69	60	81	86	54	80	65	73	76	72	86	100
64673	PRINCETON	71	51	30	49	58	67	54	63	61	52	71	73	47	69	54	64	65	62	75	82
64674	PURDIN	61	45	27	43	50	58	47	54	54	46	63	63	41	60	48	56	57	54	65	70
64676	ROTHVILLE	73	51	27	48	60	67	51	62	58	50	68	75	43	67	52	61	62	62	74	87
64679	SPICKARD	69	49	29	46	55	65	52	60	60	51	71	69	46	67	52	64	64	60	73	77
64681	SUMNER	73	51	27	48	60	67	51	62	58	50	68	75	43	67	52	61	62	62	74	87
64682	TINA	67	50	32	48	55	64	53	60	59	51	70	69	47	67	53	62	64	59	71	76
64683	TRENTON	72	55	35	52	61	70	57	65	63	55	75	75	51	73	57	66	69	64	76	82
64686	UTICA	81	56	29	53	66	73	56	69	64	55	75	83	47	74	58	67	68	68	82	96
64688	WHEELING	97	68	35	64	79	88	67	82	77	66	90	99	57	88	69	81	82	81	98	115
64689	WINSTON	86	62	35	58	71	80	60	74	69	60	81	89	52	80	63	73	75	73	88	103
64701	HARRISONVILLE	89	80	66	78	83	90	79	84	82	78	100	98	77	100	79	83	95	83	89	101
64720	ADRIAN	80	64	45	61	69	79	66	73	72	64	86	83	61	84	66	76	80	72	84	90
64722	AMORET	96	67	35	63	78	88	66	82	76	66	90	99	57	88	69	80	82	81	98	114
	MISSOURI	87	82	79	80	83	90	82	85	85	82	104	99	81	103	82	85	100	85	87	100
	UNITED STATES	100	100	100	100	100	100	100	100	100	100	100	100	100	100	100	100	100	100	100	100

MISSOURI

POPULATION CHANGE

A 64723-65049

#	POST OFFICE NAME	COUNTY FIPS CODE	POPULATION			2000-2004 ANNUAL RATE		HOUSEHOLDS					FAMILIES		
			2000	2004	2009	% Rate	State Centile	2000	2004	2009	% Annual Rate 2000-2004	2004 Average HH Size	2000	2004	% Annual Rate 2000-2004
64723	AMSTERDAM	013	768	779	797	0.3	47	284	289	296	0.4	2.70	205	205	0.0
64724	APPLETON CITY	185	1602	1480	1409	-1.9	1	665	612	582	-1.9	2.30	427	383	-2.5
64725	ARCHIE	037	1679	1762	1930	1.1	72	646	682	753	1.3	2.58	492	510	0.9
64726	BLAIRSTOWN	083	601	673	717	2.7	91	226	255	274	2.9	2.64	185	206	2.6
64728	BRONAUGH	217	577	570	566	-0.3	23	229	228	227	-0.1	2.50	167	162	-0.7
64730	BUTLER	013	9053	9307	9619	0.7	58	3612	3717	3844	0.7	2.45	2481	2498	0.2
64733	CHILHOWEE	101	962	1114	1222	3.5	96	381	443	487	3.6	2.51	279	317	3.1
64734	CLEVELAND	037	1834	2091	2396	3.1	93	669	770	890	3.4	2.72	552	625	3.0
64735	CLINTON	083	13194	13294	13497	0.2	40	5526	5605	5725	0.3	2.32	3689	3660	-0.2
64738	COLLINS	185	953	904	869	-1.2	3	395	377	365	-1.1	2.40	292	274	-1.5
64739	CREIGHTON	037	921	984	1074	1.6	80	346	372	407	1.7	2.65	265	279	1.2
64740	DEEPWATER	083	1657	1770	1844	1.6	80	708	762	798	1.7	2.32	531	558	1.2
64741	DEERFIELD	217	1061	1049	1040	-0.3	23	425	424	422	-0.1	2.47	317	310	-0.5
64742	DREXEL	037	2080	2173	2352	1.0	69	788	827	900	1.1	2.63	591	606	0.6
64744	EL DORADO SPRINGS	039	7055	7185	7394	0.4	50	2921	2992	3092	0.6	2.34	1959	1960	0.0
64745	FOSTER	013	419	421	428	0.1	37	170	170	173	0.0	2.48	126	124	-0.4
64746	FREEMAN	037	1441	1537	1700	1.5	79	517	558	622	1.8	2.75	405	429	1.4
64747	GARDEN CITY	037	3667	3955	4383	1.8	83	1379	1500	1674	2.0	2.64	1046	1113	1.5
64748	GOLDEN CITY	011	1446	1486	1536	0.6	57	585	597	615	0.5	2.47	395	395	0.0
64750	HARWOOD	217	167	162	160	-0.7	11	69	68	67	-0.3	2.38	48	46	-1.0
64752	HUME	217	781	781	790	0.0	32	295	294	297	-0.1	2.66	219	215	-0.4
64755	JASPER	097	3229	3303	3385	0.5	54	1238	1270	1303	0.6	2.57	918	921	0.1
64756	JERICO SPRINGS	039	1102	1108	1127	0.1	37	437	441	450	0.2	2.51	325	322	-0.2
64759	LAMAR	011	8436	8709	9032	0.8	61	3304	3401	3516	0.7	2.52	2306	2326	0.2
64761	LEETON	101	1316	1445	1544	2.2	87	508	561	602	2.4	2.58	377	407	1.8
64762	LIBERAL	011	1766	1801	1857	0.5	51	680	692	712	0.4	2.60	495	495	0.0
64763	LOWRY CITY	185	1396	1300	1241	-1.7	1	584	543	518	-1.7	2.27	375	339	-2.4
64767	MILO	217	560	626	659	2.7	91	211	236	249	2.7	2.64	163	179	2.2
64769	MINDENMINES	011	558	549	561	-0.4	20	207	204	207	-0.3	2.68	154	148	-0.9
64770	MONTROSE	083	780	783	793	0.1	36	346	350	357	0.3	2.24	217	213	-0.4
64771	MOUNDVILLE	217	474	469	465	-0.3	24	193	192	191	-0.1	2.44	141	137	-0.7
64772	NEVADA	217	12580	12297	12145	-0.5	16	4893	4805	4760	-0.4	2.35	3128	2991	-1.1
64776	OSCEOLA	185	5681	5874	5927	0.8	63	2389	2484	2519	0.9	2.35	1691	1717	0.4
64778	RICHARDS	217	852	845	840	-0.2	25	309	306	304	-0.2	2.76	231	224	-0.7
64779	RICH HILL	013	1837	1864	1910	0.3	47	740	752	770	0.4	2.48	484	480	-0.2
64780	ROCKVILLE	013	433	425	431	-0.4	19	179	176	180	-0.4	2.41	131	127	-0.7
64783	SCHELL CITY	217	868	868	867	0.0	32	341	343	344	0.1	2.53	248	244	-0.4
64784	SHELDON	217	1495	1663	1747	2.5	89	574	638	673	2.5	2.59	445	485	2.1
64788	URICH	083	977	1024	1054	1.1	71	402	424	439	1.3	2.42	285	294	0.7
64790	WALKER	217	569	589	596	0.8	64	220	229	234	1.0	2.57	171	175	0.6
64801	JOPLIN	097	32299	32933	33896	0.5	51	13091	13388	13799	0.5	2.37	8295	8285	0.0
64804	JOPLIN	145	34338	35039	36101	0.5	52	14235	14574	15057	0.6	2.36	9434	9449	0.0
64831	ANDERSON	119	5891	6578	7301	2.6	90	2178	2452	2732	2.8	2.63	1588	1747	2.3
64832	ASBURY	097	760	778	797	0.6	54	288	296	304	0.7	2.61	225	227	0.2
64833	AVILLA	097	221	223	226	0.2	41	81	82	84	0.3	2.72	64	64	0.0
64834	CARL JUNCTION	097	7334	7790	8134	1.4	77	2601	2777	2906	1.6	2.79	2098	2205	1.2
64835	CARTERVILLE	097	1829	1963	2064	1.7	82	691	745	785	1.8	2.63	497	522	1.2
64836	CARTHAGE	097	21993	22998	23862	1.1	70	8315	8699	9029	1.1	2.56	5896	6021	0.5
64840	DIAMOND	145	2574	2627	2695	0.5	52	944	970	1001	0.6	2.71	736	744	0.3
64842	FAIRVIEW	145	779	805	831	0.8	62	287	298	309	0.9	2.67	214	218	0.4
64843	GOODMAN	119	2810	2845	2999	0.3	44	1089	1101	1159	0.3	2.57	789	785	-0.1
64844	GRANBY	145	4510	4535	4646	0.1	37	1707	1724	1775	0.2	2.60	1277	1266	-0.2
64847	LANAGAN	119	815	812	849	-0.1	28	323	320	333	-0.2	2.54	224	220	-0.4
64848	LA RUSSELL	109	765	781	815	0.5	53	268	275	288	0.6	2.84	209	210	0.1
64850	NEOSHO	145	21158	22001	22927	0.9	66	8076	8423	8814	1.0	2.56	5802	5944	0.6
64854	NOEL	119	3294	3499	3752	1.4	77	1169	1232	1315	1.2	2.84	812	839	0.8
64855	ORONOGO	097	2589	2711	2809	1.1	70	962	1012	1052	1.2	2.64	741	764	0.7
64856	PINEVILLE	119	3837	4137	4482	1.8	83	1477	1596	1730	1.8	2.58	1079	1143	1.4
64859	REEDS	097	770	784	799	0.4	49	295	302	309	0.6	2.60	232	233	0.1
64861	ROCKY COMFORT	119	738	745	774	0.2	41	273	275	285	0.2	2.71	198	196	-0.2
64862	SARCOXIE	097	2641	2673	2722	0.3	44	1034	1050	1070	0.4	2.52	723	716	-0.2
64863	SOUTH WEST CITY	119	1534	1546	1609	0.2	40	551	550	569	0.0	2.81	402	395	-0.4
64865	SENECA	145	5087	5101	5316	0.1	34	1881	1886	1972	0.1	2.65	1418	1398	-0.3
64866	STARK CITY	145	1317	1533	1686	3.6	96	495	576	635	3.6	2.66	377	432	3.3
64867	STELLA	119	1778	1838	1924	0.8	62	668	689	720	0.7	2.65	505	512	0.3
64868	TIFF CITY	119	44	45	46	0.5	54	19	19	20	0.0	2.37	15	15	0.0
64870	WEBB CITY	097	11977	12589	13075	1.2	73	4581	4811	4992	1.2	2.54	3156	3236	0.6
64873	WENTWORTH	145	1243	1234	1266	-0.2	26	473	473	486	0.0	2.60	368	361	-0.5
64874	WHEATON	009	1138	1170	1235	0.7	58	434	446	471	0.6	2.62	317	320	0.2
65001	ARGYLE	151	437	420	428	-0.9	7	158	153	158	-0.8	2.75	117	112	-1.0
65010	ASHLAND	019	4098	4452	4885	2.0	85	1561	1701	1875	2.0	2.58	1144	1219	1.5
65011	BARNETT	141	2075	2167	2247	1.0	69	725	761	791	1.2	2.85	560	578	0.8
65013	BELLE	125	3252	3257	3315	0.0	34	1343	1355	1392	0.2	2.40	910	898	-0.3
65014	BLAND	073	2430	2511	2607	0.8	61	1006	1049	1098	1.0	2.34	704	717	0.4
65016	BONNOTS MILL	151	1417	1414	1446	-0.1	30	527	534	555	0.3	2.65	403	406	0.2
65017	BRUMLEY	131	1716	1915	2120	2.6	90	612	693	776	3.0	2.74	430	476	2.4
65018	CALIFORNIA	135	7393	7650	7928	0.8	63	2859	2969	3090	0.9	2.54	2061	2100	0.4
65020	CAMDENTON	029	10426	12202	14229	3.8	97	4280	5072	5994	4.1	2.36	3055	3538	3.5
65023	CENTERTOWN	051	1620	1665	1730	0.7	58	626	653	686	1.0	2.55	468	476	0.4
65024	CHAMOIS	151	1114	1430	1677	6.1	99	425	559	668	6.7	2.56	287	370	6.2
65025	CLARKSBURG	135	912	925	949	0.3	46	333	342	354	0.6	2.70	238	239	0.1
65026	ELDON	131	9792	10462	11325	1.6	80	4029	4315	4693	1.6	2.39	2642	2775	1.2
65032	EUGENE	051	1243	1241	1293	0.0	30	435	439	462	0.2	2.83	342	339	-0.2
65034	FORTUNA	141	581	591	605	0.4	48	200	204	209	0.5	2.84	151	151	0.0
65035	FREEBURG	151	1620	1690	1765	1.0	68	592	627	665	1.4	2.69	450	468	0.9
65037	GRAVOIS MILLS	141	3902	4104	4263	1.2	73	1786	1889	1973	1.3	2.12	1206	1248	0.8
65039	HARTSBURG	019	2064	2255	2479	2.1	87	793	875	969	2.3	2.54	616	665	1.8
65040	HENLEY	051	1177	1150	1186	-0.5	15	421	417	436	-0.2	2.76	336	327	-0.6
65041	HERMANN	073	5149	5084	5198	-0.3	22	2137	2127	2192	-0.1	2.32	1450	1413	-0.6
65042	HIGH POINT	135	70	73	76	1.0	68	24	25	27	1.0	2.92	19	20	1.2
65043	HOLTS SUMMIT	027	8504	9181	9946	1.8	83	3160	3449	3772	2.1	2.65	2392	2563	1.6
65046	JAMESTOWN	135	1188	1197	1228	0.2	40	490	497	513	0.3	2.41	327	324	-0.2
65047	KAISER	131	1022	1181	1330	3.5	96	444	523	599	3.9	2.23	298	343	3.4
65048	KOELTZTOWN	151	217	204	207	-1.4	2	78	74	76	-1.2	2.72	58	54	-1.7
65049	LAKE OZARK	131	6718	7541	8467	2.8	92	2963	3371	3830	3.1	2.23	2070	2308	2.6
	MISSOURI					0.8					0.9	2.46			0.4
	UNITED STATES					1.2					1.3	2.58			1.1

ZIP CODE #	POST OFFICE NAME	RACE (%) White 2000	White 2004	Black 2000	Black 2004	Asian/Pacific 2000	Asian/Pacific 2004	% Hispanic Origin 2000	% Hispanic Origin 2004	2004 AGE DISTRIBUTION (%) 0-4	5-9	10-14	15-19	20-24	25-44	45-64	65-84	85+	18+	MEDIAN AGE 2004	% 2004 Males	% 2004 Females
64723	AMSTERDAM	96.5	96.3	0.1	0.1	0.1	0.1	0.8	1.0	5.3	7.5	9.0	7.5	5.9	27.3	25.9	10.7	1.0	73.6	37.0	51.4	48.7
64724	APPLETON CITY	98.2	98.2	0.0	0.0	0.1	0.1	0.5	0.5	6.4	6.4	7.0	6.4	5.8	20.8	22.4	18.2	6.7	75.9	42.7	46.7	53.3
64725	ARCHIE	98.1	97.9	0.4	0.4	0.1	0.2	0.7	0.9	6.8	7.1	8.4	6.7	5.7	27.2	23.9	12.5	1.7	73.6	37.4	49.4	50.6
64726	BLAIRSTOWN	97.2	96.9	0.8	0.9	0.0	0.0	1.5	1.9	5.7	6.4	7.7	5.7	5.1	26.5	29.9	12.2	1.0	76.7	40.6	51.0	49.0
64728	BRONAUGH	98.6	98.8	0.0	0.0	0.2	0.2	0.2	0.2	6.1	6.5	6.8	5.8	5.4	25.8	26.7	15.3	1.6	76.7	40.6	50.9	49.1
64730	BUTLER	97.1	96.8	1.0	1.1	0.2	0.2	0.9	1.1	6.1	6.2	7.1	6.8	6.4	24.0	24.4	15.7	3.3	76.5	40.6	48.5	51.5
64733	CHILHOWEE	97.9	97.7	0.3	0.3	0.2	0.4	0.4	0.5	6.7	6.9	7.4	7.0	5.8	25.6	26.3	12.7	1.6	74.7	38.9	50.3	49.7
64734	CLEVELAND	96.7	96.4	0.6	0.6	0.2	0.2	1.0	1.2	5.6	6.4	7.3	6.7	5.3	24.8	31.8	11.4	0.8	76.7	41.7	51.4	48.6
64735	CLINTON	96.1	95.8	1.4	1.5	0.3	0.3	1.0	1.1	6.1	5.7	6.6	6.3	6.0	24.7	25.6	16.0	3.1	77.8	41.3	48.6	51.4
64738	COLLINS	95.7	95.6	0.1	0.1	0.5	0.6	1.3	1.3	5.9	6.1	5.8	6.3	4.8	21.1	28.8	19.6	1.8	78.4	45.1	51.1	48.9
64739	CREIGHTON	97.5	97.4	0.9	0.9	0.1	0.1	0.8	0.9	6.6	6.7	7.8	7.2	5.9	26.8	25.6	12.0	1.3	74.5	39.1	51.4	48.6
64740	DEEPWATER	97.5	97.2	0.5	0.6	0.3	0.4	0.6	0.7	4.6	5.1	5.4	4.9	4.4	22.5	32.5	19.4	1.3	82.0	47.3	51.8	48.2
64741	DEERFIELD	98.8	98.7	0.1	0.1	0.2	0.2	0.4	0.4	6.1	6.7	7.5	6.7	5.3	24.8	27.5	13.8	1.6	75.5	40.8	50.1	50.0
64742	DREXEL	97.9	97.7	0.8	0.9	0.1	0.2	1.0	1.1	8.0	6.5	8.7	6.9	5.8	25.8	25.3	11.3	1.7	72.2	37.5	50.1	49.9
64744	EL DORADO SPRINGS	96.2	95.8	0.5	0.6	0.4	0.5	1.3	1.5	6.1	6.0	6.7	7.5	6.3	23.5	24.3	16.6	3.2	76.4	40.9	48.4	51.7
64745	FOSTER	96.4	96.2	0.0	0.0	0.0	0.0	1.9	1.9	7.1	7.4	8.1	7.6	5.2	26.6	25.2	10.9	1.9	73.2	37.7	51.3	48.7
64746	FREEMAN	96.9	96.6	0.5	0.5	0.3	0.3	1.2	1.4	7.7	7.8	7.1	6.1	5.3	26.1	28.4	10.7	0.9	73.6	39.3	50.7	49.3
64747	GARDEN CITY	97.6	97.4	0.4	0.4	0.1	0.2	1.3	1.4	7.7	7.6	7.5	6.6	6.1	27.7	24.4	11.2	1.3	73.2	36.6	50.2	49.8
64748	GOLDEN CITY	96.3	96.1	0.3	0.3	0.4	0.4	1.5	1.6	6.7	6.8	7.6	6.5	7.1	25.0	23.9	14.3	2.2	75.0	38.3	50.8	49.2
64750	HARWOOD	98.8	98.2	0.0	0.0	0.0	0.0	0.6	0.6	5.6	5.6	6.8	6.2	5.6	24.1	25.9	18.5	1.9	77.8	42.3	51.9	48.2
64752	HUME	96.7	96.4	0.3	0.3	0.1	0.1	1.4	1.3	7.4	7.6	7.9	7.3	5.3	25.5	25.0	12.2	1.9	72.6	37.9	51.0	49.0
64755	JASPER	96.8	96.5	0.2	0.2	0.2	0.3	1.4	1.5	6.9	7.2	7.8	6.7	6.4	25.3	26.4	11.5	1.9	74.2	38.0	50.2	49.8
64756	JERICO SPRINGS	98.2	98.0	0.0	0.0	0.4	0.5	0.5	0.5	6.9	7.6	7.2	5.9	4.9	21.9	27.1	16.7	1.9	74.6	41.9	51.3	48.7
64759	LAMAR	97.0	96.7	0.3	0.3	0.4	0.5	1.0	1.1	7.6	7.3	7.3	6.2	6.4	24.7	24.0	13.7	2.7	73.9	38.4	48.9	51.1
64761	LEETON	97.3	97.0	0.2	0.2	0.3	0.4	0.9	1.1	7.4	7.4	7.5	7.3	6.4	25.7	26.8	10.3	1.1	73.2	37.2	50.1	49.9
64762	LIBERAL	96.9	96.7	0.2	0.2	0.2	0.3	0.7	0.8	9.3	8.7	7.3	6.5	5.9	25.8	23.0	11.4	2.1	71.0	35.0	48.6	51.4
64763	LOWRY CITY	98.1	98.0	0.1	0.2	0.1	0.1	1.8	1.9	5.4	5.3	5.6	5.3	5.0	21.7	26.4	20.2	5.1	80.2	46.3	49.6	50.4
64767	MILO	97.7	97.8	0.0	0.0	0.2	0.2	0.4	0.2	7.2	7.0	7.0	6.7	5.9	25.7	25.7	13.4	1.3	74.0	38.1	49.2	50.8
64769	MINDENMINES	97.9	97.8	0.0	0.0	0.0	0.2	0.2	0.4	8.7	8.4	7.8	5.8	5.3	26.4	24.4	11.8	1.3	71.6	37.0	50.1	49.9
64770	MONTROSE	98.5	98.3	0.1	0.1	0.5	0.6	0.0	0.0	6.1	5.9	5.4	5.9	5.9	25.7	26.1	16.7	2.4	79.2	42.3	53.5	46.5
64771	MOUNDVILLE	98.5	98.5	0.0	0.0	0.2	0.2	0.2	0.2	6.0	6.4	6.8	5.8	5.3	26.0	26.9	15.4	1.5	77.4	40.7	51.4	48.6
64772	NEVADA	96.4	96.3	0.8	0.9	0.5	0.5	1.1	1.1	6.7	6.6	7.1	8.8	6.9	24.4	23.4	13.1	3.1	74.8	37.0	47.3	52.7
64776	OSCEOLA	97.2	97.2	0.3	0.3	0.1	0.1	0.9	0.9	5.5	5.8	6.4	5.9	4.8	21.7	29.2	18.6	2.1	78.5	44.9	50.4	49.6
64778	RICHARDS	97.5	97.3	0.9	1.1	0.2	0.2	0.1	0.1	8.2	8.1	7.3	6.5	5.0	24.0	24.6	14.2	2.1	72.4	38.7	50.8	49.2
64779	RICH HILL	97.4	97.1	0.2	0.2	0.1	0.2	1.0	1.1	6.6	6.5	7.3	7.2	6.6	24.4	24.6	14.4	2.5	75.3	39.0	47.3	52.7
64780	ROCKVILLE	97.2	97.2	0.7	0.7	0.0	0.0	0.7	0.9	7.1	7.1	6.4	5.9	5.4	23.3	25.4	16.7	2.8	75.5	41.8	50.1	49.9
64783	SCHELL CITY	97.9	97.9	0.1	0.1	0.1	0.1	0.8	0.8	6.6	6.8	6.9	6.2	5.4	24.8	27.3	14.1	2.0	75.9	40.1	50.0	50.0
64784	SHELDON	97.7	97.7	0.1	0.1	0.1	0.1	0.3	0.2	7.2	7.0	7.0	7.0	6.0	25.8	25.5	13.3	1.3	73.8	37.9	49.5	50.5
64788	URICH	96.9	96.8	0.3	0.3	0.3	0.4	2.2	2.3	5.9	6.2	7.2	6.5	5.3	26.0	25.6	15.3	2.1	77.0	40.7	49.4	50.6
64790	WALKER	97.2	97.3	0.2	0.2	0.4	0.3	1.1	0.9	7.8	8.0	7.3	6.5	5.9	26.0	26.3	10.5	1.7	72.8	36.1	49.4	50.6
64801	JOPLIN	91.7	91.0	2.6	2.7	0.7	1.0	2.3	2.5	7.3	6.7	6.5	7.1	8.4	28.4	22.8	11.1	1.8	76.0	34.4	48.6	51.4
64804	JOPLIN	93.2	92.6	1.4	1.5	0.7	0.9	2.1	2.3	6.8	6.5	6.5	5.8	6.4	26.9	25.4	13.7	2.0	76.8	38.7	47.9	52.1
64831	ANDERSON	90.6	90.0	0.3	0.3	0.3	0.3	3.4	3.9	7.8	7.7	7.7	6.6	6.3	27.3	23.4	11.3	1.9	72.9	35.6	49.8	50.2
64832	ASBURY	95.9	95.4	0.3	0.4	0.3	0.4	1.1	1.4	7.6	7.8	7.7	6.6	5.7	28.4	25.8	9.4	1.0	72.6	36.4	51.7	48.3
64833	AVILLA	97.3	96.9	0.0	0.0	0.5	0.5	0.9	1.4	8.1	7.2	8.1	5.4	4.9	28.7	25.1	11.7	0.9	73.1	37.2	51.6	48.4
64834	CARL JUNCTION	95.9	95.6	0.3	0.4	0.3	0.4	1.4	1.5	6.7	7.1	8.7	7.1	6.3	28.4	25.7	9.1	0.9	72.9	36.3	49.6	50.5
64835	CARTERVILLE	96.8	96.4	0.2	0.2	0.3	0.3	0.8	1.0	6.6	6.8	8.6	7.5	6.9	28.6	24.6	9.4	1.0	73.4	34.6	49.5	50.5
64836	CARTHAGE	90.2	89.0	1.1	1.2	1.2	1.4	8.5	9.5	7.3	6.9	6.8	6.6	7.2	27.0	23.7	12.2	2.4	75.1	36.6	49.9	50.1
64840	DIAMOND	95.2	94.8	0.5	0.7	0.2	0.3	1.4	1.5	8.1	7.4	7.6	6.8	7.2	26.5	24.6	10.5	1.3	72.8	35.6	49.1	50.9
64842	FAIRVIEW	96.4	95.9	0.3	0.3	0.4	0.5	1.5	2.0	8.3	7.8	7.3	7.5	6.3	27.3	22.1	11.9	1.4	71.6	35.4	52.1	48.0
64843	GOODMAN	90.8	90.0	0.3	0.3	1.0	1.2	2.1	2.5	7.0	7.2	8.7	7.0	5.8	27.6	23.7	11.7	1.3	72.6	35.8	51.3	48.7
64844	GRANBY	95.3	95.0	0.2	0.2	0.3	0.3	1.1	1.3	7.7	7.5	7.6	6.4	6.6	27.1	23.9	11.5	1.7	73.1	36.2	49.4	50.7
64847	LANAGAN	90.1	89.3	0.1	0.1	0.1	0.1	8.1	9.5	7.1	7.1	6.8	6.3	7.0	26.0	26.6	11.7	1.4	74.9	37.5	50.0	50.0
64848	LA RUSSELL	96.7	96.5	0.1	0.1	0.0	0.0	2.0	1.9	6.5	7.0	8.2	7.3	5.9	27.0	25.7	11.1	1.2	73.6	37.2	51.0	49.0
64850	NEOSHO	92.3	91.7	0.6	0.7	0.9	1.0	3.2	3.5	7.6	7.2	7.4	7.2	6.9	26.5	23.3	11.9	2.0	73.7	35.9	48.9	51.1
64854	NOEL	80.4	78.7	0.2	0.2	0.1	0.1	34.7	38.4	9.8	8.0	7.6	6.0	7.9	30.1	20.7	9.1	0.9	70.9	32.4	52.5	47.5
64855	ORONOGO	96.4	96.1	0.1	0.1	0.2	0.2	1.1	1.3	7.6	7.6	8.0	7.0	6.7	27.5	25.4	9.3	0.9	72.8	35.4	50.3	49.7
64856	PINEVILLE	93.8	93.3	0.1	0.1	0.1	0.2	3.1	3.4	7.7	7.3	7.7	7.7	6.7	27.0	23.9	10.9	1.3	72.7	35.9	50.1	49.9
64859	REEDS	96.1	95.5	0.3	0.3	0.4	0.5	1.8	2.2	7.7	7.7	7.8	5.6	4.7	27.4	27.0	11.0	1.2	73.3	37.5	50.9	49.1
64861	ROCKY COMFORT	96.1	95.8	0.0	0.0	0.1	0.1	1.0	1.1	5.5	8.2	9.0	8.1	5.2	28.2	25.2	9.1	1.5	72.4	37.4	50.7	49.3
64862	SARCOXIE	95.8	95.5	0.2	0.3	0.2	0.2	1.4	1.6	7.6	7.6	7.9	6.4	6.0	26.5	22.9	12.8	2.2	72.6	35.7	47.1	52.9
64863	SOUTH WEST CITY	77.1	75.7	0.2	0.2	0.1	0.2	28.0	31.1	10.3	9.6	8.4	7.0	6.5	29.2	20.1	7.6	1.2	67.4	30.3	50.8	49.2
64865	SENECA	90.0	89.5	0.2	0.2	0.4	0.4	1.0	1.1	6.6	6.9	8.0	7.0	6.2	26.0	25.0	12.5	1.8	74.1	37.7	48.8	51.2
64866	STARK CITY	93.7	93.2	0.0	0.1	0.1	0.1	2.7	3.1	7.0	6.9	7.1	7.8	7.3	25.8	24.8	11.7	1.6	74.4	37.0	51.7	48.3
64867	STELLA	96.0	95.6	0.1	0.2	0.2	0.3	1.2	1.5	7.5	7.9	8.2	7.7	5.9	27.0	23.9	10.7	1.2	71.5	35.8	51.7	48.3
64868	TIFF CITY	90.9	91.1	0.0	0.0	0.0	0.0	0.0	0.0	8.9	8.9	8.9	6.7	4.4	33.3	17.8	11.1	0.0	73.3	34.4	48.9	51.1
64870	WEBB CITY	93.7	93.1	0.8	0.9	0.9	1.1	2.4	2.6	8.3	7.4	7.3	8.5	9.4	26.8	20.6	10.2	1.6	72.7	31.5	48.0	52.0
64873	WENTWORTH	97.8	97.7	0.0	0.0	0.4	0.5	1.1	1.1	5.8	6.2	7.5	7.6	5.3	24.1	28.9	13.4	1.3	76.0	40.8	50.0	50.0
64874	WHEATON	93.7	92.8	0.1	0.1	0.0	0.0	8.0	9.2	8.8	7.1	8.4	7.1	8.2	25.2	18.8	15.4	1.0	71.7	33.6	48.1	51.9
65001	ARGYLE	99.1	99.1	0.0	0.0	0.0	0.0	0.9	1.0	7.4	7.4	7.6	6.7	6.2	28.6	22.4	12.4	1.4	73.6	36.6	51.4	48.6
65010	ASHLAND	97.0	96.6	0.9	1.1	0.3	0.4	1.2	1.3	6.6	7.1	7.9	6.9	5.2	28.8	26.2	10.0	1.4	73.8	37.3	48.3	51.7
65011	BARNETT	97.5	97.3	0.1	0.2	0.2	0.2	0.9	1.0	8.5	8.5	7.7	6.3	5.2	24.4	25.2	13.1	1.2	71.4	37.6	50.1	49.9
65013	BELLE	97.4	97.1	0.2	0.2	0.1	0.1	0.9	1.0	6.5	6.5	6.5	6.4	6.1	26.7	25.4	14.4	1.7	76.7	39.3	50.2	49.8
65014	BLAND	98.1	98.1	0.1	0.1	0.1	0.1	0.7	0.8	5.5	5.7	6.3	6.8	6.2	24.2	27.0	16.2	2.1	77.9	42.1	51.0	49.0
65016	BONNOTS MILL	99.0	98.9	0.4	0.4	0.1	0.1	0.4	0.6	6.3	7.2	7.1	6.6	5.9	29.4	24.5	11.6	1.3	75.3	37.1	51.0	49.0
65017	BRUMLEY	96.8	96.5	0.4	0.4	0.1	0.1	1.6	1.7	8.0	7.7	6.7	6.6	6.8	29.2	23.3	10.6	1.1	73.6	35.2	50.9	49.1
65018	CALIFORNIA	95.1	94.5	0.6	0.6	0.4	0.4	4.8	5.4	7.4	7.2	7.4	7.0	6.8	26.8	23.1	12.1	2.5	73.8	36.3	49.2	50.8
65020	CAMDENTON	97.0	96.7	0.2	0.2	0.4	0.6	1.2	1.3	5.5	5.7	6.5	6.5	5.7	23.4	28.5	16.4	1.8	78.3	42.8	49.7	50.3
65023	CENTERTOWN	99.0	98.9	0.1	0.1	0.1	0.2	0.4	0.5	6.0	7.0	7.0	6.9	5.7	28.9	27.9	9.7	1.1	75.6	38.3	51.5	48.5
65024	CHAMOIS	98.6	98.3	0.0	0.0	0.0	0.1	1.2	1.3	6.4	6.9	7.3	6.8	6.9	24.8	23.7	14.8	2.5	75.2	37.5	49.8	50.2
65025	CLARKSBURG	98.6	98.5	0.2	0.2	0.1	0.1	2.0	2.3	8.4	8.1	8.2	7.9	6.4	26.4	23.9	9.5	1.2	70.2	33.2	50.8	49.2
65026	ELDON	98.2	98.1	0.3	0.3	0.2	0.3	1.0	1.1	6.8	6.6	6.9	6.6	7.0	25.0	24.4	13.7	3.0	75.6	38.5	48.0	52.0
65032	EUGENE	98.3	98.2	0.1	0.1	0.2	0.2	0.6	0.6	7.9	7.9	8.5	6.8	6.2	29.4	23.1	8.9	1.3	71.5	35.0	50.2	49.8
65034	FORTUNA	98.5	98.3	0.3	0.3	0.2	0.2	1.0	1.0	8.3	8.3	8.5	6.8	6.3	25.2	23.0	11.7	2.0	70.9	35.6	50.4	49.6
65035	FREEBURG	99.9	99.9	0.0	0.0	0.0	0.0	0.8	0.9	8.2	8.2	7.8	5.7	6.2	30.5	22.3	10.0	1.2	72.4	34.7	50.5	49.5
65037	GRAVOIS MILLS	97.9	97.8	0.2	0.2	0.1	0.1	0.6	0.6	3.9	4.1	4.7	4.2	3.7	18.5	32.1	26.1	2.8	84.5	53.2	49.6	50.4
65039	HARTSBURG	97.2	96.9	0.5	0.7	0.1	0.1	1.1	1.3	6.5	7.0	7.4	6.5	5.1	28.3	28.4	9.7	1.3	74.7	38.7	49.3	50.7
65040	HENLEY	98.9	98.8	0.0	0.0	0.3	0.4	0.5	0.6	8.4	8.3	8.2	7.1	6.4	29.4	23.8	7.4	1.1	70.9	34.2	50.0	50.0
65041	HERMANN	98.8	98.7	0.3	0.3	0.1	0.1	0.5	0.5	5.3	5.7	6.4	5.9	5.4	23.2	26.3	17.4	4.5	78.9	43.8	48.6	51.4
65042	HIGH POINT	98.6	97.3	0.0	0.0	0.0	0.0	0.0	1.4	6.9	8.2	8.2	6.9	5.5	27.4	24.7	12.3	0.0	72.6	37.1	50.7	49.3
65043	HOLTS SUMMIT	95.4	94.8	2.1	2.4	0.3	0.4	1.3	1.5	8.1	7.7	8.0	6.8	6.6	30.2	24.5	7.5	0.7	72.1	34.4	49.8	50.2
65046	JAMESTOWN	96.6	96.0	0.5	0.7	0.4	0.5	0.8	0.8	6.5	7.0	7.3	6.2	5.6	26.7	28.2	11.1	1.5	75.4	39.1	52.4	47.6
65047	KAISER	96.1	95.9	0.5	0.6	0.2	0.2	1.7	1.8	8.3	7.7	6.5	6.4	6.6	29.6	23.3	10.5	1.2	73.6	35.1	51.0	49.0
65048	KOELTZTOWN	99.1	99.0	0.0	0.0	0.0	0.0	0.9	0.5	7.4	7.4	7.8	7.4	6.4	27.9	21.6	12.3	2.0	72.6	36.6	50.5	49.5
65049	LAKE OZARK	97.9	97.7	0.3	0.3	0.3	0.3	1.0	1.0	5.1	5.5	5.5	5.3	4.6	22.6	35.5	15.1	0.8	80.5	45.8	49.9	50.2
	MISSOURI	84.9	84.1	11.3	11.5	1.2	1.4	2.1	2.3	6.7	6.6	7.0	7.0	7.3	27.6	24.2	11.7	1.9	75.6	36.8	48.7	51.3
	UNITED STATES	75.1	73.6	12.3	12.5	3.8	4.2	12.5	14.1	6.9	6.7	7.2	7.0	7.3	28.6	23.8	10.8	1.7	75.1	36.0	49.1	50.9

#	ZIP CODE POST OFFICE NAME	2004 Per Capita Income	2004 HH Income Base	2004 Household Income Distribution (%) Less than $25,000	$25,000 to $49,999	$50,000 to $99,999	$100,000 to $149,999	$150,000 or More	Median Household Income 2004	2009	2004 National Centile	2004 State Centile	2004 Home Value Base	2004 Home Value Distribution (%) Less than $50,000	$50,000 to $89,999	$90,000 to $174,999	$175,000 to $399,999	$400,000 or More	2004 Median Home Value
64723	AMSTERDAM	16838	289	31.1	34.6	27.0	5.5	1.7	36985	42350	35	56	242	24.4	19.0	36.8	16.1	3.7	103261
64724	APPLETON CITY	16950	612	43.6	32.8	19.4	2.6	1.5	28219	32744	9	13	433	36.0	34.6	21.7	6.7	0.9	63919
64725	ARCHIE	20262	682	22.9	33.7	35.2	6.5	1.8	45811	53190	63	79	533	7.7	23.6	47.3	17.6	3.8	109375
64726	BLAIRSTOWN	20420	255	17.7	37.7	37.7	4.3	2.8	44576	50970	60	77	210	22.9	21.0	26.2	23.3	6.7	106818
64728	BRONAUGH	17474	228	34.7	33.8	25.4	4.0	2.2	36124	41821	32	52	186	28.0	28.0	23.1	17.7	3.2	78889
64730	BUTLER	18198	3717	34.5	33.7	24.4	5.4	2.0	34821	40294	27	44	2712	22.6	28.0	32.1	15.2	2.1	88994
64733	CHILHOWEE	18230	443	30.3	34.3	28.4	5.6	1.4	38092	45633	40	61	365	25.2	22.5	34.0	17.5	0.8	94250
64734	CLEVELAND	29093	770	12.7	21.6	44.7	15.6	5.5	64512	75189	88	95	688	6.5	10.0	35.5	40.7	7.3	170205
64735	CLINTON	19481	5605	36.3	33.5	23.0	4.6	2.7	34411	40265	25	42	3977	21.1	29.1	35.6	12.7	1.5	89699
64738	COLLINS	12966	377	49.9	32.4	16.5	1.3	0.0	25057	28450	5	4	317	37.9	22.1	24.9	15.1	0.0	74524
64739	CREIGHTON	21539	372	22.6	31.5	37.1	5.7	3.2	46318	53167	65	80	315	18.4	27.3	31.4	19.4	3.5	100368
64740	DEEPWATER	19385	762	34.3	33.7	26.4	3.9	1.7	35084	40574	28	45	636	32.4	23.1	30.7	13.4	0.5	78108
64741	DEERFIELD	19022	424	36.6	27.6	28.3	5.4	2.1	36046	43004	32	51	347	19.9	22.5	33.4	22.2	2.0	104427
64742	DREXEL	20217	827	23.2	30.2	37.1	7.7	1.7	47430	54940	67	82	627	14.8	24.9	35.7	21.4	3.2	104561
64744	EL DORADO SPRINGS	15012	2992	44.3	33.8	19.0	2.3	0.6	27999	31795	9	12	2233	31.2	31.5	28.0	8.4	0.9	70906
64745	FOSTER	17692	170	36.5	32.4	29.4	1.2	0.6	35249	40155	28	46	139	35.3	20.9	27.3	14.4	2.2	74167
64746	FREEMAN	25101	558	15.2	27.4	40.9	12.2	4.3	55328	63710	80	91	485	10.3	23.1	37.3	25.0	4.3	119556
64747	GARDEN CITY	22644	1500	20.6	31.3	38.8	6.6	2.7	48679	55918	70	84	1209	13.2	23.0	40.3	20.0	3.5	113111
64748	GOLDEN CITY	14255	597	42.9	36.9	16.8	2.2	1.3	28476	32973	10	14	407	39.8	32.4	19.4	7.9	0.5	58300
64750	HARWOOD	13685	68	45.6	36.8	17.7	0.0	0.0	27801	31716	8	11	56	53.6	25.0	14.3	7.1	0.0	46667
64752	HUME	15773	294	38.8	31.3	27.6	2.0	0.3	33266	37822	22	35	239	35.6	22.2	26.8	13.4	2.1	73182
64755	JASPER	19047	1270	32.2	35.8	25.9	3.9	2.3	35376	41629	29	47	991	30.9	33.8	25.2	8.1	2.0	69950
64756	JERICO SPRINGS	14916	441	36.5	40.4	19.5	3.2	0.5	35347	40107	29	47	380	33.2	35.8	14.5	16.6	0.0	67805
64759	LAMAR	16692	3401	36.9	32.9	24.5	3.8	1.9	34646	40057	26	43	2541	24.8	31.9	32.5	10.0	0.9	82079
64761	LEETON	17644	561	27.1	38.0	29.6	4.5	0.9	38725	46305	42	63	458	26.2	30.8	28.6	13.8	0.7	81579
64762	LIBERAL	14250	692	36.0	38.9	23.3	1.5	0.4	32603	37910	20	31	535	40.0	31.8	20.4	7.1	0.8	58770
64763	LOWRY CITY	16421	543	45.1	27.8	23.0	2.4	1.7	28639	32431	10	15	410	37.8	25.6	29.8	6.8	0.0	70455
64767	MILO	16629	236	27.5	41.1	26.7	3.0	1.7	36853	43806	35	55	191	38.2	28.3	25.1	6.8	1.6	63462
64769	MINDENMINES	14951	204	36.3	33.3	27.5	1.5	1.5	34194	39766	25	40	166	29.5	29.5	28.9	9.6	2.4	72500
64770	MONTROSE	18179	350	38.9	31.1	25.7	3.7	0.6	32553	36643	19	31	278	35.6	27.3	25.2	9.0	2.9	70000
64771	MOUNDVILLE	17917	192	34.4	34.9	25.5	3.7	1.6	35956	41905	31	51	157	29.3	28.0	21.7	17.8	3.2	76429
64772	NEVADA	18407	4805	38.7	30.1	23.5	5.6	2.1	33902	40311	24	39	3230	23.8	34.3	29.3	12.0	0.7	81881
64776	OSCEOLA	16797	2484	42.6	33.5	19.7	2.8	1.4	29433	33788	11	17	2010	35.2	24.1	30.6	8.1	2.1	76179
64778	RICHARDS	13729	306	42.8	28.8	24.8	2.9	0.7	29747	34156	12	18	246	36.2	24.4	26.4	11.0	2.0	74615
64779	RICH HILL	15982	752	47.1	35.2	15.0	1.6	1.1	26669	31219	7	7	554	58.3	27.1	11.7	2.7	0.2	42203
64780	ROCKVILLE	15110	176	34.1	47.7	15.9	2.3	0.0	33709	37115	23	38	134	37.3	37.3	12.7	9.0	3.7	60769
64783	SCHELL CITY	14538	343	42.9	34.7	20.1	1.2	1.2	30076	35402	12	19	283	44.9	27.6	20.1	7.1	0.4	54833
64784	SHELDON	16992	638	27.9	40.1	27.4	3.1	1.4	36925	43590	35	56	516	37.8	28.3	25.8	7.0	1.2	64286
64788	URICH	19041	424	29.5	34.9	28.8	6.1	0.7	37479	43986	37	58	335	36.4	23.9	27.5	10.5	1.8	73750
64790	WALKER	16654	229	37.1	31.4	28.4	2.2	0.9	35146	40557	28	46	190	33.7	27.9	33.2	5.3	0.0	74000
64801	JOPLIN	19148	13388	35.9	33.2	23.5	4.9	2.6	34545	40276	26	43	8481	26.0	32.1	31.9	9.0	0.9	79187
64804	JOPLIN	24045	14574	30.2	32.7	26.3	6.2	4.6	38791	45418	42	63	10204	16.8	32.6	36.7	11.0	3.0	90665
64831	ANDERSON	15932	2452	42.0	34.6	18.6	2.5	2.2	30350	34445	13	21	1886	26.0	31.7	30.0	11.1	1.2	81049
64832	ASBURY	18762	296	27.0	30.4	34.5	7.8	0.3	44673	50805	60	77	248	26.6	21.8	34.7	14.5	2.4	92000
64833	AVILLA	16091	82	29.3	39.0	29.3	2.4	0.0	38414	45912	41	62	67	25.4	26.9	34.3	10.5	3.0	86250
64834	CARL JUNCTION	20392	2777	22.7	31.2	32.7	10.7	2.7	47028	54773	66	82	2292	12.9	37.4	34.3	14.6	0.9	89716
64835	CARTERVILLE	15006	745	33.6	39.1	24.2	2.4	0.8	34004	39746	24	39	597	43.7	40.7	13.1	2.2	0.3	53989
64836	CARTHAGE	18422	8699	32.9	35.6	24.8	4.6	2.2	35715	41355	30	49	6193	24.1	32.4	31.8	10.4	1.4	80791
64840	DIAMOND	17299	970	26.5	37.1	30.6	4.4	1.3	37913	43728	39	60	755	21.6	36.3	32.1	7.3	2.8	80083
64842	FAIRVIEW	16689	298	36.2	38.3	20.1	2.7	2.7	32601	38213	20	31	246	28.5	29.7	29.7	11.0	1.2	77000
64843	GOODMAN	14274	1101	38.2	38.1	21.0	2.1	0.7	30653	35219	14	22	887	33.6	35.1	22.0	7.4	1.9	67593
64844	GRANBY	15540	1724	32.1	38.1	26.7	2.3	0.8	35594	41266	30	48	1393	40.1	29.0	21.9	7.2	1.9	61615
64847	LANAGAN	12645	320	47.2	36.3	14.7	1.3	0.6	27061	31008	7	8	240	45.0	24.2	18.8	9.6	2.5	56000
64848	LA RUSSELL	16003	275	35.3	32.0	26.6	4.4	1.8	35522	41196	30	48	223	32.3	22.4	27.8	14.4	3.1	82500
64850	NEOSHO	18581	8423	30.8	34.1	28.0	4.9	2.2	37966	44078	39	60	6174	19.8	32.9	35.8	9.8	1.6	86406
64854	NOEL	14033	1232	37.1	40.5	18.4	2.3	1.7	31925	36530	18	28	715	25.9	36.9	24.2	11.8	1.3	76288
64855	ORONOGO	19004	1012	30.3	34.2	29.6	4.2	1.8	39489	45552	44	65	851	29.6	31.6	31.5	5.1	2.2	74077
64856	PINEVILLE	15582	1596	39.2	34.5	20.8	3.8	1.8	32069	36893	18	29	1243	34.4	29.0	23.6	10.4	2.7	70739
64859	REEDS	17236	302	32.1	35.1	26.8	4.0	2.0	36775	42857	35	54	252	25.0	26.2	31.4	14.3	3.2	88125
64861	ROCKY COMFORT	22624	275	41.8	30.2	15.3	4.7	8.0	30745	35908	14	22	226	23.9	31.4	19.0	24.8	0.9	82941
64862	SARCOXIE	15736	1050	40.5	31.6	23.3	3.1	1.5	30836	35872	14	23	787	33.6	31.4	26.9	7.8	0.4	71103
64863	SOUTH WEST CITY	11904	550	53.6	31.1	12.9	0.7	1.6	23258	26520	3	2	339	36.9	31.0	24.8	3.8	3.5	71000
64865	SENECA	18403	1886	29.3	34.8	28.5	5.3	2.2	38968	45292	43	64	1539	24.6	33.1	31.7	9.2	1.3	81082
64866	STARK CITY	16388	576	35.1	35.6	24.0	3.8	1.6	33866	39586	24	38	470	42.1	19.8	28.9	7.9	1.3	64074
64867	STELLA	16937	689	37.0	34.0	22.9	3.9	2.2	32463	36908	19	30	576	28.5	26.2	29.5	13.2	2.6	82703
64868	TIFF CITY	12722	19	52.6	26.3	21.1	0.0	0.0	23541	35000	4	3	16	31.3	25.0	25.0	18.8	0.0	80000
64870	WEBB CITY	17696	4811	36.1	32.3	24.8	5.1	1.6	33951	39514	24	39	3071	20.0	33.6	41.1	5.0	0.4	86139
64873	WENTWORTH	17212	473	32.6	39.5	22.0	3.2	2.8	35947	41538	31	50	400	30.3	19.5	33.0	16.5	0.8	90345
64874	WHEATON	13034	446	42.4	39.5	15.7	2.0	0.5	28333	32458	9	13	327	33.3	31.2	25.4	7.0	3.1	70192
65001	ARGYLE	17121	153	28.8	33.3	32.0	4.6	1.3	41806	48652	52	72	130	22.3	26.2	33.9	15.4	2.3	92857
65010	ASHLAND	24958	1701	16.3	28.6	42.9	8.8	3.5	53665	65504	78	90	1324	11.5	12.1	42.8	26.7	7.0	138587
65011	BARNETT	17788	761	31.0	33.8	26.0	4.2	5.0	37300	42880	36	57	645	23.3	26.5	32.4	14.9	3.0	90313
65013	BELLE	19215	1355	34.6	32.0	28.1	3.9	1.3	35472	41478	29	48	1055	26.2	31.0	32.4	9.0	1.4	81012
65014	BLAND	19819	1049	29.2	36.0	27.6	6.3	1.0	39406	45307	44	65	868	25.1	26.5	29.8	14.1	4.5	87742
65016	BONNOTS MILL	21884	534	22.3	30.2	37.3	8.1	2.3	47832	54342	68	83	457	11.4	20.1	43.1	20.6	4.8	124769
65017	BRUMLEY	15993	693	36.4	34.2	23.5	3.8	2.2	33237	38598	22	35	553	27.7	23.3	31.1	14.7	3.3	88103
65018	CALIFORNIA	20406	2969	27.9	32.4	31.9	5.2	2.6	42774	48215	55	74	2226	17.1	27.0	40.1	14.1	1.8	96931
65020	CAMDENTON	19004	5072	32.2	36.6	24.8	4.5	1.9	36371	42002	33	53	3928	15.7	18.0	36.6	25.6	4.2	117078
65023	CENTERTOWN	23274	653	20.5	26.5	42.7	8.3	2.0	51885	61343	75	88	549	12.8	18.4	44.3	23.1	1.5	124531
65024	CHAMOIS	16747	559	31.7	34.0	30.8	2.9	0.7	37768	44448	38	59	456	41.0	19.3	28.1	9.7	2.0	64000
65025	CLARKSBURG	17802	342	31.6	32.5	30.4	3.5	2.1	39193	44783	43	64	275	30.6	22.9	29.1	12.0	5.5	84722
65026	ELDON	17222	4315	37.9	34.4	22.2	3.4	2.2	33048	38450	21	34	2965	24.7	32.2	32.4	9.3	1.5	81031
65032	EUGENE	20820	439	23.9	23.9	41.5	8.0	2.7	51368	60298	74	87	385	16.4	14.3	44.4	22.6	2.3	118371
65034	FORTUNA	18740	204	27.9	33.3	30.9	3.9	3.9	40753	48427	49	69	170	24.1	20.6	35.3	18.8	1.2	101000
65035	FREEBURG	20517	627	21.1	35.3	36.4	5.9	1.4	46268	52241	64	80	541	15.0	19.2	42.7	20.3	2.8	109722
65037	GRAVOIS MILLS	21502	1889	34.7	36.4	20.0	5.7	3.2	33601	39037	23	37	1585	18.6	18.9	38.3	22.3	2.0	110548
65039	HARTSBURG	27481	875	12.7	25.3	45.5	12.3	4.2	60674	74508	85	93	740	8.2	10.3	44.2	30.7	6.6	149107
65040	HENLEY	23373	417	24.2	26.6	37.2	8.2	3.8	49371	59007	71	85	359	25.4	14.5	40.1	17.3	2.8	108073
65041	HERMANN	21556	2127	26.8	35.5	29.5	5.4	2.9	41700	47587	52	72	1689	14.0	26.5	40.0	15.7	3.8	102387
65042	HIGH POINT	16027	25	28.0	28.0	40.0	4.0	0.0	42376	54495	54	73	21	14.3	14.3	33.3	33.3	4.8	143750
65043	HOLTS SUMMIT	21090	3449	19.4	32.0	39.3	7.7	1.7	48774	55563	70	84	2841	19.8	12.0	52.6	14.6	1.1	111207
65046	JAMESTOWN	19056	497	26.6	39.4	29.0	3.2	1.8	40130	44940	47	67	412	26.5	27.4	31.8	12.4	1.9	84667
65047	KAISER	19469	523	36.0	34.6	23.1	4.4	1.9	32700	37750	20	32	397	28.5	21.9	31.5	14.9	3.3	89211
65048	KOELTZTOWN	17461	74	25.7	35.1	33.8	5.4	0.0	43897	50720	58	76	63	14.3	27.0	44.4	14.3	0.0	104167
65049	LAKE OZARK	33288	3371	20.4	30.4	32.6	8.5	8.1	49117	59919	70	85	2767	6.8	10.8	34.2	36.6	11.7	170819
	MISSOURI	23864		27.0	29.4	30.1	9.0	4.5	44017	52626				15.2	22.7	39.0	19.7	3.4	109184
	UNITED STATES	25866		24.7	27.1	30.8	10.9	6.5	48124	56710				10.9	15.0	33.7	30.1	10.4	145905

SPENDING POTENTIAL INDICES

MISSOURI

64723-65049 D

ZIP CODE		FINANCIAL SERVICES				THE HOME						ENTERTAINMENT						PERSONAL			
						Home Improvements		Furnishings													
#	POST OFFICE NAME	Auto Loan	Home Loan	Invest-ments	Retire-ment Plans	Home Repair	Lawn & Garden	Comput-ers & Hard-ware	Major Appli-ances	TV, Radio, Sound Equip-ment	Furni-ture	Dine out/ Carry out	Sports Equip-ment	Fees & Tickets	Toys & Games	Travel	Cable TV	Apparel & Services	Auto Repairs	Health Insur-ance	Pets & Supplies
64723	AMSTERDAM	84	58	29	51	65	74	56	69	66	57	78	82	48	75	57	71	71	68	83	97
64724	APPLETON CITY	65	48	31	46	53	63	53	59	59	50	70	66	47	66	52	62	63	59	70	72
64725	ARCHIE	82	71	56	70	75	83	71	76	75	70	91	89	68	91	71	76	86	75	83	93
64726	BLAIRSTOWN	86	77	58	73	81	87	71	79	75	71	92	94	70	94	73	77	87	77	85	102
64728	BRONAUGH	77	55	30	52	63	71	56	67	63	54	75	79	48	72	57	67	68	66	80	90
64730	BUTLER	76	56	35	53	63	72	59	67	66	57	78	78	52	75	59	69	71	67	80	86
64733	CHILHOWEE	74	65	48	62	69	74	60	67	64	60	78	80	58	79	62	66	74	66	73	87
64734	CLEVELAND	103	127	135	127	125	123	114	113	105	113	133	133	121	141	116	102	132	109	102	126
64735	CLINTON	71	58	46	55	62	71	61	66	67	59	80	76	57	78	61	69	75	66	75	80
64738	COLLINS	59	39	18	34	44	51	38	47	46	39	54	57	32	51	38	49	49	47	58	67
64739	CREIGHTON	91	81	62	77	86	92	75	83	80	75	97	99	74	99	77	82	92	81	90	107
64740	DEEPWATER	85	57	26	49	64	74	55	69	66	56	78	82	47	73	56	71	71	68	84	97
64741	DEERFIELD	76	60	41	57	65	75	63	69	69	60	82	79	57	79	63	73	76	69	81	86
64742	DREXEL	91	71	46	68	79	87	68	80	75	68	90	96	63	90	70	78	84	78	91	107
64744	EL DORADO SPRINGS	60	44	27	41	48	57	46	53	53	45	62	60	41	59	46	56	57	52	63	67
64745	FOSTER	79	55	29	52	64	72	55	68	63	54	74	81	47	72	57	66	67	67	81	94
64746	FREEMAN	106	101	85	98	105	111	93	101	96	93	117	119	93	121	96	97	113	98	105	126
64747	GARDEN CITY	95	83	64	80	87	95	80	87	85	79	103	102	78	104	81	87	97	85	94	109
64748	GOLDEN CITY	59	43	26	41	48	57	46	53	52	45	62	60	41	59	46	56	56	52	63	67
64750	HARWOOD	61	41	19	35	47	54	40	50	48	40	56	59	34	53	40	52	51	49	61	70
64752	HUME	73	52	30	50	60	68	54	64	61	52	72	75	46	69	55	64	65	63	76	85
64755	JASPER	90	63	33	57	71	81	61	74	71	61	84	89	53	81	62	76	77	73	89	104
64756	JERICO SPRINGS	71	47	21	41	54	62	46	57	55	46	65	68	39	61	46	59	59	56	70	81
64759	LAMAR	68	56	41	54	60	68	56	62	61	55	73	72	53	73	57	63	68	61	70	78
64761	LEETON	71	61	47	60	64	72	62	66	66	61	80	76	59	79	62	67	75	65	72	80
64762	LIBERAL	62	48	31	47	53	60	48	56	53	48	64	65	44	63	49	55	59	55	63	72
64763	LOWRY CITY	62	48	32	45	53	62	49	56	56	48	66	65	44	63	50	59	60	56	67	72
64767	MILO	69	58	45	58	61	69	60	64	64	59	77	73	57	77	60	65	72	63	70	76
64769	MINDENMINES	73	51	26	48	59	66	50	62	58	49	68	75	43	66	52	60	62	61	74	86
64770	MONTROSE	66	49	32	47	54	65	54	60	61	52	72	68	48	68	54	65	66	60	72	74
64771	MOUNDVILLE	78	55	30	52	63	72	55	67	63	54	74	80	48	72	57	67	68	66	80	91
64772	NEVADA	66	57	53	56	60	68	61	63	65	59	79	73	58	79	61	67	75	64	70	75
64776	OSCEOLA	69	49	28	45	55	64	50	59	58	50	69	69	44	65	51	62	63	59	72	79
64778	RICHARDS	61	46	30	44	50	60	51	56	57	48	67	63	45	63	50	60	61	56	67	68
64779	RICH HILL	65	48	31	46	53	63	53	59	59	50	70	66	47	66	52	63	64	59	70	72
64780	ROCKVILLE	68	46	21	40	52	60	45	55	54	45	63	66	38	60	45	58	57	55	68	78
64783	SCHELL CITY	64	47	28	44	52	59	47	55	54	47	64	65	42	62	47	57	59	54	65	73
64784	SHELDON	69	59	45	58	62	69	60	64	64	59	77	74	57	77	60	65	72	63	70	77
64788	URICH	74	58	39	55	63	73	62	68	68	59	81	77	56	77	61	72	74	67	80	83
64790	WALKER	67	57	44	57	60	67	59	62	62	57	75	71	56	75	58	63	71	62	68	74
64801	JOPLIN	66	61	60	61	61	67	65	65	66	63	82	76	63	81	64	66	79	66	66	74
64804	JOPLIN	85	77	68	75	80	89	78	82	82	77	100	95	76	100	79	84	96	82	89	98
64831	ANDERSON	74	54	30	49	59	68	54	63	62	54	73	74	47	69	54	66	67	63	75	84
64832	ASBURY	80	69	50	65	74	80	64	72	69	64	83	86	62	85	66	71	79	71	79	94
64833	AVILLA	70	62	48	59	66	71	58	64	61	58	75	76	57	76	59	63	71	62	69	83
64834	CARL JUNCTION	83	84	77	83	85	89	80	83	79	79	98	96	80	100	80	79	95	81	82	95
64835	CARTERVILLE	70	53	31	47	58	65	50	59	57	50	68	71	45	66	51	60	63	58	69	81
64836	CARTHAGE	75	63	49	61	66	74	65	69	69	63	84	80	61	83	64	71	79	69	76	84
64840	DIAMOND	78	63	43	60	67	75	62	69	68	61	81	81	58	80	62	70	76	68	78	88
64842	FAIRVIEW	84	56	26	49	64	73	54	68	66	55	77	81	46	73	55	71	70	67	84	97
64843	GOODMAN	67	48	25	42	53	59	46	56	53	47	63	66	40	60	46	57	58	55	66	76
64844	GRANBY	69	54	35	51	58	64	53	60	58	54	70	71	48	67	53	60	66	60	68	78
64847	LANAGAN	58	42	22	37	46	52	40	49	47	41	55	58	35	52	41	50	51	48	58	67
64848	LA RUSSELL	76	63	43	58	67	74	59	67	65	59	78	80	55	78	60	67	73	66	76	89
64850	NEOSHO	74	64	54	63	67	74	66	69	69	65	84	80	63	83	65	70	80	69	74	82
64854	NOEL	63	53	41	53	56	63	54	58	58	53	70	67	52	69	54	59	66	57	63	69
64855	ORONOGO	85	70	47	65	74	80	66	75	72	67	87	89	61	84	67	74	82	74	83	97
64856	PINEVILLE	66	54	38	51	57	63	54	60	58	54	70	69	49	66	54	59	66	60	65	74
64859	REEDS	76	61	41	57	66	73	57	66	64	58	77	79	54	76	59	66	72	65	75	88
64861	ROCKY COMFORT	115	77	35	67	87	101	75	93	90	76	106	111	63	100	76	97	96	92	115	132
64862	SARCOXIE	71	50	26	45	56	65	50	60	58	50	69	70	43	65	50	62	63	59	73	81
64863	SOUTH WEST CITY	46	41	44	40	40	46	47	45	50	46	61	53	46	60	46	50	59	47	47	50
64865	SENECA	78	67	52	66	71	78	66	72	70	66	85	84	64	85	67	72	80	70	78	88
64866	STARK CITY	82	55	26	48	62	72	53	66	64	54	75	79	45	71	54	69	68	66	81	94
64867	STELLA	85	57	26	49	64	74	55	69	66	56	78	82	47	73	56	71	71	68	84	97
64868	TIFF CITY	57	38	17	33	43	50	37	46	44	37	52	55	31	49	37	48	47	45	57	65
64870	WEBB CITY	67	60	55	60	61	68	64	65	66	62	81	76	61	80	62	65	77	65	67	75
64873	WENTWORTH	82	58	30	51	65	74	55	68	65	56	77	81	48	74	56	70	71	67	82	95
64874	WHEATON	53	45	35	45	48	54	47	50	50	46	60	57	45	60	46	50	56	49	54	59
65001	ARGYLE	74	65	50	63	68	75	63	69	67	63	81	80	61	82	64	68	77	67	74	85
65010	ASHLAND	91	98	95	98	97	100	92	94	89	92	111	109	94	114	93	87	109	92	89	106
65011	BARNETT	83	71	52	67	76	83	66	75	71	66	86	89	63	87	68	74	81	73	83	98
65013	BELLE	76	60	40	56	65	74	60	68	67	59	80	79	55	78	61	71	74	67	79	87
65014	BLAND	88	59	27	51	67	77	57	71	69	58	81	85	49	76	58	74	73	70	87	101
65016	BONNOTS MILL	99	78	50	73	86	95	74	87	82	74	98	105	68	98	77	85	91	86	100	118
65017	BRUMLEY	77	59	37	54	63	70	57	66	63	58	76	78	51	72	57	65	71	66	74	87
65018	CALIFORNIA	83	69	50	66	74	83	70	76	76	68	91	88	65	89	70	78	84	75	86	95
65020	CAMDENTON	74	59	42	56	65	73	59	67	65	58	78	78	54	76	61	68	72	67	77	86
65023	CENTERTOWN	95	85	64	80	89	96	78	87	83	78	101	103	77	103	81	85	96	84	94	112
65024	CHAMOIS	71	53	33	50	58	69	57	64	64	54	75	73	50	71	57	67	68	64	76	80
65025	CLARKSBURG	78	63	45	62	68	77	64	71	70	63	84	82	60	83	65	71	78	70	79	88
65026	ELDON	68	53	36	50	57	66	54	61	61	53	72	71	50	70	55	63	67	61	71	77
65032	EUGENE	94	84	64	80	89	95	78	86	82	78	100	102	76	102	80	84	95	84	93	111
65034	FORTUNA	92	71	45	68	80	88	68	81	76	68	91	97	62	91	71	79	84	79	93	109
65035	FREEBURG	89	79	60	75	83	89	73	81	77	73	94	96	71	96	75	79	89	79	87	104
65037	GRAVOIS MILLS	79	61	40	55	69	77	58	70	66	57	78	82	51	76	61	70	72	69	83	96
65039	HARTSBURG	92	113	119	113	111	110	101	101	94	101	118	118	107	125	103	91	118	98	91	112
65040	HENLEY	103	92	70	87	97	104	85	94	90	85	110	112	83	112	88	93	104	92	102	122
65041	HERMANN	83	65	44	62	71	82	67	75	74	65	88	87	60	85	68	77	81	75	88	96
65042	HIGH POINT	75	67	51	63	71	76	62	68	66	62	80	82	60	81	64	67	76	67	74	88
65043	HOLTS SUMMIT	85	82	70	80	83	87	78	82	78	79	96	95	76	95	78	77	93	81	81	96
65046	JAMESTOWN	72	62	48	61	65	72	62	67	66	61	80	77	60	80	62	67	75	66	73	80
65047	KAISER	73	61	42	57	63	68	58	65	62	60	75	76	53	71	58	63	71	65	70	82
65048	KOELTZTOWN	75	65	50	64	68	76	64	70	68	64	83	81	62	83	65	70	78	68	75	85
65049	LAKE OZARK	125	100	70	91	111	123	95	112	105	94	126	131	85	123	100	111	117	111	129	150
	MISSOURI	87	82	79	80	83	90	82	85	85	82	104	99	81	103	82	85	100	85	87	100
	UNITED STATES	100	100	100	100	100	100	100	100	100	100	100	100	100	100	100	100	100	100	100	100

 Copyright © 2004 ESRI BIS. All rights reserved. Reproduction by any method is prohibited.

# POST OFFICE NAME	COUNTY FIPS CODE	POPULATION 2000	2004	2009	2000-2004 ANNUAL RATE % Rate	State Centile	HOUSEHOLDS 2000	2004	2009	% Annual Rate 2000-2004	2004 Average HH Size	FAMILIES 2000	2004	% Annual Rate 2000-2004
65050 LATHAM	135	649	678	705	1.0	69	180	190	199	1.3	3.57	141	146	0.8
65051 LINN	151	4340	4416	4542	0.4	49	1673	1722	1795	0.7	2.50	1146	1156	0.2
65052 LINN CREEK	029	3686	3963	4388	1.7	82	1416	1540	1725	2.0	2.55	1078	1155	1.6
65053 LOHMAN	051	1293	1393	1484	1.8	83	466	506	544	2.0	2.75	379	404	1.5
65054 LOOSE CREEK	151	1075	1077	1102	0.0	34	395	402	417	0.4	2.65	313	315	0.2
65058 META	125	950	913	925	-0.9	7	376	364	373	-0.8	2.51	282	270	-1.0
65059 MOKANE	027	871	984	1088	2.9	92	328	374	418	3.1	2.60	257	287	2.6
65061 MORRISON	151	766	765	785	0.0	30	314	317	328	0.2	2.41	218	216	-0.2
65062 MOUNT STERLING	073	203	203	208	0.0	32	87	88	91	0.3	2.31	62	62	0.0
65063 NEW BLOOMFIELD	027	3026	3386	3726	2.7	91	1114	1256	1393	2.9	2.68	853	946	2.5
65064 OLEAN	131	958	974	1025	0.4	48	352	362	383	0.7	2.66	274	277	0.3
65065 OSAGE BEACH	029	4693	5015	5531	1.6	80	2113	2288	2559	1.9	2.14	1381	1464	1.4
65066 OWENSVILLE	073	6340	6789	7223	1.6	81	2458	2650	2839	1.8	2.53	1713	1807	1.3
65067 PORTLAND	027	432	473	515	2.2	87	177	196	216	2.4	2.41	127	137	1.8
65068 PRAIRIE HOME	053	604	609	630	0.2	40	249	253	264	0.4	2.41	189	189	0.0
65069 RHINELAND	139	1035	1068	1098	0.7	60	417	434	450	0.9	2.46	299	306	0.6
65072 ROCKY MOUNT	141	1294	1320	1348	0.5	51	611	627	642	0.6	2.11	433	436	0.2
65074 RUSSELLVILLE	051	2412	2497	2603	0.8	64	912	950	999	1.0	2.63	695	710	0.5
65075 SAINT ELIZABETH	131	761	777	819	0.5	53	246	254	270	0.8	2.90	191	194	0.4
65076 SAINT THOMAS	051	741	698	712	-1.4	2	241	230	238	-1.1	3.03	200	189	-1.3
65077 STEEDMAN	027	511	557	604	2.1	86	198	218	240	2.3	2.56	141	152	1.8
65078 STOVER	141	3447	3517	3602	0.5	51	1457	1492	1532	0.6	2.33	1009	1010	0.0
65079 SUNRISE BEACH	029	5367	5678	6217	1.3	75	2527	2706	2998	1.6	2.10	1822	1917	1.2
65080 TEBBETTS	027	1050	1134	1224	1.8	83	388	423	461	2.1	2.68	318	342	1.7
65081 TIPTON	135	3827	3824	3878	0.0	31	1083	1088	1116	0.1	2.40	718	703	-0.5
65082 TUSCUMBIA	131	1317	1354	1431	0.7	58	446	464	496	0.9	2.68	325	334	0.6
65083 ULMAN	131	627	659	706	1.2	73	240	255	276	1.4	2.55	178	186	1.0
65084 VERSAILLES	141	6408	6562	6726	0.6	54	2447	2513	2581	0.6	2.55	1708	1720	0.2
65085 WESTPHALIA	151	1224	1217	1247	-0.1	27	418	422	438	0.2	2.78	326	324	-0.1
65101 JEFFERSON CITY	051	28903	30037	31559	0.9	66	10387	10947	11699	1.2	2.36	6575	6787	0.8
65109 JEFFERSON CITY	051	35436	37123	39119	1.1	71	14075	14943	15956	1.4	2.38	9355	9689	0.8
65201 COLUMBIA	019	33912	35556	38096	1.1	71	12486	13284	14526	1.5	2.12	5123	5269	0.7
65202 COLUMBIA	019	35672	39414	43707	2.4	88	14207	15861	17735	2.6	2.45	9064	9792	1.8
65203 COLUMBIA	019	45077	48172	52515	1.6	80	18557	19951	21887	1.7	2.39	11462	11979	1.0
65211 COLUMBIA	019	229	239	257	1.0	68	146	154	167	1.3	1.55	19	19	0.0
65215 COLUMBIA	019	301	321	341	1.5	79	20	24	27	4.4	5.67	4	4	0.0
65216 COLUMBIA	019	242	242	249	0.0	32	15	15	16	0.0	2.53	6	5	-4.2
65230 ARMSTRONG	089	724	739	741	0.5	52	268	276	279	0.7	2.57	197	198	0.1
65231 AUXVASSE	027	3236	3346	3529	0.8	63	1240	1292	1373	1.0	2.56	894	912	0.5
65232 BENTON CITY	007	245	245	245	0.0	32	103	104	105	0.2	2.36	82	82	0.1
65233 BOONVILLE	053	11005	11378	11881	0.8	63	3709	3892	4132	1.1	2.41	2514	2578	0.6
65236 BRUNSWICK	041	1440	1414	1389	-0.4	19	631	623	616	-0.3	2.22	390	375	-0.9
65237 BUNCETON	053	1065	1074	1107	0.2	40	431	439	456	0.4	2.45	311	310	-0.1
65239 CAIRO	175	1246	1252	1251	0.1	37	482	489	493	0.3	2.56	366	364	-0.1
65240 CENTRALIA	007	6699	6961	7445	0.9	66	2566	2695	2908	1.2	2.55	1903	1954	0.6
65243 CLARK	175	5535	5607	5661	0.3	44	1253	1289	1318	0.7	2.99	986	998	0.3
65244 CLIFTON HILL	175	358	361	361	0.2	40	144	146	148	0.3	2.47	112	112	0.0
65246 DALTON	041	155	151	148	-0.6	14	68	67	66	-0.4	2.24	42	40	-1.1
65247 EXCELLO	121	606	588	574	-0.7	11	240	236	232	-0.4	2.49	182	175	-0.9
65248 FAYETTE	089	4717	4648	4605	-0.4	20	1690	1666	1656	-0.3	2.38	1129	1090	-0.8
65250 FRANKLIN	089	738	760	767	0.7	59	281	291	295	0.8	2.61	206	208	0.2
65251 FULTON	027	21067	21911	23161	0.9	67	6993	7382	7944	1.3	2.46	4735	4888	0.8
65254 GLASGOW	089	1738	1725	1713	-0.2	26	679	680	679	0.0	2.47	456	445	-0.6
65255 HALLSVILLE	019	3150	3311	3570	1.2	73	1227	1303	1416	1.4	2.53	943	981	0.9
65256 HARRISBURG	019	1389	1522	1673	2.2	87	527	582	643	2.4	2.61	405	437	1.8
65257 HIGBEE	089	1248	1258	1257	0.2	40	512	521	525	0.4	2.39	356	353	-0.2
65258 HOLLIDAY	137	293	374	435	5.9	99	117	152	178	6.4	2.45	85	108	5.8
65259 HUNTSVILLE	175	3399	3533	3598	0.9	66	1274	1336	1371	1.1	2.60	922	947	0.6
65260 JACKSONVILLE	175	708	736	749	0.9	66	265	277	284	1.1	2.66	204	210	0.7
65261 KEYTESVILLE	041	1327	1299	1274	-0.5	17	584	576	569	-0.3	2.24	377	362	-1.0
65262 KINGDOM CITY	027	450	460	488	0.5	53	181	187	201	0.8	2.46	146	148	0.3
65263 MADISON	137	2178	2482	2731	3.1	93	824	951	1058	3.4	2.58	622	705	3.0
65264 MARTINSBURG	007	794	821	840	0.8	63	307	320	329	1.0	2.56	240	245	0.5
65265 MEXICO	007	15470	15448	15489	0.0	30	6354	6402	6474	0.2	2.33	4229	4157	-0.4
65270 MOBERLY	175	14013	13842	13806	-0.3	23	5832	5810	5843	-0.1	2.30	3737	3627	-0.7
65274 NEW FRANKLIN	089	1724	1730	1729	0.1	35	696	702	703	0.2	2.42	479	472	-0.4
65275 PARIS	137	3278	3277	3362	0.0	31	1275	1279	1322	0.1	2.46	877	859	-0.5
65276 PILOT GROVE	053	1594	1663	1758	1.0	68	607	635	675	1.1	2.57	424	436	0.7
65279 ROCHEPORT	019	1527	1583	1690	0.9	64	596	623	669	1.1	2.54	456	466	0.5
65280 RUSH HILL	007	502	505	506	0.1	38	197	199	201	0.2	2.54	159	159	0.0
65281 SALISBURY	041	3530	3452	3383	-0.5	16	1402	1387	1373	-0.3	2.40	978	946	-0.8
65282 SANTA FE	137	703	705	721	0.1	35	275	279	288	0.3	2.52	220	219	-0.1
65283 STOUTSVILLE	137	429	434	446	0.3	43	173	177	184	0.5	2.44	134	134	0.0
65284 STURGEON	019	2340	2582	2858	2.3	88	871	974	1087	2.7	2.63	633	689	2.0
65285 THOMPSON	007	974	1024	1049	1.2	73	357	380	393	1.5	2.69	285	299	1.1
65286 TRIPLETT	041	200	196	193	-0.5	18	83	82	81	-0.3	2.39	58	56	-0.8
65287 WOOLDRIDGE	053	309	307	317	-0.2	27	118	118	123	0.0	2.60	93	92	-0.3
65301 SEDALIA	159	32078	32273	32617	0.1	38	12884	12996	13170	0.2	2.44	8533	8410	-0.3
65305 WHITEMAN AIR FORCE B	101	3843	3857	3917	0.1	36	940	953	977	0.3	3.49	910	920	0.3
65321 BLACKBURN	195	748	716	679	-1.0	5	280	269	257	-0.9	2.66	207	196	-1.3
65322 BLACKWATER	053	720	792	857	2.3	88	296	331	363	2.7	2.30	221	242	2.2
65323 CALHOUN	083	1051	1052	1060	0.0	33	414	418	424	0.2	2.52	308	305	-0.2
65324 CLIMAX SPRINGS	029	2502	2579	2808	0.7	59	1152	1201	1323	1.0	2.15	836	857	0.6
65325 COLE CAMP	015	3008	3539	3944	3.9	97	1205	1456	1649	4.6	2.39	857	1013	4.0
65326 EDWARDS	015	1727	1716	1754	-0.2	27	802	807	836	0.2	2.13	565	557	-0.3
65329 FLORENCE	141	944	970	995	0.6	57	343	353	362	0.7	2.75	269	272	0.3
65330 GILLIAM	195	490	472	449	-0.9	8	203	197	188	-0.7	2.40	139	132	-1.2
65332 GREEN RIDGE	159	1543	1510	1504	-0.5	17	567	562	563	-0.2	2.68	433	418	-0.8
65333 HOUSTONIA	159	942	984	1001	1.0	69	341	360	369	1.3	2.68	262	271	0.8
65334 HUGHESVILLE	159	745	810	844	2.0	85	261	286	300	2.2	2.79	201	216	1.7
65335 IONIA	015	222	212	212	-1.1	4	93	90	90	-0.8	2.36	71	68	-1.0
65336 KNOB NOSTER	101	5342	5445	5643	0.5	50	2042	2086	2167	0.5	2.61	1434	1428	-0.1
65337 LA MONTE	159	1970	1966	1965	-0.1	30	742	747	751	0.2	2.60	536	524	-0.5
65338 LINCOLN	015	2101	2148	2201	0.5	53	835	859	886	0.7	2.44	591	596	0.2
65339 MALTA BEND	195	605	580	551	-1.0	6	232	224	214	-0.8	2.59	172	163	-1.3
MISSOURI					0.8					0.9	2.46			0.4
UNITED STATES					1.2					1.3	2.58			1.1

ZIP CODE #	POST OFFICE NAME	RACE (%) White 2000	White 2004	Black 2000	Black 2004	Asian/Pacific 2000	Asian/Pacific 2004	% Hispanic Origin 2000	% Hispanic Origin 2004	2004 AGE DISTRIBUTION (%) 0-4	5-9	10-14	15-19	20-24	25-44	45-64	65-84	85+	18+	MEDIAN AGE 2004	% 2004 Males	% 2004 Females
65050	LATHAM	95.4	95.0	2.5	2.7	0.2	0.2	1.2	1.5	10.2	9.9	10.5	8.9	7.4	25.4	20.2	7.4	0.3	63.7	27.4	51.9	48.1
65051	LINN	98.1	97.9	0.2	0.2	0.2	0.3	0.4	0.3	6.7	6.6	7.0	6.9	7.1	28.1	22.4	12.7	2.6	76.0	36.4	51.5	48.6
65052	LINN CREEK	98.1	97.8	0.2	0.3	0.2	0.3	1.2	1.3	6.8	6.8	6.7	5.9	5.3	26.0	28.0	13.6	1.0	75.9	40.4	50.5	49.5
65053	LOHMAN	96.5	96.0	1.9	2.2	0.4	0.5	0.9	0.9	7.5	7.8	8.0	6.8	5.4	28.0	26.4	8.8	1.4	72.4	37.0	50.2	49.8
65054	LOOSE CREEK	99.2	99.2	0.4	0.5	0.0	0.0	0.3	0.3	8.0	7.9	7.3	6.3	5.8	28.8	23.5	10.9	1.6	72.8	36.1	50.1	50.0
65058	META	98.3	98.3	0.1	0.1	0.1	0.1	0.8	1.1	7.2	7.2	7.6	6.9	5.8	26.6	24.0	13.4	1.3	73.7	37.9	50.9	49.1
65059	MOKANE	98.1	97.8	0.5	0.6	0.1	0.1	0.2	0.3	7.2	7.1	7.0	6.9	6.0	29.1	25.4	10.0	1.3	74.0	37.4	49.1	50.9
65061	MORRISON	98.6	98.4	0.1	0.1	0.3	0.3	0.5	0.5	5.5	6.4	7.6	6.5	4.7	25.2	25.2	17.1	1.7	76.3	41.5	49.7	50.3
65062	MOUNT STERLING	99.0	99.0	0.0	0.0	0.0	0.0	0.0	0.5	5.4	5.9	6.9	6.4	5.4	23.7	28.1	16.8	1.5	77.8	42.9	50.3	49.8
65063	NEW BLOOMFIELD	97.1	96.8	0.9	1.0	0.2	0.3	0.5	0.6	7.5	7.5	7.9	6.8	6.2	28.9	25.2	9.0	1.1	72.9	35.8	48.4	51.7
65064	OLEAN	98.5	98.7	0.2	0.2	0.0	0.0	0.4	0.5	6.3	6.9	8.1	7.7	6.7	24.7	27.7	11.0	0.9	73.5	37.8	50.0	50.0
65065	OSAGE BEACH	97.3	97.0	0.9	0.9	0.6	0.7	0.9	1.0	4.1	4.0	4.7	4.1	4.2	24.4	34.5	18.1	1.9	84.7	47.7	49.7	50.4
65066	OWENSVILLE	98.6	98.4	0.1	0.1	0.2	0.3	0.4	0.4	6.7	6.7	7.0	6.9	6.0	25.3	24.8	14.1	2.5	75.3	39.5	48.7	51.3
65067	PORTLAND	96.8	96.6	0.2	0.2	0.0	0.0	0.9	1.1	6.8	6.3	6.3	7.0	7.0	27.5	27.7	10.4	1.1	76.1	39.4	51.0	49.1
65068	PRAIRIE HOME	97.9	97.7	0.7	0.8	0.0	0.2	0.3	0.3	6.7	7.4	7.2	6.4	4.9	26.3	27.6	11.5	2.0	74.6	39.6	50.1	49.9
65069	RHINELAND	98.0	97.9	0.7	0.7	0.1	0.2	0.8	0.8	6.4	6.8	7.5	7.5	5.3	24.3	26.4	13.8	2.1	74.6	39.9	49.8	50.2
65072	ROCKY MOUNT	98.2	98.0	0.1	0.1	0.0	0.0	0.9	1.2	3.0	3.3	3.4	3.0	3.0	17.9	36.7	28.1	1.7	88.6	55.5	51.7	48.3
65074	RUSSELLVILLE	98.2	98.0	0.1	0.1	0.1	0.1	1.0	1.2	7.4	7.7	8.6	7.3	5.7	26.8	25.1	9.9	1.6	71.8	36.2	49.7	50.3
65075	SAINT ELIZABETH	99.2	99.4	0.0	0.0	0.0	0.0	0.8	0.9	6.8	7.2	8.2	6.8	5.5	28.4	20.5	13.0	3.5	72.8	36.9	50.5	49.6
65076	SAINT THOMAS	98.8	98.6	0.4	0.6	0.3	0.4	0.3	0.4	9.9	8.7	6.9	7.5	6.2	30.5	21.9	7.7	0.7	69.8	32.5	49.4	50.6
65077	STEEDMAN	96.9	96.6	0.2	0.2	0.2	0.2	1.0	1.1	6.8	6.5	6.5	7.0	7.4	27.3	27.7	9.9	1.1	76.1	38.9	50.8	49.2
65078	STOVER	97.6	97.4	0.3	0.3	0.2	0.2	0.8	0.9	5.5	5.7	6.5	5.6	4.8	21.5	29.1	19.2	2.2	78.8	45.3	50.4	49.6
65079	SUNRISE BEACH	98.0	98.0	0.1	0.1	0.2	0.2	0.7	0.7	2.8	3.0	3.4	3.3	3.0	13.6	38.4	31.0	1.5	88.8	57.7	50.4	49.6
65080	TEBBETTS	97.1	96.7	0.7	0.7	0.2	0.4	1.6	1.9	7.1	7.1	7.8	7.1	6.5	26.4	28.5	8.7	0.9	73.6	38.1	50.1	49.9
65081	TIPTON	84.1	82.5	12.9	14.2	0.4	0.5	0.9	0.9	4.9	4.9	5.3	4.9	6.6	40.1	20.3	10.5	2.5	81.9	37.3	63.6	36.4
65082	TUSCUMBIA	97.7	97.4	0.3	0.3	0.2	0.3	0.6	0.8	6.4	6.3	6.7	6.8	6.9	26.7	24.7	13.1	2.4	76.4	38.5	51.4	48.6
65083	ULMAN	97.6	97.3	0.2	0.2	0.2	0.2	1.4	1.5	7.9	7.4	6.7	7.1	7.3	28.4	23.7	10.5	1.1	73.8	35.4	50.7	49.3
65084	VERSAILLES	96.4	96.1	1.2	1.3	0.2	0.2	1.0	1.0	7.4	7.3	7.5	6.6	5.8	24.1	23.4	15.1	2.8	73.6	38.5	47.6	52.4
65085	WESTPHALIA	99.0	98.9	0.1	0.1	0.0	0.0	0.5	0.6	7.6	7.6	7.4	6.5	6.0	28.3	22.0	11.8	2.9	73.1	37.2	50.0	50.0
65101	JEFFERSON CITY	80.9	79.8	16.0	16.8	0.8	1.0	1.2	1.3	6.1	6.0	5.9	6.9	8.8	32.9	23.4	8.8	1.3	78.6	35.2	54.5	45.5
65109	JEFFERSON CITY	89.8	88.5	6.8	7.7	1.1	1.4	1.5	1.7	6.7	6.6	6.7	6.4	6.5	29.7	24.8	10.5	2.1	76.0	36.8	48.7	51.3
65201	COLUMBIA	85.4	83.6	7.4	8.0	4.4	5.4	1.9	2.1	3.9	3.5	3.4	16.3	29.4	24.0	13.5	4.9	1.3	87.2	23.9	48.9	51.1
65202	COLUMBIA	82.5	80.7	11.5	12.5	2.3	2.8	1.9	2.1	7.5	6.9	7.0	7.0	9.0	33.6	20.4	7.4	1.3	74.6	32.0	48.8	51.2
65203	COLUMBIA	82.7	81.1	10.4	10.8	3.8	4.9	1.9	2.1	6.7	6.4	7.3	7.3	10.0	29.5	23.3	8.3	1.1	75.3	32.8	47.6	52.4
65211	COLUMBIA	85.2	82.0	1.8	2.1	10.9	13.8	3.5	3.8	0.4	0.4	0.4	6.3	57.3	30.5	3.8	0.8	0.0	98.7	23.7	51.1	49.0
65215	COLUMBIA	87.7	86.6	8.0	8.7	2.3	2.8	3.3	3.7	0.9	0.9	0.6	30.5	42.4	15.9	6.5	1.9	0.3	96.6	22.0	25.2	74.8
65216	COLUMBIA	60.7	57.4	31.0	33.5	3.3	4.1	2.1	2.1	4.1	3.7	3.3	19.0	36.0	21.5	9.1	2.9	0.4	85.1	22.8	46.3	53.7
65230	ARMSTRONG	97.0	96.8	1.7	1.9	0.1	0.1	0.7	0.7	6.2	6.4	6.5	6.1	7.0	25.0	28.2	12.5	2.2	76.7	40.4	51.3	48.7
65231	AUXVASSE	95.8	95.3	2.2	2.5	0.2	0.2	0.6	0.7	6.1	6.6	8.4	7.5	6.3	28.6	23.9	11.3	1.4	73.7	37.2	48.6	51.4
65232	BENTON CITY	98.4	98.4	0.4	0.4	0.0	0.0	0.4	0.8	6.5	6.9	6.1	5.7	6.1	24.5	26.5	16.3	1.2	76.3	41.2	50.6	49.4
65233	BOONVILLE	84.6	83.3	13.0	14.0	0.4	0.4	1.0	1.1	5.5	5.6	6.0	7.4	13.2	26.7	21.0	11.8	2.7	79.5	33.1	56.1	43.9
65236	BRUNSWICK	89.7	88.8	9.2	10.0	0.2	0.3	1.2	1.3	5.0	5.1	6.1	6.7	6.2	21.3	25.4	19.7	4.7	79.2	44.8	47.5	52.5
65237	BUNCETON	95.7	95.3	2.9	3.2	0.1	0.2	0.3	0.3	6.0	6.3	6.5	6.9	6.1	26.4	27.2	13.0	1.7	77.0	40.2	51.5	48.5
65239	CAIRO	98.6	98.6	0.0	0.0	0.2	0.2	0.6	0.5	5.5	6.1	8.4	7.6	6.1	26.1	26.9	12.1	1.3	75.4	38.7	49.5	50.5
65240	CENTRALIA	97.4	97.1	0.9	1.0	0.1	0.1	0.7	0.8	7.5	7.1	7.8	7.0	5.9	26.1	23.7	12.3	2.5	73.1	37.4	47.9	52.1
65243	CLARK	84.4	83.8	13.6	14.1	0.3	0.3	0.7	0.7	5.7	5.4	5.8	5.3	7.8	36.5	24.5	7.9	1.1	80.0	37.0	64.4	35.7
65244	CLIFTON HILL	97.2	97.2	1.1	1.1	0.0	0.0	1.1	1.1	5.3	5.5	7.8	6.7	5.8	23.3	30.8	13.3	1.7	77.3	42.2	51.5	48.5
65246	DALTON	95.5	95.4	3.9	4.0	0.0	0.0	1.3	0.7	5.3	5.3	6.0	6.0	6.6	21.9	25.8	19.2	4.0	79.5	44.3	47.7	52.3
65247	EXCELLO	96.7	96.3	1.5	1.7	0.2	0.2	1.5	1.7	6.6	6.8	7.1	6.1	5.3	25.7	28.4	12.8	1.2	75.9	40.3	52.4	47.6
65248	FAYETTE	86.1	85.4	11.6	12.3	0.2	0.2	0.7	0.8	5.4	5.3	6.0	9.4	13.4	22.5	22.3	13.0	2.9	80.0	35.4	48.2	51.8
65250	FRANKLIN	97.6	97.5	0.4	0.5	0.1	0.1	1.2	1.2	6.8	6.8	7.8	7.1	6.6	28.0	26.2	9.6	1.1	74.2	36.3	50.8	49.2
65251	FULTON	87.9	86.7	9.4	10.3	0.8	1.1	0.9	0.9	5.3	5.4	6.4	8.8	10.6	29.4	22.0	10.2	1.9	78.9	35.0	53.8	46.2
65254	GLASGOW	91.9	91.6	6.4	6.7	0.1	0.1	0.6	0.5	6.3	5.9	7.6	6.6	6.6	25.9	24.8	13.9	2.5	75.5	38.7	48.4	51.7
65255	HALLSVILLE	97.0	96.6	0.9	1.0	0.1	0.1	0.9	1.1	6.9	7.2	7.9	6.9	5.8	29.3	26.7	8.5	0.9	73.7	36.9	49.4	50.6
65256	HARRISBURG	97.1	96.8	0.6	0.6	0.2	0.3	1.2	1.3	6.4	6.6	7.4	7.5	6.4	28.9	27.9	8.0	0.9	74.8	37.4	49.9	50.1
65257	HIGBEE	97.0	96.8	1.7	1.8	0.1	0.1	1.2	1.2	6.1	6.1	6.7	6.6	6.6	25.3	28.0	12.6	2.1	77.0	40.1	50.0	50.0
65258	HOLLIDAY	99.0	99.2	0.3	0.3	0.0	0.0	0.7	0.8	9.1	8.0	5.6	6.7	6.2	25.4	23.5	13.4	2.1	73.3	37.0	50.0	50.0
65259	HUNTSVILLE	93.9	93.9	3.6	3.7	0.1	0.1	0.7	0.7	6.7	6.7	7.4	7.4	6.8	26.3	25.8	11.2	1.7	74.6	37.1	50.2	49.8
65260	JACKSONVILLE	97.6	97.6	0.1	0.1	0.6	0.5	0.7	0.8	6.1	6.5	7.6	6.9	5.4	27.5	26.5	12.5	1.0	75.4	39.1	52.9	47.2
65261	KEYTESVILLE	96.5	96.2	2.8	2.9	0.0	0.1	0.7	0.8	5.8	5.7	6.2	5.8	6.2	22.3	25.6	18.9	3.6	78.4	43.7	48.1	51.9
65262	KINGDOM CITY	96.4	96.1	2.0	2.2	0.2	0.2	0.9	1.1	6.7	6.7	7.0	7.0	5.4	29.6	25.2	11.3	1.1	75.2	38.3	50.7	49.4
65263	MADISON	98.9	98.8	0.3	0.3	0.1	0.2	1.0	1.1	8.5	7.8	6.2	7.0	5.7	24.8	24.1	13.8	2.1	73.5	37.7	50.7	49.3
65264	MARTINSBURG	98.4	98.3	0.5	0.5	0.4	0.4	0.5	0.6	7.4	7.3	7.4	7.4	6.2	26.1	26.1	11.0	1.1	73.1	37.4	48.8	51.2
65265	MEXICO	91.3	91.0	6.9	7.2	0.5	0.5	0.8	0.8	6.4	6.5	7.2	6.3	6.0	24.8	24.9	15.0	3.0	76.0	39.9	47.6	52.4
65270	MOBERLY	91.4	91.0	6.1	6.4	0.6	0.6	1.5	1.5	7.4	6.7	6.7	6.6	7.3	26.1	22.4	13.7	3.0	75.5	36.7	47.6	52.4
65274	NEW FRANKLIN	96.9	96.8	0.9	1.0	0.3	0.3	1.5	1.5	6.0	6.2	7.8	6.5	5.4	26.2	24.5	14.0	3.4	75.6	39.7	47.0	53.0
65275	PARIS	95.0	94.4	3.6	4.1	0.1	0.1	0.5	0.5	6.4	6.6	6.6	6.0	5.7	22.5	24.3	17.1	4.9	76.6	42.2	49.0	51.0
65276	PILOT GROVE	97.9	98.0	0.9	0.9	0.1	0.1	0.8	0.9	6.9	7.1	7.3	5.8	5.6	25.6	24.7	14.3	2.9	75.1	39.4	49.6	50.5
65279	ROCHEPORT	96.1	95.6	1.4	1.6	0.7	0.8	1.0	1.1	5.6	6.9	8.2	7.6	4.7	26.8	30.8	8.6	0.8	74.3	39.8	50.3	49.7
65280	RUSH HILL	98.2	98.0	0.8	0.8	0.0	0.0	0.6	0.4	8.5	7.3	5.9	5.9	6.1	24.8	24.8	15.3	1.4	74.3	40.1	52.3	47.7
65281	SALISBURY	96.7	96.4	2.5	2.7	0.1	0.2	0.5	0.5	5.2	5.2	6.3	6.6	6.3	22.0	27.0	17.1	4.4	79.2	44.0	48.4	51.6
65282	SANTA FE	97.4	97.2	1.0	1.1	0.3	0.4	0.1	0.1	4.8	4.8	7.8	7.8	5.1	25.0	31.4	12.1	1.3	77.3	42.5	52.3	47.7
65283	STOUTSVILLE	97.2	96.8	0.9	1.2	0.2	0.5	0.2	0.2	3.5	6.5	8.1	6.9	6.0	24.4	29.0	14.3	1.4	78.1	42.4	52.1	47.9
65284	STURGEON	97.1	96.8	0.6	0.7	0.2	0.3	0.7	0.9	6.8	6.6	7.2	7.5	6.6	28.1	25.3	10.1	1.9	75.0	36.8	48.9	51.1
65285	THOMPSON	98.3	98.3	0.6	0.6	0.1	0.1	0.6	0.6	6.5	6.4	9.5	7.1	4.3	27.3	27.9	10.1	1.1	73.1	38.4	51.2	48.8
65286	TRIPLETT	96.5	96.4	2.0	2.0	1.0	1.0	0.5	0.5	4.6	5.1	7.7	6.6	8.2	21.4	26.0	17.9	2.6	78.1	43.1	48.5	51.5
65287	WOOLDRIDGE	98.4	98.1	0.7	0.7	0.0	0.0	0.3	0.3	5.5	6.2	6.2	6.2	5.9	26.7	32.3	9.5	1.6	78.2	40.7	49.2	50.8
65301	SEDALIA	91.2	90.4	3.6	3.9	0.5	0.6	4.1	4.5	7.3	6.8	6.9	6.7	7.1	26.9	22.9	13.2	2.3	75.1	37.1	48.3	51.7
65305	WHITEMAN AIR FORCE B	81.8	79.6	9.7	10.7	2.2	2.9	5.7	6.4	15.5	10.1	9.1	9.2	17.9	36.7	1.5	0.1	0.0	62.6	21.7	55.2	44.9
65321	BLACKBURN	95.9	95.5	1.2	1.4	0.4	0.4	2.1	2.4	6.3	6.4	6.8	6.4	5.5	25.8	27.9	12.6	2.2	76.7	40.4	49.3	50.7
65322	BLACKWATER	98.8	98.6	0.8	1.0	0.0	0.0	0.8	0.9	6.6	6.8	7.5	5.7	5.1	26.0	25.9	13.6	2.9	75.6	40.4	50.1	49.9
65323	CALHOUN	97.8	97.5	0.1	0.1	0.3	0.4	0.5	0.5	4.6	5.3	7.2	6.7	5.1	25.8	30.0	14.0	1.3	78.7	41.9	51.6	48.4
65324	CLIMAX SPRINGS	98.4	98.3	0.4	0.5	0.1	0.1	0.7	0.8	2.9	3.2	3.5	3.7	3.5	16.5	35.6	29.8	1.3	88.1	56.4	50.2	49.8
65325	COLE CAMP	98.6	98.6	0.0	0.1	0.2	0.3	0.5	0.6	6.1	6.8	6.2	6.5	5.9	24.2	25.0	15.9	3.5	76.9	40.9	49.0	51.0
65326	EDWARDS	97.8	97.6	0.4	0.4	0.1	0.1	1.0	1.3	3.3	3.6	4.8	5.2	3.7	15.5	35.1	27.8	1.1	85.1	54.8	50.9	49.1
65329	FLORENCE	97.4	96.8	0.0	0.0	0.1	0.1	0.4	0.6	7.9	8.1	7.7	6.9	5.3	24.0	26.4	12.5	1.1	71.8	38.3	49.5	50.5
65330	GILLIAM	96.5	96.4	2.0	2.1	0.2	0.2	0.4	0.4	5.7	5.7	6.4	6.8	6.1	23.1	26.3	16.1	3.8	78.4	42.4	49.6	50.4
65332	GREEN RIDGE	96.6	96.1	0.5	0.6	0.2	0.2	2.5	2.9	7.2	7.4	7.1	6.8	6.2	26.8	25.6	11.9	1.2	74.1	37.1	50.9	49.1
65333	HOUSTONIA	97.9	97.6	0.2	0.3	0.5	0.6	0.9	1.0	6.5	6.6	7.5	7.0	6.3	25.1	25.4	13.6	1.9	74.9	39.6	49.7	50.3
65334	HUGHESVILLE	98.0	97.7	0.3	0.3	0.4	0.5	0.7	0.7	6.9	7.2	8.0	7.3	6.1	25.4	24.4	12.8	1.9	73.2	38.1	49.9	50.1
65335	IONIA	97.8	97.6	0.5	0.5	0.0	0.0	1.4	1.4	6.6	7.1	7.1	6.6	5.7	25.0	27.4	13.7	0.9	74.5	40.3	52.4	47.6
65336	KNOB NOSTER	81.9	80.3	7.3	7.8	1.6	1.9	9.1	9.9	7.4	6.8	7.3	8.5	9.8	30.8	21.5	7.4	0.6	73.5	30.9	51.8	48.2
65337	LA MONTE	92.4	91.4	0.8	1.0	0.8	1.0	6.9	7.8	6.8	6.7	7.1	7.1	6.5	28.1	24.7	11.6	1.5	75.1	36.6	50.8	49.2
65338	LINCOLN	98.4	98.3	0.1	0.1	0.1	0.1	0.9	1.0	6.6	6.6	7.1	6.4	5.8	22.4	25.0	17.1	3.1	75.2	41.7	48.9	51.1
65339	MALTA BEND	97.0	96.6	0.8	0.9	0.5	0.7	1.7	1.7	5.5	5.9	6.9	6.0	7.1	24.5	29.3	13.1	1.7	78.1	40.8	52.4	47.6
	MISSOURI	84.9	84.1	11.3	11.5	1.2	1.4	2.1	2.3	6.7	6.6	7.0	7.0	7.3	27.6	24.2	11.7	1.9	75.6	36.8	48.7	51.3
	UNITED STATES	75.1	73.6	12.3	12.5	3.8	4.2	12.5	14.1	6.9	6.7	7.2	7.0	7.3	28.6	23.8	10.8	1.7	75.1	36.0	49.1	50.9

ZIP CODE #	POST OFFICE NAME	2004 Per Capita Income	2004 HH Income Base	2004 Household Income Distribution (%) Less than $25,000	$25,000 to $49,999	$50,000 to $99,999	$100,000 to $149,999	$150,000 or More	Median Household Income 2004	2009	2004 National Centile	2004 State Centile	2004 Home Value Base	2004 Home Value Distribution (%) Less than $50,000	$50,000 to $89,999	$90,000 to $174,999	$175,000 to $399,999	$400,000 or More	2004 Median Home Value
65050	LATHAM	13651	190	22.6	44.7	24.2	6.3	2.1	40776	46938	49	69	158	26.0	18.4	31.7	20.9	3.2	97500
65051	LINN	20890	1722	27.2	31.5	33.9	5.9	1.6	44819	50423	61	78	1336	10.9	25.3	41.8	20.4	1.5	108766
65052	LINN CREEK	22861	1540	23.6	33.1	30.8	8.3	4.2	42830	51014	56	74	1286	13.9	18.1	33.8	29.6	4.7	125250
65053	LOHMAN	22465	506	16.0	32.0	40.9	8.7	2.4	51383	61114	75	87	425	5.7	11.5	45.2	35.5	2.1	141750
65054	LOOSE CREEK	22933	402	17.2	31.8	40.6	8.5	2.0	50790	57404	73	86	348	5.2	18.1	49.4	23.6	3.7	126471
65058	META	18070	364	30.5	31.9	31.0	5.8	0.8	39033	44846	43	64	313	24.0	23.0	36.1	14.1	2.9	95000
65059	MOKANE	21303	374	16.3	37.4	36.9	7.8	1.6	46821	53977	66	81	317	16.1	21.8	35.7	23.0	3.5	110278
65061	MORRISON	20089	317	27.1	37.9	29.0	3.5	2.5	41074	47024	50	70	272	27.2	23.2	28.7	16.5	4.4	89412
65062	MOUNT STERLING	20208	88	27.3	35.2	31.8	3.4	2.3	40909	46388	49	70	77	26.0	24.7	27.3	18.2	3.9	89167
65063	NEW BLOOMFIELD	21804	1256	20.8	33.8	34.0	8.0	3.5	46622	53838	65	81	1015	15.6	21.7	36.7	20.3	5.8	109044
65064	OLEAN	18231	362	35.6	24.3	31.5	4.7	3.9	40737	46717	49	69	306	12.8	25.5	39.2	18.3	4.3	105392
65065	OSAGE BEACH	30137	2288	19.2	32.9	32.7	9.0	6.2	47751	58179	68	83	1807	5.9	9.9	35.8	40.2	8.3	171085
65066	OWENSVILLE	18310	2650	32.2	33.4	27.7	4.8	1.8	37544	43066	38	58	2109	18.5	29.3	37.4	12.0	2.8	93273
65067	PORTLAND	18339	196	32.1	35.2	25.5	7.1	0.0	33874	40374	24	38	164	24.4	33.5	34.8	7.3	0.0	82353
65068	PRAIRIE HOME	20549	253	23.7	35.2	35.2	5.1	0.8	43243	48198	57	75	212	16.0	21.2	35.4	21.2	6.1	119792
65069	RHINELAND	21114	434	23.3	35.5	32.3	6.9	2.1	42865	49590	56	74	365	18.6	20.3	30.4	24.4	6.3	109570
65072	ROCKY MOUNT	23747	627	30.9	27.3	32.9	6.5	2.4	38671	46501	42	63	564	11.7	20.4	33.2	34.8	0.0	145238
65074	RUSSELLVILLE	27622	950	21.9	31.8	35.7	7.1	3.6	47409	55053	67	82	798	13.8	17.4	41.4	23.4	4.0	122137
65075	SAINT ELIZABETH	19150	254	19.7	33.1	36.2	5.9	5.1	48596	55392	69	84	212	14.6	17.9	39.2	22.2	6.1	115244
65076	SAINT THOMAS	21578	230	17.8	22.6	49.6	8.3	1.7	56373	66876	81	92	204	10.8	13.2	53.9	22.1	0.0	125000
65077	STEEDMAN	17368	218	33.0	33.9	25.2	7.8	0.0	33681	38538	23	37	182	24.2	34.1	34.1	7.7	0.0	82500
65078	STOVER	17537	1492	38.7	33.9	22.9	3.2	1.5	32159	37121	18	29	1206	30.2	23.6	34.3	11.5	0.5	83662
65079	SUNRISE BEACH	26839	2706	27.0	33.3	29.3	7.4	3.1	40915	49237	49	70	2410	11.2	11.2	38.1	33.6	5.9	150293
65080	TEBBETTS	24476	423	18.7	27.9	40.2	11.4	1.9	52314	60097	76	88	376	12.2	11.4	52.4	22.1	1.9	129348
65081	TIPTON	17540	1088	33.1	31.0	29.0	4.5	2.4	38761	44539	42	63	831	23.5	31.1	36.6	8.3	0.6	84048
65082	TUSCUMBIA	16054	464	31.3	36.4	26.9	2.8	2.6	34759	41477	27	44	398	28.4	23.1	34.2	11.1	3.3	88065
65083	ULMAN	17473	255	37.3	32.9	24.3	2.8	2.8	33676	39343	23	37	220	27.7	25.0	30.5	14.1	2.7	85714
65084	VERSAILLES	17899	2513	36.9	33.4	22.2	4.8	2.8	34371	40061	25	41	1938	21.9	31.0	33.0	12.7	1.4	85789
65085	WESTPHALIA	19585	422	16.1	35.3	39.1	7.8	1.7	48932	55247	70	84	359	6.7	16.4	56.3	18.1	2.5	120216
65101	JEFFERSON CITY	22701	10947	25.3	27.6	35.6	8.8	2.8	47407	56823	67	82	7038	6.4	18.0	49.1	24.9	1.6	124092
65109	JEFFERSON CITY	27531	14943	21.0	27.7	36.0	10.4	4.9	51108	60630	74	87	10537	5.7	13.1	53.4	25.0	2.7	125240
65201	COLUMBIA	20000	13284	40.9	27.0	22.7	6.1	3.2	31873	39264	17	27	5132	21.7	13.7	42.6	17.5	4.5	110319
65202	COLUMBIA	22285	15861	23.6	32.5	32.9	8.7	2.2	45169	55022	62	78	9232	16.3	21.1	51.5	9.5	1.6	103937
65203	COLUMBIA	29852	19951	25.3	24.4	28.8	13.7	7.8	50356	63028	73	86	11977	4.0	11.8	43.0	36.3	5.0	156133
65211	COLUMBIA	18427	154	66.9	18.8	11.7	2.0	0.7	14390	17048	1	0	4	0.0	25.0	75.0	0.0	0.0	108333
65215	COLUMBIA	8755	24	62.5	20.8	16.7	0.0	0.0	18028	22222	1	1	4	0.0	100.0	0.0	0.0	0.0	76667
65216	COLUMBIA	5670	15	73.3	26.7	0.0	0.0	0.0	17071	15000	1	1	4	25.0	75.0	0.0	0.0	0.0	70000
65230	ARMSTRONG	16504	276	35.1	31.5	28.6	4.0	0.7	37516	42606	38	58	229	31.0	21.0	30.1	14.0	3.9	85909
65231	AUXVASSE	18870	1292	26.2	36.1	31.9	4.6	1.2	41697	48317	52	72	1016	19.7	25.9	36.4	15.1	3.0	95696
65232	BENTON CITY	19358	104	31.7	35.6	26.9	3.9	1.9	37861	44451	39	60	84	27.4	28.6	27.4	16.7	0.0	78000
65233	BOONVILLE	18150	3892	28.9	34.9	30.0	5.1	1.2	40302	45134	47	67	2850	13.7	28.5	40.4	15.5	1.9	102138
65236	BRUNSWICK	20433	623	39.7	34.2	21.0	3.2	1.9	33767	38713	23	38	455	51.9	27.0	17.6	3.1	0.4	47639
65237	BUNCETON	17690	439	27.6	41.2	27.3	3.0	0.9	36852	42183	35	55	359	27.0	26.7	22.8	17.8	5.6	83250
65239	CAIRO	19589	489	26.4	33.3	30.5	8.0	1.8	42586	48658	55	73	411	29.2	28.5	28.0	11.9	2.4	77955
65240	CENTRALIA	21646	2695	25.9	31.5	33.4	6.8	2.4	43814	53790	58	76	2100	19.8	32.1	35.3	11.9	0.9	87516
65243	CLARK	15552	1289	28.9	33.0	29.3	6.0	3.0	40146	47021	47	67	1077	23.6	28.0	31.7	14.3	2.5	88226
65244	CLIFTON HILL	22189	146	24.7	34.3	30.1	6.9	4.1	43502	50513	57	75	122	32.0	20.5	32.0	12.3	3.3	86250
65246	DALTON	17725	67	37.3	38.8	19.4	4.5	0.0	33591	38884	23	36	50	52.0	26.0	20.0	2.0	0.0	48333
65247	EXCELLO	20723	236	24.6	44.5	25.4	3.8	1.7	36272	42723	33	52	199	27.1	24.1	36.2	11.6	1.0	87917
65248	FAYETTE	19018	1666	34.8	30.3	28.3	5.5	1.2	36824	43112	35	55	1194	22.9	26.0	34.3	13.4	3.4	91556
65250	FRANKLIN	16291	291	30.9	40.9	23.7	3.4	1.0	34540	40830	26	43	235	37.5	14.0	34.5	11.9	2.1	86500
65251	FULTON	19676	7382	27.6	32.3	30.6	6.7	2.9	41425	48006	51	71	5157	15.3	23.9	40.4	17.8	2.6	104954
65254	GLASGOW	17195	680	34.9	35.9	24.6	3.5	1.2	35303	41111	29	47	502	31.7	27.5	27.3	9.4	4.2	74545
65255	HALLSVILLE	22528	1303	20.2	31.0	36.2	10.4	2.2	48875	60245	70	84	1106	19.4	23.1	37.2	18.4	2.0	101012
65256	HARRISBURG	24186	582	18.4	29.7	38.8	8.9	4.1	51299	62315	74	87	495	13.1	24.9	40.2	20.8	1.0	108494
65257	HIGBEE	19724	521	35.7	32.1	27.6	3.5	1.2	33564	40178	23	36	414	53.6	17.4	20.8	5.6	2.7	45946
65258	HOLLIDAY	15938	152	37.5	36.2	21.7	3.3	1.3	32305	37135	19	29	125	36.8	35.2	19.2	8.0	0.8	63182
65259	HUNTSVILLE	17149	1336	32.5	32.9	28.8	4.8	1.1	37627	43934	38	59	1047	36.7	26.6	26.1	9.2	1.5	66188
65260	JACKSONVILLE	17020	277	26.0	41.5	27.8	3.3	1.4	39356	44742	44	65	234	24.8	19.7	36.8	15.4	3.4	103750
65261	KEYTESVILLE	18020	576	38.4	37.5	20.1	3.1	0.9	33342	38963	22	36	441	46.0	24.3	22.7	5.7	1.4	54861
65262	KINGDOM CITY	22571	187	18.7	41.7	25.7	12.3	1.6	44004	50140	59	76	155	8.4	19.4	41.3	27.7	3.2	128676
65263	MADISON	16277	951	34.7	36.4	23.3	3.8	1.8	34194	38661	25	40	782	31.7	27.4	25.3	13.9	1.7	75714
65264	MARTINSBURG	21088	320	25.3	26.9	40.3	5.0	2.5	47686	54374	68	83	272	17.3	21.7	36.0	22.4	2.6	110484
65265	MEXICO	20944	6402	31.5	32.5	26.9	6.9	2.2	37563	44445	38	58	4563	22.5	30.4	34.4	11.3	1.4	85985
65270	MOBERLY	18773	5810	36.7	33.6	23.6	4.6	1.6	33808	39257	23	38	3821	38.7	32.3	20.9	7.8	0.4	62299
65274	NEW FRANKLIN	18486	702	34.2	34.5	25.9	4.1	1.3	37506	43597	37	58	514	25.7	32.9	28.8	10.5	2.1	79130
65275	PARIS	17657	1279	32.5	37.8	26.0	2.4	1.3	35219	39558	28	46	992	29.8	32.0	25.5	11.4	1.3	75333
65276	PILOT GROVE	16782	635	33.1	35.9	25.8	4.1	1.1	36461	41793	33	53	502	18.7	34.7	29.1	15.1	2.4	86047
65279	ROCHEPORT	28618	623	15.7	25.2	37.6	14.9	6.6	56910	71065	82	92	555	7.2	18.9	38.4	27.9	7.6	133239
65280	RUSH HILL	18427	199	30.7	36.7	25.1	5.5	2.0	39174	45805	43	64	160	26.9	23.8	30.0	19.4	0.0	88571
65281	SALISBURY	19344	1387	31.3	33.2	29.7	3.3	2.5	40800	45027	49	69	1118	30.1	27.3	36.6	5.9	0.1	76000
65282	SANTA FE	17063	279	24.4	41.6	31.2	2.2	0.7	40829	45446	49	70	236	10.6	20.8	32.2	23.7	12.7	114286
65283	STOUTSVILLE	18350	177	32.2	38.4	23.7	5.1	0.6	36270	40828	33	52	146	15.1	19.2	37.7	22.6	5.5	122059
65284	STURGEON	20131	974	24.9	30.0	35.5	7.3	2.4	45436	56586	62	79	767	24.9	32.5	31.2	11.1	0.4	81172
65285	THOMPSON	18824	380	20.8	34.0	39.2	4.5	1.6	43938	51126	58	76	329	20.7	17.0	37.1	21.3	4.0	124583
65286	TRIPLETT	17175	82	36.6	36.6	20.7	4.9	1.2	34184	40167	25	40	67	26.9	22.4	41.8	7.5	1.5	90714
65287	WOOLDRIDGE	20231	118	22.0	28.0	40.7	9.3	0.0	50000	54117	72	86	105	10.5	21.9	40.0	27.6	0.0	128906
65301	SEDALIA	19180	12996	32.2	35.5	25.1	5.1	2.1	35988	41558	31	51	9195	20.9	32.3	34.4	11.2	1.3	86114
65305	WHITEMAN AIR FORCE B	12737	953	19.0	55.9	20.7	3.3	1.2	37273	42622	36	57	18	0.0	0.0	100.0	0.0	0.0	112500
65321	BLACKBURN	16555	269	36.4	32.0	24.5	5.6	1.5	37017	42750	35	56	192	43.8	21.9	25.0	7.3	2.1	58571
65322	BLACKWATER	18505	331	30.8	36.3	27.5	4.2	1.2	37315	41717	37	57	273	23.4	26.7	28.2	17.6	4.0	89722
65323	CALHOUN	18362	418	32.1	29.0	31.3	6.9	0.7	39810	45921	45	66	352	30.7	28.7	25.6	14.2	0.9	76000
65324	CLIMAX SPRINGS	22353	1201	33.5	31.6	27.7	4.1	3.1	36621	43321	34	54	1048	13.1	14.1	34.0	34.1	4.8	139615
65325	COLE CAMP	18955	1456	35.9	33.6	23.5	4.0	3.1	34352	40085	25	41	1128	24.0	23.0	38.5	12.8	1.8	92931
65326	EDWARDS	15972	807	49.8	30.6	15.9	3.1	0.6	25121	29297	5	4	688	31.7	19.9	28.9	14.0	5.5	87500
65329	FLORENCE	15711	353	35.1	31.7	27.2	6.0	0.0	34178	38568	25	40	294	17.4	23.1	40.5	14.3	4.8	98235
65330	GILLIAM	15139	197	38.1	42.6	16.8	2.5	0.0	32459	38051	19	30	143	42.0	23.8	30.1	4.2	0.0	63500
65332	GREEN RIDGE	17515	562	31.1	33.1	28.5	4.8	2.5	36982	42344	35	56	461	20.2	26.3	34.5	15.8	3.3	95323
65333	HOUSTONIA	18285	360	26.7	31.1	34.2	5.6	2.5	42024	48664	53	73	300	27.0	27.0	31.3	11.7	3.0	84545
65334	HUGHESVILLE	16538	286	30.4	31.1	32.2	4.9	1.4	38835	44384	42	64	239	26.4	28.9	30.1	11.7	2.9	83421
65335	IONIA	17878	90	33.3	36.7	25.6	4.4	0.0	33592	38602	23	37	72	23.6	13.9	41.7	20.8	0.0	116667
65336	KNOB NOSTER	19573	2086	26.4	38.4	26.8	5.6	2.9	38085	45558	40	61	1420	20.4	21.1	44.5	12.3	1.7	101792
65337	LA MONTE	15970	747	35.5	35.1	25.7	2.7	1.1	34308	39426	25	41	516	27.5	35.9	27.3	6.6	2.7	77843
65338	LINCOLN	16287	859	37.7	34.3	23.2	4.1	0.7	31876	37287	17	27	649	19.9	30.7	35.4	13.9	0.2	89514
65339	MALTA BEND	21216	224	26.3	38.4	28.1	4.5	2.7	39533	45643	44	65	173	28.3	20.2	28.9	18.5	4.1	91786
	MISSOURI	23864		27.0	29.4	30.1	9.0	4.5	44017	52626				15.2	22.7	39.0	19.7	3.4	109184
	UNITED STATES	25866		24.7	27.1	30.8	10.9	6.5	48124	56710				10.9	15.0	33.7	30.1	10.4	145905

ZIP CODE #	POST OFFICE NAME	FINANCIAL SERVICES: Auto Loan	Home Loan	Invest-ments	Retire-ment Plans	THE HOME: Home Improvements: Home Repair	Lawn & Garden	Furnishings: Comput-ers & Hard-ware	Major Appli-ances	TV, Radio, Sound Equip-ment	Furni-ture	ENTERTAINMENT: Dine out/ Carry out	Sports Equip-ment	Fees & Tickets	Toys & Games	Travel	Cable TV	PERSONAL: Apparel & Services	Auto Repairs	Health Insur-ance	Pets & Supplies
65050	LATHAM	78	69	53	66	73	79	64	71	68	64	83	85	63	85	66	70	79	69	77	91
65051	LINN	85	71	51	68	76	85	70	77	76	69	91	90	66	90	71	79	85	76	87	97
65052	LINN CREEK	97	80	58	74	87	95	76	88	83	77	100	102	70	97	79	86	94	87	98	115
65053	LOHMAN	97	90	73	88	93	98	83	90	86	84	105	107	82	107	85	87	101	88	94	113
65054	LOOSE CREEK	98	87	66	83	92	99	81	89	86	81	104	106	79	106	83	88	99	87	97	115
65058	META	73	62	47	60	66	73	60	66	65	60	78	78	58	78	61	66	74	65	73	84
65059	MOKANE	88	80	62	76	83	88	74	81	78	75	95	97	72	96	76	79	91	80	86	103
65061	MORRISON	83	64	43	59	72	81	61	73	69	60	82	86	54	81	65	73	76	72	86	100
65062	MOUNT STERLING	79	62	42	56	70	78	58	70	66	58	78	82	52	77	62	71	73	69	83	96
65063	NEW BLOOMFIELD	93	82	63	79	86	93	79	86	83	79	101	101	76	101	80	84	96	84	92	107
65064	OLEAN	82	63	41	61	70	78	63	73	70	62	84	86	57	82	64	72	77	72	83	95
65065	OSAGE BEACH	111	87	59	79	98	110	82	99	93	81	110	116	73	109	87	99	102	97	117	135
65066	OWENSVILLE	78	60	40	57	66	75	61	69	68	60	81	80	56	79	61	71	75	68	80	88
65067	PORTLAND	83	56	26	49	63	73	54	67	65	55	76	81	46	72	55	70	69	67	83	96
65068	PRAIRIE HOME	87	64	37	61	73	81	62	75	71	62	84	91	55	83	65	74	77	74	88	103
65069	RHINELAND	83	74	56	70	78	84	68	76	73	68	88	90	67	90	71	75	84	74	82	98
65072	ROCKY MOUNT	85	66	45	60	75	84	63	76	71	62	84	88	56	83	67	76	78	74	89	103
65074	RUSSELLVILLE	116	104	79	98	109	117	96	106	102	96	124	126	94	126	99	104	117	103	115	137
65075	SAINT ELIZABETH	91	81	62	77	85	92	75	83	79	75	96	99	73	98	77	81	92	81	90	107
65076	SAINT THOMAS	92	99	97	101	96	97	95	95	90	96	113	112	95	114	93	85	111	94	85	105
65077	STEEDMAN	83	56	26	48	63	73	54	68	65	55	77	81	46	72	55	70	70	67	83	96
65078	STOVER	68	53	35	50	58	67	53	61	59	52	71	71	48	69	54	63	65	60	72	79
65079	SUNRISE BEACH	95	75	51	68	84	95	71	85	80	70	95	100	63	93	75	85	88	84	101	116
65080	TEBBETTS	105	93	71	89	99	106	86	96	92	86	112	114	85	114	89	94	106	93	104	124
65081	TIPTON	63	47	29	45	52	61	49	56	55	47	65	65	43	63	49	58	60	56	67	72
65082	TUSCUMBIA	82	56	27	49	63	72	54	67	64	55	76	80	47	72	55	69	69	66	81	94
65083	ULMAN	83	57	28	50	64	73	55	68	65	56	77	81	48	73	56	70	71	67	82	95
65084	VERSAILLES	75	60	42	57	65	74	61	68	67	59	80	79	56	78	62	70	74	67	78	86
65085	WESTPHALIA	88	79	60	75	83	89	73	81	77	73	94	96	71	96	75	79	89	78	87	104
65101	JEFFERSON CITY	73	79	89	80	78	81	79	77	77	78	96	91	81	99	79	75	95	78	73	86
65109	JEFFERSON CITY	91	96	102	97	95	99	95	94	92	94	115	111	96	116	94	90	113	94	89	105
65201	COLUMBIA	66	52	64	57	51	57	73	61	71	67	89	79	65	84	64	65	85	69	57	69
65202	COLUMBIA	78	76	80	79	75	78	79	78	77	79	97	93	78	95	77	74	94	80	72	87
65203	COLUMBIA	97	102	115	105	99	102	105	100	100	104	127	119	105	126	101	96	124	102	91	110
65211	COLUMBIA	40	25	31	28	24	29	48	35	46	40	58	49	39	52	38	41	54	43	33	40
65215	COLUMBIA	34	20	26	23	20	24	40	29	38	33	48	41	32	43	32	34	45	36	27	33
65216	COLUMBIA	26	16	20	18	16	19	31	23	30	26	38	32	26	34	25	27	36	28	21	26
65230	ARMSTRONG	79	54	26	48	62	71	53	66	62	53	73	79	45	70	54	67	67	65	80	92
65231	AUXVASSE	77	68	53	66	70	76	66	71	69	66	84	83	63	82	66	69	80	70	75	86
65232	BENTON CITY	80	59	34	56	67	75	58	70	65	57	77	84	51	76	60	68	71	68	81	95
65233	BOONVILLE	64	55	44	53	58	66	56	61	60	55	73	70	53	72	57	62	68	60	68	73
65236	BRUNSWICK	76	56	35	54	62	73	60	68	68	58	80	78	53	76	60	72	73	68	82	86
65237	BUNCETON	79	55	28	50	62	71	54	66	63	54	74	79	46	71	55	67	68	65	80	92
65239	CAIRO	82	70	51	67	75	81	66	74	71	65	85	88	63	87	68	73	81	72	81	97
65240	CENTRALIA	90	75	54	72	80	89	74	82	80	73	96	95	70	95	75	82	90	80	91	103
65243	CLARK	61	53	39	50	56	61	50	55	54	50	65	65	48	65	51	55	61	54	60	70
65244	CLIFTON HILL	96	72	43	68	81	90	70	83	78	69	93	100	62	92	72	82	86	82	97	114
65246	DALTON	65	48	31	46	53	63	53	59	60	51	70	66	47	66	53	63	64	59	70	72
65247	EXCELLO	90	68	42	64	77	84	66	78	74	65	87	94	59	87	68	77	81	77	90	106
65248	FAYETTE	80	61	40	58	67	77	63	72	71	61	84	83	57	81	64	74	77	71	84	91
65250	FRANKLIN	80	54	24	46	61	70	52	65	63	53	73	77	44	69	53	67	67	64	80	92
65251	FULTON	72	68	64	67	69	75	69	71	70	68	86	82	67	85	68	70	83	71	72	82
65254	GLASGOW	67	57	45	54	62	69	56	62	61	55	74	73	54	76	58	64	70	61	71	79
65255	HALLSVILLE	91	82	63	78	85	91	76	84	80	77	98	99	74	98	78	81	93	82	89	106
65256	HARRISBURG	102	90	67	85	95	102	83	93	89	83	108	110	81	110	86	91	102	90	101	120
65257	HIGBEE	86	62	34	55	69	78	59	71	69	60	81	85	52	79	60	73	75	70	85	99
65258	HOLLIDAY	72	50	25	44	56	64	48	59	57	49	68	70	42	64	49	61	62	59	72	82
65259	HUNTSVILLE	72	60	44	58	64	71	59	66	64	59	77	77	56	77	60	66	72	65	73	82
65260	JACKSONVILLE	82	57	30	54	67	74	57	70	65	56	76	84	48	75	59	68	70	69	83	97
65261	KEYTESVILLE	68	50	31	47	55	65	53	61	60	51	71	69	47	67	53	63	64	60	72	77
65262	KINGDOM CITY	87	81	65	77	84	89	74	81	77	74	94	96	74	97	76	79	90	79	86	102
65263	MADISON	74	54	32	50	60	68	54	63	61	54	73	75	48	71	54	65	67	63	74	84
65264	MARTINSBURG	86	77	59	73	81	87	72	79	76	72	92	94	70	93	73	77	88	77	85	101
65265	MEXICO	75	67	57	64	71	79	67	71	71	65	86	82	66	88	68	74	82	70	79	86
65270	MOBERLY	61	57	56	56	58	65	60	61	62	58	77	70	59	77	60	63	73	61	64	70
65274	NEW FRANKLIN	76	55	34	53	62	72	59	67	67	57	79	77	52	75	59	71	72	67	81	85
65275	PARIS	73	55	36	53	61	71	58	66	65	56	77	76	52	74	58	68	70	65	77	83
65276	PILOT GROVE	74	54	33	52	61	70	57	65	64	55	75	76	50	72	57	67	69	65	77	85
65279	ROCHEPORT	100	114	114	114	112	112	104	105	98	104	123	124	107	128	105	95	122	102	96	119
65280	RUSH HILL	84	59	32	56	69	77	59	72	67	58	79	86	50	78	61	70	72	71	85	99
65281	SALISBURY	81	60	36	56	67	77	60	71	68	59	81	84	53	79	62	72	74	70	84	94
65282	SANTA FE	70	61	46	57	65	70	56	63	60	56	73	75	55	74	58	62	69	62	69	82
65283	STOUTSVILLE	77	59	39	54	67	75	56	68	64	56	75	80	50	74	60	68	70	67	80	93
65284	STURGEON	84	73	56	71	77	85	72	78	76	71	92	90	69	92	72	77	87	76	84	95
65285	THOMPSON	81	72	55	69	76	82	67	74	71	67	86	88	66	88	69	73	82	72	80	95
65286	TRIPLETT	74	52	27	49	60	68	51	63	59	51	69	76	44	68	53	62	63	62	75	88
65287	WOOLDRIDGE	84	75	57	71	79	85	69	77	74	69	90	92	68	92	71	76	85	75	83	99
65301	SEDALIA	69	64	59	62	66	72	65	67	67	63	83	78	63	83	65	69	79	67	71	79
65305	WHITEMAN AIR FORCE B	72	46	44	52	42	50	68	59	69	64	86	78	58	77	56	63	83	69	54	67
65321	BLACKBURN	80	56	30	53	65	73	55	68	63	54	74	82	47	73	57	66	68	67	81	94
65322	BLACKWATER	78	55	29	52	64	71	54	67	62	53	73	80	46	71	56	65	66	66	79	93
65323	CALHOUN	87	58	26	50	66	76	56	70	68	57	80	84	48	75	57	73	72	70	87	100
65324	CLIMAX SPRINGS	82	64	43	57	72	81	60	73	68	60	81	85	54	80	64	73	75	71	86	99
65325	COLE CAMP	75	58	38	56	64	73	60	68	67	58	79	78	54	77	61	70	73	67	79	86
65326	EDWARDS	58	45	31	41	51	57	43	51	48	42	57	60	38	56	45	52	53	51	61	70
65329	FLORENCE	78	55	30	52	64	71	54	66	62	53	73	80	47	72	56	65	67	65	79	92
65330	GILLIAM	59	44	29	42	48	58	49	54	55	46	64	60	43	61	48	58	59	54	64	65
65332	GREEN RIDGE	77	65	47	62	70	76	61	69	66	61	80	83	58	80	63	68	75	68	76	91
65333	HOUSTONIA	82	68	48	65	74	80	64	73	70	64	84	88	61	85	66	72	79	72	82	97
65334	HUGHESVILLE	78	63	42	60	69	75	60	69	66	59	79	83	56	79	62	68	73	68	78	92
65335	IONIA	75	56	32	50	61	69	53	63	61	53	72	75	47	70	54	64	67	62	75	87
65336	KNOB NOSTER	73	70	68	70	70	75	72	72	73	71	90	85	71	90	71	72	87	73	72	82
65337	LA MONTE	69	55	37	53	59	67	55	62	60	54	72	73	51	71	56	62	67	61	70	79
65338	LINCOLN	69	49	28	45	55	65	51	60	60	50	70	69	45	66	52	63	64	60	73	78
65339	MALTA BEND	99	69	36	66	81	91	69	85	79	68	93	102	59	91	71	83	84	84	101	118
	MISSOURI	87	82	79	80	83	90	82	85	85	82	104	99	81	103	82	85	100	85	87	100
	UNITED STATES	100	100	100	100	100	100	100	100	100	100	100	100	100	100	100	100	100	100	100	100

POPULATION CHANGE

#	POST OFFICE NAME	COUNTY FIPS CODE	POPULATION 2000	2004	2009	2000-2004 ANNUAL RATE % Rate	State Centile	HOUSEHOLDS 2000	2004	2009	% Annual Rate 2000-2004	2004 Average HH Size	FAMILIES 2000	2004	% Annual Rate 2000-2004
65340	MARSHALL	195	15383	14870	14240	-0.8	9	5688	5492	5245	-0.8	2.44	3709	3493	-1.4
65344	MIAMI	195	557	524	495	-1.4	2	215	203	193	-1.3	2.54	157	146	-1.7
65345	MORA	159	133	156	169	3.8	97	46	54	59	3.8	2.89	37	43	3.6
65347	NELSON	195	940	927	900	-0.3	21	367	364	355	-0.2	2.49	275	268	-0.6
65348	OTTERVILLE	053	1040	1102	1167	1.4	76	392	420	448	1.6	2.62	290	305	1.2
65349	SLATER	195	2755	2589	2443	-1.5	2	1160	1093	1034	-1.4	2.31	733	673	-2.0
65350	SMITHTON	159	1505	1668	1757	2.5	89	552	618	654	2.7	2.65	434	476	2.2
65351	SWEET SPRINGS	195	2418	2393	2313	-0.2	25	914	905	877	-0.2	2.52	656	637	-0.7
65354	SYRACUSE	141	582	596	610	0.6	54	218	223	229	0.5	2.67	170	171	0.1
65355	WARSAW	015	10486	10539	10718	0.1	37	4682	4753	4881	0.4	2.19	3228	3203	-0.2
65360	WINDSOR	083	4162	4228	4284	0.4	48	1655	1686	1714	0.4	2.48	1139	1132	-0.1
65401	ROLLA	161	27493	28905	30639	1.2	73	11187	11887	12743	1.4	2.30	7084	7349	0.9
65409	ROLLA	161	1007	1012	1033	0.1	37	1	1	1	0.0	3.00	0	0	0.0
65436	BEULAH	161	502	517	542	0.7	59	193	202	213	1.1	2.56	145	149	0.6
65438	BIRCH TREE	203	3577	3611	3677	0.2	41	1367	1392	1432	0.4	2.56	1016	1017	0.0
65439	BIXBY	093	494	475	469	-0.9	7	194	189	188	-0.6	2.40	144	137	-1.2
65440	BOSS	065	433	427	430	-0.3	21	171	170	173	-0.1	2.50	138	136	-0.3
65441	BOURBON	055	4850	5013	5222	0.8	62	1782	1853	1944	0.9	2.66	1293	1321	0.5
65443	BRINKTOWN	125	1126	1120	1138	-0.1	27	407	408	418	0.1	2.75	305	301	-0.3
65444	BUCYRUS	215	1251	1311	1372	1.1	71	504	535	567	1.4	2.43	381	396	0.9
65446	CHERRYVILLE	055	873	877	896	0.1	37	336	339	349	0.2	2.59	258	256	-0.2
65449	COOK STATION	055	339	342	350	0.2	41	130	132	136	0.4	2.58	97	97	0.0
65452	CROCKER	169	2706	2620	2696	-0.8	10	1102	1092	1146	-0.2	2.39	796	759	-1.1
65453	CUBA	055	8254	8587	9000	0.9	67	3272	3432	3626	1.1	2.46	2347	2413	0.7
65456	DAVISVILLE	055	345	346	353	0.1	35	131	132	136	0.2	2.62	101	100	-0.2
65457	DEVILS ELBOW	169	921	938	985	0.4	50	359	373	399	0.9	2.47	242	241	-0.1
65459	DIXON	169	6586	6699	7073	0.4	48	2542	2633	2830	0.8	2.53	1855	1864	0.1
65461	DUKE	161	154	159	166	0.8	61	62	65	68	1.1	2.45	47	48	0.5
65462	EDGAR SPRINGS	161	1116	1160	1220	0.9	66	447	470	500	1.2	2.47	328	339	0.8
65463	ELDRIDGE	105	924	1054	1145	3.2	94	354	409	447	3.5	2.57	279	318	3.1
65464	ELK CREEK	215	413	475	521	3.4	95	166	193	213	3.6	2.46	121	138	3.1
65466	EMINENCE	203	2440	2455	2499	0.1	38	1045	1063	1093	0.4	2.29	696	691	-0.2
65468	EUNICE	215	65	64	65	-0.4	20	29	29	29	0.0	2.21	22	21	-1.1
65470	FALCON	105	821	835	859	0.4	48	309	317	329	0.6	2.63	246	249	0.3
65473	FORT LEONARD WOOD	169	13877	15762	17624	3.0	93	2723	3367	4023	5.1	3.22	2390	2972	5.3
65479	HARTSHORN	215	271	265	270	-0.5	16	110	108	112	-0.4	2.45	83	80	-0.9
65483	HOUSTON	215	4483	4497	4635	0.1	35	1927	1948	2028	0.3	2.26	1284	1270	-0.3
65484	HUGGINS	215	245	254	264	0.9	64	85	89	94	1.1	2.75	65	68	1.1
65486	IBERIA	131	3893	3935	4153	0.3	42	1510	1536	1633	0.4	2.55	1113	1111	0.0
65501	JADWIN	065	417	412	415	-0.3	23	149	148	151	-0.2	2.78	118	116	-0.4
65529	JEROME	161	334	336	347	0.1	38	143	145	152	0.3	2.32	97	97	0.0
65534	LAQUEY	169	854	830	854	-0.7	12	315	313	328	-0.2	2.65	243	235	-0.8
65535	LEASBURG	055	1650	1702	1768	0.7	60	624	647	676	0.9	2.62	456	465	0.5
65536	LEBANON	105	25955	26662	27570	0.6	56	10251	10583	10999	0.8	2.49	7259	7345	0.3
65541	LENOX	065	758	748	754	-0.3	22	277	275	279	-0.2	2.66	219	215	-0.4
65542	LICKING	215	4238	5069	5694	4.3	98	1779	2158	2453	4.7	2.32	1243	1480	4.2
65543	LYNCHBURG	105	270	265	269	-0.4	19	105	104	106	-0.2	2.55	81	78	-0.9
65548	MOUNTAIN VIEW	091	4825	4761	4738	-0.3	22	1991	1985	1989	-0.1	2.35	1390	1352	-0.7
65550	NEWBURG	161	2792	2845	2962	0.4	50	1174	1207	1268	0.7	2.36	836	842	0.2
65552	PLATO	215	1642	1592	1619	-0.7	10	654	643	662	-0.4	2.47	479	463	-0.8
65555	RAYMONDVILLE	215	1351	1378	1420	0.5	51	508	523	544	0.7	2.62	370	373	0.2
65556	RICHLAND	169	4265	4147	4281	-0.7	12	1764	1752	1842	-0.2	2.34	1240	1191	-0.9
65557	ROBY	215	235	232	236	-0.3	22	102	102	105	0.0	2.27	76	75	-0.3
65559	SAINT JAMES	161	8108	8437	8870	0.9	67	3161	3317	3523	1.1	2.43	2199	2258	0.6
65560	SALEM	065	13092	13525	13961	0.8	61	5258	5482	5710	1.0	2.42	3713	3792	0.5
65564	SOLO	215	209	248	275	4.1	98	91	109	122	4.3	2.28	66	78	4.0
65565	STEELVILLE	055	4486	4555	4701	0.4	47	1779	1817	1889	0.5	2.45	1236	1237	0.0
65566	VIBURNUM	093	911	881	869	-0.8	9	341	334	333	-0.5	2.56	253	243	-0.9
65567	STOUTLAND	029	1738	1754	1875	0.2	41	662	676	731	0.5	2.58	502	505	0.1
65570	SUCCESS	215	407	419	434	0.7	59	157	164	172	1.0	2.55	118	121	0.6
65571	SUMMERSVILLE	215	1605	1537	1559	-1.0	5	636	612	626	-0.9	2.50	452	426	-1.4
65580	VICHY	125	835	852	874	0.5	52	353	362	375	0.6	2.35	263	264	0.1
65582	VIENNA	125	2103	2246	2375	1.6	80	803	876	941	2.1	2.47	559	596	1.5
65583	WAYNESVILLE	169	8312	8275	8612	-0.1	28	3198	3266	3476	0.5	2.48	2279	2247	-0.3
65584	SAINT ROBERT	169	5166	5715	6191	2.4	88	2035	2303	2547	3.0	2.47	1361	1486	2.1
65586	WESCO	055	505	507	519	0.1	36	207	210	216	0.3	2.39	152	151	-0.2
65588	WINONA	203	2460	2558	2645	0.9	66	977	1026	1072	1.2	2.49	698	718	0.7
65589	YUKON	215	409	416	434	0.4	48	151	155	163	0.6	2.68	113	114	0.2
65590	LONG LANE	059	1755	1860	1997	1.4	76	666	707	759	1.4	2.63	520	544	1.1
65591	MONTREAL	029	872	889	959	0.5	51	343	354	386	0.8	2.51	258	263	0.5
65601	ALDRICH	167	738	696	699	-1.4	2	305	290	292	-1.2	2.40	232	216	-1.7
65603	ARCOLA	057	519	517	523	-0.1	28	224	224	227	0.0	2.31	170	167	-0.4
65604	ASH GROVE	077	2811	2909	3020	0.8	63	1083	1131	1185	1.0	2.52	789	803	0.4
65605	AURORA	009	11507	11824	12480	0.6	57	4526	4654	4918	0.7	2.51	3184	3210	0.2
65606	ALTON	149	3493	3360	3336	-0.9	7	1454	1407	1405	-0.8	2.39	1029	978	-1.2
65608	AVA	067	8923	9136	9433	0.6	54	3600	3713	3864	0.7	2.43	2463	2485	0.2
65609	BAKERSFIELD	153	782	812	835	0.9	65	291	304	316	1.0	2.67	218	224	0.6
65610	BILLINGS	043	2788	3109	3609	2.6	90	1109	1249	1463	2.8	2.49	832	922	2.5
65611	BLUE EYE	209	2169	2313	2524	1.5	79	924	988	1080	1.6	2.34	699	734	1.2
65612	BOIS D ARC	077	2048	2363	2611	3.4	95	752	876	977	3.7	2.70	604	691	3.2
65613	BOLIVAR	167	15091	15649	16278	0.9	64	5423	5642	5892	0.9	2.52	3753	3825	0.5
65614	BRADLEYVILLE	213	548	563	603	0.6	57	211	218	234	0.8	2.58	163	165	0.3
65616	BRANSON	213	16877	18242	20160	1.9	84	7042	7626	8454	1.9	2.37	4764	5051	1.4
65617	BRIGHTON	167	1089	1185	1251	2.0	86	379	416	441	2.2	2.79	294	317	1.8
65618	BRIXEY	153	276	280	285	0.3	47	113	116	118	0.6	2.41	85	86	0.3
65619	BROOKLINE STATION	077	4007	4467	4835	2.6	90	1527	1724	1886	2.9	2.59	1236	1365	2.4
65620	BRUNER	043	307	527	722	13.6	100	113	196	270	13.8	2.69	88	150	13.4
65622	BUFFALO	059	7546	8025	8640	1.5	78	2918	3112	3355	1.5	2.55	2090	2185	1.1
65623	BUTTERFIELD	009	916	959	1022	1.1	70	339	356	380	1.2	2.69	249	257	0.8
65624	CAPE FAIR	209	2128	2268	2472	1.5	79	903	959	1045	1.4	2.34	678	709	1.1
65625	CASSVILLE	009	6352	7061	7820	2.5	89	2515	2816	3142	2.7	2.45	1755	1923	2.2
65626	CAULFIELD	091	1339	1389	1419	0.9	65	538	563	579	1.1	2.47	405	416	0.6
65627	CEDARCREEK	213	516	552	604	1.6	81	222	238	260	1.7	2.32	149	155	0.9
65629	CHADWICK	043	439	430	464	-0.5	18	180	178	193	-0.3	2.42	133	129	-0.7
65630	CHESTNUTRIDGE	043	300	308	335	0.6	56	115	119	130	0.8	2.59	89	90	0.3
	MISSOURI					0.8					0.9	2.46			0.4
	UNITED STATES					1.2					1.3	2.58			1.1

#	POST OFFICE NAME	RACE (%) White 2000	White 2004	Black 2000	Black 2004	Asian/Pacific 2000	Asian/Pacific 2004	% Hispanic Origin 2000	% Hispanic Origin 2004	2004 AGE DISTRIBUTION (%) 0-4	5-9	10-14	15-19	20-24	25-44	45-64	65-84	85+	18+	MEDIAN AGE 2004	% 2004 Males	% 2004 Females
65340	MARSHALL	87.7	86.5	6.6	7.1	0.7	0.8	6.2	6.8	6.5	6.3	6.6	8.2	9.4	25.4	23.3	12.0	2.4	76.8	35.5	49.1	50.9
65344	MIAMI	98.4	98.5	0.4	0.4	0.0	0.0	1.4	1.5	7.4	7.3	6.7	5.7	5.5	23.7	28.4	13.7	1.5	75.2	41.3	48.9	51.2
65345	MORA	95.5	95.5	0.8	1.3	0.0	0.6	1.5	1.3	5.8	7.1	11.5	7.7	4.5	26.9	25.6	9.6	1.3	69.9	37.5	53.2	46.8
65347	NELSON	97.6	97.3	1.4	1.5	0.1	0.1	0.5	0.5	5.1	5.6	7.0	6.6	5.2	25.2	27.1	15.2	3.0	78.0	42.3	49.8	50.2
65348	OTTERVILLE	97.8	97.6	0.7	0.8	0.1	0.1	0.9	1.0	7.3	6.9	7.0	6.4	6.7	26.0	25.6	12.5	1.6	74.9	37.7	49.6	50.4
65349	SLATER	89.7	88.9	7.6	8.2	0.2	0.2	1.3	1.4	6.1	5.9	6.2	6.6	6.8	23.9	24.3	15.7	4.4	78.0	41.2	49.1	50.9
65350	SMITHTON	96.2	95.8	0.9	1.0	0.2	0.3	1.6	1.8	7.1	7.1	9.5	8.3	6.3	26.9	21.7	11.2	2.1	71.0	35.8	49.4	50.6
65351	SWEET SPRINGS	96.0	95.5	0.9	1.0	0.7	0.9	1.2	1.4	6.1	6.2	6.8	6.8	6.1	24.0	25.3	15.7	3.1	76.4	41.0	49.6	50.4
65354	SYRACUSE	98.6	98.3	0.0	0.0	0.3	0.3	1.2	1.7	5.7	6.4	8.2	6.5	6.5	28.4	26.2	10.7	1.3	75.7	38.1	54.0	46.0
65355	WARSAW	97.7	97.5	0.2	0.2	0.1	0.2	1.0	1.1	4.2	4.5	4.6	4.9	4.4	18.8	33.2	23.4	2.1	83.7	50.9	49.6	50.4
65360	WINDSOR	97.0	96.7	0.6	0.7	0.3	0.3	0.7	0.7	7.0	6.6	6.9	6.9	6.3	25.6	23.1	14.2	3.3	75.3	38.3	48.8	51.2
65401	ROLLA	92.7	91.6	1.8	2.0	2.9	3.7	1.4	1.6	5.9	5.7	6.1	8.3	11.0	25.9	23.5	11.8	1.8	78.4	34.8	50.7	49.3
65409	ROLLA	82.3	79.2	2.9	3.1	11.0	14.0	1.6	1.7	3.8	3.0	2.7	22.8	33.0	22.2	6.4	4.2	2.0	88.9	22.7	66.6	33.4
65436	BEULAH	98.0	97.7	0.2	0.2	0.2	0.4	1.0	1.0	6.2	6.2	6.6	6.2	6.0	24.8	27.5	15.3	1.4	77.6	41.4	48.6	51.5
65438	BIRCH TREE	94.9	94.6	0.2	0.2	0.1	0.1	1.5	1.7	6.4	6.5	7.6	7.1	6.0	25.0	25.5	14.2	1.7	74.9	39.2	49.2	50.8
65439	BIXBY	98.4	98.7	0.2	0.2	0.0	0.0	0.4	0.4	6.7	6.7	7.6	6.3	5.9	24.2	25.5	14.7	2.3	74.5	39.4	48.6	51.4
65440	BOSS	97.9	97.7	0.2	0.2	0.5	0.7	1.2	1.4	6.3	6.3	6.1	6.6	6.1	24.1	29.7	13.8	0.9	76.8	41.3	50.6	49.4
65441	BOURBON	98.7	98.6	0.0	0.0	0.1	0.1	0.8	1.0	7.3	7.3	7.6	7.2	6.4	26.9	24.1	11.7	1.6	73.1	36.8	50.9	49.1
65443	BRINKTOWN	95.5	95.0	1.7	1.9	0.2	0.2	2.6	3.0	6.9	7.1	9.2	8.0	5.7	23.1	26.4	12.6	1.0	71.8	38.3	52.8	47.2
65444	BUCYRUS	97.5	97.3	0.1	0.1	0.8	1.0	0.9	1.0	6.2	6.2	6.3	6.1	6.0	23.3	28.4	15.7	1.8	77.5	42.4	49.6	50.4
65446	CHERRYVILLE	98.1	98.0	0.1	0.1	0.1	0.1	0.2	0.3	6.4	7.3	7.2	5.9	5.4	24.7	29.0	13.3	0.8	75.4	40.4	50.3	49.7
65449	COOK STATION	96.5	95.9	0.6	0.9	0.3	0.6	0.9	0.9	6.4	6.7	7.3	6.1	6.1	24.0	28.4	13.7	1.2	76.0	40.6	50.9	49.1
65452	CROCKER	96.1	95.9	0.4	0.4	0.6	0.7	1.1	1.2	6.0	6.1	6.9	6.8	6.0	25.5	27.0	14.4	1.4	76.8	40.8	50.3	49.7
65453	CUBA	98.1	97.9	0.2	0.3	0.2	0.2	1.0	1.1	6.2	6.1	6.8	6.4	6.6	24.4	25.3	15.9	2.4	77.0	40.7	49.2	50.8
65456	DAVISVILLE	98.3	98.3	0.0	0.0	0.0	0.0	0.3	0.0	6.7	7.2	7.2	5.8	5.5	24.9	27.8	13.9	1.2	75.1	40.7	49.4	50.6
65457	DEVILS ELBOW	81.2	79.2	9.1	9.9	4.8	5.8	2.6	2.8	6.9	6.5	6.9	8.0	7.3	27.5	25.5	9.2	2.2	74.3	37.1	48.5	51.5
65459	DIXON	92.7	91.7	2.8	3.2	1.2	1.5	2.0	2.2	6.7	6.7	7.4	7.0	6.8	25.7	26.1	12.2	1.6	75.0	38.3	48.7	51.3
65461	DUKE	98.1	98.7	0.0	0.0	0.0	0.0	1.3	1.3	5.7	6.3	6.9	5.7	5.7	23.9	30.2	14.5	1.3	77.4	42.3	47.2	52.8
65462	EDGAR SPRINGS	97.1	96.6	0.2	0.2	0.5	0.7	0.8	1.0	5.5	5.8	6.6	5.9	6.0	25.0	29.7	14.3	1.3	78.7	42.2	49.8	50.2
65463	ELDRIDGE	98.3	98.0	0.2	0.2	0.1	0.2	0.8	1.0	6.7	6.7	7.1	7.3	7.1	25.8	27.0	11.1	1.0	74.4	37.8	51.5	48.5
65464	ELK CREEK	95.9	95.4	0.0	0.0	0.2	0.4	1.5	1.3	5.7	6.1	7.4	6.3	5.5	21.3	30.7	15.6	1.5	77.1	43.3	50.1	49.9
65466	EMINENCE	95.8	95.6	0.2	0.2	0.0	0.0	0.6	0.6	5.5	5.5	5.6	6.3	5.7	22.7	30.4	16.1	2.3	79.9	44.1	49.7	50.3
65468	EUNICE	96.9	95.3	0.0	0.0	0.0	0.0	0.0	0.0	6.3	6.3	6.3	7.8	6.3	21.9	26.6	17.2	1.6	75.0	41.3	51.6	48.4
65470	FALCON	97.7	97.5	0.2	0.2	0.1	0.1	0.9	1.0	6.5	6.6	7.2	7.4	6.6	24.7	27.8	12.5	0.8	75.2	39.5	51.9	48.1
65473	FORT LEONARD WOOD	65.1	64.4	21.3	21.2	2.9	3.5	11.3	11.7	10.3	8.6	6.3	15.5	21.5	35.4	2.1	0.2	0.0	72.2	22.2	60.6	39.4
65479	HARTSHORN	96.3	95.9	0.0	0.0	0.0	0.0	0.4	0.4	5.3	5.7	6.4	8.3	7.6	21.5	29.1	15.1	1.1	78.1	41.5	47.6	52.5
65483	HOUSTON	96.5	96.2	0.1	0.1	0.2	0.2	1.1	1.3	5.4	5.5	6.5	6.4	6.3	22.2	27.0	17.8	2.9	78.5	43.4	47.2	52.8
65484	HUGGINS	97.6	96.9	0.0	0.4	0.4	0.4	0.8	0.8	5.1	5.9	6.7	5.5	5.5	20.1	27.6	19.7	3.9	78.7	45.8	47.6	52.4
65486	IBERIA	99.1	99.1	0.1	0.1	0.1	0.1	0.5	0.6	7.5	7.3	7.5	6.3	6.0	26.9	23.7	13.2	1.7	73.8	37.3	50.7	49.3
65501	JADWIN	95.9	95.4	0.2	0.2	0.2	0.5	0.5	0.5	6.6	6.8	7.8	6.3	5.3	25.2	26.7	13.8	1.5	75.0	40.5	50.7	49.3
65529	JEROME	96.1	95.5	0.3	0.3	0.6	0.9	1.2	1.2	3.9	6.0	6.3	7.1	4.2	26.8	31.3	13.1	1.5	78.6	42.9	52.7	47.3
65534	LAQUEY	93.2	92.7	1.8	1.9	1.1	1.2	2.7	2.9	6.8	6.5	7.4	6.8	6.3	27.5	26.8	11.5	0.7	75.1	38.4	49.6	50.4
65535	LEASBURG	98.2	98.1	0.2	0.2	0.1	0.2	0.5	0.4	6.8	6.8	7.1	7.2	6.5	25.2	26.8	12.3	1.4	75.0	38.5	49.7	50.4
65536	LEBANON	97.0	96.7	0.5	0.5	0.4	0.5	1.3	1.4	7.0	6.8	7.1	6.7	6.9	26.7	24.0	12.9	1.8	74.9	37.4	48.8	51.2
65541	LENOX	97.8	97.5	0.3	0.3	0.0	0.0	0.5	0.8	5.5	5.9	6.7	6.7	5.6	22.3	29.0	15.9	2.4	78.1	43.3	50.0	50.0
65542	LICKING	97.1	96.9	0.1	0.0	0.2	0.3	1.2	1.3	5.7	6.2	7.0	6.2	5.5	24.6	25.8	16.2	2.8	77.4	41.4	47.9	52.1
65543	LYNCHBURG	95.6	95.9	0.4	0.4	0.4	0.4	1.1	1.1	7.2	6.8	6.0	7.2	6.4	24.2	26.8	14.3	1.1	76.6	40.1	52.8	47.2
65548	MOUNTAIN VIEW	96.0	95.6	0.0	0.0	0.3	0.4	1.1	1.3	6.6	6.4	6.7	6.0	6.4	23.4	25.3	16.0	3.3	76.5	40.8	47.9	52.2
65550	NEWBURG	96.8	96.5	0.3	0.3	0.4	0.5	0.6	0.7	6.0	6.2	6.8	6.6	6.2	25.6	28.4	12.7	1.6	76.9	40.4	49.8	50.2
65552	PLATO	92.1	91.3	2.0	2.1	1.2	1.5	1.6	1.8	5.7	6.3	7.9	6.2	6.2	24.8	29.2	12.1	1.6	76.2	40.8	49.3	50.7
65555	RAYMONDVILLE	97.3	97.0	0.1	0.2	0.2	0.3	0.4	0.4	5.7	5.7	6.5	7.9	6.7	23.3	27.5	14.7	2.0	77.4	41.4	49.9	50.2
65556	RICHLAND	95.8	95.5	0.7	0.7	0.6	0.7	1.5	1.5	6.3	6.4	6.7	6.4	5.8	25.0	26.6	14.9	1.8	76.5	40.7	48.7	51.3
65557	ROBY	96.2	96.1	0.4	0.4	0.4	0.4	0.9	0.4	5.2	5.6	7.3	6.0	6.5	22.8	29.7	15.1	1.7	77.6	42.8	50.0	50.0
65559	SAINT JAMES	95.1	94.7	0.8	0.8	0.4	0.5	0.8	0.9	5.6	6.0	8.1	7.8	5.3	23.6	25.1	15.7	2.8	75.2	40.7	49.1	50.9
65560	SALEM	97.0	96.7	0.4	0.5	0.2	0.3	0.7	0.8	6.6	6.5	6.8	6.2	6.1	24.0	25.2	15.7	2.8	76.2	40.7	48.3	51.7
65564	SOLO	95.7	95.6	0.0	0.0	0.5	0.4	1.4	1.6	5.7	6.5	7.3	6.5	5.7	21.0	29.8	16.1	1.6	77.0	43.1	50.8	49.2
65565	STEELVILLE	98.2	98.1	0.1	0.1	0.3	0.3	0.5	0.5	6.8	6.9	7.4	6.7	5.9	25.8	23.4	14.8	2.2	74.7	38.3	47.8	52.2
65566	VIBURNUM	98.5	98.5	0.1	0.1	0.1	0.1	0.4	0.5	7.3	7.3	8.0	6.2	5.7	24.6	24.9	13.9	2.3	73.6	38.2	48.7	51.3
65567	STOUTLAND	97.6	97.4	0.0	0.0	0.2	0.3	0.7	0.9	5.0	5.2	6.9	8.2	6.8	25.8	27.5	13.4	1.2	77.4	40.6	52.8	47.2
65570	SUCCESS	96.8	96.7	0.0	0.0	0.5	0.7	0.7	0.5	6.0	6.0	6.9	6.4	6.7	24.8	27.9	14.1	1.2	77.6	40.9	50.6	49.4
65571	SUMMERSVILLE	97.0	96.8	0.1	0.1	0.1	0.1	0.4	0.5	7.2	7.0	7.1	7.2	6.2	23.0	25.3	15.3	1.6	74.5	38.7	49.4	50.6
65580	VICHY	97.1	96.8	0.2	0.2	0.2	0.2	1.7	2.1	5.6	6.0	6.7	6.2	5.1	24.5	28.9	15.7	1.3	77.8	42.5	52.2	47.8
65582	VIENNA	98.3	98.2	0.0	0.0	0.1	0.2	0.4	0.4	7.2	6.4	6.7	6.0	5.5	25.0	22.9	16.9	3.4	76.2	40.8	48.6	51.4
65583	WAYNESVILLE	82.6	81.2	8.7	9.2	2.8	3.4	3.4	3.7	6.5	6.6	7.3	7.8	6.5	26.9	26.9	10.5	1.0	74.4	37.7	48.2	51.8
65584	SAINT ROBERT	68.2	66.4	18.0	18.5	5.0	6.1	5.8	6.1	7.6	6.9	8.2	8.7	8.1	30.5	23.2	6.3	0.5	72.0	33.0	49.0	51.0
65586	WESCO	97.0	96.8	0.6	0.6	0.2	0.4	0.6	0.8	6.3	6.5	7.1	6.5	6.1	25.4	26.8	14.2	1.0	76.1	40.1	50.1	49.9
65588	WINONA	94.2	93.8	0.1	0.1	0.0	0.0	0.8	1.0	7.4	7.4	8.5	7.2	6.5	25.2	24.3	12.2	1.3	72.3	36.4	48.8	51.2
65589	YUKON	96.1	95.9	0.0	0.0	0.0	0.2	0.5	0.7	5.5	5.8	6.7	7.2	6.7	21.6	29.8	15.4	1.2	77.6	42.4	49.0	51.0
65590	LONG LANE	97.5	97.2	0.1	0.1	0.3	0.4	0.5	0.5	6.3	6.6	7.1	7.1	6.2	24.8	27.6	12.9	1.3	75.6	40.2	51.6	48.4
65591	MONTREAL	98.4	98.2	0.0	0.0	0.0	0.0	0.8	1.0	5.3	5.4	6.5	7.3	6.3	27.5	28.1	12.3	1.4	78.5	40.5	52.3	47.7
65601	ALDRICH	98.1	98.0	0.1	0.1	0.1	0.1	1.2	1.3	5.2	5.8	6.9	5.6	4.9	24.4	29.5	16.8	1.0	78.6	43.4	50.1	49.9
65603	ARCOLA	97.5	97.3	0.2	0.2	0.2	0.2	1.7	1.9	6.0	6.2	6.0	5.8	5.4	21.9	29.8	17.2	1.7	78.3	44.2	53.0	47.0
65604	ASH GROVE	97.6	97.4	0.2	0.2	0.1	0.1	0.7	0.8	6.5	6.8	6.9	6.6	5.6	25.2	27.2	12.5	2.8	75.3	40.1	49.5	50.5
65605	AURORA	96.2	95.9	0.2	0.2	0.2	0.3	2.3	2.5	7.6	7.3	7.4	6.6	6.4	26.1	22.9	13.4	2.2	73.5	36.8	49.3	50.7
65606	ALTON	92.8	92.3	0.1	0.2	0.1	0.1	0.9	1.0	6.1	6.3	6.5	5.9	5.7	23.0	28.5	15.9	2.2	77.6	42.6	49.5	50.5
65608	AVA	97.3	97.1	0.1	0.1	0.3	0.3	0.9	1.0	6.3	6.3	6.9	6.7	6.6	22.7	25.7	16.2	2.6	76.3	40.8	48.5	51.5
65609	BAKERSFIELD	95.9	95.4	0.1	0.3	0.0	0.0	1.0	1.1	8.3	7.9	7.3	6.5	6.5	27.5	21.8	13.2	1.1	72.5	35.0	50.4	49.6
65610	BILLINGS	97.1	96.7	0.3	0.3	0.4	0.4	0.4	0.5	6.1	6.3	6.8	6.7	5.6	26.1	27.7	12.7	2.0	76.7	40.0	49.5	50.5
65611	BLUE EYE	97.7	97.5	0.0	0.0	0.1	0.2	0.4	0.5	4.5	4.6	4.8	4.4	4.3	18.9	32.2	24.6	1.7	83.4	51.1	47.3	52.8
65612	BOIS D ARC	98.1	97.8	0.1	0.2	0.0	0.0	0.6	0.7	5.7	6.2	6.7	6.6	5.7	25.6	30.3	12.2	1.1	77.3	41.0	50.7	49.3
65613	BOLIVAR	96.9	96.5	0.6	0.7	0.3	0.4	1.4	1.6	6.8	6.3	6.3	9.6	12.4	23.3	20.0	12.8	2.5	76.3	32.5	47.5	52.5
65614	BRADLEYVILLE	97.5	97.2	0.0	0.0	0.4	0.4	0.9	1.2	6.2	6.4	5.7	5.9	6.2	25.0	27.2	15.5	2.0	78.5	41.7	51.3	48.7
65616	BRANSON	95.4	95.0	0.4	0.5	0.6	0.7	3.5	3.9	6.2	6.2	6.4	6.1	5.9	25.9	27.0	14.8	1.6	77.5	40.3	47.7	52.3
65617	BRIGHTON	97.6	97.5	0.2	0.2	0.1	0.1	1.7	1.9	7.6	7.9	7.8	8.1	5.7	27.9	24.1	10.0	0.9	71.1	35.0	51.5	48.5
65618	BRIXEY	97.8	97.9	0.0	0.0	0.0	0.0	0.7	1.1	6.1	5.4	5.0	6.4	5.4	22.1	30.4	17.9	1.4	79.3	44.8	49.3	50.7
65619	BROOKLINE STATION	96.5	95.9	0.4	0.5	0.8	1.0	1.1	1.3	8.0	7.9	6.8	5.9	5.4	30.5	26.2	8.8	0.7	73.7	36.6	49.1	51.0
65620	BRUNER	97.7	97.5	0.0	0.0	0.0	0.2	2.0	2.1	5.7	6.1	7.2	6.8	6.3	28.5	28.7	9.9	1.0	77.0	38.2	51.6	48.4
65622	BUFFALO	97.7	97.5	0.1	0.1	0.0	0.0	1.0	1.1	6.9	6.8	7.8	7.6	6.5	25.0	24.5	12.8	2.0	73.7	37.5	48.8	51.2
65623	BUTTERFIELD	90.2	89.1	0.2	0.2	0.4	0.5	12.5	14.3	8.3	8.5	8.6	6.5	6.4	28.7	23.5	8.9	0.8	70.8	34.0	49.7	50.3
65624	CAPE FAIR	97.2	97.1	0.2	0.2	0.2	0.2	1.4	1.5	4.5	5.0	5.5	5.2	4.7	21.5	32.7	19.9	1.1	81.8	47.7	50.8	49.2
65625	CASSVILLE	96.2	95.7	0.1	0.1	0.5	0.6	2.1	2.4	6.2	6.3	7.2	6.7	6.3	24.7	25.0	15.1	2.5	76.4	39.8	49.1	50.9
65626	CAULFIELD	97.9	97.6	0.3	0.4	0.1	0.1	1.3	1.4	6.1	6.0	6.1	7.0	6.9	23.8	27.4	15.1	1.7	77.6	40.9	51.7	48.3
65627	CEDARCREEK	95.2	94.9	0.4	0.4	0.4	0.4	3.5	3.6	6.3	6.0	6.7	6.5	7.3	26.1	27.5	12.3	1.3	76.8	39.7	48.7	51.3
65629	CHADWICK	97.5	97.4	0.0	0.0	0.0	0.2	0.7	0.7	5.4	5.6	7.7	7.9	7.0	26.7	27.4	11.4	0.9	76.5	38.7	48.6	51.4
65630	CHESTNUTRIDGE	97.7	97.7	0.0	0.0	0.0	0.0	1.0	1.3	6.2	6.2	7.8	7.1	6.2	28.3	27.6	9.7	1.0	76.0	37.9	49.0	51.0
	MISSOURI	84.9	84.1	11.3	11.5	1.2	1.4	2.1	2.3	6.7	6.6	7.0	7.0	7.3	27.6	24.2	11.7	1.9	75.6	36.8	48.7	51.3
	UNITED STATES	75.1	73.6	12.3	12.5	3.8	4.2	12.5	14.1	6.9	6.7	7.2	7.0	7.3	28.6	23.8	10.8	1.7	75.1	36.0	49.1	50.9

ZIP CODE #	POST OFFICE NAME	2004 Per Capita Income	2004 HH Income Base	2004 HOUSEHOLD INCOME DISTRIBUTION (%) Less than $25,000	$25,000 to $49,999	$50,000 to $99,999	$100,000 to $149,999	$150,000 or More	MEDIAN HOUSEHOLD INCOME 2004	2009	2004 National Centile	2004 State Centile	2004 Home Value Base	2004 HOME VALUE DISTRIBUTION (%) Less than $50,000	$50,000 to $89,999	$90,000 to $174,999	$175,000 to $399,999	$400,000 or More	2004 Median Home Value
65340	MARSHALL	19841	5492	31.1	33.3	26.5	6.4	2.7	37624	43717	38	59	3669	22.3	28.9	35.1	12.0	1.7	88065
65344	MIAMI	20824	203	29.6	36.0	26.6	4.9	3.0	40412	45870	48	68	156	28.9	19.9	37.8	7.1	6.4	94000
65345	MORA	18624	54	16.7	40.7	33.3	7.4	1.9	45885	53820	64	80	46	13.0	23.9	43.5	19.6	0.0	120833
65347	NELSON	20437	364	22.8	38.5	28.6	7.1	3.0	41654	47700	52	72	303	28.1	20.5	32.3	14.2	5.0	93000
65348	OTTERVILLE	19002	420	30.7	37.6	26.9	2.4	2.4	37765	43296	38	59	343	29.5	26.2	32.4	10.5	1.5	81522
65349	SLATER	15830	1093	40.0	36.1	20.6	2.4	1.0	31768	36953	17	27	786	49.6	29.8	14.5	5.1	1.0	50366
65350	SMITHTON	18179	618	22.5	42.1	28.2	5.3	1.9	38288	44208	40	62	497	20.7	33.4	32.0	11.9	2.0	84875
65351	SWEET SPRINGS	18660	905	28.3	34.1	31.2	4.5	1.9	40982	47706	50	70	702	28.9	37.3	25.9	6.3	1.6	73425
65354	SYRACUSE	21864	223	24.7	35.0	31.4	3.1	5.8	43211	50450	57	75	187	29.4	19.8	27.8	22.5	0.5	91154
65355	WARSAW	18742	4753	43.1	30.8	21.1	3.0	1.9	30169	34754	13	20	3957	25.3	31.5	31.0	11.3	1.0	82021
65360	WINDSOR	18133	1686	35.2	32.0	27.5	3.8	1.5	35113	40879	28	45	1237	28.3	36.1	27.5	7.8	0.3	71179
65401	ROLLA	20211	11887	36.5	28.2	25.9	6.4	3.0	35108	41893	28	45	7656	19.5	25.1	38.6	15.8	1.1	99028
65409	ROLLA	5248	0	0.0	0.0	0.0	0.0	0.0	0	0	0	0	0	0.0	0.0	0.0	0.0	0.0	0
65436	BEULAH	14907	202	40.6	34.2	22.3	2.5	0.5	31849	38981	17	27	175	37.7	25.7	21.1	13.1	2.3	68333
65438	BIRCH TREE	11555	1392	56.8	30.9	9.8	1.9	0.6	21963	24608	3	1	1117	49.1	26.5	18.5	4.4	1.5	51296
65439	BIXBY	18086	189	37.6	31.2	25.9	3.7	1.6	33102	38902	21	34	153	36.0	37.9	21.6	3.9	0.7	63438
65440	BOSS	18771	170	29.4	35.3	25.9	7.7	1.8	39094	44656	43	64	146	19.9	28.8	37.7	11.0	2.7	92857
65441	BOURBON	17070	1853	31.5	33.4	29.7	3.8	1.7	38160	43001	40	61	1484	19.9	30.3	34.1	13.8	2.0	89835
65443	BRINKTOWN	14100	408	34.3	39.2	23.0	3.4	0.0	33086	38933	21	34	352	27.6	17.1	38.4	11.9	5.1	94634
65444	BUCYRUS	18178	535	45.1	29.5	20.2	2.4	2.8	28415	32636	9	13	448	29.9	26.3	30.6	10.9	2.2	79091
65446	CHERRYVILLE	14840	339	40.7	37.8	16.8	2.4	2.4	32537	38148	19	30	289	29.8	32.5	26.3	8.7	2.8	71667
65449	COOK STATION	13867	132	39.4	39.4	18.9	2.3	0.0	33875	38886	24	38	113	28.3	15.9	35.4	15.9	4.4	99286
65452	CROCKER	17196	1092	35.3	35.3	25.2	3.8	0.6	34620	39131	26	43	904	33.4	29.3	29.3	6.2	1.8	72500
65453	CUBA	17625	3432	35.6	32.1	26.4	4.2	1.7	35526	40769	30	48	2620	19.5	26.6	38.6	12.7	2.6	95838
65456	DAVISVILLE	15750	132	40.2	33.3	19.7	3.0	3.8	35000	40331	28	44	112	29.5	37.5	23.2	7.1	2.7	68182
65457	DEVILS ELBOW	18635	373	32.4	33.2	29.8	3.8	0.8	36299	39274	33	53	262	14.9	20.6	56.9	7.6	0.0	103571
65459	DIXON	16738	2633	32.2	35.6	27.8	3.2	1.2	35607	40597	30	48	2085	26.5	27.7	37.7	7.5	0.7	82669
65461	DUKE	15572	65	40.0	35.4	21.5	3.1	0.0	32346	37380	19	29	56	33.9	26.8	21.4	14.3	3.6	73333
65462	EDGAR SPRINGS	15063	470	40.4	31.7	24.9	2.3	0.6	31117	36742	15	24	404	35.9	26.0	25.3	9.9	3.0	76800
65463	ELDRIDGE	14892	409	35.7	41.8	17.9	4.7	0.0	33236	39163	22	35	345	33.3	21.7	35.9	5.8	3.2	75357
65464	ELK CREEK	29563	193	38.3	34.2	18.7	3.6	5.2	31656	37555	17	26	163	32.5	27.0	22.7	16.0	1.8	71875
65466	EMINENCE	14724	1063	50.6	29.4	16.2	2.9	0.9	24639	28166	4	4	852	35.3	25.2	28.5	8.6	2.4	71373
65468	EUNICE	14482	29	48.3	37.9	10.3	3.5	0.0	26103	28596	6	6	25	40.0	16.0	40.0	4.0	0.0	75000
65470	FALCON	16610	317	35.3	35.7	24.3	4.1	0.6	34140	40506	24	40	264	21.2	21.6	26.9	20.8	9.5	100833
65473	FORT LEONARD WOOD	14069	3367	13.0	56.2	24.8	4.8	1.2	39241	44615	44	65	88	6.8	28.4	59.1	5.7	0.0	103333
65479	HARTSHORN	13117	108	48.2	36.1	12.0	3.7	0.0	26099	27668	6	6	91	44.0	20.9	27.5	7.7	0.0	61250
65483	HOUSTON	17779	1948	45.8	30.7	17.8	3.6	2.2	27011	31437	7	8	1398	24.2	31.8	31.9	11.3	0.9	82385
65484	HUGGINS	17074	89	34.8	33.7	24.7	4.5	2.3	33795	40750	23	38	74	21.6	29.7	33.8	13.5	1.4	88000
65486	IBERIA	16033	1536	33.7	37.0	25.9	2.9	0.7	36105	41708	32	52	1265	25.9	26.6	35.0	10.7	1.8	86013
65501	JADWIN	16328	148	36.5	33.8	25.0	3.4	1.4	33976	39163	24	39	123	26.8	30.1	35.0	7.3	0.8	79444
65529	JEROME	15578	145	46.2	26.2	25.5	2.1	0.0	27292	32088	8	10	108	21.3	35.2	31.5	12.0	0.0	78000
65534	LAQUEY	15945	313	35.5	36.4	24.6	2.6	1.0	32836	37348	20	33	272	37.5	15.8	32.7	11.8	2.2	84000
65535	LEASBURG	17304	647	38.2	34.6	19.9	4.2	3.1	31625	36615	17	26	516	27.1	30.2	31.2	10.1	1.4	81915
65536	LEBANON	19057	10583	36.8	32.9	22.3	5.0	3.0	33995	40475	24	39	7593	25.4	24.8	34.4	13.6	1.8	89684
65541	LENOX	16476	275	38.2	34.6	23.6	2.6	1.1	34256	39183	25	41	232	29.3	25.9	33.6	10.3	0.9	82500
65542	LICKING	15962	2158	47.4	30.1	18.3	3.1	1.1	26502	30852	6	7	1633	33.4	29.0	27.3	8.7	1.6	74457
65543	LYNCHBURG	16103	104	36.5	42.3	17.3	3.9	0.0	35428	40879	29	47	88	27.3	14.8	39.8	6.8	11.4	96364
65548	MOUNTAIN VIEW	14748	1985	47.3	35.4	13.1	3.1	1.1	26360	30441	6	7	1475	29.4	33.9	29.4	6.6	0.8	73119
65550	NEWBURG	18753	1207	35.5	34.3	25.5	3.3	1.3	33755	40457	23	38	945	35.5	29.1	26.4	7.2	1.9	72015
65552	PLATO	19403	643	35.5	28.2	29.6	4.5	2.3	35451	41368	29	48	543	23.2	22.8	39.8	8.7	5.5	97963
65555	RAYMONDVILLE	12954	523	49.3	31.7	15.1	2.7	1.2	25320	29000	5	5	428	37.9	23.1	28.3	9.6	1.2	68889
65556	RICHLAND	17233	1752	37.3	36.7	22.4	2.9	0.8	32395	36775	19	29	1405	32.1	30.5	26.8	8.9	1.7	73544
65557	ROBY	19925	102	45.1	25.5	20.6	5.9	2.9	29059	34442	10	16	86	26.7	31.4	25.6	11.6	4.7	81250
65559	SAINT JAMES	17541	3317	38.5	33.4	21.8	4.6	1.7	32572	39482	20	31	2470	20.4	31.2	34.3	12.4	1.7	88361
65560	SALEM	16561	5482	41.7	32.3	20.9	3.9	1.2	30772	36016	14	22	4024	26.7	31.0	32.9	8.0	1.3	79545
65564	SOLO	21179	109	36.7	33.9	19.3	3.7	6.4	32627	38203	20	32	92	31.5	29.4	20.7	16.3	2.2	70000
65565	STEELVILLE	16350	1817	41.8	31.0	20.6	4.1	2.4	31266	36383	16	25	1391	28.1	29.5	31.1	9.5	1.8	79279
65566	VIBURNUM	16164	334	35.9	31.4	27.5	3.9	1.2	34741	40714	26	43	268	36.2	41.4	20.9	1.5	0.0	61667
65567	STOUTLAND	17848	676	28.6	41.6	25.4	2.5	1.9	37524	43576	38	58	570	31.9	21.4	37.0	7.5	2.1	82963
65570	SUCCESS	16020	164	52.4	24.4	17.7	4.3	1.2	23366	28479	3	2	138	29.0	31.2	27.5	10.1	2.2	80000
65571	SUMMERSVILLE	11628	612	56.4	31.1	9.8	1.6	1.1	21415	24703	2	1	466	41.2	24.0	26.2	7.5	1.1	63929
65580	VICHY	18882	362	35.1	28.7	30.4	4.7	1.1	37841	44041	39	60	304	19.7	24.0	33.9	18.8	3.6	98261
65582	VIENNA	17967	876	34.3	29.9	28.9	5.9	1.0	35799	41465	31	49	694	23.8	23.5	35.5	14.1	3.2	93800
65583	WAYNESVILLE	20256	3266	28.4	30.4	32.9	7.0	1.3	42794	47036	55	74	2539	18.0	21.1	45.5	13.9	1.5	105320
65584	SAINT ROBERT	18799	2303	29.5	35.4	28.8	5.0	1.3	38521	42920	41	63	1512	24.3	15.2	52.2	8.2	0.2	100169
65586	WESCO	15587	210	40.0	37.1	18.6	3.3	1.0	32944	37836	21	33	175	30.9	20.0	31.4	13.7	4.0	88500
65588	WINONA	14149	1026	54.4	29.8	12.4	2.2	1.2	22613	25000	3	2	815	41.6	34.4	18.2	4.2	1.7	58563
65589	YUKON	13215	155	47.1	34.2	13.6	3.2	1.9	26680	31436	7	8	132	40.2	22.7	25.8	10.6	0.8	65714
65590	LONG LANE	17891	707	33.4	34.7	27.2	3.0	1.8	37323	43553	37	57	595	33.1	22.7	31.8	11.9	0.5	74500
65591	MONTREAL	16365	354	27.1	43.8	26.6	2.5	0.0	37125	43123	36	56	299	34.8	19.1	27.4	15.4	3.3	80417
65601	ALDRICH	17607	290	31.4	35.9	28.6	4.1	0.0	34538	40000	26	42	229	20.1	23.1	32.3	22.7	1.8	100431
65603	ARCOLA	16847	224	37.5	34.8	23.7	2.7	1.3	32867	36543	21	33	184	27.2	22.3	39.1	8.7	2.7	90833
65604	ASH GROVE	19275	1131	31.7	33.2	29.0	3.4	2.7	38943	46637	43	64	876	14.4	31.6	40.2	11.9	1.9	94605
65605	AURORA	16404	4654	39.5	32.9	21.7	3.5	2.4	31660	36686	17	26	3446	25.2	32.2	31.1	10.3	1.2	81380
65606	ALTON	14503	1407	52.4	31.1	12.2	2.5	1.9	23681	26375	4	3	1122	41.0	24.4	26.0	8.0	0.5	64242
65608	AVA	16478	3713	44.0	34.9	16.6	2.6	1.9	28137	31547	9	12	2796	27.7	29.3	30.6	11.6	0.9	79217
65609	BAKERSFIELD	20469	304	45.1	31.9	18.4	2.6	2.0	27790	31366	8	11	238	36.6	23.5	27.3	10.9	1.7	70625
65610	BILLINGS	20179	1249	28.8	32.7	31.1	5.0	2.4	39653	47395	45	66	975	10.9	23.6	45.6	16.8	3.1	111213
65611	BLUE EYE	21776	988	25.9	43.3	26.3	2.3	2.1	37625	43035	38	59	817	15.1	20.0	37.1	25.6	2.3	119222
65612	BOIS D ARC	19348	876	23.3	34.9	32.2	7.4	2.2	43496	50808	57	75	744	12.8	23.5	39.9	21.4	2.4	112500
65613	BOLIVAR	16012	5642	39.7	32.5	21.6	4.9	1.4	32605	37684	20	31	3699	14.3	25.3	42.2	16.3	2.0	105784
65614	BRADLEYVILLE	16632	218	34.9	43.6	15.6	3.7	2.3	33681	39149	23	37	183	32.8	19.1	27.3	17.5	3.3	87083
65616	BRANSON	23081	7626	30.6	32.4	26.2	7.2	3.6	37743	44051	38	59	5067	11.6	14.9	42.1	27.5	3.9	126878
65617	BRIGHTON	16950	416	26.0	36.1	31.3	5.3	1.4	40834	46295	49	70	333	15.9	19.5	41.1	20.4	3.0	111167
65618	BRIXEY	13471	116	44.8	37.1	16.4	1.7	0.0	28143	31499	9	12	99	32.3	25.3	28.3	10.1	4.0	79375
65619	BROOKLINE STATION	24537	1724	17.3	29.1	39.0	10.4	4.1	52713	63429	76	89	1445	9.6	20.4	52.4	16.8	0.9	112641
65620	BRUNER	15383	196	32.7	37.8	26.5	1.5	1.5	35586	42343	30	48	166	26.5	27.1	34.9	9.6	1.8	85000
65622	BUFFALO	17706	3112	39.8	33.9	20.9	3.2	2.3	30999	36545	15	24	2320	22.3	22.5	40.7	11.1	3.5	97806
65623	BUTTERFIELD	17730	356	32.3	36.5	22.8	0.8	7.6	33410	38616	22	36	284	26.1	34.5	22.9	13.4	3.2	73000
65624	CAPE FAIR	24541	959	29.8	33.2	29.6	4.7	2.7	38275	44318	40	62	810	14.6	21.9	40.1	21.0	2.5	107944
65625	CASSVILLE	19457	2816	38.2	32.1	24.3	3.4	2.1	33062	38284	21	34	2113	22.0	32.4	32.8	10.7	2.2	85470
65626	CAULFIELD	16607	563	43.7	36.8	16.3	1.8	1.4	28009	32149	9	12	471	35.2	25.5	29.3	8.3	1.7	75192
65627	CEDARCREEK	17197	238	38.7	32.8	23.5	4.6	0.4	30000	35411	12	19	193	46.6	28.5	16.6	8.3	0.0	53095
65629	CHADWICK	18225	178	35.4	37.6	21.4	3.4	2.3	32402	38776	19	30	147	21.1	29.3	34.7	12.9	2.0	89500
65630	CHESTNUTRIDGE	20164	119	30.3	32.8	28.6	5.9	2.5	38069	45928	39	61	100	19.0	21.0	37.0	22.0	1.0	109211
	MISSOURI	23864		27.0	29.4	30.1	9.0	4.5	44017	52626				15.2	22.7	39.0	19.7	3.4	109184
	UNITED STATES	25866		24.7	27.1	30.8	10.9	6.5	48124	56710				10.9	15.0	33.7	30.1	10.4	145905

ZIP CODE #	POST OFFICE NAME	FINANCIAL SERVICES: Auto Loan	FINANCIAL SERVICES: Home Loan	FINANCIAL SERVICES: Invest-ments	FINANCIAL SERVICES: Retire-ment Plans	THE HOME: Home Improvements: Home Repair	THE HOME: Home Improvements: Lawn & Garden	THE HOME: Furnishings: Comput-ers & Hard-ware	THE HOME: Furnishings: Major Appli-ances	THE HOME: Furnishings: TV, Radio, Sound Equip-ment	THE HOME: Furnishings: Furni-ture	ENTERTAINMENT: Dine out/Carry out	ENTERTAINMENT: Sports Equip-ment	ENTERTAINMENT: Fees & Tickets	ENTERTAINMENT: Toys & Games	ENTERTAINMENT: Travel	ENTERTAINMENT: Cable TV	PERSONAL: Apparel & Services	PERSONAL: Auto Repairs	PERSONAL: Health Insur-ance	PERSONAL: Pets & Supplies
65340	MARSHALL	77	66	54	64	69	79	69	73	74	67	89	84	65	87	69	76	83	73	81	87
65344	MIAMI	96	67	36	64	78	88	67	82	77	66	90	99	57	88	69	80	82	81	97	113
65345	MORA	86	77	58	73	81	87	71	79	75	71	92	94	70	94	73	77	87	77	85	101
65347	NELSON	93	66	36	61	75	84	64	78	74	64	87	94	56	85	66	78	80	77	93	109
65348	OTTERVILLE	79	66	50	65	70	79	68	73	72	67	88	84	64	86	67	74	82	72	80	88
65349	SLATER	57	49	39	45	52	59	48	53	53	47	64	61	47	66	50	56	60	52	61	66
65350	SMITHTON	78	65	48	63	69	77	65	71	70	64	84	83	61	84	65	71	79	70	79	89
65351	SWEET SPRINGS	76	65	49	63	69	76	64	70	69	63	83	82	62	83	65	70	78	69	77	87
65354	SYRACUSE	94	83	63	79	88	94	77	86	82	77	99	102	75	101	79	84	94	83	93	111
65355	WARSAW	69	54	36	49	60	68	53	62	59	52	70	72	47	69	55	63	65	61	73	82
65360	WINDSOR	73	58	41	56	62	72	60	66	66	59	79	76	56	77	60	69	73	66	76	82
65401	ROLLA	70	62	59	62	63	69	68	67	69	65	85	80	64	83	65	68	81	69	68	78
65409	ROLLA	0	0	0	0	0	0	0	0	0	0	0	0	0	0	0	0	0	0	0	0
65436	BEULAH	72	48	22	42	54	63	46	58	56	47	66	69	39	62	47	60	60	57	72	82
65438	BIRCH TREE	56	37	17	32	42	49	36	45	43	37	51	54	31	48	37	47	46	45	55	64
65439	BIXBY	81	55	27	48	62	72	54	67	65	55	76	79	47	72	55	70	69	66	82	93
65440	BOSS	89	59	27	51	67	77	57	72	69	58	81	86	49	77	58	74	74	71	88	102
65441	BOURBON	77	61	41	57	66	73	60	68	66	59	79	79	55	78	60	68	74	67	77	87
65443	BRINKTOWN	73	49	22	42	55	64	47	59	57	48	67	70	40	63	48	61	61	58	73	84
65444	BUCYRUS	80	55	28	49	62	72	55	67	65	55	77	79	47	73	56	70	70	66	82	92
65446	CHERRYVILLE	72	48	22	42	55	63	47	58	56	48	66	70	40	63	48	61	60	58	72	83
65449	COOK STATION	67	45	21	39	51	59	44	55	53	44	62	65	37	59	45	57	56	54	67	77
65452	CROCKER	72	54	32	50	60	67	52	62	59	52	70	74	47	69	53	62	65	61	72	85
65453	CUBA	75	57	36	52	63	71	56	65	63	55	75	77	50	73	57	66	69	64	76	87
65456	DAVISVILLE	78	52	24	45	59	68	50	63	61	51	71	75	43	67	51	65	65	62	77	89
65457	DEVILS ELBOW	70	64	54	64	66	72	64	67	66	64	81	77	62	80	64	66	77	67	70	78
65459	DIXON	69	56	40	53	60	68	56	63	61	55	73	73	52	71	57	64	68	62	71	79
65461	DUKE	72	48	22	41	54	63	46	58	56	47	66	69	39	62	47	60	60	57	71	82
65462	EDGAR SPRINGS	70	47	21	40	53	61	45	57	55	46	64	68	39	61	46	59	58	56	70	80
65463	ELDRIDGE	72	48	22	42	55	63	47	58	56	48	66	70	40	62	47	61	60	58	72	83
65464	ELK CREEK	137	92	42	79	104	120	89	111	107	90	125	132	75	119	90	115	114	110	136	157
65466	EMINENCE	61	42	21	37	47	55	42	51	50	42	59	60	36	55	43	53	53	51	62	69
65468	EUNICE	60	40	18	35	46	53	39	49	47	40	55	58	33	52	40	51	50	48	60	69
65470	FALCON	82	56	26	48	63	72	54	66	64	54	75	79	46	72	54	69	69	66	81	94
65473	FORT LEONARD WOOD	78	50	47	57	46	54	73	63	74	68	93	84	63	83	61	68	89	75	59	72
65479	HARTSHORN	60	40	19	35	46	53	39	49	47	40	56	58	34	53	40	51	51	48	60	69
65483	HOUSTON	67	49	31	47	54	65	54	60	61	51	71	68	47	67	53	64	65	60	72	74
65484	HUGGINS	81	58	34	54	65	76	62	71	71	60	83	81	54	79	62	75	76	71	86	91
65486	IBERIA	71	53	32	49	59	67	52	61	60	52	71	72	47	68	53	63	65	61	72	82
65501	JADWIN	86	57	26	49	65	75	55	69	67	56	78	83	47	74	56	72	71	68	85	98
65529	JEROME	68	46	21	39	52	59	44	55	53	45	62	66	37	59	45	57	57	54	68	78
65534	LAQUEY	77	53	26	47	59	69	53	64	62	53	73	75	45	69	53	67	67	63	78	88
65535	LEASBURG	83	57	29	51	65	74	56	69	67	57	78	82	48	75	57	71	71	68	84	96
65536	LEBANON	76	63	49	59	66	74	63	69	69	62	83	81	59	82	63	71	78	69	77	87
65541	LENOX	80	55	28	49	62	72	55	67	65	55	77	78	47	72	56	70	70	66	82	91
65542	LICKING	66	46	25	42	51	60	47	56	55	47	65	65	41	61	47	59	59	56	68	74
65543	LYNCHBURG	77	52	23	45	59	67	50	62	60	51	71	75	42	67	51	65	64	62	77	89
65548	MOUNTAIN VIEW	63	43	22	39	49	57	44	53	52	44	61	62	38	57	44	55	55	52	64	71
65550	NEWBURG	73	57	38	54	62	71	58	66	65	57	77	75	53	74	58	68	71	65	76	82
65552	PLATO	87	61	31	56	70	79	60	73	70	60	82	88	51	79	61	74	75	73	88	102
65555	RAYMONDVILLE	64	43	19	37	48	56	41	52	50	42	59	62	35	55	42	54	53	51	64	73
65556	RICHLAND	70	51	30	47	56	65	52	61	60	51	71	70	46	67	52	63	65	60	72	79
65557	ROBY	85	57	26	50	65	75	55	69	66	56	78	83	47	74	56	71	71	68	85	98
65559	SAINT JAMES	74	54	32	51	61	70	56	65	64	54	75	76	49	72	56	67	68	65	78	85
65560	SALEM	71	50	27	45	56	65	51	61	60	51	70	70	45	66	51	64	64	60	74	81
65564	SOLO	91	61	28	52	69	79	59	73	71	60	83	88	50	79	60	76	76	73	90	104
65565	STEELVILLE	72	50	26	46	57	66	51	61	59	50	69	72	44	66	51	63	63	61	74	83
65566	VIBURNUM	78	53	24	45	60	69	51	63	61	52	72	76	43	68	52	66	65	63	78	90
65567	STOUTLAND	87	58	26	50	66	76	56	70	68	57	80	84	48	75	57	73	72	70	87	100
65570	SUCCESS	77	52	23	45	58	67	50	62	60	51	71	74	42	67	51	65	64	62	77	88
65571	SUMMERSVILLE	51	36	20	33	40	47	37	44	43	37	51	51	32	48	37	46	46	43	53	58
65580	VICHY	82	56	27	50	64	73	55	68	65	55	76	81	47	73	56	69	69	67	83	96
65582	VIENNA	72	60	43	57	64	72	60	66	65	58	78	76	56	77	60	68	73	65	75	83
65583	WAYNESVILLE	78	71	58	69	73	79	70	74	72	69	88	86	67	86	70	73	84	74	78	88
65584	SAINT ROBERT	70	67	59	67	65	68	67	67	65	67	81	80	64	78	64	63	79	68	63	77
65586	WESCO	70	47	22	41	53	61	46	57	55	46	64	68	39	61	46	59	58	56	70	81
65588	WINONA	66	44	20	38	50	58	43	54	52	44	61	64	37	57	44	56	55	53	66	76
65589	YUKON	67	45	20	39	51	58	43	54	52	44	61	64	37	58	44	56	56	53	66	77
65590	LONG LANE	85	62	34	55	68	77	59	71	68	59	81	85	52	78	60	72	74	70	84	98
65591	MONTREAL	77	52	24	45	59	68	50	63	60	51	71	75	43	67	51	65	64	62	77	89
65601	ALDRICH	73	53	30	50	60	69	54	64	62	53	73	75	47	70	55	65	66	63	77	85
65603	ARCOLA	73	49	23	43	56	64	48	59	57	48	67	71	41	64	49	61	61	59	73	84
65604	ASH GROVE	78	66	50	65	69	78	66	72	71	65	86	83	63	85	66	72	80	70	78	87
65605	AURORA	70	54	35	51	59	66	54	61	60	54	72	72	49	69	54	63	67	61	70	79
65606	ALTON	62	43	22	38	48	56	43	52	51	43	60	61	37	57	44	55	55	52	64	71
65608	AVA	70	50	28	45	55	65	52	60	60	51	70	70	45	66	52	64	64	60	73	79
65609	BAKERSFIELD	103	69	31	59	78	90	67	83	80	68	94	99	57	89	68	87	86	82	103	118
65610	BILLINGS	83	67	47	65	73	81	66	75	72	65	86	88	62	86	67	74	81	73	83	95
65611	BLUE EYE	79	72	66	68	76	89	66	76	71	70	88	77	66	75	72	76	82	74	89	89
65612	BOIS D ARC	84	74	57	71	79	84	69	76	73	69	89	91	67	91	71	75	84	74	83	98
65613	BOLIVAR	65	51	41	50	54	62	58	59	61	55	74	70	52	71	55	62	69	61	65	71
65614	BRADLEYVILLE	81	54	25	47	61	71	52	65	63	53	74	78	44	70	53	68	67	65	81	93
65616	BRANSON	87	74	60	71	79	88	73	81	78	73	95	93	69	91	75	81	89	81	90	100
65617	BRIGHTON	76	68	53	65	70	75	64	70	67	65	82	82	62	80	65	67	78	69	73	87
65618	BRIXEY	61	41	19	35	46	53	40	49	48	40	56	59	34	53	40	51	51	49	61	70
65619	BROOKLINE STATION	95	95	85	93	95	98	88	93	88	89	109	110	88	110	89	87	105	91	91	110
65620	BRUNER	78	52	24	45	59	68	50	63	61	51	71	75	43	67	51	65	65	62	78	89
65622	BUFFALO	75	59	39	55	63	72	60	67	66	59	79	78	54	76	60	69	73	67	77	85
65623	BUTTERFIELD	90	60	27	52	68	79	58	73	70	59	82	87	50	78	59	76	75	72	89	103
65624	CAPE FAIR	101	76	47	68	85	97	72	87	83	72	98	103	64	95	76	89	91	86	104	121
65625	CASSVILLE	88	60	30	54	68	79	60	73	71	60	83	86	52	79	61	76	76	72	89	100
65626	CAULFIELD	77	52	23	45	59	67	50	62	60	51	71	75	42	67	51	65	64	62	77	89
65627	CEDARCREEK	68	53	35	48	60	67	50	60	57	50	67	71	45	66	53	61	62	59	71	83
65629	CHADWICK	80	57	30	50	64	72	54	66	64	55	76	79	48	73	56	68	69	66	80	93
65630	CHESTNUTRIDGE	89	71	47	66	77	85	67	77	74	67	89	92	63	89	69	78	84	76	88	103
	MISSOURI	87	82	79	80	83	90	82	85	85	82	104	99	81	103	82	85	100	85	87	100
	UNITED STATES	100	100	100	100	100	100	100	100	100	100	100	100	100	100	100	100	100	100	100	100

POPULATION CHANGE

#	POST OFFICE NAME	COUNTY FIPS CODE	POPULATION 2000	2004	2009	% Rate	State Centile	HOUSEHOLDS 2000	2004	2009	% Annual Rate 2000-2004	2004 Average HH Size	FAMILIES 2000	2004	% Annual Rate 2000-2004
65631	CLEVER	043	3219	3534	3938	2.2	87	1192	1310	1465	2.3	2.70	926	1006	2.0
65632	CONWAY	105	2404	2706	2940	2.8	92	927	1053	1151	3.0	2.57	698	777	2.6
65633	CRANE	209	1923	2567	3205	7.0	100	720	992	1261	7.8	2.50	482	648	7.2
65634	CROSS TIMBERS	085	667	695	733	1.0	68	284	297	314	1.1	2.33	200	205	0.6
65635	DADEVILLE	057	942	967	991	0.6	56	380	391	401	0.7	2.47	279	282	0.3
65637	DORA	153	1577	1624	1673	0.7	59	635	660	685	0.9	2.46	462	472	0.5
65638	DRURY	067	850	884	920	0.9	67	328	345	362	1.2	2.55	243	251	0.8
65640	DUNNEGAN	167	747	882	997	4.0	97	276	329	374	4.2	2.67	214	249	3.6
65641	EAGLE ROCK	009	1392	1483	1595	1.5	79	610	650	701	1.5	2.28	443	464	1.1
65644	ELKLAND	225	1384	1395	1443	0.2	40	510	518	539	0.4	2.69	392	391	-0.1
65646	EVERTON	057	2128	2270	2395	1.5	79	840	900	953	1.6	2.52	631	663	1.2
65647	EXETER	009	2626	2922	3224	2.5	89	1043	1170	1297	2.7	2.50	768	844	2.3
65648	FAIR GROVE	077	4005	4366	4661	2.1	86	1486	1643	1775	2.4	2.66	1181	1277	1.9
65649	FAIR PLAY	039	1574	1588	1619	0.2	41	653	663	679	0.4	2.40	464	458	-0.3
65650	FLEMINGTON	167	699	891	1040	5.9	99	292	371	433	5.8	2.40	234	291	5.3
65652	FORDLAND	225	1885	2045	2222	1.9	85	754	816	890	1.9	2.16	553	587	1.4
65653	FORSYTH	213	4670	5066	5570	1.9	84	2055	2238	2469	2.0	2.18	1407	1501	1.5
65654	FREISTATT	109	378	402	431	1.5	78	153	162	173	1.4	2.48	123	128	0.9
65655	GAINESVILLE	153	2086	2116	2154	0.3	47	875	891	911	0.4	2.33	615	614	0.0
65656	GALENA	209	2894	3006	3238	0.9	65	1063	1104	1191	0.9	2.71	817	840	0.7
65657	GARRISON	043	238	231	250	-0.7	11	76	74	81	-0.6	3.12	56	53	-1.3
65658	GOLDEN	009	1197	1307	1426	2.1	86	558	611	669	2.2	2.14	397	426	1.7
65660	GRAFF	229	226	243	254	1.7	82	83	91	96	2.2	2.67	67	73	2.0
65661	GREENFIELD	057	2167	2180	2217	0.1	38	902	910	927	0.2	2.26	577	568	-0.4
65662	GROVESPRING	229	1457	1447	1450	-0.2	26	553	555	560	0.1	2.61	409	402	-0.4
65663	HALF WAY	167	2194	2190	2239	0.0	30	766	768	788	0.1	2.85	601	594	-0.3
65666	HARDENVILLE	153	299	302	307	0.2	42	117	119	121	0.4	2.54	85	84	-0.3
65667	HARTVILLE	229	3017	2897	2868	-1.0	6	1197	1158	1155	-0.8	2.45	834	790	-1.3
65668	HERMITAGE	085	3196	3377	3591	1.3	75	1445	1536	1641	1.5	2.15	1010	1052	1.0
65669	HIGHLANDVILLE	043	1530	1721	1946	2.8	92	566	641	728	3.0	2.68	456	508	2.6
65672	HOLLISTER	213	7630	8248	9036	1.9	84	2889	3170	3522	2.2	2.28	1881	2012	1.6
65674	HUMANSVILLE	167	1510	1449	1477	-1.0	6	614	591	605	-0.9	2.26	395	367	-1.7
65675	HURLEY	209	658	682	734	0.9	64	238	247	266	0.9	2.76	185	192	0.9
65676	ISABELLA	153	681	689	700	0.3	44	294	299	306	0.4	2.28	208	208	0.0
65679	KIRBYVILLE	213	2377	2564	2814	1.8	83	922	992	1088	1.7	2.58	650	685	1.2
65680	KISSEE MILLS	213	962	1060	1177	2.3	88	419	462	513	2.3	2.29	305	330	1.9
65681	LAMPE	209	2289	2444	2668	1.6	79	994	1063	1162	1.6	2.30	748	786	1.2
65682	LOCKWOOD	057	2412	2418	2455	0.1	34	958	962	977	0.1	2.51	696	686	-0.3
65685	LOUISBURG	059	3345	3554	3823	1.4	78	1310	1391	1496	1.4	2.54	936	973	0.9
65686	KIMBERLING CITY	209	4735	5021	5471	1.4	77	2100	2231	2438	1.4	2.21	1592	1663	1.0
65688	BRANDSVILLE	091	102	135	155	6.8	100	42	56	65	7.0	2.41	33	43	6.4
65689	CABOOL	215	4020	4073	4196	0.3	45	1621	1656	1722	0.5	2.38	1114	1116	0.0
65690	COUCH	149	1127	1085	1078	-0.9	8	460	446	447	-0.7	2.43	354	339	-1.0
65692	KOSHKONONG	149	1140	1230	1297	1.8	83	466	502	531	1.8	2.45	349	372	1.5
65701	MC CLURG	153	7	7	8	0.0	32	4	4	4	0.0	1.75	3	3	0.0
65702	MACOMB	229	474	536	570	2.9	93	169	192	205	3.1	2.79	135	150	2.5
65704	MANSFIELD	229	3608	3642	3683	0.2	41	1394	1416	1440	0.4	2.54	1011	1006	-0.1
65705	MARIONVILLE	109	4741	4894	5174	0.8	61	1861	1928	2044	0.8	2.48	1338	1364	0.5
65706	MARSHFIELD	225	13059	14227	15359	2.0	86	4915	5382	5836	2.2	2.60	3695	3977	1.8
65707	MILLER	109	2199	2235	2339	0.4	48	877	896	941	0.5	2.49	630	629	0.0
65708	MONETT	009	11074	11553	12330	1.0	69	4205	4388	4675	1.0	2.59	2932	2996	0.5
65710	MORRISVILLE	167	820	840	868	0.6	55	310	319	330	0.7	2.59	236	239	0.3
65711	MOUNTAIN GROVE	229	9077	9127	9278	0.1	37	3707	3746	3827	0.3	2.40	2598	2569	-0.3
65712	MOUNT VERNON	109	8000	8399	8929	1.2	72	3075	3249	3471	1.3	2.47	2185	2260	0.8
65713	NIANGUA	225	2742	2892	3069	1.3	74	1044	1109	1182	1.4	2.60	809	846	1.1
65714	NIXA	043	21014	23607	26758	2.8	92	7937	8988	10269	3.0	2.60	6068	6771	2.6
65715	NOBLE	153	99	100	102	0.2	42	35	36	36	0.7	2.78	26	26	0.0
65717	NORWOOD	229	2190	2372	2484	1.9	84	783	857	903	2.2	2.76	600	644	1.7
65720	OLDFIELD	043	375	521	667	8.0	100	151	209	270	8.0	2.49	114	157	7.8
65721	OZARK	043	18848	21342	24168	3.0	93	6957	7971	9115	3.3	2.64	5331	6002	2.8
65722	PHILLIPSBURG	105	1344	1395	1443	0.9	65	498	522	544	1.1	2.64	398	411	0.8
65723	PIERCE CITY	109	3094	3220	3421	0.9	67	1181	1235	1316	1.1	2.60	864	886	0.6
65724	PITTSBURG	085	864	903	954	1.0	69	412	431	457	1.1	2.10	287	294	0.6
65725	PLEASANT HOPE	167	2386	2670	2867	2.7	91	899	1014	1094	2.9	2.63	699	774	2.4
65727	POLK	167	217	212	214	-0.6	15	73	71	72	-0.7	2.99	59	57	-0.8
65728	PONCE DE LEON	209	846	900	981	1.5	78	318	339	369	1.5	2.65	253	270	1.5
65729	PONTIAC	153	464	470	478	0.3	44	184	187	192	0.4	2.42	131	131	0.0
65730	POWELL	119	2050	2103	2210	0.6	56	783	802	841	0.6	2.62	568	572	0.2
65731	POWERSITE	213	379	407	446	1.7	82	157	168	184	1.6	2.42	111	116	1.0
65732	PRESTON	085	823	840	877	0.5	52	317	324	339	0.5	2.57	252	254	0.2
65733	PROTEM	213	316	382	443	4.6	98	136	164	190	4.5	2.33	101	120	4.1
65734	PURDY	009	3437	3528	3721	0.6	56	1283	1316	1388	0.6	2.68	944	952	0.2
65735	QUINCY	085	274	285	301	0.9	67	111	116	123	1.0	2.46	74	75	0.3
65737	REEDS SPRING	209	6800	7394	8149	2.0	85	2814	3073	3397	2.1	2.39	2082	2234	1.7
65738	REPUBLIC	077	11653	13069	14179	2.7	91	4347	4936	5416	3.0	2.61	3350	3728	2.6
65739	RIDGEDALE	213	1217	1430	1639	3.9	97	509	602	692	4.0	2.38	386	447	3.5
65740	ROCKAWAY BEACH	213	2627	2747	2963	1.1	70	1056	1104	1193	1.1	2.42	726	744	0.6
65742	ROGERSVILLE	225	10093	10994	11890	2.0	86	3854	4243	4628	2.3	2.58	3054	3306	1.9
65744	RUETER	213	170	188	210	2.4	88	74	82	91	2.4	2.29	56	61	2.0
65745	SELIGMAN	009	2040	2162	2320	1.4	76	744	792	852	1.5	2.73	523	546	1.0
65746	SEYMOUR	225	8056	8528	9039	1.4	76	2399	2556	2725	1.5	3.16	1858	1950	1.1
65747	SHELL KNOB	009	3678	3870	4156	1.2	73	1729	1820	1955	1.2	2.13	1252	1293	0.8
65752	SOUTH GREENFIELD	057	268	270	274	0.2	40	109	110	111	0.2	2.45	82	81	-0.3
65753	SPARTA	043	3672	4241	4960	3.5	95	1422	1653	1945	3.6	2.56	1081	1238	3.2
65754	SPOKANE	043	793	902	1024	3.1	93	286	327	373	3.2	2.76	234	264	2.9
65755	SQUIRES	067	558	566	580	0.3	47	228	234	242	0.6	2.39	174	176	0.3
65756	STOTTS CITY	109	586	610	647	1.0	67	220	229	243	1.0	2.66	163	167	0.6
65757	STRAFFORD	077	5496	5848	6176	1.5	78	2092	2258	2412	1.8	2.56	1610	1702	1.3
65759	TANEYVILLE	213	1259	1441	1632	3.2	94	476	546	619	3.3	2.64	347	390	2.8
65760	TECUMSEH	153	650	652	661	0.1	35	266	267	272	0.1	2.44	198	195	-0.4
65761	THEODOSIA	153	1142	1184	1224	0.9	64	527	550	571	1.0	2.15	373	381	0.5
65762	THORNFIELD	153	688	695	706	0.2	42	274	279	285	0.4	2.48	200	200	0.0
65764	TUNAS	059	1022	1069	1141	1.1	70	361	377	403	1.0	2.83	274	282	0.7
65766	UDALL	153	171	171	173	0.0	32	72	72	73	0.0	2.38	53	52	-0.5
65767	URBANA	059	940	999	1074	1.4	78	374	397	426	1.4	2.47	263	273	0.9
	MISSOURI					0.8					0.9	2.46			0.4
	UNITED STATES					1.2					1.3	2.58			1.1

ZIP CODE #	POST OFFICE NAME	RACE (%) White 2000	White 2004	Black 2000	Black 2004	Asian/Pacific 2000	Asian/Pacific 2004	% Hispanic Origin 2000	% Hispanic Origin 2004	2004 AGE DISTRIBUTION (%) 0-4	5-9	10-14	15-19	20-24	25-44	45-64	65-84	85+	18+	MEDIAN AGE 2004	% 2004 Males	% 2004 Females
65631	CLEVER	97.5	97.3	0.1	0.1	0.2	0.3	1.1	1.2	8.7	8.4	7.5	6.5	5.4	29.1	24.4	9.1	1.0	71.4	35.4	49.3	50.7
65632	CONWAY	96.7	96.3	0.2	0.2	0.4	0.4	1.6	1.9	7.8	7.6	7.4	6.9	6.1	27.2	24.2	11.7	1.2	73.1	36.5	50.0	50.0
65633	CRANE	96.9	96.7	0.1	0.1	0.1	0.1	0.8	0.9	7.8	7.8	8.3	6.1	6.5	24.6	21.1	14.4	3.5	72.3	36.7	47.2	52.8
65634	CROSS TIMBERS	97.9	97.8	0.0	0.0	0.0	0.0	0.6	0.6	5.8	5.8	7.1	5.9	5.5	19.9	29.2	19.0	2.0	77.8	45.2	50.8	49.2
65635	DADEVILLE	97.2	97.2	0.4	0.4	0.1	0.1	0.6	0.7	5.1	5.3	5.8	7.0	5.7	22.3	28.0	18.7	2.1	79.6	44.2	50.8	49.2
65637	DORA	95.6	95.1	0.4	0.5	0.2	0.3	1.0	0.9	5.5	6.0	6.8	5.4	5.5	22.0	30.2	16.9	1.7	78.3	44.1	50.5	49.5
65638	DRURY	95.8	95.6	0.2	0.2	0.4	0.5	0.7	0.8	5.9	6.2	6.7	6.5	5.9	22.2	30.8	14.8	1.1	77.2	42.8	52.2	47.9
65640	DUNNEGAN	98.1	98.1	0.0	0.0	0.0	0.0	0.8	0.9	7.1	7.3	7.0	6.4	5.0	23.1	27.4	15.5	1.1	74.6	41.1	49.2	50.8
65641	EAGLE ROCK	96.8	96.4	0.1	0.1	0.1	0.1	1.6	1.8	4.7	5.2	6.8	5.7	4.5	20.1	30.8	20.8	1.5	79.8	47.2	50.3	49.7
65644	ELKLAND	95.6	95.1	0.7	0.8	0.4	0.6	0.7	0.9	7.0	7.2	8.5	7.9	6.7	26.3	26.7	8.7	1.1	72.7	36.2	51.8	48.2
65646	EVERTON	98.3	98.2	0.1	0.2	0.1	0.1	0.8	0.8	6.2	6.5	6.9	6.1	5.9	24.0	28.7	14.3	1.4	76.7	41.4	50.3	49.7
65647	EXETER	95.4	94.9	0.3	0.2	0.2	0.2	3.1	3.6	7.2	7.3	7.3	6.7	6.1	27.3	23.6	13.4	1.1	74.1	37.3	49.3	50.7
65648	FAIR GROVE	97.2	96.8	0.2	0.3	0.1	0.2	0.9	1.1	6.8	6.9	7.5	6.8	6.1	28.0	27.6	9.2	0.9	74.5	37.8	50.4	49.6
65649	FAIR PLAY	97.2	97.1	0.3	0.3	0.1	0.1	0.8	0.7	5.5	5.7	7.3	6.8	4.6	21.2	30.5	17.1	1.5	76.9	44.3	50.6	49.4
65650	FLEMINGTON	98.1	98.0	0.1	0.1	0.3	0.3	1.3	1.2	6.1	6.5	7.1	6.2	4.9	22.9	29.0	16.1	1.4	76.3	42.8	49.8	50.2
65652	FORDLAND	90.1	89.5	6.4	6.7	0.4	0.5	1.2	1.4	5.8	6.0	6.5	6.1	6.5	35.2	23.6	9.3	1.1	77.9	36.3	57.1	42.9
65653	FORSYTH	97.7	97.5	0.3	0.3	0.1	0.2	0.8	0.9	6.0	5.8	5.5	5.1	4.6	22.3	26.9	20.8	3.1	79.8	45.6	48.5	51.5
65654	FREISTATT	96.6	96.5	0.5	0.5	0.3	0.3	2.1	2.2	9.5	9.5	9.5	6.2	5.2	26.9	21.6	10.5	1.2	67.9	33.2	52.7	47.3
65655	GAINESVILLE	97.9	97.9	0.2	0.2	0.1	0.1	1.2	1.4	5.7	5.8	6.2	6.0	5.8	22.5	27.5	17.5	3.2	78.6	43.7	48.7	51.3
65656	GALENA	97.1	97.0	0.1	0.1	0.2	0.2	0.6	0.6	7.0	7.1	6.8	5.8	5.4	26.1	27.5	13.5	0.9	75.5	39.6	50.3	49.7
65657	GARRISON	97.5	97.0	0.0	0.0	0.0	0.0	0.4	0.4	5.2	5.2	7.8	8.2	7.8	25.1	26.8	12.6	1.3	76.6	38.8	48.9	51.1
65658	GOLDEN	98.3	98.1	0.0	0.0	0.2	0.2	1.2	1.4	4.4	4.7	4.7	4.1	3.4	17.4	33.8	25.9	1.8	84.0	52.9	50.3	49.7
65660	GRAFF	98.7	98.8	0.0	0.0	0.0	0.0	0.0	0.0	6.6	7.4	7.0	7.0	4.9	24.7	28.4	13.2	0.8	74.5	39.0	51.0	49.0
65661	GREENFIELD	96.7	96.5	0.3	0.4	0.1	0.1	1.1	1.3	5.9	5.8	6.2	6.0	5.2	20.4	24.6	19.6	6.2	78.4	45.4	46.4	53.6
65662	GROVESPRING	98.0	97.9	0.1	0.1	0.1	0.1	1.1	1.2	6.6	6.8	7.1	6.6	6.2	25.2	26.3	13.8	1.6	75.7	39.7	52.0	48.0
65663	HALF WAY	97.4	97.2	0.4	0.5	0.1	0.1	1.0	1.1	8.2	8.4	8.7	6.4	5.6	26.4	23.5	11.8	1.0	70.6	35.6	51.5	48.5
65666	HARDENVILLE	97.3	97.4	0.3	0.3	0.0	0.0	1.7	1.3	6.0	6.0	6.3	5.6	6.0	22.9	28.2	16.9	2.3	77.8	43.2	50.3	49.7
65667	HARTVILLE	97.0	96.8	0.8	0.9	0.1	0.1	0.9	1.0	7.1	7.2	7.5	6.5	6.1	23.6	25.5	14.3	2.4	74.3	39.1	49.6	50.4
65668	HERMITAGE	97.3	97.1	0.0	0.0	0.1	0.2	0.8	1.0	3.6	3.6	4.6	4.7	4.3	15.4	31.5	29.7	2.6	85.3	55.5	49.1	50.9
65669	HIGHLANDVILLE	97.8	97.5	0.1	0.1	0.1	0.1	1.1	1.2	6.8	6.8	7.4	7.4	6.7	28.7	26.6	8.9	0.8	74.6	36.7	50.0	50.0
65672	HOLLISTER	96.1	95.8	0.4	0.4	0.5	0.5	2.6	2.9	5.2	5.0	5.1	8.7	13.7	25.2	22.2	12.9	2.0	81.7	34.5	48.6	51.4
65674	HUMANSVILLE	98.3	98.1	0.3	0.3	0.1	0.1	0.6	0.6	6.1	6.1	6.5	5.9	4.8	22.0	24.7	19.7	4.2	77.6	44.0	48.0	52.0
65675	HURLEY	98.0	98.0	0.0	0.0	0.2	0.2	0.3	0.4	7.8	7.9	7.9	6.5	6.3	28.6	24.8	9.4	0.9	72.4	36.4	52.4	47.7
65676	ISABELLA	97.9	97.8	0.0	0.0	0.2	0.2	0.7	0.7	4.6	4.5	4.6	4.5	5.2	18.0	30.5	26.0	2.0	83.6	51.8	50.2	49.8
65679	KIRBYVILLE	96.5	96.1	0.3	0.4	0.4	0.5	2.2	2.4	7.1	7.2	6.5	5.6	5.4	27.6	24.8	14.1	1.5	75.7	38.3	48.8	51.2
65680	KISSEE MILLS	97.5	97.5	0.0	0.0	0.1	0.1	0.5	0.6	5.0	4.9	5.7	6.1	5.0	23.9	28.8	19.3	1.4	80.5	44.6	50.2	49.8
65681	LAMPE	98.7	98.6	0.0	0.0	0.0	0.0	0.7	0.8	4.6	4.8	5.5	4.5	4.5	20.4	30.3	24.2	1.3	82.4	49.0	48.6	51.4
65682	LOCKWOOD	97.6	97.4	0.3	0.3	0.3	0.4	0.7	0.8	6.4	6.3	6.4	6.8	6.0	23.7	25.7	16.4	2.3	76.7	41.3	49.5	50.5
65685	LOUISBURG	97.2	97.0	0.2	0.2	0.1	0.1	1.1	1.2	6.6	6.7	7.1	6.8	5.9	24.1	26.1	14.9	1.9	75.4	40.0	50.2	49.8
65686	KIMBERLING CITY	98.2	98.0	0.1	0.1	0.3	0.4	1.0	1.1	3.6	3.9	4.3	4.1	3.5	16.3	33.1	28.3	3.1	85.7	54.8	47.8	52.2
65688	BRANDSVILLE	97.1	97.0	0.0	0.0	0.0	0.0	2.0	1.5	5.9	5.9	7.4	8.2	6.7	25.9	27.4	11.1	1.5	75.6	39.1	49.6	50.4
65689	CABOOL	96.4	96.0	0.2	0.2	0.6	0.8	1.0	1.1	6.6	6.7	7.1	6.7	5.3	22.6	24.9	16.4	3.7	75.4	41.3	47.7	52.3
65690	COUCH	93.6	93.0	0.0	0.0	0.4	0.6	0.9	1.0	4.9	5.4	7.3	6.4	5.8	21.7	29.9	16.8	1.9	78.5	44.0	51.9	48.1
65692	KOSHKONONG	96.0	95.8	0.1	0.1	0.2	0.2	0.8	0.8	5.0	5.4	7.5	7.1	6.1	25.4	29.1	13.2	1.4	78.0	41.1	50.2	49.8
65701	MC CLURG	100.0	100.0	0.0	0.0	0.0	0.0	0.0	0.0	0.0	0.0	0.0	0.0	28.6	71.4	0.0	0.0	0.0	100.0	28.8	57.1	42.9
65702	MACOMB	97.3	96.8	0.2	0.2	0.4	0.6	0.8	0.8	7.5	7.7	7.7	7.1	6.5	25.2	25.8	11.8	0.9	73.1	37.1	50.6	49.4
65704	MANSFIELD	97.6	97.3	0.3	0.3	0.3	0.3	0.7	0.8	7.6	6.9	7.4	7.0	6.9	24.7	23.6	14.3	1.7	73.8	37.2	48.8	51.2
65705	MARIONVILLE	97.6	97.4	0.1	0.1	0.2	0.3	0.7	0.8	7.1	7.0	7.1	6.2	5.9	26.2	23.7	14.3	2.7	75.0	39.0	49.5	50.5
65706	MARSHFIELD	97.8	97.6	0.3	0.3	0.3	0.3	1.5	1.6	7.4	7.2	7.5	7.0	6.3	27.7	23.4	11.5	2.1	73.6	36.5	48.7	51.3
65707	MILLER	98.0	98.0	0.1	0.0	0.0	0.0	0.7	0.7	6.0	6.3	8.1	6.8	6.0	25.7	24.9	14.4	1.9	75.4	39.3	50.7	49.4
65708	MONETT	91.2	90.4	0.2	0.2	0.6	0.8	9.1	9.9	8.1	7.5	7.5	6.6	6.6	26.9	21.9	12.3	2.6	72.9	35.8	49.1	51.0
65710	MORRISVILLE	97.7	97.5	0.1	0.1	0.1	0.2	1.8	2.0	7.5	7.9	8.0	7.7	5.5	26.6	24.3	11.4	1.2	71.7	36.3	50.7	49.3
65711	MOUNTAIN GROVE	97.7	97.5	0.1	0.1	0.1	0.1	0.7	0.8	6.9	6.8	6.7	7.0	6.5	23.4	24.9	15.5	2.4	75.3	39.6	47.9	52.1
65712	MOUNT VERNON	96.9	96.6	0.4	0.4	0.3	0.4	1.4	1.5	6.5	6.6	7.1	6.4	5.8	24.3	25.3	15.0	3.0	75.8	40.2	50.0	50.0
65713	NIANGUA	97.9	97.7	0.1	0.1	0.2	0.2	1.4	1.6	6.9	6.8	7.1	6.9	6.7	25.5	27.0	11.9	1.2	74.9	38.7	50.7	49.3
65714	NIXA	97.4	97.1	0.4	0.4	0.4	0.6	1.4	1.5	8.2	8.0	7.6	6.6	6.1	30.6	22.4	9.5	1.1	72.1	34.5	48.2	51.8
65715	NOBLE	98.0	99.0	0.0	0.0	0.0	0.0	0.0	0.0	6.0	6.0	7.0	6.0	6.0	23.0	27.0	17.0	2.0	75.0	42.5	51.0	49.0
65717	NORWOOD	97.3	97.1	0.3	0.3	0.3	0.4	0.5	0.5	7.1	7.2	7.5	7.1	6.3	24.4	26.5	12.7	1.2	73.8	38.3	51.2	48.8
65720	OLDFIELD	97.6	97.7	0.0	0.0	0.0	0.0	1.3	1.5	5.6	5.8	7.5	7.1	6.7	28.4	27.8	10.4	0.8	76.6	38.7	50.9	49.1
65721	OZARK	96.9	96.7	0.3	0.3	0.3	0.4	1.5	1.7	8.1	7.5	7.2	6.5	6.9	30.9	22.7	8.8	1.4	73.2	33.8	48.2	51.8
65722	PHILLIPSBURG	97.9	97.8	0.3	0.4	0.2	0.1	0.9	1.0	7.2	7.3	8.0	7.3	5.7	27.2	25.5	10.5	1.3	73.1	36.8	50.8	49.3
65723	PIERCE CITY	95.8	95.6	0.2	0.2	0.0	0.1	2.5	2.6	8.0	7.6	7.2	6.9	6.8	26.2	25.1	10.7	1.6	73.1	36.2	50.1	49.9
65724	PITTSBURG	98.2	97.9	0.0	0.0	0.1	0.2	0.7	0.8	3.8	4.0	5.0	4.8	4.2	16.2	33.6	26.6	2.0	84.6	53.9	49.6	50.4
65725	PLEASANT HOPE	97.7	97.5	0.1	0.2	0.0	0.1	0.9	1.0	6.7	6.9	7.7	7.5	6.4	28.7	25.7	9.4	1.1	74.1	37.1	50.3	49.7
65727	POLK	97.7	97.2	0.5	0.5	0.5	0.5	1.4	1.9	6.6	7.1	6.6	5.7	5.7	21.7	28.8	16.5	1.4	76.4	42.8	49.1	50.9
65728	PONCE DE LEON	97.8	97.4	0.0	0.0	0.2	0.3	0.6	0.6	7.2	7.4	7.7	6.3	5.9	26.9	27.9	9.8	0.9	73.8	37.8	50.3	49.7
65729	PONTIAC	98.1	98.1	0.0	0.0	0.0	0.0	0.7	0.6	5.1	4.9	4.7	4.9	5.3	19.2	29.4	23.4	3.2	82.3	49.5	48.3	51.7
65730	POWELL	96.5	96.3	0.1	0.1	0.3	0.4	0.8	1.0	6.9	7.4	8.4	7.6	6.1	28.4	25.8	8.8	0.7	72.7	36.6	52.4	47.6
65731	POWERSITE	96.6	96.6	0.3	0.3	0.3	0.5	1.9	2.2	7.1	6.9	6.4	5.4	5.4	27.8	24.6	14.7	1.7	76.2	38.8	48.9	51.1
65732	PRESTON	97.1	96.9	0.1	0.1	0.0	0.0	1.2	1.4	6.6	6.8	7.3	6.8	5.5	21.0	28.3	16.0	1.9	75.1	42.2	49.1	51.0
65733	PROTEM	98.4	98.7	0.0	0.0	0.0	0.0	0.3	0.3	4.7	5.0	5.5	4.5	5.2	23.6	28.8	21.2	1.6	82.5	45.9	53.4	46.6
65734	PURDY	90.4	89.2	0.1	0.1	0.2	0.3	9.3	10.5	7.5	7.5	7.9	6.9	7.1	26.9	23.3	11.3	1.6	72.8	35.4	50.3	49.7
65735	QUINCY	98.5	98.3	0.0	0.0	0.0	0.0	0.0	0.0	5.6	5.3	6.3	5.6	6.0	19.0	29.1	20.0	3.2	79.3	46.9	49.1	50.9
65737	REEDS SPRING	97.3	97.1	0.1	0.1	0.3	0.4	1.7	1.9	5.6	5.8	5.8	5.4	4.7	23.7	30.8	17.0	1.2	79.4	44.3	49.0	51.0
65738	REPUBLIC	97.4	97.0	0.2	0.3	0.4	0.6	1.0	1.1	6.9	7.0	7.6	6.8	6.4	29.2	24.2	10.1	1.7	74.0	36.1	48.1	51.9
65739	RIDGEDALE	97.1	96.9	0.7	0.7	0.3	0.5	1.4	1.6	5.5	5.7	5.0	4.3	4.1	23.9	33.6	16.6	1.3	81.3	45.9	48.6	51.4
65740	ROCKAWAY BEACH	96.4	96.2	0.1	0.1	0.0	0.0	1.3	1.5	6.8	5.9	6.5	7.0	6.8	23.0	27.2	15.5	1.4	77.2	40.8	48.9	51.1
65742	ROGERSVILLE	97.3	97.0	0.2	0.2	0.4	0.5	1.0	1.1	6.2	6.7	7.8	6.8	5.5	26.6	29.0	10.3	1.1	75.0	39.5	50.1	49.9
65744	RUETER	97.7	98.4	0.0	0.0	0.0	0.0	1.2	0.5	5.3	5.9	5.3	5.3	5.3	25.0	27.1	19.2	1.6	79.8	43.7	52.1	47.9
65745	SELIGMAN	94.6	94.0	0.1	0.1	0.2	0.2	2.8	3.2	7.1	7.2	9.0	6.7	6.6	26.8	25.4	10.4	0.8	72.5	36.1	50.9	49.1
65746	SEYMOUR	94.3	93.8	2.3	2.5	0.3	0.4	1.2	1.4	8.9	8.4	9.0	7.6	7.1	27.8	21.2	8.9	1.2	69.1	32.4	51.8	48.2
65747	SHELL KNOB	98.0	97.8	0.0	0.0	0.1	0.1	1.1	1.2	3.4	3.6	4.6	4.2	3.3	16.1	33.5	28.9	2.3	85.8	55.0	50.0	50.0
65752	SOUTH GREENFIELD	97.8	97.8	0.0	0.0	0.4	0.4	0.4	0.4	6.3	6.3	7.4	7.0	5.6	24.4	27.0	14.1	1.9	75.6	40.7	50.7	49.3
65753	SPARTA	97.8	97.7	0.1	0.1	0.2	0.2	1.2	1.4	6.3	6.7	8.1	7.3	6.2	28.3	25.8	10.0	1.1	74.4	36.7	49.4	50.6
65754	SPOKANE	98.0	97.8	0.0	0.0	0.1	0.1	0.6	0.9	7.5	7.3	7.1	7.1	6.9	27.6	26.1	9.5	0.9	73.8	36.1	49.1	50.9
65755	SQUIRES	96.8	96.8	0.0	0.0	0.0	0.0	0.2	0.2	4.8	5.1	6.7	7.4	5.5	20.3	32.7	15.9	1.6	78.5	45.1	51.1	48.9
65756	STOTTS CITY	94.4	94.1	0.3	0.5	0.0	0.0	3.8	3.9	7.9	7.9	8.4	7.4	6.6	28.9	22.3	9.8	1.0	71.5	34.1	51.8	48.2
65757	STRAFFORD	97.7	97.5	0.2	0.2	0.1	0.1	1.2	1.4	6.5	6.8	7.1	6.4	5.8	28.0	27.4	10.8	1.3	75.6	38.4	50.0	50.0
65759	TANEYVILLE	97.9	97.8	0.1	0.1	0.1	0.1	1.0	1.2	8.8	8.1	6.9	6.7	5.8	27.6	22.4	12.4	1.3	72.0	35.9	49.0	51.0
65760	TECUMSEH	97.7	97.6	0.2	0.2	0.2	0.2	0.9	0.9	5.8	6.0	5.5	5.8	5.7	22.7	30.8	16.0	1.7	79.1	43.7	51.5	48.5
65761	THEODOSIA	97.9	97.7	0.0	0.0	0.1	0.2	1.0	1.1	3.1	3.4	4.6	4.7	4.8	17.7	33.7	26.6	1.4	86.4	52.7	49.9	50.1
65762	THORNFIELD	98.1	98.0	0.0	0.0	0.2	0.3	0.6	0.6	5.9	6.0	6.5	5.5	5.6	22.3	28.1	18.4	1.7	78.4	43.8	50.2	49.8
65764	TUNAS	97.1	96.6	0.1	0.2	0.2	0.3	1.4	1.3	8.6	9.0	8.0	6.5	4.7	24.9	24.6	12.4	1.4	70.3	36.8	50.1	50.0
65766	UDALL	98.3	98.3	0.0	0.0	0.0	0.0	0.6	0.6	5.9	5.9	5.3	5.9	5.9	23.4	31.6	14.6	1.8	79.5	42.8	51.5	48.5
65767	URBANA	97.5	97.3	0.1	0.1	0.0	0.0	0.6	0.7	6.1	6.3	7.0	6.4	5.5	24.0	26.4	15.8	2.4	76.4	41.5	49.4	50.7
	MISSOURI	84.9	84.1	11.3	11.5	1.2	1.4	2.1	2.3	6.7	6.6	7.0	7.0	7.3	27.6	24.2	11.7	1.9	75.6	36.8	48.7	51.3
	UNITED STATES	75.1	73.6	12.3	12.5	3.8	4.2	12.5	14.1	6.9	6.7	7.2	7.0	7.3	28.6	23.8	10.8	1.7	75.1	36.0	49.1	50.9

#	POST OFFICE NAME	2004 Per Capita Income	2004 HH Income Base	2004 Household Income Distribution (%): Less than $25,000	$25,000 to $49,999	$50,000 to $99,999	$100,000 to $149,999	$150,000 or More	Median Household Income: 2004	2009	2004 National Centile	2004 State Centile	2004 Home Value Base	2004 Home Value Distribution (%): Less than $50,000	$50,000 to $89,999	$90,000 to $174,999	$175,000 to $399,999	$400,000 or More	2004 Median Home Value
65631	CLEVER	19119	1310	22.6	38.1	31.6	6.3	1.4	41762	49875	52	72	1098	12.2	23.7	43.6	18.4	2.1	104255
65632	CONWAY	15266	1053	38.6	33.3	24.1	3.4	0.6	32813	38675	20	32	854	30.2	24.4	32.6	11.1	1.8	83158
65633	CRANE	15468	992	44.4	30.0	19.6	3.7	2.3	28518	33391	10	14	700	27.6	25.0	32.4	14.3	0.7	85263
65634	CROSS TIMBERS	15032	297	48.5	30.3	15.8	3.7	1.7	25711	28211	5	5	250	28.4	27.6	25.2	14.8	4.0	82857
65635	DADEVILLE	16474	391	28.9	44.8	23.0	2.8	0.5	35394	40063	29	47	329	22.2	25.2	43.8	8.5	0.3	92297
65637	DORA	14866	660	42.6	37.9	15.5	2.7	1.4	29367	32881	11	16	545	19.6	27.2	37.8	12.1	3.3	96481
65638	DRURY	13572	345	44.9	37.4	14.8	2.0	0.9	26729	30106	7	8	287	27.2	23.3	29.6	17.1	2.8	88636
65640	DUNNEGAN	14046	329	40.7	35.9	21.0	2.1	0.3	31833	37718	17	27	276	33.7	20.3	27.2	18.8	0.0	82143
65641	EAGLE ROCK	17685	650	35.7	38.2	21.9	3.5	0.8	32019	36991	18	28	547	22.1	29.1	33.3	12.1	3.5	88194
65644	ELKLAND	14963	518	35.3	36.1	23.4	5.0	0.2	35267	40472	29	46	433	28.6	26.1	37.2	6.2	1.9	84875
65646	EVERTON	17323	900	33.0	37.1	24.6	3.4	1.9	36641	41045	34	54	760	23.0	24.1	32.4	18.2	2.4	94583
65647	EXETER	17632	1170	40.6	37.3	17.3	1.7	3.2	30520	35288	14	21	908	32.3	34.3	23.4	7.4	2.8	68846
65648	FAIR GROVE	23233	1643	21.1	31.8	35.7	8.6	2.7	48060	57009	68	83	1403	12.4	24.6	43.1	16.8	3.1	106734
65649	FAIR PLAY	17882	663	39.5	41.8	15.5	1.1	2.1	28608	33320	10	15	531	32.4	21.3	28.8	17.0	0.6	81522
65650	FLEMINGTON	18144	371	34.0	33.2	28.0	3.8	1.1	36224	41446	32	52	319	30.4	21.3	30.4	17.6	0.3	86765
65652	FORDLAND	19869	816	31.1	36.6	26.0	3.7	2.6	37266	43543	36	56	661	22.5	29.5	32.8	12.9	2.3	87065
65653	FORSYTH	22542	2238	33.0	35.4	25.4	4.1	2.1	35801	41831	31	49	1758	20.5	19.2	46.7	12.2	1.5	102279
65654	FREISTATT	19731	162	29.0	36.4	30.3	1.9	2.5	38155	42318	40	61	129	16.3	25.6	31.8	22.5	3.9	102885
65655	GAINESVILLE	17146	891	43.7	34.5	17.5	2.5	1.9	29250	33126	11	16	689	32.1	30.0	27.4	7.4	3.1	69727
65656	GALENA	16457	1104	37.5	34.5	21.7	3.9	2.4	32101	36943	18	29	906	32.7	19.4	30.2	16.1	1.6	86200
65657	GARRISON	12342	74	39.2	41.9	16.2	1.4	1.4	30460	37309	13	21	60	20.0	33.3	40.0	6.7	0.0	86000
65658	GOLDEN	18414	611	39.1	35.5	20.6	2.8	2.0	32197	37098	18	29	522	16.3	24.0	43.3	14.2	2.3	103750
65660	GRAFF	15088	91	45.1	31.9	16.5	2.2	4.4	27591	31689	8	10	75	26.7	24.0	24.0	18.7	6.7	87500
65661	GREENFIELD	15260	910	45.0	35.2	16.8	2.1	1.0	27774	31548	8	11	653	26.5	34.6	31.7	6.9	0.3	74554
65662	GROVESPRING	16867	555	38.4	35.7	18.0	6.0	2.0	32866	38373	20	33	457	26.7	19.0	38.1	12.3	3.9	95417
65663	HALF WAY	15097	768	34.0	35.6	24.2	4.0	2.2	34732	40287	26	43	636	21.5	28.3	31.9	15.4	2.8	90263
65666	HARDENVILLE	16938	119	42.9	31.1	19.3	3.4	3.4	31410	35373	16	25	94	30.9	28.7	29.8	8.5	2.1	72500
65667	HARTVILLE	16445	1158	45.1	30.4	18.0	4.3	2.3	28711	33542	10	15	910	26.5	23.3	34.3	12.2	3.7	90274
65668	HERMITAGE	16056	1536	41.0	42.3	13.4	2.3	1.0	28525	31740	10	14	1311	27.8	34.6	28.7	8.2	0.8	75560
65669	HIGHLANDVILLE	18310	641	25.3	35.4	33.9	4.1	1.4	41174	48799	50	70	538	12.8	16.7	43.1	24.7	2.6	117366
65672	HOLLISTER	17619	3170	38.4	36.5	20.1	3.8	1.2	30938	35745	15	23	1984	21.2	22.6	36.8	18.3	1.1	96758
65674	HUMANSVILLE	13660	591	51.1	32.0	14.4	1.5	1.0	24205	28138	4	3	439	45.1	27.8	17.3	8.9	0.9	55375
65675	HURLEY	16962	247	29.6	41.3	23.9	4.1	1.2	36091	41701	32	51	208	19.2	17.8	38.5	21.6	2.9	106250
65676	ISABELLA	20740	299	42.8	28.4	19.7	6.7	2.3	29003	33492	10	16	247	18.6	26.3	34.4	18.6	2.0	101786
65679	KIRBYVILLE	21306	992	27.8	39.6	26.6	4.2	1.7	40269	46492	47	67	791	24.8	21.5	40.3	9.9	3.5	96146
65680	KISSEE MILLS	18887	462	39.2	39.8	16.2	3.3	1.5	29660	34591	12	18	383	30.8	27.7	31.9	7.3	2.4	80714
65681	LAMPE	23544	1063	27.2	38.7	23.7	7.7	2.7	38352	44527	41	62	874	8.5	16.5	45.8	25.7	3.6	128211
65682	LOCKWOOD	17037	962	35.8	37.4	21.8	2.2	2.8	32403	36798	19	30	736	32.6	30.3	24.2	9.2	3.7	73571
65685	LOUISBURG	17117	1391	40.6	33.1	21.9	2.1	2.4	29977	34899	12	19	1097	29.2	27.8	30.0	11.8	1.3	78761
65686	KIMBERLING CITY	23781	2231	23.0	36.6	31.0	5.7	3.8	42033	49877	53	73	1887	4.4	12.8	52.1	27.3	3.4	135045
65688	BRANDSVILLE	22012	56	39.3	30.4	19.6	5.4	5.4	33186	37359	21	35	47	27.7	23.4	27.7	17.0	4.3	88333
65689	CABOOL	16780	1656	45.2	33.0	15.8	3.4	2.7	27440	32061	8	10	1205	32.0	26.1	28.4	11.5	2.0	77734
65690	COUCH	15890	446	49.8	27.1	18.8	3.1	1.1	25133	28420	5	5	369	41.7	19.8	30.4	7.3	0.8	67857
65692	KOSHKONONG	19329	502	39.6	33.7	20.1	3.4	3.2	31603	36410	17	26	418	29.7	23.2	27.5	14.4	5.3	85714
65701	MC CLURG	0	0	0.0	0.0	0.0	0.0	0.0	0	0	0	0	0	0.0	0.0	0.0	0.0	0.0	0
65702	MACOMB	13799	192	41.7	30.2	24.0	3.7	0.5	30335	35512	13	20	152	29.0	28.3	26.3	13.2	3.3	81538
65704	MANSFIELD	14408	1416	43.7	32.9	18.8	3.3	1.3	29580	33988	11	17	1033	28.9	29.3	28.7	10.9	2.1	75779
65705	MARIONVILLE	16502	1928	37.5	36.2	22.6	3.1	0.7	32612	37735	20	31	1462	25.5	26.6	34.2	12.4	1.3	87156
65706	MARSHFIELD	17717	5382	29.0	36.6	27.3	5.3	1.9	37952	44029	39	60	4070	12.9	27.7	45.6	13.1	0.7	101495
65707	MILLER	17881	896	37.7	35.5	21.4	3.2	2.1	34477	39637	26	42	688	25.6	36.1	25.7	11.1	1.6	76250
65708	MONETT	19006	4388	32.4	35.0	25.1	4.6	2.9	37251	42783	36	56	3224	13.2	34.2	36.6	14.1	1.9	93717
65710	MORRISVILLE	15527	319	34.2	36.1	25.4	4.1	0.3	35643	40609	30	48	250	28.8	22.4	35.2	12.8	0.8	88571
65711	MOUNTAIN GROVE	15098	3746	47.0	33.2	14.8	2.5	2.5	26571	30720	7	7	2650	28.6	23.4	32.6	13.1	2.3	85769
65712	MOUNT VERNON	20222	3249	31.0	35.0	25.7	5.3	3.1	37408	43171	37	58	2436	11.5	29.4	40.6	16.5	2.1	103528
65713	NIANGUA	16893	1109	31.9	38.1	23.0	5.4	1.6	35333	41006	29	47	921	24.2	27.4	31.1	16.4	1.0	87411
65714	NIXA	23172	8988	22.3	30.3	34.7	8.9	3.8	47283	56349	67	82	6549	9.4	14.2	51.9	23.1	1.4	120147
65715	NOBLE	13533	36	44.4	30.6	22.2	2.8	0.0	28137	31491	9	12	29	27.6	20.7	27.6	17.2	6.9	95000
65717	NORWOOD	13646	857	43.2	34.4	18.3	2.1	2.0	28105	32618	9	12	696	31.8	23.6	27.7	13.8	3.2	79024
65720	OLDFIELD	16260	209	33.5	38.8	23.9	2.4	1.4	34243	41069	25	41	175	25.1	28.6	36.0	9.1	1.1	85000
65721	OZARK	22956	7971	23.8	31.8	32.1	7.9	4.3	45102	52810	61	78	6041	7.2	16.6	49.5	22.5	4.1	120238
65722	PHILLIPSBURG	21124	522	25.5	38.7	27.6	3.5	4.8	40160	46871	47	67	433	20.8	29.1	35.3	13.4	1.4	90179
65723	PIERCE CITY	16536	1235	35.6	35.0	25.0	3.0	1.5	35644	40392	30	49	929	29.8	28.7	26.2	14.1	1.2	76389
65724	PITTSBURG	16852	431	40.8	38.5	17.2	3.5	0.0	28866	32414	10	15	366	28.4	31.4	30.1	8.5	1.6	76250
65725	PLEASANT HOPE	18511	1014	27.1	36.3	28.7	5.7	2.2	39672	45217	45	66	842	11.2	30.2	36.9	17.7	4.0	104167
65727	POLK	15940	71	32.4	32.4	28.2	5.6	1.4	39306	46563	44	65	63	25.4	27.0	31.8	15.9	0.0	87000
65728	PONCE DE LEON	19434	339	32.7	31.6	25.1	8.6	2.1	37949	44396	39	60	290	19.3	18.6	31.4	28.3	2.4	114583
65729	PONTIAC	18555	187	42.3	31.0	18.7	5.4	2.7	29453	32935	11	17	154	21.4	27.3	33.8	15.6	2.0	92500
65730	POWELL	16025	802	40.5	31.3	22.7	3.9	1.6	30110	33884	13	20	664	37.4	31.2	17.8	9.0	4.7	64565
65731	POWERSITE	19588	168	27.4	40.5	25.6	4.2	2.4	40311	46537	47	68	135	23.7	21.5	42.2	8.9	3.7	98125
65732	PRESTON	16855	324	35.5	29.9	27.2	4.3	3.1	34461	38873	26	42	277	11.2	24.6	39.0	23.8	1.4	109167
65733	PROTEM	16178	164	40.9	37.2	15.9	5.5	0.6	29630	33671	11	18	140	30.7	22.1	38.6	7.1	1.4	86000
65734	PURDY	14295	1316	37.4	40.0	19.3	2.3	1.1	32400	37041	19	30	1018	21.6	36.5	27.6	12.3	2.0	77717
65735	QUINCY	13407	116	54.3	27.6	14.7	3.5	0.0	22471	25982	3	2	91	33.0	27.5	23.1	13.2	3.3	74167
65737	REEDS SPRING	23625	3073	31.0	36.7	21.9	6.0	4.4	35909	41187	31	50	2483	18.0	18.2	32.5	26.0	5.3	117053
65738	REPUBLIC	19104	4936	25.8	34.4	32.1	6.6	1.2	41407	50047	51	71	3993	10.1	31.4	45.5	11.9	1.1	98122
65739	RIDGEDALE	29207	602	23.3	35.9	34.7	2.5	3.7	42789	50224	55	74	494	18.8	13.0	31.8	33.4	3.0	139231
65740	ROCKAWAY BEACH	16638	1104	43.6	39.3	14.0	1.9	1.2	27825	31993	8	11	888	42.5	35.4	17.2	3.9	1.0	59178
65742	ROGERSVILLE	30119	4243	23.3	28.8	29.9	10.4	7.6	48041	57187	68	83	3589	9.8	15.3	38.2	27.4	9.3	138186
65744	RUETER	17757	82	39.0	40.2	15.9	4.9	0.0	30732	37348	14	22	69	31.9	20.3	31.9	11.6	4.4	87000
65745	SELIGMAN	14418	792	38.3	37.1	19.6	4.0	1.0	31581	36480	17	26	639	31.3	27.5	32.9	6.1	2.2	75000
65746	SEYMOUR	12739	2556	40.2	33.4	21.7	3.5	1.3	31484	36314	16	26	2049	24.1	28.4	35.6	10.3	1.6	86699
65747	SHELL KNOB	21673	1820	37.0	35.9	21.5	3.0	2.6	32855	37665	20	33	1561	13.6	21.2	43.3	19.1	2.8	112763
65752	SOUTH GREENFIELD	16765	110	39.1	34.6	23.6	1.8	0.9	31972	36638	18	28	89	21.4	25.8	32.6	12.4	7.9	95000
65753	SPARTA	19254	1653	32.1	34.0	26.8	4.4	2.8	36483	43627	33	53	1315	17.4	27.1	36.1	18.5	0.9	98056
65754	SPOKANE	17114	327	26.6	36.1	32.7	4.0	0.6	38714	44910	42	63	273	11.7	12.1	49.8	24.2	2.2	121701
65755	SQUIRES	14757	234	41.9	37.6	16.2	3.4	0.9	30949	35194	15	23	201	21.9	17.9	37.8	21.4	1.0	98542
65756	STOTTS CITY	17606	229	38.4	36.7	16.6	4.8	3.5	33013	38915	21	34	187	36.4	21.4	30.5	10.7	1.1	73125
65757	STRAFFORD	22092	2258	23.0	35.5	30.3	8.1	3.2	43090	51198	56	74	1839	10.2	22.6	44.3	19.3	3.6	110730
65759	TANEYVILLE	15324	546	40.3	38.1	16.7	2.9	2.0	30504	35558	14	21	435	29.7	29.0	30.6	10.1	0.7	80385
65760	TECUMSEH	15294	267	42.7	38.2	13.9	3.0	2.3	29584	33412	11	18	223	29.6	29.2	30.0	8.5	2.7	74231
65761	THEODOSIA	16996	550	46.0	35.5	15.5	1.3	1.8	27174	30929	7	9	468	34.2	26.9	24.8	11.3	2.8	75161
65762	THORNFIELD	15797	279	44.4	30.8	20.8	3.2	0.7	28176	32495	9	13	228	28.1	19.3	28.1	19.3	5.3	97500
65764	TUNAS	14155	377	51.5	31.0	11.9	3.5	2.1	23525	26470	4	3	318	30.5	31.5	20.1	13.2	4.7	74231
65766	UDALL	12719	72	47.2	40.3	9.7	2.8	0.0	26240	30929	6	7	60	30.0	30.0	30.0	8.3	1.7	72500
65767	URBANA	20343	397	37.5	35.5	17.9	5.0	4.0	33015	40735	21	34	319	30.7	20.7	30.7	12.9	5.0	81000
	MISSOURI	23864		27.0	29.4	30.1	9.0	4.5	44017	52626				15.2	22.7	39.0	19.7	3.4	109184
	UNITED STATES	25866		24.7	27.1	30.8	10.9	6.5	48124	56710				10.9	15.0	33.7	30.1	10.4	145905

ZIP CODE #	POST OFFICE NAME	FINANCIAL SERVICES: Auto Loan	FINANCIAL SERVICES: Home Loan	FINANCIAL SERVICES: Invest-ments	FINANCIAL SERVICES: Retire-ment Plans	THE HOME: Home Improvements: Home Repair	THE HOME: Home Improvements: Lawn & Garden	THE HOME: Furnishings: Comput-ers & Hard-ware	THE HOME: Furnishings: Major Appli-ances	THE HOME: Furnishings: TV, Radio, Sound Equip-ment	THE HOME: Furnishings: Furni-ture	ENTERTAINMENT: Dine out/ Carry out	ENTERTAINMENT: Sports Equip-ment	ENTERTAINMENT: Fees & Tickets	ENTERTAINMENT: Toys & Games	ENTERTAINMENT: Travel	ENTERTAINMENT: Cable TV	PERSONAL: Apparel & Services	PERSONAL: Auto Repairs	PERSONAL: Health Insur-ance	PERSONAL: Pets & Supplies
65631	CLEVER	82	71	55	69	75	82	69	75	73	69	89	88	67	90	70	75	84	74	82	93
65632	CONWAY	71	51	28	46	57	64	49	59	57	50	68	70	43	65	50	60	62	58	70	82
65633	CRANE	63	47	31	45	52	62	52	58	59	50	69	65	46	65	52	62	63	58	69	70
65634	CROSS TIMBERS	58	43	27	40	47	56	46	52	52	45	62	59	41	58	46	56	56	52	63	65
65635	DADEVILLE	73	52	28	49	60	67	51	63	58	50	69	75	44	67	53	62	63	62	75	87
65637	DORA	69	46	21	40	52	60	45	56	54	45	63	67	38	60	45	58	57	55	69	79
65638	DRURY	65	44	20	38	49	57	42	53	51	43	60	63	36	56	43	55	54	52	65	75
65640	DUNNEGAN	70	47	23	43	54	62	46	58	55	47	64	69	39	62	48	58	58	57	70	81
65641	EAGLE ROCK	70	53	34	47	60	68	50	61	58	50	68	72	44	67	53	62	63	60	73	84
65644	ELKLAND	74	52	26	45	58	66	50	61	59	50	69	73	43	66	50	63	63	60	74	86
65646	EVERTON	78	57	32	52	64	72	55	66	63	55	75	79	49	73	56	66	69	65	78	91
65647	EXETER	82	56	26	48	63	72	54	67	65	55	76	80	46	72	55	70	69	66	82	95
65648	FAIR GROVE	94	91	78	88	93	97	84	90	85	84	105	107	84	108	86	85	101	88	91	110
65649	FAIR PLAY	75	55	32	49	62	71	54	65	62	53	73	76	47	71	56	66	67	64	78	89
65650	FLEMINGTON	77	56	33	52	64	72	54	67	62	54	73	79	47	72	57	66	67	66	79	92
65652	FORDLAND	80	59	35	54	65	74	58	68	67	58	79	80	52	76	59	70	73	67	80	91
65653	FORSYTH	83	67	49	64	73	82	66	75	71	67	86	85	61	80	67	74	80	74	86	95
65654	FREISTATT	76	65	51	65	68	77	67	71	71	66	86	82	64	85	66	72	81	70	77	84
65655	GAINESVILLE	68	49	29	46	55	65	52	60	60	51	70	69	46	67	52	64	64	60	72	76
65656	GALENA	82	57	29	51	64	73	55	67	65	56	77	80	48	74	56	70	70	67	81	94
65657	GARRISON	73	49	22	42	55	63	47	59	57	48	66	70	40	63	48	61	60	58	72	83
65658	GOLDEN	67	52	36	47	59	66	49	60	56	49	66	70	44	65	53	60	62	59	70	81
65660	GRAFF	75	51	24	45	58	66	49	62	59	50	69	74	42	66	51	63	63	61	75	87
65661	GREENFIELD	58	43	27	41	47	56	46	52	52	44	61	59	41	58	46	55	56	52	62	65
65662	GROVESPRING	82	56	27	49	63	72	54	67	64	55	76	80	46	72	55	69	69	66	81	94
65663	HALF WAY	73	57	37	53	62	70	56	64	62	56	75	75	51	73	56	65	69	63	74	84
65666	HARDENVILLE	78	54	27	48	60	70	54	65	64	54	75	76	47	71	54	68	68	64	79	88
65667	HARTVILLE	72	50	26	45	56	66	51	61	60	51	71	71	44	67	51	64	64	61	74	82
65668	HERMITAGE	54	48	44	43	51	61	45	52	49	47	60	53	44	53	48	53	56	51	62	62
65669	HIGHLANDVILLE	79	70	53	67	74	79	65	72	69	65	84	86	64	85	67	71	80	70	78	93
65672	HOLLISTER	61	57	55	57	59	65	58	61	59	58	73	69	56	70	59	60	70	61	63	70
65674	HUMANSVILLE	52	38	23	36	42	50	41	47	47	39	55	53	36	52	41	49	50	46	56	59
65675	HURLEY	82	62	37	56	68	76	59	70	67	60	80	84	54	79	60	71	74	69	82	95
65676	ISABELLA	73	66	60	62	70	83	62	71	67	66	82	71	62	70	67	71	77	69	83	82
65679	KIRBYVILLE	88	79	61	76	80	85	76	82	77	77	95	94	71	90	75	77	91	81	83	98
65680	KISSEE MILLS	81	55	26	48	62	71	53	66	63	54	75	79	45	71	54	68	68	65	80	93
65681	LAMPE	85	75	65	70	81	94	70	81	76	73	93	84	68	82	76	81	86	79	95	99
65682	LOCKWOOD	74	53	30	50	60	69	55	65	63	54	74	75	48	71	56	67	68	64	78	85
65685	LOUISBURG	75	54	31	49	60	70	56	65	65	55	76	75	49	72	56	69	69	65	79	85
65686	KIMBERLING CITY	80	75	72	71	79	94	69	79	73	74	91	77	70	76	75	78	85	77	92	90
65688	BRANDSVILLE	100	67	30	58	76	87	65	81	78	66	92	97	55	86	66	84	83	80	100	115
65689	CABOOL	69	50	29	46	55	65	52	60	60	51	70	69	46	67	52	64	64	60	73	78
65690	COUCH	72	49	23	42	55	63	47	59	57	48	67	70	40	63	48	61	61	58	72	83
65692	KOSHKONONG	89	60	27	52	68	78	58	72	70	59	82	86	49	77	59	75	74	71	89	102
65701	MC CLURG	0	0	0	0	0	0	0	0	0	0	0	0	0	0	0	0	0	0	0	0
65702	MACOMB	73	49	22	42	55	63	47	59	57	48	66	70	40	63	48	61	60	58	72	83
65704	MANSFIELD	65	45	25	41	51	59	47	55	54	46	64	64	41	60	47	58	58	55	67	73
65705	MARIONVILLE	70	54	35	50	59	67	53	61	60	53	71	72	49	69	54	63	66	60	71	80
65706	MARSHFIELD	74	63	48	61	67	74	62	68	66	61	80	79	59	81	63	68	76	66	75	84
65707	MILLER	75	57	36	54	63	72	58	67	65	57	77	78	52	75	59	68	71	66	78	86
65708	MONETT	78	64	49	62	68	77	67	72	72	65	87	83	63	86	67	74	82	72	80	87
65710	MORRISVILLE	71	54	33	49	58	64	52	61	58	53	70	72	46	66	52	60	65	60	69	80
65711	MOUNTAIN GROVE	63	45	26	42	50	59	47	55	54	46	63	63	41	60	47	57	58	54	66	71
65712	MOUNT VERNON	83	66	45	63	72	82	68	75	74	66	88	87	62	86	68	77	82	74	87	94
65713	NIANGUA	83	55	25	48	63	72	54	67	65	55	76	80	46	72	54	70	69	66	82	95
65714	NIXA	86	92	89	92	91	92	86	87	83	87	104	103	87	106	86	80	101	86	81	99
65715	NOBLE	66	48	29	46	55	63	47	58	54	47	64	68	42	61	49	57	58	57	69	78
65717	NORWOOD	71	48	22	41	54	62	46	57	55	47	65	69	39	61	47	60	59	57	71	81
65720	OLDFIELD	76	51	23	44	58	67	49	62	60	50	70	74	42	66	50	64	64	61	76	88
65721	OZARK	92	87	75	87	88	94	85	89	86	85	106	103	83	105	84	85	101	87	89	103
65722	PHILLIPSBURG	92	79	57	74	82	88	75	83	79	77	97	97	70	93	75	80	92	83	88	104
65723	PIERCE CITY	73	57	38	54	62	69	56	64	62	56	74	75	52	73	56	65	69	63	73	84
65724	PITTSBURG	60	47	32	42	53	59	44	53	50	44	59	62	40	59	47	54	55	53	63	73
65725	PLEASANT HOPE	78	69	53	66	73	79	64	71	68	64	83	85	63	85	66	70	79	69	77	92
65727	POLK	82	63	40	56	71	80	59	72	68	59	80	85	53	79	63	73	74	71	86	99
65728	PONCE DE LEON	83	74	56	70	78	83	68	75	72	68	88	90	67	90	70	74	83	73	82	97
65729	PONTIAC	71	61	52	58	65	77	60	68	65	62	79	70	58	70	63	69	74	66	80	79
65730	POWELL	68	60	45	57	61	65	57	63	59	59	73	73	53	69	57	59	69	62	64	76
65731	POWERSITE	75	69	54	66	69	73	66	70	66	68	82	81	62	77	65	66	79	70	70	83
65732	PRESTON	81	55	25	47	62	71	53	66	64	54	75	79	45	71	54	69	68	65	81	94
65733	PROTEM	71	48	22	41	54	62	46	57	55	47	65	68	39	61	47	60	59	57	71	81
65734	PURDY	69	49	26	44	54	62	48	58	56	48	66	68	42	63	49	60	61	57	69	78
65735	QUINCY	53	40	26	38	44	52	44	49	50	42	58	55	39	55	44	52	53	49	58	59
65737	REEDS SPRING	96	77	54	71	83	94	73	85	81	75	97	97	67	90	76	85	91	84	98	110
65738	REPUBLIC	77	71	59	70	73	77	69	74	71	69	87	87	66	85	69	70	83	73	75	88
65739	RIDGEDALE	94	98	113	102	98	103	100	99	96	99	121	116	100	118	99	93	117	100	95	108
65740	ROCKAWAY BEACH	64	59	46	57	59	62	56	60	57	58	70	69	53	66	55	56	67	60	60	71
65742	ROGERSVILLE	119	112	95	109	117	125	105	114	109	105	133	133	104	134	108	111	127	111	120	140
65744	RUETER	77	51	23	44	58	67	50	62	60	50	70	74	42	66	50	64	64	61	76	88
65745	SELIGMAN	74	50	22	43	56	65	48	60	58	49	68	72	41	64	49	62	62	59	74	85
65746	SEYMOUR	72	52	29	47	57	65	51	61	59	51	70	72	45	66	51	62	64	60	72	82
65747	SHELL KNOB	76	62	48	57	69	79	59	69	65	60	78	77	55	73	63	69	73	68	82	90
65752	SOUTH GREENFIELD	74	52	27	49	61	68	51	63	59	51	69	76	44	68	53	62	63	63	76	88
65753	SPARTA	88	65	38	59	72	80	62	74	71	63	85	88	56	82	63	75	78	73	87	101
65754	SPOKANE	76	67	51	64	71	76	62	69	66	62	80	82	61	82	64	68	76	67	75	89
65755	SQUIRES	67	45	20	39	51	58	43	54	52	44	61	64	37	58	44	56	55	53	66	77
65756	STOTTS CITY	88	59	27	51	67	77	57	71	69	58	81	85	49	77	58	74	74	71	88	101
65757	STRAFFORD	88	80	65	78	84	91	76	83	80	76	98	97	75	99	78	81	93	81	88	102
65759	TANEYVILLE	67	56	40	54	59	63	54	61	57	55	70	71	50	66	54	58	66	60	64	76
65760	TECUMSEH	70	47	21	41	53	61	45	57	55	46	64	68	39	61	46	59	59	56	70	81
65761	THEODOSIA	56	50	48	46	54	65	47	55	52	50	63	54	47	55	51	55	59	54	66	63
65762	THORNFIELD	68	51	32	48	57	65	50	60	56	50	67	69	44	63	52	59	61	59	71	79
65764	TUNAS	75	50	23	44	57	66	49	61	59	50	69	73	42	65	50	63	63	60	75	86
65766	UDALL	57	38	17	33	43	50	37	46	44	37	52	55	31	49	37	48	47	46	57	65
65767	URBANA	83	62	40	59	68	81	68	75	76	64	89	84	60	84	67	80	82	75	90	92
	MISSOURI	87	82	79	80	83	90	82	85	85	82	104	99	81	103	82	85	100	85	87	100
	UNITED STATES	100	100	100	100	100	100	100	100	100	100	100	100	100	100	100	100	100	100	100	100

ZIP CODE			POPULATION			2000-2004 ANNUAL RATE		HOUSEHOLDS					FAMILIES		
#	POST OFFICE NAME	COUNTY FIPS CODE	2000	2004	2009	% Rate	State Centile	2000	2004	2009	% Annual Rate 2000-2004	2004 Average HH Size	2000	2004	% Annual Rate 2000-2004
65768	VANZANT	067	1167	1212	1259	0.9	65	446	467	490	1.1	2.59	351	362	0.7
65769	VERONA	009	2827	3380	3859	4.3	98	992	1180	1342	4.2	2.86	763	891	3.7
65770	WALNUT GROVE	077	2457	2457	2510	0.0	32	947	958	987	0.3	2.51	715	706	-0.3
65771	WALNUT SHADE	213	1024	1059	1137	0.8	63	373	388	417	0.9	2.70	290	297	0.6
65772	WASHBURN	009	1875	1938	2051	0.8	62	715	742	788	0.9	2.61	528	540	0.5
65773	WASOLA	153	737	747	760	0.3	45	291	297	304	0.5	2.50	218	219	0.1
65774	WEAUBLEAU	085	977	1028	1092	1.2	73	392	411	436	1.1	2.50	261	267	0.5
65775	WEST PLAINS	091	22889	23056	23252	0.2	39	9077	9183	9299	0.3	2.45	6469	6422	-0.2
65777	MOODY	091	336	367	382	2.1	87	118	131	137	2.5	2.80	94	103	2.2
65778	MYRTLE	149	420	403	400	-1.0	6	169	163	163	-0.9	2.47	124	118	-1.2
65779	WHEATLAND	085	2138	2211	2324	0.8	63	949	986	1040	0.9	2.22	653	664	0.4
65781	WILLARD	077	6703	6890	7133	0.7	58	2388	2483	2599	0.9	2.69	1904	1938	0.4
65783	WINDYVILLE	059	1080	1143	1225	1.3	76	402	424	455	1.3	2.67	297	308	0.9
65784	ZANONI	153	261	264	268	0.3	43	107	109	111	0.4	2.42	81	81	0.0
65785	STOCKTON	039	5822	6004	6189	0.7	60	2391	2474	2563	0.8	2.34	1666	1688	0.3
65786	MACKS CREEK	029	2057	2163	2369	1.2	73	799	845	934	1.3	2.55	600	625	1.0
65787	ROACH	029	1886	2000	2210	1.4	77	694	752	852	1.9	2.34	508	540	1.5
65788	PEACE VALLEY	091	337	338	337	0.1	35	119	121	121	0.4	2.79	97	97	0.0
65789	POMONA	091	1520	1604	1645	1.3	74	568	607	627	1.6	2.63	447	469	1.1
65790	POTTERSVILLE	091	643	699	728	2.0	85	263	288	301	2.2	2.43	206	221	1.7
65791	THAYER	149	3777	4188	4460	2.5	89	1560	1734	1852	2.5	2.35	1051	1145	2.0
65793	WILLOW SPRINGS	091	5940	5928	6016	-0.1	30	2334	2342	2390	0.1	2.48	1674	1641	-0.5
65802	SPRINGFIELD	077	38524	39294	40983	0.5	51	15561	16023	16916	0.7	2.28	9335	9357	0.1
65803	SPRINGFIELD	077	38470	38593	40082	0.1	35	15204	15432	16223	0.4	2.38	9949	9820	-0.3
65804	SPRINGFIELD	077	35930	36139	37335	0.1	38	16716	17045	17825	0.5	2.11	9667	9482	-0.5
65806	SPRINGFIELD	077	10920	10883	11227	-0.1	29	5244	5267	5513	0.1	1.82	1555	1489	-1.0
65807	SPRINGFIELD	077	49948	52729	55671	1.3	74	20462	22079	23753	1.8	2.17	11734	12122	0.8
65809	SPRINGFIELD	077	9484	10307	11017	2.0	85	3439	3784	4088	2.3	2.67	2858	3094	1.9
65810	SPRINGFIELD	077	15507	18005	19883	3.6	96	5640	6669	7468	4.0	2.67	4512	5236	3.6
MISSOURI						0.8					0.9	2.46			0.4
UNITED STATES						1.2					1.3	2.58			1.1

#	ZIP CODE POST OFFICE NAME	RACE (%) White 2000	2004	Black 2000	2004	Asian/Pacific 2000	2004	% Hispanic Origin 2000	2004	2004 AGE DISTRIBUTION (%) 0-4	5-9	10-14	15-19	20-24	25-44	45-64	65-84	85+	18+	MEDIAN AGE 2004	% 2004 Males	% 2004 Females
65768	VANZANT	95.5	95.1	0.1	0.2	0.1	0.2	0.8	0.8	5.5	6.0	6.4	6.2	5.5	23.4	31.1	14.4	1.5	78.1	43.2	51.0	49.0
65769	VERONA	86.6	85.7	0.4	0.4	0.2	0.3	16.5	17.9	9.2	8.6	7.7	7.0	6.7	27.7	22.2	10.1	0.9	70.3	33.6	51.5	48.5
65770	WALNUT GROVE	97.8	97.6	0.2	0.2	0.1	0.1	0.6	0.7	6.0	6.4	7.1	6.6	5.5	26.4	27.1	12.8	2.2	76.3	40.3	49.5	50.5
65771	WALNUT SHADE	97.1	96.7	0.0	0.0	0.7	0.9	0.7	0.8	6.5	6.7	6.9	6.2	6.0	26.7	28.1	11.9	0.9	75.5	39.7	50.2	49.8
65772	WASHBURN	97.7	97.6	0.1	0.1	0.0	0.0	1.0	1.0	7.3	7.5	8.2	7.2	6.7	26.5	24.5	11.2	0.9	72.7	35.7	50.5	49.5
65773	WASOLA	98.2	98.0	0.0	0.0	0.0	0.1	0.7	0.8	5.9	5.8	5.5	6.4	5.5	22.2	29.9	17.3	1.6	79.0	44.2	49.5	50.5
65774	WEAUBLEAU	96.0	95.7	0.5	0.6	0.0	0.0	0.9	1.0	6.1	5.9	7.0	8.4	6.2	22.3	24.7	16.9	2.4	75.7	40.3	48.0	52.0
65775	WEST PLAINS	96.6	96.3	0.4	0.5	0.5	0.6	1.3	1.4	7.1	6.8	7.0	6.8	6.6	25.2	24.0	14.4	2.2	75.0	38.2	48.6	51.4
65777	MOODY	95.8	95.6	1.2	1.1	0.3	0.3	1.8	1.9	8.2	7.4	6.8	6.5	6.3	24.8	25.3	13.6	1.1	73.6	37.9	51.2	48.8
65778	MYRTLE	94.5	94.5	0.0	0.0	0.0	0.0	0.5	0.5	5.2	5.7	6.7	6.0	5.2	20.8	30.5	17.4	2.5	78.7	45.3	51.6	48.4
65779	WHEATLAND	98.2	98.0	0.0	0.0	0.2	0.3	0.5	0.5	3.9	3.8	4.9	5.1	5.0	16.4	31.0	26.6	3.2	84.3	53.4	49.3	50.8
65781	WILLARD	98.0	97.7	0.2	0.2	0.1	0.1	0.6	0.8	7.2	7.0	7.4	7.1	6.4	27.7	24.1	10.7	2.4	73.5	36.9	48.5	51.5
65783	WINDYVILLE	97.1	96.9	0.2	0.2	0.4	0.4	1.0	1.1	6.7	6.9	7.2	7.5	6.7	23.7	27.7	12.1	1.4	74.0	39.3	50.9	49.1
65784	ZANONI	97.3	97.0	0.4	0.4	0.0	0.0	1.2	1.1	5.7	5.7	5.3	5.7	5.7	22.0	31.4	17.1	1.5	79.2	45.0	51.5	48.5
65785	STOCKTON	96.8	96.5	0.2	0.2	0.6	0.8	1.0	1.1	5.4	5.7	6.3	7.7	5.2	19.7	28.1	19.4	2.5	77.4	45.0	49.7	50.3
65786	MACKS CREEK	98.2	98.2	0.1	0.1	0.2	0.1	1.0	1.1	5.9	6.0	7.0	6.4	6.1	24.3	27.7	15.1	1.6	76.9	41.4	51.1	48.9
65787	ROACH	97.5	97.2	0.1	0.2	0.4	0.5	0.7	0.9	4.8	5.2	5.8	4.8	5.2	21.2	32.6	19.0	1.7	81.3	47.3	50.0	50.0
65788	PEACE VALLEY	97.9	97.6	0.3	0.3	0.6	0.6	0.6	0.3	5.0	6.5	8.3	8.3	5.6	25.4	27.8	12.4	0.6	74.9	39.2	51.8	48.2
65789	POMONA	96.6	96.3	0.1	0.1	0.4	0.5	1.0	1.1	6.5	6.7	7.2	7.0	6.4	25.6	27.5	12.1	0.9	75.2	38.5	50.9	49.1
65790	POTTERSVILLE	95.2	94.9	0.0	0.0	0.2	0.1	0.6	0.6	7.4	7.7	7.4	7.4	6.7	26.6	25.5	10.4	0.7	73.1	35.4	49.6	50.4
65791	THAYER	96.4	96.1	0.1	0.1	0.1	0.2	1.3	1.5	6.8	6.5	6.4	5.8	6.1	23.2	24.7	16.5	4.1	76.7	41.1	47.0	53.0
65793	WILLOW SPRINGS	95.9	95.5	0.2	0.2	0.3	0.3	0.9	1.1	6.3	6.4	6.7	6.9	6.0	23.0	26.1	16.2	2.6	76.2	41.3	48.2	51.8
65802	SPRINGFIELD	91.7	91.0	3.5	3.7	1.0	1.2	2.5	2.8	6.7	6.3	6.1	7.7	11.1	29.5	21.1	10.1	1.4	77.5	32.9	48.9	51.1
65803	SPRINGFIELD	93.1	92.5	2.9	3.2	0.5	0.6	1.9	2.2	6.6	6.2	6.5	7.0	8.8	27.8	24.1	11.2	1.9	77.1	35.8	48.8	51.2
65804	SPRINGFIELD	94.6	93.8	1.5	1.6	1.4	1.8	1.6	1.8	5.0	4.9	5.2	5.5	9.1	25.7	24.8	17.0	2.8	81.9	40.8	47.2	52.8
65806	SPRINGFIELD	85.9	84.2	5.6	6.4	2.0	2.4	3.4	3.8	5.0	3.9	3.8	9.2	27.4	27.1	15.6	6.7	1.4	84.7	25.4	50.6	49.5
65807	SPRINGFIELD	91.8	90.8	3.1	3.4	2.0	2.5	2.3	2.5	5.8	5.1	4.9	8.3	11.6	30.0	20.1	11.4	2.8	81.4	33.2	48.6	51.4
65809	SPRINGFIELD	96.3	95.6	0.8	0.9	1.3	1.7	0.6	0.7	5.4	6.6	7.2	6.6	4.4	21.5	32.9	13.4	2.1	76.6	44.0	49.4	50.6
65810	SPRINGFIELD	95.3	94.4	0.9	0.9	1.9	2.5	1.3	1.5	6.7	7.1	7.6	6.5	5.6	29.4	26.6	9.3	1.2	74.5	37.5	49.1	50.9
	MISSOURI	84.9	84.1	11.3	11.5	1.2	1.4	2.1	2.3	6.7	6.6	7.0	7.0	7.3	27.6	24.2	11.7	1.9	75.6	36.8	48.7	51.3
	UNITED STATES	75.1	73.6	12.3	12.5	3.8	4.2	12.5	14.1	6.9	6.7	7.2	7.0	7.3	28.6	23.8	10.8	1.7	75.1	36.0	49.1	50.9

ZIP CODE		2004 Per Capita Income	2004 HH Income Base	2004 HOUSEHOLD INCOME DISTRIBUTION (%)					MEDIAN HOUSEHOLD INCOME				2004 Home Value Base	2004 HOME VALUE DISTRIBUTION (%)					2004 Median Home Value
#	POST OFFICE NAME			Less than $25,000	$25,000 to $49,999	$50,000 to $99,999	$100,000 to $149,999	$150,000 or More	2004	2009	2004 National Centile	2004 State Centile		Less than $50,000	$50,000 to $89,999	$90,000 to $174,999	$175,000 to $399,999	$400,000 or More	
65768	VANZANT	19953	467	36.2	39.6	15.9	2.4	6.0	31037	35128	15	24	379	18.2	19.8	40.9	16.9	4.2	106964
65769	VERONA	15237	1180	35.2	35.6	23.1	4.4	1.7	35190	40447	28	46	934	26.9	29.7	25.8	15.4	2.3	81867
65770	WALNUT GROVE	19264	958	26.9	35.5	30.1	5.9	1.7	40712	48102	49	69	806	19.4	25.4	40.2	12.9	2.1	96176
65771	WALNUT SHADE	19570	388	32.0	32.0	26.8	6.2	3.1	36677	42369	34	54	324	17.0	20.1	38.3	20.1	4.6	104018
65772	WASHBURN	16113	742	36.7	36.0	21.7	2.8	2.8	32995	38012	21	33	618	24.3	24.1	39.5	7.6	4.5	91852
65773	WASOLA	13394	297	44.4	35.4	18.2	1.7	0.3	28413	31895	9	13	250	32.8	22.8	27.2	12.4	4.8	80667
65774	WEAUBLEAU	12301	411	55.0	29.2	13.1	1.7	1.0	22813	25834	3	2	305	39.0	32.1	21.6	6.2	1.0	57791
65775	WEST PLAINS	17162	9183	42.1	32.4	19.8	3.4	2.4	30061	34559	12	19	6668	22.5	29.1	33.3	12.9	2.3	88399
65777	MOODY	11966	131	48.9	30.5	18.3	2.3	0.0	25647	29709	5	5	109	23.9	24.8	38.5	11.0	1.8	92500
65778	MYRTLE	12407	163	55.2	27.0	14.7	2.5	0.6	22231	25177	3	2	133	41.4	24.8	24.8	9.0	0.0	64500
65779	WHEATLAND	15606	986	47.4	32.3	16.8	2.6	0.9	26106	28967	6	6	816	25.9	29.7	31.7	10.8	2.0	82105
65781	WILLARD	19691	2483	23.3	32.2	35.7	6.1	2.7	45537	53432	63	79	2028	4.9	24.1	52.3	16.2	2.4	110151
65783	WINDYVILLE	20969	424	44.8	25.7	23.4	1.9	4.3	29525	35151	11	17	355	25.9	34.1	29.6	9.0	1.4	77424
65784	ZANONI	16620	109	44.0	32.1	19.3	1.8	2.8	30270	34532	13	20	92	31.5	25.0	30.4	10.9	2.2	77500
65785	STOCKTON	18071	2474	37.8	34.3	21.6	4.2	2.0	33097	38284	21	34	2010	24.5	27.9	32.1	14.2	1.2	86142
65786	MACKS CREEK	16350	845	34.3	36.8	22.8	4.5	1.5	34790	40492	27	44	701	27.1	27.0	28.5	15.7	1.7	82875
65787	ROACH	23932	752	30.7	30.6	26.6	7.5	4.7	40750	48096	49	69	613	10.1	17.9	28.6	37.9	5.6	147426
65788	PEACE VALLEY	15323	121	32.2	43.8	19.8	3.3	0.8	35148	40217	28	46	101	28.7	17.8	35.6	16.8	1.0	93889
65789	POMONA	16639	607	44.0	35.4	14.8	2.5	3.3	28733	33548	10	15	502	30.1	23.5	33.1	11.4	2.0	85135
65790	POTTERSVILLE	15611	288	43.1	33.7	20.1	2.4	0.7	28522	32910	10	14	240	23.3	29.6	28.3	15.8	2.9	87813
65791	THAYER	15413	1734	50.7	30.2	14.3	3.2	1.6	24558	27696	4	4	1290	38.1	29.8	22.9	7.7	1.5	67172
65793	WILLOW SPRINGS	13942	2342	48.6	31.0	17.3	2.0	1.2	25766	29556	6	6	1800	30.6	30.1	28.8	9.7	0.8	74741
65802	SPRINGFIELD	17743	16023	38.6	35.7	20.1	4.1	1.5	31970	37798	18	28	9274	20.4	40.2	32.4	6.0	1.1	78587
65803	SPRINGFIELD	18075	15432	37.5	33.5	22.2	4.9	2.0	32826	39513	20	33	9680	20.6	36.3	33.0	8.9	1.1	81594
65804	SPRINGFIELD	29575	17045	26.0	33.2	26.4	8.5	5.9	41827	50334	52	72	10773	5.4	17.6	54.1	19.9	2.9	120749
65806	SPRINGFIELD	13507	5267	67.7	22.0	8.4	1.2	0.8	17079	19795	1	1	1137	25.3	59.9	10.5	4.1	0.3	60492
65807	SPRINGFIELD	21732	22079	29.3	35.6	27.3	5.3	2.6	38581	45936	41	63	12558	5.7	27.0	59.9	7.2	0.2	101920
65809	SPRINGFIELD	46734	3784	8.2	17.8	30.7	19.7	23.7	83792	112072	96	99	3412	0.6	1.7	29.5	52.5	15.7	223750
65810	SPRINGFIELD	32158	6669	10.6	21.5	42.6	15.2	10.2	65938	81732	89	96	5594	0.5	6.3	58.6	33.0	1.7	146414
	MISSOURI	23864		27.0	29.4	30.1	9.0	4.5	44017	52626				15.2	22.7	39.0	19.7	3.4	109184
	UNITED STATES	25866		24.7	27.1	30.8	10.9	6.5	48124	56710				10.9	15.0	33.7	30.1	10.4	145905

#	POST OFFICE NAME	FINANCIAL SERVICES				THE HOME							ENTERTAINMENT						PERSONAL			
						Home Improvements		Furnishings														
		Auto Loan	Home Loan	Invest-ments	Retire-ment Plans	Home Repair	Lawn & Garden	Comput-ers & Hard-ware	Major Appli-ances	TV, Radio, Sound Equip-ment	Furni-ture	Dine out/ Carry out	Sports Equip-ment	Fees & Tickets	Toys & Games	Travel	Cable TV	Apparel & Services	Auto Repairs	Health Insur-ance	Pets & Supplies
65768	VANZANT	94	65	34	61	76	85	64	80	75	64	87	96	55	85	67	78	80	79	95	111
65769	VERONA	69	59	45	58	61	68	60	64	63	59	76	73	57	75	59	64	72	63	69	76
65770	WALNUT GROVE	80	68	49	64	73	79	64	72	69	64	83	86	61	84	65	71	78	70	79	94
65771	WALNUT SHADE	85	77	59	73	78	83	72	78	74	74	91	91	69	88	72	74	87	77	80	96
65772	WASHBURN	79	53	24	46	60	69	51	64	62	52	73	77	44	69	52	67	66	63	79	91
65773	WASOLA	62	42	20	37	48	55	41	51	49	42	58	61	35	55	42	52	52	51	62	72
65774	WEAUBLEAU	57	39	19	34	44	51	38	47	45	38	53	56	32	50	38	49	48	46	57	66
65775	WEST PLAINS	70	56	39	52	60	67	56	63	61	56	74	73	51	70	56	64	69	63	71	79
65777	MOODY	63	42	19	36	48	55	41	51	49	42	58	61	35	55	41	53	53	51	63	72
65778	MYRTLE	58	39	18	33	44	50	37	47	45	38	53	56	32	50	38	49	48	46	58	66
65779	WHEATLAND	56	45	33	42	49	58	45	52	50	44	60	58	41	57	47	54	55	51	62	65
65781	WILLARD	84	76	61	74	79	85	73	78	76	72	93	92	71	93	73	77	88	77	83	96
65783	WINDYVILLE	103	71	36	65	82	93	70	86	81	69	96	104	59	93	72	86	87	85	104	121
65784	ZANONI	76	51	23	44	57	66	49	61	59	50	69	73	42	66	50	64	63	61	75	87
65785	STOCKTON	74	54	32	50	60	70	55	64	63	54	74	75	48	71	56	67	68	64	77	85
65786	MACKS CREEK	76	54	28	47	60	69	51	63	61	52	72	75	44	68	53	65	66	63	77	89
65787	ROACH	100	78	53	71	88	100	76	90	86	75	102	104	68	99	80	92	94	89	107	120
65788	PEACE VALLEY	80	54	25	48	62	70	52	65	63	53	73	78	45	70	54	67	67	65	80	92
65789	POMONA	81	56	27	48	63	72	54	67	64	55	76	79	46	72	55	69	69	66	81	94
65790	POTTERSVILLE	71	48	22	41	54	62	46	58	56	47	64	61	43	61	48	60	59	57	71	82
65791	THAYER	60	44	28	42	49	58	48	54	55	46	64	60	41	57	45	53	59	54	65	67
65793	WILLOW SPRINGS	58	44	31	41	48	55	45	51	51	45	60	60	41	57	45	53	56	51	60	65
65802	SPRINGFIELD	59	53	53	53	53	59	59	58	60	57	74	69	56	73	57	60	71	60	59	66
65803	SPRINGFIELD	62	59	58	58	60	66	61	62	63	59	77	72	60	78	61	63	74	62	64	71
65804	SPRINGFIELD	85	83	94	85	84	91	89	87	89	87	111	102	88	109	88	88	108	90	87	97
65806	SPRINGFIELD	34	27	33	29	27	31	38	33	38	35	47	41	34	45	34	36	45	36	32	36
65807	SPRINGFIELD	69	65	71	67	65	70	71	69	70	69	88	82	69	86	68	68	85	71	67	77
65809	SPRINGFIELD	165	202	223	204	199	203	182	180	169	183	213	207	196	220	187	166	213	174	166	198
65810	SPRINGFIELD	118	135	142	138	131	130	125	123	117	127	148	145	130	151	125	111	147	122	109	136
	MISSOURI	87	82	79	80	83	90	82	85	85	82	104	99	81	103	82	85	100	85	87	100
	UNITED STATES	100	100	100	100	100	100	100	100	100	100	100	100	100	100	100	100	100	100	100	100

# POST OFFICE NAME	COUNTY FIPS CODE	POPULATION 2000	2004	2009	2000-2004 ANNUAL RATE % Rate	State Centile	HOUSEHOLDS 2000	2004	2009	% Annual Rate 2000-2004	2004 Average HH Size	FAMILIES 2000	2004	% Annual Rate 2000-2004
59001 ABSAROKEE	095	1628	1653	1688	0.4	71	671	689	710	0.6	2.36	467	473	0.3
59002 ACTON	111	79	82	84	0.9	86	31	33	34	1.5	2.48	25	26	0.9
59003 ASHLAND	087	384	384	385	0.0	57	151	152	153	0.2	2.53	104	104	0.0
59006 BALLANTINE	111	851	913	959	1.7	93	318	345	366	1.9	2.65	232	246	1.4
59007 BEARCREEK	009	394	397	398	0.2	64	177	181	184	0.5	2.19	127	128	0.2
59008 BELFRY	009	54	55	55	0.4	73	20	21	21	1.2	2.62	14	15	1.6
59010 BIGHORN	103	149	147	147	-0.3	39	57	57	57	0.0	2.58	39	38	-0.6
59011 BIG TIMBER	097	2863	3007	3187	1.2	91	1204	1271	1354	1.3	2.32	792	822	0.9
59012 BIRNEY	087	96	96	96	0.0	57	45	45	46	0.0	2.13	31	31	0.0
59014 BRIDGER	009	1728	1718	1718	-0.1	47	717	721	728	0.1	2.37	494	491	-0.1
59015 BROADVIEW	111	546	564	582	0.8	84	204	214	223	1.1	2.64	164	170	0.9
59016 BUSBY	003	1542	1607	1644	1.0	88	401	419	430	1.0	3.83	340	352	0.8
59019 COLUMBUS	095	3299	3454	3584	1.1	90	1294	1365	1428	1.3	2.48	914	951	0.9
59022 CROW AGENCY	003	2616	2669	2700	0.5	75	648	668	681	0.7	3.90	563	576	0.5
59024 CUSTER	111	335	368	391	2.2	97	137	152	163	2.5	2.42	99	108	2.1
59025 DECKER	003	145	140	140	-0.8	18	65	63	63	-0.7	2.22	44	42	-1.1
59027 EMIGRANT	067	473	479	481	0.3	70	189	196	201	0.9	2.44	122	124	0.4
59028 FISHTAIL	095	513	522	533	0.4	72	191	198	204	0.9	2.44	133	136	0.5
59029 FROMBERG	009	816	835	846	0.5	79	318	327	333	0.7	2.55	220	223	0.3
59030 GARDINER	067	1633	1602	1583	-0.5	30	801	807	814	0.2	1.98	425	418	-0.4
59031 GARRYOWEN	003	374	373	374	-0.1	50	110	111	112	0.2	3.18	100	101	0.2
59032 GRASS RANGE	027	451	446	440	-0.3	42	179	179	180	0.0	2.34	131	129	-0.4
59033 GREYCLIFF	097	414	424	444	0.6	80	146	150	157	0.6	2.83	104	106	0.5
59034 HARDIN	003	4302	4287	4286	-0.1	49	1650	1661	1673	0.2	2.53	1134	1123	-0.2
59037 HUNTLEY	111	1513	1588	1650	1.1	91	569	605	635	1.5	2.62	436	455	1.0
59038 HYSHAM	103	119	117	117	-0.4	34	48	48	48	0.0	2.44	33	32	-0.7
59039 INGOMAR	087	111	110	110	-0.2	44	49	49	50	0.0	2.22	37	36	-0.6
59041 JOLIET	009	1609	1609	1611	0.0	57	659	667	674	0.3	2.41	479	479	0.0
59043 LAME DEER	087	2932	2926	2924	-0.1	50	790	798	806	0.2	3.63	602	601	0.0
59044 LAUREL	111	9830	9960	10200	0.3	70	3829	3918	4049	0.5	2.52	2774	2787	0.1
59046 LAVINA	037	507	520	525	0.6	81	223	231	234	0.8	1.99	161	165	0.6
59047 LIVINGSTON	067	12120	12072	12024	-0.1	48	5247	5321	5397	0.3	2.24	3258	3242	-0.1
59050 LODGE GRASS	003	3041	3024	3031	-0.1	47	856	864	876	0.2	3.46	698	698	0.0
59052 MC LEOD	097	226	231	240	0.5	78	87	89	93	0.5	2.60	62	63	0.4
59053 MARTINSDALE	059	64	62	61	-0.7	20	28	27	27	-0.9	2.30	19	19	0.0
59055 MELVILLE	097	74	75	78	0.3	70	30	31	32	0.8	2.42	22	22	0.0
59057 MOLT	095	614	632	651	0.7	83	222	231	241	0.9	2.74	177	182	0.7
59058 MOSBY	033	25	25	25	0.0	57	9	9	9	0.0	2.78	6	6	0.0
59059 MUSSELSHELL	065	445	435	431	-0.5	28	176	174	174	-0.3	2.40	128	125	-0.6
59061 NYE	095	235	238	243	0.3	70	123	127	131	0.8	1.75	86	88	0.5
59062 OTTER	075	404	408	411	0.2	66	170	174	177	0.6	2.34	123	124	0.2
59063 PARK CITY	095	1648	1686	1730	0.5	79	619	643	668	0.9	2.59	491	505	0.7
59064 POMPEYS PILLAR	111	260	283	300	2.0	95	111	122	131	2.3	2.32	80	87	2.0
59065 PRAY	067	94	95	94	0.3	67	45	46	47	0.5	2.07	32	33	0.7
59067 RAPELJE	095	191	195	200	0.5	75	77	79	81	0.6	2.47	59	60	0.4
59068 RED LODGE	009	3439	3520	3562	0.6	80	1550	1609	1646	0.9	2.13	914	932	0.5
59069 REED POINT	095	451	461	474	0.5	78	176	181	187	0.7	2.55	134	136	0.4
59070 ROBERTS	009	829	833	834	0.1	61	343	349	353	0.4	2.39	250	252	0.2
59071 ROSCOE	009	116	117	117	0.2	65	50	51	51	0.5	2.27	36	37	0.7
59072 ROUNDUP	065	3992	3972	3963	-0.1	47	1670	1677	1682	0.1	2.31	1084	1070	-0.3
59074 RYEGATE	037	633	638	638	0.2	64	191	194	194	0.4	2.78	138	138	0.0
59075 SAINT XAVIER	003	189	188	188	-0.1	47	56	57	57	0.4	3.28	43	43	0.0
59076 SANDERS	103	120	118	118	-0.4	35	46	46	46	0.0	2.57	31	31	0.0
59077 SAND SPRINGS	033	76	74	72	-0.6	23	30	30	30	0.0	2.40	20	20	0.0
59078 SHAWMUT	107	290	286	279	-0.3	38	72	72	71	0.0	3.39	53	53	0.0
59079 SHEPHERD	111	2843	3176	3414	2.6	98	988	1117	1212	2.9	2.84	808	901	2.6
59085 TWO DOT	107	1669	1619	1570	-0.7	20	662	646	630	-0.6	2.10	399	383	-1.0
59086 WILSALL	067	1317	1328	1330	0.2	65	528	544	556	0.7	2.38	373	379	0.4
59087 WINNETT	069	497	506	506	0.4	73	210	218	218	0.9	2.32	137	140	0.5
59088 WORDEN	111	1157	1220	1271	1.3	92	464	496	522	1.6	2.46	333	348	1.0
59089 WYOLA	003	440	456	466	0.8	85	131	138	142	1.2	3.21	105	110	1.1
59101 BILLINGS	111	36249	36477	37391	0.2	63	15232	15410	15911	0.3	2.31	8702	8639	-0.2
59102 BILLINGS	111	44839	45889	47444	0.6	80	19048	19736	20629	0.8	2.24	12014	12162	0.3
59105 BILLINGS	111	23570	24606	25599	1.0	89	8689	9206	9685	1.4	2.65	6468	6730	0.9
59106 BILLINGS	111	7570	8312	8857	2.2	97	2592	2881	3101	2.5	2.86	2168	2389	2.3
59201 WOLF POINT	085	4763	4719	4676	-0.2	44	1676	1669	1662	-0.1	2.77	1219	1197	-0.4
59211 ANTELOPE	091	165	154	145	-1.6	2	70	67	64	-1.0	2.30	51	47	-1.9
59212 BAINVILLE	085	323	315	310	-0.6	25	139	137	136	-0.3	2.30	94	91	-0.8
59213 BROCKTON	085	922	912	903	-0.3	42	279	279	280	0.0	3.27	232	231	-0.1
59214 BROCKWAY	055	162	156	150	-0.9	15	69	68	67	-0.3	2.29	57	55	-0.8
59215 CIRCLE	055	1112	1067	1021	-1.0	14	459	449	438	-0.5	2.38	322	311	-0.8
59218 CULBERTSON	085	839	826	817	-0.4	36	338	336	335	-0.1	2.42	216	210	-0.7
59219 DAGMAR	091	224	212	200	-1.3	5	85	82	79	-0.8	2.59	59	56	-1.2
59221 FAIRVIEW	083	1349	1278	1206	-1.3	6	547	528	507	-0.8	2.42	368	351	-1.1
59222 FLAXVILLE	019	263	252	242	-1.0	13	117	115	113	-0.4	2.19	81	78	-0.9
59223 FORT PECK	105	684	661	634	-0.8	19	287	281	273	-0.5	2.35	214	207	-0.8
59225 FRAZER	105	735	703	673	-1.0	12	211	204	197	-0.8	3.43	172	165	-1.0
59226 FROID	085	416	404	398	-0.7	21	190	186	185	-0.5	2.08	125	120	-1.0
59230 GLASGOW	105	4875	4756	4589	-0.6	25	2073	2040	1989	-0.4	2.25	1331	1288	-0.8
59241 HINSDALE	105	649	614	584	-1.3	4	268	259	251	-0.8	2.37	183	174	-1.2
59242 HOMESTEAD	091	58	56	53	-0.8	18	26	25	25	-0.9	2.24	18	18	0.0
59243 LAMBERT	083	616	588	557	-1.1	10	227	220	212	-0.7	2.67	172	165	-1.0
59244 LARSLAN	105	137	125	117	-2.1	0	54	50	47	-1.8	2.46	44	41	-1.7
59247 MEDICINE LAKE	091	427	404	382	-1.3	5	182	175	168	-0.9	2.31	127	121	-1.1
59248 NASHUA	105	221	210	200	-1.2	8	84	80	78	-1.1	2.59	67	63	-1.4
59250 OPHEIM	105	247	234	222	-1.3	6	114	110	107	-0.8	2.13	77	74	-0.9
59252 OUTLOOK	091	186	175	165	-1.4	3	80	76	74	-1.2	2.29	56	53	-1.3
59253 PEERLESS	019	327	315	304	-0.9	15	137	135	133	-0.4	2.33	95	92	-0.8
59254 PLENTYWOOD	091	2410	2289	2170	-1.2	7	1008	969	931	-0.9	2.24	627	592	-1.3
59255 POPLAR	085	3545	3524	3499	-0.1	47	1035	1037	1038	0.1	3.26	788	781	-0.2
59256 RAYMOND	091	8	8	7	0.0	57	5	5	5	0.0	1.60	3	3	0.0
59257 REDSTONE	091	124	115	108	-1.8	1	56	53	51	-1.3	2.17	41	38	-1.8
59258 RESERVE	091	121	131	132	1.9	95	51	56	57	2.2	2.34	35	39	2.6
59259 RICHEY	021	379	376	365	-0.2	45	166	167	164	0.1	2.25	121	120	-0.2
59260 RICHLAND	105	125	118	112	-1.4	3	54	52	50	-0.9	2.27	37	35	-1.3
MONTANA					0.4					0.7	2.42			0.3
UNITED STATES					1.2					1.3	2.58			1.1

ZIP CODE # POST OFFICE NAME	RACE (%) White 2000	White 2004	Black 2000	Black 2004	Asian/Pacific 2000	Asian/Pacific 2004	% Hispanic Origin 2000	% Hispanic Origin 2004	2004 AGE DISTRIBUTION (%) 0-4	5-9	10-14	15-19	20-24	25-44	45-64	65-84	85+	18+	MEDIAN AGE 2004	% 2004 Males	% 2004 Females
59001 ABSAROKEE	97.2	97.0	0.1	0.1	0.2	0.2	2.6	2.8	5.8	6.1	7.3	6.4	4.8	23.5	29.5	14.2	2.4	76.1	42.5	49.9	50.1
59002 ACTON	96.2	97.6	0.0	0.0	0.0	0.0	2.5	1.2	6.1	7.3	8.5	7.3	3.7	26.8	32.9	7.3	0.0	70.7	40.0	54.9	45.1
59003 ASHLAND	80.0	78.1	0.3	0.3	0.3	0.3	4.7	4.7	7.3	8.6	9.1	6.5	5.0	26.3	30.2	6.3	0.8	71.1	36.2	51.6	48.4
59006 BALLANTINE	95.2	94.5	0.2	0.3	0.1	0.2	4.7	5.4	6.1	6.1	7.8	7.6	6.0	24.2	29.8	11.3	1.1	75.0	40.0	50.9	49.1
59007 BEARCREEK	97.7	97.2	0.3	0.3	0.3	0.3	1.5	1.5	5.5	5.8	6.1	5.8	5.0	24.4	31.0	14.9	1.5	79.1	43.6	51.1	48.9
59008 BELFRY	100.0	100.0	0.0	0.0	0.0	0.0	0.0	0.0	5.5	5.5	7.3	5.5	3.6	23.6	36.4	12.7	0.0	81.8	44.5	47.3	52.7
59010 BIGHORN	96.6	96.6	0.0	0.0	0.7	0.7	2.0	1.4	5.4	6.1	6.8	7.5	5.4	19.7	31.3	15.0	2.7	76.9	44.3	52.4	47.6
59011 BIG TIMBER	97.0	96.7	0.0	0.0	0.3	0.4	1.5	1.6	5.9	6.3	7.3	6.3	4.8	22.7	29.2	14.1	3.5	76.5	42.6	50.3	49.8
59012 BIRNEY	80.2	79.2	0.0	0.0	0.0	0.0	4.2	4.2	7.3	8.3	8.3	7.3	5.2	27.1	29.2	6.3	1.0	69.8	35.7	50.0	50.0
59014 BRIDGER	97.6	97.5	0.1	0.1	0.1	0.1	2.5	2.6	5.7	6.1	6.8	6.6	5.8	22.8	29.7	14.7	2.0	77.4	42.6	50.1	49.9
59015 BROADVIEW	95.8	95.4	0.2	0.4	0.4	0.5	2.0	2.1	6.0	7.3	9.0	7.1	3.9	26.8	30.5	8.9	0.5	72.7	39.7	52.1	47.9
59016 BUSBY	7.2	6.9	0.0	0.0	0.0	0.0	3.0	2.9	13.2	12.0	11.6	8.7	7.0	25.1	18.3	3.7	0.4	57.8	23.2	49.8	50.2
59019 COLUMBUS	96.7	96.4	0.2	0.1	0.2	0.3	1.8	2.0	5.7	6.1	7.9	7.2	5.3	24.5	29.7	11.4	2.2	75.3	41.0	50.8	49.2
59022 CROW AGENCY	16.9	16.3	0.0	0.0	0.2	0.2	1.6	1.5	10.5	9.6	10.1	10.3	8.9	24.3	20.4	5.5	0.4	63.0	25.5	49.8	50.2
59024 CUSTER	95.8	95.4	0.0	0.3	0.0	0.0	4.2	5.2	5.7	5.2	7.9	8.2	4.4	25.3	31.5	11.4	0.5	75.5	40.9	52.2	47.8
59025 DECKER	95.2	95.0	0.0	0.0	0.7	0.7	2.8	2.9	4.3	5.7	7.1	3.6	5.0	27.1	32.1	14.3	0.7	80.0	43.7	50.0	50.0
59027 EMIGRANT	95.8	95.6	1.3	1.3	0.4	0.4	1.9	1.7	6.5	6.7	6.1	6.3	4.0	23.4	36.3	10.0	0.8	76.4	43.3	48.6	51.4
59028 FISHTAIL	96.9	96.4	0.4	0.4	0.4	0.4	2.9	3.3	3.3	3.8	5.4	3.8	3.8	23.4	37.7	17.2	1.5	84.9	48.1	54.0	46.0
59029 FROMBERG	94.5	94.6	0.0	0.0	0.4	0.4	4.2	4.2	4.4	4.9	7.4	8.1	7.0	21.1	31.9	13.2	2.0	78.3	43.2	49.8	50.2
59030 GARDINER	97.3	97.1	0.4	0.4	0.3	0.3	1.3	1.3	5.6	6.3	5.3	4.2	2.7	30.9	36.2	8.5	0.3	79.5	42.3	48.9	51.1
59031 GARRYOWEN	21.4	20.6	0.0	0.0	0.3	0.3	1.1	1.1	9.1	8.3	8.3	8.6	7.5	24.7	22.8	9.7	1.1	68.1	32.4	47.2	52.8
59032 GRASS RANGE	98.7	98.7	0.0	0.0	0.0	0.0	0.4	0.7	5.4	6.3	7.9	7.0	4.7	22.4	31.4	13.9	1.1	75.3	42.8	52.0	48.0
59033 GREYCLIFF	96.9	96.5	0.0	0.0	0.5	0.7	1.7	1.9	6.1	6.4	7.8	7.3	4.5	22.4	31.4	12.3	1.9	75.2	42.4	50.7	49.3
59034 HARDIN	67.4	66.6	0.1	0.1	0.5	0.5	5.1	5.2	7.6	7.4	7.9	8.1	7.0	24.6	24.1	11.2	2.2	71.5	35.9	48.5	51.5
59037 HUNTLEY	94.9	94.3	0.3	0.3	0.3	0.4	3.8	4.2	6.1	6.6	7.9	7.4	6.3	25.1	30.0	9.7	0.9	74.9	39.5	50.4	49.6
59038 HYSHAM	96.6	96.6	0.0	0.0	0.0	0.0	1.7	1.7	5.1	6.0	6.8	7.7	5.1	20.5	32.5	13.7	2.6	76.9	44.2	53.0	47.0
59039 INGOMAR	96.4	97.3	0.0	0.0	0.0	0.0	1.8	1.8	5.5	6.4	6.4	7.3	3.6	20.9	34.6	13.6	1.8	76.4	45.0	53.6	46.4
59041 JOLIET	97.1	97.1	0.4	0.4	0.7	0.7	1.2	1.2	6.0	6.7	8.0	6.2	3.9	22.5	30.4	13.9	2.4	75.3	43.0	50.8	49.2
59043 LAME DEER	8.3	7.4	0.0	0.0	0.1	0.1	2.0	2.0	11.8	10.5	11.2	11.1	9.3	23.8	17.6	4.4	0.3	58.9	22.9	48.1	51.9
59044 LAUREL	96.5	96.1	0.2	0.2	0.4	0.5	2.2	2.5	6.7	6.9	7.4	6.7	6.0	25.3	26.9	12.0	2.0	74.6	39.0	48.9	51.1
59046 LAVINA	98.6	98.5	0.0	0.0	0.2	0.2	1.0	1.0	5.0	5.6	8.1	6.4	4.6	21.4	33.5	14.4	1.2	76.9	44.3	51.7	48.3
59047 LIVINGSTON	96.5	96.4	0.4	0.4	0.4	0.4	2.0	2.0	5.6	5.7	6.4	6.8	6.3	24.4	29.3	13.0	2.5	78.0	41.7	49.5	50.5
59050 LODGE GRASS	24.0	23.5	0.0	0.0	0.1	0.1	4.0	3.9	10.4	10.0	9.7	9.1	8.3	25.0	20.3	6.9	0.4	64.0	27.3	50.3	49.7
59052 MC LEOD	96.9	96.1	0.0	0.0	0.4	0.9	1.8	1.7	6.1	6.1	7.8	7.4	4.8	23.4	30.7	12.1	1.7	74.9	42.0	51.1	48.9
59053 MARTINSDALE	98.4	98.4	0.0	0.0	0.0	0.0	0.0	1.6	4.8	6.5	8.1	4.8	3.2	21.0	32.3	19.4	0.0	80.7	46.0	54.8	45.2
59055 MELVILLE	97.3	97.3	0.0	0.0	0.0	0.0	1.4	1.3	5.3	6.7	6.7	5.3	5.3	22.7	34.7	12.0	1.3	78.7	43.5	53.3	46.7
59057 MOLT	95.6	95.3	0.2	0.3	0.3	0.5	2.3	2.5	6.0	7.1	8.9	7.1	4.1	26.0	30.1	10.1	0.6	72.9	40.1	52.4	47.6
59058 MOSBY	100.0	100.0	0.0	0.0	0.0	0.0	0.0	0.0	8.0	8.0	8.0	8.0	8.0	32.0	28.0	0.0	0.0	76.0	31.3	48.0	52.0
59059 MUSSELSHELL	97.1	97.0	0.0	0.0	0.2	0.2	0.9	0.9	3.9	5.8	6.0	9.0	3.2	21.2	37.0	13.1	0.9	78.6	45.4	50.8	49.2
59061 NYE	97.0	97.1	0.4	0.4	0.0	0.0	3.0	3.4	3.4	3.8	5.0	3.8	3.8	22.7	37.8	18.1	1.7	85.3	48.5	54.6	45.4
59062 OTTER	96.5	96.3	0.0	0.0	0.3	0.3	0.0	0.0	7.1	7.4	6.9	5.9	4.2	21.8	31.9	13.5	1.5	75.0	43.0	50.3	49.8
59063 PARK CITY	97.4	97.0	0.1	0.2	0.2	0.2	1.1	1.3	5.6	6.2	7.1	6.8	6.4	23.7	32.4	11.0	0.8	76.4	41.5	49.9	50.1
59064 POMPEYS PILLAR	95.4	94.7	0.0	0.4	0.0	0.0	4.2	5.3	5.7	5.0	7.8	7.8	4.6	24.7	32.2	11.7	0.7	76.3	41.6	51.6	48.4
59065 PRAY	97.9	97.9	0.0	0.0	1.1	1.1	2.1	1.1	4.2	3.2	7.4	4.2	4.2	23.2	41.1	12.6	0.0	81.1	46.6	51.6	48.4
59067 RAPELJE	95.3	94.4	0.0	0.0	0.5	0.5	2.6	3.1	6.2	6.7	8.2	6.7	5.6	22.6	27.7	15.4	1.0	74.4	40.9	54.4	45.6
59068 RED LODGE	97.2	97.1	0.3	0.3	0.4	0.4	1.4	1.5	4.7	5.0	6.5	5.8	5.3	24.7	29.9	14.9	3.1	79.8	43.7	49.7	50.3
59069 REED POINT	95.8	95.4	0.0	0.0	0.2	0.2	2.4	2.8	5.4	6.3	7.8	6.5	4.8	21.9	33.2	13.0	1.1	76.1	43.2	52.9	47.1
59070 ROBERTS	98.1	98.1	0.0	0.0	0.2	0.2	0.7	0.8	4.3	5.6	8.2	7.0	2.4	24.3	32.3	13.8	2.2	77.1	44.1	52.3	47.7
59071 ROSCOE	98.3	97.4	0.0	0.0	0.0	0.0	0.9	0.0	4.3	6.0	7.7	6.8	2.6	24.8	31.6	14.5	1.7	76.9	44.0	53.0	47.0
59072 ROUNDUP	96.9	96.9	0.1	0.1	0.2	0.2	1.7	1.7	5.0	5.8	6.3	7.0	4.7	21.3	32.8	14.5	2.8	78.2	45.0	49.0	51.0
59074 RYEGATE	99.2	99.1	0.0	0.0	0.2	0.2	1.3	1.3	5.3	5.8	8.5	6.3	5.5	21.0	30.9	15.4	1.4	76.0	43.4	51.6	48.4
59075 SAINT XAVIER	48.7	47.9	0.0	0.0	0.0	0.0	9.5	9.6	9.0	9.0	8.5	7.5	6.4	28.2	22.3	9.0	0.0	68.1	33.3	51.6	48.4
59076 SANDERS	96.7	96.6	0.0	0.0	0.0	0.0	1.7	1.7	5.1	5.9	6.8	7.6	5.1	20.3	32.2	14.4	2.5	77.1	44.4	53.4	46.6
59077 SAND SPRINGS	98.7	98.7	0.0	0.0	0.0	0.0	0.0	0.0	5.4	6.8	6.8	5.4	5.4	23.0	28.4	14.9	4.1	75.7	43.0	50.0	50.0
59078 SHAWMUT	96.2	96.2	0.3	0.4	0.7	0.7	0.3	0.0	8.0	7.7	8.0	5.2	5.2	25.5	26.2	12.6	1.4	72.4	38.3	51.8	48.3
59079 SHEPHERD	96.2	95.9	0.1	0.2	0.1	0.1	1.9	2.2	7.0	7.2	8.9	7.8	6.8	27.3	27.6	6.9	0.5	72.0	36.1	51.7	48.3
59085 TWO DOT	97.3	97.3	0.1	0.1	0.2	0.3	1.4	1.4	5.6	5.9	7.7	6.6	5.1	20.2	28.2	17.0	3.6	76.3	44.0	48.9	51.1
59086 WILSALL	97.5	97.4	0.0	0.0	0.2	0.2	1.7	1.7	5.2	5.8	6.9	6.1	5.2	22.4	34.7	12.4	1.3	78.0	44.0	51.1	48.9
59087 WINNETT	99.2	99.2	0.0	0.0	0.0	0.0	1.2	1.2	6.9	7.5	6.9	5.3	4.9	22.7	28.7	16.2	0.8	75.3	41.9	52.8	47.2
59088 WORDEN	96.6	96.4	0.3	0.3	0.0	0.1	3.5	4.0	5.8	6.2	7.3	6.7	6.5	24.1	29.5	12.3	1.6	76.3	41.4	51.1	48.9
59089 WYOLA	28.6	27.9	0.0	0.0	0.2	0.2	2.5	2.4	9.0	9.0	8.3	7.2	7.5	27.2	23.3	7.7	0.9	69.1	31.7	52.4	47.6
59101 BILLINGS	87.0	86.1	0.8	0.9	0.5	0.6	7.0	7.6	7.5	6.9	7.0	6.5	7.8	31.0	23.6	8.4	1.3	74.7	34.1	50.0	50.1
59102 BILLINGS	94.9	94.5	0.4	0.4	0.6	0.7	2.3	2.6	5.9	5.8	6.3	6.6	6.6	25.1	24.3	16.1	3.4	78.4	40.5	46.7	53.4
59105 BILLINGS	94.0	93.4	0.4	0.4	0.7	0.8	2.7	3.0	7.0	7.1	7.7	7.4	6.8	27.1	27.5	8.5	0.9	73.5	36.0	49.6	50.5
59106 BILLINGS	96.3	95.8	0.2	0.2	0.9	1.1	1.9	2.1	5.7	7.3	9.9	8.5	4.3	23.2	32.3	8.1	0.6	71.0	40.6	51.1	49.0
59201 WOLF POINT	48.4	46.2	0.0	0.0	0.7	0.9	1.6	1.5	8.6	7.4	9.2	8.5	7.4	22.2	23.8	10.8	2.2	69.0	34.6	49.4	50.7
59211 ANTELOPE	97.6	96.8	0.0	0.0	0.0	0.0	1.2	1.3	5.2	5.8	5.8	5.2	5.2	21.4	31.2	18.2	2.0	79.2	45.7	51.3	48.7
59212 BAINVILLE	92.6	91.8	0.0	0.0	0.0	0.0	0.6	1.0	5.4	4.4	6.4	10.5	2.2	20.3	32.4	15.6	2.9	75.9	45.5	53.3	46.7
59213 BROCKTON	20.2	18.9	0.0	0.0	0.4	0.4	0.7	0.8	8.0	9.8	11.0	10.1	6.6	22.4	25.4	6.4	0.4	64.1	29.3	49.6	50.4
59214 BROCKWAY	98.8	98.7	0.0	0.0	0.0	0.0	0.6	0.6	3.9	5.1	7.1	7.7	5.1	25.6	27.6	17.3	0.6	79.5	43.1	50.0	50.0
59215 CIRCLE	97.5	97.4	0.5	0.5	0.0	0.0	0.9	0.9	5.5	5.9	7.1	6.8	5.3	22.2	27.9	17.1	2.1	77.1	43.2	48.6	51.4
59218 CULBERTSON	90.1	89.4	0.2	0.2	0.2	0.2	1.2	1.1	4.2	4.6	7.5	6.9	6.3	19.4	29.1	18.2	3.9	79.2	45.6	49.9	50.1
59219 DAGMAR	96.0	96.2	0.0	0.0	0.0	0.0	0.5	0.5	4.7	5.2	6.1	7.6	3.8	18.4	32.6	18.4	3.3	78.8	47.1	53.3	46.7
59221 FAIRVIEW	97.4	97.3	0.2	0.2	0.0	0.0	1.9	2.0	5.9	6.2	7.9	6.5	5.8	21.6	29.3	14.6	2.4	75.9	42.3	51.0	49.0
59222 FLAXVILLE	96.2	96.0	0.0	0.0	0.4	0.4	0.4	0.8	4.8	6.8	6.4	5.2	4.8	21.0	30.6	19.1	1.6	79.4	45.8	52.4	47.6
59223 FORT PECK	97.8	97.6	0.0	0.0	0.0	0.0	0.0	0.0	4.1	5.0	6.1	6.5	3.2	20.9	36.9	16.0	1.4	79.9	47.5	51.9	48.1
59225 FRAZER	34.8	32.4	0.1	0.1	0.0	0.0	0.3	0.3	9.3	8.8	10.0	9.4	7.7	26.3	20.5	7.5	0.6	66.0	28.9	51.1	48.9
59226 FROID	92.6	92.1	0.0	0.0	0.0	0.0	1.0	1.0	4.5	4.7	6.4	8.2	4.0	18.6	30.5	19.3	4.0	78.0	47.0	52.2	47.8
59230 GLASGOW	93.7	92.9	0.2	0.2	0.4	0.5	1.0	1.0	5.4	5.4	6.8	6.6	5.6	21.5	27.9	17.6	3.3	78.1	44.2	48.5	51.5
59241 HINSDALE	97.5	97.2	0.0	0.0	0.0	0.0	1.1	1.1	4.9	5.7	7.3	5.9	4.2	22.2	28.8	19.1	2.0	78.5	44.9	52.3	47.7
59242 HOMESTEAD	94.8	94.6	0.0	0.0	0.0	0.0	0.0	0.0	5.4	5.4	5.4	8.9	3.6	17.9	30.4	19.6	3.6	75.0	46.7	51.8	48.2
59243 LAMBERT	99.2	99.2	0.0	0.0	0.0	0.0	0.7	0.7	6.1	7.0	9.2	7.3	5.4	26.7	25.3	11.4	1.5	73.1	38.3	54.6	45.4
59244 LARSLAN	93.4	92.8	0.0	0.0	0.0	0.0	0.0	0.0	5.6	5.6	7.2	5.6	3.2	22.4	29.6	17.6	3.2	76.8	45.2	52.0	48.0
59247 MEDICINE LAKE	94.2	93.6	0.2	0.3	0.5	0.5	0.2	0.3	5.0	5.5	5.9	9.2	3.2	19.8	33.9	14.9	2.7	77.5	45.7	52.7	47.3
59248 NASHUA	67.0	65.2	0.0	0.0	0.0	0.0	0.5	0.5	7.1	7.1	9.5	9.1	6.7	25.2	25.7	8.6	1.0	69.5	34.6	50.0	50.0
59250 OPHEIM	97.6	97.4	0.0	0.0	0.0	0.0	0.8	1.3	4.7	5.6	7.3	5.6	4.3	21.4	30.3	19.2	1.7	79.1	45.8	52.6	47.4
59252 OUTLOOK	97.3	96.6	0.0	0.0	0.0	0.6	1.1	1.7	5.1	5.7	5.7	5.7	4.6	20.6	32.0	18.3	2.3	79.4	46.3	50.3	49.7
59253 PEERLESS	96.9	96.8	0.0	0.0	0.3	0.3	0.6	0.6	5.1	5.7	7.0	6.0	3.8	21.9	31.8	16.5	2.2	78.4	45.3	53.0	47.0
59254 PLENTYWOOD	97.3	96.9	0.1	0.1	0.4	0.5	1.1	1.3	4.3	4.5	6.1	6.9	5.6	19.4	28.2	20.1	5.0	80.0	46.8	48.5	51.5
59255 POPLAR	16.9	15.7	0.0	0.0	0.3	0.4	1.0	0.9	9.6	9.5	11.8	10.2	7.5	26.1	19.0	5.8	0.7	62.6	26.3	49.4	50.6
59256 RAYMOND	100.0	100.0	0.0	0.0	0.0	0.0	0.0	0.0	0.0	0.0	0.0	0.0	25.0	75.0	0.0	0.0	0.0	100.0	30.0	50.0	50.0
59257 REDSTONE	96.8	96.5	0.0	0.0	0.0	0.0	1.6	1.7	6.1	7.0	6.1	6.1	5.2	22.6	27.0	18.3	1.7	75.7	43.1	49.6	50.4
59258 RESERVE	98.4	98.5	0.0	0.0	0.0	0.0	4.1	4.6	4.6	5.3	3.8	8.4	2.3	17.6	38.2	19.9	0.0	78.6	47.4	51.9	48.1
59259 RICHEY	99.5	99.5	0.0	0.0	0.0	0.0	0.8	0.8	4.5	5.6	6.9	5.6	5.1	19.7	31.7	18.4	2.7	79.8	46.6	48.7	51.3
59260 RICHLAND	97.6	97.5	0.0	0.0	0.0	0.0	1.6	0.9	5.1	5.9	7.6	5.9	4.2	22.9	28.8	17.8	1.7	76.3	43.8	51.7	48.3
MONTANA	90.6	90.2	0.3	0.3	0.6	0.7	2.0	2.2	6.1	6.2	7.1	7.5	7.2	25.5	27.0	11.7	1.9	76.2	38.5	49.9	50.1
UNITED STATES	75.1	73.6	12.3	12.5	3.8	4.2	12.5	14.1	6.9	6.7	7.2	7.0	7.3	28.6	23.8	10.8	1.7	75.1	36.0	49.1	50.9

INCOME

#	POST OFFICE NAME	2004 Per Capita Income	2004 HH Income Base	2004 Household Income Distribution (%): Less than $25,000	$25,000 to $49,999	$50,000 to $99,999	$100,000 to $149,999	$150,000 or More	Median Household Income: 2004	2009	2004 National Centile	2004 State Centile	2004 Home Value Base	2004 Home Value Distribution (%): Less than $50,000	$50,000 to $89,999	$90,000 to $174,999	$175,000 to $399,999	$400,000 or More	2004 Median Home Value
59001	ABSAROKEE	23748	689	24.7	29.3	36.1	7.8	2.0	46868	52096	66	95	532	11.1	15.0	38.4	28.4	7.1	143015
59002	ACTON	28047	33	15.2	30.3	36.4	9.1	9.1	54545	62398	79	99	30	10.0	10.0	40.0	33.3	6.7	150000
59003	ASHLAND	15942	152	37.5	32.2	25.7	3.3	1.3	33769	36265	23	58	95	26.3	30.5	27.4	9.5	6.3	80714
59006	BALLANTINE	18818	345	32.2	28.4	31.0	7.0	1.5	40124	42089	47	86	281	15.0	22.4	40.6	17.4	4.6	110671
59007	BEARCREEK	18138	181	38.1	30.4	28.7	2.8	0.0	34345	37570	25	62	144	11.1	9.0	34.7	32.6	12.5	160417
59008	BELFRY	19402	21	19.1	33.3	42.9	4.8	0.0	47375	51350	67	96	17	0.0	0.0	17.7	58.8	23.5	243750
59010	BIGHORN	14151	57	40.4	40.4	15.8	3.5	0.0	30775	32294	14	34	43	41.9	25.6	23.3	7.0	2.3	58750
59011	BIG TIMBER	20184	1271	34.5	35.3	23.0	4.6	2.8	35444	38930	29	69	967	11.9	12.6	43.0	23.0	9.5	129849
59012	BIRNEY	19003	45	35.6	33.3	26.7	4.4	0.0	34064	38185	24	60	28	28.6	32.1	28.6	7.1	3.6	76667
59014	BRIDGER	17003	721	38.8	32.3	25.4	2.8	0.7	31658	34583	17	43	538	16.7	22.3	33.6	21.6	5.8	110507
59015	BROADVIEW	24776	214	22.4	30.8	32.2	8.4	6.1	47167	52269	66	95	189	14.3	10.1	39.7	29.1	6.9	146635
59016	BUSBY	8172	419	40.6	42.2	16.2	1.0	0.0	30528	34432	14	32	226	32.7	42.9	13.3	5.8	5.3	66250
59019	COLUMBUS	19947	1365	26.2	34.1	32.5	5.2	2.1	41993	46797	53	89	1070	12.2	12.2	43.5	26.0	6.1	130372
59022	CROW AGENCY	10067	668	40.6	25.9	29.9	3.6	0.0	32731	36143	20	53	476	43.7	25.4	21.9	2.3	6.7	63913
59024	CUSTER	17673	152	36.8	32.2	24.3	5.9	0.7	34522	36884	26	64	121	15.7	19.0	25.6	26.5	13.2	143056
59025	DECKER	12821	63	60.3	27.0	12.7	0.0	0.0	22634	25171	3	3	38	15.8	63.2	15.8	5.3	0.0	62222
59027	EMIGRANT	20722	196	32.1	37.2	20.9	6.6	3.1	36975	40476	35	77	146	13.7	8.2	24.0	40.4	13.7	190000
59028	FISHTAIL	24846	198	25.8	25.8	38.9	7.1	2.5	48223	50438	69	96	152	4.6	11.2	32.2	37.5	14.5	180357
59029	FROMBERG	17792	327	33.9	35.8	24.5	3.7	2.1	34283	37726	25	62	262	17.6	32.8	30.5	12.2	6.9	89524
59030	GARDINER	23256	807	32.1	37.1	25.7	3.8	1.4	35604	39897	30	70	449	16.5	7.8	27.0	40.3	8.5	171181
59031	GARRYOWEN	12093	111	41.4	27.9	27.0	3.6	0.0	29705	32949	12	22	86	43.0	17.4	16.3	7.0	16.3	76667
59032	GRASS RANGE	16361	179	44.7	33.0	16.2	4.5	1.7	28205	30675	9	17	139	35.3	23.7	18.0	13.0	10.1	74375
59033	GREYCLIFF	20440	150	28.0	38.0	24.7	4.0	5.3	38495	42598	41	82	114	14.0	8.8	22.8	29.8	24.6	195833
59034	HARDIN	15420	1661	39.7	34.1	21.4	3.6	1.1	31000	33848	15	36	1134	22.8	31.7	36.2	6.9	2.5	85405
59037	HUNTLEY	21981	605	26.1	27.3	34.7	9.3	2.6	47016	51496	66	95	512	11.3	16.8	52.5	17.4	2.0	116667
59038	HYSHAM	14973	48	39.6	39.6	16.7	4.2	0.0	31445	32248	16	41	36	41.7	25.0	22.2	8.3	2.8	60000
59039	INGOMAR	21566	49	34.7	26.5	30.6	6.1	2.0	38647	42376	42	83	38	23.7	15.8	31.6	15.8	13.2	112500
59041	JOLIET	16786	667	36.6	34.8	24.4	3.5	0.8	33498	36449	22	56	513	11.3	15.6	40.6	25.2	7.4	130048
59043	LAME DEER	8787	798	51.3	26.9	19.3	2.4	0.1	24113	27886	4	4	392	47.5	30.1	18.9	3.6	0.0	53846
59044	LAUREL	21186	3918	32.2	30.4	29.5	5.4	2.5	39785	44400	45	86	3045	9.9	20.1	52.2	15.9	1.9	114901
59046	LAVINA	20420	231	43.7	31.6	19.9	3.0	1.7	30409	32689	13	30	183	24.0	28.4	27.9	13.7	6.0	85500
59047	LIVINGSTON	19423	5321	37.0	34.0	21.7	4.9	2.4	33840	37611	24	58	3664	11.5	14.4	46.6	21.5	6.1	120651
59050	LODGE GRASS	9822	864	45.6	32.9	19.3	1.4	0.8	27243	30061	7	12	567	36.2	24.5	27.5	6.2	5.6	72159
59052	MC LEOD	22814	89	27.0	37.1	25.8	5.6	4.5	39531	42766	44	85	68	13.2	7.4	20.6	35.3	23.5	212500
59053	MARTINSDALE	14315	27	44.4	37.0	14.8	3.7	0.0	28592	36120	10	19	19	26.3	26.3	31.6	10.5	5.3	87500
59055	MELVILLE	18267	31	29.0	38.7	25.8	3.2	3.2	35722	40000	30	71	24	0.0	8.3	33.3	25.0	33.3	225000
59057	MOLT	21994	231	26.0	31.6	29.4	7.4	5.6	43947	48435	58	90	198	19.2	11.6	36.9	25.3	7.1	135417
59058	MOSBY	11100	9	44.4	33.3	22.2	0.0	0.0	27247	27247	7	13	7	0.0	57.1	42.9	0.0	0.0	67500
59059	MUSSELSHELL	19054	174	36.8	37.4	20.1	2.3	3.5	31607	35336	17	43	145	23.5	24.1	31.7	11.7	9.0	101500
59061	NYE	33933	127	25.2	28.4	37.0	6.3	3.2	46158	48488	64	94	98	6.1	10.2	29.6	36.7	17.4	187500
59062	OTTER	18603	174	35.6	35.1	23.0	3.5	2.9	34129	37325	24	61	133	24.8	21.8	30.8	8.3	14.3	96429
59063	PARK CITY	18603	643	25.5	36.6	31.9	4.4	1.7	41382	46001	51	88	533	16.9	13.1	40.7	25.7	3.6	125536
59064	POMPEYS PILLAR	18551	122	36.1	33.6	24.6	4.9	0.8	34426	36589	25	63	96	16.7	19.8	27.1	22.9	13.5	132143
59065	PRAY	28217	46	21.7	37.0	28.3	10.9	2.2	45000	47354	61	91	37	2.7	5.4	27.0	46.0	18.9	243750
59067	RAPELJE	16141	79	43.0	35.4	19.0	1.3	1.3	30304	33025	13	30	60	35.0	16.7	30.0	10.0	8.3	86667
59068	RED LODGE	21863	1609	31.6	33.8	27.7	5.0	2.0	37749	43168	38	80	1104	6.6	9.1	39.0	33.9	11.4	162850
59069	REED POINT	17426	181	35.4	37.0	23.2	2.8	1.7	34107	37146	24	61	141	26.2	13.5	28.4	20.6	11.4	113393
59070	ROBERTS	17249	349	34.1	39.0	22.4	3.7	0.9	33267	35805	22	55	278	18.0	19.1	24.1	28.1	10.8	130682
59071	ROSCOE	18101	51	35.3	37.3	23.5	3.9	0.0	32281	35547	19	47	41	19.5	17.1	22.0	26.8	14.6	137500
59072	ROUNDUP	16564	1677	45.9	32.2	18.2	1.9	1.9	27552	30259	8	16	1260	29.1	28.8	27.5	10.9	3.7	79783
59074	RYEGATE	13525	194	43.3	33.0	18.6	3.1	2.1	30335	33617	13	30	152	27.0	32.2	25.0	8.6	7.2	74000
59075	SAINT XAVIER	11205	57	40.4	22.8	36.8	0.0	0.0	30547	31704	14	32	40	5.0	35.0	42.5	5.0	12.5	110000
59076	SANDERS	14227	46	41.3	37.0	17.4	4.4	0.0	30854	31779	14	35	35	40.0	25.7	22.9	8.6	2.9	61667
59077	SAND SPRINGS	15948	30	40.0	40.0	16.7	3.3	0.0	30000	30000	12	28	22	40.9	18.2	18.2	4.6	18.2	70000
59078	SHAWMUT	9522	72	50.0	34.7	12.5	2.8	0.0	25000	26872	5	6	55	32.7	38.2	20.0	3.6	5.5	64167
59079	SHEPHERD	18295	1117	26.2	29.0	35.2	8.2	1.3	44278	48559	59	91	933	11.4	15.9	47.6	20.9	4.3	130175
59085	TWO DOT	15222	646	45.5	35.3	16.6	2.3	0.3	27416	30077	8	15	474	27.0	38.6	27.9	4.4	2.1	72245
59086	WILSALL	17879	544	34.2	38.2	21.0	4.8	1.8	35503	38052	30	69	424	12.5	11.8	38.4	25.9	11.3	138690
59087	WINNETT	17332	218	48.2	30.3	15.1	2.3	4.1	26180	30190	6	9	167	37.1	30.5	26.4	2.4	3.6	66538
59088	WORDEN	19355	496	37.7	31.1	24.0	4.4	2.8	35000	36715	28	66	395	19.5	12.7	47.6	16.5	3.8	115981
59089	WYOLA	10694	138	50.7	29.7	15.2	4.4	0.0	24595	27281	4	5	108	38.9	20.4	34.3	4.6	1.9	75000
59101	BILLINGS	16695	15410	42.8	31.6	21.0	3.2	1.3	30044	34289	12	28	8523	17.9	25.7	43.6	11.5	1.4	98189
59102	BILLINGS	24149	19736	26.3	31.2	32.0	6.3	4.2	43393	49419	57	90	13639	7.3	9.4	61.9	20.4	1.0	128189
59105	BILLINGS	21128	9206	23.5	31.4	34.3	7.6	3.2	45671	51236	63	93	6774	7.5	11.3	58.9	20.9	1.5	137524
59106	BILLINGS	35751	2881	14.3	23.3	32.6	15.5	14.3	65288	71561	89	100	2596	6.4	5.7	29.2	47.3	11.3	195513
59201	WOLF POINT	13903	1669	43.0	30.0	21.2	4.6	1.2	29399	33430	11	21	1096	30.7	41.7	23.2	2.9	1.6	68175
59211	ANTELOPE	20393	67	31.3	41.8	19.4	6.0	1.5	36189	39053	32	74	54	46.3	16.7	31.5	5.6	0.0	56667
59212	BAINVILLE	18584	137	39.4	36.5	16.8	3.7	3.7	30177	33340	13	29	111	49.6	23.4	18.0	5.4	3.6	50500
59213	BROCKTON	10795	279	53.4	22.2	19.0	3.9	1.4	22932	24504	3	3	213	39.9	32.4	22.5	4.2	0.9	61190
59214	BROCKWAY	17607	68	41.2	35.3	20.6	2.9	0.0	30000	34430	12	28	54	38.9	31.5	20.4	3.7	5.6	61667
59215	CIRCLE	15471	449	39.6	36.8	21.2	1.6	0.9	31186	35136	15	38	331	44.4	36.6	15.1	2.1	1.8	55781
59218	CULBERTSON	15383	336	41.7	33.9	20.8	3.3	0.3	30260	33923	13	29	248	42.7	34.7	21.4	0.8	0.4	56000
59219	DAGMAR	15947	82	35.4	42.7	15.9	6.1	0.0	32919	34523	21	54	66	62.1	16.7	18.2	1.5	1.5	36000
59221	FAIRVIEW	15194	528	40.7	34.7	21.2	2.7	0.8	30000	32769	12	28	388	37.4	33.0	20.9	7.7	1.0	62162
59222	FLAXVILLE	16459	115	45.2	33.9	17.4	2.6	0.9	27529	30727	8	16	92	42.4	31.5	14.1	6.5	5.4	61250
59223	FORT PECK	18886	281	24.2	42.0	31.7	1.8	0.4	40298	44858	47	87	237	5.1	18.1	61.6	13.9	1.3	114844
59225	FRAZER	9893	204	50.5	33.3	12.8	1.5	2.0	24744	28185	4	5	133	54.1	12.0	22.6	6.8	4.5	46944
59226	FROID	20152	186	38.2	32.8	21.0	5.9	2.2	32902	36454	21	54	155	51.6	26.5	18.7	1.3	1.9	48810
59230	GLASGOW	18916	2040	37.3	31.1	25.7	3.6	2.3	34479	38236	26	64	1505	28.4	36.3	31.0	4.4	0.0	74384
59241	HINSDALE	19183	259	39.8	30.9	22.4	3.5	3.5	31678	33961	17	44	205	37.6	29.3	21.0	7.8	4.4	64167
59242	HOMESTEAD	16250	25	40.0	40.0	16.0	4.0	0.0	31106	28586	15	37	20	60.0	15.0	25.0	0.0	0.0	37500
59243	LAMBERT	15861	220	40.9	34.6	19.1	2.3	3.2	30000	32161	12	28	174	36.2	18.4	35.6	6.3	3.5	74167
59244	LARSLAN	16840	50	44.0	34.0	10.0	8.0	4.0	26862	30340	7	10	38	50.0	2.6	31.6	5.3	10.5	50000
59247	MEDICINE LAKE	17336	175	39.4	38.3	15.4	5.7	1.1	31968	35000	18	45	138	63.0	14.5	18.1	2.9	1.5	35000
59248	NASHUA	17546	80	41.3	37.5	13.8	2.5	5.0	30000	34057	12	28	58	41.4	19.0	27.6	5.2	6.9	67500
59250	OPHEIM	20867	110	39.1	30.9	21.8	3.6	4.6	32336	33944	19	50	87	35.6	32.2	19.5	6.9	5.8	64375
59252	OUTLOOK	17350	76	35.5	39.5	19.7	5.3	0.0	35000	39062	28	66	61	42.6	21.3	31.2	4.9	0.0	61250
59253	PEERLESS	16762	135	40.7	34.8	21.5	2.2	0.7	30656	33605	14	33	108	41.7	32.4	14.8	6.5	4.6	61000
59254	PLENTYWOOD	17011	969	40.6	34.4	19.8	4.2	1.0	30423	33906	13	31	741	33.6	34.8	28.7	2.3	0.5	67891
59255	POPLAR	9506	1037	55.1	28.3	13.2	2.9	0.6	22092	25198	3	3	575	41.0	31.0	24.2	2.8	1.0	61122
59256	RAYMOND	14063	5	100.0	0.0	0.0	0.0	0.0	22500	22500	3	3	0	0.0	0.0	0.0	0.0	0.0	0
59257	REDSTONE	19043	53	32.1	43.4	18.9	5.7	0.0	36153	40293	32	74	43	41.9	14.0	39.5	4.7	0.0	65000
59258	RESERVE	16475	56	37.5	44.6	12.5	3.6	1.8	30708	32294	14	34	51	41.2	9.8	41.2	7.8	0.0	87500
59259	RICHEY	16792	167	44.3	34.1	16.2	3.0	2.4	30122	32312	13	29	132	68.9	11.4	17.4	2.3	0.0	31250
59260	RICHLAND	19601	52	40.4	30.8	23.1	3.9	1.9	31519	33600	16	42	41	41.5	24.4	19.5	9.8	4.9	62500
	MONTANA	19326		33.9	32.7	25.9	5.0	2.5	36188	40555				14.7	16.4	40.8	23.3	4.9	122379
	UNITED STATES	25866		24.7	27.1	30.8	10.9	6.5	48124	56710				10.9	15.0	33.7	30.1	10.4	145905

ZIP CODE		FINANCIAL SERVICES				THE HOME						ENTERTAINMENT						PERSONAL			
						Home Improvements		Furnishings													
#	POST OFFICE NAME	Auto Loan	Home Loan	Invest-ments	Retire-ment Plans	Home Repair	Lawn & Garden	Comput-ers & Hard-ware	Major Appli-ances	TV, Radio, Sound Equip-ment	Furni-ture	Dine out/ Carry out	Sports Equip-ment	Fees & Tickets	Toys & Games	Travel	Cable TV	Apparel & Services	Auto Repairs	Health Insur-ance	Pets & Supplies
59001	ABSAROKEE	101	72	40	68	84	94	71	87	81	70	95	104	61	94	74	85	87	86	103	121
59002	ACTON	90	113	120	113	111	109	100	100	93	100	117	117	107	125	103	90	117	96	90	111
59003	ASHLAND	64	58	46	56	58	62	56	60	56	57	70	69	53	66	55	56	67	60	59	71
59006	BALLANTINE	84	68	46	65	74	81	64	74	70	64	84	89	60	85	66	73	79	73	83	99
59007	BEARCREEK	72	50	26	47	59	66	50	61	57	49	67	74	42	66	51	60	61	61	73	85
59008	BELFRY	87	67	44	61	76	85	64	77	72	63	86	91	56	84	68	77	79	76	91	106
59010	BIGHORN	66	46	24	44	54	60	46	56	52	45	62	68	39	60	47	55	56	56	67	78
59011	BIG TIMBER	81	60	37	57	67	76	61	71	69	60	82	83	55	79	62	72	75	71	83	93
59012	BIRNEY	64	59	46	57	59	62	56	60	57	58	70	69	53	66	55	56	67	60	60	71
59014	BRIDGER	69	50	30	48	57	65	52	61	59	51	70	71	46	67	53	63	64	61	73	79
59015	BROADVIEW	91	101	100	101	102	103	92	95	88	91	110	112	95	115	94	87	108	92	90	110
59016	BUSBY	43	39	47	37	38	44	42	41	46	44	57	46	44	57	42	47	56	42	43	47
59019	COLUMBUS	83	66	45	64	72	80	66	75	72	66	86	88	60	84	67	73	80	74	83	95
59022	CROW AGENCY	56	59	57	60	58	58	56	57	54	57	68	67	56	68	56	51	66	57	52	64
59024	CUSTER	77	54	28	51	63	71	53	66	62	53	72	80	46	71	55	65	66	65	79	92
59025	DECKER	52	36	19	34	42	47	36	44	41	35	48	53	30	47	37	43	44	43	52	61
59027	EMIGRANT	90	65	38	61	75	84	63	78	72	63	85	93	55	84	66	77	78	76	92	107
59028	FISHTAIL	108	84	58	76	95	107	80	96	90	79	107	112	71	105	85	96	99	95	113	131
59029	FROMBERG	82	57	30	54	67	75	57	70	65	56	77	84	48	75	59	69	70	69	83	98
59030	GARDINER	68	62	58	60	66	71	63	67	65	61	80	79	60	80	64	66	76	67	70	81
59031	GARRYOWEN	60	56	46	54	57	61	53	57	54	53	66	67	52	67	53	54	64	56	58	69
59032	GRASS RANGE	71	50	26	47	58	65	49	61	56	48	66	73	42	65	51	59	60	60	72	84
59033	GREYCLIFF	105	73	38	69	85	95	72	89	83	71	97	107	62	95	75	87	89	88	106	124
59034	HARDIN	59	50	43	50	53	60	54	57	57	52	69	67	50	68	54	58	65	57	62	68
59037	HUNTLEY	88	85	71	82	88	92	78	85	80	78	98	100	77	101	80	81	94	82	88	105
59038	HYSHAM	66	46	24	44	54	60	46	56	52	45	62	68	39	60	47	55	56	56	67	78
59039	INGOMAR	87	61	32	58	71	80	60	75	69	60	81	90	51	80	63	73	74	73	89	104
59041	JOLIET	70	50	29	48	57	66	52	61	59	51	70	72	45	67	53	63	64	61	73	80
59043	LAME DEER	43	40	47	38	38	44	44	42	47	44	58	48	44	58	43	48	57	44	44	48
59044	LAUREL	79	76	67	74	78	84	74	78	75	73	93	90	73	93	75	76	89	77	81	92
59046	LAVINA	79	55	28	50	63	71	54	67	63	53	73	80	46	71	55	66	67	66	80	93
59047	LIVINGSTON	67	58	50	57	62	68	59	64	62	58	76	75	56	75	60	64	72	64	69	78
59050	LODGE GRASS	56	43	31	41	47	53	44	50	49	43	59	59	40	58	45	51	55	50	58	65
59052	MC LEOD	107	75	40	71	87	98	74	91	85	73	100	110	63	98	77	89	91	90	109	127
59053	MARTINSDALE	56	44	30	39	49	55	41	50	47	41	55	58	37	55	44	50	51	49	59	68
59055	MELVILLE	80	56	29	53	65	73	55	68	64	54	75	82	47	73	57	67	68	67	81	95
59057	MOLT	89	90	81	88	93	96	83	89	82	82	101	105	82	105	85	82	98	86	89	107
59058	MOSBY	56	39	20	37	45	51	38	48	44	38	52	57	33	51	40	47	47	47	57	66
59059	MUSSELSHELL	84	59	31	56	69	77	58	72	67	57	79	87	50	77	60	70	72	71	86	100
59061	NYE	106	83	57	75	93	105	78	94	88	77	105	110	70	104	83	95	97	93	111	129
59062	OTTER	79	55	29	52	64	72	54	67	63	54	74	81	46	72	56	66	67	66	80	94
59063	PARK CITY	88	61	32	58	71	80	60	75	70	60	82	90	52	80	63	73	75	74	89	104
59064	POMPEYS PILLAR	78	54	28	51	63	71	54	66	62	53	73	80	46	71	56	65	66	65	79	92
59065	PRAY	99	78	53	70	87	98	73	88	83	72	98	103	65	97	78	88	91	87	104	120
59067	RAPELJE	72	50	26	48	59	66	50	61	57	49	67	74	42	66	52	60	61	61	73	86
59068	RED LODGE	75	60	46	58	65	75	63	70	69	61	82	80	58	80	64	72	77	70	79	86
59069	REED POINT	80	56	29	53	65	73	55	68	64	55	75	83	47	73	57	67	68	68	82	95
59070	ROBERTS	75	52	27	49	61	68	51	64	59	51	69	77	44	68	53	62	63	63	76	88
59071	ROSCOE	75	52	28	50	61	68	52	64	60	51	70	77	44	69	54	63	64	63	76	89
59072	ROUNDUP	66	48	28	45	54	62	50	58	57	49	67	67	44	64	50	60	61	58	70	75
59074	RYEGATE	71	50	26	47	58	65	49	61	57	48	66	73	42	65	51	59	60	60	72	85
59075	SAINT XAVIER	63	49	33	44	55	62	46	56	52	46	62	65	41	61	49	56	57	55	66	76
59076	SANDERS	66	46	24	44	54	60	46	56	52	45	62	68	39	60	47	55	56	56	67	78
59077	SAND SPRINGS	70	49	26	46	57	64	49	60	56	48	66	72	41	64	50	59	60	59	72	84
59078	SHAWMUT	58	40	21	38	47	52	40	49	46	39	54	59	34	53	41	48	49	48	58	68
59079	SHEPHERD	76	78	72	78	77	78	74	76	72	74	89	90	73	90	73	69	87	75	71	88
59085	TWO DOT	58	42	25	40	48	55	44	51	50	43	59	60	38	56	45	53	53	51	61	67
59086	WILSALL	78	55	29	52	63	71	54	66	62	53	73	80	46	71	56	65	66	65	79	92
59087	WINNETT	73	51	27	48	59	66	50	62	58	50	68	75	43	66	52	61	62	61	74	86
59088	WORDEN	85	61	34	58	70	78	60	73	68	59	80	88	52	79	62	71	74	72	86	101
59089	WYOLA	62	43	23	41	50	57	43	53	50	42	58	64	37	57	45	52	53	52	63	73
59101	BILLINGS	55	52	53	52	52	56	55	55	56	54	69	65	54	68	54	55	67	56	54	62
59102	BILLINGS	74	79	88	79	78	83	79	78	77	78	97	90	80	97	79	76	95	78	75	86
59105	BILLINGS	78	85	85	85	83	84	81	81	77	81	97	95	82	99	80	75	95	80	75	90
59106	BILLINGS	138	165	171	166	162	163	147	147	137	147	173	172	157	181	150	134	172	142	135	166
59201	WOLF POINT	59	49	41	48	52	59	53	56	57	51	68	66	49	67	52	58	64	57	62	68
59211	ANTELOPE	85	59	31	56	69	77	58	72	67	58	79	87	50	77	61	71	72	71	86	101
59212	BAINVILLE	77	54	28	51	63	70	53	66	61	53	72	79	46	71	55	64	66	65	79	92
59213	BROCKTON	51	49	50	50	50	54	49	51	49	49	61	61	48	59	49	49	58	51	52	59
59214	BROCKWAY	73	51	27	48	59	67	50	62	58	50	68	75	43	67	52	61	62	61	74	87
59215	CIRCLE	62	45	28	43	50	59	48	55	55	46	64	63	43	61	48	58	58	55	66	70
59218	CULBERTSON	61	45	30	44	50	60	50	55	56	47	66	62	44	62	50	59	60	55	66	68
59219	DAGMAR	75	52	27	49	61	68	51	64	59	51	70	77	44	68	53	62	63	63	76	89
59221	FAIRVIEW	63	45	27	43	51	59	48	55	54	46	64	64	42	61	48	57	58	55	66	72
59222	FLAXVILLE	63	47	28	45	54	59	46	55	51	45	61	66	40	60	47	54	56	54	64	75
59223	FORT PECK	75	59	40	53	67	75	56	67	63	55	75	79	50	74	59	67	69	66	79	92
59225	FRAZER	50	42	39	40	43	49	47	48	50	45	61	56	44	60	46	51	58	49	52	56
59226	FROID	71	53	33	50	59	69	56	64	64	54	75	73	50	71	56	67	68	64	77	81
59230	GLASGOW	71	54	35	52	59	69	57	64	64	55	76	73	51	72	57	67	69	64	76	80
59241	HINSDALE	82	57	30	54	67	75	57	70	65	56	77	85	48	75	59	69	70	69	84	98
59242	HOMESTEAD	66	46	24	43	54	60	45	56	52	45	61	68	39	60	47	55	56	55	67	78
59243	LAMBERT	77	54	28	51	62	70	53	65	61	52	71	79	45	70	55	64	65	64	78	91
59244	LARSLAN	75	53	28	50	61	69	52	64	60	51	70	78	44	69	54	63	64	63	77	90
59247	MEDICINE LAKE	72	51	26	48	59	66	50	62	58	49	67	74	43	66	52	60	62	61	74	86
59248	NASHUA	76	57	40	54	63	71	60	68	66	58	79	81	53	78	60	69	74	68	77	88
59250	OPHEIM	80	56	29	53	65	73	55	68	64	55	75	83	47	73	57	67	68	68	82	95
59252	OUTLOOK	72	50	26	48	59	66	50	62	57	49	67	74	42	66	52	60	61	61	73	86
59253	PEERLESS	69	51	30	48	58	64	50	60	56	49	66	72	44	65	51	58	61	59	70	81
59254	PLENTYWOOD	67	48	28	46	54	63	50	59	57	49	67	68	44	65	51	60	61	58	70	77
59255	POPLAR	45	36	40	34	36	43	42	42	46	42	57	49	40	55	41	48	54	44	46	50
59256	RAYMOND	41	28	15	27	33	37	28	35	32	28	38	42	24	37	29	34	35	34	41	48
59257	REDSTONE	75	52	27	49	61	68	52	64	59	51	70	77	44	68	53	62	64	63	76	89
59258	RESERVE	69	49	27	47	57	63	48	59	55	48	65	71	42	64	50	58	59	58	70	82
59259	RICHEY	68	48	25	45	56	62	47	58	54	47	64	70	40	62	49	57	58	58	69	81
59260	RICHLAND	81	56	29	53	65	73	56	69	64	55	75	83	47	74	58	67	68	68	82	96
	MONTANA	72	64	57	63	66	72	65	69	68	64	83	81	62	81	65	68	79	69	72	83
	UNITED STATES	100	100	100	100	100	100	100	100	100	100	100	100	100	100	100	100	100	100	100	100

#	POST OFFICE NAME	COUNTY FIPS CODE	POPULATION 2000	2004	2009	2000-2004 ANNUAL RATE % Rate	State Centile	HOUSEHOLDS 2000	2004	2009	% Annual Rate 2000-2004	2004 Average HH Size	FAMILIES 2000	2004	% Annual Rate 2000-2004
59261	SACO	071	195	188	180	-0.9	15	70	68	67	-0.7	2.74	47	45	-1.0
59262	SAVAGE	083	1043	990	936	-1.2	7	396	384	371	-0.7	2.58	290	278	-1.0
59263	SCOBEY	019	1305	1270	1230	-0.6	22	587	582	574	-0.2	2.12	350	341	-0.6
59270	SIDNEY	083	6581	6308	6006	-1.0	13	2666	2605	2530	-0.5	2.38	1798	1728	-0.9
59274	VIDA	055	513	495	475	-0.8	16	205	201	197	-0.5	2.46	159	154	-0.8
59275	WESTBY	091	382	361	342	-1.3	4	178	172	166	-0.8	2.10	123	116	-1.4
59276	WHITETAIL	019	132	127	122	-0.9	14	58	57	56	-0.4	2.23	40	39	-0.6
59301	MILES CITY	017	10565	10284	9989	-0.6	23	4347	4267	4179	-0.4	2.31	2774	2677	-0.8
59311	ALZADA	011	90	85	79	-1.3	4	34	32	31	-1.4	2.66	26	24	-1.9
59312	ANGELA	087	42	42	42	0.0	57	20	20	20	0.0	2.10	15	15	0.0
59313	BAKER	025	2399	2337	2271	-0.6	25	962	953	942	-0.2	2.40	667	652	-0.5
59314	BIDDLE	075	464	458	457	-0.3	40	177	177	179	0.0	2.59	138	137	-0.2
59315	BLOOMFIELD	021	220	214	206	-0.7	22	81	80	78	-0.3	2.65	61	60	-0.4
59316	BOYES	011	85	80	75	-1.4	3	29	28	26	-0.8	2.86	22	21	-1.1
59317	BROADUS	075	862	853	853	-0.3	43	341	339	342	-0.1	2.42	228	223	-0.5
59318	BRUSETT	033	182	178	174	-0.5	29	79	80	80	0.3	2.23	55	55	0.0
59322	COHAGEN	033	279	270	263	-0.8	19	109	109	109	0.0	2.44	74	73	-0.3
59324	EKALAKA	011	876	836	788	-1.1	10	358	343	325	-1.0	2.39	242	228	-1.4
59326	FALLON	079	289	276	265	-1.1	10	126	123	120	-0.6	2.24	94	91	-0.8
59327	FORSYTH	087	3158	3115	3104	-0.3	39	1341	1345	1350	0.1	2.27	877	865	-0.3
59330	GLENDIVE	021	8362	7991	7639	-1.1	11	3336	3236	3140	-0.7	2.32	2262	2159	-1.1
59332	HAMMOND	011	262	247	231	-1.4	3	100	95	90	-1.2	2.60	76	72	-1.3
59336	ISMAY	017	347	339	330	-0.6	27	124	123	121	-0.2	2.76	101	99	-0.5
59337	JORDAN	033	726	707	690	-0.6	24	309	310	311	0.1	2.26	213	210	-0.3
59338	KINSEY	017	378	370	359	-0.5	29	135	134	131	-0.2	2.76	111	109	-0.4
59339	LINDSAY	021	92	88	84	-1.0	12	41	40	39	-0.6	2.17	32	31	-0.7
59341	MILDRED	079	76	73	70	-0.9	14	28	27	27	-0.9	2.70	21	20	-1.1
59343	OLIVE	075	52	53	53	0.5	74	20	20	21	0.0	2.65	14	15	1.6
59344	PLEVNA	025	377	365	354	-0.8	19	155	153	151	-0.3	2.39	119	117	-0.4
59345	POWDERVILLE	075	18	18	18	0.0	57	9	9	9	0.0	2.00	7	7	0.0
59347	ROSEBUD	087	3128	3084	3072	-0.3	38	1117	1121	1126	0.1	2.75	891	884	-0.2
59349	TERRY	079	834	805	775	-0.8	17	383	377	370	-0.4	2.07	240	232	-0.8
59351	VOLBORG	017	483	472	460	-0.5	28	189	187	184	-0.3	2.52	126	122	-0.8
59353	WIBAUX	109	1068	1058	1058	-0.2	44	421	421	421	0.0	2.43	287	283	-0.3
59354	WILLARD	025	42	41	39	-0.6	26	16	16	16	0.0	2.56	12	12	0.0
59401	GREAT FALLS	013	14682	14011	13529	-1.1	10	6571	6330	6173	-0.9	2.17	3539	3329	-1.4
59402	MALMSTROM A F B	013	2128	2025	1957	-1.2	8	679	653	636	-0.9	2.81	597	570	-1.1
59404	GREAT FALLS	013	24820	24728	24382	-0.1	48	9523	9617	9603	0.2	2.55	7069	7044	-0.1
59405	GREAT FALLS	013	29238	28729	28139	-0.4	34	12032	11963	11847	-0.1	2.31	7531	7322	-0.7
59410	AUGUSTA	049	898	880	874	-0.5	30	359	356	357	-0.2	2.34	236	229	-0.7
59411	BABB	035	538	588	613	2.1	96	178	194	202	2.1	3.03	136	146	1.7
59412	BELT	013	1649	1654	1633	0.1	59	656	662	659	0.2	2.50	455	451	-0.2
59414	BLACK EAGLE	013	924	885	855	-1.0	13	422	411	403	-0.6	2.15	283	271	-1.0
59416	BRADY	073	322	307	295	-1.1	9	131	126	121	-0.9	2.44	100	95	-1.2
59417	BROWNING	035	7832	7831	7817	0.0	57	2286	2301	2309	0.2	3.34	1839	1833	-0.1
59418	BUFFALO	027	87	86	84	-0.3	42	32	32	32	0.0	2.53	25	24	-1.0
59419	BYNUM	099	139	143	146	0.7	82	46	47	48	0.5	3.02	36	37	0.7
59420	CARTER	015	322	301	285	-1.6	2	138	130	124	-1.4	2.32	101	94	-1.7
59421	CASCADE	013	2569	2530	2475	-0.4	37	1034	1030	1019	-0.1	2.40	755	741	-0.4
59422	CHOTEAU	099	3013	3052	3092	0.3	70	1201	1219	1240	0.4	2.45	778	777	0.0
59424	COFFEE CREEK	027	130	128	126	-0.4	37	54	54	54	0.0	2.22	40	40	0.0
59425	CONRAD	073	3555	3436	3311	-0.8	19	1450	1410	1367	-0.7	2.39	987	945	-1.0
59427	CUT BANK	035	4937	4877	4845	-0.3	40	1850	1828	1816	-0.3	2.64	1288	1254	-0.6
59430	DENTON	027	567	557	548	-0.4	32	230	230	230	0.0	2.27	171	169	-0.3
59433	DUTTON	099	736	731	736	-0.2	45	302	303	308	0.1	2.41	218	216	-0.2
59434	EAST GLACIER PARK	035	47	48	49	0.5	77	23	24	25	1.0	2.00	14	14	0.0
59436	FAIRFIELD	099	1874	1889	1910	0.2	64	726	739	752	0.4	2.56	526	528	0.1
59440	FLOWEREE	013	116	110	105	-1.2	6	47	45	44	-1.0	2.44	33	31	-1.5
59441	FORESTGROVE	027	88	87	86	-0.3	42	37	37	37	0.0	2.22	27	27	0.0
59442	FORT BENTON	015	2050	1950	1864	-1.2	8	813	779	746	-1.0	2.37	554	521	-1.4
59443	FORT SHAW	013	903	900	884	-0.1	49	344	347	345	0.2	2.59	261	260	-0.1
59444	GALATA	101	68	65	64	-1.1	11	28	27	27	-0.9	2.41	21	20	-1.1
59446	GERALDINE	015	602	592	573	-0.4	35	239	238	231	-0.1	2.49	176	172	-0.5
59447	GEYSER	045	436	440	448	0.2	66	155	156	158	0.2	2.82	115	114	-0.2
59448	HEART BUTTE	073	756	746	725	-0.3	40	184	183	178	-0.1	4.00	157	155	-0.3
59450	HIGHWOOD	015	478	453	431	-1.3	6	172	165	157	-1.0	2.75	131	124	-1.3
59451	HILGER	027	743	730	718	-0.4	34	249	249	249	0.0	2.75	186	183	-0.4
59452	HOBSON	045	702	716	734	0.5	75	289	297	306	0.6	2.41	212	215	0.3
59453	JUDITH GAP	107	300	296	289	-0.3	39	119	119	117	0.0	2.12	88	87	-0.3
59454	KEVIN	101	220	229	233	1.0	87	91	93	94	0.5	2.46	67	68	0.4
59456	LEDGER	073	39	38	36	-0.6	25	12	12	11	0.0	3.17	10	10	0.0
59457	LEWISTOWN	027	8430	8280	8150	-0.4	32	3587	3577	3577	-0.1	2.22	2250	2203	-0.5
59460	LOMA	015	202	192	183	-1.2	8	87	83	80	-1.1	2.23	68	64	-1.4
59462	MOCCASIN	045	174	178	182	0.5	79	66	68	70	0.7	2.62	48	49	0.5
59463	MONARCH	013	109	109	108	0.0	57	51	51	51	0.0	2.14	39	39	0.0
59464	MOORE	027	573	564	556	-0.4	36	197	198	198	0.1	2.70	152	151	-0.2
59465	NEIHART	013	177	177	174	0.0	57	85	86	85	0.3	2.06	65	65	0.0
59466	OILMONT	101	104	102	101	-0.5	30	43	42	41	-0.6	2.43	32	31	-0.7
59467	PENDROY	099	113	115	116	0.4	72	45	46	47	0.5	2.50	35	35	0.0
59468	POWER	099	658	654	654	-0.1	47	247	248	250	0.1	2.64	187	185	-0.3
59469	RAYNESFORD	045	203	206	210	0.4	71	80	81	83	0.3	2.54	59	59	0.0
59471	ROY	027	421	416	411	-0.3	41	128	128	129	0.0	3.05	94	93	-0.3
59472	SAND COULEE	013	567	557	543	-0.4	32	201	199	196	-0.2	2.80	147	143	-0.7
59474	SHELBY	101	3813	3748	3713	-0.4	34	1428	1412	1406	-0.3	2.35	911	885	-0.7
59479	STANFORD	045	859	861	875	0.1	58	378	380	387	0.1	2.27	240	237	-0.3
59480	STOCKETT	013	541	531	518	-0.4	31	201	199	197	-0.2	2.67	148	144	-0.6
59482	SUNBURST	101	815	810	807	-0.1	47	288	284	281	-0.3	2.85	215	209	-0.5
59483	SUN RIVER	013	848	865	860	0.5	75	306	318	320	0.9	2.50	235	241	0.6
59484	SWEET GRASS	101	247	256	261	0.9	85	84	86	87	0.6	2.98	62	63	0.4
59486	VALIER	073	1656	1627	1578	-0.4	34	604	591	572	-0.5	2.75	457	442	-0.8
59487	VAUGHN	013	1028	1053	1047	0.6	81	379	393	396	0.9	2.68	284	291	0.6
59489	WINIFRED	027	331	327	323	-0.3	40	141	141	142	0.0	2.18	103	102	-0.2
59501	HAVRE	041	13074	12431	11808	-1.2	8	5308	5101	4894	-0.9	2.37	3376	3183	-1.4
59520	BIG SANDY	015	2234	2205	2143	-0.4	40	741	723	699	-0.6	2.93	558	540	-0.8
59521	BOX ELDER	041	2066	2001	1912	-0.8	20	531	524	510	-0.3	3.82	451	441	-0.5
	MONTANA					0.4					0.7	2.42			0.3
	UNITED STATES					1.2					1.3	2.58			1.1

#	POST OFFICE NAME	RACE (%) White 2000	White 2004	Black 2000	Black 2004	Asian/Pacific 2000	Asian/Pacific 2004	% Hispanic Origin 2000	% Hispanic Origin 2004	2004 AGE DISTRIBUTION (%) 0-4	5-9	10-14	15-19	20-24	25-44	45-64	65-84	85+	18+	MEDIAN AGE 2004	% 2004 Males	% 2004 Females
59261	SACO	90.8	90.4	0.0	0.5	0.0	0.0	0.5	0.5	6.4	6.9	7.5	7.5	5.3	23.9	27.7	12.8	2.1	73.9	40.6	53.2	46.8
59262	SAVAGE	98.5	98.4	0.0	0.0	0.0	0.0	1.8	2.0	5.2	5.6	9.8	8.7	5.4	21.7	30.8	11.4	1.5	73.1	41.4	52.0	48.0
59263	SCOBEY	95.8	95.8	0.0	0.0	0.3	0.3	2.2	2.2	4.0	4.7	5.6	6.1	5.8	16.8	30.7	21.3	5.0	81.6	49.6	47.4	52.6
59270	SIDNEY	95.9	95.5	0.1	0.1	0.3	0.3	2.4	2.7	6.0	6.3	7.2	8.1	6.6	23.4	26.9	13.1	2.4	75.4	40.1	49.1	50.9
59274	VIDA	95.7	95.6	0.2	0.2	0.8	0.8	1.2	1.2	5.3	6.1	7.1	6.3	3.8	18.8	33.9	17.6	1.2	77.8	46.4	52.9	47.1
59275	WESTBY	99.2	98.9	0.0	0.0	0.0	0.0	0.8	0.6	4.4	4.7	5.5	5.3	4.7	16.6	32.1	22.7	3.9	82.3	49.6	54.9	45.2
59276	WHITETAIL	96.2	96.9	0.0	0.0	0.0	0.0	0.8	0.8	4.7	6.3	6.3	5.5	4.7	21.3	32.3	17.3	1.6	78.0	45.8	53.5	46.5
59301	MILES CITY	96.8	96.6	0.1	0.1	0.3	0.4	1.6	1.8	6.1	6.2	6.9	7.1	6.6	24.3	25.6	14.5	2.7	76.5	40.3	48.8	51.2
59311	ALZADA	97.8	97.7	0.0	0.0	0.0	0.0	0.0	0.0	3.5	4.7	7.1	5.9	5.9	24.7	32.9	14.1	1.2	78.8	43.9	48.2	51.8
59312	ANGELA	97.6	97.6	0.0	0.0	0.0	0.0	2.4	2.4	4.8	4.8	4.8	7.1	4.8	23.8	31.0	19.1	0.0	85.7	45.0	54.8	45.2
59313	BAKER	98.5	98.4	0.2	0.2	0.4	0.4	0.4	0.5	5.0	5.4	7.5	7.9	5.7	22.9	26.9	16.2	2.6	76.7	42.4	50.3	49.7
59314	BIDDLE	97.8	97.8	0.0	0.0	0.0	0.0	1.1	1.1	3.3	6.8	9.6	8.1	3.7	18.8	33.0	16.2	0.7	74.9	44.9	50.0	50.0
59315	BLOOMFIELD	99.1	99.1	0.0	0.0	0.0	0.0	0.0	0.0	4.7	5.6	7.5	6.1	5.6	19.2	32.7	16.8	1.9	78.0	45.7	49.5	50.5
59316	BOYES	97.7	97.5	0.0	0.0	0.0	0.0	0.0	0.0	3.8	3.8	7.5	6.3	5.0	25.0	33.8	13.8	1.3	78.8	44.2	51.3	48.8
59317	BROADUS	97.8	97.8	0.0	0.0	0.1	0.1	0.7	0.7	6.6	6.9	6.9	5.7	4.7	21.6	26.9	17.4	3.4	75.6	43.5	48.2	51.8
59318	BRUSETT	98.9	99.4	0.0	0.0	0.0	0.0	0.6	0.6	6.7	6.7	5.6	5.6	5.1	24.2	30.3	14.0	1.7	77.5	42.3	53.9	46.1
59322	COHAGEN	99.3	99.3	0.0	0.0	0.0	0.0	0.0	0.0	6.7	7.0	5.9	5.9	5.9	21.9	27.4	15.2	4.1	75.9	42.5	52.6	47.4
59324	EKALAKA	99.1	99.0	0.1	0.1	0.0	0.0	0.6	0.6	4.0	5.1	9.5	7.9	2.2	22.0	27.9	16.5	5.0	74.8	44.6	47.4	52.6
59326	FALLON	98.3	98.2	0.0	0.0	0.0	0.0	0.7	0.7	4.7	5.4	5.8	4.4	5.1	22.5	34.8	14.9	2.5	80.8	46.1	52.9	47.1
59327	FORSYTH	95.8	95.6	0.2	0.2	0.6	0.6	1.5	1.5	5.6	5.8	6.7	6.9	5.6	19.9	31.1	15.8	2.6	77.7	44.7	50.1	49.9
59330	GLENDIVE	97.3	97.1	0.3	0.3	0.2	0.2	0.9	1.0	5.3	5.4	6.4	6.6	7.2	23.6	28.0	14.8	2.6	79.2	41.9	49.7	50.3
59332	HAMMOND	97.7	97.2	0.0	0.0	0.4	0.4	0.8	0.8	4.5	4.9	7.7	6.5	5.7	23.9	31.2	14.2	1.6	78.5	43.0	50.6	49.4
59336	ISMAY	98.9	98.8	0.0	0.0	0.3	0.3	0.9	0.9	6.8	5.6	8.9	6.8	4.7	25.1	29.5	12.1	0.6	73.8	40.4	52.5	47.5
59337	JORDAN	99.2	99.2	0.1	0.1	0.1	0.1	0.6	0.6	6.8	6.8	5.8	5.7	5.7	23.3	28.6	14.4	3.0	76.9	42.2	52.6	47.4
59338	KINSEY	98.7	98.4	0.0	0.0	0.3	0.3	1.1	1.4	7.0	5.7	8.9	6.2	4.9	25.4	29.7	11.6	0.5	73.8	40.2	52.2	47.8
59339	LINDSAY	98.9	97.7	0.0	0.0	0.0	0.0	0.0	0.0	4.6	5.7	8.0	6.8	5.7	18.2	35.2	14.8	1.1	77.3	45.4	52.3	47.7
59341	MILDRED	98.7	97.3	0.0	0.0	0.0	0.0	0.0	0.0	4.1	5.5	5.5	4.1	4.1	20.6	41.1	12.3	2.7	84.9	48.2	53.4	46.6
59343	OLIVE	96.2	96.2	0.0	0.0	0.0	0.0	0.0	0.0	7.6	7.6	7.6	5.7	3.8	20.8	32.1	13.2	1.9	77.4	43.1	47.2	52.8
59344	PLEVNA	99.2	99.2	0.0	0.0	0.5	0.6	0.3	0.0	4.4	4.7	6.6	8.8	3.6	23.8	31.8	15.6	0.8	78.4	44.1	52.3	47.7
59345	POWDERVILLE	94.4	94.4	0.0	0.0	0.0	0.0	0.0	0.0	11.1	11.1	11.1	5.6	0.0	16.7	44.4	0.0	0.0	66.7	42.5	50.0	50.0
59347	ROSEBUD	86.2	85.2	0.5	0.5	0.2	0.2	3.1	3.2	6.4	8.1	8.7	8.9	6.5	23.0	32.3	5.7	0.4	71.2	37.6	50.7	49.3
59349	TERRY	97.8	97.9	0.0	0.0	0.2	0.3	0.7	0.8	3.6	4.1	4.5	4.6	4.8	15.4	36.5	21.4	5.1	84.2	52.8	50.2	49.8
59351	VOLBORG	98.6	98.5	0.0	0.0	0.2	0.2	0.6	0.6	4.7	4.9	4.7	5.1	6.6	23.7	33.7	15.0	1.7	82.6	45.2	52.5	47.5
59353	WIBAUX	98.0	98.0	0.2	0.2	0.2	0.2	0.4	0.4	5.3	5.8	7.1	7.2	6.8	19.6	27.6	16.7	4.0	76.9	43.9	48.1	51.9
59354	WILLARD	100.0	100.0	0.0	0.0	0.0	0.0	0.0	0.0	4.9	4.9	4.9	9.8	2.4	26.8	34.2	12.2	0.0	75.6	43.5	48.8	51.2
59401	GREAT FALLS	89.1	88.3	1.0	1.0	1.0	1.2	2.7	3.0	6.6	5.9	6.5	7.4	8.2	28.5	22.5	11.3	3.1	76.6	36.2	48.7	51.3
59402	MALMSTROM A F B	83.2	81.6	6.6	7.2	2.5	3.0	7.9	8.6	15.1	10.3	7.5	9.4	19.6	36.3	1.9	0.1	0.0	64.5	22.0	54.5	45.5
59404	GREAT FALLS	92.8	92.2	0.4	0.5	0.8	0.9	1.8	2.0	5.8	6.2	7.6	7.5	5.9	25.1	28.8	12.2	1.0	75.4	40.4	50.4	49.6
59405	GREAT FALLS	88.8	88.0	1.7	1.8	1.1	1.3	2.9	3.2	7.2	6.4	6.6	6.8	8.2	25.6	22.8	13.7	2.7	75.9	36.5	48.2	51.8
59410	AUGUSTA	96.9	96.7	0.0	0.0	0.0	0.0	1.3	1.5	5.9	5.7	6.3	6.8	7.1	21.8	28.8	16.1	1.6	78.9	42.3	50.1	49.9
59411	BABB	23.4	22.3	0.0	0.0	0.0	0.0	1.5	1.5	7.5	6.8	10.4	8.2	7.8	25.9	26.4	6.6	0.5	69.2	33.7	50.5	49.5
59412	BELT	96.9	96.5	0.8	1.0	0.2	0.2	1.4	1.7	5.2	5.6	7.2	7.1	6.2	23.2	30.8	13.0	1.8	77.6	42.2	50.2	49.8
59414	BLACK EAGLE	91.0	90.5	0.2	0.2	0.3	0.5	1.4	1.5	6.7	6.9	7.0	7.0	6.2	27.7	27.5	10.2	0.9	75.0	38.1	51.9	48.1
59416	BRADY	96.0	95.1	0.3	0.3	0.3	0.3	0.6	1.0	5.2	6.2	7.8	9.5	5.5	20.2	30.3	13.4	2.0	73.9	42.7	54.1	45.9
59417	BROWNING	10.7	10.2	0.1	0.1	0.1	0.1	1.4	1.4	9.6	8.8	9.9	10.5	9.3	25.5	20.4	5.7	0.5	64.8	26.6	49.7	50.3
59418	BUFFALO	97.7	97.7	0.0	0.0	0.0	0.0	0.0	0.0	4.7	4.7	7.0	4.7	4.7	19.8	33.7	17.4	3.5	79.1	47.9	51.2	48.8
59419	BYNUM	97.1	97.2	0.0	0.0	0.0	0.0	1.4	0.7	8.4	8.4	9.8	6.3	5.6	23.8	25.2	11.2	1.4	68.5	35.3	50.4	49.7
59420	CARTER	98.5	97.7	0.3	0.3	0.6	0.7	0.3	0.3	4.7	5.3	5.7	5.7	5.3	23.3	32.9	15.3	2.0	80.4	45.1	52.2	47.8
59421	CASCADE	96.2	95.9	0.3	0.3	0.1	0.1	0.9	1.0	4.5	5.2	7.3	7.2	5.3	20.8	32.3	15.8	1.6	78.2	44.8	51.2	48.9
59422	CHOTEAU	95.2	95.0	0.1	0.1	0.1	0.1	1.2	1.3	6.1	6.5	7.4	6.8	5.4	20.8	27.3	15.8	4.0	75.3	42.8	48.1	51.9
59424	COFFEE CREEK	97.7	97.7	0.0	0.0	0.0	0.0	1.5	1.6	5.5	5.5	7.8	7.0	6.3	23.4	29.7	13.3	1.6	75.8	41.8	52.3	47.7
59425	CONRAD	96.0	95.3	0.1	0.1	0.3	0.3	0.9	1.0	5.8	5.9	7.3	8.4	6.3	21.8	25.7	15.5	3.4	75.3	41.4	48.3	51.7
59427	CUT BANK	75.4	74.4	0.1	0.1	0.2	0.3	0.9	0.9	6.9	6.8	8.0	8.4	6.7	23.1	25.3	12.8	2.2	73.2	38.2	49.0	51.0
59430	DENTON	97.7	97.5	0.0	0.0	0.2	0.2	1.6	1.8	5.2	5.4	7.5	7.2	6.1	23.0	30.0	14.2	1.4	76.8	42.3	53.0	47.0
59433	DUTTON	95.7	95.6	0.4	0.4	0.3	0.3	2.0	2.2	5.9	6.0	6.8	7.7	2.9	23.4	30.0	16.1	1.2	76.1	43.6	49.9	50.1
59434	EAST GLACIER PARK	87.2	87.5	0.0	0.0	0.0	0.0	0.0	0.0	4.2	8.3	6.3	4.2	4.2	22.9	43.8	6.3	0.0	79.2	45.0	47.9	52.1
59436	FAIRFIELD	98.4	98.3	0.1	0.1	0.0	0.0	0.4	0.4	6.8	7.3	7.4	7.4	5.9	25.1	27.2	11.7	1.4	73.9	38.7	51.3	48.7
59440	FLOWEREE	94.0	95.5	0.0	0.0	0.0	0.0	0.9	0.9	5.5	6.4	6.4	6.4	5.5	26.4	29.1	12.7	1.8	76.4	41.8	54.6	45.5
59441	FORESTGROVE	98.9	98.9	0.0	0.0	0.0	0.0	0.0	0.0	5.8	6.9	8.1	6.9	4.6	21.8	29.9	14.9	1.2	73.6	42.5	54.0	46.0
59442	FORT BENTON	97.8	97.7	0.2	0.3	0.4	0.5	0.5	0.6	4.8	5.2	6.5	7.1	6.1	21.0	27.3	17.4	4.7	78.6	44.6	49.2	50.8
59443	FORT SHAW	96.1	95.8	0.3	0.3	0.4	0.4	0.7	1.0	4.8	6.9	8.9	8.8	3.4	20.4	32.1	13.2	1.4	72.9	42.9	52.9	47.1
59444	GALATA	97.1	98.5	0.0	0.0	0.0	0.0	0.0	0.0	7.7	7.7	6.2	6.2	6.2	24.6	24.6	13.9	3.1	75.4	40.4	55.4	44.6
59446	GERALDINE	98.3	98.1	0.0	0.0	0.2	0.2	0.5	0.7	5.2	5.9	7.6	6.9	5.4	23.0	28.2	15.5	2.2	77.0	42.4	51.2	48.8
59447	GEYSER	97.5	97.3	0.0	0.0	0.2	0.2	0.7	0.7	6.8	7.1	7.5	7.1	5.9	22.7	29.1	11.8	2.1	74.6	40.8	53.4	46.6
59448	HEART BUTTE	5.7	4.7	0.1	0.1	0.3	0.4	1.1	0.9	10.5	9.3	10.6	12.7	10.3	23.5	17.3	5.6	0.3	61.4	23.4	48.0	52.0
59450	HIGHWOOD	97.5	97.1	0.2	0.2	1.3	1.6	0.6	0.7	4.6	6.4	8.4	8.8	2.9	24.1	29.8	13.3	1.8	74.8	42.3	52.5	47.5
59451	HILGER	97.7	97.5	0.0	0.0	0.1	0.1	1.6	1.8	5.3	5.3	7.4	7.3	6.2	23.2	30.0	14.0	1.4	76.7	42.1	52.9	47.1
59452	HOBSON	98.9	98.9	0.0	0.0	0.1	0.1	0.9	0.8	5.9	7.0	7.7	6.3	4.3	22.4	27.8	16.6	2.1	75.4	43.1	51.3	48.7
59453	JUDITH GAP	96.0	96.3	0.3	0.3	0.7	0.7	0.3	0.0	7.8	7.4	7.8	5.4	5.7	26.4	26.0	12.2	1.4	73.3	38.5	53.0	47.0
59454	KEVIN	95.9	96.1	0.0	0.0	0.5	0.4	1.8	1.3	7.4	7.4	8.7	8.3	6.6	23.6	25.8	10.9	1.3	71.2	36.1	50.2	49.8
59456	LEDGER	97.4	100.0	0.0	0.0	0.0	0.0	0.0	0.0	5.3	5.3	7.9	7.9	5.3	21.1	34.2	13.2	0.0	81.6	43.8	55.3	44.7
59457	LEWISTOWN	96.7	96.5	0.1	0.1	0.3	0.3	0.8	0.8	5.3	5.5	6.5	6.3	6.1	21.0	27.7	17.6	4.0	78.4	44.5	47.6	52.5
59460	LOMA	98.5	99.5	0.0	0.0	0.0	0.0	0.0	0.0	4.7	5.7	6.3	7.3	7.8	22.4	30.2	14.6	1.0	78.7	42.8	54.2	45.8
59462	MOCCASIN	98.9	99.4	0.0	0.0	0.0	0.0	0.6	0.6	5.6	6.7	7.9	6.2	3.9	24.2	27.0	16.9	1.7	75.8	42.9	50.0	50.0
59463	MONARCH	97.3	97.3	0.0	0.0	0.0	0.0	1.8	0.9	5.5	5.5	5.5	6.4	5.5	24.8	31.2	13.8	1.8	78.0	43.3	54.1	45.9
59464	MOORE	97.6	97.5	0.0	0.0	0.0	0.0	0.7	0.7	5.0	5.3	6.7	5.7	5.1	20.2	33.3	16.0	2.7	79.3	46.2	50.5	49.5
59465	NEIHART	97.2	96.1	0.0	0.0	0.0	0.0	1.1	1.7	5.1	5.7	5.7	6.8	5.7	23.2	32.2	14.1	1.7	79.1	43.8	52.0	48.0
59466	OILMONT	94.2	94.1	0.0	0.0	0.0	0.0	0.0	0.0	6.9	6.9	7.8	7.8	5.9	23.5	25.5	13.7	2.0	73.5	40.0	50.0	50.0
59467	PENDROY	97.4	97.4	0.0	0.0	0.0	0.0	1.8	1.7	7.8	7.8	8.7	7.0	6.1	22.6	27.8	10.4	1.7	70.4	37.9	53.0	47.0
59468	POWER	95.3	95.4	0.8	0.8	0.0	0.0	1.7	1.5	6.4	6.6	6.4	6.4	5.5	23.4	30.6	13.3	1.4	76.6	42.2	51.1	48.9
59469	RAYNESFORD	97.5	97.6	0.0	0.0	0.0	0.0	0.5	0.5	6.8	6.8	7.3	6.8	5.8	22.3	31.1	11.2	1.9	76.2	41.5	55.3	44.7
59471	ROY	98.8	98.6	0.0	0.0	0.0	0.0	0.5	0.7	5.3	6.3	7.7	7.0	4.6	22.6	31.7	13.9	1.0	75.5	42.9	52.4	47.6
59472	SAND COULEE	97.9	97.9	0.0	0.0	0.0	0.0	0.9	0.9	4.7	7.2	7.2	6.6	5.0	25.0	29.4	12.9	2.0	77.4	41.9	51.4	48.7
59474	SHELBY	93.3	93.1	0.2	0.2	0.4	0.4	1.2	1.2	5.1	5.3	6.7	6.7	7.6	25.9	26.2	13.7	2.8	78.3	40.7	52.1	47.9
59479	STANFORD	99.2	99.2	0.1	0.1	0.0	0.0	0.2	0.2	3.0	4.0	7.3	7.0	5.8	19.4	33.7	17.2	2.7	81.5	47.0	53.2	46.8
59480	STOCKETT	98.0	97.9	0.0	0.0	0.0	0.0	0.9	0.9	4.9	7.2	7.2	6.6	5.1	25.1	28.8	13.2	2.1	77.2	41.7	51.2	48.8
59482	SUNBURST	95.0	94.9	0.0	0.0	0.1	0.1	0.9	0.9	6.4	6.7	8.0	7.7	6.1	23.1	27.5	12.7	1.9	74.0	40.2	50.6	49.4
59483	SUN RIVER	92.5	91.9	0.5	0.6	0.4	0.4	1.3	1.5	5.7	6.5	7.8	7.4	6.2	27.8	27.8	10.3	0.7	75.4	38.1	55.0	45.0
59484	SWEET GRASS	96.0	95.7	0.0	0.0	0.4	0.4	1.6	1.6	7.4	7.4	9.0	8.6	6.3	23.1	26.2	10.9	1.2	71.5	36.3	50.8	49.2
59486	VALIER	93.2	92.5	0.0	0.0	0.0	0.0	0.9	0.9	6.4	6.6	7.7	8.1	6.2	20.4	29.3	14.0	1.4	74.3	41.2	51.0	49.0
59487	VAUGHN	94.2	93.8	0.7	0.7	0.5	0.6	1.0	1.0	7.2	7.7	8.9	7.2	5.4	26.5	25.1	11.0	1.0	71.7	37.0	51.3	48.7
59489	WINIFRED	98.8	99.1	0.0	0.0	0.0	0.0	0.3	0.0	5.5	6.1	8.0	7.0	4.9	22.3	30.9	14.1	1.2	74.6	42.6	51.7	48.3
59501	HAVRE	88.3	87.1	0.1	0.1	0.5	0.6	1.3	1.4	7.1	6.7	6.6	7.6	9.0	25.3	24.3	11.3	2.1	75.4	35.0	49.7	50.3
59520	BIG SANDY	60.7	58.8	0.0	0.0	0.1	0.1	1.0	1.1	9.8	9.2	9.1	7.2	7.8	21.7	22.1	11.3	1.9	67.3	31.4	50.5	49.5
59521	BOX ELDER	10.3	9.7	0.1	0.1	0.2	0.2	1.5	1.3	10.5	10.9	11.2	10.0	8.9	24.2	18.2	5.8	0.4	61.0	24.1	49.7	50.3
	MONTANA	90.6	90.2	0.3	0.3	0.6	0.7	2.0	2.2	6.1	6.2	7.1	7.5	7.2	25.5	27.0	11.7	1.9	76.2	38.5	49.9	50.1
	UNITED STATES	75.1	73.6	12.3	12.5	3.8	4.2	12.5	14.1	6.9	6.7	7.2	7.0	7.3	28.6	23.8	10.8	1.7	75.1	36.0	49.1	50.9

ZIP CODE # POST OFFICE NAME	2004 Per Capita Income	2004 HH Income Base	2004 HOUSEHOLD INCOME DISTRIBUTION (%) Less than $25,000	$25,000 to $49,999	$50,000 to $99,999	$100,000 to $149,999	$150,000 or More	MEDIAN HOUSEHOLD INCOME 2004	2009	2004 National Centile	2004 State Centile	2004 Home Value Base	2004 HOME VALUE DISTRIBUTION (%) Less than $50,000	$50,000 to $89,999	$90,000 to $174,999	$175,000 to $399,999	$400,000 or More	2004 Median Home Value
59261 SACO	13678	68	48.5	26.5	20.6	4.4	0.0	25872	30552	6	8	51	54.9	21.6	17.7	5.9	0.0	45000
59262 SAVAGE	14438	384	35.7	41.4	19.5	3.4	0.0	32563	35464	19	51	303	23.4	41.6	26.4	6.9	1.7	77069
59263 SCOBEY	18631	582	43.1	32.7	17.9	4.8	1.6	29474	32621	11	21	445	39.1	34.6	22.5	3.2	0.7	61413
59270 SIDNEY	18908	2605	33.4	35.5	26.3	2.8	2.0	36030	39827	32	73	1865	23.1	36.0	36.3	4.2	0.3	80475
59274 VIDA	19804	201	33.3	34.3	23.9	5.0	3.5	34463	37657	26	64	163	33.7	27.6	24.5	7.4	6.8	69583
59275 WESTBY	20610	172	32.0	45.9	15.1	5.2	1.7	32019	35394	18	45	141	60.3	18.4	19.2	2.1	0.0	39643
59276 WHITETAIL	14882	57	43.9	35.1	19.3	1.8	0.0	28309	35000	9	18	45	40.0	33.3	15.6	4.4	6.7	63750
59301 MILES CITY	17598	4267	38.9	32.9	22.5	4.5	1.3	32293	36043	19	48	2974	29.4	32.3	31.9	5.3	1.1	80199
59311 ALZADA	13811	32	40.6	34.4	18.8	6.3	0.0	31479	33615	16	42	24	41.7	4.2	16.7	8.3	29.2	100000
59312 ANGELA	19226	20	35.0	30.0	30.0	5.0	0.0	35000	45000	28	66	16	18.8	12.5	37.5	12.5	18.8	116667
59313 BAKER	17765	953	39.2	31.9	24.1	3.2	1.6	32668	36898	20	52	729	35.7	34.0	21.5	5.8	3.0	65423
59314 BIDDLE	16061	177	45.8	31.6	18.1	1.1	3.4	26977	29815	7	11	140	49.3	10.7	17.1	13.6	9.3	60000
59315 BLOOMFIELD	13890	80	42.5	35.0	17.5	3.8	1.3	30000	32652	12	28	63	47.6	19.1	28.6	1.6	3.2	53750
59316 BOYES	12516	28	42.9	32.1	21.4	3.6	0.0	32315	35000	19	49	22	31.8	4.6	9.1	4.6	50.0	350000
59317 BROADUS	16383	339	40.7	37.8	18.6	1.2	1.8	29730	32819	12	23	256	27.0	42.2	21.1	5.5	4.3	69310
59318 BRUSETT	14170	80	48.8	31.3	17.5	2.5	0.0	25722	29048	5	8	64	46.9	25.0	9.4	7.8	10.9	55000
59322 COHAGEN	15856	109	44.0	36.7	16.5	1.8	0.9	28433	32003	9	19	80	43.8	23.8	15.0	5.0	12.5	60000
59324 EKALAKA	14447	343	46.7	32.7	17.8	2.6	0.3	27195	30638	7	12	265	50.6	15.5	15.1	8.3	10.6	49063
59326 FALLON	15905	123	44.7	32.5	17.9	4.1	0.8	27474	30000	8	15	94	28.7	31.9	24.5	7.5	7.5	73750
59327 FORSYTH	19303	1345	34.5	32.8	27.1	3.9	1.6	36062	40489	32	74	953	32.1	30.8	28.2	4.5	4.4	70915
59330 GLENDIVE	17159	3236	37.9	33.1	24.4	3.6	1.1	34288	37810	25	62	2395	25.6	35.0	34.3	4.2	0.9	79029
59332 HAMMOND	13979	95	43.2	32.6	19.0	4.2	1.1	30818	33891	14	35	73	37.0	4.1	15.1	8.2	35.6	152500
59336 ISMAY	15591	123	31.7	35.0	27.6	4.9	0.8	36906	40913	35	77	101	12.9	18.8	38.6	20.8	8.9	122500
59337 JORDAN	15352	310	46.8	32.9	17.1	2.6	0.7	26972	29873	7	10	239	43.1	24.3	11.7	6.3	14.6	61563
59338 KINSEY	15620	134	29.9	35.8	28.4	4.5	1.5	37444	40773	37	79	110	11.8	19.1	40.0	20.0	9.1	122222
59339 LINDSAY	16504	40	45.0	35.0	17.5	2.5	0.0	27261	31287	8	14	32	31.3	25.0	34.4	3.1	6.3	75000
59341 MILDRED	13363	27	44.4	29.6	22.2	3.7	0.0	27247	28592	7	13	21	19.1	38.1	38.1	0.0	4.8	78333
59343 OLIVE	13349	20	35.0	40.0	25.0	0.0	0.0	32279	38596	19	47	15	26.7	20.0	33.3	6.7	13.3	95000
59344 PLEVNA	15803	153	38.6	36.6	21.6	2.0	1.3	31426	35180	16	41	122	32.8	17.2	22.1	18.0	9.8	90000
59345 POWDERVILLE	13611	9	44.4	55.6	0.0	0.0	0.0	27247	27247	7	13	7	0.0	14.3	57.1	0.0	28.6	156250
59347 ROSEBUD	21759	1121	17.6	29.3	42.0	9.6	1.6	53006	59364	77	98	897	34.3	23.5	33.3	4.7	4.1	79490
59349 TERRY	16168	377	45.6	36.1	15.9	2.1	0.3	27358	30334	8	15	302	53.0	27.2	16.6	1.7	1.7	47000
59351 VOLBORG	15972	187	37.4	34.8	23.0	3.7	1.1	33101	35337	21	54	120	26.7	9.2	27.5	10.8	25.8	129167
59353 WIBAUX	18318	421	40.6	31.6	22.6	2.9	2.4	30539	33285	14	32	309	44.0	26.2	16.8	8.7	4.2	63667
59354 WILLARD	13049	16	50.0	31.3	18.8	0.0	0.0	25000	45000	5	6	13	38.5	15.4	7.7	38.5	0.0	75000
59401 GREAT FALLS	17166	6330	42.9	33.3	19.3	3.2	1.3	29694	33879	12	22	3298	8.3	32.5	53.4	5.2	0.7	97297
59402 MALMSTROM A F B	13587	653	27.1	51.3	19.0	2.6	0.0	34891	38248	27	65	11	0.0	0.0	100.0	0.0	0.0	135938
59404 GREAT FALLS	22211	9617	25.4	32.9	30.5	6.8	4.5	43116	48198	56	89	7802	10.8	16.1	54.4	17.0	1.7	117740
59405 GREAT FALLS	19110	11963	36.8	32.2	25.2	3.8	2.0	35135	38764	28	67	6786	13.2	19.2	58.4	8.0	1.2	107648
59410 AUGUSTA	13651	356	49.4	36.0	11.2	1.4	2.0	25253	27611	5	7	255	17.3	32.9	34.5	9.4	5.9	89861
59411 BABB	12441	194	47.9	34.0	10.3	3.1	4.6	26265	28344	6	9	151	49.0	29.1	15.9	2.0	4.0	51500
59412 BELT	18764	662	34.4	34.7	23.0	4.4	3.5	33939	36160	24	59	524	23.3	25.0	31.5	14.3	5.9	93913
59414 BLACK EAGLE	19943	411	35.0	37.0	23.8	2.7	1.5	35168	38525	28	67	303	33.7	22.4	38.9	3.6	1.3	78333
59416 BRADY	20239	126	28.6	36.5	27.8	4.8	2.4	40000	44650	46	86	98	18.4	21.4	32.7	27.6	0.0	110000
59417 BROWNING	10342	2301	46.2	34.3	15.9	2.7	0.8	27027	30393	7	11	1306	26.4	31.9	33.3	6.4	2.1	80924
59418 BUFFALO	17912	32	31.3	34.4	31.3	3.1	0.0	37339	45000	37	78	26	11.5	15.4	30.8	30.8	11.5	150000
59419 BYNUM	13787	47	38.3	34.0	19.2	6.4	2.1	32324	31514	19	49	36	11.1	16.7	38.9	19.4	13.9	121429
59420 CARTER	20698	130	35.4	35.4	20.0	3.9	5.4	33169	37706	21	55	96	18.8	22.9	38.5	14.6	5.2	98889
59421 CASCADE	19274	1030	34.3	34.8	24.4	4.0	2.6	36246	38836	33	75	836	14.6	15.1	45.9	20.5	4.0	115476
59422 CHOTEAU	15412	1219	43.6	33.1	19.2	2.5	1.5	28720	31892	10	20	886	15.7	26.2	44.4	10.5	3.3	98090
59424 COFFEE CREEK	17740	54	38.9	35.2	20.4	5.6	0.0	31798	33606	17	44	41	39.0	26.8	19.5	7.3	7.3	65000
59425 CONRAD	18125	1410	38.7	28.5	26.1	5.2	1.5	34346	38763	25	63	992	19.7	29.9	41.7	8.2	0.5	90533
59427 CUT BANK	16687	1828	35.6	32.5	26.0	4.1	1.8	35968	39890	31	73	1367	24.4	37.9	32.0	4.8	1.0	78969
59430 DENTON	17378	230	37.8	36.5	20.9	3.5	1.3	32295	35000	19	48	175	34.9	24.6	25.7	8.0	6.9	73889
59433 DUTTON	16487	303	33.7	38.3	25.1	2.6	0.3	35434	38182	29	68	240	20.4	33.3	32.1	11.3	2.9	86400
59434 EAST GLACIER PARK	24838	24	37.5	4.2	58.3	0.0	0.0	64858	76604	88	100	13	61.5	0.0	38.5	0.0	0.0	36250
59436 FAIRFIELD	17281	739	30.7	36.5	27.1	4.3	1.4	35546	38791	30	70	575	11.8	22.3	41.2	21.7	3.0	112500
59440 FLOWEREE	15932	45	35.6	35.6	26.7	2.2	0.0	34064	38182	24	60	33	30.3	21.2	39.4	6.1	3.0	87500
59441 FORESTGROVE	14588	37	46.0	35.1	16.2	2.7	0.0	27285	32302	8	14	29	37.9	27.6	13.8	13.8	6.9	67500
59442 FORT BENTON	16670	779	35.0	40.1	20.5	2.8	1.5	32733	36202	20	53	607	18.1	29.7	41.9	8.2	2.1	92935
59443 FORT SHAW	16516	347	35.7	36.6	23.6	2.9	1.2	35735	37552	31	71	283	16.6	20.1	40.6	19.8	2.8	111944
59444 GALATA	13654	27	48.2	29.6	22.2	0.0	0.0	26099	28592	6	9	21	19.1	33.3	23.8	14.3	9.5	85000
59446 GERALDINE	16732	238	37.4	37.0	18.5	4.2	2.9	31765	35146	17	44	185	31.4	26.5	23.2	8.7	10.3	79545
59447 GEYSER	14916	156	41.0	37.2	12.2	6.4	3.2	32091	34483	18	47	124	35.5	11.3	34.7	10.5	8.1	94000
59448 HEART BUTTE	7577	183	50.8	33.3	13.7	2.2	0.0	24598	29632	4	5	90	34.4	18.9	31.1	12.2	3.3	80000
59450 HIGHWOOD	17071	165	27.9	35.8	29.1	5.5	1.8	40183	43400	47	87	131	15.3	16.8	35.9	23.7	8.4	119643
59451 HILGER	14470	249	38.6	36.1	20.5	3.6	1.2	31831	35114	17	45	190	33.7	24.7	26.3	8.4	6.8	76000
59452 HOBSON	17945	297	37.0	37.0	18.2	4.4	3.4	32854	35779	20	53	232	22.4	21.1	30.2	15.1	11.2	102586
59453 JUDITH GAP	14301	119	51.3	32.8	11.8	2.5	1.7	24422	26088	4	4	91	31.9	36.3	20.9	5.5	5.5	67500
59454 KEVIN	16857	93	41.9	32.3	17.2	6.5	2.2	30443	34066	13	31	70	38.6	34.3	20.0	5.7	1.4	63333
59456 LEDGER	11974	12	33.3	41.7	25.0	0.0	0.0	35000	42313	28	66	10	0.0	0.0	70.0	30.0	0.0	125000
59457 LEWISTOWN	18458	3577	37.3	34.6	22.5	4.2	1.5	32790	36243	20	53	2572	17.6	30.5	38.2	10.9	2.8	92487
59460 LOMA	23256	83	33.7	36.1	19.3	6.0	4.8	34588	35899	26	65	64	26.6	25.0	29.7	10.9	7.8	88000
59462 MOCCASIN	16479	68	39.7	35.3	17.7	2.9	4.4	31485	35730	16	42	53	20.8	20.8	32.1	15.1	11.3	105357
59463 MONARCH	20528	51	37.3	29.4	25.5	5.9	2.0	35748	37343	31	71	41	9.8	12.2	46.3	19.5	12.2	140625
59464 MOORE	16850	198	29.8	34.3	28.8	5.6	1.5	37828	41777	39	81	161	13.0	16.8	32.3	27.3	10.6	136458
59465 NEIHART	26642	86	36.1	27.9	26.7	4.7	4.7	37849	37991	39	81	70	8.6	11.4	51.4	17.1	11.4	128571
59466 OILMONT	18334	42	31.0	40.5	23.8	4.8	0.0	36515	40743	34	75	33	33.3	36.4	21.2	6.1	3.0	70833
59467 PENDROY	16756	46	37.0	41.3	15.2	2.2	4.4	32295	35544	19	48	36	16.7	27.8	30.6	19.4	5.6	104167
59468 POWER	16252	248	30.2	39.9	25.0	4.8	0.0	36728	40439	34	76	198	14.7	23.7	36.4	20.2	5.1	102000
59469 RAYNESFORD	16443	81	43.2	35.8	11.1	6.2	3.7	31111	34524	15	37	65	36.9	9.2	36.9	9.2	7.7	94167
59471 ROY	12689	128	42.2	34.4	17.2	3.9	2.3	30000	32060	12	28	100	35.0	24.0	18.0	13.0	10.0	75000
59472 SAND COULEE	16354	199	37.7	31.7	23.1	3.5	4.0	33996	36132	24	60	166	27.1	25.9	34.3	12.1	0.6	85000
59474 SHELBY	16190	1412	40.0	32.7	23.9	2.0	1.4	32033	35763	18	46	994	20.9	39.2	31.4	7.1	1.3	81140
59479 STANFORD	15499	380	46.1	34.5	16.3	2.4	0.8	28612	31297	10	20	294	36.4	34.7	22.8	2.4	3.7	66429
59480 STOCKETT	17664	199	37.2	31.2	24.1	3.5	4.0	34392	35938	25	63	165	23.6	24.2	36.4	12.7	3.0	93889
59482 SUNBURST	15397	284	33.1	38.0	22.2	4.6	2.1	36596	39357	34	76	219	35.6	33.8	19.6	6.4	4.6	67045
59483 SUN RIVER	18236	318	33.3	36.2	25.2	3.5	1.9	35886	38393	31	72	263	16.0	24.7	40.3	16.4	2.7	105053
59484 SWEET GRASS	13967	86	41.9	31.4	17.4	7.0	2.3	30894	35366	15	36	65	36.9	35.4	20.0	6.2	1.5	65000
59486 VALIER	13576	591	41.8	36.4	17.6	3.1	1.2	30426	33449	13	31	462	17.1	27.3	40.0	10.0	5.6	100676
59487 VAUGHN	15758	393	35.9	36.4	23.2	3.3	1.3	33816	36792	23	58	324	17.9	29.9	38.6	11.7	1.9	93500
59489 WINIFRED	17532	141	44.7	33.3	15.6	4.3	2.1	28223	31213	9	17	110	35.5	24.6	16.4	13.6	10.0	73333
59501 HAVRE	17720	5101	38.2	31.4	24.3	4.3	1.9	33748	37878	23	57	3297	13.9	27.9	46.1	11.4	0.7	102914
59520 BIG SANDY	13054	723	45.2	32.8	17.6	2.6	1.8	27661	30418	8	16	426	28.6	29.3	32.4	6.3	3.3	80286
59521 BOX ELDER	9946	524	40.8	32.1	22.0	4.4	0.8	30758	33819	14	34	289	53.3	30.5	12.1	4.2	0.0	45870
MONTANA	19326		33.9	32.7	25.9	5.0	2.5	36188	40555				14.7	16.4	40.8	23.3	4.9	122379
UNITED STATES	25866		24.7	27.1	30.8	10.9	6.5	48124	56710				10.9	15.0	33.7	30.1	10.4	145905

ZIP CODE #	POST OFFICE NAME	FINANCIAL SERVICES: Auto Loan	FINANCIAL SERVICES: Home Loan	FINANCIAL SERVICES: Invest-ments	FINANCIAL SERVICES: Retire-ment Plans	THE HOME: Home Improvements: Home Repair	THE HOME: Home Improvements: Lawn & Garden	THE HOME: Furnishings: Comput-ers & Hard-ware	THE HOME: Furnishings: Major Appli-ances	THE HOME: Furnishings: TV, Radio, Sound Equip-ment	THE HOME: Furnishings: Furni-ture	ENTERTAINMENT: Dine out/ Carry out	ENTERTAINMENT: Sports Equip-ment	ENTERTAINMENT: Fees & Tickets	ENTERTAINMENT: Toys & Games	ENTERTAINMENT: Travel	ENTERTAINMENT: Cable TV	PERSONAL: Apparel & Services	PERSONAL: Auto Repairs	PERSONAL: Health Insur-ance	PERSONAL: Pets & Supplies
59261	SACO	68	47	25	45	55	62	47	58	54	46	63	70	40	62	49	57	58	57	69	81
59262	SAVAGE	67	47	25	44	55	61	46	57	54	46	63	69	40	62	48	56	57	57	68	80
59263	SCOBEY	65	49	32	47	54	64	53	59	60	51	70	67	48	67	53	63	64	59	71	73
59270	SIDNEY	75	58	40	56	64	72	60	68	66	58	78	79	54	76	60	68	72	68	78	86
59274	VIDA	88	62	32	58	72	80	61	75	70	60	82	91	52	81	63	74	75	74	90	105
59275	WESTBY	78	55	29	52	64	71	54	67	62	53	73	80	46	71	56	65	66	66	79	93
59276	WHITETAIL	60	42	22	40	49	55	41	51	48	41	56	62	35	55	43	50	51	50	61	71
59301	MILES CITY	66	53	39	51	57	66	56	61	61	54	72	69	51	70	56	64	67	61	71	74
59311	ALZADA	66	46	24	44	54	60	46	57	53	45	62	68	39	61	47	55	56	56	67	79
59312	ANGELA	73	51	27	48	59	67	50	62	58	50	68	75	43	67	52	61	62	61	74	87
59313	BAKER	78	54	28	51	63	71	54	66	62	53	73	80	46	71	56	65	66	66	79	93
59314	BIDDLE	75	52	27	50	61	68	52	64	60	51	70	77	44	69	54	63	64	63	76	89
59315	BLOOMFIELD	67	47	24	44	54	61	46	57	53	46	62	69	39	61	48	56	57	56	68	79
59316	BOYES	65	45	24	43	53	59	45	55	51	44	60	66	38	59	46	54	55	54	66	77
59317	BROADUS	66	49	31	47	55	64	53	60	60	51	71	68	47	67	53	63	64	60	72	75
59318	BRUSETT	53	42	29	38	47	53	40	48	45	39	53	56	35	52	42	48	49	47	56	65
59322	COHAGEN	70	49	26	46	57	64	48	60	56	48	66	72	41	64	50	59	60	59	71	83
59324	EKALAKA	63	44	23	41	51	57	43	54	50	43	59	65	37	57	45	52	53	53	64	75
59326	FALLON	65	45	24	43	53	59	45	55	51	44	60	66	38	59	46	54	55	54	66	77
59327	FORSYTH	76	55	32	52	62	72	57	67	65	55	76	78	50	73	58	68	70	66	80	87
59330	GLENDIVE	67	53	38	51	58	65	54	61	59	53	71	72	49	69	55	61	66	61	69	78
59332	HAMMOND	66	46	24	43	53	60	45	56	52	45	61	68	39	60	47	55	56	55	67	78
59336	ISMAY	78	54	28	51	63	71	54	66	62	53	72	80	46	71	56	65	66	65	79	92
59337	JORDAN	61	45	28	42	52	58	44	53	50	43	59	63	38	58	46	53	54	52	63	73
59338	KINSEY	78	54	29	51	63	71	54	67	62	53	73	80	46	71	56	65	66	66	79	93
59339	LINDSAY	65	45	24	43	53	59	45	56	52	44	61	67	38	60	47	54	55	55	66	77
59341	MILDRED	65	46	24	43	53	60	45	56	52	45	61	67	38	60	47	55	56	55	66	78
59343	OLIVE	64	45	23	42	52	58	44	55	51	44	60	66	38	58	46	53	54	54	65	76
59344	PLEVNA	68	48	25	45	55	62	47	58	54	46	64	70	40	62	49	57	58	57	69	81
59345	POWDERVILLE	49	34	18	32	40	45	34	42	39	34	46	51	29	45	35	41	42	41	50	59
59347	ROSEBUD	94	88	72	86	89	93	82	89	83	84	102	104	79	100	82	82	98	87	89	107
59349	TERRY	56	41	26	40	46	54	45	50	50	43	59	58	40	56	45	53	54	50	60	63
59351	VOLBORG	73	51	27	48	59	66	50	62	58	50	68	75	43	67	52	61	62	61	74	87
59353	WIBAUX	76	56	34	53	62	73	59	68	67	57	78	78	52	75	59	70	72	67	81	87
59354	WILLARD	61	42	22	40	49	55	42	52	48	41	56	62	36	55	43	50	51	51	61	72
59401	GREAT FALLS	49	50	58	50	50	54	54	52	54	52	67	61	53	67	53	53	65	53	52	57
59402	MALMSTROM A F B	63	40	38	46	37	43	60	51	61	56	76	68	51	68	49	55	72	61	48	58
59404	GREAT FALLS	80	82	80	80	84	89	79	82	79	79	98	94	80	99	80	80	95	81	82	94
59405	GREAT FALLS	62	60	63	59	60	66	63	63	65	62	80	73	62	80	63	64	77	64	64	70
59410	AUGUSTA	55	43	29	39	49	55	41	49	46	40	55	57	36	54	43	49	51	48	58	67
59411	BABB	64	50	34	45	56	63	47	57	54	47	63	67	42	63	50	57	59	56	67	78
59412	BELT	79	58	35	55	65	76	61	70	69	59	82	81	54	78	62	73	74	70	84	90
59414	BLACK EAGLE	68	62	49	60	62	66	59	64	60	61	74	74	56	70	59	59	71	63	63	76
59416	BRADY	89	62	33	59	73	81	62	76	71	61	83	92	53	82	64	74	76	75	91	106
59417	BROWNING	49	45	49	44	44	49	48	48	50	48	62	55	47	61	47	50	60	49	49	55
59418	BUFFALO	85	59	31	56	69	77	58	72	67	58	79	87	50	77	60	70	72	71	86	100
59419	BYNUM	76	53	28	50	62	69	52	64	60	52	70	78	45	69	54	63	64	64	77	90
59420	CARTER	87	61	32	57	71	79	60	74	69	59	81	89	51	79	62	72	74	73	88	103
59421	CASCADE	76	61	47	58	67	79	61	70	67	62	81	76	57	73	64	71	75	69	83	86
59422	CHOTEAU	60	50	41	49	54	60	51	56	55	50	66	66	48	64	52	56	62	56	62	69
59424	COFFEE CREEK	73	51	27	48	60	67	51	63	58	50	68	75	43	67	53	61	62	62	75	87
59425	CONRAD	72	55	36	53	60	70	58	65	64	56	76	75	52	73	58	67	70	65	76	81
59427	CUT BANK	70	59	46	56	63	71	59	65	64	58	77	75	56	75	60	66	72	65	73	80
59430	DENTON	73	51	27	48	60	67	51	63	58	50	68	75	43	67	53	61	62	62	75	87
59433	DUTTON	72	50	26	47	59	66	50	61	57	49	67	74	42	66	51	60	61	61	73	85
59434	EAST GLACIER PARK	81	67	51	62	74	82	64	74	70	63	84	87	58	83	67	74	79	74	85	98
59436	FAIRFIELD	80	56	29	53	65	73	55	68	64	54	74	82	47	73	57	67	68	67	81	95
59440	FLOWEREE	66	53	36	51	57	62	52	59	55	52	67	69	47	64	52	56	63	58	64	75
59441	FORESTGROVE	59	41	22	39	48	54	41	51	47	40	55	61	35	54	42	50	50	50	60	71
59442	FORT BENTON	70	50	29	48	57	66	52	61	59	50	69	72	45	67	53	62	63	61	73	81
59443	FORT SHAW	78	54	28	51	63	71	53	66	62	53	72	80	46	71	55	65	66	65	79	92
59444	GALATA	44	46	53	48	47	49	47	47	46	47	57	55	47	56	47	44	55	47	45	51
59446	GERALDINE	75	53	28	50	61	69	52	64	60	51	70	77	44	69	54	63	64	63	76	89
59447	GEYSER	76	53	28	50	62	69	52	65	60	52	71	78	45	70	54	63	65	64	77	90
59448	HEART BUTTE	41	38	46	36	36	42	41	40	44	42	55	45	42	55	40	45	54	41	42	46
59450	HIGHWOOD	85	59	31	56	69	77	58	72	67	58	79	87	50	77	61	71	72	71	86	101
59451	HILGER	74	51	27	48	60	67	51	63	58	50	68	76	43	67	53	61	62	62	75	87
59452	HOBSON	78	55	29	52	64	71	54	67	62	53	73	80	46	72	56	65	67	66	79	93
59453	JUDITH GAP	58	40	21	38	47	52	40	49	46	39	54	59	34	53	41	48	49	48	58	68
59454	KEVIN	75	52	28	50	61	68	52	64	60	51	70	77	44	69	54	63	64	63	76	89
59456	LEDGER	69	48	25	45	56	62	47	59	55	47	64	71	40	63	49	57	58	58	70	81
59457	LEWISTOWN	69	51	32	49	57	67	55	62	62	53	73	71	49	70	55	66	67	62	74	77
59460	LOMA	96	67	35	63	78	87	66	82	76	65	89	99	56	88	69	80	81	81	97	114
59462	MOCCASIN	78	54	29	51	64	71	54	67	62	53	73	80	46	71	56	65	66	66	79	93
59463	MONARCH	75	58	39	53	66	74	55	66	62	55	74	78	49	73	59	67	69	65	78	91
59464	MOORE	84	59	31	55	68	77	58	72	67	57	78	86	49	77	60	70	71	71	85	100
59465	NEIHART	93	73	50	66	82	92	69	83	78	68	92	97	61	91	73	83	86	82	98	113
59466	OILMONT	81	56	29	53	66	73	56	69	64	55	75	83	47	74	58	67	68	68	82	96
59467	PENDROY	76	53	28	50	62	69	52	65	60	52	71	78	45	69	54	63	64	64	77	90
59468	POWER	76	55	32	53	63	70	54	66	61	54	73	79	47	71	56	64	67	65	76	89
59469	RAYNESFORD	76	53	28	50	62	69	52	65	60	52	71	78	45	69	54	63	64	64	77	90
59471	ROY	71	50	26	47	58	65	49	61	56	48	66	73	42	65	51	59	60	60	72	84
59472	SAND COULEE	82	58	32	55	68	76	57	70	66	56	77	85	49	76	59	69	71	69	84	98
59474	SHELBY	63	52	41	51	56	62	54	59	57	52	69	70	49	68	54	59	65	59	65	74
59479	STANFORD	64	44	23	42	52	58	44	54	50	43	59	65	37	58	45	53	54	53	65	75
59480	STOCKETT	84	60	34	56	70	78	59	72	68	58	79	87	51	78	61	71	73	71	86	100
59482	SUNBURST	79	55	29	52	65	72	55	68	63	54	74	82	47	73	57	66	68	67	81	94
59483	SUN RIVER	86	60	31	57	70	78	59	73	68	58	80	88	50	78	61	71	73	72	87	102
59484	SWEET GRASS	75	53	27	50	61	69	52	64	60	51	70	77	44	69	54	63	64	63	76	89
59486	VALIER	64	46	27	44	53	61	48	57	55	47	64	66	42	62	49	58	59	56	67	74
59487	VAUGHN	76	54	28	51	62	69	53	65	61	52	71	78	45	70	55	64	65	64	77	90
59489	WINIFRED	71	50	26	47	58	65	49	61	56	48	66	73	42	65	51	59	60	60	72	84
59501	HAVRE	63	57	52	56	59	64	59	61	61	58	74	72	56	74	58	61	71	62	64	72
59520	BIG SANDY	62	46	37	44	50	59	51	56	57	50	69	65	46	66	51	60	64	57	65	70
59521	BOX ELDER	55	48	51	46	48	55	51	52	55	52	69	59	51	68	51	57	66	53	55	61
	MONTANA	72	64	57	63	66	72	65	69	68	64	83	81	62	81	65	68	79	69	72	83
	UNITED STATES	100	100	100	100	100	100	100	100	100	100	100	100	100	100	100	100	100	100	100	100

POPULATION CHANGE

# POST OFFICE NAME	COUNTY FIPS CODE	POPULATION 2000	2004	2009	2000-2004 ANNUAL RATE % Rate	State Centile	HOUSEHOLDS 2000	2004	2009	% Annual Rate 2000-2004	2004 Average HH Size	FAMILIES 2000	2004	% Annual Rate 2000-2004
59522 CHESTER	051	1396	1360	1321	-0.6	25	567	558	547	-0.4	2.33	374	362	-0.8
59523 CHINOOK	005	2562	2497	2448	-0.6	25	1080	1057	1040	-0.5	2.33	691	664	-0.9
59524 DODSON	071	158	153	148	-0.8	20	51	50	49	-0.5	3.06	42	41	-0.6
59525 GILDFORD	041	310	301	288	-0.7	21	121	119	115	-0.4	2.53	85	81	-1.1
59526 HARLEM	005	2400	2362	2325	-0.4	36	787	776	765	-0.3	3.02	599	583	-0.6
59527 HAYS	005	1538	1555	1551	0.3	68	430	437	438	0.4	3.54	349	352	0.2
59528 HINGHAM	041	309	298	284	-0.9	16	113	110	107	-0.6	2.71	79	75	-1.2
59529 HOGELAND	005	131	128	126	-0.5	28	50	49	48	-0.5	2.61	38	37	-0.6
59530 INVERNESS	041	203	189	178	-1.7	1	79	75	71	-1.2	2.52	54	50	-1.8
59531 JOPLIN	051	388	381	371	-0.4	31	158	156	154	-0.3	2.43	125	122	-0.6
59532 KREMLIN	041	305	296	283	-0.7	21	124	122	118	-0.4	2.43	87	84	-0.8
59535 LLOYD	005	176	172	169	-0.5	28	73	72	71	-0.3	2.39	54	53	-0.4
59537 LORING	071	218	210	202	-0.9	15	76	74	73	-0.6	2.81	51	49	-0.9
59538 MALTA	071	3682	3522	3375	-1.0	12	1515	1470	1428	-0.7	2.34	998	952	-1.1
59540 RUDYARD	041	397	370	348	-1.6	1	178	168	160	-1.4	2.20	121	112	-1.8
59542 TURNER	005	211	206	202	-0.6	26	84	83	81	-0.3	2.48	64	63	-0.4
59544 WHITEWATER	071	95	91	88	-1.0	13	30	29	29	-0.8	3.14	20	19	-1.2
59545 WHITLASH	051	374	371	363	-0.2	45	108	108	106	0.0	3.44	86	84	-0.6
59546 ZORTMAN	071	247	233	222	-1.4	3	105	100	97	-1.1	2.33	82	78	-1.2
59601 HELENA	049	27406	27479	27704	0.1	58	12383	12555	12773	0.3	2.13	7038	6980	-0.2
59602 HELENA	049	18343	18962	19374	0.8	84	6806	7127	7348	1.1	2.65	5226	5385	0.7
59625 HELENA	049	480	479	478	-0.1	50	1	1	1	0.0	3.00	0	0	0.0
59632 BOULDER	043	1912	1957	2002	0.6	80	711	736	760	0.8	2.42	470	477	0.4
59633 CANYON CREEK	049	486	522	541	1.7	93	208	227	238	2.1	2.30	157	169	1.8
59634 CLANCY	043	4951	5274	5507	1.5	92	1763	1894	1990	1.7	2.77	1459	1553	1.5
59635 EAST HELENA	049	5994	6140	6206	0.6	81	2165	2245	2287	0.9	2.73	1666	1702	0.5
59639 LINCOLN	049	1250	1250	1243	0.0	57	551	560	562	0.4	2.23	360	357	-0.2
59641 RADERSBURG	007	155	156	154	0.2	63	67	68	68	0.4	2.29	53	54	0.4
59642 RINGLING	059	54	53	51	-0.4	31	22	22	21	0.0	2.41	15	15	0.0
59643 TOSTON	007	340	339	335	-0.1	49	138	139	139	0.2	2.43	109	109	0.0
59644 TOWNSEND	007	3327	3327	3296	0.0	57	1341	1357	1359	0.3	2.41	943	940	-0.1
59645 WHITE SULPHUR SPRING	059	1814	1803	1782	-0.1	47	753	752	747	0.0	2.36	494	485	-0.4
59647 WINSTON	007	373	375	371	0.1	62	131	133	133	0.4	2.82	105	105	0.0
59648 WOLF CREEK	049	861	962	1017	2.6	98	377	425	453	2.9	2.26	274	303	2.4
59701 BUTTE	093	33632	32827	31978	-0.6	26	14073	13853	13606	-0.4	2.29	8649	8352	-0.8
59711 ANACONDA	023	9448	9113	8690	-0.9	16	4006	3890	3735	-0.7	2.26	2537	2420	-1.1
59714 BELGRADE	031	10933	12890	14728	4.0	100	4069	4879	5635	4.4	2.64	3005	3515	3.8
59715 BOZEMAN	031	29270	30704	33386	1.1	90	11682	12389	13654	1.4	2.29	6165	6409	0.9
59717 BOZEMAN	031	808	842	872	1.0	87	33	42	50	5.8	4.02	23	28	4.7
59718 BOZEMAN	031	16029	18302	20797	3.2	99	6219	7163	8192	3.4	2.55	4061	4557	2.8
59720 CAMERON	057	319	326	329	0.5	77	144	150	152	1.0	2.17	88	90	0.5
59721 CARDWELL	043	377	388	395	0.7	83	152	158	162	0.9	2.45	111	114	0.6
59722 DEER LODGE	077	5829	5837	5886	0.0	57	1879	1899	1935	0.3	2.32	1234	1227	-0.1
59724 DELL	001	47	48	48	0.5	77	21	22	22	1.1	2.18	16	16	0.0
59725 DILLON	001	8136	8011	7867	-0.4	37	3212	3207	3194	0.0	2.35	2061	2024	-0.4
59727 DIVIDE	093	292	282	273	-0.8	18	121	118	115	-0.6	2.29	92	89	-0.8
59729 ENNIS	057	2065	2077	2081	0.1	62	946	969	979	0.6	2.11	576	579	0.1
59730 GALLATIN GATEWAY	031	2246	2335	2522	0.9	86	957	1010	1101	1.3	2.31	603	612	0.4
59731 GARRISON	077	815	830	845	0.4	73	326	332	340	0.4	2.49	235	237	0.2
59733 GOLD CREEK	077	118	123	127	1.0	88	48	51	53	1.4	2.41	36	37	0.7
59735 HARRISON	057	405	410	412	0.3	69	158	162	164	0.6	2.52	116	117	0.2
59736 JACKSON	001	232	228	223	-0.4	34	94	93	92	0.0	2.41	58	57	-0.4
59739 LIMA	001	372	355	343	-1.1	10	161	156	153	-0.7	2.28	101	97	-1.0
59741 MANHATTAN	031	4033	4419	4868	2.2	97	1507	1675	1863	2.5	2.62	1128	1225	2.0
59745 NORRIS	057	276	279	281	0.3	67	108	111	112	0.7	2.50	79	80	0.3
59747 PONY	057	176	178	179	0.3	68	68	70	70	0.7	2.53	50	51	0.5
59748 RAMSAY	093	93	95	94	0.5	77	35	36	36	0.7	2.64	27	28	0.9
59749 SHERIDAN	057	1652	1654	1651	0.0	57	726	739	744	0.4	2.19	455	454	-0.1
59750 BUTTE	093	484	494	489	0.5	75	166	171	171	0.7	2.89	129	132	0.5
59751 SILVER STAR	057	348	348	348	0.0	57	129	130	131	0.2	2.68	92	92	0.1
59752 THREE FORKS	031	3042	3158	3367	0.9	86	1195	1250	1342	1.1	2.52	841	856	0.4
59754 TWIN BRIDGES	057	1009	1008	1005	0.0	51	414	417	417	0.2	2.42	284	281	-0.3
59755 VIRGINIA CITY	057	274	274	273	0.0	57	127	130	131	0.6	2.11	84	84	0.0
59756 WARM SPRINGS	023	23	23	22	0.0	57	11	11	11	0.0	1.55	7	7	0.0
59758 WEST YELLOWSTONE	031	1654	1698	1804	0.6	81	727	754	808	0.9	2.17	423	423	0.0
59759 WHITEHALL	043	3089	3139	3206	0.4	71	1240	1273	1311	0.6	2.46	893	901	0.2
59761 WISDOM	001	224	220	215	-0.4	32	106	106	105	0.0	2.04	66	64	-0.7
59762 WISE RIVER	001	263	260	254	-0.3	42	123	124	122	0.0	2.00	81	80	-0.3
59801 MISSOULA	063	28699	28793	29803	0.1	59	12182	12371	12977	0.4	2.13	5758	5606	-0.6
59802 MISSOULA	063	17815	18368	19297	0.7	83	8050	8408	8943	1.0	2.13	3949	4005	0.3
59803 MISSOULA	063	14268	15409	16587	1.8	94	5194	5676	6170	2.1	2.69	3874	4144	1.6
59804 MISSOULA	063	7326	7714	8164	1.2	91	2819	3010	3225	1.6	2.51	1969	2053	1.0
59808 MISSOULA	063	11347	12606	13657	2.5	98	4079	4622	5081	3.0	2.64	2895	3229	2.6
59820 ALBERTON	061	1173	1281	1357	2.1	96	466	517	554	2.5	2.48	348	381	2.2
59821 ARLEE	047	2133	2113	2124	-0.2	44	816	818	829	0.1	2.58	587	579	-0.3
59823 BONNER	063	2149	2215	2314	0.7	83	854	894	946	1.1	2.48	633	649	0.6
59824 CHARLO	047	1745	1758	1774	0.2	63	563	572	579	0.4	2.67	404	405	0.1
59825 CLINTON	063	1604	1637	1707	0.5	75	607	629	664	0.8	2.60	456	463	0.4
59826 CONDON	063	585	584	604	0.0	51	251	255	267	0.4	2.29	173	172	-0.1
59827 CONNER	081	448	466	478	0.9	86	199	210	217	1.3	1.86	139	145	1.0
59828 CORVALLIS	081	4360	5004	5417	3.3	99	1636	1890	2055	3.5	2.64	1247	1425	3.2
59829 DARBY	081	2642	2667	2702	0.2	66	969	988	1009	0.5	2.55	701	703	0.1
59831 DIXON	089	471	466	461	-0.3	43	189	190	190	0.1	2.45	119	118	-0.2
59832 DRUMMOND	039	856	842	827	-0.4	35	359	357	354	-0.1	2.35	247	242	-0.5
59833 FLORENCE	081	5106	5461	5717	1.6	92	1803	1952	2060	1.9	2.80	1468	1571	1.6
59834 FRENCHTOWN	063	2161	2515	2790	3.6	100	752	887	995	4.0	2.84	611	710	3.6
59837 HALL	039	221	216	211	-0.5	28	96	95	94	-0.3	2.27	66	64	-0.7
59840 HAMILTON	081	12826	12982	13251	0.3	68	5469	5577	5725	0.5	2.28	3531	3526	0.0
59843 HELMVILLE	077	246	247	249	0.1	61	98	100	101	0.4	2.47	73	73	0.0
59844 HERON	089	666	668	663	0.1	59	269	276	279	0.6	2.41	195	196	0.1
59845 HOT SPRINGS	089	1041	1045	1039	0.1	60	489	498	502	0.4	2.06	281	280	-0.1
59846 HUSON	063	1084	1228	1344	3.0	99	421	484	535	3.3	2.54	342	388	3.0
59847 LOLO	063	4895	5132	5410	1.1	90	1752	1867	1990	1.5	2.75	1385	1452	1.1
59848 LONEPINE	089	216	217	215	0.1	61	89	91	91	0.5	2.33	51	50	-0.5
59853 NOXON	089	541	542	539	0.0	58	227	232	236	0.5	2.32	167	169	0.3
MONTANA					0.4					0.7	2.42			0.3
UNITED STATES					1.2					1.3	2.58			1.1

# ZIP CODE POST OFFICE NAME	RACE (%) White 2000	White 2004	Black 2000	Black 2004	Asian/Pacific 2000	Asian/Pacific 2004	% Hispanic Origin 2000	% Hispanic Origin 2004	2004 AGE DISTRIBUTION (%) 0-4	5-9	10-14	15-19	20-24	25-44	45-64	65-84	85+	18+	MEDIAN AGE 2004	% 2004 Males	% 2004 Females
59522 CHESTER	99.1	99.0	0.0	0.0	0.4	0.4	0.1	0.2	4.3	4.5	5.7	7.0	6.9	19.6	29.3	17.9	4.6	80.4	46.1	47.9	52.1
59523 CHINOOK	92.9	92.4	0.2	0.2	0.1	0.1	0.8	0.8	6.0	6.2	5.9	8.4	5.7	21.4	28.3	15.2	3.1	76.5	42.7	49.0	51.0
59524 DODSON	10.8	9.8	0.0	0.0	0.0	0.0	0.0	0.0	4.6	9.8	11.8	7.8	3.9	19.0	26.1	16.3	0.7	68.6	39.2	51.0	49.0
59525 GILDFORD	98.4	98.7	0.0	0.0	0.0	0.0	0.3	0.3	5.7	5.7	6.3	7.0	6.3	22.6	31.6	13.0	2.0	78.4	42.9	51.8	48.2
59526 HARLEM	31.5	30.4	0.2	0.2	0.2	0.2	1.4	1.4	10.1	9.1	9.1	8.8	8.1	23.2	21.3	8.9	1.4	65.8	29.0	47.9	52.1
59527 HAYS	4.4	4.1	0.1	0.1	0.0	0.0	0.9	0.8	10.7	11.1	12.0	9.4	9.0	24.6	16.5	6.6	0.3	60.0	23.8	50.0	50.0
59528 HINGHAM	98.7	98.7	0.0	0.0	0.0	0.0	0.3	0.3	5.7	6.0	6.7	7.1	6.0	22.5	30.5	13.4	2.0	77.5	42.6	52.0	48.0
59529 HOGELAND	94.7	93.8	0.0	0.0	0.0	0.0	0.8	0.0	6.3	7.0	7.0	6.3	4.7	26.6	27.3	13.3	1.6	75.0	40.0	52.3	47.7
59530 INVERNESS	98.5	98.4	0.0	0.0	0.0	0.0	0.0	0.0	6.4	6.4	6.9	7.4	4.8	22.2	28.6	15.3	2.1	77.3	42.7	51.9	48.2
59531 JOPLIN	99.5	99.5	0.0	0.0	0.0	0.0	0.5	0.3	6.8	6.6	6.8	8.1	6.6	24.9	26.3	12.3	1.6	74.5	38.9	52.5	47.5
59532 KREMLIN	98.7	98.7	0.0	0.0	0.0	0.0	0.3	0.3	5.7	5.7	6.4	7.1	6.4	23.0	30.4	13.2	2.0	78.0	42.4	52.7	47.3
59535 LLOYD	95.5	95.4	0.0	0.0	0.0	0.0	1.1	1.2	6.4	7.6	6.4	9.9	4.7	22.7	33.1	8.7	0.6	73.3	40.4	53.5	46.5
59537 LORING	90.8	89.1	0.5	0.5	0.0	0.5	0.9	1.4	6.7	6.7	7.1	7.6	5.7	23.3	28.1	12.9	1.9	74.3	40.8	53.8	46.2
59538 MALTA	92.3	91.7	0.1	0.1	0.4	0.5	1.2	1.3	4.8	5.5	8.0	7.6	5.6	21.5	28.6	15.1	3.3	76.4	43.3	49.7	50.3
59540 RUDYARD	98.7	98.7	0.0	0.0	0.0	0.0	0.3	0.3	6.0	6.5	6.8	7.0	4.3	21.9	29.7	16.0	1.9	77.6	43.6	50.8	49.2
59542 TURNER	94.3	94.2	0.0	0.0	0.0	0.0	0.5	0.5	5.8	6.8	8.7	5.8	5.3	25.2	27.2	13.6	1.5	74.8	39.6	52.9	47.1
59544 WHITEWATER	90.5	91.2	0.0	0.0	0.0	0.0	1.1	0.0	5.5	7.7	7.7	7.7	5.5	23.1	28.6	12.1	2.2	72.5	40.9	53.9	46.2
59545 WHITLASH	99.5	99.2	0.0	0.0	0.3	0.3	0.0	0.0	7.8	7.6	7.3	7.0	5.9	26.7	24.5	12.1	1.1	73.3	38.2	52.8	47.2
59546 ZORTMAN	93.9	93.6	0.4	0.4	0.0	0.0	2.0	2.2	5.2	6.4	9.9	9.0	2.2	24.9	30.9	10.7	0.9	71.7	41.2	51.5	48.5
59601 HELENA	94.8	94.4	0.2	0.3	0.8	0.9	1.6	1.8	5.7	5.5	6.2	6.9	8.3	24.0	29.0	12.0	2.5	78.5	40.5	47.9	52.1
59602 HELENA	96.0	95.7	0.2	0.2	0.4	0.5	1.4	1.6	6.3	6.8	7.9	7.3	5.8	26.0	30.1	9.0	0.8	74.1	39.2	50.2	49.8
59625 HELENA	94.2	93.5	0.0	0.0	3.8	4.6	1.7	1.9	0.2	0.0	0.2	39.9	52.8	2.9	2.7	1.0	0.2	98.3	20.9	45.3	54.7
59632 BOULDER	93.7	93.2	0.3	0.3	0.8	0.9	1.5	1.7	4.8	5.4	7.8	11.0	6.5	25.2	29.3	8.8	1.3	74.0	38.9	50.3	49.7
59633 CANYON CREEK	95.3	95.0	0.2	0.2	0.2	0.2	1.4	1.5	4.6	5.2	6.9	5.9	5.6	24.5	38.1	8.6	0.6	79.3	43.4	51.2	48.9
59634 CLANCY	96.9	96.6	0.1	0.1	0.4	0.5	1.4	1.6	5.3	6.5	8.7	7.9	4.0	23.5	35.3	7.9	0.9	73.9	41.9	49.8	50.3
59635 EAST HELENA	94.4	93.9	0.3	0.3	0.3	0.4	1.6	1.7	8.4	8.8	9.4	7.4	5.9	30.4	22.3	7.0	0.5	68.7	33.1	50.0	50.0
59639 LINCOLN	95.4	95.1	0.0	0.0	0.2	0.2	0.6	0.7	4.2	5.0	8.2	7.3	1.8	21.7	35.9	15.5	0.3	77.2	46.1	51.2	48.8
59641 RADERSBURG	96.1	96.8	0.7	0.6	0.0	0.0	1.3	1.3	4.5	7.1	8.3	7.1	1.3	27.6	32.7	11.5	0.0	74.4	41.8	52.6	47.4
59642 RINGLING	98.2	98.1	0.0	0.0	0.0	0.0	0.0	1.9	3.8	5.7	7.6	5.7	3.8	20.8	34.0	18.9	0.0	83.0	46.5	56.6	43.4
59643 TOSTON	96.8	97.1	0.3	0.3	0.3	0.3	0.6	0.9	4.7	6.5	7.7	6.8	2.1	25.7	34.2	11.2	1.2	75.5	43.0	51.6	48.4
59644 TOWNSEND	97.2	97.1	0.2	0.2	0.1	0.1	1.4	1.5	5.5	6.3	6.9	6.5	4.2	22.5	30.1	15.3	2.8	76.9	43.8	51.1	48.9
59645 WHITE SULPHUR SPRING	97.2	97.1	0.0	0.0	0.2	0.2	1.5	1.6	5.0	6.1	7.3	7.3	4.9	19.9	30.3	17.4	1.8	77.0	44.7	50.1	49.9
59647 WINSTON	96.5	96.3	0.5	0.5	0.3	0.3	1.1	1.1	4.8	6.7	8.8	7.2	1.6	27.5	30.7	12.5	0.3	73.9	41.3	51.5	48.5
59648 WOLF CREEK	96.2	96.0	0.1	0.2	0.1	0.2	1.5	1.7	3.2	5.0	5.4	5.8	2.6	20.1	40.2	16.9	0.7	82.0	48.7	52.7	47.3
59701 BUTTE	95.3	94.9	0.2	0.2	0.5	0.6	2.8	3.1	5.8	5.9	6.7	6.9	6.9	25.3	26.3	13.6	2.6	77.7	39.9	49.4	50.6
59711 ANACONDA	96.0	95.7	0.2	0.2	0.4	0.4	1.6	1.8	4.6	5.0	6.0	8.2	6.4	21.4	29.5	16.0	2.8	79.6	43.8	50.2	49.8
59714 BELGRADE	97.0	96.7	0.1	0.2	0.4	0.5	1.5	1.7	7.9	7.3	7.6	7.5	7.7	32.5	22.9	6.1	0.7	72.6	32.6	50.9	49.1
59715 BOZEMAN	95.6	95.2	0.3	0.3	1.4	1.7	1.4	1.6	4.6	4.4	4.9	10.2	13.7	29.5	22.9	8.2	1.6	83.0	30.8	51.8	48.2
59717 BOZEMAN	91.5	89.9	0.9	0.8	4.1	5.1	1.6	1.8	2.5	0.8	0.5	62.4	22.8	10.0	1.1	0.0	0.0	95.8	18.7	56.1	43.9
59718 BOZEMAN	96.5	96.1	0.3	0.3	0.7	0.9	1.4	1.6	6.9	6.5	6.8	6.7	9.6	33.0	22.8	7.0	0.8	76.2	31.8	51.6	48.4
59720 CAMERON	97.8	97.9	0.0	0.0	0.6	0.6	2.2	2.2	3.1	3.7	4.9	5.2	5.5	27.9	35.0	13.8	0.9	84.7	44.8	52.2	47.9
59721 CARDWELL	97.1	96.9	0.0	0.0	0.3	0.3	2.1	2.3	5.4	5.9	9.3	7.5	2.6	24.2	31.7	11.6	1.8	73.7	41.9	52.3	47.7
59722 DEER LODGE	91.4	91.1	0.6	0.6	0.5	0.5	2.2	2.2	4.3	4.4	5.1	6.8	9.1	28.5	27.3	12.4	2.2	82.3	40.2	61.0	39.0
59724 DELL	95.7	93.8	0.0	0.0	0.0	0.0	6.4	8.3	8.3	8.3	6.3	6.3	4.2	29.2	27.1	10.4	0.0	77.1	38.3	54.2	45.8
59725 DILLON	95.9	95.5	0.2	0.3	0.2	0.3	2.5	2.8	5.8	5.8	6.4	8.1	8.4	25.6	26.3	11.5	2.1	77.6	37.5	51.2	48.8
59727 DIVIDE	96.6	96.1	0.0	0.0	0.3	0.4	1.4	1.4	5.0	6.7	8.2	8.5	5.0	21.3	32.6	11.4	1.4	74.1	42.3	50.7	49.3
59729 ENNIS	97.8	97.7	0.1	0.1	0.3	0.3	1.7	1.7	4.3	4.7	5.5	5.3	5.6	24.8	32.6	14.9	2.4	81.6	45.0	50.1	49.9
59730 GALLATIN GATEWAY	97.7	97.4	0.1	0.1	0.6	0.8	1.5	1.8	5.5	5.9	5.6	4.9	3.9	34.4	30.2	8.9	0.8	79.9	39.6	53.1	46.9
59731 GARRISON	97.7	97.8	0.0	0.0	0.3	0.2	0.6	0.7	6.5	8.2	8.6	6.1	3.6	22.1	31.7	12.1	1.2	72.8	42.0	50.4	49.6
59733 GOLD CREEK	95.8	95.9	0.0	0.0	0.9	0.8	3.4	2.4	2.4	6.5	6.5	7.3	4.1	21.1	39.8	11.4	0.8	79.7	46.3	52.0	48.0
59735 HARRISON	97.3	97.1	0.0	0.0	0.3	0.2	3.2	3.4	5.1	5.6	8.5	7.8	2.2	24.6	32.0	11.7	2.4	74.9	42.4	52.2	47.8
59736 JACKSON	97.0	96.5	0.0	0.0	0.4	0.4	5.2	5.3	5.7	5.7	5.7	3.5	2.2	22.8	40.4	12.3	1.8	80.3	47.5	53.5	46.5
59739 LIMA	94.4	94.1	0.0	0.0	0.0	0.0	2.2	2.3	7.0	7.0	6.8	6.2	4.2	20.9	28.5	17.8	1.7	74.9	43.4	50.1	49.9
59741 MANHATTAN	97.9	97.7	0.0	0.1	0.4	0.5	1.1	1.3	5.6	6.7	8.7	7.9	4.7	27.1	27.4	10.2	1.6	73.6	38.4	50.9	49.1
59745 NORRIS	97.1	97.1	0.0	0.0	0.4	0.4	2.9	3.2	5.0	5.7	8.6	7.5	2.2	24.0	33.0	11.8	2.2	74.9	42.9	53.4	46.6
59747 PONY	97.2	97.2	0.0	0.0	0.0	0.0	3.4	3.4	5.1	5.6	8.4	7.9	2.3	24.2	32.6	11.8	2.3	75.3	42.7	52.8	47.2
59748 RAMSAY	98.9	99.0	0.0	0.0	0.0	0.0	1.1	1.1	4.2	6.3	8.4	9.5	4.2	27.4	29.5	10.5	0.0	73.7	40.3	49.5	50.5
59749 SHERIDAN	96.1	96.1	0.1	0.1	0.1	0.1	1.4	1.3	4.0	4.7	5.8	5.6	4.8	18.7	34.0	19.5	3.0	81.6	48.4	50.3	49.7
59750 BUTTE	98.4	98.2	0.0	0.0	0.2	0.2	1.0	1.2	4.7	7.3	8.9	9.3	4.1	26.3	29.2	9.7	0.6	73.3	39.7	51.0	49.0
59751 SILVER STAR	96.3	96.3	0.0	0.0	0.6	0.6	3.2	2.9	6.3	6.9	6.6	5.5	5.8	21.0	32.8	14.9	0.3	76.7	43.6	52.0	48.0
59752 THREE FORKS	96.5	96.2	0.2	0.2	0.5	0.6	1.8	1.9	6.4	7.1	8.5	6.9	4.8	26.0	27.2	12.0	1.1	73.4	39.3	50.8	49.2
59754 TWIN BRIDGES	97.1	97.1	0.0	0.0	0.3	0.3	1.5	1.6	5.6	6.4	7.5	6.5	5.5	20.7	33.1	14.0	0.8	76.6	43.6	49.7	50.3
59755 VIRGINIA CITY	96.4	96.4	0.0	0.0	0.0	0.0	1.5	1.1	3.7	4.7	5.8	5.5	4.4	19.3	38.3	16.8	1.5	82.5	48.0	52.9	47.1
59756 WARM SPRINGS	95.7	95.7	0.0	0.0	0.0	0.0	0.0	0.0	0.0	0.0	0.0	4.4	8.7	34.8	47.8	4.4	0.0	100.0	45.8	60.9	39.1
59758 WEST YELLOWSTONE	93.8	93.2	0.3	0.3	0.7	0.9	5.7	6.3	4.7	5.4	6.4	5.6	3.4	35.6	33.2	5.5	0.2	80.0	39.1	54.9	45.1
59759 WHITEHALL	96.1	95.8	0.1	0.1	0.4	0.5	1.7	1.8	5.2	6.0	8.3	7.0	3.8	21.6	33.1	13.1	1.9	76.0	43.8	50.9	49.1
59761 WISDOM	96.9	96.4	0.0	0.0	0.5	0.5	5.4	5.5	5.9	5.9	5.9	3.6	2.3	23.2	38.6	12.7	1.8	79.6	46.8	51.8	48.2
59762 WISE RIVER	96.2	95.8	0.0	0.0	0.4	0.4	3.8	4.2	5.0	5.8	5.4	7.7	5.0	21.5	36.2	11.9	1.5	79.2	44.7	53.9	46.2
59801 MISSOULA	92.7	92.0	0.4	0.5	1.8	2.1	1.9	2.1	5.0	4.4	4.7	11.4	16.4	29.2	19.0	8.3	1.6	82.7	28.7	49.2	50.8
59802 MISSOULA	93.4	92.8	0.3	0.3	0.8	0.9	1.8	2.0	5.2	4.6	5.2	6.8	11.3	32.2	24.2	8.8	1.7	81.3	33.7	51.0	49.0
59803 MISSOULA	96.0	95.7	0.3	0.4	0.8	1.0	1.4	1.5	6.3	6.6	7.5	7.2	7.2	27.3	28.2	8.9	1.0	75.3	36.9	49.1	50.9
59804 MISSOULA	95.7	95.1	0.1	0.1	1.1	1.4	1.2	1.3	5.3	5.5	6.4	6.9	6.8	24.4	30.2	11.8	2.7	78.5	41.4	48.8	51.2
59808 MISSOULA	92.9	92.4	0.1	0.1	1.3	1.6	1.6	1.7	6.8	6.9	8.0	7.6	6.8	29.2	24.9	8.4	1.5	73.6	35.8	50.2	49.8
59820 ALBERTON	95.9	95.8	0.4	0.5	0.3	0.3	0.6	0.6	5.2	6.1	7.0	7.1	6.3	24.9	33.3	9.5	0.6	77.4	41.0	50.6	49.4
59821 ARLEE	59.6	56.9	0.0	0.0	0.3	0.4	3.6	3.5	7.2	7.2	8.7	7.6	6.7	26.3	27.6	8.1	0.8	72.1	35.4	51.1	48.9
59823 BONNER	95.6	95.2	0.1	0.1	0.6	0.7	1.4	1.5	5.2	5.9	7.2	7.2	4.2	27.5	32.7	9.5	0.7	76.8	41.4	51.1	48.9
59824 CHARLO	67.4	66.4	0.3	0.3	0.0	0.0	1.7	1.8	8.0	7.1	7.7	13.0	10.6	23.6	20.0	8.7	1.3	70.2	28.2	50.4	49.6
59825 CLINTON	95.8	95.4	0.1	0.1	0.4	0.4	1.4	1.7	5.9	6.3	7.0	7.2	6.3	26.5	30.9	9.0	0.8	76.4	39.5	51.0	49.1
59826 CONDON	96.8	96.6	0.2	0.2	0.2	0.2	1.7	1.9	3.6	4.1	8.4	8.2	1.7	20.0	36.6	16.3	1.0	77.7	47.5	51.5	48.5
59827 CONNER	94.9	94.6	0.2	0.2	0.5	0.4	3.1	3.2	2.8	3.4	4.3	14.4	9.2	16.3	34.8	14.0	0.9	81.6	44.7	56.4	43.6
59828 CORVALLIS	96.9	96.6	0.1	0.1	0.5	0.6	2.1	2.3	5.5	6.2	8.1	7.0	5.4	23.1	29.4	13.9	1.4	75.5	41.6	50.0	50.0
59829 DARBY	94.2	93.9	0.2	0.2	0.2	0.2	2.5	2.7	4.6	5.3	6.9	9.5	6.3	20.0	33.7	12.7	1.0	77.1	43.1	52.8	47.2
59831 DIXON	56.3	55.6	0.0	0.0	0.0	0.0	3.6	3.7	7.1	6.9	7.5	6.7	5.6	26.2	27.9	11.4	0.9	74.7	38.4	50.9	49.1
59832 DRUMMOND	96.3	96.1	0.0	0.0	0.1	0.1	0.7	0.8	5.9	6.3	6.8	6.7	4.4	23.5	30.9	14.1	1.4	76.8	42.9	51.5	48.5
59833 FLORENCE	96.9	96.5	0.1	0.2	0.4	0.5	1.3	1.5	6.5	7.3	7.9	7.4	5.3	26.1	30.5	8.4	0.6	73.7	38.7	50.9	49.1
59834 FRENCHTOWN	96.1	95.8	0.1	0.1	0.5	0.6	1.2	1.4	6.4	7.3	8.5	7.1	5.5	26.7	30.4	7.5	0.6	73.4	38.6	51.4	48.6
59837 HALL	95.9	95.8	0.0	0.0	0.0	0.0	0.9	0.5	6.0	6.5	6.5	6.5	4.6	23.6	31.0	13.9	1.4	76.4	42.8	52.3	47.7
59840 HAMILTON	96.8	96.6	0.1	0.1	0.5	0.6	1.9	2.1	5.6	5.7	6.7	6.6	5.2	20.6	29.4	16.9	3.4	77.8	44.8	48.2	51.8
59843 HELMVILLE	97.2	97.6	0.0	0.0	0.0	0.0	0.8	0.8	5.3	6.9	7.7	5.3	2.4	23.1	34.4	13.4	1.6	76.1	44.7	53.9	46.2
59844 HERON	96.9	96.9	0.0	0.0	0.2	0.2	0.5	0.6	4.5	5.5	7.5	7.3	2.3	18.9	40.0	12.7	1.4	76.8	47.1	51.7	48.4
59845 HOT SPRINGS	79.0	78.1	0.2	0.2	0.2	0.2	2.4	2.3	4.7	5.3	6.4	6.9	4.2	18.2	30.3	20.2	3.8	78.5	47.8	48.7	51.3
59846 HUSON	96.3	95.9	0.1	0.2	0.5	0.6	0.9	1.1	6.2	7.1	8.1	6.8	5.1	25.8	31.7	8.6	0.7	74.4	40.3	52.0	48.1
59847 LOLO	96.6	96.3	0.2	0.2	0.4	0.6	1.1	1.3	7.8	7.9	8.3	7.4	6.7	29.6	25.4	6.5	0.5	71.6	34.2	50.1	49.9
59848 LONEPINE	79.2	77.9	0.5	0.5	0.0	0.0	2.3	2.8	4.2	4.6	6.5	6.5	4.2	18.0	30.4	21.2	4.6	79.7	49.8	47.9	52.1
59853 NOXON	96.1	96.1	0.2	0.2	0.2	0.2	0.6	0.4	3.5	5.7	7.4	8.1	2.6	19.2	38.2	14.0	1.3	76.9	46.7	52.2	47.8
MONTANA	90.6	90.2	0.3	0.3	0.6	0.7	2.0	2.2	6.1	6.2	7.1	7.5	7.2	25.5	27.0	11.7	1.9	76.2	38.5	49.9	50.1
UNITED STATES	75.1	73.6	12.3	12.5	3.8	4.2	12.5	14.1	6.9	6.7	7.2	7.0	7.3	28.6	23.8	10.8	1.7	75.1	36.0	49.1	50.9

MONTANA

INCOME

C 59522-59853

ZIP CODE #	POST OFFICE NAME	2004 Per Capita Income	2004 HH Income Base	2004 Household Income Distribution (%): Less than $25,000	$25,000 to $49,999	$50,000 to $99,999	$100,000 to $149,999	$150,000 or More	Median Household Income: 2004	2009	2004 National Centile	2004 State Centile	2004 Home Value Base	2004 Home Value Distribution (%): Less than $50,000	$50,000 to $89,999	$90,000 to $174,999	$175,000 to $399,999	$400,000 or More	2004 Median Home Value
59522	CHESTER	17750	558	40.1	29.9	24.0	4.3	1.6	32023	36774	18	46	397	22.9	34.5	34.0	7.3	1.3	76974
59523	CHINOOK	16661	1057	42.8	31.0	20.3	4.9	1.0	30030	33785	12	28	728	24.7	30.8	33.5	8.1	2.9	79839
59524	DODSON	12369	50	46.0	22.0	30.0	2.0	0.0	28163	32327	9	17	43	25.6	27.9	46.5	0.0	0.0	85000
59525	GILDFORD	16972	119	30.3	33.6	32.8	2.5	0.8	38466	42030	41	82	95	30.5	26.3	35.8	7.4	0.0	73000
59526	HARLEM	12423	776	44.9	28.6	21.7	4.1	0.8	28785	31875	10	20	435	34.9	38.2	22.1	4.1	0.7	63039
59527	HAYS	8093	437	56.5	27.9	13.7	1.6	0.2	21710	23747	2	2	239	38.9	36.4	20.9	3.8	0.0	61731
59528	HINGHAM	15988	110	30.9	34.6	30.9	2.7	0.9	37594	40274	38	80	88	31.8	27.3	31.8	9.1	0.0	70000
59529	HOGELAND	15794	49	40.8	30.6	20.4	8.2	0.0	32327	35000	19	49	29	37.9	20.7	24.1	17.2	0.0	67500
59530	INVERNESS	17486	75	34.7	40.0	17.3	6.7	1.3	33782	36197	23	58	58	32.8	36.2	20.7	6.9	3.5	66667
59531	JOPLIN	19968	156	32.1	34.0	26.9	3.9	3.2	37898	42130	39	81	121	26.5	33.9	24.8	12.4	2.5	75357
59532	KREMLIN	17686	122	29.5	34.4	32.8	2.5	0.8	38342	39300	41	82	98	30.6	25.5	35.7	8.2	0.0	74000
59535	LLOYD	16509	72	40.3	36.1	16.7	5.6	1.4	31254	33343	16	40	54	24.1	20.4	31.5	16.7	7.4	107143
59537	LORING	13297	74	48.7	25.7	21.6	4.1	0.0	25877	29425	6	8	56	51.8	19.6	23.2	5.4	0.0	48333
59538	MALTA	17929	1470	40.8	31.0	24.4	2.7	1.1	32043	36286	18	46	1058	32.2	30.5	32.9	3.6	0.8	76364
59540	RUDYARD	20125	168	35.1	37.5	17.3	7.1	3.0	33501	35874	22	56	130	36.2	30.0	22.3	8.5	3.1	67500
59542	TURNER	16487	83	41.0	32.5	20.5	6.0	0.0	31113	35364	15	37	49	38.8	20.4	22.5	18.4	0.0	65000
59544	WHITEWATER	10247	29	51.7	27.6	17.2	3.5	0.0	24012	33610	4	4	22	50.0	27.3	22.7	0.0	0.0	50000
59545	WHITLASH	10708	108	42.6	36.1	19.4	1.9	0.0	30000	32333	12	28	82	31.7	15.9	35.4	12.2	4.9	95000
59546	ZORTMAN	18316	100	40.0	29.0	27.0	4.0	0.0	30000	34639	12	28	75	34.7	21.3	32.0	10.7	1.3	69000
59601	HELENA	23442	12555	30.5	30.6	30.0	6.3	2.6	39145	44533	43	85	7360	6.9	8.2	55.4	27.3	2.3	141321
59602	HELENA	20615	7127	20.7	34.8	34.9	7.4	2.2	45264	50156	62	92	6038	14.5	8.6	44.3	29.1	3.6	143322
59625	HELENA	8919	0	0.0	0.0	0.0	0.0	0.0	0	0	0	0	0	0.0	0.0	0.0	0.0	0.0	0
59632	BOULDER	17437	736	34.1	33.6	26.8	4.1	1.5	35360	40600	29	68	534	25.1	24.5	31.3	16.1	3.0	90513
59633	CANYON CREEK	22497	227	26.0	31.3	34.4	5.3	3.1	41477	45378	51	88	186	8.1	11.8	48.4	29.6	2.2	138793
59634	CLANCY	24530	1894	14.4	24.6	44.7	12.0	4.3	59942	65829	84	99	1696	4.7	6.8	26.4	56.6	5.5	196458
59635	EAST HELENA	17222	2245	23.9	38.8	33.3	3.2	0.9	41367	46069	51	88	1794	8.3	11.7	64.1	13.8	2.2	122904
59639	LINCOLN	16322	560	42.9	39.5	15.0	1.1	1.6	29357	32049	11	21	451	16.9	24.8	42.4	11.8	4.2	100880
59641	RADERSBURG	24266	68	22.1	27.9	41.2	5.9	2.9	50000	55237	72	97	55	7.3	14.6	32.7	32.7	12.7	162500
59642	RINGLING	12877	22	45.5	40.9	13.6	0.0	0.0	30000	31091	12	28	16	6.3	37.5	25.0	25.0	6.3	100000
59643	TOSTON	22056	139	23.7	34.5	30.9	6.5	4.3	42346	47800	54	89	113	8.0	13.3	38.1	29.2	11.5	151136
59644	TOWNSEND	17075	1357	34.6	39.6	20.3	3.4	2.1	32339	35501	19	50	1027	15.0	24.1	43.3	12.3	5.4	102951
59645	WHITE SULPHUR SPRING	16295	752	40.4	37.1	18.4	3.2	0.9	31273	33843	16	40	563	21.7	30.6	33.6	10.5	3.7	87642
59647	WINSTON	19737	133	21.8	29.3	39.1	6.8	3.0	48839	52793	70	96	108	11.1	12.0	33.3	33.3	10.2	157500
59648	WOLF CREEK	19809	425	30.1	37.4	27.1	3.5	1.9	37081	40583	36	77	348	12.1	10.9	39.7	28.5	8.9	142045
59701	BUTTE	18815	13853	38.2	31.3	24.1	4.3	2.1	32628	36648	20	51	9435	18.4	29.9	38.6	12.2	1.0	92784
59711	ANACONDA	17520	3890	42.8	32.3	21.4	2.0	1.6	29781	33097	12	24	2788	18.7	30.0	42.4	8.3	0.6	92056
59714	BELGRADE	20078	4879	20.9	35.2	35.1	6.6	2.3	45505	51361	63	93	3296	9.8	6.0	47.9	30.0	6.3	156135
59715	BOZEMAN	23041	12389	31.2	30.0	26.3	8.0	4.5	39006	44515	43	84	6629	7.5	3.0	25.6	47.2	16.8	210421
59717	BOZEMAN	9297	42	64.3	28.6	7.1	0.0	0.0	18958	21749	1	2	2	0.0	0.0	50.0	50.0	0.0	175000
59718	BOZEMAN	21229	7163	21.7	36.5	32.4	6.6	2.9	44203	49186	59	91	4955	12.5	5.4	30.8	43.2	8.1	177693
59720	CAMERON	23542	150	29.3	37.3	23.3	6.0	4.0	35939	39560	31	72	105	3.8	6.7	27.6	42.9	19.1	201471
59721	CARDWELL	16361	158	39.9	35.4	19.6	3.2	1.9	31520	35497	16	42	130	12.3	16.2	37.7	25.4	8.5	121875
59722	DEER LODGE	15416	1899	36.9	39.9	18.7	2.9	1.6	32726	35736	20	52	1343	20.0	29.1	32.9	14.1	4.0	91059
59724	DELL	14932	22	50.0	36.4	13.6	0.0	0.0	25000	30000	5	6	12	0.0	16.7	41.7	16.7	25.0	150000
59725	DILLON	17960	3207	39.4	28.2	26.7	4.4	1.3	33431	38370	22	56	2166	15.1	19.9	45.0	16.4	3.6	112042
59727	DIVIDE	24618	118	27.1	29.7	32.2	6.8	4.2	45493	50287	63	92	99	7.1	13.1	31.3	38.4	10.1	170833
59729	ENNIS	22196	969	31.9	36.2	23.3	5.4	3.2	35450	39367	29	69	674	5.5	8.9	41.0	33.4	11.3	163608
59730	GALLATIN GATEWAY	28896	1010	20.7	33.1	30.2	9.3	6.7	46178	49581	64	94	734	5.0	2.5	19.1	45.8	27.7	249524
59731	GARRISON	17496	332	36.1	37.7	20.8	2.7	2.7	34157	36862	25	61	270	13.3	16.3	38.2	26.3	5.9	122449
59733	GOLD CREEK	15005	51	35.3	45.1	17.7	2.0	0.0	35248	38329	28	67	38	23.7	23.7	18.4	26.3	7.9	106250
59735	HARRISON	15904	162	34.6	39.5	21.6	2.5	1.9	35945	38026	31	73	132	10.6	12.9	39.4	28.0	9.1	129167
59736	JACKSON	16688	93	39.8	35.5	19.4	3.2	2.2	28423	32931	9	19	57	17.5	17.5	31.6	21.1	12.3	120833
59739	LIMA	14911	156	44.9	34.0	19.9	1.3	0.0	27258	30178	7	13	120	27.5	32.5	31.7	2.5	5.8	83333
59741	MANHATTAN	18717	1675	25.8	38.9	28.8	4.9	1.7	39694	42837	45	85	1310	8.8	9.1	37.3	38.0	6.8	165395
59745	NORRIS	16061	111	35.1	39.6	20.7	2.7	1.8	35652	37698	30	70	90	13.3	13.3	36.7	27.8	8.9	128125
59747	PONY	15766	70	38.6	38.6	20.0	1.4	1.4	33622	37833	23	57	57	8.8	12.3	42.1	28.1	8.8	127500
59748	RAMSAY	23147	36	19.4	30.6	38.9	8.3	2.8	50000	54495	72	97	31	6.5	12.9	48.4	29.0	3.2	134375
59749	SHERIDAN	17689	739	45.6	32.3	17.6	3.1	1.4	27058	30297	7	11	570	9.5	18.3	41.4	21.9	9.0	124029
59750	BUTTE	21112	171	19.3	31.6	38.0	8.8	2.3	49092	53745	70	97	148	5.4	14.9	43.9	31.1	4.7	139474
59751	SILVER STAR	16636	130	36.2	31.5	25.4	4.6	2.3	35437	38473	29	68	103	3.9	4.9	43.7	27.2	20.4	168056
59752	THREE FORKS	17667	1250	27.5	40.4	27.8	2.6	1.7	37751	41472	38	80	982	9.7	19.9	44.6	22.0	3.9	118750
59754	TWIN BRIDGES	17130	417	35.5	33.6	25.9	3.8	1.2	33608	36490	23	57	332	12.4	16.3	38.3	22.6	10.5	118657
59755	VIRGINIA CITY	18647	130	40.0	36.9	17.7	4.6	0.8	31206	35195	15	39	106	5.7	15.1	32.1	31.1	16.0	162500
59756	WARM SPRINGS	22638	11	36.4	27.3	36.4	0.0	0.0	37303	32290	36	78	7	0.0	57.1	42.9	0.0	0.0	85000
59758	WEST YELLOWSTONE	23536	754	32.0	35.5	23.2	6.1	3.2	36367	40000	33	75	355	18.6	0.6	17.8	45.4	17.8	213525
59759	WHITEHALL	16228	1273	37.2	34.4	25.3	2.0	1.1	34488	38997	26	64	1015	11.3	18.9	40.7	25.0	4.0	122109
59761	WISDOM	19680	106	40.6	34.9	18.9	3.8	1.9	28340	33052	9	18	65	21.5	16.9	29.2	20.0	12.3	119643
59762	WISE RIVER	21055	124	37.1	34.7	21.8	4.0	2.4	30431	33870	13	31	85	17.7	17.7	30.6	23.5	10.6	126786
59801	MISSOULA	18120	12371	42.5	31.6	20.3	4.2	1.5	29675	34052	12	22	5027	7.2	6.0	49.8	34.9	2.2	156414
59802	MISSOULA	20259	8408	43.6	28.2	19.6	5.7	2.9	29843	33575	12	24	4253	13.5	6.3	39.1	33.9	7.3	158311
59803	MISSOULA	23941	5676	16.8	27.6	41.7	9.6	4.4	54946	62282	80	99	4418	1.7	1.3	35.7	56.6	4.8	193016
59804	MISSOULA	21673	3010	22.8	32.3	36.4	5.9	2.7	45709	50739	63	93	2159	11.4	4.3	22.5	52.5	9.4	197491
59808	MISSOULA	19303	4622	27.4	29.0	35.1	5.8	2.6	43644	48109	58	90	3644	24.3	11.3	24.3	34.6	5.5	143031
59820	ALBERTON	23754	517	29.2	26.9	31.7	7.7	4.5	45203	50152	62	92	433	10.9	8.6	29.6	34.4	16.6	178409
59821	ARLEE	16508	818	39.4	30.4	22.7	6.0	1.5	32229	35534	18	47	644	18.8	9.5	35.9	28.9	7.0	132692
59823	BONNER	20190	894	25.5	38.0	28.9	5.0	2.6	39927	44308	46	86	732	8.6	6.3	33.9	39.2	12.0	178462
59824	CHARLO	13192	572	40.7	35.7	20.3	2.8	0.5	31287	34071	16	41	428	15.4	11.9	31.8	35.5	5.4	150000
59825	CLINTON	18429	629	25.9	38.6	29.9	3.8	1.8	39006	43591	43	84	509	10.4	7.3	36.4	40.3	5.7	166734
59826	CONDON	19074	255	38.0	31.8	24.3	3.1	2.8	33962	36921	24	59	207	10.1	8.2	23.7	37.2	20.8	196711
59827	CONNER	25325	210	39.5	34.3	16.2	5.7	4.3	32344	34764	19	50	170	7.1	8.8	37.1	26.5	20.6	165385
59828	CORVALLIS	17604	1890	32.7	34.2	24.7	6.5	2.0	35769	39306	31	72	1519	9.7	6.5	28.7	43.7	11.4	188455
59829	DARBY	16371	988	36.4	40.5	16.4	4.2	2.5	30835	33868	14	35	760	8.3	8.7	32.4	31.8	18.8	177841
59831	DIXON	13945	190	54.7	20.5	19.5	3.2	2.1	21774	23637	3	2	142	41.6	20.4	21.1	9.2	7.8	64444
59832	DRUMMOND	17862	357	37.5	35.0	21.3	3.9	2.2	31268	34602	16	40	276	18.8	30.8	27.9	15.2	7.3	95000
59833	FLORENCE	22030	1952	19.6	35.1	33.6	8.5	3.2	46095	51391	64	94	1658	8.8	5.6	33.5	48.3	3.9	178661
59834	FRENCHTOWN	21002	887	17.9	29.8	43.1	7.2	2.0	51767	57001	75	98	770	10.9	6.2	27.4	45.1	10.4	192213
59837	HALL	17308	95	36.8	36.8	21.1	4.2	1.1	31219	33595	16	39	73	21.9	35.6	27.4	9.6	5.5	79286
59840	HAMILTON	21461	5577	38.3	34.6	18.6	5.3	3.3	31210	35119	15	39	3908	9.1	7.8	38.8	34.0	10.3	160733
59843	HELMVILLE	14334	100	46.0	34.0	17.0	3.0	0.0	27286	30951	8	14	75	8.0	16.0	33.3	18.7	24.0	155357
59844	HERON	16963	276	37.7	38.4	17.4	4.4	2.2	32428	36064	19	51	221	14.5	12.2	37.1	26.2	10.0	141146
59845	HOT SPRINGS	14353	498	63.1	21.7	12.3	1.6	1.4	18189	20530	1	1	335	21.2	24.5	33.1	12.2	9.0	96304
59846	HUSON	23681	484	18.8	29.6	41.9	7.2	2.5	51346	56576	74	98	419	10.0	4.1	24.3	47.0	14.6	213851
59847	LOLO	21689	1867	15.5	35.7	39.5	6.2	3.1	49004	54779	70	97	1526	9.6	4.1	48.0	34.2	4.1	159831
59848	LONEPINE	12521	91	67.0	18.7	12.1	1.1	1.1	16731	18622	1	1	61	19.7	24.6	37.7	11.5	6.6	98750
59853	NOXON	17613	232	36.2	38.8	18.5	4.3	2.2	32700	35990	20	52	184	14.1	13.0	35.3	26.6	10.9	141176
	MONTANA	19326		33.9	32.7	25.9	5.0	2.5	36188	40555				14.7	16.4	40.8	23.3	4.9	122379
	UNITED STATES	25866		24.7	27.1	30.8	10.9	6.5	48124	56710				10.9	15.0	33.7	30.1	10.4	145905

ZIP CODE #	POST OFFICE NAME	FINANCIAL SERVICES: Auto Loan	Home Loan	Invest-ments	Retire-ment Plans	THE HOME: Home Improvements: Home Repair	Lawn & Garden	Furnishings: Comput-ers & Hard-ware	Major Appli-ances	TV, Radio, Sound Equip-ment	Furni-ture	ENTERTAINMENT: Dine out/ Carry out	Sports Equip-ment	Fees & Tickets	Toys & Games	Travel	Cable TV	PERSONAL: Apparel & Services	Auto Repairs	Health Insur-ance	Pets & Supplies
59522	CHESTER	71	52	32	49	58	68	55	63	62	53	73	72	49	70	56	66	67	63	75	80
59523	CHINOOK	66	48	29	46	54	63	51	58	58	49	68	67	45	65	51	61	62	58	70	75
59524	DODSON	67	49	28	46	56	62	48	58	54	47	64	70	42	63	50	56	59	57	68	80
59525	GILDFORD	78	54	28	51	63	71	54	66	62	53	72	80	46	71	56	65	66	65	79	92
59526	HARLEM	57	46	41	44	48	57	50	53	55	50	67	60	48	65	50	58	63	54	60	64
59527	HAYS	39	36	42	34	34	40	39	38	42	40	53	43	40	52	39	43	51	39	40	43
59528	HINGHAM	78	55	29	52	64	71	54	67	62	53	73	81	46	72	56	65	67	66	80	93
59529	HOGELAND	75	52	27	49	61	68	51	64	59	51	70	77	44	68	53	62	63	63	76	89
59530	INVERNESS	80	56	29	53	65	73	55	68	63	54	74	82	47	73	57	66	68	67	81	95
59531	JOPLIN	88	61	32	58	72	80	61	75	70	60	82	90	52	80	63	73	75	74	89	105
59532	KREMLIN	78	54	28	51	63	71	54	66	62	53	72	80	46	71	56	65	66	65	79	92
59535	LLOYD	71	50	26	47	58	65	49	61	57	49	66	73	42	65	51	60	61	60	72	85
59537	LORING	68	47	25	45	55	62	47	58	54	46	63	70	40	62	49	57	58	57	69	81
59538	MALTA	71	52	32	50	58	68	56	64	63	53	74	73	49	71	56	66	67	63	76	81
59540	RUDYARD	80	56	29	53	65	73	55	68	64	55	75	82	47	73	57	67	68	67	81	95
59542	TURNER	74	52	27	49	60	67	51	63	59	50	69	76	44	68	53	62	63	62	75	88
59544	WHITEWATER	58	41	21	38	47	53	40	50	46	40	54	60	34	53	42	49	49	49	59	69
59545	WHITLASH	67	46	24	44	54	61	46	57	53	45	62	68	39	61	48	55	57	56	68	79
59546	ZORTMAN	77	54	28	51	63	70	53	66	61	53	72	79	45	71	55	64	66	65	78	92
59601	HELENA	67	71	81	72	71	74	73	71	71	72	89	84	74	90	72	69	87	72	68	78
59602	HELENA	81	82	74	80	82	85	76	80	75	77	93	94	76	93	77	74	91	79	78	94
59625	HELENA	0	0	0	0	0	0	0	0	0	0	0	0	0	0	0	0	0	0	0	0
59632	BOULDER	69	61	47	59	63	69	60	65	63	60	76	75	56	73	60	63	72	64	69	78
59633	CANYON CREEK	89	68	44	65	76	84	66	79	73	66	87	94	59	86	68	76	81	78	89	105
59634	CLANCY	97	104	98	103	106	108	95	100	93	94	114	118	96	119	97	92	112	97	97	118
59635	EAST HELENA	67	70	67	70	69	71	67	68	65	67	81	79	67	82	66	63	79	67	64	76
59639	LINCOLN	62	48	33	44	54	61	46	55	52	45	61	64	41	60	49	55	57	54	65	75
59641	RADERSBURG	101	70	37	66	82	92	69	86	80	69	94	104	59	92	72	84	86	85	102	120
59642	RINGLING	53	41	28	37	46	52	39	47	44	39	52	55	35	52	41	47	49	46	55	64
59643	TOSTON	97	68	35	64	79	88	67	83	77	66	90	100	57	89	69	81	82	82	99	115
59644	TOWNSEND	70	51	31	49	57	67	54	62	61	52	72	72	48	69	55	65	66	62	74	79
59645	WHITE SULPHUR SPRING	66	49	30	46	55	63	50	59	56	48	66	68	44	64	51	60	61	58	70	78
59647	WINSTON	101	70	37	66	82	92	69	86	80	69	94	103	59	92	72	84	86	85	102	120
59648	WOLF CREEK	76	60	41	54	67	75	56	68	64	56	75	79	50	74	60	68	70	67	80	93
59701	BUTTE	62	59	58	58	60	67	61	62	63	59	77	71	60	77	61	64	74	62	66	71
59711	ANACONDA	61	51	43	49	54	63	54	58	59	52	71	66	51	69	55	62	66	58	67	69
59714	BELGRADE	76	81	77	81	79	80	76	77	73	77	91	91	76	91	75	70	89	76	71	87
59715	BOZEMAN	75	69	81	74	68	73	83	75	80	79	101	93	79	97	77	75	98	80	69	83
59717	BOZEMAN	34	20	26	23	20	24	40	29	38	33	48	40	32	43	32	34	45	36	27	33
59718	BOZEMAN	80	73	75	76	72	76	78	76	77	78	97	92	75	92	74	73	94	79	72	88
59720	CAMERON	87	68	46	61	77	86	64	77	73	64	86	90	57	85	68	78	80	76	91	106
59721	CARDWELL	73	51	27	48	59	66	50	62	58	49	68	75	43	66	52	61	62	61	74	86
59722	DEER LODGE	66	52	36	49	56	64	52	59	58	52	69	69	48	66	53	60	64	59	68	75
59724	DELL	59	41	22	39	48	54	41	50	47	40	55	61	35	54	42	49	50	50	60	70
59725	DILLON	69	56	46	54	60	68	57	63	62	57	75	74	53	74	58	64	71	64	71	80
59727	DIVIDE	103	74	41	69	85	96	72	89	83	71	97	107	62	96	75	87	89	88	106	123
59729	ENNIS	78	60	40	56	67	77	61	71	69	59	81	81	55	79	63	73	75	70	84	91
59730	GALLATIN GATEWAY	108	93	71	87	101	110	87	100	94	86	112	118	81	113	91	98	106	98	112	131
59731	GARRISON	78	56	31	52	65	72	55	67	63	54	74	81	47	72	57	66	67	66	80	93
59733	GOLD CREEK	65	46	24	43	53	60	45	56	52	45	61	67	39	60	47	55	56	55	66	78
59735	HARRISON	73	51	27	48	59	66	50	62	58	49	68	75	43	66	52	61	62	61	74	86
59736	JACKSON	69	54	37	49	61	68	51	61	57	50	68	72	45	67	54	61	63	60	72	84
59739	LIMA	58	45	31	41	51	57	43	51	48	42	57	60	38	56	45	51	53	51	61	70
59741	MANHATTAN	83	67	44	63	73	80	63	74	70	63	83	88	59	84	65	72	78	72	83	98
59745	NORRIS	73	51	27	48	59	66	50	62	58	50	68	75	43	67	52	61	62	61	74	86
59747	PONY	72	50	26	48	59	66	50	62	57	49	67	74	43	66	52	60	61	61	73	86
59748	RAMSAY	98	87	66	83	92	99	80	89	86	81	104	106	79	106	83	88	99	87	97	115
59749	SHERIDAN	67	48	28	46	55	63	51	59	57	49	68	69	44	65	51	61	62	59	71	77
59750	BUTTE	98	87	66	83	92	99	80	89	85	80	104	106	79	106	83	88	99	87	96	115
59751	SILVER STAR	81	56	29	53	66	73	56	69	64	55	75	83	47	74	58	67	68	68	82	96
59752	THREE FORKS	74	60	41	58	64	71	59	67	64	59	77	78	54	74	59	65	72	66	73	85
59754	TWIN BRIDGES	75	52	27	49	61	68	52	64	60	51	70	77	44	68	54	62	64	63	76	89
59755	VIRGINIA CITY	71	50	26	47	58	65	49	61	56	48	66	73	42	65	51	59	60	60	72	84
59756	WARM SPRINGS	68	51	34	49	56	67	56	62	63	53	74	69	50	70	56	67	68	62	74	75
59758	WEST YELLOWSTONE	80	66	69	71	67	72	74	73	75	74	94	89	69	88	70	72	90	77	71	87
59759	WHITEHALL	69	50	29	47	56	65	52	60	59	50	69	70	45	66	52	62	63	60	72	79
59761	WISDOM	69	54	37	49	61	68	51	61	57	50	68	72	45	67	54	61	63	60	72	84
59762	WISE RIVER	74	57	38	52	65	73	54	65	61	54	73	77	48	72	58	65	67	64	77	90
59801	MISSOULA	54	48	59	52	47	51	60	54	59	57	74	68	56	71	55	55	72	59	50	60
59802	MISSOULA	61	55	63	58	55	60	64	60	63	62	79	73	61	76	61	60	76	64	58	68
59803	MISSOULA	87	100	106	102	98	98	93	93	88	94	111	108	97	113	93	84	110	91	83	102
59804	MISSOULA	73	83	89	83	82	84	79	78	75	78	94	91	81	98	79	74	93	77	73	86
59808	MISSOULA	77	76	71	76	75	79	73	75	72	74	89	88	72	86	72	70	87	75	73	86
59820	ALBERTON	84	86	82	86	87	92	83	85	82	82	101	99	84	103	83	81	98	83	84	97
59821	ARLEE	68	61	47	58	63	67	58	63	60	59	73	73	55	72	58	60	70	62	65	77
59823	BONNER	82	69	51	64	75	83	65	74	70	64	85	88	61	85	68	74	80	73	84	98
59824	CHARLO	62	48	31	46	52	59	47	55	53	47	63	64	43	62	48	55	58	54	62	71
59825	CLINTON	77	68	52	65	72	78	63	70	67	63	82	84	61	83	65	69	77	68	76	91
59826	CONDON	74	58	40	52	65	74	55	66	62	54	73	77	49	73	58	66	68	65	78	90
59827	CONNER	89	70	48	63	79	88	66	79	75	65	88	93	59	87	70	80	82	78	94	109
59828	CORVALLIS	80	60	36	57	67	76	60	70	67	59	80	84	53	78	61	70	73	69	82	94
59829	DARBY	73	56	36	53	62	70	55	64	61	54	73	76	50	72	57	64	68	63	74	85
59831	DIXON	59	44	28	39	48	54	44	51	50	44	60	60	39	57	44	53	55	51	59	68
59832	DRUMMOND	75	54	30	50	62	70	53	65	60	52	71	77	45	70	55	64	65	64	77	90
59833	FLORENCE	83	97	99	97	96	95	88	89	83	88	104	105	92	109	89	81	103	86	81	100
59834	FRENCHTOWN	84	84	89	86	85	89	85	86	83	85	103	100	84	100	84	81	100	86	83	96
59837	HALL	71	50	26	47	58	65	49	61	57	49	66	73	42	65	51	59	61	60	72	84
59840	HAMILTON	83	63	41	60	70	81	65	74	72	63	86	85	58	81	66	76	78	74	88	95
59843	HELMVILLE	60	47	31	42	53	59	44	54	50	44	60	63	40	59	47	54	55	53	63	73
59844	HERON	74	52	27	49	60	68	51	63	59	51	69	76	44	68	53	62	63	62	75	88
59845	HOT SPRINGS	48	36	24	35	40	47	40	44	45	38	52	50	35	50	39	47	48	44	53	54
59846	HUSON	83	84	94	87	85	90	85	86	83	85	104	101	85	102	85	82	101	87	84	96
59847	LOLO	83	91	92	93	88	88	87	86	81	88	103	102	87	103	85	77	101	85	76	94
59848	LONEPINE	47	36	23	34	39	47	39	43	44	37	52	49	35	49	39	47	47	43	52	52
59853	NOXON	74	52	27	49	60	68	51	63	59	51	69	76	44	68	53	62	63	62	75	88
	MONTANA	72	64	57	63	66	72	65	69	68	64	83	81	62	81	65	68	79	69	72	83
	UNITED STATES	100	100	100	100	100	100	100	100	100	100	100	100	100	100	100	100	100	100	100	100

POPULATION CHANGE

ZIP CODE		COUNTY FIPS CODE	POPULATION			2000-2004 ANNUAL RATE		HOUSEHOLDS					FAMILIES		
#	POST OFFICE NAME		2000	2004	2009	% Rate	State Centile	2000	2004	2009	% Annual Rate 2000-2004	2004 Average HH Size	2000	2004	% Annual Rate 2000-2004
59854	OVANDO	077	297	300	303	0.2	67	123	125	128	0.4	2.39	91	92	0.3
59858	PHILIPSBURG	039	1571	1574	1558	0.0	58	656	662	660	0.2	2.33	409	406	-0.2
59859	PLAINS	089	3369	3388	3375	0.1	62	1381	1409	1428	0.5	2.33	938	942	0.1
59860	POLSON	047	9549	9643	9781	0.2	66	3860	3917	4000	0.4	2.42	2662	2658	0.0
59864	RONAN	047	6534	6562	6595	0.1	61	2295	2316	2338	0.2	2.74	1673	1664	-0.1
59865	SAINT IGNATIUS	047	2872	2797	2787	-0.6	24	1061	1045	1049	-0.4	2.68	748	724	-0.8
59866	SAINT REGIS	061	1099	1068	1050	-0.7	22	469	463	462	-0.3	2.30	308	299	-0.7
59868	SEELEY LAKE	063	1848	1928	2021	1.0	88	761	808	857	1.4	2.38	533	553	0.9
59870	STEVENSVILLE	081	8259	8625	8872	1.0	89	3169	3348	3471	1.3	2.55	2355	2450	0.9
59871	SULA	081	218	236	248	1.9	94	103	113	120	2.2	1.98	69	75	2.0
59872	SUPERIOR	061	2230	2229	2218	0.0	52	890	902	912	0.3	2.40	602	600	-0.1
59873	THOMPSON FALLS	089	2555	2554	2538	0.0	52	1067	1088	1102	0.5	2.31	730	732	0.1
59874	TROUT CREEK	089	1456	1462	1454	0.1	61	588	603	612	0.6	2.39	434	439	0.3
59875	VICTOR	081	3342	3587	3759	1.7	93	1323	1435	1514	1.9	2.50	982	1047	1.5
59901	KALISPELL	029	41905	43635	45817	1.0	87	16631	17489	18549	1.2	2.46	11325	11748	0.9
59910	BIG ARM	047	392	408	417	1.0	87	171	180	185	1.2	2.27	125	129	0.7
59911	BIGFORK	047	6848	7542	8048	2.3	97	2884	3233	3493	2.7	2.31	2060	2270	2.3
59912	COLUMBIA FALLS	029	11480	12192	12845	1.4	92	4288	4593	4882	1.6	2.62	3200	3380	1.3
59914	DAYTON	047	233	238	240	0.5	77	106	110	112	0.9	2.16	73	74	0.3
59915	ELMO	047	254	262	265	0.7	84	98	102	104	1.0	2.57	69	70	0.3
59916	ESSEX	029	261	252	255	-0.8	18	97	93	96	-1.0	1.84	50	47	-1.5
59917	EUREKA	053	4515	4509	4509	0.0	51	1836	1871	1909	0.5	2.38	1263	1266	0.1
59920	KILA	029	870	894	925	0.6	82	335	349	365	1.0	2.55	255	262	0.6
59922	LAKESIDE	029	1824	1998	2139	2.2	97	770	842	905	2.1	2.37	567	610	1.7
59923	LIBBY	053	10161	10134	10141	-0.1	50	4178	4236	4317	0.3	2.36	2872	2871	0.0
59925	MARION	029	725	744	769	0.6	81	272	283	297	0.9	2.54	207	212	0.6
59928	POLEBRIDGE	029	92	90	91	-0.5	29	47	46	47	-0.5	1.33	27	17	-10.3
59929	PROCTOR	047	107	116	120	1.9	95	46	50	52	2.0	2.32	33	36	2.1
59930	REXFORD	053	868	883	890	0.4	72	340	354	363	1.0	2.48	245	252	0.7
59931	ROLLINS	047	355	383	399	1.8	94	156	169	178	1.9	2.27	113	121	1.6
59932	SOMERS	029	1299	1315	1348	0.3	69	560	572	592	0.5	2.30	389	390	0.1
59935	TROY	053	3293	3319	3340	0.2	64	1410	1453	1494	0.7	2.28	955	968	0.3
59937	WHITEFISH	029	11674	12197	12764	1.0	89	4786	5073	5368	1.4	2.38	3120	3240	0.9
MONTANA						0.4					0.7	2.42			0.3
UNITED STATES						1.2					1.3	2.58			1.1

#	POST OFFICE NAME	White 2000	White 2004	Black 2000	Black 2004	Asian/Pacific 2000	Asian/Pacific 2004	% Hispanic Origin 2000	% Hispanic Origin 2004	0-4	5-9	10-14	15-19	20-24	25-44	45-64	65-84	85+	18+	MEDIAN AGE 2004	% 2004 Males	% 2004 Females
59854	OVANDO	97.0	96.3	0.3	0.3	0.3	0.3	1.4	1.3	5.0	6.7	7.7	5.7	2.7	23.3	35.3	12.3	1.3	76.0	44.4	54.0	46.0
59858	PHILIPSBURG	96.2	96.1	0.0	0.0	0.3	0.3	1.7	1.7	4.0	4.8	6.7	6.7	5.3	20.3	34.0	15.9	2.4	79.5	46.4	50.5	49.5
59859	PLAINS	94.5	94.4	0.1	0.1	0.5	0.5	2.1	2.1	5.2	5.2	6.4	7.2	4.8	20.5	32.9	15.7	2.2	78.3	45.4	49.8	50.2
59860	POLSON	77.1	75.4	0.1	0.1	0.5	0.6	2.3	2.4	6.6	6.3	7.4	7.5	6.1	21.9	27.3	14.6	2.3	74.8	41.0	48.5	51.5
59864	RONAN	59.6	57.0	0.1	0.1	0.3	0.3	3.3	3.3	8.2	7.8	8.6	8.4	7.4	24.7	23.7	9.5	1.7	69.7	32.9	49.1	50.9
59865	SAINT IGNATIUS	61.0	58.1	0.1	0.1	0.2	0.3	2.9	2.8	7.5	7.3	8.0	7.8	8.0	23.7	26.0	10.2	1.5	72.4	35.8	48.9	51.1
59866	SAINT REGIS	95.5	95.4	0.0	0.0	0.6	0.7	2.5	2.5	5.2	5.1	7.0	7.1	3.8	23.7	34.4	13.0	0.8	77.7	43.7	52.9	47.1
59868	SEELEY LAKE	96.1	95.8	0.1	0.1	0.2	0.3	1.6	1.7	5.0	5.6	8.3	7.6	2.5	26.0	32.8	11.4	0.8	75.6	42.4	52.3	47.7
59870	STEVENSVILLE	97.3	97.0	0.3	0.3	0.3	0.4	1.5	1.7	5.9	6.6	7.3	7.0	5.1	24.7	29.5	12.2	1.7	75.5	41.0	49.6	50.5
59871	SULA	95.0	94.9	0.0	0.0	0.9	0.9	3.7	4.2	3.8	4.2	4.2	6.4	4.7	17.8	40.3	17.8	0.9	83.1	50.7	52.1	47.9
59872	SUPERIOR	93.8	93.7	0.1	0.1	0.5	0.5	1.4	1.4	5.0	5.5	6.9	6.2	5.5	23.2	30.9	15.3	1.5	78.7	43.5	51.4	48.6
59873	THOMPSON FALLS	96.6	96.5	0.2	0.2	0.2	0.2	1.0	1.0	4.7	5.1	6.7	6.9	5.1	21.0	33.8	15.1	1.6	78.8	45.3	50.9	49.1
59874	TROUT CREEK	95.8	95.8	0.1	0.1	0.3	0.3	0.8	0.8	3.8	5.0	7.9	7.1	3.3	19.6	38.7	13.5	1.1	78.4	46.6	53.0	47.0
59875	VICTOR	96.6	96.3	0.1	0.1	0.3	0.3	2.4	2.7	6.0	6.7	7.3	6.5	4.7	22.9	30.2	14.6	1.2	75.7	42.4	49.9	50.1
59901	KALISPELL	96.1	95.8	0.2	0.2	0.5	0.6	1.4	1.5	6.2	6.5	7.4	7.1	6.4	25.0	27.8	11.6	1.9	75.4	39.5	48.9	51.1
59910	BIG ARM	75.3	73.3	0.0	0.0	0.3	0.5	1.0	1.2	5.6	6.4	6.4	5.4	3.9	18.9	32.8	19.1	1.5	77.7	47.1	48.3	51.7
59911	BIGFORK	96.7	96.6	0.2	0.2	0.4	0.5	1.9	2.1	3.7	5.0	6.4	6.0	4.2	20.4	36.4	16.0	1.7	80.9	47.4	50.5	50.5
59912	COLUMBIA FALLS	96.1	95.7	0.2	0.2	0.5	0.6	1.3	1.5	6.4	6.6	7.8	7.4	6.7	25.0	27.9	11.1	1.2	74.6	38.7	50.5	49.5
59914	DAYTON	73.0	70.2	0.0	0.0	0.0	0.0	0.9	0.8	5.0	5.5	5.5	4.6	3.8	16.8	31.9	24.8	2.1	81.1	51.3	47.9	52.1
59915	ELMO	72.4	69.9	0.0	0.0	0.0	0.0	0.8	0.8	5.3	6.1	6.1	4.6	4.2	17.9	32.1	21.8	1.9	79.0	49.0	47.3	52.7
59916	ESSEX	92.3	91.7	0.0	0.0	4.2	4.8	1.9	1.6	2.4	2.0	4.4	9.1	17.9	28.6	26.2	8.7	0.8	88.1	34.1	48.0	52.0
59917	EUREKA	97.0	96.9	0.1	0.1	0.4	0.4	1.4	1.4	5.5	5.8	7.1	7.9	4.6	22.6	31.3	13.7	1.6	76.2	43.0	50.4	49.6
59920	KILA	96.0	95.5	0.1	0.1	0.3	0.3	1.5	1.6	5.5	6.0	7.4	7.8	5.0	24.2	35.5	8.2	0.5	75.7	41.4	51.8	48.2
59922	LAKESIDE	97.5	97.4	0.1	0.1	0.7	0.8	1.2	1.4	6.1	6.4	6.1	5.5	3.0	22.0	33.3	16.5	1.2	77.7	45.6	49.2	50.8
59923	LIBBY	95.8	95.7	0.1	0.1	0.4	0.4	1.5	1.5	4.9	5.5	7.8	6.9	4.6	22.4	32.0	14.2	1.7	77.1	43.6	50.5	49.5
59925	MARION	95.3	95.2	0.0	0.0	0.4	0.4	1.0	1.1	4.7	5.8	7.3	10.1	4.4	22.0	36.7	8.9	0.3	74.7	42.1	55.0	45.0
59928	POLEBRIDGE	96.7	96.7	0.0	0.0	0.0	0.0	1.1	1.1	3.3	3.3	0.0	2.2	3.3	24.4	54.4	8.9	0.0	92.2	49.3	64.4	35.6
59929	PROCTOR	97.2	98.3	1.9	1.7	0.0	0.0	0.0	0.0	3.5	3.5	4.3	5.2	4.3	13.8	39.7	23.3	2.6	84.5	54.2	51.7	48.3
59930	REXFORD	96.5	96.5	0.1	0.1	0.1	0.1	2.0	2.2	5.9	6.0	6.1	7.4	5.9	22.7	32.5	12.8	0.8	76.6	42.6	51.6	48.4
59931	ROLLINS	97.5	97.9	1.7	1.6	0.0	0.0	0.3	0.3	2.9	3.9	4.4	5.0	4.4	12.8	41.3	23.0	2.4	85.4	54.9	51.4	48.6
59932	SOMERS	96.9	96.7	0.1	0.2	0.3	0.3	1.8	2.1	4.9	5.6	6.5	6.6	3.4	23.3	33.7	14.7	1.3	78.2	44.8	50.0	50.0
59935	TROY	95.7	95.7	0.2	0.2	0.3	0.3	1.3	1.3	4.2	5.0	7.6	7.2	4.0	19.3	35.6	15.9	1.2	77.4	46.4	51.8	48.2
59937	WHITEFISH	96.4	96.1	0.1	0.1	0.7	0.8	1.6	1.7	5.2	5.6	6.9	7.1	5.7	27.2	30.8	10.2	1.3	77.5	40.4	50.3	49.7
	MONTANA	90.6	90.2	0.3	0.3	0.6	0.7	2.0	2.2	6.1	6.2	7.1	7.5	7.2	25.5	27.0	11.7	1.9	76.2	38.5	49.9	50.1
	UNITED STATES	75.1	73.6	12.3	12.5	3.8	4.2	12.5	14.1	6.9	6.7	7.2	7.0	7.3	28.6	23.8	10.8	1.7	75.1	36.0	49.1	50.9

#	POST OFFICE NAME	2004 Per Capita Income	2004 HH Income Base	2004 HOUSEHOLD INCOME DISTRIBUTION (%)					MEDIAN HOUSEHOLD INCOME				2004 Home Value Base	2004 HOME VALUE DISTRIBUTION (%)					2004 Median Home Value
				Less than $25,000	$25,000 to $49,999	$50,000 to $99,999	$100,000 to $149,999	$150,000 or More	2004	2009	2004 National Centile	2004 State Centile		Less than $50,000	$50,000 to $89,999	$90,000 to $174,999	$175,000 to $399,999	$400,000 or More	
59854	OVANDO	15035	125	42.4	36.0	17.6	4.0	0.0	29708	32041	12	23	93	7.5	16.1	34.4	21.5	20.4	156250
59858	PHILIPSBURG	18053	662	41.8	32.8	19.3	2.9	3.2	29790	33491	12	24	488	21.5	20.3	35.7	17.2	5.3	100333
59859	PLAINS	15787	1409	42.1	33.6	20.4	2.8	1.1	29724	32293	12	23	1130	16.6	20.3	33.6	24.6	5.0	114865
59860	POLSON	18039	3917	40.6	32.6	20.7	3.2	2.9	30695	34058	14	33	2706	8.4	11.2	38.3	31.3	10.9	155678
59864	RONAN	15277	2316	40.7	34.2	20.3	2.5	2.4	30857	34415	14	36	1650	15.1	13.8	36.5	30.1	4.6	130556
59865	SAINT IGNATIUS	13914	1045	45.2	29.5	21.7	3.1	0.6	28390	31376	9	18	794	12.7	15.5	39.0	24.6	8.2	122024
59866	SAINT REGIS	18711	463	45.8	31.8	14.7	4.1	3.7	27281	30000	8	14	347	20.5	15.9	38.3	21.9	3.5	108789
59868	SEELEY LAKE	20521	808	29.8	39.7	23.6	3.8	3.0	36338	40106	33	75	656	11.7	16.2	32.6	31.7	7.8	148134
59870	STEVENSVILLE	19633	3348	29.7	37.7	24.6	4.7	3.3	37499	41781	37	79	2639	5.2	6.8	39.1	42.9	6.0	172814
59871	SULA	24503	113	29.2	37.2	25.7	3.5	4.4	40536	45000	48	87	90	7.8	3.3	31.1	26.7	31.1	275000
59872	SUPERIOR	16271	902	40.2	34.9	19.4	4.2	1.2	30862	34451	14	36	712	15.9	21.9	39.6	19.7	3.0	109524
59873	THOMPSON FALLS	17318	1088	37.6	38.0	18.8	3.4	2.1	31143	34930	15	38	843	12.9	23.1	40.1	18.9	5.0	110102
59874	TROUT CREEK	17667	603	37.7	34.8	20.2	4.8	2.5	31619	35526	17	43	491	11.4	13.4	39.7	24.6	10.8	132908
59875	VICTOR	19543	1435	30.4	38.9	24.9	3.6	2.3	37169	40760	36	78	1155	9.5	11.2	31.8	35.9	11.6	167420
59901	KALISPELL	19746	17489	32.1	35.4	24.9	4.5	3.1	36639	41217	34	76	12627	10.6	8.1	45.6	31.1	4.6	144507
59910	BIG ARM	18845	180	42.8	26.1	22.8	3.9	4.4	28416	31652	9	19	148	13.5	9.5	23.7	33.1	20.3	183929
59911	BIGFORK	21569	3233	31.0	33.5	27.0	5.5	3.0	37341	41412	37	79	2561	5.8	6.1	33.6	36.2	18.4	189070
59912	COLUMBIA FALLS	17409	4593	31.2	34.3	28.6	4.7	1.2	38731	43054	42	83	3537	11.4	9.0	49.0	26.8	3.8	136374
59914	DAYTON	19984	110	48.2	21.8	20.9	3.6	5.5	26507	29283	6	10	89	10.1	6.7	24.7	29.2	29.2	195833
59915	ELMO	16877	102	48.0	23.5	20.6	2.9	4.9	26095	29280	6	8	83	12.1	7.2	25.3	28.9	26.5	189063
59916	ESSEX	25454	93	21.5	33.3	38.7	3.2	3.2	45453	50000	62	92	55	9.1	14.6	34.6	25.5	16.4	143750
59917	EUREKA	15311	1871	42.0	34.4	20.6	2.6	0.4	29865	32301	12	25	1472	15.8	18.2	39.6	23.6	2.9	112749
59920	KILA	18331	349	33.8	34.1	25.2	4.6	2.3	35530	38735	30	69	286	7.0	10.8	39.2	38.1	4.9	157759
59922	LAKESIDE	22302	842	33.1	28.6	28.2	6.7	3.4	37897	41675	39	81	673	7.1	2.1	33.3	38.3	18.7	194467
59923	LIBBY	16345	4236	41.4	33.3	21.7	2.7	0.9	30659	33227	14	33	3175	19.8	24.6	37.4	15.8	2.4	97088
59925	MARION	17068	283	36.8	32.5	25.8	3.2	1.8	33849	37208	24	59	228	7.5	9.7	38.2	39.0	5.7	161957
59928	POLEBRIDGE	24332	46	60.9	13.0	10.9	15.2	0.0	18700	21491	1	1	43	0.0	0.0	20.9	79.1	0.0	217500
59929	PROCTOR	22018	50	36.0	34.0	20.0	6.0	4.0	33179	32308	21	55	41	9.8	9.8	19.5	48.8	12.2	225000
59930	REXFORD	14073	354	48.6	29.7	18.4	3.1	0.3	25622	28413	5	7	297	14.8	17.2	38.4	24.2	5.4	122384
59931	ROLLINS	22616	169	39.1	32.0	19.5	5.3	4.1	31125	33299	15	38	138	8.7	10.1	20.3	50.0	10.9	228261
59932	SOMERS	25138	572	30.8	32.5	27.5	4.0	5.2	38651	41800	42	83	459	7.4	6.3	30.9	41.6	13.7	189583
59935	TROY	13742	1453	49.4	33.7	14.3	2.2	0.4	25289	27760	5	7	1170	22.2	23.3	34.3	17.2	3.0	98525
59937	WHITEFISH	24076	5073	29.9	32.8	26.6	6.4	4.3	38961	43347	43	84	3631	9.0	5.8	35.2	39.4	10.6	174960
	MONTANA	19326		33.9	32.7	25.9	5.0	2.5	36188	40555				14.7	16.4	40.8	23.3	4.9	122379
	UNITED STATES	25866		24.7	27.1	30.8	10.9	6.5	48124	56710				10.9	15.0	33.7	30.1	10.4	145905

# POST OFFICE NAME	FINANCIAL SERVICES Auto Loan	Home Loan	Invest-ments	Retire-ment Plans	THE HOME — Home Improvements Home Repair	Lawn & Garden	Furnishings Comput-ers & Hard-ware	Major Appli-ances	TV, Radio, Sound Equip-ment	Furni-ture	ENTERTAINMENT Dine out/ Carry out	Sports Equip-ment	Fees & Tickets	Toys & Games	Travel	Cable TV	PERSONAL Apparel & Services	Auto Repairs	Health Insur-ance	Pets & Supplies
59854 OVANDO	61	48	33	43	54	61	45	55	51	45	61	64	40	60	48	55	56	54	64	75
59858 PHILIPSBURG	70	53	36	50	59	69	56	63	63	54	74	72	50	71	57	66	68	63	75	80
59859 PLAINS	63	46	28	44	52	60	48	56	55	47	65	65	42	62	49	58	59	56	67	72
59860 POLSON	73	56	39	53	62	70	58	66	64	56	76	76	52	74	59	67	71	65	76	84
59864 RONAN	68	56	41	53	59	66	57	62	61	56	74	73	52	71	57	63	69	62	69	78
59865 SAINT IGNATIUS	61	49	34	47	53	60	49	55	54	48	64	64	45	63	50	56	60	54	63	70
59866 SAINT REGIS	81	54	25	47	62	71	52	66	63	53	74	78	45	70	53	68	68	65	81	93
59868 SEELEY LAKE	83	65	44	59	73	82	61	74	69	61	82	87	55	81	65	74	77	73	87	101
59870 STEVENSVILLE	85	66	42	62	73	82	65	76	73	64	86	89	59	85	67	76	80	74	88	100
59871 SULA	85	67	45	60	75	84	63	76	71	62	84	89	56	83	67	76	78	75	90	104
59872 SUPERIOR	67	49	30	47	55	64	52	59	58	50	69	68	46	66	52	61	63	59	70	76
59873 THOMPSON FALLS	71	50	27	47	57	66	51	61	59	50	69	72	44	66	52	63	63	60	73	82
59874 TROUT CREEK	79	54	26	48	61	70	52	65	62	53	73	78	45	70	54	66	66	64	79	92
59875 VICTOR	88	62	33	59	72	80	61	75	70	60	82	90	52	81	63	74	75	74	89	104
59901 KALISPELL	74	69	61	67	71	76	67	71	69	67	84	83	65	84	68	69	81	71	73	85
59910 BIG ARM	73	56	36	51	63	71	54	65	61	53	72	75	48	71	57	65	67	64	77	87
59911 BIGFORK	83	67	50	62	75	85	64	76	71	64	85	85	59	80	68	75	79	74	89	99
59912 COLUMBIA FALLS	73	64	48	61	67	73	62	67	65	61	79	79	59	79	62	66	75	66	73	84
59914 DAYTON	73	58	39	52	65	73	54	65	61	54	73	76	48	72	58	66	68	64	77	89
59915 ELMO	73	57	39	52	64	73	55	65	62	54	73	76	49	72	58	66	68	64	77	89
59916 ESSEX	93	77	83	76	83	93	79	86	86	79	105	102	75	106	82	90	100	87	95	111
59917 EUREKA	65	46	25	42	52	60	46	55	54	46	63	65	40	60	47	57	58	55	67	75
59920 KILA	77	64	46	60	70	77	60	70	66	60	79	82	56	80	63	69	74	68	79	93
59922 LAKESIDE	90	70	48	64	79	89	66	80	75	66	89	94	59	88	71	80	83	79	95	109
59923 LIBBY	69	49	26	44	55	63	49	59	57	48	67	69	42	64	50	61	61	58	71	80
59925 MARION	76	58	37	53	66	74	55	67	63	55	74	79	49	73	58	67	68	66	79	92
59928 POLEBRIDGE	70	55	37	49	62	69	52	62	58	51	69	73	46	68	55	62	64	61	74	85
59929 PROCTOR	87	68	46	61	77	86	64	77	73	63	86	90	57	85	68	77	80	76	91	106
59930 REXFORD	66	44	20	38	50	57	42	53	51	43	60	64	36	57	43	55	55	53	66	75
59931 ROLLINS	87	68	46	62	77	86	64	77	73	64	86	91	57	85	69	78	80	76	92	106
59932 SOMERS	102	74	43	69	86	96	72	89	83	71	97	106	63	96	76	87	89	87	105	123
59935 TROY	51	39	26	37	43	51	41	47	46	40	55	53	37	52	42	49	50	46	56	59
59937 WHITEFISH	88	78	68	77	82	89	79	84	82	77	100	100	75	99	79	82	95	84	88	103
MONTANA	72	64	57	63	66	72	65	69	68	64	83	81	62	81	65	68	79	69	72	83
UNITED STATES	100	100	100	100	100	100	100	100	100	100	100	100	100	100	100	100	100	100	100	100

ZIP CODE		COUNTY FIPS CODE	POPULATION			2000-2004 ANNUAL RATE		HOUSEHOLDS					FAMILIES		
#	POST OFFICE NAME		2000	2004	2009	% Rate	State Centile	2000	2004	2009	% Annual Rate 2000-2004	2004 Average HH Size	2000	2004	% Annual Rate 2000-2004
68001	ABIE	023	176	172	175	-0.5	19	61	61	63	0.0	2.82	45	45	0.0
68002	ARLINGTON	177	2190	2298	2434	1.1	87	810	858	915	1.4	2.68	620	658	1.4
68003	ASHLAND	155	4254	4500	4775	1.3	89	1672	1788	1918	1.6	2.46	1194	1281	1.7
68004	BANCROFT	039	985	1068	1121	1.9	91	404	444	472	2.3	2.36	293	322	2.3
68005	BELLEVUE	153	23628	23782	25764	0.2	62	9458	9739	10783	0.7	2.43	6327	6524	0.7
68007	BENNINGTON	055	2335	2936	3382	5.5	99	828	1060	1237	6.0	2.76	665	845	5.8
68008	BLAIR	177	11043	11713	12462	1.4	89	4095	4406	4750	1.7	2.53	2903	3131	1.8
68010	BOYS TOWN	055	775	828	864	1.6	90	54	71	82	6.7	3.28	49	64	6.5
68014	BRUNO	023	285	278	284	-0.6	16	113	112	116	-0.2	2.48	84	83	-0.3
68015	CEDAR BLUFFS	155	1037	1051	1086	0.3	70	411	422	442	0.6	2.49	296	305	0.7
68017	CERESCO	155	1619	1648	1711	0.4	73	593	612	644	0.7	2.69	470	487	0.8
68018	COLON	155	545	558	579	0.6	77	193	200	210	0.8	2.79	150	156	0.9
68019	CRAIG	021	631	636	637	0.2	63	243	246	248	0.3	2.59	191	194	0.4
68020	DECATUR	021	895	884	882	-0.3	38	393	392	395	-0.1	2.26	287	287	0.0
68022	ELKHORN	055	9165	9911	10490	1.9	91	3035	3341	3580	2.3	2.93	2538	2777	2.1
68023	FORT CALHOUN	177	2570	2716	2888	1.3	88	939	1004	1080	1.6	2.71	758	812	1.6
68025	FREMONT	053	29337	29883	30489	0.4	73	11820	12196	12595	0.7	2.37	7924	8197	0.8
68028	GRETNA	153	5016	6473	7848	6.2	99	1737	2293	2842	6.8	2.80	1381	1820	6.7
68029	HERMAN	177	967	1064	1155	2.3	93	376	419	459	2.6	2.53	289	322	2.6
68030	HOMER	043	792	797	806	0.2	62	284	288	292	0.3	2.70	210	213	0.3
68031	HOOPER	053	1921	1896	1902	-0.3	36	758	756	765	-0.1	2.45	539	539	0.0
68033	ITHACA	155	493	510	533	0.8	82	175	182	192	0.9	2.80	137	143	1.0
68034	KENNARD	177	920	974	1037	1.4	89	333	356	382	1.6	2.74	271	290	1.6
68036	LINWOOD	023	326	318	325	-0.6	16	131	130	135	-0.2	2.45	97	96	-0.2
68037	LOUISVILLE	025	2301	2385	2519	0.9	83	891	937	1003	1.2	2.49	649	684	1.2
68038	LYONS	021	1473	1437	1427	-0.6	16	600	590	591	-0.4	2.42	407	402	-0.3
68039	MACY	173	1471	1473	1491	0.0	57	339	339	343	0.0	4.29	287	287	0.0
68040	MALMO	155	414	421	436	0.4	72	165	170	178	0.7	2.47	127	132	0.9
68041	MEAD	155	862	898	941	1.0	85	296	310	327	1.1	2.90	234	246	1.2
68044	NICKERSON	053	829	857	881	0.8	81	294	306	318	1.0	2.80	235	245	1.0
68045	OAKLAND	021	2115	2112	2112	0.0	53	833	835	839	0.1	2.46	581	584	0.1
68046	PAPILLION	153	18976	20677	23194	2.0	92	6398	7175	8246	2.7	2.82	5131	5729	2.6
68047	PENDER	173	1894	1898	1918	0.1	58	752	756	765	0.1	2.43	531	535	0.2
68048	PLATTSMOUTH	025	11892	12692	13538	1.5	90	4441	4805	5192	1.9	2.60	3255	3533	2.0
68050	PRAGUE	155	754	764	789	0.3	69	287	295	308	0.7	2.59	210	217	0.8
68055	ROSALIE	173	391	391	396	0.0	56	146	146	147	0.0	2.68	108	108	0.0
68057	SCRIBNER	053	2094	2062	2065	-0.4	33	792	786	794	-0.2	2.52	545	543	-0.1
68059	SPRINGFIELD	153	3018	3208	3529	1.5	89	1097	1194	1343	2.0	2.69	881	959	2.0
68061	TEKAMAH	021	2824	2918	2979	0.8	81	1134	1185	1220	1.0	2.43	811	850	1.1
68062	THURSTON	173	360	361	365	0.1	59	134	135	136	0.2	2.67	110	111	0.2
68064	VALLEY	055	3393	3302	3349	-0.6	13	1352	1341	1380	-0.2	2.42	937	922	-0.4
68065	VALPARAISO	155	1548	1745	1911	2.9	94	521	601	669	3.4	2.85	383	441	3.4
68066	WAHOO	155	4957	5158	5403	0.9	84	1922	2017	2133	1.1	2.48	1270	1336	1.2
68067	WALTHILL	173	1342	1358	1380	0.3	67	402	402	405	0.0	3.37	300	301	0.1
68069	WATERLOO	055	2041	2153	2246	1.3	88	857	924	980	1.8	2.32	603	646	1.6
68070	WESTON	155	796	915	1012	3.3	96	304	355	398	3.7	2.57	217	254	3.8
68071	WINNEBAGO	173	1701	1755	1803	0.7	80	478	491	502	0.6	3.54	390	401	0.7
68073	YUTAN	155	1892	1948	2030	0.7	80	631	657	692	1.0	2.96	505	526	1.0
68102	OMAHA	055	5358	5549	5744	0.8	82	2287	2451	2611	1.6	1.49	443	466	1.2
68104	OMAHA	055	34827	34827	35748	0.0	56	13922	14168	14741	0.4	2.42	8802	8864	0.2
68105	OMAHA	055	24119	23945	24370	-0.2	45	10139	10098	10345	-0.1	2.29	5095	5015	-0.4
68106	OMAHA	055	20040	19560	19834	-0.6	17	9284	9209	9465	-0.2	2.07	4832	4746	-0.4
68107	OMAHA	055	27081	26835	27257	-0.2	43	9659	9564	9750	-0.2	2.80	6267	6153	-0.4
68108	OMAHA	055	13867	13926	14245	0.1	60	5179	5217	5374	0.2	2.56	2931	2909	-0.2
68110	OMAHA	055	8522	8341	8476	-0.5	22	2932	2903	2991	-0.2	2.50	1854	1817	-0.5
68111	OMAHA	055	27249	26328	26664	-0.8	6	9604	9407	9636	-0.5	2.78	6671	6491	-0.6
68112	OMAHA	055	12039	11589	11723	-0.9	4	4426	4332	4442	-0.5	2.61	3035	2948	-0.7
68113	OFFUTT A F B	153	1463	1334	1380	-2.2	7	326	288	313	-2.9	2.70	304	269	-2.8
68114	OMAHA	055	17095	17065	17454	0.0	52	8153	8303	8621	0.4	2.02	4222	4246	0.1
68116	OMAHA	055	8710	12480	15226	8.8	100	3145	4600	5688	9.4	2.69	2411	3523	9.3
68117	OMAHA	055	8050	7835	7937	-0.6	13	3116	3093	3177	-0.2	2.50	2142	2112	-0.3
68118	OMAHA	055	8278	10239	11602	5.1	99	2510	3158	3624	5.6	3.21	2176	2741	5.6
68122	OMAHA	055	5325	6216	6849	3.7	97	1919	2252	2500	3.8	2.76	1530	1787	3.7
68123	BELLEVUE	153	24988	28021	31776	2.7	94	8191	9446	10970	3.4	2.96	6716	7714	3.3
68124	OMAHA	055	16023	15714	15995	-0.5	26	6570	6566	6780	0.0	2.29	4340	4304	-0.2
68127	OMAHA	055	22878	22906	23498	0.0	57	10004	10217	10623	0.5	2.23	5609	5665	0.2
68128	LA VISTA	153	11793	13126	14953	2.6	93	4431	5061	5897	3.2	2.59	3154	3571	3.0
68130	OMAHA	055	10713	12735	14202	4.2	98	3705	4506	5108	4.7	2.83	3114	3764	4.6
68131	OMAHA	055	14230	13754	13906	-0.8	7	5781	5604	5715	-0.7	2.15	2238	2129	-1.2
68132	OMAHA	055	13454	13055	13232	-0.7	9	6209	6111	6270	-0.4	2.07	3098	3024	-0.6
68133	PAPILLION	153	4472	5691	6853	5.8	99	1420	1802	2186	5.8	3.15	1236	1575	5.9
68134	OMAHA	055	27753	28068	29038	0.3	67	12046	12368	12947	0.6	2.25	7182	7317	0.4
68135	OMAHA	055	13182	19052	23633	9.1	100	3781	5424	6718	8.9	3.51	3550	5089	8.8
68136	OMAHA	153	2303	4544	6646	17.3	100	819	1596	2348	17.0	2.85	703	1361	16.8
68137	OMAHA	055	25144	26851	28466	1.6	90	9374	10195	10955	2.0	2.62	6892	7469	1.9
68138	OMAHA	153	12033	14638	17464	4.7	98	4143	5185	6335	5.4	2.82	3272	4064	5.2
68142	OMAHA	055	1730	1890	2015	2.1	92	648	719	776	2.5	2.63	479	529	2.4
68144	OMAHA	055	25156	25378	26145	0.2	65	9974	10266	10731	0.7	2.46	6944	7104	0.5
68147	BELLEVUE	153	10028	10082	11009	0.1	61	3699	3805	4244	0.7	2.64	2736	2813	0.7
68152	OMAHA	055	6835	6919	7101	0.3	67	2468	2543	2649	0.7	2.54	1871	1919	0.6
68154	OMAHA	055	23693	24577	25607	0.9	83	9888	10452	11045	1.3	2.33	6183	6457	1.0
68157	OMAHA	153	4842	5023	5460	0.9	83	1684	1792	1996	1.5	2.78	1378	1468	1.5
68164	OMAHA	055	25021	27840	30111	2.5	93	9765	11016	12041	2.9	2.52	6712	7535	2.8
68182	OMAHA	055	556	555	561	-0.7	52	0	0	0	0.0	0.00	0	0	0.0
68198	OMAHA	055	66	64	65	-0.7	9	0	0	0	0.0	0.00	0	0	0.0
68301	ADAMS	067	1385	1440	1506	0.9	84	503	530	561	1.2	2.61	391	412	1.2
68303	ALEXANDRIA	169	378	369	361	-0.6	17	159	158	157	-0.2	2.33	105	105	0.0
68304	ALVO	025	374	381	396	0.4	74	140	145	152	0.8	2.63	111	115	0.8
68305	AUBURN	127	4311	4299	4278	-0.1	50	1808	1829	1842	0.3	2.27	1181	1199	0.4
68307	AVOCA	025	624	629	652	0.2	63	240	244	256	0.4	2.58	180	184	0.5
68309	BARNESTON	067	122	142	158	3.6	96	53	58	65	4.1	2.40	34	41	4.5
68310	BEATRICE	067	14977	15483	16145	0.8	81	6149	6437	6797	1.1	2.26	3873	4070	1.2
68313	BEAVER CROSSING	159	828	823	846	-0.1	47	322	326	341	0.3	2.52	238	242	0.4
68314	BEE	159	492	492	504	0.0	56	177	180	187	0.4	2.73	133	136	0.5
68315	BELVIDERE	169	179	173	168	-0.8	7	77	75	74	-0.6	2.29	56	55	-0.4
	NEBRASKA					0.8					1.0	2.47			1.1
	UNITED STATES					1.2					1.3	2.58			1.1

ZIP CODE #	POST OFFICE NAME	RACE (%) White 2000	White 2004	Black 2000	Black 2004	Asian/Pacific 2000	Asian/Pacific 2004	% Hispanic Origin 2000	% Hispanic Origin 2004	2004 AGE DISTRIBUTION (%) 0-4	5-9	10-14	15-19	20-24	25-44	45-64	65-84	85+	18+	MEDIAN AGE 2004	% 2004 Males	% 2004 Females
68001	ABIE	97.2	96.5	0.0	0.0	0.0	0.0	3.4	4.1	7.0	8.7	7.0	6.4	6.4	25.0	25.6	12.8	1.2	73.3	37.5	56.4	43.6
68002	ARLINGTON	98.8	98.5	0.1	0.1	0.3	0.5	1.0	1.1	6.7	6.9	8.1	6.7	6.0	25.2	26.6	12.1	1.8	74.1	39.3	50.6	49.4
68003	ASHLAND	98.3	98.0	0.1	0.1	0.3	0.4	1.5	1.7	6.0	6.4	6.9	6.4	5.8	25.6	27.1	13.6	2.4	76.6	41.0	49.1	50.9
68004	BANCROFT	97.7	97.2	0.0	0.0	0.3	0.4	1.5	1.9	6.6	6.7	7.2	6.0	5.4	23.3	24.7	16.9	3.2	75.6	41.4	51.1	48.9
68005	BELLEVUE	85.6	83.5	6.3	6.8	2.5	3.3	5.1	6.1	7.1	6.5	7.0	7.1	7.9	29.5	22.4	11.4	1.2	75.2	34.8	49.3	50.7
68007	BENNINGTON	98.2	97.6	0.5	0.7	0.5	0.8	1.5	2.0	5.8	6.8	9.2	7.6	5.6	25.3	29.4	9.6	0.9	73.6	38.9	49.1	50.9
68008	BLAIR	97.8	97.4	0.4	0.4	0.5	0.7	1.2	1.4	6.5	6.6	7.1	7.8	8.5	25.6	24.3	11.2	2.4	75.4	36.5	49.1	50.9
68010	BOYS TOWN	66.1	61.5	21.2	24.2	0.5	0.6	7.6	9.5	7.0	5.2	21.1	48.7	6.0	11.0	0.7	0.2	0.0	24.9	16.7	67.2	32.9
68014	BRUNO	97.2	97.1	0.0	0.0	0.0	0.0	3.5	4.0	6.8	7.2	7.2	6.5	6.1	25.9	25.5	13.3	1.4	74.5	39.1	55.4	44.6
68015	CEDAR BLUFFS	98.9	98.9	0.3	0.3	0.0	0.0	0.5	0.5	5.3	6.1	7.9	7.9	5.6	24.5	27.3	13.5	1.9	75.9	40.9	51.9	48.1
68017	CERESCO	98.7	98.4	0.1	0.1	0.0	0.0	1.1	1.3	8.0	8.4	8.4	6.4	4.9	27.3	26.3	9.3	1.0	71.2	37.0	51.3	48.7
68018	COLON	97.8	97.5	0.0	0.0	0.2	0.4	1.8	2.2	6.1	7.2	8.4	7.4	5.4	23.1	27.6	13.6	1.3	73.3	40.5	51.8	48.2
68019	CRAIG	99.1	99.1	0.0	0.0	0.3	0.3	0.0	0.0	6.5	6.9	8.0	6.8	5.2	23.6	24.7	17.1	1.3	74.4	40.9	51.1	48.9
68020	DECATUR	90.6	90.3	0.5	0.5	0.2	0.2	0.9	0.9	5.7	6.3	8.0	6.3	5.0	20.5	29.8	16.5	1.9	76.1	43.8	51.1	48.9
68022	ELKHORN	98.0	97.4	0.2	0.2	0.4	0.5	1.8	2.4	7.3	8.1	9.2	8.3	5.8	26.3	26.9	7.2	1.0	70.1	35.8	49.5	50.6
68023	FORT CALHOUN	98.5	98.4	0.5	0.6	0.1	0.2	0.9	1.1	6.2	7.7	8.1	7.5	4.8	24.2	31.3	9.0	1.1	73.1	39.8	50.8	49.2
68025	FREMONT	95.5	94.8	0.5	0.5	0.7	0.9	4.2	5.0	6.3	6.2	6.4	6.9	7.6	25.8	23.6	14.3	2.9	77.4	38.5	48.3	51.7
68028	GRETNA	98.4	98.2	0.1	0.1	0.3	0.5	0.9	1.2	7.3	7.5	8.6	7.9	5.9	28.6	24.1	8.9	1.3	71.3	35.7	49.7	50.3
68029	HERMAN	99.3	99.5	0.1	0.1	0.0	0.0	0.6	0.6	6.3	6.8	7.4	6.4	4.9	24.9	29.0	12.9	1.5	75.5	41.5	52.4	47.7
68030	HOMER	95.3	94.6	0.0	0.0	0.0	0.0	3.0	3.6	6.3	6.7	8.4	7.4	5.8	25.2	24.5	13.3	2.5	73.8	38.9	51.1	48.9
68031	HOOPER	98.0	97.7	0.1	0.1	0.3	0.4	2.3	2.7	5.6	6.0	6.9	7.2	6.0	23.5	27.5	13.9	3.4	77.3	41.8	49.6	50.4
68033	ITHACA	98.8	98.8	0.0	0.0	0.0	0.0	0.8	1.0	6.7	7.3	8.0	7.5	5.1	27.1	25.5	12.0	1.0	73.3	38.9	50.8	49.2
68034	KENNARD	98.3	98.0	0.1	0.1	0.5	0.7	0.7	0.9	6.8	7.7	9.2	6.7	5.4	24.3	28.1	10.9	0.8	72.1	39.1	51.8	48.3
68036	LINWOOD	97.2	97.2	0.0	0.0	0.0	0.0	3.4	3.8	6.9	7.2	7.2	6.6	6.3	25.5	25.8	13.2	1.3	74.8	38.6	56.3	43.7
68037	LOUISVILLE	98.4	98.1	0.1	0.1	0.4	0.5	1.2	1.4	6.1	6.5	7.4	6.6	5.6	26.4	27.4	11.5	2.5	75.9	40.3	48.4	51.6
68038	LYONS	96.2	96.1	0.3	0.4	0.2	0.2	3.7	3.8	5.4	5.9	7.4	6.7	5.3	19.7	26.2	19.0	4.4	76.7	44.7	47.5	52.5
68039	MACY	9.4	8.8	0.1	0.1	0.1	0.1	2.5	2.5	14.1	11.9	12.3	10.7	8.6	22.1	13.8	6.2	0.3	54.8	20.6	48.8	51.2
68040	MALMO	98.1	98.1	0.0	0.0	0.2	0.5	1.2	1.2	7.1	7.6	8.6	7.4	4.8	21.6	25.7	15.4	1.9	72.0	40.7	50.8	49.2
68041	MEAD	98.6	98.3	0.1	0.1	0.1	0.1	1.2	1.5	7.0	7.5	8.7	7.7	5.7	27.0	24.3	11.4	0.9	71.9	37.1	50.1	49.9
68044	NICKERSON	94.0	93.1	0.4	0.4	0.0	0.0	8.2	9.5	8.8	8.3	7.6	7.5	6.2	25.8	25.2	10.0	0.7	70.6	35.2	51.9	48.1
68045	OAKLAND	98.6	98.6	0.0	0.0	0.2	0.2	0.7	0.8	5.8	6.1	7.4	7.0	5.5	20.1	24.1	19.1	5.0	76.3	43.8	48.4	51.6
68046	PAPILLION	93.6	92.4	2.2	2.5	1.4	1.9	2.7	3.4	6.7	7.4	8.8	8.4	6.7	28.4	25.6	6.8	1.3	71.6	35.2	49.1	50.9
68047	PENDER	97.4	97.4	0.2	0.2	0.1	0.1	1.5	1.5	5.5	5.9	6.6	7.4	5.9	22.2	24.1	18.8	3.7	77.6	42.6	50.4	49.6
68048	PLATTSMOUTH	97.5	97.3	0.3	0.3	0.4	0.6	1.7	2.0	7.2	7.1	7.6	6.7	6.5	26.9	25.5	10.6	2.0	74.0	37.3	48.7	51.3
68050	PRAGUE	98.8	98.4	0.0	0.0	0.1	0.1	1.1	1.3	6.4	7.1	7.7	6.3	4.5	23.7	25.7	16.4	2.4	74.9	42.0	51.6	48.4
68055	ROSALIE	80.1	79.5	0.0	0.0	0.3	0.3	2.6	2.6	8.7	9.2	9.5	7.4	4.9	25.8	20.0	13.0	1.5	67.8	34.2	51.2	48.9
68057	SCRIBNER	98.2	97.9	0.2	0.2	0.2	0.3	1.3	1.5	6.3	6.6	7.5	7.0	4.9	22.8	24.4	16.2	4.3	75.2	41.6	48.2	51.8
68059	SPRINGFIELD	98.5	98.1	0.2	0.3	0.3	0.5	1.2	1.5	5.6	6.2	7.7	6.9	6.4	25.3	30.2	10.9	0.9	76.3	40.3	50.8	49.2
68061	TEKAMAH	98.7	98.7	0.2	0.2	0.2	0.2	0.9	0.9	6.0	6.3	6.6	6.0	5.6	22.1	28.0	16.2	3.1	77.1	43.3	49.6	50.4
68062	THURSTON	98.3	98.3	0.0	0.0	0.0	0.0	0.6	0.6	7.2	6.9	7.2	5.8	5.5	28.3	22.7	15.0	1.4	75.4	38.5	50.7	49.3
68064	VALLEY	97.2	96.6	0.4	0.5	0.2	0.3	1.3	1.7	5.7	6.6	8.0	8.1	5.2	24.8	26.6	12.8	2.2	74.6	39.9	50.2	49.8
68065	VALPARAISO	98.3	97.9	0.2	0.3	0.1	0.2	1.0	1.2	6.1	6.8	8.9	7.9	5.0	26.6	25.9	11.5	1.5	72.7	38.8	51.2	48.8
68066	WAHOO	98.5	98.3	0.1	0.1	0.4	0.5	0.8	0.9	6.6	6.7	8.1	7.3	6.2	24.3	23.3	13.6	4.1	73.8	39.2	48.6	51.4
68067	WALTHILL	31.7	30.9	0.0	0.0	0.1	0.1	4.8	4.7	11.7	10.6	10.7	9.1	5.9	23.8	17.5	9.9	0.9	60.7	26.8	49.1	50.9
68069	WATERLOO	98.1	97.8	0.4	0.5	0.2	0.2	1.9	2.4	5.9	6.4	6.5	6.0	4.9	24.1	31.6	13.8	0.9	77.3	42.9	50.2	49.8
68070	WESTON	98.5	98.1	0.1	0.2	0.1	0.1	0.9	1.0	6.2	6.8	8.3	7.2	5.4	25.6	24.7	13.9	2.0	73.7	40.1	50.6	49.4
68071	WINNEBAGO	14.2	13.5	0.3	0.3	0.0	0.0	1.9	1.9	11.5	11.7	12.2	9.4	7.0	24.2	16.8	6.7	0.5	58.7	23.7	49.4	50.6
68073	YUTAN	97.6	97.4	0.1	0.1	0.3	0.4	1.1	1.4	7.1	7.4	9.5	8.2	7.3	28.2	23.1	8.3	0.9	70.7	34.1	51.3	48.7
68102	OMAHA	61.8	57.7	24.2	26.3	4.5	5.3	8.9	10.6	3.4	2.5	1.8	6.3	18.2	41.0	20.8	5.3	0.7	91.4	31.6	61.8	38.2
68104	OMAHA	68.2	65.0	26.7	29.2	1.1	1.3	3.1	3.9	8.1	7.6	7.6	7.2	7.1	29.9	21.3	9.4	1.7	72.2	33.6	47.5	52.5
68105	OMAHA	79.8	76.4	5.2	5.7	1.5	1.9	20.1	24.0	7.7	6.7	6.1	6.1	8.8	33.4	19.6	9.8	1.9	75.9	32.8	51.4	48.6
68106	OMAHA	92.8	91.2	2.3	2.7	2.1	2.7	3.5	4.5	6.2	5.6	5.3	5.2	7.7	31.2	21.6	14.2	3.0	80.2	37.2	46.1	54.0
68107	OMAHA	67.7	63.4	6.5	6.9	0.7	0.9	34.2	39.6	9.5	8.8	7.8	6.8	7.6	30.6	18.0	9.3	1.6	69.8	31.0	50.6	49.4
68108	OMAHA	73.3	68.6	3.3	3.7	1.2	1.4	27.7	33.0	8.4	7.2	6.7	7.0	9.4	32.1	18.5	8.8	1.9	73.9	31.2	51.1	48.9
68110	OMAHA	37.2	34.3	55.3	57.6	0.3	0.3	5.7	6.7	7.6	7.3	8.0	7.6	8.8	29.1	21.3	9.2	1.3	72.5	32.9	53.0	47.0
68111	OMAHA	24.0	21.4	69.7	72.1	0.5	0.5	4.0	4.7	9.1	9.1	10.3	9.4	8.0	25.8	19.1	8.2	1.0	65.7	28.3	46.6	53.4
68112	OMAHA	75.7	72.5	19.4	22.0	0.4	0.5	4.0	5.0	6.6	6.6	8.0	7.9	7.2	25.2	24.2	12.2	2.1	74.0	37.1	47.3	52.7
68113	OFFUTT A F B	72.9	69.4	13.9	14.9	2.7	3.7	8.7	10.5	9.5	3.9	3.0	15.8	46.5	19.8	1.2	0.3	0.0	82.5	21.9	59.8	40.3
68114	OMAHA	91.6	89.5	3.3	4.0	2.9	3.9	2.0	2.7	5.3	5.0	5.3	5.2	6.7	26.1	23.2	19.0	4.4	81.2	42.4	45.8	54.2
68116	OMAHA	93.5	91.9	1.6	2.0	3.0	4.0	1.6	2.1	10.4	9.1	7.4	5.3	6.1	35.5	21.5	4.4	0.3	69.6	32.3	49.6	50.4
68117	OMAHA	91.2	89.0	1.2	1.4	1.1	1.5	8.2	10.6	7.0	7.1	7.0	6.0	5.8	30.1	22.9	12.4	1.8	75.3	37.1	49.7	50.3
68118	OMAHA	95.2	94.0	1.1	1.3	2.1	2.9	1.4	1.8	6.7	9.3	11.9	10.4	4.6	25.9	27.6	3.2	0.4	64.9	34.6	49.6	50.4
68122	OMAHA	86.6	83.5	9.3	11.5	1.7	2.4	1.5	2.1	10.2	8.7	7.2	5.6	5.7	35.6	21.5	5.2	0.3	70.6	32.8	49.1	50.9
68123	BELLEVUE	82.9	80.7	8.4	9.0	3.0	3.9	5.2	6.2	10.2	9.6	8.8	7.1	8.0	35.0	17.9	3.2	0.2	66.8	28.7	49.9	50.1
68124	OMAHA	94.9	93.7	2.0	2.3	1.5	2.0	1.9	2.4	4.9	5.4	6.5	6.6	5.3	21.8	28.0	18.2	3.2	79.0	44.6	46.7	53.3
68127	OMAHA	90.8	88.6	2.3	2.7	3.0	3.9	5.1	6.6	5.8	5.4	6.2	6.9	11.0	33.2	24.1	7.1	0.4	78.7	32.3	50.9	49.1
68128	LA VISTA	90.5	89.0	2.9	3.1	2.4	3.2	4.1	4.9	8.2	7.6	8.2	7.6	8.0	35.0	20.1	5.1	0.3	71.4	30.8	48.4	51.6
68130	OMAHA	96.3	95.4	0.9	1.1	1.3	1.8	1.4	1.9	7.5	8.5	8.7	6.8	4.8	27.1	30.0	5.9	0.6	70.8	37.6	49.5	50.5
68131	OMAHA	64.6	60.5	21.1	22.7	4.7	5.9	10.7	12.8	7.1	5.4	5.4	11.8	15.3	32.3	15.8	5.9	1.2	78.8	27.2	51.0	49.0
68132	OMAHA	86.2	83.9	6.5	7.3	2.4	3.2	4.4	5.5	6.2	6.0	5.8	7.5	10.3	31.4	23.2	8.4	1.2	78.7	33.1	49.8	50.2
68133	PAPILLION	91.5	89.8	2.1	2.3	3.0	4.1	3.2	3.9	10.7	10.3	9.3	6.6	5.0	34.0	20.0	3.7	0.5	65.2	32.0	49.4	50.6
68134	OMAHA	87.6	85.0	7.3	8.7	2.2	2.9	2.5	3.2	7.1	6.3	6.0	6.0	8.2	30.4	22.4	11.6	2.1	77.2	35.0	47.1	52.9
68135	OMAHA	96.4	95.4	0.4	0.4	2.1	2.7	1.3	1.6	9.7	11.7	11.9	8.3	2.9	31.9	21.8	1.8	0.1	60.8	32.4	50.4	49.7
68136	OMAHA	97.8	97.2	0.3	0.3	0.7	1.1	1.7	2.2	10.1	9.9	8.4	5.2	4.1	33.7	22.9	5.7	0.1	68.2	34.2	49.6	50.4
68137	OMAHA	95.3	94.2	1.2	1.5	1.4	1.9	2.7	3.5	7.3	7.3	7.7	6.7	6.8	31.3	25.0	7.2	0.7	73.6	34.6	48.8	51.2
68138	OMAHA	95.4	94.4	0.8	0.9	1.0	1.5	2.8	3.5	10.7	9.5	8.3	6.7	6.1	39.5	17.2	1.9	0.1	67.3	30.3	49.6	50.4
68142	OMAHA	92.7	91.2	3.2	3.7	1.4	1.9	2.6	3.3	10.0	9.1	7.8	5.5	5.2	36.7	19.6	5.8	0.4	69.8	32.0	49.3	50.7
68144	OMAHA	94.8	93.6	1.4	1.7	1.6	2.1	2.4	3.1	6.1	6.5	7.1	6.9	6.5	26.7	26.7	12.4	1.1	76.0	38.4	48.8	51.3
68147	BELLEVUE	86.2	83.8	5.0	5.5	1.8	2.5	8.7	10.4	7.6	7.2	7.2	6.8	6.8	31.6	22.4	9.7	0.6	73.7	34.4	50.2	49.8
68152	OMAHA	72.6	68.9	23.8	27.1	0.5	0.6	1.8	2.2	7.2	6.0	6.7	7.4	6.5	20.6	28.2	13.8	3.6	75.4	41.7	46.8	53.2
68154	OMAHA	93.3	91.5	2.2	2.7	2.7	3.6	1.8	2.3	5.7	6.3	7.1	6.7	8.2	27.3	27.1	10.0	1.5	76.5	36.5	47.2	52.8
68157	OMAHA	92.6	91.2	2.3	2.5	0.7	1.0	5.7	7.1	6.8	7.2	8.0	7.6	6.6	28.2	26.1	9.4	0.3	73.2	35.4	49.2	50.8
68164	OMAHA	89.2	87.4	5.7	6.3	2.7	3.5	2.1	2.6	9.5	8.6	6.6	5.5	7.1	34.9	21.8	5.7	0.4	72.0	32.7	48.1	51.9
68182	OMAHA	91.9	89.7	2.2	2.5	3.6	5.1	1.6	2.2	3.2	5.4	5.2	25.4	12.8	13.7	22.3	10.6	1.3	84.5	24.2	49.2	50.8
68198	OMAHA	92.4	92.2	3.0	4.7	1.5	1.6	3.0	3.1	3.1	3.1	4.7	7.8	14.1	31.3	18.8	14.1	3.1	89.1	36.7	48.4	51.6
68301	ADAMS	98.8	98.6	0.1	0.1	0.2	0.4	0.6	0.6	7.6	8.1	7.6	5.4	4.2	27.5	23.8	12.2	3.7	72.9	39.1	48.0	52.0
68303	ALEXANDRIA	98.9	98.6	0.0	0.0	0.0	0.0	2.1	2.4	5.7	6.2	7.6	6.5	4.9	22.2	26.8	16.5	3.5	77.2	42.5	48.8	51.2
68304	ALVO	97.6	97.6	0.0	0.0	0.0	0.0	1.6	1.8	6.3	6.8	6.8	6.6	5.0	24.9	28.9	13.1	1.6	76.1	41.3	50.7	49.3
68305	AUBURN	97.5	97.5	0.3	0.3	0.9	0.9	0.9	0.9	5.3	5.4	6.9	7.2	6.3	22.5	26.8	15.2	4.4	77.8	42.7	47.0	53.0
68307	AVOCA	99.5	99.4	0.0	0.0	0.0	0.2	1.0	1.3	6.8	7.5	9.2	6.2	4.5	26.1	26.2	11.6	1.9	72.5	38.6	51.2	48.8
68309	BARNESTON	96.7	97.2	0.0	0.0	0.0	0.0	1.6	1.4	6.3	5.6	6.3	7.0	6.3	22.5	23.2	18.3	4.2	76.8	42.0	50.0	50.0
68310	BEATRICE	97.5	97.2	0.5	0.5	0.4	0.5	0.9	1.0	5.7	5.7	6.2	6.8	7.2	24.5	24.7	15.5	3.7	78.6	40.9	48.2	51.8
68313	BEAVER CROSSING	98.1	97.8	0.5	0.5	0.1	0.1	0.6	0.6	7.3	7.3	7.2	6.7	5.7	24.2	26.7	13.4	1.6	74.0	39.6	50.9	49.1
68314	BEE	98.2	98.4	0.0	0.0	0.4	0.4	1.0	1.0	6.3	6.7	7.9	6.5	5.7	27.4	26.6	11.4	1.4	74.8	37.9	53.7	46.3
68315	BELVIDERE	98.9	98.8	0.0	0.0	0.0	0.0	0.6	0.6	5.8	6.4	6.4	6.9	5.2	20.2	28.3	18.5	2.3	76.9	44.5	50.9	49.1
	NEBRASKA	89.6	88.4	4.0	4.2	1.3	1.8	5.5	6.4	7.0	6.9	7.2	7.3	7.6	27.5	23.5	11.2	2.1	74.8	35.7	49.4	50.6
	UNITED STATES	75.1	73.6	12.3	12.5	3.8	4.2	12.5	14.1	6.9	6.7	7.2	7.0	7.3	28.6	23.8	10.8	1.7	75.1	36.0	49.1	50.9

ZIP CODE #	POST OFFICE NAME	2004 Per Capita Income	2004 HH Income Base	2004 Household Income Distribution (%): Less than $25,000	$25,000 to $49,999	$50,000 to $99,999	$100,000 to $149,999	$150,000 or More	Median Household Income: 2004	2009	2004 National Centile	2004 State Centile	2004 Home Value Base	2004 Home Value Distribution (%): Less than $50,000	$50,000 to $89,999	$90,000 to $174,999	$175,000 to $399,999	$400,000 or More	2004 Median Home Value
68001	ABIE	15912	61	31.2	31.2	32.8	4.9	0.0	39301	41733	44	58	49	42.9	20.4	24.5	10.2	2.0	61667
68002	ARLINGTON	23774	858	14.2	29.4	40.4	13.6	2.3	54869	65413	80	91	697	9.0	14.8	45.5	24.3	6.5	124907
68003	ASHLAND	25115	1788	21.4	24.3	39.2	12.8	2.3	52956	62205	77	90	1358	11.7	23.1	41.5	21.1	2.7	113723
68004	BANCROFT	19395	444	31.3	38.1	27.3	1.6	1.8	36149	40000	32	37	335	31.9	28.7	29.9	7.2	2.4	69464
68005	BELLEVUE	25515	9739	17.6	31.0	37.1	10.8	3.4	50966	60263	74	87	6079	7.7	17.6	62.1	11.7	0.9	113618
68007	BENNINGTON	27270	1060	12.0	23.0	45.1	13.2	6.7	61216	74858	86	94	880	2.4	9.7	49.4	28.0	10.6	150245
68008	BLAIR	24333	4406	19.4	26.2	37.7	13.5	3.3	53927	64853	78	90	3266	8.2	11.8	51.0	24.7	4.4	133442
68010	BOYS TOWN	12721	71	7.0	26.8	66.2	0.0	0.0	55191	61580	80	91	0	0.0	0.0	0.0	0.0	0.0	0
68014	BRUNO	18237	112	31.3	32.1	31.3	5.4	0.0	37962	42711	39	49	89	42.7	23.6	23.6	9.0	1.1	60833
68015	CEDAR BLUFFS	19264	422	24.2	37.0	33.7	3.8	1.4	42314	49194	54	71	352	23.0	33.0	31.0	12.8	0.3	83438
68017	CERESCO	22794	612	12.1	31.2	45.9	8.2	2.6	54859	63914	79	91	521	7.5	17.5	49.1	21.1	4.8	129375
68018	COLON	20611	200	19.5	33.5	36.5	7.5	3.0	47706	53440	68	83	165	10.9	19.4	40.0	26.7	3.0	121500
68019	CRAIG	18609	246	27.2	37.0	27.6	7.3	0.8	39283	44461	44	57	191	22.0	25.7	33.5	13.6	5.2	93000
68020	DECATUR	19187	392	31.4	33.4	30.1	4.1	1.0	37471	42440	37	45	309	41.4	25.2	22.0	7.1	4.2	64688
68022	ELKHORN	35350	3341	7.3	18.6	38.1	23.7	12.3	79098	96625	95	99	2992	4.3	10.1	48.6	29.6	7.5	152500
68023	FORT CALHOUN	29722	1004	14.3	19.8	39.6	16.7	9.5	66182	78425	89	97	875	7.1	8.2	29.0	46.5	9.1	186458
68025	FREMONT	22187	12196	26.6	31.0	32.5	7.0	2.9	43356	50607	57	74	8192	11.8	25.4	48.7	13.0	1.2	102618
68028	GRETNA	28368	2293	13.6	22.0	40.9	17.7	5.8	64289	75585	88	96	1867	3.0	6.4	49.4	33.9	7.3	152664
68029	HERMAN	22880	419	17.9	33.2	35.3	11.7	1.9	48977	57040	70	84	330	12.4	17.0	37.3	29.4	3.9	119271
68030	HOMER	18976	288	26.0	33.0	32.3	6.6	2.1	43330	49444	57	74	227	17.6	34.8	35.7	11.5	0.4	86944
68031	HOOPER	19718	756	25.5	34.3	33.7	5.3	1.2	42164	49058	53	70	602	21.4	29.6	40.0	7.5	1.5	88500
68033	ITHACA	20862	182	20.9	28.0	38.5	10.4	2.2	50825	59429	74	87	151	11.9	22.5	35.1	26.5	4.0	116071
68034	KENNARD	26717	356	14.0	21.1	44.7	16.9	3.4	65003	76801	89	96	308	3.6	14.3	34.7	39.6	7.8	170556
68036	LINWOOD	18479	130	33.1	31.5	29.2	4.6	1.5	37055	42667	36	43	104	40.4	23.1	23.1	10.6	2.9	64286
68037	LOUISVILLE	25799	937	15.2	29.5	39.3	12.7	3.4	55732	64019	80	92	769	7.0	23.4	38.5	29.8	1.3	119627
68038	LYONS	17702	590	33.7	35.4	25.4	3.7	1.7	34890	40477	27	28	438	41.1	39.7	15.5	2.7	0.9	59070
68039	MACY	7749	339	48.7	31.9	17.4	1.2	0.9	25664	29497	5	1	152	44.7	27.6	23.0	4.0	0.7	56667
68040	MALMO	19811	170	24.1	35.3	34.7	5.3	0.6	41016	46387	50	65	141	12.1	17.0	47.5	19.9	3.6	116518
68041	MEAD	20468	310	21.3	28.4	36.1	11.6	2.6	50247	58873	72	86	257	13.2	23.0	37.4	23.0	3.5	109063
68044	NICKERSON	18952	306	19.9	34.6	37.3	6.2	2.0	47320	54946	67	82	227	20.7	18.5	39.2	15.9	5.7	108750
68045	OAKLAND	20240	835	29.1	35.0	27.8	5.8	2.4	38102	44950	40	50	612	26.8	32.8	32.2	6.5	1.6	76829
68046	PAPILLION	30681	7175	10.6	17.6	41.1	21.6	9.1	73183	83418	93	98	5566	1.2	2.9	59.2	34.1	2.6	157354
68047	PENDER	19129	756	28.3	39.3	26.9	3.6	2.0	36523	42428	34	40	560	21.4	33.9	35.7	8.8	0.2	83333
68048	PLATTSMOUTH	23881	4805	17.8	29.3	38.6	10.2	4.1	52145	61930	76	89	3701	13.8	20.1	39.0	24.5	2.7	113010
68050	PRAGUE	16424	295	31.2	38.3	27.5	2.4	0.7	35659	41548	30	34	240	21.7	25.4	30.4	18.8	3.8	94118
68055	ROSALIE	12504	146	41.1	38.4	19.2	1.4	0.0	28392	32276	9	5	114	50.0	27.2	13.2	9.7	0.0	50000
68057	SCRIBNER	18305	786	29.0	36.5	29.9	3.4	1.2	39882	46221	46	59	607	31.0	30.2	31.8	5.9	1.2	73625
68059	SPRINGFIELD	29876	1194	13.0	20.9	40.7	17.8	7.7	65362	77628	89	96	1007	6.2	7.1	45.0	34.4	7.5	146548
68061	TEKAMAH	20330	1185	28.5	35.1	29.7	4.1	2.5	39908	45245	46	59	927	23.2	32.3	31.1	12.1	1.4	83841
68062	THURSTON	15433	135	30.4	35.6	31.9	2.2	0.0	37657	41317	38	47	110	33.6	32.7	28.2	3.6	1.8	73571
68064	VALLEY	26183	1341	22.0	26.9	35.9	9.8	5.4	51014	63488	74	87	977	16.4	24.0	36.5	18.2	4.9	100879
68065	VALPARAISO	19789	601	19.1	32.1	39.8	6.8	2.2	49016	55686	70	84	494	15.8	25.9	37.5	19.6	1.2	103819
68066	WAHOO	19792	2017	27.0	30.8	34.2	6.5	1.4	43122	51032	56	73	1463	10.1	28.4	46.3	13.0	2.2	103161
68067	WALTHILL	12309	402	38.3	27.9	28.1	5.5	0.3	33503	39602	22	21	274	49.6	33.9	13.5	2.9	0.0	50244
68069	WATERLOO	37819	924	17.6	22.9	36.0	13.7	9.6	60098	75985	84	94	785	7.0	15.0	36.7	31.9	9.4	155758
68070	WESTON	19384	355	22.5	35.2	36.6	4.8	0.9	44440	50327	60	76	288	19.4	28.8	35.4	15.6	0.7	92778
68071	WINNEBAGO	9708	491	44.4	35.4	17.3	2.9	0.0	28071	32111	9	4	239	59.0	20.5	15.1	4.2	1.3	35536
68073	YUTAN	22306	657	14.8	31.1	38.8	11.9	3.5	53705	61914	78	90	550	4.9	21.6	53.1	17.8	2.6	108390
68102	OMAHA	18562	2451	51.3	30.2	14.0	3.0	1.5	24115	30922	4	1	123	45.5	24.4	26.0	4.1	0.0	57857
68104	OMAHA	21573	14168	25.1	34.4	31.2	7.5	1.8	42472	52938	55	71	9020	12.2	57.6	27.2	2.8	0.2	77369
68105	OMAHA	19528	10098	34.4	32.3	26.5	5.6	1.2	36231	45753	32	38	4472	12.1	45.4	40.8	1.7	0.1	84266
68106	OMAHA	27819	9209	23.9	30.8	32.7	9.1	3.5	45204	56106	62	78	5745	9.8	31.3	54.7	3.8	0.4	96087
68107	OMAHA	15908	9564	35.0	31.6	27.5	4.9	1.1	35667	44887	30	34	5910	20.7	57.8	20.9	0.5	0.2	70183
68108	OMAHA	16446	5217	33.0	36.6	24.6	4.6	1.2	35067	42849	28	30	2471	32.1	50.8	16.8	0.3	0.0	62436
68110	OMAHA	13829	2903	46.5	32.0	17.2	3.3	1.1	26739	32859	7	2	1480	62.6	29.5	7.8	0.1	0.0	38694
68111	OMAHA	12451	9407	45.9	32.8	17.9	2.5	0.9	27009	32650	7	2	4641	56.7	36.6	6.0	0.6	0.1	46409
68112	OMAHA	21002	4332	26.0	29.3	33.4	8.7	2.7	44522	55704	60	77	3211	26.0	47.8	18.7	6.5	1.1	66727
68113	OFFUTT A F B	12181	288	31.3	57.3	9.4	2.1	0.0	31061	35785	15	10	8	0.0	0.0	100.0	0.0	0.0	112500
68114	OMAHA	39273	8303	20.3	32.5	28.4	8.6	10.3	47317	58067	67	82	4414	1.0	16.9	49.8	21.4	10.8	123788
68116	OMAHA	42240	4600	4.1	13.2	41.1	25.7	15.9	87132	104520	97	99	3693	1.2	1.7	31.5	59.0	6.6	202760
68117	OMAHA	21156	3093	22.4	32.4	34.4	9.4	1.4	46824	58212	66	81	2352	8.6	44.4	45.0	1.5	0.5	88081
68118	OMAHA	39394	3158	4.8	10.5	29.9	32.5	22.4	105043	128516	99	100	2899	3.4	0.9	19.5	61.2	15.0	225071
68122	OMAHA	29960	2252	7.8	19.9	49.1	17.4	5.9	69048	83717	91	98	2049	6.6	6.3	66.1	16.8	4.2	132247
68123	BELLEVUE	23801	9446	8.8	27.8	44.2	14.2	4.9	61277	69868	86	94	5339	1.4	3.5	66.6	26.2	2.3	146829
68124	OMAHA	39143	6566	18.3	24.4	31.8	13.7	11.8	59737	74106	84	93	4610	0.7	8.9	58.3	25.6	6.6	142517
68127	OMAHA	30273	10217	15.5	32.5	35.4	11.7	5.0	51833	64220	75	89	4739	0.9	9.5	74.3	14.9	0.4	125812
68128	LA VISTA	23459	5061	14.7	29.3	44.5	9.4	2.1	53662	62975	78	90	3006	1.9	16.9	70.2	10.8	0.3	111451
68130	OMAHA	40659	4506	5.2	12.5	38.6	23.5	20.2	89469	107435	97	100	4001	0.1	2.1	52.2	36.9	8.7	169127
68131	OMAHA	17783	5604	41.5	33.3	20.3	3.2	1.7	29576	36763	11	7	1323	22.9	45.1	26.8	3.6	1.7	74752
68132	OMAHA	31387	6111	25.7	30.9	25.3	10.9	7.3	43291	53944	57	74	3014	4.7	21.1	39.4	26.6	8.2	136373
68133	PAPILLION	29325	1802	5.1	9.0	54.1	23.4	8.4	81199	94094	95	99	1565	0.4	0.4	36.3	61.7	1.2	192763
68134	OMAHA	26699	12368	19.5	30.6	37.0	10.4	2.6	49956	61912	72	86	7016	1.7	13.5	78.9	5.6	0.4	114040
68135	OMAHA	40037	5424	1.8	7.0	34.9	34.1	22.2	105569	128716	99	100	5334	0.7	1.0	28.2	62.0	8.1	224713
68136	OMAHA	34357	1596	1.6	17.8	43.4	27.1	10.1	82512	91436	96	99	1564	0.8	1.0	29.5	59.7	9.0	222909
68137	OMAHA	29905	10195	9.0	23.2	44.0	18.7	5.1	66646	81294	90	97	7728	2.7	7.9	79.7	9.0	0.7	124064
68138	OMAHA	25491	5185	6.8	19.9	56.1	14.2	3.0	65851	77087	89	96	4316	0.4	4.7	85.9	8.3	0.8	126122
68142	OMAHA	26316	719	8.2	28.4	47.2	13.5	2.8	60724	73554	85	94	648	36.6	8.3	41.5	9.9	3.7	107188
68144	OMAHA	33122	10266	13.1	24.4	38.1	16.0	8.5	63663	78402	88	96	7378	3.6	6.3	71.2	17.4	1.5	138108
68147	BELLEVUE	22710	3805	16.0	32.4	40.0	9.0	2.5	51086	60242	74	87	2866	2.1	29.5	59.7	8.2	0.5	103405
68152	OMAHA	29322	2543	21.4	23.8	31.6	15.5	7.8	55686	68735	80	92	1968	5.3	19.3	47.5	24.0	3.9	125577
68154	OMAHA	41512	10452	11.2	24.7	34.3	17.1	12.7	66144	81118	89	97	6209	0.5	3.4	55.7	33.5	6.9	164821
68157	OMAHA	25799	1792	10.6	23.0	46.9	16.0	3.6	67541	71618	86	95	1504	0.0	7.9	83.9	8.2	0.0	120861
68164	OMAHA	31646	11016	11.2	22.1	41.6	17.0	8.2	65978	80203	89	97	7827	9.5	3.5	63.8	21.7	1.5	133995
68182	OMAHA	4081	0	0.0	0.0	0.0	0.0	0.0	0	0	0	0	0	0.0	0.0	0.0	0.0	0.0	0
68198	OMAHA	1767	0	0.0	0.0	0.0	0.0	0.0	0	0	0	0	0	0.0	0.0	0.0	0.0	0.0	0
68301	ADAMS	21295	530	20.2	33.8	35.7	7.4	3.0	47012	52982	66	81	425	10.6	14.8	43.1	30.4	1.2	129808
68303	ALEXANDRIA	19006	158	32.9	32.3	28.5	4.4	1.9	35000	40281	28	29	127	53.5	29.1	12.6	2.4	2.4	46786
68304	ALVO	21463	145	20.7	28.3	39.3	8.3	3.5	50596	56003	73	87	121	11.6	18.2	41.3	24.8	4.1	115972
68305	AUBURN	21540	1829	31.0	28.1	31.7	7.2	2.1	40119	49705	46	61	1277	26.0	34.5	30.9	7.6	1.0	77427
68307	AVOCA	20778	244	18.9	32.4	41.0	7.4	0.4	49027	54814	70	84	194	19.6	26.3	32.0	20.1	2.1	98889
68309	BARNESTON	17789	58	34.5	39.7	20.7	3.5	1.7	35515	40561	30	33	43	48.8	25.6	18.6	7.0	0.0	51667
68310	BEATRICE	20706	6437	29.3	33.9	29.3	5.5	2.1	39203	45663	43	57	4439	19.6	36.0	35.5	8.2	0.7	83881
68313	BEAVER CROSSING	17350	326	30.4	34.1	29.8	4.9	0.9	39488	46631	44	58	261	31.0	24.9	33.0	8.8	2.3	84259
68314	BEE	20619	180	20.6	32.8	34.4	8.3	3.9	47958	54577	68	83	141	26.2	26.2	34.8	12.1	0.7	86111
68315	BELVIDERE	18645	75	30.7	36.0	26.7	5.3	1.3	36115	38890	32	37	59	54.2	25.4	13.6	3.4	3.4	45833
	NEBRASKA	23743		24.5	30.5	31.8	9.2	4.0	45453	54516				17.2	23.9	42.4	14.4	2.2	101398
	UNITED STATES	25866		24.7	27.1	30.8	10.9	6.5	48124	56710				10.9	15.0	33.7	30.1	10.4	145905

ZIP CODE #	POST OFFICE NAME	FINANCIAL SERVICES: Auto Loan	FINANCIAL SERVICES: Home Loan	FINANCIAL SERVICES: Investments	FINANCIAL SERVICES: Retirement Plans	THE HOME: Home Improvements: Home Repair	THE HOME: Home Improvements: Lawn & Garden	THE HOME: Furnishings: Computers & Hardware	THE HOME: Furnishings: Major Appliances	THE HOME: Furnishings: TV, Radio, Sound Equipment	THE HOME: Furnishings: Furniture	ENTERTAINMENT: Dine out/ Carry out	ENTERTAINMENT: Sports Equipment	ENTERTAINMENT: Fees & Tickets	ENTERTAINMENT: Toys & Games	ENTERTAINMENT: Travel	ENTERTAINMENT: Cable TV	PERSONAL: Apparel & Services	PERSONAL: Auto Repairs	PERSONAL: Health Insurance	PERSONAL: Pets & Supplies
68001	ABIE	81	57	30	54	66	74	56	69	64	55	76	83	48	74	58	68	69	68	82	96
68002	ARLINGTON	88	95	95	93	96	100	89	92	87	88	108	107	91	114	91	87	106	89	90	106
68003	ASHLAND	102	82	59	80	89	101	83	93	90	82	108	108	77	107	84	93	101	92	104	117
68004	BANCROFT	84	58	31	55	68	76	58	71	66	57	78	86	49	76	60	70	71	70	85	99
68005	BELLEVUE	84	87	95	88	86	90	89	87	87	88	109	103	89	110	88	85	107	88	83	97
68007	BENNINGTON	97	120	129	120	118	117	108	108	101	108	127	126	115	135	111	98	127	104	97	119
68008	BLAIR	92	88	82	87	91	97	88	92	89	86	109	108	86	110	88	89	105	91	94	108
68010	BOYS TOWN	0	0	0	0	0	0	0	0	0	0	0	0	0	0	0	0	0	0	0	0
68014	BRUNO	82	57	30	54	67	75	56	70	65	56	76	84	48	75	59	68	70	69	83	97
68015	CEDAR BLUFFS	77	63	47	63	67	76	65	71	69	64	84	81	61	83	65	71	78	69	78	86
68017	CERESCO	87	93	91	94	91	91	88	89	84	89	106	105	89	106	87	80	104	88	80	99
68018	COLON	103	73	39	69	85	95	72	88	83	71	97	107	62	95	75	87	89	87	105	123
68019	CRAIG	87	61	32	57	71	79	60	74	69	59	81	89	51	80	62	73	74	73	88	103
68020	DECATUR	78	55	29	52	64	71	54	67	62	53	73	80	46	72	56	65	67	66	79	93
68022	ELKHORN	142	167	172	171	161	160	151	149	140	154	177	174	159	182	151	134	177	146	132	164
68023	FORT CALHOUN	111	122	120	122	122	126	114	116	110	113	137	135	117	143	115	109	134	113	111	131
68025	FREMONT	74	74	76	74	75	81	75	75	76	74	94	88	75	95	75	76	91	76	76	86
68028	GRETNA	106	126	133	127	123	123	115	114	107	116	136	133	122	141	116	104	135	111	102	125
68029	HERMAN	105	73	38	69	85	96	72	90	83	72	98	108	62	96	75	88	89	88	107	125
68030	HOMER	93	66	35	62	76	85	65	80	74	64	87	96	55	86	67	78	80	79	95	111
68031	HOOPER	88	62	33	59	72	80	61	75	70	60	82	90	53	81	63	73	75	74	89	104
68033	ITHACA	97	80	56	76	87	95	76	87	83	75	99	104	71	100	78	85	93	85	97	115
68034	KENNARD	114	105	87	103	112	117	98	109	101	97	123	129	95	126	101	102	117	106	114	137
68036	LINWOOD	82	57	30	54	67	74	56	70	65	56	76	84	48	75	58	68	69	69	83	97
68037	LOUISVILLE	96	92	82	92	95	102	90	94	92	89	112	109	89	114	91	92	108	92	97	110
68038	LYONS	71	53	33	50	59	69	57	64	64	54	75	73	50	71	57	67	68	64	77	80
68039	MACY	48	38	46	35	37	44	44	44	50	45	61	51	42	59	43	52	59	47	49	53
68040	MALMO	89	62	32	58	72	81	61	76	70	60	83	91	52	81	63	74	75	75	90	105
68041	MEAD	96	84	62	79	89	96	78	87	83	78	101	104	75	103	80	85	96	85	95	113
68044	NICKERSON	88	73	52	70	79	86	69	79	75	69	90	94	65	91	71	77	85	77	88	104
68045	OAKLAND	84	62	38	59	69	81	66	76	75	64	88	87	58	84	66	79	80	75	90	96
68046	PAPILLION	120	135	141	139	131	132	127	125	119	128	151	147	132	153	126	114	149	123	112	137
68047	PENDER	79	58	36	55	65	76	62	71	70	59	82	81	54	78	62	74	75	70	84	90
68048	PLATTSMOUTH	87	91	91	91	92	96	89	90	87	88	108	105	89	110	89	86	105	89	88	101
68050	PRAGUE	77	54	28	51	63	70	53	66	61	52	72	79	45	70	55	64	65	65	78	91
68055	ROSALIE	53	44	34	44	47	53	46	49	49	45	59	56	43	58	45	49	55	48	53	59
68057	SCRIBNER	80	58	34	55	66	76	61	71	69	59	81	82	53	78	61	73	74	70	84	92
68059	SPRINGFIELD	111	121	120	122	121	125	114	116	110	114	137	134	117	141	115	108	134	113	110	130
68061	TEKAMAH	90	63	33	59	73	82	62	77	71	61	84	92	53	82	64	75	76	76	91	107
68062	THURSTON	75	52	27	49	61	68	51	64	59	51	70	77	44	68	53	62	63	63	76	89
68064	VALLEY	107	86	59	82	94	104	83	96	91	83	109	113	77	109	85	94	102	94	108	125
68065	VALPARAISO	96	76	51	73	85	92	74	86	81	73	96	103	67	96	76	83	89	85	97	115
68066	WAHOO	82	64	43	62	70	80	66	74	73	64	87	86	60	84	66	75	80	73	85	93
68067	WALTHILL	64	54	45	54	57	64	57	60	61	56	74	69	54	72	56	62	69	60	65	71
68069	WATERLOO	154	115	71	107	131	146	111	134	126	110	148	160	97	146	116	132	137	132	158	184
68070	WESTON	90	63	33	60	73	82	62	77	72	62	84	93	53	83	65	75	77	76	91	107
68071	WINNEBAGO	48	43	49	41	42	49	46	46	50	47	63	52	47	62	46	52	61	47	49	54
68073	YUTAN	97	98	92	99	98	99	94	96	91	95	114	115	93	114	93	88	111	96	90	111
68102	OMAHA	41	31	40	35	31	35	45	39	45	42	56	50	41	52	40	41	54	44	36	43
68104	OMAHA	70	72	81	73	72	76	75	73	74	74	93	86	76	94	74	72	91	74	70	81
68105	OMAHA	60	58	69	60	58	62	65	62	65	64	82	74	64	81	63	63	80	65	60	68
68106	OMAHA	76	80	96	81	79	85	84	81	83	83	104	95	85	103	83	81	102	83	78	89
68107	OMAHA	61	59	61	57	58	63	62	62	64	62	80	70	62	80	61	64	78	63	62	67
68108	OMAHA	57	55	61	55	54	59	61	59	61	59	77	69	60	76	59	60	75	61	57	64
68110	OMAHA	50	44	48	41	44	51	48	48	53	49	65	54	48	62	48	55	63	50	52	55
68111	OMAHA	48	43	51	40	41	48	47	46	51	48	64	52	47	62	46	53	62	48	50	53
68112	OMAHA	76	78	80	77	78	84	78	78	78	77	97	91	79	98	79	78	94	78	78	88
68113	OFFUTT A F B	56	36	34	41	33	39	53	46	54	50	68	61	46	61	44	49	65	54	43	52
68114	OMAHA	104	108	136	110	107	117	115	109	114	113	143	128	117	143	114	113	140	113	107	120
68116	OMAHA	161	175	183	185	167	168	167	162	155	171	198	191	171	196	162	146	195	162	141	179
68117	OMAHA	71	78	80	76	78	82	75	75	74	74	92	86	78	97	76	74	90	74	74	84
68118	OMAHA	175	206	215	212	199	199	184	182	169	189	215	211	196	219	185	162	215	176	161	201
68122	OMAHA	117	133	131	138	128	124	121	120	111	124	141	140	124	142	118	104	139	116	103	131
68123	BELLEVUE	104	98	98	104	94	97	103	99	99	103	126	120	100	121	97	93	122	103	89	111
68124	OMAHA	120	136	158	137	135	141	133	130	127	132	160	152	138	162	135	125	158	130	123	142
68127	OMAHA	93	94	107	99	91	95	99	94	95	98	120	113	98	118	95	90	118	97	86	104
68128	LA VISTA	85	89	94	93	86	87	89	86	84	90	106	103	89	105	86	79	105	87	76	95
68130	OMAHA	155	181	194	186	176	176	166	163	154	168	195	191	175	200	167	148	194	160	146	180
68131	OMAHA	55	46	59	50	46	50	60	54	60	57	75	67	56	71	55	56	73	59	51	60
68132	OMAHA	88	86	105	91	85	90	98	90	95	94	119	111	96	117	93	90	117	96	84	100
68133	PAPILLION	132	147	144	153	141	138	135	134	124	139	158	157	138	158	132	117	156	131	116	147
68134	OMAHA	81	83	96	86	82	86	88	84	85	86	107	100	88	106	86	82	105	86	78	92
68135	OMAHA	196	229	230	238	219	215	205	202	187	211	238	235	216	242	202	176	237	196	174	222
68136	OMAHA	136	159	161	166	153	150	142	140	130	147	166	163	150	168	141	123	165	136	121	154
68137	OMAHA	109	121	124	124	117	118	114	113	107	116	135	132	117	137	112	102	133	111	101	124
68138	OMAHA	103	114	113	119	109	106	105	104	97	109	123	122	108	123	102	90	122	102	89	114
68142	OMAHA	96	112	111	115	107	104	101	100	93	103	117	117	105	120	99	87	116	97	86	109
68144	OMAHA	107	123	139	124	120	124	117	115	112	117	141	134	122	144	118	109	139	114	106	126
68147	BELLEVUE	79	89	96	90	88	90	86	85	83	86	104	99	89	108	86	81	103	84	79	93
68152	OMAHA	103	113	127	112	112	119	110	110	108	110	135	125	114	136	112	107	133	109	107	121
68154	OMAHA	134	142	158	149	138	143	141	137	134	142	170	161	144	167	138	128	167	138	124	151
68157	OMAHA	95	112	118	112	109	109	104	103	98	104	123	120	108	128	105	94	122	101	93	113
68164	OMAHA	113	119	124	124	115	116	116	114	110	118	139	135	117	137	113	104	137	114	101	126
68182	OMAHA	0	0	0	0	0	0	0	0	0	0	0	0	0	0	0	0	0	0	0	0
68198	OMAHA	0	0	0	0	0	0	0	0	0	0	0	0	0	0	0	0	0	0	0	0
68301	ADAMS	102	72	39	68	84	93	71	87	81	70	96	105	61	94	74	85	87	86	103	121
68303	ALEXANDRIA	80	56	29	53	65	73	55	68	64	55	75	82	47	73	57	67	68	67	81	95
68304	ALVO	102	71	37	67	83	93	70	87	81	70	95	105	60	93	73	85	87	86	104	121
68305	AUBURN	86	62	36	59	70	81	64	75	73	62	86	88	56	83	65	77	78	75	90	99
68307	AVOCA	89	74	52	70	80	87	70	80	76	69	91	95	66	92	72	78	85	78	89	105
68309	BARNESTON	69	52	34	50	57	68	58	63	64	55	76	71	51	72	57	68	69	63	76	76
68310	BEATRICE	70	65	60	64	68	75	66	69	69	65	84	80	65	85	67	70	80	69	74	81
68313	BEAVER CROSSING	79	55	29	52	64	72	55	67	63	54	74	81	47	72	57	66	67	67	80	94
68314	BEE	88	75	58	75	79	89	77	82	82	76	99	94	74	98	76	83	93	81	89	97
68315	BELVIDERE	78	54	28	51	63	71	54	66	62	53	73	80	46	71	56	65	66	65	79	92
	NEBRASKA	88	81	77	81	83	90	83	85	84	82	104	101	80	103	82	84	100	86	87	100
	UNITED STATES	100	100	100	100	100	100	100	100	100	100	100	100	100	100	100	100	100	100	100	100

NEBRASKA

POPULATION CHANGE

A 68316-68448

# POST OFFICE NAME	COUNTY FIPS CODE	Population 2000	Population 2004	Population 2009	% Rate	State Centile	Households 2000	Households 2004	Households 2009	% Annual Rate 2000-2004	2004 Average HH Size	Families 2000	Families 2004	% Annual Rate 2000-2004
68316 BENEDICT	185	645	652	659	0.3	66	227	232	238	0.5	2.81	175	179	0.5
68317 BENNET	109	1577	1644	1735	1.0	85	596	630	672	1.3	2.61	488	516	1.3
68318 BLUE SPRINGS	067	637	633	653	-0.2	46	260	261	272	0.1	2.42	173	174	0.1
68319 BRADSHAW	185	684	683	687	0.0	53	266	270	276	0.4	2.53	214	217	0.3
68320 BROCK	127	382	376	372	-0.4	32	154	154	154	0.0	2.44	100	100	0.0
68321 BROWNVILLE	127	435	426	421	-0.5	23	183	182	181	-0.1	2.34	125	125	0.0
68322 BRUNING	169	444	433	424	-0.6	15	197	196	194	-0.1	2.21	130	130	0.0
68323 BURCHARD	133	418	400	397	-1.0	2	171	166	167	-0.7	2.41	125	122	-0.6
68324 BURR	131	210	259	297	5.1	99	95	119	137	5.4	2.18	70	87	5.3
68325 BYRON	169	332	330	325	-0.1	47	133	134	134	0.2	2.37	90	91	0.3
68326 CARLETON	169	274	267	261	-0.6	14	108	107	106	-0.2	2.50	72	72	0.0
68327 CHESTER	169	442	429	419	-0.7	10	198	195	194	-0.4	2.19	134	133	-0.2
68328 CLATONIA	067	484	485	496	0.1	58	193	197	204	0.5	2.46	150	153	0.5
68329 COOK	097	699	688	695	-0.4	32	297	296	302	-0.1	2.32	212	212	0.0
68330 CORDOVA	159	222	220	227	-0.2	43	96	97	101	0.2	2.27	71	72	0.3
68331 CORTLAND	067	829	847	876	0.5	76	327	339	356	0.9	2.48	253	263	0.9
68332 CRAB ORCHARD	097	141	139	139	-0.3	34	65	65	66	0.0	2.14	43	43	0.0
68333 CRETE	151	7565	7904	8304	1.0	86	2638	2769	2924	1.2	2.58	1745	1840	1.3
68335 DAVENPORT	169	442	426	414	-0.9	5	195	191	188	-0.5	2.23	143	140	-0.5
68336 DAVEY	109	475	461	474	-0.7	10	174	171	177	-0.4	2.70	140	137	-0.5
68337 DAWSON	147	378	368	359	-0.6	13	149	147	145	-0.3	2.50	103	102	-0.2
68338 DAYKIN	095	300	285	274	-1.2	1	128	124	120	-0.7	2.30	94	91	-0.8
68339 DENTON	109	863	989	1091	3.3	95	328	383	429	3.7	2.58	265	310	3.8
68340 DESHLER	169	1066	1059	1043	-0.2	46	449	452	451	0.2	2.26	305	308	0.2
68341 DE WITT	067	1019	1109	1193	2.0	92	413	455	494	2.3	2.44	276	305	2.4
68342 DILLER	095	598	582	566	-0.6	13	231	229	225	-0.2	2.54	168	167	-0.1
68343 DORCHESTER	151	929	927	960	-0.1	51	362	364	379	0.1	2.55	274	276	0.2
68344 DOUGLAS	131	424	528	609	5.3	99	159	200	232	5.6	2.64	117	147	5.5
68345 DU BOIS	133	292	306	313	1.1	87	127	135	140	1.5	2.27	80	85	1.4
68346 DUNBAR	131	558	582	614	1.0	85	201	210	222	1.0	2.77	156	163	1.0
68347 EAGLE	025	2231	2291	2394	0.6	78	778	807	852	0.9	2.84	625	649	0.9
68348 ELK CREEK	097	321	336	347	1.1	86	140	148	154	1.3	2.17	94	99	1.2
68349 ELMWOOD	025	1086	1091	1125	0.1	60	408	412	428	0.2	2.65	303	307	0.3
68350 ENDICOTT	095	253	244	236	-0.9	5	110	108	106	-0.4	2.26	79	78	-0.3
68351 EXETER	059	895	893	889	-0.1	51	345	346	347	0.1	2.45	222	223	0.1
68352 FAIRBURY	095	5563	5411	5237	-0.7	12	2407	2364	2310	-0.4	2.22	1526	1502	-0.4
68354 FAIRMONT	059	936	933	929	-0.1	50	368	369	370	0.1	2.41	242	244	0.2
68355 FALLS CITY	147	5886	5751	5626	-0.5	19	2465	2422	2384	-0.4	2.31	1552	1529	-0.4
68357 FILLEY	067	427	421	432	-0.3	35	172	172	179	0.0	2.45	132	133	0.2
68358 FIRTH	109	1231	1268	1321	0.7	80	417	435	458	1.0	2.80	332	346	1.0
68359 FRIEND	151	1644	1668	1729	0.3	70	638	651	677	0.5	2.48	453	464	0.6
68360 GARLAND	159	863	893	930	0.8	82	330	348	368	1.3	2.57	247	262	1.4
68361 GENEVA	059	2998	2984	2968	-0.1	48	1218	1227	1230	0.2	2.29	808	816	0.2
68362 GILEAD	169	156	153	150	-0.5	26	66	66	65	0.0	2.18	41	41	0.0
68364 GOEHNER	159	390	392	403	0.1	60	143	146	152	0.5	2.64	105	107	0.4
68365 GRAFTON	059	233	229	226	-0.4	28	95	95	94	0.0	2.40	72	72	0.0
68366 GREENWOOD	025	921	979	1041	1.5	89	353	382	412	1.9	2.56	258	280	1.9
68367 GRESHAM	185	532	540	548	0.4	71	207	212	218	0.6	2.54	156	161	0.8
68368 HALLAM	109	612	611	638	0.0	52	237	241	256	0.4	2.54	189	192	0.4
68370 HEBRON	169	2149	2107	2067	-0.5	26	877	872	866	-0.1	2.28	559	557	-0.1
68371 HENDERSON	185	1714	1713	1722	0.0	53	650	662	678	0.4	2.45	473	483	0.5
68372 HICKMAN	109	2114	2122	2202	0.1	59	726	741	778	0.5	2.86	582	593	0.4
68375 HUBBELL	169	186	181	177	-0.6	13	80	79	78	-0.3	2.27	53	53	0.0
68376 HUMBOLDT	147	1633	1637	1619	0.1	58	694	703	701	0.3	2.26	438	445	0.4
68377 JANSEN	095	489	481	468	-0.4	30	195	195	192	0.0	2.47	148	148	0.0
68378 JOHNSON	127	838	824	814	-0.4	29	371	370	370	-0.1	2.23	250	250	0.0
68380 LEWISTON	133	181	173	172	-1.1	2	73	71	71	-0.7	2.44	53	52	-0.5
68381 LIBERTY	067	234	266	293	3.1	95	86	99	110	3.4	2.63	60	69	3.3
68401 MC COOL JUNCTION	185	764	764	768	0.0	56	306	313	321	0.5	2.44	226	232	0.6
68402 MALCOLM	109	1061	1112	1168	1.1	87	366	392	419	1.6	2.64	303	323	1.5
68404 MARTELL	109	1025	1178	1302	3.3	96	393	462	518	3.9	2.55	304	357	3.9
68405 MILFORD	159	3444	3431	3519	-0.1	50	1190	1204	1258	0.3	2.57	811	824	0.4
68406 MILLIGAN	059	477	466	459	-0.6	18	216	213	212	-0.3	2.19	137	135	-0.4
68407 MURDOCK	025	824	852	893	0.8	81	318	333	353	1.1	2.56	251	264	1.2
68409 MURRAY	025	829	815	849	-0.4	29	316	315	332	-0.1	2.58	241	241	0.0
68410 NEBRASKA CITY	131	8568	8692	9060	0.3	70	3374	3442	3607	0.5	2.45	2246	2289	0.5
68413 NEHAWKA	025	432	429	444	-0.2	46	170	171	179	0.1	2.51	129	130	0.2
68414 NEMAHA	127	381	373	368	-0.5	22	158	157	157	-0.2	2.38	108	108	0.0
68415 ODELL	067	736	752	777	0.5	76	282	292	305	0.8	2.58	219	227	0.9
68416 OHIOWA	059	265	259	255	-0.5	19	123	121	120	-0.4	2.14	78	77	-0.3
68417 OTOE	131	413	418	434	0.3	67	157	160	167	0.5	2.61	117	120	0.6
68418 PALMYRA	131	1000	1175	1318	3.9	97	382	453	511	4.1	2.59	289	343	4.1
68420 PAWNEE CITY	133	1438	1412	1409	-0.4	26	629	622	625	-0.3	2.18	375	371	-0.3
68421 PERU	127	1229	1201	1187	-0.5	19	373	366	363	-0.4	2.31	216	213	-0.3
68422 PICKRELL	067	622	637	660	0.6	77	237	246	259	0.9	2.55	183	191	1.0
68423 PLEASANT DALE	159	817	830	856	0.4	71	321	332	349	0.8	2.42	242	251	0.9
68424 PLYMOUTH	095	861	844	819	-0.5	24	330	328	323	-0.1	2.57	250	249	-0.1
68428 RAYMOND	109	1214	1232	1274	0.4	71	437	450	471	0.7	2.68	362	372	0.6
68429 REYNOLDS	095	134	129	125	-0.9	4	60	59	58	-0.4	2.19	43	42	-0.6
68430 ROCA	109	1094	1128	1192	0.7	80	407	428	459	1.2	2.64	332	347	1.1
68431 RULO	147	349	344	338	-0.3	34	148	148	147	0.0	2.32	106	106	0.0
68433 SALEM	147	250	243	237	-0.7	10	112	110	108	-0.4	2.21	78	77	-0.3
68434 SEWARD	159	7687	8181	8658	1.5	89	2767	3006	3246	2.0	2.43	1874	2045	2.1
68436 SHICKLEY	059	665	652	644	-0.5	26	260	259	258	-0.1	2.51	198	197	-0.1
68437 SHUBERT	147	342	336	329	-0.4	28	133	132	131	-0.2	2.55	91	91	0.0
68439 STAPLEHURST	159	572	572	586	0.0	56	221	225	234	0.4	2.54	166	169	0.4
68440 STEELE CITY	095	156	151	145	-0.8	8	74	73	71	-0.3	2.07	53	52	-0.5
68441 STEINAUER	133	308	313	317	0.4	72	125	129	132	0.7	2.43	83	85	0.6
68442 STELLA	147	303	297	291	-0.5	24	134	133	132	-0.2	2.23	92	92	0.0
68443 STERLING	097	1037	1021	1028	-0.4	32	424	423	430	-0.1	2.41	287	288	0.1
68444 STRANG	059	131	128	126	-0.5	19	53	52	52	-0.5	2.46	36	36	0.0
68445 SWANTON	151	210	210	216	0.0	56	89	90	93	0.3	2.33	66	67	0.4
68446 SYRACUSE	131	2403	2494	2620	0.9	83	992	1041	1103	1.1	2.31	709	744	1.1
68447 TABLE ROCK	133	450	472	482	1.1	87	214	227	235	1.4	2.08	134	143	1.5
68448 TALMAGE	131	505	505	524	0.0	56	195	196	205	0.1	2.58	145	145	0.0
NEBRASKA					0.8					1.0	2.47			1.1
UNITED STATES					1.2					1.3	2.58			1.1

Copyright © 2004 ESRI BIS. All rights reserved. Reproduction by any method is prohibited.

ZIP CODE #	POST OFFICE NAME	RACE (%) White 2000	White 2004	Black 2000	Black 2004	Asian/Pacific 2000	Asian/Pacific 2004	% Hispanic Origin 2000	% Hispanic Origin 2004	2004 AGE DISTRIBUTION (%) 0-4	5-9	10-14	15-19	20-24	25-44	45-64	65-84	85+	18+	MEDIAN AGE 2004	% 2004 Males	% 2004 Females
68316	BENEDICT	98.1	97.9	0.6	0.6	0.0	0.0	0.6	0.8	6.0	6.4	8.4	7.4	5.7	23.9	27.2	13.2	1.8	74.5	40.7	50.2	49.9
68317	BENNET	98.0	97.8	0.1	0.1	0.3	0.4	0.8	0.9	6.3	7.2	8.1	6.6	5.1	24.2	30.4	11.4	0.9	74.2	40.9	51.6	48.4
68318	BLUE SPRINGS	96.9	96.4	0.2	0.2	0.5	0.6	0.8	1.0	6.6	6.5	6.5	6.2	5.7	22.6	26.1	17.4	2.5	76.5	42.1	49.0	51.0
68319	BRADSHAW	98.4	98.4	0.2	0.2	0.0	0.0	0.3	0.4	5.7	6.6	8.6	6.7	5.6	24.6	28.1	12.6	1.5	74.7	40.5	51.0	49.1
68320	BROCK	97.9	97.9	0.0	0.0	0.3	0.3	0.8	0.5	4.3	5.1	7.5	6.1	5.6	22.6	31.7	14.1	3.2	80.1	44.3	50.0	50.0
68321	BROWNVILLE	99.3	99.1	0.0	0.0	0.2	0.2	0.7	0.7	4.7	5.2	6.8	6.8	5.6	22.1	29.3	16.9	2.6	79.1	44.3	50.9	49.1
68322	BRUNING	98.9	98.6	0.0	0.0	0.0	0.0	2.3	2.5	5.8	6.5	7.4	6.5	4.9	22.2	27.3	16.2	3.5	76.0	42.5	48.7	51.3
68323	BURCHARD	98.6	98.5	0.0	0.0	0.7	0.8	0.0	0.0	5.8	6.3	6.3	6.5	5.8	19.3	28.5	18.5	3.3	78.0	45.2	51.0	49.0
68324	BURR	97.1	96.9	0.5	0.8	0.5	0.8	0.5	0.8	5.4	8.1	6.6	6.6	4.6	25.5	27.8	13.9	1.5	76.1	41.2	52.9	47.1
68325	BYRON	97.9	97.9	0.0	0.0	0.3	0.3	1.2	1.2	6.7	6.7	7.0	5.5	4.9	21.2	23.9	18.8	5.5	76.1	43.6	48.2	51.8
68326	CARLETON	98.9	98.9	0.0	0.0	0.0	0.0	1.8	1.9	6.0	6.4	7.5	6.7	4.9	22.5	26.2	16.5	3.4	75.7	42.1	49.8	50.2
68327	CHESTER	98.4	98.1	0.2	0.2	0.2	0.5	0.9	0.9	5.1	5.6	6.3	5.1	4.4	19.6	31.2	20.1	2.6	79.7	47.0	51.5	48.5
68328	CLATONIA	98.1	97.9	0.0	0.0	0.2	0.4	0.6	0.6	5.6	6.6	9.3	7.2	4.5	26.0	28.5	11.6	0.8	73.0	39.9	51.3	48.7
68329	COOK	98.4	98.4	0.0	0.0	1.1	1.2	0.3	0.4	4.8	5.5	6.7	6.7	5.7	20.2	29.7	17.9	2.9	78.8	45.3	51.6	48.4
68330	CORDOVA	97.8	97.7	0.5	0.5	0.0	0.0	0.5	0.5	7.7	7.7	7.3	6.8	5.9	23.6	25.9	13.6	1.4	72.3	38.9	50.9	49.1
68331	CORTLAND	99.3	99.1	0.1	0.1	0.1	0.2	0.5	0.6	7.1	7.6	7.3	5.8	4.6	26.1	27.3	12.8	1.5	74.4	40.2	51.1	48.9
68332	CRAB ORCHARD	98.6	99.3	0.0	0.0	0.0	0.0	0.0	0.7	5.0	6.5	7.9	5.8	5.0	24.5	28.1	14.4	2.9	76.3	42.3	47.5	52.5
68333	CRETE	88.7	86.6	0.6	0.7	2.9	3.8	11.0	12.8	7.0	6.7	6.6	9.1	11.5	24.6	21.3	10.3	3.0	75.7	32.6	50.0	50.0
68335	DAVENPORT	98.6	98.6	0.0	0.0	0.0	0.0	0.7	0.9	5.6	6.1	5.9	7.3	5.9	20.7	28.2	18.1	2.4	78.2	44.2	50.2	49.8
68336	DAVEY	97.9	97.8	0.4	0.4	0.0	0.0	1.7	2.0	5.4	6.9	8.9	7.4	4.3	25.2	28.9	11.7	1.3	73.8	40.6	51.8	48.2
68337	DAWSON	96.8	96.5	0.5	0.5	0.3	0.5	1.1	1.1	4.6	5.2	7.9	6.0	5.2	23.1	29.6	16.6	1.9	78.5	43.8	52.7	47.3
68338	DAYKIN	98.7	98.6	0.0	0.0	0.3	0.4	1.3	1.1	4.6	5.3	6.0	7.0	6.0	19.7	31.9	17.2	2.5	80.0	45.9	49.1	50.9
68339	DENTON	98.2	97.9	0.1	0.1	0.1	0.3	0.9	1.2	5.9	7.1	6.9	6.2	4.8	23.0	36.0	9.7	0.6	76.3	42.7	51.0	49.0
68340	DESHLER	98.0	97.7	0.0	0.0	0.3	0.4	1.2	1.4	6.4	6.7	6.8	5.4	5.0	21.1	24.5	18.9	5.3	76.6	44.0	48.4	51.6
68341	DE WITT	98.7	98.7	0.0	0.0	0.3	0.4	0.8	0.9	5.7	6.0	7.7	6.9	5.7	25.2	27.0	13.3	2.8	76.2	40.8	50.1	49.9
68342	DILLER	99.0	98.8	0.0	0.0	0.2	0.2	0.8	0.9	5.7	6.0	6.4	6.2	5.0	23.4	28.5	16.5	2.4	78.4	43.5	52.6	47.4
68343	DORCHESTER	98.3	97.8	0.1	0.1	0.0	0.0	2.4	2.8	6.2	6.5	8.1	6.6	5.7	26.9	25.2	12.6	2.3	75.4	39.4	51.7	48.3
68344	DOUGLAS	97.4	96.8	0.7	0.8	0.5	0.8	0.7	0.8	5.5	8.0	6.4	6.4	4.6	25.8	28.0	13.6	1.7	75.8	41.3	51.7	48.3
68345	DU BOIS	98.6	99.0	0.0	0.0	0.0	0.0	1.4	1.3	4.6	5.2	6.9	5.9	4.3	21.6	28.1	20.6	2.9	79.4	46.1	50.3	49.7
68346	DUNBAR	98.8	98.6	0.2	0.2	0.0	0.2	0.4	0.3	7.6	7.9	9.1	6.7	5.0	24.9	25.1	12.5	1.2	71.1	37.8	52.2	47.8
68347	EAGLE	98.2	98.0	0.0	0.0	0.1	0.2	1.7	2.0	8.2	8.3	8.6	7.6	5.9	29.2	24.2	7.2	0.8	70.1	34.8	50.7	49.3
68348	ELK CREEK	91.9	92.0	0.3	0.3	5.0	4.8	3.1	3.0	6.0	6.0	5.4	5.7	5.7	21.7	26.8	17.6	5.4	78.6	44.8	47.3	52.7
68349	ELMWOOD	99.1	99.0	0.1	0.1	0.3	0.4	0.4	0.4	8.0	8.4	8.3	6.3	5.0	26.1	24.3	11.3	2.3	71.0	37.7	51.5	48.5
68350	ENDICOTT	98.8	98.4	0.0	0.0	0.0	0.4	0.8	1.2	5.3	6.2	5.7	6.2	4.9	23.0	29.1	17.6	2.1	78.7	44.3	52.9	47.1
68351	EXETER	97.4	97.3	0.1	0.1	0.1	0.1	1.9	1.9	5.5	6.4	8.2	6.4	4.5	22.4	25.6	16.2	4.8	75.4	42.8	48.9	51.1
68352	FAIRBURY	98.1	97.9	0.1	0.1	0.2	0.3	1.6	1.9	5.5	5.5	6.0	6.3	5.4	21.7	25.7	18.5	5.4	79.0	44.7	47.9	52.1
68354	FAIRMONT	97.4	97.3	0.1	0.1	0.1	0.1	1.7	1.8	5.7	6.5	8.3	6.2	4.5	22.2	25.8	16.3	4.5	75.0	42.8	49.1	50.9
68355	FALLS CITY	94.9	94.5	0.1	0.1	0.2	0.2	0.9	1.0	5.9	6.1	7.3	7.1	5.8	21.9	24.3	17.4	4.3	76.0	42.3	47.7	52.3
68357	FILLEY	99.1	98.8	0.0	0.2	0.2	0.5	0.5	0.7	5.0	5.2	7.8	7.4	4.5	26.8	28.3	14.0	1.0	76.7	41.5	53.0	47.0
68358	FIRTH	98.7	98.4	0.2	0.2	0.4	0.6	0.2	0.4	8.1	8.7	8.9	6.1	4.6	26.7	21.7	11.6	3.6	70.2	36.8	47.2	52.8
68359	FRIEND	98.6	98.4	0.0	0.0	0.0	0.0	1.1	1.3	5.6	6.1	7.6	7.2	5.2	20.9	25.1	17.2	5.2	75.4	43.2	48.6	51.4
68360	GARLAND	97.6	97.2	0.1	0.1	0.1	0.1	2.2	2.7	5.4	6.3	6.9	7.1	5.9	23.9	32.6	10.8	1.2	77.4	41.9	52.1	47.9
68361	GENEVA	97.4	97.5	0.4	0.4	0.0	0.0	1.7	1.7	6.2	6.2	6.3	8.3	4.8	21.3	25.4	17.1	4.4	75.1	42.7	47.8	52.2
68362	GILEAD	99.4	99.4	0.0	0.0	0.0	0.0	0.0	0.7	5.9	5.9	6.5	5.9	5.2	18.3	25.5	20.3	6.5	77.1	46.6	49.0	51.0
68364	GOEHNER	99.0	98.7	0.3	0.3	0.3	0.3	0.5	0.3	5.9	6.4	7.9	7.1	5.4	23.5	26.8	14.5	2.6	75.0	41.4	51.3	48.7
68365	GRAFTON	98.7	99.1	0.0	0.0	0.0	0.0	0.9	0.9	7.0	7.0	7.4	6.1	5.2	23.6	26.6	15.3	1.8	73.8	41.2	51.5	48.5
68366	GREENWOOD	97.9	97.8	0.2	0.2	0.3	0.4	0.8	0.8	6.8	7.1	6.7	5.4	5.8	25.9	29.4	12.1	0.7	76.1	40.6	52.2	47.8
68367	GRESHAM	98.1	98.0	0.6	0.7	0.0	0.0	0.6	0.7	6.1	6.5	8.5	7.4	5.6	23.7	26.3	13.7	2.2	74.3	40.7	50.0	50.0
68368	HALLAM	96.2	95.4	0.0	0.0	1.8	2.3	0.8	0.8	5.2	7.7	7.0	6.2	3.0	32.7	24.6	12.0	1.6	75.6	38.0	51.1	48.9
68370	HEBRON	99.0	98.9	0.0	0.0	0.1	0.1	0.6	0.7	5.8	5.8	6.2	5.8	5.4	19.0	26.2	20.3	5.5	78.0	46.3	49.8	50.2
68371	HENDERSON	98.9	98.8	0.1	0.1	0.2	0.4	0.5	0.5	4.9	5.8	6.6	7.4	5.4	18.7	26.4	19.6	5.1	77.1	45.7	48.0	52.0
68372	HICKMAN	98.3	98.1	0.4	0.4	0.1	0.1	1.0	1.2	7.6	8.0	8.8	8.0	7.0	25.8	26.0	8.0	0.9	70.7	35.7	51.5	48.5
68375	HUBBELL	98.4	98.3	0.0	0.0	0.5	0.6	0.5	1.1	5.0	5.5	6.6	5.0	4.4	19.9	29.8	20.4	3.3	79.6	47.0	50.8	49.2
68376	HUMBOLDT	96.8	96.5	0.4	0.5	0.1	0.1	1.6	1.9	4.6	5.0	6.8	6.8	5.7	19.9	26.7	19.9	4.6	78.9	45.8	48.6	51.4
68377	JANSEN	99.4	99.2	0.0	0.0	0.2	0.2	0.6	0.6	5.2	6.0	7.7	7.1	5.6	23.5	28.5	13.9	2.5	76.7	41.9	52.2	47.8
68378	JOHNSON	98.2	97.9	0.0	0.0	0.2	0.2	0.6	0.6	4.4	5.2	7.5	6.4	5.7	22.1	31.6	14.1	3.0	78.8	44.2	50.0	50.0
68380	LEWISTON	98.3	98.3	0.0	0.0	0.6	0.6	0.0	0.0	5.8	6.4	6.4	6.4	5.8	19.1	28.3	18.5	3.5	77.5	45.2	50.9	49.1
68381	LIBERTY	97.0	97.0	0.0	0.0	0.0	0.0	1.3	1.5	6.4	6.0	6.8	6.8	6.0	22.2	24.8	17.3	3.8	75.9	41.8	48.9	51.1
68401	MC COOL JUNCTION	98.0	97.5	0.0	0.0	0.7	0.8	1.7	2.1	6.3	7.7	7.9	7.3	3.9	26.2	29.3	10.3	1.1	72.4	38.3	51.2	48.8
68402	MALCOLM	98.2	97.9	0.5	0.5	0.3	0.4	0.7	0.7	5.1	6.6	10.1	10.0	4.1	26.4	30.0	7.3	0.5	71.4	37.6	52.9	47.1
68404	MARTELL	97.8	97.3	0.1	0.1	0.3	0.3	1.2	1.4	5.9	6.9	6.8	5.6	4.7	24.3	34.1	10.4	1.4	77.0	42.5	50.8	49.2
68405	MILFORD	97.9	97.8	0.2	0.2	0.2	0.3	1.4	1.5	5.5	5.6	6.9	11.1	11.0	23.0	22.0	12.6	2.4	78.2	34.4	54.0	46.0
68406	MILLIGAN	98.3	98.5	0.0	0.0	0.2	0.2	1.9	1.9	5.8	6.0	6.7	7.1	5.4	23.4	27.0	15.9	2.8	77.7	42.4	51.1	48.9
68407	MURDOCK	97.6	97.5	0.0	0.0	0.1	0.1	1.3	1.6	6.0	6.7	7.0	6.6	5.1	24.9	29.9	12.4	1.4	76.2	41.5	50.5	49.5
68409	MURRAY	98.1	97.8	0.0	0.0	0.7	1.1	1.5	1.7	6.3	6.8	7.9	6.1	5.2	27.2	28.1	11.3	1.2	75.1	39.7	49.1	50.9
68410	NEBRASKA CITY	96.5	95.9	0.4	0.4	0.4	0.5	3.8	4.5	6.8	6.6	7.1	6.9	6.5	23.8	24.4	14.5	3.4	75.1	39.6	48.5	51.5
68413	NEHAWKA	97.5	97.0	0.0	0.0	0.7	0.9	2.3	2.8	6.3	6.8	7.9	7.2	4.9	25.9	28.9	11.2	0.9	74.8	39.9	50.4	49.7
68414	NEMAHA	99.2	99.5	0.0	0.0	0.3	0.3	0.5	0.5	4.8	4.8	6.7	6.7	5.4	22.8	29.5	16.9	2.4	79.6	44.4	50.9	49.1
68415	ODELL	98.9	98.8	0.0	0.0	0.0	0.0	0.4	0.4	5.9	6.7	8.5	6.9	5.7	23.1	26.1	15.7	1.5	74.7	41.1	50.9	49.1
68416	OHIOWA	98.5	98.5	0.0	0.0	0.0	0.0	1.9	1.9	5.8	6.2	6.6	7.3	5.4	23.6	26.3	15.8	3.1	76.8	42.2	50.2	49.8
68417	OTOE	98.8	98.6	0.0	0.0	0.0	0.2	0.5	0.5	6.5	7.2	9.3	6.7	5.5	26.1	25.6	12.0	1.2	72.7	38.0	52.4	47.6
68418	PALMYRA	98.4	98.1	0.2	0.2	0.1	0.1	1.7	2.0	6.7	7.6	7.0	6.6	4.7	26.0	28.7	11.5	1.3	74.6	39.7	52.0	48.0
68420	PAWNEE CITY	99.1	99.1	0.0	0.0	0.1	0.1	0.6	0.6	5.4	5.4	7.1	5.5	5.0	18.2	24.3	22.0	7.2	78.5	47.5	45.6	54.4
68421	PERU	96.4	96.3	1.2	1.3	0.4	0.4	2.1	2.1	3.4	3.8	5.2	14.2	29.6	17.4	17.6	7.4	1.5	85.0	24.0	50.7	49.3
68422	PICKRELL	99.2	99.1	0.0	0.2	0.2	0.2	0.5	0.6	7.2	7.5	7.2	5.5	4.4	26.7	26.8	12.6	2.0	74.4	40.2	50.4	49.6
68423	PLEASANT DALE	98.0	97.8	0.1	0.1	0.4	0.4	1.2	1.5	5.7	6.4	6.6	6.1	5.9	24.7	30.6	12.2	1.8	77.5	41.7	51.3	48.7
68424	PLYMOUTH	99.2	98.9	0.0	0.0	0.1	0.2	0.6	0.8	5.3	5.8	7.4	7.0	5.6	23.2	28.9	14.2	2.6	77.3	42.4	51.7	48.3
68428	RAYMOND	97.4	96.8	0.3	0.2	0.3	0.2	1.9	2.4	5.6	7.5	10.1	8.3	3.2	27.8	29.1	8.0	0.5	70.9	38.7	52.4	47.6
68429	REYNOLDS	99.3	99.2	0.0	0.0	0.0	0.0	0.8	0.8	5.4	5.4	6.2	5.4	4.7	22.5	30.2	17.8	2.3	78.3	45.2	52.7	47.3
68430	ROCA	98.2	97.8	0.1	0.1	0.3	0.4	1.2	1.4	6.5	7.3	8.1	6.6	5.2	24.0	30.9	10.4	1.2	74.0	40.6	50.2	49.8
68431	RULO	93.7	93.0	0.0	0.0	0.0	0.0	0.6	0.9	6.4	6.7	8.1	7.0	4.9	22.4	27.0	15.7	1.7	74.1	41.7	51.5	48.6
68433	SALEM	96.8	96.7	0.4	0.4	0.4	0.4	0.8	1.2	4.5	5.4	7.8	6.2	5.4	23.1	30.0	15.6	2.1	78.2	43.6	52.7	47.3
68434	SEWARD	97.9	97.6	0.4	0.4	0.5	0.7	1.1	1.3	5.9	5.8	6.8	8.9	11.5	24.6	21.4	11.7	3.5	77.6	33.7	48.7	51.3
68436	SHICKLEY	98.8	98.9	0.0	0.0	0.0	0.0	0.9	0.9	6.9	7.1	7.2	5.8	5.2	23.5	27.0	15.8	1.5	74.4	41.6	51.7	48.3
68437	SHUBERT	98.0	97.6	0.0	0.0	0.0	0.0	1.2	1.5	4.2	6.6	7.7	8.9	5.7	24.4	28.0	12.8	1.8	75.3	41.2	51.2	48.8
68439	STAPLEHURST	98.3	98.3	0.0	0.0	0.4	0.5	0.9	0.9	6.3	6.8	7.7	6.5	5.6	27.1	26.8	11.7	1.6	75.2	38.4	53.5	46.5
68440	STEELE CITY	98.7	99.3	0.0	0.0	0.0	0.0	0.6	0.7	6.0	6.0	6.0	6.0	5.3	23.2	27.2	17.9	2.7	78.2	43.5	52.3	47.7
68441	STEINAUER	98.7	98.7	0.0	0.0	0.3	0.3	0.7	0.6	5.1	5.8	6.4	6.1	4.8	20.8	27.5	20.5	3.2	78.9	45.8	50.8	49.2
68442	STELLA	98.0	98.0	0.0	0.0	0.0	0.0	1.3	1.7	4.0	6.4	8.1	9.1	5.7	23.6	28.3	13.1	1.7	75.4	41.2	50.8	49.2
68443	STERLING	98.3	98.2	0.2	0.2	0.6	0.6	0.6	0.6	5.4	6.0	7.3	6.0	5.0	24.3	27.8	15.7	2.6	77.6	42.8	49.1	50.9
68444	STRANG	98.5	98.4	0.0	0.0	0.0	0.0	1.5	1.6	6.3	6.3	7.0	7.0	5.5	23.4	25.8	16.4	2.3	75.8	41.8	50.8	49.2
68445	SWANTON	98.6	98.1	0.0	0.0	0.0	0.0	1.4	1.4	4.8	6.7	9.5	7.1	4.3	23.8	31.0	11.4	1.4	73.8	40.9	53.3	46.7
68446	SYRACUSE	98.9	98.6	0.0	0.0	0.2	0.3	0.5	0.6	6.0	5.9	6.5	5.2	4.5	22.2	23.1	20.9	5.7	78.2	44.8	48.1	51.9
68447	TABLE ROCK	98.7	99.2	0.0	0.0	0.0	0.0	1.3	1.3	4.7	5.3	6.8	5.7	4.2	21.8	27.5	21.0	3.0	79.5	46.1	51.1	48.9
68448	TALMAGE	99.0	98.8	0.8	0.8	0.0	0.0	0.6	0.6	7.5	7.7	6.9	6.5	5.0	23.0	26.5	14.9	2.0	73.7	40.5	53.3	46.7
	NEBRASKA	89.6	88.4	4.0	4.2	1.3	1.8	5.5	6.4	7.0	6.9	7.2	7.3	7.6	27.5	23.5	11.2	2.1	74.8	35.7	49.4	50.6
	UNITED STATES	75.1	73.6	12.3	12.5	3.8	4.2	12.5	14.1	6.9	6.7	7.2	7.0	7.3	28.6	23.8	10.8	1.7	75.1	36.0	49.1	50.9

#	POST OFFICE NAME	2004 Per Capita Income	2004 HH Income Base	2004 Household Income Distribution (%): Less than $25,000	$25,000 to $49,999	$50,000 to $99,999	$100,000 to $149,999	$150,000 or More	Median Household Income: 2004	2009	2004 National Centile	2004 State Centile	2004 Home Value Base	2004 Home Value Distribution (%): Less than $50,000	$50,000 to $89,999	$90,000 to $174,999	$175,000 to $399,999	$400,000 or More	2004 Median Home Value
68316	BENEDICT	19038	232	22.8	36.2	32.8	5.6	2.6	42165	47175	53	70	182	28.0	26.4	31.9	10.4	3.3	81111
68317	BENNET	28942	630	12.7	26.2	43.2	13.0	4.9	59504	71525	84	93	551	9.1	14.2	42.1	29.4	5.3	129521
68318	BLUE SPRINGS	17348	261	33.7	34.9	25.7	5.0	0.8	35429	40562	29	32	190	46.3	25.3	21.6	5.8	1.1	55833
68319	BRADSHAW	20813	270	19.6	37.0	37.8	4.8	0.7	45971	50870	64	80	212	16.0	23.1	36.3	17.0	7.6	103571
68320	BROCK	18949	154	31.2	31.8	30.5	5.2	1.3	38360	46330	41	52	122	30.3	21.3	32.0	13.9	2.5	83333
68321	BROWNVILLE	20257	182	31.9	28.6	31.9	5.0	2.8	40000	47372	46	60	145	38.6	31.7	13.1	11.7	4.8	61364
68322	BRUNING	19913	196	32.1	32.1	29.6	4.1	2.0	35746	39142	31	35	158	55.1	29.1	12.0	1.9	1.9	45789
68323	BURCHARD	19367	166	29.5	39.2	24.1	5.4	1.8	36369	41811	33	39	136	39.0	25.0	25.0	11.0	0.0	64545
68324	BURR	22330	119	22.7	40.3	27.7	7.6	1.7	40661	46271	48	63	98	23.5	19.4	31.6	22.5	3.1	100000
68325	BYRON	17339	134	33.6	37.3	24.6	3.7	0.8	35000	38885	28	29	107	57.9	26.2	9.4	3.7	2.8	41500
68326	CARLETON	17608	107	33.6	33.6	27.1	4.7	0.9	33944	40000	24	24	86	53.5	29.1	12.8	2.3	2.3	46667
68327	CHESTER	18183	195	36.9	37.4	20.0	4.1	1.5	31440	36112	16	13	159	55.4	23.3	17.0	2.5	1.9	42917
68328	CLATONIA	20556	197	17.3	38.6	38.6	5.1	0.5	45518	50648	63	79	159	17.0	20.8	42.1	20.1	0.0	122500
68329	COOK	20665	296	32.4	33.5	27.4	4.1	2.7	37109	42564	36	44	233	30.0	32.2	26.2	8.6	3.0	72333
68330	CORDOVA	18869	97	30.9	35.1	28.9	4.1	1.0	38053	45970	39	50	78	34.6	23.1	30.8	9.0	2.6	82500
68331	CORTLAND	20936	339	19.5	33.9	40.1	5.9	0.6	47120	53098	66	82	274	9.9	21.9	54.0	13.5	0.7	114674
68332	CRAB ORCHARD	20974	65	32.3	30.8	30.8	4.6	1.5	37359	43216	37	45	52	32.7	26.9	32.7	7.7	0.0	72500
68333	CRETE	18853	2769	28.6	29.9	32.5	7.4	1.7	42262	50057	54	70	1865	17.3	28.5	40.2	12.6	1.5	93878
68335	DAVENPORT	19074	191	33.0	35.6	25.7	4.7	1.1	34780	39532	27	27	152	54.0	25.7	13.2	4.0	3.3	47000
68336	DAVEY	26639	171	10.5	26.3	42.1	15.8	5.3	63509	75900	87	95	149	4.0	11.4	32.2	47.0	5.4	181731
68337	DAWSON	15151	147	34.0	42.9	19.7	3.4	0.0	33560	39147	23	22	117	59.8	21.4	13.7	5.1	0.0	38929
68338	DAYKIN	21871	124	26.6	38.7	25.8	5.7	3.2	37822	42977	39	48	96	39.6	16.7	34.4	6.3	3.1	68333
68339	DENTON	28198	383	10.2	21.2	46.7	17.8	4.2	64999	78252	89	96	332	2.7	6.9	41.0	45.5	3.9	173837
68340	DESHLER	18198	452	34.1	37.6	23.9	3.5	0.9	34522	39212	26	26	362	59.7	25.4	9.7	3.3	1.9	41667
68341	DE WITT	19829	455	27.0	30.8	36.0	5.3	0.9	42363	48873	54	71	358	21.5	37.4	29.9	10.1	1.1	79500
68342	DILLER	20726	229	31.4	30.1	31.9	3.9	2.6	39127	44362	43	57	189	48.7	22.2	18.5	9.0	1.6	51923
68343	DORCHESTER	17719	364	26.1	40.1	28.6	3.9	1.4	38516	44135	41	53	286	21.0	36.4	32.5	8.4	1.8	81600
68344	DOUGLAS	18463	200	23.5	40.5	27.5	7.0	1.5	40000	45846	46	60	165	21.2	18.8	33.9	23.0	3.0	104167
68345	DU BOIS	18221	135	34.8	42.2	17.0	5.2	0.7	32929	37887	21	18	110	59.1	21.8	12.7	5.5	0.9	42857
68346	DUNBAR	19025	210	20.5	31.0	39.5	8.1	1.0	48531	53377	69	83	162	13.0	23.5	27.8	33.3	2.5	135000
68347	EAGLE	25279	807	11.0	26.6	45.2	12.3	4.8	60038	68606	84	93	686	12.2	18.1	48.1	18.2	3.4	111475
68348	ELK CREEK	21226	148	31.1	35.1	24.3	7.4	2.0	39525	45907	44	59	114	29.0	36.0	28.1	7.0	0.0	68462
68349	ELMWOOD	21585	412	21.1	26.7	43.0	6.3	2.9	51230	56783	74	88	345	11.6	24.1	47.8	12.2	4.4	109464
68350	ENDICOTT	24300	108	32.4	27.8	32.4	3.7	3.7	40000	45643	46	60	89	53.9	20.2	15.7	9.0	1.1	47308
68351	EXETER	18314	346	32.1	32.1	30.9	3.5	1.5	38992	43353	43	56	272	49.6	30.2	16.5	2.6	1.1	50476
68352	FAIRBURY	24062	2364	34.8	33.0	24.8	4.4	3.1	35618	42200	30	33	1706	52.2	25.3	18.4	3.5	0.7	48645
68354	FAIRMONT	19482	369	31.2	31.7	31.2	4.1	1.9	40356	45000	47	62	289	48.4	30.8	17.0	2.8	1.0	51957
68355	FALLS CITY	18601	2422	38.3	31.0	24.7	5.0	1.0	33506	40034	22	21	1742	48.7	30.0	17.2	3.0	1.0	51325
68357	FILLEY	17942	172	25.6	40.7	30.2	3.5	0.0	37286	41992	36	44	138	18.1	26.1	35.5	19.6	0.7	97273
68358	FIRTH	21726	435	19.1	27.4	39.1	10.6	3.9	52438	63118	76	89	370	7.0	17.8	41.9	30.0	3.2	125926
68359	FRIEND	19466	651	27.2	37.8	29.0	3.4	2.6	39822	45606	45	59	519	21.8	32.4	39.1	6.2	0.6	85521
68360	GARLAND	31393	348	15.8	22.1	43.4	12.9	5.8	60000	70729	84	93	299	11.7	14.4	32.4	33.1	8.4	160511
68361	GENEVA	21182	1227	26.3	41.4	25.8	4.2	2.2	37844	43537	39	48	916	31.0	32.5	30.0	6.0	0.4	69294
68362	GILEAD	20944	66	30.3	37.9	22.7	6.1	3.0	35000	42369	28	29	49	38.8	30.6	28.6	2.0	0.0	63000
68364	GOEHNER	18718	146	25.3	29.5	37.7	6.2	1.4	46671	52397	65	81	114	17.5	30.7	42.1	9.7	0.0	91538
68365	GRAFTON	24778	95	22.1	37.9	29.5	7.4	3.2	43455	48203	57	75	73	32.9	27.4	27.4	11.0	1.4	75833
68366	GREENWOOD	23134	382	16.2	31.9	41.6	7.9	2.4	51475	60423	75	88	329	19.5	23.7	37.4	16.1	3.3	98654
68367	GRESHAM	20994	212	24.1	34.9	32.1	6.1	2.8	41944	46548	53	69	166	29.5	27.7	31.3	9.6	1.8	74444
68368	HALLAM	25046	241	17.0	30.3	40.7	7.9	4.2	51882	63544	75	89	202	8.9	33.2	44.6	11.9	1.5	98000
68370	HEBRON	23107	872	31.5	36.5	22.9	6.8	2.3	35668	42733	30	34	654	38.7	31.4	25.5	3.8	0.6	62319
68371	HENDERSON	21834	662	24.8	35.7	30.5	7.0	2.1	42890	48205	56	72	536	17.2	36.8	37.5	6.9	1.7	87162
68372	HICKMAN	22468	741	15.8	25.6	44.1	12.2	2.3	56520	67744	81	92	624	6.7	19.9	53.0	17.0	3.4	110862
68375	HUBBELL	18805	79	38.0	36.7	20.3	3.8	1.3	30935	35736	15	9	63	52.4	25.4	17.5	3.2	1.6	47000
68376	HUMBOLDT	19267	703	33.0	35.4	26.2	4.4	1.0	35360	42182	29	31	525	57.3	24.2	16.2	2.3	0.0	43125
68377	JANSEN	17596	195	28.2	38.5	28.2	4.6	0.5	38850	43382	42	55	160	33.8	30.0	26.3	6.9	3.1	67778
68378	JOHNSON	21010	370	30.8	31.6	30.5	5.1	1.9	38404	45812	41	52	293	29.0	22.9	31.7	13.7	2.7	85000
68380	LEWISTON	19116	71	29.6	38.0	23.9	5.6	2.8	36732	41741	34	41	58	39.7	25.9	22.4	12.1	0.0	64000
68381	LIBERTY	16121	99	34.3	39.4	20.2	4.0	2.0	35190	40641	28	30	73	48.0	26.0	19.2	6.9	0.0	53000
68401	MC COOL JUNCTION	18758	313	24.9	35.1	36.4	2.9	0.6	41297	45491	51	66	240	20.4	22.5	35.4	14.2	7.5	98500
68402	MALCOLM	28945	392	11.2	21.7	45.4	15.8	5.9	62336	75551	87	95	337	3.3	10.4	41.5	42.4	2.4	158796
68404	MARTELL	26539	462	13.0	24.2	47.4	11.5	3.9	61228	72646	86	94	401	7.7	16.0	43.1	29.7	3.5	137772
68405	MILFORD	20861	1204	25.4	28.3	34.1	8.0	4.2	46659	55102	65	81	842	9.4	22.8	49.1	16.6	2.1	110028
68406	MILLIGAN	18543	213	31.5	41.3	22.5	3.8	0.9	34853	38762	27	28	164	43.3	22.0	20.1	10.4	4.3	61765
68407	MURDOCK	22816	333	19.2	28.2	39.3	9.9	3.3	51636	57957	75	89	277	11.2	18.8	39.0	27.4	3.6	120357
68409	MURRAY	25233	315	13.7	23.2	49.5	10.8	2.9	59572	69621	84	93	257	14.0	21.4	47.5	16.0	1.2	104957
68410	NEBRASKA CITY	20593	3442	28.9	32.1	30.8	6.1	2.1	40779	48695	49	64	2443	22.8	30.6	33.2	13.0	0.5	85875
68413	NEHAWKA	22431	171	16.4	35.7	39.8	6.4	1.8	48622	55499	70	84	138	13.8	25.4	36.2	19.6	5.1	102632
68414	NEMAHA	19851	157	31.9	29.3	31.2	5.1	2.6	39165	47378	43	57	126	40.5	31.8	13.5	11.1	3.2	59231
68415	ODELL	20207	292	24.3	34.3	32.2	6.5	2.7	40765	45576	49	64	239	21.8	31.4	32.6	13.4	0.8	82500
68416	OHIOWA	18999	121	29.8	42.2	22.3	4.1	1.7	35657	39049	30	34	93	40.9	22.6	20.4	11.8	4.3	63500
68417	OTOE	18900	160	26.3	32.5	33.1	8.1	0.0	43183	50241	56	73	124	21.8	28.2	34.7	12.9	2.4	90000
68418	PALMYRA	24447	453	18.5	32.2	35.5	8.0	5.7	49287	58451	71	85	386	13.2	21.5	34.7	23.1	7.5	112097
68420	PAWNEE CITY	20004	622	42.0	33.8	18.5	3.1	2.7	30000	35299	12	7	463	59.4	28.7	9.1	2.8	0.0	41944
68421	PERU	16327	366	33.3	36.3	23.5	4.4	2.5	33797	41367	23	23	250	51.6	30.0	14.4	4.0	0.0	48974
68422	PICKRELL	20592	246	20.3	33.3	39.0	6.1	1.2	47043	52922	66	81	198	10.1	20.2	53.5	16.2	0.0	116429
68423	PLEASANT DALE	28158	332	14.2	26.8	41.9	12.1	5.1	56326	66078	81	92	281	12.5	11.7	41.6	28.5	5.7	147266
68424	PLYMOUTH	17227	328	27.7	38.7	27.7	4.6	1.2	38689	43349	42	54	267	35.2	28.8	26.2	6.7	3.0	67069
68428	RAYMOND	28665	450	10.0	19.1	48.0	16.9	6.0	67702	80942	90	98	395	4.3	8.6	40.3	43.3	3.5	166776
68429	REYNOLDS	24839	59	32.2	28.8	33.9	3.4	1.7	39300	45000	44	58	49	57.1	18.4	14.3	10.2	0.0	45625
68430	ROCA	28025	428	12.9	23.1	44.9	13.8	5.4	62330	75626	87	95	375	6.4	11.7	42.7	32.8	6.4	149085
68431	RULO	17501	148	35.1	37.2	24.3	2.7	0.7	33394	38834	22	20	115	31.3	21.7	27.0	13.9	6.1	84167
68433	SALEM	17366	110	33.6	42.7	20.0	3.6	0.0	33753	39474	23	23	88	60.2	21.6	13.6	4.6	0.0	38000
68434	SEWARD	23010	3006	23.0	27.5	35.8	10.4	3.3	49544	58291	71	86	2096	7.3	23.3	50.8	17.2	1.4	113361
68436	SHICKLEY	23929	259	22.4	37.5	29.3	7.7	3.1	43273	49653	57	74	199	33.7	29.2	24.6	11.6	1.0	73824
68437	SHUBERT	16656	132	36.4	31.8	25.8	6.1	0.0	32815	38963	20	18	108	59.3	23.2	12.0	5.6	0.0	37857
68439	STAPLEHURST	21872	225	21.3	32.0	35.6	7.6	3.6	47958	54367	68	83	176	25.6	27.3	35.8	10.8	0.6	85833
68440	STEELE CITY	22930	73	31.5	27.4	37.0	2.7	1.4	40444	45446	48	62	60	53.3	20.0	16.7	10.0	0.0	47500
68441	STEINAUER	17716	129	33.3	40.3	19.4	5.4	1.6	34736	38600	26	27	106	51.9	22.6	17.0	7.6	0.9	48000
68442	STELLA	18984	133	35.3	31.6	26.3	6.8	0.0	33605	39304	23	22	109	59.6	22.9	11.9	5.5	0.0	37500
68443	STERLING	18912	423	31.7	31.7	30.7	4.5	1.4	37436	43358	37	45	337	31.2	29.4	29.1	8.9	1.5	72708
68444	STRANG	17070	52	28.9	38.5	28.9	3.9	0.0	38613	43621	41	53	40	37.5	25.0	25.0	10.0	2.5	67500
68445	SWANTON	20429	90	32.2	32.2	27.8	4.4	3.3	35743	41383	31	35	72	23.6	23.6	31.9	18.1	2.8	94000
68446	SYRACUSE	22553	1041	23.7	34.3	31.0	8.8	2.1	44076	51116	59	75	831	12.6	30.8	46.0	8.9	1.7	98258
68447	TABLE ROCK	19908	227	36.1	41.4	17.2	4.9	0.4	32419	37643	19	16	185	58.4	22.2	13.0	5.4	1.1	42619
68448	TALMAGE	19346	196	32.1	31.6	27.6	6.1	2.6	38038	43763	39	49	152	32.2	21.1	24.3	20.4	2.0	80000
	NEBRASKA	23743		24.5	30.5	31.8	9.2	4.0	45453	54516				17.2	23.9	42.4	14.4	2.2	101398
	UNITED STATES	25866		24.7	27.1	30.8	10.9	6.5	48124	56710				10.9	15.0	33.7	30.1	10.4	145905

ZIP CODE #	POST OFFICE NAME	FINANCIAL SERVICES: Auto Loan	Home Loan	Invest-ments	Retire-ment Plans	THE HOME: Home Improvements: Home Repair	Lawn & Garden	Furnishings: Comput-ers & Hard-ware	Major Appli-ances	TV, Radio, Sound Equip-ment	Furni-ture	ENTERTAINMENT: Dine out/Carry out	Sports Equip-ment	Fees & Tickets	Toys & Games	Travel	Cable TV	PERSONAL: Apparel & Services	Auto Repairs	Health Insur-ance	Pets & Supplies
68316	BENEDICT	97	68	35	64	79	88	67	83	77	66	90	99	57	88	69	81	82	81	98	115
68317	BENNET	109	115	107	113	117	120	104	109	103	104	128	129	107	133	107	103	124	106	108	131
68318	BLUE SPRINGS	69	51	33	49	56	67	56	62	63	53	74	70	50	70	56	67	68	62	75	76
68319	BRADSHAW	95	67	35	63	78	87	66	81	76	65	89	98	56	87	68	79	81	80	97	113
68320	BROCK	84	58	31	55	68	76	58	71	67	57	78	86	49	76	60	70	71	70	85	99
68321	BROWNVILLE	86	60	31	57	70	78	59	73	68	58	80	88	51	78	61	72	73	72	87	102
68322	BRUNING	80	56	29	53	65	73	55	68	63	54	74	82	47	73	57	66	68	67	81	95
68323	BURCHARD	84	59	31	56	69	77	58	72	67	58	79	87	50	77	60	70	72	71	86	100
68324	BURR	88	61	32	58	72	80	61	75	70	60	82	90	52	80	63	73	75	74	89	104
68325	BYRON	67	51	33	49	55	66	56	62	63	53	74	69	50	70	55	66	67	62	74	74
68326	CARLETON	80	56	29	52	65	72	55	68	63	54	74	82	47	73	57	66	68	67	81	94
68327	CHESTER	72	50	27	48	58	66	50	61	58	49	68	74	43	66	52	60	62	61	73	85
68328	CLATONIA	92	64	33	60	74	83	63	78	73	62	85	94	54	84	65	76	78	77	93	109
68329	COOK	87	61	32	57	71	79	60	74	69	59	81	89	51	79	62	72	74	73	88	103
68330	CORDOVA	77	54	28	51	63	71	53	66	62	53	72	80	46	71	55	65	66	65	79	92
68331	CORTLAND	94	66	34	62	77	86	65	80	75	64	88	97	56	86	67	79	80	79	96	112
68332	CRAB ORCHARD	81	57	30	54	66	74	56	69	64	55	76	83	48	74	58	68	69	68	82	96
68333	CRETE	76	69	61	70	72	79	70	73	73	69	89	85	68	89	70	73	84	73	77	86
68335	DAVENPORT	77	54	28	51	63	70	53	66	61	52	72	79	45	70	55	64	65	65	78	91
68336	DAVEY	108	107	92	103	110	115	97	104	99	97	122	124	98	126	100	100	117	101	107	129
68337	DAWSON	68	48	25	45	56	62	47	58	55	47	64	70	41	63	49	57	58	58	70	81
68338	DAYKIN	91	63	33	60	74	83	63	78	72	62	85	93	54	83	65	76	77	76	92	108
68339	DENTON	94	118	125	118	115	114	105	105	97	104	122	122	112	130	107	94	122	101	94	115
68340	DESHLER	68	51	33	49	56	66	56	62	63	53	74	69	50	70	55	66	67	62	74	75
68341	DE WITT	78	63	46	63	68	77	65	71	70	64	84	83	61	83	65	72	78	70	79	88
68342	DILLER	95	67	35	63	78	87	66	81	76	65	89	98	56	87	68	79	81	80	97	113
68343	DORCHESTER	82	57	30	54	66	74	56	70	65	56	76	84	48	75	58	68	69	69	83	97
68344	DOUGLAS	88	62	32	58	72	80	61	75	70	60	82	91	52	81	63	74	75	74	90	105
68345	DU BOIS	67	50	33	48	55	66	56	61	62	53	73	68	49	69	55	66	67	61	73	74
68346	DUNBAR	95	67	35	63	78	87	66	81	76	65	89	98	56	87	68	80	81	80	97	113
68347	EAGLE	104	108	102	108	106	107	102	104	99	103	123	124	102	124	101	95	120	103	97	119
68348	ELK CREEK	85	59	31	56	69	78	59	73	68	58	79	87	50	78	61	71	72	72	86	101
68349	ELMWOOD	102	73	40	69	84	94	72	88	82	71	96	106	62	95	74	86	88	87	103	121
68350	ENDICOTT	99	69	36	66	81	90	69	85	79	68	93	102	58	91	71	83	84	84	101	118
68351	EXETER	83	58	30	55	67	76	57	71	66	56	77	85	49	76	59	69	70	70	84	98
68352	FAIRBURY	85	69	52	66	75	87	73	79	80	70	95	90	68	94	73	84	88	79	92	96
68354	FAIRMONT	87	61	32	57	71	79	60	74	69	59	81	89	51	79	62	72	74	73	88	103
68355	FALLS CITY	71	53	34	51	59	70	58	65	65	55	76	73	51	72	57	69	70	64	77	80
68357	FILLEY	79	55	29	52	65	72	55	68	63	54	74	82	47	73	57	66	68	67	81	94
68358	FIRTH	112	78	41	74	91	102	77	96	89	76	105	115	66	103	80	94	95	94	114	133
68359	FRIEND	89	62	32	58	72	81	61	76	70	60	83	91	52	81	63	74	75	75	90	105
68360	GARLAND	129	115	87	109	121	130	106	118	113	106	137	140	104	140	109	116	130	115	127	152
68361	GENEVA	87	62	36	59	71	81	64	76	73	62	86	89	56	83	65	77	78	75	90	100
68362	GILEAD	76	57	38	55	62	75	63	69	71	60	83	78	56	78	62	75	76	69	83	84
68364	GOEHNER	90	63	33	59	73	82	62	77	72	61	84	93	53	82	64	75	76	76	91	107
68365	GRAFTON	108	75	39	71	88	98	75	92	86	74	101	111	64	99	77	90	92	91	110	128
68366	GREENWOOD	95	84	64	80	89	96	78	87	83	78	101	103	76	103	80	85	96	85	94	112
68367	GRESHAM	97	67	35	64	79	88	67	82	77	66	90	99	57	88	69	81	82	81	98	115
68368	HALLAM	96	87	73	86	90	100	87	92	91	86	111	106	85	111	87	92	105	91	98	108
68370	HEBRON	89	66	43	63	73	87	73	81	81	69	96	91	64	91	72	86	87	80	97	99
68371	HENDERSON	92	67	42	64	75	88	72	82	82	69	96	94	64	92	72	86	88	82	98	103
68372	HICKMAN	88	100	102	101	98	97	93	93	87	93	109	109	95	113	93	83	108	91	83	103
68375	HUBBELL	76	54	29	51	62	70	54	65	62	53	73	78	47	71	56	65	66	65	78	89
68376	HUMBOLDT	73	54	34	52	60	71	59	66	66	56	78	75	52	74	58	70	71	66	79	81
68377	JANSEN	79	55	29	52	64	72	54	67	62	54	73	81	46	72	56	65	67	66	80	93
68378	JOHNSON	85	59	31	56	69	77	58	72	67	58	79	87	50	77	61	71	72	71	86	101
68380	LEWISTON	84	59	31	56	69	77	58	72	67	57	79	87	50	77	60	70	72	71	86	100
68381	LIBERTY	69	52	34	50	57	68	57	63	64	54	75	71	51	71	57	68	69	63	75	76
68401	MC COOL JUNCTION	83	58	30	55	67	75	57	71	66	56	77	85	49	76	59	69	70	70	84	98
68402	MALCOLM	104	129	137	129	127	125	115	115	107	115	134	134	122	143	118	104	134	111	103	127
68404	MARTELL	87	105	114	103	103	105	96	96	92	96	115	111	103	123	99	90	115	93	89	105
68405	MILFORD	90	76	57	74	80	89	76	83	81	75	98	96	72	98	76	83	92	81	90	101
68406	MILLIGAN	73	51	27	48	60	67	51	63	58	50	68	75	43	67	53	61	62	62	75	87
68407	MURDOCK	103	76	44	72	87	96	74	89	83	73	98	107	65	97	77	87	90	88	105	123
68409	MURRAY	83	101	110	99	99	101	93	92	89	92	111	107	99	118	95	87	111	90	86	101
68410	NEBRASKA CITY	81	68	51	66	72	81	69	75	74	67	89	86	65	89	69	76	83	74	83	91
68413	NEHAWKA	100	72	41	68	83	92	71	86	81	70	95	104	62	94	73	84	87	85	101	119
68414	NEMAHA	85	60	31	56	69	78	59	73	68	58	80	88	50	78	61	71	73	72	87	101
68415	ODELL	94	66	34	62	77	86	65	80	75	64	88	97	55	86	67	79	80	79	96	112
68416	OHIOWA	74	51	27	49	60	67	51	63	58	50	69	76	43	67	53	61	63	62	75	87
68417	OTOE	89	62	33	59	73	81	62	76	71	61	83	92	53	82	64	74	76	75	91	106
68418	PALMYRA	104	89	64	84	95	103	83	94	89	83	108	112	79	109	85	92	102	91	103	122
68420	PAWNEE CITY	73	54	35	52	60	71	59	66	66	56	78	75	52	74	59	70	71	66	79	81
68421	PERU	62	48	56	52	49	54	63	58	64	60	79	74	57	74	58	60	76	64	56	67
68422	PICKRELL	96	67	35	63	78	87	66	82	76	65	89	98	56	87	68	80	81	81	97	114
68423	PLEASANT DALE	111	99	77	95	105	112	92	101	97	92	118	121	90	121	95	99	113	99	109	130
68424	PLYMOUTH	80	56	29	53	65	73	55	68	64	55	75	82	47	73	57	67	68	67	81	95
68428	RAYMOND	101	126	133	126	123	122	112	112	104	112	130	131	119	139	115	101	130	108	100	123
68429	REYNOLDS	98	69	36	65	80	90	68	84	78	67	92	101	58	90	70	82	83	83	100	117
68430	ROCA	95	118	126	117	115	115	106	105	99	105	125	123	113	133	109	97	124	102	96	116
68431	RULO	74	51	27	49	60	67	51	63	58	50	69	76	43	67	53	61	63	62	75	87
68433	SALEM	69	48	25	46	56	63	48	59	55	47	65	71	41	63	50	58	59	58	70	82
68434	SEWARD	82	82	86	84	82	87	85	84	84	83	104	100	84	104	84	81	101	85	81	95
68436	SHICKLEY	109	76	40	72	89	99	75	93	87	74	102	112	64	100	78	91	93	92	111	129
68437	SHUBERT	77	54	28	51	62	70	53	65	61	52	71	79	45	70	55	64	65	64	78	91
68439	STAPLEHURST	88	74	57	73	78	88	76	81	81	74	98	93	72	97	75	82	91	80	89	97
68440	STEELE CITY	86	60	31	57	70	78	59	73	68	58	80	88	51	78	61	72	73	72	87	102
68441	STEINAUER	72	53	33	50	59	69	56	64	64	54	75	74	50	72	57	67	68	64	77	82
68442	STELLA	77	54	28	51	62	70	53	65	61	52	71	79	45	70	55	64	65	64	78	91
68443	STERLING	83	58	30	54	67	75	57	70	66	56	77	85	49	75	59	69	70	69	84	98
68444	STRANG	76	53	28	50	62	69	52	65	60	52	71	78	45	69	54	63	65	64	77	90
68445	SWANTON	86	60	32	57	70	79	59	74	69	59	80	89	51	79	62	72	73	73	88	102
68446	SYRACUSE	90	66	40	63	74	86	69	80	78	67	92	92	61	88	70	83	84	79	95	102
68447	TABLE ROCK	67	50	33	48	55	66	56	61	62	53	73	69	49	69	55	66	67	61	73	74
68448	TALMAGE	90	63	33	59	73	82	62	77	72	61	84	93	53	82	65	75	77	76	92	107
	NEBRASKA	88	81	77	81	83	90	83	85	84	82	104	101	80	103	82	84	100	86	87	100
	UNITED STATES	100	100	100	100	100	100	100	100	100	100	100	100	100	100	100	100	100	100	100	100

A 68450-68726

#	POST OFFICE NAME	COUNTY FIPS CODE	POPULATION 2000	2004	2009	2000-2004 ANNUAL RATE % Rate	State Centile	HOUSEHOLDS 2000	2004	2009	% Annual Rate 2000-2004	2004 Average HH Size	FAMILIES 2000	2004	% Annual Rate 2000-2004
68450	TECUMSEH	097	2403	2469	2525	0.6	79	1000	1034	1064	0.8	2.34	648	672	0.9
68452	ONG	035	117	116	118	-0.2	44	54	54	55	0.0	2.07	35	35	0.0
68453	TOBIAS	151	444	438	451	-0.3	36	179	178	185	-0.1	2.46	127	127	0.0
68454	UNADILLA	131	662	775	867	3.8	97	272	321	362	4.0	2.41	206	244	4.1
68455	UNION	025	777	778	809	0.0	57	290	294	309	0.3	2.65	221	224	0.3
68456	UTICA	159	1093	1103	1133	0.2	65	411	420	437	0.5	2.57	302	309	0.5
68457	VERDON	147	390	382	374	-0.5	23	158	157	156	-0.2	2.43	108	108	0.0
68458	VIRGINIA	067	149	147	151	-0.3	36	63	63	65	0.0	2.33	48	48	0.0
68460	WACO	185	795	806	816	0.3	70	298	306	314	0.6	2.63	226	232	0.6
68461	WALTON	109	610	627	652	0.7	79	220	229	241	1.0	2.74	183	190	0.9
68462	WAVERLY	109	3095	3217	3372	0.9	83	1071	1134	1206	1.4	2.79	860	908	1.3
68463	WEEPING WATER	025	1916	1968	2054	0.6	78	731	758	800	0.9	2.60	527	548	0.9
68464	WESTERN	151	578	572	590	-0.3	41	242	242	251	0.0	2.36	171	172	0.1
68465	WILBER	151	2239	2429	2608	1.9	91	906	992	1074	2.2	2.39	616	676	2.2
68466	WYMORE	067	2110	2314	2501	2.2	93	890	985	1074	2.4	2.31	611	678	2.5
68467	YORK	185	9652	9747	9859	0.2	66	3826	3926	4034	0.6	2.32	2509	2583	0.7
68502	LINCOLN	109	27293	26963	27950	-0.3	38	11320	11305	11855	0.0	2.28	6015	5968	-0.2
68503	LINCOLN	109	15902	16159	16872	0.4	72	6271	6455	6822	0.7	2.38	3067	3132	0.5
68504	LINCOLN	109	14327	15266	16527	1.5	90	6384	6988	7725	2.2	2.06	2954	3200	1.9
68505	LINCOLN	109	13701	14251	15012	0.9	84	5867	6231	6663	1.4	2.28	3811	4042	1.4
68506	LINCOLN	109	27389	28052	29517	0.6	77	11600	12056	12847	0.9	2.26	7371	7635	0.8
68507	LINCOLN	109	13188	13368	13948	0.3	70	5403	5551	5860	0.6	2.40	3522	3616	0.6
68508	LINCOLN	109	13943	14139	14551	0.3	70	4905	5039	5321	0.6	1.68	1241	1275	0.6
68510	LINCOLN	109	20923	20795	21574	-0.1	47	9450	9514	9982	0.2	2.17	5243	5265	0.1
68512	LINCOLN	109	6899	7268	7737	1.2	88	2835	3096	3381	2.1	2.11	1941	2115	2.0
68514	LINCOLN	109	162	161	172	0.0	56	59	60	65	0.4	2.70	45	45	0.0
68516	LINCOLN	109	32899	37756	42050	3.3	95	11973	13866	15588	3.5	2.71	8935	10381	3.6
68517	LINCOLN	109	449	453	481	0.2	65	157	161	174	0.6	2.81	121	121	0.0
68520	LINCOLN	109	1248	1480	1662	4.1	98	459	554	630	4.5	2.66	373	451	4.6
68521	LINCOLN	109	25363	28294	31006	2.6	93	9739	11015	12204	2.9	2.56	6363	7185	2.9
68522	LINCOLN	109	8320	9307	10126	2.7	94	2714	3142	3501	3.5	2.66	1920	2219	3.5
68523	LINCOLN	109	1078	1274	1427	4.0	98	375	449	509	4.3	2.82	299	358	4.3
68524	LINCOLN	109	4999	5162	5458	0.8	81	1503	1583	1701	1.2	3.11	1186	1233	0.9
68526	LINCOLN	109	1067	1232	1366	3.4	96	350	409	458	3.7	3.00	290	338	3.7
68527	LINCOLN	109	708	770	828	2.0	92	256	283	308	2.4	2.72	213	235	2.3
68528	LINCOLN	109	3572	4060	4483	3.1	95	1565	1817	2038	3.6	2.23	950	1099	3.5
68531	LINCOLN	109	154	155	159	0.2	62	56	57	59	0.4	2.72	46	47	0.5
68532	LINCOLN	109	493	535	574	1.9	91	185	205	223	2.4	2.61	149	165	2.4
68583	LINCOLN	109	112	133	150	4.1	98	40	48	55	4.4	2.75	22	26	4.0
68601	COLUMBUS	141	26339	26570	26784	0.2	65	10218	10443	10666	0.5	2.51	7046	7223	0.6
68620	ALBION	011	3527	3572	3655	0.3	68	1363	1396	1443	0.6	2.51	945	970	0.6
68621	AMES	053	252	265	275	1.2	87	102	109	114	1.6	2.43	79	86	2.0
68622	BARTLETT	183	227	225	225	-0.2	43	93	94	94	0.3	2.39	64	65	0.4
68623	BELGRADE	125	239	234	230	-0.5	22	104	104	104	0.0	2.25	76	76	0.0
68624	BELLWOOD	023	1160	1378	1536	4.1	98	437	527	597	4.5	2.61	322	389	4.6
68626	BRAINARD	023	672	663	679	-0.3	36	267	268	278	0.1	2.47	184	185	0.1
68627	CEDAR RAPIDS	011	691	700	716	0.3	68	286	294	306	0.7	2.38	195	202	0.8
68628	CLARKS	121	726	709	698	-0.6	17	312	309	307	-0.2	2.29	220	218	-0.2
68629	CLARKSON	037	1307	1287	1287	-0.4	33	502	491	486	-0.5	2.53	331	325	-0.4
68631	CRESTON	141	698	683	677	-0.5	21	249	248	249	-0.1	2.75	197	196	-0.1
68632	DAVID CITY	023	3850	3890	4008	0.2	66	1524	1554	1618	0.5	2.44	965	984	0.5
68633	DODGE	053	1851	1838	1841	-0.2	45	712	715	723	0.1	2.50	506	509	0.1
68635	DWIGHT	023	622	614	628	-0.3	37	249	250	259	0.1	2.46	173	173	0.0
68636	ELGIN	003	1303	1289	1272	-0.3	41	526	525	523	0.0	2.45	360	359	-0.1
68637	ERICSON	183	311	308	308	-0.2	42	135	137	137	0.4	2.25	94	95	0.3
68638	FULLERTON	125	2001	1980	1952	-0.3	41	779	781	780	0.1	2.44	548	552	0.2
68640	GENOA	125	1994	1953	1920	-0.5	23	763	759	756	-0.1	2.52	533	532	0.0
68641	HOWELLS	037	1026	1013	1012	-0.3	37	411	405	400	-0.4	2.50	296	292	-0.3
68642	HUMPHREY	141	1844	1821	1808	-0.3	38	640	643	648	0.1	2.83	482	485	0.2
68643	LEIGH	037	1003	1023	1036	0.5	74	387	396	398	0.5	2.58	282	289	0.6
68644	LINDSAY	141	1008	981	972	-0.6	13	342	338	340	-0.3	2.90	255	252	-0.3
68647	MONROE	141	954	1006	1035	1.3	88	364	394	413	1.9	2.55	265	288	2.0
68648	MORSE BLUFF	155	464	470	485	0.3	68	191	196	205	0.6	2.40	140	144	0.7
68649	NORTH BEND	053	1829	1781	1780	-0.6	14	708	697	705	-0.4	2.48	506	501	-0.2
68651	OSCEOLA	143	1393	1374	1348	-0.3	36	568	567	562	0.0	2.33	384	384	0.0
68652	PETERSBURG	011	678	687	702	0.3	69	274	281	291	0.6	2.44	193	199	0.7
68653	PLATTE CENTER	141	976	960	955	-0.4	30	358	360	364	0.1	2.66	280	282	0.2
68654	POLK	143	942	918	896	-0.6	14	387	382	377	-0.3	2.40	277	274	-0.3
68655	PRIMROSE	011	232	235	241	0.3	68	91	94	97	0.8	2.50	64	66	0.7
68658	RISING CITY	023	797	915	1008	3.3	95	307	358	400	3.7	2.56	228	265	3.6
68659	ROGERS	037	214	212	212	-0.2	42	78	77	76	-0.3	2.74	63	62	-0.4
68660	SAINT EDWARD	011	1058	1072	1096	0.3	69	415	424	439	0.5	2.42	283	290	0.6
68661	SCHUYLER	037	6819	7018	7154	0.7	80	2246	2269	2272	0.2	3.06	1590	1611	0.3
68662	SHELBY	143	1515	1495	1467	-0.3	36	601	601	597	0.0	2.49	432	433	0.1
68663	SILVER CREEK	121	626	609	598	-0.7	12	264	261	259	-0.3	2.33	177	175	-0.3
68665	SPALDING	077	962	939	918	-0.6	17	366	364	361	-0.1	2.52	249	248	-0.1
68666	STROMSBURG	143	1731	1692	1655	-0.5	20	672	662	653	-0.4	2.40	452	446	-0.3
68667	SURPRISE	023	191	185	189	-0.8	8	72	71	73	-0.3	2.61	55	54	-0.4
68669	ULYSSES	023	479	465	474	-0.7	10	178	175	181	-0.4	2.66	135	133	-0.4
68701	NORFOLK	119	30369	30992	31417	0.5	74	11682	12074	12345	0.8	2.48	7724	8015	0.9
68710	ALLEN	051	805	921	981	3.2	95	313	361	387	3.4	2.55	228	262	3.3
68711	AMELIA	089	204	205	206	0.1	60	77	79	81	0.6	2.59	60	62	0.8
68713	ATKINSON	089	2085	2082	2089	0.0	53	857	875	897	0.5	2.30	578	592	0.6
68714	BASSETT	149	1463	1438	1418	-0.4	29	644	650	657	0.2	2.17	412	417	0.3
68715	BATTLE CREEK	119	1508	1535	1548	0.4	73	557	572	581	0.6	2.68	422	436	0.8
68716	BEEMER	039	1165	1271	1336	2.1	92	445	492	523	2.4	2.53	318	352	2.4
68717	BELDEN	027	238	232	227	-0.6	15	92	91	91	-0.3	2.55	72	72	0.0
68718	BLOOMFIELD	107	2018	1970	1939	-0.6	17	848	838	832	-0.3	2.25	539	534	-0.2
68719	BRISTOW	015	288	285	281	-0.3	41	113	113	113	0.0	2.52	75	75	0.0
68720	BRUNSWICK	003	524	513	502	-0.5	22	176	175	174	-0.1	2.93	141	140	-0.2
68722	BUTTE	015	552	533	521	-0.8	5	215	210	207	-0.6	2.42	141	138	-0.5
68723	CARROLL	179	550	542	538	-0.3	34	220	220	219	-0.1	2.46	166	166	0.0
68724	CENTER	107	222	223	222	0.1	60	84	85	85	0.3	2.59	57	58	0.4
68725	CHAMBERS	089	804	801	803	-0.1	50	328	334	341	0.4	2.40	238	243	0.5
68726	CLEARWATER	003	840	822	807	-0.5	21	332	330	329	-0.1	2.49	234	233	-0.1
	NEBRASKA					0.8					1.0	2.47			1.1
	UNITED STATES					1.2					1.3	2.58			1.1

#	POST OFFICE NAME	White 2000	White 2004	Black 2000	Black 2004	Asian/Pacific 2000	Asian/Pacific 2004	% Hispanic Origin 2000	% Hispanic Origin 2004	0-4	5-9	10-14	15-19	20-24	25-44	45-64	65-84	85+	18+	MEDIAN AGE 2004	% 2004 Males	% 2004 Females
68450	TECUMSEH	90.3	90.4	0.1	0.1	3.8	3.7	4.6	4.6	5.9	6.0	6.2	6.1	5.7	22.6	25.2	17.9	4.5	77.9	43.4	47.4	52.6
68452	ONG	98.3	98.3	0.0	0.0	0.0	0.0	0.9	1.7	6.0	6.0	6.0	5.2	5.2	23.3	25.0	19.0	4.3	77.6	43.8	50.9	49.1
68453	TOBIAS	98.2	98.0	0.2	0.2	0.2	0.2	0.5	0.5	5.0	6.2	7.5	6.4	4.8	21.9	28.5	16.4	3.2	77.2	43.6	50.7	49.3
68454	UNADILLA	98.5	98.2	0.2	0.1	0.0	0.1	1.7	2.1	6.7	7.5	7.0	6.6	4.7	25.9	29.2	11.2	1.3	74.8	39.9	51.9	48.1
68455	UNION	97.3	96.8	0.0	0.0	0.6	0.9	2.2	2.6	6.3	6.8	8.0	7.3	4.9	26.1	28.9	10.8	0.9	74.4	39.8	50.5	49.5
68456	UTICA	99.2	98.9	0.1	0.1	0.2	0.3	0.3	0.4	5.6	6.3	8.3	7.3	5.4	23.4	26.5	14.5	2.9	74.8	41.4	51.3	48.7
68457	VERDON	98.0	97.6	0.0	0.0	0.0	0.0	1.0	1.3	4.2	6.5	8.1	8.6	5.5	24.4	28.3	12.8	1.6	75.1	41.2	51.1	49.0
68458	VIRGINIA	98.7	98.6	0.0	0.0	0.7	0.7	0.7	0.7	5.4	5.4	7.5	7.5	4.8	27.2	26.5	14.3	1.4	76.9	41.4	51.0	49.0
68460	WACO	98.0	97.6	0.6	0.7	0.0	0.0	0.8	1.0	6.1	6.6	8.4	7.4	5.5	24.1	26.6	13.5	1.9	74.1	40.6	49.6	50.4
68461	WALTON	97.9	97.5	0.0	0.0	0.8	1.0	1.0	1.1	5.1	6.4	7.8	6.5	5.3	21.4	34.0	12.3	1.3	76.4	43.5	51.0	49.0
68462	WAVERLY	98.1	97.8	0.1	0.1	0.2	0.4	0.9	1.1	8.0	7.9	8.3	7.2	6.4	27.6	24.3	8.8	1.5	70.8	34.8	48.5	51.5
68463	WEEPING WATER	99.1	99.0	0.1	0.1	0.2	0.3	0.6	0.8	7.2	7.4	7.6	7.1	6.1	25.3	25.9	11.5	2.1	73.5	38.4	48.3	51.7
68464	WESTERN	98.3	98.1	0.2	0.2	0.2	0.4	0.4	0.5	5.1	5.9	7.5	6.5	4.9	21.9	29.0	16.1	3.2	77.3	43.7	51.4	48.6
68465	WILBER	97.5	97.0	0.0	0.0	0.9	1.1	1.5	1.8	6.5	6.6	7.4	6.6	5.4	26.2	24.1	13.0	4.2	75.6	39.5	49.2	50.8
68466	WYMORE	96.9	96.6	0.1	0.1	0.3	0.4	1.3	1.6	6.4	6.2	6.6	6.6	5.8	22.6	24.9	17.5	3.4	76.1	42.0	49.0	51.0
68467	YORK	96.0	95.4	1.3	1.4	0.8	1.0	1.7	2.1	5.9	5.9	6.6	7.3	7.8	25.6	24.8	13.1	3.2	77.4	38.4	47.1	52.9
68502	LINCOLN	88.1	86.4	4.3	4.6	1.9	2.5	5.1	6.1	6.2	5.6	5.7	6.4	9.9	34.7	22.1	7.8	1.7	78.9	33.1	51.1	48.9
68503	LINCOLN	71.3	67.7	8.9	9.2	10.0	12.6	6.8	7.9	7.4	6.8	6.4	7.4	15.2	35.2	15.6	5.3	0.7	76.0	27.5	52.4	47.6
68504	LINCOLN	90.5	88.9	3.0	3.3	1.9	2.6	3.4	4.2	6.5	4.9	4.6	7.9	15.8	34.0	17.0	8.0	1.2	81.4	28.6	49.1	50.9
68505	LINCOLN	94.3	93.2	1.2	1.2	2.2	3.0	2.0	2.4	6.3	6.0	6.0	6.3	7.9	29.4	22.5	14.2	1.6	78.2	36.2	48.3	51.7
68506	LINCOLN	94.9	93.9	1.3	1.3	1.6	2.2	1.8	2.2	5.2	5.4	6.1	6.8	7.3	25.9	25.7	14.6	2.9	79.5	40.3	47.3	52.8
68507	LINCOLN	94.8	94.0	1.1	1.2	1.2	1.6	2.2	2.7	6.4	6.3	6.4	6.6	6.9	29.6	24.5	11.3	2.0	77.0	37.0	48.5	51.5
68508	LINCOLN	83.1	80.7	4.7	4.9	4.1	5.4	7.6	8.9	3.1	2.4	2.1	25.2	26.4	25.1	10.1	4.7	1.0	91.3	23.3	52.7	47.3
68510	LINCOLN	89.7	88.1	2.7	2.8	3.2	4.2	3.4	4.1	6.5	5.8	5.3	5.9	8.1	28.3	22.8	13.3	4.0	78.9	37.4	47.5	52.5
68512	LINCOLN	89.5	87.8	4.9	5.3	2.1	2.8	2.9	3.6	5.5	5.5	5.9	6.0	8.5	33.6	27.0	7.7	0.6	79.5	35.4	53.5	46.5
68514	LINCOLN	97.5	96.3	0.6	1.2	0.0	0.6	1.9	1.9	5.6	6.2	7.4	7.4	6.2	25.3	27.2	13.6	1.2	75.9	40.0	51.9	48.2
68516	LINCOLN	94.8	93.6	1.0	1.1	2.4	3.3	1.7	2.0	7.6	8.1	8.2	7.0	6.5	30.1	25.6	6.3	0.7	71.7	34.3	48.8	51.2
68517	LINCOLN	97.8	96.9	0.7	0.9	0.2	0.4	1.6	2.0	5.5	6.4	8.2	7.3	6.2	24.5	28.5	12.1	1.3	75.9	40.1	51.2	48.8
68520	LINCOLN	97.5	97.0	0.3	0.3	0.9	1.2	0.9	1.1	6.0	6.9	8.1	7.2	6.8	21.8	33.1	9.4	0.7	75.0	40.3	49.5	50.5
68521	LINCOLN	88.0	86.0	2.8	2.9	4.6	6.0	3.7	4.2	9.1	7.9	6.8	6.3	9.2	35.5	18.1	6.3	0.9	72.6	29.4	50.0	50.0
68522	LINCOLN	87.8	85.6	3.5	3.6	4.0	5.4	3.4	4.1	7.8	6.9	6.6	6.2	8.9	40.0	18.6	4.8	0.3	75.3	30.3	54.0	46.0
68523	LINCOLN	97.0	96.3	0.5	0.5	0.6	0.8	1.8	2.0	5.0	5.9	7.4	6.3	6.4	25.3	33.5	9.4	0.9	77.6	41.6	48.7	51.3
68524	LINCOLN	82.8	81.2	7.0	7.3	1.7	2.4	5.2	6.1	10.1	10.4	8.9	6.3	6.6	36.1	17.0	4.4	0.2	66.5	28.6	52.2	47.8
68526	LINCOLN	97.4	96.8	0.5	0.5	0.8	1.1	0.8	1.2	5.8	7.0	8.8	7.4	6.0	21.9	33.5	8.9	0.7	73.9	40.4	50.1	49.9
68527	LINCOLN	97.7	97.3	0.1	0.1	0.9	1.0	1.1	1.2	5.6	6.4	7.9	7.1	6.1	22.3	33.4	10.3	0.9	76.0	41.8	50.0	50.0
68528	LINCOLN	87.2	85.0	2.7	2.8	5.0	6.5	5.3	6.2	8.2	7.2	6.1	5.0	6.9	38.5	21.6	6.2	0.5	75.7	31.5	51.8	48.3
68531	LINCOLN	97.4	96.8	0.0	0.0	0.0	0.0	2.0	2.6	5.8	7.7	9.7	7.1	3.2	29.0	29.0	8.4	0.0	72.3	39.5	52.3	47.7
68532	LINCOLN	98.6	98.3	0.0	0.0	0.0	0.2	0.6	0.9	5.6	6.9	7.5	6.0	4.9	23.6	34.2	10.5	0.9	76.3	42.5	52.5	47.5
68583	LINCOLN	67.9	63.9	5.4	6.0	11.6	15.0	11.6	12.0	9.0	7.5	7.5	6.8	15.0	42.1	10.5	1.5	0.0	72.9	26.3	53.4	46.6
68601	COLUMBUS	93.2	92.1	0.4	0.4	0.5	0.6	7.8	9.2	7.5	7.2	7.5	7.4	7.1	26.4	23.7	11.2	2.0	73.4	36.0	49.5	50.5
68620	ALBION	99.2	99.2	0.0	0.0	0.1	0.1	0.9	1.0	6.6	6.9	8.0	7.6	5.3	22.4	24.5	15.5	3.3	73.0	40.6	49.2	50.8
68621	AMES	96.0	95.5	0.0	0.0	0.8	1.1	5.2	6.4	6.0	6.8	7.9	6.0	5.3	25.7	29.1	12.5	0.8	74.7	40.1	52.5	47.6
68622	BARTLETT	99.1	99.1	0.0	0.0	0.0	0.0	0.9	0.4	8.0	8.0	7.1	5.8	5.8	20.0	28.0	15.6	1.8	72.9	41.5	49.8	50.2
68623	BELGRADE	99.6	99.6	0.0	0.0	0.0	0.0	0.0	0.0	7.7	7.3	6.4	7.3	6.4	23.9	26.9	12.4	1.7	74.8	40.4	51.3	48.7
68624	BELLWOOD	98.5	98.3	0.1	0.1	0.2	0.2	2.0	2.4	7.6	7.5	7.0	6.5	6.1	25.0	26.9	12.1	1.5	74.1	39.1	51.8	48.2
68626	BRAINARD	98.5	98.5	0.2	0.2	0.0	0.0	1.3	1.7	7.4	7.5	7.1	6.3	5.4	23.8	25.0	15.5	1.8	74.1	40.7	52.5	47.5
68627	CEDAR RAPIDS	99.4	99.4	0.0	0.0	0.1	0.1	0.7	0.7	5.0	6.0	7.7	6.7	5.9	21.9	27.0	16.7	3.1	77.0	42.9	53.1	46.9
68628	CLARKS	98.8	98.9	0.1	0.1	0.0	0.0	0.8	0.9	6.5	7.1	7.3	5.8	4.9	23.7	25.5	16.5	2.7	75.7	41.9	49.4	50.6
68629	CLARKSON	98.6	98.4	0.0	0.0	0.1	0.1	1.9	2.3	6.1	6.5	7.2	7.2	5.6	23.5	21.8	18.0	4.1	75.0	41.5	48.5	51.5
68631	CRESTON	99.3	99.1	0.1	0.3	0.1	0.3	1.0	1.2	6.3	6.9	9.2	8.8	6.6	23.4	27.2	10.4	1.2	72.2	38.0	52.4	47.6
68632	DAVID CITY	98.5	98.2	0.1	0.2	0.3	0.3	1.3	1.5	6.6	6.7	7.4	7.0	6.0	22.8	23.9	15.8	3.9	74.5	40.4	50.0	50.1
68633	DODGE	98.2	97.8	0.0	0.0	0.2	0.2	1.4	1.7	6.5	7.1	8.2	6.5	4.7	24.1	24.7	14.8	3.5	73.8	40.4	49.7	50.3
68635	DWIGHT	98.7	98.5	0.2	0.2	0.0	0.0	1.3	1.5	7.5	7.7	7.0	6.5	5.4	23.6	25.1	15.3	2.0	74.1	40.4	52.1	47.9
68636	ELGIN	99.5	99.3	0.0	0.0	0.0	0.0	0.2	0.3	6.0	6.4	7.8	7.5	5.2	21.3	23.8	19.3	2.7	74.3	42.5	49.7	50.4
68637	ERICSON	99.0	99.0	0.0	0.0	0.0	0.0	0.6	0.7	7.1	8.1	7.8	6.2	5.8	20.1	27.0	15.9	2.0	73.1	41.2	49.7	50.3
68638	FULLERTON	97.8	97.8	0.0	0.0	0.1	0.1	1.7	1.8	5.9	6.0	7.5	6.6	6.2	20.6	25.7	18.3	3.3	76.3	43.0	50.0	50.0
68640	GENOA	98.9	98.8	0.0	0.0	0.1	0.1	0.8	0.8	6.7	6.8	7.9	7.1	6.9	21.9	24.8	15.5	2.5	73.8	40.2	52.0	48.0
68641	HOWELLS	98.0	97.6	0.0	0.0	0.4	0.5	1.5	1.8	5.7	6.3	8.4	7.9	4.8	23.4	23.7	16.3	3.5	74.6	41.2	50.2	49.9
68642	HUMPHREY	99.3	99.2	0.2	0.3	0.2	0.3	0.7	0.9	8.6	8.7	9.7	8.1	5.9	22.5	22.0	12.9	1.6	67.5	35.5	52.6	47.4
68643	LEIGH	98.0	97.6	0.1	0.1	0.1	0.1	2.7	3.3	5.9	6.5	8.5	8.5	5.5	22.5	24.5	15.8	2.4	73.2	40.6	50.7	49.3
68644	LINDSAY	98.5	98.2	0.0	0.0	0.1	0.1	1.9	2.3	6.0	6.9	9.1	8.5	6.6	21.0	27.3	13.0	1.6	72.7	39.1	53.3	46.7
68647	MONROE	98.6	98.5	0.1	0.1	0.4	0.5	0.7	0.8	6.6	6.6	6.2	6.4	6.2	25.8	26.3	14.2	1.8	76.9	40.1	50.5	49.5
68648	MORSE BLUFF	98.7	98.7	0.0	0.0	0.0	0.0	1.1	1.3	6.4	7.0	7.7	6.4	4.5	23.8	25.5	16.4	2.3	75.1	41.9	51.7	48.3
68649	NORTH BEND	99.1	99.1	0.1	0.1	0.1	0.1	1.0	1.2	4.9	5.8	8.7	8.3	4.9	22.5	26.2	15.0	3.7	74.6	41.7	48.5	51.5
68651	OSCEOLA	99.2	99.2	0.0	0.0	0.0	0.0	0.8	1.0	5.5	6.0	7.4	5.6	5.3	22.8	26.2	16.8	4.4	77.5	43.3	47.7	52.3
68652	PETERSBURG	99.0	99.0	0.0	0.0	0.0	0.0	1.0	1.0	6.0	6.4	8.6	8.6	5.2	22.4	24.3	15.7	2.8	71.6	40.7	51.7	48.3
68653	PLATTE CENTER	98.2	97.9	0.1	0.2	0.5	0.7	0.9	1.0	7.5	7.8	8.3	7.3	5.2	25.2	26.6	10.8	1.3	72.0	37.3	52.5	47.5
68654	POLK	99.0	99.0	0.0	0.0	0.0	0.0	1.2	1.3	4.7	5.6	6.9	6.3	5.9	22.3	29.2	17.0	2.2	79.0	43.9	52.8	47.2
68655	PRIMROSE	99.1	99.2	0.0	0.0	0.0	0.0	0.9	0.9	6.0	6.8	8.1	6.8	5.1	23.8	26.0	15.3	2.1	74.5	40.9	52.8	47.2
68658	RISING CITY	98.5	98.4	0.0	0.0	0.1	0.2	1.8	2.1	7.4	7.3	6.9	6.7	6.0	25.1	27.0	12.0	1.5	74.2	39.1	51.9	48.1
68659	ROGERS	96.3	95.3	0.0	0.0	0.5	0.5	5.6	6.6	5.7	8.0	9.4	9.0	3.3	28.8	25.5	9.4	0.9	71.2	39.1	54.3	45.8
68660	SAINT EDWARD	99.3	99.4	0.3	0.3	0.0	0.0	0.9	0.8	5.8	6.0	7.6	7.7	5.9	19.5	24.4	18.4	4.9	75.8	43.4	49.8	50.2
68661	SCHUYLER	73.6	70.2	0.1	0.1	0.4	0.5	38.3	43.0	8.4	8.4	7.9	6.5	7.4	29.2	20.0	10.2	2.1	71.2	32.8	52.7	47.3
68662	SHELBY	98.4	98.1	0.1	0.1	0.2	0.3	1.7	1.9	6.8	7.1	7.2	5.5	5.8	25.4	27.2	13.3	1.8	75.5	40.0	51.4	48.6
68663	SILVER CREEK	99.0	98.9	0.2	0.2	0.0	0.0	0.8	1.0	6.6	7.1	6.7	5.3	4.6	24.0	25.1	17.7	3.0	76.4	42.7	48.4	51.6
68665	SPALDING	98.7	98.5	0.1	0.1	0.0	0.0	0.8	1.0	6.3	6.6	7.9	6.5	5.4	21.3	23.6	18.7	3.6	74.9	42.1	48.6	51.4
68666	STROMSBURG	99.2	99.2	0.0	0.0	0.1	0.1	0.7	0.8	6.2	6.4	7.0	5.9	5.4	20.1	23.2	19.0	6.8	76.8	44.1	49.2	50.8
68667	SURPRISE	98.4	98.4	0.0	0.0	0.0	0.0	1.6	1.6	7.0	7.0	7.0	7.0	5.4	26.5	26.5	11.9	1.6	74.1	38.3	51.4	48.7
68669	ULYSSES	98.1	98.1	0.0	0.0	0.0	0.0	1.5	1.5	7.1	6.9	6.7	8.0	5.6	26.0	26.0	12.5	1.3	74.0	38.0	51.8	48.2
68701	NORFOLK	92.2	91.1	1.1	1.2	0.5	0.6	6.8	8.1	7.3	6.7	7.0	7.8	9.1	26.7	22.6	10.6	2.2	74.9	34.2	49.5	50.5
68710	ALLEN	97.8	97.6	0.1	0.1	0.1	0.1	1.9	2.1	7.4	7.5	7.3	6.5	4.7	24.7	26.0	13.9	2.2	73.7	39.4	50.5	49.5
68711	AMELIA	99.0	99.0	0.0	0.0	0.5	0.5	0.5	0.5	4.9	5.9	7.8	6.8	5.4	23.4	26.3	18.5	1.0	76.6	42.9	51.7	48.3
68713	ATKINSON	99.0	99.0	0.1	0.1	0.3	0.3	0.6	0.5	5.1	5.8	7.5	6.9	5.1	22.4	27.8	14.8	4.5	77.0	43.1	49.5	50.5
68714	BASSETT	98.9	98.9	0.0	0.0	0.2	0.2	0.6	0.6	5.5	5.6	5.2	6.1	5.9	20.9	27.9	18.0	4.9	79.6	45.5	47.5	52.5
68715	BATTLE CREEK	97.6	97.4	0.1	0.1	0.0	0.0	1.0	1.2	7.0	8.0	9.3	7.6	5.5	26.1	23.7	11.3	1.4	70.9	36.8	50.5	49.5
68716	BEEMER	97.5	97.1	0.0	0.0	0.3	0.3	1.6	2.1	6.9	7.0	7.2	6.3	5.2	23.2	23.6	17.2	3.5	74.7	41.2	50.9	49.1
68717	BELDEN	99.2	99.1	0.0	0.0	0.0	0.0	0.4	0.4	6.5	8.2	9.9	8.6	7.3	24.1	24.1	10.3	0.9	69.4	34.2	53.5	46.6
68718	BLOOMFIELD	94.9	94.3	0.0	0.1	0.3	0.4	0.8	1.0	4.7	5.1	6.0	5.9	5.5	19.1	26.3	22.1	5.3	80.4	47.5	47.6	52.4
68719	BRISTOW	98.6	98.6	0.0	0.0	0.4	0.4	0.0	0.0	5.3	6.0	7.4	6.7	6.0	19.3	28.1	17.9	3.5	77.2	44.6	48.8	51.2
68720	BRUNSWICK	98.9	98.8	0.0	0.0	0.2	0.2	0.0	0.0	7.2	7.2	8.6	7.4	6.0	24.2	25.0	13.3	1.2	71.9	38.8	50.3	49.7
68722	BUTTE	99.1	99.3	0.0	0.0	0.0	0.0	0.2	0.2	5.4	5.6	5.4	6.4	5.4	19.0	26.8	19.9	6.0	79.2	46.7	49.0	51.0
68723	CARROLL	97.8	97.8	0.2	0.2	0.6	0.6	0.0	0.0	6.8	7.2	8.5	7.0	5.2	23.1	26.8	13.8	1.7	73.1	40.3	52.2	47.8
68724	CENTER	79.3	78.5	0.0	0.0	0.0	0.0	0.9	0.9	6.7	7.2	7.2	7.6	5.4	21.1	24.2	17.5	3.1	73.5	41.4	50.2	49.8
68725	CHAMBERS	99.1	99.3	0.0	0.0	0.0	0.0	0.9	1.0	7.1	7.2	7.0	6.2	5.5	20.6	27.1	16.5	2.8	74.9	42.5	50.4	49.6
68726	CLEARWATER	99.3	99.2	0.1	0.1	0.1	0.2	0.1	0.1	7.4	7.5	8.4	7.8	6.2	22.6	23.5	13.5	3.0	71.8	38.4	51.5	48.5
	NEBRASKA	89.6	88.4	4.0	4.2	1.3	1.8	5.5	6.4	7.0	6.9	7.2	7.3	7.6	27.5	23.5	11.2	2.1	74.8	35.7	49.4	50.6
	UNITED STATES	75.1	73.6	12.3	12.5	3.8	4.2	12.5	14.1	6.9	6.7	7.2	7.0	7.3	28.6	23.8	10.8	1.7	75.1	36.0	49.1	50.9

#	POST OFFICE NAME	2004 Per Capita Income	2004 HH Income Base	2004 Household Income Distribution (%): Less than $25,000	$25,000 to $49,999	$50,000 to $99,999	$100,000 to $149,999	$150,000 or More	Median Household Income: 2004	2009	2004 National Centile	2004 State Centile	2004 Home Value Base	2004 Home Value Distribution (%): Less than $50,000	$50,000 to $89,999	$90,000 to $174,999	$175,000 to $399,999	$400,000 or More	2004 Median Home Value
68450	TECUMSEH	19148	1034	34.8	32.1	25.5	5.6	1.9	36854	43729	35	42	765	34.5	33.2	27.2	4.7	0.4	64408
68452	ONG	22734	54	31.5	37.0	24.1	5.6	1.9	38616	44086	41	53	42	50.0	26.2	16.7	7.1	0.0	50000
68453	TOBIAS	20416	178	28.1	39.3	27.0	2.8	2.8	37518	43855	38	46	143	46.2	24.5	16.8	9.8	2.8	54583
68454	UNADILLA	26636	321	18.4	31.8	36.1	7.8	5.9	49854	58990	72	86	274	12.8	21.9	34.3	23.0	8.0	112500
68455	UNION	21438	294	16.0	35.4	39.5	6.8	2.4	49035	55337	70	84	237	13.1	24.5	36.3	21.9	4.2	105682
68456	UTICA	19694	420	24.5	29.3	38.8	6.2	1.2	47339	53623	67	82	326	13.8	32.2	44.2	9.8	0.0	93333
68457	VERDON	17459	157	35.7	33.1	25.5	5.7	0.0	33381	39487	22	20	128	59.4	22.7	12.5	5.5	0.0	38125
68458	VIRGINIA	18648	63	27.0	38.1	31.8	3.2	0.0	37719	42330	38	47	50	22.0	26.0	30.0	20.0	2.0	92500
68460	WACO	20154	306	23.5	35.6	32.0	5.6	3.3	41635	45806	52	67	239	30.5	26.8	31.4	8.8	2.5	72273
68461	WALTON	31881	229	9.6	20.1	44.5	16.2	9.6	67459	81793	90	97	203	3.0	3.0	36.5	49.3	8.4	187917
68462	WAVERLY	24355	1134	13.8	25.4	43.3	14.2	3.3	59092	70571	84	93	910	2.1	14.2	66.8	15.5	1.4	117712
68463	WEEPING WATER	22372	758	20.5	28.9	38.5	10.0	2.1	50545	58552	73	87	592	15.5	26.4	38.9	16.7	2.5	99412
68464	WESTERN	21165	242	28.1	38.4	26.9	3.3	3.3	38077	43468	40	50	195	46.2	26.2	16.4	9.2	2.1	54688
68465	WILBER	22487	992	26.0	32.0	35.6	4.2	2.2	45054	51523	61	78	804	20.9	40.8	27.7	8.7	1.9	78723
68466	WYMORE	18300	985	34.1	37.0	22.5	5.0	1.4	35325	40835	29	31	728	47.5	26.0	19.1	6.3	1.1	53600
68467	YORK	21598	3926	25.5	35.8	30.4	5.6	2.7	41355	48149	51	66	2639	14.9	35.2	39.0	10.0	0.9	89659
68502	LINCOLN	25111	11305	27.3	32.2	28.8	7.7	4.0	41687	50982	52	68	5557	3.1	23.9	54.5	16.7	1.8	113789
68503	LINCOLN	16696	6455	39.5	34.3	21.7	3.3	1.1	31211	38481	16	11	2119	7.9	49.6	39.4	2.5	0.6	85253
68504	LINCOLN	19976	6988	31.5	38.4	25.4	3.5	1.1	35499	43384	29	32	2656	15.3	31.2	51.4	1.7	0.4	92109
68505	LINCOLN	26108	6231	20.1	30.7	36.7	9.6	3.0	49242	60023	71	85	4036	1.4	18.4	70.1	8.5	1.6	112051
68506	LINCOLN	32020	12056	14.8	29.4	35.8	12.9	7.1	54816	65890	79	91	8359	0.6	11.1	63.8	23.3	1.2	130459
68507	LINCOLN	25871	5551	19.0	29.2	38.1	10.7	2.9	51229	62937	74	88	3914	3.6	25.6	61.7	8.8	0.3	106777
68508	LINCOLN	15999	5039	55.2	28.2	13.3	2.3	1.0	21977	27248	3	1	740	23.5	45.0	28.1	2.7	0.7	73942
68510	LINCOLN	27542	9514	25.3	29.6	31.9	9.1	4.1	45307	54883	62	78	5223	0.8	16.9	68.0	13.0	1.4	116506
68512	LINCOLN	34190	3096	13.6	28.8	34.8	15.0	7.7	56218	67723	81	92	2199	1.1	9.4	63.0	22.0	4.5	129888
68514	LINCOLN	24822	60	11.7	33.3	36.7	13.3	5.0	54523	66679	79	91	47	4.3	12.8	29.8	48.9	4.3	184375
68516	LINCOLN	33466	13866	8.4	20.6	39.7	21.2	10.2	75126	89194	93	98	10588	1.1	1.9	51.2	41.2	4.5	168659
68517	LINCOLN	25278	161	11.8	30.4	38.5	13.7	5.6	58070	69534	83	92	128	5.5	11.7	29.7	46.1	7.0	185000
68520	LINCOLN	41872	554	12.1	15.0	32.9	19.7	20.4	83631	102536	96	99	484	1.2	3.3	28.5	51.9	15.1	237313
68521	LINCOLN	22864	11015	21.3	29.2	38.0	9.5	2.0	49503	60231	71	85	6883	16.6	10.6	60.5	11.9	0.4	114557
68522	LINCOLN	20954	3142	17.7	30.0	41.1	9.1	2.2	51575	61463	75	88	2230	11.0	13.4	62.7	11.3	1.5	110604
68523	LINCOLN	28419	449	12.3	17.8	40.5	19.6	9.8	71681	85238	92	98	405	5.4	6.7	17.8	59.0	11.1	224185
68524	LINCOLN	17581	1583	19.4	34.7	36.6	6.5	2.8	47606	56049	67	82	727	4.5	27.8	46.6	19.0	2.1	108810
68526	LINCOLN	37370	409	9.8	14.9	35.2	20.8	19.3	84943	103906	96	99	363	1.1	4.7	24.8	54.0	15.4	242500
68527	LINCOLN	31971	283	12.7	23.0	36.4	16.6	11.3	62714	77609	87	95	246	3.7	6.5	33.3	48.8	7.7	191000
68528	LINCOLN	29335	1817	19.9	27.7	37.2	10.1	5.2	52230	63573	76	89	1310	5.3	10.9	62.4	18.7	2.7	116706
68531	LINCOLN	27874	57	8.8	19.3	49.1	17.5	5.3	70005	83380	91	98	50	2.0	6.0	40.0	50.0	2.0	179167
68532	LINCOLN	27214	205	13.2	22.0	43.4	18.1	3.4	63628	77373	88	95	176	2.3	3.4	37.5	52.8	4.0	185000
68583	LINCOLN	12770	48	47.9	29.2	16.7	6.3	0.0	25687	31326	5	1	10	10.0	10.0	70.0	10.0	0.0	112500
68601	COLUMBUS	22248	10443	23.4	31.4	34.8	7.6	2.9	45914	53304	64	80	7667	11.4	32.6	44.5	10.6	0.9	94904
68620	ALBION	20019	1396	30.3	36.0	25.9	5.2	2.7	36923	42647	35	42	1038	23.6	32.5	30.4	11.2	2.3	81923
68621	AMES	20842	109	22.0	33.0	38.5	5.5	0.9	45376	50760	62	79	91	24.2	19.8	41.8	13.2	1.1	97857
68622	BARTLETT	17858	94	39.4	36.2	16.0	5.3	3.2	31687	36287	17	14	70	50.0	21.4	17.1	4.3	7.1	50000
68623	BELGRADE	21049	104	38.5	37.5	18.3	1.9	3.9	35482	40485	29	32	70	57.1	24.3	11.4	5.7	1.4	43750
68624	BELLWOOD	18697	527	22.2	41.2	29.0	5.9	1.7	40307	46113	47	61	425	25.2	32.2	31.8	9.2	1.7	81923
68626	BRAINARD	21073	268	23.5	38.8	28.7	7.1	1.9	41785	48016	52	68	209	31.1	28.2	29.2	9.1	2.4	80250
68627	CEDAR RAPIDS	18692	294	34.7	38.1	21.1	3.1	3.1	33944	38662	24	24	238	51.7	21.4	15.6	9.7	1.7	48750
68628	CLARKS	19266	309	30.7	38.5	26.5	2.9	1.3	37038	40567	36	43	244	42.2	26.6	20.5	7.4	3.3	60500
68629	CLARKSON	16104	491	34.8	35.0	26.9	2.4	0.8	35465	41097	29	32	377	44.0	28.9	21.2	5.3	0.5	57031
68631	CRESTON	16980	248	28.2	30.7	36.3	3.6	1.2	40413	47167	48	62	192	18.8	38.0	29.2	11.5	2.6	83158
68632	DAVID CITY	19390	1554	29.5	31.3	32.7	4.4	2.1	40051	47605	46	61	1119	27.7	35.5	29.9	6.3	0.6	77079
68633	DODGE	20537	715	28.0	39.2	25.9	3.9	3.1	38170	43860	40	51	576	27.8	32.3	27.3	9.6	3.1	70606
68635	DWIGHT	21183	250	23.2	38.4	29.6	7.2	1.6	42203	47768	54	70	195	30.8	28.2	29.2	9.2	2.6	80789
68636	ELGIN	15940	525	36.0	37.1	23.1	3.2	0.6	33537	37314	23	22	420	41.2	31.4	19.5	5.0	2.9	59487
68637	ERICSON	18937	137	38.7	38.0	15.3	5.8	2.2	31684	36010	17	14	102	52.0	20.6	17.7	2.9	6.9	48182
68638	FULLERTON	20523	781	34.8	36.1	22.2	4.4	2.6	35612	40524	30	33	590	47.0	33.4	16.8	2.2	0.7	53000
68640	GENOA	20976	759	32.7	35.1	25.6	4.4	2.4	36279	41500	33	38	576	31.1	32.1	25.9	7.5	3.5	73571
68641	HOWELLS	18700	405	27.9	40.7	24.4	4.0	3.0	38277	43675	40	51	329	35.9	27.4	26.8	8.5	1.5	67222
68642	HUMPHREY	18203	643	26.9	34.2	31.4	5.9	1.6	42118	48197	53	69	518	12.0	29.7	43.6	12.6	2.1	98431
68643	LEIGH	17627	396	31.3	33.8	31.1	2.5	1.3	38704	43530	42	54	321	35.5	34.9	19.9	8.4	1.3	65179
68644	LINDSAY	17617	338	28.4	37.0	26.9	4.4	3.3	37906	44210	39	48	267	18.0	25.5	36.3	15.0	5.2	97955
68647	MONROE	19939	394	25.4	34.5	31.7	6.9	1.5	42903	50822	56	72	329	21.9	36.8	30.4	8.8	2.1	80172
68648	MORSE BLUFF	17768	196	31.6	38.3	27.6	2.6	0.0	35405	41151	29	32	159	23.3	25.8	28.9	18.9	3.1	91250
68649	NORTH BEND	18808	697	22.8	38.5	34.3	3.3	1.2	43176	50184	56	73	531	19.2	39.7	31.8	8.5	0.8	79597
68651	OSCEOLA	22144	567	28.6	30.9	34.0	4.2	2.3	41189	47003	50	66	449	29.8	33.6	29.6	5.4	1.6	74457
68652	PETERSBURG	17252	281	33.1	37.7	23.5	3.2	2.5	34059	38225	24	25	224	49.6	26.3	11.2	8.5	4.5	50435
68653	PLATTE CENTER	20540	360	22.5	38.1	30.0	6.4	3.1	43377	50301	57	74	295	18.3	30.5	38.3	10.5	2.4	91061
68654	POLK	19977	382	23.6	40.1	31.4	3.1	1.8	40440	45367	48	62	302	43.7	19.5	25.5	8.6	2.7	62500
68655	PRIMROSE	17883	94	35.1	38.3	21.3	3.2	2.1	33139	38947	21	19	74	48.7	23.0	17.6	10.8	0.0	51429
68658	RISING CITY	18981	358	22.4	40.2	30.5	5.6	1.4	41084	47568	50	65	287	26.1	31.7	31.0	9.4	1.7	81346
68659	ROGERS	19312	77	22.1	36.4	33.8	3.9	3.9	45310	51652	62	78	61	18.0	24.6	34.4	19.7	3.3	101389
68660	SAINT EDWARD	16804	424	37.0	37.0	20.1	4.3	1.7	34071	40082	24	25	321	54.2	24.3	15.0	4.7	1.9	46932
68661	SCHUYLER	16843	2269	24.1	36.1	30.0	7.8	2.0	42390	49144	54	71	1684	27.6	36.6	30.3	5.2	0.3	75369
68662	SHELBY	21860	601	22.5	35.8	35.1	4.5	2.2	44665	50819	60	77	473	26.4	28.1	34.0	7.2	4.2	85114
68663	SILVER CREEK	18129	261	33.7	36.8	25.7	1.9	1.9	36008	39504	32	37	208	46.6	29.3	17.3	4.3	2.4	53684
68665	SPALDING	15729	364	38.5	37.4	17.9	5.0	1.4	31745	36367	17	14	290	51.0	26.6	16.6	3.1	2.8	48889
68666	STROMSBURG	20499	662	25.4	35.1	31.1	6.2	2.3	41728	49905	52	68	488	33.0	35.9	27.9	2.5	0.8	68704
68667	SURPRISE	18217	71	23.9	35.2	35.2	4.2	1.4	44527	50977	60	77	55	29.1	29.1	25.5	12.7	3.6	78333
68669	ULYSSES	17918	175	22.9	36.0	35.4	5.1	0.6	44797	50908	61	77	136	30.2	27.2	27.9	10.3	4.4	80000
68701	NORFOLK	20316	12074	27.4	31.6	31.9	7.0	2.1	41669	49575	52	68	8022	12.2	31.7	43.4	12.1	0.7	95743
68710	ALLEN	18387	361	25.5	39.3	29.9	3.6	1.7	40844	46093	49	65	288	31.9	35.8	25.7	6.6	0.0	72813
68711	AMELIA	17219	79	31.7	38.0	24.1	3.8	2.5	35364	40447	29	31	60	33.3	20.0	30.0	6.7	10.0	86667
68713	ATKINSON	18813	875	36.1	37.0	21.7	3.3	1.8	34002	38999	24	24	669	38.6	25.6	29.0	4.9	1.9	68452
68714	BASSETT	17414	650	42.5	34.5	17.9	3.5	1.7	28344	32700	9	5	483	52.2	27.5	15.3	3.7	1.2	48433
68715	BATTLE CREEK	20178	572	22.4	29.7	38.3	8.4	1.2	48370	56165	69	83	481	15.0	32.2	46.4	6.0	0.4	92288
68716	BEEMER	18094	492	32.3	37.6	26.6	1.4	2.0	36056	39786	32	37	384	31.5	27.9	28.7	8.9	3.1	70000
68717	BELDEN	17605	91	24.2	45.1	26.4	4.4	0.0	40171	45172	47	61	70	24.3	30.0	31.4	12.9	1.4	85000
68718	BLOOMFIELD	17513	838	40.7	32.8	22.3	3.0	1.2	31035	36548	15	10	628	53.7	27.9	14.7	3.5	0.3	47326
68719	BRISTOW	16124	113	39.8	32.7	21.2	3.5	2.7	31234	35734	16	11	91	61.5	23.1	13.2	2.2	0.0	35625
68720	BRUNSWICK	14272	175	36.0	37.7	21.7	2.3	2.3	32847	37741	20	18	134	27.6	23.9	25.4	22.4	0.8	87778
68722	BUTTE	13551	210	48.6	34.3	13.3	3.8	0.0	25672	30405	5	1	167	70.1	15.0	9.6	2.4	3.0	28971
68723	CARROLL	17618	220	24.6	44.1	28.2	3.2	0.0	38470	45481	41	52	174	27.6	31.6	29.9	10.9	0.0	78571
68724	CENTER	14217	85	42.4	34.1	18.8	3.5	1.2	30362	34437	13	7	62	46.8	32.3	17.7	3.2	0.0	52500
68725	CHAMBERS	16447	334	40.7	37.7	16.8	2.4	2.4	29814	35199	12	7	259	39.8	26.6	22.4	6.2	5.0	63095
68726	CLEARWATER	15892	330	38.2	34.6	21.5	5.2	0.6	34343	37974	25	25	262	53.8	21.8	16.0	7.6	0.8	46429
	NEBRASKA	23743		24.5	30.5	31.8	9.2	4.0	45453	54516				17.2	23.9	42.4	14.4	2.2	101398
	UNITED STATES	25866		24.7	27.1	30.8	10.9	6.5	48124	56710				10.9	15.0	33.7	30.1	10.4	145905

ZIP CODE #	POST OFFICE NAME	FINANCIAL SERVICES: Auto Loan	Home Loan	Invest-ments	Retire-ment Plans	THE HOME: Home Improvements: Home Repair	Lawn & Garden	Furnishings: Comput-ers & Hard-ware	Major Appli-ances	TV, Radio, Sound Equip-ment	Furni-ture	ENTERTAINMENT: Dine out/ Carry out	Sports Equip-ment	Fees & Tickets	Toys & Games	Travel	Cable TV	PERSONAL: Apparel & Services	Auto Repairs	Health Insur-ance	Pets & Supplies
68450	TECUMSEH	78	56	33	53	63	73	59	68	66	57	78	80	51	75	59	70	71	68	82	89
68452	ONG	87	61	32	57	71	79	60	74	69	59	81	89	51	79	62	72	74	73	88	103
68453	TOBIAS	91	63	33	60	74	83	63	78	72	62	85	93	54	83	65	76	77	76	92	108
68454	UNADILLA	105	90	66	86	97	104	84	95	90	84	109	113	81	111	87	93	103	92	104	123
68455	UNION	102	72	39	68	84	93	71	87	81	70	96	105	61	94	74	85	87	86	103	121
68456	UTICA	93	65	34	61	75	84	64	79	73	63	86	95	54	84	66	77	79	78	94	110
68457	VERDON	77	54	28	51	63	70	53	66	61	52	72	79	45	70	55	64	65	65	78	91
68458	VIRGINIA	78	55	30	52	63	71	55	67	63	54	74	80	47	72	56	66	67	66	80	91
68460	WACO	96	67	35	63	78	87	66	82	76	65	90	99	57	88	69	80	82	81	98	114
68461	WALTON	122	136	132	134	136	138	122	126	118	122	147	148	127	155	125	117	145	122	120	147
68462	WAVERLY	99	103	98	104	102	103	98	99	94	98	118	118	98	119	97	91	115	98	92	114
68463	WEEPING WATER	98	78	52	75	87	95	75	88	82	74	98	105	68	98	77	85	91	86	99	117
68464	WESTERN	90	63	34	60	74	82	63	77	72	62	84	93	54	83	65	75	77	76	92	107
68465	WILBER	86	72	55	71	76	86	74	80	79	72	95	91	70	94	73	80	89	78	87	96
68466	WYMORE	69	52	34	50	57	68	57	63	64	54	75	71	51	71	56	68	69	63	75	76
68467	YORK	83	66	51	64	72	81	69	76	75	67	90	89	63	88	70	78	84	76	86	95
68502	LINCOLN	78	76	91	80	75	80	86	80	84	83	105	98	84	104	83	80	103	85	75	88
68503	LINCOLN	54	49	59	52	48	53	60	55	59	57	74	67	57	72	56	56	72	59	52	60
68504	LINCOLN	58	51	61	54	51	55	63	57	62	59	78	71	59	75	59	58	75	62	54	64
68505	LINCOLN	79	85	94	85	84	88	86	83	83	84	104	98	87	107	85	81	103	84	79	92
68506	LINCOLN	97	106	121	108	105	110	106	104	102	105	128	122	109	129	106	99	126	105	97	113
68507	LINCOLN	83	90	98	92	90	92	90	88	86	88	108	104	91	111	89	83	106	88	82	97
68508	LINCOLN	44	35	47	39	35	39	49	42	49	45	61	54	45	58	44	45	59	48	40	47
68510	LINCOLN	78	81	97	83	80	85	87	83	85	85	106	99	87	107	85	82	104	86	79	91
68512	LINCOLN	104	117	125	119	114	115	112	110	106	112	134	130	115	137	111	102	132	110	99	121
68514	LINCOLN	105	93	76	90	97	105	90	97	95	89	116	116	87	117	91	96	110	96	103	123
68516	LINCOLN	125	139	147	144	135	135	132	129	124	134	156	152	136	158	130	117	155	128	114	142
68517	LINCOLN	111	100	84	97	104	112	96	103	100	95	122	123	94	124	97	101	117	101	108	129
68520	LINCOLN	151	181	191	185	176	179	160	158	148	162	188	184	174	195	163	144	188	153	144	178
68521	LINCOLN	86	81	81	85	80	84	84	83	83	85	104	99	82	101	81	79	100	85	78	94
68522	LINCOLN	78	85	92	87	84	85	85	83	81	84	102	99	86	104	84	77	101	84	75	91
68523	LINCOLN	104	130	138	130	128	126	116	115	107	115	135	135	123	144	118	104	135	111	103	128
68524	LINCOLN	74	79	87	81	78	80	81	78	77	79	97	94	81	99	79	74	96	79	72	85
68526	LINCOLN	148	184	198	188	178	179	162	159	149	164	188	185	177	197	166	144	190	154	142	176
68527	LINCOLN	132	129	112	126	133	140	118	126	120	118	147	149	120	151	121	121	142	122	129	156
68528	LINCOLN	89	98	101	100	95	95	95	94	90	95	114	111	96	115	94	85	112	94	84	103
68531	LINCOLN	99	122	129	122	120	119	109	109	101	109	127	128	116	135	112	98	127	105	98	121
68532	LINCOLN	92	115	122	115	113	111	102	102	95	102	119	119	109	127	105	92	119	98	91	113
68583	LINCOLN	48	38	50	43	38	42	53	47	52	50	66	60	48	62	48	48	64	53	43	52
68601	COLUMBUS	82	80	76	80	81	86	79	81	79	78	98	94	78	98	79	78	94	81	81	93
68620	ALBION	89	63	35	60	73	83	64	77	74	63	87	92	56	84	66	78	79	77	92	104
68621	AMES	85	69	48	66	76	82	66	75	72	65	86	90	61	87	68	74	81	74	85	100
68622	BARTLETT	77	54	28	51	63	70	53	66	61	53	72	79	46	71	55	64	66	65	79	92
68623	BELGRADE	86	60	31	57	70	78	59	73	68	58	80	88	50	78	61	71	73	72	87	102
68624	BELLWOOD	88	62	33	59	72	80	61	75	70	60	82	91	52	81	63	74	75	74	89	105
68626	BRAINARD	94	66	34	62	77	86	65	80	75	64	88	97	56	86	67	79	80	79	96	112
68627	CEDAR RAPIDS	81	56	29	53	66	73	56	69	64	55	75	83	47	74	58	67	68	68	82	96
68628	CLARKS	80	56	29	53	65	73	55	68	64	54	75	82	47	73	57	67	68	67	81	95
68629	CLARKSON	69	51	31	48	56	66	54	62	61	52	72	71	48	69	54	64	66	61	74	78
68631	CRESTON	85	59	31	56	69	77	58	72	67	58	79	87	50	77	61	71	72	71	86	100
68632	DAVID CITY	79	61	41	59	66	76	64	71	70	62	83	82	58	81	64	73	77	70	82	88
68633	DODGE	94	66	34	62	77	86	65	80	75	64	88	97	55	86	67	78	80	79	96	112
68635	DWIGHT	94	66	34	62	77	86	65	80	75	64	88	97	55	86	67	78	80	79	96	112
68636	ELGIN	71	49	26	47	57	64	49	60	56	48	66	73	42	65	51	59	60	59	72	84
68637	ERICSON	77	54	28	51	63	70	53	66	61	52	72	79	45	70	55	64	65	65	78	91
68638	FULLERTON	89	63	36	60	72	83	65	77	75	64	88	91	57	85	67	79	80	77	92	103
68640	GENOA	89	69	47	68	76	86	70	80	77	69	92	93	64	91	71	79	86	79	90	101
68641	HOWELLS	85	59	31	56	69	77	58	72	67	58	79	87	50	77	61	71	72	71	86	100
68642	HUMPHREY	93	65	34	61	76	85	64	79	74	63	87	96	55	85	67	78	79	78	95	111
68643	LEIGH	82	57	30	54	67	75	57	70	65	56	77	85	48	75	59	69	70	69	84	98
68644	LINDSAY	92	65	34	61	75	84	64	79	74	63	86	95	55	84	66	77	79	78	94	110
68647	MONROE	83	71	52	68	76	83	67	75	72	66	87	90	64	88	69	74	82	73	82	98
68648	MORSE BLUFF	77	54	28	51	63	70	53	66	61	53	72	79	45	70	55	64	65	65	78	92
68649	NORTH BEND	81	61	38	59	68	76	61	71	68	60	81	84	55	80	62	71	75	70	82	93
68651	OSCEOLA	94	67	37	63	78	87	66	81	75	65	89	97	57	87	68	79	81	80	96	112
68652	PETERSBURG	76	53	28	50	62	69	53	65	61	52	71	78	45	70	55	64	65	64	77	90
68653	PLATTE CENTER	94	73	47	70	82	89	70	83	78	70	92	100	63	92	73	80	86	82	95	111
68654	POLK	85	62	35	57	71	80	60	74	69	59	81	88	52	79	63	73	74	73	88	102
68655	PRIMROSE	81	56	30	53	66	74	56	69	64	55	75	83	48	74	58	67	69	68	82	96
68658	RISING CITY	88	61	32	58	71	80	61	75	70	60	82	90	52	80	63	73	75	74	89	104
68659	ROGERS	96	67	35	63	78	87	66	82	76	65	89	99	56	88	69	80	81	81	97	114
68660	SAINT EDWARD	68	50	32	48	56	66	55	61	62	52	72	70	48	69	55	65	66	61	73	76
68661	SCHUYLER	81	68	54	67	70	77	70	75	75	71	91	86	66	88	69	74	87	76	78	88
68662	SHELBY	96	70	41	65	81	90	68	83	78	67	92	99	59	90	71	82	84	82	99	115
68663	SILVER CREEK	77	53	28	50	62	70	53	65	61	52	71	79	45	70	55	64	65	64	78	91
68665	SPALDING	72	50	26	48	59	66	50	62	57	49	67	74	43	66	52	60	61	61	73	86
68666	STROMSBURG	84	62	39	59	69	81	67	76	75	64	89	86	59	84	67	80	81	75	90	95
68667	SURPRISE	86	60	31	57	70	78	59	73	68	59	80	88	51	78	61	72	73	72	87	102
68669	ULYSSES	86	60	31	57	70	78	59	73	68	59	80	89	51	79	62	72	73	72	87	102
68701	NORFOLK	72	71	71	72	71	76	73	73	72	71	90	85	72	90	72	71	87	73	72	82
68710	ALLEN	75	62	46	61	66	74	63	69	68	62	82	79	60	81	63	69	77	68	76	84
68711	AMELIA	81	56	30	53	66	74	56	69	64	55	75	83	48	74	58	67	69	68	82	96
68713	ATKINSON	76	55	31	52	62	71	56	67	64	55	75	78	49	73	57	68	69	66	80	88
68714	BASSETT	64	47	29	45	52	61	50	57	56	48	66	66	44	63	50	59	60	57	68	72
68715	BATTLE CREEK	87	77	59	73	82	88	71	79	76	71	92	94	70	94	74	78	88	77	86	102
68716	BEEMER	84	58	31	55	68	76	58	71	66	57	78	86	49	76	60	70	71	70	85	99
68717	BELDEN	81	57	30	54	66	74	56	69	65	55	76	83	48	74	58	68	69	68	82	96
68718	BLOOMFIELD	67	49	31	47	55	64	53	60	59	51	70	69	47	67	53	62	64	59	71	75
68719	BRISTOW	74	51	27	49	60	67	51	63	58	50	69	76	43	67	53	61	63	62	75	87
68720	BRUNSWICK	76	53	28	50	62	69	52	65	60	52	71	78	45	69	54	63	64	64	77	90
68722	BUTTE	54	40	26	39	44	53	44	49	50	42	58	55	39	55	44	52	53	49	59	60
68723	CARROLL	79	55	29	52	64	72	54	67	62	54	73	81	46	72	56	65	67	66	80	93
68724	CENTER	59	46	33	45	50	58	50	54	55	48	65	61	46	63	49	57	60	54	63	65
68725	CHAMBERS	71	50	26	47	58	65	49	61	57	49	67	73	42	65	51	60	61	60	72	85
68726	CLEARWATER	72	50	26	47	58	65	49	61	57	49	67	74	42	65	51	60	61	60	73	85
	NEBRASKA	88	81	77	81	83	90	83	85	84	82	104	101	80	103	82	84	100	86	87	100
	UNITED STATES	100	100	100	100	100	100	100	100	100	100	100	100	100	100	100	100	100	100	100	100

NEBRASKA

POPULATION CHANGE

A 68727-68850

#	POST OFFICE NAME	COUNTY FIPS CODE	POPULATION 2000	POPULATION 2004	POPULATION 2009	% Rate	State Centile	HOUSEHOLDS 2000	HOUSEHOLDS 2004	HOUSEHOLDS 2009	% Annual Rate 2000-2004	2004 Average HH Size	FAMILIES 2000	FAMILIES 2004	% Annual Rate 2000-2004
68727	COLERIDGE	027	879	852	833	-0.7	8	353	347	345	-0.4	2.32	214	212	-0.2
68728	CONCORD	051	288	280	278	-0.7	11	116	114	114	-0.4	2.46	88	86	-0.5
68729	CREIGHTON	107	1804	1803	1792	0.0	53	740	747	748	0.2	2.36	492	498	0.3
68730	CROFTON	107	2079	2049	2021	-0.3	34	791	794	794	0.1	2.57	596	599	0.1
68731	DAKOTA CITY	043	2531	2633	2712	0.9	84	846	884	910	1.0	2.95	644	674	1.1
68732	DIXON	051	300	291	288	-0.7	9	121	119	119	-0.4	2.45	91	89	-0.5
68733	EMERSON	043	1425	1419	1428	-0.1	49	540	542	547	0.1	2.59	393	395	0.1
68734	EMMET	089	185	185	185	0.0	56	65	66	68	0.4	2.80	45	46	0.5
68735	EWING	089	1140	1132	1133	-0.2	45	438	446	456	0.4	2.54	305	312	0.5
68736	FORDYCE	027	720	710	699	-0.3	35	234	235	236	0.1	3.02	187	188	0.1
68739	HARTINGTON	027	3093	3057	3019	-0.3	38	1135	1138	1139	0.1	2.64	782	786	0.1
68740	HOSKINS	179	823	814	809	-0.3	40	304	305	305	0.1	2.67	225	226	0.1
68741	HUBBARD	043	852	881	905	0.8	81	316	329	340	1.0	2.65	237	247	1.0
68742	INMAN	089	364	362	362	-0.1	47	148	151	155	0.5	2.40	104	106	0.5
68743	JACKSON	043	674	709	736	1.2	87	245	260	271	1.4	2.73	185	197	1.5
68745	LAUREL	027	1699	1649	1612	-0.7	10	658	646	640	-0.4	2.49	456	449	-0.4
68746	LYNCH	015	445	440	434	-0.3	39	202	202	201	0.0	2.18	134	135	0.2
68747	MCLEAN	139	204	200	199	-0.5	26	74	74	74	0.0	2.70	60	59	-0.4
68748	MADISON	119	3528	3559	3572	0.2	65	1132	1146	1154	0.3	2.94	838	850	0.3
68749	MAGNET	027	101	99	97	-0.5	24	47	47	46	0.0	2.11	36	36	0.0
68751	MASKELL	051	165	158	155	-1.0	3	61	59	59	-0.8	2.68	45	43	-1.1
68752	MEADOW GROVE	119	905	991	1042	2.2	92	353	392	417	2.5	2.52	262	291	2.5
68753	MILLS	103	325	320	320	-0.4	33	118	118	118	0.0	2.71	84	84	0.0
68755	NAPER	015	403	389	380	-0.8	5	175	171	169	-0.5	2.16	115	112	-0.6
68756	NELIGH	003	2128	2092	2058	-0.4	29	892	894	894	0.1	2.25	591	594	0.1
68757	NEWCASTLE	051	774	753	748	-0.7	12	308	303	304	-0.4	2.49	213	211	-0.2
68758	NEWMAN GROVE	119	1215	1174	1165	-0.8	7	478	464	464	-0.7	2.41	314	306	-0.6
68759	NEWPORT	149	293	286	281	-0.6	17	119	120	120	0.2	2.38	89	90	0.3
68760	NIOBRARA	107	1329	1334	1327	0.1	59	523	529	530	0.3	2.50	366	370	0.3
68761	OAKDALE	003	489	482	474	-0.3	34	193	193	192	0.0	2.50	140	140	0.0
68763	ONEILL	089	5369	5327	5342	-0.2	44	2156	2175	2220	0.2	2.39	1450	1466	0.3
68764	ORCHARD	003	971	951	933	-0.5	23	385	384	382	-0.1	2.46	273	273	0.0
68765	OSMOND	139	1607	1582	1572	-0.4	32	612	610	611	-0.1	2.57	447	446	-0.1
68766	PAGE	089	425	422	422	-0.2	45	174	177	182	0.4	2.38	121	124	0.6
68767	PIERCE	139	3018	3004	3006	-0.1	48	1106	1109	1118	0.1	2.65	805	808	0.1
68768	PILGER	167	1071	1018	1015	-1.2	1	411	398	403	-0.8	2.47	301	291	-0.8
68769	PLAINVIEW	139	2278	2242	2223	-0.4	32	908	902	904	-0.2	2.43	615	612	-0.1
68770	PONCA	051	1665	1639	1626	-0.4	32	614	610	610	-0.2	2.60	448	445	-0.2
68771	RANDOLPH	027	1763	1732	1707	-0.4	28	667	663	660	-0.1	2.56	477	475	-0.1
68773	ROYAL	003	454	446	439	-0.4	28	173	173	172	0.0	2.57	136	136	0.0
68774	SAINT HELENA	027	460	474	478	0.7	80	177	187	192	1.3	2.53	139	146	1.2
68776	SOUTH SIOUX CITY	043	14781	15098	15420	0.5	75	5175	5285	5395	0.5	2.81	3643	3728	0.5
68777	SPENCER	015	758	749	738	-0.3	38	311	311	309	0.0	2.40	207	207	0.0
68778	SPRINGVIEW	103	652	642	642	-0.4	33	288	287	287	-0.1	2.24	206	206	0.0
68779	STANTON	167	2863	2833	2857	-0.3	41	1063	1071	1097	0.2	2.57	794	796	0.1
68780	STUART	089	1242	1249	1256	0.1	61	458	470	482	0.6	2.58	335	344	0.6
68781	TILDEN	003	1643	1687	1705	0.6	78	620	641	654	0.8	2.55	426	442	0.9
68783	VERDIGRE	107	1043	1027	1014	-0.4	33	432	431	429	-0.1	2.27	287	287	0.0
68784	WAKEFIELD	051	2142	2083	2063	-0.7	11	772	751	745	-0.7	2.70	539	525	-0.6
68785	WATERBURY	051	250	284	302	3.1	94	94	108	116	3.3	2.63	68	79	3.6
68786	WAUSA	107	1114	1089	1072	-0.5	20	460	454	450	-0.3	2.33	332	328	-0.3
68787	WAYNE	179	6823	6798	6779	-0.1	50	2301	2308	2313	0.1	2.41	1349	1357	0.1
68788	WEST POINT	039	5397	5384	5424	-0.1	50	2039	2049	2082	0.1	2.55	1417	1428	0.2
68789	WINNETOON	107	225	225	223	0.0	56	89	90	90	0.3	2.42	59	59	0.0
68790	WINSIDE	179	803	794	788	-0.3	40	315	315	315	0.0	2.52	226	226	0.0
68791	WISNER	039	1962	1914	1914	-0.6	16	809	799	807	-0.3	2.34	537	532	-0.2
68792	WYNOT	027	490	549	575	2.7	94	191	219	234	3.3	2.51	145	166	3.2
68801	GRAND ISLAND	079	27620	27663	27848	0.0	57	10400	10449	10559	0.1	2.60	7057	7103	0.2
68803	GRAND ISLAND	079	20332	20868	21325	0.6	77	7889	8180	8425	0.9	2.47	5485	5711	1.0
68810	ALDA	079	984	1002	1017	0.4	73	353	365	374	0.8	2.74	272	281	0.8
68812	AMHERST	019	748	765	789	0.5	76	282	292	304	0.8	2.62	214	221	0.8
68813	ANSELMO	041	518	511	511	-0.3	36	188	188	190	0.0	2.72	145	145	0.0
68814	ANSLEY	041	795	787	788	-0.2	41	321	321	323	0.0	2.45	227	227	0.0
68815	ARCADIA	175	543	528	516	-0.7	11	223	219	215	-0.4	2.41	160	157	-0.4
68816	ARCHER	121	225	222	220	-0.3	36	76	76	75	0.0	2.92	61	61	0.0
68817	ASHTON	163	496	486	468	-0.5	23	207	207	205	0.0	2.35	145	145	0.0
68818	AURORA	081	5241	5236	5238	0.0	53	2011	2024	2039	0.2	2.51	1454	1467	0.2
68819	BERWYN	041	294	297	298	0.2	66	103	105	107	0.5	2.83	79	81	0.6
68820	BOELUS	093	465	463	469	-0.1	49	184	185	189	0.1	2.50	135	136	0.2
68821	BREWSTER	009	230	226	226	-0.4	28	89	89	89	0.0	2.54	63	63	0.0
68822	BROKEN BOW	041	4710	4692	4703	-0.1	50	1955	1970	1997	0.2	2.30	1267	1281	0.3
68823	BURWELL	071	1902	1863	1824	-0.5	23	813	811	808	-0.1	2.23	529	529	0.0
68824	CAIRO	079	1290	1258	1256	-0.6	15	486	479	483	-0.3	2.63	377	371	-0.4
68825	CALLAWAY	041	1152	1155	1159	0.1	58	454	458	463	0.2	2.43	318	322	0.3
68826	CENTRAL CITY	121	3944	3817	3746	-0.8	7	1538	1502	1486	-0.6	2.47	1074	1051	-0.5
68827	CHAPMAN	121	835	849	852	0.4	72	306	316	321	0.8	2.69	237	246	0.9
68828	COMSTOCK	041	323	323	324	0.0	56	138	139	141	0.2	2.32	102	103	0.2
68831	DANNEBROG	093	861	856	868	-0.1	47	320	322	329	0.2	2.66	238	239	0.1
68832	DONIPHAN	079	1865	1877	1893	0.2	62	689	702	715	0.4	2.64	529	539	0.4
68833	DUNNING	009	178	175	175	-0.4	29	81	81	81	0.0	2.16	58	58	0.0
68834	EDDYVILLE	047	180	175	174	-0.7	11	77	75	74	-0.6	2.33	57	55	-0.8
68835	ELBA	093	577	673	740	3.7	97	216	255	283	4.0	2.64	158	187	4.0
68836	ELM CREEK	019	1734	1735	1772	0.0	56	659	669	692	0.4	2.59	472	479	0.4
68837	ELYRIA	175	265	258	252	-0.6	13	110	108	106	-0.4	2.39	78	77	-0.3
68838	FARWELL	093	348	404	442	3.6	96	133	156	173	3.8	2.59	97	114	3.9
68840	GIBBON	019	2692	2749	2830	0.5	75	992	1021	1059	0.7	2.66	738	759	0.7
68841	GILTNER	081	709	715	717	0.2	64	250	254	257	0.4	2.81	203	206	0.4
68842	GREELEY	077	773	754	735	-0.6	16	302	299	296	-0.2	2.46	207	205	-0.2
68843	HAMPTON	081	952	937	933	-0.4	32	346	345	346	-0.1	2.72	278	277	-0.1
68844	HAZARD	163	264	252	240	-1.1	2	113	111	108	-0.4	2.27	83	82	-0.3
68845	KEARNEY	019	16507	17323	18141	1.1	87	6290	6709	7130	1.5	2.40	3905	4201	1.7
68846	HORDVILLE	081	418	417	416	-0.1	50	144	146	146	0.3	2.86	122	123	0.2
68847	KEARNEY	019	14526	14809	15304	0.5	74	5964	6163	6451	0.8	2.35	3651	3776	0.8
68849	KEARNEY	019	1551	1582	1608	0.5	74	27	30	32	2.5	2.57	10	11	2.3
68850	LEXINGTON	047	11926	12254	12423	0.6	79	3779	3817	3814	0.2	3.14	2758	2793	0.3
	NEBRASKA					0.8					1.0	2.47			1.1
	UNITED STATES					1.2					1.3	2.58			1.1

ZIP CODE #	POST OFFICE NAME	RACE (%) White 2000	White 2004	Black 2000	Black 2004	Asian/Pacific 2000	Asian/Pacific 2004	% Hispanic Origin 2000	% Hispanic Origin 2004	2004 AGE DISTRIBUTION (%) 0-4	5-9	10-14	15-19	20-24	25-44	45-64	65-84	85+	18+	MEDIAN AGE 2004	% 2004 Males	% 2004 Females
68727	COLERIDGE	98.8	98.8	0.0	0.0	0.0	0.0	0.5	0.4	5.4	5.8	7.3	6.7	5.9	19.0	25.2	17.8	6.9	76.8	45.0	49.3	50.7
68728	CONCORD	97.2	97.5	0.0	0.0	0.0	0.0	3.5	3.9	7.9	7.5	5.4	6.8	5.4	23.6	23.6	18.2	1.8	75.0	40.7	51.4	48.6
68729	CREIGHTON	98.3	98.2	0.3	0.3	0.2	0.2	0.6	0.7	5.2	5.7	7.4	7.0	4.6	20.0	24.9	21.0	4.2	76.4	45.0	48.8	51.3
68730	CROFTON	98.2	97.9	0.1	0.1	0.1	0.1	0.7	0.8	6.2	6.6	7.7	7.5	6.0	21.9	29.1	13.3	1.7	74.4	41.2	51.3	48.7
68731	DAKOTA CITY	75.5	72.4	0.5	0.6	4.2	5.2	28.1	31.3	9.0	8.8	9.0	8.1	7.5	28.8	20.9	7.2	0.8	68.0	30.5	51.6	48.4
68732	DIXON	98.0	98.3	0.0	0.0	0.0	0.0	2.7	2.8	7.6	6.9	6.2	6.9	5.5	23.4	25.4	16.5	1.7	75.3	40.4	50.9	49.1
68733	EMERSON	92.9	92.4	0.0	0.0	0.6	0.6	4.1	4.6	6.0	7.1	8.4	7.5	6.0	25.3	23.8	13.8	2.1	73.5	38.8	51.0	49.1
68734	EMMET	98.9	99.5	0.0	0.0	0.5	0.5	0.0	0.0	4.9	6.0	8.1	7.0	5.4	24.3	28.7	13.5	2.2	76.2	41.9	50.8	49.2
68735	EWING	99.1	99.1	0.0	0.0	0.3	0.3	0.5	0.5	6.2	6.7	7.2	6.5	5.9	20.6	28.1	16.0	2.8	76.0	42.9	51.8	48.2
68736	FORDYCE	98.8	98.6	0.3	0.3	0.0	0.0	0.7	0.7	7.2	7.5	9.3	9.9	6.8	21.6	26.6	9.7	1.6	69.7	36.3	52.1	47.9
68739	HARTINGTON	99.1	99.1	0.1	0.1	0.0	0.0	0.5	0.5	6.9	7.0	8.9	8.3	5.8	22.0	22.1	15.3	3.8	71.6	38.3	51.4	48.6
68740	HOSKINS	98.9	99.0	0.0	0.0	0.1	0.1	0.7	0.7	6.0	6.8	9.7	9.3	3.4	27.4	24.1	12.3	1.0	71.0	37.3	49.8	50.3
68741	HUBBARD	96.2	95.6	0.0	0.0	0.6	0.9	2.0	2.4	6.0	6.5	8.4	7.7	6.5	25.0	26.5	11.7	1.8	74.2	38.9	51.9	48.1
68742	INMAN	99.2	99.5	0.0	0.0	0.3	0.3	0.3	0.3	5.0	5.8	7.5	6.9	6.1	21.3	28.5	16.3	2.8	77.6	43.4	53.0	47.0
68743	JACKSON	96.9	96.3	0.0	0.0	1.0	1.4	1.3	1.6	5.9	6.2	8.6	7.9	6.9	24.8	27.4	10.9	1.4	74.6	38.7	52.6	47.4
68745	LAUREL	99.3	99.2	0.1	0.1	0.1	0.1	0.4	0.4	5.0	5.6	8.0	7.9	6.6	21.6	24.2	16.3	4.9	76.2	41.3	49.2	50.8
68746	LYNCH	98.7	98.6	0.0	0.0	0.2	0.2	0.0	0.0	5.5	5.9	7.3	6.6	5.9	19.3	28.4	17.7	3.4	77.3	44.7	48.4	51.6
68747	MCLEAN	98.0	98.5	0.0	0.0	0.0	0.0	0.5	0.5	6.5	8.0	9.0	8.0	6.5	25.0	28.0	8.0	1.0	71.0	36.8	54.0	46.0
68748	MADISON	82.0	79.2	0.5	0.5	0.2	0.3	24.3	28.1	7.9	7.2	9.0	9.6	6.2	26.0	20.0	10.9	3.3	70.1	33.8	52.8	47.2
68749	MAGNET	99.0	98.0	0.0	0.0	0.0	0.0	1.0	1.0	7.1	7.1	9.1	9.1	5.1	24.2	23.2	14.1	1.0	72.7	38.2	50.5	49.5
68751	MASKELL	99.4	100.0	0.0	0.0	0.0	0.0	0.6	0.6	5.7	6.3	7.6	7.0	5.7	21.5	31.0	13.3	1.9	76.0	41.7	49.4	50.6
68752	MEADOW GROVE	97.8	97.5	0.1	0.1	0.2	0.3	1.4	1.6	5.2	7.0	9.7	9.1	4.0	24.5	26.2	12.5	1.8	72.7	40.1	50.9	49.1
68753	MILLS	99.4	99.4	0.0	0.0	0.0	0.0	4.0	4.1	6.6	6.6	7.2	5.3	4.1	24.4	25.3	17.8	2.8	75.9	42.2	50.0	50.0
68755	NAPER	99.3	99.0	0.0	0.0	0.0	0.0	0.3	0.3	5.4	5.7	5.4	6.4	5.1	19.0	27.0	19.8	6.2	79.4	46.8	48.3	51.7
68756	NELIGH	98.8	98.6	0.0	0.0	0.0	0.0	1.3	1.6	5.9	5.8	6.1	7.2	6.4	20.1	26.2	17.0	5.3	77.4	43.9	47.7	52.3
68757	NEWCASTLE	99.5	99.5	0.0	0.0	0.1	0.1	0.5	0.5	5.7	6.5	8.9	7.8	5.1	22.6	29.1	12.2	2.1	74.1	40.2	52.7	47.3
68758	NEWMAN GROVE	92.4	90.9	0.0	0.0	0.7	0.8	10.0	12.0	6.1	6.3	7.0	8.2	6.0	20.6	23.4	16.8	5.7	74.5	42.0	49.4	50.6
68759	NEWPORT	99.7	99.7	0.0	0.0	0.0	0.0	0.3	0.4	5.9	6.3	6.3	7.7	5.6	23.1	29.4	14.0	1.8	76.6	42.1	51.8	48.3
68760	NIOBRARA	62.5	60.1	0.0	0.0	0.4	0.5	1.9	2.0	8.5	8.4	7.7	7.2	6.0	21.5	24.3	14.2	2.3	70.9	37.3	50.0	50.0
68761	OAKDALE	99.2	99.2	0.2	0.2	0.0	0.0	0.4	0.4	7.1	7.3	7.3	6.9	5.0	21.6	28.8	14.5	1.7	74.1	41.6	50.8	49.2
68763	ONEILL	98.7	98.7	0.0	0.0	0.2	0.2	0.9	0.9	6.7	7.0	7.5	6.7	5.4	22.8	25.0	15.7	3.2	74.4	41.2	48.3	51.7
68764	ORCHARD	99.2	99.0	0.0	0.0	0.0	0.1	0.4	0.5	5.8	6.2	6.4	6.8	6.0	21.1	27.3	17.3	3.1	77.2	43.6	50.4	49.6
68765	OSMOND	98.8	98.8	0.1	0.1	0.3	0.3	0.6	0.6	6.3	6.9	8.5	7.7	5.9	23.7	24.8	13.8	2.5	72.8	39.5	51.1	48.9
68766	PAGE	99.3	99.3	0.0	0.0	0.2	0.2	0.2	0.2	5.2	6.2	7.6	6.9	5.9	21.1	29.2	15.2	2.8	76.5	43.2	53.1	46.9
68767	PIERCE	99.0	98.9	0.0	0.0	0.1	0.1	0.7	0.7	6.7	6.8	7.8	7.8	7.4	24.3	24.0	12.2	2.9	73.7	37.7	49.8	50.2
68768	PILGER	98.2	98.0	0.2	0.2	0.2	0.2	0.9	1.2	5.8	7.1	7.0	6.4	5.1	23.0	27.7	14.8	3.1	75.5	41.9	50.8	49.2
68769	PLAINVIEW	98.2	98.1	0.1	0.1	0.3	0.3	0.3	0.3	6.3	6.3	7.3	7.4	6.1	22.2	22.9	16.6	5.0	75.2	41.1	48.6	51.4
68770	PONCA	97.8	97.7	0.0	0.0	0.1	0.1	1.9	1.8	6.4	6.8	8.2	6.5	5.9	23.4	26.4	13.1	3.3	74.9	39.7	50.0	50.0
68771	RANDOLPH	98.8	98.7	0.1	0.1	0.3	0.3	0.3	0.4	6.7	7.0	7.4	7.0	5.0	22.6	24.3	16.6	3.4	74.0	41.1	50.4	49.7
68773	ROYAL	98.9	98.9	0.0	0.0	0.2	0.2	0.7	0.5	5.8	6.3	8.5	8.1	6.7	22.9	26.0	14.4	1.4	73.5	40.4	52.2	47.8
68774	SAINT HELENA	99.1	99.0	0.2	0.2	0.0	0.0	0.2	0.2	7.0	7.0	8.4	9.9	6.5	21.3	27.4	11.2	1.3	71.1	37.7	53.0	47.1
68776	SOUTH SIOUX CITY	76.0	72.7	0.8	0.8	3.5	4.5	25.7	29.2	9.3	8.4	7.9	7.1	8.0	29.1	20.8	8.1	1.3	69.9	30.8	49.3	50.7
68777	SPENCER	98.7	98.7	0.0	0.0	0.3	0.3	0.0	0.0	5.3	5.9	7.3	6.5	5.9	19.2	28.3	18.0	3.5	77.3	44.9	48.7	51.3
68778	SPRINGVIEW	99.4	99.4	0.0	0.0	0.0	0.0	3.8	3.9	6.4	6.9	7.3	5.3	4.2	23.5	25.9	17.6	3.0	76.0	42.4	50.0	50.0
68779	STANTON	98.0	97.8	0.1	0.1	0.2	0.3	1.5	1.7	6.4	6.8	7.1	7.2	6.4	23.7	24.7	14.6	3.2	75.3	39.6	49.0	51.0
68780	STUART	98.7	98.7	0.0	0.0	0.3	0.3	0.3	0.4	5.4	5.7	7.9	8.3	6.4	22.5	24.2	15.9	3.8	75.4	41.3	50.4	49.6
68781	TILDEN	96.7	96.2	0.1	0.1	0.1	0.1	4.7	5.6	5.7	5.9	7.2	8.0	7.0	21.9	24.8	15.5	4.2	76.1	41.3	49.0	51.0
68783	VERDIGRE	95.0	94.6	0.0	0.0	0.0	0.0	0.9	0.9	5.5	5.7	5.7	5.7	4.6	19.6	27.8	20.5	5.0	79.3	47.2	51.5	48.5
68784	WAKEFIELD	88.7	88.3	0.1	0.1	0.4	0.4	12.1	12.5	6.6	6.4	7.0	8.2	6.7	23.8	23.0	14.6	3.8	75.0	39.2	49.0	51.0
68785	WATERBURY	98.0	98.2	0.0	0.0	0.0	0.0	1.6	2.1	7.4	6.7	7.0	6.7	4.6	24.7	26.8	14.1	2.1	74.7	40.0	50.7	49.3
68786	WAUSA	98.2	98.0	0.2	0.2	0.3	0.4	0.9	1.1	6.9	7.1	6.5	6.7	5.0	21.4	25.6	17.2	3.7	74.8	42.6	50.7	49.3
68787	WAYNE	96.3	96.3	1.3	1.3	0.4	0.4	1.6	1.7	5.0	4.5	5.0	14.1	19.7	21.2	17.5	10.2	2.8	82.6	26.0	47.1	52.9
68788	WEST POINT	93.9	92.8	0.2	0.2	0.2	0.3	9.3	11.0	7.0	6.8	7.2	6.9	6.0	23.9	22.9	15.6	3.8	74.5	39.6	50.8	49.2
68789	WINNETOON	98.2	97.8	0.0	0.4	0.0	0.0	0.9	0.9	4.9	5.3	7.1	6.7	4.4	21.3	24.4	21.3	4.4	77.3	45.2	48.9	51.1
68790	WINSIDE	98.6	98.6	0.3	0.3	0.3	0.3	0.5	0.5	7.3	7.3	8.1	7.4	5.3	26.1	23.8	13.1	1.6	72.5	38.7	49.0	51.0
68791	WISNER	98.6	98.4	0.3	0.3	0.3	0.4	0.7	0.7	6.4	6.6	7.1	6.1	5.8	23.7	24.1	16.5	3.8	76.1	41.0	50.9	49.1
68792	WYNOT	99.6	99.6	0.4	0.4	0.0	0.0	0.4	0.4	7.5	7.5	8.7	7.7	5.5	22.2	24.6	14.6	1.8	71.6	38.7	53.2	46.8
68801	GRAND ISLAND	83.7	81.2	0.4	0.4	1.5	1.9	20.9	24.0	8.5	8.0	7.3	6.6	7.6	28.2	22.1	10.1	1.7	72.4	33.5	50.2	49.8
68803	GRAND ISLAND	92.9	91.5	0.4	0.4	1.1	1.5	7.3	8.8	6.8	6.5	6.9	6.7	6.8	25.4	24.7	13.8	2.4	75.8	38.8	48.7	51.4
68810	ALDA	95.8	95.0	0.3	0.3	0.1	0.2	5.7	6.8	6.6	7.1	8.2	7.4	6.4	27.1	27.7	9.1	0.5	73.5	37.3	51.3	48.7
68812	AMHERST	99.6	99.5	0.1	0.1	0.1	0.1	0.0	0.0	5.4	7.7	9.4	6.9	3.4	28.2	24.3	13.5	1.2	72.6	38.5	52.6	47.5
68813	ANSELMO	99.0	99.2	0.0	0.0	0.4	0.4	0.4	0.4	6.5	6.9	7.4	7.8	5.9	22.5	26.6	14.7	1.8	74.2	41.1	52.8	47.2
68814	ANSLEY	99.3	99.2	0.0	0.0	0.0	0.0	1.1	1.1	7.1	7.5	7.5	6.1	4.6	23.9	24.1	17.3	1.9	74.1	40.6	50.3	49.7
68815	ARCADIA	98.9	99.1	0.2	0.2	0.0	0.0	0.9	0.8	7.6	7.4	6.8	6.3	4.0	25.6	23.1	16.9	2.5	74.1	39.9	50.4	49.6
68816	ARCHER	97.8	98.7	0.0	0.0	0.0	0.0	1.3	1.4	6.3	7.2	9.0	7.2	5.4	24.3	26.1	13.1	1.4	72.1	39.4	50.9	49.1
68817	ASHTON	99.2	99.0	0.0	0.0	0.2	0.2	0.6	0.8	5.6	5.8	6.6	6.0	4.3	22.6	28.8	17.5	2.9	78.4	44.4	52.1	47.9
68818	AURORA	98.1	98.1	0.2	0.2	0.4	0.4	1.4	1.5	7.0	7.1	7.5	6.9	6.6	23.6	23.8	13.9	3.6	73.8	39.3	48.4	51.6
68819	BERWYN	98.3	98.3	0.0	0.0	0.0	0.0	1.0	1.4	7.1	7.4	7.7	7.1	5.4	24.6	26.6	12.5	1.7	73.7	38.8	51.5	48.5
68820	BOELUS	98.7	98.7	0.2	0.2	0.2	0.2	1.1	1.5	4.8	5.4	8.0	6.9	6.1	24.4	29.8	12.5	2.2	77.5	41.4	49.7	50.3
68821	BREWSTER	99.1	99.1	0.0	0.0	0.0	0.0	0.0	0.0	5.3	6.2	7.1	5.8	4.9	26.6	26.6	15.5	2.2	77.4	42.3	50.9	49.1
68822	BROKEN BOW	98.5	98.5	0.2	0.2	0.1	0.1	0.7	0.8	6.0	6.3	7.4	6.2	5.3	21.7	25.3	17.1	4.7	76.3	42.9	47.6	52.4
68823	BURWELL	98.8	98.8	0.0	0.0	0.1	0.1	1.0	1.0	5.0	5.4	6.9	6.7	5.1	17.4	28.7	19.8	5.2	78.5	47.4	48.1	51.9
68824	CAIRO	98.8	98.4	0.1	0.1	0.0	0.0	1.8	2.3	7.6	7.6	7.2	6.9	5.7	25.3	26.9	11.3	1.7	73.5	38.5	49.4	50.6
68825	CALLAWAY	97.9	97.8	0.0	0.0	0.5	0.5	1.0	1.0	4.7	5.5	8.1	7.5	4.4	20.4	26.3	18.8	4.4	76.9	44.7	48.6	51.4
68826	CENTRAL CITY	98.3	98.2	0.3	0.3	0.4	0.5	1.2	1.2	6.4	6.7	7.8	7.2	6.2	22.9	24.2	14.7	3.9	73.9	39.7	47.9	52.1
68827	CHAPMAN	98.2	98.2	0.0	0.0	0.0	0.0	2.5	2.5	6.5	7.2	8.7	7.2	5.0	26.3	26.6	11.5	1.1	73.0	38.6	52.3	47.7
68828	COMSTOCK	99.4	99.4	0.0	0.0	0.0	0.0	0.9	0.9	6.8	7.1	9.3	6.5	5.0	22.0	23.5	18.0	1.9	72.8	40.7	52.6	47.4
68831	DANNEBROG	98.7	98.5	0.2	0.2	0.2	0.4	1.2	1.3	5.1	5.7	8.1	7.0	5.8	24.7	29.4	12.4	1.8	76.8	41.0	50.0	50.0
68832	DONIPHAN	98.1	97.8	0.1	0.1	0.1	0.1	2.5	3.1	6.7	7.3	8.0	7.4	6.1	25.8	26.9	10.4	1.5	73.2	37.9	49.6	50.5
68833	DUNNING	98.9	98.9	0.0	0.0	0.0	0.0	0.0	0.0	5.7	6.3	7.4	5.7	4.6	25.1	26.9	16.0	2.3	77.1	42.3	49.7	50.3
68834	EDDYVILLE	97.2	97.1	0.6	0.6	0.0	0.0	4.4	5.1	6.3	8.0	7.4	6.3	5.7	26.3	25.1	13.1	1.7	74.3	37.9	49.7	50.3
68835	ELBA	97.6	97.5	0.4	0.3	0.0	0.0	1.6	1.9	6.1	6.1	7.1	7.9	6.5	25.4	24.8	14.1	1.9	75.8	39.7	52.6	47.4
68836	ELM CREEK	98.0	97.7	0.0	0.0	0.1	0.2	2.5	3.1	7.1	7.7	8.8	7.0	6.0	26.9	24.8	10.7	1.1	72.1	36.0	50.2	49.8
68837	ELYRIA	98.9	98.8	0.0	0.0	0.0	0.0	1.1	1.2	7.0	7.0	7.0	6.2	4.3	24.4	24.0	17.4	2.7	74.8	40.8	50.4	49.6
68838	FARWELL	97.7	97.5	0.3	0.3	0.0	0.0	1.7	2.0	5.9	5.9	7.2	7.7	6.7	24.5	25.5	14.6	2.0	76.5	39.8	51.7	48.3
68840	GIBBON	89.3	87.7	0.2	0.2	0.2	0.2	14.9	17.4	7.9	7.7	8.1	6.9	6.1	26.2	24.2	10.9	2.1	71.8	35.8	49.8	50.2
68841	GILTNER	98.7	98.7	0.6	0.6	0.0	0.0	0.9	0.8	6.7	9.5	8.5	6.6	5.9	24.9	26.4	10.6	0.8	71.3	36.7	50.6	49.4
68842	GREELEY	97.4	97.2	1.2	1.2	0.1	0.1	0.8	0.9	6.0	6.5	8.2	6.5	5.3	21.0	25.1	17.1	4.4	74.5	42.5	51.5	48.5
68843	HAMPTON	99.1	99.2	0.1	0.1	0.0	0.0	0.3	0.3	5.7	7.0	9.3	7.9	5.2	23.1	28.5	12.3	1.1	72.7	40.8	52.6	47.4
68844	HAZARD	98.1	97.6	0.0	0.0	0.0	0.0	1.5	2.0	5.6	6.0	6.8	6.8	5.2	21.0	29.4	17.5	2.0	78.2	44.0	52.0	48.0
68845	KEARNEY	94.9	94.0	0.8	0.9	1.0	1.3	3.7	4.4	6.5	6.0	6.7	10.1	13.4	27.6	21.3	7.0	1.5	75.7	29.1	49.8	50.2
68846	HORDVILLE	99.0	99.0	0.2	0.2	0.0	0.0	0.2	0.2	6.2	7.2	8.6	6.7	5.5	22.5	29.7	12.5	1.0	73.6	40.9	53.5	46.5
68847	KEARNEY	95.9	95.3	0.4	0.4	0.6	0.8	4.5	5.4	7.4	6.7	6.4	6.2	8.6	31.3	20.7	10.3	2.4	76.0	32.8	48.9	51.1
68849	KEARNEY	93.4	92.1	1.5	1.5	2.6	3.5	2.5	2.9	1.0	1.3	1.1	51.8	30.5	8.8	3.5	1.4	0.6	96.0	19.5	46.8	53.2
68850	LEXINGTON	68.2	64.5	0.4	0.4	1.1	1.4	45.2	50.1	9.8	8.9	8.3	7.4	7.3	28.4	19.7	8.4	1.8	68.7	31.0	52.0	48.0
	NEBRASKA	89.6	88.4	4.0	4.2	1.3	1.8	5.5	6.4	7.0	6.9	7.2	7.3	7.6	27.5	23.5	11.2	2.1	74.8	35.7	49.4	50.6
	UNITED STATES	75.1	73.6	12.3	12.5	3.8	4.2	12.5	14.1	6.9	6.7	7.2	7.0	7.3	28.6	23.8	10.8	1.7	75.1	36.0	49.1	50.9

ZIP CODE #	POST OFFICE NAME	2004 Per Capita Income	2004 HH Income Base	2004 Household Income Distribution (%) Less than $25,000	$25,000 to $49,999	$50,000 to $99,999	$100,000 to $149,999	$150,000 or More	Median Household Income 2004	2009	2004 National Centile	2004 State Centile	2004 Home Value Base	2004 Home Value Distribution (%) Less than $50,000	$50,000 to $89,999	$90,000 to $174,999	$175,000 to $399,999	$400,000 or More	2004 Median Home Value
68727	COLERIDGE	17859	347	34.3	37.5	23.3	2.6	2.3	35631	40881	30	34	254	45.7	33.5	13.4	7.1	0.4	55238
68728	CONCORD	16567	114	34.2	36.0	25.4	4.4	0.0	35879	40994	31	35	89	30.3	30.3	30.3	9.0	0.0	79167
68729	CREIGHTON	15922	747	40.6	35.2	20.2	2.8	1.2	31211	35747	16	11	605	50.6	28.4	16.9	3.6	0.5	49470
68730	CROFTON	17330	794	28.7	41.2	25.3	3.8	1.0	35000	39505	28	29	639	27.7	34.7	29.7	7.7	0.2	75566
68731	DAKOTA CITY	18653	884	21.4	32.7	36.8	7.1	2.0	46421	55479	65	80	683	35.0	23.7	33.7	7.2	0.4	78256
68732	DIXON	17633	119	32.8	36.1	26.1	4.2	0.8	36580	42895	34	40	94	34.0	29.8	28.7	7.5	0.0	75000
68733	EMERSON	18328	542	28.8	33.4	31.4	5.4	1.1	41362	47151	51	67	426	25.6	35.0	28.6	9.4	1.4	77632
68734	EMMET	13405	66	37.9	37.9	21.2	3.0	0.0	33875	40000	24	23	50	44.0	30.0	24.0	2.0	0.0	57500
68735	EWING	15681	446	39.7	35.0	20.2	4.0	1.1	31791	36746	17	15	350	50.6	24.3	18.6	3.7	2.9	49474
68736	FORDYCE	14865	235	26.4	40.4	27.2	4.3	1.7	38630	42032	42	54	185	33.0	32.4	24.9	8.7	1.1	73000
68739	HARTINGTON	17661	1138	29.3	37.6	27.0	4.0	2.2	38537	43742	41	53	911	32.8	31.2	27.6	7.5	1.0	71776
68740	HOSKINS	16522	305	31.2	29.8	34.1	4.9	0.0	38812	46147	42	54	249	16.9	31.7	39.4	12.1	0.0	91346
68741	HUBBARD	21646	329	20.7	31.0	36.8	9.1	2.4	48577	56973	69	84	266	18.1	26.3	41.0	13.5	1.1	96522
68742	INMAN	16948	151	37.8	33.8	23.2	4.6	0.7	34156	39235	25	25	119	51.3	23.5	19.3	3.4	2.5	48750
68743	JACKSON	22425	260	16.9	30.0	40.4	10.8	1.9	53077	62702	77	90	214	17.3	21.5	44.9	14.5	1.9	100625
68745	LAUREL	18180	646	29.9	41.5	22.8	4.0	1.9	36386	42121	33	39	487	30.0	36.6	26.3	6.8	0.4	72125
68746	LYNCH	18706	202	39.6	33.7	21.3	3.5	2.0	31034	36454	15	10	163	60.7	23.3	12.9	3.1	0.0	36786
68747	MCLEAN	19775	74	25.7	36.5	25.7	8.1	4.1	40738	46856	49	64	57	19.3	22.8	38.6	17.5	1.8	99000
68748	MADISON	16445	1146	25.3	35.0	33.3	5.1	1.3	41650	49315	52	67	869	27.4	35.8	28.7	6.4	1.7	71917
68749	MAGNET	20581	47	25.5	44.7	25.5	2.1	2.1	37946	41530	39	49	38	34.2	10.5	23.7	29.0	2.6	112500
68751	MASKELL	17901	59	30.5	33.9	27.1	5.1	3.4	40557	46357	48	63	47	44.7	27.7	23.4	4.3	0.0	58333
68752	MEADOW GROVE	17420	392	32.1	34.7	26.5	6.4	0.3	37055	43095	36	43	310	38.7	27.1	25.8	7.4	1.0	67778
68753	MILLS	11954	118	45.8	40.7	10.2	1.7	1.7	26687	30000	7	2	90	55.6	14.4	12.2	5.6	12.2	42857
68755	NAPER	14935	171	48.5	33.9	13.5	4.1	0.0	25713	29416	5	1	136	71.3	14.0	10.3	1.5	2.9	28667
68756	NELIGH	21218	894	34.3	35.1	22.4	6.7	1.5	36001	41075	32	36	692	38.9	33.8	23.0	3.0	1.3	62338
68757	NEWCASTLE	16907	303	32.7	38.0	25.4	2.6	1.3	35090	40383	28	30	240	39.6	26.7	21.3	11.3	1.3	69286
68758	NEWMAN GROVE	20056	464	32.3	36.2	24.6	4.3	2.6	36693	43864	34	41	340	45.6	28.8	20.0	4.1	1.5	55769
68759	NEWPORT	17590	120	43.3	34.2	15.0	5.0	2.5	27839	31978	8	4	84	48.8	23.8	13.1	10.7	3.6	52000
68760	NIOBRARA	14351	529	46.1	32.7	16.5	3.8	1.0	27060	31463	7	3	337	45.7	30.9	17.8	4.2	1.5	54394
68761	OAKDALE	13140	193	39.4	45.1	14.5	0.0	1.0	28933	33577	10	5	159	74.2	15.7	7.6	0.6	1.9	26875
68763	ONEILL	18863	2175	33.9	33.3	25.5	5.0	2.3	36503	42276	34	40	1637	25.6	30.4	35.4	6.0	2.6	84306
68764	ORCHARD	15053	384	43.8	38.3	13.8	2.6	1.6	27764	32383	8	4	303	56.1	21.1	12.5	7.9	2.3	42885
68765	OSMOND	20292	610	32.8	34.9	23.8	4.6	3.9	34872	40637	27	28	475	35.0	28.0	27.2	8.6	1.3	69043
68766	PAGE	16862	177	37.9	33.3	23.2	5.1	0.6	34741	39072	26	27	139	51.8	23.7	18.0	3.6	2.9	48214
68767	PIERCE	19489	1109	28.8	32.4	30.3	6.2	2.3	40959	48793	50	65	839	23.5	32.9	34.6	8.5	0.6	81894
68768	PILGER	18523	398	25.6	40.5	27.6	5.3	1.0	39702	43804	45	59	300	27.0	27.0	34.0	9.3	2.7	84286
68769	PLAINVIEW	18216	902	35.6	35.1	23.0	3.4	2.9	32573	38994	20	17	682	37.8	34.2	20.2	7.3	0.4	63934
68770	PONCA	18598	610	25.3	36.7	31.8	4.1	2.1	40349	45792	47	61	480	21.0	31.0	38.5	8.3	1.0	87727
68771	RANDOLPH	20222	663	30.3	42.1	21.6	3.6	2.4	35641	40232	30	34	527	38.5	28.7	25.2	7.0	0.6	65345
68773	ROYAL	16239	173	37.6	37.0	20.2	2.9	2.3	32482	37615	19	16	132	31.8	17.4	27.3	18.9	4.6	90909
68774	SAINT HELENA	19419	187	25.7	36.4	31.0	4.8	2.1	40796	44147	49	64	147	34.0	29.9	24.5	9.5	2.0	68929
68776	SOUTH SIOUX CITY	18713	5285	26.2	31.5	31.6	8.5	2.3	43426	51207	57	74	3365	21.8	31.7	38.6	7.9	0.1	86662
68777	SPENCER	16737	311	39.9	34.1	20.9	3.5	1.6	30927	35976	15	9	250	62.4	23.2	12.0	2.0	0.4	35000
68778	SPRINGVIEW	14542	287	45.3	41.1	10.1	1.7	1.7	26864	30093	7	2	218	56.0	14.2	12.8	5.1	11.9	42778
68779	STANTON	17171	1071	28.8	37.0	28.4	5.0	0.8	37949	42382	39	49	783	25.7	32.3	32.6	7.9	1.5	80942
68780	STUART	18187	470	34.5	37.9	21.7	3.8	2.1	35518	40598	30	33	365	37.5	19.7	31.5	6.6	4.7	77250
68781	TILDEN	17099	641	32.1	35.3	27.3	3.7	1.6	37849	44242	39	48	463	37.2	32.8	23.3	5.6	1.1	63816
68783	VERDIGRE	15929	431	47.8	31.3	17.2	2.6	1.2	26086	30074	6	2	343	48.7	32.1	13.1	6.1	0.0	51154
68784	WAKEFIELD	17227	751	30.1	35.7	28.5	4.3	1.5	38499	45534	41	53	541	28.1	38.3	26.1	7.4	0.2	76224
68785	WATERBURY	17949	108	25.0	38.9	30.6	3.7	1.9	41304	46137	51	66	86	33.7	34.9	25.6	5.8	0.0	71111
68786	WAUSA	17649	454	34.4	38.6	22.0	3.5	1.5	33977	38422	24	24	367	46.1	25.3	15.8	10.6	2.2	54833
68787	WAYNE	18000	2308	35.1	28.0	27.8	7.2	1.9	35946	44740	31	36	1224	9.6	32.1	47.1	11.2	0.1	97391
68788	WEST POINT	19882	2049	27.7	38.7	25.9	4.6	3.2	37691	43657	38	47	1524	15.3	34.3	38.4	9.5	2.6	90479
68789	WINNETOON	15248	90	40.0	35.6	20.0	3.3	1.1	31273	33891	16	12	73	49.3	30.1	16.4	4.1	0.0	50625
68790	WINSIDE	16387	315	35.9	31.8	27.9	4.4	0.0	33716	39302	23	22	250	24.0	36.0	32.8	6.8	0.4	78750
68791	WISNER	19548	799	27.0	42.4	26.3	2.8	1.5	36976	41200	35	43	584	28.9	36.0	26.4	7.7	1.0	69167
68792	WYNOT	20329	219	27.9	38.8	26.9	4.6	1.8	38850	42994	42	55	176	38.6	28.4	22.7	9.1	1.1	64000
68801	GRAND ISLAND	20305	10449	28.2	32.8	29.6	5.9	3.5	41008	48529	50	65	6522	13.4	37.0	37.8	11.0	1.0	89687
68803	GRAND ISLAND	21233	8180	26.6	30.7	31.9	8.0	2.8	44201	51544	59	76	5694	7.9	22.9	60.0	8.4	0.8	106925
68810	ALDA	22416	365	18.4	34.5	34.8	8.5	3.8	46960	54391	66	81	288	24.7	17.0	33.0	21.5	3.8	105405
68812	AMHERST	19119	292	24.3	32.9	34.9	6.2	1.7	44509	50000	60	76	225	23.6	23.6	40.4	11.6	0.9	93611
68813	ANSELMO	14515	188	34.6	40.4	21.8	2.7	0.5	32737	37626	20	17	144	47.2	18.1	20.8	9.0	4.9	55714
68814	ANSLEY	16615	321	36.8	38.9	21.2	2.2	0.9	31159	36063	15	11	250	68.0	18.4	6.0	4.0	3.6	30263
68815	ARCADIA	17147	219	44.3	31.1	19.2	3.2	2.3	28509	33268	10	5	172	57.0	23.3	13.4	5.2	1.2	43684
68816	ARCHER	16585	76	22.4	43.4	27.6	5.3	1.3	40000	42310	46	60	59	28.8	20.3	28.8	17.0	5.1	90625
68817	ASHTON	17054	207	30.9	46.4	17.9	3.4	1.5	33949	38193	24	24	167	46.7	28.7	14.4	8.4	1.8	53929
68818	AURORA	20276	2024	24.0	36.2	31.4	6.3	2.2	42944	50169	56	72	1525	16.3	30.0	44.7	8.3	0.8	93005
68819	BERWYN	17928	105	26.7	37.1	27.6	5.7	2.9	38951	44538	43	56	83	41.0	20.5	19.3	13.3	6.0	63750
68820	BOELUS	16078	185	33.0	35.7	29.2	2.2	0.0	36324	40560	33	38	146	25.3	30.1	27.4	16.4	0.7	80000
68821	BREWSTER	13291	89	42.7	38.2	16.9	2.3	0.0	27204	30232	7	3	58	67.2	17.2	3.5	3.5	8.6	26667
68822	BROKEN BOW	20825	1970	32.4	33.9	26.0	5.8	1.9	35973	42157	31	36	1409	33.5	37.3	24.7	3.4	1.1	65629
68823	BURWELL	16693	811	41.7	32.9	20.2	4.6	0.6	30623	36040	14	8	590	47.1	26.4	20.2	5.1	1.2	53469
68824	CAIRO	18406	479	25.9	37.2	29.9	5.0	2.1	38808	44078	42	54	382	12.6	36.9	35.1	15.5	0.0	90370
68825	CALLAWAY	16959	458	36.0	34.7	24.2	3.5	1.5	35558	40206	30	33	353	32.0	27.8	29.2	8.2	2.8	78194
68826	CENTRAL CITY	19324	1502	28.6	38.8	26.5	4.4	1.7	38939	43748	43	55	1068	28.4	34.5	32.6	3.5	1.1	75729
68827	CHAPMAN	16460	316	22.2	44.6	29.4	3.2	0.6	39080	43605	43	56	246	26.4	26.0	30.9	13.0	3.7	85385
68828	COMSTOCK	24310	139	36.7	38.9	18.0	2.2	4.3	33370	37519	22	20	105	49.5	19.1	11.4	15.2	4.8	50500
68831	DANNEBROG	15623	322	32.0	36.3	28.9	2.2	0.6	36982	41418	35	43	254	23.2	29.9	29.9	15.4	1.6	84667
68832	DONIPHAN	22084	702	21.7	33.5	35.2	6.1	3.6	45122	53092	62	78	567	18.9	26.6	39.3	13.2	1.9	95426
68833	DUNNING	15621	81	42.0	37.0	18.5	2.5	0.0	27679	29722	8	3	53	67.9	17.0	3.8	3.8	7.6	25833
68834	EDDYVILLE	19466	75	30.7	38.7	24.0	4.0	2.7	35305	38929	29	31	59	42.4	27.1	20.3	10.2	0.0	62778
68835	ELBA	16171	255	29.8	42.4	22.0	3.9	2.0	36390	41337	33	39	196	35.2	25.5	26.5	10.2	2.6	70000
68836	ELM CREEK	19634	669	24.1	39.0	29.6	5.4	1.9	40711	46498	49	63	517	26.7	30.0	32.9	8.9	1.6	82500
68837	ELYRIA	17069	108	43.5	32.4	19.4	2.8	1.9	28734	33183	10	5	85	56.5	23.5	14.1	5.9	0.0	43889
68838	FARWELL	16267	156	30.1	42.3	22.4	3.9	1.3	36381	41216	33	39	120	35.0	26.7	26.7	10.8	0.8	70000
68840	GIBBON	17900	1021	26.1	36.1	32.2	4.6	1.0	40828	46739	49	64	766	20.0	33.3	40.7	4.7	1.3	86429
68841	GILTNER	23362	254	20.1	30.7	33.9	10.2	5.1	49268	54679	71	85	201	24.9	25.4	34.8	11.0	4.0	89688
68842	GREELEY	15287	299	37.1	37.1	22.1	3.0	0.7	31926	35881	18	15	235	54.9	23.8	11.9	6.0	3.4	46167
68843	HAMPTON	20950	345	15.9	35.1	38.6	7.5	2.9	49323	54520	71	85	275	19.6	30.2	34.6	12.7	2.9	90200
68844	HAZARD	17708	111	34.2	43.2	17.1	2.7	2.7	33450	37038	22	21	90	35.6	33.3	18.9	7.8	4.4	72857
68845	KEARNEY	22986	6709	26.3	30.6	30.9	8.1	4.2	43971	52039	59	75	4017	10.2	14.1	52.2	21.5	2.1	126146
68846	HORDVILLE	22465	146	15.8	33.6	34.3	11.0	5.5	50395	55024	73	86	112	20.5	21.4	38.4	17.0	2.7	101563
68847	KEARNEY	21216	6163	27.9	32.4	30.5	7.5	1.8	40603	48266	48	63	3769	20.8	22.6	45.1	11.1	0.5	96734
68849	KEARNEY	9074	30	26.7	36.7	26.7	3.3	6.7	41492	54460	51	67	11	0.0	27.3	72.7	0.0	0.0	109375
68850	LEXINGTON	16921	3817	26.7	31.6	31.3	6.9	3.4	44161	51323	59	75	2586	22.4	41.0	29.7	6.3	0.6	77010
	NEBRASKA	23743		24.5	30.5	31.8	9.2	4.0	45453	54516				17.2	23.9	42.4	14.4	2.2	101398
	UNITED STATES	25866		24.7	27.1	30.8	10.9	6.5	48124	56710				10.9	15.0	33.7	30.1	10.4	145905

ZIP CODE		FINANCIAL SERVICES				THE HOME						ENTERTAINMENT						PERSONAL			
						Home Improvements		Furnishings													
#	POST OFFICE NAME	Auto Loan	Home Loan	Invest-ments	Retire-ment Plans	Home Repair	Lawn & Garden	Comput-ers & Hard-ware	Major Appli-ances	TV, Radio, Sound Equip-ment	Furni-ture	Dine out/ Carry out	Sports Equip-ment	Fees & Tickets	Toys & Games	Travel	Cable TV	Apparel & Services	Auto Repairs	Health Insur-ance	Pets & Supplies
68727	COLERIDGE	70	52	32	50	58	68	56	63	63	53	74	72	49	70	56	66	67	63	76	79
68728	CONCORD	73	52	28	49	60	67	51	62	59	51	69	75	44	68	53	61	63	62	74	86
68729	CREIGHTON	62	46	30	44	51	60	50	56	57	48	67	63	45	63	50	60	61	56	67	69
68730	CROFTON	81	56	29	53	66	74	56	69	64	55	75	83	48	74	58	67	69	68	82	96
68731	DAKOTA CITY	88	80	62	77	81	86	76	82	77	77	95	95	72	91	75	77	91	81	83	99
68732	DIXON	77	55	30	52	63	71	54	66	62	54	73	79	47	72	56	65	67	65	78	91
68733	EMERSON	81	62	39	60	69	77	62	72	69	61	82	85	56	81	63	71	76	71	82	94
68734	EMMET	68	47	25	45	55	62	47	58	54	46	63	70	40	62	49	57	58	57	69	81
68735	EWING	72	50	26	48	59	66	50	61	57	49	67	74	42	66	52	60	61	61	73	86
68736	FORDYCE	81	57	30	54	66	74	56	69	65	55	76	84	48	74	58	68	69	68	83	96
68739	HARTINGTON	79	61	44	60	68	75	61	71	67	60	80	85	55	78	62	69	74	70	80	93
68740	HOSKINS	80	56	29	53	65	73	55	68	63	54	74	82	47	73	57	67	68	67	81	95
68741	HUBBARD	97	79	53	75	86	94	74	86	82	74	98	103	70	98	77	84	92	84	97	114
68742	INMAN	74	51	27	48	60	67	51	63	58	50	69	76	43	67	53	61	62	62	75	87
68743	JACKSON	98	87	66	83	92	99	81	89	86	81	104	106	79	106	83	88	99	87	97	115
68745	LAUREL	77	56	34	54	63	74	60	68	68	58	80	79	53	76	60	71	73	68	82	87
68746	LYNCH	74	51	27	49	60	67	51	63	59	50	69	76	43	67	53	61	63	62	75	88
68747	MCLEAN	97	68	35	64	79	88	67	82	77	66	90	99	57	88	69	81	82	81	98	115
68748	MADISON	79	65	47	64	70	78	66	73	71	65	86	84	62	85	66	73	80	71	80	90
68749	MAGNET	78	55	29	52	64	71	54	67	62	53	73	81	46	72	56	65	67	66	80	93
68751	MASKELL	87	61	32	57	71	79	60	74	69	59	81	89	51	79	62	72	74	73	88	103
68752	MEADOW GROVE	77	57	34	54	65	72	56	67	63	55	74	80	50	74	58	66	69	66	78	91
68753	MILLS	59	41	21	39	48	53	40	50	47	40	55	60	35	54	42	49	50	49	60	70
68755	NAPER	53	40	26	38	43	52	44	48	49	42	58	54	39	55	43	52	53	48	58	58
68756	NELIGH	84	60	35	57	68	79	63	74	72	61	84	86	55	81	64	75	77	73	88	96
68757	NEWCASTLE	76	53	28	50	62	69	52	65	60	52	71	78	45	69	54	63	65	64	77	90
68758	NEWMAN GROVE	81	60	39	58	67	79	66	73	74	63	87	83	58	82	65	78	79	73	88	91
68759	NEWPORT	76	53	28	50	62	69	52	65	60	52	71	78	45	69	54	63	64	64	77	90
68760	NIOBRARA	56	47	35	46	49	57	49	53	52	48	63	60	46	62	48	54	59	52	58	62
68761	OAKDALE	59	41	22	39	48	54	41	51	47	40	55	61	35	54	42	50	50	50	60	71
68763	ONEILL	79	57	33	54	64	74	59	69	67	57	78	81	51	76	60	70	72	68	82	91
68764	ORCHARD	62	45	28	43	51	60	49	55	55	47	65	63	43	62	49	58	59	55	66	69
68765	OSMOND	95	66	35	63	77	86	65	81	75	65	88	97	56	87	68	79	81	80	96	113
68766	PAGE	73	51	27	48	59	66	50	62	58	50	68	75	43	66	52	61	62	61	74	86
68767	PIERCE	92	67	39	64	77	85	66	80	74	66	88	96	58	87	68	77	81	79	93	109
68768	PILGER	82	61	36	57	69	76	59	71	66	58	78	85	52	78	61	69	72	69	82	97
68769	PLAINVIEW	75	55	34	52	61	72	59	67	66	56	78	77	52	74	59	70	71	67	80	84
68770	PONCA	88	62	33	59	72	81	61	76	70	61	83	91	52	81	64	74	75	74	90	105
68771	RANDOLPH	94	66	34	62	77	86	65	81	75	64	88	97	56	86	68	79	80	79	96	112
68773	ROYAL	75	53	28	50	61	69	52	64	60	52	71	78	45	69	54	63	64	64	77	89
68774	SAINT HELENA	89	62	33	59	72	81	61	76	71	61	83	92	52	81	64	74	76	75	90	106
68776	SOUTH SIOUX CITY	76	71	68	70	72	78	74	75	76	73	94	86	72	93	73	76	91	76	76	85
68777	SPENCER	72	51	27	48	59	66	50	62	58	50	68	74	43	67	52	61	62	61	74	86
68778	SPRINGVIEW	59	41	21	39	48	54	41	50	47	40	55	60	35	54	42	49	50	49	60	70
68779	STANTON	73	58	41	57	63	71	59	66	64	58	77	77	55	76	59	66	72	65	74	83
68780	STUART	86	60	31	57	70	78	59	73	68	59	80	88	51	79	61	72	73	72	87	102
68781	TILDEN	75	55	32	52	62	71	57	67	65	55	76	77	50	73	58	68	69	66	79	87
68783	VERDIGRE	59	45	30	43	49	58	49	54	55	47	65	61	44	61	49	58	59	54	65	65
68784	WAKEFIELD	77	61	43	60	67	75	62	70	68	61	81	81	57	80	63	70	76	69	78	88
68785	WATERBURY	76	62	46	62	66	75	64	69	68	63	83	80	60	82	64	70	77	68	77	85
68786	WAUSA	75	53	28	50	61	69	52	64	60	51	70	77	44	69	54	63	64	63	76	89
68787	WAYNE	68	57	62	61	59	64	68	65	69	65	85	81	63	82	64	66	82	70	65	76
68788	WEST POINT	86	66	43	64	72	83	68	77	75	66	89	89	61	87	68	78	82	76	88	98
68789	WINNETOON	60	45	30	43	50	59	50	55	56	48	66	62	45	62	50	59	60	55	66	67
68790	WINSIDE	75	52	27	49	61	68	52	64	59	51	70	77	44	68	53	62	63	63	76	89
68791	WISNER	84	58	31	55	68	76	58	71	66	57	78	86	49	76	60	70	71	70	85	99
68792	WYNOT	92	64	34	61	75	84	64	79	73	63	86	95	54	84	66	77	78	78	94	109
68801	GRAND ISLAND	74	73	75	73	73	78	75	75	75	74	94	88	75	94	74	74	91	76	74	84
68803	GRAND ISLAND	74	76	79	76	76	81	75	75	75	74	93	88	76	95	75	74	90	75	75	85
68810	ALDA	99	87	66	83	92	99	81	90	86	82	105	107	79	105	83	88	100	88	97	116
68812	AMHERST	91	63	33	60	74	83	62	77	72	62	84	93	53	83	65	76	77	76	92	108
68813	ANSELMO	71	50	26	47	58	65	49	61	57	49	67	73	42	65	51	60	61	60	72	85
68814	ANSLEY	67	50	31	48	55	65	54	61	61	52	71	69	48	68	54	64	65	61	73	76
68815	ARCADIA	75	52	27	49	61	68	52	64	59	51	70	77	44	68	53	62	64	63	76	89
68816	ARCHER	88	61	32	58	71	80	60	75	70	60	82	90	52	80	63	73	74	74	89	104
68817	ASHTON	68	53	36	48	60	67	50	61	57	50	67	71	45	66	54	61	63	60	72	83
68818	AURORA	86	67	45	65	74	83	68	77	75	66	89	90	62	88	69	77	82	76	88	100
68819	BERWYN	92	64	34	61	75	84	63	78	73	63	86	94	54	84	66	77	78	77	93	109
68820	BOELUS	73	51	27	48	59	66	50	62	58	50	68	75	43	67	52	61	62	61	74	86
68821	BREWSTER	61	43	22	40	50	56	42	52	49	42	57	63	36	56	44	51	52	51	62	73
68822	BROKEN BOW	78	62	48	61	68	77	65	72	71	63	85	84	60	81	66	73	78	72	82	89
68823	BURWELL	63	46	28	44	51	60	49	56	56	47	66	64	43	63	50	59	60	56	67	71
68824	CAIRO	87	61	32	58	71	80	60	75	69	60	82	90	51	80	63	73	74	74	89	104
68825	CALLAWAY	70	51	31	49	58	67	55	63	62	53	73	72	48	70	55	65	66	62	75	80
68826	CENTRAL CITY	74	63	54	63	67	75	66	71	70	65	84	82	62	82	66	71	79	71	77	84
68827	CHAPMAN	79	57	32	54	65	73	56	68	63	55	75	82	49	74	58	66	68	67	80	93
68828	COMSTOCK	102	71	37	67	83	93	70	87	81	70	95	105	60	93	73	85	87	86	104	121
68831	DANNEBROG	75	52	27	50	61	68	52	64	60	51	70	77	44	69	54	63	64	63	76	89
68832	DONIPHAN	95	83	62	79	88	95	77	86	82	77	100	103	75	102	79	85	94	84	94	112
68833	DUNNING	61	43	22	40	50	56	42	52	49	42	57	63	36	56	44	51	52	51	62	73
68834	EDDYVILLE	82	57	30	54	67	75	57	70	65	56	77	84	48	75	59	69	70	69	83	98
68835	ELBA	77	54	28	51	63	70	53	66	61	53	72	79	45	71	55	64	66	65	78	92
68836	ELM CREEK	82	68	50	67	72	81	69	75	73	68	89	87	64	88	69	75	83	74	82	92
68837	ELYRIA	74	52	27	49	60	67	51	63	59	50	69	76	43	67	53	62	63	62	75	88
68838	FARWELL	76	53	28	50	62	69	53	65	61	52	71	78	45	70	55	64	65	64	77	91
68840	GIBBON	79	64	44	62	69	77	63	71	69	62	83	83	59	82	64	71	77	70	80	91
68841	GILTNER	119	83	43	78	97	108	82	101	95	81	111	122	70	109	85	99	101	100	121	141
68842	GREELEY	69	48	25	45	56	62	47	58	54	47	64	70	40	63	49	57	58	58	70	81
68843	HAMPTON	103	72	38	68	84	94	71	88	82	70	96	106	61	94	74	86	87	87	105	122
68844	HAZARD	73	51	27	48	59	66	50	62	58	50	68	75	43	66	52	61	62	61	74	86
68845	KEARNEY	77	78	89	81	78	81	84	80	81	82	102	97	83	101	81	77	99	83	74	89
68846	HORDVILLE	116	81	42	77	94	106	80	99	92	79	108	119	68	106	83	97	99	98	118	138
68847	KEARNEY	70	71	74	71	71	75	72	72	71	71	88	84	72	89	71	69	86	72	69	81
68849	KEARNEY	77	48	60	54	47	57	91	67	89	77	111	94	75	100	73	78	104	82	63	77
68850	LEXINGTON	82	70	60	68	71	76	73	78	76	76	95	89	68	91	71	75	93	79	77	89
	NEBRASKA	88	81	77	81	83	90	83	85	84	82	104	101	80	103	82	84	100	86	87	100
	UNITED STATES	100	100	100	100	100	100	100	100	100	100	100	100	100	100	100	100	100	100	100	100

NEBRASKA
A
68852-69030

POPULATION CHANGE

ZIP CODE			POPULATION			2000-2004 ANNUAL RATE		HOUSEHOLDS					FAMILIES		
#	POST OFFICE NAME	COUNTY FIPS CODE	2000	2004	2009	% Rate	State Centile	2000	2004	2009	% Annual Rate 2000-2004	2004 Average HH Size	2000	2004	% Annual Rate 2000-2004
68852	LITCHFIELD	163	544	517	491	-1.2	1	217	211	205	-0.7	2.45	157	153	-0.6
68853	LOUP CITY	163	1556	1492	1424	-1.0	3	676	662	645	-0.5	2.17	420	412	-0.5
68854	MARQUETTE	081	784	821	842	1.1	86	295	313	323	1.4	2.62	246	261	1.4
68855	MASON CITY	041	478	482	484	0.2	64	191	195	198	0.5	2.47	146	149	0.5
68856	MERNA	041	924	931	936	0.2	63	367	374	380	0.5	2.48	278	284	0.5
68858	MILLER	019	321	322	329	0.1	59	130	133	137	0.5	2.42	94	96	0.5
68859	NORTH LOUP	175	562	549	539	-0.6	18	241	238	236	-0.3	2.31	165	164	-0.1
68860	OCONTO	041	509	514	517	0.2	66	214	218	222	0.4	2.36	159	163	0.6
68861	ODESSA	019	132	133	135	0.2	63	53	54	56	0.4	2.46	43	44	0.5
68862	ORD	175	3277	3229	3177	-0.4	33	1391	1387	1380	-0.1	2.27	896	897	0.0
68863	OVERTON	047	1209	1182	1176	-0.5	20	470	460	455	-0.5	2.57	349	342	-0.5
68864	PALMER	121	1002	1029	1040	0.6	78	386	401	409	0.9	2.51	277	288	0.9
68865	PHILLIPS	081	933	966	982	0.8	82	343	359	368	1.1	2.69	283	296	1.1
68866	PLEASANTON	019	1009	1037	1071	0.7	79	376	391	408	0.9	2.65	286	297	0.9
68869	RAVENNA	019	2042	2077	2133	0.4	72	816	836	866	0.6	2.41	556	570	0.6
68870	RIVERDALE	019	477	503	526	1.3	88	175	187	198	1.6	2.69	144	154	1.6
68871	ROCKVILLE	163	462	447	427	-0.8	7	183	182	178	-0.1	2.46	131	130	-0.2
68872	SAINT LIBORY	093	953	946	957	-0.2	45	325	328	335	0.2	2.88	257	260	0.3
68873	SAINT PAUL	093	3215	3244	3307	0.2	65	1307	1329	1367	0.4	2.41	867	884	0.5
68874	SARGENT	041	913	911	913	-0.1	51	382	385	389	0.2	2.26	252	254	0.2
68875	SCOTIA	077	637	623	608	-0.5	20	256	254	252	-0.2	2.40	175	175	0.0
68876	SHELTON	019	1772	1792	1834	0.3	66	652	660	679	0.3	2.70	480	486	0.3
68878	SUMNER	047	452	440	437	-0.6	13	179	174	172	-0.7	2.53	132	129	-0.5
68879	TAYLOR	115	712	724	724	0.4	72	289	296	296	0.6	2.45	207	212	0.6
68881	WESTERVILLE	041	175	176	176	0.1	61	66	67	68	0.4	2.63	50	50	0.0
68882	WOLBACH	077	504	493	484	-0.5	20	215	214	213	-0.1	2.26	149	149	0.0
68883	WOOD RIVER	079	2459	2455	2466	0.0	52	930	941	954	0.3	2.54	681	690	0.3
68901	HASTINGS	001	26648	26998	27484	0.3	69	10467	10668	10918	0.5	2.38	6668	6818	0.5
68920	ALMA	083	1557	1540	1528	-0.3	40	658	657	658	0.0	2.28	424	425	0.1
68922	ARAPAHOE	065	1329	1382	1411	0.9	84	569	596	609	1.1	2.26	368	387	1.2
68923	ATLANTA	137	150	154	158	0.6	78	60	62	64	0.8	2.48	47	48	0.5
68924	AXTELL	099	1296	1302	1300	0.1	60	427	434	439	0.4	2.85	320	326	0.4
68925	AYR	001	521	522	528	0.1	58	191	194	198	0.4	2.69	150	152	0.3
68926	BEAVER CITY	065	793	770	761	-0.7	10	346	339	336	-0.5	2.17	215	211	-0.4
68927	BERTRAND	137	1326	1362	1396	0.6	78	493	513	532	0.9	2.59	352	367	1.0
68928	BLADEN	181	537	521	500	-0.7	9	210	205	199	-0.6	2.54	159	155	-0.5
68929	BLOOMINGTON	061	382	368	353	-0.9	4	162	157	152	-0.7	2.31	112	109	-0.6
68930	BLUE HILL	181	1466	1437	1392	-0.5	24	561	555	542	-0.3	2.45	394	390	-0.2
68932	CAMPBELL	061	458	438	420	-1.1	2	179	171	164	-1.1	2.39	131	125	-1.1
68933	CLAY CENTER	035	1105	1113	1137	0.2	63	430	436	449	0.3	2.54	309	314	0.4
68934	DEWEESE	035	283	285	291	0.2	63	112	114	117	0.4	2.50	82	84	0.6
68935	EDGAR	035	755	748	758	-0.2	42	316	316	323	0.0	2.28	206	206	0.0
68936	EDISON	065	282	276	274	-0.5	22	109	107	107	-0.4	2.52	76	75	-0.3
68937	ELWOOD	073	2021	2094	2149	0.8	82	851	891	919	1.1	2.29	635	665	1.1
68938	FAIRFIELD	035	567	566	578	0.0	52	221	222	229	0.1	2.55	164	165	0.1
68939	FRANKLIN	061	1194	1150	1105	-0.9	4	507	491	473	-0.8	2.21	327	317	-0.7
68940	FUNK	137	526	537	548	0.5	75	194	200	207	0.7	2.68	153	159	0.9
68941	GLENVIL	035	746	765	787	0.6	77	281	291	302	0.8	2.63	212	220	0.9
68942	GUIDE ROCK	181	460	438	418	-1.2	1	224	217	210	-0.7	1.92	137	133	-0.7
68943	HARDY	129	410	400	389	-0.6	16	156	155	154	-0.2	2.58	115	114	-0.2
68944	HARVARD	035	1376	1382	1409	0.1	60	521	530	546	0.4	2.56	384	391	0.4
68945	HEARTWELL	099	235	232	230	-0.3	37	90	90	91	0.0	2.58	67	67	0.0
68946	HENDLEY	065	187	181	178	-0.8	8	69	68	67	-0.3	2.66	50	49	-0.5
68947	HILDRETH	061	625	604	580	-0.8	7	266	258	249	-0.7	2.34	193	187	-0.7
68948	HOLBROOK	065	357	346	342	-0.7	8	153	150	149	-0.5	2.31	105	103	-0.5
68949	HOLDREGE	137	6869	6944	7059	0.3	66	2750	2812	2889	0.5	2.39	1850	1897	0.6
68950	HOLSTEIN	001	416	419	424	0.2	63	159	162	165	0.4	2.59	126	128	0.4
68952	INAVALE	181	192	183	174	-1.1	1	76	73	71	-0.9	2.36	46	44	-1.0
68954	INLAND	035	113	114	116	0.2	65	45	46	47	0.5	2.43	32	33	0.7
68955	JUNIATA	001	1318	1355	1386	0.7	79	478	496	511	0.9	2.72	377	391	0.9
68956	KENESAW	001	1161	1180	1199	0.4	72	427	438	448	0.6	2.59	320	328	0.6
68957	LAWRENCE	129	596	583	568	-0.5	20	244	243	242	-0.1	2.40	170	170	0.0
68958	LOOMIS	137	654	671	687	0.6	77	255	264	274	0.8	2.52	198	205	0.8
68959	MINDEN	099	4162	4163	4152	0.0	56	1641	1656	1666	0.2	2.42	1153	1166	0.3
68960	NAPONEE	061	324	313	300	-0.8	6	136	132	128	-0.7	2.36	94	92	-0.5
68961	NELSON	129	987	965	941	-0.5	20	426	423	420	-0.2	2.21	273	272	-0.1
68964	OAK	129	270	264	257	-0.5	20	110	109	108	-0.2	2.34	70	70	0.0
68966	ORLEANS	083	689	690	688	0.0	57	297	300	302	0.2	2.30	184	186	0.3
68967	OXFORD	065	1291	1271	1261	-0.4	32	542	537	534	-0.2	2.32	377	375	-0.1
68969	RAGAN	083	99	98	98	-0.2	41	37	37	37	0.0	2.65	26	26	0.0
68970	RED CLOUD	181	1516	1455	1392	-1.0	3	680	663	643	-0.6	2.12	418	408	-0.6
68971	REPUBLICAN CITY	083	536	530	525	-0.3	40	251	250	250	-0.1	2.06	166	166	0.0
68972	RIVERTON	061	319	308	296	-0.8	5	131	128	123	-0.5	2.38	89	87	-0.5
68973	ROSELAND	001	577	576	582	0.0	52	225	228	232	0.3	2.53	177	179	0.3
68974	RUSKIN	129	292	284	276	-0.7	12	117	116	115	-0.2	2.45	87	86	-0.3
68975	SARONVILLE	035	225	223	227	-0.2	43	80	80	83	0.0	2.79	65	65	0.0
68976	SMITHFIELD	073	287	285	287	-0.2	46	121	122	124	0.2	2.32	93	93	0.0
68977	STAMFORD	083	408	405	403	-0.2	45	167	168	168	0.1	2.40	118	119	0.2
68978	SUPERIOR	129	2413	2361	2303	-0.5	21	1129	1127	1122	0.0	2.09	708	710	0.1
68979	SUTTON	035	1828	1950	2055	1.5	90	726	782	832	1.8	2.45	518	560	1.9
68980	TRUMBULL	035	407	410	417	0.2	63	143	146	150	0.5	2.75	104	106	0.5
68981	UPLAND	061	272	263	252	-0.8	7	104	101	97	-0.7	2.58	75	73	-0.6
68982	WILCOX	099	560	564	565	0.2	63	220	224	227	0.4	2.41	165	168	0.4
69001	MC COOK	145	9345	9522	9760	0.4	74	3875	4005	4161	0.8	2.31	2574	2669	0.9
69020	BARTLEY	145	509	522	537	0.6	77	191	197	204	0.7	2.65	137	141	0.7
69021	BENKELMAN	057	1510	1473	1444	-0.6	16	662	651	644	-0.4	2.16	424	417	-0.4
69022	CAMBRIDGE	065	1367	1353	1348	-0.2	41	599	598	599	0.0	2.20	377	377	0.0
69023	CHAMPION	029	569	559	553	-0.4	28	231	231	232	0.0	2.42	174	174	0.0
69024	CULBERTSON	087	1208	1169	1139	-0.8	7	487	478	472	-0.4	2.44	363	358	-0.3
69025	CURTIS	063	1212	1216	1216	0.1	59	445	451	453	0.3	2.40	282	287	0.4
69026	DANBURY	145	251	251	255	0.0	56	105	107	110	0.2	2.35	81	82	0.3
69027	ENDERS	029	212	209	206	-0.3	35	89	89	89	0.0	2.31	64	64	0.0
69028	EUSTIS	063	847	841	837	-0.2	45	343	345	347	0.1	2.44	242	244	0.2
69029	FARNAM	047	284	281	280	-0.3	41	120	119	118	-0.2	2.36	89	88	-0.3
69030	HAIGLER	057	418	414	409	-0.2	42	157	157	157	0.0	2.55	114	114	0.0
	NEBRASKA					0.8					1.0	2.47			1.1
	UNITED STATES					1.2					1.3	2.58			1.1

183-A

#	POST OFFICE NAME	RACE (%) White 2000	White 2004	Black 2000	Black 2004	Asian/Pacific 2000	Asian/Pacific 2004	% Hispanic Origin 2000	% Hispanic Origin 2004	2004 AGE DISTRIBUTION (%) 0-4	5-9	10-14	15-19	20-24	25-44	45-64	65-84	85+	18+	MEDIAN AGE 2004	% 2004 Males	% 2004 Females
68852	LITCHFIELD	99.6	99.6	0.0	0.0	0.0	0.0	1.1	1.0	6.0	6.0	6.8	5.8	4.8	21.1	30.0	16.3	3.3	78.0	44.7	50.3	49.7
68853	LOUP CITY	97.9	97.7	0.1	0.1	0.5	0.6	1.1	1.2	5.2	5.4	6.8	6.8	5.3	20.5	23.8	20.8	5.2	78.2	44.9	46.7	53.4
68854	MARQUETTE	98.5	98.4	0.1	0.1	0.1	0.1	1.0	1.1	6.9	7.9	9.6	6.6	5.2	24.0	28.3	10.5	1.0	71.0	38.4	53.0	47.0
68855	MASON CITY	98.3	98.3	0.0	0.0	0.0	0.0	0.8	1.0	7.3	7.5	7.9	7.3	5.2	24.7	25.1	13.1	2.1	72.6	38.3	51.0	49.0
68856	MERNA	99.1	99.0	0.1	0.1	0.1	0.1	0.8	0.9	5.1	5.7	8.3	7.0	5.7	22.6	29.0	14.8	1.9	76.7	42.4	51.7	48.3
68858	MILLER	100.0	100.0	0.0	0.0	0.0	0.0	0.0	0.0	6.2	6.8	7.5	6.8	5.3	25.8	28.3	12.1	1.2	75.8	39.7	55.0	45.0
68859	NORTH LOUP	97.9	97.8	0.0	0.0	0.0	0.0	1.4	1.3	5.3	6.0	7.3	6.9	4.7	20.8	28.1	18.0	2.9	77.1	44.3	50.8	49.2
68860	OCONTO	98.8	99.0	0.0	0.0	0.0	0.0	1.2	1.4	5.3	6.2	8.8	7.0	4.7	23.2	28.6	15.0	1.4	75.5	41.8	53.3	46.7
68861	ODESSA	96.2	95.5	0.0	0.0	0.8	1.5	4.6	5.3	6.8	7.5	9.0	7.5	6.8	26.3	28.6	7.5	0.0	72.2	35.9	50.4	49.6
68862	ORD	98.0	98.0	0.2	0.2	0.2	0.2	1.8	1.9	5.4	5.7	6.7	6.3	5.4	19.7	26.5	19.4	4.9	77.8	45.5	47.0	53.0
68863	OVERTON	94.7	93.5	0.2	0.3	0.3	0.3	6.4	7.9	6.9	7.4	8.5	6.9	6.1	25.6	26.3	10.7	1.7	72.9	37.6	54.0	46.0
68864	PALMER	98.5	98.5	0.1	0.1	0.1	0.1	1.6	1.7	5.6	6.1	8.4	7.3	5.8	24.3	23.8	15.7	2.9	74.7	40.8	49.8	50.2
68865	PHILLIPS	98.9	99.1	0.0	0.0	0.0	0.0	1.3	1.2	7.4	8.2	7.6	5.7	5.9	26.7	29.0	8.9	0.7	72.9	38.1	52.6	47.4
68866	PLEASANTON	98.8	98.8	0.1	0.1	0.2	0.3	0.9	1.1	6.3	6.7	7.4	6.5	5.2	25.0	27.2	14.4	1.5	75.7	40.4	51.8	48.2
68869	RAVENNA	98.9	98.7	0.1	0.1	0.2	0.3	0.8	0.9	6.1	6.4	8.0	7.3	5.8	23.6	23.6	14.6	4.6	75.0	40.0	47.0	53.0
68870	RIVERDALE	99.6	99.6	0.2	0.2	0.0	0.0	0.4	0.4	4.6	5.2	7.2	7.6	6.0	28.0	29.6	10.9	1.0	78.3	40.4	52.5	47.5
68871	ROCKVILLE	98.5	98.4	0.0	0.0	0.2	0.2	1.1	1.1	5.6	5.8	6.7	6.3	4.7	22.2	28.9	17.5	2.5	77.9	44.1	52.1	47.9
68872	SAINT LIBORY	98.5	98.5	0.1	0.1	0.0	0.0	1.3	1.4	7.7	8.0	8.4	6.7	5.4	27.0	24.7	11.5	0.6	71.9	37.2	51.4	48.6
68873	SAINT PAUL	99.0	98.9	0.3	0.4	0.1	0.2	0.8	0.9	6.8	6.5	7.6	7.5	6.5	23.2	22.6	15.8	3.6	74.3	39.5	50.0	50.0
68874	SARGENT	98.3	98.2	0.0	0.0	0.3	0.3	1.5	1.7	5.2	5.6	7.0	7.1	5.7	18.7	24.8	19.3	6.6	77.4	45.5	48.7	51.3
68875	SCOTIA	97.3	97.1	1.3	1.3	0.2	0.2	0.8	0.8	5.9	6.4	8.0	6.4	5.5	21.0	25.4	17.0	4.3	75.0	42.6	51.2	48.8
68876	SHELTON	91.3	90.0	0.6	0.6	0.0	0.0	12.6	14.9	7.8	8.0	8.5	6.9	4.9	26.6	23.7	11.6	2.1	71.1	36.9	50.0	50.0
68878	SUMNER	97.4	96.4	0.7	0.9	0.2	0.2	4.0	5.2	8.2	8.2	7.1	5.9	5.5	25.2	24.6	13.2	2.3	72.7	37.7	51.1	48.9
68879	TAYLOR	98.9	98.9	0.0	0.0	0.1	0.1	1.7	1.7	6.2	6.8	6.5	7.2	4.6	20.2	28.9	17.5	2.2	76.0	44.1	52.2	47.8
68881	WESTERVILLE	99.4	99.4	0.0	0.0	0.0	0.0	0.6	0.6	6.3	6.3	9.7	6.3	5.7	21.6	26.1	16.5	1.7	73.9	41.4	52.3	47.7
68882	WOLBACH	98.4	98.6	0.4	0.4	0.0	0.0	0.8	0.8	6.1	6.5	7.5	6.7	5.5	22.3	24.3	17.9	3.3	75.5	41.9	49.5	50.5
68883	WOOD RIVER	97.6	97.1	0.2	0.2	0.2	0.2	7.2	8.9	6.6	7.1	7.7	6.2	4.6	26.0	25.0	14.1	2.9	74.4	40.0	50.8	49.3
68901	HASTINGS	93.9	92.7	0.7	0.8	1.9	2.5	5.2	6.1	6.4	6.1	6.7	7.8	8.3	25.7	23.1	12.8	3.1	77.1	36.7	49.0	51.0
68920	ALMA	99.1	99.1	0.1	0.1	0.1	0.1	0.6	0.5	4.8	5.3	6.8	5.7	4.7	18.3	29.0	21.0	4.5	79.4	48.0	48.7	51.3
68922	ARAPAHOE	97.9	97.8	0.0	0.0	0.5	0.5	1.4	1.4	5.8	6.1	7.5	6.1	5.3	20.0	24.2	19.3	5.8	76.6	44.4	44.9	55.1
68923	ATLANTA	98.7	98.7	0.0	0.0	0.0	0.0	0.7	0.7	5.8	7.1	8.4	7.1	5.8	24.0	27.3	13.0	1.3	73.4	40.4	52.6	47.4
68924	AXTELL	98.2	98.1	0.2	0.2	0.3	0.3	1.5	1.5	7.1	7.5	7.9	6.6	5.8	27.7	25.8	10.4	1.3	72.5	37.5	52.0	48.0
68925	AYR	97.7	97.3	0.0	0.0	0.4	0.6	1.3	1.5	6.9	7.1	7.5	6.3	4.8	26.6	28.7	10.5	1.5	74.5	39.5	51.5	48.5
68926	BEAVER CITY	98.1	98.1	0.3	0.3	0.0	0.0	1.8	1.8	4.8	5.2	6.9	6.1	5.7	17.3	27.8	20.5	5.7	78.8	47.4	46.1	53.9
68927	BERTRAND	99.2	99.1	0.1	0.1	0.2	0.2	0.6	0.7	6.0	6.3	7.3	6.7	6.0	22.4	28.1	13.6	3.7	75.8	42.1	50.6	49.4
68928	BLADEN	98.9	98.5	0.0	0.0	0.4	0.6	0.2	0.4	7.3	7.5	8.8	6.9	4.4	24.6	25.5	13.8	1.2	72.0	39.4	50.1	49.9
68929	BLOOMINGTON	99.2	98.9	0.0	0.0	0.0	0.3	0.5	0.8	6.0	6.5	7.6	6.0	4.4	22.3	25.8	18.8	2.7	76.1	43.1	50.0	50.0
68930	BLUE HILL	98.0	97.6	0.2	0.2	0.5	0.6	0.7	0.8	5.5	5.8	7.6	6.3	5.0	21.2	25.5	19.0	4.2	77.0	44.1	47.7	52.3
68932	CAMPBELL	98.9	98.6	0.0	0.0	0.0	0.0	0.4	0.5	5.9	5.9	5.7	5.3	5.7	22.8	21.7	21.2	5.7	79.2	44.0	48.6	51.4
68933	CLAY CENTER	96.7	96.1	0.5	0.7	0.7	1.0	2.5	3.1	6.8	6.8	7.3	6.7	6.2	22.7	28.2	13.8	1.4	74.3	41.0	48.6	51.4
68934	DEWEESE	98.6	98.3	0.0	0.0	0.7	0.7	0.4	0.4	6.7	7.0	7.0	6.3	6.3	27.4	26.7	11.6	1.1	75.8	38.2	50.5	49.5
68935	EDGAR	98.4	98.3	0.3	0.3	0.1	0.1	0.9	1.2	5.8	5.8	6.4	5.1	4.6	22.6	26.5	18.9	4.6	78.3	44.9	51.1	48.9
68936	EDISON	98.2	97.8	0.0	0.0	0.4	0.4	0.7	0.7	6.2	6.5	6.5	6.2	5.1	21.4	28.3	17.4	2.5	76.8	43.9	50.0	50.0
68937	ELWOOD	98.5	98.3	0.1	0.1	0.3	0.3	2.1	2.4	4.9	5.3	6.8	6.0	4.6	22.2	28.3	18.7	3.3	78.8	45.2	50.5	49.5
68938	FAIRFIELD	98.6	98.6	0.2	0.2	0.0	0.0	1.2	1.4	6.0	6.4	7.1	8.0	5.3	22.8	26.5	16.1	1.9	75.6	41.6	50.2	49.8
68939	FRANKLIN	99.5	99.4	0.0	0.0	0.1	0.2	0.8	0.9	4.9	5.1	6.7	6.1	4.6	18.4	24.8	22.4	7.0	78.9	48.0	44.8	55.2
68940	FUNK	98.3	98.0	0.0	0.0	0.4	0.4	1.5	1.7	5.8	7.8	8.8	7.1	5.8	26.3	26.6	11.2	0.7	72.8	38.6	52.7	47.3
68941	GLENVIL	98.7	98.6	0.0	0.0	0.4	0.5	0.4	0.7	5.9	6.3	7.2	6.4	5.8	26.5	28.5	12.0	1.4	76.7	40.2	51.1	48.9
68942	GUIDE ROCK	98.5	98.4	0.2	0.2	0.2	0.2	0.0	0.0	4.8	4.8	5.3	5.7	4.6	21.0	30.4	20.3	3.2	81.3	47.4	50.7	49.3
68943	HARDY	98.5	98.0	0.0	0.0	0.2	0.5	1.2	1.8	5.3	5.5	7.3	6.8	6.5	21.5	28.8	16.5	2.0	78.0	43.0	50.5	49.5
68944	HARVARD	96.9	96.2	0.1	0.1	0.1	0.1	7.1	8.3	6.1	6.8	8.4	7.2	5.6	23.8	26.9	13.3	2.0	74.0	40.4	49.3	50.7
68945	HEARTWELL	95.3	95.7	0.0	0.0	0.4	0.4	3.8	4.3	6.0	6.9	7.8	5.6	5.2	25.4	30.2	12.1	0.9	75.4	41.0	53.0	47.0
68946	HENDLEY	98.4	98.3	0.0	0.0	0.0	0.0	1.6	1.7	6.6	7.2	7.7	5.5	5.0	23.8	27.1	15.5	1.7	75.1	40.6	52.5	47.5
68947	HILDRETH	99.2	99.2	0.0	0.0	0.0	0.0	0.8	0.8	5.6	6.1	7.3	6.6	5.0	25.5	26.5	15.1	2.3	76.7	41.7	51.0	49.0
68948	HOLBROOK	98.3	98.0	0.0	0.0	0.3	0.3	1.1	1.2	6.4	6.9	6.4	5.2	5.5	22.5	26.6	18.2	2.3	77.2	42.6	52.0	48.0
68949	HOLDREGE	97.3	96.9	0.2	0.2	0.3	0.4	2.8	3.4	6.4	6.7	7.1	6.5	5.9	23.7	25.2	15.0	3.6	75.7	40.8	48.4	51.6
68950	HOLSTEIN	98.6	98.6	0.0	0.0	0.0	0.0	1.2	1.4	6.9	7.2	7.6	6.4	4.8	26.7	27.7	11.2	1.4	74.0	39.4	52.7	47.3
68952	INAVALE	98.4	98.4	0.0	0.0	0.0	0.6	0.0	0.0	4.4	4.4	4.9	5.5	4.4	19.7	31.7	21.9	3.3	82.0	49.2	51.4	48.6
68954	INLAND	97.4	96.5	0.0	0.0	0.0	0.0	6.2	7.0	7.0	7.0	7.9	7.0	6.1	22.8	25.4	14.0	2.6	72.8	38.6	50.0	50.0
68955	JUNIATA	98.7	98.5	0.2	0.4	0.2	0.2	0.9	1.3	7.0	7.6	8.6	7.5	6.4	25.5	27.7	8.9	0.9	72.0	37.2	49.7	50.3
68956	KENESAW	98.8	98.7	0.0	0.0	0.0	0.0	1.3	1.6	6.8	7.5	7.8	5.4	5.0	24.8	25.7	13.9	3.1	73.9	40.2	50.7	49.3
68957	LAWRENCE	99.0	99.0	0.0	0.0	0.0	0.0	0.7	0.7	6.2	5.7	6.9	8.1	3.6	21.8	25.7	19.4	2.7	75.5	43.8	51.3	48.7
68958	LOOMIS	98.8	98.5	0.0	0.0	0.2	0.3	0.9	1.0	6.3	7.3	8.6	6.9	6.0	24.9	25.9	12.5	1.6	72.9	39.6	52.0	48.0
68959	MINDEN	97.9	97.9	0.1	0.1	0.2	0.2	2.6	2.6	6.0	6.1	6.9	6.6	5.6	24.5	25.5	14.8	4.0	76.7	41.2	48.8	51.2
68960	NAPONEE	99.1	99.0	0.0	0.0	0.0	0.3	0.6	0.6	6.1	6.7	7.7	6.1	4.2	22.4	27.2	17.9	1.9	75.7	43.0	51.1	48.9
68961	NELSON	99.2	99.1	0.0	0.0	0.1	0.1	1.1	1.2	4.6	5.0	6.2	6.6	5.7	21.9	27.8	17.4	4.9	79.6	45.0	50.6	49.4
68964	OAK	99.3	99.2	0.0	0.0	0.0	0.0	1.1	1.1	4.6	4.9	6.1	6.4	5.7	22.0	28.0	17.4	4.9	79.9	45.2	50.0	50.0
68966	ORLEANS	98.3	98.3	0.3	0.3	0.2	0.1	1.0	0.9	4.8	5.2	6.7	6.1	4.6	20.7	29.4	18.7	3.8	79.4	46.1	50.1	49.9
68967	OXFORD	98.2	98.3	0.0	0.0	0.2	0.2	0.8	0.8	6.1	6.3	6.6	6.8	5.4	21.4	28.6	16.4	2.4	76.5	43.4	50.9	49.1
68969	RAGAN	99.0	99.0	0.0	0.0	0.0	0.0	1.0	0.0	6.1	6.1	8.2	9.2	5.1	21.4	27.6	14.3	2.0	73.5	41.3	53.1	46.9
68970	RED CLOUD	97.8	97.5	0.1	0.1	0.7	1.0	0.7	0.8	4.7	5.0	6.3	6.2	4.5	18.7	26.7	21.9	5.9	79.3	48.1	49.0	51.0
68971	REPUBLICAN CITY	99.3	99.3	0.0	0.0	0.0	0.0	0.6	0.8	5.1	5.5	7.0	6.0	4.7	18.3	29.3	20.0	4.2	78.5	47.3	49.8	50.2
68972	RIVERTON	99.1	98.7	0.0	0.0	0.0	0.3	0.6	0.7	6.2	6.5	7.5	5.8	4.2	21.8	26.6	18.8	2.6	76.0	43.6	50.0	50.0
68973	ROSELAND	97.6	97.2	0.0	0.0	0.5	0.7	1.4	1.6	7.1	7.3	7.6	6.3	4.9	27.1	28.1	10.2	1.4	74.3	38.9	52.1	47.9
68974	RUSKIN	98.3	97.9	0.0	0.0	0.3	0.4	1.4	1.8	4.9	5.6	7.4	7.0	6.3	21.5	30.3	15.1	1.8	77.8	43.0	51.8	48.2
68975	SARONVILLE	96.9	96.9	0.0	0.0	0.0	0.0	3.6	4.0	4.5	7.2	9.4	8.5	3.6	26.0	29.6	10.8	0.5	72.2	40.5	52.5	47.5
68976	SMITHFIELD	99.3	99.3	0.0	0.0	0.4	0.4	0.7	0.7	6.0	6.0	5.3	5.6	4.9	21.8	29.8	19.0	1.8	79.0	45.3	51.2	48.8
68977	STAMFORD	98.8	99.0	0.0	0.0	0.0	0.0	1.2	1.0	5.7	6.2	7.7	7.7	5.4	22.5	28.2	14.8	2.0	75.3	42.0	51.9	48.2
68978	SUPERIOR	98.9	98.6	0.0	0.0	0.2	0.3	1.0	1.1	5.3	5.3	5.6	6.3	5.2	18.8	26.4	22.3	4.8	79.7	47.4	46.4	53.6
68979	SUTTON	97.9	97.7	0.1	0.1	0.3	0.4	3.2	3.7	6.2	6.3	7.5	6.8	5.2	21.6	25.4	17.1	3.9	75.4	42.7	48.1	51.9
68980	TRUMBULL	97.1	96.1	0.0	0.2	0.0	0.2	7.1	8.5	6.3	6.8	8.1	7.1	6.1	22.9	26.3	13.9	2.4	74.4	40.3	48.8	51.2
68981	UPLAND	99.3	98.9	0.0	0.0	0.0	0.0	0.7	0.4	5.7	6.1	7.2	6.5	4.9	25.5	25.9	15.6	2.7	76.0	41.8	51.0	49.1
68982	WILCOX	98.4	98.2	0.2	0.2	0.2	0.2	1.3	1.2	7.1	7.3	8.0	6.9	5.9	26.8	26.1	10.8	1.2	72.5	37.9	51.8	48.2
69001	MC COOK	97.4	97.1	0.2	0.2	0.2	0.3	2.6	3.1	6.6	6.2	6.7	6.5	7.1	23.0	24.7	16.0	3.3	76.9	40.5	48.1	51.9
69020	BARTLEY	97.8	97.1	0.4	0.4	0.2	0.4	1.8	2.3	5.9	6.3	8.2	6.9	5.6	23.8	25.9	15.7	1.7	75.1	40.7	50.8	49.2
69021	BENKELMAN	97.4	97.3	0.0	0.0	0.7	0.7	1.7	1.7	5.0	5.3	5.8	5.3	5.6	20.4	28.2	19.2	5.2	80.5	46.6	47.6	52.4
69022	CAMBRIDGE	98.8	98.7	0.0	0.0	0.2	0.2	0.7	0.7	5.1	5.5	6.6	6.1	5.3	19.4	26.8	19.9	5.4	79.1	46.4	48.9	51.1
69023	CHAMPION	98.2	98.2	0.2	0.2	0.0	0.0	1.2	1.3	5.4	5.2	7.7	6.6	4.3	23.4	32.6	13.1	1.8	76.9	43.3	50.6	49.4
69024	CULBERTSON	98.4	98.4	0.2	0.2	0.1	0.1	1.4	1.5	5.3	5.7	6.7	6.8	6.0	21.9	27.0	17.9	2.7	78.3	43.6	49.3	50.7
69025	CURTIS	97.6	97.6	0.2	0.2	0.3	0.3	1.1	1.1	6.3	5.3	6.3	8.4	12.4	22.8	21.8	13.5	3.4	78.9	34.0	48.5	51.5
69026	DANBURY	99.6	99.6	0.0	0.0	0.0	0.0	0.4	0.4	5.6	5.6	10.8	6.4	3.6	22.7	28.3	16.7	0.4	73.7	42.1	51.4	48.6
69027	ENDERS	97.6	97.6	0.0	0.0	0.0	0.0	2.4	1.9	4.8	5.3	6.7	5.7	4.8	23.0	30.1	16.8	2.9	79.4	44.8	48.8	51.2
69028	EUSTIS	98.8	98.9	0.0	0.0	0.2	0.2	1.1	1.2	6.0	6.0	6.9	7.1	6.4	21.3	29.1	14.7	2.5	76.9	42.7	52.1	47.9
69029	FARNAM	98.2	97.9	0.0	0.0	0.0	0.0	1.8	1.8	5.7	5.7	8.5	7.8	5.0	23.1	29.5	12.8	1.8	74.0	40.9	52.7	47.3
69030	HAIGLER	95.9	95.9	0.0	0.0	0.2	0.2	7.7	7.5	6.5	7.3	7.5	6.3	5.6	23.9	29.2	11.8	1.9	74.4	39.6	54.1	45.9
	NEBRASKA	89.6	88.4	4.0	4.2	1.3	1.8	5.5	6.4	7.0	6.9	7.2	7.3	7.6	27.5	23.5	11.2	2.1	74.8	35.7	49.4	50.6
	UNITED STATES	75.1	73.6	12.3	12.5	3.8	4.2	12.5	14.1	6.9	6.7	7.2	7.0	7.3	28.6	23.8	10.8	1.7	75.1	36.0	49.1	50.9

INCOME

#	POST OFFICE NAME	2004 Per Capita Income	2004 HH Income Base	2004 Household Income Distribution (%): Less than $25,000	$25,000 to $49,999	$50,000 to $99,999	$100,000 to $149,999	$150,000 or More	Median Household Income: 2004	2009	2004 National Centile	2004 State Centile	2004 Home Value Base	2004 Home Value Distribution (%): Less than $50,000	$50,000 to $89,999	$90,000 to $174,999	$175,000 to $399,999	$400,000 or More	2004 Median Home Value
68852	LITCHFIELD	15961	211	34.6	43.1	19.0	1.4	1.9	33451	37289	22	21	173	52.0	24.3	15.6	5.2	2.9	47500
68853	LOUP CITY	16556	662	42.6	33.2	21.0	2.4	0.8	29103	33521	11	5	493	52.3	32.9	10.8	3.3	0.8	48309
68854	MARQUETTE	21621	313	18.5	33.6	36.1	9.6	2.2	48161	53545	69	83	244	27.1	21.7	27.9	18.4	4.9	91765
68855	MASON CITY	20134	195	28.2	35.9	28.7	4.6	2.6	38347	44497	41	52	154	44.2	19.5	16.2	13.0	7.1	59000
68856	MERNA	19875	374	29.4	37.7	25.9	4.0	2.9	37310	42729	37	44	288	37.2	23.6	26.4	8.3	4.5	69412
68858	MILLER	19008	133	27.8	33.1	31.6	5.3	2.3	41875	47352	53	69	92	29.4	18.5	33.7	17.4	1.1	92857
68859	NORTH LOUP	16548	238	40.3	39.9	16.0	2.1	1.7	29126	34007	11	6	184	50.0	21.2	19.6	7.6	1.6	50000
68860	OCONTO	18333	218	34.4	34.4	25.7	4.1	1.4	36414	40694	33	40	165	37.6	13.3	32.1	9.1	7.9	88500
68861	ODESSA	26829	54	14.8	31.5	40.7	11.1	1.9	52891	65568	77	90	46	17.4	10.9	39.1	28.3	4.4	135000
68862	ORD	17822	1387	37.4	34.1	23.4	3.5	1.6	32158	37806	18	15	1045	44.0	29.8	21.4	4.3	0.5	57353
68863	OVERTON	17227	460	30.7	39.6	22.8	5.7	1.3	37621	42971	38	46	351	31.3	37.6	23.7	6.0	1.4	72179
68864	PALMER	17495	401	27.7	44.1	23.9	3.0	1.3	36693	40908	34	41	315	33.7	24.4	26.4	11.1	4.4	71250
68865	PHILLIPS	21266	359	17.8	38.7	32.3	7.8	3.3	44249	49586	59	76	287	34.2	23.3	33.8	8.0	0.7	79000
68866	PLEASANTON	17679	391	24.8	36.6	34.3	4.1	0.3	41812	47678	52	68	316	24.1	26.0	30.7	17.4	1.9	90000
68869	RAVENNA	18563	836	28.8	37.4	29.2	3.4	1.2	38380	45259	41	52	632	34.2	33.4	22.5	8.1	1.9	68136
68870	RIVERDALE	23315	187	16.6	31.0	41.7	7.0	3.7	51409	60378	75	88	156	17.3	18.6	34.6	26.9	2.6	119118
68871	ROCKVILLE	16315	182	32.4	46.2	17.0	2.8	1.7	33154	37619	21	19	147	41.5	30.6	16.3	8.2	3.4	61923
68872	SAINT LIBORY	17037	328	24.1	42.1	28.1	4.0	1.8	40704	45876	49	63	261	14.9	26.8	42.2	11.9	4.2	95972
68873	SAINT PAUL	19415	1329	31.7	33.2	27.1	5.9	2.2	38062	44525	39	50	978	22.8	33.5	34.1	7.1	2.6	82250
68874	SARGENT	15308	385	40.0	40.5	16.9	2.3	0.3	29378	34768	11	6	289	68.2	17.3	10.4	2.8	1.4	30795
68875	SCOTIA	15670	254	37.8	36.6	22.1	2.8	0.8	31551	35839	16	13	199	54.8	23.6	12.1	6.0	3.5	46346
68876	SHELTON	18989	660	24.9	36.7	31.8	4.7	2.0	42133	48911	53	70	533	26.1	35.8	31.9	5.4	0.8	74079
68878	SUMNER	17998	174	29.3	39.1	24.7	3.5	3.5	36031	40000	32	37	137	41.6	24.1	21.9	10.2	2.2	64643
68879	TAYLOR	14334	296	42.6	37.2	16.6	3.0	0.7	28343	31645	9	4	234	50.0	15.4	15.4	10.7	8.6	50000
68881	WESTERVILLE	21126	67	31.3	40.3	20.9	3.0	4.5	35798	40000	31	35	51	43.1	21.6	17.7	13.7	3.9	57000
68882	WOLBACH	17886	214	36.5	38.3	19.6	4.2	1.4	32578	37317	20	17	170	44.7	27.1	18.8	5.3	4.1	57500
68883	WOOD RIVER	20311	941	27.1	32.9	31.6	5.5	2.9	42529	48092	55	72	719	19.1	33.1	34.5	10.4	2.9	87232
68901	HASTINGS	21862	10668	26.5	33.6	29.7	7.1	3.0	41804	49142	52	68	7085	16.0	34.8	38.3	9.9	1.0	89224
68920	ALMA	17862	657	35.5	38.7	20.4	3.5	2.0	32668	37477	20	17	534	47.2	29.0	17.8	5.8	0.2	54412
68922	ARAPAHOE	19148	596	32.2	38.8	21.8	5.0	2.2	34881	40868	27	28	440	47.7	27.7	19.6	4.3	0.7	53846
68923	ATLANTA	21425	62	22.6	35.5	32.3	8.1	1.6	43213	50000	57	73	51	21.6	31.4	41.2	3.9	2.0	86250
68924	AXTELL	18005	434	24.2	35.9	31.8	5.5	2.5	41818	47874	52	69	336	22.9	25.3	36.3	11.6	3.9	92857
68925	AYR	19574	194	20.1	35.1	37.1	4.6	3.1	45000	50412	61	78	155	21.9	25.8	35.5	13.6	3.2	93182
68926	BEAVER CITY	18459	339	36.3	36.9	20.7	4.7	1.5	31775	36832	17	15	256	62.5	27.0	8.6	1.2	0.8	38846
68927	BERTRAND	19227	513	25.3	38.0	27.9	6.0	2.7	40509	46486	48	62	409	22.7	36.9	28.9	9.5	2.0	78289
68928	BLADEN	18040	205	27.3	42.4	22.9	5.4	2.0	37673	42047	38	47	167	42.5	25.2	27.0	4.2	1.2	59615
68929	BLOOMINGTON	16503	157	40.8	37.6	16.6	2.6	2.6	30196	33977	13	7	127	59.8	22.8	11.0	4.7	1.6	37917
68930	BLUE HILL	18053	555	32.3	33.2	28.7	4.1	1.8	37011	42334	35	43	425	31.3	36.2	26.4	5.2	0.9	70658
68932	CAMPBELL	16644	171	36.3	40.9	16.4	2.9	3.5	31155	35577	15	10	139	58.3	17.3	18.0	5.0	1.4	39250
68933	CLAY CENTER	20614	436	27.8	31.4	31.2	6.9	2.8	41305	49019	51	66	348	35.3	30.8	30.2	3.7	0.0	68108
68934	DEWEESE	18342	114	27.2	39.5	29.8	1.8	1.8	39476	45978	44	58	90	38.9	32.2	24.4	4.4	0.0	58333
68935	EDGAR	20249	316	31.0	37.3	25.3	4.4	1.9	38329	43641	40	51	247	49.0	28.3	16.6	5.7	0.4	50806
68936	EDISON	17702	107	30.8	38.3	25.2	4.7	0.9	34209	39682	25	25	78	59.0	25.6	12.8	0.0	2.6	45000
68937	ELWOOD	22173	891	25.9	36.1	29.1	5.6	3.3	41199	47622	50	66	710	18.5	29.3	40.1	10.7	1.4	92667
68938	FAIRFIELD	21280	222	31.1	35.6	25.2	5.9	2.3	36573	41575	34	40	177	43.5	41.2	14.1	1.1	0.0	55000
68939	FRANKLIN	17807	491	37.1	40.5	17.9	2.4	2.0	30756	35732	14	9	384	53.1	32.6	12.2	2.1	0.0	46842
68940	FUNK	19515	200	21.5	37.0	31.0	9.0	1.5	43049	49769	56	73	148	17.6	26.4	37.8	13.5	4.7	97500
68941	GLENVIL	18353	291	26.5	38.8	29.2	2.8	2.8	39486	44763	44	58	227	33.5	26.4	25.6	12.3	2.2	71923
68942	GUIDE ROCK	21820	217	43.3	37.8	13.8	2.8	2.3	28076	31109	9	4	171	61.4	17.0	13.5	6.4	1.8	37188
68943	HARDY	16121	155	35.5	40.0	17.4	5.8	1.3	32942	36909	21	18	125	64.0	12.8	17.6	5.6	0.0	33750
68944	HARVARD	17912	530	30.6	36.8	25.1	5.5	2.1	36835	41821	35	42	418	45.7	29.2	19.9	5.0	0.2	55000
68945	HEARTWELL	21280	90	22.2	33.3	35.6	6.7	2.2	45752	50460	63	80	69	20.3	20.3	42.0	15.9	1.5	98125
68946	HENDLEY	17724	68	29.4	41.2	22.1	4.4	2.9	36833	41737	35	41	53	43.4	32.1	13.2	7.6	3.8	58750
68947	HILDRETH	22106	258	26.7	34.9	29.5	5.4	3.5	40598	46207	48	63	206	45.2	26.7	18.0	7.3	2.9	56250
68948	HOLBROOK	20380	150	38.0	34.7	18.7	6.7	2.0	31731	36308	17	14	122	54.9	23.0	15.6	5.7	0.8	45385
68949	HOLDREGE	23732	2812	25.9	32.8	29.7	7.7	3.9	42805	51089	55	72	2084	20.0	36.9	36.7	5.6	0.9	83077
68950	HOLSTEIN	21302	162	22.8	34.0	32.1	6.2	4.9	45000	50732	61	78	128	25.0	25.8	28.1	19.5	1.6	88571
68952	INAVALE	14985	73	46.6	37.0	12.3	2.7	1.4	26574	30436	7	2	58	63.8	15.5	13.8	5.2	1.7	35000
68954	INLAND	19310	46	30.4	39.1	23.9	4.4	2.2	36108	42347	32	37	36	50.0	27.8	16.7	5.6	0.0	50000
68955	JUNIATA	19354	496	20.4	39.1	31.9	6.5	2.2	42756	49568	55	72	410	18.5	21.0	45.1	15.4	0.0	101056
68956	KENESAW	19012	438	23.1	36.3	33.1	5.7	1.8	43699	48894	58	75	348	26.4	31.6	33.1	8.9	0.0	80345
68957	LAWRENCE	16573	243	37.5	39.1	18.5	2.9	2.1	30545	34723	14	8	202	58.9	25.7	11.4	4.0	0.0	43333
68958	LOOMIS	20922	264	22.7	36.7	30.7	8.0	1.9	42522	49313	55	71	208	21.2	29.3	38.5	7.7	3.4	89375
68959	MINDEN	22109	1656	22.8	33.6	35.8	6.6	1.3	45315	52298	62	79	1251	16.8	33.7	39.9	9.0	0.6	89454
68960	NAPONEE	16054	132	40.2	37.9	16.7	2.3	3.0	30486	33617	13	8	107	62.6	20.6	10.3	4.7	1.9	35500
68961	NELSON	17775	423	32.2	44.0	19.9	3.8	0.2	34921	38639	27	28	338	55.6	23.4	15.7	4.4	0.9	44063
68964	OAK	16804	109	32.1	44.0	20.2	3.7	0.0	34709	37808	26	26	87	57.5	23.0	16.1	3.5	0.0	41875
68966	ORLEANS	18407	300	35.3	36.0	23.0	3.3	2.3	33540	38836	23	22	240	46.3	26.3	19.2	7.9	0.4	56923
68967	OXFORD	19225	537	30.9	37.2	25.7	4.3	1.9	34942	40660	27	29	403	53.4	27.5	13.2	3.2	2.7	47750
68969	RAGAN	17574	37	29.7	37.8	24.3	5.4	2.7	37315	43643	37	45	29	44.8	31.0	13.8	6.9	3.5	55000
68970	RED CLOUD	22038	663	35.6	39.5	20.4	3.5	1.1	32686	37863	20	17	485	59.0	23.9	14.2	2.5	0.4	43603
68971	REPUBLICAN CITY	19954	250	34.4	39.6	20.8	3.6	1.6	33228	38178	22	20	203	47.3	29.6	17.2	5.4	0.5	53929
68972	RIVERTON	14817	128	45.3	37.5	14.1	1.6	1.6	27269	31412	8	3	104	64.4	20.2	8.7	4.8	1.9	33571
68973	ROSELAND	20818	228	19.7	35.1	37.7	4.4	3.1	45377	51044	62	79	183	21.9	26.8	34.4	13.1	3.8	91923
68974	RUSKIN	16746	116	35.3	40.5	18.1	6.0	0.0	33159	36246	21	19	94	63.8	11.7	18.1	6.4	0.0	33750
68975	SARONVILLE	16389	80	27.5	45.0	21.3	6.3	0.0	39189	42757	43	57	62	33.9	27.4	37.1	1.6	0.0	70000
68976	SMITHFIELD	21558	122	23.8	38.5	27.9	6.6	3.3	40000	47723	46	60	95	24.2	29.5	30.5	11.6	4.2	84167
68977	STAMFORD	19215	168	29.2	38.1	26.2	3.6	3.0	37673	42119	38	47	134	41.8	31.3	14.9	9.0	3.0	58462
68978	SUPERIOR	19961	1127	39.8	37.4	18.0	2.3	2.6	30677	35384	14	9	839	56.7	25.6	16.5	1.2	0.0	45044
68979	SUTTON	20316	782	26.9	37.1	27.6	6.0	2.4	38989	45677	43	56	606	31.7	34.5	25.9	7.6	0.3	72449
68980	TRUMBULL	17013	146	30.1	36.3	26.0	5.5	2.1	36740	41850	34	41	115	47.0	29.6	17.4	6.1	0.0	53500
68981	UPLAND	19537	101	27.7	36.6	27.7	5.0	3.0	39644	44598	45	59	81	46.9	25.9	18.5	6.2	2.5	54167
68982	WILCOX	21146	224	23.7	36.2	32.1	5.8	2.2	41995	47021	53	69	175	24.6	26.9	34.9	10.9	2.9	87727
69001	MC COOK	19503	4005	31.4	35.7	25.7	5.8	1.5	37120	42318	36	44	2821	28.4	35.6	29.9	6.0	0.2	74283
69020	BARTLEY	15631	197	32.5	40.6	22.8	2.5	1.5	35928	40516	31	36	157	50.3	35.7	12.7	1.3	0.0	49706
69021	BENKELMAN	19034	651	39.9	29.3	23.5	5.2	2.0	31501	38486	16	13	496	59.7	18.6	14.3	4.8	2.6	42258
69022	CAMBRIDGE	25408	598	35.5	35.1	20.2	5.5	3.7	35465	40781	29	32	447	50.1	24.6	18.8	5.8	0.7	49875
69023	CHAMPION	18361	231	32.9	38.1	21.2	5.6	2.2	35861	42180	31	35	172	35.5	29.1	24.4	6.4	4.7	67500
69024	CULBERTSON	17817	478	35.4	32.4	24.7	5.9	1.7	34804	40759	27	28	387	51.7	33.1	11.1	3.4	0.8	48917
69025	CURTIS	16916	451	33.9	38.1	22.8	3.1	2.0	34132	40238	24	25	310	41.6	34.2	18.4	3.9	1.9	59286
69026	DANBURY	19142	107	35.5	34.6	23.4	4.7	1.9	37312	42604	37	44	85	49.4	37.7	9.4	3.5	0.0	50833
69027	ENDERS	18201	89	36.0	38.2	20.2	4.5	1.1	34589	40370	26	26	69	42.0	29.0	20.3	4.4	4.4	60833
69028	EUSTIS	23015	345	30.1	35.4	23.2	7.0	4.4	37613	44341	38	46	274	26.6	29.2	34.3	8.4	1.5	82727
69029	FARNAM	21839	119	22.7	43.7	25.2	5.0	3.4	37651	42299	38	46	86	29.1	20.9	30.2	14.0	5.8	90000
69030	HAIGLER	17614	157	36.9	31.9	22.3	7.0	1.9	32776	39236	20	17	110	56.4	20.9	19.1	2.7	0.9	43636
	NEBRASKA	23743		24.5	30.5	31.8	9.2	4.0	45453	54516				17.2	23.9	42.4	14.4	2.2	101398
	UNITED STATES	25866		24.7	27.1	30.8	10.9	6.5	48124	56710				10.9	15.0	33.7	30.1	10.4	145905

ZIP CODE #	POST OFFICE NAME	FINANCIAL SERVICES: Auto Loan	FINANCIAL SERVICES: Home Loan	FINANCIAL SERVICES: Invest-ments	FINANCIAL SERVICES: Retire-ment Plans	THE HOME: Home Improvements: Home Repair	THE HOME: Home Improvements: Lawn & Garden	THE HOME: Furnishings: Comput-ers & Hard-ware	THE HOME: Furnishings: Major Appli-ances	THE HOME: Furnishings: TV, Radio, Sound Equip-ment	THE HOME: Furnishings: Furni-ture	ENTERTAINMENT: Dine out/ Carry out	ENTERTAINMENT: Sports Equip-ment	ENTERTAINMENT: Fees & Tickets	ENTERTAINMENT: Toys & Games	ENTERTAINMENT: Travel	ENTERTAINMENT: Cable TV	PERSONAL: Apparel & Services	PERSONAL: Auto Repairs	PERSONAL: Health Insur-ance	PERSONAL: Pets & Supplies
68852	LITCHFIELD	71	49	26	47	58	64	49	60	56	48	66	73	42	65	51	59	60	59	72	84
68853	LOUP CITY	60	45	29	43	49	58	48	54	54	46	64	61	43	61	48	57	58	54	65	67
68854	MARQUETTE	103	72	37	68	83	93	71	87	82	70	96	105	60	94	73	86	87	86	104	122
68855	MASON CITY	90	63	33	59	73	82	62	77	72	61	84	92	53	82	64	75	77	76	91	106
68856	MERNA	89	62	33	59	72	81	62	76	71	61	83	91	53	82	64	75	76	75	91	105
68858	MILLER	83	58	30	55	68	76	57	71	66	57	78	86	49	76	60	69	71	70	85	99
68859	NORTH LOUP	69	48	25	46	56	63	48	59	55	47	64	71	41	63	49	58	59	58	70	82
68860	OCONTO	78	55	29	52	64	71	54	67	62	53	73	80	46	71	56	65	66	66	79	93
68861	ODESSA	92	101	101	103	98	97	96	95	90	97	114	113	97	115	94	85	112	95	84	105
68862	ORD	70	50	30	48	57	66	53	62	60	51	71	72	46	68	54	63	64	61	74	80
68863	OVERTON	80	56	29	53	65	73	55	68	64	55	75	82	47	73	57	67	68	67	81	95
68864	PALMER	80	56	29	53	65	73	55	68	64	55	75	82	47	73	57	67	68	67	81	95
68865	PHILLIPS	94	80	58	76	86	93	75	84	80	75	97	101	72	99	77	83	92	82	93	110
68866	PLEASANTON	85	59	31	56	69	77	59	72	67	58	79	87	50	77	61	71	72	71	86	101
68869	RAVENNA	75	57	38	56	63	73	60	67	66	58	79	78	54	77	60	69	73	67	78	85
68870	RIVERDALE	88	97	94	96	98	99	88	91	85	87	105	108	90	110	90	84	103	88	87	106
68871	ROCKVILLE	70	52	33	48	60	67	50	61	57	50	67	72	44	66	53	61	62	60	72	84
68872	SAINT LIBORY	89	62	32	59	72	81	61	76	71	61	83	91	52	81	64	74	76	75	90	106
68873	SAINT PAUL	82	59	33	56	67	77	60	71	69	59	81	84	52	78	61	72	74	71	85	95
68874	SARGENT	58	43	27	41	48	56	46	52	52	44	61	60	41	58	46	55	56	52	63	66
68875	SCOTIA	68	48	25	45	56	62	47	58	54	47	64	70	40	63	49	57	58	58	69	81
68876	SHELTON	83	67	49	66	73	82	69	76	74	68	90	88	64	88	69	76	83	75	84	94
68878	SUMNER	82	57	30	54	67	75	57	70	65	56	77	85	48	75	59	69	70	69	84	98
68879	TAYLOR	63	44	23	42	52	58	44	54	50	43	59	65	37	58	45	53	54	53	64	75
68881	WESTERVILLE	100	70	37	66	82	91	69	86	80	68	94	103	59	92	72	84	85	84	102	119
68882	WOLBACH	74	51	27	49	60	67	51	63	59	50	69	76	43	67	53	61	63	62	75	87
68883	WOOD RIVER	88	68	45	66	75	84	68	78	75	67	90	92	62	89	69	78	83	77	89	101
68901	HASTINGS	74	74	78	74	74	80	76	76	76	75	94	89	76	95	76	75	91	77	75	86
68920	ALMA	69	52	34	49	58	67	53	62	60	52	71	71	48	69	55	64	65	61	73	80
68922	ARAPAHOE	72	53	34	51	59	70	58	65	65	55	77	74	52	73	58	69	70	65	78	80
68923	ATLANTA	96	67	35	64	78	88	66	82	76	66	90	99	57	88	69	80	82	81	98	114
68924	AXTELL	95	66	35	63	77	86	65	81	75	65	88	97	56	87	68	79	81	80	96	113
68925	AYR	95	67	35	63	78	87	66	81	76	65	89	98	56	87	68	79	81	80	97	113
68926	BEAVER CITY	67	50	32	48	55	65	54	61	61	52	72	69	48	68	54	64	65	61	73	75
68927	BERTRAND	91	64	33	60	74	83	63	78	72	62	85	94	54	83	65	76	77	77	92	108
68928	BLADEN	83	58	30	55	67	75	57	71	66	56	77	85	49	76	59	69	70	70	84	98
68929	BLOOMINGTON	68	48	27	45	55	63	49	59	56	48	65	69	42	64	50	59	60	58	70	79
68930	BLUE HILL	76	56	34	53	62	73	59	68	67	57	79	78	52	75	60	71	72	67	81	86
68932	CAMPBELL	66	49	33	47	54	65	55	60	61	52	72	68	49	68	54	65	66	60	72	73
68933	CLAY CENTER	95	66	35	63	77	86	65	81	75	65	88	98	56	87	68	79	81	80	96	113
68934	DEWEESE	83	58	30	55	68	76	57	71	66	57	77	85	49	76	59	69	70	70	84	99
68935	EDGAR	85	59	31	56	69	78	59	73	68	58	79	87	50	78	61	71	72	72	86	101
68936	EDISON	81	57	30	54	66	74	56	69	65	55	76	84	48	74	58	68	69	68	83	97
68937	ELWOOD	92	66	38	62	76	85	64	79	74	64	87	94	56	85	67	78	80	78	94	109
68938	FAIRFIELD	98	69	36	65	80	89	68	84	78	67	91	101	58	90	70	82	83	82	100	117
68939	FRANKLIN	65	49	32	47	54	64	54	60	60	51	71	67	48	67	53	64	65	59	71	73
68940	FUNK	95	66	35	62	77	86	65	81	75	65	88	97	56	87	68	79	80	80	96	112
68941	GLENVIL	87	61	32	58	71	80	60	74	69	59	81	90	51	80	62	73	74	73	89	104
68942	GUIDE ROCK	70	52	34	50	57	68	57	64	64	55	76	72	51	72	57	68	69	63	76	78
68943	HARDY	75	52	28	50	61	68	52	64	60	51	70	77	45	69	54	63	64	63	76	88
68944	HARVARD	84	58	31	55	68	76	58	71	66	57	78	86	49	76	60	70	71	70	85	99
68945	HEARTWELL	99	69	36	65	81	90	68	85	79	68	92	102	58	91	71	83	84	83	101	118
68946	HENDLEY	85	60	31	56	69	78	59	73	68	58	80	88	50	78	61	71	73	72	87	101
68947	HILDRETH	94	65	34	62	76	85	65	80	74	64	87	96	55	86	67	78	80	79	95	111
68948	HOLBROOK	78	57	36	55	64	75	62	70	70	60	83	80	55	78	62	74	75	70	84	87
68949	HOLDREGE	98	73	46	71	82	93	75	87	84	73	100	101	67	97	76	88	92	86	101	112
68950	HOLSTEIN	100	70	36	66	81	91	69	85	79	68	93	102	59	91	71	83	85	84	101	118
68952	INAVALE	58	44	29	42	48	57	48	53	54	46	64	60	43	60	48	57	58	53	64	64
68954	INLAND	86	60	31	57	70	78	59	73	68	58	80	88	51	78	61	72	73	72	87	102
68955	JUNIATA	78	78	71	78	78	79	75	77	73	75	90	92	73	90	74	70	88	77	73	90
68956	KENESAW	91	63	33	60	74	82	62	77	72	62	84	93	53	83	65	75	77	76	92	107
68957	LAWRENCE	72	50	26	47	58	65	50	61	57	49	67	74	42	66	51	60	61	60	73	85
68958	LOOMIS	95	67	35	63	78	87	66	81	76	65	89	98	57	87	69	80	81	80	97	113
68959	MINDEN	94	68	39	64	77	89	70	83	80	68	94	97	61	91	71	84	86	82	99	109
68960	NAPONEE	68	48	26	45	55	62	48	58	55	47	64	70	41	63	49	58	59	58	70	80
68961	NELSON	72	50	26	47	59	66	50	61	57	49	67	74	42	66	51	60	61	60	73	85
68964	OAK	72	50	26	48	59	66	50	61	57	49	67	74	42	66	52	60	61	61	73	86
68966	ORLEANS	73	56	37	51	63	71	53	64	60	53	71	75	47	70	56	64	66	63	76	88
68967	OXFORD	81	57	30	54	66	74	56	69	65	55	76	84	48	74	58	68	69	68	83	97
68969	RAGAN	84	59	31	56	69	77	58	72	67	57	78	87	50	77	60	70	72	71	86	100
68970	RED CLOUD	77	58	38	55	63	76	64	70	71	60	84	79	57	79	63	75	77	70	84	85
68971	REPUBLICAN CITY	70	52	33	49	58	68	54	62	61	52	72	72	48	69	55	65	66	62	75	80
68972	RIVERTON	62	44	25	42	51	58	45	54	51	44	60	64	39	59	46	54	55	53	64	73
68973	ROSELAND	95	66	35	63	77	87	66	81	76	65	89	98	56	87	68	79	81	80	97	113
68974	RUSKIN	74	52	27	49	60	68	51	63	59	51	69	76	44	68	53	62	63	62	75	88
68975	SARONVILLE	83	58	30	55	67	75	57	70	66	56	77	85	49	76	59	69	70	69	84	98
68976	SMITHFIELD	91	63	33	60	74	83	63	78	72	62	85	93	54	83	65	76	77	76	92	108
68977	STAMFORD	84	58	31	55	68	76	58	71	67	57	78	86	49	76	60	70	71	70	85	99
68978	SUPERIOR	68	51	33	49	56	67	56	62	63	53	74	70	49	70	55	66	67	62	74	76
68979	SUTTON	91	63	33	60	74	83	63	77	72	62	85	93	53	83	65	76	77	76	92	108
68980	TRUMBULL	85	60	31	56	69	78	59	73	68	58	80	88	50	78	61	71	73	72	87	101
68981	UPLAND	91	64	34	60	74	83	64	78	73	63	86	93	55	84	66	77	78	77	93	107
68982	WILCOX	94	66	34	62	77	86	65	80	75	64	88	97	55	86	67	79	80	79	96	112
69001	MC COOK	66	61	57	60	64	71	63	66	66	61	80	75	61	80	63	67	76	65	70	76
69020	BARTLEY	75	52	27	49	61	68	52	64	60	51	70	77	44	68	54	62	64	63	76	89
69021	BENKELMAN	72	52	30	50	59	68	54	63	62	52	72	74	47	70	55	65	66	63	76	83
69022	CAMBRIDGE	85	75	70	76	79	87	79	83	82	77	99	96	75	96	78	82	94	83	88	96
69023	CHAMPION	80	56	29	53	65	73	55	69	64	55	75	83	47	73	58	67	68	68	82	95
69024	CULBERTSON	74	54	33	51	60	70	57	65	64	55	76	75	50	72	57	68	69	65	78	84
69025	CURTIS	70	52	33	49	57	68	56	63	63	54	74	71	50	71	56	67	68	63	75	78
69026	DANBURY	81	57	30	54	66	74	56	69	65	55	76	84	48	74	58	68	69	68	83	96
69027	ENDERS	75	53	29	50	61	69	54	65	62	53	72	77	46	70	55	65	66	64	77	88
69028	EUSTIS	100	72	41	67	83	93	70	86	80	69	95	103	61	93	73	85	87	85	102	119
69029	FARNAM	93	65	34	62	76	85	64	80	74	64	87	96	55	85	67	78	79	78	95	111
69030	HAIGLER	82	57	30	54	67	75	57	70	65	56	77	85	48	75	59	69	70	69	84	98
	NEBRASKA	88	81	77	81	83	90	83	85	84	82	104	101	80	103	82	84	100	86	87	100
	UNITED STATES	100	100	100	100	100	100	100	100	100	100	100	100	100	100	100	100	100	100	100	100

ZIP CODE		POPULATION			2000-2004 ANNUAL RATE		HOUSEHOLDS					FAMILIES		
# POST OFFICE NAME	COUNTY FIPS CODE	2000	2004	2009	% Rate	State Centile	2000	2004	2009	% Annual Rate 2000-2004	2004 Average HH Size	2000	2004	% Annual Rate 2000-2004
69032 HAYES CENTER	085	878	894	920	0.4	73	346	356	370	0.7	2.51	254	262	0.7
69033 IMPERIAL	029	2431	2410	2391	-0.2	44	976	984	991	0.2	2.38	679	686	0.2
69034 INDIANOLA	145	1182	1208	1240	0.5	76	469	483	500	0.7	2.50	344	355	0.7
69036 LEBANON	145	161	161	163	0.0	56	70	71	73	0.3	2.27	54	55	0.4
69037 MAX	057	136	130	126	-1.1	2	59	57	56	-0.8	2.28	39	38	-0.6
69038 MAYWOOD	063	725	721	719	-0.1	47	266	267	269	0.1	2.70	205	206	0.1
69039 MOOREFIELD	063	312	306	303	-0.5	26	125	125	125	0.0	2.37	91	91	0.0
69040 PALISADE	087	689	681	677	-0.3	39	281	283	286	0.2	2.41	202	204	0.2
69041 PARKS	057	228	226	223	-0.2	43	83	83	83	0.0	2.63	60	60	0.0
69042 STOCKVILLE	063	113	111	110	-0.4	28	50	50	50	0.0	2.22	38	38	0.0
69043 STRATTON	087	665	651	637	-0.5	22	278	277	276	-0.1	2.35	198	199	0.1
69044 TRENTON	087	739	724	710	-0.5	23	325	323	321	-0.2	2.06	194	194	0.0
69045 WAUNETA	029	856	845	837	-0.3	37	366	368	370	0.1	2.21	247	249	0.2
69046 WILSONVILLE	065	222	215	212	-0.8	8	96	94	93	-0.5	2.29	70	68	-0.7
69101 NORTH PLATTE	111	28121	28765	29593	0.5	76	11570	12040	12597	0.9	2.34	7545	7874	1.0
69120 ARNOLD	041	1050	1040	1042	-0.2	42	467	468	474	0.1	2.22	313	315	0.2
69121 ARTHUR	005	434	427	427	-0.4	30	182	182	182	0.0	2.35	136	136	0.0
69122 BIG SPRINGS	049	685	675	677	-0.4	33	302	304	311	0.2	2.22	207	209	0.2
69123 BRADY	111	1023	1036	1058	0.3	68	425	439	456	0.8	2.36	316	326	0.7
69125 BROADWATER	123	405	396	386	-0.5	20	166	164	162	-0.3	2.35	123	122	-0.2
69127 BRULE	101	752	788	834	1.1	87	318	339	366	1.5	2.32	224	240	1.6
69128 BUSHNELL	105	379	372	368	-0.4	26	151	151	151	0.0	2.46	108	108	0.0
69129 CHAPPELL	049	1451	1470	1486	0.3	69	624	643	663	0.7	2.25	407	421	0.8
69130 COZAD	047	5635	5614	5608	-0.1	50	2287	2280	2265	-0.1	2.43	1560	1558	0.0
69131 DALTON	033	586	581	583	-0.2	44	262	264	268	0.2	2.20	172	174	0.3
69132 DICKENS	111	120	122	125	0.4	72	44	46	48	1.1	2.65	33	35	1.4
69133 DIX	105	474	465	460	-0.5	26	183	183	183	0.0	2.54	131	131	0.0
69134 ELSIE	135	453	441	426	-0.6	13	170	168	165	-0.3	2.63	130	129	-0.2
69135 ELSMERE	031	110	106	105	-0.9	4	43	43	43	0.0	2.47	32	31	-0.7
69138 GOTHENBURG	047	4223	4155	4144	-0.4	30	1701	1676	1664	-0.4	2.41	1182	1166	-0.3
69140 GRANT	135	1820	1761	1695	-0.8	7	749	736	719	-0.4	2.32	493	486	-0.3
69141 GURLEY	033	459	455	457	-0.2	43	185	187	190	0.3	2.43	122	123	0.2
69142 HALSEY	171	133	131	131	-0.4	33	59	60	60	0.4	2.18	39	40	0.6
69143 HERSHEY	111	1731	1768	1814	0.5	75	660	688	719	1.0	2.55	510	532	1.0
69144 KEYSTONE	101	326	339	358	0.9	84	144	153	164	1.4	2.22	100	106	1.4
69145 KIMBALL	105	3236	3224	3219	-0.1	50	1393	1412	1425	0.3	2.24	896	910	0.3
69146 LEMOYNE	101	238	248	261	1.0	85	114	121	130	1.4	2.04	79	84	1.5
69147 LEWELLEN	069	821	824	831	0.1	59	396	405	417	0.5	1.99	260	267	0.6
69148 LISCO	069	209	206	203	-0.3	34	93	93	93	0.0	2.22	66	66	0.0
69149 LODGEPOLE	033	748	739	742	-0.3	38	319	320	325	0.1	2.31	225	226	0.1
69150 MADRID	135	523	508	489	-0.7	10	189	186	182	-0.4	2.73	144	143	-0.2
69151 MAXWELL	111	877	897	922	0.5	76	324	337	353	0.9	2.66	255	266	1.0
69152 MULLEN	091	783	788	788	0.2	62	335	341	341	0.4	2.23	220	225	0.5
69153 OGALLALA	101	6219	6448	6791	0.9	83	2559	2696	2885	1.2	2.36	1716	1814	1.3
69154 OSHKOSH	069	1444	1424	1406	-0.3	35	645	647	648	0.1	2.13	412	414	0.1
69155 PAXTON	101	1044	1122	1204	1.7	90	412	450	490	2.1	2.49	305	333	2.1
69156 POTTER	033	666	781	854	3.8	97	262	313	346	4.3	2.49	184	220	4.3
69157 PURDUM	009	179	176	176	-0.4	29	71	71	71	0.0	2.48	50	50	0.0
69161 SENECA	171	120	118	118	-0.4	30	58	59	59	0.4	2.00	39	39	0.0
69162 SIDNEY	033	7406	7472	7549	0.2	65	3058	3122	3187	0.5	2.35	1993	2037	0.5
69163 STAPLETON	113	927	929	941	0.1	58	371	381	386	0.6	2.44	274	282	0.7
69165 SUTHERLAND	111	1602	1674	1738	1.0	86	613	651	687	1.4	2.52	448	477	1.5
69166 THEDFORD	171	472	464	464	-0.4	29	205	209	209	0.5	2.22	136	139	0.5
69167 TRYON	117	533	533	533	0.0	56	202	203	203	0.1	2.63	158	159	0.2
69168 VENANGO	135	363	344	329	-1.3	0	149	144	140	-0.8	2.39	113	109	-0.8
69169 WALLACE	111	582	590	602	0.3	70	232	240	249	0.8	2.46	176	182	0.8
69170 WELLFLEET	111	313	318	326	0.4	71	116	120	125	0.8	2.65	88	92	1.1
69201 VALENTINE	031	4267	4318	4370	0.3	67	1748	1797	1851	0.7	2.36	1154	1191	0.8
69210 AINSWORTH	017	2497	2439	2381	-0.6	18	1103	1097	1090	-0.1	2.20	713	711	-0.1
69211 CODY	031	351	336	331	-1.0	2	144	141	142	-0.5	2.38	105	103	-0.5
69212 CROOKSTON	031	237	273	294	3.4	96	95	112	123	4.0	2.44	71	83	3.7
69214 JOHNSTOWN	017	343	334	325	-0.6	14	129	128	127	-0.2	2.59	83	82	-0.3
69216 KILGORE	031	228	217	214	-1.2	1	90	88	89	-0.5	2.47	65	63	-0.7
69217 LONG PINE	017	689	682	669	-0.2	41	300	302	302	0.2	2.21	202	204	0.2
69218 MERRIMAN	031	672	644	635	-1.0	3	266	261	263	-0.5	2.47	194	190	-0.5
69221 WOOD LAKE	031	191	184	182	-0.9	4	85	84	85	-0.3	2.19	64	64	0.0
69301 ALLIANCE	013	10591	10209	9805	-0.9	4	4193	4116	4022	-0.4	2.44	2875	2830	-0.4
69331 ANGORA	123	105	103	100	-0.5	26	38	38	37	0.0	2.66	29	29	0.0
69333 ASHBY	075	154	151	151	-0.5	26	62	61	61	-0.4	2.48	47	47	0.0
69334 BAYARD	123	2627	2561	2499	-0.6	15	1027	1014	999	-0.3	2.48	738	730	-0.3
69335 BINGHAM	161	200	199	197	-0.1	48	78	79	80	0.3	2.52	55	56	0.4
69336 BRIDGEPORT	123	2612	2566	2509	-0.4	28	1030	1023	1011	-0.2	2.46	701	698	-0.1
69337 CHADRON	045	7024	6785	6577	-0.8	6	2676	2626	2583	-0.4	2.22	1516	1493	-0.4
69339 CRAWFORD	045	1616	1605	1572	-0.2	46	675	681	679	0.2	2.28	447	450	0.2
69340 ELLSWORTH	161	218	217	215	-0.1	48	100	102	102	0.5	2.13	70	72	0.7
69341 GERING	157	10585	10528	10496	-0.1	47	4256	4311	4341	0.3	2.40	2969	3014	0.4
69343 GORDON	161	2529	2465	2428	-0.6	15	1041	1032	1031	-0.2	2.34	701	696	-0.2
69345 HARRISBURG	007	817	811	811	-0.2	45	310	314	314	0.3	2.58	237	241	0.4
69346 HARRISON	165	907	889	871	-0.5	24	385	382	380	-0.2	2.33	278	276	-0.2
69347 HAY SPRINGS	161	1509	1504	1495	-0.1	50	602	609	613	0.3	2.38	415	420	0.3
69348 HEMINGFORD	013	1727	1694	1640	-0.5	26	647	645	636	-0.1	2.56	469	468	-0.1
69350 HYANNIS	075	454	446	446	-0.4	28	184	182	182	-0.3	2.45	142	141	-0.2
69351 LAKESIDE	161	53	53	52	0.0	56	22	22	23	0.0	2.41	15	16	1.5
69352 LYMAN	157	723	753	768	1.0	85	269	284	291	1.3	2.65	197	208	1.3
69354 MARSLAND	045	126	140	144	2.5	93	50	57	60	3.1	2.46	38	42	2.4
69356 MINATARE	157	2176	2150	2136	-0.3	38	852	855	856	0.1	2.51	649	652	0.1
69357 MITCHELL	157	3903	3820	3783	-0.5	22	1496	1478	1471	-0.3	2.54	1092	1081	-0.2
69358 MORRILL	157	2098	2071	2056	-0.3	37	860	860	861	0.0	2.41	585	585	0.0
69360 RUSHVILLE	161	1733	1713	1697	-0.3	39	714	721	725	0.2	2.32	479	485	0.3
69361 SCOTTSBLUFF	157	17579	17574	17580	0.0	53	7193	7281	7342	0.3	2.36	4707	4782	0.4
69366 WHITMAN	031	256	251	250	-0.5	26	91	90	90	-0.3	2.79	69	69	0.0
69367 WHITNEY	045	258	280	286	1.9	91	109	122	127	2.7	2.06	81	90	2.5
NEBRASKA					0.8					1.0	2.47			1.1
UNITED STATES					1.2					1.3	2.58			1.1

POPULATION COMPOSITION

NEBRASKA

69032-69367 B

ZIP CODE #	POST OFFICE NAME	RACE (%) White 2000	White 2004	Black 2000	Black 2004	Asian/Pacific 2000	Asian/Pacific 2004	% Hispanic Origin 2000	% Hispanic Origin 2004	2004 AGE DISTRIBUTION (%) 0-4	5-9	10-14	15-19	20-24	25-44	45-64	65-84	85+	18+	MEDIAN AGE 2004	% 2004 Males	% 2004 Females
69032	HAYES CENTER	96.7	96.5	0.2	0.2	0.3	0.3	3.1	3.1	4.3	7.3	8.7	7.9	3.6	20.0	28.5	17.7	2.0	74.5	43.9	50.3	49.7
69033	IMPERIAL	98.0	98.1	0.1	0.1	0.2	0.2	4.3	4.4	6.5	6.4	7.1	6.6	5.5	22.7	26.4	15.0	3.8	75.5	41.6	48.7	51.3
69034	INDIANOLA	97.9	97.6	0.3	0.3	0.2	0.3	2.0	2.4	6.0	6.4	8.1	6.7	5.6	23.8	26.5	15.4	1.6	75.3	40.8	51.1	48.9
69036	LEBANON	99.4	99.4	0.0	0.0	0.0	0.0	0.6	0.6	5.6	5.6	8.7	6.8	3.7	23.0	28.6	17.4	0.6	75.2	42.9	50.9	49.1
69037	MAX	97.1	96.9	0.0	0.0	0.7	0.8	0.0	0.0	3.9	4.6	5.4	6.2	4.6	20.0	33.9	18.5	3.1	81.5	47.3	47.7	52.3
69038	MAYWOOD	98.8	98.9	0.0	0.0	0.1	0.1	0.7	0.7	6.7	6.8	7.5	7.4	6.7	23.2	27.3	13.0	1.5	73.5	39.6	49.9	50.1
69039	MOOREFIELD	98.4	98.0	0.3	0.3	0.3	0.3	1.0	0.7	5.2	5.6	5.6	5.9	7.5	21.6	29.1	17.7	2.0	80.7	44.1	54.9	45.1
69040	PALISADE	98.6	98.5	0.2	0.2	0.2	0.2	1.3	1.3	5.6	6.2	7.9	7.1	6.2	20.7	28.3	15.9	2.2	75.9	42.7	50.4	49.6
69041	PARKS	96.1	96.0	0.0	0.0	0.0	0.0	7.5	7.5	6.6	7.1	7.5	6.2	5.3	23.9	29.7	12.0	1.8	74.3	40.0	54.0	46.0
69042	STOCKVILLE	99.1	100.0	0.0	0.0	0.0	0.0	0.0	0.0	5.4	5.4	6.3	5.4	6.3	21.6	31.5	16.2	1.8	77.5	44.7	55.0	45.1
69043	STRATTON	98.4	98.3	0.0	0.0	0.2	0.2	0.9	0.8	4.3	5.1	6.6	6.1	6.0	18.6	30.9	19.7	2.8	80.3	46.7	51.6	48.4
69044	TRENTON	98.4	98.3	0.0	0.0	0.1	0.1	1.8	1.7	2.8	3.0	5.4	5.3	6.4	19.8	28.0	21.3	8.2	85.2	49.8	47.2	52.8
69045	WAUNETA	97.1	97.0	0.4	0.4	0.5	0.5	2.7	2.7	4.9	4.7	6.0	5.1	4.7	21.8	26.9	21.0	5.0	80.4	46.8	48.9	51.1
69046	WILSONVILLE	98.7	98.6	0.0	0.0	0.0	0.0	1.4	1.4	6.5	7.0	7.9	5.1	5.1	23.3	28.8	14.9	1.4	75.4	41.3	54.0	46.1
69101	NORTH PLATTE	94.1	93.2	0.6	0.7	0.4	0.6	6.0	7.1	6.9	6.6	7.0	7.0	7.3	25.2	25.3	12.6	2.3	75.3	37.5	49.1	50.9
69120	ARNOLD	98.9	98.9	0.0	0.0	0.0	0.0	1.1	1.2	5.6	5.9	7.1	6.9	4.7	23.0	25.9	18.1	2.9	77.1	42.9	51.0	49.0
69121	ARTHUR	96.3	96.3	0.0	0.0	0.9	0.9	1.4	1.4	5.6	5.6	6.1	6.6	4.9	27.6	24.1	17.1	2.3	78.5	41.3	49.0	51.1
69122	BIG SPRINGS	96.9	97.0	0.0	0.0	0.0	0.0	5.3	5.2	4.0	4.3	5.8	7.6	5.3	18.8	30.5	20.4	3.3	81.3	47.1	49.8	50.2
69123	BRADY	98.7	98.8	0.1	0.1	0.1	0.1	0.8	1.0	6.9	7.4	7.5	5.1	4.3	26.1	28.7	12.3	1.8	74.9	40.3	50.5	49.5
69125	BROADWATER	97.0	96.2	0.0	0.3	0.0	0.0	4.0	4.6	5.3	6.3	8.6	8.8	4.8	22.7	26.3	15.4	1.8	73.5	40.5	52.0	48.0
69127	BRULE	97.1	96.6	0.1	0.1	0.1	0.1	3.6	4.2	4.3	4.8	5.6	5.2	3.9	18.0	36.2	20.3	1.7	81.7	49.6	52.7	47.3
69128	BUSHNELL	98.2	98.1	0.0	0.0	0.0	0.0	4.0	4.0	5.4	6.2	7.3	6.5	5.4	21.8	30.1	16.1	1.3	77.2	43.5	51.3	48.7
69129	CHAPPELL	97.5	97.6	0.1	0.1	0.6	0.5	1.5	1.5	5.0	5.2	6.0	6.6	5.2	22.4	27.5	18.2	4.0	79.4	44.8	49.0	51.0
69130	COZAD	94.6	93.5	0.1	0.1	0.4	0.5	8.9	10.9	7.1	7.0	7.4	6.2	5.8	25.1	25.1	14.0	2.4	74.7	38.9	49.2	50.8
69131	DALTON	98.6	98.8	0.0	0.0	0.0	0.0	1.5	1.7	5.5	5.9	7.6	6.9	5.3	24.3	27.4	14.5	2.8	76.8	42.1	47.7	52.3
69132	DICKENS	98.3	97.5	0.0	0.0	0.0	0.0	2.5	3.3	5.7	7.4	7.4	7.4	5.7	22.1	28.7	13.1	2.5	74.6	41.1	49.2	50.8
69133	DIX	98.1	98.3	0.0	0.0	0.0	0.0	4.0	4.1	5.2	6.0	7.3	6.7	5.4	21.9	30.1	15.9	1.5	77.0	43.5	51.6	48.4
69134	ELSIE	97.1	96.8	0.0	0.0	0.4	0.5	3.5	4.1	6.8	7.3	7.7	7.5	6.6	24.9	24.7	13.2	1.4	73.5	36.8	51.7	48.3
69135	ELSMERE	98.2	98.1	0.0	0.0	0.0	0.0	0.0	0.0	7.6	8.5	7.6	6.6	4.7	26.4	26.4	11.3	0.9	70.8	36.9	54.7	45.3
69138	GOTHENBURG	97.4	96.9	0.4	0.4	0.2	0.2	3.7	4.6	8.0	8.1	7.3	6.0	5.9	23.2	23.6	14.4	3.5	72.8	37.9	47.4	52.6
69140	GRANT	98.2	98.0	0.0	0.0	0.2	0.2	1.7	1.9	5.1	5.6	6.8	6.1	5.6	20.5	28.0	16.6	5.7	78.3	45.2	49.1	50.9
69141	GURLEY	98.7	98.7	0.0	0.0	0.0	0.0	1.5	1.8	5.3	5.7	7.3	6.6	5.5	24.4	28.1	14.3	2.9	77.6	42.4	48.4	51.7
69142	HALSEY	99.3	100.0	0.0	0.0	0.0	0.0	0.8	0.8	6.1	6.1	4.6	4.6	6.1	22.1	32.8	14.5	3.1	79.4	45.2	48.1	51.9
69143	HERSHEY	96.0	95.2	0.2	0.3	0.6	0.7	4.2	4.9	5.6	6.1	7.4	7.1	5.3	24.6	30.7	11.5	1.6	76.4	41.1	50.0	50.0
69144	KEYSTONE	96.9	96.5	0.0	0.3	0.0	0.0	3.4	3.8	3.8	4.1	5.3	5.0	3.5	16.2	38.4	21.8	1.8	82.9	51.6	52.5	47.5
69145	KIMBALL	96.7	96.7	0.3	0.3	0.1	0.1	3.2	3.2	5.7	5.7	7.0	6.8	5.6	20.6	26.1	19.2	3.4	77.3	44.1	48.1	51.9
69146	LEMOYNE	97.1	96.8	0.0	0.0	0.0	0.0	3.4	3.6	3.6	4.4	5.2	5.2	3.2	16.1	38.7	21.8	1.6	83.5	51.7	52.4	47.6
69147	LEWELLEN	97.8	97.7	0.1	0.1	0.2	0.2	2.1	2.2	3.6	4.3	5.7	6.4	4.3	18.2	31.9	22.0	3.6	81.9	49.7	49.6	50.4
69148	LISCO	99.0	99.0	0.0	0.0	0.0	0.0	1.0	1.5	4.4	6.8	6.8	7.8	3.9	24.3	32.5	12.1	1.5	76.2	42.1	52.4	47.6
69149	LODGEPOLE	99.2	99.2	0.0	0.0	0.1	0.1	2.0	2.3	4.5	5.3	7.0	6.2	5.8	21.2	30.7	16.6	2.6	79.2	45.0	52.4	47.6
69150	MADRID	97.1	96.7	0.0	0.0	0.4	0.4	3.3	3.9	6.7	7.1	8.5	7.5	6.3	24.2	25.6	12.8	1.4	73.0	37.0	52.6	47.4
69151	MAXWELL	98.5	98.3	0.2	0.2	0.0	0.0	2.3	2.7	5.9	6.7	8.8	6.2	4.9	25.8	29.0	11.3	1.5	74.6	40.0	51.3	48.7
69152	MULLEN	98.7	98.7	0.0	0.0	0.1	0.1	1.0	1.0	4.6	4.8	6.6	7.4	4.6	18.4	28.1	19.9	5.7	79.4	47.0	46.2	53.8
69153	OGALLALA	96.6	96.1	0.0	0.1	0.2	0.3	4.7	5.5	6.2	6.1	7.3	7.2	6.3	23.3	25.1	15.9	2.5	75.8	40.7	48.3	51.7
69154	OSHKOSH	98.3	98.2	0.1	0.1	0.3	0.3	1.5	1.5	3.6	4.2	5.9	7.1	4.6	18.9	29.2	22.0	4.6	81.5	48.5	48.7	51.3
69155	PAXTON	97.0	96.9	0.3	0.3	0.1	0.1	2.8	3.2	7.0	7.2	7.3	6.5	4.9	23.9	27.4	14.2	1.7	74.5	40.4	49.9	50.1
69156	POTTER	98.1	98.0	0.2	0.1	0.0	0.0	2.1	2.6	7.2	7.3	7.4	6.8	5.4	24.2	27.5	12.4	1.8	73.9	40.1	51.9	48.1
69157	PURDUM	98.9	98.9	0.0	0.0	0.0	0.0	0.0	0.0	5.7	6.3	7.4	5.7	4.6	25.0	27.3	15.9	2.3	77.3	42.5	50.0	50.0
69161	SENECA	99.2	100.0	0.0	0.0	0.0	0.0	0.8	0.9	5.9	5.9	5.1	4.2	5.9	21.2	34.8	14.4	2.5	80.5	46.0	51.7	48.3
69162	SIDNEY	95.6	94.8	0.2	0.2	0.6	0.7	5.3	6.3	6.9	6.6	6.2	7.0	7.4	24.8	24.4	14.1	2.6	75.8	38.7	48.8	51.2
69163	STAPLETON	98.6	98.6	0.1	0.1	0.0	0.0	1.0	1.1	5.4	5.9	6.9	6.7	5.8	21.6	31.4	14.2	2.1	77.9	43.4	50.8	49.2
69165	SUTHERLAND	96.4	95.9	0.1	0.1	0.2	0.2	3.9	4.5	5.8	6.2	7.1	6.8	5.6	23.2	27.5	14.9	2.9	76.7	41.8	50.5	49.5
69166	THEDFORD	99.4	99.6	0.0	0.0	0.0	0.0	0.9	0.9	5.8	6.3	5.2	4.7	5.8	22.0	32.1	14.9	3.2	79.7	45.1	49.8	50.2
69167	TRYON	97.9	97.9	0.0	0.0	0.4	0.4	1.5	1.5	7.7	7.5	6.2	6.6	5.6	21.8	27.2	14.6	2.8	74.7	41.0	50.3	49.7
69168	VENANGO	96.7	96.8	0.0	0.0	0.0	0.0	2.8	3.2	5.2	6.7	8.4	6.7	5.5	23.3	31.1	11.9	1.2	74.7	40.5	53.2	46.8
69169	WALLACE	98.5	98.3	0.0	0.0	0.0	0.0	2.4	3.1	6.4	6.8	8.0	7.6	5.6	23.1	28.6	12.0	1.9	74.2	40.0	49.8	50.2
69170	WELLFLEET	98.7	98.7	0.0	0.0	0.0	0.0	2.2	2.8	6.3	6.6	7.6	7.2	5.4	23.3	29.6	12.3	1.9	75.2	40.8	49.7	50.3
69201	VALENTINE	94.0	93.9	0.0	0.0	0.5	0.5	0.9	0.9	6.3	6.5	7.1	7.3	5.8	23.3	25.7	14.8	3.1	75.1	40.2	48.8	51.2
69210	AINSWORTH	98.6	98.6	0.0	0.0	0.3	0.3	0.8	0.8	5.6	6.0	6.5	6.4	5.2	22.0	27.0	17.5	3.9	77.2	43.9	49.8	50.2
69211	CODY	94.0	93.8	0.3	0.3	0.3	0.3	1.4	1.8	5.7	6.3	7.7	7.1	5.4	23.8	26.5	15.8	1.8	75.9	41.2	51.2	48.8
69212	CROOKSTON	92.8	92.7	0.0	0.0	0.4	0.4	0.4	0.4	7.3	7.3	6.6	7.0	5.9	24.2	27.8	12.1	1.8	74.4	38.2	50.2	49.8
69214	JOHNSTOWN	98.5	98.5	0.0	0.0	0.3	0.3	0.9	0.6	6.0	6.0	6.6	6.3	5.4	22.2	26.7	17.1	3.9	76.7	43.3	50.0	50.0
69216	KILGORE	93.0	92.6	0.4	0.5	0.4	0.5	1.3	0.9	4.6	5.1	8.8	8.3	5.5	22.6	27.2	16.1	1.8	76.0	42.1	50.7	49.3
69217	LONG PINE	98.8	98.8	0.0	0.0	0.3	0.3	1.0	1.0	5.1	5.4	6.2	6.3	5.0	21.3	28.0	18.5	4.3	78.5	45.5	49.9	50.2
69218	MERRIMAN	94.9	95.0	0.2	0.2	0.3	0.3	1.2	1.1	5.9	6.4	7.9	7.1	5.1	24.5	26.9	14.6	1.6	75.3	40.4	52.3	47.7
69221	WOOD LAKE	95.8	96.2	0.0	0.0	0.0	0.0	1.6	1.1	8.2	8.7	6.5	4.9	4.4	27.7	24.5	13.6	1.6	73.4	37.5	52.2	47.8
69301	ALLIANCE	90.2	88.9	0.4	0.5	0.6	0.8	8.1	9.5	6.8	6.7	7.2	7.4	7.9	23.4	27.2	11.2	2.4	74.5	37.8	49.7	50.3
69331	ANGORA	96.2	96.1	0.0	0.0	0.0	0.0	4.8	4.9	5.8	5.8	7.8	7.8	4.9	22.3	29.1	14.6	1.9	74.8	42.2	52.4	47.6
69333	ASHBY	98.7	99.3	0.0	0.0	0.0	0.0	1.3	1.3	5.3	6.6	9.3	9.9	2.7	23.8	30.5	11.3	0.7	72.2	40.2	53.6	46.4
69334	BAYARD	93.9	92.8	0.0	0.1	0.3	0.4	10.2	12.1	5.9	5.9	6.8	7.3	6.3	22.8	28.0	14.5	2.6	76.7	41.6	50.3	49.7
69335	BINGHAM	97.0	97.5	0.0	0.0	0.0	0.0	1.5	1.0	6.5	7.0	7.0	6.0	5.0	24.6	28.1	14.1	1.5	75.4	41.1	53.8	46.2
69336	BRIDGEPORT	93.2	92.2	0.1	0.1	0.2	0.3	10.7	12.4	6.3	6.5	7.3	7.6	5.8	23.1	25.8	15.0	2.6	75.0	40.4	49.2	50.8
69337	CHADRON	93.1	92.4	0.9	0.9	0.4	0.6	2.6	3.0	5.1	4.7	5.0	12.1	19.1	20.5	20.2	11.2	2.2	81.5	28.1	49.2	50.8
69339	CRAWFORD	94.2	93.7	0.3	0.3	0.1	0.1	2.0	2.2	5.1	5.4	7.2	7.2	6.2	20.9	26.5	17.8	3.9	77.5	43.6	46.9	53.2
69340	ELLSWORTH	96.3	96.8	0.0	0.0	0.0	0.0	1.4	0.9	6.9	7.4	7.4	5.5	5.5	24.9	26.7	14.3	1.4	74.7	40.4	53.5	46.5
69341	GERING	90.9	89.3	0.1	0.1	0.3	0.4	14.5	17.1	6.5	6.3	6.7	6.7	6.9	24.0	26.1	13.9	2.8	76.3	40.0	47.6	52.5
69343	GORDON	86.2	85.8	0.0	0.0	0.3	0.3	1.2	1.3	6.0	6.4	7.7	7.1	6.0	20.8	25.2	16.9	4.0	74.9	41.7	48.2	51.9
69345	HARRISBURG	95.8	95.8	0.1	0.1	0.1	0.1	5.6	5.7	4.8	6.7	11.1	6.5	2.0	22.9	30.2	14.7	1.1	72.8	41.8	52.2	47.8
69346	HARRISON	98.4	98.2	0.0	0.0	0.1	0.1	1.2	1.2	5.0	5.4	6.1	6.3	5.7	21.3	30.3	18.3	1.7	79.9	45.2	52.5	47.5
69347	HAY SPRINGS	93.1	93.0	0.1	0.1	0.1	0.1	1.7	1.7	5.6	5.4	5.1	6.1	6.9	19.4	28.2	19.1	4.4	80.2	45.9	50.0	50.0
69348	HEMINGFORD	95.4	94.6	0.0	0.0	0.1	0.1	4.3	5.3	5.6	6.4	8.3	7.4	5.3	21.8	28.0	14.8	2.3	74.7	41.7	51.7	48.4
69350	HYANNIS	98.7	98.7	0.0	0.0	0.2	0.2	1.3	1.1	5.2	6.1	9.2	10.3	2.5	23.1	30.0	12.8	0.9	72.0	41.1	53.8	46.2
69351	LAKESIDE	96.2	96.2	0.0	0.0	0.0	0.0	0.0	0.0	7.6	7.6	7.6	5.7	3.8	26.4	28.3	13.2	0.0	77.4	39.4	52.8	47.2
69352	LYMAN	83.8	80.6	0.0	0.0	1.8	2.3	21.3	25.1	8.0	8.4	8.5	6.4	4.5	24.2	24.8	13.6	1.7	71.1	37.9	48.7	51.3
69354	MARSLAND	96.8	96.4	0.0	0.0	0.0	0.0	1.6	1.4	4.3	5.0	6.4	6.4	5.0	19.3	33.6	17.9	2.1	80.0	47.3	52.9	47.1
69356	MINATARE	90.7	89.1	0.6	0.6	0.1	0.1	11.8	14.1	7.1	7.1	7.3	6.9	6.7	26.0	25.8	12.1	1.1	74.4	37.2	49.7	50.3
69357	MITCHELL	91.2	89.6	0.1	0.1	0.9	1.3	13.4	15.8	5.9	6.5	7.8	6.7	6.2	24.3	26.7	13.7	2.2	75.5	39.6	48.5	51.5
69358	MORRILL	92.0	90.4	0.1	0.1	1.1	1.4	10.9	13.1	4.9	5.8	7.2	6.9	5.9	23.4	27.8	16.1	1.9	77.7	42.4	49.1	50.9
69360	RUSHVILLE	84.5	84.1	0.1	0.1	0.1	0.1	1.7	1.8	5.9	6.4	7.1	6.0	5.7	21.5	27.9	16.5	3.2	76.8	42.9	49.3	50.7
69361	SCOTTSBLUFF	84.1	82.4	0.4	0.4	0.7	0.9	20.8	23.4	6.9	6.6	7.0	6.9	7.2	23.8	23.9	14.7	2.9	75.3	38.2	47.4	52.6
69366	WHITMAN	98.4	98.4	0.0	0.0	0.4	0.4	1.2	1.2	5.2	6.4	9.2	9.6	2.8	23.9	29.5	12.4	1.2	72.9	40.6	53.4	46.6
69367	WHITNEY	93.8	92.9	1.9	2.1	0.4	0.7	1.9	2.5	4.3	4.6	5.7	12.1	7.5	21.4	27.9	14.6	1.8	77.9	40.3	54.6	45.4
	NEBRASKA	89.6	88.4	4.0	4.2	1.3	1.8	5.5	6.4	7.0	6.9	7.2	7.3	7.6	27.5	23.5	11.2	2.1	74.8	35.7	49.4	50.6
	UNITED STATES	75.1	73.6	12.3	12.5	3.8	4.2	12.5	14.1	6.9	6.7	7.2	7.0	7.3	28.6	23.8	10.8	1.7	75.1	36.0	49.1	50.9

INCOME

ZIP CODE #	POST OFFICE NAME	2004 Per Capita Income	2004 HH Income Base	2004 HOUSEHOLD INCOME DISTRIBUTION (%) Less than $25,000	$25,000 to $49,999	$50,000 to $99,999	$100,000 to $149,999	$150,000 or More	MEDIAN HOUSEHOLD INCOME 2004	2009	2004 National Centile	2004 State Centile	2004 Home Value Base	2004 HOME VALUE DISTRIBUTION (%) Less than $50,000	$50,000 to $89,999	$90,000 to $174,999	$175,000 to $399,999	$400,000 or More	2004 Median Home Value
69032	HAYES CENTER	15642	356	39.3	35.7	19.4	4.2	1.4	29306	33935	11	6	266	50.0	24.1	14.3	6.8	4.9	50000
69033	IMPERIAL	22052	984	28.8	34.4	25.7	7.5	3.7	38951	46411	43	56	778	28.3	34.8	31.0	5.1	0.8	75000
69034	INDIANOLA	17245	483	31.7	39.1	24.4	3.1	1.7	36672	41319	34	41	383	46.2	36.3	15.1	2.4	0.0	53537
69036	LEBANON	19894	71	36.6	32.4	23.9	4.2	2.8	37732	41119	38	48	56	48.2	37.5	10.7	3.6	0.0	52500
69037	MAX	16699	57	43.9	28.1	22.8	3.5	1.8	28309	35000	9	4	45	57.8	8.9	15.6	11.1	6.7	41250
69038	MAYWOOD	20285	267	26.2	40.8	25.8	3.8	3.4	38183	43616	40	51	201	28.9	30.9	26.9	10.0	3.5	72917
69039	MOOREFIELD	22833	125	30.4	36.0	20.8	7.2	5.6	38295	45279	40	51	96	30.2	25.0	28.1	13.5	3.1	80000
69040	PALISADE	16921	283	41.7	33.9	17.7	3.5	3.2	30469	35218	13	8	220	47.3	30.5	13.2	7.3	1.8	54615
69041	PARKS	17069	83	34.9	32.5	22.9	7.2	2.4	34524	39529	26	26	58	56.9	20.7	20.7	1.7	0.0	43333
69042	STOCKVILLE	26011	50	26.0	38.0	24.0	8.0	4.0	40000	46543	46	60	39	25.6	23.1	33.3	12.8	5.1	91667
69043	STRATTON	17725	277	38.3	33.9	20.6	4.7	2.5	31053	36122	15	10	218	43.1	30.7	19.3	3.7	3.2	58824
69044	TRENTON	17183	323	41.2	35.3	20.1	3.1	0.3	29525	34667	11	6	240	61.3	29.2	8.3	1.3	0.0	42286
69045	WAUNETA	19355	368	31.3	40.2	22.0	4.6	1.9	34386	39507	25	26	297	52.5	29.0	14.8	3.7	0.0	48077
69046	WILSONVILLE	20760	94	29.8	40.4	21.3	4.3	4.3	36971	42359	35	42	73	42.5	30.1	15.1	8.2	4.1	59167
69101	NORTH PLATTE	22707	12040	29.2	30.0	29.6	8.2	3.0	41510	50272	51	67	8265	19.6	29.8	40.4	9.0	1.2	90639
69120	ARNOLD	19530	468	37.6	33.1	24.4	3.6	1.3	31198	35573	15	11	362	45.9	26.8	16.9	5.0	5.5	55556
69121	ARTHUR	18722	182	36.8	33.5	21.4	4.4	3.9	31386	37116	16	13	114	47.4	25.4	21.1	5.3	0.9	55000
69122	BIG SPRINGS	20718	304	32.9	34.9	25.0	5.3	2.0	36292	43059	33	38	235	36.2	27.7	29.4	5.1	1.7	67667
69123	BRADY	18405	439	31.7	37.4	25.3	4.1	1.6	34933	40331	27	29	335	29.9	28.4	29.6	10.2	2.1	76750
69125	BROADWATER	18197	164	35.4	41.5	16.5	4.3	2.4	31841	36852	17	15	117	46.2	19.7	21.4	11.1	1.7	57500
69127	BRULE	20348	339	32.2	34.2	26.3	5.3	2.1	38072	44495	40	50	277	24.2	27.4	36.5	9.4	2.5	87750
69128	BUSHNELL	17119	151	38.4	34.4	19.2	4.0	4.0	31189	35602	15	11	122	53.3	21.3	13.1	10.7	1.6	47647
69129	CHAPPELL	20908	643	29.7	35.0	27.7	5.3	2.3	38927	45980	42	55	513	38.4	36.3	19.1	5.7	0.6	59015
69130	COZAD	22057	2280	29.0	34.2	28.4	4.7	3.6	38820	45593	42	54	1629	30.5	37.1	24.9	6.9	0.7	70179
69131	DALTON	22882	264	32.6	33.0	25.0	6.4	3.0	33731	38601	23	23	218	36.7	29.8	23.4	7.8	2.3	64800
69132	DICKENS	20837	46	28.3	30.4	28.3	10.9	2.2	45000	50000	61	78	36	27.8	38.9	30.6	2.8	0.0	70000
69133	DIX	16598	183	38.3	35.0	19.1	3.8	3.8	31243	35857	16	12	148	52.7	21.6	14.2	10.1	1.4	47895
69134	ELSIE	22719	168	23.2	33.9	28.0	11.3	3.6	45632	52963	63	79	129	55.0	17.8	16.3	7.0	3.9	47045
69135	ELSMERE	14882	43	30.2	46.5	20.9	2.3	0.0	30535	36689	14	8	16	25.0	18.8	12.5	6.3	37.5	125000
69138	GOTHENBURG	20088	1676	29.1	34.4	28.8	5.9	1.8	40893	47773	49	65	1223	22.9	35.7	36.3	4.3	0.8	80321
69140	GRANT	21133	736	32.7	32.3	26.5	6.3	2.2	37716	45595	38	47	557	29.8	35.9	31.1	2.7	0.5	71413
69141	GURLEY	20574	187	34.2	32.6	24.6	5.9	2.7	33086	38365	21	19	154	37.7	31.2	23.4	6.5	1.3	63684
69142	HALSEY	18074	60	40.0	31.7	25.0	3.3	0.0	33190	37819	21	19	46	58.7	23.9	13.0	4.4	0.0	40000
69143	HERSHEY	23313	688	20.6	29.9	37.1	8.7	3.6	49544	59924	71	86	570	14.9	26.0	39.7	17.2	2.3	101563
69144	KEYSTONE	21061	153	33.3	34.0	26.1	4.6	2.0	37528	44445	38	46	128	25.8	27.3	35.9	8.6	2.3	85556
69145	KIMBALL	22074	1412	32.0	34.6	26.1	4.9	2.5	35294	42030	29	31	1027	42.6	33.4	20.0	4.0	0.1	59684
69146	LEMOYNE	22803	121	31.4	33.9	27.3	5.0	2.5	38608	44308	41	53	102	25.5	26.5	38.2	7.8	2.0	87143
69147	LEWELLEN	20777	405	37.5	33.6	22.5	4.7	1.7	32327	37449	19	16	314	37.9	29.3	27.1	4.5	1.3	65238
69148	LISCO	17778	93	37.6	39.8	18.3	2.2	2.2	31613	35368	17	13	51	35.3	41.2	21.6	2.0	0.0	66250
69149	LODGEPOLE	20635	320	32.2	36.3	24.1	4.7	2.8	34799	39472	27	27	256	37.5	34.0	21.5	5.5	1.6	62667
69150	MADRID	21265	186	23.7	35.0	27.4	10.2	3.8	44318	52015	59	76	143	51.8	18.2	18.2	7.7	4.2	48913
69151	MAXWELL	18978	337	29.7	27.6	34.7	6.2	1.8	41912	49045	53	69	258	27.9	21.7	33.3	13.2	3.9	90769
69152	MULLEN	17618	341	37.0	39.9	18.2	2.4	2.6	30648	35080	14	9	263	49.8	26.6	17.1	1.5	4.9	50227
69153	OGALLALA	20694	2696	30.5	35.3	27.2	5.1	2.0	37374	43515	37	45	1898	20.8	39.3	33.0	5.4	1.5	80545
69154	OSHKOSH	17886	647	40.7	33.9	20.1	4.5	0.9	29349	34141	11	6	475	45.5	31.0	21.1	2.3	0.2	55119
69155	PAXTON	18360	450	33.3	36.0	25.6	4.0	1.1	35787	40379	31	35	345	35.9	33.0	21.2	6.1	3.8	71000
69156	POTTER	19066	313	33.6	31.6	27.5	4.2	3.2	33951	38875	24	24	222	46.0	23.9	20.3	8.1	1.8	55294
69157	PURDUM	13724	71	42.3	38.0	16.9	2.8	0.0	27462	30927	8	3	47	63.8	19.2	4.3	4.3	8.5	29167
69161	SENECA	19725	59	40.7	30.5	25.4	3.4	0.0	32340	37966	19	16	45	57.8	24.4	13.3	4.4	0.0	41250
69162	SIDNEY	21002	3122	28.3	34.7	27.7	6.7	2.5	39114	47191	43	56	2219	25.4	42.3	25.0	5.9	1.4	69508
69163	STAPLETON	18974	381	26.8	42.0	24.2	5.8	1.3	38139	43326	40	50	292	32.9	23.0	31.2	9.6	3.4	80556
69165	SUTHERLAND	20739	651	24.6	30.1	35.2	7.8	2.3	46254	54101	64	80	520	12.1	36.4	42.1	7.5	1.9	91702
69166	THEDFORD	17730	209	39.2	32.1	24.4	4.3	0.0	33266	37795	22	20	160	55.0	23.8	13.8	6.3	1.3	44286
69167	TRYON	14812	203	40.4	32.5	21.2	5.9	0.0	30182	36584	13	7	135	47.4	31.1	14.1	2.2	5.2	52692
69168	VENANGO	20322	144	27.8	36.8	29.2	4.2	2.1	37497	43987	37	46	113	43.4	21.2	26.6	6.2	2.7	60455
69169	WALLACE	23057	240	26.7	32.9	27.5	10.0	2.9	44090	51191	59	75	187	30.0	35.8	26.7	4.8	2.7	69167
69170	WELLFLEET	20648	120	28.3	31.7	28.3	10.0	1.7	42364	48654	54	71	92	27.2	37.0	28.3	4.4	3.3	72500
69201	VALENTINE	19112	1797	35.1	32.7	24.2	6.2	1.8	34779	41637	27	27	1149	26.5	33.3	29.5	7.6	3.1	79853
69210	AINSWORTH	18936	1097	39.0	36.7	18.8	3.7	1.9	31562	36559	17	13	842	44.7	31.0	19.4	4.2	0.8	56164
69211	CODY	18017	141	37.6	35.5	19.9	5.0	2.1	31003	36837	15	10	82	50.0	17.1	14.6	4.9	13.4	50000
69212	CROOKSTON	20293	112	30.4	33.0	25.0	9.8	1.8	39205	44603	43	57	84	38.1	23.8	29.8	8.3	0.0	67500
69214	JOHNSTOWN	16055	128	39.1	36.7	18.8	3.1	2.3	31340	36253	16	12	98	44.9	31.6	19.4	4.1	0.0	56250
69216	KILGORE	16511	88	38.6	35.2	20.5	5.7	0.0	30621	35367	14	8	60	58.3	16.7	11.7	5.0	8.3	43750
69217	LONG PINE	19051	302	37.4	38.7	18.5	3.0	2.3	33014	38019	21	18	236	47.5	28.8	18.2	5.1	0.4	52857
69218	MERRIMAN	17030	261	36.8	36.4	20.3	4.6	1.9	31382	36556	16	12	140	46.4	17.9	12.9	5.7	17.1	57143
69221	WOOD LAKE	21808	84	36.9	36.9	19.1	2.4	4.8	31268	38619	16	12	34	32.4	11.8	20.6	8.8	26.5	125000
69301	ALLIANCE	22391	4116	25.4	29.6	34.2	8.4	2.4	45645	54226	63	80	2927	23.4	34.3	35.6	6.0	0.6	82209
69331	ANGORA	14640	38	36.8	36.8	21.1	5.3	0.0	33158	39062	21	19	26	42.3	19.2	23.1	15.4	0.0	70000
69333	ASHBY	16833	61	31.2	42.6	21.3	3.3	1.6	35921	40438	31	36	38	52.6	23.7	13.2	5.3	5.3	46667
69334	BAYARD	17856	1014	34.8	29.8	29.6	4.8	1.0	36505	42743	34	40	764	37.4	33.1	21.6	6.8	1.1	64429
69335	BINGHAM	15666	79	32.9	41.8	21.5	3.8	0.0	35264	39189	28	30	51	47.1	19.6	21.6	5.9	5.9	53750
69336	BRIDGEPORT	16944	1023	35.3	36.5	23.2	4.2	0.9	33469	39241	22	21	744	45.2	30.7	17.6	5.5	1.1	55806
69337	CHADRON	21104	2626	37.6	27.7	23.9	8.0	2.9	33779	42574	23	23	1409	32.4	34.5	25.6	6.6	0.9	73007
69339	CRAWFORD	20119	681	34.8	36.6	22.8	4.1	1.8	33552	40873	23	22	497	52.7	27.0	12.3	5.6	2.4	47589
69340	ELLSWORTH	18445	102	32.4	43.1	20.6	3.9	0.0	35348	39366	29	31	68	48.5	19.1	20.6	7.4	4.4	52000
69341	GERING	20921	4311	31.2	32.5	25.4	8.8	2.1	38905	46073	42	55	3152	19.5	37.4	36.5	6.2	0.4	83636
69343	GORDON	17263	1032	39.2	33.3	21.7	4.0	1.8	31621	36589	17	14	744	44.2	31.7	18.7	3.5	1.9	57049
69345	HARRISBURG	18443	314	31.5	32.8	28.3	4.1	3.2	37174	46207	36	44	200	30.0	30.0	25.5	14.5	0.0	78000
69346	HARRISON	18909	382	35.9	36.7	20.2	5.2	2.1	31688	36972	17	14	266	41.4	25.6	17.3	6.4	9.4	60000
69347	HAY SPRINGS	17047	609	36.5	36.0	22.8	3.8	1.0	35238	40244	28	30	456	48.7	27.2	16.7	5.0	2.4	51875
69348	HEMINGFORD	21464	645	27.8	31.0	34.0	4.5	2.8	40499	47087	48	62	500	31.6	32.4	24.6	8.4	3.0	69423
69350	HYANNIS	17101	182	30.2	40.7	25.3	1.7	2.2	36921	40290	35	42	122	59.0	22.1	13.9	3.3	1.6	40000
69351	LAKESIDE	15330	22	36.4	45.5	13.6	4.6	0.0	32290	43612	19	16	15	46.7	26.7	20.0	0.0	6.7	55000
69352	LYMAN	16492	284	39.1	33.1	19.0	6.3	2.5	32431	37757	19	16	217	47.9	20.3	18.9	10.1	2.8	55000
69354	MARSLAND	19804	57	28.1	36.8	26.3	5.3	3.5	37963	42343	39	49	44	31.8	25.0	18.2	15.9	9.1	80000
69356	MINATARE	16923	855	37.2	35.0	21.5	4.6	1.8	34732	40063	26	26	580	40.0	24.7	24.0	10.0	1.4	62745
69357	MITCHELL	20043	1478	31.0	33.4	25.6	6.6	3.4	38033	45837	39	49	1064	23.7	29.0	35.9	9.8	1.7	86667
69358	MORRILL	21850	860	31.6	34.2	25.9	5.2	3.0	36247	43086	33	38	601	30.0	37.9	20.6	9.7	1.8	69928
69360	RUSHVILLE	17802	721	35.4	35.8	23.3	4.4	1.1	33397	38348	22	20	530	44.7	30.4	19.3	4.0	1.7	56667
69361	SCOTTSBLUFF	22113	7281	33.9	30.5	25.9	6.3	3.4	36405	44214	33	39	4553	20.2	32.1	36.7	10.3	0.9	87424
69366	WHITMAN	15115	90	31.1	40.0	25.6	2.2	1.1	36315	40000	33	38	54	55.6	22.2	11.1	3.7	7.4	42500
69367	WHITNEY	21111	122	27.9	37.7	27.9	4.9	1.6	38176	44651	40	51	95	32.6	27.4	22.1	13.7	4.2	75000
	NEBRASKA	23743		24.5	30.5	31.8	9.2	4.0	45453	54516				17.2	23.9	42.4	14.4	2.2	101398
	UNITED STATES	25866		24.7	27.1	30.8	10.9	6.5	48124	56710				10.9	15.0	33.7	30.1	10.4	145905

# ZIP CODE / POST OFFICE NAME	FINANCIAL SERVICES				THE HOME						ENTERTAINMENT						PERSONAL			
					Home Improvements		Furnishings													
	Auto Loan	Home Loan	Invest-ments	Retire-ment Plans	Home Repair	Lawn & Garden	Comput-ers & Hard-ware	Major Appli-ances	TV, Radio, Sound Equip-ment	Furni-ture	Dine out/ Carry out	Sports Equip-ment	Fees & Tickets	Toys & Games	Travel	Cable TV	Apparel & Services	Auto Repairs	Health Insur-ance	Pets & Supplies
69032 HAYES CENTER	71	50	26	47	58	65	49	61	56	48	66	73	42	65	51	59	60	60	72	84
69033 IMPERIAL	96	67	35	64	78	88	66	82	77	66	90	99	57	88	69	80	82	81	98	114
69034 INDIANOLA	78	54	29	51	63	71	54	66	62	53	73	80	46	71	56	65	66	65	79	92
69036 LEBANON	82	57	30	54	66	74	56	70	65	56	64	71	41	63	49	57	59	58	70	82
69037 MAX	69	48	25	45	56	63	48	59	55	47	64	71	41	63	49	57	59	58	70	82
69038 MAYWOOD	99	69	36	65	81	90	68	84	79	67	92	102	58	90	71	83	84	83	101	118
69039 MOOREFIELD	92	72	49	66	80	92	70	83	79	69	94	96	63	92	73	84	87	82	98	110
69040 PALISADE	74	51	27	49	60	67	51	63	59	50	69	76	43	67	53	61	63	62	75	87
69041 PARKS	82	57	30	54	67	75	57	70	65	56	77	85	48	75	59	69	70	69	84	98
69042 STOCKVILLE	100	76	48	69	86	97	72	88	82	72	97	104	64	96	76	87	90	87	104	121
69043 STRATTON	75	53	28	50	61	69	52	64	60	51	70	77	44	69	54	63	64	63	77	90
69044 TRENTON	60	45	28	43	49	58	48	54	54	46	64	62	43	61	48	57	58	54	65	68
69045 WAUNETA	71	53	34	51	58	69	58	65	65	55	77	73	51	72	58	69	70	64	77	79
69046 WILSONVILLE	86	60	31	57	70	78	59	73	68	59	80	88	51	78	61	72	73	72	87	102
69101 NORTH PLATTE	76	73	73	73	75	80	75	76	76	74	94	89	73	94	75	76	91	77	78	88
69120 ARNOLD	79	55	29	52	64	72	54	67	62	53	73	81	46	72	56	65	67	66	80	93
69121 ARTHUR	80	55	29	52	65	72	55	68	63	54	74	82	47	73	57	66	68	67	81	94
69122 BIG SPRINGS	83	58	31	55	68	76	57	71	66	57	78	85	49	76	60	69	71	70	84	99
69123 BRADY	79	55	29	52	64	72	54	67	62	54	73	81	46	72	56	66	67	66	80	93
69125 BROADWATER	78	55	29	52	64	71	54	67	62	53	73	81	46	72	56	65	67	66	80	93
69127 BRULE	81	62	41	57	71	79	59	72	67	59	80	84	53	78	63	72	74	71	85	98
69128 BUSHNELL	76	53	28	50	62	70	53	65	61	52	71	78	45	70	55	64	65	64	77	91
69129 CHAPPELL	77	58	37	55	64	76	63	70	71	60	83	79	56	79	63	75	76	70	84	86
69130 COZAD	86	72	54	69	77	86	72	79	78	70	93	92	68	94	73	80	87	78	89	99
69131 DALTON	91	64	33	60	74	83	63	78	72	62	85	94	54	83	65	76	77	77	93	108
69132 DICKENS	100	70	37	66	81	91	69	85	79	68	93	103	59	91	72	83	85	84	102	119
69133 DIX	76	53	28	50	62	70	53	65	61	52	71	78	45	70	55	64	65	64	77	91
69134 ELSIE	108	75	39	71	88	98	74	92	86	74	101	111	64	99	77	90	92	91	110	128
69135 ELSMERE	66	46	24	44	54	60	46	57	53	45	62	68	39	61	47	55	56	56	67	79
69138 GOTHENBURG	83	63	41	61	70	79	64	74	71	63	84	87	58	83	65	73	78	73	85	96
69140 GRANT	85	62	36	59	70	81	64	75	73	62	86	87	56	83	65	77	77	76	92	98
69141 GURLEY	91	63	33	60	74	83	62	77	72	62	84	93	53	83	65	76	77	76	92	108
69142 HALSEY	71	50	26	47	58	65	49	61	57	49	67	73	42	65	51	60	61	60	73	85
69143 HERSHEY	108	75	39	71	88	98	75	92	86	74	101	111	64	99	77	90	92	91	110	128
69144 KEYSTONE	79	62	42	56	70	79	59	71	66	58	79	83	52	77	62	71	73	69	83	96
69145 KIMBALL	76	65	57	65	69	77	69	73	72	67	87	84	65	84	68	74	82	73	80	86
69146 LEMOYNE	79	62	42	56	70	79	59	71	66	58	79	83	52	78	62	71	73	70	83	97
69147 LEWELLEN	70	53	34	49	59	68	54	63	61	53	72	72	48	70	55	65	66	62	75	81
69148 LISCO	71	50	26	47	58	65	49	61	57	49	66	73	42	65	51	59	61	60	72	85
69149 LODGEPOLE	86	60	31	57	70	78	59	73	68	59	80	89	51	79	62	72	73	72	87	102
69150 MADRID	105	73	38	69	85	96	72	90	83	72	98	108	62	96	75	88	89	88	107	125
69151 MAXWELL	91	64	33	60	74	83	63	78	73	62	85	94	54	83	65	76	78	77	93	109
69152 MULLEN	72	50	26	48	59	66	50	62	57	49	67	74	42	66	52	60	61	61	73	86
69153 OGALLALA	83	64	42	62	70	79	64	74	71	63	84	87	58	83	65	73	78	73	84	95
69154 OSHKOSH	64	47	30	45	52	62	51	58	58	49	68	66	45	64	51	61	62	57	69	72
69155 PAXTON	83	58	31	55	67	76	57	71	66	56	77	85	49	76	59	69	70	70	84	98
69156 POTTER	86	60	31	57	70	78	59	73	68	59	80	88	51	79	62	72	73	72	87	102
69157 PURDUM	62	43	22	41	50	56	42	52	49	42	57	63	36	56	44	51	52	52	63	73
69161 SENECA	71	50	26	47	58	65	49	61	57	49	67	73	42	65	51	60	61	60	72	85
69162 SIDNEY	79	64	49	63	70	78	67	74	72	65	86	87	62	85	67	73	81	73	81	92
69163 STAPLETON	82	60	35	57	69	76	58	71	66	58	78	85	51	77	61	69	72	70	83	97
69165 SUTHERLAND	95	67	35	63	78	87	66	81	76	65	89	98	56	87	68	80	81	80	97	113
69166 THEDFORD	71	50	26	47	58	65	49	61	57	49	66	73	42	65	51	59	61	60	72	85
69167 TRYON	70	49	26	46	57	64	49	60	56	48	66	72	41	64	50	59	60	59	71	84
69168 VENANGO	88	61	32	58	71	80	61	75	70	60	82	90	52	80	63	73	75	74	89	104
69169 WALLACE	103	72	37	68	83	93	71	87	81	70	96	105	60	94	73	86	87	86	104	122
69170 WELLFLEET	99	69	36	65	81	90	68	84	79	67	92	102	58	90	71	83	84	83	101	118
69201 VALENTINE	77	56	34	53	63	73	59	68	67	57	79	79	52	76	60	71	72	68	82	87
69210 AINSWORTH	76	53	28	50	62	69	52	64	60	52	70	78	45	69	54	63	64	64	77	90
69211 CODY	78	54	28	51	63	71	54	66	62	53	72	80	46	71	56	65	66	65	79	92
69212 CROOKSTON	90	62	33	59	73	82	62	76	71	61	83	92	53	82	64	75	76	75	91	106
69214 JOHNSTOWN	75	53	28	50	61	69	52	64	60	51	70	77	44	69	54	63	64	63	76	89
69216 KILGORE	74	51	27	49	60	67	51	63	59	50	69	76	43	67	53	61	63	62	75	87
69217 LONG PINE	77	54	28	51	62	70	53	65	61	52	72	79	45	70	55	64	65	64	78	91
69218 MERRIMAN	76	53	28	50	62	69	52	65	60	52	71	78	45	69	54	63	65	64	77	90
69221 WOOD LAKE	86	60	32	57	70	79	60	74	69	59	81	89	51	79	62	72	73	73	88	103
69301 ALLIANCE	88	74	57	72	79	86	74	82	79	73	95	96	69	94	75	80	89	81	89	101
69331 ANGORA	71	50	26	47	58	65	49	61	57	48	66	73	42	65	51	59	60	60	72	85
69333 ASHBY	75	53	28	50	61	69	52	64	60	51	70	77	44	69	54	63	64	63	77	90
69334 BAYARD	75	55	33	52	62	72	58	67	66	56	77	77	51	74	59	69	71	67	80	86
69335 BINGHAM	71	50	26	47	58	65	49	61	57	49	67	73	42	65	51	60	61	60	73	85
69336 BRIDGEPORT	70	52	32	49	58	68	55	63	62	53	73	72	48	70	55	66	67	63	75	80
69337 CHADRON	74	59	63	62	61	68	74	70	75	69	92	86	67	88	69	72	88	75	70	82
69339 CRAWFORD	78	57	35	55	64	75	61	70	69	59	81	80	54	77	61	73	74	69	83	88
69340 ELLSWORTH	71	50	26	47	58	65	49	61	56	48	66	73	42	65	51	59	60	60	72	84
69341 GERING	78	67	57	66	71	79	69	74	73	68	88	86	65	86	69	74	83	74	81	89
69343 GORDON	66	49	32	47	54	65	55	60	61	52	72	68	49	68	54	65	66	60	72	73
69345 HARRISBURG	86	60	31	57	70	79	59	73	68	59	80	89	51	79	62	72	73	72	88	102
69346 HARRISON	80	56	29	53	65	73	55	68	63	54	74	82	47	73	57	66	68	67	81	95
69347 HAY SPRINGS	70	51	30	48	57	67	53	62	60	51	71	72	46	68	54	64	65	62	74	81
69348 HEMINGFORD	101	70	37	66	82	92	69	86	80	69	94	104	59	92	72	84	86	85	102	120
69350 HYANNIS	76	53	28	50	62	69	52	65	60	52	71	78	45	69	54	63	64	64	77	90
69351 LAKESIDE	67	47	24	44	54	61	46	57	53	46	62	69	39	61	48	56	57	56	68	79
69352 LYMAN	81	55	26	49	63	72	54	67	64	54	75	80	46	72	55	68	68	66	82	94
69354 MARSLAND	88	61	32	58	72	80	61	75	70	60	82	90	52	80	63	73	75	74	89	105
69356 MINATARE	73	53	31	50	60	69	55	64	63	53	73	75	48	71	56	66	67	64	77	84
69357 MITCHELL	90	64	36	61	73	84	66	78	75	64	88	92	57	85	67	79	80	77	93	104
69358 MORRILL	90	65	39	62	73	85	68	79	78	66	91	92	60	87	69	82	83	79	95	103
69360 RUSHVILLE	70	51	32	49	58	67	55	63	62	53	73	72	48	69	55	65	66	62	75	80
69361 SCOTTSBLUFF	74	72	74	71	73	78	74	75	75	73	93	87	73	92	74	74	90	76	75	85
69366 WHITMAN	76	53	28	50	62	69	53	65	61	52	71	78	45	70	55	64	65	64	77	91
69367 WHITNEY	83	58	30	55	68	76	57	71	66	57	77	85	49	76	59	69	71	70	84	99
NEBRASKA	88	81	77	81	83	90	83	85	84	82	104	101	80	103	82	84	100	86	87	100
UNITED STATES	100	100	100	100	100	100	100	100	100	100	100	100	100	100	100	100	100	100	100	100

POPULATION CHANGE

# ZIP CODE / POST OFFICE NAME	COUNTY FIPS CODE	POPULATION 2000	2004	2009	2000-2004 ANNUAL RATE % Rate	State Centile	HOUSEHOLDS 2000	2004	2009	% Annual Rate 2000-2004	2004 Average HH Size	FAMILIES 2000	2004	% Annual Rate 2000-2004
89001 ALAMO	017	947	939	919	-0.2	18	344	346	343	0.1	2.71	255	255	0.0
89005 BOULDER CITY	003	15082	16233	19045	1.8	42	6450	6920	8077	1.7	2.31	4321	4577	1.4
89008 CALIENTE	017	1343	1317	1287	-0.5	14	502	497	491	-0.2	2.28	301	297	-0.3
89011 HENDERSON	003	169	220	283	6.4	85	78	101	129	6.3	2.18	63	81	6.1
89012 HENDERSON	003	16235	26665	38628	12.4	92	6870	11165	16008	12.1	2.39	4872	7826	11.8
89013 GOLDFIELD	009	355	365	365	0.7	28	174	183	183	1.2	1.97	93	97	1.0
89014 HENDERSON	003	35322	41028	50572	3.6	66	13704	15740	19209	3.3	2.60	9009	10242	3.1
89015 HENDERSON	003	64729	76273	94482	3.9	67	23085	26979	33113	3.7	2.81	17190	19901	3.5
89017 HIKO	017	149	148	145	-0.2	19	48	48	48	0.0	3.08	36	36	0.0
89018 INDIAN SPRINGS	003	3237	3261	3544	0.2	22	597	606	717	0.4	2.46	393	389	-0.2
89019 JEAN	003	2455	4589	6909	15.9	95	952	1804	2717	16.2	2.46	615	1181	16.6
89020 AMARGOSA VALLEY	023	2454	2330	2353	-1.2	8	1028	976	990	-1.2	2.39	594	556	-1.5
89027 MESQUITE	003	9163	11954	15392	6.5	86	3422	4481	5752	6.6	2.65	2519	3255	6.2
89029 LAUGHLIN	003	7133	8153	9917	3.2	61	3208	3657	4420	3.1	2.22	2007	2241	2.6
89030 NORTH LAS VEGAS	003	54137	60171	71835	2.5	55	14129	15449	18231	2.1	3.81	11108	12007	1.9
89031 NORTH LAS VEGAS	003	34707	52928	73625	10.4	91	11307	16760	22820	9.7	3.16	9100	13369	9.5
89032 NORTH LAS VEGAS	003	27312	38941	52682	8.7	89	8787	12484	16767	8.6	3.12	7062	9930	8.4
89033 NORTH LAS VEGAS	003	8	26	48	32.0	99	5	16	30	31.5	1.63	3	10	32.8
89040 OVERTON	003	9243	10249	12246	2.5	52	3053	3362	3980	2.3	3.05	2335	2550	2.1
89041 PAHRUMP	023	164	173	180	1.3	33	80	85	89	1.4	2.01	56	59	1.2
89043 PIOCHE	017	1726	1726	1700	0.0	20	646	657	657	0.4	2.37	419	423	0.2
89045 ROUND MOUNTAIN	023	1756	1622	1634	-1.9	5	635	597	608	-1.4	2.72	446	414	-1.7
89046 SEARCHLIGHT	003	1082	1222	1426	2.9	58	599	688	829	3.3	1.27	229	104	-17.0
89047 SILVERPEAK	009	531	546	546	0.7	28	233	243	243	1.0	2.25	141	146	0.8
89048 PAHRUMP	023	14159	16404	18005	3.5	65	5936	6933	7661	3.7	2.36	4112	4772	3.6
89049 TONOPAH	023	3226	2860	2853	-2.8	2	1338	1198	1207	-2.6	2.25	815	721	-2.8
89052 HENDERSON	003	13757	21215	29485	10.7	92	5654	8613	11837	10.4	2.46	3938	5904	10.0
89060 PAHRUMP	023	7340	8270	8910	2.9	58	2991	3410	3703	3.1	2.41	2084	2345	2.8
89061 PAHRUMP	023	2968	3584	3995	4.5	73	1146	1396	1567	4.8	2.57	854	1032	4.6
89074 HENDERSON	003	46803	58815	74627	5.5	79	17549	21955	27656	5.4	2.67	12488	15456	5.2
89084 NORTH LAS VEGAS	003	10	33	60	32.4	100	5	16	30	31.5	2.06	3	11	35.8
89101 LAS VEGAS	003	50281	55583	65834	2.4	51	15858	17178	20271	1.9	2.95	8457	9094	1.7
89102 LAS VEGAS	003	36229	40244	48272	2.5	54	14117	15446	18305	2.1	2.59	8035	8697	1.9
89103 LAS VEGAS	003	44496	49942	60037	2.8	57	19285	21528	25664	2.6	2.32	10670	11612	2.0
89104 LAS VEGAS	003	35126	40327	49438	3.3	62	13390	15039	18174	2.8	2.66	7756	8728	2.8
89106 LAS VEGAS	003	25620	29267	35505	3.2	60	8791	9975	12046	3.0	2.82	5470	6127	2.8
89107 LAS VEGAS	003	36748	39611	47001	1.8	43	13186	14114	16594	1.6	2.80	8665	9098	1.2
89108 LAS VEGAS	003	68984	78798	95569	3.2	60	25010	28443	34264	3.1	2.75	16882	18899	2.7
89109 LAS VEGAS	003	40981	45314	54610	2.4	51	19061	20753	24735	2.0	2.18	8322	8791	1.3
89110 LAS VEGAS	003	64181	74114	90696	3.4	63	20203	23099	27991	3.2	3.19	15526	17605	3.0
89113 LAS VEGAS	003	8475	10814	13815	5.9	81	3581	4512	5700	5.6	2.40	2309	2862	5.2
89115 LAS VEGAS	003	54091	62038	75084	3.3	61	17272	19634	23620	3.1	3.08	12750	14359	2.8
89117 LAS VEGAS	003	50552	64864	83466	6.0	83	20976	26783	34176	5.9	2.42	13460	16864	5.5
89118 LAS VEGAS	003	18075	22397	28301	5.2	77	7858	9632	12037	4.9	2.32	4289	5219	4.7
89119 LAS VEGAS	003	45926	50675	60797	2.3	49	20044	21898	26019	2.1	2.29	9670	10299	1.5
89120 LAS VEGAS	003	21762	23551	28030	1.9	45	8534	9231	10923	1.9	2.53	5544	5891	1.4
89121 LAS VEGAS	003	60538	67107	80211	2.5	52	25141	27740	32925	2.3	2.40	15014	16282	1.9
89122 LAS VEGAS	003	29045	34822	43207	4.4	71	11835	14159	17461	4.3	2.45	7502	8793	3.8
89123 LAS VEGAS	003	47581	69099	95479	9.2	89	18030	25969	35492	9.0	2.66	12520	17842	8.7
89124 LAS VEGAS	003	3837	5240	6934	7.6	88	1227	1693	2259	7.9	2.86	825	1134	7.8
89128 LAS VEGAS	003	36319	44775	56286	5.1	77	14351	17614	21977	4.9	2.54	9636	11673	4.6
89129 LAS VEGAS	003	32832	42409	54938	6.2	84	11736	15069	19378	6.1	2.80	8934	11367	5.8
89130 LAS VEGAS	003	24077	30796	39622	6.0	82	8907	11336	14479	5.8	2.70	6838	8642	5.7
89131 LAS VEGAS	003	11041	20178	30202	15.2	95	3508	6556	9834	15.9	2.95	2813	5222	15.7
89134 LAS VEGAS	003	25100	31704	40510	5.7	80	11428	14427	18351	5.6	2.19	8403	10509	5.4
89135 LAS VEGAS	003	3539	7645	12099	19.9	98	1490	3207	5039	19.8	2.38	1055	2240	19.4
89139 LAS VEGAS	003	2310	4547	6951	17.3	96	821	1617	2457	17.3	2.80	621	1208	17.0
89141 LAS VEGAS	003	274	557	861	18.2	97	98	198	305	18.0	2.81	68	135	17.5
89142 LAS VEGAS	003	22981	29552	37869	6.1	83	7413	9383	11859	5.7	3.15	5844	7344	5.5
89143 LAS VEGAS	003	2368	4190	6142	14.4	94	800	1410	2053	14.3	2.97	635	1104	13.9
89144 LAS VEGAS	003	11081	18448	26851	12.7	93	4351	7081	10142	12.1	2.61	3128	5049	11.9
89145 LAS VEGAS	003	24737	29396	36594	4.1	68	9545	11451	14249	4.4	2.57	6481	7637	3.9
89146 LAS VEGAS	003	17495	19132	22746	2.1	47	7017	7611	8982	1.9	2.47	4412	4742	1.7
89147 LAS VEGAS	003	39610	53106	70537	7.1	87	15055	20168	26612	7.1	2.63	10352	13693	6.8
89148 LAS VEGAS	003	1041	2782	4750	26.0	98	422	1126	1910	26.0	2.47	309	815	25.6
89149 LAS VEGAS	003	11302	14306	18208	5.7	80	4136	5279	6711	5.9	2.69	3306	4157	5.5
89154 LAS VEGAS	003	1861	2085	2430	2.7	56	376	438	531	3.7	3.54	128	145	3.0
89156 LAS VEGAS	003	23204	27902	34641	4.4	72	7945	9512	11750	4.3	2.87	5808	6881	4.1
89191 NELLIS AFB	003	1481	1816	2229	4.9	76	1	1	2	0.0	3.00	1	1	0.0
89301 ELY	033	8587	8430	8236	-0.4	15	3025	3014	2986	-0.1	2.45	1978	1960	-0.2
89310 AUSTIN	015	481	376	321	-5.6	1	230	183	158	-5.2	2.01	143	112	-5.6
89311 BAKER	033	228	222	218	-0.6	13	114	107	102	-1.5	2.07	73	4	-49.5
89316 EUREKA	011	1110	1048	979	-1.3	6	434	412	387	-1.2	2.52	282	267	-1.3
89317 LUND	033	366	354	343	-0.8	12	143	141	138	-0.3	2.14	110	108	-0.4
89403 DAYTON	019	7807	9477	11616	4.7	75	2902	3529	4326	4.7	2.68	2174	2632	4.6
89404 DENIO	013	149	147	145	-0.3	17	68	68	67	0.0	2.16	50	49	-0.5
89405 EMPIRE	031	273	269	287	-0.4	17	81	80	87	-0.3	2.39	49	46	-1.5
89406 FALLON	001	23914	24407	24875	0.5	24	8894	9089	9270	0.5	2.64	6451	6566	0.4
89408 FERNLEY	019	8674	10780	13410	5.3	78	3192	3988	4973	5.4	2.70	2398	2981	5.3
89409 GABBS	023	503	425	421	-3.9	2	203	174	174	-3.6	2.44	133	113	-3.8
89410 GARDNERVILLE	005	7466	8823	10502	4.0	67	3056	3618	4337	4.1	2.40	2099	2492	4.1
89412 GERLACH	031	640	657	717	0.6	27	271	281	309	0.9	2.16	169	170	0.1
89413 GLENBROOK	005	5778	6128	6897	1.4	36	2575	2765	3149	1.7	2.21	1544	1641	1.4
89414 GOLCONDA	013	413	426	428	0.7	29	161	164	164	0.4	2.60	123	125	0.4
89415 HAWTHORNE	021	3954	3710	3434	-1.5	5	1743	1672	1588	-1.0	2.19	1102	1050	-1.1
89418 IMLAY	027	746	796	848	1.5	39	306	326	346	1.5	2.44	230	244	1.4
89419 LOVELOCK	027	4936	5049	5215	0.5	26	1340	1387	1452	0.8	2.62	907	934	0.7
89420 LUNING	021	287	265	244	-1.9	4	159	151	143	-1.2	1.75	86	81	-1.4
89423 MINDEN	005	8512	10334	12454	4.7	75	3283	4047	4939	5.1	2.54	2593	3168	4.8
89424 NIXON	031	458	480	528	1.1	33	146	154	170	1.3	3.12	102	107	1.1
89425 OROVADA	013	1089	1042	1014	-1.0	10	379	364	354	-1.0	2.80	267	255	-1.1
89426 PARADISE VALLEY	013	299	289	283	-0.8	11	116	112	110	-0.8	2.50	82	79	-0.9
89427 SCHURZ	021	830	838	802	0.2	23	295	306	299	0.9	2.55	192	198	0.7
89429 SILVER SPRINGS	019	6676	7945	9677	4.3	69	2530	3024	3695	4.3	2.58	1790	2126	4.1
89430 SMITH	019	462	499	580	1.8	44	167	181	212	1.9	2.73	124	134	1.8
NEVADA					4.1					3.9	2.64			3.8
UNITED STATES					1.2					1.3	2.58			1.1

ZIP CODE #	POST OFFICE NAME	RACE (%) White 2000	White 2004	Black 2000	Black 2004	Asian/Pacific 2000	Asian/Pacific 2004	% Hispanic Origin 2000	% Hispanic Origin 2004	2004 AGE DISTRIBUTION (%) 0-4	5-9	10-14	15-19	20-24	25-44	45-64	65-84	85+	18+	MEDIAN AGE 2004	% 2004 Males	% 2004 Females
89001	ALAMO	93.0	92.9	0.1	0.1	0.2	0.2	3.9	3.8	7.0	7.0	7.6	8.6	7.6	18.7	27.1	15.4	1.0	73.1	39.9	50.8	49.2
89005	BOULDER CITY	94.5	93.9	0.7	0.8	0.9	0.9	4.4	5.5	3.8	4.3	6.0	6.2	4.8	18.9	31.0	22.0	3.1	81.8	49.1	49.6	50.4
89008	CALIENTE	88.3	88.1	1.9	2.0	0.7	0.7	6.7	6.8	6.2	6.7	8.5	15.3	4.8	17.1	24.5	14.8	2.2	66.0	36.2	48.3	51.7
89011	HENDERSON	91.7	90.9	1.2	1.8	2.4	2.3	5.9	7.3	4.1	3.6	3.6	3.6	3.2	21.4	44.6	15.5	0.5	85.9	50.4	50.5	49.6
89012	HENDERSON	87.1	85.4	2.9	3.3	4.8	4.7	7.1	9.3	7.0	6.6	5.7	4.2	4.7	33.1	23.8	14.4	0.7	78.2	38.2	49.1	50.9
89013	GOLDFIELD	93.2	93.4	0.3	0.3	0.3	0.3	5.1	4.9	4.4	3.3	3.8	5.5	4.9	17.8	36.7	21.6	1.9	85.2	50.7	54.5	45.5
89014	HENDERSON	80.6	79.1	4.9	5.2	5.7	5.6	12.3	14.8	6.3	6.1	7.0	7.2	8.7	30.9	24.5	8.6	0.7	76.3	34.6	49.3	50.7
89015	HENDERSON	86.2	84.7	3.5	3.8	2.2	2.1	12.4	15.0	7.6	7.4	7.8	6.6	6.1	29.0	24.6	10.1	0.9	73.1	36.0	49.9	50.1
89017	HIKO	93.3	93.2	0.0	0.0	0.0	0.0	4.0	4.7	6.8	6.8	7.4	9.5	7.4	17.6	27.0	16.2	1.4	73.0	40.6	51.4	48.7
89018	INDIAN SPRINGS	71.9	70.6	21.3	22.0	2.0	1.9	11.9	14.2	3.1	2.9	3.5	5.8	11.9	44.2	23.1	5.3	0.4	87.8	35.8	77.9	22.1
89019	JEAN	88.2	88.8	3.5	2.9	2.0	1.6	9.0	10.5	4.4	4.9	6.2	5.9	4.8	23.4	36.0	13.7	0.9	81.0	45.3	52.4	47.6
89020	AMARGOSA VALLEY	83.2	80.7	0.1	0.1	1.0	0.9	19.2	22.2	7.8	6.6	7.5	7.5	5.9	22.7	29.3	11.9	0.8	73.1	39.1	52.2	47.8
89027	MESQUITE	80.0	77.5	0.7	0.7	1.4	1.2	25.2	29.1	8.0	6.4	6.2	6.4	6.0	21.3	26.4	18.2	1.1	75.3	40.9	50.8	49.2
89029	LAUGHLIN	88.9	87.3	2.9	3.0	2.5	2.6	10.6	13.1	4.6	4.2	5.5	5.9	6.8	20.3	31.7	20.2	0.9	82.4	47.0	49.3	50.7
89030	NORTH LAS VEGAS	46.8	46.3	19.1	17.8	1.6	1.4	62.7	66.9	11.4	10.1	9.9	8.2	8.7	30.5	14.8	5.7	0.8	63.8	26.0	52.4	47.6
89031	NORTH LAS VEGAS	69.7	67.6	13.4	14.2	5.8	5.4	14.0	16.9	9.9	9.1	8.6	6.3	5.8	36.6	18.2	5.3	0.3	68.5	31.3	49.9	50.1
89032	NORTH LAS VEGAS	56.1	54.4	26.7	27.4	5.4	4.9	17.6	20.5	9.7	9.2	9.0	6.7	6.0	33.6	19.3	6.1	0.3	67.9	31.2	48.7	51.3
89033	NORTH LAS VEGAS	87.5	84.6	12.5	7.7	0.0	0.0	0.0	3.9	3.9	7.7	7.7	7.7	7.7	26.9	26.9	11.5	0.0	80.8	37.5	50.0	50.0
89040	OVERTON	85.1	83.5	0.5	0.6	1.0	0.9	14.8	17.7	8.1	7.8	9.2	8.6	6.6	23.0	23.3	12.1	1.2	69.5	35.1	51.0	49.0
89041	PAHRUMP	91.5	91.3	1.2	1.2	0.6	0.6	7.9	8.7	5.2	4.6	5.8	5.2	5.2	19.1	31.8	22.0	1.2	80.9	48.3	52.0	48.0
89043	PIOCHE	93.0	92.9	2.7	2.7	0.2	0.2	5.1	5.2	6.3	6.1	5.9	6.2	5.8	22.4	30.1	15.5	1.9	78.1	43.0	54.8	45.2
89045	ROUND MOUNTAIN	84.1	82.7	0.1	0.1	0.2	0.2	8.0	9.1	8.1	7.5	9.0	9.0	8.4	27.1	24.9	5.4	0.6	69.9	32.2	52.5	47.5
89046	SEARCHLIGHT	68.4	65.8	13.6	14.3	5.3	5.0	14.3	17.2	0.7	0.8	1.3	1.1	2.8	32.4	43.0	16.8	1.2	96.6	50.1	71.9	28.2
89047	SILVERPEAK	72.9	72.3	0.0	0.0	0.2	0.2	14.3	14.3	4.8	5.0	7.0	7.3	8.1	22.5	28.9	15.2	1.3	78.9	41.6	56.6	43.4
89048	PAHRUMP	91.0	90.3	1.4	1.4	1.4	1.3	7.1	8.2	5.1	5.3	6.5	5.8	4.4	19.8	29.1	22.6	1.4	79.3	47.3	50.1	49.9
89049	TONOPAH	89.7	88.9	1.7	1.8	0.7	0.7	6.1	6.9	6.9	7.0	7.3	6.4	6.1	26.7	29.3	9.2	1.2	74.6	38.9	54.5	45.5
89052	HENDERSON	85.6	84.4	3.3	3.6	5.7	5.6	7.9	10.0	7.1	6.7	5.4	4.1	4.3	36.3	25.7	10.0	0.4	78.3	37.3	49.6	50.4
89060	PAHRUMP	91.7	91.1	1.0	1.0	1.0	0.9	7.8	8.9	5.8	5.6	5.6	5.6	4.7	19.4	31.4	20.7	1.2	79.5	47.1	51.4	48.6
89061	PAHRUMP	89.3	88.5	1.8	1.8	1.3	1.2	9.4	10.7	6.1	6.5	6.8	5.6	3.6	20.5	30.0	20.1	1.0	77.2	45.7	51.1	48.9
89074	HENDERSON	84.0	82.9	3.7	4.0	5.9	5.7	9.2	11.3	6.2	6.4	7.3	6.6	6.3	30.3	26.5	9.6	0.9	76.0	37.4	48.9	51.1
89084	NORTH LAS VEGAS	80.0	84.9	10.0	9.1	0.0	0.0	0.0	6.1	6.1	6.1	9.1	6.1	6.1	27.3	24.2	12.1	3.0	78.8	39.2	48.5	51.5
89101	LAS VEGAS	53.2	51.4	12.0	11.6	4.0	3.4	53.4	58.6	9.2	7.6	7.4	6.8	9.0	34.3	18.2	6.9	0.7	72.2	30.4	58.2	41.8
89102	LAS VEGAS	64.0	62.6	7.5	7.5	6.1	5.3	38.6	42.7	8.0	6.8	6.6	6.1	8.0	29.4	20.8	12.8	1.6	75.1	34.3	51.9	48.1
89103	LAS VEGAS	69.9	67.6	6.5	6.9	9.2	8.6	22.7	27.2	6.5	5.6	5.6	5.4	8.1	30.9	24.2	12.4	1.3	79.2	36.8	50.8	49.2
89104	LAS VEGAS	68.5	66.7	6.3	6.4	7.6	6.8	33.6	38.5	6.8	6.4	6.6	6.2	6.7	26.8	24.7	14.3	1.6	76.5	38.4	51.6	48.4
89106	LAS VEGAS	35.3	34.6	44.4	43.5	3.2	3.0	29.6	32.9	9.2	8.3	8.2	6.9	8.2	29.2	20.0	9.0	0.9	70.2	31.1	51.5	48.5
89107	LAS VEGAS	73.4	71.1	6.6	6.8	4.2	3.9	25.2	29.3	7.3	7.1	7.7	6.6	6.9	28.8	22.3	12.0	1.4	73.8	35.4	50.0	50.0
89108	LAS VEGAS	68.3	66.1	12.4	12.9	4.6	4.3	21.7	25.2	8.2	7.6	7.7	7.0	8.1	31.0	21.2	8.4	0.9	72.5	32.3	49.7	50.3
89109	LAS VEGAS	65.7	64.5	9.3	9.4	6.7	6.0	35.3	39.6	6.6	5.4	5.0	5.2	8.4	32.1	23.6	12.3	1.5	80.2	36.8	55.3	44.7
89110	LAS VEGAS	61.1	59.6	11.3	11.4	6.4	5.8	36.0	40.3	9.2	8.7	8.8	7.8	7.9	30.1	19.8	7.2	0.5	68.5	29.9	50.2	49.8
89113	LAS VEGAS	78.5	76.8	4.0	4.4	9.7	9.5	10.0	12.7	5.5	4.9	5.2	5.9	8.1	29.8	28.4	11.3	1.0	81.1	38.8	49.3	50.7
89115	LAS VEGAS	56.3	54.8	20.4	20.2	3.7	3.4	33.2	37.1	11.5	9.9	8.9	7.6	10.8	31.8	15.3	4.0	0.3	65.6	25.7	51.9	48.1
89117	LAS VEGAS	78.0	76.5	5.9	6.4	9.0	8.9	9.1	11.2	5.9	5.8	6.1	5.7	6.3	31.3	26.4	11.5	1.0	78.8	38.1	49.1	50.9
89118	LAS VEGAS	72.1	71.0	6.5	6.8	10.2	9.4	14.5	17.3	6.0	5.1	5.6	6.7	10.3	32.9	24.0	8.8	0.7	79.6	34.3	51.1	48.9
89119	LAS VEGAS	65.9	63.9	8.4	8.7	7.2	6.6	32.2	37.1	7.0	6.0	5.8	6.4	9.7	33.9	21.1	9.2	1.0	78.2	33.0	53.1	46.9
89120	LAS VEGAS	80.3	78.8	4.4	4.7	5.1	4.9	15.8	18.6	5.4	5.5	6.0	5.4	6.6	29.4	28.0	12.5	1.3	79.9	39.1	49.7	50.3
89121	LAS VEGAS	78.1	76.2	6.2	6.6	4.3	4.0	19.3	23.2	5.8	5.4	5.7	5.4	7.0	26.0	26.6	16.2	1.9	79.9	41.2	49.4	50.7
89122	LAS VEGAS	74.4	72.3	7.9	8.5	3.9	3.5	21.1	24.7	6.9	6.5	6.7	5.8	6.0	27.4	23.2	16.3	1.2	76.4	38.3	49.6	50.4
89123	LAS VEGAS	78.6	76.9	3.8	4.2	9.1	9.0	12.7	15.8	7.6	7.0	6.6	5.6	5.9	36.2	22.5	8.1	0.6	75.3	34.5	49.9	50.1
89124	LAS VEGAS	83.7	83.4	5.2	5.0	3.3	3.2	7.8	9.5	3.9	4.2	4.2	3.8	3.4	26.8	38.1	14.7	0.8	85.4	46.9	55.9	44.1
89128	LAS VEGAS	77.6	76.3	7.9	8.4	7.0	6.7	9.7	11.9	6.9	6.8	7.4	6.5	6.5	31.6	23.8	9.8	0.7	74.8	36.0	49.0	51.1
89129	LAS VEGAS	80.7	79.4	7.0	7.3	5.6	5.4	9.0	11.1	8.3	8.2	7.5	6.1	5.3	32.5	22.2	9.2	0.6	72.2	35.3	48.7	51.4
89130	LAS VEGAS	83.3	81.5	6.4	7.2	3.6	3.6	9.5	11.8	7.5	7.4	6.9	5.2	4.1	30.5	25.1	12.4	0.9	74.8	38.2	48.9	51.1
89131	LAS VEGAS	82.4	80.9	6.3	7.0	3.4	3.2	11.0	13.3	9.0	8.4	7.7	5.9	4.9	37.0	20.9	5.6	0.5	70.9	33.2	50.6	49.4
89134	LAS VEGAS	89.4	88.8	2.6	2.9	5.1	5.0	3.8	4.8	4.0	4.2	4.4	3.4	2.0	16.4	24.7	38.5	2.3	85.0	60.2	47.2	52.8
89135	LAS VEGAS	78.9	77.8	4.0	4.4	10.5	10.1	8.1	10.0	7.4	7.1	5.2	3.8	3.7	36.3	26.8	9.3	0.4	78.0	37.8	50.8	49.3
89139	LAS VEGAS	91.3	90.4	1.5	1.7	1.6	1.5	6.8	8.6	4.8	5.5	6.5	5.9	4.5	23.2	35.4	13.3	1.0	79.5	44.8	51.2	48.9
89141	LAS VEGAS	92.7	91.6	1.5	1.4	1.5	1.3	7.7	9.5	4.9	5.4	6.6	6.6	5.0	22.4	35.0	13.3	0.7	79.0	44.5	50.1	49.9
89142	LAS VEGAS	66.1	64.5	9.2	9.6	11.5	10.8	21.8	25.9	8.6	8.0	8.5	7.4	7.5	32.4	20.2	6.9	0.5	70.3	31.6	49.1	50.9
89143	LAS VEGAS	82.0	80.6	5.6	6.1	4.3	4.1	10.5	12.8	10.1	9.1	7.1	5.7	5.2	37.3	20.0	5.2	0.5	70.3	32.4	50.5	49.5
89144	LAS VEGAS	81.1	80.6	4.5	4.8	8.1	7.5	6.8	8.5	8.2	7.4	7.0	4.9	3.8	36.1	23.5	8.8	0.4	74.3	36.5	48.9	51.1
89145	LAS VEGAS	79.3	77.8	6.7	7.2	5.0	4.8	11.7	13.8	6.3	6.3	7.1	6.3	6.5	30.4	25.5	10.9	0.7	76.4	37.2	49.2	50.8
89146	LAS VEGAS	76.6	75.2	6.5	6.8	6.6	6.1	14.1	17.0	5.3	5.0	5.4	6.2	7.3	27.9	29.1	12.8	1.2	80.9	40.4	49.9	50.1
89147	LAS VEGAS	70.3	69.0	4.6	5.0	15.0	14.4	12.9	15.2	6.5	6.2	6.3	5.7	6.6	33.7	24.7	9.6	0.7	77.5	36.3	49.3	50.7
89148	LAS VEGAS	72.4	71.1	3.9	4.3	13.5	12.9	11.1	13.5	7.1	6.7	6.0	5.5	5.4	34.3	26.4	8.2	0.4	76.8	36.5	49.5	50.5
89149	LAS VEGAS	88.7	87.6	4.3	4.8	2.7	2.6	6.4	7.8	5.5	6.6	7.1	5.9	3.8	25.4	32.7	12.2	0.8	76.8	42.7	49.6	50.5
89154	LAS VEGAS	65.3	63.7	10.2	10.8	12.4	11.6	16.4	19.8	3.0	3.2	1.8	21.5	17.8	20.6	15.7	13.9	2.5	90.4	27.0	51.2	48.8
89156	LAS VEGAS	72.1	70.0	10.3	10.8	4.6	4.4	17.7	20.9	7.9	7.2	7.7	6.9	7.3	33.0	21.8	7.8	0.5	73.0	33.1	48.9	51.1
89191	NELLIS AFB	67.9	65.8	14.9	15.8	5.8	5.5	12.4	14.9	11.5	9.1	6.6	6.8	20.0	36.1	8.5	1.4	0.0	70.4	24.0	58.0	42.0
89301	ELY	86.6	85.9	3.7	3.8	1.0	1.0	11.1	12.5	6.0	6.2	6.8	6.5	6.8	27.9	25.7	12.5	1.7	76.9	38.4	55.5	44.5
89310	AUSTIN	90.6	88.8	1.5	1.9	0.6	0.8	8.1	9.6	2.1	4.0	5.9	5.6	4.3	17.0	44.7	14.1	2.4	84.3	50.5	51.3	48.7
89311	BAKER	72.8	71.6	18.4	18.9	0.9	0.5	15.4	16.2	2.7	3.2	3.2	4.1	10.8	49.1	22.5	4.1	0.5	88.3	35.3	81.5	18.5
89316	EUREKA	88.8	88.3	0.5	0.5	0.9	1.0	9.6	10.0	5.6	6.0	7.7	7.9	5.3	26.0	28.5	11.9	1.0	75.2	40.7	50.7	49.3
89317	LUND	89.1	88.1	5.2	5.4	1.6	1.7	4.9	5.7	5.7	5.7	5.7	8.5	6.5	32.2	26.6	8.5	0.9	77.4	36.9	55.1	44.9
89403	DAYTON	90.7	89.7	0.4	0.5	1.0	0.9	10.1	11.7	6.7	7.1	7.8	6.7	5.5	26.3	28.0	11.3	0.6	73.9	39.0	50.4	49.6
89404	DENIO	85.2	85.0	0.7	0.7	0.7	0.7	20.1	19.7	6.8	7.5	8.2	6.8	4.8	32.0	24.5	8.8	0.7	73.5	36.9	51.0	49.0
89405	EMPIRE	82.4	80.7	0.0	0.0	0.4	0.4	37.7	42.8	4.8	4.5	3.4	6.3	9.3	32.0	24.9	10.4	4.5	84.4	38.1	62.5	37.6
89406	FALLON	84.2	83.5	1.6	1.7	2.9	2.9	8.7	9.8	8.2	7.5	7.7	7.2	7.4	26.5	23.5	10.8	1.3	72.3	34.8	50.1	49.9
89408	FERNLEY	90.2	89.3	0.5	0.5	0.9	0.8	8.8	10.2	8.0	7.9	7.9	6.8	6.2	28.2	24.8	9.5	0.7	72.0	35.4	50.1	49.9
89409	GABBS	73.6	71.8	0.0	0.0	1.0	1.2	6.6	7.3	5.9	5.9	8.0	8.2	5.7	22.1	28.2	15.1	0.9	75.3	41.2	50.4	49.7
89410	GARDNERVILLE	91.8	91.2	0.3	0.4	1.0	1.0	8.6	9.5	4.8	5.3	7.0	6.8	4.4	22.1	30.4	17.0	2.2	78.2	44.7	49.7	50.3
89412	GERLACH	88.9	87.7	0.0	0.0	0.3	0.3	18.3	21.0	5.0	5.3	5.3	6.4	6.9	29.1	30.4	9.6	2.0	80.8	40.1	55.7	44.3
89413	GLENBROOK	89.7	89.2	0.6	0.6	3.4	3.4	9.0	9.9	3.5	4.1	6.4	5.1	4.4	24.4	36.6	14.5	1.1	82.6	46.1	52.8	47.2
89414	GOLCONDA	86.2	85.9	0.2	0.2	0.5	0.5	19.6	19.5	9.4	9.2	9.2	8.0	6.3	28.6	23.2	5.6	0.5	67.4	31.6	53.8	46.2
89415	HAWTHORNE	85.3	85.1	5.6	5.8	1.1	1.2	8.5	9.5	5.0	5.1	6.1	6.5	5.5	20.2	29.9	19.2	2.5	79.7	46.1	49.5	50.5
89418	IMLAY	86.7	85.6	0.1	0.1	0.7	0.6	15.3	17.2	8.2	8.3	8.8	8.2	5.8	25.5	26.5	8.2	0.6	69.9	35.3	51.0	49.0
89419	LOVELOCK	75.1	73.7	7.2	7.4	0.8	0.8	20.3	22.5	5.7	5.9	6.4	6.7	8.5	35.6	22.7	7.4	1.2	78.1	35.1	64.7	35.3
89420	LUNING	93.7	94.3	1.1	1.1	0.0	0.0	3.1	3.4	2.3	2.6	4.2	4.9	3.8	17.0	35.9	26.8	2.6	88.3	55.1	54.0	46.0
89423	MINDEN	94.6	94.1	0.2	0.2	1.1	1.1	5.4	6.3	4.6	5.5	7.4	7.0	4.0	21.6	32.2	16.5	1.4	77.9	45.0	49.5	50.6
89424	NIXON	23.1	22.9	0.0	0.0	0.4	0.4	8.5	9.8	8.3	8.3	10.0	9.4	6.3	26.0	21.0	9.0	1.7	67.5	31.9	49.6	50.4
89425	OROVADA	58.0	58.3	0.2	0.2	0.3	0.3	17.5	17.5	6.2	7.7	9.3	7.9	5.5	23.5	28.8	10.6	0.6	71.4	38.0	52.6	47.4
89426	PARADISE VALLEY	79.6	78.9	0.3	0.4	0.3	0.4	24.8	24.2	6.2	8.0	9.7	8.0	4.8	23.2	29.1	10.4	0.7	70.6	38.4	54.0	46.0
89427	SCHURZ	12.8	14.4	2.1	2.4	0.2	0.2	10.0	11.2	7.5	8.1	9.2	14.1	6.7	21.1	23.0	9.3	1.0	64.4	29.1	52.7	47.3
89429	SILVER SPRINGS	91.3	90.7	0.9	1.0	0.7	0.7	4.8	5.5	5.3	6.0	7.6	6.6	4.7	25.0	29.8	14.3	0.8	76.9	42.1	49.6	50.4
89430	SMITH	86.4	85.2	0.2	0.2	0.2	0.2	20.6	23.3	3.6	5.6	8.0	6.2	3.6	22.4	34.3	15.0	1.2	78.2	45.3	51.7	48.3
	NEVADA	75.2	73.9	6.8	7.0	4.9	4.8	19.7	22.0	7.3	6.9	7.1	6.5	7.0	29.9	23.8	10.6	1.0	74.8	35.6	50.6	49.4
	UNITED STATES	75.1	73.6	12.3	12.5	3.8	4.2	12.5	14.1	6.9	6.7	7.2	7.0	7.3	28.6	23.8	10.8	1.7	75.1	36.0	49.1	50.9

INCOME

ZIP CODE #	POST OFFICE NAME	2004 Per Capita Income	2004 HH Income Base	2004 HOUSEHOLD INCOME DISTRIBUTION (%) Less than $25,000	$25,000 to $49,999	$50,000 to $99,999	$100,000 to $149,999	$150,000 or More	MEDIAN HOUSEHOLD INCOME 2004	2009	2004 National Centile	2004 State Centile	2004 Home Value Base	2004 HOME VALUE DISTRIBUTION (%) Less than $50,000	$50,000 to $89,999	$90,000 to $174,999	$175,000 to $399,999	$400,000 or More	2004 Median Home Value
89001	ALAMO	18972	346	26.9	23.4	41.3	8.4	0.0	49677	56154	71	54	286	12.6	22.4	42.7	22.4	0.0	114286
89005	BOULDER CITY	35056	6920	18.8	24.6	34.0	14.7	8.0	58172	71396	83	69	5349	9.5	4.3	23.7	51.1	11.4	204759
89008	CALIENTE	21009	497	40.9	27.0	26.4	4.0	1.8	31983	39242	18	9	354	28.3	26.8	36.7	7.6	0.6	84375
89011	HENDERSON	67207	101	4.0	15.8	38.6	17.8	23.8	82150	105248	96	98	94	0.0	0.0	8.5	60.6	30.9	305263
89012	HENDERSON	38274	11165	10.2	19.7	40.6	18.1	11.4	71168	83806	92	90	8238	0.6	0.3	12.5	79.4	7.2	232372
89013	GOLDFIELD	23649	183	32.2	29.5	28.4	9.8	0.0	37917	43501	39	19	120	32.5	35.0	30.8	1.7	0.0	68333
89014	HENDERSON	30661	15740	12.6	28.3	37.2	13.0	8.9	59115	69520	84	71	8835	0.5	1.1	32.3	62.3	3.9	197577
89015	HENDERSON	24855	26979	17.3	23.9	40.8	13.2	4.8	58361	68134	83	70	20472	5.4	4.0	45.4	42.4	2.7	167982
89017	HIKO	16795	48	27.1	25.0	41.7	6.3	0.0	47382	54460	67	47	40	10.0	22.5	47.5	20.0	0.0	113889
89018	INDIAN SPRINGS	23578	606	14.7	34.5	42.4	7.1	1.3	50555	59794	73	55	358	32.1	5.0	40.2	19.0	3.6	110938
89019	JEAN	30186	1804	18.9	25.7	32.5	11.3	11.5	54586	65455	79	62	1485	8.8	14.8	34.3	33.9	8.2	143750
89020	AMARGOSA VALLEY	22404	976	32.6	27.9	28.7	7.3	3.6	41761	47545	52	32	663	18.7	25.3	45.4	4.4	6.2	97182
89027	MESQUITE	25074	4481	19.0	34.5	32.4	8.2	6.0	46970	57185	66	45	2875	3.0	1.9	55.9	33.2	6.0	162149
89029	LAUGHLIN	24124	3657	22.5	35.5	33.2	5.6	3.2	42307	50517	54	33	1335	4.0	14.2	48.0	32.4	1.4	145422
89030	NORTH LAS VEGAS	12736	15449	34.5	35.3	24.1	3.6	2.6	34486	39612	26	12	7342	10.8	18.3	67.4	3.3	0.3	105945
89031	NORTH LAS VEGAS	22995	16760	7.6	21.9	52.0	15.6	2.9	65005	76223	89	83	14535	0.6	0.3	51.4	47.4	0.4	173074
89032	NORTH LAS VEGAS	21655	12484	13.9	24.7	45.4	12.9	3.2	60046	69110	84	73	9984	1.6	1.6	54.6	42.0	0.2	168254
89033	NORTH LAS VEGAS	29677	16	0.0	62.5	37.5	0.0	0.0	46399	54916	65	44	12	0.0	0.0	75.0	0.0	25.0	150000
89040	OVERTON	18971	3362	22.2	31.9	33.0	9.9	3.0	46286	55062	65	42	2654	15.4	8.7	38.7	34.4	2.8	146217
89041	PAHRUMP	25135	85	23.5	42.4	23.5	7.1	3.5	40235	45271	47	28	72	2.8	9.7	55.6	29.2	2.8	137500
89043	PIOCHE	19168	657	40.2	20.1	32.1	5.6	2.0	37772	46364	38	18	528	25.0	13.8	41.9	15.0	4.4	105585
89045	ROUND MOUNTAIN	23137	597	14.4	25.3	48.2	10.9	1.2	56571	66590	81	66	464	46.3	35.8	15.1	2.8	0.0	54474
89046	SEARCHLIGHT	34899	688	30.5	31.7	28.6	6.1	3.1	40411	48355	48	29	357	31.1	11.8	45.7	5.9	5.6	99808
89047	SILVERPEAK	20994	243	30.0	30.0	32.1	7.0	0.8	38534	46612	41	22	170	39.4	27.7	27.1	5.9	0.0	62857
89048	PAHRUMP	21241	6933	29.9	33.2	27.0	7.6	2.4	39126	44757	43	25	5490	7.3	12.3	53.2	25.5	1.8	135384
89049	TONOPAH	22361	1198	28.3	27.6	35.5	7.7	0.9	45122	51124	62	39	731	25.7	35.8	34.2	4.2	0.0	82387
89052	HENDERSON	40300	8613	9.2	18.6	39.2	20.2	12.8	75944	90332	94	94	6284	2.3	0.4	10.8	75.5	11.1	257747
89060	PAHRUMP	19669	3410	31.0	33.3	27.3	6.9	1.4	38324	43936	40	21	2853	5.6	16.6	52.6	22.5	2.7	130900
89061	PAHRUMP	19755	1396	22.1	37.5	32.3	6.5	1.6	43040	50435	56	35	1193	7.5	7.6	46.2	36.8	1.9	154744
89074	HENDERSON	35589	21955	10.7	19.8	38.5	18.3	12.7	70825	85941	92	89	16432	0.5	1.6	27.0	61.4	9.6	212057
89084	NORTH LAS VEGAS	23382	16	0.0	62.5	37.5	0.0	0.0	46399	54916	65	44	12	0.0	0.0	75.0	0.0	25.0	150000
89101	LAS VEGAS	13621	17178	49.6	30.4	15.5	3.1	1.5	25209	29044	5	3	3972	3.9	13.2	79.5	3.0	0.4	113873
89102	LAS VEGAS	20253	15446	34.3	30.9	24.5	6.0	4.4	36310	42381	33	16	5611	7.5	4.9	52.7	29.8	5.1	152068
89103	LAS VEGAS	22029	21528	26.4	35.4	28.8	7.0	2.5	40650	46425	48	30	8303	18.3	10.7	43.8	26.8	0.3	132196
89104	LAS VEGAS	18965	15039	32.9	28.2	29.9	6.6	2.5	40116	47905	46	27	8856	20.1	4.2	59.6	15.8	0.3	132783
89106	LAS VEGAS	15078	9975	41.0	31.2	22.1	4.6	1.2	31657	37478	17	8	3876	4.9	10.5	72.5	11.4	0.8	123835
89107	LAS VEGAS	21600	14114	24.2	30.6	33.0	7.8	4.3	45746	53203	63	40	8930	0.6	2.9	76.9	16.1	3.5	142836
89108	LAS VEGAS	22094	28443	20.5	30.6	35.6	9.9	3.3	49005	57058	70	52	14973	0.8	3.9	66.7	27.7	1.0	150997
89109	LAS VEGAS	21272	20753	39.2	35.4	18.5	4.2	2.8	31191	35802	15	8	4064	11.1	12.9	42.1	26.5	7.4	136199
89110	LAS VEGAS	19210	23099	21.5	30.1	34.9	9.3	4.4	48550	56872	69	51	15002	10.1	6.9	54.8	25.4	2.9	140596
89113	LAS VEGAS	50722	4512	13.3	23.1	35.2	13.3	15.1	64054	72948	88	82	3082	1.2	2.1	21.4	53.2	22.1	230366
89115	LAS VEGAS	14254	19634	33.0	36.5	25.4	4.0	1.1	34840	40452	27	14	7410	27.1	10.6	55.4	6.6	0.4	108256
89117	LAS VEGAS	36706	26783	15.1	25.9	35.3	13.4	10.3	60042	71255	84	73	14893	0.9	0.8	18.8	64.0	15.6	234790
89118	LAS VEGAS	26071	9632	23.0	32.8	31.4	8.6	4.2	45876	53182	64	42	3221	0.0	1.4	43.1	43.3	12.3	188436
89119	LAS VEGAS	19037	21898	36.2	35.8	21.5	4.9	1.6	33046	38043	21	11	5471	2.5	14.3	49.2	32.9	1.2	152370
89120	LAS VEGAS	31266	9231	16.0	25.6	35.8	14.0	8.6	58566	70411	83	70	6211	0.1	4.7	46.7	39.8	8.7	172313
89121	LAS VEGAS	23934	27740	23.5	32.9	31.3	8.2	4.1	44278	51460	59	36	16394	17.2	4.4	53.7	23.2	1.6	138837
89122	LAS VEGAS	20097	14159	27.7	33.0	31.8	5.6	1.8	40621	47589	48	30	8784	13.9	21.8	54.8	9.5	0.0	109885
89123	LAS VEGAS	30113	25969	11.1	22.9	42.9	16.4	6.7	64703	76962	88	83	19195	2.9	2.5	22.2	68.1	4.4	210129
89124	LAS VEGAS	34077	1693	12.1	19.5	35.3	19.3	13.8	71880	88730	92	91	1408	6.3	6.8	17.4	52.8	16.8	244444
89128	LAS VEGAS	31395	17614	12.2	26.6	37.4	15.3	8.5	60684	72657	85	77	11169	0.4	4.3	39.7	50.1	5.6	183944
89129	LAS VEGAS	32044	15069	7.7	20.0	40.9	20.5	10.9	72886	88698	92	92	12682	0.7	0.3	25.6	66.1	7.4	209480
89130	LAS VEGAS	29498	11336	8.3	20.1	46.4	19.5	5.9	68127	81332	90	88	9976	0.0	0.0	33.9	63.9	2.2	193230
89131	LAS VEGAS	29405	6556	5.3	20.4	51.0	16.9	6.5	70138	83539	91	89	6242	0.9	0.4	30.2	62.2	6.4	194096
89134	LAS VEGAS	48481	14427	15.5	20.7	32.3	16.3	15.2	67260	80692	90	86	13215	0.3	0.1	12.8	69.2	17.6	244886
89135	LAS VEGAS	39948	3207	9.1	14.1	46.6	20.5	9.7	76787	93838	94	95	2388	0.0	1.0	12.6	70.8	15.7	231423
89139	LAS VEGAS	29609	1617	18.0	20.6	34.8	14.5	12.1	63632	79321	88	81	1437	3.2	7.4	18.9	57.6	12.9	255915
89141	LAS VEGAS	27558	198	18.2	25.3	32.3	12.1	12.1	55721	66848	80	65	169	7.7	14.8	33.7	35.5	8.3	148864
89142	LAS VEGAS	21918	9383	9.2	27.4	45.9	14.1	3.4	60463	70345	85	74	6930	0.0	6.7	59.8	32.7	0.8	158763
89143	LAS VEGAS	29275	1410	8.0	17.2	48.3	18.9	7.6	75559	86047	93	93	1348	1.4	0.2	23.4	64.7	10.3	206962
89144	LAS VEGAS	42438	7081	5.4	17.5	38.7	24.1	14.3	81443	104084	95	98	5724	0.0	0.0	19.4	66.0	14.6	224212
89145	LAS VEGAS	32154	11451	13.0	27.8	37.1	14.0	8.2	59406	70424	84	72	7827	0.6	3.1	59.3	28.6	8.3	160655
89146	LAS VEGAS	29936	7611	17.6	29.9	30.1	13.7	8.7	52316	63187	76	58	4186	0.8	0.8	42.3	42.8	13.3	198796
89147	LAS VEGAS	32192	20168	11.7	23.8	40.7	15.6	8.2	63248	75805	87	80	14075	1.9	1.6	36.5	54.6	5.4	190822
89148	LAS VEGAS	50439	1126	6.8	19.2	38.9	20.3	14.8	79390	98082	95	96	864	0.0	0.8	17.9	64.5	16.8	238308
89149	LAS VEGAS	39567	5279	8.6	15.5	35.0	23.9	17.0	84292	107450	96	99	4797	2.7	0.0	15.9	64.2	17.2	269737
89154	LAS VEGAS	13465	438	47.5	32.4	16.9	2.3	0.9	26047	30053	6	4	0	0.0	0.0	0.0	0.0	0.0	0
89156	LAS VEGAS	21228	9512	15.7	31.9	41.1	8.8	2.5	51929	60459	75	57	6405	4.2	10.8	58.5	25.8	0.7	148855
89191	NELLIS AFB	3515	0	0.0	0.0	0.0	0.0	0.0	0	0	0	0	0	0.0	0.0	0.0	0.0	0.0	0
89301	ELY	20857	3014	29.9	29.3	33.2	5.7	2.0	41709	47970	52	31	2284	19.6	32.2	37.4	9.2	1.6	87375
89310	AUSTIN	18360	183	38.3	32.8	26.8	2.2	0.0	36893	42996	35	17	146	39.0	19.2	37.0	4.8	0.0	58889
89311	BAKER	37731	107	28.0	22.4	36.5	1.9	11.2	44538	52190	60	38	83	9.6	19.3	19.3	39.8	12.1	187500
89316	EUREKA	21778	412	27.9	23.8	36.4	9.7	2.2	48426	55199	69	50	315	23.2	26.0	35.2	13.3	2.2	91087
89317	LUND	25724	141	10.6	44.0	34.8	7.8	2.8	45856	51461	63	41	124	8.1	23.4	47.6	21.0	0.0	106250
89403	DAYTON	22766	3529	15.3	35.5	40.8	5.5	3.0	49500	55582	71	53	2904	3.6	6.2	57.0	29.3	3.9	156619
89404	DENIO	31184	68	13.2	25.0	45.6	10.3	5.9	61165	69554	85	77	52	3.9	1.9	53.9	40.4	0.0	150000
89405	EMPIRE	17962	80	33.8	50.0	11.3	5.0	0.0	30406	35727	13	6	34	0.0	47.1	5.9	35.3	11.8	100000
89406	FALLON	22542	9089	21.7	32.2	34.8	7.6	3.7	46621	53363	65	45	6299	12.0	8.2	48.6	28.3	3.0	144925
89408	FERNLEY	21025	3988	19.4	31.0	40.0	7.7	1.9	49729	55933	71	55	3199	7.7	9.3	49.0	31.4	2.7	150122
89409	GABBS	14848	174	41.4	32.8	22.4	2.3	1.2	30000	33495	12	5	118	71.2	5.1	18.6	5.1	0.0	32500
89410	GARDNERVILLE	32065	3618	20.4	21.7	39.3	12.9	5.7	57545	67801	82	67	2788	5.5	2.8	19.2	57.9	14.6	238966
89412	GERLACH	21322	281	27.4	35.2	30.3	4.3	2.9	37937	50414	39	20	111	27.0	25.2	35.1	9.9	2.7	86875
89413	GLENBROOK	49478	2765	18.0	23.0	30.1	11.7	17.3	60507	74663	85	75	1889	6.9	4.9	4.2	28.8	55.2	448762
89414	GOLCONDA	23298	164	15.2	28.7	47.0	6.1	3.1	52326	59535	76	59	135	19.3	19.3	46.7	11.1	3.7	105603
89415	HAWTHORNE	21013	1672	30.7	31.5	30.9	5.8	1.1	39061	43667	43	23	1243	28.5	35.3	34.4	1.5	0.4	74908
89418	IMLAY	22593	326	28.8	23.6	39.0	7.1	1.5	47956	53068	68	48	264	14.0	23.5	38.3	18.6	5.7	116406
89419	LOVELOCK	21349	1387	26.5	30.6	34.5	6.4	2.1	45153	50044	62	39	981	24.6	17.2	42.5	14.5	1.2	103486
89420	LUNING	23211	151	35.1	39.7	18.5	4.0	2.7	33980	38251	24	11	119	31.9	26.9	36.1	5.0	0.0	76111
89423	MINDEN	32666	4047	11.5	17.3	47.3	18.1	5.9	68033	81591	90	87	3509	0.5	0.7	4.6	78.0	16.2	268696
89424	NIXON	13989	154	34.4	31.8	27.3	4.6	2.0	35808	42353	31	14	110	26.4	24.6	24.6	20.0	4.6	88889
89425	OROVADA	16819	364	38.5	20.3	34.6	5.2	1.4	39325	45995	44	26	276	25.7	17.8	25.4	30.1	1.1	108000
89426	PARADISE VALLEY	20753	112	32.1	18.8	42.0	6.3	0.9	48244	56821	69	49	79	10.1	17.7	29.1	40.5	2.5	147500
89427	SCHURZ	14444	306	45.4	31.7	19.0	3.3	0.7	27182	31393	7	5	232	17.7	37.1	36.6	4.3	4.3	83529
89429	SILVER SPRINGS	19930	3024	29.6	32.6	28.7	6.4	2.7	38698	43981	42	23	2548	5.4	28.7	54.3	11.6	0.1	111253
89430	SMITH	25837	181	24.3	22.1	37.6	7.2	8.8	52520	61712	76	60	129	2.3	5.4	13.2	47.3	31.8	283696
	NEVADA	26208		20.5	27.7	34.5	11.4	5.9	51572	61335				5.9	5.6	38.5	43.5	6.6	175101
	UNITED STATES	25866		24.7	27.1	30.8	10.9	6.5	48124	56710				10.9	15.0	33.7	30.1	10.4	145905

ZIP CODE #	POST OFFICE NAME	FINANCIAL SERVICES: Auto Loan	FINANCIAL SERVICES: Home Loan	FINANCIAL SERVICES: Investments	FINANCIAL SERVICES: Retirement Plans	THE HOME: Home Improvements: Home Repair	THE HOME: Home Improvements: Lawn & Garden	THE HOME: Furnishings: Computers & Hardware	THE HOME: Furnishings: Major Appliances	THE HOME: Furnishings: TV, Radio, Sound Equipment	THE HOME: Furnishings: Furniture	ENTERTAINMENT: Dine out/ Carry out	ENTERTAINMENT: Sports Equipment	ENTERTAINMENT: Fees & Tickets	ENTERTAINMENT: Toys & Games	ENTERTAINMENT: Travel	ENTERTAINMENT: Cable TV	PERSONAL: Apparel & Services	PERSONAL: Auto Repairs	PERSONAL: Health Insurance	PERSONAL: Pets & Supplies
89001	ALAMO	93	65	34	61	76	85	64	79	74	63	87	96	55	85	67	78	79	78	95	111
89005	BOULDER CITY	112	119	126	115	121	134	112	118	112	115	140	126	115	132	117	115	135	116	124	130
89008	CALIENTE	76	57	38	55	63	75	62	69	70	59	82	78	56	78	62	74	75	69	83	84
89011	HENDERSON	222	207	199	197	220	259	192	218	203	206	252	214	194	210	209	217	236	212	255	249
89012	HENDERSON	132	143	139	145	140	144	129	134	124	136	156	148	133	149	130	120	152	130	127	147
89013	GOLDFIELD	75	56	37	54	62	74	63	69	70	59	82	77	56	78	62	74	75	69	82	83
89014	HENDERSON	112	115	126	122	111	113	116	112	110	118	140	134	116	137	112	104	138	114	99	124
89015	HENDERSON	99	104	101	105	102	105	99	100	96	101	121	116	100	120	99	94	118	99	95	112
89017	HIKO	94	65	34	62	76	85	65	80	74	64	87	96	55	86	67	78	80	79	95	111
89018	INDIAN SPRINGS	20	15	12	15	15	17	17	17	18	17	22	21	15	20	16	17	21	18	18	21
89019	JEAN	118	108	87	104	109	116	103	111	105	106	130	126	98	121	103	104	124	111	112	131
89020	AMARGOSA VALLEY	85	77	62	74	78	83	74	79	75	76	92	91	70	87	73	74	89	79	80	94
89027	MESQUITE	99	94	92	93	96	108	91	97	93	94	116	103	91	104	94	95	110	96	104	110
89029	LAUGHLIN	70	73	90	73	72	81	75	74	76	75	95	83	76	93	77	77	93	75	76	82
89030	NORTH LAS VEGAS	70	60	58	58	59	62	66	67	69	70	86	74	62	81	62	66	86	70	63	72
89031	NORTH LAS VEGAS	104	117	113	122	111	108	106	105	97	110	124	123	109	124	103	91	122	103	89	115
89032	NORTH LAS VEGAS	96	104	104	107	99	99	97	96	92	101	117	112	100	117	95	88	115	95	85	106
89033	NORTH LAS VEGAS	77	70	55	67	70	74	67	72	68	69	83	83	63	79	66	67	80	71	71	85
89040	OVERTON	92	81	67	76	85	94	77	86	81	79	99	96	73	93	79	84	94	85	94	104
89041	PAHRUMP	76	72	70	66	74	87	67	76	71	72	88	76	67	76	71	75	83	74	86	84
89043	PIOCHE	73	56	38	52	63	73	57	66	65	56	76	76	51	74	59	69	70	66	79	86
89045	ROUND MOUNTAIN	100	91	71	88	91	96	87	93	88	89	109	108	82	103	86	87	104	93	93	111
89046	SEARCHLIGHT	72	70	74	64	73	89	65	75	70	70	86	70	66	73	71	75	80	72	88	81
89047	SILVERPEAK	89	59	27	51	67	78	57	72	69	59	81	86	49	77	58	75	74	71	88	102
89048	PAHRUMP	77	69	61	66	72	82	68	75	71	69	87	79	65	79	69	74	82	74	83	86
89049	TONOPAH	80	66	49	64	69	78	68	74	73	67	87	84	63	83	67	74	82	74	81	88
89052	HENDERSON	144	156	150	160	152	154	142	145	134	148	170	163	145	163	141	129	165	141	134	160
89060	PAHRUMP	75	65	52	62	67	75	65	70	68	65	83	78	61	77	65	69	78	70	76	83
89061	PAHRUMP	81	74	58	71	74	78	70	75	71	72	88	87	66	83	69	70	84	75	75	89
89074	HENDERSON	133	148	154	155	143	142	138	136	128	142	163	159	143	163	136	121	161	134	119	149
89084	NORTH LAS VEGAS	77	70	55	67	70	74	67	72	68	69	83	83	63	79	66	67	80	71	71	85
89101	LAS VEGAS	50	44	49	44	43	47	51	49	53	52	66	57	48	64	48	51	66	53	48	53
89102	LAS VEGAS	71	68	82	70	66	72	74	72	75	75	94	83	73	92	72	73	93	75	69	78
89103	LAS VEGAS	67	67	89	70	65	71	72	69	73	73	92	81	73	93	71	72	91	72	66	76
89104	LAS VEGAS	68	69	79	67	67	74	70	70	71	72	90	78	70	87	70	71	88	72	70	76
89106	LAS VEGAS	58	51	57	49	50	56	56	56	60	57	75	63	55	72	55	61	73	58	58	63
89107	LAS VEGAS	79	85	101	86	83	88	86	84	85	86	107	97	88	109	86	83	106	85	79	92
89108	LAS VEGAS	86	84	90	87	81	85	88	85	86	88	108	101	86	105	84	82	106	88	78	94
89109	LAS VEGAS	60	54	78	57	53	60	67	61	68	65	86	74	65	85	64	67	84	66	59	67
89110	LAS VEGAS	87	86	88	86	84	87	87	87	86	89	108	100	86	105	84	83	107	88	81	95
89113	LAS VEGAS	167	197	210	203	189	188	176	175	162	183	206	203	186	209	176	154	205	170	152	191
89115	LAS VEGAS	64	56	54	56	54	58	62	60	62	62	78	71	58	74	58	60	76	63	57	67
89117	LAS VEGAS	124	128	146	135	124	128	129	125	123	131	156	147	130	153	125	117	153	127	112	138
89118	LAS VEGAS	85	80	95	86	77	82	88	83	85	89	109	101	86	104	83	81	106	88	75	92
89119	LAS VEGAS	60	52	66	56	51	55	64	58	63	62	80	72	60	77	59	60	78	64	54	65
89120	LAS VEGAS	106	110	130	113	108	114	115	110	111	114	140	130	115	139	112	107	138	113	103	121
89121	LAS VEGAS	77	80	93	81	79	85	82	80	81	82	102	93	83	101	82	80	100	82	77	88
89122	LAS VEGAS	71	69	70	68	69	75	69	71	69	70	87	79	68	82	69	69	83	71	72	80
89123	LAS VEGAS	112	122	128	128	117	117	117	114	109	119	139	135	119	138	113	103	137	114	99	125
89124	LAS VEGAS	155	142	125	136	148	163	134	148	139	138	171	165	130	161	139	143	163	146	159	178
89128	LAS VEGAS	111	118	127	124	114	116	116	113	110	118	139	134	117	137	113	104	137	114	101	124
89129	LAS VEGAS	128	141	141	147	135	133	131	129	121	135	154	151	134	153	128	114	152	127	112	142
89130	LAS VEGAS	113	123	124	126	121	123	114	115	108	117	136	131	117	134	114	104	134	113	106	128
89131	LAS VEGAS	125	142	137	148	135	131	128	127	117	133	149	148	132	150	125	109	147	123	108	139
89134	LAS VEGAS	152	160	165	155	161	179	145	157	146	154	183	162	151	167	153	149	175	152	165	172
89135	LAS VEGAS	137	154	149	161	147	142	139	138	127	145	162	161	143	162	136	119	160	134	117	151
89139	LAS VEGAS	118	125	122	122	125	131	117	121	114	118	142	138	118	139	118	113	139	119	117	137
89141	LAS VEGAS	123	113	88	108	113	119	107	115	109	110	134	133	101	126	106	107	129	115	114	136
89142	LAS VEGAS	99	106	106	111	101	100	101	99	94	104	119	117	102	118	97	88	117	99	85	109
89143	LAS VEGAS	125	141	136	147	134	129	127	126	116	132	148	147	131	148	124	108	146	123	107	138
89144	LAS VEGAS	155	176	183	184	167	164	161	158	149	167	189	186	167	191	158	140	187	155	136	173
89145	LAS VEGAS	113	121	134	125	117	120	119	116	114	121	144	137	121	144	117	109	142	117	105	128
89146	LAS VEGAS	102	102	119	108	99	106	107	103	104	108	132	122	107	128	104	99	129	107	95	114
89147	LAS VEGAS	119	126	133	132	121	123	123	120	116	126	148	142	124	146	120	110	145	121	107	132
89148	LAS VEGAS	179	202	194	211	192	185	182	181	167	190	212	211	187	213	177	155	210	176	153	197
89149	LAS VEGAS	149	168	171	169	165	170	152	155	144	156	182	173	159	178	154	141	178	150	146	171
89154	LAS VEGAS	48	38	49	42	37	41	52	46	52	49	65	59	48	61	47	47	63	52	42	51
89156	LAS VEGAS	87	89	87	90	87	89	87	87	84	88	106	102	86	104	85	81	103	87	81	97
89191	NELLIS AFB	0	0	0	0	0	0	0	0	0	0	0	0	0	0	0	0	0	0	0	0
89301	ELY	77	61	42	59	66	76	63	70	70	62	83	80	58	81	63	72	77	69	80	86
89310	AUSTIN	69	46	22	40	52	60	45	56	54	46	63	67	38	60	46	58	58	55	68	79
89311	BAKER	0	0	0	0	0	0	0	0	0	0	0	0	0	0	0	0	0	0	0	0
89316	EUREKA	87	80	62	77	80	84	76	81	77	78	95	94	72	90	75	76	91	81	81	97
89317	LUND	89	79	60	75	84	90	73	81	78	73	95	97	72	97	76	80	90	79	88	105
89403	DAYTON	97	89	69	85	89	94	84	91	86	87	106	105	80	100	83	85	101	90	90	108
89404	DENIO	94	103	102	105	100	99	98	97	92	99	116	116	98	117	96	87	114	97	86	107
89405	EMPIRE	69	47	21	40	53	61	45	56	54	46	64	67	38	60	46	58	58	56	69	79
89406	FALLON	90	83	73	82	84	90	83	86	84	83	104	101	80	102	82	83	100	86	86	102
89408	FERNLEY	86	84	73	83	83	86	80	83	79	82	98	97	78	95	79	77	95	83	79	96
89409	GABBS	59	44	29	42	48	58	49	54	55	46	64	60	43	61	48	58	59	54	64	65
89410	GARDNERVILLE	109	112	111	110	114	123	108	112	108	107	133	125	109	130	110	109	128	110	115	126
89412	GERLACH	86	57	26	50	65	75	55	69	67	57	79	83	47	74	56	72	71	69	85	98
89413	GLENBROOK	168	151	144	147	158	176	147	160	154	149	189	182	142	179	152	158	180	160	173	196
89414	GOLCONDA	96	88	69	84	88	93	84	90	85	86	105	104	79	99	83	84	100	89	89	106
89415	HAWTHORNE	69	59	48	57	63	73	62	67	68	60	81	75	59	78	63	71	75	66	77	78
89418	IMLAY	88	80	63	77	80	85	76	82	77	79	95	95	72	90	75	76	92	82	81	97
89419	LOVELOCK	63	56	50	55	56	63	59	60	62	58	76	70	57	74	58	62	72	61	63	69
89420	LUNING	66	49	33	47	54	65	55	60	61	52	72	67	49	68	54	65	66	60	72	73
89423	MINDEN	112	129	136	128	129	134	117	120	112	119	141	135	123	141	122	112	138	116	116	133
89424	NIXON	69	63	50	61	63	67	60	65	61	62	75	75	57	71	59	60	72	64	64	77
89425	OROVADA	72	65	57	62	65	70	64	68	67	66	82	77	62	77	63	67	79	68	69	79
89426	PARADISE VALLEY	82	75	59	72	75	79	72	77	72	74	89	88	68	84	70	71	86	76	76	91
89427	SCHURZ	48	42	46	42	42	48	50	47	52	48	64	55	48	63	48	52	62	49	49	52
89429	SILVER SPRINGS	82	74	58	72	74	79	71	76	72	73	89	88	67	84	70	71	85	76	75	90
89430	SMITH	128	89	47	84	104	116	88	109	102	87	119	131	75	117	91	107	109	107	130	152
	NEVADA	97	98	104	100	96	101	98	98	96	100	121	113	98	119	96	93	119	99	92	109
	UNITED STATES	100	100	100	100	100	100	100	100	100	100	100	100	100	100	100	100	100	100	100	100

ZIP CODE		COUNTY FIPS CODE	POPULATION			2000-2004 ANNUAL RATE		HOUSEHOLDS					FAMILIES		
#	POST OFFICE NAME		2000	2004	2009	% Rate	State Centile	2000	2004	2009	% Annual Rate 2000-2004	2004 Average HH Size	2000	2004	% Annual Rate 2000-2004
89431	SPARKS	031	36050	37707	41906	1.1	31	13690	14363	15969	1.1	2.60	8464	8696	0.6
89433	SUN VALLEY	031	19579	21073	23598	1.8	42	6421	6910	7725	1.7	3.05	4807	5111	1.5
89434	SPARKS	031	21957	24533	28460	2.6	55	8228	9219	10683	2.7	2.63	5710	6322	2.4
89436	SPARKS	031	21724	31741	41294	9.3	90	7320	10641	13795	9.2	2.98	6106	8802	9.0
89440	VIRGINIA CITY	029	1254	1336	1411	1.5	39	574	619	660	1.8	2.16	389	417	1.7
89442	WADSWORTH	031	974	1020	1123	1.1	32	362	383	423	1.3	2.66	254	264	0.9
89444	WELLINGTON	019	2537	2818	3275	2.5	54	1100	1232	1443	2.7	2.28	791	879	2.5
89445	WINNEMUCCA	013	15169	15222	15168	0.1	21	5326	5351	5342	0.1	2.81	3859	3865	0.0
89447	YERINGTON	019	8072	8575	9843	1.4	36	3151	3367	3893	1.6	2.44	2143	2273	1.4
89451	INCLINE VILLAGE	031	9988	10566	11696	1.3	35	4192	4466	4954	1.5	2.34	2749	2878	1.1
89460	GARDNERVILLE	005	13763	15093	17291	2.2	48	5188	5764	6681	2.5	2.61	3925	4329	2.3
89501	RENO	031	2694	2868	3171	1.5	37	1524	1650	1847	1.9	1.61	389	405	1.0
89502	RENO	031	44855	47793	53413	1.5	39	18083	19234	21464	1.5	2.47	10127	10554	1.0
89503	RENO	031	30003	32419	36340	1.8	45	12696	13841	15602	2.1	2.25	6254	6648	1.5
89506	RENO	031	32785	39053	46098	4.2	70	11328	13695	16276	4.6	2.79	8563	10207	4.2
89509	RENO	031	42203	45742	51815	1.9	46	19039	20764	23574	2.1	2.19	10997	11855	1.8
89510	RENO	031	1248	1274	1385	0.5	25	483	494	537	0.5	2.58	366	368	0.1
89511	RENO	031	18430	22355	26601	4.7	73	7114	8668	10325	4.8	2.55	5177	6269	4.6
89512	RENO	031	24465	25864	28758	1.3	34	8959	9525	10634	1.5	2.60	5078	5282	0.9
89521	RENO	031	10291	12296	14636	4.3	70	4124	5003	5989	4.7	2.46	2819	3413	4.6
89523	RENO	031	18375	24108	29831	6.6	86	7087	9314	11524	6.6	2.58	4823	6245	6.3
89701	CARSON CITY	510	25846	27679	29511	1.6	41	8886	9626	10344	1.9	2.57	6191	6664	1.8
89703	CARSON CITY	510	9800	10197	10760	0.9	30	4414	4625	4895	1.1	2.18	2723	2847	1.1
89704	WASHOE VALLEY	031	4115	4406	4915	1.6	40	1619	1760	1975	2.0	2.50	1189	1274	1.6
89705	CARSON CITY	005	4271	4944	5812	3.5	64	1622	1906	2265	3.9	2.59	1259	1469	3.7
89706	CARSON CITY	019	19145	20982	23163	2.2	48	7736	8397	9207	2.0	2.48	4999	5411	1.9
89801	ELKO	007	20289	19842	19469	-0.5	14	7379	7223	7081	-0.5	2.71	5185	5055	-0.6
89815	SPRING CREEK	007	12563	13080	13104	1.0	30	4146	4337	4348	1.1	3.01	3430	3563	0.9
89820	BATTLE MOUNTAIN	015	5327	4805	4363	-2.4	3	1871	1706	1563	-2.2	2.77	1385	1257	-2.3
89821	CRESCENT VALLEY	011	527	498	465	-1.3	7	224	212	199	-1.3	2.35	152	144	-1.3
89822	CARLIN	007	2316	2199	2123	-1.2	8	795	755	726	-1.2	2.72	583	549	-1.4
89823	DEETH	007	242	280	300	3.5	64	99	113	121	3.2	2.36	74	85	3.3
89825	JACKPOT	007	665	643	624	-0.8	11	218	211	204	-0.8	2.94	127	121	-1.1
89831	MOUNTAIN CITY	007	1350	1289	1250	-1.1	9	433	413	400	-1.1	2.60	279	264	-1.3
89833	RUBY VALLEY	007	68	67	66	-0.4	17	31	31	30	0.0	1.94	21	21	0.0
89834	TUSCARORA	007	6	6	5	0.0	20	4	4	4	0.0	1.25	2	1	-15.1
89835	WELLS	007	7792	7928	7862	0.4	23	2533	2547	2508	0.1	3.06	1791	1788	0.0

NEVADA						4.1					3.9	2.64			3.8
UNITED STATES						1.2					1.3	2.58			1.1

# ZIP CODE	POST OFFICE NAME	White 2000	White 2004	Black 2000	Black 2004	Asian/Pacific 2000	Asian/Pacific 2004	% Hispanic Origin 2000	% Hispanic Origin 2004	0-4	5-9	10-14	15-19	20-24	25-44	45-64	65-84	85+	18+	MEDIAN AGE 2004	% 2004 Males	% 2004 Females
89431	SPARKS	73.6	71.0	2.7	2.8	5.3	5.0	27.3	31.7	7.8	6.9	7.0	6.5	7.6	29.9	22.5	10.6	1.2	74.6	34.4	50.2	49.8
89433	SUN VALLEY	79.9	77.6	2.2	2.3	2.9	2.8	21.0	24.9	8.9	8.5	8.3	7.2	6.8	30.8	21.8	7.3	0.5	70.1	32.4	50.4	49.6
89434	SPARKS	82.3	80.4	2.3	2.5	6.5	6.7	11.3	13.4	6.0	6.1	7.5	7.5	7.3	27.2	26.8	10.1	1.6	75.8	37.8	48.2	51.8
89436	SPARKS	88.3	87.6	1.1	1.2	3.0	3.0	6.6	8.2	8.7	8.7	8.6	6.5	4.6	33.1	24.0	5.4	0.5	69.7	34.9	49.2	50.8
89440	VIRGINIA CITY	93.5	93.0	0.2	0.3	0.8	0.8	4.8	5.4	4.7	5.3	5.6	5.4	4.2	23.2	38.9	11.8	0.9	80.7	45.7	51.5	48.5
89442	WADSWORTH	23.0	22.8	0.1	0.1	0.4	0.4	8.5	9.9	8.3	8.4	9.5	9.5	6.4	26.3	21.0	8.8	1.8	67.8	31.9	49.3	50.7
89444	WELLINGTON	90.3	89.4	0.4	0.5	0.9	0.8	11.8	13.4	3.6	4.4	5.4	5.6	4.0	19.0	33.7	22.9	1.4	82.9	50.0	51.9	48.1
89445	WINNEMUCCA	85.0	84.7	0.5	0.5	0.7	0.7	18.8	18.8	8.4	8.1	8.3	7.6	6.9	28.5	24.6	6.9	0.7	70.1	33.7	52.2	47.8
89447	YERINGTON	82.7	81.2	0.9	1.0	0.4	0.4	17.5	20.0	6.4	6.2	6.7	9.2	5.9	20.9	23.8	18.5	2.4	74.6	40.8	52.1	47.9
89451	INCLINE VILLAGE	91.0	89.9	0.5	0.5	1.7	1.7	12.1	14.4	4.6	4.8	5.8	5.6	5.6	25.9	34.6	12.7	0.5	81.5	43.6	52.1	47.9
89460	GARDNERVILLE	91.3	90.7	0.3	0.3	1.2	1.2	6.8	7.9	5.9	6.3	7.9	7.5	6.1	24.7	28.2	12.5	1.0	75.2	40.1	50.2	49.8
89501	RENO	74.5	73.1	4.6	5.0	11.8	11.7	13.2	15.7	2.8	2.6	2.3	5.8	8.0	28.2	32.7	16.1	1.5	90.4	45.2	61.4	38.6
89502	RENO	68.8	66.2	2.4	2.5	4.5	4.2	33.1	36.9	8.2	7.0	6.2	6.5	8.7	31.5	21.8	9.1	1.0	75.0	32.8	51.9	48.1
89503	RENO	82.2	80.7	1.8	2.0	7.2	7.2	10.2	12.4	5.2	4.7	5.2	7.8	11.8	30.6	23.2	10.0	1.5	82.0	34.0	51.8	48.2
89506	RENO	85.2	83.9	1.8	1.9	2.5	2.4	11.5	13.5	7.8	7.5	8.2	7.9	6.6	30.5	24.8	6.4	0.4	71.7	34.2	50.9	49.1
89509	RENO	86.7	85.9	1.5	1.5	4.2	4.1	9.9	11.5	5.0	5.2	5.7	5.5	5.8	24.2	30.2	15.9	2.6	80.8	44.1	49.2	50.8
89510	RENO	77.9	77.1	0.8	0.9	0.8	0.8	4.1	5.0	4.7	5.7	8.2	7.1	4.2	22.8	33.4	12.5	1.4	76.8	43.5	51.3	48.7
89511	RENO	92.2	91.6	0.9	1.0	2.6	2.6	5.3	6.4	5.6	6.3	7.1	6.4	5.6	23.4	32.6	11.7	1.3	77.0	42.4	49.6	50.4
89512	RENO	64.2	62.6	5.8	5.8	8.8	8.1	32.1	36.2	8.3	7.1	6.8	7.7	9.6	28.6	20.2	10.5	1.3	74.1	31.8	51.5	48.5
89521	RENO	91.1	90.0	1.0	1.3	2.9	3.3	5.7	6.8	6.4	6.6	6.3	5.6	5.4	29.7	29.3	9.9	0.8	77.3	39.5	49.2	50.8
89523	RENO	86.2	85.1	1.3	1.3	7.1	7.3	6.4	7.9	6.7	6.7	7.2	7.2	7.4	31.7	25.5	6.9	0.7	75.1	34.5	49.3	50.8
89701	CARSON CITY	83.4	82.5	3.0	3.1	2.0	2.0	16.2	17.8	6.3	5.9	6.6	6.8	7.7	29.0	25.3	11.2	1.3	77.2	37.3	54.2	45.8
89703	CARSON CITY	91.1	90.8	0.4	0.4	1.9	1.8	5.8	6.6	4.0	4.7	6.2	5.9	4.6	19.9	32.7	19.2	3.0	81.4	48.0	49.0	51.0
89704	WASHOE VALLEY	95.6	95.1	0.4	0.5	1.0	1.0	3.5	4.3	4.3	5.2	6.4	5.5	4.7	21.9	39.8	11.3	0.9	80.7	46.0	49.8	50.2
89705	CARSON CITY	91.0	90.1	0.4	0.4	0.9	0.9	9.1	10.5	6.5	7.1	7.6	6.6	4.8	25.1	28.3	13.3	0.8	74.6	40.7	49.0	51.0
89706	CARSON CITY	85.7	84.4	0.7	0.8	1.7	1.7	15.5	17.6	7.5	6.7	6.7	6.0	6.8	26.7	24.2	13.4	1.9	75.4	37.6	48.9	51.1
89801	ELKO	81.9	81.8	0.3	0.3	1.1	1.1	19.2	18.9	8.6	7.9	8.6	7.7	7.6	29.7	22.5	6.4	1.0	69.9	31.9	51.1	48.9
89815	SPRING CREEK	91.1	90.8	0.3	0.3	0.5	0.5	8.2	8.2	8.4	8.3	9.4	8.3	7.1	29.2	24.5	4.6	0.3	68.7	32.1	50.7	49.3
89820	BATTLE MOUNTAIN	83.9	82.7	0.1	0.1	0.4	0.4	19.5	21.6	8.0	7.8	9.8	8.0	7.2	26.0	26.3	6.3	0.6	68.9	33.4	51.2	48.8
89821	CRESCENT VALLEY	90.1	89.6	0.4	0.4	0.6	0.6	9.7	10.0	6.6	7.0	8.2	6.8	4.8	25.1	27.7	13.3	0.4	73.7	40.0	52.4	47.6
89822	CARLIN	90.2	89.9	1.8	1.8	0.6	0.6	8.4	8.5	7.7	7.2	7.5	7.7	7.4	30.9	23.9	7.1	0.6	73.0	34.6	54.7	45.3
89823	DEETH	88.8	89.3	0.4	0.4	0.4	0.4	14.1	12.9	7.9	7.5	7.5	7.9	7.1	28.9	25.0	7.5	0.7	72.1	33.4	54.3	45.7
89825	JACKPOT	68.0	67.3	0.0	0.0	0.3	0.3	44.4	44.3	8.4	7.6	8.1	8.6	10.6	30.3	21.6	4.8	0.0	71.2	29.0	51.8	48.2
89831	MOUNTAIN CITY	35.2	33.8	2.7	2.6	0.6	0.5	11.8	11.3	5.3	6.1	8.0	18.4	4.7	23.3	24.1	9.5	0.9	66.7	32.8	58.5	41.5
89833	RUBY VALLEY	80.9	82.1	4.4	4.5	0.0	0.0	13.2	11.9	6.0	6.0	7.5	7.5	7.5	31.3	26.9	7.5	0.0	74.6	36.3	59.7	40.3
89834	TUSCARORA	83.3	100.0	0.0	0.0	0.0	0.0	16.7	16.7	0.0	0.0	0.0	0.0	33.3	66.7	0.0	0.0	0.0	100.0	27.5	50.0	50.0
89835	WELLS	74.7	74.3	1.1	1.1	0.6	0.6	42.6	43.0	10.4	8.9	8.7	8.3	9.0	28.7	20.6	5.1	0.3	67.0	28.0	53.4	46.6
	NEVADA	75.2	73.9	6.8	7.0	4.9	4.8	19.7	22.0	7.3	6.9	7.1	6.5	7.0	29.9	23.8	10.6	1.0	74.8	35.6	50.6	49.4
	UNITED STATES	75.1	73.6	12.3	12.5	3.8	4.2	12.5	14.1	6.9	6.7	7.2	7.0	7.3	28.6	23.8	10.8	1.7	75.1	36.0	49.1	50.9

#	POST OFFICE NAME	2004 Per Capita Income	2004 HH Income Base	2004 HOUSEHOLD INCOME DISTRIBUTION (%)					MEDIAN HOUSEHOLD INCOME				2004 Home Value Base	2004 HOME VALUE DISTRIBUTION (%)					2004 Median Home Value
				Less than $25,000	$25,000 to $49,999	$50,000 to $99,999	$100,000 to $149,999	$150,000 or More	2004	2009	2004 National Centile	2004 State Centile		Less than $50,000	$50,000 to $89,999	$90,000 to $174,999	$175,000 to $399,999	$400,000 or More	
89431	SPARKS	20222	14363	25.4	34.3	32.4	6.2	1.7	42489	49893	55	33	7271	7.9	5.9	57.1	28.1	1.1	152299
89433	SUN VALLEY	17699	6910	17.9	36.0	38.1	6.5	1.5	47151	54772	66	46	5404	11.3	14.5	52.3	21.7	0.2	128236
89434	SPARKS	28333	9219	12.0	27.4	41.3	15.1	4.2	60571	72161	85	76	6358	1.4	3.1	34.4	59.4	1.8	186781
89436	SPARKS	31443	10641	5.4	14.5	47.2	23.1	9.9	78653	95258	95	95	9948	2.6	0.7	9.4	82.3	5.0	237546
89440	VIRGINIA CITY	30498	619	16.2	29.6	39.4	10.7	4.2	55102	65431	80	63	510	6.5	1.4	37.3	42.2	12.8	187019
89442	WADSWORTH	16323	383	34.2	31.9	27.2	5.0	1.8	35909	42756	31	15	275	25.5	24.7	26.6	19.3	4.0	89783
89444	WELLINGTON	24672	1232	29.7	29.6	28.3	7.3	5.2	38287	44961	40	20	993	7.4	8.9	40.5	31.7	11.6	161146
89445	WINNEMUCCA	22784	5351	17.9	27.6	41.1	10.2	3.3	53889	61551	78	61	4052	12.7	15.5	47.5	22.3	2.1	125670
89447	YERINGTON	21674	3367	29.9	36.2	24.7	4.4	4.9	37187	42353	36	17	2445	13.4	14.6	47.4	19.3	5.3	124217
89451	INCLINE VILLAGE	68865	4466	10.6	14.9	31.2	17.0	26.3	85034	116073	96	100	3225	1.2	1.6	5.4	23.8	67.9	598322
89460	GARDNERVILLE	30625	5764	14.2	27.8	36.3	13.8	8.1	57248	67386	82	67	4279	1.6	1.3	21.9	55.8	19.4	221879
89501	RENO	29003	1650	54.7	26.3	11.6	3.6	3.8	22729	26542	3	2	183	0.0	21.9	23.5	39.9	14.8	181641
89502	RENO	20732	19234	29.2	33.6	27.5	7.1	2.6	39070	45652	43	24	7735	14.3	12.0	33.6	36.7	3.5	156415
89503	RENO	24161	13841	27.8	28.8	31.5	8.5	3.3	44335	52004	60	37	6590	6.0	2.4	33.5	57.4	0.7	183551
89506	RENO	23600	13695	11.8	28.8	44.6	12.1	2.8	58112	67622	83	68	11039	9.8	7.9	41.2	40.0	1.2	161284
89509	RENO	47120	20764	18.4	21.7	29.6	15.2	15.1	62859	78390	87	78	12580	1.6	1.2	9.3	60.3	27.6	299566
89510	RENO	28488	494	11.9	22.9	43.7	15.6	5.9	65466	81870	89	84	438	4.8	6.9	23.3	51.6	13.5	232308
89511	RENO	48810	8668	10.2	18.9	31.2	20.2	19.5	80484	102244	95	97	6683	2.3	2.3	6.7	52.5	36.2	342028
89512	RENO	16744	9525	38.9	32.2	21.5	5.5	1.9	32467	38307	19	10	3689	12.0	16.4	50.5	20.4	0.6	125102
89521	RENO	33996	5003	11.1	22.9	40.1	18.5	7.4	67349	82497	90	86	3765	3.6	2.5	17.5	72.3	4.1	240463
89523	RENO	31668	9314	11.3	23.3	40.8	17.5	7.0	65830	78712	89	85	6609	4.1	1.6	10.4	77.9	6.1	233154
89701	CARSON CITY	23591	9626	19.9	29.2	36.6	10.8	3.5	50712	59598	73	56	6254	4.6	4.8	32.6	55.3	2.6	185510
89703	CARSON CITY	35558	4625	22.4	22.9	30.7	14.3	9.7	55389	66408	80	64	3466	5.4	2.5	13.7	58.6	19.9	270238
89704	WASHOE VALLEY	36851	1760	14.5	18.9	35.9	21.2	9.6	72072	87381	92	92	1565	4.1	2.2	27.4	52.3	14.0	206614
89705	CARSON CITY	29351	1906	11.6	22.4	46.5	13.1	6.4	63137	75414	87	79	1604	0.6	2.5	26.1	61.7	9.2	213054
89706	CARSON CITY	21509	8397	25.7	32.7	32.3	7.0	2.4	42837	50014	56	34	5304	15.3	10.4	37.3	35.3	1.7	152966
89801	ELKO	23013	7223	18.6	24.7	41.8	11.6	3.4	55145	62115	80	64	5204	15.4	7.7	41.9	32.3	2.7	147704
89815	SPRING CREEK	22877	4337	11.4	20.4	51.6	13.7	3.0	63200	71383	87	80	3795	5.0	10.8	50.0	31.2	3.0	152489
89820	BATTLE MOUNTAIN	19851	1706	19.6	27.1	44.8	8.1	0.4	52307	56874	76	58	1358	25.6	23.9	40.3	9.7	0.4	90556
89821	CRESCENT VALLEY	21926	212	33.0	22.6	34.0	7.6	2.8	43914	51047	58	36	178	29.2	27.0	24.7	14.0	5.1	79167
89822	CARLIN	21761	755	16.2	26.8	44.8	10.9	1.5	54092	61011	78	61	591	21.5	17.1	47.0	12.5	1.9	109777
89823	DEETH	24586	113	15.9	35.4	36.3	8.0	4.4	48967	55136	70	52	89	21.4	22.5	46.1	9.0	1.1	110938
89825	JACKPOT	14023	211	22.3	52.6	22.8	2.4	0.0	34696	41715	26	13	93	54.8	18.3	16.1	9.7	1.1	45000
89831	MOUNTAIN CITY	16111	413	43.1	33.2	17.4	5.8	0.5	31103	37762	15	7	249	40.6	25.3	20.9	10.4	2.8	68750
89833	RUBY VALLEY	26860	31	16.1	35.5	45.2	3.2	0.0	47394	52915	67	48	23	17.4	17.4	34.8	26.1	4.4	129167
89834	TUSCARORA	4104	0	0.0	0.0	0.0	0.0	0.0	0	55000	0	0	0	0.0	0.0	0.0	0.0	0.0	0
89835	WELLS	15747	2547	25.0	37.5	30.8	5.5	1.1	40191	46629	47	27	1628	28.3	21.7	33.1	15.3	1.6	90000
	NEVADA	26208		20.5	27.7	34.5	11.4	5.9	51572	61335				5.9	5.6	38.5	43.5	6.6	175101
	UNITED STATES	25866		24.7	27.1	30.8	10.9	6.5	48124	56710				10.9	15.0	33.7	30.1	10.4	145905

SPENDING POTENTIAL INDICES

89431-89835 **D**

ZIP CODE #	POST OFFICE NAME	FINANCIAL SERVICES				THE HOME						ENTERTAINMENT						PERSONAL			
						Home Improvements		Furnishings													
		Auto Loan	Home Loan	Invest-ments	Retire-ment Plans	Home Repair	Lawn & Garden	Comput-ers & Hard-ware	Major Appli-ances	TV, Radio, Sound Equip-ment	Furni-ture	Dine out/ Carry out	Sports Equip-ment	Fees & Tickets	Toys & Games	Travel	Cable TV	Apparel & Services	Auto Repairs	Health Insur-ance	Pets & Supplies
89431 SPARKS		70	72	80	73	71	75	75	73	75	74	93	86	76	94	74	73	91	75	70	80
89433 SUN VALLEY		83	78	67	77	77	81	76	79	75	78	94	92	73	89	74	73	91	79	76	92
89434 SPARKS		104	110	117	113	107	109	108	106	103	109	130	125	109	129	106	98	128	107	96	117
89436 SPARKS		133	151	147	157	144	140	137	135	125	142	159	158	141	160	133	117	158	132	115	148
89440 VIRGINIA CITY		104	94	74	89	99	107	87	96	92	87	112	113	86	113	90	94	106	94	104	123
89442 WADSWORTH		69	63	49	61	63	67	60	65	61	62	75	74	57	71	59	60	72	64	64	76
89444 WELLINGTON		89	76	67	70	83	98	72	86	80	76	97	88	70	86	78	85	89	83	101	102
89445 WINNEMUCCA		98	94	80	92	93	97	90	94	89	92	111	109	87	107	88	87	107	93	91	109
89447 YERINGTON		84	65	46	63	71	84	71	78	78	67	93	88	64	88	70	82	85	77	92	94
89451 INCLINE VILLAGE		243	230	230	221	242	265	218	237	226	218	276	276	214	277	227	232	266	234	251	294
89460 GARDNERVILLE		110	125	128	125	123	123	114	115	108	116	136	134	119	140	115	105	134	112	106	129
89501 RENO		62	53	74	56	53	61	69	61	71	65	88	75	65	85	65	69	85	68	63	68
89502 RENO		72	66	73	69	65	69	73	71	73	74	92	84	71	89	70	69	90	75	66	78
89503 RENO		72	70	85	73	69	74	80	74	78	77	98	89	78	97	76	75	96	78	69	81
89506 RENO		94	99	98	101	97	97	95	95	90	96	113	111	95	113	93	86	111	94	86	106
89509 RENO		136	146	174	147	144	156	148	144	144	147	181	167	152	179	148	142	178	147	139	158
89510 RENO		100	116	116	115	114	114	106	106	99	105	124	124	109	129	106	97	123	103	98	119
89511 RENO		169	193	212	200	187	191	181	176	169	183	215	206	191	216	181	163	214	175	159	195
89512 RENO		61	54	58	54	53	57	60	59	62	61	77	69	57	73	57	60	76	62	57	66
89521 RENO		120	128	125	130	124	125	120	120	114	122	144	141	121	143	118	109	141	119	109	135
89523 RENO		117	125	128	132	120	119	119	117	111	123	142	138	121	140	115	104	139	116	101	128
89701 CARSON CITY		76	80	85	80	80	84	80	80	79	79	98	92	81	100	80	78	96	80	77	88
89703 CARSON CITY		102	113	128	112	112	121	110	109	108	109	135	125	114	136	112	108	132	109	108	120
89704 WASHOE VALLEY		128	144	143	142	142	144	131	134	125	132	156	155	135	160	133	122	154	130	125	151
89705 CARSON CITY		104	117	121	118	114	115	110	110	103	111	131	128	112	132	110	99	129	109	99	120
89706 CARSON CITY		77	75	76	75	75	80	75	77	75	76	94	88	74	90	75	74	91	77	75	86
89801 ELKO		90	92	89	93	90	93	89	90	86	90	108	105	89	107	88	83	106	90	84	101
89815 SPRING CREEK		102	107	97	109	104	104	99	101	94	102	118	117	99	116	97	89	115	99	91	113
89820 BATTLE MOUNTAIN		87	80	62	76	80	84	76	81	77	78	95	94	72	89	75	76	91	81	81	96
89821 CRESCENT VALLEY		82	75	58	72	75	79	71	76	72	73	89	88	67	84	70	71	86	76	76	91
89822 CARLIN		94	85	67	82	85	90	81	87	82	84	102	101	77	96	80	81	98	87	87	103
89823 DEETH		94	82	62	78	85	92	78	87	82	80	100	101	73	95	79	82	95	86	91	108
89825 JACKPOT		60	51	56	55	50	54	58	56	57	58	73	68	54	68	54	55	70	60	52	65
89831 MOUNTAIN CITY		54	47	46	45	48	54	52	52	55	50	67	61	49	66	51	56	65	54	57	61
89833 RUBY VALLEY		95	66	35	63	77	87	66	81	76	65	89	98	56	87	68	79	81	80	97	113
89834 TUSCARORA		0	0	0	0	0	0	0	0	0	0	0	0	0	0	0	0	0	0	0	0
89835 WELLS		77	66	51	65	68	73	65	71	67	66	83	82	61	79	64	67	79	71	73	86
NEVADA		97	98	104	100	96	101	98	98	96	100	121	113	98	119	96	93	119	99	92	109
UNITED STATES		100	100	100	100	100	100	100	100	100	100	100	100	100	100	100	100	100	100	100	100

Copyright © 2004 ESRI BIS. All rights reserved. Reproduction by any method is prohibited.

#	POST OFFICE NAME	COUNTY FIPS CODE	POPULATION 2000	POPULATION 2004	POPULATION 2009	2000-2004 ANNUAL RATE % Rate	2000-2004 ANNUAL RATE State Centile	HOUSEHOLDS 2000	HOUSEHOLDS 2004	HOUSEHOLDS 2009	% Annual Rate 2000-2004	2004 Average HH Size	FAMILIES 2000	FAMILIES 2004	% Annual Rate 2000-2004
03031	AMHERST	011	10651	11698	12710	2.2	79	3553	3937	4314	2.4	2.97	3035	3353	2.4
03032	AUBURN	015	4682	5050	5493	1.8	63	1580	1732	1908	2.2	2.91	1322	1445	2.1
03033	BROOKLINE	011	4181	4664	5107	2.6	91	1343	1502	1652	2.7	3.11	1147	1279	2.6
03034	CANDIA	015	4078	4361	4721	1.6	49	1412	1535	1685	2.0	2.84	1153	1249	1.9
03036	CHESTER	015	3776	4506	5159	4.3	99	1207	1454	1682	4.5	3.07	1003	1205	4.4
03037	DEERFIELD	015	3604	4054	4506	2.8	93	1203	1370	1540	3.1	2.94	965	1095	3.0
03038	DERRY	015	34223	36017	38746	1.2	30	12388	13153	14284	1.4	2.72	8834	9333	1.3
03042	EPPING	015	5445	6045	6674	2.5	87	2036	2295	2568	2.9	2.63	1466	1645	2.8
03043	FRANCESTOWN	011	1469	1607	1741	2.1	77	548	607	666	2.4	2.65	416	458	2.3
03044	FREMONT	015	3552	3871	4231	2.0	74	1180	1297	1430	2.3	2.96	995	1090	2.2
03045	GOFFSTOWN	011	12800	13458	14305	1.2	29	4369	4654	5010	1.5	2.71	3243	3438	1.4
03046	DUNBARTON	013	2332	2578	2854	2.4	86	842	940	1053	2.6	2.74	676	754	2.6
03047	GREENFIELD	011	1732	1770	1845	0.5	8	589	612	647	0.9	2.66	426	440	0.8
03048	GREENVILLE	011	3324	3464	3660	1.0	19	1292	1365	1458	1.3	2.54	870	913	1.1
03049	HOLLIS	011	7058	7705	8346	2.1	76	2455	2704	2954	2.3	2.85	2036	2235	2.2
03051	HUDSON	011	23007	24365	26067	1.4	39	8073	8677	9393	1.7	2.79	6291	6720	1.6
03052	LITCHFIELD	011	7281	8024	8732	2.3	84	2318	2584	2839	2.6	3.11	2001	2224	2.5
03053	LONDONDERRY	015	23122	24906	27069	1.8	62	7592	8262	9073	2.0	3.01	6292	6831	2.0
03054	MERRIMACK	011	25188	26996	29057	1.6	52	8852	9651	10521	2.1	2.79	7000	7571	1.9
03055	MILFORD	011	13619	14383	15316	1.3	36	5229	5583	6003	1.6	2.55	3570	3787	1.4
03057	MONT VERNON	011	1975	2182	2376	2.4	86	673	756	833	2.8	2.86	559	625	2.7
03060	NASHUA	011	29539	30519	32247	0.8	13	12175	12715	13569	1.0	2.35	7072	7341	0.9
03062	NASHUA	011	26222	27005	28435	0.7	12	9989	10411	11075	1.0	2.55	6973	7227	0.9
03063	NASHUA	011	16175	16147	16884	0.0	2	6721	6800	7197	0.3	2.33	4280	4311	0.2
03064	NASHUA	011	14654	15072	15933	0.7	11	5725	5948	6347	0.9	2.52	3755	3897	0.9
03070	NEW BOSTON	011	4209	4765	5261	3.0	95	1460	1677	1873	3.3	2.84	1184	1354	3.2
03071	NEW IPSWICH	011	4147	4633	5078	2.6	91	1316	1492	1653	3.0	3.09	1060	1196	2.9
03076	PELHAM	011	10914	11918	12914	2.1	76	3606	3992	4373	2.4	2.99	2983	3291	2.3
03077	RAYMOND	015	9521	9965	10665	1.1	23	3441	3658	3966	1.5	2.72	2528	2675	1.3
03079	SALEM	015	27773	28852	30997	0.9	17	10278	10831	11785	1.2	2.65	7507	7880	1.2
03082	LYNDEBOROUGH	011	1407	1541	1672	2.2	78	497	551	605	2.5	2.80	373	411	2.3
03084	TEMPLE	011	1274	1296	1351	0.4	5	429	442	465	0.7	2.90	341	350	0.6
03086	WILTON	011	3766	3975	4228	1.3	34	1421	1513	1623	1.5	2.63	1032	1093	1.4
03087	WINDHAM	015	10696	12002	13326	2.8	92	3565	4062	4568	3.1	2.94	3016	3426	3.0
03101	MANCHESTER	011	2629	2825	3042	1.7	56	1519	1614	1743	1.4	1.63	481	509	1.3
03102	MANCHESTER	011	29913	31010	32774	0.9	15	12729	13367	14296	1.2	2.22	7201	7497	1.0
03103	MANCHESTER	011	37150	38805	41247	1.0	21	14359	15102	16182	1.2	2.51	8939	9321	1.0
03104	MANCHESTER	011	31593	32977	35021	1.0	21	13173	13909	14936	1.3	2.28	7668	8046	1.1
03106	HOOKSETT	013	12071	13414	14857	2.5	88	4247	4833	5468	3.1	2.60	3097	3515	3.0
03109	MANCHESTER	011	9334	9803	10446	1.2	28	3575	3796	4087	1.4	2.54	2526	2660	1.2
03110	BEDFORD	011	18423	20488	22450	2.5	88	6307	7162	7974	3.0	2.80	5163	5837	2.9
03216	ANDOVER	013	2138	2257	2440	1.3	34	835	899	987	1.8	2.49	618	663	1.7
03217	ASHLAND	009	2392	2558	2842	1.6	49	1027	1121	1271	2.1	2.28	643	700	2.0
03218	BARNSTEAD	001	1380	1524	1701	2.4	85	503	567	644	2.9	2.69	392	441	2.8
03220	BELMONT	001	6888	7368	8119	1.6	50	2714	2965	3332	2.1	2.48	1918	2087	2.0
03221	BRADFORD	013	1517	1603	1732	1.3	37	589	635	698	1.8	2.49	424	456	1.7
03222	BRISTOL	009	4980	5575	6343	2.7	92	1992	2275	2639	3.2	2.44	1404	1601	3.1
03223	CAMPTON	009	5038	5488	6155	2.0	72	2113	2353	2692	2.6	2.33	1401	1554	2.5
03224	CANTERBURY	013	1945	2127	2341	2.1	77	738	821	918	2.5	2.58	581	645	2.5
03225	CENTER BARNSTEAD	001	2871	3250	3687	3.0	95	1058	1220	1408	3.4	2.66	815	937	3.3
03226	CENTER HARBOR	001	728	743	798	0.5	7	314	328	359	1.0	2.25	223	232	0.9
03227	CENTER SANDWICH	003	1013	1043	1127	0.7	12	444	465	510	1.1	2.24	308	321	1.0
03229	CONTOOCOOK	013	5452	5784	6269	1.4	41	2100	2264	2491	1.8	2.55	1559	1677	1.7
03230	DANBURY	013	1071	1125	1213	1.2	28	438	469	513	1.6	2.40	312	334	1.6
03234	EPSOM	013	3934	4218	4588	1.7	53	1461	1598	1769	2.1	2.57	1083	1182	2.1
03235	FRANKLIN	013	8513	8936	9650	1.2	27	3359	3582	3928	1.5	2.43	2225	2368	1.5
03237	GILMANTON	001	2038	2225	2478	2.1	76	791	887	1009	2.7	2.50	618	691	2.7
03240	GRAFTON	009	1066	1156	1294	1.9	67	425	472	540	2.5	2.45	293	323	2.3
03241	HEBRON	009	657	712	797	1.9	66	282	312	356	2.4	2.28	204	226	2.4
03242	HENNIKER	013	4296	4618	5018	1.7	58	1541	1691	1878	2.2	2.48	994	1089	2.2
03243	HILL	013	1008	1109	1225	2.3	82	388	434	487	2.7	2.56	276	308	2.6
03244	HILLSBORO	011	6984	7157	7488	0.6	8	2684	2793	2960	0.9	2.50	1862	1925	0.8
03246	LACONIA	001	16258	17614	19638	1.9	66	6654	7388	8439	2.5	2.27	4132	4570	2.4
03249	GILFORD	001	7205	7814	8674	1.9	67	2937	3239	3659	2.3	2.41	2129	2340	2.3
03251	LINCOLN	009	1271	1368	1526	1.8	60	583	638	725	2.1	2.14	325	355	2.1
03253	MEREDITH	001	5914	6804	7779	3.4	97	2441	2866	3343	3.9	2.33	1690	1978	3.8
03254	MOULTONBOROUGH	003	4735	5218	5842	2.3	84	1986	2236	2551	2.8	2.32	1445	1621	2.7
03255	NEWBURY	013	2305	2445	2648	1.4	41	933	1010	1113	1.9	2.42	679	734	1.9
03256	NEW HAMPTON	001	2162	2335	2587	1.8	63	810	889	1003	2.2	2.62	598	654	2.1
03257	NEW LONDON	013	4221	4454	4778	1.3	33	1623	1759	1941	1.9	2.13	1089	1178	1.9
03258	CHICHESTER	013	2308	2569	2854	2.6	89	843	955	1078	3.0	2.68	654	739	2.9
03259	NORTH SANDWICH	003	282	290	313	0.7	11	123	129	141	1.1	2.25	85	89	1.1
03261	NORTHWOOD	015	3770	3934	4206	1.0	21	1399	1476	1595	1.3	2.66	1042	1094	1.2
03262	NORTH WOODSTOCK	009	892	892	973	0.0	3	389	395	441	0.4	2.11	223	225	0.2
03263	PITTSFIELD	013	4020	4277	4642	1.5	44	1530	1655	1824	1.9	2.58	1082	1168	1.8
03264	PLYMOUTH	009	7803	8501	9419	2.0	74	2436	2756	3181	3.0	2.47	1474	1662	2.9
03266	RUMNEY	009	2289	2443	2710	1.5	46	874	948	1073	1.9	2.55	610	662	1.9
03268	SALISBURY	013	1075	1127	1214	1.1	25	406	434	475	1.6	2.60	305	326	1.6
03269	SANBORNTON	001	2604	2865	3204	2.3	82	982	1107	1265	2.9	2.59	760	854	2.8
03275	SUNCOOK	013	11742	12298	13238	1.1	24	4561	4858	5312	1.5	2.52	3127	3322	1.4
03276	TILTON	013	7784	8220	8918	1.3	36	2971	3197	3535	1.7	2.48	2021	2171	1.7
03278	WARNER	013	3501	3719	4026	1.4	42	1336	1445	1591	1.9	2.48	947	1020	1.8
03279	WARREN	009	839	914	1025	2.0	74	336	374	428	2.6	2.44	216	239	2.4
03280	WASHINGTON	019	882	993	1094	2.8	94	365	420	472	3.4	2.36	274	313	3.2
03281	WEARE	011	7947	8616	9302	1.9	67	2677	2919	3172	2.1	2.95	2156	2342	2.0
03282	WENTWORTH	009	700	749	833	1.6	50	278	303	343	2.1	2.47	196	213	2.0
03284	SPRINGFIELD	019	810	871	938	1.7	58	330	362	398	2.2	2.41	245	268	2.1
03287	WILMOT	013	1154	1242	1355	1.7	59	456	499	553	2.1	2.49	327	357	2.1
03290	NOTTINGHAM	015	3621	3945	4313	2.0	74	1296	1430	1581	2.3	2.76	1020	1121	2.3
03301	CONCORD	013	31760	34151	37496	1.7	58	12717	14027	15792	2.3	2.21	7301	7994	2.2
03303	CONCORD	013	14204	15109	16400	1.5	43	5423	5871	6485	1.9	2.47	3720	4024	1.9
03304	BOW	013	6917	7475	8175	1.8	64	2236	2431	2684	2.0	3.07	1984	2155	2.0
03307	LOUDON	013	4449	4844	5319	2.0	71	1609	1786	1994	2.5	2.71	1255	1391	2.5
03431	KEENE	005	24383	25646	27430	1.2	30	9749	10526	11542	1.8	2.22	5635	6062	1.7
03440	ANTRIM	011	2498	2575	2704	0.7	13	953	994	1055	1.0	2.58	640	663	0.8
	NEW HAMPSHIRE					1.5					1.9	2.49			1.8
	UNITED STATES					1.2					1.3	2.58			1.1

ZIP CODE #	POST OFFICE NAME	RACE (%) White 2000	White 2004	Black 2000	Black 2004	Asian/Pacific 2000	Asian/Pacific 2004	% Hispanic Origin 2000	% Hispanic Origin 2004	2004 AGE DISTRIBUTION (%) 0-4	5-9	10-14	15-19	20-24	25-44	45-64	65-84	85+	18+	MEDIAN AGE 2004	% 2004 Males	% 2004 Females
03031	AMHERST	97.0	96.5	0.4	0.5	1.4	1.8	1.0	1.2	6.0	7.4	9.2	8.4	4.6	22.5	33.0	8.1	0.7	71.9	40.8	50.2	49.8
03032	AUBURN	98.3	98.0	0.2	0.3	0.4	0.6	0.9	1.1	6.8	7.5	8.3	6.9	5.2	28.2	30.4	6.1	0.6	73.0	38.9	51.1	49.0
03033	BROOKLINE	97.9	97.6	0.1	0.2	0.7	0.9	0.9	1.1	8.8	9.8	9.9	7.1	4.1	28.9	25.8	5.1	0.5	66.9	36.8	50.2	49.8
03034	CANDIA	98.1	97.9	0.4	0.4	0.6	0.8	0.9	1.0	6.7	7.4	7.8	6.0	4.6	29.3	30.5	7.2	0.6	74.3	39.1	50.3	49.7
03036	CHESTER	97.9	97.7	0.3	0.3	0.3	0.4	0.8	1.0	8.1	8.8	8.9	6.7	5.1	27.8	27.4	6.6	0.6	70.1	37.0	49.0	51.0
03037	DEERFIELD	98.5	98.5	0.2	0.2	0.1	0.2	0.3	0.4	7.1	7.8	8.3	7.1	4.7	28.5	29.0	6.7	0.8	72.3	38.1	48.5	51.5
03038	DERRY	96.1	95.5	0.9	1.0	1.1	1.4	1.9	2.2	7.2	7.2	8.6	7.9	7.3	31.1	24.1	5.8	0.8	72.0	34.1	49.5	50.5
03042	EPPING	97.1	96.8	0.3	0.3	0.4	0.6	0.8	0.9	6.9	7.3	7.7	6.4	5.8	31.1	25.3	8.7	0.9	74.2	37.3	49.2	50.8
03043	FRANCESTOWN	97.3	97.1	0.1	0.1	0.3	0.4	0.5	0.6	5.5	6.9	8.7	6.9	3.4	24.5	31.3	11.3	1.6	74.4	41.5	51.5	48.5
03044	FREMONT	98.1	97.9	0.1	0.1	0.3	0.4	0.8	0.9	8.6	8.9	8.1	5.7	4.1	32.4	24.5	6.8	0.8	70.5	36.9	49.0	51.0
03045	GOFFSTOWN	98.4	98.2	0.3	0.3	0.3	0.4	0.7	0.8	5.8	6.3	7.2	7.3	7.2	27.6	25.8	10.8	1.9	76.2	39.0	47.7	52.3
03046	DUNBARTON	98.4	98.3	0.1	0.1	0.5	0.6	0.3	0.4	7.5	8.6	8.4	5.5	3.4	29.1	29.9	7.3	0.3	71.9	39.4	50.2	49.8
03047	GREENFIELD	97.3	97.1	0.7	0.7	0.2	0.3	0.7	0.9	5.5	6.5	8.1	9.9	6.1	30.2	26.7	6.1	0.9	73.3	36.3	50.5	49.5
03048	GREENVILLE	97.9	97.8	0.2	0.3	0.6	0.7	0.8	0.8	6.5	6.9	7.6	6.8	5.6	28.4	28.0	9.2	1.1	74.7	38.9	50.8	49.2
03049	HOLLIS	96.6	96.0	0.4	0.5	1.7	2.1	0.9	1.1	6.4	8.3	8.8	7.0	3.2	24.4	32.9	8.0	1.0	71.8	41.3	50.0	50.0
03051	HUDSON	96.4	95.8	0.8	1.0	1.2	1.5	1.6	1.8	7.3	7.6	8.0	6.5	5.2	31.6	25.2	7.7	0.9	73.0	36.9	49.5	50.5
03052	LITCHFIELD	97.7	97.4	0.5	0.6	0.6	0.7	0.8	1.0	9.1	9.6	9.6	6.8	4.4	33.2	23.3	3.8	0.3	67.4	34.7	50.1	49.9
03053	LONDONDERRY	96.9	96.5	0.6	0.6	1.2	1.5	1.5	1.7	7.4	8.4	9.6	8.0	5.2	28.4	27.0	5.7	0.4	69.2	36.1	49.2	50.8
03054	MERRIMACK	96.6	96.0	0.7	0.8	1.6	2.0	1.1	1.3	6.8	7.3	8.3	7.2	5.4	29.7	27.7	7.1	0.6	73.1	37.4	49.7	50.3
03055	MILFORD	96.8	96.3	0.9	1.0	0.9	1.2	1.2	1.4	7.2	7.2	7.8	7.1	6.4	30.4	24.3	8.2	1.5	73.1	36.1	49.3	50.8
03057	MONT VERNON	98.6	98.4	0.2	0.2	0.3	0.4	0.6	0.7	5.7	8.3	9.0	7.5	2.7	28.2	29.2	8.5	1.0	71.7	40.1	51.3	48.7
03060	NASHUA	86.1	84.4	2.7	2.8	2.8	3.4	11.0	12.3	6.8	6.3	7.4	6.9	7.6	31.7	20.4	10.7	2.2	75.5	34.8	48.9	51.1
03062	NASHUA	90.1	88.3	1.6	1.7	6.1	7.6	2.4	2.8	6.2	6.5	7.3	6.4	5.6	28.6	27.3	10.4	1.7	75.9	39.0	49.5	50.5
03063	NASHUA	90.6	89.1	1.8	2.0	4.5	5.6	3.5	3.9	6.1	5.9	6.2	5.8	7.4	32.3	25.5	9.9	1.1	78.8	36.7	49.8	50.2
03064	NASHUA	92.7	91.9	1.8	1.8	1.8	2.3	6.5	7.0	6.7	6.5	7.3	7.0	6.3	30.0	24.6	10.5	1.2	75.3	37.0	49.3	50.7
03070	NEW BOSTON	98.0	97.8	0.4	0.4	0.4	0.5	0.6	0.8	7.3	8.2	8.8	6.6	4.4	29.3	29.3	5.7	0.5	71.2	37.9	50.2	49.8
03071	NEW IPSWICH	98.5	98.3	0.2	0.2	0.4	0.5	0.8	0.9	8.8	9.1	9.1	8.1	6.0	27.6	23.4	7.2	0.7	67.9	32.9	51.0	49.0
03076	PELHAM	97.3	96.9	0.4	0.5	1.0	1.4	1.0	1.1	7.4	7.9	8.0	6.5	4.9	30.5	26.1	8.0	0.8	72.7	37.5	49.4	50.6
03077	RAYMOND	97.8	97.6	0.6	0.6	0.2	0.3	0.8	0.9	7.1	7.1	7.5	7.7	6.8	31.1	25.2	6.8	0.7	73.5	35.5	49.7	50.3
03079	SALEM	95.0	94.3	0.6	0.6	2.3	2.9	2.0	2.2	6.3	6.6	7.3	6.3	5.2	28.6	27.5	11.0	1.4	75.8	39.7	49.8	50.2
03082	LYNDEBOROUGH	98.2	97.9	0.2	0.2	0.3	0.4	1.7	2.0	6.0	6.9	7.9	6.0	5.2	28.2	32.3	6.6	1.0	74.8	39.4	50.8	49.3
03084	TEMPLE	97.8	97.5	0.4	0.4	0.5	0.6	0.6	0.8	5.6	6.9	9.0	7.5	4.7	26.3	30.6	8.3	1.1	73.8	39.4	51.6	48.4
03086	WILTON	97.6	97.3	0.4	0.4	0.5	0.7	0.8	0.9	6.4	6.9	8.0	6.5	5.4	28.0	28.1	9.4	1.3	74.6	38.9	48.8	51.2
03087	WINDHAM	96.9	96.3	0.3	0.4	1.7	2.1	1.0	1.2	6.7	8.2	8.9	6.7	3.9	27.2	31.0	6.5	0.9	71.7	39.5	50.5	49.5
03101	MANCHESTER	78.2	76.6	5.3	5.5	3.4	4.1	16.0	17.6	6.5	5.4	5.4	6.0	10.1	33.9	23.0	8.2	1.5	80.0	33.8	54.2	45.8
03102	MANCHESTER	92.8	91.9	1.9	2.0	2.1	2.7	3.1	3.6	6.4	5.7	5.9	7.0	10.5	30.6	20.7	11.1	2.1	78.6	34.1	48.7	51.3
03103	MANCHESTER	90.5	89.1	2.4	2.5	2.6	3.3	6.9	8.0	7.3	6.6	7.1	7.3	7.9	31.0	21.6	9.9	1.4	74.8	34.3	49.6	50.4
03104	MANCHESTER	92.7	91.6	2.0	2.2	2.2	2.9	3.1	3.6	5.9	5.8	6.1	6.8	7.0	30.8	23.9	11.2	2.6	78.3	37.4	48.0	52.0
03106	HOOKSETT	96.3	95.7	0.7	0.8	1.8	2.3	1.5	1.7	6.2	6.6	7.0	8.2	9.1	27.9	25.0	9.1	1.0	76.7	36.4	49.8	50.2
03109	MANCHESTER	96.3	95.7	0.7	0.8	1.4	1.9	1.3	1.5	6.9	7.0	7.4	6.7	4.9	31.1	24.3	10.0	1.8	74.4	37.4	49.0	51.0
03110	BEDFORD	97.4	96.9	0.3	0.4	1.3	1.7	0.9	1.0	6.9	8.2	8.8	6.1	3.6	24.7	29.5	10.2	2.0	72.0	40.7	49.3	50.7
03216	ANDOVER	98.2	98.2	0.4	0.4	0.1	0.1	0.2	0.2	5.9	6.5	6.8	5.6	5.0	25.1	31.7	12.1	1.2	77.2	41.9	50.1	49.9
03217	ASHLAND	97.5	97.3	0.4	0.4	0.6	0.8	0.7	0.8	6.4	6.4	6.3	6.7	6.3	27.4	27.1	12.3	1.2	76.8	38.7	47.8	52.2
03218	BARNSTEAD	98.6	98.6	0.4	0.4	0.1	0.1	0.4	0.5	5.6	6.2	7.1	6.9	5.3	24.8	32.8	10.2	1.1	76.8	41.5	50.3	49.7
03220	BELMONT	97.5	97.3	0.2	0.2	0.5	0.7	1.0	1.1	5.4	5.9	7.1	6.9	5.8	28.2	29.0	10.8	1.0	77.4	40.0	49.4	50.6
03221	BRADFORD	97.3	97.2	0.3	0.3	0.1	0.2	1.1	1.2	4.9	5.8	7.1	7.1	5.6	25.2	31.5	12.0	0.9	77.7	41.3	49.8	50.2
03222	BRISTOL	96.9	96.5	0.2	0.2	1.0	1.3	0.7	0.9	5.4	5.6	6.6	6.6	5.3	26.0	29.7	13.3	1.6	78.5	41.8	49.5	50.5
03223	CAMPTON	97.8	97.5	0.1	0.2	0.6	0.8	0.6	0.6	4.9	5.4	7.2	7.3	5.6	27.6	29.4	11.8	0.9	78.0	40.2	49.7	50.3
03224	CANTERBURY	98.6	98.4	0.3	0.3	0.3	0.5	0.5	0.6	5.0	6.4	7.1	6.3	4.1	22.1	37.9	10.0	1.4	77.2	44.5	48.1	51.9
03225	CENTER BARNSTEAD	97.4	97.1	0.7	0.8	0.8	1.0	0.7	0.8	6.2	7.0	7.8	6.4	5.2	27.3	29.5	10.0	0.7	75.0	39.5	51.1	48.9
03226	CENTER HARBOR	98.8	98.5	0.0	0.0	0.8	0.9	1.0	1.1	4.2	4.7	5.9	5.4	4.7	21.7	35.9	16.0	1.5	81.3	47.0	50.2	49.8
03227	CENTER SANDWICH	97.8	97.8	0.6	0.7	0.3	0.4	0.5	0.6	3.7	4.7	6.1	6.1	4.2	15.9	36.3	19.9	3.0	81.6	49.6	47.5	52.5
03229	CONTOOCOOK	98.5	98.4	0.1	0.1	0.3	0.4	0.5	0.6	5.0	6.4	8.5	6.8	3.8	22.2	33.8	12.1	1.5	75.5	43.6	48.6	51.5
03230	DANBURY	99.5	99.6	0.2	0.2	0.0	0.0	0.5	0.5	4.4	5.1	7.0	6.1	5.4	25.6	32.7	12.2	1.5	79.8	43.1	50.3	49.7
03234	EPSOM	98.6	98.5	0.1	0.1	0.3	0.4	0.5	0.5	5.9	6.5	7.0	6.1	4.0	28.8	27.6	11.6	2.5	76.7	40.8	47.9	52.1
03235	FRANKLIN	97.1	96.9	0.4	0.4	0.5	0.7	1.2	1.3	7.1	5.8	6.6	7.4	7.3	26.0	24.8	12.5	2.5	75.8	38.2	48.5	51.5
03237	GILMANTON	98.6	98.6	0.1	0.1	0.2	0.2	0.3	0.3	5.0	5.8	6.9	6.0	5.0	27.0	32.3	10.8	1.1	78.5	42.2	50.7	49.3
03240	GRAFTON	98.4	98.2	0.2	0.2	0.3	0.4	0.5	0.5	6.2	6.6	6.2	7.4	4.8	28.2	31.1	9.0	0.5	76.5	39.8	52.3	47.8
03241	HEBRON	97.0	96.6	0.3	0.3	0.6	0.8	0.2	0.1	5.1	5.2	6.9	6.7	4.6	22.6	31.2	15.5	2.3	78.2	44.3	51.1	48.9
03242	HENNIKER	96.6	96.3	0.5	0.5	1.1	1.3	0.8	1.0	5.3	5.8	7.0	9.9	11.4	28.7	24.2	6.8	1.0	77.4	32.7	51.0	49.0
03243	HILL	99.0	98.9	0.1	0.1	0.5	0.6	0.2	0.3	4.5	7.2	7.9	7.6	4.8	28.4	29.5	8.7	1.4	75.1	40.5	51.2	48.8
03244	HILLSBORO	97.7	97.4	0.2	0.3	0.7	0.9	0.7	0.8	5.9	6.6	7.6	7.2	5.9	27.1	27.8	10.5	1.3	75.2	39.0	49.7	50.3
03246	LACONIA	96.8	96.5	0.6	0.6	0.8	0.9	1.0	1.1	5.4	5.3	6.4	6.5	7.2	26.7	25.8	13.9	2.8	78.9	39.9	48.8	51.2
03249	GILFORD	98.3	98.1	0.2	0.2	0.5	0.6	0.6	0.7	5.1	5.9	6.8	6.1	4.2	22.2	32.1	16.0	1.6	78.2	44.8	47.9	52.1
03251	LINCOLN	97.3	96.9	0.0	0.0	1.1	1.4	0.8	0.9	4.6	4.7	5.1	5.6	5.6	23.8	32.9	15.6	2.0	82.2	45.3	50.4	49.6
03253	MEREDITH	97.9	97.7	0.2	0.2	0.6	0.8	0.5	0.6	4.8	5.3	6.6	6.3	4.9	23.5	31.6	14.5	2.6	79.1	44.2	49.6	50.4
03254	MOULTONBOROUGH	98.5	98.4	0.1	0.1	0.6	0.7	0.6	0.7	3.6	4.8	6.5	6.3	3.5	20.3	35.3	18.3	1.4	80.7	48.1	49.7	50.3
03255	NEWBURY	98.1	97.9	0.3	0.3	0.2	0.3	1.1	1.3	4.1	4.9	7.1	6.6	3.8	24.7	32.8	14.5	1.4	79.2	44.4	50.1	49.9
03256	NEW HAMPTON	97.5	97.4	0.3	0.3	0.3	0.4	0.7	0.7	5.7	6.5	8.1	5.8	5.1	26.9	29.3	11.6	1.0	75.8	40.4	49.6	50.4
03257	NEW LONDON	98.3	98.1	0.2	0.2	0.8	1.0	0.6	0.8	2.9	3.4	4.0	9.7	12.9	13.1	26.0	23.2	4.9	87.2	48.6	44.2	55.8
03258	CHICHESTER	98.1	98.1	0.2	0.2	0.2	0.2	0.7	0.7	6.2	6.8	7.8	6.2	4.2	29.4	29.2	9.3	0.9	75.4	39.7	50.6	49.4
03259	NORTH SANDWICH	97.9	97.6	0.7	0.7	0.4	0.3	0.4	0.3	3.8	4.5	6.2	5.9	4.5	15.9	36.9	19.7	2.8	81.4	49.7	47.2	52.8
03261	NORTHWOOD	97.6	97.3	0.3	0.3	0.8	1.0	0.5	0.6	6.1	6.6	7.5	7.0	6.0	28.9	28.6	8.8	0.6	75.4	38.5	50.0	50.0
03262	NORTH WOODSTOCK	97.4	97.2	0.1	0.1	0.2	0.2	0.6	0.6	5.5	5.5	6.5	6.6	6.2	26.7	26.1	15.1	1.8	78.6	40.9	48.3	51.7
03263	PITTSFIELD	97.4	97.2	0.4	0.4	0.1	0.1	1.1	1.3	7.0	6.8	7.7	7.8	6.8	29.0	24.4	9.5	1.0	73.5	35.7	48.3	51.7
03264	PLYMOUTH	96.9	96.5	0.4	0.5	0.7	0.9	1.2	1.4	4.1	4.2	5.1	16.7	21.7	18.1	20.5	8.7	1.1	83.1	24.6	50.0	50.1
03266	RUMNEY	97.7	97.4	0.4	0.4	0.5	0.6	0.4	0.5	4.6	6.4	7.9	6.6	4.5	23.5	30.5	14.1	1.9	76.1	42.8	50.9	49.1
03268	SALISBURY	97.9	97.9	0.7	0.6	0.4	0.4	0.7	0.6	5.9	6.3	6.9	5.4	5.6	25.9	32.4	10.6	1.1	77.6	41.6	51.4	48.6
03269	SANBORNTON	98.2	97.9	0.2	0.2	0.5	0.6	0.4	0.5	5.1	6.0	7.4	6.5	5.3	25.7	32.6	10.5	0.8	77.5	41.9	49.4	50.6
03275	SUNCOOK	97.8	97.6	0.4	0.5	0.4	0.5	0.7	0.9	6.5	6.7	7.6	7.2	6.6	29.4	25.7	9.2	1.2	74.7	37.4	49.3	50.7
03276	TILTON	97.5	97.3	0.1	0.1	0.5	0.7	0.9	1.1	5.5	5.8	7.5	7.4	7.2	27.4	27.0	10.7	1.5	76.6	38.8	49.6	50.4
03278	WARNER	98.2	98.1	0.1	0.1	0.3	0.4	0.8	0.9	5.0	5.4	6.8	7.5	6.2	24.4	31.0	11.7	2.0	78.5	42.0	49.8	50.2
03279	WARREN	96.1	95.8	0.1	0.1	0.8	1.1	0.1	0.1	5.0	5.5	6.8	6.9	5.6	28.6	27.4	12.5	1.9	78.5	40.0	50.2	49.8
03280	WASHINGTON	98.2	98.3	0.0	0.0	0.0	0.0	1.5	1.5	4.8	5.5	6.7	5.1	3.3	22.0	32.8	18.6	1.1	79.8	46.8	51.1	48.9
03281	WEARE	98.3	98.0	0.2	0.2	0.4	0.6	0.7	0.8	7.8	8.3	9.0	7.5	5.6	31.8	25.2	4.6	0.4	70.2	35.3	50.2	49.8
03282	WENTWORTH	97.6	97.3	0.4	0.4	0.3	0.4	0.4	0.4	2.9	5.5	9.9	8.5	4.3	27.4	27.5	12.7	1.3	75.2	40.6	50.7	49.3
03284	SPRINGFIELD	98.9	98.6	0.0	0.0	0.3	0.3	0.7	0.9	5.4	6.0	7.0	4.6	4.4	28.5	31.6	10.9	1.7	77.8	41.5	49.3	50.8
03287	WILMOT	98.3	98.1	0.1	0.1	0.7	0.9	0.3	0.2	5.5	6.4	8.0	6.5	4.4	22.9	32.4	12.7	1.3	76.1	43.0	48.8	51.2
03290	NOTTINGHAM	98.4	98.1	0.2	0.2	0.6	0.8	0.7	0.8	6.4	7.1	8.3	6.7	3.9	28.8	31.4	6.8	0.6	73.7	40.1	50.5	49.5
03301	CONCORD	95.3	94.7	1.1	1.2	1.6	2.0	1.5	1.6	5.5	5.4	6.2	6.6	7.2	29.2	25.2	11.3	3.5	78.8	39.0	49.6	50.4
03303	CONCORD	97.0	96.6	0.6	0.6	0.9	1.2	1.1	1.3	6.4	6.4	7.2	6.8	7.0	30.6	24.3	9.3	1.9	75.8	36.5	49.3	50.7
03304	BOW	97.8	97.4	0.1	0.2	1.0	1.3	0.5	0.5	6.2	8.1	10.2	8.4	3.7	23.6	31.0	8.2	0.7	69.8	40.3	50.1	50.0
03307	LOUDON	98.2	98.0	0.3	0.3	0.5	0.6	0.6	0.7	7.0	7.6	8.0	6.2	5.0	28.4	29.1	8.2	0.6	73.4	38.7	49.7	50.3
03431	KEENE	97.7	97.5	0.4	0.4	0.7	0.9	0.8	0.9	4.2	4.5	5.7	10.2	11.6	24.3	24.3	12.8	2.5	81.7	36.8	47.3	52.7
03440	ANTRIM	98.0	97.9	0.2	0.3	0.4	0.5	0.8	0.9	5.6	6.0	10.5	8.0	5.7	24.7	28.2	10.3	1.1	72.2	38.7	49.6	50.4
	NEW HAMPSHIRE	96.0	95.6	0.7	0.8	1.3	1.7	1.7	1.9	6.1	6.4	7.2	7.2	6.6	27.8	26.5	10.6	1.6	76.2	38.4	49.2	50.8
	UNITED STATES	75.1	73.6	12.3	12.5	3.8	4.2	12.5	14.1	6.9	6.7	7.2	7.0	7.3	28.6	23.8	10.8	1.7	75.1	36.0	49.1	50.9

ZIP CODE #	POST OFFICE NAME	2004 Per Capita Income	2004 HH Income Base	2004 HOUSEHOLD INCOME DISTRIBUTION (%) Less than $25,000	$25,000 to $49,999	$50,000 to $99,999	$100,000 to $149,999	$150,000 or More	MEDIAN HOUSEHOLD INCOME 2004	2009	2004 National Centile	2004 State Centile	2004 Home Value Base	2004 HOME VALUE DISTRIBUTION (%) Less than $50,000	$50,000 to $89,999	$90,000 to $174,999	$175,000 to $399,999	$400,000 or More	2004 Median Home Value
03031	AMHERST	44706	3937	5.5	11.5	28.5	27.1	27.4	106265	133411	99	99	3626	1.0	1.0	7.1	58.3	32.6	328733
03032	AUBURN	35574	1732	7.0	14.1	47.1	19.1	12.8	78205	93599	94	90	1593	0.0	0.4	26.5	61.6	11.5	223949
03033	BROOKLINE	36290	1502	6.8	12.3	39.8	27.7	13.5	87485	107135	97	96	1377	0.8	1.1	10.3	77.9	10.0	270426
03034	CANDIA	30278	1535	8.4	21.4	43.1	19.4	7.8	71344	85666	92	84	1410	2.6	1.2	24.5	66.0	5.7	215094
03036	CHESTER	28363	1454	10.3	15.5	40.0	26.3	8.0	78903	95895	95	92	1343	1.1	0.0	11.1	74.0	13.8	261578
03037	DEERFIELD	29963	1370	8.2	18.5	46.4	17.7	9.3	70500	84041	91	83	1211	0.7	1.5	22.1	67.5	8.3	225498
03038	DERRY	26447	13153	13.1	25.0	41.4	15.1	5.5	62672	75436	87	71	8375	3.8	4.0	29.5	61.0	1.8	195211
03042	EPPING	24795	2295	16.3	22.1	44.9	13.1	3.7	58913	71288	83	65	1753	8.6	5.9	31.7	49.5	4.3	181898
03043	FRANCESTOWN	36046	607	7.4	17.3	39.9	22.9	12.5	76260	97037	94	88	532	0.0	0.0	29.1	51.9	19.0	227941
03044	FREMONT	28656	1297	6.6	18.3	49.9	17.7	7.6	71376	84187	92	84	1138	0.4	2.5	18.4	74.6	4.2	229545
03045	GOFFSTOWN	28986	4654	11.8	21.0	41.5	18.8	6.9	67022	82309	90	77	3841	0.2	3.1	31.5	61.6	3.6	202090
03046	DUNBARTON	32800	940	8.9	16.1	44.3	20.6	10.1	75370	89274	93	87	855	0.9	1.6	17.4	69.8	10.2	248611
03047	GREENFIELD	25268	612	12.3	28.9	40.7	13.2	4.9	57602	70674	82	63	518	0.8	1.2	36.3	55.0	6.8	197101
03048	GREENVILLE	27014	1365	16.2	29.9	36.6	12.0	5.3	53701	66862	78	52	1040	18.4	10.2	31.3	36.9	3.3	144595
03049	HOLLIS	58653	2704	8.9	12.7	22.3	21.7	34.4	111916	144202	99	100	2497	0.8	2.2	6.9	37.3	52.8	414300
03051	HUDSON	30832	8677	8.9	18.4	42.6	20.5	9.6	73401	88515	93	86	6929	1.4	2.2	16.9	75.3	4.2	234200
03052	LITCHFIELD	29695	2584	6.0	13.0	44.2	27.8	9.0	82931	101404	96	94	2316	2.3	2.9	7.9	83.7	3.3	241500
03053	LONDONDERRY	32342	8262	7.8	14.2	43.1	22.2	12.8	80183	97363	95	93	7279	1.7	3.7	20.3	67.3	7.0	228294
03054	MERRIMACK	33061	9651	6.5	14.7	43.3	23.9	11.7	79563	97175	95	92	8094	1.9	1.5	23.1	67.0	6.5	221928
03055	MILFORD	29755	5583	12.7	24.8	40.6	15.3	6.5	61109	75170	85	68	3621	4.9	4.3	25.4	61.6	3.8	206371
03057	MONT VERNON	39192	756	6.5	14.0	36.0	25.8	17.7	87256	112743	97	95	694	3.8	2.7	11.1	63.3	19.2	279918
03060	NASHUA	25734	12715	26.3	25.8	32.4	11.0	4.5	47721	59762	68	28	4998	0.5	2.1	36.6	59.9	0.9	189527
03062	NASHUA	35995	10411	9.2	16.6	39.9	22.2	12.1	76859	94859	94	89	7583	5.9	5.3	16.3	63.4	9.1	219424
03063	NASHUA	34560	6800	11.9	20.9	40.2	18.4	8.7	67576	83630	90	79	4387	2.0	3.0	28.7	61.9	4.4	206088
03064	NASHUA	29969	5948	18.6	23.1	33.8	16.7	7.8	59928	76326	84	67	3650	0.5	0.6	18.0	72.8	8.2	222585
03070	NEW BOSTON	32174	1677	7.5	18.0	44.4	19.4	10.7	75991	91367	94	88	1494	0.9	1.9	18.1	64.7	14.3	233500
03071	NEW IPSWICH	25071	1492	12.1	24.3	44.9	11.8	6.9	62430	75828	87	70	1286	2.0	4.7	34.1	57.4	1.7	190000
03076	PELHAM	31395	3992	7.8	15.5	42.3	24.5	9.9	78410	96162	95	91	3520	0.2	0.5	7.9	80.4	10.9	275360
03077	RAYMOND	22037	3658	14.5	28.7	44.6	10.4	1.8	55323	66007	80	57	2856	6.8	10.5	42.5	39.6	0.6	154167
03079	SALEM	32481	10831	13.5	20.2	36.8	18.6	11.0	68476	83963	91	79	8471	3.8	4.7	12.3	67.4	11.8	241965
03082	LYNDEBOROUGH	35396	551	8.9	20.3	42.5	20.2	8.2	70145	84937	91	82	483	0.2	3.7	24.8	60.3	11.0	221218
03084	TEMPLE	27542	442	11.1	22.4	40.1	19.0	7.5	68072	82550	90	79	380	0.0	1.6	23.4	61.8	13.2	226220
03086	WILTON	33343	1513	14.5	22.1	38.0	12.4	13.0	64568	80113	88	74	1151	0.5	2.5	26.2	59.7	11.1	216353
03087	WINDHAM	49052	4062	5.4	9.2	27.8	28.1	29.5	110671	137393	99	99	3804	0.3	0.0	4.9	58.0	36.7	346730
03101	MANCHESTER	22574	1614	49.0	29.4	16.5	2.4	2.7	25640	33053	5	0	140	0.0	22.1	46.4	30.7	0.7	143478
03102	MANCHESTER	24979	13367	24.3	30.9	34.2	7.8	2.9	45706	56215	63	25	5444	1.5	2.1	52.5	43.2	0.7	165856
03103	MANCHESTER	21260	15102	26.2	29.5	34.7	7.2	2.4	44240	54433	59	16	7471	0.8	2.4	51.7	44.2	1.0	169367
03104	MANCHESTER	32481	13909	19.0	26.4	34.9	12.7	7.0	54340	68115	79	52	6866	0.3	0.8	27.8	65.9	5.2	211232
03106	HOOKSETT	30869	4833	11.2	20.0	41.1	19.3	8.4	70593	84900	91	83	3762	3.6	1.6	26.1	65.2	3.5	207506
03109	MANCHESTER	26703	3796	14.2	20.2	47.2	15.9	2.5	64434	77693	88	74	3001	1.3	3.3	40.1	53.6	1.7	182643
03110	BEDFORD	47595	7162	5.8	9.6	33.0	25.4	26.1	101876	127161	98	98	6223	0.1	0.5	4.5	59.9	35.0	342783
03216	ANDOVER	26446	899	15.8	27.3	41.4	11.4	4.2	54840	65831	79	54	746	1.2	6.6	45.4	40.8	6.0	167941
03217	ASHLAND	24669	1121	28.2	31.9	29.1	7.5	3.4	40742	49325	49	9	695	8.1	10.4	45.3	29.9	6.3	144124
03218	BARNSTEAD	26702	567	12.2	29.5	39.0	13.8	5.6	56421	67430	81	58	496	1.8	6.1	42.7	45.8	3.6	173881
03220	BELMONT	24357	2965	19.2	27.4	40.7	8.8	3.9	52598	61004	76	46	2391	10.3	17.6	43.5	26.3	2.4	136487
03221	BRADFORD	30146	635	15.9	28.2	40.0	11.2	4.7	56043	67509	81	58	530	1.9	5.9	34.0	50.2	8.1	190714
03222	BRISTOL	25894	2275	22.0	32.2	31.3	9.3	5.2	46420	56145	65	26	1704	4.6	8.2	48.6	33.8	4.8	149606
03223	CAMPTON	23796	2353	22.3	34.4	32.0	7.4	3.9	44229	53165	59	16	1671	9.2	8.4	42.8	35.1	4.4	154896
03224	CANTERBURY	34381	821	8.3	20.1	41.4	20.5	9.7	69478	87661	91	80	741	0.3	1.8	24.7	61.3	12.0	222790
03225	CENTER BARNSTEAD	24083	1220	13.3	29.8	43.7	8.9	4.3	54488	63334	79	53	1047	0.9	5.9	57.8	34.0	1.4	151610
03226	CENTER HARBOR	35019	328	17.1	25.3	36.0	11.6	10.1	61072	75735	85	67	276	0.4	4.7	23.2	58.0	13.8	237255
03227	CENTER SANDWICH	28373	465	23.7	22.2	40.0	8.0	6.2	53432	63160	78	48	382	2.4	2.6	22.5	54.2	18.3	244167
03229	CONTOOCOOK	38183	2264	11.8	18.7	38.2	17.6	13.7	70058	88644	91	82	1933	0.1	4.0	25.3	57.1	13.6	232154
03230	DANBURY	22331	469	21.8	35.6	32.4	8.1	2.1	44317	52957	59	17	402	8.5	9.2	58.5	21.1	2.7	135127
03234	EPSOM	26969	1598	15.4	23.3	42.4	13.9	4.9	59737	72815	84	66	1337	11.0	7.3	34.6	43.7	3.4	170282
03235	FRANKLIN	20382	3582	31.0	29.2	31.8	6.2	1.9	39881	48642	46	8	2089	4.8	10.4	66.5	17.5	0.8	129827
03237	GILMANTON	28764	887	11.7	25.4	46.0	10.5	6.4	58801	69617	83	64	785	0.6	4.0	40.4	47.9	7.1	185286
03240	GRAFTON	20693	472	22.0	35.8	33.9	6.6	1.7	44824	51428	61	19	403	6.7	16.1	49.6	25.8	1.7	130492
03241	HEBRON	29979	312	22.8	27.9	32.1	11.9	5.5	49225	61122	71	33	256	3.9	11.7	42.2	33.6	8.6	151190
03242	HENNIKER	31538	1691	21.1	20.6	36.0	14.8	7.5	59476	74647	84	65	1201	7.0	2.8	35.9	49.2	5.1	183415
03243	HILL	25489	434	16.4	26.7	42.4	11.1	3.5	54809	65916	79	54	372	3.5	11.6	55.7	24.2	5.1	140404
03244	HILLSBORO	24819	2793	20.1	25.8	39.3	10.9	4.0	53229	65224	77	48	2143	9.4	10.2	46.6	31.7	2.2	146045
03246	LACONIA	23712	7388	27.0	31.6	31.3	7.3	2.9	42816	50420	55	13	4297	0.5	5.8	58.3	30.5	4.9	150979
03249	GILFORD	41483	3239	15.8	27.1	34.0	12.3	10.9	57502	73481	82	62	2763	12.2	3.9	29.0	43.4	11.6	190415
03251	LINCOLN	21388	638	37.5	28.8	23.8	7.8	2.0	33948	39415	24	1	405	6.4	9.1	44.7	30.6	9.1	150298
03253	MEREDITH	31008	2866	18.7	31.1	30.2	10.4	9.7	50273	62699	72	39	2171	8.1	5.6	29.4	40.5	16.4	198965
03254	MOULTONBOROUGH	32748	2236	16.7	29.9	33.2	12.7	7.5	53438	68247	78	49	1894	1.0	1.8	26.0	42.4	28.8	245833
03255	NEWBURY	35919	1010	11.2	25.5	40.0	14.9	8.5	63404	77508	87	72	857	0.0	2.2	27.4	50.1	20.3	229883
03256	NEW HAMPTON	25734	889	16.5	26.6	41.7	10.6	4.6	55059	65708	80	56	759	3.2	5.7	38.3	46.4	6.5	181108
03257	NEW LONDON	54728	1759	11.2	19.9	26.6	19.9	22.4	79435	115157	95	92	1482	0.6	0.5	5.7	54.3	38.8	342361
03258	CHICHESTER	29675	955	10.2	24.0	43.8	14.6	7.5	64607	77736	88	75	839	2.9	3.5	33.9	56.0	3.8	192188
03259	NORTH SANDWICH	28258	129	24.0	21.7	40.3	7.8	6.2	53457	63311	78	49	106	2.8	1.9	22.6	54.7	17.9	246875
03261	NORTHWOOD	26103	1476	13.8	28.1	40.7	12.5	4.9	58336	69276	83	63	1245	3.5	8.7	42.3	42.0	3.6	167675
03262	NORTH WOODSTOCK	23897	395	27.1	32.9	30.6	6.1	3.3	41686	50436	52	12	263	6.5	9.1	55.1	25.5	3.8	140561
03263	PITTSFIELD	26682	1655	23.8	33.0	31.0	8.2	4.1	45447	54043	62	23	1099	6.3	8.0	51.5	30.7	3.6	145391
03264	PLYMOUTH	23090	2756	29.3	27.8	28.7	8.9	5.3	44606	53321	60	18	1703	10.6	8.0	39.2	35.6	6.5	156144
03266	RUMNEY	22598	948	25.7	30.4	32.7	7.6	3.6	45148	52933	62	21	753	2.9	9.4	49.0	32.8	5.8	149151
03268	SALISBURY	27429	434	12.2	22.4	45.6	15.7	4.2	62198	75432	86	69	396	1.8	2.8	43.9	46.5	5.1	177542
03269	SANBORNTON	28461	1107	12.9	29.5	40.2	10.8	6.6	57009	68151	82	61	958	1.6	1.8	34.0	54.9	7.7	196154
03275	SUNCOOK	24123	4858	17.3	28.8	39.6	11.8	2.6	53580	64812	78	50	3387	13.8	5.2	40.3	39.8	0.9	161766
03276	TILTON	22535	3197	18.9	31.3	40.0	8.1	1.7	49762	59068	71	36	2165	8.9	11.5	50.5	25.7	3.4	140584
03278	WARNER	28349	1445	15.6	31.2	35.6	12.2	5.3	52844	64483	77	46	1115	4.0	6.1	33.9	46.0	10.0	187788
03279	WARREN	20362	374	26.5	38.0	25.9	5.9	3.7	39223	46347	43	4	302	10.3	19.2	52.7	17.2	0.7	113194
03280	WASHINGTON	24769	420	18.8	30.7	38.6	8.6	3.3	50322	58954	73	39	387	3.9	8.3	40.8	40.1	7.0	169575
03281	WEARE	26396	2919	9.4	20.7	46.4	18.3	5.2	67161	80764	90	78	2545	4.9	3.3	27.7	61.4	2.7	193698
03282	WENTWORTH	22980	303	20.1	30.0	38.3	8.3	3.3	49837	58491	72	37	255	3.1	8.6	51.4	36.9	0.0	151736
03284	SPRINGFIELD	28111	362	13.3	34.8	36.5	9.9	5.5	52108	61634	76	45	304	6.3	12.5	31.3	45.4	4.6	175000
03287	WILMOT	30378	499	13.4	29.3	36.3	12.2	8.8	57082	69618	82	62	432	0.7	0.5	22.0	59.3	17.6	234848
03290	NOTTINGHAM	29276	1430	9.9	17.4	49.7	19.0	4.0	69798	82340	91	81	1293	0.9	2.0	26.7	62.1	8.4	211140
03301	CONCORD	27702	14027	22.9	28.9	32.4	10.5	5.3	48206	58760	69	30	7264	8.3	3.4	39.3	43.5	5.5	173436
03303	CONCORD	23818	5871	18.7	28.2	41.0	9.6	2.4	51876	61271	75	44	3917	9.1	9.9	45.2	33.9	1.9	150884
03304	BOW	35762	2431	6.9	8.2	40.3	27.4	17.2	90998	110654	97	97	2312	0.1	0.2	10.5	75.3	13.9	276082
03307	LOUDON	29118	1786	11.0	23.0	47.3	14.1	4.7	62669	75363	87	71	1586	6.2	7.9	36.1	46.9	2.9	174685
03431	KEENE	26116	10526	26.8	28.9	30.9	8.5	4.9	44513	53428	60	17	6277	6.3	3.3	48.4	37.4	4.6	162087
03440	ANTRIM	22942	994	23.6	22.6	39.8	10.8	3.1	53115	65187	77	47	732	2.2	6.2	53.8	33.6	4.2	153606
	NEW HAMPSHIRE	29464		17.9	24.8	36.4	13.6	7.4	57516	70005				4.4	5.2	30.9	50.1	9.4	196454
	UNITED STATES	25866		24.7	27.1	30.8	10.9	6.5	48124	56710				10.9	15.0	33.7	30.1	10.4	145905

ZIP CODE #	POST OFFICE NAME	FINANCIAL SERVICES: Auto Loan	FINANCIAL SERVICES: Home Loan	FINANCIAL SERVICES: Invest-ments	FINANCIAL SERVICES: Retire-ment Plans	THE HOME: Home Improvements: Home Repair	THE HOME: Home Improvements: Lawn & Garden	THE HOME: Furnishings: Comput-ers & Hard-ware	THE HOME: Furnishings: Major Appli-ances	THE HOME: Furnishings: TV, Radio, Sound Equip-ment	THE HOME: Furnishings: Furni-ture	ENTERTAINMENT: Dine out/ Carry out	ENTERTAINMENT: Sports Equip-ment	ENTERTAINMENT: Fees & Tickets	ENTERTAINMENT: Toys & Games	ENTERTAINMENT: Travel	ENTERTAINMENT: Cable TV	PERSONAL: Apparel & Services	PERSONAL: Auto Repairs	PERSONAL: Health Insur-ance	PERSONAL: Pets & Supplies
03031	AMHERST	174	217	235	222	211	211	192	188	175	194	223	218	209	233	195	170	224	181	167	208
03032	AUBURN	140	168	172	170	163	159	150	149	138	152	175	175	158	182	151	132	174	144	131	164
03033	BROOKLINE	162	183	176	191	174	168	165	163	151	172	192	191	170	192	160	140	190	159	138	178
03034	CANDIA	114	137	143	138	134	132	124	124	116	124	145	145	130	152	125	111	145	120	110	136
03036	CHESTER	114	141	150	141	139	137	126	126	117	126	147	147	134	156	129	113	147	121	112	139
03037	DEERFIELD	115	143	151	143	140	138	127	127	118	127	148	149	135	158	130	115	148	122	114	141
03038	DERRY	101	106	112	111	103	103	105	102	99	107	126	122	106	125	102	94	124	103	91	112
03042	EPPING	99	94	81	93	96	101	90	95	91	90	113	112	89	113	90	91	108	93	95	113
03043	FRANCESTOWN	124	154	164	154	151	149	137	137	127	137	160	160	146	171	141	124	160	132	123	151
03044	FREMONT	122	138	133	144	131	127	125	123	114	130	145	144	128	145	121	106	143	120	105	135
03045	GOFFSTOWN	105	130	140	130	127	126	117	116	109	116	137	136	124	145	119	106	136	112	104	128
03046	DUNBARTON	122	146	149	149	141	138	130	130	120	132	152	152	137	158	131	115	151	125	113	143
03047	GREENFIELD	97	107	107	109	103	102	102	100	95	102	120	119	102	121	99	90	118	100	88	110
03048	GREENVILLE	101	101	90	100	102	107	96	100	95	96	118	116	95	118	96	94	114	98	99	116
03049	HOLLIS	219	272	297	280	264	268	241	236	221	244	281	272	264	290	246	215	282	228	212	261
03051	HUDSON	123	132	129	135	129	130	124	124	118	126	148	146	126	150	122	113	145	122	113	140
03052	LITCHFIELD	129	149	147	154	143	139	134	133	123	138	156	156	139	159	132	116	155	129	115	146
03053	LONDONDERRY	134	157	159	161	151	148	142	140	130	145	165	164	148	169	141	124	164	137	122	154
03054	MERRIMACK	121	145	157	147	142	141	134	132	124	134	157	155	140	164	135	120	156	129	118	145
03055	MILFORD	102	115	122	117	112	112	111	109	104	110	132	129	113	135	110	100	130	108	97	119
03057	MONT VERNON	146	182	193	182	179	176	162	162	150	162	189	189	173	202	166	146	189	156	145	179
03060	NASHUA	82	82	93	84	81	87	87	84	87	86	109	99	88	109	86	85	106	86	82	93
03062	NASHUA	129	135	145	140	134	138	133	132	128	134	161	156	134	160	132	123	157	133	123	148
03063	NASHUA	113	116	128	121	112	117	118	114	113	118	143	135	118	141	114	108	141	116	104	127
03064	NASHUA	98	110	127	109	108	114	109	106	106	107	132	124	112	136	109	104	130	106	100	116
03070	NEW BOSTON	125	148	149	151	143	139	133	132	122	135	154	154	139	159	132	116	153	128	115	145
03071	NEW IPSWICH	117	115	101	113	116	120	107	113	107	108	133	134	107	135	108	106	128	111	111	135
03076	PELHAM	123	151	158	152	148	145	135	135	125	135	158	158	143	167	137	121	157	130	120	149
03077	RAYMOND	92	87	73	86	87	91	84	88	84	85	104	102	81	101	83	82	100	88	86	102
03079	SALEM	120	130	133	129	129	132	122	123	118	122	148	144	125	152	123	116	145	121	117	140
03082	LYNDEBOROUGH	129	160	170	160	157	155	143	142	132	142	166	166	152	177	146	128	166	137	127	157
03084	TEMPLE	104	130	138	130	127	125	116	115	107	115	135	135	123	144	118	104	135	111	103	127
03086	WILTON	122	132	128	132	132	137	124	127	121	123	150	147	127	155	125	119	146	123	122	144
03087	WINDHAM	195	233	246	237	228	233	207	205	192	209	243	238	223	251	211	188	243	199	189	232
03101	MANCHESTER	49	43	60	45	42	49	54	49	56	52	70	59	52	68	52	55	68	54	50	54
03102	MANCHESTER	77	75	85	78	75	80	81	78	80	80	101	93	80	100	79	78	98	81	75	86
03103	MANCHESTER	71	74	82	74	73	78	77	74	76	75	95	87	77	97	76	75	93	76	72	82
03104	MANCHESTER	101	103	122	107	101	107	109	104	107	108	135	124	109	133	107	103	132	108	98	115
03106	HOOKSETT	113	126	132	128	124	125	119	119	114	120	143	140	122	146	119	110	140	117	109	132
03109	MANCHESTER	92	107	110	107	104	104	98	98	93	99	117	113	103	121	99	90	116	95	89	107
03110	BEDFORD	179	213	234	218	207	212	195	190	181	197	230	220	209	236	197	176	230	186	173	210
03216	ANDOVER	108	92	68	86	100	108	86	98	93	86	112	116	82	113	89	97	106	96	109	129
03217	ASHLAND	88	73	58	70	79	89	75	83	81	73	97	96	69	96	76	84	91	83	93	104
03218	BARNSTEAD	111	104	86	98	109	117	95	106	100	95	121	124	93	124	99	102	116	103	113	134
03220	BELMONT	96	87	67	83	89	95	82	89	85	83	104	104	79	102	82	85	99	88	92	110
03221	BRADFORD	97	116	126	113	114	117	107	107	103	106	129	124	114	137	110	102	129	104	101	118
03222	BRISTOL	106	84	59	77	94	106	80	95	90	80	107	111	73	106	85	96	100	94	111	128
03223	CAMPTON	94	74	50	67	83	93	70	84	79	69	93	98	62	92	74	84	87	83	99	115
03224	CANTERBURY	116	143	152	144	141	139	128	128	119	128	149	150	136	159	131	115	149	123	114	141
03225	CENTER BARNSTEAD	97	94	83	92	96	99	89	94	89	89	110	111	87	110	89	88	106	93	93	113
03226	CENTER HARBOR	134	105	72	95	118	133	99	119	112	98	133	140	89	131	106	120	124	118	141	163
03227	CENTER SANDWICH	108	85	58	76	95	107	80	96	90	79	107	113	71	106	85	97	100	95	114	132
03229	CONTOOCOOK	126	153	166	151	151	155	139	139	132	139	165	160	148	173	144	130	164	135	130	153
03230	DANBURY	85	77	59	73	81	86	71	78	75	71	91	93	70	93	73	77	87	76	84	100
03234	EPSOM	101	102	101	103	103	107	99	101	97	99	121	120	98	121	99	95	117	101	98	117
03235	FRANKLIN	78	65	52	63	69	77	67	73	73	66	88	84	63	86	67	74	82	72	80	89
03237	GILMANTON	108	106	95	102	111	117	97	106	99	97	121	124	96	124	101	101	117	103	110	131
03240	GRAFTON	83	67	49	64	74	83	66	75	73	65	87	87	61	86	68	76	81	74	86	97
03241	HEBRON	116	91	62	82	102	115	86	103	97	85	115	121	77	114	92	104	107	102	122	141
03242	HENNIKER	108	115	137	120	114	117	121	114	115	118	145	139	121	146	118	110	143	118	104	126
03243	HILL	104	93	71	88	98	105	86	95	91	86	111	113	84	113	88	93	105	93	103	123
03244	HILLSBORO	94	90	80	88	92	96	87	91	88	86	108	108	85	110	87	87	104	90	91	109
03246	LACONIA	81	72	66	70	76	85	75	79	79	73	96	91	72	96	75	81	91	79	86	94
03249	GILFORD	144	150	141	145	153	159	138	146	137	138	170	170	139	174	142	138	165	142	145	173
03251	LINCOLN	78	61	42	55	69	77	58	69	65	57	77	81	51	76	61	70	72	68	82	95
03253	MEREDITH	116	100	79	96	108	119	96	108	103	95	124	125	91	125	100	107	117	106	119	137
03254	MOULTONBOROUGH	129	101	69	91	114	128	96	115	108	95	128	135	85	127	102	116	119	113	136	158
03255	NEWBURY	149	115	76	104	130	146	109	132	124	108	146	155	97	144	116	132	136	130	156	181
03256	NEW HAMPTON	115	90	59	85	101	111	86	102	96	86	114	121	79	114	89	100	106	100	116	137
03257	NEW LONDON	206	185	166	174	199	232	172	198	185	182	227	203	170	196	186	197	212	193	233	236
03258	CHICHESTER	113	122	116	120	123	126	111	115	109	111	135	136	114	141	113	108	132	112	112	136
03259	NORTH SANDWICH	108	84	58	76	95	107	80	96	90	79	107	112	71	105	85	96	99	95	113	131
03261	NORTHWOOD	106	102	87	97	106	113	93	102	96	93	117	120	92	120	97	98	113	99	107	128
03262	NORTH WOODSTOCK	88	69	47	62	78	87	65	78	74	64	87	92	58	86	69	79	81	77	93	107
03263	PITTSFIELD	108	92	72	91	96	108	94	100	100	92	121	115	90	120	93	101	113	99	109	119
03264	PLYMOUTH	93	77	74	77	80	90	89	87	91	84	112	106	81	108	85	90	106	91	92	106
03266	RUMNEY	96	77	54	72	85	95	74	87	83	74	99	101	68	97	77	87	92	85	100	114
03268	SALISBURY	93	115	122	115	113	111	103	102	95	102	119	120	109	127	105	92	119	99	92	113
03269	SANBORNTON	120	103	75	96	111	121	95	109	104	95	125	129	91	126	99	108	118	106	122	144
03275	SUNCOOK	85	87	89	88	87	91	87	87	85	86	106	102	87	107	86	83	103	87	83	98
03276	TILTON	86	80	69	78	83	88	77	82	80	77	98	97	75	99	78	80	93	81	85	100
03278	WARNER	123	96	61	90	107	117	92	108	102	91	121	129	83	121	95	106	113	106	124	146
03279	WARREN	78	66	51	66	69	78	68	73	72	67	87	83	65	87	67	73	82	71	79	86
03280	WASHINGTON	99	78	53	70	88	99	73	89	83	73	99	104	66	97	78	89	92	87	105	121
03281	WEARE	110	124	121	128	118	115	114	113	105	117	133	132	116	134	111	98	131	110	97	123
03282	WENTWORTH	102	72	39	68	83	93	71	87	82	71	96	105	62	94	74	86	88	86	103	120
03284	SPRINGFIELD	108	96	73	92	102	109	89	99	95	89	115	118	87	118	92	97	109	96	107	128
03287	WILMOT	99	121	127	121	120	118	108	109	101	108	127	128	115	135	111	98	126	105	98	121
03290	NOTTINGHAM	105	130	137	130	128	126	116	116	108	116	136	136	123	144	119	105	135	112	104	128
03301	CONCORD	86	89	102	91	88	94	92	90	90	91	113	105	92	113	91	89	110	91	86	99
03303	CONCORD	83	86	87	87	86	89	85	85	83	84	104	101	85	106	85	81	101	85	81	96
03304	BOW	144	179	192	182	174	174	159	156	146	159	184	182	172	194	162	141	185	151	140	173
03307	LOUDON	108	123	126	124	119	118	115	114	107	115	135	134	117	138	114	102	133	112	101	125
03431	KEENE	84	80	86	80	81	88	86	84	87	83	108	100	84	108	84	86	104	86	85	96
03440	ANTRIM	96	79	58	75	85	96	78	88	85	77	102	101	73	101	80	88	96	86	99	111
	NEW HAMPSHIRE	106	107	107	107	108	113	105	106	104	104	129	125	105	130	105	103	125	106	105	123
	UNITED STATES	100	100	100	100	100	100	100	100	100	100	100	100	100	100	100	100	100	100	100	100

POPULATION CHANGE

ZIP CODE			POPULATION			2000-2004 ANNUAL RATE		HOUSEHOLDS					FAMILIES		
#	POST OFFICE NAME	COUNTY FIPS CODE	2000	2004	2009	% Rate	State Centile	2000	2004	2009	% Annual Rate 2000-2004	2004 Average HH Size	2000	2004	% Annual Rate 2000-2004
03441	ASHUELOT	005	498	521	560	1.1	22	199	213	233	1.6	2.45	136	145	1.5
03442	BENNINGTON	011	1404	1442	1511	0.6	9	553	577	612	1.0	2.50	357	369	0.8
03443	CHESTERFIELD	005	675	725	785	1.7	54	259	282	310	2.0	2.57	191	207	1.9
03444	DUBLIN	005	1440	1493	1582	0.9	15	543	576	623	1.4	2.47	405	429	1.4
03445	SULLIVAN	005	733	911	1062	5.3	100	273	347	413	5.8	2.62	193	245	5.8
03446	SWANZEY	005	5973	6301	6761	1.3	33	2268	2431	2653	1.7	2.59	1612	1722	1.6
03447	FITZWILLIAM	005	1903	2045	2216	1.7	56	739	809	892	2.2	2.52	517	563	2.0
03448	GILSUM	005	794	808	852	0.4	6	315	328	353	1.0	2.44	232	242	1.0
03449	HANCOCK	011	1676	1667	1740	-0.1	2	682	685	721	0.1	2.43	478	477	-0.1
03450	HARRISVILLE	005	1071	1065	1126	-0.1	2	449	458	494	0.5	2.33	306	311	0.4
03451	HINSDALE	005	4213	4386	4673	1.0	17	1684	1778	1923	1.3	2.47	1133	1193	1.2
03452	JAFFREY	005	5507	5785	6187	1.2	29	2135	2278	2477	1.5	2.46	1475	1569	1.5
03455	MARLBOROUGH	005	2310	2432	2608	1.2	31	959	1029	1123	1.7	2.36	656	703	1.6
03456	MARLOW	005	747	790	848	1.3	38	292	315	345	1.8	2.51	222	239	1.8
03457	NELSON	005	471	577	668	4.9	100	181	225	266	5.3	2.56	127	158	5.3
03458	PETERBOROUGH	011	6315	6489	6807	0.6	10	2512	2615	2778	1.0	2.36	1662	1716	0.8
03461	RINDGE	005	5626	6125	6637	2.0	71	1550	1755	1970	3.0	2.84	1179	1331	2.9
03462	SPOFFORD	005	1416	1539	1677	2.0	69	559	618	684	2.4	2.49	408	450	2.3
03464	STODDARD	005	864	906	969	1.1	25	367	394	430	1.7	2.30	246	263	1.6
03465	TROY	005	2094	2213	2378	1.3	37	787	843	920	1.6	2.63	567	605	1.5
03466	WEST CHESTERFIELD	005	1299	1361	1455	1.1	25	491	522	567	1.5	2.61	365	387	1.4
03467	WESTMORELAND	005	1748	1847	1971	1.3	36	576	626	687	2.0	2.53	445	482	1.9
03470	WINCHESTER	005	4843	5145	5552	1.4	42	1763	1906	2094	1.9	2.65	1263	1361	1.8
03561	LITTLETON	009	6003	6624	7473	2.3	84	2573	2897	3334	2.8	2.27	1627	1825	2.7
03570	BERLIN	007	10382	10304	10472	-0.2	1	4573	4629	4803	0.3	2.18	2914	2938	0.2
03574	BETHLEHEM	009	2166	2376	2673	2.2	79	911	1025	1180	2.8	2.29	581	652	2.8
03576	COLEBROOK	007	4163	4434	4660	1.5	45	1717	1888	2037	2.3	2.26	1076	1178	2.2
03579	ERROL	007	363	360	364	-0.2	0	164	167	173	0.4	2.01	118	120	0.4
03580	FRANCONIA	009	1086	1193	1342	2.2	80	459	517	594	2.8	2.22	296	332	2.7
03581	GORHAM	007	3274	3322	3404	0.3	4	1449	1503	1574	0.9	2.21	915	947	0.8
03582	GROVETON	007	2576	2684	2778	1.0	18	1045	1113	1177	1.5	2.41	694	737	1.4
03583	JEFFERSON	007	940	957	978	0.4	6	380	397	415	1.0	2.41	275	286	0.9
03584	LANCASTER	007	3659	3772	3893	0.7	13	1423	1503	1588	1.3	2.41	965	1016	1.2
03585	LISBON	009	2962	3202	3577	1.9	64	1222	1352	1542	2.4	2.35	835	922	2.4
03588	MILAN	007	1656	1672	1703	0.2	4	667	690	719	0.8	2.39	487	503	0.8
03590	NORTH STRATFORD	007	982	985	998	0.1	3	415	426	442	0.6	2.31	268	275	0.6
03592	PITTSBURG	007	1142	1196	1240	1.1	24	499	534	566	1.6	2.23	348	371	1.5
03593	RANDOLPH	007	238	243	249	0.5	7	105	110	115	1.1	2.18	73	76	1.0
03598	WHITEFIELD	007	3599	3626	3690	0.2	4	1468	1511	1571	0.7	2.35	994	1021	0.6
03602	ALSTEAD	005	2700	2813	2991	1.0	18	1066	1135	1230	1.5	2.47	747	792	1.4
03603	CHARLESTOWN	019	4842	5151	5513	1.5	44	1956	2116	2306	1.9	2.42	1356	1462	1.8
03605	LEMPSTER	019	1328	1408	1504	1.4	40	521	568	621	2.1	2.47	375	407	2.0
03607	SOUTH ACWORTH	019	371	386	408	0.9	17	153	163	176	1.5	2.37	113	119	1.2
03608	WALPOLE	005	2725	2816	2986	0.8	14	1133	1185	1274	1.1	2.37	781	813	1.0
03609	NORTH WALPOLE	005	593	602	634	0.4	5	251	259	276	0.7	2.32	161	165	0.6
03740	BATH	009	885	958	1071	1.9	65	347	383	436	2.4	2.50	249	274	2.3
03741	CANAAN	009	3635	3897	4336	1.7	53	1400	1533	1740	2.2	2.54	1013	1107	2.1
03743	CLAREMONT	019	14131	14505	15315	0.6	9	5983	6284	6783	1.2	2.26	3657	3819	1.0
03745	CORNISH	019	1597	1653	1743	0.8	14	614	651	701	1.4	2.54	441	465	1.3
03748	ENFIELD	009	5014	5273	5806	1.2	29	2156	2323	2612	1.8	2.26	1424	1532	1.7
03750	ETNA	009	977	1074	1210	2.3	81	369	411	470	2.6	2.59	292	325	2.6
03752	GOSHEN	019	710	748	796	1.2	31	266	287	312	1.8	2.58	209	225	1.8
03753	GRANTHAM	019	2305	2544	2776	2.4	85	981	1107	1235	2.9	2.30	752	846	2.8
03755	HANOVER	009	9837	10408	11230	1.3	39	2447	2720	3113	2.5	2.41	1456	1615	2.5
03765	HAVERHILL	009	331	353	391	1.5	46	148	162	183	2.2	2.10	107	117	2.1
03766	LEBANON	009	8519	9423	10648	2.4	87	3711	4200	4852	3.0	2.19	2080	2339	2.8
03768	LYME	009	1920	2116	2389	2.3	84	782	877	1009	2.7	2.40	544	609	2.7
03770	MERIDEN	019	196	211	227	1.8	60	74	81	89	2.2	2.60	59	65	2.3
03771	MONROE	009	759	824	922	2.0	69	310	345	394	2.6	2.39	227	252	2.5
03773	NEWPORT	019	7449	7767	8224	1.0	19	2928	3115	3365	1.5	2.43	1994	2111	1.4
03774	NORTH HAVERHILL	009	1674	1905	2180	3.1	96	639	747	876	3.7	2.43	420	490	3.7
03777	ORFORD	009	850	914	1018	1.7	58	366	402	457	2.2	2.27	243	266	2.2
03779	PIERMONT	009	719	773	861	1.7	58	297	326	370	2.2	2.37	198	216	2.1
03780	PIKE	009	677	721	798	1.5	45	241	263	298	2.1	2.65	174	190	2.1
03781	PLAINFIELD	019	2157	2326	2506	1.8	62	821	904	994	2.3	2.57	640	703	2.2
03782	SUNAPEE	019	3050	3241	3467	1.4	42	1295	1412	1546	2.1	2.30	880	955	1.9
03784	WEST LEBANON	009	3798	4164	4687	2.2	78	1664	1856	2128	2.6	2.21	1008	1126	2.6
03785	WOODSVILLE	009	2187	2506	2890	3.3	96	887	1053	1248	4.1	2.24	548	651	4.1
03801	PORTSMOUTH	015	21543	22041	23446	0.5	8	10162	10557	11394	0.9	2.03	5067	5234	0.8
03809	ALTON	001	3700	4121	4639	2.6	90	1491	1691	1937	3.0	2.44	1059	1197	2.9
03810	ALTON BAY	001	193	210	234	2.0	71	82	91	103	2.5	2.31	56	62	2.4
03811	ATKINSON	015	6262	6968	7704	2.6	89	2346	2654	2974	3.0	2.62	1800	2028	2.9
03812	BARTLETT	003	1676	1789	1968	1.6	46	740	806	904	2.0	2.19	473	512	1.9
03813	CENTER CONWAY	003	2829	3002	3297	1.4	41	1157	1250	1397	1.8	2.40	788	847	1.7
03814	CENTER OSSIPEE	003	3415	3734	4158	2.1	76	1368	1530	1740	2.7	2.38	927	1032	2.6
03815	CENTER STRAFFORD	017	509	599	685	3.9	98	177	212	247	4.3	2.82	140	168	4.4
03816	CENTER TUFTONBORO	003	1239	1341	1488	1.9	65	521	579	656	2.5	2.32	375	416	2.5
03817	CHOCORUA	003	283	297	324	1.1	26	123	132	146	1.7	2.24	79	84	1.5
03818	CONWAY	003	2271	2356	2555	0.9	16	981	1037	1146	1.3	2.26	601	632	1.2
03819	DANVILLE	015	3922	4304	4723	2.2	79	1390	1542	1710	2.5	2.79	1093	1208	2.4
03820	DOVER	017	28474	30040	32576	1.3	33	12146	13046	14405	1.7	2.24	6933	7443	1.7
03824	DURHAM	017	16732	18021	19543	1.8	62	4324	4833	5450	2.7	2.77	2655	2932	2.4
03825	BARRINGTON	017	7099	7916	8807	2.6	90	2599	2948	3333	3.0	2.68	1954	2207	2.9
03826	EAST HAMPSTEAD	015	2959	3087	3299	1.0	20	1090	1153	1248	1.3	2.68	761	801	1.2
03827	EAST KINGSTON	015	2592	2785	3022	1.7	54	914	995	1093	2.0	2.80	739	802	1.9
03830	EAST WAKEFIELD	003	1102	1306	1516	4.1	98	453	547	647	4.5	2.39	324	390	4.5
03833	EXETER	015	19109	20141	21690	1.3	32	7458	7946	8668	1.5	2.43	5020	5338	1.5
03835	FARMINGTON	017	5739	6310	6973	2.3	81	2125	2386	2683	2.8	2.63	1516	1694	2.7
03836	FREEDOM	003	1311	1564	1823	4.2	99	606	742	884	4.9	2.10	405	494	4.8
03837	GILMANTON IRON WORKS	001	1049	1196	1362	3.1	96	387	453	528	3.8	2.64	292	340	3.7
03838	GLEN	003	69	74	81	1.7	54	28	30	34	1.6	2.43	18	19	1.3
03839	ROCHESTER	017	3389	3677	4032	1.9	68	1293	1435	1604	2.5	2.56	943	1042	2.4
03840	GREENLAND	015	3232	3458	3743	1.6	50	1212	1316	1443	2.0	2.61	898	969	1.8
03841	HAMPSTEAD	015	5537	5843	6298	1.3	33	2023	2164	2361	1.6	2.70	1574	1675	1.5
03842	HAMPTON	015	14822	15877	17213	1.6	51	6411	6962	7643	2.0	2.26	4005	4311	1.8
	NEW HAMPSHIRE					1.5					1.9	2.49			1.8
	UNITED STATES					1.2					1.3	2.58			1.1

ZIP CODE #	POST OFFICE NAME	RACE (%) White 2000	White 2004	Black 2000	Black 2004	Asian/Pacific 2000	Asian/Pacific 2004	% Hispanic Origin 2000	% Hispanic Origin 2004	2004 AGE DISTRIBUTION (%) 0-4	5-9	10-14	15-19	20-24	25-44	45-64	65-84	85+	18+	MEDIAN AGE 2004	% 2004 Males	% 2004 Females
03441	ASHUELOT	97.8	97.5	0.4	0.4	0.0	0.2	0.4	0.4	6.0	6.3	7.3	6.7	6.0	28.4	26.1	11.9	1.3	76.4	38.4	50.1	49.9
03442	BENNINGTON	98.0	97.9	0.1	0.1	0.4	0.4	0.6	0.8	6.1	6.0	8.0	8.6	7.8	28.9	26.5	7.4	0.8	74.8	36.2	49.2	50.8
03443	CHESTERFIELD	97.9	97.8	0.3	0.3	0.2	0.1	0.7	0.7	5.1	5.9	7.6	7.0	5.1	24.3	32.4	11.5	1.1	76.8	42.1	51.2	48.8
03444	DUBLIN	97.3	96.7	0.4	0.4	1.0	1.2	1.2	1.4	4.6	5.7	6.3	6.8	4.4	22.7	35.0	12.8	1.7	78.8	44.7	49.9	50.1
03445	SULLIVAN	98.1	98.1	0.3	0.3	0.1	0.2	0.8	0.8	6.0	6.6	7.1	6.5	4.5	27.7	31.1	9.7	0.9	76.2	40.3	50.3	49.7
03446	SWANZEY	98.4	98.2	0.2	0.2	0.5	0.7	0.5	0.6	5.9	6.6	7.4	6.9	5.0	28.3	27.2	11.7	1.2	75.9	39.4	49.5	50.5
03447	FITZWILLIAM	97.5	97.5	0.4	0.4	0.3	0.3	0.8	0.9	5.1	5.8	7.2	7.1	4.8	26.2	32.4	10.4	1.0	77.4	41.5	50.7	49.3
03448	GILSUM	98.4	98.1	0.0	0.0	0.3	0.3	0.9	1.2	4.0	5.1	6.4	6.3	4.2	24.3	34.9	13.1	1.7	80.3	44.9	49.4	50.6
03449	HANCOCK	98.4	98.1	0.2	0.2	0.4	0.5	0.4	0.6	4.6	5.4	7.8	7.2	4.1	21.4	31.0	16.4	2.2	77.7	44.7	47.4	52.6
03450	HARRISVILLE	97.8	97.8	0.1	0.1	0.3	0.4	0.6	0.5	5.0	5.9	7.0	6.6	4.8	21.0	34.9	13.2	1.7	77.9	44.9	48.0	52.0
03451	HINSDALE	97.5	97.3	0.4	0.5	0.6	0.7	0.5	0.5	5.4	6.0	8.0	7.4	5.7	28.3	27.0	10.5	1.7	75.8	38.4	48.7	51.3
03452	JAFFREY	97.3	97.0	0.4	0.5	0.7	0.9	0.6	0.6	6.2	6.5	7.6	6.7	5.6	27.1	24.7	12.8	2.9	75.3	39.0	48.3	51.7
03455	MARLBOROUGH	98.5	98.3	0.2	0.2	0.4	0.4	0.6	0.7	5.0	5.7	6.9	6.1	5.1	27.5	28.9	12.6	2.3	78.6	41.3	48.4	51.6
03456	MARLOW	98.8	98.9	0.0	0.0	0.0	0.0	1.1	1.1	6.6	7.1	6.3	6.2	4.3	26.3	30.3	11.8	1.1	76.1	40.9	51.5	48.5
03457	NELSON	98.1	97.8	0.2	0.4	0.2	0.4	0.9	0.9	5.9	6.6	6.9	6.4	4.5	27.6	31.4	9.9	0.9	76.6	40.5	50.4	49.6
03458	PETERBOROUGH	97.0	96.6	0.6	0.7	1.3	1.6	0.8	1.0	5.4	5.7	7.2	7.8	5.7	21.1	27.4	15.8	4.1	76.5	43.3	46.3	53.7
03461	RINDGE	97.3	97.0	1.1	1.2	0.3	0.4	0.9	1.0	5.9	6.4	6.7	14.3	14.3	22.9	21.8	7.1	0.6	76.8	27.0	51.1	48.9
03462	SPOFFORD	97.7	97.6	0.2	0.3	0.1	0.1	0.6	0.8	4.7	5.7	7.6	6.6	4.7	25.8	33.0	10.4	1.5	78.0	41.8	50.0	50.0
03464	STODDARD	96.9	96.7	0.4	0.3	0.6	0.7	0.6	0.7	4.3	5.9	5.9	4.4	3.1	27.9	33.4	14.2	0.9	81.4	44.2	50.8	49.2
03465	TROY	98.5	98.4	0.1	0.1	0.2	0.2	1.2	1.5	5.9	6.2	7.4	7.3	6.2	28.6	27.9	9.5	1.0	76.0	38.4	48.3	51.7
03466	WEST CHESTERFIELD	97.8	97.7	0.2	0.2	0.2	0.3	0.4	0.5	5.0	6.1	7.9	7.1	4.5	23.7	32.9	12.0	1.0	76.6	42.8	51.4	48.6
03467	WESTMORELAND	97.8	97.5	0.3	0.4	0.8	1.0	0.9	1.0	3.7	4.4	5.3	6.3	5.3	24.7	31.3	14.8	4.2	82.7	45.1	49.5	50.5
03470	WINCHESTER	97.4	97.2	0.3	0.3	0.3	0.4	0.8	0.9	6.2	6.6	7.7	6.8	5.6	27.6	26.3	11.6	1.6	75.3	38.7	49.6	50.4
03561	LITTLETON	96.6	96.2	0.4	0.4	0.9	1.1	1.5	1.7	5.6	5.7	6.8	6.9	6.1	25.4	28.5	12.9	1.9	77.5	40.7	47.5	52.5
03570	BERLIN	98.3	98.1	0.2	0.2	0.4	0.5	0.7	0.7	5.2	5.2	6.1	6.0	5.9	23.4	25.9	18.6	3.8	79.8	43.8	47.9	52.1
03574	BETHLEHEM	97.0	96.8	0.1	0.2	0.3	0.4	0.8	0.9	5.2	5.4	6.7	7.5	4.8	28.2	30.9	10.2	1.0	77.6	40.5	50.8	49.2
03576	COLEBROOK	98.5	98.4	0.0	0.0	0.2	0.3	0.4	0.4	4.8	5.5	6.6	5.7	5.6	25.7	28.8	15.2	2.1	79.1	42.6	50.3	49.7
03579	ERROL	98.4	98.3	0.0	0.0	0.3	0.3	0.6	0.6	4.2	4.4	5.8	5.6	3.3	22.8	31.9	18.1	3.9	82.2	47.3	49.7	50.3
03580	FRANCONIA	97.9	97.5	0.1	0.1	0.9	1.1	0.3	0.4	3.5	4.1	5.6	5.4	4.6	20.2	36.9	16.1	3.6	83.3	48.7	48.6	51.4
03581	GORHAM	97.3	97.1	0.1	0.1	1.1	1.4	0.4	0.4	4.2	5.1	6.5	6.7	5.0	25.0	28.7	16.6	2.3	79.7	43.7	49.6	50.5
03582	GROVETON	98.1	98.0	0.0	0.0	0.4	0.5	0.5	0.6	4.9	5.4	7.6	7.9	6.2	25.8	26.0	14.6	1.5	77.1	40.7	49.0	51.0
03583	JEFFERSON	98.3	98.3	0.0	0.0	0.2	0.2	0.1	0.1	4.7	5.2	6.2	6.8	2.9	24.4	35.7	12.3	1.8	79.1	44.9	51.2	48.8
03584	LANCASTER	98.1	98.0	0.1	0.1	0.3	0.3	0.7	0.8	6.3	6.4	7.2	7.1	5.9	24.1	26.7	13.5	2.9	75.8	40.3	47.9	52.2
03585	LISBON	98.3	98.2	0.0	0.0	0.2	0.3	0.3	0.3	5.6	6.0	7.0	6.6	4.8	24.9	30.5	13.0	1.7	77.2	42.1	49.1	50.9
03588	MILAN	98.8	98.7	0.1	0.2	0.1	0.1	0.1	0.1	4.7	5.6	7.1	6.5	4.4	23.9	33.5	13.0	1.4	78.7	43.8	50.9	49.1
03590	NORTH STRATFORD	96.4	96.0	0.0	0.0	0.5	0.6	0.6	0.6	5.5	5.5	6.4	8.4	6.6	23.5	30.4	12.5	1.3	78.0	41.1	47.3	52.7
03592	PITTSBURG	97.6	97.3	0.1	0.1	0.0	0.0	0.9	1.1	4.4	4.5	4.4	5.4	4.5	22.0	35.9	17.8	1.2	83.0	48.1	52.3	47.7
03593	RANDOLPH	97.9	97.9	0.4	0.4	0.4	0.8	0.8	0.8	3.7	4.5	5.8	7.0	4.5	23.5	34.2	14.8	2.1	81.1	45.6	51.4	48.6
03598	WHITEFIELD	97.8	97.6	0.3	0.4	0.4	0.5	1.2	1.4	5.2	5.5	6.8	6.7	6.0	24.2	29.0	14.0	2.7	78.3	42.6	49.6	50.4
03602	ALSTEAD	98.5	98.3	0.2	0.2	0.4	0.5	0.4	0.5	5.6	6.2	7.0	6.2	5.6	24.9	31.1	11.9	1.4	77.3	41.9	51.4	48.6
03603	CHARLESTOWN	98.5	98.3	0.3	0.4	0.1	0.2	0.6	0.7	5.7	6.1	7.3	6.5	5.4	25.4	28.8	13.0	1.8	76.5	41.1	49.2	50.8
03605	LEMPSTER	97.1	97.1	0.2	0.2	0.2	0.2	0.5	0.6	5.1	6.0	7.2	6.6	4.6	23.0	33.2	12.6	1.6	77.7	43.5	50.5	49.5
03607	SOUTH ACWORTH	96.8	96.9	0.8	0.8	0.3	0.3	1.1	1.0	4.7	6.0	7.0	7.5	4.9	20.0	34.2	14.5	1.3	77.7	45.0	50.3	49.7
03608	WALPOLE	98.6	98.5	0.2	0.1	0.1	0.1	0.6	0.6	5.7	6.0	7.0	7.4	5.5	22.8	27.6	15.5	2.4	76.4	42.2	48.2	51.9
03609	NORTH WALPOLE	97.0	96.7	0.2	0.2	0.7	0.8	0.0	0.0	7.6	6.8	5.8	5.5	6.3	27.4	24.9	13.5	2.2	76.7	38.4	47.7	52.3
03740	BATH	98.2	98.1	0.1	0.1	0.0	0.0	0.3	0.5	4.6	5.0	6.4	5.9	6.2	22.1	33.1	15.2	1.6	80.4	44.9	48.6	51.4
03741	CANAAN	98.1	98.0	0.1	0.2	0.4	0.5	0.5	0.6	6.1	6.8	7.1	7.4	4.8	27.7	29.6	9.5	1.0	75.3	39.2	49.7	50.4
03743	CLAREMONT	97.8	97.6	0.3	0.3	0.6	0.8	0.5	0.6	5.9	5.7	6.3	6.8	6.4	26.7	25.7	13.8	2.6	77.9	40.0	48.6	51.5
03745	CORNISH	97.8	97.4	0.3	0.4	0.3	0.4	0.5	0.6	4.8	5.8	6.7	7.6	4.4	22.9	35.0	11.6	1.3	77.1	43.8	50.3	49.7
03748	ENFIELD	98.0	97.7	0.1	0.1	0.8	1.0	0.7	0.8	6.0	6.2	6.1	5.1	5.0	30.1	29.4	10.9	1.2	78.5	40.0	48.7	51.3
03750	ETNA	96.2	95.4	0.2	0.2	2.5	3.2	0.7	0.7	4.9	6.6	8.3	7.2	3.5	19.4	34.9	13.3	2.0	75.0	45.1	49.6	50.4
03752	GOSHEN	97.0	97.1	0.0	0.0	0.1	0.1	0.4	0.4	3.9	4.7	7.6	6.8	6.6	24.6	29.6	14.7	1.6	79.7	42.8	49.5	50.5
03753	GRANTHAM	98.2	98.0	0.2	0.2	0.4	0.6	0.6	0.7	4.8	5.5	6.1	4.8	3.3	22.8	29.9	21.7	1.3	80.5	46.8	48.5	51.5
03755	HANOVER	87.1	85.1	1.9	2.0	7.3	9.1	2.7	3.0	2.7	3.3	4.1	19.5	26.2	14.2	16.6	10.9	2.6	87.2	23.9	49.7	50.3
03765	HAVERHILL	98.8	98.6	0.3	0.3	0.3	0.6	0.6	0.9	5.1	6.0	7.7	8.5	4.8	23.5	29.8	13.0	1.7	75.1	41.8	49.6	50.4
03766	LEBANON	95.2	94.2	0.7	0.8	2.3	3.1	1.3	1.5	5.3	5.1	6.1	6.5	7.6	28.8	26.4	11.5	2.6	79.7	38.8	47.5	52.6
03768	LYME	98.4	98.3	0.4	0.4	0.5	0.7	0.4	0.5	5.2	6.2	7.4	6.9	4.3	22.1	32.0	13.9	2.0	76.5	43.7	49.4	50.6
03770	MERIDEN	97.5	97.2	0.0	0.0	0.5	1.0	0.0	0.0	4.7	6.6	8.5	6.2	4.3	26.5	33.2	9.0	1.0	75.8	41.9	50.2	49.8
03771	MONROE	97.9	97.8	0.1	0.1	0.1	0.2	0.1	0.1	3.5	4.1	5.7	6.9	5.1	23.3	33.6	16.5	1.2	82.4	45.7	49.8	50.2
03773	NEWPORT	98.1	98.0	0.1	0.1	0.3	0.4	0.6	0.6	6.0	6.4	7.2	6.7	5.7	27.0	25.8	12.9	2.3	75.9	39.3	49.7	50.3
03774	NORTH HAVERHILL	98.3	98.0	0.4	0.5	0.4	0.5	0.7	0.7	4.9	5.4	6.6	7.0	5.6	26.0	27.3	14.3	2.9	78.2	41.2	49.8	50.2
03777	ORFORD	97.5	97.3	0.1	0.1	0.5	0.7	0.9	1.1	6.4	6.6	6.0	4.9	4.7	27.0	30.2	12.5	1.8	77.9	41.5	50.0	50.0
03779	PIERMONT	97.6	97.2	0.1	0.1	0.6	0.7	1.0	1.2	6.2	6.6	6.1	4.9	4.7	27.0	30.4	12.3	1.8	78.0	41.6	50.2	49.8
03780	PIKE	98.8	98.8	0.2	0.3	0.3	0.4	0.7	0.8	5.0	6.0	7.9	7.9	5.0	23.7	30.0	12.9	1.7	75.3	41.8	49.4	50.6
03781	PLAINFIELD	98.1	97.9	0.3	0.3	0.4	0.5	0.4	0.4	5.7	6.8	7.5	5.8	4.3	25.9	33.0	9.9	1.1	76.4	41.9	51.2	48.8
03782	SUNAPEE	98.0	97.9	0.2	0.2	0.4	0.5	0.5	0.5	4.2	5.2	6.5	7.0	5.5	24.3	29.9	15.9	1.6	79.7	43.5	50.5	49.6
03784	WEST LEBANON	92.4	91.3	1.1	1.3	3.7	4.6	2.4	2.7	7.8	6.8	6.7	6.9	8.2	29.1	21.6	11.0	1.9	74.4	34.4	46.5	53.6
03785	WOODSVILLE	97.8	97.5	0.5	0.6	0.4	0.4	0.6	0.7	4.9	5.1	5.8	6.2	6.2	27.0	26.1	15.4	3.3	80.3	41.2	49.6	50.4
03801	PORTSMOUTH	93.6	92.7	2.1	2.3	2.4	3.1	1.4	1.5	4.7	4.5	5.1	5.3	6.3	32.6	25.4	13.4	2.7	82.5	40.0	48.7	51.3
03809	ALTON	98.8	98.7	0.1	0.1	0.3	0.4	0.5	0.6	6.0	6.4	6.5	5.6	4.4	24.1	31.5	14.1	1.5	77.7	43.3	50.1	49.9
03810	ALTON BAY	98.5	98.1	0.0	0.0	0.5	0.5	1.0	0.5	5.7	6.2	6.2	5.2	3.8	23.8	31.9	15.7	1.4	78.6	44.4	48.6	51.4
03811	ATKINSON	97.6	97.3	0.3	0.3	1.2	1.5	0.7	0.8	6.1	7.0	7.1	5.9	3.7	24.9	32.5	11.8	1.1	76.1	42.6	48.9	51.1
03812	BARTLETT	98.5	98.3	0.1	0.1	0.3	0.4	0.5	0.5	4.9	5.1	5.9	4.9	3.8	25.4	33.5	15.5	1.1	80.8	45.1	50.0	50.0
03813	CENTER CONWAY	98.0	97.8	0.1	0.1	0.7	1.0	0.3	0.4	5.7	6.4	7.0	6.1	5.7	26.6	29.4	12.0	1.1	76.8	40.8	49.0	51.0
03814	CENTER OSSIPEE	97.7	97.6	0.3	0.3	0.2	0.3	0.4	0.4	4.7	5.8	7.5	7.2	4.7	24.8	29.2	14.6	1.6	77.4	42.3	50.7	49.3
03815	CENTER STRAFFORD	98.4	98.2	0.2	0.2	0.4	0.3	0.4	0.7	5.8	7.4	10.4	9.0	2.3	31.2	26.7	6.7	0.5	69.8	37.9	50.3	49.8
03816	CENTER TUFTONBORO	98.1	98.1	0.0	0.0	0.3	0.4	0.4	0.5	4.9	5.0	5.2	5.3	3.9	19.7	35.1	19.0	2.1	81.6	48.7	49.0	51.0
03817	CHOCORUA	98.2	97.6	0.0	0.3	0.4	0.3	0.7	0.7	5.7	6.1	7.1	5.7	4.4	26.3	30.6	12.5	1.7	77.4	42.1	50.8	49.2
03818	CONWAY	98.1	98.0	0.1	0.1	0.4	0.6	0.4	0.4	5.4	5.7	6.8	6.6	5.6	25.0	30.0	13.3	1.7	78.4	41.8	49.6	50.4
03819	DANVILLE	97.6	97.3	0.6	0.7	0.4	0.5	0.9	1.0	8.2	8.2	8.3	6.4	5.1	32.0	24.1	7.0	0.7	70.9	36.1	50.7	49.3
03820	DOVER	94.6	93.8	1.1	1.2	2.4	3.0	1.1	1.2	5.7	5.3	6.1	6.3	8.2	32.4	22.6	11.0	2.4	79.0	36.3	48.2	51.8
03824	DURHAM	94.9	94.1	0.7	0.8	2.9	3.6	1.2	1.4	3.4	3.9	4.9	21.8	26.2	16.1	17.0	6.1	0.8	84.6	23.1	46.4	53.6
03825	BARRINGTON	98.0	97.8	0.3	0.3	0.5	0.7	1.0	1.1	6.3	7.0	7.9	7.1	4.8	30.8	28.9	6.7	0.6	74.0	38.0	50.8	49.2
03826	EAST HAMPSTEAD	98.0	97.7	0.2	0.3	0.7	0.9	0.7	0.9	6.3	6.6	7.8	7.3	6.0	27.5	29.2	8.5	0.8	74.6	39.2	49.3	50.7
03827	EAST KINGSTON	98.0	98.0	0.3	0.3	0.5	0.5	0.4	0.4	5.9	7.5	8.0	5.7	2.9	29.1	31.4	8.3	1.2	74.8	40.6	48.0	52.0
03830	EAST WAKEFIELD	98.3	98.1	0.1	0.2	0.3	0.3	0.5	0.5	6.0	6.3	6.5	6.0	4.2	23.3	30.9	15.9	1.0	77.4	43.6	50.2	49.8
03833	EXETER	97.2	96.8	0.5	0.5	0.9	1.2	0.9	1.0	5.8	6.3	7.1	6.6	5.0	26.3	27.4	12.1	3.4	76.5	41.1	48.1	51.9
03835	FARMINGTON	98.2	98.1	0.0	0.0	0.1	0.2	1.0	1.1	6.4	6.6	8.1	7.8	6.2	28.2	26.4	9.2	1.2	74.0	37.3	49.5	50.5
03836	FREEDOM	99.2	99.0	0.2	0.2	0.1	0.1	0.0	0.0	3.9	4.4	4.9	3.8	2.9	20.9	34.0	23.7	1.5	84.0	50.4	49.2	50.8
03837	GILMANTON IRON WORKS	98.6	98.6	0.1	0.1	0.1	0.1	0.3	0.4	5.4	6.0	7.1	6.8	5.4	25.7	31.5	11.0	1.2	77.1	41.7	49.6	50.4
03838	GLEN	98.6	100.0	0.0	0.0	0.0	0.0	0.0	0.0	5.4	5.4	5.4	5.4	2.7	23.0	35.1	17.6	0.0	81.1	46.7	48.7	51.4
03839	ROCHESTER	97.7	97.4	0.5	0.5	0.7	0.9	0.7	0.8	7.6	7.3	7.0	6.6	6.6	32.8	24.2	7.4	0.6	73.9	35.3	51.2	48.8
03840	GREENLAND	97.8	97.4	0.3	0.4	1.2	1.6	0.7	0.8	6.8	7.2	7.9	6.0	4.2	27.7	28.2	11.0	1.1	73.8	40.3	47.8	52.2
03841	HAMPSTEAD	98.7	98.5	0.2	0.2	0.5	0.7	0.8	0.9	5.8	7.2	9.6	6.9	4.2	26.5	29.2	9.7	0.9	72.6	40.0	49.7	50.3
03842	HAMPTON	97.6	97.3	0.4	0.5	0.9	1.2	0.9	1.1	5.7	5.9	6.3	5.5	4.8	26.0	30.1	14.0	1.7	78.6	42.6	48.4	51.6
	NEW HAMPSHIRE	96.0	95.6	0.7	0.8	1.3	1.7	1.7	1.9	6.1	6.4	7.2	7.2	6.6	27.8	26.5	10.6	1.6	76.2	38.4	49.2	50.8
	UNITED STATES	75.1	73.6	12.3	12.5	3.8	4.2	12.5	14.1	6.9	6.7	7.2	7.0	7.3	28.6	23.8	10.8	1.7	75.1	36.0	49.1	50.9

ZIP CODE #	POST OFFICE NAME	2004 Per Capita Income	2004 HH Income Base	2004 Household Income Distribution (%) Less than $25,000	$25,000 to $49,999	$50,000 to $99,999	$100,000 to $149,999	$150,000 or More	Median Household Income 2004	2009	2004 National Centile	2004 State Centile	2004 Home Value Base	2004 Home Value Distribution (%) Less than $50,000	$50,000 to $89,999	$90,000 to $174,999	$175,000 to $399,999	$400,000 or More	2004 Median Home Value
03441	ASHUELOT	19990	213	26.8	32.4	33.8	5.2	1.9	41596	48775	52	12	162	16.7	15.4	46.9	16.7	4.3	123864
03442	BENNINGTON	23774	577	17.0	27.9	41.3	12.7	1.2	53700	65665	78	51	364	4.1	4.1	57.1	31.9	2.8	152419
03443	CHESTERFIELD	29089	282	15.6	26.2	38.7	12.8	6.7	60823	70012	85	67	248	0.4	4.4	30.2	55.2	9.7	206863
03444	DUBLIN	35451	576	16.2	22.2	37.2	13.7	10.8	62623	76606	87	71	474	0.4	1.3	19.0	54.9	24.5	265942
03445	SULLIVAN	31558	347	19.9	25.1	36.6	11.8	6.6	55013	64433	80	55	298	2.7	8.4	41.6	40.9	6.4	169444
03446	SWANZEY	23626	2431	18.8	29.5	37.8	10.3	3.7	51469	61339	75	43	1904	6.9	10.1	38.9	40.4	3.6	162716
03447	FITZWILLIAM	27594	809	17.3	27.4	38.2	11.5	5.6	54982	65405	80	54	685	5.0	5.8	47.9	38.3	3.1	159176
03448	GILSUM	27460	328	14.3	27.4	43.3	9.5	5.5	56469	66771	81	59	284	3.2	5.6	40.9	46.8	3.5	175641
03449	HANCOCK	37331	685	12.3	24.5	35.5	18.4	9.3	65100	81700	89	75	572	1.4	1.9	17.3	58.9	20.5	255882
03450	HARRISVILLE	32343	458	14.0	29.0	39.5	10.7	6.8	55665	65721	80	58	393	1.0	4.3	28.8	53.7	12.2	206176
03451	HINSDALE	19453	1778	23.9	35.3	35.3	5.1	0.5	41017	47763	50	9	1360	15.9	9.9	51.6	21.0	1.5	133696
03452	JAFFREY	26001	2278	19.7	28.1	36.8	8.8	6.6	51402	61368	75	43	1520	4.9	6.1	43.2	37.2	8.7	168800
03455	MARLBOROUGH	25686	1029	18.5	30.2	40.8	7.3	3.2	50882	59715	74	41	812	4.6	4.9	57.4	27.2	5.9	146719
03456	MARLOW	22163	315	12.7	35.6	45.1	5.4	1.3	50978	60087	74	42	267	6.0	10.1	52.8	31.1	0.0	142287
03457	NELSON	31066	225	20.0	26.2	36.0	11.6	6.2	53608	63684	78	51	193	2.6	7.3	42.5	40.9	6.7	170109
03458	PETERBOROUGH	30590	2615	16.8	25.4	34.8	15.0	8.1	56974	72786	82	61	1800	0.0	1.0	31.7	58.1	9.2	206542
03461	RINDGE	24705	1755	10.8	29.1	41.9	11.5	6.7	57808	68042	82	63	1507	5.3	3.5	38.4	48.3	4.5	179167
03462	SPOFFORD	32540	618	16.8	26.9	31.7	16.2	8.4	56573	70068	81	60	508	0.0	3.7	28.9	50.6	16.7	215657
03464	STODDARD	23259	394	23.9	31.5	33.0	9.4	2.3	44116	52291	59	15	340	1.5	3.2	42.1	42.7	10.6	182639
03465	TROY	21331	843	22.8	28.9	39.5	6.6	2.1	48635	57403	70	32	656	6.0	8.1	56.3	28.2	1.5	143333
03466	WEST CHESTERFIELD	31321	522	15.7	23.2	40.6	12.5	8.1	63731	75570	88	73	465	1.1	4.3	29.3	55.5	9.9	208663
03467	WESTMORELAND	30300	626	10.4	24.0	42.5	14.7	8.5	65542	78095	89	75	551	0.5	0.2	25.4	60.6	13.3	219190
03470	WINCHESTER	20053	1906	23.8	30.9	36.0	7.1	2.3	46579	53864	65	27	1513	8.7	7.1	50.3	29.2	4.8	143565
03561	LITTLETON	23141	2897	31.9	26.8	31.0	6.1	4.2	40647	48412	48	8	1845	6.9	15.6	43.5	29.2	4.8	143125
03570	BERLIN	18250	4629	38.9	31.1	25.2	3.9	0.8	32724	36447	20	1	2862	12.4	36.4	46.9	3.4	1.0	91018
03574	BETHLEHEM	25364	1025	28.3	31.0	27.1	8.9	4.7	41103	50359	50	10	729	6.3	11.9	52.0	25.5	4.3	138629
03576	COLEBROOK	20744	1888	33.9	32.0	26.5	5.5	2.1	36639	41799	34	3	1412	11.8	18.5	48.2	19.5	2.1	118300
03579	ERROL	25845	167	28.7	31.7	30.5	4.8	4.2	38105	44656	40	3	135	11.1	17.8	47.4	18.5	5.2	126563
03580	FRANCONIA	28968	517	22.1	29.8	32.7	10.4	5.0	48596	59197	69	31	410	0.7	3.2	29.5	47.3	19.3	220455
03581	GORHAM	20925	1503	31.8	31.9	29.9	4.9	1.5	38377	44023	41	4	1110	12.0	19.8	48.2	19.7	0.3	115775
03582	GROVETON	16746	1113	35.5	36.0	25.0	2.5	1.0	34824	38791	27	2	826	17.8	28.1	44.9	8.4	0.9	95667
03583	JEFFERSON	23444	397	23.2	32.2	35.8	5.5	3.3	46763	53971	66	27	330	5.8	13.0	46.1	26.7	8.5	140254
03584	LANCASTER	22598	1503	25.9	33.9	26.5	11.6	2.2	45410	51618	62	22	1085	10.1	16.2	49.4	20.0	4.3	117552
03585	LISBON	23876	1352	22.5	33.0	34.5	6.5	3.6	45536	53432	63	24	1039	2.8	14.0	46.5	29.9	6.8	145116
03588	MILAN	24557	690	20.4	34.1	37.0	5.9	2.6	45520	52767	63	24	604	7.6	16.2	55.0	20.2	1.0	125647
03590	NORTH STRATFORD	18129	426	33.3	36.6	27.2	2.1	0.7	36252	40785	33	2	331	17.2	24.2	44.7	13.6	0.3	100605
03592	PITTSBURG	21440	534	24.9	33.9	35.0	5.4	0.8	43556	50236	57	14	450	5.6	17.1	51.6	22.0	3.8	129598
03593	RANDOLPH	26141	110	18.2	32.7	37.3	9.1	2.7	49091	54534	70	33	90	1.1	4.4	46.7	41.1	6.7	167857
03598	WHITEFIELD	21234	1511	27.9	33.1	30.6	6.5	2.0	40603	46746	48	8	1139	9.1	16.9	47.8	22.7	3.5	127770
03602	ALSTEAD	25440	1135	18.6	33.0	35.5	8.4	4.5	48747	57655	70	32	927	6.6	8.9	46.9	31.4	6.3	147569
03603	CHARLESTOWN	22373	2116	23.4	34.0	34.6	6.3	1.8	43183	50307	56	13	1687	19.0	14.7	50.8	14.5	1.0	112028
03605	LEMPSTER	23666	568	19.9	39.3	33.3	3.9	3.7	45308	52362	62	22	494	6.3	12.4	54.1	25.3	2.0	138480
03607	SOUTH ACWORTH	23432	163	24.5	35.0	30.7	5.5	4.3	43320	51247	57	14	134	5.2	8.2	50.8	32.1	3.7	147414
03608	WALPOLE	29286	1185	18.1	28.2	36.3	11.1	6.4	53498	63855	78	50	887	1.7	2.9	33.3	44.5	17.6	197584
03609	NORTH WALPOLE	24807	259	20.9	31.3	36.7	5.8	5.4	48037	57781	68	29	163	4.3	11.0	68.7	14.1	1.8	124107
03740	BATH	24135	383	19.6	30.8	36.8	8.9	3.9	49709	58523	71	36	324	4.6	10.5	40.4	37.4	7.1	160938
03741	CANAAN	24276	1533	20.7	31.9	35.5	9.4	2.5	48138	56787	69	29	1275	6.9	11.0	43.8	35.9	2.4	148393
03743	CLAREMONT	24106	6284	30.4	31.6	29.5	5.8	2.8	39560	45908	45	7	3715	6.0	10.7	64.6	17.2	1.6	123475
03745	CORNISH	28210	651	18.0	19.1	42.9	12.9	7.2	61387	73342	86	68	566	2.5	5.3	41.2	42.4	8.7	177586
03748	ENFIELD	28914	2323	17.0	25.7	44.6	9.0	3.8	54652	65157	79	53	1715	6.6	5.1	42.3	43.5	2.5	165293
03750	ETNA	56736	411	4.6	12.4	20.7	28.7	33.6	119739	158084	99	100	368	0.0	0.0	2.2	47.8	50.0	400000
03752	GOSHEN	25296	287	20.6	30.3	34.8	9.4	4.9	49338	58644	71	34	256	2.3	11.3	47.7	35.6	3.1	151613
03753	GRANTHAM	39132	1107	8.8	19.4	43.4	16.9	11.6	70793	86925	92	83	967	0.2	3.6	19.8	57.5	18.9	242474
03755	HANOVER	38030	2720	13.6	14.0	27.3	19.9	25.3	87580	125107	97	96	1762	0.0	0.7	3.7	47.3	48.3	392500
03765	HAVERHILL	24698	162	22.2	32.7	35.2	7.4	2.5	45000	51100	61	21	134	6.7	17.9	49.3	23.1	3.0	125000
03766	LEBANON	27398	4200	22.5	28.0	34.7	10.1	4.7	49568	60701	71	35	2162	6.1	7.3	32.7	50.9	3.1	182880
03768	LYME	47024	877	11.2	25.0	30.7	16.4	16.8	67379	93784	90	78	711	1.7	3.0	18.7	45.0	31.7	284420
03770	MERIDEN	34459	81	6.2	28.4	39.5	13.6	12.4	66574	80908	89	77	71	1.4	1.4	40.9	43.7	12.7	193750
03771	MONROE	24980	345	16.8	33.6	40.0	6.1	3.5	49651	58390	71	35	303	1.0	7.9	51.8	35.6	3.6	159069
03773	NEWPORT	21453	3115	24.9	32.2	33.2	7.6	2.0	43992	51543	59	15	2280	7.7	12.5	57.8	21.4	0.7	128387
03774	NORTH HAVERHILL	19864	747	27.2	32.5	32.0	6.6	1.7	41954	48451	53	13	545	9.2	14.1	53.2	20.9	2.6	127104
03777	ORFORD	30408	402	17.2	32.1	36.6	8.7	5.5	50606	61253	73	41	332	1.8	10.5	39.2	38.0	10.5	171951
03779	PIERMONT	29112	326	16.9	32.5	36.2	8.9	5.5	50484	61120	73	40	269	2.2	10.4	38.3	38.3	10.8	173106
03780	PIKE	19782	263	22.8	32.7	35.4	6.8	2.3	44864	51639	61	20	217	6.0	18.0	49.8	23.0	3.2	125481
03781	PLAINFIELD	32745	904	12.7	22.9	40.9	13.1	10.4	63880	77617	88	73	788	3.2	3.1	34.1	49.9	9.8	196839
03782	SUNAPEE	38662	1412	14.7	25.7	37.9	12.4	9.3	56763	68775	81	60	1127	3.6	3.6	30.7	43.1	19.0	210253
03784	WEST LEBANON	37559	1856	20.1	29.9	32.9	10.8	6.3	50039	61961	72	38	896	1.7	3.9	31.3	60.8	2.3	193671
03785	WOODSVILLE	20975	1053	29.0	31.9	31.1	6.5	1.6	41066	47364	50	10	720	10.3	11.1	54.6	21.5	2.5	130435
03801	PORTSMOUTH	34661	10557	20.5	23.8	35.0	13.4	7.3	56529	74652	81	59	5492	3.1	1.0	15.7	60.5	19.7	248888
03809	ALTON	31849	1691	20.5	29.0	34.1	9.9	6.5	50448	60747	73	40	1379	2.2	6.0	34.2	44.2	13.5	200539
03810	ALTON BAY	29340	91	23.1	30.8	28.6	11.0	6.6	47875	56872	68	28	73	0.0	2.7	37.0	43.8	16.4	208929
03811	ATKINSON	37292	2654	9.4	15.3	35.5	23.0	16.9	82760	103259	96	94	2357	0.5	0.0	3.8	75.3	20.5	294167
03812	BARTLETT	26406	806	24.4	27.7	34.9	8.6	4.5	48024	56489	68	29	615	1.8	4.6	36.3	39.5	17.9	196875
03813	CENTER CONWAY	23154	1250	24.2	32.6	30.2	8.6	4.3	45051	52746	61	21	1002	10.5	10.7	43.9	28.0	6.9	143567
03814	CENTER OSSIPEE	21652	1530	29.3	35.1	26.8	5.7	3.1	39235	45561	44	5	1217	15.2	14.1	43.0	21.7	6.0	133953
03815	CENTER STRAFFORD	24749	212	10.4	23.6	47.2	14.2	4.7	63462	75704	87	72	188	0.5	3.7	33.0	58.5	4.3	198077
03816	CENTER TUFTONBORO	30484	579	16.9	28.8	36.6	10.4	7.3	53024	64855	77	47	492	3.9	3.3	23.4	49.6	19.9	237975
03817	CHOCORUA	24547	132	28.8	31.1	30.3	6.1	3.8	41527	47998	51	11	104	10.6	7.7	43.3	32.7	5.8	148529
03818	CONWAY	22100	1037	30.5	35.2	26.6	4.2	3.5	39532	46274	44	6	745	7.1	9.5	49.0	30.7	3.6	145608
03819	DANVILLE	26697	1542	7.8	19.5	52.5	17.3	2.9	66406	78127	89	76	1399	8.9	12.7	10.4	64.1	3.9	217255
03820	DOVER	29372	13046	19.1	28.4	34.7	12.3	5.7	52531	64177	76	46	6606	3.4	2.3	31.6	55.9	6.8	197742
03824	DURHAM	25549	4833	21.9	16.9	32.6	16.7	12.0	62250	75996	86	70	2906	4.2	0.7	7.4	72.3	15.5	271184
03825	BARRINGTON	24625	2948	10.8	28.0	43.9	14.5	2.8	59644	68954	84	66	2504	10.0	4.8	27.0	55.2	3.0	190741
03826	EAST HAMPSTEAD	36918	1153	12.7	17.8	39.2	17.9	12.5	73485	89975	93	86	879	2.5	2.5	15.7	67.1	12.2	250503
03827	EAST KINGSTON	35073	995	7.7	18.3	38.6	22.5	12.9	76458	93556	94	89	909	2.3	0.8	10.6	61.1	25.3	296429
03830	EAST WAKEFIELD	26427	547	20.7	31.1	33.1	9.3	5.9	48600	58025	69	31	457	0.9	5.5	46.0	39.4	8.3	170139
03833	EXETER	33012	7946	16.0	21.5	37.3	15.9	9.3	62010	77522	86	69	5867	9.3	6.6	14.8	54.7	14.6	236114
03835	FARMINGTON	20551	2386	25.9	29.4	32.9	9.8	2.0	46454	54467	65	26	1686	8.9	10.7	57.0	21.0	2.4	130120
03836	FREEDOM	28391	742	23.2	31.3	32.1	7.7	5.8	46065	54414	64	25	634	3.2	3.8	26.8	51.6	14.7	214141
03837	GILMANTON IRON WORKS	28367	453	17.4	26.9	34.9	10.2	10.6	55066	68083	80	56	398	0.0	3.8	44.0	42.7	9.6	180000
03838	GLEN	22103	30	23.3	33.3	30.0	10.0	3.3	45000	56262	61	21	23	0.0	0.0	30.4	47.8	21.7	241667
03839	ROCHESTER	24492	1435	15.1	32.3	39.3	10.8	2.5	52078	61470	76	44	1013	10.1	4.4	49.5	34.0	2.1	148315
03840	GREENLAND	39211	1316	9.2	14.0	43.5	17.8	15.6	76431	95645	94	88	1078	1.3	0.0	8.4	56.9	33.5	310101
03841	HAMPSTEAD	37432	2164	9.6	16.4	34.7	24.1	15.3	82959	105996	96	95	1898	2.6	3.6	12.1	68.0	13.7	277193
03842	HAMPTON	37867	6962	15.3	20.3	36.7	17.0	10.9	66087	83621	89	76	4774	1.1	2.2	8.8	67.2	20.7	271871
	NEW HAMPSHIRE	29464		17.9	24.8	36.4	13.6	7.4	57516	70005				4.4	5.2	30.9	50.1	9.4	196454
	UNITED STATES	25866		24.7	27.1	30.8	10.9	6.5	48124	56710				10.9	15.0	33.7	30.1	10.4	145905

SPENDING POTENTIAL INDICES NEW HAMPSHIRE
03441-03842 D

ZIP CODE #	POST OFFICE NAME	FINANCIAL SERVICES: Auto Loan	Home Loan	Invest-ments	Retire-ment Plans	THE HOME: Home Improvements: Home Repair	Lawn & Garden	Furnishings: Comput-ers & Hard-ware	Major Appli-ances	TV, Radio, Sound Equip-ment	Furni-ture	ENTERTAINMENT: Dine out/Carry out	Sports Equip-ment	Fees & Tickets	Toys & Games	Travel	Cable TV	PERSONAL: Apparel & Services	Auto Repairs	Health Insur-ance	Pets & Supplies
03441	ASHUELOT	77	67	53	66	69	76	67	72	70	67	85	82	64	83	66	70	81	71	75	85
03442	BENNINGTON	83	91	91	93	88	87	87	86	81	87	102	102	87	103	85	76	101	85	75	94
03443	CHESTERFIELD	97	121	128	121	119	117	108	107	100	107	125	126	115	134	110	97	125	103	96	119
03444	DUBLIN	117	145	154	146	143	141	130	129	120	129	151	151	138	161	133	117	151	125	116	143
03445	SULLIVAN	133	118	90	112	125	134	109	121	116	109	141	144	107	144	112	119	134	118	131	156
03446	SWANZEY	88	90	84	87	91	96	85	88	85	84	105	102	86	109	86	85	102	86	88	103
03447	FITZWILLIAM	114	97	71	90	105	115	90	103	98	90	118	122	85	119	94	102	111	101	116	136
03448	GILSUM	107	96	75	91	101	109	89	98	94	89	115	117	88	117	92	97	109	96	106	126
03449	HANCOCK	117	141	159	140	140	147	129	130	122	130	154	147	138	156	135	122	152	126	124	142
03450	HARRISVILLE	127	100	69	91	113	126	94	114	107	94	127	133	85	125	101	114	118	112	134	155
03451	HINSDALE	77	67	51	64	69	75	65	71	68	66	83	82	62	80	65	69	79	70	75	86
03452	JAFFREY	102	89	69	87	93	103	88	95	93	87	113	110	85	113	88	95	106	93	103	116
03455	MARLBOROUGH	90	86	74	81	89	97	81	87	86	80	105	101	82	110	84	88	100	85	94	106
03456	MARLOW	89	79	60	75	84	90	73	81	78	73	95	97	72	97	75	80	90	79	88	105
03457	NELSON	129	113	85	106	120	129	104	117	112	104	135	139	101	138	108	115	128	114	128	152
03458	PETERBOROUGH	105	103	103	105	105	113	104	106	105	103	129	123	104	130	104	104	124	105	106	120
03461	RINDGE	115	110	100	108	114	120	104	111	107	104	131	132	104	134	106	107	126	109	113	136
03462	SPOFFORD	122	119	106	114	125	132	109	119	112	108	136	140	107	140	114	114	131	116	125	148
03464	STODDARD	91	71	49	64	80	90	67	81	76	66	90	95	60	89	72	81	84	80	96	111
03465	TROY	89	78	60	75	82	90	75	82	79	74	96	96	73	97	76	81	91	80	89	102
03466	WEST CHESTERFIELD	106	132	140	132	129	128	118	117	109	117	137	137	125	146	120	106	137	113	105	130
03467	WESTMORELAND	108	134	142	134	132	130	120	119	111	119	140	140	127	149	123	108	139	115	107	132
03470	WINCHESTER	84	75	59	73	78	85	72	78	76	72	92	91	70	92	73	77	87	77	83	96
03561	LITTLETON	82	71	57	69	74	82	72	77	76	70	92	89	68	91	72	77	87	76	83	93
03570	BERLIN	55	53	53	51	55	62	55	56	58	53	71	62	55	73	56	60	68	55	62	63
03574	BETHLEHEM	82	82	85	83	83	89	82	83	82	81	102	98	82	103	82	82	98	83	83	95
03576	COLEBROOK	73	64	52	61	68	77	63	69	68	62	82	79	60	83	65	71	77	68	77	86
03579	ERROL	91	71	49	64	80	90	67	81	76	67	90	95	60	89	72	81	84	80	96	111
03580	FRANCONIA	112	87	57	79	98	110	82	99	93	81	110	117	73	109	87	99	102	98	118	136
03581	GORHAM	76	60	40	57	65	74	61	69	67	59	80	80	55	78	61	70	74	68	80	88
03582	GROVETON	58	56	51	53	59	65	54	57	57	53	70	66	55	74	56	60	67	56	63	69
03583	JEFFERSON	91	80	61	76	85	92	74	83	79	74	96	98	72	98	77	81	91	81	90	107
03584	LANCASTER	88	73	54	71	78	88	74	81	80	72	96	93	70	95	74	83	90	80	91	100
03585	LISBON	96	74	48	69	82	92	72	84	81	72	97	99	66	95	74	85	90	83	97	111
03588	MILAN	96	83	62	78	89	96	77	87	83	77	100	103	74	102	80	86	95	85	96	113
03590	NORTH STRATFORD	71	56	38	50	63	70	53	63	59	52	70	74	47	70	56	64	66	62	75	87
03592	PITTSBURG	81	64	43	58	72	81	60	72	68	60	81	85	54	80	64	73	75	71	86	99
03593	RANDOLPH	97	76	52	69	86	97	72	87	81	71	97	102	64	95	77	87	90	85	103	119
03598	WHITEFIELD	84	65	42	60	71	81	65	75	73	64	87	86	59	84	66	77	81	74	87	96
03602	ALSTEAD	96	92	79	89	94	98	86	91	87	86	108	108	85	109	87	87	104	90	93	111
03603	CHARLESTOWN	87	78	60	74	81	86	73	80	76	74	93	94	70	92	74	77	89	79	84	100
03605	LEMPSTER	95	82	61	77	88	96	76	86	82	76	99	102	73	101	79	85	94	84	96	113
03607	SOUTH ACWORTH	94	74	51	67	83	93	70	84	79	69	93	98	63	92	74	84	87	82	98	114
03608	WALPOLE	102	97	87	91	102	112	93	101	98	92	120	116	92	122	97	102	114	99	110	122
03609	NORTH WALPOLE	74	81	85	76	81	90	80	79	82	77	102	88	84	111	82	86	99	77	85	87
03740	BATH	109	76	40	72	89	99	75	93	87	74	102	112	64	100	78	91	93	92	111	130
03741	CANAAN	99	87	67	83	92	100	82	90	87	81	105	107	80	107	84	89	100	88	98	116
03743	CLAREMONT	83	72	61	70	76	85	75	79	80	73	96	90	72	95	75	82	91	79	87	93
03745	CORNISH	94	115	121	115	113	112	103	103	96	102	120	120	109	128	105	93	120	99	93	114
03748	ENFIELD	91	95	99	97	95	99	93	94	91	93	114	110	94	115	93	89	111	93	89	105
03750	ETNA	193	237	262	240	232	238	212	210	197	214	249	240	230	256	218	193	249	203	193	231
03752	GOSHEN	105	93	71	89	99	106	86	96	92	86	112	114	85	114	89	94	106	93	104	124
03753	GRANTHAM	152	121	83	109	135	151	113	135	127	112	151	159	102	150	120	136	141	133	159	184
03755	HANOVER	158	165	248	176	159	172	182	164	179	180	226	199	188	233	178	174	224	172	152	182
03765	HAVERHILL	95	67	35	63	78	87	66	81	76	65	89	98	56	87	68	80	81	80	97	113
03766	LEBANON	80	86	101	89	85	88	87	85	84	87	106	100	89	107	87	81	105	86	78	93
03768	LYME	153	167	185	168	169	177	160	162	155	159	194	189	164	197	164	154	190	161	157	184
03770	MERIDEN	117	145	154	145	142	140	129	129	120	129	151	151	138	161	132	116	150	124	115	142
03771	MONROE	96	85	65	81	90	96	79	87	84	79	102	104	77	104	81	86	97	85	94	113
03773	NEWPORT	80	72	60	69	74	82	71	75	75	70	92	88	70	93	72	77	87	74	81	91
03774	NORTH HAVERHILL	83	60	37	57	68	79	64	73	72	62	85	85	56	81	64	76	78	73	88	94
03777	ORFORD	125	87	46	83	102	114	86	107	99	85	117	129	74	114	89	104	106	105	127	149
03779	PIERMONT	125	87	46	82	102	114	86	106	99	85	116	128	74	114	89	104	106	105	127	148
03780	PIKE	96	67	35	63	78	87	66	82	76	65	89	98	56	87	68	80	81	80	97	114
03781	PLAINFIELD	109	136	144	136	134	132	121	121	112	121	141	142	129	151	124	109	141	117	108	134
03782	SUNAPEE	139	123	101	114	133	146	116	131	124	115	150	153	110	152	122	130	142	129	146	170
03784	WEST LEBANON	118	112	133	121	108	114	122	116	118	123	150	140	119	144	116	111	147	122	104	129
03785	WOODSVILLE	78	59	38	56	65	77	64	71	71	61	84	80	56	80	63	76	77	71	85	88
03801	PORTSMOUTH	93	98	126	103	97	102	103	98	100	102	126	117	105	129	102	98	124	101	92	108
03809	ALTON	130	105	74	97	116	129	99	116	110	98	131	137	91	131	104	116	123	114	134	156
03810	ALTON BAY	115	90	61	81	101	114	85	102	96	84	114	120	76	112	91	103	106	101	121	140
03811	ATKINSON	127	155	170	156	152	151	141	140	131	140	165	164	149	175	144	127	165	136	126	154
03812	BARTLETT	99	77	53	70	87	98	73	88	83	72	98	103	65	97	78	88	91	87	104	120
03813	CENTER CONWAY	94	74	50	68	83	92	71	84	79	70	94	99	63	92	74	83	87	83	97	113
03814	CENTER OSSIPEE	86	67	46	62	74	85	67	78	75	65	89	89	60	87	69	80	82	77	92	101
03815	CENTER STRAFFORD	92	112	118	112	109	108	101	100	93	101	118	118	106	124	102	90	117	97	89	111
03816	CENTER TUFTONBORO	124	92	55	85	105	118	88	108	101	87	119	128	77	117	93	107	109	106	128	149
03817	CHOCORUA	94	73	50	66	83	93	69	83	78	69	93	98	62	92	74	84	86	82	98	114
03818	CONWAY	85	65	43	60	73	82	64	75	72	63	85	88	57	83	67	76	79	75	89	100
03819	DANVILLE	107	121	116	126	115	111	109	108	100	113	127	126	112	127	106	93	125	105	91	118
03820	DOVER	89	91	106	95	90	94	98	93	94	95	118	112	97	118	95	89	116	96	85	102
03824	DURHAM	111	106	120	112	103	109	123	110	117	117	148	136	118	143	114	109	144	117	99	122
03825	BARRINGTON	91	102	104	104	99	98	96	95	90	97	113	113	98	115	95	85	112	94	84	105
03826	EAST HAMPSTEAD	129	160	169	160	157	154	142	142	132	142	166	166	151	176	145	128	166	137	127	157
03827	EAST KINGSTON	127	159	168	159	156	153	141	141	131	141	165	165	150	176	145	127	165	136	126	156
03830	EAST WAKEFIELD	107	84	57	76	95	106	79	95	90	78	106	112	71	105	84	96	99	94	113	130
03833	EXETER	111	122	132	124	121	124	118	117	113	117	141	138	120	144	118	110	139	117	109	130
03835	FARMINGTON	86	74	56	72	78	86	73	80	78	72	94	92	69	92	73	79	88	78	86	98
03836	FREEDOM	101	79	54	72	89	101	75	90	85	74	100	106	67	99	80	91	93	89	107	123
03837	GILMANTON IRON WORKS	127	100	69	91	112	126	94	113	106	93	126	132	85	125	100	113	117	111	133	154
03838	GLEN	92	72	49	65	81	91	68	82	77	67	91	96	61	90	72	82	85	81	97	112
03839	ROCHESTER	86	93	96	95	90	91	91	89	86	91	109	107	92	110	89	82	107	90	80	98
03840	GREENLAND	133	166	176	166	163	161	148	148	137	147	172	173	158	184	151	133	172	142	132	163
03841	HAMPSTEAD	131	163	173	163	160	158	146	145	135	145	169	170	155	181	149	131	169	140	130	160
03842	HAMPTON	122	124	128	122	128	135	118	124	119	118	147	145	118	149	122	120	143	123	125	147
	NEW HAMPSHIRE	106	107	107	107	108	113	105	106	104	104	129	125	105	130	105	103	125	106	105	123
	UNITED STATES	100	100	100	100	100	100	100	100	100	100	100	100	100	100	100	100	100	100	100	100

# ZIP CODE POST OFFICE NAME	COUNTY FIPS CODE	POPULATION 2000	2004	2009	2000-2004 ANNUAL RATE % Rate	State Centile	HOUSEHOLDS 2000	2004	2009	% Annual Rate 2000-2004	2004 Average HH Size	FAMILIES 2000	2004	% Annual Rate 2000-2004
03844 HAMPTON FALLS	015	1880	2010	2175	1.6	49	704	765	839	2.0	2.63	546	591	1.9
03845 INTERVALE	003	1418	1524	1684	1.7	56	637	699	787	2.2	2.17	382	417	2.1
03846 JACKSON	003	850	908	1000	1.6	47	384	418	468	2.0	2.16	244	264	1.9
03848 KINGSTON	015	5912	6318	6838	1.6	47	2144	2327	2550	2.0	2.71	1650	1784	1.9
03849 MADISON	003	1692	1815	2004	1.7	54	656	712	798	2.0	2.55	470	509	1.9
03851 MILTON	017	3325	3653	4032	2.2	80	1238	1387	1557	2.7	2.63	923	1030	2.6
03852 MILTON MILLS	017	525	578	639	2.3	83	195	220	247	2.9	2.63	143	160	2.7
03853 MIRROR LAKE	003	623	678	753	2.0	71	290	324	368	2.6	2.09	207	231	2.6
03854 NEW CASTLE	015	1007	1046	1115	0.9	17	442	461	495	1.0	2.25	313	324	0.8
03855 NEW DURHAM	017	2386	2807	3210	3.9	97	879	1057	1232	4.4	2.65	671	804	4.4
03856 NEWFIELDS	015	1560	1701	1860	2.1	75	521	571	628	2.2	2.98	435	475	2.1
03857 NEWMARKET	015	8062	8677	9423	1.7	59	3390	3701	4069	2.1	2.34	1958	2122	1.9
03858 NEWTON	015	4209	4546	4948	1.8	63	1484	1623	1786	2.1	2.80	1146	1249	2.1
03860 NORTH CONWAY	003	4174	4372	4770	1.1	25	1843	1964	2182	1.5	2.16	1044	1107	1.4
03862 NORTH HAMPTON	015	4188	4511	4904	1.8	62	1648	1799	1979	2.1	2.51	1217	1322	2.0
03864 OSSIPEE	003	1716	1870	2075	2.0	74	640	715	813	2.6	2.46	457	509	2.6
03865 PLAISTOW	015	7747	8094	8657	1.0	22	2871	3047	3302	1.4	2.65	2149	2270	1.3
03867 ROCHESTER	017	21806	23053	25027	1.3	38	8802	9495	10494	1.8	2.40	5822	6243	1.7
03868 ROCHESTER	017	4918	5166	5605	1.2	28	1950	2094	2315	1.7	2.46	1372	1465	1.6
03869 ROLLINSFORD	017	2482	2561	2736	0.7	13	965	1018	1107	1.3	2.52	672	706	1.2
03870 RYE	015	5189	5530	5973	1.5	45	2179	2354	2575	1.8	2.32	1464	1572	1.5
03872 SANBORNVILLE	003	3261	3664	4148	2.8	93	1278	1463	1685	3.2	2.50	930	1061	3.2
03873 SANDOWN	015	5099	5532	6033	1.9	68	1682	1850	2041	2.3	2.97	1371	1502	2.2
03874 SEABROOK	015	8036	9022	10024	2.8	92	3475	3926	4397	2.9	2.30	2188	2454	2.7
03875 SILVER LAKE	003	488	516	565	1.3	38	204	219	244	1.7	2.35	144	154	1.6
03878 SOMERSWORTH	017	11328	12132	13238	1.6	51	4620	5048	5607	2.1	2.40	3021	3281	2.0
03882 EFFINGHAM	003	250	264	288	1.3	36	106	115	129	1.9	2.16	73	79	1.9
03883 SOUTH TAMWORTH	003	137	143	155	1.0	21	52	55	61	1.3	2.60	34	36	1.4
03884 STRAFFORD	017	1784	2018	2262	2.9	94	638	737	840	3.5	2.74	509	586	3.4
03885 STRATHAM	015	6403	6963	7607	2.0	70	2320	2538	2796	2.1	2.74	1755	1911	2.0
03886 TAMWORTH	003	1774	1862	2031	1.2	27	755	807	896	1.6	2.30	487	518	1.5
03887 UNION	017	1830	1967	2153	1.7	56	656	720	802	2.2	2.73	492	537	2.1
03890 WEST OSSIPEE	003	368	394	434	1.6	50	160	174	196	2.0	2.26	111	120	1.9
03894 WOLFEBORO	003	6334	7038	7908	2.5	88	2678	3020	3449	2.9	2.30	1801	2022	2.8
NEW HAMPSHIRE					1.5					1.9	2.49			1.8
UNITED STATES					1.2					1.3	2.58			1.1

#	ZIP CODE POST OFFICE NAME	RACE (%) White		Black		Asian/Pacific		% Hispanic Origin		2004 AGE DISTRIBUTION (%) 0-4	5-9	10-14	15-19	20-24	25-44	45-64	65-84	85+	18+	MEDIAN AGE 2004	% 2004 Males	% 2004 Females
		2000	2004	2000	2004	2000	2004	2000	2004													
03844	HAMPTON FALLS	98.5	98.3	0.1	0.1	0.7	1.0	0.7	0.8	6.2	7.7	7.8	5.7	3.1	21.0	35.1	12.1	1.3	74.7	44.0	50.2	49.8
03845	INTERVALE	97.9	97.8	0.1	0.1	0.4	0.5	0.4	0.4	4.6	4.8	6.0	6.9	4.9	27.0	31.0	13.6	1.3	80.1	42.6	50.7	49.3
03846	JACKSON	98.6	98.4	0.2	0.2	0.5	0.6	0.1	0.1	4.3	5.1	6.3	5.0	2.8	23.6	33.8	18.0	1.3	80.7	46.9	48.6	51.4
03848	KINGSTON	98.0	97.7	0.3	0.3	0.5	0.6	0.8	1.0	5.8	6.8	7.7	6.7	4.5	29.6	29.9	7.9	1.1	75.6	39.7	49.3	50.7
03849	MADISON	97.7	97.6	0.1	0.1	0.2	0.2	0.7	0.8	4.2	5.8	8.6	7.8	3.4	27.3	31.2	10.4	1.3	76.1	41.4	51.2	48.8
03851	MILTON	97.9	97.9	0.2	0.2	0.2	0.2	0.3	0.4	6.1	6.7	8.1	7.0	5.6	28.5	27.8	9.3	1.0	74.6	38.5	49.7	50.3
03852	MILTON MILLS	97.1	96.9	0.2	0.2	0.8	1.0	0.8	1.0	5.2	6.4	8.1	7.6	4.7	26.1	29.8	11.4	0.7	74.6	40.7	49.5	50.5
03853	MIRROR LAKE	98.7	98.7	0.0	0.0	0.2	0.2	0.3	0.4	4.3	4.4	4.4	4.6	3.5	17.3	36.1	23.2	2.2	83.8	52.0	48.8	51.2
03854	NEW CASTLE	97.8	97.6	0.6	0.7	0.5	0.7	0.5	0.6	3.8	5.1	5.4	5.2	2.5	18.9	32.8	24.1	2.3	82.8	50.8	49.0	51.0
03855	NEW DURHAM	98.2	97.9	0.2	0.3	0.5	0.6	0.5	0.5	6.3	7.2	8.1	6.2	4.5	27.6	29.3	10.1	0.8	74.2	40.1	51.6	48.5
03856	NEWFIELDS	97.9	97.7	0.1	0.1	0.8	1.1	0.5	0.5	9.1	9.8	9.2	5.8	4.0	28.9	25.3	7.1	0.9	68.3	38.1	49.2	50.9
03857	NEWMARKET	94.2	93.3	0.6	0.7	3.0	3.8	1.7	1.9	6.1	5.8	6.2	6.0	8.2	37.4	21.8	7.6	1.0	78.2	33.8	49.5	50.5
03858	NEWTON	97.9	97.8	0.7	0.7	0.1	0.1	1.3	1.5	7.6	7.9	8.2	6.6	4.9	32.0	25.3	6.7	0.8	72.2	36.4	49.5	50.5
03860	NORTH CONWAY	96.8	96.6	0.4	0.4	0.9	1.1	0.5	0.6	4.9	5.2	5.8	6.6	5.6	26.8	27.9	13.8	3.3	79.9	41.9	48.2	51.8
03862	NORTH HAMPTON	98.4	98.2	0.3	0.3	0.6	0.8	0.8	0.9	4.4	6.1	7.1	5.9	3.8	23.3	34.4	13.6	1.4	78.5	44.7	48.5	51.5
03864	OSSIPEE	98.6	98.5	0.1	0.1	0.2	0.3	0.4	0.4	4.7	5.7	7.4	6.8	4.9	23.1	29.7	14.8	2.9	77.9	43.5	49.9	50.1
03865	PLAISTOW	98.3	98.1	0.2	0.2	0.5	0.7	1.3	1.5	6.6	7.0	7.4	6.2	5.3	29.0	27.3	10.1	1.0	75.1	38.8	48.9	51.2
03867	ROCHESTER	97.1	96.7	0.5	0.5	1.0	1.3	0.9	1.0	6.7	6.7	7.1	6.4	5.8	28.8	25.0	11.8	1.8	75.5	38.1	48.5	51.5
03868	ROCHESTER	97.3	97.0	0.6	0.7	0.5	0.6	0.9	1.1	6.9	6.5	6.7	6.9	6.9	28.1	25.3	11.8	1.0	74.6	37.5	49.3	50.7
03869	ROLLINSFORD	97.7	97.4	0.7	0.9	0.6	0.7	0.6	0.7	6.7	6.8	7.3	5.9	5.7	30.0	25.3	11.2	1.1	75.5	37.7	49.8	50.2
03870	RYE	98.7	98.6	0.1	0.1	0.5	0.6	0.6	0.7	4.6	5.3	7.0	6.3	4.1	20.7	32.7	16.3	3.2	78.7	46.1	47.6	52.4
03872	SANBORNVILLE	98.3	98.1	0.1	0.1	0.2	0.2	0.6	0.7	5.8	6.5	6.9	6.3	4.6	25.0	30.2	13.7	1.2	76.8	42.1	49.5	50.5
03873	SANDOWN	98.4	98.3	0.2	0.2	0.2	0.2	0.6	0.7	7.6	8.0	8.9	7.6	5.9	30.8	25.5	4.9	0.8	70.5	35.6	51.0	49.0
03874	SEABROOK	97.5	97.3	0.4	0.4	0.5	0.7	0.9	1.0	5.7	5.6	5.7	5.2	4.7	28.4	27.5	15.8	1.5	79.9	41.8	50.0	50.1
03875	SILVER LAKE	98.4	98.1	0.2	0.2	0.2	0.4	0.6	0.8	4.5	5.8	8.0	6.6	3.7	26.0	32.0	12.0	1.6	77.3	42.8	50.4	49.6
03878	SOMERSWORTH	96.2	95.8	0.6	0.6	1.0	1.3	1.6	1.8	7.3	6.6	7.4	7.0	6.9	30.4	22.7	10.3	1.3	74.6	35.6	48.2	51.8
03882	EFFINGHAM	98.4	97.7	0.4	0.4	0.4	0.4	0.4	0.8	4.6	6.1	8.7	8.7	4.6	26.9	27.7	11.7	1.1	74.6	39.7	52.3	47.7
03883	SOUTH TAMWORTH	98.5	98.6	0.0	0.0	0.0	0.0	0.7	0.7	4.9	6.3	7.0	6.3	4.2	25.9	30.1	13.3	2.1	77.6	42.3	50.4	49.7
03884	STRAFFORD	98.7	98.4	0.1	0.1	0.2	0.3	0.7	0.9	5.6	6.7	8.6	8.0	4.3	27.2	31.4	7.4	0.8	73.6	39.7	50.4	49.7
03885	STRATHAM	98.0	97.6	0.2	0.2	0.8	1.1	0.6	0.7	6.4	7.7	8.8	7.0	3.8	27.1	29.6	8.9	0.7	72.6	40.1	48.8	51.2
03886	TAMWORTH	98.2	98.0	0.2	0.2	0.2	0.3	0.7	0.8	5.6	6.2	7.1	5.8	4.4	26.6	30.1	12.6	1.6	77.6	42.0	51.2	48.8
03887	UNION	98.6	98.5	0.1	0.1	0.4	0.6	0.3	0.4	7.2	7.2	7.3	7.1	6.0	28.9	25.4	10.1	0.9	73.7	38.7	51.9	48.1
03890	WEST OSSIPEE	98.4	98.0	0.3	0.3	0.3	0.5	0.5	0.5	4.6	6.1	7.4	6.1	3.8	24.9	32.2	13.5	1.5	77.7	43.6	51.3	48.7
03894	WOLFEBORO	99.1	98.9	0.2	0.2	0.4	0.5	0.6	0.7	4.5	4.9	6.1	6.0	4.7	19.7	30.9	19.8	3.5	80.6	47.4	47.5	52.5
	NEW HAMPSHIRE	96.0	95.6	0.7	0.8	1.3	1.7	1.7	1.9	6.1	6.4	7.2	7.2	6.6	27.8	26.5	10.6	1.6	76.2	38.4	49.2	50.8
	UNITED STATES	75.1	73.6	12.3	12.5	3.8	4.2	12.5	14.1	6.9	6.7	7.2	7.0	7.3	28.6	23.8	10.8	1.7	75.1	36.0	49.1	50.9

C 03844-03894

#	POST OFFICE NAME	2004 Per Capita Income	2004 HH Income Base	2004 HOUSEHOLD INCOME DISTRIBUTION (%)					MEDIAN HOUSEHOLD INCOME				2004 Home Value Base	2004 HOME VALUE DISTRIBUTION (%)					2004 Median Home Value
				Less than $25,000	$25,000 to $49,999	$50,000 to $99,999	$100,000 to $149,999	$150,000 or More	2004	2009	2004 National Centile	2004 State Centile		Less than $50,000	$50,000 to $89,999	$90,000 to $174,999	$175,000 to $399,999	$400,000 or More	
03844	HAMPTON FALLS	44960	765	7.6	17.4	31.4	21.6	22.1	89015	113177	97	96	687	0.3	0.2	2.6	45.0	52.0	410547
03845	INTERVALE	26181	699	24.6	31.6	32.6	7.2	4.0	45501	53654	63	23	484	2.3	3.9	41.5	43.0	9.3	179741
03846	JACKSON	29740	418	22.7	26.1	34.0	9.6	7.7	50945	61191	74	42	338	2.1	4.4	23.4	44.4	25.7	250000
03848	KINGSTON	36080	2327	9.4	20.5	38.6	21.1	10.4	72015	89257	92	85	2023	0.5	2.5	17.4	70.9	8.7	232972
03849	MADISON	25163	712	20.7	29.1	38.1	8.2	4.1	50186	59122	72	38	1114	11.4	10.0	47.0	30.6	1.0	139238
03851	MILTON	21470	1387	17.0	32.7	41.1	6.5	2.7	50174	57708	72	38	1114	11.4	10.0	47.0	30.6	1.0	139238
03852	MILTON MILLS	21244	220	10.9	39.6	39.6	6.8	3.2	44801	54580	61	19	182	2.8	6.6	53.9	35.7	1.1	156250
03853	MIRROR LAKE	37812	324	16.1	28.7	32.1	13.3	9.9	55020	73499	80	55	277	4.0	2.5	18.8	47.3	27.4	264744
03854	NEW CASTLE	94198	461	5.4	17.1	26.7	15.2	35.6	101810	148039	98	98	409	0.0	0.0	0.2	10.3	89.5	853618
03855	NEW DURHAM	26098	1057	14.7	25.8	43.6	12.0	3.9	58512	68041	83	64	928	2.1	7.3	41.7	44.4	4.5	172573
03856	NEWFIELDS	34838	571	7.4	11.2	44.5	22.9	14.0	82215	99255	96	93	515	0.0	0.0	10.7	57.3	32.0	294063
03857	NEWMARKET	26844	3701	21.0	24.8	39.4	10.7	4.1	53538	65062	78	50	1917	4.9	4.1	29.3	55.4	6.4	198392
03858	NEWTON	27031	1623	10.7	20.3	45.1	19.8	4.1	69707	83605	91	81	1400	0.6	2.9	11.4	81.9	3.1	229406
03860	NORTH CONWAY	25094	1964	33.2	29.5	24.5	8.0	4.7	38114	45926	40	4	1250	11.7	6.5	37.2	37.9	6.7	162862
03862	NORTH HAMPTON	43469	1799	10.1	17.3	36.1	21.4	15.1	76903	99259	94	90	1565	3.1	9.8	10.0	44.2	32.8	287950
03864	OSSIPEE	21004	715	26.4	34.8	29.2	7.1	2.4	39393	46120	44	6	563	7.8	13.3	40.9	29.7	8.4	146029
03865	PLAISTOW	30271	3047	10.9	21.3	41.3	18.7	7.8	72618	86211	92	85	2408	0.0	1.5	17.8	70.3	10.5	231567
03867	ROCHESTER	22870	9495	24.4	30.9	33.6	8.1	3.0	46026	53640	64	25	6390	13.2	7.8	48.0	29.4	1.6	139722
03868	ROCHESTER	21565	2094	21.4	35.5	33.9	7.2	2.1	44595	51650	60	18	1517	18.8	15.6	50.3	15.0	0.3	115263
03869	ROLLINSFORD	29550	1018	18.1	26.0	39.9	9.6	6.4	55236	65772	80	57	708	0.9	0.7	34.2	55.1	9.2	194129
03870	RYE	48100	2354	14.5	15.9	33.5	15.7	20.4	74541	96552	93	87	1804	2.8	0.6	4.1	31.3	61.3	487179
03872	SANBORNVILLE	26838	1463	21.5	27.3	35.5	8.8	7.0	50958	60965	74	42	1235	0.5	4.1	43.6	44.1	7.7	178318
03873	SANDOWN	32423	1850	8.7	16.8	42.8	22.4	9.4	78235	90651	94	91	1644	0.5	0.5	24.6	70.7	3.7	215789
03874	SEABROOK	25195	3926	20.9	29.2	36.9	10.2	2.7	49876	60980	72	37	2654	4.3	15.3	21.3	46.6	12.4	206563
03875	SILVER LAKE	26263	219	21.5	29.2	36.5	7.8	5.0	49407	57762	71	34	179	3.4	6.2	40.2	41.3	8.9	175500
03878	SOMERSWORTH	22699	5048	22.2	29.9	38.5	7.9	1.5	48371	55821	69	30	2906	12.3	7.4	49.6	30.4	0.3	144086
03882	EFFINGHAM	23526	115	26.1	37.4	26.1	7.8	2.6	41115	47089	50	11	93	1.1	16.1	52.7	28.0	2.2	142188
03883	SOUTH TAMWORTH	18351	55	32.7	30.9	27.3	7.3	1.8	39297	42978	44	5	41	7.3	7.3	51.2	29.3	4.9	139583
03884	STRAFFORD	29687	737	7.7	21.0	45.9	20.0	5.4	68604	80459	91	80	641	1.9	1.7	30.1	60.4	5.9	204441
03885	STRATHAM	41068	2538	7.5	14.1	34.7	25.2	18.5	89413	111764	97	97	2281	0.0	0.0	10.7	63.0	26.3	294987
03886	TAMWORTH	22751	807	31.4	31.7	27.5	6.1	3.4	39634	46330	45	7	625	9.4	8.0	44.0	31.8	6.7	147552
03887	UNION	21976	720	16.3	35.1	37.5	7.4	3.8	49085	57759	70	33	633	2.4	8.4	62.9	25.6	0.8	139674
03890	WEST OSSIPEE	26474	174	25.3	31.0	32.2	6.3	5.2	44446	53252	60	17	143	6.3	7.7	40.6	35.0	10.5	165441
03894	WOLFEBORO	34017	3020	22.4	25.4	31.4	11.2	9.6	52117	66613	76	45	2376	0.9	1.7	26.7	51.0	19.7	234578
	NEW HAMPSHIRE	29464		17.9	24.8	36.4	13.6	7.4	57516	70005				4.4	5.2	30.9	50.1	9.4	196454
	UNITED STATES	25866		24.7	27.1	30.8	10.9	6.5	48124	56710				10.9	15.0	33.7	30.1	10.4	145905

#	POST OFFICE NAME	FINANCIAL SERVICES				THE HOME						ENTERTAINMENT						PERSONAL			
						Home Improvements		Furnishings													
		Auto Loan	Home Loan	Invest-ments	Retire-ment Plans	Home Repair	Lawn & Garden	Comput-ers & Hard-ware	Major Appli-ances	TV, Radio, Sound Equip-ment	Furni-ture	Dine out/ Carry out	Sports Equip-ment	Fees & Tickets	Toys & Games	Travel	Cable TV	Apparel & Services	Auto Repairs	Health Insur-ance	Pets & Supplies
03844	HAMPTON FALLS	153	191	203	191	187	185	170	170	158	169	198	199	181	211	174	153	198	163	152	187
03845	INTERVALE	97	76	52	68	85	96	71	86	81	71	96	101	64	95	76	86	89	85	102	118
03846	JACKSON	109	86	58	77	96	108	81	97	91	80	108	114	72	107	86	98	101	96	115	133
03848	KINGSTON	128	155	164	155	152	151	141	140	132	141	166	164	148	175	143	127	165	136	126	154
03849	MADISON	109	85	58	77	96	108	80	97	91	80	108	113	72	106	86	97	100	95	115	133
03851	MILTON	91	81	61	77	85	91	75	83	79	75	96	98	73	98	77	81	92	80	89	107
03852	MILTON MILLS	89	80	61	76	84	90	74	82	78	74	95	97	72	97	76	80	90	79	88	105
03853	MIRROR LAKE	135	105	69	95	118	133	99	120	113	98	133	141	88	131	105	120	123	118	142	164
03854	NEW CASTLE	258	348	477	341	339	366	303	300	282	310	357	338	344	376	323	285	363	288	279	326
03855	NEW DURHAM	105	100	88	98	103	108	95	102	96	95	118	120	92	118	96	96	114	101	102	123
03856	NEWFIELDS	149	168	162	175	160	154	152	150	139	158	177	176	156	177	148	129	175	146	127	164
03857	NEWMARKET	90	82	95	90	79	83	92	87	89	93	113	106	89	107	86	83	110	92	78	97
03858	NEWTON	104	119	120	121	114	113	110	109	103	112	130	128	113	132	109	97	123	107	96	119
03860	NORTH CONWAY	86	72	62	69	76	85	73	80	78	72	95	94	68	93	74	80	90	81	87	101
03862	NORTH HAMPTON	138	173	199	171	169	173	156	155	146	156	184	178	168	196	161	144	185	150	142	169
03864	OSSIPEE	85	70	51	67	76	85	69	78	76	68	91	90	64	90	71	79	85	77	88	99
03865	PLAISTOW	105	125	133	125	122	123	116	115	109	115	137	134	121	144	117	105	136	112	104	126
03867	ROCHESTER	83	76	66	74	78	85	76	79	78	74	96	93	74	97	76	79	92	79	83	95
03868	ROCHESTER	82	74	60	73	75	82	73	78	75	73	93	90	70	90	73	75	88	77	80	91
03869	ROLLINSFORD	105	103	103	103	105	110	105	105	105	102	130	126	104	133	104	102	126	106	104	122
03870	RYE	154	166	181	165	168	182	157	163	154	160	193	180	162	184	163	155	187	160	164	179
03872	SANBORNVILLE	111	92	66	85	101	111	86	100	95	86	114	118	80	114	90	100	107	98	114	134
03873	SANDOWN	134	157	156	161	150	146	141	140	129	144	164	163	146	168	139	122	163	135	121	153
03874	SEABROOK	89	78	67	76	81	89	79	84	83	78	101	99	75	100	79	83	96	84	89	102
03875	SILVER LAKE	105	82	56	74	93	104	78	93	88	77	104	109	69	103	83	94	97	92	110	128
03878	SOMERSWORTH	76	75	77	75	75	80	77	77	77	76	96	90	76	96	76	76	93	78	76	86
03882	EFFINGHAM	88	69	47	62	78	88	65	79	74	65	87	92	58	86	70	79	81	77	93	107
03883	SOUTH TAMWORTH	81	63	43	57	71	80	60	72	68	59	80	84	54	79	64	72	75	71	85	99
03884	STRAFFORD	106	131	139	131	129	127	117	117	108	117	136	137	124	145	120	105	136	112	104	129
03885	STRATHAM	154	184	190	191	177	175	164	161	149	168	190	187	175	195	163	142	190	156	140	177
03886	TAMWORTH	89	70	48	63	79	88	66	79	74	65	88	93	59	87	70	80	82	78	94	108
03887	UNION	96	86	65	81	90	97	79	88	84	79	102	104	78	104	81	86	97	85	95	113
03890	WEST OSSIPEE	102	80	54	72	90	101	75	90	85	74	101	106	67	99	80	91	94	89	107	124
03894	WOLFEBORO	123	107	89	100	115	132	103	117	112	103	135	129	98	129	109	118	127	115	134	145
	NEW HAMPSHIRE	106	107	107	107	108	113	105	106	104	104	129	125	105	130	105	103	125	106	105	123
	UNITED STATES	100	100	100	100	100	100	100	100	100	100	100	100	100	100	100	100	100	100	100	100

POPULATION CHANGE

#	POST OFFICE NAME	COUNTY FIPS CODE	POPULATION 2000	2004	2009	2000-2004 ANNUAL RATE % Rate	State Centile	HOUSEHOLDS 2000	2004	2009	% Annual Rate 2000-2004	2004 Average HH Size	FAMILIES 2000	2004	% Annual Rate 2000-2004
07001	AVENEL	023	16650	17071	17607	0.6	50	4849	4948	5108	0.5	2.79	3537	3630	0.6
07002	BAYONNE	017	61842	60175	59530	-0.6	1	25545	24899	24644	-0.6	2.41	16022	15749	-0.4
07003	BLOOMFIELD	013	47663	47866	48218	0.1	27	19012	19188	19443	0.2	2.47	12042	12254	0.4
07004	FAIRFIELD	013	6993	7206	7324	0.7	56	2276	2380	2443	1.1	2.99	1965	2060	1.1
07005	BOONTON	027	15971	16392	17159	0.6	50	5814	5956	6229	0.6	2.69	4191	4321	0.7
07006	CALDWELL	013	26455	26596	26793	0.1	28	9471	9624	9779	0.4	2.58	6841	7006	0.6
07008	CARTERET	023	20814	21037	21618	0.3	34	7073	7153	7349	0.3	2.88	5240	5330	0.4
07009	CEDAR GROVE	013	12496	12480	12550	0.0	20	4476	4531	4604	0.3	2.53	3289	3351	0.4
07010	CLIFFSIDE PARK	003	23110	24596	25668	1.5	77	10067	10712	11195	1.5	2.29	6068	6538	1.8
07011	CLIFTON	031	37443	37570	37990	0.1	26	13195	13068	13088	-0.2	2.85	9139	9094	-0.1
07012	CLIFTON	031	10753	10781	10929	0.1	25	4814	4818	4867	0.0	2.23	2870	2885	0.1
07013	CLIFTON	031	25474	25990	26633	0.5	45	10181	10365	10583	0.4	2.51	7012	7176	0.6
07014	CLIFTON	031	4868	5139	5348	1.3	74	1968	2072	2146	1.2	2.48	1273	1347	1.3
07016	CRANFORD	039	22692	22392	22579	-0.3	8	8438	8287	8310	-0.4	2.64	6252	6172	-0.3
07017	EAST ORANGE	013	39232	38878	39140	-0.2	11	14506	14483	14691	0.0	2.63	8930	8987	0.2
07018	EAST ORANGE	013	31039	31712	32379	0.5	47	12010	12331	12659	0.6	2.53	7157	7415	0.8
07020	EDGEWATER	003	7677	10080	11782	6.6	100	3836	4991	5818	6.4	2.02	1973	2600	6.7
07021	ESSEX FELLS	013	1969	1963	1962	-0.1	18	663	664	668	0.0	2.95	543	546	0.1
07022	FAIRVIEW	003	13675	13789	13923	0.2	32	5026	5024	5052	0.0	2.74	3307	3337	0.2
07023	FANWOOD	039	7141	7156	7252	0.1	24	2565	2559	2580	-0.1	2.76	2045	2051	0.1
07024	FORT LEE	003	35422	36679	38007	0.8	59	16535	17066	17684	0.8	2.15	9402	9814	1.0
07026	GARFIELD	003	29857	30487	31146	0.5	46	11280	11436	11643	0.3	2.66	7444	7614	0.5
07027	GARWOOD	039	4266	4168	4190	-0.6	2	1778	1731	1731	-0.6	2.41	1159	1137	-0.5
07028	GLEN RIDGE	013	7385	7221	7192	-0.5	3	2497	2453	2456	-0.4	2.94	2009	1984	-0.3
07029	HARRISON	017	16902	16394	16162	-0.7	1	5928	5727	5635	-0.8	2.86	4262	4147	-0.6
07030	HOBOKEN	017	38577	40337	41311	1.1	68	19418	20386	20916	1.2	1.92	6842	7298	1.5
07031	NORTH ARLINGTON	003	15181	15046	15140	-0.2	11	6392	6365	6418	-0.1	2.36	4129	4146	0.1
07032	KEARNY	017	40412	39676	39289	-0.4	4	13514	13230	13077	-0.5	2.81	9790	9661	-0.3
07033	KENILWORTH	039	7864	7759	7823	-0.3	8	2925	2871	2877	-0.4	2.70	2169	2143	-0.3
07034	LAKE HIAWATHA	027	9255	9439	9861	0.5	44	3687	3741	3900	0.3	2.52	2384	2437	0.5
07035	LINCOLN PARK	027	10989	11228	11779	0.5	47	4047	4153	4373	0.6	2.54	2726	2818	0.8
07036	LINDEN	039	40811	41496	42502	0.4	40	15711	15971	16214	0.3	2.59	10456	10651	0.4
07039	LIVINGSTON	013	27528	27648	27864	0.1	27	9348	9497	9654	0.4	2.90	7977	8129	0.5
07040	MAPLEWOOD	013	23721	23853	24106	0.1	28	8385	8438	8554	0.2	2.81	6348	6417	0.3
07041	MILLBURN	013	6908	6910	6948	0.0	22	2755	2756	2779	0.0	2.50	1920	1926	0.1
07042	MONTCLAIR	013	26739	26918	27236	0.2	29	10592	10683	10855	0.2	2.47	6427	6552	0.5
07043	MONTCLAIR	013	12041	12061	12205	0.0	23	4444	4519	4623	0.4	2.61	3292	3365	0.5
07044	VERONA	013	13995	14176	14412	0.3	36	5820	5961	6116	0.6	2.37	3854	3977	0.7
07045	MONTVILLE	027	9801	11013	12017	2.8	94	3539	3986	4354	2.8	2.73	2771	3128	2.9
07046	MOUNTAIN LAKES	027	4358	4412	4572	0.3	36	1368	1382	1430	0.2	3.18	1202	1215	0.3
07047	NORTH BERGEN	017	60224	60662	60800	0.2	30	22442	22620	22679	0.2	2.65	14787	14962	0.3
07050	ORANGE	013	32280	32493	32951	0.2	29	11320	11449	11670	0.3	2.80	7582	7733	0.5
07052	WEST ORANGE	013	44806	45234	45721	0.2	33	16466	16788	17102	0.5	2.63	11663	11931	0.5
07054	PARSIPPANY	027	27561	28795	30467	1.0	68	10831	11303	11935	1.0	2.53	7210	7553	1.1
07055	PASSAIC	031	67683	69930	72054	0.8	57	19421	19820	20243	0.5	3.50	14419	14780	0.6
07057	WALLINGTON	003	11583	11473	11548	-0.2	11	4752	4683	4702	-0.3	2.45	3043	3027	-0.1
07058	PINE BROOK	027	5328	6191	6878	3.6	97	1916	2242	2498	3.8	2.75	1465	1721	3.9
07059	WARREN	035	14303	15911	17569	2.5	93	4644	5214	5795	2.8	3.03	3948	4441	2.8
07060	PLAINFIELD	039	43309	44703	46664	0.8	57	14002	14264	14782	0.4	3.06	9595	9846	0.6
07062	PLAINFIELD	039	13019	13437	13926	0.8	57	4460	4568	4705	0.6	2.92	3326	3422	0.7
07063	PLAINFIELD	039	12356	12465	12832	0.2	32	3799	3837	3947	0.2	3.25	3006	3046	0.3
07064	PORT READING	023	3723	3829	3946	0.7	53	1300	1341	1384	0.7	2.86	1030	1068	0.7
07065	RAHWAY	039	26536	26841	27337	0.3	34	10042	10089	10205	0.1	2.64	6737	6832	0.3
07066	CLARK	039	14400	14380	14583	0.0	20	5525	5516	5572	0.0	2.58	4072	4080	0.1
07067	COLONIA	023	18012	17822	18143	-0.3	10	6253	6209	6332	-0.2	2.87	5130	5120	-0.1
07068	ROSELAND	013	5247	5393	5479	0.7	53	2126	2216	2274	1.0	2.43	1511	1585	1.1
07069	WATCHUNG	035	6172	6807	7478	2.3	91	2308	2578	2858	2.6	2.58	1791	2007	2.7
07070	RUTHERFORD	003	18110	17893	18006	-0.3	9	7055	6991	7047	-0.2	2.52	4672	4676	0.0
07071	LYNDHURST	003	19383	19354	19545	0.0	19	7877	7901	7998	0.1	2.44	5205	5269	0.3
07072	CARLSTADT	003	5999	5992	6039	0.0	20	2428	2433	2456	0.1	2.46	1614	1632	0.3
07073	EAST RUTHERFORD	003	8682	8786	8908	0.3	35	3625	3678	3733	0.3	2.35	2146	2201	0.6
07074	MOONACHIE	003	2754	2754	2770	0.0	22	1041	1039	1045	-0.1	2.65	708	713	0.1
07075	WOOD RIDGE	003	7584	7491	7544	-0.3	9	3001	2984	3014	-0.1	2.51	2122	2127	0.1
07076	SCOTCH PLAINS	039	22920	23505	24134	0.6	50	8457	8643	8831	0.5	2.70	6344	6514	0.6
07077	SEWAREN	023	2781	2738	2775	-0.4	5	1022	1006	1019	-0.4	2.72	766	758	-0.3
07078	SHORT HILLS	013	12870	12771	12810	-0.2	13	4263	4244	4276	-0.1	3.01	3685	3668	-0.1
07079	SOUTH ORANGE	013	17015	17303	17520	0.4	41	5535	5686	5806	0.6	2.68	3777	3908	0.8
07080	SOUTH PLAINFIELD	023	21788	22083	22707	0.3	38	7142	7243	7450	0.3	3.01	5851	5956	0.4
07081	SPRINGFIELD	039	14634	14983	15317	0.6	48	6145	6268	6373	0.5	2.38	4111	4231	0.7
07082	TOWACO	027	4835	5323	5778	2.3	91	1625	1787	1940	2.3	2.97	1367	1508	2.3
07083	UNION	039	50829	51964	53256	0.5	48	18153	18356	18652	0.3	2.76	13192	13428	0.4
07086	WEEHAWKEN	017	13300	13070	13031	-0.4	4	5913	5821	5808	-0.4	2.24	3022	3014	-0.1
07087	UNION CITY	017	67306	66865	66461	-0.2	14	22941	22681	22488	-0.3	2.93	16111	16047	-0.1
07088	VAUXHALL	039	3364	3399	3445	0.2	33	1247	1254	1264	0.1	2.71	872	882	0.3
07090	WESTFIELD	039	29662	30149	30889	0.4	39	10623	10747	10949	0.3	2.78	8182	8315	0.4
07092	MOUNTAINSIDE	039	6609	6695	6807	0.3	36	2438	2461	2489	0.2	2.61	1928	1956	0.3
07093	WEST NEW YORK	017	54426	54080	53911	-0.2	14	19999	19778	19682	-0.3	2.73	13112	13083	-0.1
07094	SECAUCUS	017	15931	15980	15966	0.1	25	6214	6239	6233	0.1	2.41	3948	4000	0.3
07095	WOODBRIDGE	023	18112	19874	21521	2.2	90	7255	8003	8692	2.3	2.46	4888	5432	2.5
07102	NEWARK	013	10368	10539	10685	0.4	40	3966	4127	4252	0.9	1.98	1535	1610	1.1
07103	NEWARK	013	33292	33844	34463	0.4	40	10674	10937	11231	0.6	2.83	7059	7264	0.7
07104	NEWARK	013	51358	51229	51771	-0.1	18	16445	16597	16926	0.2	2.89	11064	11214	0.3
07105	NEWARK	013	44685	46074	47066	0.7	56	15463	16031	16469	0.9	2.87	11355	11842	1.0
07106	NEWARK	013	34253	34303	34728	0.0	23	11463	11589	11802	0.3	2.96	8333	8468	0.4
07107	NEWARK	013	35891	37625	38845	1.1	70	11942	12492	12928	1.1	2.97	8330	8797	1.3
07108	NEWARK	013	25366	24985	25243	-0.4	5	8681	8591	8729	-0.2	2.89	5909	5909	0.0
07109	BELLEVILLE	013	35693	35790	36023	0.1	25	13630	13732	13897	0.2	2.59	9035	9172	0.4
07110	NUTLEY	013	27262	27834	28461	0.5	46	10849	11206	11567	0.8	2.48	7342	7603	0.7
07111	IRVINGTON	013	60835	61837	63200	0.4	40	22050	22714	23421	0.7	2.71	14415	14850	0.7
07112	NEWARK	013	25849	25903	26127	0.1	24	9170	9304	9473	0.3	2.78	6354	6490	0.5
07114	NEWARK	013	11754	11884	12018	0.3	34	3350	3403	3474	0.4	2.51	1906	1958	0.6
07201	ELIZABETH	039	27657	28519	29290	0.7	56	8301	8519	8701	0.6	3.09	6054	6247	0.9
07202	ELIZABETH	039	37062	38794	40174	1.1	69	13204	13629	13969	0.8	2.82	8881	9240	0.9
07203	ROSELLE	039	21172	21574	22091	0.4	43	7482	7543	7652	0.2	2.85	5196	5274	0.4
07204	ROSELLE PARK	039	13203	13084	13192	-0.2	11	5101	5032	5041	-0.3	2.60	3389	3370	-0.1
	NEW JERSEY					0.8					0.9	2.68			1.0
	UNITED STATES					1.2					1.3	2.58			1.1

#	POST OFFICE NAME	RACE (%) White 2000	White 2004	Black 2000	Black 2004	Asian/Pacific 2000	Asian/Pacific 2004	% Hispanic Origin 2000	% Hispanic Origin 2004	2004 AGE DISTRIBUTION (%) 0-4	5-9	10-14	15-19	20-24	25-44	45-64	65-84	85+	18+	MEDIAN AGE 2004	% 2004 Males	% 2004 Females
07001	AVENEL	53.9	50.1	19.9	20.1	18.3	20.8	9.9	11.9	6.1	5.8	5.8	5.3	6.2	39.3	23.0	7.7	0.9	79.1	36.4	57.3	42.7
07002	BAYONNE	78.6	75.8	5.5	5.7	4.2	4.9	17.8	21.6	5.9	5.6	6.4	6.5	6.9	28.9	24.4	13.2	2.3	78.2	38.5	47.5	52.6
07003	BLOOMFIELD	69.7	65.6	12.0	13.1	8.5	9.6	14.5	17.8	5.9	5.8	6.1	5.8	6.4	32.0	24.5	11.4	2.1	78.8	37.9	47.7	52.3
07004	FAIRFIELD	95.7	94.6	0.5	0.6	2.8	3.5	3.5	4.6	5.5	6.0	6.4	5.7	4.8	27.0	27.7	14.9	2.1	78.6	41.9	48.7	51.3
07005	BOONTON	86.8	84.5	2.7	3.0	6.8	8.1	4.8	6.1	6.6	7.0	6.8	5.8	4.5	28.9	27.1	11.5	2.0	76.1	39.9	49.7	50.3
07006	CALDWELL	89.1	87.2	5.1	5.7	4.2	5.0	3.2	4.2	6.1	6.6	6.5	5.7	5.2	27.9	25.7	13.5	2.8	77.4	40.3	48.8	51.2
07008	CARTERET	68.9	65.2	9.5	9.5	8.3	9.6	23.3	27.7	6.2	6.3	7.6	7.0	7.0	28.0	23.5	12.5	2.0	75.5	37.4	48.8	51.2
07009	CEDAR GROVE	90.2	88.0	2.9	3.5	5.4	6.6	3.2	4.3	5.3	5.7	5.7	4.5	3.9	25.7	26.6	17.9	4.7	80.3	44.5	46.6	53.4
07010	CLIFFSIDE PARK	77.9	74.8	1.8	2.0	12.1	14.0	18.1	20.9	4.8	4.7	5.0	4.5	5.4	32.0	25.4	15.6	2.6	82.8	41.2	48.3	51.7
07011	CLIFTON	66.2	60.2	4.6	5.1	4.6	5.0	32.2	39.7	6.6	6.3	7.2	6.7	7.4	30.7	22.4	10.0	2.8	75.9	35.8	47.9	52.1
07012	CLIFTON	84.4	80.4	2.2	2.9	8.9	10.8	7.8	10.8	5.5	5.6	5.2	4.4	4.5	28.0	25.6	17.4	3.8	81.0	43.1	48.0	52.0
07013	CLIFTON	86.0	82.3	1.3	1.6	7.4	9.1	8.6	11.8	5.2	5.3	5.4	5.4	5.2	26.6	26.8	16.9	3.2	80.8	43.0	47.6	52.4
07014	CLIFTON	78.9	73.6	2.5	3.1	10.2	11.9	14.7	20.0	6.4	6.3	5.7	4.4	4.9	30.8	25.6	13.4	2.4	78.9	40.0	47.6	52.4
07016	CRANFORD	93.5	92.2	2.8	3.2	2.2	2.6	4.0	5.1	6.3	6.6	6.6	5.9	4.5	26.2	26.3	14.4	3.2	76.8	41.5	47.5	52.5
07017	EAST ORANGE	4.6	4.1	88.2	88.3	0.6	0.6	5.3	5.8	7.7	7.9	8.0	7.0	6.8	29.0	21.9	10.3	1.4	72.1	33.8	45.0	55.0
07018	EAST ORANGE	3.3	2.9	90.6	90.7	0.4	0.4	4.1	4.5	7.8	7.6	8.1	7.2	7.1	28.0	21.5	11.2	1.6	72.2	33.8	44.7	55.3
07020	EDGEWATER	67.1	62.8	3.5	4.1	23.2	26.0	10.5	12.4	5.2	4.7	4.1	4.1	5.5	40.7	25.9	8.9	0.9	83.5	38.3	48.8	51.3
07021	ESSEX FELLS	97.0	96.2	0.5	0.6	1.0	1.3	1.2	1.6	8.6	10.2	8.1	5.2	2.7	22.2	28.4	13.0	1.7	69.6	41.2	49.2	50.8
07022	FAIRVIEW	72.6	69.5	1.7	1.8	5.4	6.1	36.3	41.1	6.5	5.9	5.8	5.9	8.1	34.5	20.3	11.4	1.8	78.5	35.0	51.7	48.3
07023	FANWOOD	88.3	86.3	5.1	5.8	4.4	5.3	3.8	4.8	8.1	8.4	7.2	5.5	3.5	27.2	26.0	12.0	2.3	72.7	39.8	47.9	52.1
07024	FORT LEE	62.8	58.4	1.7	1.9	31.5	35.1	7.9	9.4	5.1	5.1	5.0	4.5	4.5	29.2	26.0	17.7	3.0	82.1	43.1	46.6	53.4
07026	GARFIELD	82.1	79.5	3.0	3.3	2.7	3.2	20.1	23.5	6.1	5.8	6.5	6.5	7.4	32.0	22.8	11.0	2.0	77.7	36.2	48.9	51.1
07027	GARWOOD	95.9	94.9	0.4	0.4	1.4	1.7	4.9	6.4	5.7	5.5	5.9	5.8	5.5	31.8	24.0	13.6	2.3	79.4	39.5	48.5	51.5
07028	GLEN RIDGE	87.5	85.1	6.6	7.7	3.3	4.0	3.5	4.6	8.7	9.9	8.8	6.1	3.6	25.5	27.2	8.7	1.6	68.5	38.6	49.1	50.9
07029	HARRISON	66.3	63.0	1.1	1.1	10.6	11.5	38.4	43.9	6.6	5.8	5.8	6.6	8.6	34.8	22.0	8.7	1.1	77.9	34.3	51.1	48.9
07030	HOBOKEN	80.8	78.8	4.3	4.0	4.4	5.2	20.2	23.5	3.2	2.6	2.9	4.2	13.3	50.5	14.5	7.7	1.1	89.3	31.4	51.2	48.8
07031	NORTH ARLINGTON	89.6	87.6	0.5	0.5	5.6	6.8	10.6	12.8	4.6	4.4	5.2	5.3	6.2	29.6	25.9	15.9	3.0	82.6	41.6	47.3	52.7
07032	KEARNY	75.7	73.1	4.0	3.9	5.6	6.2	27.3	32.4	5.8	5.5	6.0	6.6	8.2	34.6	22.6	9.2	1.5	78.9	35.2	51.7	48.3
07033	KENILWORTH	91.0	89.3	2.5	2.8	3.1	3.7	8.8	11.1	5.6	5.7	6.3	5.5	5.2	29.5	25.1	14.5	2.5	79.0	40.4	48.6	51.4
07034	LAKE HIAWATHA	79.4	76.1	2.8	3.1	12.4	14.7	7.4	9.2	6.0	5.9	6.1	5.7	6.4	34.6	25.5	9.1	0.8	78.6	37.1	49.5	50.5
07035	LINCOLN PARK	90.1	88.0	1.7	2.0	5.3	6.4	5.8	7.4	5.6	5.7	5.8	5.0	4.6	30.7	27.1	12.8	2.7	79.6	41.1	48.0	52.0
07036	LINDEN	67.2	64.4	22.0	23.0	2.3	2.7	14.0	16.8	5.9	5.9	6.5	6.3	6.4	28.6	24.6	13.1	2.7	77.9	38.7	47.6	52.4
07039	LIVINGSTON	82.7	79.2	1.2	1.4	14.5	17.4	2.5	3.4	6.8	7.6	7.6	6.3	4.1	23.5	28.4	13.9	2.0	73.9	41.8	48.7	51.3
07040	MAPLEWOOD	59.0	54.6	32.5	35.6	2.9	3.2	5.2	6.5	7.5	8.1	7.8	6.8	5.1	26.8	26.3	9.4	2.2	72.2	38.3	47.7	52.3
07041	MILLBURN	88.9	86.5	1.4	1.6	7.9	9.5	2.9	3.9	7.4	8.1	7.6	6.2	3.9	27.3	26.9	10.6	2.1	72.8	39.8	48.3	51.8
07042	MONTCLAIR	47.7	44.4	43.4	45.7	3.0	3.3	5.7	6.8	6.2	6.5	7.4	6.8	6.0	29.4	25.4	10.0	2.4	75.5	37.9	46.2	53.8
07043	MONTCLAIR	87.7	85.2	5.4	6.5	3.9	4.7	4.0	5.2	7.4	8.6	7.8	6.5	4.3	24.4	29.5	9.9	1.6	72.4	40.3	47.3	52.7
07044	VERONA	92.9	91.1	1.8	2.2	3.4	4.2	3.4	4.6	6.3	6.8	6.6	5.2	3.8	25.4	27.1	15.3	3.4	77.0	42.7	47.3	52.7
07045	MONTVILLE	86.7	84.1	0.8	0.9	11.2	13.4	2.5	3.2	6.7	7.6	7.5	5.4	3.3	26.6	29.7	11.7	1.6	74.6	41.3	47.9	52.1
07046	MOUNTAIN LAKES	93.0	91.4	0.4	0.5	5.3	6.5	1.7	2.2	7.0	9.0	11.5	8.9	3.5	17.7	31.6	9.8	1.0	66.6	41.0	49.6	50.5
07047	NORTH BERGEN	67.3	65.6	2.9	2.8	7.0	7.4	55.7	60.5	6.3	5.8	6.4	6.4	7.2	31.4	22.8	11.6	2.1	77.7	36.8	48.0	52.0
07050	ORANGE	13.3	12.2	74.7	75.3	1.4	1.5	12.8	13.9	8.5	8.0	7.8	7.2	7.2	30.8	20.5	8.6	1.4	71.3	32.5	46.5	53.5
07052	WEST ORANGE	67.5	63.4	17.6	19.4	8.1	9.4	9.9	12.0	6.5	6.7	6.6	5.8	5.2	27.2	25.0	13.5	3.6	76.5	40.3	47.1	52.9
07054	PARSIPPANY	70.6	66.5	3.1	3.3	21.4	24.5	8.0	9.6	6.0	5.9	5.8	5.5	5.6	32.5	25.6	11.5	1.6	78.9	38.7	49.0	51.0
07055	PASSAIC	35.7	32.5	13.7	13.5	5.6	5.6	62.3	66.8	9.7	8.5	8.4	7.8	9.1	30.8	17.8	6.8	1.1	69.0	28.7	50.1	50.0
07057	WALLINGTON	87.6	85.7	2.7	2.9	5.0	5.8	6.7	8.2	5.2	5.1	5.2	5.2	6.8	32.5	25.8	12.1	2.2	81.5	38.8	48.4	51.6
07058	PINE BROOK	75.4	71.2	1.6	1.8	21.2	25.0	2.9	3.6	7.1	7.0	7.1	5.1	5.0	34.0	25.7	8.3	0.8	75.6	36.1	49.7	50.3
07059	WARREN	86.3	83.7	1.3	1.5	10.7	12.9	3.2	4.1	6.9	8.4	9.0	6.7	3.6	23.8	29.6	10.7	1.2	71.1	40.8	49.7	50.3
07060	PLAINFIELD	38.1	36.4	39.4	38.9	2.6	2.8	32.9	36.5	7.9	7.3	7.3	6.8	7.6	32.9	21.2	7.6	1.4	73.3	33.2	49.9	50.1
07062	PLAINFIELD	26.0	24.6	62.7	63.1	1.3	1.4	17.4	19.3	7.4	7.6	7.8	6.5	5.9	30.7	23.6	9.4	1.3	73.1	35.7	47.5	52.5
07063	PLAINFIELD	29.4	28.9	56.8	55.8	2.1	2.4	19.2	21.3	8.1	7.8	8.3	7.3	7.0	30.4	21.8	8.4	0.9	71.3	33.5	48.1	51.9
07064	PORT READING	86.8	84.4	4.1	4.4	4.9	5.9	7.7	9.8	6.2	6.1	6.6	6.1	5.8	30.3	24.1	13.5	1.3	77.3	38.4	49.0	51.0
07065	RAHWAY	60.2	56.9	27.0	28.5	3.6	4.1	13.9	16.5	6.2	6.2	7.1	6.3	6.1	29.8	24.2	12.2	2.0	76.6	38.1	47.9	52.1
07066	CLARK	95.6	94.6	0.3	0.4	2.8	3.4	3.7	4.8	5.2	5.7	6.3	5.5	4.3	25.3	26.7	17.8	3.3	79.5	43.7	47.6	52.4
07067	COLONIA	85.9	83.5	4.8	5.2	6.4	7.8	5.0	6.5	6.3	6.5	6.8	6.3	5.1	26.2	26.5	14.7	1.7	76.4	41.0	48.2	51.8
07068	ROSELAND	93.4	91.9	0.7	0.9	4.7	5.8	2.3	3.1	5.8	6.4	6.1	4.5	3.2	23.5	29.2	18.8	2.6	78.9	45.4	45.8	54.2
07069	WATCHUNG	84.8	82.2	3.2	3.6	9.7	11.4	3.0	3.8	5.6	6.4	6.8	5.3	3.5	23.9	30.8	15.5	2.2	77.8	44.1	48.7	51.3
07070	RUTHERFORD	82.0	79.2	2.7	3.0	11.4	13.4	8.6	10.2	5.3	5.3	6.1	5.8	5.8	30.7	26.7	12.2	2.2	79.9	39.8	48.0	52.0
07071	LYNDHURST	89.9	88.0	0.6	0.7	5.4	6.5	9.0	11.0	5.0	5.0	5.6	5.5	6.0	31.0	25.2	14.3	2.4	81.1	40.2	47.8	52.2
07072	CARLSTADT	88.9	86.6	1.4	1.6	6.2	7.5	8.0	9.8	5.1	5.0	5.3	5.5	6.1	32.2	25.7	13.1	1.8	81.3	39.7	48.5	51.5
07073	EAST RUTHERFORD	79.7	76.5	3.7	4.1	10.7	12.6	10.6	12.7	5.5	5.2	5.4	5.4	5.9	33.7	25.3	11.6	2.1	80.5	38.8	48.9	51.1
07074	MOONACHIE	85.7	83.0	0.9	1.1	6.6	7.9	12.7	15.2	4.8	5.0	5.8	6.6	5.7	28.1	28.1	14.3	1.6	80.4	41.8	49.1	50.9
07075	WOOD RIDGE	91.0	89.1	0.8	1.0	5.1	6.2	7.3	8.9	6.0	6.3	6.2	5.2	4.2	28.8	26.8	14.2	2.4	78.3	41.5	47.8	52.2
07076	SCOTCH PLAINS	79.0	76.3	11.2	12.2	7.2	8.5	3.9	4.9	7.5	7.8	7.1	5.6	3.8	28.3	25.8	12.3	2.0	73.9	39.8	47.9	52.1
07077	SEWAREN	86.9	84.7	4.9	5.4	4.3	5.2	9.7	12.4	5.8	5.8	6.6	6.5	6.6	28.7	26.8	11.7	1.5	77.7	39.0	48.5	51.5
07078	SHORT HILLS	88.8	86.4	1.1	1.3	8.7	10.6	1.6	2.1	8.6	10.4	9.9	6.7	2.8	21.6	27.9	10.7	1.5	66.6	40.0	48.8	51.3
07079	SOUTH ORANGE	59.8	55.3	31.9	35.1	3.9	4.5	4.9	6.1	5.6	6.5	6.6	10.8	10.2	24.3	24.1	9.9	2.0	77.6	35.4	48.0	52.0
07080	SOUTH PLAINFIELD	77.7	74.3	8.6	9.2	7.6	9.1	8.7	11.0	6.1	6.5	7.5	6.7	5.6	27.9	25.8	12.1	1.8	75.7	39.0	49.0	51.0
07081	SPRINGFIELD	89.3	87.4	4.1	4.6	4.7	5.8	4.2	5.2	6.0	6.2	5.9	5.0	4.1	26.0	26.6	16.9	3.3	78.7	43.1	47.2	52.8
07082	TOWACO	90.1	88.0	0.5	0.6	7.8	9.5	2.2	2.9	6.4	7.6	8.1	5.8	3.5	25.9	29.9	11.7	1.1	74.1	41.2	49.0	51.0
07083	UNION	71.5	68.2	15.5	16.8	8.2	9.4	9.3	11.5	5.5	5.8	6.6	6.9	6.7	27.4	24.5	13.6	3.1	78.4	39.7	47.0	53.0
07086	WEEHAWKEN	73.2	70.6	3.6	3.6	4.8	5.2	40.4	46.0	4.7	4.1	4.8	4.9	7.6	40.3	21.5	10.5	1.5	83.6	36.2	48.8	51.2
07087	UNION CITY	58.4	57.6	3.6	3.4	2.2	2.2	82.2	85.2	7.4	6.7	7.1	7.1	8.4	33.0	20.3	8.9	1.1	74.6	32.8	50.3	49.7
07088	VAUXHALL	8.0	7.1	85.0	85.6	1.6	1.7	4.1	4.5	6.3	6.9	8.2	6.9	5.4	27.6	24.3	12.2	2.2	74.4	38.1	44.9	55.1
07090	WESTFIELD	90.0	88.2	3.9	4.5	4.1	4.9	2.8	3.6	7.6	8.5	8.3	6.3	3.9	25.5	26.6	11.3	2.1	71.4	39.7	48.0	52.0
07092	MOUNTAINSIDE	95.1	94.0	0.9	1.1	2.9	3.5	3.0	3.9	5.9	6.7	6.2	4.7	2.8	21.1	27.8	20.5	4.2	77.8	46.6	47.3	52.7
07093	WEST NEW YORK	60.9	59.9	3.5	3.3	3.2	3.4	76.5	79.6	6.8	6.0	6.3	6.4	8.2	33.6	20.3	11.0	1.4	77.3	34.2	49.2	50.8
07094	SECAUCUS	78.5	75.7	4.5	4.6	11.8	13.8	12.3	14.9	5.1	5.2	5.4	5.7	5.1	31.0	26.1	14.2	2.3	80.7	40.8	49.5	50.5
07095	WOODBRIDGE	76.7	72.1	7.1	7.9	11.2	13.8	10.0	12.5	6.4	5.9	5.9	5.6	5.8	32.3	24.1	11.9	2.1	78.4	38.0	48.0	52.1
07102	NEWARK	17.8	16.4	62.9	62.9	2.1	2.2	24.6	26.4	5.0	4.4	4.7	7.9	11.0	32.5	20.9	12.2	1.5	82.9	35.4	53.9	46.1
07103	NEWARK	7.1	6.7	83.8	83.5	0.9	0.9	12.0	13.1	8.4	8.6	9.1	10.0	9.9	26.0	18.3	8.6	1.3	68.2	28.1	46.1	54.0
07104	NEWARK	39.2	38.0	23.9	23.2	1.7	1.7	63.2	66.3	8.0	7.2	7.6	8.5	9.4	30.8	18.8	8.4	1.5	72.8	30.9	49.3	50.7
07105	NEWARK	71.9	68.5	5.5	5.7	0.5	0.5	35.7	42.0	6.6	5.8	5.9	6.1	8.9	36.9	21.4	7.5	0.9	78.3	33.2	51.7	48.3
07106	NEWARK	9.4	8.4	81.3	81.9	2.8	2.9	6.6	7.4	8.2	8.1	8.7	7.6	7.9	30.0	21.2	7.7	0.8	70.5	31.3	45.9	54.2
07107	NEWARK	27.2	25.6	40.0	38.9	1.7	1.6	45.8	50.0	8.8	7.9	8.4	8.0	8.5	30.4	18.7	8.3	1.0	70.2	30.1	47.9	52.1
07108	NEWARK	2.3	2.3	92.0	91.5	0.2	0.2	7.3	8.0	8.7	9.0	10.1	9.4	8.0	25.9	18.8	9.0	1.0	66.4	28.6	43.6	56.4
07109	BELLEVILLE	69.4	65.1	5.4	5.8	11.3	12.6	23.8	28.7	5.9	5.6	6.2	6.4	7.1	31.9	23.9	11.2	1.9	78.5	37.0	48.4	51.6
07110	NUTLEY	87.9	85.2	1.9	2.2	7.2	8.6	6.8	8.9	5.4	5.6	6.5	6.2	5.3	29.1	26.4	13.3	2.2	78.7	40.3	47.3	52.7
07111	IRVINGTON	9.1	8.4	81.6	81.7	1.2	1.3	8.4	9.3	8.0	7.7	7.9	6.9	7.6	31.4	22.5	7.2	0.9	72.3	32.5	46.7	53.3
07112	NEWARK	1.3	1.3	94.4	94.1	0.5	0.5	3.8	4.2	8.5	8.3	8.7	7.6	6.8	29.4	20.9	9.2	0.7	69.8	32.1	44.5	55.5
07114	NEWARK	18.3	17.4	55.7	54.3	0.6	0.6	35.2	38.5	6.0	5.7	6.3	6.0	9.6	40.3	18.6	7.0	0.6	78.5	32.1	61.6	38.5
07201	ELIZABETH	44.2	43.4	33.5	32.4	1.2	1.2	44.2	48.5	7.7	7.1	7.5	7.6	9.1	32.9	20.0	7.2	0.9	73.5	31.7	52.3	47.8
07202	ELIZABETH	64.2	61.7	10.1	10.1	3.4	3.5	52.0	57.6	7.1	6.7	7.1	6.7	7.9	31.9	21.1	9.7	1.9	75.2	34.3	48.9	51.1
07203	ROSELLE	35.6	33.2	51.3	52.4	2.8	3.0	17.1	19.5	6.6	6.5	7.2	7.1	7.4	29.1	23.9	10.5	1.6	75.4	35.9	46.9	53.1
07204	ROSELLE PARK	80.9	77.9	2.4	2.7	9.1	10.3	16.3	20.0	5.9	5.8	6.4	6.4	6.5	31.8	25.0	10.4	1.8	78.2	37.5	48.9	51.1
	NEW JERSEY	72.6	70.5	13.6	13.8	5.8	6.6	13.3	15.0	6.6	6.7	7.1	6.5	6.3	28.8	24.6	11.5	1.9	75.6	37.7	48.6	51.4
	UNITED STATES	75.1	73.6	12.3	12.5	3.8	4.2	12.5	14.1	6.9	6.7	7.2	7.0	7.3	28.6	23.8	10.8	1.7	75.1	36.0	49.1	50.9

#	POST OFFICE NAME	2004 Per Capita Income	2004 HH Income Base	2004 Household Income Distribution (%): Less than $25,000	$25,000 to $49,999	$50,000 to $99,999	$100,000 to $149,999	$150,000 or More	Median Household Income: 2004	2009	2004 National Centile	2004 State Centile	2004 Home Value Base	2004 Home Value Distribution (%): Less than $50,000	$50,000 to $89,999	$90,000 to $174,999	$175,000 to $399,999	$400,000 or More	2004 Median Home Value
07001	AVENEL	23631	4948	15.4	23.8	38.2	17.7	4.9	60769	69093	85	39	2786	7.9	3.7	14.9	72.8	0.7	209028
07002	BAYONNE	24310	24899	27.7	26.5	29.6	11.6	4.5	45658	51605	63	15	10764	0.5	0.8	9.1	81.2	8.4	262533
07003	BLOOMFIELD	30165	19188	17.0	23.6	36.1	15.6	7.7	61099	72761	85	40	10662	0.6	0.3	10.6	84.0	4.5	249984
07004	FAIRFIELD	38758	2380	7.4	14.0	28.5	26.2	23.9	100161	122126	98	87	2230	0.0	0.0	0.9	45.5	53.6	414038
07005	BOONTON	42119	5956	9.9	17.2	31.5	20.7	20.8	84861	101696	96	75	4424	0.5	0.1	2.8	53.0	43.6	377873
07006	CALDWELL	48052	9624	10.1	13.6	29.9	21.0	25.4	92819	114246	97	82	7531	0.1	0.2	2.3	44.8	52.7	414457
07008	CARTERET	21650	7153	22.3	25.4	34.9	13.7	3.8	52279	59580	76	24	4761	4.9	0.7	23.1	70.6	0.7	200940
07009	CEDAR GROVE	45491	4531	10.2	16.2	29.7	22.0	22.0	87774	108090	97	78	3634	0.2	0.4	2.0	62.3	35.2	363183
07010	CLIFFSIDE PARK	33484	10712	22.3	26.7	28.6	11.9	10.6	51289	60528	74	23	5237	0.3	1.3	4.1	60.3	34.1	346571
07011	CLIFTON	20852	13068	24.0	27.6	32.9	12.1	3.4	48524	55595	69	19	6557	0.2	0.6	4.4	90.7	4.1	257709
07012	CLIFTON	31545	4818	20.0	27.4	32.2	14.3	6.1	52577	60103	76	24	2753	0.2	0.1	0.6	88.2	10.9	279154
07013	CLIFTON	31871	10365	16.1	21.6	34.0	18.4	9.9	66385	76792	89	50	7658	0.3	0.2	3.3	77.0	19.3	294179
07014	CLIFTON	30823	2072	16.0	20.4	38.0	16.6	9.0	63858	73090	88	45	1446	0.6	0.0	3.3	90.5	5.7	266446
07016	CRANFORD	38865	8287	10.2	15.4	33.6	22.8	17.9	85107	102348	96	76	6889	0.1	0.3	4.1	63.2	32.4	349436
07017	EAST ORANGE	20010	14483	34.4	27.6	25.1	8.7	4.2	38303	44291	40	7	4092	1.8	2.6	32.8	61.0	1.8	192057
07018	EAST ORANGE	17542	12331	40.2	28.9	23.0	5.9	2.0	32379	36857	19	3	3164	1.8	3.2	36.6	56.7	1.7	186894
07020	EDGEWATER	50667	4991	13.5	18.3	32.8	19.1	16.2	73826	89405	93	61	2137	1.6	0.4	4.2	63.9	29.9	296495
07021	ESSEX FELLS	99017	664	2.9	6.0	17.0	16.3	57.8	175454	220573	100	100	638	0.0	0.0	0.2	7.5	92.3	930288
07022	FAIRVIEW	22006	5024	25.9	29.9	29.0	11.4	3.8	45393	52707	62	15	1999	0.0	1.1	6.3	76.9	15.8	288251
07023	FANWOOD	41856	2559	7.5	13.0	30.9	24.7	23.8	96718	114175	98	85	2354	0.0	0.0	3.2	73.8	23.0	342638
07024	FORT LEE	44895	17066	19.1	20.0	29.2	17.1	14.6	65712	78069	89	48	9626	3.3	7.0	18.3	37.9	33.5	289609
07026	GARFIELD	22623	11436	24.3	27.9	32.6	11.7	3.5	48068	55566	68	18	5003	0.1	0.6	6.0	84.0	9.3	271746
07027	GARWOOD	31642	1731	16.4	24.9	33.1	17.6	8.0	59731	69984	84	38	1056	0.0	0.0	4.7	86.9	8.3	284783
07028	GLEN RIDGE	58347	2453	6.4	12.0	22.7	20.2	38.7	118902	150000	99	95	2216	0.2	0.7	4.3	47.6	47.2	388750
07029	HARRISON	20656	5727	26.0	28.0	31.2	10.8	4.0	45559	51427	63	15	1873	1.1	0.6	17.5	70.6	10.1	251136
07030	HOBOKEN	53266	20386	19.6	15.7	28.5	18.9	17.3	75013	90854	93	63	4899	0.0	0.5	3.0	50.0	46.5	384930
07031	NORTH ARLINGTON	28191	6365	19.6	24.3	35.0	16.6	4.5	57059	65588	82	32	3411	0.0	0.2	2.0	85.4	12.4	289341
07032	KEARNY	23920	13230	19.4	28.3	33.7	12.5	6.0	52223	59501	76	23	6702	0.3	0.3	11.0	80.5	7.8	257719
07033	KENILWORTH	28003	2871	13.6	24.2	38.3	17.6	6.3	66542	78602	89	50	2233	0.0	0.3	2.9	91.5	5.4	270641
07034	LAKE HIAWATHA	32235	3741	9.5	22.3	43.5	17.2	7.6	66692	79172	90	51	2332	0.7	1.2	7.0	82.6	8.5	260979
07035	LINCOLN PARK	35271	4153	8.5	18.3	41.0	19.5	12.7	77345	89310	94	66	3170	0.3	0.3	7.3	75.4	16.7	282328
07036	LINDEN	24095	15917	21.0	27.7	35.2	12.4	3.7	51075	58936	74	22	9137	1.2	0.9	14.8	80.1	3.1	227735
07039	LIVINGSTON	58298	9497	5.1	12.0	26.5	22.1	34.4	112959	141719	99	93	8976	1.0	0.2	1.0	40.3	57.6	445255
07040	MAPLEWOOD	44410	8438	9.2	15.8	30.3	21.1	23.6	89333	109344	97	79	6751	0.2	0.7	6.0	59.5	33.7	329591
07041	MILLBURN	57474	2756	7.1	13.4	31.0	20.0	28.5	96827	122956	98	85	1891	0.0	0.0	2.2	26.0	71.8	511913
07042	MONTCLAIR	46126	10683	16.0	20.1	28.8	17.9	17.2	70768	87618	92	57	5378	0.2	0.7	6.0	52.4	40.8	357241
07043	MONTCLAIR	73715	4519	6.4	9.5	21.4	20.2	42.5	129809	161102	100	97	3826	0.3	0.1	2.2	27.5	69.9	499869
07044	VERONA	54437	5961	13.7	15.5	27.6	19.6	23.6	85853	107221	96	77	4604	0.1	0.3	5.0	57.3	37.3	362167
07045	MONTVILLE	53250	3986	9.2	10.7	24.6	19.7	35.8	110003	130399	99	92	3783	0.4	4.1	3.1	27.2	65.2	495605
07046	MOUNTAIN LAKES	80495	1382	4.9	7.0	17.5	18.2	52.4	158466	193137	100	100	1312	1.0	0.0	0.5	9.7	88.8	747143
07047	NORTH BERGEN	24651	22620	26.0	28.3	28.3	11.1	6.3	46298	52586	65	16	8942	1.1	3.1	11.4	68.9	15.6	267485
07050	ORANGE	19543	11449	29.7	30.6	27.6	8.8	3.3	41570	48095	52	11	3534	2.4	3.2	33.3	57.6	3.5	198223
07052	WEST ORANGE	42592	16788	13.7	18.4	28.2	19.9	19.8	79390	98085	95	69	11931	0.8	0.4	5.8	67.2	25.8	311171
07054	PARSIPPANY	34037	11303	12.7	20.6	35.0	19.6	12.2	72165	85050	92	58	6145	0.9	0.3	2.8	59.0	37.1	362220
07055	PASSAIC	14145	19820	32.1	32.4	25.8	6.8	2.9	37024	41589	36	6	5697	0.3	1.1	18.0	75.3	5.4	235043
07057	WALLINGTON	28931	4683	20.1	28.4	33.4	13.1	5.0	51224	58847	74	22	2059	0.0	0.0	3.3	78.8	17.9	304136
07058	PINE BROOK	45355	2242	6.9	11.5	34.1	20.8	26.8	95354	112883	98	84	1446	0.2	0.7	0.6	22.0	76.5	523666
07059	WARREN	57606	5214	5.2	11.6	25.2	18.4	39.6	117191	137522	99	95	4755	0.0	0.6	1.6	18.6	79.3	638611
07060	PLAINFIELD	21882	14264	23.0	24.3	32.8	13.4	6.6	52532	60330	76	24	6668	0.4	2.3	17.7	73.5	6.1	224439
07062	PLAINFIELD	26168	4568	17.6	23.4	34.6	15.7	8.7	58723	68186	83	36	3063	0.7	1.7	28.5	64.7	4.5	201460
07063	PLAINFIELD	22605	3837	16.3	24.9	36.8	16.1	5.9	59710	68874	84	38	2612	0.5	0.9	28.3	69.4	0.9	203424
07064	PORT READING	28450	1341	10.3	21.5	41.6	17.8	8.8	68155	78100	90	54	1080	0.4	0.7	10.8	87.6	0.5	231719
07065	RAHWAY	25372	10089	19.8	23.6	37.2	14.0	5.4	56790	65411	81	32	6579	0.7	0.5	19.9	76.8	2.1	216413
07066	CLARK	34820	5516	10.5	20.3	36.3	21.4	11.5	75368	87131	93	64	4640	0.2	0.3	2.8	71.8	25.0	325498
07067	COLONIA	32242	6209	10.9	18.4	37.7	21.8	11.2	74834	84857	93	62	5567	0.2	0.2	3.8	84.4	11.4	272022
07068	ROSELAND	51465	2216	9.0	11.5	33.0	24.2	22.3	92920	114884	97	82	1832	0.0	0.0	1.9	39.1	59.0	439709
07069	WATCHUNG	71537	2578	5.9	12.7	25.5	19.4	36.5	113338	135887	99	94	2080	0.0	0.0	0.6	18.6	80.8	639474
07070	RUTHERFORD	36294	6991	13.7	20.1	33.3	20.1	12.8	72501	85002	92	59	4629	1.0	1.0	3.7	71.6	22.7	331335
07071	LYNDHURST	30232	7901	18.1	22.7	35.7	16.7	6.8	59552	68924	84	37	4643	0.4	0.4	3.4	80.1	15.7	289293
07072	CARLSTADT	32928	2433	17.7	22.6	34.9	15.3	9.6	61252	71675	86	41	1343	0.8	0.5	1.5	75.1	22.2	328992
07073	EAST RUTHERFORD	33522	3678	19.9	23.0	35.0	13.2	9.0	56004	65314	81	30	1734	0.5	0.0	4.0	77.4	18.1	295397
07074	MOONACHIE	28613	1039	15.1	28.0	34.9	13.1	8.9	56112	65548	81	30	826	29.1	4.0	3.2	47.5	16.3	242632
07075	WOOD RIDGE	34301	2984	11.6	18.3	38.9	20.4	10.7	70554	83249	91	56	2323	0.6	0.1	3.4	85.0	10.9	292843
07076	SCOTCH PLAINS	48397	8643	9.1	13.6	31.1	21.4	24.8	92329	110965	97	81	6868	0.1	0.5	4.5	48.7	46.3	385544
07077	SEWAREN	26842	1006	20.5	20.6	33.1	18.5	7.4	64627	73332	88	46	797	0.6	0.8	15.2	79.9	3.5	225369
07078	SHORT HILLS	113870	4244	2.7	6.3	14.5	12.0	64.4	213989	269297	100	100	3865	0.0	0.3	0.9	4.2	94.6	1000001
07079	SOUTH ORANGE	51975	5686	12.2	13.6	24.8	18.8	30.6	98280	125624	98	86	4189	0.4	0.2	4.0	46.5	48.9	394560
07080	SOUTH PLAINFIELD	28480	7243	11.2	17.6	40.2	21.8	9.3	74346	84023	93	62	6489	0.3	0.0	7.4	86.6	5.7	249421
07081	SPRINGFIELD	43070	6268	12.6	16.0	33.1	21.2	17.1	81753	97309	95	72	4606	0.7	0.6	4.6	55.2	38.9	364410
07082	TOWACO	46410	1787	6.9	8.2	27.9	27.6	29.4	110771	130959	99	93	1682	0.6	0.7	2.1	30.9	65.8	483072
07083	UNION	28752	18356	16.3	20.6	36.0	17.9	9.2	66876	78700	90	52	14098	0.8	0.7	5.5	88.4	4.7	265745
07086	WEEHAWKEN	33702	5821	21.6	23.0	32.1	14.6	8.6	56089	65523	81	30	1836	0.0	2.5	7.4	53.2	36.9	354198
07087	UNION CITY	15433	22681	37.2	33.5	21.7	5.5	2.2	33266	36788	22	4	4843	1.0	2.7	13.3	72.8	10.2	249439
07088	VAUXHALL	22961	1254	22.9	29.7	32.4	11.2	3.8	48018	55470	68	17	779	1.3	5.7	31.6	59.3	2.2	196310
07090	WESTFIELD	57121	10747	9.1	12.2	23.9	21.1	33.8	110570	132169	99	92	8684	0.2	0.2	2.3	29.4	67.8	506668
07092	MOUNTAINSIDE	56767	2461	9.9	13.4	22.2	23.2	31.5	109420	131626	99	92	2228	0.0	0.0	0.3	20.5	79.2	528307
07093	WEST NEW YORK	18216	19778	35.8	30.6	23.1	6.8	3.7	36018	40222	32	5	4832	0.8	2.5	19.4	59.6	17.7	257696
07094	SECAUCUS	36799	6239	19.4	18.5	33.0	16.0	13.1	65565	75452	89	48	3932	0.2	0.1	5.7	69.7	24.4	318805
07095	WOODBRIDGE	30833	8003	16.6	20.5	36.9	17.8	8.2	65226	75146	89	47	5543	0.4	0.6	20.3	76.6	2.1	220145
07102	NEWARK	15088	4127	66.1	20.6	10.1	1.6	1.7	15014	17058	1	0	285	2.1	4.6	21.4	67.0	4.9	223311
07103	NEWARK	13561	10937	53.0	22.8	18.2	4.0	2.0	22370	25541	3	1	2638	4.8	9.3	47.2	37.3	1.3	152071
07104	NEWARK	15433	16597	41.8	27.3	21.7	6.9	2.4	31379	36308	16	3	4019	1.2	3.2	24.4	67.0	4.2	222407
07105	NEWARK	17746	16031	32.5	29.8	27.5	7.5	2.6	39159	45543	43	8	4531	1.5	0.8	13.1	63.3	21.3	285238
07106	NEWARK	16818	11589	33.6	28.8	27.1	8.0	2.6	37185	43209	36	6	3914	1.1	1.3	39.1	56.5	1.9	187908
07107	NEWARK	13887	12492	45.9	25.8	20.8	5.0	2.4	28027	32724	9	2	3319	1.7	5.0	27.6	63.6	2.1	206385
07108	NEWARK	12384	8591	53.9	23.6	17.5	3.4	1.6	21458	24619	2	1	1860	5.2	9.1	46.2	38.3	1.1	154898
07109	BELLEVILLE	25740	13732	18.9	27.0	36.1	13.2	4.8	53733	63627	78	26	7098	1.4	1.8	18.4	76.9	1.4	223070
07110	NUTLEY	33212	11206	16.6	19.0	35.9	18.0	10.6	67107	80684	90	52	7591	0.8	1.0	6.5	77.1	14.7	284408
07111	IRVINGTON	19537	22714	29.5	31.2	29.2	7.8	2.3	40776	46508	49	10	7222	1.1	1.9	36.0	59.4	1.6	190417
07112	NEWARK	16826	9304	36.0	32.1	23.4	5.8	2.7	33788	38629	23	4	2934	2.1	2.0	36.6	55.6	3.6	187687
07114	NEWARK	12569	3403	64.2	17.8	15.0	2.4	0.6	15341	17195	1	0	458	3.7	4.2	36.7	46.3	9.2	185593
07201	ELIZABETH	16029	8519	31.6	33.6	25.6	6.9	2.3	36557	41829	34	6	2617	0.5	2.6	23.6	69.4	4.0	222086
07202	ELIZABETH	17997	13629	31.1	30.1	29.0	7.4	2.5	39707	46047	45	9	4114	2.9	2.3	16.9	71.4	6.6	233017
07203	ROSELLE	24486	7543	18.3	24.5	36.8	15.0	5.4	56335	64608	81	31	4534	0.3	1.9	28.8	68.0	1.0	196358
07204	ROSELLE PARK	27376	5032	15.1	26.4	37.7	14.5	6.4	61443	71324	86	41	3113	0.0	0.6	10.0	85.9	3.5	237021
	NEW JERSEY	31614		18.6	22.5	32.1	15.5	11.4	61437	70239				1.5	2.7	19.7	54.4	21.8	255213
	UNITED STATES	25866		24.7	27.1	30.8	10.9	6.5	48124	56710				10.9	15.0	33.7	30.1	10.4	145905

ZIP CODE #	POST OFFICE NAME	FINANCIAL SERVICES: Auto Loan	Home Loan	Investments	Retirement Plans	THE HOME: Home Improvements: Home Repair	Lawn & Garden	Furnishings: Computers & Hardware	Major Appliances	TV, Radio, Sound Equipment	Furniture	ENTERTAINMENT: Dine out/ Carry out	Sports Equipment	Fees & Tickets	Toys & Games	Travel	Cable TV	PERSONAL: Apparel & Services	Auto Repairs	Health Insurance	Pets & Supplies
07001	AVENEL	93	101	122	105	100	103	103	101	99	103	125	120	104	125	103	94	123	104	91	109
07002	BAYONNE	72	77	108	77	75	83	82	78	84	81	106	90	84	110	83	86	105	81	78	85
07003	BLOOMFIELD	93	107	142	106	103	111	106	102	105	107	132	118	111	139	108	105	132	104	97	111
07004	FAIRFIELD	142	187	227	180	183	192	166	166	157	167	197	188	181	209	175	158	198	161	154	179
07005	BOONTON	140	181	229	178	175	182	165	162	156	166	196	187	178	209	171	154	198	159	146	174
07006	CALDWELL	159	201	258	197	196	207	185	182	176	186	222	209	200	234	193	176	222	179	169	197
07008	CARTERET	82	89	106	84	87	94	86	87	88	88	111	97	89	116	88	90	110	87	85	96
07009	CEDAR GROVE	150	189	233	184	184	194	174	171	166	174	209	196	187	220	181	166	209	168	160	185
07010	CLIFFSIDE PARK	91	97	163	98	92	104	107	98	112	107	142	115	111	152	109	115	142	104	97	108
07011	CLIFTON	75	82	109	79	79	85	83	80	84	85	107	91	85	112	84	85	107	82	77	87
07012	CLIFTON	88	102	125	99	100	109	99	97	99	98	123	110	104	128	102	100	122	97	96	106
07013	CLIFTON	99	120	146	115	117	126	113	111	110	113	138	126	120	146	117	111	138	110	107	120
07014	CLIFTON	97	112	132	110	110	117	108	107	106	108	133	121	113	138	110	106	132	106	102	116
07016	CRANFORD	127	159	198	155	155	164	148	145	142	148	179	166	159	189	154	143	179	143	137	157
07017	EAST ORANGE	71	67	82	64	64	75	72	70	77	74	97	79	74	95	72	80	94	73	74	80
07018	EAST ORANGE	60	56	68	53	54	63	61	59	65	62	81	66	62	79	60	67	79	61	63	67
07020	EDGEWATER	134	130	200	143	125	137	146	135	147	149	187	162	149	190	143	144	185	143	126	150
07021	ESSEX FELLS	354	477	653	467	465	502	416	412	387	425	490	463	472	515	443	391	497	396	383	447
07022	FAIRVIEW	69	73	131	72	70	80	83	75	89	82	113	88	85	123	85	93	114	81	76	83
07023	FANWOOD	139	189	236	180	183	190	166	165	157	167	196	189	182	214	175	157	199	160	150	177
07024	FORT LEE	121	133	183	140	133	140	139	135	134	137	168	162	140	168	141	130	166	140	126	146
07026	GARFIELD	76	83	109	80	79	86	84	81	85	85	108	92	86	113	85	86	108	83	78	88
07027	GARWOOD	97	112	134	112	111	116	109	107	105	108	132	124	113	136	111	104	130	107	101	116
07028	GLEN RIDGE	217	282	325	283	272	277	247	242	227	250	288	278	273	306	255	223	292	233	215	264
07029	HARRISON	67	72	131	71	68	78	81	74	87	81	111	86	83	122	83	91	112	79	74	81
07030	HOBOKEN	131	125	235	142	118	133	148	132	153	151	195	161	154	204	146	153	193	141	124	147
07031	NORTH ARLINGTON	84	95	113	93	93	102	94	92	93	93	117	105	98	120	96	94	115	92	91	100
07032	KEARNY	84	93	133	91	89	98	96	91	98	97	125	104	99	133	97	100	125	94	88	100
07033	KENILWORTH	96	111	124	106	110	119	106	106	105	105	132	118	112	137	110	107	130	104	106	115
07034	LAKE HIAWATHA	108	115	140	118	111	117	117	113	113	119	144	133	119	144	115	109	142	116	102	124
07035	LINCOLN PARK	117	140	170	141	137	140	134	130	127	133	160	153	140	167	136	124	159	130	119	142
07036	LINDEN	79	86	108	83	84	92	87	84	89	87	112	95	90	116	89	91	111	86	85	93
07039	LIVINGSTON	196	279	369	263	269	284	241	239	227	244	284	269	270	312	257	230	290	230	218	255
07040	MAPLEWOOD	161	193	228	193	188	194	180	176	170	181	215	204	191	223	183	166	215	174	161	192
07041	MILLBURN	172	223	313	220	214	227	206	199	196	208	247	230	226	268	215	197	250	196	180	214
07042	MONTCLAIR	148	158	224	164	153	166	164	155	163	166	206	182	172	212	164	162	204	159	147	172
07043	MONTCLAIR	242	317	401	314	308	323	280	276	261	284	329	315	311	348	293	259	333	267	251	300
07044	VERONA	161	200	253	194	196	209	183	183	176	185	221	206	197	229	192	178	221	179	174	198
07045	MONTVILLE	178	238	304	234	231	241	210	206	195	213	247	236	233	264	220	195	250	200	187	223
07046	MOUNTAIN LAKES	311	417	570	409	407	439	365	361	340	373	430	407	413	452	388	343	436	348	336	392
07047	NORTH BERGEN	76	77	145	74	72	84	88	82	97	92	125	93	89	132	89	103	126	88	83	90
07050	ORANGE	71	67	96	65	65	75	75	71	80	76	102	81	76	103	75	83	100	75	74	80
07052	WEST ORANGE	136	172	226	165	166	177	161	157	157	162	197	179	173	211	167	158	198	156	147	169
07054	PARSIPPANY	104	128	180	129	124	129	124	120	119	125	150	141	131	160	127	117	151	121	107	128
07055	PASSAIC	60	60	98	57	57	65	67	64	73	70	93	72	67	97	67	76	94	67	64	69
07057	WALLINGTON	90	97	125	95	94	102	99	96	100	100	127	109	102	132	100	101	127	98	93	105
07058	PINE BROOK	161	186	234	187	178	187	180	174	172	183	218	204	188	224	180	168	218	176	155	189
07059	WARREN	217	288	361	286	279	292	251	247	232	255	294	281	281	311	263	231	298	238	224	269
07060	PLAINFIELD	84	90	127	87	86	95	93	90	96	96	123	102	96	127	94	98	123	93	87	98
07062	PLAINFIELD	100	107	129	104	104	114	107	104	108	108	136	117	112	138	108	110	134	105	104	116
07063	PLAINFIELD	96	105	119	102	103	110	103	101	102	104	129	115	107	131	104	103	127	101	99	112
07064	PORT READING	103	123	141	122	121	124	116	114	111	115	140	133	123	147	119	109	139	113	106	125
07065	RAHWAY	87	95	112	94	93	99	96	93	94	95	118	107	98	121	96	94	117	94	90	101
07066	CLARK	115	136	155	132	135	144	127	127	124	127	155	143	135	160	133	125	153	125	125	138
07067	COLONIA	113	144	173	138	141	148	131	130	126	131	158	148	142	169	137	127	158	127	123	140
07068	ROSELAND	144	202	267	189	194	204	178	176	169	179	212	199	197	235	189	172	216	171	160	186
07069	WATCHUNG	218	311	422	296	300	319	267	265	250	271	314	298	302	343	286	253	321	254	241	283
07070	RUTHERFORD	109	141	192	138	136	143	132	128	126	132	159	149	142	172	137	126	160	127	117	137
07071	LYNDHURST	94	106	125	104	104	113	104	102	103	103	130	116	109	134	106	104	128	102	101	112
07072	CARLSTADT	103	117	143	119	115	121	116	113	112	115	141	132	120	145	117	110	139	114	106	123
07073	EAST RUTHERFORD	100	109	143	110	107	115	112	108	112	112	141	125	115	145	113	112	140	111	104	118
07074	MOONACHIE	99	121	137	113	117	123	107	109	103	109	129	125	113	136	111	104	129	106	102	121
07075	WOOD RIDGE	104	133	163	127	129	136	122	120	118	122	148	137	132	159	127	118	148	118	113	130
07076	SCOTCH PLAINS	161	204	260	201	198	207	188	185	178	189	224	214	202	237	195	177	225	182	168	199
07077	SEWAREN	94	107	125	105	104	110	103	102	101	104	128	116	107	132	105	101	126	102	97	111
07078	SHORT HILLS	412	560	761	546	544	584	487	482	454	497	574	543	552	609	519	458	583	463	445	522
07079	SOUTH ORANGE	185	235	313	232	227	240	218	212	208	219	262	245	236	280	226	208	264	210	194	229
07080	SOUTH PLAINFIELD	108	134	155	130	131	135	123	121	117	123	147	139	131	158	127	116	148	119	112	132
07081	SPRINGFIELD	125	157	196	151	153	163	146	144	141	145	177	163	156	188	152	143	177	142	137	155
07082	TOWACO	172	228	275	226	220	227	198	195	183	201	231	223	221	247	206	181	235	187	174	212
07083	UNION	100	119	146	114	116	124	113	111	111	114	140	126	120	147	117	112	139	111	107	120
07086	WEEHAWKEN	88	89	177	96	84	97	105	93	112	106	142	113	110	155	106	115	143	101	91	104
07087	UNION CITY	52	51	100	46	48	57	59	56	68	63	88	62	59	92	60	73	89	60	58	61
07088	VAUXHALL	85	85	94	81	83	95	84	84	88	87	111	90	89	107	86	92	108	85	90	96
07090	WESTFIELD	195	253	324	250	245	256	229	224	215	231	271	257	251	290	238	214	274	219	203	242
07092	MOUNTAINSIDE	193	235	280	232	233	244	218	218	207	218	260	249	231	268	226	206	258	213	205	235
07093	WEST NEW YORK	57	57	110	53	53	63	65	61	74	69	96	69	65	100	67	80	97	66	64	67
07094	SECAUCUS	114	136	166	132	133	142	130	128	127	130	160	146	138	168	134	128	159	127	123	138
07095	WOODBRIDGE	97	108	136	110	106	112	109	105	106	108	134	124	113	139	110	105	132	107	99	115
07102	NEWARK	38	34	52	34	33	39	41	38	44	41	56	44	41	55	41	46	54	42	41	42
07103	NEWARK	52	44	56	41	43	51	51	50	57	52	70	56	50	67	50	59	68	52	54	57
07104	NEWARK	52	52	95	48	49	57	59	56	66	62	86	63	59	89	60	71	86	60	57	61
07105	NEWARK	55	58	119	56	55	65	68	62	76	69	97	72	70	107	70	81	99	67	64	68
07106	NEWARK	65	61	85	58	59	69	67	65	73	69	92	73	69	93	68	77	90	67	68	74
07107	NEWARK	51	47	81	43	45	53	54	52	62	57	79	58	54	80	54	66	79	56	55	58
07108	NEWARK	49	42	53	40	41	49	48	47	53	49	66	53	48	63	47	55	64	49	51	54
07109	BELLEVILLE	83	91	125	88	87	95	93	89	95	94	121	101	96	127	94	97	121	92	87	97
07110	NUTLEY	104	120	148	120	117	124	118	114	114	117	144	133	123	148	120	114	142	115	108	125
07111	IRVINGTON	69	66	89	64	63	73	72	69	78	74	98	78	74	99	72	80	96	72	72	78
07112	NEWARK	64	58	70	55	56	66	63	62	69	65	86	69	65	84	63	71	84	64	66	71
07114	NEWARK	38	33	48	30	32	38	38	37	43	39	54	41	37	52	38	46	53	39	41	42
07201	ELIZABETH	59	58	104	53	54	64	65	62	74	69	96	69	65	99	66	79	96	67	65	68
07202	ELIZABETH	58	59	111	54	55	65	67	63	76	71	98	71	67	103	68	81	99	68	65	69
07203	ROSELLE	91	100	117	97	97	105	98	96	98	99	123	109	102	126	99	98	122	97	94	106
07204	ROSELLE PARK	91	103	124	101	100	106	101	98	99	102	125	113	104	129	102	98	124	99	93	107
	NEW JERSEY	110	123	153	121	120	128	120	118	119	121	150	136	125	155	123	120	149	119	114	130
	UNITED STATES	100	100	100	100	100	100	100	100	100	100	100	100	100	100	100	100	100	100	100	100

POPULATION CHANGE

#	POST OFFICE NAME	COUNTY FIPS CODE	POPULATION 2000	2004	2009	2000-2004 ANNUAL RATE % Rate	State Centile	HOUSEHOLDS 2000	2004	2009	% Annual Rate 2000-2004	2004 Average HH Size	FAMILIES 2000	2004	% Annual Rate 2000-2004
07205	HILLSIDE	039	22442	22620	23091	0.2	31	7405	7414	7515	0.0	3.05	5738	5768	0.1
07206	ELIZABETH	039	22887	23514	24264	0.6	52	6769	6904	7072	0.5	3.39	5320	5452	0.6
07208	ELIZABETH	039	32841	35382	37547	1.8	83	12164	12935	13570	1.5	2.72	7891	8434	1.6
07302	JERSEY CITY	017	34571	34676	34978	0.1	25	15663	15706	15829	0.1	2.18	7267	7392	0.4
07304	JERSEY CITY	017	42064	42822	43253	0.4	42	14320	14468	14561	0.2	2.92	9698	9895	0.5
07305	JERSEY CITY	017	58384	60658	62547	0.9	62	20137	21034	21736	1.0	2.85	14412	15137	1.2
07306	JERSEY CITY	017	55560	55811	56407	0.1	27	20710	20686	20842	0.0	2.63	12579	12681	0.2
07307	JERSEY CITY	017	45571	48081	49619	1.3	74	15956	16725	17203	1.1	2.86	10872	11497	1.3
07310	JERSEY CITY	017	3905	4659	5122	4.2	97	1846	2167	2353	3.8	2.10	807	984	4.8
07401	ALLENDALE	003	6692	6818	6945	0.4	43	2108	2156	2200	0.5	3.02	1794	1843	0.6
07403	BLOOMINGDALE	031	7634	7489	7526	-0.5	3	2855	2802	2810	-0.4	2.63	2081	2052	-0.3
07405	BUTLER	027	16781	17711	18730	1.3	74	5930	6263	6625	1.3	2.82	4713	4982	1.3
07407	ELMWOOD PARK	003	18949	19444	19908	0.6	50	7098	7278	7448	0.6	2.67	5084	5251	0.8
07410	FAIR LAWN	003	31613	31703	32158	0.1	25	11797	11872	12065	0.2	2.66	8899	9004	0.3
07416	FRANKLIN	037	5704	5837	6143	0.5	48	2089	2150	2281	0.7	2.69	1457	1506	0.8
07417	FRANKLIN LAKES	003	10409	10707	10920	0.7	54	3318	3425	3499	0.8	3.12	2957	3061	0.8
07418	GLENWOOD	037	2351	2463	2610	1.1	70	728	772	827	1.4	3.19	629	669	1.5
07419	HAMBURG	037	6794	7925	8930	3.7	97	2603	3080	3513	4.0	2.57	1907	2268	4.2
07420	HASKELL	031	5046	5171	5291	0.6	49	1569	1611	1646	0.6	2.95	1237	1274	0.7
07421	HEWITT	031	7688	7944	8194	0.8	57	2696	2790	2871	0.8	2.84	2066	2147	0.9
07422	HIGHLAND LAKES	037	7408	7741	8244	1.0	68	2497	2648	2854	1.4	2.92	2009	2137	1.5
07423	HO HO KUS	003	4060	3994	4011	-0.4	5	1433	1414	1422	-0.3	2.81	1199	1188	-0.2
07424	LITTLE FALLS	031	21963	22165	22538	0.2	33	8991	9064	9184	0.2	2.43	5835	5916	0.3
07430	MAHWAH	003	24062	25672	26773	1.5	79	9340	9892	10327	1.4	2.46	6288	6720	1.6
07432	MIDLAND PARK	003	6945	6848	6893	-0.3	7	2612	2588	2613	-0.2	2.64	1883	1880	0.0
07435	NEWFOUNDLAND	031	2404	2591	2740	1.8	84	881	950	1004	1.8	2.69	688	746	1.9
07436	OAKLAND	003	12466	13206	13730	1.4	75	4255	4528	4720	1.5	2.87	3567	3805	1.5
07438	OAK RIDGE	027	11736	12035	12501	0.6	50	4122	4223	4380	0.6	2.84	3283	3375	0.7
07439	OGDENSBURG	037	2625	2599	2710	-0.2	10	874	875	922	0.0	2.97	700	703	0.1
07440	PEQUANNOCK	027	4610	4626	4762	0.1	26	1632	1636	1684	0.1	2.82	1281	1291	0.2
07442	POMPTON LAKES	031	10640	10848	11066	0.5	44	3949	4032	4103	0.5	2.69	2805	2877	0.6
07444	POMPTON PLAINS	027	9218	9384	9739	0.4	42	3373	3435	3567	0.4	2.73	2527	2585	0.5
07446	RAMSEY	003	14293	14217	14311	-0.1	16	5298	5284	5326	-0.1	2.67	3932	3946	0.1
07450	RIDGEWOOD	003	24942	24630	24775	-0.3	9	8605	8508	8563	-0.3	2.87	6779	6735	-0.2
07452	GLEN ROCK	003	11529	11372	11434	-0.3	8	3972	3917	3937	-0.3	2.89	3317	3286	-0.2
07456	RINGWOOD	031	12372	12224	12304	-0.3	9	4102	4062	4082	-0.2	2.99	3441	3416	-0.2
07457	RIVERDALE	027	2498	2681	2855	1.7	82	919	985	1049	1.7	2.69	672	723	1.7
07458	SADDLE RIVER	003	11007	11547	11908	1.1	71	3632	3824	3951	1.2	2.99	3184	3364	1.3
07460	STOCKHOLM	037	3686	4204	4660	3.1	96	1282	1473	1645	3.3	2.85	993	1149	3.5
07461	SUSSEX	037	19026	20579	22199	1.9	85	6338	6911	7515	2.1	2.98	5102	5584	2.2
07462	VERNON	037	6596	7272	7945	2.3	91	2536	2818	3111	2.5	2.58	1739	1942	2.6
07463	WALDWICK	003	9625	9548	9619	-0.2	12	3429	3414	3446	-0.1	2.80	2679	2680	0.0
07465	WANAQUE	031	5255	5236	5287	-0.1	17	1885	1879	1892	-0.1	2.79	1461	1460	0.0
07470	WAYNE	031	53036	55076	57025	0.9	61	18441	19144	19769	0.9	2.75	14135	14755	1.0
07480	WEST MILFORD	031	15940	16898	17612	1.4	76	5522	5870	6108	1.5	2.84	4352	4633	1.5
07481	WYCKOFF	003	16518	16837	17191	0.5	43	5544	5668	5797	0.5	2.88	4636	4762	0.6
07501	PATERSON	031	34868	35462	36214	0.4	41	10280	10412	10591	0.3	3.14	6984	7101	0.4
07502	PATERSON	031	15371	15690	15981	0.5	45	4818	4857	4901	0.2	3.23	3708	3750	0.3
07503	PATERSON	031	19060	19423	19816	0.4	43	5890	5939	6010	0.2	3.26	4350	4407	0.3
07504	PATERSON	031	13189	13474	13868	0.5	47	3758	3843	3947	0.5	3.50	3044	3124	0.6
07505	PATERSON	031	2440	2395	2402	-0.4	3	746	725	725	-0.7	2.52	432	424	-0.4
07506	HAWTHORNE	031	18236	18121	18270	-0.2	14	7264	7215	7253	-0.2	2.51	4936	4925	-0.1
07508	HALEDON	031	22994	23235	23575	0.3	34	7587	7632	7710	0.1	2.88	5722	5776	0.2
07512	TOTOWA	031	9889	9832	9910	-0.1	15	3537	3516	3537	-0.1	2.63	2643	2637	-0.1
07513	PATERSON	031	13071	13242	13533	0.3	37	3530	3531	3576	0.0	3.75	2948	2956	0.1
07514	PATERSON	031	18657	18727	19031	0.1	26	6242	6267	6346	0.1	2.95	4418	4462	0.2
07522	PATERSON	031	20030	20897	21643	1.0	66	5864	6065	6243	0.8	3.42	4571	4764	1.0
07524	PATERSON	031	12625	13020	13432	0.7	56	3614	3713	3812	0.6	3.50	2922	3011	0.7
07601	HACKENSACK	003	42644	44923	46885	1.2	73	18106	19068	19945	1.2	2.27	9557	10164	1.5
07603	BOGOTA	003	8247	8185	8262	-0.2	13	2872	2852	2880	-0.2	2.85	2124	2123	-0.0
07604	HASBROUCK HEIGHTS	003	11823	11968	12230	0.3	36	4620	4694	4807	0.4	2.55	3188	3258	0.5
07605	LEONIA	003	9004	9044	9142	0.1	27	3298	3297	3325	0.0	2.74	2451	2467	0.2
07606	SOUTH HACKENSACK	003	2217	2230	2251	0.1	29	793	800	810	0.2	2.79	580	590	0.4
07607	MAYWOOD	003	9513	9612	9778	0.2	33	3706	3760	3833	0.3	2.55	2623	2677	0.5
07608	TETERBORO	003	18	18	18	0.0	22	7	7	7	0.0	2.57	5	5	0.0
07620	ALPINE	003	2181	2270	2330	1.0	64	705	738	759	1.1	3.07	620	651	1.2
07621	BERGENFIELD	003	26685	27778	28762	1.0	64	9179	9509	9816	0.8	2.91	6891	7167	0.9
07624	CLOSTER	003	8392	8461	8593	0.2	31	2792	2824	2873	0.3	2.97	2324	2360	0.4
07626	CRESSKILL	003	7784	7738	7786	-0.1	15	2641	2634	2657	-0.1	2.90	2173	2176	0.0
07627	DEMAREST	003	4784	4720	4743	-0.3	8	1584	1570	1581	-0.2	3.00	1373	1367	-0.1
07628	DUMONT	003	17271	17413	17721	0.2	31	6237	6303	6424	0.3	2.76	4672	4756	0.4
07630	EMERSON	003	7197	7091	7122	-0.4	6	2373	2346	2362	-0.3	2.90	1964	1952	-0.1
07631	ENGLEWOOD	003	26131	26051	26312	-0.1	18	9251	9223	9318	-0.1	2.79	6470	6499	0.1
07632	ENGLEWOOD CLIFFS	003	5424	5509	5607	0.4	39	1850	1886	1925	0.5	2.90	1587	1625	0.6
07640	HARRINGTON PARK	003	4917	4987	5078	0.3	38	1660	1692	1727	0.5	2.93	1423	1454	0.5
07641	HAWORTH	003	3379	3322	3337	-0.4	4	1130	1115	1123	-0.3	2.97	968	959	-0.2
07642	HILLSDALE	003	9863	9844	9933	-0.1	19	3429	3436	3475	0.1	2.85	2794	2811	0.1
07643	LITTLE FERRY	003	10816	10882	11020	0.1	29	4372	4377	4421	0.0	2.49	2790	2823	0.3
07644	LODI	003	23971	24633	25236	0.6	52	9528	9791	10030	0.6	2.50	6100	6320	0.8
07645	MONTVALE	003	7026	7148	7250	0.4	42	2504	2552	2591	0.5	2.80	1996	2045	0.6
07646	NEW MILFORD	003	16390	16302	16436	-0.1	16	6342	6332	6396	0.0	2.53	4273	4297	0.1
07647	NORTHVALE	003	4859	4856	4891	0.0	21	1651	1655	1670	0.1	2.83	1296	1308	0.2
07648	NORWOOD	003	5558	5816	5987	1.1	68	1756	1847	1907	1.2	3.03	1481	1564	1.3
07649	ORADELL	003	8026	7908	7954	-0.4	6	2779	2750	2772	-0.3	2.82	2290	2276	-0.1
07650	PALISADES PARK	003	16758	17375	17851	0.9	60	6112	6273	6410	0.6	2.77	4363	4513	0.8
07652	PARAMUS	003	25737	26174	26722	0.4	41	8082	8263	8466	0.5	2.99	6779	6955	0.6
07656	PARK RIDGE	003	8747	8734	8794	0.0	20	3178	3185	3212	0.1	2.66	2404	2425	0.2
07657	RIDGEFIELD	003	10622	11040	11353	0.9	62	3950	4085	4189	0.8	2.70	2894	3016	1.0
07660	RIDGEFIELD PARK	003	12926	13024	13239	0.2	30	5049	5106	5200	0.3	2.54	3269	3331	0.4
07661	RIVER EDGE	003	10777	11161	11501	0.8	60	4064	4192	4312	0.7	2.66	3049	3168	0.9
07662	ROCHELLE PARK	003	5538	5414	5428	-0.5	3	2065	2021	2029	-0.5	2.52	1397	1379	-0.2
07663	SADDLE BROOK	003	13148	13140	13336	0.0	21	5060	5075	5163	0.1	2.57	3578	3611	0.2
07666	TEANECK	003	39120	38602	38918	-0.3	8	13357	13177	13288	-0.3	2.86	10024	9942	-0.2
07670	TENAFLY	003	13671	13552	13638	-0.2	11	4731	4684	4712	-0.2	2.86	3831	3812	-0.1
07675	WESTWOOD	003	26192	26839	27462	0.6	49	9625	9893	10148	0.7	2.68	7164	7423	0.8
	NEW JERSEY					0.8					0.9	2.68			1.0
	UNITED STATES					1.2					1.3	2.58			1.1

ZIP CODE #	POST OFFICE NAME	RACE (%) White 2000	White 2004	Black 2000	Black 2004	Asian/Pacific 2000	Asian/Pacific 2004	% Hispanic Origin 2000	% Hispanic Origin 2004	2004 AGE DISTRIBUTION (%) 0-4	5-9	10-14	15-19	20-24	25-44	45-64	65-84	85+	18+	MEDIAN AGE 2004	% 2004 Males	% 2004 Females
07205	HILLSIDE	39.0	37.3	47.8	47.8	3.5	3.9	14.3	16.7	6.4	6.5	7.5	7.0	6.9	29.0	25.3	10.0	1.4	75.4	36.5	46.9	53.1
07206	ELIZABETH	50.2	49.4	21.5	20.3	0.6	0.6	61.5	65.5	9.3	8.8	8.8	8.3	8.7	30.4	17.8	7.0	0.9	68.2	28.9	49.0	51.0
07208	ELIZABETH	60.0	57.5	18.7	19.2	3.5	3.7	42.7	47.5	7.4	6.9	7.2	6.7	7.5	32.5	21.8	8.6	1.4	74.6	33.8	48.8	51.2
07302	JERSEY CITY	45.3	42.2	17.3	16.8	17.9	19.5	27.9	31.5	5.8	4.6	4.8	5.2	8.6	44.3	18.7	7.1	1.0	81.9	33.3	51.6	48.4
07304	JERSEY CITY	20.6	20.1	46.6	44.4	12.1	12.9	25.8	29.1	7.7	7.3	8.4	7.9	8.2	30.3	21.1	8.1	1.0	71.9	31.7	47.6	52.4
07305	JERSEY CITY	23.2	22.4	51.6	49.7	12.1	13.4	17.4	19.8	7.5	7.3	7.9	7.3	7.3	29.7	22.1	9.5	1.4	72.9	33.7	45.9	54.1
07306	JERSEY CITY	37.1	34.7	16.0	15.0	23.0	24.6	29.2	32.9	6.7	6.1	6.8	6.9	7.9	33.9	21.0	9.2	1.5	76.7	33.7	50.6	49.4
07307	JERSEY CITY	47.4	44.1	6.4	6.1	14.5	15.3	45.0	49.7	7.2	6.6	7.6	7.4	8.3	33.0	20.7	8.0	1.2	74.2	32.4	49.0	51.0
07310	JERSEY CITY	40.9	36.7	13.5	15.3	35.0	34.8	14.4	19.2	6.5	3.0	2.7	3.7	11.5	55.1	14.5	2.9	0.1	85.6	30.9	52.3	47.7
07401	ALLENDALE	92.5	90.7	0.4	0.4	6.1	7.6	2.5	3.2	6.8	8.2	9.5	6.6	3.7	22.7	28.0	11.0	3.4	70.8	41.1	48.3	51.7
07403	BLOOMINGDALE	95.5	94.2	0.4	0.6	2.2	2.8	4.4	6.2	6.5	6.6	6.6	5.2	4.9	30.9	26.1	11.6	1.7	77.0	39.4	49.5	50.5
07405	BUTLER	95.3	94.2	0.6	0.7	2.5	3.1	3.6	4.6	6.7	7.6	7.8	6.1	4.2	27.0	28.9	10.5	1.2	74.0	40.0	49.7	50.3
07407	ELMWOOD PARK	82.5	79.7	2.2	2.4	7.8	9.2	13.4	15.9	5.8	5.6	6.0	6.0	6.2	30.0	24.8	13.2	2.4	79.0	39.1	47.9	52.2
07410	FAIR LAWN	91.5	89.9	0.7	0.8	4.9	6.0	5.5	6.7	5.2	5.8	6.8	6.2	5.0	24.5	28.1	15.5	3.0	78.4	42.9	47.4	52.6
07416	FRANKLIN	95.0	94.2	0.7	0.7	1.5	1.9	4.4	5.3	6.9	6.7	7.6	7.1	6.3	28.5	25.3	9.9	1.7	74.2	37.8	47.4	52.7
07417	FRANKLIN LAKES	91.4	89.5	0.9	1.1	6.3	7.8	2.8	3.4	6.6	8.1	8.9	6.9	3.9	21.6	31.5	11.5	1.1	71.6	41.5	49.4	50.6
07418	GLENWOOD	96.4	95.7	0.6	0.7	0.9	1.1	3.2	4.0	6.3	7.3	9.3	8.4	5.6	26.8	29.5	6.2	0.7	71.9	37.7	49.5	50.5
07419	HAMBURG	94.1	93.1	0.9	1.0	2.1	2.5	4.0	4.8	6.5	6.7	7.4	6.0	5.1	29.7	27.7	10.0	1.0	75.5	38.7	48.3	51.7
07420	HASKELL	88.8	85.8	1.9	2.4	3.8	4.7	6.5	9.1	6.4	6.4	6.9	6.3	5.6	28.1	23.8	12.6	3.8	76.1	39.5	48.8	51.2
07421	HEWITT	94.1	92.2	1.3	1.8	0.9	1.3	4.2	6.2	7.1	7.7	8.6	6.8	5.1	31.5	26.9	5.8	0.7	72.2	37.0	50.3	49.7
07422	HIGHLAND LAKES	96.5	95.9	0.8	0.9	0.4	0.5	3.8	4.6	6.6	7.4	9.1	7.4	5.2	29.7	27.6	6.2	0.8	72.2	37.0	49.8	50.2
07423	HO HO KUS	92.7	91.2	0.6	0.7	5.4	6.6	2.0	2.4	7.9	9.2	8.2	5.6	2.5	22.6	28.6	13.5	1.8	70.6	41.7	48.2	51.8
07424	LITTLE FALLS	89.1	86.1	2.1	2.7	4.0	5.0	7.7	10.8	5.6	5.4	5.4	5.2	6.0	31.2	25.1	14.2	1.9	80.7	39.9	47.6	52.4
07430	MAHWAH	87.9	85.8	2.2	2.4	6.3	7.7	4.3	5.2	6.7	7.2	6.5	6.9	6.5	28.6	26.1	10.6	1.1	76.6	38.6	47.6	52.4
07432	MIDLAND PARK	95.8	95.0	0.4	0.5	2.2	2.8	3.7	4.6	7.1	7.3	6.9	5.8	4.5	28.1	26.1	12.2	2.0	75.0	39.7	48.9	51.2
07435	NEWFOUNDLAND	94.6	93.0	1.7	2.1	1.2	1.6	3.3	4.8	7.5	8.1	7.8	5.8	4.1	30.0	26.9	8.7	1.1	72.6	38.1	51.6	48.4
07436	OAKLAND	94.8	93.5	0.8	0.9	2.7	3.5	3.9	4.9	7.5	8.0	7.1	5.6	3.9	27.3	27.2	11.7	1.7	73.7	40.3	48.9	51.1
07438	OAK RIDGE	96.5	95.7	0.7	0.8	1.2	1.5	2.9	3.8	7.7	8.2	7.8	5.9	4.2	29.4	27.4	8.6	0.9	72.4	38.2	49.4	50.6
07439	OGDENSBURG	97.5	97.0	0.2	0.2	0.7	0.9	4.2	5.2	7.1	7.5	8.5	7.2	5.7	29.0	26.2	7.9	0.9	72.3	36.6	50.6	49.4
07440	PEQUANNOCK	96.9	96.2	0.4	0.4	1.8	2.2	3.3	4.3	6.8	7.2	7.3	6.6	4.8	26.8	25.9	13.0	1.7	74.6	40.3	48.9	51.1
07442	POMPTON LAKES	93.0	90.8	1.2	1.6	3.0	3.8	5.7	8.3	6.8	6.9	6.9	6.1	5.3	29.7	25.2	11.5	1.7	75.6	38.3	48.1	52.0
07444	POMPTON PLAINS	96.5	95.7	0.3	0.3	2.0	2.5	2.8	3.6	6.6	7.1	7.6	6.6	4.9	26.0	26.9	12.4	1.9	74.3	40.3	48.0	52.1
07446	RAMSEY	91.6	89.8	0.8	0.9	5.9	7.2	2.9	3.6	7.3	7.8	7.7	6.1	4.2	27.0	28.2	10.3	1.4	72.8	39.8	48.4	51.6
07450	RIDGEWOOD	87.8	85.6	1.6	1.8	8.7	10.5	3.8	4.6	7.4	8.6	8.8	7.1	4.1	23.6	28.1	10.3	2.0	70.5	39.8	48.2	51.8
07452	GLEN ROCK	90.1	88.1	1.8	2.1	6.5	8.0	2.7	3.4	7.8	9.1	8.8	6.2	3.3	23.3	28.0	11.4	2.1	70.0	40.8	49.0	51.0
07456	RINGWOOD	93.9	92.1	1.6	2.1	1.2	1.6	4.3	6.2	7.2	8.0	7.6	6.2	4.4	28.2	29.0	8.3	0.9	73.0	38.6	50.0	50.0
07457	RIVERDALE	93.4	92.1	1.1	1.2	2.7	3.3	4.4	5.7	6.0	6.5	7.4	5.9	5.2	30.1	27.5	10.3	1.2	76.9	38.6	48.9	51.1
07458	SADDLE RIVER	90.8	88.8	0.9	1.0	6.6	8.2	2.3	2.9	6.6	8.3	8.9	6.7	3.4	20.4	30.6	13.4	1.7	71.6	42.6	48.8	51.2
07460	STOCKHOLM	96.9	96.4	0.6	0.6	0.7	0.9	2.5	3.1	7.5	8.1	8.2	6.4	4.2	29.0	28.3	7.4	1.0	72.1	38.2	50.3	49.7
07461	SUSSEX	97.0	96.4	0.7	0.8	0.8	1.0	2.8	3.5	6.6	7.3	8.9	7.8	5.6	26.9	27.9	8.0	1.1	72.1	37.3	49.3	50.7
07462	VERNON	96.2	95.5	0.9	1.0	0.8	1.0	4.4	5.4	6.7	6.8	7.8	6.8	7.2	32.5	25.7	6.1	0.5	74.2	34.9	51.4	48.6
07463	WALDWICK	92.7	91.1	0.6	0.7	4.5	5.6	5.3	6.6	7.4	7.8	7.6	5.5	4.3	28.1	24.7	12.9	1.7	73.6	39.3	48.8	51.2
07465	WANAQUE	92.5	90.0	1.1	1.6	3.4	4.4	4.3	6.3	6.9	7.1	6.9	5.4	5.1	30.8	28.9	7.8	1.1	75.8	38.2	47.4	52.6
07470	WAYNE	90.3	87.5	1.5	2.0	5.7	7.1	5.1	7.1	6.0	6.6	6.9	6.9	5.5	24.7	26.7	14.1	2.6	76.8	41.2	47.6	52.5
07480	WEST MILFORD	95.4	94.0	1.3	1.7	1.1	1.4	3.0	4.4	6.8	7.4	7.7	6.2	4.5	28.9	28.3	8.9	1.3	73.9	39.1	49.5	50.5
07481	WYCKOFF	94.5	93.3	0.5	0.5	3.7	4.7	2.3	2.9	6.9	8.2	8.6	6.5	3.6	21.7	28.5	12.9	3.0	72.0	42.1	47.9	52.1
07501	PATERSON	28.3	26.7	32.9	31.8	1.4	1.4	54.8	58.3	8.8	8.0	8.2	8.2	9.2	31.1	18.5	7.3	0.9	70.4	29.6	51.1	49.0
07502	PATERSON	48.8	44.4	17.2	17.9	5.2	5.1	46.7	52.8	8.3	7.6	8.0	7.2	7.8	30.7	20.3	8.8	1.5	71.9	32.6	48.1	51.9
07503	PATERSON	47.4	43.2	9.0	9.1	2.5	2.5	54.9	61.4	8.5	7.7	8.2	8.0	8.2	31.4	19.5	7.5	1.0	71.0	31.0	49.9	50.1
07504	PATERSON	14.8	13.9	58.9	58.2	0.8	0.7	32.8	35.3	7.2	7.1	8.3	7.6	8.0	30.3	23.4	7.6	0.6	72.9	33.0	46.7	53.3
07505	PATERSON	28.5	26.4	31.8	31.1	2.9	2.7	54.5	58.5	6.6	5.8	5.8	7.4	8.5	32.6	24.3	8.3	0.8	77.5	35.4	54.0	46.1
07506	HAWTHORNE	93.8	91.9	0.8	1.0	1.9	2.4	7.4	10.4	6.3	6.2	6.1	5.7	5.5	30.7	24.9	12.4	2.3	77.9	39.1	48.0	52.1
07508	HALEDON	78.1	73.8	6.9	8.0	3.2	3.6	19.4	24.2	6.6	6.7	7.2	7.0	8.4	28.3	21.7	11.8	2.4	75.6	35.6	47.2	52.8
07512	TOTOWA	93.4	91.3	1.1	1.4	2.3	2.9	6.4	9.0	4.5	4.9	5.5	5.2	4.8	28.0	26.3	17.8	3.2	82.0	43.3	47.2	52.8
07513	PATERSON	33.6	31.6	22.9	21.9	0.9	0.8	67.3	71.2	8.4	8.2	8.7	8.0	9.1	31.0	20.2	5.8	0.7	70.0	29.7	47.9	52.1
07514	PATERSON	20.9	19.0	51.6	51.4	0.7	0.7	34.9	37.9	7.9	7.6	8.1	7.3	7.6	29.4	21.0	9.3	1.8	71.9	32.8	45.4	54.6
07522	PATERSON	26.8	25.7	43.4	42.3	3.4	3.2	45.2	49.1	9.7	9.2	9.7	8.6	8.5	30.0	18.0	5.6	0.7	66.4	27.8	47.3	52.7
07524	PATERSON	26.2	24.2	27.3	26.3	0.4	0.4	63.5	67.3	9.1	8.6	9.4	8.2	8.3	31.3	18.3	6.3	0.6	68.1	29.0	49.4	50.6
07601	HACKENSACK	52.7	50.3	24.6	24.9	7.5	8.4	25.9	28.3	5.7	5.2	5.1	5.0	6.8	35.5	24.0	10.8	2.0	81.1	37.6	49.6	50.5
07603	BOGOTA	75.7	72.5	5.7	6.2	7.8	9.0	21.3	24.9	6.4	6.5	7.3	7.1	6.2	29.3	26.0	9.8	1.3	75.3	37.3	47.6	52.4
07604	HASBROUCK HEIGHTS	87.3	84.9	2.1	2.3	6.8	8.2	8.3	10.1	5.7	5.8	6.2	6.3	5.9	27.4	26.9	13.4	2.5	78.5	40.6	48.2	51.8
07605	LEONIA	65.6	61.2	2.4	2.5	26.0	29.6	12.8	14.7	5.7	6.2	7.2	6.4	5.4	25.7	29.4	12.3	1.9	77.0	41.3	48.2	51.8
07606	SOUTH HACKENSACK	82.3	79.5	2.5	2.7	6.0	7.2	15.4	18.2	5.7	5.6	5.8	5.5	6.1	31.9	23.3	14.3	1.8	79.6	38.0	49.1	50.9
07607	MAYWOOD	84.6	81.8	2.8	3.1	7.2	8.7	11.7	14.1	6.4	6.4	6.0	5.3	4.7	28.1	26.6	13.4	3.1	77.9	40.9	46.7	53.3
07608	TETERBORO	77.8	72.2	5.6	5.6	5.6	5.6	22.2	22.2	11.1	11.1	11.1	11.1	11.1	44.4	0.0	0.0	0.0	66.7	22.5	50.0	50.0
07620	ALPINE	77.4	73.4	1.5	1.7	19.1	22.8	2.5	3.1	4.6	6.2	8.2	7.0	3.7	20.0	33.7	15.1	1.5	76.2	45.2	50.6	49.4
07621	BERGENFIELD	63.2	58.5	6.8	7.4	20.3	23.1	16.9	19.5	6.7	6.8	7.4	6.5	5.7	28.1	25.6	11.3	1.8	75.1	38.3	48.0	52.0
07624	CLOSTER	75.3	71.1	0.9	1.0	21.5	25.4	4.1	4.8	6.3	7.3	8.5	6.9	4.5	23.9	29.0	12.0	1.7	73.1	41.3	49.2	50.8
07626	CRESSKILL	78.0	74.1	0.9	1.0	18.7	22.2	4.0	4.8	6.6	7.5	7.9	6.1	4.2	23.0	27.8	14.3	2.7	73.8	42.1	48.1	51.9
07627	DEMAREST	77.3	73.2	0.5	0.6	20.2	24.0	3.5	4.1	5.8	7.4	9.4	7.6	4.1	20.3	30.4	13.2	1.7	72.4	42.5	49.0	51.0
07628	DUMONT	83.8	80.7	1.5	1.7	11.0	13.2	8.4	10.1	6.6	6.9	7.2	6.2	5.1	28.2	24.7	13.1	2.0	75.4	39.5	48.3	51.7
07630	EMERSON	89.6	87.4	0.9	1.0	7.9	9.7	4.6	5.7	6.7	7.2	6.6	5.4	4.0	25.1	25.8	15.4	3.9	76.0	42.1	47.8	52.2
07631	ENGLEWOOD	42.4	41.1	39.1	39.0	5.3	5.8	21.8	23.4	6.8	6.9	6.9	6.2	5.6	28.8	25.3	11.8	1.8	75.6	38.2	47.0	53.0
07632	ENGLEWOOD CLIFFS	67.2	62.4	1.4	1.5	29.3	33.8	4.9	5.6	5.6	6.2	6.1	5.2	3.9	22.9	27.7	20.1	2.4	78.7	45.1	47.4	52.6
07640	HARRINGTON PARK	83.2	79.7	0.7	0.8	14.9	18.1	2.6	3.2	6.8	8.0	8.1	6.6	4.3	22.4	30.0	12.3	1.5	72.7	41.4	48.5	51.5
07641	HAWORTH	88.0	85.5	1.2	1.4	9.2	11.2	2.7	3.3	6.6	8.0	8.7	6.8	3.7	20.9	30.7	12.9	1.8	71.6	42.3	49.4	50.6
07642	HILLSDALE	92.4	90.8	0.9	1.0	5.1	6.3	4.2	5.2	7.2	7.6	7.3	6.0	4.3	25.7	27.2	12.9	1.9	73.8	40.7	48.6	51.4
07643	LITTLE FERRY	68.8	65.4	4.7	4.9	17.1	19.0	15.2	17.8	6.2	5.7	5.8	5.7	6.3	32.6	25.2	11.2	1.3	79.0	38.1	48.7	51.3
07644	LODI	78.2	75.2	3.6	3.8	8.9	10.2	18.0	21.1	6.4	6.0	6.0	5.7	6.5	32.6	23.1	11.7	2.0	78.2	37.2	47.5	52.5
07645	MONTVALE	92.8	91.2	0.4	0.5	5.4	6.6	3.1	3.9	6.7	7.5	7.7	6.0	4.5	24.8	28.9	12.9	1.1	74.2	41.0	49.2	50.8
07646	NEW MILFORD	78.6	75.0	2.6	2.9	14.8	17.5	8.1	9.6	6.3	6.3	6.2	5.2	4.7	28.8	25.5	14.2	2.9	77.9	40.6	48.3	51.7
07647	NORTHVALE	83.4	80.2	1.0	1.1	13.3	15.9	4.7	5.8	5.6	5.8	6.2	6.8	5.5	26.1	26.4	14.9	2.8	77.8	41.7	50.0	50.0
07648	NORWOOD	78.0	73.8	0.8	1.0	18.9	22.5	3.0	3.7	5.7	6.6	7.8	6.8	4.4	24.1	28.4	13.1	3.1	75.4	42.2	46.9	53.1
07649	ORADELL	90.1	88.0	0.5	0.6	8.1	9.9	3.1	3.8	6.2	7.0	7.3	6.3	4.0	23.5	28.8	14.5	2.6	75.3	42.5	48.1	51.9
07650	PALISADES PARK	48.7	44.3	1.3	1.4	41.0	44.7	16.0	17.5	6.6	6.0	5.2	4.7	6.0	35.9	23.0	11.2	1.5	79.6	37.1	49.5	50.5
07652	PARAMUS	79.2	75.3	1.1	1.3	17.2	20.6	4.9	5.9	5.2	5.8	6.9	6.4	4.8	22.5	26.6	18.3	3.5	77.7	44.0	48.5	51.6
07656	PARK RIDGE	93.5	92.1	0.9	1.0	3.9	4.8	5.3	6.5	6.7	7.2	6.8	5.2	4.1	25.7	27.6	13.7	3.0	75.8	41.9	48.3	51.7
07657	RIDGEFIELD	74.3	70.4	0.9	0.9	18.4	21.3	14.7	17.0	5.3	5.5	7.0	5.9	5.7	29.0	25.0	14.2	2.5	78.5	40.2	48.6	51.5
07660	RIDGEFIELD PARK	78.1	74.9	4.2	4.6	7.9	9.3	22.2	25.8	5.8	5.7	6.4	6.4	6.3	31.6	24.9	11.4	1.5	78.1	38.3	48.0	52.0
07661	RIVER EDGE	84.3	81.6	1.0	1.1	12.6	14.8	5.3	6.3	7.1	7.3	6.5	5.9	4.4	26.1	26.2	13.9	2.6	75.2	41.0	47.8	52.2
07662	ROCHELLE PARK	90.1	88.0	0.5	0.5	6.0	7.3	8.6	10.5	5.5	5.7	5.6	4.6	4.3	26.5	25.2	16.3	6.4	80.3	43.5	46.1	53.9
07663	SADDLE BROOK	90.7	89.0	1.4	1.5	4.7	5.7	6.3	7.7	5.6	5.7	5.8	5.6	5.1	28.9	26.0	14.8	2.6	79.5	41.1	47.3	52.7
07666	TEANECK	56.2	53.2	28.8	30.0	7.2	8.2	10.5	12.0	6.3	6.8	7.6	7.7	6.6	24.2	26.4	12.1	2.3	75.0	38.8	47.4	52.6
07670	TENAFLY	76.8	72.9	1.0	1.1	19.1	22.4	4.7	5.6	6.4	7.5	8.3	7.1	5.2	21.0	29.2	13.2	2.3	73.0	42.0	48.2	51.8
07675	WESTWOOD	87.9	85.6	2.8	3.0	7.3	9.0	4.3	5.3	6.6	7.1	7.0	6.0	4.3	25.9	27.9	12.7	2.4	75.3	41.2	48.0	52.0
	NEW JERSEY	72.6	70.5	13.6	13.8	5.8	6.6	13.3	15.0	6.6	6.7	7.1	6.5	6.3	28.8	24.6	11.5	1.9	75.6	37.7	48.6	51.4
	UNITED STATES	75.1	73.6	12.3	12.5	3.8	4.2	12.5	14.1	6.9	6.7	7.2	7.0	7.3	28.6	23.8	10.8	1.7	75.1	36.0	49.1	50.9

INCOME

ZIP CODE #	POST OFFICE NAME	2004 Per Capita Income	2004 HH Income Base	2004 Household Income Distribution (%): Less than $25,000	$25,000 to $49,999	$50,000 to $99,999	$100,000 to $149,999	$150,000 or More	Median Household Income: 2004	2009	2004 National Centile	2004 State Centile	2004 Home Value Base	2004 Home Value Distribution (%): Less than $50,000	$50,000 to $89,999	$90,000 to $174,999	$175,000 to $399,999	$400,000 or More	2004 Median Home Value
07205	HILLSIDE	24675	7414	14.4	22.7	40.2	14.6	8.1	63210	73313	87	44	5057	0.1	0.9	22.4	73.5	3.1	212792
07206	ELIZABETH	12719	6904	39.3	29.9	23.7	4.9	2.2	33518	37640	22	4	2276	1.9	3.1	27.1	65.5	2.4	210292
07208	ELIZABETH	20064	12935	27.3	30.3	29.5	9.1	3.7	42656	49093	55	12	4232	0.8	0.9	12.4	78.1	7.9	242451
07302	JERSEY CITY	38254	15706	24.4	22.6	27.2	13.9	11.9	53880	64247	78	26	3457	2.8	4.2	13.5	51.1	28.4	282151
07304	JERSEY CITY	16747	14468	37.7	28.4	24.1	6.9	3.0	34343	38251	25	5	4371	2.4	4.5	37.3	53.0	2.9	184646
07305	JERSEY CITY	20527	21034	31.3	25.3	28.0	10.0	5.4	42500	47506	55	11	8904	1.7	2.1	26.0	65.5	4.7	213980
07306	JERSEY CITY	19064	20686	33.8	31.1	24.2	7.6	3.4	37269	41548	36	7	5018	1.3	3.9	29.5	61.8	3.5	203915
07307	JERSEY CITY	18918	16725	27.0	31.0	29.9	9.1	3.0	42455	47921	54	11	5512	0.8	1.8	21.1	72.3	4.0	225155
07310	JERSEY CITY	57477	2167	16.1	19.0	25.7	15.4	23.9	75523	86219	93	64	265	5.7	6.4	2.3	52.5	33.2	345062
07401	ALLENDALE	56210	2156	4.2	11.0	26.7	20.2	37.9	121292	143919	99	96	1950	0.3	0.7	0.0	14.8	84.2	626649
07403	BLOOMINGDALE	32586	2802	6.6	21.2	44.3	18.6	9.2	72925	82270	92	60	2114	0.0	0.0	4.5	86.0	9.6	267978
07405	BUTLER	44742	6263	10.1	16.5	30.9	20.3	22.3	86356	102825	97	77	5245	0.3	0.2	3.6	49.4	46.5	385041
07407	ELMWOOD PARK	26217	7278	18.9	23.8	35.5	16.4	5.4	58722	67598	83	35	4421	0.4	0.3	4.1	81.1	14.1	288270
07410	FAIR LAWN	39031	11872	12.6	16.4	32.6	22.9	15.4	80782	96438	95	70	9638	0.2	0.2	2.2	74.7	22.8	328750
07416	FRANKLIN	22893	2150	18.3	30.9	35.5	11.7	3.6	50700	57672	73	21	1550	6.5	2.2	36.3	52.8	2.2	183193
07417	FRANKLIN LAKES	78389	3425	6.1	8.8	16.0	18.1	50.9	153074	188441	100	99	3257	0.0	0.0	0.0	5.4	94.6	924763
07418	GLENWOOD	29334	772	6.4	14.9	41.5	26.8	10.5	81237	90621	95	71	720	0.0	0.0	8.6	85.3	6.1	237716
07419	HAMBURG	31072	3080	10.3	22.1	41.5	17.6	8.6	67534	76256	90	53	2380	0.2	0.4	26.1	66.1	7.3	215970
07420	HASKELL	24467	1611	12.2	19.8	46.2	17.3	4.5	66899	77067	90	52	1304	0.0	0.5	7.2	88.7	3.7	228265
07421	HEWITT	29569	2790	10.7	18.5	39.0	23.3	8.6	74580	84773	93	62	2470	0.0	0.5	16.6	77.4	5.6	230640
07422	HIGHLAND LAKES	28219	2648	10.0	16.6	47.2	19.3	7.0	74716	81696	93	62	2444	0.0	0.4	24.6	71.0	4.1	214840
07423	HO HO KUS	84639	1414	5.0	10.4	16.3	18.6	49.7	149003	182450	100	99	1295	0.0	0.0	0.2	7.3	92.5	705220
07424	LITTLE FALLS	36445	9064	13.4	22.8	36.0	17.5	10.3	66335	77113	89	50	5784	0.4	0.0	4.2	74.9	20.5	302065
07430	MAHWAH	54808	9892	8.8	15.5	30.0	20.5	25.3	91435	109062	97	81	8266	0.9	1.5	4.3	43.2	50.2	401379
07432	MIDLAND PARK	38548	2588	9.9	16.5	32.9	25.4	15.2	84677	102279	96	75	2025	0.0	0.0	1.3	56.0	42.7	380201
07435	NEWFOUNDLAND	40004	950	5.3	14.0	37.3	24.4	19.1	89332	105924	97	79	815	0.0	0.0	1.8	65.5	32.6	341770
07436	OAKLAND	40819	4528	4.9	12.6	32.7	28.2	21.6	99492	113955	98	87	4184	0.0	0.0	2.1	57.7	40.2	371754
07438	OAK RIDGE	33420	4223	6.5	16.7	40.0	25.3	11.6	82180	96572	96	73	3815	0.4	1.3	8.7	68.4	21.3	290006
07439	OGDENSBURG	27441	875	12.5	16.5	44.8	19.7	6.6	68524	77035	91	54	762	1.4	0.0	19.4	77.3	1.8	216471
07440	PEQUANNOCK	35335	1636	12.1	14.8	38.1	21.6	13.4	78498	93182	95	68	1422	0.0	0.0	2.7	64.6	32.7	346053
07442	POMPTON LAKES	30330	4032	12.0	19.0	40.9	20.6	7.7	72846	82091	92	60	3031	0.0	0.4	6.9	83.4	9.2	267484
07444	POMPTON PLAINS	38664	3435	8.5	16.8	34.4	21.7	18.6	84925	101875	96	75	3123	0.2	1.0	4.3	55.0	39.5	367279
07446	RAMSEY	49947	5284	6.8	14.4	27.6	22.6	28.7	101962	119476	98	88	4335	0.2	1.3	3.8	33.1	61.6	461179
07450	RIDGEWOOD	63984	8508	8.5	10.2	22.4	20.0	38.9	119951	144667	99	96	6975	0.3	0.3	0.8	22.2	76.4	582654
07452	GLEN ROCK	54490	3917	5.5	11.4	23.3	23.7	36.2	117374	139086	99	95	3638	0.9	0.0	0.0	28.6	70.5	477443
07456	RINGWOOD	36366	4062	7.3	11.0	37.1	27.4	17.2	91275	104987	97	81	3839	0.0	0.0	3.1	76.7	20.2	290766
07457	RIVERDALE	37880	985	10.1	18.0	35.8	23.8	12.4	78256	90911	95	68	821	0.0	0.0	2.4	79.8	17.8	307517
07458	SADDLE RIVER	85701	3824	4.9	8.0	17.5	19.2	50.4	151539	188818	100	99	3635	0.0	0.3	0.6	2.6	96.5	1000001
07460	STOCKHOLM	29883	1473	11.9	19.5	39.4	21.9	7.3	70789	78746	92	57	1351	0.0	1.6	18.5	71.3	8.7	226430
07461	SUSSEX	26547	6911	12.4	23.7	38.0	18.3	7.6	65852	74278	89	49	5849	0.1	0.1	17.4	70.6	11.7	241434
07462	VERNON	28641	2818	12.0	24.5	43.5	15.3	4.8	63898	70001	88	45	1920	0.0	2.7	31.9	60.2	5.2	206175
07463	WALDWICK	36172	3414	8.9	15.4	35.7	24.2	15.9	84236	102227	96	75	3009	0.8	0.2	0.5	69.7	28.8	349724
07465	WANAQUE	34095	1879	8.6	16.1	40.8	22.3	12.3	78000	89476	94	67	1509	0.0	0.0	4.8	85.2	9.9	290752
07470	WAYNE	41241	19144	10.4	14.7	29.2	23.4	22.3	91218	106164	97	80	16040	0.6	0.6	3.5	42.9	52.5	411498
07480	WEST MILFORD	33788	5870	8.8	15.1	38.8	24.9	12.4	83046	97065	96	74	5406	0.6	0.3	7.8	79.2	12.1	264223
07481	WYCKOFF	60361	5668	6.6	11.1	23.9	18.7	39.8	118987	143433	99	95	5256	0.1	0.5	0.2	13.3	85.9	630534
07501	PATERSON	11983	10412	46.2	29.3	19.9	3.6	1.0	27281	30297	8	2	2362	1.1	4.6	22.6	69.2	2.5	213900
07502	PATERSON	19009	4857	23.5	28.8	30.1	12.7	4.9	47746	54448	68	17	2543	2.1	2.4	14.9	77.9	2.7	216053
07503	PATERSON	15063	5939	35.0	31.0	24.8	6.5	2.8	36236	40786	32	6	2087	1.2	1.1	21.1	74.5	2.2	222701
07504	PATERSON	17535	3843	24.6	26.5	31.7	12.1	5.1	48742	54075	70	19	1780	1.1	0.5	12.5	78.7	7.3	244235
07505	PATERSON	12361	725	55.3	30.3	12.0	1.5	0.8	21250	22880	2	1	42	9.5	0.0	11.9	38.1	40.5	350000
07506	HAWTHORNE	29911	7215	14.1	25.4	37.1	15.0	8.4	61223	69849	86	40	4669	0.2	0.0	1.9	76.6	21.4	303432
07508	HALEDON	26757	7632	18.2	22.6	34.0	15.1	10.1	60937	69198	85	39	5035	0.6	0.0	6.1	69.4	23.9	292588
07512	TOTOWA	30523	3516	16.8	21.1	34.3	18.0	9.8	66317	77463	89	49	2850	0.3	0.0	4.7	76.1	19.0	296196
07513	PATERSON	14677	3531	28.2	31.0	29.7	7.1	4.0	41189	46019	50	11	1226	1.0	0.2	13.9	81.8	3.2	239337
07514	PATERSON	16652	6267	31.1	32.3	27.7	6.4	2.5	37876	42347	39	7	2253	6.7	2.0	18.2	69.2	3.9	220617
07522	PATERSON	13086	6065	36.0	31.3	25.1	6.1	1.5	35157	39213	28	5	1813	1.7	4.0	28.1	65.9	0.4	208057
07524	PATERSON	13263	3713	34.4	30.8	27.3	5.8	1.7	36160	40385	32	5	1046	0.3	1.8	16.5	79.0	2.4	232828
07601	HACKENSACK	31651	19068	18.7	25.4	34.9	13.6	7.3	55346	65410	80	29	6619	0.7	4.6	20.0	64.6	10.2	250018
07603	BOGOTA	29681	2852	11.3	24.6	36.4	17.7	10.1	67860	79265	90	53	1972	0.4	0.6	4.3	89.1	5.7	257566
07604	HASBROUCK HEIGHTS	34426	4694	14.4	17.4	35.1	21.6	11.6	73129	85745	92	60	3138	0.9	0.4	1.3	79.2	18.3	328469
07605	LEONIA	41277	3297	13.1	16.6	30.2	21.1	19.1	82105	100389	96	72	2215	0.9	0.1	4.5	41.0	53.6	416987
07606	SOUTH HACKENSACK	32369	800	10.8	29.1	33.0	15.4	11.8	62880	75000	87	43	428	0.0	0.0	1.9	62.4	35.8	337113
07607	MAYWOOD	32437	3760	13.9	19.3	37.0	20.8	9.0	70992	82376	92	57	2646	0.3	0.0	0.8	84.8	14.1	302962
07608	TETERBORO	22361	7	0.0	42.9	57.1	0.0	0.0	62635	85714	87	43	4	0.0	0.0	0.0	50.0	50.0	400000
07620	ALPINE	102642	738	8.0	8.1	16.5	16.3	51.1	154502	192961	100	99	667	0.2	0.5	0.0	4.5	94.9	1000001
07621	BERGENFIELD	28621	9509	12.5	21.4	34.9	21.9	9.3	70167	82126	91	56	6788	0.4	0.4	3.6	85.6	10.1	279138
07624	CLOSTER	43649	2824	6.7	12.3	31.8	21.5	27.8	98286	115623	98	87	2503	1.8	1.5	0.3	25.4	71.0	521883
07626	CRESSKILL	49818	2634	7.9	13.2	30.4	24.2	24.3	97024	113721	98	85	2363	1.5	1.5	1.0	39.6	56.4	428424
07627	DEMAREST	67028	1570	6.2	12.7	22.6	21.5	37.1	118760	142111	99	95	1441	0.4	0.5	0.5	22.6	76.0	570697
07628	DUMONT	31188	6303	14.5	16.6	37.6	21.0	10.2	72696	84461	92	59	4741	0.4	0.2	0.8	86.3	12.4	296681
07630	EMERSON	39776	2346	8.8	16.1	33.9	22.6	18.7	85372	103166	96	76	2165	0.3	0.4	0.3	52.9	46.1	389503
07631	ENGLEWOOD	44755	9223	17.2	20.2	28.7	15.9	17.9	67262	79887	90	53	5606	0.1	0.1	7.7	59.2	32.8	297965
07632	ENGLEWOOD CLIFFS	74815	1886	8.5	11.6	18.9	20.2	40.9	125239	153102	99	97	1725	0.2	1.0	0.5	6.6	91.7	783390
07640	HARRINGTON PARK	48762	1692	5.2	11.6	27.1	27.3	28.8	108496	127069	99	91	1579	0.6	0.7	1.5	20.5	76.6	518885
07641	HAWORTH	56751	1115	5.2	10.6	26.9	18.0	39.3	116414	138865	99	94	1054	1.0	0.8	0.0	14.3	84.0	589888
07642	HILLSDALE	41753	3436	8.6	13.2	31.0	23.1	24.2	94693	111451	98	83	3048	0.4	0.0	0.3	40.5	58.8	437640
07643	LITTLE FERRY	27755	4377	15.4	28.4	34.7	14.7	6.9	55137	63478	80	29	2030	0.3	0.0	9.6	74.3	15.8	287778
07644	LODI	24941	9791	21.5	29.9	31.0	12.9	4.6	48719	56348	70	19	4521	2.8	0.7	5.5	78.2	12.8	282051
07645	MONTVALE	55858	2552	6.6	10.3	27.9	25.0	30.2	108001	128794	99	91	2137	0.0	0.7	3.2	24.5	71.6	509793
07646	NEW MILFORD	35136	6332	13.2	20.9	34.4	18.6	12.9	68650	82119	91	54	4183	0.4	0.1	1.1	74.7	23.8	338273
07647	NORTHVALE	34335	1655	10.5	18.3	32.3	25.2	13.7	82412	96666	96	73	1292	0.0	0.5	0.5	57.2	41.7	375955
07648	NORWOOD	48863	1847	8.0	13.6	24.5	25.0	28.9	106037	127238	99	90	1644	0.5	1.6	1.5	25.4	71.0	523605
07649	ORADELL	45801	2750	7.5	13.4	26.6	23.4	29.1	104206	124600	98	89	2423	0.3	0.2	0.3	25.7	73.6	496374
07650	PALISADES PARK	26033	6273	22.0	23.9	30.5	15.6	7.9	54459	63954	79	27	2674	2.2	1.1	1.7	53.5	41.5	372044
07652	PARAMUS	34525	8263	9.3	16.3	31.8	23.8	18.8	86658	103790	97	77	7477	0.8	0.4	0.6	39.6	58.7	434924
07656	PARK RIDGE	48539	3185	7.4	15.6	28.4	24.4	24.4	97051	111995	98	86	2619	0.4	0.0	1.5	33.9	64.2	460668
07657	RIDGEFIELD	30603	4085	18.5	25.2	30.0	15.5	10.8	59590	71150	84	37	2392	0.3	0.3	2.9	57.7	38.8	365195
07660	RIDGEFIELD PARK	28273	5106	17.0	25.1	34.2	17.1	6.7	59001	68761	84	36	2806	2.1	0.3	7.8	82.2	7.6	268488
07661	RIVER EDGE	38360	4192	10.4	19.8	31.7	19.7	18.5	80443	96052	95	70	3171	0.2	0.5	0.8	58.2	40.4	377806
07662	ROCHELLE PARK	29474	2021	15.3	17.9	39.8	18.8	8.2	68785	79643	91	55	1473	1.0	0.0	1.2	87.3	10.5	289467
07663	SADDLE BROOK	31847	5075	14.2	17.2	38.5	21.6	8.6	72803	83860	92	60	3787	0.2	0.2	2.3	85.0	12.4	305219
07666	TEANECK	37662	13177	11.4	14.4	33.8	20.2	20.3	83386	99527	96	74	10123	0.3	0.2	2.5	70.9	26.1	317710
07670	TENAFLY	65116	4684	10.0	11.6	24.6	18.6	35.2	107636	128191	99	90	3858	0.7	0.6	0.9	20.7	77.1	610222
07675	WESTWOOD	46505	9893	9.9	14.7	31.0	21.7	22.7	88375	105312	97	79	7888	0.3	0.3	1.2	37.2	61.1	460483
	NEW JERSEY	31614		18.6	22.5	32.1	15.5	11.4	61437	70239				1.5	2.7	19.7	54.4	21.8	255213
	UNITED STATES	25866		24.7	27.1	30.8	10.9	6.5	48124	56710				10.9	15.0	33.7	30.1	10.4	145905

ZIP CODE #	POST OFFICE NAME	FINANCIAL SERVICES: Auto Loan	Home Loan	Invest-ments	Retire-ment Plans	THE HOME: Home Improvements: Home Repair	Lawn & Garden	Furnishings: Comput-ers & Hard-ware	Major Appli-ances	TV, Radio, Sound Equip-ment	Furni-ture	ENTERTAINMENT: Dine out/ Carry out	Sports Equip-ment	Fees & Tickets	Toys & Games	Travel	Cable TV	PERSONAL: Apparel & Services	Auto Repairs	Health Insur-ance	Pets & Supplies
07205	HILLSIDE	99	107	126	102	103	112	104	103	105	107	134	115	109	136	106	107	133	104	101	114
07206	ELIZABETH	51	49	90	45	46	54	56	54	64	60	83	59	56	85	57	69	83	57	56	59
07208	ELIZABETH	62	66	121	63	63	72	74	68	80	75	103	78	76	111	76	85	104	73	69	75
07302	JERSEY CITY	100	100	189	107	94	108	117	105	124	118	157	127	121	168	118	127	157	113	102	117
07304	JERSEY CITY	58	59	99	57	56	65	67	62	72	67	92	72	68	96	68	76	91	66	64	69
07305	JERSEY CITY	75	76	106	76	74	82	82	79	84	82	106	91	83	108	82	85	105	82	77	87
07306	JERSEY CITY	55	59	117	59	56	65	69	62	75	68	95	74	71	105	71	79	96	67	63	68
07307	JERSEY CITY	60	63	124	61	59	69	73	66	81	74	103	77	74	113	75	86	105	72	68	73
07310	JERSEY CITY	152	146	275	161	138	156	172	154	180	177	230	186	177	240	170	182	229	166	148	172
07401	ALLENDALE	225	288	342	292	279	288	252	247	231	257	294	283	281	307	261	228	297	238	223	272
07403	BLOOMINGDALE	110	131	154	131	128	131	124	122	118	124	149	142	131	156	126	115	148	121	110	133
07405	BUTLER	159	200	242	200	194	201	181	177	170	183	215	205	197	226	187	168	216	173	162	193
07407	ELMWOOD PARK	88	99	124	96	96	103	98	95	98	98	124	108	102	130	100	100	124	96	93	104
07410	FAIR LAWN	122	166	214	157	161	169	148	146	141	148	177	165	162	193	156	143	179	142	134	156
07416	FRANKLIN	84	90	94	90	89	91	89	87	86	88	108	103	90	110	88	84	105	88	82	97
07417	FRANKLIN LAKES	298	401	531	394	390	415	349	345	324	356	410	390	394	435	370	326	417	331	317	374
07418	GLENWOOD	122	152	162	153	148	147	135	134	124	135	157	156	145	166	138	121	157	129	120	148
07419	HAMBURG	108	123	132	126	120	119	116	114	108	117	137	135	119	140	115	103	135	113	101	125
07420	HASKELL	95	114	126	113	112	114	107	105	101	106	128	122	113	135	109	100	127	103	97	115
07421	HEWITT	116	133	134	136	129	126	122	121	113	124	143	143	126	146	121	107	142	119	106	133
07422	HIGHLAND LAKES	113	131	133	133	127	124	120	119	111	121	140	140	124	144	119	106	139	116	104	131
07423	HO HO KUS	284	392	535	379	380	407	339	336	317	346	400	378	385	428	363	320	407	323	309	363
07424	LITTLE FALLS	112	129	158	128	127	135	126	123	123	126	155	143	132	161	129	123	153	124	118	134
07430	MAHWAH	182	213	259	217	208	215	202	197	190	204	241	231	213	246	204	185	240	196	179	216
07432	MIDLAND PARK	125	159	196	157	155	160	146	144	138	146	173	167	156	184	151	136	174	141	131	155
07435	NEWFOUNDLAND	142	177	189	179	172	171	157	155	144	158	182	180	169	191	160	139	183	149	138	171
07436	OAKLAND	142	194	235	186	187	192	169	168	158	170	199	192	186	217	178	158	201	161	151	180
07438	OAK RIDGE	128	153	157	155	149	146	138	137	127	139	161	160	144	167	138	122	160	133	120	151
07439	OGDENSBURG	104	128	139	127	126	126	117	116	110	116	138	135	124	147	120	108	138	112	106	127
07440	PEQUANNOCK	124	155	184	153	153	158	143	141	135	143	170	162	152	178	148	134	170	138	131	153
07442	POMPTON LAKES	101	127	152	125	124	127	117	115	111	116	139	133	125	149	120	109	139	113	105	125
07444	POMPTON PLAINS	129	171	204	165	166	169	151	150	142	151	178	173	164	193	158	140	179	145	135	162
07446	RAMSEY	161	214	272	209	208	215	192	189	181	193	227	218	209	245	201	180	229	184	170	203
07450	RIDGEWOOD	222	299	389	291	289	303	264	260	247	267	311	297	293	335	278	247	316	252	236	280
07452	GLEN ROCK	194	259	318	254	251	260	226	223	210	229	265	254	251	283	237	209	269	215	202	242
07456	RINGWOOD	137	178	200	175	173	173	157	156	146	157	183	181	169	198	162	143	184	150	139	171
07457	RIVERDALE	131	150	185	155	148	152	149	144	141	148	178	172	153	182	149	137	176	145	131	157
07458	SADDLE RIVER	312	421	577	413	410	443	367	364	342	375	432	409	417	455	391	345	439	349	338	395
07460	STOCKHOLM	111	137	146	138	135	133	123	122	114	122	143	143	130	152	125	110	143	118	110	135
07461	SUSSEX	105	123	129	123	121	121	114	113	107	113	134	133	118	141	115	104	133	110	103	125
07462	VERNON	105	102	113	109	99	102	108	104	103	109	131	125	105	127	102	97	128	108	92	115
07463	WALDWICK	117	165	214	156	159	166	144	143	136	145	170	163	159	188	153	137	173	138	129	152
07465	WANAQUE	117	151	180	148	147	149	137	135	128	136	161	157	146	173	141	126	162	131	121	146
07470	WAYNE	142	183	229	178	178	186	167	164	158	167	199	187	181	213	174	158	200	160	151	176
07480	WEST MILFORD	126	154	165	154	151	152	139	138	130	139	163	160	148	172	142	127	163	133	126	152
07481	WYCKOFF	214	292	380	283	283	299	254	251	236	258	298	284	285	320	269	238	303	241	229	271
07501	PATERSON	44	42	73	39	40	46	48	46	54	50	69	51	48	71	48	57	69	49	48	50
07502	PATERSON	71	77	131	72	73	83	82	78	89	86	115	88	84	122	85	95	116	82	79	85
07503	PATERSON	59	60	101	55	56	64	65	62	72	69	93	70	65	97	66	76	94	66	63	68
07504	PATERSON	77	81	113	76	77	87	83	81	88	86	112	90	86	115	85	92	112	83	82	89
07505	PATERSON	33	33	63	29	30	36	38	36	43	40	56	39	37	58	38	47	57	39	37	39
07506	HAWTHORNE	96	110	133	111	108	113	107	105	104	107	130	123	111	134	109	102	129	105	98	114
07508	HALEDON	100	116	141	112	112	120	111	109	109	113	138	123	116	144	113	110	138	109	104	119
07512	TOTOWA	105	124	138	120	123	132	117	117	114	116	143	131	124	148	121	115	141	114	115	127
07513	PATERSON	66	63	115	57	59	69	72	69	82	77	106	76	71	109	72	88	107	74	72	75
07514	PATERSON	60	58	96	55	55	65	66	62	73	68	93	71	67	96	67	77	92	67	65	69
07522	PATERSON	55	51	89	47	48	57	59	56	67	62	86	63	59	87	59	71	86	60	59	62
07524	PATERSON	55	53	99	48	49	59	61	58	70	65	90	64	60	93	61	75	91	62	60	63
07601	HACKENSACK	89	94	148	96	90	100	102	95	105	103	134	111	105	140	103	107	133	100	92	105
07603	BOGOTA	109	126	147	125	123	127	121	119	117	121	147	138	126	154	123	115	147	118	110	129
07604	HASBROUCK HEIGHTS	105	135	174	131	131	138	125	123	120	125	150	141	135	161	130	120	151	121	113	132
07605	LEONIA	133	173	234	175	172	173	166	163	152	163	191	196	172	200	171	146	192	164	141	171
07606	SOUTH HACKENSACK	116	132	150	126	128	138	126	125	126	127	158	140	132	164	129	127	157	125	123	136
07607	MAYWOOD	100	127	160	121	122	129	117	115	114	118	143	130	125	154	121	115	144	114	107	124
07608	TETERBORO	75	83	98	79	79	84	80	79	80	83	102	89	82	105	80	80	102	80	74	86
07620	ALPINE	382	514	705	504	502	541	448	444	418	459	528	499	509	556	478	421	536	427	413	483
07621	BERGENFIELD	98	126	172	119	121	129	117	114	115	119	146	130	126	159	122	117	148	114	106	123
07624	CLOSTER	149	218	283	205	209	216	186	184	174	188	218	209	209	245	198	176	224	177	163	195
07626	CRESSKILL	165	243	328	227	233	245	208	206	194	210	244	232	234	273	223	198	250	197	184	218
07627	DEMAREST	231	335	453	315	322	340	287	284	268	290	337	320	324	372	307	272	345	272	256	302
07628	DUMONT	103	134	169	128	130	138	122	121	118	122	147	137	132	159	128	119	148	118	113	129
07630	EMERSON	138	190	243	178	184	193	168	167	160	169	200	189	184	220	178	162	203	162	154	177
07631	ENGLEWOOD	158	178	243	174	172	189	175	170	176	179	223	192	186	231	180	180	223	172	166	187
07632	ENGLEWOOD CLIFFS	260	358	488	346	347	372	310	307	289	316	365	346	351	390	331	292	372	295	283	332
07640	HARRINGTON PARK	169	239	301	229	229	237	206	202	191	208	240	230	229	266	217	191	245	194	180	216
07641	HAWORTH	193	281	380	264	270	285	241	238	225	244	283	269	272	314	258	229	290	229	215	253
07642	HILLSDALE	142	194	242	185	188	195	170	169	160	171	201	193	187	219	180	161	203	164	154	181
07643	LITTLE FERRY	88	98	124	100	97	100	99	97	95	99	121	114	100	122	99	92	120	100	88	104
07644	LODI	79	86	110	85	84	91	88	85	88	88	111	97	90	115	89	89	110	87	83	93
07645	MONTVALE	180	256	345	242	246	261	222	220	209	225	263	248	249	290	237	213	268	212	200	234
07646	NEW MILFORD	105	137	185	132	132	140	127	124	123	127	155	142	137	168	133	125	157	123	115	133
07647	NORTHVALE	113	163	215	153	156	162	142	140	133	142	167	159	157	187	150	135	171	135	124	148
07648	NORWOOD	172	254	342	237	243	256	217	214	203	219	254	242	244	284	232	206	261	206	193	227
07649	ORADELL	156	211	273	203	205	216	187	185	175	188	221	210	206	237	197	176	223	179	169	198
07650	PALISADES PARK	85	100	148	113	104	99	109	106	97	104	122	136	104	120	109	88	122	112	86	110
07652	PARAMUS	122	176	229	164	169	177	152	151	143	153	179	170	169	199	162	145	183	145	136	159
07656	PARK RIDGE	151	211	282	198	203	214	187	184	179	188	224	209	207	248	199	182	228	180	168	195
07657	RIDGEFIELD	101	124	160	118	118	126	116	114	114	118	145	129	124	154	120	115	146	114	106	122
07660	RIDGEFIELD PARK	94	103	124	103	100	105	102	100	100	103	127	115	105	130	102	99	126	101	93	109
07661	RIVER EDGE	121	163	207	158	159	163	147	145	137	146	172	168	158	185	154	136	174	142	130	155
07662	ROCHELLE PARK	97	115	132	112	113	120	108	108	105	108	132	123	115	138	112	106	130	106	104	117
07663	SADDLE BROOK	102	123	148	119	120	128	116	114	113	116	142	131	123	149	120	114	141	113	110	124
07666	TEANECK	133	168	217	161	162	173	155	152	150	156	188	172	167	199	161	151	189	150	142	164
07670	TENAFLY	215	309	419	294	298	311	269	267	250	271	314	305	299	345	287	251	321	258	237	282
07675	WESTWOOD	154	196	250	192	191	202	179	176	170	180	214	202	194	226	187	170	215	173	164	191
	NEW JERSEY	110	123	153	121	120	128	120	118	119	121	150	136	125	155	123	120	149	119	114	130
	UNITED STATES	100	100	100	100	100	100	100	100	100	100	100	100	100	100	100	100	100	100	100	100

ZIP CODE		COUNTY FIPS CODE	POPULATION			2000-2004 ANNUAL RATE		HOUSEHOLDS					FAMILIES		
#	POST OFFICE NAME		2000	2004	2009	% Rate	State Centile	2000	2004	2009	% Annual Rate 2000-2004	2004 Average HH Size	2000	2004	% Annual Rate 2000-2004
07676	TSHP OF WASHINGTON	003	8970	9129	9261	0.4	42	3227	3297	3352	0.5	2.77	2696	2767	0.6
07677	WOODCLIFF LAKE	003	5665	5786	5921	0.5	47	1796	1840	1887	0.6	3.07	1580	1623	0.6
07701	RED BANK	025	23722	23819	24601	0.1	27	9944	9991	10333	0.1	2.34	5851	5871	0.1
07702	SHREWSBURY	025	3604	3850	4071	1.6	80	1214	1289	1358	1.4	2.97	1021	1086	1.5
07703	FORT MONMOUTH	025	491	871	1262	14.4	100	61	171	284	27.5	3.46	58	163	27.5
07704	FAIR HAVEN	025	5940	5952	6117	0.1	24	2001	1992	2041	-0.1	2.98	1656	1653	0.0
07711	ALLENHURST	025	1872	1840	1884	-0.4	4	726	713	731	-0.4	2.58	514	506	-0.4
07712	ASBURY PARK	025	39340	41988	44771	1.5	79	15679	16635	17685	1.4	2.50	9607	10212	1.5
07716	ATLANTIC HIGHLANDS	025	8403	8410	8663	0.0	23	3283	3292	3396	0.1	2.49	2169	2177	0.1
07717	AVON BY THE SEA	025	2266	2247	2306	-0.2	12	1054	1046	1074	-0.2	2.15	541	539	-0.1
07718	BELFORD	025	6191	6274	6504	0.3	37	2120	2151	2231	0.3	2.91	1751	1783	0.4
07719	BELMAR	025	21905	22644	23741	0.8	58	8954	9222	9654	0.7	2.44	5510	5744	1.0
07720	BRADLEY BEACH	025	4793	4728	4843	-0.3	8	2297	2268	2325	-0.3	2.08	1086	1077	-0.2
07721	CLIFFWOOD	025	2656	2666	2756	0.1	26	964	960	989	-0.1	2.77	677	676	0.0
07722	COLTS NECK	025	10668	11244	11811	1.3	73	3026	3200	3372	1.3	3.35	2719	2877	1.3
07723	DEAL	025	1541	1516	1555	-0.4	5	580	571	586	-0.4	2.64	380	375	-0.3
07724	EATONTOWN	025	23201	23504	24390	0.3	37	9194	9370	9744	0.5	2.46	5873	5983	0.4
07726	ENGLISHTOWN	025	39823	42443	45081	1.5	78	12976	13877	14761	1.6	3.04	10791	11574	1.7
07727	FARMINGDALE	025	5940	6550	7093	2.3	91	2023	2217	2392	2.2	2.93	1511	1663	2.3
07728	FREEHOLD	025	51240	56183	60573	2.2	90	17956	19672	21171	2.2	2.77	13336	14677	2.3
07730	HAZLET	025	18678	19006	19776	0.4	42	6332	6447	6712	0.4	2.91	5095	5197	0.5
07731	HOWELL	025	37891	40244	42516	1.4	76	11834	12545	13227	1.4	3.20	9948	10583	1.5
07732	HIGHLANDS	025	5438	5402	5541	-0.2	14	2645	2631	2701	-0.1	2.04	1312	1312	0.0
07733	HOLMDEL	025	15240	15875	16615	1.0	65	4762	4979	5224	1.1	3.10	4186	4373	1.0
07734	KEANSBURG	025	13536	13808	14391	0.5	45	4759	4867	5078	0.5	2.79	3297	3380	0.6
07735	KEYPORT	025	20792	21134	21946	0.4	39	7573	7696	7990	0.4	2.72	5175	5287	0.5
07737	LEONARDO	025	4421	4591	4792	0.9	61	1505	1561	1628	0.9	2.94	1204	1255	1.0
07738	LINCROFT	025	6220	6223	6396	0.0	22	2111	2113	2173	0.0	2.91	1709	1712	0.0
07739	LITTLE SILVER	025	6256	6152	6305	-0.4	5	2258	2224	2280	-0.4	2.77	1834	1809	-0.3
07740	LONG BRANCH	025	31604	32899	34483	1.0	64	12666	13185	13815	1.0	2.48	7307	7623	1.0
07746	MARLBORO	025	17259	18093	18996	1.1	70	5414	5670	5949	1.1	3.17	4827	5065	1.1
07747	MATAWAN	023	28892	30763	32738	1.5	78	10866	11497	12193	1.3	2.66	7925	8445	1.5
07748	MIDDLETOWN	025	28051	28240	29260	0.2	29	9501	9590	9946	0.2	2.94	7656	7735	0.2
07750	MONMOUTH BEACH	025	3590	3670	3820	0.5	48	1632	1663	1729	0.4	2.21	975	997	0.5
07751	MORGANVILLE	025	17090	18747	20124	2.2	90	5306	5817	6239	2.2	3.19	4679	5134	2.2
07753	NEPTUNE	025	34917	36086	37701	0.8	58	13188	13652	14281	0.8	2.54	9050	9403	0.9
07755	OAKHURST	025	6620	6573	6747	-0.2	13	2301	2287	2350	-0.1	2.87	1858	1849	-0.1
07756	OCEAN GROVE	025	4263	4322	4495	0.3	38	2332	2374	2481	0.4	1.67	787	807	0.6
07757	OCEANPORT	025	5483	5562	5744	0.3	38	2030	2064	2134	0.4	2.69	1543	1572	0.4
07758	PORT MONMOUTH	025	5166	5455	5778	1.3	75	1727	1820	1926	1.2	2.99	1354	1432	1.3
07760	RUMSON	025	9938	9981	10257	0.1	27	3812	3824	3929	0.1	2.60	2633	2649	0.1
07762	SPRING LAKE	025	9527	9544	9804	0.0	23	4339	4343	4463	0.0	2.17	2547	2557	0.1
07764	WEST LONG BRANCH	025	8378	8364	8584	0.0	19	2512	2506	2586	-0.1	2.75	1900	1897	0.1
07801	DOVER	027	25142	26020	27300	0.8	58	7854	8000	8329	0.4	3.21	5766	5896	0.5
07803	MINE HILL	027	3679	3705	3826	0.2	30	1365	1372	1415	0.1	2.70	1041	1050	0.2
07821	ANDOVER	037	9547	10190	10919	1.6	79	3350	3617	3914	1.8	2.79	2638	2854	1.9
07822	AUGUSTA	037	838	884	938	1.3	74	268	287	310	1.6	2.88	224	240	1.6
07823	BELVIDERE	041	7079	7631	8291	1.8	84	2812	3063	3356	2.0	2.46	1917	2100	2.2
07825	BLAIRSTOWN	041	9121	9724	10500	1.5	78	3235	3491	3801	1.8	2.77	2564	2776	1.9
07826	BRANCHVILLE	037	5772	5917	6214	0.6	50	2066	2139	2270	0.8	2.68	1569	1629	0.9
07827	MONTAGUE	037	3747	3892	4107	0.9	62	1400	1470	1565	1.2	2.64	994	1046	1.2
07828	BUDD LAKE	027	12659	13022	13720	0.7	54	4904	5004	5251	0.5	2.60	3353	3451	0.7
07830	CALIFON	019	6017	6231	6537	0.8	60	2174	2268	2396	1.0	2.74	1773	1855	1.1
07832	COLUMBIA	041	4266	4474	4783	1.1	71	1483	1569	1690	1.3	2.83	1194	1268	1.4
07834	DENVILLE	027	17217	17709	18524	0.7	54	6529	6719	7033	0.7	2.59	4691	4847	0.8
07836	FLANDERS	027	12201	12692	13308	0.9	63	4364	4527	4738	0.9	2.80	3263	3395	0.9
07838	GREAT MEADOWS	041	2892	3073	3304	1.4	77	964	1035	1122	1.7	2.94	788	848	1.7
07840	HACKETTSTOWN	041	27516	29678	32181	1.8	84	10759	11658	12713	1.9	2.49	7236	7863	2.0
07843	HOPATCONG	037	12764	12917	13508	0.3	35	4581	4688	4951	0.5	2.76	3413	3503	0.6
07847	KENVIL	027	1495	1573	1658	1.2	72	554	584	616	1.3	2.65	401	426	1.2
07848	LAFAYETTE	037	4684	4895	5172	1.0	68	1466	1538	1638	1.1	2.98	1187	1248	1.2
07849	LAKE HOPATCONG	027	7338	7723	8142	1.2	72	2740	2880	3032	1.2	2.68	2010	2122	1.3
07850	LANDING	027	6833	7198	7651	1.2	73	2390	2524	2683	1.3	2.85	1752	1856	1.4
07851	LAYTON	037	539	577	618	1.6	81	199	214	231	1.7	2.70	145	156	1.7
07852	LEDGEWOOD	027	2425	2562	2710	1.3	75	1059	1122	1187	1.4	2.27	810	858	1.4
07853	LONG VALLEY	027	12367	13245	14147	1.6	81	3902	4175	4457	1.6	3.15	3367	3605	1.6
07856	MOUNT ARLINGTON	027	3463	3872	4216	2.7	94	1490	1678	1833	2.8	2.29	987	1118	3.0
07857	NETCONG	027	3252	3629	4004	2.6	93	1374	1524	1676	2.5	2.38	891	996	2.7
07860	NEWTON	027	25029	25976	27439	0.9	61	9176	9616	10267	1.1	2.60	6613	6981	1.3
07863	OXFORD	041	3759	4054	4392	1.8	84	1344	1464	1601	2.0	2.69	977	1068	2.1
07865	PORT MURRAY	041	2506	2736	2979	2.1	89	869	953	1044	2.2	2.79	699	768	2.2
07866	ROCKAWAY	027	21807	23304	24839	1.6	80	7849	8380	8927	1.6	2.78	6020	6443	1.6
07869	RANDOLPH	027	24592	26597	28526	1.9	85	8637	9276	9905	1.7	2.86	6777	7320	1.8
07871	SPARTA	037	19140	20036	21328	1.1	69	6606	6942	7440	1.2	2.88	5347	5645	1.3
07874	STANHOPE	037	8869	9242	9769	1.0	65	3086	3247	3464	1.2	2.84	2397	2531	1.3
07876	SUCCASUNNA	027	11285	11377	11772	0.2	31	3665	3692	3816	0.2	3.07	3010	3038	0.2
07882	WASHINGTON	041	14323	14858	15824	0.9	61	5316	5562	5963	1.1	2.66	3784	3966	1.1
07885	WHARTON	027	9768	10035	10458	0.6	52	3648	3735	3885	0.6	2.68	2490	2564	0.7
07901	SUMMIT	039	21800	22161	22738	0.4	40	8131	8235	8400	0.3	2.69	5816	5896	0.3
07920	BASKING RIDGE	035	24815	26370	28440	1.4	77	9377	10021	10869	1.6	2.56	6603	7090	1.7
07921	BEDMINSTER	035	7882	8771	9692	2.6	93	4068	4624	5173	3.1	1.90	1998	2288	3.2
07922	BERKELEY HEIGHTS	039	12574	12559	12695	0.0	20	4187	4161	4181	-0.2	2.93	3468	3461	-0.1
07924	BERNARDSVILLE	035	7205	7588	8138	1.2	73	2671	2832	3054	1.4	2.68	2009	2139	1.5
07927	CEDAR KNOLLS	027	3407	3689	3950	1.9	86	1210	1310	1402	1.9	2.81	937	1018	2.0
07928	CHATHAM	027	17999	18314	19039	0.4	42	6920	7011	7273	0.3	2.59	5042	5132	0.4
07930	CHESTER	027	8159	8977	9693	2.3	91	2678	2939	3155	2.2	2.99	2219	2450	2.4
07931	FAR HILLS	035	4117	4397	4730	1.6	79	1459	1573	1704	1.8	2.71	1122	1214	1.9
07932	FLORHAM PARK	027	8425	8855	9513	1.2	71	3018	3169	3392	1.2	2.69	2319	2456	1.4
07933	GILLETTE	027	3334	3314	3422	-0.1	15	1234	1225	1264	-0.2	2.70	974	970	-0.1
07934	GLADSTONE	035	1369	1453	1563	1.4	76	501	534	578	1.5	2.61	379	406	1.6
07935	GREEN VILLAGE	027	432	429	442	-0.2	14	122	121	125	-0.2	3.40	84	83	-0.3
07936	EAST HANOVER	027	11712	12126	12709	0.8	59	4017	4161	4358	0.8	2.90	3335	3462	0.8
07940	MADISON	027	16759	17118	17815	0.5	47	5603	5710	5966	0.5	2.54	3852	3950	0.6
07945	MENDHAM	027	9343	9727	10212	1.0	64	3136	3254	3412	0.9	2.91	2543	2649	1.0
07946	MILLINGTON	027	3040	3162	3328	0.9	63	1049	1090	1147	0.9	2.90	845	881	1.0
	NEW JERSEY					0.8					0.9	2.68			1.0
	UNITED STATES					1.2					1.3	2.58			1.1

POPULATION COMPOSITION

NEW JERSEY

07676-07946 B

ZIP CODE		RACE (%)						% Hispanic Origin		2004 AGE DISTRIBUTION (%)										MEDIAN AGE	% 2004 Males	% 2004 Females
#	POST OFFICE NAME	White 2000	White 2004	Black 2000	Black 2004	Asian/Pacific 2000	Asian/Pacific 2004	2000	2004	0-4	5-9	10-14	15-19	20-24	25-44	45-64	65-84	85+	18+	2004		
07676	TSHP OF WASHINGTON	92.0	90.3	1.0	1.1	5.6	6.9	3.3	4.2	6.7	7.1	6.5	5.1	3.6	25.3	27.8	16.6	1.5	76.6	42.7	47.8	52.3
07677	WOODCLIFF LAKE	93.8	92.4	0.9	1.0	4.5	5.6	2.4	2.9	6.7	8.4	9.6	6.8	3.9	20.2	30.5	11.7	2.4	70.7	42.1	48.0	52.0
07701	RED BANK	82.0	80.2	10.6	11.2	2.1	2.5	9.9	11.6	6.1	6.0	5.8	5.3	5.4	27.7	24.6	15.2	3.8	78.9	41.0	47.8	52.2
07702	SHREWSBURY	96.4	95.7	0.7	0.9	1.7	2.0	2.0	2.5	8.2	9.3	9.4	6.5	4.0	23.4	27.4	10.0	1.8	68.5	39.3	49.9	50.1
07703	FORT MONMOUTH	69.3	71.8	21.0	18.7	1.8	1.2	11.8	13.6	2.2	5.2	12.3	21.0	12.9	27.0	19.3	0.2	0.0	73.9	23.6	61.8	38.2
07704	FAIR HAVEN	93.7	92.7	4.2	4.9	1.0	1.2	1.4	1.7	8.6	9.9	9.9	7.2	3.6	23.7	26.6	9.1	1.4	66.7	38.3	48.9	51.1
07711	ALLENHURST	96.4	95.7	1.0	1.2	1.0	1.3	1.3	1.7	6.0	6.5	6.0	5.9	4.8	25.8	30.2	12.8	2.0	77.8	42.1	49.7	50.3
07712	ASBURY PARK	56.7	54.3	31.0	31.8	4.7	5.4	9.8	11.4	7.3	7.2	7.7	6.8	6.8	28.2	24.4	10.1	1.6	73.6	35.9	47.5	52.5
07716	ATLANTIC HIGHLANDS	91.4	90.0	4.7	5.2	1.8	2.2	3.3	4.2	5.7	6.2	6.3	5.5	4.3	27.4	29.3	13.0	2.3	78.2	42.1	48.4	51.6
07717	AVON BY THE SEA	97.1	96.4	0.6	0.7	0.9	1.1	2.4	3.1	5.0	4.9	5.0	5.1	4.5	25.8	27.7	19.1	2.9	81.8	44.8	49.1	50.9
07718	BELFORD	96.2	95.3	0.4	0.5	1.6	2.0	3.9	5.0	6.9	7.0	7.3	6.3	5.8	29.0	26.4	10.2	1.0	74.9	38.1	49.3	50.7
07719	BELMAR	94.2	93.2	2.0	2.2	1.3	1.6	3.8	4.7	6.1	6.4	7.0	6.2	5.2	28.8	27.2	11.2	1.8	76.6	39.8	48.9	51.1
07720	BRADLEY BEACH	88.2	86.2	3.9	4.4	1.5	1.8	12.8	15.4	5.5	5.0	5.1	5.1	6.1	34.8	25.9	10.7	1.8	81.5	38.5	49.9	50.2
07721	CLIFFWOOD	54.2	51.1	35.2	37.0	6.0	6.8	9.5	10.9	7.2	6.6	7.4	6.2	6.8	34.9	23.1	7.4	0.5	75.2	35.0	48.7	51.3
07722	COLTS NECK	90.1	88.7	4.3	4.6	3.6	4.3	3.2	3.9	7.7	8.6	9.0	7.1	7.1	23.7	26.2	9.8	0.9	70.7	37.2	50.8	49.2
07723	DEAL	94.6	93.5	1.0	1.2	0.4	0.5	4.0	5.0	5.2	5.4	5.9	6.7	5.2	21.0	23.4	23.6	3.8	79.1	45.6	48.0	52.0
07724	EATONTOWN	73.9	71.0	13.4	14.2	7.6	9.0	5.7	6.8	7.0	7.0	7.0	5.6	5.1	31.0	24.7	10.8	1.9	75.5	38.0	48.6	51.4
07726	ENGLISHTOWN	91.2	89.4	2.2	2.5	4.9	6.0	3.6	4.6	6.8	8.1	9.3	7.3	4.4	25.3	27.3	9.5	2.2	70.9	39.3	48.3	51.7
07727	FARMINGDALE	91.3	89.6	3.4	3.9	2.3	2.8	4.6	5.8	7.5	7.8	8.0	6.2	4.9	29.1	25.7	9.7	1.1	72.5	38.0	49.2	50.8
07728	FREEHOLD	84.5	82.5	6.9	7.5	4.4	5.2	9.9	11.3	7.0	7.3	7.3	5.9	5.2	28.6	25.5	11.1	2.2	74.6	38.8	49.4	50.6
07730	HAZLET	92.0	90.4	1.1	1.3	4.5	5.4	5.8	7.3	6.5	6.8	7.4	6.6	5.4	26.4	26.8	12.6	1.6	75.1	39.7	47.6	52.4
07731	HOWELL	89.6	87.8	3.7	4.2	3.7	4.3	5.7	7.0	8.1	8.5	9.1	7.6	5.7	29.1	25.4	6.0	0.7	69.3	35.3	49.2	50.8
07732	HIGHLANDS	94.8	93.9	1.7	2.1	1.1	1.3	4.0	5.1	5.0	4.9	6.0	5.2	6.0	31.9	28.6	10.8	1.7	81.1	40.5	50.1	49.9
07733	HOLMDEL	80.6	77.3	0.6	0.7	17.1	20.1	2.4	3.0	5.6	7.2	8.8	7.8	4.5	21.3	31.5	11.1	2.4	73.2	42.2	48.0	52.0
07734	KEANSBURG	93.8	92.8	1.9	2.1	1.3	1.6	7.5	9.3	6.9	6.7	7.5	7.2	7.4	28.9	24.2	9.9	1.3	74.4	35.8	48.8	51.2
07735	KEYPORT	87.5	85.6	6.2	6.9	1.9	2.2	9.5	11.7	6.4	6.5	7.2	6.9	6.2	30.2	25.2	9.9	1.6	75.7	37.4	49.4	50.6
07737	LEONARDO	97.1	96.5	0.6	0.7	1.0	1.2	3.7	4.6	6.3	6.9	7.8	6.5	4.9	28.3	30.0	8.4	0.9	75.0	39.4	49.8	50.3
07738	LINCROFT	93.1	91.7	0.8	1.0	4.5	5.5	2.5	3.2	6.3	7.3	8.5	7.1	4.6	22.0	30.0	12.1	2.2	73.1	41.9	49.1	50.9
07739	LITTLE SILVER	97.2	96.5	0.3	0.3	1.5	1.9	1.3	1.7	7.1	8.0	8.0	6.5	3.7	21.4	29.3	13.9	1.9	72.6	42.4	48.5	51.5
07740	LONG BRANCH	68.3	66.6	18.5	18.8	1.7	1.9	20.5	23.0	6.8	6.4	6.8	6.2	7.1	31.2	22.7	11.0	1.8	76.3	35.8	48.6	51.4
07746	MARLBORO	86.2	83.6	1.8	2.0	10.8	13.0	2.2	2.7	6.4	7.6	8.8	7.5	4.7	24.1	30.4	9.4	1.1	72.3	40.1	49.7	50.3
07747	MATAWAN	82.2	79.0	5.2	6.0	9.6	11.4	5.5	6.8	7.0	7.2	7.0	5.3	4.7	30.3	26.3	10.7	1.5	75.5	38.9	48.3	51.7
07748	MIDDLETOWN	94.5	93.4	0.9	1.1	3.3	3.9	3.4	4.2	6.8	7.4	7.8	6.7	5.3	26.2	28.7	9.8	1.3	73.9	39.2	48.8	51.2
07750	MONMOUTH BEACH	97.7	97.2	0.5	0.6	0.9	1.0	1.9	2.4	5.6	6.2	5.7	4.6	3.2	23.1	31.4	17.7	2.5	79.7	45.9	47.2	52.8
07751	MORGANVILLE	81.2	78.3	2.4	2.6	14.6	16.9	3.7	4.5	8.3	9.2	8.9	6.4	3.9	28.2	26.9	7.6	0.7	69.5	37.6	49.4	50.7
07753	NEPTUNE	59.4	56.9	33.7	35.3	2.1	2.5	5.9	6.8	6.6	6.6	7.0	6.4	6.8	28.0	24.5	12.1	2.1	76.0	38.1	47.7	52.3
07755	OAKHURST	95.2	94.2	0.8	1.0	2.4	2.9	2.1	2.7	6.6	7.0	8.0	7.2	5.6	24.3	27.0	12.7	1.5	73.8	39.7	48.9	51.1
07756	OCEAN GROVE	93.0	91.7	3.9	4.7	1.0	1.1	3.8	4.7	3.1	2.6	2.7	2.7	5.0	29.8	30.2	16.4	7.5	89.9	47.3	45.5	54.5
07757	OCEANPORT	97.6	97.2	0.6	0.7	0.7	0.8	1.5	1.9	5.9	6.8	7.6	6.8	4.3	21.8	30.7	14.0	2.0	75.4	43.1	47.7	52.3
07758	PORT MONMOUTH	95.7	94.8	1.2	1.4	1.0	1.1	6.1	7.7	7.0	7.4	8.2	6.9	5.8	29.3	25.2	8.9	1.3	73.0	36.6	48.5	51.6
07760	RUMSON	96.7	96.0	0.7	0.8	1.4	1.8	2.1	2.6	6.3	7.5	8.6	6.6	4.1	24.9	29.5	10.8	1.7	73.1	40.5	49.1	50.9
07762	SPRING LAKE	97.9	97.5	0.8	0.9	0.4	0.4	1.6	2.1	4.6	5.2	6.0	5.0	3.6	20.0	27.7	23.6	4.4	81.1	49.1	45.9	54.1
07764	WEST LONG BRANCH	94.1	93.0	2.3	2.6	1.3	1.6	3.1	3.8	5.0	5.5	6.9	15.1	12.5	18.4	22.6	12.1	2.0	78.9	32.9	46.8	53.2
07801	DOVER	71.6	69.4	6.9	6.8	3.6	3.9	47.3	52.7	7.1	6.9	6.8	6.0	6.9	33.9	22.1	8.7	1.5	75.6	35.1	50.9	49.1
07803	MINE HILL	90.4	88.6	3.4	3.8	2.6	3.1	8.7	11.0	8.3	8.3	7.1	4.6	3.9	29.9	24.5	12.3	1.1	73.4	39.0	48.5	51.5
07821	ANDOVER	95.7	95.1	0.9	1.0	1.2	1.4	3.3	4.0	7.2	7.8	7.7	6.3	4.6	28.6	29.1	7.5	1.1	73.2	38.6	50.3	49.7
07822	AUGUSTA	97.3	96.8	0.5	0.6	0.8	1.0	1.8	2.2	4.9	5.7	7.5	7.6	5.8	23.0	32.5	11.1	2.2	77.0	42.5	50.2	49.8
07823	BELVIDERE	97.2	96.7	0.9	0.9	0.6	0.7	2.2	2.7	6.0	6.5	7.5	6.3	5.2	26.8	26.5	13.3	2.0	76.1	40.6	49.0	51.0
07825	BLAIRSTOWN	97.9	97.5	0.4	0.4	0.6	0.7	2.1	2.6	5.9	6.8	7.5	6.6	4.5	24.9	31.4	11.0	1.5	75.6	41.7	49.8	50.2
07826	BRANCHVILLE	98.2	97.8	0.4	0.4	0.4	0.5	1.8	2.2	4.8	5.6	7.5	7.2	5.2	23.5	31.3	12.3	2.6	77.4	42.9	48.8	51.2
07827	MONTAGUE	95.5	94.9	1.7	1.8	0.6	0.8	3.1	3.8	6.8	7.0	7.9	7.0	5.3	27.5	26.7	10.9	0.9	73.8	38.5	51.5	48.5
07828	BUDD LAKE	86.3	84.3	3.8	4.1	5.7	6.6	7.4	9.2	7.8	7.5	7.1	6.6	6.3	33.2	23.8	6.8	0.8	73.4	35.1	49.4	50.6
07830	CALIFON	97.4	96.9	0.5	0.6	1.2	1.4	1.5	2.0	6.4	7.6	8.2	6.4	3.4	24.6	32.9	9.6	1.0	73.4	41.5	49.0	51.0
07832	COLUMBIA	97.7	97.2	0.4	0.4	0.6	0.8	1.8	2.3	6.5	7.3	7.9	6.1	4.4	27.1	28.3	10.8	1.4	74.0	40.4	50.2	49.8
07834	DENVILLE	91.3	89.6	1.2	1.4	5.8	7.0	2.9	3.7	6.9	7.2	6.6	5.4	4.1	27.5	27.2	11.8	3.4	75.9	41.0	48.3	51.7
07836	FLANDERS	87.6	85.5	3.7	4.1	6.2	7.4	4.2	5.3	9.1	9.5	8.1	5.6	4.0	33.1	24.5	5.6	0.5	69.5	35.5	50.6	49.4
07838	GREAT MEADOWS	97.3	96.8	0.5	0.5	0.8	0.9	2.5	3.1	7.3	8.3	9.1	6.9	4.5	27.5	28.4	7.1	0.9	70.6	37.8	49.8	50.2
07840	HACKETTSTOWN	92.6	91.4	1.6	1.8	2.6	3.1	5.4	6.7	6.6	6.7	7.1	6.4	5.9	29.6	26.2	9.6	2.0	75.7	38.3	48.2	51.9
07843	HOPATCONG	93.4	92.4	1.9	2.1	1.7	2.0	5.8	7.1	7.1	7.4	7.5	6.1	5.0	32.7	26.7	6.9	0.7	74.2	37.0	50.3	49.7
07847	KENVIL	91.8	90.3	2.1	2.4	2.9	3.6	8.8	10.9	6.1	6.6	7.4	6.0	5.0	31.3	24.2	11.4	2.1	76.1	38.6	48.8	51.2
07848	LAFAYETTE	95.6	94.8	1.3	1.5	1.8	2.2	2.7	3.3	6.1	7.0	8.4	6.2	4.0	25.8	29.3	10.8	2.5	74.3	41.0	48.4	51.6
07849	LAKE HOPATCONG	95.8	94.9	0.8	0.9	0.9	1.1	4.4	5.7	6.2	6.9	7.7	5.9	4.8	29.6	29.7	8.3	1.0	75.5	39.4	49.9	50.1
07850	LANDING	91.8	90.2	2.5	2.9	3.1	3.8	6.6	8.3	7.4	7.6	7.3	5.7	5.1	31.2	26.5	8.5	0.8	74.2	37.7	47.9	52.1
07851	LAYTON	97.8	97.6	0.4	0.4	0.6	0.7	1.3	1.4	5.2	6.2	8.2	6.2	4.7	24.6	31.2	12.0	1.7	76.3	42.3	50.8	49.2
07852	LEDGEWOOD	93.0	91.6	1.8	2.1	3.8	4.6	3.8	4.9	6.9	7.7	7.4	6.0	4.2	28.5	28.2	9.6	1.5	73.8	39.8	48.5	51.5
07853	LONG VALLEY	96.6	95.8	0.8	0.9	1.6	2.0	2.0	2.6	6.8	8.2	9.1	7.0	4.4	25.3	31.1	6.8	1.3	71.2	39.6	49.3	50.7
07856	MOUNT ARLINGTON	91.4	89.8	1.6	1.9	4.0	4.9	4.9	6.1	6.5	6.5	6.4	5.4	4.9	31.2	27.8	10.5	1.1	77.4	39.4	47.7	52.3
07857	NETCONG	92.5	91.2	2.2	2.3	2.2	2.7	7.9	10.1	6.3	6.1	6.5	6.8	6.7	30.1	24.4	11.5	1.8	77.1	37.8	49.0	51.0
07860	NEWTON	95.3	94.6	1.7	1.8	1.3	1.6	2.6	3.2	6.0	6.6	7.3	6.8	5.2	26.7	28.5	10.7	2.1	75.7	40.0	48.7	51.3
07863	OXFORD	96.5	95.9	1.1	1.2	0.6	0.7	2.9	3.7	6.5	7.1	8.0	6.3	4.4	29.1	25.7	10.7	2.2	74.3	39.4	48.7	51.3
07865	PORT MURRAY	89.1	88.7	8.3	8.3	0.7	0.8	2.5	2.8	5.9	6.8	7.7	7.2	5.2	24.7	29.6	10.6	2.3	74.9	41.0	48.8	51.2
07866	ROCKAWAY	89.3	87.1	1.9	2.3	6.0	7.3	6.2	7.8	7.3	7.6	7.4	6.0	4.7	29.8	27.1	9.2	1.0	73.8	38.3	49.2	50.8
07869	RANDOLPH	85.5	83.2	2.4	2.6	9.2	10.8	5.0	6.1	7.3	8.5	8.8	6.5	4.2	28.3	28.5	7.2	0.8	71.0	37.8	49.6	50.4
07871	SPARTA	96.6	96.0	0.4	0.4	1.4	1.8	2.6	3.2	7.6	8.5	9.1	6.7	4.1	26.3	28.9	7.8	1.1	70.3	39.0	49.2	50.8
07874	STANHOPE	93.7	92.7	1.5	1.7	1.9	2.2	4.5	5.5	7.0	7.4	7.7	6.2	5.2	30.7	28.8	6.4	0.6	74.0	37.3	48.2	51.8
07876	SUCCASUNNA	93.4	91.9	1.3	1.5	4.0	5.0	3.2	4.2	6.5	7.3	8.4	6.7	4.8	26.1	28.9	9.9	1.4	73.3	40.2	48.9	51.1
07882	WASHINGTON	93.8	92.9	2.8	3.1	1.2	1.5	3.1	3.9	6.7	6.9	8.2	7.3	5.9	28.5	26.0	9.1	1.4	73.4	37.7	49.4	50.6
07885	WHARTON	86.4	84.4	3.5	3.8	2.7	3.1	16.5	19.7	7.0	7.1	7.2	6.0	5.4	30.9	25.0	9.9	1.5	75.0	37.7	48.6	51.4
07901	SUMMIT	87.8	85.8	4.2	4.7	4.6	5.4	9.9	12.3	8.3	8.6	7.7	5.8	3.9	28.8	24.3	10.9	1.8	71.6	38.0	48.7	51.3
07920	BASKING RIDGE	89.5	87.6	1.4	1.6	7.6	9.1	2.7	3.4	7.4	8.7	8.5	5.8	2.9	25.8	28.3	10.8	1.7	71.2	40.6	48.9	51.2
07921	BEDMINSTER	90.0	88.0	1.8	2.1	6.5	7.9	3.8	4.9	5.4	5.4	4.8	4.4	4.2	34.6	29.5	10.6	1.1	81.5	40.9	45.8	54.2
07922	BERKELEY HEIGHTS	90.0	88.0	1.0	1.1	7.6	9.2	3.8	4.9	7.8	8.5	7.7	5.7	3.3	25.2	25.7	13.6	2.6	72.2	40.7	47.8	52.2
07924	BERNARDSVILLE	94.0	92.7	0.3	0.3	2.6	3.2	6.0	7.6	7.2	8.3	7.8	5.8	3.5	25.4	29.3	11.5	1.4	72.8	41.0	49.2	50.8
07927	CEDAR KNOLLS	90.1	87.9	1.1	1.2	7.3	9.0	3.8	4.9	5.8	5.9	5.9	6.8	5.2	26.9	29.1	12.5	1.9	77.8	41.0	49.8	50.2
07928	CHATHAM	94.7	93.5	0.3	0.3	3.9	4.8	2.3	3.0	8.4	9.0	7.7	5.7	3.4	26.4	26.3	11.4	1.9	71.1	39.8	47.8	52.2
07930	CHESTER	95.1	94.1	1.1	1.3	2.3	2.8	3.4	4.3	7.0	8.4	8.6	6.8	3.9	23.4	30.8	9.9	1.3	70.8	40.8	49.5	50.5
07931	FAR HILLS	92.8	91.6	1.8	2.0	4.2	5.0	3.3	4.2	7.0	8.4	7.6	5.5	3.1	25.6	30.3	11.0	1.6	73.2	41.4	48.8	51.2
07932	FLORHAM PARK	94.1	93.1	1.0	1.1	3.9	4.7	2.1	2.6	6.1	6.3	6.2	5.7	4.2	23.0	27.9	17.5	3.1	77.6	44.0	46.7	53.3
07933	GILLETTE	92.4	90.8	0.4	0.5	4.9	6.0	3.5	4.6	6.7	7.5	7.9	5.8	3.3	25.3	30.2	11.9	1.5	74.0	41.6	48.1	51.9
07934	GLADSTONE	95.4	94.6	2.3	2.6	1.1	1.3	3.6	4.5	7.3	8.5	8.0	5.4	2.8	27.1	28.2	10.9	1.9	72.4	40.6	48.8	51.2
07935	GREEN VILLAGE	94.2	93.0	0.5	0.5	4.4	5.4	2.1	2.6	7.0	7.2	7.2	5.8	3.7	23.8	27.3	13.5	4.4	74.1	42.2	48.3	51.8
07936	EAST HANOVER	87.2	84.5	0.6	0.7	10.9	13.4	2.7	3.5	6.1	6.6	6.4	5.2	4.4	26.5	28.6	14.7	1.6	77.6	42.0	48.3	51.7
07940	MADISON	89.8	88.0	3.0	3.3	4.0	4.8	5.9	7.5	5.8	6.1	6.2	11.2	11.3	24.9	21.6	10.9	2.0	78.7	34.8	47.6	52.4
07945	MENDHAM	96.2	95.4	0.7	0.8	2.0	2.5	2.1	2.7	6.8	8.4	8.9	7.1	3.6	20.2	30.8	12.3	2.1	71.0	42.2	48.4	51.6
07946	MILLINGTON	94.1	92.7	0.2	0.3	4.3	5.4	2.9	3.7	8.0	9.2	8.4	5.2	2.9	25.8	27.3	11.7	1.5	70.8	40.6	48.7	51.3
	NEW JERSEY	72.6	70.5	13.6	13.8	5.8	6.6	13.3	15.0	6.6	6.7	7.1	6.5	6.3	28.8	24.6	11.5	1.9	75.6	37.7	48.6	51.4
	UNITED STATES	75.1	73.6	12.3	12.5	3.8	4.2	12.5	14.1	6.9	6.7	7.2	7.0	7.3	28.6	23.8	10.8	1.7	75.1	36.0	49.1	50.9

ZIP CODE #	POST OFFICE NAME	2004 Per Capita Income	2004 HH Income Base	2004 Household Income Distribution (%): Less than $25,000	$25,000 to $49,999	$50,000 to $99,999	$100,000 to $149,999	$150,000 or More	Median Household Income: 2004	2009	2004 National Centile	2004 State Centile	2004 Home Value Base	2004 Home Value Distribution (%): Less than $50,000	$50,000 to $89,999	$90,000 to $174,999	$175,000 to $399,999	$400,000 or More	2004 Median Home Value
07676	TSHP OF WASHINGTON	47015	3297	6.3	16.0	29.7	23.7	24.2	95786	112093	98	84	3166	0.0	0.2	0.3	36.2	63.3	445027
07677	WOODCLIFF LAKE	67933	1840	6.0	12.3	17.0	18.0	46.6	139305	168257	100	98	1749	0.0	0.5	0.9	8.4	90.2	689688
07701	RED BANK	36833	9991	17.1	21.6	31.9	18.1	11.3	66537	77959	89	50	6863	0.3	0.4	15.3	55.4	28.5	300237
07702	SHREWSBURY	44015	1289	5.9	15.8	29.4	19.3	29.6	97558	114037	98	86	1222	0.0	0.0	0.9	46.5	52.6	412075
07703	FORT MONMOUTH	25414	171	0.0	0.0	42.7	56.1	1.2	102681	124571	98	88	43	0.0	0.0	0.0	93.0	7.0	350000
07704	FAIR HAVEN	54723	1992	7.5	12.3	26.1	20.8	33.3	108984	129612	99	91	1854	0.0	0.0	1.3	28.6	70.1	503690
07711	ALLENHURST	48377	713	8.0	10.4	31.3	26.5	23.8	100427	116855	98	87	570	0.0	0.0	2.5	40.2	57.4	443299
07712	ASBURY PARK	27646	16635	29.4	25.2	25.0	11.5	8.9	44487	51743	60	13	7302	0.4	1.6	13.6	55.7	28.7	296286
07716	ATLANTIC HIGHLANDS	45617	3292	11.2	18.5	31.5	22.6	16.3	80123	96670	95	70	2382	0.0	0.8	6.4	56.6	36.3	329067
07717	AVON BY THE SEA	49320	1046	14.4	23.4	28.6	16.1	17.5	67223	80571	90	52	658	0.0	0.0	2.6	27.7	69.8	567734
07718	BELFORD	31341	2151	8.5	19.8	39.8	19.0	13.0	76040	87107	94	65	1929	0.6	0.2	6.3	84.8	8.2	267204
07719	BELMAR	36251	9222	15.0	21.9	33.4	18.3	11.4	66164	78994	89	49	6508	0.8	0.5	9.4	56.9	32.4	306224
07720	BRADLEY BEACH	30359	2268	23.2	33.3	29.5	10.2	3.9	45963	53083	64	15	1042	0.0	1.6	18.8	60.8	18.8	260563
07721	CLIFFWOOD	28268	960	11.8	26.2	37.7	16.9	7.5	61119	71815	85	40	619	0.0	1.6	15.8	79.3	3.2	225368
07722	COLTS NECK	63153	3200	4.6	11.3	18.7	17.6	47.8	143229	165296	100	99	3026	0.3	0.0	2.3	7.7	89.7	710662
07723	DEAL	42185	571	25.9	15.1	25.7	17.0	16.3	64819	79060	88	47	388	0.0	0.0	1.6	19.9	78.6	747253
07724	EATONTOWN	33321	9370	13.9	23.3	34.2	17.7	11.0	65607	77051	89	48	5625	4.4	4.3	8.7	58.6	24.0	285136
07726	ENGLISHTOWN	38751	13877	11.7	13.5	27.5	23.8	23.6	94312	110953	98	83	12748	0.2	0.8	11.5	38.4	49.1	395357
07727	FARMINGDALE	30239	2217	14.5	21.6	33.0	20.0	10.9	68500	82335	91	54	1735	1.3	0.0	7.7	57.4	33.6	297031
07728	FREEHOLD	34164	19672	13.7	18.6	32.6	19.9	15.2	75346	87715	93	64	16219	1.2	1.6	13.8	51.4	32.0	301829
07730	HAZLET	30262	6447	12.1	18.8	38.3	21.2	9.6	75305	85273	93	63	5542	3.5	2.0	6.6	78.2	9.7	286636
07731	HOWELL	28955	12545	9.0	15.4	41.2	22.9	11.5	78869	91291	95	68	11170	1.3	1.8	10.4	75.2	11.3	279220
07732	HIGHLANDS	36218	2631	20.9	26.6	32.7	11.7	8.2	52218	61023	76	23	1473	4.6	2.9	26.1	55.7	10.9	216900
07733	HOLMDEL	60450	4979	8.4	9.8	18.7	20.4	42.8	130016	152906	100	97	4719	1.0	2.7	4.5	15.5	76.3	651038
07734	KEANSBURG	20875	4867	27.1	25.4	31.2	12.3	4.0	46751	54429	66	17	3012	3.3	2.5	38.9	52.2	3.1	184685
07735	KEYPORT	25591	7696	17.4	24.7	36.7	15.6	5.5	58386	67503	83	34	5317	0.3	0.9	22.1	74.1	2.7	215345
07737	LEONARDO	35726	1561	7.1	15.6	39.5	22.4	15.3	81399	96754	95	71	1394	0.7	0.1	9.0	66.4	23.7	286759
07738	LINCROFT	44107	2113	14.7	10.0	23.5	25.3	26.6	102900	120220	98	89	1762	0.3	0.0	0.3	33.4	66.0	489776
07739	LITTLE SILVER	55306	2224	4.4	11.2	29.7	23.2	31.5	107937	128319	99	91	2141	0.0	0.0	0.4	28.2	71.4	499026
07740	LONG BRANCH	23741	13185	28.4	28.3	28.4	9.8	5.1	43379	50717	57	12	5910	0.5	1.2	21.3	61.1	15.9	231432
07746	MARLBORO	46711	5670	6.9	11.0	24.2	24.5	33.4	114578	134064	99	94	5510	0.5	1.0	1.3	29.5	67.7	471158
07747	MATAWAN	37353	11497	11.6	15.1	35.8	23.0	14.6	80920	93658	95	71	9024	0.2	2.1	11.0	68.9	17.9	291958
07748	MIDDLETOWN	40159	9590	10.4	12.8	34.3	21.5	21.0	87158	103332	97	78	7990	0.2	0.1	4.5	50.3	44.9	376949
07750	MONMOUTH BEACH	62860	1663	7.8	13.8	32.4	20.8	25.2	91838	110104	97	81	1354	0.7	0.0	9.7	34.0	55.7	444767
07751	MORGANVILLE	46234	5817	7.6	9.6	25.6	25.0	32.2	112672	132502	99	93	5582	0.6	1.4	3.7	33.2	61.2	459674
07753	NEPTUNE	26626	13652	19.1	25.2	34.5	15.4	5.9	56373	65788	81	31	9373	0.6	0.9	19.2	73.5	5.8	228344
07755	OAKHURST	32214	2287	9.0	16.9	37.5	23.7	12.9	81303	95710	95	71	2062	0.0	0.2	3.3	72.7	23.7	318862
07756	OCEAN GROVE	30510	2374	32.9	31.7	23.3	6.9	5.1	36459	42515	33	6	1088	0.0	0.0	28.0	54.5	17.5	240426
07757	OCEANPORT	41040	2064	9.8	16.7	33.8	21.2	18.6	83345	98153	96	74	1740	0.4	0.0	1.8	53.9	43.9	374217
07758	PORT MONMOUTH	32685	1820	13.5	21.4	37.8	17.5	9.8	67574	79022	90	53	1511	0.0	0.5	11.7	79.4	8.5	256090
07760	RUMSON	84292	3824	9.4	12.7	24.4	15.6	37.9	109428	129646	99	92	3001	0.0	0.0	4.7	24.3	71.0	639955
07762	SPRING LAKE	51830	4343	16.4	20.3	30.4	17.2	15.8	68112	79055	90	54	3073	0.7	0.1	1.8	37.1	60.3	474122
07764	WEST LONG BRANCH	34293	2506	14.1	16.2	32.5	18.8	18.4	77969	93074	94	67	2094	0.2	0.0	3.4	63.1	33.2	336691
07801	DOVER	23358	8000	16.8	21.3	36.7	17.8	7.5	62794	72182	87	43	4806	0.3	1.1	8.9	82.0	7.7	248104
07803	MINE HILL	31382	1372	11.3	19.2	41.8	17.7	10.1	72334	83311	92	59	1170	0.8	0.2	7.7	86.1	5.3	243009
07821	ANDOVER	36901	3617	8.5	15.0	38.3	22.3	16.0	82778	94557	96	73	3144	0.2	0.0	12.8	67.9	19.2	263925
07822	AUGUSTA	30279	287	10.1	16.0	36.6	27.5	9.8	82059	92645	96	72	263	0.0	0.0	6.8	77.2	16.0	307732
07823	BELVIDERE	27805	3063	20.6	21.8	37.6	14.0	5.9	58687	64441	83	35	2314	0.6	1.3	24.8	65.8	7.6	221707
07825	BLAIRSTOWN	33201	3491	12.7	17.9	39.0	20.0	10.4	73682	81755	93	61	3063	0.2	0.4	7.0	65.5	26.9	309539
07826	BRANCHVILLE	28365	2139	16.6	20.5	37.3	17.8	7.8	65856	75245	89	49	1849	0.3	0.8	13.0	70.7	15.2	257779
07827	MONTAGUE	24258	1470	22.3	26.6	34.6	12.8	3.7	51151	58935	74	22	1106	1.5	4.5	32.8	58.0	3.3	196986
07828	BUDD LAKE	29762	5004	10.7	24.8	40.6	15.9	8.0	64789	74873	88	47	2814	0.0	0.0	14.2	70.2	15.6	266700
07830	CALIFON	61559	2268	8.2	11.2	27.0	20.5	33.1	106486	127001	99	90	2036	0.4	0.1	2.3	39.5	57.8	467234
07832	COLUMBIA	28415	1569	11.2	19.2	42.7	19.6	7.3	71793	78953	92	58	1397	2.0	0.0	10.2	67.5	20.3	293427
07834	DENVILLE	46244	6719	8.0	16.0	33.2	22.3	20.6	87117	103372	97	77	5686	0.1	0.0	3.5	62.4	34.0	341880
07836	FLANDERS	37402	4527	3.8	17.3	38.7	24.1	16.0	85368	102593	96	76	2967	0.0	0.0	1.6	61.0	37.5	349865
07838	GREAT MEADOWS	28127	1035	9.7	17.2	44.3	22.0	6.9	76441	83163	94	66	942	0.4	0.5	12.6	70.3	16.1	280789
07840	HACKETTSTOWN	34787	11658	12.2	22.0	36.6	18.3	10.9	68027	76192	90	54	7847	0.4	0.3	12.2	67.6	19.5	256640
07843	HOPATCONG	30694	4688	10.6	19.5	43.9	18.3	7.6	71327	79043	92	58	4100	0.2	0.5	26.2	67.9	5.2	211773
07847	KENVIL	29305	584	15.2	23.1	34.1	17.0	10.6	64901	76919	88	47	483	2.3	0.0	9.9	79.3	8.5	238836
07848	LAFAYETTE	33853	1538	7.5	15.7	35.4	22.2	19.2	85948	97402	96	77	1296	0.7	0.7	13.1	50.2	35.3	317316
07849	LAKE HOPATCONG	31827	2880	10.1	18.6	43.4	18.8	9.1	72824	83543	92	60	2507	1.0	0.7	18.0	70.8	9.7	237885
07850	LANDING	28409	2524	10.9	20.0	41.3	19.4	8.4	69803	81096	91	56	2016	0.0	0.2	7.5	86.8	5.5	238964
07851	LAYTON	27385	214	15.9	21.0	42.5	14.0	6.5	62631	71782	87	43	190	0.5	1.6	19.5	71.1	7.4	228571
07852	LEDGEWOOD	47700	1122	7.8	16.4	34.0	22.6	19.3	87417	104111	97	78	1012	0.6	0.2	4.9	62.1	32.2	322078
07853	LONG VALLEY	42453	4175	6.0	9.6	25.7	29.1	29.6	111843	131441	99	93	3794	0.2	0.9	1.2	43.3	54.5	421701
07856	MOUNT ARLINGTON	38547	1678	10.9	19.9	38.4	21.0	9.7	75414	85554	93	64	1212	1.4	1.3	9.0	78.6	9.7	260891
07857	NETCONG	27802	1524	16.9	26.3	36.6	15.8	4.4	56899	66298	82	32	879	0.0	0.3	19.1	75.0	5.6	224352
07860	NEWTON	29825	9616	15.7	20.8	37.7	16.9	8.9	65824	73953	89	49	7273	0.8	1.0	17.3	67.2	13.6	238132
07863	OXFORD	26202	1464	15.7	21.8	41.2	16.3	5.1	62975	70656	87	43	1258	4.9	2.8	28.3	56.9	7.1	212121
07865	PORT MURRAY	31858	953	9.1	19.7	35.7	22.7	12.8	79424	88120	95	69	855	0.6	2.0	9.0	60.9	27.5	294833
07866	ROCKAWAY	36374	8380	9.1	14.0	37.6	23.5	15.8	84191	100780	96	75	6833	0.2	0.4	4.1	77.6	17.7	299469
07869	RANDOLPH	51582	9276	5.0	12.3	27.7	21.1	34.0	109761	129207	99	92	7045	0.2	0.1	1.1	31.8	66.9	490175
07871	SPARTA	42142	6942	8.8	10.6	31.8	25.2	23.6	97524	108751	98	86	6229	0.3	0.0	5.2	57.7	36.8	341738
07874	STANHOPE	31405	3247	6.3	18.2	44.4	20.0	11.1	77095	84734	94	66	2813	0.2	0.1	21.4	71.7	6.6	229068
07876	SUCCASUNNA	36605	3692	7.9	14.3	32.1	26.2	19.6	92875	109838	97	82	3400	1.0	0.2	2.1	67.9	28.8	336976
07882	WASHINGTON	29768	5562	15.4	22.2	36.3	18.2	7.9	64562	71212	88	46	4051	1.2	0.4	25.6	61.9	10.9	222508
07885	WHARTON	29146	3735	14.5	22.3	35.9	19.3	8.0	66705	77813	90	51	2662	1.7	0.8	12.0	75.3	10.3	249311
07901	SUMMIT	76273	8235	10.9	11.6	23.6	18.0	35.8	108601	130972	99	91	5709	0.1	0.3	1.5	22.5	75.6	664355
07920	BASKING RIDGE	69897	10021	6.5	9.9	24.8	20.2	38.7	118695	139577	99	95	8438	0.0	0.5	2.8	30.6	66.1	523560
07921	BEDMINSTER	63194	4624	9.7	15.5	35.4	18.3	21.1	83177	101521	96	74	3615	0.9	3.2	12.6	57.1	26.3	288403
07922	BERKELEY HEIGHTS	50761	4161	6.7	9.9	23.9	21.4	38.1	120095	141383	99	96	3825	0.3	0.4	0.6	25.4	73.2	484218
07924	BERNARDSVILLE	87892	2832	6.4	11.8	24.5	16.6	40.7	120315	145198	99	96	2308	0.0	0.4	3.3	22.1	74.3	628107
07927	CEDAR KNOLLS	39448	1310	7.2	17.3	29.9	24.4	21.3	91137	108325	97	80	1163	0.4	0.9	2.3	51.4	45.0	380500
07928	CHATHAM	75479	7011	5.4	10.9	24.6	20.3	38.8	120045	144798	99	96	5780	0.1	0.5	1.0	22.7	75.7	588953
07930	CHESTER	65394	2939	6.0	11.5	22.3	18.9	41.3	124351	147140	99	97	2624	0.5	0.8	0.2	21.4	77.2	616144
07931	FAR HILLS	82910	1573	5.7	11.4	21.4	16.3	45.2	132806	157640	100	98	1347	0.4	1.3	2.3	15.1	80.9	687132
07932	FLORHAM PARK	48534	3169	7.3	16.7	24.7	22.4	28.9	102021	120558	98	88	2641	0.0	0.3	0.6	31.7	67.3	475745
07933	GILLETTE	55999	1225	9.1	14.3	24.2	19.2	33.1	104348	124156	98	89	1093	0.6	0.0	0.9	37.0	61.5	466755
07934	GLADSTONE	70072	534	5.6	11.6	29.0	19.1	34.6	108215	129758	99	91	427	0.2	0.0	1.2	16.4	82.2	658405
07935	GREEN VILLAGE	52871	121	9.1	16.5	24.8	18.2	31.4	98790	131994	98	87	84	0.0	0.0	0.0	16.7	83.3	770833
07936	EAST HANOVER	38393	4161	7.5	13.6	33.5	25.1	20.4	91996	109299	97	81	3868	0.3	1.2	2.9	31.5	64.1	463562
07940	MADISON	49280	5710	10.5	15.2	26.0	20.2	28.2	96037	115251	98	85	3864	0.0	0.0	0.2	22.1	77.7	559478
07945	MENDHAM	64719	3254	8.2	9.1	18.8	18.0	45.9	137600	163622	100	98	2960	0.0	0.8	0.1	15.2	83.9	676585
07946	MILLINGTON	55423	1090	7.4	10.9	24.0	21.1	36.5	113838	135206	99	94	993	0.5	0.3	0.4	30.4	68.4	487321
	NEW JERSEY	31614		18.6	22.5	32.1	15.5	11.4	61437	70239				1.5	2.7	19.7	54.4	21.8	255213
	UNITED STATES	25866		24.7	27.1	30.8	10.9	6.5	48124	56710				10.9	15.0	33.7	30.1	10.4	145905

ZIP CODE #	POST OFFICE NAME	FINANCIAL SERVICES: Auto Loan	FINANCIAL SERVICES: Home Loan	FINANCIAL SERVICES: Invest-ments	FINANCIAL SERVICES: Retire-ment Plans	THE HOME: Home Improvements: Home Repair	THE HOME: Home Improvements: Lawn & Garden	THE HOME: Furnishings: Comput-ers & Hard-ware	THE HOME: Furnishings: Major Appli-ances	THE HOME: Furnishings: TV, Radio, Sound Equip-ment	THE HOME: Furnishings: Furni-ture	ENTERTAINMENT: Dine out/ Carry out	ENTERTAINMENT: Sports Equip-ment	ENTERTAINMENT: Fees & Tickets	ENTERTAINMENT: Toys & Games	ENTERTAINMENT: Travel	ENTERTAINMENT: Cable TV	PERSONAL: Apparel & Services	PERSONAL: Auto Repairs	PERSONAL: Health Insur-ance	PERSONAL: Pets & Supplies
07676	TSHP OF WASHINGTON	151	214	277	202	207	217	185	184	174	187	218	208	206	240	197	176	222	177	167	196
07677	WOODCLIFF LAKE	253	348	476	338	338	363	302	299	282	308	356	337	342	380	322	285	362	287	276	323
07701	RED BANK	115	125	146	124	124	135	122	123	121	123	152	137	127	151	125	122	149	122	122	135
07702	SHREWSBURY	148	219	295	204	210	221	187	185	175	189	220	209	211	245	200	178	225	177	166	196
07703	FORT MONMOUTH	151	167	161	175	159	154	153	151	141	159	179	178	157	179	148	131	177	148	128	165
07704	FAIR HAVEN	195	269	345	260	260	271	234	231	217	236	274	263	261	298	247	218	278	222	208	249
07711	ALLENHURST	144	205	266	194	197	204	179	176	167	180	210	201	198	233	189	168	214	170	157	187
07712	ASBURY PARK	92	94	114	95	91	99	98	94	98	99	124	110	100	123	97	98	122	97	92	105
07716	ATLANTIC HIGHLANDS	144	174	216	175	170	176	166	162	158	165	199	189	175	208	169	156	198	161	148	176
07717	AVON BY THE SEA	146	153	170	153	155	170	147	152	146	151	183	167	150	172	153	148	177	151	157	170
07718	BELFORD	117	144	156	142	141	142	131	130	123	130	155	151	139	164	134	121	154	126	119	142
07719	BELMAR	114	131	155	133	129	134	127	124	122	126	154	144	133	158	129	120	152	124	116	136
07720	BRADLEY BEACH	84	86	105	90	84	89	91	87	89	91	113	104	92	112	89	86	110	90	81	96
07721	CLIFFWOOD	108	113	121	117	110	112	114	111	109	114	137	133	114	137	111	103	135	113	100	122
07722	COLTS NECK	277	357	439	357	347	364	314	310	290	319	368	352	349	384	328	288	371	298	284	339
07723	DEAL	175	156	136	145	168	193	145	167	156	150	191	178	141	173	156	167	179	163	194	205
07724	EATONTOWN	111	120	139	124	116	121	120	116	115	120	145	136	122	145	118	111	143	118	106	127
07726	ENGLISHTOWN	160	188	201	190	184	191	168	169	158	172	200	190	181	201	173	156	198	164	159	186
07727	FARMINGDALE	121	140	145	142	136	136	129	128	120	130	152	149	134	155	129	115	150	125	114	140
07728	FREEHOLD	129	148	162	147	144	150	137	137	131	139	165	156	143	167	139	129	163	135	128	151
07730	HAZLET	119	136	140	133	134	138	126	127	121	125	151	146	131	157	128	120	149	124	121	141
07731	HOWELL	127	149	151	153	144	141	135	133	124	137	157	156	141	162	134	118	156	130	116	146
07732	HIGHLANDS	95	103	127	105	101	108	106	102	104	105	131	121	108	133	106	102	129	105	97	111
07733	HOLMDEL	243	311	380	310	302	314	274	271	254	280	322	309	302	336	285	251	324	262	245	295
07734	KEANSBURG	77	81	90	81	81	86	83	81	83	81	103	95	85	106	83	82	101	82	80	89
07735	KEYPORT	91	102	117	103	100	104	100	98	97	100	122	115	103	125	101	94	120	98	92	107
07737	LEONARDO	131	168	192	163	163	166	150	148	141	150	178	171	163	192	155	140	179	144	135	161
07738	LINCROFT	169	208	228	212	204	207	186	184	172	188	218	211	202	225	191	168	218	178	167	202
07739	LITTLE SILVER	180	249	315	236	242	253	218	217	205	219	257	245	240	280	231	207	261	209	198	231
07740	LONG BRANCH	76	77	100	78	76	82	84	80	84	83	106	94	84	107	83	84	105	83	78	88
07746	MARLBORO	202	236	251	240	233	244	210	212	198	216	251	236	227	248	217	197	248	205	203	237
07747	MATAWAN	128	154	179	154	151	156	142	141	135	144	170	162	151	176	146	133	170	139	130	154
07748	MIDDLETOWN	153	183	210	183	178	184	170	167	160	170	202	194	180	209	173	157	201	164	154	183
07750	MONMOUTH BEACH	178	212	251	207	210	224	195	198	189	198	237	222	207	239	204	190	234	194	192	216
07751	MORGANVILLE	200	241	258	248	233	234	215	212	197	220	250	245	231	257	217	189	250	205	187	233
07753	NEPTUNE	92	99	109	99	97	102	98	96	96	98	121	111	100	122	98	95	118	96	92	106
07755	OAKHURST	115	149	175	144	146	150	132	132	124	132	156	150	143	167	138	124	156	127	122	143
07756	OCEAN GROVE	68	70	94	71	69	78	75	72	76	74	96	82	77	95	76	77	93	74	73	79
07757	OCEANPORT	137	174	203	167	171	179	157	157	150	157	188	177	169	198	164	151	187	152	149	170
07758	PORT MONMOUTH	132	146	150	145	145	150	139	140	135	138	168	163	143	174	141	133	165	138	134	156
07760	RUMSON	264	344	473	339	333	353	314	306	297	318	375	352	345	401	328	298	379	300	280	330
07762	SPRING LAKE	146	166	204	163	165	181	159	160	157	161	197	178	168	197	165	159	193	159	160	174
07764	WEST LONG BRANCH	134	160	181	156	158	167	150	149	145	148	181	169	159	190	155	145	179	146	144	162
07801	DOVER	96	107	137	103	103	110	105	103	106	108	135	115	108	140	106	106	135	104	97	111
07803	MINE HILL	103	135	160	129	130	134	121	119	115	120	144	137	131	157	126	114	145	116	110	129
07821	ANDOVER	137	162	175	164	159	159	149	148	140	149	176	174	156	184	151	135	175	144	134	164
07822	AUGUSTA	117	145	155	144	142	142	130	129	121	129	152	151	138	160	133	118	151	125	117	143
07823	BELVIDERE	97	97	92	96	100	107	96	99	97	93	119	114	96	122	97	98	115	97	101	113
07825	BLAIRSTOWN	120	148	158	148	146	145	132	132	123	132	155	154	141	164	136	120	154	128	119	146
07826	BRANCHVILLE	105	116	118	113	118	123	107	111	106	106	131	128	111	136	111	106	128	108	110	128
07827	MONTAGUE	91	92	87	91	93	100	90	92	90	88	111	106	91	114	90	90	107	90	93	105
07828	BUDD LAKE	110	109	120	116	105	108	113	108	108	114	137	130	112	133	108	101	134	112	96	121
07830	CALIFON	214	275	326	274	268	275	242	240	224	244	283	276	266	299	252	221	285	231	218	263
07832	COLUMBIA	106	129	137	129	127	126	116	116	108	116	136	136	123	144	118	105	135	112	104	128
07834	DENVILLE	148	192	235	186	187	194	173	171	164	173	206	197	187	220	180	163	207	167	157	185
07836	FLANDERS	143	158	174	165	153	156	152	147	142	154	181	174	158	182	150	136	180	147	131	163
07838	GREAT MEADOWS	108	134	142	134	132	130	120	119	111	119	139	140	127	149	122	108	139	115	107	132
07840	HACKETTSTOWN	117	130	146	134	128	131	127	124	120	126	152	146	130	154	126	116	150	124	114	137
07843	HOPATCONG	115	132	136	134	129	127	123	122	114	123	144	144	126	148	122	109	143	120	108	134
07847	KENVIL	100	122	133	120	120	121	112	111	106	111	133	129	119	142	115	104	133	108	102	121
07848	LAFAYETTE	139	169	178	171	164	162	151	150	140	153	177	175	160	185	153	135	176	145	132	165
07849	LAKE HOPATCONG	116	133	136	135	129	128	124	123	115	124	146	145	127	149	123	110	144	121	109	135
07850	LANDING	107	122	138	125	120	121	117	114	110	117	139	136	121	143	117	106	138	114	103	126
07851	LAYTON	93	114	126	111	111	114	105	104	101	104	126	120	112	134	108	99	126	101	97	113
07852	LEDGEWOOD	140	174	188	174	170	170	156	155	146	156	183	180	168	194	160	142	184	149	140	170
07853	LONG VALLEY	177	220	238	226	213	215	194	190	177	196	225	220	212	235	198	172	227	183	169	210
07856	MOUNT ARLINGTON	114	134	157	137	132	134	128	125	121	127	152	149	133	158	129	117	151	125	113	137
07857	NETCONG	88	96	110	98	93	97	95	92	91	95	116	109	98	117	95	88	114	93	85	102
07860	NEWTON	103	120	133	120	118	121	113	112	108	113	136	131	119	141	115	106	134	110	103	123
07863	OXFORD	95	111	116	111	108	108	103	102	97	103	122	120	107	127	103	93	121	100	92	112
07865	PORT MURRAY	116	144	155	144	141	141	130	128	121	129	152	150	139	162	133	118	152	124	116	141
07866	ROCKAWAY	130	162	183	161	157	158	145	144	136	147	171	166	155	182	148	133	172	140	128	156
07869	RANDOLPH	189	231	286	238	223	230	212	205	199	216	252	238	232	265	217	195	254	201	185	225
07871	SPARTA	157	196	219	199	190	193	175	171	162	177	205	198	190	215	179	158	206	166	154	189
07874	STANHOPE	118	141	149	142	138	136	129	128	120	129	152	151	135	158	130	116	151	125	114	141
07876	SUCCASUNNA	140	184	212	180	178	180	162	160	150	162	189	185	176	204	168	148	191	154	143	174
07882	WASHINGTON	103	119	132	121	118	119	114	112	108	113	136	132	119	142	115	105	135	111	103	123
07885	WHARTON	101	117	134	118	115	118	112	110	107	112	135	129	117	140	113	105	134	109	101	120
07901	SUMMIT	249	322	423	314	312	330	293	287	277	296	350	329	319	371	305	277	353	282	263	310
07920	BASKING RIDGE	234	291	349	294	283	292	263	258	244	267	309	298	285	320	270	239	310	252	234	282
07921	BEDMINSTER	147	156	272	170	148	163	171	155	172	174	218	187	181	232	171	172	218	162	143	171
07922	BERKELEY HEIGHTS	180	252	323	243	242	253	217	214	202	220	254	243	243	277	230	202	259	206	192	230
07924	BERNARDSVILLE	284	378	505	368	367	390	335	331	315	341	397	376	373	423	354	316	403	321	304	357
07927	CEDAR KNOLLS	127	183	237	171	176	184	158	157	149	159	186	177	176	206	169	151	190	151	142	166
07928	CHATHAM	231	320	424	308	309	325	281	277	264	284	331	316	312	361	297	265	337	268	250	297
07930	CHESTER	242	322	424	315	314	336	282	281	264	287	333	316	316	350	300	266	337	270	261	304
07931	FAR HILLS	276	376	512	366	365	392	328	324	306	334	386	366	370	411	349	309	392	312	299	351
07932	FLORHAM PARK	154	221	284	207	213	222	191	190	180	192	225	214	212	249	204	182	229	183	172	201
07933	GILLETTE	178	252	319	242	242	250	217	213	201	219	253	243	242	279	229	202	259	205	190	229
07934	GLADSTONE	216	314	425	295	302	319	269	266	252	272	316	300	304	350	288	256	324	256	240	283
07935	GREEN VILLAGE	210	309	417	289	296	312	264	261	247	267	310	295	298	346	283	251	318	251	235	277
07936	EAST HANOVER	130	181	235	173	175	181	160	157	150	161	189	180	176	208	169	151	192	153	141	168
07940	MADISON	174	211	282	213	205	217	202	195	193	203	243	228	215	255	207	191	243	195	180	212
07945	MENDHAM	233	316	411	309	306	323	274	271	254	279	322	307	309	343	290	255	327	260	247	293
07946	MILLINGTON	203	264	317	265	255	264	231	226	212	235	269	259	257	283	239	209	272	218	204	248
	NEW JERSEY	110	123	153	121	120	128	120	118	119	121	150	136	125	155	123	120	149	119	114	130
	UNITED STATES	100	100	100	100	100	100	100	100	100	100	100	100	100	100	100	100	100	100	100	100

# POST OFFICE NAME	COUNTY FIPS CODE	POPULATION 2000	2004	2009	2000-2004 ANNUAL RATE % Rate	State Centile	HOUSEHOLDS 2000	2004	2009	% Annual Rate 2000-2004	2004 Average HH Size	FAMILIES 2000	2004	% Annual Rate 2000-2004
07950 MORRIS PLAINS	027	17936	18265	18998	0.4	42	6670	6776	7045	0.4	2.58	4746	4844	0.5
07960 MORRISTOWN	027	42761	44096	46113	0.7	56	16198	16637	17386	0.6	2.53	10401	10697	0.7
07974 NEW PROVIDENCE	039	12108	11956	12043	-0.3	9	4478	4399	4403	-0.4	2.67	3370	3331	-0.3
07976 NEW VERNON	027	549	549	563	0.0	22	204	204	209	0.0	2.69	165	165	0.0
07980 STIRLING	027	2672	2684	2785	0.1	27	954	957	992	0.1	2.80	719	724	0.2
07981 WHIPPANY	027	8392	8626	9016	0.7	53	3152	3239	3383	0.6	2.66	2360	2438	0.8
08002 CHERRY HILL	007	20507	20680	20844	0.2	32	8101	8259	8403	0.5	2.42	5411	5536	0.5
08003 CHERRY HILL	007	30709	31316	31855	0.5	44	10731	11121	11450	0.8	2.76	8752	9078	0.9
08004 ATCO	007	12403	12764	13069	0.7	55	4307	4500	4660	1.0	2.79	3306	3456	1.1
08005 BARNEGAT	029	16901	19650	22607	3.6	97	6083	7025	8059	3.5	2.77	4607	5355	3.6
08007 BARRINGTON	007	5378	5441	5474	0.3	34	2264	2315	2350	0.5	2.35	1380	1417	0.6
08008 BEACH HAVEN	029	8556	8997	9836	1.2	72	4158	4366	4772	1.2	2.06	2545	2690	1.3
08009 BERLIN	007	11906	12977	13630	2.1	87	4292	4737	5026	2.4	2.72	3201	3541	2.4
08010 BEVERLY	005	10608	11076	11685	1.0	66	4144	4346	4615	1.1	2.55	2818	2980	1.3
08012 BLACKWOOD	007	39206	42611	45983	2.0	87	14524	15907	17281	2.2	2.63	10230	11267	2.3
08014 BRIDGEPORT	015	631	697	754	2.4	91	240	268	294	2.6	2.58	165	184	2.6
08015 BROWNS MILLS	005	21068	21508	22490	0.5	46	7421	7642	8061	0.7	2.81	5546	5733	0.8
08016 BURLINGTON	005	30760	33590	36309	2.1	89	11238	12329	13425	2.2	2.64	7982	8818	2.4
08019 CHATSWORTH	005	607	614	637	0.3	34	185	189	199	0.5	3.03	144	147	0.5
08020 CLARKSBORO	015	2293	2585	2831	2.9	95	794	912	1014	3.3	2.73	618	713	3.4
08021 CLEMENTON	007	46150	47503	48809	0.7	55	18505	19085	19688	0.7	2.48	11714	12151	0.9
08022 COLUMBUS	005	6218	8377	10058	7.3	100	2431	3287	3970	7.4	2.55	1866	2531	7.4
08026 GIBBSBORO	007	2434	2406	2402	-0.3	9	828	829	836	0.0	2.87	664	666	0.1
08027 GIBBSTOWN	015	4831	4888	5066	0.3	35	1851	1897	1989	0.6	2.57	1381	1422	0.7
08028 GLASSBORO	015	20150	20426	21248	0.3	38	6546	6684	7045	0.5	2.67	4309	4422	0.6
08029 GLENDORA	007	4919	4783	4766	-0.7	1	1950	1922	1936	-0.3	2.49	1301	1284	-0.3
08030 GLOUCESTER CITY	007	14031	13892	13966	-0.2	10	5231	5233	5306	0.0	2.65	3478	3491	0.1
08031 BELLMAWR	007	11268	10969	10948	-0.6	2	4450	4383	4417	-0.4	2.50	3138	3102	-0.3
08032 GRENLOCH	015	510	525	549	0.7	55	167	171	179	0.6	3.07	155	159	0.6
08033 HADDONFIELD	007	17430	17291	17346	-0.2	12	7294	7275	7341	-0.1	2.36	4845	4857	0.1
08034 CHERRY HILL	007	18402	18344	18445	-0.1	18	7283	7340	7454	0.2	2.47	5152	5210	0.3
08035 HADDON HEIGHTS	007	7498	7299	7270	-0.6	2	3017	2971	2988	-0.4	2.45	2027	2003	-0.3
08036 HAINESPORT	005	4200	5417	6354	6.2	99	1470	1908	2253	6.3	2.83	1158	1505	6.4
08037 HAMMONTON	001	23256	24231	25447	1.0	65	7960	8371	8851	1.2	2.72	5837	6173	1.3
08041 JOBSTOWN	005	483	534	579	2.4	92	169	187	205	2.4	2.86	136	152	2.7
08043 VOORHEES	007	28128	28577	28933	0.4	39	10488	10678	10870	0.4	2.59	7072	7280	0.5
08045 LAWNSIDE	007	2620	2599	2601	-0.2	14	983	986	995	0.1	2.64	670	674	0.1
08046 WILLINGBORO	005	33194	33145	34488	0.0	20	10782	10844	11376	0.1	3.04	8828	8905	0.2
08048 LUMBERTON	005	584	669	738	3.3	96	330	377	419	3.2	1.67	212	245	3.5
08049 MAGNOLIA	007	5566	5480	5493	-0.4	5	2139	2131	2156	-0.1	2.56	1509	1512	0.1
08050 MANAHAWKIN	029	20461	23677	27193	3.5	96	7803	8979	10282	3.4	2.61	5940	6887	3.5
08051 MANTUA	015	10104	10597	11205	1.1	71	4179	4452	4771	1.5	2.38	2751	2948	1.6
08052 MAPLE SHADE	005	19101	19186	19994	0.1	27	8471	8567	9008	0.3	2.21	4726	4794	0.3
08053 MARLTON	005	42075	45668	49505	2.0	86	15647	17091	18673	2.1	2.66	11289	12429	2.3
08054 MOUNT LAUREL	005	40292	43408	46600	1.8	83	16594	18051	19550	2.0	2.38	11086	12113	2.1
08055 MEDFORD	005	27212	28172	29755	0.8	59	9729	10131	10779	1.0	2.76	7745	8086	1.0
08056 MICKLETON	015	2669	2902	3120	2.0	87	937	1034	1124	2.3	2.80	768	851	2.4
08057 MOORESTOWN	005	19425	20259	21404	1.0	66	7113	7439	7910	1.1	2.68	5390	5679	1.2
08059 MOUNT EPHRAIM	007	5478	5252	5217	-1.0	0	2208	2136	2139	-0.8	2.45	1440	1399	-0.7
08060 MOUNT HOLLY	005	33212	34688	36713	1.0	67	12011	12587	13412	1.1	2.70	8495	8951	1.2
08061 MOUNT ROYAL	015	528	619	691	3.8	97	188	229	262	4.8	2.45	144	177	5.0
08062 MULLICA HILL	015	11047	12557	13821	3.1	95	3624	4139	4590	3.2	3.00	2960	3392	3.3
08063 NATIONAL PARK	015	3304	3214	3321	-0.7	1	1148	1132	1184	-0.3	2.82	894	883	-0.3
08065 PALMYRA	005	7006	7483	8002	1.6	79	2964	3177	3415	1.7	2.35	1823	1966	1.8
08066 PAULSBORO	015	8242	8309	8668	0.2	31	3439	3527	3730	0.6	2.35	2131	2183	0.6
08067 PEDRICKTOWN	033	1733	1784	1833	0.7	55	627	654	679	1.0	2.72	496	518	1.0
08068 PEMBERTON	005	7227	7176	7451	-0.2	13	2638	2632	2758	-0.1	2.56	1781	1790	0.1
08069 PENNS GROVE	033	12825	12707	12891	-0.1	11	5047	5051	5174	0.0	2.49	3351	3365	0.1
08070 PENNSVILLE	033	13003	12949	13147	-0.1	16	5241	5280	5414	0.2	2.44	3663	3698	0.2
08071 PITMAN	015	9674	9637	9966	-0.1	17	3608	3627	3794	0.1	2.57	2532	2557	0.2
08075 RIVERSIDE	005	26478	27204	28545	0.6	52	9952	10309	10912	0.8	2.63	7159	7450	0.9
08077 RIVERTON	005	17216	17678	18534	0.6	51	6081	6278	6633	0.8	2.77	4846	5026	0.9
08078 RUNNEMEDE	007	8388	8098	8055	-0.8	1	3320	3241	3253	-0.6	2.49	2239	2194	-0.5
08079 SALEM	033	12577	12693	12992	0.2	33	4985	5079	5245	0.4	2.46	3390	3471	0.6
08080 SEWELL	015	36507	39558	42834	1.9	86	11835	13097	14420	2.4	3.01	9821	10813	2.3
08081 SICKLERVILLE	007	42950	46208	48267	1.7	83	14066	15169	15917	1.8	3.04	11304	12240	1.9
08083 SOMERDALE	007	9419	9234	9233	-0.5	3	3596	3562	3594	-0.2	2.59	2590	2580	-0.1
08084 STRATFORD	007	7445	7271	7253	-0.6	2	2797	2766	2786	-0.3	2.58	1967	1949	-0.2
08085 SWEDESBORO	015	10774	13034	14894	4.6	98	3582	4342	4993	4.6	2.99	2887	3545	5.0
08086 THOROFARE	015	5387	5791	6294	1.7	82	2184	2378	2614	2.0	2.43	1419	1550	2.1
08087 TUCKERTON	029	20663	24184	27985	3.8	97	8089	9399	10826	3.6	2.55	5687	6660	3.8
08088 VINCENTOWN	005	24722	25798	27148	1.0	66	9278	9742	10330	1.2	2.63	7036	7419	1.3
08089 WATERFORD WORKS	007	4179	4265	4348	0.5	45	1402	1452	1497	0.8	2.84	1092	1131	0.8
08090 WENONAH	015	8357	8165	8447	-0.6	4	2965	2936	3074	-0.2	2.75	2343	2327	-0.2
08091 WEST BERLIN	007	5219	5142	5131	-0.4	6	1866	1859	1873	-0.1	2.76	1351	1350	0.0
08092 WEST CREEK	029	3145	3273	3552	0.9	63	1178	1226	1329	0.9	2.67	831	868	1.0
08093 WESTVILLE	015	10073	10545	11213	1.1	69	4001	4215	4523	1.2	2.49	2511	2664	1.4
08094 WILLIAMSTOWN	015	32967	34678	36911	1.2	72	11875	12627	13575	1.5	2.73	8956	9564	1.6
08096 WOODBURY	015	32662	34773	37331	1.5	77	12344	13311	14475	1.8	2.54	8561	9259	1.9
08097 WOODBURY HEIGHTS	015	3129	3112	3229	-0.1	16	1076	1084	1138	0.2	2.86	862	871	0.2
08098 WOODSTOWN	033	8637	8893	9132	0.7	55	3037	3156	3270	0.9	2.65	2237	2328	0.9
08102 CAMDEN	007	9866	9727	9745	-0.3	7	2557	2545	2579	-0.1	3.00	1630	1631	0.0
08103 CAMDEN	007	15528	15108	15076	-0.6	1	4593	4495	4524	-0.5	2.94	3196	3143	-0.4
08104 CAMDEN	007	24362	24000	24072	-0.4	6	8106	7983	8035	-0.4	2.97	5773	5713	-0.3
08105 CAMDEN	007	28222	28031	28292	-0.2	14	8371	8388	8537	0.1	3.34	6408	6439	0.1
08106 AUDUBON	007	10284	10185	10219	-0.2	10	4169	4163	4211	0.0	2.44	2690	2697	0.1
08107 OAKLYN	007	13480	13256	13238	-0.4	5	5593	5531	5563	-0.3	2.40	3235	3217	-0.1
08108 COLLINGSWOOD	007	17727	17473	17473	-0.3	6	7268	7235	7299	-0.1	2.40	4532	4528	0.0
08109 MERCHANTVILLE	007	22777	22730	22911	-0.1	19	8460	8487	8616	0.1	2.60	5820	5872	0.2
08110 PENNSAUKEN	007	18772	18653	18695	-0.2	14	6032	5991	6026	-0.2	3.11	4682	4660	-0.1
08201 ABSECON	001	9159	9592	10154	1.1	69	3348	3511	3721	1.1	2.68	2472	2604	1.2
08202 AVALON	009	2234	2300	2425	0.7	55	1090	1134	1208	0.9	2.00	701	732	1.0
08203 BRIGANTINE	001	12594	12550	12977	-0.1	17	5473	5470	5663	0.0	2.29	3338	3355	0.1
08204 CAPE MAY	009	19377	20102	21276	0.9	61	8029	8420	9009	1.1	2.32	5335	5617	1.2
08205 ABSECON	001	25931	28325	30636	2.1	89	8824	9732	10582	2.3	2.68	6316	6986	2.4
NEW JERSEY					0.8					0.9	2.68			1.0
UNITED STATES					1.2					1.3	2.58			1.1

#	POST OFFICE NAME	RACE (%) White 2000	White 2004	Black 2000	Black 2004	Asian/Pacific 2000	Asian/Pacific 2004	% Hispanic Origin 2000	% Hispanic Origin 2004	2004 AGE DISTRIBUTION (%) 0-4	5-9	10-14	15-19	20-24	25-44	45-64	65-84	85+	18+	MEDIAN AGE 2004	% 2004 Males	% 2004 Females
07950	MORRIS PLAINS	83.8	81.1	2.8	3.1	11.1	13.2	4.1	5.1	6.2	6.5	6.0	5.2	4.3	30.1	28.5	11.7	1.5	78.1	40.5	49.8	50.2
07960	MORRISTOWN	79.9	78.0	10.1	10.3	3.7	4.4	13.7	16.1	6.2	6.5	6.0	5.4	5.2	30.6	25.8	12.1	2.2	78.0	39.4	48.8	51.2
07974	NEW PROVIDENCE	89.4	87.2	1.1	1.2	7.9	9.5	3.5	4.6	7.4	8.0	7.5	5.9	3.8	26.5	25.6	13.1	2.2	73.0	40.4	48.3	51.7
07976	NEW VERNON	97.5	96.9	0.2	0.2	0.7	0.9	2.4	2.9	5.3	7.1	7.8	5.8	2.7	18.6	33.0	17.3	2.4	75.4	46.6	48.6	51.4
07980	STIRLING	92.1	90.5	0.5	0.6	4.9	6.0	3.9	5.0	7.6	7.8	7.5	5.7	4.4	28.1	26.2	11.3	1.5	73.5	39.6	47.9	52.1
07981	WHIPPANY	88.2	85.8	1.1	1.3	9.2	11.2	3.6	4.6	6.6	6.9	6.3	5.0	3.7	28.8	26.6	14.2	1.8	76.8	41.1	48.0	52.0
08002	CHERRY HILL	83.9	80.3	5.4	6.4	7.9	9.7	3.4	4.8	5.2	5.4	6.0	5.6	4.9	24.3	25.5	18.2	5.1	79.7	44.2	46.7	53.4
08003	CHERRY HILL	83.4	79.9	4.2	5.0	11.2	13.6	1.8	2.4	5.7	6.7	7.6	6.5	4.4	22.7	30.9	13.4	2.1	75.6	42.8	48.2	51.8
08004	ATCO	86.9	83.5	10.0	12.6	0.9	1.1	2.4	3.5	6.8	6.8	7.0	6.7	6.1	30.6	26.4	7.9	1.7	75.1	36.9	49.3	50.7
08005	BARNEGAT	95.0	94.1	2.1	2.3	1.0	1.2	3.8	4.7	6.3	6.5	7.6	6.8	5.3	24.0	25.2	16.6	1.8	75.3	41.0	48.0	52.0
08007	BARRINGTON	91.6	89.5	4.4	5.4	1.3	1.6	2.7	3.9	5.8	5.8	6.3	5.5	5.8	29.6	23.4	15.2	2.6	78.8	39.4	47.5	52.5
08008	BEACH HAVEN	98.1	97.7	0.3	0.3	0.6	0.6	3.0	3.7	3.1	3.4	3.8	3.3	3.1	18.6	31.4	29.5	3.9	87.7	55.6	48.2	51.8
08009	BERLIN	86.9	84.5	8.6	10.0	1.6	2.0	3.3	4.6	6.6	6.5	7.1	6.6	5.9	29.7	25.7	10.5	1.5	75.6	37.4	49.6	50.4
08010	BEVERLY	67.4	63.1	23.1	25.9	2.7	3.1	6.1	7.4	6.1	6.3	6.9	6.7	6.5	28.3	25.9	12.2	1.3	76.8	38.5	48.0	52.0
08012	BLACKWOOD	86.5	83.7	8.3	9.7	2.6	3.3	3.0	4.0	6.1	6.0	6.7	6.7	7.0	29.4	25.1	11.2	1.8	77.0	37.4	48.2	51.8
08014	BRIDGEPORT	96.8	96.6	2.5	2.7	0.3	0.4	1.0	1.2	7.0	7.0	8.3	6.3	5.0	27.3	23.2	13.2	2.6	73.3	38.3	51.1	48.9
08015	BROWNS MILLS	69.7	65.9	19.3	21.3	3.4	3.9	8.2	9.8	6.6	6.6	7.7	7.5	7.4	28.6	25.7	9.3	0.6	74.4	36.0	48.5	51.5
08016	BURLINGTON	68.4	64.9	24.7	27.1	3.0	3.5	3.8	4.7	8.0	7.8	7.1	5.8	5.1	30.7	22.2	10.9	2.4	73.3	37.1	47.6	52.4
08019	CHATSWORTH	94.6	93.8	1.3	1.5	0.2	0.2	5.1	6.0	4.9	6.0	8.1	7.2	5.4	25.2	30.6	9.8	2.8	76.1	41.1	48.5	51.5
08020	CLARKSBORO	93.6	92.6	4.2	4.7	0.7	0.9	1.7	2.1	5.7	6.0	5.9	6.2	4.8	24.4	28.6	15.5	3.0	78.4	43.2	46.7	53.3
08021	CLEMENTON	73.3	68.9	19.6	22.5	2.6	3.0	4.9	6.3	6.7	6.4	7.0	6.8	7.4	32.0	24.2	8.5	1.0	75.8	34.9	48.0	52.0
08022	COLUMBUS	94.6	93.6	2.3	2.6	1.9	2.3	1.8	2.4	4.9	5.7	5.9	4.8	3.7	20.4	25.8	26.5	2.5	80.5	48.3	48.2	51.8
08026	GIBBSBORO	94.0	92.4	2.8	3.5	1.1	1.3	2.4	3.5	5.7	6.2	6.9	7.0	5.9	26.0	27.1	14.1	1.1	77.1	40.1	49.8	50.3
08027	GIBBSTOWN	94.6	93.8	3.3	3.7	0.7	0.8	1.6	1.9	6.0	5.9	5.7	6.0	6.2	26.3	26.2	15.4	2.2	78.8	41.3	48.8	51.2
08028	GLASSBORO	73.3	71.4	20.7	21.8	2.4	2.8	3.9	4.5	6.3	6.1	6.2	10.9	17.7	24.7	18.5	8.4	1.0	77.7	27.1	48.1	51.9
08029	GLENDORA	97.5	96.7	0.6	0.7	0.4	0.5	1.6	2.3	5.2	5.2	5.9	6.1	6.4	26.8	25.1	16.6	2.7	80.1	41.6	47.4	52.6
08030	GLOUCESTER CITY	94.8	93.5	2.2	2.5	0.8	1.0	2.7	3.9	6.6	6.5	7.4	7.1	7.3	28.2	23.7	11.7	1.5	75.1	36.7	48.6	51.4
08031	BELLMAWR	92.8	91.0	1.2	1.4	3.1	3.7	3.5	4.9	5.0	5.3	6.0	5.8	5.6	28.0	26.5	16.3	1.6	80.2	41.6	49.2	50.8
08032	GRENLOCH	90.0	88.4	3.5	3.8	5.7	6.7	1.2	1.3	9.5	9.7	10.9	7.4	4.0	31.1	22.9	3.8	0.8	64.2	33.6	49.1	50.9
08033	HADDONFIELD	95.6	94.5	1.5	1.8	1.5	1.8	1.7	2.4	5.6	6.3	7.3	6.8	4.9	23.0	28.6	14.8	2.9	76.4	42.7	47.2	52.9
08034	CHERRY HILL	87.7	84.9	3.9	4.7	6.2	7.6	2.7	3.8	5.5	6.0	6.5	6.0	4.6	25.0	26.3	17.8	2.4	78.0	42.8	47.9	52.1
08035	HADDON HEIGHTS	98.0	97.4	0.4	0.5	0.7	0.9	1.1	1.5	6.0	6.2	6.4	6.6	5.2	24.7	27.4	14.9	2.7	77.1	41.7	46.8	53.2
08036	HAINESPORT	93.8	92.6	2.9	3.3	1.8	2.1	2.2	2.8	7.4	8.0	7.3	5.5	4.5	27.2	27.9	11.1	1.2	73.4	40.4	48.6	51.5
08037	HAMMONTON	84.8	81.9	5.1	5.8	1.0	1.2	13.5	16.7	5.7	5.9	6.6	6.1	5.7	29.0	25.7	13.0	2.4	78.2	39.7	50.5	49.5
08041	JOBSTOWN	94.0	92.5	1.5	1.7	2.7	3.4	2.3	3.0	5.4	6.6	7.5	6.9	5.4	26.6	28.3	11.4	1.9	76.0	40.4	48.7	51.3
08043	VOORHEES	78.3	74.2	8.0	9.3	11.5	13.7	2.5	3.4	6.2	6.8	7.5	6.7	5.7	28.4	27.3	9.0	2.4	75.0	38.3	47.9	52.1
08045	LAWNSIDE	1.7	1.5	93.7	93.7	0.6	0.7	2.4	2.8	3.9	4.7	7.7	7.1	6.6	21.7	28.0	18.0	2.4	79.4	43.9	45.5	54.5
08046	WILLINGBORO	24.9	21.9	66.5	68.8	1.8	1.9	6.1	6.9	6.1	6.7	7.9	7.6	6.2	24.0	27.1	13.5	0.9	74.4	39.3	47.2	52.8
08048	LUMBERTON	89.0	87.0	6.9	7.9	1.7	1.9	2.9	3.7	6.9	7.0	6.7	5.1	4.2	25.7	22.9	16.9	4.6	76.2	41.9	46.3	53.7
08049	MAGNOLIA	78.0	74.2	16.7	19.1	1.3	1.6	3.9	5.4	6.9	7.0	7.1	5.7	6.0	30.5	23.7	12.0	1.2	75.5	37.5	48.6	51.4
08050	MANAHAWKIN	96.8	96.1	0.8	0.9	1.0	1.2	2.5	3.1	6.7	6.7	6.8	5.5	4.8	25.9	24.9	16.3	2.3	76.3	40.9	48.5	51.5
08051	MANTUA	93.8	92.7	3.4	3.9	1.3	1.6	1.4	1.7	7.7	7.3	6.3	5.4	5.5	32.1	24.1	10.6	1.1	75.6	37.0	47.5	52.5
08052	MAPLE SHADE	83.2	80.8	7.2	7.9	6.1	7.2	4.5	5.5	5.5	5.2	5.6	5.6	6.1	33.9	22.7	13.3	2.1	80.3	38.1	49.0	51.0
08053	MARLTON	91.2	89.4	3.1	3.7	4.1	5.1	2.0	2.5	7.2	7.5	7.6	6.3	5.1	31.0	25.7	8.5	1.1	73.5	37.0	48.3	51.7
08054	MOUNT LAUREL	87.1	84.8	6.9	8.0	3.8	4.6	2.2	2.8	5.9	6.1	6.5	5.5	5.1	28.4	26.4	14.7	1.4	77.8	40.8	47.2	52.9
08055	MEDFORD	96.9	96.1	0.8	1.0	1.4	1.7	1.2	1.5	6.2	7.1	7.7	6.5	4.6	24.3	31.1	10.6	2.0	74.8	41.4	48.4	51.6
08056	MICKLETON	95.9	95.2	2.3	2.5	0.6	0.7	1.1	1.3	5.4	6.3	8.0	7.6	5.4	23.7	31.4	10.9	1.3	75.0	41.4	49.1	50.9
08057	MOORESTOWN	89.3	87.1	5.7	6.6	3.2	4.0	1.8	2.2	6.3	7.3	8.5	7.1	4.4	22.0	28.3	13.2	3.0	73.2	41.9	47.2	52.8
08059	MOUNT EPHRAIM	97.1	96.3	0.6	0.7	0.8	1.0	2.1	3.0	5.8	5.8	6.3	6.0	5.3	27.8	26.3	14.0	2.7	78.5	40.9	48.1	51.9
08060	MOUNT HOLLY	73.3	69.9	17.7	19.6	3.1	3.7	6.5	7.8	7.3	7.4	7.8	7.0	6.2	30.6	23.5	9.0	1.2	73.0	36.1	48.7	51.3
08061	MOUNT ROYAL	93.2	92.3	4.4	4.9	0.6	0.8	1.9	2.3	6.8	6.5	5.2	5.7	4.4	26.7	25.2	13.9	5.8	77.7	41.7	45.1	54.9
08062	MULLICA HILL	94.7	93.9	3.1	3.5	0.6	0.8	2.1	2.6	8.1	8.8	9.3	6.8	4.4	29.7	25.0	7.0	0.9	69.1	36.6	49.7	50.3
08063	NATIONAL PARK	98.3	98.1	0.1	0.1	0.3	0.3	1.4	1.7	5.9	5.7	6.5	8.1	8.1	27.9	25.3	11.5	1.1	77.0	37.7	49.7	50.3
08065	PALMYRA	80.8	76.9	14.5	17.4	1.4	1.8	3.2	4.1	5.8	5.8	6.6	6.3	6.0	29.4	26.4	12.1	1.7	78.1	39.6	48.3	51.7
08066	PAULSBORO	69.7	68.4	25.9	26.6	0.6	0.8	3.9	4.5	7.0	7.1	7.6	6.5	6.7	29.6	22.5	11.5	1.4	74.3	35.5	47.3	52.7
08067	PEDRICKTOWN	86.8	84.3	9.6	11.2	0.2	0.2	4.2	5.4	5.4	6.1	7.3	6.3	5.8	26.4	30.4	10.8	1.5	77.1	41.0	50.3	49.7
08068	PEMBERTON	61.2	57.7	29.4	31.6	2.6	3.0	9.3	10.9	5.5	5.4	6.0	6.9	8.0	29.3	24.0	13.4	1.5	79.0	37.7	50.9	49.1
08069	PENNS GROVE	67.6	64.5	24.9	26.8	0.8	0.9	9.0	10.5	7.1	6.8	7.4	6.9	7.1	26.5	24.1	12.2	2.0	74.5	36.6	47.2	52.8
08070	PENNSVILLE	96.6	95.9	1.1	1.3	1.0	1.2	1.6	2.1	5.8	5.9	6.4	6.1	5.7	26.9	27.2	14.1	1.9	78.2	40.7	48.0	52.0
08071	PITMAN	97.0	96.6	1.0	1.1	0.6	0.8	1.5	1.8	5.9	6.1	7.2	6.9	6.4	25.9	26.4	12.2	3.0	76.5	39.6	46.3	53.7
08075	RIVERSIDE	86.6	84.6	7.1	8.0	1.9	2.3	3.4	4.2	6.3	6.3	7.0	6.4	6.6	30.3	25.0	10.7	1.4	76.4	37.3	49.2	50.8
08077	RIVERTON	92.0	90.8	4.6	5.1	1.7	2.2	1.5	1.9	5.0	5.6	7.1	6.9	4.8	23.0	27.7	17.6	2.3	77.7	43.6	48.4	51.6
08078	RUNNEMEDE	92.0	90.1	3.6	4.3	1.5	1.9	3.5	5.0	5.9	5.6	6.2	6.6	6.7	28.6	25.3	13.3	1.8	78.2	38.9	48.2	51.8
08079	SALEM	64.6	62.6	31.4	33.0	0.3	0.4	3.0	3.5	7.3	7.3	7.9	6.3	5.8	25.1	25.0	13.3	2.1	73.6	38.4	47.2	52.9
08080	SEWELL	90.3	89.1	4.7	5.1	3.4	4.0	2.0	2.4	6.5	7.3	8.8	7.8	6.1	28.2	27.2	7.3	0.9	72.4	36.3	48.7	51.3
08081	SICKLERVILLE	68.4	65.0	26.2	28.4	2.2	2.6	3.4	4.6	8.9	8.9	8.9	7.3	6.0	32.2	21.9	5.4	0.6	68.7	32.8	48.6	51.4
08083	SOMERDALE	80.9	77.5	13.3	15.5	2.8	3.4	3.2	4.4	5.6	5.9	6.7	6.3	5.5	28.7	27.6	12.5	1.3	78.0	39.9	48.7	51.3
08084	STRATFORD	88.9	86.9	6.4	7.3	2.3	2.8	3.6	4.9	6.2	6.2	6.9	6.8	6.4	27.7	23.9	14.0	1.9	76.5	38.9	48.8	51.2
08085	SWEDESBORO	83.0	81.8	12.0	12.4	1.4	1.6	4.3	5.0	8.9	8.9	8.4	6.9	5.5	32.0	23.0	5.7	0.8	69.4	34.5	49.2	50.8
08086	THOROFARE	90.2	88.1	7.1	8.6	1.1	1.4	1.5	1.9	5.8	5.8	6.3	6.5	6.4	30.2	26.9	11.1	0.9	78.2	38.6	48.6	51.4
08087	TUCKERTON	96.5	95.7	0.7	0.8	0.6	0.7	3.2	4.1	5.9	6.2	7.2	6.0	5.6	25.7	25.9	15.6	1.8	76.9	41.0	48.5	51.5
08088	VINCENTOWN	96.7	96.0	1.4	1.7	0.7	0.8	1.4	1.9	5.1	6.0	7.0	6.5	4.4	23.6	29.1	15.8	2.5	77.6	43.5	48.9	51.1
08089	WATERFORD WORKS	73.8	69.4	22.0	25.1	0.7	0.9	3.1	4.4	4.8	5.5	6.8	6.6	5.8	26.3	31.2	11.6	1.3	78.5	41.3	50.1	49.9
08090	WENONAH	89.1	87.9	8.8	9.6	0.8	1.0	1.7	2.0	6.5	6.8	7.1	6.2	5.2	26.9	25.6	14.3	1.4	75.8	39.9	48.6	51.4
08091	WEST BERLIN	82.7	79.8	11.7	13.4	2.7	3.2	4.8	6.4	6.6	6.7	7.2	6.8	5.9	29.4	24.5	11.7	1.4	75.4	37.4	50.2	49.8
08092	WEST CREEK	98.0	97.6	0.4	0.4	0.8	1.0	1.8	2.2	5.6	5.8	7.6	6.7	5.3	24.4	28.4	14.7	1.7	77.0	41.8	49.3	50.7
08093	WESTVILLE	83.5	80.8	11.2	12.8	1.2	1.4	4.4	5.4	6.4	6.0	6.8	7.1	7.3	31.1	22.7	11.2	1.4	76.4	36.3	48.4	51.7
08094	WILLIAMSTOWN	84.8	82.9	11.0	12.0	1.2	1.4	3.3	4.0	6.7	6.8	7.2	6.4	5.9	28.5	25.7	11.5	1.3	75.2	37.9	48.4	51.6
08096	WOODBURY	84.8	83.0	11.5	12.6	1.4	1.8	2.6	3.1	6.2	6.2	6.7	6.1	6.0	29.0	24.2	13.2	2.2	77.0	38.8	47.7	52.3
08097	WOODBURY HEIGHTS	91.6	90.8	6.3	6.8	1.0	1.1	1.3	1.6	6.0	6.3	7.3	6.8	5.8	26.7	26.9	12.9	1.4	75.9	39.6	48.1	51.9
08098	WOODSTOWN	85.1	83.1	12.2	13.7	0.8	0.9	2.4	3.0	5.2	5.7	7.1	7.1	6.2	26.4	27.0	12.5	2.7	77.5	40.4	49.6	50.4
08102	CAMDEN	19.6	18.3	48.6	46.9	1.1	1.1	53.2	56.9	7.3	6.7	8.1	9.4	11.3	31.9	16.8	7.4	1.1	72.9	29.1	55.1	44.9
08103	CAMDEN	11.7	11.2	69.9	68.3	0.4	0.5	26.1	29.0	7.6	7.5	9.0	9.2	10.2	28.8	17.6	9.0	1.1	70.6	29.7	49.9	50.1
08104	CAMDEN	16.2	14.5	64.5	63.3	1.1	1.1	23.3	27.0	10.3	9.8	10.5	8.9	8.2	26.9	17.7	6.9	0.8	63.9	26.6	45.6	54.4
08105	CAMDEN	18.8	17.9	37.7	35.3	4.7	4.5	53.9	58.4	10.2	9.5	10.0	9.5	9.4	28.1	17.7	5.4	0.4	64.6	26.0	48.1	51.9
08106	AUDUBON	97.5	96.8	0.5	0.7	0.8	1.0	1.4	2.0	5.4	5.7	6.8	7.1	6.1	28.0	25.6	12.8	2.6	77.6	40.0	47.6	52.4
08107	OAKLYN	79.5	75.9	9.5	10.6	5.0	5.8	7.7	10.2	5.9	5.8	6.8	6.8	6.9	29.5	23.1	12.8	2.5	77.3	37.8	48.0	52.0
08108	COLLINGSWOOD	93.0	91.0	2.7	3.4	1.8	2.2	3.4	4.8	5.8	5.9	6.6	6.4	6.4	28.7	25.7	11.8	2.8	77.6	39.0	47.4	52.6
08109	MERCHANTVILLE	75.7	71.3	14.6	16.4	3.3	3.8	8.0	10.8	6.0	6.2	7.1	6.8	5.5	26.8	24.7	14.4	2.7	76.5	40.0	47.4	52.7
08110	PENNSAUKEN	43.5	39.4	32.6	33.2	6.7	7.0	22.9	27.5	7.0	7.3	8.9	8.7	7.6	29.0	22.2	8.3	1.1	71.3	33.2	48.4	51.6
08201	ABSECON	73.7	70.7	14.4	15.3	7.1	8.4	5.9	6.9	6.4	6.7	7.2	6.1	5.2	27.7	25.9	13.0	1.9	75.8	39.6	47.9	52.1
08202	AVALON	98.2	97.9	0.6	0.7	0.6	0.7	0.6	0.7	2.8	3.2	4.3	3.5	2.5	15.3	34.7	30.4	3.4	87.4	57.7	49.3	50.7
08203	BRIGANTINE	83.2	80.1	3.9	4.5	5.8	6.8	9.4	11.6	5.5	5.6	6.4	5.4	5.0	26.9	27.2	16.5	1.6	79.3	42.3	48.8	51.2
08204	CAPE MAY	94.5	93.6	3.0	3.4	0.6	0.7	2.1	2.6	4.4	4.8	6.3	6.5	6.0	20.9	27.3	20.5	3.4	80.8	45.8	47.7	52.3
08205	ABSECON	75.5	71.2	10.2	11.6	9.0	10.9	6.4	7.9	6.4	6.4	7.8	9.4	11.1	27.5	23.0	7.6	0.7	75.1	32.8	47.8	52.2
	NEW JERSEY	72.6	70.5	13.6	13.8	5.8	6.6	13.3	15.0	6.6	6.7	7.1	6.5	6.3	28.8	24.6	11.5	1.9	75.6	37.7	48.6	51.4
	UNITED STATES	75.1	73.6	12.3	12.5	3.8	4.2	12.5	14.1	6.9	6.7	7.2	7.0	7.3	28.6	23.8	10.8	1.7	75.1	36.0	49.1	50.9

#	POST OFFICE NAME	2004 Per Capita Income	2004 HH Income Base	2004 HOUSEHOLD INCOME DISTRIBUTION (%) Less than $25,000	$25,000 to $49,999	$50,000 to $99,999	$100,000 to $149,999	$150,000 or More	MEDIAN HOUSEHOLD INCOME 2004	2009	2004 National Centile	2004 State Centile	2004 Home Value Base	2004 HOME VALUE DISTRIBUTION (%) Less than $50,000	$50,000 to $89,999	$90,000 to $174,999	$175,000 to $399,999	$400,000 or More	2004 Median Home Value
07950	MORRIS PLAINS	48313	6776	5.8	11.2	30.6	26.6	25.9	103496	120930	98	89	5419	0.4	2.0	5.5	41.7	50.4	401926
07960	MORRISTOWN	55364	16637	11.1	15.4	26.8	19.8	26.9	92093	110850	97	81	11120	0.3	0.8	4.0	34.6	60.4	468147
07974	NEW PROVIDENCE	52326	4399	6.6	13.9	27.9	21.9	29.6	102838	125199	98	88	3509	0.5	0.3	0.5	28.8	70.0	477539
07976	NEW VERNON	92496	204	5.4	9.8	27.0	16.2	41.7	121707	149086	99	97	189	0.0	0.0	0.0	2.1	97.9	1000001
07980	STIRLING	39356	957	7.2	24.6	28.8	18.8	20.6	78435	93263	95	68	709	0.6	1.1	0.6	53.5	44.3	378796
07981	WHIPPANY	45620	3239	7.1	16.0	32.2	21.5	23.2	89555	106997	97	79	3007	0.4	0.7	4.5	41.0	53.3	414608
08002	CHERRY HILL	29036	8259	20.6	23.5	34.1	15.2	6.7	56235	62342	81	31	6097	2.3	3.0	32.6	61.3	0.9	189379
08003	CHERRY HILL	43931	11121	9.9	13.1	29.5	22.4	25.2	94959	108404	98	84	9975	0.5	0.7	11.4	74.1	13.3	259920
08004	ATCO	25734	4500	15.7	22.3	40.0	16.7	5.3	62332	69282	87	42	3794	0.8	2.8	57.3	37.4	1.7	163079
08005	BARNEGAT	22458	7025	18.0	27.3	38.7	12.5	3.5	53594	60582	78	26	6199	5.5	3.8	32.6	54.6	3.4	188897
08007	BARRINGTON	24766	2315	22.5	31.1	31.7	12.6	2.2	46424	51933	65	16	1499	1.1	0.1	77.7	20.3	0.8	148542
08008	BEACH HAVEN	36506	4366	21.1	27.2	30.5	12.0	9.2	51799	59162	75	23	3618	0.1	0.2	1.1	37.4	61.1	475468
08009	BERLIN	26394	4737	16.3	23.2	40.3	14.9	5.3	60766	67895	85	39	3742	1.0	2.6	45.5	49.0	1.9	176271
08010	BEVERLY	24252	4346	18.8	28.8	37.2	12.2	2.9	52115	58844	76	23	2830	0.3	11.6	50.8	35.9	1.5	157887
08012	BLACKWOOD	26330	15907	15.4	25.9	39.2	14.4	5.2	58589	64281	83	35	11071	0.5	3.0	51.7	44.1	0.8	168580
08014	BRIDGEPORT	39142	268	26.1	35.1	20.5	6.7	11.6	39158	43897	43	8	197	4.1	7.1	62.4	25.9	0.5	146875
08015	BROWNS MILLS	21769	7642	17.0	28.3	40.3	12.0	2.4	53854	60789	78	26	6030	6.3	6.6	68.7	18.0	0.4	139157
08016	BURLINGTON	26814	12329	17.3	23.0	37.2	16.2	6.4	61228	67987	86	41	8925	1.2	5.0	34.7	56.8	2.2	192453
08019	CHATSWORTH	26898	189	11.6	22.2	40.2	20.1	5.8	66795	76584	90	51	162	2.5	3.1	34.6	51.9	8.0	197222
08020	CLARKSBORO	26676	912	14.4	24.7	36.0	17.4	7.6	63075	68551	87	44	806	0.0	1.0	25.6	72.1	1.4	208626
08021	CLEMENTON	22276	19085	23.7	32.2	32.5	8.8	2.8	44830	50227	61	13	10568	2.0	11.7	65.9	20.1	0.3	131823
08022	COLUMBUS	31506	3287	14.1	25.1	35.2	14.7	10.9	61188	68113	86	40	3085	0.3	0.8	15.8	67.5	15.6	235773
08026	GIBBSBORO	29332	829	13.5	23.2	40.8	13.0	9.5	63764	72488	88	45	755	1.3	2.4	54.7	34.4	7.2	164487
08027	GIBBSTOWN	27860	1897	14.4	27.8	37.6	16.0	4.1	57660	63888	82	34	1587	0.5	0.6	57.8	40.8	0.3	164503
08028	GLASSBORO	21146	6684	24.2	27.5	33.6	11.1	3.5	48361	53359	69	19	3975	0.5	2.4	55.3	40.6	1.2	163638
08029	GLENDORA	23974	1922	28.6	25.2	32.1	9.5	4.7	46739	52393	66	16	1494	0.4	3.0	76.6	19.6	0.4	146795
08030	GLOUCESTER CITY	19264	5233	28.6	30.7	30.9	8.3	1.5	41324	46604	51	11	3590	6.4	21.7	65.4	6.0	0.5	111412
08031	BELLMAWR	22701	4383	21.1	29.8	37.4	9.6	2.1	49221	55556	71	20	3336	1.7	3.8	80.7	13.9	0.0	137989
08032	GRENLOCH	36062	171	5.3	11.1	35.7	27.5	20.5	95863	103885	98	84	167	1.2	0.0	13.2	74.9	10.8	275625
08033	HADDONFIELD	44831	7275	14.8	20.1	28.1	18.3	18.7	75396	83121	93	64	5390	0.4	0.3	17.1	57.3	24.9	265894
08034	CHERRY HILL	37150	7340	12.9	19.3	37.6	17.7	12.4	72125	80038	92	58	5976	0.5	1.4	28.2	67.7	2.2	199366
08035	HADDON HEIGHTS	31758	2971	18.0	22.7	35.2	15.5	8.6	62064	67742	86	42	2282	0.0	0.2	32.3	65.6	1.9	198415
08036	HAINESPORT	32283	1908	11.5	18.9	38.1	19.8	11.7	75708	82550	93	65	1677	1.9	2.5	30.5	49.9	15.3	211889
08037	HAMMONTON	22790	8371	20.6	28.7	35.4	11.4	3.9	50715	56384	73	22	6545	0.5	3.0	43.0	48.8	4.8	181124
08041	JOBSTOWN	39687	187	10.2	15.0	40.6	19.8	14.4	78321	89921	95	68	166	0.0	0.0	9.6	78.3	12.1	258929
08043	VOORHEES	39460	10678	13.8	17.9	32.1	17.8	18.4	76980	87082	94	66	7368	0.6	3.4	21.3	55.8	18.9	248979
08045	LAWNSIDE	21539	986	32.0	19.9	31.1	13.3	3.8	47455	51344	67	17	675	0.9	7.7	63.0	25.8	2.7	144493
08046	WILLINGBORO	24977	10844	9.8	21.9	45.7	17.0	5.7	66639	75338	90	51	9855	0.3	1.3	76.5	21.6	0.3	142865
08048	LUMBERTON	42336	377	24.4	17.0	32.9	17.8	8.0	64286	70452	88	46	241	2.1	0.4	15.8	71.0	10.8	244149
08049	MAGNOLIA	23382	2131	21.5	26.9	37.5	10.9	3.2	51279	58621	74	22	1647	0.7	0.7	84.1	14.4	0.1	138583
08050	MANAHAWKIN	28983	8979	15.3	24.7	39.5	15.2	5.3	59296	66467	84	37	8116	0.3	1.1	22.1	70.1	6.4	227080
08051	MANTUA	27962	4452	15.4	26.8	41.1	12.4	4.4	56703	62581	81	32	3641	2.2	7.5	57.3	31.4	1.6	148018
08052	MAPLE SHADE	27091	8567	18.3	32.5	36.1	9.9	3.2	49344	54630	71	20	4323	0.3	5.9	66.8	26.7	0.3	149076
08053	MARLTON	33171	17091	9.1	20.5	38.7	21.3	10.4	74924	82882	93	63	12992	0.3	1.3	23.8	68.6	6.0	219253
08054	MOUNT LAUREL	36821	18051	11.1	21.8	37.0	19.3	10.8	69833	77070	91	56	14701	0.3	1.5	31.9	57.7	8.5	210318
08055	MEDFORD	43368	10131	7.6	12.8	35.1	22.9	21.5	89870	102425	97	80	8589	0.0	1.2	7.4	68.2	23.2	288457
08056	MICKLETON	30233	1034	12.8	21.9	31.9	21.7	11.8	73206	77170	93	61	941	0.0	0.6	20.3	71.9	7.1	228775
08057	MOORESTOWN	49559	7439	11.0	16.1	29.2	16.8	26.9	86694	97605	97	77	6001	0.3	0.7	13.3	41.5	44.3	354600
08059	MOUNT EPHRAIM	23820	2136	23.6	27.3	33.8	13.0	2.4	49251	55301	71	20	1767	1.7	1.7	83.9	12.7	0.0	137360
08060	MOUNT HOLLY	26451	12587	15.2	24.7	38.9	15.4	5.7	61404	67317	86	41	8752	1.6	4.3	43.2	47.5	3.4	176679
08061	MOUNT ROYAL	27317	229	13.1	28.4	37.1	16.2	5.2	61112	66926	85	40	203	0.0	0.0	30.1	69.0	1.0	208224
08062	MULLICA HILL	31623	4139	11.7	19.1	32.2	25.4	11.6	79714	87550	95	69	3597	1.9	0.6	19.1	65.5	12.9	250042
08063	NATIONAL PARK	20875	1132	18.8	27.0	43.0	8.9	2.2	52959	59902	77	25	903	1.6	4.2	80.5	13.7	0.0	136044
08065	PALMYRA	26353	3177	15.5	30.2	39.4	12.8	2.2	54392	60350	79	27	2151	0.0	2.2	62.2	35.6	0.0	159463
08066	PAULSBORO	21261	3527	28.5	33.6	28.9	7.0	2.0	40894	45289	49	10	1833	3.6	17.1	65.1	13.4	0.8	116071
08067	PEDRICKTOWN	27772	654	18.0	19.0	43.0	14.7	5.4	63004	69336	87	44	571	0.4	6.3	51.5	39.8	2.1	157115
08068	PEMBERTON	25857	2632	19.2	28.3	35.9	11.9	4.8	52710	58523	76	25	1494	1.0	2.8	54.5	38.4	3.4	164701
08069	PENNS GROVE	19690	5051	33.2	27.9	28.8	8.4	1.7	38343	41113	41	8	3107	5.3	13.7	64.0	16.7	0.3	122224
08070	PENNSVILLE	24969	5280	18.9	27.9	38.8	11.8	2.6	52835	58452	77	25	4121	4.0	2.9	62.4	30.1	0.7	146671
08071	PITMAN	25684	3627	15.7	29.6	34.7	14.8	5.2	54291	60335	79	26	2696	0.0	1.5	50.3	46.7	1.6	172917
08075	RIVERSIDE	26033	10309	15.9	26.2	38.8	14.1	5.0	58945	64882	84	36	7165	0.3	2.1	37.2	59.0	1.4	189200
08077	RIVERTON	32210	6278	9.8	21.6	38.1	19.7	11.0	74457	81457	93	62	5759	0.2	0.5	19.0	75.9	4.6	224002
08078	RUNNEMEDE	22047	3241	22.6	33.3	31.9	9.4	2.9	45149	51126	62	14	2256	0.4	3.5	83.5	12.7	0.0	140622
08079	SALEM	20760	5079	31.1	29.5	29.2	7.6	2.7	40146	43094	47	9	3244	6.0	14.5	47.9	28.7	2.9	137632
08080	SEWELL	29482	13097	9.3	18.5	41.4	20.2	10.7	74244	80062	93	61	11691	0.8	1.4	31.2	62.7	3.9	204413
08081	SICKLERVILLE	24898	15169	12.0	21.4	42.9	17.7	6.0	66816	75783	90	51	13117	1.1	7.3	47.2	43.4	1.1	166479
08083	SOMERDALE	27632	3562	17.7	25.7	35.8	14.0	6.9	57971	64430	83	34	2701	1.4	2.3	59.9	36.0	0.4	155599
08084	STRATFORD	25401	2766	16.3	25.4	41.5	11.5	5.2	56694	63747	81	32	2090	0.0	1.5	64.6	33.6	0.3	160245
08085	SWEDESBORO	29157	4342	10.7	17.9	39.3	23.0	9.1	75587	83781	93	64	3775	0.3	1.6	41.3	49.9	6.9	188731
08086	THOROFARE	26307	2378	15.4	30.5	38.0	13.2	3.0	53377	59311	77	25	1578	5.8	4.9	53.2	35.4	0.7	154779
08087	TUCKERTON	23263	9399	20.5	29.8	36.3	10.9	2.6	49772	55424	71	21	7321	1.7	3.0	51.2	41.2	2.9	167475
08088	VINCENTOWN	32374	9742	16.4	21.6	33.5	17.6	10.9	65647	73892	89	48	9032	5.1	4.5	27.8	52.4	10.2	210283
08089	WATERFORD WORKS	24288	1452	18.4	24.0	36.6	15.6	5.4	58616	64854	83	35	1277	6.7	3.5	50.2	38.7	0.9	158799
08090	WENONAH	27973	2936	14.0	23.1	41.7	15.5	5.7	62597	70286	87	42	2606	0.2	0.9	58.1	38.3	2.5	162830
08091	WEST BERLIN	25985	1859	17.4	25.0	37.2	15.2	5.3	60861	67014	85	39	1471	0.8	1.6	67.1	30.5	0.0	153619
08092	WEST CREEK	26444	1226	27.5	28.5	26.4	12.4	5.2	43549	48522	57	12	1000	5.9	3.7	28.2	51.5	10.7	210303
08093	WESTVILLE	21629	4215	24.6	30.2	35.0	8.9	1.3	44966	49782	61	13	2499	1.5	3.6	76.8	17.7	0.5	138005
08094	WILLIAMSTOWN	23198	12627	19.5	25.5	38.2	13.4	3.5	54586	60544	79	27	10456	7.1	2.9	52.6	36.1	1.3	157798
08096	WOODBURY	25161	13313	21.7	24.4	36.3	13.5	4.2	53729	59942	78	26	9771	0.3	3.7	55.5	38.9	1.8	158439
08097	WOODBURY HEIGHTS	26947	1084	16.9	22.1	35.6	18.8	6.6	64832	70858	88	47	986	0.0	1.1	44.3	52.7	1.8	179555
08098	WOODSTOWN	27826	3156	15.0	28.2	34.3	15.8	6.8	60433	63267	85	38	2422	0.9	3.3	33.8	53.2	8.8	201373
08102	CAMDEN	10232	2545	61.2	23.4	13.4	1.5	0.5	17082	19204	1	1	849	58.5	33.7	7.2	0.0	0.6	44106
08103	CAMDEN	11947	4495	49.6	30.7	16.4	2.1	1.2	25201	27565	5	1	2253	46.6	40.6	11.4	1.5	0.0	51997
08104	CAMDEN	11924	7983	48.9	30.0	18.0	2.2	0.9	25651	27962	5	2	3803	36.5	51.4	10.0	1.7	0.4	57634
08105	CAMDEN	10511	8388	45.6	32.3	18.7	2.5	0.8	28099	30590	9	2	3483	28.0	54.3	15.5	2.1	0.2	60687
08106	AUDUBON	27878	4163	20.6	26.8	38.4	10.0	4.1	52005	58743	75	23	2826	2.0	3.7	70.0	23.6	0.7	149187
08107	OAKLYN	23412	5531	26.5	30.3	31.7	8.1	3.4	43037	47520	56	12	3044	1.9	14.1	67.3	16.3	0.5	135370
08108	COLLINGSWOOD	29334	7235	16.5	27.7	37.1	12.5	6.3	55435	62083	80	29	4932	0.2	3.0	57.7	38.7	0.4	160419
08109	MERCHANTVILLE	25025	8487	21.2	25.8	36.1	12.4	4.5	52988	59706	77	25	6177	1.4	4.1	65.2	28.6	0.7	152132
08110	PENNSAUKEN	18136	5991	21.4	30.4	36.4	9.4	2.5	48247	53749	69	18	4526	1.6	11.8	79.9	6.4	0.3	123026
08201	ABSECON	25646	3511	13.2	31.9	36.5	12.2	6.3	54379	59909	79	27	2641	0.6	2.5	35.8	57.4	3.8	190212
08202	AVALON	60303	1134	13.8	23.5	30.6	9.8	22.3	66518	78367	89	50	983	0.0	0.2	1.6	18.6	79.6	641284
08203	BRIGANTINE	27027	5470	24.2	27.8	32.5	10.6	4.9	48310	53223	69	18	3446	0.6	2.4	23.8	63.6	9.7	224098
08204	CAPE MAY	28129	8420	23.8	32.4	29.2	9.5	5.2	45214	50990	62	14	6439	0.7	2.8	38.2	43.4	14.9	195358
08205	ABSECON	24452	9732	15.3	27.7	38.9	13.5	4.6	55321	60553	80	29	6885	1.0	7.5	32.3	54.8	4.5	194514
	NEW JERSEY	31614		18.6	22.5	32.1	15.5	11.4	61437	70239				1.5	2.7	19.7	54.4	21.8	255213
	UNITED STATES	25866		24.7	27.1	30.8	10.9	6.5	48124	56710				10.9	15.0	33.7	30.1	10.4	145905

ZIP CODE #	POST OFFICE NAME	FINANCIAL SERVICES: Auto Loan	FINANCIAL SERVICES: Home Loan	FINANCIAL SERVICES: Invest-ments	FINANCIAL SERVICES: Retire-ment Plans	THE HOME: Home Improvements: Home Repair	THE HOME: Home Improvements: Lawn & Garden	THE HOME: Furnishings: Comput-ers & Hard-ware	THE HOME: Furnishings: Major Appli-ances	THE HOME: Furnishings: TV, Radio, Sound Equip-ment	THE HOME: Furnishings: Furni-ture	ENTERTAINMENT: Dine out/ Carry out	ENTERTAINMENT: Sports Equip-ment	ENTERTAINMENT: Fees & Tickets	ENTERTAINMENT: Toys & Games	ENTERTAINMENT: Travel	ENTERTAINMENT: Cable TV	PERSONAL: Apparel & Services	PERSONAL: Auto Repairs	PERSONAL: Health Insur-ance	PERSONAL: Pets & Supplies
07950	MORRIS PLAINS	151	198	280	194	190	201	183	177	176	185	222	204	201	242	191	177	224	175	160	190
07960	MORRISTOWN	177	212	305	214	205	221	205	197	200	208	254	228	221	267	212	201	255	197	184	215
07974	NEW PROVIDENCE	164	233	304	222	224	233	202	199	189	204	237	227	225	263	214	190	242	192	178	212
07976	NEW VERNON	301	406	556	398	395	427	353	350	329	362	416	394	401	438	377	332	423	336	325	380
07980	STIRLING	135	171	215	170	167	171	159	155	150	159	188	181	170	200	163	147	189	153	139	167
07981	WHIPPANY	137	202	265	187	194	202	173	172	163	174	203	194	193	228	185	165	208	165	154	181
08002	CHERRY HILL	90	105	126	103	103	110	101	100	99	101	124	114	106	128	104	99	123	99	95	108
08003	CHERRY HILL	154	192	229	191	188	195	176	173	166	176	209	199	190	219	181	164	209	169	159	188
08004	ATCO	97	111	117	112	108	109	104	104	98	105	124	122	107	127	104	94	122	102	94	114
08005	BARNEGAT	85	94	98	92	93	99	88	90	86	90	108	100	91	106	90	86	105	88	88	98
08007	BARRINGTON	75	82	96	81	81	88	82	80	82	81	102	92	85	105	84	82	100	81	80	88
08008	BEACH HAVEN	127	100	69	91	113	127	94	114	107	94	127	132	85	124	101	114	118	112	134	155
08009	BERLIN	94	110	117	109	108	110	103	102	99	102	124	118	108	130	104	97	122	100	95	112
08010	BEVERLY	79	88	101	88	87	91	88	86	86	87	108	100	91	112	89	85	107	86	82	94
08012	BLACKWOOD	92	102	115	104	100	103	100	98	96	100	121	115	103	123	100	93	119	98	90	107
08014	BRIDGEPORT	130	142	149	134	143	159	140	138	145	135	180	154	148	195	145	150	174	136	149	153
08015	BROWNS MILLS	82	92	98	91	90	93	87	87	84	87	106	101	90	108	88	82	104	86	82	96
08016	BURLINGTON	96	106	114	106	104	108	102	101	99	103	125	116	106	128	102	97	123	100	96	111
08019	CHATSWORTH	114	133	135	132	132	132	119	121	113	119	141	142	125	149	122	111	140	117	112	138
08020	CLARKSBORO	95	112	122	108	111	117	104	104	102	103	127	118	111	133	108	103	125	102	102	114
08021	CLEMENTON	75	77	87	80	75	79	80	77	78	80	98	92	80	97	78	74	96	79	71	85
08022	COLUMBUS	109	123	131	119	123	132	111	117	109	114	137	126	117	134	117	111	133	113	118	128
08026	GIBBSBORO	107	128	142	124	126	132	120	119	116	119	146	136	127	154	124	116	144	116	115	130
08027	GIBBSTOWN	94	105	111	102	105	113	100	101	100	99	124	115	105	129	103	101	121	99	102	112
08028	GLASSBORO	80	81	89	82	79	83	85	81	83	84	105	96	85	104	83	80	102	83	77	90
08029	GLENDORA	83	81	78	78	84	95	82	85	86	79	105	95	82	107	84	89	100	83	93	96
08030	GLOUCESTER CITY	68	70	73	68	71	78	71	71	73	69	90	81	73	95	72	74	87	71	74	80
08031	BELLMAWR	72	82	92	78	81	89	79	78	80	78	99	88	84	104	82	81	97	77	80	86
08032	GRENLOCH	156	180	178	187	172	168	162	159	148	167	188	186	169	190	159	139	187	155	137	175
08033	HADDONFIELD	134	161	196	161	159	167	152	149	145	152	182	171	162	188	156	144	181	147	141	163
08034	CHERRY HILL	115	140	172	137	136	144	132	129	127	132	159	149	140	166	136	126	159	128	121	140
08035	HADDON HEIGHTS	99	113	132	111	112	120	110	108	108	109	136	124	115	140	113	109	133	108	107	118
08036	HAINESPORT	118	143	155	142	141	144	131	130	124	130	155	150	139	164	134	122	154	126	121	143
08037	HAMMONTON	84	92	95	89	92	98	88	89	88	87	109	102	91	114	90	89	107	88	90	100
08041	JOBSTOWN	147	183	195	184	180	178	163	162	151	163	190	190	174	202	167	146	190	156	145	179
08043	VOORHEES	141	153	175	160	149	155	151	146	143	151	181	171	156	181	149	138	179	147	134	161
08045	LAWNSIDE	78	77	85	73	75	87	77	77	81	79	101	82	81	97	79	84	99	77	83	88
08046	WILLINGBORO	97	116	128	113	114	118	108	107	104	108	131	122	115	137	111	103	130	105	102	117
08048	LUMBERTON	107	97	96	98	99	111	102	104	106	100	131	119	100	129	101	107	124	105	109	119
08049	MAGNOLIA	77	85	95	85	85	88	86	84	84	84	105	98	88	110	86	82	103	84	80	91
08050	MANAHAWKIN	108	114	110	111	116	120	105	111	104	106	129	127	106	131	108	104	126	108	110	129
08051	MANTUA	91	99	107	101	98	100	95	95	91	95	115	112	97	117	95	89	112	94	88	107
08052	MAPLE SHADE	82	81	95	84	80	86	86	83	85	86	108	97	87	108	84	83	105	85	79	91
08053	MARLTON	122	135	143	140	130	131	128	126	120	131	153	148	132	154	126	115	151	125	112	138
08054	MOUNT LAUREL	122	133	143	137	130	134	127	126	120	129	152	145	131	151	126	116	150	125	116	138
08055	MEDFORD	156	189	212	192	186	189	173	171	161	174	204	198	185	211	177	157	203	167	155	187
08056	MICKLETON	109	134	144	133	132	133	121	121	114	120	143	140	129	152	124	112	142	117	112	133
08057	MOORESTOWN	170	209	250	207	206	218	191	190	181	192	228	216	206	234	199	181	227	186	180	207
08059	MOUNT EPHRAIM	75	86	94	82	85	92	82	82	81	80	101	92	86	107	85	83	100	80	83	89
08060	MOUNT HOLLY	99	104	111	106	101	105	104	101	100	104	126	119	105	127	102	97	124	102	94	112
08061	MOUNT ROYAL	89	105	115	100	104	111	98	98	97	97	121	110	104	126	102	98	119	96	98	107
08062	MULLICA HILL	129	151	158	155	147	145	138	137	128	140	162	161	144	167	138	123	161	134	121	151
08063	NATIONAL PARK	75	88	96	85	87	91	83	82	82	82	102	94	88	109	85	82	101	80	80	90
08065	PALMYRA	80	91	105	91	89	93	89	87	86	88	108	101	92	111	89	84	107	87	81	95
08066	PAULSBORO	70	65	69	65	65	72	70	68	72	69	90	79	69	90	69	72	87	70	70	77
08067	PEDRICKTOWN	96	116	129	114	114	116	108	107	103	107	129	123	115	138	111	101	129	104	99	116
08068	PEMBERTON	87	95	113	94	94	100	96	94	95	95	120	108	99	123	97	95	118	95	91	103
08069	PENNS GROVE	66	66	71	64	66	74	69	68	71	67	87	77	69	89	69	72	85	68	71	76
08070	PENNSVILLE	80	90	97	87	89	95	86	86	85	85	106	98	90	110	88	86	104	84	86	94
08071	PITMAN	86	101	112	99	100	104	95	94	92	94	115	109	101	120	98	91	114	93	90	103
08075	RIVERSIDE	91	100	110	101	99	103	98	96	95	97	119	112	101	123	98	93	117	96	91	105
08077	RIVERTON	117	136	152	134	135	143	127	128	123	127	154	144	134	157	132	123	152	125	124	140
08078	RUNNEMEDE	72	77	82	75	78	85	77	77	78	75	97	87	79	101	78	79	94	76	79	85
08079	SALEM	70	69	73	66	69	77	71	71	74	70	91	81	71	90	71	75	88	72	75	81
08080	SEWELL	123	141	143	143	136	136	128	128	120	131	151	148	133	153	128	115	150	124	115	141
08081	SICKLERVILLE	107	118	118	121	114	113	110	109	103	113	130	127	112	130	108	97	128	108	97	120
08083	SOMERDALE	92	106	116	104	105	111	101	100	99	100	124	115	107	130	104	99	122	99	98	110
08084	STRATFORD	86	94	109	94	92	98	94	92	92	94	116	106	97	118	94	91	114	92	88	101
08085	SWEDESBORO	122	137	135	140	131	130	127	125	119	129	150	146	130	153	124	113	148	122	111	137
08086	THOROFARE	89	92	98	94	91	94	91	91	89	92	111	107	92	112	90	85	109	91	84	102
08087	TUCKERTON	85	86	84	84	87	93	82	86	83	82	102	99	82	103	84	83	99	85	87	100
08088	VINCENTOWN	116	132	138	130	132	139	120	124	116	122	145	137	126	145	124	116	142	120	122	137
08089	WATERFORD WORKS	92	104	114	102	102	108	98	98	96	99	121	110	104	124	100	97	119	96	95	109
08090	WENONAH	99	120	131	118	118	121	110	110	105	110	132	126	117	140	113	104	131	107	102	120
08091	WEST BERLIN	96	106	110	104	106	111	101	102	99	100	124	117	105	129	103	99	121	100	99	114
08092	WEST CREEK	112	96	76	90	104	115	92	105	100	91	120	122	87	121	96	104	113	103	118	134
08093	WESTVILLE	72	74	82	74	73	78	77	75	76	76	96	87	77	97	76	75	93	76	73	82
08094	WILLIAMSTOWN	88	95	96	94	94	99	90	91	87	90	109	104	92	110	91	86	107	90	89	101
08096	WOODBURY	85	94	104	94	93	97	92	91	90	92	112	105	95	115	93	88	111	91	87	99
08097	WOODBURY HEIGHTS	98	118	131	115	116	119	110	109	105	109	132	125	117	140	113	104	132	106	102	118
08098	WOODSTOWN	97	114	130	114	113	116	108	107	104	107	131	124	114	137	111	103	130	105	100	117
08102	CAMDEN	32	29	49	27	27	33	34	32	38	35	49	37	34	49	34	40	48	35	34	36
08103	CAMDEN	45	41	55	38	40	47	45	44	50	47	63	49	46	61	45	52	61	46	48	50
08104	CAMDEN	48	42	52	40	41	48	48	47	52	49	65	53	48	63	47	54	63	49	50	53
08105	CAMDEN	43	40	70	36	37	44	46	44	53	49	67	49	46	68	46	56	67	47	46	49
08106	AUDUBON	87	99	114	98	98	104	97	95	95	95	119	110	101	124	99	94	117	95	92	104
08107	OAKLYN	72	78	93	77	76	82	79	77	79	78	99	89	82	102	80	79	98	78	76	84
08108	COLLINGSWOOD	90	102	123	104	101	105	101	99	98	100	123	116	105	126	102	96	121	99	93	108
08109	MERCHANTVILLE	86	95	105	93	94	100	93	92	92	91	115	106	96	119	95	92	112	91	91	101
08110	PENNSAUKEN	72	80	94	78	78	83	79	78	79	79	100	89	82	104	80	79	98	78	75	85
08201	ABSECON	91	102	114	100	100	105	98	97	96	98	121	111	102	124	99	95	119	96	93	107
08202	AVALON	207	162	111	146	183	205	153	184	173	152	205	216	137	202	163	185	191	181	218	252
08203	BRIGANTINE	88	87	90	83	89	96	84	88	87	84	107	102	84	109	87	89	104	88	91	105
08204	CAPE MAY	98	91	84	87	96	106	89	96	93	88	114	110	87	113	92	96	109	95	104	115
08205	ABSECON	93	98	109	102	95	97	98	95	94	99	119	114	99	119	96	90	117	97	86	105
	NEW JERSEY	110	123	153	121	120	128	120	118	119	121	150	136	125	155	123	120	149	119	114	130
	UNITED STATES	100	100	100	100	100	100	100	100	100	100	100	100	100	100	100	100	100	100	100	100

NEW JERSEY

A 08210-08701

POPULATION CHANGE

# POST OFFICE NAME	COUNTY FIPS CODE	POPULATION 2000	POPULATION 2004	POPULATION 2009	2000-2004 ANNUAL RATE % Rate	2000-2004 State Centile	HOUSEHOLDS 2000	HOUSEHOLDS 2004	HOUSEHOLDS 2009	% Annual Rate 2000-2004	2004 Average HH Size	FAMILIES 2000	FAMILIES 2004	% Annual Rate 2000-2004
08210 CAPE MAY COURT HOUSE	009	15574	17106	18652	2.2	90	5459	6091	6733	2.6	2.65	4006	4483	2.7
08215 EGG HARBOR CITY	001	11626	12453	13332	1.6	81	4288	4602	4932	1.7	2.67	3075	3315	1.8
08221 LINWOOD	001	7090	7450	7869	1.2	71	2622	2786	2960	1.4	2.62	1938	2059	1.4
08223 MARMORA	009	3985	4153	4410	1.0	65	1477	1550	1660	1.1	2.67	1137	1196	1.2
08225 NORTHFIELD	001	7909	8248	8675	1.0	66	2904	3047	3214	1.1	2.64	2163	2278	1.2
08226 OCEAN CITY	009	15378	15724	16512	0.5	48	7464	7731	8209	0.8	2.00	4007	4173	1.0
08230 OCEAN VIEW	009	6138	6671	7276	2.0	87	2072	2276	2506	2.2	2.91	1635	1800	2.3
08232 PLEASANTVILLE	001	18172	18700	19555	0.7	55	6076	6226	6498	0.6	2.93	4147	4264	0.7
08234 EGG HARBOR TOWNSHIP	001	29911	33174	36107	2.5	92	10862	12045	13094	2.5	2.75	7886	8759	2.5
08241 PORT REPUBLIC	001	1065	1177	1284	2.4	92	379	419	454	2.4	2.80	242	270	2.6
08242 RIO GRANDE	009	2772	3006	3261	1.9	86	1141	1256	1379	2.3	2.38	734	811	2.4
08243 SEA ISLE CITY	009	2680	2849	3055	1.5	77	1306	1405	1523	1.7	2.03	759	820	1.8
08244 SOMERS POINT	001	11647	11880	12413	0.5	45	4940	5057	5289	0.6	2.31	2967	3050	0.7
08247 STONE HARBOR	009	1204	1231	1292	0.5	48	632	653	693	0.8	1.85	356	370	0.9
08248 STRATHMERE	009	175	181	191	0.8	58	93	97	103	1.0	1.87	55	58	1.3
08251 VILLAS	009	9754	10258	10947	1.2	72	4023	4244	4552	1.3	2.41	2691	2854	1.4
08260 WILDWOOD	009	15326	15615	16375	0.4	43	6936	7147	7572	0.7	2.17	4058	4203	0.8
08270 WOODBINE	009	8338	8619	9104	0.8	58	2643	2762	2953	1.1	2.89	2049	2148	1.1
08302 BRIDGETON	011	45935	46163	46691	0.1	28	14120	14138	14374	0.0	2.82	10237	10303	0.2
08310 BUENA	001	1571	1659	1765	1.3	75	678	711	755	1.1	2.30	478	505	1.3
08311 CEDARVILLE	011	1680	1756	1806	1.1	68	559	587	607	1.2	2.91	426	449	1.2
08312 CLAYTON	015	6655	6751	7048	0.3	38	2296	2354	2482	0.6	2.86	1754	1804	0.7
08314 DELMONT	011	247	247	249	0.0	22	92	99	105	1.7	1.62	69	63	-2.1
08317 DOROTHY	001	1188	1451	1656	4.8	99	380	467	535	5.0	3.08	300	368	4.9
08318 ELMER	033	12216	13166	13894	1.8	84	4230	4601	4898	2.0	2.82	3349	3655	2.1
08319 ESTELL MANOR	001	1193	1457	1663	4.8	99	412	507	580	5.0	2.85	325	398	4.9
08322 FRANKLINVILLE	015	9773	10518	11271	1.7	83	3277	3566	3861	2.0	2.95	2656	2897	2.1
08323 GREENWICH	011	332	354	368	1.5	78	115	123	129	1.6	2.88	87	94	1.8
08324 HEISLERVILLE	011	182	181	182	-0.1	16	60	60	61	0.0	3.02	46	46	0.0
08326 LANDISVILLE	001	1660	1677	1754	0.2	33	594	602	631	0.3	2.75	429	437	0.4
08327 LEESBURG	011	396	393	396	-0.2	13	144	144	146	0.0	2.73	110	111	0.2
08328 MALAGA	015	1514	1500	1551	-0.2	11	522	522	546	0.0	2.86	402	403	0.1
08330 MAYS LANDING	001	21854	23420	25041	1.6	81	7695	8303	8911	1.8	2.70	5440	5886	1.9
08332 MILLVILLE	011	39493	39608	40161	0.1	25	13389	13491	13771	0.2	2.66	9508	9646	0.3
08340 MILMAY	011	812	844	882	0.9	62	294	308	323	1.1	2.70	221	232	1.2
08341 MINOTOLA	001	1504	1543	1618	0.6	50	604	626	659	0.9	2.46	374	389	1.0
08343 MONROEVILLE	033	4589	4681	4907	0.5	45	1630	1676	1776	0.7	2.75	1252	1294	0.8
08344 NEWFIELD	015	6160	6221	6445	0.2	33	2003	2047	2150	0.5	2.81	1575	1616	0.6
08345 NEWPORT	011	1161	1158	1169	-0.1	18	501	505	514	0.2	2.29	336	339	0.2
08346 NEWTONVILLE	001	653	717	776	2.2	90	180	199	215	2.4	3.58	136	151	2.5
08349 PORT NORRIS	011	2474	2505	2551	0.3	36	856	873	894	0.5	2.86	629	644	0.6
08350 RICHLAND	001	772	825	878	1.6	80	269	288	308	1.6	2.81	202	217	1.7
08353 SHILOH	011	367	349	348	-1.2	0	131	125	126	-1.1	2.79	106	102	-0.9
08360 VINELAND	011	39726	41444	43103	1.0	66	14298	15065	15788	1.2	2.70	9994	10583	1.4
08361 VINELAND	011	16516	16972	17409	0.6	52	5764	6001	6217	1.0	2.62	4267	4457	1.0
08401 ATLANTIC CITY	001	40517	41694	43919	0.7	55	15848	16263	17111	0.6	2.47	8708	8967	0.7
08402 MARGATE CITY	001	8199	8086	8348	-0.3	7	3987	3954	4096	-0.2	2.04	2305	2298	-0.1
08403 LONGPORT	001	1150	1134	1174	-0.3	7	584	579	601	-0.2	1.96	347	347	0.0
08406 VENTNOR CITY	001	12910	13129	13663	0.4	41	5480	5571	5794	0.4	2.36	3256	3326	0.5
08501 ALLENTOWN	025	4765	5702	6421	4.3	98	1669	1987	2233	4.2	2.87	1334	1602	4.4
08502 BELLE MEAD	035	9275	11095	12719	4.3	98	2860	3446	3971	4.5	3.21	2467	2979	4.5
08505 BORDENTOWN	005	14566	15911	17186	2.1	89	5873	6432	6987	2.2	2.46	4045	4480	2.4
08510 CLARKSBURG	025	1939	2164	2339	2.6	93	620	691	741	2.6	3.13	549	612	2.6
08511 COOKSTOWN	005	1254	1257	1277	0.1	25	216	218	226	0.2	2.93	175	177	0.3
08512 CRANBURY	023	6556	7414	8042	2.9	95	2300	2565	2762	2.6	2.87	1750	1963	2.7
08514 CREAM RIDGE	025	2997	3726	4309	5.3	99	1060	1322	1531	5.3	2.81	879	1095	5.3
08515 CROSSWICKS	005	366	399	429	2.1	87	131	140	150	1.6	2.85	109	117	1.7
08518 FLORENCE	005	4777	4872	5067	0.5	44	1907	1960	2056	0.7	2.46	1253	1294	0.8
08520 HIGHTSTOWN	021	29476	31811	33921	1.8	85	11088	11979	12802	1.8	2.63	7701	8356	1.9
08525 HOPEWELL	021	5033	5038	5169	0.0	23	1904	1925	1991	0.3	2.54	1447	1468	0.3
08526 IMLAYSTOWN	025	139	178	206	6.0	99	54	69	81	5.9	2.57	43	56	6.4
08527 JACKSON	029	42755	48473	55114	3.0	95	14154	16030	18231	3.0	3.00	11245	12787	3.1
08530 LAMBERTVILLE	019	7583	7868	8281	0.9	61	2982	3118	3314	1.1	2.39	1787	1899	1.4
08533 NEW EGYPT	029	6421	7349	8374	3.2	96	2180	2488	2829	3.2	2.95	1724	1973	3.2
08534 PENNINGTON	021	11325	12551	13540	2.5	92	4103	4600	4996	2.7	2.67	3275	3683	2.8
08535 PERRINEVILLE	025	2026	2254	2433	2.5	93	554	615	661	2.5	3.62	497	552	2.5
08536 PLAINSBORO	023	17730	21253	24314	4.4	98	7686	9193	9924	3.5	2.39	4420	5101	3.4
08540 PRINCETON	021	43526	46814	49728	1.7	82	14913	16212	17404	2.0	2.44	10231	11205	2.2
08542 PRINCETON	021	3909	3929	4043	0.1	28	1545	1554	1606	0.1	2.33	765	776	0.3
08544 PRINCETON	021	9	11	13	4.8	99	7	8	9	3.2	1.38	2	3	10.0
08550 PRINCETON JUNCTION	021	17648	19739	21408	2.7	94	5482	6144	6683	2.7	3.21	4828	5432	2.8
08551 RINGOES	019	4670	4941	5263	1.3	75	1564	1657	1772	1.4	2.97	1246	1321	1.4
08553 ROCKY HILL	035	662	670	703	0.3	35	284	291	307	0.6	2.30	190	196	0.7
08554 ROEBLING	005	3796	3893	4075	0.6	50	1442	1487	1567	0.7	2.62	1018	1054	0.8
08556 ROSEMONT	019	85	85	88	0.0	22	33	33	35	0.0	2.58	25	25	0.1
08558 SKILLMAN	035	5167	5987	6744	3.5	96	1729	2007	2267	3.6	2.95	1364	1588	3.6
08559 STOCKTON	019	5286	5602	5950	1.4	76	1969	2101	2246	1.5	2.66	1522	1630	1.6
08560 TITUSVILLE	021	3550	3676	3826	0.8	59	1325	1386	1453	1.1	2.60	1026	1076	1.1
08562 WRIGHTSTOWN	005	7173	7621	8165	1.4	77	2530	2727	2966	1.8	2.58	1920	2060	1.7
08608 TRENTON	021	1153	1161	1189	0.2	29	430	435	450	0.3	2.31	263	267	0.4
08609 TRENTON	021	13564	13887	14419	0.6	48	4396	4530	4731	0.7	2.96	2920	3013	0.7
08610 TRENTON	021	29978	29984	30761	0.0	22	12212	12302	12693	0.2	2.43	8053	8142	0.3
08611 TRENTON	021	26828	27047	27748	0.2	31	9116	9150	9402	0.1	2.70	5532	5572	0.2
08618 TRENTON	021	40532	40403	41439	-0.1	18	13390	13458	13942	0.1	2.60	8415	8486	0.2
08619 TRENTON	021	20835	20781	21296	-0.1	18	8246	8293	8557	0.1	2.46	5611	5661	0.2
08620 TRENTON	021	15868	15993	16434	0.2	30	4566	4643	4831	0.4	2.72	3462	3525	0.4
08628 TRENTON	021	8511	9176	9801	1.8	84	3414	3704	3984	1.9	2.33	2190	2398	2.2
08629 TRENTON	021	11293	11386	11704	0.2	31	4051	4088	4211	0.2	2.78	2837	2872	0.3
08638 TRENTON	021	23838	24407	25434	0.6	48	8689	8932	9343	0.7	2.68	5920	6122	0.8
08640 TRENTON	005	6837	7261	7479	1.4	76	842	879	951	1.0	3.09	711	765	1.7
08641 TRENTON	005	5046	4940	5085	-0.5	3	1127	1108	1155	-0.4	3.89	1105	1087	-0.4
08648 TRENTON	021	27494	29031	30499	1.3	75	10216	10950	11633	1.7	2.44	6751	7255	1.7
08690 TRENTON	021	19445	19623	20209	0.2	32	7178	7300	7567	0.4	2.65	5339	5446	0.5
08691 TRENTON	021	12390	13564	14530	2.3	89	4711	5153	5525	2.1	2.62	3412	3741	2.2
08701 LAKEWOOD	029	60296	67203	75783	2.6	93	19862	21830	24480	2.3	2.97	13344	14788	2.5
NEW JERSEY					0.8					0.9	2.68			1.0
UNITED STATES					1.2					1.3	2.58			1.1

#	POST OFFICE NAME	RACE (%) White 2000	White 2004	Black 2000	Black 2004	Asian/Pacific 2000	Asian/Pacific 2004	% Hispanic Origin 2000	% Hispanic Origin 2004	2004 AGE DISTRIBUTION (%) 0-4	5-9	10-14	15-19	20-24	25-44	45-64	65-84	85+	18+	MEDIAN AGE 2004	% 2004 Males	% 2004 Females
08210	CAPE MAY COURT HOUSE	87.1	85.6	9.6	10.5	1.4	1.7	1.6	2.0	6.2	6.7	7.5	6.8	4.9	25.5	25.6	13.9	3.0	75.4	40.7	48.3	51.7
08215	EGG HARBOR CITY	79.7	77.0	9.0	9.8	1.9	2.4	13.0	15.1	6.6	6.9	7.9	7.2	5.7	26.4	25.3	12.2	1.8	74.1	38.6	48.6	51.4
08221	LINWOOD	95.2	94.1	1.1	1.3	2.4	3.0	1.8	2.3	5.0	6.0	8.2	6.9	4.1	19.9	30.5	15.9	3.6	76.0	45.0	46.6	53.4
08223	MARMORA	97.8	97.3	0.7	0.8	0.7	0.9	1.2	1.6	5.6	6.6	8.2	7.1	4.6	24.7	29.1	12.3	1.8	74.4	41.2	48.2	51.8
08225	NORTHFIELD	91.6	89.6	2.6	3.1	2.6	3.2	4.3	5.6	5.4	6.2	7.9	6.6	4.5	24.7	26.7	15.3	2.8	76.0	42.2	47.6	52.4
08226	OCEAN CITY	93.6	92.7	4.3	4.8	0.6	0.8	2.0	2.5	3.4	3.5	4.8	5.1	5.3	21.0	30.6	22.2	4.3	85.1	49.7	46.3	53.7
08230	OCEAN VIEW	97.9	97.5	0.4	0.5	0.8	1.0	1.3	1.6	6.0	7.0	8.8	7.4	4.5	23.7	28.5	12.2	1.9	73.4	41.1	47.4	52.6
08232	PLEASANTVILLE	26.2	23.7	56.4	57.2	2.1	2.3	21.9	24.3	7.8	7.9	9.2	7.6	6.8	27.7	21.4	9.6	2.2	70.4	33.6	46.8	53.3
08234	EGG HARBOR TOWNSHIP	79.7	76.0	10.3	11.7	5.0	6.2	6.7	8.3	7.3	7.7	8.4	6.3	5.4	29.5	26.2	8.3	1.0	72.6	36.7	48.6	51.4
08241	PORT REPUBLIC	90.0	87.8	4.1	4.9	2.7	3.3	2.9	3.8	5.3	5.4	6.1	5.5	4.9	27.1	28.9	15.5	1.4	79.8	42.7	47.1	52.9
08242	RIO GRANDE	89.7	88.0	5.8	6.5	0.9	1.1	2.9	3.8	4.7	4.9	6.8	5.9	6.3	23.8	26.0	18.8	2.8	80.0	43.6	47.4	52.6
08243	SEA ISLE CITY	97.9	97.6	0.3	0.3	0.4	0.5	1.1	1.4	3.3	3.0	4.4	4.4	4.6	18.1	33.9	25.4	3.0	86.2	53.0	48.0	52.0
08244	SOMERS POINT	85.7	82.7	7.0	8.2	3.2	4.0	6.0	7.6	6.0	5.8	6.5	6.6	6.4	28.2	25.6	12.7	2.4	77.6	39.6	47.1	53.0
08247	STONE HARBOR	97.9	97.6	1.5	1.6	0.1	0.1	0.6	0.7	2.4	2.8	3.3	3.4	3.0	13.0	35.6	31.1	5.5	89.2	58.0	46.9	53.1
08248	STRATHMERE	97.7	96.7	0.0	0.0	1.1	1.7	1.7	2.2	1.1	0.0	1.1	2.2	2.2	18.2	33.7	38.1	3.3	96.7	61.3	51.4	48.6
08251	VILLAS	94.9	94.1	2.5	2.8	0.4	0.5	2.5	3.1	6.3	6.4	7.7	6.9	5.8	25.2	23.4	16.2	2.0	75.4	39.7	48.2	51.8
08260	WILDWOOD	86.9	85.5	6.5	6.7	0.6	0.7	8.1	9.9	5.3	5.0	5.7	5.7	5.8	23.2	26.9	19.5	2.9	80.5	44.5	48.0	52.0
08270	WOODBINE	82.2	81.0	11.6	11.9	0.3	0.4	8.4	9.7	7.3	6.7	7.8	7.0	5.9	28.8	26.9	8.6	1.1	73.9	37.1	52.9	47.1
08302	BRIDGETON	55.7	53.2	30.9	31.6	1.1	1.3	14.8	17.0	6.5	6.3	6.9	6.7	7.4	31.7	21.8	11.0	1.7	76.2	35.1	54.2	45.8
08310	BUENA	71.3	67.0	20.9	23.7	0.2	0.2	11.8	14.6	5.6	5.9	7.4	7.1	5.7	24.4	25.5	16.3	2.2	76.6	41.0	48.7	51.3
08311	CEDARVILLE	81.5	78.5	9.8	11.0	0.5	0.6	8.2	10.2	6.0	7.2	8.1	6.6	5.4	29.2	25.9	10.4	1.3	74.4	37.2	50.7	49.3
08312	CLAYTON	80.2	78.2	15.1	16.4	0.7	0.8	3.3	3.9	7.7	7.6	8.1	6.9	6.7	30.6	23.3	8.4	0.9	72.5	33.9	47.8	52.2
08314	DELMONT	69.2	68.4	23.9	24.3	0.0	0.0	6.9	8.5	4.5	4.5	4.9	3.6	4.9	46.6	22.3	8.1	0.8	83.8	36.8	68.0	32.0
08317	DOROTHY	93.9	92.6	4.0	4.8	0.3	0.3	1.6	2.1	6.1	6.8	7.7	7.1	5.1	25.3	26.5	13.8	1.6	74.6	40.6	48.5	51.6
08318	ELMER	90.0	88.6	6.5	7.3	0.6	0.7	3.1	3.9	5.4	5.9	7.3	7.4	6.6	26.0	29.1	10.7	1.6	76.7	39.7	49.5	50.5
08319	ESTELL MANOR	94.0	92.7	3.9	4.8	0.3	0.3	1.6	2.2	6.0	6.9	7.8	7.1	5.1	25.3	26.5	13.8	1.6	74.6	40.6	48.5	51.5
08322	FRANKLINVILLE	90.7	89.6	6.7	7.3	0.4	0.5	2.8	3.4	6.5	6.9	7.7	7.4	6.1	29.0	26.6	8.9	0.9	74.2	37.5	50.2	49.8
08323	GREENWICH	90.7	89.0	4.8	5.4	0.3	0.3	1.5	2.0	5.1	5.9	6.5	5.9	5.1	23.2	33.3	13.0	2.0	79.1	43.6	49.2	50.9
08324	HEISLERVILLE	95.6	95.6	1.1	1.1	0.0	0.0	1.7	1.7	6.1	7.2	7.7	5.5	5.0	27.6	26.5	12.7	1.7	75.7	39.8	50.3	49.7
08326	LANDISVILLE	74.0	70.0	8.1	8.9	0.5	0.6	29.3	35.1	6.8	6.9	7.3	7.5	8.5	29.7	22.4	9.5	1.4	74.4	34.0	50.8	49.3
08327	LEESBURG	95.7	95.2	1.3	1.3	0.0	0.0	1.5	1.8	6.4	6.9	7.9	5.9	4.8	29.0	26.0	12.0	1.3	75.1	39.3	49.9	50.1
08328	MALAGA	87.3	86.3	8.1	8.5	0.5	0.5	4.4	5.2	7.5	6.9	7.1	7.8	8.4	30.9	23.2	7.7	0.6	73.8	33.5	49.5	50.5
08330	MAYS LANDING	72.3	68.7	18.7	20.6	3.2	3.8	7.8	9.5	6.9	6.9	7.6	7.2	7.0	31.8	23.6	7.9	1.0	74.1	35.4	49.5	50.5
08332	MILLVILLE	73.6	70.9	18.1	19.2	0.7	0.8	10.0	12.1	6.3	6.2	7.2	6.9	6.5	32.3	23.3	9.9	1.4	76.0	35.7	52.3	47.7
08340	MILMAY	90.6	88.7	4.4	5.2	0.3	0.2	5.1	6.6	4.4	5.0	6.4	6.5	5.6	26.8	32.1	11.5	1.8	79.9	42.4	48.2	51.8
08341	MINOTOLA	79.3	75.8	7.5	8.4	0.5	0.6	18.7	22.5	6.0	6.1	6.7	7.0	6.6	27.2	22.4	15.6	2.5	76.6	38.7	47.4	52.6
08343	MONROEVILLE	92.5	91.3	4.2	4.6	0.2	0.3	3.1	4.0	5.6	6.3	7.5	6.6	5.8	26.3	28.7	11.5	1.7	76.2	40.5	50.1	49.9
08344	NEWFIELD	82.9	81.3	11.5	12.2	0.4	0.5	9.1	10.9	5.4	5.9	7.1	6.8	5.8	31.3	26.1	10.1	1.5	77.4	38.0	51.7	48.3
08345	NEWPORT	91.0	89.6	4.9	5.5	0.3	0.4	3.5	4.4	5.5	5.9	6.7	6.3	5.5	23.1	27.9	17.8	1.4	78.0	42.9	51.9	48.1
08346	NEWTONVILLE	50.5	45.8	39.5	43.0	0.2	0.3	12.9	15.2	6.0	6.8	9.1	8.5	5.9	25.7	25.4	11.2	1.5	72.5	37.2	49.0	51.1
08349	PORT NORRIS	71.5	68.4	24.1	26.4	0.2	0.3	3.7	4.6	6.0	6.4	7.9	7.4	6.5	25.6	24.9	13.6	1.8	75.0	39.1	48.9	51.1
08350	RICHLAND	80.1	76.9	13.6	15.3	0.3	0.2	8.0	10.1	4.7	5.2	6.7	6.7	5.9	25.6	31.4	11.9	1.9	78.8	42.2	48.4	51.6
08353	SHILOH	92.9	91.4	3.5	4.0	0.3	0.6	2.5	3.4	6.0	6.3	6.3	6.3	5.2	25.5	29.5	12.9	2.0	77.9	41.5	49.3	50.7
08360	VINELAND	62.0	59.6	15.0	15.0	0.9	1.0	37.3	41.2	6.7	6.6	7.6	7.2	7.2	27.6	23.0	11.9	2.1	74.6	36.0	48.5	51.5
08361	VINELAND	84.6	82.0	6.9	7.6	1.9	2.2	11.3	14.3	5.0	5.5	6.6	6.4	5.3	26.3	28.5	14.3	2.2	78.5	41.9	45.8	54.2
08401	ATLANTIC CITY	26.7	24.7	44.2	43.5	10.5	11.3	25.0	27.7	7.4	7.2	7.5	6.5	6.8	29.0	21.5	12.2	2.0	74.0	35.2	49.1	50.9
08402	MARGATE CITY	95.7	94.7	0.9	1.0	1.6	2.1	2.7	3.5	3.5	4.0	5.0	4.1	3.8	20.2	30.2	25.5	3.7	84.8	51.1	47.1	52.9
08403	LONGPORT	98.3	97.9	0.1	0.1	1.3	1.7	0.6	0.8	3.3	3.5	3.9	2.7	2.1	15.6	36.2	28.1	4.7	87.7	56.9	46.8	53.2
08406	VENTNOR CITY	77.1	72.9	2.9	3.3	7.5	8.8	17.1	20.8	5.5	5.4	5.7	5.6	5.7	27.7	24.9	16.9	2.7	80.1	41.6	47.8	52.2
08501	ALLENTOWN	92.6	91.5	3.6	3.9	1.1	1.4	2.6	3.3	7.5	8.3	7.8	6.1	4.2	27.6	28.7	8.7	1.1	72.2	39.3	49.5	50.5
08502	BELLE MEAD	81.3	78.1	2.2	2.4	14.5	17.1	2.1	2.7	8.2	9.5	11.0	7.8	4.4	25.5	27.5	5.6	0.5	66.2	36.0	49.2	50.8
08505	BORDENTOWN	87.2	85.2	7.6	8.6	2.5	3.0	2.7	3.4	6.1	6.3	6.4	5.9	5.3	30.8	27.1	10.8	1.3	77.6	39.3	48.6	51.4
08510	CLARKSBURG	92.7	91.3	2.5	2.9	3.3	4.0	3.6	4.5	7.4	9.0	10.1	7.1	3.8	25.5	30.1	6.2	0.8	68.6	39.0	48.8	51.2
08511	COOKSTOWN	59.9	57.8	27.5	28.2	1.6	1.8	14.8	16.7	3.0	3.4	4.5	3.8	5.0	50.8	23.8	5.7	0.0	86.8	37.4	74.2	25.8
08512	CRANBURY	80.4	76.7	3.9	4.3	11.7	14.3	8.0	9.5	7.1	8.9	9.0	6.9	3.6	28.3	26.9	8.1	1.3	70.2	38.2	49.0	51.0
08514	CREAM RIDGE	95.1	94.2	1.5	1.7	1.2	1.4	3.6	4.6	6.8	7.7	7.9	6.0	4.1	27.3	29.8	9.1	1.1	73.5	40.2	49.8	50.2
08515	CROSSWICKS	95.4	94.2	2.2	2.5	0.8	1.3	1.6	2.3	6.8	7.8	6.8	5.8	4.0	25.1	31.8	10.8	1.3	74.9	41.7	49.1	50.9
08518	FLORENCE	80.8	78.1	13.9	15.7	2.7	3.2	1.8	2.2	5.7	6.1	7.0	6.7	7.1	29.3	24.9	11.7	1.6	77.1	38.1	48.2	51.9
08520	HIGHTSTOWN	75.4	71.7	8.7	10.1	8.3	9.2	14.3	17.1	7.4	7.1	6.4	5.5	5.8	32.8	25.9	7.5	1.7	75.7	36.7	49.1	50.9
08525	HOPEWELL	93.4	91.9	3.0	3.7	1.5	1.8	1.9	2.6	5.5	6.5	7.4	6.4	4.3	25.5	31.9	11.1	1.5	76.1	42.3	50.5	49.5
08526	IMLAYSTOWN	96.4	95.5	0.7	1.1	1.4	1.1	3.6	5.6	6.2	6.7	6.7	5.6	4.5	24.7	33.7	10.1	1.7	77.0	42.7	50.0	50.0
08527	JACKSON	91.2	90.0	3.9	4.3	2.1	2.5	5.8	7.1	8.2	8.3	8.3	6.6	5.1	30.5	22.8	9.1	1.2	71.0	36.3	48.9	51.1
08530	LAMBERTVILLE	91.9	90.6	5.3	6.1	1.0	1.2	2.4	3.0	4.0	4.5	5.4	5.4	5.2	28.3	32.6	13.0	1.6	82.9	43.6	51.3	48.7
08533	NEW EGYPT	93.8	92.7	2.3	2.6	0.8	0.9	4.0	4.9	6.9	7.3	8.5	6.9	5.7	30.1	25.7	8.1	0.8	72.8	37.3	49.8	50.2
08534	PENNINGTON	89.4	87.1	4.3	5.1	4.6	5.6	2.4	3.2	7.4	8.3	8.2	6.5	4.6	25.6	27.9	10.4	1.1	71.6	39.5	49.1	50.9
08535	PERRINEVILLE	91.7	90.1	3.1	3.6	3.5	4.2	3.5	4.4	8.2	9.8	10.4	6.5	3.4	26.5	28.7	5.8	0.8	67.1	38.2	50.0	50.0
08536	PLAINSBORO	56.1	50.9	8.3	8.8	31.8	36.0	4.8	6.0	7.3	7.5	7.2	5.6	6.7	41.9	21.0	2.6	0.2	74.4	32.4	50.4	49.6
08540	PRINCETON	79.6	76.3	5.2	5.9	11.3	13.1	4.8	6.0	5.4	5.7	6.0	9.7	10.7	27.2	23.9	10.2	1.4	79.6	34.8	49.6	50.4
08542	PRINCETON	70.1	65.6	12.1	13.4	4.5	5.0	19.0	22.9	5.7	4.7	4.2	5.3	7.9	35.6	20.2	12.6	3.9	82.7	36.3	49.8	50.2
08544	PRINCETON	77.8	81.8	11.1	18.2	0.0	0.0	0.0	0.0	0.0	9.1	9.1	9.1	18.2	36.4	18.2	0.0	0.0	81.8	40.6	36.4	63.6
08550	PRINCETON JUNCTION	71.6	67.6	2.5	3.0	23.8	26.9	2.7	3.4	6.4	8.3	10.7	8.5	4.6	22.4	31.9	6.7	0.6	68.8	39.6	49.4	50.6
08551	RINGOES	95.1	94.1	1.1	1.2	2.3	2.8	2.1	2.6	6.6	7.6	8.0	6.5	4.1	26.0	31.0	8.8	1.4	73.2	40.5	49.4	50.6
08553	ROCKY HILL	95.2	94.5	1.4	1.5	1.1	1.2	3.9	5.1	5.4	6.0	6.6	5.1	3.0	24.3	31.2	16.1	2.4	78.8	44.8	49.3	50.8
08554	ROEBLING	90.6	89.0	6.0	6.9	1.5	1.8	2.5	3.1	6.5	6.8	8.0	6.6	6.3	30.1	24.7	9.5	1.7	74.8	37.2	47.0	53.0
08556	ROSEMONT	97.7	96.5	0.0	0.0	1.2	1.2	2.4	1.2	4.7	4.7	5.9	5.9	4.7	22.4	35.3	14.1	2.4	78.8	45.8	52.9	47.1
08558	SKILLMAN	88.2	86.0	2.0	2.2	8.2	9.9	2.3	3.0	8.3	9.7	8.7	5.9	2.9	27.4	28.2	8.0	0.8	68.9	38.8	49.2	50.8
08559	STOCKTON	97.9	97.5	0.3	0.4	0.9	1.1	1.1	1.5	5.4	6.3	7.3	6.0	4.2	24.7	34.2	10.6	1.4	77.0	43.0	49.5	50.5
08560	TITUSVILLE	94.4	93.3	2.5	3.0	1.7	2.0	1.6	2.1	5.3	6.0	6.6	6.3	5.1	22.4	31.5	14.9	1.8	78.2	44.0	49.8	50.2
08562	WRIGHTSTOWN	80.5	78.0	11.1	12.3	2.6	2.9	6.0	7.2	6.8	7.4	7.4	7.3	11.0	30.4	21.5	7.7	0.6	74.5	32.3	53.5	46.5
08608	TRENTON	24.4	23.8	55.5	54.7	0.5	0.5	38.0	40.2	8.1	7.8	9.5	8.0	8.7	34.5	19.6	3.7	0.1	69.4	29.8	53.1	46.9
08609	TRENTON	22.5	20.1	58.9	60.1	1.6	1.5	22.7	24.7	8.0	7.8	8.9	8.2	8.1	29.0	20.3	8.7	1.0	70.4	31.3	49.4	50.6
08610	TRENTON	82.6	79.6	10.5	12.1	1.9	2.2	7.6	9.6	5.8	5.8	6.2	5.6	5.7	29.3	25.0	14.4	2.2	78.7	40.0	47.6	52.4
08611	TRENTON	51.6	47.4	23.8	24.7	1.3	1.4	36.0	40.9	7.3	6.8	7.0	6.1	7.6	34.0	19.0	10.0	2.3	75.3	33.5	53.2	46.8
08618	TRENTON	31.4	29.4	62.0	63.3	1.3	1.5	6.3	7.1	6.5	6.7	7.2	10.8	10.7	26.3	20.8	9.4	1.6	75.5	31.5	46.6	53.4
08619	TRENTON	89.6	87.6	4.3	5.0	3.1	3.6	3.7	4.9	5.3	5.5	6.0	5.9	5.4	26.7	27.0	15.2	3.1	79.5	42.0	47.3	52.7
08620	TRENTON	76.4	74.6	16.1	16.8	1.8	2.1	6.7	7.9	4.9	5.3	5.6	6.2	18.1	27.5	21.8	9.6	1.1	81.1	31.2	59.7	40.3
08628	TRENTON	80.1	76.0	14.5	17.4	2.8	3.4	3.4	4.3	4.8	5.0	4.9	4.6	5.3	30.1	28.3	14.1	2.9	82.2	42.3	48.8	51.2
08629	TRENTON	55.6	51.5	29.2	31.0	1.4	1.5	18.9	22.2	7.1	7.0	7.7	7.2	7.0	31.3	21.9	9.3	1.5	73.9	34.5	49.0	51.0
08638	TRENTON	44.8	42.4	46.4	48.0	1.4	1.5	10.3	11.4	6.0	6.5	7.2	6.8	6.6	27.7	24.5	13.0	1.8	76.1	37.9	48.2	51.8
08640	TRENTON	61.3	58.5	34.1	36.2	1.4	1.6	22.6	25.5	4.9	4.4	4.1	2.4	9.7	56.8	16.6	1.1	0.0	85.1	33.2	81.5	18.5
08641	TRENTON	68.5	64.2	19.3	21.5	2.9	3.4	8.7	10.6	14.5	11.3	9.6	6.5	19.4	37.0	1.6	0.1	0.0	61.7	22.1	54.7	45.3
08648	TRENTON	78.7	75.5	9.7	11.1	8.0	9.1	4.7	6.0	5.5	5.6	5.9	8.7	8.8	27.6	24.5	11.3	2.2	79.3	37.1	46.8	53.3
08690	TRENTON	92.4	90.9	2.0	2.4	3.7	4.4	2.5	3.4	5.3	5.8	7.0	6.5	5.4	26.4	28.7	13.0	1.9	77.9	41.3	47.3	52.8
08691	TRENTON	91.4	89.6	2.6	3.2	4.0	4.7	2.6	3.4	8.2	8.7	7.8	5.1	3.5	30.2	26.8	8.9	0.9	71.8	38.8	48.0	52.0
08701	LAKEWOOD	78.8	76.9	12.0	12.6	1.4	1.7	14.8	16.9	12.0	8.7	7.3	5.7	8.0	22.5	16.5	15.7	3.7	68.6	31.1	47.9	52.1
	NEW JERSEY	72.6	70.5	13.6	13.8	5.8	6.6	13.3	15.0	6.6	6.7	7.1	6.5	6.3	28.8	24.6	11.5	1.9	75.6	37.7	48.6	51.4
	UNITED STATES	75.1	73.6	12.3	12.5	3.8	4.2	12.5	14.1	6.9	6.7	7.2	7.0	7.3	28.6	23.8	10.8	1.7	75.1	36.0	49.1	50.9

ZIP CODE #	POST OFFICE NAME	2004 Per Capita Income	2004 HH Income Base	2004 HOUSEHOLD INCOME DISTRIBUTION (%) Less than $25,000	$25,000 to $49,999	$50,000 to $99,999	$100,000 to $149,999	$150,000 or More	MEDIAN HOUSEHOLD INCOME 2004	2009	2004 National Centile	2004 State Centile	2004 Home Value Base	2004 HOME VALUE DISTRIBUTION (%) Less than $50,000	$50,000 to $89,999	$90,000 to $174,999	$175,000 to $399,999	$400,000 or More	2004 Median Home Value
08210	CAPE MAY COURT HOUSE	23339	6091	21.8	25.8	35.9	11.8	4.7	52333	58630	76	24	5202	4.9	4.7	33.9	51.9	4.7	190545
08215	EGG HARBOR CITY	21836	4602	24.9	25.8	37.2	9.6	2.6	49211	53223	71	20	3406	2.1	3.6	49.7	39.5	5.1	165043
08221	LINWOOD	36733	2786	14.7	22.8	34.6	14.4	13.5	63827	70925	88	45	2463	0.0	0.0	18.7	59.7	21.6	249058
08223	MARMORA	33251	1550	14.3	29.2	31.9	15.0	9.6	59047	68842	84	36	1402	1.9	1.4	8.1	75.2	13.5	258333
08225	NORTHFIELD	29331	3047	14.7	22.7	41.2	14.2	7.2	62156	69394	86	42	2783	0.3	0.7	32.3	63.9	2.8	199707
08226	OCEAN CITY	38715	7731	22.6	28.7	27.1	10.9	10.7	48863	55889	70	19	5091	0.2	0.3	11.9	50.2	37.4	330840
08230	OCEAN VIEW	31803	2276	15.0	19.7	35.7	17.5	12.1	69882	79931	91	56	2066	1.7	1.7	15.8	67.1	13.7	249691
08232	PLEASANTVILLE	16630	6226	28.1	34.1	29.8	6.6	1.5	40374	43606	47	10	3503	1.5	8.0	75.0	15.4	0.1	135754
08234	EGG HARBOR TOWNSHIP	24993	12045	16.5	27.2	37.8	13.3	5.2	56294	61215	81	31	10053	11.0	7.2	27.4	50.0	4.5	185096
08241	PORT REPUBLIC	25450	419	15.3	27.9	38.0	13.6	5.3	55718	60647	80	30	303	0.7	8.9	23.4	59.1	7.9	217208
08242	RIO GRANDE	21215	1256	39.7	28.7	24.1	4.7	2.8	31434	33593	16	3	924	19.4	16.2	34.2	28.3	2.0	131507
08243	SEA ISLE CITY	35428	1405	23.5	26.1	25.8	14.3	10.4	50543	57373	73	21	1087	0.0	0.9	3.7	46.1	49.3	395588
08244	SOMERS POINT	25157	5057	20.8	32.9	34.6	8.7	3.0	46270	50984	64	16	3005	0.2	1.5	38.1	58.1	2.2	187940
08247	STONE HARBOR	54632	653	21.3	21.4	30.6	13.2	13.5	60075	69178	84	38	556	0.0	0.2	3.2	19.2	77.3	624088
08248	STRATHMERE	49107	97	4.1	16.5	40.2	29.9	9.3	83443	96614	96	74	85	0.0	0.0	0.0	51.8	48.2	393750
08251	VILLAS	20102	4244	31.0	36.4	25.5	5.1	2.0	37436	42106	37	7	3309	0.5	10.6	70.7	17.6	0.7	126489
08260	WILDWOOD	21333	7147	37.9	31.3	21.6	6.4	2.8	32588	35295	20	3	4094	0.7	5.6	35.0	51.2	7.6	198499
08270	WOODBINE	22028	2762	21.6	22.9	37.8	12.5	5.2	54771	61335	79	28	2169	0.7	4.8	35.9	53.0	5.6	192333
08302	BRIDGETON	17799	14138	32.1	28.6	28.7	8.2	2.5	39909	43396	46	9	9264	7.2	16.8	52.8	21.4	1.8	122265
08310	BUENA	22850	711	31.9	28.4	32.1	4.8	2.8	40534	44770	48	10	581	8.4	11.2	55.4	24.3	0.7	134186
08311	CEDARVILLE	20164	587	22.2	27.3	42.4	5.8	2.4	50331	55192	73	21	525	2.9	21.3	60.6	15.2	0.0	117299
08312	CLAYTON	23070	2354	15.1	29.0	36.7	15.3	3.9	56142	62483	81	31	1844	0.4	6.6	63.9	29.0	0.0	141149
08314	DELMONT	26941	99	27.3	35.4	23.2	9.1	5.1	39315	44321	44	8	84	14.3	31.0	46.4	8.3	0.0	96667
08317	DOROTHY	20524	467	18.4	27.0	37.9	13.7	3.0	54797	60105	79	28	434	2.5	3.7	40.6	49.8	3.5	181364
08318	ELMER	24485	4601	14.7	25.3	41.5	14.4	4.2	60199	64997	85	38	4030	10.2	5.7	38.8	41.4	3.9	165891
08319	ESTELL MANOR	22151	507	18.3	27.0	38.1	13.6	3.0	54773	60394	79	28	471	2.3	3.4	40.3	50.3	3.6	182708
08322	FRANKLINVILLE	22928	3566	16.0	22.7	42.4	15.9	3.1	61195	67044	86	40	3186	1.6	5.5	51.5	39.9	1.5	162898
08323	GREENWICH	22185	123	17.9	22.8	42.3	13.8	3.3	57277	62198	82	33	107	5.6	6.5	48.6	35.5	3.7	152885
08324	HEISLERVILLE	17977	60	23.3	35.0	30.0	10.0	1.7	45000	47986	61	14	51	9.8	31.4	51.0	7.8	0.0	97500
08326	LANDISVILLE	18001	602	33.2	25.9	31.7	5.7	3.5	40255	43764	47	9	411	0.0	2.9	71.5	24.6	1.0	144752
08327	LEESBURG	19871	144	24.3	35.4	27.8	9.7	2.8	43896	50000	58	13	123	8.1	30.9	52.9	7.3	0.8	99643
08328	MALAGA	21991	522	15.1	28.5	41.6	13.2	1.5	57357	63663	82	33	420	6.2	2.6	65.2	24.8	1.2	146398
08330	MAYS LANDING	23810	8303	15.0	29.4	41.0	10.7	3.9	54419	59865	79	27	5872	1.4	7.8	48.4	38.5	4.0	159127
08332	MILLVILLE	20192	13491	27.4	30.3	30.8	8.5	3.0	43703	47747	58	13	9343	9.6	23.0	51.9	14.9	0.5	110717
08340	MILMAY	21504	308	22.7	30.5	35.1	9.1	2.6	47353	51942	67	17	264	5.7	8.0	41.7	43.6	1.1	155556
08341	MINOTOLA	18880	626	38.8	25.6	25.9	7.5	2.2	35299	38061	29	5	379	0.0	1.9	58.3	38.0	1.9	163542
08343	MONROEVILLE	22102	1676	20.3	24.0	41.1	12.2	2.5	54686	60608	79	28	1452	8.5	7.4	35.7	43.3	5.1	171695
08344	NEWFIELD	23248	2047	18.5	25.7	39.2	12.5	4.1	54978	61424	80	29	1759	5.5	6.5	54.6	31.3	2.2	147718
08345	NEWPORT	21233	505	28.5	37.4	26.5	5.7	1.8	37819	41301	39	7	459	12.2	31.8	47.7	7.6	0.7	95729
08346	NEWTONVILLE	17628	199	22.6	30.7	38.7	4.0	4.0	44747	47828	61	13	157	1.3	8.9	71.3	17.2	1.3	138221
08349	PORT NORRIS	17708	873	26.9	33.5	31.0	6.6	2.0	43648	47195	58	12	721	10.5	32.3	49.0	6.8	1.4	95365
08350	RICHLAND	20962	288	24.0	31.3	33.0	7.6	4.2	45000	50000	61	14	243	4.9	5.4	42.8	46.1	0.8	165625
08353	SHILOH	29274	125	15.2	16.0	46.4	16.8	5.6	64257	73120	88	46	109	1.8	7.3	54.1	29.4	7.3	149342
08360	VINELAND	18252	15065	32.1	30.9	28.0	6.8	2.2	38522	42275	41	8	9140	8.3	12.5	65.2	13.5	0.4	118534
08361	VINELAND	28233	6001	18.0	26.2	35.3	13.1	7.4	56827	61677	82	32	4745	3.4	3.9	56.4	34.5	1.8	152665
08401	ATLANTIC CITY	17025	16263	43.3	30.8	18.9	4.5	2.6	28986	31315	10	2	4539	3.8	14.5	50.9	27.1	3.7	139052
08402	MARGATE CITY	37621	3954	24.4	26.7	28.0	11.2	9.6	48656	53044	70	19	2818	0.0	0.4	9.3	65.3	25.1	286595
08403	LONGPORT	57978	579	17.8	24.9	27.3	9.3	20.7	58671	67521	83	35	496	0.0	0.4	5.2	42.7	51.6	412121
08406	VENTNOR CITY	24873	5571	26.1	29.5	30.5	9.3	4.6	44991	48886	61	14	3148	0.3	2.4	32.5	56.3	8.6	203750
08501	ALLENTOWN	34343	1987	8.5	17.2	35.5	22.7	16.2	81927	97747	96	72	1712	1.0	0.2	4.7	56.3	37.9	341076
08502	BELLE MEAD	54570	3446	3.7	8.2	18.6	24.7	44.9	138871	163960	100	98	3034	0.2	0.4	0.1	18.7	80.6	569019
08505	BORDENTOWN	31366	6432	12.8	22.1	39.7	18.1	7.3	65610	73973	89	48	4830	0.7	1.1	35.2	58.7	4.4	195850
08510	CLARKSBURG	42501	691	7.7	11.1	31.8	26.6	22.7	98941	115577	98	87	660	0.0	0.0	1.5	29.9	68.6	540426
08511	COOKSTOWN	20385	218	20.2	16.1	36.2	21.1	6.4	69633	76486	91	55	196	0.0	0.0	27.0	70.4	2.6	205385
08512	CRANBURY	47831	2565	10.2	15.2	25.6	21.6	27.3	97438	110142	98	86	2040	1.7	2.1	9.4	38.8	48.0	390191
08514	CREAM RIDGE	35025	1322	10.1	16.2	36.2	23.1	14.5	80692	94118	95	70	1177	1.4	0.9	3.9	52.6	41.1	365625
08515	CROSSWICKS	38042	140	6.4	10.7	37.1	28.6	17.1	93514	106582	98	83	128	0.0	0.0	4.7	68.8	26.6	295652
08518	FLORENCE	25319	1960	17.2	30.7	36.1	12.4	3.7	52619	58664	76	25	1272	5.0	10.2	41.8	42.6	0.5	162209
08520	HIGHTSTOWN	32812	11979	11.7	18.3	39.7	18.4	11.9	71320	82868	92	57	7829	1.8	4.7	27.8	57.0	8.7	208896
08525	HOPEWELL	47031	1925	5.8	15.8	30.7	25.7	22.0	95679	113138	98	84	1576	0.0	0.0	5.0	48.2	46.8	387250
08526	IMLAYSTOWN	39775	69	13.0	14.5	33.3	21.7	17.4	79947	98816	95	70	60	0.0	0.0	0.0	53.3	46.7	388889
08527	JACKSON	27581	16030	12.6	19.1	39.5	20.9	8.0	70893	78984	92	57	13623	4.0	2.8	12.7	67.2	13.3	249285
08530	LAMBERTVILLE	39236	3118	15.1	19.1	32.7	17.8	15.4	72512	84508	92	59	2301	0.0	0.6	2.8	68.3	28.3	293373
08533	NEW EGYPT	24280	2488	12.3	24.3	40.5	19.7	3.2	64557	71204	88	46	2007	4.3	1.6	15.6	65.6	12.9	246206
08534	PENNINGTON	57431	4600	4.2	14.1	28.4	23.7	29.6	105099	125141	99	89	4222	0.4	2.3	3.4	47.5	46.4	386496
08535	PERRINEVILLE	38265	615	7.3	10.4	27.2	26.8	28.3	106931	125867	99	90	586	0.0	0.2	1.7	29.0	69.1	537281
08536	PLAINSBORO	40284	8885	8.0	18.9	40.4	18.4	14.3	75905	84419	94	65	3373	2.1	1.9	19.2	45.3	31.4	295955
08540	PRINCETON	56720	16212	10.5	14.0	24.7	18.7	32.2	101771	120493	98	88	11674	0.3	0.8	4.6	35.0	59.3	464510
08542	PRINCETON	41800	1554	16.3	17.0	32.8	17.1	16.8	72246	88863	92	58	685	0.0	2.0	8.0	43.4	46.6	383904
08544	PRINCETON	53773	8	0.0	12.5	87.5	0.0	0.0	80000	80868	95	70	0	0.0	0.0	0.0	0.0	0.0	0
08550	PRINCETON JUNCTION	58844	6144	5.0	7.9	15.7	23.8	47.6	144157	167171	100	99	5407	0.3	0.4	1.3	22.2	75.8	535516
08551	RINGOES	39948	1657	7.7	13.4	33.2	23.8	21.9	92617	109704	97	82	1440	0.3	0.1	4.8	49.0	45.8	382571
08553	ROCKY HILL	55344	291	8.3	15.8	28.9	22.3	24.7	92671	110378	97	82	207	0.0	0.0	4.4	44.9	50.7	403000
08554	ROEBLING	25573	1487	18.4	21.3	39.7	15.9	4.7	60340	67267	85	38	1133	0.5	7.7	63.8	27.4	0.6	139990
08556	ROSEMONT	44072	33	15.2	12.1	30.3	18.2	24.2	85660	108072	96	76	29	0.0	0.0	0.0	37.9	62.1	487500
08558	SKILLMAN	56450	2007	5.8	10.3	19.4	25.0	39.6	128682	152012	100	97	1798	0.2	0.0	1.1	36.7	62.0	475524
08559	STOCKTON	41891	2101	11.0	14.3	33.5	20.1	21.0	84998	102401	96	76	1807	0.3	0.5	2.4	48.9	47.9	391720
08560	TITUSVILLE	48744	1386	6.8	12.1	33.1	24.3	23.7	96428	112657	98	85	1253	0.0	0.0	3.8	65.0	31.3	334497
08562	WRIGHTSTOWN	24214	2727	18.2	30.1	33.9	13.6	4.1	52235	58132	76	24	1608	17.4	4.7	13.0	51.6	13.3	229520
08608	TRENTON	12401	435	56.3	31.7	10.3	1.6	0.0	21753	24613	2	1	63	15.9	30.2	31.8	22.2	0.0	101136
08609	TRENTON	15303	4530	38.1	28.3	25.9	5.5	2.1	34159	39026	25	5	1760	4.2	29.4	59.9	6.3	0.1	107678
08610	TRENTON	26872	12302	19.0	26.1	36.7	14.3	3.9	54796	63334	79	28	8888	0.5	5.2	46.6	46.6	1.1	171706
08611	TRENTON	16974	9150	37.4	30.6	24.4	5.8	1.9	33514	38123	22	4	3940	5.2	35.2	55.1	4.3	0.2	95959
08618	TRENTON	19059	13458	31.9	28.1	28.4	8.8	2.9	40492	46201	48	10	6787	3.0	16.0	46.5	33.1	1.5	144804
08619	TRENTON	30631	8293	17.5	21.3	36.8	16.9	7.5	63734	74582	88	45	5853	0.1	0.9	19.9	76.2	2.9	220712
08620	TRENTON	26810	4643	10.0	23.8	36.9	21.0	8.3	69726	80083	91	55	3609	0.0	0.3	15.7	78.0	6.1	223843
08628	TRENTON	36172	3704	11.9	18.9	38.1	17.7	13.3	73182	84724	93	60	2681	0.0	0.7	14.0	78.1	7.2	258501
08629	TRENTON	20943	4088	19.3	33.9	34.3	9.7	2.8	48036	55324	68	18	2722	1.0	11.8	75.8	10.6	0.8	121800
08638	TRENTON	22585	8932	25.7	28.5	30.5	11.3	4.1	46319	52779	65	16	5892	3.6	13.7	38.5	42.7	1.6	161175
08640	TRENTON	15450	879	9.7	53.1	33.6	3.3	0.3	45741	51477	63	15	39	0.0	18.0	61.5	20.5	0.0	139375
08641	TRENTON	11456	1108	22.0	49.0	26.7	2.3	0.0	37586	42605	38	7	11	0.0	0.0	100.0	0.0	0.0	127083
08648	TRENTON	36759	10950	14.1	18.2	35.0	18.7	14.1	74019	85262	93	61	7498	0.3	2.4	23.2	57.0	17.0	240000
08690	TRENTON	32947	7300	8.0	17.2	43.2	21.6	10.0	75634	86583	93	65	6320	0.4	0.6	23.2	70.4	5.4	225912
08691	TRENTON	39778	5153	10.5	14.2	35.6	22.5	17.2	82839	97217	96	73	4437	2.8	0.4	20.1	45.9	30.8	285321
08701	LAKEWOOD	18543	21830	32.8	26.2	27.6	9.0	4.4	39602	44061	45	9	13867	1.2	8.4	31.0	51.1	8.3	203347
	NEW JERSEY	31614		18.6	22.5	32.1	15.5	11.4	61437	70239				1.5	2.7	19.7	54.4	21.8	255213
	UNITED STATES	25866		24.7	27.1	30.8	10.9	6.5	48124	56710				10.9	15.0	33.7	30.1	10.4	145905

ZIP CODE #	POST OFFICE NAME	FINANCIAL SERVICES: Auto Loan	FINANCIAL SERVICES: Home Loan	FINANCIAL SERVICES: Investments	FINANCIAL SERVICES: Retirement Plans	THE HOME: Home Improvements: Home Repair	THE HOME: Home Improvements: Lawn & Garden	THE HOME: Furnishings: Computers & Hardware	THE HOME: Furnishings: Major Appliances	THE HOME: Furnishings: TV, Radio, Sound Equipment	THE HOME: Furnishings: Furniture	ENTERTAINMENT: Dine out/ Carry out	ENTERTAINMENT: Sports Equipment	ENTERTAINMENT: Fees & Tickets	ENTERTAINMENT: Toys & Games	ENTERTAINMENT: Travel	ENTERTAINMENT: Cable TV	PERSONAL: Apparel & Services	PERSONAL: Auto Repairs	PERSONAL: Health Insurance	PERSONAL: Pets & Supplies
08210	CAPE MAY COURT HOUSE	89	92	91	90	93	99	88	91	88	88	109	103	89	109	90	88	106	90	92	103
08215	EGG HARBOR CITY	78	84	88	82	84	89	82	82	82	81	102	94	85	106	83	82	100	81	82	91
08221	LINWOOD	126	147	166	147	146	153	139	139	132	139	167	159	146	169	143	131	164	136	132	151
08223	MARMORA	136	126	111	119	135	148	118	132	124	117	150	152	114	150	124	129	143	129	144	166
08225	NORTHFIELD	99	120	133	117	118	122	111	111	107	111	134	127	118	141	115	106	133	108	105	120
08226	OCEAN CITY	128	104	80	96	115	129	100	116	111	99	133	136	91	131	106	118	124	115	135	155
08230	OCEAN VIEW	138	139	126	138	143	147	128	137	127	129	157	161	128	160	131	126	152	133	135	164
08232	PLEASANTVILLE	66	62	74	59	60	69	66	64	71	68	89	72	68	88	66	73	87	66	68	74
08234	EGG HARBOR TOWNSHIP	95	102	106	103	100	102	99	98	94	99	119	115	100	119	98	91	116	98	90	109
08241	PORT REPUBLIC	92	105	126	109	103	105	103	100	98	103	124	120	106	127	103	95	122	101	91	110
08242	RIO GRANDE	76	66	60	66	70	79	70	74	73	68	89	83	66	84	70	75	83	74	81	85
08243	SEA ISLE CITY	122	96	65	86	108	121	90	109	102	89	121	127	81	119	96	109	112	107	128	148
08244	SOMERS POINT	78	81	94	82	81	87	83	82	83	82	103	96	84	104	83	82	100	83	81	91
08247	STONE HARBOR	174	136	93	123	153	172	128	155	145	127	172	181	115	170	137	155	160	152	183	212
08248	STRATHMERE	155	122	83	110	137	154	115	138	130	114	154	162	103	152	123	139	143	136	164	189
08251	VILLAS	77	63	48	60	68	78	65	71	71	62	84	82	59	83	66	74	79	71	82	89
08260	WILDWOOD	78	61	43	55	69	77	58	70	66	58	79	81	52	77	62	71	73	69	83	95
08270	WOODBINE	79	90	100	88	87	90	86	85	84	86	105	98	90	109	87	83	104	84	80	94
08302	BRIDGETON	67	67	70	64	67	73	68	68	70	68	87	78	69	88	68	71	85	69	70	77
08310	BUENA	72	77	82	74	78	87	72	77	73	74	91	81	75	88	76	75	88	74	80	84
08311	CEDARVILLE	83	83	78	79	86	94	80	83	84	78	103	95	82	109	83	87	99	81	89	98
08312	CLAYTON	91	98	100	99	96	98	95	94	91	95	115	110	97	117	94	88	112	93	87	104
08314	DELMONT	58	39	18	34	44	51	38	47	46	38	54	56	32	51	38	49	49	47	58	67
08317	DOROTHY	80	98	108	95	96	98	90	89	86	90	109	103	96	115	93	85	108	87	83	97
08318	ELMER	101	103	94	99	105	110	95	100	96	95	118	117	97	123	98	97	115	97	101	119
08319	ESTELL MANOR	80	97	108	95	95	98	90	89	86	89	108	103	96	115	93	85	108	87	83	97
08322	FRANKLINVILLE	92	105	106	103	104	106	95	97	92	95	114	113	100	121	98	91	113	94	92	111
08323	GREENWICH	85	97	101	94	96	99	90	91	87	89	109	105	94	115	92	87	108	88	87	102
08324	HEISLERVILLE	102	68	31	59	77	89	66	83	80	67	94	99	56	88	67	86	85	82	102	117
08326	LANDISVILLE	69	67	68	68	68	72	71	70	71	69	87	83	70	89	69	69	84	71	69	78
08327	LEESBURG	102	68	31	59	77	89	66	83	80	67	94	99	56	88	67	86	85	82	102	117
08328	MALAGA	86	96	99	97	94	93	91	90	86	92	108	107	93	110	90	82	107	89	80	99
08330	MAYS LANDING	90	92	100	96	89	91	93	90	89	94	113	108	93	111	90	84	111	92	81	100
08332	MILLVILLE	79	75	70	72	77	84	75	78	79	74	97	90	75	98	76	80	93	77	82	91
08340	MILMAY	79	88	89	85	88	91	81	83	80	81	100	97	85	105	83	80	98	81	81	95
08341	MINOTOLA	72	58	46	57	62	72	64	68	69	61	82	77	58	79	63	71	76	68	77	80
08343	MONROEVILLE	93	90	76	86	93	98	82	89	84	82	104	105	83	107	85	85	100	86	92	110
08344	NEWFIELD	87	102	111	100	101	104	95	95	92	95	115	110	101	121	98	91	114	93	90	105
08345	NEWPORT	77	66	52	60	72	80	63	71	69	62	83	83	59	84	66	73	78	70	82	93
08346	NEWTONVILLE	80	97	107	95	95	97	90	89	86	89	108	103	96	115	92	85	108	87	83	97
08349	PORT NORRIS	74	69	61	64	72	81	67	72	73	66	89	82	67	93	70	77	85	70	81	87
08350	RICHLAND	75	91	101	89	89	91	84	84	81	84	101	96	90	108	87	80	101	81	78	91
08353	SHILOH	103	126	139	123	123	126	116	115	111	116	140	133	124	149	120	110	139	112	107	126
08360	VINELAND	64	66	85	63	65	72	67	67	71	68	89	75	68	92	69	73	88	68	68	75
08361	VINELAND	103	112	118	110	112	119	107	108	106	106	132	125	111	136	110	107	129	107	108	122
08401	ATLANTIC CITY	53	50	78	48	49	57	57	54	63	57	79	62	58	81	58	66	77	58	58	62
08402	MARGATE CITY	116	108	101	102	114	129	102	113	107	104	132	123	100	123	108	113	125	111	127	137
08403	LONGPORT	189	153	110	139	171	191	144	171	161	143	191	200	131	189	153	171	179	168	199	230
08406	VENTNOR CITY	76	78	100	76	78	87	81	80	84	80	104	92	82	108	83	86	102	82	82	91
08501	ALLENTOWN	130	157	168	159	154	152	142	141	132	143	166	166	150	175	144	127	166	137	126	155
08502	BELLE MEAD	231	288	313	298	279	281	254	247	231	258	294	286	279	306	258	224	297	239	220	274
08505	BORDENTOWN	102	116	127	118	114	116	111	109	106	111	133	128	115	138	112	103	132	108	100	119
08510	CLARKSBURG	175	218	237	225	211	213	192	188	175	195	223	217	211	232	196	170	225	181	167	208
08511	COOKSTOWN	97	120	128	120	118	116	107	107	99	107	125	125	114	133	110	96	125	103	96	118
08512	CRANBURY	179	216	250	221	209	214	199	194	185	201	235	227	213	243	202	180	235	191	174	213
08514	CREAM RIDGE	129	159	169	160	156	154	142	141	131	142	165	165	151	175	145	127	165	136	126	156
08515	CROSSWICKS	141	175	186	175	172	169	156	156	145	156	182	182	166	194	160	140	182	150	139	172
08518	FLORENCE	81	91	103	90	89	93	89	87	87	88	109	101	93	114	90	86	108	87	83	95
08520	HIGHTSTOWN	116	126	145	130	123	128	125	122	119	126	151	143	128	152	124	115	149	123	111	134
08525	HOPEWELL	151	191	229	188	187	194	175	173	165	175	207	199	187	218	181	163	207	169	159	187
08526	IMLAYSTOWN	133	165	175	165	162	160	147	147	137	147	172	172	157	183	151	133	171	142	131	162
08527	JACKSON	119	129	124	130	126	127	118	120	113	121	142	139	121	142	118	109	139	118	112	135
08530	LAMBERTVILLE	123	147	175	149	145	148	140	137	132	139	166	161	146	172	142	129	165	136	125	149
08533	NEW EGYPT	95	112	118	113	109	109	104	103	97	103	122	121	108	128	104	93	121	100	92	113
08534	PENNINGTON	201	252	281	255	245	251	224	220	207	226	262	252	245	273	230	203	263	212	200	242
08535	PERRINEVILLE	184	229	249	237	222	224	202	197	184	205	234	228	222	243	205	178	236	190	175	218
08536	PLAINSBORO	134	132	165	144	127	133	140	132	135	143	172	158	141	169	134	128	169	137	118	147
08540	PRINCETON	196	237	316	241	229	241	226	216	215	228	271	253	242	286	230	212	272	215	197	236
08542	PRINCETON	120	134	231	139	127	141	144	132	148	145	187	158	152	204	147	151	188	139	126	145
08544	PRINCETON	118	105	80	100	111	120	97	108	104	97	126	129	96	129	100	106	120	105	117	139
08550	PRINCETON JUNCTION	247	310	343	319	300	304	273	266	249	277	317	307	301	329	279	242	319	257	237	295
08551	RINGOES	158	193	202	196	187	185	172	170	158	174	200	198	183	209	174	152	200	164	151	188
08553	ROCKY HILL	164	198	223	196	197	207	181	182	171	182	216	206	193	219	189	171	214	177	174	198
08554	ROEBLING	87	95	107	96	94	96	97	94	93	94	117	112	98	121	96	90	115	95	87	102
08556	ROSEMONT	146	176	199	175	175	184	162	162	153	162	192	184	172	195	168	152	191	158	155	177
08558	SKILLMAN	221	276	299	284	266	269	243	237	221	246	281	274	267	292	247	214	284	228	210	262
08559	STOCKTON	145	177	196	180	174	177	161	159	149	161	189	184	172	196	164	146	188	154	145	175
08560	TITUSVILLE	164	201	229	198	199	209	183	184	173	184	218	208	195	222	191	173	216	179	174	200
08562	WRIGHTSTOWN	91	93	93	94	91	94	93	91	90	91	112	109	92	113	90	87	110	92	85	103
08608	TRENTON	38	31	42	29	30	36	38	36	42	38	52	41	37	50	36	43	51	39	39	41
08609	TRENTON	61	55	69	53	54	62	62	60	67	63	83	67	62	82	61	69	81	62	63	67
08610	TRENTON	84	93	105	91	93	100	92	91	92	91	115	104	96	119	94	92	112	90	90	99
08611	TRENTON	57	55	85	54	53	61	64	60	69	63	86	69	64	89	64	71	85	64	62	66
08618	TRENTON	67	65	78	63	64	72	69	67	72	70	90	76	70	89	69	74	88	69	70	76
08619	TRENTON	96	111	132	109	109	117	108	106	106	107	132	121	113	137	110	106	131	105	103	115
08620	TRENTON	105	122	135	122	120	123	116	114	111	115	139	133	121	144	117	109	138	113	107	125
08628	TRENTON	111	126	152	126	125	133	124	121	121	123	151	140	129	155	126	120	149	122	117	132
08629	TRENTON	76	80	90	77	79	86	81	79	83	80	104	90	84	108	82	84	102	80	81	88
08638	TRENTON	80	83	98	80	82	90	84	83	87	85	108	93	87	109	86	88	106	84	84	92
08640	TRENTON	78	49	47	57	45	54	73	63	75	68	93	84	63	83	61	68	89	75	59	72
08641	TRENTON	68	43	41	50	40	47	65	56	66	60	82	74	55	73	53	60	78	66	51	63
08648	TRENTON	124	134	160	138	132	140	135	131	131	135	165	153	139	166	135	128	163	133	124	144
08690	TRENTON	118	133	144	136	130	132	127	124	120	127	152	146	131	155	126	116	150	123	113	137
08691	TRENTON	144	170	174	175	163	161	152	150	139	156	177	174	161	180	151	132	176	145	131	165
08701	LAKEWOOD	77	77	85	76	77	84	78	79	78	79	98	88	78	94	78	78	95	79	79	86
	NEW JERSEY	110	123	153	121	120	128	120	118	119	121	150	136	125	155	123	120	149	119	114	130
	UNITED STATES	100	100	100	100	100	100	100	100	100	100	100	100	100	100	100	100	100	100	100	100

POPULATION CHANGE

#	POST OFFICE NAME	COUNTY FIPS CODE	POPULATION 2000	2004	2009	2000-2004 ANNUAL RATE % Rate	State Centile	HOUSEHOLDS 2000	2004	2009	% Annual Rate 2000-2004	2004 Average HH Size	FAMILIES 2000	2004	% Annual Rate 2000-2004
08721	BAYVILLE	029	17604	19525	21971	2.5	92	6372	7068	7948	2.5	2.72	4805	5332	2.5
08722	BEACHWOOD	029	10531	11381	12594	1.8	85	3521	3804	4205	1.8	2.99	2856	3096	1.9
08723	BRICK	029	31872	33205	36028	1.0	65	12470	12990	14084	1.0	2.55	8835	9240	1.1
08724	BRICK	029	43110	45714	50041	1.4	76	16503	17484	19128	1.4	2.58	11589	12326	1.5
08730	BRIELLE	025	4930	4910	5034	-0.1	16	1951	1943	1993	-0.1	2.53	1423	1420	-0.1
08731	FORKED RIVER	029	18433	19900	22038	1.8	85	6990	7545	8348	1.8	2.63	5297	5739	1.9
08733	LAKEHURST	029	2980	3061	3285	0.6	51	955	984	1062	0.7	2.93	734	759	0.8
08734	LANOKA HARBOR	029	6910	7399	8147	1.6	81	2344	2506	2754	1.6	2.95	1947	2085	1.6
08735	LAVALLETTE	029	4445	4654	5067	1.1	69	2180	2282	2488	1.1	1.98	1271	1340	1.3
08736	MANASQUAN	025	13135	13817	14586	1.2	72	5196	5457	5753	1.2	2.52	3614	3829	1.4
08738	MANTOLOKING	029	1352	1452	1601	1.7	82	662	711	783	1.7	2.03	446	481	1.8
08740	OCEAN GATE	029	1915	1966	2117	0.6	51	770	790	851	0.6	2.49	506	521	0.7
08741	PINE BEACH	029	2440	2636	2916	1.8	85	935	1009	1116	1.8	2.61	694	753	1.9
08742	POINT PLEASANT BEACH	029	26266	27318	29599	0.9	63	10610	11028	11943	0.9	2.44	7010	7327	1.1
08750	SEA GIRT	025	3818	3821	3934	0.0	23	1634	1639	1690	0.1	2.33	1078	1085	0.2
08751	SEASIDE HEIGHTS	029	4921	5339	5918	1.9	86	2345	2555	2838	2.0	2.05	1155	1267	2.2
08752	SEASIDE PARK	029	2927	3091	3378	1.3	75	1468	1549	1692	1.3	2.00	792	841	1.4
08753	TOMS RIVER	029	65025	68333	74600	1.2	71	23685	24900	27178	1.2	2.71	17518	18488	1.3
08755	TOMS RIVER	029	22479	25332	28615	2.9	95	8477	9693	11038	3.2	2.51	6298	7209	3.2
08757	TOMS RIVER	029	33468	36425	40669	2.0	87	17240	18899	21161	2.2	1.91	10288	11343	2.3
08758	WARETOWN	029	5221	5906	6685	2.9	95	1967	2224	2517	2.9	2.63	1396	1584	3.0
08759	MANCHESTER TOWNSHIP	029	30289	33133	36932	2.1	89	17547	19223	21452	2.2	1.70	8527	9397	2.3
08801	ANNANDALE	019	7639	8012	8428	1.1	71	2341	2490	2656	1.5	2.75	1805	1929	1.6
08802	ASBURY	019	3841	4189	4533	2.1	88	1304	1434	1562	2.3	2.92	1088	1198	2.3
08804	BLOOMSBURY	019	2143	2290	2465	1.6	80	790	849	919	1.7	2.69	648	700	1.8
08805	BOUND BROOK	035	12224	12704	13530	0.9	62	4346	4508	4804	0.9	2.80	3063	3193	1.0
08807	BRIDGEWATER	035	36517	39015	42254	1.6	80	13278	14328	15628	1.8	2.68	9928	10725	1.8
08809	CLINTON	019	5102	5578	6047	2.1	89	2205	2426	2645	2.3	2.25	1344	1496	2.6
08810	DAYTON	023	7182	7834	8319	2.1	88	2322	2522	2670	2.0	3.11	1940	2117	2.1
08812	DUNELLEN	035	12032	13127	14138	2.1	88	4168	4572	4945	2.2	2.80	3068	3400	2.5
08816	EAST BRUNSWICK	023	45493	46727	48484	0.6	51	15960	16404	17021	0.7	2.83	12707	13123	0.8
08817	EDISON	023	45195	45740	47023	0.3	35	16283	16478	16923	0.3	2.71	11718	11935	0.4
08820	EDISON	023	37323	38855	40581	1.0	64	12697	13296	13917	1.1	2.91	10361	10852	1.1
08822	FLEMINGTON	019	28019	30142	32299	1.7	82	10177	11034	11907	1.9	2.70	7647	8315	2.0
08823	FRANKLIN PARK	035	6699	7508	8320	2.7	94	2823	3175	3527	2.8	2.34	1821	2057	2.9
08824	KENDALL PARK	023	12287	12533	12913	0.5	45	3976	4046	4164	0.4	3.10	3304	3386	0.6
08825	FRENCHTOWN	019	4805	4893	5105	0.4	42	1722	1767	1859	0.6	2.73	1247	1285	0.7
08826	GLEN GARDNER	019	6091	6366	6701	1.0	68	2156	2284	2433	1.4	2.66	1562	1657	1.4
08827	HAMPTON	019	4740	4884	5126	0.7	56	1586	1651	1754	1.0	2.67	1248	1313	1.2
08828	HELMETTA	023	1814	1978	2097	2.1	88	743	817	870	2.3	2.42	493	546	2.4
08829	HIGH BRIDGE	019	3776	3735	3872	-0.3	9	1428	1426	1490	-0.1	2.62	1051	1054	0.1
08830	ISELIN	023	16504	16412	16775	-0.1	16	5940	5910	6041	-0.1	2.77	4461	4503	0.2
08831	MONROE TOWNSHIP	023	34346	37034	39640	1.8	84	14840	15926	16983	1.7	2.25	9888	10824	2.2
08832	KEASBEY	023	2485	2556	2662	0.7	54	913	946	989	0.8	2.70	625	648	0.9
08833	LEBANON	019	9046	9695	10356	1.6	81	3181	3441	3707	1.9	2.78	2561	2769	1.9
08835	MANVILLE	035	10330	10501	11096	0.4	40	4108	4223	4493	0.7	2.49	2754	2844	0.8
08836	MARTINSVILLE	035	3635	3796	4052	1.0	66	1288	1357	1459	1.2	2.76	1127	1189	1.3
08837	EDISON	023	14840	15256	15766	0.7	53	6089	6272	6479	0.7	2.31	3751	3893	0.9
08840	METUCHEN	023	15445	15634	16051	0.3	36	5817	5897	6059	0.3	2.65	4254	4342	0.5
08844	HILLSBOROUGH	035	37068	39519	42801	1.5	78	12793	13720	14929	1.7	2.86	9901	10666	1.8
08846	MIDDLESEX	023	13693	13718	14024	0.0	23	5036	5056	5173	0.1	2.71	3731	3765	0.2
08848	MILFORD	019	8270	8599	9090	0.9	62	3001	3137	3337	1.1	2.73	2394	2512	1.1
08850	MILLTOWN	023	8365	8350	8488	0.0	19	3082	3088	3143	0.1	2.70	2346	2364	0.2
08852	MONMOUTH JUNCTION	023	13599	15186	16361	2.6	94	5251	5873	6328	2.7	2.58	3555	3986	2.7
08853	NESHANIC STATION	035	5363	5511	5833	0.6	52	1788	1853	1975	0.8	2.97	1505	1568	1.0
08854	PISCATAWAY	023	50937	53253	55703	1.1	68	16692	17581	18459	1.2	2.82	12435	13155	1.3
08857	OLD BRIDGE	023	36072	37579	39462	1.0	65	12848	13396	14080	1.0	2.78	9569	10007	1.1
08859	PARLIN	023	20098	20894	21918	0.9	62	7527	7896	8321	1.1	2.64	5526	5787	1.1
08861	PERTH AMBOY	023	50188	50842	52416	0.3	37	15642	15730	16146	0.1	3.19	11499	11637	0.3
08863	FORDS	023	13337	13405	13814	0.1	28	5087	5071	5201	-0.1	2.64	3553	3567	0.1
08865	PHILLIPSBURG	041	28821	30188	32483	1.1	70	11262	11864	12847	1.2	2.51	7732	8192	1.4
08867	PITTSTOWN	019	6482	6717	7005	0.8	60	1598	1672	1767	1.1	3.14	1327	1392	1.1
08869	RARITAN	035	6338	6473	6832	0.5	47	2556	2630	2790	0.7	2.46	1671	1729	0.8
08872	SAYREVILLE	023	18109	18616	19294	0.7	53	6593	6773	7002	0.6	2.73	4830	4991	0.8
08873	SOMERSET	035	41500	43847	47331	1.3	75	15513	16515	17943	1.5	2.60	10435	11159	1.6
08876	SOMERVILLE	035	22933	23515	24887	0.6	50	8629	8920	9509	0.8	2.57	5807	6033	0.9
08879	SOUTH AMBOY	023	22513	22896	23655	0.4	41	8272	8463	8768	0.5	2.69	5829	6012	0.7
08880	SOUTH BOUND BROOK	035	4475	4617	4899	0.7	57	1625	1676	1783	0.7	2.75	1101	1141	0.8
08882	SOUTH RIVER	023	15282	15304	15631	0.0	23	5591	5593	5709	0.0	2.72	3974	4000	0.2
08884	SPOTSWOOD	023	7788	8064	8318	0.8	59	3069	3184	3286	0.9	2.53	2140	2238	1.1
08886	STEWARTSVILLE	041	5006	6292	7377	5.5	99	1632	2053	2412	5.6	3.04	1376	1737	5.6
08887	THREE BRIDGES	019	817	812	842	-0.1	15	441	442	462	0.1	1.81	188	187	-0.1
08889	WHITEHOUSE STATION	019	9204	9872	10600	1.7	81	3321	3585	3872	1.8	2.74	2602	2825	2.0
08901	NEW BRUNSWICK	023	48588	50767	52714	1.0	68	13058	13426	13864	0.7	3.30	7202	7492	0.9
08902	NORTH BRUNSWICK	023	36717	38506	40303	1.1	71	13796	14466	15128	1.1	2.58	9475	10011	1.3
08904	HIGHLAND PARK	023	13976	14453	15039	0.8	58	5812	6016	6254	0.8	2.40	3381	3518	0.9
	NEW JERSEY					0.8					0.9	2.68			1.0
	UNITED STATES					1.2					1.3	2.58			1.1

ZIP CODE #	POST OFFICE NAME	RACE (%) White 2000	White 2004	Black 2000	Black 2004	Asian/Pacific 2000	Asian/Pacific 2004	% Hispanic Origin 2000	% Hispanic Origin 2004	2004 AGE DISTRIBUTION (%) 0-4	5-9	10-14	15-19	20-24	25-44	45-64	65-84	85+	18+	MEDIAN AGE 2004	% 2004 Males	% 2004 Females
08721	BAYVILLE	95.9	95.1	1.4	1.5	0.8	1.0	3.8	4.7	5.8	6.0	6.7	6.4	5.5	27.1	25.8	15.0	1.7	77.5	40.4	48.5	51.5
08722	BEACHWOOD	95.4	94.6	1.2	1.3	1.2	1.4	4.3	5.4	6.9	7.5	8.4	6.8	5.7	30.2	25.6	8.1	0.9	72.9	36.2	49.1	50.9
08723	BRICK	95.4	94.5	0.9	1.1	1.2	1.5	4.7	5.9	6.1	6.4	6.9	5.9	5.4	27.4	25.6	14.2	2.1	77.0	40.1	48.4	51.7
08724	BRICK	96.0	95.3	1.1	1.2	1.2	1.5	3.3	4.1	6.3	6.5	7.1	5.8	4.8	26.4	25.1	14.8	3.2	76.5	41.0	46.9	53.1
08730	BRIELLE	93.1	91.8	3.5	4.1	0.7	0.8	3.3	4.2	6.9	7.3	6.5	5.7	4.0	22.0	29.3	16.5	1.9	75.8	43.6	47.8	52.2
08731	FORKED RIVER	97.9	97.4	0.4	0.5	0.5	0.7	2.2	2.8	6.1	6.5	7.1	6.2	4.8	25.9	26.7	14.8	2.0	76.5	41.1	48.9	51.1
08733	LAKEHURST	81.4	79.5	9.9	10.5	2.9	3.4	8.1	9.8	8.8	7.6	7.3	7.2	7.7	35.2	19.1	6.4	0.7	72.2	31.4	53.9	46.1
08734	LANOKA HARBOR	97.8	97.3	0.2	0.3	0.6	0.8	2.0	2.6	6.3	6.8	8.0	7.3	5.8	26.8	28.2	9.8	1.0	74.4	38.5	48.7	51.3
08735	LAVALLETTE	98.4	98.1	0.2	0.2	0.3	0.4	1.6	2.0	3.0	3.0	3.1	2.8	2.6	16.8	31.6	31.6	5.6	89.3	58.2	47.2	52.8
08736	MANASQUAN	97.8	97.2	0.4	0.5	0.9	1.1	2.7	3.3	6.1	6.6	6.9	5.9	4.5	24.4	28.1	15.5	2.0	76.6	42.5	48.7	51.3
08738	MANTOLOKING	99.3	99.1	0.5	0.6	0.2	0.2	0.6	0.7	1.5	1.7	2.5	2.5	1.8	12.5	41.9	32.5	3.1	93.0	59.8	49.8	50.2
08740	OCEAN GATE	96.6	95.9	1.0	1.1	1.0	1.2	2.4	3.0	7.0	6.8	7.6	6.8	6.2	28.9	23.3	11.7	1.7	74.5	37.3	47.2	52.8
08741	PINE BEACH	98.2	97.9	0.3	0.3	0.7	0.9	2.5	3.1	5.3	6.0	6.9	5.7	4.8	25.0	29.4	15.0	2.0	78.3	43.0	48.6	51.4
08742	POINT PLEASANT BEACH	97.5	96.9	0.3	0.4	0.7	0.8	2.8	3.5	5.4	5.7	6.6	5.9	5.1	26.7	28.1	14.0	2.5	78.4	41.9	48.6	51.4
08750	SEA GIRT	98.7	98.4	0.2	0.2	0.6	0.8	1.3	1.6	5.2	6.1	6.4	5.4	3.5	19.1	28.8	21.2	4.3	78.8	47.8	47.4	52.6
08751	SEASIDE HEIGHTS	93.1	92.4	2.6	2.8	0.6	0.8	7.1	8.4	5.8	5.4	5.5	5.0	6.4	29.4	26.2	14.1	2.3	80.4	40.3	50.2	49.8
08752	SEASIDE PARK	97.8	97.6	0.3	0.3	0.6	0.7	2.1	2.6	4.5	4.2	3.3	3.0	3.9	23.0	31.4	23.2	3.5	86.1	50.1	48.9	51.2
08753	TOMS RIVER	94.2	93.2	1.4	1.6	2.1	2.6	4.7	5.8	5.8	6.0	6.9	6.4	6.0	27.2	27.6	12.1	2.0	77.4	39.8	48.5	51.5
08755	TOMS RIVER	91.5	90.1	2.7	3.0	3.8	4.4	4.3	5.3	5.1	5.4	6.1	5.6	4.5	22.1	23.9	24.6	2.7	79.7	45.9	47.0	53.0
08757	TOMS RIVER	92.9	92.4	4.6	4.7	0.7	0.9	3.1	3.7	2.4	2.5	2.8	2.6	2.3	11.0	16.1	50.7	9.8	90.8	70.6	43.3	56.7
08758	WARETOWN	97.4	96.9	0.7	0.8	0.4	0.6	3.1	3.8	5.9	6.1	7.5	7.5	5.4	28.0	25.9	11.9	1.9	75.8	39.1	49.8	50.3
08759	MANCHESTER TOWNSHIP	96.3	95.8	2.0	2.2	0.6	0.7	1.7	2.2	1.4	1.5	1.7	1.7	1.5	7.3	17.0	53.1	14.7	94.3	72.8	40.3	59.7
08801	ANNANDALE	82.9	81.4	10.8	11.2	2.2	2.7	5.3	6.2	5.8	7.1	7.4	6.3	10.9	27.8	27.6	6.5	0.7	76.0	35.2	56.7	43.3
08802	ASBURY	97.6	97.2	0.9	0.9	0.8	1.0	1.2	1.5	6.3	7.7	8.6	6.6	4.2	26.0	32.0	7.8	0.9	73.1	40.5	50.6	49.4
08804	BLOOMSBURY	97.3	96.6	0.8	0.9	0.7	0.9	1.8	2.3	9.0	9.5	8.0	5.3	3.8	28.7	26.5	8.3	0.9	69.9	38.1	49.0	51.0
08805	BOUND BROOK	84.1	82.0	2.3	2.4	3.4	3.8	29.8	33.9	6.8	6.4	6.0	5.8	6.9	34.0	21.5	11.0	1.6	77.3	36.2	51.5	48.5
08807	BRIDGEWATER	83.8	80.9	2.4	2.7	11.4	13.5	5.1	6.6	7.5	7.9	7.2	5.3	4.1	30.0	25.3	10.6	2.1	73.7	38.9	48.0	52.0
08809	CLINTON	92.9	91.8	2.0	2.1	3.1	3.7	3.3	4.0	6.0	6.7	6.7	5.4	4.3	32.5	28.8	8.7	1.0	76.9	39.5	48.1	52.0
08810	DAYTON	63.8	59.4	9.3	9.6	23.4	26.9	5.0	6.2	8.2	8.9	9.3	6.8	4.6	32.8	24.2	4.7	0.4	69.2	35.0	48.2	51.8
08812	DUNELLEN	85.0	82.4	3.6	3.8	5.5	6.7	10.5	12.9	7.0	7.1	7.3	5.9	5.2	29.7	25.1	10.7	2.0	74.8	38.5	49.2	50.8
08816	EAST BRUNSWICK	77.2	73.4	2.9	3.0	16.6	19.6	4.3	5.3	5.9	6.5	7.6	6.8	5.3	26.4	29.2	11.0	1.3	75.6	40.3	48.5	51.6
08817	EDISON	60.1	56.9	8.3	8.2	26.2	28.7	8.4	10.2	7.0	6.1	6.1	6.0	6.8	35.1	22.4	9.4	1.1	77.3	34.7	49.5	50.5
08820	EDISON	53.8	48.5	5.2	5.5	38.4	43.1	3.0	3.7	6.0	6.3	6.7	6.3	5.7	27.5	29.0	11.3	1.2	77.0	40.0	48.6	51.4
08822	FLEMINGTON	93.2	92.0	1.4	1.5	3.0	3.6	3.8	4.6	6.8	7.6	8.2	6.5	4.6	27.9	28.6	8.4	1.5	72.9	39.1	48.7	51.3
08823	FRANKLIN PARK	58.0	53.6	18.6	19.9	19.5	22.0	5.1	6.1	8.5	7.7	6.0	4.7	5.0	38.2	22.0	6.9	1.0	74.8	35.8	47.9	52.1
08824	KENDALL PARK	74.9	70.8	5.3	5.6	16.9	20.1	4.3	5.3	8.2	8.6	9.1	6.7	5.0	28.3	25.4	8.1	0.7	69.5	36.5	48.3	51.7
08825	FRENCHTOWN	97.0	96.5	0.6	0.7	0.9	1.1	2.0	2.5	6.6	7.1	7.5	6.5	4.5	27.2	29.5	9.8	1.5	74.8	40.5	49.8	50.2
08826	GLEN GARDNER	96.6	96.0	0.8	0.9	1.2	1.4	2.3	2.8	6.3	7.1	7.7	6.2	4.2	28.1	29.3	9.5	1.5	74.8	40.3	49.0	51.0
08827	HAMPTON	91.7	90.6	5.0	5.5	1.1	1.3	3.0	3.7	6.7	7.5	7.6	6.2	5.1	29.7	28.2	8.0	1.0	74.2	38.3	48.8	51.3
08828	HELMETTA	93.2	91.8	2.4	2.7	2.5	3.0	5.4	6.9	6.7	6.7	5.9	5.2	4.7	38.9	25.3	5.9	0.7	77.4	37.2	49.3	50.7
08829	HIGH BRIDGE	96.2	95.6	0.8	0.9	1.5	1.8	2.1	2.6	8.2	8.3	7.2	6.1	4.5	31.8	27.0	6.2	0.8	72.1	37.2	48.7	51.4
08830	ISELIN	64.3	59.9	6.1	6.3	25.5	29.0	5.4	6.7	6.1	5.7	6.1	5.7	6.0	31.9	24.7	12.5	1.3	78.7	38.2	49.1	51.0
08831	MONROE TOWNSHIP	91.5	90.1	3.9	4.4	2.4	2.8	3.8	4.8	4.5	4.9	4.7	4.9	3.1	18.8	20.3	33.0	5.8	82.8	53.9	46.1	53.9
08832	KEASBEY	38.5	37.2	22.5	21.3	10.0	10.6	39.0	41.8	8.8	8.8	7.9	6.0	7.1	38.9	16.7	5.4	0.5	70.5	30.8	48.4	51.6
08833	LEBANON	94.8	94.0	1.3	1.3	2.7	3.3	1.8	2.3	7.2	8.3	7.9	6.2	3.7	23.9	31.7	10.0	1.2	72.5	41.3	49.7	50.3
08835	MANVILLE	96.0	95.1	0.5	0.5	1.4	1.6	5.4	7.0	5.1	5.2	6.1	5.7	5.7	29.7	25.2	15.4	2.0	80.2	40.9	49.2	50.8
08836	MARTINSVILLE	92.2	90.7	0.9	1.0	5.9	7.2	1.9	2.5	6.7	8.4	9.0	6.3	3.3	21.9	30.9	12.0	1.6	71.3	42.2	49.3	50.7
08837	EDISON	72.1	68.4	7.0	7.4	15.8	18.3	8.5	10.5	5.7	5.2	5.3	5.1	5.5	32.9	22.3	14.7	3.3	80.6	39.4	48.5	51.5
08840	METUCHEN	81.7	78.7	5.4	5.9	9.6	11.5	4.6	5.9	6.3	6.7	6.8	5.8	4.6	28.2	26.9	13.1	1.6	76.5	40.6	47.9	52.1
08844	HILLSBOROUGH	86.1	83.5	3.7	4.2	7.3	8.8	4.7	6.0	7.6	8.2	8.4	6.7	5.1	30.3	26.4	6.6	0.8	71.4	36.7	49.5	50.5
08846	MIDDLESEX	87.3	84.7	3.4	3.6	4.2	5.1	9.0	11.6	6.5	6.6	6.9	6.3	5.4	28.7	25.8	12.2	1.7	76.1	39.1	48.8	51.2
08848	MILFORD	97.7	97.3	0.4	0.4	0.5	0.6	1.8	2.2	5.9	7.1	8.1	6.0	3.8	24.5	30.6	12.3	1.8	75.1	42.2	49.9	50.1
08850	MILLTOWN	93.3	91.9	0.9	1.0	3.6	4.4	3.5	4.5	5.5	6.0	7.0	6.3	4.9	26.4	28.3	13.8	1.9	77.6	41.6	48.9	51.2
08852	MONMOUTH JUNCTION	68.9	64.6	9.5	10.1	17.8	20.7	5.8	7.3	8.0	7.8	7.4	5.5	5.7	37.0	23.0	5.2	0.6	73.4	34.4	48.3	51.7
08853	NESHANIC STATION	90.6	88.9	2.1	2.3	6.1	7.3	2.3	2.9	7.8	9.0	8.6	5.6	3.5	29.5	28.7	6.6	0.8	71.0	38.1	50.2	49.8
08854	PISCATAWAY	48.7	44.6	20.3	20.6	25.0	27.9	7.9	9.4	6.1	6.0	6.0	9.1	8.4	31.6	23.3	8.6	0.9	78.4	34.4	49.5	50.6
08857	OLD BRIDGE	81.8	79.0	4.4	4.7	10.0	11.6	7.4	9.4	6.8	6.9	7.2	6.3	5.7	30.8	25.1	9.9	1.3	75.2	37.5	48.8	51.2
08859	PARLIN	76.7	72.9	6.5	7.3	12.2	14.4	8.3	10.5	6.4	6.5	6.9	6.0	5.5	31.3	25.1	11.2	1.2	76.5	38.1	48.9	51.1
08861	PERTH AMBOY	47.7	45.2	9.8	9.3	2.0	2.1	67.2	71.5	8.1	7.6	8.1	7.5	8.4	31.0	19.6	8.4	1.4	71.8	31.6	49.8	50.2
08863	FORDS	70.9	66.8	6.4	6.7	17.4	20.1	9.3	11.6	6.6	5.9	5.9	5.8	6.0	32.8	23.3	12.1	1.7	78.3	37.4	48.3	51.8
08865	PHILLIPSBURG	94.3	93.6	2.2	2.4	0.9	1.2	3.7	4.4	6.8	6.8	7.3	6.5	5.6	26.8	24.2	13.4	2.6	75.0	39.2	48.0	52.0
08867	PITTSTOWN	86.2	84.4	9.8	10.8	1.3	1.5	4.4	5.3	5.2	6.0	6.6	5.7	4.1	34.3	28.2	8.3	1.5	78.6	39.9	43.9	56.1
08869	RARITAN	87.7	85.5	0.9	1.1	8.3	9.8	8.4	10.5	7.4	7.2	6.2	4.9	5.0	32.7	22.1	12.4	2.2	76.0	38.0	48.0	52.0
08872	SAYREVILLE	71.1	68.4	12.4	12.7	11.8	13.4	7.8	9.7	7.2	7.0	6.6	5.9	5.8	33.0	23.9	9.2	1.5	75.5	36.1	49.2	50.8
08873	SOMERSET	53.8	50.5	28.0	29.0	11.4	13.1	8.8	10.3	6.8	6.6	6.3	5.6	5.4	33.0	24.3	10.1	1.9	76.8	37.5	47.8	52.2
08876	SOMERVILLE	80.3	78.2	7.8	8.1	6.7	7.7	10.4	12.4	7.6	7.6	6.9	5.1	5.0	31.9	24.2	10.2	1.5	74.7	37.7	49.6	50.5
08879	SOUTH AMBOY	83.8	81.7	5.0	5.4	6.1	6.9	7.4	9.4	6.2	6.3	7.0	6.6	6.0	31.1	24.9	10.5	1.4	76.4	37.6	49.5	50.5
08880	SOUTH BOUND BROOK	78.0	75.3	7.8	8.2	4.2	4.6	22.8	27.1	6.3	6.3	7.2	5.6	6.4	34.4	23.9	8.6	1.5	77.0	36.5	51.6	48.5
08882	SOUTH RIVER	83.6	80.9	6.1	6.5	3.6	4.3	9.7	12.3	6.7	6.4	6.5	5.8	6.2	31.7	23.0	11.6	2.1	77.0	37.2	49.7	50.3
08884	SPOTSWOOD	93.8	92.5	1.5	1.7	2.9	3.7	4.4	5.7	5.9	6.1	6.4	5.7	5.5	27.5	26.0	15.0	1.9	78.1	40.8	48.7	51.3
08886	STEWARTSVILLE	94.0	92.9	2.1	2.5	2.0	2.5	3.5	4.3	10.7	11.1	9.1	5.4	3.2	31.2	22.4	5.7	1.2	65.5	35.1	49.0	51.1
08887	THREE BRIDGES	91.8	90.3	0.5	0.5	6.5	7.8	3.4	4.2	5.1	4.9	5.2	4.8	4.9	39.4	24.8	9.5	1.5	81.4	38.7	46.2	53.8
08889	WHITEHOUSE STATION	95.4	94.4	0.7	0.9	2.2	2.8	2.0	2.5	7.1	8.0	7.7	5.3	3.4	26.8	30.5	9.9	1.2	73.5	40.7	49.4	50.6
08901	NEW BRUNSWICK	48.9	46.4	23.0	22.2	5.4	6.0	39.0	43.2	7.1	5.7	5.2	11.7	24.3	27.6	12.2	5.4	0.9	79.2	24.2	49.6	50.4
08902	NORTH BRUNSWICK	63.0	58.9	15.2	15.6	14.1	16.4	10.4	12.7	6.6	6.4	6.3	6.1	6.4	33.9	24.1	9.2	1.1	77.0	36.3	49.7	50.3
08904	HIGHLAND PARK	72.4	69.9	8.0	8.0	13.3	14.5	8.3	10.2	5.8	5.5	6.5	6.6	7.5	33.9	22.6	9.9	1.8	78.2	35.6	48.4	51.6
	NEW JERSEY	72.6	70.5	13.6	13.8	5.8	6.6	13.3	15.0	6.6	6.7	7.1	6.5	6.3	28.8	24.6	11.5	1.9	75.6	37.7	48.6	51.4
	UNITED STATES	75.1	73.6	12.3	12.5	3.8	4.2	12.5	14.1	6.9	6.7	7.2	7.0	7.3	28.6	23.8	10.8	1.7	75.1	36.0	49.1	50.9

ZIP CODE #	POST OFFICE NAME	2004 Per Capita Income	2004 HH Income Base	2004 Household Income Distribution (%): Less than $25,000	$25,000 to $49,999	$50,000 to $99,999	$100,000 to $149,999	$150,000 or More	Median Household Income: 2004	2009	2004 National Centile	2004 State Centile	2004 Home Value Base	2004 Home Value Distribution (%): Less than $50,000	$50,000 to $89,999	$90,000 to $174,999	$175,000 to $399,999	$400,000 or More	2004 Median Home Value
08721	BAYVILLE	25272	7068	18.0	26.9	36.0	13.9	5.2	55857	61336	81	30	5989	1.0	0.1	26.0	66.2	6.8	215323
08722	BEACHWOOD	24576	3804	9.5	25.6	43.9	15.4	5.6	63461	71030	87	44	3350	0.0	0.4	35.6	63.7	0.4	188365
08723	BRICK	27177	12990	16.6	27.2	37.3	13.6	5.3	55680	61698	80	30	10189	0.2	0.2	22.4	68.8	8.4	222440
08724	BRICK	27874	17484	17.5	24.6	37.3	13.8	6.8	58554	64056	83	34	14497	0.8	2.7	26.5	62.0	7.9	221525
08730	BRIELLE	42236	1943	13.1	15.1	33.6	19.0	19.2	78494	94510	95	68	1597	0.9	0.4	0.8	38.2	59.6	454821
08731	FORKED RIVER	26778	7545	16.1	25.2	38.2	15.7	4.8	59394	66100	84	37	6683	0.0	0.6	26.1	65.5	7.9	213909
08733	LAKEHURST	19608	984	21.4	32.1	34.6	8.9	3.0	47536	53057	67	17	608	5.1	6.3	56.3	29.0	3.5	147256
08734	LANOKA HARBOR	25720	2506	10.5	23.7	40.7	19.7	5.4	69452	78479	91	55	2243	0.0	0.3	21.8	67.1	10.9	237975
08735	LAVALLETTE	35546	2282	21.8	28.8	30.0	10.7	8.8	49361	56621	71	21	1924	0.6	0.4	3.9	40.4	54.8	431507
08736	MANASQUAN	42572	5457	9.9	16.4	33.5	22.1	18.1	84155	102123	96	75	4447	0.4	0.2	1.0	38.8	59.6	452198
08738	MANTOLOKING	70890	711	13.4	17.0	29.5	15.5	24.6	82045	94064	96	72	640	1.3	0.0	0.8	18.3	79.7	723837
08740	OCEAN GATE	22142	790	25.3	30.1	32.7	8.7	3.2	45631	51370	63	15	522	0.0	0.6	50.8	46.2	2.5	173465
08741	PINE BEACH	29136	1009	14.9	23.7	37.3	17.6	6.5	63477	69606	87	44	882	1.0	0.2	14.2	72.1	12.5	244978
08742	POINT PLEASANT BEACH	31496	11028	17.6	22.4	35.4	15.5	9.2	61360	67310	86	41	8223	0.2	0.3	5.7	69.6	24.2	288988
08750	SEA GIRT	60571	1639	10.3	15.3	28.7	22.2	23.5	90920	108648	97	80	1374	0.1	0.3	1.4	18.6	79.6	705556
08751	SEASIDE HEIGHTS	22572	2555	40.0	28.3	21.4	8.0	2.4	32941	35906	21	3	1131	0.4	1.6	24.1	58.3	15.7	241583
08752	SEASIDE PARK	34467	1549	21.9	28.9	26.4	14.4	8.5	49291	55282	71	20	986	0.0	0.0	7.0	63.0	30.0	337061
08753	TOMS RIVER	27797	24900	18.0	22.4	35.8	15.6	8.3	61743	67301	86	42	20079	0.1	1.3	19.0	69.2	10.4	238391
08755	TOMS RIVER	28826	9693	19.4	23.7	35.3	14.3	7.4	57078	61886	82	33	8687	6.5	4.2	12.3	61.8	15.1	259114
08757	TOMS RIVER	23417	18899	33.8	39.6	21.6	3.4	1.6	33669	38012	23	4	17436	1.2	2.3	58.2	38.0	0.3	160514
08758	WARETOWN	25284	2224	18.1	31.5	33.4	11.0	6.1	50310	56601	72	21	1803	0.5	1.5	47.5	43.8	6.7	175957
08759	MANCHESTER TOWNSHIP	25480	19223	40.4	34.4	18.5	4.4	2.3	29919	33387	12	3	17624	15.3	24.1	36.0	23.7	1.0	111988
08801	ANNANDALE	44612	2490	4.7	6.8	30.4	27.7	30.4	111217	130267	99	93	2243	0.0	0.0	7.3	36.4	56.3	436658
08802	ASBURY	38575	1434	6.2	14.6	35.3	25.3	18.6	89683	104754	97	80	1312	0.7	0.0	6.7	50.2	42.4	372067
08804	BLOOMSBURY	37340	849	8.1	17.1	36.8	25.1	13.0	82169	98057	96	73	764	0.4	0.3	8.9	62.3	28.1	311640
08805	BOUND BROOK	29974	4508	15.3	27.7	31.4	14.9	10.7	57550	66615	82	33	2511	0.0	0.2	11.8	71.7	16.3	262957
08807	BRIDGEWATER	44338	14328	8.4	12.2	32.6	23.3	23.5	93649	110510	98	83	11767	0.3	1.2	7.4	47.0	44.2	369961
08809	CLINTON	43913	2426	9.3	18.7	34.3	21.3	16.5	79709	94287	95	69	1864	0.4	0.9	20.1	52.3	26.4	309465
08810	DAYTON	33154	2522	4.5	14.8	38.1	28.2	14.4	89161	103230	97	79	2247	0.5	1.1	11.2	71.3	15.8	259428
08812	DUNELLEN	37124	4572	12.0	19.4	35.8	18.2	14.6	74423	86125	93	62	3606	0.2	0.2	7.3	73.2	19.1	264242
08816	EAST BRUNSWICK	38160	16404	9.6	15.8	34.3	22.3	18.1	83426	96887	96	74	13940	1.1	1.4	10.8	61.8	24.9	301104
08817	EDISON	30615	16478	11.5	19.4	40.5	19.3	9.3	70303	80190	91	56	9784	2.9	1.8	12.2	78.0	5.1	232157
08820	EDISON	40434	13296	11.1	12.6	29.8	22.9	23.7	93303	106319	97	83	10367	0.9	0.5	2.0	61.3	35.3	350661
08822	FLEMINGTON	43560	11034	9.4	17.5	29.1	20.8	23.2	87756	104047	97	78	8824	0.2	0.2	7.3	48.8	43.5	369285
08823	FRANKLIN PARK	41811	3175	7.4	18.5	40.1	19.3	14.8	77809	93901	94	67	2108	0.5	1.8	23.4	52.5	21.8	238876
08824	KENDALL PARK	34301	4046	8.8	13.5	29.3	29.0	19.4	96669	111402	98	85	3577	2.2	0.6	3.9	68.1	25.2	294706
08825	FRENCHTOWN	34017	1767	15.3	17.4	35.7	17.5	14.2	75695	85700	93	65	1402	0.0	0.1	4.4	63.8	31.7	335101
08826	GLEN GARDNER	36062	2284	9.5	15.6	37.6	19.7	17.6	81214	94888	95	71	1855	0.0	0.2	14.6	51.3	33.9	329028
08827	HAMPTON	38372	1651	12.3	13.3	29.9	23.1	21.4	89322	105273	97	79	1363	0.7	0.2	4.5	49.2	45.4	379373
08828	HELMETTA	31105	817	9.9	19.5	49.3	18.2	3.1	67153	76981	90	52	723	0.0	0.3	49.1	47.2	3.5	176339
08829	HIGH BRIDGE	34193	1426	7.2	19.2	43.6	20.1	9.9	76827	87745	94	66	1183	0.0	0.4	16.0	78.9	4.7	244303
08830	ISELIN	30373	5910	12.3	19.3	38.5	20.1	9.8	72296	82156	92	59	4488	0.4	0.4	14.9	82.4	1.9	225480
08831	MONROE TOWNSHIP	34761	15926	15.6	25.3	33.4	16.6	9.1	61651	69942	86	42	14594	0.6	2.1	20.2	62.1	15.1	244757
08832	KEASBEY	24157	946	22.1	22.3	38.8	11.6	5.2	57382	64833	82	33	192	4.7	0.0	35.4	59.9	0.0	188571
08833	LEBANON	59990	3441	4.3	8.3	30.1	23.5	33.8	112676	132255	99	93	3082	0.4	0.2	1.8	36.9	60.8	469895
08835	MANVILLE	27213	4223	16.0	26.4	37.2	16.1	4.3	57553	66601	82	34	2882	0.5	0.4	12.6	85.9	0.8	223118
08836	MARTINSVILLE	65025	1357	6.3	7.7	15.9	25.9	44.2	138755	163909	100	98	1316	0.2	0.2	2.3	19.8	77.5	582785
08837	EDISON	31402	6272	16.2	22.6	37.4	16.5	7.4	63160	71206	87	44	3239	2.5	7.4	11.2	74.7	4.2	241633
08840	METUCHEN	40073	5897	10.5	16.4	34.2	22.8	16.2	81541	92692	95	72	4900	0.3	0.1	7.9	72.7	19.0	278133
08844	HILLSBOROUGH	38536	13720	6.5	12.1	34.8	26.5	20.2	93795	111346	98	83	11210	0.2	0.5	9.8	53.9	35.7	343242
08846	MIDDLESEX	32663	5056	12.6	22.6	37.8	18.2	8.8	66529	76120	89	50	3765	0.6	0.6	7.3	86.4	5.1	247415
08848	MILFORD	34368	3137	10.6	16.9	38.0	21.7	12.8	77585	92284	94	67	2827	0.1	0.2	8.1	64.1	27.5	310099
08850	MILLTOWN	35814	3088	11.2	16.7	36.8	23.0	12.5	77810	87671	94	67	2647	0.0	0.2	5.4	81.9	12.5	276126
08852	MONMOUTH JUNCTION	38767	5873	7.9	16.1	40.8	20.6	14.7	79868	92005	95	69	3600	6.3	0.9	17.9	53.8	21.1	259940
08853	NESHANIC STATION	47471	1853	6.6	12.1	23.1	24.2	33.9	114361	134453	99	94	1640	0.0	0.0	0.6	32.2	67.3	477322
08854	PISCATAWAY	31063	17581	10.3	18.3	39.5	20.7	11.2	75111	84150	93	63	12125	0.4	0.9	10.9	78.8	9.0	251743
08857	OLD BRIDGE	30314	13396	11.4	20.5	38.1	19.8	10.2	72153	80561	92	58	9152	0.1	0.0	8.3	83.7	7.9	252053
08859	PARLIN	28335	7896	13.4	23.0	38.7	18.6	6.3	65253	73929	89	48	5138	0.9	0.1	11.5	83.0	4.6	228784
08861	PERTH AMBOY	16840	15730	28.4	30.2	29.7	8.9	2.9	42226	47309	54	11	7036	0.1	1.6	32.5	64.1	1.7	197174
08863	FORDS	30941	5071	13.8	20.9	37.1	19.3	9.0	67041	77282	90	52	3322	0.5	0.1	12.1	85.5	1.8	233625
08865	PHILLIPSBURG	23709	11864	26.4	25.2	34.4	10.4	3.6	48355	53632	69	18	8255	0.5	4.1	42.5	49.1	3.9	181567
08867	PITTSTOWN	35927	1672	8.1	12.3	27.0	27.4	25.2	103588	121731	98	89	1520	0.0	0.0	1.7	36.5	61.8	472764
08869	RARITAN	31558	2630	15.2	25.9	34.9	14.9	9.2	57659	67454	82	34	1713	0.0	0.4	6.8	76.6	16.3	272604
08872	SAYREVILLE	27888	6773	12.7	23.4	40.5	16.6	6.8	64458	74396	88	46	4364	0.4	0.1	13.7	79.3	6.6	231784
08873	SOMERSET	34631	16515	11.3	18.2	37.5	20.4	12.6	76123	88359	94	66	11195	0.6	0.5	13.6	76.3	9.0	245276
08876	SOMERVILLE	36171	8920	14.8	16.7	33.5	19.0	15.9	75345	87232	93	63	5922	1.6	0.4	7.5	60.3	30.3	297503
08879	SOUTH AMBOY	26575	8463	16.3	24.4	39.1	15.2	5.0	59698	67105	84	37	5311	0.2	0.9	23.7	71.2	3.9	212874
08880	SOUTH BOUND BROOK	25111	1676	18.1	26.6	36.6	14.4	4.3	54922	63519	80	28	964	1.0	1.0	21.7	75.3	0.9	207125
08882	SOUTH RIVER	26909	5593	17.9	24.7	35.1	15.5	6.7	59273	66416	84	36	3962	0.9	0.7	19.8	72.3	6.3	222447
08884	SPOTSWOOD	29011	3184	20.5	21.1	34.2	17.9	6.3	60580	68698	85	39	2544	2.4	7.2	15.3	71.5	3.6	219904
08886	STEWARTSVILLE	36547	2053	9.3	15.0	33.4	25.6	16.8	88246	101996	97	78	1875	0.5	0.5	7.3	56.9	34.8	335779
08887	THREE BRIDGES	50967	442	20.6	18.1	30.8	18.3	12.2	69050	82232	91	55	262	0.0	0.0	76.3	19.9	3.8	153438
08889	WHITEHOUSE STATION	50176	3585	6.0	10.9	29.0	25.2	28.9	106264	126036	99	90	3288	0.8	0.3	2.4	44.0	52.4	414338
08901	NEW BRUNSWICK	16668	13426	29.7	31.0	27.1	8.4	3.7	39867	45638	45	9	3708	1.4	1.4	37.8	57.6	1.9	189113
08902	NORTH BRUNSWICK	32887	14466	13.0	20.8	38.3	16.8	11.1	67330	76421	90	53	9381	0.5	2.9	19.1	62.4	15.0	248182
08904	HIGHLAND PARK	32832	6016	18.1	24.8	32.4	13.8	11.0	59220	66271	84	36	2855	1.3	0.1	10.5	68.2	19.9	265797
	NEW JERSEY	31614		18.6	22.5	32.1	15.5	11.4	61437	70239				1.5	2.7	19.7	54.4	21.8	255213
	UNITED STATES	25866		24.7	27.1	30.8	10.9	6.5	48124	56710				10.9	15.0	33.7	30.1	10.4	145905

SPENDING POTENTIAL INDICES

08721-08904 **D**

# ZIP CODE / POST OFFICE NAME	FINANCIAL SERVICES				THE HOME						ENTERTAINMENT						PERSONAL			
					Home Improvements		Furnishings													
	Auto Loan	Home Loan	Invest-ments	Retire-ment Plans	Home Repair	Lawn & Garden	Comput-ers & Hard-ware	Major Appli-ances	TV, Radio, Sound Equip-ment	Furni-ture	Dine out/ Carry out	Sports Equip-ment	Fees & Tickets	Toys & Games	Travel	Cable TV	Apparel & Services	Auto Repairs	Health Insur-ance	Pets & Supplies
08721 BAYVILLE	93	106	111	104	105	110	97	100	94	99	118	111	102	119	100	94	116	97	97	110
08722 BEACHWOOD	97	114	121	113	111	111	106	105	100	106	126	122	110	131	107	97	125	103	95	115
08723 BRICK	91	103	112	102	102	106	99	98	95	98	120	113	102	122	100	94	118	97	94	108
08724 BRICK	98	108	116	107	107	113	102	104	99	103	125	117	105	124	104	99	122	102	101	114
08730 BRIELLE	135	167	200	167	164	171	153	151	144	153	181	174	164	188	158	142	181	148	140	165
08731 FORKED RIVER	95	106	110	102	106	112	98	101	97	98	121	114	102	124	102	98	118	98	101	113
08733 LAKEHURST	83	78	79	80	77	83	84	81	83	82	104	97	82	103	80	81	101	84	78	91
08734 LANOKA HARBOR	103	118	121	117	116	117	108	109	103	108	129	127	113	135	110	101	128	106	101	122
08735 LAVALLETTE	119	97	72	88	107	122	91	108	101	91	121	122	84	115	97	108	113	106	127	142
08736 MANASQUAN	141	165	187	163	164	171	152	153	146	153	183	177	160	189	157	145	181	150	146	171
08738 MANTOLOKING	240	195	145	178	217	246	183	218	204	185	245	247	168	233	196	218	228	214	257	288
08740 OCEAN GATE	85	75	62	69	81	90	72	80	78	70	95	92	69	97	76	83	89	79	92	102
08741 PINE BEACH	97	114	126	110	113	121	107	107	105	106	131	120	113	137	111	106	129	104	106	117
08742 POINT PLEASANT BEACH	102	115	128	114	115	121	109	110	106	109	133	127	114	137	112	106	131	109	106	123
08750 SEA GIRT	182	221	257	218	219	233	200	202	190	202	239	226	215	241	209	190	237	196	194	221
08751 SEASIDE HEIGHTS	70	59	53	56	62	70	63	66	68	61	82	77	59	81	63	70	78	67	73	81
08752 SEASIDE PARK	117	91	62	83	103	116	86	104	98	85	116	122	77	114	92	104	108	102	123	142
08753 TOMS RIVER	99	115	126	114	113	118	108	108	104	108	130	123	113	133	110	103	128	106	103	118
08755 TOMS RIVER	105	108	109	104	110	123	100	108	102	104	127	113	103	118	106	105	121	105	116	121
08757 TOMS RIVER	64	64	67	59	66	78	59	67	63	63	78	65	61	68	64	66	73	65	76	73
08758 WARETOWN	85	99	107	96	98	104	94	93	93	92	116	106	100	124	97	94	114	91	92	102
08759 MANCHESTER TOWNSHIP	63	61	64	57	64	77	57	65	61	61	75	63	58	64	62	65	71	63	76	71
08801 ANNANDALE	178	219	243	226	213	216	197	192	181	199	230	223	214	238	200	176	231	187	172	212
08802 ASBURY	148	184	199	188	179	179	163	160	149	164	189	185	177	198	166	144	190	154	142	177
08804 BLOOMSBURY	136	159	166	163	154	154	146	144	135	148	171	168	153	175	146	129	170	141	128	158
08805 BOUND BROOK	103	116	162	115	113	123	118	113	119	118	151	130	123	159	120	121	150	115	110	124
08807 BRIDGEWATER	154	189	222	187	182	187	172	170	162	175	204	196	183	214	176	159	205	167	153	184
08809 CLINTON	126	151	185	152	147	153	144	140	137	144	173	163	152	180	146	135	172	139	129	152
08810 DAYTON	146	167	164	174	159	155	150	149	137	156	175	174	156	176	147	129	173	144	127	163
08812 DUNELLEN	133	163	194	160	157	162	150	148	144	152	182	169	160	192	154	142	183	146	134	160
08816 EAST BRUNSWICK	137	173	203	171	167	171	156	153	146	158	184	177	167	194	160	143	185	150	137	166
08817 EDISON	106	123	157	126	121	124	122	119	115	121	145	142	125	148	123	111	144	121	106	128
08820 EDISON	143	186	236	190	184	184	172	170	157	171	197	202	182	206	178	151	199	168	147	181
08822 FLEMINGTON	157	184	207	189	178	181	171	167	160	173	203	195	181	208	172	154	202	165	149	183
08823 FRANKLIN PARK	141	160	154	167	152	147	144	143	132	150	168	167	148	168	140	123	166	139	121	156
08824 KENDALL PARK	138	170	191	171	164	166	153	150	143	155	180	173	164	188	156	139	181	146	135	164
08825 FRENCHTOWN	121	147	164	149	144	144	135	133	126	135	159	157	143	167	137	122	158	130	120	146
08826 GLEN GARDNER	134	152	162	157	148	147	143	140	134	144	169	165	148	172	142	127	168	139	124	155
08827 HAMPTON	153	167	167	171	166	173	155	156	149	155	186	180	163	190	156	146	183	151	149	176
08828 HELMETTA	109	106	114	114	102	104	110	106	105	113	134	127	108	128	104	98	131	109	93	117
08829 HIGH BRIDGE	121	143	147	146	139	137	130	129	120	131	151	151	136	157	130	115	151	125	113	142
08830 ISELIN	102	128	165	129	127	128	123	121	114	121	143	144	127	148	126	110	143	122	107	128
08831 MONROE TOWNSHIP	111	118	125	115	120	132	109	117	110	114	137	123	114	128	115	112	132	113	122	128
08832 KEASBEY	85	79	120	79	75	84	90	85	95	94	123	99	88	121	87	96	121	92	83	94
08833 LEBANON	218	270	317	275	263	269	243	238	224	246	284	275	264	295	248	219	285	231	214	261
08835 MANVILLE	86	99	110	97	98	104	96	94	94	94	118	109	100	123	98	94	116	93	92	103
08836 MARTINSVILLE	224	296	384	294	288	306	259	255	240	264	303	289	291	319	273	239	308	245	234	279
08837 EDISON	99	103	129	107	100	107	107	103	105	108	132	121	109	132	106	102	130	106	96	113
08840 METUCHEN	128	166	209	160	161	168	152	149	144	152	181	171	163	195	158	144	183	147	136	160
08844 HILLSBOROUGH	151	169	185	176	163	165	161	156	150	163	191	184	166	192	158	143	189	156	138	172
08846 MIDDLESEX	112	134	153	128	131	139	125	125	122	124	152	142	132	162	129	123	152	122	120	136
08848 MILFORD	121	149	163	149	146	148	135	133	126	135	159	154	145	167	138	124	159	129	122	147
08850 MILLTOWN	121	148	170	143	145	153	138	136	132	136	166	156	146	174	142	133	165	134	130	148
08852 MONMOUTH JUNCTION	146	142	150	152	137	141	146	141	139	149	177	168	144	170	138	130	173	145	125	158
08853 NESHANIC STATION	185	232	254	239	224	226	204	199	186	207	237	230	224	247	208	180	239	192	177	220
08854 PISCATAWAY	112	136	179	140	134	135	133	129	123	131	156	156	137	161	135	118	156	131	113	138
08857 OLD BRIDGE	110	126	148	127	122	128	121	118	116	121	147	137	127	152	122	114	146	118	109	129
08859 PARLIN	95	109	137	109	105	111	106	103	104	107	132	119	111	139	108	104	131	103	96	113
08861 PERTH AMBOY	64	64	112	60	60	69	71	68	79	76	103	76	71	106	72	84	103	73	69	74
08863 FORDS	100	120	151	121	120	124	118	116	112	115	141	136	122	147	113	111	139	116	108	124
08865 PHILLIPSBURG	78	84	92	82	84	90	84	83	85	82	105	95	87	110	85	85	103	83	83	91
08867 PITTSTOWN	171	211	231	215	207	209	188	186	174	190	220	214	204	229	193	170	221	180	168	205
08869 RARITAN	101	114	130	114	111	117	111	108	108	111	135	125	115	138	112	106	133	108	103	118
08872 SAYREVILLE	103	111	131	113	108	113	109	107	106	110	134	124	112	135	108	103	131	107	100	118
08873 SOMERSET	121	137	156	138	133	137	130	128	125	132	158	149	135	161	131	122	156	127	118	140
08876 SOMERVILLE	125	143	162	145	138	143	135	132	129	137	163	153	142	166	136	126	162	131	121	145
08879 SOUTH AMBOY	92	104	121	103	102	107	102	99	100	101	125	115	106	131	103	99	124	100	95	109
08880 SOUTH BOUND BROOK	89	104	118	101	101	104	98	97	95	99	120	110	103	126	100	94	120	96	90	105
08882 SOUTH RIVER	93	108	126	103	106	113	103	102	102	103	128	115	109	136	106	103	127	101	99	110
08884 SPOTSWOOD	96	108	120	105	107	115	103	104	102	103	127	116	108	129	106	102	124	103	104	113
08886 STEWARTSVILLE	156	179	178	184	174	170	161	161	150	165	189	189	168	194	160	142	187	156	142	179
08887 THREE BRIDGES	137	117	137	131	112	120	136	128	133	139	171	156	129	157	125	124	165	138	115	143
08889 WHITEHOUSE STATION	183	224	239	229	217	217	199	197	183	202	232	228	214	241	202	177	232	190	174	217
08901 NEW BRUNSWICK	73	64	91	66	62	70	81	72	83	79	105	87	77	104	76	81	103	70	70	80
08902 NORTH BRUNSWICK	116	128	143	130	124	128	124	121	119	125	150	141	127	152	123	116	148	122	112	133
08904 HIGHLAND PARK	96	106	162	110	102	111	112	104	112	112	142	124	116	150	113	112	141	108	99	115
NEW JERSEY	110	123	153	121	120	128	120	118	119	121	150	136	125	155	123	120	149	119	114	130
UNITED STATES	100	100	100	100	100	100	100	100	100	100	100	100	100	100	100	100	100	100	100	100

POPULATION CHANGE

#	POST OFFICE NAME	COUNTY FIPS CODE	POPULATION 2000	2004	2009	2000-2004 ANNUAL RATE % Rate	State Centile	HOUSEHOLDS 2000	2004	2009	% Annual Rate 2000-2004	2004 Average HH Size	FAMILIES 2000	2004	% Annual Rate 2000-2004
87001	ALGODONES	043	1176	1264	1408	1.7	77	303	336	385	2.5	3.76	260	285	2.2
87002	BELEN	061	20518	21260	23161	0.8	49	7683	8159	9065	1.4	2.57	5545	5783	1.0
87004	BERNALILLO	043	10551	11169	12366	1.4	67	3264	3534	4003	1.9	3.16	2494	2665	1.6
87005	BLUEWATER	006	2116	2211	2278	1.0	56	754	816	868	1.9	2.59	552	587	1.5
87006	BOSQUE	053	463	506	551	2.1	84	175	195	217	2.6	2.56	130	143	2.3
87007	CASA BLANCA	006	2890	2918	2959	0.2	28	795	818	848	0.7	3.51	678	690	0.4
87008	CEDAR CREST	001	2794	2920	3055	1.0	56	1156	1248	1338	1.8	2.33	866	912	1.2
87009	CEDARVALE	057	123	125	135	0.4	33	53	55	61	0.9	2.27	38	39	0.6
87010	CERRILLOS	049	947	955	984	0.2	26	458	475	501	0.9	2.01	297	297	0.0
87012	COYOTE	039	20	19	20	-1.2	1	9	9	9	0.0	1.89	7	7	0.0
87013	CUBA	043	2254	2198	2400	-0.6	5	750	753	845	0.1	2.92	555	548	-0.3
87014	CUBERO	006	9796	10032	10236	0.6	39	3005	3174	3333	1.3	3.07	2298	2390	0.9
87015	EDGEWOOD	049	11955	13239	14426	2.4	88	4187	4747	5281	3.0	2.79	3272	3641	2.6
87016	ESTANCIA	057	4366	4686	5132	1.7	76	1407	1547	1739	2.3	2.69	1051	1136	1.9
87017	GALLINA	039	967	958	977	-0.2	14	353	362	381	0.6	2.57	266	268	0.2
87018	COUNSELOR	043	619	613	662	-0.2	14	259	265	294	0.5	2.31	181	181	0.0
87020	GRANTS	006	11102	11088	11211	0.0	18	3825	3925	4076	0.6	2.66	2800	2826	0.2
87023	JARALES	061	1193	1458	1717	4.8	99	388	477	566	5.0	3.06	302	366	4.6
87024	JEMEZ PUEBLO	043	2234	2294	2495	0.6	44	579	613	685	1.4	3.73	493	516	1.1
87025	JEMEZ SPRINGS	043	1398	1517	1693	1.9	80	553	622	717	2.8	2.35	388	429	2.4
87026	LAGUNA	006	1819	1943	2064	1.6	73	470	519	565	2.4	3.74	381	414	2.0
87027	LA JARA	043	60	60	64	0.0	21	27	28	31	0.9	2.14	19	19	0.0
87028	LA JOYA	053	158	169	180	1.6	74	73	80	87	2.2	2.11	51	55	1.8
87029	LINDRITH	039	560	543	550	-0.7	3	185	186	194	0.1	2.56	138	136	-0.3
87031	LOS LUNAS	061	36281	41260	46877	3.1	92	11746	13600	15712	3.5	2.96	9240	10537	3.1
87035	MORIARTY	057	8086	8827	9807	2.1	83	2902	3238	3666	2.6	2.72	2131	2336	2.2
87036	MOUNTAINAIR	057	1594	1651	1784	0.8	49	641	677	745	1.3	2.44	412	426	0.8
87041	PENA BLANCA	043	1340	1374	1492	0.6	41	413	437	488	1.3	3.12	330	345	1.1
87042	PERALTA	061	3240	3217	3463	-0.2	16	1132	1148	1256	0.3	2.80	888	886	-0.1
87043	PLACITAS	043	3774	4328	4989	3.3	94	1621	1924	2284	4.1	2.25	1195	1397	3.7
87044	PONDEROSA	043	439	475	530	1.9	79	169	189	217	2.7	2.46	120	131	2.1
87045	PREWITT	031	1451	1514	1559	1.0	55	401	429	451	1.6	3.53	333	352	1.3
87046	REGINA	043	6	6	6	0.0	21	3	3	3	0.0	2.00	3	3	0.0
87047	SANDIA PARK	001	4498	5132	5654	3.2	93	1743	2052	2319	3.9	2.50	1315	1517	3.4
87048	CORRALES	001	7660	8079	8859	1.3	64	2943	3180	3570	1.8	2.54	2166	2304	1.5
87052	SANTO DOMINGO PUEBLO	043	3213	3463	3874	1.8	78	574	635	728	2.4	5.44	527	581	2.3
87053	SAN YSIDRO	043	905	924	1018	0.5	35	248	264	300	1.5	3.46	203	213	1.1
87056	STANLEY	049	1066	1093	1137	0.6	41	370	390	415	1.3	2.80	247	252	0.5
87059	TIJERAS	001	7998	8482	8946	1.4	68	3028	3295	3552	2.0	2.57	2307	2456	1.5
87060	TOME	061	184	216	248	3.8	97	61	74	87	4.7	2.85	48	57	4.1
87062	VEGUITA	053	2055	2254	2448	2.2	85	678	758	839	2.7	2.93	504	553	2.2
87063	WILLARD	057	340	366	403	1.8	77	139	153	172	2.3	2.39	95	102	1.7
87068	BOSQUE FARMS	001	5125	5268	5648	0.7	45	1843	1945	2126	1.3	2.69	1441	1497	0.9
87083	COCHITI LAKE	043	394	411	451	1.0	54	205	222	251	1.9	1.85	125	132	1.3
87102	ALBUQUERQUE	001	21756	21105	21618	-0.7	4	8140	8061	8449	-0.2	2.38	4151	3948	-1.2
87104	ALBUQUERQUE	001	11513	11393	11786	-0.3	13	4828	4901	5187	0.4	2.27	2821	2773	-0.4
87105	ALBUQUERQUE	001	54896	54441	56287	-0.2	15	18156	18458	19504	0.4	2.94	13791	13717	-0.1
87106	ALBUQUERQUE	001	23899	23297	23997	-0.6	5	11253	11230	11814	-0.1	1.99	4834	4591	-1.2
87107	ALBUQUERQUE	001	30967	31565	33123	0.5	34	12455	13047	14013	1.1	2.38	7892	8000	0.3
87108	ALBUQUERQUE	001	38263	37754	39078	-0.3	12	16768	16866	17795	0.1	2.17	10229	10181	-1.0
87109	ALBUQUERQUE	001	39196	39112	40717	-0.1	18	17031	17459	18600	0.6	2.22	10240	10364	0.3
87110	ALBUQUERQUE	001	40168	41400	43746	0.7	46	18065	19088	20602	1.3	2.15	14986	15649	1.0
87111	ALBUQUERQUE	001	54514	57110	60574	1.1	60	23797	25749	27992	1.9	2.19	14986	15649	1.0
87112	ALBUQUERQUE	001	43672	43701	45537	0.0	22	18343	18916	20187	0.7	2.30	11865	11851	0.0
87113	ALBUQUERQUE	001	7346	8147	8960	2.5	89	2801	3187	3591	3.1	2.51	1883	2099	2.6
87114	ALBUQUERQUE	001	31648	40944	48468	6.3	100	11875	15602	18754	6.6	2.58	8372	10815	6.2
87116	ALBUQUERQUE	001	3540	4463	5239	5.6	99	1087	1397	1679	6.1	3.06	965	1224	5.8
87117	KIRTLAND AFB	001	712	622	632	-3.1	0	227	195	202	-3.5	2.45	149	107	-7.5
87118	ALBUQUERQUE	001	941	1027	1148	2.1	83	256	284	327	2.5	3.22	202	221	2.1
87120	ALBUQUERQUE	001	44897	51915	57673	3.5	95	16508	19415	21922	3.9	2.63	12109	13918	3.3
87121	ALBUQUERQUE	001	37760	45281	51325	4.4	99	11680	14415	16723	5.1	3.13	9332	11265	4.5
87122	ALBUQUERQUE	001	13037	15184	16928	3.7	96	4780	5721	6525	4.3	2.64	3809	4476	3.9
87123	ALBUQUERQUE	001	36195	37394	39369	0.8	48	15135	16043	17260	1.4	2.31	9630	9911	0.7
87124	RIO RANCHO	043	37454	41788	47772	2.6	90	13829	15780	18470	3.2	2.62	10037	11224	2.7
87131	ALBUQUERQUE	001	1943	2076	2176	1.6	73	340	487	602	8.8	1.13	29	40	7.9
87144	RIO RANCHO	043	14923	19380	23729	6.3	100	5344	7043	8795	6.7	2.73	4206	5469	6.4
87301	GALLUP	031	39951	41196	42556	0.7	47	12264	12882	13545	1.2	3.14	9244	9587	0.9
87310	BRIMHALL	031	105	101	101	-0.9	2	41	41	42	0.0	2.46	31	30	-0.8
87312	CONTINENTAL DIVIDE	031	1122	1166	1197	0.9	52	298	318	334	1.5	3.67	241	254	1.2
87313	CROWNPOINT	031	7231	7514	7742	0.9	52	2009	2145	2257	1.6	3.50	1570	1648	1.2
87315	FENCE LAKE	006	164	166	168	0.3	30	73	76	79	1.0	2.18	51	52	0.5
87320	MEXICAN SPRINGS	031	1088	1165	1215	1.6	74	282	311	331	2.3	3.75	223	241	1.8
87321	RAMAH	031	589	593	599	0.2	25	191	198	204	0.9	2.99	148	151	0.5
87323	THOREAU	031	4605	4818	4974	1.1	58	1290	1381	1453	1.6	3.49	977	1026	1.2
87325	TOHATCHI	031	7370	7634	7876	0.8	49	1987	2118	2232	1.5	3.60	1564	1640	1.1
87327	ZUNI	031	7748	7676	7745	-0.2	14	1847	1880	1938	0.4	4.05	1637	1656	0.3
87328	NAVAJO	031	2929	2967	3029	0.3	30	709	744	778	1.1	3.99	587	606	0.8
87401	FARMINGTON	045	48207	50167	53073	0.9	54	16508	17541	18970	1.4	2.83	12220	12809	1.1
87402	FARMINGTON	045	8507	8905	9407	1.1	59	3052	3287	3560	1.8	2.71	2400	2543	1.4
87410	AZTEC	045	14763	16077	17286	2.0	82	5176	5762	6330	2.6	2.70	3921	4287	2.1
87412	BLANCO	045	947	1040	1122	2.2	86	369	417	462	2.9	2.49	275	305	2.5
87413	BLOOMFIELD	045	12618	13830	14911	2.2	84	4260	4804	5310	2.9	2.87	3344	3716	2.5
87415	FLORA VISTA	045	2072	2190	2311	1.3	65	744	809	875	2.0	2.65	583	624	1.6
87416	FRUITLAND	045	468	490	514	1.1	59	141	150	161	1.5	3.23	118	125	1.4
87417	KIRTLAND	045	5815	5936	6172	0.5	35	1699	1770	1880	1.0	3.35	1427	1471	0.7
87418	LA PLATA	045	653	671	699	0.6	44	224	235	250	1.1	2.86	174	180	0.8
87419	NAVAJO DAM	045	74	82	88	2.4	88	30	34	38	3.0	2.41	22	25	3.1
87420	SHIPROCK	045	18888	19293	20037	0.5	36	5262	5530	5891	1.2	3.49	4248	4406	0.9
87421	WATERFLOW	045	789	806	840	0.5	36	246	257	273	1.0	3.12	198	204	0.7
87501	SANTA FE	049	16447	16198	16868	-0.4	10	8351	8519	9103	0.5	1.87	4065	3969	-0.6
87505	SANTA FE	049	31634	32909	34859	0.9	53	13895	14930	16238	1.7	2.13	7535	7815	0.9
87506	SANTA FE	049	10796	11357	12122	1.2	61	4432	4808	5259	1.9	2.36	3095	3280	1.4
87507	SANTA FE	049	36594	41258	45326	2.9	90	13174	15125	16917	3.3	2.72	9020	10126	2.8
87508	SANTA FE	049	14534	15951	17227	2.2	85	5491	6284	7000	3.2	2.41	3838	4281	2.6
87510	ABIQUIU	039	2579	2735	2867	1.4	68	919	1013	1098	2.3	2.69	643	695	1.9
	NEW MEXICO					1.2					1.8	2.57			1.3
	UNITED STATES					1.2					1.3	2.58			1.1

ZIP CODE #	POST OFFICE NAME	RACE (%) White 2000	White 2004	Black 2000	Black 2004	Asian/Pacific 2000	Asian/Pacific 2004	% Hispanic Origin 2000	% Hispanic Origin 2004	2004 AGE DISTRIBUTION (%) 0-4	5-9	10-14	15-19	20-24	25-44	45-64	65-84	85+	18+	MEDIAN AGE 2004	% 2004 Males	% 2004 Females
87001	ALGODONES	17.2	13.8	0.1	0.1	0.1	0.2	17.8	12.7	9.2	8.7	9.3	9.3	7.8	30.1	19.2	5.7	0.6	67.1	29.0	50.3	49.7
87002	BELEN	71.4	70.8	1.6	1.6	0.4	0.4	57.4	58.0	7.1	7.0	7.6	7.1	6.3	25.4	24.2	13.4	1.9	73.9	37.4	48.7	51.3
87004	BERNALILLO	46.7	44.2	0.6	0.6	0.2	0.2	56.0	54.5	8.3	8.5	8.7	8.7	7.7	27.8	21.8	7.9	0.7	69.1	31.2	48.6	51.4
87005	BLUEWATER	47.5	45.6	0.4	0.4	0.2	0.3	19.6	19.5	7.6	7.6	8.6	8.1	6.9	22.8	25.6	10.9	1.9	71.2	36.4	50.5	49.5
87006	BOSQUE	69.6	68.8	0.7	0.8	0.4	0.4	58.1	58.7	9.1	8.5	8.3	8.5	6.9	26.3	23.7	7.9	0.8	68.6	31.7	51.0	49.0
87007	CASA BLANCA	1.8	1.5	0.1	0.1	0.0	0.0	3.7	3.2	9.1	8.9	9.9	8.2	7.9	26.2	19.7	8.4	1.8	67.1	29.1	47.8	52.2
87008	CEDAR CREST	90.8	90.1	0.5	0.6	1.1	1.2	16.6	17.3	3.9	6.0	7.6	6.0	2.8	25.8	36.8	10.3	0.8	78.6	44.1	51.1	48.9
87009	CEDARVALE	69.1	68.8	0.0	0.0	0.0	0.0	56.9	56.8	5.6	5.6	4.8	6.4	5.6	20.8	29.6	19.2	2.4	79.2	45.8	53.6	46.4
87010	CERRILLOS	86.5	86.0	0.3	0.3	0.7	0.7	20.9	21.8	4.4	6.5	7.9	7.2	3.5	26.6	34.1	9.0	0.8	75.9	42.1	50.1	50.0
87012	COYOTE	70.0	73.7	0.0	0.0	0.0	0.0	55.0	57.9	0.0	5.3	5.3	5.3	10.5	10.5	36.8	15.8	10.5	89.5	51.3	36.8	63.2
87013	CUBA	26.2	22.3	0.2	0.2	0.2	0.2	35.3	31.7	6.9	8.6	9.4	10.0	8.3	22.3	23.9	9.7	0.9	68.8	31.4	49.1	50.9
87014	CUBERO	30.2	29.1	0.6	0.6	0.1	0.1	24.2	24.0	8.1	7.9	9.0	8.3	7.8	25.9	22.9	9.3	0.9	69.8	32.2	49.9	50.2
87015	EDGEWOOD	84.7	84.0	0.7	0.8	0.5	0.6	21.9	22.7	6.7	7.2	9.4	8.5	6.6	28.2	26.8	6.2	0.5	71.4	36.1	49.8	50.2
87016	ESTANCIA	74.4	73.8	4.0	4.1	0.5	0.5	43.5	44.5	6.5	6.9	7.9	6.7	6.4	28.8	26.6	9.1	1.1	74.7	36.6	55.6	44.4
87017	GALLINA	44.0	43.2	0.4	0.4	0.1	0.1	81.1	81.5	5.5	6.1	8.3	8.3	6.9	23.6	25.5	13.1	2.9	75.2	38.4	49.4	50.6
87018	COUNSELOR	59.9	54.8	0.3	0.3	0.3	0.3	59.5	56.1	5.2	5.1	7.8	7.0	4.1	21.9	33.3	14.2	1.5	76.8	44.3	49.8	50.2
87020	GRANTS	54.8	53.2	1.6	1.6	0.9	1.0	50.5	50.4	8.2	7.4	7.6	7.4	7.6	27.0	23.4	10.7	0.8	72.4	34.2	48.1	51.9
87023	JARALES	58.3	55.7	1.1	1.3	0.2	0.2	54.2	53.8	8.4	8.2	9.5	8.3	6.0	27.9	23.0	8.3	0.5	68.7	32.8	49.9	50.1
87024	JEMEZ PUEBLO	9.0	9.1	0.0	0.0	0.1	0.1	5.7	5.5	7.8	7.6	9.5	9.5	8.0	26.9	22.8	7.0	1.0	69.4	30.9	48.4	51.6
87025	JEMEZ SPRINGS	70.0	66.6	0.3	0.3	0.8	0.9	32.6	33.8	5.1	5.1	6.3	6.9	4.3	22.7	36.9	10.8	1.9	78.3	44.7	48.5	51.6
87026	LAGUNA	6.1	6.7	0.2	0.3	0.0	0.0	8.4	8.9	10.0	9.5	12.4	11.1	8.2	27.3	16.8	4.4	0.3	61.1	24.3	47.4	52.7
87027	LA JARA	66.7	61.7	0.0	0.0	0.0	0.0	56.7	55.0	5.0	3.3	6.7	5.0	3.3	23.3	35.0	16.7	1.7	81.7	47.0	50.0	50.0
87028	LA JOYA	74.7	73.4	0.6	1.2	0.0	0.0	52.5	53.3	5.9	5.9	8.3	7.1	5.3	22.5	31.4	12.4	1.2	75.2	41.1	50.9	49.1
87029	LINDRITH	70.5	69.6	0.0	0.0	0.0	0.0	55.2	56.0	4.1	4.6	6.6	5.5	6.5	19.9	29.5	17.1	6.3	81.4	46.8	48.8	51.2
87031	LOS LUNAS	63.7	63.1	1.2	1.3	0.5	0.6	57.5	58.2	8.6	8.1	8.7	8.0	7.6	29.5	22.1	6.9	0.6	69.7	31.9	51.1	48.9
87035	MORIARTY	74.4	73.5	0.8	0.8	0.4	0.5	33.1	34.1	7.4	7.3	9.1	9.2	7.3	26.6	24.5	8.0	0.7	70.6	33.8	49.7	50.4
87036	MOUNTAINAIR	65.9	65.0	1.3	1.3	0.4	0.4	48.2	49.2	7.5	7.4	7.8	7.0	6.1	20.5	26.2	15.4	2.4	73.1	39.2	48.0	52.0
87041	PENA BLANCA	11.8	9.0	0.5	0.4	0.1	0.1	36.8	30.4	8.9	7.9	8.7	8.4	9.1	26.4	20.1	9.4	1.2	69.3	30.7	48.0	52.0
87042	PERALTA	65.2	64.5	0.6	0.6	0.3	0.3	46.0	46.5	6.4	6.9	8.9	7.4	6.3	26.7	26.5	10.2	0.9	73.2	37.3	49.1	50.9
87043	PLACITAS	83.7	81.5	0.7	0.6	0.5	0.5	20.4	21.9	4.1	5.5	5.3	4.8	2.6	21.1	43.6	12.2	0.9	82.0	47.9	48.5	51.5
87044	PONDEROSA	58.8	55.6	0.2	0.2	0.5	0.6	41.5	42.1	6.3	5.5	6.3	7.0	5.5	23.6	34.5	9.9	1.5	76.2	42.7	51.0	49.1
87045	PREWITT	13.8	12.6	0.5	0.5	0.1	0.1	4.7	4.3	11.0	10.2	10.7	10.8	8.1	21.5	20.5	6.7	0.5	61.4	24.5	48.0	52.1
87046	REGINA	0.0	0.0	0.0	0.0	16.7	16.7	0.0	0.0	0.0	0.0	0.0	33.3	16.7	0.0	50.0	0.0	0.0	66.7	37.5	50.0	50.0
87047	SANDIA PARK	89.1	88.3	0.6	0.6	0.7	0.8	17.9	18.9	5.2	6.3	7.6	6.3	3.4	26.3	36.3	8.0	0.6	76.5	42.9	51.1	48.9
87048	CORRALES	85.4	83.8	0.7	0.7	0.9	1.0	26.2	27.3	4.8	5.8	7.4	6.6	4.9	22.8	35.6	11.2	0.9	77.9	43.7	47.9	52.1
87052	SANTO DOMINGO PUEBLO	2.4	1.7	0.0	0.0	0.0	0.1	5.2	3.9	9.6	9.8	10.8	10.1	10.5	25.5	17.9	5.5	0.5	63.9	24.7	51.0	49.0
87053	SAN YSIDRO	19.7	19.9	0.1	0.1	0.2	0.2	10.1	11.0	8.1	7.6	8.7	8.7	7.6	27.0	23.8	7.7	1.0	70.2	31.9	48.7	51.3
87056	STANLEY	83.8	83.2	0.3	0.3	0.6	0.6	25.1	26.1	4.7	6.5	7.3	7.0	3.9	27.5	33.8	8.7	0.7	76.4	41.7	49.8	50.2
87059	TIJERAS	85.2	84.5	0.4	0.4	0.6	0.7	23.8	24.8	6.3	7.1	8.1	7.0	4.5	26.0	33.4	7.1	0.5	74.0	40.7	51.1	48.9
87060	TOME	67.4	66.7	0.5	0.5	0.0	0.5	54.9	56.5	6.5	6.5	7.4	7.4	6.5	28.2	25.5	10.2	1.9	74.5	37.5	50.5	49.5
87062	VEGUITA	70.0	69.2	0.6	0.8	0.2	0.3	58.4	59.1	8.4	8.8	8.3	8.7	7.4	26.3	23.6	7.9	0.8	68.7	31.6	51.2	48.8
87063	WILLARD	65.6	64.8	0.6	0.6	0.3	0.3	56.5	57.9	7.9	6.8	6.3	6.8	5.7	20.8	26.8	16.1	2.7	75.7	42.1	53.6	46.5
87068	BOSQUE FARMS	61.0	61.0	0.6	0.7	0.2	0.2	27.6	28.3	6.1	6.6	8.2	7.9	5.5	24.5	28.9	11.4	1.1	74.0	39.8	49.2	50.8
87083	COCHITI LAKE	78.4	73.7	0.5	0.5	1.3	1.2	10.2	10.2	2.0	2.9	3.2	3.9	2.4	15.1	38.7	29.4	2.4	89.8	55.6	49.2	50.9
87102	ALBUQUERQUE	57.7	57.1	4.2	4.3	0.7	0.8	69.4	69.7	6.6	6.3	6.2	7.1	10.0	31.9	21.0	9.1	1.8	76.9	33.1	52.3	47.7
87104	ALBUQUERQUE	67.7	67.0	1.2	1.3	0.7	0.8	61.6	62.6	6.0	5.9	6.3	7.2	6.8	26.0	27.1	13.0	1.7	77.5	39.4	47.8	52.2
87105	ALBUQUERQUE	54.7	54.2	1.5	1.6	0.5	0.6	76.6	77.4	7.9	7.7	8.1	7.9	7.6	27.3	23.0	9.6	1.0	71.5	33.2	49.5	50.5
87106	ALBUQUERQUE	70.3	69.1	4.6	4.7	4.8	5.3	28.7	29.3	5.5	4.6	4.7	7.0	14.1	33.1	20.7	8.4	1.9	82.1	31.7	49.4	50.6
87107	ALBUQUERQUE	69.6	68.8	1.6	1.7	0.7	0.8	55.5	56.6	5.8	6.0	6.8	8.3	7.1	25.5	27.1	11.8	1.5	76.1	38.3	48.9	51.1
87108	ALBUQUERQUE	66.0	64.9	4.4	4.6	2.8	3.1	45.3	45.8	7.8	6.4	5.9	6.0	8.8	30.2	21.8	10.2	2.9	76.6	34.5	49.2	50.8
87109	ALBUQUERQUE	76.5	75.2	2.6	2.7	2.8	3.2	27.1	27.9	5.7	5.6	6.3	6.8	8.3	28.0	25.5	12.2	1.7	78.5	37.7	47.4	52.6
87110	ALBUQUERQUE	78.5	77.2	2.5	2.6	2.2	2.6	31.5	32.6	5.3	5.1	5.7	6.0	7.0	26.8	24.9	16.4	2.8	80.4	41.2	47.9	52.1
87111	ALBUQUERQUE	85.7	84.7	1.9	2.0	2.8	3.2	17.8	18.5	4.5	4.7	6.1	6.7	6.9	24.7	29.6	14.2	2.6	80.8	42.7	47.9	52.2
87112	ALBUQUERQUE	79.5	78.3	2.8	2.9	2.8	3.2	27.4	28.2	6.1	6.2	6.6	6.2	6.2	27.6	26.0	13.4	1.7	77.3	39.5	48.1	51.9
87113	ALBUQUERQUE	72.5	71.4	1.6	1.7	2.8	3.5	43.9	44.4	7.9	7.4	6.8	6.4	7.2	32.0	21.6	9.2	1.6	74.2	34.0	48.3	51.7
87114	ALBUQUERQUE	75.8	74.3	2.9	3.0	1.5	1.8	37.4	37.6	8.8	7.9	6.9	6.0	7.0	34.8	20.8	7.0	0.8	72.7	32.6	49.2	50.9
87116	ALBUQUERQUE	71.8	70.6	9.2	9.3	3.4	4.0	18.0	18.8	17.2	11.1	7.3	5.4	17.4	39.6	1.8	0.2	0.0	61.7	22.6	51.5	48.5
87117	KIRTLAND AFB	70.8	69.6	10.1	10.1	3.2	3.7	18.0	18.8	12.4	9.5	6.3	9.0	30.7	30.7	1.5	0.0	0.0	69.9	22.1	60.3	39.7
87118	ALBUQUERQUE	74.4	74.5	9.0	8.7	3.4	4.1	16.2	16.6	11.6	9.6	11.1	7.9	14.9	39.5	5.1	0.1	0.2	63.1	23.3	55.2	44.8
87120	ALBUQUERQUE	70.0	68.8	3.0	3.2	1.6	1.8	44.5	45.6	8.8	8.4	7.8	6.8	6.7	34.0	22.0	5.0	0.4	70.8	32.6	48.2	51.8
87121	ALBUQUERQUE	48.4	48.0	3.5	3.7	0.6	0.7	77.2	77.5	10.9	9.8	9.2	8.2	9.1	32.4	16.1	4.0	0.3	65.1	26.5	48.9	51.1
87122	ALBUQUERQUE	89.5	88.4	1.0	1.1	3.3	4.0	13.1	14.0	4.8	6.4	8.3	7.5	4.7	21.9	34.4	10.8	1.2	75.7	43.1	49.6	50.4
87123	ALBUQUERQUE	70.9	69.8	4.3	4.4	3.6	4.1	33.0	33.4	7.0	6.6	6.6	6.2	7.5	28.0	25.2	11.4	1.6	76.1	36.7	48.4	51.6
87124	RIO RANCHO	78.1	75.7	2.6	2.6	1.6	1.7	27.3	28.5	6.9	6.9	7.6	7.3	6.8	27.2	23.8	11.4	2.4	74.2	37.0	48.1	51.9
87131	ALBUQUERQUE	79.1	77.7	2.6	2.6	2.4	2.6	19.8	20.8	1.1	0.3	0.9	38.0	37.9	8.9	4.6	5.1	3.3	96.4	21.3	48.3	51.7
87144	RIO RANCHO	78.0	75.4	2.8	2.8	1.8	2.0	30.2	31.3	9.2	8.8	8.6	6.8	5.8	33.4	20.7	6.4	0.4	69.1	32.7	49.2	50.8
87301	GALLUP	25.4	23.9	0.7	0.6	0.8	0.9	21.3	20.5	9.2	8.7	10.0	9.6	8.5	26.1	20.3	6.8	0.8	66.1	28.2	48.5	51.5
87310	BRIMHALL	1.0	1.0	0.0	0.0	0.0	0.0	0.0	0.0	10.9	8.9	11.9	11.9	6.9	23.8	17.8	7.9	0.0	60.4	24.6	47.5	52.5
87312	CONTINENTAL DIVIDE	21.5	20.9	0.0	0.0	0.2	0.3	5.4	5.4	8.3	8.2	11.2	10.2	8.7	23.9	22.5	6.8	0.2	65.6	27.9	48.6	51.4
87313	CROWNPOINT	4.7	4.3	0.2	0.2	0.2	0.2	1.2	1.1	9.6	9.9	12.0	10.5	8.5	24.7	18.0	6.2	0.7	61.5	24.7	48.0	52.1
87315	FENCE LAKE	53.1	51.8	0.0	0.0	0.0	0.0	40.9	41.0	6.6	6.6	6.6	6.0	6.0	25.3	28.9	12.7	1.2	76.5	40.4	51.8	48.2
87320	MEXICAN SPRINGS	0.1	0.1	0.0	0.0	0.2	0.2	0.6	0.6	9.6	8.9	9.9	10.3	8.4	27.4	17.9	7.0	0.7	65.3	26.8	48.1	51.9
87321	RAMAH	58.1	56.0	0.0	0.0	0.7	0.7	6.1	5.9	7.3	7.4	9.6	9.8	8.8	21.9	24.6	9.6	1.0	70.0	32.2	51.6	48.4
87323	THOREAU	10.4	9.7	0.1	0.1	0.2	0.2	4.4	4.1	10.2	9.7	11.8	10.8	9.7	24.1	17.4	5.9	0.4	61.7	23.9	48.5	51.5
87325	TOHATCHI	1.8	1.6	0.1	0.1	0.1	0.1	1.3	1.2	9.5	9.3	11.7	11.0	8.3	25.3	17.9	6.2	0.8	62.5	25.1	48.7	51.3
87327	ZUNI	3.2	2.8	0.1	0.1	0.1	0.1	2.1	1.9	8.5	8.7	10.2	9.8	8.5	30.3	18.1	5.3	0.7	66.2	28.0	47.8	52.2
87328	NAVAJO	2.5	2.2	0.0	0.0	0.0	0.0	0.7	0.6	13.0	12.2	13.2	10.4	8.5	24.9	14.1	3.3	0.4	54.9	20.7	47.3	52.8
87401	FARMINGTON	56.1	53.3	0.7	0.7	0.4	0.5	16.2	15.9	8.7	8.0	8.5	8.8	8.5	26.3	21.6	8.5	1.2	69.5	30.9	49.3	50.7
87402	FARMINGTON	79.6	77.4	0.5	0.5	0.6	0.7	15.8	15.7	6.8	7.2	7.9	8.2	7.2	26.0	27.1	9.2	0.5	73.0	36.1	49.6	50.4
87410	AZTEC	81.1	79.0	0.3	0.4	0.2	0.3	17.9	18.1	7.4	7.2	8.1	7.9	8.1	27.8	23.5	8.9	1.0	72.5	33.6	50.8	49.2
87412	BLANCO	61.1	60.4	0.1	0.1	0.1	0.1	36.1	36.8	7.7	7.8	8.1	6.5	6.5	27.1	24.5	10.7	1.1	72.1	34.9	52.3	47.7
87413	BLOOMFIELD	63.4	60.8	0.3	0.3	0.3	0.3	28.7	28.6	8.4	8.0	8.5	8.5	7.5	27.1	22.7	8.3	0.9	69.6	32.1	49.4	50.6
87415	FLORA VISTA	83.9	82.2	0.3	0.4	0.2	0.3	16.3	16.7	6.1	6.5	8.0	7.2	6.9	24.4	28.3	11.3	1.4	74.7	38.8	50.3	49.7
87416	FRUITLAND	54.5	49.4	0.2	0.2	0.4	0.4	9.0	8.2	8.0	8.0	8.6	8.8	9.4	23.9	24.7	8.4	0.4	70.4	30.4	51.4	48.6
87417	KIRTLAND	42.0	37.1	0.2	0.3	0.3	0.3	9.5	8.7	9.3	8.7	9.0	9.1	9.4	27.0	21.3	5.8	0.5	67.3	27.9	49.4	50.6
87418	LA PLATA	81.3	78.7	0.5	0.5	0.3	0.5	10.4	10.4	8.2	8.2	7.8	7.3	7.2	27.4	27.3	6.3	0.5	71.4	34.8	53.5	46.5
87419	NAVAJO DAM	67.6	65.9	0.0	0.0	0.0	0.0	40.5	41.5	7.3	7.3	8.5	4.9	6.1	26.8	24.4	13.4	1.2	73.2	36.3	52.4	47.6
87420	SHIPROCK	1.7	1.4	0.1	0.1	0.1	0.1	1.0	0.9	8.9	9.2	10.6	9.9	8.5	26.1	18.7	7.3	0.7	65.0	27.2	48.8	51.2
87421	WATERFLOW	50.6	45.4	0.1	0.1	0.4	0.4	9.9	9.2	7.3	6.8	9.3	11.0	8.3	24.6	25.8	6.6	0.3	70.4	30.5	50.0	50.0
87501	SANTA FE	81.5	81.0	0.6	0.7	1.0	1.1	36.7	37.1	3.4	3.6	3.9	4.6	5.1	24.3	34.1	18.0	3.0	86.2	48.0	46.9	53.1
87505	SANTA FE	77.8	76.8	0.6	0.6	1.5	1.7	42.3	43.4	4.4	4.5	5.4	6.6	7.5	25.3	31.6	12.8	2.0	82.0	42.4	47.9	52.1
87506	SANTA FE	59.2	58.7	0.4	0.5	0.4	0.5	45.8	45.1	6.0	6.1	6.5	5.9	5.4	24.4	31.7	13.0	1.0	77.7	42.2	49.6	50.4
87507	SANTA FE	65.7	64.9	0.7	0.8	1.0	1.1	69.5	70.1	8.9	8.0	7.7	7.3	7.8	32.3	21.3	6.1	0.7	70.9	31.5	49.4	50.6
87508	SANTA FE	83.1	83.0	1.0	1.0	0.7	0.8	34.1	33.8	5.0	6.0	7.0	5.8	4.5	26.0	36.4	8.9	0.4	78.1	42.7	50.5	49.5
87510	ABIQUIU	48.0	47.3	0.2	0.2	0.2	0.2	79.6	79.9	6.7	6.8	7.9	7.8	7.1	27.2	27.0	8.3	1.2	73.6	35.5	49.1	50.9
	NEW MEXICO	66.8	65.8	1.9	2.0	1.1	1.3	42.1	42.7	7.3	7.1	7.6	7.7	7.7	26.9	23.9	10.4	1.4	73.4	34.9	49.2	50.9
	UNITED STATES	75.1	73.6	12.3	12.5	3.8	4.2	12.5	14.1	6.9	6.7	7.2	7.0	7.3	28.6	23.8	10.8	1.7	75.1	36.0	49.1	50.9

ZIP CODE #	POST OFFICE NAME	2004 Per Capita Income	2004 HH Income Base	2004 Household Income Distribution (%) Less than $25,000	$25,000 to $49,999	$50,000 to $99,999	$100,000 to $149,999	$150,000 or More	Median Household Income 2004	2009	2004 National Centile	2004 State Centile	2004 Home Value Base	2004 Home Value Distribution (%) Less than $50,000	$50,000 to $89,999	$90,000 to $174,999	$175,000 to $399,999	$400,000 or More	2004 Median Home Value
87001	ALGODONES	14220	336	32.4	33.3	23.2	7.1	3.9	37121	42438	36	75	312	28.9	15.7	27.9	19.2	8.3	103571
87002	BELEN	17537	8159	33.9	35.3	24.3	4.8	1.7	35024	39399	28	63	6362	14.4	24.3	46.4	13.3	1.7	100371
87004	BERNALILLO	13843	3534	34.8	32.5	27.0	4.9	0.7	36284	41805	33	70	2771	23.1	29.1	36.2	10.5	1.0	87500
87005	BLUEWATER	14201	816	41.4	36.2	18.3	3.7	0.5	29607	32638	11	33	648	41.2	25.5	20.2	12.2	0.9	65806
87006	BOSQUE	14373	195	43.6	32.3	21.5	2.6	0.0	28499	32502	10	29	154	32.5	19.5	31.8	14.3	2.0	85000
87007	CASA BLANCA	10648	818	40.5	30.9	26.3	2.2	0.1	31758	35427	17	44	634	39.3	34.1	19.2	6.2	1.3	69787
87008	CEDAR CREST	37475	1248	14.7	21.1	33.7	20.0	10.4	70563	84670	91	99	1100	8.9	6.6	26.5	51.0	7.1	191241
87009	CEDARVALE	13390	55	50.9	38.2	9.1	1.8	0.0	24609	27538	4	11	45	51.1	20.0	22.2	4.4	2.2	49286
87010	CERRILLOS	31974	475	22.3	24.6	32.4	15.0	5.7	52447	63827	76	94	400	4.8	9.8	27.3	40.0	18.3	193750
87012	COYOTE	17563	9	44.4	33.3	22.2	0.0	0.0	27247	27247	7	20	8	12.5	37.5	25.0	25.0	0.0	90000
87013	CUBA	8891	753	62.0	22.4	13.8	1.3	0.4	15195	18116	1	1	615	53.3	15.9	20.5	8.8	1.5	34457
87014	CUBERO	12156	3174	43.0	33.7	19.3	3.0	1.0	28861	32283	10	30	2575	47.0	24.5	19.9	7.0	1.6	54435
87015	EDGEWOOD	22948	4747	15.3	28.8	39.5	12.7	3.5	54669	64847	79	95	4218	6.0	11.7	42.7	36.2	3.4	145955
87016	ESTANCIA	18498	1547	39.4	33.4	19.7	3.4	4.2	31863	35151	17	44	1261	22.4	25.2	29.3	17.7	5.3	94538
87017	GALLINA	12805	362	50.6	28.2	17.7	2.8	0.8	24512	26527	4	10	320	39.7	27.5	20.6	9.7	2.5	68696
87018	COUNSELOR	16886	265	44.5	26.8	22.3	6.4	0.0	32980	38342	21	53	209	21.5	35.4	30.1	12.0	1.0	81944
87020	GRANTS	15378	3925	37.7	34.5	22.6	3.5	1.7	32527	36299	19	49	2633	27.9	40.0	26.6	5.1	0.5	73339
87023	JARALES	16279	477	37.3	37.5	19.5	2.1	3.6	31139	35738	15	40	421	33.5	18.3	39.0	8.1	1.2	86739
87024	JEMEZ PUEBLO	11804	613	35.2	31.2	27.4	4.6	1.6	34940	39710	27	59	566	35.7	23.0	24.6	14.1	2.7	70435
87025	JEMEZ SPRINGS	28317	622	23.5	26.5	29.9	13.3	6.8	50000	56527	72	91	498	8.0	11.2	34.3	38.2	8.2	164286
87026	LAGUNA	8138	519	54.1	29.9	14.3	1.0	0.8	22142	26502	3	5	495	66.7	13.5	15.4	4.0	0.4	31324
87027	LA JARA	19254	28	46.4	21.4	21.4	10.7	0.0	35000	47394	28	63	23	21.7	39.1	26.1	13.0	0.0	78750
87028	LA JOYA	25860	80	36.3	27.5	27.5	3.8	5.0	35899	40956	31	68	66	25.8	25.8	28.8	15.2	4.6	88000
87029	LINDRITH	15772	186	41.4	32.8	19.4	4.8	1.6	31182	35369	15	40	158	26.0	27.2	18.4	26.0	2.5	84444
87031	LOS LUNAS	16019	13600	29.8	34.2	28.5	5.8	1.8	38874	44131	42	78	10931	13.7	21.6	44.3	18.4	1.9	107170
87035	MORIARTY	16174	3238	33.5	35.3	25.6	4.6	1.0	35112	39627	28	64	2654	19.2	22.0	46.6	10.8	1.4	101244
87036	MOUNTAINAIR	15514	677	45.9	36.0	13.7	1.6	2.7	27031	30505	7	20	505	33.1	26.3	24.8	12.3	3.6	70179
87041	PENA BLANCA	14124	437	39.6	29.3	24.0	5.0	2.1	32108	37365	18	45	327	21.1	25.7	40.1	13.2	0.0	93387
87042	PERALTA	19723	1148	23.1	33.3	35.0	5.8	2.8	44019	50543	59	85	966	4.9	17.2	47.9	24.4	5.6	124863
87043	PLACITAS	42375	1924	13.3	25.1	33.4	16.0	12.3	61845	71393	86	98	1710	4.4	3.0	12.3	51.6	28.7	290502
87044	PONDEROSA	27136	189	16.4	31.2	34.4	13.2	4.8	53733	59304	78	95	156	10.3	11.5	34.0	39.1	5.1	160938
87045	PREWITT	8314	429	60.6	26.6	8.6	1.9	2.3	18322	21345	1	2	363	74.9	11.6	7.4	4.1	1.9	24875
87046	REGINA	6250	3	100.0	0.0	0.0	0.0	0.0	12500	12500	1	1	3	33.3	66.7	0.0	0.0	0.0	52500
87047	SANDIA PARK	37511	2052	11.1	20.0	37.5	18.7	12.7	70325	84864	91	99	1837	3.8	6.7	40.1	35.4	14.0	173717
87048	CORRALES	39192	3180	13.7	22.4	30.2	17.6	16.1	71656	83614	92	99	2623	3.6	3.2	17.4	49.3	26.6	292217
87052	SANTO DOMINGO PUEBLO	6710	635	42.2	35.4	18.0	3.3	1.1	28987	33355	10	30	586	34.3	27.0	28.3	7.2	3.2	74762
87053	SAN YSIDRO	15053	264	28.4	30.3	32.2	6.4	2.7	40909	46234	49	80	242	18.2	30.6	30.6	17.8	2.9	91071
87056	STANLEY	23031	390	23.1	26.4	34.6	11.0	4.9	50273	59225	72	91	324	4.6	10.5	30.9	42.0	12.0	183553
87059	TIJERAS	29800	3295	16.0	21.6	38.3	16.1	8.0	64141	77212	88	98	2969	9.0	8.4	32.9	43.5	6.1	174172
87060	TOME	14663	74	43.2	31.1	20.3	2.7	2.7	30000	35446	12	35	60	15.0	16.7	31.7	31.7	5.0	115000
87062	VEGUITA	12101	758	45.7	30.9	20.8	2.5	0.1	27587	33702	8	23	594	34.2	18.5	31.1	14.0	2.2	82000
87063	WILLARD	12239	153	52.3	31.4	15.0	1.3	0.0	23640	26277	4	9	128	45.3	25.0	21.1	3.1	5.5	54286
87068	BOSQUE FARMS	21676	1945	23.1	32.4	34.1	6.5	3.8	44237	50264	59	85	1761	9.8	13.9	45.4	27.7	3.3	134695
87083	COCHITI LAKE	29927	222	18.0	34.7	36.0	9.9	1.4	43626	48249	58	84	190	0.0	0.0	83.7	16.3	0.0	141544
87102	ALBUQUERQUE	15234	8061	49.6	30.3	15.6	2.9	1.6	25178	29661	5	14	3403	9.5	36.0	42.3	11.2	1.1	93344
87104	ALBUQUERQUE	25854	4901	37.6	25.6	22.7	8.0	6.2	36604	44272	34	72	3028	10.5	12.4	46.2	26.6	4.3	137302
87105	ALBUQUERQUE	15688	18458	34.7	33.3	25.0	5.2	1.8	35131	40877	28	64	13066	9.6	22.8	54.7	12.0	0.9	106434
87106	ALBUQUERQUE	23454	11230	41.1	28.7	19.7	6.7	3.8	30852	36689	14	38	4489	5.8	9.6	48.8	33.6	2.3	151602
87107	ALBUQUERQUE	25042	13047	32.4	29.7	23.7	7.9	6.4	38950	46191	43	78	8397	8.5	13.0	46.4	24.4	7.7	128365
87108	ALBUQUERQUE	18734	16866	42.3	32.3	18.8	4.2	2.4	29745	34762	12	34	6104	4.8	11.5	65.5	17.3	1.0	123365
87109	ALBUQUERQUE	27246	17459	24.3	31.5	28.5	11.1	4.7	44745	52262	61	86	10264	10.1	5.2	44.9	39.6	0.3	161556
87110	ALBUQUERQUE	25775	19088	26.8	32.2	29.4	8.3	3.4	42077	49828	53	82	11505	1.8	7.9	66.7	22.6	1.0	139756
87111	ALBUQUERQUE	36053	25749	16.2	26.0	32.8	15.5	9.6	59503	70692	84	97	16360	0.5	1.7	42.0	48.6	7.2	183159
87112	ALBUQUERQUE	25508	18916	23.3	31.5	31.4	9.4	4.5	45876	53491	64	88	12227	1.4	3.9	71.7	21.0	1.9	140518
87113	ALBUQUERQUE	22371	3187	24.7	32.4	31.5	7.7	3.6	44680	53786	60	86	2407	23.5	16.5	32.0	27.3	0.7	116862
87114	ALBUQUERQUE	27166	15602	15.3	26.6	39.2	13.2	5.6	58090	69531	83	96	11052	5.1	3.4	47.0	41.7	2.8	168678
87116	ALBUQUERQUE	12932	1397	24.9	50.1	24.2	0.6	0.2	34175	38394	25	56	21	0.0	0.0	100.0	0.0	0.0	156250
87117	KIRTLAND AFB	13873	195	48.7	32.3	17.4	1.5	0.0	25424	28321	5	14	5	0.0	0.0	100.0	0.0	0.0	159375
87118	ALBUQUERQUE	20915	284	20.8	34.2	34.9	3.9	6.3	47469	55278	67	88	5	0.0	0.0	100.0	0.0	0.0	162500
87120	ALBUQUERQUE	27038	19415	12.0	26.0	42.8	14.9	4.2	61207	73790	86	97	14922	0.4	2.4	64.9	31.4	0.9	156291
87121	ALBUQUERQUE	15123	14415	26.5	39.4	28.6	3.8	1.6	38565	45159	41	77	11247	17.5	16.3	61.6	4.4	0.2	104918
87122	ALBUQUERQUE	52138	5721	5.0	11.4	27.9	27.6	28.1	107549	129873	99	100	5094	0.0	0.0	6.6	63.0	30.4	310162
87123	ALBUQUERQUE	25235	16043	28.5	31.2	27.2	8.7	4.5	41115	48605	50	81	10444	21.3	6.5	43.5	26.1	2.6	130569
87124	RIO RANCHO	23357	15780	17.3	31.6	39.0	9.3	2.8	50831	57099	74	92	11948	1.1	8.5	72.3	17.7	0.4	131825
87131	ALBUQUERQUE	17499	487	67.4	21.2	6.0	5.3	0.2	16762	20738	1	1	9	0.0	0.0	0.0	100.0	0.0	225000
87144	RIO RANCHO	23239	7043	9.9	30.6	48.1	8.4	2.9	56285	64595	81	96	6085	1.6	7.8	67.7	21.1	1.8	136740
87301	GALLUP	14483	12882	39.6	29.4	22.9	5.3	2.8	32674	37825	20	50	9088	39.9	18.2	30.1	10.0	1.9	75116
87310	BRIMHALL	12969	41	51.2	26.8	22.0	0.0	0.0	23596	30000	4	9	36	61.1	27.8	8.3	2.8	0.0	30000
87312	CONTINENTAL DIVIDE	11556	318	45.6	28.6	19.5	4.1	2.2	28335	33186	9	29	235	63.0	10.6	14.0	12.3	0.0	32031
87313	CROWNPOINT	8503	2145	54.5	28.0	15.8	1.5	0.3	21598	25603	2	5	1280	66.4	20.0	9.0	3.7	0.9	31250
87315	FENCE LAKE	16348	76	51.3	29.0	17.1	2.6	0.0	23853	28335	4	10	63	39.7	20.6	30.2	6.4	3.2	68333
87320	MEXICAN SPRINGS	8124	311	53.1	25.4	19.6	1.3	0.6	22285	25769	3	6	290	65.5	11.4	15.2	5.2	2.8	33500
87321	RAMAH	14282	198	40.9	24.8	27.3	4.0	3.0	36751	42029	35	73	162	43.8	16.7	26.5	13.0	0.0	72500
87323	THOREAU	8708	1381	53.2	28.5	16.7	1.0	0.6	22619	27010	3	6	965	68.7	18.9	8.4	2.5	1.6	26652
87325	TOHATCHI	9162	2118	49.8	28.1	19.7	1.9	0.4	25156	29225	5	13	1719	63.4	21.3	11.5	3.9	0.0	33929
87327	ZUNI	8169	1880	50.5	30.9	15.0	2.3	1.4	24578	28726	4	11	1318	44.3	29.7	15.9	7.4	2.8	60889
87328	NAVAJO	6518	744	57.3	29.3	12.1	1.2	0.1	18908	21955	1	2	242	69.0	13.2	12.0	4.6	1.2	32308
87401	FARMINGTON	17466	17541	32.4	32.2	26.4	6.3	2.6	37116	42528	36	74	12182	24.7	18.5	40.7	14.5	1.7	97871
87402	FARMINGTON	25093	3287	20.4	26.6	38.1	10.3	4.7	52981	60310	77	95	2595	6.6	15.0	47.4	28.0	3.0	130415
87410	AZTEC	18659	5762	27.2	32.3	32.0	6.6	2.0	42565	49632	55	84	4570	19.4	21.9	40.8	15.7	2.3	100948
87412	BLANCO	24304	417	30.7	26.1	29.0	9.6	4.6	44678	51824	60	86	343	19.5	20.7	40.2	17.5	2.0	99306
87413	BLOOMFIELD	17828	4804	26.9	36.4	29.1	5.5	2.2	40072	46315	46	79	3807	25.7	23.2	36.3	14.0	0.8	91293
87415	FLORA VISTA	21191	809	28.7	26.6	32.6	10.1	2.0	44221	51487	59	85	665	13.8	16.8	35.9	26.5	6.9	121484
87416	FRUITLAND	17205	150	22.0	26.0	44.0	5.3	2.7	51840	58562	75	94	125	18.4	13.6	50.4	10.4	7.2	112500
87417	KIRTLAND	16929	1770	23.0	25.6	40.6	8.3	2.5	51211	59320	74	93	1449	18.8	28.2	44.8	7.2	1.0	91986
87418	LA PLATA	20971	235	20.9	28.5	39.6	8.1	3.0	50292	57357	72	92	197	25.9	12.2	41.6	18.3	2.0	114224
87419	NAVAJO DAM	26235	34	38.2	17.7	26.5	14.7	2.9	45000	56283	61	87	28	10.7	25.0	39.3	21.4	3.6	106250
87420	SHIPROCK	8811	5530	53.5	28.3	15.6	2.2	0.5	22509	26345	3	6	3867	62.0	19.8	12.5	4.5	1.3	35599
87421	WATERFLOW	16184	257	31.1	26.9	34.6	3.9	3.5	40206	47035	47	79	210	23.8	26.7	31.0	15.2	3.3	88571
87501	SANTA FE	41366	8519	25.8	25.9	28.1	10.3	9.9	48297	58485	69	89	5203	1.0	2.2	11.4	47.6	37.9	315162
87505	SANTA FE	33539	14930	22.0	28.0	30.0	11.7	8.3	49928	60711	72	91	8813	1.2	0.8	15.6	57.8	24.6	253527
87506	SANTA FE	33115	4808	25.2	25.2	24.8	13.4	11.4	49484	59921	71	90	3898	14.9	7.7	14.0	25.1	38.4	270531
87507	SANTA FE	20063	15125	25.5	33.3	29.7	7.8	3.8	42520	51136	55	83	10477	24.6	8.0	21.1	41.8	4.6	163877
87508	SANTA FE	33698	6284	14.1	20.0	39.1	16.5	10.3	67440	81913	90	98	5360	2.6	2.6	10.2	60.4	24.2	278944
87510	ABIQUIU	17754	1013	36.1	29.6	26.1	5.6	2.6	35466	40995	29	66	821	21.8	15.6	30.2	24.4	8.0	114977
	NEW MEXICO	20647		31.7	30.6	26.4	7.4	3.8	38669	45233				18.9	17.7	37.6	21.5	4.4	113735
	UNITED STATES	25866		24.7	27.1	30.8	10.9	6.5	48124	56710				10.9	15.0	33.7	30.1	10.4	145905

SPENDING POTENTIAL INDICES NEW MEXICO
87001-87510 D

ZIP CODE #	POST OFFICE NAME	FINANCIAL SERVICES: Auto Loan	FINANCIAL SERVICES: Home Loan	FINANCIAL SERVICES: Invest-ments	FINANCIAL SERVICES: Retire-ment Plans	THE HOME: Home Improvements: Home Repair	THE HOME: Home Improvements: Lawn & Garden	THE HOME: Furnishings: Comput-ers & Hard-ware	THE HOME: Furnishings: Major Appli-ances	THE HOME: Furnishings: TV, Radio, Sound Equip-ment	THE HOME: Furnishings: Furni-ture	ENTERTAINMENT: Dine out/ Carry out	ENTERTAINMENT: Sports Equip-ment	ENTERTAINMENT: Fees & Tickets	ENTERTAINMENT: Toys & Games	ENTERTAINMENT: Travel	ENTERTAINMENT: Cable TV	PERSONAL: Apparel & Services	PERSONAL: Auto Repairs	PERSONAL: Health Insur-ance	PERSONAL: Pets & Supplies
87001	ALGODONES	80	74	64	69	71	74	74	79	76	80	95	85	69	86	71	73	94	80	74	83
87002	BELEN	69	62	54	59	63	70	61	66	64	63	79	73	59	74	62	66	76	66	70	77
87004	BERNALILLO	64	60	60	57	58	62	60	62	62	63	78	70	57	74	59	62	77	63	61	70
87005	BLUEWATER	58	48	39	44	51	58	48	53	53	47	64	63	44	63	49	55	60	54	61	69
87006	BOSQUE	59	53	42	51	53	56	51	55	52	52	64	63	48	60	50	51	61	54	54	65
87007	CASA BLANCA	58	48	40	46	50	57	49	53	54	50	66	61	47	65	49	56	62	53	59	65
87008	CEDAR CREST	113	139	151	138	137	139	125	125	117	125	147	145	133	154	129	115	147	121	116	138
87009	CEDARVALE	57	38	17	33	43	50	37	46	45	38	52	55	32	50	38	48	48	46	57	66
87010	CERRILLOS	84	103	109	103	101	100	92	92	86	92	108	108	98	115	94	84	108	89	83	102
87012	COYOTE	53	40	26	38	44	53	44	49	50	42	59	55	40	55	44	53	53	49	58	59
87013	CUBA	39	33	30	30	32	37	35	37	38	37	47	40	33	42	34	39	45	38	39	41
87014	CUBERO	58	50	41	47	51	56	50	54	53	51	65	62	47	62	50	54	62	54	57	65
87015	EDGEWOOD	93	101	94	103	97	96	92	93	87	95	109	109	93	108	90	82	107	91	83	104
87016	ESTANCIA	86	70	48	67	74	80	68	77	72	69	87	90	62	84	68	73	82	76	82	98
87017	GALLINA	41	38	61	34	37	44	43	42	49	45	62	47	41	63	43	53	62	45	46	47
87018	COUNSELOR	64	52	38	47	56	62	50	59	56	51	67	67	45	64	52	58	64	58	65	75
87020	GRANTS	60	55	52	54	56	61	57	59	59	56	72	68	55	71	57	59	69	59	60	68
87023	JARALES	79	72	56	69	72	76	69	74	70	71	86	85	65	81	68	69	83	74	73	88
87024	JEMEZ PUEBLO	69	59	47	54	59	63	59	65	63	63	78	71	54	70	58	62	76	66	65	73
87025	JEMEZ SPRINGS	115	90	62	81	101	114	85	102	96	84	114	120	76	113	91	103	106	101	121	140
87026	LAGUNA	42	38	40	37	37	42	43	41	45	42	55	48	41	54	41	45	53	43	43	46
87027	LA JARA	70	55	37	50	62	69	52	62	59	51	69	73	46	69	55	63	65	61	74	85
87028	LA JOYA	87	79	62	76	79	84	76	81	76	78	94	94	71	89	75	75	91	81	80	96
87029	LINDRITH	65	49	33	47	54	64	55	60	61	52	72	67	49	68	54	65	66	60	72	72
87031	LOS LUNAS	74	69	56	67	69	72	66	70	66	68	82	81	63	79	65	65	79	70	68	82
87035	MORIARTY	70	64	50	62	64	68	61	65	62	63	76	76	58	72	60	61	73	65	65	77
87036	MOUNTAINAIR	61	47	34	45	52	62	50	56	56	49	67	61	46	61	51	59	61	56	67	67
87041	PENA BLANCA	63	61	57	57	60	64	61	64	62	64	78	69	59	73	60	61	77	64	62	68
87042	PERALTA	85	82	69	79	82	85	77	82	77	79	95	94	75	92	77	75	92	81	79	95
87043	PLACITAS	123	151	165	151	149	151	137	137	128	136	161	158	145	167	141	125	160	132	126	150
87044	PONDEROSA	106	92	77	84	98	109	87	99	95	88	115	114	82	115	91	100	110	98	110	127
87045	PREWITT	55	37	17	32	42	48	36	45	43	36	51	53	30	48	36	46	46	44	55	63
87046	REGINA	16	20	21	20	20	20	18	18	17	18	21	21	19	22	18	16	21	17	16	20
87047	SANDIA PARK	123	151	161	153	148	147	135	134	125	136	158	156	144	166	138	121	158	130	120	148
87048	CORRALES	133	156	167	158	153	155	143	143	134	145	169	165	150	172	145	130	168	139	130	156
87052	SANTO DOMINGO PUEBLO	56	49	41	45	47	49	50	54	52	54	65	57	46	57	47	50	65	55	51	56
87053	SAN YSIDRO	85	72	53	67	78	86	67	77	73	67	88	91	64	89	70	77	83	76	87	102
87056	STANLEY	91	100	96	99	99	100	92	94	88	93	110	109	93	111	92	86	108	92	87	107
87059	TIJERAS	105	121	122	121	119	119	110	111	103	110	130	129	114	134	111	100	128	108	101	124
87060	TOME	66	60	47	58	60	64	58	62	58	59	72	71	55	68	57	58	69	62	61	73
87062	VEGUITA	56	51	40	49	51	54	49	53	50	50	61	61	46	58	48	49	59	52	52	62
87063	WILLARD	55	37	17	32	42	48	36	45	43	36	50	53	31	48	36	46	46	44	55	63
87068	BOSQUE FARMS	80	86	86	85	85	88	82	83	80	82	100	96	83	102	83	79	98	82	79	93
87083	COCHITI LAKE	70	82	91	78	81	88	77	78	77	77	96	86	82	100	81	79	94	76	79	84
87102	ALBUQUERQUE	50	44	44	43	42	46	50	49	50	50	63	56	46	58	46	48	62	52	46	52
87104	ALBUQUERQUE	80	82	91	80	80	86	83	83	84	84	105	94	83	104	83	83	104	84	81	90
87105	ALBUQUERQUE	67	64	60	60	61	64	64	67	65	68	82	73	61	77	62	64	82	68	63	71
87106	ALBUQUERQUE	63	59	74	62	58	63	70	64	69	67	87	78	67	84	66	66	84	69	60	71
87107	ALBUQUERQUE	79	82	92	81	81	87	84	83	83	84	105	95	84	104	83	82	103	84	80	90
87108	ALBUQUERQUE	55	52	61	54	51	55	59	56	59	58	74	67	57	73	57	57	73	59	53	61
87109	ALBUQUERQUE	81	84	97	86	83	89	87	85	85	86	107	99	88	106	86	83	105	87	81	93
87110	ALBUQUERQUE	72	76	91	76	75	82	79	76	79	78	99	89	81	100	79	78	97	78	75	84
87111	ALBUQUERQUE	105	117	134	119	115	120	114	112	109	114	138	130	118	139	115	106	136	112	104	123
87112	ALBUQUERQUE	76	84	97	85	83	87	84	82	82	83	103	96	87	105	84	80	101	82	78	89
87113	ALBUQUERQUE	82	85	82	87	83	85	81	82	78	83	97	95	81	95	80	75	95	81	76	92
87114	ALBUQUERQUE	99	107	110	110	103	104	102	101	96	104	122	118	104	121	100	91	120	100	90	111
87116	ALBUQUERQUE	63	40	38	46	37	44	60	52	61	56	76	69	51	68	49	55	73	61	48	59
87117	KIRTLAND AFB	53	34	32	39	31	37	50	43	51	47	64	58	43	57	41	47	61	51	40	49
87118	ALBUQUERQUE	112	71	68	82	65	77	106	91	108	99	135	122	91	120	87	98	129	108	85	104
87120	ALBUQUERQUE	102	112	112	117	107	105	105	103	97	108	123	121	107	123	102	91	122	102	89	113
87121	ALBUQUERQUE	69	66	65	65	63	66	67	67	66	70	84	77	65	80	64	64	83	69	62	74
87122	ALBUQUERQUE	185	220	241	224	214	219	199	197	185	203	234	226	212	237	202	180	233	192	180	217
87123	ALBUQUERQUE	79	83	91	83	82	88	83	83	82	83	103	95	84	101	83	81	100	83	81	91
87124	RIO RANCHO	86	94	96	96	91	92	89	88	84	90	106	103	91	106	88	80	104	87	80	97
87131	ALBUQUERQUE	37	38	44	40	38	40	39	39	38	39	47	45	39	46	39	36	46	39	37	42
87144	RIO RANCHO	91	102	99	106	97	94	93	92	85	96	109	108	95	109	91	80	107	90	79	101
87301	GALLUP	66	63	61	61	62	66	64	65	64	65	80	74	62	77	62	63	78	66	63	72
87310	BRIMHALL	49	43	36	40	41	43	44	47	46	48	57	50	40	51	42	44	57	48	44	49
87312	CONTINENTAL DIVIDE	64	54	50	50	54	63	57	60	63	58	76	66	54	69	56	65	73	61	66	70
87313	CROWNPOINT	45	40	36	38	39	43	41	43	43	43	53	48	39	49	40	43	52	44	43	49
87315	FENCE LAKE	55	51	43	49	51	54	50	52	50	51	62	60	48	59	49	50	60	52	52	61
87320	MEXICAN SPRINGS	47	41	34	38	39	41	42	45	43	45	54	48	38	48	40	42	54	46	42	47
87321	RAMAH	68	62	49	60	62	66	59	63	60	61	74	73	56	70	58	59	71	63	63	75
87323	THOREAU	47	41	35	39	41	44	42	44	43	43	54	50	39	50	41	43	52	45	45	51
87325	TOHATCHI	50	45	41	43	44	47	46	48	47	47	59	54	44	55	45	46	57	48	47	54
87327	ZUNI	50	44	38	42	43	46	45	48	47	48	59	53	42	54	44	46	57	49	47	53
87328	NAVAJO	37	31	37	29	30	35	35	35	39	37	48	40	34	45	34	39	47	37	37	40
87401	FARMINGTON	72	69	66	68	69	73	69	71	70	70	87	82	68	84	68	69	84	72	70	80
87402	FARMINGTON	94	103	102	102	102	104	96	98	93	96	116	114	98	119	97	91	114	96	92	111
87410	AZTEC	80	73	57	70	73	78	70	75	71	72	88	87	66	83	69	71	84	75	75	89
87412	BLANCO	98	85	64	80	88	95	81	90	85	83	104	104	75	99	82	86	99	90	95	112
87413	BLOOMFIELD	81	74	58	71	74	78	71	76	72	73	89	87	67	83	70	71	85	76	75	90
87415	FLORA VISTA	90	82	64	79	82	87	78	84	79	81	98	97	74	92	77	78	94	84	83	100
87416	FRUITLAND	89	81	63	78	81	85	77	83	78	79	96	95	73	91	76	77	92	82	82	98
87417	KIRTLAND	90	82	64	79	82	87	78	84	79	81	98	97	74	92	77	78	94	84	83	100
87418	LA PLATA	95	87	68	84	87	92	83	89	84	85	104	103	78	98	82	83	99	88	88	105
87419	NAVAJO DAM	105	87	63	81	94	103	83	95	89	83	108	111	75	104	85	93	101	94	105	123
87420	SHIPROCK	47	40	35	37	40	44	42	44	45	43	55	49	39	50	40	45	53	45	46	50
87421	WATERFLOW	80	73	57	70	73	77	70	75	71	72	87	86	66	82	69	70	84	75	74	89
87501	SANTA FE	104	108	132	110	108	117	111	109	110	111	138	125	112	136	112	109	134	111	108	121
87505	SANTA FE	93	103	132	105	102	108	103	101	101	103	128	117	106	130	105	101	126	102	96	110
87506	SANTA FE	112	111	112	109	112	123	108	113	110	110	136	127	108	132	110	111	131	112	116	128
87507	SANTA FE	79	76	76	75	75	78	77	78	77	79	96	89	75	92	75	74	95	80	74	86
87508	SANTA FE	114	131	134	132	128	131	119	119	112	120	141	139	124	144	120	109	140	116	110	134
87510	ABIQUIU	63	60	86	55	57	65	64	63	70	67	89	71	62	89	64	73	89	66	65	72
	NEW MEXICO	77	74	75	73	73	78	75	76	75	76	94	87	73	91	74	74	92	77	75	86
	UNITED STATES	100	100	100	100	100	100	100	100	100	100	100	100	100	100	100	100	100	100	100	100

NEW MEXICO

POPULATION CHANGE

A 87513-88045

# POST OFFICE NAME	COUNTY FIPS CODE	POPULATION 2000	2004	2009	2000-2004 ANNUAL RATE % Rate	State Centile	HOUSEHOLDS 2000	2004	2009	% Annual Rate 2000-2004	2004 Average HH Size	FAMILIES 2000	2004	% Annual Rate 2000-2004
87513 ARROYO HONDO	055	2200	2359	2509	1.7	74	945	1055	1163	2.6	2.23	561	611	2.0
87514 ARROYO SECO	055	1028	1119	1200	2.0	82	483	547	608	3.0	2.04	280	309	2.4
87520 CHAMA	039	1353	1388	1428	0.6	41	532	566	603	1.5	2.39	361	377	1.0
87521 CHAMISAL	055	597	607	627	0.4	33	240	254	272	1.3	2.39	167	174	1.0
87522 CHIMAYO	039	4965	4954	5074	-0.1	18	1913	1983	2099	0.9	2.50	1360	1381	0.4
87524 COSTILLA	055	547	579	612	1.4	67	212	233	255	2.3	2.48	121	129	1.5
87527 DIXON	039	1505	1541	1585	0.6	39	660	699	743	1.4	2.18	452	470	0.9
87528 DULCE	039	3213	3223	3282	0.1	23	999	1034	1087	0.8	3.09	744	758	0.4
87530 EL RITO	039	1000	1058	1107	1.3	66	351	386	418	2.3	2.73	245	264	1.8
87531 EMBUDO	039	5003	5418	5744	1.9	79	1785	1983	2161	2.5	2.72	1297	1415	2.1
87532 ESPANOLA	039	17544	17469	17977	-0.1	16	6613	6778	7169	0.6	2.57	4706	4734	0.1
87535 GLORIETA	049	990	1042	1097	1.2	61	371	403	434	2.0	2.48	249	263	1.3
87537 HERNANDEZ	039	1028	1116	1185	2.0	80	355	397	434	2.7	2.81	256	281	2.2
87539 LA MADERA	039	278	297	312	1.6	73	116	129	140	2.5	2.30	82	89	2.0
87540 LAMY	049	798	882	956	2.4	87	351	399	442	3.1	2.21	237	261	2.3
87544 LOS ALAMOS	028	18343	18910	19753	0.7	47	7497	7875	8370	1.2	2.39	5341	5512	0.7
87549 OJO CALIENTE	055	977	1076	1161	2.3	87	526	608	683	3.5	1.77	253	285	2.8
87552 PECOS	047	3833	4051	4170	1.3	65	1407	1543	1641	2.2	2.56	995	1068	1.7
87553 PENASCO	055	1262	1265	1301	0.1	23	494	515	549	1.0	2.46	347	355	0.5
87556 QUESTA	055	3448	3613	3795	1.1	60	1448	1580	1721	2.1	2.29	927	988	1.5
87557 RANCHOS DE TAOS	055	3843	4231	4565	2.3	86	1546	1760	1961	3.1	2.38	976	1087	2.6
87560 RIBERA	047	2182	2317	2392	1.4	69	804	884	942	2.3	2.61	584	630	1.8
87564 SAN CRISTOBAL	055	421	445	470	1.3	65	191	210	230	2.3	2.12	114	123	1.8
87565 SAN JOSE	047	1341	1403	1437	1.1	58	489	531	562	2.0	2.63	352	375	1.5
87566 SAN JUAN PUEBLO	039	5772	5990	6202	0.9	50	1911	2044	2181	1.6	2.87	1454	1530	1.2
87567 SANTA CRUZ	049	316	311	322	-0.4	9	121	123	131	0.4	2.53	87	86	-0.3
87571 TAOS	055	14021	14636	15398	1.0	55	5927	6388	6941	1.8	2.25	3560	3745	1.2
87573 TERERRO	047	118	121	122	0.6	41	57	60	63	1.2	1.87	39	41	1.2
87575 TIERRA AMARILLA	039	1936	1958	2007	0.3	29	768	807	857	1.2	2.34	538	554	0.7
87579 VADITO	055	1350	1347	1391	-0.1	18	526	547	585	0.9	2.46	372	380	0.5
87580 VALDEZ	055	270	290	309	1.7	76	133	149	164	2.7	1.93	76	83	2.1
87581 VALLECITOS	039	620	662	697	1.6	72	265	294	320	2.5	2.25	186	203	2.1
87701 LAS VEGAS	047	21116	20943	21137	-0.2	15	7732	7886	8194	0.5	2.50	5107	5099	0.0
87711 ANTON CHICO	019	294	348	437	4.1	98	106	130	169	4.9	2.61	73	88	4.5
87713 CHACON	033	240	253	269	1.3	63	85	93	102	2.1	2.72	59	63	1.6
87714 CIMARRON	007	2609	2850	3056	2.1	83	1112	1244	1367	2.7	2.28	777	854	2.3
87715 CLEVELAND	033	342	360	383	1.2	61	125	136	149	2.0	2.65	87	93	1.6
87718 EAGLE NEST	007	631	712	776	2.9	91	271	313	349	3.5	2.26	191	217	3.1
87722 GUADALUPITA	033	33	34	35	0.7	45	11	12	13	2.1	2.67	7	7	0.0
87724 LA LOMA	019	239	283	355	4.1	98	92	113	146	5.0	2.43	63	76	4.5
87728 MAXWELL	007	404	415	429	0.6	44	170	180	192	1.4	1.92	121	125	0.8
87729 MIAMI	007	72	74	76	0.7	45	33	35	37	1.4	1.74	23	24	1.0
87730 MILLS	021	34	34	34	0.0	21	15	15	15	0.0	2.20	9	9	0.0
87731 MONTEZUMA	047	51	53	54	0.9	52	17	18	19	1.4	2.67	12	12	0.0
87732 MORA	033	3433	3621	3850	1.3	64	1344	1464	1606	2.0	2.47	948	1013	1.6
87733 MOSQUERO	021	233	229	229	-0.4	8	110	112	112	0.4	2.04	69	68	-0.3
87734 OCATE	033	410	420	439	0.6	39	165	174	188	1.3	2.30	109	112	0.6
87740 RATON	007	8453	8520	8792	0.2	25	3506	3636	3854	0.9	2.30	2342	2375	0.3
87742 ROCIADA	047	812	905	959	2.6	90	318	364	396	3.2	2.49	234	262	2.7
87743 ROY	021	454	446	446	-0.4	7	208	212	212	0.5	2.10	130	130	0.0
87745 SAPELLO	047	3	3	4	0.0	21	2	2	2	0.0	1.50	1	1	0.0
87746 SOLANO	021	73	72	72	-0.3	11	31	32	32	0.8	2.25	19	19	0.0
87747 SPRINGER	007	2013	2039	2095	0.3	30	726	753	794	0.9	2.50	520	529	0.4
87750 VALMORA	033	163	167	174	0.6	39	61	64	69	1.1	2.48	40	41	0.6
87752 WAGON MOUND	033	561	574	599	0.5	38	228	240	259	1.2	2.27	149	154	0.8
87801 SOCORRO	053	11190	11491	12065	0.6	44	4340	4577	4927	1.3	2.39	2792	2877	0.7
87820 ARAGON	003	191	195	200	0.5	35	82	87	93	1.4	2.23	53	55	0.9
87821 DATIL	003	627	643	662	0.6	41	277	295	315	1.5	2.18	187	195	1.0
87823 LEMITAR	053	607	647	693	1.5	71	238	260	285	2.1	2.49	165	176	1.5
87825 MAGDALENA	053	3229	3391	3599	1.2	60	1013	1090	1183	1.7	3.11	743	787	1.4
87827 PIE TOWN	003	649	666	685	0.6	42	292	311	332	1.5	2.14	197	205	0.9
87828 POLVADERA	053	26	28	30	1.8	78	13	14	16	1.8	2.00	9	10	2.5
87829 QUEMADO	003	320	328	338	0.6	40	129	137	146	1.4	2.39	87	91	1.1
87830 RESERVE	003	1363	1393	1429	0.5	36	616	655	698	1.5	2.12	396	412	0.9
87831 SAN ACACIA	053	568	606	648	1.5	72	213	233	255	2.1	2.60	148	158	1.6
87901 TRUTH OR CONSEQUENCE	051	10194	10733	11431	1.2	62	4848	5198	5627	1.7	2.01	2790	2915	1.0
87930 ARREY	051	867	919	980	1.4	67	271	293	317	1.9	3.14	177	186	1.2
87931 CABALLO	051	1422	1498	1591	1.2	63	634	679	732	1.6	2.21	413	430	1.0
87933 DERRY	051	146	169	189	3.5	95	52	61	70	3.8	2.77	36	41	3.1
87936 GARFIELD	013	562	603	660	1.7	75	174	188	208	1.8	3.21	146	155	1.4
87937 HATCH	013	3405	3691	4064	1.9	79	1045	1140	1268	2.1	3.24	809	868	1.7
87940 RINCON	013	619	702	790	3.0	92	187	213	243	3.1	3.30	159	179	2.8
87941 SALEM	013	1001	1074	1176	1.7	75	251	270	299	1.7	3.98	210	223	1.4
87942 WILLIAMSBURG	051	120	138	153	3.3	94	53	62	70	3.8	2.21	36	41	3.1
87943 WINSTON	051	163	172	182	1.3	64	75	80	86	1.5	2.15	49	51	1.0
88001 LAS CRUCES	013	36955	38324	41757	0.9	50	13507	14298	15918	1.4	2.51	8329	8619	0.8
88002 WHITE SANDS MISSILE	013	1382	1246	1311	-2.4	1	461	426	457	-1.8	2.92	371	338	-2.2
88005 LAS CRUCES	013	26455	28753	31852	2.0	81	9826	10885	12289	2.4	2.54	6555	7111	1.9
88007 LAS CRUCES	013	21257	23096	25480	2.0	81	7515	8396	9482	2.6	2.63	5758	6317	2.2
88008 SANTA TERESA	013	5233	5813	6482	2.5	89	1602	1819	2066	3.0	3.17	1300	1451	2.6
88011 LAS CRUCES	013	17341	20492	23764	4.0	97	7219	8644	10180	4.3	2.33	4518	5301	3.8
88012 LAS CRUCES	013	15904	18320	20828	3.4	94	5312	6186	7121	3.7	2.96	4052	4646	3.3
88020 ANIMAS	023	626	590	561	-1.4	1	251	245	240	-0.6	2.41	174	166	-1.1
88021 ANTHONY	013	16113	17355	19052	1.8	78	4485	4904	5462	2.1	3.54	3873	4193	1.9
88022 ARENAS VALLEY	017	1051	1068	1072	0.4	33	399	418	432	1.1	2.55	279	286	0.6
88023 BAYARD	017	3151	3090	3059	-0.5	6	1232	1250	1277	0.3	2.38	897	894	-0.1
88025 BUCKHORN	017	1054	1100	1118	1.0	55	446	483	507	1.9	2.28	307	326	1.4
88026 SANTA CLARA	017	2218	2189	2170	-0.3	12	802	816	835	0.4	2.68	569	568	0.0
88030 DEMING	029	25016	26025	26929	0.9	53	9397	9907	10349	1.3	2.60	6592	6820	0.8
88039 GLENWOOD	003	393	402	412	0.5	37	188	200	213	1.5	2.00	121	126	1.0
88041 HANOVER	017	426	430	429	0.2	27	184	191	196	0.9	2.20	129	131	0.4
88042 HILLSBORO	051	358	377	400	1.2	62	180	193	207	1.7	1.95	117	122	1.0
88043 HURLEY	017	2195	2170	2158	-0.3	13	767	780	797	0.4	2.69	552	551	0.0
88044 LA MESA	013	4009	4199	4539	1.1	60	1279	1374	1516	1.7	3.04	1024	1084	1.1
88045 LORDSBURG	023	5306	5225	5063	-0.4	10	1901	1922	1911	0.3	2.67	1369	1360	-0.2
NEW MEXICO					1.2					1.8	2.57			1.3
UNITED STATES					1.2					1.3	2.58			1.1

ZIP CODE #	POST OFFICE NAME	RACE (%) White 2000	White 2004	Black 2000	Black 2004	Asian/Pacific 2000	Asian/Pacific 2004	% Hispanic Origin 2000	% Hispanic Origin 2004	2004 AGE DISTRIBUTION (%) 0-4	5-9	10-14	15-19	20-24	25-44	45-64	65-84	85+	18+	MEDIAN AGE 2004	% 2004 Males	% 2004 Females
87513	ARROYO HONDO	77.2	76.3	0.2	0.2	0.4	0.5	49.2	50.1	5.0	5.7	5.7	5.6	5.0	26.5	34.9	10.5	1.1	79.9	42.9	50.6	49.4
87514	ARROYO SECO	80.9	79.8	0.2	0.2	0.4	0.5	44.0	45.2	4.7	5.5	5.4	5.3	4.7	26.9	36.2	10.6	0.9	80.9	43.7	50.9	49.2
87520	CHAMA	70.9	69.9	0.8	1.0	0.7	0.7	65.3	65.6	5.3	5.6	6.1	5.8	5.0	24.1	31.5	15.4	1.2	78.8	43.7	50.9	49.1
87521	CHAMISAL	51.6	50.6	0.3	0.3	0.5	0.5	79.9	79.9	5.1	5.8	7.4	6.8	6.3	23.2	30.2	13.3	2.0	77.8	42.3	51.1	48.9
87522	CHIMAYO	51.2	50.8	0.2	0.2	0.3	0.3	86.9	87.2	6.0	6.3	7.1	7.4	6.8	28.0	26.2	11.0	1.3	76.1	37.2	50.2	49.8
87524	COSTILLA	70.4	69.1	0.2	0.2	0.9	0.9	47.5	48.5	4.7	5.0	5.7	6.7	4.0	23.1	36.1	13.1	1.6	80.1	45.4	50.1	49.9
87527	DIXON	69.1	68.2	0.4	0.5	0.1	0.2	75.5	75.7	5.5	5.9	6.7	6.0	5.5	26.4	30.4	12.7	0.9	78.3	41.4	50.3	49.7
87528	DULCE	11.2	10.0	0.1	0.1	0.1	0.1	15.2	13.8	9.5	9.3	10.7	10.0	7.6	27.2	19.5	5.9	0.3	64.2	27.4	48.0	52.0
87530	EL RITO	48.3	47.6	0.2	0.2	0.1	0.2	78.5	78.9	6.6	6.8	7.8	7.8	7.3	26.7	27.8	7.9	1.2	73.6	35.6	49.1	51.0
87531	EMBUDO	59.0	58.3	0.3	0.4	0.1	0.2	85.9	86.1	7.9	7.6	7.9	8.0	7.1	29.6	22.6	8.3	0.9	71.8	33.2	49.8	50.2
87532	ESPANOLA	64.2	63.6	0.5	0.5	0.3	0.3	76.2	76.0	7.0	7.0	7.7	7.5	7.5	27.2	25.2	9.9	1.1	73.8	35.0	48.8	51.2
87535	GLORIETA	80.1	79.6	0.2	0.2	0.6	0.7	49.2	50.2	4.9	5.3	7.1	7.0	5.2	27.5	34.8	7.5	0.7	77.2	41.0	49.1	50.9
87537	HERNANDEZ	68.2	67.7	0.2	0.3	0.5	0.5	85.6	85.8	9.0	8.0	7.4	7.1	7.4	29.8	21.2	9.1	1.2	71.3	31.9	52.0	48.0
87539	LA MADERA	44.2	43.8	0.0	0.0	0.4	0.3	82.0	82.2	6.4	6.7	8.4	7.4	6.7	28.3	25.3	9.4	1.4	73.7	35.8	49.5	50.5
87540	LAMY	84.8	84.5	0.4	0.3	0.9	1.0	23.6	23.8	4.9	6.4	7.1	6.1	3.4	24.6	37.6	9.4	0.5	77.4	43.7	48.6	51.4
87544	LOS ALAMOS	90.3	89.4	0.4	0.4	3.8	4.4	11.8	12.1	5.4	6.3	7.7	7.0	4.3	24.2	32.1	11.8	1.3	76.1	42.3	50.1	50.0
87549	OJO CALIENTE	71.3	69.9	0.4	0.4	0.5	0.6	44.3	45.6	5.8	6.0	5.4	6.1	3.8	27.5	33.2	11.3	0.9	79.1	42.3	50.4	49.6
87552	PECOS	65.1	64.8	0.4	0.4	0.4	0.5	75.9	76.8	6.3	6.5	8.0	7.8	7.3	28.8	26.7	8.0	0.7	74.2	36.0	51.1	48.9
87553	PENASCO	28.6	27.7	0.2	0.2	0.2	0.3	82.3	81.0	5.5	6.0	8.3	6.8	5.5	25.0	28.2	12.7	2.1	76.1	40.5	50.3	49.7
87556	QUESTA	62.4	61.4	0.4	0.4	0.3	0.3	61.0	61.8	5.8	6.0	6.5	6.8	5.2	24.5	32.2	11.7	1.3	77.5	42.1	49.9	50.1
87557	RANCHOS DE TAOS	72.2	70.9	0.4	0.5	0.6	0.6	66.0	66.9	6.1	6.5	7.5	7.2	5.3	25.9	29.2	11.0	1.4	75.4	39.6	48.5	51.6
87560	RIBERA	43.0	42.5	0.7	0.8	0.2	0.2	83.1	83.6	6.4	7.0	7.4	7.7	6.6	25.6	27.2	10.9	1.2	74.2	37.6	50.8	49.2
87564	SAN CRISTOBAL	79.3	78.2	1.2	1.4	0.0	0.0	32.8	33.7	5.6	4.9	5.6	5.6	4.9	24.5	37.3	10.8	0.7	80.5	44.3	51.9	48.1
87565	SAN JOSE	61.0	60.5	0.8	0.8	0.6	0.7	73.5	74.3	6.5	7.1	8.5	7.3	5.9	27.3	27.2	9.4	0.8	73.3	37.1	49.5	50.5
87566	SAN JUAN PUEBLO	61.2	60.3	0.5	0.5	0.2	0.2	74.7	73.5	7.9	7.6	8.5	8.5	7.7	30.0	21.2	7.8	0.8	70.8	31.4	49.2	50.9
87567	SANTA CRUZ	58.9	58.5	0.6	0.6	0.6	0.6	76.6	77.5	6.1	6.4	7.7	7.4	6.8	28.0	26.4	10.3	1.0	75.9	37.2	51.5	48.6
87571	TAOS	63.2	62.1	0.3	0.4	0.6	0.7	54.1	54.9	5.6	6.0	6.7	6.9	6.2	26.2	29.2	11.5	1.8	77.2	40.3	48.3	51.7
87573	TERERRO	61.9	61.2	0.9	0.8	0.0	0.0	68.6	69.4	5.0	5.0	6.6	6.6	4.1	28.1	33.1	10.7	0.8	78.5	42.1	52.9	47.1
87575	TIERRA AMARILLA	65.8	65.0	0.7	0.9	0.9	1.0	68.2	68.5	5.3	5.7	6.8	6.5	4.8	24.6	30.4	14.6	1.4	77.8	42.7	51.3	48.7
87579	VADITO	36.2	35.8	0.4	0.5	0.4	0.4	84.5	84.6	6.7	6.9	8.3	5.9	5.8	24.7	26.9	13.1	1.7	74.5	40.1	49.6	50.4
87580	VALDEZ	81.9	81.0	0.4	0.3	0.4	0.3	43.3	44.1	4.5	5.2	5.5	5.5	5.2	27.6	35.2	10.3	1.0	81.0	43.1	51.0	49.0
87581	VALLECITOS	45.3	44.7	0.2	0.2	0.3	0.3	80.7	81.0	6.5	7.0	8.6	7.4	6.3	28.0	26.0	8.9	1.4	73.3	35.8	50.0	50.0
87701	LAS VEGAS	55.1	54.4	0.9	1.0	0.7	0.8	79.6	80.1	7.0	6.4	7.2	9.3	9.4	24.9	23.5	10.7	1.7	74.6	33.9	48.5	51.5
87711	ANTON CHICO	29.3	29.0	0.3	0.3	0.7	0.6	87.1	87.6	5.8	5.8	7.2	6.9	6.6	23.3	26.4	17.0	1.2	77.3	42.1	51.4	48.6
87713	CHACON	55.8	55.7	0.0	0.0	0.4	0.4	85.4	85.8	5.9	5.9	6.7	7.1	7.1	22.9	28.1	14.6	1.6	76.7	41.0	51.0	49.0
87714	CIMARRON	84.4	83.8	0.2	0.2	0.3	0.4	31.0	31.4	4.1	6.0	7.7	7.1	3.9	22.6	34.5	13.1	1.1	77.3	44.2	52.0	48.0
87715	CLEVELAND	54.1	53.3	0.0	0.0	0.3	0.6	87.1	88.1	6.4	6.4	6.7	6.9	6.9	22.8	28.6	13.9	1.4	76.4	40.8	49.4	50.6
87718	EAGLE NEST	88.1	86.9	0.2	0.3	0.5	0.6	15.9	16.9	4.1	6.2	6.6	5.8	3.0	22.2	39.2	12.2	0.8	79.2	46.2	52.4	47.6
87722	GUADALUPITA	63.6	61.8	0.0	0.0	0.0	0.0	69.7	67.7	5.9	5.9	5.9	11.8	5.9	23.5	23.5	17.7	0.0	73.5	37.5	52.9	47.1
87724	LA LOMA	29.3	29.0	0.4	0.4	0.4	0.7	87.0	87.3	5.7	6.0	7.4	7.1	6.7	22.6	26.5	16.6	1.4	76.7	42.0	51.6	48.4
87728	MAXWELL	86.1	85.5	1.7	1.7	0.5	0.5	42.3	44.3	3.6	5.1	6.5	22.2	2.9	20.2	26.3	11.6	1.7	70.4	36.5	60.0	40.0
87729	MIAMI	86.1	85.1	1.4	1.4	0.0	0.0	41.7	44.6	4.1	5.4	6.8	21.6	2.7	18.9	25.7	12.2	2.7	68.9	36.3	59.5	40.5
87730	MILLS	85.3	85.3	0.0	0.0	0.0	0.0	44.1	47.1	2.9	5.9	5.9	5.9	5.9	20.6	26.5	23.5	2.9	85.3	47.5	50.0	50.0
87731	MONTEZUMA	60.8	58.5	2.0	1.9	2.0	1.9	62.8	62.3	7.6	7.6	7.6	13.2	7.6	24.5	26.4	5.7	0.0	69.8	31.3	50.9	49.1
87732	MORA	58.5	58.1	0.1	0.1	0.1	0.1	85.1	85.5	6.8	6.6	6.8	7.2	6.8	23.3	27.1	13.9	1.5	75.3	40.1	50.5	49.5
87733	MOSQUERO	84.1	83.8	0.4	0.4	0.0	0.0	45.1	45.4	3.1	3.9	6.1	5.7	5.7	18.3	30.6	22.7	3.9	83.4	49.9	50.2	49.8
87734	OCATE	62.2	61.7	0.0	0.0	0.0	0.0	69.5	70.5	5.0	6.0	6.0	9.5	6.0	19.8	30.2	15.5	2.1	76.2	43.5	52.4	47.6
87740	RATON	79.8	79.2	0.2	0.2	0.4	0.4	52.3	53.8	6.2	6.5	7.0	6.6	5.9	23.0	27.2	14.8	2.9	76.2	41.3	48.9	51.1
87742	ROCIADA	59.4	58.6	0.1	0.1	0.3	0.3	64.4	65.5	5.6	6.4	7.2	5.6	5.4	22.4	33.6	12.7	1.0	76.8	43.1	50.7	49.3
87743	ROY	84.4	84.1	0.4	0.5	0.0	0.0	44.9	45.1	3.1	4.0	5.8	5.4	5.4	17.7	30.5	24.0	4.0	83.6	50.7	50.5	49.6
87745	SAPELLO	66.7	66.7	0.0	0.0	0.0	0.0	66.7	66.7	0.0	0.0	0.0	0.0	66.7	33.3	0.0	0.0	0.0	100.0	23.8	66.7	33.3
87746	SOLANO	84.9	84.7	0.0	0.0	0.0	0.0	45.2	45.8	2.8	4.2	5.6	5.6	4.2	18.1	29.2	26.4	4.2	87.5	51.7	48.6	51.4
87747	SPRINGER	81.9	81.4	0.6	0.6	0.2	0.2	60.0	61.7	5.4	5.8	6.8	12.6	4.6	22.1	23.9	15.8	3.0	73.2	39.4	53.5	46.5
87750	VALMORA	62.0	61.7	0.0	0.0	0.0	0.0	68.1	68.9	4.8	5.4	6.0	9.6	6.0	19.8	30.5	15.6	2.4	76.7	43.9	52.1	47.9
87752	WAGON MOUND	62.0	61.5	0.0	0.0	0.0	0.0	68.5	69.0	5.1	5.9	5.8	9.2	6.1	19.9	30.3	15.7	2.1	76.5	43.6	51.9	48.1
87801	SOCORRO	68.0	66.9	0.7	0.8	1.8	2.1	54.0	54.7	6.7	6.0	6.9	9.6	11.1	24.9	22.7	10.7	1.3	75.9	32.3	51.3	48.7
87820	ARAGON	88.0	87.7	0.5	0.5	0.5	0.5	23.6	23.6	4.6	5.1	5.6	5.6	4.1	18.0	34.9	20.0	2.1	81.0	49.5	50.3	49.7
87821	DATIL	87.2	87.3	0.2	0.2	1.1	1.1	13.6	13.5	3.4	5.3	6.2	7.2	2.3	18.4	41.4	14.8	1.1	79.5	48.6	51.0	49.0
87823	LEMITAR	74.3	73.7	0.8	0.8	0.2	0.2	48.6	49.3	5.6	6.2	8.2	6.8	5.1	23.8	30.5	12.7	1.2	75.7	40.9	50.1	49.9
87825	MAGDALENA	35.5	34.3	0.3	0.3	0.0	0.0	23.2	22.7	8.2	8.8	10.0	8.9	7.4	25.2	21.5	9.0	1.0	67.1	30.0	48.3	51.7
87827	PIE TOWN	87.4	87.4	0.2	0.2	1.1	1.1	13.6	13.5	3.3	5.3	6.2	7.1	2.3	18.9	41.1	14.9	1.1	79.7	48.6	51.4	48.7
87828	POLVADERA	73.1	75.0	0.0	0.0	0.0	0.0	53.9	53.6	7.1	7.1	7.1	7.1	7.1	28.6	28.6	7.1	0.0	78.6	35.0	50.0	50.0
87829	QUEMADO	87.2	87.2	0.3	0.3	0.9	0.9	13.8	13.7	3.4	5.2	6.4	7.0	2.4	18.6	40.9	15.2	0.9	79.3	48.5	50.6	49.4
87830	RESERVE	88.1	88.2	0.4	0.4	0.4	0.4	23.8	23.8	4.6	5.1	5.3	5.2	4.0	18.0	35.3	20.6	2.1	81.4	50.4	51.3	48.7
87831	SAN ACACIA	74.5	73.8	0.9	0.8	0.2	0.2	50.5	51.3	5.6	6.1	8.3	6.9	5.1	23.6	30.4	12.7	1.3	75.9	41.1	50.0	50.0
87901	TRUTH OR CONSEQUENCE	86.7	86.2	0.6	0.6	0.2	0.3	24.9	25.5	4.5	4.4	5.1	5.4	5.1	17.0	29.2	25.6	3.7	82.4	51.3	49.6	50.4
87930	ARREY	87.8	87.3	0.1	0.1	0.4	0.4	31.4	32.4	5.4	5.4	6.6	6.2	5.1	18.1	30.6	21.1	1.4	78.6	47.3	51.9	48.1
87931	CABALLO	87.6	87.1	0.1	0.1	0.4	0.5	32.4	33.4	5.6	5.6	6.7	6.3	5.1	18.4	30.2	20.6	1.4	78.2	46.6	52.1	47.9
87933	DERRY	89.7	89.9	0.0	0.0	0.0	0.0	19.2	19.5	3.6	3.6	4.7	4.7	4.1	14.2	33.7	29.0	2.4	84.6	55.8	50.3	49.7
87936	GARFIELD	42.0	41.1	0.4	0.5	0.2	0.2	82.7	83.4	9.6	9.0	10.8	11.4	9.1	21.7	19.1	8.5	0.8	63.4	25.1	50.9	49.1
87937	HATCH	45.8	44.9	0.2	0.3	0.2	0.2	80.0	81.2	9.8	9.0	11.1	10.0	6.7	23.9	18.8	10.1	0.7	63.8	28.0	48.6	51.4
87940	RINCON	51.7	51.0	0.2	0.3	0.0	0.0	80.9	82.2	9.8	9.1	10.7	10.8	8.3	22.9	19.0	8.7	0.7	63.7	26.1	49.6	50.4
87941	SALEM	42.1	41.2	0.3	0.4	0.2	0.3	82.6	83.6	9.7	8.9	10.9	11.7	8.9	22.1	18.8	8.2	0.8	63.2	25.0	51.3	48.7
87942	WILLIAMSBURG	90.0	89.1	0.0	0.0	0.0	0.0	20.0	20.3	2.9	2.9	4.4	4.4	4.4	15.2	36.2	27.5	2.2	86.2	56.2	49.3	50.7
87943	WINSTON	87.7	87.8	0.0	0.0	0.0	0.0	32.5	33.1	5.8	5.8	7.0	6.4	5.2	19.2	29.7	19.8	1.2	77.3	45.4	52.9	47.1
88001	LAS CRUCES	63.5	63.0	2.9	3.0	1.5	1.6	59.7	60.6	7.7	6.5	6.6	11.1	15.5	25.8	16.0	9.7	1.1	75.3	26.5	48.2	51.8
88002	WHITE SANDS MISSILE	72.0	70.3	11.3	11.7	3.7	4.3	17.5	18.4	12.8	8.9	10.3	6.6	6.7	38.4	14.7	1.5	0.1	64.4	27.4	52.0	48.0
88005	LAS CRUCES	72.2	71.3	1.5	1.6	0.6	0.7	53.9	55.3	7.0	6.3	7.2	7.5	8.5	27.0	23.5	11.8	1.3	75.0	35.1	49.7	50.3
88007	LAS CRUCES	71.9	71.1	1.1	1.2	0.4	0.5	54.1	55.4	6.6	6.6	7.9	7.6	7.4	27.0	25.1	10.7	1.2	74.2	35.9	50.6	49.4
88008	SANTA TERESA	78.1	77.8	0.9	1.1	0.4	0.5	73.3	73.3	9.2	8.6	8.5	8.5	6.4	28.1	21.8	8.2	0.7	68.2	32.2	48.9	51.1
88011	LAS CRUCES	78.9	77.6	1.7	1.8	2.2	2.5	33.5	34.8	5.5	5.6	6.1	7.1	9.5	24.4	25.4	14.0	2.5	79.2	38.8	47.9	52.1
88012	LAS CRUCES	65.3	63.9	1.7	1.9	0.5	0.6	59.5	61.6	8.7	8.2	9.1	8.8	8.3	28.0	21.1	7.3	0.5	68.6	30.2	49.8	50.2
88020	ANIMAS	93.0	92.4	0.0	0.0	0.0	0.0	22.8	24.1	7.6	7.5	8.1	7.5	5.8	23.2	27.8	11.4	1.2	72.2	38.4	52.7	47.3
88021	ANTHONY	62.3	61.9	0.3	0.4	0.3	0.3	90.7	91.3	10.0	9.5	10.4	9.6	8.5	25.9	18.0	7.5	0.6	64.3	26.4	48.7	51.4
88022	ARENAS VALLEY	75.7	75.5	0.4	0.4	0.1	0.1	47.9	48.2	8.2	7.6	8.2	7.5	8.0	26.3	24.3	9.0	1.0	71.5	33.2	49.3	50.8
88023	BAYARD	68.4	68.3	0.3	0.3	0.0	0.0	78.5	78.5	6.5	6.4	7.4	7.4	6.6	21.4	24.8	16.9	2.6	74.5	40.3	47.5	52.5
88025	BUCKHORN	95.9	95.9	0.6	0.6	0.0	0.0	8.7	8.9	4.8	5.4	5.5	7.5	5.2	18.1	34.6	16.7	2.3	79.7	47.1	52.1	47.9
88026	SANTA CLARA	64.8	64.6	0.4	0.4	0.1	0.1	78.9	79.0	9.7	8.4	7.7	7.7	7.3	23.4	21.0	13.7	1.1	68.9	32.4	47.9	52.1
88030	DEMING	74.3	73.7	0.9	1.0	0.3	0.4	57.7	58.6	8.1	7.7	8.2	7.6	6.6	21.9	21.7	16.5	1.9	71.2	36.6	48.7	51.3
88039	GLENWOOD	88.0	88.3	0.3	0.3	0.3	0.3	23.9	23.6	4.7	5.2	5.5	5.2	4.0	17.9	34.8	20.7	2.0	80.6	50.1	50.8	49.3
88041	HANOVER	81.0	80.9	0.2	0.2	0.2	0.2	43.4	43.7	5.4	5.8	6.5	7.2	5.4	20.0	29.5	17.9	2.3	78.1	44.8	51.2	48.8
88042	HILLSBORO	87.7	87.3	0.0	0.0	0.6	0.5	32.4	33.4	5.6	5.6	6.6	6.4	5.0	18.6	30.2	20.7	1.3	78.5	46.6	52.5	47.5
88043	HURLEY	74.2	74.1	0.2	0.2	0.1	0.1	56.3	56.1	6.5	6.7	7.5	6.0	5.4	22.0	25.0	18.0	2.9	75.3	41.6	48.8	51.2
88044	LA MESA	69.6	69.1	0.3	0.3	0.2	0.2	83.3	84.2	7.3	7.1	8.1	8.3	8.0	25.7	23.1	11.2	1.1	72.3	34.4	50.1	49.9
88045	LORDSBURG	82.7	82.3	0.5	0.5	0.4	0.4	60.0	60.7	8.0	7.6	9.0	8.0	7.5	23.8	22.6	11.8	1.6	70.3	34.4	49.9	50.1
	NEW MEXICO	66.8	65.8	1.9	2.0	1.1	1.3	42.1	42.7	7.3	7.1	7.6	7.7	7.7	26.9	23.9	10.4	1.4	73.4	34.9	49.2	50.9
	UNITED STATES	75.1	73.6	12.3	12.5	3.8	4.2	12.5	14.1	6.9	6.7	7.2	7.0	7.3	28.6	23.8	10.8	1.7	75.1	36.0	49.1	50.9

ZIP CODE				2004 HOUSEHOLD INCOME DISTRIBUTION (%)					MEDIAN HOUSEHOLD INCOME					2004 HOME VALUE DISTRIBUTION (%)					
#	POST OFFICE NAME	2004 Per Capita Income	2004 HH Income Base	Less than $25,000	$25,000 to $49,999	$50,000 to $99,999	$100,000 to $149,999	$150,000 or More	2004	2009	2004 National Centile	2004 State Centile	2004 Home Value Base	Less than $50,000	$50,000 to $89,999	$90,000 to $174,999	$175,000 to $399,999	$400,000 or More	2004 Median Home Value
87513	ARROYO HONDO	22179	1055	38.1	33.2	21.7	3.5	3.5	32431	38325	19	48	822	14.2	6.7	23.1	37.8	18.1	205000
87514	ARROYO SECO	24828	547	36.0	35.8	20.7	3.7	3.8	32822	38858	20	51	435	14.7	7.1	18.6	38.4	21.2	220098
87520	CHAMA	20478	566	33.4	37.1	21.2	5.0	3.4	36007	42474	32	68	460	18.0	22.8	33.3	20.9	5.0	106818
87521	CHAMISAL	15772	254	40.9	29.5	25.2	3.9	0.4	34252	38196	25	57	223	26.0	18.8	26.5	26.0	2.7	100500
87522	CHIMAYO	18938	1983	38.0	31.5	22.7	4.7	3.1	33343	38858	22	54	1648	16.3	17.3	32.8	28.2	5.5	121094
87524	COSTILLA	14651	233	45.9	31.8	19.7	2.6	0.0	27591	33784	8	23	198	28.3	17.7	26.8	19.7	7.6	97273
87527	DIXON	17961	699	39.8	32.5	23.0	4.0	0.7	31204	35278	15	41	604	16.2	15.6	38.6	26.5	3.2	118519
87528	DULCE	12877	1034	42.3	30.2	22.7	3.7	1.2	29297	34013	11	31	671	47.4	25.6	21.0	5.1	0.9	53571
87530	EL RITO	17877	386	35.8	29.3	26.9	5.4	2.6	35937	41858	31	68	312	20.5	15.4	30.1	25.0	9.0	118023
87531	EMBUDO	18339	1983	33.3	32.1	25.8	7.3	1.5	34712	40535	26	59	1631	24.7	16.0	31.2	22.9	5.3	110759
87532	ESPANOLA	18390	6778	35.9	29.4	25.4	7.0	2.4	35697	41616	30	67	5105	22.6	10.2	30.8	30.2	6.1	127878
87535	GLORIETA	30285	403	22.6	24.1	31.5	12.7	9.2	52650	62166	76	94	321	10.6	17.8	20.6	42.1	9.0	176862
87537	HERNANDEZ	16487	397	34.3	37.5	21.7	4.8	1.8	32785	38459	20	51	326	38.3	7.7	26.7	21.8	5.5	102041
87539	LA MADERA	18334	129	40.3	31.0	22.5	4.7	1.6	32317	37979	19	47	106	28.3	17.9	26.4	22.6	4.7	96667
87540	LAMY	37458	399	16.8	21.6	37.1	12.0	12.5	58935	71045	83	96	342	3.2	5.9	17.3	51.5	22.2	251282
87544	LOS ALAMOS	42081	7875	8.2	13.6	35.2	28.1	15.0	88391	105263	97	100	6234	4.5	1.7	14.7	57.0	22.2	275339
87549	OJO CALIENTE	18377	608	57.4	28.1	12.7	0.7	1.2	19770	22381	2	3	524	39.9	14.9	22.0	18.1	5.2	77188
87552	PECOS	17314	1543	32.7	34.4	27.0	5.0	1.0	36656	43064	34	73	1219	20.2	13.5	40.0	23.2	3.0	116969
87553	PENASCO	13365	515	48.5	29.5	19.6	2.1	0.2	26248	29904	6	16	429	27.7	24.0	31.5	16.1	0.7	85313
87556	QUESTA	18753	1580	42.3	31.1	20.0	3.5	3.0	30616	35497	14	38	1271	23.3	14.5	32.8	23.5	5.9	114665
87557	RANCHOS DE TAOS	20979	1760	36.9	34.8	17.8	6.4	4.0	35068	40701	28	63	1355	12.5	5.3	31.3	40.2	10.7	176941
87560	RIBERA	14292	884	46.8	29.9	18.7	3.9	0.8	26546	30060	6	18	744	28.1	23.8	30.5	14.1	3.5	86889
87564	SAN CRISTOBAL	29774	210	33.3	27.6	22.9	7.1	9.1	40988	47602	50	80	155	8.4	8.4	29.7	41.3	12.3	183088
87565	SAN JOSE	15710	531	43.1	26.4	22.6	6.4	1.5	31201	36176	15	41	453	23.6	15.5	34.0	24.3	2.7	112076
87566	SAN JUAN PUEBLO	14118	2044	38.1	33.3	22.8	4.7	1.2	32003	37350	18	45	1578	23.4	20.7	34.2	21.2	0.5	98532
87567	SANTA CRUZ	23984	123	26.8	26.0	28.5	11.4	7.3	47905	57121	68	89	102	20.6	4.9	22.6	39.2	12.8	182143
87571	TAOS	19992	6388	42.6	29.5	19.8	4.2	4.0	30247	35640	13	35	4649	14.0	7.7	31.0	38.0	9.3	165996
87573	TERERRO	24118	60	26.7	33.3	33.3	6.7	0.0	38878	44436	42	78	49	10.2	18.4	42.9	24.5	4.1	120833
87575	TIERRA AMARILLA	20169	807	35.3	35.7	21.1	4.7	3.2	34949	41004	27	60	659	16.2	22.0	35.7	21.1	5.0	108817
87579	VADITO	15033	547	44.2	29.3	21.9	3.7	0.9	30368	34280	13	36	457	26.5	15.8	26.3	30.0	1.5	104847
87580	VALDEZ	29032	149	36.9	35.6	19.5	3.4	4.7	32466	39562	19	48	115	10.4	7.0	20.0	38.3	24.4	232692
87581	VALLECITOS	18714	294	39.8	31.0	22.5	4.8	2.0	32991	38283	21	53	243	27.2	18.1	28.4	21.8	4.5	98846
87701	LAS VEGAS	15898	7886	43.6	30.5	19.9	4.1	1.9	28790	32855	10	30	5279	24.0	20.2	42.3	12.0	1.5	98779
87711	ANTON CHICO	10224	130	56.2	31.5	10.8	1.5	0.0	19176	23053	2	3	108	53.7	25.9	12.0	3.7	4.6	46667
87713	CHACON	13778	93	40.9	32.3	22.6	3.2	1.1	29671	35000	12	33	78	30.8	16.7	34.6	16.7	1.3	96667
87714	CIMARRON	24175	1244	27.9	34.6	27.3	6.4	3.9	40118	46209	46	79	966	11.6	22.9	29.7	27.9	8.0	116541
87715	CLEVELAND	13475	136	41.2	33.1	22.1	2.9	0.7	28301	32109	9	28	108	33.3	17.6	31.5	13.0	4.6	86667
87718	EAGLE NEST	27994	313	23.6	31.6	31.3	8.0	5.4	45972	53349	64	88	236	5.9	16.5	26.3	39.8	11.4	178571
87722	GUADALUPITA	13019	12	50.0	25.0	25.0	0.0	0.0	25000	27290	5	13	10	60.0	0.0	40.0	0.0	0.0	46667
87724	LA LOMA	10884	113	56.6	31.9	10.6	0.9	0.0	19283	22963	2	3	94	55.3	25.5	10.6	4.3	4.3	45455
87728	MAXWELL	22012	180	33.9	33.9	25.6	5.0	1.7	34527	38374	26	58	146	22.6	21.9	31.5	16.4	7.5	98000
87729	MIAMI	23735	35	37.1	31.4	25.7	5.7	0.0	33622	41146	23	55	28	21.4	17.9	39.3	14.3	7.1	104167
87730	MILLS	16482	15	40.0	33.3	26.7	0.0	0.0	32320	32320	19	48	12	58.3	41.7	0.0	0.0	0.0	40000
87731	MONTEZUMA	15748	18	27.8	38.9	27.8	5.6	0.0	35000	42361	28	63	14	7.1	21.4	50.0	21.4	0.0	112500
87732	MORA	14554	1464	45.4	33.2	15.9	3.5	2.1	27309	30820	8	21	1204	28.4	19.6	34.7	12.0	5.3	93750
87733	MOSQUERO	19952	112	42.9	29.5	20.5	4.5	2.7	29357	35000	11	32	87	58.6	17.2	11.5	8.1	4.6	39500
87734	OCATE	15756	174	50.6	25.9	19.0	3.5	1.2	24645	27546	4	11	138	44.9	17.4	17.4	12.3	8.0	60000
87740	RATON	18430	3636	36.4	35.6	22.5	3.6	1.9	32855	37086	20	52	2589	16.6	37.7	31.3	12.3	2.1	85373
87742	ROCIADA	17805	364	45.9	30.8	18.4	3.3	1.7	28084	32219	9	26	291	21.3	21.3	24.4	22.3	10.7	106439
87743	ROY	19371	212	42.9	29.7	21.2	4.3	1.9	29320	33721	11	31	165	61.2	16.4	10.9	7.3	4.2	37750
87745	SAPELLO	0	0	0.0	0.0	0.0	0.0	0.0	0	0	0	0	0	0.0	0.0	0.0	0.0	0.0	0
87746	SOLANO	17883	32	43.8	31.3	18.8	6.3	0.0	28125	35000	9	26	25	52.0	16.0	16.0	12.0	4.0	47500
87747	SPRINGER	16522	753	34.9	35.9	23.5	4.4	1.3	31793	35801	17	44	565	30.1	37.4	23.7	6.4	2.5	70102
87750	VALMORA	14610	64	53.1	25.0	18.8	3.1	0.0	23341	27260	3	8	50	46.0	16.0	18.0	12.0	8.0	60000
87752	WAGON MOUND	15825	240	52.5	24.6	18.8	3.3	0.8	23546	26873	4	8	189	48.2	16.9	16.4	11.6	6.9	53889
87801	SOCORRO	17071	4577	46.7	25.9	19.0	6.3	2.1	27393	33008	8	22	2875	22.3	27.4	36.8	12.2	1.3	90377
87820	ARAGON	16905	87	44.8	31.0	19.5	3.5	1.2	28015	32310	9	25	71	23.9	22.5	33.8	15.5	4.2	95000
87821	DATIL	15703	295	47.8	30.5	17.6	4.1	0.0	26632	30346	7	18	242	30.2	15.7	27.7	20.7	5.8	96250
87823	LEMITAR	21607	260	36.9	27.3	27.3	3.5	5.0	36132	41725	32	70	213	25.4	24.9	28.2	15.5	6.1	89643
87825	MAGDALENA	11108	1090	53.0	25.1	17.6	2.8	1.5	23052	26570	3	7	863	38.8	25.1	23.2	8.5	4.4	66493
87827	PIE TOWN	15982	311	48.2	30.2	17.7	3.9	0.0	26294	30219	6	16	255	29.8	14.9	29.0	20.8	5.5	97941
87828	POLVADERA	18036	14	42.9	28.6	28.6	0.0	0.0	30000	40000	12	35	12	16.7	33.3	33.3	16.7	0.0	90000
87829	QUEMADO	14336	137	48.2	29.9	18.3	3.7	0.0	26405	30994	6	17	112	30.4	16.1	26.8	21.4	5.4	95000
87830	RESERVE	17834	655	44.3	30.5	20.0	3.8	1.4	28356	32351	9	29	534	23.4	21.9	33.3	15.5	5.8	97353
87831	SAN ACACIA	20785	233	36.5	27.5	27.5	3.4	5.2	36364	41657	33	71	192	25.5	25.0	29.2	15.1	5.2	89231
87901	TRUTH OR CONSEQUENCE	18011	5198	47.7	31.8	15.9	2.9	1.8	26138	29352	6	16	3836	29.9	32.3	27.6	8.8	1.4	73543
87930	ARREY	11262	293	43.0	38.6	14.0	3.4	1.0	27501	30497	8	23	242	24.8	23.6	38.0	13.6	0.0	92000
87931	CABALLO	15519	679	43.3	39.0	13.4	3.2	1.0	27310	30233	8	21	560	25.7	24.1	38.2	12.0	0.0	90213
87933	DERRY	17040	61	36.1	31.2	23.0	6.6	3.3	35554	40000	30	66	51	9.8	23.5	41.2	25.5	0.0	113750
87936	GARFIELD	12480	188	55.3	26.1	13.8	3.2	1.6	21244	25000	2	4	144	47.9	28.5	10.4	10.4	2.8	52727
87937	HATCH	12950	1140	51.9	29.0	13.3	3.3	2.5	23768	27009	4	10	727	51.6	26.1	17.6	3.7	1.0	47262
87940	RINCON	11091	213	52.1	33.3	9.9	3.3	1.4	23690	27517	4	9	163	67.5	14.7	12.3	3.7	1.8	29853
87941	SALEM	10108	270	55.2	25.9	13.3	3.3	2.2	21461	25107	2	5	206	47.1	28.6	10.2	11.2	2.9	53529
87942	WILLIAMSBURG	20420	62	35.5	33.9	22.6	6.5	1.6	33615	37345	23	54	52	17.3	25.0	34.6	23.1	0.0	103571
87943	WINSTON	13983	80	47.5	37.5	12.5	2.5	0.0	25831	29344	6	15	66	25.8	24.2	37.9	12.1	0.0	90000
88001	LAS CRUCES	14294	14298	47.7	29.4	18.8	2.9	1.3	26477	30704	6	18	7292	21.0	43.9	30.6	4.4	0.1	78385
88002	WHITE SANDS MISSILE	20068	426	10.6	39.7	42.0	6.3	1.4	49712	57282	71	90	19	0.0	26.3	15.8	57.9	0.0	305000
88005	LAS CRUCES	19952	10885	32.6	30.2	27.3	7.2	2.7	38620	45344	41	77	7321	20.6	21.8	39.9	15.3	2.4	100408
88007	LAS CRUCES	22091	8396	28.4	30.0	29.6	8.1	3.9	42631	50200	55	84	6799	25.4	16.8	35.1	19.2	3.6	104844
88008	SANTA TERESA	20584	1819	20.1	28.3	33.5	13.8	4.2	51653	61312	75	93	1518	13.3	19.6	38.7	26.3	2.2	113797
88011	LAS CRUCES	26736	8644	25.7	25.6	32.2	10.8	5.8	48458	57861	69	90	5557	8.2	8.1	44.1	36.8	2.8	153059
88012	LAS CRUCES	15573	6186	29.8	38.3	27.6	3.6	0.8	37003	43719	35	74	4831	30.0	23.2	41.1	5.4	0.3	84852
88020	ANIMAS	18420	245	42.5	25.7	22.5	5.3	4.1	31330	36689	16	42	154	33.1	20.1	31.2	9.1	6.5	81667
88021	ANTHONY	9695	4904	46.7	33.1	15.9	3.5	0.8	26396	30141	6	17	3470	43.2	31.8	15.7	8.2	1.1	59476
88022	ARENAS VALLEY	17545	418	32.1	33.7	27.0	6.0	1.2	38154	44103	40	76	315	24.8	14.6	48.3	10.2	2.2	108777
88023	BAYARD	13831	1250	49.0	33.6	14.6	1.8	1.0	25457	28481	5	14	951	29.4	38.7	27.3	3.6	1.0	70758
88025	BUCKHORN	19513	483	34.6	37.9	18.2	7.9	1.5	35073	39750	28	64	399	12.5	23.6	36.1	21.8	6.0	117378
88026	SANTA CLARA	11882	816	49.8	31.5	16.5	1.8	0.4	25121	28308	5	13	587	29.5	35.8	31.2	2.9	0.7	72966
88030	DEMING	12852	9907	53.3	27.3	16.1	1.9	1.5	22958	26126	3	7	7335	39.6	31.6	23.2	5.0	0.6	64765
88039	GLENWOOD	18856	200	44.5	30.0	20.0	4.0	1.5	28251	31728	9	28	163	23.3	22.1	33.1	15.3	6.1	97500
88041	HANOVER	18777	191	38.2	35.1	22.5	2.1	2.1	32491	36767	19	49	158	24.7	21.5	37.3	12.7	3.8	100000
88042	HILLSBORO	17436	193	44.0	38.9	13.0	3.1	1.0	27027	30317	7	19	159	25.8	23.9	38.4	12.0	0.0	90385
88043	HURLEY	13649	780	37.7	40.1	19.1	2.3	0.8	31123	35424	15	40	601	25.6	39.1	25.6	7.3	2.3	72500
88044	LA MESA	13311	1374	44.3	32.8	15.7	4.7	2.6	28230	32159	9	27	1075	36.7	24.7	26.7	10.1	1.8	74841
88045	LORDSBURG	14265	1922	46.3	30.4	17.9	3.9	1.6	27771	32358	8	24	1311	40.0	39.0	18.8	1.8	0.5	61560
	NEW MEXICO	20647		31.7	30.6	26.4	7.4	3.8	38669	45233				18.9	17.7	37.6	21.5	4.4	113735
	UNITED STATES	25866		24.7	27.1	30.8	10.9	6.5	48124	56710				10.9	15.0	33.7	30.1	10.4	145905

#	POST OFFICE NAME	FINANCIAL SERVICES: Auto Loan	FINANCIAL SERVICES: Home Loan	FINANCIAL SERVICES: Investments	FINANCIAL SERVICES: Retirement Plans	THE HOME: Home Improvements: Home Repair	THE HOME: Home Improvements: Lawn & Garden	THE HOME: Furnishings: Computers & Hardware	THE HOME: Furnishings: Major Appliances	THE HOME: Furnishings: TV, Radio, Sound Equipment	THE HOME: Furnishings: Furniture	ENTERTAINMENT: Dine out/Carry out	ENTERTAINMENT: Sports Equipment	ENTERTAINMENT: Fees & Tickets	ENTERTAINMENT: Toys & Games	ENTERTAINMENT: Travel	ENTERTAINMENT: Cable TV	PERSONAL: Apparel & Services	PERSONAL: Auto Repairs	PERSONAL: Health Insurance	PERSONAL: Pets & Supplies
87513	ARROYO HONDO	83	67	47	61	74	82	63	74	70	63	84	87	57	82	66	74	78	74	85	99
87514	ARROYO SECO	86	67	46	61	76	85	64	77	72	63	85	90	57	84	68	77	79	75	91	105
87520	CHAMA	84	65	45	59	74	83	62	74	70	61	83	87	55	82	66	75	77	73	88	102
87521	CHAMISAL	44	42	83	38	40	47	49	47	57	53	73	51	48	76	50	61	74	50	49	51
87522	CHIMAYO	57	57	98	52	53	61	63	60	70	67	90	67	62	93	63	74	91	64	61	65
87524	COSTILLA	61	47	32	43	52	60	47	55	53	46	62	63	42	61	49	56	58	54	65	72
87527	DIXON	45	44	86	40	41	49	51	49	59	55	76	54	50	79	52	64	77	52	51	53
87528	DULCE	64	57	43	54	58	62	54	59	56	55	68	69	51	65	54	56	65	59	61	72
87530	EL RITO	66	62	83	58	60	67	65	66	71	69	90	74	63	90	65	74	89	68	67	75
87531	EMBUDO	70	66	79	62	64	71	67	69	72	71	91	78	65	89	67	74	89	71	70	79
87532	ESPANOLA	58	58	92	54	55	63	63	61	69	66	89	69	63	91	64	73	89	64	62	67
87535	GLORIETA	111	116	111	117	113	114	111	112	105	112	132	131	110	131	108	100	130	111	101	125
87537	HERNANDEZ	65	61	75	57	59	65	62	64	67	65	85	72	60	84	62	69	83	65	64	73
87539	LA MADERA	49	48	93	43	44	53	55	52	63	59	82	58	54	85	56	68	83	56	54	57
87540	LAMY	117	130	128	131	127	130	118	119	112	120	140	138	123	142	119	109	139	116	111	135
87544	LOS ALAMOS	130	154	184	157	151	156	145	141	137	145	173	164	154	178	148	134	172	140	131	155
87549	OJO CALIENTE	52	39	26	38	43	52	44	48	49	41	58	54	39	54	43	52	53	48	58	58
87552	PECOS	72	62	47	59	64	69	60	66	63	62	77	76	55	73	60	63	74	66	69	81
87553	PENASCO	38	37	72	33	35	41	43	41	49	46	64	45	42	66	43	53	64	44	42	44
87556	QUESTA	63	54	61	50	56	64	56	60	62	57	77	68	52	77	57	66	75	61	66	73
87557	RANCHOS DE TAOS	80	73	57	70	73	77	69	74	70	71	87	86	65	82	68	69	83	74	74	88
87560	RIBERA	43	42	81	38	39	47	48	46	56	52	73	51	48	75	49	60	73	50	48	50
87564	SAN CRISTOBAL	106	85	61	77	94	104	80	95	89	80	107	111	72	105	85	95	100	94	110	127
87565	SAN JOSE	64	56	46	51	54	57	56	61	59	61	74	65	52	66	54	57	73	62	59	65
87566	SAN JUAN PUEBLO	49	49	82	45	46	53	54	52	60	57	77	58	54	79	54	63	77	55	52	56
87567	SANTA CRUZ	79	87	103	84	83	89	85	84	85	88	108	93	87	111	85	84	108	85	78	91
87571	TAOS	60	60	78	58	58	64	62	61	65	63	82	71	62	82	63	66	81	63	61	69
87573	TERERRO	79	62	42	56	70	78	58	70	66	58	78	82	52	77	62	71	73	69	83	96
87575	TIERRA AMARILLA	75	61	56	55	67	76	60	69	68	61	83	80	55	83	63	73	79	69	80	91
87579	VADITO	43	42	81	37	39	46	48	46	56	52	72	50	47	74	49	60	73	49	48	50
87580	VALDEZ	95	75	51	68	84	95	71	85	80	70	95	100	63	93	75	85	88	84	101	116
87581	VALLECITOS	49	48	91	43	45	53	55	52	63	59	82	58	54	84	55	68	82	56	55	57
87701	LAS VEGAS	51	49	74	46	47	54	53	52	58	56	74	59	52	75	53	61	74	55	54	59
87711	ANTON CHICO	30	30	58	27	28	33	34	32	39	37	51	36	34	53	35	43	52	35	34	35
87713	CHACON	43	42	82	38	39	47	49	46	56	52	73	51	48	75	49	61	74	50	48	50
87714	CIMARRON	92	76	54	70	82	90	71	83	78	72	94	97	65	91	74	81	88	82	93	109
87715	CLEVELAND	41	40	78	36	37	44	46	44	53	50	69	49	46	72	47	58	70	48	46	48
87718	EAGLE NEST	108	84	57	76	95	107	80	96	90	79	107	112	71	105	85	96	99	94	113	131
87722	GUADALUPITA	40	39	77	35	37	43	45	43	52	49	68	48	45	70	46	56	68	46	45	47
87724	LA LOMA	30	30	58	27	28	33	34	32	39	37	51	36	34	53	35	42	51	35	34	35
87728	MAXWELL	81	57	30	54	66	74	56	69	64	55	76	83	48	74	58	68	69	68	82	96
87729	MIAMI	81	57	30	53	66	74	56	69	64	55	75	83	48	74	58	68	69	68	82	96
87730	MILLS	60	45	29	43	49	59	49	55	55	47	65	61	44	61	49	58	59	54	65	67
87731	MONTEZUMA	69	59	43	55	62	67	56	63	59	56	72	73	51	69	57	60	68	62	68	80
87732	MORA	42	41	79	36	38	45	47	44	54	50	70	49	46	72	47	58	71	48	46	48
87733	MOSQUERO	66	49	33	47	54	65	55	60	61	52	72	68	49	68	54	65	66	60	72	73
87734	OCATE	42	41	80	37	38	45	47	45	55	51	71	50	47	73	48	59	71	48	47	49
87740	RATON	60	57	57	54	57	64	59	60	61	59	76	68	57	74	59	62	73	61	63	68
87742	ROCIADA	75	59	40	53	66	74	56	67	63	55	74	78	50	74	59	67	69	66	79	91
87743	ROY	66	49	33	47	54	65	55	60	61	52	72	67	49	68	54	65	66	60	72	73
87745	SAPELLO	0	0	0	0	0	0	0	0	0	0	0	0	0	0	0	0	0	0	0	0
87746	SOLANO	65	49	32	47	53	64	54	59	61	51	71	67	48	67	53	64	65	59	71	72
87747	SPRINGER	69	51	32	49	57	67	55	62	62	52	73	71	48	69	55	65	66	62	74	78
87750	VALMORA	42	41	80	37	38	45	47	45	54	51	71	49	46	73	48	59	71	48	47	49
87752	WAGON MOUND	42	41	79	37	38	45	47	45	54	50	70	49	46	73	48	59	71	48	47	49
87801	SOCORRO	62	53	48	53	54	59	58	59	59	57	73	69	54	69	56	58	70	61	60	68
87820	ARAGON	64	50	34	45	57	63	47	57	54	47	63	67	42	63	50	57	59	56	67	78
87821	DATIL	58	46	31	41	51	58	43	52	49	43	58	61	38	57	46	52	54	51	61	71
87823	LEMITAR	86	78	61	75	78	82	74	80	75	77	93	92	70	88	73	74	89	79	79	95
87825	MAGDALENA	54	45	35	43	46	52	47	51	50	48	61	57	43	57	46	51	58	51	54	58
87827	PIE TOWN	58	46	31	41	51	58	43	52	49	43	58	61	38	57	46	52	54	51	61	71
87828	POLVADERA	57	52	41	50	52	55	50	54	50	51	62	62	47	59	49	50	60	53	53	63
87829	QUEMADO	58	46	31	41	51	58	43	52	49	43	58	61	38	57	46	52	54	51	61	71
87830	RESERVE	64	50	34	45	57	64	47	57	54	47	64	67	42	63	51	57	59	56	67	78
87831	SAN ACACIA	86	78	61	75	78	83	75	80	76	77	93	93	71	88	74	75	90	80	80	95
87901	TRUTH OR CONSEQUENCE	56	49	43	46	52	62	48	54	52	49	64	55	46	56	51	56	59	53	64	62
87930	ARREY	65	45	23	39	51	58	43	54	52	44	61	63	38	57	44	56	56	53	66	75
87931	CABALLO	64	43	20	37	49	56	42	52	50	43	59	62	36	56	42	54	54	52	64	74
87933	DERRY	72	67	64	63	71	83	62	70	65	66	81	69	63	68	67	70	76	68	82	80
87936	GARFIELD	61	54	45	50	52	54	55	59	57	60	72	63	50	63	52	55	71	60	56	62
87937	HATCH	64	57	47	52	54	57	58	62	60	63	75	66	53	66	55	58	74	63	58	65
87940	RINCON	56	49	41	46	47	50	50	54	52	55	65	58	46	58	48	50	65	55	51	57
87941	SALEM	62	54	45	50	52	55	55	60	57	60	72	63	51	64	53	55	71	61	56	62
87942	WILLIAMSBURG	70	64	59	60	68	80	59	68	63	63	78	67	59	66	64	67	73	66	80	78
87943	WINSTON	57	38	17	33	43	49	37	46	44	37	52	55	31	49	37	48	47	45	56	65
88001	LAS CRUCES	52	46	46	45	45	48	52	50	52	51	65	59	48	60	49	49	63	53	48	55
88002	WHITE SANDS MISSILE	94	60	57	69	55	65	89	77	90	83	113	102	76	101	73	83	108	91	71	87
88005	LAS CRUCES	74	71	70	69	70	75	72	73	72	73	90	84	69	87	71	71	88	74	72	83
88007	LAS CRUCES	89	85	75	82	85	90	82	87	82	85	102	97	79	96	81	81	99	86	86	98
88008	SANTA TERESA	92	101	99	101	98	97	94	95	89	97	112	108	95	112	92	85	111	93	85	103
88011	LAS CRUCES	85	88	101	91	87	92	91	88	87	90	110	105	91	107	89	84	107	90	84	97
88012	LAS CRUCES	69	67	60	65	65	68	65	67	64	67	80	77	62	76	63	62	78	68	64	76
88020	ANIMAS	80	56	29	53	65	73	55	68	64	55	75	82	47	73	57	67	68	67	82	95
88021	ANTHONY	52	44	38	42	44	46	47	50	49	50	62	55	43	57	45	47	61	51	47	54
88022	ARENAS VALLEY	71	65	51	62	65	69	62	66	63	64	77	76	59	73	61	62	74	66	66	79
88023	BAYARD	51	43	34	40	43	47	45	49	48	47	59	52	41	53	43	47	57	49	49	53
88025	BUCKHORN	72	54	36	52	59	71	60	66	67	57	79	74	53	74	59	71	72	66	79	79
88026	SANTA CLARA	49	43	36	40	42	44	44	47	45	47	57	51	40	50	42	44	56	48	45	50
88030	DEMING	53	43	33	40	44	48	45	49	48	47	59	54	41	54	44	48	57	50	51	56
88039	GLENWOOD	64	50	34	45	57	64	47	57	54	47	64	67	42	63	50	57	59	56	67	78
88041	HANOVER	67	51	33	49	55	66	56	61	63	53	74	69	50	69	55	66	67	61	73	74
88042	HILLSBORO	64	43	19	37	49	56	41	52	50	42	59	62	35	56	42	54	53	51	64	74
88043	HURLEY	57	47	37	45	49	56	49	54	53	50	65	58	45	59	49	54	61	54	59	61
88044	LA MESA	62	55	45	51	52	55	55	60	58	60	72	64	51	64	53	55	72	61	56	62
88045	LORDSBURG	59	53	43	50	52	54	52	57	54	56	67	62	49	61	51	52	66	57	54	62
	NEW MEXICO	77	74	75	73	73	78	75	76	75	76	94	87	73	91	74	74	92	77	75	86
	UNITED STATES	100	100	100	100	100	100	100	100	100	100	100	100	100	100	100	100	100	100	100	100

# POST OFFICE NAME	COUNTY FIPS CODE	POPULATION 2000	2004	2009	% Rate	State Centile	HOUSEHOLDS 2000	2004	2009	% Annual Rate 2000-2004	2004 Average HH Size	FAMILIES 2000	2004	% Annual Rate 2000-2004
88047 MESILLA PARK	013	1560	1763	1985	2.9	91	507	582	666	3.3	3.03	420	476	3.0
88048 MESQUITE	013	3217	3304	3586	0.6	44	865	908	1003	1.2	3.64	766	797	0.9
88049 MIMBRES	017	1206	1217	1214	0.2	27	481	500	513	0.9	2.43	336	343	0.5
88061 SILVER CITY	017	19701	19795	19902	0.1	24	7835	8137	8440	0.9	2.38	5442	5543	0.4
88063 SUNLAND PARK	013	10720	11508	12601	1.7	76	2720	2997	3348	2.3	3.84	2436	2662	2.1
88072 VADO	013	2833	2830	3056	0.0	19	763	779	856	0.5	3.63	690	697	0.2
88081 CHAPARRAL	013	10172	11064	12021	2.0	81	2921	3242	3590	2.5	3.40	2438	2672	2.2
88101 CLOVIS	009	41494	41679	42209	0.1	24	15426	15821	16344	0.6	2.57	10888	10971	0.2
88103 CANNON AFB	009	547	601	631	2.2	86	189	218	236	3.4	2.44	143	162	3.0
88112 BROADVIEW	009	88	102	110	3.5	95	38	45	50	4.1	2.27	28	33	3.9
88113 CAUSEY	041	93	99	104	1.5	71	33	36	38	2.1	2.75	26	27	0.9
88114 CROSSROADS	025	19	19	19	0.0	21	8	8	9	0.0	2.38	6	6	0.0
88116 ELIDA	041	489	497	511	0.4	33	204	211	220	0.8	2.36	158	161	0.4
88118 FLOYD	041	249	252	260	0.3	29	96	99	103	0.7	2.55	75	76	0.3
88119 FORT SUMNER	011	1921	1942	1973	0.3	28	793	816	843	0.7	2.29	519	522	0.1
88120 GRADY	009	276	320	345	3.5	96	112	133	147	4.1	2.41	83	96	3.5
88121 HOUSE	037	147	145	142	-0.3	11	66	67	67	0.4	2.01	48	47	-0.5
88123 LINGO	041	49	52	55	1.4	69	16	17	18	1.4	3.06	13	13	0.0
88124 MELROSE	009	1167	1132	1123	-0.7	4	477	473	479	-0.2	2.35	332	318	-1.0
88125 MILNESAND	041	18	19	20	1.3	64	5	5	6	0.0	3.80	4	4	0.0
88126 PEP	041	119	127	134	1.5	72	54	58	62	1.7	2.19	42	45	1.6
88130 PORTALES	041	16712	17233	17969	0.7	47	6133	6407	6761	1.0	2.57	4149	4248	0.6
88132 ROGERS	041	283	301	318	1.5	70	94	101	108	1.7	2.98	73	78	1.6
88133 SAINT VRAIN	009	27	26	26	-0.9	3	10	10	10	0.0	2.60	8	7	-3.1
88134 TAIBAN	011	117	118	120	0.2	26	38	39	41	0.6	3.03	28	29	0.8
88135 TEXICO	009	1528	1585	1625	0.9	50	547	579	605	1.4	2.74	412	425	0.7
88136 YESO	011	205	207	210	0.2	28	93	96	100	0.8	2.16	70	71	0.3
88201 ROSWELL	005	23838	23632	23537	-0.2	15	9478	9599	9686	0.3	2.41	6578	6545	-0.1
88203 ROSWELL	005	30111	29765	29612	-0.3	13	10764	10833	10882	0.2	2.68	7613	7506	-0.3
88210 ARTESIA	015	16021	16159	16274	0.2	26	5916	6088	6248	0.7	2.64	4319	4362	0.2
88213 CAPROCK	025	25	25	26	0.0	21	11	11	12	0.0	2.27	8	8	0.0
88220 CARLSBAD	015	33190	33121	33372	-0.1	18	12632	12893	13269	0.5	2.52	9089	9122	0.1
88230 DEXTER	005	4772	4886	4926	0.6	39	1448	1507	1534	0.9	3.18	1206	1240	0.7
88231 EUNICE	025	2889	2915	2992	0.2	27	1059	1093	1147	0.8	2.67	807	820	0.4
88232 HAGERMAN	005	1868	1815	1791	-0.7	4	614	605	602	-0.4	2.99	473	459	-0.7
88240 HOBBS	025	31657	32159	33415	0.4	31	11185	11639	12377	0.9	2.65	8152	8329	0.5
88242 HOBBS	025	5007	5562	6018	2.5	89	1749	1985	2198	3.0	2.68	1438	1614	2.8
88250 HOPE	015	212	219	223	0.8	48	89	94	98	1.3	2.33	70	73	1.0
88252 JAL	025	2114	2100	2154	-0.2	16	794	807	846	0.4	2.52	597	596	0.0
88253 LAKE ARTHUR	005	958	976	983	0.4	34	302	313	319	0.9	3.12	243	248	0.5
88256 LOVING	015	2026	2080	2110	0.6	42	678	713	740	1.2	2.92	531	550	0.8
88260 LOVINGTON	025	12257	12806	13453	1.0	56	4294	4600	4945	1.6	2.73	3265	3441	1.2
88264 MALJAMAR	025	62	63	65	0.4	33	23	24	25	1.0	2.63	19	19	0.0
88265 MONUMENT	025	185	221	248	4.3	98	73	89	102	4.8	2.48	56	67	4.3
88267 TATUM	025	1296	1301	1331	0.1	23	503	519	544	0.7	2.51	367	371	0.3
88301 CARRIZOZO	027	1464	1512	1636	0.8	47	617	654	727	1.4	2.19	404	418	0.8
88310 ALAMOGORDO	035	41009	41921	43619	0.5	37	15763	16429	17426	1.0	2.53	11268	11530	0.5
88314 BENT	035	316	336	353	1.5	70	119	130	139	2.1	2.58	85	91	1.6
88316 CAPITAN	027	2420	2645	2957	2.1	84	983	1100	1261	2.7	2.38	696	765	2.3
88317 CLOUDCROFT	035	2699	2930	3110	2.0	80	1181	1312	1420	2.5	2.23	859	936	2.0
88318 CORONA	027	417	422	453	0.3	29	166	173	190	1.0	2.44	114	116	0.4
88321 ENCINO	057	125	123	133	-0.4	9	57	58	63	0.4	2.10	42	42	0.0
88324 GLENCOE	027	61	67	75	2.2	86	29	33	38	3.1	2.03	22	25	3.1
88330 HOLLOMAN AIR FORCE B	035	2076	2136	2189	0.7	45	393	425	453	1.9	3.18	380	410	1.8
88336 HONDO	027	258	268	293	0.9	51	100	107	120	1.6	2.50	71	74	1.0
88337 LA LUZ	035	2541	2547	2602	0.1	23	1046	1082	1134	0.8	2.35	766	778	0.4
88339 MAYHILL	035	883	949	1001	1.7	77	383	422	455	2.3	2.25	274	297	1.9
88340 MESCALERO	035	3155	3280	3396	0.9	53	854	920	978	1.8	3.56	711	757	1.5
88341 NOGAL	027	545	570	622	1.1	58	227	244	273	1.7	2.24	167	176	1.2
88343 PICACHO	027	44	46	50	1.1	57	17	18	20	1.4	2.56	12	13	1.9
88344 PINON	035	109	114	118	1.1	58	45	48	50	1.5	2.38	32	33	0.7
88345 RUIDOSO	027	13071	14472	16304	2.4	88	5641	6404	7391	3.0	2.25	3841	4274	2.6
88346 RUIDOSO DOWNS	027	474	535	608	2.9	91	173	200	233	3.5	2.67	127	144	3.0
88347 SACRAMENTO	035	59	59	60	0.0	21	31	32	33	0.8	1.84	22	22	0.0
88348 SAN PATRICIO	027	469	488	532	0.9	54	169	181	202	1.6	2.70	120	126	1.2
88351 TINNIE	027	181	188	205	0.9	51	77	82	92	1.5	2.29	55	57	0.8
88352 TULAROSA	035	5233	5418	5622	0.8	48	2018	2142	2273	1.4	2.53	1418	1475	0.9
88353 VAUGHN	019	616	702	866	3.1	93	264	309	392	3.8	2.27	180	206	3.2
88354 WEED	035	190	191	194	0.1	24	79	82	85	0.9	2.32	55	56	0.4
88401 TUCUMCARI	037	7888	7666	7489	-0.7	4	3243	3229	3224	-0.1	2.32	2165	2110	-0.6
88410 AMISTAD	059	156	153	148	-0.5	6	58	58	58	0.0	2.64	43	42	-0.6
88411 BARD	037	12	12	12	0.0	21	6	6	6	0.0	2.00	4	4	0.0
88414 CAPULIN	059	59	58	56	-0.4	8	25	25	25	0.0	2.32	18	18	0.0
88415 CLAYTON	059	3143	3010	2867	-1.0	2	1316	1289	1256	-0.5	2.32	869	834	-1.0
88416 CONCHAS DAM	047	344	365	377	1.4	68	166	180	190	1.9	2.03	112	119	1.4
88417 CUERVO	009	91	104	124	3.2	93	41	52	68	5.8	1.38	30	25	-4.2
88418 DES MOINES	059	297	292	281	-0.4	8	120	121	119	0.2	2.41	88	87	-0.3
88419 FOLSOM	059	144	142	136	-0.3	11	63	63	62	0.0	2.25	46	46	0.0
88421 GARITA	047	80	85	88	1.4	69	38	41	43	1.8	2.07	26	27	0.9
88422 GLADSTONE	059	42	41	40	-0.6	5	19	19	19	0.0	2.16	14	14	0.0
88424 GRENVILLE	059	194	191	183	-0.4	9	85	86	84	0.3	2.22	62	62	0.0
88426 LOGAN	037	1205	1227	1223	0.4	33	524	549	561	1.1	2.23	370	381	0.7
88427 MC ALISTER	037	142	140	138	-0.3	11	55	56	56	0.4	2.38	40	40	0.0
88430 NARA VISA	037	125	127	127	0.4	31	56	59	60	1.2	2.15	40	41	0.6
88431 NEWKIRK	047	102	108	112	1.4	67	33	36	38	2.1	3.00	22	24	2.1
88434 SAN JON	037	581	592	589	0.4	34	231	242	247	1.1	2.45	163	168	0.7
88435 SANTA ROSA	019	3440	3994	4902	3.6	96	1152	1408	1824	4.8	2.50	799	958	4.4
88436 SEDAN	059	111	109	105	-0.4	7	36	36	36	0.0	3.03	26	26	0.0
88437 SENECA	059	47	46	44	-0.5	6	19	19	19	0.0	2.42	14	14	0.0
88439 TREMENTINA	047	142	151	156	1.5	70	69	75	79	2.0	2.01	47	49	1.0
NEW MEXICO					1.2					1.8	2.57			1.3
UNITED STATES					1.2					1.3	2.58			1.1

ZIP CODE #	POST OFFICE NAME	RACE (%) White 2000	White 2004	Black 2000	Black 2004	Asian/Pacific 2000	Asian/Pacific 2004	% Hispanic Origin 2000	% Hispanic Origin 2004	2004 AGE DISTRIBUTION (%) 0-4	5-9	10-14	15-19	20-24	25-44	45-64	65-84	85+	18+	MEDIAN AGE 2004	% 2004 Males	% 2004 Females
88047	MESILLA PARK	68.3	68.1	0.6	0.7	0.5	0.6	70.9	71.8	9.1	8.5	9.5	8.6	8.5	26.8	21.4	7.1	0.7	67.7	29.4	49.7	50.3
88048	MESQUITE	57.2	56.7	0.4	0.5	0.2	0.3	90.7	91.1	9.6	9.1	10.0	9.9	9.0	26.7	18.8	6.5	0.5	65.3	26.7	49.6	50.4
88049	MIMBRES	82.3	82.1	0.3	0.3	0.6	0.6	40.2	40.6	5.5	5.8	6.3	7.2	5.5	20.1	29.6	17.9	2.1	78.0	44.7	50.9	49.1
88061	SILVER CITY	76.6	76.5	0.6	0.6	0.4	0.4	42.7	42.8	7.0	6.6	6.6	7.1	7.2	23.1	26.5	14.1	1.8	75.6	39.1	48.8	51.3
88063	SUNLAND PARK	68.8	68.5	0.5	0.6	0.0	0.0	97.5	97.6	10.1	9.6	10.2	9.4	8.8	26.5	17.3	7.7	0.4	64.4	26.3	48.4	51.7
88072	VADO	53.1	52.3	1.1	1.3	0.1	0.1	92.0	92.3	10.2	9.7	10.5	9.9	8.8	26.5	17.6	6.4	0.5	63.6	25.7	50.4	49.6
88081	CHAPARRAL	70.5	69.6	1.3	1.4	0.5	0.6	71.5	72.4	9.5	9.6	11.0	10.1	7.1	27.4	19.0	6.0	0.3	63.0	27.1	49.8	50.2
88101	CLOVIS	71.9	71.0	7.1	7.3	2.0	2.2	31.1	31.9	9.1	7.7	7.6	7.8	9.8	27.4	19.2	9.9	1.6	71.2	30.6	49.5	50.5
88103	CANNON AFB	68.9	66.9	12.1	12.7	5.9	6.7	12.6	13.5	14.3	8.7	5.5	8.5	29.1	32.6	1.3	0.0	0.0	69.2	22.2	56.2	43.8
88112	BROADVIEW	94.3	93.1	0.0	0.0	0.0	0.0	8.0	8.8	5.9	5.9	6.9	5.9	4.9	21.6	29.4	17.7	2.0	75.5	44.4	53.9	46.1
88113	CAUSEY	82.8	81.8	1.1	1.0	0.0	0.0	22.6	23.2	7.1	8.1	12.1	6.1	6.1	25.3	21.2	12.1	2.0	66.7	33.8	48.5	51.5
88114	CROSSROADS	68.4	73.7	0.0	0.0	0.0	0.0	31.6	31.6	5.3	5.3	10.5	10.5	10.5	26.3	31.6	0.0	0.0	79.0	36.3	36.8	63.2
88116	ELIDA	88.8	88.3	0.2	0.2	0.0	0.0	20.9	21.5	6.2	6.6	7.9	5.8	6.4	22.7	28.0	14.9	1.4	75.7	40.4	50.5	49.5
88118	FLOYD	88.8	88.5	0.0	0.0	0.0	0.0	21.3	21.8	6.0	6.8	7.9	6.0	6.8	23.0	27.0	15.1	1.6	75.4	40.0	50.4	49.6
88119	FORT SUMNER	83.8	83.9	0.1	0.1	0.1	0.1	37.6	37.5	5.3	5.6	6.9	6.3	5.1	20.5	23.2	21.9	5.3	78.6	45.4	48.3	51.7
88120	GRADY	93.8	93.4	0.0	0.0	0.0	0.0	8.0	8.8	5.6	5.6	7.5	6.6	5.3	23.8	27.2	16.9	1.6	77.5	42.3	51.6	48.4
88121	HOUSE	94.6	94.5	0.0	0.0	1.4	1.4	8.8	9.7	3.5	4.1	6.2	4.8	4.1	20.7	29.7	18.6	8.3	82.8	49.3	49.7	50.3
88123	LINGO	81.6	78.9	0.0	1.9	0.0	0.0	22.5	23.1	7.7	7.7	11.5	7.7	5.8	26.9	23.1	9.6	0.0	73.1	31.3	51.9	48.1
88124	MELROSE	92.8	92.2	0.4	0.4	0.6	0.6	10.7	11.7	5.7	6.0	6.9	7.3	6.9	21.1	27.3	15.8	3.0	76.4	42.0	49.5	50.5
88125	MILNESAND	83.3	84.2	0.0	0.0	0.0	0.0	22.2	21.1	10.5	10.5	10.5	10.5	5.3	42.1	10.5	0.0	0.0	68.4	26.3	52.6	47.4
88126	PEP	82.4	81.1	0.8	0.8	0.0	0.0	22.7	23.6	7.1	7.9	13.4	6.3	5.5	26.0	22.1	10.2	1.6	66.9	32.8	48.0	52.0
88130	PORTALES	73.2	72.3	1.7	1.8	0.7	0.8	34.2	35.1	7.9	7.0	7.7	9.2	11.3	26.4	18.9	10.1	1.5	73.2	29.2	49.0	51.0
88132	ROGERS	82.7	81.7	1.1	1.0	0.0	0.0	23.0	22.9	7.6	8.3	9.3	7.3	6.0	25.9	23.3	11.0	1.3	70.8	33.9	50.5	49.5
88133	SAINT VRAIN	92.6	96.2	0.0	0.0	0.0	0.0	7.4	7.7	3.9	7.7	7.7	7.7	3.9	30.8	23.1	15.4	0.0	80.8	37.5	50.0	50.0
88134	TAIBAN	84.6	83.9	0.0	0.0	0.9	0.9	23.9	23.7	6.8	5.9	5.9	5.9	5.9	23.7	27.1	17.0	1.7	76.3	41.9	52.5	47.5
88135	TEXICO	67.3	66.5	3.9	3.9	0.6	0.7	36.9	37.7	7.3	7.1	8.4	8.6	6.9	26.4	22.7	11.6	1.1	71.9	35.9	50.6	49.4
88136	YESO	85.4	85.0	0.0	0.0	1.0	1.0	20.0	20.3	6.8	6.3	4.8	5.8	5.8	23.7	29.5	16.4	1.0	79.2	42.8	54.1	45.9
88201	ROSWELL	82.1	81.5	1.1	1.2	0.8	0.9	29.8	30.5	6.0	6.1	6.9	7.5	6.6	22.2	26.3	15.6	2.8	76.6	41.3	48.5	51.5
88203	ROSWELL	65.6	64.7	3.0	3.1	0.5	0.6	51.3	52.4	8.3	7.8	8.1	8.1	8.4	25.6	20.9	11.1	1.7	70.9	32.0	49.2	50.8
88210	ARTESIA	74.0	73.2	1.2	1.3	0.3	0.3	42.3	43.4	8.0	7.7	8.1	8.1	7.3	24.2	23.4	11.6	1.8	71.3	35.2	49.1	50.9
88213	CAPROCK	72.0	72.0	0.0	0.0	0.0	0.0	32.0	32.0	8.0	8.0	8.0	8.0	8.0	28.0	28.0	4.0	0.0	76.0	32.5	48.0	52.0
88220	CARLSBAD	78.1	77.5	1.8	1.9	0.7	0.8	35.4	36.2	7.3	7.1	7.4	7.0	7.2	23.7	25.3	12.8	2.3	73.9	37.6	48.8	51.2
88230	DEXTER	63.5	62.5	0.8	0.9	0.2	0.2	58.1	59.4	7.7	7.6	9.7	8.9	8.0	26.8	22.0	8.7	0.6	69.2	31.9	51.5	48.5
88231	EUNICE	72.8	71.6	1.1	1.2	0.1	0.1	37.0	38.7	7.7	7.1	8.3	8.1	7.4	27.1	21.9	11.6	1.0	71.8	34.6	50.2	49.9
88232	HAGERMAN	68.7	67.9	0.3	0.3	0.4	0.4	60.4	61.5	8.9	9.0	10.9	9.1	7.0	23.5	20.2	10.3	1.1	65.3	30.4	50.2	49.8
88240	HOBBS	65.1	64.4	6.4	6.5	0.5	0.6	40.5	41.2	8.3	7.6	7.9	7.9	8.3	26.7	21.3	10.7	1.4	71.7	32.6	50.1	50.0
88242	HOBBS	83.8	82.9	1.1	1.1	0.5	0.6	20.4	21.2	7.0	7.0	8.1	8.4	7.4	28.7	24.9	7.8	0.7	72.6	34.8	52.0	48.0
88250	HOPE	77.8	76.7	0.5	0.9	0.0	0.0	34.0	34.7	6.9	7.3	8.2	9.1	7.3	26.5	25.1	8.7	0.9	72.2	35.2	51.6	48.4
88252	JAL	67.4	65.9	0.6	0.6	0.1	0.1	40.4	42.2	6.5	6.3	7.4	8.0	7.4	21.3	25.4	16.2	1.5	75.1	40.1	48.3	51.7
88253	LAKE ARTHUR	69.5	68.6	0.6	0.7	0.3	0.3	52.5	53.9	8.9	9.4	10.1	8.8	6.2	26.4	20.8	8.7	0.6	65.3	31.2	52.3	47.8
88256	LOVING	65.2	64.4	0.3	0.4	0.2	0.2	66.8	68.1	8.2	7.9	9.2	8.3	7.7	23.3	24.0	10.4	1.0	69.6	32.8	50.3	49.7
88260	LOVINGTON	63.9	62.3	2.5	2.7	0.4	0.5	46.8	48.6	8.2	7.7	8.1	8.5	7.9	25.2	22.0	10.9	1.4	70.6	32.6	49.6	50.4
88264	MALJAMAR	82.3	79.4	1.6	1.6	0.0	0.0	21.0	23.8	6.4	6.4	7.9	7.9	6.4	22.2	28.6	12.7	1.6	74.6	39.4	52.4	47.6
88265	MONUMENT	83.8	82.8	0.5	0.5	0.5	0.5	22.2	23.5	6.8	6.8	6.8	7.7	6.3	24.9	27.6	12.2	0.9	75.6	38.3	51.6	48.4
88267	TATUM	68.3	66.8	0.7	0.7	0.1	0.1	34.0	35.7	5.2	6.3	8.8	8.2	5.3	25.3	24.2	14.8	2.0	74.6	39.7	49.6	50.4
88301	CARRIZOZO	77.5	76.9	0.5	0.6	0.1	0.1	44.0	45.1	5.3	5.7	6.8	5.6	4.4	22.0	29.0	18.9	2.4	78.8	45.2	51.3	48.7
88310	ALAMOGORDO	76.4	75.4	5.0	5.2	1.6	1.9	31.0	31.8	7.7	7.0	7.6	7.5	7.5	28.0	21.9	11.6	1.2	73.1	34.6	49.5	50.5
88314	BENT	74.1	72.9	0.3	0.3	0.3	0.3	38.9	40.2	6.3	6.9	7.4	7.1	5.7	23.2	28.9	13.1	1.5	74.7	41.3	49.1	50.9
88316	CAPITAN	88.7	88.2	0.5	0.6	0.4	0.5	19.3	20.0	5.4	5.6	6.6	7.6	4.7	21.1	33.4	14.4	1.4	77.6	44.4	50.3	49.7
88317	CLOUDCROFT	93.1	92.7	0.2	0.2	0.4	0.4	15.4	15.7	4.3	4.7	6.9	6.6	3.6	19.8	35.1	18.4	0.8	79.2	47.4	50.8	49.2
88318	CORONA	80.8	80.1	0.0	0.0	0.2	0.2	30.2	30.8	5.9	6.4	6.6	5.2	4.7	19.9	34.1	14.9	2.1	77.5	45.6	50.2	49.8
88321	ENCINO	71.2	70.7	0.0	0.0	0.0	0.0	56.0	56.9	4.1	4.1	4.9	5.7	4.9	21.1	33.3	19.5	2.4	82.1	47.7	54.5	45.5
88324	GLENCOE	88.5	88.1	0.0	0.0	0.0	0.0	16.4	16.4	3.0	3.0	6.0	6.0	3.0	16.4	41.8	20.9	0.0	88.1	52.9	47.8	52.2
88330	HOLLOMAN AIR FORCE B	73.3	72.0	13.2	13.6	3.4	3.9	12.4	13.0	8.2	6.5	5.9	10.1	34.8	30.3	3.9	0.4	0.0	76.6	22.8	61.1	38.9
88336	HONDO	66.3	65.3	0.8	0.8	0.0	0.0	62.0	63.4	5.6	5.6	7.5	8.2	5.6	22.0	29.5	13.8	2.2	76.9	42.5	50.4	49.6
88337	LA LUZ	88.1	87.5	0.3	0.3	0.7	0.8	21.5	22.1	6.1	6.4	6.9	6.3	5.3	22.4	31.5	14.2	1.0	76.8	42.9	49.2	50.8
88339	MAYHILL	96.2	95.8	0.1	0.1	0.2	0.2	9.2	9.7	3.4	4.3	7.2	6.6	2.3	19.5	36.9	19.1	0.7	80.2	48.7	50.7	49.3
88340	MESCALERO	4.9	4.0	0.2	0.2	0.1	0.1	11.3	9.8	10.0	10.5	11.6	11.0	9.4	28.1	16.0	3.1	0.2	60.6	23.7	47.6	52.4
88341	NOGAL	87.9	87.4	0.2	0.4	0.0	0.0	22.2	22.8	5.1	4.6	7.0	9.5	3.3	22.6	33.0	13.3	1.6	77.0	43.8	52.6	47.4
88343	PICACHO	65.9	67.4	0.0	0.0	0.0	0.0	63.6	60.9	4.4	4.4	8.7	8.7	6.5	21.7	30.4	13.0	2.2	82.6	42.5	52.2	47.8
88344	PINON	90.8	89.5	0.0	0.0	0.0	0.0	15.6	15.8	3.5	4.4	6.1	6.1	5.3	17.5	34.2	21.1	1.8	80.7	49.0	53.5	46.5
88345	RUIDOSO	84.6	83.9	0.3	0.3	0.4	0.4	22.0	23.0	5.0	5.2	6.4	5.9	4.8	21.2	32.2	18.1	1.3	79.9	46.0	48.2	51.8
88346	RUIDOSO DOWNS	80.4	79.3	0.4	0.4	0.4	0.4	28.5	29.7	5.8	5.8	6.7	6.4	6.2	21.5	31.6	15.5	0.6	77.9	43.3	48.8	51.2
88347	SACRAMENTO	96.6	98.3	0.0	0.0	0.0	0.0	6.8	6.8	3.4	5.1	8.5	6.8	3.4	17.0	39.0	17.0	0.0	79.7	48.5	50.9	49.2
88348	SAN PATRICIO	66.1	65.6	0.6	0.8	0.0	0.0	62.1	62.9	5.3	5.7	7.4	8.2	5.5	22.1	29.5	13.9	2.3	76.6	42.6	50.2	49.8
88351	TINNIE	66.3	65.4	0.6	1.1	0.0	0.0	61.9	62.8	5.3	5.3	7.5	8.5	5.3	22.9	29.8	13.3	2.1	75.5	42.6	48.9	51.1
88352	TULAROSA	74.8	73.6	0.6	0.7	0.6	0.7	41.7	42.2	6.7	7.0	7.9	7.1	5.7	23.2	27.1	13.7	1.5	73.9	40.2	47.8	52.2
88353	VAUGHN	51.5	51.0	0.0	0.0	0.0	0.0	84.7	85.2	7.3	7.1	6.8	4.6	6.0	23.1	26.2	17.0	2.0	76.1	41.0	45.9	54.1
88354	WEED	97.4	97.4	0.0	0.0	0.0	0.0	7.4	7.3	2.6	4.7	7.3	6.3	2.6	17.8	37.7	19.9	1.1	81.2	50.1	51.8	48.2
88401	TUCUMCARI	79.6	78.8	1.0	1.1	1.1	1.3	43.6	44.7	6.0	5.8	7.0	7.0	6.5	22.4	27.3	15.6	2.6	76.8	41.6	48.7	51.3
88410	AMISTAD	87.2	86.9	0.0	0.0	0.6	0.7	18.0	19.6	7.2	7.2	7.2	5.9	5.2	22.9	28.1	15.0	1.3	74.5	41.5	51.6	48.4
88411	BARD	91.7	91.7	0.0	0.0	0.0	0.0	16.7	25.0	0.0	0.0	0.0	0.0	16.7	41.7	41.7	0.0	0.0	100.0	35.0	33.3	66.7
88414	CAPULIN	86.4	86.2	0.0	0.0	0.0	0.0	17.0	19.0	6.9	6.9	6.9	6.9	5.2	24.1	29.3	13.8	0.0	79.3	40.0	51.7	48.3
88415	CLAYTON	78.1	77.4	0.0	0.0	0.4	0.4	40.8	41.9	6.1	6.1	7.7	7.3	6.7	21.4	26.1	16.0	2.7	75.2	41.0	49.0	51.0
88416	CONCHAS DAM	70.4	69.6	0.0	0.0	0.3	0.3	50.0	51.0	5.5	5.8	6.0	4.9	2.7	21.4	33.4	17.8	2.5	79.5	47.3	51.2	48.8
88417	CUERVO	68.1	67.3	3.3	3.9	1.1	1.0	67.0	68.3	4.8	4.8	5.8	6.7	8.7	39.4	21.2	7.7	1.0	78.9	35.5	69.2	30.8
88418	DES MOINES	87.2	86.3	0.0	0.0	0.7	0.7	18.2	18.8	7.2	7.2	7.2	6.2	5.1	23.3	27.4	15.1	1.4	74.3	41.1	50.7	49.3
88419	FOLSOM	86.8	86.6	0.0	0.0	0.7	0.7	18.1	19.0	7.0	7.0	7.0	6.3	5.6	23.2	28.9	13.4	1.4	74.7	40.9	51.4	48.6
88421	GARITA	70.0	69.4	0.0	0.0	0.0	0.0	50.0	50.6	4.7	5.9	5.9	4.7	2.4	22.4	34.1	17.7	2.4	81.2	47.9	49.4	50.6
88422	GLADSTONE	88.1	87.8	0.0	0.0	0.0	0.0	19.1	19.5	7.3	7.3	7.3	4.9	4.9	24.4	29.3	14.6	0.0	78.1	41.9	46.3	53.7
88424	GRENVILLE	87.1	85.9	0.0	0.0	0.5	1.1	18.0	18.9	6.8	6.8	6.8	5.8	5.2	23.0	29.8	14.1	1.6	75.9	42.2	51.8	48.2
88426	LOGAN	90.0	89.6	0.2	0.2	0.1	0.1	19.8	20.8	4.9	5.4	6.9	6.4	5.4	19.6	29.0	20.5	2.1	79.0	46.0	47.8	52.2
88427	MC ALISTER	93.7	93.6	0.0	0.0	0.7	1.4	10.6	11.4	3.6	4.3	6.4	5.0	5.0	21.4	29.3	19.3	5.7	81.4	47.7	51.4	48.6
88430	NARA VISA	90.4	89.8	0.0	0.0	0.0	0.0	20.0	21.3	4.7	5.5	7.1	6.3	5.5	18.9	29.1	20.5	2.4	78.0	46.3	47.2	52.8
88431	NEWKIRK	70.6	70.4	0.0	0.0	0.0	0.0	50.0	50.9	5.6	6.5	6.5	5.6	2.8	20.4	30.6	19.4	2.8	76.9	46.9	53.7	46.3
88434	SAN JON	90.2	89.5	0.2	0.2	0.2	0.2	19.8	20.8	4.7	5.4	6.8	6.4	5.4	19.6	29.1	20.4	2.2	79.1	46.1	48.3	51.7
88435	SANTA ROSA	58.0	57.5	1.7	1.7	0.7	0.8	80.1	80.5	5.4	5.6	6.5	8.0	7.3	30.6	23.4	11.2	1.9	77.2	37.7	55.2	44.8
88436	SEDAN	87.4	86.2	0.0	0.0	0.9	0.9	18.0	19.3	7.3	7.3	7.3	6.4	5.5	22.9	25.7	15.6	1.8	72.5	40.3	52.3	47.7
88437	SENECA	87.2	87.0	0.0	0.0	0.0	0.0	17.0	17.4	8.7	8.7	8.7	6.5	4.4	21.7	28.3	13.0	0.0	73.9	40.0	50.0	50.0
88439	TREMENTINA	70.4	70.2	0.0	0.0	0.0	0.0	50.0	50.3	5.3	6.0	6.0	5.3	3.3	21.9	31.1	18.5	2.7	79.5	46.5	52.3	47.7
	NEW MEXICO	66.8	65.8	1.9	2.0	1.1	1.3	42.1	42.7	7.3	7.1	7.6	7.7	7.7	26.9	23.9	10.4	1.4	73.4	34.9	49.2	50.9
	UNITED STATES	75.1	73.6	12.3	12.5	3.8	4.2	12.5	14.1	6.9	6.7	7.2	7.0	7.3	28.6	23.8	10.8	1.7	75.1	36.0	49.1	50.9

#	POST OFFICE NAME	2004 Per Capita Income	2004 HH Income Base	2004 Household Income Distribution (%): Less than $25,000	$25,000 to $49,999	$50,000 to $99,999	$100,000 to $149,999	$150,000 or More	Median Household Income: 2004	2009	2004 National Centile	2004 State Centile	2004 Home Value Base	2004 Home Value Distribution (%): Less than $50,000	$50,000 to $89,999	$90,000 to $174,999	$175,000 to $399,999	$400,000 or More	2004 Median Home Value
88047	MESILLA PARK	16084	582	38.7	27.3	22.0	8.4	3.6	32257	37561	18	46	436	40.1	13.8	27.8	15.4	3.0	79048
88048	MESQUITE	9227	908	47.1	35.8	14.3	2.2	0.6	26073	29717	6	15	648	59.3	18.5	18.2	2.8	1.2	40164
88049	MIMBRES	17482	500	37.0	34.2	24.4	1.8	2.6	33908	37732	24	55	415	23.9	20.5	38.3	13.3	4.1	102610
88061	SILVER CITY	18590	8137	36.4	33.4	22.9	4.7	2.6	34281	38871	25	57	6016	15.4	16.8	43.5	22.1	2.2	112311
88063	SUNLAND PARK	7054	2997	57.8	30.0	10.7	1.4	0.1	21054	24369	2	4	2025	48.2	40.4	9.6	1.0	0.8	51712
88072	VADO	9453	779	44.0	35.2	18.7	2.1	0.0	27790	32126	8	24	582	57.2	28.0	13.6	1.2	0.0	44400
88081	CHAPARRAL	9849	3242	50.5	35.0	11.2	2.8	0.5	24695	28446	4	12	2496	39.7	34.5	20.0	5.8	0.0	60874
88101	CLOVIS	17845	15821	37.3	34.1	21.6	4.3	2.7	32604	37098	20	50	9523	24.1	35.8	32.3	7.2	0.7	77952
88103	CANNON AFB	13985	218	45.4	40.4	11.0	2.8	0.5	26934	30584	7	19	4	75.0	0.0	25.0	0.0	0.0	40000
88112	BROADVIEW	24073	45	31.1	35.6	22.2	6.7	4.4	37333	40000	37	76	37	21.6	29.7	35.1	10.8	2.7	88750
88113	CAUSEY	18838	36	33.3	38.9	19.4	2.8	5.6	31491	38170	16	42	29	24.1	20.7	44.8	10.3	0.0	97500
88114	CROSSROADS	11711	8	50.0	37.5	12.5	0.0	0.0	25000	27247	5	13	6	66.7	0.0	33.3	0.0	0.0	45000
88116	ELIDA	21572	211	38.9	31.3	24.2	3.3	2.4	31548	34662	16	43	145	21.4	33.1	32.4	11.0	2.1	83500
88118	FLOYD	15764	99	41.4	30.3	24.2	3.0	1.0	29672	36135	12	33	68	22.1	32.4	35.3	10.3	0.0	84000
88119	FORT SUMNER	16008	816	45.8	30.9	19.1	3.4	0.7	27902	31412	8	24	639	42.3	25.4	25.4	6.1	0.9	59340
88120	GRADY	22616	133	32.3	33.8	23.3	6.8	3.8	36428	39651	33	71	109	23.9	28.4	33.0	11.0	3.7	87917
88121	HOUSE	23820	67	31.3	32.8	28.4	4.5	3.0	35558	42370	30	66	52	32.7	32.7	28.9	3.9	1.9	70000
88123	LINGO	12212	17	35.3	41.2	17.7	5.9	0.0	30659	33060	14	38	14	35.7	21.4	42.9	0.0	0.0	80000
88124	MELROSE	17969	473	38.5	35.5	21.6	3.6	0.9	32170	35257	18	45	375	46.1	31.2	17.6	3.2	1.9	52843
88125	MILNESAND	6579	5	20.0	80.0	0.0	0.0	0.0	28290	26965	9	28	4	0.0	0.0	100.0	0.0	0.0	112500
88126	PEP	22795	58	34.5	36.2	20.7	3.5	5.2	32803	36129	20	51	46	30.4	19.6	37.0	10.9	2.2	90000
88130	PORTALES	16600	6407	42.9	30.9	20.1	3.9	2.2	29398	33672	11	32	3907	33.7	33.3	25.4	7.0	0.6	68297
88132	ROGERS	22988	101	34.7	36.6	18.8	4.0	5.9	32532	36711	19	49	81	29.6	18.5	38.3	9.9	3.7	92500
88133	SAINT VRAIN	18462	10	20.0	40.0	40.0	0.0	0.0	45000	45000	61	87	8	25.0	25.0	50.0	0.0	0.0	90000
88134	TAIBAN	12438	39	35.9	38.5	23.1	2.6	0.0	30410	31672	13	36	25	40.0	8.0	16.0	16.0	20.0	95000
88135	TEXICO	14356	579	41.3	34.9	19.5	2.9	1.4	29721	32886	12	34	454	42.1	33.9	17.8	4.6	1.5	56923
88136	YESO	17946	96	34.4	37.5	24.0	3.1	1.0	31064	33448	15	39	61	37.7	8.2	18.0	21.3	14.8	102083
88201	ROSWELL	22401	9599	32.7	31.9	24.7	6.9	3.7	37089	43031	36	74	7196	28.1	20.2	36.4	13.5	1.8	92828
88203	ROSWELL	14787	10833	43.7	33.1	18.8	2.8	1.7	28164	32153	9	26	7296	38.2	39.9	18.4	3.1	0.4	59260
88210	ARTESIA	16261	6088	37.7	31.8	24.6	4.2	1.8	33976	39101	24	56	4507	28.2	35.3	27.0	8.7	0.8	75011
88213	CAPROCK	14700	11	36.4	45.5	18.2	0.0	0.0	32290	35000	19	46	9	33.3	44.4	22.2	0.0	0.0	57500
88220	CARLSBAD	20181	12893	33.7	32.4	25.6	5.2	3.1	36500	41955	34	71	9501	23.9	38.6	27.3	9.1	1.2	76518
88230	DEXTER	13681	1507	37.3	33.1	25.0	3.1	1.6	33755	39083	23	55	1147	41.8	33.0	18.5	5.2	1.6	56217
88231	EUNICE	16713	1093	34.1	34.2	26.4	3.5	1.7	35309	39801	29	65	849	55.7	29.8	13.4	0.7	0.4	46353
88232	HAGERMAN	12121	605	45.1	32.6	19.3	2.0	1.0	27405	31428	8	22	425	49.4	30.1	12.7	6.8	0.9	50500
88240	HOBBS	16475	11639	40.0	31.9	21.3	4.6	2.3	31623	36193	17	43	7852	41.5	32.5	22.2	3.6	0.2	59433
88242	HOBBS	19350	1985	23.0	29.7	38.6	7.7	1.0	48046	54984	68	89	1676	24.6	28.3	35.5	10.4	1.2	83846
88250	HOPE	24305	94	30.9	26.6	34.0	5.3	3.2	41567	52602	52	81	76	27.6	25.0	31.6	13.2	2.6	86000
88252	JAL	17720	807	33.6	36.2	23.5	3.7	3.0	35355	40212	29	65	632	71.7	17.9	8.5	1.4	0.5	34681
88253	LAKE ARTHUR	13861	313	35.1	35.1	24.6	3.2	1.9	34864	40904	27	59	243	46.5	27.6	18.5	5.8	1.7	53542
88256	LOVING	13953	713	40.8	32.1	23.0	2.4	1.7	30594	34891	14	37	567	45.3	29.5	20.1	5.1	0.0	55096
88260	LOVINGTON	15304	4600	38.7	34.9	21.0	3.9	1.5	31199	35165	15	41	3388	40.5	34.6	19.8	5.0	0.1	58610
88264	MALJAMAR	17145	24	25.0	50.0	20.8	4.2	0.0	37313	41122	37	75	20	20.0	25.0	45.0	10.0	0.0	100000
88265	MONUMENT	15165	89	41.6	30.3	28.1	0.0	0.0	30442	33420	13	37	71	40.9	25.4	32.4	1.4	0.0	59286
88267	TATUM	16058	519	38.9	33.7	23.3	2.9	1.2	30887	34363	15	39	413	60.5	21.1	12.4	2.7	3.4	42750
88301	CARRIZOZO	17947	654	43.6	33.8	18.5	2.9	1.2	29084	34087	10	31	485	43.3	31.8	19.0	4.1	1.9	57222
88310	ALAMOGORDO	17399	16429	32.5	36.1	25.8	4.5	1.2	35164	39447	28	65	10852	22.1	32.0	36.2	8.8	0.9	85203
88314	BENT	15587	130	36.9	36.9	20.0	6.2	0.0	34370	38302	25	58	108	25.9	31.5	33.3	7.4	1.9	80000
88316	CAPITAN	18962	1100	37.7	32.9	21.8	5.2	2.4	32251	37594	18	46	908	15.1	28.0	40.3	12.3	4.3	98182
88317	CLOUDCROFT	21467	1312	29.8	35.4	27.4	5.4	2.0	36763	41423	35	73	1070	14.6	20.8	38.8	23.5	2.3	113286
88318	CORONA	28321	173	35.3	29.5	26.6	5.2	3.5	36272	40504	33	70	135	36.3	26.7	32.6	3.0	1.5	68333
88321	ENCINO	15217	58	44.8	44.8	5.2	5.2	0.0	25973	28117	6	15	47	46.8	17.0	25.5	6.4	4.3	57500
88324	GLENCOE	30336	33	15.2	33.3	36.4	12.1	3.0	51421	63158	75	93	28	3.6	3.6	35.7	35.7	21.4	200000
88330	HOLLOMAN AIR FORCE B	14757	425	15.5	58.8	20.0	5.7	0.0	41077	45633	50	80	33	81.8	18.2	0.0	0.0	0.0	35938
88336	HONDO	16349	107	38.3	36.5	17.8	4.7	2.8	32625	36127	20	50	85	21.2	10.6	32.9	18.8	16.5	126563
88337	LA LUZ	19632	1082	29.4	35.7	28.9	4.8	1.2	36593	40909	34	72	900	17.6	22.7	36.1	22.3	1.3	108813
88339	MAYHILL	21380	422	31.0	35.3	27.0	4.7	1.9	38207	43780	40	76	346	12.4	16.2	48.0	20.5	2.9	116456
88340	MESCALERO	9580	920	46.9	31.9	17.7	2.8	0.8	26784	30378	7	19	521	47.0	33.6	12.7	6.3	0.4	52039
88341	NOGAL	22176	244	33.2	27.9	30.3	6.2	2.5	37174	44367	36	75	198	11.6	23.7	38.4	18.2	8.1	127500
88343	PICACHO	13750	18	44.4	33.3	16.7	5.6	0.0	30000	30000	12	35	14	14.3	0.0	42.9	14.3	28.6	150000
88344	PINON	20307	48	35.4	37.5	20.8	2.1	4.2	30858	33855	14	39	40	32.5	27.5	30.0	7.5	2.5	75000
88345	RUIDOSO	25403	6404	28.5	30.9	27.2	8.7	4.6	41589	49548	52	82	5082	11.1	18.1	39.9	25.8	5.2	120192
88346	RUIDOSO DOWNS	20873	200	24.5	37.0	27.5	8.5	2.5	41122	49084	50	81	157	15.9	19.1	32.5	22.9	9.6	116477
88347	SACRAMENTO	19068	32	40.6	37.5	18.8	3.1	0.0	35000	38629	28	63	26	19.2	15.4	53.9	11.5	0.0	106250
88348	SAN PATRICIO	15174	181	40.3	35.9	17.1	4.4	2.2	31564	36769	17	43	144	20.1	9.7	34.7	18.8	16.7	126923
88351	TINNIE	17946	82	39.0	36.6	18.3	4.9	1.2	32312	37335	19	47	65	23.1	10.8	29.2	20.0	16.9	131250
88352	TULAROSA	15358	2142	36.3	36.8	22.5	4.1	0.3	33390	37186	22	54	1726	28.3	34.0	27.9	8.5	1.3	74908
88353	VAUGHN	13625	309	52.8	27.8	17.2	1.6	0.7	23146	26626	3	8	236	60.2	30.1	6.4	0.0	3.4	42258
88354	WEED	15476	82	40.2	37.8	19.5	1.2	1.2	35000	37991	28	63	68	20.6	16.2	48.5	10.3	4.4	106250
88401	TUCUMCARI	17879	3229	46.3	28.1	20.6	2.8	2.2	27171	31091	7	20	2228	36.9	30.7	22.8	7.3	2.3	63818
88410	AMISTAD	17446	58	36.2	27.6	29.3	5.2	1.7	36125	35000	32	69	45	26.7	40.0	15.6	11.1	6.7	69167
88411	BARD	9375	6	66.7	33.3	0.0	0.0	0.0	20000	25000	2	4	5	20.0	40.0	40.0	0.0	0.0	67500
88414	CAPULIN	19837	25	36.0	28.0	24.0	8.0	4.0	36115	38610	32	69	19	21.1	47.4	15.8	10.5	5.3	71667
88415	CLAYTON	16298	1289	40.3	35.9	20.3	2.3	1.2	30424	34523	13	36	928	36.9	33.9	22.4	5.5	1.3	63626
88416	CONCHAS DAM	20921	180	32.8	40.6	18.9	6.7	1.1	36012	40504	32	69	142	36.6	24.7	20.4	18.3	0.0	73333
88417	CUERVO	23587	52	36.5	38.5	19.2	3.9	1.9	35000	35000	28	63	37	35.1	27.0	24.3	13.5	0.0	68750
88418	DES MOINES	18913	121	38.0	27.3	26.5	5.8	2.5	34644	38821	26	58	94	25.5	37.2	18.1	12.8	6.4	73000
88419	FOLSOM	20418	63	39.7	27.0	27.0	4.8	1.6	32959	40000	21	52	49	26.5	38.8	18.4	10.2	6.1	69286
88421	GARITA	20565	41	34.2	41.5	19.5	4.9	0.0	34060	39070	24	56	32	34.4	25.0	18.8	21.9	0.0	80000
88422	GLADSTONE	21327	19	31.6	26.3	36.8	5.3	0.0	42361	42361	54	83	15	13.3	53.3	20.0	6.7	6.7	75000
88424	GRENVILLE	20481	86	37.2	26.7	27.9	5.8	2.3	35000	37848	28	63	67	26.9	40.3	17.9	10.5	4.5	68500
88426	LOGAN	15930	549	44.1	33.9	18.8	2.7	0.6	28040	32190	9	25	447	42.7	28.2	24.2	3.4	1.6	62660
88427	MC ALISTER	21114	56	33.9	30.4	28.6	5.4	1.8	35000	45000	28	63	44	31.8	29.6	27.3	6.8	4.6	70000
88430	NARA VISA	16448	59	45.8	32.2	18.6	3.4	0.0	27280	33613	8	21	48	43.8	27.1	25.0	2.1	2.1	62000
88431	NEWKIRK	14056	36	36.1	41.7	16.7	5.6	0.0	33153	40000	21	53	28	35.7	25.0	25.0	14.3	0.0	70000
88434	SAN JON	14764	242	43.8	33.9	19.0	2.9	0.4	28209	32614	9	27	197	42.1	27.9	24.9	3.1	2.0	63250
88435	SANTA ROSA	13458	1408	44.0	36.7	17.1	1.7	0.6	27979	30772	9	25	1028	32.1	32.0	27.7	7.7	0.5	72245
88436	SEDAN	15200	36	38.9	25.0	27.8	5.6	2.8	35000	35000	28	63	28	25.0	46.4	14.3	10.7	3.6	70000
88437	SENECA	19009	19	31.6	26.3	36.8	5.3	0.0	42361	42361	54	83	15	13.3	53.3	20.0	6.7	6.7	75000
88439	TREMENTINA	21020	75	33.3	41.3	18.7	5.3	1.3	35561	39440	30	67	59	35.6	25.4	20.3	18.6	0.0	75000
	NEW MEXICO	20647		31.7	30.6	26.4	7.4	3.8	38669	45233				18.9	17.7	37.6	21.5	4.4	113735
	UNITED STATES	25866		24.7	27.1	30.8	10.9	6.5	48124	56710				10.9	15.0	33.7	30.1	10.4	145905

#	POST OFFICE NAME	FINANCIAL SERVICES				THE HOME						ENTERTAINMENT						PERSONAL			
						Home Improvements		Furnishings													
		Auto Loan	Home Loan	Invest-ments	Retire-ment Plans	Home Repair	Lawn & Garden	Comput-ers & Hard-ware	Major Appli-ances	TV, Radio, Sound Equip-ment	Furni-ture	Dine out/ Carry out	Sports Equip-ment	Fees & Tickets	Toys & Games	Travel	Cable TV	Apparel & Services	Auto Repairs	Health Insur-ance	Pets & Supplies
88047	MESILLA PARK	77	69	55	66	68	72	67	72	69	70	85	81	63	79	66	67	83	73	70	82
88048	MESQUITE	51	44	38	42	43	44	46	49	48	50	61	53	43	55	44	46	60	50	45	51
88049	MIMBRES	69	52	34	50	56	68	57	63	64	54	75	70	51	71	57	68	69	63	75	76
88061	SILVER CITY	68	60	51	57	62	69	60	65	64	61	78	73	57	73	60	65	74	65	70	76
88063	SUNLAND PARK	41	36	31	34	34	36	37	39	39	40	49	43	35	45	35	37	49	41	37	41
88072	VADO	51	44	40	42	43	44	48	49	49	51	62	54	44	58	45	47	62	51	45	52
88081	CHAPARRAL	51	44	39	42	43	45	46	48	48	49	60	54	43	56	44	46	60	50	46	52
88101	CLOVIS	66	63	62	62	62	67	65	65	66	65	82	75	64	80	63	65	79	66	64	73
88103	CANNON AFB	54	35	33	40	32	37	51	44	52	48	65	59	44	58	42	48	63	52	41	50
88112	BROADVIEW	99	69	36	65	80	90	68	84	78	67	92	101	58	90	71	82	84	83	100	117
88113	CAUSEY	94	65	34	62	76	85	65	80	74	64	87	96	55	86	67	78	80	79	95	111
88114	CROSSROADS	50	35	18	33	41	46	35	43	40	34	47	52	30	46	36	42	43	42	51	60
88116	ELIDA	92	64	34	61	75	84	63	78	73	63	86	94	54	84	66	77	78	77	93	109
88118	FLOYD	73	51	27	48	59	66	50	62	58	49	68	75	43	66	52	61	62	61	74	86
88119	FORT SUMNER	62	45	28	43	51	59	48	55	55	46	64	63	42	61	48	58	58	55	66	70
88120	GRADY	98	69	36	65	80	90	68	84	78	67	92	101	58	90	70	82	84	83	100	117
88121	HOUSE	89	62	33	59	73	81	62	76	71	61	83	92	53	81	64	74	76	75	91	106
88123	LINGO	68	47	25	45	55	62	47	58	54	46	63	69	40	62	48	56	57	57	69	80
88124	MELROSE	71	52	32	50	58	68	56	64	63	53	74	73	49	71	56	66	67	63	76	81
88125	MILNESAND	45	32	17	30	37	41	31	39	36	31	42	46	27	41	32	38	38	38	46	54
88126	PEP	90	63	33	60	73	82	62	77	72	62	84	93	53	82	65	75	77	76	92	107
88130	PORTALES	65	55	51	54	56	62	60	61	62	59	76	72	56	73	58	61	73	63	63	71
88132	ROGERS	124	87	45	82	101	113	85	106	98	84	116	127	73	113	89	103	105	104	126	147
88133	SAINT VRAIN	87	61	32	57	71	79	60	74	69	59	81	89	51	79	62	72	74	73	88	103
88134	TAIBAN	68	47	25	45	55	62	47	58	54	47	64	69	40	62	49	57	58	57	69	80
88135	TEXICO	61	54	44	51	53	56	54	58	56	57	69	64	50	63	52	54	68	59	56	65
88136	YESO	70	49	26	47	57	64	48	60	56	48	65	72	42	64	50	58	60	59	71	83
88201	ROSWELL	79	75	72	73	77	83	75	79	77	75	95	89	73	92	75	77	91	79	81	90
88203	ROSWELL	59	52	45	50	52	58	55	57	58	55	71	65	51	67	53	58	68	58	59	65
88210	ARTESIA	66	59	49	56	60	64	59	63	61	60	75	71	56	72	58	61	73	63	64	73
88213	CAPROCK	60	42	22	40	49	55	42	51	48	41	56	62	36	55	43	50	51	51	61	72
88220	CARLSBAD	75	71	65	68	71	77	71	74	72	72	90	83	69	86	70	72	87	74	75	83
88230	DEXTER	67	60	49	56	58	61	60	64	62	64	77	70	55	69	58	60	76	65	62	70
88231	EUNICE	75	58	40	54	62	67	58	67	64	61	77	77	52	72	58	64	74	68	72	82
88232	HAGERMAN	56	49	41	45	47	50	50	54	52	54	65	57	46	57	47	50	64	55	51	56
88240	HOBBS	63	60	57	58	59	63	60	62	62	62	77	70	59	74	59	61	75	63	61	69
88242	HOBBS	74	76	69	75	76	78	71	74	69	72	86	85	70	85	71	68	84	72	70	85
88250	HOPE	91	82	63	78	82	87	78	84	79	80	98	97	73	92	77	79	94	84	84	101
88252	JAL	73	58	42	55	61	70	62	68	68	62	82	75	56	76	61	70	77	69	76	78
88253	LAKE ARTHUR	67	59	48	55	58	61	59	64	61	64	77	69	55	69	57	59	76	65	61	69
88256	LOVING	62	55	46	51	53	55	56	60	58	61	73	64	51	64	53	56	72	62	57	63
88260	LOVINGTON	66	56	44	53	56	60	57	62	60	60	74	68	52	67	55	59	72	63	62	70
88264	MALJAMAR	81	57	30	54	66	74	56	69	65	55	76	84	48	74	58	68	69	68	83	97
88265	MONUMENT	60	55	43	53	55	58	52	56	53	54	65	65	49	61	51	52	63	56	55	66
88267	TATUM	69	50	30	47	56	65	52	61	59	51	70	70	46	67	53	62	64	60	72	78
88301	CARRIZOZO	65	48	31	46	53	63	53	59	59	50	70	67	47	66	52	63	64	59	70	72
88310	ALAMOGORDO	66	60	54	59	60	65	62	63	63	62	78	73	59	75	60	62	75	64	63	72
88314	BENT	64	55	41	53	57	62	55	60	58	55	70	68	51	66	55	58	66	60	63	71
88316	CAPITAN	75	63	44	60	66	71	61	68	64	61	77	80	55	74	61	64	73	67	72	85
88317	CLOUDCROFT	81	63	43	58	71	79	60	72	68	60	81	85	54	80	64	72	76	72	84	98
88318	CORONA	125	87	46	82	102	114	86	107	99	85	116	128	74	114	89	104	106	105	127	148
88321	ENCINO	60	41	19	35	46	52	39	49	47	40	55	58	33	52	40	50	50	48	59	69
88324	GLENCOE	104	82	56	74	92	104	77	93	87	77	104	109	69	102	82	93	96	92	110	127
88330	HOLLOMAN AIR FORCE B	74	47	45	54	43	51	70	61	71	66	89	81	60	80	58	65	85	72	56	69
88336	HONDO	74	52	27	49	60	67	51	63	59	50	69	76	44	68	53	62	63	62	75	88
88337	LA LUZ	77	64	46	61	67	73	62	69	65	63	79	81	57	76	62	66	75	69	74	87
88339	MAYHILL	82	64	44	58	72	81	60	73	68	60	81	85	54	80	64	73	75	72	86	99
88340	MESCALERO	47	40	48	38	39	46	47	45	51	47	63	52	46	61	46	52	61	48	48	51
88341	NOGAL	90	63	34	60	73	83	63	77	73	62	85	92	54	83	65	77	78	76	92	106
88343	PICACHO	64	44	23	42	52	58	44	54	51	43	59	65	37	58	45	53	54	53	65	75
88344	PINON	83	63	41	58	72	81	60	73	69	60	81	86	53	80	64	73	75	72	87	101
88345	RUIDOSO	95	78	56	71	85	95	73	86	81	74	97	99	67	94	77	85	91	85	99	114
88346	RUIDOSO DOWNS	92	78	57	73	82	90	74	84	79	74	95	97	68	92	75	81	90	83	91	107
88347	SACRAMENTO	60	47	32	42	53	59	44	53	50	44	59	62	39	58	47	53	55	55	63	73
88348	SAN PATRICIO	74	52	27	49	60	67	51	63	59	50	69	76	44	68	53	62	63	62	75	88
88351	TINNIE	74	52	27	49	61	68	51	63	59	51	69	77	44	68	53	62	63	63	76	88
88352	TULAROSA	61	54	42	52	54	58	54	58	55	55	68	65	50	63	52	54	65	58	58	67
88353	VAUGHN	36	35	68	31	33	39	40	38	46	43	60	42	40	62	41	50	61	41	40	42
88354	WEED	61	48	33	43	54	61	45	54	51	45	61	64	40	60	48	55	56	54	64	74
88401	TUCUMCARI	66	51	39	49	55	64	56	61	62	54	74	69	50	70	55	64	69	62	70	73
88410	AMISTAD	83	58	30	55	68	76	57	71	66	57	78	86	49	76	60	69	71	70	85	99
88411	BARD	32	25	17	23	28	32	24	28	27	23	32	33	21	31	25	28	29	28	34	39
88414	CAPULIN	83	58	30	55	68	76	57	71	66	57	78	86	49	76	60	69	71	70	85	99
88415	CLAYTON	62	46	30	44	51	61	50	56	57	48	67	64	45	63	50	60	61	56	67	69
88416	CONCHAS DAM	72	56	38	51	64	71	53	64	60	53	71	75	48	70	57	64	66	63	76	88
88417	CUERVO	60	55	43	53	55	58	52	56	53	54	65	65	49	62	52	52	63	56	56	66
88418	DES MOINES	83	58	30	54	67	75	57	70	66	56	77	85	49	75	59	69	70	69	84	98
88419	FOLSOM	83	58	30	55	68	76	57	71	66	57	78	86	49	76	60	69	71	70	85	99
88421	GARITA	72	57	39	51	64	72	53	64	61	53	72	75	48	71	57	65	67	63	76	88
88422	GLADSTONE	83	58	30	55	68	76	57	71	66	57	78	86	49	76	60	69	71	70	85	99
88424	GRENVILLE	82	57	30	54	67	75	57	70	65	56	77	85	48	75	59	69	70	69	84	98
88426	LOGAN	60	47	32	43	53	60	45	54	51	44	60	63	40	59	48	54	56	53	64	74
88427	MC ALISTER	92	64	34	61	75	84	63	78	73	62	85	94	54	84	66	76	78	77	93	109
88430	NARA VISA	60	47	32	42	53	60	44	54	50	44	60	63	40	59	47	54	55	53	63	73
88431	NEWKIRK	72	56	38	51	63	71	53	64	60	52	71	75	47	70	56	64	66	63	75	87
88434	SAN JON	61	48	33	43	54	61	45	55	51	45	61	64	40	60	48	55	56	54	65	75
88435	SANTA ROSA	42	40	64	37	38	44	44	43	49	46	63	48	43	63	44	52	62	45	44	48
88436	SEDAN	83	58	30	55	68	76	57	71	66	57	78	86	49	76	60	69	71	70	85	99
88437	SENECA	83	58	30	55	68	76	57	71	66	57	78	86	49	76	60	69	71	70	85	99
88439	TREMENTINA	72	56	38	51	63	71	53	64	60	53	71	75	47	70	57	64	66	63	76	87
	NEW MEXICO	77	74	75	73	73	78	75	76	75	76	94	87	73	91	74	74	92	77	75	86
	UNITED STATES	100	100	100	100	100	100	100	100	100	100	100	100	100	100	100	100	100	100	100	100

NEW YORK — POPULATION CHANGE

A 06390-10524

# POST OFFICE NAME	COUNTY FIPS CODE	POPULATION 2000	2004	2009	% Rate	State Centile	HOUSEHOLDS 2000	2004	2009	% Annual Rate 2000-2004	2004 Average HH Size	FAMILIES 2000	2004	% Annual Rate 2000-2004
06390 FISHERS ISLAND	103	289	279	285	-0.8	2	138	134	137	-0.7	2.08	78	75	-0.9
10001 NEW YORK	061	18094	19892	21036	2.3	95	9464	10475	11074	2.4	1.71	2765	2980	1.8
10002 NEW YORK	061	84857	88033	90313	0.9	73	31510	32287	32809	0.6	2.68	18663	18915	0.3
10003 NEW YORK	061	54227	54181	54357	0.0	26	29870	29535	29379	-0.3	1.61	7298	7103	-0.6
10004 NEW YORK	061	1363	1459	1511	1.6	89	686	729	750	1.4	1.85	240	249	0.9
10005 NEW YORK	061	903	1128	1257	5.4	100	535	669	741	5.4	1.65	96	118	5.0
10006 NEW YORK	061	1419	1756	1952	5.1	100	811	1010	1122	5.3	1.65	213	258	4.6
10007 NEW YORK	061	4420	4532	4569	0.6	61	1614	1651	1659	0.5	2.03	739	746	0.2
10009 NEW YORK	061	58598	61521	63805	1.2	81	29144	30519	31444	1.1	1.99	11672	11833	0.3
10010 NEW YORK	061	24126	26210	27734	2.0	93	14425	15553	16324	1.8	1.61	4169	4423	1.4
10011 NEW YORK	061	46193	45600	45747	-0.3	14	28332	27766	27627	-0.5	1.56	6589	6356	-0.8
10012 NEW YORK	061	25580	26245	26759	0.6	62	13408	13670	13844	0.5	1.80	4290	4337	0.3
10013 NEW YORK	061	25792	27111	27782	1.2	82	10848	11338	11535	1.0	2.20	5549	5779	1.0
10014 NEW YORK	061	32699	32886	33178	0.1	37	20553	20528	20562	0.0	1.57	4678	4595	-0.4
10016 NEW YORK	061	52487	54683	55986	1.0	77	31220	32247	32738	0.8	1.60	8149	8321	0.5
10017 NEW YORK	061	15593	16099	16322	0.8	69	10489	10816	10918	0.7	1.47	2582	2616	0.3
10018 NEW YORK	061	4662	5381	5913	3.4	99	2142	2533	2814	4.0	1.85	630	733	3.6
10019 NEW YORK	061	38125	39337	40244	0.7	68	23389	23829	24147	0.4	1.63	6328	6428	0.4
10021 NEW YORK	061	103118	100953	100761	-0.5	6	62265	60527	59966	-0.7	1.65	20677	19878	-0.9
10022 NEW YORK	061	31790	31348	31285	-0.3	12	20541	20114	19925	-0.5	1.55	6584	6337	-0.9
10023 NEW YORK	061	63431	62594	62675	-0.3	13	38315	37472	37237	-0.5	1.62	11847	11537	-0.6
10024 NEW YORK	061	60634	56776	55623	-1.5	1	33352	31025	30188	-1.7	1.80	12283	11288	-2.0
10025 NEW YORK	061	95103	93435	93632	-0.4	9	46326	45108	44854	-0.6	1.97	18986	18309	-0.9
10026 NEW YORK	061	30792	31472	32219	0.5	59	12263	12563	12848	0.6	2.43	6694	6706	0.0
10027 NEW YORK	061	59436	61349	62565	0.8	69	22777	23383	23696	0.6	2.29	11053	11257	0.4
10028 NEW YORK	061	48162	48411	48866	0.1	36	28017	27938	28004	-0.1	1.72	9876	9705	-0.4
10029 NEW YORK	061	76826	77780	78767	0.3	46	28445	28595	28737	0.1	2.62	17260	17220	-0.1
10030 NEW YORK	061	25003	25531	25831	0.5	57	10427	10585	10643	0.4	2.35	5519	5536	0.1
10031 NEW YORK	061	59893	62511	64346	1.0	78	20772	21496	21969	0.8	2.87	12556	12904	0.7
10032 NEW YORK	061	63496	65367	66376	0.7	66	20779	21096	21202	0.4	3.01	13260	13400	0.3
10033 NEW YORK	061	58605	58451	58600	-0.1	25	19212	18857	18699	-0.4	3.06	12712	12500	-0.4
10034 NEW YORK	061	42030	43070	43855	0.6	61	15346	15643	15832	0.5	2.75	9732	9809	0.2
10035 NEW YORK	061	33381	34057	34424	0.5	56	11407	11618	11685	0.4	2.64	6773	6816	0.2
10036 NEW YORK	061	17205	19015	20064	2.4	96	10204	11204	11738	2.2	1.63	2213	2420	2.1
10037 NEW YORK	061	16383	16104	16084	-0.4	9	8325	8108	8032	-0.6	1.92	3688	3552	-0.4
10038 NEW YORK	061	15092	15389	15699	0.5	55	6327	6509	6645	0.7	2.10	2940	2886	-0.4
10039 NEW YORK	061	22045	20679	20317	-1.5	1	9017	8368	8147	-1.7	2.44	5437	5004	-1.9
10040 NEW YORK	061	46325	46672	47345	0.2	40	16115	15995	16031	-0.2	2.85	10612	10535	-0.2
10044 NEW YORK	061	9520	9112	8968	-1.0	1	3203	3000	2914	-1.5	2.33	1739	1615	-1.7
10128 NEW YORK	061	55430	55270	55837	-0.1	24	30252	29885	29913	-0.3	1.83	11451	11275	-0.4
10280 NEW YORK	061	6537	7070	7294	1.9	92	3647	3901	3987	1.6	1.80	1488	1572	1.3
10301 STATEN ISLAND	085	39484	42486	45614	1.7	91	14742	16045	17423	2.0	2.48	8800	9515	1.9
10302 STATEN ISLAND	085	16317	17105	18097	1.1	81	5484	5738	6088	1.1	2.95	3882	4039	0.9
10303 STATEN ISLAND	085	21096	22627	24172	1.7	89	6616	7068	7563	1.6	3.16	5033	5361	1.5
10304 STATEN ISLAND	085	38814	40503	42718	1.0	78	13128	13759	14610	1.1	2.84	9367	9773	1.0
10305 STATEN ISLAND	085	38364	41414	44302	1.8	92	14105	15282	16439	1.9	2.64	9697	10462	1.8
10306 STATEN ISLAND	085	53540	55283	57930	0.8	69	19932	20790	21979	1.0	2.64	14416	14972	0.9
10307 STATEN ISLAND	085	11666	12861	13959	2.3	95	4044	4516	4952	2.6	2.84	3060	3403	2.5
10308 STATEN ISLAND	085	28555	28997	30023	0.4	50	10290	10583	11068	0.7	2.73	8002	8201	0.6
10309 STATEN ISLAND	085	27236	29994	32462	2.3	95	8841	9898	10850	2.7	2.91	7003	7804	2.6
10310 STATEN ISLAND	085	22389	23309	24580	1.0	76	7957	8350	8871	1.1	2.77	5586	5819	1.0
10312 STATEN ISLAND	085	58430	61462	65048	1.2	83	19890	21156	22609	1.5	2.90	15964	16926	1.4
10314 STATEN ISLAND	085	87837	89784	93640	0.5	59	31312	32333	34025	0.8	2.73	23242	23884	0.6
10451 BRONX	005	39907	41085	42860	0.7	66	14302	14734	15352	0.7	2.73	9239	9437	0.5
10452 BRONX	005	71975	76331	80028	1.4	87	22740	24171	25356	1.5	3.10	16833	17821	1.4
10453 BRONX	005	77211	77252	78376	0.0	29	24259	24374	24780	0.1	3.12	17978	17958	0.0
10454 BRONX	005	35454	36644	37720	0.8	70	11626	12044	12402	0.8	2.97	7869	8106	0.7
10455 BRONX	005	36708	38587	40100	1.2	82	11746	12401	12916	1.3	3.00	8404	8836	1.2
10456 BRONX	005	80066	84644	88267	1.3	85	26374	28025	29292	1.4	2.96	18538	19577	1.3
10457 BRONX	005	68520	71881	74277	1.1	81	21714	22854	23661	1.2	3.03	15593	16339	1.1
10458 BRONX	005	77722	80856	83641	0.9	75	25308	26302	27182	0.9	2.96	17291	17861	0.8
10459 BRONX	005	37898	39182	40396	0.8	70	12127	12535	12926	0.8	3.07	8781	9025	0.7
10460 BRONX	005	54433	56460	58166	0.9	73	18309	19049	19659	0.9	2.94	13133	13585	0.8
10461 BRONX	005	50001	49661	50126	-0.2	20	20350	20247	20480	-0.1	2.33	12235	12092	-0.3
10462 BRONX	005	70623	74241	77314	1.2	82	27717	28953	30002	1.0	2.55	17833	18488	0.9
10463 BRONX	005	69931	71928	74140	0.7	64	28819	29727	30701	0.7	2.34	17131	17451	0.4
10464 BRONX	005	4634	4748	4858	0.6	61	2093	2170	2234	0.9	2.18	1185	1218	0.7
10465 BRONX	005	42515	42932	43639	0.2	42	16078	16325	16648	0.4	2.56	11152	11261	0.2
10466 BRONX	005	69840	70724	72284	0.3	47	24078	24484	25084	0.4	2.85	17231	17397	0.2
10467 BRONX	005	94562	94426	95581	0.0	26	34843	34618	34956	-0.2	2.65	22567	22241	-0.3
10468 BRONX	005	73683	74681	76131	0.3	48	24294	24535	24971	0.2	2.96	17126	17226	0.1
10469 BRONX	005	62465	61983	62565	-0.2	19	21610	21511	21760	-0.1	2.76	15327	15178	-0.2
10470 BRONX	005	15323	14903	14894	-0.7	4	6257	6088	6090	-0.6	2.42	3753	3624	-0.8
10471 BRONX	005	24874	24544	24927	-0.3	13	10313	10130	10295	-0.4	2.12	5653	5558	-0.4
10472 BRONX	005	64863	65690	67376	0.3	47	21740	22084	22683	0.4	2.96	15862	15988	0.2
10473 BRONX	005	56170	57387	58950	0.5	58	19434	20030	20679	0.7	2.84	14188	14499	0.5
10474 BRONX	005	24134	24408	24589	0.3	45	3409	3522	3590	0.8	3.07	2488	2553	0.6
10475 BRONX	005	38150	37306	37437	-0.5	6	16949	16658	16663	-0.4	2.19	9942	9700	-0.6
10501 AMAWALK	119	787	870	921	2.4	96	232	257	272	2.4	3.38	218	240	2.3
10502 ARDSLEY	119	5492	5508	5603	0.1	33	1810	1816	1849	0.1	3.01	1541	1542	0.0
10504 ARMONK	119	7102	7671	8023	1.8	92	2331	2531	2654	2.0	2.99	2021	2187	1.9
10505 BALDWIN PLACE	119	138	161	176	3.7	99	38	45	49	4.1	3.58	31	37	4.3
10506 BEDFORD	119	5438	5805	6065	1.6	88	1788	1910	1997	1.6	3.03	1543	1645	1.5
10507 BEDFORD HILLS	119	6082	6160	6233	0.3	47	1881	1911	1938	0.4	2.71	1301	1316	0.3
10509 BREWSTER	079	19325	20197	21282	1.0	79	6794	7138	7578	1.2	2.77	5051	5278	1.0
10510 BRIARCLIFF MANOR	119	9803	10207	10509	1.0	76	3176	3323	3431	1.1	2.82	2598	2710	0.9
10511 BUCHANAN	119	2206	2233	2281	0.3	46	820	832	852	0.3	2.67	615	620	0.2
10512 CARMEL	079	22104	23148	24407	1.1	80	7760	8225	8764	1.4	2.78	5900	6222	1.3
10514 CHAPPAQUA	119	12434	12500	12677	0.1	36	4007	4025	4081	0.1	3.07	3467	3476	0.1
10516 COLD SPRING	079	5078	5238	5509	0.7	68	2094	2172	2297	0.9	2.40	1378	1428	0.8
10518 CROSS RIVER	119	720	717	721	-0.1	22	227	226	227	-0.1	3.17	190	189	-0.1
10520 CROTON ON HUDSON	119	12418	12760	13081	0.6	64	4936	5066	5195	0.6	2.42	3216	3290	0.5
10522 DOBBS FERRY	119	10563	10763	10931	0.4	54	3775	3849	3914	0.5	2.55	2556	2590	0.3
10523 ELMSFORD	119	8257	8234	8311	-0.1	24	2861	2848	2870	-0.1	2.89	2126	2107	-0.2
10524 GARRISON	079	4503	4569	4729	0.3	49	1552	1591	1665	0.6	2.75	1209	1234	0.5
NEW YORK					0.4					0.5	2.60			0.4
UNITED STATES					1.2					1.3	2.58			1.1

ZIP CODE #	POST OFFICE NAME	RACE (%) White 2000	White 2004	Black 2000	Black 2004	Asian/Pacific 2000	Asian/Pacific 2004	% Hispanic Origin 2000	% Hispanic Origin 2004	2004 AGE DISTRIBUTION (%) 0-4	5-9	10-14	15-19	20-24	25-44	45-64	65-84	85+	18+	MEDIAN AGE 2004	% 2004 Males	% 2004 Females
06390	FISHERS ISLAND	95.5	94.3	1.0	1.4	1.0	1.4	1.4	1.8	3.9	4.7	6.8	6.8	4.7	25.1	31.2	14.3	2.5	80.3	44.1	51.6	48.4
10001	NEW YORK	64.2	60.6	9.5	10.0	14.8	16.4	20.2	23.2	2.6	2.3	2.7	6.2	9.8	39.1	23.5	11.4	2.5	90.7	37.9	49.4	50.6
10002	NEW YORK	26.1	24.0	7.6	7.4	49.3	50.4	26.8	28.5	4.9	4.8	5.6	6.5	7.7	31.7	23.5	13.3	2.1	80.9	37.8	49.7	50.3
10003	NEW YORK	77.6	72.5	4.4	5.3	12.2	15.0	7.6	9.9	2.4	1.8	1.9	6.1	12.7	44.4	21.7	7.9	1.1	92.8	34.4	48.3	51.7
10004	NEW YORK	73.0	67.6	6.5	7.5	12.6	15.0	7.6	9.7	4.7	3.0	1.9	1.7	7.3	55.2	23.4	2.7	0.0	89.5	34.9	57.0	43.0
10005	NEW YORK	67.4	60.6	3.2	3.9	22.7	27.3	7.4	9.7	2.0	0.7	0.7	1.6	24.2	59.0	11.0	0.8	0.0	96.1	29.7	59.4	40.6
10006	NEW YORK	76.7	71.6	6.6	8.1	9.8	11.9	6.7	8.8	3.9	1.0	1.3	0.7	10.8	65.3	15.1	1.8	0.1	93.3	33.3	59.6	40.4
10007	NEW YORK	66.2	61.9	10.1	10.7	19.1	22.1	14.8	16.9	5.0	4.3	3.8	3.8	6.6	47.9	23.7	4.6	0.4	85.1	36.0	59.4	40.6
10009	NEW YORK	60.0	55.7	10.5	10.9	10.2	11.8	30.2	33.3	4.3	4.2	4.5	5.1	7.5	38.3	23.6	10.6	2.1	84.2	37.2	47.3	52.7
10010	NEW YORK	78.6	74.1	6.1	6.9	9.4	11.7	9.0	11.4	2.9	2.2	2.1	3.2	8.8	41.3	25.1	12.1	2.4	91.6	38.4	46.1	53.9
10011	NEW YORK	81.9	77.9	5.4	6.6	6.2	7.7	12.1	15.1	2.7	2.1	2.2	2.7	5.5	45.0	27.4	10.7	1.7	91.8	40.0	51.7	48.3
10012	NEW YORK	71.2	65.3	2.8	3.3	20.1	24.0	7.3	9.5	2.8	2.3	2.6	3.2	10.6	44.3	23.0	10.1	1.2	90.7	35.9	50.1	49.9
10013	NEW YORK	46.9	43.0	5.0	5.2	43.0	46.2	4.9	5.9	4.1	4.1	4.5	5.2	7.6	33.4	27.3	12.0	1.6	84.8	40.1	51.3	48.7
10014	NEW YORK	88.3	85.1	2.8	3.4	4.9	6.3	6.1	8.3	2.5	1.9	1.9	2.3	5.1	48.9	26.7	9.4	1.4	92.5	38.9	51.5	48.5
10016	NEW YORK	77.7	73.2	5.3	6.0	11.9	14.6	7.9	9.9	2.7	1.8	1.7	2.9	9.7	45.0	24.6	10.4	1.3	92.5	37.0	46.4	53.7
10017	NEW YORK	75.9	70.7	3.5	4.2	16.7	20.4	5.5	7.2	2.7	1.6	1.3	1.3	6.3	45.8	28.5	11.2	1.3	93.7	39.9	45.4	54.6
10018	NEW YORK	53.5	47.0	12.2	15.4	21.0	22.5	21.5	24.6	3.3	2.1	2.1	5.4	12.0	47.9	21.5	5.5	0.3	91.0	34.1	53.8	46.2
10019	NEW YORK	72.6	67.5	5.7	6.5	10.8	12.8	17.9	22.3	2.8	2.0	2.2	2.8	6.7	45.8	24.2	11.8	1.7	91.5	38.4	51.2	48.8
10021	NEW YORK	89.4	86.3	1.5	1.9	6.5	8.5	4.7	6.4	4.3	3.4	2.7	2.4	4.3	40.0	26.4	14.1	2.5	88.1	40.7	44.2	55.8
10022	NEW YORK	89.8	86.9	1.2	1.5	6.6	8.5	4.7	6.5	2.9	2.3	1.7	1.8	3.7	35.6	29.5	19.6	2.9	92.1	46.5	45.8	54.2
10023	NEW YORK	82.4	78.5	5.4	6.2	7.4	9.5	7.9	10.0	3.9	3.0	2.6	2.9	5.6	41.8	25.4	12.5	2.3	89.0	39.4	46.8	53.2
10024	NEW YORK	83.1	79.2	6.0	7.1	4.3	5.4	11.1	14.3	4.8	4.1	3.8	3.8	4.9	37.4	28.0	11.2	2.0	85.0	40.2	46.9	53.1
10025	NEW YORK	60.8	55.4	16.2	17.6	6.5	7.5	25.6	30.5	4.5	4.0	4.4	5.5	8.3	35.0	25.3	11.2	1.9	84.3	37.8	47.1	52.9
10026	NEW YORK	8.1	7.5	75.6	75.3	1.4	1.5	20.7	22.1	7.8	7.6	8.5	7.1	6.9	32.4	20.1	8.4	1.2	71.8	33.0	47.4	52.6
10027	NEW YORK	25.8	22.8	53.0	53.6	6.2	6.9	21.5	24.0	5.9	5.8	6.5	9.1	11.1	32.1	19.3	8.9	1.4	78.3	31.6	47.0	53.1
10028	NEW YORK	90.5	87.7	1.4	1.7	5.3	6.9	4.3	5.9	4.5	4.0	3.5	3.2	5.2	39.8	26.0	12.0	1.9	86.1	39.0	45.0	55.0
10029	NEW YORK	29.1	28.2	34.0	32.7	4.0	4.1	56.0	59.2	7.2	7.0	8.1	8.0	8.5	30.2	19.2	10.3	1.5	72.9	32.1	46.8	53.2
10030	NEW YORK	4.5	4.4	82.2	81.6	0.8	0.9	17.3	18.4	7.8	7.9	9.1	7.6	6.8	30.1	20.6	8.7	1.3	70.7	33.0	46.4	53.6
10031	NEW YORK	14.7	14.1	38.7	37.5	1.4	1.3	59.8	62.1	7.0	6.8	7.8	7.1	7.9	32.6	21.2	8.6	1.1	74.3	33.2	48.3	51.7
10032	NEW YORK	19.6	18.0	22.6	21.6	3.3	3.3	70.6	73.6	6.8	6.5	7.3	7.1	8.6	32.3	21.4	8.9	1.2	75.2	32.9	48.0	52.1
10033	NEW YORK	34.1	30.7	8.2	8.1	1.6	1.6	75.2	79.4	6.6	6.4	7.5	7.5	8.8	31.2	22.0	8.9	1.2	75.4	33.5	48.4	51.6
10034	NEW YORK	30.6	28.2	10.7	10.2	1.9	1.9	74.0	77.4	7.3	7.0	7.5	7.1	8.0	32.6	21.7	7.8	1.1	74.0	33.0	46.9	53.2
10035	NEW YORK	21.1	20.8	47.6	46.1	1.0	1.0	50.9	53.6	7.2	7.3	8.3	7.8	7.9	31.4	19.9	9.1	1.2	72.7	32.7	49.8	50.3
10036	NEW YORK	67.7	62.3	11.2	12.7	7.8	9.0	20.5	25.3	3.0	2.3	2.3	3.0	7.3	43.6	27.6	10.1	0.9	90.8	39.4	57.0	43.0
10037	NEW YORK	2.6	2.6	89.1	88.7	0.5	0.5	11.2	11.9	5.6	5.7	6.8	5.8	5.3	27.8	24.2	15.7	3.3	78.4	40.3	41.4	58.6
10038	NEW YORK	47.7	44.9	9.9	9.7	31.2	33.5	18.5	18.8	3.3	3.0	3.6	8.8	15.9	28.4	19.7	14.2	3.1	87.8	34.5	46.6	53.5
10039	NEW YORK	4.9	5.0	79.9	78.9	0.7	0.7	20.1	21.5	7.9	7.5	9.1	8.4	7.4	27.7	19.6	10.8	1.7	70.4	32.5	44.4	55.7
10040	NEW YORK	31.7	29.2	8.9	9.1	2.2	2.2	75.8	78.9	7.2	7.0	7.7	7.1	7.4	30.5	21.0	9.6	2.5	74.0	34.0	46.4	53.6
10044	NEW YORK	49.2	42.7	27.3	30.2	10.9	12.4	14.4	17.4	4.8	4.0	5.0	7.1	9.6	25.1	26.5	15.0	3.0	83.1	41.1	47.8	52.2
10128	NEW YORK	84.1	80.8	4.9	5.6	6.4	7.8	8.5	10.9	4.6	4.1	3.9	3.8	7.2	39.4	25.1	10.4	1.5	85.0	37.4	45.6	54.4
10280	NEW YORK	74.5	68.9	3.5	4.1	17.9	22.1	5.4	7.0	6.4	5.5	4.1	2.6	3.9	46.9	26.0	4.4	0.3	82.5	37.4	50.3	49.7
10301	STATEN ISLAND	57.9	54.9	23.4	24.3	6.7	7.8	18.0	19.7	6.6	6.2	6.8	7.2	8.0	29.7	23.3	10.2	2.0	76.5	35.5	48.2	51.9
10302	STATEN ISLAND	60.3	56.4	19.3	20.8	2.9	3.3	25.8	28.9	7.6	7.4	8.1	7.7	7.7	29.2	21.7	9.2	1.5	72.2	33.0	49.3	50.7
10303	STATEN ISLAND	41.1	37.8	35.9	36.9	4.5	5.0	27.8	30.4	8.8	8.9	9.7	8.7	7.7	28.6	19.6	7.1	1.0	67.0	29.9	47.3	52.7
10304	STATEN ISLAND	51.3	48.4	30.0	31.0	6.0	6.8	18.4	20.2	7.6	7.6	8.1	7.7	7.2	28.4	22.4	9.5	1.6	72.0	34.3	47.7	52.3
10305	STATEN ISLAND	82.6	79.3	3.8	4.3	6.3	7.8	13.8	16.6	6.4	6.2	6.8	6.5	7.0	29.8	24.1	11.4	1.8	76.7	37.2	48.6	51.4
10306	STATEN ISLAND	92.1	90.2	1.1	1.3	3.4	4.4	8.3	10.3	6.1	6.1	6.8	6.1	6.0	28.3	25.3	13.2	2.0	77.1	39.3	47.9	52.2
10307	STATEN ISLAND	95.3	94.2	0.7	0.8	2.2	2.8	5.3	6.7	8.2	8.0	7.9	6.9	6.1	31.4	23.3	7.5	0.9	71.5	35.2	49.7	50.3
10308	STATEN ISLAND	95.2	93.9	0.3	0.4	2.6	3.2	5.4	6.8	6.5	6.7	7.0	6.2	5.9	29.0	26.6	11.0	1.2	75.9	38.3	48.6	51.4
10309	STATEN ISLAND	91.0	88.8	2.6	3.3	3.8	4.7	6.3	7.9	6.9	7.0	7.5	6.7	6.0	32.4	25.1	7.5	0.8	74.2	35.8	50.6	49.4
10310	STATEN ISLAND	61.2	58.6	22.0	22.5	4.0	4.7	19.5	21.6	7.3	7.9	8.8	7.4	6.5	27.9	23.4	9.3	1.5	71.4	34.7	47.4	52.6
10312	STATEN ISLAND	93.2	91.3	0.7	0.9	3.9	5.0	5.7	7.2	6.2	6.5	7.2	6.4	6.0	30.0	27.6	9.2	1.0	76.3	37.4	48.6	51.4
10314	STATEN ISLAND	80.7	77.1	3.4	3.9	10.7	12.9	9.0	10.7	6.2	6.3	6.9	6.4	6.4	28.2	26.9	11.0	1.9	76.7	38.3	48.1	51.9
10451	BRONX	19.6	20.3	45.5	43.4	1.6	1.7	55.6	57.9	7.9	8.6	9.6	8.7	7.5	26.6	20.9	9.1	1.1	68.5	30.8	45.3	54.7
10452	BRONX	16.5	17.1	36.1	34.3	1.5	1.5	64.5	66.4	10.5	9.7	9.9	8.1	8.1	31.0	17.5	4.9	0.3	65.0	27.5	46.8	53.2
10453	BRONX	15.6	16.0	41.8	39.9	1.2	1.3	59.9	61.8	10.0	9.5	10.2	8.9	8.5	29.9	17.8	4.8	0.4	64.8	26.9	46.5	53.5
10454	BRONX	24.5	25.3	29.9	28.1	0.6	0.6	73.2	75.0	9.5	9.1	10.5	9.1	8.6	27.3	17.9	7.3	0.6	65.4	27.1	46.2	53.8
10455	BRONX	22.6	23.2	28.0	26.1	0.8	0.8	74.4	76.5	9.4	8.8	9.8	9.1	8.8	28.1	18.5	7.0	0.6	66.6	27.9	47.1	52.9
10456	BRONX	14.3	14.7	51.5	49.8	0.9	1.0	50.4	52.2	9.5	9.4	10.3	8.9	7.9	28.3	18.2	6.6	0.7	65.3	27.9	45.7	54.3
10457	BRONX	17.1	17.4	36.1	34.7	2.0	2.1	61.9	63.6	10.4	9.7	9.8	8.3	8.3	29.2	17.8	5.9	0.6	65.1	27.4	46.4	53.6
10458	BRONX	31.4	30.0	23.1	22.4	4.8	5.1	58.9	61.7	9.6	8.9	9.2	9.2	10.0	30.2	16.5	5.7	0.8	67.7	27.0	47.5	52.5
10459	BRONX	24.0	24.5	31.6	30.4	0.9	0.9	71.6	72.7	9.5	8.9	10.0	8.9	8.4	28.1	18.2	7.2	0.9	66.2	28.1	46.7	53.3
10460	BRONX	24.5	24.7	34.0	32.7	1.6	1.6	65.2	67.2	9.6	9.2	10.3	8.5	8.4	29.3	17.5	6.5	0.6	65.7	27.7	45.9	54.1
10461	BRONX	72.6	69.4	4.8	4.9	7.6	8.8	26.2	30.2	5.8	5.3	5.7	5.3	7.3	31.7	22.6	13.7	2.7	80.0	38.0	47.8	52.2
10462	BRONX	37.2	34.7	28.2	27.5	7.5	8.4	41.4	45.1	7.4	7.2	7.8	6.8	6.9	31.5	21.6	9.1	1.7	73.3	34.2	46.6	53.4
10463	BRONX	52.3	49.8	17.6	17.4	4.8	5.6	40.5	43.7	6.3	6.2	6.6	5.9	6.5	28.5	22.7	13.6	3.7	77.2	38.0	45.1	54.9
10464	BRONX	89.8	87.5	2.0	2.4	3.4	4.4	8.9	11.4	4.9	5.2	6.1	5.2	4.1	26.0	30.4	15.7	2.4	80.5	44.2	48.0	52.0
10465	BRONX	78.7	76.2	7.1	7.4	1.8	2.2	24.9	29.2	5.8	5.8	6.5	6.3	6.9	28.4	24.0	14.1	2.3	78.2	38.8	47.4	52.7
10466	BRONX	11.5	11.2	72.3	71.7	2.3	2.5	19.6	20.8	7.7	7.7	8.4	7.5	7.4	28.7	22.2	9.2	1.3	71.6	33.3	44.5	55.5
10467	BRONX	30.2	28.9	36.9	36.1	5.5	5.9	42.0	45.1	8.4	8.0	8.3	7.1	7.4	31.1	19.7	8.6	1.6	71.1	32.1	46.4	53.6
10468	BRONX	25.0	24.5	26.7	25.7	5.0	5.3	63.4	65.7	9.4	8.9	9.1	7.4	7.6	30.7	18.9	6.5	1.6	68.2	30.0	46.9	53.1
10469	BRONX	27.2	26.0	57.6	57.2	2.9	3.4	19.0	21.0	6.6	6.3	7.4	7.2	6.9	27.0	22.6	13.4	2.7	75.4	37.2	45.0	55.0
10470	BRONX	56.5	55.0	32.1	32.4	3.1	3.4	11.4	12.8	6.7	6.2	6.0	5.8	6.0	33.7	21.1	12.8	1.9	77.6	36.5	46.7	53.4
10471	BRONX	75.6	72.0	9.2	9.9	5.3	6.5	16.0	19.0	4.7	4.4	4.6	8.1	6.9	24.4	25.2	16.7	5.2	83.1	42.7	45.4	54.7
10472	BRONX	26.4	26.8	31.1	29.8	4.4	4.5	62.5	64.4	9.1	8.6	9.0	8.0	8.3	29.7	19.3	7.2	0.8	68.4	29.5	46.8	53.3
10473	BRONX	24.0	24.8	45.1	43.0	1.2	1.3	54.1	56.5	7.4	7.9	9.2	8.6	7.7	26.1	22.4	9.6	1.1	70.3	32.4	44.8	55.2
10474	BRONX	18.7	18.5	48.9	47.7	0.7	0.7	47.7	49.9	5.2	4.6	4.8	10.8	14.5	44.0	13.1	2.8	0.2	80.4	29.8	69.2	30.8
10475	BRONX	26.8	25.2	59.6	60.0	1.0	1.1	24.3	26.6	5.2	5.9	6.6	5.6	4.8	25.5	26.6	16.5	3.2	78.7	42.7	42.5	57.5
10501	AMAWALK	96.1	95.2	0.9	1.2	2.2	2.8	2.2	2.8	8.9	9.8	8.6	5.4	4.0	25.9	29.5	7.5	0.5	69.0	38.9	50.5	49.5
10502	ARDSLEY	84.0	80.7	2.1	2.5	11.7	14.2	4.0	5.1	5.5	7.1	8.8	6.9	3.8	21.1	30.9	14.4	1.5	73.5	43.2	48.8	51.2
10504	ARMONK	92.7	90.8	1.5	1.8	4.2	5.3	3.2	4.2	6.9	8.7	10.0	6.9	3.5	21.7	30.5	10.8	0.9	69.5	40.9	49.2	50.8
10505	BALDWIN PLACE	94.9	93.2	2.2	3.1	0.7	1.2	2.9	3.7	8.7	9.9	8.7	5.6	3.7	29.2	26.7	7.5	0.0	68.9	37.7	49.7	50.3
10506	BEDFORD	96.1	95.0	0.8	1.0	2.3	3.0	2.6	3.4	7.7	9.7	10.2	6.8	2.9	21.7	29.8	10.5	0.8	67.5	40.5	49.9	50.1
10507	BEDFORD HILLS	81.0	78.1	10.9	12.0	2.5	3.0	12.9	15.7	6.4	6.5	6.0	7.5	6.3	33.5	23.2	9.3	1.4	76.8	37.1	45.2	54.8
10509	BREWSTER	92.6	91.5	2.1	2.3	1.7	2.1	8.0	9.5	6.8	7.5	7.6	6.1	5.3	29.7	27.0	8.9	1.1	74.0	38.3	50.8	49.2
10510	BRIARCLIFF MANOR	90.3	87.9	1.9	2.3	5.5	6.9	3.9	5.0	6.9	8.2	8.7	7.6	5.4	21.7	27.7	11.4	2.4	72.0	40.5	47.0	53.0
10511	BUCHANAN	96.2	95.3	0.7	0.8	1.2	1.5	3.5	4.5	6.6	6.9	7.1	6.6	5.9	28.8	25.5	10.7	2.0	75.6	38.3	49.7	50.3
10512	CARMEL	94.0	92.9	1.4	1.6	1.1	1.4	6.2	7.6	6.7	7.3	7.7	6.3	4.9	28.9	27.4	9.3	1.4	74.1	38.9	49.5	50.6
10514	CHAPPAQUA	91.3	89.1	1.3	1.5	5.8	7.3	2.7	3.5	7.5	9.5	10.2	7.6	3.8	21.0	31.0	8.8	0.7	67.9	39.9	49.7	50.4
10516	COLD SPRING	95.8	94.9	0.7	0.7	1.0	1.2	3.4	4.3	5.9	6.7	7.2	5.5	4.2	25.4	30.7	12.5	1.9	76.7	42.4	49.1	51.0
10518	CROSS RIVER	94.2	92.6	1.3	1.5	2.8	3.6	3.5	4.5	7.5	9.8	10.7	6.8	2.9	23.6	31.4	6.7	0.6	67.4	39.7	48.5	51.5
10520	CROTON ON HUDSON	90.9	88.7	2.7	3.3	2.5	3.1	5.8	7.5	6.6	7.2	7.1	5.3	3.7	23.4	28.8	14.0	4.0	75.5	43.2	47.0	53.0
10522	DOBBS FERRY	80.6	77.0	7.4	8.5	7.7	9.3	7.0	8.7	5.1	6.8	8.1	8.8	5.7	24.0	26.5	12.1	3.0	74.6	40.0	49.0	51.1
10523	ELMSFORD	55.2	50.8	25.7	27.5	7.3	8.4	18.1	20.8	6.8	6.9	6.7	6.2	6.0	30.4	24.4	11.4	1.3	75.8	37.7	48.9	51.2
10524	GARRISON	95.3	94.6	1.7	1.8	1.3	1.6	4.3	5.2	6.3	7.3	7.2	5.7	3.5	24.9	32.4	11.5	1.3	75.2	42.5	48.4	51.6
	NEW YORK	68.0	65.9	15.9	16.2	5.6	6.4	15.1	16.7	6.5	6.5	7.1	7.0	7.1	28.9	24.0	11.2	1.8	75.8	36.7	48.3	51.7
	UNITED STATES	75.1	73.6	12.3	12.5	3.8	4.2	12.5	14.1	6.9	6.7	7.2	7.0	7.3	28.6	23.8	10.8	1.7	75.1	36.0	49.1	50.9

INCOME

ZIP CODE #	POST OFFICE NAME	2004 Per Capita Income	2004 HH Income Base	2004 HOUSEHOLD INCOME DISTRIBUTION (%) Less than $25,000	$25,000 to $49,999	$50,000 to $99,999	$100,000 to $149,999	$150,000 or More	MEDIAN HOUSEHOLD INCOME 2004	2009	2004 National Centile	2004 State Centile	2004 Home Value Base	2004 HOME VALUE DISTRIBUTION (%) Less than $50,000	$50,000 to $89,999	$90,000 to $174,999	$175,000 to $399,999	$400,000 or More	2004 Median Home Value
06390	FISHERS ISLAND	35919	134	18.7	23.9	35.1	10.5	11.9	60000	69789	84	75	76	0.0	0.0	0.0	43.4	56.6	422727
10001	NEW YORK	47792	10475	26.7	21.4	24.4	11.9	15.6	52504	73220	76	66	2966	32.8	1.2	8.3	15.8	41.9	269022
10002	NEW YORK	16973	32287	46.2	25.4	19.3	5.5	3.6	28224	35778	9	4	4909	8.8	2.4	26.7	50.0	12.1	197485
10003	NEW YORK	71834	29535	16.2	17.1	27.7	16.1	23.0	76075	108554	94	88	9213	0.1	0.2	5.8	37.0	56.9	469478
10004	NEW YORK	85610	729	7.3	14.1	21.3	18.1	39.2	120571	160444	99	98	174	0.0	0.0	28.7	62.1	9.2	239130
10005	NEW YORK	73659	669	12.0	13.3	23.2	26.2	25.4	102338	137883	98	96	66	0.0	0.0	18.2	81.8	0.0	228947
10006	NEW YORK	89902	1010	9.7	9.8	26.3	25.0	29.2	105168	138030	99	97	7	0.0	0.0	0.0	100.0	0.0	275000
10007	NEW YORK	77291	1651	12.9	12.0	16.8	16.7	41.6	123256	167608	99	98	544	0.7	0.6	5.9	26.8	66.0	578629
10009	NEW YORK	34371	30519	29.5	22.7	27.3	12.1	8.4	47658	61667	68	57	3099	10.7	2.7	14.0	37.6	35.0	305386
10010	NEW YORK	77144	15553	14.1	16.7	29.9	16.8	22.5	77563	107849	94	89	4577	4.9	0.0	7.8	40.4	47.0	379956
10011	NEW YORK	84457	27766	16.6	15.3	27.9	16.3	23.9	78045	110931	94	89	10398	2.9	0.2	7.1	34.6	55.3	456065
10012	NEW YORK	62343	13670	21.5	15.4	27.0	16.9	19.2	70222	100156	91	84	3150	1.8	0.0	5.3	22.4	70.5	843668
10013	NEW YORK	59545	11338	30.0	20.7	18.1	10.6	20.6	48929	65267	70	60	3280	1.2	0.3	4.9	14.2	79.5	1000001
10014	NEW YORK	92576	20528	13.4	15.5	27.9	16.0	27.3	84684	120610	96	92	6232	0.1	0.2	6.3	26.1	67.3	627763
10016	NEW YORK	81135	32247	16.0	15.0	26.3	17.2	25.6	82236	118103	96	91	8872	0.3	0.4	9.7	42.9	46.7	381254
10017	NEW YORK	88820	10816	13.2	14.4	28.4	18.6	25.4	87707	122716	97	93	3534	0.2	0.6	12.4	44.3	42.5	360972
10018	NEW YORK	49341	2533	21.4	20.5	28.5	14.5	15.0	58846	80138	83	73	501	1.4	0.0	7.0	37.1	54.5	475000
10019	NEW YORK	82202	23829	19.1	18.0	24.4	15.1	23.4	70626	102753	91	85	5036	0.5	1.2	7.8	27.6	62.9	531355
10021	NEW YORK	122720	60527	10.8	13.2	27.6	15.3	33.2	95963	136710	98	95	23599	0.3	0.1	4.9	25.3	69.5	656712
10022	NEW YORK	130599	20114	9.6	13.1	26.0	17.2	34.1	102492	143967	98	96	9379	0.4	0.1	5.3	27.1	67.1	602204
10023	NEW YORK	112469	37472	13.3	15.0	23.2	16.4	32.0	95350	136381	98	95	15348	0.6	0.2	3.3	27.0	68.9	623003
10024	NEW YORK	104788	31025	14.4	13.0	23.0	16.1	33.5	98541	140460	98	96	11721	1.1	0.2	3.1	19.6	76.0	734243
10025	NEW YORK	49184	45108	23.6	18.7	26.9	13.6	17.2	60888	82973	85	75	12345	2.3	0.3	7.4	31.6	58.4	491257
10026	NEW YORK	16607	12563	50.4	24.4	16.8	5.3	3.2	24719	30837	4	3	1259	4.8	2.6	18.6	41.1	33.0	269872
10027	NEW YORK	20290	23383	47.3	23.8	17.9	5.9	5.1	27514	35395	8	4	2533	4.9	3.6	34.1	31.4	26.0	196132
10028	NEW YORK	114143	27938	10.1	14.0	26.4	16.1	33.4	98724	137629	98	96	10815	0.8	0.1	4.3	23.2	71.7	710716
10029	NEW YORK	19616	28595	47.4	25.7	17.5	4.9	4.6	27210	34543	7	4	2465	13.0	1.8	7.2	19.2	58.9	519199
10030	NEW YORK	15371	10585	55.3	24.9	14.4	3.1	2.3	21090	26319	2	2	1011	8.0	2.8	4.2	36.7	48.4	386694
10031	NEW YORK	14295	21496	45.6	27.7	19.2	5.1	2.4	28314	35565	9	4	1833	19.5	3.8	11.1	18.6	47.0	334706
10032	NEW YORK	15432	21096	42.7	28.3	20.7	5.8	2.6	30929	38506	15	5	1539	19.8	1.8	12.4	37.2	28.9	248422
10033	NEW YORK	18447	18857	36.4	27.9	24.5	7.4	3.8	36085	44298	32	17	1585	6.1	2.0	26.9	39.8	25.2	236321
10034	NEW YORK	16247	15643	37.8	29.8	24.1	6.4	1.9	34614	42723	26	12	1320	16.7	14.2	42.0	25.1	2.1	126594
10035	NEW YORK	12707	11618	59.5	21.8	13.3	3.6	1.8	17959	22405	1	1	648	13.3	5.1	14.0	36.7	30.9	315068
10036	NEW YORK	49927	11204	28.9	21.0	25.4	11.4	13.4	50194	72974	72	62	1405	1.6	3.1	12.7	33.5	49.0	393350
10037	NEW YORK	20841	8108	41.8	32.3	19.1	5.0	1.9	31117	37708	15	5	488	55.5	4.5	19.3	6.6	14.1	37656
10038	NEW YORK	33200	6509	36.7	20.9	19.5	10.5	12.5	39624	53572	45	33	1914	23.4	1.3	9.4	32.8	33.2	268269
10039	NEW YORK	13426	8368	56.4	25.1	14.2	2.4	2.0	20608	25417	2	2	507	44.4	7.3	13.2	7.9	27.2	85952
10040	NEW YORK	15280	15995	40.3	29.5	22.9	5.2	2.1	32592	40239	20	7	1172	25.2	3.4	25.4	37.7	8.3	157971
10044	NEW YORK	32934	3000	25.4	17.7	27.4	15.5	14.0	59022	78181	84	74	410	51.5	11.5	7.8	22.2	7.1	49294
10128	NEW YORK	102715	29885	14.5	13.7	25.6	15.3	30.9	89720	128778	97	94	10221	1.0	0.1	3.2	22.6	73.0	825191
10280	NEW YORK	110940	3901	8.7	9.8	18.4	18.5	44.6	134211	181153	100	99	826	0.0	0.0	1.1	38.3	60.7	457516
10301	STATEN ISLAND	28368	16045	22.7	24.5	31.4	12.9	8.5	53135	63306	77	67	6704	1.2	2.7	8.5	57.3	30.3	311126
10302	STATEN ISLAND	21008	5738	27.5	22.8	33.2	11.8	4.7	49553	58192	71	61	2989	0.7	0.7	8.9	81.4	8.3	249704
10303	STATEN ISLAND	18541	7068	27.0	24.9	32.7	11.0	4.4	47465	55323	67	57	3712	1.1	1.4	18.0	76.7	2.9	223333
10304	STATEN ISLAND	25155	13759	30.8	22.1	26.3	12.3	8.6	46617	55013	65	55	6659	0.5	0.2	11.2	55.1	33.1	299633
10305	STATEN ISLAND	26198	15282	25.0	21.2	33.4	13.8	6.6	54382	63694	79	69	8282	0.6	0.3	6.9	72.6	19.7	292670
10306	STATEN ISLAND	29898	20790	19.6	18.9	34.9	17.3	9.4	63491	74927	87	79	13518	0.4	0.3	4.9	63.5	30.9	340499
10307	STATEN ISLAND	31317	4516	11.9	16.7	38.9	20.8	11.8	72349	85100	92	86	3305	0.2	0.0	2.3	46.9	50.6	404067
10308	STATEN ISLAND	31057	10583	11.9	20.5	39.3	17.5	10.7	69789	80682	91	84	8075	0.3	0.1	3.5	66.0	30.0	340889
10309	STATEN ISLAND	32162	9898	11.9	18.9	37.3	19.2	12.7	73076	84554	92	86	7607	0.3	0.1	2.3	46.5	50.9	404629
10310	STATEN ISLAND	24334	8350	27.0	20.2	30.7	15.2	7.0	54373	64421	79	69	4480	0.5	0.7	5.1	74.8	19.0	288345
10312	STATEN ISLAND	31507	21156	10.9	16.6	39.9	21.1	11.6	76072	87615	94	88	17216	0.1	0.1	3.8	60.9	35.2	348817
10314	STATEN ISLAND	29843	32333	16.1	19.1	37.2	17.5	10.1	66604	78264	90	82	21757	0.5	0.6	8.0	66.8	24.1	312919
10451	BRONX	12538	14734	54.6	25.7	15.7	2.6	1.4	21721	24229	2	2	1942	42.3	13.2	18.4	22.5	3.6	69385
10452	BRONX	10525	24171	52.2	29.0	15.6	2.0	1.2	23249	26429	3	3	897	20.3	5.6	12.2	52.3	9.7	216542
10453	BRONX	11506	24374	52.2	27.0	16.4	3.1	1.4	23316	26543	3	3	1286	5.1	1.1	10.6	76.4	6.8	277103
10454	BRONX	10261	12044	63.6	21.5	11.7	2.1	1.2	16203	18584	1	1	560	3.6	3.0	19.8	67.5	6.1	242991
10455	BRONX	11083	12401	54.5	27.9	13.2	2.7	1.7	21899	24819	3	2	844	5.7	1.0	14.5	69.1	9.8	273514
10456	BRONX	11368	28025	58.0	23.7	14.3	2.5	1.6	19458	22120	2	1	1906	5.0	4.9	27.0	54.9	8.1	218777
10457	BRONX	11546	22854	54.2	25.7	15.1	3.5	1.5	21610	24567	2	2	1607	5.0	0.8	12.1	73.9	8.3	272465
10458	BRONX	11955	26302	50.0	27.7	17.6	3.6	1.2	25038	28403	5	3	1563	3.9	3.9	17.0	66.4	8.8	254677
10459	BRONX	11069	12535	57.5	23.8	14.5	2.7	1.5	20033	22796	2	1	1630	5.8	2.1	21.3	64.5	6.3	242125
10460	BRONX	11559	19049	53.3	26.5	15.9	3.1	1.1	22567	25636	3	2	2052	3.6	5.6	10.7	64.2	15.9	289474
10461	BRONX	24033	20247	28.7	25.9	30.5	11.3	3.6	44817	52023	61	50	7470	0.9	1.0	4.5	74.9	18.7	315223
10462	BRONX	18906	28953	32.4	31.3	27.2	6.8	2.2	37685	42987	38	23	7025	11.2	17.7	14.6	45.3	11.2	234114
10463	BRONX	26376	29727	29.7	26.0	28.5	9.3	6.5	44202	51315	59	48	8497	12.3	9.1	21.9	43.0	13.6	201623
10464	BRONX	36817	2170	19.5	16.3	35.9	17.2	11.1	66509	78515	89	82	1272	0.5	0.0	1.2	47.3	51.0	404362
10465	BRONX	24791	16325	27.6	21.3	31.2	14.2	5.7	51193	59702	74	65	9188	0.3	0.7	6.5	75.3	17.1	307554
10466	BRONX	19093	24484	32.9	25.0	27.7	10.5	4.0	41374	47389	51	39	8953	0.4	0.5	4.1	78.1	16.8	293541
10467	BRONX	16071	34618	39.8	29.7	23.3	5.3	1.9	32427	36808	19	7	4989	9.2	3.7	12.5	57.7	16.9	284088
10468	BRONX	13909	24535	43.5	28.2	22.4	4.1	1.9	30237	34103	13	5	2290	26.3	12.7	15.3	35.6	10.1	140570
10469	BRONX	22828	21511	26.9	25.1	30.4	12.2	5.4	47900	55520	68	58	10315	0.5	0.4	2.9	78.7	17.5	305556
10470	BRONX	24204	6088	27.4	28.2	29.5	9.9	5.0	43845	50653	58	47	2156	1.4	2.9	4.9	68.0	22.8	316997
10471	BRONX	42188	10130	18.7	19.3	32.0	15.5	14.6	64396	76685	88	80	4293	1.0	5.5	23.1	34.3	36.2	286922
10472	BRONX	13125	22084	48.4	27.3	18.2	4.5	1.7	26117	29576	6	4	3650	3.6	0.6	4.1	73.8	17.8	320109
10473	BRONX	14796	20030	42.1	26.6	23.4	6.1	1.9	31460	35413	16	6	4825	1.6	0.6	9.2	76.9	11.6	285127
10474	BRONX	11467	3522	61.6	23.0	13.0	2.1	0.4	17707	20295	1	1	316	14.9	0.0	15.2	57.0	13.0	258929
10475	BRONX	24140	16658	25.3	29.8	34.7	8.5	1.7	45501	52261	63	52	7149	73.2	1.4	10.0	9.2	6.3	20545
10501	AMAWALK	47092	257	2.3	5.1	21.0	26.5	45.1	139753	166494	100	99	249	0.0	0.0	0.8	19.3	79.9	554907
10502	ARDSLEY	58510	1816	4.8	8.0	23.5	22.7	41.0	127975	162608	100	98	1682	0.0	0.2	0.8	19.9	79.1	555195
10504	ARMONK	92141	2531	3.5	7.2	21.0	15.9	52.5	159047	209640	100	100	2338	0.0	0.0	0.6	3.7	95.7	915330
10505	BALDWIN PLACE	33416	45	4.4	6.7	33.3	26.7	28.9	108944	147494	99	97	43	0.0	0.0	2.3	65.1	32.6	331818
10506	BEDFORD	105121	1910	3.2	4.9	15.2	17.0	59.7	181313	230130	100	100	1758	0.0	0.3	0.7	5.0	94.1	919428
10507	BEDFORD HILLS	53620	1911	13.0	13.9	30.2	17.1	25.9	85812	113883	96	92	1231	0.0	0.0	4.3	36.8	58.9	463663
10509	BREWSTER	33712	7138	10.3	16.9	37.7	20.9	14.3	77878	90695	94	89	5588	0.5	0.3	6.4	69.2	23.6	303283
10510	BRIARCLIFF MANOR	77127	3323	7.7	6.1	18.2	16.4	51.6	154196	197905	100	99	2941	0.1	0.1	2.1	14.4	83.2	659058
10511	BUCHANAN	37736	832	10.6	17.4	39.7	17.1	15.3	72807	91441	92	86	626	0.0	0.3	7.0	77.6	15.0	310246
10512	CARMEL	36257	8225	10.1	15.6	35.2	23.3	15.9	81367	96082	95	91	6769	0.1	0.1	9.9	69.5	20.3	273877
10514	CHAPPAQUA	98577	4025	3.8	5.1	15.5	14.2	61.5	194568	250185	100	100	3677	0.2	0.4	0.6	10.9	88.0	773559
10516	COLD SPRING	43320	2172	15.7	15.4	32.7	18.9	17.4	74207	88563	93	87	1616	2.2	1.7	6.5	54.9	34.7	330812
10518	CROSS RIVER	83871	226	2.7	5.8	15.5	16.8	59.3	182019	227062	100	100	214	0.0	0.9	0.0	23.4	75.7	653846
10520	CROTON ON HUDSON	48783	5066	13.6	15.4	26.5	20.0	24.5	86699	114392	97	93	3458	0.7	3.0	4.1	42.8	49.5	398052
10522	DOBBS FERRY	45343	3849	12.1	17.7	27.2	17.4	25.6	84197	112904	96	92	2476	0.0	0.2	5.9	30.9	62.9	466183
10523	ELMSFORD	37969	2848	10.5	17.4	32.7	19.3	20.2	81432	104716	95	91	1919	0.1	0.2	5.9	60.1	33.7	347391
10524	GARRISON	46316	1591	5.5	12.9	35.8	25.3	20.4	92371	107657	97	95	1403	1.1	0.7	2.5	56.2	39.4	347340
	NEW YORK	28049		26.3	24.3	29.3	11.5	8.6	49309	58077				4.6	8.6	27.2	39.9	19.8	219050
	UNITED STATES	25866		24.7	27.1	30.8	10.9	6.5	48124	56710				10.9	15.0	33.7	30.1	10.4	145905

SPENDING POTENTIAL INDICES NEW YORK
06390-10524 D

# ZIP CODE	POST OFFICE NAME	FINANCIAL SERVICES: Auto Loan	Home Loan	Investments	Retirement Plans	THE HOME: Home Improvements: Home Repair	Lawn & Garden	Furnishings: Computers & Hardware	Major Appliances	TV, Radio, Sound Equipment	Furniture	ENTERTAINMENT: Dine out/Carry out	Sports Equipment	Fees & Tickets	Toys & Games	Travel	Cable TV	PERSONAL: Apparel & Services	Auto Repairs	Health Insurance	Pets & Supplies
06390	FISHERS ISLAND	127	99	68	90	112	126	94	113	106	93	126	132	84	124	100	113	117	111	134	155
10001	NEW YORK	103	103	199	111	97	111	121	108	128	122	163	130	126	175	122	131	163	117	105	120
10002	NEW YORK	52	56	101	58	55	60	64	59	66	63	84	71	64	90	65	68	85	63	57	64
10003	NEW YORK	162	155	292	179	147	165	183	162	188	187	239	200	191	251	180	186	237	174	152	182
10004	NEW YORK	218	207	362	236	196	218	242	217	246	247	313	267	249	322	236	242	310	233	201	243
10005	NEW YORK	156	149	281	172	141	158	176	156	181	180	230	192	184	241	173	179	228	168	146	175
10006	NEW YORK	196	187	348	215	177	198	221	196	227	226	288	242	230	301	217	224	286	211	183	220
10007	NEW YORK	250	263	449	293	254	275	290	265	286	293	363	325	303	377	290	280	361	279	242	292
10009	NEW YORK	82	81	158	87	77	88	96	86	102	97	130	103	99	139	96	104	130	92	84	95
10010	NEW YORK	160	155	295	176	146	165	183	162	189	186	240	199	191	254	181	189	239	174	153	181
10011	NEW YORK	170	163	307	186	155	174	193	171	199	197	253	210	201	266	191	198	251	184	162	192
10012	NEW YORK	146	143	268	162	136	151	168	149	172	170	219	184	175	231	166	171	218	161	140	166
10013	NEW YORK	170	190	298	211	190	194	203	192	191	201	241	239	207	245	204	181	241	201	167	206
10014	NEW YORK	186	178	335	205	169	189	211	186	216	215	275	230	220	288	207	214	273	200	174	209
10016	NEW YORK	169	164	311	186	155	174	193	171	199	197	254	210	202	268	191	199	252	184	161	191
10017	NEW YORK	166	159	296	182	151	169	187	167	192	191	244	204	195	255	185	191	242	178	157	186
10018	NEW YORK	125	113	197	130	108	121	141	124	143	140	181	155	141	184	135	139	179	135	115	138
10019	NEW YORK	169	163	308	185	154	173	192	170	198	196	252	209	200	265	190	198	251	183	160	190
10021	NEW YORK	256	258	463	290	246	274	291	262	295	297	375	318	308	393	290	293	373	277	245	292
10022	NEW YORK	257	252	456	285	239	268	289	260	295	295	375	316	303	392	287	294	372	276	245	290
10023	NEW YORK	234	225	426	258	213	239	266	236	274	271	348	290	278	366	262	272	346	253	221	263
10024	NEW YORK	237	232	437	262	220	247	271	241	279	276	355	295	284	375	269	279	353	258	227	269
10025	NEW YORK	115	118	235	124	111	128	139	123	149	140	190	148	144	207	141	154	190	134	122	137
10026	NEW YORK	45	46	93	46	44	52	55	49	61	55	77	58	57	85	57	65	78	54	51	55
10027	NEW YORK	55	56	111	56	53	62	67	60	73	67	93	70	68	100	67	76	93	65	60	66
10028	NEW YORK	247	249	448	280	237	264	282	253	285	287	362	308	297	380	280	283	361	268	236	282
10029	NEW YORK	59	60	118	57	56	66	69	64	78	72	100	73	70	106	71	83	101	69	66	70
10030	NEW YORK	41	42	81	41	40	47	49	44	54	49	68	52	50	75	50	58	69	48	46	50
10031	NEW YORK	46	47	94	44	44	52	55	50	61	56	79	57	55	85	56	66	80	54	52	55
10032	NEW YORK	53	53	105	49	49	58	61	57	70	64	90	64	61	95	62	75	91	62	59	62
10033	NEW YORK	65	64	127	60	60	71	75	70	85	79	109	79	75	115	76	91	110	75	72	76
10034	NEW YORK	50	51	102	48	48	56	59	55	67	62	86	62	60	92	60	72	87	59	56	60
10035	NEW YORK	39	37	69	35	35	42	44	41	49	46	63	46	43	65	44	53	63	44	43	45
10036	NEW YORK	100	99	189	108	94	107	117	104	123	118	156	126	121	167	117	125	156	112	101	116
10037	NEW YORK	46	47	89	46	45	52	55	50	60	55	77	58	56	83	56	64	77	54	52	56
10038	NEW YORK	91	91	148	97	89	98	108	97	109	105	138	119	107	142	106	108	136	105	93	107
10039	NEW YORK	39	37	67	36	35	42	44	41	49	45	62	47	44	65	45	52	62	44	43	45
10040	NEW YORK	50	50	98	46	46	55	57	54	65	61	85	60	57	89	58	70	85	58	56	59
10044	NEW YORK	96	104	218	103	98	115	123	108	135	121	172	129	127	194	127	144	174	119	111	120
10128	NEW YORK	230	240	434	261	229	256	268	242	274	272	348	291	284	371	270	276	348	255	230	269
10280	NEW YORK	253	242	456	279	229	257	286	253	294	292	373	312	299	391	282	291	370	272	237	283
10301	STATEN ISLAND	89	96	144	98	93	101	102	96	104	102	132	113	106	139	103	105	131	100	93	106
10302	STATEN ISLAND	81	85	99	83	83	90	87	85	89	87	111	97	89	113	87	89	109	86	84	94
10303	STATEN ISLAND	80	77	92	74	74	82	81	80	85	83	107	91	82	106	80	86	105	82	79	89
10304	STATEN ISLAND	88	96	143	94	93	104	101	96	104	101	131	110	105	138	103	107	131	99	95	105
10305	STATEN ISLAND	89	95	122	94	92	101	98	94	100	98	126	109	101	129	99	100	124	97	93	103
10306	STATEN ISLAND	101	117	135	115	114	121	112	110	109	112	138	126	117	142	114	109	136	110	106	120
10307	STATEN ISLAND	122	139	144	142	135	133	129	128	121	131	152	151	133	155	128	115	150	126	113	140
10308	STATEN ISLAND	110	133	143	131	130	132	121	121	115	121	145	139	129	152	124	113	144	117	111	132
10309	STATEN ISLAND	130	153	159	156	148	146	139	138	129	141	163	161	145	167	139	123	161	134	121	151
10310	STATEN ISLAND	86	96	120	94	94	101	96	93	95	96	119	107	100	123	97	95	118	94	89	102
10312	STATEN ISLAND	118	146	157	145	142	143	131	130	123	131	155	151	140	163	134	120	154	126	118	143
10314	STATEN ISLAND	104	124	145	120	120	126	116	115	113	117	142	130	122	149	119	113	142	113	108	124
10451	BRONX	40	38	72	36	36	43	45	42	51	47	66	47	45	68	45	54	66	46	44	46
10452	BRONX	37	37	71	33	34	41	42	40	49	45	63	44	42	65	43	53	64	43	42	44
10453	BRONX	42	40	77	36	38	45	47	44	54	50	70	49	46	72	47	58	70	48	46	48
10454	BRONX	35	34	65	30	32	37	39	37	45	42	58	41	39	60	39	49	59	40	39	40
10455	BRONX	38	37	72	33	35	41	43	41	49	46	64	45	42	66	43	53	65	44	42	44
10456	BRONX	39	38	73	35	35	42	44	41	50	47	65	46	44	68	45	54	65	45	43	45
10457	BRONX	40	39	76	35	37	43	45	43	52	48	67	48	45	70	46	56	68	46	45	47
10458	BRONX	40	40	78	37	37	44	47	43	53	49	68	49	46	72	47	57	69	47	45	47
10459	BRONX	40	38	73	35	36	43	44	42	51	47	66	47	44	68	45	55	66	45	44	46
10460	BRONX	39	38	74	34	36	42	44	42	51	47	66	46	44	68	45	55	66	45	44	46
10461	BRONX	70	72	109	72	70	79	80	75	83	79	105	87	81	109	81	85	104	79	75	82
10462	BRONX	53	56	112	54	53	62	65	59	72	66	92	68	67	101	67	77	93	64	60	65
10463	BRONX	73	75	132	73	72	83	85	79	92	86	117	91	86	124	86	96	117	84	80	87
10464	BRONX	103	115	144	118	113	119	115	111	112	115	141	131	119	144	116	110	139	113	105	122
10465	BRONX	81	90	113	87	88	96	90	88	90	90	114	100	93	117	92	92	113	89	87	96
10466	BRONX	67	68	105	66	65	76	74	70	79	75	101	79	76	105	75	83	100	73	73	78
10467	BRONX	47	50	98	48	47	55	58	52	64	58	82	61	59	89	59	68	82	57	54	58
10468	BRONX	48	47	90	44	44	52	54	51	61	57	79	57	54	83	55	66	80	55	53	56
10469	BRONX	82	86	113	82	82	93	88	85	92	90	116	95	91	119	89	95	115	87	87	95
10470	BRONX	71	75	114	75	73	83	82	77	85	81	108	89	84	112	83	88	107	80	78	85
10471	BRONX	120	128	184	131	124	137	136	129	138	136	174	150	140	179	137	139	172	134	126	141
10472	BRONX	45	44	86	40	41	49	51	48	58	54	76	53	50	79	51	63	76	52	50	52
10473	BRONX	50	49	89	45	46	54	55	52	63	59	81	58	55	84	56	67	81	56	54	58
10474	BRONX	31	30	57	27	28	33	34	33	40	37	51	36	34	53	35	43	52	35	34	36
10475	BRONX	67	71	95	71	70	78	75	72	76	74	96	82	77	97	76	77	94	74	72	79
10501	AMAWALK	210	262	284	270	253	255	231	225	210	234	267	260	253	278	234	203	269	216	199	249
10502	ARDSLEY	208	291	397	280	282	301	252	249	235	256	296	281	285	320	269	238	302	239	228	268
10504	ARMONK	345	455	591	452	443	470	398	392	368	406	466	444	448	489	419	368	473	377	360	428
10505	BALDWIN PLACE	157	196	213	203	190	192	173	168	157	175	200	195	190	208	176	152	202	162	150	187
10506	BEDFORD	386	520	713	510	507	548	453	449	422	464	534	505	515	562	483	426	543	432	417	488
10507	BEDFORD HILLS	168	210	277	207	204	218	196	192	188	197	237	220	212	249	204	188	237	190	180	208
10509	BREWSTER	124	150	160	152	146	146	137	135	127	137	160	158	145	167	138	123	160	131	121	148
10510	BRIARCLIFF MANOR	278	379	516	367	368	395	332	328	311	337	392	369	374	418	353	314	398	316	303	354
10511	BUCHANAN	128	153	177	152	150	153	145	142	138	144	174	166	152	182	147	135	173	141	131	155
10512	CARMEL	131	160	177	161	157	157	146	145	137	146	172	169	155	181	149	133	172	141	130	159
10514	CHAPPAQUA	374	499	666	492	486	520	435	430	404	445	511	485	492	538	461	406	519	413	397	469
10516	COLD SPRING	134	157	185	160	156	162	150	148	142	150	179	172	157	182	153	139	177	146	137	161
10518	CROSS RIVER	322	434	594	425	423	456	378	374	352	386	445	421	429	469	403	355	452	360	348	407
10520	CROTON ON HUDSON	150	183	234	182	178	188	174	168	166	174	209	195	186	220	178	165	210	168	156	183
10522	DOBBS FERRY	151	188	244	187	183	193	177	172	168	177	212	200	189	223	182	167	212	171	159	186
10523	ELMSFORD	136	168	206	162	162	169	156	153	150	158	190	175	165	201	160	149	190	152	141	165
10524	GARRISON	170	210	228	211	207	209	189	188	175	189	221	217	202	231	194	172	220	182	171	207
	NEW YORK	95	100	134	99	98	107	103	100	105	103	133	116	105	138	104	107	131	102	99	112
	UNITED STATES	100	100	100	100	100	100	100	100	100	100	100	100	100	100	100	100	100	100	100	100

NEW YORK
POPULATION CHANGE

A 10526-10980

#	POST OFFICE NAME	COUNTY FIPS CODE	POPULATION 2000	2004	2009	2000-2004 ANNUAL RATE % Rate	State Centile	HOUSEHOLDS 2000	2004	2009	% Annual Rate 2000-2004	2004 Average HH Size	FAMILIES 2000	2004	% Annual Rate 2000-2004
10526	GOLDENS BRIDGE	119	2000	2003	2010	0.0	30	688	687	688	0.0	2.88	555	553	-0.1
10527	GRANITE SPRINGS	119	1394	1479	1536	1.4	87	437	465	483	1.5	3.18	401	425	1.4
10528	HARRISON	119	11843	12441	12945	1.2	82	4382	4615	4808	1.2	2.69	3235	3393	1.1
10530	HARTSDALE	119	12295	13423	14182	2.1	94	5602	6101	6437	2.0	2.20	3532	3844	2.0
10532	HAWTHORNE	119	7039	7131	7229	0.3	48	1816	1846	1878	0.4	2.91	1358	1378	0.3
10533	IRVINGTON	119	7630	7781	7970	0.5	55	2836	2895	2967	0.5	2.66	2022	2056	0.4
10535	JEFFERSON VALLEY	119	372	330	325	-2.8	0	122	109	107	-2.6	3.03	98	87	-2.8
10536	KATONAH	119	12431	12694	12911	0.5	57	3723	3810	3880	0.5	3.04	3066	3128	0.5
10537	LAKE PEEKSKILL	079	1634	1753	1867	1.7	90	607	659	708	2.0	2.66	441	477	1.9
10538	LARCHMONT	119	16541	16436	16598	-0.2	20	6120	6087	6151	-0.1	2.69	4549	4503	-0.2
10541	MAHOPAC	079	26900	28140	29768	1.1	79	8666	9152	9770	1.3	3.06	7182	7555	1.2
10543	MAMARONECK	119	20345	20654	21029	0.4	50	7708	7802	7934	0.3	2.61	5352	5395	0.2
10546	MILLWOOD	119	1013	994	996	-0.4	8	363	357	359	-0.4	2.73	311	305	-0.5
10547	MOHEGAN LAKE	119	8359	8700	8968	1.0	76	2762	2882	2976	1.0	2.84	2132	2215	0.9
10548	MONTROSE	119	3978	3757	3742	-1.3	1	1380	1303	1299	-1.3	2.65	1008	947	-1.5
10549	MOUNT KISCO	119	15547	16014	16426	0.7	66	5826	5980	6124	0.6	2.63	3985	4093	0.6
10550	MOUNT VERNON	119	37776	37636	38046	-0.1	23	13736	13674	13821	-0.1	2.72	9129	9042	-0.2
10552	MOUNT VERNON	119	19178	19236	19508	0.1	33	8230	8291	8418	0.2	2.29	4848	4840	0.0
10553	MOUNT VERNON	119	11339	11350	11441	0.0	30	3721	3724	3768	0.0	3.03	2664	2651	-0.1
10560	NORTH SALEM	119	5091	5384	5574	1.3	86	1729	1836	1906	1.4	2.80	1351	1429	1.3
10562	OSSINING	119	31155	31583	32161	0.3	48	10658	10832	11069	0.4	2.62	7209	7280	0.2
10566	PEEKSKILL	119	22450	23228	23815	0.8	71	8699	8975	9192	0.7	2.56	5348	5473	0.6
10567	CORTLANDT MANOR	119	18318	19289	20021	1.2	83	5823	6149	6390	1.3	3.07	4874	5135	1.2
10570	PLEASANTVILLE	119	12897	12811	12923	-0.2	20	4321	4299	4342	-0.1	2.82	3266	3236	-0.2
10573	PORT CHESTER	119	36265	37037	37787	0.5	57	12594	12821	13060	0.4	2.86	8766	8887	0.3
10576	POUND RIDGE	119	5169	5309	5420	0.7	63	1898	1957	2001	0.7	2.70	1535	1578	0.7
10577	PURCHASE	119	3553	3860	4048	2.0	93	785	865	915	2.3	3.56	683	751	2.3
10578	PURDYS	119	790	842	873	1.5	88	274	293	304	1.6	2.85	233	248	1.5
10579	PUTNAM VALLEY	079	8138	8363	8704	0.6	64	2797	2908	3057	0.9	2.85	2204	2284	0.8
10580	RYE	119	17157	17197	17425	0.1	31	6203	6215	6295	0.2	2.76	4621	4615	0.0
10583	SCARSDALE	119	37995	38096	38627	0.1	32	13328	13457	13678	0.2	2.82	10624	10624	0.0
10588	SHRUB OAK	119	1986	2243	2416	2.9	98	702	785	843	2.7	2.86	579	644	2.5
10589	SOMERS	119	7145	8289	9158	3.6	99	3296	3800	4169	3.4	2.13	2145	2451	3.2
10590	SOUTH SALEM	119	6450	6569	6656	0.4	53	2228	2279	2316	0.5	2.88	1810	1845	0.5
10591	TARRYTOWN	119	21510	21916	22302	0.4	54	8256	8425	8579	0.5	2.54	5358	5434	0.3
10594	THORNWOOD	119	5112	5299	5439	0.9	72	1594	1660	1708	1.0	3.04	1334	1387	0.9
10595	VALHALLA	119	5882	6218	6475	1.3	85	1856	1977	2070	1.5	2.86	1467	1561	1.5
10597	WACCABUC	119	699	707	716	0.3	45	234	238	241	0.4	2.97	196	199	0.4
10598	YORKTOWN HEIGHTS	119	29072	28556	28911	-0.4	9	10161	10018	10145	-0.3	2.82	7959	7828	-0.4
10601	WHITE PLAINS	119	9318	10045	10548	1.8	91	4274	4646	4881	2.0	2.05	1995	2142	1.7
10603	WHITE PLAINS	119	15771	16444	17040	1.0	77	6427	6648	6858	0.8	2.44	3936	4042	0.6
10604	WEST HARRISON	119	10374	10761	11119	0.9	73	3812	3951	4085	0.9	2.60	2601	2685	0.8
10605	WHITE PLAINS	119	18402	18741	19180	0.4	53	7320	7501	7698	0.6	2.47	4928	5009	0.4
10606	WHITE PLAINS	119	14937	15519	15947	0.9	74	5001	5173	5305	0.8	2.91	3343	3430	0.6
10607	WHITE PLAINS	119	6783	7432	7925	2.2	94	2224	2437	2598	2.2	3.02	1747	1916	2.2
10701	YONKERS	119	62595	64262	66101	0.6	63	22266	22886	23553	0.7	2.77	15085	15390	0.5
10703	YONKERS	119	22924	22705	22808	-0.2	16	8413	8319	8354	-0.3	2.65	5700	5602	-0.4
10704	YONKERS	119	29103	28679	28824	-0.3	12	11935	11775	11841	-0.3	2.43	7635	7498	-0.4
10705	YONKERS	119	35946	37473	38758	1.0	77	12525	13021	13442	0.9	2.88	8637	8913	0.7
10706	HASTINGS ON HUDSON	119	8614	8446	8467	-0.5	8	3472	3413	3424	-0.4	2.46	2418	2366	-0.5
10707	TUCKAHOE	119	9073	9027	9101	-0.1	22	3626	3621	3658	0.0	2.49	2460	2444	-0.2
10708	BRONXVILLE	119	23713	24250	24960	0.5	59	10296	10598	10948	0.7	2.20	6069	6198	0.5
10709	EASTCHESTER	119	8517	8466	8550	-0.1	21	3397	3379	3414	-0.1	2.50	2349	2336	-0.1
10710	YONKERS	119	25631	25889	26370	0.2	43	10337	10463	10653	0.3	2.46	7018	7089	0.2
10801	NEW ROCHELLE	119	36141	36718	37417	0.4	50	12687	12789	12980	0.2	2.82	8370	8378	0.0
10803	PELHAM	119	12982	12696	12724	-0.5	6	4530	4434	4445	-0.5	2.79	3382	3294	-0.6
10804	NEW ROCHELLE	119	13721	13594	13691	-0.2	16	4701	4656	4688	-0.2	2.91	3871	3826	-0.3
10805	NEW ROCHELLE	119	17256	17472	17714	0.3	46	7078	7164	7267	0.3	2.28	3971	3981	0.1
10901	SUFFERN	087	22863	23303	23999	0.5	55	8482	8644	8906	0.5	2.65	5918	6009	0.4
10913	BLAUVELT	087	5313	5262	5332	-0.2	16	1582	1570	1596	-0.2	3.10	1284	1270	-0.3
10916	CAMPBELL HALL	071	3932	4380	4860	2.6	97	1234	1383	1540	2.7	3.10	1031	1150	2.6
10917	CENTRAL VALLEY	071	1550	1639	1772	1.3	85	556	592	642	1.5	2.76	427	449	1.2
10918	CHESTER	071	11480	12304	13390	1.6	89	3672	3948	4326	1.7	2.90	2822	3017	1.6
10919	CIRCLEVILLE	071	533	535	569	0.1	34	184	186	198	0.3	2.87	139	140	0.2
10920	CONGERS	087	9106	9754	10303	1.6	89	2978	3215	3411	1.8	2.99	2423	2596	1.6
10921	FLORIDA	071	4479	4791	5184	1.6	89	1468	1594	1747	2.0	2.65	1057	1138	1.8
10923	GARNERVILLE	087	7401	7337	7452	-0.2	18	2481	2474	2520	-0.1	2.93	1881	1859	-0.3
10924	GOSHEN	071	11920	12790	13903	1.7	90	3904	4239	4656	2.0	2.73	2820	3049	1.9
10925	GREENWOOD LAKE	071	5093	5312	5702	1.0	77	2034	2129	2289	1.1	2.49	1325	1373	0.8
10926	HARRIMAN	071	3116	3416	3764	2.2	94	1217	1351	1505	2.5	2.52	850	931	2.2
10927	HAVERSTRAW	087	10117	10122	10309	0.0	29	2816	2816	2870	0.0	3.42	2169	2156	-0.1
10928	HIGHLAND FALLS	071	5369	5518	5899	0.7	64	2241	2314	2481	0.8	2.38	1390	1419	0.5
10930	HIGHLAND MILLS	071	7529	8282	9138	2.3	95	2450	2707	2994	2.4	3.05	2052	2258	2.3
10931	HILLBURN	087	881	857	867	-0.7	4	273	268	271	-0.7	3.23	222	215	-0.8
10940	MIDDLETOWN	071	42753	45835	50050	1.7	89	15422	16622	18225	1.8	2.69	10387	11121	1.6
10941	MIDDLETOWN	071	13163	13575	14554	0.7	68	4754	4937	5317	0.9	2.73	3456	3566	0.7
10950	MONROE	071	38663	43179	48119	2.6	97	10505	11640	12935	2.4	3.63	8783	9719	2.4
10952	MONSEY	087	30244	31612	33027	1.1	79	7483	7820	8170	1.0	3.97	6361	6630	1.0
10954	NANUET	087	22253	22907	23667	0.7	65	7925	8177	8442	0.7	2.73	5862	6012	0.6
10956	NEW CITY	087	31831	32145	33102	0.2	42	10115	10255	10585	0.3	3.06	8755	8853	0.3
10958	NEW HAMPTON	071	2688	2940	3233	2.1	94	931	1023	1129	2.2	2.83	747	815	2.1
10960	NYACK	087	14680	14673	15010	0.0	27	6027	6027	6174	0.0	2.33	3379	3373	0.0
10962	ORANGEBURG	087	5365	5411	5535	0.2	40	1717	1750	1803	0.5	2.67	1290	1301	0.2
10963	OTISVILLE	071	4280	4790	5124	2.7	97	791	907	1022	3.3	2.88	591	672	3.1
10964	PALISADES	087	1453	1421	1438	-0.5	6	560	547	554	-0.6	2.59	375	365	-0.6
10965	PEARL RIVER	087	14664	14358	14546	-0.5	7	5334	5236	5313	-0.4	2.73	4032	3939	-0.6
10968	PIERMONT	087	2404	2466	2529	0.6	61	1103	1137	1170	0.7	2.17	625	638	0.5
10969	PINE ISLAND	071	1084	1314	1522	4.6	100	386	472	550	4.9	2.75	281	343	4.8
10970	POMONA	087	9011	9639	10139	1.6	89	3289	3542	3740	1.8	2.65	2378	2538	1.5
10973	SLATE HILL	071	2091	2371	2657	3.0	98	693	791	890	3.2	2.98	569	646	3.0
10974	SLOATSBURG	087	3353	3338	3410	-0.1	22	1129	1129	1157	0.0	2.89	897	893	-0.1
10975	SOUTHFIELDS	071	425	470	519	2.4	96	197	219	243	2.5	2.12	134	148	2.4
10976	SPARKILL	087	1413	1613	1754	3.2	98	296	346	382	3.7	3.83	211	247	3.8
10977	SPRING VALLEY	087	49062	52849	55758	1.8	91	13477	14420	15156	1.6	3.57	10837	11526	1.5
10980	STONY POINT	087	12714	13097	13500	0.7	66	4330	4468	4612	0.7	2.91	3417	3509	0.6
	NEW YORK					0.4					0.5	2.60			0.4
	UNITED STATES					1.2					1.3	2.58			1.1

ZIP CODE #	POST OFFICE NAME	RACE (%) White 2000	White 2004	Black 2000	Black 2004	Asian/Pacific 2000	Asian/Pacific 2004	% Hispanic Origin 2000	% Hispanic Origin 2004	2004 AGE DISTRIBUTION (%) 0-4	5-9	10-14	15-19	20-24	25-44	45-64	65-84	85+	18+	MEDIAN AGE 2004	% 2004 Males	% 2004 Females
10526	GOLDENS BRIDGE	95.4	94.1	1.7	2.1	2.3	3.0	2.6	3.4	6.1	7.7	11.3	7.4	3.4	24.6	31.3	7.2	0.8	69.5	39.9	49.2	50.8
10527	GRANITE SPRINGS	96.2	95.1	0.9	1.2	1.7	2.2	2.6	3.4	8.3	9.2	8.5	5.7	3.9	26.1	30.0	7.8	0.7	70.3	39.1	49.4	50.6
10528	HARRISON	89.2	86.7	0.6	0.8	7.6	9.3	5.5	7.0	6.7	7.2	7.8	6.4	4.9	27.1	25.0	12.9	2.0	74.2	39.6	47.7	52.3
10530	HARTSDALE	76.3	72.1	7.4	8.6	12.3	14.3	8.1	10.0	5.9	6.1	5.3	4.4	3.8	26.9	29.7	16.1	1.9	79.9	43.7	46.3	53.8
10532	HAWTHORNE	80.1	77.8	13.9	15.0	3.5	4.0	7.5	9.1	4.9	5.2	5.9	8.5	7.8	31.7	22.2	11.6	2.2	78.3	36.5	54.8	45.2
10533	IRVINGTON	86.4	83.4	2.5	2.9	7.9	9.6	4.4	5.7	7.4	8.6	8.1	6.0	3.6	25.4	27.8	11.6	1.6	71.9	40.0	48.0	52.0
10535	JEFFERSON VALLEY	90.9	88.5	2.2	2.4	4.6	5.8	5.9	7.6	6.7	7.6	8.2	7.9	4.9	25.5	28.8	9.7	0.9	72.1	39.4	49.4	50.6
10536	KATONAH	89.5	87.6	5.8	6.5	2.2	2.7	5.1	6.3	7.1	8.3	8.3	7.8	4.1	26.3	27.6	8.8	1.6	70.8	39.1	47.6	52.4
10537	LAKE PEEKSKILL	94.8	93.9	1.7	1.8	1.1	1.4	9.3	11.3	5.5	6.3	8.3	6.6	5.4	30.2	28.4	8.1	1.1	75.8	38.9	49.6	50.4
10538	LARCHMONT	92.6	90.9	1.8	2.1	3.1	3.8	4.8	6.1	7.8	8.9	8.6	6.4	3.5	24.7	27.0	11.3	1.9	70.4	39.6	48.0	52.0
10541	MAHOPAC	94.8	93.9	1.0	1.1	1.3	1.6	5.5	6.7	7.0	7.4	7.9	6.7	5.4	28.1	27.6	8.9	1.0	73.5	38.3	49.6	50.4
10543	MAMARONECK	85.1	82.2	3.9	4.5	3.8	4.5	16.3	19.9	6.1	6.5	7.2	6.0	5.3	28.7	25.0	12.5	2.5	76.2	39.3	48.1	51.9
10546	MILLWOOD	88.9	86.2	2.7	3.3	6.8	8.5	3.6	4.6	6.8	8.7	10.0	7.6	3.2	22.4	31.8	8.9	0.7	68.6	40.5	50.2	49.8
10547	MOHEGAN LAKE	84.7	81.8	6.6	7.6	2.7	3.2	10.6	13.3	7.3	7.7	7.6	8.6	5.5	28.6	25.0	8.3	1.4	71.9	36.7	49.8	50.2
10548	MONTROSE	90.1	87.6	4.0	4.8	2.7	3.4	5.8	7.5	6.1	6.7	7.2	5.8	4.4	25.0	29.7	13.3	1.8	76.2	42.1	51.0	49.0
10549	MOUNT KISCO	83.7	81.1	4.3	4.8	3.8	4.5	16.9	19.8	6.9	7.4	7.3	6.8	5.5	28.6	26.1	10.2	1.2	74.2	38.0	50.0	50.0
10550	MOUNT VERNON	18.3	16.7	68.6	69.3	1.9	2.1	11.8	13.2	7.8	7.6	8.2	7.5	7.5	28.5	22.1	9.4	1.4	71.8	33.8	45.2	54.9
10552	MOUNT VERNON	60.3	55.6	27.5	30.2	3.5	4.0	9.7	11.6	5.6	5.4	5.0	4.9	5.1	29.8	26.0	14.6	3.6	80.8	41.6	45.5	54.5
10553	MOUNT VERNON	9.2	8.2	84.0	84.6	0.8	0.9	6.5	7.1	6.9	6.8	8.2	7.6	7.1	27.8	23.8	10.4	1.5	73.5	35.7	44.8	55.2
10560	NORTH SALEM	95.4	94.3	0.8	0.9	1.0	1.3	3.6	4.8	7.2	8.1	7.6	5.7	3.3	25.1	28.3	11.3	3.6	73.2	41.5	47.9	52.1
10562	OSSINING	66.9	63.8	16.4	17.3	4.4	5.0	22.6	25.7	6.0	6.1	6.1	5.5	5.9	33.4	24.6	10.4	2.1	78.3	38.0	52.6	47.4
10566	PEEKSKILL	57.1	52.7	25.5	27.5	2.4	2.7	21.9	25.3	7.4	7.2	7.1	5.7	5.7	32.7	23.0	9.8	1.5	74.8	36.2	48.6	51.4
10567	CORTLANDT MANOR	86.5	83.6	6.1	7.3	2.9	3.6	8.1	10.3	7.7	8.4	8.5	7.2	4.6	26.2	27.5	8.7	1.3	70.7	38.3	49.5	50.5
10570	PLEASANTVILLE	90.7	88.4	2.2	2.7	4.0	4.9	5.8	7.4	6.9	8.1	8.3	8.5	5.7	24.1	26.9	10.1	1.5	71.7	38.4	49.7	50.3
10573	PORT CHESTER	68.1	65.3	5.6	5.7	2.6	3.1	36.7	40.3	7.1	6.6	6.5	5.9	6.9	31.8	22.0	11.0	2.3	76.3	36.3	50.0	50.0
10576	POUND RIDGE	95.4	94.1	1.3	1.6	1.7	2.2	2.5	3.3	6.9	8.5	8.0	5.9	3.1	22.2	32.7	11.7	1.0	72.4	42.6	48.9	51.1
10577	PURCHASE	87.8	85.0	4.1	4.8	4.3	5.3	5.4	6.9	7.8	8.4	8.2	10.5	10.9	22.6	20.9	9.4	1.3	72.9	29.1	46.9	53.1
10578	PURDYS	96.8	95.8	0.5	0.7	0.8	1.0	2.3	3.1	8.2	8.8	7.8	5.5	3.7	24.8	28.5	11.5	1.2	71.1	40.8	48.8	51.2
10579	PUTNAM VALLEY	94.5	93.6	1.6	1.8	0.8	1.0	5.6	6.8	6.9	7.5	7.3	6.4	4.4	28.5	29.8	8.3	1.1	74.2	39.3	49.7	50.3
10580	RYE	89.7	87.3	1.4	1.6	6.2	7.7	5.1	6.4	8.2	9.3	9.3	6.4	3.5	24.9	25.1	11.6	1.9	69.0	38.9	48.4	51.6
10583	SCARSDALE	84.7	81.3	1.9	2.3	11.5	14.1	3.1	4.0	6.9	8.3	8.8	6.6	3.5	21.7	29.1	13.2	2.0	71.6	41.8	47.9	52.1
10588	SHRUB OAK	91.9	90.2	2.8	3.4	1.9	2.2	8.1	10.4	7.5	8.0	8.2	7.3	5.5	26.4	28.0	8.5	0.6	71.7	38.1	48.8	51.2
10589	SOMERS	95.5	94.2	1.5	1.7	2.0	2.8	2.1	2.7	4.7	5.3	4.5	4.2	2.0	16.9	29.2	29.1	4.2	82.3	53.9	44.8	55.2
10590	SOUTH SALEM	95.2	93.9	1.0	1.2	2.0	2.5	2.3	3.0	7.5	8.8	9.2	7.1	3.8	21.8	32.9	8.2	0.6	69.6	40.8	49.3	50.7
10591	TARRYTOWN	73.0	69.7	6.4	7.0	5.0	6.0	28.1	31.1	7.1	6.7	6.2	6.1	6.4	33.0	22.2	10.6	1.7	76.6	36.4	47.6	52.4
10594	THORNWOOD	91.3	89.2	2.8	3.4	3.4	4.2	5.5	7.0	6.8	7.5	7.3	8.0	4.9	25.7	25.5	12.8	1.6	72.6	39.0	49.4	50.6
10595	VALHALLA	90.7	89.5	4.7	4.9	2.9	3.5	4.5	5.6	6.2	6.4	6.2	5.8	5.0	28.4	24.4	14.6	3.1	77.7	40.6	50.5	49.5
10597	WACCABUC	95.1	94.1	1.1	1.4	2.0	2.6	2.9	3.8	6.9	9.1	10.6	6.9	3.1	21.5	33.0	8.4	0.6	68.7	41.0	47.4	52.6
10598	YORKTOWN HEIGHTS	92.1	90.2	2.2	2.7	3.5	4.3	4.8	6.1	6.7	7.5	8.2	6.6	4.4	24.2	28.1	12.0	2.4	73.1	41.0	47.7	52.3
10601	WHITE PLAINS	48.0	45.2	27.5	27.6	5.1	5.9	29.4	32.4	5.6	5.3	5.6	4.9	6.8	34.2	21.9	12.5	3.2	80.7	37.7	45.6	54.4
10603	WHITE PLAINS	56.6	51.7	29.1	31.8	5.0	5.6	13.3	15.8	6.3	6.2	6.2	5.4	5.6	30.3	25.6	12.5	2.0	78.1	39.5	46.7	53.3
10604	WEST HARRISON	80.1	77.8	8.9	9.3	3.7	4.3	13.3	16.0	6.8	6.7	6.7	6.7	6.5	30.8	22.2	11.8	1.9	76.3	36.8	46.6	53.4
10605	WHITE PLAINS	78.8	75.8	9.4	10.3	4.1	5.0	12.7	14.8	6.0	6.5	6.3	5.3	4.3	25.4	28.9	15.1	2.2	77.9	42.7	47.0	53.0
10606	WHITE PLAINS	58.4	55.2	16.9	17.6	3.8	4.3	35.7	39.5	6.3	6.2	6.3	5.8	6.9	32.1	22.9	10.7	2.9	77.7	36.8	49.7	50.3
10607	WHITE PLAINS	49.5	45.1	33.0	35.0	8.0	8.9	13.2	15.3	5.9	6.5	6.4	5.5	4.8	27.1	28.4	14.1	1.5	77.9	41.4	48.3	51.7
10701	YONKERS	42.8	39.9	28.0	28.4	3.3	3.7	34.6	37.5	8.1	7.9	8.2	7.6	7.5	29.7	20.3	9.2	1.6	71.1	32.4	47.1	52.9
10703	YONKERS	63.3	59.7	17.4	18.3	4.0	4.6	22.4	25.7	6.7	6.3	6.9	6.7	6.7	27.4	22.1	14.2	2.9	76.0	37.5	46.4	53.6
10704	YONKERS	83.9	80.5	4.6	5.3	4.5	5.4	11.0	13.8	5.9	5.5	5.2	4.5	5.2	32.1	23.6	15.3	2.7	80.7	39.7	48.0	52.0
10705	YONKERS	46.4	43.3	16.6	16.7	5.7	6.1	44.5	48.3	8.1	7.9	8.4	7.6	7.8	30.3	19.4	9.2	1.3	71.1	31.8	48.0	52.0
10706	HASTINGS ON HUDSON	88.9	86.3	2.3	2.7	5.3	6.6	4.3	5.5	5.0	6.5	8.3	6.5	3.8	22.0	32.2	13.9	2.0	75.5	43.8	47.9	52.1
10707	TUCKAHOE	80.1	76.5	7.1	8.0	7.8	9.4	7.3	9.0	7.3	7.4	6.5	5.7	4.6	29.8	23.6	13.2	2.0	75.4	38.9	47.8	52.2
10708	BRONXVILLE	88.8	86.2	3.8	4.5	4.0	5.1	6.5	8.3	5.4	5.7	5.5	5.8	5.5	25.9	27.5	15.7	2.8	80.6	42.6	45.0	55.0
10709	EASTCHESTER	90.6	88.3	0.7	0.8	5.9	7.4	3.4	4.4	6.1	6.7	6.8	5.3	4.2	24.7	26.6	16.6	3.0	77.1	42.9	46.9	53.1
10710	YONKERS	73.3	69.7	10.6	11.4	9.8	11.3	11.0	13.4	5.3	5.5	5.4	4.9	4.8	26.1	26.4	18.7	3.0	80.8	43.7	46.8	53.2
10801	NEW ROCHELLE	56.2	53.4	27.9	28.8	3.0	3.4	28.0	31.2	7.0	6.7	7.2	7.5	7.7	29.7	21.4	10.9	1.9	74.9	34.6	48.5	51.6
10803	PELHAM	86.5	83.8	5.4	6.3	4.0	4.9	6.1	7.8	6.9	7.7	8.0	6.4	4.4	24.9	26.4	12.3	3.0	73.1	40.3	48.2	51.8
10804	NEW ROCHELLE	86.6	83.7	7.9	9.5	2.9	3.7	3.8	4.8	6.8	7.7	8.2	6.5	3.7	20.7	29.1	15.1	2.4	72.8	42.8	48.4	51.6
10805	NEW ROCHELLE	71.9	67.9	13.6	15.2	3.9	4.5	21.3	25.2	5.8	5.2	5.1	6.7	7.5	30.4	22.2	13.1	4.0	80.8	38.3	45.5	54.5
10901	SUFFERN	89.5	87.6	3.2	3.5	2.9	3.6	8.2	10.0	6.4	7.0	7.5	6.4	4.9	25.8	26.6	13.0	2.5	74.8	40.3	47.9	52.1
10913	BLAUVELT	88.5	85.9	1.7	1.9	7.1	8.8	5.6	7.0	7.0	7.2	7.4	7.1	6.1	24.4	22.8	15.8	2.2	74.4	39.2	47.0	53.0
10916	CAMPBELL HALL	93.9	92.3	1.9	2.3	1.4	1.8	4.5	5.9	6.6	7.5	8.4	7.2	4.9	25.1	29.5	9.2	1.8	72.9	40.0	48.5	51.5
10917	CENTRAL VALLEY	94.1	92.4	0.8	1.0	1.7	2.1	7.1	9.1	6.7	7.1	8.5	6.6	5.9	27.2	27.5	8.9	1.7	73.3	38.4	50.5	49.5
10918	CHESTER	87.6	85.5	6.7	7.5	2.5	3.0	9.8	12.1	6.9	7.4	7.7	6.3	4.9	30.4	28.1	7.4	0.9	74.0	38.6	52.7	47.3
10919	CIRCLEVILLE	92.7	91.0	2.4	2.8	1.7	2.1	3.4	4.5	6.4	6.9	6.9	5.6	5.4	27.3	29.7	10.3	1.5	76.5	40.2	50.1	49.9
10920	CONGERS	84.1	80.6	2.0	2.2	9.6	11.8	7.6	9.4	7.0	7.3	7.1	6.3	5.4	28.6	27.2	10.0	1.2	74.6	38.4	48.9	51.1
10921	FLORIDA	93.5	92.0	3.1	3.7	0.6	0.7	5.7	7.3	5.7	6.3	6.7	6.0	4.4	23.0	25.8	15.2	7.0	77.5	43.7	44.8	55.2
10923	GARNERVILLE	77.3	74.1	7.2	7.6	3.3	3.9	21.0	24.8	6.5	6.6	7.3	6.6	6.1	30.5	25.6	10.0	0.9	75.5	37.0	48.6	51.4
10924	GOSHEN	88.6	86.6	6.6	7.5	1.8	2.3	7.5	9.3	5.5	6.3	7.5	7.7	6.0	27.2	25.6	10.7	3.5	75.7	38.9	51.0	49.1
10925	GREENWOOD LAKE	95.2	94.1	1.0	1.2	1.0	1.3	5.5	7.1	6.2	6.5	7.5	6.1	5.6	30.3	28.0	8.7	1.2	75.7	39.1	51.1	48.9
10926	HARRIMAN	88.5	86.0	2.9	3.4	4.3	5.3	8.3	10.5	7.1	7.3	8.3	6.9	5.7	31.7	24.4	7.5	1.1	72.5	36.5	50.1	49.9
10927	HAVERSTRAW	46.0	43.0	12.1	11.9	1.2	1.4	59.3	63.5	7.4	7.1	8.3	8.2	8.9	29.2	19.8	8.9	2.3	72.4	32.1	48.4	51.6
10928	HIGHLAND FALLS	82.1	78.8	9.2	10.7	1.9	2.3	9.3	11.5	5.8	6.0	7.1	6.5	5.6	28.8	25.7	12.7	1.8	77.1	39.5	49.4	50.6
10930	HIGHLAND MILLS	90.8	88.8	3.1	3.7	2.0	2.5	7.7	9.7	8.4	8.7	8.7	7.2	5.3	27.4	26.5	7.1	0.8	69.6	36.4	48.7	51.3
10931	HILLBURN	49.0	44.8	11.1	11.9	5.0	5.6	5.6	6.3	8.4	8.2	7.7	7.5	5.4	26.7	23.1	11.1	2.0	71.1	35.7	45.2	54.8
10940	MIDDLETOWN	75.2	71.9	11.9	13.1	1.7	2.0	19.6	22.9	7.3	7.1	7.7	7.2	7.0	28.4	23.7	9.7	1.9	73.4	35.5	48.7	51.3
10941	MIDDLETOWN	81.2	77.8	9.0	10.4	2.9	3.5	12.6	15.4	6.5	6.7	7.7	7.3	6.4	29.8	26.8	7.9	1.0	74.4	36.3	48.9	51.1
10950	MONROE	94.0	92.9	1.7	1.9	1.4	1.7	5.6	6.9	11.9	10.3	10.2	10.3	8.5	23.0	19.6	5.6	0.7	61.6	24.4	51.5	48.5
10952	MONSEY	90.5	88.8	4.7	5.3	2.6	3.1	3.5	4.4	12.3	10.7	11.0	9.6	7.5	21.4	18.9	7.7	1.0	59.9	24.3	50.0	50.0
10954	NANUET	74.3	70.7	12.0	12.9	9.0	10.8	8.1	9.8	6.7	6.9	6.9	6.2	5.8	28.3	26.0	11.8	1.5	75.7	38.6	48.2	51.8
10956	NEW CITY	85.1	82.5	4.6	4.9	7.0	8.6	5.8	7.2	6.3	6.9	7.4	6.5	5.0	24.0	30.5	12.0	1.4	75.0	41.3	49.0	51.0
10958	NEW HAMPTON	91.9	90.0	2.7	3.2	1.8	2.2	6.7	8.6	6.0	6.9	7.9	7.9	5.3	26.7	27.8	10.5	1.0	73.8	39.0	50.0	50.0
10960	NYACK	70.5	67.8	19.2	20.2	4.0	4.7	7.5	8.9	5.3	5.1	5.5	6.6	7.4	29.1	27.3	12.0	1.6	80.6	39.6	47.6	52.4
10962	ORANGEBURG	74.2	70.3	7.2	7.6	15.1	18.1	7.2	8.7	5.1	5.3	6.3	6.0	4.8	25.4	27.8	17.4	1.9	79.4	43.4	50.9	49.1
10963	OTISVILLE	70.8	68.6	23.5	24.7	1.9	2.1	19.5	22.0	3.2	3.8	5.3	4.3	7.8	45.3	24.3	5.4	0.7	85.1	36.6	73.0	27.0
10964	PALISADES	87.1	84.2	0.8	0.9	9.7	12.0	5.2	6.6	6.7	7.7	7.7	5.7	3.4	22.7	28.0	12.7	5.4	73.8	42.5	46.8	53.2
10965	PEARL RIVER	94.8	93.5	0.6	0.7	3.2	4.0	3.6	4.6	6.6	6.9	7.5	6.1	4.7	27.2	25.6	14.0	1.4	75.0	40.0	48.2	51.8
10968	PIERMONT	78.4	75.4	4.7	5.2	8.0	9.0	11.8	14.1	4.7	5.1	5.8	4.6	5.1	29.9	32.3	11.2	1.3	81.8	42.2	50.4	49.6
10969	PINE ISLAND	95.9	94.9	0.9	1.2	0.7	0.9	5.2	6.9	6.4	7.5	8.7	7.1	4.6	25.0	30.8	8.6	1.4	72.5	39.9	49.9	50.2
10970	POMONA	79.6	76.4	8.6	9.5	5.6	6.8	10.3	12.7	6.4	6.5	6.1	5.7	5.1	27.9	29.9	10.8	1.7	77.4	40.4	47.7	52.3
10973	SLATE HILL	94.0	92.5	1.5	1.8	1.7	2.2	4.4	5.6	6.8	7.5	8.5	7.1	5.6	27.5	27.5	8.6	0.9	72.1	37.8	50.3	49.7
10974	SLOATSBURG	91.2	89.6	3.5	4.0	2.4	3.0	5.5	7.0	7.3	7.6	7.1	6.2	5.0	28.0	26.8	10.3	1.7	73.9	38.5	50.5	49.6
10975	SOUTHFIELDS	91.3	89.4	1.4	1.7	4.5	5.7	3.5	4.5	5.5	5.7	6.0	5.3	4.5	29.6	30.2	11.9	1.3	78.9	41.9	50.6	49.4
10976	SPARKILL	85.2	82.0	3.0	3.4	6.2	7.6	7.4	9.4	7.2	6.9	6.1	6.6	10.7	24.5	19.2	14.0	4.8	77.7	35.6	45.5	54.5
10977	SPRING VALLEY	51.2	48.7	33.6	34.3	6.7	7.6	11.5	12.9	10.0	9.1	9.3	8.3	7.5	26.2	20.5	7.8	1.3	66.3	29.5	49.6	50.4
10980	STONY POINT	94.2	92.8	1.4	1.6	1.5	1.9	6.9	8.7	6.9	7.4	7.8	6.2	4.9	27.3	26.7	11.5	1.3	73.8	39.2	49.6	50.4
	NEW YORK	68.0	65.9	15.9	16.2	5.6	6.4	15.1	16.7	6.5	6.5	7.1	7.0	7.1	28.9	24.0	11.2	1.8	75.8	36.7	48.3	51.7
	UNITED STATES	75.1	73.6	12.3	12.5	3.8	4.2	12.5	14.1	6.9	6.7	7.2	7.0	7.3	28.6	23.8	10.8	1.7	75.1	36.0	49.1	50.9

#	ZIP CODE POST OFFICE NAME	2004 Per Capita Income	2004 HH Income Base	2004 HOUSEHOLD INCOME DISTRIBUTION (%) Less than $25,000	$25,000 to $49,999	$50,000 to $99,999	$100,000 to $149,999	$150,000 or More	MEDIAN HOUSEHOLD INCOME 2004	2009	2004 National Centile	2004 State Centile	2004 Home Value Base	2004 HOME VALUE DISTRIBUTION (%) Less than $50,000	$50,000 to $89,999	$90,000 to $174,999	$175,000 to $399,999	$400,000 or More	2004 Median Home Value
10526	GOLDENS BRIDGE	80498	687	4.1	6.8	17.3	21.0	50.8	153044	203955	100	99	617	0.0	0.0	1.1	23.0	75.9	602700
10527	GRANITE SPRINGS	47494	465	6.5	6.7	18.9	26.2	41.7	132708	162693	100	99	438	0.0	0.0	1.4	26.9	71.7	511834
10528	HARRISON	56916	4615	11.5	15.8	26.9	17.5	28.3	89261	118502	97	94	2969	0.1	0.7	2.7	13.5	82.9	647843
10530	HARTSDALE	57998	6101	9.2	15.0	29.8	19.9	26.1	91838	119730	97	95	4633	0.2	2.0	18.8	36.4	42.7	353375
10532	HAWTHORNE	29324	1846	11.0	16.9	29.3	25.2	17.7	84878	110127	96	92	1484	1.1	0.1	0.5	39.6	58.8	434031
10533	IRVINGTON	75242	2895	7.9	10.5	25.4	19.2	37.0	112065	146525	99	98	2200	0.0	0.3	7.5	23.4	68.8	553683
10535	JEFFERSON VALLEY	39703	109	11.9	10.1	24.8	25.7	27.5	104085	131305	98	97	88	0.0	0.0	0.0	60.2	39.8	368966
10536	KATONAH	62166	3810	5.1	8.6	23.3	18.8	44.2	129868	166637	100	98	3308	0.0	0.1	0.6	15.2	84.1	643184
10537	LAKE PEEKSKILL	30814	659	11.5	20.0	41.7	18.1	8.7	73149	84366	93	86	555	0.0	0.0	21.8	77.3	0.9	210731
10538	LARCHMONT	92100	6087	7.6	9.5	19.9	13.3	49.8	148728	199950	100	99	4748	0.1	1.0	5.6	11.2	82.1	743761
10541	MAHOPAC	34857	9152	7.9	14.7	34.7	24.8	17.8	87354	103212	97	93	7943	0.3	0.3	3.3	65.4	30.7	343773
10543	MAMARONECK	52358	7802	14.3	18.1	28.1	15.6	23.9	77772	103682	94	89	4845	0.3	1.3	7.5	26.3	64.6	497180
10546	MILLWOOD	105549	357	2.2	6.7	18.5	12.9	59.7	174390	224111	100	100	327	0.0	0.0	0.3	15.3	84.4	685748
10547	MOHEGAN LAKE	34949	2882	8.1	16.5	35.0	23.3	17.0	84114	105295	96	92	2283	0.3	0.6	5.7	76.4	17.0	292221
10548	MONTROSE	32308	1303	17.9	16.4	31.9	21.0	13.0	73532	92743	93	86	1049	0.0	0.0	9.7	69.4	20.9	273361
10549	MOUNT KISCO	65066	5980	13.7	14.7	24.7	15.5	31.5	91687	122905	97	94	3944	0.8	2.1	8.4	26.3	62.4	499187
10550	MOUNT VERNON	18835	13674	33.4	27.8	26.2	9.2	3.4	39004	47814	43	29	3609	0.6	0.6	7.5	70.1	21.2	297064
10552	MOUNT VERNON	38163	8291	17.1	22.3	32.9	15.1	12.6	63094	78998	87	78	4349	7.7	10.9	9.9	29.7	41.8	357861
10553	MOUNT VERNON	25087	3724	23.7	21.8	31.6	15.5	7.4	54846	68660	79	70	1688	0.7	1.5	5.7	62.1	30.0	332535
10560	NORTH SALEM	64476	1836	5.2	11.3	22.9	26.8	33.8	117617	151232	99	98	1605	0.0	0.0	2.5	34.3	63.2	478044
10562	OSSINING	38266	10832	15.1	19.6	29.5	17.2	18.6	71253	91737	92	85	6598	0.3	1.2	5.2	61.6	31.7	337143
10566	PEEKSKILL	26647	8975	22.3	24.3	32.8	13.8	6.8	54558	68492	79	69	4528	0.7	2.7	19.7	72.0	5.0	221429
10567	CORTLANDT MANOR	37541	6149	6.2	12.6	33.8	23.4	24.1	95206	119008	98	95	5548	0.1	0.1	3.1	64.5	32.2	331224
10570	PLEASANTVILLE	59671	4299	7.3	13.1	22.1	21.1	36.5	114713	149139	99	98	3502	0.4	0.6	2.3	26.2	70.6	528558
10573	PORT CHESTER	34853	12821	19.3	20.2	29.1	14.9	16.5	64210	82658	88	79	7105	1.6	1.5	3.5	38.1	55.4	432002
10576	POUND RIDGE	99803	1957	3.1	6.5	18.2	17.3	54.9	168030	218967	100	100	1793	0.0	0.7	1.5	9.2	88.7	833207
10577	PURCHASE	87903	865	3.7	4.7	13.4	18.2	60.0	188712	244837	100	100	793	0.0	0.0	0.0	4.5	95.5	984023
10578	PURDYS	40608	293	4.8	10.2	36.5	28.0	20.5	97118	121555	98	96	280	0.0	0.0	0.0	44.3	55.7	427119
10579	PUTNAM VALLEY	40133	2908	8.9	12.4	35.8	24.1	18.8	87250	103566	97	93	2604	0.0	0.3	5.5	69.5	24.7	317085
10580	RYE	107576	6215	7.2	9.3	19.0	17.5	47.1	139566	189332	100	99	4756	0.6	0.0	2.5	12.7	84.2	864899
10583	SCARSDALE	93154	13457	5.3	8.6	20.3	15.9	49.9	149542	190178	100	99	11903	0.2	0.8	8.0	12.5	78.5	684801
10588	SHRUB OAK	37262	785	8.5	11.0	36.3	29.6	14.7	90848	110824	97	94	686	0.0	0.0	3.5	76.4	20.1	318327
10589	SOMERS	53255	3800	9.1	15.4	30.4	21.2	23.9	88937	120527	97	94	3531	0.0	0.0	1.4	52.7	45.9	384803
10590	SOUTH SALEM	64059	2279	4.2	8.7	25.0	23.1	39.1	121091	155476	99	98	2029	0.0	0.2	2.3	23.0	74.6	584618
10591	TARRYTOWN	44618	8425	13.4	18.4	30.8	17.5	19.9	75808	99576	94	88	4073	0.0	0.9	6.8	36.0	56.3	438548
10594	THORNWOOD	42191	1660	8.1	12.8	29.3	23.7	26.1	99612	127110	98	96	1488	0.3	0.1	1.0	25.5	73.1	518952
10595	VALHALLA	38533	1977	6.6	13.9	32.4	23.9	23.2	94225	122014	98	95	1687	0.2	0.2	0.6	29.6	69.4	487333
10597	WACCABUC	75235	238	2.9	6.7	19.8	23.1	47.5	142831	183077	100	99	223	0.0	0.0	0.0	16.1	83.9	650974
10598	YORKTOWN HEIGHTS	41308	10018	11.3	13.1	26.4	24.1	25.1	98077	126227	98	96	8969	0.0	0.0	3.9	61.1	35.0	355733
10601	WHITE PLAINS	29424	4646	29.9	23.8	30.2	9.8	6.4	46093	57274	64	53	1421	4.8	12.2	42.6	32.4	8.0	150091
10603	WHITE PLAINS	38235	6648	16.5	18.3	33.8	17.5	13.9	72108	91256	92	85	3916	0.6	1.4	14.7	59.1	24.2	291442
10604	WEST HARRISON	49791	3951	15.7	17.7	31.1	17.0	18.4	74753	95244	93	87	2345	0.7	0.1	6.0	16.7	76.6	556770
10605	WHITE PLAINS	57552	7501	12.1	14.6	25.6	16.8	30.9	93924	124512	98	95	5560	0.6	4.0	9.6	17.8	68.1	537162
10606	WHITE PLAINS	32861	5173	19.0	19.2	30.8	15.2	15.8	65459	84625	89	81	2440	0.5	2.0	7.5	45.2	44.8	380793
10607	WHITE PLAINS	44784	2437	7.4	11.6	25.2	24.8	31.0	108952	138620	99	97	2142	0.5	0.0	1.5	52.2	45.9	385805
10701	YONKERS	21008	22886	34.9	23.9	26.4	9.7	5.1	39592	49885	45	32	6529	1.2	3.9	17.1	54.8	23.1	296621
10703	YONKERS	25077	8319	28.2	20.9	31.4	13.6	6.0	51128	64808	74	64	3796	1.4	4.2	12.9	63.0	18.6	277252
10704	YONKERS	33950	11775	17.1	20.6	35.5	18.1	8.6	64725	80961	88	80	6363	1.3	3.0	7.9	60.5	27.5	332810
10705	YONKERS	22150	13021	31.8	25.4	25.9	10.5	6.4	41408	52927	51	39	4081	2.6	5.7	12.0	58.1	21.7	299821
10706	HASTINGS ON HUDSON	68063	3413	8.6	12.5	26.3	17.4	35.2	105153	138129	99	97	2454	0.2	1.3	6.3	17.8	74.5	579505
10707	TUCKAHOE	43304	3621	14.8	15.9	31.5	22.3	15.6	78674	101057	95	90	2259	0.0	0.8	6.7	39.2	53.3	415762
10708	BRONXVILLE	66269	10598	13.5	15.7	29.2	16.2	25.5	82788	106464	96	91	7041	1.7	8.2	19.2	24.9	46.2	356742
10709	EASTCHESTER	50135	3379	11.8	17.2	29.1	17.5	24.3	83489	108963	96	92	2541	0.2	0.6	13.7	21.6	64.0	487965
10710	YONKERS	34642	10463	17.2	19.7	32.2	19.3	11.7	67084	85633	90	82	6936	1.1	7.0	13.6	49.3	29.0	332343
10801	NEW ROCHELLE	27308	12789	28.0	22.0	28.1	13.0	9.0	50035	64761	72	62	5332	0.7	2.4	9.2	51.0	36.8	357125
10803	PELHAM	66274	4434	8.7	13.9	24.7	17.1	35.7	105610	138773	99	97	3376	0.2	1.2	5.2	22.7	70.7	576247
10804	NEW ROCHELLE	74140	4656	4.8	6.4	19.2	18.9	50.7	151449	190909	100	99	4321	0.1	0.2	2.9	11.7	85.2	622038
10805	NEW ROCHELLE	33118	7164	21.2	21.6	34.3	14.5	8.4	57366	73861	82	72	2541	1.2	7.7	16.8	36.1	38.2	313150
10901	SUFFERN	39811	8644	14.6	14.7	30.8	21.8	18.1	81173	99544	95	91	6357	1.1	2.0	6.4	54.7	35.7	338417
10913	BLAUVELT	37916	1570	9.2	11.0	31.0	23.6	25.2	97316	115740	98	96	1396	0.4	0.0	0.5	49.8	49.3	397881
10916	CAMPBELL HALL	31870	1383	9.0	15.1	38.0	21.1	16.8	81162	92980	95	91	1249	0.3	0.2	4.4	75.6	19.5	290401
10917	CENTRAL VALLEY	32396	592	9.6	18.4	38.7	20.3	13.0	76943	87604	94	89	426	0.0	0.0	8.0	73.2	18.8	297561
10918	CHESTER	29832	3948	10.4	15.2	41.8	19.4	13.4	76212	85593	94	88	3070	0.4	0.5	18.2	63.8	17.0	265341
10919	CIRCLEVILLE	23618	186	11.3	14.5	61.8	10.2	2.2	63335	74075	87	79	157	0.0	0.0	29.3	61.8	8.9	222297
10920	CONGERS	35499	3215	7.0	13.7	35.5	23.6	20.3	89684	107615	97	94	2750	0.2	0.0	1.9	67.6	30.3	356640
10921	FLORIDA	25371	1594	20.8	17.1	38.5	16.4	7.2	63313	73826	87	79	1260	0.3	0.2	19.5	68.2	11.8	237152
10923	GARNERVILLE	26935	2474	12.3	19.9	38.0	21.8	8.0	68957	84217	91	84	1786	2.2	1.1	7.1	79.8	9.9	282407
10924	GOSHEN	30127	4239	15.6	20.5	36.3	14.9	12.8	67405	78050	90	82	3137	0.3	0.0	12.2	70.4	17.1	262363
10925	GREENWOOD LAKE	28760	2129	19.5	20.9	37.4	15.9	6.3	60776	69735	85	75	1516	0.1	1.4	37.4	52.9	8.3	191313
10926	HARRIMAN	31041	1351	11.0	23.6	42.4	15.0	8.0	66498	77050	89	82	900	4.2	1.2	26.7	58.3	9.6	228212
10927	HAVERSTRAW	17719	2816	26.7	24.1	30.9	14.2	4.2	49222	60461	71	61	1208	0.0	1.1	25.6	68.0	5.4	214262
10928	HIGHLAND FALLS	27793	2314	15.0	27.2	38.8	14.5	4.5	57822	66433	82	72	1386	7.9	2.2	16.7	65.4	7.8	217963
10930	HIGHLAND MILLS	33360	2707	7.5	12.7	39.2	26.2	14.4	86504	99940	97	93	2338	1.0	0.4	7.5	78.4	12.6	270922
10931	HILLBURN	22913	265	12.5	23.0	42.3	14.7	7.6	62764	75339	87	78	212	0.0	0.0	17.5	79.3	3.3	228000
10940	MIDDLETOWN	23533	16622	25.1	24.8	35.0	10.8	4.4	50085	57239	72	62	9673	0.8	2.5	44.7	50.0	2.0	177996
10941	MIDDLETOWN	25766	4937	14.0	20.5	46.4	14.0	5.0	62421	71980	87	77	3250	2.4	1.7	22.7	68.6	4.6	217773
10950	MONROE	20004	11640	23.4	19.1	32.1	17.4	8.0	60738	68609	85	75	8102	1.1	1.3	14.2	73.5	10.1	252196
10952	MONSEY	23480	7820	22.5	17.4	26.5	16.6	17.0	65940	82167	89	81	4966	0.1	0.3	3.6	52.9	43.0	376903
10954	NANUET	36804	8177	11.0	14.5	34.8	23.5	16.2	82520	100392	96	91	5924	0.7	0.5	6.3	64.5	28.0	332938
10956	NEW CITY	43234	10255	7.2	9.8	29.4	25.7	27.9	105094	126280	99	97	9150	0.3	0.1	0.9	47.4	51.4	407107
10958	NEW HAMPTON	26258	1023	15.8	20.5	40.3	16.8	6.6	66862	77428	90	82	883	0.9	0.9	16.8	71.5	10.0	233513
10960	NYACK	43870	6027	13.9	19.5	31.9	18.9	15.9	73391	90120	93	86	3372	0.0	0.3	6.4	48.0	45.3	381175
10962	ORANGEBURG	36793	1750	12.1	18.9	29.8	18.4	20.7	81219	97810	95	91	1373	0.7	0.2	5.0	48.4	45.8	387390
10963	OTISVILLE	19251	907	15.2	24.9	37.5	18.7	3.6	60975	70314	85	75	741	0.8	2.7	34.3	58.2	4.1	196755
10964	PALISADES	61735	547	22.9	7.9	22.1	19.4	27.8	92173	115637	97	95	437	0.0	0.0	1.6	37.8	60.6	489423
10965	PEARL RIVER	37673	5236	10.5	15.5	31.2	25.2	17.7	85755	105548	96	92	4094	0.0	0.0	2.3	61.9	35.8	361927
10968	PIERMONT	53480	1137	9.7	20.8	32.1	19.8	17.7	75943	91289	94	88	725	0.0	0.6	12.0	30.3	57.1	462048
10969	PINE ISLAND	30507	472	19.9	22.3	29.5	16.3	12.1	59123	69496	84	74	387	0.0	0.0	16.5	62.0	21.5	245707
10970	POMONA	36531	3542	11.6	19.3	33.4	19.9	15.8	75563	89715	93	88	2738	4.8	2.7	19.6	40.2	32.7	294192
10973	SLATE HILL	24561	791	14.0	23.0	38.1	19.5	5.4	65955	76797	89	81	689	2.2	0.3	14.4	71.3	11.9	245468
10974	SLOATSBURG	33425	1129	7.4	17.8	35.8	24.3	14.7	80895	98021	95	91	941	0.2	0.3	5.4	78.8	15.3	272374
10975	SOUTHFIELDS	44545	219	9.6	21.0	36.1	16.0	17.4	68359	80486	90	83	154	0.0	1.3	13.0	60.4	25.3	298333
10976	SPARKILL	26030	346	11.0	16.2	33.0	23.7	16.2	80103	100000	95	90	276	1.1	0.0	2.5	53.6	42.8	381651
10977	SPRING VALLEY	22014	14420	20.0	21.7	31.7	16.4	10.2	61249	73853	86	76	8184	4.3	3.1	8.4	67.6	16.5	285634
10980	STONY POINT	33655	4468	11.2	15.9	35.1	21.7	16.1	81979	98601	96	91	3760	3.2	1.0	4.6	64.5	26.8	328642
	NEW YORK	28049		26.3	24.3	29.3	11.5	8.6	49309	58077				4.6	8.6	27.2	39.9	19.8	219050
	UNITED STATES	25866		24.7	27.1	30.8	10.9	6.5	48124	56710				10.9	15.0	33.7	30.1	10.4	145905

ZIP CODE #	POST OFFICE NAME	FINANCIAL SERVICES: Auto Loan	FINANCIAL SERVICES: Home Loan	FINANCIAL SERVICES: Invest-ments	FINANCIAL SERVICES: Retire-ment Plans	THE HOME: Home Improvements: Home Repair	THE HOME: Home Improvements: Lawn & Garden	THE HOME: Furnishings: Comput-ers & Hard-ware	THE HOME: Furnishings: Major Appli-ances	THE HOME: Furnishings: TV, Radio, Sound Equip-ment	THE HOME: Furnishings: Furni-ture	ENTERTAINMENT: Dine out/ Carry out	ENTERTAINMENT: Sports Equip-ment	ENTERTAINMENT: Fees & Tickets	ENTERTAINMENT: Toys & Games	ENTERTAINMENT: Travel	ENTERTAINMENT: Cable TV	PERSONAL: Apparel & Services	PERSONAL: Auto Repairs	PERSONAL: Health Insur-ance	PERSONAL: Pets & Supplies
10526	GOLDENS BRIDGE	283	382	523	374	372	402	332	330	310	340	392	370	378	412	354	313	398	316	306	358
10527	GRANITE SPRINGS	193	247	293	251	240	248	217	213	199	221	253	244	241	264	224	196	256	205	192	234
10528	HARRISON	183	243	320	236	235	247	219	215	207	221	260	247	240	279	230	207	263	211	196	231
10530	HARTSDALE	154	189	264	189	183	194	182	175	176	183	222	204	195	237	188	176	223	175	161	189
10532	HAWTHORNE	104	146	187	137	141	148	127	127	121	128	151	143	141	166	136	122	153	122	116	134
10533	IRVINGTON	240	324	436	314	314	335	287	283	270	291	341	322	320	365	304	272	345	275	260	305
10535	JEFFERSON VALLEY	158	197	214	204	191	193	174	169	158	176	201	196	191	209	177	153	203	163	150	188
10536	KATONAH	236	323	421	315	312	330	280	276	260	285	328	313	315	352	296	261	334	265	251	299
10537	LAKE PEEKSKILL	104	124	143	124	122	124	118	115	112	117	141	135	124	148	120	110	140	114	106	126
10538	LARCHMONT	301	397	527	390	386	409	355	349	333	359	420	399	393	445	373	332	424	340	320	378
10541	MAHOPAC	136	171	192	170	167	168	154	153	144	154	180	178	164	192	158	140	181	148	138	167
10543	MAMARONECK	168	206	273	201	199	212	196	190	190	197	240	219	209	254	202	191	241	190	178	206
10546	MILLWOOD	355	478	655	468	466	503	416	413	388	426	490	464	473	516	444	391	498	396	383	448
10547	MOHEGAN LAKE	132	160	184	163	157	158	149	146	139	148	175	172	157	184	151	135	175	143	131	160
10548	MONTROSE	105	141	174	132	136	145	126	125	121	125	151	140	137	165	133	124	152	121	118	133
10549	MOUNT KISCO	211	261	354	256	253	273	246	239	238	248	300	273	265	318	256	240	302	238	225	259
10550	MOUNT VERNON	65	63	93	61	61	70	70	66	76	71	95	76	72	98	71	79	94	70	69	75
10552	MOUNT VERNON	110	123	161	122	120	132	124	120	124	124	156	138	129	160	127	125	154	122	117	131
10553	MOUNT VERNON	100	101	125	97	98	112	104	101	109	106	138	112	109	137	106	113	135	104	106	115
10560	NORTH SALEM	237	304	359	304	295	306	268	264	249	272	315	301	297	332	278	246	318	254	240	288
10562	OSSINING	122	146	209	143	141	152	143	138	142	144	180	159	152	192	148	145	181	139	131	150
10566	PEEKSKILL	88	95	121	94	92	98	97	93	97	97	122	108	99	126	97	96	121	96	89	102
10567	CORTLANDT MANOR	148	191	218	191	185	187	168	166	155	169	196	192	184	210	174	152	198	160	148	181
10570	PLEASANTVILLE	208	283	375	272	273	289	250	246	236	253	297	280	278	320	264	237	301	239	226	265
10573	PORT CHESTER	119	139	207	133	133	147	139	133	142	141	180	151	146	191	143	147	181	136	130	145
10576	POUND RIDGE	331	441	590	435	430	460	385	381	358	393	453	430	436	476	408	359	459	366	352	415
10577	PURCHASE	458	620	849	606	604	651	539	535	503	552	636	601	612	671	575	507	646	513	496	580
10578	PURDYS	150	181	204	179	180	189	166	166	157	166	197	188	176	200	172	156	195	162	159	181
10579	PUTNAM VALLEY	149	184	202	184	180	181	166	164	154	166	194	191	177	204	169	150	194	159	148	180
10580	RYE	360	470	649	464	457	491	423	415	399	431	505	472	472	533	446	402	510	404	385	451
10583	SCARSDALE	317	412	589	409	399	430	375	365	356	382	449	416	419	478	395	358	455	357	337	396
10588	SHRUB OAK	139	173	185	175	169	168	154	152	141	154	178	177	165	189	157	137	179	146	136	168
10589	SOMERS	172	167	164	160	174	201	153	171	159	163	199	171	157	170	165	168	187	166	194	194
10590	SOUTH SALEM	233	302	370	304	293	306	265	260	243	270	309	297	296	323	275	241	313	250	236	285
10591	TARRYTOWN	136	160	243	157	153	167	161	153	163	162	206	178	170	221	166	166	207	157	146	166
10594	THORNWOOD	160	213	261	204	208	217	189	188	178	190	224	213	206	239	199	179	225	182	174	202
10595	VALHALLA	136	189	243	180	183	190	167	165	157	168	197	188	183	216	176	158	200	160	149	176
10597	WACCABUC	270	364	499	357	355	383	317	315	296	325	374	354	360	394	338	298	380	302	292	342
10598	YORKTOWN HEIGHTS	147	188	222	186	183	190	168	166	157	169	198	189	183	209	175	156	199	161	152	180
10601	WHITE PLAINS	79	77	122	81	74	83	87	80	90	88	114	95	89	116	86	91	113	85	79	90
10603	WHITE PLAINS	118	131	183	134	127	138	134	127	132	134	167	148	140	173	135	132	166	130	121	140
10604	WEST HARRISON	162	198	267	195	193	205	190	184	185	190	233	213	203	248	197	186	233	184	173	200
10605	WHITE PLAINS	176	213	286	209	208	225	202	197	197	204	249	225	218	261	210	199	249	197	189	215
10606	WHITE PLAINS	114	130	204	127	125	139	135	127	139	136	176	146	142	190	139	144	178	132	125	139
10607	WHITE PLAINS	160	218	285	205	209	221	193	191	184	196	232	215	212	253	204	186	236	186	174	203
10701	YONKERS	69	73	122	71	69	79	80	75	85	81	109	86	82	115	81	89	109	79	75	82
10703	YONKERS	83	90	125	86	87	97	93	89	97	93	121	102	97	128	95	100	121	92	90	98
10704	YONKERS	105	117	145	116	115	125	117	114	116	116	145	130	121	149	119	116	143	115	112	124
10705	YONKERS	74	79	135	75	75	86	86	81	93	89	119	92	88	126	88	98	120	86	82	89
10706	HASTINGS ON HUDSON	201	263	361	257	255	272	240	234	228	242	287	267	264	308	252	229	290	229	216	252
10707	TUCKAHOE	135	155	205	156	150	161	154	148	150	154	189	173	161	196	156	149	188	151	139	161
10708	BRONXVILLE	189	216	285	217	211	230	213	206	209	213	263	237	225	269	219	210	261	208	200	226
10709	EASTCHESTER	152	190	242	182	186	201	177	175	173	177	216	197	191	230	186	176	216	172	168	188
10710	YONKERS	106	125	158	122	122	131	121	118	119	121	149	135	127	155	124	120	149	119	114	128
10801	NEW ROCHELLE	96	103	147	101	100	111	108	103	111	108	140	119	112	147	110	114	140	107	102	113
10803	PELHAM	231	291	395	289	283	303	269	262	256	272	323	301	294	339	281	256	325	258	244	285
10804	NEW ROCHELLE	255	355	480	341	344	367	308	305	287	313	362	343	347	390	328	291	369	293	280	328
10805	NEW ROCHELLE	96	101	160	105	97	108	110	102	113	111	143	120	115	151	111	115	143	108	100	113
10901	SUFFERN	136	159	195	162	156	164	153	149	146	153	184	173	161	190	156	144	183	149	139	163
10913	BLAUVELT	151	196	235	189	192	202	176	175	167	176	209	198	191	222	185	168	210	170	165	189
10916	CAMPBELL HALL	130	162	172	162	159	157	144	143	133	144	168	168	154	178	147	129	168	138	128	158
10917	CENTRAL VALLEY	109	139	176	137	136	140	129	126	122	129	153	147	138	164	133	120	154	124	113	136
10918	CHESTER	120	142	151	145	138	138	130	129	121	131	153	151	137	158	131	116	152	126	114	141
10919	CIRCLEVILLE	86	104	115	102	102	105	97	96	92	96	116	111	103	124	99	91	116	93	89	104
10920	CONGERS	128	178	219	170	170	174	154	152	143	155	180	174	169	198	161	142	183	146	134	162
10921	FLORIDA	86	105	113	103	103	105	95	95	91	95	114	110	102	120	98	90	113	92	89	104
10923	GARNERVILLE	104	117	136	117	114	118	113	111	110	114	139	129	117	142	114	107	138	111	102	122
10924	GOSHEN	110	130	146	131	128	130	122	120	115	121	144	141	127	150	124	112	143	118	111	132
10925	GREENWOOD LAKE	93	109	121	109	106	108	103	102	98	103	124	119	107	128	104	95	122	101	92	111
10926	HARRIMAN	108	121	122	123	117	116	114	113	107	115	135	134	115	136	112	101	133	112	99	124
10927	HAVERSTRAW	74	75	123	69	71	81	82	79	90	86	116	87	82	119	83	95	116	83	80	85
10928	HIGHLAND FALLS	84	98	114	97	96	101	94	92	91	94	115	107	99	119	96	91	114	92	88	101
10930	HIGHLAND MILLS	137	164	171	168	159	157	148	146	136	150	172	171	156	179	148	130	172	142	128	161
10931	HILLBURN	94	114	126	111	112	114	106	104	101	105	127	121	113	135	108	99	126	102	97	114
10940	MIDDLETOWN	85	90	102	91	89	93	92	89	90	90	112	105	93	114	91	88	110	90	85	98
10941	MIDDLETOWN	98	104	110	107	101	103	102	100	97	103	123	119	103	123	100	93	121	101	90	111
10950	MONROE	98	109	114	109	107	107	105	104	100	106	126	121	107	131	104	96	126	103	94	113
10952	MONSEY	120	140	170	139	136	142	133	131	129	135	163	150	140	169	135	127	164	131	120	142
10954	NANUET	123	159	202	153	154	162	145	143	139	146	175	164	157	187	152	140	176	141	132	154
10956	NEW CITY	165	217	267	211	211	220	192	190	180	194	227	216	211	242	201	180	229	184	174	205
10958	NEW HAMPTON	99	117	124	116	114	114	108	107	101	108	128	125	113	134	109	98	127	105	97	117
10960	NYACK	133	153	194	154	150	158	151	146	146	151	184	170	157	189	153	144	183	148	136	159
10962	ORANGEBURG	138	165	182	161	162	173	152	152	147	152	185	171	163	191	158	148	183	148	148	166
10963	OTISVILLE	79	97	106	95	95	96	89	88	84	88	106	102	94	112	91	82	105	85	81	96
10964	PALISADES	198	246	307	241	241	252	229	228	219	229	274	263	243	287	237	217	273	224	210	244
10965	PEARL RIVER	124	162	202	157	157	164	147	145	140	147	175	167	159	189	153	140	176	142	133	156
10968	PIERMONT	156	161	196	171	157	164	168	161	162	169	205	194	169	202	164	154	201	167	146	178
10969	PINE ISLAND	110	137	146	138	134	133	122	121	112	122	142	141	131	150	124	109	142	116	108	133
10970	POMONA	132	146	170	149	143	149	142	139	135	143	170	163	146	171	142	131	169	139	127	154
10973	SLATE HILL	108	110	99	107	112	116	101	106	101	101	125	126	102	129	103	101	121	103	106	129
10974	SLOATSBURG	121	158	185	153	153	156	140	139	132	140	165	160	152	179	146	130	166	134	126	151
10975	SOUTHFIELDS	122	139	172	144	137	141	138	133	131	137	165	159	142	169	138	127	163	135	121	146
10976	SPARKILL	148	155	180	162	156	163	158	157	152	157	191	184	158	187	157	147	186	158	150	171
10977	SPRING VALLEY	101	112	143	109	108	116	111	108	112	113	141	123	115	147	112	112	141	110	103	118
10980	STONY POINT	128	154	167	153	151	156	140	140	133	140	167	160	149	173	144	131	166	136	131	154
	NEW YORK	95	100	134	99	98	107	103	100	105	103	133	116	105	138	104	107	131	102	99	112
	UNITED STATES	100	100	100	100	100	100	100	100	100	100	100	100	100	100	100	100	100	100	100	100

POPULATION CHANGE

#	POST OFFICE NAME	COUNTY FIPS CODE	POPULATION 2000	POPULATION 2004	POPULATION 2009	2000-2004 ANNUAL RATE % Rate	2000-2004 ANNUAL RATE State Centile	HOUSEHOLDS 2000	HOUSEHOLDS 2004	HOUSEHOLDS 2009	HOUSEHOLDS % Annual Rate 2000-2004	HOUSEHOLDS 2004 Average HH Size	FAMILIES 2000	FAMILIES 2004	FAMILIES % Annual Rate 2000-2004
10983	TAPPAN	087	5802	5922	6112	0.5	56	2048	2122	2209	0.8	2.67	1649	1693	0.6
10984	THIELLS	087	2809	2923	3080	0.9	75	884	921	972	1.0	3.09	758	789	1.0
10985	THOMPSON RIDGE	071	77	83	90	1.8	91	22	24	26	2.1	3.46	18	20	2.5
10986	TOMKINS COVE	087	1772	1758	1785	-0.2	18	596	593	602	-0.1	2.96	463	456	-0.4
10987	TUXEDO PARK	071	2958	3245	3576	2.2	95	1164	1284	1419	2.3	2.52	848	928	2.1
10989	VALLEY COTTAGE	087	9163	9424	9728	0.7	64	3328	3457	3579	0.9	2.63	2389	2464	0.7
10990	WARWICK	071	19361	20943	22898	1.9	92	6551	7115	7814	2.0	2.80	4929	5338	1.9
10992	WASHINGTONVILLE	071	10211	11085	12157	2.0	93	3342	3639	4010	2.0	3.04	2641	2862	1.9
10993	WEST HAVERSTRAW	087	6115	5991	6067	-0.5	7	2176	2128	2153	-0.5	2.79	1494	1449	-0.7
10994	WEST NYACK	087	6964	6976	7153	0.0	30	2246	2256	2318	0.1	3.08	1876	1877	0.0
10996	WEST POINT	071	7126	7357	7675	0.8	69	993	1054	1150	1.4	3.55	936	992	1.4
10998	WESTTOWN	071	3285	3682	4102	2.7	97	1088	1224	1366	2.8	3.00	868	970	2.7
11001	FLORAL PARK	059	28952	28649	28660	-0.3	15	10078	9953	9941	-0.3	2.87	7621	7500	-0.4
11003	ELMONT	059	41106	41387	41621	0.2	38	12531	12488	12483	-0.1	3.30	9927	9863	-0.2
11004	GLEN OAKS	081	11305	11040	11047	-0.6	5	4358	4225	4198	-0.7	2.58	2933	2832	-0.8
11005	FLORAL PARK	081	2634	3396	3869	6.2	100	1647	2165	2478	6.7	1.55	629	810	6.1
11010	FRANKLIN SQUARE	059	23651	23436	23454	-0.2	17	8201	8112	8113	-0.3	2.88	6359	6264	-0.4
11020	GREAT NECK	059	5391	5412	5461	0.1	34	1800	1797	1808	0.0	2.84	1502	1492	-0.2
11021	GREAT NECK	059	17045	18031	18707	1.3	86	7617	8010	8241	1.2	2.23	4542	4778	1.2
11023	GREAT NECK	059	8855	8860	8912	0.0	29	3203	3183	3191	-0.2	2.77	2529	2505	-0.2
11024	GREAT NECK	059	7953	7963	7983	0.0	30	2299	2284	2279	-0.2	3.20	1887	1870	-0.2
11030	MANHASSET	059	17373	17346	17437	0.0	26	5900	5888	5912	-0.1	2.87	4907	4882	-0.1
11040	NEW HYDE PARK	059	39721	39432	39556	-0.2	19	13710	13584	13610	-0.2	2.90	10988	10851	-0.3
11042	NEW HYDE PARK	059	513	511	511	-0.1	23	0	0	0	0.0	0.00	0	0	0.0
11050	PORT WASHINGTON	059	28599	29081	29471	0.4	51	10470	10624	10733	0.3	2.72	7819	7919	0.3
11096	INWOOD	059	8037	8221	8357	0.5	59	2610	2645	2676	0.3	3.10	1933	1950	0.2
11101	LONG ISLAND CITY	081	27161	28196	29125	0.9	74	10019	10339	10606	0.7	2.62	5842	5969	0.5
11102	ASTORIA	081	34378	35163	35851	0.5	59	12811	13122	13326	0.6	2.67	7561	7666	0.3
11103	ASTORIA	081	44580	44616	44821	0.0	30	17944	17844	17800	-0.1	2.50	10032	9918	-0.3
11104	SUNNYSIDE	081	26294	26229	26381	-0.1	25	11129	11017	10996	-0.2	2.38	6066	5966	-0.4
11105	ASTORIA	081	40703	40318	40217	-0.2	16	16519	16355	16243	-0.2	2.46	9907	9743	-0.4
11106	ASTORIA	081	41031	41539	41953	0.3	46	16986	16985	16979	0.0	2.43	9337	9310	-0.1
11201	BROOKLYN	047	47775	48831	49899	0.5	59	21561	22069	22555	0.6	1.94	8970	9082	0.3
11203	BROOKLYN	047	84174	84438	85325	0.1	33	27757	27856	28090	0.1	2.97	20556	20541	0.0
11204	BROOKLYN	047	73977	73449	73728	-0.2	19	25361	25054	25033	-0.3	2.93	18484	18174	-0.4
11205	BROOKLYN	047	38398	38638	39196	0.2	38	14333	14428	14618	0.2	2.50	7848	7810	-0.1
11206	BROOKLYN	047	66808	73780	79889	2.4	95	21583	23493	25129	2.0	3.06	15139	16499	2.0
11207	BROOKLYN	047	89595	92038	94355	0.6	63	28739	29523	30216	0.6	3.06	21471	21959	0.5
11208	BROOKLYN	047	89018	89633	90740	0.2	38	26535	26638	26887	0.1	3.33	20933	20946	0.0
11209	BROOKLYN	047	70169	70266	70707	0.0	30	31650	31516	31562	-0.1	2.22	16977	16778	-0.3
11210	BROOKLYN	047	71687	70261	70212	-0.5	7	23629	22983	22830	-0.7	3.05	17227	16699	-0.7
11211	BROOKLYN	047	84202	88696	92277	1.2	83	27556	28921	29933	1.1	3.05	17342	18108	1.0
11212	BROOKLYN	047	86997	86407	86814	-0.2	20	29134	28954	29043	-0.2	2.90	21100	20878	-0.3
11213	BROOKLYN	047	63150	65230	66965	0.8	70	21734	22450	23003	0.8	2.86	14649	15076	0.7
11214	BROOKLYN	047	83492	84921	86319	0.4	52	31652	32030	32411	0.3	2.62	21709	21841	0.1
11215	BROOKLYN	047	62532	64907	66653	0.9	74	27125	28157	28856	0.9	2.29	13448	13843	0.7
11216	BROOKLYN	047	55227	55806	56617	0.3	43	21583	21727	21959	0.2	2.52	12537	12551	0.0
11217	BROOKLYN	047	36203	36084	36248	-0.1	24	16070	16003	16043	-0.1	2.16	6975	6882	-0.3
11218	BROOKLYN	047	72038	73540	74705	0.5	57	24651	24878	25080	0.2	2.93	16318	16372	0.1
11219	BROOKLYN	047	86486	86752	87284	0.1	33	26654	26454	26414	-0.2	3.23	19386	19160	-0.3
11220	BROOKLYN	047	91538	91876	92224	0.1	34	28053	27967	27920	-0.1	3.27	20915	20750	-0.2
11221	BROOKLYN	047	73955	76701	78734	0.9	73	24451	25311	25902	0.8	2.96	16926	17448	0.7
11222	BROOKLYN	047	39328	41465	42949	1.3	84	15854	16651	17180	1.2	2.48	8745	9130	1.0
11223	BROOKLYN	047	79405	79319	80070	0.0	26	29239	29034	29156	-0.2	2.72	20481	20215	-0.3
11224	BROOKLYN	047	51209	49732	49582	-0.7	3	20154	19455	19334	-0.8	2.47	12791	12293	-0.9
11225	BROOKLYN	047	63526	65622	67958	0.8	70	23379	24106	24894	0.7	2.72	15721	16110	0.6
11226	BROOKLYN	047	110432	111514	113279	0.2	42	37200	37514	38042	0.2	2.95	26476	26599	0.1
11228	BROOKLYN	047	41239	40060	39872	-0.7	3	16053	15544	15411	-0.8	2.56	10920	10521	-0.9
11229	BROOKLYN	047	80064	79750	80304	-0.1	23	30378	30032	30056	-0.3	2.65	21042	20670	-0.4
11230	BROOKLYN	047	82723	85241	87573	0.7	67	29050	29627	30227	0.5	2.86	19564	19906	0.4
11231	BROOKLYN	047	32974	33891	34700	0.7	64	14972	15423	15802	0.7	2.19	7709	7847	0.4
11232	BROOKLYN	047	28205	29038	29406	0.7	66	8589	8608	8677	0.1	3.13	6143	6123	-0.1
11233	BROOKLYN	047	64703	65806	67336	0.4	52	23342	23662	24114	0.3	2.74	15426	15588	0.3
11234	BROOKLYN	047	84644	83648	83935	-0.3	14	30378	29859	29828	-0.4	2.80	22728	22257	-0.5
11235	BROOKLYN	047	76525	78849	80752	0.7	67	31659	32190	32679	0.4	2.40	19482	19688	0.3
11236	BROOKLYN	047	96116	95303	95663	-0.2	18	31666	30939	30771	-0.6	3.02	24145	23506	-0.6
11237	BROOKLYN	047	47594	49907	51608	1.1	81	13678	14281	14695	1.0	3.49	11011	11454	0.9
11238	BROOKLYN	047	46114	48399	50418	1.1	81	19809	20823	21665	1.2	2.28	9654	10023	0.9
11239	BROOKLYN	047	14188	13582	13454	-1.0	1	5888	5611	5576	-1.1	2.36	3484	3298	-1.3
11354	FLUSHING	081	54011	56069	57515	0.9	74	19481	20276	20744	1.0	2.67	13210	13696	0.9
11355	FLUSHING	081	82807	86318	88491	1.0	77	28591	29666	30228	0.9	2.88	20332	21030	0.8
11356	COLLEGE POINT	081	20011	19983	20068	0.0	26	7087	7064	7059	-0.1	2.83	5226	5186	-0.2
11357	WHITESTONE	081	37451	36081	35752	-0.9	2	14536	13986	13802	-0.9	2.55	10385	9953	-1.0
11358	FLUSHING	081	38090	37608	37582	-0.3	14	13937	13761	13696	-0.3	2.73	10055	9865	-0.5
11360	BAYSIDE	081	19580	19016	19132	-0.7	3	9047	8718	8701	-0.9	2.17	5420	5249	-0.8
11361	BAYSIDE	081	26300	25960	25937	-0.3	13	9794	9662	9618	-0.3	2.63	6594	6475	-0.4
11362	LITTLE NECK	081	17589	17303	17265	-0.4	10	7072	6947	6903	-0.4	2.47	4941	4833	-0.5
11363	LITTLE NECK	081	6554	6476	6496	-0.3	14	2519	2481	2473	-0.4	2.61	1771	1730	-0.6
11364	OAKLAND GARDENS	081	35522	36135	36817	0.4	52	13944	14197	14422	0.4	2.54	9719	9836	0.3
11365	FRESH MEADOWS	081	37738	37859	38516	0.1	33	13997	13934	14072	-0.1	2.71	10138	10055	-0.2
11366	FRESH MEADOWS	081	15646	15590	15715	-0.1	24	5558	5514	5523	-0.2	2.79	4096	4036	-0.4
11367	FLUSHING	081	40143	41628	42651	0.9	73	15323	15883	16213	0.9	2.61	10429	10719	0.7
11368	CORONA	081	97578	96414	96240	-0.3	14	27133	26548	26263	-0.5	3.61	20796	20269	-0.6
11369	EAST ELMHURST	081	38025	39101	39713	0.7	64	11629	11803	11862	0.4	3.26	8704	8801	0.3
11370	EAST ELMHURST	081	30911	30431	30380	-0.4	10	10357	10116	10022	-0.6	3.01	7684	7473	-0.7
11372	JACKSON HEIGHTS	081	67063	71558	74730	1.5	88	23750	24918	25720	1.1	2.87	15254	15914	1.0
11373	ELMHURST	081	104234	106089	107611	0.4	53	31909	32043	32162	0.1	3.29	23045	23047	0.0
11374	REGO PARK	081	42953	44961	46433	1.1	80	19028	19793	20292	0.9	2.27	11151	11520	0.8
11375	FOREST HILLS	081	71185	73108	74823	0.6	63	33582	34520	35187	0.7	2.10	18141	18430	0.4
11377	WOODSIDE	081	91734	92557	93282	0.2	41	33070	33090	33087	0.0	2.79	21054	20961	-0.1
11378	MASPETH	081	33315	33828	34254	0.4	50	12803	12968	13067	0.3	2.59	8725	8806	0.2
11379	MIDDLE VILLAGE	081	34882	34633	34661	-0.2	19	14114	14012	13971	-0.2	2.43	9412	9302	-0.3
11385	RIDGEWOOD	081	99443	100759	101978	0.3	48	35467	35472	35532	0.0	2.84	25184	25099	-0.1
11411	CAMBRIA HEIGHTS	081	20882	20554	20452	-0.4	10	6566	6465	6407	-0.4	3.18	5343	5248	-0.4
11412	SAINT ALBANS	081	37531	37332	37393	-0.1	21	11581	11537	11516	-0.1	3.23	8889	8824	-0.2
	NEW YORK					0.4					0.5	2.60			0.4
	UNITED STATES					1.2					1.3	2.58			1.1

ZIP CODE #	POST OFFICE NAME	RACE (%) White 2000	White 2004	Black 2000	Black 2004	Asian/Pacific 2000	Asian/Pacific 2004	% Hispanic Origin 2000	% Hispanic Origin 2004	2004 AGE DISTRIBUTION (%) 0-4	5-9	10-14	15-19	20-24	25-44	45-64	65-84	85+	18+	MEDIAN AGE 2004	% 2004 Males	% 2004 Females
10983	TAPPAN	85.0	82.0	1.5	1.7	10.2	12.3	6.6	8.3	7.0	7.2	6.6	6.1	5.9	24.3	24.7	16.1	2.2	75.7	40.7	47.7	52.4
10984	THIELLS	85.9	83.7	5.5	6.1	4.0	4.9	13.3	16.1	5.8	6.1	7.2	7.1	5.7	27.4	31.8	8.5	0.6	76.3	39.1	50.6	49.4
10985	THOMPSON RIDGE	97.4	95.2	1.3	1.2	0.0	1.2	5.2	7.2	7.2	7.2	9.6	8.4	4.8	25.3	27.7	8.4	1.2	68.7	38.2	49.4	50.6
10986	TOMKINS COVE	94.2	92.8	0.9	1.0	0.9	1.1	6.2	8.0	7.0	7.2	7.6	6.5	5.0	29.0	27.8	8.7	1.1	74.2	38.2	48.3	51.7
10987	TUXEDO PARK	92.9	91.2	1.3	1.5	3.0	3.8	4.4	5.7	5.4	6.3	6.2	5.2	3.7	27.7	32.6	11.7	1.1	78.5	42.4	49.7	50.3
10989	VALLEY COTTAGE	80.8	77.1	5.8	6.5	9.1	11.1	6.8	8.4	5.7	6.0	6.1	5.7	5.1	26.9	29.5	12.2	2.8	78.5	41.7	47.9	52.1
10990	WARWICK	89.2	87.7	6.1	6.5	1.0	1.2	7.0	8.5	6.4	7.2	8.5	6.9	4.8	26.3	27.7	10.5	1.8	73.5	40.0	50.3	49.7
10992	WASHINGTONVILLE	89.5	87.3	4.6	5.4	1.4	1.7	9.3	11.7	7.2	7.9	9.2	7.9	5.5	27.5	25.5	8.2	1.1	70.5	36.7	49.7	50.3
10993	WEST HAVERSTRAW	59.5	56.0	16.1	16.3	4.5	4.9	33.2	38.0	7.8	7.2	7.6	7.8	7.0	27.9	21.2	11.6	1.9	72.5	35.3	48.0	52.0
10994	WEST NYACK	85.2	82.3	3.8	4.1	8.0	9.8	5.8	7.3	6.5	7.0	6.8	6.1	4.7	25.6	29.1	12.9	1.2	75.5	40.9	48.5	51.6
10996	WEST POINT	82.3	78.9	9.1	10.7	3.5	4.2	6.6	8.2	7.7	5.9	4.3	16.4	42.4	19.4	3.9	0.1	0.0	80.2	21.9	69.2	30.8
10998	WESTTOWN	95.9	94.7	1.4	1.7	0.6	0.9	4.7	6.2	6.7	7.1	8.6	8.0	5.5	27.2	27.8	8.0	1.0	72.3	37.8	49.1	51.0
11001	FLORAL PARK	80.0	76.9	4.6	4.9	10.2	12.2	8.1	9.7	6.2	6.5	6.9	6.4	5.5	26.6	26.7	13.0	2.3	76.4	40.2	48.2	51.8
11003	ELMONT	46.7	42.9	34.5	36.5	8.6	9.5	13.2	14.9	6.4	6.5	7.7	7.5	6.8	28.7	24.3	10.4	1.8	75.0	36.6	47.4	52.6
11004	GLEN OAKS	60.4	54.2	4.6	4.9	29.8	35.0	7.7	8.8	5.5	5.9	6.2	5.4	5.2	27.6	26.8	14.8	2.6	79.0	41.3	46.7	53.3
11005	FLORAL PARK	89.5	88.8	2.6	2.7	6.2	6.6	1.6	1.7	0.9	1.3	1.4	1.1	1.1	7.2	20.1	55.0	11.9	95.7	72.5	37.8	62.2
11010	FRANKLIN SQUARE	93.0	91.3	0.6	0.7	3.4	4.3	6.4	8.1	6.0	6.3	6.5	5.7	4.8	28.5	24.5	15.0	2.8	77.7	40.3	47.7	52.3
11020	GREAT NECK	70.8	66.1	12.2	13.8	12.9	15.4	6.1	7.0	4.8	5.8	7.7	6.7	4.8	19.4	27.6	18.4	4.8	77.5	45.5	46.3	53.7
11021	GREAT NECK	87.8	85.0	2.1	2.4	6.6	8.2	6.4	8.0	5.4	5.7	5.7	5.0	4.3	25.5	26.8	17.4	4.2	80.0	43.9	46.1	53.9
11023	GREAT NECK	89.2	86.7	1.5	1.8	5.1	6.3	5.3	6.5	6.6	7.2	7.6	6.7	5.1	21.6	27.6	15.2	2.5	74.5	41.7	48.7	51.4
11024	GREAT NECK	87.0	84.2	2.5	3.0	4.1	5.1	6.9	8.4	5.9	6.5	7.7	8.9	9.1	21.2	25.6	13.2	1.9	75.4	37.6	52.4	47.7
11030	MANHASSET	87.6	84.7	2.5	3.0	8.2	10.3	3.5	4.4	6.7	7.8	7.6	6.1	3.7	21.5	27.7	16.2	2.8	73.8	42.9	48.2	51.8
11040	NEW HYDE PARK	77.0	72.7	1.2	1.3	18.4	21.9	6.2	7.5	5.6	6.0	6.5	5.9	5.0	24.9	27.0	16.3	2.9	78.3	42.6	47.6	52.4
11042	NEW HYDE PARK	77.4	72.6	5.9	6.9	16.0	19.8	1.8	2.2	2.0	2.9	5.1	4.7	2.9	12.7	20.4	32.7	16.6	86.3	64.2	40.9	59.1
11050	PORT WASHINGTON	84.1	81.0	2.2	2.5	8.4	10.2	11.7	13.9	6.7	7.4	7.5	5.6	4.4	26.4	27.7	12.5	1.9	74.8	40.5	48.3	51.7
11096	INWOOD	53.2	48.5	26.5	28.9	2.1	2.4	25.6	28.8	7.3	7.0	8.3	7.9	6.8	28.7	21.1	11.2	1.7	72.7	35.2	46.6	53.4
11101	LONG ISLAND CITY	39.0	37.1	23.8	21.9	12.1	13.7	35.9	39.1	7.0	6.2	6.7	6.3	8.3	37.0	20.4	7.2	0.9	76.4	32.9	51.3	48.7
11102	ASTORIA	50.4	47.3	10.2	9.6	14.6	16.7	31.9	34.4	6.6	6.2	6.5	5.5	7.4	39.1	19.2	8.1	1.3	77.4	33.1	50.1	49.9
11103	ASTORIA	63.2	58.5	1.4	1.4	14.1	16.3	25.5	29.0	5.7	5.1	5.1	4.6	6.9	42.0	20.3	9.2	1.3	81.6	34.8	51.0	49.1
11104	SUNNYSIDE	57.6	53.1	2.0	2.0	24.0	27.1	29.9	32.8	5.4	5.0	5.0	4.8	6.4	37.8	23.6	10.3	1.7	81.8	37.1	50.2	49.8
11105	ASTORIA	69.5	65.3	2.0	2.0	10.8	12.7	20.6	23.6	5.3	4.8	4.9	5.0	7.1	37.9	21.6	11.9	1.6	82.2	36.0	49.8	50.2
11106	ASTORIA	52.4	48.1	8.2	8.2	17.0	19.2	29.9	33.2	6.0	5.5	5.4	5.3	7.2	37.6	20.7	10.4	2.0	80.1	35.2	49.8	50.2
11201	BROOKLYN	62.6	59.4	20.7	21.3	6.8	7.9	14.4	16.7	4.6	3.8	3.9	5.0	8.0	39.9	23.2	9.8	1.9	85.0	36.6	50.8	49.2
11203	BROOKLYN	4.2	3.6	90.3	90.7	1.0	1.0	4.9	5.1	6.8	6.6	7.3	7.2	8.0	28.7	24.3	10.1	1.0	75.0	34.7	44.3	55.7
11204	BROOKLYN	74.4	69.4	0.3	0.4	19.2	22.9	7.8	9.6	7.2	6.6	7.6	7.6	7.7	27.3	21.8	12.5	1.8	74.1	34.5	49.1	50.9
11205	BROOKLYN	21.6	19.8	55.9	56.0	2.9	3.2	28.8	30.9	7.4	6.8	7.5	8.2	10.4	32.1	18.7	8.1	1.0	74.3	30.5	46.1	53.9
11206	BROOKLYN	25.4	25.9	34.7	32.1	4.5	4.7	53.3	55.3	9.2	8.3	9.4	8.5	9.4	28.2	18.5	7.8	0.8	67.9	28.3	46.9	53.1
11207	BROOKLYN	9.2	8.9	65.0	64.8	1.1	1.1	34.7	35.4	9.1	8.8	9.8	8.8	8.5	28.3	19.2	7.0	0.6	67.0	28.5	44.9	55.2
11208	BROOKLYN	15.1	14.6	43.7	43.2	5.6	5.8	44.7	46.3	8.9	8.7	9.6	8.9	8.7	29.1	19.4	6.2	0.6	67.4	28.6	47.0	53.0
11209	BROOKLYN	78.2	73.5	1.7	1.8	10.1	12.5	11.0	13.7	5.6	5.3	5.4	4.9	5.7	33.3	24.3	13.2	2.4	80.9	39.0	48.2	51.9
11210	BROOKLYN	36.1	33.7	54.2	55.7	3.7	4.2	7.4	8.2	7.9	7.6	8.4	7.7	7.5	27.6	23.1	9.0	1.2	71.4	32.9	46.2	53.8
11211	BROOKLYN	63.2	59.4	4.8	5.3	2.2	2.5	36.1	40.3	10.5	8.5	9.0	8.7	9.5	29.5	16.1	7.2	1.0	66.8	27.1	49.5	50.5
11212	BROOKLYN	3.7	3.6	85.7	85.4	0.7	0.7	13.9	14.3	9.0	8.9	10.0	9.1	8.2	27.3	19.6	7.3	0.7	66.4	28.6	43.3	56.7
11213	BROOKLYN	12.6	10.6	79.7	81.3	0.7	0.7	8.3	9.0	8.1	7.9	9.0	8.6	8.5	28.2	20.1	8.5	1.1	69.9	30.4	44.4	55.6
11214	BROOKLYN	71.7	66.0	0.7	0.8	21.1	25.5	8.5	10.4	5.5	5.1	5.8	6.0	6.9	29.2	23.8	15.1	2.6	80.1	39.1	48.2	51.9
11215	BROOKLYN	68.3	63.8	8.0	9.0	5.7	6.7	26.3	30.2	5.9	5.1	5.4	5.4	7.5	40.2	22.5	7.1	1.1	80.5	34.5	48.0	52.0
11216	BROOKLYN	2.1	2.0	89.3	89.3	1.2	1.2	7.9	8.2	7.9	7.6	8.3	7.4	7.4	30.7	21.2	8.3	1.2	71.7	32.7	45.6	54.4
11217	BROOKLYN	47.6	43.2	31.2	33.2	4.0	4.6	25.5	28.4	5.5	4.6	5.0	5.6	7.8	41.0	22.4	7.1	1.1	81.6	34.7	48.0	52.0
11218	BROOKLYN	55.9	50.4	12.6	14.0	14.4	16.3	19.3	22.4	7.9	7.1	7.6	7.2	8.0	29.9	21.2	9.4	1.7	73.0	32.9	49.4	50.6
11219	BROOKLYN	71.5	67.6	1.0	1.1	16.3	18.5	12.0	13.9	10.8	8.2	8.7	8.2	8.5	24.8	17.6	11.2	2.2	67.4	28.8	49.8	50.2
11220	BROOKLYN	36.1	33.2	3.1	3.2	29.1	30.5	46.1	48.4	8.0	7.1	7.6	7.1	8.6	32.7	20.1	7.9	1.0	73.1	31.7	49.9	50.1
11221	BROOKLYN	9.8	9.7	61.5	60.9	1.1	1.0	37.7	38.6	9.3	8.8	9.5	8.4	8.4	28.6	18.9	7.3	0.9	67.4	29.0	45.9	54.1
11222	BROOKLYN	80.4	76.6	1.5	1.7	3.9	4.6	19.5	23.8	5.0	4.7	5.1	5.0	7.3	35.1	26.1	10.4	1.2	82.5	37.2	50.5	49.5
11223	BROOKLYN	74.8	70.7	4.1	4.0	14.6	17.7	9.6	11.3	6.5	5.9	6.8	6.8	7.3	27.4	23.1	13.9	2.2	76.7	37.1	48.2	51.8
11224	BROOKLYN	55.3	53.1	29.2	29.8	3.8	4.2	18.0	19.9	5.9	6.2	7.3	7.2	6.8	22.3	23.2	17.5	3.6	76.1	40.1	45.2	54.8
11225	BROOKLYN	7.2	6.3	85.3	86.0	0.8	0.9	9.2	9.5	7.4	7.3	7.7	7.4	7.9	29.3	23.1	9.1	0.9	73.1	33.3	43.8	56.2
11226	BROOKLYN	6.4	5.9	80.0	79.9	2.7	2.8	13.9	14.6	8.2	7.8	8.2	7.5	8.3	30.1	22.4	6.9	0.7	71.3	31.6	44.6	55.4
11228	BROOKLYN	81.3	76.9	0.3	0.3	13.2	16.3	6.6	8.3	5.9	5.6	5.8	5.5	6.2	30.1	23.7	14.6	2.7	79.5	39.2	47.9	52.1
11229	BROOKLYN	75.3	70.9	4.7	5.0	14.8	17.8	6.7	8.2	5.6	5.4	6.5	6.6	6.8	26.3	25.4	14.7	2.7	78.4	39.9	47.6	52.4
11230	BROOKLYN	73.7	69.1	6.9	7.9	11.9	14.1	7.9	9.8	8.0	6.9	7.9	7.4	7.7	25.4	21.5	12.6	2.6	72.7	34.3	48.9	51.1
11231	BROOKLYN	62.5	60.1	17.8	17.5	3.0	3.7	25.3	28.2	6.1	5.4	6.2	5.8	6.7	39.3	20.5	8.7	1.4	78.8	34.7	46.5	53.5
11232	BROOKLYN	43.6	41.1	6.0	6.5	10.9	11.0	64.3	67.7	7.7	6.8	7.5	7.0	9.6	37.0	17.7	5.9	0.7	73.9	30.4	53.8	46.2
11233	BROOKLYN	3.4	3.3	87.8	87.6	0.5	0.6	12.0	12.5	8.9	8.8	9.6	8.2	7.9	28.2	19.3	8.2	1.0	67.8	30.0	43.6	56.4
11234	BROOKLYN	59.1	55.1	33.6	36.2	3.1	3.7	7.0	8.3	6.3	6.2	7.0	6.8	6.9	27.6	26.0	11.8	1.6	76.5	37.8	46.4	53.6
11235	BROOKLYN	76.6	71.7	2.4	2.8	12.8	15.7	9.6	11.8	4.7	4.4	5.0	5.7	6.6	25.8	26.0	18.1	3.7	82.6	43.5	47.8	52.2
11236	BROOKLYN	17.1	14.4	71.6	73.4	4.0	4.4	8.8	9.5	7.3	7.3	8.2	7.9	7.6	29.0	23.1	8.3	1.2	72.3	33.6	44.6	55.4
11237	BROOKLYN	26.8	26.5	10.5	10.0	5.6	5.7	79.3	81.2	10.1	9.1	9.6	8.3	9.7	32.1	15.9	4.8	0.4	66.3	26.7	49.8	50.2
11238	BROOKLYN	18.2	15.6	68.5	70.1	3.5	3.9	11.6	12.6	6.1	5.6	6.0	6.1	8.4	37.6	21.1	8.0	1.2	78.8	33.7	46.2	53.8
11239	BROOKLYN	37.9	32.7	44.9	48.1	4.0	4.5	18.4	20.7	5.0	5.1	7.0	7.6	8.2	23.8	23.4	17.5	2.6	78.3	39.7	42.8	57.2
11354	FLUSHING	42.6	38.5	3.7	3.5	42.8	46.6	18.4	19.3	5.5	5.2	5.4	5.0	6.2	30.6	24.8	13.8	3.6	81.0	40.2	47.4	52.6
11355	FLUSHING	27.1	24.0	5.6	5.3	53.6	56.6	20.3	21.3	5.8	5.5	5.9	5.7	6.9	32.9	24.9	10.9	1.6	79.5	37.6	48.9	51.1
11356	COLLEGE POINT	69.4	64.8	1.2	1.2	15.5	18.2	24.3	28.0	6.7	6.3	6.9	6.5	6.5	31.3	23.5	10.9	1.4	76.2	36.6	48.1	51.9
11357	WHITESTONE	82.6	78.7	0.4	0.5	12.7	15.7	8.0	9.8	5.2	5.1	5.2	5.1	5.4	27.5	26.2	17.3	3.1	81.5	42.7	47.7	52.3
11358	FLUSHING	64.8	59.5	1.0	1.0	25.8	30.0	14.3	16.3	5.6	5.5	5.7	5.4	6.1	31.7	25.8	12.2	1.9	79.9	38.9	48.2	51.8
11360	BAYSIDE	79.0	73.7	1.3	1.4	16.9	21.6	5.7	6.9	4.2	4.3	4.5	3.8	3.5	24.5	29.4	22.6	3.3	84.6	48.5	46.0	54.0
11361	BAYSIDE	66.9	61.8	4.0	4.0	21.9	26.0	12.0	13.8	5.3	5.2	5.7	5.5	6.1	31.9	25.2	12.3	2.9	80.5	39.3	48.1	51.9
11362	LITTLE NECK	71.6	66.5	1.0	1.1	23.5	27.9	6.8	8.1	4.4	4.7	5.3	5.3	5.1	24.8	29.2	18.2	3.0	82.2	45.2	46.8	53.2
11363	LITTLE NECK	74.3	68.9	0.5	0.5	20.7	25.3	7.6	9.1	4.4	5.0	5.8	5.7	4.9	27.1	30.1	14.9	2.2	81.2	43.3	48.0	52.0
11364	OAKLAND GARDENS	58.6	53.0	2.5	2.5	33.8	38.8	8.0	9.0	4.8	5.0	5.8	5.8	5.9	26.9	28.1	15.1	2.6	80.8	42.4	47.5	52.5
11365	FRESH MEADOWS	53.9	48.0	7.5	7.7	30.5	35.6	12.4	13.7	6.1	6.0	6.4	5.7	6.0	29.6	25.3	12.6	2.3	78.0	39.1	47.6	52.4
11366	FRESH MEADOWS	48.9	43.6	12.3	12.4	30.7	35.3	10.8	11.8	5.6	5.5	6.0	5.9	6.4	27.6	26.3	13.9	2.8	79.3	40.3	47.8	52.2
11367	FLUSHING	59.6	54.8	11.7	12.5	15.9	18.4	15.5	17.7	7.0	6.6	6.6	6.3	6.9	29.3	22.9	12.5	2.0	76.0	36.1	47.0	53.0
11368	CORONA	35.8	35.0	17.6	17.1	10.1	10.7	64.5	66.0	8.2	7.2	7.3	7.1	9.6	35.4	18.3	6.1	0.9	73.3	30.4	51.3	48.7
11369	EAST ELMHURST	29.6	29.0	31.9	30.7	7.7	8.3	50.2	52.7	7.2	6.8	7.6	7.3	8.0	30.6	21.3	9.7	1.4	74.1	33.5	47.5	52.6
11370	EAST ELMHURST	53.8	50.5	1.4	1.4	20.5	22.1	37.8	40.6	6.7	6.3	6.5	5.8	7.1	33.3	22.5	10.7	1.3	77.1	35.7	49.7	50.3
11372	JACKSON HEIGHTS	50.0	47.7	2.8	2.8	17.7	19.0	55.6	58.4	6.2	5.7	5.9	5.5	7.3	34.4	23.3	10.2	1.5	79.0	35.8	50.4	49.7
11373	ELMHURST	32.3	30.4	2.1	2.0	38.6	40.3	46.1	47.0	6.5	6.0	6.1	5.6	7.6	37.1	22.0	8.3	0.9	78.3	34.2	51.6	48.4
11374	REGO PARK	64.8	59.5	2.6	2.8	24.0	28.0	13.6	15.6	4.8	4.5	4.8	5.2	6.3	31.1	26.1	14.7	2.7	83.0	40.8	47.0	53.0
11375	FOREST HILLS	71.4	66.8	2.6	2.8	19.7	23.2	10.8	12.6	4.6	4.3	4.3	4.4	5.2	31.2	26.4	16.2	3.4	84.2	42.5	46.4	53.6
11377	WOODSIDE	44.1	40.7	3.3	3.2	29.3	31.7	37.2	39.4	6.0	5.5	5.8	5.3	7.0	37.1	22.1	9.9	1.4	79.7	35.5	50.0	50.0
11378	MASPETH	81.5	78.0	0.8	0.8	6.6	8.0	18.7	22.3	6.1	5.7	5.8	5.7	6.5	31.5	23.8	12.4	2.5	79.0	37.9	47.8	52.2
11379	MIDDLE VILLAGE	87.0	84.3	0.7	0.8	6.7	8.3	9.8	12.0	5.0	4.9	5.4	5.2	5.8	29.6	25.4	15.8	2.9	81.6	41.4	47.1	52.9
11385	RIDGEWOOD	65.4	61.8	2.1	2.1	6.3	7.2	38.0	42.3	7.3	6.8	7.4	6.9	8.0	32.1	20.9	9.3	1.4	74.4	33.4	48.8	51.2
11411	CAMBRIA HEIGHTS	2.8	2.5	91.6	91.5	0.5	0.6	4.1	4.4	5.7	6.0	7.1	6.8	6.1	28.2	26.4	12.7	1.1	77.0	38.6	44.6	55.4
11412	SAINT ALBANS	1.3	1.2	93.7	93.5	0.6	0.6	3.6	3.8	6.5	6.9	8.0	7.5	6.7	27.9	23.0	12.1	1.4	74.0	36.1	44.3	55.7
	NEW YORK	68.0	65.9	15.9	16.2	5.6	6.4	15.1	16.7	6.5	6.5	7.1	7.0	7.1	28.9	24.0	11.2	1.8	75.8	36.7	48.3	51.7
	UNITED STATES	75.1	73.6	12.3	12.5	3.8	4.2	12.5	14.1	6.9	6.7	7.2	7.0	7.3	28.6	23.8	10.8	1.7	75.1	36.0	49.1	50.9

INCOME

ZIP CODE #	POST OFFICE NAME	2004 Per Capita Income	2004 HH Income Base	2004 Household Income Distribution (%): Less than $25,000	$25,000 to $49,999	$50,000 to $99,999	$100,000 to $149,999	$150,000 or More	Median Household Income: 2004	2009	2004 National Centile	2004 State Centile	2004 Home Value Base	2004 Home Value Distribution (%): Less than $50,000	$50,000 to $89,999	$90,000 to $174,999	$175,000 to $399,999	$400,000 or More	2004 Median Home Value
10983	TAPPAN	38452	2122	7.3	14.1	33.9	26.7	18.1	90074	109363	97	94	1939	1.1	0.2	1.0	53.2	44.5	383071
10984	THIELLS	34770	921	6.5	8.4	35.7	29.1	20.3	98695	116303	98	96	806	0.0	0.0	5.8	72.1	22.1	340945
10985	THOMPSON RIDGE	17892	24	20.8	20.8	41.7	12.5	4.2	56180	66506	81	71	20	0.0	0.0	15.0	75.0	10.0	233333
10986	TOMKINS COVE	36239	593	11.0	12.1	35.6	25.8	15.5	87219	106569	97	93	521	0.2	0.0	7.1	44.5	48.2	392636
10987	TUXEDO PARK	46752	1284	10.1	17.6	32.9	19.9	19.6	79883	91525	95	90	974	0.2	0.4	5.3	39.9	54.1	429197
10989	VALLEY COTTAGE	40244	3457	6.3	16.0	35.6	24.0	18.1	86361	103835	97	93	2746	0.0	0.2	12.3	64.3	23.2	324615
10990	WARWICK	30748	7115	14.1	19.5	34.9	19.8	11.6	73667	83250	93	87	5771	0.2	0.1	13.4	67.4	19.0	261262
10992	WASHINGTONVILLE	29300	3639	10.7	18.9	37.5	23.0	10.0	75127	84708	93	87	3044	3.9	1.5	13.7	72.9	7.9	256821
10993	WEST HAVERSTRAW	20664	2128	26.1	24.5	31.9	14.8	2.7	49191	59505	70	60	1050	0.0	0.0	21.8	75.5	2.7	210367
10994	WEST NYACK	46628	2256	7.1	9.7	25.7	25.5	32.0	111940	132948	99	98	2011	0.2	0.3	1.2	47.3	51.1	405059
10996	WEST POINT	17235	1054	5.6	19.5	54.6	17.5	2.9	65070	75978	89	80	15	0.0	0.0	0.0	0.0	100.0	1000001
10998	WESTTOWN	24178	1224	13.2	25.3	41.1	14.8	5.7	61480	70858	86	76	1012	1.5	0.4	23.9	66.7	7.5	223541
11001	FLORAL PARK	33829	9953	12.8	15.8	34.6	21.5	15.3	78921	94357	95	90	7811	0.4	0.2	2.3	54.0	43.1	380165
11003	ELMONT	25890	12488	15.3	17.9	35.7	20.5	10.6	72195	85523	92	85	9513	0.3	0.1	1.7	85.1	12.9	311665
11004	GLEN OAKS	30857	4225	17.1	21.2	35.1	17.7	8.9	63031	75163	87	78	2807	0.4	4.6	27.8	42.3	24.9	318576
11005	FLORAL PARK	63514	2165	19.5	20.0	30.4	12.8	17.4	66261	83570	89	82	1804	0.0	0.4	4.4	37.6	57.5	456667
11010	FRANKLIN SQUARE	28656	8112	14.4	17.5	37.2	20.3	10.6	71734	85937	92	85	6740	0.3	0.1	0.7	69.0	30.0	358798
11020	GREAT NECK	61767	1797	8.4	14.1	20.7	20.0	36.9	114585	138273	99	98	1588	0.0	0.3	0.6	9.8	89.4	774425
11021	GREAT NECK	62651	8010	12.0	16.1	28.1	16.8	27.0	84984	105959	96	92	5417	0.6	0.8	10.5	25.6	62.6	558247
11023	GREAT NECK	58529	3183	10.8	11.7	23.2	19.3	35.0	107956	132056	99	97	2585	0.5	1.2	2.2	6.3	89.7	771847
11024	GREAT NECK	71809	2284	12.2	10.7	17.8	15.9	43.4	125418	152377	100	98	1929	0.1	0.0	2.2	9.7	88.0	1000001
11030	MANHASSET	86047	5888	6.2	8.2	18.5	18.0	49.2	147040	174692	100	99	5349	0.0	0.2	0.1	3.7	96.1	995738
11040	NEW HYDE PARK	36572	13584	12.3	15.7	32.3	21.4	18.4	81293	100036	95	91	12127	0.5	0.3	2.1	39.0	58.1	428690
11042	NEW HYDE PARK	5323	0	0.0	0.0	0.0	0.0	0.0	0	0	0	0	0	0.0	0.0	0.0	0.0	0.0	0
11050	PORT WASHINGTON	58348	10624	11.0	13.7	24.6	17.7	33.0	101349	124859	98	96	7236	0.4	0.4	0.7	12.7	85.8	654090
11096	INWOOD	18440	2645	28.9	23.6	32.4	11.7	3.4	47841	57905	68	58	1246	0.0	0.2	6.5	81.1	12.3	290448
11101	LONG ISLAND CITY	19681	10339	38.7	26.4	22.8	7.5	4.7	34251	40687	25	10	1777	0.8	1.1	12.5	59.4	26.2	298450
11102	ASTORIA	20056	13122	32.9	28.0	27.7	7.4	4.1	39426	45786	44	31	2538	1.2	1.0	3.0	44.3	50.6	402577
11103	ASTORIA	21300	17844	28.8	28.7	31.7	8.0	2.8	43173	49961	56	45	3786	0.7	0.7	2.7	38.9	56.9	431566
11104	SUNNYSIDE	22543	11017	29.5	29.7	29.9	7.2	3.7	42207	48277	54	42	1738	4.0	9.7	18.2	42.7	25.4	317375
11105	ASTORIA	23295	16355	29.3	27.2	29.0	9.7	4.7	43512	50828	57	46	4985	0.5	0.9	2.1	46.6	49.8	399362
11106	ASTORIA	20969	16985	34.3	27.8	26.3	8.9	2.7	38470	44432	41	27	3383	0.9	4.0	27.4	34.6	33.2	326421
11201	BROOKLYN	57003	22069	19.8	18.0	27.3	14.8	20.1	67770	87352	90	83	7771	5.0	2.3	13.1	31.9	47.6	375566
11203	BROOKLYN	18392	27856	29.7	27.7	29.6	9.3	3.6	42277	49794	54	42	10848	1.0	0.5	4.5	82.3	11.6	282236
11204	BROOKLYN	17930	25054	37.7	25.0	24.8	8.8	3.6	36705	43001	34	19	8143	2.9	1.1	1.6	41.1	53.3	417421
11205	BROOKLYN	19399	14428	42.0	25.1	21.6	6.8	4.6	32998	39982	21	8	3115	10.7	4.0	18.0	32.1	35.3	273452
11206	BROOKLYN	11607	23493	54.1	25.1	16.0	3.0	1.8	21860	25376	3	2	2520	17.9	2.9	6.4	56.4	16.5	260516
11207	BROOKLYN	12780	29523	47.8	26.1	19.5	4.7	2.0	26702	31085	7	4	7521	1.6	0.7	15.1	76.2	6.5	250728
11208	BROOKLYN	13056	26638	41.7	28.7	21.9	5.7	2.1	31296	36212	16	6	7509	1.8	0.3	9.5	81.3	7.1	262326
11209	BROOKLYN	31754	31516	25.6	24.1	30.3	12.1	8.0	50328	59157	73	63	9840	0.9	2.4	11.5	32.6	52.6	415546
11210	BROOKLYN	22158	22983	26.8	25.8	29.5	11.3	6.8	47268	55398	67	56	9217	0.6	2.2	5.2	53.2	38.9	356600
11211	BROOKLYN	13160	28921	47.4	26.1	19.8	5.0	1.8	27113	32073	7	4	4237	3.3	1.9	7.7	55.7	31.4	328745
11212	BROOKLYN	12466	28954	52.1	24.3	18.0	4.0	1.6	23397	27127	3	3	4625	4.0	0.5	9.1	73.9	12.5	254055
11213	BROOKLYN	14775	22450	43.6	28.7	20.8	4.7	2.1	29996	34402	12	5	4101	3.2	1.3	7.0	64.5	24.0	312715
11214	BROOKLYN	19746	32030	36.7	24.6	26.1	8.7	3.9	38019	44516	39	25	9262	3.6	2.0	5.9	39.4	49.2	396818
11215	BROOKLYN	39897	28157	18.8	20.3	31.5	15.6	13.9	64491	81390	88	80	9550	0.8	0.4	6.0	35.0	57.8	476327
11216	BROOKLYN	16855	21727	46.0	26.9	19.5	5.1	2.6	28007	32504	9	4	4403	1.7	1.3	9.8	68.9	18.3	285978
11217	BROOKLYN	37688	16003	22.7	19.9	32.1	13.7	11.6	59083	75060	84	74	4074	0.5	1.3	7.2	23.6	67.3	580264
11218	BROOKLYN	19083	24878	34.0	25.3	27.3	9.0	4.5	40914	47892	49	37	6783	1.6	3.4	11.9	46.8	36.3	348281
11219	BROOKLYN	14434	26454	44.0	25.6	20.0	7.1	3.2	30015	35035	12	5	6592	2.1	0.8	3.5	32.3	61.4	465104
11220	BROOKLYN	15033	27967	38.5	27.8	23.8	6.6	3.3	34312	40079	25	11	7096	7.1	1.8	4.4	53.5	33.3	349078
11221	BROOKLYN	12130	25311	51.7	25.1	17.5	4.0	1.6	23676	27361	4	3	5567	1.9	1.5	8.3	76.1	12.3	281691
11222	BROOKLYN	20186	16651	32.8	30.8	26.0	7.8	2.6	37918	43899	39	24	3775	1.6	0.7	3.6	58.2	36.0	352760
11223	BROOKLYN	19390	29034	38.1	24.7	24.2	8.4	4.7	36987	43477	35	20	9396	2.2	2.0	4.3	46.1	45.5	385082
11224	BROOKLYN	16245	19455	51.3	22.8	18.4	5.1	2.4	23871	28155	4	3	4240	35.7	2.6	6.6	43.4	11.8	195522
11225	BROOKLYN	17913	24106	37.5	30.7	23.0	5.7	3.1	33639	38769	23	9	4120	2.5	1.7	6.8	60.9	28.2	325083
11226	BROOKLYN	14951	37514	38.4	30.9	22.9	5.4	2.3	33089	38360	21	8	4517	1.0	1.6	7.8	64.4	25.3	300932
11228	BROOKLYN	26440	15544	26.3	23.5	30.1	13.1	7.1	50290	59335	72	63	7994	1.1	1.2	1.4	38.0	58.2	435428
11229	BROOKLYN	21953	30032	32.8	23.1	27.6	10.6	5.9	42454	50622	54	43	12473	2.8	4.6	6.9	55.2	30.6	337818
11230	BROOKLYN	19478	29627	36.8	23.6	25.3	8.9	5.4	37742	44374	38	23	8791	2.3	2.6	8.8	33.1	53.3	422480
11231	BROOKLYN	38863	15423	27.7	19.4	27.5	12.9	12.5	53806	68327	78	68	4016	0.5	0.4	5.3	25.9	68.0	572056
11232	BROOKLYN	13879	8608	40.3	29.5	22.9	5.7	1.7	32210	37422	18	7	2047	2.8	6.1	11.7	58.7	20.8	290724
11233	BROOKLYN	13689	23662	49.2	25.0	19.1	4.8	1.9	25628	29868	5	3	5325	2.2	1.6	11.6	71.5	13.1	279386
11234	BROOKLYN	26135	29859	21.1	20.7	34.2	16.3	7.7	60198	70043	85	75	18987	0.4	0.7	2.5	68.1	28.3	334008
11235	BROOKLYN	21575	32190	39.6	23.3	23.9	8.6	4.7	34716	40754	26	12	10596	4.3	5.6	15.3	43.6	31.2	315992
11236	BROOKLYN	19335	30939	26.2	25.6	32.3	11.9	4.0	47873	55685	68	58	13981	1.5	0.3	3.0	69.9	25.4	333207
11237	BROOKLYN	10941	14281	48.8	29.6	16.9	3.2	1.6	25719	29434	5	3	1512	2.6	0.5	4.4	80.7	11.8	275410
11238	BROOKLYN	28054	20823	26.9	26.1	29.3	11.4	6.3	46856	57256	66	55	5223	0.6	1.7	10.3	47.2	40.3	350442
11239	BROOKLYN	14694	5611	55.3	23.4	16.6	3.3	1.5	19750	23479	2	1	160	3.8	1.9	5.0	68.8	20.6	240000
11354	FLUSHING	20963	20276	30.1	28.0	27.9	9.4	4.6	42256	48629	54	42	8310	3.1	10.0	24.3	27.2	35.3	311022
11355	FLUSHING	18391	29666	31.3	28.3	28.6	8.3	3.6	40759	46692	49	37	8642	4.6	7.2	17.7	40.7	29.9	310304
11356	COLLEGE POINT	24992	7064	21.3	24.7	32.8	13.8	7.5	54590	63655	79	70	3617	0.9	0.5	1.8	65.8	31.0	349891
11357	WHITESTONE	30862	13986	17.7	22.0	35.0	15.9	9.4	62795	73736	87	78	9581	0.6	1.3	9.2	40.1	48.9	395419
11358	FLUSHING	26853	13761	19.6	23.0	33.4	15.0	9.0	59693	69212	84	74	7905	1.1	1.6	2.3	40.4	54.5	420824
11360	BAYSIDE	40062	8718	16.1	21.7	34.1	16.5	11.6	65529	75984	89	81	6051	0.7	1.0	20.1	35.9	42.3	324432
11361	BAYSIDE	29884	9662	16.3	20.7	36.1	17.4	9.5	64453	76754	88	80	5332	0.9	1.1	4.8	40.9	52.3	412639
11362	LITTLE NECK	34990	6947	17.8	18.1	34.9	17.1	12.2	67859	79497	90	83	5550	0.9	3.5	28.1	22.6	44.9	361202
11363	LITTLE NECK	40071	2481	10.9	16.3	36.0	16.7	20.2	78227	92103	94	89	1811	0.2	0.9	4.8	26.3	67.9	549620
11364	OAKLAND GARDENS	29526	14197	16.6	23.6	35.6	15.4	8.8	61183	71293	86	76	9325	1.4	5.9	24.0	30.8	37.8	340703
11365	FRESH MEADOWS	27644	13934	16.9	23.9	36.0	16.2	7.1	61046	71122	85	76	6946	5.5	1.7	2.7	48.7	41.5	373694
11366	FRESH MEADOWS	31104	5514	15.0	22.4	31.1	17.7	13.8	67842	79969	90	83	3386	1.9	1.4	1.9	43.4	51.5	406443
11367	FLUSHING	23242	15883	26.1	26.3	31.1	10.8	5.7	47265	54873	67	56	6760	2.9	7.8	18.0	44.4	26.8	316791
11368	CORONA	13924	26548	31.6	30.4	27.8	7.6	2.6	38813	44383	42	28	6013	3.5	4.0	7.0	49.6	35.9	352651
11369	EAST ELMHURST	17107	11803	27.9	27.7	33.3	8.2	2.9	44256	50736	59	48	5952	2.1	6.1	10.8	66.5	14.6	291736
11370	EAST ELMHURST	21144	10116	21.2	29.5	32.3	11.5	5.5	49327	57079	71	61	4184	1.4	0.3	7.1	51.2	40.1	370642
11372	JACKSON HEIGHTS	19248	24918	26.8	30.5	30.9	8.1	3.7	43408	49834	57	45	6980	4.5	19.3	34.3	26.2	15.7	140573
11373	ELMHURST	16329	32043	29.4	30.3	28.6	8.2	3.5	41632	47373	52	40	7952	4.0	5.5	12.1	44.0	34.4	335983
11374	REGO PARK	26021	19793	28.6	25.4	30.9	9.8	5.3	45629	52617	63	52	6529	3.7	10.9	29.2	33.6	22.7	213984
11375	FOREST HILLS	36965	34520	21.5	21.9	32.9	14.1	9.7	58871	69283	83	73	13467	1.5	4.4	27.6	36.9	29.6	261085
11377	WOODSIDE	19101	33090	28.3	31.0	29.3	8.3	3.0	42176	48222	53	42	9140	7.5	6.4	13.7	44.0	28.4	320484
11378	MASPETH	23702	12968	24.4	26.5	32.7	11.7	4.7	49003	57186	70	60	6412	0.9	0.8	2.9	70.4	25.1	332087
11379	MIDDLE VILLAGE	27830	14012	22.7	22.1	33.7	14.7	6.8	56125	65237	81	71	7873	0.6	0.3	1.7	58.8	38.6	371914
11385	RIDGEWOOD	18555	35472	30.1	29.6	29.8	7.9	2.7	40961	46974	50	37	11649	1.2	0.4	3.1	76.7	18.7	325398
11411	CAMBRIA HEIGHTS	26571	6465	11.9	21.4	39.9	17.9	8.9	67887	78695	90	83	5285	0.6	0.1	2.3	92.9	4.2	271988
11412	SAINT ALBANS	21467	11537	22.2	24.1	34.4	13.2	6.2	54232	62836	79	69	8056	0.5	0.3	5.7	88.7	4.9	255669
	NEW YORK	28049		26.3	24.3	29.3	11.5	8.6	49309	58077				4.6	8.6	27.2	39.9	19.8	219050
	UNITED STATES	25866		24.7	27.1	30.8	10.9	6.5	48124	56710				10.9	15.0	33.7	30.1	10.4	145905

ZIP CODE	FINANCIAL SERVICES				THE HOME						ENTERTAINMENT						PERSONAL			
					Home Improvements		Furnishings													
# POST OFFICE NAME	Auto Loan	Home Loan	Invest-ments	Retire-ment Plans	Home Repair	Lawn & Garden	Comput-ers & Hard-ware	Major Appli-ances	TV, Radio, Sound Equip-ment	Furni-ture	Dine out/ Carry out	Sports Equip-ment	Fees & Tickets	Toys & Games	Travel	Cable TV	Apparel & Services	Auto Repairs	Health Insur-ance	Pets & Supplies
10983 TAPPAN	127	169	212	162	164	171	151	150	143	151	179	171	164	192	158	143	180	146	137	160
10984 THIELLS	141	173	189	173	171	174	156	157	146	156	184	180	166	192	161	144	183	152	145	172
10985 THOMPSON RIDGE	80	100	106	100	98	97	89	89	83	89	104	104	95	111	91	80	104	86	80	98
10986 TOMKINS COVE	139	173	185	173	169	167	155	154	144	154	180	181	164	192	158	139	180	149	138	170
10987 TUXEDO PARK	150	186	221	187	182	186	170	167	159	170	200	195	182	210	174	155	200	163	152	183
10989 VALLEY COTTAGE	130	170	218	164	164	172	155	151	147	155	185	173	168	200	161	148	187	149	139	163
10990 WARWICK	116	138	152	140	135	136	127	125	119	128	151	146	135	157	129	116	150	123	114	138
10992 WASHINGTONVILLE	122	138	144	140	135	136	128	128	121	129	152	150	132	155	129	117	150	126	116	142
10993 WEST HAVERSTRAW	79	73	87	70	73	85	79	79	85	77	105	90	76	107	79	89	101	81	86	91
10994 WEST NYACK	168	235	309	223	227	239	205	203	193	207	242	229	228	265	218	195	247	196	185	216
10996 WEST POINT	118	75	72	86	68	81	111	96	113	104	141	128	95	127	92	103	135	113	89	109
10998 WESTTOWN	93	115	124	114	113	113	104	103	97	104	123	121	111	131	107	95	122	100	94	114
11001 FLORAL PARK	116	152	194	145	147	154	139	137	132	139	166	157	149	178	145	132	168	135	125	146
11003 ELMONT	106	130	159	123	125	132	121	119	118	123	149	134	128	159	124	119	150	118	111	128
11004 GLEN OAKS	99	113	148	115	112	118	115	112	111	113	140	132	117	142	117	109	138	115	105	120
11005 FLORAL PARK	143	140	150	128	146	177	130	149	139	140	173	141	133	147	142	149	161	144	174	161
11010 FRANKLIN SQUARE	102	125	146	119	123	133	116	116	114	115	142	130	124	151	122	116	141	113	114	125
11020 GREAT NECK	224	292	382	282	284	307	259	257	246	264	311	288	289	326	274	250	313	249	243	280
11021 GREAT NECK	174	210	288	212	204	218	201	195	193	203	243	226	216	254	207	192	243	194	181	212
11023 GREAT NECK	190	269	365	257	260	276	231	229	216	235	272	258	262	296	248	219	278	220	209	246
11024 GREAT NECK	288	407	553	389	393	419	351	347	327	356	412	391	397	448	375	332	421	333	317	372
11030 MANHASSET	306	407	551	399	397	427	359	355	336	366	424	400	403	447	380	338	430	342	330	385
11040 NEW HYDE PARK	125	170	217	160	165	173	151	150	143	151	180	169	165	196	160	145	182	145	138	159
11042 NEW HYDE PARK	0	0	0	0	0	0	0	0	0	0	0	0	0	0	0	0	0	0	0	0
11050 PORT WASHINGTON	191	251	331	240	241	256	226	222	216	229	273	251	247	293	237	218	277	218	205	239
11096 INWOOD	74	77	96	74	74	82	79	77	82	80	103	87	81	105	80	83	102	79	77	85
11101 LONG ISLAND CITY	57	56	103	55	53	62	66	60	73	67	92	71	68	98	67	77	92	65	62	67
11102 ASTORIA	59	62	125	61	58	68	73	65	80	73	102	77	75	113	75	85	103	71	67	72
11103 ASTORIA	57	62	127	61	58	68	72	64	79	72	101	76	75	114	75	85	102	70	66	71
11104 SUNNYSIDE	57	62	129	62	58	68	73	64	80	72	102	77	76	115	76	85	103	71	66	72
11105 ASTORIA	63	67	134	67	64	74	78	70	85	78	109	83	81	121	81	90	110	76	71	78
11106 ASTORIA	56	59	119	58	56	66	69	62	76	69	97	73	71	107	71	81	98	68	64	69
11201 BROOKLYN	153	145	266	162	137	155	172	153	178	175	226	187	178	236	169	178	224	165	146	171
11203 BROOKLYN	65	67	111	66	64	75	74	69	80	75	102	79	77	108	77	85	102	73	72	78
11204 BROOKLYN	58	64	119	65	61	69	73	66	77	72	97	79	74	107	75	80	98	72	65	73
11205 BROOKLYN	61	57	101	58	54	63	68	62	73	69	93	73	69	96	68	76	92	67	63	69
11206 BROOKLYN	42	40	74	37	38	44	47	44	53	49	68	49	46	71	47	56	68	47	45	48
11207 BROOKLYN	49	45	72	42	43	51	52	50	58	54	74	56	52	74	52	62	73	53	53	56
11208 BROOKLYN	52	50	90	46	47	56	58	54	65	60	83	61	58	86	58	69	83	58	57	60
11209 BROOKLYN	80	86	158	87	82	94	98	88	104	97	132	105	101	144	100	108	132	95	88	98
11210 BROOKLYN	76	84	149	83	80	92	92	85	99	92	125	99	97	137	96	104	126	90	86	94
11211 BROOKLYN	47	47	86	46	44	51	54	50	59	56	76	58	55	80	55	62	76	54	50	55
11212 BROOKLYN	45	42	67	40	40	47	49	45	54	49	68	52	49	70	49	57	67	49	48	51
11213 BROOKLYN	49	49	89	48	47	55	57	52	63	57	80	61	59	86	58	67	80	56	55	59
11214 BROOKLYN	57	62	119	62	59	68	71	64	76	70	97	76	73	108	74	80	98	70	65	71
11215 BROOKLYN	110	109	211	120	103	117	129	114	135	130	172	139	134	184	129	137	171	123	110	128
11216 BROOKLYN	51	50	85	48	48	56	58	54	64	58	80	62	59	84	58	67	80	57	57	61
11217 BROOKLYN	102	99	189	110	94	106	118	105	123	120	157	127	122	165	117	124	156	113	100	117
11218 BROOKLYN	61	66	132	66	62	72	76	68	83	76	106	81	79	118	79	88	107	74	69	76
11219 BROOKLYN	50	55	111	55	52	60	64	57	69	63	88	69	66	98	66	73	89	62	57	63
11220 BROOKLYN	55	59	111	58	56	63	67	62	72	68	92	73	68	99	69	76	93	67	61	68
11221 BROOKLYN	46	42	66	38	39	47	48	46	54	50	68	51	48	68	47	57	67	49	48	51
11222 BROOKLYN	54	58	119	58	55	64	68	60	75	67	95	72	71	107	70	80	96	66	62	67
11223 BROOKLYN	59	64	119	64	61	69	73	66	77	72	99	78	75	108	75	81	99	71	66	73
11224 BROOKLYN	48	47	78	46	45	53	55	51	59	55	75	59	55	78	55	62	74	55	53	56
11225 BROOKLYN	52	56	117	56	53	62	66	58	73	65	92	69	69	105	69	78	94	64	60	65
11226 BROOKLYN	47	51	105	50	48	57	60	53	66	59	84	63	62	94	62	70	85	58	55	59
11228 BROOKLYN	82	91	132	91	89	98	95	91	96	95	122	105	98	128	97	98	121	94	89	99
11229 BROOKLYN	68	74	122	75	72	80	81	76	84	80	106	90	83	113	83	86	106	80	74	83
11230 BROOKLYN	62	68	127	67	64	74	76	69	82	76	104	81	79	116	79	87	105	74	70	76
11231 BROOKLYN	105	101	190	110	96	109	119	107	125	122	160	128	122	167	118	127	159	115	103	119
11232 BROOKLYN	49	49	97	45	46	54	57	53	65	60	84	60	57	89	58	70	85	58	55	58
11233 BROOKLYN	50	44	60	42	43	50	51	49	56	52	70	55	51	69	50	58	68	51	52	56
11234 BROOKLYN	92	105	132	101	101	110	102	100	102	104	129	112	107	134	104	104	129	101	97	109
11235 BROOKLYN	58	64	118	64	61	69	72	65	76	71	97	78	74	107	74	80	98	70	65	72
11236 BROOKLYN	72	75	111	72	71	81	80	76	85	82	108	86	82	113	81	88	108	80	76	84
11237 BROOKLYN	44	43	84	39	40	48	50	47	57	53	74	52	49	77	50	62	75	51	49	51
11238 BROOKLYN	76	76	143	81	72	83	90	80	95	90	121	97	93	130	90	98	121	87	79	90
11239 BROOKLYN	44	39	57	41	39	46	49	45	52	47	64	52	48	63	48	52	62	49	49	50
11354 FLUSHING	66	76	119	80	76	78	82	78	79	80	100	95	82	104	83	77	100	82	70	83
11355 FLUSHING	60	67	119	72	67	70	76	71	75	74	96	88	76	102	78	75	96	76	64	76
11356 COLLEGE POINT	87	99	134	95	95	102	98	95	100	101	127	108	102	135	100	101	128	97	90	103
11357 WHITESTONE	100	116	144	113	113	122	112	110	110	112	138	124	118	144	115	111	137	110	106	119
11358 FLUSHING	86	104	152	105	102	106	105	101	101	104	128	121	108	135	108	100	129	105	91	108
11360 BAYSIDE	110	120	155	121	119	130	123	120	122	122	154	138	127	155	126	123	151	123	118	131
11361 BAYSIDE	95	113	163	115	111	116	114	110	110	113	139	130	118	147	117	109	140	112	99	117
11362 LITTLE NECK	104	132	169	131	131	135	125	124	118	123	147	146	131	155	130	116	147	124	113	131
11363 LITTLE NECK	125	155	229	160	151	157	152	145	143	151	180	174	161	190	156	140	182	147	128	156
11364 OAKLAND GARDENS	92	106	145	115	109	108	111	109	102	108	128	135	109	126	112	95	127	114	94	115
11365 FRESH MEADOWS	89	103	153	111	105	105	110	106	103	107	130	132	109	132	112	98	130	112	92	112
11366 FRESH MEADOWS	102	126	185	131	126	126	128	123	119	125	150	151	129	158	131	115	152	128	107	130
11367 FLUSHING	72	78	124	79	76	84	85	79	87	84	110	93	87	117	87	89	110	84	78	87
11368 CORONA	57	57	114	53	53	63	66	61	75	69	97	70	67	103	68	81	98	67	64	67
11369 EAST ELMHURST	66	67	118	63	63	74	75	70	83	77	106	79	76	112	76	88	106	75	73	78
11370 EAST ELMHURST	73	79	136	77	75	85	87	80	93	87	118	93	90	128	89	97	119	86	81	89
11372 JACKSON HEIGHTS	59	63	131	62	60	70	74	67	82	75	105	78	77	117	77	88	107	73	69	74
11373 ELMHURST	60	67	121	71	66	71	76	71	77	75	98	87	76	105	78	77	98	76	65	76
11374 REGO PARK	65	71	137	73	68	77	82	74	86	81	110	90	84	121	84	89	111	80	72	81
11375 FOREST HILLS	92	98	174	103	94	104	110	100	113	110	143	120	113	154	111	114	144	107	96	110
11377 WOODSIDE	59	64	122	64	61	69	73	67	78	73	99	80	75	109	75	81	101	72	66	73
11378 MASPETH	78	85	111	82	82	89	86	83	87	87	111	94	88	115	87	89	110	85	81	91
11379 MIDDLE VILLAGE	84	94	128	92	91	101	95	92	97	95	122	105	100	128	98	99	121	94	91	100
11385 RIDGEWOOD	60	63	115	61	60	70	71	66	78	72	99	76	73	107	73	82	100	70	67	72
11411 CAMBRIA HEIGHTS	115	116	129	110	113	130	114	114	120	118	150	122	121	145	118	125	147	115	122	130
11412 SAINT ALBANS	95	94	104	89	92	106	94	94	99	97	124	100	99	119	96	103	121	94	101	107
NEW YORK	95	100	134	99	98	107	103	100	105	103	133	116	105	138	104	107	131	102	99	112
UNITED STATES	100	100	100	100	100	100	100	100	100	100	100	100	100	100	100	100	100	100	100	100

POPULATION CHANGE

ZIP CODE			POPULATION			2000-2004 ANNUAL RATE		HOUSEHOLDS					FAMILIES		
#	POST OFFICE NAME	COUNTY FIPS CODE	2000	2004	2009	% Rate	State Centile	2000	2004	2009	% Annual Rate 2000-2004	2004 Average HH Size	2000	2004	% Annual Rate 2000-2004
11413	SPRINGFIELD GARDENS	081	43165	43113	43294	0.0	26	13598	13599	13612	0.0	3.16	10767	10731	-0.1
11414	HOWARD BEACH	081	29514	28832	28639	-0.6	5	11813	11551	11434	-0.5	2.49	8204	7984	-0.6
11415	KEW GARDENS	081	18813	18919	19095	0.1	37	7841	7867	7901	0.1	2.29	4300	4278	-0.1
11416	OZONE PARK	081	24106	24062	24125	0.0	26	7408	7257	7179	-0.5	3.31	5839	5703	-0.6
11417	OZONE PARK	081	30027	30453	30750	0.3	49	9768	9759	9742	0.0	3.12	7467	7441	-0.1
11418	RICHMOND HILL	081	37448	37739	38037	0.2	40	11671	11614	11583	-0.1	3.22	8481	8425	-0.2
11419	SOUTH RICHMOND HILL	081	46244	46408	46492	0.1	33	12661	12598	12516	-0.1	3.68	10713	10635	-0.2
11420	SOUTH OZONE PARK	081	47672	47263	47115	-0.2	18	13887	13720	13599	-0.3	3.42	11328	11160	-0.4
11421	WOODHAVEN	081	34846	35766	36311	0.6	63	11348	11503	11562	0.3	3.10	8422	8503	0.2
11422	ROSEDALE	081	30985	30292	30109	-0.5	6	9568	9335	9232	-0.6	3.24	7593	7384	-0.7
11423	HOLLIS	081	31605	31414	31443	-0.1	21	9784	9692	9646	-0.2	3.17	7463	7378	-0.3
11426	BELLEROSE	081	18824	18689	18655	-0.2	19	6361	6268	6214	-0.4	2.80	4634	4557	-0.4
11427	QUEENS VILLAGE	081	22106	22038	22148	-0.1	24	7640	7606	7605	-0.1	2.88	5669	5614	-0.2
11428	QUEENS VILLAGE	081	18707	18452	18373	-0.3	13	5411	5306	5247	-0.5	3.47	4512	4413	-0.5
11429	QUEENS VILLAGE	081	28720	28242	28157	-0.4	10	8021	7886	7830	-0.4	3.56	6668	6538	-0.5
11430	JAMAICA	081	1971	2026	2060	0.7	64	224	239	248	1.5	3.82	183	195	1.5
11432	JAMAICA	081	56159	56595	57109	0.2	40	18212	18327	18424	0.2	2.95	12686	12701	0.0
11433	JAMAICA	081	28092	28703	29201	0.5	58	8771	8963	9084	0.5	3.16	6372	6489	0.4
11434	JAMAICA	081	58749	59197	59778	0.2	40	20423	20502	20612	0.1	2.82	13972	14019	0.1
11435	JAMAICA	081	55333	55632	56158	0.1	37	18170	18174	18241	0.0	3.01	12737	12666	0.1
11436	JAMAICA	081	19537	19218	19158	-0.4	10	5908	5815	5778	-0.4	3.30	4718	4627	-0.5
11501	MINEOLA	059	19434	19434	19615	0.0	28	7542	7528	7583	0.0	2.58	5009	4976	-0.2
11507	ALBERTSON	059	7441	7474	7556	0.1	35	2469	2482	2508	0.1	3.01	2062	2066	0.1
11509	ATLANTIC BEACH	059	4232	4304	4362	0.4	52	2001	2053	2083	0.6	2.06	1250	1263	0.2
11510	BALDWIN	059	32343	32701	33113	0.3	44	10867	10962	11086	0.2	2.98	8560	8603	0.1
11514	CARLE PLACE	059	4872	4779	4773	-0.5	8	1780	1746	1744	-0.5	2.73	1276	1245	-0.6
11516	CEDARHURST	059	6745	6717	6735	-0.1	22	2474	2456	2459	-0.2	2.73	1795	1773	-0.3
11518	EAST ROCKAWAY	059	11127	11040	11071	-0.2	19	4287	4264	4279	-0.1	2.57	3034	3004	-0.2
11520	FREEPORT	059	44232	44535	44914	0.2	38	13610	13593	13629	0.0	3.23	10005	9942	-0.2
11530	GARDEN CITY	059	26440	26610	26825	0.2	38	9102	9178	9261	0.2	2.82	7214	7251	0.1
11542	GLEN COVE	059	27441	27986	28454	0.5	55	9750	9966	10136	0.5	2.72	6882	6992	0.4
11545	GLEN HEAD	059	13016	13238	13421	0.4	52	4420	4490	4537	0.4	2.94	3652	3701	0.3
11548	GREENVALE	059	2489	2468	2467	-0.2	18	449	441	439	-0.4	2.78	333	326	-0.5
11550	HEMPSTEAD	059	58969	61337	62888	0.9	75	15976	16417	16697	0.6	3.45	11792	12067	0.5
11552	WEST HEMPSTEAD	059	23050	23073	23185	0.0	30	7321	7313	7338	0.0	3.14	5942	5918	-0.1
11553	UNIONDALE	059	23531	24753	25529	1.2	83	6180	6454	6631	1.0	3.69	4958	5161	1.0
11554	EAST MEADOW	059	37705	38930	39821	0.8	69	12258	12732	13061	0.9	2.93	9706	10022	0.8
11557	HEWLETT	059	8098	8110	8162	0.0	30	2892	2892	2909	0.0	2.80	2341	2334	-0.1
11558	ISLAND PARK	059	8553	8765	8932	0.6	61	3011	3089	3150	0.6	2.74	2262	2316	0.6
11559	LAWRENCE	059	8079	8160	8257	0.2	43	2659	2661	2673	0.0	3.06	2048	2042	-0.1
11560	LOCUST VALLEY	059	6616	6579	6590	-0.1	21	2338	2322	2324	-0.2	2.81	1771	1752	-0.3
11561	LONG BEACH	059	41091	41595	42196	0.3	46	17255	17498	17725	0.3	2.27	9677	9699	0.1
11563	LYNBROOK	059	23329	23063	23077	-0.3	15	8567	8462	8454	-0.3	2.68	6116	6011	-0.4
11565	MALVERNE	059	9065	8946	8947	-0.3	13	3153	3111	3110	-0.3	2.87	2577	2533	-0.4
11566	MERRICK	059	35475	35619	36006	0.1	35	11777	11822	11943	0.1	3.01	10029	10053	0.1
11568	OLD WESTBURY	059	4060	4241	4350	1.0	78	1010	1060	1089	1.1	3.35	911	955	1.1
11570	ROCKVILLE CENTRE	059	28178	28516	28894	0.3	45	10202	10344	10481	0.3	2.72	7326	7368	0.1
11572	OCEANSIDE	059	31315	31508	31804	0.1	37	10769	10831	10913	0.1	2.90	8747	8769	0.1
11575	ROOSEVELT	059	15881	16252	16537	0.5	60	4101	4189	4258	0.5	3.86	3400	3463	0.4
11576	ROSLYN	059	13317	13059	13041	-0.5	8	4814	4720	4698	-0.5	2.71	3811	3720	-0.5
11577	ROSLYN HEIGHTS	059	10796	11241	11703	1.0	76	3718	3861	4012	0.9	2.90	3105	3207	0.8
11579	SEA CLIFF	059	5049	4981	4980	-0.3	13	2007	1977	1976	-0.4	2.50	1351	1324	-0.5
11580	VALLEY STREAM	059	38068	38644	39150	0.4	50	12699	12814	12942	0.2	3.00	9792	9853	0.2
11581	VALLEY STREAM	059	21249	21610	21885	0.4	52	7432	7531	7614	0.3	2.87	5957	6015	0.2
11590	WESTBURY	059	42861	43841	44631	0.5	59	12604	12759	12923	0.3	3.42	10042	10130	0.2
11596	WILLISTON PARK	059	10683	10505	10520	-0.4	10	3724	3665	3673	-0.4	2.86	2919	2863	-0.5
11598	WOODMERE	059	13390	13860	14235	0.8	71	4292	4453	4582	0.9	3.04	3543	3653	0.7
11691	FAR ROCKAWAY	081	55677	55981	56351	0.1	37	17632	17593	17578	-0.1	3.00	12076	12004	-0.1
11692	ARVERNE	081	14939	16342	17676	2.1	94	4586	4997	5386	2.0	3.02	3350	3682	2.3
11693	FAR ROCKAWAY	081	11194	10965	10903	-0.5	7	4197	4105	4059	-0.5	2.65	2773	2696	-0.7
11694	ROCKAWAY PARK	081	19241	18995	18926	-0.3	14	7830	7746	7694	-0.3	2.26	4492	4413	-0.4
11697	BREEZY POINT	081	4226	4226	4254	0.0	28	1796	1798	1804	0.0	2.35	1167	1161	-0.1
11701	AMITYVILLE	103	25337	26299	27587	0.9	74	8364	8689	9150	0.9	2.95	5772	5981	0.8
11702	BABYLON	103	15235	15498	16057	0.4	52	5505	5643	5888	0.6	2.70	3979	4061	0.5
11703	NORTH BABYLON	103	16516	16596	17159	0.1	36	5709	5772	5998	0.2	2.87	4379	4414	0.2
11704	WEST BABYLON	103	40069	41366	43438	0.8	69	13115	13589	14342	0.8	3.00	10064	10403	0.8
11705	BAYPORT	103	8648	8985	9454	0.9	74	3217	3376	3575	1.1	2.65	2300	2408	1.1
11706	BAY SHORE	103	61182	62883	65538	0.7	64	18828	19380	20271	0.7	3.20	14272	14641	0.6
11709	BAYVILLE	059	7090	7063	7093	-0.1	23	2547	2535	2531	-0.1	2.75	1897	1883	-0.2
11710	BELLMORE	059	34074	34206	34473	0.1	34	11408	11462	11543	0.1	2.97	9320	9336	0.0
11713	BELLPORT	103	9014	9669	10484	1.7	89	2666	2895	3173	2.0	3.25	2088	2259	1.9
11714	BETHPAGE	059	23168	23091	23179	-0.1	24	8016	7996	8027	-0.1	2.88	6284	6251	-0.1
11715	BLUE POINT	103	4407	4562	4765	0.8	71	1571	1635	1717	0.9	2.76	1178	1222	0.9
11716	BOHEMIA	103	10375	11275	12143	2.0	93	3490	3797	4103	2.0	2.88	2686	2929	2.1
11717	BRENTWOOD	103	50600	52877	55487	1.0	79	11830	12238	12809	0.8	4.25	10231	10567	0.8
11718	BRIGHTWATERS	103	3216	3261	3363	0.3	49	1119	1139	1181	0.4	2.85	895	909	0.4
11719	BROOKHAVEN	103	3042	3104	3202	0.5	56	1035	1075	1127	0.9	2.47	793	824	0.9
11720	CENTEREACH	103	27859	29167	30792	1.1	80	8403	8864	9421	1.3	3.23	7166	7540	1.2
11721	CENTERPORT	103	5923	6211	6568	1.1	81	2205	2324	2469	1.2	2.66	1687	1772	1.2
11722	CENTRAL ISLIP	103	31305	34222	36816	2.1	94	8446	9342	10153	2.4	3.59	6631	7228	2.1
11724	COLD SPRING HARBOR	103	2511	2505	2568	-0.1	25	819	818	842	0.0	3.06	709	707	-0.1
11725	COMMACK	103	29827	30202	31348	0.3	46	9579	9764	10201	0.5	3.04	8300	8445	0.4
11726	COPIAGUE	103	18849	19313	20125	0.6	61	6013	6138	6403	0.5	3.12	4323	4396	0.4
11727	CORAM	103	27465	28886	30503	1.2	82	10187	10795	11461	1.4	2.66	7377	7775	1.2
11729	DEER PARK	103	27872	28448	29698	0.5	56	9365	9648	10147	0.7	2.94	7298	7498	0.6
11730	EAST ISLIP	103	16407	16467	16967	0.1	34	5340	5385	5580	0.2	3.02	4366	4389	0.1
11731	EAST NORTHPORT	103	30011	29901	30808	-0.1	23	9926	9944	10305	0.1	2.96	8230	8225	0.0
11732	EAST NORWICH	059	3508	3553	3630	0.3	47	1203	1214	1237	0.2	2.90	938	935	-0.1
11733	EAST SETAUKET	103	18291	18811	19619	0.7	64	6147	6357	6664	0.9	2.94	4910	5063	0.7
11735	FARMINGDALE	103	32182	32775	33480	0.4	53	10815	11020	11251	0.4	2.92	8269	8390	0.3
11738	FARMINGVILLE	103	17386	18513	19657	1.5	88	5262	5635	6016	1.6	3.28	4491	4795	1.6
11740	GREENLAWN	103	10106	10220	10556	0.3	44	3582	3645	3787	0.4	2.73	2608	2643	0.3
11741	HOLBROOK	103	28072	29284	30863	1.0	77	9162	9645	10237	1.2	3.03	7486	7834	1.1
11742	HOLTSVILLE	103	11218	12466	13555	2.5	96	3760	4176	4550	2.5	2.98	2972	3309	2.6
11743	HUNTINGTON	103	42299	42910	44574	0.3	49	14997	15261	15922	0.4	2.79	11489	11668	0.4
	NEW YORK					0.4					0.5	2.60			0.4
	UNITED STATES					1.2					1.3	2.58			1.1

ZIP CODE #	POST OFFICE NAME	RACE (%) White 2000	White 2004	Black 2000	Black 2004	Asian/Pacific 2000	Asian/Pacific 2004	% Hispanic Origin 2000	% Hispanic Origin 2004	2004 AGE DISTRIBUTION (%) 0-4	5-9	10-14	15-19	20-24	25-44	45-64	65-84	85+	18+	MEDIAN AGE 2004	% 2004 Males	% 2004 Females
11413	SPRINGFIELD GARDENS	2.8	2.6	91.5	91.3	0.6	0.6	4.5	4.7	6.1	6.5	7.5	7.0	6.6	29.0	25.3	10.9	0.9	75.5	36.7	45.6	54.4
11414	HOWARD BEACH	91.2	89.4	1.1	1.2	3.3	4.1	10.5	12.9	4.9	5.0	5.3	4.9	4.9	27.0	26.3	19.2	2.6	81.8	43.6	46.9	53.1
11415	KEW GARDENS	66.2	61.9	7.7	8.3	12.4	14.5	20.6	23.5	6.3	5.4	5.4	5.6	7.5	34.3	22.9	10.6	2.1	79.7	36.4	48.9	51.1
11416	OZONE PARK	42.7	39.4	7.0	6.9	13.9	15.4	41.3	44.3	8.0	7.3	8.1	7.7	8.3	31.9	19.9	7.7	1.2	72.1	31.7	48.2	51.8
11417	OZONE PARK	50.1	46.1	4.5	4.5	14.8	16.7	28.1	31.2	7.5	7.0	7.3	6.5	7.7	32.3	21.8	8.7	1.2	74.3	33.9	48.7	51.3
11418	RICHMOND HILL	42.5	39.3	8.5	8.3	16.3	18.1	36.1	38.8	7.6	6.9	7.5	7.2	8.4	32.5	21.3	7.6	1.1	73.9	32.8	49.7	50.3
11419	SOUTH RICHMOND HILL	18.6	17.3	15.5	14.9	24.9	26.6	24.8	25.9	7.5	7.0	7.7	7.8	8.6	32.8	21.5	6.4	0.6	73.1	32.0	49.6	50.4
11420	SOUTH OZONE PARK	20.5	19.1	35.3	34.4	13.0	14.2	22.7	24.2	7.3	7.0	7.7	7.7	7.8	31.0	22.4	8.4	0.9	73.4	33.4	48.1	51.9
11421	WOODHAVEN	48.5	44.8	5.1	5.1	13.9	15.6	43.2	46.7	7.0	6.6	7.6	7.4	7.8	30.9	21.9	9.0	1.7	74.3	34.2	48.1	51.9
11422	ROSEDALE	12.4	11.0	76.2	76.6	2.4	2.7	8.6	9.3	6.8	6.7	8.0	7.6	7.2	30.0	24.4	8.3	1.0	73.6	35.1	45.3	54.8
11423	HOLLIS	19.7	18.1	40.3	39.7	18.4	20.2	16.7	17.7	6.7	6.5	6.9	6.7	7.2	29.2	24.2	10.6	2.0	75.7	36.4	46.4	53.6
11426	BELLEROSE	60.8	55.4	5.8	6.1	24.0	28.1	12.9	14.8	5.8	5.9	6.6	5.9	5.4	29.7	26.4	12.0	2.2	78.1	39.7	48.9	51.1
11427	QUEENS VILLAGE	39.3	36.4	22.2	21.7	20.4	23.1	17.1	18.5	6.0	6.0	6.7	6.4	6.5	27.3	26.1	12.5	2.4	77.4	38.9	46.4	53.6
11428	QUEENS VILLAGE	28.5	26.0	23.5	23.0	22.6	24.8	23.2	24.8	6.7	6.6	7.5	7.2	7.7	30.3	25.0	8.0	1.0	74.9	34.5	47.9	52.2
11429	QUEENS VILLAGE	7.4	7.0	77.9	77.3	3.6	4.0	10.8	11.6	6.9	7.1	8.3	7.6	7.0	28.9	23.5	9.7	1.0	73.1	34.5	45.3	54.7
11430	JAMAICA	13.4	12.4	63.6	63.7	4.2	4.4	24.4	25.5	14.7	11.7	9.9	8.8	9.0	27.1	13.0	5.4	0.4	58.2	22.7	44.8	55.2
11432	JAMAICA	28.6	26.2	21.6	21.3	25.4	27.6	24.5	25.9	6.8	6.2	6.4	6.9	7.6	31.7	23.3	9.4	1.8	77.1	35.2	48.3	51.7
11433	JAMAICA	3.8	3.8	82.6	82.1	2.6	2.8	10.2	10.7	7.6	7.5	8.7	8.7	7.9	27.4	21.2	9.8	1.3	70.9	32.4	45.2	54.8
11434	JAMAICA	2.4	2.2	92.0	91.8	0.6	0.7	4.8	5.1	6.7	6.9	8.0	7.2	6.4	27.5	23.8	12.1	1.6	74.0	36.9	44.4	55.6
11435	JAMAICA	27.6	25.7	32.6	32.1	14.6	16.1	29.2	30.8	7.3	6.8	7.1	6.6	7.6	33.0	21.9	8.7	1.1	74.9	33.7	48.6	51.4
11436	JAMAICA	1.7	1.6	89.6	89.2	1.2	1.3	6.6	7.0	7.4	7.5	8.6	8.4	7.7	27.8	21.6	10.0	1.1	71.4	33.4	45.6	54.4
11501	MINEOLA	86.5	83.5	1.0	1.2	4.5	5.5	12.9	16.0	6.0	5.9	5.5	5.2	5.6	31.9	24.5	13.3	2.0	79.4	39.3	48.2	51.8
11507	ALBERTSON	77.9	73.6	0.5	0.6	18.2	21.8	4.4	5.4	5.8	6.6	7.1	6.2	4.7	22.8	28.6	15.9	2.3	76.6	43.0	48.1	51.9
11509	ATLANTIC BEACH	91.1	89.0	6.0	7.2	0.8	1.0	3.8	4.8	6.3	7.0	6.5	5.8	4.3	19.9	28.5	19.0	2.7	76.5	45.2	48.3	51.7
11510	BALDWIN	72.1	68.3	17.7	19.6	3.6	4.3	10.2	12.1	6.6	6.9	7.5	6.8	5.7	27.5	26.7	10.9	1.6	74.8	38.9	47.7	52.3
11514	CARLE PLACE	90.1	87.7	1.9	2.3	5.3	6.6	7.5	9.4	5.7	5.9	6.5	6.1	5.7	29.0	26.6	12.3	2.2	78.1	40.0	47.8	52.2
11516	CEDARHURST	91.1	89.0	1.3	1.5	3.0	3.7	7.9	9.7	7.8	7.3	6.7	6.2	4.8	25.1	25.3	14.7	2.1	74.4	39.3	47.7	52.3
11518	EAST ROCKAWAY	95.8	94.7	0.5	0.6	1.6	2.0	5.6	7.2	6.3	6.6	6.9	5.8	5.1	27.9	26.8	12.6	2.0	76.5	40.3	47.9	52.1
11520	FREEPORT	42.5	39.4	33.1	34.2	1.4	1.6	33.3	36.0	6.9	6.9	7.7	7.2	6.9	30.3	23.6	9.2	1.5	74.2	35.3	48.2	51.9
11530	GARDEN CITY	93.9	92.4	1.5	1.7	3.3	4.2	3.3	4.1	6.7	7.7	7.8	7.2	4.9	22.1	26.9	14.6	2.3	74.0	41.2	47.6	52.5
11542	GLEN COVE	80.7	77.6	6.3	7.0	4.1	4.9	19.6	23.1	6.2	6.0	6.0	5.5	6.0	29.1	23.9	14.1	3.2	78.5	39.6	48.1	51.9
11545	GLEN HEAD	91.4	89.2	1.2	1.5	5.1	6.4	3.7	4.7	6.4	7.5	8.4	6.4	4.0	22.6	29.1	13.8	1.8	73.4	42.0	47.8	52.2
11548	GREENVALE	67.8	62.6	11.7	13.3	10.8	12.6	11.8	13.8	2.9	2.7	3.3	23.3	30.4	15.7	14.4	6.2	1.2	89.0	22.9	45.3	54.7
11550	HEMPSTEAD	27.7	25.9	51.0	51.5	1.4	1.5	30.9	33.0	7.9	7.4	7.3	9.1	10.2	30.8	18.6	7.4	1.4	73.6	30.2	48.1	51.9
11552	WEST HEMPSTEAD	73.2	70.2	16.3	17.3	4.3	5.2	9.3	11.2	6.8	7.2	8.0	6.5	5.4	27.4	24.4	12.4	2.0	73.9	38.2	48.5	51.5
11553	UNIONDALE	26.7	24.1	56.0	57.7	2.2	2.3	22.6	23.9	6.7	6.9	7.9	6.9	6.6	29.2	23.1	10.6	2.1	74.3	35.6	47.6	52.5
11554	EAST MEADOW	85.3	82.3	4.3	5.0	6.7	8.2	7.0	8.6	6.0	6.3	6.7	6.4	5.7	28.2	24.7	14.4	1.7	77.1	39.6	49.5	50.5
11557	HEWLETT	91.5	89.4	0.9	1.1	4.7	5.9	6.2	7.8	5.5	6.3	7.8	7.4	4.9	21.3	29.9	14.8	2.1	75.5	43.0	47.8	52.2
11558	ISLAND PARK	91.1	89.2	0.9	1.0	1.5	1.9	13.6	16.6	5.9	6.0	5.9	5.3	5.7	28.7	27.7	13.0	1.8	78.9	40.8	48.0	52.0
11559	LAWRENCE	86.9	85.0	5.8	6.5	1.8	2.3	8.1	9.6	7.8	8.4	9.6	8.2	5.9	21.4	23.8	12.8	2.2	69.0	35.8	49.0	51.0
11560	LOCUST VALLEY	90.3	88.2	2.3	2.7	2.6	3.3	9.2	11.3	6.8	7.5	7.0	5.9	4.2	26.1	28.0	12.8	1.7	74.7	40.5	48.8	51.2
11561	LONG BEACH	85.9	83.8	5.4	6.0	2.2	2.6	11.5	13.7	4.8	5.0	5.6	5.3	5.2	30.3	26.8	13.7	3.3	81.4	41.4	48.4	51.6
11563	LYNBROOK	92.2	90.2	1.0	1.2	3.0	3.7	8.0	10.0	5.8	6.1	6.7	5.8	4.8	27.5	25.4	14.7	3.2	77.7	41.2	47.3	52.7
11565	MALVERNE	92.2	90.4	1.8	2.1	3.0	3.8	6.2	7.8	6.2	6.8	6.5	5.8	4.5	24.6	29.4	13.9	2.3	76.8	42.3	48.2	51.8
11566	MERRICK	94.7	93.3	0.7	0.9	2.5	3.2	3.7	4.7	6.7	7.5	7.9	6.4	4.4	25.1	28.3	12.3	1.5	73.9	40.6	48.4	51.6
11568	OLD WESTBURY	67.6	62.0	14.7	17.0	11.6	13.6	7.3	8.8	5.1	6.0	7.4	13.8	12.2	19.2	24.3	11.1	1.0	77.5	33.5	46.4	53.6
11570	ROCKVILLE CENTRE	83.2	81.2	11.1	11.9	1.4	1.8	7.7	9.2	6.4	7.1	7.4	6.6	5.1	24.0	27.3	13.2	2.8	74.8	41.0	46.6	53.4
11572	OCEANSIDE	94.9	93.7	0.5	0.7	1.8	2.3	6.1	7.6	5.9	6.5	7.5	6.5	4.8	25.0	27.9	14.2	1.8	76.0	41.5	48.2	51.8
11575	ROOSEVELT	8.3	7.7	78.9	79.2	0.6	0.6	15.9	16.4	8.1	8.1	8.9	7.7	7.1	29.6	21.8	8.2	0.6	70.0	32.3	46.8	53.2
11576	ROSLYN	85.6	82.4	1.3	1.5	10.5	12.7	3.2	4.0	5.6	7.1	7.7	6.0	3.3	21.5	29.8	16.5	2.4	75.6	44.2	48.4	51.6
11577	ROSLYN HEIGHTS	84.1	81.1	3.9	4.1	8.7	10.6	4.6	5.8	6.8	8.0	8.3	6.2	4.0	22.9	28.1	13.7	2.1	72.9	41.3	48.9	51.1
11579	SEA CLIFF	94.8	93.5	1.7	2.1	1.3	1.6	4.8	6.1	5.2	6.3	7.6	6.4	4.0	23.9	31.7	12.5	2.5	76.9	43.1	48.9	51.1
11580	VALLEY STREAM	68.9	64.5	14.9	16.7	8.1	9.5	13.0	15.4	6.1	6.4	7.1	6.5	5.8	27.7	25.2	12.8	2.4	76.3	39.1	47.2	52.8
11581	VALLEY STREAM	81.9	78.9	7.0	7.6	7.3	9.0	6.8	8.4	5.7	6.3	7.1	6.7	5.4	24.4	27.4	15.0	2.0	76.7	41.5	48.0	52.0
11590	WESTBURY	60.3	57.7	23.3	24.0	5.5	6.4	21.8	24.3	6.8	6.8	7.3	6.5	6.5	29.8	23.7	11.1	1.5	75.2	36.1	49.1	50.9
11596	WILLISTON PARK	89.1	86.6	0.4	0.4	8.5	10.4	3.8	4.8	6.3	6.9	7.2	5.9	4.8	26.3	26.7	13.6	2.4	75.9	40.7	47.4	52.6
11598	WOODMERE	93.2	91.2	1.6	2.1	3.0	3.9	4.1	5.2	7.2	7.7	8.3	7.1	5.0	21.6	26.5	14.3	2.4	72.3	40.3	48.8	51.2
11691	FAR ROCKAWAY	28.2	26.5	53.4	53.4	1.7	1.9	23.2	25.3	8.6	8.1	9.0	7.8	7.6	26.1	19.9	10.7	2.2	69.5	31.7	45.7	54.3
11692	ARVERNE	16.9	16.7	68.8	67.9	0.9	1.1	16.4	18.1	7.8	7.6	9.0	8.3	7.8	27.0	19.8	10.5	2.4	70.5	32.5	46.3	53.7
11693	FAR ROCKAWAY	57.8	55.6	30.3	30.8	2.0	2.4	15.3	17.5	7.3	8.2	9.0	7.8	6.3	27.1	23.4	9.6	1.4	70.5	34.5	46.3	53.7
11694	ROCKAWAY PARK	88.0	86.0	5.7	6.3	2.4	3.0	8.2	10.1	5.7	5.9	5.8	5.5	5.0	25.9	26.2	16.7	3.4	79.2	42.6	48.7	51.3
11697	BREEZY POINT	99.2	99.1	0.1	0.1	0.4	0.5	1.2	1.6	5.4	5.9	6.3	4.6	4.1	22.7	27.7	20.2	3.1	79.5	45.7	46.8	53.2
11701	AMITYVILLE	49.5	46.9	40.1	41.6	1.3	1.4	12.1	13.7	6.6	7.1	8.0	6.8	6.0	28.6	24.0	10.8	2.2	74.1	37.1	47.1	52.9
11702	BABYLON	92.9	91.3	2.5	3.0	1.6	2.0	5.0	6.3	6.6	6.9	7.1	6.2	4.9	28.7	26.6	11.1	1.7	75.2	39.4	48.5	51.5
11703	NORTH BABYLON	91.9	90.0	2.1	2.5	2.1	2.7	7.5	9.5	6.8	7.0	7.1	5.6	4.9	30.5	24.4	12.4	1.5	75.6	38.7	48.1	51.9
11704	WEST BABYLON	82.1	80.5	11.6	11.8	2.0	2.5	8.0	9.9	7.0	7.0	7.5	6.6	5.6	29.6	23.5	11.4	1.8	74.3	37.3	47.6	52.4
11705	BAYPORT	96.1	95.0	0.9	1.1	1.2	1.5	3.9	5.1	7.4	7.7	7.1	5.7	4.5	27.4	26.3	12.3	1.6	74.0	39.5	47.7	52.3
11706	BAY SHORE	67.0	63.9	13.9	14.8	2.2	2.5	28.5	31.8	7.2	7.2	8.0	7.2	6.7	30.2	22.6	9.8	1.1	73.2	35.2	49.3	50.7
11709	BAYVILLE	96.2	95.1	0.3	0.4	1.6	2.0	4.6	6.0	6.0	6.6	6.9	6.0	4.7	27.1	28.6	12.3	1.9	76.4	41.1	49.2	50.8
11710	BELLMORE	94.3	92.8	1.2	1.5	2.6	3.3	3.9	5.0	6.7	7.2	7.6	6.0	4.7	27.1	26.5	12.7	1.6	74.6	39.9	48.7	51.3
11713	BELLPORT	63.7	63.4	23.3	22.6	2.0	2.2	14.4	15.6	7.2	7.6	8.7	6.9	6.0	27.4	25.3	9.7	1.2	72.2	35.9	48.7	51.3
11714	BETHPAGE	94.7	93.4	0.4	0.4	2.6	3.2	5.0	6.4	6.3	6.6	6.6	5.8	4.5	28.0	24.4	16.0	1.8	76.9	40.5	48.0	52.0
11715	BLUE POINT	96.4	95.5	0.7	0.9	1.1	1.4	4.4	5.7	7.0	7.3	7.4	7.2	4.5	27.1	27.3	10.7	1.7	73.3	39.6	49.2	50.8
11716	BOHEMIA	94.2	92.9	1.1	1.3	2.4	3.0	4.8	6.0	6.0	6.3	7.1	6.1	5.1	29.9	26.3	10.7	2.5	76.7	39.2	49.9	50.2
11717	BRENTWOOD	48.2	45.2	18.3	18.6	2.1	2.3	53.1	57.2	8.1	7.9	8.7	7.9	7.6	31.5	19.7	7.7	1.0	70.4	31.5	50.1	49.9
11718	BRIGHTWATERS	94.5	93.3	2.0	2.3	1.5	1.8	4.4	5.5	7.7	8.3	7.2	6.0	4.6	25.8	28.8	10.3	1.4	72.8	39.6	48.2	51.8
11719	BROOKHAVEN	84.5	81.8	10.0	11.7	0.8	1.0	7.1	8.8	6.9	7.4	6.4	5.2	4.4	26.2	27.1	12.7	3.8	75.9	41.0	47.0	53.0
11720	CENTEREACH	91.9	89.8	2.0	2.4	3.3	4.3	6.9	8.8	7.0	7.2	7.9	6.7	6.1	30.4	24.8	8.2	1.6	73.6	36.2	49.8	50.2
11721	CENTERPORT	97.5	96.9	0.3	0.3	1.2	1.5	2.1	2.8	7.3	8.1	7.4	5.2	3.1	25.7	30.1	11.6	1.6	73.7	41.6	48.5	51.5
11722	CENTRAL ISLIP	48.0	45.0	27.5	28.0	2.9	3.2	36.1	39.7	7.8	7.9	8.5	7.9	7.9	30.6	21.4	7.5	0.7	71.3	32.1	49.2	50.8
11724	COLD SPRING HARBOR	96.8	96.1	0.2	0.2	1.6	2.0	1.8	2.4	6.7	8.7	9.8	7.5	3.7	21.4	30.6	10.3	1.2	69.9	40.9	48.5	51.5
11725	COMMACK	94.5	93.1	0.6	0.7	3.7	4.7	3.0	3.9	7.5	8.0	7.6	5.9	4.0	26.7	24.9	13.5	2.0	72.9	40.0	48.3	51.7
11726	COPIAGUE	69.1	65.4	15.4	16.4	1.8	2.1	22.4	26.3	6.6	6.6	7.1	6.5	6.3	29.8	23.6	11.1	2.3	75.7	37.0	48.6	51.4
11727	CORAM	80.5	77.8	10.0	10.9	3.5	4.3	10.1	12.2	7.4	7.2	6.7	5.6	5.4	32.2	25.3	9.0	1.1	75.2	36.4	48.1	51.9
11729	DEER PARK	83.1	81.0	9.3	9.8	2.9	3.6	7.8	9.5	6.9	7.0	7.4	6.3	4.9	29.7	22.8	13.7	1.3	74.7	38.2	48.5	51.5
11730	EAST ISLIP	96.4	95.5	0.5	0.6	1.4	1.7	3.7	4.8	7.2	7.7	8.7	6.9	4.9	27.9	24.6	10.6	1.5	71.9	38.1	49.1	50.9
11731	EAST NORTHPORT	93.7	92.1	1.0	1.2	3.7	4.7	3.4	4.4	7.5	7.8	7.3	5.7	4.1	28.1	25.4	12.5	1.6	73.7	39.7	49.2	50.8
11732	EAST NORWICH	92.5	90.6	1.5	2.0	4.4	5.4	3.2	4.0	6.2	6.8	6.6	5.7	4.4	25.2	28.8	14.6	1.8	76.6	42.2	47.5	52.5
11733	EAST SETAUKET	88.9	86.4	1.4	1.7	7.7	9.5	3.6	4.6	6.5	7.5	8.0	6.5	5.6	26.2	28.8	9.9	1.0	73.7	38.8	49.1	50.9
11735	FARMINGDALE	87.4	85.2	3.9	4.3	3.6	4.3	8.9	10.8	6.9	6.9	7.1	6.4	5.6	29.8	23.4	12.3	1.6	75.3	38.1	49.3	50.8
11738	FARMINGVILLE	93.6	91.9	1.3	1.6	1.8	2.2	8.4	10.7	7.4	7.6	8.1	6.8	5.8	32.4	24.9	6.3	0.7	72.6	34.9	49.7	50.3
11740	GREENLAWN	89.9	87.9	5.1	5.8	2.6	3.2	4.5	5.6	6.6	7.2	7.7	6.0	4.3	24.3	26.0	14.4	3.6	74.5	41.6	46.7	53.3
11741	HOLBROOK	93.9	92.4	1.3	1.6	2.9	3.6	6.0	7.6	7.2	7.4	7.3	5.8	5.3	31.6	26.9	7.7	0.8	74.5	36.4	48.6	51.4
11742	HOLTSVILLE	94.7	93.4	1.1	1.3	1.4	1.8	7.4	9.4	8.1	8.1	7.6	6.0	5.2	32.7	24.3	7.3	0.7	72.4	35.7	48.8	51.2
11743	HUNTINGTON	87.9	85.9	6.5	7.3	2.4	3.0	5.1	6.2	6.8	7.4	7.2	5.7	4.2	26.9	28.3	11.9	1.6	74.9	40.7	48.7	51.3
	NEW YORK	68.0	65.9	15.9	16.2	5.6	6.4	15.1	16.7	6.5	6.5	7.1	7.0	7.1	28.9	24.0	11.2	1.8	75.8	36.7	48.3	51.7
	UNITED STATES	75.1	73.6	12.3	12.5	3.8	4.2	12.5	14.1	6.9	6.7	7.2	7.0	7.3	28.6	23.8	10.8	1.7	75.1	36.0	49.1	50.9

#	ZIP CODE POST OFFICE NAME	2004 Per Capita Income	2004 HH Income Base	2004 HOUSEHOLD INCOME DISTRIBUTION (%) Less than $25,000	$25,000 to $49,999	$50,000 to $99,999	$100,000 to $149,999	$150,000 or More	MEDIAN HOUSEHOLD INCOME 2004	2009	2004 National Centile	2004 State Centile	2004 Home Value Base	2004 HOME VALUE DISTRIBUTION (%) Less than $50,000	$50,000 to $89,999	$90,000 to $174,999	$175,000 to $399,999	$400,000 or More	2004 Median Home Value
11413	SPRINGFIELD GARDENS	23639	13599	14.1	23.9	38.9	16.1	7.0	63003	72797	87	78	9982	0.4	0.2	3.7	89.6	6.1	270871
11414	HOWARD BEACH	29352	11551	20.6	22.6	35.4	14.2	7.2	58302	67021	83	73	7901	0.4	4.8	19.8	23.4	51.6	410162
11415	KEW GARDENS	29118	7867	21.1	25.7	35.5	11.6	6.2	53343	62590	77	68	2141	0.4	7.1	20.7	36.5	35.2	297204
11416	OZONE PARK	16893	7257	27.2	28.4	32.1	9.0	3.4	45258	51831	62	51	3230	1.0	0.1	2.4	80.7	15.9	293099
11417	OZONE PARK	18811	9759	25.2	26.9	33.4	11.2	3.3	47450	54789	67	57	5047	0.8	0.2	2.4	83.5	13.0	286196
11418	RICHMOND HILL	17725	11614	26.3	29.0	32.1	8.7	4.0	44762	51560	61	50	4275	0.6	1.1	4.4	69.7	24.2	324761
11419	SOUTH RICHMOND HILL	16563	12598	24.0	28.7	32.8	10.0	4.5	47259	54202	67	56	6252	0.3	0.0	3.0	84.6	12.1	284161
11420	SOUTH OZONE PARK	18933	13720	21.1	25.7	36.0	12.4	4.9	53341	61068	77	68	9003	0.4	0.1	3.4	86.3	9.9	271476
11421	WOODHAVEN	19122	11503	24.4	25.9	34.2	11.7	3.9	49762	57131	71	62	5762	1.9	4.8	5.4	77.6	10.4	273283
11422	ROSEDALE	23662	9335	14.2	21.4	39.1	17.9	7.5	65845	77087	89	81	6416	0.5	1.1	3.2	84.6	10.6	282566
11423	HOLLIS	21755	9692	20.0	28.5	31.0	12.9	7.7	51589	59926	75	65	5440	3.8	6.6	5.6	58.8	25.1	286932
11426	BELLEROSE	27487	6268	16.2	21.1	37.1	17.5	8.1	65233	76967	89	81	4608	0.6	2.9	6.3	70.0	20.2	329862
11427	QUEENS VILLAGE	27619	7606	16.4	25.7	34.2	14.1	9.6	59427	67942	84	74	4772	0.6	9.7	11.8	49.0	29.0	304381
11428	QUEENS VILLAGE	21300	5306	14.1	22.6	39.8	16.8	6.7	64293	75092	88	80	3820	0.1	0.9	2.9	89.8	6.2	278942
11429	QUEENS VILLAGE	20035	7886	16.1	23.8	38.6	14.5	7.0	60574	68952	85	75	5379	0.1	0.3	2.7	91.8	5.1	268584
11430	JAMAICA	15275	239	19.7	27.6	32.6	12.6	7.5	53232	61988	77	67	166	0.6	1.2	12.7	82.5	3.0	236111
11432	JAMAICA	22225	18327	23.8	27.2	30.9	10.2	7.8	48937	57059	70	60	7120	2.4	2.9	6.5	50.0	38.2	352902
11433	JAMAICA	15088	8963	37.7	25.4	26.9	7.2	2.8	36277	41843	33	17	4133	1.7	1.0	10.0	80.1	7.2	244597
11434	JAMAICA	20916	20502	24.6	27.2	33.5	10.6	4.1	48297	55651	69	59	10509	3.0	1.0	9.4	80.6	6.0	244000
11435	JAMAICA	18577	18174	25.5	30.1	31.4	9.7	3.3	45026	51687	61	50	6350	2.0	6.1	20.1	58.2	13.7	247497
11436	JAMAICA	17526	5815	28.9	26.5	30.8	9.9	4.0	44333	51236	60	48	3876	1.1	0.5	13.6	81.7	3.0	228911
11501	MINEOLA	34955	7528	13.7	17.6	37.4	20.1	11.2	70716	85529	92	85	4714	0.0	0.1	7.0	50.7	42.2	378783
11507	ALBERTSON	45279	2482	9.6	12.4	29.0	19.9	29.1	97490	119379	98	96	2310	0.2	1.3	0.7	26.5	71.3	501712
11509	ATLANTIC BEACH	40683	2053	34.7	15.7	20.7	15.3	13.6	48881	60954	70	60	1247	0.0	0.0	0.2	29.2	70.7	546615
11510	BALDWIN	35019	10962	10.7	15.1	34.1	22.2	17.9	83375	100683	96	92	9318	0.2	0.0	2.8	75.8	21.2	328220
11514	CARLE PLACE	38112	1746	16.6	10.8	36.1	22.9	13.7	80541	96097	95	90	1296	0.5	0.0	1.6	57.1	40.7	373684
11516	CEDARHURST	38612	2456	17.3	17.8	29.3	16.2	19.5	69752	86693	91	84	1740	0.1	1.4	2.8	29.9	65.8	475691
11518	EAST ROCKAWAY	34900	4264	14.5	19.9	33.0	19.5	13.1	68647	83489	91	83	3088	0.2	1.4	8.4	49.9	40.1	362454
11520	FREEPORT	24298	13593	16.7	21.9	35.0	17.4	8.9	64066	77090	88	79	8793	0.4	3.4	5.9	79.8	10.5	277216
11530	GARDEN CITY	62056	9178	7.8	10.2	25.4	22.3	34.3	111171	134473	99	98	8297	0.2	0.2	1.9	13.5	84.2	642759
11542	GLEN COVE	31874	9966	16.6	21.1	33.3	16.4	12.7	65258	78947	89	81	6034	0.2	0.5	4.6	42.2	52.5	411903
11545	GLEN HEAD	69151	4490	9.3	11.3	23.7	19.6	36.2	111034	134462	99	98	4006	0.0	0.1	0.3	11.4	88.3	701464
11548	GREENVALE	38721	441	9.8	13.4	31.8	20.0	25.2	87233	111954	97	93	338	0.0	0.0	1.5	28.7	69.8	575758
11550	HEMPSTEAD	19462	16417	23.5	23.7	32.0	14.0	6.8	53244	64274	77	67	7062	0.4	0.6	5.9	86.5	6.7	265927
11552	WEST HEMPSTEAD	31230	7313	10.5	15.9	35.4	23.9	14.2	80659	97748	95	91	6458	0.1	0.3	2.7	71.4	25.6	340491
11553	UNIONDALE	21781	6454	16.7	17.9	36.6	18.8	10.0	68844	81328	91	83	5104	0.2	0.0	4.1	92.1	3.7	265292
11554	EAST MEADOW	32461	12732	11.4	17.5	35.8	21.0	14.3	76712	91541	94	88	11081	0.2	0.0	3.2	74.5	22.1	335386
11557	HEWLETT	65471	2892	9.4	11.8	26.5	18.3	34.0	104693	127954	98	97	2510	0.2	0.3	3.7	30.0	65.8	505484
11558	ISLAND PARK	33039	3089	18.8	12.8	35.6	21.2	11.7	75214	90539	93	87	2241	0.6	0.2	1.0	66.0	32.1	351747
11559	LAWRENCE	56107	2661	18.0	17.4	16.8	14.1	33.8	91330	114943	97	94	1965	0.1	1.0	5.9	16.4	76.6	721577
11560	LOCUST VALLEY	71495	2322	11.1	16.1	24.1	14.2	34.5	96104	120237	98	95	1832	0.0	0.2	0.7	18.2	81.0	643638
11561	LONG BEACH	39255	17498	16.0	18.4	34.7	17.2	13.8	67958	82772	90	83	9857	0.1	0.3	7.7	51.5	40.4	362043
11563	LYNBROOK	32897	8462	16.2	17.7	33.6	21.3	11.3	71940	86064	92	85	6094	0.4	1.2	5.1	65.0	28.3	349097
11565	MALVERNE	38528	3111	9.5	9.9	35.3	26.8	18.5	92257	111245	97	95	2914	0.0	0.6	1.3	56.2	41.8	380167
11566	MERRICK	40743	11822	7.8	10.9	30.3	26.5	24.5	101178	121517	98	96	11062	0.1	0.1	1.0	46.6	52.2	410717
11568	OLD WESTBURY	83842	1060	4.0	6.5	17.8	15.8	55.9	174771	209280	100	100	963	0.0	0.0	1.9	2.6	95.5	1000001
11570	ROCKVILLE CENTRE	47304	10344	13.2	13.8	27.8	19.6	25.6	89047	107410	97	94	7429	0.1	0.4	5.5	28.1	66.0	498225
11572	OCEANSIDE	36434	10831	11.6	14.8	31.0	23.8	18.8	85890	105081	96	92	9516	0.1	0.0	2.3	56.0	41.5	375745
11575	ROOSEVELT	19882	4189	15.4	22.4	36.6	18.1	7.5	64964	76724	88	80	3087	0.6	0.4	9.8	86.3	3.0	242668
11576	ROSLYN	79818	4720	5.9	9.7	19.1	16.6	48.7	145271	171600	100	99	4193	0.2	0.7	7.9	4.7	86.5	853737
11577	ROSLYN HEIGHTS	54083	3861	8.9	11.7	23.4	19.7	36.2	112599	135126	99	98	3432	0.2	0.3	0.4	15.4	83.7	637160
11579	SEA CLIFF	49588	1977	11.3	14.3	28.0	22.5	24.0	91418	113065	97	94	1492	0.0	0.0	0.6	20.5	78.9	581739
11580	VALLEY STREAM	29647	12814	14.1	18.0	35.4	21.3	11.1	73677	87565	93	87	10403	0.5	0.6	1.6	80.9	16.5	328226
11581	VALLEY STREAM	34546	7531	11.8	17.7	33.8	20.9	15.9	78352	94407	95	90	6196	0.5	0.2	1.4	57.5	40.5	370182
11590	WESTBURY	28721	12759	11.4	16.7	34.5	22.3	15.1	79575	94417	95	90	9953	0.3	0.1	2.6	69.7	27.3	332662
11596	WILLISTON PARK	41256	3665	10.0	14.7	29.9	24.8	20.7	90869	110299	97	94	3139	0.2	0.2	0.0	35.9	63.7	451561
11598	WOODMERE	55256	4453	8.6	11.6	23.2	21.0	35.6	110850	133250	99	97	3836	0.2	0.4	2.5	17.9	78.9	579787
11691	FAR ROCKAWAY	14725	17593	41.2	27.0	23.2	6.3	2.4	32596	37865	20	7	4092	1.2	0.4	5.1	75.8	17.6	286461
11692	ARVERNE	15204	4997	38.0	28.0	23.4	8.1	2.4	34497	41156	26	11	1762	10.4	0.3	8.6	77.8	2.8	238171
11693	FAR ROCKAWAY	20179	4105	35.3	25.9	27.2	9.0	2.7	40208	46018	47	35	2004	27.8	2.1	15.9	47.9	6.3	190909
11694	ROCKAWAY PARK	33263	7746	25.1	20.7	29.5	14.7	10.1	55159	64367	80	70	3657	6.5	1.6	3.7	26.0	62.1	476162
11697	BREEZY POINT	35481	1798	18.8	18.6	34.5	17.3	10.7	66697	78015	90	82	1755	0.2	0.4	4.3	55.4	39.7	355296
11701	AMITYVILLE	25639	8689	17.5	22.8	35.4	14.6	9.7	61485	71727	86	76	6186	5.5	1.4	10.8	70.0	12.3	252034
11702	BABYLON	37980	5643	9.7	17.1	36.7	20.5	16.1	78619	91373	95	90	4343	0.1	0.1	3.3	65.6	30.9	326398
11703	NORTH BABYLON	27997	5772	11.7	20.0	41.3	18.9	8.2	70089	81432	91	84	4736	0.2	0.3	2.9	92.1	4.5	272135
11704	WEST BABYLON	25586	13589	14.8	17.9	40.8	19.4	7.0	67857	79783	90	83	10334	0.2	0.3	5.9	90.7	2.9	261625
11705	BAYPORT	37527	3376	16.0	12.0	32.1	23.3	16.7	82770	98433	96	91	2526	0.0	0.0	1.5	67.3	31.2	338521
11706	BAY SHORE	24678	19380	17.1	21.4	37.3	15.5	8.7	62826	73108	87	78	13737	0.7	0.6	10.6	79.2	9.0	240039
11709	BAYVILLE	41253	2535	12.3	14.6	34.5	19.8	18.8	80651	100200	95	91	2010	0.4	0.0	0.8	31.6	67.2	468317
11710	BELLMORE	34297	11462	9.3	15.1	34.9	23.0	17.7	83858	101406	96	92	10144	0.1	0.0	1.7	61.9	36.3	362843
11713	BELLPORT	26805	2895	14.9	17.6	39.3	17.1	11.1	69694	80914	91	84	2271	0.0	1.1	17.4	68.3	13.1	243123
11714	BETHPAGE	33122	7996	12.9	17.4	34.5	20.9	14.3	75257	90916	93	87	6856	0.2	0.1	3.9	70.7	25.1	340007
11715	BLUE POINT	33470	1635	9.7	14.1	41.2	21.4	13.6	79540	92442	95	90	1368	0.0	0.0	3.7	73.8	22.5	300792
11716	BOHEMIA	28889	3797	13.1	22.7	33.8	20.3	10.2	70804	82346	92	85	3061	2.2	8.7	3.7	71.4	14.0	279866
11717	BRENTWOOD	17346	12238	13.7	22.5	40.5	17.6	5.7	64262	72921	88	80	9301	0.3	0.2	13.4	85.0	1.0	223583
11718	BRIGHTWATERS	43757	1139	5.8	14.9	30.8	21.1	27.4	96625	114116	98	95	1016	0.0	0.0	1.8	55.0	43.2	374632
11719	BROOKHAVEN	34786	1075	9.0	16.4	40.3	17.3	17.0	76802	87974	94	88	905	0.0	0.2	7.1	63.8	29.0	313409
11720	CENTEREACH	27514	8864	9.6	15.0	43.2	21.0	11.3	76637	88118	94	88	7754	0.1	0.0	5.8	87.7	6.4	256337
11721	CENTERPORT	50885	2324	5.4	8.7	31.8	24.0	30.1	105583	125637	99	97	2119	0.4	0.0	0.2	22.9	76.5	511108
11722	CENTRAL ISLIP	20550	9342	16.7	20.1	41.6	14.4	7.3	63311	72314	87	79	6968	0.3	0.4	21.8	75.5	2.0	217989
11724	COLD SPRING HARBOR	77986	818	3.1	7.2	24.6	15.2	50.0	150000	165797	100	99	754	0.0	0.0	0.7	8.0	91.4	856183
11725	COMMACK	35542	9764	8.5	11.8	33.3	26.2	20.3	93300	110073	97	95	9069	0.1	0.0	0.7	55.1	44.1	384768
11726	COPIAGUE	22951	6138	18.9	22.5	37.2	13.7	7.8	59487	67693	84	74	4280	0.1	0.0	9.3	84.2	6.4	242381
11727	CORAM	29144	10795	13.2	19.6	40.7	19.5	7.0	68576	79866	91	83	7372	0.5	1.2	9.2	84.6	4.5	245601
11729	DEER PARK	28481	9648	13.9	18.3	39.7	19.5	8.6	67856	79741	90	83	7771	0.2	0.0	2.7	92.1	5.0	274245
11730	EAST ISLIP	33366	5385	10.1	15.8	37.4	23.8	12.9	80059	93397	95	90	4635	0.0	0.0	2.0	71.5	26.5	302551
11731	EAST NORTHPORT	35847	9944	7.9	14.3	34.1	25.0	18.7	88861	105311	97	94	9007	0.2	0.0	0.5	57.4	42.0	378002
11732	EAST NORWICH	54908	1214	9.0	11.5	24.1	25.8	29.7	108350	130860	99	97	1017	0.5	0.0	0.5	18.1	80.9	566691
11733	EAST SETAUKET	48308	6357	10.2	10.5	27.0	20.7	31.6	104230	124578	98	97	5540	0.1	0.1	0.5	42.3	57.2	437044
11735	FARMINGDALE	30870	11020	11.0	17.8	38.4	20.2	12.6	75265	88300	93	88	8726	0.3	1.0	3.6	77.9	17.2	323922
11738	FARMINGVILLE	27777	5635	6.9	17.7	41.1	21.5	12.8	77023	88625	94	89	4734	0.2	0.1	7.0	87.5	5.3	261903
11740	GREENLAWN	35096	3645	17.2	14.8	30.1	20.4	17.5	77870	91523	94	89	2920	0.1	0.0	1.8	48.3	49.8	399214
11741	HOLBROOK	31924	9645	8.3	15.5	40.7	22.3	13.1	80337	93085	95	90	7609	0.6	0.6	3.6	85.3	9.9	279472
11742	HOLTSVILLE	27052	4176	10.3	18.5	42.6	21.3	7.3	73220	84531	93	86	3347	0.2	1.0	9.8	82.3	6.8	263639
11743	HUNTINGTON	53342	15261	9.3	12.7	28.3	19.4	30.3	99312	116166	98	96	12846	0.1	0.1	1.9	35.1	62.9	484431
	NEW YORK	28049		26.3	24.3	29.3	11.5	8.6	49309	58077				4.6	8.6	27.2	39.9	19.8	219050
	UNITED STATES	25866		24.7	27.1	30.8	10.9	6.5	48124	56710				10.9	15.0	33.7	30.1	10.4	145905

ZIP CODE #	POST OFFICE NAME	FINANCIAL SERVICES: Auto Loan	FINANCIAL SERVICES: Home Loan	FINANCIAL SERVICES: Invest-ments	FINANCIAL SERVICES: Retire-ment Plans	THE HOME: Home Improvements: Home Repair	THE HOME: Home Improvements: Lawn & Garden	THE HOME: Furnishings: Comput-ers & Hard-ware	THE HOME: Furnishings: Major Appli-ances	THE HOME: Furnishings: TV, Radio, Sound Equip-ment	THE HOME: Furnishings: Furni-ture	ENTERTAINMENT: Dine out/ Carry out	ENTERTAINMENT: Sports Equip-ment	ENTERTAINMENT: Fees & Tickets	ENTERTAINMENT: Toys & Games	ENTERTAINMENT: Travel	ENTERTAINMENT: Cable TV	PERSONAL: Apparel & Services	PERSONAL: Auto Repairs	PERSONAL: Health Insur-ance	PERSONAL: Pets & Supplies
11413	SPRINGFIELD GARDENS	103	102	112	96	99	115	101	101	106	105	134	108	106	128	104	111	130	102	109	116
11414	HOWARD BEACH	94	106	124	103	105	114	102	102	102	103	128	114	107	129	106	103	126	102	102	111
11415	KEW GARDENS	76	80	163	82	75	88	94	83	102	94	129	100	98	144	96	107	131	91	84	93
11416	OZONE PARK	63	67	125	65	63	73	76	69	82	77	105	80	78	116	78	87	107	75	70	76
11417	OZONE PARK	69	76	121	74	72	80	81	75	85	82	108	87	83	117	82	88	109	79	74	83
11418	RICHMOND HILL	61	67	136	66	63	73	78	69	85	77	108	82	81	122	80	91	110	75	71	77
11419	SOUTH RICHMOND HILL	70	77	131	76	74	82	84	78	88	84	112	91	87	122	86	91	113	83	76	85
11420	SOUTH OZONE PARK	85	91	109	87	87	95	90	88	91	93	116	98	93	118	91	92	115	90	86	97
11421	WOODHAVEN	68	72	131	69	68	79	80	74	87	81	111	85	82	121	83	93	112	80	77	82
11422	ROSEDALE	102	109	126	104	105	114	106	105	108	110	137	116	110	138	107	108	136	106	102	116
11423	HOLLIS	84	93	137	92	90	98	97	92	99	98	125	107	100	132	99	101	126	96	89	101
11426	BELLEROSE	97	118	153	118	116	119	115	113	109	114	137	133	118	142	117	106	137	114	101	120
11427	QUEENS VILLAGE	97	111	157	109	108	118	112	108	112	113	142	123	116	149	115	114	142	111	105	117
11428	QUEENS VILLAGE	96	106	127	103	102	108	104	103	103	107	131	116	106	135	104	102	131	104	95	111
11429	QUEENS VILLAGE	97	99	111	94	96	108	97	97	101	101	127	105	102	125	99	104	125	98	100	109
11430	JAMAICA	90	90	99	86	88	101	89	89	93	92	117	95	94	113	91	97	114	90	95	101
11432	JAMAICA	75	85	149	87	83	90	94	87	95	92	121	105	95	131	96	97	122	93	82	94
11433	JAMAICA	64	60	75	57	58	68	65	63	70	66	88	70	66	86	65	73	85	65	67	72
11434	JAMAICA	81	80	89	76	78	90	80	80	85	83	107	86	84	103	82	88	104	81	86	92
11435	JAMAICA	65	68	119	67	65	75	77	71	82	77	105	82	79	112	78	86	105	76	72	79
11436	JAMAICA	79	76	87	73	74	86	78	78	83	81	105	84	82	102	79	86	102	79	83	89
11501	MINEOLA	111	131	176	129	126	134	128	123	126	129	159	142	135	168	131	126	159	124	115	134
11507	ALBERTSON	160	220	284	207	213	227	193	192	184	194	230	216	214	251	206	187	233	185	179	205
11509	ATLANTIC BEACH	108	114	148	116	114	126	120	115	120	118	150	133	124	150	122	121	147	119	116	126
11510	BALDWIN	122	168	214	159	162	168	149	147	141	149	177	168	163	194	157	142	179	143	133	157
11514	CARLE PLACE	121	168	220	160	162	168	149	147	141	150	177	169	163	195	157	141	179	143	131	156
11516	CEDARHURST	127	159	205	154	155	166	150	147	145	150	182	167	160	193	156	147	182	146	139	158
11518	EAST ROCKAWAY	111	137	168	133	134	141	128	126	124	128	155	144	137	164	133	124	155	124	119	136
11520	FREEPORT	96	112	155	106	107	116	109	106	111	112	141	120	115	149	112	114	142	108	102	115
11530	GARDEN CITY	216	286	372	274	279	299	253	253	240	257	302	283	280	320	269	244	304	245	237	272
11542	GLEN COVE	109	130	168	125	125	134	124	121	123	126	155	138	131	164	128	124	155	122	115	131
11545	GLEN HEAD	234	339	458	319	326	344	290	287	271	294	341	324	328	377	311	275	349	276	260	306
11548	GREENVALE	222	272	351	275	267	279	256	250	241	257	305	292	274	317	263	238	304	248	229	272
11550	HEMPSTEAD	84	89	133	85	85	96	93	90	99	96	126	101	96	132	95	104	126	93	90	99
11552	WEST HEMPSTEAD	114	159	205	147	152	161	139	138	133	140	167	155	154	183	148	136	169	133	127	147
11553	UNIONDALE	107	117	136	112	113	123	113	112	114	116	144	124	118	146	115	115	143	112	110	123
11554	EAST MEADOW	114	149	181	141	146	154	132	133	127	133	159	149	144	169	140	128	159	129	126	143
11557	HEWLETT	223	293	377	282	284	302	260	259	246	265	311	291	287	330	274	248	314	251	239	278
11558	ISLAND PARK	119	139	163	136	135	142	131	130	127	133	160	147	137	165	134	126	160	129	122	141
11559	LAWRENCE	208	270	352	260	262	281	244	241	233	246	293	273	268	311	256	235	295	235	225	260
11560	LOCUST VALLEY	245	319	418	309	309	327	288	284	273	292	344	322	315	367	301	273	348	277	260	305
11561	LONG BEACH	114	132	174	132	128	137	131	126	128	131	161	147	137	168	133	128	160	128	119	137
11563	LYNBROOK	108	137	168	131	133	141	126	125	122	126	153	142	135	163	132	123	153	122	118	134
11565	MALVERNE	134	178	217	171	174	182	158	157	149	158	187	178	172	199	166	149	188	152	146	169
11566	MERRICK	143	202	260	192	195	203	175	173	164	177	206	197	195	227	186	165	210	167	156	185
11568	OLD WESTBURY	395	532	729	522	519	560	464	459	432	474	546	517	527	575	494	436	555	441	427	499
11570	ROCKVILLE CENTRE	161	195	249	192	189	202	184	179	179	185	225	205	198	235	190	179	225	178	170	195
11572	OCEANSIDE	127	170	210	162	165	173	151	150	143	151	179	170	164	193	159	144	180	145	138	160
11575	ROOSEVELT	105	105	117	100	102	117	104	104	109	108	137	111	110	133	107	113	134	105	111	118
11576	ROSLYN	261	361	493	349	350	375	313	310	292	319	368	349	354	395	334	295	375	297	285	334
11577	ROSLYN HEIGHTS	185	257	345	245	248	263	223	221	210	227	265	249	251	288	238	213	270	213	202	237
11579	SEA CLIFF	144	201	264	191	193	201	179	175	168	179	211	202	195	233	188	169	214	171	157	186
11580	VALLEY STREAM	106	139	176	131	134	142	126	125	122	127	153	141	137	166	132	123	154	122	116	133
11581	VALLEY STREAM	120	155	191	148	150	159	141	139	135	141	169	158	152	180	147	136	170	136	130	150
11590	WESTBURY	118	153	195	144	147	155	139	137	135	141	170	155	150	183	145	136	171	135	127	147
11596	WILLISTON PARK	135	194	259	183	186	195	169	167	159	170	199	190	188	221	179	160	203	161	149	177
11598	WOODMERE	197	272	355	260	263	278	237	235	222	240	280	265	264	303	252	224	285	226	214	252
11691	FAR ROCKAWAY	53	53	89	51	50	59	61	56	66	61	83	65	62	88	61	69	83	60	58	62
11692	ARVERNE	62	55	75	52	53	62	63	60	69	64	86	68	63	85	62	71	84	63	64	69
11693	FAR ROCKAWAY	65	67	102	65	64	73	74	69	79	73	99	81	76	105	75	81	98	73	70	77
11694	ROCKAWAY PARK	99	113	144	112	111	120	112	109	110	111	138	125	117	142	114	111	137	109	105	118
11697	BREEZY POINT	136	113	89	104	125	142	106	125	117	108	141	139	99	132	114	125	132	123	147	162
11701	AMITYVILLE	99	110	130	106	107	117	107	105	107	108	134	118	113	136	109	108	133	105	104	117
11702	BABYLON	126	161	199	155	157	164	147	146	141	147	177	167	158	190	154	142	178	143	136	158
11703	NORTH BABYLON	101	124	144	122	121	124	115	113	109	114	138	131	122	146	118	108	137	111	105	123
11704	WEST BABYLON	98	117	133	114	114	119	110	108	106	109	133	124	116	140	112	106	132	106	103	118
11705	BAYPORT	123	153	188	149	149	157	142	140	136	142	171	160	152	181	147	136	171	138	131	151
11706	BAY SHORE	103	115	134	112	112	119	112	110	111	113	140	126	116	144	113	110	138	111	106	121
11709	BAYVILLE	130	190	249	177	182	190	163	162	153	164	192	183	182	215	174	156	196	156	145	171
11710	BELLMORE	120	165	209	156	160	167	145	144	138	146	172	164	160	189	154	139	175	139	132	154
11713	BELLPORT	116	133	151	131	130	138	124	124	121	127	152	140	132	155	128	121	151	122	119	137
11714	BETHPAGE	115	151	186	142	147	157	135	135	130	135	162	151	147	174	143	132	163	131	129	145
11715	BLUE POINT	111	152	184	145	147	150	133	132	125	133	156	152	146	172	140	124	158	127	118	142
11716	BOHEMIA	111	130	143	130	129	133	120	121	115	121	144	138	126	147	124	113	142	118	115	133
11717	BRENTWOOD	96	104	129	99	99	106	102	101	104	107	133	113	105	137	103	105	133	103	96	109
11718	BRIGHTWATERS	159	195	231	196	192	199	179	178	168	180	212	205	192	220	185	166	212	174	164	194
11719	BROOKHAVEN	121	147	164	145	145	150	135	135	128	135	161	154	144	167	140	127	160	131	127	147
11720	CENTEREACH	116	142	152	142	139	139	129	128	121	128	152	150	137	161	132	117	151	124	116	141
11721	CENTERPORT	155	226	305	212	217	229	193	191	181	196	227	216	218	252	207	184	233	184	173	203
11722	CENTRAL ISLIP	98	108	125	105	103	109	104	103	103	107	131	116	107	135	105	102	131	104	96	112
11724	COLD SPRING HARBOR	289	389	534	381	379	409	339	336	316	347	400	378	385	421	362	319	406	323	312	365
11725	COMMACK	133	176	213	170	172	179	156	155	146	157	184	176	170	196	164	147	185	150	143	167
11726	COPIAGUE	91	107	126	104	105	111	101	101	99	102	124	114	107	130	104	99	124	99	95	109
11727	CORAM	104	117	127	118	113	116	112	110	107	112	135	128	115	137	111	104	133	109	101	121
11729	DEER PARK	107	127	143	123	124	130	119	118	115	118	145	135	126	152	122	115	144	116	112	128
11730	EAST ISLIP	129	161	181	158	158	161	145	145	137	145	172	166	155	182	150	135	172	140	133	158
11731	EAST NORTHPORT	126	175	222	166	169	175	153	152	144	154	180	173	168	198	162	144	183	147	136	162
11732	EAST NORWICH	196	254	319	248	248	261	229	227	216	230	271	259	249	286	240	215	273	221	209	245
11733	EAST SETAUKET	178	233	279	231	226	232	205	201	189	207	239	232	226	255	213	187	242	194	181	220
11735	FARMINGDALE	109	141	178	135	137	144	129	127	125	129	156	145	140	169	135	125	157	125	118	137
11738	FARMINGVILLE	120	145	154	146	142	141	131	131	122	131	154	153	139	162	133	118	153	127	117	144
11740	GREENLAWN	116	148	192	143	144	152	139	135	134	137	167	155	149	180	144	135	168	134	127	145
11741	HOLBROOK	125	154	168	155	151	151	139	138	130	139	163	162	148	173	142	126	163	134	124	152
11742	HOLTSVILLE	108	128	134	129	124	123	117	115	109	117	137	135	122	143	117	104	136	113	103	127
11743	HUNTINGTON	179	240	312	231	232	245	213	211	201	215	253	239	235	273	224	202	257	204	192	226
	NEW YORK	95	100	134	99	98	107	103	100	105	103	133	116	105	138	104	107	131	102	99	112
	UNITED STATES	100	100	100	100	100	100	100	100	100	100	100	100	100	100	100	100	100	100	100	100

# POST OFFICE NAME	COUNTY FIPS CODE	POPULATION 2000	POPULATION 2004	POPULATION 2009	2000-2004 ANNUAL RATE % Rate	2000-2004 ANNUAL RATE State Centile	HOUSEHOLDS 2000	HOUSEHOLDS 2004	HOUSEHOLDS 2009	% Annual Rate 2000-2004	2004 Average HH Size	FAMILIES 2000	FAMILIES 2004	% Annual Rate 2000-2004
11746 HUNTINGTON STATION	103	64169	65487	68107	0.5	56	20589	21030	21943	0.5	3.08	16657	16964	0.4
11747 MELVILLE	103	15839	17205	18478	2.0	93	5272	5795	6280	2.3	2.86	4272	4669	2.1
11749 ISLANDIA	103	3882	3881	4004	0.0	27	1369	1370	1417	0.0	2.83	968	963	-0.1
11751 ISLIP	103	15071	15406	15996	0.5	59	5112	5249	5475	0.6	2.92	3963	4053	0.5
11752 ISLIP TERRACE	103	9602	9526	9815	-0.2	18	2914	2907	3011	-0.1	3.27	2464	2453	-0.1
11753 JERICHO	059	11234	11387	11548	0.3	48	3906	3967	4016	0.4	2.83	3317	3355	0.3
11754 KINGS PARK	103	18862	19158	19907	0.4	50	6370	6497	6789	0.5	2.86	4855	4926	0.3
11755 LAKE GROVE	103	11211	11533	11984	0.7	65	3707	3827	3995	0.8	2.99	2979	3068	0.7
11756 LEVITTOWN	059	43596	43212	43327	-0.2	17	13919	13794	13831	-0.2	3.13	11446	11313	-0.3
11757 LINDENHURST	103	46361	46722	48259	0.2	40	15175	15366	15953	0.3	3.02	11842	11960	0.2
11758 MASSAPEQUA	059	55164	55036	55385	-0.1	25	18161	18132	18243	0.0	3.03	15012	14947	-0.1
11762 MASSAPEQUA PARK	059	24025	24033	24229	0.0	29	7830	7835	7901	0.0	3.05	6694	6681	-0.1
11763 MEDFORD	103	24984	26620	28264	1.5	88	7604	8133	8678	1.6	3.22	6280	6711	1.6
11764 MILLER PLACE	103	11240	12268	13164	2.1	94	3591	3936	4244	2.2	3.09	2939	3208	2.1
11765 MILL NECK	059	471	463	462	-0.4	9	162	159	158	-0.4	2.91	126	123	-0.6
11766 MOUNT SINAI	103	9429	10314	11098	2.1	94	2868	3152	3408	2.3	3.26	2402	2639	2.2
11767 NESCONSET	103	13799	14667	15569	1.5	87	4362	4656	4969	1.6	3.11	3607	3837	1.5
11768 NORTHPORT	103	22100	22435	23343	0.4	50	7886	8048	8420	0.5	2.74	6129	6239	0.4
11769 OAKDALE	103	9508	9781	10215	0.7	65	3550	3682	3871	0.9	2.61	2548	2633	0.8
11770 OCEAN BEACH	103	176	186	195	1.3	85	79	84	89	1.5	2.19	49	51	1.0
11771 OYSTER BAY	059	10678	11178	11534	1.1	80	4126	4317	4446	1.1	2.56	2887	3015	1.0
11772 PATCHOGUE	103	42395	44166	46525	1.0	77	15146	15771	16646	1.0	2.75	10403	10826	0.9
11776 PORT JEFFERSON STATI	103	23228	24606	26091	1.4	86	7627	8129	8667	1.5	2.98	5807	6192	1.5
11777 PORT JEFFERSON	103	9031	9403	9831	1.0	76	3389	3552	3742	1.1	2.49	2313	2414	1.0
11778 ROCKY POINT	103	11895	12836	13685	1.8	92	4130	4465	4776	1.9	2.87	3146	3384	1.7
11779 RONKONKOMA	103	38835	40572	42870	1.0	78	12924	13599	14462	1.2	2.95	9999	10453	1.1
11780 SAINT JAMES	103	14986	15565	16293	0.9	74	5160	5392	5680	1.0	2.80	3996	4166	1.0
11782 SAYVILLE	103	15645	15816	16390	0.3	44	5237	5324	5550	0.4	2.90	4075	4133	0.3
11783 SEAFORD	059	21964	21979	22102	0.0	30	7292	7295	7333	0.0	3.00	5933	5915	-0.1
11784 SELDEN	103	23847	24913	26243	1.0	78	7401	7780	8226	1.2	3.20	6001	6277	1.1
11786 SHOREHAM	103	6239	6440	6735	0.8	69	1968	2031	2131	0.7	3.17	1615	1664	0.7
11787 SMITHTOWN	103	34083	35193	36828	0.8	69	11362	11830	12478	1.0	2.90	9391	9761	0.9
11788 HAUPPAUGE	103	16814	17002	17692	0.3	44	5841	5956	6240	0.5	2.83	4635	4717	0.3
11789 SOUND BEACH	103	7069	7378	7730	1.0	78	2477	2593	2728	1.1	2.83	1862	1943	1.0
11790 STONY BROOK	103	17703	17901	18400	0.3	44	4723	4827	5029	0.5	2.85	3725	3800	0.5
11791 SYOSSET	059	24243	24419	24714	0.2	39	8062	8110	8189	0.1	2.98	6885	6904	0.1
11792 WADING RIVER	103	7555	8339	9010	2.4	95	2607	2918	3187	2.7	2.80	2018	2250	2.6
11793 WANTAGH	059	33112	32922	33101	-0.1	21	11161	11097	11156	-0.1	2.96	9145	9067	-0.2
11794 STONY BROOK	103	2629	2628	2631	0.0	27	24	24	25	0.0	5.08	19	19	0.0
11795 WEST ISLIP	103	27071	27133	28037	0.1	31	8336	8403	8733	0.2	3.18	7133	7177	0.1
11796 WEST SAYVILLE	103	4211	4359	4564	0.8	71	1434	1495	1574	1.0	2.85	1088	1131	0.9
11797 WOODBURY	059	9144	9184	9234	0.1	35	2897	2898	2889	0.0	2.83	2340	2336	0.0
11798 WYANDANCH	103	15031	16017	16993	1.5	88	3813	4049	4302	1.4	3.92	3191	3383	1.4
11801 HICKSVILLE	059	39751	39444	39543	-0.2	19	13250	13130	13155	-0.2	2.99	10415	10283	-0.3
11803 PLAINVIEW	059	27857	28271	28725	0.4	50	9241	9393	9549	0.4	2.96	7907	8017	0.3
11804 OLD BETHPAGE	059	5012	4924	4917	-0.4	9	1747	1712	1708	-0.5	2.81	1480	1447	-0.5
11901 RIVERHEAD	103	22069	23630	25384	1.6	89	8511	9168	9903	1.8	2.51	5630	6020	1.6
11933 CALVERTON	103	7314	8201	8956	2.7	98	2587	2956	3279	3.2	2.42	1717	1936	2.9
11934 CENTER MORICHES	103	6940	7505	8035	1.9	92	2378	2576	2768	1.9	2.86	1818	1965	1.9
11935 CUTCHOGUE	103	3972	4179	4407	1.2	83	1586	1680	1783	1.4	2.44	1117	1179	1.3
11937 EAST HAMPTON	103	14802	16241	17497	2.2	95	6028	6599	7119	2.2	2.45	3768	4099	2.0
11939 EAST MARION	103	756	760	780	0.1	36	329	333	344	0.3	2.28	222	224	0.2
11940 EAST MORICHES	103	4427	4753	5056	1.7	90	1496	1623	1742	1.9	2.87	1166	1260	1.8
11941 EASTPORT	103	3900	4084	4284	1.1	80	1494	1560	1638	1.0	2.56	1079	1123	0.9
11942 EAST QUOGUE	103	5024	5318	5628	1.4	86	2002	2118	2244	1.3	2.51	1350	1422	1.2
11944 GREENPORT	103	3693	3843	4020	0.9	75	1509	1578	1661	1.1	2.33	896	932	0.9
11946 HAMPTON BAYS	103	12529	13463	14324	1.7	90	4999	5343	5683	1.6	2.49	3170	3372	1.5
11948 LAUREL	103	729	812	881	2.6	97	292	327	356	2.7	2.47	220	246	2.7
11949 MANORVILLE	103	11518	13455	14968	3.7	99	4263	4957	5515	3.6	2.70	3039	3534	3.6
11950 MASTIC	103	14782	15625	16474	1.3	85	4202	4461	4727	1.4	3.48	3563	3771	1.3
11951 MASTIC BEACH	103	12828	13584	14336	1.4	86	4084	4334	4589	1.4	3.12	3109	3288	1.3
11952 MATTITUCK	103	4470	4712	5001	1.3	84	1748	1849	1971	1.3	2.54	1305	1376	1.3
11953 MIDDLE ISLAND	103	11396	12944	14298	3.0	98	4285	4939	5516	3.4	2.55	2970	3414	3.3
11954 MONTAUK	103	3849	4173	4459	1.9	93	1591	1719	1838	1.8	2.42	991	1067	1.8
11955 MORICHES	103	2313	2896	3362	5.4	100	1116	1399	1631	5.5	2.05	670	871	6.4
11957 ORIENT	103	709	735	767	0.9	72	330	344	361	1.0	2.13	206	214	0.9
11958 PECONIC	103	576	651	710	2.9	98	233	264	290	3.0	2.45	167	188	2.8
11961 RIDGE	103	12080	12775	13546	1.3	85	5123	5444	5794	1.4	2.30	3243	3420	1.3
11963 SAG HARBOR	103	8293	8928	9537	1.8	91	3696	3988	4274	1.9	2.24	2206	2373	1.7
11964 SHELTER ISLAND	103	1183	1254	1323	1.4	87	508	540	573	1.5	2.32	335	355	1.4
11965 SHELTER ISLAND HEIGH	103	1045	1100	1158	1.2	83	488	514	541	1.2	2.14	321	336	1.1
11967 SHIRLEY	103	24440	25413	26583	0.9	75	7172	7499	7886	1.1	3.38	5973	6231	1.0
11968 SOUTHAMPTON	103	11738	12603	13397	1.7	90	4615	4982	5328	1.8	2.41	2875	3089	1.7
11971 SOUTHOLD	103	5430	6094	6642	2.8	98	2309	2582	2817	2.7	2.35	1598	1781	2.6
11976 WATER MILL	103	2508	2766	2987	2.3	95	1051	1167	1266	2.5	2.36	700	774	2.4
11977 WESTHAMPTON	103	2206	2481	2702	2.8	98	865	972	1062	2.8	2.48	613	686	2.7
11978 WESTHAMPTON BEACH	103	3732	3977	4206	1.5	88	1427	1520	1613	1.5	2.46	890	944	1.4
11980 YAPHANK	103	4210	4543	4834	1.8	92	1315	1432	1538	2.0	2.85	956	1040	2.0
12007 ALCOVE	001	205	212	215	0.8	70	71	74	77	1.0	2.86	54	56	0.9
12008 ALPLAUS	093	450	440	436	-0.5	6	180	179	179	-0.1	2.43	128	126	-0.4
12009 ALTAMONT	001	7480	7332	7346	-0.5	7	2826	2808	2851	-0.2	2.55	2024	1998	-0.3
12010 AMSTERDAM	057	29058	29439	29757	0.3	48	12124	12406	12667	0.5	2.31	7633	7761	0.3
12015 ATHENS	039	3113	3447	3804	2.4	96	1242	1400	1572	2.9	2.29	852	955	2.7
12017 AUSTERLITZ	021	317	321	332	0.3	47	126	130	136	0.7	2.47	85	87	0.6
12018 AVERILL PARK	083	7659	7825	7950	0.5	58	2854	2960	3048	0.9	2.64	2110	2172	0.5
12019 BALLSTON LAKE	091	13556	14119	14998	1.0	76	5075	5379	5806	1.4	2.62	3892	4083	1.1
12020 BALLSTON SPA	091	28252	29397	30967	0.9	75	10666	11230	11996	1.2	2.57	7636	7974	1.0
12022 BERLIN	083	831	812	811	-0.5	5	316	313	317	-0.2	2.59	218	215	-0.3
12023 BERNE	001	1846	1853	1853	0.1	34	707	721	730	0.5	2.57	524	530	0.3
12024 BRAINARD	021	176	182	190	0.8	70	71	75	79	1.3	2.43	50	52	0.9
12025 BROADALBIN	035	5363	5585	5737	1.0	76	2101	2212	2300	1.2	2.52	1510	1582	1.1
12027 BURNT HILLS	091	3493	3560	3720	0.5	55	1293	1336	1415	0.8	2.66	1001	1029	0.7
12028 BUSKIRK	115	1808	1864	1911	0.7	67	640	670	697	1.1	2.71	477	496	0.9
12029 CANAAN	021	1309	1337	1381	0.5	57	433	450	474	0.9	2.34	280	288	0.7
12031 CARLISLE	095	54	75	89	8.0	100	18	25	30	8.0	3.00	13	18	8.0
NEW YORK					0.4					0.5	2.60			0.4
UNITED STATES					1.2					1.3	2.58			1.1

ZIP CODE #	POST OFFICE NAME	RACE (%) White 2000	White 2004	Black 2000	Black 2004	Asian/Pacific 2000	Asian/Pacific 2004	% Hispanic Origin 2000	% Hispanic Origin 2004	2004 AGE DISTRIBUTION (%) 0-4	5-9	10-14	15-19	20-24	25-44	45-64	65-84	85+	18+	MEDIAN AGE 2004	% 2004 Males	% 2004 Females
11746	HUNTINGTON STATION	80.9	77.8	6.6	7.4	4.8	6.0	12.3	14.4	7.2	7.5	7.5	6.4	5.2	28.5	25.8	10.6	1.3	73.7	38.0	49.7	50.3
11747	MELVILLE	89.9	87.4	2.2	2.6	5.4	6.9	3.7	4.7	7.3	7.8	7.1	5.6	3.8	26.9	27.1	12.6	1.7	73.9	40.3	49.2	50.8
11749	ISLANDIA	65.8	61.8	16.6	18.0	8.0	9.3	21.5	24.9	7.6	7.2	6.6	6.1	5.8	34.7	24.2	7.3	0.6	74.9	35.6	48.5	51.5
11751	ISLIP	90.6	88.5	3.3	3.9	2.0	2.6	8.1	10.1	7.7	7.9	8.0	6.5	5.1	29.4	24.5	9.7	1.2	72.2	37.0	49.0	51.0
11752	ISLIP TERRACE	94.4	93.1	1.5	1.7	1.4	1.7	7.2	9.1	7.3	7.7	8.6	7.4	5.7	29.7	22.9	9.7	1.0	71.7	36.1	49.2	50.8
11753	JERICHO	87.1	84.2	1.3	1.5	10.2	12.6	2.3	2.9	6.2	7.1	7.6	6.4	3.9	21.7	30.5	15.4	1.3	74.8	43.4	48.5	51.5
11754	KINGS PARK	95.7	94.5	0.8	1.0	1.8	2.4	3.2	4.1	7.4	7.6	7.3	5.7	4.4	28.6	24.3	12.2	2.6	74.1	39.2	48.5	51.5
11755	LAKE GROVE	91.7	89.9	1.5	1.7	4.6	5.6	4.9	6.2	7.5	7.6	7.5	6.4	5.0	32.2	24.6	8.3	1.0	73.2	36.2	49.6	50.4
11756	LEVITTOWN	93.8	92.3	0.5	0.7	3.0	3.8	7.4	9.3	6.5	6.9	8.0	6.7	5.6	28.4	25.7	11.1	1.1	74.4	38.2	48.7	51.4
11757	LINDENHURST	93.0	91.3	1.6	1.9	1.5	1.9	7.9	10.0	6.9	7.2	7.8	6.5	5.3	31.1	24.0	10.1	1.1	74.1	37.1	49.0	51.0
11758	MASSAPEQUA	91.6	90.4	4.5	4.9	1.5	1.9	4.5	5.5	6.8	7.2	7.5	5.9	4.6	27.8	25.5	13.2	1.4	74.7	39.7	48.5	51.5
11762	MASSAPEQUA PARK	97.1	96.3	0.3	0.4	1.6	2.1	3.0	3.8	7.1	7.5	7.5	5.7	4.3	26.4	25.1	14.7	1.8	74.2	40.3	48.4	51.6
11763	MEDFORD	83.0	80.7	9.7	10.4	1.4	1.7	11.1	13.7	7.2	7.5	8.0	6.7	6.0	30.9	25.2	7.5	1.0	73.2	35.1	49.2	50.8
11764	MILLER PLACE	96.7	95.9	0.4	0.5	1.3	1.7	3.2	4.2	7.6	8.3	8.5	6.7	5.0	28.0	27.7	7.2	1.1	71.1	37.2	49.4	50.6
11765	MILL NECK	94.3	92.4	0.9	1.1	3.0	3.7	4.5	6.1	7.1	8.2	7.8	5.6	3.2	23.5	28.9	13.4	2.2	73.0	41.6	49.2	50.8
11766	MOUNT SINAI	94.4	93.2	1.5	1.8	1.9	2.4	4.3	5.5	7.1	7.9	9.0	7.1	5.1	28.2	27.3	7.0	1.3	71.4	36.5	48.9	51.1
11767	NESCONSET	94.3	92.9	1.0	1.2	3.0	3.8	4.0	5.1	7.3	7.7	7.6	5.9	4.4	31.1	26.2	8.3	1.5	73.6	37.6	49.2	50.8
11768	NORTHPORT	96.7	95.9	0.7	0.8	1.5	1.9	2.3	3.0	6.6	7.5	7.3	5.5	3.7	25.2	30.2	12.7	1.4	74.9	42.0	49.7	50.3
11769	OAKDALE	96.7	95.9	1.3	1.5	1.0	1.2	2.9	3.8	6.0	6.3	6.9	5.9	5.0	27.4	27.6	13.5	1.5	77.5	40.7	47.7	52.3
11770	OCEAN BEACH	96.0	95.7	0.0	0.0	2.3	2.7	2.3	3.2	3.2	4.3	7.5	5.9	3.8	24.2	35.0	15.1	1.1	81.2	45.6	53.8	46.2
11771	OYSTER BAY	90.9	88.6	2.6	3.2	2.9	3.7	8.9	10.9	6.1	6.6	6.9	6.2	4.6	26.1	28.1	13.3	2.1	76.4	41.4	48.3	51.7
11772	PATCHOGUE	86.0	83.6	4.6	5.1	1.6	2.0	13.8	16.5	6.8	6.8	7.0	6.1	5.8	31.1	24.6	9.9	2.0	75.6	37.1	49.3	50.8
11776	PORT JEFFERSON STATI	89.7	87.5	2.3	2.7	3.4	4.1	8.6	10.9	7.5	7.5	7.5	6.0	5.4	32.0	23.5	9.3	1.3	73.8	36.3	49.0	51.0
11777	PORT JEFFERSON	92.0	90.1	1.6	1.9	3.5	4.4	5.0	6.3	5.1	5.4	5.9	6.2	5.2	27.4	29.2	13.0	2.7	79.5	41.9	48.6	51.4
11778	ROCKY POINT	95.9	94.8	0.6	0.7	1.1	1.4	4.7	6.1	8.4	8.4	8.5	6.9	5.3	32.1	22.4	6.8	1.2	70.3	34.5	49.8	50.2
11779	RONKONKOMA	93.5	92.0	1.1	1.3	2.5	3.1	6.3	8.0	6.8	6.9	7.2	6.3	5.6	31.0	25.7	9.1	1.6	75.2	37.3	48.9	51.1
11780	SAINT JAMES	97.1	96.3	0.4	0.4	1.4	1.8	3.2	4.2	6.7	7.5	7.8	5.7	3.8	24.9	25.0	14.4	4.2	74.3	41.7	47.6	52.4
11782	SAYVILLE	96.0	94.8	0.7	0.8	2.0	2.6	2.9	3.7	6.9	7.3	8.0	6.7	5.0	27.6	26.3	10.2	2.1	73.4	38.8	48.2	51.9
11783	SEAFORD	97.0	96.2	0.3	0.4	1.6	2.0	3.5	4.5	6.9	7.2	7.2	6.0	5.0	27.5	26.1	12.6	1.5	74.9	39.6	48.4	51.6
11784	SELDEN	92.1	90.1	2.0	2.4	2.4	3.0	8.1	10.2	7.4	7.4	8.1	7.1	6.2	31.7	23.2	8.0	1.0	72.7	35.1	49.0	51.0
11786	SHOREHAM	95.9	94.8	1.0	1.2	1.6	2.0	3.5	4.5	6.4	7.4	8.3	6.0	4.4	23.7	26.0	15.7	2.2	73.9	41.4	48.7	51.3
11787	SMITHTOWN	96.1	95.1	0.6	0.7	2.0	2.5	3.4	4.4	7.5	7.8	7.4	5.7	4.1	27.4	25.5	12.4	2.3	73.6	39.7	48.4	51.6
11788	HAUPPAUGE	92.3	90.4	1.4	1.6	4.1	5.2	4.7	6.0	6.5	6.8	6.8	5.6	4.6	29.3	27.4	12.0	0.9	76.3	39.6	49.6	50.4
11789	SOUND BEACH	95.9	94.9	0.7	0.9	1.5	1.9	3.6	4.5	7.5	7.8	8.2	6.6	5.7	33.3	23.0	6.7	1.2	72.2	34.9	49.4	50.6
11790	STONY BROOK	78.2	75.6	5.0	5.3	13.7	15.6	4.2	4.9	5.3	5.8	6.1	13.2	15.1	21.8	21.2	10.1	1.4	79.5	30.3	49.8	50.2
11791	SYOSSET	85.6	82.3	0.7	0.8	12.1	14.9	2.8	3.5	6.3	7.4	7.9	6.7	4.2	23.2	29.4	13.5	1.6	73.8	41.6	48.9	51.1
11792	WADING RIVER	95.2	94.1	1.9	2.2	1.1	1.4	3.6	4.6	6.4	7.5	8.4	6.5	4.3	27.2	29.2	9.3	1.3	73.5	39.3	50.0	50.0
11793	WANTAGH	95.7	94.6	0.6	0.7	2.2	2.8	3.8	4.9	7.3	7.7	7.4	6.0	4.7	26.2	26.4	12.8	1.5	73.7	40.0	48.5	51.5
11794	STONY BROOK	36.3	31.3	17.2	17.8	36.9	40.4	10.6	11.6	0.3	0.3	0.5	39.0	52.1	6.1	1.1	0.5	0.1	98.1	21.0	49.6	50.4
11795	WEST ISLIP	97.0	96.2	0.4	0.4	1.1	1.4	3.4	4.4	7.2	7.9	8.7	6.8	4.6	27.6	24.5	11.0	1.8	71.8	38.3	49.0	51.0
11796	WEST SAYVILLE	97.4	96.7	0.6	0.7	1.1	1.4	2.4	3.1	6.8	7.1	8.1	6.6	5.4	27.2	26.5	10.7	1.6	73.6	38.8	48.1	51.9
11797	WOODBURY	90.9	88.6	1.0	1.2	7.0	8.9	1.4	1.8	5.2	6.5	8.1	6.0	3.3	21.3	28.4	15.4	5.9	75.8	44.8	46.8	53.2
11798	WYANDANCH	19.3	17.5	68.9	69.9	1.4	1.5	15.0	16.1	8.6	8.9	9.9	8.9	7.6	28.0	20.7	6.8	0.6	66.9	29.7	47.4	52.6
11801	HICKSVILLE	85.3	82.2	0.7	0.9	8.9	10.9	9.5	11.6	6.1	6.3	6.6	5.6	5.3	29.2	25.3	13.9	1.7	77.6	39.9	48.8	51.2
11803	PLAINVIEW	93.5	91.7	0.4	0.5	4.8	6.1	2.7	3.5	6.3	7.1	7.2	6.2	4.3	23.5	28.2	15.3	1.9	75.4	42.3	48.5	51.5
11804	OLD BETHPAGE	94.7	93.3	1.2	1.5	3.0	3.9	1.8	2.4	6.1	6.8	7.4	5.7	4.3	23.7	27.8	16.7	1.6	76.0	42.8	48.2	51.8
11901	RIVERHEAD	75.6	72.1	18.7	21.1	0.9	1.2	8.3	9.9	6.1	6.3	6.7	6.0	5.7	25.2	24.9	16.0	3.2	77.1	41.1	48.2	51.8
11933	CALVERTON	82.3	81.3	12.8	12.9	0.9	1.1	7.6	8.9	5.5	5.9	6.0	5.7	5.9	31.7	23.7	14.0	1.6	79.6	39.2	54.5	45.5
11934	CENTER MORICHES	90.0	88.2	5.1	5.9	1.1	1.3	6.9	8.7	7.6	7.5	6.7	6.0	5.2	30.5	24.6	10.2	1.8	74.2	37.7	49.4	50.6
11935	CUTCHOGUE	94.1	92.8	2.0	2.3	0.6	0.8	5.2	6.5	4.2	4.9	6.7	5.7	4.2	21.5	30.9	18.8	3.0	80.4	46.7	49.6	50.4
11937	EAST HAMPTON	89.0	86.7	3.5	4.1	1.3	1.6	12.9	15.9	5.1	5.5	6.3	5.8	4.8	24.6	30.9	14.9	2.1	79.4	43.8	49.7	50.3
11939	EAST MARION	95.2	94.1	0.9	1.2	0.9	1.2	2.9	3.8	4.3	5.1	6.1	4.2	3.3	20.0	29.5	24.0	3.6	82.0	50.1	50.0	50.0
11940	EAST MORICHES	94.5	93.1	1.6	2.0	1.6	2.0	5.6	7.1	6.8	7.3	8.1	6.0	4.8	27.9	27.2	10.0	1.8	73.5	39.0	49.7	50.4
11941	EASTPORT	94.5	93.2	1.6	2.0	1.4	1.7	5.5	7.0	5.7	6.5	7.8	5.9	4.1	26.8	29.3	11.8	2.2	76.0	41.4	49.7	50.3
11942	EAST QUOGUE	94.9	93.7	1.4	1.7	0.7	0.9	4.7	6.0	6.2	6.9	6.8	5.4	4.3	25.5	30.1	12.7	2.1	76.7	42.1	49.5	50.6
11944	GREENPORT	82.8	80.3	10.4	11.7	0.7	0.8	12.2	14.7	5.6	5.3	6.5	5.9	5.1	21.1	26.1	19.5	4.9	79.3	45.4	46.3	53.7
11946	HAMPTON BAYS	92.9	91.3	0.9	1.1	0.8	1.0	12.5	15.6	6.3	6.5	5.9	4.6	4.6	30.2	26.1	13.5	2.4	78.6	40.6	49.9	50.1
11948	LAUREL	97.1	96.4	1.2	1.6	0.0	0.0	2.3	3.0	5.1	5.9	8.1	5.5	4.4	23.8	28.3	16.5	2.3	78.0	43.3	50.3	49.8
11949	MANORVILLE	96.2	95.3	1.2	1.5	0.7	0.9	4.3	5.5	8.0	8.2	7.8	6.2	4.5	29.2	23.1	11.6	1.5	71.9	37.8	49.2	50.8
11950	MASTIC	84.7	82.2	6.0	6.9	1.2	1.5	12.5	15.5	8.1	8.1	9.1	8.1	7.4	31.4	22.3	4.9	0.5	69.8	30.8	49.9	50.1
11951	MASTIC BEACH	88.8	86.5	4.6	5.4	0.7	0.9	10.1	12.7	8.3	8.2	9.1	7.6	7.2	29.9	22.7	6.3	1.0	69.9	32.2	49.7	50.3
11952	MATTITUCK	96.7	95.9	1.2	1.5	0.5	0.6	2.4	3.1	5.5	6.1	6.9	6.3	5.0	22.4	29.1	16.2	2.6	77.6	43.7	48.6	51.4
11953	MIDDLE ISLAND	80.5	77.9	12.1	13.3	2.5	3.0	7.3	8.8	7.4	7.0	6.0	5.5	6.2	30.0	24.2	11.9	1.8	76.2	37.6	47.5	52.5
11954	MONTAUK	87.0	84.5	0.9	1.0	0.8	1.0	23.9	28.7	4.9	5.2	5.8	5.6	4.9	31.3	27.3	13.7	1.3	80.6	41.0	51.2	48.8
11955	MORICHES	94.9	94.5	1.3	1.2	1.8	2.1	4.0	4.6	3.7	2.8	2.7	2.4	5.2	26.4	28.6	26.7	1.6	89.2	50.2	50.1	49.9
11957	ORIENT	97.3	96.9	0.6	0.7	1.3	1.5	1.0	1.2	4.1	4.5	5.3	4.5	2.6	12.7	33.5	27.2	5.7	83.0	56.3	48.8	51.2
11958	PECONIC	92.5	90.6	1.6	1.8	1.0	1.2	4.9	6.3	4.6	5.1	6.1	5.7	4.2	21.7	33.6	16.9	2.2	81.0	46.4	51.0	49.0
11961	RIDGE	92.5	91.4	3.8	4.2	0.9	1.1	3.8	4.7	5.7	6.2	6.7	5.6	4.1	23.1	21.2	22.4	5.1	77.8	44.1	45.5	54.5
11963	SAG HARBOR	90.4	89.2	5.4	5.8	1.0	1.2	4.9	6.2	4.7	5.3	5.8	4.6	3.2	22.4	32.7	18.6	2.6	81.3	47.2	48.7	51.3
11964	SHELTER ISLAND	95.0	93.7	1.0	1.2	0.6	0.7	3.2	4.2	4.9	5.6	6.6	4.5	3.1	22.7	31.5	17.9	3.3	80.2	46.7	48.9	51.1
11965	SHELTER ISLAND HEIGH	97.8	97.3	0.4	0.5	0.4	0.6	1.4	1.8	3.3	3.9	5.0	3.0	3.0	13.0	36.1	27.6	5.2	86.2	55.6	47.6	52.5
11967	SHIRLEY	89.6	87.4	3.6	4.2	1.3	1.6	10.9	13.7	7.6	8.0	9.2	7.4	6.6	31.1	23.4	6.1	0.7	70.6	32.7	49.6	50.4
11968	SOUTHAMPTON	83.6	81.7	6.7	7.5	1.2	1.4	9.2	11.3	5.4	5.5	5.4	7.1	6.4	25.0	27.7	15.0	2.5	80.5	42.1	48.5	51.5
11971	SOUTHOLD	96.6	95.7	0.9	1.1	0.2	0.3	2.6	3.3	5.1	5.5	6.0	5.3	3.6	20.8	27.7	21.9	4.3	80.0	47.5	47.9	52.1
11976	WATER MILL	95.2	94.3	2.7	3.2	0.8	1.1	3.2	4.2	4.4	5.4	6.3	4.9	3.5	20.9	35.0	17.8	1.8	80.7	47.5	50.0	50.0
11977	WESTHAMPTON	95.2	94.2	1.9	2.1	1.0	1.3	3.6	4.5	6.5	6.9	7.0	6.1	5.0	26.2	28.3	11.7	2.4	75.7	40.7	49.5	50.5
11978	WESTHAMPTON BEACH	84.5	81.4	6.9	8.1	1.3	1.7	10.1	12.6	5.1	5.2	6.4	6.9	5.5	26.2	25.8	15.3	3.6	78.7	41.7	49.9	50.1
11980	YAPHANK	88.0	85.7	8.2	9.6	1.4	1.8	8.4	10.5	6.0	6.5	6.4	5.9	5.3	31.5	27.7	9.1	1.5	77.6	38.4	51.8	48.3
12007	ALCOVE	98.5	98.6	0.5	0.5	0.0	0.5	1.0	1.4	5.7	6.1	7.6	8.5	6.1	25.9	29.7	9.4	0.9	75.0	39.3	51.9	48.1
12008	ALPLAUS	97.3	96.6	0.2	0.2	2.0	2.5	1.1	1.6	5.5	6.4	7.7	6.6	3.9	24.8	27.1	15.9	2.3	75.2	42.1	50.0	50.0
12009	ALTAMONT	95.5	94.2	1.6	2.0	1.2	1.6	1.3	1.7	5.6	6.2	8.1	7.3	5.3	26.6	28.2	10.6	2.1	74.9	40.1	48.4	51.6
12010	AMSTERDAM	92.8	92.4	1.7	1.8	0.6	0.6	10.9	11.4	6.1	5.9	6.8	6.4	5.9	24.6	24.8	15.7	3.8	77.1	41.1	47.1	52.9
12015	ATHENS	90.5	89.0	5.3	5.9	0.8	1.0	3.5	4.2	5.4	5.5	6.2	6.1	6.6	26.5	28.1	13.8	1.8	79.3	41.3	51.1	48.9
12017	AUSTERLITZ	98.1	97.5	0.3	0.6	0.3	0.6	0.6	0.9	4.7	5.3	6.2	5.0	4.1	20.9	35.5	16.8	1.6	80.4	47.2	52.0	48.0
12018	AVERILL PARK	98.0	97.5	0.3	0.4	0.4	0.6	0.9	1.1	5.6	6.3	7.6	7.4	5.3	27.0	30.1	9.7	1.0	75.7	40.2	49.5	50.5
12019	BALLSTON LAKE	96.8	96.2	0.7	0.8	1.3	1.6	0.9	1.0	5.7	6.5	7.6	6.8	4.8	26.0	30.1	11.4	1.2	75.6	40.7	50.2	49.9
12020	BALLSTON SPA	96.6	96.0	1.0	1.1	0.6	0.8	1.7	2.1	7.8	7.7	7.4	6.2	5.7	31.3	24.2	8.3	1.4	73.0	36.2	49.2	50.8
12022	BERLIN	97.8	97.4	0.0	0.0	0.1	0.1	1.0	1.4	6.3	6.7	7.4	7.6	5.4	23.9	28.6	12.2	2.0	75.3	40.9	49.8	50.3
12023	BERNE	97.5	96.8	0.7	0.8	0.6	0.7	0.9	1.1	5.7	6.2	6.9	6.6	5.5	26.3	31.1	10.7	1.1	77.3	41.0	49.3	50.7
12024	BRAINARD	96.6	96.2	1.1	1.1	1.1	1.1	1.1	1.1	4.4	5.0	6.6	6.6	3.9	22.0	35.2	14.8	1.7	79.7	45.8	49.5	50.6
12025	BROADALBIN	98.3	98.0	0.5	0.6	0.2	0.3	1.0	1.3	5.7	6.5	8.2	6.7	5.4	27.1	26.8	12.3	1.4	75.1	39.7	49.9	50.2
12027	BURNT HILLS	98.8	98.6	0.2	0.2	0.4	0.5	0.6	0.7	5.6	6.5	7.6	7.3	5.0	22.8	30.5	12.8	1.8	75.5	42.0	49.6	50.4
12028	BUSKIRK	97.7	97.3	0.7	0.8	0.2	0.3	0.9	1.2	6.7	7.0	7.5	7.3	6.1	26.2	26.6	10.8	1.8	73.9	38.3	49.4	50.6
12029	CANAAN	86.3	84.1	9.8	11.3	0.8	1.0	2.6	3.1	3.9	4.8	9.4	20.0	2.9	17.9	28.4	11.3	1.4	63.9	37.6	59.7	40.3
12031	CARLISLE	98.2	98.7	0.0	0.0	0.0	0.0	1.9	2.7	8.0	8.0	8.0	6.7	4.0	29.3	25.3	9.3	1.3	69.3	37.9	52.0	48.0
	NEW YORK	68.0	65.9	15.9	16.2	5.6	6.4	15.1	16.7	6.5	6.5	7.1	7.0	7.1	28.9	24.0	11.2	1.8	75.8	36.7	48.3	51.7
	UNITED STATES	75.1	73.6	12.3	12.5	3.8	4.2	12.5	14.1	6.9	6.7	7.2	7.0	7.3	28.6	23.8	10.8	1.7	75.1	36.0	49.1	50.9

#	ZIP CODE / POST OFFICE NAME	2004 Per Capita Income	2004 HH Income Base	2004 HOUSEHOLD INCOME DISTRIBUTION (%) Less than $25,000	$25,000 to $49,999	$50,000 to $99,999	$100,000 to $149,999	$150,000 or More	MEDIAN HOUSEHOLD INCOME 2004	2009	2004 National Centile	2004 State Centile	2004 Home Value Base	2004 HOME VALUE DISTRIBUTION (%) Less than $50,000	$50,000 to $89,999	$90,000 to $174,999	$175,000 to $399,999	$400,000 or More	2004 Median Home Value
11746	HUNTINGTON STATION	38143	21030	9.8	15.7	31.5	20.8	22.3	86479	102188	97	93	17340	0.3	0.1	2.0	49.4	48.1	391606
11747	MELVILLE	50164	5795	8.2	12.2	26.9	22.0	30.8	104174	123705	98	97	5059	0.6	0.1	1.1	30.4	67.8	501148
11749	ISLANDIA	26617	1370	13.6	22.6	41.9	13.7	8.3	64057	75401	88	79	796	0.0	0.5	6.9	89.1	3.5	253390
11751	ISLIP	30684	5249	11.3	16.6	38.8	21.6	11.7	75639	87007	93	88	3916	1.2	0.3	4.4	74.6	19.5	281954
11752	ISLIP TERRACE	26813	2907	6.9	18.9	44.5	19.9	9.7	74892	85508	93	87	2558	0.2	0.2	3.3	92.4	4.0	273409
11753	JERICHO	57040	3967	6.9	9.6	21.7	23.0	38.8	120617	145031	99	98	3525	0.1	0.7	0.0	10.6	88.6	633923
11754	KINGS PARK	33336	6497	13.4	15.1	34.4	22.5	14.5	79603	92702	95	90	5253	0.1	0.1	2.2	65.4	32.3	350267
11755	LAKE GROVE	31250	3827	8.9	17.1	38.7	21.1	14.4	77597	90949	94	89	3088	0.0	0.0	4.1	76.8	19.1	294891
11756	LEVITTOWN	28569	13794	8.0	15.9	43.2	23.0	9.9	77513	91163	94	89	12197	0.1	0.0	1.6	92.3	5.9	291983
11757	LINDENHURST	26767	15366	12.8	19.5	40.7	18.8	8.2	68682	80257	91	83	12346	0.2	0.1	5.0	90.3	4.5	262989
11758	MASSAPEQUA	34793	18132	9.9	13.5	34.3	24.3	18.1	86680	105207	97	93	16184	0.3	0.0	0.7	56.7	42.2	378978
11762	MASSAPEQUA PARK	34880	7835	6.6	14.3	34.9	27.0	17.2	90098	108703	97	94	7536	0.1	0.0	0.4	63.5	35.9	369024
11763	MEDFORD	25421	8133	9.3	16.6	44.6	21.6	7.9	75263	86033	93	87	7124	0.2	0.1	14.7	80.8	4.2	229607
11764	MILLER PLACE	31711	3936	6.9	11.8	40.2	27.6	13.5	86763	102944	97	93	3507	0.2	1.1	2.6	71.8	24.3	307736
11765	MILL NECK	110933	159	10.7	8.2	17.0	15.1	49.1	145743	175091	100	99	133	0.0	0.0	0.0	8.3	91.7	1000001
11766	MOUNT SINAI	34435	3152	5.9	12.1	36.9	25.0	20.1	92339	107636	97	95	2855	0.1	0.1	2.0	63.3	34.5	349485
11767	NESCONSET	34451	4656	7.0	12.0	34.2	27.0	19.8	94060	110308	98	95	3933	0.0	0.1	2.4	63.0	34.5	359756
11768	NORTHPORT	50264	8048	7.6	11.9	28.7	22.2	29.7	102850	122160	98	96	6956	0.1	0.1	0.4	26.6	72.8	524374
11769	OAKDALE	36250	3682	16.6	13.9	34.3	17.8	17.4	76287	89004	94	88	3017	0.0	0.5	9.6	63.1	26.8	331053
11770	OCEAN BEACH	54392	84	13.1	21.4	27.4	17.9	20.2	72771	88803	92	86	67	0.0	0.0	0.0	28.4	71.6	485294
11771	OYSTER BAY	67894	4317	12.6	12.8	30.4	14.4	29.8	86132	105224	96	92	3103	0.0	0.8	5.2	17.2	76.8	649178
11772	PATCHOGUE	27019	15771	17.6	20.5	37.9	16.3	7.7	63373	74961	87	79	10505	0.4	1.4	13.6	78.8	5.8	235375
11776	PORT JEFFERSON STATI	27780	8129	11.4	18.1	40.7	20.2	9.5	72096	84059	92	85	6520	0.2	0.9	7.3	85.6	6.1	258830
11777	PORT JEFFERSON	44268	3552	11.9	16.2	31.7	17.2	23.1	79313	95468	95	90	2627	0.0	0.0	0.9	48.6	50.6	403033
11778	ROCKY POINT	26903	4465	14.6	21.8	39.9	16.6	7.1	64861	76466	88	80	3529	0.3	0.5	17.0	75.9	6.3	228365
11779	RONKONKOMA	27603	13599	14.4	16.4	41.6	18.8	8.8	70880	81993	92	85	10484	0.1	0.2	7.8	87.5	4.5	259797
11780	SAINT JAMES	43879	5392	11.1	14.4	30.9	20.6	23.0	87267	102807	97	93	4867	0.0	0.0	1.2	51.1	47.6	391400
11782	SAYVILLE	34461	5324	11.9	15.3	32.2	23.5	17.1	83778	99611	96	92	4562	0.3	0.3	2.8	69.7	26.9	327491
11783	SEAFORD	34733	7295	9.9	13.6	35.5	24.8	16.2	86173	104175	96	93	6584	0.1	0.0	1.4	61.2	37.4	370186
11784	SELDEN	23982	7780	11.7	20.5	42.5	19.1	6.1	66206	78028	89	81	6301	0.3	0.3	10.1	87.9	1.5	235294
11786	SHOREHAM	31540	2031	10.3	11.6	35.9	23.2	19.0	87789	103963	97	93	1905	0.1	0.6	7.2	64.6	27.5	320019
11787	SMITHTOWN	37817	11830	9.0	12.6	33.2	24.6	20.6	90880	107184	97	94	10345	0.0	0.2	1.1	50.9	47.8	393160
11788	HAUPPAUGE	37204	5956	7.2	13.8	36.6	24.6	17.8	86919	103557	97	93	4900	0.1	0.4	2.2	51.6	45.6	387209
11789	SOUND BEACH	24718	2593	14.9	20.8	43.2	16.5	4.7	62939	75032	87	78	2041	0.4	0.0	12.1	84.3	3.2	232156
11790	STONY BROOK	35532	4827	8.1	11.9	30.6	24.9	24.5	98721	115749	98	96	4419	0.3	0.0	1.5	58.6	39.7	372757
11791	SYOSSET	57025	8110	7.1	9.1	26.5	22.4	34.9	112323	135452	99	98	7560	0.5	0.3	0.2	17.0	82.0	567037
11792	WADING RIVER	31338	2918	13.2	16.4	36.2	20.5	13.7	76210	88689	94	88	2641	3.1	1.0	7.3	60.5	28.2	305656
11793	WANTAGH	36904	11097	8.8	12.2	35.9	25.4	17.7	88289	106556	97	93	10118	0.3	0.0	1.0	63.5	35.3	366622
11794	STONY BROOK	14051	24	8.3	12.5	29.2	29.2	20.8	100000	103392	98	96	23	0.0	0.0	0.0	73.9	26.1	350000
11795	WEST ISLIP	33991	8403	6.8	12.9	40.7	22.3	17.3	85132	100097	96	92	7824	0.1	0.0	1.7	70.1	28.1	332664
11796	WEST SAYVILLE	29377	1495	11.9	16.4	39.9	21.3	10.6	75221	86655	93	87	1187	0.0	0.2	4.9	80.4	14.6	281233
11797	WOODBURY	74595	2898	6.9	5.8	20.0	19.3	48.0	143524	170742	100	99	2334	0.0	0.2	0.0	8.6	91.3	804740
11798	WYANDANCH	19168	4049	18.7	25.7	31.1	14.0	10.5	59178	66509	84	74	2662	0.3	1.0	21.6	69.5	7.6	242193
11801	HICKSVILLE	30946	13130	11.1	16.2	38.6	21.1	13.0	77124	91608	94	89	11141	0.4	0.1	0.8	79.3	19.4	330579
11803	PLAINVIEW	42989	9393	8.4	11.0	28.0	26.8	25.8	103320	125200	98	97	8756	0.2	0.2	0.2	32.1	67.4	461116
11804	OLD BETHPAGE	44710	1712	11.7	8.1	27.5	25.3	27.5	103996	126659	98	97	1540	0.3	0.4	0.3	26.7	72.3	476786
11901	RIVERHEAD	24522	9168	25.5	28.8	29.9	10.7	5.1	45420	53810	62	51	6488	6.6	4.7	20.1	58.5	10.1	217401
11933	CALVERTON	31762	2956	21.1	25.2	29.8	17.5	6.4	54966	66521	80	70	2386	9.9	8.5	11.3	56.3	14.0	235214
11934	CENTER MORICHES	26050	2576	11.9	18.5	46.4	17.0	6.2	67918	79191	90	83	2067	0.0	0.2	10.0	76.9	12.9	255141
11935	CUTCHOGUE	39512	1680	17.9	16.6	35.0	14.6	16.0	69428	81081	91	84	1443	0.0	0.4	1.8	52.4	45.5	381178
11937	EAST HAMPTON	39596	6599	17.9	21.8	29.8	15.4	15.0	64455	77048	88	80	5182	0.7	1.3	3.0	36.2	58.7	459371
11939	EAST MARION	28363	333	21.3	27.9	36.9	10.2	3.6	50895	60344	74	64	276	0.0	0.0	2.5	71.0	26.5	316667
11940	EAST MORICHES	29930	1623	13.3	16.0	38.6	20.5	11.8	72899	84683	92	86	1417	0.9	0.4	5.7	76.3	16.7	279249
11941	EASTPORT	37421	1560	14.8	17.8	34.0	18.8	14.7	69352	83150	91	84	1306	1.3	0.1	6.6	55.3	36.8	325431
11942	EAST QUOGUE	38128	2118	15.3	18.0	37.0	18.6	11.1	69743	83230	91	84	1781	3.1	0.6	3.0	49.4	43.9	369693
11944	GREENPORT	26226	1578	29.0	26.9	30.2	8.4	5.6	40754	50507	49	37	1054	0.8	0.2	13.5	64.8	20.8	265610
11946	HAMPTON BAYS	31795	5343	19.0	22.9	35.0	15.2	8.0	57537	67805	82	72	3984	0.8	0.7	6.1	73.7	18.8	283004
11948	LAUREL	35429	327	17.1	19.3	36.1	18.4	9.2	66071	79059	89	81	283	0.0	0.4	3.2	62.2	34.3	331538
11949	MANORVILLE	32500	4957	12.6	18.3	40.2	20.8	8.2	73341	84993	93	86	3917	0.3	0.9	10.4	67.0	21.4	289637
11950	MASTIC	21082	4461	14.8	23.3	42.1	15.7	4.1	60999	71337	85	76	3637	1.8	0.5	43.3	53.8	0.6	180360
11951	MASTIC BEACH	20047	4334	19.0	27.2	38.5	12.1	3.1	54071	63232	78	69	3232	0.2	0.7	59.6	38.4	1.2	162177
11952	MATTITUCK	29637	1849	18.6	20.3	34.4	18.3	8.3	63880	76173	88	79	1584	0.0	0.3	1.6	68.3	29.7	324471
11953	MIDDLE ISLAND	26749	4939	14.8	26.2	38.3	14.7	6.0	59426	67459	84	74	3366	1.1	4.9	22.6	69.1	2.3	221875
11954	MONTAUK	29149	1719	24.2	25.0	29.8	13.0	8.1	51034	62144	74	64	1115	0.4	0.9	1.4	37.1	60.3	453256
11955	MORICHES	40233	1399	15.8	15.9	38.3	22.4	7.6	74480	86741	93	87	771	0.0	0.0	3.6	76.8	19.6	299390
11957	ORIENT	36765	344	19.8	26.7	32.0	9.6	11.9	53102	65791	77	67	296	0.0	0.0	2.0	43.9	54.1	429268
11958	PECONIC	27203	264	16.3	27.7	36.7	13.3	6.1	54640	65227	79	70	214	0.0	0.0	0.5	55.1	44.4	373913
11961	RIDGE	29589	5444	24.4	22.7	32.5	13.3	7.2	53338	65623	77	68	4651	0.6	1.3	22.5	68.3	7.4	226796
11963	SAG HARBOR	43723	3988	14.7	22.6	33.6	14.9	14.1	65820	78617	89	81	3215	0.1	0.3	1.8	33.8	64.0	511571
11964	SHELTER ISLAND	29485	540	18.5	31.3	30.4	12.2	7.6	50201	59623	72	63	439	0.0	0.0	1.8	47.6	50.6	403086
11965	SHELTER ISLAND HEIGH	44508	514	15.2	18.7	31.9	17.9	16.3	74681	89587	93	87	451	0.0	0.0	2.2	29.7	68.1	493678
11967	SHIRLEY	22549	7499	12.2	22.1	42.8	17.3	5.7	65395	77168	89	81	6248	0.2	0.2	32.3	64.9	2.4	196704
11968	SOUTHAMPTON	40145	4982	17.4	23.6	28.8	15.3	14.9	63007	76038	87	78	3892	1.3	0.1	2.8	34.3	61.5	484688
11971	SOUTHOLD	34874	2582	20.5	25.5	26.8	19.2	8.0	58502	72285	83	73	2129	0.0	0.0	1.7	61.7	36.6	350608
11976	WATER MILL	64382	1167	12.3	13.6	29.7	17.5	26.9	88897	105896	97	94	1049	0.0	0.1	1.8	12.6	85.5	808654
11977	WESTHAMPTON	43988	972	14.2	19.3	25.1	23.5	17.9	81141	99729	95	91	747	0.4	0.5	7.2	32.3	59.6	452574
11978	WESTHAMPTON BEACH	38089	1520	20.3	19.9	30.3	14.9	14.6	64003	77349	88	79	1046	2.4	0.6	4.3	40.0	52.8	420567
11980	YAPHANK	28411	1432	9.0	14.0	44.0	24.7	8.2	77858	90559	94	89	1233	0.0	0.0	15.4	81.9	2.7	221391
12007	ALCOVE	29035	74	6.8	24.3	51.4	12.2	5.4	66271	80274	89	82	65	0.0	7.7	46.2	44.6	1.5	164583
12008	ALPLAUS	31376	179	8.9	17.3	50.3	19.6	3.9	68996	80334	91	84	164	0.0	6.1	51.8	42.1	0.0	167073
12009	ALTAMONT	30498	2808	14.4	23.4	37.6	15.6	8.9	64233	76064	88	79	2102	2.8	1.4	40.3	50.6	5.0	182294
12010	AMSTERDAM	19500	12406	36.3	30.1	25.9	5.7	2.0	34828	38794	27	12	7835	10.5	28.6	45.3	14.6	1.0	105127
12015	ATHENS	26181	1400	25.1	31.6	29.8	8.4	5.1	45181	51040	62	51	1085	6.4	6.5	52.4	31.2	3.4	143820
12017	AUSTERLITZ	38237	130	16.9	26.9	33.9	9.2	13.1	54818	63965	79	70	110	1.8	2.7	24.6	47.3	23.6	235294
12018	AVERILL PARK	28099	2960	14.6	25.1	39.8	13.2	7.3	61774	68692	86	76	2520	4.2	4.5	46.2	42.2	3.0	166103
12019	BALLSTON LAKE	32669	5379	9.4	21.6	40.7	18.7	9.6	70965	81309	92	85	4233	1.4	1.3	32.1	62.3	3.0	190980
12020	BALLSTON SPA	26133	11230	16.2	26.9	39.1	13.7	4.2	56429	64440	81	71	8673	7.1	5.4	51.9	33.7	1.9	151904
12022	BERLIN	20095	313	24.9	35.1	32.3	6.1	1.6	42553	48827	55	43	255	7.8	14.5	59.6	14.9	3.1	116211
12023	BERNE	24709	721	16.4	31.2	39.1	8.7	4.6	52227	60649	76	66	626	4.8	6.4	54.6	32.8	1.4	146087
12024	BRAINARD	33958	75	14.7	22.7	37.3	16.0	9.3	61799	72277	86	77	64	0.0	4.7	29.7	50.0	15.6	216667
12025	BROADALBIN	21468	2212	22.8	34.3	33.5	6.2	3.2	44859	50412	61	50	1828	8.2	16.5	48.8	24.6	1.9	130898
12027	BURNT HILLS	28838	1336	12.1	22.5	40.4	20.4	4.6	67693	77555	90	83	1146	1.2	1.0	51.2	44.2	2.4	170815
12028	BUSKIRK	22282	670	21.3	29.6	37.3	7.6	4.2	49355	55394	71	61	549	8.0	10.0	50.3	29.7	2.0	142006
12029	CANAAN	34746	450	16.7	24.0	32.0	15.6	11.8	60737	71984	85	75	376	1.6	1.3	25.0	52.1	20.0	237879
12031	CARLISLE	16233	25	20.0	36.0	40.0	4.0	0.0	43618	52915	58	46	21	4.8	14.3	57.1	23.8	0.0	122500
	NEW YORK	28049		26.3	24.3	29.3	11.5	8.6	49309	58077				4.6	8.6	27.2	39.9	19.8	219050
	UNITED STATES	25866		24.7	27.1	30.8	10.9	6.5	48124	56710				10.9	15.0	33.7	30.1	10.4	145905

SPENDING POTENTIAL INDICES

NEW YORK

11746-12031 D

ZIP CODE #	POST OFFICE NAME	FINANCIAL SERVICES: Auto Loan	FINANCIAL SERVICES: Home Loan	FINANCIAL SERVICES: Investments	FINANCIAL SERVICES: Retirement Plans	THE HOME: Home Improvements: Home Repair	THE HOME: Home Improvements: Lawn & Garden	THE HOME: Furnishings: Computers & Hardware	THE HOME: Furnishings: Major Appliances	THE HOME: Furnishings: TV, Radio, Sound Equipment	THE HOME: Furnishings: Furniture	ENTERTAINMENT: Dine out/ Carry out	ENTERTAINMENT: Sports Equipment	ENTERTAINMENT: Fees & Tickets	ENTERTAINMENT: Toys & Games	ENTERTAINMENT: Travel	ENTERTAINMENT: Cable TV	PERSONAL: Apparel & Services	PERSONAL: Auto Repairs	PERSONAL: Health Insurance	PERSONAL: Pets & Supplies
11746	HUNTINGTON STATION	143	187	240	179	180	189	168	165	160	170	202	188	183	218	175	161	205	162	151	178
11747	MELVILLE	183	239	287	233	232	240	211	210	197	214	248	239	230	263	220	196	250	203	190	226
11749	ISLANDIA	95	108	141	109	105	108	107	103	105	107	133	122	111	142	108	104	133	104	95	114
11751	ISLIP	117	138	152	138	136	138	129	128	122	129	154	149	135	160	131	119	152	126	117	140
11752	ISLIP TERRACE	111	135	149	132	132	135	125	124	120	124	150	143	133	160	128	118	150	121	115	135
11753	JERICHO	200	262	336	257	254	268	233	230	218	237	276	262	257	291	244	218	279	223	210	249
11754	KINGS PARK	120	150	178	149	146	150	138	135	131	138	164	157	148	174	142	129	164	133	124	147
11755	LAKE GROVE	120	145	169	144	141	144	135	133	128	136	161	155	142	168	137	125	160	131	120	145
11756	LEVITTOWN	106	145	177	137	140	144	128	126	121	128	151	144	140	166	134	121	153	122	115	135
11757	LINDENHURST	103	125	137	122	122	125	116	114	111	115	139	132	123	148	118	109	139	112	106	125
11758	MASSAPEQUA	126	167	206	159	163	171	150	149	143	150	179	169	163	193	158	144	180	144	138	159
11762	MASSAPEQUA PARK	124	174	222	163	168	176	152	151	144	152	180	170	168	198	161	146	182	145	138	160
11763	MEDFORD	108	130	138	129	127	127	118	118	111	118	140	137	125	147	120	108	139	115	107	130
11764	MILLER PLACE	130	157	167	158	154	153	142	141	132	143	166	165	150	174	144	128	166	137	127	155
11765	MILL NECK	391	526	722	516	513	554	459	455	427	469	540	511	521	569	489	431	549	437	422	494
11766	MOUNT SINAI	148	179	195	182	175	178	162	160	150	163	190	185	173	197	165	146	190	155	145	176
11767	NESCONSET	130	178	216	172	172	175	155	153	144	156	181	176	171	198	162	143	184	147	136	165
11768	NORTHPORT	167	227	288	219	220	229	199	197	186	201	234	224	220	253	210	187	238	190	179	212
11769	OAKDALE	120	147	167	142	145	152	135	135	130	135	163	153	145	172	141	131	162	132	130	147
11770	OCEAN BEACH	204	160	109	144	180	202	151	182	171	149	202	213	135	200	161	182	188	179	215	248
11771	OYSTER BAY	215	271	352	268	264	279	251	246	238	252	300	283	271	314	260	236	300	242	227	266
11772	PATCHOGUE	96	111	131	110	108	113	107	105	103	107	130	121	111	136	108	102	130	104	98	114
11776	PORT JEFFERSON STATI	108	128	143	128	125	127	120	118	114	120	143	137	126	150	121	111	142	116	108	129
11777	PORT JEFFERSON	140	180	229	177	175	183	165	162	156	165	196	188	178	208	171	155	197	159	148	175
11778	ROCKY POINT	105	120	124	122	117	115	112	111	105	113	132	131	115	135	111	100	131	110	98	122
11779	RONKONKOMA	107	126	139	126	123	125	118	116	111	117	140	136	123	146	119	108	139	114	106	128
11780	SAINT JAMES	158	200	239	192	196	207	177	180	169	180	212	200	192	220	186	170	211	173	171	195
11782	SAYVILLE	122	163	198	157	158	162	145	144	137	145	171	165	158	187	152	136	173	139	130	155
11783	SEAFORD	123	170	211	161	164	171	149	148	141	149	176	168	163	193	157	142	178	143	135	158
11784	SELDEN	100	118	127	117	115	117	110	109	104	110	131	127	116	138	112	102	131	107	100	119
11786	SHOREHAM	129	158	181	152	156	165	140	144	135	143	169	159	151	173	148	136	167	139	139	157
11787	SMITHTOWN	136	179	216	173	174	181	159	158	150	160	188	180	173	201	167	150	189	153	145	170
11788	HAUPPAUGE	126	167	219	161	162	170	151	148	144	152	180	169	165	195	159	144	182	145	136	159
11789	SOUND BEACH	97	108	108	110	104	103	102	101	96	103	121	120	103	122	100	90	119	101	89	111
11790	STONY BROOK	137	199	261	187	191	199	172	169	161	173	201	192	191	224	183	162	206	163	151	180
11791	SYOSSET	198	283	374	267	273	287	244	242	229	246	287	273	273	316	261	232	293	233	219	257
11792	WADING RIVER	115	138	150	138	134	136	127	126	120	128	152	147	134	158	129	117	151	123	115	138
11793	WANTAGH	125	181	233	168	174	181	156	155	147	157	184	175	173	205	166	149	187	149	140	164
11794	STONY BROOK	119	177	239	165	170	176	153	151	143	153	178	173	170	201	163	144	183	146	133	159
11795	WEST ISLIP	136	174	201	170	171	174	156	155	146	156	184	179	168	197	162	145	185	150	142	169
11796	WEST SAYVILLE	107	130	151	129	127	130	122	120	115	121	145	140	128	153	124	113	145	118	110	130
11797	WOODBURY	280	378	518	370	368	397	329	326	307	337	388	367	374	408	351	309	394	313	303	354
11798	WYANDANCH	97	106	131	100	102	112	104	102	107	106	134	115	110	139	106	109	133	103	100	113
11801	HICKSVILLE	110	148	185	138	142	150	131	130	126	132	158	147	144	173	139	128	160	127	121	139
11803	PLAINVIEW	152	210	267	199	203	214	183	182	173	184	216	206	202	237	194	175	220	176	167	195
11804	OLD BETHPAGE	162	201	238	198	199	210	182	182	171	183	216	205	196	221	190	171	215	177	173	198
11901	RIVERHEAD	92	85	79	81	88	99	85	90	89	84	109	100	83	105	86	92	103	89	98	105
11933	CALVERTON	129	119	102	114	122	132	113	124	116	116	143	140	109	136	115	118	137	122	129	147
11934	CENTER MORICHES	97	117	126	115	114	115	108	107	102	107	128	124	114	135	110	100	128	104	98	117
11935	CUTCHOGUE	161	132	102	123	146	167	125	147	138	128	166	162	117	153	133	147	154	144	174	189
11937	EAST HAMPTON	165	129	88	117	146	164	122	147	138	121	164	172	109	162	130	148	152	145	174	201
11939	EAST MARION	110	86	59	78	97	109	81	98	92	80	109	115	73	108	87	98	101	96	116	134
11940	EAST MORICHES	114	137	148	137	135	137	125	125	117	125	147	144	132	152	128	114	146	121	114	137
11941	EASTPORT	154	138	112	134	146	155	130	145	136	131	165	170	123	164	133	138	157	142	153	182
11942	EAST QUOGUE	137	141	136	135	146	155	130	139	132	130	162	161	131	166	136	134	157	136	144	167
11944	GREENPORT	99	79	62	74	86	98	82	91	91	80	109	105	75	106	84	95	102	91	105	115
11946	HAMPTON BAYS	113	113	114	109	116	126	109	114	112	108	137	132	109	140	113	114	133	113	119	134
11948	LAUREL	120	123	140	128	125	131	126	126	122	125	152	147	125	149	125	118	148	127	121	139
11949	MANORVILLE	117	135	146	136	132	135	126	125	120	127	151	144	132	155	127	117	149	123	116	137
11950	MASTIC	102	113	114	114	109	108	107	106	100	108	127	125	108	128	105	95	125	105	94	116
11951	MASTIC BEACH	83	92	99	93	90	91	91	88	86	90	109	105	92	112	90	83	107	89	81	96
11952	MATTITUCK	109	109	105	104	113	122	102	110	105	102	128	126	102	130	107	107	124	108	115	131
11953	MIDDLE ISLAND	96	100	105	101	100	105	98	99	96	100	120	113	99	117	98	94	117	99	96	110
11954	MONTAUK	120	94	64	85	106	119	89	107	100	88	119	125	79	117	95	107	111	105	126	146
11955	MORICHES	124	110	117	114	112	126	115	119	117	120	148	130	113	130	115	116	141	121	123	134
11957	ORIENT	132	105	73	95	118	132	99	119	111	98	132	139	89	131	105	119	123	117	139	161
11958	PECONIC	114	89	61	80	100	113	84	101	95	83	113	118	75	111	90	102	105	100	120	138
11961	RIDGE	99	100	100	96	102	114	94	102	96	98	119	107	95	110	98	98	113	99	109	112
11963	SAG HARBOR	164	131	95	119	147	166	124	148	138	124	165	169	113	159	132	148	154	145	174	197
11964	SHELTER ISLAND	116	91	62	82	103	115	86	103	97	85	115	121	77	114	92	104	107	102	122	142
11965	SHELTER ISLAND HEIGH	162	127	86	114	143	160	119	144	135	118	160	169	107	158	127	144	149	142	170	197
11967	SHIRLEY	103	117	121	118	114	114	110	109	104	111	131	129	113	134	110	99	129	108	98	120
11968	SOUTHAMPTON	154	138	121	129	148	163	131	147	141	130	170	170	126	170	138	147	162	145	163	187
11971	SOUTHOLD	122	117	112	110	123	140	109	121	114	112	141	130	109	132	116	120	133	118	135	143
11976	WATER MILL	237	221	190	212	234	252	202	225	210	203	256	261	198	257	212	217	246	219	242	285
11977	WESTHAMPTON	160	165	157	160	170	176	153	162	153	152	188	191	153	194	158	154	183	159	163	194
11978	WESTHAMPTON BEACH	159	130	99	120	144	160	126	146	138	124	165	171	115	164	132	145	155	144	167	193
11980	YAPHANK	111	137	147	137	135	134	123	123	115	123	144	143	131	154	126	112	144	119	111	135
12007	ALCOVE	105	128	141	125	125	128	119	117	113	118	142	135	126	152	122	112	142	114	109	128
12008	ALPLAUS	97	113	125	108	112	122	107	107	107	106	133	120	114	138	112	109	130	105	109	117
12009	ALTAMONT	101	120	139	121	118	120	113	111	107	113	135	131	119	140	115	104	134	110	102	122
12010	AMSTERDAM	65	60	58	57	61	69	62	64	66	60	80	73	61	81	63	68	77	64	69	74
12015	ATHENS	85	89	90	84	90	99	85	88	88	84	108	99	88	113	88	90	105	86	92	100
12017	AUSTERLITZ	151	130	105	121	142	157	122	141	133	122	159	164	115	158	129	139	150	138	159	184
12018	AVERILL PARK	97	117	124	117	115	115	107	106	100	106	126	124	112	133	108	97	125	103	96	117
12019	BALLSTON LAKE	113	130	144	132	128	131	123	122	116	123	147	141	128	149	124	113	145	120	112	134
12020	BALLSTON SPA	95	102	102	103	100	102	97	97	93	98	117	113	98	117	96	90	114	96	90	108
12022	BERLIN	70	72	71	69	73	82	72	72	75	69	92	81	74	98	73	77	89	71	78	81
12023	BERNE	94	93	83	89	96	101	86	92	88	86	108	109	86	111	89	89	104	90	95	113
12024	BRAINARD	108	126	137	124	125	131	117	118	112	117	141	134	123	144	121	112	139	115	113	129
12025	BROADALBIN	89	73	53	68	80	89	70	81	77	69	92	94	65	92	73	81	86	79	92	106
12027	BURNT HILLS	98	119	133	118	117	118	110	109	104	109	131	127	116	137	112	102	130	106	100	119
12028	BUSKIRK	102	84	58	80	90	98	80	92	86	81	104	108	74	102	82	88	98	90	100	118
12029	CANAAN	141	132	127	128	139	150	128	138	132	127	162	163	123	163	132	135	155	137	145	170
12031	CARLISLE	78	69	53	66	73	79	64	71	68	64	83	85	63	85	66	70	79	69	77	92
	NEW YORK	95	100	134	99	98	107	103	100	105	103	133	116	105	138	104	107	131	102	99	112
	UNITED STATES	100	100	100	100	100	100	100	100	100	100	100	100	100	100	100	100	100	100	100	100

# ZIP CODE POST OFFICE NAME	COUNTY FIPS CODE	POPULATION			2000-2004 ANNUAL RATE		HOUSEHOLDS					FAMILIES		
		2000	2004	2009	% Rate	State Centile	2000	2004	2009	% Annual Rate 2000-2004	2004 Average HH Size	2000	2004	% Annual Rate 2000-2004
12032 CAROGA LAKE	041	654	652	651	-0.1	24	295	299	303	0.3	2.18	195	196	0.1
12033 CASTLETON ON HUDSON	083	7855	8026	8196	0.5	58	2975	3077	3180	0.8	2.57	2200	2262	0.7
12035 CENTRAL BRIDGE	095	787	782	786	-0.2	20	286	289	295	0.3	2.71	211	212	0.1
12036 CHARLOTTEVILLE	095	142	145	147	0.5	57	58	60	62	0.8	2.42	39	41	1.2
12037 CHATHAM	021	4153	4302	4498	0.8	72	1744	1828	1937	1.1	2.34	1143	1190	1.0
12041 CLARKSVILLE	001	109	107	106	-0.4	8	37	37	37	0.0	2.89	27	27	0.0
12042 CLIMAX	039	291	304	325	1.0	78	109	115	125	1.3	2.64	82	86	1.1
12043 COBLESKILL	095	8047	8096	8171	0.1	37	2870	2934	3012	0.5	2.30	1754	1780	0.4
12046 COEYMANS HOLLOW	001	632	656	668	0.9	74	218	229	236	1.2	2.86	166	173	1.0
12047 COHOES	001	18175	18142	18170	0.0	26	7934	8020	8126	0.3	2.23	4577	4584	0.0
12051 COXSACKIE	039	6781	7012	7358	0.8	70	1589	1693	1843	1.5	2.63	1003	1059	1.3
12052 CROPSEYVILLE	083	1402	1441	1464	0.7	64	532	555	572	1.0	2.60	394	408	0.8
12053 DELANSON	093	4482	4625	4693	0.7	68	1615	1687	1730	1.0	2.74	1255	1304	0.9
12054 DELMAR	001	15867	16255	16544	0.6	61	6328	6543	6730	0.8	2.45	4430	4563	0.7
12056 DUANESBURG	093	2352	2455	2500	1.0	78	905	957	986	1.3	2.56	682	716	1.2
12057 EAGLE BRIDGE	115	2229	2245	2271	0.2	39	822	841	865	0.5	2.64	607	617	0.4
12058 EARLTON	039	1531	1594	1705	1.0	76	593	626	678	1.3	2.55	414	434	1.1
12059 EAST BERNE	001	1959	1950	1939	-0.1	22	735	743	749	0.3	2.62	550	552	0.1
12060 EAST CHATHAM	021	1456	1519	1593	1.0	77	594	648	668	1.3	2.29	391	411	1.2
12061 EAST GREENBUSH	083	8470	8613	8794	0.4	51	3193	3289	3400	0.7	2.53	2219	2268	0.5
12062 EAST NASSAU	083	1687	1682	1707	-0.1	24	642	650	669	0.3	2.59	469	471	0.1
12064 EAST WORCESTER	077	516	520	521	0.2	40	205	210	213	0.6	2.48	137	139	0.2
12065 CLIFTON PARK	091	38502	41085	43986	1.5	88	15524	16844	18317	1.9	2.42	10478	11247	1.7
12066 ESPERANCE	057	2124	2115	2125	-0.1	22	782	790	804	0.2	2.67	581	584	0.1
12067 FEURA BUSH	001	1801	1820	1824	0.3	43	670	689	700	0.7	2.63	484	494	0.5
12068 FONDA	057	3664	3577	3546	-0.6	5	1392	1376	1380	-0.3	2.58	1001	986	-0.4
12070 FORT JOHNSON	057	1675	1660	1653	-0.2	17	657	661	666	0.1	2.26	460	461	0.1
12071 FULTONHAM	095	229	226	227	-0.3	13	99	100	101	0.2	2.21	70	69	-0.3
12072 FULTONVILLE	057	2592	2551	2533	-0.4	10	949	946	951	-0.1	2.53	687	683	-0.1
12074 GALWAY	091	3107	3289	3520	1.4	86	1160	1250	1360	1.8	2.63	883	945	1.6
12075 GHENT	021	3249	3410	3589	1.1	81	1172	1247	1332	1.5	2.61	855	904	1.3
12076 GILBOA	095	1411	1399	1405	-0.2	18	587	591	603	0.2	2.34	420	420	0.2
12077 GLENMONT	001	5591	5774	5897	0.8	69	2047	2129	2198	0.9	2.64	1601	1659	0.8
12078 GLOVERSVILLE	035	23854	24066	24309	0.2	41	9807	10000	10215	0.5	2.32	6233	6314	0.3
12083 GREENVILLE	039	3611	3876	4150	1.7	90	1447	1577	1712	2.0	2.46	994	1074	1.8
12084 GUILDERLAND	001	4178	4336	4401	0.9	74	2085	2182	2237	1.1	1.93	1175	1216	0.8
12086 HAGAMAN	035	1188	1192	1204	0.1	33	468	475	485	0.4	2.50	335	340	0.4
12087 HANNACROIX	039	1452	1531	1641	1.3	84	543	581	632	1.6	2.60	404	430	1.5
12090 HOOSICK FALLS	083	5995	5993	6037	0.0	27	2355	2379	2423	0.2	2.49	1621	1623	0.0
12092 HOWES CAVE	095	1401	1403	1417	0.0	30	552	561	575	0.4	2.50	393	397	0.2
12093 JEFFERSON	095	1654	1753	1863	1.4	87	669	721	777	1.8	2.39	471	505	1.7
12094 JOHNSONVILLE	083	2008	2152	2242	1.6	89	689	748	789	2.0	2.88	527	568	1.8
12095 JOHNSTOWN	035	12837	12649	12634	-0.4	11	4842	4816	4865	-0.1	2.48	3137	3101	-0.3
12106 KINDERHOOK	021	2580	2667	2785	0.8	70	1052	1107	1174	1.2	2.41	735	769	1.1
12108 LAKE PLEASANT	041	528	517	507	-0.5	7	225	224	223	-0.1	2.24	148	147	-0.2
12110 LATHAM	001	18519	18466	18483	-0.1	24	7120	7195	7290	0.3	2.47	4936	4954	0.1
12115 MALDEN BRIDGE	021	83	88	94	1.4	87	41	44	47	1.7	2.00	29	31	1.6
12116 MARYLAND	077	1616	1634	1638	0.3	44	676	692	703	0.6	2.36	455	463	0.4
12117 MAYFIELD	035	3096	3110	3126	0.1	36	1209	1232	1255	0.4	2.51	860	877	0.3
12118 MECHANICVILLE	091	12252	12641	13277	0.7	68	5116	5342	5686	1.0	2.36	3330	3456	0.9
12120 MEDUSA	001	553	576	590	1.0	76	218	230	239	1.3	2.47	149	156	1.1
12121 MELROSE	083	1878	1897	1916	0.2	43	673	690	707	0.6	2.75	555	567	0.5
12122 MIDDLEBURGH	095	4060	4071	4101	0.1	32	1666	1695	1733	0.4	2.38	1103	1115	0.3
12123 NASSAU	083	5317	5471	5612	0.7	65	2085	2175	2261	1.0	2.52	1486	1537	0.8
12125 NEW LEBANON	021	1384	1490	1589	1.8	91	545	596	646	2.1	2.39	362	393	2.0
12130 NIVERVILLE	021	875	883	913	0.2	41	333	341	358	0.6	2.57	243	247	0.4
12131 NORTH BLENHEIM	095	80	79	80	-0.3	14	32	32	33	0.0	1.75	22	22	0.0
12134 NORTHVILLE	041	3745	3955	4123	1.3	85	1579	1696	1797	1.7	2.33	1091	1166	1.6
12136 OLD CHATHAM	021	903	946	995	1.1	81	378	401	427	1.4	2.35	256	270	1.3
12137 PATTERSONVILLE	093	1467	1520	1545	0.8	72	545	572	587	1.1	2.64	412	429	1.0
12138 PETERSBURG	083	3216	3248	3278	0.2	42	1213	1244	1272	0.6	2.61	879	894	0.4
12139 PISECO	041	221	222	220	0.1	36	94	95	96	0.3	2.34	66	66	0.0
12140 POESTENKILL	083	1202	1219	1231	0.3	49	461	474	484	0.7	2.55	341	348	0.5
12143 RAVENA	001	6159	6041	6009	-0.5	8	2392	2375	2390	-0.2	2.51	1639	1614	-0.4
12144 RENSSELAER	083	18320	18561	18840	0.3	48	7645	7853	8075	0.6	2.35	4870	4960	0.4
12147 RENSSELAERVILLE	001	495	481	476	-0.7	4	207	205	205	-0.2	2.30	139	136	-0.5
12148 REXFORD	091	3187	3644	4029	3.2	99	1232	1433	1610	3.6	2.54	938	1084	3.5
12149 RICHMONDVILLE	095	2400	2387	2401	-0.1	21	957	965	985	0.2	2.47	671	673	0.1
12150 ROTTERDAM JUNCTION	093	855	864	864	0.3	43	342	350	354	0.6	2.47	211	214	0.3
12151 ROUND LAKE	091	117	115	120	-0.4	9	50	50	53	0.0	2.30	42	42	0.0
12153 SAND LAKE	083	819	808	808	-0.3	13	320	321	326	0.1	2.52	236	235	-0.1
12154 SCHAGHTICOKE	083	2934	2941	2975	0.1	32	1073	1089	1116	0.4	2.70	832	839	0.2
12155 SCHENEVUS	077	2047	2125	2189	0.9	74	827	871	910	1.2	2.42	568	594	1.1
12156 SCHODACK LANDING	083	858	891	917	0.9	74	330	346	360	1.1	2.57	259	271	1.1
12157 SCHOHARIE	095	4309	4312	4346	0.0	30	1644	1666	1704	0.3	2.54	1157	1167	0.2
12158 SELKIRK	001	6344	6512	6625	0.6	63	2272	2374	2450	1.0	2.62	1652	1713	0.9
12159 SLINGERLANDS	001	8049	8833	9259	2.2	95	3225	3637	3889	2.9	2.41	1844	2056	2.6
12160 SLOANSVILLE	095	894	987	1054	2.4	95	323	360	388	2.6	2.74	240	266	2.5
12164 SPECULATOR	041	348	340	334	-0.6	5	163	162	161	-0.1	2.04	108	106	-0.4
12165 SPENCERTOWN	021	113	118	124	1.0	78	48	51	54	1.4	2.31	34	36	1.4
12166 SPRAKERS	057	1599	1609	1624	0.2	38	588	600	613	0.5	2.68	440	447	0.4
12167 STAMFORD	025	2840	3063	3433	1.8	91	1106	1218	1398	2.3	2.38	739	806	2.1
12168 STEPHENTOWN	083	2098	2163	2201	0.7	67	841	878	905	1.0	2.46	608	630	0.8
12169 STEPHENTOWN	083	316	326	333	0.7	68	119	125	129	1.2	2.61	84	87	0.8
12170 STILLWATER	091	5209	5401	5672	0.9	73	1900	1998	2129	1.2	2.70	1423	1486	1.0
12173 STUYVESANT	021	2271	2315	2403	0.5	55	864	895	944	0.8	2.58	650	671	0.7
12175 SUMMIT	095	745	753	761	0.3	43	206	213	220	0.8	3.09	141	145	0.7
12176 SURPRISE	039	167	172	184	0.7	66	71	74	80	1.0	2.32	51	53	0.9
12180 TROY	083	52397	52350	52940	0.0	26	20802	21002	21502	0.2	2.29	11806	11847	0.1
12182 TROY	083	14260	14546	14800	0.5	56	5920	6118	6300	0.8	2.35	3703	3798	0.6
12183 TROY	001	2249	2552	2716	3.0	98	1059	1223	1322	3.5	2.09	573	654	3.2
12184 VALATIE	021	7266	7613	8022	1.1	81	2746	2934	3146	1.6	2.49	1946	2066	1.1
12185 VALLEY FALLS	083	1968	2020	2064	0.6	63	714	743	769	0.9	2.72	543	562	0.8
12186 VOORHEESVILLE	001	6420	6581	6675	0.6	61	2498	2609	2685	1.0	2.52	1921	1994	0.9
12187 WARNERVILLE	095	715	717	723	0.1	33	284	289	296	0.4	2.48	202	204	0.2
NEW YORK					0.4					0.5	2.60			0.4
UNITED STATES					1.2					1.3	2.58			1.1

ZIP CODE #	POST OFFICE NAME	RACE (%) White 2000	White 2004	Black 2000	Black 2004	Asian/Pacific 2000	Asian/Pacific 2004	% Hispanic Origin 2000	% Hispanic Origin 2004	2004 AGE DISTRIBUTION (%) 0-4	5-9	10-14	15-19	20-24	25-44	45-64	65-84	85+	18+	MEDIAN AGE 2004	% 2004 Males	% 2004 Females
12032	CAROGA LAKE	98.9	98.8	0.0	0.0	0.5	0.6	0.3	0.3	5.1	4.5	6.9	6.1	4.0	24.1	32.5	15.3	1.5	79.5	44.6	52.0	48.0
12033	CASTLETON ON HUDSON	97.7	97.1	0.6	0.7	0.5	0.7	1.4	1.8	5.6	6.2	7.9	6.8	4.9	25.6	28.3	12.5	2.2	75.8	40.9	48.7	51.4
12035	CENTRAL BRIDGE	97.7	97.4	0.3	0.3	0.4	0.5	1.4	1.7	5.6	6.1	7.9	6.9	6.7	27.6	28.6	9.3	1.2	76.1	38.1	50.3	49.7
12036	CHARLOTTEVILLE	97.2	97.2	1.4	1.4	0.0	0.0	1.4	0.7	6.2	6.9	5.5	4.8	4.1	21.4	35.9	14.5	0.7	77.2	45.6	51.7	48.3
12037	CHATHAM	96.4	95.7	1.4	1.7	0.5	0.6	1.2	1.5	5.5	6.0	7.0	6.4	4.9	23.6	30.5	13.7	2.4	77.2	42.9	48.8	51.2
12041	CLARKSVILLE	98.2	97.2	0.0	0.0	0.9	0.9	0.9	0.9	5.6	6.5	6.5	5.6	4.7	27.1	29.0	13.1	1.9	75.7	42.1	50.5	49.5
12042	CLIMAX	97.3	96.7	0.3	0.7	0.0	0.0	1.0	1.3	5.6	5.9	6.6	6.9	5.6	26.3	29.6	12.2	1.3	77.3	40.8	50.3	49.7
12043	COBLESKILL	95.3	94.5	1.8	2.1	0.9	1.1	2.4	3.0	4.5	4.5	6.0	16.2	10.8	20.3	22.6	12.3	2.8	80.6	34.2	49.0	51.0
12046	COEYMANS HOLLOW	98.4	98.0	0.5	0.6	0.2	0.5	1.3	1.7	5.5	6.1	7.5	7.9	6.1	25.3	30.8	9.8	1.1	76.4	40.3	50.8	49.2
12047	COHOES	94.7	93.5	2.2	2.6	1.2	1.5	2.0	2.4	6.1	5.9	6.5	6.1	6.6	27.5	24.7	14.0	2.5	77.7	39.1	46.9	53.1
12051	COXSACKIE	68.9	66.8	22.9	23.9	0.7	0.8	12.5	14.0	4.3	4.3	4.8	12.3	19.6	27.3	18.7	7.6	1.2	82.8	28.3	66.2	33.8
12052	CROPSEYVILLE	98.0	97.7	0.1	0.1	0.2	0.3	0.5	0.6	6.2	6.5	6.5	6.9	6.0	26.7	30.6	9.9	0.8	76.7	39.5	50.5	49.5
12053	DELANSON	97.8	97.2	0.5	0.6	0.3	0.4	0.7	0.9	5.9	6.7	7.9	6.8	5.0	26.8	30.6	9.3	1.1	75.1	40.3	50.3	49.7
12054	DELMAR	96.3	95.3	1.2	1.4	1.4	1.8	1.4	1.8	5.9	6.6	7.5	7.3	5.2	21.9	30.1	12.8	2.8	75.0	42.3	47.6	52.4
12056	DUANESBURG	98.0	97.4	0.3	0.3	0.3	0.4	0.9	1.1	4.2	5.1	7.8	7.0	5.5	25.5	32.9	10.8	1.3	78.5	42.3	49.9	50.1
12057	EAGLE BRIDGE	97.2	96.5	0.9	1.3	0.5	0.6	0.9	1.2	5.2	5.8	7.1	6.5	5.9	26.0	29.1	13.1	1.3	77.6	41.4	50.2	49.8
12058	EARLTON	97.7	97.1	0.9	1.1	0.1	0.1	2.0	2.6	6.5	6.7	7.2	7.1	5.1	25.9	27.6	12.7	1.3	75.2	40.0	50.6	49.4
12059	EAST BERNE	98.0	97.4	0.4	0.5	0.4	0.5	0.8	1.0	5.4	6.2	7.3	7.2	5.3	25.9	30.6	11.0	1.2	76.7	41.1	49.5	50.5
12060	EAST CHATHAM	94.1	93.1	2.9	3.3	1.2	1.5	1.2	1.5	4.9	5.8	7.3	9.9	4.3	21.7	32.2	12.2	1.7	74.5	42.4	50.6	49.4
12061	EAST GREENBUSH	95.2	94.2	2.2	2.5	1.6	2.1	1.3	1.7	5.6	6.1	6.9	6.4	5.1	27.0	28.8	11.4	2.7	77.2	40.9	47.0	53.0
12062	EAST NASSAU	96.7	95.9	1.0	1.2	0.6	0.8	1.0	1.3	5.5	6.0	7.3	7.1	5.7	26.6	29.8	11.0	1.1	76.8	40.8	49.6	50.4
12064	EAST WORCESTER	96.7	96.4	0.8	1.0	0.4	0.4	0.8	1.2	5.8	6.2	6.5	6.0	5.6	22.9	31.4	13.9	1.9	78.1	43.0	50.2	49.8
12065	CLIFTON PARK	94.4	93.2	1.5	1.6	2.5	3.2	1.7	2.0	6.5	6.7	7.0	6.2	5.4	29.8	27.9	9.7	1.1	75.8	38.5	49.0	51.0
12066	ESPERANCE	98.0	97.7	0.5	0.6	0.3	0.3	1.0	1.2	6.3	6.8	7.5	6.3	5.8	26.9	28.2	10.8	1.3	75.3	39.5	50.7	49.3
12067	FEURA BUSH	97.8	97.2	0.4	0.6	0.6	0.7	1.3	1.7	6.2	6.7	7.0	6.8	5.1	25.6	30.3	11.2	1.3	75.9	41.0	50.3	49.7
12068	FONDA	97.4	97.3	0.4	0.5	0.7	0.8	1.5	1.5	6.0	6.0	7.2	6.8	6.5	25.9	27.1	12.7	1.8	76.3	39.8	48.3	51.7
12070	FORT JOHNSON	92.7	91.9	5.6	6.1	0.2	0.2	3.5	3.9	4.3	5.1	7.2	11.5	5.2	23.4	28.4	12.7	2.2	74.0	40.4	51.3	48.7
12071	FULTONHAM	97.8	98.2	1.3	1.3	0.0	0.0	1.3	1.3	6.2	6.6	5.8	5.8	5.3	24.8	31.4	12.8	1.3	77.9	41.4	50.9	49.1
12072	FULTONVILLE	95.8	95.6	1.9	2.0	0.9	0.9	2.2	2.3	5.1	5.6	7.6	7.1	6.4	28.4	26.5	11.8	1.5	77.2	38.8	51.7	48.3
12074	GALWAY	98.3	97.9	0.2	0.3	0.4	0.5	1.2	1.5	5.5	6.2	7.5	6.6	5.0	26.5	30.7	10.9	1.2	76.6	41.2	50.1	49.9
12075	GHENT	96.9	96.2	1.1	1.3	0.3	0.4	1.3	1.7	5.0	5.7	7.2	6.3	5.0	24.1	29.7	13.6	3.4	78.1	43.1	49.7	50.3
12076	GILBOA	96.0	95.4	1.2	1.4	0.3	0.4	2.3	2.8	5.2	5.2	5.4	5.4	5.7	22.6	33.1	15.9	1.6	81.1	45.4	49.4	50.6
12077	GLENMONT	93.4	92.1	3.3	3.8	1.9	2.5	2.1	2.6	7.3	7.9	8.6	9.0	5.3	24.0	27.5	9.2	1.1	69.8	37.7	48.8	51.3
12078	GLOVERSVILLE	95.5	94.8	1.9	2.2	0.6	0.7	1.7	2.1	6.1	6.1	6.9	6.4	6.4	26.4	25.1	13.8	3.0	76.8	39.7	48.6	51.4
12083	GREENVILLE	97.5	96.7	0.5	0.6	0.7	0.9	1.5	2.0	5.2	5.8	7.6	7.1	5.2	23.7	27.7	15.6	2.2	76.8	42.3	48.0	52.0
12084	GUILDERLAND	86.3	83.3	3.7	4.4	8.1	9.9	2.5	3.0	5.4	5.5	6.5	5.7	5.4	31.6	25.7	11.5	2.7	78.7	39.1	47.1	52.9
12086	HAGAMAN	98.2	98.1	0.2	0.2	0.5	0.6	1.5	1.7	5.6	6.0	6.8	6.0	5.3	24.9	28.5	14.7	2.1	77.8	42.2	49.8	50.3
12087	HANNACROIX	97.5	96.8	0.6	0.7	0.4	0.5	1.4	1.9	5.4	5.8	7.2	6.9	5.0	24.5	31.4	12.0	2.0	77.3	42.4	49.1	50.9
12090	HOOSICK FALLS	97.9	97.4	0.5	0.6	0.4	0.6	0.9	1.2	6.5	6.5	7.1	6.9	6.3	25.9	25.2	13.2	2.4	75.7	39.5	47.8	52.2
12092	HOWES CAVE	97.9	97.4	0.4	0.4	0.3	0.4	1.1	1.4	5.4	6.0	7.8	6.9	5.9	26.2	29.1	11.2	1.5	76.5	39.5	49.0	51.0
12093	JEFFERSON	96.1	95.7	2.1	2.3	0.1	0.1	1.8	2.1	5.7	5.7	6.0	5.9	5.2	22.9	32.5	14.7	1.5	78.8	44.1	51.0	49.0
12094	JOHNSONVILLE	97.9	97.4	0.6	0.7	0.2	0.2	0.5	0.6	7.4	7.3	7.9	7.8	6.6	29.0	24.9	8.4	0.8	72.7	35.3	50.4	49.6
12095	JOHNSTOWN	94.6	93.7	2.4	2.7	1.0	1.3	1.9	2.3	5.5	5.6	6.8	7.6	6.4	26.4	25.3	13.6	2.8	76.8	39.4	49.5	50.5
12106	KINDERHOOK	98.0	97.4	0.5	0.6	0.5	0.8	1.1	1.4	5.0	5.6	7.4	6.8	5.0	23.3	30.9	14.3	1.8	77.8	43.1	48.3	51.7
12108	LAKE PLEASANT	97.5	97.1	1.0	1.2	0.4	0.4	1.1	1.0	5.0	4.8	4.5	4.5	4.3	24.0	31.0	19.7	2.3	82.6	46.9	51.5	48.6
12110	LATHAM	91.0	88.9	2.6	3.1	4.6	5.7	1.8	2.2	4.9	5.2	6.6	6.9	6.9	27.1	27.3	13.1	2.1	78.7	40.4	47.7	52.3
12115	MALDEN BRIDGE	96.4	95.5	1.2	1.1	1.2	1.1	0.0	1.1	3.4	4.6	6.8	5.7	2.3	18.2	40.9	15.9	2.3	79.6	50.0	48.9	51.1
12116	MARYLAND	98.3	97.9	0.5	0.6	0.1	0.2	1.9	2.3	4.1	4.6	6.5	5.5	4.6	25.3	33.1	14.5	1.8	81.6	44.7	48.5	51.5
12117	MAYFIELD	98.6	98.4	0.4	0.5	0.0	0.0	1.0	1.2	4.9	6.3	7.3	7.8	6.4	25.1	29.7	11.0	1.7	76.6	40.5	50.2	49.8
12118	MECHANICVILLE	97.5	97.1	0.5	0.6	0.7	0.8	1.1	1.3	6.4	6.5	7.2	6.5	6.1	29.5	24.6	11.5	1.9	75.9	38.0	48.7	51.3
12120	MEDUSA	96.4	95.5	2.0	2.4	0.2	0.4	1.1	1.4	5.9	6.3	6.1	6.9	5.6	21.0	32.5	13.9	1.9	76.7	43.8	49.5	50.5
12121	MELROSE	98.4	97.9	0.4	0.5	0.6	0.8	0.8	0.9	5.5	6.3	7.6	7.1	5.4	25.9	29.5	11.8	0.9	76.2	40.6	49.7	50.3
12122	MIDDLEBURGH	97.2	96.7	0.7	0.8	0.2	0.2	1.9	2.3	5.5	5.7	6.6	6.2	6.2	25.1	28.8	14.2	1.7	78.3	41.5	49.2	50.9
12123	NASSAU	96.8	96.0	1.0	1.2	0.5	0.7	1.5	1.9	5.3	5.7	7.2	7.2	5.7	27.4	29.8	10.2	1.4	77.3	40.3	49.6	50.4
12125	NEW LEBANON	95.5	94.4	1.3	1.5	1.5	2.0	1.2	1.4	5.1	6.0	7.1	9.9	5.0	22.8	30.7	12.0	1.5	75.0	41.2	48.7	51.3
12130	NIVERVILLE	97.5	97.1	0.8	0.9	0.3	0.5	0.5	0.7	5.0	5.4	6.9	7.0	5.1	27.0	31.0	11.8	0.8	78.3	41.2	50.6	49.4
12131	NORTH BLENHEIM	80.0	78.5	16.3	17.7	0.0	0.0	8.8	12.7	3.8	2.5	5.1	5.1	17.7	31.7	21.5	11.4	1.3	84.8	34.5	64.6	35.4
12134	NORTHVILLE	98.4	98.1	0.2	0.3	0.3	0.4	1.0	1.2	5.3	5.6	6.1	5.3	5.3	23.7	31.8	15.0	1.9	79.8	44.1	50.0	50.0
12136	OLD CHATHAM	96.6	96.0	1.2	1.4	0.8	1.0	0.7	0.7	3.9	5.8	7.2	7.0	3.1	22.6	35.9	12.8	1.7	78.3	45.2	50.0	50.0
12137	PATTERSONVILLE	98.4	98.0	0.3	0.3	0.4	0.5	0.7	1.0	5.4	6.0	7.3	7.0	5.4	26.9	31.5	9.7	0.8	76.7	41.0	51.9	48.1
12138	PETERSBURG	98.3	97.9	0.1	0.2	0.5	0.7	0.6	0.8	6.4	6.7	7.3	7.0	5.6	26.1	28.4	11.5	1.2	75.2	39.7	50.4	49.6
12139	PISECO	99.1	99.1	0.0	0.0	0.0	0.0	0.0	0.5	3.6	3.6	3.6	6.3	5.0	20.3	39.2	17.1	1.4	85.6	49.7	50.5	49.6
12140	POESTENKILL	98.3	97.9	0.2	0.3	0.4	0.6	0.5	0.6	5.0	5.9	8.2	6.6	5.2	28.0	29.8	10.5	0.8	76.0	40.4	50.3	49.7
12143	RAVENA	93.9	92.4	2.5	3.0	0.5	0.7	3.6	4.5	7.0	6.9	7.3	7.0	6.7	28.6	24.2	10.7	1.6	74.3	36.7	48.5	51.5
12144	RENSSELAER	92.0	90.6	4.5	5.2	1.6	2.0	1.6	2.0	6.2	6.1	6.9	6.6	6.1	27.9	26.4	12.0	1.7	76.6	39.1	47.7	52.3
12147	RENSSELAERVILLE	94.8	93.6	2.2	2.7	0.0	0.0	1.4	1.9	4.4	5.4	5.6	7.7	4.2	22.3	34.9	13.9	1.7	78.8	45.3	51.8	48.2
12148	REXFORD	95.1	94.2	0.8	0.9	2.3	2.9	1.4	1.8	7.4	8.4	8.2	5.8	3.6	26.3	27.8	10.7	1.7	72.3	39.6	48.3	51.7
12149	RICHMONDVILLE	96.8	96.2	0.8	0.9	0.5	0.6	1.6	1.9	7.0	7.3	7.5	5.9	5.1	26.7	26.0	13.1	1.4	74.4	38.9	50.9	49.1
12150	ROTTERDAM JUNCTION	97.8	97.1	0.7	0.8	0.7	1.0	1.3	1.5	4.5	4.4	5.3	7.3	6.5	26.3	28.9	14.9	1.9	81.4	42.4	49.0	51.0
12151	ROUND LAKE	96.6	96.5	0.9	0.9	1.7	1.7	0.9	0.9	6.1	7.0	7.0	6.1	4.4	24.4	30.4	13.9	0.9	74.8	42.3	50.4	49.6
12153	SAND LAKE	98.5	98.0	0.0	0.0	0.4	0.5	1.0	1.5	5.5	6.1	7.3	7.4	5.3	24.9	32.1	10.6	0.9	76.2	41.3	49.0	51.0
12154	SCHAGHTICOKE	98.2	97.9	0.6	0.7	0.3	0.3	0.6	0.8	6.5	7.0	8.3	7.4	5.6	26.9	26.9	10.4	1.1	73.6	38.4	50.3	49.7
12155	SCHENEVUS	98.3	97.9	0.4	0.4	0.3	0.4	1.2	1.6	5.8	6.0	7.1	6.0	5.9	24.9	28.7	13.5	2.2	77.3	41.5	50.6	49.4
12156	SCHODACK LANDING	97.7	97.1	0.8	1.0	0.4	0.5	1.4	1.9	6.4	7.0	8.5	6.7	4.8	28.4	26.8	10.2	1.1	73.6	38.5	50.2	49.8
12157	SCHOHARIE	98.4	98.1	0.4	0.4	0.1	0.2	1.1	1.4	5.8	6.2	7.4	6.9	6.0	25.3	27.2	13.0	2.3	76.3	40.4	48.5	51.6
12158	SELKIRK	92.4	90.9	4.3	5.0	1.2	1.6	2.4	2.9	6.8	6.9	7.1	8.8	6.2	26.9	25.9	10.2	1.2	73.5	37.0	49.0	51.0
12159	SLINGERLANDS	91.5	89.3	2.3	2.8	4.9	6.1	1.9	2.3	5.4	5.8	6.8	6.1	5.2	27.0	28.3	11.9	3.5	78.0	41.3	47.0	53.1
12160	SLOANSVILLE	98.0	97.8	0.5	0.5	0.3	0.4	1.6	1.8	7.1	7.7	8.1	6.6	5.8	27.5	26.4	9.7	1.1	73.0	37.7	51.0	49.0
12164	SPECULATOR	97.4	97.4	1.2	1.2	0.3	0.3	0.9	1.2	5.0	5.0	4.7	4.7	4.4	23.5	30.3	20.0	2.4	82.4	46.8	50.9	49.1
12165	SPENCERTOWN	96.5	95.8	1.8	1.7	0.9	0.9	0.9	1.7	3.4	5.1	6.8	5.9	4.2	19.5	34.8	18.6	1.7	79.7	48.0	49.2	50.9
12166	SPRAKERS	98.1	98.0	0.5	0.5	0.3	0.3	1.1	1.2	5.5	6.3	7.8	7.0	5.3	25.9	29.3	11.6	1.2	76.0	40.6	51.0	49.0
12167	STAMFORD	96.8	96.2	0.8	0.9	0.6	0.7	2.5	3.1	5.5	5.6	6.1	6.0	5.3	21.6	28.6	17.7	3.8	78.9	45.1	48.2	51.8
12168	STEPHENTOWN	98.2	97.9	0.3	0.4	0.2	0.2	1.1	1.4	6.4	6.8	7.6	6.6	5.3	27.4	28.9	10.3	0.8	75.2	39.4	48.9	51.1
12169	STEPHENTOWN	98.4	98.2	0.3	0.3	0.0	0.0	1.3	1.5	6.4	6.8	7.7	6.8	5.5	27.0	28.8	10.1	0.9	75.5	39.0	49.7	50.3
12170	STILLWATER	98.0	97.7	0.5	0.5	0.5	0.7	0.7	0.9	6.7	6.9	7.9	6.6	6.1	28.8	26.2	9.7	1.1	74.4	37.8	50.1	50.0
12173	STUYVESANT	97.5	96.9	1.1	1.3	0.4	0.4	1.1	1.4	6.2	6.6	7.9	7.0	5.7	26.5	28.7	10.1	1.5	74.9	38.9	49.2	50.8
12175	SUMMIT	90.1	89.1	7.4	8.0	0.1	0.1	4.7	5.4	5.2	5.2	5.3	5.2	8.2	26.2	29.6	13.7	1.5	81.0	40.7	56.3	43.7
12176	SURPRISE	97.6	97.1	0.0	0.6	1.2	1.2	1.2	2.3	5.2	5.8	7.0	7.6	5.8	22.7	29.1	14.5	2.3	76.7	42.5	48.8	51.2
12180	TROY	82.7	80.3	9.8	10.7	3.5	4.3	3.6	4.3	6.1	5.6	5.8	9.4	11.1	26.5	21.2	11.7	2.4	78.8	33.9	49.7	50.4
12182	TROY	91.1	89.5	5.0	5.8	1.0	1.2	2.7	3.3	6.0	5.9	6.9	6.9	7.3	26.9	25.0	13.1	2.1	76.9	38.4	47.9	52.1
12183	TROY	96.9	96.0	1.3	1.7	0.4	0.4	0.8	0.9	6.1	5.6	5.7	5.5	7.1	31.2	24.3	12.3	2.2	79.4	37.7	48.9	51.1
12184	VALATIE	96.8	96.1	1.0	1.2	1.0	1.3	1.4	1.7	5.5	6.2	7.1	6.3	4.6	25.9	29.1	12.6	2.8	77.0	41.7	48.3	51.8
12185	VALLEY FALLS	97.7	97.4	0.5	0.5	0.3	0.4	1.0	1.2	7.1	7.5	8.3	7.3	6.0	27.1	26.3	9.3	1.2	72.6	37.1	50.0	50.1
12186	VOORHEESVILLE	97.9	97.4	0.5	0.6	0.6	0.8	0.7	1.0	5.0	6.1	8.0	6.9	4.2	23.1	32.7	12.8	1.3	76.3	43.2	48.4	51.6
12187	WARNERVILLE	98.5	98.2	0.3	0.4	0.4	0.4	1.3	1.7	6.3	6.6	6.6	5.7	4.7	25.1	29.7	13.8	1.5	77.0	41.5	51.2	48.8
	NEW YORK	68.0	65.9	15.9	16.2	5.6	6.4	15.1	16.7	6.5	6.5	7.1	7.0	7.1	28.9	24.0	11.2	1.8	75.8	36.7	48.3	51.7
	UNITED STATES	75.1	73.6	12.3	12.5	3.8	4.2	12.5	14.1	6.9	6.7	7.2	7.0	7.3	28.6	23.8	10.8	1.7	75.1	36.0	49.1	50.9

ZIP CODE #	POST OFFICE NAME	2004 Per Capita Income	2004 HH Income Base	2004 HOUSEHOLD INCOME DISTRIBUTION (%) Less than $25,000	$25,000 to $49,999	$50,000 to $99,999	$100,000 to $149,999	$150,000 or More	MEDIAN HOUSEHOLD INCOME 2004	2009	2004 National Centile	2004 State Centile	2004 Home Value Base	2004 HOME VALUE DISTRIBUTION (%) Less than $50,000	$50,000 to $89,999	$90,000 to $174,999	$175,000 to $399,999	$400,000 or More	2004 Median Home Value
12032	CAROGA LAKE	22237	299	30.4	37.1	25.1	4.7	2.7	37668	41412	38	23	268	11.2	30.6	39.2	16.0	3.0	104032
12033	CASTLETON ON HUDSON	28783	3077	14.0	22.7	41.1	15.6	6.6	63019	71884	87	78	2503	5.0	2.9	46.9	43.8	1.3	167836
12035	CENTRAL BRIDGE	20021	289	21.1	33.6	35.6	7.6	2.1	46327	51346	65	54	231	5.2	12.6	63.2	17.3	1.7	120833
12036	CHARLOTTEVILLE	19065	60	30.0	33.3	31.7	5.0	0.0	42301	47839	54	42	52	11.5	23.1	46.2	19.2	0.0	110000
12037	CHATHAM	30612	1828	22.2	30.1	31.8	8.5	7.4	48143	54790	69	58	1393	9.5	4.0	33.2	42.6	10.8	181454
12041	CLARKSVILLE	24977	37	18.9	27.0	32.4	13.5	8.1	54570	61530	79	70	32	0.0	0.0	62.5	37.5	0.0	150000
12042	CLIMAX	21800	115	17.4	30.4	40.0	10.4	1.7	51367	57879	74	65	99	2.0	4.0	50.5	38.4	5.1	162500
12043	COBLESKILL	20535	2934	33.6	29.4	26.9	7.0	3.2	37416	41178	37	22	1867	5.3	11.3	57.8	24.5	1.1	128482
12046	COEYMANS HOLLOW	28364	229	6.6	23.1	51.5	12.2	6.6	67736	77994	90	83	202	1.0	6.4	47.0	44.1	1.5	162500
12047	COHOES	22379	8020	32.5	29.0	28.0	7.2	3.3	38869	45100	42	29	4236	1.3	9.1	70.7	18.4	0.5	125576
12051	COXSACKIE	17323	1693	29.9	30.7	30.0	7.0	2.4	40219	45157	47	35	1087	5.6	4.7	55.3	32.2	2.2	149315
12052	CROPSEYVILLE	24697	555	17.1	29.4	39.1	10.5	4.0	52991	61159	77	67	492	3.3	10.4	54.7	31.3	0.4	140464
12053	DELANSON	25426	1687	13.5	24.7	41.1	15.8	4.9	61386	69511	86	76	1485	3.4	8.2	50.9	35.2	2.4	154297
12054	DELMAR	39312	6543	9.3	22.4	34.8	18.9	14.6	73423	85755	93	86	5191	0.2	0.3	31.2	65.1	3.3	196315
12056	DUANESBURG	27503	957	13.6	25.9	39.5	16.3	4.7	61143	70266	85	76	819	3.4	6.1	51.3	38.0	1.2	156715
12057	EAGLE BRIDGE	21079	841	25.2	37.9	25.8	7.7	3.3	40921	45531	49	37	709	9.2	6.8	56.4	25.8	1.8	133638
12058	EARLTON	20028	626	23.0	36.1	32.6	6.1	2.2	43957	48987	59	48	495	6.7	10.3	50.9	30.7	1.4	147024
12059	EAST BERNE	25900	743	18.0	26.2	38.6	11.6	5.5	55918	65212	81	71	648	7.3	5.6	50.2	35.7	1.4	150000
12060	EAST CHATHAM	32842	628	17.0	29.5	33.9	11.2	8.4	53575	61221	78	68	508	3.9	1.8	31.9	48.6	13.8	205319
12061	EAST GREENBUSH	30379	3289	10.9	27.8	35.7	17.5	8.2	63090	71221	87	78	2451	2.2	4.0	41.4	48.7	3.7	178585
12062	EAST NASSAU	24086	650	19.9	28.6	37.9	10.2	3.5	51085	57741	74	64	529	6.6	8.5	49.0	33.8	2.1	147738
12064	EAST WORCESTER	17511	210	34.8	33.8	25.7	3.8	1.9	35687	38855	30	15	176	11.9	14.8	55.1	15.3	2.8	120000
12065	CLIFTON PARK	34589	16844	12.2	25.2	36.4	15.5	10.8	64425	74279	88	80	11862	8.2	1.6	31.0	55.5	3.7	187381
12066	ESPERANCE	20922	790	19.6	32.4	37.6	8.5	1.9	48096	53788	69	58	681	12.9	17.5	48.5	20.3	0.9	116150
12067	FEURA BUSH	32433	689	15.7	23.7	37.6	13.9	9.1	62756	72434	87	78	582	4.6	3.3	47.8	36.6	7.7	162308
12068	FONDA	19643	1376	28.1	33.5	29.3	6.8	2.3	41220	46088	50	38	1104	16.3	19.9	48.4	15.2	0.2	111788
12070	FORT JOHNSON	25670	661	17.4	37.8	30.7	8.6	5.5	43519	49775	57	46	573	9.3	24.3	41.5	24.1	0.9	116346
12071	FULTONHAM	19519	100	36.0	33.0	25.0	5.0	1.0	35547	38630	30	15	85	10.6	16.5	44.7	27.1	1.2	122115
12072	FULTONVILLE	19746	946	25.9	33.1	34.5	4.3	2.2	41999	47486	53	41	755	23.3	23.8	40.7	12.1	0.1	95119
12074	GALWAY	25262	1250	19.0	23.6	43.0	10.7	3.7	56108	63749	81	71	1085	3.2	6.4	50.2	37.7	2.5	156638
12075	GHENT	27150	1247	19.3	28.2	36.4	7.9	8.3	52611	60467	76	66	1024	2.4	3.9	36.8	49.5	7.3	184669
12076	GILBOA	21086	591	30.8	35.2	25.2	6.3	2.5	37627	42485	38	23	509	15.3	21.6	41.3	18.9	3.0	112340
12077	GLENMONT	34606	2129	8.8	20.2	35.4	22.4	13.2	77350	90427	94	89	1775	0.3	1.0	24.6	70.3	3.8	211159
12078	GLOVERSVILLE	18760	10000	37.3	31.1	24.7	4.9	2.1	33926	37123	24	10	6677	9.0	29.9	49.0	10.7	1.4	103712
12083	GREENVILLE	23025	1577	25.8	27.3	35.2	8.5	3.2	46127	52084	64	53	1226	1.4	5.3	50.2	40.6	2.5	163062
12084	GUILDERLAND	41959	2182	13.3	22.6	38.9	15.1	10.2	65999	77473	89	81	941	0.0	0.0	26.3	65.8	8.0	243899
12086	HAGAMAN	21910	475	23.0	28.8	37.5	8.8	1.9	48246	54510	69	59	405	3.5	14.6	53.1	27.2	1.7	138766
12087	HANNACROIX	23065	581	14.6	31.2	43.4	8.8	2.1	53184	60128	77	67	498	1.4	6.2	44.8	46.2	1.4	169231
12090	HOOSICK FALLS	22823	2379	24.4	32.9	34.2	6.0	2.5	44376	50229	60	49	1736	4.3	12.2	61.8	20.5	1.3	123422
12092	HOWES CAVE	22592	561	22.3	36.2	29.4	8.7	3.4	42272	46969	54	42	438	8.0	13.2	56.2	19.2	3.4	119811
12093	JEFFERSON	21866	721	30.1	32.7	26.8	6.0	4.4	39069	43691	43	30	606	9.7	19.1	48.5	20.6	2.0	118750
12094	JOHNSONVILLE	19920	748	19.3	26.5	45.5	7.9	0.9	53118	59719	77	67	624	13.3	10.1	48.6	27.2	0.8	134709
12095	JOHNSTOWN	18145	4816	34.5	32.9	25.4	5.7	1.7	36867	40643	35	20	3284	6.8	25.8	50.5	16.0	0.9	114043
12106	KINDERHOOK	28999	1107	16.4	25.6	38.8	13.0	6.2	57822	65505	82	72	927	1.8	3.0	28.4	59.3	7.4	204044
12108	LAKE PLEASANT	22457	224	32.1	39.3	19.6	5.4	3.6	34754	38910	27	12	177	4.0	9.6	46.3	31.6	8.5	151974
12110	LATHAM	31132	7195	12.3	24.7	40.3	14.0	8.7	62493	72714	87	77	5232	1.2	0.6	51.5	44.4	2.3	170864
12115	MALDEN BRIDGE	48343	44	9.1	18.2	43.2	18.2	11.4	75000	85676	93	87	39	0.0	0.0	18.0	61.5	20.5	242500
12116	MARYLAND	20683	692	30.1	33.4	27.8	6.9	1.9	38321	43023	40	26	576	9.4	17.9	51.0	21.4	0.4	128261
12117	MAYFIELD	19632	1232	28.5	35.8	29.1	4.5	2.2	39043	43420	43	29	997	7.1	24.2	42.1	23.0	3.6	125846
12118	MECHANICVILLE	22901	5342	22.7	33.4	33.1	8.2	2.6	45219	51651	62	51	3509	9.7	6.4	59.0	22.6	2.4	136896
12120	MEDUSA	22990	230	22.2	31.3	35.7	7.0	3.9	46265	53907	64	53	194	3.1	9.8	57.7	27.3	2.1	138889
12121	MELROSE	24164	690	18.1	18.1	47.8	13.5	2.5	63932	73448	88	79	627	1.3	5.6	53.0	36.8	3.4	159311
12122	MIDDLEBURGH	20499	1695	31.2	32.6	28.7	5.4	2.1	37572	42102	38	23	1307	8.7	16.2	56.7	17.0	1.4	117577
12123	NASSAU	25537	2175	17.3	31.1	36.6	10.3	4.6	51423	58365	75	65	1718	7.8	5.9	52.3	31.1	2.9	143168
12125	NEW LEBANON	24314	596	19.6	30.9	36.6	9.4	3.5	49539	56600	71	61	445	7.9	2.9	33.3	47.9	8.1	189096
12130	NIVERVILLE	26099	341	12.9	29.3	41.4	13.5	2.9	55975	63119	81	71	297	3.4	3.4	59.6	31.0	2.7	152123
12131	NORTH BLENHEIM	25235	32	25.0	34.4	28.1	6.3	6.3	43162	47321	56	45	29	3.5	17.2	55.2	24.1	0.0	119643
12134	NORTHVILLE	21942	1696	28.0	33.6	29.7	6.1	2.7	41418	46382	51	39	1358	5.9	14.5	48.2	28.3	3.1	136241
12136	OLD CHATHAM	38725	401	15.7	26.9	33.7	11.5	12.2	57669	66867	82	72	334	0.6	1.2	24.9	53.3	20.1	234783
12137	PATTERSONVILLE	26343	572	12.8	24.0	44.6	14.5	4.2	62716	71065	87	77	503	2.0	9.0	41.0	44.5	3.6	172031
12138	PETERSBURG	23362	1244	22.0	28.6	35.8	10.7	3.0	49353	55401	71	61	1062	6.4	15.8	55.8	20.5	1.4	128505
12139	PISECO	24056	95	29.5	35.8	23.2	8.4	3.2	39052	44296	43	29	85	7.1	7.1	51.8	30.6	3.5	144271
12140	POESTENKILL	25649	474	15.4	26.4	44.9	9.3	4.0	62467	67847	87	77	404	2.7	5.9	43.8	46.0	1.5	168590
12143	RAVENA	24289	2375	20.8	30.1	34.4	11.3	3.3	49277	57238	71	61	1675	8.9	4.6	64.5	21.0	1.0	137730
12144	RENSSELAER	26364	7853	20.9	31.0	34.0	10.7	3.5	48113	54647	69	58	5259	1.3	7.0	65.1	25.5	1.1	138138
12147	RENSSELAERVILLE	27194	205	21.5	26.3	38.1	8.3	5.9	52662	60258	76	66	173	2.3	5.8	52.0	37.0	2.9	151974
12148	REXFORD	36652	1433	12.4	16.9	35.0	23.0	12.8	79390	91709	95	90	1241	0.3	0.7	28.0	63.7	7.3	215909
12149	RICHMONDVILLE	19072	965	28.6	38.1	25.9	5.4	2.0	38465	42795	41	27	735	12.0	16.3	50.9	20.0	0.8	116233
12150	ROTTERDAM JUNCTION	22731	350	24.3	27.1	36.9	8.6	3.1	47623	55609	67	57	239	0.0	8.0	58.6	33.5	0.0	144207
12151	ROUND LAKE	42340	50	6.0	20.0	36.0	22.0	16.0	79830	85546	95	90	46	0.0	0.0	17.4	82.6	0.0	202500
12153	SAND LAKE	31619	321	14.0	20.3	39.6	14.0	12.2	64575	73731	88	80	285	7.4	7.7	50.5	31.9	2.5	146627
12154	SCHAGHTICOKE	23997	1089	20.8	27.6	36.0	11.9	3.7	51528	58892	75	65	886	4.7	5.6	50.2	35.1	4.3	157971
12155	SCHENEVUS	19192	871	32.2	36.5	24.2	5.1	2.1	36377	40437	33	18	689	10.9	19.5	51.5	16.3	1.9	119935
12156	SCHODACK LANDING	26180	346	11.0	30.4	42.2	11.9	4.6	57322	65831	82	72	298	2.0	3.7	40.9	51.3	2.0	178472
12157	SCHOHARIE	21265	1666	24.9	32.9	31.0	8.0	3.2	42993	48068	56	44	1279	10.7	9.8	53.7	23.9	2.0	131164
12158	SELKIRK	26638	2374	14.2	28.3	38.8	12.9	5.8	57030	65540	82	72	1785	8.0	2.4	60.9	27.2	1.6	143396
12159	SLINGERLANDS	37176	3637	15.5	25.4	31.3	15.0	12.8	61698	71764	86	76	2202	0.6	0.5	37.9	53.1	7.9	201232
12160	SLOANSVILLE	19635	360	21.1	33.6	36.9	6.9	1.4	46336	51635	65	54	306	9.5	18.3	52.9	19.0	0.3	115217
12164	SPECULATOR	24699	162	31.5	38.3	21.0	5.6	3.7	35676	39780	30	15	128	2.3	10.9	46.9	32.0	7.8	150000
12165	SPENCERTOWN	51345	51	13.7	23.5	35.3	9.8	17.7	63124	72019	87	78	43	0.0	0.0	23.3	58.1	18.6	232500
12166	SPRAKERS	18905	600	25.3	33.3	33.3	6.3	1.7	42154	47447	53	42	522	25.1	20.7	39.5	12.8	1.9	98148
12167	STAMFORD	21268	1218	34.2	33.0	24.2	5.3	3.3	36577	40554	34	19	887	8.2	14.7	49.5	25.8	1.8	130703
12168	STEPHENTOWN	21782	878	20.8	33.5	38.2	6.0	1.5	47605	53152	67	57	725	10.6	10.1	52.6	25.9	0.8	134983
12169	STEPHENTOWN	20669	125	19.2	35.2	38.4	6.4	0.8	47839	53073	68	58	103	11.7	8.7	54.4	24.3	1.0	133125
12170	STILLWATER	21687	1998	20.0	29.2	38.2	10.1	2.5	50732	57710	73	63	1615	10.0	7.4	58.8	22.1	1.7	136294
12173	STUYVESANT	23470	895	16.2	29.8	40.0	10.8	3.1	53281	60704	77	67	717	5.2	3.8	50.8	36.7	3.6	157449
12175	SUMMIT	15114	213	29.6	34.7	28.6	5.6	1.4	41835	47332	52	41	187	10.2	23.5	45.5	19.8	1.1	110985
12176	SURPRISE	24281	74	28.4	24.3	36.5	4.1	6.8	48184	53981	69	59	62	0.0	8.1	40.3	51.6	0.0	177083
12180	TROY	22202	21002	33.4	26.4	29.1	7.6	3.6	39007	44469	43	29	10547	3.4	9.1	62.1	23.8	1.8	139097
12182	TROY	21404	6118	30.1	31.4	29.6	6.6	2.2	39827	45143	45	33	3543	4.1	10.8	68.1	16.0	1.0	124667
12183	TROY	20591	1223	26.7	42.8	27.7	2.3	0.5	37215	42612	36	21	620	1.1	7.9	86.0	5.0	0.0	116489
12184	VALATIE	29433	2934	16.1	25.8	37.2	12.9	8.1	60000	68160	84	75	2349	3.1	2.1	30.5	56.8	7.6	199816
12185	VALLEY FALLS	23191	743	20.2	24.4	40.5	12.0	3.0	54922	61445	80	70	603	11.1	7.3	45.3	33.7	2.7	147962
12186	VOORHEESVILLE	36918	2609	10.3	21.1	39.2	18.7	10.7	70505	83629	91	84	2291	0.8	0.8	42.6	49.8	6.0	182444
12187	WARNERVILLE	20880	289	26.3	32.5	31.1	6.6	3.5	42083	46358	53	41	233	4.7	13.3	51.5	29.2	1.3	134470
	NEW YORK	28049		26.3	24.3	29.3	11.5	8.6	49309	58077				4.6	8.6	27.2	39.9	19.8	219050
	UNITED STATES	25866		24.7	27.1	30.8	10.9	6.5	48124	56710				10.9	15.0	33.7	30.1	10.4	145905

ZIP CODE		FINANCIAL SERVICES				THE HOME						ENTERTAINMENT						PERSONAL			
						Home Improvements		Furnishings													
#	POST OFFICE NAME	Auto Loan	Home Loan	Invest-ments	Retire-ment Plans	Home Repair	Lawn & Garden	Comput-ers & Hard-ware	Major Appli-ances	TV, Radio, Sound Equip-ment	Furni-ture	Dine out/ Carry out	Sports Equip-ment	Fees & Tickets	Toys & Games	Travel	Cable TV	Apparel & Services	Auto Repairs	Health Insur-ance	Pets & Supplies
12032	CAROGA LAKE	82	65	44	58	73	82	61	73	69	60	82	86	54	81	65	74	76	72	87	100
12033	CASTLETON ON HUDSON	99	113	119	111	113	118	105	106	102	104	127	121	110	133	108	102	125	103	104	119
12035	CENTRAL BRIDGE	83	78	65	76	80	85	74	79	76	74	93	93	73	94	75	76	89	77	81	95
12036	CHARLOTTEVILLE	79	61	40	55	69	77	58	70	66	57	78	82	51	76	61	70	72	69	83	96
12037	CHATHAM	111	100	84	97	105	115	98	106	102	97	124	121	94	121	99	103	118	104	112	127
12041	CLARKSVILLE	116	103	78	98	109	117	95	106	101	95	123	126	93	126	98	104	117	103	114	136
12042	CLIMAX	92	82	63	78	87	93	76	84	81	76	98	100	74	100	78	83	93	82	91	109
12043	COBLESKILL	71	68	70	67	69	76	70	71	72	69	88	83	70	89	70	72	85	72	73	82
12046	COEYMANS HOLLOW	104	125	136	121	123	126	115	115	111	114	139	133	122	148	118	109	138	112	108	126
12047	COHOES	65	68	77	67	67	74	71	69	72	69	89	79	72	91	71	72	87	70	70	75
12051	COXSACKIE	76	70	63	68	72	79	70	74	73	69	89	86	68	89	70	74	85	73	78	87
12052	CROPSEYVILLE	105	89	66	83	96	105	83	95	90	83	109	112	79	110	87	94	103	93	106	125
12053	DELANSON	93	110	113	109	109	109	99	100	94	99	117	117	104	124	101	92	116	97	93	112
12054	DELMAR	126	149	169	150	147	153	139	138	132	139	166	159	147	169	142	129	164	136	129	151
12056	DUANESBURG	91	113	121	113	111	110	101	101	94	101	119	118	108	126	104	92	118	97	91	111
12057	EAGLE BRIDGE	88	76	59	75	80	89	76	82	80	75	97	94	73	97	76	82	92	80	88	99
12058	EARLTON	84	71	51	68	75	81	68	76	72	69	87	90	63	85	69	73	83	75	81	96
12059	EAST BERNE	87	106	115	103	104	105	97	96	92	96	116	112	103	123	99	91	115	94	89	106
12060	EAST CHATHAM	106	112	122	113	113	120	109	111	108	109	134	130	110	136	111	107	131	111	108	126
12061	EAST GREENBUSH	101	118	137	119	116	120	112	110	107	112	135	129	118	139	114	105	133	109	103	121
12062	EAST NASSAU	88	92	89	90	92	97	87	89	87	87	107	104	89	111	88	86	104	88	88	103
12064	EAST WORCESTER	76	55	31	49	61	71	55	65	64	54	75	76	48	71	56	68	69	65	79	88
12065	CLIFTON PARK	114	124	137	127	122	126	121	119	116	121	146	141	123	146	120	112	143	120	110	133
12066	ESPERANCE	87	81	66	78	85	90	75	82	78	75	95	97	74	98	77	79	91	79	86	103
12067	FEURA BUSH	131	124	105	120	130	137	115	126	119	115	145	149	114	149	119	120	139	123	131	156
12068	FONDA	75	71	63	67	74	81	68	73	72	67	88	84	68	91	71	75	84	72	80	88
12070	FORT JOHNSON	84	91	90	88	91	96	85	87	84	84	105	102	88	109	87	84	102	85	87	101
12071	FULTONHAM	74	58	39	52	65	73	54	66	62	54	73	77	49	72	58	66	68	65	78	90
12072	FULTONVILLE	78	70	58	65	74	82	67	73	73	66	88	85	67	91	69	76	84	72	81	91
12074	GALWAY	102	95	81	89	100	108	88	97	93	88	113	114	86	115	92	96	108	95	105	123
12075	GHENT	117	101	77	97	108	117	96	107	102	95	124	127	92	125	98	105	117	105	117	138
12076	GILBOA	84	66	45	60	74	83	62	75	70	62	83	88	56	82	66	75	78	74	89	102
12077	GLENMONT	123	150	161	153	145	146	134	131	123	136	157	153	145	162	136	119	157	127	117	145
12078	GLOVERSVILLE	63	58	56	55	59	67	60	62	64	58	78	71	59	79	61	65	74	62	67	72
12083	GREENVILLE	81	81	78	77	84	90	77	82	79	76	97	94	77	100	80	81	94	80	86	97
12084	GUILDERLAND	106	122	149	126	120	124	119	116	113	119	143	138	123	146	120	110	141	117	106	127
12086	HAGAMAN	72	80	85	76	80	88	76	77	76	75	95	87	79	98	79	79	92	76	80	87
12087	HANNACROIX	89	89	80	86	91	96	82	87	83	82	103	103	83	106	84	84	99	85	89	106
12090	HOOSICK FALLS	81	80	75	76	83	91	77	80	81	75	99	92	79	105	80	83	95	78	86	95
12092	HOWES CAVE	84	79	70	77	81	89	78	81	80	77	98	93	77	99	78	82	94	80	86	96
12093	JEFFERSON	89	70	48	63	79	89	66	80	75	65	89	93	59	87	70	80	82	78	94	109
12094	JOHNSONVILLE	90	83	67	79	85	90	78	84	80	79	98	98	76	97	79	80	94	83	86	103
12095	JOHNSTOWN	63	62	64	60	64	70	63	63	65	61	80	73	64	84	64	67	77	63	67	73
12106	KINDERHOOK	95	106	110	104	107	112	98	101	95	98	118	116	101	121	101	95	116	98	99	114
12108	LAKE PLEASANT	86	68	46	61	76	86	64	77	72	63	86	90	57	85	68	77	80	76	91	105
12110	LATHAM	101	119	137	119	117	121	112	111	107	112	135	129	118	138	115	105	133	110	104	121
12115	MALDEN BRIDGE	124	150	169	149	149	157	138	138	130	138	164	156	146	166	143	130	162	135	132	151
12116	MARYLAND	85	63	39	59	72	81	61	74	70	61	82	88	54	81	64	74	76	73	88	103
12117	MAYFIELD	81	65	47	59	72	81	63	73	71	62	85	85	58	85	66	76	79	72	85	96
12118	MECHANICVILLE	77	78	74	75	78	84	75	77	76	75	94	89	76	96	76	76	91	76	78	88
12120	MEDUSA	99	75	47	68	85	95	71	87	81	71	96	103	63	95	75	86	89	86	103	120
12121	MELROSE	84	103	113	101	101	103	95	94	90	94	113	109	101	121	97	89	113	91	87	103
12122	MIDDLEBURGH	72	67	59	62	71	79	65	70	70	63	85	80	64	88	68	73	80	69	79	86
12123	NASSAU	83	95	104	94	95	98	92	90	89	90	111	105	96	117	93	87	110	89	86	99
12125	NEW LEBANON	84	83	84	84	84	90	83	85	84	82	104	99	83	104	83	83	100	84	85	96
12130	NIVERVILLE	85	104	114	101	101	104	96	95	92	95	115	110	102	123	98	90	115	92	88	103
12131	NORTH BLENHEIM	88	69	47	63	78	88	65	79	74	65	88	92	58	87	70	79	82	78	93	108
12134	NORTHVILLE	85	68	48	63	76	85	65	77	73	65	87	89	59	86	69	77	81	76	89	102
12136	OLD CHATHAM	152	123	88	118	136	150	118	138	129	117	154	164	109	152	123	133	144	135	156	181
12137	PATTERSONVILLE	91	111	117	110	110	110	100	100	94	99	118	117	106	125	102	92	117	97	92	111
12138	PETERSBURG	96	85	68	82	90	98	81	89	86	81	105	104	79	106	83	88	99	87	96	112
12139	PISECO	95	75	51	67	84	95	71	85	80	70	95	99	63	93	75	85	88	84	100	116
12140	POESTENKILL	93	101	96	99	102	104	91	95	89	91	111	112	94	116	94	89	109	92	92	112
12143	RAVENA	90	82	74	82	85	94	86	88	88	83	108	102	83	108	85	88	103	88	92	102
12144	RENSSELAER	80	90	104	91	89	93	89	87	86	88	108	102	92	112	90	85	107	87	82	95
12147	RENSSELAERVILLE	111	82	49	76	94	105	79	96	90	78	106	115	69	105	83	96	98	95	114	133
12148	REXFORD	123	134	154	137	134	141	133	132	129	132	161	154	136	161	134	126	158	132	127	144
12149	RICHMONDVILLE	79	62	43	57	68	77	60	70	68	60	81	82	56	81	62	72	76	69	82	92
12150	ROTTERDAM JUNCTION	71	83	92	79	82	90	78	79	78	78	97	88	83	101	82	80	95	77	80	85
12151	ROUND LAKE	129	150	161	147	149	155	138	140	132	139	166	159	145	168	142	131	164	136	134	154
12153	SAND LAKE	107	124	127	124	123	125	114	115	108	113	135	134	119	142	116	106	133	111	107	128
12154	SCHAGHTICOKE	87	98	101	95	98	101	91	92	89	90	111	107	95	117	93	88	109	90	89	105
12155	SCHENEVUS	78	59	38	55	66	76	60	70	68	58	80	81	53	77	62	72	73	69	83	92
12156	SCHODACK LANDING	101	99	86	95	102	107	91	97	93	91	115	115	92	119	94	94	111	95	101	120
12157	SCHOHARIE	84	74	59	71	77	86	74	79	78	73	94	91	70	93	74	80	89	79	87	96
12158	SELKIRK	96	108	110	106	107	111	101	102	98	100	123	117	105	129	103	98	120	99	98	113
12159	SLINGERLANDS	123	130	146	135	129	134	129	127	124	129	156	150	131	155	128	120	153	128	119	142
12160	SLOANSVILLE	83	78	65	76	81	85	73	78	75	73	92	93	72	94	74	75	88	77	81	97
12164	SPECULATOR	87	68	46	61	76	86	64	77	72	63	86	90	57	85	68	77	80	76	91	105
12165	SPENCERTOWN	153	184	208	183	184	193	169	170	160	170	201	192	180	204	176	159	199	165	162	185
12166	SPRAKERS	87	69	44	63	75	83	65	75	72	65	87	90	60	86	66	76	81	74	86	101
12167	STAMFORD	85	65	43	61	71	84	68	77	76	65	90	87	61	86	69	81	83	76	92	97
12168	STEPHENTOWN	85	74	57	72	78	86	72	78	76	71	93	91	70	94	73	78	88	77	85	97
12169	STEPHENTOWN	84	74	59	73	77	85	74	79	77	73	94	91	71	94	73	78	89	77	84	94
12170	STILLWATER	92	82	65	80	86	94	79	86	83	78	101	101	77	102	80	84	95	84	92	107
12173	STUYVESANT	86	90	87	87	91	95	84	87	84	83	104	102	86	108	86	84	101	85	87	102
12175	SUMMIT	80	63	43	57	71	80	59	72	67	59	80	84	53	79	63	72	74	71	85	98
12176	SURPRISE	101	72	39	68	83	93	71	87	81	70	95	105	61	93	73	85	87	86	103	120
12180	TROY	69	69	82	70	68	74	76	72	75	74	94	85	75	94	74	74	92	75	70	79
12182	TROY	65	69	78	68	69	75	71	69	72	69	89	80	73	93	72	72	87	70	70	76
12183	TROY	56	59	66	59	59	62	62	59	61	59	76	70	63	79	61	59	74	60	58	65
12184	VALATIE	111	108	97	106	112	119	102	110	104	102	128	128	101	131	105	105	123	107	113	132
12185	VALLEY FALLS	91	93	87	90	95	99	86	91	87	86	108	106	88	112	89	88	105	88	92	108
12186	VOORHEESVILLE	124	145	152	143	144	147	132	133	126	132	158	154	139	164	135	125	156	129	126	149
12187	WARNERVILLE	85	69	51	65	76	85	67	77	74	66	88	91	62	88	70	77	82	76	89	102
	NEW YORK	95	100	134	99	98	107	103	100	105	103	133	116	105	138	104	107	131	102	99	112
	UNITED STATES	100	100	100	100	100	100	100	100	100	100	100	100	100	100	100	100	100	100	100	100

POPULATION CHANGE

# ZIP CODE / POST OFFICE NAME	COUNTY FIPS CODE	POPULATION 2000	2004	2009	2000-2004 ANNUAL RATE % Rate	State Centile	HOUSEHOLDS 2000	2004	2009	% Annual Rate 2000-2004	2004 Average HH Size	FAMILIES 2000	2004	% Annual Rate 2000-2004
12188 WATERFORD	091	10785	10872	11330	0.2	40	4372	4471	4730	0.5	2.42	2847	2888	0.3
12189 WATERVLIET	001	16460	16878	17132	0.6	61	7596	7867	8069	0.8	2.05	4127	4226	0.6
12190 WELLS	041	737	723	710	-0.5	8	322	322	322	0.0	2.18	205	203	-0.2
12192 WEST COXSACKIE	039	1953	2017	2139	0.8	69	748	787	851	1.2	2.29	551	577	1.1
12193 WESTERLO	001	2154	2134	2122	-0.2	16	818	824	831	0.2	2.59	600	600	0.0
12194 WEST FULTON	095	147	146	146	-0.2	20	61	62	63	0.4	1.65	42	40	-1.1
12196 WEST SAND LAKE	083	2820	2873	2908	0.4	54	1050	1084	1112	0.8	2.61	794	813	0.6
12197 WORCESTER	077	2324	2334	2328	0.1	35	949	965	976	0.4	2.41	638	645	0.3
12198 WYNANTSKILL	083	7336	7548	7717	0.7	65	2817	2941	3049	1.0	2.54	2056	2128	0.8
12202 ALBANY	001	9850	9894	9952	0.1	35	4517	4554	4619	0.2	2.10	2101	2102	0.0
12203 ALBANY	001	32647	32593	32870	0.0	26	12168	12341	12643	0.3	2.05	5806	5777	-0.1
12204 ALBANY	001	6489	6553	6614	0.2	42	2995	3059	3122	0.5	2.08	1607	1625	0.3
12205 ALBANY	001	25805	26341	26817	0.5	56	10848	11249	11608	0.9	2.30	7023	7247	0.7
12206 ALBANY	001	16231	15639	15505	-0.9	2	6883	6681	6690	-0.7	2.27	3433	3285	-1.0
12207 ALBANY	001	2018	1961	1954	-0.7	4	1214	1179	1183	-0.7	1.54	406	395	-0.6
12208 ALBANY	001	21119	20954	21010	-0.2	19	9410	9461	9600	0.1	2.10	4235	4202	-0.2
12209 ALBANY	001	10129	10235	10322	0.3	43	4427	4519	4610	0.5	2.21	2517	2543	0.2
12210 ALBANY	001	9763	9379	9348	-0.9	2	4951	4831	4882	-0.6	1.88	1657	1571	-1.3
12211 ALBANY	001	13907	13856	13889	-0.1	23	4592	4646	4724	0.3	2.71	3296	3319	0.2
12302 SCHENECTADY	093	26853	27106	27237	0.2	41	10634	10849	11009	0.5	2.41	7445	7530	0.3
12303 SCHENECTADY	001	28185	27916	27786	-0.2	16	11466	11462	11513	0.0	2.42	7764	7710	-0.2
12304 SCHENECTADY	093	20889	20694	20650	-0.2	16	8357	8356	8415	0.0	2.40	5193	5132	-0.3
12305 SCHENECTADY	093	5906	5729	5674	-0.7	3	2436	2345	2329	-0.9	1.52	609	572	-1.5
12306 SCHENECTADY	093	24276	24423	24517	0.1	37	10028	10172	10292	0.3	2.40	6739	6787	0.2
12307 SCHENECTADY	093	6914	6385	6248	-1.9	0	2734	2539	2501	-1.7	2.50	1479	1353	-2.1
12308 SCHENECTADY	093	13241	13454	13628	0.4	50	5790	5924	6045	0.5	2.23	3129	3179	0.4
12309 SCHENECTADY	093	29962	30612	31006	0.5	58	11255	11639	11916	0.8	2.51	8083	8298	0.6
12401 KINGSTON	111	35192	35976	37306	0.5	59	14679	15145	15878	0.7	2.30	8684	8905	0.6
12404 ACCORD	111	3818	3929	4074	0.7	65	1443	1503	1577	1.0	2.60	991	1025	0.8
12405 ACRA	039	609	642	692	1.3	84	255	271	295	1.4	2.35	173	183	1.3
12406 ARKVILLE	111	735	791	899	1.7	91	343	374	434	2.1	1.98	209	226	1.9
12409 BEARSVILLE	111	1029	1033	1057	0.1	34	490	499	518	0.4	2.04	274	277	0.3
12410 BIG INDIAN	111	561	536	544	-1.1	1	253	245	252	-0.8	2.13	148	142	-1.0
12411 BLOOMINGTON	111	375	377	386	0.1	37	145	148	154	0.5	2.51	97	98	0.2
12412 BOICEVILLE	111	497	522	545	1.2	82	205	218	231	1.5	2.39	141	149	1.3
12413 CAIRO	039	2958	3117	3356	1.2	83	1252	1330	1447	1.4	2.32	805	850	1.3
12414 CATSKILL	039	11073	11767	12761	1.4	87	4433	4774	5254	1.8	2.37	2835	3038	1.6
12416 CHICHESTER	111	232	231	236	-0.1	22	118	119	124	0.2	1.85	57	57	0.0
12418 CORNWALLVILLE	039	459	478	510	1.0	76	181	191	207	1.3	2.43	127	134	1.3
12419 COTTEKILL	111	701	695	711	-0.2	18	274	276	286	0.2	2.51	168	169	0.1
12421 DENVER	025	191	215	253	2.8	98	85	97	117	3.2	2.22	57	65	3.1
12422 DURHAM	039	264	275	294	1.0	77	104	110	119	1.3	2.42	74	78	1.3
12423 EAST DURHAM	039	1032	1074	1148	0.9	75	449	474	514	1.3	2.25	303	319	1.2
12424 EAST JEWETT	039	335	347	370	0.8	72	145	152	164	1.1	2.28	99	104	1.2
12427 ELKA PARK	039	864	880	918	0.4	53	227	234	250	0.7	2.76	145	148	0.5
12428 ELLENVILLE	111	7220	7175	7370	-0.2	20	2588	2597	2700	0.1	2.61	1739	1734	-0.1
12430 FLEISCHMANNS	025	1335	1531	1804	3.3	99	572	661	788	3.5	2.32	363	415	3.2
12431 FREEHOLD	039	1271	1318	1407	0.9	73	485	506	546	1.0	2.60	341	354	0.9
12433 GLENFORD	111	664	657	672	-0.3	15	293	295	306	0.2	2.20	200	200	0.0
12435 GREENFIELD PARK	111	324	308	312	-1.2	1	126	119	122	-1.3	2.40	84	79	-1.4
12439 HENSONVILLE	039	170	177	189	1.0	76	78	82	89	1.2	2.16	48	50	1.0
12440 HIGH FALLS	111	1760	1776	1828	0.2	41	756	774	808	0.6	2.26	480	487	0.3
12442 HUNTER	039	412	427	455	0.8	72	168	176	189	1.1	2.43	111	116	1.0
12443 HURLEY	111	3885	3853	3966	-0.2	18	1557	1567	1635	0.2	2.44	1112	1116	0.1
12444 JEWETT	039	369	381	406	0.8	69	148	154	167	0.9	2.47	103	107	0.9
12446 KERHONKSON	111	5116	5173	5322	0.3	44	1999	2041	2127	0.5	2.32	1340	1360	0.4
12448 LAKE HILL	111	44	43	43	-0.5	5	19	19	19	0.0	2.21	10	10	0.0
12449 LAKE KATRINE	111	3645	3805	3973	1.0	78	1251	1330	1414	1.5	2.46	869	919	1.3
12450 LANESVILLE	039	814	840	894	0.7	68	384	399	428	0.9	2.11	216	222	0.7
12451 LEEDS	039	1478	1609	1764	2.0	93	605	670	745	2.4	2.40	406	447	2.3
12454 MAPLECREST	039	410	423	450	0.7	68	157	164	177	1.0	2.58	104	108	0.9
12455 MARGARETVILLE	025	2505	2771	3214	2.4	96	980	1104	1310	2.8	2.35	596	667	2.7
12456 MOUNT MARION	111	583	622	656	1.5	88	211	229	244	1.9	2.72	162	174	1.7
12457 MOUNT TREMPER	111	1119	1099	1122	-0.4	9	500	500	517	0.0	2.15	278	275	-0.3
12458 NAPANOCH	111	3230	3190	3242	-0.3	14	824	819	846	-0.1	2.92	575	568	-0.3
12460 OAK HILL	039	437	459	488	1.2	82	158	169	182	1.6	2.64	111	118	1.5
12461 OLIVEBRIDGE	111	1775	1827	1889	0.7	65	715	746	781	1.0	2.42	470	488	0.9
12463 PALENVILLE	039	1333	1355	1428	0.4	51	526	541	578	0.7	2.39	351	359	0.5
12464 PHOENICIA	111	1259	1281	1326	0.4	52	577	594	622	0.7	2.12	330	337	0.5
12465 PINE HILL	111	289	274	284	-1.3	1	134	128	135	-1.1	2.07	78	75	-0.9
12466 PORT EWEN	111	3223	3237	3303	0.1	35	1305	1331	1376	0.5	2.43	870	880	0.3
12468 PRATTSVILLE	039	1515	1633	1786	1.8	91	605	664	738	2.2	2.45	411	445	1.9
12469 PRESTON HOLLOW	001	722	751	771	0.9	75	309	326	338	1.3	2.28	209	219	1.1
12470 PURLING	039	547	578	623	1.3	85	200	214	233	1.6	2.67	135	143	1.4
12472 ROSENDALE	111	1634	1635	1673	0.0	29	710	722	749	0.4	2.25	448	453	0.3
12473 ROUND TOP	039	580	625	681	1.8	91	230	251	277	2.1	2.44	155	168	1.9
12474 ROXBURY	025	2239	2480	2894	2.4	96	968	1092	1296	2.9	2.26	645	723	2.7
12477 SAUGERTIES	111	20307	21419	22538	1.3	84	7678	8205	8752	1.6	2.47	5178	5503	1.4
12480 SHANDAKEN	039	442	473	503	1.6	89	186	201	216	1.8	2.35	114	122	1.6
12481 SHOKAN	111	1590	1658	1726	1.0	77	643	682	720	1.4	2.41	444	468	1.3
12482 SOUTH CAIRO	039	565	613	670	1.9	93	251	275	304	2.2	2.23	169	183	1.9
12484 STONE RIDGE	111	2890	2918	2993	0.2	42	1139	1165	1209	0.5	2.49	777	790	0.4
12485 TANNERSVILLE	039	989	1015	1074	0.6	62	440	455	488	0.8	2.06	272	279	0.6
12486 TILLSON	111	1593	1592	1626	0.0	27	595	604	626	0.4	2.64	394	398	0.2
12487 ULSTER PARK	111	3657	3730	3846	0.5	56	1337	1386	1455	0.9	2.43	878	906	0.7
12491 WEST HURLEY	111	1945	1968	2037	0.3	45	800	824	865	0.7	2.34	533	544	0.5
12492 WEST KILL	039	378	471	553	5.3	100	175	221	262	5.6	2.13	104	130	5.4
12494 WEST SHOKAN	111	701	743	780	1.4	87	296	317	336	1.6	2.34	201	213	1.4
12495 WILLOW	111	353	342	348	-0.7	3	171	168	174	-0.4	2.00	94	92	-0.5
12496 WINDHAM	039	1350	1394	1485	0.8	69	601	629	678	1.1	2.22	381	397	1.0
12498 WOODSTOCK	111	4474	4698	4947	1.2	82	2078	2234	2393	1.7	2.09	1157	1231	1.5
12501 AMENIA	027	2522	2611	2727	0.8	71	986	1033	1089	1.1	2.49	668	693	0.9
12502 ANCRAM	021	873	910	954	1.0	77	378	400	425	1.3	2.25	267	281	1.2
12503 ANCRAMDALE	021	931	987	1045	1.4	87	356	383	411	1.7	2.58	258	276	1.6
12507 BARRYTOWN	027	255	264	274	0.8	71	76	80	84	1.2	2.80	51	53	0.9
NEW YORK					0.4					0.5	2.60			0.4
UNITED STATES					1.2					1.3	2.58			1.1

ZIP CODE #	POST OFFICE NAME	RACE (%) White 2000	White 2004	Black 2000	Black 2004	Asian/Pacific 2000	Asian/Pacific 2004	% Hispanic Origin 2000	% Hispanic Origin 2004	2004 AGE DISTRIBUTION (%) 0-4	5-9	10-14	15-19	20-24	25-44	45-64	65-84	85+	18+	MEDIAN AGE 2004	% 2004 Males	% 2004 Females
12188	WATERFORD	97.0	96.4	0.7	0.8	1.1	1.3	1.0	1.3	6.0	6.0	6.7	6.4	6.0	30.3	25.5	11.7	1.5	77.4	38.6	48.1	51.9
12189	WATERVLIET	90.8	88.8	3.9	4.8	2.7	3.3	3.0	3.7	6.2	5.5	6.2	7.5	9.8	29.2	21.8	11.7	2.2	78.5	35.1	47.3	52.7
12190	WELLS	96.6	96.5	0.5	0.6	0.3	0.3	0.3	0.3	3.7	4.3	6.4	5.5	5.0	20.2	33.9	18.3	2.8	81.5	47.8	50.6	49.4
12192	WEST COXSACKIE	90.7	89.0	6.0	7.0	0.5	0.6	4.2	5.3	4.8	5.3	6.7	6.7	6.8	27.1	29.2	11.1	2.2	79.3	40.9	53.2	46.9
12193	WESTERLO	98.3	97.7	0.7	0.8	0.3	0.4	0.7	1.1	6.1	6.8	7.9	6.4	4.7	25.3	30.1	11.0	1.6	74.9	40.9	49.3	50.7
12194	WEST FULTON	80.3	78.8	15.7	17.1	0.0	0.0	9.5	10.3	2.7	3.4	4.8	6.2	15.8	30.8	22.6	11.6	2.1	86.3	35.4	63.7	36.3
12196	WEST SAND LAKE	98.7	98.4	0.3	0.3	0.5	0.7	0.8	1.0	5.6	6.5	7.9	6.9	4.8	24.1	30.9	11.1	2.1	75.7	41.5	48.1	51.9
12197	WORCESTER	97.9	97.6	0.5	0.5	0.3	0.4	1.0	1.3	5.5	5.9	7.2	6.8	5.8	23.5	29.0	14.2	2.1	76.9	42.1	48.8	51.2
12198	WYNANTSKILL	97.1	96.4	0.8	0.9	0.7	1.0	0.7	0.9	5.9	6.4	6.9	6.8	4.9	26.4	28.1	12.8	1.8	76.3	40.5	48.4	51.6
12202	ALBANY	36.3	31.8	53.8	57.5	1.4	1.6	9.2	10.1	8.2	7.7	8.1	7.1	8.7	30.9	19.9	7.7	1.6	71.7	31.5	46.2	53.8
12203	ALBANY	84.1	80.9	7.9	9.3	4.8	5.9	3.8	4.7	3.5	3.5	4.0	15.5	17.8	22.6	18.7	11.4	3.1	86.4	30.1	47.4	52.6
12204	ALBANY	68.9	64.5	23.3	26.2	4.1	5.0	3.7	4.4	5.7	5.4	6.6	5.9	6.1	26.5	26.3	14.2	3.2	78.5	40.5	46.8	53.2
12205	ALBANY	91.2	89.1	4.3	5.2	2.7	3.4	1.7	2.1	5.1	5.4	6.2	5.6	5.0	26.9	26.6	16.5	2.7	79.8	42.4	48.0	52.0
12206	ALBANY	45.2	41.5	45.2	47.8	3.0	3.4	6.4	7.2	7.5	7.0	7.7	7.4	10.8	27.8	19.7	10.5	1.8	73.3	31.8	48.8	51.2
12207	ALBANY	30.7	26.7	60.4	63.7	2.2	2.5	7.0	7.6	6.6	6.0	6.6	6.1	5.3	26.9	26.1	13.3	3.2	77.0	39.7	50.3	49.7
12208	ALBANY	80.9	77.3	11.4	13.5	3.5	4.2	3.7	4.5	4.4	4.5	5.0	6.5	12.0	30.6	21.7	12.4	2.9	82.8	35.6	47.3	52.7
12209	ALBANY	72.0	68.1	20.6	23.4	2.6	3.1	5.2	6.1	6.4	6.1	6.6	6.1	6.5	30.3	22.6	12.8	2.7	77.2	37.6	46.0	54.0
12210	ALBANY	42.0	39.5	48.4	49.8	2.6	3.0	7.2	8.0	6.8	5.6	5.7	5.5	14.0	35.9	19.0	6.1	1.3	78.8	30.3	50.6	49.4
12211	ALBANY	89.2	87.2	5.1	5.7	3.7	4.6	2.5	3.0	4.9	5.2	6.3	8.2	9.0	21.8	27.5	14.9	2.2	79.8	41.0	47.8	52.2
12302	SCHENECTADY	97.3	96.7	0.7	0.9	0.9	1.1	1.2	1.6	5.1	5.7	7.0	6.5	4.9	23.5	28.5	15.4	3.5	77.9	43.4	47.7	52.3
12303	SCHENECTADY	91.6	90.0	4.6	5.3	1.0	1.2	2.5	3.1	6.0	6.5	7.7	6.6	5.2	26.0	26.1	13.6	2.3	75.6	40.2	47.7	52.4
12304	SCHENECTADY	78.8	75.8	13.2	14.8	2.8	3.4	4.7	5.5	6.9	6.9	7.3	6.8	5.8	26.9	23.4	13.0	3.0	74.6	38.4	48.0	52.0
12305	SCHENECTADY	76.5	72.7	14.2	16.1	4.1	5.0	4.6	5.6	2.9	2.2	2.1	15.7	20.3	27.5	19.3	8.3	1.9	91.9	29.7	56.1	43.9
12306	SCHENECTADY	96.4	95.5	1.4	1.7	0.7	0.9	1.4	1.8	6.0	6.2	6.8	6.1	5.3	27.3	26.1	14.0	2.1	77.2	40.4	48.7	51.3
12307	SCHENECTADY	43.3	39.1	42.5	45.2	1.4	1.5	13.1	14.6	9.7	8.9	10.2	8.9	7.2	26.6	19.4	7.8	1.4	66.0	29.3	47.1	52.9
12308	SCHENECTADY	82.9	79.4	9.4	11.0	1.6	2.0	5.4	6.7	7.1	6.5	6.9	6.4	7.8	29.9	20.8	11.8	2.7	75.5	35.0	47.1	52.9
12309	SCHENECTADY	89.6	87.3	3.6	4.4	4.7	5.8	2.0	2.6	5.6	6.3	7.2	6.7	4.6	23.4	29.0	14.0	3.2	76.4	42.7	48.5	51.6
12401	KINGSTON	84.9	82.8	9.4	10.4	1.4	1.8	5.2	6.3	6.0	6.0	6.9	6.7	6.4	26.1	25.6	13.6	2.7	76.9	40.1	47.8	52.2
12404	ACCORD	93.8	92.7	2.1	2.4	0.7	0.8	4.1	5.0	5.8	6.6	7.9	7.3	5.2	26.7	29.6	9.7	1.1	74.9	39.7	50.4	49.6
12405	ACRA	97.5	97.0	0.3	0.3	0.2	0.3	2.6	3.4	5.3	5.5	7.2	7.0	5.3	23.2	27.9	16.7	2.0	77.7	42.8	48.6	51.4
12406	ARKVILLE	96.3	95.6	0.7	0.8	1.0	1.3	4.0	5.1	4.6	5.1	5.9	4.7	3.7	21.9	30.1	20.0	4.2	81.4	48.0	48.8	51.2
12409	BEARSVILLE	94.3	93.2	1.1	1.3	1.6	1.9	2.4	3.0	3.1	3.4	4.9	5.0	2.7	19.9	43.1	15.6	2.2	85.2	50.7	50.4	49.6
12410	BIG INDIAN	95.2	94.4	0.9	1.1	1.1	1.3	2.5	3.2	4.9	4.3	5.6	5.2	3.7	23.9	35.8	15.1	1.5	81.9	46.1	50.9	49.1
12411	BLOOMINGTON	96.5	95.8	1.1	1.3	0.5	0.5	1.1	1.3	6.4	6.6	6.4	7.7	6.1	26.8	27.3	10.9	1.9	75.1	39.2	50.1	49.9
12412	BOICEVILLE	97.0	96.6	0.4	0.4	1.0	1.2	2.6	3.1	4.8	6.1	7.5	6.7	3.3	24.9	33.1	11.5	2.1	76.8	43.4	49.2	50.8
12413	CAIRO	96.0	95.0	0.7	0.9	0.4	0.5	4.7	6.1	5.7	5.9	7.6	7.1	5.6	23.3	26.4	16.3	2.3	76.6	41.7	47.6	52.4
12414	CATSKILL	89.5	87.4	6.3	7.6	0.7	0.8	4.0	5.0	6.1	5.9	6.5	6.5	5.6	24.5	26.9	14.8	3.2	77.4	41.5	47.9	52.2
12416	CHICHESTER	95.7	94.4	0.9	0.9	0.4	0.9	3.5	3.9	3.0	3.9	5.6	6.1	5.2	23.4	33.3	16.0	3.5	84.0	46.6	49.4	50.7
12418	CORNWALLVILLE	98.5	98.3	0.0	0.0	0.4	0.4	1.1	1.3	5.2	5.4	7.1	5.9	4.2	22.6	32.0	15.7	1.9	78.7	44.7	50.2	49.8
12419	COTTEKILL	93.9	92.8	2.6	2.9	0.3	0.4	2.9	3.6	3.9	5.2	7.5	7.9	5.5	28.2	31.5	9.2	1.2	78.9	40.6	49.5	50.5
12421	DENVER	96.9	96.3	0.5	0.9	0.5	0.9	2.6	3.7	6.5	6.1	4.7	4.7	4.7	19.5	34.0	19.5	0.5	80.0	47.0	48.8	51.2
12422	DURHAM	98.5	98.2	0.0	0.0	0.4	0.4	0.8	1.1	4.7	5.5	7.3	5.8	4.4	22.6	32.0	16.0	1.8	78.6	44.9	50.6	49.5
12423	EAST DURHAM	98.3	97.8	0.1	0.2	0.5	0.7	1.7	2.2	5.0	5.5	6.3	5.8	4.5	22.8	31.3	17.0	1.8	79.5	45.1	50.2	49.8
12424	EAST JEWETT	97.9	97.7	0.0	0.0	0.9	0.9	2.7	3.5	3.8	5.5	8.1	5.2	2.9	21.9	34.6	16.1	2.0	79.8	46.6	50.7	49.3
12427	ELKA PARK	98.0	97.6	0.1	0.1	0.2	0.2	1.0	1.4	7.5	9.3	9.1	6.1	4.3	22.3	28.0	11.4	2.1	70.0	38.6	49.9	50.1
12428	ELLENVILLE	73.2	70.1	11.5	12.3	1.3	1.5	22.1	25.7	6.1	6.3	7.4	7.4	6.8	28.2	25.3	10.7	1.8	75.6	37.2	49.4	50.6
12430	FLEISCHMANNS	96.6	96.1	0.6	0.7	0.9	1.1	6.5	7.9	5.4	5.9	7.1	4.8	3.8	23.4	30.4	17.2	2.0	78.6	44.8	49.1	51.0
12431	FREEHOLD	96.9	96.1	0.3	0.4	1.0	1.4	2.1	2.7	6.3	6.6	7.4	6.8	5.2	23.6	27.2	15.4	1.7	75.5	41.6	48.6	51.4
12433	GLENFORD	95.3	94.4	1.1	1.2	1.2	1.5	2.9	3.8	3.2	3.8	5.5	5.3	4.4	19.9	37.6	18.9	1.4	84.0	49.8	49.2	50.8
12435	GREENFIELD PARK	81.2	78.6	9.0	9.7	0.6	0.7	11.4	14.0	4.9	5.5	5.8	6.2	5.8	27.6	31.8	11.4	1.0	79.9	41.5	50.3	49.7
12439	HENSONVILLE	98.2	97.7	0.6	0.6	0.0	0.0	1.8	2.8	4.5	5.1	6.8	6.8	5.1	20.3	31.1	18.6	1.7	79.1	45.8	47.5	52.5
12440	HIGH FALLS	95.7	94.8	1.6	1.9	0.2	0.3	3.2	4.0	5.0	5.5	5.7	6.3	5.2	25.7	33.2	12.2	1.4	79.9	42.9	48.7	51.3
12442	HUNTER	97.6	97.0	0.2	0.5	0.7	0.9	3.2	4.0	4.2	5.6	7.7	4.9	2.8	22.3	34.9	15.9	1.6	79.9	46.5	50.1	49.9
12443	HURLEY	96.0	95.2	1.3	1.6	1.1	1.4	1.8	2.3	4.6	5.5	6.8	6.5	4.5	22.1	31.6	17.1	1.3	78.8	45.0	48.6	51.4
12444	JEWETT	97.6	97.1	0.3	0.3	0.8	1.1	3.0	3.7	3.9	5.8	7.9	5.0	2.9	23.1	33.9	15.8	1.8	79.8	45.9	50.1	49.9
12446	KERHONKSON	87.5	85.9	6.6	7.1	0.8	1.0	8.4	10.0	5.4	5.6	6.7	7.0	6.3	30.5	25.8	11.3	1.4	78.1	38.6	54.6	45.4
12448	LAKE HILL	95.5	93.0	2.3	2.3	2.3	2.3	2.3	2.3	2.3	4.7	4.7	4.7	4.7	23.3	39.5	14.0	2.3	88.4	48.1	48.8	51.2
12449	LAKE KATRINE	93.0	91.7	3.0	3.4	2.0	2.4	1.7	2.1	5.4	5.7	6.4	6.1	5.1	25.6	26.7	14.6	4.5	78.6	42.5	46.5	53.5
12450	LANESVILLE	96.6	95.7	1.1	1.4	0.3	0.2	3.1	4.2	5.6	5.7	6.6	5.6	3.8	21.9	33.1	16.2	1.6	78.6	45.5	51.9	48.1
12451	LEEDS	96.6	95.7	1.0	1.4	0.3	0.4	3.2	4.0	5.5	5.8	7.0	6.7	5.6	24.2	28.1	15.1	1.9	77.5	42.0	49.0	51.0
12454	MAPLECREST	98.5	98.1	0.0	0.0	0.0	0.2	1.7	2.1	3.3	4.3	7.3	6.6	4.3	18.4	37.1	17.0	1.7	80.9	48.5	47.8	52.3
12455	MARGARETVILLE	94.1	93.0	0.6	0.7	0.5	0.7	6.0	7.3	4.2	4.9	6.5	5.9	3.7	19.9	30.0	20.5	4.5	80.4	48.1	48.3	51.8
12456	MOUNT MARION	95.5	95.0	4.0	4.5	0.0	0.0	0.9	1.0	6.9	6.6	6.4	6.4	7.1	27.5	25.7	12.4	1.0	76.2	39.3	47.1	52.9
12457	MOUNT TREMPER	95.0	94.1	1.2	1.4	1.0	1.3	2.6	3.2	3.5	3.6	6.0	6.4	4.2	20.8	39.0	14.7	1.9	83.0	47.7	49.2	50.8
12458	NAPANOCH	76.6	74.2	15.0	15.9	0.8	1.0	12.4	14.6	4.4	4.6	5.5	5.3	6.6	37.7	24.6	10.1	1.3	82.1	38.2	61.6	38.4
12460	OAK HILL	98.4	98.3	0.2	0.2	0.2	0.4	0.9	1.1	5.2	5.5	7.0	5.7	4.6	22.4	32.2	15.5	2.0	78.7	44.7	50.1	49.9
12461	OLIVEBRIDGE	96.4	95.7	0.6	0.7	1.2	1.5	2.1	2.7	4.5	5.4	7.7	6.0	3.8	22.8	34.5	13.1	2.1	78.0	44.8	50.0	50.0
12463	PALENVILLE	96.2	95.4	0.6	0.7	0.9	1.1	2.1	2.8	6.9	6.8	7.5	6.5	5.1	26.8	27.8	11.4	1.3	74.8	40.1	48.7	51.3
12464	PHOENICIA	94.9	93.9	1.2	1.4	1.1	1.4	2.9	3.8	4.5	4.6	6.9	6.3	4.1	21.5	35.2	15.0	2.0	80.1	46.0	49.5	50.5
12465	PINE HILL	94.8	94.2	0.7	0.7	1.4	1.8	3.5	4.7	4.4	4.7	5.1	3.7	4.0	24.1	33.9	18.3	1.8	83.6	47.4	51.1	48.9
12466	PORT EWEN	93.3	91.9	2.8	3.2	1.3	1.6	1.9	2.5	5.8	6.2	7.5	6.6	5.3	26.8	28.3	11.9	1.5	76.3	40.6	46.9	53.1
12468	PRATTSVILLE	98.1	97.6	0.1	0.2	0.4	0.5	1.8	2.3	5.9	6.5	6.4	5.6	4.3	24.4	29.1	15.7	2.2	77.6	42.9	47.9	52.1
12469	PRESTON HOLLOW	96.5	95.9	1.8	2.1	0.3	0.3	1.3	1.3	5.7	6.1	6.0	6.5	5.5	21.4	32.4	14.4	2.0	77.5	44.1	49.7	50.3
12470	PURLING	97.4	96.7	0.7	1.0	0.2	0.4	2.4	2.9	5.7	6.1	8.0	8.0	6.1	24.4	26.8	13.0	2.1	74.9	39.7	49.7	50.4
12472	ROSENDALE	96.0	95.3	1.7	1.9	0.4	0.6	2.4	3.0	6.1	6.4	7.0	7.0	5.8	28.1	27.9	10.0	1.7	76.0	39.0	49.3	50.7
12473	ROUND TOP	97.9	97.4	0.5	0.6	0.2	0.2	3.1	4.3	6.1	6.1	7.5	8.2	5.8	23.4	25.8	14.9	2.4	75.5	40.7	47.8	52.2
12474	ROXBURY	97.4	96.8	0.5	0.5	0.6	0.7	1.3	1.7	5.9	5.7	4.9	5.0	5.0	21.3	32.7	17.8	1.7	80.5	46.4	49.5	50.5
12477	SAUGERTIES	92.1	90.9	4.0	4.3	0.8	1.0	4.6	5.5	5.5	5.8	7.1	6.8	6.2	29.1	26.3	11.7	1.4	77.3	39.3	51.4	48.7
12480	SHANDAKEN	93.9	92.4	1.4	1.5	2.0	2.5	2.9	3.6	4.7	5.7	7.6	5.9	3.8	19.0	34.0	17.3	1.9	78.2	46.8	48.4	51.6
12481	SHOKAN	96.9	96.3	0.9	1.1	1.1	1.5	2.8	3.5	3.7	5.0	8.1	7.4	4.9	23.8	32.9	12.5	1.8	77.9	43.5	50.6	49.4
12482	SOUTH CAIRO	96.6	95.8	1.1	1.5	0.2	0.3	3.2	3.9	5.6	5.9	7.2	6.9	5.7	24.5	27.6	14.9	2.0	77.2	41.6	48.8	51.2
12484	STONE RIDGE	95.8	94.8	1.1	1.3	0.9	1.2	2.3	2.9	4.8	5.7	7.4	6.7	4.5	23.8	33.7	12.1	1.5	77.8	43.5	49.0	51.0
12485	TANNERSVILLE	96.4	95.6	0.5	0.7	0.2	0.2	2.1	2.8	5.1	5.8	7.4	6.6	5.3	21.7	30.3	15.4	2.5	77.7	43.6	50.5	49.5
12486	TILLSON	96.9	96.2	1.2	1.4	0.4	0.6	2.3	3.0	7.0	7.2	7.5	6.3	5.1	27.9	26.0	11.1	1.8	74.4	39.0	48.9	51.1
12487	ULSTER PARK	95.3	94.5	2.0	2.3	0.7	0.8	1.9	2.4	5.8	6.4	7.8	6.6	5.6	26.8	29.1	10.5	1.4	76.0	39.7	49.3	50.8
12491	WEST HURLEY	94.7	93.7	1.8	2.0	1.8	2.2	2.1	2.7	4.2	5.2	6.2	6.8	4.4	19.8	34.6	17.2	1.8	79.8	47.1	48.6	51.4
12492	WEST KILL	97.6	97.0	0.0	0.0	0.5	0.6	1.3	2.1	4.5	4.9	5.5	4.9	4.0	20.4	35.2	18.1	2.6	82.0	48.4	46.3	53.7
12494	WEST SHOKAN	96.7	96.1	0.3	0.3	0.6	0.9	2.9	3.6	5.8	5.8	6.6	5.3	2.6	25.3	34.7	11.7	2.3	77.8	44.3	49.4	50.6
12495	WILLOW	94.6	93.6	1.4	1.5	1.4	1.8	2.0	2.9	2.3	3.2	6.1	6.1	4.4	17.5	42.7	15.8	1.8	84.5	50.4	48.0	52.1
12496	WINDHAM	97.9	97.4	0.5	0.7	0.2	0.2	2.1	2.7	4.3	5.3	7.0	6.7	4.7	21.4	30.9	17.7	2.1	79.3	45.4	48.5	51.5
12498	WOODSTOCK	94.3	93.2	1.3	1.5	1.6	2.0	2.7	3.4	3.1	3.8	5.6	5.8	4.2	19.4	39.0	16.9	2.2	83.5	49.4	48.1	51.9
12501	AMENIA	92.6	91.2	2.9	3.4	0.5	0.7	3.6	4.5	5.9	6.1	7.6	6.5	6.2	25.7	27.0	13.4	1.7	76.4	40.2	49.3	50.7
12502	ANCRAM	97.9	97.5	0.7	0.9	0.2	0.3	0.9	1.1	4.3	4.8	6.9	6.2	4.2	24.4	32.3	14.7	2.2	79.7	44.6	51.1	48.9
12503	ANCRAMDALE	97.6	97.3	1.1	1.2	0.1	0.2	1.0	1.1	4.5	5.3	7.0	6.8	4.3	24.5	30.8	14.6	2.3	78.8	43.8	51.3	48.7
12507	BARRYTOWN	94.5	93.6	1.2	1.1	2.0	2.7	2.8	3.4	4.9	4.9	6.1	10.6	14.8	22.0	23.9	11.0	1.9	80.3	33.2	47.7	52.3
	NEW YORK	68.0	65.9	15.9	16.2	5.6	6.4	15.1	16.7	6.5	6.5	7.1	7.0	7.1	28.9	24.0	11.2	1.8	75.8	36.7	48.3	51.7
	UNITED STATES	75.1	73.6	12.3	12.5	3.8	4.2	12.5	14.1	6.9	6.7	7.2	7.0	7.3	28.6	23.8	10.8	1.7	75.1	36.0	49.1	50.9

#	Post Office Name	2004 Per Capita Income	2004 HH Income Base	2004 Household Income Distribution (%): Less than $25,000	$25,000 to $49,999	$50,000 to $99,999	$100,000 to $149,999	$150,000 or More	Median Household Income: 2004	2009	2004 National Centile	2004 State Centile	2004 Home Value Base	2004 Home Value Distribution (%): Less than $50,000	$50,000 to $89,999	$90,000 to $174,999	$175,000 to $399,999	$400,000 or More	2004 Median Home Value
12188	WATERFORD	26996	4471	16.7	30.4	38.0	10.7	4.3	52632	60514	76	66	2990	1.5	3.7	63.7	30.1	1.0	150044
12189	WATERVLIET	23384	7867	29.0	34.4	28.4	6.1	2.2	39012	44592	43	29	3701	1.7	5.4	68.7	23.8	0.5	133377
12190	WELLS	18531	322	39.1	33.2	20.5	6.8	0.3	32104	35209	18	7	263	5.7	14.5	51.7	25.1	3.0	131618
12192	WEST COXSACKIE	25390	787	15.8	35.2	36.9	8.6	3.6	49387	56235	71	61	671	5.1	6.1	48.9	38.5	1.5	152500
12193	WESTERLO	23119	824	19.9	30.5	39.9	7.2	2.6	49763	57567	71	62	704	4.3	7.4	55.5	30.7	2.1	144253
12194	WEST FULTON	25875	62	25.8	33.9	30.7	4.8	4.8	44057	48360	59	48	56	10.7	19.6	41.1	25.0	3.6	121429
12196	WEST SAND LAKE	31043	1084	21.7	16.3	37.6	13.5	11.0	59725	68534	84	74	906	0.4	2.4	41.2	52.0	4.0	182297
12197	WORCESTER	18749	965	34.8	33.8	25.1	4.6	1.8	34275	38078	25	11	767	11.0	12.5	59.3	15.7	1.6	124771
12198	WYNANTSKILL	26567	2941	15.6	25.1	41.4	14.0	3.9	62409	69912	87	77	2503	1.8	2.6	55.5	36.2	3.9	159035
12202	ALBANY	15596	4554	53.5	27.1	16.0	2.6	0.8	22871	25508	3	2	1248	7.4	24.9	59.9	6.6	1.2	104508
12203	ALBANY	26608	12341	26.4	26.1	31.6	10.4	5.5	47319	54948	67	56	6623	0.4	1.7	59.2	37.2	1.4	158322
12204	ALBANY	31509	3059	26.1	30.0	30.1	6.1	7.8	44386	51087	60	49	1250	2.7	8.7	57.3	18.5	12.8	139235
12205	ALBANY	26876	11249	19.0	26.2	39.8	11.4	3.6	53987	62913	78	69	8595	2.2	2.0	70.6	24.7	0.5	145294
12206	ALBANY	17266	6681	48.0	26.9	19.6	4.0	1.4	26532	30313	6	4	2194	4.3	21.1	61.2	12.7	0.6	116318
12207	ALBANY	15998	1179	68.9	18.9	9.1	1.4	1.7	13445	16170	1	1	156	1.9	21.8	69.9	6.4	0.0	112946
12208	ALBANY	27039	9461	28.2	28.6	29.6	8.4	5.2	43109	50208	56	45	4665	0.4	2.2	64.2	32.3	1.0	151320
12209	ALBANY	24091	4519	25.5	31.7	31.9	7.9	2.9	43876	50452	58	47	2724	1.0	3.1	82.5	12.9	0.5	131644
12210	ALBANY	21093	4831	46.7	29.5	15.4	5.1	3.2	27189	32423	7	4	1056	2.7	12.9	48.8	33.9	1.8	144326
12211	ALBANY	33027	4646	14.2	19.6	34.0	18.2	14.1	70649	83049	91	85	3808	0.4	1.3	36.0	54.3	8.0	194431
12302	SCHENECTADY	28845	10849	15.8	26.0	39.3	13.6	5.2	58278	66334	83	73	8738	2.0	4.7	63.7	28.9	0.7	146139
12303	SCHENECTADY	26371	11462	23.6	28.3	32.9	9.4	5.8	48110	55735	69	58	8427	1.9	13.3	52.2	31.2	1.4	142240
12304	SCHENECTADY	20004	8356	32.1	29.9	31.0	5.1	1.9	38497	44052	41	27	4910	3.4	23.1	62.4	11.1	0.0	110747
12305	SCHENECTADY	19697	2345	52.7	27.3	13.4	4.3	2.2	22581	25334	3	2	387	5.4	26.6	47.0	19.4	1.6	111925
12306	SCHENECTADY	23952	10172	22.4	30.9	33.9	10.0	2.8	46372	53714	65	54	7494	1.3	10.4	63.8	23.9	0.6	133770
12307	SCHENECTADY	11276	2539	60.1	26.6	11.0	1.3	0.9	19336	21579	2	1	685	23.1	50.7	23.2	2.6	0.4	67500
12308	SCHENECTADY	20916	5924	34.4	32.2	25.7	5.6	2.1	36556	41455	34	19	2689	2.5	18.2	70.3	9.0	0.0	113310
12309	SCHENECTADY	35548	11639	13.0	18.8	37.8	17.8	12.6	73098	82626	92	86	9259	0.3	1.9	42.4	52.3	3.1	183707
12401	KINGSTON	22984	15145	31.4	29.7	27.5	7.7	3.8	39269	44634	44	30	8623	3.6	6.0	55.7	31.7	3.0	146724
12404	ACCORD	27764	1503	19.9	27.6	37.1	10.1	5.3	51814	57797	75	65	1235	3.9	6.3	35.7	48.6	5.5	182173
12405	ACRA	21896	271	29.5	32.1	26.6	9.6	2.2	39182	44482	43	30	198	4.0	8.6	57.6	27.8	2.0	140948
12406	ARKVILLE	23124	374	34.5	32.9	24.1	5.9	2.7	35379	39598	29	14	288	3.8	6.6	54.2	29.5	5.9	144718
12409	BEARSVILLE	40091	499	20.8	21.6	33.5	9.8	14.2	58290	69249	83	73	402	0.0	0.3	25.4	49.8	24.6	247458
12410	BIG INDIAN	25783	245	31.0	32.2	26.5	5.3	4.9	37609	42864	38	23	196	3.6	10.2	49.0	32.1	5.1	147143
12411	BLOOMINGTON	25089	148	29.1	19.6	37.8	6.1	7.4	50852	58226	74	64	118	11.9	1.7	54.2	30.5	1.7	141667
12412	BOICEVILLE	27350	218	17.9	24.3	41.7	10.1	6.0	55790	64797	80	71	177	1.1	1.7	43.5	46.9	6.8	179779
12413	CAIRO	23194	1330	33.9	30.4	25.9	6.0	3.8	37060	41552	36	21	853	2.2	7.7	58.0	30.5	1.5	145954
12414	CATSKILL	20817	4774	34.5	30.0	25.2	6.5	3.7	36682	41100	34	19	3159	3.8	9.3	53.9	29.6	3.3	142333
12416	CHICHESTER	35076	119	38.7	22.7	17.7	13.5	7.6	32873	36993	21	8	77	3.9	1.3	54.6	37.7	2.6	159375
12418	CORNWALLVILLE	21659	191	26.2	37.2	26.7	7.3	2.6	40761	46636	49	37	155	7.7	6.5	47.1	32.9	5.8	145673
12419	COTTEKILL	22548	276	21.7	30.1	36.2	9.1	2.9	48410	55859	69	59	181	3.9	2.8	34.3	56.4	2.8	190278
12421	DENVER	25825	97	32.0	32.0	20.6	10.3	5.2	38053	43077	39	25	83	4.8	2.4	47.0	37.4	8.4	166250
12422	DURHAM	21982	110	23.6	39.1	26.4	8.2	2.7	42874	50700	56	44	90	6.7	6.7	48.9	32.2	5.6	143333
12423	EAST DURHAM	22388	474	32.9	30.8	28.9	5.5	1.9	36006	40761	32	16	381	9.7	6.6	43.3	36.2	4.2	149833
12424	EAST JEWETT	26676	152	25.7	30.9	28.3	7.9	7.2	45404	51596	62	51	126	3.2	6.4	37.3	45.2	7.9	185000
12427	ELKA PARK	16172	234	31.2	28.6	32.1	6.0	2.1	39004	44013	43	29	188	0.0	2.1	59.6	36.7	1.6	147807
12428	ELLENVILLE	17883	2597	39.4	24.6	26.0	7.8	2.2	36606	41527	34	19	1456	7.1	10.4	51.9	28.2	2.3	142283
12430	FLEISCHMANNS	19415	661	37.7	35.0	19.2	5.0	3.2	33578	37086	23	9	520	1.7	8.3	52.9	31.2	6.0	145168
12431	FREEHOLD	21200	506	25.1	32.8	29.5	8.1	4.6	43520	49205	57	46	396	0.5	5.8	50.8	39.7	3.3	157051
12433	GLENFORD	31780	295	21.4	28.5	31.2	10.9	8.1	50238	58211	72	63	252	0.0	0.0	30.6	62.3	7.1	197273
12435	GREENFIELD PARK	22135	119	28.6	22.7	36.1	11.8	0.8	48652	55581	70	60	93	3.2	6.5	41.9	44.1	4.3	172321
12439	HENSONVILLE	26441	82	30.5	30.5	24.4	8.5	6.1	40906	45573	49	37	60	0.0	3.3	38.3	51.7	6.7	190625
12440	HIGH FALLS	27580	774	25.2	27.7	31.9	8.5	6.7	45861	52714	63	53	586	2.1	1.0	43.5	42.0	11.4	182463
12442	HUNTER	24288	176	28.4	29.6	27.3	8.0	6.8	44224	49659	59	48	138	4.4	6.5	38.4	44.2	6.5	177500
12443	HURLEY	29688	1567	16.0	25.0	37.0	13.9	8.2	58777	67468	83	73	1370	3.5	1.7	40.7	51.7	2.5	178915
12444	JEWETT	24147	154	26.6	29.9	29.2	7.8	6.5	45404	50784	62	51	128	5.5	6.3	37.5	44.5	6.3	177273
12446	KERHONKSON	22004	2041	26.5	32.9	30.2	7.6	2.7	44263	50283	59	48	1512	4.4	6.6	49.7	35.1	4.2	151857
12448	LAKE HILL	37568	19	5.3	31.6	31.6	21.1	10.5	70624	70624	91	84	16	0.0	0.0	31.3	37.5	31.3	275000
12449	LAKE KATRINE	22936	1330	17.3	33.2	35.4	10.5	3.5	49533	56583	71	61	947	9.5	2.9	52.5	33.3	1.9	147935
12450	LANESVILLE	24837	399	39.6	27.1	24.1	4.3	5.0	35837	41825	31	16	249	5.6	7.2	46.6	34.9	5.6	150521
12451	LEEDS	23979	670	31.3	25.5	29.0	8.8	5.4	43012	47443	56	44	545	5.5	11.6	48.8	31.9	2.2	148828
12454	MAPLECREST	23818	164	26.2	32.9	27.4	6.7	6.7	42571	49179	55	43	137	0.7	5.1	42.3	43.1	8.8	179808
12455	MARGARETVILLE	20298	1104	33.8	27.5	28.1	8.2	2.5	36024	40140	32	16	857	4.2	6.5	51.0	31.7	6.5	147253
12456	MOUNT MARION	15895	229	17.5	57.6	20.5	3.1	1.3	36037	42399	32	16	203	0.0	10.3	84.2	2.5	3.0	117031
12457	MOUNT TREMPER	35412	500	24.4	28.6	26.0	11.0	10.0	45773	52485	63	52	392	1.5	5.1	38.0	38.0	17.4	190909
12458	NAPANOCH	16127	819	33.8	25.2	30.8	9.4	0.9	43392	49824	57	45	672	10.6	10.0	50.5	28.4	0.6	139172
12460	OAK HILL	20277	169	23.7	37.3	28.4	7.7	3.0	43322	49321	57	45	139	6.5	7.2	51.8	30.2	4.3	140104
12461	OLIVEBRIDGE	23109	746	22.8	32.3	31.4	10.7	2.8	46469	52655	65	54	626	1.9	3.4	37.5	53.5	3.7	186480
12463	PALENVILLE	24537	541	23.1	33.1	29.0	11.5	3.3	44926	50314	61	50	382	1.8	2.4	56.5	38.0	1.3	149747
12464	PHOENICIA	24847	594	35.0	33.5	20.5	6.9	4.0	35475	40504	29	15	437	4.6	8.7	56.5	28.6	1.6	143382
12465	PINE HILL	27812	128	28.9	34.4	24.2	7.0	5.5	38153	44742	40	25	102	2.9	6.9	45.1	36.3	8.8	162500
12466	PORT EWEN	25702	1331	23.1	28.9	30.5	11.1	6.3	46907	54100	66	55	1049	2.8	7.8	49.3	37.9	2.2	159598
12468	PRATTSVILLE	19679	664	30.4	37.7	22.9	5.1	3.9	35315	40083	29	14	563	9.8	8.9	42.8	34.3	4.3	143414
12469	PRESTON HOLLOW	23833	326	23.9	32.8	33.1	6.8	3.4	43636	50471	58	46	276	5.4	12.3	54.0	26.1	2.2	135000
12470	PURLING	28303	214	26.6	29.9	36.9	2.8	3.7	42368	47375	54	43	143	0.0	0.7	73.4	25.9	0.0	147837
12472	ROSENDALE	26214	722	23.0	25.4	38.2	9.4	4.0	51182	58483	74	64	524	5.7	2.7	55.9	33.8	1.9	149107
12473	ROUND TOP	20184	251	23.1	35.5	31.1	10.4	0.0	44066	49560	59	48	194	1.0	5.7	60.8	32.5	0.0	145902
12474	ROXBURY	22837	1092	33.7	30.3	22.2	11.0	2.8	35921	40365	31	16	890	4.4	9.9	47.6	31.2	6.9	143033
12477	SAUGERTIES	23413	8205	23.2	30.0	34.5	9.7	2.6	47139	53767	66	56	6069	2.4	3.5	51.6	40.0	2.5	162043
12480	SHANDAKEN	19698	201	31.3	41.3	19.4	6.0	2.0	36994	42345	35	21	151	5.3	8.0	61.6	23.2	2.0	139527
12481	SHOKAN	25777	682	19.5	25.7	39.2	11.3	4.4	54097	62195	79	69	563	0.9	2.7	43.9	46.7	5.9	177665
12482	SOUTH CAIRO	26875	275	31.3	24.4	30.6	8.7	5.1	43548	48100	57	46	220	4.6	10.9	52.3	30.5	1.8	148256
12484	STONE RIDGE	26333	1165	21.8	27.9	34.4	9.8	6.1	50286	56868	72	63	969	0.9	1.2	26.8	62.1	8.9	217857
12485	TANNERSVILLE	21652	455	32.5	30.8	29.2	5.5	2.0	38345	43488	41	26	327	0.9	1.5	49.5	45.6	2.5	170724
12486	TILLSON	22242	604	21.7	24.8	40.4	10.4	2.7	52337	59632	76	66	470	3.0	2.1	58.1	34.7	2.1	156765
12487	ULSTER PARK	24367	1386	19.8	22.5	43.1	10.5	4.1	54890	62935	80	70	999	1.7	8.0	41.7	44.2	4.3	172029
12491	WEST HURLEY	29662	824	22.5	22.9	33.1	12.6	8.9	53786	61070	78	68	693	0.6	3.0	39.7	54.1	2.6	185473
12492	WEST KILL	24565	221	38.0	29.4	20.4	6.8	5.4	33440	39210	22	9	187	3.7	9.1	46.5	35.8	4.8	148828
12494	WEST SHOKAN	26492	317	12.9	32.5	38.8	12.9	2.8	53129	60238	77	67	268	2.6	1.5	38.1	47.8	10.1	190909
12495	WILLOW	49013	168	11.9	29.8	27.4	16.1	14.9	62616	72490	87	77	137	0.0	2.2	26.3	40.9	30.7	283929
12496	WINDHAM	25085	629	32.8	29.9	24.3	7.6	5.4	38489	43821	41	27	472	3.0	4.0	41.5	46.0	5.5	177778
12498	WOODSTOCK	36816	2234	24.1	22.4	31.4	11.7	10.4	53939	63116	78	68	1689	0.8	0.5	20.3	63.8	14.7	232215
12501	AMENIA	27545	1033	16.8	32.6	35.9	11.4	3.2	50645	59557	73	63	699	1.9	1.7	24.8	60.9	10.7	213889
12502	ANCRAM	30879	400	19.3	30.8	35.5	7.5	7.0	50000	56474	72	62	325	3.1	4.9	29.2	48.9	13.9	202049
12503	ANCRAMDALE	25996	383	18.0	30.3	36.3	8.1	7.3	50986	57581	74	64	315	5.7	6.4	32.7	42.5	12.7	186458
12507	BARRYTOWN	23311	80	22.5	21.3	33.8	15.0	7.5	58095	67520	83	73	66	1.5	1.5	24.2	53.0	19.7	223684
	NEW YORK	28049		26.3	24.3	29.3	11.5	8.6	49309	58077				4.6	8.6	27.2	39.9	19.8	219050
	UNITED STATES	25866		24.7	27.1	30.8	10.9	6.5	48124	56710				10.9	15.0	33.7	30.1	10.4	145905

SPENDING POTENTIAL INDICES

NEW YORK

12188-12507 **D**

#	POST OFFICE NAME	FINANCIAL SERVICES: Auto Loan	FINANCIAL SERVICES: Home Loan	FINANCIAL SERVICES: Invest-ments	FINANCIAL SERVICES: Retire-ment Plans	THE HOME: Home Improvements: Home Repair	THE HOME: Home Improvements: Lawn & Garden	THE HOME: Furnishings: Comput-ers & Hard-ware	THE HOME: Furnishings: Major Appli-ances	THE HOME: Furnishings: TV, Radio, Sound Equip-ment	THE HOME: Furnishings: Furni-ture	ENTERTAINMENT: Dine out/ Carry out	ENTERTAINMENT: Sports Equip-ment	ENTERTAINMENT: Fees & Tickets	ENTERTAINMENT: Toys & Games	ENTERTAINMENT: Travel	ENTERTAINMENT: Cable TV	PERSONAL: Apparel & Services	PERSONAL: Auto Repairs	PERSONAL: Health Insur-ance	PERSONAL: Pets & Supplies
12188	WATERFORD	86	96	105	96	94	97	94	92	91	93	114	108	97	118	94	88	112	92	86	101
12189	WATERVLIET	64	64	76	65	63	69	70	66	70	68	88	78	70	88	69	69	86	69	66	73
12190	WELLS	69	54	37	49	61	69	51	62	58	51	68	72	46	68	54	62	64	61	73	84
12192	WEST COXSACKIE	90	91	83	87	93	97	84	89	85	84	104	104	85	108	86	86	101	87	90	107
12193	WESTERLO	92	87	72	83	90	96	80	87	83	80	102	103	80	105	83	85	98	85	92	109
12194	WEST FULTON	87	68	47	62	77	86	64	78	73	64	86	91	58	85	69	78	80	76	92	106
12196	WEST SAND LAKE	104	128	140	126	126	127	117	116	110	116	139	134	124	147	120	108	138	113	107	127
12197	WORCESTER	77	57	35	52	63	73	58	68	67	57	79	78	52	75	59	71	72	67	81	88
12198	WYNANTSKILL	86	105	115	102	103	106	96	96	92	96	116	110	103	122	99	91	115	93	90	105
12202	ALBANY	44	39	51	38	38	43	46	43	49	46	61	50	45	59	44	49	59	46	45	49
12203	ALBANY	82	81	98	84	80	87	92	84	89	88	112	102	90	111	88	86	109	89	81	93
12204	ALBANY	86	90	111	90	89	98	94	91	95	93	119	104	96	119	94	96	116	93	91	100
12205	ALBANY	79	91	103	88	90	97	88	87	87	87	109	99	92	113	90	88	107	86	86	95
12206	ALBANY	53	47	58	47	46	53	56	52	58	54	73	62	55	71	54	58	70	56	54	58
12207	ALBANY	33	28	40	28	28	33	34	32	37	34	46	37	34	45	34	38	45	35	35	36
12208	ALBANY	78	72	91	77	71	78	86	79	85	82	106	97	83	103	82	80	104	85	74	87
12209	ALBANY	69	76	85	75	75	80	77	75	76	75	95	87	79	98	77	75	93	75	73	81
12210	ALBANY	55	45	59	47	44	50	58	53	60	56	75	64	55	71	54	58	73	58	52	59
12211	ALBANY	118	144	171	139	141	149	135	133	130	134	163	152	143	171	139	130	162	131	126	144
12302	SCHENECTADY	92	106	118	104	105	111	100	100	97	100	122	115	105	126	103	97	120	99	97	110
12303	SCHENECTADY	84	93	100	91	92	98	90	89	89	89	111	103	94	115	92	90	109	89	89	99
12304	SCHENECTADY	64	65	73	64	65	71	68	67	69	67	86	77	69	87	68	70	84	68	68	74
12305	SCHENECTADY	47	39	53	43	39	45	52	46	53	49	66	57	49	63	49	51	64	52	46	51
12306	SCHENECTADY	75	83	89	81	83	89	81	80	81	79	100	91	84	105	83	81	98	79	80	88
12307	SCHENECTADY	38	33	43	31	32	37	39	37	42	39	52	42	38	51	38	43	51	39	39	42
12308	SCHENECTADY	61	61	71	62	61	67	67	64	68	65	84	75	67	85	66	67	82	66	64	70
12309	SCHENECTADY	118	139	161	138	137	143	131	130	126	131	158	149	138	162	135	124	156	128	123	141
12401	KINGSTON	72	73	81	72	73	80	75	74	76	74	95	86	76	96	76	77	92	75	76	83
12404	ACCORD	118	101	76	97	108	116	96	108	102	96	123	128	90	121	98	103	116	107	116	138
12405	ACRA	84	64	43	61	71	83	68	77	77	65	90	87	61	86	69	81	83	76	92	95
12406	ARKVILLE	79	62	42	56	70	79	60	71	67	59	80	83	53	78	63	72	74	70	84	96
12409	BEARSVILLE	114	124	131	120	126	139	114	120	113	117	141	128	119	132	120	116	136	117	126	134
12410	BIG INDIAN	94	74	50	67	83	94	70	84	79	69	94	98	62	92	74	84	87	83	99	115
12411	BLOOMINGTON	82	92	112	95	92	94	91	89	87	91	110	106	94	112	92	85	108	90	82	98
12412	BOICEVILLE	98	96	85	94	100	104	89	97	90	89	110	114	88	114	92	91	106	94	98	118
12413	CAIRO	88	66	43	63	73	86	72	80	81	69	95	90	64	90	72	85	87	80	96	98
12414	CATSKILL	73	67	61	64	69	77	68	72	72	67	88	82	66	88	69	74	84	71	78	84
12416	CHICHESTER	113	89	61	80	100	113	84	101	95	83	112	118	75	111	89	101	105	99	119	138
12418	CORNWALLVILLE	90	71	48	64	80	90	67	81	76	66	90	94	60	89	71	81	83	79	95	110
12419	COTTEKILL	72	83	102	86	82	84	82	79	78	81	98	95	84	101	82	75	97	80	72	87
12421	DENVER	97	76	52	69	86	96	72	87	81	71	96	101	64	95	77	87	90	85	102	118
12422	DURHAM	91	72	49	65	81	91	68	81	76	67	91	95	60	89	72	82	84	80	96	111
12423	EAST DURHAM	86	67	46	61	76	85	63	76	72	63	85	89	57	84	68	77	79	75	90	104
12424	EAST JEWETT	103	81	55	73	91	102	76	92	86	76	102	108	68	101	81	92	95	91	109	126
12427	ELKA PARK	80	63	43	57	71	79	59	71	67	59	79	83	53	78	63	71	74	70	84	97
12428	ELLENVILLE	69	59	55	57	61	69	65	66	69	63	84	77	61	83	64	71	80	68	72	78
12430	FLEISCHMANNS	76	60	41	54	67	76	56	68	64	56	76	80	50	75	60	68	70	67	80	93
12431	FREEHOLD	97	69	39	66	79	90	70	84	80	69	94	100	61	92	72	84	86	83	101	114
12433	GLENFORD	90	109	123	108	109	114	100	101	95	100	119	114	107	121	104	94	118	98	96	110
12435	GREENFIELD PARK	88	73	55	71	78	88	73	81	79	72	95	93	69	94	74	81	89	79	90	100
12439	HENSONVILLE	97	76	52	69	85	96	72	86	81	71	96	101	64	95	76	87	89	85	102	118
12440	HIGH FALLS	86	92	95	88	94	102	86	90	87	86	107	102	89	110	90	89	105	88	93	104
12442	HUNTER	100	78	53	71	88	99	74	89	84	73	99	104	66	98	79	89	92	88	105	122
12443	HURLEY	94	111	122	108	110	115	103	103	100	102	125	117	109	130	106	100	123	101	100	113
12444	JEWETT	101	79	54	72	89	101	75	90	85	74	100	106	67	99	80	91	93	89	107	123
12446	KERHONKSON	74	63	50	60	68	76	62	69	67	61	81	79	59	81	64	70	76	68	77	86
12448	LAKE HILL	109	131	148	130	131	137	120	121	114	121	143	137	128	145	125	113	142	118	115	132
12449	LAKE KATRINE	79	86	98	86	85	90	85	84	84	85	105	97	88	107	86	83	103	84	81	93
12450	LANESVILLE	89	70	47	63	78	88	66	79	74	65	88	93	59	87	70	79	82	78	93	108
12451	LEEDS	98	74	48	72	83	93	75	87	83	74	99	102	68	98	76	86	91	85	99	113
12454	MAPLECREST	104	82	56	74	92	103	77	93	87	76	103	109	69	102	82	93	96	91	110	127
12455	MARGARETVILLE	82	63	43	58	71	81	62	73	70	61	83	85	56	81	65	75	77	72	87	97
12456	MOUNT MARION	55	60	63	57	61	68	60	59	62	57	77	66	63	83	62	64	74	58	63	65
12457	MOUNT TREMPER	114	112	105	107	118	127	104	113	106	104	130	130	103	131	109	110	125	111	120	138
12458	NAPANOCH	72	68	62	63	72	79	64	71	68	64	83	81	63	84	68	71	79	69	78	87
12460	OAK HILL	92	72	49	65	81	91	68	82	77	67	91	96	61	90	72	82	85	81	97	112
12461	OLIVEBRIDGE	97	73	46	70	83	92	72	86	80	71	95	103	63	94	74	83	88	84	99	116
12463	PALENVILLE	91	81	70	81	84	93	83	87	86	81	105	100	80	105	82	87	99	86	91	101
12464	PHOENICIA	90	71	48	64	79	89	67	80	75	66	89	94	59	88	71	80	83	79	95	110
12465	PINE HILL	99	78	53	70	88	99	74	89	83	73	99	104	66	97	78	89	92	87	105	121
12466	PORT EWEN	89	92	90	90	93	97	86	89	86	86	107	106	88	111	88	86	104	88	89	106
12468	PRATTSVILLE	82	64	44	58	72	81	61	73	69	60	81	85	54	80	65	73	76	72	86	100
12469	PRESTON HOLLOW	94	72	46	65	81	91	68	83	78	68	92	98	60	90	72	83	85	82	98	114
12470	PURLING	123	92	61	89	101	121	102	112	114	97	135	126	91	127	101	121	123	112	135	136
12472	ROSENDALE	76	88	106	90	86	89	85	83	81	85	102	98	89	105	86	79	101	83	76	91
12473	ROUND TOP	80	60	40	58	66	79	67	73	75	63	88	82	59	83	66	79	80	73	88	88
12474	ROXBURY	88	69	47	62	77	87	65	78	73	64	87	91	58	86	69	78	81	77	92	107
12477	SAUGERTIES	82	86	85	83	87	92	82	84	82	81	102	99	84	106	84	82	99	83	85	98
12480	SHANDAKEN	78	62	42	56	69	78	58	70	66	57	78	82	52	77	62	70	72	69	83	96
12481	SHOKAN	80	98	106	96	96	97	89	88	84	89	106	103	95	113	92	83	106	86	81	97
12482	SOUTH CAIRO	102	77	49	74	86	97	78	90	87	76	103	106	70	101	79	90	95	89	104	117
12484	STONE RIDGE	104	90	73	87	98	106	87	98	93	86	112	116	82	113	90	95	106	96	107	124
12485	TANNERSVILLE	78	61	42	55	69	77	58	70	65	57	77	81	52	76	62	70	72	68	82	95
12486	TILLSON	74	88	102	88	87	89	84	82	80	84	101	97	88	106	85	78	100	82	76	90
12487	ULSTER PARK	79	95	108	95	94	95	89	88	84	88	106	102	94	111	91	82	105	86	81	96
12491	WEST HURLEY	96	105	107	101	106	113	97	100	97	97	120	115	101	123	101	98	117	98	101	115
12492	WEST KILL	89	70	47	63	78	88	66	79	74	65	88	93	59	87	70	79	82	78	94	108
12494	WEST SHOKAN	112	78	41	74	91	102	77	96	89	77	105	115	66	103	80	94	95	94	114	133
12495	WILLOW	128	154	174	153	153	161	141	142	134	142	168	161	150	170	147	133	167	138	135	155
12496	WINDHAM	94	74	50	67	83	94	70	84	79	69	94	98	62	92	74	84	87	83	99	115
12498	WOODSTOCK	103	114	128	113	115	124	108	110	106	110	133	122	112	129	112	107	130	109	111	122
12501	AMENIA	88	99	106	94	99	108	96	95	98	93	121	107	102	131	99	100	118	93	99	105
12502	ANCRAM	122	91	56	84	104	117	87	106	100	87	118	126	77	116	92	106	108	105	126	147
12503	ANCRAMDALE	121	85	44	80	99	110	84	103	96	83	113	125	71	111	87	101	103	102	123	144
12507	BARRYTOWN	91	103	118	104	102	108	101	99	96	100	121	114	104	121	102	94	119	99	94	108
	NEW YORK	95	100	134	99	98	107	103	100	105	103	133	116	105	138	104	107	131	102	99	112
	UNITED STATES	100	100	100	100	100	100	100	100	100	100	100	100	100	100	100	100	100	100	100	100

 Copyright © 2004 ESRI BIS. All rights reserved. Reproduction by any method is prohibited.

NEW YORK

POPULATION CHANGE

A 12508-12776

| ZIP CODE | | COUNTY FIPS CODE | POPULATION | | | 2000-2004 ANNUAL RATE | | HOUSEHOLDS | | | | | FAMILIES | | |
#	POST OFFICE NAME		2000	2004	2009	% Rate	State Centile	2000	2004	2009	% Annual Rate 2000-2004	2004 Average HH Size	2000	2004	% Annual Rate 2000-2004
12508	BEACON	027	18547	19678	21020	1.4	87	6066	6627	7276	2.1	2.54	4000	4271	1.6
12513	CLAVERACK	021	415	460	497	2.5	96	173	197	218	3.1	2.07	120	136	3.0
12514	CLINTON CORNERS	027	2762	3085	3346	2.6	97	1009	1144	1255	3.0	2.64	726	819	2.9
12515	CLINTONDALE	111	1018	1051	1092	0.8	69	376	395	416	1.2	2.65	235	244	0.9
12516	COPAKE	021	1679	1748	1830	1.0	76	671	711	756	1.4	2.33	451	475	1.2
12517	COPAKE FALLS	021	356	362	374	0.4	51	154	159	167	0.8	2.16	106	109	0.7
12518	CORNWALL	071	6040	6583	7245	2.1	94	2331	2541	2800	2.1	2.58	1648	1781	1.8
12520	CORNWALL ON HUDSON	071	3151	3168	3342	0.1	37	1211	1224	1295	0.3	2.58	831	831	0.0
12521	CRARYVILLE	021	1470	1499	1552	0.5	55	593	614	647	0.8	2.38	407	418	0.6
12522	DOVER PLAINS	027	4868	5125	5399	1.2	83	1874	1992	2119	1.5	2.54	1274	1346	1.3
12523	ELIZAVILLE	021	1908	1958	2042	0.6	62	772	806	854	1.0	2.34	528	548	0.9
12524	FISHKILL	027	13455	14115	14907	1.1	81	4952	5272	5651	1.5	2.37	3157	3340	1.3
12525	GARDINER	111	3225	3458	3656	1.7	89	1223	1327	1421	1.9	2.58	876	946	1.8
12526	GERMANTOWN	021	3598	3813	4040	1.4	86	1407	1512	1625	1.7	2.46	953	1017	1.5
12528	HIGHLAND	111	13681	14133	14677	0.8	70	5071	5322	5612	1.1	2.47	3373	3517	1.0
12529	HILLSDALE	021	2964	3015	3119	0.4	52	1118	1153	1211	0.7	2.57	759	777	0.6
12531	HOLMES	027	3414	3713	3978	1.7	93	1143	1262	1367	2.4	2.88	877	965	2.3
12533	HOPEWELL JUNCTION	027	22472	24275	25961	1.8	92	7369	8049	8686	2.1	3.01	6121	6660	2.0
12534	HUDSON	021	20512	21105	22078	0.7	65	8167	8511	9043	1.0	2.32	5072	5254	0.8
12538	HYDE PARK	027	13718	13911	14449	0.3	49	5224	5360	5634	0.6	2.46	3591	3664	0.5
12540	LAGRANGEVILLE	027	6532	6757	7037	0.8	71	2165	2261	2375	1.0	2.92	1778	1849	0.9
12542	MARLBORO	111	5225	5473	5717	1.1	81	1916	2027	2140	1.3	2.70	1348	1419	1.2
12543	MAYBROOK	071	3118	3743	4318	4.4	99	1054	1273	1473	4.5	2.93	790	944	4.3
12545	MILLBROOK	027	4771	4807	4956	0.2	40	1791	1822	1898	0.4	2.51	1167	1181	0.3
12546	MILLERTON	027	2918	2987	3096	0.6	60	1102	1143	1199	0.9	2.50	749	772	0.7
12547	MILTON	111	2655	2809	2961	1.3	86	959	1026	1093	1.6	2.74	687	733	1.5
12548	MODENA	111	1263	1359	1440	1.7	91	463	507	544	2.2	2.67	337	366	2.0
12549	MONTGOMERY	071	8944	9926	11022	2.5	96	3045	3382	3759	2.5	2.89	2379	2634	2.4
12550	NEWBURGH	071	52477	54938	59153	1.1	80	17807	18664	20134	1.1	2.87	12723	13249	1.0
12553	NEW WINDSOR	071	22500	23555	25537	1.1	80	8381	8807	9574	1.2	2.65	6010	6270	1.0
12561	NEW PALTZ	111	17031	17860	18650	1.1	81	6010	6443	6861	1.7	2.37	3365	3564	1.4
12563	PATTERSON	079	8237	9098	9835	2.4	95	2541	2859	3140	2.8	2.86	1925	2158	2.7
12564	PAWLING	027	6448	6919	7354	1.7	90	2459	2673	2872	2.0	2.54	1708	1849	1.9
12566	PINE BUSH	111	9502	10353	11203	2.0	94	3417	3755	4096	2.2	2.66	2566	2800	2.1
12567	PINE PLAINS	027	2894	2904	2985	0.1	33	1125	1144	1189	0.4	2.53	793	800	0.2
12569	PLEASANT VALLEY	027	9282	9880	10459	1.5	88	3516	3773	4025	1.7	2.60	2569	2746	1.6
12570	POUGHQUAG	027	6063	7044	7804	3.6	99	1947	2293	2568	3.9	3.04	1593	1867	3.3
12571	RED HOOK	027	12461	12833	13320	0.7	66	3495	3661	3866	1.1	2.87	2484	2590	1.0
12572	RHINEBECK	027	9727	10180	10644	1.1	80	3756	4002	4252	1.5	2.19	2339	2476	1.4
12575	ROCK TAVERN	071	1485	1787	2065	4.5	100	485	586	682	4.6	3.04	407	489	4.4
12577	SALISBURY MILLS	071	1625	1764	1947	2.0	93	513	557	615	2.0	3.15	420	453	1.8
12578	SALT POINT	027	1956	2129	2280	2.0	93	704	775	838	2.3	2.73	526	576	2.2
12580	STAATSBURG	027	3957	4079	4280	0.7	67	1471	1544	1641	1.2	2.60	1108	1156	1.0
12581	STANFORDVILLE	027	2334	2604	2822	2.6	97	938	1064	1168	3.0	2.34	653	737	2.9
12582	STORMVILLE	027	4433	5070	5570	3.2	99	1384	1605	1782	3.6	3.15	1185	1370	3.5
12583	TIVOLI	027	2263	2387	2506	1.3	84	862	929	996	1.8	2.02	543	581	1.6
12585	VERBANK	027	1165	1207	1257	0.8	72	392	409	429	1.0	2.76	327	340	0.9
12586	WALDEN	071	11721	12612	13798	1.7	91	4154	4483	4912	1.8	2.78	3078	3295	1.6
12589	WALLKILL	111	14651	15489	16320	1.3	85	4205	4530	4857	1.8	2.94	3177	3404	1.6
12590	WAPPINGERS FALLS	027	34949	35289	36652	0.2	42	12841	13122	13773	0.5	2.66	9187	9354	0.4
12592	WASSAIC	027	1019	1071	1125	1.2	82	401	428	454	1.6	2.46	268	283	1.3
12594	WINGDALE	027	4216	4364	4548	0.8	71	1422	1481	1556	1.0	2.82	1047	1085	0.8
12601	POUGHKEEPSIE	027	44053	45362	47406	0.7	66	15727	16371	17320	1.0	2.50	9326	9586	0.7
12603	POUGHKEEPSIE	027	37489	38472	40263	0.6	62	14250	14731	15554	0.8	2.52	10042	10338	0.7
12604	POUGHKEEPSIE	027	1995	2008	2037	0.2	38	47	48	50	0.5	2.56	31	32	0.8
12701	MONTICELLO	105	12483	12927	13528	0.8	72	4869	5092	5392	1.1	2.42	3002	3117	0.9
12719	BARRYVILLE	105	878	926	976	1.3	84	337	360	385	1.6	2.42	230	244	1.4
12720	BETHEL	105	96	98	101	0.5	57	39	40	42	0.6	2.40	24	25	1.0
12721	BLOOMINGBURG	105	5912	6244	6670	1.3	85	2063	2198	2366	1.5	2.83	1552	1644	1.4
12723	CALLICOON	105	2159	2280	2404	1.3	85	750	812	874	1.9	2.37	512	551	1.7
12725	CLARYVILLE	111	252	236	239	-1.5	1	102	97	100	-1.2	2.35	61	57	-1.6
12726	COCHECTON	105	1239	1277	1332	0.7	67	495	518	548	1.1	2.44	338	351	0.9
12727	COCHECTON CENTER	105	20	20	21	0.0	28	11	11	12	0.0	1.82	8	8	0.0
12729	CUDDEBACKVILLE	071	2565	2637	2815	0.7	64	935	967	1036	0.8	2.72	697	716	0.6
12732	ELDRED	105	951	1004	1059	1.3	84	376	403	432	1.7	2.31	255	271	1.4
12733	FALLSBURG	105	873	916	963	1.1	81	210	220	234	1.1	3.34	130	135	0.9
12734	FERNDALE	105	1482	1485	1547	0.1	31	563	568	599	0.2	2.40	367	368	0.1
12736	FREMONT CENTER	105	237	237	245	0.0	28	99	100	105	0.2	2.37	69	70	0.3
12737	GLEN SPEY	105	1513	1624	1730	1.7	90	606	654	703	1.8	2.48	415	446	1.7
12738	GLEN WILD	105	155	158	165	0.5	55	59	61	64	0.8	2.56	40	41	0.6
12740	GRAHAMSVILLE	105	1700	1794	1899	1.3	84	673	714	763	1.4	2.51	495	524	1.4
12741	HANKINS	105	224	224	231	0.0	28	90	91	96	0.3	2.46	63	63	0.0
12742	HARRIS	105	189	192	199	0.4	50	84	87	91	0.8	2.03	54	55	0.4
12743	HIGHLAND LAKE	105	345	358	375	0.9	73	142	149	158	1.1	2.40	97	102	1.2
12745	HORTONVILLE	105	47	51	54	1.9	93	16	18	20	2.8	1.89	11	12	2.1
12746	HUGUENOT	071	1063	1175	1301	2.4	96	380	423	470	2.6	2.78	273	301	2.3
12747	HURLEYVILLE	105	2713	2736	2826	0.2	40	890	909	953	0.5	2.65	594	603	0.4
12748	JEFFERSONVILLE	105	2022	2087	2178	0.8	69	796	830	875	1.0	2.45	535	554	0.8
12750	KENOZA LAKE	105	77	80	83	0.9	74	33	35	36	1.4	2.26	23	24	1.0
12751	KIAMESHA LAKE	105	284	335	376	4.0	99	121	143	162	4.0	2.34	82	96	3.8
12752	LAKE HUNTINGTON	105	148	151	157	0.5	56	74	77	81	0.9	1.96	50	51	0.5
12754	LIBERTY	105	6488	6806	7200	1.1	81	2548	2712	2910	1.5	2.37	1523	1608	1.3
12758	LIVINGSTON MANOR	105	4489	4532	4688	0.2	41	1719	1758	1841	0.5	2.55	1172	1192	0.4
12759	LOCH SHELDRAKE	105	1365	1377	1427	0.2	41	503	513	538	0.5	2.57	344	349	0.3
12760	LONG EDDY	025	597	639	715	1.6	89	239	259	293	1.9	2.46	170	183	1.8
12762	MONGAUP VALLEY	105	234	226	232	-0.8	2	100	97	101	-0.7	2.12	65	63	-0.7
12763	MOUNTAIN DALE	105	1019	1040	1082	0.5	56	379	391	411	0.7	2.60	264	271	0.6
12764	NARROWSBURG	105	1710	1732	1788	0.3	47	696	714	746	0.6	2.32	445	454	0.5
12765	NEVERSINK	105	1282	1367	1452	1.5	88	454	487	521	1.7	2.81	344	366	1.5
12766	NORTH BRANCH	105	552	565	588	0.6	60	215	222	233	0.8	2.53	143	147	0.7
12768	PARKSVILLE	105	1165	1198	1245	0.7	64	404	423	448	1.1	2.39	255	264	0.8
12770	POND EDDY	105	324	344	364	1.4	87	130	139	148	1.6	2.47	91	97	1.5
12771	PORT JERVIS	071	13694	14489	15665	1.3	86	5227	5557	6025	1.5	2.59	3463	3650	1.3
12775	ROCK HILL	105	1805	1921	2040	1.5	88	737	795	854	1.8	2.41	504	540	1.6
12776	ROSCOE	025	2574	2705	2917	1.2	82	1042	1113	1218	1.6	2.34	685	726	1.4
	NEW YORK					0.4					0.5	2.60			0.4
	UNITED STATES					1.2					1.3	2.58			1.1

ZIP CODE #	POST OFFICE NAME	RACE (%) White 2000	White 2004	Black 2000	Black 2004	Asian/Pacific 2000	Asian/Pacific 2004	% Hispanic Origin 2000	% Hispanic Origin 2004	2004 AGE DISTRIBUTION (%) 0-4	5-9	10-14	15-19	20-24	25-44	45-64	65-84	85+	18+	MEDIAN AGE 2004	% 2004 Males	% 2004 Females
12508	BEACON	65.7	62.7	22.3	23.4	1.4	1.9	17.2	19.3	6.0	6.0	6.7	6.8	7.2	33.6	23.2	9.1	1.4	77.0	36.4	53.9	46.1
12513	CLAVERACK	87.7	85.7	10.4	12.0	0.5	0.4	4.3	5.2	3.7	3.9	5.4	14.8	6.5	20.9	25.0	17.4	2.4	77.0	41.1	54.4	45.7
12514	CLINTON CORNERS	94.9	94.0	2.0	2.3	1.1	1.3	2.4	3.0	5.2	6.3	7.1	5.8	3.8	25.6	32.9	12.0	1.4	77.4	43.0	50.6	49.4
12515	CLINTONDALE	91.1	89.7	4.3	4.9	1.0	1.1	6.3	7.7	5.9	5.8	7.0	6.2	5.8	26.5	26.8	14.2	1.8	77.5	40.7	48.7	51.3
12516	COPAKE	97.0	96.3	0.8	0.9	0.1	0.2	1.3	1.8	4.1	4.6	7.0	5.2	3.8	26.1	28.0	18.5	2.6	80.8	44.4	50.5	49.5
12517	COPAKE FALLS	96.1	95.3	0.8	1.1	0.0	0.3	2.3	3.3	4.4	5.3	8.3	6.1	4.4	27.6	28.5	13.8	1.7	78.7	41.6	52.5	47.5
12518	CORNWALL	94.3	93.0	1.2	1.5	1.4	1.7	5.6	7.2	6.7	7.1	8.2	6.6	4.9	26.8	27.1	11.0	1.6	73.3	39.5	47.3	52.7
12520	CORNWALL ON HUDSON	96.2	95.3	0.6	0.7	0.7	0.8	4.2	5.4	5.6	5.9	7.6	7.9	6.0	23.5	27.6	13.5	2.3	75.4	41.3	47.4	52.7
12521	CRARYVILLE	96.3	95.6	1.6	1.9	0.3	0.4	2.5	3.1	3.9	5.5	7.3	7.2	3.7	24.2	30.8	15.5	2.0	78.5	44.1	50.8	49.2
12522	DOVER PLAINS	94.4	93.2	1.9	2.2	0.9	1.1	4.4	5.5	6.2	6.6	7.6	6.8	5.4	27.3	26.3	12.1	1.8	75.3	39.7	50.4	49.6
12523	ELIZAVILLE	97.2	96.6	1.2	1.4	0.4	0.6	2.2	2.6	4.9	5.6	7.6	5.5	4.2	26.2	28.1	15.2	2.8	78.0	42.5	49.6	50.4
12524	FISHKILL	83.7	82.0	9.3	9.8	3.0	3.7	8.2	9.4	5.3	5.4	6.2	5.6	5.6	30.3	25.9	13.3	2.5	79.8	40.6	52.6	47.4
12525	GARDINER	93.2	91.9	2.3	2.6	0.8	1.0	6.6	8.1	6.2	6.8	8.0	6.6	4.7	29.7	28.2	8.8	1.0	74.4	38.8	50.7	49.3
12526	GERMANTOWN	96.8	96.1	1.3	1.5	0.4	0.6	1.8	2.2	5.1	5.5	7.7	6.9	5.1	24.5	27.7	15.1	2.6	77.4	42.2	48.7	51.3
12528	HIGHLAND	90.1	88.4	4.6	5.2	1.2	1.5	6.5	7.8	6.1	6.1	7.3	7.8	5.9	28.2	24.8	11.1	2.6	75.1	38.2	48.6	51.4
12529	HILLSDALE	96.8	96.2	0.7	0.8	0.3	0.4	2.3	3.0	4.9	5.7	7.6	6.2	4.5	23.4	31.0	14.5	2.1	78.0	43.5	50.6	49.4
12531	HOLMES	95.5	94.5	1.1	1.3	1.1	1.5	3.9	4.8	7.0	7.5	8.0	7.3	5.3	26.5	27.9	8.6	1.9	72.9	38.6	49.5	50.5
12533	HOPEWELL JUNCTION	91.8	90.0	2.5	3.0	3.0	3.7	4.7	5.8	7.7	8.3	8.6	6.8	5.2	27.3	27.2	8.1	0.9	70.9	37.2	49.7	50.3
12534	HUDSON	83.1	81.1	10.9	11.9	1.4	1.6	4.6	5.5	5.8	5.5	6.5	6.8	6.3	25.9	25.7	14.8	2.7	77.9	40.6	50.1	49.9
12538	HYDE PARK	91.2	89.5	4.1	4.8	1.4	1.8	3.4	4.1	5.8	6.1	7.3	8.0	7.0	25.9	25.4	12.6	1.9	76.4	38.7	49.4	50.6
12540	LAGRANGEVILLE	93.9	92.5	2.0	2.4	1.9	2.4	3.4	4.3	6.5	7.4	8.8	7.0	4.6	26.7	28.3	9.7	1.0	72.6	39.4	49.8	50.2
12542	MARLBORO	95.1	94.2	2.5	2.9	0.3	0.4	4.0	5.1	6.3	6.7	8.0	6.8	5.6	28.2	26.1	10.9	1.5	74.9	38.5	49.3	50.7
12543	MAYBROOK	82.8	79.7	9.0	10.3	1.2	1.4	12.7	15.6	7.7	7.7	8.7	8.9	7.7	29.2	23.2	6.0	1.1	70.2	32.3	48.5	51.5
12545	MILLBROOK	94.5	93.4	2.9	3.4	0.7	0.9	3.7	4.6	5.4	6.2	7.1	7.4	4.6	24.3	28.2	14.5	2.3	75.7	42.0	48.6	51.4
12546	MILLERTON	95.7	94.7	2.0	2.4	0.6	0.7	3.2	4.1	4.0	4.7	7.4	9.7	6.1	25.0	29.1	12.1	1.9	78.5	41.0	49.6	50.5
12547	MILTON	93.3	92.0	3.4	3.9	0.4	0.5	4.0	5.0	6.2	6.7	7.8	6.4	5.6	29.5	27.1	9.4	1.3	75.3	38.3	49.5	50.5
12548	MODENA	90.5	88.8	3.6	4.1	0.5	0.6	11.6	14.3	6.3	6.5	7.8	7.1	6.3	28.1	26.5	10.2	1.3	75.1	37.9	50.8	49.2
12549	MONTGOMERY	93.6	92.0	2.6	3.2	0.7	0.9	5.9	7.7	6.8	7.3	8.3	7.0	5.5	28.4	26.4	9.2	1.3	72.8	37.6	49.5	50.5
12550	NEWBURGH	61.7	59.1	21.5	22.1	1.5	1.8	24.0	26.7	8.4	7.7	8.1	7.8	8.0	27.1	21.7	9.7	1.5	71.3	33.1	48.1	52.0
12553	NEW WINDSOR	84.7	82.2	6.8	7.6	1.9	2.3	11.0	13.5	6.9	7.0	7.6	6.7	5.9	28.1	25.2	11.0	1.6	74.3	37.8	49.4	50.6
12561	NEW PALTZ	85.3	83.0	5.0	5.5	3.3	3.9	7.0	8.4	4.2	4.7	5.6	11.4	17.5	23.6	22.6	9.0	1.4	82.4	30.7	47.1	52.9
12563	PATTERSON	91.1	89.8	3.7	4.0	1.3	1.6	7.0	8.4	6.4	7.1	7.9	6.5	5.4	33.6	25.5	6.8	0.8	74.3	36.8	51.3	48.8
12564	PAWLING	93.6	92.4	1.9	2.1	1.4	1.7	5.3	6.5	5.6	6.3	7.5	6.4	4.7	26.1	27.3	14.0	2.3	76.5	41.5	49.1	50.9
12566	PINE BUSH	95.1	94.2	1.7	1.9	0.6	0.8	4.3	5.5	6.0	6.7	8.2	7.2	5.8	28.9	26.8	9.3	1.1	74.3	38.1	50.5	49.5
12567	PINE PLAINS	96.5	95.9	0.9	1.0	0.7	0.8	1.4	1.7	4.9	5.4	7.0	7.4	5.6	25.0	29.3	13.4	1.9	77.7	42.1	48.3	51.7
12569	PLEASANT VALLEY	94.9	93.8	2.1	2.5	1.0	1.2	2.9	3.6	6.3	6.7	7.7	6.7	5.0	27.3	28.6	10.5	1.2	74.9	39.7	49.4	50.6
12570	POUGHQUAG	94.4	93.2	2.0	2.3	1.7	2.1	4.9	6.1	7.8	8.2	8.6	6.9	5.2	28.1	26.4	8.0	0.9	71.0	37.5	50.3	49.7
12571	RED HOOK	84.6	82.7	9.1	9.9	1.6	2.0	6.5	7.6	4.8	5.2	6.7	7.5	7.7	31.4	25.5	10.1	1.1	78.9	37.7	56.6	43.4
12572	RHINEBECK	91.0	89.6	4.8	5.3	1.3	1.6	4.4	5.3	4.2	4.8	6.2	6.6	4.9	24.5	28.2	15.9	4.8	80.5	44.3	50.0	50.0
12575	ROCK TAVERN	92.3	90.5	3.0	3.6	0.9	1.2	6.5	8.3	7.3	8.0	8.8	7.6	5.7	27.8	27.4	6.6	1.0	70.6	36.6	50.3	49.7
12577	SALISBURY MILLS	92.8	91.3	2.5	3.0	1.2	1.4	7.0	8.8	7.6	8.3	9.1	7.6	5.6	27.0	26.8	7.2	0.9	70.2	36.8	49.6	50.4
12578	SALT POINT	95.8	94.7	1.5	1.8	0.7	0.9	2.1	2.7	6.3	6.9	7.8	6.4	4.4	26.9	30.8	9.3	1.2	74.8	40.4	50.2	49.8
12580	STAATSBURG	94.4	93.3	2.5	2.9	0.8	1.0	2.3	2.8	5.4	6.6	7.6	6.6	4.4	26.1	32.0	10.3	1.1	76.1	41.5	49.7	50.3
12581	STANFORDVILLE	92.9	91.8	3.0	3.3	1.1	1.5	3.4	4.1	4.7	5.7	6.8	5.8	4.4	26.7	32.1	12.4	1.3	79.0	42.7	52.0	48.0
12582	STORMVILLE	94.4	93.2	2.0	2.4	1.7	2.1	3.3	4.1	7.5	8.0	8.0	7.0	5.4	28.1	28.7	6.5	0.8	71.9	37.3	49.9	50.1
12583	TIVOLI	92.4	90.8	2.0	2.4	2.6	3.2	3.3	4.1	5.2	4.5	6.1	11.7	18.3	25.0	19.9	8.2	1.1	80.9	27.5	47.5	52.5
12585	VERBANK	94.1	92.7	2.3	2.7	1.1	1.6	3.7	4.5	6.6	7.4	8.3	7.0	5.1	26.7	28.1	9.8	1.2	73.1	39.5	50.2	49.8
12586	WALDEN	92.6	90.8	2.7	3.2	0.6	0.7	7.4	9.5	7.0	7.3	8.4	7.4	6.3	28.2	24.3	9.7	1.4	72.6	36.3	48.9	51.2
12589	WALLKILL	84.1	82.6	8.5	8.7	1.0	1.2	12.7	14.7	5.9	6.3	7.1	6.4	6.5	34.5	25.0	7.3	1.0	76.7	36.3	55.2	44.8
12590	WAPPINGERS FALLS	86.8	84.2	4.9	5.7	4.0	4.9	7.3	9.0	6.6	6.7	7.3	6.6	6.0	29.3	25.7	10.4	1.4	75.1	37.7	49.6	50.4
12592	WASSAIC	93.9	92.6	3.3	4.0	0.4	0.6	3.5	4.4	5.1	5.4	7.0	7.5	7.4	25.2	28.5	11.9	2.1	77.7	40.7	49.2	50.8
12594	WINGDALE	85.4	83.6	9.2	10.1	1.2	1.4	6.3	7.5	6.7	7.4	9.1	9.9	5.2	29.6	24.1	7.2	0.9	70.6	35.5	52.2	47.8
12601	POUGHKEEPSIE	63.9	60.7	25.7	27.4	2.8	3.4	8.6	10.0	6.6	6.2	6.9	10.1	11.5	26.6	20.2	10.1	1.8	76.1	31.5	48.5	51.5
12603	POUGHKEEPSIE	84.0	81.3	8.0	9.1	4.4	5.3	5.2	6.2	6.2	6.4	7.4	7.3	7.4	25.6	25.5	12.6	1.7	75.9	38.8	48.2	51.8
12604	POUGHKEEPSIE	78.5	74.6	7.0	8.0	9.1	11.0	5.5	6.6	6.1	3.2	4.0	21.3	30.6	18.7	10.8	4.4	0.9	85.2	22.5	44.4	55.6
12701	MONTICELLO	71.3	68.7	18.8	20.0	1.7	2.0	15.8	18.3	6.4	6.1	7.3	7.4	6.3	24.4	27.3	13.3	1.6	75.5	39.5	49.2	50.9
12719	BARRYVILLE	93.6	92.6	3.4	3.9	0.9	1.0	4.2	5.2	4.8	5.0	6.2	5.8	4.9	24.4	32.9	14.2	1.9	80.2	44.4	50.3	49.7
12720	BETHEL	93.8	92.9	2.1	2.0	0.0	0.0	8.3	11.2	5.1	6.1	7.1	6.1	4.1	24.5	29.6	15.3	2.0	76.5	43.1	51.0	49.0
12721	BLOOMINGBURG	94.7	93.5	1.9	2.2	0.9	1.1	5.4	6.9	6.8	7.0	8.4	8.0	6.3	27.6	26.4	8.6	0.9	72.7	36.9	50.0	50.0
12723	CALLICOON	86.2	84.3	10.7	12.0	0.9	1.1	6.9	8.4	4.2	4.3	5.7	17.6	9.5	19.8	24.5	12.7	1.7	74.6	36.1	50.5	49.5
12725	CLARYVILLE	94.8	93.6	0.8	0.9	1.2	1.7	2.4	3.0	4.7	4.7	5.1	4.2	4.7	25.0	32.6	17.4	1.7	83.1	46.0	50.9	49.2
12726	COCHECTON	95.8	95.1	1.5	1.7	0.7	0.8	2.5	3.2	4.5	5.1	6.7	6.4	4.2	24.5	32.2	14.8	1.6	79.4	44.2	50.6	49.4
12727	COCHECTON CENTER	95.0	100.0	0.0	0.0	0.0	0.0	0.0	0.0	0.0	0.0	10.0	10.0	5.0	20.0	40.0	15.0	0.0	90.0	47.5	50.0	50.0
12729	CUDDEBACKVILLE	95.0	93.9	2.2	2.7	0.4	0.4	4.6	5.8	6.3	7.0	8.2	6.6	5.1	28.1	28.4	9.6	0.6	74.2	38.8	50.7	49.3
12732	ELDRED	92.9	91.7	4.0	4.7	1.0	0.9	4.9	6.1	4.6	4.7	5.9	6.0	5.0	24.9	33.1	13.9	2.0	80.7	44.4	50.3	49.7
12733	FALLSBURG	81.0	78.1	13.3	15.1	1.0	1.2	10.0	12.1	8.8	8.2	8.8	10.8	11.4	22.8	19.5	8.5	1.1	68.6	26.4	53.8	46.2
12734	FERNDALE	84.1	81.8	7.2	8.1	1.4	1.7	13.8	16.6	5.2	5.3	6.4	7.3	6.2	26.6	28.5	13.4	1.1	78.1	41.1	51.5	48.5
12736	FREMONT CENTER	94.9	94.1	1.7	1.7	0.8	1.3	1.3	1.7	7.2	6.3	5.9	5.9	5.1	22.4	30.0	15.6	1.7	76.4	43.1	50.6	49.4
12737	GLEN SPEY	96.8	96.1	0.2	0.3	0.9	1.2	2.1	2.7	5.5	6.0	8.1	6.4	5.1	23.0	28.5	15.6	1.9	76.5	42.8	47.5	52.5
12738	GLEN WILD	89.0	87.3	3.9	4.4	1.9	1.9	8.4	10.8	5.1	5.7	7.0	7.0	5.7	25.3	30.4	12.7	1.3	77.9	41.3	50.6	49.4
12740	GRAHAMSVILLE	97.2	96.6	0.2	0.2	0.4	0.4	2.2	2.8	6.0	7.0	8.5	6.3	4.7	25.2	29.0	12.0	1.3	74.4	40.7	49.6	50.5
12741	HANKINS	94.6	93.8	1.8	1.8	0.9	1.3	0.9	1.3	7.6	6.3	5.8	5.8	4.9	22.3	29.9	15.6	1.8	77.2	43.2	51.8	48.2
12742	HARRIS	88.9	87.0	5.8	6.8	2.1	2.6	9.0	10.9	4.7	5.2	5.7	5.7	4.7	25.5	30.7	16.2	1.6	80.7	43.9	50.5	49.5
12743	HIGHLAND LAKE	97.1	96.7	1.2	1.1	0.6	0.6	1.2	1.4	5.3	5.6	6.4	5.9	4.2	21.5	33.5	15.6	2.0	78.2	45.7	50.0	50.0
12745	HORTONVILLE	76.6	72.6	21.3	23.5	2.1	2.0	10.6	13.7	3.9	3.9	3.9	29.4	13.7	15.7	19.6	9.8	0.0	70.6	23.2	52.9	47.1
12746	HUGUENOT	94.8	93.5	1.7	2.0	0.6	0.8	3.9	5.0	6.8	7.1	7.7	7.3	6.3	26.1	25.3	12.3	1.1	73.7	37.8	48.0	52.0
12747	HURLEYVILLE	82.6	80.0	9.1	10.2	1.3	1.5	11.5	13.8	6.5	6.5	7.0	8.3	8.4	25.1	26.2	10.9	1.0	75.1	36.8	49.2	50.8
12748	JEFFERSONVILLE	94.8	93.8	1.8	2.1	0.5	0.5	3.7	4.6	5.2	5.8	7.0	6.1	5.6	23.5	28.7	15.3	2.9	78.0	42.9	49.3	50.7
12750	KENOZA LAKE	94.8	92.5	2.6	3.8	0.0	1.3	2.6	2.5	5.0	6.3	7.5	6.3	5.0	23.8	31.3	13.8	1.3	77.5	42.0	53.8	46.3
12751	KIAMESHA LAKE	81.3	78.8	11.3	12.5	2.8	3.3	12.0	14.6	5.4	5.7	7.8	7.5	6.6	23.9	26.3	15.8	1.2	76.7	40.7	47.5	52.5
12752	LAKE HUNTINGTON	96.6	96.7	0.7	1.3	0.7	0.7	1.4	2.0	4.6	5.3	6.6	6.6	4.0	26.5	31.1	13.9	1.3	79.5	42.9	51.7	48.3
12754	LIBERTY	82.4	79.8	10.0	11.2	1.6	2.0	11.1	13.4	5.7	5.6	7.3	7.7	6.7	23.6	25.5	14.7	3.1	76.4	40.7	47.6	52.4
12758	LIVINGSTON MANOR	90.2	88.5	4.2	4.7	0.9	1.1	7.6	9.3	6.4	6.2	7.6	7.0	6.3	23.5	27.9	13.6	1.6	75.3	40.5	49.5	50.5
12759	LOCH SHELDRAKE	81.8	79.2	8.2	9.1	0.8	1.0	12.5	14.9	7.3	7.6	6.6	9.1	9.0	23.8	23.8	12.0	0.9	73.1	34.8	48.1	51.9
12760	LONG EDDY	96.0	95.2	1.2	1.4	0.8	1.1	1.2	1.4	5.8	6.0	7.0	7.0	4.9	23.0	28.5	16.3	1.6	76.8	42.6	50.9	49.1
12762	MONGAUP VALLEY	90.6	89.8	3.4	3.5	1.3	1.8	18.0	21.7	5.8	5.8	5.8	6.2	5.8	29.2	26.1	14.2	1.3	80.1	39.4	50.4	49.6
12763	MOUNTAIN DALE	85.8	83.8	6.6	7.3	0.6	0.8	13.8	16.7	5.5	5.8	7.7	8.2	7.5	25.1	27.4	12.2	0.7	75.6	38.7	52.3	47.7
12764	NARROWSBURG	90.3	88.5	5.9	6.8	0.8	1.0	3.3	4.1	5.4	5.6	6.1	5.8	4.2	21.7	30.8	18.0	2.5	79.0	45.8	51.0	49.0
12765	NEVERSINK	96.6	95.8	0.7	0.8	0.2	0.2	2.3	2.9	6.7	7.4	8.5	6.9	5.1	25.2	27.7	11.3	1.2	73.1	39.2	49.1	50.9
12766	NORTH BRANCH	95.1	94.0	0.5	0.7	0.7	0.9	4.9	6.0	6.0	6.2	6.9	5.1	4.8	23.7	30.6	14.3	2.3	77.9	43.2	49.2	50.8
12768	PARKSVILLE	86.9	85.1	8.8	9.8	0.9	1.1	10.4	12.4	4.5	4.8	6.8	6.1	6.2	29.5	27.1	13.0	2.1	79.6	40.9	52.8	47.2
12770	POND EDDY	96.6	95.6	0.3	0.3	1.5	1.7	1.5	1.7	5.8	6.4	7.9	5.2	4.4	24.1	30.2	14.5	1.5	76.5	42.9	49.7	50.3
12771	PORT JERVIS	91.7	89.9	3.4	4.0	0.7	1.0	6.3	8.0	7.4	7.1	7.8	7.2	6.8	26.5	23.9	11.5	1.9	73.1	36.6	48.3	51.7
12775	ROCK HILL	94.1	92.8	1.2	1.4	2.1	2.7	4.2	5.4	6.3	6.6	6.9	5.6	4.1	24.3	30.7	14.4	1.2	76.5	42.7	49.8	50.2
12776	ROSCOE	95.8	95.1	1.2	1.4	0.7	0.8	2.9	3.6	5.2	5.4	6.3	5.8	4.8	22.2	28.5	18.4	3.5	79.4	45.2	49.5	50.5
	NEW YORK	68.0	65.9	15.9	16.2	5.6	6.4	15.1	16.7	6.5	6.5	7.1	7.0	7.1	28.9	24.0	11.2	1.8	75.8	36.7	48.3	51.7
	UNITED STATES	75.1	73.6	12.3	12.5	3.8	4.2	12.5	14.1	6.9	6.7	7.2	7.0	7.3	28.6	23.8	10.8	1.7	75.1	36.0	49.1	50.9

INCOME

#	POST OFFICE NAME	2004 Per Capita Income	2004 HH Income Base	2004 Household Income Distribution (%): Less than $25,000	$25,000 to $49,999	$50,000 to $99,999	$100,000 to $149,999	$150,000 or More	Median Household Income: 2004	2009	2004 National Centile	2004 State Centile	2004 Home Value Base	2004 Home Value Distribution (%): Less than $50,000	$50,000 to $89,999	$90,000 to $174,999	$175,000 to $399,999	$400,000 or More	2004 Median Home Value
12508	BEACON	22801	6627	21.2	26.2	37.6	11.2	3.8	52504	60500	76	66	3784	1.2	1.4	36.8	58.9	1.7	190314
12513	CLAVERACK	29679	197	21.8	25.9	39.6	5.6	7.1	51300	57812	74	65	167	6.0	2.4	46.1	41.9	3.6	162500
12514	CLINTON CORNERS	34113	1144	11.4	22.9	36.5	18.9	10.4	68977	81249	91	84	911	0.3	0.7	9.4	69.4	20.2	266401
12515	CLINTONDALE	19660	395	25.8	33.4	30.9	8.4	1.5	42309	47183	54	43	282	6.4	11.4	32.6	47.2	2.5	174074
12516	COPAKE	28515	711	19.0	35.4	32.6	6.8	6.2	46876	53427	66	55	567	0.2	1.4	50.4	40.2	7.8	171314
12517	COPAKE FALLS	30870	159	22.6	28.9	33.3	8.8	6.3	48640	54518	70	60	122	1.6	2.5	36.1	46.7	13.1	195000
12518	CORNWALL	33556	2541	16.9	18.2	35.4	19.3	10.2	65934	76854	89	81	1876	1.5	1.6	18.1	61.9	17.0	244713
12520	CORNWALL ON HUDSON	32326	1224	18.6	20.3	33.3	18.1	9.7	63123	73498	87	78	911	0.0	0.3	11.9	74.5	13.3	245962
12521	CRARYVILLE	30267	614	26.2	24.6	32.4	10.1	6.7	49095	55736	70	60	494	1.6	3.4	32.6	48.0	14.4	201744
12522	DOVER PLAINS	26283	1992	20.6	28.7	34.2	12.0	4.5	50633	58643	73	63	1524	14.7	8.1	21.8	49.3	6.1	189310
12523	ELIZAVILLE	26527	806	22.5	38.8	27.4	7.1	4.2	42707	48391	55	43	617	5.0	8.9	31.6	49.4	5.0	184821
12524	FISHKILL	29739	5272	16.6	23.2	36.9	14.9	8.3	61183	70289	86	76	3657	1.5	1.8	16.9	73.5	6.3	228073
12525	GARDINER	26929	1327	14.3	27.5	40.2	12.9	5.1	56817	63035	81	72	1086	5.0	1.3	15.9	73.1	4.7	220288
12526	GERMANTOWN	26716	1512	23.2	30.5	29.7	11.2	5.4	47342	54114	67	56	1153	4.4	4.1	30.5	50.9	10.1	196083
12528	HIGHLAND	25800	5322	19.0	26.3	36.2	13.3	5.1	55665	63642	80	71	3621	2.2	2.5	31.1	59.4	4.9	195854
12529	HILLSDALE	26648	1153	24.4	30.0	29.9	9.5	6.2	45723	52583	63	52	897	1.1	3.1	35.0	45.8	14.9	198197
12531	HOLMES	31122	1262	7.8	16.6	44.5	19.3	11.8	73789	84630	93	87	1071	0.3	0.0	9.0	72.4	18.4	279082
12533	HOPEWELL JUNCTION	33685	8049	9.7	15.8	37.1	22.0	15.5	80994	92707	95	91	7101	0.9	0.6	9.8	69.4	19.3	295566
12534	HUDSON	21421	8511	33.3	31.0	27.1	5.0	3.6	37332	41995	37	22	5244	6.5	5.7	54.0	29.7	4.1	145185
12538	HYDE PARK	26590	5360	18.1	25.7	37.8	13.5	4.9	55529	64430	80	71	3942	3.7	2.7	27.7	61.2	4.7	199569
12540	LAGRANGEVILLE	33164	2261	8.6	16.9	41.3	20.2	13.1	77551	89344	94	89	2037	0.2	0.4	5.9	72.7	20.9	291547
12542	MARLBORO	24654	2027	21.7	24.1	36.1	12.6	5.5	54045	61769	78	69	1501	1.2	1.1	20.6	74.1	3.1	219715
12543	MAYBROOK	22159	1273	14.5	25.4	43.9	13.5	2.8	59954	67919	84	74	818	0.7	1.2	52.6	44.6	0.9	167355
12545	MILLBROOK	35105	1822	17.7	24.4	30.5	15.5	12.0	61011	72184	85	76	1155	0.6	0.0	7.0	65.9	26.5	284875
12546	MILLERTON	28180	1143	21.5	30.6	34.9	8.5	4.5	48337	56100	69	59	853	3.8	1.6	32.8	50.4	11.4	201271
12547	MILTON	25075	1026	19.5	23.7	37.7	13.1	6.0	55716	63331	80	71	783	1.9	1.5	17.0	75.6	4.0	229751
12548	MODENA	22517	507	19.9	34.3	32.7	7.9	5.1	45792	51504	63	52	408	17.4	8.6	27.7	44.9	1.5	165625
12549	MONTGOMERY	25337	3382	10.9	27.1	38.9	16.8	6.3	63920	75088	88	79	2820	1.2	1.1	23.8	66.4	7.5	220050
12550	NEWBURGH	21610	18664	24.7	26.7	32.5	11.3	4.9	48547	56733	69	59	10896	1.2	2.9	33.1	56.8	6.1	199493
12553	NEW WINDSOR	26557	8807	14.6	28.4	36.6	14.6	5.8	57838	66228	83	73	6211	5.3	1.7	23.0	67.1	2.9	211326
12561	NEW PALTZ	23951	6443	29.8	23.2	30.4	10.8	5.8	46368	52323	65	54	4008	1.5	3.5	22.9	62.3	9.9	212116
12563	PATTERSON	30323	2859	7.8	18.0	41.7	19.7	12.8	75363	87573	93	88	2358	1.1	0.5	12.7	69.4	16.4	262335
12564	PAWLING	36303	2673	13.1	19.4	40.4	16.0	11.0	66893	77870	90	82	2007	0.5	0.2	8.8	70.6	20.0	274386
12566	PINE BUSH	24599	3755	18.0	25.2	39.1	12.9	4.7	58796	66344	83	73	3036	0.4	2.7	29.0	62.0	6.0	208132
12567	PINE PLAINS	28321	1144	20.3	33.0	30.9	8.9	6.9	47616	55091	67	57	821	1.7	2.2	38.9	44.5	12.8	190658
12569	PLEASANT VALLEY	30173	3773	13.8	24.0	36.9	15.8	9.5	64051	75261	88	79	2980	5.1	2.2	13.3	66.8	12.7	246280
12570	POUGHQUAG	31069	2293	5.4	18.8	43.7	22.2	9.9	78830	89290	95	90	1971	1.4	0.9	5.5	75.8	16.4	293984
12571	RED HOOK	22962	3661	20.0	26.1	33.0	13.2	7.7	54561	63414	79	69	2853	2.8	1.1	23.7	60.9	11.5	221861
12572	RHINEBECK	34846	4002	18.4	22.7	33.3	15.3	10.3	61602	72072	86	76	2892	1.6	0.5	12.7	66.2	19.1	256116
12575	ROCK TAVERN	25279	586	15.4	21.0	35.2	18.3	10.2	65118	76197	89	80	531	3.4	1.5	9.2	67.8	18.1	279773
12577	SALISBURY MILLS	31896	557	5.2	20.5	41.7	23.3	9.3	76438	86137	94	88	484	0.0	1.0	14.9	72.7	11.4	242336
12578	SALT POINT	32961	775	11.7	20.5	39.9	16.1	11.7	69019	80568	91	84	660	2.9	1.4	11.2	69.6	15.0	258716
12580	STAATSBURG	33026	1544	11.2	19.7	39.1	19.8	10.3	72159	83415	92	85	1333	1.3	0.8	22.3	62.3	13.4	221774
12581	STANFORDVILLE	35737	1064	12.3	26.6	35.6	16.8	8.7	62953	75191	87	78	773	0.1	0.9	9.3	69.7	19.9	267735
12582	STORMVILLE	34378	1605	4.9	14.1	40.8	26.2	14.1	85812	99041	96	92	1445	0.5	0.1	3.5	74.2	21.7	321893
12583	TIVOLI	28363	929	25.4	23.5	33.4	11.7	6.0	50956	60598	74	64	604	1.7	1.3	25.8	62.8	8.4	218345
12585	VERBANK	31790	409	5.4	19.8	42.3	20.1	12.5	75823	87496	94	88	367	0.0	0.3	6.0	75.2	18.5	291768
12586	WALDEN	23042	4483	19.9	27.1	34.4	14.8	3.8	52981	61674	77	67	3342	4.2	1.4	35.0	55.2	4.3	191773
12589	WALLKILL	22014	4530	15.3	25.4	40.4	13.6	5.3	58927	66469	83	74	3561	3.7	1.9	18.5	69.6	6.3	222042
12590	WAPPINGERS FALLS	29899	13122	13.7	22.6	37.0	18.3	8.5	65421	76309	89	81	9116	2.5	2.2	13.8	75.6	5.9	237342
12592	WASSAIC	27131	428	21.0	36.2	29.7	8.6	4.4	41666	48595	52	40	285	5.3	4.2	27.4	57.2	6.0	199671
12594	WINGDALE	23841	1481	12.4	22.4	48.7	13.0	3.4	61664	71140	86	76	1227	6.2	1.6	19.7	68.4	4.1	220283
12601	POUGHKEEPSIE	20664	16371	34.6	25.7	26.5	9.6	3.7	38272	44290	40	26	7691	2.2	2.7	36.5	55.6	3.1	193225
12603	POUGHKEEPSIE	32340	14731	14.4	20.6	37.4	17.8	9.8	66987	78091	90	82	11038	0.8	1.1	18.9	72.1	7.0	226785
12604	POUGHKEEPSIE	8652	48	16.7	20.8	39.6	12.5	10.4	62500	79209	87	77	29	0.0	0.0	10.3	89.7	0.0	230357
12701	MONTICELLO	21392	5092	38.5	24.7	25.3	7.5	4.1	36318	41115	33	18	2717	5.1	10.3	56.3	26.2	2.2	138594
12719	BARRYVILLE	25870	360	25.6	28.3	33.6	7.8	4.7	46544	53006	65	55	299	0.3	4.0	42.8	50.5	2.3	179087
12720	BETHEL	49266	40	32.5	30.0	20.0	5.0	12.5	40000	50000	46	34	32	0.0	15.6	31.3	43.8	9.4	178571
12721	BLOOMINGBURG	22172	2198	21.0	23.1	38.8	13.0	4.1	54670	63162	79	70	1773	10.6	7.0	30.0	48.5	4.0	180179
12723	CALLICOON	21985	812	26.6	31.8	30.7	8.6	2.3	42049	49053	53	41	648	0.9	5.3	50.9	36.3	6.6	160625
12725	CLARYVILLE	24357	97	26.8	33.0	27.8	7.2	5.2	39679	44297	45	33	77	5.2	6.5	44.2	35.1	9.1	158929
12726	COCHECTON	23935	518	28.0	29.0	32.2	7.0	3.9	43989	50424	59	48	430	4.2	7.2	43.7	42.1	2.8	160135
12727	COCHECTON CENTER	20625	11	36.4	36.4	27.3	0.0	0.0	32290	35000	19	7	9	0.0	0.0	44.4	55.6	0.0	179167
12729	CUDDEBACKVILLE	21324	967	20.3	25.4	43.1	9.0	2.2	53195	61172	77	67	789	5.6	7.0	45.4	39.3	2.8	165234
12732	ELDRED	27155	403	26.8	28.3	33.0	7.0	5.0	45107	52560	61	51	335	0.3	4.2	42.7	50.2	2.7	179095
12733	FALLSBURG	10298	220	60.5	21.8	15.0	1.4	1.4	20599	22292	2	2	94	5.3	14.9	60.6	19.2	0.0	132895
12734	FERNDALE	20106	568	29.8	34.0	25.9	7.9	2.5	37972	43226	39	24	398	13.8	10.3	42.2	31.4	2.3	139091
12736	FREMONT CENTER	21163	100	31.0	30.0	32.0	5.0	2.0	37342	43387	37	22	81	2.5	12.4	43.2	35.8	6.2	158750
12737	GLEN SPEY	22469	654	28.0	27.8	30.6	9.5	4.1	46342	52772	65	54	520	1.0	4.0	42.3	49.0	3.7	179023
12738	GLEN WILD	21213	61	29.5	32.8	23.0	9.8	4.9	40558	51191	48	36	45	4.4	6.7	44.4	37.8	6.7	159375
12740	GRAHAMSVILLE	24420	714	18.1	31.8	35.3	10.1	4.8	50153	58357	72	62	586	4.6	2.4	37.2	45.9	9.9	186039
12741	HANKINS	20356	91	30.8	29.7	31.9	5.5	2.2	38371	41868	41	26	74	2.7	12.2	41.9	36.5	6.8	161111
12742	HARRIS	32491	87	24.1	29.9	29.9	9.2	6.9	46936	55001	66	55	57	1.8	3.5	52.6	42.1	0.0	158929
12743	HIGHLAND LAKE	26979	149	23.5	32.2	30.9	9.4	4.0	46322	54960	65	54	125	0.8	5.6	45.6	45.6	2.4	170536
12745	HORTONVILLE	21090	18	16.7	50.0	27.8	5.6	0.0	38478	45000	41	27	14	0.0	0.0	64.3	35.7	0.0	150000
12746	HUGUENOT	19691	423	22.9	29.6	36.6	8.3	2.6	47985	54123	68	58	353	9.4	10.8	47.0	32.6	0.3	146406
12747	HURLEYVILLE	17263	909	42.0	22.4	26.8	6.6	2.1	33860	37411	24	10	530	14.2	7.2	51.3	25.7	1.7	139516
12748	JEFFERSONVILLE	24085	830	31.7	28.9	26.1	7.7	5.5	40870	47489	49	37	642	2.2	6.2	50.9	35.1	5.6	148311
12750	KENOZA LAKE	30009	35	28.6	28.6	28.6	8.6	5.7	45739	53453	63	52	28	0.0	3.6	60.7	32.1	3.6	144444
12751	KIAMESHA LAKE	21688	143	31.5	25.2	33.6	7.7	2.1	41268	47089	51	39	91	0.0	28.6	45.1	26.4	0.0	133036
12752	LAKE HUNTINGTON	27340	77	28.6	28.6	33.8	6.5	2.6	44313	52380	59	48	63	3.2	6.4	46.0	42.9	1.6	160417
12754	LIBERTY	20224	2712	36.4	27.5	25.4	7.2	3.5	34778	39111	27	12	1551	7.0	6.1	59.2	26.6	1.2	138932
12758	LIVINGSTON MANOR	18376	1758	32.9	34.2	24.3	6.3	2.2	37049	42051	36	21	1261	4.1	10.1	56.0	28.6	1.3	141927
12759	LOCH SHELDRAKE	21475	513	31.8	26.5	29.0	9.0	3.7	44171	50423	59	48	332	28.3	6.3	34.6	29.8	0.9	131757
12760	LONG EDDY	18627	259	35.9	32.1	25.5	4.6	1.9	34054	37966	24	10	215	10.2	20.0	42.8	22.8	4.2	131071
12762	MONGAUP VALLEY	25851	97	37.1	22.7	26.8	9.3	4.1	36928	44450	35	20	74	5.4	13.5	31.1	43.2	6.8	175000
12763	MOUNTAIN DALE	20289	391	23.8	35.0	28.4	10.0	2.8	43091	49284	56	44	282	8.5	8.9	53.2	29.4	0.0	126389
12764	NARROWSBURG	22176	714	29.1	28.3	33.2	7.1	2.2	43850	50626	58	47	586	4.3	3.9	53.8	33.6	4.4	151974
12765	NEVERSINK	21026	487	21.6	26.5	39.6	9.7	2.7	51727	58985	75	65	411	5.4	4.6	44.5	37.0	8.5	160081
12766	NORTH BRANCH	22159	222	27.5	30.2	31.5	4.5	6.3	44539	51515	60	49	180	1.1	8.3	46.1	35.6	8.9	160294
12768	PARKSVILLE	17990	423	36.9	31.7	21.5	7.6	2.4	35061	40000	28	13	315	4.8	6.4	55.6	30.5	2.9	147627
12770	POND EDDY	24021	139	22.3	30.2	31.7	10.1	5.8	48397	55251	69	59	115	0.9	6.1	40.0	50.4	2.6	179605
12771	PORT JERVIS	20540	5557	29.3	29.0	31.2	8.0	2.5	41123	47972	50	38	3416	2.5	7.0	54.1	34.1	2.3	150525
12775	ROCK HILL	27995	795	19.0	27.3	37.2	8.2	8.3	52871	61106	77	67	641	0.6	3.7	37.0	50.2	8.4	189919
12776	ROSCOE	19588	1113	32.7	32.7	27.9	4.6	2.1	36744	41450	34	20	876	5.4	12.6	51.5	24.7	5.9	135253
	NEW YORK	28049		26.3	24.3	29.3	11.5	8.6	49309	58077				4.6	8.6	27.2	39.9	19.8	219050
	UNITED STATES	25866		24.7	27.1	30.8	10.9	6.5	48124	56710				10.9	15.0	33.7	30.1	10.4	145905

ZIP CODE #	POST OFFICE NAME	FINANCIAL SERVICES: Auto Loan	FINANCIAL SERVICES: Home Loan	FINANCIAL SERVICES: Investments	FINANCIAL SERVICES: Retirement Plans	THE HOME: Home Improvements: Home Repair	THE HOME: Home Improvements: Lawn & Garden	THE HOME: Furnishings: Computers & Hardware	THE HOME: Furnishings: Major Appliances	THE HOME: Furnishings: TV, Radio, Sound Equipment	THE HOME: Furnishings: Furniture	ENTERTAINMENT: Dine out/Carry out	ENTERTAINMENT: Sports Equipment	ENTERTAINMENT: Fees & Tickets	ENTERTAINMENT: Toys & Games	ENTERTAINMENT: Travel	ENTERTAINMENT: Cable TV	PERSONAL: Apparel & Services	PERSONAL: Auto Repairs	PERSONAL: Health Insurance	PERSONAL: Pets & Supplies
12508	BEACON	85	84	85	83	84	92	87	87	88	85	108	100	86	109	86	88	105	87	88	98
12513	CLAVERACK	83	97	107	92	96	105	92	92	91	91	114	103	97	118	96	94	112	90	93	100
12514	CLINTON CORNERS	117	140	161	143	138	139	132	129	124	131	156	153	138	162	133	120	155	128	117	142
12515	CLINTONDALE	72	73	79	71	74	84	72	76	73	73	91	81	73	86	74	74	87	75	80	83
12516	COPAKE	116	91	61	82	102	115	86	103	97	85	115	121	76	113	91	104	107	102	122	141
12517	COPAKE FALLS	117	91	62	83	103	116	86	104	98	85	116	122	77	114	92	104	107	102	123	142
12518	CORNWALL	116	133	146	132	131	136	123	124	118	125	149	142	128	151	126	117	146	122	117	137
12520	CORNWALL ON HUDSON	110	125	142	127	125	130	119	119	114	120	143	137	123	144	121	112	141	118	113	131
12521	CRARYVILLE	123	96	66	89	108	121	93	110	104	92	124	129	84	122	98	111	115	108	129	147
12522	DOVER PLAINS	100	95	86	93	97	105	93	98	95	93	117	111	91	113	94	95	111	97	101	113
12523	ELIZAVILLE	107	81	52	75	91	104	81	95	92	79	108	111	72	105	84	97	100	94	113	126
12524	FISHKILL	96	109	130	110	108	113	107	105	104	106	131	122	112	135	109	103	129	105	100	115
12525	GARDINER	94	106	114	108	104	103	101	100	95	101	120	118	103	122	100	91	118	99	89	109
12526	GERMANTOWN	106	87	64	83	94	106	89	98	97	86	116	113	82	113	90	101	108	97	112	122
12528	HIGHLAND	87	97	110	99	96	99	95	93	91	94	114	110	97	118	95	89	112	93	87	103
12529	HILLSDALE	117	92	63	83	103	116	87	104	98	86	117	122	78	115	92	105	108	103	123	141
12531	HOLMES	118	147	156	147	144	142	131	130	121	130	152	152	139	162	134	117	152	125	116	144
12533	HOPEWELL JUNCTION	134	163	173	166	159	158	147	145	135	147	171	170	156	179	149	131	171	141	129	160
12534	HUDSON	68	66	68	63	67	75	68	69	71	67	87	78	68	87	69	73	84	69	74	78
12538	HYDE PARK	88	101	111	99	99	104	96	95	92	95	116	109	100	119	98	91	114	94	91	104
12540	LAGRANGEVILLE	128	158	168	159	156	153	141	141	131	141	165	165	150	176	145	127	165	136	126	156
12542	MARLBORO	91	98	101	98	99	103	94	95	92	93	114	111	96	117	95	92	111	94	93	107
12543	MAYBROOK	88	94	100	97	92	93	95	92	90	94	113	110	95	115	93	85	112	93	83	101
12545	MILLBROOK	116	135	160	137	134	140	130	128	124	130	157	148	136	160	133	123	155	127	120	139
12546	MILLERTON	94	105	113	100	105	115	100	101	101	99	125	113	105	131	104	104	122	99	105	112
12547	MILTON	88	108	117	107	106	107	98	98	92	98	116	114	105	124	101	90	116	95	89	107
12548	MODENA	92	88	77	85	88	95	83	89	84	86	104	99	81	97	84	84	100	88	90	102
12549	MONTGOMERY	97	113	121	114	112	112	106	105	100	105	126	123	111	132	107	97	125	103	96	116
12550	NEWBURGH	83	88	98	87	86	91	89	87	88	89	110	101	90	112	88	87	109	88	84	96
12553	NEW WINDSOR	95	104	111	104	103	107	100	100	98	100	122	117	103	126	101	96	120	99	95	112
12561	NEW PALTZ	81	84	96	86	83	87	90	84	86	87	108	101	89	107	87	82	106	87	79	93
12563	PATTERSON	120	144	156	145	141	141	133	131	124	132	156	154	139	164	134	120	155	128	118	145
12564	PAWLING	121	143	161	144	141	143	134	132	127	134	159	154	141	166	136	124	158	130	122	146
12566	PINE BUSH	93	100	99	100	100	102	94	96	91	94	114	112	96	117	95	89	111	94	90	108
12567	PINE PLAINS	117	95	70	90	105	117	93	107	102	92	122	126	86	122	97	107	114	106	123	139
12569	PLEASANT VALLEY	108	121	121	120	120	123	112	114	108	112	134	132	116	139	113	106	132	111	107	128
12570	POUGHQUAG	129	154	157	157	149	145	138	137	127	140	160	160	144	167	138	121	159	132	120	151
12571	RED HOOK	97	105	112	105	105	111	101	102	100	100	124	119	104	127	103	99	121	101	99	115
12572	RHINEBECK	110	125	142	124	125	134	118	120	115	119	144	134	123	143	122	115	141	118	118	131
12575	ROCK TAVERN	101	123	130	123	121	120	111	110	103	110	129	129	117	137	113	100	129	107	99	122
12577	SALISBURY MILLS	136	163	167	166	158	155	146	145	135	148	170	170	153	177	147	129	169	140	127	160
12578	SALT POINT	121	144	148	143	141	141	129	130	121	129	152	152	136	159	132	118	151	126	119	145
12580	STAATSBURG	112	139	148	138	136	135	125	124	116	124	146	145	133	156	128	113	146	120	112	137
12581	STANFORDVILLE	110	126	154	130	124	127	124	121	118	123	149	144	128	153	125	115	147	122	110	132
12582	STORMVILLE	141	176	188	178	172	171	156	155	144	157	182	181	168	192	160	140	182	149	138	171
12583	TIVOLI	89	80	95	85	80	87	96	89	95	92	119	109	92	115	90	90	116	95	85	99
12585	VERBANK	118	147	156	147	145	143	131	131	122	131	153	153	140	163	134	118	153	126	117	145
12586	WALDEN	89	94	94	93	94	98	91	92	90	90	111	107	92	115	91	89	109	90	89	104
12589	WALLKILL	94	105	108	105	102	103	98	98	93	99	118	115	100	120	98	90	116	97	89	109
12590	WAPPINGERS FALLS	104	120	136	121	118	121	115	113	109	114	138	132	119	142	116	107	136	112	104	124
12592	WASSAIC	87	94	99	89	95	105	93	92	96	89	119	103	98	129	96	100	115	90	99	102
12594	WINGDALE	100	102	93	101	101	103	96	99	94	97	117	117	95	117	95	91	114	98	93	114
12601	POUGHKEEPSIE	71	70	85	70	69	76	76	73	77	75	96	85	76	95	75	77	94	75	72	81
12603	POUGHKEEPSIE	105	127	148	126	125	129	119	117	113	118	143	136	126	149	122	112	142	115	109	128
12604	POUGHKEEPSIE	98	113	139	117	111	114	112	108	106	111	134	129	115	137	112	103	132	109	98	118
12701	MONTICELLO	80	67	65	63	71	80	70	75	76	69	93	87	66	91	71	79	88	76	83	93
12719	BARRYVILLE	109	86	58	77	97	109	81	97	92	80	108	114	72	107	86	98	101	96	115	133
12720	BETHEL	204	160	109	144	180	202	151	182	171	149	202	213	135	200	161	182	188	179	215	248
12721	BLOOMINGBURG	87	95	95	94	94	96	89	90	86	89	108	106	91	110	90	84	106	89	85	102
12723	CALLICOON	87	76	62	70	83	92	72	82	79	72	95	95	68	95	76	83	89	81	94	106
12725	CLARYVILLE	99	77	53	70	87	98	73	88	83	72	98	103	65	97	78	88	91	87	104	120
12726	COCHECTON	100	78	53	70	88	99	74	89	83	73	99	104	66	97	78	89	92	87	105	121
12727	COCHECTON CENTER	64	50	34	45	56	63	47	57	53	47	63	66	42	62	50	57	59	56	67	77
12729	CUDDEBACKVILLE	84	83	77	82	84	89	81	84	82	81	101	97	81	103	81	81	97	83	84	96
12732	ELDRED	111	87	59	78	98	110	82	99	93	81	110	115	73	108	87	99	102	97	116	135
12733	FALLSBURG	47	40	37	38	41	47	43	44	46	42	56	52	40	55	43	47	53	45	49	54
12734	FERNDALE	79	66	53	62	73	80	65	74	70	64	85	87	60	84	67	73	80	73	83	96
12736	FREMONT CENTER	85	67	45	60	75	84	63	76	71	62	84	89	56	83	67	76	78	75	90	104
12737	GLEN SPEY	95	74	51	67	84	94	70	84	79	69	94	99	63	93	75	85	87	83	100	115
12738	GLEN WILD	92	72	49	65	82	92	68	82	77	68	92	96	61	90	73	83	85	81	97	113
12740	GRAHAMSVILLE	110	78	42	73	90	101	76	94	88	76	103	114	66	101	80	92	94	93	112	131
12741	HANKINS	85	67	45	60	75	84	63	76	71	62	84	89	56	83	67	76	78	75	90	104
12742	HARRIS	117	92	63	83	104	117	87	105	98	86	117	123	78	115	93	105	108	103	124	143
12743	HIGHLAND LAKE	110	86	59	78	97	109	81	98	92	80	109	114	73	107	87	98	101	96	116	134
12745	HORTONVILLE	81	63	43	57	71	80	60	72	67	59	80	84	53	79	64	72	74	71	85	98
12746	HUGUENOT	87	79	62	76	79	84	76	81	77	78	95	94	72	90	75	76	91	81	81	96
12747	HURLEYVILLE	77	62	46	57	68	77	60	70	67	59	80	82	55	79	63	71	75	69	81	93
12748	JEFFERSONVILLE	97	77	56	72	85	97	78	89	87	76	103	102	71	99	80	91	95	88	103	113
12750	KENOZA LAKE	116	91	62	82	102	115	86	103	97	85	115	121	77	113	91	104	107	102	122	141
12751	KIAMESHA LAKE	86	68	46	61	76	86	64	77	72	63	85	90	57	84	68	77	79	76	91	105
12752	LAKE HUNTINGTON	91	71	49	64	80	90	67	81	76	67	90	95	60	89	72	81	84	80	96	111
12754	LIBERTY	67	63	68	63	64	72	68	68	71	66	87	79	67	86	68	71	83	70	72	77
12758	LIVINGSTON MANOR	74	61	48	56	65	74	62	68	68	60	82	78	58	81	63	72	77	68	79	85
12759	LOCH SHELDRAKE	95	75	51	67	84	94	70	85	80	70	94	99	63	93	75	85	88	83	100	116
12760	LONG EDDY	78	61	42	55	69	77	58	69	65	57	77	81	51	76	61	70	72	68	82	95
12762	MONGAUP VALLEY	97	76	52	69	86	96	72	87	81	71	96	101	64	95	77	87	90	85	102	118
12763	MOUNTAIN DALE	90	71	48	64	80	90	67	80	75	66	89	94	60	88	71	81	83	79	95	110
12764	NARROWSBURG	89	70	47	63	78	88	66	79	74	65	88	93	59	87	70	79	82	78	93	108
12765	NEVERSINK	93	80	69	78	87	94	78	87	83	78	101	104	73	100	81	85	95	87	95	111
12766	NORTH BRANCH	78	78	86	81	79	85	80	81	79	79	98	94	79	95	80	77	94	81	80	90
12768	PARKSVILLE	71	58	49	54	64	72	58	66	64	57	77	77	54	76	61	68	73	66	76	86
12770	POND EDDY	101	79	54	71	89	100	75	90	84	74	100	105	67	99	80	90	93	88	106	123
12771	PORT JERVIS	74	73	73	71	74	80	74	75	76	73	94	86	75	96	75	77	91	75	77	85
12775	ROCK HILL	115	90	61	81	101	114	85	102	96	84	114	120	76	112	90	102	106	101	121	140
12776	ROSCOE	75	60	43	56	65	75	61	69	67	59	80	79	55	77	62	71	74	69	80	87
	NEW YORK	95	100	134	99	98	107	103	100	105	103	133	116	105	138	104	107	131	102	99	112
	UNITED STATES	100	100	100	100	100	100	100	100	100	100	100	100	100	100	100	100	100	100	100	100

# POST OFFICE NAME	COUNTY FIPS CODE	POPULATION 2000	POPULATION 2004	POPULATION 2009	2000-2004 ANNUAL RATE % Rate	2000-2004 ANNUAL RATE State Centile	HOUSEHOLDS 2000	HOUSEHOLDS 2004	HOUSEHOLDS 2009	% Annual Rate 2000-2004	2004 Average HH Size	FAMILIES 2000	FAMILIES 2004	% Annual Rate 2000-2004
12777 FORESTBURGH	105	707	755	802	1.6	89	282	305	329	1.9	2.46	191	206	1.8
12779 SOUTH FALLSBURG	105	1439	1436	1486	-0.1	25	568	573	600	0.2	2.40	366	366	0.0
12780 SPARROW BUSH	071	2228	2315	2482	0.9	74	869	908	976	1.0	2.55	618	640	0.8
12782 SUNDOWN	111	181	167	168	-1.9	0	77	72	74	-1.6	2.22	44	41	-1.7
12783 SWAN LAKE	105	1653	1728	1820	1.1	79	545	582	626	1.6	2.66	366	387	1.3
12786 WHITE LAKE	105	704	694	714	-0.3	12	268	267	279	-0.1	2.43	172	170	-0.3
12787 WHITE SULPHUR SPRING	105	81	85	90	1.1	81	32	34	36	1.4	2.50	23	24	1.0
12788 WOODBOURNE	105	2606	2663	2739	0.5	58	643	677	719	1.2	2.40	444	464	1.0
12789 WOODRIDGE	105	2408	2474	2558	0.6	64	656	688	729	1.1	2.45	398	416	1.1
12790 WURTSBORO	105	5615	5837	6116	0.9	75	2264	2382	2523	1.2	2.44	1531	1599	1.0
12791 YOUNGSVILLE	105	678	692	717	0.5	56	285	294	309	0.7	2.35	196	201	0.6
12792 YULAN	105	272	285	299	1.1	81	116	123	131	1.4	2.23	79	83	1.2
12801 GLENS FALLS	113	14152	14331	14843	0.3	47	6192	6368	6705	0.7	2.21	3371	3432	0.4
12803 SOUTH GLENS FALLS	091	7141	7227	7507	0.3	45	2958	3042	3209	0.7	2.37	1940	1982	0.5
12804 QUEENSBURY	113	24120	25339	26619	1.2	82	9380	10043	10742	1.6	2.49	6745	7171	1.5
12808 ADIRONDACK	113	346	350	361	0.3	45	164	169	177	0.8	2.07	114	117	0.6
12809 ARGYLE	115	3435	3606	3736	1.2	81	1224	1309	1381	1.6	2.66	929	988	1.5
12810 ATHOL	113	636	652	675	0.6	61	246	256	270	0.9	2.53	177	183	0.8
12812 BLUE MOUNTAIN LAKE	041	254	251	247	-0.3	14	115	115	115	0.0	2.15	72	71	-0.3
12814 BOLTON LANDING	113	1401	1418	1459	0.3	45	628	648	678	0.7	2.19	408	417	0.5
12815 BRANT LAKE	113	1067	1081	1112	0.3	48	448	462	484	0.7	2.34	312	320	0.6
12816 CAMBRIDGE	115	4325	4344	4398	0.1	35	1710	1745	1797	0.5	2.42	1184	1201	0.3
12817 CHESTERTOWN	113	2099	2126	2186	0.3	47	902	929	973	0.7	2.17	611	625	0.5
12819 CLEMONS	115	369	386	399	1.1	79	140	149	157	1.5	2.59	103	109	1.3
12821 COMSTOCK	115	3106	3182	3235	0.6	61	135	147	157	2.0	2.56	101	110	2.0
12822 CORINTH	091	5355	5549	5846	0.8	72	2110	2223	2381	1.2	2.49	1475	1546	1.1
12823 COSSAYUNA	115	206	210	214	0.5	55	82	85	88	0.9	2.47	63	65	0.7
12824 DIAMOND POINT	113	847	869	900	0.6	62	373	389	410	1.0	2.23	266	276	0.9
12827 FORT ANN	115	3765	3768	3820	0.0	30	1400	1446	1504	0.8	2.20	1066	1096	0.7
12828 FORT EDWARD	115	7800	7889	8077	0.3	45	2909	2995	3121	0.7	2.56	2101	2152	0.6
12831 GANSEVOORT	091	15062	16658	18088	2.4	96	5101	5756	6366	2.9	2.75	3879	4355	2.8
12832 GRANVILLE	115	7029	7089	7187	0.2	40	2650	2719	2808	0.6	2.50	1847	1883	0.5
12833 GREENFIELD CENTER	091	5552	5711	5968	0.7	65	2035	2133	2266	1.1	2.67	1514	1576	1.0
12834 GREENWICH	115	6447	6495	6622	0.2	39	2506	2565	2661	0.6	2.53	1781	1814	0.4
12835 HADLEY	091	2569	2977	3313	3.5	99	1013	1196	1353	4.0	2.47	734	860	3.8
12836 HAGUE	113	895	903	926	0.2	41	388	396	412	0.5	2.28	271	275	0.4
12837 HAMPTON	115	704	712	723	0.3	45	258	266	275	0.7	2.62	186	190	0.5
12838 HARTFORD	115	633	655	672	0.8	71	225	236	247	1.1	2.78	178	186	1.0
12839 HUDSON FALLS	115	12154	12313	12539	0.3	48	4886	5039	5224	0.7	2.40	3219	3303	0.6
12842 INDIAN LAKE	041	1217	1196	1175	-0.4	9	536	534	532	-0.1	2.20	353	350	-0.2
12843 JOHNSBURG	113	1281	1319	1369	0.7	66	501	526	556	1.2	2.45	349	364	1.0
12844 KATTSKILL BAY	115	253	252	260	-0.1	23	124	127	133	0.6	1.98	93	94	0.3
12845 LAKE GEORGE	113	4847	5188	5504	1.6	89	2052	2230	2405	2.0	2.31	1381	1493	1.9
12846 LAKE LUZERNE	113	3219	3358	3512	1.0	77	1264	1333	1413	1.3	2.51	884	926	1.1
12847 LONG LAKE	041	852	832	815	-0.6	5	387	385	384	-0.1	2.10	237	234	-0.3
12849 MIDDLE GRANVILLE	115	283	287	292	0.3	49	105	109	113	0.9	2.52	79	81	0.6
12850 MIDDLE GROVE	091	2338	2433	2566	0.9	75	854	904	969	1.4	2.69	643	676	1.2
12851 MINERVA	031	264	274	291	0.9	74	104	109	118	1.1	2.51	73	76	1.0
12852 NEWCOMB	031	481	489	514	0.4	51	211	219	235	0.9	2.21	141	146	0.8
12853 NORTH CREEK	113	1985	2030	2095	0.5	59	814	849	895	1.0	2.07	542	560	0.8
12854 NORTH GRANVILLE	115	123	122	123	-0.2	18	48	48	50	0.0	2.54	35	35	0.0
12855 NORTH HUDSON	031	266	271	285	0.4	54	114	118	126	0.8	2.30	77	79	0.6
12857 OLMSTEDVILLE	031	580	601	638	0.8	72	237	249	268	1.2	2.40	166	173	1.0
12858 PARADOX	031	13	14	14	1.8	91	6	6	7	0.0	2.33	4	4	0.0
12859 PORTER CORNERS	091	1632	1705	1797	1.0	78	608	647	693	1.5	2.63	466	493	1.3
12860 POTTERSVILLE	113	709	716	731	0.2	42	76	78	82	0.6	6.90	55	56	0.4
12861 PUTNAM STATION	115	560	586	605	1.1	79	208	222	233	1.5	2.64	153	162	1.4
12863 ROCK CITY FALLS	091	529	538	558	0.4	52	202	207	217	0.6	2.60	146	148	0.3
12865 SALEM	115	3386	3565	3707	1.2	83	1287	1380	1462	1.7	2.54	920	980	1.5
12866 SARATOGA SPRINGS	091	34099	35729	38005	1.1	81	13827	14721	15950	1.5	2.27	8261	8820	1.6
12870 SCHROON LAKE	031	1696	1754	1861	0.8	70	708	741	795	1.1	2.32	454	472	0.9
12871 SCHUYLERVILLE	091	4414	4650	4940	1.2	83	1703	1831	1980	1.7	2.51	1189	1270	1.6
12872 SEVERANCE	031	6	6	7	0.0	28	3	3	3	0.0	2.00	2	2	0.0
12873 SHUSHAN	115	760	756	764	-0.1	22	323	326	335	0.2	2.29	210	210	0.0
12878 STONY CREEK	113	678	690	712	0.4	52	270	279	292	0.8	2.46	189	194	0.6
12883 TICONDEROGA	031	5220	5463	5832	1.1	80	2055	2178	2358	1.4	2.45	1373	1448	1.3
12885 WARRENSBURG	113	4913	5066	5262	0.7	67	1969	2059	2172	1.1	2.43	1354	1405	0.9
12886 WEVERTOWN	113	34	35	36	0.7	65	16	17	18	1.4	2.06	12	13	1.9
12887 WHITEHALL	115	4911	5007	5117	0.5	55	1949	2021	2103	0.9	2.46	1342	1381	0.7
12901 PLATTSBURGH	019	32566	32961	33777	0.3	45	12876	13310	13942	1.0	2.25	7280	7447	0.5
12903 PLATTSBURGH	019	104	80	78	-6.0	0	59	47	46	-5.2	1.70	25	20	-5.1
12910 ALTONA	019	2428	2515	2585	0.8	72	631	661	693	1.1	2.69	462	483	1.1
12911 KEESEVILLE	031	73	77	81	1.3	84	30	32	34	1.5	2.38	21	22	1.1
12912 AU SABLE FORKS	019	2198	2258	2348	0.6	64	864	902	955	1.0	2.50	607	631	0.9
12913 BLOOMINGDALE	031	1038	1066	1125	0.6	63	418	434	465	0.9	2.45	271	280	0.8
12914 BOMBAY	033	955	989	1040	0.8	72	375	395	422	1.2	2.50	256	268	1.1
12916 BRUSHTON	033	2253	2333	2453	0.8	71	890	937	1002	1.2	2.48	615	643	1.1
12917 BURKE	033	1335	1408	1488	1.3	84	483	515	554	1.5	2.65	361	384	1.5
12918 CADYVILLE	019	2371	2360	2393	-0.1	22	865	876	905	0.3	2.58	647	653	0.2
12919 CHAMPLAIN	019	2877	2916	2991	0.3	48	1186	1225	1280	0.8	2.36	797	818	0.7
12920 CHATEAUGAY	033	2563	2754	2875	1.7	90	938	984	1049	1.1	2.42	633	659	1.0
12921 CHAZY	019	2611	2846	3016	2.1	94	976	1083	1170	2.5	2.60	711	787	2.4
12922 CHILDWOLD	089	36	36	36	0.0	28	20	20	21	0.0	1.80	13	13	0.0
12923 CHURUBUSCO	019	717	773	815	1.8	91	265	291	312	2.2	2.66	197	214	2.0
12924 KEESEVILLE	019	221	207	208	-1.5	1	82	78	80	-1.2	2.65	57	54	-1.3
12926 CONSTABLE	033	2119	2259	2412	1.5	88	793	858	931	1.9	2.62	586	630	1.7
12928 CROWN POINT	031	2101	2152	2272	0.6	61	792	824	883	0.9	2.59	575	596	0.9
12930 DICKINSON CENTER	033	548	563	589	0.6	64	220	230	244	1.1	2.45	163	169	0.9
12932 ELIZABETHTOWN	031	1397	1428	1501	0.5	59	523	544	583	0.9	2.38	344	356	0.8
12934 ELLENBURG CENTER	019	1369	1348	1366	-0.4	11	454	456	471	0.1	2.88	313	312	-0.1
12935 ELLENBURG DEPOT	019	1451	1454	1477	0.1	31	547	557	576	0.4	2.51	388	393	0.3
12936 ESSEX	031	365	374	394	0.6	61	150	156	167	0.9	2.39	100	103	0.7
12937 FORT COVINGTON	033	1507	1546	1618	0.6	61	575	600	637	1.0	2.58	432	448	0.9
12941 JAY	031	1319	1388	1487	1.2	83	528	564	613	1.6	2.45	372	396	1.5
12942 KEENE	031	540	557	589	0.7	68	228	238	256	1.0	2.24	143	149	1.0
NEW YORK					0.4					0.5	2.60			0.4
UNITED STATES					1.2					1.3	2.58			1.1

#	POST OFFICE NAME	RACE (%) White 2000	White 2004	Black 2000	Black 2004	Asian/Pacific 2000	Asian/Pacific 2004	% Hispanic Origin 2000	% Hispanic Origin 2004	2004 AGE DISTRIBUTION (%) 0-4	5-9	10-14	15-19	20-24	25-44	45-64	65-84	85+	18+	MEDIAN AGE 2004	% 2004 Males	% 2004 Females
12777	FORESTBURGH	95.6	94.7	2.0	2.4	0.0	0.0	4.8	6.1	5.6	5.7	6.2	5.4	4.6	23.6	31.7	15.1	2.1	79.2	44.4	47.8	52.2
12779	SOUTH FALLSBURG	73.7	70.9	15.9	17.3	1.7	2.0	16.3	18.7	7.2	7.0	7.3	7.1	7.5	24.2	25.9	12.4	1.4	74.1	38.0	49.7	50.4
12780	SPARROW BUSH	97.1	96.3	0.7	0.9	0.8	1.0	2.6	3.4	6.1	6.4	7.2	6.7	5.8	27.0	28.4	11.0	1.4	76.2	40.4	50.6	49.4
12782	SUNDOWN	94.5	94.0	0.6	0.6	1.7	1.8	2.2	3.6	4.2	4.2	4.8	3.6	4.2	24.6	34.7	18.0	1.8	84.4	47.7	51.5	48.5
12783	SWAN LAKE	88.3	86.9	6.2	6.8	0.8	0.9	11.9	14.0	4.9	5.3	5.6	5.3	5.1	26.6	32.0	13.7	1.6	80.9	43.5	53.0	47.1
12786	WHITE LAKE	91.9	90.6	2.8	3.2	0.9	1.0	14.5	17.6	5.8	5.9	6.2	6.1	5.3	26.5	28.0	14.7	1.6	78.5	41.1	51.0	49.0
12787	WHITE SULPHUR SPRING	93.8	90.6	3.7	4.7	0.0	1.2	4.9	5.9	5.9	4.7	8.2	5.9	7.1	24.7	29.4	11.8	2.4	78.8	41.1	51.8	48.2
12788	WOODBOURNE	69.5	67.7	23.0	23.9	0.9	1.0	14.2	16.1	3.9	4.3	4.9	4.6	5.1	42.0	27.0	7.4	0.8	83.7	38.3	68.9	31.1
12789	WOODRIDGE	66.2	63.4	22.0	23.0	1.7	2.1	18.8	21.6	4.1	4.2	5.1	4.8	5.6	39.3	25.3	10.7	1.0	83.6	38.7	64.9	35.1
12790	WURTSBORO	93.3	92.1	2.2	2.6	1.2	1.5	4.4	5.5	6.7	6.8	7.0	6.4	5.3	26.9	27.1	12.6	1.3	75.7	39.6	50.7	49.3
12791	YOUNGSVILLE	96.8	95.7	0.7	0.9	1.0	1.3	4.6	5.8	4.9	5.5	6.1	5.8	5.1	23.0	33.8	14.0	1.9	80.1	44.8	49.1	50.9
12792	YULAN	94.9	93.3	2.6	3.2	0.7	1.1	2.9	4.2	4.9	5.3	6.3	6.0	4.6	23.5	32.6	14.7	2.1	79.3	44.7	49.8	50.2
12801	GLENS FALLS	96.5	96.0	1.3	1.4	0.5	0.6	1.4	1.7	5.9	5.6	7.1	7.3	7.5	29.9	23.6	11.0	2.2	77.0	36.7	48.3	51.7
12803	SOUTH GLENS FALLS	98.6	98.3	0.5	0.5	0.2	0.2	0.6	0.8	6.0	6.1	6.8	6.4	5.9	27.8	24.7	14.7	1.6	76.9	39.7	47.7	52.3
12804	QUEENSBURY	97.5	97.0	0.6	0.7	0.7	0.9	1.2	1.4	5.8	6.3	7.6	6.6	5.1	25.7	27.3	13.5	2.2	76.1	40.9	47.9	52.1
12808	ADIRONDACK	98.6	98.0	0.3	0.3	0.3	0.3	0.6	0.3	2.6	4.3	8.3	7.1	3.4	21.1	34.0	17.4	1.7	80.0	47.0	50.6	49.4
12809	ARGYLE	98.8	98.5	0.3	0.3	0.0	0.1	1.0	1.3	5.2	6.0	8.1	7.1	5.0	27.1	27.3	11.9	2.4	76.1	39.8	48.9	51.1
12810	ATHOL	97.5	97.4	0.3	0.3	0.5	0.6	0.9	1.1	4.8	6.1	8.0	7.2	4.9	26.2	28.1	13.5	1.2	76.1	41.0	51.5	48.5
12812	BLUE MOUNTAIN LAKE	98.4	98.8	0.0	0.0	0.0	0.0	1.6	1.6	3.6	4.0	6.0	4.4	3.6	21.5	35.1	19.5	2.4	83.3	49.4	47.0	53.0
12814	BOLTON LANDING	98.0	97.7	0.7	0.8	0.3	0.4	0.6	0.7	3.9	4.4	5.7	4.9	4.2	21.7	36.3	16.7	2.3	83.0	48.2	50.1	49.9
12815	BRANT LAKE	98.6	98.4	0.2	0.2	0.2	0.3	0.5	0.6	2.7	4.4	8.3	7.1	3.2	21.6	34.0	17.2	1.6	79.7	46.7	50.4	49.6
12816	CAMBRIDGE	97.8	97.2	0.7	0.8	0.4	0.5	1.1	1.5	5.6	6.1	7.7	6.8	5.2	24.2	27.4	14.7	2.3	75.5	41.3	48.7	51.3
12817	CHESTERTOWN	98.6	98.4	0.1	0.1	0.4	0.5	0.5	0.6	5.4	5.3	5.3	8.4	6.1	22.0	29.6	16.1	1.9	80.4	43.4	50.1	50.0
12819	CLEMONS	99.5	99.7	0.0	0.0	0.0	0.0	0.5	1.0	5.4	6.2	7.3	6.7	4.4	24.6	29.5	14.5	1.3	76.7	42.2	51.8	48.2
12821	COMSTOCK	51.3	46.7	37.3	40.3	0.5	0.5	19.1	21.8	2.1	2.1	2.4	9.3	18.1	46.1	16.1	3.6	0.3	90.9	31.3	81.8	18.2
12822	CORINTH	98.2	98.0	0.3	0.3	0.3	0.3	0.8	0.8	6.1	6.1	7.0	7.2	6.3	26.6	26.0	13.0	1.8	76.6	39.2	49.2	50.8
12823	COSSAYUNA	98.5	98.1	0.0	0.5	0.5	0.5	0.5	0.5	5.7	5.7	7.6	6.2	5.2	24.8	30.5	12.9	1.4	77.1	41.9	49.1	51.0
12824	DIAMOND POINT	98.0	97.6	0.4	0.4	0.7	1.0	1.3	1.5	4.0	4.6	5.6	5.1	3.7	21.4	36.4	17.6	1.6	82.5	48.3	51.0	49.0
12827	FORT ANN	87.5	86.0	9.0	9.9	0.1	0.2	4.9	5.9	5.3	5.7	6.4	7.3	7.8	32.2	25.7	8.9	0.7	78.9	36.7	58.8	41.2
12828	FORT EDWARD	98.0	97.6	0.6	0.7	0.4	0.5	0.7	0.9	5.8	6.2	7.6	6.8	5.6	28.7	25.4	12.0	1.8	76.0	38.6	49.4	50.6
12831	GANSEVOORT	94.0	93.3	3.4	3.6	0.5	0.7	2.3	2.7	7.0	7.4	7.5	6.4	5.5	31.8	26.4	7.4	0.7	73.9	36.9	52.1	47.9
12832	GRANVILLE	97.5	97.0	0.7	0.9	0.3	0.4	0.9	1.1	6.5	6.7	7.6	6.9	5.5	26.1	24.9	13.1	2.7	74.8	38.7	49.6	50.4
12833	GREENFIELD CENTER	97.5	97.1	0.6	0.7	0.3	0.4	1.1	1.4	6.4	6.9	8.0	7.0	6.0	29.5	26.8	8.6	0.9	74.2	37.3	50.3	49.7
12834	GREENWICH	98.0	97.6	0.4	0.5	0.7	0.8	0.6	0.8	6.0	6.3	7.2	6.9	5.9	24.8	28.1	13.1	1.8	76.0	40.7	48.8	51.2
12835	HADLEY	98.0	97.6	0.7	0.7	0.2	0.2	0.4	0.5	5.5	5.5	6.4	6.5	6.4	25.4	29.0	13.9	1.4	78.4	41.5	50.2	49.9
12836	HAGUE	98.4	98.3	0.1	0.1	0.1	0.1	0.5	0.6	3.2	3.8	5.8	5.8	4.5	19.6	30.6	24.1	2.7	83.5	50.0	48.2	51.8
12837	HAMPTON	98.3	98.2	0.6	0.6	0.1	0.3	1.0	1.3	6.3	6.6	7.3	7.6	5.3	27.1	27.4	11.1	1.3	74.7	38.8	49.7	50.3
12838	HARTFORD	97.3	97.0	0.6	0.9	0.0	0.0	0.8	0.8	7.0	7.3	7.8	7.0	5.2	28.6	27.2	8.7	1.2	73.4	37.8	51.5	48.6
12839	HUDSON FALLS	98.0	97.6	0.5	0.6	0.2	0.3	0.7	0.8	6.0	6.0	7.0	7.1	6.7	28.2	24.4	12.9	1.7	76.6	38.1	48.2	51.8
12842	INDIAN LAKE	97.9	97.7	0.4	0.4	0.1	0.1	1.2	1.3	4.4	4.6	5.8	4.9	4.5	22.6	32.1	18.7	2.3	81.5	47.0	49.8	50.2
12843	JOHNSBURG	98.1	97.8	0.3	0.3	0.4	0.5	0.2	0.3	4.8	5.2	6.6	5.7	4.8	26.6	28.9	15.0	2.5	80.0	42.9	49.0	51.0
12844	KATTSKILL BAY	98.8	98.4	0.0	0.0	0.4	0.4	0.8	0.4	4.0	4.8	7.1	7.1	4.0	21.8	34.1	15.9	1.2	79.4	45.5	50.0	50.0
12845	LAKE GEORGE	97.8	97.5	0.5	0.5	0.6	0.8	0.9	1.0	4.5	5.2	6.3	6.0	5.0	23.3	33.1	14.8	1.9	80.0	44.9	50.0	50.0
12846	LAKE LUZERNE	97.8	97.4	0.3	0.3	0.3	0.4	1.0	1.3	5.5	5.8	7.4	7.1	4.8	28.1	27.0	13.0	1.3	76.5	40.3	49.7	50.3
12847	LONG LAKE	97.4	97.2	0.6	0.6	0.4	0.4	1.1	1.2	3.4	3.9	4.5	4.8	4.9	19.6	38.3	18.5	2.2	84.6	50.0	50.0	50.0
12849	MIDDLE GRANVILLE	98.2	97.6	0.4	0.7	0.4	0.4	0.7	1.1	6.6	7.0	7.0	7.0	5.2	25.1	27.5	12.2	2.4	74.6	40.3	50.9	49.1
12850	MIDDLE GROVE	97.7	97.3	0.6	0.7	0.4	0.5	1.4	1.7	6.3	6.9	8.3	7.0	5.5	29.9	27.2	8.2	0.7	74.2	37.5	50.4	49.6
12851	MINERVA	97.0	96.4	0.4	0.4	0.0	0.0	0.0	0.0	4.0	4.4	6.6	7.7	5.5	24.8	28.8	16.8	1.5	80.7	43.3	52.2	47.8
12852	NEWCOMB	95.2	94.5	0.0	0.0	0.0	0.0	0.4	0.4	4.5	5.1	5.5	5.3	4.3	16.6	29.0	26.8	2.9	80.8	52.4	47.7	52.4
12853	NORTH CREEK	97.8	97.4	0.2	0.2	0.5	0.6	1.0	1.3	4.7	4.9	5.8	11.5	7.8	23.0	25.7	13.9	2.6	81.2	39.2	47.7	52.3
12854	NORTH GRANVILLE	97.6	98.4	0.0	0.0	0.8	0.8	0.0	0.0	4.9	4.9	7.4	7.4	4.9	27.1	31.2	11.5	0.8	79.5	40.6	47.5	52.5
12855	NORTH HUDSON	94.7	94.1	0.0	0.0	0.4	0.4	0.0	0.0	5.2	5.2	8.9	6.3	4.8	21.0	31.7	14.8	2.2	76.8	43.8	50.2	49.8
12857	OLMSTEDVILLE	96.9	96.5	0.3	0.3	0.2	0.2	0.2	0.2	4.0	4.5	6.5	7.5	5.3	24.6	29.3	16.8	1.5	80.5	43.6	51.9	48.1
12858	PARADOX	100.0	100.0	0.0	0.0	0.0	0.0	0.0	0.0	0.0	0.0	14.3	0.0	0.0	28.6	57.1	0.0	0.0	85.7	46.3	42.9	57.1
12859	PORTER CORNERS	97.9	97.4	0.5	0.6	0.3	0.4	0.8	1.1	6.5	6.9	8.1	7.4	5.8	29.2	26.8	8.6	0.9	73.7	37.5	50.4	49.6
12860	POTTERSVILLE	96.5	96.1	0.3	0.3	0.9	1.1	1.7	2.2	4.5	4.8	5.7	20.3	12.3	18.4	22.6	10.3	1.1	81.4	27.9	48.2	51.8
12861	PUTNAM STATION	99.5	99.7	0.0	0.0	0.0	0.0	0.7	1.0	5.3	6.1	7.2	6.7	4.4	24.2	30.0	14.7	1.4	77.3	42.7	51.2	48.8
12863	ROCK CITY FALLS	95.3	94.2	0.8	0.7	0.6	0.9	2.5	3.0	8.2	7.4	7.8	7.4	8.0	31.0	23.1	6.5	0.6	72.1	32.4	50.2	49.8
12865	SALEM	97.8	97.2	0.8	1.0	0.2	0.3	0.8	1.0	5.1	5.6	7.8	7.4	5.9	26.2	27.0	13.6	1.4	76.8	40.2	50.4	49.6
12866	SARATOGA SPRINGS	94.4	93.6	2.6	2.9	0.9	1.1	1.7	2.0	5.5	5.4	6.0	8.2	8.8	26.9	25.7	11.1	2.5	79.4	37.7	48.1	51.9
12870	SCHROON LAKE	98.1	97.7	0.8	1.0	0.2	0.2	0.5	0.7	4.1	4.5	6.7	6.5	5.6	24.5	29.2	16.7	2.3	80.7	43.8	47.3	52.7
12871	SCHUYLERVILLE	97.7	97.3	1.0	1.1	0.2	0.3	1.1	1.3	6.7	6.6	7.0	7.2	6.9	28.7	25.6	9.9	1.6	75.3	37.3	49.7	50.3
12872	SEVERANCE	100.0	100.0	0.0	0.0	0.0	0.0	0.0	0.0	0.0	0.0	0.0	0.0	33.3	66.7	0.0	0.0	0.0	100.0	27.5	50.0	50.0
12873	SHUSHAN	98.3	97.9	0.9	1.1	0.5	0.7	0.9	1.2	4.0	4.5	6.1	6.9	5.0	21.8	34.0	15.3	2.4	80.6	45.9	51.5	48.5
12878	STONY CREEK	97.5	97.0	0.3	0.3	0.4	0.6	0.7	1.0	4.9	5.8	6.8	6.5	5.5	25.2	29.9	14.1	1.3	78.0	42.3	51.9	48.1
12883	TICONDEROGA	98.1	97.8	0.5	0.6	0.3	0.4	0.4	0.5	6.2	6.3	7.8	7.3	5.8	24.4	26.0	14.1	2.2	74.8	39.6	48.5	51.6
12885	WARRENSBURG	98.1	97.7	0.2	0.2	0.5	0.6	0.5	0.7	5.5	5.9	7.3	6.6	5.6	26.9	28.3	12.2	1.9	76.7	40.4	48.2	51.8
12886	WEVERTOWN	97.1	100.0	0.0	0.0	0.0	0.0	0.0	0.0	5.7	5.7	5.7	5.7	5.7	25.7	31.4	14.3	0.0	82.9	42.5	51.4	48.6
12887	WHITEHALL	97.8	97.4	0.5	0.6	0.2	0.3	1.3	1.7	6.6	6.4	7.0	6.9	6.9	25.9	25.1	13.8	1.5	76.0	38.6	49.1	50.9
12901	PLATTSBURGH	94.7	93.6	1.9	2.3	1.2	1.4	1.7	2.1	5.0	4.9	5.8	10.1	13.1	25.7	22.5	11.3	1.9	80.6	34.0	47.9	52.1
12903	PLATTSBURGH	93.3	90.0	4.8	7.5	0.0	0.0	1.9	2.5	11.3	7.5	2.5	3.8	6.3	26.3	26.3	15.0	1.3	76.3	40.7	56.3	43.8
12910	ALTONA	77.4	77.3	15.5	15.2	0.2	0.2	10.4	10.9	3.8	4.0	5.8	6.2	8.6	40.8	22.1	7.9	0.8	82.6	35.9	64.9	35.1
12911	KEESEVILLE	97.3	96.1	1.4	1.3	0.0	0.0	2.7	2.6	5.2	5.2	6.5	9.1	7.8	27.3	24.7	13.0	1.3	75.3	38.8	46.8	53.3
12912	AU SABLE FORKS	98.5	98.1	0.2	0.3	0.1	0.2	0.6	0.8	5.9	6.1	6.9	7.7	5.2	26.4	26.6	13.7	1.6	76.3	40.2	49.0	51.0
12913	BLOOMINGDALE	97.4	96.9	0.4	0.5	0.2	0.3	1.0	1.4	5.4	5.6	7.3	7.9	6.3	25.1	29.3	11.6	1.5	76.7	40.8	49.9	50.1
12914	BOMBAY	82.9	79.7	0.4	0.5	0.1	0.1	0.9	1.4	6.2	6.6	7.7	7.3	5.8	26.2	27.5	11.4	1.4	74.9	38.6	47.9	52.1
12916	BRUSHTON	97.3	96.4	0.4	0.5	0.3	0.4	0.8	1.1	5.5	6.0	7.2	7.2	6.3	25.9	28.1	12.3	1.6	76.8	39.5	49.6	50.4
12917	BURKE	96.3	95.2	1.1	1.5	0.1	0.1	1.4	2.0	7.0	7.1	7.8	6.7	5.8	27.1	26.3	11.1	1.3	73.4	37.8	52.6	47.4
12918	CADYVILLE	95.4	94.8	2.6	2.9	0.3	0.3	1.8	2.3	5.3	5.9	8.0	7.8	5.3	29.8	26.2	10.6	1.1	75.6	38.1	51.2	48.8
12919	CHAMPLAIN	97.9	97.5	0.5	0.6	0.4	0.5	0.9	1.1	5.6	6.0	7.9	6.5	6.0	26.9	25.9	13.6	1.6	76.5	40.2	49.1	50.9
12920	CHATEAUGAY	91.7	89.1	4.7	6.2	0.2	0.3	4.6	6.5	4.9	5.0	6.5	7.1	6.6	32.9	25.0	10.8	1.2	79.3	38.0	56.2	43.8
12921	CHAZY	97.7	97.3	0.3	0.5	0.4	0.5	0.7	0.9	6.3	6.5	7.8	7.0	5.8	27.5	26.3	11.7	1.3	75.0	39.0	49.2	50.8
12922	CHILDWOLD	97.2	100.0	0.0	0.0	0.0	0.0	0.0	0.0	5.6	5.6	5.6	5.6	5.6	16.7	36.1	19.4	0.0	83.3	47.5	52.8	47.2
12923	CHURUBUSCO	98.3	98.1	0.3	0.4	0.1	0.1	0.3	0.5	4.1	6.3	8.0	8.5	3.5	28.2	26.3	13.6	1.4	75.3	39.3	53.0	47.0
12924	KEESEVILLE	99.1	98.1	0.5	0.5	0.5	0.5	0.5	1.5	5.8	5.8	8.2	5.8	4.8	26.6	26.6	14.0	2.4	76.3	41.2	49.8	50.2
12926	CONSTABLE	97.3	96.7	0.3	0.4	0.1	0.1	0.4	0.6	5.6	6.7	8.5	7.6	4.7	30.1	25.7	10.4	0.7	74.5	37.6	51.3	48.7
12928	CROWN POINT	97.5	96.9	0.1	0.1	0.4	0.5	0.1	0.2	7.2	7.0	7.2	7.5	5.8	24.5	26.4	13.0	1.5	74.2	39.1	50.5	49.5
12930	DICKINSON CENTER	97.5	97.0	0.4	0.5	0.2	0.2	0.6	0.5	4.6	6.9	6.0	6.8	5.0	26.1	29.7	13.5	1.4	78.2	41.4	51.9	48.1
12932	ELIZABETHTOWN	98.0	97.5	0.5	0.6	0.4	0.6	0.4	0.5	4.8	6.1	7.6	6.2	4.1	22.3	28.2	15.6	5.0	76.5	44.2	50.1	49.9
12934	ELLENBURG CENTER	96.8	96.0	1.5	1.8	0.3	0.5	1.4	1.9	4.7	5.3	6.7	6.5	5.9	27.1	27.7	14.2	1.9	78.9	41.1	51.0	49.0
12935	ELLENBURG DEPOT	95.3	94.2	2.5	3.0	0.2	0.3	1.7	2.1	5.5	5.9	7.2	8.3	5.1	30.6	25.3	10.9	1.2	75.9	38.3	53.5	46.5
12936	ESSEX	99.5	99.5	0.0	0.0	0.0	0.0	0.3	0.3	3.5	4.6	7.5	7.2	4.0	21.9	30.8	17.9	2.7	78.9	45.9	50.8	49.2
12937	FORT COVINGTON	91.4	89.5	0.5	0.7	0.5	0.7	1.1	1.6	6.0	6.3	7.4	7.6	5.8	24.5	27.2	14.2	1.1	75.7	40.3	48.0	52.0
12941	JAY	98.4	98.1	0.3	0.4	0.4	0.5	0.6	0.8	6.2	6.4	7.3	5.9	4.0	26.6	29.3	12.9	1.4	76.2	41.3	49.3	50.7
12942	KEENE	98.7	98.2	0.2	0.2	0.6	0.7	0.4	0.5	4.1	3.8	8.8	7.4	3.2	20.8	32.0	15.4	4.5	78.6	46.0	46.1	53.9
	NEW YORK	68.0	65.9	15.9	16.2	5.6	6.4	15.1	16.7	6.5	6.5	7.1	7.0	7.1	28.9	24.0	11.2	1.8	75.8	36.7	48.3	51.7
	UNITED STATES	75.1	73.6	12.3	12.5	3.8	4.2	12.5	14.1	6.9	6.7	7.2	7.0	7.3	28.6	23.8	10.8	1.7	75.1	36.0	49.1	50.9

INCOME

#	POST OFFICE NAME	2004 Per Capita Income	2004 HH Income Base	2004 Household Income Distribution (%): Less than $25,000	$25,000 to $49,999	$50,000 to $99,999	$100,000 to $149,999	$150,000 or More	Median Household Income: 2004	2009	2004 National Centile	2004 State Centile	2004 Home Value Base	2004 Home Value Distribution (%): Less than $50,000	$50,000 to $89,999	$90,000 to $174,999	$175,000 to $399,999	$400,000 or More	2004 Median Home Value
12777	FORESTBURGH	33841	305	18.4	21.3	41.0	10.5	8.9	60576	69661	85	75	266	0.8	3.4	26.3	55.6	13.9	199074
12779	SOUTH FALLSBURG	22203	573	36.8	21.6	27.9	8.9	4.7	37532	42531	38	23	307	2.0	5.9	59.9	28.7	3.6	148505
12780	SPARROW BUSH	21973	908	23.7	29.2	34.7	8.0	4.4	48157	54413	69	59	745	12.6	7.3	42.4	35.8	1.9	153005
12782	SUNDOWN	26448	72	26.4	33.3	26.4	8.3	5.6	40000	46564	46	34	57	0.0	7.0	49.1	35.1	8.8	160417
12783	SWAN LAKE	22748	582	30.2	34.7	21.0	9.3	4.8	37121	42327	36	21	465	1.3	11.2	37.4	44.7	5.4	175171
12786	WHITE LAKE	32770	267	34.1	24.7	25.5	7.9	7.9	40287	46476	47	35	209	2.9	13.4	29.7	46.4	7.7	182083
12787	WHITE SULPHUR SPRING	16952	34	26.5	47.1	23.5	2.9	0.0	36079	41092	32	17	28	0.0	10.7	53.6	35.7	0.0	160714
12788	WOODBOURNE	19853	677	28.8	29.0	28.2	9.0	5.0	38594	43548	41	27	541	8.1	9.8	50.1	26.3	5.7	138209
12789	WOODRIDGE	18956	688	32.7	26.9	26.7	10.2	3.5	37646	42870	38	23	387	4.1	11.9	63.1	19.4	1.6	133367
12790	WURTSBORO	22282	2382	23.8	35.1	29.5	7.8	3.9	42599	49268	55	43	1826	8.0	7.5	49.2	34.7	0.6	147126
12791	YOUNGSVILLE	23237	294	27.9	30.6	28.9	8.8	3.7	45000	52206	61	50	244	0.4	4.5	58.2	35.3	1.6	152143
12792	YULAN	28563	123	25.2	30.1	31.7	8.1	4.9	45849	53195	63	53	103	1.0	3.9	43.7	48.5	2.9	176875
12801	GLENS FALLS	20372	6368	36.2	32.1	25.0	4.5	2.3	33561	37462	23	9	3171	0.9	9.3	76.4	12.9	0.6	121142
12803	SOUTH GLENS FALLS	20956	3042	27.2	35.5	28.9	6.7	1.6	40821	46121	49	37	2170	3.6	11.9	72.9	11.2	0.4	125283
12804	QUEENSBURY	27585	10043	17.7	30.8	34.1	11.5	5.9	51319	57975	74	65	7805	3.3	4.5	50.5	38.1	3.7	160808
12808	ADIRONDACK	26880	169	29.6	32.0	29.0	4.7	4.7	41141	46149	50	38	145	8.3	14.5	44.1	26.2	6.9	134868
12809	ARGYLE	22684	1309	21.2	36.3	34.3	5.2	3.0	44671	49406	60	49	1118	4.9	15.9	58.4	20.3	0.5	128886
12810	ATHOL	18046	256	29.7	36.3	27.7	4.7	1.6	38545	42622	41	27	217	5.1	16.1	60.4	18.0	0.5	122250
12812	BLUE MOUNTAIN LAKE	21098	115	31.3	34.8	25.2	5.2	3.5	36246	39646	33	17	91	4.4	6.6	51.7	36.3	1.1	149405
12814	BOLTON LANDING	28975	648	21.6	27.2	37.7	9.4	4.2	50825	56610	74	64	524	1.5	2.7	41.4	42.6	11.8	186500
12815	BRANT LAKE	23774	462	29.9	32.7	28.8	4.8	3.9	40619	46193	48	36	396	8.3	14.9	43.7	26.3	6.8	133824
12816	CAMBRIDGE	22063	1745	26.7	32.7	30.0	7.4	3.3	43587	48018	58	46	1354	7.1	10.8	54.1	23.9	4.1	138229
12817	CHESTERTOWN	22142	929	29.5	35.0	27.2	5.2	3.1	40219	45705	47	35	754	8.8	19.0	46.0	24.5	1.7	126550
12819	CLEMONS	21105	149	27.5	28.2	31.5	10.7	2.0	42050	47378	53	41	126	12.7	19.1	43.7	15.9	8.7	114130
12821	COMSTOCK	11343	147	25.2	36.7	29.3	5.4	3.4	42593	46815	55	43	117	3.4	21.4	64.1	10.3	0.9	117083
12822	CORINTH	19125	2223	29.0	34.8	28.4	5.9	1.9	39285	44645	44	31	1672	9.5	17.6	56.8	13.9	2.3	114041
12823	COSSAYUNA	24671	85	24.7	27.1	37.7	5.9	4.7	47390	50000	67	56	73	4.1	12.3	56.2	24.7	2.7	130147
12824	DIAMOND POINT	33902	389	20.8	23.9	36.3	11.1	8.0	53942	61549	78	69	319	2.5	4.7	32.3	41.4	19.1	197635
12827	FORT ANN	23990	1446	22.5	32.4	35.7	6.0	3.5	46468	51595	65	54	1207	4.5	15.6	51.5	23.4	5.1	133076
12828	FORT EDWARD	22079	2995	24.3	33.2	33.2	6.7	2.6	43930	49543	58	47	2299	6.1	16.4	60.3	16.6	0.6	118098
12831	GANSEVOORT	23821	5756	17.8	25.8	40.4	11.9	4.2	56205	63544	81	71	4905	11.1	5.6	46.0	35.8	1.6	151461
12832	GRANVILLE	19172	2719	30.8	33.1	28.7	5.4	1.9	39580	42767	45	32	2068	8.5	26.7	52.6	11.2	1.1	105535
12833	GREENFIELD CENTER	21316	2133	20.5	33.2	34.5	8.4	3.4	47402	53011	67	57	1773	13.6	8.4	43.3	32.6	2.1	142619
12834	GREENWICH	21903	2565	25.9	32.0	32.0	6.4	3.8	43725	48097	58	47	1939	4.5	7.8	56.0	28.4	3.4	141702
12835	HADLEY	21662	1196	25.0	34.7	31.4	5.9	2.9	42635	49012	55	43	958	8.0	15.3	52.1	22.9	1.7	124758
12836	HAGUE	30305	396	28.0	28.5	30.8	6.3	6.3	44177	49778	59	48	338	3.3	8.3	47.6	27.2	13.6	152206
12837	HAMPTON	19029	266	22.9	38.0	30.8	7.5	0.8	42209	46829	54	42	228	9.7	25.0	50.4	14.0	0.9	106098
12838	HARTFORD	19334	236	23.7	30.1	36.9	6.8	2.5	47198	52802	67	56	198	5.6	13.1	55.1	24.2	2.0	133871
12839	HUDSON FALLS	20737	5039	31.0	33.4	28.7	5.1	1.8	37876	41806	39	24	3327	4.9	18.4	65.8	10.9	0.0	111770
12842	INDIAN LAKE	21192	534	35.0	32.8	24.5	4.9	2.8	35310	39304	29	14	431	4.4	7.2	59.6	26.7	2.1	141354
12843	JOHNSBURG	19142	526	36.7	33.7	23.2	4.0	2.5	34289	38046	25	11	434	16.6	17.1	45.2	18.9	2.3	110061
12844	KATTSKILL BAY	34411	127	19.7	29.1	34.7	10.2	6.3	50818	59572	74	64	111	2.7	8.1	36.9	33.3	18.9	181944
12845	LAKE GEORGE	28453	2230	19.9	30.9	33.1	10.9	5.2	49374	56384	71	61	1715	3.4	4.9	40.3	40.4	11.0	178347
12846	LAKE LUZERNE	18856	1333	29.5	35.9	29.3	3.5	1.8	39570	43400	45	32	1101	10.0	11.4	62.5	14.7	1.5	125052
12847	LONG LAKE	22998	385	37.4	27.0	27.5	4.4	3.6	33071	36807	21	8	307	3.6	5.9	45.9	35.5	9.1	164145
12849	MIDDLE GRANVILLE	18506	109	25.7	41.3	26.6	6.4	0.0	41530	46006	51	40	95	8.4	31.6	51.6	7.4	1.1	98636
12850	MIDDLE GROVE	21638	904	20.5	34.4	34.4	7.6	3.1	46664	52361	65	55	765	11.1	8.4	52.0	27.3	1.2	138528
12851	MINERVA	17603	109	36.7	32.1	23.9	6.4	0.9	32627	36538	20	7	91	13.2	16.5	49.5	20.9	0.0	126974
12852	NEWCOMB	19338	219	35.6	33.3	25.1	5.9	0.0	35741	39309	31	15	186	1.1	7.5	75.3	16.1	0.0	133984
12853	NORTH CREEK	21161	849	33.1	33.2	27.2	4.4	2.1	37852	42850	39	24	675	11.1	16.0	49.3	20.4	3.1	119982
12854	NORTH GRANVILLE	19738	48	18.8	41.7	31.3	8.3	0.0	45711	50000	63	52	41	19.5	22.0	41.5	17.1	0.0	98750
12855	NORTH HUDSON	17860	118	33.1	39.0	22.9	5.1	0.0	31471	34604	16	6	99	18.2	21.2	53.5	4.0	3.0	97500
12857	OLMSTEDVILLE	18326	249	36.1	31.7	24.9	6.0	1.2	33115	35904	21	8	206	12.6	15.5	49.5	21.8	0.5	129444
12858	PARADOX	6964	6	100.0	0.0	0.0	0.0	0.0	16902	20878	1	1	4	0.0	0.0	100.0	0.0	0.0	125000
12859	PORTER CORNERS	21842	647	22.6	27.8	38.5	8.0	3.1	49724	55632	71	61	554	7.8	11.6	52.4	26.0	2.4	133750
12860	POTTERSVILLE	9090	78	24.4	39.7	28.2	3.9	3.9	41517	48192	51	40	65	13.9	18.5	44.6	20.0	3.1	114773
12861	PUTNAM STATION	20654	222	27.9	27.9	30.6	11.3	2.3	41694	45206	52	40	187	12.3	18.2	44.9	16.6	8.0	115203
12863	ROCK CITY FALLS	19285	207	18.4	44.4	28.5	6.8	1.9	41968	46348	53	41	163	35.6	13.5	37.4	13.5	0.0	91667
12865	SALEM	21220	1380	21.0	36.3	33.1	6.4	3.2	44346	49665	60	48	1127	7.7	19.6	53.9	17.1	1.7	117239
12866	SARATOGA SPRINGS	30475	14721	23.3	24.2	33.7	12.0	6.7	52451	60784	76	66	9416	5.4	3.2	40.8	44.2	6.3	176201
12870	SCHROON LAKE	17417	741	40.8	30.8	22.8	4.3	1.4	31588	34624	17	6	549	3.6	7.1	55.6	30.1	3.6	144981
12871	SCHUYLERVILLE	22803	1831	24.4	28.6	35.2	8.3	3.6	47033	53276	66	55	1360	3.6	11.8	62.4	20.4	1.8	132508
12872	SEVERANCE	0	0	0.0	0.0	0.0	0.0	0.0	0	0	0	0	2	0.0	0.0	100.0	0.0	0.0	137500
12873	SHUSHAN	24300	326	29.1	30.7	26.7	8.9	4.6	41128	45928	50	38	271	8.1	17.3	45.0	26.2	3.3	123864
12878	STONY CREEK	17751	279	32.6	35.8	25.1	5.4	1.1	37087	40951	36	21	237	5.5	17.3	61.2	16.0	0.0	117457
12883	TICONDEROGA	18393	2178	31.4	34.2	28.2	4.8	1.4	36995	40759	35	21	1563	4.9	17.3	57.3	17.9	2.6	122763
12885	WARRENSBURG	17765	2059	37.2	31.8	25.0	4.5	1.6	34573	38210	26	11	1544	10.0	16.3	56.4	16.2	1.2	117681
12886	WEVERTOWN	17143	17	29.4	52.9	17.7	0.0	0.0	33988	38072	24	10	15	20.0	20.0	40.0	20.0	0.0	97500
12887	WHITEHALL	19519	2021	30.3	32.3	28.9	7.6	0.9	39352	42995	44	31	1439	10.1	37.9	41.5	9.7	0.9	92169
12901	PLATTSBURGH	21043	13310	35.2	28.0	27.6	6.2	3.1	36720	41008	34	20	7562	9.7	8.8	48.0	30.3	3.3	146041
12903	PLATTSBURGH	20032	47	48.9	21.3	29.8	0.0	0.0	35745	30000	31	15	15	0.0	0.0	100.0	0.0	0.0	132955
12910	ALTONA	16284	661	30.7	27.1	36.5	5.3	0.5	41847	47099	52	41	541	15.9	20.9	51.8	10.9	0.6	106675
12911	KEESEVILLE	21243	32	25.0	34.4	37.5	3.1	0.0	45000	50000	61	50	23	0.0	13.0	73.9	13.0	0.0	131944
12912	AU SABLE FORKS	19087	902	32.7	35.5	24.7	4.7	2.4	36772	41146	35	20	704	6.5	20.2	56.7	15.1	1.6	116887
12913	BLOOMINGDALE	21134	434	27.4	29.5	33.2	7.8	2.1	42822	46927	55	44	313	9.3	16.0	44.7	27.5	2.6	135381
12914	BOMBAY	15890	395	42.8	32.9	20.0	3.0	1.3	30676	33267	14	5	310	31.9	25.8	33.6	7.4	1.3	76190
12916	BRUSHTON	15547	937	43.2	29.8	22.1	4.5	0.4	30037	33091	12	5	708	25.0	32.1	35.6	6.8	0.6	78333
12917	BURKE	16703	515	30.1	36.7	27.6	3.7	1.9	37429	41407	37	22	427	13.6	30.4	41.0	13.6	1.4	99808
12918	CADYVILLE	21488	876	18.0	29.9	43.3	7.7	1.1	51392	57324	75	65	728	6.7	12.8	54.8	25.3	0.4	133896
12919	CHAMPLAIN	21724	1225	31.5	29.4	30.2	6.6	2.3	40619	45587	48	36	942	9.8	16.2	55.6	17.0	1.4	120157
12920	CHATEAUGAY	17001	984	34.6	33.9	26.8	3.9	0.8	36536	40333	34	19	777	16.0	35.7	38.2	9.4	0.8	87596
12921	CHAZY	21806	1083	25.0	26.7	36.8	8.2	3.3	47830	52669	68	57	862	6.0	10.8	53.0	27.3	2.9	139498
12922	CHILDWOLD	21944	20	30.0	40.0	30.0	0.0	0.0	35000	43604	28	13	17	23.5	23.5	41.2	11.8	0.0	95000
12923	CHURUBUSCO	14273	291	40.6	32.0	24.4	2.1	1.0	31647	35796	17	6	246	22.4	32.9	35.4	8.9	0.4	81875
12924	KEESEVILLE	14890	78	38.5	35.9	20.5	3.9	1.3	33160	37323	21	8	63	3.2	23.8	63.5	7.9	1.6	114423
12926	CONSTABLE	17292	858	35.2	32.9	26.0	4.4	1.5	35297	38669	29	14	712	20.9	28.5	43.3	6.6	0.7	90727
12928	CROWN POINT	19679	824	31.2	35.3	27.3	4.4	1.8	37117	40758	36	21	647	10.7	20.4	52.6	15.8	0.6	116431
12930	DICKINSON CENTER	17562	230	38.3	31.7	24.8	3.5	1.7	35000	38294	28	13	196	17.9	39.3	38.3	3.6	1.0	79524
12932	ELIZABETHTOWN	19405	544	33.1	32.7	27.4	4.0	2.8	36795	40767	35	20	414	7.3	13.8	53.4	23.9	1.7	125000
12934	ELLENBURG CENTER	15906	456	33.1	33.8	25.7	5.5	2.0	36417	40981	33	18	378	12.4	27.0	44.4	14.0	2.1	100316
12935	ELLENBURG DEPOT	18084	557	32.3	31.4	29.6	5.9	0.7	39278	44414	44	31	464	25.7	22.6	41.2	9.9	0.7	92500
12936	ESSEX	21665	156	25.6	37.8	26.3	8.3	1.9	40446	45250	48	35	130	6.2	11.5	40.0	33.1	9.2	143750
12937	FORT COVINGTON	16812	600	35.0	35.7	23.5	4.7	1.2	35305	38969	29	14	474	24.9	31.7	34.8	6.8	1.9	78958
12941	JAY	19090	564	29.6	35.6	28.9	3.7	2.1	40189	44614	47	35	461	4.6	13.5	51.8	27.1	3.0	129968
12942	KEENE	20370	238	29.4	32.4	32.4	4.2	1.7	38540	42580	41	27	197	3.1	3.1	36.6	48.2	9.1	190104
	NEW YORK	28049		26.3	24.3	29.3	11.5	8.6	49309	58077				4.6	8.6	27.2	39.9	19.8	219050
	UNITED STATES	25866		24.7	27.1	30.8	10.9	6.5	48124	56710				10.9	15.0	33.7	30.1	10.4	145905

ZIP CODE		FINANCIAL SERVICES				THE HOME						ENTERTAINMENT						PERSONAL			
						Home Improvements		Furnishings													
#	POST OFFICE NAME	Auto Loan	Home Loan	Invest-ments	Retire-ment Plans	Home Repair	Lawn & Garden	Comput-ers & Hard-ware	Major Appli-ances	TV, Radio, Sound Equip-ment	Furni-ture	Dine out/ Carry out	Sports Equip-ment	Fees & Tickets	Toys & Games	Travel	Cable TV	Apparel & Services	Auto Repairs	Health Insur-ance	Pets & Supplies
12777	FORESTBURGH	142	111	76	100	125	141	105	126	119	104	140	148	94	139	112	127	131	124	149	173
12779	SOUTH FALLSBURG	79	74	74	73	77	84	74	78	77	73	94	92	72	94	76	78	90	78	81	94
12780	SPARROW BUSH	89	80	62	76	84	90	74	81	79	74	96	97	73	98	76	81	91	79	88	104
12782	SUNDOWN	102	80	55	72	90	101	75	91	85	75	101	106	67	100	80	91	94	90	107	124
12783	SWAN LAKE	107	84	57	76	95	107	79	96	90	79	107	112	71	105	85	96	99	94	113	131
12786	WHITE LAKE	141	110	75	100	124	140	104	125	118	103	140	147	93	138	111	126	130	123	148	171
12787	WHITE SULPHUR SPRING	78	54	27	47	61	70	52	64	62	53	73	77	45	69	53	67	66	64	79	91
12788	WOODBOURNE	83	62	39	59	70	78	61	73	68	60	81	88	54	80	63	71	75	72	85	99
12789	WOODRIDGE	85	67	45	60	75	84	63	76	71	62	84	88	56	83	67	76	78	74	89	103
12790	WURTSBORO	91	73	51	68	80	89	70	82	78	70	93	96	64	91	73	81	87	81	94	108
12791	YOUNGSVILLE	93	73	49	66	82	92	69	83	78	68	92	97	61	91	73	83	86	81	98	113
12792	YULAN	110	86	59	78	97	109	81	98	92	81	109	115	73	108	87	98	102	97	116	134
12801	GLENS FALLS	59	60	70	61	60	64	65	62	64	63	81	74	65	82	64	63	79	64	60	68
12803	SOUTH GLENS FALLS	70	69	65	67	71	78	69	71	71	67	87	81	69	89	70	72	83	70	75	82
12804	QUEENSBURY	94	103	109	103	102	106	98	98	95	98	119	114	101	121	99	94	117	97	94	110
12808	ADIRONDACK	94	74	50	67	83	94	70	84	79	69	94	98	62	92	74	84	87	83	99	115
12809	ARGYLE	100	86	63	80	92	100	80	90	86	79	104	107	76	105	83	89	98	88	100	118
12810	ATHOL	81	59	33	55	68	76	57	70	66	57	77	84	49	76	60	69	71	69	83	97
12812	BLUE MOUNTAIN LAKE	77	61	41	55	68	77	57	69	65	57	77	81	51	76	61	69	71	68	81	94
12814	BOLTON LANDING	108	84	57	76	95	107	80	96	90	79	107	112	71	105	85	96	99	94	113	131
12815	BRANT LAKE	94	74	50	67	83	94	70	84	79	69	94	98	62	92	74	84	87	83	99	115
12816	CAMBRIDGE	87	71	52	69	77	87	72	80	78	70	94	92	67	92	73	81	87	79	90	99
12817	CHESTERTOWN	83	65	44	59	73	82	62	74	70	61	83	86	55	81	66	75	77	73	87	100
12819	CLEMONS	93	73	50	66	82	92	69	83	78	68	92	97	61	91	73	83	85	81	98	113
12821	COMSTOCK	2	2	2	2	2	2	2	2	2	2	3	3	2	3	2	2	2	2	2	3
12822	CORINTH	70	66	58	62	69	76	64	68	68	62	83	78	64	86	66	70	79	67	75	83
12823	COSSAYUNA	98	87	66	83	92	98	80	89	85	80	104	106	79	106	83	87	99	87	96	115
12824	DIAMOND POINT	128	101	69	91	113	127	95	114	107	94	127	134	85	126	101	115	118	113	135	156
12827	FORT ANN	69	59	44	55	64	69	55	63	60	55	72	74	52	73	57	62	68	61	70	82
12828	FORT EDWARD	82	81	74	77	83	91	77	81	81	76	99	93	79	104	80	83	95	79	87	96
12831	GANSEVOORT	102	101	88	100	100	103	94	98	92	97	115	114	93	112	93	90	111	97	93	114
12832	GRANVILLE	77	64	46	61	68	77	64	71	70	63	84	82	60	82	65	72	78	70	80	88
12833	GREENFIELD CENTER	87	83	72	82	84	87	79	83	79	80	98	98	77	96	79	78	95	83	82	98
12834	GREENWICH	81	78	68	74	81	88	74	79	78	73	96	91	75	100	77	81	92	77	86	96
12835	HADLEY	87	71	52	68	77	87	71	80	77	70	93	92	66	92	72	80	86	78	90	101
12836	HAGUE	117	92	63	83	103	116	87	104	98	86	116	122	77	115	92	105	108	103	123	143
12837	HAMPTON	80	71	54	68	76	81	66	73	70	66	85	87	65	87	68	72	81	71	79	95
12838	HARTFORD	86	77	58	73	81	87	71	78	75	71	91	93	69	93	73	77	87	76	85	101
12839	HUDSON FALLS	67	69	72	67	69	75	70	69	71	68	88	80	71	92	70	72	86	69	71	78
12842	INDIAN LAKE	80	62	43	56	70	79	59	71	67	58	79	83	53	78	63	71	73	70	84	97
12843	JOHNSBURG	80	63	43	57	71	79	59	71	67	59	79	83	53	78	63	72	74	70	84	98
12844	KATTSKILL BAY	116	91	62	82	102	115	85	103	97	85	115	121	76	113	91	103	107	101	122	141
12845	LAKE GEORGE	106	88	66	82	96	108	86	98	95	84	113	113	79	111	89	100	106	97	113	126
12846	LAKE LUZERNE	78	63	45	59	69	78	61	71	68	61	81	82	56	80	64	71	76	70	81	92
12847	LONG LAKE	83	65	44	59	73	82	61	74	69	61	82	86	55	81	65	74	76	73	87	101
12849	MIDDLE GRANVILLE	76	67	51	64	71	76	62	69	66	62	80	82	61	82	64	68	76	67	75	89
12850	MIDDLE GROVE	91	84	68	80	87	92	78	85	81	79	100	100	77	100	80	82	95	83	89	106
12851	MINERVA	75	59	40	53	66	74	56	67	63	55	74	78	50	73	59	67	69	66	79	91
12852	NEWCOMB	73	57	39	51	64	72	54	65	61	53	72	76	48	71	57	65	67	64	77	89
12853	NORTH CREEK	78	61	42	55	69	78	58	70	66	57	78	82	52	77	62	70	72	69	82	95
12854	NORTH GRANVILLE	80	72	54	68	76	81	66	73	70	66	85	87	65	87	68	72	81	71	79	95
12855	NORTH HUDSON	70	55	37	49	61	69	51	62	58	51	69	73	46	68	55	62	64	61	73	85
12857	OLMSTEDVILLE	75	59	40	53	66	74	55	67	63	55	74	78	49	73	59	67	69	66	79	91
12858	PARADOX	28	22	15	20	24	27	20	25	23	20	27	29	18	27	22	25	25	24	29	34
12859	PORTER CORNERS	87	85	73	83	86	89	79	84	80	80	98	99	79	100	80	79	95	82	83	101
12860	POTTERSVILLE	89	69	47	63	78	88	66	79	74	65	88	92	59	87	70	79	82	78	93	108
12861	PUTNAM STATION	92	73	49	65	82	92	68	82	77	68	92	96	61	91	73	83	85	81	97	113
12863	ROCK CITY FALLS	80	73	57	70	73	77	69	74	70	71	87	86	66	82	68	69	83	74	74	88
12865	SALEM	84	76	61	72	80	87	72	79	77	71	93	92	71	96	74	79	88	77	86	99
12866	SARATOGA SPRINGS	97	101	115	103	100	105	103	100	100	102	126	119	104	127	102	98	123	102	95	112
12870	SCHROON LAKE	69	54	37	49	61	68	51	61	58	51	68	72	46	67	54	62	64	60	73	84
12871	SCHUYLERVILLE	82	82	76	80	83	90	80	82	81	79	101	93	81	104	81	82	97	80	85	93
12872	SEVERANCE	0	0	0	0	0	0	0	0	0	0	0	0	0	0	0	0	0	0	0	0
12873	SHUSHAN	73	82	88	78	82	89	78	79	78	77	97	88	82	100	81	80	95	77	81	87
12878	STONY CREEK	76	57	36	52	65	73	55	67	62	54	74	79	48	73	58	66	68	66	79	92
12883	TICONDEROGA	69	59	49	57	63	71	61	66	66	59	79	76	58	79	62	68	74	66	74	80
12885	WARRENSBURG	70	56	40	55	60	69	58	64	63	57	76	73	54	74	58	65	70	63	72	78
12886	WEVERTOWN	60	47	32	42	53	59	44	53	50	44	59	62	40	59	47	54	55	53	63	73
12887	WHITEHALL	70	65	58	62	68	76	64	68	69	63	83	78	64	87	66	71	79	67	75	81
12901	PLATTSBURGH	68	65	71	66	65	71	70	68	70	69	87	81	69	86	69	69	85	70	67	77
12903	PLATTSBURGH	54	42	29	40	45	54	46	50	51	44	60	56	41	57	46	54	55	50	59	60
12910	ALTONA	81	63	39	57	68	75	60	70	67	61	80	83	54	77	61	70	75	69	79	93
12911	KEESEVILLE	81	71	54	68	74	81	68	75	73	68	88	87	66	89	69	74	83	73	81	93
12912	AU SABLE FORKS	79	60	40	56	67	78	62	71	70	60	83	81	56	80	64	75	76	71	85	90
12913	BLOOMINGDALE	93	66	36	62	77	86	65	80	74	64	87	96	56	86	67	78	80	79	95	111
12914	BOMBAY	75	50	23	43	57	65	48	61	58	49	69	72	41	65	49	63	62	60	75	86
12916	BRUSHTON	66	48	29	45	54	62	50	58	57	49	67	67	44	64	50	61	62	57	69	75
12917	BURKE	70	59	45	58	62	70	61	65	65	59	78	75	58	77	60	66	73	64	71	78
12918	CADYVILLE	76	79	75	77	80	83	74	77	74	74	91	89	75	94	75	73	89	75	76	90
12919	CHAMPLAIN	82	68	50	66	73	82	69	75	74	67	89	87	65	88	69	77	84	74	85	93
12920	CHATEAUGAY	69	54	37	53	59	68	56	63	62	55	74	72	51	72	57	65	68	62	72	78
12921	CHAZY	91	80	61	77	84	91	76	83	80	76	98	98	74	99	77	82	93	81	90	105
12922	CHILDWOLD	67	53	36	47	59	66	50	60	56	49	66	70	44	66	53	60	62	59	71	82
12923	CHURUBUSCO	71	48	23	42	54	62	46	58	56	47	65	69	40	62	47	60	59	57	71	82
12924	KEESEVILLE	64	48	32	46	52	63	53	58	59	50	70	65	47	66	52	63	64	58	70	70
12926	CONSTABLE	68	65	60	65	65	69	64	66	63	65	79	77	62	75	63	62	76	66	65	76
12928	CROWN POINT	81	66	49	65	70	81	69	75	75	67	90	85	65	88	69	77	84	74	84	89
12930	DICKINSON CENTER	73	57	38	51	64	72	54	65	61	53	72	76	48	71	57	65	67	64	77	89
12932	ELIZABETHTOWN	77	61	43	58	66	76	63	70	70	61	83	80	58	80	64	73	77	70	82	87
12934	ELLENBURG CENTER	77	61	42	56	68	76	59	69	66	58	78	80	53	77	61	69	73	68	80	92
12935	ELLENBURG DEPOT	79	60	39	56	66	74	59	69	66	59	79	80	53	76	60	69	73	68	79	91
12936	ESSEX	87	69	49	63	78	87	66	78	74	65	87	91	59	87	70	78	82	77	91	105
12937	FORT COVINGTON	75	54	32	50	60	70	56	65	64	55	76	75	49	72	56	68	69	64	78	84
12941	JAY	79	62	42	56	70	79	59	71	66	58	79	83	52	78	63	71	73	70	84	97
12942	KEENE	78	61	42	55	69	78	58	70	66	57	78	82	52	77	62	70	72	69	83	95
	NEW YORK	95	100	134	99	98	107	103	100	105	103	133	116	105	138	104	107	131	102	99	112
	UNITED STATES	100	100	100	100	100	100	100	100	100	100	100	100	100	100	100	100	100	100	100	100

ZIP CODE			POPULATION			2000-2004 ANNUAL RATE		HOUSEHOLDS					FAMILIES		
#	POST OFFICE NAME	COUNTY FIPS CODE	2000	2004	2009	% Rate	State Centile	2000	2004	2009	% Annual Rate 2000-2004	2004 Average HH Size	2000	2004	% Annual Rate 2000-2004
12943	KEENE VALLEY	031	521	538	569	0.8	69	213	223	239	1.1	2.31	134	139	0.9
12944	KEESEVILLE	031	4373	4540	4776	0.9	74	1717	1811	1938	1.3	2.48	1228	1289	1.2
12945	LAKE CLEAR	033	433	451	475	1.0	76	171	181	194	1.4	2.47	108	114	1.3
12946	LAKE PLACID	031	6434	7047	7658	2.2	94	2299	2600	2914	2.9	2.18	1294	1453	2.8
12949	LAWRENCEVILLE	089	141	144	147	0.5	57	46	48	49	1.0	3.00	34	36	1.4
12950	LEWIS	031	537	554	588	0.7	68	219	230	247	1.2	2.41	157	164	1.0
12952	LYON MOUNTAIN	019	469	468	474	-0.1	25	223	227	235	0.4	1.81	152	154	0.3
12953	MALONE	033	16393	16755	17349	0.5	59	4636	4849	5168	1.1	2.37	3000	3117	0.9
12955	LYON MOUNTAIN	019	298	294	299	-0.3	13	134	135	140	0.2	2.15	91	91	0.0
12956	MINEVILLE	031	2013	2096	2222	1.0	76	716	766	834	1.6	2.36	484	516	1.5
12957	MOIRA	033	1390	1440	1514	0.8	72	537	566	604	1.3	2.52	377	394	1.0
12958	MOOERS	019	1791	1824	1869	0.4	53	671	691	719	0.7	2.64	495	508	0.6
12959	MOOERS FORKS	019	1357	1351	1372	-0.1	22	495	500	515	0.2	2.70	372	374	0.1
12960	MORIAH	031	927	964	1027	0.9	75	364	386	418	1.4	2.49	243	256	1.2
12961	MORIAH CENTER	031	180	184	194	0.5	59	67	70	75	1.0	2.61	46	47	0.5
12962	MORRISONVILLE	019	5478	5566	5691	0.4	50	2033	2112	2202	0.9	2.60	1520	1571	0.8
12964	NEW RUSSIA	031	187	192	203	0.6	63	69	72	77	1.0	2.67	51	53	0.9
12965	NICHOLVILLE	089	100	100	101	0.0	28	39	40	41	0.6	2.50	29	29	0.0
12966	NORTH BANGOR	033	2746	2903	3087	1.3	85	986	1060	1145	1.7	2.71	745	797	1.6
12967	NORTH LAWRENCE	089	959	989	1012	0.7	68	365	383	399	1.1	2.58	272	285	1.1
12969	OWLS HEAD	033	408	439	471	1.7	91	174	190	207	2.1	2.29	119	129	1.9
12970	PAUL SMITHS	033	817	829	849	0.3	49	114	119	127	1.0	3.30	73	76	1.0
12972	PERU	019	5654	5958	6214	1.2	83	2071	2224	2363	1.7	2.65	1562	1670	1.6
12973	PIERCEFIELD	089	114	113	114	-0.2	17	49	50	51	0.5	2.26	31	32	0.8
12974	PORT HENRY	031	1732	1875	2040	1.9	92	736	810	896	2.3	2.29	473	518	2.2
12978	REDFORD	019	338	351	362	0.9	74	117	124	130	1.4	2.83	87	92	1.3
12979	ROUSES POINT	019	2408	2518	2616	1.1	79	1026	1089	1149	1.4	2.28	638	672	1.2
12980	SAINT REGIS FALLS	033	1479	1539	1618	0.9	75	594	627	669	1.3	2.45	409	429	1.1
12981	SARANAC	019	6691	6756	6840	0.2	42	1437	1487	1545	0.8	2.66	1053	1084	0.7
12983	SARANAC LAKE	033	8109	8492	8984	1.1	80	3318	3537	3815	1.5	2.15	1815	1922	1.4
12985	SCHUYLER FALLS	019	878	913	943	0.9	75	324	344	363	1.4	2.65	244	258	1.3
12986	TUPPER LAKE	033	6319	6554	6887	0.9	73	2512	2644	2823	1.2	2.34	1581	1652	1.0
12987	UPPER JAY	031	116	122	131	1.2	82	49	52	56	1.4	2.35	33	35	1.4
12989	VERMONTVILLE	033	1796	1857	1937	0.8	70	571	606	650	1.4	2.34	384	404	1.2
12992	WEST CHAZY	019	4642	4766	4928	0.6	63	1699	1784	1883	1.2	2.66	1288	1347	1.1
12993	WESTPORT	031	1869	1904	2001	0.4	54	795	823	879	0.8	2.26	517	533	0.7
12996	WILLSBORO	031	2096	2170	2305	0.8	71	898	945	1019	1.2	2.28	612	641	1.1
12997	WILMINGTON	031	1057	1107	1184	1.1	80	431	456	494	1.3	2.43	285	301	1.3
13021	AUBURN	011	41714	41695	41970	0.0	27	16312	16517	16865	0.3	2.35	10268	10339	0.2
13026	AURORA	011	1652	1679	1691	0.4	50	547	565	578	0.8	2.53	384	393	0.6
13027	BALDWINSVILLE	067	28959	30285	31036	1.1	79	11398	12091	12568	1.4	2.49	7895	8316	1.2
13028	BERNHARDS BAY	075	1260	1286	1322	0.5	56	465	483	504	0.9	2.66	342	353	0.8
13029	BREWERTON	067	5450	5367	5328	-0.4	11	2075	2083	2102	0.1	2.58	1518	1512	-0.1
13030	BRIDGEPORT	053	4180	4094	4086	-0.5	7	1630	1631	1656	0.0	2.51	1169	1160	-0.2
13031	CAMILLUS	067	15342	15542	15656	0.3	48	6159	6363	6521	0.8	2.44	4364	4475	0.6
13032	CANASTOTA	053	12230	12381	12515	0.3	46	4812	4945	5063	0.6	2.50	3333	3403	0.5
13033	CATO	011	4089	4246	4325	0.9	74	1413	1486	1535	1.2	2.86	1115	1164	1.0
13034	CAYUGA	011	2111	2124	2131	0.1	37	793	813	828	0.6	2.61	598	608	0.4
13035	CAZENOVIA	053	8380	8572	8701	0.5	59	3022	3140	3229	0.9	2.55	2164	2236	0.8
13036	CENTRAL SQUARE	075	8201	8482	8853	0.8	71	3222	3378	3576	1.1	2.51	2241	2341	1.0
13037	CHITTENANGO	053	8337	8548	8733	0.6	61	3136	3271	3390	1.0	2.59	2297	2382	0.9
13039	CICERO	067	15041	16409	17200	2.1	94	5470	6093	6504	2.6	2.69	4117	4539	2.3
13040	CINCINNATUS	023	3109	3137	3185	0.2	41	1145	1171	1205	0.5	2.66	844	858	0.4
13041	CLAY	067	9608	9680	9693	0.2	40	3266	3362	3426	0.7	2.88	2647	2706	0.5
13042	CLEVELAND	065	2412	2416	2440	0.0	30	897	913	934	0.4	2.65	678	685	0.2
13044	CONSTANTIA	075	2725	2733	2783	0.1	33	995	1015	1049	0.5	2.69	738	747	0.3
13045	CORTLAND	023	28854	28998	29314	0.1	36	10861	11081	11380	0.5	2.34	6222	6297	0.3
13052	DE RUYTER	053	2066	2145	2203	0.9	74	687	725	755	1.3	2.73	502	525	1.1
13053	DRYDEN	109	4792	5065	5332	1.3	85	1803	1950	2093	1.9	2.53	1197	1281	1.6
13054	DURHAMVILLE	065	1644	1653	1658	0.1	37	583	596	602	0.5	2.77	435	441	0.3
13057	EAST SYRACUSE	067	14912	15354	15644	0.7	66	6297	6630	6883	1.2	2.30	3971	4150	1.0
13060	ELBRIDGE	067	2854	2787	2761	-0.6	5	1134	1128	1137	-0.1	2.47	831	820	-0.3
13061	ERIEVILLE	053	1140	1124	1125	-0.3	12	436	438	445	0.1	2.47	320	318	-0.2
13063	FABIUS	067	2122	2140	2134	0.2	40	720	739	748	0.6	2.89	558	569	0.5
13066	FAYETTEVILLE	067	12302	12450	12549	0.3	45	4964	5096	5212	0.6	2.42	3459	3536	0.5
13068	FREEVILLE	109	5331	5448	5661	0.5	58	2053	2133	2252	0.9	2.50	1340	1375	0.6
13069	FULTON	075	24470	24959	25830	0.5	56	9513	9841	10336	0.8	2.52	6437	6612	0.6
13071	GENOA	011	1080	1048	1042	-0.7	3	403	398	402	-0.3	2.63	300	294	-0.5
13072	GEORGETOWN	053	810	866	904	1.6	89	284	313	334	2.3	2.58	204	223	2.1
13073	GROTON	109	5919	6315	6719	1.5	88	2201	2378	2566	1.8	2.61	1580	1692	1.6
13074	HANNIBAL	075	4874	5273	5593	1.9	92	1729	1903	2050	2.3	2.72	1289	1408	2.1
13076	HASTINGS	075	1999	2162	2294	1.9	92	705	777	838	2.3	2.78	539	590	2.2
13077	HOMER	023	6774	6833	6902	0.2	40	2600	2663	2731	0.6	2.54	1869	1902	0.4
13078	JAMESVILLE	067	8225	8718	8970	1.4	87	3006	3272	3437	2.0	2.51	2165	2326	1.7
13080	JORDAN	067	3755	3771	3780	0.1	35	1400	1438	1468	0.6	2.62	1031	1049	0.4
13081	KING FERRY	011	1083	1084	1085	0.0	30	411	418	425	0.4	2.47	298	301	0.2
13082	KIRKVILLE	053	5120	5287	5407	0.8	69	1944	2048	2130	1.2	2.56	1443	1512	1.1
13083	LACONA	075	1996	2069	2148	0.9	72	764	805	849	1.2	2.57	541	565	1.0
13084	LA FAYETTE	067	4264	4254	4232	-0.1	25	1570	1603	1624	0.5	2.65	1183	1198	0.3
13088	LIVERPOOL	067	22324	21771	21561	-0.6	4	9776	9772	9861	0.0	2.21	5869	5795	-0.3
13090	LIVERPOOL	067	30735	30987	31293	0.2	40	11434	11716	12025	0.6	2.64	8317	8503	0.5
13092	LOCKE	011	2696	2777	2840	0.7	66	1000	1052	1095	1.2	2.63	760	794	1.0
13101	MC GRAW	023	2495	2542	2576	0.4	54	911	940	965	0.7	2.69	683	700	0.6
13103	MALLORY	075	763	781	807	0.6	60	246	256	268	0.9	3.05	192	199	0.9
13104	MANLIUS	067	14429	14764	14875	0.5	60	5455	5659	5784	0.9	2.60	4026	4146	0.7
13108	MARCELLUS	067	5917	5841	5804	-0.3	14	2212	2226	2251	0.2	2.62	1642	1640	0.0
13110	MARIETTA	067	2171	2167	2157	0.0	26	825	841	853	0.5	2.58	623	629	0.2
13111	MARTVILLE	011	1857	1898	1927	0.5	59	633	655	673	0.8	2.90	485	497	0.6
13112	MEMPHIS	067	1781	1814	1837	0.4	53	659	687	710	1.0	2.64	488	506	0.9
13114	MEXICO	075	6905	7056	7259	0.5	58	2562	2664	2783	0.9	2.65	1859	1918	0.8
13116	MINOA	067	3377	3235	3189	-1.0	1	1267	1245	1251	-0.4	2.54	947	923	-0.6
13118	MORAVIA	011	6647	6709	6796	0.2	41	1936	1990	2053	0.7	2.61	1389	1419	0.5
13120	NEDROW	067	3457	3488	3494	0.2	41	1040	1046	1054	0.1	3.31	821	821	0.0
13122	NEW WOODSTOCK	053	1002	1019	1029	0.4	52	372	384	392	0.8	2.65	284	291	0.5
13124	NORTH PITCHER	017	130	128	130	-0.4	11	46	46	47	0.0	2.67	35	35	0.0
	NEW YORK					0.4					0.5	2.60			0.4
	UNITED STATES					1.2					1.3	2.58			1.1

ZIP CODE #	POST OFFICE NAME	RACE (%) White 2000	White 2004	Black 2000	Black 2004	Asian/Pacific 2000	Asian/Pacific 2004	% Hispanic Origin 2000	% Hispanic Origin 2004	2004 AGE DISTRIBUTION (%) 0-4	5-9	10-14	15-19	20-24	25-44	45-64	65-84	85+	18+	MEDIAN AGE 2004	% 2004 Males	% 2004 Females
12943	KEENE VALLEY	98.7	98.7	0.0	0.0	0.4	0.6	0.4	0.4	4.1	3.7	9.1	7.3	3.4	21.0	32.2	15.1	4.3	78.6	45.8	46.1	53.9
12944	KEESEVILLE	97.6	97.1	0.6	0.7	0.2	0.3	1.1	1.4	5.8	5.9	7.4	7.3	5.8	27.0	27.6	12.3	1.1	76.3	40.0	49.1	50.9
12945	LAKE CLEAR	97.2	96.2	0.5	0.4	0.9	1.3	0.7	1.1	5.1	5.3	6.7	6.4	5.5	26.4	32.4	10.2	2.0	78.3	41.7	49.9	50.1
12946	LAKE PLACID	87.0	85.9	8.9	9.5	1.1	1.3	5.9	6.8	4.2	4.2	5.2	5.8	6.6	35.9	24.1	11.6	2.5	82.7	38.9	57.6	42.4
12949	LAWRENCEVILLE	98.6	98.6	0.0	0.0	0.0	0.0	1.4	1.4	7.6	7.6	8.3	7.6	5.6	25.7	25.7	10.4	1.4	71.5	36.4	49.3	50.7
12950	LEWIS	99.3	99.1	0.2	0.2	0.0	0.0	0.0	0.2	6.0	6.7	8.7	7.0	3.8	28.5	28.0	10.3	1.1	73.3	39.3	52.5	47.5
12952	LYON MOUNTAIN	88.5	85.9	7.3	8.8	0.6	0.6	3.8	5.1	4.1	4.3	4.7	6.4	5.8	31.0	27.6	14.3	1.9	83.3	42.3	55.6	44.4
12953	MALONE	75.8	73.4	16.9	18.1	0.6	0.7	10.2	11.8	3.8	3.8	4.8	5.5	8.8	39.3	22.0	10.1	2.1	84.3	36.8	62.9	37.1
12955	LYON MOUNTAIN	97.7	97.3	0.7	0.7	0.3	0.7	1.0	1.0	4.4	5.1	6.8	6.5	5.8	25.5	28.9	15.0	2.0	79.6	42.0	49.0	51.0
12956	MINEVILLE	90.8	89.5	6.1	6.7	0.5	0.6	5.7	6.9	4.7	5.1	6.0	5.5	9.4	32.4	23.6	11.9	1.6	80.7	36.0	56.7	43.3
12957	MOIRA	96.6	95.8	0.6	0.8	0.1	0.2	0.8	1.1	6.5	6.7	7.4	6.8	5.8	27.6	27.3	10.7	1.3	75.1	37.9	49.9	50.1
12958	MOOERS	98.6	98.3	0.2	0.4	0.1	0.1	0.9	1.3	5.8	6.0	7.4	7.9	6.1	29.6	24.5	11.5	1.2	76.0	37.7	50.7	49.3
12959	MOOERS FORKS	97.5	96.9	0.2	0.2	0.4	0.5	0.7	1.0	6.5	6.6	7.6	7.1	5.6	30.3	24.9	10.6	0.9	75.0	37.3	51.7	48.3
12960	MORIAH	97.7	97.3	0.3	0.3	0.7	0.8	1.1	1.4	5.9	6.0	7.2	6.2	5.7	25.2	26.0	15.7	2.1	76.9	40.9	49.9	50.1
12961	MORIAH CENTER	97.8	96.7	0.6	0.5	0.6	1.1	0.6	0.5	4.9	5.4	7.6	6.0	7.1	25.5	27.7	14.1	1.6	78.8	40.4	50.5	49.5
12962	MORRISONVILLE	97.2	96.5	1.2	1.6	0.3	0.4	1.1	1.5	5.7	6.2	7.4	7.8	6.3	26.7	28.1	10.6	1.1	75.3	39.1	50.3	49.7
12964	NEW RUSSIA	97.3	96.9	0.5	1.0	1.1	1.6	0.0	0.0	4.2	7.8	8.9	6.8	3.7	20.8	30.7	13.5	3.7	73.4	43.6	50.5	49.5
12965	NICHOLVILLE	98.0	98.0	0.0	0.0	0.0	0.0	0.0	1.0	6.0	7.0	8.0	6.0	5.0	26.0	27.0	13.0	2.0	73.0	39.4	50.0	50.0
12966	NORTH BANGOR	96.9	96.1	0.6	0.6	0.3	0.4	1.4	1.9	6.4	6.4	7.7	7.4	6.2	28.4	25.7	10.8	1.0	74.7	37.3	50.8	49.2
12967	NORTH LAWRENCE	98.4	98.3	0.0	0.0	0.1	0.1	0.8	1.1	6.6	7.4	8.0	7.3	5.7	26.5	27.3	10.3	1.0	73.4	37.0	49.8	50.3
12969	OWLS HEAD	98.3	98.2	0.0	0.0	0.0	0.0	0.5	0.5	3.6	5.5	5.9	7.3	3.9	25.1	33.5	14.1	1.1	80.2	44.2	53.1	46.9
12970	PAUL SMITHS	79.3	74.1	18.6	23.5	1.2	1.5	0.5	0.7	2.8	2.2	3.0	18.2	24.1	27.7	17.0	4.5	0.5	89.5	24.9	68.3	31.7
12972	PERU	97.7	97.0	0.7	0.9	0.6	0.7	0.9	1.2	5.7	6.2	8.3	7.8	5.7	27.3	26.2	11.6	1.2	74.5	38.9	48.3	51.7
12973	PIERCEFIELD	97.4	96.5	0.0	0.0	0.0	0.9	0.9	1.8	4.4	4.4	4.4	5.3	4.4	20.4	36.3	18.6	1.8	84.1	48.4	51.3	48.7
12974	PORT HENRY	97.8	97.3	0.2	0.3	0.6	0.9	1.7	2.2	6.4	6.2	6.7	6.1	5.2	24.9	25.1	17.1	2.2	76.5	41.2	49.1	50.9
12978	REDFORD	98.5	98.0	0.0	0.0	0.3	0.6	1.2	1.7	5.7	6.3	9.1	7.7	5.4	29.6	24.2	11.1	0.9	73.8	38.2	49.6	50.4
12979	ROUSES POINT	97.6	97.1	0.6	0.8	0.3	0.4	1.1	1.4	6.3	6.6	7.4	5.8	5.6	26.6	26.7	13.2	1.8	76.0	39.4	48.6	51.4
12980	SAINT REGIS FALLS	98.3	98.0	0.1	0.1	0.1	0.1	0.2	0.3	4.9	5.4	7.7	7.7	5.6	24.4	29.0	13.7	1.6	77.3	41.4	51.3	48.7
12981	SARANAC	69.0	66.1	22.8	24.4	0.7	0.8	11.6	13.2	3.5	3.9	5.0	5.7	8.3	46.2	20.5	6.1	0.7	84.1	35.2	69.9	30.2
12983	SARANAC LAKE	93.0	91.8	4.2	4.8	0.7	0.8	3.0	3.8	4.9	4.7	6.0	6.1	8.7	29.4	26.3	11.6	2.5	81.1	39.3	52.6	47.4
12985	SCHUYLER FALLS	98.2	97.6	0.3	0.4	0.2	0.3	1.1	1.4	4.9	6.8	9.2	8.7	3.7	30.9	25.5	9.6	0.7	73.2	38.3	50.7	49.3
12986	TUPPER LAKE	97.6	96.8	1.2	1.7	0.1	0.1	0.6	0.8	5.3	5.1	6.7	7.8	7.2	26.3	25.3	13.7	2.6	77.7	39.8	50.6	49.4
12987	UPPER JAY	98.3	99.2	0.0	0.0	0.0	0.0	0.0	0.0	6.6	6.6	6.6	7.4	6.6	24.6	27.1	13.9	0.8	75.4	39.4	47.5	52.5
12989	VERMONTVILLE	89.1	86.4	8.6	10.8	0.6	0.7	0.5	0.7	3.8	3.9	6.5	12.6	12.8	28.0	22.7	8.8	0.8	81.4	34.9	58.8	41.2
12992	WEST CHAZY	98.3	97.9	0.4	0.5	0.4	0.6	0.7	1.0	5.7	6.2	8.0	7.5	6.2	29.6	27.0	9.1	0.7	75.5	37.9	49.7	50.3
12993	WESTPORT	97.6	97.1	0.5	0.5	0.5	0.7	1.1	1.5	4.6	5.1	6.7	6.0	4.0	22.6	32.4	15.9	2.8	79.6	45.6	50.1	49.9
12996	WILLSBORO	98.6	98.3	0.2	0.3	0.0	0.0	0.4	0.5	4.1	4.9	7.1	6.0	4.4	25.5	27.5	18.1	2.4	79.9	43.7	50.1	49.9
12997	WILMINGTON	98.6	98.5	0.1	0.1	0.1	0.1	0.7	0.8	7.2	7.2	7.3	6.9	5.7	26.7	25.4	12.7	0.8	73.9	37.4	48.7	51.3
13021	AUBURN	91.6	90.4	5.4	6.1	0.6	0.7	2.2	2.6	6.1	5.8	6.5	6.5	7.0	27.1	24.3	13.8	2.9	77.5	39.2	50.1	50.0
13026	AURORA	96.1	95.2	0.7	0.8	1.3	1.6	1.2	1.6	5.6	4.9	6.0	11.3	10.7	22.9	25.9	11.2	1.6	80.2	36.0	43.4	56.6
13027	BALDWINSVILLE	96.6	95.7	0.9	1.2	0.9	1.3	0.8	1.2	6.5	7.0	7.9	6.8	5.4	27.2	27.3	10.6	1.2	74.1	39.0	48.6	51.4
13028	BERNHARDS BAY	98.3	97.9	0.2	0.3	0.1	0.1	0.6	0.7	6.0	6.6	8.6	7.7	5.9	27.8	27.6	9.1	0.7	73.3	37.7	51.9	48.1
13029	BREWERTON	97.7	97.1	0.6	0.8	0.3	0.3	0.9	1.2	7.2	7.6	8.6	6.8	5.5	28.9	24.4	10.1	1.0	72.5	37.3	48.8	51.2
13030	BRIDGEPORT	97.3	96.7	0.7	0.9	0.3	0.5	0.6	0.8	5.6	6.2	7.3	6.8	5.6	27.2	28.0	12.5	0.8	76.3	40.4	50.4	49.6
13031	CAMILLUS	96.6	95.6	0.9	1.1	1.2	1.5	0.8	1.1	5.8	6.2	6.9	6.6	5.4	24.5	26.4	16.5	1.8	77.0	41.8	47.9	52.1
13032	CANASTOTA	97.9	97.6	0.6	0.6	0.3	0.3	0.7	0.9	6.7	6.8	7.1	6.3	5.6	27.2	26.8	12.1	1.6	75.4	39.4	49.3	50.7
13033	CATO	97.3	96.7	0.4	0.6	0.2	0.2	0.8	1.0	6.6	6.8	8.4	8.0	6.1	28.3	26.5	8.4	0.8	73.1	37.1	50.3	49.7
13034	CAYUGA	98.3	97.9	0.3	0.4	0.1	0.2	0.9	1.2	6.2	6.5	7.3	7.4	5.7	25.4	27.5	12.5	1.6	75.3	39.6	49.6	50.4
13035	CAZENOVIA	97.5	97.1	0.9	1.0	0.4	0.6	1.3	1.6	6.1	6.4	7.4	8.5	7.3	23.2	27.7	11.7	1.8	75.8	39.5	47.9	52.1
13036	CENTRAL SQUARE	97.7	97.3	0.3	0.4	0.4	0.5	0.6	0.7	6.0	6.3	8.1	7.2	5.9	29.4	25.5	10.5	1.1	75.2	37.9	49.6	50.4
13037	CHITTENANGO	98.0	97.6	0.4	0.4	0.4	0.4	0.6	0.7	6.4	6.9	7.9	7.1	5.9	27.2	27.2	9.9	1.6	74.0	38.2	48.3	51.7
13039	CICERO	96.2	95.1	1.3	1.6	0.9	1.2	1.0	1.3	8.1	8.2	8.1	6.6	5.3	30.3	24.7	8.0	0.7	71.5	36.3	49.1	50.9
13040	CINCINNATUS	98.1	97.8	0.2	0.3	0.1	0.1	1.2	1.5	6.8	7.0	8.1	7.3	5.3	27.3	25.9	11.1	1.2	73.4	38.2	50.0	50.1
13041	CLAY	92.3	90.4	3.6	4.6	1.3	1.6	1.3	1.8	7.8	7.8	8.4	7.0	5.7	31.6	25.3	6.1	0.4	71.6	35.1	48.9	51.1
13042	CLEVELAND	97.7	97.3	0.3	0.4	0.3	0.5	0.8	0.9	6.0	6.5	8.2	7.5	5.7	27.7	27.7	9.8	1.0	74.2	38.2	50.9	49.1
13044	CONSTANTIA	98.2	97.9	0.2	0.3	0.2	0.2	0.2	0.2	5.4	6.2	8.3	7.1	4.5	28.6	28.3	10.8	1.0	75.6	39.5	51.6	48.4
13045	CORTLAND	96.2	95.6	1.2	1.3	0.6	0.8	1.5	1.8	5.5	5.3	5.8	11.0	14.3	23.9	21.4	10.9	2.1	80.0	32.0	47.8	52.2
13052	DE RUYTER	91.8	90.3	5.5	6.4	0.2	0.3	2.8	3.5	6.1	6.4	7.4	7.0	6.8	29.6	25.2	10.2	1.3	75.9	37.3	53.5	46.5
13053	DRYDEN	95.8	95.0	1.6	1.8	0.6	0.8	1.7	2.1	5.8	6.8	7.1	9.3	8.1	26.1	26.9	8.9	1.1	75.5	36.2	50.3	49.7
13054	DURHAMVILLE	97.7	97.2	0.4	0.4	0.2	0.4	0.6	0.7	5.9	6.2	7.4	7.1	5.4	26.5	28.2	12.3	0.9	76.0	39.9	50.5	49.6
13057	EAST SYRACUSE	95.0	93.7	1.3	1.7	1.6	2.1	1.0	1.3	5.3	5.7	6.9	6.6	5.5	25.7	26.7	15.9	1.8	77.8	41.9	47.5	52.6
13060	ELBRIDGE	97.6	96.9	0.5	0.6	0.4	0.5	1.1	1.5	6.4	6.8	7.6	7.2	5.4	26.4	26.8	12.1	1.2	74.6	39.6	49.7	50.3
13061	ERIEVILLE	97.4	97.1	0.9	1.0	0.2	0.2	1.4	1.7	5.6	6.1	9.3	10.4	5.3	26.4	27.4	8.6	0.9	73.3	37.7	51.2	48.8
13063	FABIUS	98.0	97.4	0.4	0.5	0.3	0.4	1.2	1.5	7.0	7.8	8.6	7.1	5.0	26.5	27.9	9.0	1.0	72.2	38.0	49.7	50.3
13066	FAYETTEVILLE	94.3	92.7	1.0	1.2	3.3	4.3	1.2	1.6	5.6	6.4	7.7	7.0	4.3	20.8	30.0	15.7	2.5	75.6	43.9	47.3	52.7
13068	FREEVILLE	95.6	94.6	1.2	1.4	1.1	1.5	1.3	1.6	6.4	6.8	7.5	7.7	6.7	29.3	25.8	8.8	1.0	74.2	36.1	49.7	50.3
13069	FULTON	97.4	96.9	0.6	0.6	0.3	0.4	1.4	1.7	7.2	6.9	7.6	7.1	7.0	27.3	24.3	11.0	1.7	74.0	36.4	49.0	51.0
13071	GENOA	97.3	96.6	0.7	0.9	0.4	0.4	2.1	2.8	5.4	6.3	8.4	8.4	5.5	26.9	26.4	11.6	1.0	74.3	38.5	51.4	48.6
13072	GEORGETOWN	92.6	91.3	4.9	5.5	0.3	0.4	2.6	3.4	6.9	7.0	7.4	7.2	6.5	29.6	24.3	10.1	1.2	74.4	36.6	52.7	47.3
13073	GROTON	97.2	96.6	0.7	0.9	0.4	0.6	0.8	1.1	5.8	6.1	7.9	8.1	6.8	25.7	27.0	11.0	1.5	74.8	38.6	49.4	50.6
13074	HANNIBAL	97.8	97.4	0.4	0.4	0.2	0.2	0.9	1.2	6.9	7.2	8.6	8.6	7.7	27.9	24.5	7.7	0.8	72.3	34.2	50.3	49.7
13076	HASTINGS	97.8	97.4	0.2	0.3	0.2	0.1	0.8	1.1	6.7	7.0	8.7	7.3	6.2	30.8	24.1	8.5	0.7	73.2	36.3	50.5	49.5
13077	HOMER	98.1	97.8	0.4	0.4	0.3	0.4	0.7	0.9	5.9	6.3	7.7	7.3	6.4	26.0	27.5	11.4	1.6	75.7	39.1	48.7	51.4
13078	JAMESVILLE	91.9	89.8	3.2	4.0	2.2	3.0	0.8	1.1	5.6	6.6	7.4	6.4	4.5	23.6	27.8	13.7	4.4	76.0	42.7	48.8	51.2
13080	JORDAN	98.0	97.4	0.3	0.4	0.5	0.6	1.0	1.3	6.2	6.4	7.6	7.8	6.7	26.2	26.7	11.1	1.4	74.9	38.8	49.8	50.2
13081	KING FERRY	96.5	95.9	0.3	0.3	0.5	0.6	2.2	2.9	4.8	6.9	9.7	9.2	5.9	23.6	25.9	12.2	1.8	73.0	38.6	48.8	51.2
13082	KIRKVILLE	98.2	97.8	0.2	0.3	0.3	0.4	0.4	0.5	5.6	6.2	6.9	6.8	5.4	26.3	29.4	12.3	1.2	76.9	41.1	49.5	50.5
13083	LACONA	98.4	98.2	0.1	0.1	0.1	0.1	0.8	1.0	6.1	6.4	8.1	6.8	5.9	26.8	27.5	11.1	1.3	75.1	38.9	50.1	49.9
13084	LA FAYETTE	96.0	95.1	0.4	0.5	0.7	0.9	0.5	0.6	5.6	6.5	8.0	7.8	5.3	24.3	30.7	10.6	1.1	75.0	40.8	50.4	49.6
13088	LIVERPOOL	92.6	90.7	2.7	3.4	2.6	3.4	1.5	1.9	5.4	5.4	5.9	5.7	6.0	29.3	25.6	14.2	2.4	79.8	40.0	47.2	52.9
13090	LIVERPOOL	91.0	88.9	4.2	5.2	2.4	3.0	1.5	1.9	7.4	7.6	7.9	7.1	6.7	30.1	25.2	7.4	0.6	72.5	35.0	48.5	51.5
13092	LOCKE	97.8	97.4	0.7	0.8	0.4	0.5	0.9	1.1	6.4	6.7	7.9	8.1	6.7	27.4	26.5	9.4	0.9	73.8	37.3	50.3	49.7
13101	MC GRAW	97.8	97.4	0.2	0.3	0.1	0.1	0.6	0.8	6.4	6.7	8.0	7.3	6.7	27.0	25.3	11.3	1.3	74.2	37.4	49.5	50.5
13103	MALLORY	97.4	96.8	0.1	0.3	0.3	0.3	0.5	0.6	6.7	7.8	9.7	7.9	5.4	31.0	23.6	7.2	0.8	70.6	35.0	50.8	49.2
13104	MANLIUS	94.1	92.5	0.9	1.2	3.6	4.6	1.1	1.4	6.4	7.6	8.8	7.0	4.6	22.0	30.6	11.4	1.6	72.6	41.5	48.6	51.4
13108	MARCELLUS	98.3	98.0	0.4	0.5	0.3	0.3	0.9	1.2	5.9	6.6	8.2	7.7	5.8	23.8	28.8	12.0	1.4	74.5	40.3	48.3	51.7
13110	MARIETTA	97.6	97.0	0.5	0.6	0.4	0.6	0.3	0.4	6.6	7.2	8.4	7.3	5.2	26.1	28.2	10.1	0.9	73.2	38.9	50.5	49.5
13111	MARTVILLE	98.2	97.8	0.1	0.2	0.2	0.2	0.5	0.7	6.5	6.7	8.5	9.0	6.9	27.5	25.2	9.0	0.7	72.7	36.2	51.8	48.2
13112	MEMPHIS	98.3	97.8	0.4	0.6	0.3	0.3	0.5	0.7	5.9	6.2	6.9	6.6	6.0	27.0	29.0	11.2	1.3	77.0	40.3	50.2	49.8
13114	MEXICO	98.1	97.8	0.2	0.2	0.3	0.4	0.8	1.0	6.4	6.7	8.3	7.6	6.5	28.3	26.3	9.0	0.9	73.6	36.9	49.9	50.1
13116	MINOA	96.7	95.7	0.5	0.7	1.3	1.6	0.5	0.8	5.2	5.8	7.7	6.7	6.1	25.4	28.1	12.4	2.6	76.9	41.1	46.8	53.2
13118	MORAVIA	82.4	80.7	13.2	14.2	0.4	0.5	6.3	7.3	4.6	5.1	6.3	6.2	7.8	36.2	24.1	8.5	1.3	80.1	36.6	61.0	39.0
13120	NEDROW	69.3	66.2	3.2	4.0	0.4	0.5	0.8	1.0	10.0	10.1	10.3	8.3	6.1	24.6	20.9	8.4	1.4	64.3	30.9	50.4	49.6
13122	NEW WOODSTOCK	98.0	97.6	0.6	0.7	0.4	0.6	0.8	1.0	6.9	7.5	8.0	7.0	4.9	24.7	29.0	10.5	1.7	73.3	40.1	50.4	49.6
13124	NORTH PITCHER	96.2	95.3	3.1	3.1	0.0	0.0	1.5	2.3	5.5	7.0	7.8	7.0	7.8	28.1	26.6	8.6	1.6	75.0	36.7	53.1	46.9
	NEW YORK	68.0	65.9	15.9	16.2	5.6	6.4	15.1	16.7	6.5	6.5	7.1	7.0	7.1	28.9	24.0	11.2	1.8	75.8	36.7	48.3	51.7
	UNITED STATES	75.1	73.6	12.3	12.5	3.8	4.2	12.5	14.1	6.9	6.7	7.2	7.0	7.3	28.6	23.8	10.8	1.7	75.1	36.0	49.1	50.9

ZIP CODE #	POST OFFICE NAME	2004 Per Capita Income	2004 HH Income Base	2004 HOUSEHOLD INCOME DISTRIBUTION (%) Less than $25,000	$25,000 to $49,999	$50,000 to $99,999	$100,000 to $149,999	$150,000 or More	MEDIAN HOUSEHOLD INCOME 2004	2009	2004 National Centile	2004 State Centile	2004 Home Value Base	2004 HOME VALUE DISTRIBUTION (%) Less than $50,000	$50,000 to $89,999	$90,000 to $174,999	$175,000 to $399,999	$400,000 or More	2004 Median Home Value
12943	KEENE VALLEY	19697	223	29.6	32.3	33.2	4.0	0.9	38535	43132	41	27	185	1.1	2.7	36.2	51.4	8.7	195109
12944	KEESEVILLE	20333	1811	28.4	34.0	28.3	6.7	2.6	41496	46459	51	39	1426	10.1	15.9	54.7	17.1	2.2	124698
12945	LAKE CLEAR	21890	181	23.8	32.6	30.9	11.1	1.7	43829	48874	58	47	151	4.0	13.9	39.1	39.7	3.3	154808
12946	LAKE PLACID	20757	2600	30.9	35.3	25.0	6.1	2.7	38162	42333	40	25	1624	7.7	4.4	36.3	39.4	12.3	179116
12949	LAWRENCEVILLE	13781	48	35.4	33.3	29.2	2.1	0.0	35000	40550	28	13	39	15.4	28.2	46.2	7.7	2.6	96250
12950	LEWIS	20003	230	26.5	38.3	30.0	3.9	1.3	39683	43135	45	33	191	12.0	14.7	44.5	27.2	1.6	123897
12952	LYON MOUNTAIN	25516	227	30.0	30.4	31.3	7.1	1.3	42192	48044	53	42	195	29.2	21.0	37.4	11.8	0.5	89286
12953	MALONE	17210	4849	38.1	32.2	22.8	3.8	3.1	32344	36030	19	7	3294	12.3	30.6	44.0	12.2	0.9	100687
12955	LYON MOUNTAIN	21425	135	33.3	34.1	25.9	5.2	1.5	35743	41006	31	15	112	12.5	26.8	43.8	14.3	2.7	100000
12956	MINEVILLE	21847	766	36.0	30.4	26.4	3.9	3.3	36082	39383	32	17	580	11.9	22.9	49.7	15.3	0.2	107857
12957	MOIRA	15026	566	41.5	33.9	20.3	3.9	0.4	30325	33613	13	5	448	27.9	30.8	35.3	5.8	0.2	73793
12958	MOOERS	18845	691	26.9	34.2	31.0	6.8	1.2	43767	49219	58	47	578	11.6	14.5	58.3	14.7	0.9	117210
12959	MOOERS FORKS	16334	500	33.8	32.8	27.2	5.4	0.8	40699	46188	49	36	418	18.4	23.7	46.7	11.2	0.0	99706
12960	MORIAH	22479	386	34.5	33.7	24.6	3.1	4.2	35642	39078	30	15	287	11.5	24.4	54.0	10.1	0.0	105664
12961	MORIAH CENTER	17783	70	38.6	31.4	24.3	1.4	4.3	32821	39308	20	8	53	11.3	26.4	52.8	9.4	0.0	103409
12962	MORRISONVILLE	22955	2112	21.2	27.8	38.7	9.7	2.8	50916	56464	74	64	1711	9.4	10.4	47.5	30.8	1.9	139194
12964	NEW RUSSIA	19388	72	25.0	30.6	34.7	6.9	2.8	42845	48002	56	44	58	1.7	8.6	63.8	24.1	1.7	136765
12965	NICHOLVILLE	16125	40	35.0	25.0	37.5	2.5	0.0	40000	38640	46	34	32	18.8	34.4	40.6	6.3	0.0	85000
12966	NORTH BANGOR	15324	1060	36.6	34.2	24.1	4.2	1.0	33879	37437	24	10	880	24.1	30.7	39.6	5.1	0.6	81923
12967	NORTH LAWRENCE	15956	383	34.2	33.9	29.0	2.4	0.5	35782	40075	31	16	312	18.3	28.5	42.0	10.3	1.0	93448
12969	OWLS HEAD	19822	190	28.4	36.8	29.0	3.2	2.6	38808	43361	42	28	163	17.8	27.0	36.2	17.8	1.2	100521
12970	PAUL SMITHS	14795	119	24.4	27.7	38.7	8.4	0.8	48085	52782	68	58	96	11.5	7.3	49.0	27.1	5.2	132143
12972	PERU	21696	2224	25.4	32.3	31.6	6.0	4.7	42235	47114	54	42	1816	9.3	10.9	48.1	30.0	1.7	139510
12973	PIERCEFIELD	19890	50	26.0	36.0	36.0	2.0	0.0	40000	44298	46	34	42	16.7	23.8	42.9	11.9	4.8	105000
12974	PORT HENRY	22962	810	36.2	33.3	24.0	3.5	3.1	34599	37399	26	12	593	10.6	23.3	55.3	10.8	0.0	107255
12978	REDFORD	17335	124	22.6	36.3	34.7	5.7	0.8	42615	47072	55	43	106	11.3	16.0	62.3	9.4	0.9	120588
12979	ROUSES POINT	22211	1089	29.8	31.2	29.9	6.4	2.6	41185	46701	50	38	678	5.0	13.4	62.7	17.0	1.9	128636
12980	SAINT REGIS FALLS	17533	627	38.0	30.3	25.8	5.1	0.8	35237	38529	28	14	477	27.3	27.7	27.0	14.7	3.4	79828
12981	SARANAC	17710	1487	22.9	30.3	37.7	7.7	1.4	47428	53196	67	57	1190	8.0	14.2	60.0	17.1	0.8	126375
12983	SARANAC LAKE	20693	3537	36.8	29.3	24.4	6.8	2.8	36072	39935	32	17	2053	4.6	13.7	49.4	27.7	4.5	138142
12985	SCHUYLER FALLS	21791	344	24.1	35.5	30.8	5.8	3.8	43296	47792	57	45	294	6.8	15.3	51.7	24.5	1.7	132627
12986	TUPPER LAKE	18842	2644	33.5	27.7	33.7	4.5	0.7	39043	42929	43	29	1727	4.1	17.4	58.3	18.4	1.9	127627
12987	UPPER JAY	22570	52	28.9	32.7	30.8	5.8	1.9	41124	45000	50	38	39	0.0	12.8	51.3	35.9	0.0	142188
12989	VERMONTVILLE	19938	606	25.7	29.9	37.0	6.1	1.3	45770	51069	63	52	514	12.1	11.5	45.7	26.9	3.9	132667
12992	WEST CHAZY	17719	1784	32.0	29.2	31.8	5.3	1.7	40675	46024	48	36	1498	13.4	13.2	52.2	19.8	1.5	128783
12993	WESTPORT	24441	823	26.3	32.6	30.4	6.4	4.4	42124	47005	53	41	641	3.6	12.0	45.1	30.3	9.1	144707
12996	WILLSBORO	23558	945	28.2	36.4	27.0	6.2	2.2	40788	44960	49	37	781	7.9	18.7	45.5	24.3	3.6	123917
12997	WILMINGTON	20470	456	34.2	32.5	23.7	6.8	2.9	37365	41396	37	22	322	6.8	14.0	41.3	33.5	4.4	142000
13021	AUBURN	20870	16517	32.6	29.6	28.5	6.9	2.5	39100	43109	43	30	10743	4.4	30.5	47.6	16.3	1.2	106430
13026	AURORA	22123	565	19.7	33.5	34.2	9.0	3.7	46399	52084	65	54	457	6.6	17.5	46.0	24.7	5.3	129953
13027	BALDWINSVILLE	27947	12091	19.1	24.1	36.6	13.5	6.8	57851	66653	83	73	8893	2.4	15.2	56.8	24.6	1.0	123252
13028	BERNHARDS BAY	17907	483	26.5	32.7	34.8	5.8	0.2	41515	46333	51	40	412	19.4	27.7	42.7	9.0	1.2	93000
13029	BREWERTON	24984	2083	18.6	23.3	43.9	11.3	2.9	57925	65803	83	73	1696	1.8	11.9	64.8	21.1	0.5	122019
13030	BRIDGEPORT	23784	1631	21.2	30.2	36.9	9.3	2.5	48945	56568	70	60	1310	3.8	28.5	49.9	17.0	0.8	114787
13031	CAMILLUS	28253	6363	17.5	26.0	39.0	12.7	4.8	56577	65194	81	71	4905	0.7	7.7	70.2	20.6	0.8	133713
13032	CANASTOTA	21308	4945	24.6	31.3	34.3	7.8	2.0	44507	50623	60	49	3733	6.8	24.8	48.7	18.9	0.9	111055
13033	CATO	20091	1486	21.4	31.0	38.4	6.9	2.3	47906	53132	68	58	1271	11.6	24.9	48.5	13.3	1.7	107583
13034	CAYUGA	21147	813	25.0	31.7	32.8	7.9	2.6	45407	50443	62	51	681	14.0	22.5	49.5	12.0	2.1	104320
13035	CAZENOVIA	31711	3140	17.1	24.0	33.3	13.8	11.9	60448	70899	85	75	2561	2.9	7.8	38.9	42.1	8.3	175733
13036	CENTRAL SQUARE	21060	3378	24.6	32.3	34.5	6.8	1.8	43731	49805	58	47	2583	10.9	20.3	56.5	11.9	0.5	108986
13037	CHITTENANGO	25504	3271	19.1	30.9	33.8	10.7	5.6	50097	57575	72	62	2628	7.2	20.0	55.9	15.8	1.1	116519
13039	CICERO	26981	6093	14.9	23.2	42.7	14.6	4.7	62633	72479	87	77	5115	0.6	9.7	69.5	20.0	0.2	132000
13040	CINCINNATUS	18290	1171	27.3	37.5	29.0	4.4	1.9	39653	43823	45	33	957	12.6	25.5	48.8	12.4	0.6	101326
13041	CLAY	24323	3362	10.9	26.4	44.5	14.3	3.9	62145	70837	86	77	3052	1.1	16.7	71.7	10.1	0.5	116450
13042	CLEVELAND	19333	913	25.2	30.2	35.1	8.9	0.7	43049	47798	56	44	780	14.1	24.1	48.6	12.3	0.9	105072
13044	CONSTANTIA	18190	1015	22.7	33.5	37.6	6.1	0.1	44193	49835	59	48	858	18.2	20.9	41.1	18.7	1.2	108333
13045	CORTLAND	18764	11081	38.5	29.6	24.5	5.3	2.1	33377	36992	22	8	6108	3.7	10.3	65.5	19.4	1.2	126503
13052	DE RUYTER	17611	725	29.4	34.5	30.8	3.5	1.9	38814	43248	42	29	586	22.5	26.8	37.5	12.8	0.3	90930
13053	DRYDEN	22000	1950	24.8	28.3	34.9	8.9	3.1	46932	53341	66	55	1335	7.3	6.1	52.1	33.1	1.4	146146
13054	DURHAMVILLE	18552	596	22.0	33.4	38.8	4.4	1.5	45610	50806	63	52	500	8.0	26.0	55.6	9.4	1.0	108193
13057	EAST SYRACUSE	27225	6630	23.5	29.3	32.9	9.2	5.1	47283	54941	67	56	5030	2.7	20.0	61.3	15.9	0.1	113302
13060	ELBRIDGE	23434	1128	23.0	31.7	34.2	7.5	3.6	46430	53915	65	54	961	18.9	10.0	48.8	21.4	0.8	119612
13061	ERIEVILLE	25163	438	17.1	28.3	40.0	10.7	3.9	53512	61391	78	68	370	5.1	15.4	52.7	25.7	1.1	131897
13063	FABIUS	22998	739	14.2	30.6	39.5	10.4	5.3	55586	63790	80	71	629	1.1	17.8	55.3	24.8	1.0	133125
13066	FAYETTEVILLE	44188	5096	12.8	20.8	30.8	17.1	18.5	74003	86285	93	87	4163	2.3	4.8	40.7	44.6	7.5	179768
13068	FREEVILLE	23106	2133	23.1	28.7	35.4	9.5	3.3	48044	54544	68	58	1518	9.8	7.1	50.1	31.0	2.0	145308
13069	FULTON	19455	9841	31.7	31.3	28.3	6.1	2.6	38098	42619	40	25	6716	14.6	34.6	43.0	7.3	0.5	90781
13071	GENOA	19379	398	23.1	35.2	36.4	4.0	1.3	43711	48643	58	46	327	14.7	31.8	40.1	11.3	2.1	93710
13072	GEORGETOWN	17926	313	29.7	36.7	28.8	3.5	1.3	37394	41949	37	22	254	27.2	26.8	33.9	11.8	0.4	83333
13073	GROTON	21219	2378	22.8	31.4	36.0	8.0	1.9	46925	53754	66	55	1847	6.9	14.0	62.1	16.4	0.6	123692
13074	HANNIBAL	19201	1903	28.1	35.4	26.0	7.5	3.1	39458	44395	44	32	1545	24.5	28.2	40.2	6.6	0.5	85278
13076	HASTINGS	19222	777	24.5	28.6	38.5	7.6	0.9	47820	53213	68	57	668	14.4	22.0	54.6	8.1	0.9	101923
13077	HOMER	22844	2663	23.1	32.3	31.3	10.1	3.2	45358	51162	62	51	2062	5.8	8.4	59.6	24.2	2.0	135052
13078	JAMESVILLE	36546	3272	13.3	22.0	33.6	16.0	15.1	69425	81432	91	84	2686	4.5	7.1	42.3	40.4	5.6	165702
13080	JORDAN	22354	1438	22.7	31.8	33.4	9.1	3.1	46364	53324	65	54	1165	11.8	20.3	53.2	14.2	0.5	108915
13081	KING FERRY	25876	418	19.1	31.3	34.9	9.8	4.8	49501	53734	71	61	346	9.0	19.4	43.4	25.1	3.2	124091
13082	KIRKVILLE	23971	2048	19.1	29.3	37.8	10.9	2.8	51799	59308	75	65	1804	14.6	22.3	49.7	12.7	0.7	108431
13083	LACONA	18584	805	31.3	30.4	29.7	7.2	1.4	38973	43341	43	29	640	18.8	26.7	41.7	12.5	0.3	95179
13084	LA FAYETTE	27553	1603	16.8	27.7	36.2	11.7	7.5	57093	65870	82	72	1385	3.0	16.5	50.4	27.9	2.2	133757
13088	LIVERPOOL	27085	9772	22.7	29.8	33.9	9.1	4.5	47505	54436	67	57	5991	1.3	14.0	74.7	9.5	0.6	114807
13090	LIVERPOOL	26582	11716	13.4	27.0	40.5	14.7	4.4	60183	68247	85	75	8461	4.5	9.0	70.3	16.1	0.2	124475
13092	LOCKE	19548	1052	24.1	36.9	31.7	5.7	1.7	42151	46612	53	42	875	23.4	22.2	43.5	10.1	0.8	95500
13101	MC GRAW	23026	940	23.6	33.6	33.8	5.9	3.1	43732	49476	58	47	730	6.3	21.1	59.6	12.2	0.8	113088
13103	MALLORY	16822	256	25.8	28.1	38.3	5.9	2.0	46063	51106	64	53	221	27.2	25.3	41.2	6.3	0.0	86071
13104	MANLIUS	40318	5659	13.8	20.4	31.4	16.4	18.1	72311	84263	92	86	4515	0.4	4.5	32.8	55.2	7.1	193192
13108	MARCELLUS	29765	2226	15.7	24.6	41.3	11.7	6.7	59423	67719	84	74	1825	1.0	8.2	62.4	26.9	1.5	144071
13110	MARIETTA	26459	841	12.5	33.5	39.0	10.5	4.5	53535	61325	78	68	722	2.8	14.0	54.9	26.9	1.5	129907
13111	MARTVILLE	15575	655	28.4	38.6	27.0	5.3	0.6	37902	42306	39	24	541	16.1	37.2	34.6	10.9	1.3	85625
13112	MEMPHIS	25155	687	19.1	27.2	37.4	9.5	6.8	53678	62384	78	68	585	8.4	18.1	51.1	21.0	1.4	120752
13114	MEXICO	19918	2664	25.9	29.9	34.5	8.0	1.6	45810	51356	63	52	2164	15.4	26.5	49.7	8.0	0.4	98286
13116	MINOA	23497	1245	18.6	30.5	37.9	10.0	3.1	51076	59305	74	64	947	0.6	17.7	80.0	1.6	0.0	108791
13118	MORAVIA	17812	1990	26.0	35.0	32.2	4.6	2.2	42164	46484	53	42	1592	16.6	25.7	43.7	12.2	1.8	99609
13120	NEDROW	21633	1046	15.1	28.3	37.1	12.8	6.7	59075	66542	84	74	892	3.1	20.7	54.5	21.1	0.6	131410
13122	NEW WOODSTOCK	31822	384	14.8	29.2	35.2	10.7	10.2	56828	65346	82	72	323	9.9	13.9	35.9	36.8	3.4	142130
13124	NORTH PITCHER	16697	46	37.0	32.6	23.9	4.4	2.2	35000	39074	28	13	37	29.7	27.0	37.8	5.4	0.0	77500
	NEW YORK	28049		26.3	24.3	29.3	11.5	8.6	49309	58077				4.6	8.6	27.2	39.9	19.8	219050
	UNITED STATES	25866		24.7	27.1	30.8	10.9	6.5	48124	56710				10.9	15.0	33.7	30.1	10.4	145905

ZIP CODE #	POST OFFICE NAME	FINANCIAL SERVICES: Auto Loan	FINANCIAL SERVICES: Home Loan	FINANCIAL SERVICES: Invest-ments	FINANCIAL SERVICES: Retire-ment Plans	THE HOME: Home Improvements: Home Repair	THE HOME: Home Improvements: Lawn & Garden	THE HOME: Furnishings: Comput-ers & Hard-ware	THE HOME: Furnishings: Major Appli-ances	THE HOME: Furnishings: TV, Radio, Sound Equip-ment	THE HOME: Furnishings: Furni-ture	ENTERTAINMENT: Dine out/ Carry out	ENTERTAINMENT: Sports Equip-ment	ENTERTAINMENT: Fees & Tickets	ENTERTAINMENT: Toys & Games	ENTERTAINMENT: Travel	ENTERTAINMENT: Cable TV	PERSONAL: Apparel & Services	PERSONAL: Auto Repairs	PERSONAL: Health Insur-ance	PERSONAL: Pets & Supplies
12943	KEENE VALLEY	78	61	42	55	69	78	58	70	65	57	78	82	52	77	62	70	72	69	82	95
12944	KEESEVILLE	82	68	50	64	73	82	67	75	73	66	87	87	62	86	68	76	81	74	85	96
12945	LAKE CLEAR	91	72	50	66	81	91	69	82	77	68	92	95	62	91	73	82	85	80	96	110
12946	LAKE PLACID	60	57	58	56	59	64	58	60	60	57	74	71	57	75	59	60	71	61	62	71
12949	LAWRENCEVILLE	65	55	42	54	58	65	56	60	60	55	73	69	54	72	56	61	68	60	66	72
12950	LEWIS	75	64	50	64	67	76	66	70	70	65	85	80	63	84	65	71	79	69	76	83
12952	LYON MOUNTAIN	83	65	45	60	73	82	62	74	70	62	83	86	56	82	66	74	77	73	87	99
12953	MALONE	58	49	40	48	53	59	50	55	54	49	65	64	47	65	51	56	61	55	62	67
12955	LYON MOUNTAIN	79	61	40	56	69	78	58	70	66	57	78	83	52	77	62	70	72	69	83	96
12956	MINEVILLE	84	72	57	66	76	87	72	79	80	70	96	90	69	97	74	84	90	78	91	96
12957	MOIRA	72	48	22	41	54	62	46	58	56	47	65	69	39	62	47	60	60	57	71	82
12958	MOOERS	86	68	44	63	72	79	65	75	71	67	86	88	59	81	65	73	81	74	82	96
12959	MOOERS FORKS	73	62	44	58	64	69	59	66	62	61	76	77	55	72	59	63	72	66	69	82
12960	MORIAH	75	76	75	72	78	88	77	78	81	74	99	87	79	105	79	84	95	76	85	87
12961	MORIAH CENTER	60	65	69	62	66	73	64	64	67	62	83	71	68	90	67	69	80	62	69	70
12962	MORRISONVILLE	87	89	82	87	90	95	83	87	83	83	102	101	84	105	84	83	99	84	87	102
12964	NEW RUSSIA	88	69	47	62	77	87	65	78	73	64	87	91	58	86	69	78	81	77	92	107
12965	NICHOLVILLE	67	53	38	50	59	66	52	60	58	52	69	70	48	68	54	61	64	59	69	78
12966	NORTH BANGOR	66	54	41	53	58	65	55	60	59	55	72	70	52	71	55	61	67	60	66	73
12967	NORTH LAWRENCE	69	54	36	51	58	66	54	61	60	54	72	71	50	70	54	62	67	60	70	78
12969	OWLS HEAD	77	61	41	55	68	77	57	69	65	57	77	81	51	76	61	69	71	68	81	94
12970	PAUL SMITHS	90	70	48	63	79	89	66	80	75	66	89	93	59	88	71	80	83	79	94	109
12972	PERU	88	79	66	77	82	92	79	84	83	77	101	96	77	101	79	84	95	82	90	100
12973	PIERCEFIELD	76	60	41	54	67	76	56	68	64	56	76	80	50	75	60	68	70	67	80	93
12974	PORT HENRY	78	68	58	65	72	84	72	75	78	69	94	84	69	94	73	81	88	75	86	88
12978	REDFORD	77	65	51	65	68	77	67	72	71	66	86	82	64	85	67	72	81	71	78	85
12979	ROUSES POINT	75	70	61	68	73	80	69	72	73	68	89	83	69	92	70	75	85	71	78	86
12980	SAINT REGIS FALLS	73	57	39	52	64	72	54	65	61	53	72	76	48	71	58	65	67	64	77	89
12981	SARANAC	61	57	49	56	60	65	55	59	57	55	70	69	54	71	56	58	67	58	62	72
12983	SARANAC LAKE	64	57	56	56	59	65	61	62	63	59	78	74	58	77	60	64	74	64	66	75
12985	SCHUYLER FALLS	94	80	59	75	86	94	75	85	81	75	98	101	71	99	78	85	93	83	95	112
12986	TUPPER LAKE	71	58	44	54	63	73	59	66	65	57	78	75	55	77	61	69	72	65	77	82
12987	UPPER JAY	90	70	48	64	79	89	66	80	75	66	89	94	59	88	71	80	83	79	95	109
12989	VERMONTVILLE	87	68	46	61	77	86	64	77	73	64	86	91	57	85	68	78	80	76	91	106
12992	WEST CHAZY	74	68	55	66	70	74	64	69	66	65	81	81	62	80	65	66	78	68	71	85
12993	WESTPORT	83	77	69	73	81	91	75	81	79	74	96	93	73	97	78	83	92	80	89	99
12996	WILLSBORO	89	72	51	67	79	88	70	80	77	69	92	93	64	91	72	81	86	79	92	105
12997	WILMINGTON	82	63	42	59	70	81	65	74	73	63	86	85	58	83	66	77	79	74	88	96
13021	AUBURN	68	68	73	67	69	75	70	70	72	68	89	81	71	91	71	72	86	70	72	79
13026	AURORA	90	85	75	80	89	96	80	87	83	79	101	102	78	104	83	86	97	86	93	108
13027	BALDWINSVILLE	93	103	114	105	102	104	100	98	96	100	121	115	103	124	100	94	119	98	92	108
13028	BERNHARDS BAY	77	67	50	64	72	77	63	70	67	63	81	83	61	83	64	69	77	68	76	91
13029	BREWERTON	86	98	103	98	96	97	93	92	88	92	111	108	95	114	93	85	109	91	84	101
13030	BRIDGEPORT	87	85	76	81	88	95	81	85	84	80	103	99	82	108	83	86	99	83	90	102
13031	CAMILLUS	88	103	115	101	101	107	98	97	95	97	119	111	103	123	100	95	118	96	94	106
13032	CANASTOTA	81	74	61	70	77	85	71	77	76	70	92	89	70	94	73	78	88	75	84	94
13033	CATO	92	82	63	78	86	92	76	84	80	76	98	100	74	99	78	82	93	82	90	108
13034	CAYUGA	83	78	66	74	81	88	74	79	78	73	95	92	74	98	76	80	91	78	85	97
13035	CAZENOVIA	113	124	136	124	124	130	119	119	116	118	145	139	122	148	121	115	142	118	115	135
13036	CENTRAL SQUARE	84	73	57	71	76	83	72	77	75	71	92	90	69	91	72	76	87	76	82	94
13037	CHITTENANGO	98	97	87	95	98	103	92	96	92	92	114	113	92	116	92	91	110	94	96	114
13039	CICERO	102	111	110	113	109	110	104	104	99	106	125	122	106	126	103	96	122	102	96	117
13040	CINCINNATUS	80	66	47	63	70	77	65	72	70	65	85	84	61	83	65	72	79	71	79	90
13041	CLAY	95	110	112	110	107	106	101	101	95	102	119	118	105	123	101	91	118	98	90	111
13042	CLEVELAND	82	73	56	69	77	83	67	75	72	67	87	89	66	89	69	73	83	73	81	96
13044	CONSTANTIA	79	70	53	66	74	79	65	72	69	65	83	85	63	85	66	70	79	70	78	92
13045	CORTLAND	63	58	63	59	58	64	65	63	66	63	81	75	63	80	63	64	79	65	63	71
13052	DE RUYTER	81	66	47	63	71	78	65	72	70	64	84	85	60	83	65	73	79	71	81	92
13053	DRYDEN	74	84	96	86	84	85	81	80	77	80	96	94	83	100	81	75	95	79	73	88
13054	DURHAMVILLE	75	73	65	69	75	82	69	73	73	68	89	84	70	94	71	75	85	71	79	88
13057	EAST SYRACUSE	86	90	92	88	91	98	88	89	88	86	109	102	90	112	90	89	106	88	91	100
13060	ELBRIDGE	80	87	86	85	86	89	82	83	80	82	99	96	83	101	83	78	98	82	79	94
13061	ERIEVILLE	92	95	90	95	94	95	90	92	87	91	109	109	89	109	89	84	106	91	86	106
13063	FABIUS	96	101	95	100	102	104	93	96	91	93	113	114	95	117	94	90	110	94	93	113
13066	FAYETTEVILLE	137	165	195	165	163	171	154	152	146	154	183	174	163	188	159	145	182	150	144	166
13068	FREEVILLE	80	84	90	86	82	84	84	82	81	84	102	99	84	102	82	77	100	84	76	92
13069	FULTON	72	67	61	65	68	74	68	70	70	67	86	81	66	86	68	71	83	70	73	82
13071	GENOA	83	67	48	66	72	81	68	76	74	67	89	88	63	88	68	76	83	74	84	94
13072	GEORGETOWN	79	62	41	58	67	76	61	70	68	60	81	82	56	80	62	71	75	69	81	91
13073	GROTON	85	77	65	76	81	87	76	81	79	75	96	95	74	98	76	79	92	80	85	98
13074	HANNIBAL	87	73	53	69	76	82	70	78	74	72	91	91	65	86	70	75	86	78	83	98
13076	HASTINGS	85	77	60	74	79	84	72	79	75	74	92	92	70	90	73	75	88	78	81	97
13077	HOMER	81	85	84	83	86	91	81	83	81	80	100	97	83	104	83	81	98	81	83	96
13078	JAMESVILLE	127	145	155	144	144	150	135	136	130	134	162	157	141	167	138	129	160	133	131	152
13080	JORDAN	87	84	74	82	85	92	81	85	82	80	101	98	80	103	81	83	97	83	87	99
13081	KING FERRY	112	87	58	79	98	110	82	99	93	82	110	116	73	109	87	99	102	98	117	135
13082	KIRKVILLE	91	91	82	88	91	95	86	90	85	87	106	104	85	106	86	85	103	88	88	104
13083	LACONA	77	63	47	61	69	77	63	71	69	62	82	82	58	81	64	71	77	70	80	90
13084	LA FAYETTE	100	112	112	110	112	115	102	105	100	102	124	123	107	131	105	99	122	102	101	121
13088	LIVERPOOL	79	87	99	88	85	90	86	84	83	85	105	98	88	107	86	82	103	84	79	92
13090	LIVERPOOL	98	105	109	107	101	103	101	100	96	103	122	118	103	121	99	92	120	100	90	111
13092	LOCKE	82	74	57	71	75	80	71	76	72	72	89	88	67	85	70	72	85	76	77	91
13101	MC GRAW	90	88	79	84	90	98	85	88	88	84	108	102	85	112	86	90	104	87	94	105
13103	MALLORY	82	74	58	72	74	79	71	76	72	73	89	88	67	84	70	71	85	76	76	90
13104	MANLIUS	137	159	180	160	157	163	150	148	143	150	180	171	158	186	153	141	179	146	140	163
13108	MARCELLUS	102	117	128	116	116	120	110	110	107	110	134	128	115	140	113	106	132	109	106	123
13110	MARIETTA	91	106	110	106	103	103	99	98	93	99	117	115	102	121	98	89	116	96	87	107
13111	MARTVILLE	72	65	51	63	66	70	62	67	63	64	78	77	59	74	62	63	75	66	67	80
13112	MEMPHIS	90	99	101	97	98	103	94	95	92	93	114	109	97	118	95	91	112	93	91	106
13114	MEXICO	85	73	54	70	76	84	70	78	75	70	91	91	67	90	71	77	86	76	84	97
13116	MINOA	77	92	101	90	91	95	85	85	82	85	103	97	91	108	88	82	102	83	82	93
13118	MORAVIA	62	50	34	47	54	60	50	56	54	49	65	65	45	62	50	56	61	56	63	71
13120	NEDROW	96	110	113	109	108	111	102	101	99	102	124	116	107	131	103	98	122	99	97	111
13122	NEW WOODSTOCK	120	130	123	127	131	133	117	122	115	117	142	144	121	149	120	114	139	118	118	144
13124	NORTH PITCHER	83	57	29	50	65	74	55	68	66	56	77	81	47	74	57	71	70	68	84	96
	NEW YORK	95	100	134	99	98	107	103	100	105	103	133	116	105	138	104	107	131	102	99	112
	UNITED STATES	100	100	100	100	100	100	100	100	100	100	100	100	100	100	100	100	100	100	100	100

# POST OFFICE NAME	COUNTY FIPS CODE	POPULATION 2000	2004	2009	2000-2004 ANNUAL RATE % Rate	State Centile	HOUSEHOLDS 2000	2004	2009	% Annual Rate 2000-2004	2004 Average HH Size	FAMILIES 2000	2004	% Annual Rate 2000-2004
13126 OSWEGO	075	37221	37860	39026	0.4	52	13522	13949	14623	0.7	2.45	8483	8710	0.6
13131 PARISH	075	3732	3828	3973	0.6	61	1306	1362	1434	1.0	2.81	1009	1045	0.8
13132 PENNELLVILLE	075	4481	4563	4688	0.4	53	1624	1685	1759	0.9	2.71	1248	1286	0.7
13135 PHOENIX	075	6034	6069	6177	0.1	37	2305	2359	2442	0.6	2.57	1644	1672	0.4
13136 PITCHER	017	592	591	602	0.0	26	205	208	214	0.3	2.73	153	154	0.2
13140 PORT BYRON	011	4954	4977	4990	0.1	36	1800	1842	1877	0.5	2.70	1347	1369	0.4
13141 PREBLE	023	861	828	824	-0.9	2	319	312	315	-0.5	2.65	231	225	-0.6
13142 PULASKI	075	7108	7351	7624	0.8	70	2748	2884	3034	1.1	2.54	1899	1975	0.9
13143 RED CREEK	117	3380	3404	3429	0.2	39	1052	1076	1099	0.5	2.89	751	763	0.4
13144 RICHLAND	075	1191	1228	1271	0.7	67	388	407	428	1.1	2.83	289	300	0.9
13145 SANDY CREEK	075	1562	1553	1588	-0.1	21	633	640	665	0.3	2.43	421	421	0.0
13146 SAVANNAH	117	2366	2345	2365	-0.2	17	844	845	862	0.0	2.69	632	630	-0.1
13147 SCIPIO CENTER	011	1619	1608	1605	-0.2	20	594	601	610	0.3	2.68	444	446	0.1
13148 SENECA FALLS	099	10763	10792	11065	0.1	32	4329	4401	4579	0.4	2.38	2860	2887	0.2
13152 SKANEATELES	067	8756	8778	8782	0.1	32	3432	3505	3566	0.5	2.50	2500	2535	0.3
13155 SOUTH OTSELIC	017	666	671	682	0.2	40	240	244	252	0.4	2.71	185	188	0.4
13156 STERLING	011	2351	2277	2260	-0.8	3	960	944	951	-0.4	2.41	676	659	-0.6
13158 TRUXTON	023	1419	1407	1409	-0.2	18	510	512	520	0.1	2.74	388	388	0.0
13159 TULLY	067	5285	5273	5266	-0.1	25	1981	2009	2039	0.3	2.60	1454	1464	0.2
13160 UNION SPRINGS	011	1894	1921	1932	0.3	49	729	752	768	0.7	2.55	520	531	0.5
13164 WARNERS	067	1428	1452	1462	0.4	51	523	544	558	0.9	2.67	404	417	0.8
13165 WATERLOO	099	11153	11144	11384	0.0	26	4257	4323	4484	0.4	2.49	2939	2962	0.2
13166 WEEDSPORT	011	5844	5843	5844	0.0	28	2155	2188	2222	0.4	2.64	1567	1578	0.2
13167 WEST MONROE	075	3782	3886	4032	0.6	64	1321	1384	1460	1.1	2.81	1018	1061	1.0
13202 SYRACUSE	067	5495	5261	5189	-1.0	1	2396	2300	2290	-1.0	1.90	904	853	-1.4
13203 SYRACUSE	067	15846	15814	15897	-0.1	25	7427	7480	7612	0.2	2.02	3237	3233	0.0
13204 SYRACUSE	067	21260	20609	20412	-0.7	3	8745	8593	8631	-0.4	2.36	4714	4561	-0.8
13205 SYRACUSE	067	20386	19918	19826	-0.5	5	7797	7720	7794	-0.2	2.50	4638	4531	-0.6
13206 SYRACUSE	067	16566	16150	16050	-0.6	4	7812	7767	7847	-0.1	2.07	4009	3924	-0.5
13207 SYRACUSE	067	14828	14511	14427	-0.5	6	5566	5522	5564	-0.2	2.61	3770	3703	-0.4
13208 SYRACUSE	067	21127	21306	21455	0.2	40	9037	9214	9399	0.5	2.30	4962	5002	0.2
13209 SYRACUSE	067	13548	13648	13768	0.2	39	5581	5715	5855	0.6	2.39	3671	3734	0.4
13210 SYRACUSE	067	24779	24233	24086	-0.5	6	9426	9344	9432	-0.2	2.11	3286	3201	-0.6
13211 SYRACUSE	067	6400	6345	6325	-0.2	18	2634	2656	2690	0.2	2.39	1677	1669	-0.1
13212 SYRACUSE	067	20812	20594	20572	-0.3	15	8527	8640	8797	0.3	2.37	5753	5775	0.1
13214 SYRACUSE	067	8865	9033	9154	0.4	54	3128	3265	3377	1.0	2.28	2068	2143	0.7
13215 SYRACUSE	067	14404	14757	14955	0.6	61	5217	5414	5562	0.9	2.61	3727	3840	0.7
13219 SYRACUSE	067	15587	15410	15410	-0.3	15	6230	6315	6437	0.3	2.39	4388	4394	0.0
13224 SYRACUSE	067	9424	9258	9205	-0.4	9	3936	3939	3986	0.0	2.31	2466	2439	-0.3
13244 SYRACUSE	067	2119	2123	2124	0.0	30	35	36	37	0.7	3.61	4	4	0.0
13301 ALDER CREEK	065	50	50	50	0.0	28	24	24	24	0.0	1.92	16	16	0.0
13302 ALTMAR	075	1722	1944	2111	2.9	98	596	685	755	3.3	2.81	447	510	3.2
13303 AVA	065	1346	1328	1321	-0.3	13	509	509	510	0.0	2.61	385	383	-0.1
13304 BARNEVELD	065	1793	1786	1782	-0.1	23	699	706	709	0.2	2.52	515	517	0.1
13308 BLOSSVALE	065	5139	5086	5060	-0.2	16	2020	2024	2028	0.1	2.34	1406	1398	-0.1
13309 BOONVILLE	065	6518	6495	6496	-0.1	24	2486	2516	2542	0.3	2.51	1736	1744	0.1
13310 BOUCKVILLE	053	305	316	324	0.8	72	133	143	150	1.7	1.83	96	103	1.7
13314 BROOKFIELD	053	132	133	134	0.2	40	47	48	49	0.5	2.77	36	37	0.7
13315 BURLINGTON FLATS	077	1372	1415	1432	0.7	68	503	525	539	1.0	2.67	381	396	0.9
13316 CAMDEN	065	6992	6983	6976	0.0	26	2557	2592	2611	0.3	2.66	1856	1870	0.2
13317 CANAJOHARIE	057	3840	3843	3841	0.0	30	1501	1516	1530	0.2	2.51	1034	1040	0.1
13318 CASSVILLE	065	1892	1911	1918	0.2	43	664	679	685	0.5	2.81	507	516	0.4
13319 CHADWICKS	065	743	738	735	-0.2	20	299	302	303	0.2	2.44	217	217	0.0
13320 CHERRY VALLEY	077	1899	1928	1934	0.4	50	741	763	775	0.7	2.52	547	559	0.5
13322 CLAYVILLE	043	1275	1296	1308	0.4	51	463	478	487	0.8	2.71	348	358	0.7
13323 CLINTON	065	12051	12096	12127	0.1	34	4149	4218	4260	0.4	2.43	2742	2769	0.2
13324 COLD BROOK	043	1929	2003	2045	0.9	74	745	790	816	1.4	2.53	533	559	1.1
13325 CONSTABLEVILLE	049	978	981	990	0.1	33	366	374	385	0.5	2.62	258	262	0.4
13326 COOPERSTOWN	077	5590	5603	5596	0.1	31	2278	2307	2331	0.3	2.28	1433	1442	0.2
13327 CROGHAN	049	1975	2013	2048	0.5	55	697	722	747	0.8	2.79	540	557	0.7
13328 DEANSBORO	065	1106	1112	1113	0.1	37	425	436	440	0.6	2.27	299	305	0.5
13329 DOLGEVILLE	043	3887	3829	3806	-0.4	11	1558	1556	1558	0.0	2.44	1069	1060	-0.2
13331 EAGLE BAY	043	708	701	697	-0.2	16	313	315	315	0.2	2.17	199	198	-0.1
13332 EARLVILLE	053	2819	2785	2802	-0.3	14	1055	1056	1077	0.0	2.60	758	753	-0.2
13333 EAST SPRINGFIELD	077	114	116	117	0.4	52	44	45	46	0.5	2.58	32	33	0.7
13334 EATON	053	1343	1364	1383	0.4	50	482	501	518	0.9	2.10	336	348	0.8
13335 EDMESTON	077	1606	1695	1740	1.3	84	571	613	638	1.7	2.65	419	447	1.5
13337 FLY CREEK	077	770	762	754	-0.3	15	313	313	314	0.0	2.43	218	216	-0.2
13338 FORESTPORT	043	1326	1309	1300	-0.3	14	570	572	573	0.1	2.28	373	371	-0.1
13339 FORT PLAIN	057	6411	6378	6363	-0.1	22	2467	2475	2493	0.1	2.56	1714	1713	0.1
13340 FRANKFORT	043	8123	8166	8193	0.1	36	3249	3310	3351	0.4	2.46	2295	2327	0.3
13342 GARRATTSVILLE	077	103	107	108	0.9	74	46	48	50	1.0	2.23	34	35	0.7
13343 GLENFIELD	049	1949	2005	2055	0.7	65	768	802	836	1.0	2.50	562	584	0.9
13345 GREIG	049	453	458	464	0.3	44	183	188	194	0.6	2.43	132	135	0.5
13346 HAMILTON	053	5564	5713	5856	0.6	63	1537	1626	1713	1.3	2.25	919	982	1.6
13348 HARTWICK	077	1550	1561	1559	0.2	39	578	589	596	0.4	2.65	425	431	0.3
13350 HERKIMER	043	9941	9841	9790	-0.2	16	4128	4129	4131	0.0	2.26	2400	2379	-0.2
13353 HOFFMEISTER	041	151	152	150	0.2	38	65	66	66	0.4	2.30	46	46	0.1
13354 HOLLAND PATENT	065	3637	3651	3655	0.1	34	1328	1352	1363	0.4	2.68	991	1002	0.3
13355 HUBBARDSVILLE	053	736	820	872	2.6	97	264	298	320	2.9	2.72	194	216	2.6
13357 ILION	043	11256	11310	11338	0.1	36	4428	4500	4541	0.4	2.48	2968	2994	0.2
13360 INLET	041	406	403	398	-0.2	19	188	191	193	0.4	2.10	129	130	0.2
13361 JORDANVILLE	043	729	750	760	0.7	65	269	281	287	1.0	2.63	201	209	0.9
13363 LEE CENTER	065	2293	2268	2254	-0.3	15	855	859	861	0.1	2.64	650	650	0.0
13365 LITTLE FALLS	043	9378	9061	8919	-0.8	2	3887	3797	3763	-0.6	2.34	2435	2363	-0.7
13367 LOWVILLE	049	8343	8534	8715	0.5	59	3167	3290	3417	0.9	2.53	2202	2277	0.8
13368 LYONS FALLS	049	1053	1040	1046	-0.3	14	401	403	412	0.1	2.57	282	282	0.0
13402 MADISON	053	1692	1742	1786	0.7	66	668	700	727	1.1	2.47	461	479	0.9
13403 MARCY	065	8032	8094	8121	0.2	40	1445	1493	1518	0.8	2.78	1102	1134	0.7
13406 MIDDLEVILLE	043	283	280	278	-0.3	15	104	104	105	0.0	2.63	80	79	-0.3
13407 MOHAWK	043	5589	5466	5420	-0.5	6	2222	2202	2198	-0.2	2.43	1503	1481	-0.4
13408 MORRISVILLE	053	3973	4029	4079	0.3	49	1009	1039	1068	0.7	3.11	715	731	0.5
13409 MUNNSVILLE	053	2069	2273	2395	2.2	95	735	824	882	2.7	2.68	562	626	2.6
13411 NEW BERLIN	017	3443	3505	3571	0.4	53	1296	1336	1381	0.7	2.56	905	928	0.6
13413 NEW HARTFORD	065	16053	16174	16235	0.2	40	6403	6554	6634	0.6	2.32	4235	4298	0.4
NEW YORK					0.4					0.5	2.60			0.4
UNITED STATES					1.2					1.3	2.58			1.1

#	POST OFFICE NAME	RACE (%) White 2000	White 2004	Black 2000	Black 2004	Asian/Pacific 2000	Asian/Pacific 2004	% Hispanic Origin 2000	% Hispanic Origin 2004	2004 AGE DISTRIBUTION (%) 0-4	5-9	10-14	15-19	20-24	25-44	45-64	65-84	85+	18+	MEDIAN AGE 2004	% 2004 Males	% 2004 Females
13126	OSWEGO	95.8	95.0	1.1	1.2	0.8	1.0	2.2	2.7	5.3	5.5	6.8	10.3	13.3	24.6	22.1	10.2	1.9	78.3	33.0	48.4	51.6
13131	PARISH	98.6	98.4	0.3	0.3	0.1	0.2	0.5	0.6	6.7	6.9	8.6	7.9	6.8	29.0	24.3	9.0	0.8	72.9	36.1	49.8	50.2
13132	PENNELLVILLE	97.7	97.3	0.4	0.5	0.3	0.4	0.8	0.9	6.4	6.8	8.1	7.4	6.1	28.1	27.6	8.9	0.7	73.7	37.9	50.9	49.1
13135	PHOENIX	97.4	96.9	0.5	0.6	0.6	0.7	1.1	1.3	6.5	6.7	7.5	7.6	6.3	26.5	27.7	10.1	1.1	74.4	38.4	49.2	50.8
13136	PITCHER	96.1	95.4	2.7	3.1	0.2	0.2	2.0	2.4	6.1	6.8	6.9	7.8	6.8	28.1	26.1	10.2	1.4	75.1	37.2	53.6	46.4
13140	PORT BYRON	97.5	97.0	0.6	0.7	0.1	0.2	1.0	1.3	6.4	6.4	7.4	7.6	6.7	27.1	26.1	11.0	1.2	75.2	38.0	49.0	51.0
13141	PREBLE	98.6	98.4	0.2	0.2	0.2	0.2	0.5	0.5	6.0	6.9	7.5	7.0	5.9	24.2	31.3	10.3	1.0	75.2	40.2	51.5	48.6
13142	PULASKI	98.3	98.0	0.2	0.2	0.3	0.4	0.7	0.8	6.7	6.7	8.2	7.3	6.8	26.1	25.7	11.0	1.6	73.9	37.3	49.5	50.5
13143	RED CREEK	91.4	90.3	5.7	6.3	0.2	0.2	3.4	4.1	6.3	6.3	7.6	7.9	6.8	31.6	24.2	8.6	0.9	74.7	35.9	54.9	45.1
13144	RICHLAND	97.7	97.4	0.8	1.0	0.1	0.1	1.1	1.3	6.4	6.8	8.6	7.7	6.1	26.8	27.6	9.5	0.5	72.8	36.8	54.6	45.4
13145	SANDY CREEK	98.0	97.6	0.1	0.2	0.1	0.1	0.5	0.6	5.7	6.1	7.4	6.4	5.2	26.8	26.9	13.8	1.7	76.7	40.7	50.6	49.5
13146	SAVANNAH	94.3	93.3	3.1	3.5	0.3	0.3	1.8	2.3	7.0	7.3	7.9	7.0	6.4	27.5	24.9	10.8	1.3	73.4	36.4	51.2	48.8
13147	SCIPIO CENTER	97.7	97.0	0.2	0.3	0.5	0.7	1.4	2.0	4.9	6.1	9.1	9.0	6.0	25.6	27.6	10.8	0.9	73.9	38.2	50.5	49.5
13148	SENECA FALLS	96.2	95.5	0.8	0.8	1.3	1.7	1.3	1.5	5.7	5.7	6.8	6.9	6.7	28.0	25.1	13.4	1.9	77.3	38.5	49.6	50.4
13152	SKANEATELES	98.9	98.7	0.1	0.2	0.3	0.4	0.4	0.5	5.0	6.1	7.6	7.5	4.4	21.0	31.8	14.6	2.1	76.3	44.1	49.4	50.6
13155	SOUTH OTSELIC	97.6	97.3	0.9	0.9	0.2	0.2	2.4	3.0	7.9	7.9	7.9	7.5	7.0	26.8	24.1	10.0	0.9	71.7	35.7	52.2	47.8
13156	STERLING	98.3	97.9	0.1	0.1	0.0	0.0	0.5	0.7	5.5	6.0	7.4	6.0	4.8	24.8	30.1	14.1	1.3	77.3	42.0	50.4	49.6
13158	TRUXTON	97.5	96.9	0.3	0.4	0.2	0.2	0.9	1.1	6.8	7.4	9.1	7.3	6.0	27.2	25.8	9.2	1.1	72.1	36.6	50.7	49.3
13159	TULLY	97.1	96.5	0.5	0.6	0.5	0.7	0.9	1.2	6.8	7.5	8.3	7.2	5.0	26.8	28.0	9.4	1.0	72.7	38.3	49.4	50.6
13160	UNION SPRINGS	98.1	97.6	0.7	0.8	0.2	0.3	0.7	0.8	5.3	5.6	7.5	7.1	5.5	25.6	27.1	14.7	1.6	77.0	41.1	48.8	51.2
13164	WARNERS	98.3	97.9	0.3	0.4	0.2	0.2	0.8	1.0	6.1	6.5	6.8	7.0	6.0	26.1	28.9	11.2	1.5	76.5	39.8	51.0	49.0
13165	WATERLOO	97.3	96.9	0.8	0.8	0.4	0.6	1.5	1.8	5.8	6.2	7.4	6.5	5.6	25.9	26.5	13.6	2.6	76.6	40.2	47.9	52.1
13166	WEEDSPORT	97.7	97.1	0.3	0.4	0.4	0.6	0.7	0.9	6.6	6.8	8.3	7.8	6.4	27.1	25.0	10.6	1.3	73.4	37.3	49.0	51.0
13167	WEST MONROE	97.4	96.9	0.2	0.2	0.3	0.4	0.4	0.5	6.3	7.9	9.3	8.1	4.9	31.2	24.9	6.7	0.7	71.2	35.3	51.9	48.1
13202	SYRACUSE	28.3	24.8	59.5	61.8	5.0	5.6	9.6	10.6	10.0	6.6	6.7	7.9	11.4	33.8	17.2	5.8	0.7	72.9	28.3	53.1	46.9
13203	SYRACUSE	75.2	70.9	13.8	16.4	4.3	5.0	3.9	4.8	6.6	5.8	6.2	6.0	8.5	30.2	21.4	11.9	3.3	78.0	35.8	48.1	52.0
13204	SYRACUSE	63.5	59.4	21.8	24.1	0.7	0.8	13.1	14.9	9.5	8.4	8.7	7.5	7.9	28.6	18.6	9.3	1.5	68.7	30.3	47.8	52.2
13205	SYRACUSE	41.4	37.7	50.5	53.3	2.0	2.5	3.3	3.6	7.4	7.8	9.1	8.1	6.9	23.9	20.4	13.1	3.5	70.3	34.7	45.0	55.0
13206	SYRACUSE	88.1	85.6	6.9	8.4	1.2	1.5	2.4	3.0	6.1	5.7	6.0	5.5	6.2	30.9	23.8	13.6	2.2	78.9	38.9	47.2	52.8
13207	SYRACUSE	59.1	55.6	33.7	36.5	0.5	0.7	4.4	5.0	7.9	8.2	9.5	8.2	6.7	26.6	22.8	9.0	1.3	69.3	33.3	46.0	54.0
13208	SYRACUSE	81.5	78.3	6.9	8.2	5.6	6.6	3.1	3.8	7.6	7.0	7.2	6.7	7.0	28.6	21.1	12.4	2.6	74.1	35.6	47.3	52.7
13209	SYRACUSE	96.6	95.9	0.7	0.9	0.5	0.7	1.6	2.1	6.3	6.4	7.0	6.4	5.9	26.5	25.1	14.5	2.1	76.5	39.7	46.9	53.1
13210	SYRACUSE	64.4	59.9	22.9	25.3	7.4	8.7	4.4	5.1	4.1	3.9	4.5	15.3	30.9	21.9	11.7	5.8	1.8	84.8	23.6	48.2	51.8
13211	SYRACUSE	94.3	92.8	1.8	2.3	0.8	1.0	2.1	2.8	5.8	5.8	7.3	7.5	6.7	28.4	23.0	13.4	2.1	76.4	38.2	48.2	51.8
13212	SYRACUSE	95.1	93.9	1.7	2.2	1.1	1.4	0.9	1.2	6.0	6.2	6.9	6.2	5.7	26.7	25.1	15.2	2.1	77.1	40.3	47.5	52.5
13214	SYRACUSE	82.9	79.6	11.2	13.2	3.0	3.8	1.9	2.4	4.7	5.2	5.7	11.6	11.5	18.7	23.4	15.8	3.5	81.0	38.9	45.4	54.6
13215	SYRACUSE	95.5	94.4	1.5	1.9	1.3	1.7	1.1	1.4	5.8	6.8	8.0	6.9	4.9	23.3	27.0	13.7	3.7	75.0	41.8	48.2	51.8
13219	SYRACUSE	96.7	95.7	0.9	1.1	0.9	1.2	1.1	1.5	5.3	5.8	6.5	6.1	4.7	22.3	26.3	19.1	3.8	78.4	44.6	46.6	53.4
13224	SYRACUSE	56.0	51.2	36.9	40.6	2.8	3.4	3.1	3.5	6.2	6.5	8.1	7.2	5.8	24.3	26.8	13.1	2.1	74.4	39.2	46.4	53.6
13244	SYRACUSE	85.0	81.2	5.0	6.2	5.8	7.3	4.1	5.3	0.1	0.1	0.1	63.5	34.5	1.2	0.4	0.2	0.0	99.3	18.9	46.2	53.8
13301	ALDER CREEK	100.0	100.0	0.0	0.0	0.0	0.0	0.0	0.0	6.0	4.0	4.0	4.0	4.0	28.0	28.0	16.0	6.0	86.0	45.0	46.0	54.0
13302	ALTMAR	98.1	97.9	0.4	0.4	0.2	0.2	0.6	0.7	7.7	7.9	9.0	7.6	6.7	26.7	25.4	8.3	0.9	70.7	34.8	48.7	51.3
13303	AVA	97.7	97.1	0.5	0.5	0.4	0.5	0.6	0.8	5.8	6.3	8.4	6.9	5.7	28.0	26.1	11.3	1.5	75.3	39.3	51.5	48.5
13304	BARNEVELD	98.1	97.5	0.5	0.6	0.5	0.6	0.4	0.5	5.5	6.2	7.9	7.5	5.7	24.4	29.3	12.5	1.1	75.7	40.9	49.9	50.1
13308	BLOSSVALE	93.3	92.5	4.1	4.4	0.5	0.6	2.7	3.2	5.6	5.9	7.3	6.5	6.5	30.6	26.3	10.3	1.0	77.1	37.9	54.0	46.1
13309	BOONVILLE	99.1	98.9	0.2	0.2	0.1	0.2	0.2	0.3	5.7	5.8	6.7	7.6	6.4	26.6	25.3	13.4	2.4	76.7	39.9	49.5	50.5
13310	BOUCKVILLE	91.8	90.8	5.6	6.0	1.0	1.3	1.3	1.9	5.4	5.4	6.7	13.9	11.1	23.1	20.6	11.4	2.5	78.2	32.1	49.7	50.3
13314	BROOKFIELD	97.7	97.7	0.8	0.8	0.0	0.0	0.0	0.8	6.8	6.8	7.5	8.3	6.0	27.8	26.3	9.8	0.8	73.7	36.3	48.1	51.9
13315	BURLINGTON FLATS	97.2	96.6	0.5	0.6	0.3	0.4	1.5	1.9	5.5	6.0	7.8	8.5	5.1	26.9	26.1	12.5	1.6	75.3	39.1	50.5	49.5
13316	CAMDEN	98.1	97.6	0.4	0.5	0.4	0.5	0.7	1.0	6.2	6.4	7.8	7.4	6.6	26.5	26.4	11.3	1.4	74.7	38.3	50.6	49.4
13317	CANAJOHARIE	97.1	97.0	0.6	0.6	0.5	0.5	1.2	1.2	5.8	6.1	7.9	7.5	6.1	24.9	25.8	13.7	2.2	75.0	39.6	48.8	51.2
13318	CASSVILLE	97.5	97.0	0.6	0.8	0.6	0.8	1.0	1.2	7.2	7.4	9.7	8.5	5.2	29.3	24.0	8.2	0.5	70.1	35.6	50.9	49.1
13319	CHADWICKS	96.1	94.9	0.7	0.8	2.7	3.7	0.4	0.7	5.2	5.8	7.6	7.3	5.2	22.9	29.0	15.5	1.6	76.2	42.5	47.8	52.2
13320	CHERRY VALLEY	98.5	98.1	0.1	0.1	0.4	0.5	1.0	1.1	4.2	6.2	9.1	8.7	4.1	24.9	27.9	13.4	1.6	73.9	41.3	50.2	49.8
13322	CLAYVILLE	98.5	98.2	0.3	0.4	0.2	0.3	0.5	0.7	5.7	6.4	8.4	7.8	5.6	25.6	28.9	10.3	1.2	74.5	39.2	50.9	49.1
13323	CLINTON	96.6	95.8	1.1	1.3	1.1	1.4	1.2	1.6	3.8	4.3	6.2	11.9	11.7	20.0	25.6	13.6	2.9	81.4	39.0	48.1	51.9
13324	COLD BROOK	97.3	96.9	0.5	0.6	0.5	0.6	0.6	0.7	5.6	6.3	7.6	7.0	5.3	27.8	28.9	10.6	0.9	75.7	39.5	52.0	48.0
13325	CONSTABLEVILLE	99.3	99.3	0.0	0.0	0.1	0.2	0.1	0.1	6.5	6.4	7.3	7.2	5.8	27.1	25.2	13.2	1.2	74.5	38.8	49.0	51.0
13326	COOPERSTOWN	97.2	96.6	0.8	0.8	0.8	1.1	1.6	1.9	4.6	5.1	7.0	6.8	5.0	22.1	28.6	16.7	4.1	78.7	44.6	47.8	52.2
13327	CROGHAN	98.9	98.7	0.2	0.2	0.3	0.3	0.6	0.8	6.1	6.6	9.1	9.2	6.4	26.7	24.4	10.3	1.2	72.2	36.2	50.0	50.0
13328	DEANSBORO	97.4	96.8	0.9	1.1	0.6	0.8	0.9	1.3	4.6	4.8	6.3	12.1	12.7	23.1	24.6	10.3	1.5	79.7	34.9	49.6	50.4
13329	DOLGEVILLE	97.8	97.6	0.4	0.4	0.4	0.5	0.8	0.9	6.0	6.1	6.8	6.8	6.6	25.0	27.2	13.4	2.2	76.6	39.7	49.3	50.7
13331	EAGLE BAY	97.9	97.3	0.7	1.0	0.3	0.3	0.7	1.0	3.9	4.4	6.4	5.7	4.6	26.0	31.4	15.4	2.3	81.5	44.5	49.5	50.5
13332	EARLVILLE	98.0	97.7	0.7	0.9	0.3	0.4	1.1	1.4	6.0	6.8	8.3	8.0	5.6	26.3	26.7	11.3	1.2	74.2	38.4	49.2	50.8
13333	EAST SPRINGFIELD	98.3	99.1	0.0	0.0	0.0	0.0	0.9	0.9	4.3	6.0	8.6	8.6	4.3	25.9	27.6	12.9	1.7	75.0	41.5	48.3	51.7
13334	EATON	91.7	90.5	5.4	6.1	0.9	1.2	1.9	2.1	4.3	4.6	7.0	19.6	13.3	20.3	19.4	9.8	1.8	79.7	26.5	51.0	49.1
13335	EDMESTON	98.2	97.8	0.4	0.5	0.1	0.1	1.0	1.3	6.8	7.3	7.8	6.3	5.0	27.5	25.3	12.5	1.7	74.1	38.3	50.7	49.3
13337	FLY CREEK	98.3	98.0	0.8	0.9	0.3	0.3	0.8	1.1	4.3	5.9	7.2	7.4	4.5	20.5	34.1	14.2	2.0	77.4	45.1	50.0	50.0
13338	FORESTPORT	98.5	98.2	0.4	0.5	0.2	0.2	0.1	0.2	5.1	5.5	6.2	5.5	4.2	23.2	32.1	17.0	1.2	79.6	45.2	50.9	49.1
13339	FORT PLAIN	98.4	98.3	0.2	0.3	0.5	0.5	1.0	1.0	6.2	6.3	7.2	7.0	5.9	25.5	25.7	14.2	2.2	75.7	39.6	49.5	50.5
13340	FRANKFORT	97.9	97.4	0.4	0.5	0.2	0.3	0.9	1.1	5.6	5.9	7.3	6.6	5.8	26.3	26.5	13.4	2.5	77.0	40.5	47.8	52.2
13342	GARRATTSVILLE	97.1	96.3	1.0	0.9	0.0	0.9	1.9	1.9	5.6	5.6	6.5	7.5	5.6	24.3	30.8	12.2	1.9	76.6	41.6	46.7	53.3
13343	GLENFIELD	98.2	97.9	0.3	0.4	0.7	0.8	0.6	0.8	6.1	6.3	8.0	6.9	5.3	26.9	26.4	13.2	1.0	75.2	39.7	51.1	48.9
13345	GREIG	98.7	98.5	0.7	0.7	0.4	0.4	0.2	0.4	6.1	6.6	7.4	6.3	5.2	25.1	28.0	14.2	1.1	75.8	40.8	50.0	50.0
13346	HAMILTON	93.2	92.2	2.2	2.3	2.6	3.1	1.9	2.3	3.0	3.1	5.0	25.8	21.9	15.3	16.8	7.7	1.5	85.8	23.0	48.2	51.8
13348	HARTWICK	98.0	97.6	0.5	0.5	0.6	0.8	1.1	1.4	4.8	5.8	8.7	9.4	4.5	24.2	28.5	12.4	1.7	74.4	40.6	50.2	49.8
13350	HERKIMER	96.8	96.3	1.0	1.1	1.0	1.3	1.2	1.4	4.8	4.6	6.1	6.4	9.5	23.8	23.5	17.1	4.3	81.5	41.0	47.6	52.4
13353	HOFFMEISTER	99.3	98.7	0.0	0.0	0.0	0.0	0.0	0.7	4.0	3.3	4.0	6.6	5.3	21.1	36.2	17.8	2.0	84.9	48.8	52.0	48.0
13354	HOLLAND PATENT	97.8	97.2	0.5	0.6	0.4	0.6	0.5	0.6	6.1	6.9	8.3	7.3	5.1	25.8	28.2	11.3	1.1	73.8	39.5	50.2	49.9
13355	HUBBARDSVILLE	98.1	97.8	0.5	0.5	0.4	0.5	0.8	1.0	5.9	5.9	7.9	7.2	5.4	25.5	29.2	11.8	1.3	75.5	39.8	50.9	49.2
13357	ILION	97.6	97.2	0.6	0.6	0.2	0.3	1.4	1.7	6.6	6.5	7.5	7.2	7.2	25.5	24.6	12.5	2.4	74.9	37.7	47.2	52.8
13360	INLET	96.3	96.3	0.0	0.0	0.3	0.3	2.5	2.5	6.0	6.0	4.7	3.0	3.0	25.8	30.8	18.6	2.2	81.4	46.1	51.1	48.9
13361	JORDANVILLE	97.8	97.5	0.4	0.4	0.7	0.8	0.6	0.8	5.9	6.5	8.1	7.7	6.0	26.1	26.1	12.0	1.5	74.4	39.1	53.3	46.7
13363	LEE CENTER	97.8	97.3	0.6	0.7	0.3	0.4	0.7	0.9	6.0	6.4	8.6	7.6	6.2	28.2	25.5	10.2	1.2	74.1	37.1	50.2	49.8
13365	LITTLE FALLS	98.1	97.7	0.4	0.4	0.5	0.6	0.5	0.6	6.0	6.1	7.0	6.2	6.3	24.6	25.9	14.9	3.2	77.2	40.8	48.6	51.4
13367	LOWVILLE	97.8	97.4	0.6	0.6	0.5	0.6	0.7	0.9	6.1	6.2	7.6	7.4	6.2	25.7	24.3	13.6	3.0	75.4	39.4	48.5	51.5
13368	LYONS FALLS	98.9	98.8	0.5	0.5	0.0	0.0	0.2	0.2	6.4	6.6	7.2	6.8	6.5	23.8	27.5	13.7	1.4	75.5	40.3	50.7	49.3
13402	MADISON	97.8	97.2	0.3	0.3	0.8	1.0	0.8	1.0	6.7	6.6	6.3	6.4	5.6	26.7	27.7	12.7	1.3	76.1	39.6	50.1	49.9
13403	MARCY	65.3	63.7	24.5	25.0	0.6	0.7	15.5	17.1	2.6	2.8	3.7	4.6	12.2	44.8	21.6	7.3	0.6	88.6	36.0	72.9	27.1
13406	MIDDLEVILLE	98.2	98.6	0.4	0.4	0.0	0.0	0.4	0.4	5.7	6.4	6.8	7.1	6.4	27.1	27.1	12.1	1.1	76.8	39.3	50.4	49.6
13407	MOHAWK	98.6	98.4	0.5	0.5	0.2	0.2	1.2	1.5	5.5	5.8	6.9	6.4	6.0	26.1	27.8	13.5	2.0	78.0	40.8	50.2	49.8
13408	MORRISVILLE	92.4	91.3	4.9	5.4	0.8	1.0	1.6	1.9	4.7	4.8	7.2	18.0	12.7	21.4	20.6	9.2	1.6	78.9	28.0	51.0	49.0
13409	MUNNSVILLE	95.8	95.2	1.2	1.3	0.4	0.6	0.9	1.1	8.0	7.7	7.3	8.2	7.0	27.5	23.2	9.9	1.2	72.2	35.3	50.6	49.4
13411	NEW BERLIN	98.3	98.0	0.3	0.3	0.2	0.3	0.9	1.2	6.3	6.6	7.4	6.7	5.0	24.8	26.6	14.0	2.7	75.5	40.4	48.6	51.4
13413	NEW HARTFORD	95.8	94.7	0.9	1.1	2.5	3.2	0.8	1.0	4.9	5.3	6.4	6.4	4.7	21.4	27.3	18.6	5.0	79.0	45.7	46.4	53.6
	NEW YORK	68.0	65.9	15.9	16.2	5.6	6.4	15.1	16.7	6.5	6.5	7.1	7.0	7.1	28.9	24.0	11.2	1.8	75.8	36.7	48.3	51.7
	UNITED STATES	75.1	73.6	12.3	12.5	3.8	4.2	12.5	14.1	6.9	6.7	7.2	7.0	7.3	28.6	23.8	10.8	1.7	75.1	36.0	49.1	50.9

#	POST OFFICE NAME	2004 Per Capita Income	2004 HH Income Base	2004 Household Income Distribution (%): Less than $25,000	$25,000 to $49,999	$50,000 to $99,999	$100,000 to $149,999	$150,000 or More	Median Household Income: 2004	2009	2004 National Centile	2004 State Centile	2004 Home Value Base	2004 Home Value Distribution (%): Less than $50,000	$50,000 to $89,999	$90,000 to $174,999	$175,000 to $399,999	$400,000 or More	2004 Median Home Value
13126	OSWEGO	19790	13949	34.5	27.2	27.8	8.0	2.6	38074	42645	40	25	9146	12.1	25.3	45.7	16.5	0.4	106234
13131	PARISH	18284	1362	25.0	32.1	34.6	7.3	1.0	43827	48834	58	47	1136	18.0	26.9	46.7	8.4	0.0	95370
13132	PENNELLVILLE	20202	1685	21.5	31.7	36.7	8.1	2.0	47397	53155	67	57	1438	18.3	18.4	50.8	11.9	0.6	106406
13135	PHOENIX	25117	2359	25.4	31.3	29.3	7.9	6.2	44942	50824	61	50	1785	10.4	23.9	46.3	18.3	1.1	107657
13136	PITCHER	16067	208	37.5	33.7	22.6	4.3	1.9	34245	37695	25	10	171	29.8	29.8	32.2	8.2	0.0	72273
13140	PORT BYRON	17328	1842	27.3	36.0	30.4	5.4	0.9	40000	43598	46	34	1472	20.3	32.1	38.3	9.0	0.3	86635
13141	PREBLE	22680	312	16.4	33.3	36.9	10.9	2.6	50224	56212	72	63	264	8.0	8.0	48.9	33.0	2.3	142157
13142	PULASKI	18930	2884	32.3	29.4	29.2	7.7	1.4	39744	43984	45	33	1961	11.1	32.1	48.4	7.9	0.5	96974
13143	RED CREEK	15774	1076	30.8	31.8	31.3	4.5	1.7	39641	44412	45	33	852	19.5	33.7	38.9	7.2	0.8	86301
13144	RICHLAND	16167	407	31.0	30.2	32.4	5.9	0.5	39461	44337	44	32	326	19.3	39.0	39.3	2.5	0.0	79722
13145	SANDY CREEK	19760	640	34.8	27.7	29.7	5.6	2.2	36485	40713	33	18	470	15.1	30.9	37.0	17.0	0.0	98261
13146	SAVANNAH	18584	845	27.5	30.2	35.5	5.8	1.1	43532	49186	57	46	695	24.9	34.5	34.0	6.3	0.3	77609
13147	SCIPIO CENTER	19285	601	23.6	31.5	37.4	6.5	1.0	46081	51165	64	53	502	13.8	24.9	42.0	16.9	2.4	105526
13148	SENECA FALLS	21140	4401	30.7	27.7	32.7	6.9	2.1	41846	46474	52	41	2979	4.7	14.1	60.8	19.4	1.0	126954
13152	SKANEATELES	33134	3505	15.9	23.7	35.7	13.1	11.6	62208	72086	86	77	3004	2.1	5.9	38.0	44.4	9.6	183108
13155	SOUTH OTSELIC	16400	244	33.2	35.3	25.4	4.1	2.1	35412	39685	29	14	198	26.3	24.2	41.4	8.1	0.0	88750
13156	STERLING	19712	944	26.8	38.0	28.1	6.4	0.7	39488	43743	44	32	768	15.1	35.6	35.9	11.3	2.1	89057
13158	TRUXTON	17304	512	27.9	34.2	32.2	3.9	1.8	41036	45468	50	38	419	15.0	19.1	51.1	14.3	0.5	108386
13159	TULLY	26922	2009	16.9	29.6	34.2	11.9	7.4	53272	60983	77	67	1631	5.5	10.6	47.4	34.5	2.2	142337
13160	UNION SPRINGS	23691	752	22.6	26.6	37.8	9.0	4.0	50645	55668	73	63	592	10.0	20.4	42.6	25.5	1.5	117457
13164	WARNERS	25128	544	14.9	25.0	40.8	15.3	4.0	60987	69446	85	75	465	0.7	14.6	68.0	16.6	0.2	118786
13165	WATERLOO	18973	4323	29.4	33.1	30.0	6.3	1.2	39332	43603	44	31	3226	8.7	21.6	52.6	16.2	0.9	116192
13166	WEEDSPORT	21019	2188	22.7	36.8	31.5	6.7	2.2	42689	47491	55	43	1741	26.8	18.9	42.7	10.3	1.3	96802
13167	WEST MONROE	18864	1384	22.9	29.8	39.2	5.6	2.4	46258	51452	64	53	1177	24.8	22.7	44.6	7.8	0.1	93933
13202	SYRACUSE	12755	2300	73.5	17.1	6.7	1.2	1.5	11398	13742	1	1	110	39.1	31.8	19.1	10.0	0.0	63077
13203	SYRACUSE	20034	7480	44.4	32.9	15.7	4.5	2.5	28440	32372	9	4	2390	10.5	31.8	43.4	14.0	0.3	97222
13204	SYRACUSE	14649	8593	52.1	28.0	16.2	2.6	1.1	23526	26487	4	3	2898	18.1	47.3	31.4	2.9	0.2	76952
13205	SYRACUSE	14981	7720	48.8	28.0	18.0	3.9	1.3	25726	29292	5	3	3432	12.5	48.7	37.4	1.3	0.2	80660
13206	SYRACUSE	22174	7767	36.5	29.3	27.1	5.3	1.9	35804	41114	31	16	4167	4.7	32.1	61.4	1.7	0.0	96453
13207	SYRACUSE	21157	5522	31.2	28.3	28.8	8.6	3.2	41810	47191	52	41	3438	5.4	42.2	46.8	5.6	0.1	92019
13208	SYRACUSE	17270	9214	42.2	33.3	19.2	4.1	1.2	29967	34114	12	5	4554	6.7	43.8	48.0	1.3	0.2	89633
13209	SYRACUSE	23100	5715	24.0	33.3	31.6	7.9	3.2	43796	50734	58	47	4213	3.4	22.9	64.6	8.6	0.5	107293
13210	SYRACUSE	16078	9344	56.3	21.9	15.5	4.4	1.9	20917	23150	2	2	2373	5.9	21.4	65.6	7.1	0.1	106851
13211	SYRACUSE	22040	2656	28.2	32.0	30.7	6.7	2.3	39951	46130	46	34	1867	1.6	56.7	40.2	1.6	0.0	86118
13212	SYRACUSE	24093	8640	23.1	31.0	34.4	8.2	3.3	46419	53773	65	54	6424	0.5	22.5	69.8	7.1	0.1	105352
13214	SYRACUSE	30315	3265	21.9	20.5	32.9	14.9	9.8	60306	69431	85	75	2492	0.4	4.9	65.7	28.6	0.6	150472
13215	SYRACUSE	30225	5414	16.3	21.3	38.1	14.2	10.1	62507	72175	87	77	4148	0.9	4.9	46.3	45.7	2.2	171276
13219	SYRACUSE	26151	6315	20.6	24.8	38.2	13.1	3.4	55014	63414	80	70	5624	0.9	8.0	74.5	16.5	0.1	121643
13224	SYRACUSE	28387	3939	28.4	23.8	29.1	9.8	9.0	48117	54442	69	58	2511	0.8	18.0	58.2	21.9	1.1	129566
13244	SYRACUSE	13170	36	69.4	30.6	0.0	0.0	0.0	15000	14192	1	1	2	0.0	100.0	0.0	0.0	0.0	55000
13301	ALDER CREEK	23211	24	37.5	25.0	33.3	4.2	0.0	35000	40000	28	13	17	11.8	35.3	41.2	11.8	0.0	95000
13302	ALTMAR	18379	685	29.6	34.2	29.8	4.5	1.9	37979	42514	39	24	579	23.7	38.7	32.3	5.2	0.2	74149
13303	AVA	21101	509	25.0	32.8	33.4	5.9	3.0	44284	49115	59	48	425	19.1	24.2	42.1	13.4	1.2	100158
13304	BARNEVELD	28828	706	16.0	29.9	39.4	9.8	5.0	53626	60740	78	68	612	12.4	13.6	48.0	24.7	1.3	125543
13308	BLOSSVALE	21073	2024	26.7	33.0	31.6	5.6	3.2	40488	45244	48	36	1643	21.7	25.1	42.9	9.6	0.7	95297
13309	BOONVILLE	18074	2516	31.0	33.6	29.8	4.7	1.0	38507	42499	41	27	1917	14.8	31.0	44.2	9.6	0.5	95031
13310	BOUCKVILLE	27887	143	29.4	38.5	23.1	4.9	4.2	36924	41122	35	20	115	22.6	23.5	47.0	7.0	0.0	95625
13314	BROOKFIELD	15492	48	33.3	35.4	27.1	2.1	2.1	33852	37950	24	9	40	40.0	35.0	17.5	7.5	0.0	62000
13315	BURLINGTON FLATS	17872	525	26.1	36.2	31.4	5.0	1.3	40727	45390	49	36	449	9.4	21.8	44.5	22.3	2.0	121828
13316	CAMDEN	19916	2592	29.0	30.2	33.5	5.2	2.2	41620	46961	52	40	2044	11.8	30.6	45.5	11.8	0.3	99064
13317	CANAJOHARIE	19121	1516	33.1	31.6	26.1	6.2	3.1	36405	41353	33	18	1103	11.7	37.8	36.5	12.2	1.9	90696
13318	CASSVILLE	16829	679	28.3	38.0	25.2	6.6	1.9	37657	42710	38	23	545	37.4	19.5	29.2	13.6	0.4	76912
13319	CHADWICKS	36940	302	15.9	24.5	35.4	10.6	13.6	62176	70367	86	77	258	7.0	9.3	55.0	27.5	1.2	140341
13320	CHERRY VALLEY	21090	763	27.7	33.8	30.3	5.0	3.3	40569	45359	48	36	635	7.4	14.2	46.5	28.2	3.8	136748
13322	CLAYVILLE	17833	478	25.5	36.0	31.0	6.9	0.6	41219	46137	50	38	399	7.0	25.3	51.4	14.8	1.5	114787
13323	CLINTON	25780	4218	21.1	28.8	33.7	10.8	5.6	50065	56501	72	62	3225	11.4	13.9	48.9	23.7	2.1	127887
13324	COLD BROOK	17330	790	33.2	36.8	23.7	5.1	1.3	35491	39021	29	15	678	26.1	26.4	33.9	12.7	0.9	86667
13325	CONSTABLEVILLE	17317	374	32.9	33.7	27.8	3.7	1.9	38045	41183	39	25	311	18.0	23.2	44.1	11.9	2.9	101225
13326	COOPERSTOWN	26321	2307	26.7	34.0	25.0	7.1	7.2	41560	48229	52	40	1682	4.9	7.6	36.7	38.0	12.8	177708
13327	CROGHAN	15951	722	32.6	34.9	26.7	4.4	1.4	37850	41390	39	24	597	11.6	21.3	48.7	16.3	2.2	110375
13328	DEANSBORO	23812	436	27.3	30.3	31.7	6.9	3.9	43526	49502	57	46	332	9.9	25.6	47.6	15.7	1.2	109420
13329	DOLGEVILLE	15967	1556	34.8	38.9	23.1	2.8	0.4	34421	37912	25	11	1150	20.4	46.5	28.3	4.4	0.4	70513
13331	EAGLE BAY	22735	315	27.6	37.1	26.0	5.1	4.1	39026	43511	43	29	250	4.8	9.6	39.6	35.2	10.8	164130
13332	EARLVILLE	18730	1056	27.9	37.6	26.8	4.9	2.8	38502	42767	41	27	863	20.9	31.2	36.0	11.4	0.6	86023
13333	EAST SPRINGFIELD	19612	45	31.1	33.3	26.7	6.7	2.2	37333	45000	37	22	37	2.7	13.5	56.8	24.3	2.7	137500
13334	EATON	23131	501	26.0	35.5	28.7	7.2	2.6	40315	45311	47	35	372	19.6	21.8	49.5	8.9	0.3	102703
13335	EDMESTON	18770	613	31.0	32.0	28.4	6.0	2.6	40055	43877	46	34	503	13.3	24.3	46.7	14.3	1.4	109578
13337	FLY CREEK	34308	313	18.5	30.0	32.6	7.7	11.2	51000	58395	74	64	264	1.1	5.7	39.8	35.2	18.2	189063
13338	FORESTPORT	20482	572	28.3	37.6	29.2	3.7	1.2	38190	43440	40	25	490	21.2	26.1	34.9	17.1	0.6	96500
13339	FORT PLAIN	17098	2475	37.3	31.7	24.9	4.1	2.0	32801	36598	20	8	1864	24.8	36.7	28.4	9.2	0.9	77679
13340	FRANKFORT	19215	3310	28.6	32.9	32.3	5.1	1.2	41290	45471	51	39	2509	13.8	26.9	46.9	11.9	0.5	103900
13342	GARRATTSVILLE	21694	48	29.2	35.4	27.1	6.3	2.1	38188	43200	40	25	41	4.9	17.1	48.8	26.8	2.4	127083
13343	GLENFIELD	17612	802	31.7	38.7	23.3	4.5	1.9	36384	40192	33	18	665	12.8	25.4	44.1	16.4	1.4	105811
13345	GREIG	17559	188	33.5	34.6	27.7	3.7	0.5	36506	40315	34	18	159	16.4	23.9	39.0	18.2	2.5	104167
13346	HAMILTON	21928	1626	28.4	28.7	28.0	9.4	5.5	43053	48676	56	44	1095	11.4	17.2	40.6	29.9	0.9	128533
13348	HARTWICK	19343	589	31.8	33.1	27.5	4.8	2.9	38476	43039	41	27	492	8.5	14.0	48.6	24.8	4.1	127813
13350	HERKIMER	19123	4129	42.4	25.6	25.5	4.9	1.7	31449	34660	16	6	2456	11.7	34.9	41.3	11.5	0.7	94019
13353	HOFFMEISTER	24295	66	30.3	34.9	24.2	7.6	3.0	39055	41839	43	29	59	8.5	8.5	49.2	30.5	3.4	144167
13354	HOLLAND PATENT	27097	1352	15.8	31.8	38.5	8.5	5.3	52000	58370	75	66	1171	16.6	12.3	50.8	18.7	1.6	118258
13355	HUBBARDSVILLE	19250	298	26.9	32.9	29.5	7.1	3.7	41535	46756	51	40	250	24.4	22.4	30.0	22.0	1.2	95714
13357	ILION	16746	4500	37.8	28.5	29.0	4.1	0.6	36316	40143	33	18	3024	15.1	38.4	37.3	9.0	0.2	86429
13360	INLET	24837	191	31.9	40.8	15.7	4.7	6.8	35433	40106	29	14	155	6.5	3.2	33.6	38.7	18.1	203125
13361	JORDANVILLE	16352	281	31.0	38.4	26.7	2.5	1.4	36400	40272	33	18	233	23.2	28.8	31.3	15.0	1.7	87353
13363	LEE CENTER	18885	859	22.4	38.1	31.7	6.6	1.3	40623	45251	48	36	703	23.2	27.5	39.4	10.0	0.0	89082
13365	LITTLE FALLS	17485	3797	40.5	33.2	21.1	3.9	1.3	31401	34464	16	6	2579	23.8	33.5	32.1	9.9	0.7	79895
13367	LOWVILLE	17458	3290	34.9	31.4	27.7	4.4	1.6	36988	40577	35	20	2428	6.6	19.3	55.9	15.2	2.9	116651
13368	LYONS FALLS	17216	403	37.7	31.0	25.3	3.7	2.2	33822	37137	24	9	316	13.0	26.9	43.7	13.9	2.5	103500
13402	MADISON	18359	700	34.7	34.1	23.3	5.0	2.9	35093	38758	28	13	562	19.6	29.0	34.3	16.6	0.5	91905
13403	MARCY	18321	1493	15.4	30.9	39.9	9.7	4.1	53011	59151	77	67	1260	1.4	11.9	57.9	28.3	0.4	134811
13406	MIDDLEVILLE	19734	104	24.0	33.7	36.5	3.9	1.9	45000	50338	61	50	89	19.1	23.6	44.9	12.4	0.0	100625
13407	MOHAWK	17929	2202	32.7	37.1	25.0	4.1	1.2	37191	41048	36	21	1686	16.0	39.7	38.7	5.6	0.1	84892
13408	MORRISVILLE	16462	1039	25.2	35.1	29.9	7.5	2.2	41151	46666	50	38	783	18.5	22.1	49.2	10.0	0.3	103146
13409	MUNNSVILLE	19343	824	27.2	32.8	32.8	5.2	2.1	40194	45588	47	35	664	17.5	26.5	46.2	9.2	0.6	96061
13411	NEW BERLIN	17078	1336	37.9	29.9	25.4	4.9	2.0	32774	35969	20	7	1023	20.0	24.4	43.4	11.3	0.8	97434
13413	NEW HARTFORD	30348	6554	23.5	25.2	31.7	10.8	8.9	51375	57621	75	65	4979	4.5	11.7	55.7	26.0	2.2	134700
	NEW YORK	28049		26.3	24.3	29.3	11.5	8.6	49309	58077				4.6	8.6	27.2	39.9	19.8	219050
	UNITED STATES	25866		24.7	27.1	30.8	10.9	6.5	48124	56710				10.9	15.0	33.7	30.1	10.4	145905

ZIP CODE		FINANCIAL SERVICES				THE HOME						ENTERTAINMENT						PERSONAL			
						Home Improvements		Furnishings													
#	POST OFFICE NAME	Auto Loan	Home Loan	Invest-ments	Retire-ment Plans	Home Repair	Lawn & Garden	Comput-ers & Hard-ware	Major Appli-ances	TV, Radio, Sound Equip-ment	Furni-ture	Dine out/ Carry out	Sports Equip-ment	Fees & Tickets	Toys & Games	Travel	Cable TV	Apparel & Services	Auto Repairs	Health Insur-ance	Pets & Supplies
13126	OSWEGO	72	67	68	67	68	74	71	71	72	69	89	83	69	87	70	71	86	72	71	81
13131	PARISH	82	73	56	70	77	82	69	75	72	69	88	89	67	88	70	73	84	74	80	95
13132	PENNELLVILLE	88	78	59	74	82	88	72	80	77	72	93	95	71	95	74	79	89	78	87	103
13135	PHOENIX	92	91	88	89	93	99	89	91	91	88	112	106	90	115	90	92	109	90	94	107
13136	PITCHER	82	56	28	49	64	73	54	67	64	55	76	80	46	72	55	69	69	66	82	95
13140	PORT BYRON	72	65	53	61	67	74	63	68	66	63	81	78	61	81	64	68	77	67	73	83
13141	PREBLE	96	86	67	82	90	97	80	88	84	80	102	105	77	104	82	86	97	87	95	113
13142	PULASKI	78	62	44	60	68	78	64	71	70	62	84	82	59	82	65	73	78	70	82	89
13143	RED CREEK	81	62	38	56	67	75	59	69	66	60	79	82	53	76	60	70	74	69	80	93
13144	RICHLAND	73	61	47	60	65	73	62	68	67	61	81	78	59	80	63	68	76	67	75	82
13145	SANDY CREEK	81	64	44	58	71	80	61	72	68	60	81	84	54	80	64	73	75	71	85	98
13146	SAVANNAH	83	71	51	66	75	82	66	74	71	66	86	88	63	87	68	73	81	72	82	97
13147	SCIPIO CENTER	88	67	42	64	74	83	67	78	74	66	89	92	60	87	68	77	82	77	89	101
13148	SENECA FALLS	75	69	61	68	72	80	70	73	73	68	89	84	68	89	70	74	84	73	79	86
13152	SKANEATELES	110	125	134	122	126	133	116	119	113	115	141	135	121	145	121	114	139	116	117	133
13155	SOUTH OTSELIC	71	59	45	58	62	71	60	65	65	59	78	75	57	77	60	66	73	64	72	79
13156	STERLING	84	62	37	55	70	79	59	72	68	60	81	85	52	78	62	73	75	71	86	99
13158	TRUXTON	76	68	53	65	70	75	64	70	66	65	81	82	62	80	65	67	78	69	72	86
13159	TULLY	99	106	103	105	106	108	99	101	97	99	120	120	101	124	100	95	118	100	97	117
13160	UNION SPRINGS	106	78	46	74	89	99	77	92	87	76	102	111	67	101	79	90	94	91	108	126
13164	WARNERS	85	104	114	101	101	103	96	95	91	95	115	109	102	122	98	90	114	92	88	103
13165	WATERLOO	74	65	53	62	68	75	64	69	68	63	83	81	62	84	65	70	78	68	76	85
13166	WEEDSPORT	89	79	62	76	82	88	75	82	78	76	96	96	73	95	76	79	91	81	86	101
13167	WEST MONROE	85	76	59	73	77	82	72	78	74	74	91	91	69	88	72	74	87	78	80	95
13202	SYRACUSE	32	26	36	27	26	30	34	31	36	33	45	37	32	43	32	36	43	34	32	35
13203	SYRACUSE	54	51	62	51	51	57	58	55	60	56	75	65	57	74	57	60	72	58	57	61
13204	SYRACUSE	45	40	49	40	39	45	47	45	50	46	62	53	46	60	45	50	60	47	46	50
13205	SYRACUSE	50	47	58	45	46	53	52	50	55	52	69	57	52	68	51	57	67	52	53	56
13206	SYRACUSE	60	62	72	62	62	67	65	63	66	63	82	74	66	84	65	65	80	64	63	70
13207	SYRACUSE	73	75	87	75	74	80	78	76	79	78	99	88	80	100	78	78	97	77	75	84
13208	SYRACUSE	52	52	58	50	52	58	56	54	58	54	72	62	56	73	56	59	69	55	57	59
13209	SYRACUSE	73	78	83	76	77	83	78	77	78	76	97	88	80	100	78	78	95	77	77	85
13210	SYRACUSE	48	38	49	41	37	42	54	45	53	49	67	58	49	63	48	49	64	51	43	51
13211	SYRACUSE	68	73	78	71	74	80	74	72	75	71	93	82	77	100	75	76	90	72	75	79
13212	SYRACUSE	73	83	94	81	82	87	81	80	80	80	100	92	85	104	83	80	98	79	78	87
13214	SYRACUSE	99	111	129	109	110	118	110	108	108	108	134	124	113	137	111	108	132	108	105	117
13215	SYRACUSE	105	122	136	122	120	123	116	114	111	115	139	133	121	144	117	108	138	113	106	125
13219	SYRACUSE	80	94	104	90	93	100	89	88	87	88	109	100	94	113	92	88	107	87	88	96
13224	SYRACUSE	87	90	110	91	89	96	94	91	94	94	118	106	96	117	94	93	116	93	88	100
13244	SYRACUSE	25	15	19	17	15	18	30	22	29	25	36	30	24	32	24	25	34	26	20	25
13301	ALDER CREEK	75	57	38	54	62	74	62	69	70	59	82	77	55	78	62	74	75	69	82	84
13302	ALTMAR	92	67	39	60	75	86	64	78	75	65	89	93	57	85	67	80	81	77	94	108
13303	AVA	78	81	80	79	82	86	76	79	76	76	94	93	78	97	78	76	92	77	79	92
13304	BARNEVELD	93	112	122	109	109	112	104	103	99	103	125	119	110	132	106	98	124	100	96	112
13308	BLOSSVALE	72	63	49	59	67	73	60	66	64	59	78	77	58	78	62	66	74	65	73	84
13309	BOONVILLE	74	59	41	56	64	73	61	67	67	59	80	78	56	77	61	70	74	67	78	84
13310	BOUCKVILLE	88	75	58	75	78	89	77	82	82	76	99	94	74	98	76	83	93	81	89	97
13314	BROOKFIELD	68	62	49	60	62	66	59	64	60	61	74	74	56	70	59	59	71	63	63	76
13315	BURLINGTON FLATS	80	65	45	62	71	78	62	71	68	62	81	85	58	82	64	70	76	70	80	94
13316	CAMDEN	82	74	61	70	78	85	70	77	75	70	92	90	70	94	73	78	87	75	84	96
13317	CANAJOHARIE	68	66	62	62	69	76	65	68	69	63	84	77	66	89	67	71	81	66	74	79
13318	CASSVILLE	75	69	55	66	70	73	65	70	66	67	81	82	62	78	65	65	78	70	70	84
13319	CHADWICKS	115	139	156	137	138	143	128	128	122	128	154	146	137	159	133	121	152	125	121	140
13320	CHERRY VALLEY	94	68	39	64	79	88	66	82	76	66	90	97	58	88	70	80	82	80	97	113
13322	CLAYVILLE	84	64	40	61	72	79	62	73	69	61	82	88	56	81	64	72	76	72	84	99
13323	CLINTON	94	97	103	95	98	106	95	97	95	95	118	110	96	116	97	96	114	97	99	110
13324	COLD BROOK	72	59	42	55	64	72	57	65	63	56	75	76	52	74	59	66	70	64	75	86
13325	CONSTABLEVILLE	84	58	29	50	65	75	56	69	66	56	78	82	48	74	57	71	71	68	84	97
13326	COOPERSTOWN	96	81	68	79	87	99	83	91	89	82	108	104	78	104	85	93	101	91	102	111
13327	CROGHAN	75	59	41	54	66	74	56	67	63	56	75	78	51	74	60	67	70	66	78	90
13328	DEANSBORO	75	80	85	77	81	88	79	78	81	77	100	89	83	107	81	83	97	77	82	88
13329	DOLGEVILLE	64	50	34	46	54	63	51	57	57	50	68	66	47	67	51	61	63	57	68	73
13331	EAGLE BAY	84	66	45	60	75	84	62	75	71	62	84	88	56	83	67	75	78	74	89	103
13332	EARLVILLE	85	63	38	59	71	80	62	74	70	61	83	88	55	82	64	74	77	73	87	100
13333	EAST SPRINGFIELD	91	64	33	60	74	83	63	78	73	62	85	94	54	84	65	76	78	77	93	109
13334	EATON	90	72	51	68	79	89	71	81	78	70	93	95	65	92	73	82	87	80	93	106
13335	EDMESTON	91	64	33	60	74	83	63	78	72	62	85	93	54	83	65	76	77	76	93	108
13337	FLY CREEK	144	109	71	103	124	140	106	128	119	107	142	146	95	133	111	125	130	125	151	169
13338	FORESTPORT	79	62	43	56	70	79	59	71	66	58	79	83	53	78	63	71	73	70	83	96
13339	FORT PLAIN	66	59	49	54	62	70	58	63	63	57	77	72	57	79	60	67	73	62	71	76
13340	FRANKFORT	68	66	62	64	67	74	66	68	67	65	83	77	65	82	66	68	79	67	71	78
13342	GARRATTSVILLE	85	63	37	60	72	79	61	74	69	61	82	89	54	81	63	72	75	72	86	101
13343	GLENFIELD	73	59	42	55	65	73	57	66	63	56	75	77	52	74	59	66	70	65	75	86
13345	GREIG	72	57	39	51	64	72	53	64	61	53	72	75	48	71	57	65	67	63	76	88
13346	HAMILTON	82	80	88	81	81	87	84	83	85	82	105	99	83	106	84	83	102	85	83	96
13348	HARTWICK	91	65	37	62	75	84	65	78	74	64	87	94	56	85	67	77	80	77	93	107
13350	HERKIMER	62	56	58	55	58	65	61	61	64	59	78	70	59	78	61	65	75	62	66	70
13353	HOFFMEISTER	95	74	51	67	84	94	70	85	79	70	94	99	63	93	75	85	87	83	100	116
13354	HOLLAND PATENT	98	111	115	108	110	113	103	104	100	102	125	121	107	131	105	99	123	101	99	117
13355	HUBBARDSVILLE	75	78	74	76	78	81	74	76	73	74	90	88	74	91	74	72	88	75	74	87
13357	ILION	57	56	57	54	57	63	58	58	60	56	74	66	58	76	58	61	71	58	62	66
13360	INLET	89	70	47	63	78	88	66	79	74	65	88	93	59	87	70	79	82	78	94	108
13361	JORDANVILLE	79	55	28	50	62	71	54	66	63	54	74	79	46	71	55	67	67	65	79	91
13363	LEE CENTER	70	69	73	71	70	75	71	72	70	70	87	83	70	85	70	69	83	72	71	80
13365	LITTLE FALLS	63	53	45	51	57	64	55	59	60	53	72	68	52	72	55	62	68	59	67	72
13367	LOWVILLE	70	60	46	56	64	72	59	65	64	58	76	75	56	77	60	66	72	64	74	82
13368	LYONS FALLS	68	60	50	55	64	72	58	64	63	57	76	74	56	78	61	67	72	63	73	81
13402	MADISON	68	62	53	62	64	71	63	66	65	62	79	75	61	80	63	66	75	65	69	76
13403	MARCY	69	84	90	82	83	85	76	76	73	76	91	88	81	96	79	72	91	74	72	84
13406	MIDDLEVILLE	84	74	57	71	79	84	69	76	73	69	89	91	67	91	71	75	85	74	83	98
13407	MOHAWK	62	61	57	59	63	69	60	62	62	58	76	71	61	80	61	64	73	61	66	73
13408	MORRISVILLE	87	72	53	68	79	87	69	79	76	69	91	92	65	91	72	79	85	78	89	103
13409	MUNNSVILLE	82	70	54	69	73	82	71	76	76	70	92	88	68	91	71	77	86	75	83	91
13411	NEW BERLIN	77	55	31	50	61	71	56	66	65	55	76	77	49	73	56	69	70	65	79	87
13413	NEW HARTFORD	97	106	115	104	106	115	102	104	101	102	126	117	105	127	105	102	123	103	105	115
	NEW YORK	95	100	134	99	98	107	103	100	105	103	133	116	105	138	104	107	131	102	99	112
	UNITED STATES	100	100	100	100	100	100	100	100	100	100	100	100	100	100	100	100	100	100	100	100

NEW YORK

POPULATION CHANGE

A 13415-13669

# POST OFFICE NAME	COUNTY FIPS CODE	POPULATION 2000	2004	2009	% Rate	State Centile	HOUSEHOLDS 2000	2004	2009	% Annual Rate 2000-2004	2004 Average HH Size	FAMILIES 2000	2004	% Annual Rate 2000-2004
13415 NEW LISBON	077	95	98	100	0.7	68	39	41	42	1.2	2.39	28	30	1.6
13416 NEWPORT	043	2328	2318	2310	-0.1	22	844	853	857	0.3	2.67	625	628	0.1
13417 NEW YORK MILLS	065	3166	3200	3218	0.3	43	1537	1571	1589	0.5	2.03	768	778	0.3
13418 NORTH BROOKFIELD	053	162	163	164	0.1	37	51	52	53	0.5	3.13	37	38	0.6
13420 OLD FORGE	043	1190	1173	1163	-0.3	12	527	526	525	0.0	2.19	332	329	-0.2
13421 ONEIDA	053	13836	13938	14076	0.2	39	5548	5658	5781	0.5	2.40	3542	3586	0.3
13424 ORISKANY	065	2959	3007	3026	0.4	50	951	983	998	0.8	2.59	699	719	0.7
13425 ORISKANY FALLS	065	2007	2043	2058	0.4	53	770	796	809	0.8	2.56	554	568	0.6
13428 PALATINE BRIDGE	057	1895	1927	1933	0.4	51	723	739	748	0.5	2.55	519	528	0.4
13431 POLAND	043	1896	1866	1851	-0.4	10	716	716	718	0.0	2.61	525	522	-0.1
13433 PORT LEYDEN	049	1436	1444	1461	0.1	37	533	545	562	0.5	2.63	386	392	0.4
13437 REDFIELD	075	509	527	545	0.8	71	200	210	221	1.2	2.51	145	151	1.0
13438 REMSEN	065	4527	4670	4743	0.7	68	1738	1824	1869	1.1	2.55	1246	1295	0.9
13439 RICHFIELD SPRINGS	077	4040	3993	3962	-0.3	15	1587	1591	1596	0.1	2.49	1103	1097	-0.1
13440 ROME	065	44919	44802	44856	-0.1	25	17306	17470	17619	0.2	2.38	11182	11227	0.1
13450 ROSEBOOM	077	205	211	213	0.7	65	78	82	84	1.2	2.32	57	59	0.8
13452 SAINT JOHNSVILLE	035	4851	4848	4846	0.0	27	1880	1902	1924	0.3	2.47	1282	1290	0.2
13454 SALISBURY CENTER	043	583	569	562	-0.6	5	198	196	196	-0.2	2.90	146	144	-0.3
13456 SAUQUOIT	065	4290	4407	4461	0.6	64	1616	1687	1721	1.0	2.59	1199	1244	0.9
13459 SHARON SPRINGS	095	2078	2169	2252	1.0	78	771	819	864	1.4	2.58	558	591	1.4
13460 SHERBURNE	017	4287	4344	4458	0.3	48	1707	1748	1818	0.6	2.48	1151	1170	0.4
13461 SHERRILL	065	3144	3089	3062	-0.4	9	1263	1258	1255	-0.1	2.45	880	871	-0.2
13464 SMYRNA	017	1600	1702	1800	1.5	87	541	583	625	1.8	2.90	398	426	1.6
13468 SPRINGFIELD CENTER	077	534	542	543	0.4	50	211	217	221	0.7	2.50	148	152	0.6
13469 STITTVILLE	065	678	671	667	-0.2	16	252	251	252	-0.1	1.83	196	194	-0.2
13470 STRATFORD	035	779	736	728	-1.3	1	288	276	276	-1.0	2.62	205	196	-1.1
13471 TABERG	065	3391	3649	3781	1.7	91	1192	1306	1370	2.2	2.76	892	970	2.0
13473 TURIN	049	910	897	903	-0.3	12	333	334	342	0.1	2.69	234	234	0.0
13475 VAN HORNESVILLE	043	17	18	19	1.4	86	8	9	9	2.8	2.00	6	7	3.7
13476 VERNON	065	3246	3290	3307	0.3	48	1288	1324	1344	0.7	2.48	917	937	0.5
13477 VERNON CENTER	065	1171	1186	1191	0.3	47	426	438	444	0.7	2.69	303	309	0.5
13478 VERONA	065	3198	3262	3297	0.5	56	1199	1242	1265	0.8	2.61	918	945	0.7
13480 WATERVILLE	065	4146	4113	4097	-0.2	18	1496	1501	1504	0.1	2.68	1097	1093	-0.1
13482 WEST BURLINGTON	077	33	34	35	0.7	66	11	12	12	2.1	2.83	8	9	2.8
13483 WESTDALE	065	239	241	242	0.2	40	90	92	93	0.5	2.62	68	69	0.3
13485 WEST EDMESTON	053	1194	1219	1235	0.5	57	424	440	452	0.9	2.77	324	334	0.8
13486 WESTERNVILLE	065	632	621	617	-0.4	9	228	228	228	0.0	2.72	174	173	-0.1
13488 WESTFORD	077	152	154	155	0.3	48	57	59	60	0.8	2.61	41	42	0.6
13489 WEST LEYDEN	049	564	578	590	0.6	61	197	205	213	0.9	2.82	142	148	1.0
13490 WESTMORELAND	065	1086	1153	1185	1.4	87	380	410	425	1.8	2.81	291	312	1.7
13491 WEST WINFIELD	077	4029	4048	4056	0.1	36	1493	1521	1539	0.4	2.66	1119	1132	0.3
13492 WHITESBORO	065	11822	11696	11638	-0.3	15	4835	4855	4868	0.1	2.40	3325	3314	-0.1
13493 WILLIAMSTOWN	075	2070	2174	2271	1.2	82	726	774	820	1.5	2.81	540	571	1.3
13494 WOODGATE	065	339	333	330	-0.4	9	147	147	147	0.0	2.27	96	95	-0.3
13495 YORKVILLE	065	2169	2102	2072	-0.7	3	921	902	894	-0.5	2.20	559	543	-0.7
13501 UTICA	065	36037	35552	35354	-0.3	13	14645	14508	14459	-0.2	2.32	8420	8282	-0.4
13502 UTICA	065	32844	32254	32023	-0.4	8	13730	13651	13649	-0.1	2.23	8179	8038	-0.4
13601 WATERTOWN	045	38180	38211	38836	0.0	30	15059	15302	15798	0.4	2.38	9504	9572	0.2
13602 FORT DRUM	045	4651	4636	4636	-0.1	24	12	7	7	-11.9	3.00	10	6	-11.3
13603 WATERTOWN	045	7472	8400	9008	2.8	98	2241	2540	2754	3.0	3.31	2193	2483	3.0
13605 ADAMS	045	4694	4668	4723	-0.1	21	1822	1842	1893	0.3	2.53	1286	1288	0.1
13606 ADAMS CENTER	045	2571	2621	2679	0.5	55	940	972	1008	0.8	2.68	681	697	0.6
13607 ALEXANDRIA BAY	045	2068	2088	2124	0.2	42	899	925	957	0.7	2.20	590	601	0.4
13608 ANTWERP	045	1737	1728	1742	-0.1	22	614	621	636	0.3	2.78	448	450	0.1
13611 BELLEVILLE	045	106	111	115	1.1	80	34	36	38	1.4	3.08	25	27	1.8
13612 BLACK RIVER	045	2682	2800	2899	1.0	78	1034	1097	1154	1.4	2.55	744	783	1.2
13613 BRASHER FALLS	089	2265	2280	2308	0.2	38	915	938	967	0.6	2.43	623	635	0.5
13614 BRIER HILL	089	485	490	495	0.2	43	205	211	217	0.7	2.32	143	146	0.5
13616 CALCIUM	045	2015	2121	2196	1.2	83	648	692	728	1.6	3.07	551	586	1.5
13617 CANTON	089	10956	11102	11284	0.3	48	3412	3526	3661	0.8	2.41	2191	2248	0.6
13618 CAPE VINCENT	045	1689	1713	1739	0.3	49	726	751	775	0.8	2.25	503	515	0.6
13619 CARTHAGE	049	11539	11447	11575	-0.2	18	4341	4377	4496	0.2	2.58	3105	3105	0.0
13620 CASTORLAND	049	2319	2330	2352	0.1	36	818	838	862	0.6	2.77	627	640	0.5
13621 CHASE MILLS	089	592	630	654	1.5	87	228	247	262	1.9	2.51	161	173	1.7
13622 CHAUMONT	045	2394	2425	2465	0.3	47	913	944	977	0.8	2.55	654	669	0.5
13624 CLAYTON	045	6000	6139	6262	0.5	60	1916	2014	2101	1.2	2.41	1349	1403	0.9
13625 COLTON	089	2445	2556	2636	1.1	79	989	1053	1105	1.5	2.43	684	723	1.3
13626 COPENHAGEN	049	2245	2270	2304	0.3	44	783	805	832	0.7	2.68	590	604	0.6
13630 DE KALB JUNCTION	089	1313	1373	1416	1.1	79	472	502	527	1.5	2.69	345	364	1.3
13633 DE PEYSTER	089	185	220	243	4.2	99	52	63	71	4.6	3.49	40	49	4.9
13634 DEXTER	045	3874	3795	3822	-0.5	7	1439	1435	1469	-0.1	2.63	1054	1043	-0.3
13635 EDWARDS	089	1123	1106	1112	-0.4	11	419	419	428	0.0	2.64	317	314	-0.2
13636 ELLISBURG	045	322	336	346	1.0	78	110	116	122	1.3	2.90	83	87	1.1
13637 EVANS MILLS	045	3816	4072	4248	1.5	88	1324	1437	1525	2.0	2.82	1024	1103	1.8
13638 FELTS MILLS	045	274	289	299	1.3	84	105	113	119	1.7	2.56	76	81	1.5
13639 FINE	089	287	279	280	-0.7	4	101	101	103	0.0	2.72	75	74	-0.3
13640 WELLESLEY ISLAND	045	324	337	347	0.9	75	159	169	177	1.5	1.93	101	106	1.1
13642 GOUVERNEUR	089	9920	10057	10298	0.3	48	3412	3510	3661	0.7	2.56	2376	2437	0.6
13646 HAMMOND	089	2418	2561	2662	1.4	86	972	1055	1120	2.0	2.43	686	739	1.8
13648 HARRISVILLE	049	2326	2499	2622	1.7	90	890	971	1037	2.1	2.57	681	740	2.0
13650 HENDERSON	045	1388	1384	1404	-0.1	24	577	585	602	0.3	2.36	418	420	0.1
13652 HERMON	089	1824	1830	1843	0.1	33	664	680	697	0.6	2.65	480	487	0.3
13654 HEUVELTON	089	2630	2750	2842	1.1	79	891	944	989	1.4	2.89	656	691	1.2
13655 HOGANSBURG	033	2782	2915	3085	1.1	81	948	1006	1080	1.4	2.89	699	738	1.3
13656 LA FARGEVILLE	045	2444	2440	2467	0.0	26	851	864	887	0.4	2.82	654	660	0.2
13658 LISBON	089	1979	1989	2024	0.1	36	706	724	750	0.6	2.73	529	538	0.4
13659 LORRAINE	045	504	506	512	0.1	34	193	197	202	0.5	2.54	147	149	0.3
13660 MADRID	089	2070	2233	2340	1.8	91	721	794	848	2.3	2.69	526	573	2.0
13661 MANNSVILLE	045	1598	1617	1641	0.3	45	567	584	603	0.7	2.76	435	444	0.5
13662 MASSENA	089	16588	16750	17059	0.2	42	6874	7043	7288	0.6	2.32	4421	4497	0.4
13665 NATURAL BRIDGE	049	834	809	813	-0.7	3	312	308	315	-0.3	2.63	235	230	-0.5
13666 NEWTON FALLS	089	274	265	266	-0.8	3	104	103	105	-0.2	2.56	71	70	-0.3
13667 NORFOLK	089	3857	3989	4091	0.8	70	1531	1615	1686	1.3	2.46	1078	1128	1.1
13668 NORWOOD	089	3547	3580	3621	0.2	41	1387	1427	1471	0.7	2.47	980	997	0.4
13669 OGDENSBURG	089	18001	17647	17730	-0.5	7	6215	6167	6307	-0.2	2.43	4062	4005	-0.3
NEW YORK					0.4					0.5	2.60			0.4
UNITED STATES					1.2					1.3	2.58			1.1

ZIP CODE #	POST OFFICE NAME	RACE (%) White 2000	White 2004	Black 2000	Black 2004	Asian/Pacific 2000	Asian/Pacific 2004	% Hispanic Origin 2000	% Hispanic Origin 2004	2004 AGE DISTRIBUTION (%) 0-4	5-9	10-14	15-19	20-24	25-44	45-64	65-84	85+	18+	MEDIAN AGE 2004	% 2004 Males	% 2004 Females
13415	NEW LISBON	97.9	96.9	1.1	1.0	0.0	1.0	2.1	1.0	6.1	6.1	6.1	7.1	5.1	24.5	30.6	12.2	2.0	75.5	41.9	50.0	50.0
13416	NEWPORT	98.5	98.3	0.3	0.3	0.0	0.0	0.5	0.6	5.3	6.5	7.7	7.8	5.4	26.6	26.9	12.2	1.5	75.2	39.0	49.6	50.4
13417	NEW YORK MILLS	98.1	97.6	0.4	0.5	0.4	0.5	1.1	1.5	4.9	4.7	5.1	5.3	5.6	27.5	23.3	18.5	5.0	82.2	42.7	45.5	54.5
13418	NORTH BROOKFIELD	98.8	98.2	0.6	0.6	0.6	0.6	0.0	0.0	7.4	6.1	8.0	9.2	5.5	27.6	26.4	8.6	1.2	72.4	36.5	51.5	48.5
13420	OLD FORGE	98.2	97.8	0.5	0.7	0.2	0.3	0.8	1.0	3.9	4.6	6.8	6.1	4.3	25.5	31.6	15.2	2.0	80.5	44.3	49.3	50.7
13421	ONEIDA	96.6	96.1	0.7	0.8	0.4	0.6	0.8	0.9	6.1	6.2	7.4	7.2	6.7	27.3	25.0	11.9	2.3	75.6	38.3	48.7	51.4
13424	ORISKANY	93.0	91.6	4.5	5.3	0.7	0.9	2.5	3.3	4.6	5.0	6.3	7.3	6.7	29.2	26.7	11.0	3.3	79.7	39.9	52.3	47.7
13425	ORISKANY FALLS	98.1	97.5	0.4	0.4	0.7	0.9	0.6	0.8	5.7	5.9	7.2	7.8	7.2	27.7	26.0	11.1	1.6	76.4	38.2	50.0	50.0
13428	PALATINE BRIDGE	97.8	97.7	0.6	0.7	0.5	0.6	0.5	0.5	6.5	6.4	6.8	7.3	5.9	24.7	25.1	14.7	2.8	75.8	39.9	48.9	51.1
13431	POLAND	98.5	98.2	0.2	0.3	0.4	0.5	0.6	0.8	5.6	6.7	7.9	7.2	4.7	26.2	26.8	13.2	1.8	75.0	40.0	50.0	50.0
13433	PORT LEYDEN	98.7	98.6	0.2	0.2	0.0	0.0	0.4	0.5	6.4	6.4	8.0	8.0	7.0	27.0	24.3	11.3	1.6	74.1	36.6	50.1	49.9
13437	REDFIELD	98.4	98.3	0.2	0.2	0.2	0.2	1.2	1.3	6.6	7.2	9.1	7.8	6.5	26.0	25.2	10.6	1.0	71.9	36.4	49.9	50.1
13438	REMSEN	98.2	97.8	0.4	0.5	0.4	0.6	0.3	0.3	5.7	6.0	7.3	7.9	6.2	26.5	28.4	10.9	1.1	75.7	39.7	49.8	50.2
13439	RICHFIELD SPRINGS	97.5	97.1	0.5	0.6	0.6	0.7	0.6	0.7	5.3	5.6	6.8	6.7	6.0	22.6	28.5	16.2	2.3	78.2	42.9	49.6	50.4
13440	ROME	90.5	89.0	5.7	6.4	0.8	1.0	3.7	4.4	5.8	5.9	6.6	6.4	6.6	27.7	24.8	13.9	2.4	77.8	39.3	50.7	49.3
13450	ROSEBOOM	96.6	95.7	1.0	1.4	1.0	1.0	1.0	1.4	5.2	6.2	6.6	6.2	4.7	24.6	26.5	15.2	4.7	77.7	42.3	50.2	49.8
13452	SAINT JOHNSVILLE	98.6	98.5	0.3	0.3	0.2	0.2	0.9	1.0	5.8	6.1	7.0	6.9	6.5	25.0	26.2	13.8	2.7	76.7	40.4	49.6	50.4
13454	SALISBURY CENTER	98.3	98.1	0.2	0.2	0.3	0.5	0.2	0.4	6.2	6.3	7.6	8.1	7.6	26.7	26.2	10.4	1.1	75.2	37.1	51.3	48.7
13456	SAUQUOIT	97.8	97.2	0.4	0.5	0.8	1.0	0.6	0.8	5.0	5.7	8.4	7.5	5.4	25.4	28.6	12.1	1.8	75.8	40.6	48.6	51.4
13459	SHARON SPRINGS	98.0	97.7	0.5	0.6	0.1	0.1	1.6	2.0	6.0	7.2	8.4	7.5	4.8	25.9	24.3	13.9	2.0	73.6	39.2	50.0	50.0
13460	SHERBURNE	98.7	98.4	0.2	0.3	0.1	0.2	0.8	1.0	6.2	6.7	7.8	7.2	5.5	25.5	26.7	12.8	1.8	74.6	39.3	48.8	51.2
13461	SHERRILL	98.0	97.6	0.2	0.3	0.6	0.8	0.8	1.0	6.0	6.4	7.6	7.3	5.4	22.4	28.1	14.3	2.5	75.1	41.6	46.9	53.1
13464	SMYRNA	98.4	98.2	0.3	0.3	0.1	0.1	0.6	0.8	7.0	7.2	8.1	7.6	6.2	27.6	25.2	10.1	1.1	72.6	36.3	50.4	49.6
13468	SPRINGFIELD CENTER	98.9	98.5	0.2	0.2	0.4	0.4	0.4	0.6	4.6	5.2	6.6	7.8	5.2	23.4	30.4	14.8	2.0	78.4	43.3	50.0	50.0
13469	STITTVILLE	76.4	74.2	15.9	17.0	0.6	0.6	10.8	12.2	3.7	4.0	6.3	6.3	7.6	40.7	23.7	7.3	0.5	82.3	36.4	65.6	34.4
13470	STRATFORD	97.4	97.2	0.9	1.0	0.1	0.1	1.3	1.5	4.9	5.3	6.7	7.9	6.4	25.8	29.8	13.2	0.8	77.7	41.2	53.3	46.7
13471	TABERG	97.1	96.4	1.9	2.3	0.1	0.1	0.8	1.0	6.3	6.7	8.7	8.5	6.4	29.8	24.1	8.7	0.9	72.8	35.7	52.4	47.6
13473	TURIN	98.9	98.8	0.1	0.1	0.0	0.1	0.2	0.2	6.7	6.6	7.5	7.3	6.6	25.0	26.1	13.0	1.3	74.5	39.2	50.8	49.2
13475	VAN HORNESVILLE	100.0	100.0	0.0	0.0	0.0	0.0	0.0	0.0	11.1	11.1	11.1	11.1	5.6	22.2	27.8	0.0	0.0	66.7	30.0	55.6	44.4
13476	VERNON	97.9	97.4	0.5	0.6	0.4	0.5	0.7	1.0	5.8	6.1	8.0	7.1	5.9	26.4	27.2	11.9	1.5	75.6	39.6	49.4	50.6
13477	VERNON CENTER	98.0	97.4	0.5	0.7	0.6	0.8	0.9	1.1	6.8	6.9	7.6	6.9	5.7	27.7	26.5	10.6	1.4	74.5	38.2	50.4	49.6
13478	VERONA	97.4	96.9	0.6	0.7	0.5	0.7	0.6	0.6	5.7	6.1	7.5	7.1	5.7	27.7	26.9	12.1	1.2	76.2	39.3	51.0	49.1
13480	WATERVILLE	98.3	98.0	0.4	0.5	0.4	0.5	0.6	0.8	6.6	6.7	8.5	8.2	6.4	24.9	24.6	12.0	2.1	72.9	37.8	49.2	50.8
13482	WEST BURLINGTON	97.0	97.1	0.0	0.0	0.0	0.0	0.0	0.0	5.9	5.9	5.9	8.8	5.9	29.4	23.5	14.7	0.0	82.4	38.3	50.0	50.0
13483	WESTDALE	98.7	98.3	0.4	0.4	0.4	0.4	0.4	0.4	7.5	7.5	7.9	7.9	6.6	27.0	24.5	10.4	0.8	72.2	37.2	51.0	49.0
13485	WEST EDMESTON	98.0	97.7	0.7	0.7	0.2	0.3	0.7	0.8	7.0	7.1	7.7	8.0	5.8	26.5	26.3	10.5	1.2	73.2	36.6	49.0	51.0
13486	WESTERNVILLE	97.8	97.4	0.5	0.5	0.3	0.5	0.6	1.0	6.0	6.3	8.1	6.9	5.6	28.2	26.6	11.0	1.5	75.4	39.5	51.9	48.2
13488	WESTFORD	98.7	98.7	0.0	0.0	0.7	0.7	1.3	1.3	5.2	5.8	7.8	7.1	5.2	24.7	29.9	13.0	1.3	76.6	41.8	51.3	48.7
13489	WEST LEYDEN	99.3	99.3	0.4	0.4	0.0	0.0	0.4	0.4	5.4	5.4	7.6	9.7	7.3	29.4	24.2	10.0	1.0	76.0	37.9	51.6	48.4
13490	WESTMORELAND	97.9	97.3	0.9	1.1	0.3	0.4	1.1	1.5	5.2	6.0	8.4	7.9	5.8	27.5	27.3	10.6	1.3	75.6	39.6	50.8	49.2
13491	WEST WINFIELD	98.6	98.3	0.3	0.3	0.3	0.4	0.6	0.7	6.5	7.2	8.3	7.6	5.6	26.4	25.4	11.8	1.3	73.0	37.6	50.1	49.9
13492	WHITESBORO	98.3	97.9	0.4	0.5	0.5	0.6	1.0	1.3	5.3	5.7	6.9	6.4	5.5	24.8	27.1	16.1	2.2	78.2	42.2	47.5	52.5
13493	WILLIAMSTOWN	97.4	97.0	0.8	0.9	0.1	0.2	0.9	1.2	6.7	7.2	9.2	7.9	6.6	28.2	24.8	8.8	0.6	72.0	35.8	50.6	49.4
13494	WOODGATE	98.5	98.2	0.3	0.3	0.3	0.3	0.0	0.3	5.1	5.4	6.0	5.4	4.2	22.8	32.1	17.7	1.2	79.9	45.7	50.5	49.6
13495	YORKVILLE	98.3	97.8	0.5	0.6	0.4	0.6	1.2	1.6	5.5	5.3	5.5	6.4	6.2	25.1	24.6	17.0	4.4	79.8	41.8	45.8	54.2
13501	UTICA	76.2	73.2	14.6	15.9	3.1	3.7	6.4	7.7	6.9	6.6	7.2	7.4	6.6	24.5	21.4	15.5	4.0	75.1	38.0	47.1	52.9
13502	UTICA	87.6	85.5	8.1	9.3	1.0	1.3	3.8	4.8	6.1	5.7	6.3	7.0	7.7	26.3	23.7	14.7	2.6	78.2	38.8	47.7	52.3
13601	WATERTOWN	89.8	88.4	5.0	5.5	1.1	1.3	3.5	4.2	7.4	6.6	7.0	6.7	7.6	29.0	22.2	11.3	2.3	75.0	35.3	49.2	50.8
13602	FORT DRUM	63.0	59.6	21.6	22.9	2.7	3.2	13.4	15.3	0.0	0.0	0.1	15.8	58.0	25.5	0.6	0.0	0.0	99.7	22.9	89.8	10.2
13603	WATERTOWN	64.9	61.6	18.6	19.7	3.3	3.9	13.2	15.1	19.3	11.0	7.2	5.1	15.9	39.1	2.4	0.1	0.0	59.7	22.4	49.1	50.9
13605	ADAMS	98.1	97.8	0.3	0.3	0.2	0.3	0.8	0.9	6.4	6.5	7.3	6.9	6.2	26.8	26.3	12.0	1.5	75.3	39.3	49.3	50.7
13606	ADAMS CENTER	97.8	97.4	0.6	0.7	0.4	0.6	0.7	0.9	6.7	6.9	8.1	7.8	6.3	27.2	25.8	10.0	1.3	73.3	37.7	49.8	50.3
13607	ALEXANDRIA BAY	98.7	98.5	0.3	0.3	0.1	0.1	0.8	0.9	4.3	4.7	5.7	5.8	5.0	22.3	31.9	17.4	3.0	81.5	46.4	48.9	51.1
13608	ANTWERP	97.8	97.4	0.5	0.6	0.3	0.5	1.0	1.2	6.1	6.6	9.2	7.7	6.1	27.6	26.5	9.3	0.9	73.2	36.7	50.8	49.3
13611	BELLEVILLE	98.1	99.1	0.0	0.0	0.0	0.0	1.9	1.8	4.5	8.1	9.0	9.0	3.6	25.2	24.3	14.4	1.8	73.0	39.2	50.5	49.6
13612	BLACK RIVER	93.4	92.3	2.4	2.7	1.7	2.0	1.8	2.2	5.8	6.5	7.8	7.7	6.0	29.7	25.2	10.3	1.1	74.9	37.5	49.3	50.7
13613	BRASHER FALLS	97.0	96.4	0.2	0.3	0.4	0.4	0.8	1.1	6.0	6.1	6.9	6.5	6.2	26.5	27.5	12.6	1.7	76.8	39.8	49.5	50.5
13614	BRIER HILL	97.9	97.6	0.2	0.2	0.0	0.0	0.4	0.4	5.7	6.3	7.4	5.5	4.3	24.7	30.4	14.7	1.0	76.9	42.4	49.8	50.2
13616	CALCIUM	82.3	80.1	10.5	11.5	1.3	1.7	6.6	7.8	11.3	9.7	8.4	6.2	8.9	30.7	19.2	5.1	0.4	66.7	28.0	49.8	50.2
13617	CANTON	94.9	93.8	2.5	3.1	0.7	0.9	1.3	1.7	4.3	4.4	5.6	15.3	16.1	21.9	20.8	9.7	1.9	82.0	29.1	50.1	49.9
13618	CAPE VINCENT	97.5	97.2	0.9	0.9	0.4	0.5	0.8	1.1	3.9	4.2	5.7	6.1	5.0	22.1	32.0	19.0	2.1	82.3	47.0	49.0	51.0
13619	CARTHAGE	93.3	92.3	2.7	2.9	1.0	1.2	2.4	2.8	7.2	7.0	8.0	7.4	6.6	27.7	23.9	10.6	1.6	73.3	35.8	48.9	51.1
13620	CASTORLAND	97.6	97.3	0.7	0.9	0.1	0.2	0.8	0.9	6.9	7.1	7.8	7.0	7.0	27.1	26.1	10.0	1.1	74.0	36.5	50.1	49.9
13621	CHASE MILLS	98.0	97.8	0.3	0.5	0.3	0.5	0.7	0.8	5.6	5.7	7.0	7.5	3.7	26.4	30.5	12.7	1.1	76.7	41.1	50.2	49.8
13622	CHAUMONT	97.2	96.8	1.0	1.1	0.1	0.2	0.8	1.1	4.5	6.0	7.8	8.6	5.1	25.3	27.7	13.6	1.5	76.5	41.4	50.2	49.8
13624	CLAYTON	82.5	81.5	12.7	13.0	0.3	0.4	8.1	9.1	4.5	4.7	5.8	5.5	6.7	35.7	24.3	11.1	1.7	81.3	38.5	59.3	40.7
13625	COLTON	98.7	98.5	0.1	0.1	0.3	0.3	0.7	1.0	5.1	5.6	7.1	6.6	4.8	25.1	30.8	13.7	1.3	77.7	42.5	51.1	48.9
13626	COPENHAGEN	94.2	93.4	3.0	3.2	0.3	0.4	2.7	3.2	6.9	7.0	7.8	7.1	6.6	31.1	24.3	8.4	0.8	74.0	35.1	53.7	46.3
13630	DE KALB JUNCTION	98.2	97.8	0.4	0.6	0.2	0.2	0.5	0.5	7.0	7.5	9.0	8.6	6.3	26.8	24.7	9.3	0.7	71.1	34.0	50.2	49.8
13633	DE PEYSTER	98.4	98.2	1.1	0.9	0.0	0.0	0.0	0.5	7.7	8.2	9.1	9.1	6.4	25.5	23.6	10.0	0.5	69.6	33.1	52.3	47.7
13634	DEXTER	97.9	97.5	0.3	0.3	0.3	0.4	0.6	0.7	5.9	6.3	7.9	7.3	6.4	27.5	25.9	11.7	1.2	75.3	38.7	48.5	51.5
13635	EDWARDS	98.1	97.7	0.5	0.5	0.1	0.1	0.8	1.0	6.1	6.5	8.6	8.0	5.7	26.7	24.8	12.8	1.0	74.1	37.7	49.0	51.0
13636	ELLISBURG	97.8	97.6	0.3	0.6	0.3	0.3	1.2	1.8	5.4	8.0	9.2	10.4	4.8	25.9	23.2	11.6	1.5	70.5	36.5	50.0	50.0
13637	EVANS MILLS	77.5	75.1	12.0	12.9	1.7	1.9	8.9	10.4	12.0	9.7	8.3	7.4	9.6	34.4	13.7	4.5	0.4	65.5	26.2	50.6	49.4
13638	FELTS MILLS	93.1	91.7	2.9	3.5	0.7	0.7	2.2	3.1	7.3	7.3	8.0	6.6	6.9	29.4	25.3	8.7	0.7	73.4	35.3	50.5	49.5
13639	FINE	97.6	97.1	0.0	0.0	0.7	0.7	0.0	0.0	5.7	5.4	5.0	4.7	6.8	24.7	30.1	16.1	1.4	81.0	43.5	48.4	51.6
13640	WELLESLEY ISLAND	98.8	98.5	0.3	0.3	0.0	0.0	0.6	0.6	3.6	3.9	5.0	5.3	4.5	20.2	33.2	20.5	3.9	84.0	49.6	48.1	51.9
13642	GOUVERNEUR	89.3	87.6	6.8	7.8	0.4	0.5	4.4	5.4	6.6	6.7	7.1	6.6	7.2	31.6	22.7	10.1	1.4	75.4	35.2	54.1	45.9
13646	HAMMOND	97.4	97.1	0.5	0.6	0.1	0.1	0.6	0.8	5.8	6.4	7.2	6.2	5.0	25.3	28.7	14.0	1.5	76.8	41.1	50.5	49.5
13648	HARRISVILLE	98.2	97.8	0.0	0.0	0.3	0.5	0.5	0.7	6.1	7.1	7.8	7.3	5.0	26.5	28.7	10.4	1.2	74.0	38.3	50.8	49.2
13650	HENDERSON	98.6	98.3	0.1	0.1	0.1	0.1	0.9	1.1	5.1	6.3	7.7	6.9	4.7	25.2	27.5	15.1	1.5	76.5	41.5	49.4	50.6
13652	HERMON	98.6	98.1	0.4	0.7	0.4	0.6	0.2	0.4	6.3	6.7	7.7	7.4	6.7	26.5	27.8	9.7	1.2	74.2	37.4	50.6	49.4
13654	HEUVELTON	98.0	97.6	0.5	0.6	0.2	0.3	0.3	0.4	7.5	7.7	8.4	7.7	6.3	25.9	24.9	10.5	1.1	71.4	35.8	49.9	50.1
13655	HOGANSBURG	4.6	4.0	0.0	0.0	0.0	0.0	0.7	0.8	8.3	8.1	9.6	9.3	7.3	27.9	21.2	7.2	0.9	68.0	30.7	49.6	50.4
13656	LA FARGEVILLE	96.1	95.4	1.2	1.3	0.5	0.6	1.3	1.7	7.3	7.5	8.7	7.1	6.2	29.1	24.4	8.7	1.1	71.9	35.7	50.4	49.6
13658	LISBON	98.2	97.7	0.2	0.4	0.2	0.2	0.7	1.0	6.6	6.9	7.9	6.8	6.3	27.4	26.8	10.3	1.1	74.3	38.1	50.0	50.0
13659	LORRAINE	98.6	98.4	0.2	0.2	0.0	0.2	0.6	1.0	7.3	7.3	7.9	7.7	5.9	27.5	25.9	9.3	1.2	72.5	37.2	52.8	47.2
13660	MADRID	97.7	97.2	1.1	1.3	0.3	0.4	0.7	0.9	5.5	6.4	8.4	6.9	4.4	28.3	27.9	11.0	1.2	75.0	39.4	50.4	49.6
13661	MANNSVILLE	97.6	97.2	0.6	0.6	0.5	0.7	1.1	1.3	7.0	7.7	8.8	8.4	5.8	27.8	24.1	9.3	1.2	71.3	36.1	49.2	50.8
13662	MASSENA	95.2	94.6	0.3	0.4	0.5	0.7	1.1	1.5	5.8	5.8	6.5	6.8	6.1	25.1	26.6	15.2	2.3	77.6	41.2	47.8	52.2
13665	NATURAL BRIDGE	96.2	95.7	0.5	0.5	0.5	0.6	1.1	1.2	6.7	7.5	8.9	8.0	4.2	28.1	26.6	9.4	0.6	71.6	36.9	50.2	49.8
13666	NEWTON FALLS	95.3	94.7	0.0	0.0	0.0	0.0	1.5	1.9	4.2	6.4	7.2	9.4	3.4	24.9	27.9	15.1	1.5	75.5	41.7	50.2	49.8
13667	NORFOLK	96.9	96.2	0.4	0.6	0.8	1.0	0.8	1.1	6.1	6.1	6.5	7.1	6.1	26.2	27.3	13.3	1.4	76.8	39.9	49.8	50.2
13668	NORWOOD	98.2	97.9	0.3	0.4	0.5	0.7	0.5	0.6	5.8	6.0	7.0	6.7	7.2	26.5	28.3	11.4	1.2	76.9	38.6	49.4	50.6
13669	OGDENSBURG	89.3	88.5	6.9	7.2	0.6	0.7	4.4	5.0	5.0	5.1	6.5	6.5	7.3	31.1	24.7	11.7	2.1	79.3	38.2	54.0	46.1
	NEW YORK	68.0	65.9	15.9	16.2	5.6	6.4	15.1	16.7	6.5	6.5	7.1	7.0	7.1	28.9	24.0	11.2	1.8	75.8	36.7	48.3	51.7
	UNITED STATES	75.1	73.6	12.3	12.5	3.8	4.2	12.5	14.1	6.9	6.7	7.2	7.0	7.3	28.6	23.8	10.8	1.7	75.1	36.0	49.1	50.9

ZIP CODE #	POST OFFICE NAME	2004 Per Capita Income	2004 HH Income Base	2004 Household Income Distribution (%): Less than $25,000	$25,000 to $49,999	$50,000 to $99,999	$100,000 to $149,999	$150,000 or More	Median Household Income: 2004	2009	2004 National Centile	2004 State Centile	2004 Home Value Base	2004 Home Value Distribution (%): Less than $50,000	$50,000 to $89,999	$90,000 to $174,999	$175,000 to $399,999	$400,000 or More	2004 Median Home Value
13415	NEW LISBON	19989	41	31.7	34.2	26.8	4.9	2.4	34277	40000	25	11	35	5.7	17.1	54.3	22.9	0.0	120833
13416	NEWPORT	17752	853	28.1	33.8	31.9	5.2	1.1	41458	45284	51	39	716	17.3	25.4	44.3	12.4	0.6	102241
13417	NEW YORK MILLS	20703	1571	38.1	34.6	20.9	5.1	1.3	32802	36164	20	8	760	1.5	22.0	66.1	10.5	0.0	112033
13418	NORTH BROOKFIELD	12714	52	32.7	38.5	26.9	1.9	0.0	35000	37957	28	13	44	38.6	31.8	22.7	4.6	2.3	65000
13420	OLD FORGE	22468	526	27.4	38.0	25.9	5.3	3.4	39194	44050	43	30	405	4.0	8.9	43.0	36.3	7.9	162228
13421	ONEIDA	22261	5658	30.2	32.2	28.1	5.7	3.8	39871	44682	46	33	3585	6.0	26.9	53.3	13.4	0.5	106661
13424	ORISKANY	19860	983	23.6	29.8	37.0	7.7	1.8	47275	53111	67	56	800	4.3	20.5	60.4	14.1	0.8	114413
13425	ORISKANY FALLS	19779	796	27.0	38.1	27.4	4.7	2.9	39228	45137	44	30	622	14.8	32.5	42.6	9.5	0.6	93696
13428	PALATINE BRIDGE	20401	739	32.3	31.5	27.7	4.3	4.1	36220	40685	32	17	598	26.3	36.0	26.1	11.0	0.7	76481
13431	POLAND	20280	716	27.0	34.6	27.9	8.2	2.2	42007	46373	53	41	600	12.5	22.7	47.0	17.5	0.3	112090
13433	PORT LEYDEN	15570	545	35.4	35.6	24.6	3.3	1.1	35133	38450	28	13	432	27.3	29.4	34.0	8.6	0.7	78000
13437	REDFIELD	17354	210	31.4	37.1	27.1	4.3	0.0	36046	40388	32	16	169	26.0	29.0	39.1	5.9	0.0	79667
13438	REMSEN	20326	1824	24.7	35.1	32.2	5.9	2.1	41708	46904	52	40	1496	16.6	27.3	41.4	13.8	0.8	100687
13439	RICHFIELD SPRINGS	19095	1591	30.9	34.3	28.2	5.0	1.8	38094	42197	40	25	1248	9.5	20.3	49.0	18.4	2.8	116768
13440	ROME	21619	17470	30.1	30.4	30.1	6.5	2.9	40497	45482	48	36	11357	10.0	33.2	47.4	8.8	0.7	96853
13450	ROSEBOOM	24622	82	24.4	37.8	26.8	6.1	4.9	42305	49079	54	42	67	9.0	9.0	46.3	26.9	9.0	139773
13452	SAINT JOHNSVILLE	16636	1902	35.3	35.1	25.0	3.3	1.3	35207	39408	28	14	1465	22.7	35.8	32.4	8.1	1.2	78287
13454	SALISBURY CENTER	13905	196	33.2	38.8	24.5	2.6	1.0	36041	39596	32	16	164	22.0	41.5	32.3	3.7	0.6	77000
13456	SAUQUOIT	23434	1687	20.1	30.8	34.9	10.3	3.9	49109	55098	70	60	1421	11.3	13.3	53.6	21.1	0.7	126670
13459	SHARON SPRINGS	21611	819	27.7	34.1	30.5	4.5	3.2	41139	45456	50	38	662	10.6	19.6	50.9	17.7	1.2	112418
13460	SHERBURNE	18152	1748	38.0	28.7	26.3	4.6	2.4	34888	37999	27	12	1308	19.8	21.6	44.3	13.5	0.9	100291
13461	SHERRILL	25595	1258	21.1	25.5	38.8	11.1	3.4	53664	60408	78	68	983	0.0	6.9	68.1	24.6	0.4	129658
13464	SMYRNA	15742	583	30.7	38.8	24.4	4.1	2.1	36837	40807	35	20	484	26.2	27.9	34.5	10.7	0.6	81667
13468	SPRINGFIELD CENTER	18765	217	30.0	35.9	27.2	4.6	2.3	38908	43543	42	29	173	6.4	15.0	42.2	29.5	6.9	139500
13469	STITTVILLE	27535	251	11.6	38.3	39.0	8.4	2.8	50199	55844	72	63	213	5.6	19.3	56.3	17.8	0.9	115675
13470	STRATFORD	14684	276	39.1	33.7	23.9	2.2	1.1	32079	35891	18	7	227	26.4	28.2	37.0	8.4	0.0	80455
13471	TABERG	16948	1306	27.2	36.1	31.1	4.3	1.3	39329	44181	44	31	1070	33.9	23.6	34.1	8.4	0.0	77179
13473	TURIN	17017	334	36.2	32.9	24.0	3.9	3.0	35000	38287	28	13	263	12.9	26.6	47.2	11.0	2.3	102644
13475	VAN HORNESVILLE	14028	9	44.4	44.4	11.1	0.0	0.0	27247	27247	7	4	8	12.5	37.5	50.0	0.0	0.0	90000
13476	VERNON	23074	1324	24.9	32.0	34.3	6.7	2.0	44490	49618	60	49	1016	10.7	18.9	55.6	13.8	1.0	112293
13477	VERNON CENTER	18701	438	27.9	36.1	29.5	4.6	2.1	41017	45779	50	38	348	16.7	22.4	45.4	14.7	0.9	104583
13478	VERONA	21188	1242	15.9	33.3	44.9	4.8	1.1	50453	56121	73	63	1056	5.8	28.5	57.0	8.3	0.4	106017
13480	WATERVILLE	19707	1501	27.3	33.0	30.0	6.9	2.8	41566	46752	52	40	1107	15.2	22.6	49.1	12.9	0.3	104764
13482	WEST BURLINGTON	16028	12	25.0	41.7	33.3	0.0	0.0	40000	40000	46	34	10	0.0	40.0	40.0	20.0	0.0	100000
13483	WESTDALE	18019	92	30.4	32.6	32.6	3.3	1.1	40000	45373	46	34	76	29.0	31.6	31.6	7.9	0.0	78750
13485	WEST EDMESTON	15728	440	33.2	35.2	25.7	3.6	2.3	35113	38574	28	13	369	30.6	31.2	29.0	8.4	0.8	72419
13486	WESTERNVILLE	20034	228	27.2	31.1	32.9	5.7	3.1	44303	48904	59	48	191	17.8	25.1	42.4	13.6	1.1	101042
13488	WESTFORD	17484	59	28.8	35.6	28.8	5.1	1.7	37966	42343	39	24	51	11.8	15.7	51.0	21.6	0.0	126042
13489	WEST LEYDEN	16323	205	28.8	37.1	27.8	4.9	1.5	38351	42338	41	26	174	14.9	24.1	45.4	13.2	2.3	100000
13490	WESTMORELAND	21521	410	13.9	24.4	49.5	10.7	1.5	57028	63490	82	72	364	3.6	19.2	62.9	12.4	1.9	115278
13491	WEST WINFIELD	17979	1521	28.2	36.0	28.9	4.8	2.1	37941	41830	39	24	1245	15.6	29.3	39.0	14.8	1.4	98141
13492	WHITESBORO	24134	4855	22.5	29.5	34.3	9.9	3.8	48102	54218	69	58	3825	3.4	19.9	57.8	18.5	0.4	118079
13493	WILLIAMSTOWN	16029	774	29.8	37.5	27.3	4.9	0.5	36249	40693	33	17	638	28.2	31.4	35.6	4.9	0.0	74000
13494	WOODGATE	20682	147	27.9	38.1	29.9	3.4	0.7	38214	43744	40	26	126	22.2	27.0	34.1	16.7	0.0	92000
13495	YORKVILLE	19853	902	32.5	32.7	28.5	5.9	0.4	37770	43133	38	24	624	2.4	44.2	50.3	2.7	0.3	92333
13501	UTICA	18145	14508	48.3	26.9	17.9	4.2	2.8	26116	29050	6	4	7064	18.5	39.5	34.1	7.1	0.9	79890
13502	UTICA	18699	13651	39.5	29.2	25.0	4.8	1.5	32446	36209	19	7	8249	15.6	36.1	43.3	4.6	0.4	88282
13601	WATERTOWN	19117	15302	37.9	30.2	24.3	5.3	2.3	34357	37714	25	11	8404	8.2	21.3	51.5	17.9	1.2	115588
13602	FORT DRUM	13747	7	0.0	0.0	100.0	0.0	0.0	61875	66942	86	77	0	0.0	0.0	0.0	0.0	0.0	0
13603	WATERTOWN	12833	2540	23.5	48.9	24.8	1.9	0.9	35852	40235	31	16	12	33.3	50.0	0.0	16.7	0.0	75000
13605	ADAMS	20041	1842	29.3	32.3	29.0	7.0	2.5	39463	43526	44	32	1402	10.6	21.3	48.8	17.6	1.9	117459
13606	ADAMS CENTER	21800	972	25.1	30.9	32.5	8.4	3.1	44382	48600	60	49	768	13.0	15.0	46.5	20.4	5.1	124569
13607	ALEXANDRIA BAY	21482	925	35.0	29.8	25.4	6.7	3.0	38145	42262	40	25	709	10.9	15.9	46.3	21.2	5.8	125500
13608	ANTWERP	17090	621	31.7	35.3	26.4	4.4	2.3	37718	41255	38	23	503	18.5	27.8	40.2	12.9	0.6	95441
13611	BELLEVILLE	18609	36	33.3	27.8	25.0	5.6	8.3	40000	45000	46	34	28	17.9	25.0	46.4	10.7	0.0	103125
13612	BLACK RIVER	20249	1097	25.2	33.6	32.6	6.7	2.0	43263	48188	57	45	778	12.1	12.7	56.7	18.4	0.1	120808
13613	BRASHER FALLS	18910	938	38.0	30.9	23.6	5.7	1.9	33934	36840	24	10	731	23.8	25.9	42.7	7.5	0.1	90385
13614	BRIER HILL	23065	211	29.9	37.4	24.6	4.7	3.3	38848	42329	42	29	176	20.5	22.2	36.4	17.6	3.4	99286
13616	CALCIUM	14397	692	29.2	43.4	22.0	4.8	0.7	36764	39825	35	20	355	16.1	13.2	49.6	21.1	0.0	115278
13617	CANTON	19288	3526	30.3	31.3	29.0	7.6	1.8	40538	44663	48	36	2370	15.9	16.7	43.7	22.4	1.3	115288
13618	CAPE VINCENT	21583	751	29.4	33.2	29.4	5.6	2.4	39842	44835	45	33	622	9.2	18.2	42.6	26.5	3.5	126989
13619	CARTHAGE	16449	4377	37.2	31.0	25.6	4.8	1.4	35036	38259	28	13	2858	12.3	21.6	49.9	14.7	1.5	109203
13620	CASTORLAND	16051	838	30.9	35.6	28.4	3.6	1.6	39008	42776	43	29	673	7.3	18.6	56.2	16.2	1.8	117870
13621	CHASE MILLS	19729	247	29.2	32.4	29.6	6.5	2.4	39474	43636	44	32	206	14.1	27.7	35.0	22.3	1.0	106481
13622	CHAUMONT	20792	944	27.3	35.0	29.9	5.5	2.3	41398	46316	51	39	785	9.2	17.8	48.3	22.9	1.8	121898
13624	CLAYTON	18889	2014	28.3	34.7	29.4	5.6	2.0	39318	43458	44	31	1532	8.8	14.5	48.7	23.2	4.8	127834
13625	COLTON	21530	1053	26.6	34.5	30.7	6.6	1.7	42032	46832	53	41	864	16.0	18.9	41.3	21.4	2.4	123387
13626	COPENHAGEN	17649	805	30.2	29.8	32.9	5.6	1.5	41766	45000	52	41	645	9.6	19.8	48.4	19.4	2.8	114838
13630	DE KALB JUNCTION	15550	502	33.5	34.9	27.3	3.8	0.6	36333	40195	33	18	399	22.8	30.3	36.1	10.8	0.0	82647
13633	DE PEYSTER	12594	63	36.5	36.5	20.6	3.2	3.2	34296	39306	25	11	53	18.9	32.1	34.0	15.1	0.0	88333
13634	DEXTER	18334	1435	29.2	34.2	29.6	5.8	1.2	41235	45388	51	39	1176	7.8	15.8	54.9	20.2	1.2	121146
13635	EDWARDS	15130	419	40.8	32.9	22.0	2.9	1.4	33074	36137	21	8	336	31.3	31.6	33.3	3.0	0.9	72414
13636	ELLISBURG	19494	116	31.9	27.6	26.7	6.0	7.8	41545	45926	51	40	92	14.1	26.1	43.5	14.1	2.2	104545
13637	EVANS MILLS	15339	1437	28.7	42.5	23.9	4.0	0.9	36090	39247	32	17	717	6.8	18.0	55.9	19.3	0.0	118963
13638	FELTS MILLS	18050	113	25.7	38.1	30.1	5.3	0.9	40275	46435	47	35	81	13.6	19.8	60.5	6.2	0.0	107386
13639	FINE	16656	101	30.7	33.7	31.7	3.0	1.0	39596	43820	45	33	84	33.3	41.7	20.2	3.6	1.2	59333
13640	WELLESLEY ISLAND	25212	169	33.7	30.2	24.3	7.7	4.1	39081	43500	43	30	127	7.1	8.7	51.2	25.2	7.9	137500
13642	GOUVERNEUR	15258	3510	38.5	34.6	23.3	2.4	1.2	32493	35906	19	7	2449	16.5	32.0	41.2	9.5	0.9	91995
13646	HAMMOND	16282	1055	40.6	35.6	19.2	3.7	1.0	30342	33178	13	5	852	19.0	24.4	39.0	15.7	1.9	101128
13648	HARRISVILLE	17183	971	32.4	35.6	26.0	4.4	1.5	36347	39805	33	18	813	22.4	28.9	38.4	9.2	1.1	87558
13650	HENDERSON	22013	585	28.0	34.5	27.2	5.6	4.6	40047	44863	46	34	486	10.3	23.1	42.2	20.4	4.1	118373
13652	HERMON	15811	680	31.0	36.9	28.1	3.5	0.4	37080	40964	36	21	564	23.1	28.4	37.2	10.6	0.7	86800
13654	HEUVELTON	15491	944	34.5	35.1	24.8	4.0	1.6	34922	38462	27	12	759	18.3	26.8	43.4	11.3	0.3	96048
13655	HOGANSBURG	13906	1006	38.6	34.4	22.3	3.9	0.9	35051	37440	28	13	648	2.3	2.3	63.1	32.3	0.0	144372
13656	LA FARGEVILLE	17477	864	29.3	34.0	31.7	3.7	1.3	38700	42417	42	28	705	13.6	24.1	45.8	14.9	1.6	110156
13658	LISBON	16848	724	28.2	37.6	28.9	4.3	1.1	38609	42477	41	28	590	19.7	15.6	42.4	19.8	2.5	113208
13659	LORRAINE	19587	197	27.9	32.0	32.5	4.6	3.1	41736	45455	52	40	169	16.6	27.2	34.3	20.7	1.2	101875
13660	MADRID	16798	794	33.1	31.4	30.7	3.7	1.1	37431	41621	37	22	639	16.7	27.9	39.1	15.0	1.3	96635
13661	MANNSVILLE	19235	584	28.4	27.9	33.4	6.5	3.8	45334	50057	62	51	484	14.7	30.2	40.5	13.6	1.0	96250
13662	MASSENA	20268	7043	35.7	30.5	26.0	5.5	2.3	35649	39692	30	15	4802	7.2	15.8	57.3	18.3	1.5	123148
13665	NATURAL BRIDGE	15898	308	34.1	34.7	28.3	2.3	0.7	33857	37683	24	10	255	30.6	26.7	37.7	5.1	0.0	69138
13666	NEWTON FALLS	15371	103	35.9	35.9	25.2	2.9	0.0	34136	37873	24	10	77	37.7	32.5	19.5	7.8	2.6	57917
13667	NORFOLK	19170	1615	34.8	30.0	28.2	5.5	1.6	36235	40000	32	17	1259	15.7	27.6	41.0	14.9	1.0	99194
13668	NORWOOD	19393	1427	29.0	32.8	31.8	5.2	1.2	40781	46225	49	37	1085	15.6	23.9	45.4	14.5	0.7	101822
13669	OGDENSBURG	17953	6167	37.3	31.5	24.2	4.7	2.4	34351	37961	25	11	4141	18.7	28.1	39.5	11.7	2.0	94529
	NEW YORK	28049		26.3	24.3	29.3	11.5	8.6	49309	58077				4.6	8.6	27.2	39.9	19.8	219050
	UNITED STATES	25866		24.7	27.1	30.8	10.9	6.5	48124	56710				10.9	15.0	33.7	30.1	10.4	145905

ZIP CODE #	POST OFFICE NAME	FINANCIAL SERVICES: Auto Loan	Home Loan	Invest-ments	Retire-ment Plans	THE HOME: Home Improvements: Home Repair	Lawn & Garden	Furnishings: Comput-ers & Hard-ware	Major Appli-ances	TV, Radio, Sound Equip-ment	Furni-ture	ENTERTAINMENT: Dine out/ Carry out	Sports Equip-ment	Fees & Tickets	Toys & Games	Travel	Cable TV	PERSONAL: Apparel & Services	Auto Repairs	Health Insur-ance	Pets & Supplies
13415	NEW LISBON	87	60	31	56	70	79	59	73	69	59	81	88	51	79	61	73	74	73	88	103
13416	NEWPORT	81	64	42	61	71	78	61	71	67	61	81	86	56	81	63	70	75	70	81	96
13417	NEW YORK MILLS	60	54	56	54	56	64	58	59	61	56	75	67	56	74	58	63	71	60	65	68
13418	NORTH BROOKFIELD	63	58	45	56	58	61	55	59	56	57	69	68	52	65	54	55	66	59	59	70
13420	OLD FORGE	84	66	45	59	74	83	62	75	70	62	83	88	56	82	66	75	77	74	88	102
13421	ONEIDA	75	74	73	71	75	82	75	75	77	73	95	87	75	98	75	78	92	75	79	86
13424	ORISKANY	71	78	82	74	78	86	75	75	77	73	95	84	79	101	78	79	92	74	79	84
13425	ORISKANY FALLS	72	71	66	67	73	80	69	71	72	67	88	81	70	94	71	74	85	70	77	84
13428	PALATINE BRIDGE	80	70	58	64	74	84	69	75	76	68	92	86	67	94	71	80	87	74	86	93
13431	POLAND	87	70	49	68	76	85	70	79	76	69	91	92	65	90	71	78	85	78	88	100
13433	PORT LEYDEN	76	52	25	45	59	68	50	62	60	51	70	74	43	67	51	64	64	62	76	88
13437	REDFIELD	74	58	39	52	65	73	55	66	62	54	73	77	49	72	58	66	68	65	78	90
13438	REMSEN	79	72	60	70	75	82	70	76	74	69	90	87	68	91	71	75	85	74	81	91
13439	RICHFIELD SPRINGS	81	60	37	56	68	78	61	72	69	60	82	84	54	79	63	73	75	71	86	95
13440	ROME	70	71	77	69	71	78	73	72	74	71	92	83	74	94	73	75	89	73	74	81
13450	ROSEBOOM	98	75	50	70	83	97	79	89	88	76	104	101	70	100	80	94	96	89	106	113
13452	SAINT JOHNSVILLE	67	54	39	49	58	66	54	60	60	53	72	69	50	72	55	64	67	60	71	76
13454	SALISBURY CENTER	76	51	23	44	58	66	49	61	59	50	70	73	42	66	50	64	63	61	76	87
13456	SAUQUOIT	81	93	97	91	92	95	86	87	83	85	104	101	90	109	88	82	102	85	83	98
13459	SHARON SPRINGS	94	75	51	72	81	91	74	84	81	73	97	99	69	96	75	83	90	83	94	108
13460	SHERBURNE	77	57	35	53	63	73	58	67	66	57	78	78	52	76	59	70	72	66	80	87
13461	SHERRILL	88	89	85	86	90	98	87	90	89	85	109	103	87	111	88	90	105	89	93	102
13464	SMYRNA	73	63	47	58	67	74	60	67	65	59	79	78	58	80	61	68	74	65	75	85
13468	SPRINGFIELD CENTER	85	59	31	56	69	77	58	72	67	58	79	87	50	77	61	71	72	71	86	101
13469	STITTVILLE	49	51	47	50	52	53	46	49	46	46	57	58	47	59	48	46	55	47	48	59
13470	STRATFORD	67	51	32	45	57	64	48	58	55	48	65	69	42	64	51	59	60	57	70	80
13471	TABERG	72	68	58	66	68	72	65	69	66	67	81	80	62	77	65	64	78	69	68	81
13473	TURIN	71	61	49	57	65	73	60	66	66	59	80	76	58	81	62	69	75	65	75	82
13475	VAN HORNESVILLE	53	35	16	31	40	46	34	43	41	35	48	51	29	46	35	44	44	42	53	61
13476	VERNON	87	78	64	77	81	90	79	83	82	77	100	95	76	100	78	83	95	82	88	97
13477	VERNON CENTER	79	67	53	67	71	79	69	74	73	68	89	84	66	88	68	74	83	72	80	87
13478	VERONA	84	80	68	77	83	88	74	80	77	74	94	94	74	97	76	78	90	78	83	99
13480	WATERVILLE	77	75	68	71	77	84	72	75	75	71	93	87	73	96	74	77	89	74	80	89
13482	WEST BURLINGTON	73	65	49	62	68	73	60	66	64	60	77	79	59	79	62	65	73	65	72	86
13483	WESTDALE	85	62	34	55	69	77	59	71	68	60	81	85	52	78	60	73	75	70	85	98
13485	WEST EDMESTON	71	61	45	59	63	68	59	65	62	60	75	76	55	71	59	62	71	65	68	80
13486	WESTERNVILLE	80	80	72	77	82	87	74	79	76	74	93	93	75	97	76	76	90	77	81	96
13488	WESTFORD	77	61	41	55	68	77	57	69	65	57	77	81	51	76	61	69	71	68	82	94
13489	WEST LEYDEN	74	61	46	59	66	74	61	68	66	60	80	78	58	79	62	68	75	67	76	84
13490	WESTMORELAND	77	93	102	91	91	93	86	85	82	85	104	99	92	110	88	81	103	83	80	94
13491	WEST WINFIELD	76	64	48	63	68	75	65	70	69	64	84	81	61	82	65	70	78	69	76	85
13492	WHITESBORO	75	84	92	82	83	89	82	81	81	80	101	92	85	105	84	82	99	80	81	89
13493	WILLIAMSTOWN	80	59	34	52	66	75	56	68	65	56	77	81	49	74	58	69	71	67	82	95
13494	WOODGATE	79	62	42	56	70	79	59	71	66	58	79	83	53	78	63	71	73	70	84	97
13495	YORKVILLE	59	61	62	58	62	70	61	61	64	59	79	68	63	84	63	67	76	60	67	69
13501	UTICA	57	54	61	53	54	61	60	58	62	58	77	66	59	76	59	63	74	60	61	64
13502	UTICA	56	57	62	55	56	62	59	58	60	58	74	66	60	75	59	60	72	59	59	64
13601	WATERTOWN	66	60	61	60	60	66	65	64	67	63	83	77	63	81	63	66	79	67	65	74
13602	FORT DRUM	100	63	61	73	58	69	95	81	96	88	120	109	81	107	78	88	115	96	75	93
13603	WATERTOWN	68	43	41	50	40	47	65	56	66	60	82	74	55	73	53	60	78	66	52	63
13605	ADAMS	79	68	54	65	72	81	68	74	73	66	88	85	65	89	69	75	83	73	82	91
13606	ADAMS CENTER	93	81	62	78	85	93	79	86	83	78	101	100	76	102	79	85	96	84	93	106
13607	ALEXANDRIA BAY	79	62	42	57	69	79	61	71	69	60	82	82	55	80	64	73	76	71	84	94
13608	ANTWERP	79	63	45	59	70	79	61	71	68	60	81	83	56	80	64	72	75	70	82	94
13611	BELLEVILLE	104	72	38	68	84	95	72	89	82	71	97	107	61	95	74	87	88	87	105	123
13612	BLACK RIVER	80	70	56	69	73	81	70	75	74	69	90	87	68	90	70	75	85	74	81	90
13613	BRASHER FALLS	82	57	30	51	64	75	58	69	68	58	80	81	50	76	58	73	73	69	84	94
13614	BRIER HILL	91	71	49	64	80	90	67	81	76	66	90	95	60	89	72	81	84	80	96	111
13616	CALCIUM	71	45	43	52	41	49	67	58	68	63	85	77	57	76	55	62	82	68	54	66
13617	CANTON	76	67	62	67	70	77	70	72	73	68	89	85	67	88	69	73	84	73	76	86
13618	CAPE VINCENT	81	63	43	57	71	80	60	72	68	59	80	84	53	79	64	72	74	71	85	98
13619	CARTHAGE	63	55	51	55	57	64	59	60	62	57	76	69	57	76	58	63	72	60	65	70
13620	CASTORLAND	70	59	46	59	62	70	61	65	65	60	78	74	58	78	60	66	73	64	70	77
13621	CHASE MILLS	78	68	52	64	72	80	66	72	71	65	86	84	64	87	67	74	81	71	81	91
13622	CHAUMONT	88	71	50	65	78	88	68	80	76	67	90	93	62	89	71	80	84	78	92	106
13624	CLAYTON	64	50	34	45	56	63	47	57	53	47	63	66	42	62	50	57	59	56	67	78
13625	COLTON	88	70	48	65	78	86	67	79	74	66	88	93	60	87	70	78	82	77	91	106
13626	COPENHAGEN	76	66	51	64	70	77	64	70	68	63	82	82	62	83	65	70	78	69	76	88
13630	DE KALB JUNCTION	67	55	41	54	59	66	57	62	61	56	74	71	53	72	56	62	69	61	68	75
13633	DE PEYSTER	83	55	25	48	63	72	54	67	65	55	76	80	46	72	54	70	69	66	82	95
13634	DEXTER	79	65	49	61	71	79	63	72	69	62	83	84	59	82	65	72	77	71	81	93
13635	EDWARDS	75	50	23	43	57	66	49	61	59	50	69	73	41	65	49	63	63	60	75	86
13636	ELLISBURG	100	73	41	69	83	93	71	86	81	70	95	104	62	94	74	84	88	85	101	119
13637	EVANS MILLS	69	50	44	54	47	54	64	59	65	61	81	75	56	74	56	61	77	66	56	68
13638	FELTS MILLS	72	61	48	61	64	73	63	67	67	62	81	77	60	80	63	68	76	66	73	80
13639	FINE	58	63	67	60	64	71	63	62	65	60	80	69	66	87	65	67	78	61	67	68
13640	WELLESLEY ISLAND	84	66	45	59	74	83	62	75	70	61	83	87	55	82	66	75	77	74	88	102
13642	GOUVERNEUR	59	52	45	50	54	61	54	57	58	53	70	65	52	69	54	59	66	56	62	67
13646	HAMMOND	67	53	36	47	59	67	50	60	56	49	66	70	44	66	53	60	62	59	71	82
13648	HARRISVILLE	78	58	34	51	65	74	55	67	64	55	75	79	48	73	57	68	69	66	81	93
13650	HENDERSON	90	68	44	62	77	87	65	79	74	64	87	93	58	86	69	79	81	78	94	108
13652	HERMON	66	56	44	56	59	66	57	61	61	56	74	70	55	73	57	62	69	60	67	73
13654	HEUVELTON	76	58	38	55	63	72	58	67	65	58	78	78	53	76	59	68	72	66	77	86
13655	HOGANSBURG	55	51	56	51	51	56	57	55	58	55	72	65	56	72	56	58	70	57	56	61
13656	LA FARGEVILLE	80	68	50	64	73	80	64	73	70	64	84	86	61	84	67	73	79	71	82	94
13658	LISBON	78	61	42	59	67	74	60	70	66	60	79	83	54	77	61	67	73	69	78	91
13659	LORRAINE	80	66	48	65	70	79	67	74	72	66	87	85	63	86	67	74	81	73	81	90
13660	MADRID	72	59	43	57	62	72	62	67	67	60	80	76	57	76	61	69	74	67	76	80
13661	MANNSVILLE	88	73	52	69	79	86	70	79	75	69	91	93	66	91	71	78	85	77	88	102
13662	MASSENA	68	64	61	60	66	73	64	67	68	63	84	76	64	85	65	71	80	66	73	78
13665	NATURAL BRIDGE	67	55	42	54	59	67	56	62	60	55	72	71	52	72	56	62	68	61	69	76
13666	NEWTON FALLS	67	52	36	47	59	66	49	59	56	49	66	70	44	65	53	60	62	59	70	81
13667	NORFOLK	82	62	37	56	68	77	60	70	69	60	82	83	55	79	61	73	75	70	83	94
13668	NORWOOD	76	64	50	64	68	76	66	70	70	64	84	81	63	84	65	71	79	69	77	84
13669	OGDENSBURG	64	61	60	59	63	70	62	64	65	61	80	73	62	82	63	67	77	64	69	74
	NEW YORK	95	100	134	99	98	107	103	100	105	103	133	116	105	138	104	107	131	102	99	112
	UNITED STATES	100	100	100	100	100	100	100	100	100	100	100	100	100	100	100	100	100	100	100	100

ZIP CODE		COUNTY FIPS CODE	POPULATION			2000-2004 ANNUAL RATE		HOUSEHOLDS					FAMILIES		
#	POST OFFICE NAME		2000	2004	2009	% Rate	State Centile	2000	2004	2009	% Annual Rate 2000-2004	2004 Average HH Size	2000	2004	% Annual Rate 2000-2004
13670	OSWEGATCHIE	089	566	552	553	-0.6	4	234	233	239	-0.1	2.27	162	160	-0.3
13672	PARISHVILLE	089	332	334	338	0.1	37	137	140	145	0.5	2.39	99	101	0.5
13673	PHILADELPHIA	045	2729	2783	2832	0.5	55	953	989	1021	0.9	2.81	721	742	0.7
13675	PLESSIS	045	66	65	66	-0.4	11	24	24	25	0.0	2.71	18	18	0.0
13676	POTSDAM	089	15069	15247	15492	0.3	45	5242	5412	5613	0.8	2.30	2960	3035	0.6
13679	REDWOOD	045	1721	1701	1716	-0.3	15	659	664	681	0.2	2.56	462	462	0.0
13680	RENSSELAER FALLS	089	1180	1237	1279	1.1	81	402	430	453	1.6	2.82	296	315	1.5
13681	RICHVILLE	089	1047	1130	1186	1.8	92	390	433	464	2.5	2.49	294	324	2.3
13682	RODMAN	045	906	924	942	0.5	55	307	317	327	0.8	2.66	245	252	0.7
13684	RUSSELL	089	907	904	910	-0.1	24	348	354	363	0.4	2.55	253	255	0.2
13685	SACKETS HARBOR	045	2052	2123	2190	0.8	71	913	965	1013	1.3	2.19	574	601	1.1
13687	SOUTH COLTON	089	300	317	329	1.3	85	124	134	141	1.8	2.37	84	90	1.6
13690	STAR LAKE	089	820	792	793	-0.8	2	346	342	349	-0.3	2.30	227	222	-0.5
13691	THERESA	045	2711	2756	2809	0.4	51	956	990	1024	0.8	2.78	708	727	0.6
13693	THREE MILE BAY	045	267	271	275	0.4	50	121	125	129	0.8	2.16	84	86	0.6
13694	WADDINGTON	089	1545	1589	1624	0.7	64	641	671	698	1.1	2.34	427	443	0.9
13695	WANAKENA	089	191	187	187	-0.5	6	74	74	75	0.0	2.38	48	48	0.0
13696	WEST STOCKHOLM	089	274	272	274	-0.2	19	105	107	110	0.4	2.54	77	77	0.0
13697	WINTHROP	089	2458	2522	2581	0.6	62	951	996	1038	1.1	2.53	689	717	0.9
13699	POTSDAM	089	1491	1473	1472	-0.3	14	100	95	96	-1.2	2.56	36	34	-1.3
13730	AFTON	017	2921	2991	3077	0.6	60	1166	1214	1269	1.0	2.46	821	849	0.8
13731	ANDES	025	1058	1175	1372	2.5	96	482	544	647	2.9	2.15	307	344	2.7
13732	APALACHIN	107	8240	8590	8865	1.0	77	2966	3138	3287	1.3	2.74	2384	2512	1.2
13733	BAINBRIDGE	017	5277	5372	5519	0.4	53	2072	2143	2235	0.8	2.50	1445	1486	0.7
13734	BARTON	107	2772	2856	2909	0.7	66	999	1043	1079	1.0	2.74	748	775	0.8
13736	BERKSHIRE	107	2523	2530	2551	0.1	33	931	950	974	0.5	2.66	686	695	0.3
13739	BLOOMVILLE	025	1165	1287	1492	2.4	95	434	490	582	2.9	2.49	307	344	2.7
13740	BOVINA CENTER	025	568	636	745	2.7	97	233	263	313	2.9	2.42	162	183	2.9
13743	CANDOR	107	4404	4505	4598	0.5	59	1689	1758	1823	1.0	2.56	1221	1261	0.8
13744	CASTLE CREEK	007	1179	1193	1192	0.3	45	437	450	455	0.7	2.65	320	327	0.5
13746	CHENANGO FORKS	007	3000	2937	2923	-0.5	6	1137	1136	1147	0.0	2.58	832	827	-0.1
13748	CONKLIN	007	4030	4007	3972	-0.1	21	1519	1534	1541	0.2	2.61	1129	1132	0.1
13750	DAVENPORT	025	904	1014	1192	2.7	98	362	413	494	3.2	2.46	252	286	3.0
13751	DAVENPORT CENTER	025	173	194	228	2.7	98	66	75	90	3.1	2.59	46	52	2.9
13752	DE LANCEY	025	906	1013	1187	2.7	97	394	448	534	3.1	2.24	260	293	2.9
13753	DELHI	025	5332	5775	6536	1.9	93	1752	1976	2348	2.9	2.32	1127	1264	2.7
13754	DEPOSIT	007	3441	3699	4061	1.7	90	1388	1521	1699	2.2	2.43	931	1008	1.9
13755	DOWNSVILLE	025	1175	1317	1545	2.7	97	493	559	665	3.0	2.33	325	366	2.8
13756	EAST BRANCH	025	737	825	968	2.7	97	282	321	382	3.1	2.57	195	220	2.9
13757	EAST MEREDITH	025	1265	1411	1652	2.6	97	501	569	678	3.0	2.48	356	402	2.9
13760	ENDICOTT	007	44109	43766	43518	-0.2	19	18751	18814	18906	0.1	2.30	11959	11955	0.0
13775	FRANKLIN	025	1729	1914	2231	2.4	96	681	763	903	2.7	2.50	475	529	2.6
13776	GILBERTSVILLE	077	442	448	449	0.3	48	195	200	203	0.6	2.23	137	140	0.5
13777	GLEN AUBREY	007	818	838	841	0.6	61	278	289	294	0.9	2.90	212	219	0.8
13778	GREENE	017	5588	5874	6161	1.2	82	2220	2372	2525	1.6	2.47	1523	1615	1.4
13780	GUILFORD	017	952	994	1030	1.0	78	377	401	422	1.5	2.29	267	282	1.3
13782	HAMDEN	025	709	790	925	2.6	97	304	344	411	3.0	2.29	205	230	2.7
13783	HANCOCK	025	2583	2848	3315	2.3	95	1077	1210	1433	2.8	2.35	693	775	2.7
13786	HARPERSFIELD	025	223	249	291	2.6	97	83	94	112	3.0	2.64	62	70	2.9
13787	HARPURSVILLE	007	3894	3939	3953	0.3	45	1383	1423	1447	0.7	2.76	1033	1057	0.5
13788	HOBART	025	655	716	827	2.1	94	263	293	345	2.6	2.34	188	208	2.4
13790	JOHNSON CITY	007	19521	19064	18771	-0.6	5	8474	8377	8337	-0.3	2.19	4720	4628	-0.5
13795	KIRKWOOD	007	3736	3670	3617	-0.4	9	1464	1463	1461	0.0	2.51	1057	1048	-0.2
13796	LAURENS	077	1484	1491	1488	0.1	36	582	594	601	0.5	2.51	422	427	0.3
13797	LISLE	007	2617	2626	2613	0.1	33	934	950	955	0.4	2.76	698	706	0.3
13801	MC DONOUGH	017	1330	1358	1390	0.5	57	519	539	560	0.9	2.50	375	387	0.7
13802	MAINE	007	398	384	376	-0.8	2	141	138	137	-0.5	2.78	107	104	-0.7
13803	MARATHON	023	3929	4156	4320	1.3	86	1440	1545	1631	1.7	2.69	1073	1144	1.5
13804	MASONVILLE	025	437	491	576	2.8	98	161	185	221	3.3	2.56	122	139	3.1
13806	MERIDALE	025	42	47	54	2.7	97	19	21	26	2.4	2.19	14	15	1.6
13807	MILFORD	077	1591	1588	1579	0.0	26	600	607	611	0.3	2.58	422	424	0.1
13808	MORRIS	077	1679	1685	1680	0.1	33	672	681	686	0.3	2.47	481	483	0.1
13809	MOUNT UPTON	017	1743	1747	1766	0.1	31	678	691	709	0.5	2.53	477	483	0.3
13810	MOUNT VISION	077	1273	1307	1320	0.6	63	496	516	528	0.9	2.53	354	366	0.8
13811	NEWARK VALLEY	107	4359	4391	4428	0.2	39	1589	1628	1668	0.6	2.66	1200	1222	0.4
13812	NICHOLS	107	2468	2473	2490	0.1	31	924	942	963	0.5	2.59	691	701	0.3
13813	NINEVEH	007	749	743	738	-0.2	18	283	285	288	0.2	2.59	211	212	0.1
13815	NORWICH	017	14189	14373	14733	0.3	47	5798	5944	6174	0.6	2.31	3608	3676	0.4
13820	ONEONTA	077	20888	21041	21316	0.2	39	7295	7450	7666	0.5	2.23	3947	4007	0.4
13825	OTEGO	077	3697	3605	3555	-0.6	4	1442	1428	1428	-0.2	2.49	1024	1008	-0.4
13826	OUAQUAGA	007	217	213	210	-0.4	8	83	83	83	0.0	2.57	62	61	-0.4
13827	OWEGO	107	11309	11403	11626	0.2	40	4508	4606	4763	0.5	2.44	3104	3157	0.4
13830	OXFORD	017	5070	5272	5466	0.9	75	1838	1943	2045	1.3	2.60	1318	1385	1.2
13832	PLYMOUTH	017	374	402	425	1.7	90	131	142	152	1.9	2.83	98	106	1.9
13833	PORT CRANE	007	4643	4795	4839	0.8	69	1775	1868	1912	1.2	2.57	1302	1362	1.1
13834	PORTLANDVILLE	077	156	154	152	-0.3	14	64	64	64	0.0	2.41	41	40	-0.6
13835	RICHFORD	107	1301	1314	1329	0.2	42	487	500	513	0.6	2.63	356	363	0.5
13838	SIDNEY	025	4445	4891	5669	2.3	95	1896	2118	2498	2.6	2.27	1164	1291	2.5
13839	SIDNEY CENTER	025	1557	1745	2047	2.7	97	598	682	815	3.1	2.54	438	497	3.0
13841	SMITHVILLE FLATS	017	389	458	506	3.9	99	138	166	186	4.4	2.73	105	126	4.4
13842	SOUTH KORTRIGHT	025	355	388	444	2.1	94	93	105	125	2.9	3.22	64	72	2.8
13843	SOUTH NEW BERLIN	077	2170	2213	2263	0.5	55	831	861	893	0.8	2.57	611	629	0.7
13844	SOUTH PLYMOUTH	017	779	775	786	-0.1	22	201	202	208	0.1	3.41	148	148	0.0
13846	TREADWELL	025	247	273	319	2.4	96	104	117	138	2.8	2.33	75	84	2.7
13849	UNADILLA	025	5256	5421	5703	0.7	68	2089	2187	2336	1.1	2.47	1477	1538	1.0
13850	VESTAL	007	26522	26423	26314	-0.1	23	8510	8597	8656	0.2	2.42	5920	5922	0.0
13856	WALTON	025	6571	7581	9029	3.4	99	2783	3273	3968	3.9	2.30	1842	2153	3.7
13859	WELLS BRIDGE	077	206	204	202	-0.2	16	83	83	84	0.0	2.46	59	59	0.0
13861	WEST ONEONTA	077	499	492	487	-0.3	12	201	201	202	0.0	2.43	134	133	-0.2
13862	WHITNEY POINT	007	4191	4201	4178	0.1	32	1544	1574	1586	0.5	2.67	1130	1144	0.3
13863	WILLET	023	471	468	469	-0.2	20	176	177	180	0.1	2.64	134	134	0.0
13864	WILLSEYVILLE	107	1151	1123	1135	-0.6	4	472	469	482	-0.2	2.39	322	317	-0.4
13865	WINDSOR	007	6470	6416	6350	-0.2	18	2366	2378	2380	0.1	2.70	1764	1761	0.0
13901	BINGHAMTON	007	19797	19467	19234	-0.4	10	8724	8705	8707	-0.1	2.21	4981	4925	-0.3
13903	BINGHAMTON	007	19482	19299	19137	-0.2	16	7985	8021	8049	0.1	2.40	5140	5131	0.0
	NEW YORK					0.4					0.5	2.60			0.4
	UNITED STATES					1.2					1.3	2.58			1.1

POPULATION COMPOSITION

NEW YORK

13670-13903 **B**

#	POST OFFICE NAME	RACE (%) White 2000	White 2004	Black 2000	Black 2004	Asian/Pacific 2000	Asian/Pacific 2004	% Hispanic Origin 2000	% Hispanic Origin 2004	2004 AGE DISTRIBUTION (%) 0-4	5-9	10-14	15-19	20-24	25-44	45-64	65-84	85+	18+	MEDIAN AGE 2004	% 2004 Males	% 2004 Females
13670	OSWEGATCHIE	97.5	96.9	0.7	0.9	0.2	0.4	0.2	0.2	4.4	4.5	6.0	6.7	6.9	23.7	29.4	17.0	1.5	80.6	43.6	50.4	49.6
13672	PARISHVILLE	98.8	98.8	0.3	0.3	0.3	0.3	0.3	0.3	3.9	4.8	8.1	5.1	4.8	24.3	31.7	16.8	0.6	79.6	44.4	49.7	50.3
13673	PHILADELPHIA	90.4	88.9	4.2	4.7	1.1	1.4	3.6	4.3	8.9	8.1	9.0	8.2	8.8	29.7	19.1	7.3	1.0	69.1	29.7	49.3	50.7
13675	PLESSIS	97.0	98.5	1.5	1.5	0.0	0.0	0.0	0.0	6.2	7.7	9.2	6.2	4.6	30.8	29.2	6.2	0.0	73.9	37.1	49.2	50.8
13676	POTSDAM	94.8	93.6	1.4	1.7	2.3	2.9	1.2	1.6	4.5	4.6	5.4	13.7	20.5	21.1	19.2	9.3	1.7	81.9	26.1	49.5	50.5
13679	REDWOOD	98.3	97.9	0.5	0.6	0.1	0.1	0.9	1.2	5.6	6.2	8.1	6.7	5.8	27.1	27.6	11.5	1.5	75.9	39.7	50.2	49.8
13680	RENSSELAER FALLS	97.3	96.7	0.6	0.8	0.3	0.3	0.9	1.2	7.0	7.1	8.6	8.3	7.3	26.8	23.2	10.4	1.4	71.9	35.0	50.3	49.7
13681	RICHVILLE	94.2	93.5	3.4	3.8	0.3	0.4	2.1	2.5	7.2	7.4	8.9	8.0	6.6	28.0	23.8	9.5	0.8	71.4	34.0	52.5	47.5
13682	RODMAN	91.1	90.3	5.6	6.0	0.2	0.2	3.6	4.2	5.1	5.8	7.6	7.1	6.6	32.7	26.3	8.0	0.8	77.2	37.4	55.8	44.2
13684	RUSSELL	98.7	98.5	0.2	0.2	0.2	0.2	0.3	0.6	6.4	6.9	7.9	7.0	6.0	26.3	27.5	11.1	1.0	74.3	38.3	49.3	50.7
13685	SACKETS HARBOR	97.3	96.8	0.3	0.4	0.4	0.5	1.4	1.7	5.6	5.7	5.8	6.4	7.3	32.1	25.2	11.0	1.1	78.8	36.9	52.3	47.7
13687	SOUTH COLTON	99.0	99.1	0.0	0.0	0.0	0.0	0.7	1.0	4.4	4.7	6.3	5.4	4.7	23.0	33.1	16.7	1.6	80.8	45.9	50.2	49.8
13690	STAR LAKE	96.3	95.7	0.5	0.8	0.4	0.5	1.1	1.4	4.9	5.3	5.9	8.6	4.3	24.6	29.4	15.9	1.0	78.3	42.9	49.0	51.0
13691	THERESA	97.3	96.9	1.2	1.4	0.3	0.4	0.8	1.0	6.7	6.9	8.5	7.7	6.9	29.7	25.4	7.8	0.5	73.2	35.7	51.7	48.3
13693	THREE MILE BAY	98.1	98.2	0.4	0.4	0.4	0.4	0.4	0.7	3.7	4.1	5.9	6.3	4.8	21.4	32.1	19.6	2.2	82.3	47.5	47.6	52.4
13694	WADDINGTON	98.4	98.1	0.2	0.3	0.3	0.3	0.4	0.6	5.6	5.9	6.2	5.9	4.9	26.1	29.3	14.4	2.0	78.3	42.1	49.0	51.0
13695	WANAKENA	97.4	97.3	1.1	1.6	0.0	0.0	0.0	0.0	2.7	3.7	6.4	8.0	7.0	21.9	32.1	16.6	1.6	81.3	45.1	54.6	45.5
13696	WEST STOCKHOLM	97.8	98.2	0.4	0.4	0.0	0.0	0.4	0.4	5.5	6.3	8.8	6.6	6.3	26.1	28.3	11.4	0.7	75.0	38.4	47.4	52.6
13697	WINTHROP	97.9	97.5	0.3	0.3	0.2	0.3	0.5	0.8	6.3	6.8	7.5	7.7	5.9	27.5	26.3	11.1	1.0	74.7	37.3	50.0	50.0
13699	POTSDAM	91.2	89.0	2.8	3.5	3.6	4.5	1.5	1.9	0.8	0.5	0.5	41.6	49.0	4.9	2.2	0.6	0.1	96.5	20.7	71.0	29.0
13730	AFTON	98.7	98.5	0.2	0.2	0.1	0.1	1.0	1.2	4.9	6.9	8.4	7.5	5.1	26.0	27.0	12.5	1.7	74.6	39.9	50.2	49.8
13731	ANDES	97.1	96.6	0.4	0.5	0.6	0.8	1.9	2.4	4.3	4.5	5.3	4.5	4.3	20.3	33.8	20.9	2.2	83.2	49.4	51.4	48.6
13732	APALACHIN	96.9	96.3	0.6	0.7	0.9	1.2	1.1	1.3	6.3	6.9	8.1	7.7	5.7	24.5	28.7	11.5	0.6	73.8	39.8	49.7	50.3
13733	BAINBRIDGE	98.5	98.2	0.3	0.3	0.3	0.3	1.1	1.3	5.7	6.3	7.4	6.9	5.8	25.5	28.1	12.8	1.5	76.2	40.5	50.2	49.8
13734	BARTON	97.9	97.4	0.2	0.3	0.2	0.3	1.1	1.2	7.1	7.4	8.8	7.5	6.3	27.8	24.0	10.3	0.8	72.1	36.4	50.3	49.8
13736	BERKSHIRE	98.2	97.9	0.6	0.7	0.2	0.3	0.5	0.6	6.6	6.9	7.3	7.1	6.2	26.6	28.5	9.7	1.2	74.9	38.4	50.4	49.6
13739	BLOOMVILLE	92.7	92.0	4.5	5.0	0.4	0.5	2.8	3.3	5.8	6.1	7.2	10.3	4.6	23.2	26.0	14.8	1.9	72.3	39.7	51.9	48.1
13740	BOVINA CENTER	98.4	97.8	0.2	0.2	0.4	0.5	2.8	3.8	3.8	4.4	5.0	6.0	4.6	22.8	31.3	20.4	1.7	83.2	47.8	50.6	49.4
13743	CANDOR	97.3	96.8	0.8	0.8	0.2	0.2	1.0	1.3	7.0	7.0	7.8	7.2	6.3	26.7	25.4	11.3	1.4	73.7	37.7	49.2	50.8
13744	CASTLE CREEK	97.1	96.5	1.0	1.2	0.6	0.8	0.7	1.0	5.6	5.9	7.2	8.6	6.3	25.6	28.3	11.6	1.1	76.0	40.2	50.8	49.2
13746	CHENANGO FORKS	98.0	97.6	0.6	0.8	0.2	0.2	0.7	1.0	5.9	6.4	7.9	7.7	6.2	25.3	28.5	11.1	1.1	74.8	39.9	50.9	49.1
13748	CONKLIN	97.6	97.1	0.9	1.0	0.2	0.3	0.9	1.3	5.6	6.1	7.9	8.2	5.8	25.1	27.5	12.6	1.2	75.1	40.0	49.4	50.6
13750	DAVENPORT	98.0	97.5	0.6	0.7	0.1	0.1	1.0	1.3	6.1	6.5	6.8	5.9	5.1	25.1	29.1	14.1	1.3	76.9	41.4	50.5	49.5
13751	DAVENPORT CENTER	97.7	97.4	0.6	0.5	0.0	0.0	0.6	0.5	6.2	6.7	6.7	5.2	5.2	24.7	31.4	12.9	1.0	77.3	41.8	51.0	49.0
13752	DE LANCEY	97.6	97.2	0.2	0.2	0.3	0.5	1.0	1.4	4.4	4.7	5.3	5.6	4.8	21.8	30.3	20.3	2.6	82.0	47.0	50.6	49.4
13753	DELHI	92.9	92.1	3.7	3.9	1.1	1.4	2.5	2.9	3.3	3.8	5.6	16.2	11.2	18.7	24.0	13.9	3.5	83.9	36.6	50.2	49.9
13754	DEPOSIT	97.6	97.0	0.8	1.0	0.4	0.6	2.0	2.4	6.5	6.5	7.1	6.9	6.1	23.5	26.3	15.0	2.2	75.8	40.7	48.9	51.1
13755	DOWNSVILLE	98.8	98.7	0.2	0.2	0.2	0.2	0.8	1.0	6.2	6.1	6.0	5.5	5.0	23.3	27.6	17.7	2.7	78.5	43.7	48.4	51.6
13756	EAST BRANCH	96.5	95.6	1.0	1.2	1.0	1.2	1.6	2.1	5.2	5.8	7.2	7.3	5.1	23.3	28.2	16.6	1.3	77.2	42.4	50.6	49.5
13757	EAST MEREDITH	98.3	98.0	0.3	0.4	0.2	0.2	1.1	1.4	5.2	6.0	7.5	6.6	5.9	24.6	30.3	12.3	1.6	77.3	40.8	50.5	49.5
13760	ENDICOTT	94.6	93.6	2.1	2.3	1.7	2.2	1.2	1.4	5.8	5.9	6.7	6.1	5.7	26.4	25.8	15.2	2.3	77.8	40.9	48.0	52.0
13775	FRANKLIN	98.3	98.1	0.7	0.7	0.2	0.3	0.7	0.9	5.5	5.5	6.7	7.7	6.0	23.6	28.8	14.2	2.0	77.0	41.6	50.4	49.6
13776	GILBERTSVILLE	97.3	96.9	0.7	0.9	0.2	0.2	1.1	1.3	3.8	5.8	8.7	7.6	4.2	23.2	31.0	13.8	1.8	76.8	43.0	48.2	51.8
13777	GLEN AUBREY	97.7	97.0	0.4	0.5	0.2	0.4	0.7	1.1	6.6	6.9	8.6	8.2	6.6	27.7	26.1	8.5	0.8	72.9	36.2	49.8	50.2
13778	GREENE	98.4	98.0	0.3	0.3	0.3	0.4	0.7	1.0	5.7	6.1	7.4	7.4	6.5	24.9	27.9	12.4	1.7	76.1	40.3	49.7	50.3
13780	GUILFORD	97.5	97.0	0.8	0.9	0.3	0.3	1.1	1.3	5.2	5.6	6.9	5.9	5.4	23.2	27.7	16.6	3.3	78.6	43.4	51.6	48.4
13782	HAMDEN	97.6	97.3	0.1	0.1	0.1	0.1	1.1	1.5	5.1	5.3	5.8	6.2	4.8	21.8	31.5	17.6	1.9	79.5	45.6	49.2	50.8
13783	HANCOCK	97.0	96.4	0.6	0.7	0.4	0.5	2.6	3.1	5.0	5.4	6.6	6.5	5.3	22.6	28.5	17.9	2.2	78.8	44.0	49.1	50.9
13786	HARPERSFIELD	97.3	96.8	0.9	1.2	0.0	0.0	2.2	2.8	5.2	5.6	6.8	6.4	4.0	23.7	29.7	17.3	1.2	77.5	43.9	48.6	51.4
13787	HARPURSVILLE	98.0	97.6	0.3	0.3	0.4	0.6	0.8	0.9	6.3	6.7	7.9	8.4	6.4	25.4	27.6	10.3	1.1	73.6	38.4	50.3	49.7
13788	HOBART	95.4	94.6	2.0	2.4	0.5	0.6	1.8	2.2	6.4	6.3	5.6	6.4	5.5	24.6	26.5	16.2	2.5	76.4	41.9	49.9	50.1
13790	JOHNSON CITY	90.4	88.8	2.6	2.8	4.3	5.3	2.0	2.3	5.7	5.3	5.8	6.1	7.1	27.1	23.4	14.8	4.6	79.7	40.1	47.1	52.9
13795	KIRKWOOD	97.5	97.1	0.8	0.9	0.5	0.6	0.6	0.7	5.9	6.2	7.2	6.6	5.3	26.3	26.6	14.6	1.3	76.6	40.7	49.9	50.1
13796	LAURENS	96.9	96.2	0.3	0.3	0.2	0.3	1.4	1.7	5.0	5.6	7.7	6.8	5.8	24.5	31.5	11.7	1.5	77.5	41.6	49.0	51.0
13797	LISLE	98.2	97.8	0.3	0.4	0.1	0.1	0.5	0.7	6.9	7.4	9.0	8.1	6.0	27.8	24.2	9.7	1.0	71.9	35.7	50.1	49.9
13801	MC DONOUGH	97.2	96.8	1.1	1.2	0.2	0.2	1.3	1.5	5.2	7.4	7.6	7.7	5.1	26.7	28.1	11.3	0.9	74.2	39.0	52.4	47.6
13802	MAINE	97.7	97.1	0.3	0.3	0.3	0.5	0.8	1.0	5.5	6.0	8.3	8.1	6.8	28.1	26.8	9.4	1.0	75.0	38.0	51.3	48.7
13803	MARATHON	98.4	98.0	0.5	0.6	0.1	0.1	0.5	0.6	7.1	7.2	8.6	7.8	6.6	26.3	25.5	10.0	1.1	72.4	36.5	50.2	49.8
13804	MASONVILLE	96.1	95.3	2.5	3.1	0.2	0.2	2.1	2.9	5.9	6.3	6.7	7.9	4.9	24.2	27.5	15.1	1.4	74.5	40.9	54.6	45.4
13806	MERIDALE	97.6	100.0	0.0	0.0	0.0	0.0	0.0	2.1	4.3	6.4	8.5	8.5	6.4	25.5	23.4	12.8	4.3	76.6	38.1	53.2	46.8
13807	MILFORD	97.4	97.0	0.5	0.5	0.8	1.0	1.6	1.9	5.2	6.0	7.9	7.6	5.2	25.0	29.5	12.3	1.3	75.8	40.8	48.8	51.2
13808	MORRIS	96.8	96.4	0.7	0.8	0.3	0.4	1.6	2.0	5.8	6.7	8.3	6.7	4.9	25.5	28.2	12.2	1.8	75.0	40.3	48.3	51.7
13809	MOUNT UPTON	96.7	96.1	1.0	1.1	0.2	0.3	0.9	1.1	5.4	5.7	6.8	7.1	6.0	26.1	28.4	13.2	1.3	77.9	40.9	50.5	49.5
13810	MOUNT VISION	97.3	96.8	0.6	0.7	0.4	0.5	1.5	1.8	5.5	6.0	7.3	7.4	5.8	24.0	29.8	12.5	1.8	76.6	41.3	48.8	51.2
13811	NEWARK VALLEY	97.9	97.6	0.5	0.5	0.3	0.4	0.7	0.8	6.6	6.9	7.9	7.4	6.8	26.5	26.8	10.0	1.2	74.3	37.9	50.8	49.2
13812	NICHOLS	99.1	98.9	0.4	0.4	0.2	0.2	0.8	1.0	6.5	6.6	7.4	7.5	5.9	25.0	26.9	12.8	1.5	74.9	39.8	49.8	50.2
13813	NINEVEH	97.9	97.7	0.8	0.8	0.0	0.0	0.7	0.7	5.9	6.5	7.9	8.6	5.9	26.2	26.5	11.3	1.1	73.5	38.5	50.7	49.3
13815	NORWICH	96.7	96.2	1.4	1.5	0.5	0.7	1.1	1.4	6.3	6.4	7.3	6.9	6.0	25.3	25.0	13.8	3.1	75.6	39.5	47.4	52.6
13820	ONEONTA	92.3	91.2	4.0	4.4	1.2	1.5	3.3	3.9	3.8	4.1	4.6	14.6	20.6	19.3	19.9	10.9	2.1	83.7	27.1	46.8	53.2
13825	OTEGO	97.5	97.0	1.0	1.1	0.4	0.5	1.2	1.4	5.1	5.6	7.6	8.3	5.8	24.5	29.1	12.3	1.7	76.0	40.8	48.6	51.4
13826	OUAQUAGA	98.2	98.6	0.0	0.0	0.5	0.5	1.4	1.4	5.6	6.1	8.0	8.0	7.0	23.9	29.1	11.3	0.9	74.7	40.4	50.7	49.3
13827	OWEGO	96.9	96.4	0.7	0.7	0.8	1.0	1.2	1.4	5.6	5.7	6.5	7.2	6.9	25.2	27.6	13.5	1.9	77.7	40.8	49.5	50.5
13830	OXFORD	97.6	97.2	0.8	1.0	0.3	0.4	1.1	1.3	5.7	5.9	7.2	7.3	6.1	23.6	27.4	14.5	2.4	76.8	41.4	50.6	49.4
13832	PLYMOUTH	98.1	98.0	0.0	0.0	0.3	0.3	1.3	1.5	9.0	8.5	8.2	8.0	6.7	26.4	23.6	9.0	0.8	69.4	34.1	50.0	50.0
13833	PORT CRANE	97.7	97.2	0.7	0.8	0.1	0.2	1.0	1.4	5.9	6.4	7.7	7.0	5.6	24.9	29.0	12.1	1.4	75.5	40.8	50.7	49.3
13834	PORTLANDVILLE	97.4	97.4	1.3	1.3	0.0	0.0	2.6	3.3	3.3	3.9	5.8	4.6	3.9	24.0	37.0	15.6	2.0	83.1	47.7	46.8	53.3
13835	RICHFORD	98.5	98.3	0.6	0.7	0.0	0.0	0.5	0.6	6.2	6.6	9.3	8.5	7.2	28.2	24.3	8.7	1.0	72.8	35.6	50.2	49.9
13838	SIDNEY	96.0	95.3	0.9	1.1	0.9	1.1	1.5	1.8	6.4	6.3	7.3	7.1	6.2	23.0	24.8	15.8	3.1	75.3	40.5	47.2	52.8
13839	SIDNEY CENTER	96.7	96.1	1.2	1.4	0.3	0.4	1.2	1.4	5.3	5.9	7.8	7.0	4.7	24.6	28.4	14.9	1.4	76.3	41.7	51.0	49.1
13841	SMITHVILLE FLATS	98.5	98.3	0.3	0.2	0.3	0.4	0.5	0.7	6.6	6.8	7.9	6.8	5.7	26.0	28.2	11.4	0.9	74.7	39.5	53.3	46.7
13842	SOUTH KORTRIGHT	83.4	81.4	11.6	12.9	0.9	1.0	4.8	5.4	5.2	5.4	8.5	18.3	2.8	20.6	24.5	13.4	1.3	64.7	35.7	56.2	43.8
13843	SOUTH NEW BERLIN	97.6	97.1	0.6	0.7	0.3	0.5	1.2	1.5	5.9	6.6	7.8	7.3	5.0	24.9	29.4	11.9	1.3	75.1	40.7	49.0	51.0
13844	SOUTH PLYMOUTH	91.4	90.5	6.6	7.2	0.1	0.3	4.6	5.6	5.9	6.5	7.1	6.3	6.3	31.2	26.2	9.4	1.0	76.3	37.6	56.9	43.1
13846	TREADWELL	98.8	98.5	0.4	0.7	0.4	0.4	0.8	1.1	5.9	5.5	5.5	5.9	5.5	22.7	30.4	16.1	2.6	80.2	44.3	49.8	50.2
13849	UNADILLA	97.2	96.6	0.9	1.1	0.3	0.3	1.3	1.6	5.9	6.3	7.9	7.1	5.6	24.7	27.0	13.9	1.6	75.5	40.3	50.0	50.1
13850	VESTAL	87.1	84.6	2.2	2.4	8.3	10.3	2.4	2.9	4.2	4.6	5.7	17.0	11.9	18.2	22.2	13.8	2.5	82.2	34.5	47.5	52.5
13856	WALTON	97.8	97.4	0.4	0.5	0.4	0.5	1.1	1.4	5.0	5.1	6.2	6.7	6.0	23.2	30.0	15.3	2.3	79.2	43.5	48.5	51.5
13859	WELLS BRIDGE	97.1	96.6	1.0	1.0	0.0	0.5	1.5	1.5	7.4	7.4	7.8	7.8	5.4	24.5	24.5	14.2	1.0	72.6	38.6	49.0	51.0
13861	WEST ONEONTA	97.4	96.8	0.8	0.8	0.2	0.2	1.6	2.0	3.9	4.7	5.3	5.5	3.3	21.3	33.9	19.1	3.1	81.9	48.3	47.6	52.4
13862	WHITNEY POINT	97.8	97.3	0.4	0.4	0.4	0.5	0.8	1.0	5.8	6.6	8.7	8.7	7.0	26.3	25.9	10.1	1.1	73.4	37.4	49.8	50.2
13863	WILLET	98.3	98.1	0.0	0.0	0.2	0.2	0.0	0.0	7.5	7.5	7.9	7.9	5.8	28.6	24.2	10.0	0.6	72.0	36.5	52.6	47.4
13864	WILLSEYVILLE	97.0	96.3	1.0	1.3	0.5	0.7	0.7	1.0	6.8	6.8	6.4	6.5	5.7	27.5	28.1	11.0	1.3	75.8	39.4	49.6	50.4
13865	WINDSOR	98.0	97.6	0.6	0.6	0.3	0.4	0.8	0.9	6.5	6.8	8.6	7.9	6.0	25.0	27.2	10.9	1.1	73.1	38.9	49.9	50.1
13901	BINGHAMTON	90.6	89.0	4.9	5.5	1.4	1.8	2.1	2.5	5.7	5.7	7.0	6.9	6.9	24.2	26.2	15.0	2.5	77.5	41.0	48.7	51.3
13903	BINGHAMTON	88.2	86.8	6.2	6.6	1.9	2.3	2.6	3.1	6.6	6.7	7.5	6.4	6.1	26.2	25.9	12.8	1.9	75.3	38.8	47.8	52.3
	NEW YORK	68.0	65.9	15.9	16.2	5.6	6.4	15.1	16.7	6.5	6.5	7.1	7.0	7.1	28.9	24.0	11.2	1.8	75.8	36.7	48.3	51.7
	UNITED STATES	75.1	73.6	12.3	12.5	3.8	4.2	12.5	14.1	6.9	6.7	7.2	7.0	7.3	28.6	23.8	10.8	1.7	75.1	36.0	49.1	50.9

INCOME

#	POST OFFICE NAME	2004 Per Capita Income	2004 HH Income Base	2004 Household Income Distribution (%): Less than $25,000	$25,000 to $49,999	$50,000 to $99,999	$100,000 to $149,999	$150,000 or More	Median Household Income: 2004	2009	2004 National Centile	2004 State Centile	2004 Home Value Base	2004 Home Value Distribution (%): Less than $50,000	$50,000 to $89,999	$90,000 to $174,999	$175,000 to $399,999	$400,000 or More	2004 Median Home Value
13670	OSWEGATCHIE	18081	233	36.1	38.2	20.6	3.4	1.7	33730	37462	23	9	196	33.7	32.7	26.5	4.6	2.6	66471
13672	PARISHVILLE	20359	140	29.3	42.1	21.4	5.0	2.1	36596	41106	34	19	117	16.2	23.9	40.2	16.2	3.4	109375
13673	PHILADELPHIA	15304	989	35.9	31.6	27.3	3.6	1.6	34520	37347	26	11	608	12.2	24.0	50.2	13.5	0.2	106504
13675	PLESSIS	14930	24	33.3	37.5	25.0	4.2	0.0	35000	36115	28	13	20	15.0	25.0	55.0	5.0	0.0	100000
13676	POTSDAM	18350	5412	40.2	28.3	22.9	6.2	2.3	32475	35486	19	7	3037	12.5	18.8	44.1	23.4	1.3	122085
13679	REDWOOD	17443	664	35.5	32.5	25.5	5.3	1.2	35503	38781	30	15	516	15.7	27.7	42.1	13.4	1.2	99189
13680	RENSSELAER FALLS	14678	430	35.4	34.4	25.6	4.2	0.5	36128	40079	32	17	313	20.8	25.2	42.8	10.9	0.3	95208
13681	RICHVILLE	16492	433	36.0	34.9	24.7	3.0	1.4	34901	38253	27	12	341	20.5	30.2	38.1	10.9	0.3	88333
13682	RODMAN	18644	317	24.9	34.7	31.6	6.3	2.5	42352	46909	54	43	274	10.2	17.5	43.8	25.9	2.6	127907
13684	RUSSELL	16625	354	35.0	33.3	27.4	3.4	0.9	35367	38629	29	14	294	23.5	29.6	36.7	9.5	0.7	84375
13685	SACKETS HARBOR	25239	965	26.1	28.8	36.6	6.0	2.5	46122	51804	64	53	619	13.3	12.8	50.7	21.7	1.6	127626
13687	SOUTH COLTON	23614	134	26.9	36.6	26.9	6.7	3.0	41361	47916	51	39	112	9.8	16.1	48.2	23.2	2.7	135185
13690	STAR LAKE	20611	342	36.6	26.0	30.1	6.1	1.2	36755	40534	35	20	251	30.7	30.3	28.7	9.6	0.8	68269
13691	THERESA	17304	990	28.8	37.3	26.3	5.7	2.0	40000	43553	46	34	809	21.9	25.0	41.9	10.5	0.7	94180
13693	THREE MILE BAY	22519	125	29.6	33.6	28.8	5.6	2.4	39685	44688	45	33	103	7.8	18.5	43.7	27.2	2.9	127500
13694	WADDINGTON	23214	671	28.8	31.6	30.4	6.1	3.1	40057	44870	46	34	482	12.9	21.8	46.5	17.0	1.9	113816
13695	WANAKENA	15887	74	37.8	41.9	14.9	4.1	1.4	31660	32320	17	6	63	33.3	28.6	28.6	4.8	4.8	71000
13696	WEST STOCKHOLM	17661	107	33.6	28.0	31.8	4.7	1.9	34708	38758	26	12	89	13.5	31.5	39.3	14.6	1.1	95000
13697	WINTHROP	17180	996	34.7	31.9	27.5	5.2	0.6	34259	37764	25	10	797	17.8	27.1	40.9	13.4	0.8	97364
13699	POTSDAM	13218	95	59.0	24.2	15.8	1.1	0.0	17530	20000	1	1	23	8.7	13.0	65.2	13.0	0.0	126563
13730	AFTON	19043	1214	29.3	37.4	26.6	5.4	1.2	38302	42121	40	26	998	11.7	24.0	49.9	13.2	1.2	109412
13731	ANDES	24027	544	31.1	33.6	24.6	6.4	4.2	38465	43336	41	27	458	5.7	9.2	40.2	36.9	8.1	159459
13732	APALACHIN	26928	3138	14.1	27.6	38.2	13.3	6.8	57025	64480	82	72	2737	8.5	16.2	59.1	15.5	0.8	121167
13733	BAINBRIDGE	19702	2143	28.9	33.3	30.5	5.1	2.2	40413	44617	48	35	1731	12.7	22.9	45.8	16.6	2.0	110245
13734	BARTON	18329	1043	28.4	34.7	26.0	8.2	2.8	39300	43507	44	31	846	24.2	33.6	33.6	7.5	1.2	75932
13736	BERKSHIRE	19231	950	27.6	33.9	30.8	5.6	2.1	41566	45959	52	40	782	19.8	29.5	40.0	10.1	0.5	90862
13739	BLOOMVILLE	18240	490	30.0	37.8	26.1	4.1	2.0	38232	42074	40	26	409	12.0	14.4	47.4	22.0	4.2	128163
13740	BOVINA CENTER	23258	263	20.5	34.6	33.5	8.0	3.4	45161	51935	62	51	223	5.8	5.4	48.4	31.4	9.0	158712
13743	CANDOR	20203	1758	27.5	35.0	28.2	6.1	3.2	40379	44663	47	35	1394	24.1	29.7	39.3	6.9	0.0	83765
13744	CASTLE CREEK	20793	450	23.8	34.4	30.4	7.6	3.8	43859	49221	58	47	372	19.1	24.5	45.2	11.0	0.3	95455
13746	CHENANGO FORKS	19700	1136	27.2	32.8	29.9	8.4	1.8	41979	46620	53	41	966	27.0	20.8	38.1	13.5	0.6	94038
13748	CONKLIN	19437	1534	25.6	34.2	28.9	9.8	1.4	41503	46880	51	39	1299	24.6	29.8	41.5	4.2	0.0	85551
13750	DAVENPORT	21279	413	32.0	36.6	23.7	5.1	2.7	35786	39833	31	16	337	17.2	10.1	50.7	19.3	2.7	127568
13751	DAVENPORT CENTER	17925	75	30.7	40.0	22.7	5.3	1.3	36604	40632	34	19	61	14.8	6.6	57.4	19.7	1.6	132031
13752	DE LANCEY	24587	448	25.7	36.6	29.7	5.4	2.7	41850	47453	52	41	354	8.8	9.6	46.1	30.2	5.4	139925
13753	DELHI	22128	1976	28.6	33.6	28.0	7.0	2.8	39457	44664	44	32	1405	6.3	9.1	47.1	33.6	3.8	146924
13754	DEPOSIT	18264	1521	37.2	33.0	22.6	4.7	2.6	34152	37392	25	10	1122	14.4	29.1	42.3	12.5	1.7	98090
13755	DOWNSVILLE	17327	559	35.8	35.8	23.8	3.9	0.7	34570	38087	26	11	433	10.6	18.0	53.1	15.0	3.2	117045
13756	EAST BRANCH	16984	321	35.5	35.5	22.7	4.4	1.9	33646	36649	23	9	271	13.3	23.6	45.0	13.7	4.4	115625
13757	EAST MEREDITH	22442	569	28.3	35.9	27.8	5.5	2.6	39408	43898	44	31	474	11.0	10.8	46.2	28.3	3.8	135494
13760	ENDICOTT	24643	18814	27.9	29.8	29.3	8.8	4.2	42815	48768	55	44	12755	5.0	26.4	53.0	14.8	0.7	108079
13775	FRANKLIN	20295	763	27.3	35.9	26.7	8.3	1.8	38800	43289	42	28	605	7.4	9.9	52.6	27.1	3.0	136101
13776	GILBERTSVILLE	24420	200	25.0	33.0	32.5	6.5	3.0	43818	49749	58	47	172	8.1	14.0	48.3	27.3	2.3	130000
13777	GLEN AUBREY	17213	289	26.3	37.0	30.1	5.2	1.4	40784	45472	49	37	249	36.1	24.1	32.1	6.4	1.2	73824
13778	GREENE	19378	2372	29.1	35.0	27.0	7.5	1.5	39366	43698	44	31	1818	12.7	18.5	43.4	24.3	1.2	122054
13780	GUILFORD	17282	401	32.9	38.7	24.9	3.0	0.5	33787	37732	23	9	340	13.8	30.0	42.4	13.2	0.6	99130
13782	HAMDEN	21766	344	29.9	34.0	27.9	5.8	2.3	38108	43094	40	25	283	11.3	11.3	47.4	25.8	4.2	134868
13783	HANCOCK	19289	1210	36.9	31.5	24.6	5.6	1.5	33229	36079	22	8	900	11.6	27.3	43.3	14.8	3.0	110950
13786	HARPERSFIELD	19015	94	31.9	34.0	27.7	4.3	2.1	36523	39205	34	19	79	5.1	20.3	49.4	24.1	1.3	127206
13787	HARPURSVILLE	18372	1423	24.5	36.1	31.9	5.3	2.2	42901	48207	56	44	1200	27.0	29.7	34.4	8.3	0.7	78788
13788	HOBART	21816	293	24.6	35.2	31.7	6.1	2.4	42768	47569	55	44	236	7.2	11.4	53.0	25.4	3.0	136404
13790	JOHNSON CITY	19800	8377	37.7	30.6	24.1	5.6	2.0	33007	37282	21	8	4833	10.2	46.5	36.3	6.7	0.4	84205
13795	KIRKWOOD	19613	1463	25.2	36.2	31.4	5.1	2.1	40685	46804	49	36	1097	14.2	31.0	43.0	11.2	0.6	93571
13796	LAURENS	19486	594	26.6	33.8	32.2	5.7	1.7	39574	44281	45	32	480	9.0	15.0	51.7	22.7	1.7	128283
13797	LISLE	16583	950	28.0	38.8	28.1	3.7	1.4	37572	41877	38	23	793	36.1	27.9	31.9	3.8	0.4	70982
13801	MC DONOUGH	17331	539	34.7	36.2	24.5	2.8	1.9	35664	39183	30	15	462	26.4	30.7	29.4	12.8	0.7	76250
13802	MAINE	18280	138	15.2	42.0	37.0	5.8	0.0	45401	50206	62	51	118	17.0	30.5	47.5	5.1	0.0	93000
13803	MARATHON	17702	1545	26.7	37.9	28.2	5.8	1.4	38534	43066	41	27	1210	11.7	21.1	51.5	14.5	1.3	106492
13804	MASONVILLE	16199	185	34.6	37.3	21.6	6.0	0.5	33426	36865	22	9	157	10.2	15.9	50.3	21.0	2.6	131090
13806	MERIDALE	20440	21	28.6	38.1	28.6	4.8	0.0	38596	42330	41	28	17	5.9	5.9	47.1	41.2	0.0	156250
13807	MILFORD	18283	607	31.6	35.9	24.4	5.4	2.6	38289	42025	40	26	492	10.6	17.3	50.8	16.3	5.1	120787
13808	MORRIS	20047	681	31.6	33.3	27.3	5.4	2.4	37936	42187	39	24	539	10.4	15.6	53.8	18.0	2.2	120724
13809	MOUNT UPTON	17883	691	29.1	41.1	23.7	3.8	2.3	37332	41800	37	22	575	17.4	24.7	43.3	14.1	0.5	99286
13810	MOUNT VISION	19044	516	29.7	34.7	27.7	5.4	2.5	37892	42730	39	24	415	9.9	14.5	47.2	26.5	1.9	127183
13811	NEWARK VALLEY	19813	1628	23.0	35.3	32.4	6.6	2.7	44487	48820	60	49	1360	16.4	30.5	44.6	7.9	0.6	93590
13812	NICHOLS	18406	942	23.1	42.7	26.8	5.5	1.9	40849	45693	49	37	766	15.5	37.6	42.2	4.3	0.4	85556
13813	NINEVEH	17610	285	30.2	39.3	24.2	4.2	2.1	39383	43989	44	31	238	28.6	33.6	27.7	9.2	0.8	74231
13815	NORWICH	19727	5944	37.1	30.2	24.2	6.0	2.5	34404	37775	25	11	3935	18.7	21.5	42.7	16.1	1.0	102966
13820	ONEONTA	19220	7450	40.2	27.2	24.2	5.5	2.8	31937	35245	18	6	4238	8.3	11.6	57.2	21.3	1.7	128828
13825	OTEGO	17738	1428	31.0	36.2	26.1	5.7	1.0	36250	40724	33	17	1132	14.6	11.7	51.3	21.4	1.1	126697
13826	OUAQUAGA	19946	83	28.9	32.5	26.5	7.2	4.8	37747	42351	38	24	69	31.9	24.6	34.8	8.7	0.0	81000
13827	OWEGO	21874	4606	27.3	29.3	32.1	8.8	2.6	43237	48066	57	45	3242	15.7	26.2	45.2	12.5	0.4	99161
13830	OXFORD	18088	1943	29.4	33.5	29.3	6.3	1.5	39116	43474	43	30	1564	15.0	24.7	45.1	14.4	0.8	105586
13832	PLYMOUTH	15474	142	32.4	36.6	23.9	4.2	2.8	35000	38170	28	13	118	33.9	23.7	33.9	8.5	0.0	73750
13833	PORT CRANE	21130	1868	22.2	37.5	30.0	8.4	1.9	42753	48449	55	44	1598	31.2	20.3	38.4	10.1	0.1	87928
13834	PORTLANDVILLE	20869	64	31.3	28.1	31.3	7.8	1.6	38206	41550	40	26	54	11.1	14.8	53.7	20.4	0.0	128846
13835	RICHFORD	17535	500	29.2	35.6	30.4	3.6	1.2	38767	43067	42	28	402	30.1	29.4	34.8	5.5	0.3	74167
13838	SIDNEY	17170	2118	38.3	37.0	19.8	3.4	1.6	31483	34238	16	6	1340	7.3	25.8	57.2	9.1	0.7	107787
13839	SIDNEY CENTER	19519	682	28.3	37.1	26.1	5.7	2.8	37748	41624	38	24	583	10.3	18.2	48.9	20.6	2.1	124868
13841	SMITHVILLE FLATS	15104	166	23.5	53.0	20.5	3.0	0.0	36959	41199	35	20	140	18.6	32.9	33.6	15.0	0.0	88000
13842	SOUTH KORTRIGHT	13314	105	33.3	38.1	23.8	2.9	1.9	35371	40320	29	14	89	9.0	15.7	49.4	22.5	3.4	129167
13843	SOUTH NEW BERLIN	20591	861	28.9	31.9	29.3	7.1	2.8	40611	44616	48	36	726	15.4	20.3	41.6	20.8	1.9	113288
13844	SOUTH PLYMOUTH	13385	202	34.7	32.7	26.2	4.0	2.5	35889	39145	31	16	166	29.5	21.1	39.8	9.6	0.0	88333
13846	TREADWELL	19908	117	28.2	31.6	35.0	4.3	0.9	39647	43639	45	33	93	3.2	10.8	51.6	30.1	4.3	141447
13849	UNADILLA	19765	2187	27.5	39.0	26.3	5.1	2.2	38676	43185	42	28	1814	15.7	17.6	50.1	15.5	1.1	114613
13850	VESTAL	28041	8597	20.9	23.7	33.7	13.5	8.2	56433	63817	81	71	6693	5.3	17.8	53.7	20.2	2.9	122005
13856	WALTON	19605	3273	36.0	32.8	24.6	4.1	2.4	33869	37127	24	10	2332	10.6	15.6	48.7	21.4	3.8	127506
13859	WELLS BRIDGE	17181	83	27.7	42.2	25.3	4.8	0.0	35365	40745	29	14	69	14.5	11.6	52.2	21.7	0.0	122500
13861	WEST ONEONTA	20909	201	30.4	25.9	32.3	10.5	1.0	39354	45000	44	31	173	10.4	14.5	43.4	30.1	1.7	130357
13862	WHITNEY POINT	18101	1574	27.2	35.3	30.7	5.2	1.7	40364	45765	47	35	1271	27.4	29.9	38.4	4.0	0.3	80365
13863	WILLET	18275	177	26.0	44.6	23.7	4.0	1.7	38656	43649	42	28	143	15.4	28.7	42.7	13.3	0.0	96538
13864	WILLSEYVILLE	24050	469	24.7	33.9	30.9	5.8	4.7	45602	51208	63	52	374	20.3	23.0	40.4	16.0	0.3	102652
13865	WINDSOR	18662	2378	24.6	35.0	32.6	5.8	2.1	43258	48712	57	45	1954	23.5	28.4	39.4	8.5	0.3	87824
13901	BINGHAMTON	21225	8705	39.3	26.8	23.4	7.7	2.9	35440	40166	29	15	4990	10.3	28.9	50.1	10.3	0.3	100067
13903	BINGHAMTON	23485	8021	30.7	28.7	29.4	6.8	4.5	41511	46904	51	40	5330	8.2	37.4	40.5	13.2	0.8	94177
	NEW YORK	28049		26.3	24.3	29.3	11.5	8.6	49309	58077				4.6	8.6	27.2	39.9	19.8	219050
	UNITED STATES	25866		24.7	27.1	30.8	10.9	6.5	48124	56710				10.9	15.0	33.7	30.1	10.4	145905

ZIP CODE #	POST OFFICE NAME	FINANCIAL SERVICES: Auto Loan	FINANCIAL SERVICES: Home Loan	FINANCIAL SERVICES: Invest-ments	FINANCIAL SERVICES: Retire-ment Plans	THE HOME: Home Improvements: Home Repair	THE HOME: Home Improvements: Lawn & Garden	THE HOME: Furnishings: Comput-ers & Hard-ware	THE HOME: Furnishings: Major Appli-ances	THE HOME: Furnishings: TV, Radio, Sound Equip-ment	THE HOME: Furnishings: Furni-ture	ENTERTAINMENT: Dine out/ Carry out	ENTERTAINMENT: Sports Equip-ment	ENTERTAINMENT: Fees & Tickets	ENTERTAINMENT: Toys & Games	ENTERTAINMENT: Travel	ENTERTAINMENT: Cable TV	PERSONAL: Apparel & Services	PERSONAL: Auto Repairs	PERSONAL: Health Insur-ance	PERSONAL: Pets & Supplies
13670	OSWEGATCHIE	63	56	48	52	61	68	54	60	59	53	71	69	53	74	57	62	68	59	68	76
13672	PARISHVILLE	71	66	59	61	70	79	64	69	69	63	84	79	63	88	67	73	80	68	78	85
13673	PHILADELPHIA	69	50	40	52	50	59	61	60	65	59	79	73	54	73	56	63	74	65	63	71
13675	PLESSIS	63	54	42	54	56	64	55	59	59	54	71	67	53	70	55	60	67	58	64	70
13676	POTSDAM	66	55	55	56	56	63	64	62	66	61	81	75	59	78	61	64	77	65	64	73
13679	REDWOOD	73	57	40	54	63	73	58	66	65	57	77	76	53	75	60	68	71	66	77	85
13680	RENSSELAER FALLS	67	54	39	53	58	66	56	61	60	55	72	71	52	71	56	62	67	60	68	75
13681	RICHVILLE	69	53	36	50	57	65	54	61	61	54	73	71	50	70	54	63	67	61	70	77
13682	RODMAN	88	67	41	63	75	83	65	77	72	64	86	92	58	85	67	76	80	76	89	105
13684	RUSSELL	70	56	39	53	60	68	56	63	62	55	74	73	52	72	56	64	69	62	71	79
13685	SACKETS HARBOR	78	79	83	78	81	86	77	80	77	76	95	94	76	96	78	77	92	80	80	95
13687	SOUTH COLTON	95	74	51	67	84	94	70	84	79	69	94	99	63	93	75	85	87	83	100	115
13690	STAR LAKE	80	63	43	57	71	80	59	72	67	59	80	84	53	79	63	72	74	71	85	98
13691	THERESA	77	67	51	64	70	76	65	71	68	66	83	83	61	80	65	69	79	71	75	88
13693	THREE MILE BAY	83	65	44	58	73	82	61	74	69	61	82	86	55	81	65	74	76	72	87	101
13694	WADDINGTON	73	76	75	72	77	85	75	76	78	73	96	85	78	102	77	81	93	74	81	85
13695	WANAKENA	65	51	35	46	57	64	48	58	54	47	64	67	43	63	51	58	60	57	68	79
13696	WEST STOCKHOLM	70	60	46	59	62	71	61	65	65	60	79	75	59	78	61	66	74	65	71	77
13697	WINTHROP	71	57	41	55	61	69	58	64	63	57	76	74	54	75	58	65	71	63	71	79
13699	POTSDAM	37	30	36	32	30	33	43	36	42	38	52	46	38	50	38	38	50	40	33	40
13730	AFTON	79	61	40	58	66	75	61	69	68	61	82	81	56	79	61	71	76	69	80	89
13731	ANDES	88	69	47	62	78	87	65	78	74	64	87	92	58	86	69	79	81	77	93	107
13732	APALACHIN	100	113	115	112	112	114	104	105	100	103	125	124	108	132	106	99	124	103	99	120
13733	BAINBRIDGE	88	63	35	58	70	80	62	74	72	63	85	88	55	82	63	76	78	73	88	100
13734	BARTON	87	68	44	63	72	80	66	75	72	67	87	88	59	82	66	74	81	75	83	98
13736	BERKSHIRE	81	73	57	70	76	82	68	75	72	69	87	89	67	88	70	73	83	73	79	95
13739	BLOOMVILLE	78	61	42	55	69	77	58	69	65	57	78	81	52	77	62	70	72	68	82	94
13740	BOVINA CENTER	95	75	51	68	84	95	71	85	80	70	95	99	63	93	75	85	88	84	100	116
13743	CANDOR	91	68	40	63	76	84	66	78	74	66	88	93	59	86	67	78	82	77	91	106
13744	CASTLE CREEK	81	81	74	78	83	87	75	79	76	75	94	93	76	98	77	77	91	77	81	96
13746	CHENANGO FORKS	80	73	58	69	76	81	68	74	71	68	87	88	66	88	69	73	83	73	80	94
13748	CONKLIN	71	75	72	72	74	79	71	72	71	71	88	83	72	90	72	71	86	71	72	83
13750	DAVENPORT	87	69	49	64	77	87	67	78	74	66	89	91	61	88	70	79	83	77	91	104
13751	DAVENPORT CENTER	79	62	42	56	69	78	58	70	66	58	78	82	52	77	62	70	73	69	83	96
13752	DE LANCEY	94	73	50	66	83	93	69	83	78	69	93	98	62	92	74	84	86	82	99	114
13753	DELHI	85	77	68	74	81	90	76	82	80	75	97	95	73	97	78	83	92	81	90	99
13754	DEPOSIT	68	58	46	54	62	71	59	64	65	57	78	73	56	77	60	68	72	64	75	79
13755	DOWNSVILLE	67	51	34	48	56	66	53	60	59	51	70	69	47	67	54	63	64	60	72	77
13756	EAST BRANCH	74	58	39	52	65	73	55	66	62	54	73	77	49	72	58	66	68	65	78	90
13757	EAST MEREDITH	98	72	42	67	82	92	70	85	80	69	94	101	60	92	73	84	86	84	101	118
13760	ENDICOTT	75	81	89	79	81	87	80	80	80	79	100	91	83	102	82	80	97	79	80	88
13775	FRANKLIN	85	64	40	59	71	83	66	76	75	64	88	88	58	84	67	79	81	76	91	98
13776	GILBERTSVILLE	88	78	59	74	82	88	72	80	77	72	93	95	71	95	74	78	88	78	86	103
13777	GLEN AUBREY	79	72	56	69	73	77	69	74	70	70	86	86	65	82	68	69	83	73	74	89
13778	GREENE	77	65	48	63	68	76	64	70	69	63	83	81	61	83	64	71	78	69	77	87
13780	GUILFORD	75	51	24	45	58	66	49	61	59	50	69	74	42	66	50	63	63	61	75	87
13782	HAMDEN	85	66	45	60	75	84	63	75	71	62	84	88	56	83	67	76	78	74	89	103
13783	HANCOCK	75	57	38	53	63	74	59	68	67	57	79	77	53	76	60	71	72	67	81	86
13786	HARPERSFIELD	85	67	45	60	75	84	63	76	71	63	85	89	57	83	67	76	79	75	90	103
13787	HARPURSVILLE	81	72	55	69	75	81	68	74	72	69	87	87	66	87	69	73	83	73	79	93
13788	HOBART	87	68	46	62	76	86	66	78	74	65	88	91	59	86	69	79	82	77	92	104
13790	JOHNSON CITY	59	59	64	58	59	65	62	61	63	60	78	71	62	79	62	63	76	62	62	68
13795	KIRKWOOD	69	68	66	66	69	75	69	70	70	67	86	81	68	87	69	71	83	70	73	80
13796	LAURENS	78	67	50	64	71	78	65	72	70	64	84	84	62	85	66	72	79	70	79	90
13797	LISLE	73	66	52	64	66	70	63	68	64	65	79	79	60	75	63	63	76	68	68	81
13801	MC DONOUGH	76	57	35	51	64	72	54	66	62	54	74	77	47	72	57	67	68	65	79	91
13802	MAINE	82	73	55	69	77	82	67	74	71	67	87	89	66	88	69	73	82	72	80	96
13803	MARATHON	75	65	50	63	68	75	64	70	68	64	83	81	62	83	64	70	78	68	76	85
13804	MASONVILLE	71	55	37	50	62	70	52	63	59	52	70	74	47	69	56	63	65	62	75	86
13806	MERIDALE	83	58	30	54	67	75	57	70	66	56	77	85	49	75	59	69	70	69	84	98
13807	MILFORD	77	61	43	60	66	76	63	70	69	62	82	81	58	81	63	71	76	69	80	87
13808	MORRIS	83	63	39	60	70	80	65	74	72	63	86	86	57	83	65	76	79	74	87	96
13809	MOUNT UPTON	84	57	28	51	65	74	56	69	66	56	78	83	48	74	57	70	71	68	84	97
13810	MOUNT VISION	83	63	39	60	70	78	62	73	69	61	82	86	56	81	64	72	76	72	84	97
13811	NEWARK VALLEY	83	75	61	73	78	83	72	77	74	72	91	91	70	92	72	75	87	76	81	95
13812	NICHOLS	72	67	57	64	69	77	66	69	69	64	84	79	65	87	67	71	80	68	75	82
13813	NINEVEH	74	61	44	58	65	73	61	67	66	60	79	78	57	78	61	68	74	66	75	84
13815	NORWICH	69	62	55	59	64	72	62	66	66	61	81	76	61	81	63	68	77	66	72	79
13820	ONEONTA	69	57	54	58	59	67	66	65	68	62	83	77	61	80	63	67	78	68	69	76
13825	OTEGO	75	59	40	55	64	71	57	66	64	57	76	77	53	75	58	66	71	64	75	86
13826	OUAQUAGA	82	73	56	69	77	83	67	75	72	67	87	89	66	89	69	73	83	73	81	97
13827	OWEGO	78	75	69	72	77	83	74	77	76	73	93	89	73	95	74	77	90	76	80	90
13830	OXFORD	72	65	54	61	69	76	63	68	68	62	82	79	62	85	65	71	78	67	76	84
13832	PLYMOUTH	75	57	35	53	62	71	57	65	64	57	76	76	51	74	57	67	70	64	76	85
13833	PORT CRANE	84	78	64	75	80	85	73	79	76	74	93	93	72	93	74	76	89	78	82	97
13834	PORTLANDVILLE	85	67	46	60	75	85	63	76	71	62	84	89	56	83	67	76	79	75	90	104
13835	RICHFORD	73	67	52	64	67	71	63	68	65	65	79	79	60	76	63	64	76	68	69	82
13838	SIDNEY	52	52	57	50	52	59	54	53	56	53	70	61	55	72	55	58	68	54	57	60
13839	SIDNEY CENTER	86	65	42	58	72	82	63	74	72	63	85	87	57	83	65	77	79	73	88	100
13841	SMITHVILLE FLATS	78	52	24	45	59	68	50	63	61	51	71	75	43	67	51	65	65	62	77	89
13842	SOUTH KORTRIGHT	72	57	39	51	64	72	54	65	61	53	72	76	48	71	57	65	67	64	76	88
13843	SOUTH NEW BERLIN	87	74	52	69	79	86	69	78	75	69	90	93	66	91	71	77	85	76	87	103
13844	SOUTH PLYMOUTH	72	60	46	59	64	72	61	67	66	60	79	76	58	79	61	67	74	66	73	81
13846	TREADWELL	84	59	31	55	68	77	58	72	67	57	78	86	49	77	60	70	71	71	85	100
13849	UNADILLA	82	65	44	59	71	79	63	72	70	63	84	85	58	83	64	74	79	71	84	96
13850	VESTAL	102	112	125	112	112	118	110	108	107	108	134	125	113	137	111	106	131	108	105	120
13856	WALTON	76	57	38	54	63	73	59	68	66	58	78	78	53	75	60	70	72	67	79	87
13859	WELLS BRIDGE	68	60	46	57	64	68	56	62	59	56	72	74	55	73	57	61	68	60	67	80
13861	WEST ONEONTA	65	75	83	71	74	81	71	71	71	70	88	80	75	92	74	73	87	70	73	78
13862	WHITNEY POINT	76	68	53	66	70	76	65	71	68	65	84	82	63	83	66	69	79	70	75	86
13863	WILLET	90	61	30	54	69	79	59	73	71	60	83	87	51	79	60	76	76	73	89	103
13864	WILLSEYVILLE	86	86	76	84	86	88	81	84	79	82	99	98	79	97	80	78	96	83	81	98
13865	WINDSOR	80	70	55	66	73	80	67	74	71	67	87	86	64	86	68	73	82	73	80	92
13901	BINGHAMTON	61	65	74	64	64	69	67	65	67	65	83	75	68	86	67	67	82	65	65	71
13903	BINGHAMTON	74	79	88	78	79	84	80	78	80	78	99	90	82	102	80	80	97	78	78	86
	NEW YORK	95	100	134	99	98	107	103	100	105	103	133	116	105	138	104	107	131	102	99	112
	UNITED STATES	100	100	100	100	100	100	100	100	100	100	100	100	100	100	100	100	100	100	100	100

POPULATION CHANGE

ZIP CODE		COUNTY FIPS CODE	POPULATION			2000-2004 ANNUAL RATE		HOUSEHOLDS					FAMILIES		
#	POST OFFICE NAME		2000	2004	2009	% Rate	State Centile	2000	2004	2009	% Annual Rate 2000-2004	2004 Average HH Size	2000	2004	% Annual Rate 2000-2004
13904	BINGHAMTON	007	9187	9067	8966	-0.3	13	3626	3619	3615	-0.1	2.38	2312	2292	-0.2
13905	BINGHAMTON	007	27842	27406	27098	-0.4	10	11952	11889	11870	-0.1	2.18	5890	5770	-0.5
14001	AKRON	029	9307	9409	9429	0.3	44	3703	3765	3790	0.4	2.50	2610	2641	0.3
14004	ALDEN	029	12110	12229	12255	0.2	42	3885	3959	3989	0.4	2.64	2955	2991	0.3
14005	ALEXANDER	037	1824	1825	1820	0.0	29	637	646	652	0.3	2.83	488	492	0.2
14006	ANGOLA	029	10900	10898	10879	0.0	28	4193	4219	4231	0.2	2.57	2956	2952	0.0
14008	APPLETON	063	1557	1596	1606	0.6	61	530	548	558	0.8	2.89	409	420	0.6
14009	ARCADE	121	5583	5628	5661	0.2	40	2189	2241	2289	0.6	2.51	1516	1544	0.4
14011	ATTICA	121	8081	8144	8206	0.2	40	2234	2283	2338	0.5	2.64	1637	1665	0.4
14012	BARKER	063	2477	2439	2410	-0.4	11	870	863	859	-0.2	2.81	686	677	-0.3
14013	BASOM	037	1908	1915	1911	0.1	34	667	678	684	0.4	2.82	479	484	0.2
14020	BATAVIA	037	22957	22959	22934	0.0	28	9078	9187	9276	0.3	2.37	5740	5778	0.2
14024	BLISS	121	1612	1589	1585	-0.3	12	573	574	583	0.0	2.77	438	437	-0.1
14025	BOSTON	029	2821	2871	2889	0.4	52	1060	1085	1097	0.6	2.65	802	815	0.4
14026	BOWMANSVILLE	029	620	668	691	1.8	91	242	263	273	2.0	2.40	197	214	2.0
14028	BURT	063	2147	2175	2178	0.3	48	851	873	884	0.6	2.49	602	612	0.4
14030	CHAFFEE	029	1495	1459	1439	-0.6	5	554	545	542	-0.4	2.68	424	415	-0.5
14031	CLARENCE	029	9038	9198	9244	0.4	52	3305	3367	3391	0.4	2.59	2367	2392	0.3
14032	CLARENCE CENTER	029	5377	5578	5676	0.9	73	1789	1871	1918	1.1	2.98	1492	1553	1.0
14033	COLDEN	029	2418	2404	2394	-0.1	21	908	908	909	0.0	2.64	681	676	-0.2
14034	COLLINS	029	6105	6076	6054	-0.1	22	829	824	821	-0.1	2.76	610	603	-0.3
14036	CORFU	037	5166	5179	5179	0.1	32	1873	1897	1915	0.3	2.73	1396	1408	0.2
14037	COWLESVILLE	121	1183	1162	1157	-0.4	9	415	414	419	-0.1	2.80	333	331	-0.1
14039	DALE	121	73	72	72	-0.3	13	28	28	28	0.0	2.57	22	22	0.0
14040	DARIEN CENTER	037	2235	2227	2219	-0.1	24	773	781	788	0.2	2.84	618	622	0.2
14041	DAYTON	009	113	111	110	-0.4	9	37	37	37	0.0	3.00	27	27	0.0
14042	DELEVAN	009	5090	5074	5058	-0.1	24	1977	1992	2005	0.2	2.54	1359	1362	0.1
14043	DEPEW	029	25545	25123	24933	-0.4	10	10243	10119	10081	-0.3	2.47	7009	6880	-0.4
14047	DERBY	029	6774	6662	6607	-0.4	10	2482	2457	2448	-0.2	2.69	1846	1818	-0.4
14048	DUNKIRK	013	16147	16082	16048	-0.1	23	6549	6590	6625	0.2	2.37	4059	4056	0.0
14051	EAST AMHERST	029	18110	19430	20065	1.7	90	6162	6649	6907	1.8	2.92	5066	5444	1.7
14052	EAST AURORA	029	17550	17448	17357	-0.1	21	6651	6654	6650	0.0	2.57	4843	4821	-0.1
14054	EAST BETHANY	037	1368	1386	1389	0.3	48	507	522	529	0.7	2.65	398	408	0.6
14055	EAST CONCORD	029	1536	1506	1488	-0.5	8	537	530	527	-0.3	2.84	413	405	-0.5
14057	EDEN	029	8362	8226	8142	-0.4	10	2951	2920	2901	-0.3	2.75	2306	2270	-0.4
14058	ELBA	037	2347	2286	2253	-0.6	4	823	809	805	-0.4	2.79	646	631	-0.6
14059	ELMA	029	9144	8928	8803	-0.6	5	3409	3349	3317	-0.4	2.66	2684	2625	-0.5
14060	FARMERSVILLE STATION	003	547	544	545	-0.1	21	198	200	202	0.2	2.71	143	143	0.0
14062	FORESTVILLE	013	3399	3460	3486	0.4	53	1299	1337	1357	0.7	2.57	961	983	0.5
14063	FREDONIA	013	14690	14595	14553	-0.2	20	5080	5098	5116	0.1	2.34	2991	2976	-0.1
14065	FREEDOM	009	1851	1911	1936	0.8	69	640	671	688	1.1	2.85	494	515	1.0
14066	GAINESVILLE	121	1817	1763	1753	-0.7	3	652	644	653	-0.3	2.74	507	499	-0.4
14067	GASPORT	063	5528	5443	5386	-0.4	11	1985	1983	1986	0.0	2.70	1512	1502	-0.2
14068	GETZVILLE	029	6579	7295	7656	2.5	96	2186	2454	2593	2.8	2.86	1662	1861	2.7
14069	GLENWOOD	029	755	749	744	-0.2	18	300	300	300	0.0	2.50	228	227	-0.1
14070	GOWANDA	009	5452	5411	5381	-0.2	19	2191	2191	2191	0.0	2.32	1378	1367	-0.2
14072	GRAND ISLAND	029	18621	18853	18922	0.3	46	6898	7017	7071	0.4	2.67	5219	5285	0.3
14075	HAMBURG	029	41706	42505	42828	0.5	55	16333	16762	16970	0.6	2.49	11362	11576	0.4
14080	HOLLAND	029	4525	4531	4524	0.0	30	1658	1671	1676	0.2	2.71	1238	1241	0.1
14081	IRVING	029	3772	3772	3763	0.0	28	1370	1376	1377	0.1	2.71	944	942	-0.1
14082	JAVA CENTER	121	501	495	494	-0.3	14	185	186	188	0.1	2.66	136	135	-0.2
14083	JAVA VILLAGE	121	230	222	221	-0.8	2	76	75	75	-0.3	2.96	56	55	-0.4
14085	LAKE VIEW	029	5726	6221	6462	2.0	93	1969	2151	2243	2.1	2.87	1576	1715	2.0
14086	LANCASTER	029	30278	31077	31425	0.6	62	11478	11794	11973	0.6	2.60	8166	8376	0.6
14091	LAWTONS	029	1119	1111	1102	-0.2	19	379	379	377	0.0	2.90	290	289	-0.1
14092	LEWISTON	063	11156	11150	11108	0.0	27	4488	4540	4571	0.3	2.40	3200	3221	0.2
14094	LOCKPORT	063	49959	51009	51422	0.5	57	19920	20581	20977	0.8	2.43	13151	13494	0.6
14098	LYNDONVILLE	073	2954	2958	2957	0.0	30	1080	1094	1105	0.3	2.70	793	798	0.2
14101	MACHIAS	009	1977	2016	2031	0.5	55	700	722	734	0.7	2.64	503	516	0.6
14102	MARILLA	029	1653	1604	1578	-0.7	3	556	543	536	-0.6	2.95	465	452	-0.7
14103	MEDINA	073	11552	11396	11323	-0.4	11	4376	4345	4357	-0.2	2.53	2981	2943	-0.3
14105	MIDDLEPORT	063	4449	4364	4308	-0.5	8	1662	1645	1640	-0.2	2.65	1233	1212	-0.4
14108	NEWFANE	063	5973	6089	6120	0.5	55	2175	2241	2275	0.7	2.64	1623	1661	0.6
14109	NIAGARA UNIVERSITY	063	1347	1325	1317	-0.4	10	0	0	0	0.0	0.00	0	0	0.0
14111	NORTH COLLINS	029	2849	2795	2761	-0.5	8	1085	1071	1062	-0.3	2.59	781	766	-0.5
14113	NORTH JAVA	121	701	705	706	0.1	37	251	256	261	0.5	2.75	188	191	0.4
14120	NORTH TONAWANDA	063	43531	43202	42924	-0.2	19	17334	17397	17471	0.1	2.47	11806	11781	-0.1
14125	OAKFIELD	037	3731	3659	3619	-0.5	8	1335	1321	1319	-0.3	2.76	998	983	-0.4
14127	ORCHARD PARK	029	28064	28676	28940	0.5	58	10460	10757	10910	0.7	2.60	7760	7936	0.5
14129	PERRYSBURG	009	1650	1633	1621	-0.2	16	617	618	620	0.0	2.57	445	443	-0.1
14131	RANSOMVILLE	063	5999	6014	5995	0.1	32	2155	2194	2214	0.4	2.68	1641	1660	0.3
14132	SANBORN	063	5847	5973	6007	0.5	57	2182	2261	2302	0.8	2.63	1654	1706	0.7
14134	SARDINIA	029	85	84	83	-0.3	14	30	30	30	0.0	2.80	23	23	0.0
14136	SILVER CREEK	013	5378	5422	5444	0.2	40	2113	2146	2168	0.4	2.40	1461	1474	0.2
14138	SOUTH DAYTON	009	1823	1773	1749	-0.7	4	661	651	648	-0.4	2.71	472	462	-0.5
14139	SOUTH WALES	029	2119	2104	2089	-0.2	19	820	819	817	0.0	2.57	617	613	-0.2
14141	SPRINGVILLE	029	7942	7867	7802	-0.2	16	3052	3044	3033	-0.1	2.51	2099	2079	-0.2
14143	STAFFORD	037	1282	1343	1368	1.1	81	485	515	531	1.4	2.61	363	383	1.3
14145	STRYKERSVILLE	121	1523	1599	1601	0.8	70	526	551	569	1.1	2.85	412	429	1.0
14150	TONAWANDA	029	44751	44773	44776	0.0	29	18933	19101	19212	0.2	2.34	12442	12452	0.0
14167	VARYSBURG	121	1770	1792	1804	0.3	46	662	681	698	0.7	2.63	497	509	0.6
14170	WEST FALLS	029	2335	2281	2250	-0.6	5	887	872	865	-0.4	2.60	676	661	-0.5
14171	WEST VALLEY	009	2191	2245	2265	0.6	61	839	873	892	0.9	2.57	614	635	0.8
14172	WILSON	063	3227	3283	3296	0.4	52	1241	1277	1294	0.7	2.57	926	947	0.5
14174	YOUNGSTOWN	063	5560	5473	5414	-0.4	10	2159	2155	2157	0.0	2.53	1572	1558	-0.2
14201	BUFFALO	029	13634	13559	13591	-0.1	21	6302	6328	6392	0.1	2.04	2670	2611	-0.5
14202	BUFFALO	029	3856	3876	3879	0.1	36	1671	1687	1692	0.2	1.46	417	412	-0.3
14203	BUFFALO	029	1156	1118	1104	-0.8	3	595	579	576	-0.6	1.59	170	162	-1.1
14204	BUFFALO	029	9701	9546	9520	-0.4	10	4527	4470	4472	-0.3	2.12	2350	2280	-0.7
14206	BUFFALO	029	22959	22628	22444	-0.3	12	10270	10180	10131	-0.2	2.22	5928	5820	-0.4
14207	BUFFALO	029	22838	22922	22951	0.1	34	9769	9804	9825	0.1	2.33	5567	5537	-0.1
14208	BUFFALO	029	13293	13393	13471	0.2	40	5138	5181	5218	0.2	2.33	2942	2950	0.1
14209	BUFFALO	029	7849	8025	8150	0.5	59	3853	3904	3951	0.3	1.94	1482	1521	0.6
14210	BUFFALO	029	16605	16164	15973	-0.6	4	6731	6568	6535	-0.5	2.45	4194	4073	-0.7
14211	BUFFALO	029	29454	28018	27418	-1.2	1	11823	11274	11053	-1.1	2.46	7277	6867	-1.4
	NEW YORK					0.4					0.5	2.60			0.4
	UNITED STATES					1.2					1.3	2.58			1.1

ZIP CODE #	POST OFFICE NAME	RACE (%) White 2000	White 2004	Black 2000	Black 2004	Asian/Pacific 2000	Asian/Pacific 2004	% Hispanic Origin 2000	% Hispanic Origin 2004	2004 AGE DISTRIBUTION (%) 0-4	5-9	10-14	15-19	20-24	25-44	45-64	65-84	85+	18+	MEDIAN AGE 2004	% 2004 Males	% 2004 Females
13904	BINGHAMTON	90.4	89.1	4.5	4.8	0.9	1.1	3.1	3.7	6.2	6.2	6.4	6.6	5.8	25.4	26.1	14.0	3.3	77.2	41.1	47.9	52.1
13905	BINGHAMTON	85.9	83.5	6.5	7.2	3.8	4.7	3.4	4.1	5.1	4.7	5.5	6.1	13.4	24.8	22.6	14.2	3.7	81.4	37.2	48.3	51.8
14001	AKRON	98.1	97.5	0.4	0.5	0.1	0.2	0.6	0.7	5.8	6.2	7.1	6.2	5.4	27.0	26.4	14.0	1.9	77.0	40.5	49.1	50.9
14004	ALDEN	92.1	90.6	5.9	7.0	0.3	0.4	2.4	2.8	4.9	5.4	6.1	6.0	5.8	28.4	26.9	13.7	2.9	79.9	41.3	53.5	46.5
14005	ALEXANDER	98.6	98.4	0.3	0.3	0.3	0.3	0.4	0.6	7.4	7.6	8.8	7.5	5.0	28.0	24.6	10.1	1.1	71.7	36.9	49.9	50.1
14006	ANGOLA	97.4	96.7	0.5	0.7	0.2	0.2	1.1	1.6	5.8	6.1	7.5	7.7	5.9	26.0	27.7	11.9	1.6	76.0	39.6	48.6	51.4
14008	APPLETON	95.3	94.4	1.3	1.6	0.3	0.3	2.1	2.5	5.6	7.0	9.3	8.6	5.1	26.7	25.8	10.5	1.4	72.5	37.8	51.1	48.9
14009	ARCADE	98.8	98.4	0.2	0.3	0.3	0.4	0.7	1.1	5.9	6.1	7.8	7.3	6.4	26.7	26.6	11.6	1.6	75.7	38.7	49.4	50.6
14011	ATTICA	79.9	77.8	15.4	16.7	0.3	0.3	6.8	7.9	4.7	4.9	5.9	5.4	8.2	39.0	23.1	7.8	1.1	81.3	36.0	63.1	37.0
14012	BARKER	97.3	96.7	0.7	0.9	0.4	0.5	1.3	1.6	6.6	7.7	8.5	7.9	5.4	25.3	27.4	10.1	1.2	72.2	37.6	51.1	48.9
14013	BASOM	83.5	82.7	1.4	1.5	0.3	0.3	2.0	2.4	6.1	7.3	9.0	8.2	7.2	27.1	23.2	11.3	0.7	72.6	36.1	50.6	49.5
14020	BATAVIA	92.2	91.1	4.1	4.5	0.9	1.1	1.9	2.3	6.0	5.8	6.6	6.8	7.0	26.8	24.1	13.8	3.1	77.4	39.1	48.6	51.4
14024	BLISS	97.7	97.1	0.4	0.6	0.5	0.6	0.4	0.6	6.2	7.6	8.9	8.3	5.6	26.9	25.9	9.6	1.2	71.9	37.1	50.6	49.4
14025	BOSTON	99.0	98.6	0.3	0.4	0.1	0.1	0.9	1.3	6.1	6.7	7.5	6.4	5.4	27.0	29.3	10.5	1.1	75.7	39.8	50.7	49.3
14026	BOWMANSVILLE	97.4	96.6	1.0	1.5	0.5	0.8	0.8	1.1	5.8	6.6	7.8	7.6	4.8	24.3	26.5	12.9	3.7	74.7	41.5	48.1	52.0
14028	BURT	96.8	96.2	0.6	0.8	0.4	0.5	1.5	1.8	5.3	6.1	6.9	7.0	5.7	24.5	30.0	13.2	1.3	77.4	41.7	50.9	49.2
14030	CHAFFEE	97.5	96.8	0.3	0.5	0.3	0.3	0.7	0.9	6.3	6.8	8.2	7.3	5.6	26.2	28.2	10.2	1.2	74.0	38.5	50.2	49.8
14031	CLARENCE	97.7	97.0	0.5	0.7	0.9	1.2	0.7	0.9	4.9	5.8	7.7	6.8	4.2	21.3	28.3	16.4	4.7	77.1	44.6	47.2	52.8
14032	CLARENCE CENTER	97.6	96.8	0.6	0.8	0.7	0.8	1.0	1.3	7.4	8.5	8.9	6.9	4.7	26.2	26.8	9.5	1.1	70.6	38.3	49.8	50.2
14033	COLDEN	98.5	98.0	0.1	0.1	0.4	0.5	0.5	0.8	5.2	6.0	7.5	7.0	4.8	25.8	31.1	11.6	1.0	76.8	41.5	49.8	50.2
14034	COLLINS	60.0	53.0	29.9	35.6	0.3	0.3	15.2	17.4	2.6	2.6	2.5	3.2	9.8	55.3	18.9	4.5	0.6	90.4	35.7	81.3	18.8
14036	CORFU	98.3	97.9	0.3	0.4	0.1	0.2	0.5	0.7	6.0	6.6	8.4	7.2	5.7	27.1	26.2	11.6	1.1	74.3	38.8	49.6	50.5
14037	COWLESVILLE	99.1	98.8	0.0	0.0	0.3	0.3	0.3	0.3	5.2	5.6	6.5	6.3	5.7	28.0	30.0	11.6	1.1	79.1	41.1	51.1	48.9
14039	DALE	98.6	98.6	0.0	0.0	0.0	0.0	0.0	0.0	4.2	6.9	9.7	8.3	2.8	29.2	26.4	11.1	1.4	70.8	40.0	51.4	48.6
14040	DARIEN CENTER	98.9	98.8	0.1	0.1	0.0	0.0	0.3	0.3	5.5	6.5	8.8	7.3	5.3	28.1	26.5	11.1	0.9	74.4	39.1	52.7	47.3
14041	DAYTON	97.4	97.3	0.0	0.0	0.0	0.0	0.0	0.0	5.4	7.2	9.9	8.1	3.6	27.9	26.1	10.8	0.9	72.1	38.1	50.5	49.6
14042	DELEVAN	98.5	98.1	0.2	0.3	0.3	0.4	0.8	1.0	7.1	6.9	7.3	7.3	7.2	26.6	25.7	10.6	1.4	74.4	36.8	50.4	49.6
14043	DEPEW	97.7	96.8	0.8	1.2	0.5	0.6	0.7	1.0	5.5	5.6	6.2	5.9	5.5	27.1	27.1	15.4	1.9	79.0	41.3	48.1	51.9
14047	DERBY	98.3	97.8	0.3	0.4	0.3	0.4	1.3	1.9	5.7	6.1	7.2	7.1	6.2	26.3	29.5	10.3	1.6	76.4	39.7	48.6	51.4
14048	DUNKIRK	85.0	83.0	4.4	4.7	0.3	0.3	16.8	19.7	6.0	6.0	7.1	6.7	6.5	25.1	24.6	14.7	3.4	77.0	39.6	47.8	52.2
14051	EAST AMHERST	92.2	89.8	1.6	2.3	5.1	6.4	0.9	1.3	6.5	7.8	8.9	7.2	4.6	24.0	31.3	8.9	0.7	71.9	40.1	48.9	51.1
14052	EAST AURORA	98.9	98.4	0.2	0.3	0.3	0.5	0.6	0.8	5.7	6.4	7.5	6.6	4.8	23.9	28.8	14.1	2.5	76.1	42.3	48.5	51.5
14054	EAST BETHANY	97.1	96.7	0.8	0.9	0.2	0.3	0.4	0.4	5.8	6.1	7.1	6.9	6.6	27.1	28.0	11.6	0.9	77.1	39.4	51.8	48.2
14055	EAST CONCORD	98.1	97.5	0.4	0.6	0.3	0.4	0.8	1.1	5.8	6.6	8.2	6.9	5.1	26.0	30.2	10.3	1.1	74.9	39.8	49.9	50.1
14057	EDEN	98.3	97.8	0.4	0.6	0.2	0.3	1.0	1.4	5.4	6.5	8.2	7.4	4.7	26.1	27.5	12.2	2.1	75.0	40.5	49.8	50.2
14058	ELBA	93.3	92.0	1.7	1.9	0.1	0.1	5.2	6.4	6.7	7.1	8.0	6.7	5.6	27.1	27.2	10.7	0.9	74.1	38.2	51.1	49.0
14059	ELMA	99.1	98.7	0.1	0.1	0.3	0.3	0.6	0.8	5.0	6.1	7.5	6.4	4.6	23.0	30.5	15.2	1.6	77.0	43.5	49.3	50.7
14060	FARMERSVILLE STATION	98.5	98.0	0.2	0.2	0.2	0.4	0.9	1.1	7.2	7.2	7.4	7.4	6.4	25.4	25.7	12.3	1.1	73.9	37.7	50.2	49.8
14062	FORESTVILLE	97.4	96.8	0.3	0.4	0.2	0.3	1.4	1.9	5.6	6.2	6.8	6.5	5.1	26.2	29.3	12.9	1.4	77.2	40.9	50.7	49.3
14063	FREDONIA	94.9	94.0	2.4	2.7	0.8	1.0	2.6	3.2	3.7	3.9	5.1	15.6	16.9	21.8	20.6	10.6	1.8	83.3	28.1	47.2	52.8
14065	FREEDOM	98.5	98.2	0.2	0.2	0.2	0.3	0.9	1.1	7.2	7.2	8.1	8.0	7.3	26.8	26.0	8.8	0.7	72.6	35.8	51.1	48.9
14066	GAINESVILLE	97.8	97.2	0.4	0.6	0.7	0.8	0.6	0.9	5.3	7.7	9.9	9.2	4.9	27.4	26.2	8.5	0.9	70.4	36.8	50.9	49.1
14067	GASPORT	97.0	96.3	0.7	0.9	0.4	0.5	0.8	1.0	6.0	6.5	7.4	6.6	5.7	27.2	27.4	11.7	1.5	75.9	39.5	50.0	50.0
14068	GETZVILLE	91.4	88.7	2.0	2.8	5.0	6.4	1.1	1.4	5.7	6.7	8.5	7.1	4.5	23.9	29.6	10.3	3.7	74.1	41.5	47.1	52.9
14069	GLENWOOD	98.7	98.3	0.3	0.4	0.1	0.3	0.5	0.7	5.7	6.3	7.3	7.1	4.9	26.0	31.5	10.4	0.7	76.1	41.0	51.5	48.5
14070	GOWANDA	84.3	82.9	1.0	1.3	0.2	0.2	1.7	2.0	6.7	6.2	6.5	6.3	5.7	25.6	24.4	15.5	3.3	76.6	40.8	49.7	50.3
14072	GRAND ISLAND	95.8	94.3	1.7	2.4	1.2	1.5	1.1	1.5	5.9	6.9	7.8	6.9	4.9	25.2	30.5	10.8	1.1	74.8	40.6	49.3	50.7
14075	HAMBURG	98.2	97.6	0.4	0.6	0.4	0.5	1.2	1.6	5.6	6.0	7.1	6.4	5.6	24.8	28.3	13.5	2.6	77.2	41.5	47.4	52.6
14080	HOLLAND	98.3	97.7	0.4	0.6	0.3	0.4	0.4	0.6	6.1	6.7	8.0	6.8	5.6	28.7	27.8	9.1	1.1	74.9	38.2	50.1	49.9
14081	IRVING	63.3	62.0	0.7	1.0	0.1	0.1	1.7	2.0	7.0	6.7	7.5	8.0	6.4	26.4	24.4	11.9	1.8	73.7	37.2	47.6	52.4
14082	JAVA CENTER	99.0	99.0	0.2	0.2	0.0	0.0	0.4	0.6	6.9	7.1	7.1	6.7	6.1	29.1	26.1	10.1	1.0	75.4	37.4	50.5	49.5
14083	JAVA VILLAGE	99.6	99.6	0.0	0.0	0.0	0.0	0.4	0.9	6.3	7.2	6.8	7.2	5.9	27.5	27.9	10.4	0.9	74.3	38.3	51.4	48.7
14085	LAKE VIEW	99.1	98.8	0.1	0.1	0.2	0.3	1.0	1.3	7.1	7.5	8.3	7.7	5.2	27.2	26.4	9.7	0.8	72.3	37.8	50.0	50.0
14086	LANCASTER	98.1	97.3	0.8	1.2	0.4	0.6	0.7	1.0	6.6	6.8	7.2	6.4	5.3	27.9	26.2	11.6	1.9	75.3	39.3	48.3	51.7
14091	LAWTONS	70.5	70.0	0.5	0.6	0.2	0.2	1.2	1.5	7.9	7.2	7.5	7.7	5.9	28.4	23.5	10.4	1.5	72.7	36.4	48.6	51.4
14092	LEWISTON	95.4	94.8	1.0	1.2	0.7	0.9	0.8	0.9	4.7	5.1	6.1	6.9	5.7	21.6	29.0	17.9	3.0	80.1	44.9	47.5	52.5
14094	LOCKPORT	92.9	91.6	4.3	5.0	0.7	0.9	1.5	1.8	6.6	6.6	7.2	7.0	6.5	27.7	25.5	11.2	1.8	75.2	37.8	48.8	51.2
14098	LYNDONVILLE	97.0	96.9	0.9	1.0	0.3	0.3	1.1	1.2	6.2	6.6	7.7	8.1	6.6	24.2	27.7	11.4	1.6	74.5	39.6	50.2	49.8
14101	MACHIAS	98.1	97.7	0.2	0.3	0.2	0.2	0.9	1.1	5.4	5.5	6.9	6.6	6.3	23.6	28.0	14.2	3.5	78.0	42.1	50.1	50.0
14102	MARILLA	99.2	99.0	0.1	0.1	0.2	0.3	0.9	1.2	5.8	6.4	7.4	7.4	5.9	24.2	30.4	11.9	0.8	76.1	40.7	49.1	50.9
14103	MEDINA	90.7	90.1	5.8	6.3	0.5	0.5	2.8	3.0	6.9	6.5	7.4	8.4	6.7	24.8	24.1	12.7	2.6	74.1	37.6	48.1	51.9
14105	MIDDLEPORT	97.8	97.3	0.6	0.7	0.5	0.6	1.1	1.3	6.9	6.9	6.9	7.4	6.3	26.2	26.5	11.5	1.4	74.8	38.6	49.3	50.7
14108	NEWFANE	97.7	97.2	0.6	0.8	0.2	0.3	0.6	0.8	6.3	6.4	7.3	6.7	6.2	26.2	25.8	12.5	2.8	75.6	39.5	48.9	51.1
14109	NIAGARA UNIVERSITY	91.8	89.8	4.6	5.7	1.2	1.4	2.3	3.0	0.7	0.3	1.1	51.9	37.1	4.5	3.3	1.0	0.2	95.3	19.6	41.1	58.9
14111	NORTH COLLINS	94.2	92.9	0.5	0.7	0.7	0.9	2.5	3.2	5.2	6.2	8.3	7.1	5.0	27.6	26.2	12.5	1.8	75.8	39.5	49.3	50.7
14113	NORTH JAVA	98.2	97.9	0.3	0.4	0.3	0.3	0.3	0.4	7.2	7.4	7.5	6.7	6.4	29.5	23.8	10.5	1.0	73.8	36.6	50.4	49.7
14120	NORTH TONAWANDA	97.8	97.3	0.4	0.5	0.5	0.7	1.0	1.2	5.7	5.9	6.8	6.6	6.5	26.8	26.8	13.0	2.0	77.6	40.1	48.9	51.1
14125	OAKFIELD	96.8	96.3	1.1	1.2	0.2	0.3	1.2	1.5	6.0	6.3	8.5	7.7	7.3	27.3	24.8	11.1	1.2	74.5	37.3	48.9	51.1
14127	ORCHARD PARK	97.6	96.8	0.5	0.7	1.0	1.4	1.0	1.3	5.4	6.1	7.4	6.9	5.1	22.7	29.4	14.5	2.5	76.5	42.7	48.2	51.8
14129	PERRYSBURG	85.2	84.2	0.4	0.4	0.1	0.1	0.9	1.0	6.3	5.8	5.9	6.9	6.1	26.7	27.5	13.4	1.5	77.6	40.5	49.9	50.2
14131	RANSOMVILLE	97.5	97.0	0.5	0.7	0.2	0.3	0.8	1.1	5.5	6.0	7.4	6.9	5.7	26.5	27.7	12.9	1.4	76.9	40.4	49.8	50.2
14132	SANBORN	94.2	93.7	1.4	1.6	0.5	0.6	0.7	0.9	5.9	6.8	8.0	7.2	5.5	27.4	25.4	12.6	1.3	74.7	39.0	49.5	50.5
14134	SARDINIA	98.8	97.6	0.0	1.2	0.0	0.0	0.0	1.2	6.0	6.0	9.5	6.0	4.8	25.0	31.0	10.7	1.2	72.6	40.0	48.8	51.2
14136	SILVER CREEK	96.6	96.0	0.5	0.7	0.2	0.3	1.8	2.3	5.7	5.8	7.0	7.3	6.2	24.6	25.5	13.9	4.1	76.7	40.8	47.5	52.5
14138	SOUTH DAYTON	97.6	97.2	0.2	0.3	0.1	0.1	1.0	1.2	6.7	8.7	8.9	7.7	6.0	25.2	24.9	9.9	2.2	70.6	35.3	49.4	50.6
14139	SOUTH WALES	98.5	98.1	0.1	0.1	0.4	0.5	0.6	0.8	6.0	6.8	7.2	5.9	5.1	25.7	30.3	11.7	1.3	76.4	41.3	49.3	50.7
14141	SPRINGVILLE	98.3	97.7	0.5	0.7	0.3	0.4	1.2	1.7	6.0	6.2	7.3	6.9	5.8	25.7	26.8	12.8	2.5	76.0	40.3	48.8	51.2
14143	STAFFORD	97.2	96.8	1.2	1.3	0.4	0.5	0.2	0.2	4.6	5.3	7.0	6.0	6.0	25.8	30.5	13.3	1.4	79.5	41.8	50.3	49.7
14145	STRYKERSVILLE	99.8	99.7	0.1	0.2	0.1	0.1	0.1	0.2	7.6	7.7	7.6	6.6	6.1	28.5	23.4	11.3	1.3	73.4	36.4	51.6	48.4
14150	TONAWANDA	96.2	95.1	1.3	1.8	1.2	1.5	1.1	1.5	5.2	5.3	6.3	6.3	6.1	25.3	25.9	17.8	1.9	79.3	42.1	48.3	51.7
14167	VARYSBURG	99.2	99.1	0.1	0.1	0.2	0.2	0.3	0.5	5.4	6.5	7.8	7.7	4.7	27.7	29.1	10.3	1.0	75.3	39.3	50.3	49.7
14170	WEST FALLS	98.5	97.9	0.2	0.3	0.6	0.9	0.7	0.9	5.8	6.6	7.2	7.1	4.9	24.0	30.7	12.3	1.5	75.8	41.9	49.9	50.2
14171	WEST VALLEY	97.4	97.0	1.1	1.3	0.1	0.2	0.8	1.0	6.1	6.5	7.6	7.1	5.2	26.9	29.1	10.2	1.3	75.3	39.5	50.3	49.7
14172	WILSON	97.7	97.3	0.4	0.5	0.2	0.3	0.8	1.1	5.5	6.1	7.4	7.3	5.0	25.3	29.3	12.2	2.0	76.2	41.3	49.4	50.6
14174	YOUNGSTOWN	97.6	97.0	0.4	0.5	0.6	0.7	0.8	1.0	5.2	5.6	7.1	7.1	5.6	23.7	30.1	13.9	1.7	77.7	42.4	49.2	50.9
14201	BUFFALO	43.5	38.6	26.5	29.7	2.0	2.0	37.0	39.1	8.1	7.2	7.1	6.4	8.3	29.1	21.5	10.1	2.3	74.1	33.0	48.1	52.0
14202	BUFFALO	61.9	55.0	33.3	39.5	1.0	1.2	5.3	6.2	1.9	1.5	1.5	7.4	12.1	39.1	21.8	13.0	1.7	91.7	37.2	61.1	38.9
14203	BUFFALO	23.0	19.0	70.9	75.0	0.1	0.1	5.1	5.1	4.7	6.5	7.6	6.4	5.2	24.8	26.1	16.9	1.9	76.9	42.4	56.3	43.7
14204	BUFFALO	19.5	18.0	74.0	75.3	0.5	0.5	7.6	8.1	7.2	7.7	8.1	7.5	6.1	24.0	23.7	14.0	1.7	72.5	37.2	44.8	55.2
14206	BUFFALO	88.3	87.2	9.3	10.0	0.5	0.6	1.5	2.0	5.9	5.8	6.4	5.9	5.8	27.4	24.1	16.2	2.6	78.4	40.4	47.7	52.3
14207	BUFFALO	84.3	80.6	6.4	8.1	1.0	1.3	8.6	10.6	7.5	7.1	8.0	7.4	7.3	28.0	21.7	11.4	1.7	73.0	34.8	48.1	51.9
14208	BUFFALO	11.7	9.3	85.0	87.4	0.6	0.6	1.7	1.8	5.8	6.4	7.7	10.8	9.6	20.2	19.8	16.2	3.4	75.8	35.8	43.3	56.7
14209	BUFFALO	42.3	35.9	53.0	59.1	1.2	1.3	3.2	3.6	5.7	5.6	5.9	5.6	9.0	27.8	22.3	14.4	3.8	79.5	37.8	45.8	54.2
14210	BUFFALO	91.9	90.0	3.6	4.4	0.5	0.6	5.2	6.6	8.0	7.6	7.8	7.1	7.3	29.8	20.9	10.5	1.2	72.3	34.2	48.4	51.6
14211	BUFFALO	24.4	21.8	71.6	74.0	1.1	1.2	2.0	2.1	8.4	8.3	9.2	8.4	6.5	25.7	21.1	10.8	1.6	68.8	32.7	46.0	54.0
	NEW YORK	68.0	65.9	15.9	16.2	5.6	6.4	15.1	16.7	6.5	6.5	7.1	7.0	7.1	28.9	24.0	11.2	1.8	75.8	36.7	48.3	51.7
	UNITED STATES	75.1	73.6	12.3	12.5	3.8	4.2	12.5	14.1	6.9	6.7	7.2	7.0	7.3	28.6	23.8	10.8	1.7	75.1	36.0	49.1	50.9

ZIP CODE #	POST OFFICE NAME	2004 Per Capita Income	2004 HH Income Base	2004 HOUSEHOLD INCOME DISTRIBUTION (%) Less than $25,000	$25,000 to $49,999	$50,000 to $99,999	$100,000 to $149,999	$150,000 or More	MEDIAN HOUSEHOLD INCOME 2004	2009	2004 National Centile	2004 State Centile	2004 Home Value Base	2004 HOME VALUE DISTRIBUTION (%) Less than $50,000	$50,000 to $89,999	$90,000 to $174,999	$175,000 to $399,999	$400,000 or More	2004 Median Home Value
13904	BINGHAMTON	19580	3619	32.6	34.5	25.8	4.9	2.2	36908	41971	35	20	2435	10.3	46.5	34.6	7.7	0.9	84954
13905	BINGHAMTON	21180	11889	42.7	27.7	21.3	5.3	2.9	30765	33672	14	5	5656	8.8	34.8	45.7	10.0	0.7	96766
14001	AKRON	21046	3765	22.3	32.3	37.3	6.9	1.3	45841	52065	63	52	2986	8.1	15.1	59.2	17.3	0.2	124917
14004	ALDEN	21854	3959	19.2	28.3	40.1	8.5	3.9	51849	58813	75	65	3332	6.2	7.3	63.6	22.2	0.6	137451
14005	ALEXANDER	21191	646	19.7	32.2	40.3	5.9	2.0	48340	52708	69	59	541	5.4	21.3	61.0	10.7	1.7	105804
14006	ANGOLA	20442	4219	24.3	33.5	30.5	10.0	1.7	42185	48941	53	42	3342	9.1	24.3	55.3	10.6	0.7	107697
14008	APPLETON	19497	548	20.1	32.1	37.6	8.6	1.6	48438	54615	69	59	462	5.6	21.0	59.7	13.0	0.7	110926
14009	ARCADE	18937	2241	26.8	35.9	30.0	6.6	0.7	39880	43365	46	33	1797	10.1	14.0	47.7	27.3	1.0	132795
14011	ATTICA	19411	2283	21.6	29.6	39.5	6.9	2.4	49041	53123	70	60	1772	2.5	10.7	64.5	20.9	1.4	135083
14012	BARKER	20043	863	21.3	32.1	33.5	10.9	2.2	47786	53825	68	57	710	6.2	23.2	60.1	9.6	0.9	107949
14013	BASOM	15543	678	30.8	33.5	31.3	4.1	0.3	38146	41719	40	25	566	22.6	32.9	35.7	8.1	0.7	82439
14020	BATAVIA	20455	9187	31.4	32.5	28.4	4.9	2.7	38203	42024	40	25	5910	8.5	26.7	54.0	10.6	0.1	103058
14024	BLISS	20368	574	24.6	40.6	27.9	4.4	2.6	40381	44657	47	35	482	7.1	26.4	52.7	12.7	1.2	108516
14025	BOSTON	23255	1085	19.2	31.4	35.1	10.2	4.1	49456	57554	71	61	892	1.0	6.7	61.6	29.3	1.5	144158
14026	BOWMANSVILLE	31789	263	14.5	17.5	43.0	17.1	8.0	70866	81257	92	85	237	0.8	3.8	42.2	53.2	0.0	179464
14028	BURT	23117	873	14.3	34.7	41.7	7.8	1.5	50815	57318	73	64	726	6.6	22.0	58.8	12.4	0.1	110632
14030	CHAFFEE	19509	545	22.6	36.0	31.9	7.5	2.0	43656	49714	58	46	460	6.7	15.0	63.9	13.7	0.7	124202
14031	CLARENCE	35550	3367	17.3	18.8	34.6	15.4	13.9	67247	78104	90	82	2792	11.5	1.6	36.0	43.1	7.8	176935
14032	CLARENCE CENTER	32146	1871	8.3	19.7	40.6	16.1	15.3	73451	84557	93	86	1682	0.1	1.3	39.4	53.2	6.0	195833
14033	COLDEN	25672	908	16.9	30.3	36.2	10.4	6.3	53878	61369	78	68	787	3.1	8.3	57.1	29.1	2.5	146417
14034	COLLINS	16010	824	27.7	26.6	34.8	6.4	4.5	43687	50541	58	46	687	12.4	34.5	41.9	11.2	0.0	92905
14036	CORFU	19618	1897	18.9	35.4	37.9	5.9	1.9	46702	51739	66	55	1538	2.5	13.8	67.9	14.9	0.9	123309
14037	COWLESVILLE	21666	414	17.2	29.2	42.5	6.5	4.6	52341	58396	76	66	365	3.0	6.3	53.7	35.6	1.4	157008
14039	DALE	21520	28	21.4	32.1	35.7	10.7	0.0	48155	52070	69	59	25	4.0	16.0	60.0	20.0	0.0	127083
14040	DARIEN CENTER	20414	781	13.4	31.6	44.8	8.7	1.4	52946	57291	77	67	678	1.0	12.2	60.0	26.1	0.6	131048
14041	DAYTON	15181	37	35.1	32.4	24.3	5.4	2.7	34054	38635	24	10	31	9.7	22.6	48.4	19.4	0.0	110938
14042	DELEVAN	17175	1992	33.0	35.2	26.1	4.2	1.5	35371	39290	29	14	1538	23.5	17.2	48.4	10.2	0.7	104762
14043	DEPEW	23457	10119	21.4	29.7	36.8	9.4	2.7	48807	55848	70	60	7675	3.0	8.7	78.7	9.6	0.0	120498
14047	DERBY	24236	2457	16.4	25.6	42.1	12.0	3.9	59043	67370	84	74	2077	9.0	17.6	60.7	12.3	0.4	113744
14048	DUNKIRK	18102	6590	39.8	31.8	22.6	3.5	2.3	32052	35215	18	6	4227	23.7	40.4	29.3	6.1	0.5	75058
14051	EAST AMHERST	42975	6649	6.3	13.4	35.9	21.5	23.0	90841	105241	97	94	6232	0.1	3.2	26.4	62.8	7.5	213514
14052	EAST AURORA	27424	6654	17.3	24.8	37.7	14.2	6.1	58600	67190	83	73	5613	6.0	4.5	50.3	36.4	2.8	158662
14054	EAST BETHANY	21854	522	14.9	35.4	39.3	8.4	1.9	49725	54922	71	62	435	6.9	27.4	54.5	10.6	0.7	110694
14055	EAST CONCORD	20285	530	20.8	32.8	34.9	8.3	3.2	47139	53737	66	56	455	4.0	13.0	64.4	18.0	0.7	126006
14057	EDEN	26459	2920	14.9	25.0	41.7	11.4	7.0	61233	70151	86	76	2555	0.5	5.0	64.3	29.1	1.1	145777
14058	ELBA	20378	809	18.3	30.9	40.2	8.2	2.5	50536	55753	73	63	691	8.0	24.6	62.8	4.2	0.4	107386
14059	ELMA	30877	3349	15.5	22.3	38.3	14.3	9.7	62736	74278	87	78	2977	0.9	2.7	42.5	49.5	4.3	181209
14060	FARMERSVILLE STATION	15213	200	32.0	40.0	24.0	3.5	0.5	33855	37305	24	10	165	17.0	24.9	45.5	12.7	0.0	102232
14062	FORESTVILLE	19601	1337	23.9	35.8	32.3	6.2	1.8	42910	47573	56	44	1123	13.8	28.1	43.1	13.5	1.4	99526
14063	FREDONIA	20093	5098	30.3	30.7	28.7	7.7	2.6	39129	43201	43	30	3297	8.3	17.4	53.4	19.7	1.3	118159
14065	FREEDOM	15628	671	27.7	39.1	27.6	4.5	1.2	36349	40561	33	18	559	13.4	22.5	45.4	17.9	0.7	111458
14066	GAINESVILLE	17128	644	24.8	39.6	30.1	4.2	1.2	39368	42666	44	31	537	10.1	25.9	50.7	12.3	1.1	106486
14067	GASPORT	20949	1983	17.2	34.0	37.8	8.0	3.0	48678	54800	70	60	1701	2.9	20.9	65.9	10.4	0.0	114134
14068	GETZVILLE	28943	2454	17.9	14.1	33.8	21.8	12.4	74489	85182	93	87	2056	0.1	5.7	34.5	59.0	0.6	191337
14069	GLENWOOD	27556	300	17.0	33.7	35.0	6.7	7.7	49418	56538	71	61	261	3.5	10.7	61.3	22.6	1.9	136029
14070	GOWANDA	18430	2191	35.2	33.8	23.6	6.4	1.0	35206	38712	28	14	1561	11.8	37.4	44.5	6.3	0.1	91033
14072	GRAND ISLAND	30939	7017	14.1	21.8	37.8	17.2	9.2	66922	78024	90	82	6023	0.8	6.5	54.4	36.2	2.1	156143
14075	HAMBURG	26209	16762	18.4	27.5	36.5	13.4	4.2	54263	62056	79	69	13183	5.9	4.6	65.0	23.9	0.6	134251
14080	HOLLAND	21592	1671	19.6	28.6	38.9	10.7	2.2	51593	58939	75	65	1384	5.1	10.5	55.4	28.5	0.6	140709
14081	IRVING	18851	1376	29.1	36.5	25.9	7.3	1.2	39634	44913	45	33	1057	16.8	30.6	39.6	12.5	0.6	92969
14082	JAVA CENTER	21501	186	19.4	35.0	34.4	8.1	3.2	47168	51916	66	56	158	1.3	8.9	57.0	31.0	1.9	143902
14083	JAVA VILLAGE	19465	75	17.3	33.3	37.3	9.3	2.7	49594	54406	71	61	64	0.0	4.7	60.9	31.3	3.1	150000
14085	LAKE VIEW	29396	2151	10.1	18.3	50.9	16.8	3.9	67230	77408	90	82	2006	0.4	5.3	70.0	22.6	1.7	140078
14086	LANCASTER	25271	11794	18.5	24.0	40.2	13.4	3.9	57327	65467	82	72	9561	0.8	6.8	61.0	30.8	0.6	145867
14091	LAWTONS	19029	379	25.6	33.3	30.9	6.3	4.0	43400	48258	57	45	320	11.6	25.6	49.7	13.1	0.0	106132
14092	LEWISTON	29950	4540	20.8	22.1	36.3	13.4	7.3	57438	65197	82	72	3674	0.9	5.6	63.7	27.1	2.8	144196
14094	LOCKPORT	23788	20581	26.5	28.4	31.6	10.0	3.5	45445	51118	62	51	14214	10.2	22.7	51.7	14.7	0.7	110925
14098	LYNDONVILLE	17793	1094	24.5	35.3	34.4	5.3	0.6	43209	47220	57	45	911	13.8	37.7	41.6	6.5	0.4	88579
14101	MACHIAS	16929	722	34.8	32.3	24.5	6.9	1.5	36293	39760	33	18	575	14.8	19.3	44.7	19.5	1.7	111690
14102	MARILLA	29723	543	9.4	25.1	48.4	13.8	3.3	64503	72602	88	80	494	0.0	4.5	50.6	44.9	0.0	168056
14103	MEDINA	19239	4345	31.6	32.8	27.6	5.6	2.4	37356	41108	37	22	3037	14.8	43.8	37.1	4.1	0.3	81317
14105	MIDDLEPORT	20058	1645	20.7	35.8	35.2	6.4	1.9	45501	51451	63	52	1296	7.3	30.3	55.8	6.7	0.0	101286
14108	NEWFANE	21122	2241	20.9	32.0	36.6	7.5	3.0	47044	52933	66	56	1821	5.8	23.1	62.6	8.3	0.2	108119
14109	NIAGARA UNIVERSITY	12040	0	0.0	0.0	0.0	0.0	0.0	0	0	0	0	0	0.0	0.0	0.0	0.0	0.0	0
14111	NORTH COLLINS	21701	1071	23.1	30.8	35.2	8.3	2.6	47549	54397	67	57	866	3.1	24.9	58.8	12.6	0.6	109954
14113	NORTH JAVA	21213	256	20.7	30.5	37.1	7.8	3.9	48910	52987	70	60	214	1.9	5.1	57.9	33.6	1.4	146371
14120	NORTH TONAWANDA	22959	17397	24.8	28.3	34.6	9.5	2.8	47120	53524	66	56	12696	2.8	16.6	64.7	15.8	0.2	120025
14125	OAKFIELD	18700	1321	23.2	33.5	34.4	7.4	1.4	45959	50835	64	53	1044	7.2	36.9	48.7	6.5	0.8	93758
14127	ORCHARD PARK	33152	10757	13.7	23.1	34.8	16.4	12.1	65446	76620	89	81	8550	0.9	3.3	44.6	46.6	4.6	177336
14129	PERRYSBURG	17839	618	28.5	36.9	27.5	5.5	1.6	37692	41405	38	23	500	12.6	24.6	47.6	14.6	0.6	111364
14131	RANSOMVILLE	23462	2194	18.8	27.7	38.5	10.6	4.4	52578	59804	76	66	1837	9.4	13.7	57.6	18.8	0.5	125795
14132	SANBORN	22858	2261	21.0	28.5	35.8	10.9	3.8	50389	56864	73	63	1871	1.9	6.8	65.3	25.8	0.2	139809
14134	SARDINIA	19555	30	23.3	33.3	33.3	6.7	3.3	45000	50000	61	50	25	4.0	16.0	60.0	20.0	0.0	127500
14136	SILVER CREEK	20515	2146	26.7	35.6	28.3	7.1	2.2	40141	44855	47	35	1673	14.4	28.8	47.0	9.4	0.5	97500
14138	SOUTH DAYTON	17345	651	32.7	36.1	25.8	4.0	1.4	35583	38816	30	15	525	18.1	32.0	38.5	10.1	1.3	89865
14139	SOUTH WALES	26763	819	15.9	26.6	38.6	13.8	5.1	58888	66595	83	74	712	9.3	4.2	44.2	38.1	4.2	159722
14141	SPRINGVILLE	21507	3044	24.7	32.2	32.3	7.4	3.3	44431	50537	60	49	2246	7.3	16.3	61.0	14.7	0.8	117185
14143	STAFFORD	23950	515	16.5	28.4	41.2	9.3	4.7	54419	60491	79	69	449	3.8	27.2	59.0	9.6	0.5	112146
14145	STRYKERSVILLE	21421	551	13.6	39.4	37.2	7.1	2.7	47969	52373	68	58	468	0.0	3.9	52.6	40.8	2.8	163636
14150	TONAWANDA	22919	19101	24.7	31.9	33.5	7.9	2.0	44801	51236	61	50	14140	1.3	17.1	77.7	3.8	0.1	111544
14167	VARYSBURG	20364	681	24.2	31.4	37.3	4.7	2.4	44859	48870	61	50	574	5.6	14.1	49.7	28.9	1.7	139908
14170	WEST FALLS	29385	872	13.0	24.9	38.0	16.5	7.7	63845	75369	88	79	773	1.3	4.8	57.1	32.1	4.8	156204
14171	WEST VALLEY	21677	873	21.8	35.2	34.7	5.8	2.5	44883	49485	61	50	728	7.3	12.9	54.0	23.9	1.9	131903
14172	WILSON	22812	1277	18.0	32.1	39.7	8.0	2.2	49912	56246	72	62	1079	8.0	17.8	59.2	14.7	0.3	118213
14174	YOUNGSTOWN	27779	2155	17.6	27.8	35.9	12.7	6.0	54784	61988	79	70	1800	5.5	9.1	60.1	24.1	1.2	137048
14201	BUFFALO	14911	6328	64.0	19.0	12.8	2.6	1.6	16718	19226	1	1	1305	19.4	42.7	30.3	7.4	0.3	75669
14202	BUFFALO	25868	1687	49.9	26.1	13.3	3.3	7.5	25053	28046	5	3	346	5.8	8.1	38.4	34.7	13.0	170652
14203	BUFFALO	12330	579	78.4	15.7	4.2	1.0	0.7	11307	13139	1	0	51	58.8	35.3	5.9	0.0	0.0	48043
14204	BUFFALO	13648	4470	63.1	21.6	11.2	2.4	1.7	16811	18794	1	1	1417	38.9	26.3	33.9	1.0	0.0	66815
14206	BUFFALO	17410	10180	42.1	32.7	21.1	3.3	0.8	30526	34414	14	5	6350	16.1	44.8	38.4	0.8	0.0	81029
14207	BUFFALO	15275	9804	47.6	30.3	18.8	2.5	0.8	26417	29718	6	4	4416	17.7	63.8	17.8	0.8	0.0	71257
14208	BUFFALO	14897	5181	50.6	29.7	15.5	2.8	1.4	24587	27291	4	3	2568	35.6	46.2	17.5	0.6	0.2	62861
14209	BUFFALO	21268	3904	51.8	26.5	13.8	3.5	4.4	23836	27503	4	3	1163	24.2	19.1	30.0	22.4	4.4	99235
14210	BUFFALO	15422	6588	42.2	30.9	23.2	3.2	0.5	30076	34151	12	5	3335	20.4	40.9	38.1	0.6	0.0	81895
14211	BUFFALO	13137	11274	53.9	28.6	14.9	1.6	0.9	22343	25079	3	2	5133	44.1	36.8	17.4	1.6	0.1	55963
	NEW YORK	28049		26.3	24.3	29.3	11.5	8.6	49309	58077				4.6	8.6	27.2	39.9	19.8	219050
	UNITED STATES	25866		24.7	27.1	30.8	10.9	6.5	48124	56710				10.9	15.0	33.7	30.1	10.4	145905

ZIP CODE #	POST OFFICE NAME	FINANCIAL SERVICES: Auto Loan	Home Loan	Invest-ments	Retire-ment Plans	THE HOME: Home Improvements: Home Repair	Lawn & Garden	Furnishings: Comput-ers & Hard-ware	Major Appli-ances	TV, Radio, Sound Equip-ment	Furni-ture	ENTERTAINMENT: Dine out/ Carry out	Sports Equip-ment	Fees & Tickets	Toys & Games	Travel	Cable TV	PERSONAL: Apparel & Services	Auto Repairs	Health Insur-ance	Pets & Supplies
13904	BINGHAMTON	65	64	65	62	65	71	65	66	68	64	83	76	66	85	66	69	81	66	69	75
13905	BINGHAMTON	64	59	67	60	59	66	68	64	69	65	85	77	65	84	65	67	82	68	65	72
14001	AKRON	77	74	65	71	77	84	71	75	75	70	91	87	71	94	73	77	87	73	81	90
14004	ALDEN	85	91	90	88	91	96	85	87	84	84	105	101	88	109	87	84	102	85	86	101
14005	ALEXANDER	90	88	77	87	89	93	83	87	83	83	103	103	82	104	83	82	99	86	86	105
14006	ANGOLA	73	75	74	72	76	83	72	75	74	71	92	85	74	95	74	76	88	73	78	85
14008	APPLETON	84	83	73	79	85	90	77	81	78	76	96	96	77	100	79	79	93	79	84	100
14009	ARCADE	78	64	46	61	69	77	62	70	68	62	82	82	59	81	64	71	77	69	79	90
14011	ATTICA	69	75	75	72	75	79	70	72	70	70	87	83	73	91	72	71	85	70	72	82
14012	BARKER	89	77	60	76	81	90	76	82	81	75	98	96	73	98	77	82	92	81	89	101
14013	BASOM	74	61	42	56	65	71	57	65	62	57	75	77	54	75	58	65	70	63	73	86
14020	BATAVIA	67	68	72	67	69	74	69	69	70	67	87	80	70	90	70	70	84	69	70	77
14024	BLISS	93	78	56	74	84	91	73	83	79	73	96	99	70	97	76	82	90	81	92	109
14025	BOSTON	85	92	91	89	93	96	85	88	85	85	105	103	88	110	88	85	103	86	87	102
14026	BOWMANSVILLE	102	127	135	127	125	123	114	113	105	113	132	133	121	141	116	102	132	109	101	125
14028	BURT	78	82	82	78	83	90	79	80	81	77	101	91	83	107	82	83	97	78	84	92
14030	CHAFFEE	84	75	57	71	78	84	69	76	73	69	89	91	68	90	71	75	85	75	82	98
14031	CLARENCE	127	141	147	138	142	153	134	136	132	132	163	153	138	166	138	133	159	133	137	151
14032	CLARENCE CENTER	124	154	165	154	151	150	138	137	128	137	161	160	147	171	141	125	161	132	123	151
14033	COLDEN	95	102	99	98	102	107	94	97	93	94	116	113	97	122	97	94	114	95	96	113
14034	COLLINS	21	26	28	25	25	26	24	23	23	24	29	27	25	30	24	22	28	23	22	26
14036	CORFU	86	76	58	72	81	86	71	78	75	71	91	93	69	93	73	77	87	76	85	101
14037	COWLESVILLE	85	91	89	88	92	95	84	87	84	84	104	102	87	109	87	84	102	85	86	101
14039	DALE	89	79	60	75	83	89	73	81	77	73	94	96	72	96	75	79	90	79	88	104
14040	DARIEN CENTER	84	86	80	83	87	92	79	83	80	79	99	98	81	103	82	81	96	81	84	100
14041	DAYTON	82	58	30	54	67	75	57	70	65	56	77	85	49	75	59	69	70	69	84	98
14042	DELEVAN	73	60	42	56	63	69	58	65	63	59	76	76	54	73	58	64	71	64	71	82
14043	DEPEW	74	86	94	83	85	90	82	81	80	81	101	92	86	105	84	81	99	80	80	89
14047	DERBY	83	100	110	97	98	101	93	92	89	92	112	106	99	119	96	89	111	90	87	100
14048	DUNKIRK	59	57	58	55	58	65	59	59	62	57	77	68	60	79	60	64	74	60	64	67
14051	EAST AMHERST	166	203	221	209	196	197	182	177	167	184	212	207	196	219	184	161	212	172	158	196
14052	EAST AURORA	93	110	116	108	109	111	101	101	97	100	121	117	106	127	104	96	120	99	96	113
14054	EAST BETHANY	83	86	80	83	87	92	79	83	80	79	99	98	81	103	82	81	96	81	84	100
14055	EAST CONCORD	92	82	63	78	87	93	76	84	81	76	98	100	74	100	78	83	93	82	91	109
14057	EDEN	94	114	124	111	112	114	105	104	100	104	126	121	111	134	108	99	125	101	97	114
14058	ELBA	82	85	80	82	86	90	78	82	79	78	98	96	80	102	81	79	95	80	83	98
14059	ELMA	105	128	140	126	126	129	117	117	112	116	140	134	125	148	121	110	139	113	109	128
14060	FARMERSVILLE STATION	73	54	32	48	60	68	51	62	59	51	70	74	45	68	53	63	65	62	75	86
14062	FORESTVILLE	75	71	62	68	74	81	68	72	71	67	87	84	68	91	70	73	84	70	78	88
14063	FREDONIA	69	66	68	67	67	72	70	69	70	68	87	83	68	87	69	69	84	71	69	79
14065	FREEDOM	78	60	36	54	64	71	57	67	64	59	77	79	51	73	58	66	71	66	76	88
14066	GAINESVILLE	78	65	45	61	70	76	61	70	66	61	80	83	57	80	63	68	75	68	78	92
14067	GASPORT	82	84	78	81	86	90	78	82	79	78	97	96	80	101	80	79	94	80	83	98
14068	GETZVILLE	111	135	146	137	132	133	122	121	113	122	142	140	130	149	124	110	142	117	109	133
14069	GLENWOOD	103	101	89	97	104	109	93	99	95	93	117	117	94	122	96	97	113	97	103	122
14070	GOWANDA	63	56	49	53	58	67	59	61	63	56	76	69	57	76	59	65	71	61	69	71
14072	GRAND ISLAND	107	130	142	130	128	128	119	118	112	118	141	137	126	149	122	109	140	115	108	130
14075	HAMBURG	87	98	105	96	97	101	93	93	91	92	113	108	97	118	95	90	112	92	90	104
14080	HOLLAND	85	84	76	80	87	93	79	83	82	78	101	97	81	106	82	84	97	81	88	100
14081	IRVING	78	71	61	68	74	81	69	75	73	69	89	86	67	88	70	74	85	74	79	90
14082	JAVA CENTER	93	80	60	76	86	93	75	84	80	75	97	100	72	99	77	83	92	82	93	110
14083	JAVA VILLAGE	92	82	63	78	87	93	76	84	81	76	98	100	74	100	78	83	93	82	91	109
14085	LAKE VIEW	109	135	145	135	133	132	122	121	114	121	143	141	130	152	125	111	143	117	109	133
14086	LANCASTER	90	100	103	100	99	101	94	94	91	94	113	109	97	118	95	89	111	92	89	105
14091	LAWTONS	78	78	77	74	78	84	75	77	77	75	95	89	76	98	76	78	93	76	79	91
14092	LEWISTON	94	109	121	107	108	114	103	102	100	102	125	117	108	130	106	100	124	101	100	112
14094	LOCKPORT	79	84	87	83	84	88	83	82	82	81	102	96	84	104	83	81	99	82	81	93
14098	LYNDONVILLE	71	66	59	62	70	78	64	69	68	62	83	79	63	87	67	72	79	68	77	85
14101	MACHIAS	79	59	37	53	67	75	56	68	65	56	77	80	50	75	59	69	71	67	81	94
14102	MARILLA	114	142	151	142	139	137	126	126	117	126	147	148	135	157	129	114	147	121	113	139
14103	MEDINA	71	67	61	64	69	77	67	70	71	65	86	79	67	89	68	73	82	69	76	81
14105	MIDDLEPORT	77	75	69	71	78	85	72	75	75	71	92	87	73	97	74	77	89	73	81	90
14108	NEWFANE	83	79	69	76	82	89	76	81	80	75	98	93	77	101	78	81	93	79	86	97
14109	NIAGARA UNIVERSITY	0	0	0	0	0	0	0	0	0	0	0	0	0	0	0	0	0	0	0	0
14111	NORTH COLLINS	74	83	87	80	83	88	79	79	78	77	98	90	83	104	81	79	96	77	79	88
14113	NORTH JAVA	95	82	61	78	88	95	77	86	82	76	99	102	74	101	79	84	94	84	94	112
14120	NORTH TONAWANDA	75	83	89	81	83	87	80	80	79	79	98	92	83	103	82	79	96	79	78	89
14125	OAKFIELD	76	74	66	71	77	82	70	74	72	69	89	86	71	92	72	74	85	72	78	90
14127	ORCHARD PARK	113	133	146	131	132	138	124	123	120	123	150	141	132	157	128	119	148	120	119	136
14129	PERRYSBURG	64	66	65	64	67	73	64	66	65	63	80	74	65	82	66	66	78	65	68	74
14131	RANSOMVILLE	87	95	95	92	95	100	88	90	87	88	108	105	92	114	91	87	106	88	89	104
14132	SANBORN	78	90	96	87	89	93	85	84	83	83	104	97	90	111	87	84	102	82	83	93
14134	SARDINIA	88	78	59	74	83	88	72	80	77	72	93	95	71	95	74	79	89	78	87	103
14136	SILVER CREEK	72	68	62	66	70	77	69	71	72	67	88	82	68	90	69	73	84	71	76	82
14138	SOUTH DAYTON	76	62	46	61	66	75	63	69	68	62	82	80	59	81	63	70	77	68	76	85
14139	SOUTH WALES	88	107	117	105	105	106	98	97	93	98	117	113	105	125	101	91	117	95	90	107
14141	SPRINGVILLE	77	78	74	74	80	87	74	77	77	73	95	89	76	99	77	79	91	76	82	91
14143	STAFFORD	79	96	106	94	94	96	89	88	85	88	107	102	95	114	91	84	107	86	82	96
14145	STRYKERSVILLE	98	87	66	83	92	99	81	89	86	81	104	106	79	106	83	88	99	87	97	115
14150	TONAWANDA	69	77	86	74	76	83	75	74	75	74	94	84	79	98	77	77	92	74	76	81
14167	VARYSBURG	86	76	58	73	81	87	71	78	75	71	91	93	69	93	73	77	87	76	85	101
14170	WEST FALLS	98	120	132	118	117	119	110	108	104	109	131	125	117	139	112	102	131	105	100	118
14171	WEST VALLEY	89	79	60	75	84	90	74	82	78	73	95	97	72	97	76	80	90	79	88	105
14172	WILSON	84	84	78	80	86	93	80	83	82	78	102	96	81	107	82	85	98	81	88	99
14174	YOUNGSTOWN	89	109	121	106	107	110	100	100	96	100	120	115	107	127	103	95	120	97	93	109
14201	BUFFALO	40	34	51	34	33	38	43	39	46	43	58	47	41	56	41	46	57	43	40	44
14202	BUFFALO	62	55	75	58	55	62	69	63	70	65	88	75	66	85	66	69	85	68	64	69
14203	BUFFALO	21	18	26	19	18	22	23	21	25	22	31	25	23	30	23	25	30	23	23	24
14204	BUFFALO	40	35	42	32	34	40	39	39	43	39	53	43	39	51	39	45	51	40	43	44
14206	BUFFALO	51	52	55	49	53	59	53	53	56	52	69	59	55	71	54	58	66	53	57	59
14207	BUFFALO	48	44	49	43	44	50	50	48	53	49	65	56	49	65	49	53	63	50	50	53
14208	BUFFALO	50	42	46	39	42	50	48	47	53	48	64	52	47	59	46	55	62	49	53	55
14209	BUFFALO	56	51	67	51	51	59	58	56	62	58	77	64	58	75	58	63	75	59	60	63
14210	BUFFALO	50	49	53	48	49	54	53	51	55	51	68	60	53	69	53	55	66	53	53	57
14211	BUFFALO	45	39	45	36	38	45	44	43	48	44	59	48	43	57	43	50	57	45	48	49
	NEW YORK	95	100	134	99	98	107	103	100	105	103	133	116	105	138	104	107	131	102	99	112
	UNITED STATES	100	100	100	100	100	100	100	100	100	100	100	100	100	100	100	100	100	100	100	100

# POST OFFICE NAME	COUNTY FIPS CODE	POPULATION 2000	POPULATION 2004	POPULATION 2009	2000-2004 ANNUAL RATE % Rate	2000-2004 ANNUAL RATE State Centile	HOUSEHOLDS 2000	HOUSEHOLDS 2004	HOUSEHOLDS 2009	% Annual Rate 2000-2004	2004 Average HH Size	FAMILIES 2000	FAMILIES 2004	% Annual Rate 2000-2004
14212 BUFFALO	029	15574	14848	14564	-1.1	1	6935	6596	6466	-1.2	2.25	3776	3571	-1.3
14213 BUFFALO	029	28469	28726	28890	0.2	41	10469	10559	10629	0.2	2.49	5985	5949	-0.1
14214 BUFFALO	029	22531	22130	21952	-0.4	9	8688	8568	8523	-0.3	2.33	4579	4430	-0.8
14215 BUFFALO	029	44307	43781	43529	-0.3	14	17331	17128	17050	-0.3	2.51	11082	10864	-0.5
14216 BUFFALO	029	23165	23156	23127	0.0	27	10650	10717	10752	0.2	2.14	5609	5568	-0.2
14217 BUFFALO	029	24328	24024	23926	-0.3	14	10535	10439	10428	-0.2	2.25	6197	6077	-0.5
14218 BUFFALO	029	20249	19626	19308	-0.7	3	8641	8422	8319	-0.6	2.30	5146	4972	-0.8
14219 BUFFALO	029	13222	12686	12427	-1.0	1	5445	5254	5167	-0.8	2.40	3495	3341	-1.1
14220 BUFFALO	029	26445	25486	25023	-0.9	2	10439	10108	9960	-0.8	2.45	6612	6350	-1.0
14221 BUFFALO	029	52023	53290	53918	0.6	61	20810	21481	21859	0.8	2.40	14158	14493	0.6
14222 BUFFALO	029	12836	12533	12391	-0.6	5	7069	6912	6848	-0.5	1.74	2232	2150	-0.9
14223 BUFFALO	029	24370	23725	23376	-0.6	4	10196	9979	9868	-0.5	2.35	6695	6506	-0.7
14224 BUFFALO	029	40940	40327	40003	-0.4	11	16233	16081	16015	-0.2	2.47	11326	11152	-0.4
14225 BUFFALO	029	35359	35232	35152	-0.1	24	15507	15510	15526	0.0	2.26	9920	9841	-0.2
14226 BUFFALO	029	29357	29296	29244	-0.1	25	12538	12599	12638	0.1	2.28	7886	7843	-0.1
14227 BUFFALO	029	24213	24212	24185	0.0	28	10257	10297	10320	0.1	2.31	6672	6674	0.0
14228 BUFFALO	029	18183	18250	18297	0.1	34	7512	7601	7672	0.3	2.34	4543	4542	0.0
14260 BUFFALO	029	4443	4443	4443	0.0	28	0	0	0	0.00	0.00	0	0	0.0
14301 NIAGARA FALLS	063	13807	13357	13124	-0.8	3	6291	6122	6064	-0.6	2.11	3285	3163	-0.9
14303 NIAGARA FALLS	063	7285	6942	6778	-1.1	1	3447	3302	3248	-1.0	2.08	1786	1692	-1.3
14304 NIAGARA FALLS	063	30482	30260	30070	-0.2	19	12699	12772	12841	0.1	2.34	8324	8301	-0.1
14305 NIAGARA FALLS	063	19086	18416	18057	-0.8	2	7713	7516	7440	-0.6	2.42	5051	4885	-0.8
14410 ADAMS BASIN	055	156	169	176	1.9	93	52	57	60	2.2	2.96	42	46	2.2
14411 ALBION	073	14157	14263	14394	0.2	40	4700	4784	4879	0.4	2.60	3217	3255	0.3
14414 AVON	051	6482	6615	6807	0.5	56	2527	2605	2706	0.7	2.51	1716	1756	0.5
14415 BELLONA	123	68	69	71	0.3	49	28	29	30	0.8	2.38	21	21	0.0
14416 BERGEN	037	3209	3161	3130	-0.4	11	1210	1207	1208	-0.1	2.61	871	864	-0.2
14418 BRANCHPORT	123	1394	1395	1410	0.0	30	534	540	549	0.3	2.57	387	388	0.1
14420 BROCKPORT	055	19737	19814	19936	0.1	34	6612	6746	6884	0.5	2.58	4307	4354	0.3
14422 BYRON	037	2839	2845	2841	0.1	31	1003	1017	1026	0.3	2.80	763	770	0.2
14423 CALEDONIA	051	4863	4916	5072	0.3	44	1795	1826	1897	0.4	2.68	1353	1369	0.3
14424 CANANDAIGUA	069	24543	25416	26463	0.8	72	9775	10235	10783	1.1	2.41	6349	6617	1.0
14425 FARMINGTON	069	9663	9798	10098	0.3	49	3529	3624	3779	0.6	2.70	2630	2686	0.5
14427 CASTILE	121	1973	2078	2142	1.2	83	762	818	857	1.7	2.50	550	586	1.5
14428 CHURCHVILLE	055	7679	7639	7659	-0.1	22	2721	2735	2771	0.1	2.78	2081	2079	0.0
14432 CLIFTON SPRINGS	069	5914	5980	6141	0.3	44	2197	2241	2326	0.5	2.57	1514	1532	0.3
14433 CLYDE	117	4808	4772	4820	-0.2	19	1776	1782	1820	0.1	2.66	1272	1267	-0.1
14435 CONESUS	051	2565	2621	2699	0.5	58	964	999	1041	0.8	2.54	729	751	0.7
14437 DANSVILLE	051	12306	12501	12846	0.4	50	3844	3932	4083	0.5	2.75	2672	2721	0.4
14441 DRESDEN	123	297	309	318	0.9	75	115	120	125	1.0	2.55	85	88	0.8
14445 EAST ROCHESTER	055	8893	8690	8676	-0.5	5	3419	3378	3409	-0.3	2.36	2055	2013	-0.5
14450 FAIRPORT	055	41196	42237	43094	0.6	61	15827	16452	16993	0.9	2.54	11577	11999	0.9
14454 GENESEO	051	10419	10891	11299	1.1	79	2834	3048	3241	1.7	2.42	1547	1655	1.6
14456 GENEVA	069	20404	20820	21548	0.5	56	7736	7991	8385	0.8	2.38	4830	4946	0.6
14462 GROVELAND	051	536	545	555	0.4	51	190	201	212	1.3	1.06	135	34	-27.7
14464 HAMLIN	055	7880	7794	7785	-0.3	15	2745	2752	2783	0.1	2.82	2118	2115	0.0
14466 HEMLOCK	069	1582	1586	1626	0.1	32	563	570	591	0.3	2.78	450	454	0.2
14467 HENRIETTA	055	8859	8884	8935	0.1	33	3309	3368	3430	0.4	2.63	2487	2520	0.3
14468 HILTON	055	16443	16656	16851	0.3	47	5704	5858	6001	0.6	2.81	4506	4609	0.5
14469 BLOOMFIELD	069	6220	6424	6661	0.8	69	2331	2439	2558	1.1	2.62	1741	1813	1.0
14470 HOLLEY	073	8933	8973	9018	0.1	36	2861	2905	2950	0.4	2.66	2063	2081	0.2
14471 HONEOYE	069	2870	2878	2955	0.1	33	1185	1205	1254	0.4	2.39	818	826	0.2
14472 HONEOYE FALLS	055	7953	8103	8196	0.4	54	2989	3085	3157	0.8	2.59	2235	2294	0.6
14475 IONIA	069	220	241	258	2.2	94	82	91	98	2.5	2.65	64	71	2.5
14476 KENDALL	073	2222	2211	2201	-0.1	22	771	777	781	0.2	2.85	627	629	0.1
14477 KENT	073	2123	2249	2314	1.4	86	742	792	821	1.6	2.82	569	605	1.5
14478 KEUKA PARK	123	1325	1350	1375	0.4	54	307	318	328	0.8	3.07	213	220	0.8
14480 LAKEVILLE	051	197	213	226	1.9	92	86	94	100	2.1	2.24	61	66	1.9
14481 LEICESTER	051	3676	3686	3738	0.1	32	698	714	743	0.5	3.36	528	538	0.4
14482 LE ROY	037	9084	8912	8821	-0.5	8	3502	3481	3483	-0.1	2.50	2405	2377	-0.3
14485 LIMA	051	4528	4606	4725	0.4	52	1560	1607	1669	0.7	2.55	1110	1137	0.6
14486 LINWOOD	051	291	294	301	0.2	43	100	102	106	0.5	2.88	76	78	0.6
14487 LIVONIA	051	6230	6594	6930	1.4	86	2280	2441	2591	1.6	2.68	1684	1794	1.5
14489 LYONS	117	7613	7496	7541	-0.4	11	2846	2837	2889	-0.1	2.57	1905	1884	-0.3
14502 MACEDON	117	9507	10034	10417	1.3	84	3460	3686	3866	1.5	2.72	2655	2819	1.4
14504 MANCHESTER	069	1422	1404	1434	-0.3	14	630	630	651	0.0	2.23	409	406	-0.2
14505 MARION	117	5106	5096	5139	-0.1	25	1802	1818	1854	0.2	2.80	1383	1388	0.1
14506 MENDON	055	1227	1232	1235	0.1	35	413	419	424	0.3	2.94	350	354	0.3
14507 MIDDLESEX	123	1378	1375	1395	-0.1	25	514	517	528	0.1	2.61	376	376	0.0
14510 MOUNT MORRIS	051	5194	5216	5340	0.1	35	2019	2041	2109	0.3	2.39	1306	1312	0.1
14512 NAPLES	069	4556	4824	5057	1.4	86	1818	1952	2071	1.7	2.46	1264	1347	1.5
14513 NEWARK	117	14692	14598	14733	-0.2	20	5677	5701	5818	0.1	2.45	3825	3813	-0.1
14514 NORTH CHILI	055	4597	4809	4921	1.1	79	1673	1776	1842	1.4	2.45	1185	1251	1.3
14516 NORTH ROSE	117	2360	2423	2485	0.6	63	891	928	964	1.0	2.60	651	674	0.8
14517 NUNDA	051	2648	2764	2883	1.0	78	1005	1061	1117	1.3	2.56	741	779	1.2
14519 ONTARIO	117	11076	11423	11688	0.7	68	4101	4287	4442	1.1	2.66	3094	3218	0.9
14521 OVID	099	3803	4342	4766	3.2	99	1143	1346	1516	3.9	2.62	757	892	3.9
14522 PALMYRA	117	8753	9023	9249	0.7	67	3428	3565	3692	0.9	2.52	2368	2451	0.8
14525 PAVILION	037	3049	3038	3031	-0.1	23	1068	1078	1088	0.2	2.82	833	837	0.1
14526 PENFIELD	055	19955	20330	20611	0.4	54	7400	7642	7844	0.8	2.61	5571	5710	0.6
14527 PENN YAN	123	13076	13233	13471	0.3	45	5010	5095	5216	0.4	2.48	3362	3399	0.3
14530 PERRY	121	5809	5842	5877	0.1	37	2265	2305	2351	0.4	2.31	1579	1600	0.3
14532 PHELPS	069	4301	4312	4422	0.1	32	1680	1707	1771	0.4	2.52	1203	1215	0.2
14533 PIFFARD	051	2375	2403	2461	0.3	45	871	892	922	0.6	2.65	649	665	0.6
14534 PITTSFORD	055	30287	30828	31345	0.4	53	10905	11240	11564	0.7	2.70	8720	8967	0.7
14536 PORTAGEVILLE	121	716	724	730	0.3	44	272	279	286	0.6	2.59	202	207	0.6
14541 ROMULUS	099	1810	2080	2288	3.3	99	641	753	845	3.9	2.68	481	564	3.8
14543 RUSH	055	3266	3248	3258	-0.1	21	1137	1149	1168	0.3	2.60	873	877	0.1
14544 RUSHVILLE	123	2038	2097	2159	0.7	65	760	786	814	0.8	2.64	563	580	0.7
14545 SCOTTSBURG	051	274	298	318	2.0	93	105	116	125	2.4	2.57	81	89	2.2
14546 SCOTTSVILLE	055	5402	5322	5321	-0.4	11	2134	2136	2164	0.0	2.48	1474	1466	-0.1
14548 SHORTSVILLE	069	4204	4218	4337	0.1	33	1571	1593	1655	0.3	2.63	1147	1157	0.2
14550 SILVER SPRINGS	121	1736	1706	1701	-0.4	9	675	675	683	0.0	2.52	469	466	-0.2
14551 SODUS	117	5814	5813	5894	0.0	28	2164	2186	2241	0.2	2.62	1498	1503	0.1
14555 SODUS POINT	117	1187	1175	1183	-0.2	16	503	505	515	0.1	2.33	345	343	-0.1
NEW YORK					0.4					0.5	2.60			0.4
UNITED STATES					1.2					1.3	2.58			1.1

ZIP CODE #	POST OFFICE NAME	RACE (%) White 2000	White 2004	Black 2000	Black 2004	Asian/Pacific 2000	Asian/Pacific 2004	% Hispanic Origin 2000	% Hispanic Origin 2004	2004 AGE DISTRIBUTION (%) 0-4	5-9	10-14	15-19	20-24	25-44	45-64	65-84	85+	18+	MEDIAN AGE 2004	% 2004 Males	% 2004 Females
14212	BUFFALO	50.3	45.5	45.3	50.0	1.5	1.5	1.8	1.9	8.2	7.9	7.6	6.7	6.5	26.7	21.7	12.8	2.0	72.1	35.5	47.0	53.0
14213	BUFFALO	56.0	49.4	19.0	22.7	3.0	3.3	26.1	29.5	8.4	7.4	7.8	9.4	12.3	28.0	17.7	7.5	1.5	71.7	28.0	47.6	52.4
14214	BUFFALO	55.4	50.6	38.3	42.1	2.8	3.4	2.7	3.3	5.4	5.4	6.0	9.8	16.0	24.8	20.9	10.0	1.7	79.3	30.4	47.5	52.5
14215	BUFFALO	23.3	19.4	71.7	75.4	1.9	1.9	2.3	2.4	7.9	8.3	9.1	7.7	8.2	26.6	21.6	9.1	1.5	69.9	31.8	45.4	54.6
14216	BUFFALO	84.6	80.0	9.7	13.0	1.3	1.7	4.2	5.4	5.9	5.7	6.1	5.8	6.6	31.1	24.3	12.2	2.4	78.8	37.7	46.9	53.2
14217	BUFFALO	97.0	95.9	1.0	1.4	0.7	0.9	1.3	1.7	5.7	5.7	6.0	5.9	5.8	27.1	25.1	15.0	3.7	79.0	41.1	46.0	54.0
14218	BUFFALO	84.9	83.0	9.0	9.9	0.3	0.4	4.8	5.9	6.9	6.5	6.8	6.6	6.1	26.5	22.6	15.7	2.4	75.8	38.5	48.1	51.9
14219	BUFFALO	96.9	95.8	0.7	1.1	0.4	0.5	2.7	3.7	6.0	5.9	6.7	6.3	6.4	29.0	24.6	13.2	1.8	77.5	38.3	48.2	51.8
14220	BUFFALO	95.0	93.4	1.0	1.4	0.6	0.8	4.5	6.0	7.0	6.5	6.6	6.7	6.7	28.6	22.3	13.4	2.3	75.8	37.2	47.3	52.7
14221	BUFFALO	92.8	90.5	2.1	2.9	3.9	5.1	1.0	1.4	5.0	5.5	6.5	6.1	4.7	21.5	27.7	18.8	4.3	79.1	45.5	46.5	53.6
14222	BUFFALO	83.2	78.2	10.6	14.1	1.8	2.2	4.7	6.0	3.5	3.0	3.3	4.1	10.1	37.4	23.8	11.7	3.0	87.8	37.3	49.0	51.0
14223	BUFFALO	96.0	94.7	1.3	1.9	1.2	1.6	1.3	1.8	5.4	5.7	6.5	6.3	5.5	24.5	26.0	16.9	3.2	78.4	42.4	46.4	53.7
14224	BUFFALO	98.1	97.4	0.5	0.7	0.5	0.7	0.8	1.1	5.1	5.4	6.3	6.1	5.5	24.9	28.1	16.3	2.4	79.4	42.9	47.7	52.3
14225	BUFFALO	95.6	94.2	2.5	3.5	0.6	0.8	1.0	1.3	5.8	5.8	5.9	5.4	5.3	26.6	23.6	19.0	2.7	79.2	41.9	46.8	53.2
14226	BUFFALO	88.0	84.6	5.9	7.8	4.1	5.1	1.6	2.1	5.9	5.8	6.0	6.3	7.1	25.2	25.1	15.5	3.1	78.8	40.6	46.3	53.7
14227	BUFFALO	96.2	94.9	1.7	2.3	1.1	1.4	1.0	1.4	4.9	5.0	5.5	5.3	5.5	27.1	27.0	16.9	3.0	81.5	42.8	47.0	53.0
14228	BUFFALO	85.6	82.0	5.3	6.9	7.1	8.6	1.8	2.3	5.6	5.4	6.5	6.7	7.9	29.7	23.8	11.3	3.1	78.1	36.7	48.0	52.0
14260	BUFFALO	76.6	70.5	9.8	13.1	12.7	15.3	2.3	2.9	0.0	0.0	0.0	52.8	45.1	2.0	0.1	0.0	0.0	99.8	19.7	55.1	44.9
14301	NIAGARA FALLS	73.7	70.2	20.0	22.7	0.8	1.0	2.8	3.2	6.8	6.4	6.8	6.6	6.9	26.1	20.9	15.6	3.9	76.1	38.4	45.1	54.9
14303	NIAGARA FALLS	72.2	68.3	20.4	23.5	0.7	0.7	3.1	3.5	6.7	6.3	6.5	6.1	6.4	27.2	22.5	14.9	3.3	76.8	38.9	47.9	52.1
14304	NIAGARA FALLS	94.5	93.4	2.4	2.9	0.9	1.1	1.0	1.2	5.3	5.5	6.5	6.2	5.9	26.9	26.3	15.3	2.2	78.9	41.1	48.2	51.8
14305	NIAGARA FALLS	65.0	62.5	30.3	32.3	0.4	0.5	1.9	2.1	7.0	7.0	8.1	7.5	7.1	25.0	22.9	13.5	2.1	73.5	36.8	46.7	53.3
14410	ADAMS BASIN	96.8	95.9	1.3	1.8	0.6	1.2	1.3	1.8	6.5	6.5	9.5	7.7	4.7	28.4	29.0	7.7	0.0	71.6	37.5	50.3	49.7
14411	ALBION	83.7	83.4	10.9	11.1	0.4	0.4	6.0	6.2	6.3	6.3	7.3	6.9	7.2	31.3	22.2	10.5	2.1	75.9	36.0	54.1	45.9
14414	AVON	95.8	95.0	1.5	1.8	0.7	0.9	1.4	1.8	6.1	6.2	7.1	7.4	7.2	26.8	25.6	11.8	1.9	75.6	38.7	48.6	51.4
14415	BELLONA	98.5	100.0	0.0	0.0	0.0	0.0	0.0	0.0	8.7	7.3	5.8	7.3	5.8	23.2	24.6	14.5	2.9	73.9	39.4	52.2	47.8
14416	BERGEN	97.3	96.8	0.3	0.4	0.5	0.7	1.0	1.3	7.0	7.1	7.4	6.4	6.0	28.3	26.1	10.3	1.5	74.5	38.0	50.8	49.2
14418	BRANCHPORT	98.6	98.4	0.5	0.5	0.1	0.1	0.6	0.8	5.3	5.9	7.5	5.9	5.6	24.0	32.0	12.5	1.2	77.3	42.6	51.2	48.8
14420	BROCKPORT	93.0	91.1	3.2	4.0	1.0	1.2	2.8	3.8	5.0	5.4	6.6	11.9	15.5	24.2	21.9	8.0	1.6	78.9	29.7	48.7	51.3
14422	BYRON	96.1	95.3	0.4	0.4	0.4	0.5	3.3	4.1	6.7	6.9	7.7	7.7	6.1	28.7	26.4	9.2	0.7	74.1	37.4	49.9	50.1
14423	CALEDONIA	94.4	93.4	3.3	3.9	0.6	0.8	0.9	1.1	6.9	7.0	7.2	7.1	6.3	27.7	26.5	10.2	1.1	74.1	38.1	50.1	49.9
14424	CANANDAIGUA	96.8	96.2	1.1	1.2	0.6	0.8	1.0	1.3	5.6	5.9	7.1	6.5	6.0	25.7	27.4	13.3	2.4	77.2	40.7	48.9	51.1
14425	FARMINGTON	96.4	95.7	1.1	1.3	1.0	1.3	1.2	1.6	7.4	7.4	8.0	7.3	6.7	29.3	27.3	6.0	0.6	72.8	35.5	48.8	51.2
14427	CASTILE	98.4	98.0	0.5	0.7	0.3	0.4	0.5	0.7	5.3	6.0	7.9	8.0	6.6	27.1	25.3	12.2	1.5	75.4	39.1	50.2	49.8
14428	CHURCHVILLE	96.3	95.3	1.5	1.9	0.7	0.9	0.9	1.3	6.1	6.7	8.6	7.3	5.7	27.6	28.3	8.8	0.9	73.7	38.4	50.0	50.0
14432	CLIFTON SPRINGS	97.7	97.2	0.7	0.8	0.3	0.3	1.2	1.4	6.0	6.3	7.5	7.3	5.9	27.4	25.5	11.4	2.8	75.4	39.1	49.2	50.8
14433	CLYDE	94.3	93.4	3.2	3.7	0.1	0.2	1.4	1.7	7.0	7.2	7.7	7.2	6.6	26.0	24.1	12.2	1.9	73.5	37.2	49.1	50.9
14435	CONESUS	96.7	96.3	1.6	1.8	0.1	0.2	0.9	1.0	5.3	6.0	8.2	8.4	4.9	30.3	27.1	9.0	0.8	74.9	38.4	51.2	48.8
14437	DANSVILLE	89.1	87.8	7.4	8.1	0.5	0.6	4.1	4.9	5.4	5.5	6.5	6.1	7.2	31.3	26.0	10.7	1.4	78.7	38.2	55.6	44.4
14441	DRESDEN	97.0	96.8	0.0	0.0	0.0	0.0	3.4	4.2	5.8	6.8	6.8	5.5	6.5	22.0	29.5	15.2	1.9	76.4	42.1	51.8	48.2
14445	EAST ROCHESTER	95.6	94.3	1.5	2.0	1.0	1.3	2.3	3.1	5.7	5.7	6.5	9.1	9.2	28.2	22.5	11.5	1.7	78.4	35.6	46.9	53.1
14450	FAIRPORT	93.9	92.0	1.7	2.2	2.9	3.8	1.4	2.0	6.6	7.4	7.8	6.6	4.8	25.8	29.0	10.5	1.7	73.8	40.1	48.3	51.7
14454	GENESEO	92.9	91.6	2.6	2.9	2.5	3.0	2.6	3.2	3.2	3.1	3.7	20.7	27.9	17.6	15.4	7.0	1.5	87.6	23.5	43.9	56.1
14456	GENEVA	86.2	84.4	7.3	8.0	1.2	1.4	6.2	7.3	5.9	5.9	7.0	9.3	9.8	23.5	23.2	12.9	2.5	77.1	36.0	47.5	52.5
14462	GROVELAND	60.3	56.3	32.3	34.9	0.2	0.2	15.1	17.4	1.7	2.0	3.3	3.3	9.4	53.4	22.2	4.4	0.4	90.8	36.5	80.0	20.0
14464	HAMLIN	96.9	95.9	1.0	1.3	0.3	0.4	1.6	2.3	7.0	7.4	8.8	8.0	6.6	29.1	26.0	6.4	0.7	71.7	35.1	49.4	50.6
14466	HEMLOCK	98.0	97.6	0.3	0.4	0.3	0.4	0.8	1.0	5.9	7.1	8.6	8.3	5.9	27.4	28.3	7.8	0.8	72.6	38.3	50.1	49.9
14467	HENRIETTA	87.6	84.4	6.2	7.8	3.4	4.2	2.5	3.3	6.1	6.7	7.9	7.1	5.4	28.3	27.1	10.3	1.1	74.4	38.3	48.3	51.7
14468	HILTON	96.7	95.8	1.4	1.8	0.7	0.8	1.2	1.6	6.5	7.0	8.5	8.1	5.9	27.0	27.3	8.6	1.3	72.8	37.9	49.3	50.7
14469	BLOOMFIELD	98.5	98.2	0.4	0.4	0.2	0.3	0.9	1.2	6.4	6.7	7.7	6.4	5.0	27.5	29.1	10.1	1.2	75.1	39.6	49.8	50.2
14470	HOLLEY	88.2	87.5	9.8	10.3	0.3	0.3	4.6	4.9	6.0	6.1	7.0	6.7	6.4	35.3	23.8	8.0	0.9	76.9	36.5	43.3	56.7
14471	HONEOYE	98.5	98.1	0.2	0.2	0.4	0.5	0.8	1.0	4.8	5.5	7.2	6.0	4.9	26.3	32.4	11.5	1.4	78.7	42.4	50.7	49.3
14472	HONEOYE FALLS	97.4	96.6	0.9	1.1	0.9	1.1	1.0	1.4	5.6	6.7	8.5	7.1	4.7	23.9	31.4	9.9	2.3	74.1	41.5	48.9	51.1
14475	IONIA	99.1	98.8	0.0	0.0	0.0	0.4	0.9	1.2	5.8	6.6	7.9	5.4	5.4	26.6	30.7	10.8	0.8	76.4	40.8	51.0	49.0
14476	KENDALL	96.8	96.6	0.8	0.9	0.2	0.2	1.3	1.5	6.2	6.5	7.6	8.6	6.6	23.3	29.3	10.9	1.0	74.4	39.8	51.3	48.7
14477	KENT	94.9	94.6	2.5	2.6	0.2	0.2	1.5	1.7	5.4	6.9	9.0	8.4	4.0	27.8	28.3	9.3	0.9	73.2	38.6	51.2	48.8
14478	KEUKA PARK	98.1	97.9	0.8	0.9	0.3	0.4	0.6	0.7	3.6	4.2	4.7	19.6	16.4	14.7	22.7	13.0	1.1	84.4	27.3	42.7	57.3
14480	LAKEVILLE	98.0	97.7	0.5	0.5	0.5	0.5	1.0	0.5	6.6	6.6	8.5	7.0	5.6	25.8	27.7	10.3	1.9	73.2	39.2	49.3	50.7
14481	LEICESTER	74.4	71.7	20.2	22.1	0.1	0.2	10.0	11.5	4.0	4.3	4.6	5.6	8.0	43.3	21.7	7.7	0.8	84.0	36.0	68.2	31.8
14482	LE ROY	96.1	95.4	1.8	2.1	0.4	0.5	0.8	0.9	6.1	6.5	7.0	6.8	5.9	27.0	26.2	12.0	2.5	75.9	39.2	48.8	51.2
14485	LIMA	96.8	96.2	1.0	1.2	0.5	0.7	1.3	1.6	4.9	5.0	7.1	8.1	9.6	29.0	26.1	8.8	1.4	78.8	36.5	49.5	50.5
14486	LINWOOD	97.9	97.6	0.3	0.3	0.3	0.7	1.0	1.0	6.5	6.8	7.5	6.1	5.4	27.2	27.9	11.2	1.4	75.9	39.8	50.0	50.0
14487	LIVONIA	97.8	97.3	0.5	0.6	0.4	0.5	0.8	1.0	6.6	6.9	8.4	7.8	6.1	25.9	27.5	9.5	1.4	72.4	38.4	49.2	50.8
14489	LYONS	90.1	88.7	6.8	7.7	0.5	0.6	2.3	2.8	5.7	6.1	7.5	7.4	6.5	26.0	26.4	12.5	1.9	76.1	39.3	48.9	51.1
14502	MACEDON	97.1	96.5	0.8	0.9	0.8	1.0	1.5	1.8	8.3	8.4	7.9	6.6	5.3	30.4	24.8	7.6	0.7	71.3	36.1	49.6	50.4
14504	MANCHESTER	97.3	96.7	0.4	0.4	0.3	0.3	1.2	1.5	5.1	5.5	6.5	6.5	5.9	24.6	28.4	15.2	2.4	78.9	42.4	49.4	50.6
14505	MARION	97.8	97.4	0.9	1.0	0.3	0.3	1.4	1.7	6.5	6.9	8.6	7.7	6.0	27.6	26.6	9.0	1.3	73.0	37.4	48.6	51.4
14506	MENDON	97.3	96.6	0.4	0.5	1.7	2.3	0.8	1.1	6.3	8.0	9.1	7.4	3.8	22.4	33.0	9.3	0.7	71.5	41.4	50.4	49.6
14507	MIDDLESEX	98.6	98.3	0.2	0.3	0.2	0.2	0.7	0.9	5.5	6.3	8.6	7.1	5.9	23.6	29.8	12.3	1.0	74.9	40.8	50.6	49.4
14510	MOUNT MORRIS	93.5	92.4	2.5	2.8	0.6	0.7	4.8	5.9	5.9	5.9	6.8	6.7	7.0	28.6	24.6	11.4	3.0	77.0	38.3	50.6	49.4
14512	NAPLES	97.9	97.5	0.3	0.4	0.5	0.6	0.7	0.9	5.3	6.0	7.4	6.7	5.2	25.1	30.6	12.1	1.7	77.0	41.7	49.6	50.4
14513	NEWARK	91.3	89.9	4.0	4.4	0.5	0.6	5.6	6.8	6.3	6.3	7.2	7.1	6.7	25.5	25.2	12.9	3.0	75.7	39.2	48.1	51.9
14514	NORTH CHILI	94.0	92.2	3.0	3.8	1.2	1.6	2.0	2.7	6.2	5.6	6.9	8.2	9.7	27.4	20.6	13.0	2.4	78.1	35.2	47.0	53.1
14516	NORTH ROSE	95.7	95.0	1.8	2.0	0.2	0.3	1.5	1.9	5.3	5.7	7.6	7.0	5.6	25.6	28.8	12.8	1.7	76.8	41.0	49.4	50.6
14517	NUNDA	97.8	97.3	0.6	0.7	0.2	0.3	1.1	1.4	7.1	7.0	7.6	7.0	6.5	27.0	25.2	10.9	1.7	73.4	37.2	49.1	50.9
14519	ONTARIO	96.4	95.7	1.3	1.4	0.6	0.8	1.2	1.5	7.1	7.5	8.3	6.9	5.5	29.0	26.5	8.3	1.0	72.5	37.5	50.6	49.4
14521	OVID	82.0	80.9	13.0	13.3	0.4	0.5	6.3	7.1	5.3	5.6	7.1	7.0	8.0	32.4	22.9	10.0	1.7	77.5	35.8	56.5	43.6
14522	PALMYRA	97.5	97.1	0.4	0.5	0.4	0.5	0.8	1.0	6.2	6.5	7.3	6.9	6.1	27.5	27.1	10.8	1.5	75.8	38.8	49.7	50.3
14525	PAVILION	97.4	97.0	0.6	0.7	0.3	0.5	0.6	0.8	6.2	7.0	8.2	7.4	6.1	27.4	26.4	10.3	1.1	73.8	38.0	50.7	49.3
14526	PENFIELD	92.9	90.9	2.2	2.8	3.5	4.5	1.5	2.0	5.8	6.7	7.9	6.8	4.6	24.5	29.7	12.0	2.0	74.8	41.6	47.9	52.1
14527	PENN YAN	98.0	97.7	0.4	0.5	0.3	0.4	0.9	1.1	6.5	6.7	7.0	7.4	6.7	22.6	25.7	14.7	2.6	75.6	40.2	48.7	51.3
14530	PERRY	92.0	90.8	5.2	5.8	0.5	0.6	3.4	4.3	5.9	5.8	6.8	6.6	7.5	30.6	24.1	11.0	1.8	77.3	36.8	53.3	46.7
14532	PHELPS	98.2	97.9	0.2	0.3	0.2	0.2	1.3	1.5	6.0	6.8	7.8	7.4	5.7	27.3	26.7	10.9	1.4	74.5	38.3	48.8	51.2
14533	PIFFARD	97.4	96.8	1.1	1.4	0.6	0.7	0.8	1.1	6.2	6.6	7.2	6.7	5.5	27.4	28.1	11.0	1.2	75.3	39.8	50.8	49.2
14534	PITTSFORD	91.8	89.5	2.2	2.7	4.8	6.0	1.3	1.8	6.0	7.5	8.5	6.6	3.8	20.1	31.9	13.6	2.1	73.3	43.6	48.3	51.8
14536	PORTAGEVILLE	97.9	97.5	0.3	0.3	0.1	0.1	0.6	0.7	6.2	6.5	7.9	7.7	6.5	25.8	27.1	11.1	1.2	74.3	39.0	49.3	50.7
14541	ROMULUS	95.4	94.6	2.7	3.0	0.4	0.5	1.4	1.7	5.9	6.9	8.4	7.4	5.7	24.2	27.0	12.8	1.8	73.9	39.4	50.0	50.1
14543	RUSH	90.9	88.7	5.9	7.4	1.2	1.5	2.2	2.9	4.7	6.3	8.3	10.9	3.6	24.7	29.1	11.2	1.3	71.5	40.6	53.7	46.3
14544	RUSHVILLE	97.6	97.0	0.5	0.6	0.3	0.5	0.9	1.2	7.1	7.3	8.2	7.3	5.7	25.3	27.3	10.6	1.2	72.5	38.1	50.6	49.4
14545	SCOTTSBURG	96.7	95.6	0.7	0.7	0.7	1.0	0.4	0.7	4.7	5.7	7.7	6.0	5.0	25.5	31.2	12.8	1.3	77.9	42.6	50.7	49.3
14546	SCOTTSVILLE	92.0	89.9	4.6	5.8	1.0	1.3	2.2	3.1	6.0	6.6	7.4	7.3	5.2	29.7	26.1	10.5	1.3	75.2	37.7	48.2	51.8
14548	SHORTSVILLE	98.0	97.6	0.2	0.3	0.3	0.3	1.2	1.4	6.0	6.3	7.4	6.4	5.5	27.8	27.8	11.3	1.5	76.2	39.7	49.8	50.2
14550	SILVER SPRINGS	98.1	97.8	0.2	0.2	0.4	0.4	1.0	1.2	5.3	6.5	7.7	6.3	4.9	28.1	26.8	12.8	1.5	76.3	39.9	49.5	50.5
14551	SODUS	85.8	84.0	9.9	11.0	0.6	0.7	2.9	3.4	6.3	6.5	7.7	7.3	6.3	25.9	26.4	11.6	2.1	75.0	38.7	48.7	51.4
14555	SODUS POINT	93.9	92.9	3.4	3.8	0.3	0.3	1.6	2.1	5.3	6.2	7.3	6.2	4.5	25.5	31.7	11.9	1.5	77.4	41.9	50.9	49.1
	NEW YORK	68.0	65.9	15.9	16.2	5.6	6.4	15.1	16.7	6.5	6.5	7.1	7.0	7.1	28.9	24.0	11.2	1.8	75.8	36.7	48.3	51.7
	UNITED STATES	75.1	73.6	12.3	12.5	3.8	4.2	12.5	14.1	6.9	6.7	7.2	7.0	7.3	28.6	23.8	10.8	1.7	75.1	36.0	49.1	50.9

#	POST OFFICE NAME	2004 Per Capita Income	2004 HH Income Base	2004 Household Income Distribution (%): Less than $25,000	$25,000 to $49,999	$50,000 to $99,999	$100,000 to $149,999	$150,000 or More	Median Household Income: 2004	2009	2004 National Centile	2004 State Centile	2004 Home Value Base	2004 Home Value Distribution (%): Less than $50,000	$50,000 to $89,999	$90,000 to $174,999	$175,000 to $399,999	$400,000 or More	2004 Median Home Value
14212	BUFFALO	12418	6596	57.0	28.0	13.3	1.3	0.4	20319	22859	2	1	2824	41.3	28.2	29.7	0.7	0.0	64876
14213	BUFFALO	12886	10559	55.6	25.4	16.4	1.9	0.7	21665	24340	2	2	3577	29.8	46.7	21.3	2.2	0.0	65328
14214	BUFFALO	20071	8568	39.1	25.7	24.7	6.8	3.6	34419	39694	25	11	4063	9.4	23.5	54.7	11.6	0.8	110752
14215	BUFFALO	16262	17128	42.1	30.6	22.0	4.1	1.3	30243	33230	13	5	9081	16.8	56.8	25.2	1.1	0.1	71179
14216	BUFFALO	23051	10717	33.5	30.8	26.3	6.3	3.2	37556	42695	38	23	5253	0.9	13.1	76.7	7.8	1.5	117338
14217	BUFFALO	24157	10439	25.8	29.0	34.6	7.7	2.9	44606	51337	60	49	7019	1.7	14.0	80.4	3.7	0.2	111213
14218	BUFFALO	19372	8422	38.1	29.9	26.2	4.1	1.8	33864	38665	24	10	4973	10.1	27.0	58.9	4.0	0.0	102097
14219	BUFFALO	22035	5254	23.1	34.6	32.4	7.2	2.6	43743	50604	58	47	3437	2.2	16.4	75.3	5.7	0.4	112033
14220	BUFFALO	19853	10108	29.6	32.9	29.3	6.7	1.6	39855	45581	45	33	6786	2.5	36.3	60.3	1.0	0.0	96325
14221	BUFFALO	35481	21481	15.3	20.9	35.8	15.5	12.5	66340	76814	89	82	16830	0.9	4.7	54.5	37.3	2.6	162280
14222	BUFFALO	32439	6912	34.9	26.8	23.5	8.1	6.8	37952	44861	39	24	2418	1.0	10.3	53.6	30.1	4.9	146966
14223	BUFFALO	24103	9979	23.4	28.8	36.0	9.1	2.9	47961	54525	68	58	7917	0.6	11.2	82.1	5.8	0.3	116277
14224	BUFFALO	24136	16081	20.1	27.1	39.3	11.0	2.6	52403	60191	76	66	12864	1.5	9.6	73.1	15.4	0.4	130893
14225	BUFFALO	21934	15510	28.0	34.6	30.4	5.3	1.8	39520	45150	44	32	11715	4.2	20.7	72.9	2.1	0.2	104927
14226	BUFFALO	30519	12599	23.7	25.5	32.7	10.1	8.0	50839	57612	74	64	8958	0.8	12.5	65.9	19.0	1.8	124058
14227	BUFFALO	24755	10297	24.1	30.0	34.4	9.2	2.3	46839	53651	66	55	7074	2.9	6.3	82.2	8.5	0.1	121688
14228	BUFFALO	25593	7601	23.9	27.8	32.5	11.6	4.2	48219	55182	69	59	4334	0.4	8.2	65.1	25.9	0.4	147453
14260	BUFFALO	13716	0	0.0	0.0	0.0	0.0	0.0	0	0	0	0	0	0.0	0.0	0.0	0.0	0.0	0
14301	NIAGARA FALLS	14505	6122	54.2	28.5	14.5	2.1	0.7	22275	24651	3	2	2662	24.2	55.7	19.8	0.3	0.0	66225
14303	NIAGARA FALLS	15016	3302	53.8	28.7	14.3	2.2	0.9	22692	25016	3	2	1540	20.5	64.1	14.7	0.7	0.0	65239
14304	NIAGARA FALLS	22290	12772	26.6	30.4	33.9	7.3	1.8	43812	50141	58	47	9717	11.8	28.4	49.4	9.6	0.7	98616
14305	NIAGARA FALLS	18019	7516	43.4	27.7	21.7	4.9	2.3	29775	32939	12	4	4500	19.7	41.1	35.5	3.6	0.1	77055
14410	ADAMS BASIN	25128	57	5.3	22.8	50.9	14.0	7.0	69221	76077	91	84	49	0.0	2.0	59.2	38.8	0.0	159722
14411	ALBION	17227	4784	32.4	31.4	29.9	5.1	1.3	38210	41473	40	26	3386	20.8	32.5	42.3	4.2	0.2	86028
14414	AVON	23561	2605	26.9	25.8	35.5	8.1	3.8	46462	51096	65	54	1958	19.5	3.4	59.6	15.6	1.9	122074
14415	BELLONA	19684	29	27.6	31.0	37.9	3.5	0.0	37287	41492	36	21	23	0.0	13.0	69.6	13.0	4.4	130357
14416	BERGEN	24062	1207	17.0	29.6	41.0	9.4	3.0	53649	59328	78	68	972	2.3	22.8	66.8	7.8	0.3	114507
14418	BRANCHPORT	17396	540	32.4	35.4	25.6	5.0	1.7	37426	40864	37	22	457	9.9	21.2	42.2	23.2	3.5	123941
14420	BROCKPORT	22394	6746	22.0	25.0	38.5	11.5	3.0	52752	60666	77	66	4414	5.0	11.9	62.6	20.1	0.4	127413
14422	BYRON	22092	1017	18.5	25.6	44.1	7.6	4.3	54187	60138	79	69	877	7.3	22.6	58.5	11.1	0.6	111328
14423	CALEDONIA	21996	1826	19.7	31.3	36.6	9.7	2.7	48882	53794	70	60	1500	9.7	9.7	66.1	13.8	0.7	119830
14424	CANANDAIGUA	25627	10235	23.1	29.0	33.6	9.4	4.9	48215	54549	69	59	7002	7.0	9.9	52.9	26.5	3.7	140278
14425	FARMINGTON	24007	3624	15.3	29.1	40.8	12.8	2.0	54991	62065	80	70	2794	15.0	5.1	65.4	14.2	0.5	123239
14427	CASTILE	18917	818	30.1	37.3	26.3	4.8	1.6	38612	42033	41	28	621	6.8	18.4	61.0	10.1	3.7	117894
14428	CHURCHVILLE	26153	2735	13.3	23.7	43.7	14.3	5.0	62806	72387	87	78	2343	3.9	6.1	65.1	24.4	0.5	138019
14432	CLIFTON SPRINGS	21208	2241	24.3	30.1	37.2	6.3	2.1	46084	51016	64	53	1661	19.2	21.6	51.1	7.8	0.5	98829
14433	CLYDE	17862	1782	30.9	30.4	31.8	4.9	2.0	38534	43667	41	27	1352	15.8	46.4	32.8	4.5	0.4	78984
14435	CONESUS	26787	999	17.2	29.2	37.9	11.3	4.3	52795	58100	77	66	873	6.9	14.3	54.2	23.7	0.9	130697
14437	DANSVILLE	17319	3932	29.4	32.5	30.6	6.1	1.5	41164	45927	50	38	2913	10.4	34.6	47.8	6.9	0.4	94803
14441	DRESDEN	19235	120	29.2	34.2	30.8	3.3	2.5	40997	45279	50	37	99	11.1	11.1	49.5	25.3	3.0	123214
14445	EAST ROCHESTER	22633	3378	24.6	31.5	33.0	8.1	2.8	44470	51635	60	49	2104	2.6	21.0	67.9	8.2	0.3	108497
14450	FAIRPORT	37349	16452	11.8	17.2	37.4	19.6	14.1	77257	88166	94	89	13128	0.6	3.8	42.5	50.0	3.2	180171
14454	GENESEO	21629	3048	28.8	25.0	30.5	10.4	5.2	46597	51383	65	55	1671	1.1	5.5	60.1	30.6	2.7	148433
14456	GENEVA	20595	7991	30.1	30.3	30.3	7.0	2.4	39514	44283	44	32	4939	7.3	27.8	48.1	15.5	1.4	105542
14462	GROVELAND	31446	201	16.9	32.3	38.3	8.5	4.0	50506	56957	73	63	158	1.9	17.1	55.7	22.2	3.2	131000
14464	HAMLIN	22044	2752	19.6	26.1	40.7	11.1	2.6	54947	63276	80	70	2304	19.7	6.5	61.3	12.3	0.2	115234
14466	HEMLOCK	22556	570	14.9	27.4	45.1	10.2	2.5	56552	63410	81	71	504	5.6	11.9	56.0	26.6	0.0	134706
14467	HENRIETTA	28906	3368	11.8	22.9	43.7	16.1	5.5	64748	76812	88	80	2571	0.0	1.6	77.3	20.0	1.2	142070
14468	HILTON	24806	5858	11.6	26.1	44.6	13.5	4.2	61417	70349	86	76	4907	0.5	5.3	73.0	20.5	0.7	134062
14469	BLOOMFIELD	26166	2439	17.6	29.4	36.0	12.3	4.7	53315	60088	77	68	2071	13.7	10.3	50.9	23.9	1.3	129261
14470	HOLLEY	19436	2905	17.1	36.8	38.2	5.8	2.1	46483	51576	65	55	2363	20.7	24.1	44.7	10.2	0.3	96256
14471	HONEOYE	27799	1205	17.8	29.1	39.6	9.9	3.6	52502	59068	76	66	993	9.6	14.7	49.8	25.1	0.9	129774
14472	HONEOYE FALLS	39319	3085	13.5	17.7	32.8	18.7	17.2	77019	88028	94	89	2543	2.5	4.3	35.0	50.1	8.1	193886
14475	IONIA	22789	91	17.6	34.1	33.0	13.2	2.2	48637	55102	70	59	80	21.3	17.5	35.0	23.8	2.5	118750
14476	KENDALL	24903	777	14.2	31.8	36.8	11.8	5.4	53430	59138	78	68	677	0.4	12.1	67.2	20.2	0.0	128584
14477	KENT	20396	792	17.4	32.5	40.0	7.1	3.0	50092	54623	72	62	693	5.3	24.8	58.9	11.0	0.0	109070
14478	KEUKA PARK	17505	318	23.6	30.5	34.3	7.6	4.1	43634	49356	58	46	266	3.4	4.5	40.2	44.0	7.9	179630
14480	LAKEVILLE	27820	94	19.2	24.5	44.7	8.5	3.2	54454	63005	79	69	69	7.3	10.1	60.9	21.7	0.0	129464
14481	LEICESTER	15023	714	21.6	36.8	34.5	5.9	1.3	45272	50815	62	51	592	18.1	19.9	51.5	9.8	0.7	100954
14482	LE ROY	22258	3481	21.7	32.4	35.9	8.1	2.0	46095	51133	64	53	2569	4.1	21.7	64.0	9.8	0.5	114396
14485	LIMA	21912	1607	18.8	29.3	39.6	10.6	1.8	51843	58018	75	65	1206	9.3	4.4	66.4	18.5	1.4	136000
14486	LINWOOD	18542	102	20.6	29.4	43.1	5.9	1.0	50000	55327	72	62	85	3.5	21.2	63.5	11.8	0.0	113125
14487	LIVONIA	23273	2441	17.4	24.4	46.4	9.4	2.4	56406	62960	81	71	1870	6.5	10.5	62.4	20.5	0.1	126090
14489	LYONS	21039	2837	25.2	30.9	35.9	5.9	2.1	44604	50178	60	49	2055	15.4	44.4	34.8	4.4	1.1	78788
14502	MACEDON	24625	3686	13.7	26.9	42.4	13.7	3.3	59764	65754	84	74	3104	7.2	4.9	65.2	22.0	0.8	140481
14504	MANCHESTER	21281	630	24.9	38.1	31.8	4.6	0.6	40117	44192	46	35	491	25.7	21.0	49.9	3.5	0.0	92426
14505	MARION	20900	1818	18.3	27.2	42.8	9.5	2.2	52897	59459	77	67	1518	8.0	10.9	66.1	14.8	0.3	117467
14506	MENDON	45056	419	5.7	14.3	33.9	19.1	27.0	92827	109598	97	95	399	0.0	3.8	22.6	58.4	15.3	231329
14507	MIDDLESEX	22200	517	23.2	33.3	31.9	7.2	4.5	44759	49836	61	50	447	5.2	13.4	54.1	24.2	3.1	132392
14510	MOUNT MORRIS	18964	2041	30.8	35.6	27.1	4.5	2.0	37690	41893	38	23	1380	17.0	33.4	43.3	5.1	1.2	89608
14512	NAPLES	22413	1952	25.4	32.2	32.5	6.6	3.3	43486	48811	57	45	1619	8.3	20.3	48.6	19.8	3.0	119810
14513	NEWARK	20605	5701	30.8	29.3	31.8	5.8	2.4	40688	45602	49	36	3768	11.5	32.0	49.9	5.8	0.9	95867
14514	NORTH CHILI	26742	1776	14.7	33.2	37.1	10.4	4.7	51984	60370	75	66	1230	0.0	0.0	85.1	14.6	0.3	133693
14516	NORTH ROSE	20334	928	23.2	31.5	36.1	7.8	1.5	46458	52112	65	54	767	12.3	32.3	43.8	10.4	1.2	96288
14517	NUNDA	19974	1061	23.0	36.0	33.7	6.2	1.1	43359	49046	57	45	809	16.2	41.3	35.7	6.4	0.4	83763
14519	ONTARIO	25897	4287	17.2	26.8	36.6	14.4	5.1	57836	62901	82	73	3670	11.9	2.0	62.8	22.7	0.7	139495
14521	OVID	18879	1346	27.5	34.6	28.5	6.4	3.1	39653	45000	45	33	1003	7.5	22.2	45.4	21.0	3.9	122850
14522	PALMYRA	22806	3565	21.7	28.1	39.5	8.2	2.5	50131	55867	72	62	2662	10.1	13.9	63.8	11.5	0.7	114526
14525	PAVILION	20864	1078	15.7	32.3	41.2	9.2	1.7	51255	56194	74	65	892	6.1	22.9	55.7	13.7	1.7	112785
14526	PENFIELD	34926	7642	12.3	19.4	36.3	18.6	13.4	72621	84151	92	86	6502	0.1	1.0	53.9	42.5	2.6	167194
14527	PENN YAN	19466	5095	31.6	33.9	27.4	4.6	2.6	37314	41450	37	22	3732	6.6	12.9	51.3	24.0	5.3	133758
14530	PERRY	21343	2305	28.3	32.8	32.4	5.1	1.4	41897	45674	53	41	1686	2.7	24.7	60.2	10.9	1.5	113701
14532	PHELPS	24299	1707	18.8	30.8	38.3	9.6	2.6	50364	56490	73	63	1348	9.3	21.4	58.0	11.0	0.3	108657
14533	PIFFARD	21931	892	19.6	33.1	38.0	6.7	2.6	46377	50842	65	54	746	2.1	22.3	66.0	9.7	0.0	114091
14534	PITTSFORD	47640	11240	7.7	13.0	32.6	21.9	24.8	93507	109641	98	95	10261	0.6	2.1	23.7	63.7	10.1	220217
14536	PORTAGEVILLE	17380	279	30.1	42.3	21.5	4.7	1.4	37323	40950	37	22	224	12.5	24.6	50.9	11.2	0.9	104902
14541	ROMULUS	20521	753	23.6	34.0	30.0	9.2	3.2	44730	50445	60	50	629	9.2	14.9	38.2	32.9	4.8	140434
14543	RUSH	30985	1149	9.2	19.2	41.7	23.9	5.9	73141	84487	92	86	986	0.0	4.5	50.0	43.2	2.3	168642
14544	RUSHVILLE	23706	786	19.9	35.1	32.1	7.1	5.9	45928	51395	64	53	656	7.6	17.4	49.7	20.4	4.9	123589
14545	SCOTTSBURG	21499	116	19.8	33.6	36.2	7.8	2.6	47617	53538	67	57	106	9.4	26.4	54.7	9.4	0.0	105208
14546	SCOTTSVILLE	28479	2136	15.0	24.4	39.0	16.2	5.5	60796	70229	85	75	1540	4.0	9.0	68.4	18.3	0.3	126534
14548	SHORTSVILLE	22447	1593	18.7	33.0	38.3	8.0	2.0	48509	54035	69	59	1340	14.4	15.0	57.8	11.6	1.2	110759
14550	SILVER SPRINGS	18370	675	25.6	37.5	30.8	5.8	0.3	40992	43899	50	37	527	13.1	26.4	49.3	10.1	1.1	103875
14551	SODUS	20139	2186	28.3	29.2	32.5	7.9	2.1	43845	49784	58	47	1679	12.8	32.7	45.7	8.0	0.8	94048
14555	SODUS POINT	23645	505	25.4	34.7	29.3	7.7	3.0	43248	48596	57	45	417	15.1	22.5	45.1	14.9	2.4	103434
	NEW YORK	28049		26.3	24.3	29.3	11.5	8.6	49309	58077				4.6	8.6	27.2	39.9	19.8	219050
	UNITED STATES	25866		24.7	27.1	30.8	10.9	6.5	48124	56710				10.9	15.0	33.7	30.1	10.4	145905

ZIP CODE #	POST OFFICE NAME	FINANCIAL SERVICES: Auto Loan	Home Loan	Invest-ments	Retire-ment Plans	THE HOME: Home Improvements: Home Repair	Lawn & Garden	Furnishings: Comput-ers & Hard-ware	Major Appli-ances	TV, Radio, Sound Equip-ment	Furni-ture	ENTERTAINMENT: Dine out/ Carry out	Sports Equip-ment	Fees & Tickets	Toys & Games	Travel	Cable TV	PERSONAL: Apparel & Services	Auto Repairs	Health Insur-ance	Pets & Supplies
14212	BUFFALO	38	34	39	32	34	39	38	38	42	38	51	42	38	50	38	43	49	39	41	42
14213	BUFFALO	43	38	48	38	37	42	45	42	47	44	59	50	44	58	43	48	58	45	44	47
14214	BUFFALO	64	62	77	64	61	67	69	66	70	68	87	78	69	86	67	68	85	69	64	73
14215	BUFFALO	56	51	60	49	50	57	56	54	59	57	74	62	56	73	55	61	72	56	57	62
14216	BUFFALO	64	67	81	68	67	71	71	68	70	69	88	80	72	90	71	69	86	70	66	75
14217	BUFFALO	70	77	88	76	77	82	78	76	77	76	96	88	80	100	79	77	94	76	75	83
14218	BUFFALO	59	61	65	58	61	68	62	61	64	60	80	69	64	83	63	66	77	61	65	68
14219	BUFFALO	70	75	81	74	75	81	75	74	74	73	93	84	77	96	76	75	90	74	74	81
14220	BUFFALO	62	67	73	64	67	73	67	66	68	65	85	75	70	89	68	69	83	66	68	72
14221	BUFFALO	112	130	151	129	128	136	123	122	119	123	150	139	130	152	127	119	148	121	118	134
14222	BUFFALO	76	71	95	76	70	77	85	77	84	82	105	95	82	103	81	80	103	83	74	86
14223	BUFFALO	73	83	92	80	83	89	80	79	79	79	99	90	84	104	83	80	97	78	80	87
14224	BUFFALO	77	88	98	86	88	94	84	84	83	84	104	95	89	108	87	84	102	83	84	92
14225	BUFFALO	64	70	77	67	70	78	69	69	70	68	87	76	72	90	71	72	85	68	72	75
14226	BUFFALO	91	99	118	98	97	105	100	97	99	99	124	113	103	125	101	98	122	99	95	106
14227	BUFFALO	77	82	90	81	82	88	81	81	80	80	100	92	83	102	82	81	98	81	81	91
14228	BUFFALO	80	83	100	85	81	88	87	84	85	86	108	98	88	107	86	83	105	86	80	92
14260	BUFFALO	0	0	0	0	0	0	0	0	0	0	0	0	0	0	0	0	0	0	0	0
14301	NIAGARA FALLS	41	39	44	37	38	44	43	41	45	42	56	47	43	56	42	46	54	42	44	46
14303	NIAGARA FALLS	42	39	43	37	38	44	44	42	46	42	57	48	43	56	43	48	55	44	46	47
14304	NIAGARA FALLS	72	75	74	72	76	82	72	74	74	71	91	84	75	95	74	75	88	72	77	84
14305	NIAGARA FALLS	58	58	67	55	57	65	60	59	63	60	78	67	62	80	61	65	76	60	63	66
14410	ADAMS BASIN	97	120	128	120	118	116	107	107	99	107	125	125	114	133	110	96	125	103	96	118
14411	ALBION	65	64	61	61	65	72	63	65	66	61	81	74	64	84	65	68	78	64	70	75
14414	AVON	93	81	64	79	85	94	80	86	85	79	103	101	78	103	81	86	97	85	93	106
14415	BELLONA	75	67	51	63	71	76	62	68	66	62	80	82	61	81	64	67	76	67	74	88
14416	BERGEN	97	92	76	89	95	100	85	92	87	85	107	109	84	110	87	88	103	90	95	114
14418	BRANCHPORT	75	61	43	56	67	74	57	67	63	57	76	79	52	75	60	67	71	66	77	90
14420	BROCKPORT	80	86	97	88	85	88	89	85	85	87	107	101	89	108	87	82	105	86	78	93
14422	BYRON	90	93	84	90	95	98	85	89	85	84	105	105	86	109	87	85	102	87	90	108
14423	CALEDONIA	82	87	86	86	88	92	83	85	82	82	102	98	85	105	84	81	99	83	83	96
14424	CANANDAIGUA	87	90	93	89	91	97	88	89	87	87	109	103	89	109	89	87	106	89	89	101
14425	FARMINGTON	92	99	97	99	98	98	93	94	89	94	111	110	94	112	92	86	109	93	86	106
14427	CASTILE	70	65	58	62	68	75	65	68	68	63	83	77	64	86	66	70	79	66	74	80
14428	CHURCHVILLE	98	112	116	111	110	112	104	104	99	104	124	122	108	130	105	97	123	102	96	116
14432	CLIFTON SPRINGS	86	77	63	75	80	87	75	81	78	75	95	94	72	94	76	80	91	80	86	98
14433	CLYDE	70	66	58	63	69	76	64	68	68	63	83	78	64	87	66	70	79	66	74	82
14435	CONESUS	104	92	70	88	97	104	85	94	90	85	110	113	84	112	88	93	105	92	102	122
14437	DANSVILLE	70	68	62	65	71	77	65	69	69	64	84	79	67	89	67	71	81	67	74	82
14441	DRESDEN	83	65	45	59	74	83	62	74	70	61	83	87	55	82	66	75	77	73	88	102
14445	EAST ROCHESTER	71	77	89	78	77	80	80	77	78	78	97	91	81	100	79	75	96	78	73	84
14450	FAIRPORT	124	148	167	150	145	148	137	135	129	137	163	157	146	169	140	126	162	132	124	148
14454	GENESEO	77	72	89	76	71	77	88	77	85	83	107	97	84	105	82	80	104	84	72	86
14456	GENEVA	68	69	75	68	69	75	71	70	72	69	89	82	71	90	71	72	87	71	71	79
14462	GROVELAND	0	0	0	0	0	0	0	0	0	0	0	0	0	0	0	0	0	0	0	0
14464	HAMLIN	96	91	76	88	93	98	84	91	86	85	106	108	83	108	86	87	102	89	93	112
14466	HEMLOCK	88	96	95	96	96	97	89	91	85	89	106	107	91	110	90	83	105	89	85	104
14467	HENRIETTA	103	117	121	117	114	114	110	109	104	110	131	128	113	134	110	99	129	108	98	119
14468	HILTON	94	106	111	107	105	106	100	100	96	100	120	118	104	125	101	93	119	99	92	111
14469	BLOOMFIELD	102	103	92	100	104	108	95	100	95	95	117	118	96	121	96	95	114	97	100	120
14470	HOLLEY	86	76	59	74	79	85	73	79	76	74	93	93	71	92	74	77	89	78	84	97
14471	HONEOYE	109	91	66	85	100	110	85	99	94	85	112	117	80	113	90	98	105	97	112	131
14472	HONEOYE FALLS	135	159	179	163	156	159	148	145	139	148	175	171	157	181	150	135	174	143	132	161
14475	IONIA	97	86	66	82	91	98	80	88	84	80	103	105	78	105	82	87	98	86	95	114
14476	KENDALL	91	109	119	106	107	109	101	100	97	100	121	116	107	129	103	95	121	98	94	110
14477	KENT	89	81	66	79	85	92	77	84	81	77	99	98	76	101	79	83	94	82	89	104
14478	KEUKA PARK	88	82	75	80	86	92	78	85	81	78	99	100	77	101	81	83	95	84	89	105
14480	LAKEVILLE	79	97	107	94	95	97	89	88	85	89	107	102	95	114	92	84	107	86	82	96
14481	LEICESTER	83	75	58	72	77	83	70	77	73	71	90	90	68	88	71	74	85	76	80	96
14482	LE ROY	78	81	80	79	82	87	78	80	78	77	97	93	80	101	80	79	94	78	80	91
14485	LIMA	76	89	102	91	88	88	84	83	80	84	100	98	88	104	85	77	99	82	75	91
14486	LINWOOD	68	82	91	80	81	82	76	75	73	76	92	87	81	97	78	72	91	73	70	82
14487	LIVONIA	81	96	104	95	94	95	90	89	85	89	107	103	94	113	91	83	107	87	81	97
14489	LYONS	81	76	65	71	79	87	73	78	78	71	95	90	73	99	75	81	90	76	86	95
14502	MACEDON	92	104	106	105	102	101	96	96	91	97	114	113	99	118	96	87	113	94	87	107
14504	MANCHESTER	70	68	60	65	68	73	66	68	67	66	83	78	65	83	66	67	80	67	70	79
14505	MARION	94	82	62	78	87	94	78	86	83	77	100	101	75	102	79	85	95	84	93	109
14506	MENDON	173	216	232	220	210	210	191	188	175	192	222	219	207	234	195	170	223	181	168	208
14507	MIDDLESEX	103	76	45	72	86	96	74	89	83	73	99	107	65	98	76	87	91	87	103	122
14510	MOUNT MORRIS	64	62	56	59	63	68	60	62	62	60	76	71	60	78	61	63	73	61	65	73
14512	NAPLES	83	76	66	72	80	89	74	80	78	73	95	92	72	97	76	81	91	79	88	98
14513	NEWARK	73	69	66	67	71	78	70	72	73	69	90	84	70	92	71	75	86	72	77	85
14514	NORTH CHILI	87	103	114	99	102	109	97	97	95	96	119	109	103	124	100	96	117	94	96	105
14516	NORTH ROSE	91	71	46	65	78	87	67	79	75	67	90	94	61	89	70	80	84	78	92	108
14517	NUNDA	81	70	54	69	73	82	70	75	74	69	90	87	67	90	70	75	84	74	81	91
14519	ONTARIO	99	102	94	102	103	108	97	100	96	96	119	116	98	121	97	95	115	97	98	114
14521	OVID	82	68	52	64	73	84	70	77	77	67	92	87	65	91	71	81	86	76	89	94
14522	PALMYRA	87	80	69	78	82	89	79	83	82	78	100	97	77	101	79	83	96	82	87	100
14525	PAVILION	92	85	68	81	89	94	78	86	82	78	100	102	78	103	81	84	96	83	91	108
14526	PENFIELD	119	144	162	145	141	144	133	131	124	132	157	152	140	163	135	122	156	128	120	144
14527	PENN YAN	79	64	47	61	69	79	65	72	71	63	85	83	60	83	66	75	79	72	83	91
14530	PERRY	63	63	62	60	65	71	62	64	65	61	80	73	63	84	64	66	77	63	68	74
14532	PHELPS	89	89	81	87	90	96	85	88	86	84	106	103	85	108	86	86	102	87	90	104
14533	PIFFARD	86	86	78	83	88	93	80	84	81	79	100	99	81	104	82	82	97	82	86	102
14534	PITTSFORD	166	206	237	206	201	208	186	184	174	187	220	211	201	229	192	172	220	179	169	201
14536	PORTAGEVILLE	72	63	48	61	67	72	60	66	64	60	77	78	58	78	61	65	73	64	71	83
14541	ROMULUS	96	72	45	67	82	92	70	84	79	69	94	100	62	93	73	84	87	83	99	114
14543	RUSH	111	134	143	134	131	132	122	121	113	122	143	141	128	149	124	110	142	118	110	133
14544	RUSHVILLE	104	86	61	80	93	103	81	93	89	81	107	110	76	107	84	93	100	92	106	123
14545	SCOTTSBURG	89	79	60	75	83	89	73	81	77	73	94	96	71	96	75	79	89	79	87	104
14546	SCOTTSVILLE	95	106	114	107	105	107	101	101	97	101	122	119	104	125	102	95	120	100	94	113
14548	SHORTSVILLE	91	84	70	81	87	94	80	86	83	80	102	101	79	103	81	84	97	84	90	105
14550	SILVER SPRINGS	67	65	58	61	68	74	62	66	66	61	80	76	63	84	64	68	77	64	71	79
14551	SODUS	85	71	53	69	76	85	71	78	76	70	92	90	67	91	71	78	86	76	86	97
14555	SODUS POINT	93	73	50	66	82	93	69	83	78	68	93	97	62	91	74	83	86	82	98	114
	NEW YORK	95	100	134	99	98	107	103	100	105	103	133	116	105	138	104	107	131	102	99	112
	UNITED STATES	100	100	100	100	100	100	100	100	100	100	100	100	100	100	100	100	100	100	100	100

NEW YORK
 14559-14807

POPULATION CHANGE

ZIP CODE			POPULATION			2000-2004 ANNUAL RATE		HOUSEHOLDS					FAMILIES		
#	POST OFFICE NAME	COUNTY FIPS CODE	2000	2004	2009	% Rate	State Centile	2000	2004	2009	% Annual Rate 2000-2004	2004 Average HH Size	2000	2004	% Annual Rate 2000-2004
14559	SPENCERPORT	055	15894	16079	16316	0.3	45	5799	5948	6110	0.6	2.69	4403	4491	0.5
14560	SPRINGWATER	069	2361	2355	2410	-0.1	25	916	925	960	0.2	2.53	652	656	0.1
14561	STANLEY	069	2967	3045	3146	0.6	62	1027	1062	1107	0.8	2.84	799	822	0.7
14564	VICTOR	069	9980	11197	12130	2.7	98	3690	4199	4607	3.1	2.62	2749	3110	3.0
14568	WALWORTH	117	6273	6614	6855	1.3	84	2112	2249	2356	1.5	2.94	1681	1783	1.4
14569	WARSAW	121	6012	5979	5976	-0.1	21	2322	2344	2380	0.2	2.37	1513	1518	0.1
14571	WATERPORT	073	1289	1278	1270	-0.2	18	492	493	494	0.1	2.59	344	342	-0.1
14572	WAYLAND	101	5152	5216	5282	0.3	46	1970	2018	2066	0.6	2.56	1392	1419	0.5
14580	WEBSTER	055	43437	45985	47678	1.4	86	16713	17978	18898	1.7	2.53	12084	12886	1.5
14586	WEST HENRIETTA	055	7322	7702	7911	1.2	83	2490	2664	2775	1.6	2.64	1589	1677	1.3
14589	WILLIAMSON	117	7953	8131	8294	0.5	59	3039	3149	3253	0.8	2.56	2252	2317	0.7
14590	WOLCOTT	117	5810	5866	5945	0.2	42	2250	2299	2356	0.5	2.45	1559	1582	0.4
14591	WYOMING	121	1970	1978	1983	0.1	35	698	709	721	0.4	2.72	547	554	0.3
14604	ROCHESTER	055	1324	1297	1294	-0.5	7	930	911	914	-0.5	1.23	124	119	-1.0
14605	ROCHESTER	055	14554	14067	14047	-0.8	2	5036	4913	4954	-0.6	2.77	3366	3260	-0.8
14606	ROCHESTER	055	29779	29308	29340	-0.4	10	11465	11415	11549	-0.1	2.56	7580	7495	-0.3
14607	ROCHESTER	055	16544	16902	17302	0.5	57	10014	10338	10696	0.8	1.56	1987	2011	0.3
14608	ROCHESTER	055	12832	12958	13270	0.2	42	5448	5589	5797	0.6	2.29	2810	2854	0.4
14609	ROCHESTER	055	43340	42411	42383	-0.5	6	17667	17457	17616	-0.3	2.41	10961	10738	-0.5
14610	ROCHESTER	055	14496	14745	15066	0.4	52	7018	7229	7475	0.7	2.00	3408	3466	0.4
14611	ROCHESTER	055	18287	19056	19821	1.0	77	6673	7050	7421	1.3	2.65	4181	4366	1.0
14612	ROCHESTER	055	35233	35079	35552	-0.1	22	13874	14093	14504	0.4	2.46	9269	9316	0.1
14613	ROCHESTER	055	15629	16327	16842	1.0	78	5865	6117	6340	1.0	2.64	3592	3713	0.8
14614	ROCHESTER	055	939	947	952	0.2	40	21	25	27	4.2	1.64	0	0	
14615	ROCHESTER	055	15307	15228	15329	-0.1	22	6712	6738	6848	0.1	2.25	3860	3844	-0.1
14616	ROCHESTER	055	28059	29194	30045	0.9	75	11478	12090	12584	1.2	2.39	7703	8053	1.1
14617	ROCHESTER	055	23899	24240	24640	0.3	49	9939	10208	10498	0.6	2.37	6712	6835	0.4
14618	ROCHESTER	055	21839	21522	21630	-0.3	12	8889	8804	8932	-0.2	2.26	5560	5480	-0.3
14619	ROCHESTER	055	15343	15494	15705	0.2	42	5595	5682	5801	0.4	2.70	3726	3766	0.3
14620	ROCHESTER	055	25231	25235	25489	0.0	28	11122	11243	11491	0.3	1.97	4545	4529	-0.1
14621	ROCHESTER	055	35133	34770	35072	-0.2	16	13039	12966	13174	-0.1	2.61	7955	7840	-0.3
14622	ROCHESTER	055	12013	11782	11802	-0.5	8	5234	5200	5274	-0.2	2.26	3327	3291	-0.3
14623	ROCHESTER	055	25818	26446	27031	0.6	61	8545	8951	9321	1.1	2.30	4676	4869	1.0
14624	ROCHESTER	055	38204	38762	39242	0.3	49	14338	14743	15108	0.7	2.60	10631	10888	0.6
14625	ROCHESTER	055	11071	11302	11480	0.5	57	4623	4761	4886	0.7	2.37	3165	3231	0.5
14626	ROCHESTER	055	28709	30094	31032	1.1	81	11134	11877	12424	1.5	2.50	7918	8393	1.4
14627	ROCHESTER	055	2423	2425	2426	0.0	30	11	11	11	0.0	2.73	5	5	0.0
14642	ROCHESTER	055	453	418	411	-1.9	0	291	270	269	-1.8	1.37	93	81	-3.2
14701	JAMESTOWN	013	42992	42430	42186	-0.3	13	17973	17930	17967	-0.1	2.31	11135	11015	-0.3
14706	ALLEGANY	009	7725	7853	7915	0.4	51	2496	2581	2635	0.8	2.48	1712	1763	0.7
14708	ALMA	003	179	175	175	-0.5	6	66	66	66	0.0	2.65	50	50	0.0
14709	ANGELICA	003	1631	1593	1585	-0.6	5	650	646	653	-0.2	2.47	452	446	-0.3
14710	ASHVILLE	013	3995	4084	4121	0.5	59	1504	1552	1578	0.7	2.63	1141	1174	0.7
14711	BELFAST	003	1695	1798	1854	1.4	87	658	709	742	1.8	2.54	446	478	1.6
14712	BEMUS POINT	013	3470	3479	3478	0.1	32	1429	1444	1453	0.3	2.36	996	1000	0.1
14714	BLACK CREEK	003	567	569	571	0.1	33	185	188	192	0.4	3.03	133	135	0.4
14715	BOLIVAR	003	3013	2988	2996	-0.2	18	1132	1140	1158	0.2	2.60	809	810	0.0
14716	BROCTON	013	3474	3458	3447	-0.1	22	870	874	877	0.1	2.70	602	601	0.0
14717	CANEADEA	003	848	874	890	0.7	67	336	351	362	1.0	2.47	228	236	0.8
14718	CASSADAGA	013	2404	2405	2403	0.0	29	918	929	935	0.3	2.59	654	657	0.1
14719	CATTARAUGUS	009	3710	3825	3879	0.7	67	1376	1435	1470	1.0	2.66	979	1015	0.9
14721	CERES	003	326	341	348	1.1	79	127	135	140	1.5	2.53	93	99	1.5
14723	CHERRY CREEK	013	1424	1427	1426	0.1	31	507	513	517	0.3	2.77	393	396	0.2
14724	CLYMER	013	2292	2478	2572	1.9	92	808	883	922	2.1	2.81	634	689	2.0
14726	CONEWANGO VALLEY	009	2192	2128	2100	-0.7	3	599	592	592	-0.3	3.59	467	460	-0.4
14727	CUBA	003	5323	5447	5536	0.5	60	2064	2136	2198	0.8	2.52	1452	1495	0.7
14728	DEWITTVILLE	013	1302	1300	1298	0.0	26	496	501	503	0.2	2.45	344	345	0.1
14729	EAST OTTO	009	1017	1046	1060	0.7	64	380	398	408	1.1	2.63	274	285	0.9
14731	ELLICOTTVILLE	009	1756	1764	1763	0.1	36	787	803	810	0.5	2.18	478	484	0.3
14733	FALCONER	013	3873	3831	3810	-0.3	15	1641	1635	1636	-0.1	2.33	1072	1061	-0.2
14735	FILLMORE	003	2763	2755	2756	-0.1	24	1040	1054	1070	0.3	2.59	743	749	0.2
14736	FINDLEY LAKE	013	367	369	369	0.1	37	164	167	169	0.4	2.21	121	123	0.4
14737	FRANKLINVILLE	009	4291	4286	4274	0.0	26	1633	1646	1656	0.2	2.59	1173	1175	0.0
14738	FREWSBURG	013	3797	3951	4021	0.9	75	1416	1496	1533	1.3	2.60	1068	1122	1.2
14739	FRIENDSHIP	003	3084	3109	3136	0.2	40	1190	1215	1242	0.5	2.52	820	832	0.3
14740	GERRY	013	1164	1190	1202	0.5	59	403	414	421	0.6	2.64	311	318	0.5
14741	GREAT VALLEY	009	2023	2036	2041	0.2	38	777	793	805	0.5	2.55	544	552	0.3
14743	HINSDALE	009	2106	2245	2311	1.5	88	796	861	897	1.9	2.59	582	626	1.7
14744	HOUGHTON	003	2288	2426	2503	1.4	87	483	540	576	2.7	2.84	328	365	2.6
14747	KENNEDY	013	2592	2594	2592	0.0	30	972	985	993	0.3	2.63	733	739	0.2
14748	KILL BUCK	009	648	624	612	-0.9	2	264	258	256	-0.5	2.37	183	178	-0.7
14750	LAKEWOOD	013	4446	4485	4500	0.2	41	1918	1957	1978	0.5	2.29	1249	1268	0.4
14753	LIMESTONE	009	1347	1342	1336	-0.1	23	524	530	534	0.3	2.48	361	361	0.0
14754	LITTLE GENESEE	003	790	801	805	0.3	49	291	300	306	0.7	2.67	222	228	0.6
14755	LITTLE VALLEY	009	2895	2873	2860	-0.2	19	1080	1085	1090	0.1	2.53	766	764	-0.1
14757	MAYVILLE	013	3665	3592	3553	-0.5	7	1492	1478	1474	-0.2	2.32	1016	999	-0.4
14760	OLEAN	009	20324	20070	19968	-0.3	14	8345	8344	8389	0.0	2.30	5124	5085	-0.2
14767	PANAMA	013	1936	1995	2020	0.7	67	660	686	699	0.9	2.91	529	547	0.8
14769	PORTLAND	013	1212	1195	1185	-0.3	12	462	460	460	-0.1	2.59	322	319	-0.2
14770	PORTVILLE	003	3006	3005	3004	0.0	27	1156	1174	1188	0.4	2.56	836	844	0.2
14772	RANDOLPH	009	4265	4293	4297	0.2	38	1553	1587	1608	0.5	2.63	1114	1132	0.4
14775	RIPLEY	013	2820	2745	2709	-0.6	4	1066	1051	1047	-0.3	2.61	769	753	-0.5
14777	RUSHFORD	003	403	387	384	-1.0	1	163	159	159	-0.6	2.43	111	107	-0.9
14779	SALAMANCA	009	7702	7437	7310	-0.8	2	3101	3018	2990	-0.6	2.41	2034	1964	-0.8
14781	SHERMAN	013	2264	2249	2239	-0.2	20	809	810	812	0.0	2.77	592	589	-0.1
14782	SINCLAIRVILLE	013	2979	2993	2996	0.1	36	1025	1042	1051	0.4	2.69	777	785	0.2
14784	STOCKTON	013	970	974	975	0.1	35	335	340	343	0.4	2.79	259	262	0.3
14787	WESTFIELD	013	5515	5513	5506	0.0	27	2194	2213	2224	0.2	2.44	1509	1512	0.1
14801	ADDISON	101	5404	5405	5453	0.0	28	2008	2031	2070	0.3	2.66	1439	1448	0.2
14802	ALFRED	003	3698	3780	3824	0.5	59	438	470	491	1.7	3.78	208	221	1.4
14803	ALFRED STATION	003	1646	1670	1685	0.3	49	641	671	693	1.1	1.63	353	365	0.8
14804	ALMOND	003	1457	1484	1495	0.4	53	569	588	602	0.8	2.40	383	394	0.7
14805	ALPINE	097	1223	1225	1239	0.0	30	476	484	497	0.4	2.53	337	340	0.2
14806	ANDOVER	003	2198	2193	2195	-0.1	25	842	850	863	0.2	2.57	592	594	0.1
14807	ARKPORT	101	3028	3071	3106	0.3	49	1185	1214	1241	0.6	2.53	854	870	0.4
	NEW YORK					0.4					0.5	2.60			0.4
	UNITED STATES					1.2					1.3	2.58			1.1

ZIP CODE #	POST OFFICE NAME	RACE (%) White 2000	White 2004	Black 2000	Black 2004	Asian/Pacific 2000	Asian/Pacific 2004	% Hispanic Origin 2000	% Hispanic Origin 2004	2004 AGE DISTRIBUTION (%) 0-4	5-9	10-14	15-19	20-24	25-44	45-64	65-84	85+	18+	MEDIAN AGE 2004	% 2004 Males	% 2004 Females
14559	SPENCERPORT	97.0	96.2	0.9	1.2	0.7	0.9	1.4	1.8	5.7	6.3	7.8	7.3	5.7	27.4	29.0	9.7	1.1	75.6	39.3	49.3	50.7
14560	SPRINGWATER	97.4	96.9	0.4	0.5	0.6	0.7	0.7	0.9	5.1	5.9	7.4	6.2	4.9	25.8	31.6	11.9	1.2	77.5	42.2	50.6	49.4
14561	STANLEY	98.2	97.8	0.5	0.6	0.2	0.2	1.2	1.5	5.9	6.6	8.0	7.8	5.5	24.5	28.7	11.5	1.6	74.6	40.2	49.8	50.3
14564	VICTOR	96.5	95.7	0.9	1.0	1.1	1.4	1.6	2.0	6.8	7.6	8.0	6.6	4.4	26.4	28.8	10.4	1.2	73.6	39.9	49.5	50.5
14568	WALWORTH	96.7	96.0	0.9	1.0	0.9	1.1	1.5	1.8	8.3	8.5	8.5	6.8	5.6	30.8	24.6	6.3	0.6	70.3	35.4	50.1	49.9
14569	WARSAW	96.9	96.2	0.8	1.0	0.9	1.1	0.9	1.1	5.8	5.9	6.7	6.8	6.6	26.1	24.5	13.4	4.2	77.4	39.8	48.0	52.0
14571	WATERPORT	94.5	94.1	3.4	3.8	0.1	0.1	1.1	1.3	6.1	6.5	7.0	6.7	5.8	24.9	30.2	11.7	1.1	76.3	41.0	53.3	46.7
14572	WAYLAND	97.3	96.8	0.8	0.9	0.5	0.6	0.8	0.9	5.7	6.1	7.9	7.8	6.8	25.1	27.7	11.6	1.4	74.9	39.6	49.8	50.2
14580	WEBSTER	94.9	93.4	1.7	2.2	2.0	2.5	1.6	2.1	6.1	6.8	7.5	6.4	4.6	26.3	27.8	12.6	1.9	75.3	40.7	48.3	51.7
14586	WEST HENRIETTA	84.3	80.5	7.7	9.5	5.2	6.5	3.0	4.0	6.0	5.7	7.1	10.7	15.5	28.9	20.0	5.5	0.7	77.2	29.1	53.2	46.8
14589	WILLIAMSON	93.3	92.2	4.0	4.6	0.5	0.6	1.8	2.2	5.7	6.4	7.9	7.4	5.9	25.8	27.8	11.4	1.7	75.1	39.9	49.4	50.6
14590	WOLCOTT	93.4	92.4	3.4	3.8	0.2	0.2	3.4	4.1	6.2	6.3	7.3	6.9	6.3	27.0	26.3	12.1	1.5	75.6	38.8	51.3	48.7
14591	WYOMING	96.2	95.6	1.6	1.8	0.2	0.2	1.0	1.4	5.5	6.3	8.4	7.8	5.8	28.9	25.5	10.8	1.1	74.4	37.8	51.9	48.1
14604	ROCHESTER	53.9	48.0	31.7	35.2	2.3	2.8	14.8	17.5	4.2	2.8	1.9	3.0	9.3	27.0	28.1	20.5	3.2	90.5	46.1	46.7	53.4
14605	ROCHESTER	16.7	15.6	59.4	58.9	0.9	1.0	32.3	34.2	10.1	10.5	11.1	9.9	9.1	25.9	16.8	6.2	0.5	62.5	24.7	46.1	53.9
14606	ROCHESTER	73.2	69.6	15.5	17.3	3.9	4.5	8.3	9.9	7.1	7.0	7.9	7.1	6.4	27.9	23.1	11.6	1.9	73.5	36.5	47.8	52.2
14607	ROCHESTER	79.7	75.5	13.3	15.9	2.4	3.0	4.3	5.5	3.0	2.1	2.4	3.3	15.0	46.0	18.8	6.4	3.0	91.0	31.9	52.5	47.5
14608	ROCHESTER	21.8	19.0	67.1	69.0	1.7	1.7	11.0	12.0	9.5	8.9	8.9	7.5	7.6	28.9	20.3	7.6	0.9	68.2	29.9	47.0	53.0
14609	ROCHESTER	63.0	59.2	27.6	29.9	0.9	1.0	10.3	12.1	7.8	7.6	7.9	6.7	6.1	29.2	22.1	10.6	2.2	72.7	35.5	46.7	53.3
14610	ROCHESTER	90.2	88.0	5.7	6.9	1.8	2.2	2.4	3.2	4.9	4.9	5.0	4.7	6.2	29.1	26.3	13.9	5.0	82.2	41.8	46.6	53.4
14611	ROCHESTER	23.4	20.5	69.0	71.2	1.3	1.5	7.2	8.0	8.9	8.9	10.3	8.8	7.1	27.0	20.7	7.6	0.8	66.5	29.5	46.7	53.3
14612	ROCHESTER	92.6	90.7	3.6	4.4	1.3	1.6	2.7	3.6	6.1	6.3	7.1	6.8	6.1	26.7	27.5	11.3	2.1	76.3	39.5	48.2	51.8
14613	ROCHESTER	56.5	50.9	30.2	33.6	2.0	2.2	11.7	14.1	9.4	8.9	9.7	8.2	7.8	30.1	19.1	5.9	0.9	66.8	29.2	48.4	51.6
14614	ROCHESTER	37.1	31.2	62.0	67.8	0.2	0.2	1.0	1.1	0.1	0.1	0.1	10.4	17.9	60.1	9.7	1.5	0.2	96.3	31.4	98.3	1.7
14615	ROCHESTER	79.9	75.8	11.8	14.1	2.2	2.7	7.2	9.2	6.9	6.5	6.8	6.4	6.7	31.2	23.5	10.5	1.6	75.9	36.0	48.3	51.8
14616	ROCHESTER	94.1	92.5	2.4	3.1	1.1	1.4	2.4	3.3	5.9	6.1	6.9	6.8	5.8	26.9	25.2	14.1	2.4	76.7	39.7	47.8	52.2
14617	ROCHESTER	94.9	93.5	2.2	2.8	1.1	1.3	2.2	2.9	5.0	5.5	6.7	6.7	5.0	22.6	28.5	16.4	3.6	78.3	44.0	46.9	53.1
14618	ROCHESTER	90.0	87.6	2.7	3.3	5.6	6.9	1.9	2.5	4.8	5.4	6.1	8.0	6.6	22.2	27.9	15.1	3.8	79.8	42.8	45.6	54.4
14619	ROCHESTER	25.5	21.2	69.5	73.4	0.8	0.9	2.8	3.2	7.8	8.0	9.5	8.3	7.3	27.9	23.5	6.9	1.1	69.6	32.5	45.6	54.4
14620	ROCHESTER	73.5	68.9	15.0	17.4	6.2	7.3	5.0	6.3	5.0	4.4	4.8	5.2	11.7	32.8	20.2	11.1	4.8	82.9	35.3	48.0	52.0
14621	ROCHESTER	32.8	29.3	43.8	44.8	2.3	2.4	26.3	29.3	9.0	8.6	9.7	8.7	7.6	25.3	19.0	9.0	3.3	67.4	30.3	45.9	54.1
14622	ROCHESTER	95.4	94.2	2.2	2.8	0.8	1.0	2.1	2.8	5.1	5.6	6.1	5.5	4.5	25.4	27.3	17.3	3.3	79.8	43.7	46.9	53.1
14623	ROCHESTER	80.1	75.9	7.2	8.8	9.1	11.0	3.4	4.4	4.2	4.0	4.3	13.4	20.0	26.8	16.3	9.0	2.0	85.0	27.5	54.3	45.7
14624	ROCHESTER	91.0	88.6	5.8	7.3	1.3	1.7	1.9	2.5	5.8	6.2	7.3	6.6	5.8	27.4	27.3	12.0	1.7	76.6	39.5	48.7	51.3
14625	ROCHESTER	94.6	93.2	1.6	2.1	2.5	3.1	1.5	2.0	5.3	6.2	7.0	6.1	4.1	22.6	31.0	15.6	2.2	77.3	44.3	48.5	51.5
14626	ROCHESTER	93.3	91.4	3.1	3.9	1.8	2.3	2.5	3.4	5.5	6.2	7.3	6.6	5.1	25.7	26.5	14.7	2.5	76.7	41.2	47.8	52.2
14627	ROCHESTER	73.1	67.7	4.8	5.7	17.3	20.8	5.0	6.3	0.1	0.1	0.0	60.1	37.5	1.9	0.1	0.0	0.0	99.2	19.1	57.5	42.5
14642	ROCHESTER	60.5	54.1	6.6	7.7	29.1	33.7	5.1	6.0	4.6	1.9	1.4	4.6	27.8	47.1	8.9	3.1	0.7	91.9	26.9	54.1	45.9
14701	JAMESTOWN	93.2	92.1	2.6	3.0	0.5	0.6	3.9	4.8	6.9	6.5	6.8	6.8	6.8	25.4	24.7	13.6	2.6	75.6	38.6	48.1	51.9
14706	ALLEGANY	96.5	95.7	0.8	0.9	1.1	1.4	0.9	1.2	4.1	4.4	5.5	12.5	17.4	19.3	24.2	11.0	1.7	82.4	32.0	47.6	52.4
14708	ALMA	98.3	98.3	0.0	0.0	0.6	0.6	0.0	0.0	5.7	6.9	7.4	6.9	5.1	22.9	30.3	13.7	1.1	76.0	41.7	49.7	50.3
14709	ANGELICA	98.0	97.7	0.3	0.3	0.1	0.3	0.4	0.4	6.5	6.7	7.2	6.9	5.7	25.1	27.0	13.4	1.6	75.4	39.8	50.7	49.3
14710	ASHVILLE	98.4	98.1	0.3	0.3	0.1	0.2	0.6	0.8	5.8	6.2	7.3	7.5	6.0	23.3	30.1	12.5	1.4	76.1	41.2	50.3	49.7
14711	BELFAST	98.3	98.1	0.1	0.1	0.2	0.3	0.8	0.9	6.5	7.0	9.3	8.1	5.6	25.7	24.7	11.5	1.7	72.1	36.6	50.4	49.6
14712	BEMUS POINT	98.4	98.1	0.2	0.3	0.2	0.3	0.9	1.2	4.5	5.2	6.8	6.4	4.4	20.4	31.7	17.9	2.8	79.5	46.3	49.4	50.6
14714	BLACK CREEK	98.4	98.1	0.2	0.4	0.0	0.2	0.9	0.7	6.0	6.9	9.8	7.4	5.3	24.8	26.7	11.8	1.4	72.6	38.9	49.9	50.1
14715	BOLIVAR	98.5	98.3	0.4	0.4	0.2	0.2	0.2	0.2	7.1	6.8	7.8	8.7	6.3	25.3	23.9	12.1	2.0	73.0	37.0	49.4	50.6
14716	BROCTON	77.0	74.4	16.9	18.4	0.0	0.0	11.5	13.7	4.1	4.2	5.0	8.9	13.6	36.3	18.4	8.3	1.2	82.9	31.9	62.2	37.9
14717	CANEADEA	98.5	98.3	0.1	0.1	0.2	0.2	1.1	1.1	6.3	6.6	8.7	8.1	6.4	24.1	24.6	13.3	1.8	73.6	37.8	50.1	49.9
14718	CASSADAGA	97.6	97.0	0.2	0.2	0.3	0.5	1.6	2.0	5.6	6.0	7.3	6.9	6.2	24.6	28.7	13.1	1.8	77.0	41.0	49.9	50.1
14719	CATTARAUGUS	98.6	98.3	0.2	0.2	0.1	0.1	0.9	1.2	6.9	7.1	8.1	7.7	6.4	24.9	26.1	11.7	1.1	72.9	37.7	50.6	49.4
14721	CERES	99.1	98.8	0.0	0.0	0.0	0.0	1.8	2.4	4.1	5.9	10.0	10.0	4.7	27.0	27.9	9.7	0.9	73.3	39.0	51.6	48.4
14723	CHERRY CREEK	97.3	96.6	0.1	0.3	0.3	0.4	1.8	2.5	5.8	7.6	10.2	9.5	4.9	27.4	24.1	9.8	0.7	70.1	36.2	50.1	49.9
14724	CLYMER	98.8	98.6	0.1	0.2	0.3	0.3	0.3	0.4	8.7	8.5	8.7	6.5	5.5	26.7	23.2	11.1	1.1	70.1	35.0	51.1	48.9
14726	CONEWANGO VALLEY	98.5	98.2	0.1	0.2	0.1	0.1	0.4	0.5	10.6	10.5	10.1	9.8	6.6	23.1	20.6	7.7	1.0	62.5	27.4	50.5	49.5
14727	CUBA	97.9	97.5	0.4	0.4	0.3	0.4	0.8	1.0	5.9	6.2	7.4	7.5	6.4	23.6	27.8	13.2	2.1	75.8	40.4	48.8	51.2
14728	DEWITTVILLE	96.2	95.5	1.7	1.9	0.2	0.2	1.0	1.2	5.0	5.1	5.9	6.7	6.0	24.2	28.7	16.5	1.9	79.9	43.0	51.0	49.0
14729	EAST OTTO	98.8	98.6	0.1	0.2	0.2	0.3	0.5	0.5	6.2	6.5	7.3	6.4	6.5	26.4	29.5	10.2	1.0	76.3	39.0	51.0	49.0
14731	ELLICOTTVILLE	97.7	97.4	0.2	0.2	0.2	0.3	1.1	1.4	4.7	5.1	5.5	5.4	4.8	22.2	34.4	16.7	1.3	81.2	46.3	49.6	50.5
14733	FALCONER	98.1	97.6	0.5	0.6	0.2	0.3	1.1	1.5	5.3	5.5	7.0	6.6	5.9	24.4	25.7	16.8	2.8	78.1	42.1	48.5	51.6
14735	FILLMORE	98.0	97.7	0.2	0.2	0.3	0.4	0.7	0.9	6.6	6.7	7.8	8.0	6.9	24.5	26.0	11.9	1.5	74.1	37.4	49.7	50.3
14736	FINDLEY LAKE	98.6	98.4	0.3	0.3	0.3	0.3	0.8	1.1	3.8	4.9	7.9	6.8	4.9	24.9	30.9	14.9	1.1	78.9	43.0	50.7	49.3
14737	FRANKLINVILLE	98.4	98.1	0.1	0.1	0.2	0.3	0.6	0.8	6.4	6.4	7.7	7.9	6.6	25.1	26.3	12.3	1.5	74.2	38.4	49.4	50.6
14738	FREWSBURG	98.9	98.6	0.2	0.3	0.2	0.3	0.4	0.5	5.3	5.7	7.5	7.5	6.0	23.9	27.5	14.4	2.3	76.5	41.8	48.8	51.2
14739	FRIENDSHIP	97.4	97.0	0.8	0.9	0.2	0.2	0.6	0.6	6.2	6.6	7.6	7.6	5.9	26.3	25.1	12.8	1.9	74.7	38.3	50.7	49.3
14740	GERRY	98.3	97.9	0.3	0.3	0.1	0.2	0.7	1.0	5.7	5.9	7.5	6.7	6.5	24.0	25.3	13.9	4.5	76.6	41.4	48.2	51.9
14741	GREAT VALLEY	96.7	96.4	0.6	0.6	0.4	0.5	0.7	0.9	5.4	5.7	6.3	7.2	5.6	24.5	30.3	14.1	1.1	77.9	42.2	52.0	48.0
14743	HINSDALE	97.4	96.8	0.5	0.6	0.3	0.5	0.7	0.8	5.4	5.8	7.6	7.2	6.1	24.1	30.0	13.0	0.9	76.5	41.1	50.7	49.4
14744	HOUGHTON	96.2	95.4	1.1	1.3	0.9	1.2	2.1	2.6	4.7	4.0	5.2	14.6	26.3	21.4	13.2	8.3	2.4	83.7	24.1	44.6	55.4
14747	KENNEDY	98.2	97.8	0.6	0.7	0.1	0.2	0.9	1.2	5.4	5.8	8.1	7.5	6.8	25.9	27.4	12.3	0.9	76.0	39.9	50.7	49.3
14748	KILL BUCK	89.5	88.1	0.9	1.0	1.1	1.3	0.8	1.0	4.3	5.0	7.4	8.2	5.0	26.0	27.4	16.2	0.6	77.4	41.5	52.4	47.6
14750	LAKEWOOD	97.9	97.5	0.6	0.7	0.6	0.8	0.7	0.9	4.8	5.5	6.8	6.2	5.0	22.3	29.9	16.8	2.8	79.0	44.6	48.1	51.9
14753	LIMESTONE	93.2	92.3	1.6	1.7	0.3	0.3	0.8	1.0	5.7	6.1	6.9	8.3	6.6	25.0	26.5	14.6	0.4	75.6	39.0	51.0	49.0
14754	LITTLE GENESEE	99.0	98.9	0.1	0.1	0.0	0.0	0.4	0.5	7.7	7.5	6.9	7.4	6.6	27.3	25.3	10.1	1.1	73.4	36.0	49.4	50.6
14755	LITTLE VALLEY	96.1	95.4	1.0	1.0	0.3	0.4	0.9	1.2	6.2	5.9	6.9	7.4	6.0	27.9	26.4	12.0	1.4	76.4	39.2	52.4	47.7
14757	MAYVILLE	96.6	96.0	1.4	1.5	0.5	0.6	1.2	1.4	4.7	4.9	6.4	6.9	6.0	23.9	28.5	16.7	1.9	79.7	43.1	51.0	49.0
14760	OLEAN	94.3	93.4	2.8	3.1	0.9	1.2	1.1	1.3	6.0	6.0	6.7	7.1	7.5	24.8	25.1	14.0	2.8	76.9	38.9	47.4	52.6
14767	PANAMA	98.7	98.4	0.3	0.3	0.1	0.1	0.5	0.6	7.8	7.7	8.3	7.6	6.2	26.1	25.0	10.3	1.1	71.6	35.7	50.3	49.7
14769	PORTLAND	97.2	96.7	0.3	0.3	0.0	0.0	1.7	2.2	6.4	6.6	7.9	7.5	6.4	25.2	26.0	12.1	1.8	74.5	38.4	49.5	50.5
14770	PORTVILLE	98.3	97.9	0.5	0.6	0.1	0.1	0.9	1.2	5.0	5.8	8.1	8.0	6.1	25.1	28.0	12.6	1.5	76.2	40.2	49.4	50.6
14772	RANDOLPH	97.2	96.7	0.7	0.8	0.2	0.3	0.6	0.7	6.7	7.0	7.6	8.6	6.2	23.8	26.1	12.5	1.6	72.6	38.0	50.3	49.7
14775	RIPLEY	98.1	97.7	0.2	0.2	0.1	0.2	1.4	1.9	6.0	6.3	7.9	6.7	6.3	26.3	25.6	13.2	1.6	75.6	38.6	51.1	48.9
14777	RUSHFORD	98.8	99.0	0.0	0.0	0.0	0.0	0.7	0.8	6.2	5.9	5.7	6.7	6.5	22.2	26.9	18.1	1.8	78.3	42.8	48.6	51.4
14779	SALAMANCA	81.2	79.5	0.6	0.7	0.3	0.4	1.8	2.1	7.8	6.8	7.1	7.0	6.9	24.6	23.9	13.8	2.1	73.7	37.6	48.3	51.8
14781	SHERMAN	98.2	97.9	0.2	0.2	0.4	0.5	0.6	0.8	6.7	7.1	7.9	6.9	6.0	25.0	27.5	11.4	1.5	73.9	38.7	50.2	49.8
14782	SINCLAIRVILLE	98.4	97.9	0.2	0.2	0.1	0.2	0.9	1.2	5.9	6.2	7.8	6.8	5.8	25.0	25.3	13.2	4.0	75.9	40.5	48.5	51.6
14784	STOCKTON	96.3	95.7	1.4	1.6	0.3	0.3	1.9	2.4	6.7	6.7	8.3	8.5	6.3	25.4	25.6	11.4	1.2	73.1	37.2	49.0	51.0
14787	WESTFIELD	97.0	96.3	0.3	0.3	0.5	0.7	2.5	3.3	5.7	5.9	8.0	7.0	5.4	23.9	26.8	14.3	3.1	75.8	41.3	48.5	51.5
14801	ADDISON	98.1	97.7	0.3	0.4	0.3	0.4	0.6	0.9	7.0	7.0	7.6	7.3	7.1	26.9	25.6	10.4	1.3	74.0	36.3	49.3	50.7
14802	ALFRED	91.9	90.5	3.4	3.7	2.5	3.2	2.2	2.5	1.7	1.9	2.4	30.7	37.9	9.9	10.3	4.6	0.7	92.3	21.8	56.7	43.3
14803	ALFRED STATION	94.1	92.9	2.1	2.4	2.0	2.5	1.6	1.9	3.1	3.3	4.4	22.6	27.1	14.4	16.6	7.5	1.0	86.5	23.1	53.5	46.5
14804	ALMOND	96.6	96.1	0.4	0.5	1.9	2.4	0.6	0.7	4.3	5.9	7.8	11.1	8.2	23.1	27.8	10.8	1.2	76.9	37.4	51.6	48.4
14805	ALPINE	97.1	96.8	0.5	0.6	0.2	0.2	1.2	1.5	6.8	7.0	7.8	6.0	5.6	28.3	26.8	10.5	1.2	74.5	37.7	50.8	49.2
14806	ANDOVER	98.2	97.8	0.2	0.2	0.3	0.4	1.1	1.3	7.0	6.9	7.2	7.2	7.3	23.7	27.2	12.0	1.6	74.8	38.2	49.5	50.5
14807	ARKPORT	98.0	97.6	0.3	0.3	0.3	0.4	1.0	1.1	5.5	7.0	7.8	7.3	5.7	23.9	27.4	13.2	2.1	74.7	40.6	48.9	51.1
	NEW YORK	68.0	65.9	15.9	16.2	5.6	6.4	15.1	16.7	6.5	6.5	7.1	7.0	7.1	28.9	24.0	11.2	1.8	75.8	36.7	48.3	51.7
	UNITED STATES	75.1	73.6	12.3	12.5	3.8	4.2	12.5	14.1	6.9	6.7	7.2	7.0	7.3	28.6	23.8	10.8	1.7	75.1	36.0	49.1	50.9

#	POST OFFICE NAME	2004 Per Capita Income	2004 HH Income Base	2004 Household Income Distribution (%): Less than $25,000	$25,000 to $49,999	$50,000 to $99,999	$100,000 to $149,999	$150,000 or More	Median Household Income: 2004	2009	2004 National Centile	2004 State Centile	2004 Home Value Base	2004 Home Value Distribution (%): Less than $50,000	$50,000 to $89,999	$90,000 to $174,999	$175,000 to $399,999	$400,000 or More	2004 Median Home Value
14559	SPENCERPORT	27749	5948	11.2	24.6	42.7	15.7	5.9	64187	75211	88	79	4963	1.2	3.0	64.0	30.4	1.4	146199
14560	SPRINGWATER	24231	925	21.1	29.4	38.9	8.0	2.6	49540	54559	71	61	803	14.0	21.5	47.3	16.8	0.4	107517
14561	STANLEY	19498	1062	19.3	34.5	34.7	10.5	1.1	46833	52398	66	55	893	4.8	16.2	63.8	14.1	1.0	113264
14564	VICTOR	37026	4199	12.1	23.4	34.2	14.3	16.0	66235	77865	89	82	3524	1.2	9.6	42.7	37.0	9.5	166460
14568	WALWORTH	23945	2249	12.9	21.1	46.8	15.1	4.2	64300	72034	88	80	1993	7.9	4.7	64.6	22.5	0.3	138977
14569	WARSAW	19638	2344	33.8	29.4	30.5	4.4	1.9	40546	43704	48	36	1610	4.1	11.5	64.9	18.8	0.8	123064
14571	WATERPORT	19571	493	22.1	38.5	31.2	6.5	1.6	45040	50199	61	50	408	5.6	32.4	50.3	11.3	0.5	104839
14572	WAYLAND	20425	2018	24.9	32.3	35.4	6.1	1.4	45232	50847	62	51	1596	14.0	19.8	55.4	10.2	0.6	107441
14580	WEBSTER	31500	17978	13.5	21.8	38.9	17.2	8.7	65795	76832	89	81	14201	0.9	2.5	57.7	36.9	1.9	159386
14586	WEST HENRIETTA	24177	2664	18.1	20.6	41.8	16.7	2.9	60479	70484	85	75	1799	0.5	3.1	81.6	13.6	1.2	135321
14589	WILLIAMSON	23515	3149	20.4	24.8	41.5	10.0	3.3	54586	61258	79	70	2577	4.5	13.5	67.8	13.5	0.7	117970
14590	WOLCOTT	19739	2299	30.1	31.0	30.7	5.9	2.3	40019	44842	46	34	1795	19.2	33.8	40.1	6.0	1.0	86656
14591	WYOMING	19701	709	19.6	34.6	37.4	6.6	1.8	47060	51657	66	56	599	6.2	15.9	60.9	16.0	1.0	123769
14604	ROCHESTER	17418	911	74.9	13.0	9.8	1.1	1.3	10516	12736	1	0	13	0.0	0.0	7.7	76.9	15.4	268750
14605	ROCHESTER	10016	4913	63.2	24.9	9.0	1.9	1.1	17726	20315	1	1	1021	38.5	43.2	15.2	2.6	0.5	58453
14606	ROCHESTER	19674	11415	30.0	29.6	31.1	7.2	2.1	41324	47650	51	39	7058	5.9	25.6	65.0	3.3	0.2	106034
14607	ROCHESTER	30780	10338	37.3	31.3	20.7	6.7	4.1	34409	41117	25	11	1691	0.4	17.2	44.9	34.2	3.3	148264
14608	ROCHESTER	14714	5589	57.3	24.9	13.8	2.5	1.5	20947	24002	2	2	1408	26.7	35.3	33.3	4.7	0.0	71308
14609	ROCHESTER	20062	17457	32.5	30.3	28.9	6.5	1.9	39098	44713	43	30	10557	3.7	39.7	53.7	2.7	0.2	94213
14610	ROCHESTER	43449	7229	22.0	27.2	29.2	10.7	11.0	50889	60898	74	64	3934	0.4	13.0	53.2	25.7	7.8	140839
14611	ROCHESTER	12862	7050	51.1	25.9	19.9	2.6	0.5	24248	27705	4	3	2876	20.9	58.9	19.2	1.0	0.0	67491
14612	ROCHESTER	26464	14093	21.3	24.2	37.1	12.5	4.9	54306	62299	79	69	9552	0.6	10.4	63.6	24.9	0.5	137924
14613	ROCHESTER	16169	6117	40.9	29.5	24.1	4.2	1.4	31683	36108	17	6	2453	9.2	64.3	22.9	3.5	0.1	74771
14614	ROCHESTER	13439	25	84.0	16.0	0.0	0.0	0.0	8333	9643	0	0	0	0.0	0.0	0.0	0.0	0.0	0
14615	ROCHESTER	24459	6738	28.4	34.5	28.1	6.3	2.8	39087	44390	43	30	3628	1.2	35.6	57.7	5.2	0.2	98817
14616	ROCHESTER	24789	12090	17.8	33.8	36.8	9.3	2.3	48544	56684	69	59	9323	0.9	12.4	79.8	6.9	0.1	113099
14617	ROCHESTER	30321	10208	16.2	25.6	39.9	12.8	5.5	58887	67411	83	73	8421	0.6	3.6	83.2	12.2	0.4	124577
14618	ROCHESTER	40431	8804	11.5	20.2	36.6	17.1	14.7	70883	82697	92	85	6348	0.0	5.5	49.0	39.8	5.7	168141
14619	ROCHESTER	18551	5682	28.7	31.0	31.9	6.8	1.6	41293	46573	51	39	3389	3.8	62.8	32.1	1.3	0.0	81185
14620	ROCHESTER	23821	11243	36.8	29.0	23.7	7.0	3.5	35049	40709	28	13	4137	2.4	30.8	55.0	11.3	0.5	108175
14621	ROCHESTER	13405	12966	51.7	27.1	17.1	2.8	1.3	23876	27310	4	3	4823	19.9	60.2	18.6	1.1	0.3	67894
14622	ROCHESTER	26152	5200	21.1	33.1	33.0	9.4	3.5	47033	54559	66	55	4271	1.2	12.2	77.4	8.6	0.7	114263
14623	ROCHESTER	21940	8951	22.4	30.5	35.9	8.9	2.4	47625	54304	67	57	4747	1.3	5.8	86.1	6.7	0.3	118968
14624	ROCHESTER	28175	14743	14.3	24.5	41.5	14.3	5.3	61906	72240	86	77	12436	1.1	5.2	78.3	15.2	0.1	129984
14625	ROCHESTER	36733	4761	14.3	22.1	35.1	16.9	11.7	67441	79207	90	83	4127	13.2	3.8	44.8	37.0	1.3	154846
14626	ROCHESTER	27777	11877	15.6	27.6	37.4	13.5	5.9	57237	66711	82	72	9538	0.4	3.3	72.5	23.3	0.6	139488
14627	ROCHESTER	13899	11	27.3	36.4	18.2	0.0	18.2	42313	47321	54	43	0	0.0	0.0	0.0	0.0	0.0	0
14642	ROCHESTER	28040	270	41.9	31.1	21.1	3.7	2.2	31672	35988	17	6	65	0.0	0.0	100.0	0.0	0.0	113010
14701	JAMESTOWN	18737	17930	40.1	29.9	23.2	4.7	2.1	32194	35530	18	7	10876	21.6	40.0	30.4	7.5	0.5	75966
14706	ALLEGANY	19136	2581	30.3	31.0	29.6	7.3	1.8	41491	45525	51	39	2058	18.8	15.0	42.9	21.7	1.6	125616
14708	ALMA	17236	66	27.3	37.9	28.8	4.6	1.5	37303	42838	36	21	56	21.4	26.8	44.6	7.1	0.0	93333
14709	ANGELICA	17856	646	33.9	39.2	22.5	2.9	1.6	34886	37975	27	12	528	21.4	31.1	42.8	4.6	0.2	86061
14710	ASHVILLE	21841	1552	24.0	35.0	30.1	7.5	3.5	42973	48295	56	44	1310	19.5	28.5	39.4	10.4	2.3	92571
14711	BELFAST	16775	709	37.9	34.4	23.1	3.2	1.3	32747	35840	20	7	549	23.9	31.3	39.7	3.8	1.3	82297
14712	BEMUS POINT	23950	1444	23.6	32.3	31.2	9.0	4.0	45477	51223	63	52	1194	17.4	15.2	35.1	25.3	7.0	122531
14714	BLACK CREEK	15932	188	31.4	36.7	26.6	3.7	1.6	36587	40589	34	19	155	16.8	29.0	44.5	9.7	0.0	95909
14715	BOLIVAR	15055	1140	38.1	35.4	22.7	3.1	0.8	33216	36131	22	8	856	29.8	34.9	32.1	3.0	0.1	68652
14716	BROCTON	14101	874	38.7	32.2	26.2	3.0	0.0	31802	34785	17	6	675	24.6	37.9	32.0	5.2	0.3	75743
14717	CANEADEA	16514	351	37.6	36.5	21.7	3.4	0.9	31975	35154	18	6	273	22.3	30.8	38.8	7.0	1.1	85000
14718	CASSADAGA	20133	929	23.4	38.5	29.9	6.2	1.9	42450	47794	54	43	787	21.2	28.8	37.1	11.9	0.9	89918
14719	CATTARAUGUS	17393	1435	28.9	38.1	26.8	4.6	1.5	36615	40806	34	19	1188	16.3	27.0	42.9	12.5	1.3	100000
14721	CERES	20831	135	25.2	34.1	34.8	5.2	0.7	44605	48226	60	49	117	25.6	22.2	35.9	15.4	0.9	94167
14723	CHERRY CREEK	16295	513	31.6	31.8	31.6	3.7	1.4	37186	40862	36	21	417	32.4	33.6	25.7	8.4	0.0	71250
14724	CLYMER	16790	883	27.2	39.0	28.1	3.6	2.2	39059	42963	43	30	726	22.3	32.5	35.0	9.9	0.3	83750
14726	CONEWANGO VALLEY	12949	592	34.1	35.3	24.3	3.6	2.7	35096	38756	28	13	490	24.9	25.5	40.4	8.4	0.8	89394
14727	CUBA	17616	2136	32.9	34.2	27.5	3.9	1.5	36639	40603	34	19	1661	18.7	29.1	40.8	10.6	0.8	93476
14728	DEWITTVILLE	21434	501	31.3	31.7	25.4	7.2	4.4	38647	43115	42	28	400	17.5	19.8	34.3	20.8	7.8	108654
14729	EAST OTTO	18584	398	25.4	39.7	28.4	5.0	1.5	37595	41666	38	23	338	8.9	21.9	50.3	17.8	1.2	118359
14731	ELLICOTTVILLE	26141	803	25.3	31.0	30.8	8.1	4.9	45364	50419	62	51	623	7.7	9.0	38.2	38.5	6.6	155449
14733	FALCONER	20585	1635	32.2	30.8	29.5	5.6	1.9	39227	42955	44	30	1149	14.2	50.0	30.1	5.4	0.4	77854
14735	FILLMORE	16009	1054	36.3	36.3	22.2	3.5	1.6	33520	37042	22	9	804	19.2	28.2	45.2	6.8	0.6	93387
14736	FINDLEY LAKE	23535	167	21.0	42.5	27.5	6.0	3.0	42463	48122	54	43	142	12.0	23.9	31.7	30.3	2.1	119118
14737	FRANKLINVILLE	16666	1646	31.8	36.0	26.9	4.4	0.9	37222	41110	36	21	1304	18.9	29.5	41.6	9.7	0.4	92121
14738	FREWSBURG	19624	1496	23.2	35.8	32.2	6.6	2.3	43278	48585	57	45	1232	9.6	29.7	47.0	12.3	1.5	101613
14739	FRIENDSHIP	15764	1215	39.1	35.5	21.7	2.8	0.9	32070	35150	18	6	927	26.9	33.4	34.0	5.2	0.5	73769
14740	GERRY	18290	414	30.7	33.1	29.2	4.8	2.2	39146	43496	43	30	351	28.8	28.8	35.0	6.8	0.6	78654
14741	GREAT VALLEY	18817	793	29.3	36.3	27.1	4.9	2.4	39326	43024	44	31	680	17.5	21.8	39.3	20.3	1.2	107426
14743	HINSDALE	17533	861	30.7	34.4	29.5	4.1	1.4	38349	42009	41	26	731	21.8	19.6	43.2	13.8	1.6	107060
14744	HOUGHTON	14496	540	35.4	31.3	27.0	5.9	0.4	36672	40604	34	19	347	7.8	17.0	54.2	20.2	0.9	125625
14747	KENNEDY	18269	985	28.6	37.6	27.1	5.1	1.6	37486	41793	37	22	819	33.7	32.8	24.4	8.8	0.2	68333
14748	KILL BUCK	17635	258	35.3	31.0	29.5	3.1	1.2	36899	40493	35	20	222	34.2	17.1	36.5	12.2	0.0	86250
14750	LAKEWOOD	27787	1957	24.4	30.5	29.9	8.0	7.2	44622	50959	60	49	1555	11.1	25.1	45.9	14.6	3.3	114116
14753	LIMESTONE	16322	530	38.1	31.5	25.9	3.8	0.8	32491	35742	19	7	414	30.4	32.6	31.2	5.6	0.2	70000
14754	LITTLE GENESEE	15679	300	32.3	35.7	28.7	3.3	0.0	38191	42211	40	25	244	31.2	34.0	29.1	5.7	0.0	70455
14755	LITTLE VALLEY	17734	1085	32.3	34.7	27.4	4.5	1.2	35763	39252	31	16	825	14.3	31.4	39.4	13.8	1.1	96339
14757	MAYVILLE	22704	1478	29.2	31.1	28.6	7.2	3.9	41577	46979	52	40	1161	16.6	22.9	32.4	20.6	7.5	107335
14760	OLEAN	19725	8344	36.5	31.0	25.4	5.2	2.0	34857	37957	27	12	5417	10.0	26.8	49.2	13.3	0.7	108547
14767	PANAMA	17321	686	28.3	36.6	27.1	5.1	2.9	37857	42303	39	24	580	22.4	32.9	37.8	6.2	0.7	83261
14769	PORTLAND	16198	460	34.8	33.7	25.2	6.1	0.2	34821	37930	27	12	342	26.9	38.9	29.2	5.0	0.0	71290
14770	PORTVILLE	19613	1174	27.6	35.9	29.0	4.9	2.7	38626	42695	42	28	958	18.7	25.7	45.0	10.3	0.3	98852
14772	RANDOLPH	17699	1587	31.4	33.9	28.0	4.8	1.9	37355	40849	37	22	1252	15.0	28.9	44.9	10.6	0.6	98261
14775	RIPLEY	17807	1051	30.4	38.1	26.4	4.4	0.9	35680	39030	30	15	826	28.5	37.5	24.7	8.5	0.9	68571
14777	RUSHFORD	15704	159	35.2	42.1	18.9	3.8	0.0	30583	33876	14	5	129	18.6	31.8	39.5	10.1	0.0	89286
14779	SALAMANCA	15318	3018	44.1	31.8	20.4	2.8	0.9	28973	31454	10	4	1913	22.6	38.1	29.5	9.2	0.5	76871
14781	SHERMAN	16604	810	28.6	38.2	26.5	5.2	1.5	38703	42609	42	28	624	23.6	35.6	27.4	12.8	0.6	76613
14782	SINCLAIRVILLE	17372	1042	30.5	32.7	30.4	4.5	1.8	39044	43106	43	29	860	28.4	28.3	33.7	9.3	0.4	80000
14784	STOCKTON	19006	340	29.4	35.3	26.8	5.9	2.7	39127	44238	43	30	278	29.9	26.3	28.8	14.8	0.4	81053
14787	WESTFIELD	18346	2213	34.7	31.7	25.6	6.6	1.4	36177	39343	32	17	1617	14.2	29.2	40.0	15.4	1.2	98022
14801	ADDISON	17198	2031	34.1	32.1	26.2	5.5	2.1	36163	40721	32	17	1568	18.9	24.9	40.8	14.5	0.9	97760
14802	ALFRED	13648	470	40.4	25.1	22.3	7.9	4.3	33850	36507	24	9	239	8.4	12.6	45.6	33.5	0.0	143622
14803	ALFRED STATION	26031	671	36.2	28.3	24.4	7.2	3.9	36696	40057	34	19	400	12.5	19.3	43.8	24.5	0.0	127431
14804	ALMOND	22607	588	29.6	28.7	31.1	7.0	3.6	41386	45854	51	39	439	16.9	18.2	47.6	16.6	0.7	116604
14805	ALPINE	18958	484	24.2	40.1	30.4	4.3	1.0	39581	44149	45	32	399	18.6	17.8	48.4	14.3	1.0	109964
14806	ANDOVER	20425	850	32.7	35.2	24.4	5.1	2.7	36342	40456	33	18	648	20.8	33.2	36.0	9.9	0.2	84583
14807	ARKPORT	19556	1214	28.8	34.2	29.3	5.5	2.1	39353	43771	44	31	1009	16.8	22.6	41.8	17.6	1.2	105301
	NEW YORK	28049		26.3	24.3	29.3	11.5	8.6	49309	58077				4.6	8.6	27.2	39.9	19.8	219050
	UNITED STATES	25866		24.7	27.1	30.8	10.9	6.5	48124	56710				10.9	15.0	33.7	30.1	10.4	145905

ZIP CODE		FINANCIAL SERVICES				THE HOME						ENTERTAINMENT						PERSONAL			
						Home Improvements		Furnishings													
#	POST OFFICE NAME	Auto Loan	Home Loan	Invest-ments	Retire-ment Plans	Home Repair	Lawn & Garden	Comput-ers & Hard-ware	Major Appli-ances	TV, Radio, Sound Equip-ment	Furni-ture	Dine out/ Carry out	Sports Equip-ment	Fees & Tickets	Toys & Games	Travel	Cable TV	Apparel & Services	Auto Repairs	Health Insur-ance	Pets & Supplies
14559	SPENCERPORT	100	116	122	116	115	116	106	107	101	106	127	126	111	133	108	99	126	104	99	121
14560	SPRINGWATER	101	85	61	79	92	101	79	91	87	79	104	108	74	105	83	91	98	89	103	121
14561	STANLEY	84	79	67	77	82	88	76	81	78	75	96	94	75	97	77	79	91	79	84	97
14564	VICTOR	123	158	180	156	154	155	141	140	131	141	165	163	152	177	145	129	166	135	125	153
14568	WALWORTH	100	110	106	112	108	107	101	102	95	102	120	120	103	122	100	91	118	99	92	115
14569	WARSAW	70	65	61	65	68	72	65	68	67	64	82	80	64	82	65	66	79	68	70	80
14571	WATERPORT	82	67	50	65	73	82	67	75	73	66	88	87	62	87	68	76	82	74	85	95
14572	WAYLAND	84	73	55	70	77	85	69	77	74	69	90	90	67	91	71	76	85	75	84	98
14580	WEBSTER	104	120	135	120	118	122	115	113	110	114	138	131	119	143	116	108	137	112	106	124
14586	WEST HENRIETTA	86	98	117	101	96	98	96	93	91	96	115	112	99	118	96	88	114	94	85	102
14589	WILLIAMSON	95	88	70	84	92	97	81	88	84	81	103	105	80	105	83	86	98	86	94	112
14590	WOLCOTT	83	65	44	60	72	81	63	73	70	62	84	86	57	83	65	74	78	72	85	98
14591	WYOMING	84	74	57	71	79	84	69	76	73	69	89	91	67	91	71	75	84	74	83	98
14604	ROCHESTER	28	24	35	25	24	29	32	28	33	30	41	34	30	40	30	33	40	31	30	31
14605	ROCHESTER	37	31	44	28	29	35	37	35	42	38	52	40	36	50	36	43	51	38	38	40
14606	ROCHESTER	66	69	77	67	68	74	71	69	72	70	89	80	73	92	71	72	87	70	69	76
14607	ROCHESTER	65	56	86	63	55	61	73	64	73	70	92	80	70	90	68	69	90	71	60	72
14608	ROCHESTER	47	38	48	36	37	44	46	45	51	47	63	51	44	59	44	52	61	48	48	51
14609	ROCHESTER	64	65	76	64	64	70	68	66	69	67	87	76	70	88	68	70	85	67	66	73
14610	ROCHESTER	112	124	157	126	122	131	125	121	123	125	155	141	130	158	127	122	153	123	117	133
14611	ROCHESTER	47	42	50	40	41	47	47	46	51	47	63	52	46	61	46	52	61	47	48	52
14612	ROCHESTER	85	96	107	96	94	98	94	92	91	92	114	107	97	117	94	89	112	92	87	100
14613	ROCHESTER	58	54	62	53	53	59	60	58	62	59	78	68	60	77	59	62	76	60	59	64
14614	ROCHESTER	0	0	0	0	0	0	0	0	0	0	0	0	0	0	0	0	0	0	0	0
14615	ROCHESTER	73	75	84	75	74	80	79	76	79	77	98	88	79	100	78	78	96	77	75	83
14616	ROCHESTER	77	86	94	84	86	92	84	83	83	82	104	95	88	109	86	84	102	82	83	91
14617	ROCHESTER	94	107	117	104	107	114	101	102	99	101	124	115	106	126	104	100	121	100	102	112
14618	ROCHESTER	123	142	172	143	140	149	137	135	132	137	166	156	144	170	140	131	165	135	128	147
14619	ROCHESTER	67	66	77	65	64	71	70	68	72	70	91	78	71	90	69	72	88	70	68	76
14620	ROCHESTER	65	60	76	63	59	65	71	66	71	69	89	80	69	86	68	68	87	71	64	73
14621	ROCHESTER	47	42	54	41	41	48	48	46	52	48	65	53	48	64	47	53	63	49	49	52
14622	ROCHESTER	76	85	95	81	84	92	83	82	83	81	104	92	87	108	85	85	101	81	84	90
14623	ROCHESTER	74	71	85	73	70	76	83	75	81	79	102	92	80	100	78	77	99	80	71	83
14624	ROCHESTER	95	113	122	110	111	115	105	104	101	104	126	120	110	133	107	100	125	102	99	114
14625	ROCHESTER	117	133	144	130	132	139	123	125	119	124	149	142	128	150	126	119	147	122	120	139
14626	ROCHESTER	92	106	113	104	104	108	99	99	96	99	121	113	104	126	101	95	119	97	95	108
14627	ROCHESTER	110	67	85	76	66	80	130	95	126	110	158	133	106	142	104	111	148	117	89	109
14642	ROCHESTER	56	45	58	50	44	49	62	54	61	58	77	70	56	72	56	56	75	62	50	61
14701	JAMESTOWN	59	59	62	57	59	65	61	60	63	59	77	70	61	79	61	63	75	61	62	68
14706	ALLEGANY	77	69	59	65	72	79	69	72	72	67	88	86	66	88	69	74	84	72	78	90
14708	ALMA	82	59	34	52	67	76	57	69	66	57	78	82	49	75	59	71	72	68	84	96
14709	ANGELICA	74	59	40	53	66	74	55	66	63	55	74	78	50	73	59	67	69	65	78	90
14710	ASHVILLE	96	78	55	72	86	95	73	86	81	73	97	102	68	97	77	85	91	85	99	115
14711	BELFAST	71	55	37	51	62	71	54	64	61	53	73	74	49	71	57	65	67	63	76	85
14712	BEMUS POINT	98	75	49	69	85	95	72	86	81	71	96	102	64	95	76	86	89	85	101	118
14714	BLACK CREEK	82	64	44	58	72	81	60	73	68	60	81	85	54	80	64	73	75	72	86	100
14715	BOLIVAR	60	53	43	49	56	63	51	56	56	51	68	65	50	70	53	59	65	55	64	70
14716	BROCTON	29	31	33	30	32	35	31	31	32	30	40	34	33	43	32	33	39	30	33	34
14717	CANEADEA	68	53	36	49	59	67	52	61	59	51	70	71	47	68	55	63	65	61	72	81
14718	CASSADAGA	84	71	54	67	76	84	69	77	74	68	89	90	65	90	71	77	84	76	86	98
14719	CATTARAUGUS	77	62	43	59	67	75	60	69	66	60	80	81	56	79	61	69	74	67	77	89
14721	CERES	84	75	57	71	79	85	69	77	74	69	90	92	68	91	71	76	85	75	83	99
14723	CHERRY CREEK	71	60	47	60	63	71	62	66	65	61	79	75	59	79	61	66	74	65	71	78
14724	CLYMER	85	60	32	56	69	78	59	73	68	58	79	87	50	78	61	71	73	72	86	101
14726	CONEWANGO VALLEY	82	62	37	56	68	76	59	69	67	59	80	83	53	78	60	71	74	68	81	95
14727	CUBA	73	60	43	54	65	73	57	66	63	56	76	77	53	76	59	67	71	65	77	88
14728	DEWITTVILLE	89	69	46	64	76	87	70	80	78	68	93	92	63	90	71	83	86	79	94	103
14729	EAST OTTO	77	66	51	65	70	78	66	71	70	65	85	83	63	85	66	71	80	70	78	87
14731	ELLICOTTVILLE	97	76	52	69	86	96	72	86	81	71	96	101	64	95	77	87	89	85	102	118
14733	FALCONER	64	68	68	64	69	76	66	67	68	64	84	75	69	90	68	71	82	65	71	76
14735	FILLMORE	69	54	37	51	59	67	54	62	60	54	72	72	50	70	55	63	67	61	71	79
14736	FINDLEY LAKE	88	69	47	62	78	88	65	79	74	65	87	92	58	86	70	79	81	77	93	107
14737	FRANKLINVILLE	67	58	48	54	63	70	57	63	62	55	74	73	54	77	59	65	70	62	72	80
14738	FREWSBURG	74	72	65	68	75	82	69	73	73	67	89	84	70	93	71	75	85	71	79	88
14739	FRIENDSHIP	68	50	31	46	56	65	51	60	59	50	69	69	45	66	52	62	63	59	72	78
14740	GERRY	84	68	46	62	73	80	64	73	70	64	85	87	60	84	65	74	79	72	83	97
14741	GREAT VALLEY	79	65	47	61	70	78	63	71	69	62	82	83	58	82	65	71	77	70	81	92
14743	HINSDALE	77	62	42	56	68	75	58	68	65	58	77	80	53	77	60	68	72	67	78	92
14744	HOUGHTON	59	47	59	52	46	52	64	57	63	60	79	72	58	74	57	59	77	64	53	64
14747	KENNEDY	77	68	52	65	72	78	63	70	67	63	82	84	62	83	65	69	78	69	77	91
14748	KILL BUCK	72	57	38	53	62	68	54	62	60	54	72	74	50	71	55	63	67	61	71	84
14750	LAKEWOOD	83	92	98	88	93	101	88	89	89	87	111	100	92	116	92	91	108	87	92	100
14753	LIMESTONE	72	54	31	48	59	66	51	61	59	51	70	73	46	68	52	62	64	60	72	84
14754	LITTLE GENESEE	66	60	47	57	63	67	55	61	59	55	72	72	55	74	57	60	68	59	66	77
14755	LITTLE VALLEY	73	59	42	57	64	73	60	67	66	59	79	77	56	77	61	69	73	66	77	84
14757	MAYVILLE	89	69	46	65	76	87	70	80	78	68	93	93	63	90	71	82	86	79	94	103
14760	OLEAN	65	61	61	60	63	70	64	64	66	62	81	75	63	83	64	67	78	65	68	74
14767	PANAMA	86	68	44	64	75	82	65	76	71	64	85	91	60	86	67	74	80	74	86	101
14769	PORTLAND	59	57	54	54	60	67	57	59	60	55	74	67	57	78	59	63	70	58	65	70
14770	PORTVILLE	80	68	51	66	72	80	67	73	72	66	87	86	64	87	68	74	82	72	81	92
14772	RANDOLPH	72	64	52	60	68	76	62	68	67	61	81	78	60	83	64	70	77	67	76	85
14775	RIPLEY	68	63	56	61	65	73	64	66	67	62	82	75	63	84	64	69	78	65	72	77
14777	RUSHFORD	65	51	35	46	57	64	48	58	54	48	64	68	43	63	51	58	60	57	68	79
14779	SALAMANCA	53	49	45	47	51	58	51	52	54	49	66	59	50	67	51	56	62	52	58	61
14781	SHERMAN	75	61	44	59	66	74	61	68	66	60	80	79	57	79	62	68	74	67	76	86
14782	SINCLAIRVILLE	80	63	42	59	68	76	62	70	69	62	82	82	57	81	62	71	76	69	80	91
14784	STOCKTON	97	68	35	61	77	87	66	81	78	67	92	96	58	88	68	83	84	80	98	112
14787	WESTFIELD	65	61	54	58	64	71	61	64	65	59	79	73	60	81	62	67	75	63	71	76
14801	ADDISON	78	59	37	55	64	74	59	68	67	59	80	79	54	77	59	70	74	67	79	89
14802	ALFRED	72	49	62	55	48	56	83	65	81	73	101	88	70	92	69	72	96	77	60	73
14803	ALFRED STATION	77	58	62	62	59	67	80	71	81	73	100	90	71	94	71	76	95	79	70	82
14804	ALMOND	88	72	57	70	77	87	74	81	80	73	97	94	69	95	75	82	90	81	90	101
14805	ALPINE	79	64	45	61	68	77	63	71	69	63	83	82	59	82	64	72	78	70	79	90
14806	ANDOVER	85	69	50	67	73	83	71	77	76	69	92	89	66	90	70	78	86	76	86	94
14807	ARKPORT	73	71	64	68	72	78	68	72	70	68	86	82	67	86	69	71	82	71	75	84
	NEW YORK	95	100	134	99	98	107	103	100	105	103	133	116	105	138	104	107	131	102	99	112
	UNITED STATES	100	100	100	100	100	100	100	100	100	100	100	100	100	100	100	100	100	100	100	100

POPULATION CHANGE

#	POST OFFICE NAME	COUNTY FIPS CODE	POPULATION			2000-2004 ANNUAL RATE		HOUSEHOLDS					FAMILIES		
			2000	2004	2009	% Rate	State Centile	2000	2004	2009	% Annual Rate 2000-2004	2004 Average HH Size	2000	2004	% Annual Rate 2000-2004
14808	ATLANTA	101	158	159	160	0.2	38	66	67	68	0.4	2.37	48	49	0.5
14809	AVOCA	101	2667	2806	2898	1.2	83	983	1049	1097	1.5	2.64	693	736	1.4
14810	BATH	101	12277	12419	12606	0.3	45	4911	5047	5198	0.6	2.33	3064	3114	0.4
14812	BEAVER DAMS	097	3824	3929	3994	0.6	64	1267	1320	1359	1.0	2.83	981	1016	0.8
14813	BELMONT	003	2299	2268	2261	-0.3	13	911	913	923	0.1	2.26	607	605	-0.1
14814	BIG FLATS	015	1676	1720	1740	0.6	62	653	678	691	0.9	2.54	512	530	0.8
14815	BRADFORD	097	947	970	989	0.6	61	363	379	393	1.0	2.42	263	273	0.9
14816	BREESPORT	015	828	823	821	-0.1	21	292	295	297	0.2	2.77	223	224	0.1
14817	BROOKTONDALE	109	2066	2170	2283	1.2	82	802	857	916	1.6	2.49	524	553	1.3
14818	BURDETT	097	1796	1859	1908	0.8	71	712	749	780	1.2	2.48	511	535	1.1
14819	CAMERON	101	708	720	729	0.4	52	263	271	277	0.7	2.66	196	200	0.5
14820	CAMERON MILLS	101	921	948	966	0.7	65	301	313	323	0.9	3.03	228	237	0.9
14821	CAMPBELL	101	3432	3502	3558	0.5	56	1283	1328	1367	0.8	2.63	949	976	0.7
14822	CANASERAGA	003	1196	1228	1245	0.6	63	448	466	478	0.9	2.64	328	340	0.9
14823	CANISTEO	101	3969	3942	3957	-0.2	20	1556	1562	1585	0.1	2.52	1085	1083	0.0
14824	CAYUTA	097	610	604	610	-0.2	16	238	240	245	0.2	2.52	185	185	0.0
14825	CHEMUNG	015	833	901	934	1.9	92	297	326	341	2.2	2.72	230	251	2.1
14826	COHOCTON	101	2654	2681	2710	0.2	43	988	1009	1031	0.5	2.65	713	723	0.3
14830	CORNING	101	19444	19333	19442	-0.1	21	8264	8289	8419	0.1	2.31	5123	5112	-0.1
14836	DALTON	051	1050	1060	1083	0.2	41	385	392	405	0.4	2.70	291	296	0.4
14837	DUNDEE	123	5308	5432	5556	0.5	60	1899	1960	2021	0.8	2.69	1363	1399	0.6
14838	ERIN	015	1862	1946	1989	1.0	79	679	720	743	1.4	2.70	550	580	1.3
14839	GREENWOOD	101	744	760	771	0.5	57	281	291	300	0.8	2.61	206	212	0.7
14840	HAMMONDSPORT	101	3495	3589	3667	0.6	63	1487	1549	1603	1.0	2.26	1047	1084	0.8
14841	HECTOR	097	874	898	919	0.6	64	353	369	383	1.1	2.43	242	251	0.9
14842	HIMROD	123	742	753	766	0.4	50	253	257	263	0.4	2.93	201	204	0.4
14843	HORNELL	101	13500	13499	13616	0.0	28	5384	5439	5545	0.2	2.42	3427	3437	0.1
14845	HORSEHEADS	015	20353	20417	20434	0.1	33	7922	8053	8136	0.4	2.46	5649	5714	0.3
14846	HUNT	051	824	843	868	0.5	60	302	312	324	0.8	2.70	229	236	0.7
14847	INTERLAKEN	099	2261	2266	2322	0.1	31	878	896	932	0.5	2.49	596	602	0.2
14850	ITHACA	109	63328	65509	68611	0.8	71	23610	24919	26699	1.3	2.18	10473	10977	1.1
14853	ITHACA	109	8	8	8	0.0	28	5	5	6	0.0	1.60	2	2	0.0
14855	JASPER	101	918	915	919	-0.1	24	293	296	301	0.2	3.09	235	237	0.2
14858	LINDLEY	101	1812	1791	1799	-0.3	15	650	650	661	0.0	2.76	505	503	-0.1
14859	LOCKWOOD	107	1105	1145	1167	0.8	72	392	410	423	1.1	2.79	297	309	0.9
14860	LODI	099	1019	1073	1128	1.2	83	395	422	450	1.6	2.54	279	296	1.4
14861	LOWMAN	015	1396	1507	1561	1.8	92	544	596	624	2.2	2.52	411	447	2.0
14864	MILLPORT	015	1342	1319	1307	-0.4	9	529	526	526	-0.1	2.43	383	378	-0.3
14865	MONTOUR FALLS	097	2737	2757	2793	0.2	39	1072	1094	1124	0.5	2.38	708	718	0.3
14867	NEWFIELD	109	5509	5712	5972	0.9	73	2221	2333	2472	1.2	2.45	1482	1537	0.9
14869	ODESSA	097	1357	1358	1374	0.0	30	516	524	538	0.4	2.56	362	366	0.3
14870	PAINTED POST	101	9253	9812	10203	1.4	87	3802	4069	4276	1.6	2.37	2549	2708	1.4
14871	PINE CITY	015	5092	5163	5197	0.3	49	1946	1996	2026	0.6	2.58	1487	1521	0.5
14872	PINE VALLEY	015	476	472	469	-0.2	18	197	198	198	0.1	2.38	138	138	0.0
14873	PRATTSBURGH	101	2721	2752	2781	0.3	45	1064	1091	1117	0.6	2.52	742	757	0.5
14874	PULTENEY	101	237	235	235	-0.2	18	97	97	99	0.0	2.42	65	64	-0.4
14877	REXVILLE	101	490	493	496	0.1	37	175	179	183	0.5	2.75	130	132	0.4
14878	ROCK STREAM	097	819	823	834	0.1	36	318	324	333	0.4	2.48	241	245	0.4
14879	SAVONA	101	1958	1965	1983	0.1	33	753	766	783	0.4	2.55	541	547	0.3
14880	SCIO	003	1953	1909	1914	-0.5	6	720	719	734	0.0	2.45	514	511	-0.1
14881	SLATERVILLE SPRINGS	109	156	161	168	0.8	69	78	82	87	1.2	1.96	52	54	0.9
14882	LANSING	109	4023	4157	4330	0.8	70	1506	1582	1676	1.2	2.48	1052	1092	0.9
14883	SPENCER	107	3809	3921	4018	0.7	65	1463	1530	1592	1.1	2.56	1032	1071	0.9
14884	SWAIN	003	372	386	392	0.9	73	152	160	165	1.2	2.41	101	106	1.1
14885	TROUPSBURG	101	779	800	814	0.6	63	281	292	301	0.9	2.74	215	222	0.8
14886	TRUMANSBURG	109	6458	6625	6852	0.6	61	2537	2651	2788	1.0	2.47	1744	1805	0.8
14889	VAN ETTEN	015	1437	1424	1414	-0.2	17	564	567	569	0.1	2.51	397	395	-0.1
14891	WATKINS GLEN	097	4592	4659	4734	0.3	49	1873	1919	1973	0.6	2.36	1240	1262	0.4
14892	WAVERLY	107	8359	8367	8451	0.0	30	3321	3363	3440	0.3	2.41	2196	2210	0.2
14894	WELLSBURG	015	2636	2681	2702	0.4	52	632	659	674	1.0	2.63	440	455	0.8
14895	WELLSVILLE	003	9983	9769	9730	-0.5	6	4077	4033	4068	-0.3	2.36	2605	2560	-0.4
14897	WHITESVILLE	003	879	890	895	0.3	46	334	343	349	0.6	2.59	246	251	0.5
14898	WOODHULL	101	1457	1476	1492	0.3	48	486	499	510	0.6	2.96	365	373	0.5
14901	ELMIRA	015	16434	16115	15977	-0.5	8	6368	6332	6340	-0.1	2.27	3659	3584	-0.5
14903	ELMIRA	015	7487	7392	7335	-0.3	14	3189	3189	3194	0.0	2.31	2011	1993	-0.2
14904	ELMIRA	015	16652	16324	16152	-0.5	7	6747	6678	6661	-0.2	2.42	4304	4223	-0.5
14905	ELMIRA	015	10846	10672	10577	-0.4	10	3856	3819	3808	-0.2	2.28	2384	2342	-0.4
	NEW YORK					0.4					0.5	2.60			0.4
	UNITED STATES					1.2					1.3	2.58			1.1

#	POST OFFICE NAME	White 2000	White 2004	Black 2000	Black 2004	Asian/Pacific 2000	Asian/Pacific 2004	% Hispanic Origin 2000	% Hispanic Origin 2004	0-4	5-9	10-14	15-19	20-24	25-44	45-64	65-84	85+	18+	MEDIAN AGE 2004	% 2004 Males	% 2004 Females
14808	ATLANTA	98.1	98.1	0.0	0.0	0.0	0.0	0.0	0.0	6.3	6.3	7.6	8.2	7.6	23.9	28.3	10.1	1.9	74.8	39.3	49.1	50.9
14809	AVOCA	97.4	96.9	1.1	1.2	0.3	0.4	0.9	1.0	5.3	6.3	9.1	7.9	6.4	24.7	26.0	12.5	1.9	73.7	38.3	50.5	49.5
14810	BATH	96.0	95.3	1.8	2.0	0.8	0.9	0.8	0.9	5.4	5.5	6.2	6.9	6.6	23.5	26.6	16.6	2.8	78.5	42.3	50.4	49.6
14812	BEAVER DAMS	94.8	94.0	3.2	3.5	0.4	0.5	1.8	2.0	6.0	6.7	7.4	9.3	8.3	25.7	26.0	9.7	0.8	74.8	36.1	51.7	48.3
14813	BELMONT	96.7	96.3	1.4	1.6	0.4	0.4	0.8	0.9	5.8	5.9	6.7	10.3	9.8	23.9	23.7	12.1	1.9	77.6	35.7	52.2	47.8
14814	BIG FLATS	95.6	94.5	1.5	1.7	1.7	2.2	0.9	1.2	5.6	6.6	7.9	6.9	4.8	22.9	30.3	13.7	1.3	75.5	42.2	49.2	50.8
14815	BRADFORD	94.2	93.4	3.2	3.5	0.5	0.6	2.2	2.6	5.4	6.2	7.4	8.6	7.8	23.3	27.7	12.6	1.0	76.3	39.0	53.3	46.7
14816	BREESPORT	97.5	97.0	0.9	1.0	0.9	1.1	0.4	0.5	5.4	6.0	7.5	8.3	5.2	25.8	28.7	12.2	1.1	75.9	40.6	50.1	49.9
14817	BROOKTONDALE	93.2	92.1	3.5	4.0	0.7	0.9	2.2	2.8	5.5	6.1	7.7	8.3	6.8	26.2	28.9	9.3	1.2	75.0	38.4	49.9	50.1
14818	BURDETT	98.1	97.7	0.5	0.6	0.2	0.3	0.5	0.7	5.4	6.0	7.5	5.7	5.0	25.2	32.8	11.1	1.2	77.2	42.0	51.0	49.0
14819	CAMERON	98.2	97.9	0.1	0.1	0.1	0.1	0.3	0.3	5.0	5.4	9.4	8.5	6.3	27.6	27.2	9.7	0.8	74.9	37.9	52.1	47.9
14820	CAMERON MILLS	97.9	97.7	0.2	0.2	0.1	0.1	0.4	0.6	5.9	6.3	9.0	8.2	6.4	27.4	26.5	9.5	0.7	73.6	37.1	51.2	48.8
14821	CAMPBELL	98.3	98.0	0.4	0.5	0.3	0.4	0.4	0.5	6.5	6.8	7.7	7.3	6.1	27.4	26.2	11.0	0.9	74.3	38.0	49.9	50.1
14822	CANASERAGA	97.7	97.3	0.1	0.1	0.1	0.1	1.0	1.3	6.4	6.9	7.6	7.7	5.2	25.3	28.0	11.7	1.1	74.3	39.5	51.0	49.0
14823	CANISTEO	98.3	98.0	0.2	0.2	0.5	0.5	0.8	1.0	5.5	6.5	7.7	7.4	5.9	24.0	27.1	13.4	2.1	75.2	39.9	48.8	51.2
14824	CAYUTA	96.1	95.2	1.0	1.2	0.5	0.5	1.0	1.3	6.1	6.5	7.0	6.5	6.3	25.5	29.0	11.9	1.3	76.7	39.9	49.5	50.5
14825	CHEMUNG	97.6	97.0	0.5	0.7	0.2	0.2	0.8	1.2	7.2	7.3	7.7	7.1	5.4	27.2	25.3	11.4	1.3	72.9	37.6	50.4	49.6
14826	COHOCTON	97.4	97.1	0.5	0.6	0.3	0.3	0.3	0.3	6.0	6.7	8.2	7.5	6.0	27.0	25.6	11.3	1.7	74.2	38.3	50.0	50.0
14830	CORNING	94.8	94.0	2.5	2.7	1.3	1.7	0.8	0.9	6.1	6.2	7.0	6.8	6.4	26.6	25.6	13.1	2.2	76.4	39.0	48.0	52.0
14836	DALTON	97.3	97.1	0.3	0.3	0.3	0.3	0.5	0.7	6.9	7.4	7.2	6.7	5.8	25.3	28.7	10.9	1.3	74.4	38.6	51.2	48.8
14837	DUNDEE	97.3	96.9	1.0	1.1	0.3	0.4	1.0	1.3	7.6	7.5	8.3	7.6	6.0	22.6	24.9	13.9	1.7	71.5	38.1	49.5	50.5
14838	ERIN	98.6	98.2	0.2	0.2	0.4	0.5	0.4	0.6	6.2	6.7	7.2	6.6	6.0	28.2	28.9	9.2	0.9	75.9	38.1	51.6	48.4
14839	GREENWOOD	98.3	97.8	0.3	0.3	0.1	0.3	0.3	0.3	7.9	7.4	6.5	7.0	7.2	24.5	26.6	11.7	1.3	73.8	36.7	51.6	48.4
14840	HAMMONDSPORT	97.8	97.4	0.6	0.7	0.5	0.6	0.4	0.5	4.7	5.0	6.0	5.5	4.4	21.3	33.0	17.7	2.4	80.7	46.9	49.6	50.4
14841	HECTOR	98.2	97.9	0.9	1.0	0.5	0.6	1.3	1.7	5.0	6.0	7.0	5.9	4.3	22.8	34.3	12.8	1.8	77.5	44.4	50.5	49.6
14842	HIMROD	96.2	95.8	1.6	1.7	0.1	0.1	0.5	0.7	9.7	9.6	8.8	5.6	6.5	24.0	22.6	12.4	0.9	68.4	34.2	50.6	49.4
14843	HORNELL	96.5	96.0	1.7	1.9	0.7	0.8	1.1	1.3	6.7	6.5	7.2	7.2	6.9	24.8	23.9	14.2	2.7	75.2	38.2	47.8	52.2
14845	HORSEHEADS	96.1	95.1	1.2	1.4	1.6	2.0	0.7	0.9	5.5	5.8	6.7	6.7	5.5	23.5	27.8	15.8	2.9	77.8	42.7	47.3	52.7
14846	HUNT	97.8	97.6	0.1	0.1	0.1	0.2	0.4	0.5	8.0	8.0	7.8	7.2	5.9	25.7	26.3	9.9	1.2	71.7	36.4	50.3	49.7
14847	INTERLAKEN	97.1	96.8	0.7	0.7	0.2	0.2	1.4	1.6	5.1	5.7	7.3	6.8	5.3	22.3	31.5	14.1	2.0	77.1	43.3	49.2	50.8
14850	ITHACA	80.4	77.0	4.6	4.9	10.7	13.0	3.9	4.6	3.7	3.5	4.0	15.6	23.2	23.5	17.4	7.6	1.5	86.1	25.0	49.4	50.6
14853	ITHACA	87.5	87.5	0.0	0.0	12.5	12.5	0.0	0.0	0.0	0.0	0.0	37.5	62.5	0.0	0.0	0.0	0.0	100.0	21.0	75.0	25.0
14855	JASPER	98.3	97.8	0.3	0.3	0.7	0.9	0.2	0.3	7.4	7.4	9.0	9.2	8.4	25.3	23.1	9.5	0.8	70.6	32.0	50.9	49.1
14858	LINDLEY	98.2	97.8	0.6	0.6	0.2	0.2	0.7	0.8	6.8	7.4	8.9	6.2	5.6	28.3	27.4	8.5	0.8	72.9	36.2	50.5	49.5
14859	LOCKWOOD	97.9	97.5	0.2	0.3	0.6	0.8	0.7	0.8	7.1	7.6	9.0	7.4	5.6	26.8	25.9	9.4	1.2	71.5	36.3	51.1	48.9
14860	LODI	95.8	95.3	0.5	0.6	0.5	0.5	2.3	2.7	5.7	6.4	9.0	5.7	3.9	25.5	29.0	13.3	1.5	74.6	40.5	52.4	47.6
14861	LOWMAN	97.7	97.2	0.6	0.8	0.2	0.3	0.4	0.5	5.6	5.9	6.8	7.1	5.5	26.2	29.7	12.0	1.2	77.2	40.5	52.2	47.8
14864	MILLPORT	97.8	97.3	0.4	0.5	0.2	0.2	0.9	1.2	5.2	5.6	6.2	6.0	5.5	23.1	29.8	15.9	2.6	78.5	43.9	49.2	50.8
14865	MONTOUR FALLS	97.8	97.5	0.7	0.8	0.3	0.3	0.5	0.7	5.1	5.0	6.1	5.8	6.1	23.7	27.1	16.9	4.4	80.1	44.0	47.0	53.0
14867	NEWFIELD	95.7	94.8	1.2	1.4	0.5	0.6	1.2	1.6	6.6	6.9	8.2	6.6	6.0	29.5	27.2	8.0	1.1	74.3	36.8	48.7	51.3
14869	ODESSA	97.1	96.4	0.4	0.5	0.0	0.1	0.9	1.1	5.9	6.1	7.4	6.8	7.0	26.0	28.7	10.8	1.3	75.9	39.1	48.5	51.5
14870	PAINTED POST	93.4	92.2	2.0	2.3	3.5	4.3	1.2	1.4	6.6	6.3	6.9	6.1	5.5	24.7	26.4	14.7	2.9	76.5	41.3	48.1	51.9
14871	PINE CITY	98.6	98.2	0.5	0.6	0.3	0.4	0.5	0.6	4.9	5.5	7.1	6.7	5.6	22.7	31.2	14.6	1.8	78.4	43.5	49.2	50.8
14872	PINE VALLEY	97.9	97.5	0.2	0.2	0.3	0.4	0.6	0.6	7.2	7.0	7.0	6.4	6.1	26.1	28.2	11.2	0.9	74.6	38.2	51.3	48.7
14873	PRATTSBURGH	97.0	96.4	1.2	1.3	0.1	0.1	1.3	1.6	6.0	6.4	8.0	7.1	5.8	24.9	27.8	12.9	1.2	75.3	39.6	50.2	49.9
14874	PULTENEY	99.6	99.6	0.0	0.0	0.0	0.0	1.3	0.9	5.5	6.4	7.2	6.4	4.3	22.1	33.2	13.6	1.3	76.6	43.7	50.6	49.4
14877	REXVILLE	98.8	98.8	0.0	0.0	0.2	0.2	0.8	0.8	6.3	6.5	7.1	6.1	6.5	24.8	30.4	11.4	1.0	76.5	40.1	50.1	49.9
14878	ROCK STREAM	96.2	95.6	1.5	1.6	0.5	0.7	1.0	1.0	6.9	7.1	7.2	7.8	6.0	23.3	26.1	14.3	1.3	73.8	39.1	50.4	49.6
14879	SAVONA	98.1	97.8	0.4	0.5	0.3	0.4	0.5	0.6	6.5	6.5	7.7	7.1	6.6	26.9	27.1	10.6	1.0	74.8	37.8	50.0	50.0
14880	SCIO	96.9	96.4	0.8	0.9	0.6	0.7	0.5	0.6	5.9	5.9	7.1	6.9	7.1	23.4	25.8	14.5	3.4	77.0	40.4	49.2	50.8
14881	SLATERVILLE SPRINGS	93.6	92.6	1.9	2.5	1.3	1.9	1.3	1.2	4.4	5.6	8.7	6.8	5.0	26.1	31.7	10.6	1.2	77.0	41.3	46.6	53.4
14882	LANSING	91.8	90.3	4.9	5.6	0.8	1.0	2.1	2.6	4.8	6.0	8.9	12.4	5.1	24.5	27.1	10.3	0.9	70.5	37.8	50.4	49.6
14883	SPENCER	96.9	96.3	0.8	0.9	0.5	0.6	1.4	1.7	6.8	7.0	7.6	7.1	6.2	27.3	27.5	9.4	1.2	74.0	37.9	49.3	50.7
14884	SWAIN	96.2	95.3	0.8	0.8	0.3	0.3	1.1	1.3	6.0	6.5	6.0	5.4	5.4	22.3	31.1	15.8	1.6	78.5	43.9	52.3	47.7
14885	TROUPSBURG	98.0	97.8	0.1	0.1	0.5	0.5	1.3	1.6	9.3	8.1	8.0	6.9	6.5	25.9	24.0	10.5	0.9	70.5	34.1	48.5	51.5
14886	TRUMANSBURG	96.8	96.1	1.0	1.1	0.6	0.7	1.2	1.5	5.1	6.1	8.6	7.3	5.2	24.5	30.2	11.5	1.6	75.4	41.1	48.8	51.2
14889	VAN ETTEN	98.5	98.1	0.3	0.4	0.2	0.3	0.5	0.8	7.1	7.2	7.7	7.2	5.5	26.3	27.3	10.3	1.5	73.5	37.7	49.6	50.4
14891	WATKINS GLEN	97.1	96.6	0.9	1.0	0.6	0.7	1.0	1.3	6.2	6.1	6.5	7.3	6.4	24.0	26.3	14.9	2.5	76.7	40.6	48.5	51.5
14892	WAVERLY	98.0	97.7	0.4	0.5	0.4	0.5	1.0	1.2	6.5	6.6	7.2	6.4	6.0	26.4	24.4	13.7	2.9	75.5	39.3	47.9	52.1
14894	WELLSBURG	70.4	70.3	23.5	23.1	0.1	0.1	10.4	11.2	3.7	4.1	5.1	4.8	11.8	40.3	20.2	9.3	0.8	84.5	34.0	67.8	32.2
14895	WELLSVILLE	97.0	96.4	0.4	0.5	1.0	1.3	0.6	0.8	6.1	6.1	6.5	6.5	6.1	24.1	26.2	15.4	3.1	77.3	41.3	48.3	51.7
14897	WHITESVILLE	98.8	98.5	0.3	0.3	0.1	0.1	0.5	0.6	6.1	6.3	7.6	7.1	6.6	23.2	26.6	14.6	1.9	75.7	40.3	50.8	49.2
14898	WOODHULL	97.3	96.9	0.5	0.5	0.6	0.6	1.2	1.4	8.2	8.0	8.3	6.8	6.4	27.4	23.9	9.8	1.3	71.3	33.7	50.0	50.0
14901	ELMIRA	83.5	81.1	12.1	13.7	0.6	0.7	1.9	2.3	7.2	6.2	6.2	8.1	10.9	25.6	20.9	12.3	2.7	76.8	34.0	47.6	52.4
14903	ELMIRA	96.7	96.0	1.1	1.3	0.8	1.0	0.7	0.9	5.2	5.7	6.9	7.3	6.4	25.6	26.0	15.0	2.0	77.8	40.5	47.5	52.5
14904	ELMIRA	92.2	90.7	5.0	5.9	0.3	0.3	1.5	1.9	6.8	6.8	7.8	7.2	7.2	25.9	22.8	13.5	2.1	74.0	37.0	47.4	52.6
14905	ELMIRA	81.2	79.1	13.4	14.5	1.2	1.4	4.5	5.4	5.3	5.1	5.2	5.9	8.4	31.4	24.3	12.1	2.4	81.0	37.9	56.1	43.9
	NEW YORK	68.0	65.9	15.9	16.2	5.6	6.4	15.1	16.7	6.5	6.5	7.1	7.0	7.1	28.9	24.0	11.2	1.8	75.8	36.7	48.3	51.7
	UNITED STATES	75.1	73.6	12.3	12.5	3.8	4.2	12.5	14.1	6.9	6.7	7.2	7.0	7.3	28.6	23.8	10.8	1.7	75.1	36.0	49.1	50.9

#	POST OFFICE NAME	2004 Per Capita Income	2004 HH Income Base	Less than $25,000	$25,000 to $49,999	$50,000 to $99,999	$100,000 to $149,999	$150,000 or More	2004	2009	2004 National Centile	2004 State Centile	2004 Home Value Base	Less than $50,000	$50,000 to $89,999	$90,000 to $174,999	$175,000 to $399,999	$400,000 or More	2004 Median Home Value
14808	ATLANTA	19096	67	31.3	31.3	28.4	6.0	3.0	39435	42840	44	32	56	16.1	30.4	39.3	12.5	1.8	95000
14809	AVOCA	16687	1049	32.0	35.0	28.2	3.2	1.6	35270	39279	29	14	818	13.1	30.4	43.3	12.2	1.0	98030
14810	BATH	19645	5047	34.6	33.1	24.2	5.7	2.4	35992	40262	32	16	3392	17.3	17.6	47.4	17.1	0.6	112928
14812	BEAVER DAMS	18737	1320	23.7	34.8	33.2	5.8	2.5	42132	46639	53	42	1126	20.2	25.5	40.0	13.9	0.4	96282
14813	BELMONT	18212	913	37.2	32.3	25.4	4.3	0.8	35256	38279	28	14	664	22.6	32.5	37.1	7.5	0.3	81905
14814	BIG FLATS	27893	678	12.5	27.9	40.6	12.1	6.9	58426	65596	83	73	577	4.7	12.8	56.3	25.7	0.5	132095
14815	BRADFORD	17884	379	29.6	37.7	27.7	4.5	0.5	38240	42788	40	26	320	15.3	22.2	48.8	12.8	0.9	104630
14816	BREESPORT	22232	295	15.6	27.1	42.7	13.2	1.4	55456	62374	80	70	248	8.9	25.4	51.6	13.3	0.8	108750
14817	BROOKTONDALE	24498	857	23.6	26.6	34.7	11.9	3.3	49794	57354	72	62	593	4.2	10.1	45.0	38.6	2.0	156250
14818	BURDETT	23114	749	23.1	36.2	31.2	7.1	2.4	43620	48944	58	46	627	5.9	18.3	45.0	27.6	3.2	135150
14819	CAMERON	19005	271	32.5	33.6	26.9	3.3	3.7	37188	41067	36	21	216	24.1	24.5	35.7	14.8	0.9	91875
14820	CAMERON MILLS	15685	313	31.6	34.5	28.1	3.8	1.9	37484	41901	37	22	255	22.8	20.8	38.4	16.9	1.2	98684
14821	CAMPBELL	20501	1328	25.1	33.8	31.5	7.4	2.3	43054	48065	56	44	1130	18.7	17.9	43.5	19.2	0.8	110405
14822	CANASERAGA	16792	466	33.5	36.1	24.9	4.3	1.3	36052	39833	32	16	376	16.0	34.3	41.8	6.9	1.1	89667
14823	CANISTEO	17097	1562	33.4	32.8	29.1	4.3	0.5	38494	42515	41	27	1181	13.6	33.5	44.7	8.0	0.3	93194
14824	CAYUTA	20934	240	22.1	39.6	32.1	2.5	3.8	39254	44022	44	30	200	16.0	25.0	50.0	9.0	0.0	99474
14825	CHEMUNG	16936	326	25.8	39.6	29.1	4.9	0.6	39459	43890	44	32	279	30.1	36.2	25.5	7.5	0.7	71833
14826	COHOCTON	17531	1009	30.4	34.4	28.0	5.7	1.6	38751	43079	42	28	823	12.4	28.6	46.2	12.2	0.7	102109
14830	CORNING	25315	8289	29.9	28.9	27.3	8.1	5.8	41153	46559	50	38	5438	6.1	16.3	51.7	23.3	2.7	125154
14836	DALTON	17625	392	26.3	36.5	31.1	5.1	1.0	42131	47248	53	42	336	15.5	39.6	36.3	7.1	1.6	83704
14837	DUNDEE	16724	1960	35.6	33.8	24.8	3.8	2.0	33565	36742	23	9	1456	8.9	19.0	48.5	19.4	4.2	120018
14838	ERIN	19351	720	20.4	35.7	37.2	5.6	1.1	46145	51178	64	53	641	35.6	25.6	30.7	7.6	0.5	73163
14839	GREENWOOD	15441	291	37.5	35.4	21.7	4.5	1.0	33426	36600	22	9	234	29.1	23.9	29.5	16.7	0.9	82222
14840	HAMMONDSPORT	24662	1549	25.1	34.0	29.5	7.1	4.4	42694	48882	55	43	1297	9.6	17.1	43.4	26.1	3.8	128790
14841	HECTOR	25554	369	25.2	29.8	29.5	10.3	5.2	46317	52255	65	53	310	11.3	13.9	38.4	30.0	6.5	140000
14842	HIMROD	17679	257	23.4	37.0	31.5	5.5	2.7	43545	47760	57	46	222	22.5	18.9	22.5	16.7	19.4	109677
14843	HORNELL	18318	5439	39.1	29.8	24.3	5.1	1.7	33601	37503	23	9	3555	14.9	34.6	39.8	10.2	0.6	90582
14845	HORSEHEADS	24032	8053	22.9	29.7	34.2	8.9	4.3	47345	53193	67	56	6266	10.1	24.1	51.5	13.4	1.0	109106
14846	HUNT	16425	312	30.8	33.7	30.8	4.2	0.6	38309	42055	40	26	260	19.2	37.7	37.7	4.6	0.8	80000
14847	INTERLAKEN	22098	896	25.7	36.7	26.8	7.8	3.0	40295	44821	47	35	728	9.3	21.4	45.6	20.7	2.9	119130
14850	ITHACA	25153	24919	35.4	25.0	24.1	8.8	6.8	38496	45040	41	27	10870	3.8	3.1	37.0	48.7	7.4	187875
14853	ITHACA	78750	5	20.0	0.0	0.0	40.0	40.0	141449	134826	100	99	2	0.0	0.0	0.0	100.0	0.0	275000
14855	JASPER	15064	296	29.4	38.2	24.0	6.4	2.0	36997	41639	35	21	242	22.3	26.0	29.3	21.1	1.2	92857
14858	LINDLEY	17544	650	27.1	34.5	31.9	5.2	1.4	41080	46217	50	38	568	19.2	21.8	39.6	18.5	0.9	108553
14859	LOCKWOOD	16667	410	28.1	43.2	24.2	2.0	2.7	40000	44276	46	34	339	34.8	21.2	38.1	4.7	1.2	76176
14860	LODI	19212	422	25.1	36.5	30.6	6.6	1.2	41134	46057	50	38	364	14.0	22.8	36.8	22.8	3.6	114024
14861	LOWMAN	21003	596	25.8	36.9	31.4	3.9	2.0	40644	44882	48	36	508	33.7	28.2	31.3	5.5	1.4	72381
14864	MILLPORT	23403	526	28.7	28.9	29.5	7.0	5.9	44429	49060	60	49	444	16.2	19.4	42.1	21.4	0.9	121250
14865	MONTOUR FALLS	18877	1094	32.8	32.6	27.3	5.7	1.6	36773	40585	35	20	772	13.7	17.0	52.7	15.5	1.0	113889
14867	NEWFIELD	19821	2333	27.5	34.1	32.1	4.9	1.4	41227	46269	51	39	1808	14.1	11.0	59.3	14.7	0.9	125909
14869	ODESSA	19296	524	27.1	32.3	32.3	7.6	0.8	40754	45613	49	37	394	10.9	17.3	57.1	13.5	1.3	118310
14870	PAINTED POST	28504	4069	26.3	27.7	28.5	10.6	7.0	45522	51988	63	52	3023	10.9	10.1	51.2	21.8	6.0	133498
14871	PINE CITY	24526	1996	16.3	34.8	34.6	10.6	3.7	49143	56395	70	60	1741	8.3	28.5	55.0	7.8	0.5	103481
14872	PINE VALLEY	19913	198	30.8	36.9	24.2	6.1	2.0	38243	42877	40	26	164	37.2	14.0	39.0	9.8	0.0	86667
14873	PRATTSBURGH	17505	1091	31.8	36.9	26.6	3.3	1.5	36224	39968	32	17	900	16.4	26.4	41.4	13.8	1.9	101433
14874	PULTENEY	18902	97	27.8	39.2	26.8	4.1	2.1	38809	43636	42	28	81	16.1	17.3	33.3	25.9	7.4	123611
14877	REXVILLE	14514	179	35.8	33.5	26.8	3.9	0.0	36116	39764	32	17	144	20.8	22.9	30.6	20.8	4.9	98182
14878	ROCK STREAM	20427	324	25.9	37.4	29.6	4.6	2.5	40000	43919	46	34	271	11.8	20.3	46.5	19.6	1.9	118438
14879	SAVONA	17594	766	26.4	42.4	25.1	5.2	0.9	38130	42889	40	25	605	17.7	25.8	41.5	14.6	0.5	96695
14880	SCIO	16978	719	34.1	34.6	26.8	4.3	0.1	36292	39512	33	18	557	19.9	38.2	38.4	3.2	0.2	78558
14881	SLATERVILLE SPRINGS	33170	82	29.3	29.3	23.2	12.2	6.1	45544	53038	63	52	65	7.7	7.7	44.6	38.5	1.5	156944
14882	LANSING	26802	1582	18.2	24.0	38.4	13.7	5.6	56737	65137	81	72	1217	4.9	5.5	49.6	32.5	7.5	153304
14883	SPENCER	19448	1530	25.4	36.0	32.0	5.2	1.5	42824	47986	55	44	1221	17.2	27.1	44.3	11.1	0.3	96435
14884	SWAIN	17141	160	36.3	29.4	30.6	3.1	0.6	36023	39297	32	16	133	19.6	26.3	48.1	5.3	0.8	97857
14885	TROUPSBURG	14841	292	36.6	30.8	28.8	2.7	1.0	34714	37762	26	12	234	16.7	23.5	31.6	26.1	2.1	111765
14886	TRUMANSBURG	23469	2651	25.1	29.8	32.3	8.7	4.1	44611	51273	60	49	2053	8.6	9.6	43.3	35.9	2.6	147817
14889	VAN ETTEN	16841	567	33.5	33.7	28.9	3.4	0.5	34828	38113	27	12	427	28.3	32.8	29.0	9.1	0.7	75000
14891	WATKINS GLEN	19555	1919	33.6	32.3	26.9	4.6	2.5	36544	40138	34	19	1357	10.1	16.7	52.9	19.1	1.3	119492
14892	WAVERLY	17733	3363	33.9	33.5	27.9	4.0	0.8	36567	40560	34	19	2296	20.1	33.1	41.1	5.6	0.1	86158
14894	WELLSBURG	17125	659	28.8	31.4	33.7	4.0	2.1	39587	43898	45	32	541	46.8	23.1	26.3	3.5	0.4	57000
14895	WELLSVILLE	20060	4033	38.5	28.7	24.4	5.8	2.6	33802	36935	23	9	2761	19.3	31.5	39.2	9.2	0.8	88799
14897	WHITESVILLE	16871	343	32.7	36.2	28.0	2.3	0.9	36279	40319	33	18	284	24.3	40.5	26.8	8.5	0.0	74000
14898	WOODHULL	14235	499	36.1	32.7	25.9	3.8	1.6	34432	38078	25	11	410	22.4	23.2	34.2	19.3	1.0	96429
14901	ELMIRA	17189	6332	44.1	30.2	20.3	3.4	2.1	29778	32435	12	5	3146	29.2	50.2	15.8	3.8	1.0	65970
14903	ELMIRA	21584	3189	30.4	32.0	28.1	6.6	3.0	38740	42639	42	28	2090	12.0	44.4	30.7	11.5	1.4	82941
14904	ELMIRA	16800	6678	37.1	34.9	23.8	3.2	1.0	33618	37157	23	9	4052	34.1	53.9	11.6	0.4	0.0	57445
14905	ELMIRA	25023	3819	26.0	28.0	29.9	10.0	6.1	46185	52148	64	53	2620	2.5	28.9	50.5	15.5	2.6	112310
	NEW YORK	28049		26.3	24.3	29.3	11.5	8.6	49309	58077				4.6	8.6	27.2	39.9	19.8	219050
	UNITED STATES	25866		24.7	27.1	30.8	10.9	6.5	48124	56710				10.9	15.0	33.7	30.1	10.4	145905

# ZIP CODE / POST OFFICE NAME	Auto Loan	Home Loan	Invest-ments	Retire-ment Plans	Home Repair	Lawn & Garden	Comput-ers & Hard-ware	Major Appli-ances	TV, Radio, Sound Equip-ment	Furni-ture	Dine out/ Carry out	Sports Equip-ment	Fees & Tickets	Toys & Games	Travel	Cable TV	Apparel & Services	Auto Repairs	Health Insur-ance	Pets & Supplies
14808 ATLANTA	71	60	47	60	63	71	62	66	66	61	80	75	59	79	61	67	75	65	72	78
14809 AVOCA	77	59	36	54	65	72	56	66	63	56	76	79	51	74	57	67	70	65	77	90
14810 BATH	72	62	54	59	66	74	62	68	67	62	81	76	60	78	63	69	77	67	76	81
14812 BEAVER DAMS	89	74	52	69	78	86	71	79	77	71	93	93	67	91	71	79	87	78	88	102
14813 BELMONT	67	52	40	51	56	65	58	61	63	55	75	71	52	72	56	64	69	62	69	74
14814 BIG FLATS	94	108	114	106	108	112	100	101	96	99	121	116	105	125	103	96	119	98	98	113
14815 BRADFORD	79	56	30	49	64	73	54	66	64	54	75	79	47	72	56	68	69	66	81	93
14816 BREESPORT	90	89	80	89	91	97	86	90	86	85	106	103	86	108	86	86	102	88	90	104
14817 BROOKTONDALE	85	89	96	90	90	93	86	87	85	86	106	104	87	108	87	84	103	87	84	101
14818 BURDETT	95	78	56	72	86	95	73	86	81	73	97	101	68	96	77	85	91	84	98	114
14819 CAMERON	93	64	32	56	73	83	62	77	74	63	87	91	53	83	63	79	79	76	94	108
14820 CAMERON MILLS	87	62	32	54	69	78	59	72	69	60	82	86	52	78	60	74	75	71	86	100
14821 CAMPBELL	89	75	54	70	80	88	70	79	77	70	92	94	67	93	72	79	87	78	89	104
14822 CANASERAGA	70	59	45	58	62	70	60	65	64	59	77	74	57	77	60	65	72	64	71	79
14823 CANISTEO	64	58	50	54	61	69	58	62	62	56	75	70	56	77	59	65	71	61	70	75
14824 CAYUTA	96	68	36	60	76	86	65	80	77	66	91	95	57	87	67	82	83	78	96	111
14825 CHEMUNG	79	60	38	56	65	74	60	69	68	60	81	80	55	78	60	70	75	68	79	89
14826 COHOCTON	71	64	52	61	67	74	62	67	66	61	81	78	61	82	63	68	76	66	73	82
14830 CORNING	82	82	84	81	83	89	82	83	83	81	103	98	82	105	83	82	99	83	83	96
14836 DALTON	70	66	65	66	69	74	66	69	67	65	82	81	64	81	66	67	78	69	72	82
14837 DUNDEE	76	58	38	54	64	74	58	68	66	57	78	78	52	75	60	70	72	67	80	88
14838 ERIN	83	76	59	73	77	82	71	77	73	72	90	90	68	88	71	73	86	76	79	94
14839 GREENWOOD	75	51	24	45	58	66	49	62	59	50	69	74	42	66	50	63	63	61	75	87
14840 HAMMONDSPORT	96	75	50	67	84	95	71	85	80	70	95	100	63	94	75	86	88	84	101	117
14841 HECTOR	106	82	55	75	93	104	78	94	88	77	104	110	69	103	83	94	97	93	111	129
14842 HIMROD	88	69	47	62	77	87	65	78	73	64	87	92	58	86	69	78	81	77	92	107
14843 HORNELL	63	59	56	58	61	68	62	63	64	60	79	73	60	79	62	66	75	63	68	73
14845 HORSEHEADS	82	87	88	85	88	94	83	85	83	82	103	97	85	107	85	84	101	84	86	97
14846 HUNT	67	60	53	60	63	69	61	65	63	60	77	75	58	76	61	64	73	64	69	77
14847 INTERLAKEN	91	73	52	69	81	91	71	83	79	70	94	98	65	94	74	82	88	82	95	109
14850 ITHACA	81	74	92	79	73	79	90	81	88	85	110	100	85	106	84	83	107	87	76	90
14853 ITHACA	178	109	137	123	107	129	211	154	204	178	255	215	172	229	168	180	240	189	143	176
14855 JASPER	84	59	31	56	69	77	58	72	67	57	79	86	50	77	60	70	72	71	85	100
14858 LINDLEY	78	69	52	65	71	76	65	71	68	66	83	84	62	81	65	69	79	70	75	89
14859 LOCKWOOD	77	65	46	61	67	73	62	69	66	64	81	81	58	76	62	67	76	69	74	86
14860 LODI	85	63	39	58	72	81	61	74	70	60	82	88	54	81	64	74	76	73	88	102
14861 LOWMAN	96	69	37	61	76	87	66	80	77	67	91	95	58	88	67	82	84	79	96	111
14864 MILLPORT	104	73	39	68	84	95	72	88	83	71	98	106	62	95	74	87	89	87	105	122
14865 MONTOUR FALLS	65	62	57	59	64	73	62	65	66	60	80	73	62	81	64	69	76	64	72	76
14867 NEWFIELD	75	71	60	69	71	74	68	71	68	70	84	83	65	80	67	66	81	71	69	83
14869 ODESSA	78	67	52	66	70	79	67	72	71	66	87	83	65	86	67	73	81	71	79	87
14870 PAINTED POST	100	97	93	95	100	109	93	99	95	94	117	112	93	115	95	97	113	97	103	115
14871 PINE CITY	84	94	98	90	94	100	88	89	88	87	109	102	92	114	91	89	107	87	90	101
14872 PINE VALLEY	77	67	50	65	69	74	65	71	67	66	82	83	60	78	64	67	78	71	73	87
14873 PRATTSBURGH	73	57	39	53	64	73	57	66	64	56	76	76	51	74	59	68	70	65	78	86
14874 PULTENEY	78	61	42	55	69	77	57	69	65	57	77	81	51	76	61	69	72	68	82	95
14877 REXVILLE	70	52	33	47	59	67	50	61	57	50	68	71	44	66	52	61	63	60	72	84
14878 ROCK STREAM	79	71	58	68	75	82	68	74	72	68	88	86	67	89	70	74	84	73	80	92
14879 SAVONA	73	60	43	54	64	73	58	66	65	57	78	76	55	79	59	69	73	65	76	85
14880 SCIO	75	52	29	49	60	68	54	64	62	53	73	76	46	70	54	65	66	64	77	87
14881 SLATERVILLE SPRINGS	104	93	71	88	98	105	86	95	91	86	111	113	84	113	88	93	105	93	103	123
14882 LANSING	105	99	83	95	104	111	92	100	95	92	116	118	91	119	95	97	112	97	105	125
14883 SPENCER	78	71	57	69	73	78	68	73	70	69	86	85	66	85	68	70	82	72	75	88
14884 SWAIN	70	55	37	50	62	70	52	62	59	51	70	73	46	69	55	63	65	62	74	85
14885 TROUPSBURG	72	52	30	49	60	67	51	62	58	50	69	74	44	67	53	61	63	61	74	86
14886 TRUMANSBURG	83	85	84	84	85	89	81	84	81	82	100	99	81	101	82	80	98	84	82	98
14889 VAN ETTEN	67	58	44	56	61	67	57	62	61	56	74	72	55	74	57	62	69	61	67	76
14891 WATKINS GLEN	71	62	51	59	66	74	62	67	67	61	81	77	60	81	63	70	77	66	76	81
14892 WAVERLY	65	58	47	56	60	67	59	62	62	58	76	71	56	75	59	64	71	62	68	73
14894 WELLSBURG	83	68	47	62	71	79	65	74	71	66	86	86	60	82	65	73	81	73	81	95
14895 WELLSVILLE	78	61	43	58	66	77	63	71	70	61	83	81	58	81	64	74	77	70	82	88
14897 WHITESVILLE	82	55	25	48	63	72	53	67	64	54	75	80	45	71	54	69	69	66	82	94
14898 WOODHULL	79	53	25	47	61	69	52	64	62	52	72	77	44	69	53	66	66	64	79	91
14901 ELMIRA	54	51	57	50	51	57	56	54	58	54	72	63	55	72	55	58	70	56	56	61
14903 ELMIRA	64	71	79	69	71	76	70	69	70	68	88	79	73	93	72	71	86	68	69	76
14904 ELMIRA	55	54	57	52	55	61	57	56	59	55	73	64	57	75	57	61	70	57	60	63
14905 ELMIRA	81	88	102	87	88	95	89	87	88	88	110	100	92	112	90	88	108	88	86	96
NEW YORK	95	100	134	99	98	107	103	100	105	103	133	116	105	138	104	107	131	102	99	112
UNITED STATES	100	100	100	100	100	100	100	100	100	100	100	100	100	100	100	100	100	100	100	100

NORTH CAROLINA POPULATION CHANGE

A 27006-27332

# POST OFFICE NAME	COUNTY FIPS CODE	Population 2000	2004	2009	% Rate	State Centile	Households 2000	2004	2009	% Annual Rate 2000-2004	2004 Average HH Size	Families 2000	2004	% Annual Rate 2000-2004
27006 ADVANCE	059	10904	12892	14850	4.0	93	4347	5183	6021	4.2	2.47	3355	3951	3.9
27007 ARARAT	171	2179	2449	2668	2.8	82	819	933	1025	3.1	2.62	658	742	2.9
27009 BELEWS CREEK	067	2375	2299	2378	-0.8	1	938	915	952	-0.6	2.51	733	706	-0.9
27011 BOONVILLE	197	5140	5570	6068	1.9	62	2062	2252	2470	2.1	2.47	1531	1651	1.8
27012 CLEMMONS	067	21969	24418	26554	2.5	77	8256	9238	10099	2.7	2.61	6439	7115	2.4
27013 CLEVELAND	159	6102	6731	7415	2.3	73	2217	2457	2722	2.5	2.73	1694	1854	2.2
27016 DANBURY	169	1855	1928	2052	0.9	34	705	745	804	1.3	2.55	531	554	1.0
27017 DOBSON	171	8510	8888	9331	1.0	37	3207	3375	3576	1.2	2.58	2386	2476	0.9
27018 EAST BEND	197	7244	7873	8586	2.0	64	2893	3175	3491	2.2	2.47	2111	2287	1.9
27019 GERMANTON	169	4143	4400	4725	1.4	51	1641	1761	1911	1.7	2.48	1240	1313	1.4
27020 HAMPTONVILLE	197	6084	6481	6997	1.5	52	2357	2529	2748	1.7	2.56	1767	1871	1.4
27021 KING	169	15793	17249	18892	2.1	68	6171	6874	7662	2.6	2.47	4574	5030	2.3
27022 LAWSONVILLE	169	1615	1674	1780	0.9	32	653	687	741	1.2	2.43	493	513	0.9
27023 LEWISVILLE	067	9918	10708	11479	1.8	60	3843	4171	4488	2.0	2.57	2995	3206	1.6
27024 LOWGAP	171	2534	2848	3104	2.8	82	1005	1153	1276	3.3	2.42	756	856	3.0
27025 MADISON	157	11157	11516	11961	0.8	28	4390	4607	4859	1.1	2.47	3221	3339	0.9
27027 MAYODAN	157	4181	4286	4413	0.6	24	1872	1944	2028	0.9	2.20	1178	1203	0.5
27028 MOCKSVILLE	059	23584	25243	27770	1.6	55	9251	10024	11150	1.9	2.49	6791	7258	1.6
27030 MOUNT AIRY	171	38500	39662	41436	0.7	27	15504	16153	17057	1.0	2.41	11040	11345	0.6
27040 PFAFFTOWN	067	9601	10254	10932	1.6	54	3674	3946	4226	1.7	2.58	2899	3073	1.4
27041 PILOT MOUNTAIN	171	6412	6864	7358	1.6	55	2664	2902	3154	2.0	2.36	1939	2075	1.6
27042 PINE HALL	169	645	668	709	0.8	32	259	273	294	1.3	2.45	189	196	0.9
27043 PINNACLE	171	6024	6428	6878	1.5	53	2342	2530	2738	1.8	2.54	1784	1903	1.5
27045 RURAL HALL	067	7869	8243	8748	1.1	39	3285	3474	3710	1.3	2.37	2349	2445	1.0
27046 SANDY RIDGE	169	1951	2059	2208	1.3	47	779	835	908	1.7	2.47	576	609	1.3
27047 SILOAM	171	1053	1135	1208	1.8	59	413	450	484	2.0	2.52	328	353	1.7
27048 STONEVILLE	157	8390	8611	8874	0.6	25	3288	3432	3591	1.0	2.51	2472	2544	0.7
27050 TOBACCOVILLE	067	3931	4062	4263	0.8	29	1575	1645	1740	1.0	2.47	1196	1232	0.7
27051 WALKERTOWN	067	6677	6853	7162	0.6	25	2656	2751	2893	0.8	2.47	1996	2032	0.4
27052 WALNUT COVE	169	10363	10781	11590	0.9	35	4081	4298	4683	1.2	2.47	2958	3072	0.9
27053 WESTFIELD	169	2833	2945	3132	0.9	34	1111	1168	1258	1.2	2.50	831	863	0.9
27054 WOODLEAF	159	2482	2875	3206	3.5	89	917	1066	1193	3.6	2.70	700	802	3.3
27055 YADKINVILLE	197	13415	14087	15126	1.2	42	5252	5573	6044	1.4	2.45	3842	4027	1.1
27101 WINSTON SALEM	067	20156	19999	20665	-0.2	7	8371	8292	8613	-0.2	2.15	4153	4026	-0.7
27103 WINSTON SALEM	067	26614	28413	30508	1.6	53	11982	12870	13883	1.7	2.17	6913	7278	1.2
27104 WINSTON SALEM	067	26934	27610	28997	0.6	24	12567	13002	13740	0.8	2.10	7304	7378	0.2
27105 WINSTON SALEM	067	39681	40204	42044	0.3	16	15065	15303	16055	0.4	2.57	10150	10121	-0.1
27106 WINSTON SALEM	067	42047	44164	46677	1.2	42	16850	17808	18955	1.3	2.28	10350	10687	0.8
27107 WINSTON SALEM	057	38773	41835	44865	1.8	60	14738	16008	17272	2.0	2.57	10698	11457	1.6
27110 WINSTON SALEM	067	750	753	756	0.1	12	0	0	0	0.0	0.00	0	0	0.0
27127 WINSTON SALEM	067	24827	26377	28122	1.4	51	10215	10915	11693	1.6	2.38	6762	7065	1.0
27203 ASHEBORO	151	20052	20677	21841	0.7	27	8138	8392	8903	0.7	2.39	5117	5183	0.3
27205 ASHEBORO	151	30379	32284	34563	1.4	51	11449	12285	13267	1.7	2.60	8800	9332	1.4
27207 BEAR CREEK	037	3390	3873	4555	3.2	86	1321	1533	1827	3.6	2.50	1008	1158	3.3
27208 BENNETT	037	1874	2151	2490	3.3	87	746	869	1016	3.7	2.48	561	645	3.3
27209 BISCOE	123	4161	4366	4663	1.1	40	1431	1512	1631	1.3	2.81	1060	1105	1.0
27212 BLANCH	033	1931	1969	2052	0.5	21	547	575	616	1.2	2.60	406	422	0.9
27214 BROWNS SUMMIT	081	8089	8816	9559	2.1	66	3071	3396	3728	2.4	2.58	2275	2489	2.1
27215 BURLINGTON	001	33084	34771	37642	1.2	42	14238	15103	16485	1.4	2.28	9105	9473	0.9
27217 BURLINGTON	001	34674	36195	39059	1.0	37	13201	13870	15077	1.2	2.55	9316	9650	0.8
27229 CANDOR	123	2972	3154	3391	1.4	50	1032	1094	1183	1.4	2.85	774	811	1.1
27231 CEDAR GROVE	135	1857	1891	2038	0.4	19	700	722	785	0.7	2.62	518	527	0.4
27233 CLIMAX	151	2871	2936	3084	0.5	23	1088	1128	1197	0.9	2.60	853	873	0.6
27235 COLFAX	081	2210	2704	3093	4.9	96	843	1044	1208	5.2	2.59	640	782	4.8
27239 DENTON	057	8736	9409	10055	1.8	59	3375	3676	3970	2.0	2.53	2560	2750	1.7
27242 EAGLE SPRINGS	125	2020	2120	2267	1.1	40	729	775	840	1.5	2.54	548	574	1.1
27243 EFLAND	135	3402	3653	3997	1.7	57	1347	1462	1611	2.0	2.50	1003	1074	1.6
27244 ELON	001	11501	12527	13649	2.0	65	3721	4167	4652	2.7	2.54	2549	2805	2.3
27248 FRANKLINVILLE	151	3845	4429	4934	3.4	88	1488	1732	1947	3.6	2.55	1130	1297	3.3
27249 GIBSONVILLE	081	10338	11270	12228	2.1	66	4026	4464	4905	2.5	2.51	2999	3284	2.2
27252 GOLDSTON	037	1991	2163	2478	2.0	64	819	903	1048	2.3	2.38	590	644	1.7
27253 GRAHAM	001	25307	27957	30892	2.4	74	10130	11278	12553	2.6	2.44	7066	7755	2.2
27258 HAW RIVER	001	5845	6485	7213	2.5	76	2389	2679	3005	2.7	2.40	1735	1923	2.5
27260 HIGH POINT	081	25417	25625	26851	0.2	13	9413	9590	10164	0.4	2.60	6299	6296	0.0
27262 HIGH POINT	081	22977	22939	23915	0.0	10	9270	9324	9832	0.1	2.32	5891	5804	-0.4
27263 HIGH POINT	151	17509	18376	19560	1.1	40	7163	7633	8220	1.5	2.39	5096	5343	1.1
27265 HIGH POINT	081	32912	37108	40986	2.9	82	13233	15018	16736	3.0	2.46	9349	10551	2.9
27278 HILLSBOROUGH	135	21976	23453	25556	1.5	53	8443	9139	10055	1.9	2.52	6114	6520	1.5
27281 JACKSON SPRINGS	125	3372	3679	4019	2.1	68	1072	1190	1319	2.5	3.04	824	903	2.2
27282 JAMESTOWN	081	13322	15142	16782	3.1	85	5154	5951	6683	3.4	2.54	3907	4448	3.1
27283 JULIAN	081	3124	3216	3377	0.7	27	1219	1278	1361	1.1	2.52	955	987	0.8
27284 KERNERSVILLE	067	42195	46013	49743	2.1	67	16787	18432	20030	2.2	2.48	12333	13369	1.9
27288 EDEN	157	25042	24794	25198	-0.2	6	10318	10343	10653	0.1	2.36	7128	7042	-0.3
27291 LEASBURG	033	1862	1970	2104	1.3	48	745	801	869	1.7	2.46	540	573	1.4
27292 LEXINGTON	057	39105	40121	41964	0.6	25	15380	15973	16905	0.9	2.46	10897	11177	0.6
27295 LEXINGTON	057	35141	36674	38549	1.0	36	13959	14763	15701	1.3	2.46	10301	10751	1.0
27298 LIBERTY	151	9398	10070	10865	1.6	56	3659	3955	4301	1.9	2.54	2694	2866	1.5
27299 LINWOOD	057	4384	4876	5282	2.5	77	1674	1889	2070	2.9	2.55	1251	1389	2.1
27301 MC LEANSVILLE	081	5705	6212	6717	2.0	65	2135	2363	2591	2.4	2.58	1638	1788	2.1
27302 MEBANE	001	21176	23125	25455	2.1	68	8238	9120	10137	2.4	2.52	6005	6547	2.1
27305 MILTON	033	1580	1803	2000	3.2	86	571	663	748	3.6	2.70	430	493	3.3
27306 MOUNT GILEAD	123	5687	6146	6735	1.8	61	2203	2430	2707	2.3	2.50	1629	1774	2.0
27310 OAK RIDGE	081	3741	4162	4527	2.5	78	1296	1460	1605	2.8	2.85	1076	1198	2.6
27311 PELHAM	033	3952	4039	4262	0.5	22	1550	1614	1732	1.0	2.50	1141	1173	0.7
27312 PITTSBORO	037	14218	16170	18949	3.1	85	5926	6862	8160	3.5	2.32	4098	4676	3.2
27313 PLEASANT GARDEN	081	6557	6935	7385	1.3	48	2473	2657	2866	1.7	2.59	1971	2095	1.5
27314 PROSPECT HILL	033	822	844	885	0.6	26	328	343	366	1.1	2.44	247	255	0.8
27315 PROVIDENCE	033	1745	1872	2030	1.7	57	732	798	879	2.1	2.35	532	572	1.7
27316 RAMSEUR	151	6934	7425	7991	1.6	55	2642	2840	3074	1.7	2.61	1940	2052	1.3
27317 RANDLEMAN	151	15093	16174	17451	1.6	56	5886	6360	6914	1.8	2.53	4369	4664	1.6
27320 REIDSVILLE	157	38270	39790	41441	0.9	34	15144	16001	16915	1.3	2.44	10787	11226	0.9
27325 ROBBINS	125	6516	6857	7377	1.2	44	2483	2625	2844	1.3	2.61	1792	1864	0.9
27326 RUFFIN	157	3591	3545	3626	-0.3	5	1428	1437	1495	0.2	2.45	1033	1025	-0.2
27330 SANFORD	105	32258	33479	35265	0.9	33	12021	12554	13300	1.0	2.60	8605	8864	0.7
27332 SANFORD	105	23589	25947	28537	2.3	72	8833	9728	10715	2.3	2.66	6605	7193	2.0
NORTH CAROLINA					1.9					2.2	2.46			1.8
UNITED STATES					1.2					1.3	2.58			1.1

ZIP CODE #	POST OFFICE NAME	RACE (%) White 2000	White 2004	Black 2000	Black 2004	Asian/Pacific 2000	Asian/Pacific 2004	% Hispanic Origin 2000	% Hispanic Origin 2004	2004 AGE DISTRIBUTION (%) 0-4	5-9	10-14	15-19	20-24	25-44	45-64	65-84	85+	18+	MEDIAN AGE 2004	% 2004 Males	% 2004 Females
27006	ADVANCE	95.7	95.1	2.7	3.0	0.4	0.4	1.4	1.9	5.8	6.5	7.0	5.3	4.3	25.4	30.4	13.3	2.0	77.1	42.5	49.2	50.8
27007	ARARAT	94.5	93.4	0.7	0.8	0.2	0.2	5.9	7.5	6.9	7.0	7.2	6.1	6.5	31.2	25.6	8.7	1.0	75.3	35.6	51.0	49.0
27009	BELEWS CREEK	90.2	88.6	7.5	8.4	0.1	0.1	1.9	2.6	7.1	7.4	6.6	5.2	4.1	31.0	28.2	9.4	1.0	75.5	38.8	50.0	50.0
27011	BOONVILLE	92.7	92.0	3.7	3.6	0.2	0.3	4.9	6.3	6.5	6.7	7.1	5.8	5.2	29.3	25.5	12.6	1.4	76.2	38.7	49.7	50.3
27012	CLEMMONS	92.4	91.2	4.6	5.0	1.4	1.6	1.8	2.5	6.3	7.0	8.2	6.3	4.3	28.4	28.7	9.6	1.3	74.4	39.5	48.7	51.3
27013	CLEVELAND	80.8	79.0	16.1	17.2	0.5	0.6	2.6	3.3	7.4	7.4	8.0	6.8	5.9	30.0	24.1	9.4	1.1	72.8	35.6	49.8	50.2
27016	DANBURY	96.1	95.3	1.5	1.7	0.2	0.3	2.5	3.2	5.6	6.2	6.7	5.3	5.7	28.2	28.3	12.6	1.6	78.3	40.2	49.7	50.3
27017	DOBSON	85.9	83.5	2.1	2.1	0.1	0.1	15.6	19.1	7.1	7.0	6.7	5.9	6.4	30.4	24.0	11.1	1.3	75.6	36.1	52.0	48.0
27018	EAST BEND	94.5	93.8	2.4	2.5	0.3	0.4	4.3	5.4	6.4	6.6	7.1	6.3	5.4	29.4	26.9	10.8	1.2	76.1	38.9	50.0	50.0
27019	GERMANTON	94.7	94.1	3.6	3.8	0.2	0.2	1.2	1.6	6.0	6.3	7.0	6.1	4.9	28.8	28.1	11.7	1.2	76.9	39.9	49.3	50.7
27020	HAMPTONVILLE	93.8	92.4	1.1	1.1	0.2	0.2	8.7	11.3	7.0	7.1	7.2	5.9	5.5	29.5	25.0	11.6	1.2	75.1	37.0	51.0	49.0
27021	KING	97.2	96.8	1.2	1.3	0.3	0.4	1.5	1.9	6.7	6.8	7.1	6.0	5.4	29.7	26.7	10.2	1.5	75.7	38.1	49.0	51.0
27022	LAWSONVILLE	95.5	94.9	1.6	1.7	0.2	0.2	3.3	4.2	5.4	6.0	6.6	5.4	5.8	27.9	28.9	12.5	1.4	78.6	40.6	49.7	50.3
27023	LEWISVILLE	92.7	91.6	4.6	5.1	1.2	1.4	1.3	1.9	6.8	7.3	7.4	6.3	5.0	28.2	29.3	8.9	0.7	74.6	39.4	49.2	50.8
27024	LOWGAP	96.8	96.2	0.6	0.6	0.0	0.0	2.2	2.7	6.0	6.4	6.6	6.7	5.3	29.3	26.9	11.8	1.1	76.6	38.2	51.1	48.9
27025	MADISON	82.7	82.1	14.7	14.8	0.3	0.4	2.3	2.9	6.2	6.4	6.5	5.7	5.4	29.1	26.3	12.4	2.0	77.4	39.4	49.6	50.4
27027	MAYODAN	89.0	88.1	7.5	7.6	0.3	0.4	3.5	4.5	5.7	5.6	5.9	5.3	5.4	27.6	26.2	15.9	2.4	79.6	41.4	47.5	52.5
27028	MOCKSVILLE	88.1	87.2	8.6	8.9	0.3	0.4	4.4	5.7	6.7	6.8	6.9	5.9	5.6	29.0	25.7	12.1	1.5	76.1	38.1	49.7	50.3
27030	MOUNT AIRY	90.1	89.0	5.4	5.5	1.0	1.2	5.1	6.6	6.4	6.5	6.7	5.9	5.5	27.9	24.9	14.3	2.1	76.9	39.2	48.9	51.1
27040	PFAFFTOWN	90.0	88.8	7.9	8.7	0.5	0.6	1.2	1.7	5.5	6.4	7.2	6.1	4.4	24.6	31.6	12.9	1.4	77.1	42.9	48.8	51.2
27041	PILOT MOUNTAIN	93.3	92.3	3.8	4.2	0.3	0.3	2.7	3.3	6.1	6.3	6.6	6.2	5.4	28.5	27.0	12.3	1.7	77.3	39.3	48.6	51.4
27042	PINE HALL	86.2	84.6	11.8	12.9	0.2	0.2	1.7	2.3	6.6	6.4	6.3	5.7	5.5	31.7	27.0	9.3	1.5	77.4	37.8	48.8	51.2
27043	PINNACLE	95.1	94.5	2.8	3.0	0.1	0.1	2.1	2.7	6.2	6.4	7.1	5.9	5.4	29.5	27.6	10.9	1.1	76.7	39.0	49.9	50.1
27045	RURAL HALL	83.7	82.2	12.1	12.6	0.4	0.4	3.5	4.6	6.1	6.4	6.6	5.5	4.7	29.0	27.2	13.4	1.1	77.5	40.5	48.6	51.4
27046	SANDY RIDGE	95.9	95.2	1.6	1.8	0.6	0.6	2.9	3.7	4.8	5.4	6.8	5.6	5.4	30.7	27.3	12.5	1.5	79.5	39.8	49.8	50.2
27047	SILOAM	95.7	95.1	1.3	1.4	0.2	0.3	2.0	2.5	6.5	6.4	6.2	5.4	5.6	32.4	25.6	10.8	1.1	77.7	37.6	52.1	47.9
27048	STONEVILLE	81.9	80.9	13.1	13.0	0.3	0.3	6.4	7.7	6.2	6.6	7.0	5.7	5.2	28.6	28.0	11.4	1.3	76.7	39.1	49.7	50.3
27050	TOBACCOVILLE	91.6	90.5	6.7	7.5	0.2	0.3	1.6	2.2	6.6	6.9	7.1	6.3	5.5	29.3	27.6	9.9	1.0	75.6	38.6	49.3	50.7
27051	WALKERTOWN	83.7	82.0	13.6	14.8	0.3	0.4	1.6	2.3	6.7	6.9	6.6	5.7	4.9	29.8	25.9	12.2	1.3	76.3	39.0	48.7	51.3
27052	WALNUT COVE	86.6	86.2	11.6	11.7	0.2	0.2	1.4	1.9	6.5	6.7	6.7	5.8	5.1	29.4	26.4	11.8	1.6	76.4	38.9	49.1	50.9
27053	WESTFIELD	91.5	90.6	6.5	7.0	0.1	0.1	2.4	3.1	6.8	7.1	6.7	5.8	5.3	28.1	27.1	11.4	1.6	75.7	38.8	49.5	50.5
27054	WOODLEAF	76.0	73.4	19.1	20.6	0.2	0.2	5.4	7.1	7.2	7.3	7.7	7.0	5.8	29.8	24.0	10.0	1.1	73.4	35.7	50.3	49.7
27055	YADKINVILLE	92.2	91.3	3.2	3.2	0.2	0.2	8.1	10.1	6.8	6.8	6.6	5.4	5.0	29.1	25.1	13.1	2.1	76.5	39.0	49.7	50.3
27101	WINSTON SALEM	37.0	35.3	56.3	56.7	0.6	0.7	7.3	9.1	6.5	6.3	6.3	7.3	9.0	31.5	21.5	10.0	1.7	77.5	34.1	48.6	51.4
27103	WINSTON SALEM	75.8	73.5	16.3	17.1	2.2	2.5	7.2	9.0	6.3	5.9	5.6	5.1	6.4	31.5	22.9	13.7	2.5	79.0	38.0	46.6	53.5
27104	WINSTON SALEM	86.6	85.1	9.5	10.2	1.9	2.2	2.7	3.7	5.1	5.6	6.3	5.8	5.4	26.9	27.5	15.1	2.4	79.5	41.7	46.4	53.6
27105	WINSTON SALEM	30.9	30.0	62.0	61.8	0.3	0.4	10.4	12.2	7.2	7.2	7.8	6.8	7.0	27.9	22.2	11.9	2.1	73.8	35.4	47.4	52.6
27106	WINSTON SALEM	71.5	69.5	22.2	22.9	1.4	1.7	6.8	8.5	5.9	5.9	6.2	9.0	10.8	26.2	22.1	11.5	2.4	78.5	34.5	47.3	52.7
27107	WINSTON SALEM	61.6	60.8	31.2	30.8	0.3	0.4	10.1	11.8	7.2	7.1	7.1	6.4	6.5	30.2	24.1	10.6	0.9	74.8	36.0	48.5	51.5
27110	WINSTON SALEM	0.8	0.7	98.4	98.4	0.0	0.0	0.8	0.8	0.0	0.0	0.9	60.4	33.9	2.9	1.9	0.0	0.0	98.8	19.1	32.9	67.1
27127	WINSTON SALEM	66.3	64.3	26.4	26.9	1.2	1.4	7.7	9.6	7.7	7.2	6.7	5.8	6.4	32.2	22.3	10.6	1.3	75.0	35.4	47.5	52.5
27203	ASHEBORO	74.8	73.3	13.3	12.8	1.4	1.6	20.7	25.6	7.8	7.1	6.4	6.0	7.4	30.6	20.1	12.2	2.4	75.4	34.2	49.4	50.7
27205	ASHEBORO	92.0	90.8	3.0	3.1	0.6	0.7	5.7	7.3	6.6	6.8	7.1	6.3	5.4	29.0	26.4	11.0	1.4	75.5	38.1	49.6	50.4
27207	BEAR CREEK	81.1	80.1	16.6	17.0	0.2	0.2	2.9	3.8	5.4	5.9	6.8	6.4	5.4	26.6	29.4	12.7	1.4	77.9	40.8	49.6	50.4
27208	BENNETT	91.5	91.0	6.5	6.5	0.2	0.2	2.0	2.6	6.0	6.2	6.0	5.4	5.1	27.9	27.5	13.9	2.0	78.4	40.6	50.3	49.7
27209	BISCOE	67.7	65.5	16.6	15.7	0.7	0.8	23.9	29.5	7.7	7.8	7.4	6.6	6.7	28.9	22.1	10.6	2.2	72.9	34.0	49.7	50.3
27212	BLANCH	48.5	47.3	48.7	49.4	0.4	0.6	1.6	2.0	5.5	5.5	5.1	4.9	7.1	34.0	25.1	11.0	1.7	80.7	37.6	58.3	41.8
27214	BROWNS SUMMIT	71.0	69.5	25.4	26.3	0.3	0.4	3.2	4.1	7.1	7.1	7.1	6.0	6.1	31.7	24.6	9.5	0.9	75.0	35.8	50.1	49.9
27215	BURLINGTON	82.5	81.3	11.8	11.9	1.7	2.0	5.8	7.2	5.8	5.9	6.4	6.0	5.9	28.2	24.9	14.6	2.3	78.1	39.4	47.6	52.4
27217	BURLINGTON	57.6	56.2	34.1	33.9	0.8	0.9	10.2	12.6	6.8	6.6	7.0	6.5	5.8	29.1	23.6	12.5	2.0	75.5	37.4	48.5	51.5
27229	CANDOR	53.9	51.8	28.1	26.4	0.6	0.6	25.7	31.4	9.1	8.5	7.7	6.0	7.2	29.0	21.0	10.0	1.4	71.0	32.0	51.2	48.8
27231	CEDAR GROVE	68.3	66.4	26.0	27.0	0.2	0.2	5.0	6.0	5.5	6.1	6.8	6.3	4.8	29.1	29.8	10.3	1.3	77.6	40.4	48.9	51.1
27233	CLIMAX	94.9	94.1	2.6	2.8	0.2	0.2	1.5	2.0	6.1	6.5	7.1	6.4	5.2	28.6	28.6	10.4	1.1	76.3	39.7	49.5	50.5
27235	COLFAX	92.9	91.4	4.1	4.9	1.6	2.1	1.3	1.7	6.7	7.1	7.5	6.3	5.1	31.0	26.5	8.9	1.0	74.8	38.0	49.4	50.6
27239	DENTON	98.3	98.0	0.4	0.4	0.3	0.3	1.0	1.3	6.0	6.3	7.0	6.2	5.7	29.0	27.1	11.0	1.7	76.9	38.8	49.5	50.5
27242	EAGLE SPRINGS	60.6	58.8	32.4	32.7	0.3	0.3	7.6	9.8	6.9	7.2	9.4	11.3	5.8	26.0	22.7	9.5	1.3	67.6	33.1	50.5	49.5
27243	EFLAND	70.0	69.4	26.4	26.3	0.4	0.4	3.3	4.2	6.4	6.9	7.3	6.0	5.0	30.2	28.1	9.2	0.9	75.6	38.4	48.2	51.8
27244	ELON	85.4	84.2	12.3	13.0	0.8	0.9	1.7	2.3	4.5	5.0	5.7	16.4	14.3	21.5	21.6	9.6	1.4	81.6	30.1	47.0	53.0
27248	FRANKLINVILLE	93.7	92.4	2.0	2.2	0.2	0.2	4.3	5.9	7.3	7.1	7.1	6.6	5.8	29.0	26.0	10.1	1.0	74.4	37.1	50.2	49.8
27249	GIBSONVILLE	79.6	77.8	17.1	18.2	0.4	0.5	2.7	3.4	6.1	6.4	6.8	6.0	5.0	28.8	27.6	11.7	1.6	77.0	39.7	49.0	51.0
27252	GOLDSTON	78.0	76.9	20.3	21.1	0.1	0.1	1.5	1.9	4.7	5.2	6.0	5.6	4.8	25.6	32.2	14.2	1.8	80.9	43.7	49.3	50.7
27253	GRAHAM	79.4	78.1	15.0	15.1	0.6	0.7	8.8	11.1	7.0	6.8	6.6	6.0	6.0	30.8	24.0	11.4	1.4	76.0	36.7	48.7	51.3
27258	HAW RIVER	83.6	81.6	12.3	13.3	0.4	0.5	5.2	6.7	6.7	7.0	7.1	6.0	5.2	31.1	25.6	10.1	1.3	75.5	37.5	48.6	51.4
27260	HIGH POINT	28.3	26.2	62.7	63.5	3.7	4.1	6.4	7.6	8.4	7.9	8.2	7.3	7.0	28.6	21.3	9.7	1.7	71.1	33.0	47.2	52.8
27262	HIGH POINT	70.3	67.9	22.0	23.0	2.3	2.7	6.4	8.0	6.6	6.3	6.4	7.0	7.7	27.7	22.5	13.2	2.6	77.2	36.9	47.8	52.3
27263	HIGH POINT	87.9	86.7	6.3	6.5	2.8	3.3	2.5	3.3	6.4	6.4	6.6	5.6	5.7	30.2	25.5	12.4	1.4	77.4	38.2	49.5	50.5
27265	HIGH POINT	81.2	79.7	14.2	14.8	2.3	2.8	2.4	3.0	6.7	6.7	6.8	5.9	5.9	30.8	25.8	10.1	1.3	76.2	37.6	48.5	51.5
27278	HILLSBOROUGH	78.9	78.2	17.1	17.1	0.7	0.8	3.0	3.8	6.0	6.5	7.5	6.4	5.0	29.4	28.7	9.3	1.1	76.0	38.9	49.1	50.9
27281	JACKSON SPRINGS	65.0	64.4	24.8	23.5	0.3	0.3	14.2	17.0	7.1	7.1	7.8	6.7	6.0	25.5	23.7	14.7	1.4	73.5	37.2	50.7	49.3
27282	JAMESTOWN	81.3	78.5	12.2	13.3	4.3	5.6	2.0	2.7	7.6	7.8	7.4	5.8	4.4	33.2	24.6	8.7	0.7	73.6	36.7	48.8	51.3
27283	JULIAN	95.7	95.2	3.0	3.4	0.3	0.4	0.9	1.1	5.6	6.1	6.4	5.8	4.8	28.1	29.4	12.5	1.4	78.4	41.3	50.2	49.8
27284	KERNERSVILLE	88.3	86.6	7.2	7.8	1.0	1.3	4.1	5.2	6.7	6.8	6.8	6.3	5.6	30.3	26.6	9.9	1.0	75.9	37.8	49.3	50.7
27288	EDEN	78.1	77.0	19.7	20.3	0.3	0.4	2.2	2.8	6.0	6.0	6.3	6.0	5.7	26.9	26.2	14.8	2.3	78.0	40.3	47.2	52.8
27291	LEASBURG	74.5	74.0	23.8	24.0	0.1	0.1	1.5	1.9	5.0	5.6	7.3	6.0	5.2	26.2	29.8	13.1	1.8	78.2	41.7	49.1	50.9
27292	LEXINGTON	79.3	78.6	15.5	15.3	1.0	1.2	5.2	6.3	6.7	6.5	6.6	6.1	6.3	29.6	25.7	11.1	1.4	76.5	37.6	49.4	50.6
27295	LEXINGTON	91.7	90.8	4.2	4.5	1.6	1.8	2.2	2.8	6.3	6.6	6.9	5.7	5.2	29.9	26.0	12.1	1.4	76.7	38.9	49.4	50.6
27298	LIBERTY	84.0	82.8	11.0	11.3	0.2	0.3	6.0	7.7	6.3	6.7	7.1	6.2	5.4	29.5	26.0	11.4	1.4	76.0	38.1	50.5	49.5
27299	LINWOOD	96.3	95.7	1.6	1.7	0.5	0.6	1.3	1.8	6.4	6.8	7.8	6.3	5.6	32.9	24.8	8.4	1.0	74.9	36.0	50.5	49.5
27301	MC LEANSVILLE	79.8	77.5	16.7	18.3	0.5	0.6	2.7	3.6	6.6	6.9	7.2	6.3	5.3	30.9	26.3	9.9	0.8	75.5	37.5	50.3	49.7
27302	MEBANE	75.1	73.7	21.2	21.9	0.4	0.5	3.9	5.1	6.8	7.0	7.2	6.2	5.6	30.7	25.2	10.2	1.2	75.1	37.3	48.8	51.2
27305	MILTON	46.4	45.3	50.8	51.5	0.7	0.8	2.0	2.4	6.3	6.4	6.9	6.3	6.2	26.8	29.0	11.1	1.0	76.6	39.1	48.8	51.3
27306	MOUNT GILEAD	53.6	52.5	40.4	40.5	3.8	4.4	2.3	2.7	6.1	6.3	6.6	6.0	5.4	24.8	28.6	14.7	1.6	77.5	41.7	49.3	50.7
27310	OAK RIDGE	92.9	92.0	4.6	5.0	0.5	0.6	1.8	2.5	6.0	7.1	8.6	7.6	4.0	29.0	29.6	7.1	1.0	73.2	39.3	49.6	50.4
27311	PELHAM	71.8	71.4	26.4	26.7	0.1	0.1	1.8	2.2	5.2	5.5	6.6	6.4	5.4	28.0	29.2	12.4	1.4	78.8	40.8	49.4	50.6
27312	PITTSBORO	78.6	77.6	18.0	18.3	0.5	0.6	3.1	4.0	5.6	6.1	5.9	5.3	4.5	27.4	28.3	15.0	1.9	78.9	42.2	48.4	51.6
27313	PLEASANT GARDEN	91.0	89.9	6.7	7.3	0.2	0.2	1.3	1.8	6.1	6.5	7.0	6.2	4.6	27.9	29.9	10.4	1.4	76.5	40.6	48.8	51.2
27314	PROSPECT HILL	69.7	69.2	28.6	28.8	0.1	0.1	1.5	1.8	5.5	6.0	7.8	5.9	5.3	27.7	28.9	11.6	1.2	76.9	40.3	50.1	49.9
27315	PROVIDENCE	85.4	85.5	12.6	12.3	0.1	0.1	1.3	1.6	5.1	5.5	6.0	5.7	6.2	26.6	29.3	14.3	1.3	80.1	42.2	49.4	50.6
27316	RAMSEUR	81.0	78.8	12.2	12.8	0.4	0.5	8.6	11.0	7.2	7.1	7.2	6.2	6.0	29.3	23.9	11.7	1.5	74.9	36.5	50.1	49.9
27317	RANDLEMAN	92.1	90.9	4.0	4.3	0.3	0.4	5.5	7.0	7.3	7.2	7.0	6.3	5.9	30.8	24.8	9.8	1.0	74.6	36.4	49.7	50.3
27320	REIDSVILLE	70.3	69.3	26.4	26.8	0.4	0.4	3.0	3.8	6.1	6.3	6.8	6.0	5.6	27.9	26.8	12.7	1.8	77.0	39.5	48.6	51.4
27325	ROBBINS	78.3	75.2	7.6	7.8	0.3	0.3	18.4	22.5	7.4	6.9	6.6	6.8	7.3	28.2	22.5	12.9	1.6	75.1	35.7	50.5	49.5
27326	RUFFIN	75.6	74.8	21.7	21.9	0.1	0.1	3.2	4.2	5.8	6.0	6.1	5.7	5.6	28.3	27.9	13.0	1.6	78.7	40.3	50.3	49.7
27330	SANFORD	67.9	66.1	22.7	22.6	0.9	1.0	11.8	14.5	7.0	6.9	6.9	6.6	6.9	28.5	24.6	11.0	1.7	75.3	36.7	49.4	50.6
27332	SANFORD	72.9	71.3	18.1	18.0	0.7	0.9	9.5	11.5	7.6	7.2	7.4	6.6	6.6	30.7	22.5	10.6	0.8	73.8	35.0	49.7	50.3
	NORTH CAROLINA	72.1	71.2	21.6	21.6	1.5	1.8	4.7	5.9	6.7	6.6	6.8	6.7	7.1	29.8	24.2	10.8	1.4	76.2	36.2	49.2	50.8
	UNITED STATES	75.1	73.6	12.3	12.5	3.8	4.2	12.5	14.1	6.9	6.7	7.2	7.0	7.3	28.6	23.8	10.8	1.7	75.1	36.0	49.1	50.9

ZIP CODE #	POST OFFICE NAME	2004 Per Capita Income	2004 HH Income Base	2004 HOUSEHOLD INCOME DISTRIBUTION (%) Less than $25,000	$25,000 to $49,999	$50,000 to $99,999	$100,000 to $149,999	$150,000 or More	MEDIAN HOUSEHOLD INCOME 2004	2009	2004 National Centile	2004 State Centile	2004 Home Value Base	2004 HOME VALUE DISTRIBUTION (%) Less than $50,000	$50,000 to $89,999	$90,000 to $174,999	$175,000 to $399,999	$400,000 or More	2004 Median Home Value
27006	ADVANCE	31566	5183	17.2	25.4	33.9	13.1	10.5	57962	67795	83	91	4563	12.9	8.6	31.6	36.5	10.4	166022
27007	ARARAT	17935	933	29.6	35.3	28.7	4.0	2.5	40451	46145	48	54	768	19.5	26.7	40.1	13.3	0.4	94462
27009	BELEWS CREEK	24017	915	18.9	29.0	39.8	9.5	2.8	51357	58410	74	87	806	14.9	18.1	41.9	22.6	2.5	119309
27011	BOONVILLE	20207	2252	30.6	34.3	27.2	5.2	2.7	38816	44142	42	47	1809	20.3	24.8	39.1	14.0	1.9	95173
27012	CLEMMONS	31870	9238	11.5	22.3	39.4	16.2	10.6	66858	77929	90	96	7801	4.4	5.2	44.8	42.3	3.4	168153
27013	CLEVELAND	19497	2457	25.2	30.9	35.3	6.5	2.2	43670	49249	58	69	2038	21.9	21.4	39.5	15.8	1.4	101727
27016	DANBURY	17819	745	31.1	33.2	31.0	3.1	1.6	39104	44045	43	48	616	29.6	27.1	29.7	12.0	1.6	79828
27017	DOBSON	18505	3375	35.3	30.3	28.0	4.4	2.0	35868	40168	31	34	2628	24.6	21.7	37.2	15.0	1.6	97153
27018	EAST BEND	21444	3175	25.1	32.3	32.7	7.8	2.1	43295	48935	57	68	2637	25.9	19.0	35.2	18.2	1.7	97445
27019	GERMANTON	21116	1761	24.9	34.6	31.7	6.8	2.0	42597	48112	55	66	1473	18.7	18.3	42.2	19.7	1.2	111068
27020	HAMPTONVILLE	20329	2529	27.6	33.5	30.5	6.3	2.2	41301	46826	51	60	2064	23.1	26.5	35.8	13.0	1.6	90533
27021	KING	22749	6874	23.3	29.1	36.7	8.2	2.8	47913	53264	68	83	5426	14.2	20.8	49.4	14.1	1.5	108971
27022	LAWSONVILLE	18936	687	32.2	33.0	29.6	2.9	2.3	37758	42772	38	43	568	28.7	26.8	29.4	13.7	1.4	81622
27023	LEWISVILLE	32609	4171	11.8	22.0	40.1	16.0	10.1	66393	77454	89	95	3447	4.4	7.3	47.2	34.2	6.8	159689
27024	LOWGAP	17510	1153	34.9	36.9	22.8	3.9	1.6	33795	37632	23	24	950	27.3	28.6	33.5	8.8	1.8	81385
27025	MADISON	19187	4607	29.5	34.0	29.4	5.4	1.8	40153	45582	47	53	3654	21.1	23.9	40.3	13.6	1.1	97038
27027	MAYODAN	17701	1944	38.2	34.5	23.4	3.2	0.7	31702	35549	17	17	1310	26.0	37.1	29.5	7.3	0.2	76929
27028	MOCKSVILLE	21490	10024	28.1	33.0	29.0	7.1	2.7	40341	46553	47	54	7949	20.3	23.9	38.4	14.8	2.7	99697
27030	MOUNT AIRY	19607	16153	35.0	34.5	23.4	4.3	2.8	34766	38752	27	29	12064	20.1	29.8	35.8	12.6	1.7	90119
27040	PFAFFTOWN	30209	3946	13.5	21.8	42.0	14.7	8.0	63599	73609	88	94	3530	4.3	8.2	54.5	30.8	2.2	145300
27041	PILOT MOUNTAIN	21755	2902	29.3	32.1	29.4	6.3	2.9	40881	46531	49	57	2221	18.6	22.4	42.3	14.7	2.1	105007
27042	PINE HALL	16032	273	40.7	34.4	19.8	2.2	2.9	28812	33080	10	9	223	24.7	30.9	35.0	9.4	0.0	86429
27043	PINNACLE	21851	2530	24.7	32.2	33.5	7.9	1.7	44547	50000	60	73	2080	19.2	16.9	39.4	20.9	3.6	114213
27045	RURAL HALL	24367	3474	22.3	30.4	36.3	8.2	2.8	47759	54945	68	82	2711	8.3	19.5	59.5	11.6	1.1	113704
27046	SANDY RIDGE	19997	835	31.4	34.1	27.9	2.6	4.0	37432	42819	37	41	699	32.9	23.9	35.1	8.2	0.0	75469
27047	SILOAM	19403	450	32.0	30.7	29.3	5.8	2.2	37391	42177	37	41	371	23.2	21.0	37.2	18.6	0.0	95513
27048	STONEVILLE	19682	3432	26.1	33.4	33.0	5.7	1.9	41797	47267	52	61	2767	21.7	23.2	43.0	11.4	0.7	96159
27050	TOBACCOVILLE	24001	1645	18.6	30.3	41.0	7.8	2.3	50642	57878	73	86	1380	12.9	14.4	58.6	13.0	1.2	114345
27051	WALKERTOWN	22557	2751	22.7	28.1	39.5	8.0	1.7	49169	56322	70	85	2255	12.6	26.1	52.4	8.3	0.6	103552
27052	WALNUT COVE	19770	4298	26.6	34.1	33.5	4.6	1.2	42037	47111	53	62	3512	21.8	24.0	40.8	12.9	0.6	95906
27053	WESTFIELD	17785	1168	36.0	32.9	25.4	3.3	2.4	35257	40000	28	31	961	25.7	30.0	33.0	10.0	1.4	83588
27054	WOODLEAF	18341	1066	24.0	34.4	35.5	5.1	1.0	43594	48721	58	69	861	25.1	21.3	39.3	12.2	2.2	95526
27055	YADKINVILLE	21633	5573	27.6	31.7	31.2	6.3	3.2	41337	47046	51	60	4505	19.9	22.6	39.7	16.2	1.7	99404
27101	WINSTON SALEM	17306	8292	47.3	28.6	17.6	4.6	1.9	26529	30965	6	4	2986	15.3	30.3	42.7	10.3	1.3	94498
27103	WINSTON SALEM	27727	12870	22.7	28.8	35.2	9.4	3.9	48605	56740	69	84	7876	6.2	13.2	62.3	17.9	0.4	123811
27104	WINSTON SALEM	45593	13002	16.5	26.9	28.9	11.9	15.8	58474	68115	83	92	8040	2.0	8.5	34.6	40.0	15.0	192148
27105	WINSTON SALEM	17597	15303	38.0	30.0	25.3	4.9	1.8	33881	39116	24	25	8287	13.7	39.5	41.3	4.9	0.6	86706
27106	WINSTON SALEM	31499	17808	23.9	26.4	29.3	11.1	9.3	49650	57491	71	85	10327	4.5	9.6	47.7	30.2	8.0	152960
27107	WINSTON SALEM	19861	16008	28.1	31.5	31.4	7.0	2.0	41757	48192	52	61	11284	15.6	25.1	46.6	11.9	0.9	103485
27110	WINSTON SALEM	12109	0	0.0	0.0	0.0	0.0	0.0	0	0	0	0	0	0.0	0.0	0.0	0.0	0.0	0
27127	WINSTON SALEM	22570	10915	24.4	30.1	35.9	7.2	2.4	45701	53551	63	77	7427	10.7	23.7	58.4	7.1	0.2	107629
27203	ASHEBORO	18260	8392	35.9	34.4	24.0	4.0	1.7	34576	38646	26	27	4633	16.4	30.5	45.5	7.0	0.5	92771
27205	ASHEBORO	22226	12285	22.3	34.2	32.5	7.0	4.1	45080	50331	61	75	10197	16.1	20.9	43.8	17.1	2.1	107552
27207	BEAR CREEK	19637	1533	29.4	29.2	33.6	5.5	2.3	43079	49579	56	67	1280	20.6	25.6	32.6	18.8	2.4	95326
27208	BENNETT	19700	869	30.0	29.0	32.0	7.3	1.7	39408	44750	44	49	740	16.8	24.2	42.8	16.2	0.0	103393
27209	BISCOE	17904	1512	32.5	36.1	24.8	4.0	2.5	36038	41192	32	35	1154	29.3	37.0	26.7	6.4	0.6	73600
27212	BLANCH	16979	575	33.4	28.5	30.3	5.9	1.9	40174	45460	47	53	475	19.2	29.5	37.3	13.1	1.1	91383
27214	BROWNS SUMMIT	22748	3396	22.5	32.3	32.7	8.5	4.0	46760	53690	66	80	2632	16.9	18.7	40.0	20.2	4.3	111722
27215	BURLINGTON	26799	15103	24.1	29.7	32.2	8.9	5.1	46072	52588	64	78	9796	8.0	14.8	42.2	31.3	3.7	137848
27217	BURLINGTON	17770	13870	33.3	32.4	28.3	4.7	1.3	36962	42115	35	40	9652	20.3	27.0	42.0	9.2	1.5	93094
27229	CANDOR	15310	1094	36.0	34.9	23.9	2.8	2.4	34111	38676	24	25	865	31.0	39.1	25.2	4.4	0.4	69177
27231	CEDAR GROVE	24109	722	25.5	18.7	36.3	15.5	4.0	54816	66020	79	89	591	11.5	14.0	42.3	25.0	7.1	128977
27233	CLIMAX	20964	1128	23.4	33.2	34.0	7.5	2.0	44681	50217	60	73	952	14.9	22.7	46.1	13.3	2.9	107794
27235	COLFAX	28911	1044	13.8	24.1	36.7	18.2	7.2	62409	73553	87	93	894	4.4	7.3	49.7	32.7	6.0	155426
27239	DENTON	18646	3676	30.2	32.5	30.9	4.8	1.6	40659	46001	48	55	2995	24.9	25.9	34.8	12.7	1.7	88848
27242	EAGLE SPRINGS	15270	775	40.1	34.2	22.3	1.2	2.2	30351	34546	13	13	585	32.0	28.2	26.2	10.6	3.1	76574
27243	EFLAND	23370	1462	22.4	28.9	34.9	10.9	2.9	48599	58775	69	84	1193	13.1	14.2	44.9	23.4	4.4	123992
27244	ELON	22233	4167	27.3	27.8	29.9	9.4	5.6	45381	51196	62	76	3157	15.6	17.7	36.4	25.8	4.6	119132
27248	FRANKLINVILLE	19591	1732	29.6	35.3	28.6	4.7	1.7	39146	43760	43	48	1435	24.2	28.9	35.8	9.8	1.3	86520
27249	GIBSONVILLE	25661	4464	20.7	27.5	35.7	10.8	5.4	51398	59368	75	87	3543	8.9	20.8	40.9	25.3	4.0	121076
27252	GOLDSTON	20612	903	30.6	29.4	31.6	6.5	2.0	41252	47900	51	59	747	24.4	27.7	32.7	14.1	1.2	86961
27253	GRAHAM	22023	11278	24.6	33.5	32.5	6.8	2.7	43693	49860	58	70	8018	17.2	17.7	43.3	19.0	2.9	112949
27258	HAW RIVER	22207	2679	24.1	36.1	31.8	5.5	2.5	43408	49664	57	68	2205	29.9	14.7	35.8	17.7	1.9	99264
27260	HIGH POINT	14151	9590	47.6	29.7	18.2	2.9	1.5	26703	30475	7	4	4131	20.1	52.3	26.1	1.3	0.2	71541
27262	HIGH POINT	25505	9324	29.5	31.6	26.7	5.9	6.3	40651	47047	48	55	5612	6.6	30.3	39.7	19.0	4.5	109375
27263	HIGH POINT	21355	7633	26.3	34.8	30.6	6.5	1.8	41291	47084	51	60	5496	12.1	29.7	48.0	9.5	0.8	99848
27265	HIGH POINT	30695	15018	15.1	26.0	38.2	13.2	7.6	59087	68984	84	92	11080	3.6	10.1	53.3	29.1	4.0	144875
27278	HILLSBOROUGH	28181	9139	18.9	26.9	34.6	13.6	6.0	53759	65067	78	88	7130	15.6	10.5	36.6	30.3	7.0	140527
27281	JACKSON SPRINGS	17068	1190	29.4	30.5	29.7	7.8	2.6	41165	48034	50	58	965	23.4	26.5	27.9	19.3	2.9	90106
27282	JAMESTOWN	38190	5951	10.8	16.7	37.7	21.3	13.5	77088	91858	94	98	4834	2.3	4.2	38.8	49.6	5.1	181865
27283	JULIAN	22761	1278	22.5	29.6	35.1	9.4	3.4	48068	55107	68	83	1099	7.5	16.4	50.5	22.0	3.6	125446
27284	KERNERSVILLE	27774	18432	17.3	27.0	37.9	12.4	5.5	55277	64243	80	89	13358	8.4	9.9	50.8	28.8	2.2	141646
27288	EDEN	17750	10343	39.7	30.9	23.5	3.9	2.0	32429	36519	19	19	7317	22.6	34.6	34.0	8.4	0.5	81051
27291	LEASBURG	22368	801	26.3	34.0	29.6	6.0	4.1	43023	48728	56	67	665	11.6	27.7	38.4	19.9	2.6	107813
27292	LEXINGTON	19652	15973	31.7	30.9	29.3	5.8	2.3	38534	43913	41	46	11145	17.3	25.8	42.7	12.2	2.0	99070
27295	LEXINGTON	22177	14763	25.5	30.1	35.3	7.1	2.1	44899	50641	61	74	11716	16.8	16.9	49.4	15.8	1.1	112612
27298	LIBERTY	20712	3955	25.3	31.4	34.9	6.3	2.1	44931	49805	61	74	3207	17.3	22.1	43.2	15.7	1.8	105233
27299	LINWOOD	19725	1889	20.8	39.5	34.0	4.4	1.2	43149	49002	56	67	1523	25.1	22.4	43.5	8.6	0.5	92810
27301	MC LEANSVILLE	22551	2363	21.7	28.7	37.6	8.6	3.4	49625	57003	71	85	1967	18.9	16.5	52.1	10.9	1.6	111649
27302	MEBANE	22072	9120	25.0	30.4	32.7	8.7	3.1	45256	52203	62	75	6952	17.2	14.8	41.5	24.2	2.4	117518
27305	MILTON	16372	663	34.8	25.9	35.0	3.6	0.6	37591	41782	38	42	520	21.9	36.0	36.4	5.8	0.0	79818
27306	MOUNT GILEAD	19075	2430	37.6	27.9	26.6	4.1	3.7	34174	38961	25	26	1960	28.0	30.5	26.9	9.7	4.9	78895
27310	OAK RIDGE	35016	1460	8.8	16.6	40.8	19.1	14.6	76903	88137	94	98	1310	1.9	6.7	31.1	47.3	13.1	208470
27311	PELHAM	19886	1614	29.3	31.5	33.0	5.0	1.2	41199	46244	50	59	1301	20.5	28.4	37.3	12.0	1.8	91436
27312	PITTSBORO	30925	6862	22.1	24.1	34.9	11.1	7.7	53748	62875	78	88	5479	10.7	10.0	30.0	41.7	7.7	173121
27313	PLEASANT GARDEN	26756	2657	16.6	25.6	39.7	14.1	4.0	56156	64265	81	90	2268	9.5	15.4	44.8	28.4	1.9	135069
27314	PROSPECT HILL	19027	343	26.8	35.0	32.9	2.9	2.3	38914	43279	42	47	278	16.2	27.3	47.8	8.6	0.0	98571
27315	PROVIDENCE	20275	798	31.0	29.3	35.0	3.5	1.3	40125	44744	47	53	649	17.1	31.0	37.6	13.1	1.2	92404
27316	RAMSEUR	18064	2840	31.6	32.5	29.9	4.1	1.9	39933	44683	46	51	2241	22.4	24.7	37.2	12.9	2.9	92823
27317	RANDLEMAN	20017	6360	27.0	35.9	29.9	5.1	2.1	39857	45387	45	50	4944	24.0	25.1	38.1	12.0	0.8	91146
27320	REIDSVILLE	20344	16001	31.4	32.5	27.1	6.0	3.0	38131	43476	40	45	11664	16.7	27.4	40.5	14.3	1.2	98381
27325	ROBBINS	16535	2625	36.5	29.6	28.6	4.0	1.3	35503	39474	30	32	2064	34.2	28.8	27.6	8.9	0.5	70222
27326	RUFFIN	18278	1437	29.5	33.5	31.0	5.5	0.5	39069	44799	43	48	1121	13.7	32.4	40.0	12.1	1.9	94495
27330	SANFORD	21468	12554	28.1	30.4	28.7	9.0	3.8	42192	48120	53	63	8587	13.1	21.1	44.5	18.9	2.4	111421
27332	SANFORD	21303	9728	24.7	31.2	33.9	7.7	2.7	45566	52105	63	76	7746	19.0	17.9	45.2	16.5	1.4	106466
	NORTH CAROLINA	23743		27.0	29.8	30.1	8.5	4.7	43794	50711				14.5	20.0	39.7	21.7	4.1	115673
	UNITED STATES	25866		24.7	27.1	30.8	10.9	6.5	48124	56710				10.9	15.0	33.7	30.1	10.4	145905

ZIP CODE #	POST OFFICE NAME	FINANCIAL SERVICES: Auto Loan	Home Loan	Investments	Retirement Plans	THE HOME: Home Improvements: Home Repair	Lawn & Garden	Furnishings: Computers & Hardware	Major Appliances	TV, Radio, Sound Equipment	Furniture	ENTERTAINMENT: Dine out/ Carry out	Sports Equipment	Fees & Tickets	Toys & Games	Travel	Cable TV	PERSONAL: Apparel & Services	Auto Repairs	Health Insurance	Pets & Supplies
27006	ADVANCE	116	116	107	115	117	121	109	114	108	110	134	134	109	134	110	106	130	112	111	134
27007	ARARAT	76	67	50	63	71	76	62	69	66	62	80	82	60	82	64	68	76	67	75	89
27009	BELEWS CREEK	94	87	71	84	91	96	81	88	84	81	103	105	80	105	83	85	98	86	92	110
27011	BOONVILLE	81	66	48	64	71	79	67	73	72	66	87	85	63	86	67	74	81	72	81	91
27012	CLEMMONS	116	131	132	132	128	131	120	120	113	121	143	140	125	146	121	110	141	117	111	135
27013	CLEVELAND	85	76	59	73	78	83	73	79	75	73	92	91	69	90	73	75	88	78	81	96
27016	DANBURY	86	58	26	50	65	75	55	69	67	57	79	83	47	74	56	72	71	69	86	99
27017	DOBSON	86	64	37	57	70	78	61	72	69	62	83	86	54	79	62	73	77	72	84	98
27018	EAST BEND	88	75	54	71	78	84	71	79	75	73	91	92	67	88	71	76	87	78	83	99
27019	GERMANTON	87	72	51	68	77	85	68	77	75	68	90	92	65	90	70	77	85	76	86	101
27020	HAMPTONVILLE	92	69	41	63	75	84	66	78	75	68	90	92	60	86	67	79	83	77	90	104
27021	KING	87	81	66	79	83	89	77	83	79	77	97	96	75	98	78	80	93	81	86	100
27022	LAWSONVILLE	87	58	26	50	66	76	56	70	68	57	79	84	48	75	57	73	72	69	86	99
27023	LEWISVILLE	116	134	134	136	131	129	120	121	112	122	141	141	126	146	121	108	140	117	108	135
27024	LOWGAP	80	54	25	47	61	70	52	65	63	53	74	77	44	70	53	67	67	64	80	92
27025	MADISON	79	64	44	60	69	76	62	70	68	62	82	82	58	81	63	71	77	69	79	91
27027	MAYODAN	58	52	44	49	55	62	52	56	57	51	69	63	51	70	53	59	65	55	63	67
27028	MOCKSVILLE	88	73	53	69	77	85	71	79	77	71	93	93	67	92	72	79	88	78	87	100
27030	MOUNT AIRY	81	62	42	58	67	76	62	70	69	62	83	83	56	80	62	72	77	70	81	92
27040	PFAFFTOWN	108	121	119	119	121	124	110	113	106	109	132	132	114	139	113	106	130	109	108	130
27041	PILOT MOUNTAIN	83	70	52	68	74	81	69	76	74	69	89	88	65	87	69	75	84	75	82	94
27042	PINE HALL	74	49	22	43	56	65	48	60	58	49	68	71	41	64	49	62	61	59	74	85
27043	PINNACLE	92	78	55	73	82	89	73	82	79	74	95	97	69	94	74	81	90	81	90	106
27045	RURAL HALL	88	81	67	79	84	91	79	84	82	78	100	97	77	101	79	83	95	82	89	101
27046	SANDY RIDGE	93	62	28	54	70	81	60	75	72	61	85	90	51	80	61	78	77	74	92	107
27047	SILOAM	92	62	28	53	70	80	60	74	72	61	84	89	51	80	61	77	77	74	92	106
27048	STONEVILLE	83	67	45	63	72	80	64	73	71	64	85	86	60	84	65	73	79	72	82	96
27050	TOBACCOVILLE	92	86	72	84	88	93	81	87	82	82	102	102	79	102	82	82	98	85	88	106
27051	WALKERTOWN	85	79	67	76	82	89	76	81	79	75	97	94	75	98	77	80	92	79	86	98
27052	WALNUT COVE	86	66	40	60	71	79	63	74	71	64	84	87	56	81	63	74	78	73	84	99
27053	WESTFIELD	81	58	30	51	64	73	55	67	65	57	77	80	48	73	56	69	71	67	80	93
27054	WOODLEAF	79	71	56	69	72	77	68	73	69	69	85	85	65	82	67	69	82	73	74	88
27055	YADKINVILLE	92	72	46	67	78	87	69	80	77	70	93	94	64	91	70	81	86	79	91	105
27101	WINSTON SALEM	47	42	51	42	41	46	48	46	50	48	63	54	47	60	46	50	61	49	47	52
27103	WINSTON SALEM	81	87	98	88	86	90	87	85	85	86	106	100	89	107	87	83	104	86	81	94
27104	WINSTON SALEM	127	138	167	141	136	145	138	134	134	138	169	156	143	168	139	131	166	136	127	147
27105	WINSTON SALEM	63	58	64	56	58	66	63	62	66	63	82	70	63	80	62	68	80	64	66	70
27106	WINSTON SALEM	102	106	123	110	104	110	109	105	106	108	133	125	110	132	107	102	130	108	99	116
27107	WINSTON SALEM	75	70	66	69	71	77	71	73	73	70	90	85	70	90	71	74	87	73	75	85
27110	WINSTON SALEM	0	0	0	0	0	0	0	0	0	0	0	0	0	0	0	0	0	0	0	0
27127	WINSTON SALEM	73	77	83	78	76	79	77	76	75	77	95	89	78	96	77	74	93	76	72	84
27203	ASHEBORO	65	57	52	56	59	66	61	62	64	59	78	72	59	78	60	65	75	63	67	72
27205	ASHEBORO	92	83	65	79	86	92	78	85	81	79	100	100	75	99	79	82	95	84	89	106
27207	BEAR CREEK	89	65	36	58	72	81	62	74	71	62	85	89	55	82	63	76	78	73	88	103
27208	BENNETT	91	62	29	54	70	80	60	74	71	61	84	88	51	80	61	77	77	73	91	105
27209	BISCOE	93	65	33	57	72	83	63	77	74	64	88	91	55	84	64	79	80	76	92	106
27212	BLANCH	86	59	29	52	66	76	57	70	68	58	80	84	49	76	58	73	73	70	86	98
27214	BROWNS SUMMIT	87	85	81	85	85	89	82	84	82	83	102	100	82	102	82	80	99	84	82	99
27215	BURLINGTON	85	86	91	86	86	92	86	87	86	86	107	101	87	107	86	86	104	87	86	99
27217	BURLINGTON	71	61	50	58	64	70	61	66	66	61	80	77	59	79	61	67	76	66	71	81
27229	CANDOR	82	55	25	48	62	72	53	66	64	54	75	79	45	71	54	69	69	66	82	94
27231	CEDAR GROVE	96	89	75	88	93	100	86	92	89	85	109	107	85	110	87	90	104	90	96	110
27233	CLIMAX	87	79	61	75	80	86	74	80	76	75	94	94	71	92	74	77	90	79	83	99
27235	COLFAX	112	115	102	114	115	116	104	109	102	106	127	128	106	130	105	100	124	106	105	129
27239	DENTON	86	61	33	54	68	77	59	71	69	60	82	85	52	78	60	73	75	70	85	98
27242	EAGLE SPRINGS	74	49	22	43	56	65	48	60	58	49	68	71	41	64	49	62	61	59	74	85
27243	EFLAND	91	83	67	81	86	92	80	86	82	80	101	100	77	100	80	83	96	84	89	104
27244	ELON	93	82	72	80	84	91	86	86	87	84	108	104	81	105	83	86	103	88	88	104
27248	FRANKLINVILLE	90	66	36	59	72	81	63	76	73	64	86	90	56	82	64	77	80	75	89	103
27249	GIBSONVILLE	100	91	74	89	95	103	87	94	91	87	111	110	86	112	88	92	106	92	100	115
27252	GOLDSTON	91	63	31	55	71	81	60	75	72	61	84	89	52	81	62	76	77	74	91	105
27253	GRAHAM	80	76	69	73	77	83	74	77	76	74	94	91	74	95	75	77	91	77	80	92
27258	HAW RIVER	89	74	52	70	78	85	71	80	76	72	92	94	66	89	71	78	87	79	86	102
27260	HIGH POINT	50	45	51	43	44	51	50	49	54	50	66	56	49	64	49	55	64	51	52	56
27262	HIGH POINT	84	81	86	81	82	89	85	85	87	84	107	99	84	106	84	86	104	86	86	95
27263	HIGH POINT	81	69	55	67	72	80	69	74	73	68	89	87	66	89	69	75	84	74	80	91
27265	HIGH POINT	107	112	115	116	109	112	109	108	104	110	131	127	110	131	107	100	129	108	98	121
27278	HILLSBOROUGH	101	108	106	107	107	111	102	103	99	102	123	120	103	125	102	97	120	102	99	117
27281	JACKSON SPRINGS	89	71	49	65	76	86	67	78	74	70	90	88	62	82	69	78	84	77	90	100
27282	JAMESTOWN	137	153	152	158	147	145	141	140	131	145	166	164	145	168	139	124	164	137	122	154
27283	JULIAN	92	82	62	78	86	93	76	84	80	76	98	100	74	100	78	82	93	81	91	108
27284	KERNERSVILLE	98	102	102	104	102	105	98	99	95	98	119	116	99	120	98	93	116	98	94	113
27288	EDEN	67	55	43	52	59	66	56	61	61	55	74	71	52	73	56	64	69	61	69	76
27291	LEASBURG	96	74	45	67	81	90	69	82	79	70	94	98	63	92	71	83	87	81	96	112
27292	LEXINGTON	78	65	50	61	68	76	64	71	70	64	85	83	61	84	65	72	80	70	78	89
27295	LEXINGTON	88	77	58	73	81	88	73	80	78	73	94	95	70	94	74	80	89	79	87	102
27298	LIBERTY	86	72	52	69	77	84	70	78	75	70	91	91	66	90	70	77	86	76	85	98
27299	LINWOOD	81	73	56	69	75	80	68	74	71	69	87	87	66	85	69	71	83	73	77	92
27301	MC LEANSVILLE	92	84	67	81	86	92	80	86	83	80	101	101	77	100	80	83	97	85	89	105
27302	MEBANE	89	77	61	75	79	86	76	82	79	76	97	95	72	95	75	80	92	81	86	99
27305	MILTON	75	58	38	54	62	71	58	66	64	57	77	76	53	75	58	67	71	65	75	84
27306	MOUNT GILEAD	87	62	32	54	69	79	59	73	70	60	82	86	51	79	61	75	75	72	88	102
27310	OAK RIDGE	136	161	165	165	155	153	145	143	133	147	169	168	152	174	145	127	168	139	126	158
27311	PELHAM	91	64	34	57	72	81	62	75	72	62	86	90	54	82	63	77	78	74	90	105
27312	PITTSBORO	107	106	97	104	108	115	100	106	100	101	124	119	100	121	102	101	120	104	108	123
27313	PLEASANT GARDEN	106	103	88	99	106	111	94	101	96	94	118	120	95	122	97	97	114	98	104	125
27314	PROSPECT HILL	82	62	36	56	68	76	59	70	67	59	80	83	53	78	60	71	74	69	82	96
27315	PROVIDENCE	87	62	32	54	69	78	59	72	69	60	82	86	52	79	60	74	75	71	86	100
27316	RAMSEUR	79	63	43	60	68	76	62	70	68	62	82	82	57	80	62	70	76	69	78	90
27317	RANDLEMAN	82	70	52	67	73	80	69	75	72	69	88	87	65	86	68	73	83	74	80	92
27320	REIDSVILLE	81	67	51	63	71	80	66	73	72	66	87	85	62	85	67	75	82	72	82	92
27325	ROBBINS	77	55	30	49	60	68	54	65	63	56	75	76	47	70	54	67	70	65	76	87
27326	RUFFIN	77	59	36	54	64	72	58	67	65	58	78	79	53	76	58	68	72	66	78	88
27330	SANFORD	82	79	75	78	80	85	78	80	80	78	98	94	78	98	78	79	95	80	81	93
27332	SANFORD	89	81	67	79	83	88	78	84	80	80	98	96	75	94	78	80	94	83	85	100
	NORTH CAROLINA	90	81	73	80	83	90	81	85	84	82	103	100	79	101	81	84	99	85	88	102
	UNITED STATES	100	100	100	100	100	100	100	100	100	100	100	100	100	100	100	100	100	100	100	100

ZIP CODE		COUNTY FIPS CODE	POPULATION			2000-2004 ANNUAL RATE		HOUSEHOLDS					FAMILIES		
#	POST OFFICE NAME		2000	2004	2009	% Rate	State Centile	2000	2004	2009	% Annual Rate 2000-2004	2004 Average HH Size	2000	2004	% Annual Rate 2000-2004
27341	SEAGROVE	151	5160	5418	5768	1.2	41	2019	2139	2298	1.4	2.53	1528	1596	1.0
27343	SEMORA	145	1696	1784	1911	1.2	43	669	717	780	1.6	2.46	486	514	1.3
27344	SILER CITY	037	16023	18135	21199	3.0	83	5847	6625	7786	3.0	2.71	4229	4729	2.7
27349	SNOW CAMP	001	4974	5842	6681	3.9	92	1900	2255	2600	4.1	2.59	1436	1677	3.7
27350	SOPHIA	151	6413	6559	6941	0.5	23	2444	2543	2722	0.9	2.57	1937	1989	0.6
27355	STALEY	151	2149	2217	2371	0.7	28	837	872	941	1.0	2.54	630	649	0.7
27356	STAR	123	3207	3327	3536	0.9	32	1299	1365	1469	1.2	2.42	912	945	0.8
27357	STOKESDALE	157	5916	6338	6678	1.6	56	2264	2467	2637	2.0	2.55	1722	1851	1.7
27358	SUMMERFIELD	081	9021	10263	11250	3.1	85	3328	3838	4258	3.4	2.67	2687	3058	3.1
27360	THOMASVILLE	057	41982	43945	46496	1.1	38	16761	17727	18948	1.3	2.45	12056	12558	1.0
27370	TRINITY	151	15461	16340	17444	1.3	47	5811	6237	6734	1.7	2.60	4567	4844	1.4
27371	TROY	123	8609	9221	9941	1.6	56	3145	3443	3788	2.2	2.43	2263	2446	1.9
27376	WEST END	125	7555	8208	8962	2.0	64	3099	3409	3765	2.3	2.39	2359	2558	1.9
27377	WHITSETT	081	3581	3890	4190	2.0	64	1454	1608	1756	2.4	2.42	1096	1193	2.0
27379	YANCEYVILLE	033	5530	5837	6209	1.3	47	1946	2095	2283	1.8	2.46	1358	1442	1.4
27401	GREENSBORO	081	18729	17848	18273	-1.1	1	7466	7170	7456	-1.0	2.19	3907	3656	-1.6
27403	GREENSBORO	081	19750	19395	20036	-0.4	4	8370	8317	8700	-0.2	2.22	4022	3872	-0.9
27405	GREENSBORO	081	39443	40532	42721	0.6	26	15955	16577	17668	0.9	2.41	10011	10197	0.4
27406	GREENSBORO	081	49988	51975	54926	0.9	34	19520	20645	22127	1.3	2.45	13551	14052	0.9
27407	GREENSBORO	081	42770	44901	47528	1.2	41	17080	18152	19433	1.4	2.44	10890	11301	0.9
27408	GREENSBORO	081	17543	17957	18860	0.6	24	8048	8395	8945	1.0	2.13	4982	5077	0.5
27409	GREENSBORO	081	13632	16027	17931	3.9	92	6499	7732	8748	4.2	2.03	3129	3652	3.7
27410	GREENSBORO	081	45669	49686	53553	2.0	64	19577	21659	23665	2.4	2.24	12554	13590	1.9
27411	GREENSBORO	081	1207	1205	1209	0.0	10	0	0	0	0.0	0.00	0	0	0.0
27413	GREENSBORO	081	2929	2933	2938	0.0	11	17	18	20	1.4	3.39	3	3	0.0
27455	GREENSBORO	081	20811	24044	26741	3.5	89	8684	10139	11394	3.7	2.35	5538	6339	3.2
27501	ANGIER	085	12701	14892	17424	3.8	91	4773	5637	6641	4.0	2.58	3385	3943	3.7
27502	APEX	183	18265	23374	29085	6.0	98	6488	8399	10521	6.3	2.78	4980	6329	5.8
27503	BAHAMA	063	3585	4132	4732	3.4	88	1367	1602	1857	3.8	2.51	1084	1259	3.6
27504	BENSON	101	13651	15935	18854	3.7	91	5338	6252	7419	3.8	2.54	3764	4354	3.5
27505	BROADWAY	085	4621	5065	5664	2.2	71	1729	1908	2143	2.4	2.65	1297	1416	2.1
27507	BULLOCK	077	1754	1979	2253	2.9	83	658	756	875	3.3	2.62	497	564	3.0
27508	BUNN	069	1975	2158	2450	2.1	69	623	690	798	2.4	2.83	439	479	2.1
27509	BUTNER	077	9130	10345	11088	3.0	83	1698	1936	2256	3.1	2.53	1180	1326	2.8
27510	CARRBORO	135	13541	14187	15284	1.1	39	6407	6741	7294	1.2	2.09	2562	2613	0.5
27511	CARY	183	44677	49392	57454	2.4	74	16896	18803	21964	2.6	2.61	12058	13226	2.2
27513	CARY	183	36022	44243	54474	5.0	96	13722	16895	20853	5.0	2.61	8994	10815	4.4
27514	CHAPEL HILL	135	30194	32734	35779	1.9	63	10756	11994	13460	2.6	2.17	4942	5308	1.7
27516	CHAPEL HILL	135	30907	35131	39645	3.1	85	11597	13272	15108	3.2	2.47	6545	7426	3.0
27517	CHAPEL HILL	037	17771	19660	22203	2.4	75	7879	8852	10118	2.8	2.17	4675	5128	2.2
27519	CARY	183	11058	14888	18990	7.3	100	3695	4920	6241	7.0	3.03	3084	4062	6.7
27520	CLAYTON	101	31348	38267	45969	4.8	96	11574	14227	17169	5.0	2.68	8860	10736	4.6
27521	COATS	085	5751	6370	7296	2.4	75	2216	2458	2828	2.5	2.56	1566	1714	2.2
27522	CREEDMOOR	077	7713	9238	10952	4.3	94	3100	3767	4531	4.7	2.43	2194	2625	4.3
27523	APEX	037	7198	9054	11176	5.6	98	2898	3684	4578	5.8	2.44	2181	2741	5.5
27524	FOUR OAKS	101	9596	10886	12620	3.0	84	3824	4370	5093	3.2	2.47	2658	2987	2.8
27525	FRANKLINTON	069	10577	11777	13633	2.6	78	4022	4522	5285	2.8	2.60	2917	3235	2.5
27526	FUQUAY VARINA	085	23246	27103	32118	3.7	90	8563	10091	12040	3.9	2.67	6511	7542	3.5
27529	GARNER	183	30277	34925	41398	3.4	88	11512	13431	16037	3.7	2.58	8488	9712	3.2
27530	GOLDSBORO	191	37762	38133	38998	0.2	15	14480	14807	15359	0.5	2.41	9745	9854	0.3
27531	GOLDSBORO	191	2192	2110	2101	-0.9	1	343	331	335	-0.8	5.03	327	315	-0.9
27534	GOLDSBORO	191	30915	31662	32392	0.6	24	11956	12466	12966	1.0	2.45	8617	8835	0.3
27536	HENDERSON	181	18395	18617	19314	0.3	16	7213	7405	7790	0.6	2.44	4743	4774	0.2
27537	HENDERSON	181	22344	24200	25994	1.9	62	8168	8992	9798	2.3	2.66	6250	6788	2.0
27539	APEX	183	11567	14581	18049	5.6	98	4270	5450	6794	5.9	2.67	3386	4246	5.5
27540	HOLLY SPRINGS	183	12742	15542	18795	4.6	95	4633	5696	6983	5.0	2.71	3597	4339	4.5
27541	HURDLE MILLS	145	3250	3481	3783	1.6	56	1267	1378	1517	2.0	2.52	953	1021	1.6
27542	KENLY	101	8051	8505	9473	1.3	47	3201	3407	3822	1.5	2.50	2293	2405	1.1
27544	KITTRELL	181	2694	2834	3048	1.2	43	1054	1128	1230	1.6	2.51	829	878	1.4
27545	KNIGHTDALE	183	16027	19920	24521	5.3	97	5884	7385	9146	5.5	2.68	4395	5402	5.0
27546	LILLINGTON	085	16392	18365	20866	2.7	81	5581	6409	7439	3.3	2.57	3870	4375	2.9
27549	LOUISBURG	069	20048	21973	25190	2.2	71	7497	8343	9707	2.6	2.52	5319	5841	2.2
27551	MACON	185	3165	3213	3317	0.4	18	1296	1345	1419	0.9	2.38	931	953	0.6
27553	MANSON	185	2358	2437	2530	0.8	29	890	935	987	1.2	2.61	641	663	0.8
27557	MIDDLESEX	127	6992	7468	8186	1.6	54	2684	2892	3195	1.8	2.58	1959	2077	1.4
27559	MONCURE	037	1944	2088	2376	1.7	57	758	827	953	2.1	2.52	542	583	1.7
27560	MORRISVILLE	183	9320	13118	17026	8.4	100	4021	5706	7438	8.6	2.30	2770	3812	7.8
27562	NEW HILL	037	1786	2135	2576	4.3	93	686	830	1010	4.6	2.57	505	605	4.3
27563	NORLINA	185	4058	4081	4186	0.1	13	1421	1463	1540	0.7	2.38	974	987	0.3
27565	OXFORD	077	23562	25564	28832	1.9	63	8820	9725	11149	2.3	2.57	6361	6928	2.0
27569	PRINCETON	101	6272	6868	7678	2.2	70	2476	2751	3110	2.5	2.46	1841	2014	2.1
27571	ROLESVILLE	183	943	1083	1280	3.3	87	359	416	493	3.5	2.60	284	322	3.0
27572	ROUGEMONT	145	6093	6797	7553	2.6	79	2282	2584	2906	3.0	2.61	1762	1969	2.7
27573	ROXBORO	145	10951	11338	11938	0.8	31	4606	4840	5174	1.2	2.29	2963	3056	0.7
27574	ROXBORO	145	13596	14218	15069	1.1	38	5190	5524	5952	1.5	2.55	3906	4104	1.2
27576	SELMA	101	16914	18841	21666	2.6	78	6532	7317	8448	2.7	2.57	4614	5046	2.3
27577	SMITHFIELD	101	19161	21008	23865	2.2	71	7365	8177	9403	2.5	2.40	4803	5237	2.1
27581	STEM	077	2287	2561	2929	2.7	80	864	978	1134	3.0	2.58	670	749	2.7
27583	TIMBERLAKE	145	5167	5591	6028	1.9	61	1986	2184	2389	2.3	2.55	1535	1669	2.0
27587	WAKE FOREST	183	29874	35865	43346	4.4	94	10836	13125	15957	4.6	2.71	8387	9980	4.2
27589	WARRENTON	185	9689	10053	10471	0.9	32	3700	3927	4186	1.4	2.50	2612	2731	1.1
27591	WENDELL	183	14741	16744	19625	3.0	84	5503	6328	7472	3.3	2.62	4051	4564	2.9
27592	WILLOW SPRING	183	9887	12069	14614	4.8	96	3647	4492	5469	5.0	2.68	2770	3348	4.6
27596	YOUNGSVILLE	069	9455	11753	14343	5.3	97	3598	4512	5553	5.5	2.60	2689	3323	5.1
27597	ZEBULON	183	17710	19607	22625	2.4	75	6667	7466	8685	2.7	2.60	4861	5338	2.2
27601	RALEIGH	183	9811	9954	11065	0.3	17	3389	3491	3981	0.7	2.40	1786	1750	-0.5
27603	RALEIGH	183	33040	37764	44663	3.2	86	12601	14513	17312	3.4	2.45	7633	8671	3.1
27604	RALEIGH	183	32249	36207	42636	2.8	81	13424	15227	18065	3.0	2.34	8275	9196	2.5
27605	RALEIGH	183	3752	3863	4312	0.7	27	2280	2378	2685	1.0	1.54	540	531	-0.4
27606	RALEIGH	183	41488	44907	51468	1.9	62	14998	16625	19564	2.5	2.31	6922	7398	1.6
27607	RALEIGH	183	18656	20306	23302	2.0	65	7286	8195	9719	2.8	2.14	3627	3924	1.9
27608	RALEIGH	183	10210	10255	11404	0.1	12	5030	5108	5735	0.4	1.95	2448	2389	-0.6
27609	RALEIGH	183	32964	34819	39670	1.3	47	14722	15798	18157	1.7	2.20	8481	8783	0.8
27610	RALEIGH	183	43685	49206	57641	2.8	82	15027	17154	20337	3.2	2.71	10389	11577	2.6
27612	RALEIGH	183	27671	32554	39096	3.9	92	12658	15179	18423	4.4	2.13	6749	7653	3.0
	NORTH CAROLINA					1.9					2.2	2.46			1.8
	UNITED STATES					1.2					1.3	2.58			1.1

#	POST OFFICE NAME	RACE (%) White 2000	White 2004	Black 2000	Black 2004	Asian/Pacific 2000	Asian/Pacific 2004	% Hispanic Origin 2000	% Hispanic Origin 2004	2004 AGE DISTRIBUTION (%) 0-4	5-9	10-14	15-19	20-24	25-44	45-64	65-84	85+	18+	MEDIAN AGE 2004	% 2004 Males	% 2004 Females
27341	SEAGROVE	91.9	91.0	5.9	6.3	0.2	0.2	2.0	2.7	6.7	6.6	6.8	6.2	5.8	29.0	26.1	11.8	1.2	76.2	38.0	50.3	49.7
27343	SEMORA	57.4	55.3	40.5	42.2	0.3	0.4	2.1	2.5	5.4	5.7	6.6	6.3	5.4	26.9	30.9	11.8	1.1	78.1	41.4	50.9	49.1
27344	SILER CITY	64.0	61.3	19.1	18.2	0.6	0.6	22.4	27.4	7.1	6.8	6.6	6.1	6.5	31.1	23.1	11.4	1.5	75.8	35.8	50.8	49.2
27349	SNOW CAMP	91.4	90.4	6.1	6.6	0.2	0.2	2.5	3.3	6.5	6.9	7.3	6.2	5.0	30.0	26.4	10.4	1.3	75.5	38.3	50.9	49.1
27350	SOPHIA	96.6	96.0	1.2	1.3	0.3	0.4	1.2	1.6	6.0	6.6	7.4	6.6	5.4	30.5	28.0	8.7	0.9	75.9	38.1	51.0	49.0
27355	STALEY	86.2	84.8	9.4	9.8	0.2	0.3	4.8	6.3	6.2	6.7	7.2	6.0	5.3	29.0	27.2	11.2	1.2	76.1	38.7	51.3	48.7
27356	STAR	91.6	90.3	3.9	4.0	0.4	0.5	5.6	7.3	6.9	6.6	6.2	6.6	6.5	28.4	25.8	11.8	1.4	76.5	37.1	50.3	49.7
27357	STOKESDALE	91.8	91.0	5.2	5.5	0.3	0.4	2.7	3.4	7.1	7.4	7.4	6.1	4.9	32.5	24.8	8.7	1.1	74.3	36.9	50.3	49.7
27358	SUMMERFIELD	92.8	91.8	4.5	4.8	0.6	0.7	1.6	2.2	6.4	7.2	8.0	6.3	4.7	29.0	28.8	8.9	0.9	74.5	39.0	49.7	50.3
27360	THOMASVILLE	84.1	82.9	12.0	12.3	0.5	0.6	3.8	5.0	7.0	6.9	6.7	5.7	5.6	29.9	24.4	12.1	1.8	75.9	37.7	48.4	51.6
27370	TRINITY	95.1	94.7	2.9	3.0	0.6	0.7	0.9	1.2	6.3	6.6	6.7	6.1	5.4	30.0	27.9	9.9	1.2	76.6	38.8	49.4	50.6
27371	TROY	74.8	73.4	19.4	19.6	1.8	2.2	4.5	5.8	6.4	6.5	6.5	5.3	6.0	30.3	25.4	12.2	1.6	77.4	37.7	53.1	46.9
27376	WEST END	81.6	80.8	16.0	16.5	0.3	0.3	1.4	1.7	4.7	5.1	5.8	5.1	4.1	21.3	27.7	24.5	1.6	81.1	47.6	48.7	51.4
27377	WHITSETT	89.1	87.7	8.5	9.4	0.2	0.3	1.3	1.8	6.5	6.8	6.4	5.4	4.9	30.2	27.5	11.3	1.0	76.9	38.9	50.2	49.8
27379	YANCEYVILLE	51.1	50.1	46.5	47.1	0.1	0.2	1.5	1.8	5.6	5.9	6.5	5.6	6.0	30.0	26.2	12.7	1.8	78.7	39.0	53.2	46.8
27401	GREENSBORO	23.1	22.5	71.9	71.7	1.1	1.2	3.7	4.5	5.4	5.4	6.1	12.7	11.0	26.9	20.1	10.7	1.8	79.7	31.7	47.2	52.9
27403	GREENSBORO	72.5	70.3	18.4	19.1	4.1	4.7	4.8	6.0	5.1	4.8	4.9	7.8	16.2	31.1	20.0	8.5	1.6	82.3	31.4	48.9	51.1
27405	GREENSBORO	42.3	40.9	50.5	50.8	2.1	2.4	5.4	6.6	7.2	7.0	7.4	6.7	8.0	30.0	21.6	10.7	1.6	74.4	34.0	47.7	52.3
27406	GREENSBORO	42.0	40.4	53.3	54.2	1.3	1.6	2.5	3.1	6.6	6.8	7.2	6.9	6.5	28.8	25.0	10.8	1.5	75.6	36.6	46.6	53.5
27407	GREENSBORO	62.8	60.4	25.3	25.8	5.8	6.7	6.7	8.2	7.2	6.7	6.6	5.9	7.4	34.6	21.5	8.8	1.3	76.0	33.9	49.2	50.8
27408	GREENSBORO	87.3	85.9	9.6	10.4	1.0	1.2	2.3	3.0	5.9	5.8	5.5	5.3	5.2	27.2	26.7	16.4	2.1	79.5	41.7	47.4	52.6
27409	GREENSBORO	72.2	70.4	20.8	21.5	2.8	3.3	5.0	6.2	5.2	4.8	5.4	5.5	9.2	39.4	21.8	7.1	1.7	81.5	33.0	48.8	51.2
27410	GREENSBORO	85.3	83.6	9.5	10.3	2.7	3.3	2.5	3.2	5.7	5.8	6.2	6.5	6.5	29.0	26.1	12.0	2.1	78.4	38.9	48.0	52.0
27411	GREENSBORO	0.7	0.6	97.4	97.2	0.1	0.1	1.2	1.4	0.3	0.3	0.4	61.9	31.2	3.5	1.6	0.7	0.2	98.6	19.0	48.5	51.5
27413	GREENSBORO	63.5	60.5	31.7	33.7	2.6	3.1	2.1	2.7	0.1	0.0	0.0	63.6	33.9	2.2	0.1	0.0	0.0	99.6	18.9	29.2	70.9
27455	GREENSBORO	78.7	76.3	17.9	19.6	1.5	1.8	2.1	2.7	6.9	6.9	6.6	5.6	5.7	32.5	25.6	9.2	1.1	76.2	37.0	47.6	52.4
27501	ANGIER	77.5	75.5	13.7	13.8	0.6	0.7	10.7	13.3	7.9	7.7	7.0	6.6	6.8	33.9	21.2	8.1	0.9	73.9	33.5	50.2	49.8
27502	APEX	81.0	79.1	12.0	12.5	3.4	3.9	3.8	5.0	9.4	9.2	8.0	5.4	4.4	38.5	20.0	4.4	0.6	69.7	33.4	49.7	50.3
27503	BAHAMA	84.2	82.6	13.2	14.3	0.8	0.9	1.9	2.5	5.1	6.2	7.1	5.9	4.3	25.2	33.6	11.2	1.7	77.8	42.9	49.9	50.1
27504	BENSON	82.0	81.1	12.0	11.6	0.3	0.3	6.1	7.7	7.7	7.4	7.0	5.8	5.9	32.3	23.3	9.6	1.1	74.4	35.3	49.5	50.5
27505	BROADWAY	78.6	77.5	15.6	15.7	0.3	0.4	7.0	8.6	7.6	7.3	7.3	6.7	6.6	30.7	23.6	9.3	1.0	73.8	34.9	50.2	49.8
27507	BULLOCK	54.1	52.7	43.3	44.2	0.2	0.2	2.9	3.5	6.5	6.8	7.2	6.6	5.6	27.9	25.8	12.4	1.2	75.5	38.4	48.8	51.2
27508	BUNN	52.7	50.6	43.0	44.4	0.3	0.3	5.6	6.9	6.8	6.7	7.7	7.1	7.7	34.7	22.2	6.3	0.8	74.6	33.6	54.2	45.8
27509	BUTNER	49.6	48.6	43.4	43.6	0.7	0.9	6.5	8.0	3.8	3.9	4.2	7.2	11.9	40.8	22.0	5.7	0.6	84.3	34.1	70.4	29.6
27510	CARRBORO	70.0	68.2	15.7	15.3	5.1	5.7	13.0	15.5	5.0	4.5	4.8	5.3	15.3	44.6	15.6	4.3	0.8	82.8	29.1	49.3	50.8
27511	CARY	84.4	82.9	5.9	5.9	5.5	6.5	5.7	6.8	6.1	6.7	7.8	6.8	6.2	30.1	27.6	7.9	0.9	75.0	36.9	49.6	50.4
27513	CARY	79.2	77.1	7.4	7.5	10.1	11.8	3.4	4.3	8.2	7.8	7.4	6.2	6.5	39.8	20.3	3.4	0.4	72.8	32.6	49.9	50.1
27514	CHAPEL HILL	79.2	77.0	10.1	10.4	7.3	8.7	3.1	4.0	3.4	3.3	4.5	20.9	20.6	22.9	16.6	6.6	1.2	86.0	24.4	44.5	55.5
27516	CHAPEL HILL	79.6	78.4	13.2	13.0	4.0	4.8	3.7	4.8	5.1	5.3	6.4	9.3	12.3	31.4	23.1	6.2	0.9	79.6	31.2	48.6	51.4
27517	CHAPEL HILL	82.5	80.3	8.9	9.6	5.2	6.0	4.0	5.3	4.9	4.8	5.4	5.3	5.9	32.0	25.8	13.6	2.2	81.3	39.1	47.3	52.8
27519	CARY	84.4	82.2	4.7	4.9	8.6	10.2	2.4	3.1	11.1	11.3	9.6	5.8	3.4	37.4	18.6	2.7	0.2	64.1	33.0	49.8	50.2
27520	CLAYTON	79.1	77.3	14.9	15.4	0.6	0.6	6.7	8.5	8.8	8.3	7.3	5.7	5.6	35.9	21.3	6.4	0.7	72.1	33.8	49.9	50.1
27521	COATS	81.5	80.0	12.1	12.3	0.5	0.5	9.4	11.7	7.2	6.9	7.0	7.0	8.1	32.1	22.2	8.7	0.8	75.1	33.5	50.3	49.7
27522	CREEDMOOR	77.5	76.4	19.5	20.0	0.4	0.4	2.0	2.5	7.2	7.2	7.1	5.5	5.0	32.4	25.0	9.6	1.1	75.1	37.1	49.3	50.7
27523	APEX	85.3	83.4	7.8	8.2	4.3	5.2	2.8	3.7	9.1	9.2	7.7	5.0	3.6	36.7	20.5	6.3	2.0	70.7	35.3	49.2	50.9
27524	FOUR OAKS	83.2	81.2	9.4	9.8	0.3	0.3	10.3	12.9	7.1	7.4	6.8	5.6	5.9	31.4	24.6	10.1	1.1	75.2	36.0	50.4	49.6
27525	FRANKLINTON	61.6	60.8	33.1	33.0	0.4	0.4	5.2	6.3	7.6	7.5	7.1	6.0	5.8	31.5	24.4	9.0	1.0	74.1	35.9	49.6	50.4
27526	FUQUAY VARINA	79.4	78.0	15.9	16.4	0.5	0.6	5.6	7.2	8.1	7.9	7.7	6.3	5.4	33.6	22.0	7.9	1.1	72.3	34.8	49.1	50.9
27529	GARNER	70.9	68.6	24.1	25.6	0.8	0.9	4.5	5.5	7.5	7.4	7.2	6.1	5.8	33.3	23.8	8.1	0.8	74.1	35.6	48.9	51.1
27530	GOLDSBORO	53.1	53.4	43.7	42.9	0.7	0.8	2.4	3.0	6.7	6.8	6.9	6.3	6.4	28.7	24.6	12.2	1.4	75.7	37.4	49.2	50.8
27531	GOLDSBORO	68.8	66.3	22.4	23.4	2.1	2.4	6.2	7.8	13.2	9.1	7.1	6.0	19.9	40.6	3.9	0.3	0.0	68.4	23.7	58.4	41.6
27534	GOLDSBORO	65.9	63.9	27.8	28.7	2.0	2.4	4.1	5.1	6.8	6.5	6.9	6.6	8.4	29.7	23.2	11.0	1.0	76.0	35.2	49.9	50.1
27536	HENDERSON	39.0	38.1	56.9	56.9	0.7	0.8	5.5	6.7	7.3	7.2	7.6	7.1	6.3	26.0	22.5	13.8	2.3	73.7	36.4	45.7	54.3
27537	HENDERSON	55.7	54.5	41.2	41.8	0.3	0.3	4.0	5.0	6.7	7.0	8.0	7.4	6.5	29.0	25.3	9.2	0.9	73.9	35.3	49.2	50.8
27539	APEX	84.1	82.4	10.7	11.3	1.9	2.3	4.0	5.1	8.3	8.7	8.5	6.3	4.7	33.9	24.8	4.4	0.4	70.4	35.1	50.4	49.6
27540	HOLLY SPRINGS	76.4	74.8	19.1	19.9	1.1	1.3	3.2	4.3	9.6	9.1	7.6	5.8	4.6	37.8	20.5	4.5	0.5	70.0	33.4	49.6	50.4
27541	HURDLE MILLS	79.9	79.4	16.8	16.9	0.1	0.1	3.4	4.2	5.5	6.0	6.7	5.9	5.1	29.0	28.9	11.6	1.3	78.1	40.4	50.6	49.4
27542	KENLY	78.4	76.5	16.7	17.3	0.1	0.2	6.5	8.5	6.4	6.6	7.3	6.1	6.1	29.2	26.0	11.3	1.2	76.1	37.5	49.8	50.2
27544	KITTRELL	57.7	55.9	40.9	42.5	0.1	0.1	1.3	1.6	6.6	6.9	7.6	6.3	6.0	28.6	27.3	10.0	0.9	75.2	37.6	48.4	51.6
27545	KNIGHTDALE	66.7	63.5	26.0	27.7	1.1	1.3	6.9	8.7	8.5	8.2	7.9	6.4	5.9	36.3	20.8	5.3	0.6	71.2	32.9	49.3	50.8
27546	LILLINGTON	69.6	68.2	24.8	25.2	0.8	1.0	5.0	6.3	6.4	6.2	6.7	8.3	9.6	31.2	20.9	9.6	1.3	76.9	33.3	50.8	49.2
27549	LOUISBURG	61.3	59.7	35.4	36.3	0.3	0.4	4.2	5.1	6.2	6.3	6.7	6.8	6.4	28.8	25.6	11.4	1.8	76.9	38.1	48.7	51.3
27551	MACON	50.6	49.6	38.7	39.1	0.2	0.2	1.2	1.4	4.3	4.7	6.2	6.1	5.2	20.8	34.2	16.9	1.5	81.0	46.5	48.9	51.1
27553	MANSON	25.6	24.7	71.8	72.2	0.0	0.0	3.1	3.6	5.8	6.3	7.8	7.1	6.4	25.0	27.2	13.1	1.4	75.8	39.0	46.9	53.1
27557	MIDDLESEX	67.8	66.2	24.9	25.0	0.2	0.2	9.8	11.9	7.6	7.7	7.4	6.4	6.7	30.2	23.6	9.6	0.8	73.4	34.6	49.1	50.9
27559	MONCURE	69.8	68.1	25.6	26.5	0.5	0.5	2.8	3.7	5.7	6.2	6.8	5.8	4.7	29.3	30.0	10.1	1.4	77.7	40.3	50.3	49.7
27560	MORRISVILLE	82.2	79.9	7.6	8.2	7.5	8.6	2.8	3.8	8.6	8.5	8.1	5.9	5.3	36.9	21.9	4.5	0.4	71.2	33.9	50.4	49.6
27562	NEW HILL	83.0	81.4	12.3	12.9	1.1	1.4	4.2	5.6	8.6	8.2	6.7	5.1	4.4	34.2	23.8	7.7	1.2	72.9	35.8	50.4	49.6
27563	NORLINA	42.7	41.5	55.3	56.1	0.2	0.2	1.4	1.6	4.7	5.1	6.6	6.2	7.9	32.1	23.2	12.5	1.8	79.8	37.2	55.0	45.0
27565	OXFORD	53.8	52.4	42.1	42.7	0.3	0.3	4.2	5.2	6.1	6.6	7.5	6.6	5.3	27.0	26.1	12.9	1.9	75.6	39.2	48.1	51.9
27569	PRINCETON	85.5	84.4	11.6	12.1	0.1	0.2	3.3	4.1	6.6	6.7	6.8	5.9	6.1	30.5	25.8	10.5	1.1	76.3	37.3	49.6	50.5
27571	ROLESVILLE	78.4	77.3	18.4	18.7	0.6	0.7	2.9	3.8	7.6	7.8	8.6	6.5	5.5	32.8	23.6	7.0	0.7	72.1	35.6	50.4	49.6
27572	ROUGEMONT	83.4	82.0	13.8	14.7	0.3	0.4	2.2	2.9	5.8	6.4	7.0	6.0	4.8	29.1	29.8	9.9	1.2	77.0	40.0	49.7	50.3
27573	ROXBORO	54.7	53.4	41.5	42.2	0.2	0.3	2.9	3.5	6.7	6.4	6.7	6.0	5.9	27.1	24.3	14.6	2.4	76.6	39.0	45.8	54.2
27574	ROXBORO	70.8	69.6	26.5	27.3	0.1	0.1	1.6	2.0	6.0	6.3	6.6	5.8	5.2	28.3	28.1	12.3	1.5	77.4	40.2	49.5	50.5
27576	SELMA	68.5	66.9	22.5	22.4	0.2	0.2	12.4	15.0	7.5	7.3	7.2	6.0	6.3	30.7	23.7	10.2	1.2	74.5	35.1	49.4	50.6
27577	SMITHFIELD	71.9	71.0	22.0	21.7	0.5	0.5	8.3	10.4	6.4	6.3	6.3	5.7	6.0	29.7	24.4	13.3	2.1	77.5	38.2	50.1	49.9
27581	STEM	83.4	82.0	12.9	13.6	0.4	0.4	3.2	4.2	6.5	6.9	8.0	6.6	5.5	32.4	26.1	7.3	0.6	74.5	36.7	51.7	48.3
27583	TIMBERLAKE	82.2	81.3	15.3	15.7	0.2	0.2	1.3	1.6	6.8	7.1	7.2	5.8	5.0	32.1	25.8	9.4	0.8	75.1	37.6	49.6	50.4
27587	WAKE FOREST	83.6	82.7	12.4	12.5	1.3	1.5	2.7	3.6	8.5	8.5	8.2	6.2	5.1	33.8	22.9	6.0	0.8	70.8	34.5	49.4	50.7
27589	WARRENTON	30.2	29.3	61.2	61.6	0.1	0.2	1.7	2.0	6.4	6.6	7.2	7.1	5.9	25.9	24.0	14.6	2.4	75.3	39.2	47.9	52.1
27591	WENDELL	72.4	70.3	22.6	23.4	0.4	0.5	5.7	7.4	7.7	7.6	7.5	6.7	6.0	32.4	23.5	7.7	0.9	73.1	34.8	48.8	51.2
27592	WILLOW SPRING	86.7	85.1	8.3	8.7	0.4	0.4	5.2	6.8	8.5	8.3	7.7	5.9	5.6	36.0	21.8	5.9	0.5	71.9	33.9	50.3	49.7
27596	YOUNGSVILLE	83.3	81.5	12.6	13.5	0.5	0.6	4.4	5.7	8.5	8.2	7.1	5.6	5.3	34.4	23.5	6.9	0.6	72.9	35.2	50.0	50.0
27597	ZEBULON	69.7	68.4	25.4	25.7	0.4	0.5	6.6	8.2	7.3	7.3	7.3	6.3	6.0	31.3	24.4	9.1	1.1	74.2	36.0	49.4	50.6
27601	RALEIGH	14.2	14.3	80.5	79.6	0.5	0.5	5.7	7.0	8.2	7.6	7.3	10.2	11.4	27.9	17.3	8.7	1.5	73.0	28.8	47.1	52.9
27603	RALEIGH	68.7	66.6	23.4	23.8	1.6	1.8	7.6	9.8	6.7	6.2	6.4	6.2	8.2	37.0	21.9	6.8	0.6	77.3	33.8	53.1	46.9
27604	RALEIGH	57.6	56.3	32.1	31.9	4.0	4.5	7.2	8.6	7.5	6.8	6.2	6.3	7.1	37.1	21.0	7.3	0.7	76.0	33.8	48.8	51.2
27605	RALEIGH	88.8	87.6	7.4	8.0	1.4	1.6	1.8	2.4	2.0	1.4	1.6	3.3	11.9	47.3	21.4	9.5	1.6	93.5	34.9	50.9	49.1
27606	RALEIGH	75.4	73.5	12.9	12.9	6.1	7.0	6.7	8.3	4.2	3.9	4.1	14.0	24.3	29.4	15.4	4.3	0.4	85.4	24.9	54.5	45.5
27607	RALEIGH	82.3	80.6	9.1	9.2	5.0	6.1	3.9	4.9	4.1	3.9	4.2	12.4	13.7	30.3	19.9	9.5	2.0	85.2	31.7	47.8	52.2
27608	RALEIGH	91.5	90.7	5.8	6.0	0.9	1.0	2.3	3.0	5.5	5.2	5.1	4.2	4.9	34.3	24.8	12.1	3.8	81.5	39.3	46.0	54.0
27609	RALEIGH	77.0	75.0	14.8	15.4	2.5	2.9	9.0	11.1	5.8	5.4	5.6	5.6	7.8	33.1	23.4	12.0	1.2	79.9	36.3	49.1	50.9
27610	RALEIGH	24.0	24.0	68.0	66.6	0.6	0.7	9.1	11.0	7.3	7.2	7.5	7.6	8.1	32.7	21.2	7.6	0.9	73.8	32.5	46.7	53.3
27612	RALEIGH	82.7	80.7	11.0	11.7	3.1	3.8	4.5	5.9	5.6	5.1	5.0	5.2	8.7	37.0	23.1	8.7	1.6	81.2	34.4	48.8	51.2
	NORTH CAROLINA	72.1	71.2	21.6	21.6	1.5	1.8	4.7	5.9	6.7	6.6	6.8	6.7	7.1	29.8	24.2	10.8	1.4	76.2	36.2	49.2	50.8
	UNITED STATES	75.1	73.6	12.3	12.5	3.8	4.2	12.5	14.1	6.9	6.7	7.2	7.0	7.3	28.6	23.8	10.8	1.7	75.1	36.0	49.1	50.9

#	POST OFFICE NAME	2004 Per Capita Income	2004 HH Income Base	2004 Household Income Distribution (%) Less than $25,000	$25,000 to $49,999	$50,000 to $99,999	$100,000 to $149,999	$150,000 or More	Median Household Income 2004	2009	2004 National Centile	2004 State Centile	2004 Home Value Base	2004 Home Value Distribution (%) Less than $50,000	$50,000 to $89,999	$90,000 to $174,999	$175,000 to $399,999	$400,000 or More	2004 Median Home Value
27341	SEAGROVE	18383	2139	29.1	33.3	31.9	4.6	1.1	41199	46319	50	59	1808	26.7	25.8	35.3	10.3	1.9	87013
27343	SEMORA	21698	717	32.8	32.1	26.6	4.9	3.6	37913	42746	39	44	582	16.2	30.4	30.2	20.6	2.6	93448
27344	SILER CITY	18523	6625	29.5	34.0	27.4	6.7	2.4	39841	45757	45	50	4937	20.8	24.3	36.8	14.8	3.4	96322
27349	SNOW CAMP	20491	2255	21.4	32.6	36.3	8.2	1.6	46218	51837	64	79	1932	19.8	19.0	39.0	18.9	3.4	105824
27350	SOPHIA	20818	2543	23.1	34.7	33.6	6.8	1.7	44056	48862	59	71	2137	22.8	19.5	43.6	12.5	1.6	98144
27355	STALEY	19540	872	25.1	29.9	39.7	4.2	1.0	45909	51145	64	78	725	17.5	28.1	40.8	9.1	4.4	95727
27356	STAR	19208	1365	34.7	31.9	27.8	3.8	1.8	35998	41298	32	35	1110	32.5	26.4	31.2	8.4	1.5	75506
27357	STOKESDALE	23456	2467	18.9	28.1	41.3	8.7	3.0	51769	58816	75	88	2060	19.5	10.6	51.5	15.3	3.1	118546
27358	SUMMERFIELD	32001	3838	16.5	19.8	36.0	17.1	10.6	66326	76963	89	95	3339	6.9	8.4	37.2	37.1	10.5	169318
27360	THOMASVILLE	20362	17727	30.1	32.5	30.5	5.1	1.9	39823	45411	45	50	12481	16.0	25.2	46.2	12.0	0.6	98968
27370	TRINITY	21817	6237	21.7	31.9	36.9	6.8	2.7	47018	52371	66	81	5187	15.7	18.2	49.7	14.4	2.0	110306
27371	TROY	20770	3443	34.3	30.2	26.6	5.4	3.5	37379	43322	37	41	2576	19.3	30.2	33.5	13.7	3.3	90903
27376	WEST END	27833	3409	17.7	31.0	37.2	7.5	6.7	50954	58999	74	86	2949	11.4	13.0	35.6	32.4	7.6	147072
27377	WHITSETT	24249	1608	23.2	30.9	32.7	7.7	5.5	46409	52426	65	79	1362	22.4	17.1	38.3	19.5	2.8	107485
27379	YANCEYVILLE	16796	2095	38.8	30.4	25.3	4.0	1.6	33621	37658	23	23	1555	22.6	28.6	39.6	8.6	0.6	88347
27401	GREENSBORO	17803	7170	41.8	32.9	19.0	4.3	2.0	29416	34123	11	10	2867	7.4	41.0	38.0	12.1	1.5	91409
27403	GREENSBORO	25715	8317	30.4	29.9	26.2	8.3	5.2	40761	47822	49	56	4274	2.3	29.5	40.3	24.6	3.4	116613
27405	GREENSBORO	20187	16577	33.1	33.6	25.3	5.6	2.5	36194	41944	32	36	8623	12.3	34.0	44.9	6.0	2.8	93025
27406	GREENSBORO	21852	20645	26.3	32.5	30.8	7.7	2.8	41986	48764	53	62	13348	10.4	21.4	52.9	14.2	1.1	108405
27407	GREENSBORO	26916	18152	21.1	29.9	34.4	9.3	5.4	49038	56804	70	84	9795	2.9	15.0	58.8	19.2	4.1	124729
27408	GREENSBORO	46368	8395	17.5	26.4	29.9	10.4	15.8	56885	66470	82	91	5975	0.3	9.5	47.5	27.6	15.1	156378
27409	GREENSBORO	30171	7732	19.8	35.2	31.4	8.6	4.9	45698	52452	63	77	3641	2.6	27.1	43.0	20.1	7.3	124370
27410	GREENSBORO	38878	21659	12.7	23.8	34.6	16.9	11.9	65684	77175	89	95	14059	0.8	2.6	42.4	47.1	7.1	182943
27411	GREENSBORO	11562	0	0.0	0.0	0.0	0.0	0.0	0	0	0	0	0	0.0	0.0	0.0	0.0	0.0	0
27413	GREENSBORO	12825	18	5.6	33.3	61.1	0.0	0.0	54216	60990	79	89	0	0.0	0.0	0.0	0.0	0.0	0
27455	GREENSBORO	33269	10139	14.9	25.3	37.1	14.1	8.7	59714	69221	84	92	6843	1.5	8.4	53.4	29.3	7.4	152096
27501	ANGIER	20415	5637	25.8	31.6	33.3	6.6	2.8	43778	49131	58	70	4261	17.7	13.1	49.8	17.6	1.9	114718
27502	APEX	31263	8399	10.0	17.0	39.8	23.3	9.9	76241	87291	94	98	7105	5.9	3.2	28.1	58.9	4.0	198018
27503	BAHAMA	39733	1602	11.6	20.5	35.3	16.3	16.4	68091	78519	90	96	1420	3.1	3.9	32.0	43.9	17.0	197794
27504	BENSON	19433	6252	29.7	29.9	32.3	6.2	2.0	40243	46420	47	54	4684	19.4	18.7	48.6	12.1	1.3	106162
27505	BROADWAY	20712	1908	25.8	35.0	32.0	5.3	1.9	40083	45887	46	52	1541	25.9	21.9	37.4	13.6	1.2	93750
27507	BULLOCK	18130	756	32.9	35.5	26.5	3.4	1.7	36262	41343	33	36	616	21.6	37.0	34.7	5.8	0.8	80185
27508	BUNN	15892	690	33.3	28.4	31.9	5.1	1.3	40698	46118	49	55	529	31.0	28.2	33.1	6.4	1.3	77083
27509	BUTNER	17471	1936	26.5	30.8	31.2	7.5	4.0	44800	51933	61	74	1392	31.7	14.6	45.3	8.5	0.0	98667
27510	CARRBORO	24561	6741	31.6	34.0	22.0	8.9	3.5	36871	44302	35	39	1929	3.2	10.0	33.0	49.3	4.5	180760
27511	CARY	37982	18803	9.2	20.1	34.1	21.5	15.0	77536	89815	94	98	13865	2.6	1.1	28.8	54.2	13.4	219296
27513	CARY	36681	16895	8.0	17.4	39.7	20.9	14.0	78102	90890	94	98	10264	0.5	1.8	28.9	59.3	9.4	213023
27514	CHAPEL HILL	31776	11994	36.8	19.0	18.3	10.1	15.9	41552	52038	51	60	4895	5.3	2.2	15.1	48.9	28.6	284581
27516	CHAPEL HILL	31014	13272	22.4	22.7	28.1	14.5	12.3	56741	70444	81	90	7997	7.2	5.6	28.8	44.1	14.3	205286
27517	CHAPEL HILL	46626	8852	15.0	21.4	32.7	15.5	15.4	66533	79791	89	95	5477	5.5	1.7	23.4	45.6	23.8	233713
27519	CARY	36830	4920	5.0	10.5	35.1	33.0	16.4	99027	114396	98	99	4287	1.3	1.5	10.4	77.0	9.8	261193
27520	CLAYTON	25509	14227	17.2	24.6	42.6	11.5	4.2	56869	63242	82	90	11544	12.0	9.5	51.2	25.1	2.3	135281
27521	COATS	19231	2458	34.1	31.5	27.2	5.6	1.7	36010	40726	32	35	1734	22.7	22.6	40.2	13.5	1.0	96136
27522	CREEDMOOR	24188	3767	24.5	28.8	33.8	9.4	3.5	45989	52378	64	78	2938	17.6	15.3	42.8	22.1	2.1	117121
27523	APEX	39081	3684	8.4	15.7	38.6	25.9	11.5	81568	96381	95	99	2937	5.0	2.5	16.3	68.8	7.3	234280
27524	FOUR OAKS	20063	4370	31.5	27.7	32.5	6.7	1.7	40109	45613	46	52	3296	22.2	23.8	43.3	10.2	0.6	94963
27525	FRANKLINTON	19819	4522	27.6	29.2	34.5	6.6	2.0	43672	49421	58	70	3587	22.9	26.0	35.2	14.9	1.0	91808
27526	FUQUAY VARINA	25384	10091	17.9	27.4	36.1	13.5	5.1	54939	63980	80	89	7842	7.2	8.2	49.7	31.7	3.3	147780
27529	GARNER	25415	13431	15.3	28.6	39.1	13.9	3.1	56118	64700	81	90	10371	6.9	8.2	60.0	23.6	1.3	138525
27530	GOLDSBORO	19240	14807	36.1	31.2	24.9	5.3	2.5	34689	39271	26	28	9280	16.2	31.7	42.4	9.5	0.3	91986
27531	GOLDSBORO	9080	331	21.2	56.2	20.5	1.8	0.3	36050	40325	32	35	12	66.7	33.3	0.0	0.0	0.0	30000
27534	GOLDSBORO	22495	12466	25.3	34.5	30.3	6.6	3.3	42503	48087	55	65	7925	17.7	22.9	41.8	15.6	2.0	103160
27536	HENDERSON	17330	7405	47.6	27.5	17.9	3.7	3.4	26586	30135	7	4	3848	23.0	32.6	29.7	13.1	1.6	84119
27537	HENDERSON	18629	8992	30.2	34.7	26.4	6.5	2.3	38695	43766	42	47	7147	26.3	26.7	33.7	11.7	1.6	85687
27539	APEX	36676	5450	7.7	17.6	38.3	23.3	13.1	80217	93423	95	99	4688	7.1	2.9	29.4	51.1	9.5	206163
27540	HOLLY SPRINGS	29863	5696	11.9	22.9	40.1	16.4	8.8	67392	78578	90	96	4848	6.7	6.8	39.0	40.7	6.8	169394
27541	HURDLE MILLS	25410	1378	22.8	28.0	34.3	9.9	5.0	49279	56432	71	85	1168	8.3	20.0	44.6	22.8	4.4	130061
27542	KENLY	17848	3407	36.3	30.8	25.8	5.3	1.8	35607	40476	30	33	2560	25.5	27.3	36.2	10.2	0.9	85590
27544	KITTRELL	28353	1128	23.8	39.5	28.2	4.2	4.4	42653	48096	55	66	907	26.6	28.9	35.9	6.6	2.0	83400
27545	KNIGHTDALE	24602	7385	13.9	28.4	42.1	12.4	3.2	57312	66625	82	91	6034	10.5	6.2	64.6	17.9	0.8	134561
27546	LILLINGTON	19315	6409	31.2	31.1	28.7	6.3	2.7	39875	45205	46	51	4537	20.2	23.1	38.6	16.5	1.6	101247
27549	LOUISBURG	18738	8343	30.7	31.7	30.3	5.7	1.6	39514	44570	44	49	6342	21.8	23.7	38.5	14.7	1.3	96667
27551	MACON	20368	1345	34.9	28.3	27.2	7.3	2.2	37347	42819	37	41	1107	24.1	21.3	33.3	18.2	3.1	98707
27553	MANSON	15119	935	44.9	26.5	24.4	2.3	1.9	29317	32795	11	10	760	31.5	24.3	31.8	11.6	0.8	69318
27557	MIDDLESEX	18221	2892	33.3	32.1	27.2	4.6	2.8	37299	42771	36	40	2239	25.4	26.0	38.9	6.6	3.1	87237
27559	MONCURE	21851	827	23.0	33.6	33.7	5.9	3.8	43772	50479	58	70	673	24.1	25.1	30.0	18.1	2.7	92200
27560	MORRISVILLE	47682	5706	8.8	14.9	34.5	20.7	21.1	84699	96530	96	99	3399	1.7	2.0	13.5	52.5	30.3	305712
27562	NEW HILL	27069	830	16.9	23.9	38.2	15.3	5.8	60576	69566	85	93	708	11.4	11.9	32.5	38.3	5.9	161513
27563	NORLINA	15835	1463	43.3	30.6	22.0	2.1	2.1	29971	33179	12	11	1063	36.9	31.9	23.3	7.3	0.6	67022
27565	OXFORD	20143	9725	31.6	29.0	29.8	6.4	3.2	41169	46881	50	58	7161	14.0	25.0	42.3	16.5	2.2	106788
27569	PRINCETON	19213	2751	29.2	35.8	27.2	6.0	1.8	39923	45443	46	51	2098	24.0	27.8	38.5	9.5	0.2	88020
27571	ROLESVILLE	26036	416	14.7	23.8	43.3	14.4	3.9	61004	70407	85	93	349	9.5	6.9	51.3	28.9	3.4	145179
27572	ROUGEMONT	27017	2584	19.8	24.1	37.5	12.5	6.1	55445	63496	80	90	2200	7.6	17.2	39.0	29.8	6.5	139483
27573	ROXBORO	19189	4840	39.2	29.6	26.1	3.5	1.7	32385	37043	19	19	2831	17.5	29.1	42.0	10.8	0.6	93851
27574	ROXBORO	21306	5524	25.2	32.5	34.8	5.0	2.5	44285	49806	59	72	4517	10.9	28.2	41.8	17.1	2.1	104243
27576	SELMA	17102	7317	35.3	31.6	27.1	4.7	1.3	35781	40689	31	34	4945	23.4	26.0	40.3	9.6	0.8	90854
27577	SMITHFIELD	21118	8177	35.0	29.8	26.4	5.7	3.1	36697	41821	34	38	5313	12.7	21.4	46.7	17.5	1.7	112443
27581	STEM	21919	978	21.2	27.6	43.3	6.1	1.8	50890	58063	74	86	820	13.1	19.5	46.2	18.5	2.7	115823
27583	TIMBERLAKE	22938	2184	23.2	27.1	40.3	6.2	3.2	49717	55047	71	85	1855	11.6	19.1	48.5	20.0	0.8	114566
27587	WAKE FOREST	29051	13125	15.5	21.7	38.1	16.6	8.2	63964	74292	88	94	10029	7.9	7.6	35.8	41.1	7.6	171935
27589	WARRENTON	14754	3927	44.3	34.2	17.7	2.2	1.7	28270	31742	9	7	3012	39.9	28.8	26.3	4.0	1.1	64826
27591	WENDELL	21972	6328	21.4	27.1	39.6	9.8	2.2	51026	59444	74	87	4995	11.4	12.6	55.7	18.5	1.8	120226
27592	WILLOW SPRING	23203	4492	15.1	29.5	42.2	10.3	2.9	53795	62195	78	88	3812	14.0	12.6	50.6	21.5	1.4	129974
27596	YOUNGSVILLE	23425	4512	15.5	31.3	41.1	9.3	2.7	52382	59299	76	88	3810	15.6	14.2	49.2	19.3	1.6	122978
27597	ZEBULON	21724	7466	26.4	28.3	33.0	9.2	3.1	45310	51601	62	75	5686	14.1	17.9	47.4	17.6	2.9	114316
27601	RALEIGH	13984	3491	57.2	24.7	12.7	2.9	2.4	20104	24400	2	1	925	13.3	24.5	32.7	25.4	4.1	111152
27603	RALEIGH	24205	14513	23.9	28.8	32.6	11.4	3.4	47276	56303	67	82	9015	12.9	8.2	49.1	28.0	1.9	141282
27604	RALEIGH	27246	15227	15.5	29.3	40.0	11.2	4.1	54712	64736	79	89	9534	4.3	3.3	63.2	27.0	2.1	149845
27605	RALEIGH	40600	2378	22.5	31.3	32.0	9.3	5.0	45970	56950	64	78	783	0.9	4.2	25.2	54.9	14.8	219954
27606	RALEIGH	25809	16625	25.1	29.6	27.8	12.0	5.5	45367	52554	62	76	6374	3.5	3.6	37.6	46.5	8.9	191488
27607	RALEIGH	33527	8195	18.2	24.0	31.4	16.0	10.4	60394	70039	85	93	4347	1.2	1.8	19.2	62.1	15.7	237727
27608	RALEIGH	46785	5108	17.8	24.1	27.5	15.4	15.2	60543	71633	85	93	3145	0.3	1.3	14.6	45.8	38.0	311203
27609	RALEIGH	35215	15798	15.2	28.2	34.4	14.5	7.7	57133	66034	82	91	8759	0.3	2.0	41.5	45.8	10.5	184573
27610	RALEIGH	18974	17154	25.7	33.2	31.0	7.8	2.3	42485	50327	55	65	10209	11.0	14.8	59.2	14.2	0.8	119794
27612	RALEIGH	39905	15179	12.5	24.4	35.3	16.8	11.1	63456	73372	87	94	7649	0.7	1.9	20.0	63.9	13.5	230902
	NORTH CAROLINA	23743		27.0	29.8	30.1	8.5	4.7	43794	50711				14.5	20.0	39.7	21.7	4.1	115673
	UNITED STATES	25866		24.7	27.1	30.8	10.9	6.5	48124	56710				10.9	15.0	33.7	30.1	10.4	145905

ZIP CODE		FINANCIAL SERVICES				THE HOME						ENTERTAINMENT						PERSONAL			
						Home Improvements		Furnishings													
#	POST OFFICE NAME	Auto Loan	Home Loan	Invest-ments	Retire-ment Plans	Home Repair	Lawn & Garden	Comput-ers & Hard-ware	Major Appli-ances	TV, Radio, Sound Equip-ment	Furni-ture	Dine out/ Carry out	Sports Equip-ment	Fees & Tickets	Toys & Games	Travel	Cable TV	Apparel & Services	Auto Repairs	Health Insur-ance	Pets & Supplies
27341	SEAGROVE	87	59	28	51	67	76	57	71	68	58	80	84	49	76	58	73	73	70	86	100
27343	SEMORA	95	70	42	62	79	90	67	81	77	67	91	96	58	89	70	83	84	80	98	113
27344	SILER CITY	86	67	44	62	72	80	65	75	73	66	87	88	60	85	66	76	81	74	85	98
27349	SNOW CAMP	85	76	59	73	78	83	72	78	74	73	91	92	69	89	72	75	87	77	81	97
27350	SOPHIA	86	77	59	73	80	85	72	79	75	73	92	93	70	91	73	76	88	77	83	99
27355	STALEY	88	66	39	60	72	80	63	75	72	64	86	89	57	82	64	75	79	74	86	101
27356	STAR	88	59	27	51	67	77	57	71	69	58	80	85	49	76	58	74	73	70	87	100
27357	STOKESDALE	93	86	73	84	87	93	83	88	84	84	104	103	80	100	82	84	99	88	89	105
27358	SUMMERFIELD	120	134	132	134	133	136	120	123	115	121	144	144	126	150	123	114	142	119	117	142
27360	THOMASVILLE	78	68	56	66	71	78	68	73	72	67	87	85	65	86	68	73	83	72	78	88
27370	TRINITY	93	80	58	75	85	92	74	84	80	75	97	99	72	98	76	83	92	82	92	109
27371	TROY	80	63	42	59	68	77	61	70	68	61	82	83	57	80	62	71	76	69	81	92
27376	WEST END	104	95	83	91	99	111	89	99	93	93	115	106	88	103	93	96	109	97	109	117
27377	WHITSETT	94	84	65	81	87	93	79	86	82	80	101	101	76	99	80	83	96	85	90	107
27379	YANCEYVILLE	69	50	26	44	55	62	47	58	55	48	66	69	42	63	48	59	60	57	69	80
27401	GREENSBORO	55	49	59	48	48	55	57	54	60	56	75	62	56	71	55	60	72	57	56	61
27403	GREENSBORO	77	74	90	77	73	79	88	79	85	83	107	97	84	105	82	81	104	84	74	87
27405	GREENSBORO	67	64	71	64	63	70	69	67	70	68	88	78	69	87	68	70	85	69	68	75
27406	GREENSBORO	75	76	81	75	75	80	76	76	76	76	95	88	77	95	76	75	93	77	74	86
27407	GREENSBORO	93	92	100	96	90	94	96	93	93	96	117	110	95	115	92	89	114	95	86	103
27408	GREENSBORO	126	148	175	147	147	156	141	140	136	140	171	160	149	175	145	136	168	138	135	152
27409	GREENSBORO	88	83	95	90	81	85	90	86	87	91	111	104	88	106	85	82	108	90	78	96
27410	GREENSBORO	121	129	145	135	126	131	128	125	122	129	154	147	130	152	126	117	152	126	114	137
27411	GREENSBORO	0	0	0	0	0	0	0	0	0	0	0	0	0	0	0	0	0	0	0	0
27413	GREENSBORO	73	48	61	54	47	55	84	65	82	73	102	88	71	93	69	73	97	77	60	73
27455	GREENSBORO	105	118	132	122	115	117	114	111	107	115	136	132	117	138	113	103	134	111	100	122
27501	ANGIER	83	74	60	73	75	81	74	77	76	74	93	90	70	90	72	75	89	77	79	91
27502	APEX	124	140	137	146	134	129	127	126	116	132	148	147	131	148	124	109	146	123	107	137
27503	BAHAMA	132	163	177	163	159	161	146	145	136	146	171	167	157	179	150	133	171	140	132	159
27504	BENSON	75	70	60	69	70	75	69	72	70	69	86	83	67	85	68	70	83	71	73	84
27505	BROADWAY	88	80	62	76	81	85	75	81	77	77	95	95	72	91	75	76	91	80	82	99
27507	BULLOCK	89	60	27	52	68	78	58	72	70	59	82	86	49	77	59	75	74	71	89	103
27508	BUNN	73	67	52	64	67	70	64	68	64	65	79	79	60	75	63	63	76	68	68	81
27509	BUTNER	74	67	53	65	67	71	64	69	65	66	80	79	61	76	63	64	77	68	68	82
27510	CARRBORO	72	58	71	64	57	62	79	68	77	74	97	88	72	91	70	70	93	77	62	76
27511	CARY	136	151	166	157	146	149	144	140	135	146	172	165	150	172	143	129	170	140	126	155
27513	CARY	138	145	147	154	138	137	140	137	131	145	167	162	141	163	134	122	164	137	118	151
27514	CHAPEL HILL	106	96	133	105	94	103	120	105	117	114	147	131	115	144	111	111	143	114	97	117
27516	CHAPEL HILL	109	109	125	116	106	110	118	110	113	116	143	134	117	139	112	106	140	115	99	122
27517	CHAPEL HILL	131	144	206	151	141	151	147	140	144	148	182	165	154	187	149	142	180	143	131	154
27519	CARY	159	181	175	189	172	166	163	161	149	169	190	189	168	190	159	139	188	157	137	176
27520	CLAYTON	99	106	100	109	103	103	99	99	93	101	117	116	99	117	97	89	115	98	89	111
27521	COATS	77	66	52	65	68	76	68	72	71	67	87	83	65	85	67	71	82	72	76	85
27522	CREEDMOOR	92	83	66	81	84	91	81	86	83	82	102	100	77	97	80	83	97	86	88	102
27523	APEX	136	151	151	157	145	143	140	138	129	144	164	162	143	163	137	121	161	136	121	151
27524	FOUR OAKS	80	68	52	65	70	77	67	73	71	68	87	85	63	83	67	72	82	73	77	89
27525	FRANKLINTON	82	74	58	70	75	80	70	76	73	72	89	88	67	86	70	73	85	75	78	92
27526	FUQUAY VARINA	102	101	88	101	101	105	95	99	94	96	117	115	95	117	95	93	113	97	96	114
27529	GARNER	91	100	103	102	97	97	95	94	90	96	114	111	97	115	94	86	112	93	84	103
27530	GOLDSBORO	69	62	59	59	62	69	64	66	67	65	82	74	62	79	63	68	79	66	69	76
27531	GOLDSBORO	66	42	40	48	38	45	62	53	63	58	79	71	53	70	51	57	75	63	49	61
27534	GOLDSBORO	83	78	72	77	78	84	79	80	79	78	98	94	76	96	77	78	95	81	80	93
27536	HENDERSON	63	53	51	50	55	64	57	60	63	57	77	68	55	72	57	66	73	61	67	71
27537	HENDERSON	83	69	48	64	72	78	66	74	71	67	86	87	61	82	66	72	81	73	80	94
27539	APEX	140	158	153	165	151	147	143	142	131	148	167	166	147	167	140	123	165	138	121	156
27540	HOLLY SPRINGS	118	129	120	132	123	121	117	118	109	122	138	137	119	137	114	103	136	115	103	131
27541	HURDLE MILLS	103	92	71	87	96	103	85	94	90	85	109	112	83	110	87	92	104	92	101	120
27542	KENLY	75	59	40	56	63	71	59	66	64	59	77	77	54	75	59	66	72	65	74	84
27544	KITTRELL	118	100	71	94	103	111	96	106	101	98	123	124	89	117	95	102	117	106	112	133
27545	KNIGHTDALE	98	103	94	105	100	100	95	97	90	98	113	112	95	112	93	86	111	95	87	108
27546	LILLINGTON	76	67	56	66	67	73	70	71	70	69	87	83	65	84	67	69	83	71	71	83
27549	LOUISBURG	82	64	41	58	68	77	62	72	69	63	83	84	56	80	63	72	77	71	82	94
27551	MACON	86	63	38	56	71	81	60	74	70	61	83	86	53	79	63	75	76	73	89	101
27553	MANSON	74	50	23	43	56	65	48	60	58	49	68	72	41	64	49	62	62	59	74	85
27557	MIDDLESEX	81	64	42	59	68	74	62	70	67	63	81	83	56	77	61	69	76	70	78	91
27559	MONCURE	87	79	62	76	81	86	75	81	77	76	95	94	72	93	75	78	91	80	84	98
27560	MORRISVILLE	154	174	177	182	167	165	160	157	147	165	187	183	166	188	157	138	186	154	135	172
27562	NEW HILL	104	103	93	106	102	106	99	101	97	100	120	117	98	119	97	94	116	99	97	115
27563	NORLINA	73	49	22	42	56	64	47	59	57	48	67	71	40	64	48	62	61	59	73	84
27565	OXFORD	82	70	55	65	73	82	69	76	75	69	91	87	66	89	70	78	86	75	84	94
27569	PRINCETON	77	66	48	63	68	74	65	71	68	65	83	81	60	78	64	69	78	70	75	86
27571	ROLESVILLE	98	107	101	109	103	102	98	98	92	101	116	116	99	116	96	87	114	96	87	110
27572	ROUGEMONT	105	104	93	102	105	112	98	103	98	98	121	119	98	122	99	99	117	101	104	121
27573	ROXBORO	73	56	39	52	60	70	58	65	65	57	78	75	53	75	58	69	72	65	76	82
27574	ROXBORO	90	76	54	71	81	88	71	80	77	71	93	96	68	94	73	80	88	79	89	105
27576	SELMA	68	58	48	56	60	66	60	63	64	60	78	74	57	75	59	64	74	64	68	76
27577	SMITHFIELD	80	70	58	68	73	81	71	76	75	71	91	87	68	88	71	77	86	75	82	90
27581	STEM	89	81	63	78	81	86	77	83	78	79	96	96	73	91	76	77	93	82	82	98
27583	TIMBERLAKE	95	84	63	80	85	91	80	87	83	82	101	101	75	96	79	82	97	87	89	106
27587	WAKE FOREST	114	126	121	130	121	119	115	115	107	118	135	134	117	135	112	101	133	112	100	127
27589	WARRENTON	70	47	21	40	53	61	45	56	54	46	64	67	38	60	46	58	58	56	69	80
27591	WENDELL	86	85	77	85	84	88	82	84	80	83	100	98	80	99	81	78	97	83	81	96
27592	WILLOW SPRING	93	97	87	98	94	94	89	91	85	92	107	106	89	104	87	81	104	89	83	103
27596	YOUNGSVILLE	94	92	79	92	91	93	86	90	84	89	105	104	84	101	85	81	102	89	85	104
27597	ZEBULON	90	78	61	75	81	89	77	83	81	77	99	97	73	96	77	82	93	82	88	102
27601	RALEIGH	47	40	50	38	39	47	47	46	51	47	63	52	46	59	45	53	61	48	49	52
27603	RALEIGH	85	86	93	90	84	86	89	86	86	89	108	102	88	106	86	82	105	87	79	95
27604	RALEIGH	90	93	100	98	90	91	94	91	89	95	113	108	93	111	90	84	111	92	80	100
27605	RALEIGH	83	78	138	89	75	83	93	83	95	94	120	103	96	124	91	93	119	90	77	93
27606	RALEIGH	89	75	92	82	73	80	100	85	97	92	121	109	92	115	89	89	117	95	78	95
27607	RALEIGH	101	103	133	108	100	107	115	104	111	111	139	128	114	139	110	105	137	110	96	116
27608	RALEIGH	117	134	181	137	130	139	134	128	129	134	163	150	140	169	135	128	162	130	119	140
27609	RALEIGH	108	104	125	112	101	108	112	107	109	114	139	128	111	133	108	104	136	112	98	119
27610	RALEIGH	73	72	76	72	70	75	73	72	73	74	92	83	73	90	72	72	90	73	70	81
27612	RALEIGH	118	114	143	124	111	118	124	117	120	125	153	141	123	149	119	115	150	123	107	130
	NORTH CAROLINA	90	81	73	80	83	90	81	85	84	82	103	100	79	101	81	84	99	85	88	102
	UNITED STATES	100	100	100	100	100	100	100	100	100	100	100	100	100	100	100	100	100	100	100	100

NORTH CAROLINA

A 27613-27924

POPULATION CHANGE

ZIP CODE			POPULATION			2000-2004 ANNUAL RATE		HOUSEHOLDS					FAMILIES		
#	POST OFFICE NAME	COUNTY FIPS CODE	2000	2004	2009	% Rate	State Centile	2000	2004	2009	% Annual Rate 2000-2004	2004 Average HH Size	2000	2004	% Annual Rate 2000-2004
27613	RALEIGH	183	32700	39680	48213	4.7	95	13226	16114	19661	4.8	2.46	8519	10238	4.4
27614	RALEIGH	183	11600	15581	20007	7.2	99	3906	5347	6935	7.7	2.91	3371	4513	7.1
27615	RALEIGH	183	39426	43852	51005	2.5	78	15462	17423	20421	2.9	2.50	10624	11658	2.2
27616	RALEIGH	183	21979	28924	36719	6.7	99	8035	10539	13376	6.6	2.74	5583	7267	6.4
27617	RALEIGH	183	3597	4673	5851	6.4	99	1281	1690	2141	6.7	2.77	1086	1414	6.4
27695	RALEIGH	183	4	5	6	5.4	97	1	1	2	0.0	3.00	0	0	0.0
27701	DURHAM	063	23660	24185	26357	0.5	22	9220	9403	10291	0.5	2.48	4806	4772	-0.2
27703	DURHAM	063	32305	36148	41113	2.7	80	11943	13453	15396	2.8	2.68	8400	9263	2.3
27704	DURHAM	063	26865	28894	32039	1.7	58	10764	11670	13034	1.9	2.44	6969	7424	1.5
27705	DURHAM	063	42197	45090	49671	1.6	54	17103	18584	20842	2.0	2.13	8815	9288	1.2
27707	DURHAM	063	39886	42344	46851	1.4	50	16036	17215	19268	1.7	2.33	9329	9801	1.2
27709	DURHAM	063	25	27	31	1.8	60	9	10	11	2.5	2.60	4	5	5.4
27712	DURHAM	063	16817	18929	21488	2.8	82	6220	7119	8175	3.2	2.62	4959	5629	3.0
27713	DURHAM	063	32351	39816	47835	5.0	96	13843	17073	20598	5.1	2.31	8287	10060	4.7
27801	ROCKY MOUNT	065	22701	22790	22927	0.1	12	8103	8216	8355	0.3	2.74	5896	5903	0.0
27803	ROCKY MOUNT	127	22012	22325	23445	0.3	17	8554	8783	9334	0.6	2.52	6085	6151	0.3
27804	ROCKY MOUNT	127	25503	26503	28109	0.9	34	10205	10755	11563	1.2	2.38	6791	7046	0.9
27805	AULANDER	015	2037	1994	1989	-0.5	3	808	809	825	0.0	2.46	572	565	-0.3
27806	AURORA	013	2747	2735	2785	-0.1	8	1146	1161	1204	0.3	2.36	791	786	-0.2
27807	BAILEY	127	5312	5717	6145	1.7	59	1979	2143	2322	1.9	2.67	1457	1554	1.5
27808	BATH	013	2130	2149	2212	0.2	14	908	933	977	0.6	2.30	663	671	0.3
27809	BATTLEBORO	127	4885	5014	5161	0.6	26	1753	1830	1913	1.0	2.60	1352	1394	0.7
27810	BELHAVEN	013	3941	3864	3928	-0.5	4	1645	1646	1707	0.0	2.32	1141	1124	-0.4
27812	BETHEL	147	2674	2669	2841	0.0	10	1020	1032	1115	0.3	2.58	726	723	-0.1
27814	BLOUNTS CREEK	013	1968	2195	2368	2.6	79	812	923	1015	3.1	2.38	601	673	2.7
27816	CASTALIA	069	2516	2853	3247	3.0	84	958	1101	1268	3.3	2.58	701	794	3.0
27817	CHOCOWINITY	013	5862	6168	6449	1.2	43	2325	2503	2672	1.8	2.46	1734	1841	1.4
27818	COMO	091	1421	1500	1607	1.3	47	567	613	671	1.9	2.41	409	436	1.5
27820	CONWAY	131	3159	3154	3175	0.0	10	1308	1332	1369	0.4	2.36	882	885	0.1
27821	EDWARD	013	106	106	108	0.0	11	45	46	47	0.5	2.30	31	31	0.0
27822	ELM CITY	195	8294	8871	9464	1.6	54	3199	3473	3752	2.0	2.54	2430	2603	1.6
27823	ENFIELD	083	8800	8884	8963	0.2	15	3122	3212	3301	0.7	2.73	2263	2296	0.3
27824	ENGELHARD	095	1725	1761	1832	0.5	22	710	740	788	1.0	2.38	454	465	0.6
27826	FAIRFIELD	095	1102	1125	1160	0.5	22	213	223	237	1.1	3.87	148	153	0.8
27828	FARMVILLE	147	8768	8847	9375	0.2	14	3391	3479	3747	0.6	2.52	2391	2414	0.2
27829	FOUNTAIN	147	1568	1596	1692	0.4	19	628	646	693	0.7	2.47	467	473	0.3
27830	FREMONT	191	4291	4121	4143	-1.0	1	1687	1644	1677	-0.6	2.47	1182	1131	-1.0
27831	GARYSBURG	131	3680	3731	3783	0.3	17	1444	1495	1549	0.8	2.48	1008	1030	0.5
27832	GASTON	131	2987	3044	3089	0.5	20	1228	1283	1333	1.0	2.37	853	879	0.7
27834	GREENVILLE	147	43901	47867	53183	2.1	67	16720	18682	21204	2.7	2.47	10561	11519	2.1
27837	GRIMESLAND	147	3971	4323	4756	2.0	65	1516	1667	1856	2.3	2.59	1122	1216	1.9
27839	HALIFAX	083	4238	4184	4163	-0.3	5	1295	1299	1314	0.1	2.34	894	883	-0.3
27840	HAMILTON	117	927	861	846	-1.7	0	344	327	328	-1.2	2.57	257	241	-1.5
27842	HENRICO	131	1325	1352	1374	0.5	21	651	682	712	1.1	1.98	465	480	0.8
27843	HOBGOOD	065	1857	1832	1819	-0.3	5	700	704	711	0.1	2.60	520	516	-0.2
27844	HOLLISTER	083	2529	2528	2525	0.0	10	943	966	987	0.6	2.62	694	703	0.3
27845	JACKSON	131	1948	1936	1946	-0.2	7	756	766	786	0.3	2.09	503	501	-0.1
27846	JAMESVILLE	117	2770	2744	2731	-0.2	6	1079	1085	1096	0.1	2.51	806	802	-0.1
27847	KELFORD	015	421	414	412	-0.4	4	151	152	155	0.2	2.72	98	96	-0.5
27849	LEWISTON WOODVILLE	015	1719	1711	1715	-0.1	8	618	625	639	0.3	2.73	423	421	-0.1
27850	LITTLETON	083	6245	6895	7312	2.4	74	2721	3046	3283	2.7	2.26	1930	2130	2.4
27851	LUCAMA	195	4786	4987	5221	1.0	35	1850	1954	2072	1.3	2.55	1378	1433	0.9
27852	MACCLESFIELD	065	4175	4277	4325	0.6	24	1587	1644	1683	0.8	2.60	1190	1217	0.5
27853	MARGARETTSVILLE	131	402	400	402	-0.1	7	143	144	147	0.2	2.78	102	102	0.1
27855	MURFREESBORO	091	5842	5956	6275	0.5	21	2304	2395	2576	0.9	2.47	1600	1640	0.6
27856	NASHVILLE	127	15086	16323	17616	1.9	61	5445	6008	6596	2.3	2.56	4074	4437	2.0
27857	OAK CITY	117	1554	1451	1428	-1.6	0	628	602	605	-1.0	2.41	434	409	-1.4
27858	GREENVILLE	147	45027	48588	53188	1.8	60	18255	20025	22355	2.2	2.23	9393	10153	1.9
27860	PANTEGO	013	1954	1945	1982	-0.1	8	761	774	805	0.4	2.46	555	555	0.0
27862	PENDLETON	131	1164	1167	1174	0.1	12	452	461	473	0.5	2.52	321	323	0.2
27863	PIKEVILLE	191	8378	8696	8953	0.9	33	3194	3374	3528	1.3	2.57	2408	2500	0.9
27864	PINETOPS	065	4737	4686	4666	-0.3	6	1822	1837	1859	0.2	2.55	1331	1325	-0.1
27865	PINETOWN	013	2005	2125	2246	1.4	49	778	847	916	2.0	2.48	571	611	1.6
27866	PLEASANT HILL	131	580	589	596	0.4	18	207	216	225	1.0	2.55	147	152	0.8
27869	RICH SQUARE	131	3051	3022	3036	-0.2	6	987	999	1027	0.3	2.57	657	654	-0.1
27870	ROANOKE RAPIDS	083	28239	28257	28376	0.0	11	11345	11538	11784	0.4	2.42	7753	7765	0.0
27871	ROBERSONVILLE	117	4848	4638	4618	-1.0	1	1880	1837	1864	-0.5	2.52	1300	1250	-0.9
27872	ROXOBEL	015	698	695	695	-0.1	8	296	301	308	0.4	2.31	193	193	0.0
27873	SARATOGA	195	207	207	214	0.0	11	89	90	95	0.3	2.30	62	62	0.1
27874	SCOTLAND NECK	083	5359	5246	5230	-0.5	3	2080	2078	2111	0.0	2.46	1361	1337	-0.4
27875	SCRANTON	095	1195	1228	1272	0.6	26	479	509	546	1.4	1.80	335	352	1.2
27876	SEABOARD	131	1520	1599	1653	1.2	43	625	672	711	1.7	2.38	412	436	1.3
27880	SIMS	195	2080	2128	2206	0.5	23	785	816	856	0.9	2.60	586	600	0.6
27882	SPRING HOPE	127	6117	7030	7873	3.3	88	2376	2763	3129	3.6	2.54	1744	2000	3.3
27883	STANTONSBURG	195	2731	2844	2972	1.0	35	1083	1144	1210	1.3	2.49	785	816	0.9
27884	STOKES	147	785	824	901	1.2	41	298	320	356	1.7	2.58	228	242	1.4
27885	SWANQUARTER	095	1107	1129	1171	0.5	21	437	457	486	1.1	2.27	294	304	0.8
27886	TARBORO	065	18987	18929	19010	-0.1	9	7127	7196	7312	0.2	2.55	5076	5053	-0.1
27888	WALSTONBURG	079	3095	3146	3273	0.4	18	1105	1132	1188	0.6	2.77	839	852	0.4
27889	WASHINGTON	013	25967	27012	28443	0.9	35	10480	11092	11807	1.3	2.39	7306	7632	1.0
27890	WELDON	083	2377	2268	2239	-1.1	1	898	869	870	-0.8	2.53	618	589	-1.1
27891	WHITAKERS	127	5414	5604	5866	0.8	31	1960	2061	2186	1.2	2.70	1443	1498	0.9
27892	WILLIAMSTON	117	15653	16152	16439	0.7	28	6159	6450	6669	1.1	2.46	4446	4592	0.8
27893	WILSON	195	42121	42954	44685	0.5	21	16201	16687	17555	0.7	2.47	10544	10663	0.3
27896	WILSON	195	13993	15567	16879	2.5	78	5561	6268	6874	2.9	2.46	4141	4594	2.5
27897	WOODLAND	091	2680	2708	2770	0.2	15	1053	1088	1138	0.8	2.48	725	738	0.2
27909	ELIZABETH CITY	139	34897	36664	39079	1.2	42	12907	13823	15025	1.6	2.48	9094	9603	1.3
27910	AHOSKIE	091	11905	12497	13337	1.2	41	4700	5029	5475	1.6	2.43	3261	3439	1.3
27916	AYDLETT	053	486	542	641	2.6	79	196	221	263	2.9	2.45	144	160	2.5
27917	BARCO	053	980	1068	1236	2.0	66	340	380	452	2.7	2.55	243	267	2.2
27919	BELVIDERE	143	1564	1543	1563	-0.3	5	636	642	664	0.2	2.40	469	468	-0.1
27921	CAMDEN	029	3098	3599	4264	3.6	90	1196	1409	1693	3.9	2.55	918	1069	3.7
27922	COFIELD	091	670	716	772	1.6	54	285	312	344	2.2	2.29	198	214	1.9
27923	COINJOCK	053	553	613	720	2.5	76	233	261	309	2.7	2.32	172	190	2.4
27924	COLERAIN	015	3288	3429	3518	1.0	36	1307	1395	1463	1.5	2.46	930	979	1.2
	NORTH CAROLINA					1.9					2.2	2.46			1.8
	UNITED STATES					1.2					1.3	2.58			1.1

ZIP CODE #	POST OFFICE NAME	RACE (%) White 2000	White 2004	Black 2000	Black 2004	Asian/Pacific 2000	Asian/Pacific 2004	% Hispanic Origin 2000	% Hispanic Origin 2004	2004 AGE DISTRIBUTION (%) 0-4	5-9	10-14	15-19	20-24	25-44	45-64	65-84	85+	18+	MEDIAN AGE 2004	% 2004 Males	% 2004 Females
27613	RALEIGH	85.0	83.5	8.5	8.8	4.2	4.9	2.8	3.7	6.7	6.9	7.1	6.6	7.0	36.1	25.2	4.2	0.3	75.2	34.4	49.3	50.7
27614	RALEIGH	87.6	84.4	8.0	10.2	2.6	3.2	1.9	2.8	7.3	8.5	9.2	7.0	4.0	26.9	30.5	6.1	0.6	70.5	38.5	50.0	50.0
27615	RALEIGH	82.7	80.8	10.7	11.4	3.6	4.2	3.7	4.7	6.3	6.7	7.5	6.7	5.8	29.6	28.7	7.4	1.4	75.2	37.7	48.4	51.6
27616	RALEIGH	56.8	56.2	31.8	31.0	3.6	4.1	9.5	11.0	9.4	8.8	7.8	6.3	7.1	38.6	17.9	3.8	0.3	70.2	31.4	50.3	49.7
27617	RALEIGH	86.7	85.1	7.0	7.5	4.2	4.9	2.3	3.1	8.3	8.7	8.3	7.0	5.0	33.7	25.3	3.5	0.2	70.3	35.4	49.2	50.8
27695	RALEIGH	75.0	80.0	0.0	20.0	0.0	0.0	0.0	0.0	0.0	0.0	0.0	40.0	60.0	0.0	0.0	0.0	0.0	100.0	20.8	0.0	100.0
27701	DURHAM	25.4	24.7	62.7	61.2	0.8	0.8	15.0	18.1	7.8	7.2	7.1	7.4	9.1	34.4	18.6	7.1	1.4	74.0	31.2	50.8	49.3
27703	DURHAM	40.1	39.6	51.1	50.0	1.2	1.5	10.1	12.3	8.3	7.7	7.5	6.5	7.1	34.6	20.4	7.1	0.7	72.6	32.4	49.0	51.0
27704	DURHAM	41.0	38.8	52.0	52.8	1.1	1.2	6.7	8.6	7.1	7.3	7.4	6.5	6.5	31.7	22.3	9.6	1.6	74.2	34.5	46.2	53.8
27705	DURHAM	66.7	63.3	20.5	21.5	5.7	6.5	7.7	9.9	5.3	4.8	4.8	10.8	13.2	30.9	19.6	8.9	1.9	82.2	31.6	49.5	50.5
27707	DURHAM	42.5	42.0	48.0	46.9	2.9	3.3	8.9	11.1	6.5	6.1	6.2	7.8	9.9	32.4	21.0	8.7	1.4	77.7	32.7	47.7	52.4
27709	DURHAM	64.0	66.7	20.0	18.5	8.0	7.4	8.0	11.1	7.4	7.4	7.4	7.4	7.4	33.3	25.9	3.7	0.0	77.8	31.3	48.2	51.9
27712	DURHAM	81.4	80.0	14.9	15.8	2.1	2.4	1.3	1.7	5.1	6.1	7.1	5.9	4.3	25.2	32.4	12.1	1.9	77.9	42.9	48.2	51.8
27713	DURHAM	54.1	52.2	34.7	34.9	7.3	8.2	3.7	4.8	7.6	6.7	5.8	4.8	6.9	41.0	20.8	5.6	0.8	76.8	33.2	47.6	52.5
27801	ROCKY MOUNT	23.1	23.5	75.6	75.3	0.2	0.2	1.1	1.0	7.5	7.8	8.9	7.4	6.3	26.3	24.2	10.4	1.2	71.2	35.1	45.6	54.4
27803	ROCKY MOUNT	59.1	57.8	38.5	39.5	0.3	0.4	1.5	1.7	7.1	7.3	8.1	6.5	5.6	27.5	24.9	11.6	1.5	73.6	37.4	46.6	53.4
27804	ROCKY MOUNT	61.9	60.9	33.5	33.7	1.4	1.6	2.6	3.1	6.2	6.1	7.0	6.7	7.4	28.5	24.7	11.6	1.8	76.9	36.8	47.4	52.6
27805	AULANDER	44.3	43.2	54.1	54.9	0.1	0.1	1.3	1.6	6.1	6.8	8.1	6.9	5.7	26.8	24.2	13.7	1.8	74.5	38.5	47.6	52.4
27806	AURORA	49.0	47.0	49.7	51.5	0.0	0.0	1.2	1.4	5.1	5.6	7.4	6.5	5.6	22.0	28.6	16.8	2.6	78.1	43.6	48.2	51.8
27807	BAILEY	68.0	65.9	21.7	21.9	0.1	0.1	11.3	13.5	7.8	7.6	6.9	6.2	6.1	30.8	24.1	9.8	0.8	73.9	35.5	50.4	49.6
27808	BATH	85.2	84.2	13.3	13.9	0.1	0.1	1.3	1.7	4.1	4.6	5.9	4.9	4.3	22.9	33.3	18.3	1.6	82.4	47.0	48.9	51.1
27809	BATTLEBORO	47.2	46.6	50.4	50.9	0.2	0.3	1.8	1.9	6.4	6.8	7.7	6.7	6.0	29.8	26.9	8.8	0.8	75.2	37.2	45.0	55.0
27810	BELHAVEN	58.3	57.7	39.8	40.1	0.3	0.3	3.5	4.4	5.6	6.6	6.6	5.4	5.1	23.5	28.9	15.9	2.4	77.7	42.9	47.8	52.2
27812	BETHEL	47.3	45.9	50.2	51.1	0.2	0.3	2.7	3.4	6.5	6.9	7.4	6.7	6.3	24.0	26.8	14.0	1.5	75.2	39.3	47.1	52.9
27814	BLOUNTS CREEK	63.6	63.6	34.5	34.3	0.3	0.3	1.1	1.4	4.3	4.9	5.2	5.7	4.8	21.1	37.7	14.9	1.4	81.9	47.5	49.2	50.8
27816	CASTALIA	63.3	61.8	32.2	32.8	0.2	0.3	3.7	4.6	6.1	6.3	7.0	6.6	5.5	30.3	25.8	11.2	1.4	76.6	38.5	50.6	49.4
27817	CHOCOWINITY	73.4	72.2	24.6	25.5	0.1	0.1	2.6	3.3	6.1	6.3	6.7	5.9	5.9	26.1	30.6	11.3	1.0	77.1	40.0	49.8	50.2
27818	COMO	27.6	26.9	71.6	72.2	0.1	0.1	1.2	1.3	6.1	6.4	7.1	6.3	6.3	23.3	29.0	13.5	2.0	76.3	41.8	47.0	53.0
27820	CONWAY	58.1	57.2	40.9	41.6	0.4	0.4	0.4	0.4	6.1	6.5	7.1	6.1	5.4	24.5	27.6	14.8	2.0	76.5	41.4	47.3	52.7
27821	EDWARD	49.1	47.2	50.0	51.9	0.0	0.0	0.9	0.9	4.7	4.7	5.7	6.6	4.7	21.7	34.0	16.0	1.9	82.1	46.4	47.2	52.8
27822	ELM CITY	65.1	63.1	32.9	34.4	0.2	0.2	2.2	2.9	6.4	7.4	7.2	6.0	5.9	27.0	27.5	11.7	1.1	75.4	38.7	48.5	51.5
27823	ENFIELD	16.4	16.5	79.2	78.9	0.1	0.1	1.1	1.2	6.8	7.2	8.7	7.7	6.3	25.2	24.4	12.1	1.6	72.5	36.4	47.3	52.8
27824	ENGELHARD	54.0	53.0	44.0	44.6	0.2	0.2	3.3	4.0	5.1	5.8	8.6	6.4	5.2	24.4	27.1	14.8	2.6	76.4	41.7	47.1	52.9
27826	FAIRFIELD	59.7	58.6	37.9	38.8	0.4	0.4	1.9	2.2	4.3	4.8	6.0	4.8	7.7	37.2	23.1	10.8	1.3	81.7	37.0	62.0	38.0
27828	FARMVILLE	51.3	50.0	43.8	44.3	0.3	0.3	5.0	6.1	6.6	6.7	7.6	7.0	5.8	26.5	25.8	12.4	1.8	74.6	37.9	46.6	53.4
27829	FOUNTAIN	63.4	61.7	34.6	35.9	0.1	0.1	2.3	2.9	6.6	6.8	6.8	6.5	5.7	26.1	27.5	12.5	1.6	76.0	39.9	47.2	52.8
27830	FREMONT	69.0	67.8	27.2	27.5	0.4	0.4	3.3	4.3	6.2	6.4	7.5	6.8	5.8	26.6	25.4	13.9	1.4	75.2	39.0	47.8	52.2
27831	GARYSBURG	20.4	20.0	77.9	78.1	0.1	0.1	0.8	0.9	5.6	6.2	7.9	7.4	5.9	24.7	27.5	13.1	1.6	75.5	39.2	46.6	53.4
27832	GASTON	37.2	36.5	61.2	61.7	0.0	0.0	1.0	1.2	6.3	6.5	7.2	6.4	5.2	24.7	28.2	14.2	1.3	76.0	40.6	47.7	52.3
27834	GREENVILLE	43.1	42.6	52.2	51.8	1.0	1.2	3.9	4.7	7.8	6.8	7.0	7.1	9.3	32.3	20.5	7.9	1.3	74.5	31.2	47.1	52.9
27837	GRIMESLAND	67.7	65.9	27.2	27.5	0.2	0.2	5.5	7.2	6.9	6.9	7.5	6.9	6.0	31.0	24.8	9.2	0.9	74.6	35.7	50.6	49.4
27839	HALIFAX	28.2	27.4	69.9	70.3	0.2	0.3	1.3	1.7	3.8	4.1	5.1	5.3	8.7	36.5	24.2	10.9	1.5	83.8	37.2	61.4	38.7
27840	HAMILTON	40.2	38.7	58.7	60.2	0.1	0.1	2.4	2.4	4.7	5.1	6.9	7.9	7.0	21.0	30.2	15.3	2.0	78.8	43.1	46.0	54.0
27842	HENRICO	64.7	63.9	34.6	35.1	0.2	0.4	0.5	0.7	2.7	3.2	4.1	3.6	3.2	18.2	37.9	25.8	1.3	87.9	54.6	50.2	49.9
27843	HOBGOOD	39.7	39.0	58.9	59.4	0.2	0.2	1.6	1.9	5.9	6.0	7.3	6.8	6.7	26.1	27.1	12.8	1.5	76.9	39.3	48.5	51.5
27844	HOLLISTER	4.9	4.8	45.1	44.2	0.1	0.2	1.3	1.4	7.7	7.5	8.0	7.2	6.7	27.5	24.2	10.3	1.0	72.4	34.8	48.9	51.2
27845	JACKSON	35.6	35.0	63.4	63.8	0.1	0.1	0.4	0.6	4.8	5.0	5.9	6.2	6.9	29.9	24.8	14.3	2.4	80.8	39.5	54.2	45.8
27846	JAMESVILLE	66.8	65.6	30.0	30.7	0.0	0.0	2.8	3.5	5.8	6.4	7.5	6.1	5.5	26.7	28.1	12.3	1.7	76.3	39.7	48.4	51.6
27847	KELFORD	28.5	27.8	69.4	69.8	0.0	0.0	1.2	1.2	6.8	7.3	8.2	7.5	6.0	23.0	25.1	14.3	1.9	73.4	38.1	47.1	52.9
27849	LEWISTON WOODVILLE	17.7	17.4	81.2	81.4	0.1	0.1	0.9	1.0	6.5	6.7	8.2	7.5	6.5	25.7	26.0	11.1	1.8	73.8	37.2	47.2	52.8
27850	LITTLETON	52.2	50.2	43.8	45.5	0.2	0.3	0.8	1.0	4.6	5.0	5.9	5.1	4.7	20.6	33.2	19.1	1.7	81.3	47.8	48.0	52.1
27851	LUCAMA	79.9	77.7	16.7	18.0	0.3	0.4	3.8	5.2	6.5	6.4	7.0	6.4	6.2	28.6	26.8	11.0	1.2	76.3	37.9	49.4	50.6
27852	MACCLESFIELD	66.0	64.9	31.9	33.0	0.1	0.1	3.0	3.0	6.4	6.6	7.1	6.2	5.8	27.6	27.4	11.9	1.0	76.1	38.6	49.3	50.7
27853	MARGARETTSVILLE	48.8	48.0	49.0	49.8	0.0	0.0	0.8	0.8	6.8	7.3	8.5	6.8	5.3	23.5	26.0	14.3	1.8	73.0	40.7	47.5	52.5
27855	MURFREESBORO	36.7	36.2	60.8	60.9	0.3	0.4	2.3	2.8	5.9	6.1	7.8	7.6	6.8	24.8	26.0	13.2	1.9	75.1	38.4	47.5	52.5
27856	NASHVILLE	64.0	63.5	33.1	33.1	0.4	0.4	2.6	3.3	6.0	6.3	6.8	6.2	5.8	30.7	26.2	10.5	1.5	77.0	38.2	51.0	49.0
27857	OAK CITY	38.9	37.4	59.1	60.2	0.1	0.1	3.4	4.1	4.8	5.2	7.1	7.0	5.3	22.3	29.2	17.5	1.7	78.6	43.8	48.2	51.8
27858	GREENVILLE	80.7	79.3	14.9	15.4	1.8	2.2	2.3	3.0	5.0	4.7	5.1	12.8	17.6	27.6	18.4	7.8	1.0	82.1	27.5	48.0	52.0
27860	PANTEGO	68.4	66.7	29.2	30.2	0.1	0.1	3.5	4.5	5.7	5.9	6.3	6.0	5.1	25.0	29.0	14.5	2.6	78.5	42.0	48.9	51.1
27862	PENDLETON	52.9	52.0	44.5	45.1	0.3	0.3	1.5	1.6	5.9	6.4	8.1	6.5	5.6	24.9	25.1	15.3	2.2	75.5	40.7	48.7	51.3
27863	PIKEVILLE	83.3	81.8	13.5	14.4	0.8	1.0	2.5	3.2	8.0	7.9	7.6	6.2	5.5	32.3	22.7	9.0	0.8	72.5	35.2	50.0	50.0
27864	PINETOPS	62.6	62.2	36.2	36.5	0.0	0.0	1.7	1.7	6.4	6.8	7.2	6.5	6.0	27.4	27.6	11.4	0.9	75.7	38.2	48.7	51.3
27865	PINETOWN	88.1	87.9	10.4	10.4	0.2	0.1	2.6	3.4	5.6	5.7	6.0	5.8	4.9	25.4	29.2	15.4	2.0	79.2	42.7	47.8	52.2
27866	PLEASANT HILL	33.6	32.8	65.3	66.0	0.0	0.0	0.3	0.3	4.1	4.8	6.5	5.8	4.6	22.6	32.3	17.2	2.4	80.7	46.1	48.2	51.8
27869	RICH SQUARE	28.8	28.1	69.3	69.7	0.0	0.0	1.1	1.3	4.8	4.9	6.0	6.7	6.8	25.9	24.1	16.6	4.3	80.2	41.8	50.2	49.8
27870	ROANOKE RAPIDS	60.6	59.4	37.0	37.8	1.0	1.2	0.8	1.0	6.5	6.7	7.7	7.1	5.9	27.1	24.8	12.5	1.8	74.7	38.0	46.7	53.3
27871	ROBERSONVILLE	35.2	33.9	62.3	63.2	0.4	0.4	2.2	2.9	6.2	6.4	7.2	6.6	6.5	24.3	26.9	14.2	1.8	76.2	40.1	46.7	53.3
27872	ROXOBEL	27.4	26.6	70.8	71.2	0.0	0.0	0.9	1.0	6.6	7.1	8.2	7.2	6.2	24.2	25.5	13.2	1.9	73.7	37.9	47.5	52.5
27873	SARATOGA	57.0	55.1	39.6	41.1	0.0	0.0	3.9	4.8	5.3	5.3	6.3	5.8	6.8	26.6	29.0	14.0	1.0	79.2	41.3	48.8	51.2
27874	SCOTLAND NECK	28.3	28.2	70.0	69.8	0.1	0.1	1.7	2.0	6.2	6.4	8.1	7.3	6.1	22.9	24.5	16.2	2.5	74.8	40.3	46.3	53.7
27875	SCRANTON	58.7	57.6	39.0	39.8	0.3	0.4	1.5	2.0	4.2	4.6	5.8	4.6	8.0	38.0	23.1	10.5	1.2	82.3	36.9	63.2	36.8
27876	SEABOARD	32.4	31.3	66.5	67.4	0.2	0.3	0.4	0.3	7.5	7.6	7.5	7.1	6.3	21.7	25.6	14.5	2.1	73.1	40.3	46.0	54.0
27880	SIMS	76.5	73.5	16.0	16.6	0.1	0.1	10.6	14.1	6.3	6.6	6.9	6.6	5.9	28.2	28.1	10.2	1.2	75.9	38.0	50.1	49.9
27882	SPRING HOPE	61.8	60.8	34.2	34.4	0.1	0.2	4.8	6.0	6.4	6.6	7.0	6.1	6.1	28.2	26.5	11.8	1.3	76.3	38.6	48.7	51.3
27883	STANTONSBURG	63.1	60.6	33.2	34.6	0.1	0.1	5.0	6.7	6.2	6.1	6.3	6.8	6.6	27.4	26.8	12.8	1.2	77.2	39.5	49.8	50.2
27884	STOKES	67.9	66.8	29.9	30.8	0.0	0.0	3.1	3.9	6.2	6.4	6.7	6.7	5.7	26.9	28.8	11.7	1.0	76.7	39.6	51.1	48.9
27885	SWANQUARTER	60.9	59.9	36.2	36.9	0.7	0.9	2.3	2.6	4.4	4.4	5.0	6.6	6.2	22.8	27.8	17.5	5.3	81.8	45.4	45.7	54.3
27886	TARBORO	51.3	50.8	44.3	44.8	0.2	0.2	5.4	5.4	6.1	6.1	6.9	6.9	6.7	26.7	25.8	12.8	2.1	76.6	38.9	47.5	52.5
27888	WALSTONBURG	53.3	51.7	35.6	35.0	0.1	0.1	14.2	17.5	8.4	7.8	7.2	7.5	7.1	28.1	22.1	10.7	1.1	72.1	34.0	49.9	50.1
27889	WASHINGTON	67.0	66.0	29.9	30.3	0.3	0.4	3.9	4.8	6.6	6.5	6.5	6.2	6.0	26.1	26.7	13.6	1.9	76.6	39.4	47.3	52.7
27890	WELDON	28.1	27.4	70.4	70.9	0.2	0.2	0.6	0.8	7.0	7.6	8.4	7.3	5.3	22.9	22.3	16.0	3.2	72.1	39.1	46.1	53.9
27891	WHITAKERS	36.0	34.8	60.7	61.5	0.2	0.2	2.0	2.3	5.9	6.3	7.7	6.9	6.3	28.1	26.9	10.8	1.2	75.8	38.3	49.5	50.5
27892	WILLIAMSTON	56.9	55.8	41.2	42.0	0.3	0.4	1.8	2.3	6.6	6.7	7.3	6.5	5.8	25.9	26.1	13.3	1.8	75.3	39.1	46.2	53.8
27893	WILSON	41.4	40.4	52.6	52.4	0.4	0.4	8.2	10.1	7.3	7.0	7.2	7.1	7.4	27.6	23.0	11.8	1.6	74.4	35.2	47.5	52.5
27896	WILSON	83.2	81.5	13.2	14.2	1.0	1.1	2.3	2.9	6.0	6.5	6.8	5.7	5.3	27.2	29.4	11.9	1.2	76.9	40.5	48.2	51.8
27897	WOODLAND	46.6	45.6	52.0	52.8	0.0	0.0	0.8	1.0	6.8	6.9	7.5	7.0	5.3	24.1	25.3	15.0	2.0	74.2	39.8	46.7	53.3
27909	ELIZABETH CITY	56.9	56.0	40.1	40.5	0.9	1.1	1.2	1.5	6.4	6.1	6.8	7.4	8.2	27.6	23.6	11.9	1.9	76.6	36.6	48.7	51.3
27910	AHOSKIE	39.1	38.3	57.4	57.8	0.4	0.5	1.4	1.5	5.3	5.6	7.1	7.1	6.6	24.0	27.3	14.7	2.2	77.6	41.2	45.6	54.5
27916	AYDLETT	94.7	93.9	2.5	2.6	0.2	0.4	1.4	1.9	4.8	5.5	6.5	6.1	4.8	27.5	26.9	15.9	2.0	79.7	42.0	48.2	51.9
27917	BARCO	79.6	78.2	15.9	16.7	0.6	0.8	3.8	4.9	6.4	6.4	6.7	6.4	5.2	29.8	24.0	12.0	3.4	76.9	38.1	49.6	50.4
27919	BELVIDERE	75.8	75.1	23.1	23.7	0.3	0.5	0.4	0.5	5.1	5.3	6.0	6.4	6.0	25.0	28.7	15.1	2.5	79.8	42.5	48.7	51.3
27921	CAMDEN	79.5	78.9	19.2	19.6	0.1	0.1	0.7	0.9	5.7	6.1	7.2	6.7	4.9	26.4	29.0	12.9	1.2	76.9	41.5	49.0	51.0
27922	COFIELD	32.8	32.1	64.5	65.1	0.2	0.1	1.0	1.1	4.6	5.0	7.3	6.8	5.9	27.7	27.8	13.6	1.4	78.6	40.9	46.0	54.1
27923	COINJOCK	92.8	92.2	4.0	4.2	0.2	0.2	2.0	2.6	4.9	5.7	6.7	6.2	4.6	28.7	25.6	15.2	2.5	79.3	41.4	48.1	51.9
27924	COLERAIN	44.5	43.0	54.1	55.5	0.0	0.0	1.3	1.4	6.7	6.8	6.7	6.1	5.9	24.4	25.9	15.7	1.8	76.1	40.5	47.7	52.3
	NORTH CAROLINA	72.1	71.2	21.6	21.6	1.5	1.8	4.7	5.9	6.7	6.6	6.8	6.7	7.1	29.8	24.2	10.8	1.4	76.2	36.2	49.2	50.8
	UNITED STATES	75.1	73.6	12.3	12.5	3.8	4.2	12.5	14.1	6.9	6.7	7.2	7.0	7.3	28.6	23.8	10.8	1.7	75.1	36.0	49.1	50.9

ZIP CODE #	POST OFFICE NAME	2004 Per Capita Income	2004 HH Income Base	2004 HOUSEHOLD INCOME DISTRIBUTION (%) Less than $25,000	$25,000 to $49,999	$50,000 to $99,999	$100,000 to $149,999	$150,000 or More	MEDIAN HOUSEHOLD INCOME 2004	2009	2004 National Centile	2004 State Centile	2004 Home Value Base	2004 HOME VALUE DISTRIBUTION (%) Less than $50,000	$50,000 to $89,999	$90,000 to $174,999	$175,000 to $399,999	$400,000 or More	2004 Median Home Value
27613	RALEIGH	39674	16114	9.2	18.1	37.3	21.3	14.2	77153	89355	94	98	10580	0.8	0.7	20.1	68.0	10.4	232072
27614	RALEIGH	46738	5347	7.3	11.3	28.9	25.6	27.0	103266	112471	98	100	4859	0.8	0.3	17.8	55.6	25.5	290413
27615	RALEIGH	40935	17423	9.6	21.6	33.6	19.3	16.0	75835	85601	94	97	11993	0.6	1.0	20.3	61.3	16.8	244808
27616	RALEIGH	25507	10539	13.5	26.4	40.9	14.8	4.4	60464	70360	85	93	7412	10.5	3.8	51.6	31.8	2.4	148504
27617	RALEIGH	45891	1690	3.7	8.8	34.3	30.1	23.2	103637	118735	98	100	1624	0.5	0.3	10.0	74.9	14.4	246448
27695	RALEIGH	3910	0	0.0	0.0	0.0	0.0	0.0	0	0	0	0	0	0.0	0.0	0.0	0.0	0.0	0
27701	DURHAM	17587	9403	45.8	28.3	17.6	5.3	3.0	27408	32283	8	6	2676	8.4	28.2	40.7	20.6	2.1	109888
27703	DURHAM	20989	13453	25.3	28.5	33.7	9.9	2.7	46233	54637	64	79	7912	7.6	16.5	56.0	18.9	1.0	123123
27704	DURHAM	20407	11670	27.5	30.9	32.6	7.3	1.7	43198	50533	56	67	6702	4.3	21.6	65.8	7.8	0.6	112744
27705	DURHAM	27035	18584	28.3	28.8	27.3	9.7	6.0	42251	49232	54	63	8562	4.7	8.1	44.9	36.6	5.8	157696
27707	DURHAM	29942	17215	25.6	27.7	27.7	10.3	8.8	46830	54453	66	80	8307	2.5	12.7	40.2	35.7	9.0	163003
27709	DURHAM	21039	10	10.0	50.0	40.0	0.0	0.0	42176	47321	53	63	3	0.0	0.0	100.0	0.0	0.0	112500
27712	DURHAM	34571	7119	9.0	18.2	42.0	20.4	10.4	72829	84145	92	97	6552	1.4	2.1	49.4	42.5	4.6	171037
27713	DURHAM	32885	17073	12.7	23.8	39.0	17.7	6.8	64389	75991	88	95	9868	1.8	5.2	46.5	44.6	1.9	169008
27801	ROCKY MOUNT	14420	8216	42.5	32.3	20.8	2.8	1.6	30479	34112	13	14	4816	24.1	43.4	29.7	2.4	0.5	75661
27803	ROCKY MOUNT	20972	8783	35.7	25.2	27.0	8.2	4.0	37581	43705	38	42	5828	18.0	22.3	40.7	16.5	2.5	104127
27804	ROCKY MOUNT	26657	10755	24.8	29.9	31.0	9.8	4.5	45274	52659	62	75	6624	15.2	17.6	45.1	18.0	4.1	113272
27805	AULANDER	14111	809	49.2	25.6	21.4	3.0	0.9	25532	27605	5	3	589	31.9	41.9	23.6	2.6	0.0	65852
27806	AURORA	15493	1161	46.9	25.1	23.6	3.6	0.8	27206	30561	7	6	877	41.4	32.2	21.0	5.5	0.0	57865
27807	BAILEY	18865	2143	31.6	30.9	29.9	4.8	2.8	39551	45754	45	49	1675	29.1	26.8	35.6	7.2	1.3	80529
27808	BATH	26879	933	26.5	30.7	28.6	9.2	5.0	41464	48492	51	60	788	23.5	21.5	33.5	18.3	3.3	98333
27809	BATTLEBORO	20108	1830	33.7	26.2	30.0	6.6	3.6	38054	43473	39	45	1427	24.4	27.3	33.4	13.1	1.9	86824
27810	BELHAVEN	17449	1646	47.3	25.4	21.9	2.7	2.7	26838	30382	7	5	1192	36.2	23.6	26.7	12.3	1.3	68488
27812	BETHEL	17666	1032	41.2	28.3	24.3	4.6	1.7	32925	37701	21	20	738	25.6	42.1	24.0	8.3	0.0	75347
27814	BLOUNTS CREEK	21952	923	35.0	27.0	26.8	8.5	2.8	42221	49278	54	63	774	28.8	24.9	19.9	22.2	4.1	84314
27816	CASTALIA	16726	1101	39.2	27.9	27.0	4.3	1.6	33234	37862	22	22	874	41.5	23.0	27.0	7.6	0.9	63800
27817	CHOCOWINITY	20357	2503	33.1	31.4	25.8	6.6	3.1	36095	42557	32	35	2029	28.3	33.6	23.2	12.2	2.6	74436
27818	COMO	17453	613	37.7	26.1	32.6	2.6	1.0	33258	37506	22	22	482	44.2	40.5	12.7	2.7	0.0	55185
27820	CONWAY	20251	1332	41.7	29.9	20.1	5.7	2.7	31109	36163	15	15	1058	33.7	43.6	19.4	2.8	0.5	63945
27821	EDWARD	18309	46	43.5	28.3	21.7	6.5	0.0	40000	47354	46	51	38	26.3	34.2	31.6	7.9	0.0	80000
27822	ELM CITY	19067	3473	31.9	30.1	30.5	5.1	2.4	38904	44683	42	47	2781	22.4	30.5	35.3	10.5	1.3	86877
27823	ENFIELD	13225	3212	47.8	29.7	18.2	3.3	1.0	26334	29518	6	4	2152	38.9	35.1	21.6	4.0	0.6	60405
27824	ENGELHARD	14825	740	49.2	28.0	16.6	4.7	1.5	25425	27168	5	2	557	39.0	33.0	22.3	5.2	0.5	62411
27826	FAIRFIELD	10220	223	40.8	39.0	16.1	3.1	0.9	30417	33388	13	13	183	50.8	20.8	27.9	0.6	0.0	49118
27828	FARMVILLE	20327	3479	37.2	29.7	23.7	6.0	3.4	35250	40377	28	31	2316	21.2	34.3	35.8	7.5	1.2	84391
27829	FOUNTAIN	17522	646	43.8	24.9	25.1	4.2	2.0	30507	35210	14	14	462	31.4	40.0	20.6	6.7	1.3	69583
27830	FREMONT	18425	1644	37.4	31.5	24.5	5.0	1.8	33296	36710	22	22	1223	27.2	33.6	33.9	4.6	0.7	75472
27831	GARYSBURG	15914	1495	47.0	26.7	20.7	3.9	1.7	27150	31278	7	5	1110	39.9	36.6	20.5	2.9	0.2	57943
27832	GASTON	15937	1283	45.4	30.4	20.5	2.3	1.3	28226	32450	9	7	915	45.1	31.0	14.3	7.9	1.6	54890
27834	GREENVILLE	18329	18682	38.2	30.4	23.6	5.6	2.3	33546	39362	23	23	8654	23.2	33.0	34.1	7.8	1.9	83030
27837	GRIMESLAND	19872	1667	29.9	26.7	33.2	8.7	1.6	43934	51110	58	71	1347	25.0	31.3	30.7	12.0	1.0	79162
27839	HALIFAX	13881	1299	47.3	32.5	17.3	2.0	0.9	26551	29828	6	4	957	39.2	37.7	19.8	2.7	0.6	59673
27840	HAMILTON	15338	327	39.5	30.6	23.9	5.2	0.9	30793	35000	14	15	251	37.5	36.7	20.7	5.2	0.0	67353
27842	HENRICO	33794	682	27.7	28.6	31.4	8.5	3.8	44740	52449	61	74	602	16.3	14.6	24.1	39.7	5.3	142045
27843	HOBGOOD	15718	704	42.5	27.8	24.0	4.0	1.7	30082	33366	12	12	569	37.3	40.8	20.9	0.9	0.2	62846
27844	HOLLISTER	13797	966	57.0	22.9	16.1	3.0	1.0	20000	22358	2	1	695	49.6	31.1	15.5	3.7	0.0	50291
27845	JACKSON	19526	766	42.4	28.1	22.7	5.1	1.7	31021	35792	15	15	591	30.1	41.0	24.4	4.2	0.3	67075
27846	JAMESVILLE	19401	1085	36.8	28.4	27.2	4.5	3.1	36849	42620	35	39	864	34.1	27.8	33.9	4.2	0.0	74179
27847	KELFORD	12723	152	52.6	33.6	11.2	0.7	2.0	23541	27083	4	1	115	49.6	34.8	9.6	5.2	0.9	50455
27849	LEWISTON WOODVILLE	13032	625	49.4	29.0	17.8	2.6	1.3	25278	28392	5	2	479	44.7	36.5	15.7	2.9	0.2	55313
27850	LITTLETON	22041	3046	34.4	29.9	24.2	7.7	3.8	36522	42421	34	37	2431	21.1	22.6	27.6	25.0	3.7	101563
27851	LUCAMA	19332	1954	29.3	32.6	30.6	5.5	2.0	40852	46431	49	57	1510	29.5	30.3	34.5	5.4	0.2	78768
27852	MACCLESFIELD	17487	1644	34.1	35.6	23.7	4.5	2.0	36108	40585	32	35	1304	31.4	38.5	26.6	2.9	0.5	67872
27853	MARGARETTSVILLE	13157	144	46.5	31.9	18.8	1.4	1.4	27300	32327	8	6	114	47.4	28.1	21.9	2.6	0.0	55000
27855	MURFREESBORO	17467	2395	40.7	30.6	20.5	5.5	2.7	31657	36050	17	17	1708	39.9	29.5	23.5	7.0	0.1	61010
27856	NASHVILLE	20417	6008	29.6	29.0	30.3	7.5	3.6	41991	48499	53	62	4648	20.7	23.6	39.3	15.3	1.2	99147
27857	OAK CITY	15409	602	47.3	27.7	18.3	4.3	2.3	26324	29801	6	4	450	25.6	42.0	24.9	5.3	2.2	76875
27858	GREENVILLE	25306	20025	34.4	24.3	26.7	9.6	5.0	39521	46518	44	49	10362	9.8	18.2	46.1	22.8	3.1	122823
27860	PANTEGO	20554	774	36.1	28.3	28.0	4.9	2.7	33744	39150	23	24	642	38.0	27.7	25.9	7.8	0.6	63500
27862	PENDLETON	15588	461	47.9	26.3	19.7	4.1	2.0	27335	31580	8	6	369	37.9	37.1	19.8	4.9	0.3	59674
27863	PIKEVILLE	20960	3374	24.5	35.2	31.9	6.3	2.1	42571	47358	55	65	2748	23.0	26.6	42.3	6.9	1.2	90356
27864	PINETOPS	18529	1837	31.6	31.9	29.8	5.1	1.6	38619	43450	41	47	1334	26.3	36.0	31.3	6.2	0.2	76815
27865	PINETOWN	20987	847	31.3	31.2	29.4	5.4	2.7	40927	47652	49	57	709	32.7	27.8	26.1	12.3	1.1	74149
27866	PLEASANT HILL	16051	216	39.4	35.2	17.6	7.9	0.0	33623	37559	23	23	175	33.7	32.0	32.6	1.7	0.0	64688
27869	RICH SQUARE	15008	999	44.0	30.3	20.0	4.9	0.7	28657	33032	10	8	739	37.2	42.2	17.1	3.3	0.3	58670
27870	ROANOKE RAPIDS	17060	11538	40.9	28.8	23.9	4.6	1.8	31562	36030	17	16	7963	24.5	34.6	32.5	7.6	0.8	80102
27871	ROBERSONVILLE	15416	1837	47.0	28.9	18.5	4.5	1.1	26644	29956	7	4	1297	30.8	42.8	22.1	4.2	0.2	70392
27872	ROXOBEL	15295	301	49.8	32.9	14.0	1.3	2.0	25077	27587	5	2	229	51.1	34.9	9.2	4.4	0.4	49306
27873	SARATOGA	16258	90	43.3	30.0	24.4	1.1	1.1	30000	35448	12	12	67	20.9	50.8	25.4	3.0	0.0	71875
27874	SCOTLAND NECK	15078	2078	51.6	29.5	13.0	3.3	2.6	23931	26823	4	2	1335	36.5	39.9	18.4	4.5	0.8	59918
27875	SCRANTON	18285	509	38.7	41.1	16.1	3.3	0.8	30851	33566	14	15	422	53.6	17.5	28.7	0.2	0.0	46429
27876	SEABOARD	19240	672	48.5	24.6	20.1	4.6	2.2	26055	30184	6	3	505	36.8	33.5	26.5	3.2	0.0	65357
27880	SIMS	19117	816	28.9	29.3	33.8	5.6	2.3	42341	48046	54	64	657	26.9	24.7	37.4	10.1	0.9	87614
27882	SPRING HOPE	19330	2763	32.8	31.4	27.9	5.7	2.1	38210	43657	40	46	2104	26.9	28.0	32.0	10.7	2.4	83795
27883	STANTONSBURG	17121	1144	34.7	33.0	26.0	5.2	1.2	35207	39923	28	30	895	18.8	40.0	36.8	4.4	0.1	81990
27884	STOKES	22321	320	32.2	25.9	31.3	7.5	3.1	40841	47392	49	56	260	20.4	50.0	24.2	5.0	0.4	73000
27885	SWANQUARTER	17227	457	37.2	29.1	28.7	4.8	0.2	33856	37256	24	25	365	29.6	46.3	17.0	7.1	0.0	70614
27886	TARBORO	18500	7196	33.6	31.3	27.1	5.5	2.6	37529	42151	38	42	5032	26.4	35.5	31.2	6.0	1.0	76132
27888	WALSTONBURG	15693	1132	31.5	40.4	22.5	4.3	1.3	37441	42548	37	41	843	36.4	25.6	31.4	3.4	3.1	78981
27889	WASHINGTON	18777	11092	36.9	30.4	24.7	6.1	1.8	34607	40105	26	28	7942	22.3	29.2	32.7	14.0	1.7	87908
27890	WELDON	15858	869	45.8	34.6	14.0	1.8	3.7	27147	30718	7	5	510	28.2	46.5	17.5	7.8	0.0	66197
27891	WHITAKERS	16620	2061	32.6	34.5	27.9	3.8	1.3	38005	43404	39	44	1615	37.0	31.5	25.3	5.5	0.8	65795
27892	WILLIAMSTON	17487	6450	38.5	28.9	26.0	5.1	1.5	33047	38263	21	21	4744	25.4	38.2	29.1	6.6	0.6	76286
27893	WILSON	16403	16687	43.4	29.7	21.0	3.7	2.2	29501	34249	11	10	8718	17.1	36.6	37.6	7.5	1.3	86705
27896	WILSON	32451	6268	15.9	24.3	39.3	11.8	8.7	59239	67926	84	92	4931	4.5	11.5	48.4	32.3	3.3	142572
27897	WOODLAND	16751	1088	46.2	27.0	19.8	5.2	1.8	27783	31692	8	7	813	37.0	41.7	18.6	2.2	0.5	62612
27909	ELIZABETH CITY	17335	13823	37.4	31.1	24.5	5.0	2.1	33850	38640	24	24	9305	18.0	28.2	41.1	11.5	1.2	94586
27910	AHOSKIE	18423	5029	43.6	30.4	19.5	3.9	2.6	29054	32708	10	9	3421	29.2	38.3	25.4	6.2	0.9	71658
27916	AYDLETT	23871	221	19.5	34.4	33.5	6.8	5.9	47969	54940	68	83	179	15.6	9.5	38.0	32.4	4.5	144886
27917	BARCO	14027	380	33.4	46.1	19.5	1.1	0.0	34388	38594	25	26	261	36.0	19.9	39.9	4.2	0.0	78333
27919	BELVIDERE	16032	642	38.0	35.8	23.2	2.8	0.2	35163	39030	28	30	526	28.7	27.4	39.0	4.9	0.0	81351
27921	CAMDEN	21615	1409	22.1	33.3	31.0	11.1	2.4	43921	51406	58	71	1196	10.5	15.9	47.1	26.5	0.0	126190
27922	COFIELD	14279	312	52.2	30.5	14.1	2.6	0.6	23718	26425	4	1	246	43.9	40.2	13.0	2.9	0.0	56250
27923	COINJOCK	25128	261	18.0	36.0	33.7	6.5	5.8	47937	54714	68	83	208	16.8	6.7	38.0	34.6	3.9	146875
27924	COLERAIN	16969	1395	46.1	31.0	17.0	4.0	1.9	26874	30580	7	5	1064	31.5	42.4	21.9	3.5	0.8	67600
	NORTH CAROLINA	23743		27.0	29.8	30.1	8.5	4.7	43794	50711				14.5	20.0	39.7	21.7	4.1	115673
	UNITED STATES	25866		24.7	27.1	30.8	10.9	6.5	48124	56710				10.9	15.0	33.7	30.1	10.4	145905

ZIP CODE #	POST OFFICE NAME	FINANCIAL SERVICES: Auto Loan	Home Loan	Invest-ments	Retire-ment Plans	THE HOME: Home Improvements: Home Repair	Lawn & Garden	Furnishings: Comput-ers & Hard-ware	Major Appli-ances	TV, Radio, Sound Equip-ment	Furni-ture	ENTERTAINMENT: Dine out/ Carry out	Sports Equip-ment	Fees & Tickets	Toys & Games	Travel	Cable TV	PERSONAL: Apparel & Services	Auto Repairs	Health Insur-ance	Pets & Supplies
27613	RALEIGH	140	150	152	158	143	142	143	139	133	147	169	165	145	167	138	124	167	139	121	154
27614	RALEIGH	184	222	236	229	214	213	197	194	180	202	229	225	212	235	198	173	230	188	170	213
27615	RALEIGH	142	153	171	161	148	152	149	145	140	151	178	171	153	176	146	134	176	146	130	160
27616	RALEIGH	101	108	108	114	103	101	102	100	95	106	121	118	104	119	99	88	119	100	86	110
27617	RALEIGH	182	206	198	215	196	189	186	184	170	193	216	215	191	216	181	158	214	179	156	201
27695	RALEIGH	0	0	0	0	0	0	0	0	0	0	0	0	0	0	0	0	0	0	0	0
27701	DURHAM	60	51	65	52	50	57	63	58	66	62	82	70	60	78	59	65	79	63	59	66
27703	DURHAM	78	78	85	78	76	80	80	78	80	80	100	91	80	99	78	78	98	80	75	87
27704	DURHAM	69	69	75	69	68	73	71	69	71	71	89	81	71	88	70	70	87	71	68	78
27705	DURHAM	85	80	94	85	79	85	90	85	88	88	111	103	88	108	86	84	108	90	80	94
27707	DURHAM	97	97	119	100	95	103	103	99	102	103	129	116	104	126	101	100	126	102	95	110
27709	DURHAM	76	72	83	77	70	74	80	76	78	79	99	92	78	96	76	73	96	80	69	83
27712	DURHAM	120	143	153	144	141	142	131	131	123	131	155	151	138	161	133	120	154	127	120	143
27713	DURHAM	108	105	122	113	101	105	111	106	107	113	136	127	110	132	106	101	133	110	95	118
27801	ROCKY MOUNT	59	51	49	47	51	59	53	55	58	54	71	61	52	67	53	61	68	56	61	66
27803	ROCKY MOUNT	81	72	65	68	73	81	71	76	76	72	93	87	70	91	71	78	89	76	82	92
27804	ROCKY MOUNT	92	89	90	90	89	95	91	91	91	91	114	107	90	112	90	90	110	92	90	104
27805	AULANDER	65	44	20	38	50	57	42	53	51	43	60	63	36	57	43	55	55	52	65	75
27806	AURORA	66	46	23	40	51	60	46	55	54	46	63	65	39	60	46	58	58	55	67	75
27807	BAILEY	87	68	43	62	72	80	65	76	72	67	87	89	59	82	65	75	81	75	84	99
27808	BATH	104	83	58	76	93	104	78	93	88	78	104	109	71	104	83	93	97	92	109	126
27809	BATTLEBORO	84	70	57	65	73	83	70	77	78	71	94	88	67	90	70	81	88	76	87	96
27810	BELHAVEN	67	50	36	46	55	65	53	60	60	52	71	68	48	67	53	64	66	60	71	76
27812	BETHEL	72	60	49	54	63	72	60	66	66	60	80	75	57	77	60	70	76	66	76	83
27814	BLOUNTS CREEK	88	70	51	64	77	89	66	79	74	68	89	87	61	82	70	79	83	77	94	102
27816	CASTALIA	81	54	25	47	62	71	53	66	63	54	75	79	45	70	53	68	68	65	81	93
27817	CHOCOWINITY	87	68	44	62	73	82	64	75	72	66	87	86	59	80	66	75	80	75	86	98
27818	COMO	80	53	24	46	60	70	51	64	62	52	73	77	44	69	52	67	66	64	79	91
27820	CONWAY	90	60	27	52	68	79	58	73	70	59	82	87	50	78	59	76	75	72	90	103
27821	EDWARD	72	56	38	51	63	71	53	64	60	52	71	75	47	70	56	64	66	63	75	87
27822	ELM CITY	83	66	43	60	71	78	62	72	69	63	83	86	58	82	63	72	78	71	82	96
27823	ENFIELD	62	44	29	39	48	57	46	53	54	46	64	61	41	59	46	58	59	53	64	70
27824	ENGELHARD	57	43	28	41	47	56	47	52	53	45	62	58	42	59	47	56	57	52	62	63
27826	FAIRFIELD	68	46	21	40	52	60	45	56	54	45	63	66	38	60	45	58	57	55	68	78
27828	FARMVILLE	82	68	54	64	72	81	68	74	74	68	90	86	65	89	68	77	85	74	83	93
27829	FOUNTAIN	81	55	26	48	62	71	53	66	63	54	75	78	45	71	54	68	68	65	81	93
27830	FREMONT	80	60	36	55	65	74	59	69	66	59	79	81	53	76	59	69	73	68	79	91
27831	GARYSBURG	70	49	29	43	54	63	49	59	59	50	69	68	43	64	49	63	64	59	71	79
27832	GASTON	65	47	32	41	51	59	48	55	56	48	67	64	43	62	48	60	62	56	67	73
27834	GREENVILLE	68	58	59	59	58	64	64	64	66	65	83	76	61	78	61	65	79	67	64	75
27837	GRIMESLAND	88	71	47	65	74	81	68	77	74	69	89	91	62	85	68	75	84	77	84	99
27839	HALIFAX	45	31	17	27	34	40	30	37	37	31	43	44	26	40	31	39	39	37	45	51
27840	HAMILTON	75	50	23	43	57	65	48	60	58	49	68	72	41	65	49	63	62	60	74	86
27842	HENRICO	113	89	62	81	100	113	84	101	95	84	113	117	76	110	90	101	105	100	120	137
27843	HOBGOOD	77	52	23	44	58	67	50	62	60	51	71	74	42	67	51	65	64	62	77	88
27844	HOLLISTER	68	46	21	39	52	59	44	55	53	45	62	66	37	59	45	57	57	54	68	78
27845	JACKSON	72	53	38	48	57	68	57	64	66	57	78	72	51	72	56	70	72	64	77	80
27846	JAMESVILLE	83	65	42	60	69	78	64	73	71	64	85	85	58	80	64	73	79	73	82	94
27847	KELFORD	65	44	20	38	49	57	42	53	51	43	60	63	36	56	43	55	54	52	65	75
27849	LEWISTON WOODVILLE	67	45	20	39	51	58	43	54	52	44	61	65	37	58	44	56	56	54	67	77
27850	LITTLETON	86	65	43	59	72	84	63	75	72	64	86	84	57	79	65	77	79	74	90	98
27851	LUCAMA	85	66	42	61	71	79	64	74	71	65	85	87	58	81	64	74	79	73	83	97
27852	MACCLESFIELD	81	59	34	54	65	73	58	68	66	58	79	81	51	75	58	70	73	68	80	92
27853	MARGARETTSVILLE	69	46	21	40	52	60	44	56	54	45	63	66	38	60	45	58	57	55	69	79
27855	MURFREESBORO	72	56	37	53	60	68	57	64	63	57	75	74	52	71	57	66	70	64	73	81
27856	NASHVILLE	87	73	53	68	78	86	70	79	77	70	92	93	66	91	71	80	87	78	88	101
27857	OAK CITY	62	45	28	43	50	59	49	55	56	47	65	63	43	62	49	59	60	55	66	69
27858	GREENVILLE	82	74	83	78	73	78	89	80	86	84	108	99	83	103	82	80	104	86	74	90
27860	PANTEGO	94	64	32	59	74	84	63	78	74	63	87	94	54	84	65	79	79	77	95	110
27862	PENDLETON	74	50	22	43	56	65	48	60	58	49	68	72	41	64	49	62	62	59	74	85
27863	PIKEVILLE	86	78	61	75	78	83	74	80	75	76	93	92	70	88	74	75	89	79	80	95
27864	PINETOPS	84	63	37	57	68	76	61	71	68	62	82	84	54	77	61	71	76	71	81	95
27865	PINETOWN	96	67	34	59	76	86	64	79	76	65	90	95	56	86	66	81	82	78	96	111
27866	PLEASANT HILL	76	52	27	45	58	67	51	63	61	52	72	74	44	68	52	66	66	62	77	87
27869	RICH SQUARE	67	48	33	43	52	62	51	58	59	51	70	66	46	65	51	63	65	58	70	75
27870	ROANOKE RAPIDS	67	54	40	50	58	66	54	60	60	54	73	70	51	71	55	63	68	60	69	76
27871	ROBERSONVILLE	71	49	26	42	54	63	48	59	57	49	68	69	42	63	48	62	62	58	72	81
27872	ROXOBEL	66	45	20	38	50	58	43	54	52	44	61	64	37	58	44	56	55	53	66	76
27873	SARATOGA	70	47	21	41	53	61	45	57	55	46	64	68	39	61	46	59	59	56	70	81
27874	SCOTLAND NECK	60	45	36	41	47	57	49	54	56	49	67	60	45	61	48	60	62	54	64	66
27875	SCRANTON	68	46	21	39	52	60	44	55	53	45	63	66	38	59	45	57	57	55	68	78
27876	SEABOARD	72	55	49	48	56	68	59	64	69	61	83	71	56	75	58	74	78	66	77	79
27880	SIMS	87	66	40	60	73	81	63	74	72	63	85	89	57	83	64	75	79	73	87	101
27882	SPRING HOPE	86	64	39	59	70	79	63	74	71	64	85	87	57	82	63	75	79	73	85	97
27883	STANTONSBURG	77	54	28	48	60	69	53	64	62	54	74	76	46	70	54	66	67	64	77	88
27884	STOKES	103	76	44	68	83	92	73	87	83	75	99	103	65	94	74	87	92	86	100	116
27885	SWANQUARTER	65	49	32	47	53	64	54	59	60	51	71	66	48	67	53	64	65	59	71	71
27886	TARBORO	74	65	55	62	67	74	64	69	68	64	83	79	62	81	65	70	79	69	74	84
27888	WALSTONBURG	76	59	36	54	62	69	56	65	62	58	75	77	51	71	56	64	70	65	73	85
27889	WASHINGTON	70	62	52	59	64	71	61	66	65	62	79	74	59	75	61	66	75	65	71	79
27890	WELDON	57	52	57	48	51	59	54	55	59	56	73	60	55	70	54	62	71	56	60	64
27891	WHITAKERS	81	59	33	53	64	73	57	68	65	58	78	80	50	74	57	69	72	67	79	92
27892	WILLIAMSTON	73	56	38	52	60	69	56	64	63	56	76	74	52	72	56	66	70	63	74	82
27893	WILSON	60	53	51	50	54	61	56	57	60	55	73	66	54	71	55	61	70	58	62	67
27896	WILSON	115	117	116	117	119	126	112	116	111	112	138	135	113	139	114	111	134	114	116	134
27897	WOODLAND	78	52	24	45	59	68	51	63	61	52	72	76	43	68	52	66	65	63	78	90
27909	ELIZABETH CITY	67	58	51	56	59	66	60	63	63	60	77	72	57	75	59	64	73	63	67	75
27910	AHOSKIE	76	57	38	51	61	72	58	66	67	58	79	76	52	75	58	71	73	66	79	86
27916	AYDLETT	105	75	42	70	87	97	73	90	84	72	99	108	63	97	76	88	90	89	107	125
27917	BARCO	57	52	41	50	52	55	50	53	50	51	62	62	47	59	49	50	60	53	53	63
27919	BELVIDERE	72	48	23	42	55	63	47	59	57	48	67	70	40	63	48	61	61	58	72	82
27921	CAMDEN	95	72	45	69	81	90	71	83	79	70	94	99	64	93	73	82	87	82	96	112
27922	COFIELD	62	41	19	36	47	54	40	50	48	41	57	60	34	53	41	52	51	49	61	71
27923	COINJOCK	104	76	43	72	86	96	74	90	84	74	99	108	64	97	76	87	91	89	105	123
27924	COLERAIN	78	53	24	46	60	69	51	63	61	52	72	76	43	68	52	66	65	63	78	90
	NORTH CAROLINA	90	81	73	80	83	90	81	85	84	82	103	100	79	101	81	84	99	85	88	102
	UNITED STATES	100	100	100	100	100	100	100	100	100	100	100	100	100	100	100	100	100	100	100	100

# POST OFFICE NAME	COUNTY FIPS CODE	POPULATION 2000	2004	2009	2000-2004 ANNUAL RATE % Rate	State Centile	HOUSEHOLDS 2000	2004	2009	% Annual Rate 2000-2004	2004 Average HH Size	FAMILIES 2000	2004	% Annual Rate 2000-2004
27925 COLUMBIA	177	3952	3922	3859	-0.2	7	1453	1474	1481	0.3	2.36	999	999	0.0
27926 CORAPEAKE	073	1748	1834	1936	1.1	40	646	687	737	1.5	2.67	494	520	1.2
27927 COROLLA	053	648	897	1173	8.0	100	314	442	586	8.4	2.03	205	284	8.0
27928 CRESWELL	187	2153	2166	2141	0.1	13	845	866	873	0.6	2.49	635	643	0.3
27929 CURRITUCK	053	631	819	1039	6.3	99	240	315	405	6.6	2.57	195	253	6.3
27932 EDENTON	041	12351	12545	12760	0.4	18	4729	4877	5036	0.7	2.43	3386	3448	0.4
27935 EURE	073	1543	1612	1699	1.0	37	604	639	681	1.3	2.51	449	469	1.0
27937 GATES	073	3159	3317	3504	1.2	41	1158	1230	1315	1.4	2.70	889	934	1.2
27938 GATESVILLE	073	1457	1484	1538	0.4	19	472	488	514	0.8	2.73	344	350	0.4
27939 GRANDY	053	1613	1854	2222	3.3	88	681	791	958	3.6	2.34	491	564	3.3
27941 HARBINGER	053	766	887	1068	3.5	89	302	354	430	3.8	2.51	222	257	3.5
27942 HARRELLSVILLE	091	1228	1327	1440	1.8	61	497	548	606	2.3	2.42	351	381	2.0
27944 HERTFORD	143	10109	10598	11140	1.1	40	4130	4413	4727	1.6	2.37	2996	3158	1.3
27946 HOBBSVILLE	073	890	919	962	0.8	29	363	382	406	1.2	2.41	265	275	0.9
27947 JARVISBURG	053	537	626	756	3.7	90	192	226	276	3.9	2.77	140	163	3.6
27948 KILL DEVIL HILLS	055	9276	10857	13087	3.8	91	3980	4723	5768	4.1	2.29	2440	2843	3.7
27949 KITTY HAWK	055	6022	6855	8152	3.1	86	2573	2956	3552	3.3	2.31	1871	2125	3.0
27950 KNOTTS ISLAND	053	1825	2237	2767	4.9	96	688	851	1063	5.1	2.63	518	632	4.8
27953 MANNS HARBOR	055	147	160	187	2.0	65	57	63	74	2.4	2.54	43	47	2.1
27954 MANTEO	055	5197	6108	7380	3.9	92	2107	2511	3073	4.2	2.41	1465	1721	3.9
27956 MAPLE	053	286	312	361	2.1	68	93	104	124	2.7	2.71	66	73	2.4
27957 MERRY HILL	015	1005	993	991	-0.3	5	405	411	419	0.4	2.42	289	290	0.1
27958 MOYOCK	053	7590	8712	10452	3.3	87	2712	3142	3808	3.5	2.77	1893	2199	3.3
27959 NAGS HEAD	055	6763	7862	9434	3.6	90	2956	3489	4248	4.0	2.21	219	232	3.6
27960 OCRACOKE	095	769	814	864	1.4	49	370	400	434	1.9	2.04	219	232	1.4
27962 PLYMOUTH	187	7793	7557	7359	-0.7	2	3068	3037	3018	-0.2	2.43	2206	2153	-0.6
27964 POINT HARBOR	053	376	446	543	4.1	93	161	193	237	4.4	2.31	117	138	4.0
27965 POPLAR BRANCH	053	570	657	788	3.4	88	217	253	307	3.7	2.60	158	182	3.4
27966 POWELLS POINT	053	1019	1208	1469	4.1	93	401	479	589	4.3	2.52	291	344	4.0
27970 ROPER	187	3902	3890	3830	-0.1	9	1514	1545	1555	0.5	2.52	1106	1112	0.1
27973 SHAWBORO	053	710	785	912	2.4	74	288	323	382	2.7	2.40	214	237	2.4
27974 SHILOH	029	1094	1236	1443	2.9	83	415	475	562	3.2	2.59	317	358	2.9
27976 SOUTH MILLS	029	2293	2522	2907	2.3	72	895	1001	1171	2.7	2.52	670	741	2.4
27978 STUMPY POINT	055	1035	1129	1313	2.1	68	403	446	526	2.4	2.53	306	335	2.2
27979 SUNBURY	073	1741	1802	1889	0.8	31	669	704	748	1.2	2.56	500	520	0.9
27980 TYNER	041	1848	1839	1838	-0.1	8	719	731	744	0.4	2.51	525	524	0.0
27981 WANCHESE	055	1527	1773	2129	3.6	90	614	723	879	3.9	2.45	433	504	3.6
27983 WINDSOR	015	10259	10244	10286	0.0	10	4018	4102	4214	0.5	2.45	2824	2841	0.1
27986 WINTON	091	1535	1702	1868	2.5	76	610	696	785	3.2	2.34	415	467	2.8
28001 ALBEMARLE	167	27190	27630	28821	0.4	18	10796	11047	11626	0.5	2.41	7477	7527	0.2
28006 ALEXIS	071	741	820	900	2.4	75	291	327	364	2.8	2.51	230	257	2.7
28012 BELMONT	071	18639	18898	19496	0.3	17	7305	7528	7894	0.7	2.42	5160	5240	0.4
28016 BESSEMER CITY	071	12673	13345	14025	1.2	44	4906	5250	5601	1.6	2.54	3629	3829	1.3
28018 BOSTIC	161	4962	5223	5491	1.2	44	1971	2112	2257	1.6	2.44	1442	1522	1.3
28020 CASAR	045	2367	2492	2619	1.2	44	969	1037	1105	1.6	2.40	721	761	1.3
28021 CHERRYVILLE	071	12828	13270	13960	0.8	30	5068	5320	5671	1.2	2.44	3703	3833	0.8
28023 CHINA GROVE	159	12787	13600	14456	1.5	51	4876	5236	5607	1.7	2.59	3701	3916	1.3
28025 CONCORD	025	41204	45749	52438	2.5	76	15636	17495	20194	2.7	2.56	11239	12385	2.3
28027 CONCORD	025	38495	46066	54810	4.3	94	14280	17262	20703	4.6	2.63	10781	12881	4.3
28031 CORNELIUS	119	14139	17056	20408	4.5	95	5957	7266	8788	4.8	2.35	3959	4708	4.2
28032 CRAMERTON	071	2154	2262	2370	1.2	42	898	957	1019	1.5	2.35	576	605	1.2
28033 CROUSE	109	2290	2399	2603	1.1	39	864	915	1003	1.4	2.62	684	715	1.1
28034 DALLAS	071	15551	16263	16990	1.1	38	6031	6428	6829	1.5	2.49	4492	4724	1.2
28036 DAVIDSON	119	9838	11274	13007	3.3	87	3105	3730	4477	4.4	2.55	2343	2747	3.8
28037 DENVER	109	12155	14154	16439	3.7	90	4728	5578	6548	4.0	2.52	3671	4276	3.7
28040 ELLENBORO	161	7353	7728	8118	1.2	42	2978	3178	3387	1.5	2.41	2163	2272	1.2
28043 FOREST CITY	161	21190	21412	22310	0.3	15	8586	8810	9321	0.6	2.37	5974	6044	0.3
28052 GASTONIA	071	36319	36731	38068	0.3	16	13527	13830	14519	0.5	2.62	8893	8965	0.2
28054 GASTONIA	071	33143	33540	34666	0.3	16	13766	14157	14865	0.7	2.30	8375	9057	1.9
28056 GASTONIA	071	28789	31101	33142	1.8	60	10656	11695	12649	2.2	2.65	804	868	1.8
28071 GOLD HILL	159	2770	2987	3224	1.8	59	1051	1147	1251	2.1	2.55	804	868	1.8
28073 GROVER	045	4935	5533	6019	2.7	81	1868	2123	2337	3.1	2.61	1396	1565	2.7
28075 HARRISBURG	025	8181	9822	11678	4.4	94	2837	3444	4127	4.7	2.83	2390	2876	4.5
28078 HUNTERSVILLE	119	27715	33784	40592	4.8	95	10226	12746	15565	5.3	2.61	7674	9371	4.8
28079 INDIAN TRAIL	179	15925	20613	27222	6.3	99	5743	7537	10052	6.6	2.73	4654	6027	6.3
28080 IRON STATION	109	6689	7615	8754	3.1	86	2433	2808	3263	3.4	2.71	1914	2184	3.2
28081 KANNAPOLIS	025	23231	24390	26682	1.2	41	9060	9604	10588	1.4	2.51	6453	6714	0.9
28083 KANNAPOLIS	025	20283	21399	23735	1.3	46	8313	8840	9872	1.5	2.39	5574	5812	1.0
28086 KINGS MOUNTAIN	045	26878	28295	29883	1.2	44	10191	10852	11592	1.5	2.58	7659	8058	1.2
28088 LANDIS	159	3079	3085	3189	0.1	12	1241	1248	1298	0.1	2.47	870	858	-0.3
28090 LAWNDALE	045	8766	9159	9617	1.0	37	3337	3534	3754	1.4	2.56	2521	2632	1.0
28091 LILESVILLE	007	2950	3029	3157	0.6	26	1162	1213	1283	1.0	2.50	836	861	0.7
28092 LINCOLNTON	109	34053	37254	42025	2.1	70	12799	14133	16108	2.4	2.58	9450	10316	2.1
28097 LOCUST	167	2819	3054	3276	1.9	62	1073	1183	1286	2.3	2.58	826	899	2.0
28098 LOWELL	071	2904	2964	3059	0.5	21	1192	1235	1293	0.8	2.40	837	853	0.5
28103 MARSHVILLE	179	9416	10776	13394	3.2	87	3477	4043	5087	3.6	2.64	2651	3041	3.3
28104 MATTHEWS	179	16055	19999	25866	5.3	97	5565	6980	9084	5.5	2.86	4652	5788	5.3
28105 MATTHEWS	119	30366	35545	41885	3.8	91	11063	13196	15794	4.2	2.67	8210	9658	3.9
28107 MIDLAND	025	5233	5773	6580	2.3	73	1949	2168	2484	2.5	2.66	1521	1667	2.2
28110 MONROE	179	35278	43285	55707	4.9	96	12357	15307	19865	5.2	2.81	9597	11755	4.9
28112 MONROE	179	23057	26570	33070	3.4	88	8128	9444	11863	3.6	2.76	6115	6988	3.2
28114 MOORESBORO	045	7302	7958	8553	2.0	66	2929	3235	3520	2.4	2.46	2139	2328	2.0
28115 MOORESVILLE	097	24266	28319	32918	3.7	90	9309	10987	12899	4.0	2.55	6724	7816	3.6
28117 MOORESVILLE	097	19346	23807	28578	5.0	96	7418	9178	11088	5.1	2.59	5803	7081	4.8
28119 MORVEN	007	2107	2214	2328	1.2	42	752	798	849	1.4	2.77	567	595	1.1
28120 MOUNT HOLLY	071	15185	16032	16870	1.3	47	6051	6526	6992	1.8	2.43	4372	4637	1.4
28124 MOUNT PLEASANT	025	6486	7669	8982	4.0	93	2333	2794	3304	4.3	2.66	1863	2201	4.0
28125 MOUNT ULLA	159	2090	2321	2529	2.5	76	797	893	981	2.7	2.58	605	670	2.4
28127 NEW LONDON	167	7181	7560	8028	1.2	44	2498	2692	2909	1.8	2.66	1914	2035	1.5
28128 NORWOOD	167	7601	8014	8464	1.3	45	3010	3225	3446	1.6	2.48	2219	2341	1.3
28129 OAKBORO	167	5786	6182	6631	1.6	54	2250	2431	2633	1.8	2.54	1728	1844	1.5
28133 PEACHLAND	007	2796	2941	3087	1.2	43	1052	1123	1199	1.6	2.46	795	840	1.3
28134 PINEVILLE	119	7387	8573	10023	3.6	90	2802	3338	3985	4.2	2.46	1818	2129	3.8
28135 POLKTON	007	8474	8793	9171	0.9	32	2768	2935	3124	1.4	2.67	2032	2125	1.1
28137 RICHFIELD	159	2989	3161	3336	1.3	48	1028	1108	1187	1.8	2.58	748	795	1.4
NORTH CAROLINA					1.9					2.2	2.46			1.8
UNITED STATES					1.2					1.3	2.58			1.1

ZIP CODE #	POST OFFICE NAME	RACE (%) White 2000	White 2004	Black 2000	Black 2004	Asian/Pacific 2000	Asian/Pacific 2004	% Hispanic Origin 2000	% Hispanic Origin 2004	2004 AGE DISTRIBUTION (%) 0-4	5-9	10-14	15-19	20-24	25-44	45-64	65-84	85+	18+	MEDIAN AGE 2004	% 2004 Males	% 2004 Females
27925	COLUMBIA	56.0	55.7	39.9	40.2	0.8	0.8	3.6	3.7	5.0	5.0	6.2	6.5	7.2	28.9	25.4	13.5	2.2	79.6	39.9	53.3	46.7
27926	CORAPEAKE	69.7	68.8	27.5	28.0	0.5	0.6	1.7	2.0	6.2	6.6	8.1	7.6	5.4	28.1	25.7	10.7	1.5	74.4	38.6	49.3	50.7
27927	COROLLA	97.4	97.1	1.2	1.3	0.3	0.3	0.6	0.8	3.0	2.6	3.2	3.0	3.1	19.7	52.2	13.0	0.7	89.0	52.4	51.2	48.8
27928	CRESWELL	62.3	60.9	32.5	32.9	0.4	0.4	4.0	4.9	5.6	5.8	6.7	6.1	6.0	26.0	26.4	15.5	1.8	78.1	40.7	49.9	50.1
27929	CURRITUCK	96.7	96.6	1.3	1.2	0.2	0.2	1.6	1.7	5.3	6.0	6.1	6.1	3.9	25.4	32.6	13.6	1.1	78.3	43.5	51.9	48.1
27932	EDENTON	58.8	58.1	39.4	39.7	0.3	0.4	1.5	1.9	5.9	6.0	6.7	7.0	7.2	23.2	25.7	15.7	2.5	77.6	40.7	47.0	53.0
27935	EURE	76.6	76.0	22.0	22.6	0.3	0.4	0.6	0.7	5.8	6.7	8.0	6.3	4.7	26.1	27.7	13.1	1.6	75.4	40.1	49.0	51.0
27937	GATES	52.8	52.0	45.6	46.2	0.1	0.2	0.6	0.7	6.1	7.1	9.0	7.0	4.7	27.3	25.8	11.8	1.2	73.3	38.4	49.4	50.6
27938	GATESVILLE	48.0	47.0	50.6	51.5	0.1	0.2	0.3	0.4	5.7	6.2	7.4	6.9	5.0	27.2	23.9	15.0	3.0	76.7	40.4	51.4	48.6
27939	GRANDY	89.0	88.1	8.0	8.5	0.6	0.7	0.6	0.9	5.6	5.7	6.2	6.0	5.2	26.8	28.5	15.0	1.1	78.9	41.7	48.9	51.1
27941	HARBINGER	94.1	93.8	4.7	5.0	0.1	0.2	0.7	1.0	5.5	5.2	7.3	5.1	4.9	27.4	28.5	14.7	1.5	78.8	42.3	49.7	50.3
27942	HARRELLSVILLE	41.5	40.7	57.8	58.6	0.1	0.1	0.7	0.9	4.8	4.9	6.3	6.9	7.2	24.1	28.6	15.8	1.6	80.3	42.7	45.7	54.3
27944	HERTFORD	70.3	69.6	28.5	29.0	0.3	0.3	0.6	0.8	5.3	5.3	6.2	6.4	5.7	22.5	28.3	17.9	2.3	79.0	43.9	48.0	52.0
27946	HOBBSVILLE	57.6	56.7	41.2	42.1	0.3	0.4	0.8	1.1	4.5	6.4	7.8	7.2	3.9	28.0	26.1	14.2	2.0	76.8	40.5	48.9	51.1
27947	JARVISBURG	87.0	85.9	10.4	11.0	0.4	0.3	0.7	1.1	6.1	6.1	6.7	6.2	5.4	28.8	26.8	12.8	1.1	77.3	39.7	48.1	51.9
27948	KILL DEVIL HILLS	96.6	96.1	0.6	0.6	0.6	0.7	2.6	3.4	5.4	6.0	6.6	5.4	4.8	34.0	26.7	10.5	0.7	78.5	38.8	51.0	49.0
27949	KITTY HAWK	98.2	97.9	0.5	0.5	0.3	0.4	1.2	1.5	4.8	5.2	5.6	4.9	2.7	22.3	35.1	18.5	1.0	81.4	47.5	50.1	49.9
27950	KNOTTS ISLAND	98.7	98.5	0.1	0.0	0.4	0.5	1.0	1.4	5.5	6.0	7.8	7.2	5.5	29.1	29.3	8.9	0.8	76.3	39.0	50.8	49.2
27953	MANNS HARBOR	95.2	94.4	0.7	0.6	0.0	0.0	4.8	6.3	6.9	7.5	6.3	5.6	5.0	28.1	27.5	11.9	1.3	75.6	38.9	51.3	48.8
27954	MANTEO	82.9	82.2	12.7	12.7	0.2	0.2	3.7	4.6	5.6	5.9	6.5	6.3	5.8	27.1	30.3	11.3	1.2	78.0	40.7	50.1	50.0
27956	MAPLE	79.4	78.2	16.1	16.7	0.4	1.0	3.9	4.8	6.4	6.4	6.4	6.1	5.1	30.5	23.7	12.2	3.2	77.2	38.0	50.0	50.0
27957	MERRY HILL	52.8	52.1	46.4	47.1	0.0	0.0	0.6	0.7	4.8	5.4	6.6	6.3	5.1	24.3	30.4	15.3	1.7	79.4	43.4	48.1	51.9
27958	MOYOCK	89.8	89.1	8.0	8.2	0.5	0.6	1.5	2.0	6.9	7.0	7.8	7.3	6.3	28.2	26.6	9.1	1.0	73.9	37.6	50.2	49.8
27959	NAGS HEAD	97.5	97.1	0.6	0.7	0.6	0.7	1.1	1.4	4.2	4.5	5.8	5.2	4.0	28.5	31.8	14.3	1.7	82.1	43.8	50.2	49.8
27960	OCRACOKE	96.1	95.7	1.7	1.7	0.3	0.3	2.0	2.5	4.3	4.4	3.2	2.6	3.0	28.0	37.6	15.0	2.0	86.5	48.0	50.1	49.9
27962	PLYMOUTH	44.7	43.8	53.0	53.4	0.5	0.6	2.0	2.4	7.2	7.0	7.5	6.7	5.9	22.8	27.3	13.3	2.4	74.0	39.6	46.3	53.7
27964	POINT HARBOR	89.4	88.6	9.0	9.6	0.0	0.0	1.3	1.6	6.5	6.3	7.0	6.1	5.8	30.0	26.2	11.0	1.1	76.2	39.0	48.7	51.4
27965	POPLAR BRANCH	87.9	86.9	9.1	9.6	0.5	0.6	0.7	0.8	5.6	5.6	6.2	6.1	5.2	27.7	28.2	14.3	1.1	78.7	41.2	48.4	51.6
27966	POWELLS POINT	89.5	88.7	8.9	9.5	0.1	0.1	1.2	1.5	6.5	6.4	7.0	6.0	6.0	29.4	26.3	11.3	1.1	76.2	38.7	48.2	51.8
27970	ROPER	48.2	47.1	49.5	50.2	0.2	0.2	1.9	2.4	5.9	6.2	6.8	6.3	6.1	24.1	29.8	13.4	1.5	77.3	41.1	48.7	51.3
27973	SHAWBORO	80.4	79.4	17.8	18.5	0.3	0.4	1.4	1.7	5.9	6.0	6.0	6.0	5.0	26.6	29.0	13.5	2.0	78.5	41.6	49.8	50.2
27974	SHILOH	87.4	86.6	8.3	8.3	2.6	3.2	0.6	0.7	7.1	7.0	6.1	6.2	4.9	28.2	25.3	13.5	1.6	76.3	38.2	49.8	50.2
27976	SOUTH MILLS	78.5	77.9	19.2	19.6	0.4	0.5	0.7	0.8	5.1	5.5	6.8	6.5	5.0	29.0	28.6	12.1	1.4	78.6	40.9	49.8	50.2
27978	STUMPY POINT	95.0	94.0	0.6	0.6	0.0	0.0	5.1	6.5	7.3	7.2	5.9	5.6	5.3	28.2	27.0	12.3	1.2	76.3	39.1	50.0	50.0
27979	SUNBURY	54.5	53.7	43.7	44.2	0.3	0.4	0.7	0.9	5.8	6.3	8.0	6.9	5.4	26.5	26.1	13.0	2.1	75.7	40.3	47.7	52.3
27980	TYNER	69.3	67.5	28.6	29.9	0.5	0.7	1.5	1.9	5.8	6.1	7.3	5.8	6.0	24.0	27.8	15.2	2.0	77.2	41.6	49.3	50.7
27981	WANCHESE	98.1	97.9	0.3	0.3	0.1	0.2	1.8	2.4	5.1	5.4	6.0	6.5	6.7	31.6	26.9	10.6	1.2	79.6	38.8	51.2	48.8
27983	WINDSOR	34.9	34.4	63.8	64.1	0.2	0.2	0.9	1.1	6.4	6.6	7.2	6.9	6.1	24.7	26.2	14.0	2.0	75.6	39.9	47.1	52.9
27986	WINTON	29.6	28.7	65.7	66.2	0.6	0.7	1.4	1.6	6.4	6.6	6.7	6.9	5.9	27.6	28.0	10.7	1.1	75.7	37.9	46.9	53.1
28001	ALBEMARLE	80.9	79.7	14.1	14.4	3.1	3.7	1.4	1.7	6.7	6.7	7.2	6.5	5.8	27.7	23.7	13.7	2.3	75.4	38.1	48.4	51.6
28006	ALEXIS	90.2	89.8	8.1	8.2	0.1	0.1	0.8	1.0	5.6	6.8	8.2	7.4	4.9	29.6	27.8	8.9	0.7	74.5	37.4	50.6	49.4
28012	BELMONT	89.2	88.0	6.2	6.5	2.2	2.6	2.5	3.1	6.2	6.2	6.4	6.2	6.6	29.9	25.8	11.1	1.6	77.7	38.0	48.8	51.2
28016	BESSEMER CITY	88.4	87.6	9.1	9.6	0.4	0.5	2.6	3.3	7.2	7.2	7.3	6.1	5.7	31.9	24.0	9.9	0.7	74.5	35.5	49.0	51.0
28018	BOSTIC	96.6	96.3	2.2	2.4	0.3	0.4	0.8	1.0	5.7	6.2	7.3	6.1	5.7	27.6	26.7	13.2	1.7	77.0	39.3	49.6	50.4
28020	CASAR	97.7	97.5	1.2	1.2	0.0	0.0	1.9	2.3	5.2	5.6	6.5	5.4	5.5	28.7	28.6	13.2	1.4	79.5	40.5	50.6	49.4
28021	CHERRYVILLE	88.9	87.9	9.3	10.0	0.5	0.6	2.0	2.5	6.2	6.4	6.7	5.7	5.2	28.1	25.9	13.7	2.1	77.0	39.8	49.1	50.9
28023	CHINA GROVE	90.6	89.6	5.3	5.5	0.8	0.9	4.7	5.8	6.6	6.6	6.8	6.2	6.1	29.8	25.1	11.3	1.5	76.2	37.7	49.4	50.6
28025	CONCORD	80.8	80.3	14.2	13.7	0.7	0.8	6.6	8.1	7.1	6.8	7.0	6.4	6.7	30.5	23.4	10.6	1.6	75.4	35.9	49.1	50.9
28027	CONCORD	85.1	83.8	9.9	10.3	1.4	1.7	5.5	6.8	7.9	7.6	7.4	6.3	6.1	32.5	23.3	8.0	1.0	73.2	34.6	49.7	50.3
28031	CORNELIUS	92.6	91.4	4.7	5.2	1.3	1.6	2.5	3.4	6.5	6.7	6.2	5.1	4.8	32.5	29.6	8.1	0.6	77.5	39.0	50.5	49.5
28032	CRAMERTON	94.6	93.8	2.7	3.1	0.7	0.9	0.9	1.2	6.3	6.5	6.7	5.8	6.3	31.3	23.5	11.9	1.6	76.9	36.2	47.9	52.1
28033	CROUSE	94.7	94.0	2.4	2.5	0.6	0.8	5.0	6.5	7.0	7.0	7.4	6.4	5.6	31.9	25.1	8.6	0.9	74.6	36.5	50.2	49.8
28034	DALLAS	89.4	88.9	9.0	9.3	0.3	0.3	1.6	2.1	6.6	6.6	6.9	6.4	5.7	30.6	25.7	10.6	0.9	75.9	37.0	50.0	50.0
28036	DAVIDSON	89.2	88.1	7.6	8.0	1.3	1.7	2.0	2.8	6.5	6.7	7.4	9.6	11.6	25.3	22.7	8.5	1.8	76.2	33.5	49.4	50.6
28037	DENVER	95.1	94.7	3.3	3.5	0.4	0.4	1.2	1.7	6.1	6.6	7.2	5.6	4.2	30.7	28.4	10.4	0.8	76.6	39.5	50.2	49.8
28040	ELLENBORO	94.0	93.5	4.5	4.7	0.2	0.3	1.1	1.4	6.5	6.7	7.3	5.8	5.8	29.0	25.5	11.8	1.7	75.8	37.8	49.0	51.0
28043	FOREST CITY	80.6	79.7	16.7	17.1	0.5	0.6	3.0	3.7	6.7	6.6	6.9	5.9	5.8	27.6	24.1	14.1	2.4	76.2	38.4	47.3	52.7
28052	GASTONIA	64.5	63.7	32.6	32.8	0.5	0.5	4.8	5.8	7.7	7.5	7.6	6.4	6.3	29.0	23.0	11.1	1.4	73.3	34.9	47.8	52.2
28054	GASTONIA	79.1	77.8	16.2	16.8	1.5	1.8	5.2	6.4	6.1	6.0	6.2	5.8	6.4	29.6	23.8	13.9	2.2	78.3	38.0	47.1	52.9
28056	GASTONIA	89.7	88.6	7.1	7.5	1.1	1.4	2.0	2.7	6.5	6.7	7.3	6.6	5.9	29.8	27.4	9.1	0.8	75.4	37.7	49.1	50.9
28071	GOLD HILL	96.6	96.3	1.5	1.6	0.4	0.5	1.0	1.3	6.0	6.4	7.1	7.7	6.5	29.4	26.4	9.7	0.9	76.1	37.4	51.5	48.5
28073	GROVER	83.0	81.9	14.8	15.6	0.5	0.5	1.2	1.6	8.5	8.4	7.6	6.2	5.4	32.0	23.4	7.7	0.8	71.6	33.6	50.0	50.0
28075	HARRISBURG	92.0	91.0	5.6	6.2	1.1	1.3	1.1	1.5	6.4	7.9	8.8	6.2	3.9	30.2	27.8	8.0	0.8	72.7	38.7	49.3	50.7
28078	HUNTERSVILLE	88.2	86.3	7.9	8.7	1.4	1.7	3.8	5.4	9.1	8.8	7.3	5.6	5.1	35.7	21.6	5.6	1.0	71.2	34.4	49.4	50.6
28079	INDIAN TRAIL	91.5	90.1	4.9	5.5	1.0	1.2	2.3	3.3	9.0	8.6	7.6	5.7	5.1	35.0	21.8	6.8	0.5	71.3	34.2	49.5	50.5
28080	IRON STATION	88.6	88.1	9.2	9.3	0.3	0.4	1.9	2.5	6.4	7.1	7.7	6.5	5.3	31.3	26.5	8.5	0.8	74.7	37.0	50.2	49.8
28081	KANNAPOLIS	83.0	81.5	11.6	12.0	1.0	1.2	5.4	6.9	7.2	6.8	6.9	6.1	6.0	30.6	23.1	11.7	1.8	75.5	36.7	49.1	50.9
28083	KANNAPOLIS	76.9	74.7	18.3	19.5	0.7	0.8	5.6	7.3	6.5	6.2	6.3	5.6	6.2	28.7	23.1	14.6	2.8	77.7	38.5	48.2	51.8
28086	KINGS MOUNTAIN	80.6	79.6	16.3	16.8	1.5	1.8	1.4	1.8	7.0	7.1	7.6	6.2	5.4	29.1	25.1	11.1	1.4	74.4	37.2	48.7	51.3
28088	LANDIS	88.2	86.6	6.5	6.9	1.0	1.3	7.7	9.8	6.6	6.6	6.8	5.7	6.0	28.5	23.2	14.7	1.9	76.8	38.3	49.3	50.7
28090	LAWNDALE	84.4	83.7	14.1	14.5	0.1	0.1	2.0	2.5	6.7	6.8	7.0	6.2	5.8	28.5	25.2	12.4	1.5	75.7	38.1	49.2	50.8
28091	LILESVILLE	46.1	44.9	52.6	53.8	0.3	0.4	0.6	0.7	6.5	7.0	7.8	6.7	6.1	26.0	26.5	12.0	1.5	74.6	38.3	47.9	52.1
28092	LINCOLNTON	87.8	86.8	7.7	7.8	0.4	0.4	8.9	11.4	6.4	6.5	6.9	6.4	5.9	29.7	25.3	11.6	1.6	76.3	37.6	49.5	50.5
28097	LOCUST	95.7	95.2	1.5	1.6	0.1	0.2	2.8	3.3	6.6	7.0	7.4	5.9	4.9	30.6	25.3	11.3	1.0	75.3	38.0	50.9	49.1
28098	LOWELL	92.1	91.6	5.4	5.5	0.8	1.0	1.9	2.4	6.8	6.6	6.4	5.6	6.1	29.5	23.9	13.2	1.9	76.9	37.8	47.0	53.0
28103	MARSHVILLE	78.5	77.4	19.7	20.4	0.2	0.2	1.8	2.5	6.8	7.0	7.5	6.5	5.7	28.7	25.5	10.6	1.6	74.6	37.2	49.6	50.4
28104	MATTHEWS	92.3	91.2	4.5	4.9	0.9	1.1	2.0	2.9	7.6	8.2	8.6	6.7	4.9	30.2	26.8	6.7	0.5	71.4	36.7	50.2	49.9
28105	MATTHEWS	86.2	83.9	8.4	9.4	2.8	3.4	3.4	4.7	7.2	7.4	7.9	6.8	6.2	31.1	25.0	7.0	1.3	73.1	35.7	48.5	51.5
28107	MIDLAND	93.2	92.3	4.8	5.3	0.2	0.2	1.8	2.4	6.0	7.1	7.6	6.2	5.1	29.0	27.7	10.4	1.0	75.4	38.7	50.5	49.5
28110	MONROE	78.4	77.8	14.3	13.7	0.6	0.8	11.1	13.3	8.7	8.3	7.5	6.1	6.3	33.6	20.8	7.9	0.9	71.8	33.1	50.5	49.5
28112	MONROE	77.2	75.3	17.3	17.9	0.3	0.4	9.7	12.7	7.5	7.4	7.2	6.4	5.9	29.5	23.6	11.0	1.5	73.9	36.0	49.8	50.2
28114	MOORESBORO	92.1	91.6	6.6	6.9	0.3	0.4	1.4	1.7	6.4	6.6	7.1	5.9	5.5	28.8	25.5	12.8	1.4	76.3	38.3	50.0	50.0
28115	MOORESVILLE	84.6	83.1	12.2	13.1	1.0	1.2	2.2	2.9	7.1	7.2	7.6	6.7	6.1	30.6	23.1	10.1	1.5	73.9	35.7	49.2	50.8
28117	MOORESVILLE	93.9	93.3	3.7	3.8	1.2	1.4	1.1	1.5	7.2	7.8	7.7	5.4	3.6	30.5	27.5	9.7	0.7	73.8	39.2	50.6	49.4
28119	MORVEN	27.9	26.9	71.1	72.0	0.0	0.0	0.5	0.5	8.7	8.6	9.1	7.4	6.1	27.4	22.9	8.9	0.9	68.9	33.1	45.8	54.2
28120	MOUNT HOLLY	88.4	87.1	8.4	8.9	1.6	2.0	1.4	1.9	6.0	6.1	6.6	5.8	5.7	30.1	26.2	12.0	1.4	77.7	38.7	48.8	51.2
28124	MOUNT PLEASANT	93.7	93.0	4.6	5.0	0.6	0.7	0.7	1.0	6.3	6.7	6.9	5.9	5.1	30.5	26.9	10.4	1.3	76.3	38.6	51.1	48.9
28125	MOUNT ULLA	88.9	87.7	7.8	8.2	0.2	0.2	3.3	4.2	7.5	7.3	7.3	6.8	5.6	30.0	24.3	9.9	1.3	73.6	36.3	50.8	49.3
28127	NEW LONDON	81.2	80.3	16.5	16.9	1.1	1.3	0.7	0.9	5.2	5.7	7.0	6.0	5.5	28.4	28.7	12.1	1.3	78.5	40.1	52.1	47.9
28128	NORWOOD	80.9	79.2	14.6	15.4	1.3	1.6	3.2	4.0	5.4	5.8	7.0	6.1	5.8	27.2	27.8	13.4	1.4	78.0	40.2	50.1	49.9
28129	OAKBORO	92.9	92.2	5.1	5.3	0.1	0.1	2.1	2.8	6.2	6.2	6.1	6.2	5.6	29.4	26.2	12.7	1.5	77.7	39.0	50.4	49.6
28133	PEACHLAND	75.1	74.3	20.9	21.1	2.0	2.4	1.3	1.6	6.5	6.6	7.0	6.1	6.3	30.3	24.5	11.0	1.7	76.2	37.0	52.4	47.6
28134	PINEVILLE	75.0	72.6	16.1	16.6	2.8	3.3	7.7	10.2	8.1	7.4	7.1	6.3	7.4	37.9	16.8	7.2	1.8	73.6	32.3	48.7	51.3
28135	POLKTON	50.1	49.1	48.2	49.0	0.4	0.5	0.9	1.1	6.3	6.4	6.7	6.2	6.7	32.4	23.9	10.1	1.4	76.9	36.2	54.2	45.8
28137	RICHFIELD	91.8	91.1	5.1	5.4	1.2	1.5	1.2	1.5	6.3	6.4	5.8	10.1	10.2	26.4	24.0	9.9	1.0	77.6	34.1	50.7	49.3
	NORTH CAROLINA	72.1	71.2	21.6	21.6	1.5	1.8	4.7	5.9	6.7	6.6	6.8	6.7	7.1	29.8	24.2	10.8	1.4	76.2	36.2	49.2	50.8
	UNITED STATES	75.1	73.6	12.3	12.5	3.8	4.2	12.5	14.1	6.9	6.7	7.2	7.0	7.3	28.6	23.8	10.8	1.7	75.1	36.0	49.1	50.9

#	POST OFFICE NAME	2004 Per Capita Income	2004 HH Income Base	2004 Household Income Distribution (%): Less than $25,000	$25,000 to $49,999	$50,000 to $99,999	$100,000 to $149,999	$150,000 or More	Median Household Income: 2004	2009	2004 National Centile	2004 State Centile	2004 Home Value Base	2004 Home Value Distribution (%): Less than $50,000	$50,000 to $89,999	$90,000 to $174,999	$175,000 to $399,999	$400,000 or More	2004 Median Home Value
27925	COLUMBIA	16329	1474	45.2	30.6	19.4	2.8	2.0	28004	31654	9	7	1132	36.9	37.5	19.3	5.3	1.0	60505
27926	CORAPEAKE	18841	687	27.4	38.9	28.4	3.4	2.0	40850	46474	49	56	561	27.1	26.2	37.3	9.5	0.0	85595
27927	COROLLA	78966	442	25.1	10.9	33.5	10.0	20.6	66343	78601	89	95	379	0.0	0.0	13.7	48.6	37.7	321186
27928	CRESWELL	18137	866	38.3	31.9	21.9	4.5	3.4	33344	37976	22	22	684	29.8	36.8	24.3	7.5	1.6	72429
27929	CURRITUCK	25727	315	15.2	22.5	43.5	14.6	4.1	59543	66031	84	92	279	5.4	9.0	28.7	46.6	10.4	186890
27932	EDENTON	17255	4877	37.1	30.9	26.6	4.1	1.2	33884	37889	24	25	3432	20.1	27.0	34.2	15.7	3.2	93778
27935	EURE	19146	639	31.5	26.0	35.1	6.3	1.3	39631	45084	45	50	516	24.4	36.6	27.5	10.7	0.8	76429
27937	GATES	17263	1230	39.9	27.0	26.8	3.7	2.6	36340	40991	33	36	993	32.8	30.1	32.4	4.6	0.0	71833
27938	GATESVILLE	19238	488	28.5	29.7	32.4	7.6	1.8	42266	47278	54	63	401	27.2	25.4	36.2	11.2	0.0	86111
27939	GRANDY	19020	791	34.0	34.9	23.6	5.8	1.6	34797	40000	27	29	626	10.4	27.3	48.1	12.9	1.3	107974
27941	HARBINGER	20714	354	23.2	39.3	29.1	5.4	3.1	41998	48276	53	62	294	7.8	4.4	51.4	30.3	6.1	148558
27942	HARRELLSVILLE	16270	548	46.0	33.0	17.0	2.4	1.6	26890	30581	7	5	437	41.4	44.6	11.7	2.3	0.0	57500
27944	HERTFORD	17654	4413	39.8	32.8	22.1	3.9	1.4	31756	35444	17	17	3412	23.0	30.1	29.7	14.5	2.8	85661
27946	HOBBSVILLE	20536	382	29.8	29.3	31.4	8.6	0.8	40611	45000	48	55	319	21.6	33.5	30.1	14.7	0.0	84844
27947	JARVISBURG	16846	226	30.1	37.2	25.2	6.2	1.3	37042	42691	36	40	178	6.7	21.4	54.5	16.3	1.1	117073
27948	KILL DEVIL HILLS	25463	4723	19.5	35.9	33.4	6.8	4.4	45736	52135	63	77	3452	5.2	6.8	58.0	27.3	2.7	138690
27949	KITTY HAWK	36914	2956	13.7	26.2	36.7	13.1	10.4	60279	71581	85	93	2504	1.6	3.1	23.2	56.5	15.6	230690
27950	KNOTTS ISLAND	20615	851	28.6	27.6	33.6	7.3	2.9	43533	48052	57	69	699	12.5	18.5	40.2	26.3	2.6	116708
27953	MANNS HARBOR	16287	63	36.5	34.9	23.8	4.8	0.0	37971	41146	39	44	50	32.0	10.0	36.0	22.0	0.0	104167
27954	MANTEO	23584	2511	29.9	29.4	28.9	6.5	5.4	41659	47061	52	61	1882	9.9	11.9	40.3	28.4	9.5	146339
27956	MAPLE	13209	104	33.7	46.2	19.2	1.0	0.0	34420	39051	25	27	71	36.6	19.7	39.4	4.2	0.0	77500
27957	MERRY HILL	19664	411	29.9	33.1	27.7	7.1	2.2	39905	46723	46	51	329	26.1	38.9	24.6	10.3	0.0	68953
27958	MOYOCK	21247	3142	22.3	27.4	40.5	7.2	2.6	50228	57016	72	86	2654	18.7	13.4	43.9	21.8	2.2	121491
27959	NAGS HEAD	29384	3489	19.8	30.7	34.7	8.9	5.9	49532	56729	71	85	2715	5.4	7.3	42.3	36.0	9.1	163866
27960	OCRACOKE	21972	400	22.3	45.3	26.5	6.0	0.0	37525	43257	38	42	322	4.4	3.4	31.4	59.3	1.6	209615
27962	PLYMOUTH	16703	3037	45.0	26.7	20.7	5.8	1.8	29153	33253	11	9	2081	28.6	32.5	34.0	4.5	0.4	76335
27964	POINT HARBOR	22337	193	23.8	38.3	30.1	4.2	3.6	41589	47506	52	61	154	6.5	5.2	64.9	20.1	3.3	126786
27965	POPLAR BRANCH	17213	253	32.4	36.0	23.7	6.7	1.2	35817	41129	31	34	200	8.0	26.5	48.5	16.0	1.0	112500
27966	POWELLS POINT	20517	479	23.6	38.2	30.1	4.4	3.8	41831	47405	52	61	383	6.8	5.5	63.2	21.2	3.4	128750
27970	ROPER	18611	1545	35.5	32.8	24.3	4.9	2.6	35161	39972	28	30	1237	23.9	37.6	30.9	6.2	1.4	79745
27973	SHAWBORO	20670	323	26.6	30.3	34.4	8.1	0.6	42826	49452	55	66	263	12.9	18.6	46.0	22.1	0.4	112500
27974	SHILOH	20851	475	25.5	31.6	28.8	10.7	3.4	44231	51112	59	72	385	20.0	26.2	43.9	9.9	0.0	97632
27976	SOUTH MILLS	21059	1001	24.5	32.9	31.5	7.6	3.6	43841	50626	58	70	846	10.6	23.6	47.5	17.4	0.8	117944
27978	STUMPY POINT	16319	446	37.7	36.1	22.4	3.8	0.0	36413	41658	33	36	353	28.3	9.9	38.0	23.8	0.0	111563
27979	SUNBURY	17928	704	34.1	31.4	26.9	5.7	2.0	37436	42294	37	41	578	29.4	24.7	34.8	11.1	0.0	82941
27980	TYNER	17667	731	36.1	31.1	28.2	3.2	1.5	35231	39242	28	30	597	24.1	31.7	33.0	11.2	0.0	83947
27981	WANCHESE	20999	723	20.9	35.3	34.6	8.0	1.2	41581	46746	52	61	597	17.1	16.3	54.3	12.4	0.0	116964
27983	WINDSOR	17094	4102	45.8	28.1	19.6	4.0	2.5	27662	31307	8	7	3090	31.1	41.9	22.0	4.7	0.3	67461
27986	WINTON	14534	696	51.6	29.2	15.1	2.6	1.6	24124	26989	4	2	478	36.6	38.7	18.8	5.7	0.2	60000
28001	ALBEMARLE	20127	11047	34.6	30.6	27.7	4.9	2.3	37058	42057	36	40	7958	13.3	29.7	41.4	14.5	1.1	98824
28006	ALEXIS	21589	327	20.2	34.3	35.2	9.5	0.9	45427	50270	62	76	277	17.3	20.9	43.3	16.6	1.8	106389
28012	BELMONT	24451	7528	21.6	31.8	33.4	10.1	3.2	47055	54265	66	82	5586	13.6	20.2	47.6	15.6	3.1	112487
28016	BESSEMER CITY	18913	5250	27.6	34.5	31.0	5.7	1.2	40181	45980	47	53	3890	16.7	32.4	43.6	6.8	0.4	90769
28018	BOSTIC	16949	2112	36.7	33.2	25.5	3.8	0.8	33570	37629	23	23	1721	23.9	30.9	34.9	9.5	0.8	84310
28020	CASAR	19598	1037	33.4	31.5	27.3	5.2	2.6	36553	41453	34	38	859	25.6	30.0	30.6	13.2	0.6	82971
28021	CHERRYVILLE	21486	5320	28.0	32.1	29.9	7.0	3.0	40230	45753	47	54	4194	15.4	29.9	40.7	12.0	2.1	95198
28023	CHINA GROVE	20036	5236	26.0	32.5	33.0	6.2	2.3	42435	47647	54	65	4231	14.2	27.1	45.2	11.0	2.4	99645
28025	CONCORD	23477	17495	22.7	30.3	33.3	9.3	4.4	46999	53852	66	81	12273	11.5	18.9	45.6	21.4	2.6	120789
28027	CONCORD	26172	17262	15.3	26.2	40.1	12.8	5.6	57978	65478	83	91	13313	13.0	12.9	40.5	30.5	3.2	141081
28031	CORNELIUS	56210	7266	9.5	17.1	31.0	17.9	24.6	84388	102732	96	99	5573	0.5	3.4	25.7	37.7	32.7	268660
28032	CRAMERTON	23073	957	24.9	35.5	29.2	6.4	4.1	42431	49724	54	65	610	15.7	47.4	25.7	8.4	2.8	77024
28033	CROUSE	19485	915	22.5	35.1	36.4	5.0	1.0	45428	50812	62	76	751	14.4	24.9	47.8	11.5	1.5	100419
28034	DALLAS	20863	6428	25.8	33.5	32.4	6.4	2.0	42785	48355	55	66	4720	16.8	30.0	44.2	8.5	0.5	93458
28036	DAVIDSON	39490	3730	12.2	18.8	29.1	18.6	21.4	78884	92913	95	99	3019	3.4	6.8	19.0	44.7	26.2	275159
28037	DENVER	29463	5578	14.7	27.2	36.3	14.1	7.7	58451	65673	83	92	4760	8.9	8.6	34.5	35.5	12.5	168283
28040	ELLENBORO	17271	3178	35.6	34.4	25.3	3.9	0.8	35017	39123	28	29	2525	30.0	29.2	32.8	7.6	0.4	77873
28043	FOREST CITY	18539	8810	38.9	31.2	23.7	4.1	2.1	32059	36257	18	18	6134	24.6	31.1	35.3	8.4	0.5	81959
28052	GASTONIA	16527	13830	37.1	30.9	26.1	4.3	1.6	34453	39175	26	27	8589	17.4	38.6	39.3	4.6	0.2	84217
28054	GASTONIA	23960	14157	27.8	30.6	29.2	8.5	3.9	42499	48266	55	65	7902	7.8	28.5	50.4	11.8	1.5	107351
28056	GASTONIA	27021	11695	18.3	26.9	35.7	12.4	6.7	55253	62357	80	89	9321	10.5	16.2	46.1	24.0	3.3	120552
28071	GOLD HILL	20746	1147	22.0	36.0	32.7	6.1	3.2	42200	48226	53	63	950	17.0	27.3	35.9	17.4	2.5	102254
28073	GROVER	17877	2123	28.9	36.0	30.1	4.1	0.9	39943	45394	46	51	1672	28.2	30.3	36.4	4.6	0.5	78367
28075	HARRISBURG	29661	3444	8.5	18.2	45.3	20.1	8.0	74453	82051	93	97	3226	4.7	4.3	38.0	50.2	2.7	180713
28078	HUNTERSVILLE	34528	12746	10.5	18.6	36.1	24.1	10.8	77148	89673	94	98	9801	3.1	4.1	29.0	58.4	5.4	203704
28079	INDIAN TRAIL	26892	7537	11.3	25.5	42.8	15.3	5.1	61312	69159	86	93	6702	6.1	5.9	48.3	35.5	4.3	154842
28080	IRON STATION	19387	2808	21.2	34.7	35.3	6.9	1.9	45281	50280	62	75	2356	15.9	26.3	42.3	14.9	0.6	99946
28081	KANNAPOLIS	19916	9604	29.3	32.9	28.9	6.8	2.1	40466	45831	48	54	6750	13.4	30.3	41.6	13.8	1.0	97414
28083	KANNAPOLIS	19467	8840	31.3	33.0	28.8	5.0	1.8	38219	43708	40	46	5860	9.7	35.9	44.7	9.1	0.6	94214
28086	KINGS MOUNTAIN	19886	10852	29.6	30.8	31.1	6.2	2.3	40903	46133	49	57	8301	18.4	24.3	43.0	12.9	1.4	99305
28088	LANDIS	18302	1248	31.5	33.2	29.9	4.9	0.6	39184	44337	43	49	970	15.4	27.1	46.2	11.3	0.0	97935
28090	LAWNDALE	17176	3534	32.1	35.6	26.5	4.6	1.3	37092	41911	36	40	2838	28.4	29.6	31.1	10.2	0.7	79211
28091	LILESVILLE	18050	1213	40.7	25.8	27.2	5.3	1.0	32148	35839	18	18	947	32.0	34.3	29.5	3.2	1.1	73114
28092	LINCOLNTON	19123	14133	27.5	32.9	31.5	6.1	1.9	41952	47086	53	62	10477	15.6	27.3	43.2	13.0	0.9	98789
28097	LOCUST	21552	1183	21.5	31.9	37.1	6.7	2.9	47256	53043	67	82	987	11.7	18.0	49.3	20.1	0.9	115709
28098	LOWELL	18368	1235	28.3	37.9	30.0	3.7	0.2	38184	44746	40	45	789	16.0	40.9	41.7	1.4	0.0	82324
28103	MARSHVILLE	20277	4043	24.6	29.0	37.1	6.6	2.8	46256	52069	64	79	3283	14.4	21.5	40.2	21.1	2.9	112580
28104	MATTHEWS	33360	6980	9.1	20.8	37.8	20.0	12.2	71591	81063	92	96	6268	2.0	5.9	35.7	43.0	13.3	193738
28105	MATTHEWS	32905	13196	9.4	18.4	43.5	19.7	9.1	71604	83351	92	97	9639	1.2	0.9	40.1	52.7	5.1	187525
28107	MIDLAND	24634	2168	16.4	25.7	40.1	13.9	3.9	56193	64065	81	90	1825	10.0	13.9	43.0	29.6	3.6	130549
28110	MONROE	22196	15307	19.3	29.6	37.1	10.3	3.7	50975	58525	74	87	11332	9.9	11.6	48.2	26.9	3.4	134263
28112	MONROE	22740	9444	22.7	28.2	36.5	8.1	4.6	49104	55371	70	85	6904	7.9	16.0	51.2	22.3	2.7	130228
28114	MOORESBORO	19865	3235	36.9	31.2	25.6	3.8	2.5	34243	38279	25	26	2623	29.9	30.9	29.2	9.2	0.8	75843
28115	MOORESVILLE	22208	10987	24.0	31.9	33.4	7.5	3.2	44218	50497	59	72	7891	9.3	16.4	45.0	27.0	2.4	126445
28117	MOORESVILLE	39762	9178	10.9	19.1	39.7	17.1	13.2	72782	82445	92	97	7930	1.5	3.6	20.3	52.8	21.8	253200
28119	MORVEN	13212	798	45.6	33.1	18.2	2.5	0.6	27521	30785	8	6	609	50.6	31.0	14.9	3.5	0.0	49557
28120	MOUNT HOLLY	24516	6526	23.0	28.6	37.2	9.0	2.2	48345	54753	69	83	4801	11.3	24.0	47.1	16.7	0.9	108991
28124	MOUNT PLEASANT	23564	2794	17.3	27.3	38.9	13.8	2.8	53946	60898	78	88	2349	11.8	16.3	40.0	27.9	4.0	122590
28125	MOUNT ULLA	20949	893	20.7	33.3	36.7	7.6	1.7	47229	53630	67	82	758	17.7	16.9	40.1	23.1	2.2	119845
28127	NEW LONDON	23641	2692	26.5	30.6	30.0	6.3	6.5	44148	50481	59	72	2258	15.5	24.2	40.0	16.2	4.1	105260
28128	NORWOOD	19885	3225	29.0	31.8	32.0	5.2	2.0	41248	46660	51	59	2573	19.2	30.2	30.9	15.4	4.4	90859
28129	OAKBORO	21588	2431	25.1	30.5	35.5	6.5	2.4	45349	50890	62	75	2016	10.6	24.6	46.1	17.3	1.5	109383
28133	PEACHLAND	21561	1123	27.6	31.0	33.3	5.1	3.0	42513	48036	55	65	923	23.1	26.8	36.5	9.6	4.0	90300
28134	PINEVILLE	24800	3338	17.6	30.6	36.1	12.0	3.7	51604	60308	75	87	1889	5.0	6.6	57.8	26.8	3.8	142926
28135	POLKTON	16866	2935	36.6	33.5	24.6	3.0	2.3	34033	38594	24	25	2336	33.1	32.9	23.9	7.3	2.8	68564
28137	RICHFIELD	18727	1108	23.9	40.6	27.0	5.3	3.2	40863	46527	49	57	895	19.2	24.7	37.0	15.5	3.6	100754
	NORTH CAROLINA	23743		27.0	29.8	30.1	8.5	4.7	43794	50711				14.5	20.0	39.7	21.7	4.1	115673
	UNITED STATES	25866		24.7	27.1	30.8	10.9	6.5	48124	56710				10.9	15.0	33.7	30.1	10.4	145905

#	POST OFFICE NAME	FINANCIAL SERVICES: Auto Loan	FINANCIAL SERVICES: Home Loan	FINANCIAL SERVICES: Invest-ments	FINANCIAL SERVICES: Retire-ment Plans	THE HOME: Home Improvements: Home Repair	THE HOME: Home Improvements: Lawn & Garden	THE HOME: Furnishings: Comput-ers & Hard-ware	THE HOME: Furnishings: Major Appli-ances	THE HOME: Furnishings: TV, Radio, Sound Equip-ment	THE HOME: Furnishings: Furni-ture	ENTERTAINMENT: Dine out/ Carry out	ENTERTAINMENT: Sports Equip-ment	ENTERTAINMENT: Fees & Tickets	ENTERTAINMENT: Toys & Games	ENTERTAINMENT: Travel	ENTERTAINMENT: Cable TV	PERSONAL: Apparel & Services	PERSONAL: Auto Repairs	PERSONAL: Health Insur-ance	PERSONAL: Pets & Supplies
27925	COLUMBIA	65	48	35	44	52	62	52	58	60	51	71	65	47	65	51	64	65	58	69	72
27926	CORAPEAKE	87	68	44	63	72	80	66	76	72	67	87	89	59	82	66	74	81	75	84	98
27927	COROLLA	272	213	145	192	240	270	201	242	227	199	270	283	180	266	214	243	251	239	286	331
27928	CRESWELL	85	57	26	49	64	74	55	69	67	56	78	82	47	74	56	72	71	68	85	97
27929	CURRITUCK	87	107	113	107	105	104	96	96	89	95	112	112	101	119	98	86	111	92	86	106
27932	EDENTON	71	54	37	49	59	68	55	63	63	54	74	72	49	71	55	66	69	63	75	82
27935	EURE	89	62	30	54	69	79	59	73	70	61	83	87	51	79	60	75	76	72	88	102
27937	GATES	80	64	42	59	67	73	61	70	66	63	80	82	56	76	61	68	76	69	76	90
27938	GATESVILLE	91	69	45	65	76	88	72	81	80	70	95	93	65	92	72	85	88	80	95	102
27939	GRANDY	77	58	37	53	66	74	56	68	64	55	75	80	49	74	59	67	69	67	80	93
27941	HARBINGER	91	68	40	64	76	84	66	79	74	66	88	95	58	86	68	77	81	78	91	107
27942	HARRELLSVILLE	74	50	23	43	56	65	48	60	58	49	68	72	41	64	49	62	62	59	74	85
27944	HERTFORD	69	54	38	51	59	69	55	62	62	54	73	70	51	69	56	65	68	62	74	78
27946	HOBBSVILLE	82	69	48	64	74	80	64	73	70	64	84	87	61	85	66	72	79	71	81	96
27947	JARVISBURG	80	62	40	58	69	76	60	71	66	60	79	84	54	77	62	69	74	70	80	94
27948	KILL DEVIL HILLS	97	79	57	75	87	95	76	88	83	76	99	104	69	98	79	85	93	87	98	116
27949	KITTY HAWK	142	115	86	107	128	146	109	129	121	111	145	144	101	135	116	129	135	127	153	168
27950	KNOTTS ISLAND	84	80	66	77	79	82	76	80	75	78	94	93	73	90	75	74	90	80	78	93
27953	MANNS HARBOR	75	52	27	49	61	68	52	64	59	51	70	77	44	68	54	62	64	63	76	89
27954	MANTEO	93	80	60	76	85	92	75	85	80	76	97	99	71	96	77	82	92	83	92	108
27956	MAPLE	57	52	41	50	52	55	50	53	50	51	62	62	47	59	49	50	60	53	53	63
27957	MERRY HILL	84	62	37	55	70	79	59	72	68	59	81	85	52	78	62	73	74	71	87	100
27958	MOYOCK	90	87	73	84	88	92	81	86	82	82	101	101	79	100	81	82	97	85	87	104
27959	NAGS HEAD	111	87	60	79	98	111	82	99	93	82	111	116	74	109	88	100	103	98	117	136
27960	OCRACOKE	76	59	41	54	67	75	56	68	63	56	75	79	50	74	60	68	70	67	80	92
27962	PLYMOUTH	66	51	40	47	54	63	53	59	60	53	72	69	49	69	53	63	68	59	68	75
27964	POINT HARBOR	85	73	53	70	75	80	70	77	73	71	89	90	65	84	70	73	84	77	80	95
27965	POPLAR BRANCH	78	58	35	53	66	74	56	68	64	55	75	81	49	74	59	68	69	67	81	94
27966	POWELLS POINT	85	73	52	70	75	81	70	78	73	71	89	91	64	85	70	73	84	77	81	96
27970	ROPER	88	59	27	51	67	77	57	71	69	58	81	85	48	76	58	74	73	71	88	101
27973	SHAWBORO	74	70	62	69	72	78	69	72	71	69	87	83	68	87	69	71	83	71	74	83
27974	SHILOH	86	68	47	66	73	86	73	80	81	70	96	90	67	92	72	84	88	79	93	96
27976	SOUTH MILLS	85	76	58	72	80	86	70	78	74	70	90	92	69	92	72	76	86	75	84	100
27978	STUMPY POINT	75	52	27	49	61	68	52	64	59	51	70	77	44	68	53	62	64	63	76	89
27979	SUNBURY	83	60	32	53	66	74	58	69	67	59	79	82	51	75	58	70	73	69	82	95
27980	TYNER	84	56	25	48	63	73	54	68	65	55	77	81	46	72	55	70	70	67	83	96
27981	WANCHESE	82	75	58	72	75	79	71	76	72	73	89	88	67	84	70	71	86	76	76	91
27983	WINDSOR	73	52	33	45	56	66	53	62	63	54	74	72	47	69	53	67	68	62	75	82
27986	WINTON	65	43	20	37	49	56	42	52	50	42	59	62	35	56	42	54	54	52	64	74
28001	ALBEMARLE	76	65	54	63	68	77	66	71	71	65	86	82	64	86	66	73	82	70	78	86
28006	ALEXIS	86	78	60	74	80	86	73	80	76	74	93	94	70	92	74	76	89	78	83	99
28012	BELMONT	86	87	84	86	88	93	84	86	84	83	104	101	85	107	85	84	101	85	86	100
28016	BESSEMER CITY	79	66	48	62	69	76	64	71	69	65	83	82	60	81	64	70	79	70	77	88
28018	BOSTIC	76	54	29	48	60	68	52	63	60	52	71	75	45	69	53	64	66	62	75	87
28020	CASAR	83	62	37	56	69	77	59	71	68	60	81	84	54	79	61	72	75	69	83	97
28021	CHERRYVILLE	88	71	48	67	76	85	69	78	76	69	91	92	64	90	70	79	85	77	89	101
28023	CHINA GROVE	82	72	57	69	76	82	69	75	73	69	89	89	68	90	70	75	85	74	81	95
28025	CONCORD	87	87	85	86	87	92	85	87	85	85	105	102	85	105	85	84	102	87	85	100
28027	CONCORD	102	103	98	106	102	104	99	100	96	101	120	117	99	120	97	92	117	99	93	113
28031	CORNELIUS	175	200	237	207	194	200	191	186	179	193	227	218	200	230	191	173	226	185	167	204
28032	CRAMERTON	78	75	73	75	76	83	76	77	77	75	96	89	76	97	76	77	92	77	78	88
28033	CROUSE	81	74	57	70	75	80	70	75	71	71	88	88	66	85	70	71	84	74	77	92
28034	DALLAS	84	71	54	68	75	82	70	76	75	69	91	90	66	90	70	77	86	75	83	96
28036	DAVIDSON	154	176	186	178	174	179	161	161	153	162	192	188	170	197	164	150	190	157	152	183
28037	DENVER	107	114	107	112	113	116	105	108	102	106	127	127	106	129	106	100	124	106	104	125
28040	ELLENBORO	77	54	27	47	60	68	52	63	61	53	72	75	45	68	52	65	66	63	76	88
28043	FOREST CITY	75	57	38	52	61	70	57	65	65	57	77	77	52	75	57	68	72	65	76	85
28052	GASTONIA	63	56	55	54	58	65	59	61	63	58	77	70	58	77	59	65	74	61	66	72
28054	GASTONIA	77	76	83	77	76	82	79	78	79	78	99	91	79	98	78	78	96	79	77	88
28056	GASTONIA	105	107	99	105	108	112	100	104	99	100	123	122	100	125	101	98	119	102	102	123
28071	GOLD HILL	89	74	51	69	78	85	70	79	76	71	92	93	65	89	71	78	86	78	87	102
28073	GROVER	81	63	39	58	67	74	60	70	67	62	80	82	54	76	61	69	75	69	79	92
28075	HARRISBURG	118	136	135	140	131	127	123	122	113	126	143	143	127	146	121	106	142	118	105	134
28078	HUNTERSVILLE	131	138	137	144	133	134	132	131	125	135	158	153	133	156	128	118	154	130	116	145
28079	INDIAN TRAIL	104	118	116	122	113	110	107	106	99	111	125	125	110	126	105	93	124	104	91	117
28080	IRON STATION	84	76	58	72	78	83	71	77	74	72	90	91	68	89	72	74	86	76	81	96
28081	KANNAPOLIS	78	68	56	66	71	78	68	73	72	67	88	85	66	88	68	74	83	72	78	88
28083	KANNAPOLIS	69	63	55	61	65	73	64	67	67	62	82	76	63	83	64	69	78	66	72	78
28086	KINGS MOUNTAIN	85	70	51	65	74	82	67	76	73	68	89	89	63	87	68	76	84	75	84	98
28088	LANDIS	67	61	52	60	63	71	62	65	65	60	80	74	61	81	62	67	75	64	70	75
28090	LAWNDALE	78	59	35	53	64	71	56	66	64	58	76	78	50	72	57	66	71	66	76	89
28091	LILESVILLE	85	57	26	49	64	74	55	69	66	56	78	82	47	73	56	71	71	68	85	97
28092	LINCOLNTON	83	67	46	63	72	80	65	74	71	65	86	86	61	84	66	74	80	72	82	94
28097	LOCUST	89	79	60	75	84	90	73	81	78	73	95	97	72	97	76	80	90	79	88	105
28098	LOWELL	65	59	51	58	61	69	61	63	64	59	78	72	59	79	61	65	74	62	68	73
28103	MARSHVILLE	90	73	50	68	79	87	70	79	77	70	92	94	66	92	71	80	86	78	89	104
28104	MATTHEWS	131	153	157	157	148	147	139	137	128	141	162	160	146	166	138	122	161	133	120	151
28105	MATTHEWS	125	133	139	140	128	129	129	126	121	132	153	149	130	151	125	113	151	126	111	139
28107	MIDLAND	105	93	72	89	99	106	87	97	92	87	111	115	84	113	89	94	106	94	104	124
28110	MONROE	92	91	83	90	91	95	87	90	87	88	108	106	86	108	87	86	105	89	89	105
28112	MONROE	97	88	74	86	92	99	86	91	89	85	109	108	84	111	87	90	105	90	96	112
28114	MOORESBORO	88	64	35	57	71	80	61	73	71	62	84	88	54	81	62	75	77	72	88	102
28115	MOORESVILLE	86	80	68	79	82	88	78	82	80	78	99	96	76	98	78	81	94	81	85	98
28117	MOORESVILLE	140	167	171	171	161	158	150	148	137	152	174	173	158	180	150	131	173	143	129	163
28119	MORVEN	69	46	21	40	52	60	45	56	54	45	63	67	38	60	45	58	57	55	69	79
28120	MOUNT HOLLY	89	85	75	82	87	94	82	86	84	81	104	100	81	106	83	86	99	85	90	103
28124	MOUNT PLEASANT	102	91	69	86	96	103	84	93	89	84	108	111	82	110	86	91	103	91	100	120
28125	MOUNT ULLA	87	78	60	74	81	86	73	80	76	73	93	94	70	92	74	77	88	78	84	100
28127	NEW LONDON	108	88	61	82	95	105	83	96	92	83	110	113	78	110	86	96	103	94	109	126
28128	NORWOOD	79	66	51	64	71	78	66	73	71	65	86	85	62	84	66	73	80	72	81	91
28129	OAKBORO	88	77	59	74	82	88	73	80	77	72	94	95	71	95	74	79	89	78	87	102
28133	PEACHLAND	80	64	46	62	69	78	65	72	71	65	86	83	61	84	65	73	80	71	81	89
28134	PINEVILLE	90	88	94	95	84	86	91	88	87	93	110	105	90	106	86	81	108	90	77	97
28135	POLKTON	83	55	25	48	63	72	54	67	65	55	76	80	46	72	54	69	69	66	82	95
28137	RICHFIELD	79	68	53	66	71	78	67	73	71	67	86	84	64	85	67	72	81	72	78	89
	NORTH CAROLINA	90	81	73	80	83	90	81	85	84	82	103	100	79	101	81	84	99	85	88	102
	UNITED STATES	100	100	100	100	100	100	100	100	100	100	100	100	100	100	100	100	100	100	100	100

NORTH CAROLINA POPULATION CHANGE

A 28138-28385

#	POST OFFICE NAME	COUNTY FIPS CODE	POPULATION 2000	POPULATION 2004	POPULATION 2009	% Rate	State Centile	HOUSEHOLDS 2000	HOUSEHOLDS 2004	HOUSEHOLDS 2009	% Annual Rate 2000-2004	2004 Average HH Size	FAMILIES 2000	FAMILIES 2004	% Annual Rate 2000-2004
28138	ROCKWELL	159	9865	10496	11214	1.5	52	3711	3990	4295	1.7	2.60	2835	3007	1.4
28139	RUTHERFORDTON	161	17117	18198	19336	1.5	51	6566	7077	7625	1.8	2.48	4794	5105	1.5
28144	SALISBURY	159	26154	26052	26974	-0.1	8	10072	10092	10548	0.1	2.35	6307	6208	-0.4
28146	SALISBURY	159	25374	26909	28607	1.4	50	10035	10792	11583	1.7	2.46	7369	7783	1.3
28147	SALISBURY	159	21859	24220	26239	2.4	75	7958	8936	9782	2.8	2.57	5788	6412	2.4
28150	SHELBY	045	28391	28446	29338	0.1	12	11127	11295	11795	0.4	2.44	6472	6819	1.2
28152	SHELBY	045	23449	24714	26100	1.2	45	8881	9493	10160	1.6	2.49	6472	6819	1.2
28159	SPENCER	159	3185	3090	3171	-0.7	2	1244	1211	1251	-0.6	2.44	792	754	-1.2
28160	SPINDALE	161	3713	3637	3731	-0.5	3	1517	1506	1568	-0.2	2.27	981	954	-0.7
28163	STANFIELD	167	5418	5971	6459	2.3	73	2008	2240	2448	2.6	2.67	3484	3909	2.8
28164	STANLEY	071	12033	13442	14762	2.6	80	4521	5138	5726	3.1	2.61	1815	2067	3.1
28166	TROUTMAN	097	6169	7037	8100	3.2	86	2444	2827	3290	3.5	2.49	740	772	1.0
28167	UNION MILLS	161	2555	2658	2777	0.9	35	998	1056	1120	1.3	2.47	2731	3027	2.5
28168	VALE	109	9407	10436	11714	2.5	76	3577	4023	4564	2.8	2.59	5087	6772	7.0
28170	WADESBORO	007	8948	9175	9556	0.6	24	3470	3624	3841	1.0	2.45	2437	2508	0.7
28173	WAXHAW	179	17665	23592	31551	7.0	99	6038	8099	10886	7.2	2.91	1527	1835	4.4
28174	WINGATE	179	6279	7436	9286	4.1	93	2079	2543	3274	4.9	2.64	686	881	6.1
28202	CHARLOTTE	119	5027	6543	8223	6.4	99	2445	3229	4135	6.8	1.67	2095	2169	0.8
28203	CHARLOTTE	119	9928	10469	11735	1.3	46	4656	5043	5772	1.9	2.03	871	859	-0.3
28204	CHARLOTTE	119	5390	5514	6095	0.5	23	2538	2675	3044	1.2	1.84	10302	10527	0.5
28205	CHARLOTTE	119	45918	48074	53862	1.1	38	19104	20156	22830	1.3	2.34	2852	2817	-0.3
28206	CHARLOTTE	119	12508	12515	13761	0.0	11	4347	4418	4936	0.4	2.73	1982	1974	-0.1
28207	CHARLOTTE	119	7714	7805	8544	0.3	16	3542	3636	4053	0.6	2.01	8727	8819	0.3
28208	CHARLOTTE	119	35788	36550	40732	0.5	22	13030	13531	15306	0.9	2.66	4504	4654	0.8
28209	CHARLOTTE	119	19985	21121	23715	1.3	47	10203	10999	12545	1.8	1.91	10094	10812	1.6
28210	CHARLOTTE	119	41215	44987	51252	2.1	68	18657	20684	23887	2.5	2.16	7311	7628	1.0
28211	CHARLOTTE	119	27757	29026	32527	1.1	38	12010	12887	14728	1.7	2.21	8277	8813	1.5
28212	CHARLOTTE	119	35367	38408	43809	2.0	63	14878	16383	18930	2.3	2.33	5760	6838	4.1
28213	CHARLOTTE	119	24731	29700	35514	4.4	94	9160	11177	13554	4.8	2.64	5795	7020	4.6
28214	CHARLOTTE	119	20543	24753	29955	4.5	95	7829	9623	11820	5.0	2.57	10654	11838	2.5
28215	CHARLOTTE	119	41367	46011	53117	2.5	78	14956	16853	19703	2.9	2.71	7791	8948	3.3
28216	CHARLOTTE	119	29769	33859	39614	3.1	85	10989	12811	15315	3.7	2.50	4729	5311	2.8
28217	CHARLOTTE	119	19527	22162	26011	3.0	84	7080	8150	9687	3.4	2.72	9221	10449	3.0
28226	CHARLOTTE	119	33287	37602	43810	2.9	83	13636	15759	18678	3.5	2.37	11080	12381	2.7
28227	CHARLOTTE	119	40579	45303	52208	2.6	79	15516	17663	20673	3.1	2.56	4072	4793	3.9
28262	CHARLOTTE	119	22639	26090	30289	3.4	88	7497	9038	10888	4.5	2.51	10832	13667	5.6
28269	CHARLOTTE	119	42416	53440	65300	5.6	98	16138	20642	25557	6.0	2.57	7657	8810	3.4
28270	CHARLOTTE	119	26938	30759	35828	3.2	86	10158	11821	13978	3.6	2.60	4764	5696	4.3
28273	CHARLOTTE	119	18388	21987	26208	4.3	94	7039	8604	10430	4.8	2.54	8	8	0.0
28274	CHARLOTTE	119	401	404	434	0.2	13	14	14	16	0.0	2.57	9891	12864	6.4
28277	CHARLOTTE	119	35344	45854	57211	6.3	99	13327	17579	22223	6.7	2.60	1980	2511	5.8
28278	CHARLOTTE	119	6572	8329	10254	5.7	98	2615	3351	4171	6.0	2.49	4145	4000	-0.8
28301	FAYETTEVILLE	051	18164	17630	17817	-0.7	2	6809	6723	6939	-0.3	2.25	8608	8414	-0.5
28303	FAYETTEVILLE	051	31549	30703	31194	-0.6	2	12746	12681	13129	-0.1	2.42	10036	10075	0.1
28304	FAYETTEVILLE	051	36622	36564	37629	0.0	10	13772	14012	14673	0.4	2.59	1701	1666	-0.5
28305	FAYETTEVILLE	051	6524	6479	6622	-0.2	7	3137	3176	3301	0.3	2.03	8466	9322	2.3
28306	FAYETTEVILLE	051	30599	33505	35941	2.2	70	11412	12662	13786	2.5	2.63	3135	3058	-0.6
28307	FORT BRAGG	051	13263	13009	13092	-0.5	4	3229	3156	3236	-0.5	2.27	488	483	-0.2
28308	POPE A F B	051	2583	2536	2559	-0.4	4	501	497	512	-0.2	3.50	1167	1137	-0.6
28310	FORT BRAGG	093	16209	15894	15992	-0.5	4	1194	1165	1195	-0.6	2.56	8935	9266	0.9
28311	FAYETTEVILLE	051	33076	34096	35231	0.7	27	12489	13158	13861	1.2	2.53	4713	4779	0.3
28312	FAYETTEVILLE	051	16713	16881	17353	0.2	15	6409	6574	6868	0.6	2.53	12726	13914	2.1
28314	FAYETTEVILLE	051	47916	52276	55953	2.1	68	17250	19125	20793	2.5	2.73	2523	2712	1.7
28315	ABERDEEN	125	8788	9452	10340	1.7	58	3600	3937	4372	2.1	2.29	1254	1280	0.5
28318	AUTRYVILLE	163	4306	4385	4551	0.4	19	1686	1743	1831	0.8	2.52	2484	2640	1.4
28320	BLADENBORO	017	8494	8961	9472	1.3	46	3593	3877	4187	1.8	2.29	625	677	1.9
28323	BUNNLEVEL	085	2266	2457	2760	1.9	63	836	917	1039	2.2	2.68	2606	3030	3.6
28326	CAMERON	085	9509	11137	12880	3.8	91	3439	4047	4703	3.9	2.74	4076	4318	1.4
28327	CARTHAGE	125	13980	14929	16146	1.6	54	5455	5867	6400	1.7	2.49	6737	7077	1.2
28328	CLINTON	163	25634	27023	28738	1.3	45	9535	10168	10930	1.5	2.54	3117	3213	0.7
28333	DUDLEY	191	11766	12188	12604	0.8	32	4189	4377	4576	1.0	2.78	6292	6865	2.1
28334	DUNN	163	22998	25170	28063	2.2	70	9016	9987	11253	2.4	2.48	2922	3002	0.6
28337	ELIZABETHTOWN	017	11153	11446	11869	0.6	25	4334	4525	4784	1.0	2.42	1160	1169	0.2
28338	ELLERBE	153	4109	4152	4230	0.3	15	1650	1688	1740	0.5	2.45	2086	2173	1.0
28339	ERWIN	085	7606	7983	8846	1.1	40	3009	3186	3558	1.4	2.65	3090	3135	0.3
28340	FAIRMONT	155	11603	11702	12149	0.2	14	4253	4376	4621	0.7	2.65	1103	1276	3.5
28341	FAISON	163	4201	4877	5482	3.6	90	1539	1809	2055	3.9	2.67	450	457	0.4
28343	GIBSON	165	1711	1727	1743	0.2	15	621	640	659	0.7	2.69	928	1050	3.3
28344	GODWIN	163	3687	4153	4520	2.8	82	1209	1387	1532	3.3	2.92	3456	3555	0.7
28345	HAMLET	153	12616	13014	13513	0.7	28	4927	5154	5422	1.1	2.49	352	409	3.6
28347	HOFFMAN	153	2369	2698	2923	3.1	86	468	551	611	3.9	3.80	6850	7497	2.2
28348	HOPE MILLS	051	25308	27658	29434	2.1	69	9022	10022	10840	2.5	2.74	870	912	1.1
28349	KENANSVILLE	061	3641	3793	4063	1.0	35	1220	1295	1411	1.4	2.68	1503	1482	-0.3
28351	LAUREL HILL	165	5511	5410	5418	-0.4	4	2077	2082	2126	0.1	2.60	6791	6931	0.5
28352	LAURINBURG	165	25348	25766	26295	0.4	18	9452	9766	10138	0.8	2.54	960	990	0.7
28356	LINDEN	051	3314	3392	3479	0.6	24	1244	1299	1357	1.0	2.61	758	804	1.4
28357	LUMBER BRIDGE	155	2915	3099	3335	1.5	51	991	1066	1160	1.7	2.90	9539	9852	0.8
28358	LUMBERTON	155	36660	37861	39919	0.8	29	13612	14259	15266	1.1	2.54	3385	3522	0.9
28360	LUMBERTON	155	13101	13546	14182	0.8	30	4475	4714	5016	1.2	2.81	172	213	5.2
28363	MARSTON	153	540	650	723	4.5	95	223	281	321	5.6	2.01	3464	3672	1.4
28364	MAXTON	155	13109	13739	14491	1.1	40	4525	4849	5205	1.6	2.82	4011	4144	0.8
28365	MOUNT OLIVE	061	15273	15853	16633	0.9	33	5758	6037	6396	1.1	2.55	1213	1294	1.5
28366	NEWTON GROVE	163	4601	4935	5347	1.7	57	1699	1839	2010	1.9	2.65	614	634	0.8
28369	ORRUM	155	2160	2217	2321	0.6	25	842	867	923	1.1	2.55	1150	1302	3.0
28371	PARKTON	155	4250	4839	5305	3.1	86	1456	1670	1851	3.3	2.87	2894	3054	1.3
28372	PEMBROKE	155	11589	12098	12741	1.0	37	3905	4174	4488	1.6	2.69	523	553	1.3
28373	PINEBLUFF	125	1867	1990	2151	1.5	52	723	777	847	1.7	2.55	3718	4302	3.5
28374	PINEHURST	125	10859	12565	14176	3.5	89	5016	5887	6725	3.8	2.07	6607	7642	3.5
28376	RAEFORD	093	25623	29508	34273	3.4	88	8616	10069	11857	3.7	2.86	2979	3115	1.1
28377	RED SPRINGS	093	11820	12389	13288	1.1	40	3946	4181	4535	1.4	2.93	7295	7428	0.4
28379	ROCKINGHAM	153	26421	26795	27552	0.3	17	10412	10742	11218	0.7	2.42	1857	1921	0.8
28382	ROSEBORO	163	6455	6673	7030	0.8	29	2497	2617	2786	1.1	2.55	2171	2231	0.6
28383	ROWLAND	155	8129	8280	8618	0.4	19	2901	3021	3203	1.0	2.73	2777	3047	2.2
28384	SAINT PAULS	155	10661	11778	12874	2.4	74	3759	4180	4617	2.5	2.79	789	807	0.5
28385	SALEMBURG	163	2868	2942	3067	0.6	25	1078	1117	1175	0.8	2.62			
	NORTH CAROLINA					1.9					2.2	2.46			1.8
	UNITED STATES					1.2					1.3	2.58			1.1

#	POST OFFICE NAME	RACE (%) White 2000	White 2004	Black 2000	Black 2004	Asian/Pacific 2000	Asian/Pacific 2004	% Hispanic Origin 2000	% Hispanic Origin 2004	2004 AGE DISTRIBUTION (%) 0-4	5-9	10-14	15-19	20-24	25-44	45-64	65-84	85+	18+	MEDIAN AGE 2004	% 2004 Males	% 2004 Females
28138	ROCKWELL	96.5	96.0	1.4	1.6	0.4	0.5	1.3	1.8	6.6	6.9	7.5	6.6	5.7	30.3	24.9	10.3	1.2	74.8	37.1	49.9	50.1
28139	RUTHERFORDTON	89.4	88.8	8.9	9.2	0.3	0.4	1.4	1.8	6.0	6.4	7.0	6.0	5.7	27.1	26.2	13.6	2.1	76.9	39.6	48.8	51.2
28144	SALISBURY	53.8	52.8	41.6	42.0	1.3	1.6	3.8	4.5	6.5	6.3	6.5	7.1	8.6	24.9	22.9	14.5	2.8	77.3	37.5	48.1	51.9
28146	SALISBURY	89.9	88.6	7.3	7.9	0.7	0.8	2.8	3.9	6.6	6.7	6.7	6.1	5.7	28.6	25.6	12.2	1.9	76.3	38.6	49.3	50.7
28147	SALISBURY	79.8	78.1	14.2	14.8	1.2	1.4	5.7	7.1	6.7	6.6	6.7	6.3	6.9	31.3	24.5	9.6	1.4	76.2	36.1	51.6	48.4
28150	SHELBY	66.8	66.3	31.5	31.7	0.4	0.5	1.4	1.7	6.1	6.4	7.2	6.4	5.6	26.2	25.6	13.9	2.5	76.4	39.6	47.6	52.5
28152	SHELBY	77.7	76.5	19.8	20.7	0.6	0.7	1.6	2.0	6.6	6.6	7.0	7.8	7.4	28.1	24.2	11.0	1.3	76.0	35.7	48.5	51.5
28159	SPENCER	71.0	68.6	23.0	24.3	0.5	0.7	6.4	7.8	6.4	6.2	6.3	6.6	6.3	27.7	23.1	14.1	3.2	77.0	38.5	49.0	51.0
28160	SPINDALE	72.2	70.6	25.9	27.1	0.5	0.6	1.0	1.4	5.6	5.6	6.0	6.2	5.8	28.4	24.7	15.3	2.5	79.2	40.1	49.7	50.3
28163	STANFIELD	97.1	96.5	0.6	0.7	0.3	0.4	6.1	7.6	6.8	7.0	7.8	6.5	5.5	31.1	25.0	9.4	0.9	74.3	36.7	51.1	48.9
28164	STANLEY	91.0	90.8	7.4	7.3	0.4	0.4	0.9	1.2	6.8	7.0	7.3	6.2	5.5	30.4	26.0	9.9	1.0	75.2	37.2	49.7	50.3
28166	TROUTMAN	86.3	85.4	12.3	12.9	0.3	0.4	0.7	1.0	6.1	6.6	7.1	5.8	5.3	30.0	26.5	11.4	1.2	76.7	38.7	49.4	50.6
28167	UNION MILLS	91.0	90.0	7.6	8.4	0.2	0.2	1.2	1.5	5.8	6.2	7.2	6.2	5.7	27.0	27.9	12.4	1.5	76.8	40.0	50.0	50.0
28168	VALE	94.0	93.4	3.5	3.6	0.7	0.9	2.1	2.6	6.3	6.5	7.3	6.1	6.0	30.4	26.7	9.7	1.0	76.2	37.6	50.7	49.3
28170	WADESBORO	47.3	46.7	51.1	51.5	0.5	0.6	0.8	0.9	6.4	6.5	7.1	6.0	6.4	24.7	25.1	15.0	2.8	76.4	39.7	45.5	54.6
28173	WAXHAW	90.2	88.9	7.7	8.5	0.6	0.7	1.6	2.4	8.3	8.8	8.8	6.8	4.6	29.5	25.2	7.5	0.7	69.7	36.6	49.4	50.6
28174	WINGATE	68.5	65.5	27.4	29.4	0.3	0.3	5.6	7.7	7.4	7.4	6.6	9.6	12.1	29.0	20.2	6.9	0.8	75.3	29.4	50.2	49.8
28202	CHARLOTTE	41.3	34.0	55.2	62.4	1.2	1.2	1.6	1.7	4.6	5.3	4.3	4.5	9.3	42.1	20.5	8.2	1.2	83.6	33.9	56.5	43.5
28203	CHARLOTTE	55.1	54.3	42.6	43.0	0.8	0.9	1.5	1.9	6.1	5.8	5.8	5.9	6.6	36.7	22.7	8.9	1.5	78.6	35.3	47.7	52.4
28204	CHARLOTTE	59.2	56.9	37.6	39.5	1.0	1.1	1.5	2.0	5.8	4.6	4.6	6.5	8.9	40.6	19.7	7.3	2.1	82.2	33.4	47.8	52.2
28205	CHARLOTTE	46.6	43.7	39.5	39.9	3.9	4.3	12.6	15.8	7.0	6.4	6.6	6.4	8.6	35.9	19.1	8.4	1.7	76.3	32.9	50.1	49.9
28206	CHARLOTTE	11.9	12.3	78.7	76.9	1.7	1.8	12.3	14.8	8.4	8.3	9.0	8.1	8.5	30.8	19.5	6.7	0.9	69.6	30.2	49.1	50.9
28207	CHARLOTTE	95.9	95.2	2.9	3.4	0.5	0.7	0.8	1.1	6.2	6.9	5.8	6.2	5.6	26.5	26.2	14.0	2.6	78.0	40.6	46.1	53.9
28208	CHARLOTTE	21.0	19.6	71.6	71.8	2.5	2.8	5.6	7.1	7.7	8.0	8.9	8.0	7.6	30.2	21.1	7.8	0.9	70.6	31.8	48.1	51.9
28209	CHARLOTTE	81.3	78.5	9.3	10.0	2.6	3.0	9.5	12.2	5.3	4.7	4.6	4.2	6.3	39.2	22.1	11.4	2.3	83.0	37.0	48.1	51.9
28210	CHARLOTTE	79.2	76.8	10.9	11.3	4.0	4.6	8.5	11.0	5.8	5.5	5.8	5.8	7.2	34.0	23.4	10.8	1.7	79.3	36.4	48.9	51.1
28211	CHARLOTTE	82.7	81.1	12.7	13.3	2.3	2.8	3.1	4.0	6.1	6.2	6.2	5.3	5.0	30.2	25.3	13.5	2.3	77.9	39.3	47.7	52.3
28212	CHARLOTTE	48.8	46.2	39.0	39.9	4.3	4.7	12.5	15.1	7.5	6.5	6.5	6.6	10.4	37.7	17.6	6.3	1.0	75.8	30.8	48.8	51.3
28213	CHARLOTTE	36.0	35.1	47.0	45.4	3.9	4.7	15.1	17.4	7.4	6.7	6.8	7.0	12.0	35.9	18.8	5.0	0.4	75.4	29.7	52.4	47.6
28214	CHARLOTTE	71.3	69.3	21.7	22.9	4.2	4.5	2.7	3.6	7.0	7.1	7.1	6.2	5.3	30.9	25.1	10.5	0.8	74.9	37.3	49.1	50.9
28215	CHARLOTTE	44.5	42.9	44.8	44.8	3.3	3.6	9.2	11.0	7.9	7.7	7.7	6.8	7.3	34.5	20.9	6.6	0.7	72.5	32.9	49.3	50.7
28216	CHARLOTTE	36.6	38.8	59.3	56.3	1.5	1.9	3.3	3.9	7.0	7.0	7.1	7.5	7.2	30.0	22.4	10.5	1.2	75.1	35.4	47.7	52.3
28217	CHARLOTTE	29.9	28.5	56.6	56.2	2.9	3.2	17.9	20.6	7.4	6.8	7.5	7.1	8.9	34.4	20.6	6.8	0.4	74.1	31.6	50.2	49.8
28226	CHARLOTTE	89.0	87.0	5.3	5.9	3.5	4.3	2.8	4.0	6.0	6.5	7.1	6.0	5.2	29.0	28.4	10.1	1.7	76.4	39.2	48.1	51.9
28227	CHARLOTTE	73.9	71.2	19.8	21.4	2.3	2.6	5.3	6.9	7.0	7.1	7.3	6.5	6.0	32.7	25.0	7.8	0.7	74.6	35.7	48.6	51.4
28262	CHARLOTTE	60.7	57.6	27.8	29.1	6.0	7.1	5.9	7.2	6.3	5.2	4.9	13.2	21.1	33.2	13.0	2.8	0.5	81.0	24.9	51.1	48.9
28269	CHARLOTTE	63.7	61.5	28.4	29.1	4.7	5.6	3.5	4.5	9.1	8.3	7.2	5.7	6.5	39.4	19.1	4.3	0.5	71.9	32.2	49.3	50.7
28270	CHARLOTTE	89.8	88.1	5.3	5.9	2.9	3.6	2.6	3.6	7.4	7.8	8.1	6.8	6.0	28.6	27.9	6.9	0.5	72.5	36.7	48.5	51.5
28273	CHARLOTTE	61.5	58.1	28.6	30.2	5.7	6.6	5.5	7.1	8.4	7.8	7.1	5.9	6.4	40.1	20.3	3.7	0.5	73.1	32.8	48.6	51.4
28274	CHARLOTTE	94.8	93.8	3.0	3.5	1.0	1.2	1.3	1.7	5.5	6.2	4.5	13.4	13.4	22.8	21.3	11.9	1.2	80.7	33.1	43.1	56.9
28277	CHARLOTTE	89.7	87.8	4.3	4.8	4.2	5.1	2.8	3.9	7.8	8.2	7.9	6.4	4.8	33.8	25.8	5.0	0.4	72.0	35.8	49.3	50.7
28278	CHARLOTTE	86.5	83.9	9.1	10.4	2.1	2.9	2.1	2.9	7.1	7.1	5.9	4.8	4.0	33.8	28.3	8.6	0.6	77.0	38.7	51.2	48.8
28301	FAYETTEVILLE	17.5	17.3	79.0	78.8	0.7	0.8	1.9	2.2	7.0	6.1	6.5	9.8	9.2	22.8	20.9	15.2	2.6	76.7	35.8	45.3	54.7
28303	FAYETTEVILLE	51.8	50.2	36.9	36.8	3.8	4.4	7.1	8.5	7.7	7.0	6.9	6.6	8.0	31.1	22.3	9.7	0.7	74.5	32.8	48.7	51.3
28304	FAYETTEVILLE	58.8	57.3	31.0	31.0	2.4	2.8	7.0	8.5	7.9	7.4	7.6	7.4	7.5	31.8	21.1	8.5	0.7	72.6	32.7	47.8	52.2
28305	FAYETTEVILLE	70.9	69.6	24.6	25.3	0.8	1.0	2.8	3.5	5.2	5.3	5.7	5.7	6.0	26.4	26.4	16.6	2.8	80.4	42.2	46.4	53.6
28306	FAYETTEVILLE	65.7	64.6	25.3	25.4	1.4	1.6	4.5	5.6	8.1	7.9	8.2	7.1	6.2	31.8	22.6	7.7	0.6	71.2	33.8	48.7	51.3
28307	FORT BRAGG	57.5	55.5	25.8	25.2	2.8	3.2	15.6	18.8	11.4	8.2	5.0	9.9	31.8	32.2	1.5	0.2	0.0	74.0	22.5	67.9	32.1
28308	POPE A F B	77.0	75.3	14.1	14.2	2.9	3.4	6.2	7.7	11.8	9.8	7.0	7.2	16.9	45.5	1.7	0.1	0.0	69.0	24.2	62.0	38.0
28310	FORT BRAGG	58.1	56.1	25.3	24.6	2.7	3.1	15.8	19.0	11.4	8.1	4.9	9.9	32.3	32.2	1.2	0.1	0.0	74.2	22.4	68.3	31.7
28311	FAYETTEVILLE	53.3	52.1	38.8	38.8	1.9	2.3	5.9	7.1	8.1	7.6	7.3	7.8	9.1	32.8	20.5	6.5	0.4	72.9	30.5	49.2	50.8
28312	FAYETTEVILLE	64.6	63.5	28.7	29.1	0.6	0.7	2.6	3.2	6.4	6.5	7.1	6.3	5.8	28.0	27.2	11.4	1.3	76.1	38.7	48.6	51.4
28314	FAYETTEVILLE	44.8	43.1	43.2	43.1	3.4	3.9	8.9	10.8	8.8	7.8	8.0	7.8	9.3	35.5	17.7	4.9	0.2	70.8	29.3	49.3	50.7
28315	ABERDEEN	70.1	69.5	24.1	23.9	0.7	0.8	3.6	4.6	5.8	5.9	6.3	6.2	6.5	27.4	25.3	15.0	1.6	78.4	39.8	50.7	49.3
28318	AUTRYVILLE	85.6	84.3	8.7	9.0	0.3	0.3	6.2	8.0	7.1	7.1	7.1	5.6	5.9	31.1	25.0	10.2	0.8	75.3	36.0	50.2	49.9
28320	BLADENBORO	76.6	75.4	21.3	22.2	0.1	0.2	1.4	1.7	6.4	6.5	6.1	5.3	5.6	27.2	28.1	13.3	1.5	77.9	40.0	49.1	51.0
28323	BUNNLEVEL	50.8	49.2	43.3	44.2	0.6	0.7	3.4	4.1	8.1	7.7	8.5	6.8	7.6	32.5	20.9	7.2	0.7	71.6	31.9	50.1	49.9
28326	CAMERON	72.9	71.1	20.9	21.5	0.6	0.7	4.9	6.2	8.9	8.3	8.5	7.4	7.3	33.3	19.2	6.7	0.5	69.8	31.1	50.1	49.9
28327	CARTHAGE	85.7	84.6	11.5	12.0	0.3	0.4	2.3	3.0	6.0	6.2	7.0	6.0	5.3	26.3	24.9	16.1	2.2	77.0	40.7	48.6	51.4
28328	CLINTON	54.4	53.1	34.4	33.8	0.5	0.6	10.5	12.9	7.3	7.0	6.7	6.3	6.2	28.7	23.6	12.2	2.0	75.3	36.6	49.3	50.7
28333	DUDLEY	46.8	43.9	43.1	44.3	0.6	0.7	10.6	12.6	7.7	7.3	8.0	8.0	8.4	29.5	23.1	7.6	0.5	72.1	32.1	49.3	50.7
28334	DUNN	70.1	69.3	24.2	24.1	0.4	0.5	4.9	6.0	7.0	7.0	7.3	6.2	5.9	28.1	24.7	12.2	1.7	74.9	37.0	48.1	51.9
28337	ELIZABETHTOWN	54.6	53.5	41.1	41.3	0.2	0.2	4.7	5.8	6.5	6.7	7.1	6.4	6.5	25.6	25.7	13.5	2.1	75.8	38.5	48.5	51.5
28338	ELLERBE	64.9	63.9	30.5	30.7	0.6	0.6	7.7	9.7	6.3	6.7	7.5	6.7	5.6	28.2	24.6	12.8	1.6	75.5	37.7	49.4	50.6
28339	ERWIN	71.6	70.5	24.6	25.1	0.2	0.2	3.4	4.3	6.3	6.7	6.9	6.7	5.8	27.9	24.6	13.5	1.7	76.1	38.1	48.6	51.4
28340	FAIRMONT	31.0	29.9	37.8	37.7	0.2	0.2	1.9	2.2	7.2	7.6	8.1	7.1	6.5	26.2	24.6	11.6	1.1	72.7	35.6	47.6	52.4
28341	FAISON	47.5	45.7	32.9	31.8	0.2	0.2	23.7	27.7	7.1	7.5	7.3	6.9	7.1	30.5	21.8	10.6	1.3	73.7	34.1	51.0	49.0
28343	GIBSON	49.1	48.0	40.0	40.8	0.1	0.2	1.1	1.2	7.5	7.5	8.9	7.6	6.8	27.7	23.8	9.3	0.9	71.3	33.8	48.5	51.5
28344	GODWIN	72.3	70.9	18.3	18.4	0.5	0.6	10.2	12.1	6.7	6.9	7.4	6.6	6.1	30.8	23.7	10.2	1.5	74.7	35.5	50.7	49.3
28345	HAMLET	60.3	60.3	34.9	34.3	0.4	0.5	1.2	1.5	7.0	7.1	7.7	6.6	5.7	26.4	25.1	12.6	1.7	74.1	37.5	48.5	51.5
28347	HOFFMAN	53.4	52.5	41.9	42.2	0.8	0.9	3.9	4.7	5.9	6.0	6.2	10.9	15.1	30.1	17.7	7.3	0.9	78.3	27.7	59.0	41.0
28348	HOPE MILLS	69.9	68.3	21.1	21.6	1.0	1.2	5.2	6.5	8.3	8.1	8.6	7.3	6.4	33.4	20.6	6.7	0.6	70.5	32.6	48.4	51.6
28349	KENANSVILLE	53.5	52.1	41.5	41.9	0.2	0.2	5.5	6.9	5.9	6.3	6.7	6.5	5.8	28.7	25.6	12.4	2.2	77.3	38.7	50.2	49.8
28351	LAUREL HILL	63.1	61.5	25.4	26.5	0.2	0.2	1.1	1.3	7.3	7.3	8.1	7.6	7.0	28.7	24.9	8.5	0.7	72.8	34.5	48.4	51.6
28352	LAURINBURG	50.7	50.0	38.8	38.8	0.7	0.8	1.2	1.4	7.2	7.1	7.6	7.6	7.5	25.9	24.9	10.8	1.6	73.7	35.4	46.7	53.3
28356	LINDEN	74.9	73.9	21.1	21.6	0.6	0.7	2.5	3.2	6.9	7.3	7.5	6.9	5.3	29.3	27.5	8.8	0.4	73.7	37.4	50.1	49.9
28357	LUMBER BRIDGE	43.7	42.4	36.3	36.3	0.3	0.3	4.0	4.7	7.9	7.8	8.6	7.8	7.3	29.2	23.2	7.7	0.5	70.8	32.6	50.4	49.6
28358	LUMBERTON	49.9	48.8	29.4	29.2	0.7	0.8	3.9	4.8	7.7	7.3	7.3	7.0	7.2	28.9	22.7	10.5	1.5	73.4	34.5	48.2	51.8
28360	LUMBERTON	25.5	25.1	11.1	10.8	0.2	0.2	7.7	9.0	8.1	7.8	8.2	7.1	8.1	31.5	21.8	6.8	0.6	71.6	31.5	51.7	48.3
28363	MARSTON	62.6	62.0	31.5	31.4	1.1	1.4	3.0	3.5	6.8	6.8	6.6	8.8	11.5	29.7	21.4	7.7	0.8	76.3	30.6	56.0	44.0
28364	MAXTON	11.0	10.5	25.2	24.6	0.3	0.4	1.2	1.4	8.6	8.6	8.8	7.9	7.2	29.1	22.1	7.1	0.6	69.0	30.9	48.0	52.0
28365	MOUNT OLIVE	64.2	62.7	25.7	25.1	0.2	0.3	13.0	15.8	6.6	6.3	6.8	7.5	7.9	27.9	23.3	12.0	1.7	76.2	35.9	49.4	50.6
28366	NEWTON GROVE	71.7	69.7	17.9	18.0	0.1	0.1	15.2	18.2	6.7	6.8	6.9	6.6	6.4	30.1	24.0	11.1	1.4	75.7	35.8	50.6	49.4
28369	ORRUM	59.9	58.2	23.4	24.0	0.2	0.2	2.6	2.9	6.2	6.5	7.0	6.0	6.5	28.2	27.0	11.9	0.8	76.4	38.0	49.8	50.2
28371	PARKTON	61.5	60.0	27.5	27.7	0.8	0.9	6.1	7.4	9.3	8.4	8.5	8.4	7.8	32.6	18.9	5.4	0.5	68.5	30.1	49.9	50.1
28372	PEMBROKE	9.9	9.2	4.9	4.8	0.4	0.4	1.6	1.9	8.3	7.8	7.4	9.4	10.0	27.1	20.7	8.3	0.9	72.3	29.8	48.9	51.1
28373	PINEBLUFF	69.6	68.1	25.6	26.3	0.6	0.7	3.1	3.9	7.7	7.6	8.2	7.2	6.4	30.5	23.3	8.1	0.9	72.0	34.4	48.7	51.3
28374	PINEHURST	90.4	89.6	7.8	8.3	0.7	0.9	1.1	1.5	3.5	3.6	3.5	3.1	2.4	15.6	28.7	35.5	4.2	87.4	59.5	46.9	53.1
28376	RAEFORD	47.2	46.2	39.9	39.6	1.1	1.2	7.9	9.5	9.6	8.6	7.7	6.8	7.5	34.0	18.3	6.9	0.7	70.0	30.6	50.2	49.8
28377	RED SPRINGS	23.1	22.2	33.6	32.2	0.4	0.5	8.1	9.6	9.2	8.4	8.4	7.5	8.1	27.6	20.8	9.0	1.0	69.5	30.6	48.8	51.2
28379	ROCKINGHAM	68.3	67.1	27.2	27.8	0.9	1.1	2.8	3.4	6.9	6.7	7.1	6.8	6.8	27.8	24.1	12.3	1.5	75.3	36.5	48.7	51.3
28382	ROSEBORO	64.5	63.5	29.9	30.0	0.4	0.4	5.2	6.4	7.0	6.9	6.8	6.1	6.1	28.5	25.9	11.4	1.2	75.5	37.2	49.7	50.3
28383	ROWLAND	12.5	11.7	27.1	26.8	0.1	0.1	1.1	1.2	7.6	7.4	8.1	7.7	7.3	27.8	24.1	8.9	1.0	72.0	33.5	47.8	52.2
28384	SAINT PAULS	51.1	49.0	28.4	28.5	0.4	0.4	10.5	12.3	8.0	7.6	7.5	6.9	7.4	30.1	23.1	8.5	0.9	72.8	33.2	50.6	49.4
28385	SALEMBURG	67.0	65.6	27.0	27.3	0.3	0.4	6.9	8.6	7.2	7.2	6.7	5.6	5.9	28.3	25.1	12.4	1.6	75.4	37.5	49.3	50.7
	NORTH CAROLINA	72.1	71.2	21.6	21.6	1.5	1.8	4.7	5.9	6.7	6.6	6.8	6.7	7.1	29.8	24.2	10.8	1.4	76.2	36.2	49.2	50.8
	UNITED STATES	75.1	73.6	12.3	12.5	3.8	4.2	12.5	14.1	6.9	6.7	7.2	7.0	7.3	28.6	23.8	10.8	1.7	75.1	36.0	49.1	50.9

ZIP CODE #	POST OFFICE NAME	2004 Per Capita Income	2004 HH Income Base	2004 HOUSEHOLD INCOME DISTRIBUTION (%) Less than $25,000	$25,000 to $49,999	$50,000 to $99,999	$100,000 to $149,999	$150,000 or More	MEDIAN HOUSEHOLD INCOME 2004	2009	2004 National Centile	2004 State Centile	2004 Home Value Base	2004 HOME VALUE DISTRIBUTION (%) Less than $50,000	$50,000 to $89,999	$90,000 to $174,999	$175,000 to $399,999	$400,000 or More	2004 Median Home Value
28138	ROCKWELL	20505	3990	21.3	34.8	35.5	6.2	2.2	44732	50351	60	74	3271	13.4	23.3	44.7	17.1	1.6	106280
28139	RUTHERFORDTON	19893	7077	31.7	31.2	28.1	6.1	2.9	39072	44450	43	48	5482	22.8	23.6	36.2	15.6	1.8	95751
28144	SALISBURY	21109	10092	36.4	30.7	23.2	5.9	3.8	35500	40368	29	32	5673	10.2	28.9	40.5	16.1	4.3	104162
28146	SALISBURY	21624	10792	24.7	31.8	33.8	7.6	2.1	44655	50217	60	73	8398	14.2	19.9	46.9	17.0	2.0	110712
28147	SALISBURY	21793	8936	22.7	32.7	33.5	8.2	2.9	45459	51017	62	76	6643	17.5	17.7	48.0	15.2	1.6	110993
28150	SHELBY	21231	11295	34.5	29.9	25.6	5.3	4.7	36592	41497	34	38	7827	15.4	29.0	36.8	15.6	3.2	97082
28152	SHELBY	19575	9493	28.8	32.2	31.3	5.6	2.1	40946	46534	49	57	7039	15.0	30.5	42.0	12.0	0.5	94831
28159	SPENCER	20339	1211	29.2	32.3	31.5	4.0	3.0	41373	47942	51	60	838	10.0	39.0	40.3	9.4	1.2	90684
28160	SPINDALE	15571	1506	48.2	30.9	16.5	3.3	1.1	26008	29252	6	3	1026	25.1	40.4	31.8	2.8	0.0	71354
28163	STANFIELD	21465	2240	26.3	29.3	34.5	6.3	3.5	44103	50000	59	71	1857	16.5	15.0	43.7	22.8	2.1	117082
28164	STANLEY	22496	5138	18.6	34.6	36.0	8.6	2.2	47271	54171	67	82	4104	13.8	22.4	44.8	18.2	0.9	107618
28166	TROUTMAN	25106	2827	20.8	31.5	35.1	8.7	3.9	48321	54939	69	83	2363	7.7	20.7	41.8	25.8	4.0	122424
28167	UNION MILLS	15997	1056	35.5	35.3	24.9	4.1	0.2	33162	37153	21	21	879	24.6	30.3	29.4	14.7	1.1	84014
28168	VALE	19271	4023	24.1	35.1	33.9	4.9	2.0	43546	48621	57	69	3309	20.3	23.5	40.4	14.1	1.7	99049
28170	WADESBORO	17452	3624	40.6	33.0	20.5	3.4	2.6	30516	34425	14	14	2506	24.3	36.8	29.5	8.8	0.6	78327
28173	WAXHAW	30543	8099	11.8	22.1	38.2	17.7	10.3	66749	76436	90	96	7218	4.6	7.8	31.0	42.4	14.2	195067
28174	WINGATE	19701	2543	27.3	28.2	35.9	6.0	2.6	44219	50241	59	72	1866	12.0	19.6	52.7	15.2	0.5	113326
28202	CHARLOTTE	32705	3229	39.8	20.6	22.9	9.3	7.4	36186	45212	32	35	920	1.5	7.2	35.7	39.2	16.4	198214
28203	CHARLOTTE	38408	5043	33.3	20.8	23.5	9.6	12.9	43293	51462	57	68	2119	2.4	11.3	18.6	45.6	22.2	237009
28204	CHARLOTTE	29336	2675	33.6	25.0	25.6	9.6	6.1	38041	46935	39	45	682	1.8	4.1	33.4	49.9	10.9	196471
28205	CHARLOTTE	20537	20156	29.0	36.0	27.4	5.1	2.4	37806	44200	39	43	8081	4.0	25.0	55.1	14.4	1.5	111704
28206	CHARLOTTE	13622	4418	41.8	38.4	16.7	1.9	1.2	28529	33073	10	8	1381	18.5	56.3	23.5	1.5	0.1	73854
28207	CHARLOTTE	87783	3636	10.6	17.0	19.6	15.7	37.1	107242	130743	99	100	2531	0.8	0.9	9.2	25.2	64.0	554652
28208	CHARLOTTE	15159	13531	38.2	35.2	22.5	3.2	1.0	31133	35967	15	15	5743	11.9	51.7	35.4	0.8	0.3	80195
28209	CHARLOTTE	39138	10999	19.3	28.1	33.0	11.1	8.5	52349	61865	76	88	5527	0.5	5.2	45.0	37.9	11.4	173596
28210	CHARLOTTE	41679	20684	14.9	27.5	34.1	11.5	12.1	57862	66917	83	91	11327	0.8	3.6	42.2	40.2	13.3	183246
28211	CHARLOTTE	47686	12887	15.7	21.5	29.6	16.0	17.2	68030	80482	90	96	7537	0.3	3.1	20.3	53.8	22.5	258115
28212	CHARLOTTE	20733	16383	22.3	39.6	31.6	5.3	1.2	41346	47449	51	60	5955	1.0	13.0	81.4	4.2	0.4	121566
28213	CHARLOTTE	21806	11177	23.0	29.4	35.7	9.1	2.7	47509	55890	67	82	6297	6.5	18.6	55.7	18.8	0.5	125796
28214	CHARLOTTE	25548	9623	14.8	28.7	41.5	10.9	4.1	55564	64931	80	90	8188	7.7	12.8	61.2	15.6	2.7	131246
28215	CHARLOTTE	22872	16853	17.1	31.3	37.3	10.8	3.5	51336	60191	74	87	11450	3.6	13.4	62.8	18.6	1.6	128301
28216	CHARLOTTE	22540	12811	24.9	28.2	33.5	9.9	3.4	46831	55383	66	80	9120	5.0	21.2	54.1	16.0	3.7	124060
28217	CHARLOTTE	20498	8150	24.3	36.4	30.5	6.6	2.3	42403	49087	54	64	4012	3.7	38.0	52.2	5.7	0.3	97551
28226	CHARLOTTE	50389	15759	8.9	20.5	33.4	17.8	19.4	75857	87928	94	97	11290	0.6	3.1	29.3	47.0	20.1	219096
28227	CHARLOTTE	26465	17663	13.1	29.0	40.8	12.8	4.2	56323	64495	81	90	13266	3.6	7.6	65.4	21.5	1.9	134405
28262	CHARLOTTE	26492	9038	14.6	27.3	38.8	13.1	6.2	57896	67275	83	91	4152	2.9	3.7	59.2	30.7	3.5	158762
28269	CHARLOTTE	31978	20642	12.9	19.9	39.1	18.2	9.9	68979	81755	91	96	13934	1.2	6.7	41.4	48.3	2.4	175897
28270	CHARLOTTE	44940	11821	6.6	17.2	33.9	21.4	21.0	85912	101182	96	99	8889	0.7	0.9	22.8	58.3	17.4	258574
28273	CHARLOTTE	28165	8604	9.9	24.9	46.2	15.2	3.8	63243	73941	87	94	5746	2.1	6.3	67.0	24.0	0.6	147473
28274	CHARLOTTE	9450	14	0.0	7.1	28.6	21.4	42.9	125000	171651	99	100	10	0.0	0.0	0.0	20.0	80.0	750000
28277	CHARLOTTE	48817	17579	6.1	13.0	33.3	24.7	23.0	95227	110945	98	99	13589	0.8	0.4	22.1	55.6	21.2	247204
28278	CHARLOTTE	37457	3351	10.8	18.0	39.5	19.8	12.0	75646	87390	93	97	3068	3.7	5.3	27.9	50.3	12.8	195603
28301	FAYETTEVILLE	14812	6723	55.2	26.2	13.9	3.2	1.5	21345	24144	2	1	3108	16.1	47.9	33.0	2.5	0.6	79744
28303	FAYETTEVILLE	25132	12681	23.4	36.9	27.3	7.5	5.0	43036	48334	56	67	7393	5.6	25.8	52.0	13.2	3.4	106310
28304	FAYETTEVILLE	20735	14012	21.2	36.0	33.6	6.6	2.6	44849	50905	61	74	9197	4.4	40.1	47.9	7.5	0.2	93787
28305	FAYETTEVILLE	34855	3176	32.0	25.9	24.2	8.3	9.6	39161	43216	43	49	1856	4.4	20.5	37.8	29.9	7.4	138857
28306	FAYETTEVILLE	20698	12662	27.3	30.7	31.7	7.3	2.9	42734	48492	55	66	9525	17.7	31.2	39.0	11.7	0.5	91323
28307	FORT BRAGG	15220	3156	28.5	48.1	21.5	1.5	0.4	32953	36614	21	20	82	7.3	39.0	53.7	0.0	0.0	91875
28308	POPE A F B	12373	497	12.5	69.4	15.1	0.6	2.4	35313	39518	29	31	7	0.0	100.0	0.0	0.0	0.0	65000
28310	FORT BRAGG	8734	1165	28.2	48.4	21.5	1.6	0.4	33030	36609	21	21	15	6.7	40.0	53.3	0.0	0.0	91667
28311	FAYETTEVILLE	21688	13158	24.2	32.6	30.8	9.6	2.9	44543	49765	60	73	7556	6.0	26.5	50.9	15.4	1.1	108327
28312	FAYETTEVILLE	21710	6574	30.0	32.2	27.6	6.2	4.0	40123	44635	47	53	5209	22.6	28.7	33.9	13.5	1.3	88159
28314	FAYETTEVILLE	20052	19125	19.2	37.2	35.3	6.2	2.1	45728	51265	63	77	11084	5.2	26.5	63.5	4.1	0.8	102600
28315	ABERDEEN	24112	3937	29.3	30.4	28.5	7.5	4.3	40749	46789	49	56	2912	14.5	21.1	39.8	19.0	5.7	116419
28318	AUTRYVILLE	18103	1743	34.7	32.5	25.5	5.3	2.0	37080	41966	36	40	1434	37.7	31.4	25.5	4.7	0.7	68857
28320	BLADENBORO	17661	3877	42.7	29.8	21.7	4.0	1.8	30169	34382	13	13	3034	29.2	37.5	28.8	4.3	0.2	69291
28323	BUNNLEVEL	17188	917	32.6	31.3	30.4	4.1	1.5	38614	44775	41	47	684	32.8	20.5	35.5	11.3	0.0	84634
28326	CAMERON	18605	4047	26.7	33.8	31.6	5.8	2.1	40681	47244	49	55	3096	27.6	24.3	39.4	8.2	0.6	87489
28327	CARTHAGE	22461	5867	27.3	29.7	31.4	8.4	3.3	44007	50461	59	71	4772	16.1	18.7	34.6	26.9	3.8	120933
28328	CLINTON	18079	10168	38.2	29.4	24.1	5.3	3.0	34654	39385	26	28	7209	21.7	32.2	32.7	12.1	1.4	85707
28333	DUDLEY	16220	4377	30.2	41.2	24.4	2.7	1.6	35568	41197	30	32	3321	39.4	38.5	19.4	2.3	0.5	58622
28334	DUNN	19102	9987	38.4	28.0	25.0	5.3	3.3	34764	38812	27	28	7100	19.2	28.1	39.2	12.0	1.5	93445
28337	ELIZABETHTOWN	17931	4525	42.8	26.4	23.3	4.3	3.3	30151	34840	13	13	3371	32.5	35.1	23.7	7.3	1.5	70571
28338	ELLERBE	15145	1688	45.3	30.3	19.9	2.7	1.8	27836	31307	8	7	1310	36.0	37.0	21.5	4.3	1.2	61304
28339	ERWIN	18163	3186	38.2	30.1	24.7	4.7	2.2	34683	38061	26	28	2371	22.3	36.0	33.7	7.1	0.9	81778
28340	FAIRMONT	14106	4376	44.1	30.8	20.6	3.2	1.3	28977	31823	10	9	3184	40.0	30.0	25.5	4.3	0.1	58855
28341	FAISON	15634	1809	38.9	29.5	25.0	4.8	1.8	31550	35283	16	16	1321	32.6	31.7	25.8	9.6	0.3	72895
28343	GIBSON	15858	640	42.5	27.8	25.0	3.1	1.6	29766	34662	12	11	478	42.3	36.6	14.2	6.7	0.2	60175
28344	GODWIN	15199	1387	29.1	36.6	28.7	4.6	0.9	37726	42565	38	43	1135	24.1	32.4	35.4	7.7	0.4	82933
28345	HAMLET	16134	5154	38.8	33.7	21.7	4.6	1.2	32310	36286	19	19	3789	36.6	41.5	17.9	3.3	0.7	61793
28347	HOFFMAN	13437	551	33.6	32.3	24.7	5.3	4.2	36455	41950	33	37	442	33.3	25.8	26.2	13.1	1.6	78571
28348	HOPE MILLS	18130	10022	27.3	32.0	34.2	5.2	1.4	43212	48070	57	67	7560	15.5	34.5	42.8	7.1	0.2	89989
28349	KENANSVILLE	17157	1295	34.5	33.8	24.3	4.8	2.7	35555	40088	30	32	1033	28.9	25.4	35.9	8.8	1.0	82054
28351	LAUREL HILL	15573	2082	39.4	31.7	24.3	3.2	1.4	31330	36946	16	16	1610	35.7	44.0	15.2	5.1	0.0	62990
28352	LAURINBURG	19030	9766	36.7	28.1	26.0	5.8	3.4	35664	42029	30	33	6522	22.0	34.7	31.8	11.0	0.6	81705
28356	LINDEN	23385	1299	26.4	28.6	29.8	9.5	5.8	44189	48425	59	72	1101	18.4	28.5	35.9	16.8	0.4	93807
28357	LUMBER BRIDGE	14483	1066	38.9	30.8	25.3	3.3	1.7	33280	36939	22	22	864	37.2	29.8	28.4	4.4	0.4	67971
28358	LUMBERTON	17095	14259	39.5	30.2	23.1	5.1	2.1	32224	36469	18	18	9646	32.5	33.6	25.7	7.1	1.1	71648
28360	LUMBERTON	15197	4714	37.8	31.8	23.1	5.9	1.5	33649	38193	23	23	3589	36.1	32.5	26.9	3.2	1.2	66342
28363	MARSTON	25282	281	29.9	32.7	26.0	6.4	5.0	39081	42913	43	48	233	27.0	29.6	28.3	14.2	0.9	81842
28364	MAXTON	13776	4849	45.2	32.0	18.5	2.6	1.8	28495	31594	10	8	3588	41.5	37.0	18.3	3.2	0.0	57153
28365	MOUNT OLIVE	17367	6037	38.1	31.3	24.2	4.5	2.0	33026	36740	21	21	4397	29.5	31.5	28.9	9.9	0.3	77445
28366	NEWTON GROVE	18870	1839	31.7	29.6	29.5	6.1	3.1	40199	45274	47	53	1398	24.3	30.0	36.0	9.3	0.4	84915
28369	ORRUM	17478	867	36.2	33.6	23.2	5.0	2.1	33068	36854	21	21	693	40.7	32.5	20.6	6.2	0.0	63154
28371	PARKTON	17866	1670	27.3	31.7	33.7	6.4	1.0	43293	49738	57	68	1336	21.6	31.1	42.0	4.5	0.8	87040
28372	PEMBROKE	14974	4174	40.4	31.7	22.0	4.4	1.5	31224	34519	16	16	3065	34.9	35.1	23.2	6.2	0.6	67768
28373	PINEBLUFF	20396	777	29.5	33.1	29.6	5.5	2.3	40044	46226	46	52	612	26.1	24.4	42.0	6.2	1.3	89434
28374	PINEHURST	48797	5887	12.3	24.1	36.1	14.9	12.6	63165	75128	87	94	5071	2.7	3.8	25.5	51.7	16.3	221725
28376	RAEFORD	15697	10069	31.3	35.8	26.7	4.8	1.4	36688	40627	34	38	7585	21.3	30.2	40.7	7.3	0.5	88123
28377	RED SPRINGS	14261	4181	42.0	31.2	20.3	4.5	2.1	29991	33148	12	12	3097	36.9	34.3	23.3	5.1	0.5	63290
28379	ROCKINGHAM	17195	10742	40.8	29.9	23.1	4.2	2.0	31185	35341	15	15	7611	33.4	37.1	23.3	6.0	0.2	68961
28382	ROSEBORO	17777	2617	36.7	33.9	22.7	4.7	2.1	35078	39929	28	30	2071	28.0	35.5	30.6	5.3	0.6	74899
28383	ROWLAND	14165	3021	44.5	30.6	20.9	2.8	1.3	29401	32499	11	10	2348	50.0	29.8	18.1	2.2	0.0	50059
28384	SAINT PAULS	13790	4180	43.0	30.2	22.6	3.6	0.7	29772	33015	12	11	3114	31.0	35.6	28.7	4.3	0.4	71000
28385	SALEMBURG	18175	1117	35.5	30.4	25.0	6.5	2.8	36468	41535	33	37	855	24.8	39.1	26.7	8.2	1.3	76127
	NORTH CAROLINA	23743		27.0	29.8	30.1	8.5	4.7	43794	50711				14.5	20.0	39.7	21.7	4.1	115673
	UNITED STATES	25866		24.7	27.1	30.8	10.9	6.5	48124	56710				10.9	15.0	33.7	30.1	10.4	145905

ZIP CODE #	POST OFFICE NAME	FINANCIAL SERVICES: Auto Loan	Home Loan	Invest-ments	Retire-ment Plans	THE HOME: Home Improvements: Home Repair	Lawn & Garden	Furnishings: Comput-ers & Hard-ware	Major Appli-ances	TV, Radio, Sound Equip-ment	Furni-ture	ENTERTAINMENT: Dine out/ Carry out	Sports Equip-ment	Fees & Tickets	Toys & Games	Travel	Cable TV	PERSONAL: Apparel & Services	Auto Repairs	Health Insur-ance	Pets & Supplies
28138	ROCKWELL	85	75	58	73	77	84	73	79	76	73	93	91	70	91	73	76	88	77	83	95
28139	RUTHERFORDTON	83	68	48	62	73	81	65	74	72	65	86	87	61	85	66	75	81	73	84	96
28144	SALISBURY	74	68	70	66	69	77	71	72	74	70	91	84	70	90	71	75	88	73	76	84
28146	SALISBURY	86	74	56	70	78	85	71	79	76	71	92	92	68	91	72	78	87	77	86	99
28147	SALISBURY	89	80	67	78	82	88	79	83	81	79	99	98	75	97	78	81	95	83	85	101
28150	SHELBY	83	68	55	65	72	81	70	76	76	69	92	88	66	89	70	79	87	76	85	94
28152	SHELBY	77	67	55	64	70	77	66	72	71	66	86	84	64	86	67	73	82	71	78	88
28159	SPENCER	68	70	70	67	71	79	70	70	72	67	89	78	72	95	71	75	86	69	75	78
28160	SPINDALE	63	44	25	40	49	58	46	54	53	45	62	62	40	59	46	56	57	53	65	71
28163	STANFIELD	92	82	62	78	85	91	76	84	80	77	98	99	74	97	78	81	93	83	89	106
28164	STANLEY	96	82	59	77	87	94	77	86	83	77	101	102	74	101	79	86	95	85	95	111
28166	TROUTMAN	96	91	75	88	93	99	85	91	87	86	107	107	84	108	86	87	103	89	94	111
28167	UNION MILLS	74	50	24	44	57	65	49	60	58	49	68	72	42	65	49	62	62	60	74	85
28168	VALE	84	69	47	64	74	80	65	74	71	66	86	88	61	84	66	73	80	73	83	97
28170	WADESBORO	69	54	40	50	58	68	56	63	64	55	76	71	52	74	57	68	71	62	74	78
28173	WAXHAW	128	139	132	140	137	139	126	128	120	128	151	150	130	154	126	117	148	125	120	148
28174	WINGATE	83	75	62	75	77	84	74	79	77	74	94	91	72	94	74	77	89	78	82	93
28202	CHARLOTTE	68	66	109	72	63	70	75	69	78	77	98	83	78	101	74	77	97	73	66	77
28203	CHARLOTTE	104	98	144	102	95	107	111	104	116	112	145	122	112	145	109	117	142	110	105	117
28204	CHARLOTTE	75	68	113	74	65	75	81	74	85	82	107	89	82	108	79	86	105	79	74	83
28205	CHARLOTTE	66	63	76	67	62	66	70	66	69	69	87	80	69	85	67	66	85	69	62	73
28206	CHARLOTTE	52	45	51	42	44	51	51	50	55	51	68	56	50	66	50	57	66	52	54	56
28207	CHARLOTTE	229	280	414	286	271	295	266	255	255	271	323	295	293	339	276	255	325	253	237	279
28208	CHARLOTTE	56	52	59	50	50	57	56	55	59	57	74	62	56	72	55	60	72	56	56	62
28209	CHARLOTTE	101	103	124	108	101	107	108	104	105	108	133	124	108	131	106	102	130	107	98	115
28210	CHARLOTTE	125	127	146	133	124	131	130	127	126	132	159	149	131	155	128	121	156	130	118	140
28211	CHARLOTTE	140	154	193	158	151	160	153	149	148	154	187	174	159	188	154	145	185	150	139	163
28212	CHARLOTTE	69	64	73	69	62	66	70	67	68	71	87	81	68	83	67	64	85	71	61	75
28213	CHARLOTTE	83	79	82	81	77	81	82	81	82	84	103	94	81	99	79	78	101	83	75	90
28214	CHARLOTTE	96	99	91	98	98	101	92	95	91	93	113	112	92	114	92	89	110	94	92	110
28215	CHARLOTTE	86	92	95	95	89	89	90	88	86	91	108	104	91	108	88	81	107	89	79	97
28216	CHARLOTTE	80	84	88	83	81	87	81	81	81	83	101	91	84	100	81	81	99	80	79	90
28217	CHARLOTTE	79	74	83	78	72	77	80	77	79	81	100	92	79	96	76	76	97	80	72	86
28226	CHARLOTTE	158	183	213	187	180	185	173	170	163	174	205	198	181	209	175	158	204	168	155	187
28227	CHARLOTTE	94	101	107	104	98	99	98	96	93	99	118	114	99	118	96	88	116	97	87	107
28262	CHARLOTTE	104	94	103	103	91	94	107	99	103	107	130	121	102	123	98	94	126	105	87	110
28269	CHARLOTTE	120	122	123	128	117	119	119	117	114	123	144	138	120	141	115	108	141	118	105	131
28270	CHARLOTTE	158	185	197	191	179	180	169	166	156	172	199	194	179	202	169	150	198	162	147	183
28273	CHARLOTTE	103	111	111	116	106	104	105	103	98	108	124	122	106	123	101	91	122	102	89	113
28274	CHARLOTTE	238	320	439	314	312	337	279	276	260	285	328	311	317	346	297	262	333	265	257	300
28277	CHARLOTTE	174	203	217	212	195	194	185	181	170	190	217	211	195	221	184	162	216	177	158	199
28278	CHARLOTTE	130	147	146	150	143	144	134	134	126	136	158	155	139	160	134	121	156	130	122	149
28301	FAYETTEVILLE	49	41	43	39	42	50	46	47	51	46	62	52	44	58	45	53	59	48	53	55
28303	FAYETTEVILLE	82	85	95	86	83	88	87	85	85	87	107	99	88	107	86	83	105	86	81	94
28304	FAYETTEVILLE	73	79	84	80	77	79	78	76	75	78	94	90	79	95	77	72	92	77	70	84
28305	FAYETTEVILLE	92	99	118	97	98	108	99	98	100	99	125	111	103	126	101	102	122	98	99	108
28306	FAYETTEVILLE	82	79	71	78	79	83	76	79	76	77	94	92	74	92	75	75	91	79	78	92
28307	FORT BRAGG	63	40	38	46	37	43	60	51	60	56	76	68	51	68	49	55	72	61	47	58
28308	POPE A F B	69	44	42	50	40	47	65	56	66	61	82	75	56	74	53	60	79	66	52	64
28310	FORT BRAGG	63	40	38	46	37	43	60	51	61	56	76	69	51	68	49	55	73	61	48	59
28311	FAYETTEVILLE	79	75	78	78	72	76	81	77	79	80	99	94	79	97	76	75	97	80	71	86
28312	FAYETTEVILLE	87	78	62	74	79	85	76	81	78	77	96	94	72	93	75	79	92	81	84	97
28314	FAYETTEVILLE	81	71	72	76	68	72	81	75	79	79	99	93	77	95	74	74	97	81	69	84
28315	ABERDEEN	85	78	67	76	80	88	78	82	80	78	98	93	75	94	78	81	94	82	87	96
28318	AUTRYVILLE	80	61	37	55	65	73	59	69	66	60	79	81	52	74	59	68	73	68	78	91
28320	BLADENBORO	75	51	24	45	58	66	50	62	60	50	70	73	43	66	51	64	64	61	75	86
28323	BUNNLEVEL	73	66	52	64	66	71	64	68	65	65	80	79	60	76	63	64	76	68	69	81
28326	CAMERON	81	74	58	72	74	78	71	76	71	73	88	88	67	83	70	70	85	75	75	90
28327	CARTHAGE	89	79	65	76	82	91	76	84	80	78	98	93	73	90	77	81	92	83	90	100
28328	CLINTON	74	63	50	60	65	72	63	68	67	63	81	78	59	78	63	68	77	68	73	83
28333	DUDLEY	71	65	52	63	65	69	62	67	63	64	78	77	59	74	62	63	75	66	67	79
28334	DUNN	76	63	48	60	66	74	64	70	69	64	83	80	60	80	64	71	78	70	77	85
28337	ELIZABETHTOWN	72	56	43	52	60	69	57	64	64	57	77	75	52	74	58	68	72	64	74	83
28338	ELLERBE	70	47	22	41	53	61	45	56	54	46	64	67	39	60	46	58	58	56	69	80
28339	ERWIN	71	59	44	56	62	71	60	66	66	59	79	75	57	78	60	68	74	65	74	80
28340	FAIRMONT	64	48	32	43	51	59	48	55	55	49	66	64	43	61	48	58	61	55	65	72
28341	FAISON	73	56	35	51	60	67	54	63	60	55	72	74	49	68	54	62	67	62	71	82
28343	GIBSON	74	58	37	53	61	68	56	64	61	57	74	75	50	70	56	63	69	64	71	83
28344	GODWIN	74	63	45	59	65	70	59	66	63	61	77	78	56	74	60	64	73	66	70	83
28345	HAMLET	66	51	38	46	54	63	52	58	59	52	71	67	48	67	52	63	66	58	69	75
28347	HOFFMAN	82	75	59	72	75	79	72	77	73	74	90	89	68	85	71	72	86	77	76	91
28348	HOPE MILLS	76	74	64	72	73	75	70	73	69	72	86	85	68	83	69	67	83	73	70	85
28349	KENANSVILLE	79	63	42	59	67	74	62	70	68	63	82	81	56	77	62	70	76	70	78	89
28351	LAUREL HILL	72	54	31	48	58	65	51	61	58	53	70	72	46	66	52	61	65	61	70	82
28352	LAURINBURG	73	66	61	64	67	74	67	70	70	67	86	81	65	83	66	71	83	71	74	83
28356	LINDEN	109	82	48	74	89	98	78	92	88	79	105	109	69	101	78	92	97	91	106	124
28357	LUMBER BRIDGE	67	61	48	59	61	64	58	62	59	60	73	72	55	69	57	58	70	62	62	74
28358	LUMBERTON	65	60	56	57	60	66	60	63	63	61	77	71	59	75	60	64	75	63	65	73
28360	LUMBERTON	71	60	44	57	62	67	57	64	61	59	74	75	54	71	57	61	70	63	67	80
28363	MARSTON	89	78	58	74	79	84	74	81	77	76	94	94	70	89	74	77	90	81	83	99
28364	MAXTON	67	49	33	44	53	61	50	57	57	50	68	67	45	64	50	60	63	58	67	76
28365	MOUNT OLIVE	75	59	39	54	62	70	58	66	65	59	78	77	53	74	58	67	72	66	75	85
28366	NEWTON GROVE	84	67	45	63	71	79	66	75	72	67	87	87	60	82	66	75	81	75	83	95
28369	ORRUM	83	57	27	49	64	73	55	68	65	56	77	81	47	73	56	70	70	67	83	95
28371	PARKTON	79	77	65	76	76	78	72	76	71	75	89	88	70	85	71	69	86	75	72	88
28372	PEMBROKE	70	51	33	46	55	63	53	60	60	52	72	71	47	68	52	63	67	60	70	80
28373	PINEBLUFF	77	78	71	78	77	78	74	76	72	76	90	89	73	88	73	69	88	76	71	86
28374	PINEHURST	157	146	140	139	155	182	135	154	143	145	178	151	137	148	147	153	167	150	180	176
28376	RAEFORD	71	62	52	62	61	65	64	65	64	64	80	77	60	75	61	63	76	66	64	76
28377	RED SPRINGS	65	58	47	54	59	64	57	61	60	57	73	70	54	71	57	61	70	61	64	73
28379	ROCKINGHAM	69	55	39	50	58	66	55	62	61	55	73	72	51	71	55	64	68	61	70	79
28382	ROSEBORO	77	59	40	55	63	71	59	67	66	59	79	79	54	76	59	68	74	67	76	87
28383	ROWLAND	67	50	32	45	54	61	49	58	57	51	68	67	44	63	49	60	63	57	67	76
28384	SAINT PAULS	66	51	34	47	54	60	50	57	56	51	67	67	46	64	50	57	63	57	64	74
28385	SALEMBURG	76	63	46	61	66	75	65	70	70	63	84	80	60	81	64	72	78	70	78	85
	NORTH CAROLINA	90	81	73	80	83	90	81	85	84	82	103	100	79	101	81	84	99	85	88	102
	UNITED STATES	100	100	100	100	100	100	100	100	100	100	100	100	100	100	100	100	100	100	100	100

#	POST OFFICE NAME	COUNTY FIPS CODE	POPULATION 2000	2004	2009	2000-2004 ANNUAL RATE % Rate	State Centile	HOUSEHOLDS 2000	2004	2009	% Annual Rate 2000-2004	2004 Average HH Size	FAMILIES 2000	2004	% Annual Rate 2000-2004
28386	SHANNON	155	5373	6016	6633	2.7	80	1731	1954	2176	2.9	3.08	1314	1463	2.6
28387	SOUTHERN PINES	125	12801	13243	14185	0.8	30	5539	5789	6275	1.0	2.21	3467	3577	0.7
28390	SPRING LAKE	085	19862	20033	21345	0.2	14	7553	7736	8350	0.6	2.59	5234	5277	0.2
28391	STEDMAN	051	4711	4864	5029	0.8	28	1821	1916	2015	1.2	2.54	1390	1442	0.9
28392	TAR HEEL	017	2027	2121	2216	1.1	38	793	849	906	1.6	2.49	578	610	1.3
28393	TURKEY	163	1988	1992	2051	0.1	12	731	740	769	0.3	2.69	539	539	0.0
28394	VASS	125	4720	5157	5645	2.1	69	1906	2115	2347	2.5	2.38	1334	1456	2.1
28395	WADE	051	2228	2416	2570	1.9	63	881	982	1066	2.6	2.39	646	707	2.2
28396	WAGRAM	165	3070	3203	3282	1.0	36	1120	1194	1247	1.5	2.68	826	868	1.2
28398	WARSAW	061	6633	6995	7565	1.3	46	2537	2707	2955	1.5	2.51	1780	1874	1.2
28399	WHITE OAK	017	1823	1961	2080	1.7	58	684	749	809	2.2	2.62	500	540	1.8
28401	WILMINGTON	129	22030	22689	24277	0.7	27	9748	10223	11156	1.1	2.12	4934	4993	0.3
28403	WILMINGTON	129	30094	30973	33048	0.7	26	13800	14516	15853	1.2	1.97	6040	6093	0.2
28405	WILMINGTON	129	24937	26695	29095	1.6	55	10346	11404	12737	2.3	2.31	6987	7549	1.8
28409	WILMINGTON	129	26528	29177	32078	2.3	72	10121	11286	12606	2.6	2.58	7885	8672	2.3
28411	WILMINGTON	129	18517	22856	26668	5.1	97	7489	9481	11297	5.7	2.41	5458	6765	5.2
28412	WILMINGTON	129	23498	25568	27943	2.0	65	10152	11345	12686	2.7	2.23	6367	6922	2.0
28420	ASH	019	4100	4567	5429	2.6	78	1555	1760	2127	3.0	2.58	1167	1304	2.7
28421	ATKINSON	141	1522	1657	1863	2.0	65	634	704	804	2.5	2.35	439	480	2.1
28422	BOLIVIA	019	4707	6068	7765	6.2	98	1802	2386	3126	6.8	2.51	1368	1796	6.6
28423	BOLTON	047	2339	2382	2437	0.4	19	872	905	943	0.9	2.61	646	662	0.6
28425	BURGAW	141	9781	10656	11927	2.0	66	3438	3827	4384	2.6	2.52	2492	2738	2.2
28428	CAROLINA BEACH	129	5189	5118	5368	-0.3	5	2534	2560	2743	0.2	1.98	1430	1400	-0.5
28429	CASTLE HAYNE	129	7076	7154	7610	0.3	15	2658	2747	2983	0.8	2.57	574	592	0.7
28430	CERRO GORDO	047	2069	2115	2179	0.5	22	794	829	871	1.0	2.55	1546	1691	2.1
28431	CHADBOURN	047	5681	6191	6649	2.0	66	2253	2498	2730	2.5	2.47	796	840	1.3
28432	CLARENDON	047	2725	2855	2986	1.1	39	1073	1149	1226	1.6	2.48	796	840	1.3
28433	CLARKTON	017	4884	4968	5109	0.4	18	1906	1977	2074	0.9	2.49	1333	1364	0.5
28434	COUNCIL	017	1682	1684	1729	0.0	11	690	709	745	0.6	2.37	484	490	0.3
28435	CURRIE	141	2189	2409	2722	2.3	73	867	975	1120	2.8	2.44	625	693	2.5
28436	DELCO	047	1789	1892	1975	1.3	48	688	745	794	1.9	2.54	529	567	1.7
28438	EVERGREEN	047	2097	2096	2137	0.0	10	814	829	862	0.4	2.53	599	603	0.2
28439	FAIR BLUFF	047	1954	1943	1976	-0.1	7	806	819	849	0.4	2.34	531	531	0.0
28441	GARLAND	163	2791	2846	2984	0.5	21	1029	1064	1129	0.8	2.61	756	772	0.5
28442	HALLSBORO	047	1836	1831	1866	-0.1	9	761	776	806	0.5	2.33	516	517	0.1
28443	HAMPSTEAD	141	10534	11752	13387	2.6	79	4418	4990	5752	2.9	2.36	3301	3676	2.6
28444	HARRELLS	163	1769	1923	2098	2.0	64	664	727	800	2.2	2.62	475	512	1.8
28445	HOLLY RIDGE	133	4266	4545	5016	1.5	52	1839	1981	2214	1.8	2.28	1228	1301	1.4
28447	IVANHOE	017	626	726	810	3.6	89	238	278	314	3.7	2.55	175	202	3.4
28448	KELLY	017	968	1009	1052	1.0	36	427	453	482	1.4	2.23	284	296	1.0
28449	KURE BEACH	129	1458	1557	1680	1.6	54	704	771	851	2.2	2.02	444	474	1.6
28450	LAKE WACCAMAW	047	2289	2406	2504	1.2	42	848	911	968	1.7	2.40	589	624	1.4
28451	LELAND	019	15990	18006	21539	2.8	82	6003	6872	8363	3.2	2.61	4418	5000	3.0
28452	LONGWOOD	019	211	230	270	2.1	66	71	79	94	2.5	2.89	56	61	2.0
28453	MAGNOLIA	061	3564	3922	4321	2.3	73	1222	1343	1484	2.3	2.82	887	962	1.9
28454	MAPLE HILL	141	2387	2584	2872	1.9	62	887	977	1102	2.3	2.64	647	704	2.0
28455	NAKINA	047	1729	1741	1777	0.2	13	679	697	724	0.6	2.50	493	499	0.3
28456	RIEGELWOOD	047	3319	3331	3424	0.1	12	1262	1297	1360	0.7	2.56	959	974	0.4
28457	ROCKY POINT	141	7902	8530	9593	1.8	60	2976	3236	3676	2.0	2.63	2197	2361	1.7
28458	ROSE HILL	061	5476	5660	6078	0.8	29	2052	2134	2305	0.9	2.64	1484	1522	0.6
28460	SNEADS FERRY	133	5516	6175	6916	2.7	80	2373	2693	3059	3.0	2.29	1640	1837	2.7
28461	SOUTHPORT	019	9004	11173	14039	5.2	97	3924	4957	6343	5.7	2.24	2782	3452	5.2
28462	SUPPLY	019	10325	12122	14797	3.9	91	4447	5295	6570	4.2	2.27	3182	3739	3.9
28463	TABOR CITY	047	7323	7484	7666	0.5	22	2798	2901	3018	0.9	2.55	1965	2007	0.5
28464	TEACHEY	061	1679	1872	2085	2.6	78	639	722	812	2.9	2.58	460	513	2.6
28465	OAK ISLAND	019	6782	7570	9012	2.6	79	3192	3625	4391	3.0	2.09	2238	2459	2.7
28466	WALLACE	061	8216	8508	9147	0.8	32	3196	3355	3645	1.2	2.50	1824	2058	2.9
28467	CALABASH	019	5238	5914	7086	2.9	83	2528	2903	3542	3.3	2.04	1824	2058	2.9
28468	SUNSET BEACH	019	2637	3998	5496	10.3	100	1264	1938	2703	10.6	2.06	935	1419	10.3
28469	OCEAN ISLE BEACH	019	4049	5027	6304	5.2	97	1832	2307	2940	5.6	2.18	1299	1611	5.2
28470	SHALLOTTE	019	7172	8461	10327	4.0	92	2761	3336	4169	4.6	2.45	2004	2396	4.3
28472	WHITEVILLE	047	20035	20277	20774	0.3	16	7811	8045	8394	0.7	2.40	5414	5495	0.4
28478	WILLARD	141	5096	6133	7276	4.5	94	1962	2406	2900	4.9	2.51	1435	1738	4.6
28479	WINNABOW	019	2793	3073	3620	2.3	72	1015	1137	1369	2.7	2.61	762	842	2.4
28480	WRIGHTSVILLE BEACH	129	2564	2736	3031	1.5	53	1258	1368	1545	2.0	1.98	580	607	1.1
28501	KINSTON	107	21306	20838	21081	-0.5	3	8885	8837	9091	-0.1	2.28	5533	5393	-0.6
28504	KINSTON	107	21857	22385	22896	0.6	24	8592	8969	9333	1.0	2.40	6074	6238	0.6
28508	ALBERTSON	061	2206	2610	2988	4.0	93	739	869	996	3.9	3.00	550	639	3.6
28510	ARAPAHOE	137	1399	1529	1658	2.1	69	601	670	739	2.6	2.27	434	477	2.3
28511	ATLANTIC	031	817	800	833	-0.5	3	362	360	383	-0.1	1.93	246	240	-0.6
28512	ATLANTIC BEACH	031	3684	3595	3763	-0.6	2	1915	1916	2046	0.0	1.87	1172	1147	-0.5
28513	AYDEN	147	8562	8757	9389	0.5	23	3447	3596	3922	1.0	2.42	2351	2410	0.4
28515	BAYBORO	137	3007	3057	3193	0.4	18	1007	1040	1109	0.8	2.55	700	713	0.4
28516	BEAUFORT	031	10965	11444	12183	1.0	36	4700	5009	5432	1.5	2.26	3212	3361	1.1
28518	BEULAVILLE	061	6768	7184	7814	1.4	50	2625	2822	3101	1.7	2.52	1927	2045	1.4
28520	CEDAR ISLAND	031	324	315	329	-0.7	2	136	135	144	-0.2	2.33	98	96	-0.5
28521	CHINQUAPIN	061	1520	1515	1606	-0.1	9	625	633	679	0.3	2.39	463	464	0.1
28523	COVE CITY	049	2475	2607	2743	1.2	45	963	1032	1104	1.6	2.53	724	767	1.4
28525	DEEP RUN	107	3038	3331	3533	2.2	71	1155	1278	1374	2.4	2.60	880	962	2.1
28526	DOVER	049	2222	2199	2246	-0.2	6	901	908	945	0.2	2.42	664	661	-0.1
28527	ERNUL	049	534	537	547	0.1	13	202	207	216	0.6	2.02	149	151	0.3
28528	GLOUCESTER	031	462	472	496	0.5	22	197	206	220	1.1	2.29	146	151	0.8
28529	GRANTSBORO	137	1867	1975	2102	1.3	48	724	780	846	1.8	2.39	526	559	1.4
28530	GRIFTON	147	6139	6226	6504	0.3	17	2369	2432	2572	0.6	2.53	1714	1733	0.3
28531	HARKERS ISLAND	031	1525	1465	1528	-0.9	1	661	652	696	-0.3	2.24	498	484	-0.7
28532	HAVELOCK	049	27463	27655	28413	0.2	13	8321	8542	8966	0.6	2.80	6679	6767	0.3
28537	HOBUCKEN	137	215	201	207	-1.6	1	98	93	98	-1.2	2.16	67	63	-1.4
28538	HOOKERTON	079	3111	3892	4545	5.4	98	1150	1462	1730	5.8	2.66	859	1074	5.4
28539	HUBERT	133	13696	14763	16262	1.8	59	4546	4969	5575	2.1	2.75	3470	3752	1.9
28540	JACKSONVILLE	133	46841	49300	53796	1.2	44	15994	17190	19181	1.7	2.67	11684	12429	1.5
28543	TARAWA TERRACE	133	6401	6314	6683	-0.3	5	1908	1909	2076	0.0	2.77	1865	1864	0.0
28544	MIDWAY PARK	133	6036	6250	6842	0.8	31	2216	2335	2597	1.2	2.67	1744	1807	0.8
28546	JACKSONVILLE	133	32666	36323	40855	2.5	77	11821	13305	15168	2.8	2.70	9042	10075	2.6
28547	CAMP LEJEUNE	133	19201	19372	19807	0.2	14	1432	1492	1621	1.0	4.06	1418	1477	1.0
28551	LA GRANGE	107	11786	12266	12629	0.9	35	4554	4827	5051	1.4	2.50	3258	3396	1.0
	NORTH CAROLINA					1.9					2.2	2.46			1.8
	UNITED STATES					1.2					1.3	2.58			1.1

ZIP CODE #	POST OFFICE NAME	RACE (%) White		Black		Asian/Pacific		% Hispanic Origin		2004 AGE DISTRIBUTION (%)										MEDIAN AGE		
		2000	2004	2000	2004	2000	2004	2000	2004	0-4	5-9	10-14	15-19	20-24	25-44	45-64	65-84	85+	18+	2004	% 2004 Males	% 2004 Females
28386	SHANNON	24.1	24.6	14.9	13.8	0.2	0.2	15.3	18.1	9.7	8.5	8.4	8.0	9.0	30.2	19.7	5.9	0.5	68.5	28.5	50.9	49.1
28387	SOUTHERN PINES	72.6	72.0	24.6	24.7	0.8	0.9	2.1	2.8	5.4	5.4	6.2	5.7	5.5	22.7	24.6	19.9	4.7	79.5	44.4	45.5	54.5
28390	SPRING LAKE	50.9	50.1	36.9	36.0	2.7	3.1	9.1	10.9	10.5	8.7	7.6	7.3	9.2	34.7	16.4	5.3	0.4	69.0	28.1	50.5	49.6
28391	STEDMAN	81.9	80.7	13.1	13.6	0.4	0.5	2.1	2.7	6.1	6.3	6.7	6.9	6.6	29.5	27.0	10.1	0.7	76.7	38.4	49.9	50.1
28392	TAR HEEL	52.1	50.8	43.9	44.6	0.3	0.3	3.5	4.3	5.7	6.1	7.4	6.0	6.2	30.8	26.2	10.2	1.3	77.1	37.3	47.2	52.9
28393	TURKEY	52.7	50.6	37.7	37.9	0.6	0.7	8.1	9.9	7.2	7.2	7.8	7.4	6.2	27.9	22.3	12.3	1.7	73.2	36.2	50.6	49.5
28394	VASS	84.0	82.6	11.1	11.6	0.4	0.6	3.9	5.1	6.4	6.3	6.2	6.0	5.4	28.5	24.6	14.0	2.7	77.5	39.6	49.4	50.6
28395	WADE	71.7	71.0	24.4	24.7	0.5	0.6	1.8	2.2	5.6	6.0	6.8	5.8	5.6	27.0	27.6	13.8	1.7	77.7	40.7	49.0	51.0
28396	WAGRAM	39.1	37.9	46.4	47.2	0.2	0.2	1.3	1.4	7.7	7.8	8.4	6.5	6.5	26.0	26.5	9.6	1.0	72.0	35.2	48.6	51.4
28398	WARSAW	39.9	38.4	48.8	48.1	0.5	0.6	13.0	15.7	8.2	8.0	7.6	6.2	5.9	28.1	22.6	12.0	1.5	72.4	34.9	48.2	51.8
28399	WHITE OAK	64.4	63.2	29.0	29.0	0.1	0.2	9.7	12.1	7.6	7.2	6.6	6.0	6.0	29.7	26.6	9.5	0.8	75.0	36.2	51.3	48.7
28401	WILMINGTON	45.5	43.4	50.9	52.4	0.4	0.5	2.9	3.6	6.3	6.1	6.2	5.9	7.0	30.9	23.0	12.1	2.5	78.0	36.4	47.0	53.0
28403	WILMINGTON	82.7	81.6	13.4	13.8	1.2	1.4	3.0	3.8	4.7	4.2	4.2	11.5	14.7	29.3	18.1	11.3	2.1	84.7	30.2	47.3	52.7
28405	WILMINGTON	76.6	75.9	20.6	20.8	0.8	0.9	1.6	2.0	5.9	6.1	6.2	5.9	7.0	29.4	25.9	12.6	1.0	78.4	37.9	48.5	51.5
28409	WILMINGTON	91.9	91.0	5.6	5.9	1.1	1.4	1.1	1.4	5.5	6.4	7.3	6.5	4.5	26.4	30.9	11.7	0.9	76.7	41.4	48.9	51.1
28411	WILMINGTON	88.2	86.7	9.6	10.7	0.8	0.9	1.3	1.7	6.5	6.6	6.3	4.9	4.8	32.9	26.7	10.1	1.3	77.5	38.0	49.3	50.8
28412	WILMINGTON	88.8	87.8	7.5	7.7	1.3	1.5	2.6	3.3	6.0	5.7	5.8	5.5	6.6	31.9	24.1	12.9	1.6	79.3	37.3	47.2	52.8
28420	ASH	72.0	70.4	23.3	23.8	0.5	0.5	6.7	8.6	6.9	6.7	7.1	6.4	6.6	29.1	24.7	11.5	1.1	75.5	36.8	49.5	50.5
28421	ATKINSON	55.9	54.9	40.5	41.2	0.3	0.3	2.3	2.8	5.5	5.9	6.4	5.7	5.4	26.8	28.3	14.1	1.8	78.8	41.3	49.4	50.6
28422	BOLIVIA	72.0	70.9	25.3	26.1	0.3	0.4	0.9	1.0	5.3	5.3	6.2	6.2	6.3	23.0	31.1	15.7	0.9	79.4	43.4	49.4	50.6
28423	BOLTON	39.5	38.5	35.4	35.4	0.1	0.1	1.3	1.6	7.0	7.0	7.4	7.0	6.8	26.2	26.2	11.1	1.5	74.4	36.9	47.6	52.4
28425	BURGAW	59.7	58.3	36.3	36.8	0.1	0.1	4.4	5.5	6.0	6.2	6.6	6.3	6.4	29.8	25.1	11.7	2.0	77.2	38.0	50.8	49.2
28428	CAROLINA BEACH	97.1	96.6	1.1	1.2	0.4	0.5	0.8	1.0	3.5	3.2	4.5	4.3	4.0	28.1	37.7	13.4	1.3	86.1	46.3	50.7	49.3
28429	CASTLE HAYNE	70.3	68.7	26.9	28.1	0.2	0.2	1.8	2.4	6.3	6.6	7.1	6.9	6.5	29.5	27.7	8.7	0.7	75.5	37.4	49.6	50.4
28430	CERRO GORDO	75.9	74.5	20.4	21.0	0.4	0.5	3.1	3.9	6.9	6.8	7.1	5.9	7.0	27.1	25.7	12.3	1.3	75.7	37.5	48.2	51.8
28431	CHADBOURN	54.3	53.5	42.1	42.6	0.3	0.3	1.5	1.7	7.3	7.3	7.6	6.5	6.9	25.4	25.3	12.5	1.3	73.7	37.0	48.0	52.0
28432	CLARENDON	89.2	88.6	8.0	8.1	0.2	0.2	2.1	2.7	6.7	6.8	7.3	6.2	6.0	29.0	25.8	11.2	1.1	75.5	37.3	49.3	50.8
28433	CLARKTON	47.1	45.8	47.6	48.4	0.1	0.1	3.0	3.7	7.0	7.3	7.5	6.7	6.2	26.2	25.6	12.3	1.3	73.9	37.8	48.0	52.0
28434	COUNCIL	29.3	28.1	61.4	62.0	0.0	0.0	2.6	2.9	6.1	6.9	7.7	6.4	5.5	24.8	27.0	14.1	1.5	74.9	40.0	47.7	52.3
28435	CURRIE	63.2	61.6	30.2	30.7	0.4	0.4	4.8	5.9	5.9	6.4	7.7	6.6	6.1	28.7	27.2	10.6	0.8	75.8	37.9	49.7	50.3
28436	DELCO	61.0	60.8	30.3	30.4	0.1	0.1	1.7	2.1	6.7	7.0	7.2	6.5	6.7	26.4	27.2	11.5	1.0	75.2	37.4	49.1	51.0
28438	EVERGREEN	66.2	65.0	30.6	31.1	0.1	0.2	2.1	2.8	6.0	6.1	6.5	6.6	7.2	26.5	28.4	11.3	1.5	77.7	39.2	48.5	51.5
28439	FAIR BLUFF	53.4	52.4	43.8	44.4	0.0	0.0	1.8	2.3	6.3	6.4	6.8	6.4	5.7	25.8	25.7	14.9	1.9	76.4	40.3	46.4	53.6
28441	GARLAND	46.8	44.7	42.5	42.7	0.1	0.1	11.8	14.2	7.5	7.7	8.0	6.0	6.4	28.7	22.9	11.5	1.4	73.0	34.3	50.0	50.0
28442	HALLSBORO	59.0	58.3	34.3	34.5	0.3	0.3	1.4	1.8	5.9	6.1	7.2	7.4	6.8	26.8	26.1	12.0	1.7	76.2	38.3	48.7	51.3
28443	HAMPSTEAD	89.6	88.8	8.5	8.9	0.2	0.3	1.4	1.8	5.2	5.3	5.8	4.9	4.2	23.6	30.9	19.1	1.0	80.6	45.6	50.1	49.9
28444	HARRELLS	33.2	30.9	58.5	59.4	0.5	0.6	8.6	10.1	6.5	6.7	7.4	6.6	6.5	26.8	25.5	12.5	1.6	75.6	38.1	49.8	50.2
28445	HOLLY RIDGE	93.0	92.6	3.9	3.9	0.7	0.8	1.8	2.2	5.6	5.4	5.7	5.7	5.9	27.6	30.1	13.2	1.0	79.6	41.2	49.6	50.4
28447	IVANHOE	37.9	34.6	54.8	56.9	0.3	0.3	8.2	9.6	6.5	6.6	7.3	6.9	6.3	26.0	26.3	12.5	1.5	75.5	38.7	50.3	49.7
28448	KELLY	60.0	58.6	37.0	37.8	0.2	0.2	2.9	3.8	5.5	6.1	5.2	4.3	5.4	24.0	32.7	15.0	2.1	80.8	44.8	48.2	51.8
28449	KURE BEACH	97.9	97.6	0.3	0.4	0.3	0.3	0.8	1.2	3.2	3.5	3.9	3.0	2.9	22.8	41.6	18.1	1.2	87.6	50.8	48.5	51.5
28450	LAKE WACCAMAW	61.3	59.9	19.7	19.8	0.1	0.2	1.3	1.6	5.8	6.0	6.2	6.0	5.0	24.3	27.3	15.8	3.6	78.1	42.4	46.8	53.2
28451	LELAND	70.8	69.2	23.7	24.4	0.4	0.4	4.5	5.7	7.7	7.4	7.5	6.8	6.8	31.3	24.0	8.0	0.6	73.3	34.0	49.9	50.1
28452	LONGWOOD	56.9	55.7	40.3	41.3	0.5	0.4	4.7	6.5	5.2	5.2	6.5	6.1	5.7	25.7	28.7	15.7	1.3	79.1	41.9	48.7	51.3
28453	MAGNOLIA	40.1	37.6	38.6	37.2	0.2	0.2	23.7	28.4	8.5	8.0	7.3	6.7	7.2	30.3	21.3	9.9	1.0	72.1	32.7	51.2	48.8
28454	MAPLE HILL	62.2	62.1	34.9	34.3	0.4	0.5	1.9	2.5	7.7	7.2	6.7	6.4	7.5	29.0	24.2	10.2	1.2	74.6	34.5	50.2	49.8
28455	NAKINA	89.1	88.3	7.2	7.2	0.0	0.1	6.2	7.8	6.6	6.5	6.0	6.7	6.0	29.2	24.9	13.1	1.0	77.1	38.0	49.7	50.3
28456	RIEGELWOOD	36.1	35.5	54.2	53.7	0.0	0.0	4.0	4.9	6.8	6.8	7.0	6.6	6.5	25.9	27.3	11.9	1.4	75.3	38.1	47.6	52.4
28457	ROCKY POINT	73.1	72.0	20.8	20.8	0.2	0.3	6.9	8.2	7.0	6.9	7.5	6.9	6.7	30.9	24.8	8.5	0.8	74.3	35.5	50.7	49.3
28458	ROSE HILL	46.2	44.3	39.9	39.1	0.3	0.3	17.1	20.6	7.8	7.5	7.0	6.5	6.2	29.5	22.8	11.4	1.4	73.8	35.1	49.4	50.6
28460	SNEADS FERRY	92.5	91.8	4.2	4.3	0.8	1.0	1.6	2.0	5.5	5.4	5.4	4.6	4.9	29.5	29.2	14.7	0.9	80.9	41.3	50.8	49.2
28461	SOUTHPORT	85.9	85.5	11.9	12.0	0.5	0.6	0.9	1.2	4.8	5.2	5.7	5.3	4.6	23.1	32.1	17.7	1.6	81.0	45.9	48.7	51.3
28462	SUPPLY	87.0	86.3	10.6	10.9	0.2	0.2	1.6	2.1	5.2	5.5	5.6	4.9	4.6	23.4	30.9	18.7	1.1	80.6	45.5	49.6	50.4
28463	TABOR CITY	64.1	62.9	32.5	33.1	0.1	0.1	3.3	4.2	7.4	7.3	7.4	6.6	6.7	26.2	24.2	12.8	1.4	73.8	36.4	47.8	52.2
28464	TEACHEY	44.8	43.4	47.6	47.3	0.1	0.2	11.4	14.0	7.5	7.3	6.6	6.3	5.7	27.9	23.9	13.6	1.3	74.9	37.3	46.5	53.5
28465	OAK ISLAND	98.1	97.8	0.4	0.4	0.2	0.2	0.8	1.0	3.4	3.7	3.7	3.5	3.5	19.4	38.5	23.2	1.1	87.1	52.6	48.7	51.3
28466	WALLACE	61.4	59.6	29.2	29.1	0.2	0.3	11.3	13.8	7.1	6.9	6.7	5.8	6.2	27.4	24.2	13.8	1.9	75.6	38.0	48.0	52.0
28467	CALABASH	87.5	86.4	10.4	11.0	0.3	0.4	2.4	3.2	3.0	3.2	3.6	3.3	2.5	15.3	28.6	38.5	2.0	88.1	60.5	48.4	51.6
28468	SUNSET BEACH	93.1	92.3	4.4	4.8	0.3	0.4	2.2	2.8	2.7	3.0	2.8	2.7	2.9	14.6	38.5	31.4	1.5	89.9	58.6	49.7	50.3
28469	OCEAN ISLE BEACH	93.2	92.5	3.8	3.9	0.2	0.2	2.3	2.9	4.0	4.1	4.1	3.7	3.6	20.1	34.4	25.1	1.0	85.7	52.6	48.9	51.1
28470	SHALLOTTE	82.1	81.4	14.0	14.0	0.4	0.4	3.9	5.0	5.8	5.9	6.6	6.5	6.4	24.9	27.0	15.6	1.5	78.3	41.1	49.0	51.0
28472	WHITEVILLE	65.3	64.3	30.4	30.8	0.4	0.5	2.0	2.5	6.4	6.3	6.8	6.4	6.3	27.7	25.8	12.6	1.7	76.6	38.5	48.9	51.1
28478	WILLARD	63.4	62.8	32.7	32.6	0.1	0.1	4.6	5.7	6.1	6.1	7.2	6.4	6.3	29.3	26.0	11.5	1.2	76.7	38.0	50.6	49.4
28479	WINNABOW	80.2	78.9	16.1	16.9	0.2	0.3	1.9	2.5	6.2	6.5	7.5	6.1	5.4	29.3	26.4	10.7	2.1	76.3	38.4	49.0	51.0
28480	WRIGHTSVILLE BEACH	98.1	97.8	0.3	0.4	0.6	0.7	0.7	0.8	2.9	2.4	2.5	3.6	7.8	36.8	27.1	15.4	1.4	90.6	40.2	55.7	44.3
28501	KINSTON	33.2	33.4	64.9	64.5	0.3	0.3	1.5	1.8	6.7	6.7	7.1	6.4	6.1	23.4	25.4	15.7	2.5	75.5	40.4	45.4	54.6
28504	KINSTON	70.9	68.5	25.9	27.7	0.6	0.8	3.2	4.0	5.7	6.0	6.4	6.8	6.0	26.2	28.3	13.5	1.0	77.5	40.4	49.1	50.9
28508	ALBERTSON	65.0	61.0	6.8	6.4	0.5	0.5	36.2	42.2	9.4	8.1	7.2	7.4	8.7	33.0	18.1	7.5	0.7	71.0	30.0	54.0	46.1
28510	ARAPAHOE	78.4	78.4	19.4	19.1	0.4	0.5	2.5	3.2	4.1	4.5	6.0	5.0	3.7	22.0	33.1	20.1	1.6	82.3	48.3	49.5	50.5
28511	ATLANTIC	98.0	97.9	0.2	0.3	0.1	0.1	0.9	1.1	4.4	4.5	4.6	4.9	3.4	22.0	27.5	21.4	7.4	83.0	49.9	50.3	49.8
28512	ATLANTIC BEACH	98.5	98.3	0.4	0.4	0.5	0.6	0.8	1.1	1.7	2.0	2.3	2.4	2.9	18.9	39.0	28.8	2.0	92.6	56.5	50.2	49.8
28513	AYDEN	61.1	60.1	35.3	35.5	0.3	0.3	3.7	4.6	6.3	6.4	7.1	6.7	6.1	26.4	26.4	12.7	1.9	76.0	38.8	47.6	52.5
28515	BAYBORO	51.4	50.1	46.2	47.1	0.3	0.3	1.5	1.9	5.0	5.2	6.4	6.2	6.4	28.7	26.2	13.7	2.2	79.4	40.4	53.8	46.2
28516	BEAUFORT	83.6	82.6	14.1	14.7	0.3	0.3	1.9	2.3	4.9	5.4	5.7	5.7	4.7	26.1	31.3	14.7	1.4	80.4	43.4	49.0	51.0
28518	BEULAVILLE	76.1	74.7	17.1	16.9	0.1	0.2	7.1	9.0	6.7	6.8	7.2	5.9	5.9	29.0	25.2	11.9	1.3	75.6	37.2	49.5	50.5
28520	CEDAR ISLAND	98.8	98.7	0.6	0.6	0.3	0.3	0.0	0.0	4.4	4.8	5.1	3.8	3.8	26.4	33.3	16.5	1.9	83.5	46.1	50.5	49.5
28521	CHINQUAPIN	79.8	79.4	17.8	17.7	0.1	0.1	2.9	3.6	6.1	6.3	6.7	5.5	5.0	27.9	26.3	14.5	1.7	77.2	40.1	50.8	49.2
28523	COVE CITY	62.5	61.3	35.2	36.0	0.2	0.3	1.8	2.2	5.5	5.9	7.3	6.3	5.7	25.7	30.2	12.0	1.5	77.5	41.1	48.7	51.3
28525	DEEP RUN	83.4	80.9	9.4	10.3	0.1	0.2	8.6	10.6	7.5	7.4	7.7	7.1	6.3	29.8	23.3	9.7	1.1	73.0	35.5	49.7	50.3
28526	DOVER	59.8	58.8	38.1	38.7	0.2	0.3	3.2	4.1	4.8	5.1	6.6	5.4	6.1	25.6	30.1	14.9	1.5	80.3	42.7	48.5	51.5
28527	ERNUL	74.0	73.2	23.6	24.0	0.2	0.4	1.9	2.4	4.5	4.8	5.0	4.8	7.3	38.4	26.1	8.6	0.6	82.3	37.8	62.2	37.8
28528	GLOUCESTER	99.1	99.2	0.0	0.0	0.2	0.2	0.0	0.2	4.2	4.7	6.8	5.9	3.6	25.6	33.3	14.0	1.9	80.7	44.5	48.7	51.3
28529	GRANTSBORO	80.5	79.7	17.0	17.5	0.5	0.6	1.0	1.4	5.1	5.5	5.7	5.8	5.3	26.8	28.5	15.4	2.0	80.1	42.2	52.4	47.7
28530	GRIFTON	64.1	62.6	33.2	34.2	0.2	0.2	3.0	3.7	6.5	6.9	7.2	6.6	5.6	26.8	26.9	12.4	1.1	75.1	39.1	50.1	49.9
28531	HARKERS ISLAND	98.6	98.4	0.0	0.0	0.2	0.3	0.1	0.1	3.1	3.6	4.6	4.5	3.8	21.0	37.3	20.4	1.7	85.5	50.1	48.9	51.1
28532	HAVELOCK	68.0	66.1	22.2	22.5	2.4	2.8	7.8	9.7	10.6	6.9	6.0	7.6	20.6	29.3	13.6	4.9	0.4	73.3	24.6	55.5	44.5
28537	HOBUCKEN	98.6	98.5	0.5	0.5	0.0	0.0	0.9	1.0	4.5	5.5	6.0	5.0	3.5	22.4	32.3	17.9	3.0	80.6	47.0	45.3	54.7
28538	HOOKERTON	50.1	49.1	42.8	42.2	0.1	0.1	7.3	9.1	8.1	7.8	7.1	6.2	6.7	27.5	25.1	10.4	1.0	73.2	35.9	48.0	52.0
28539	HUBERT	84.4	83.0	7.8	8.0	1.6	1.8	5.0	6.3	8.6	7.6	7.4	8.8	11.9	34.2	15.9	5.2	0.4	72.1	27.7	53.8	46.2
28540	JACKSONVILLE	69.3	68.2	21.9	21.6	1.9	2.2	6.4	7.9	9.1	7.3	6.8	9.1	13.5	30.8	16.3	6.7	0.6	73.0	27.2	52.2	47.8
28543	TARAWA TERRACE	60.5	57.8	21.1	20.7	1.6	1.9	17.0	20.6	25.0	7.2	1.7	12.5	32.0	21.2	0.5	0.0	0.0	65.7	20.6	57.9	42.1
28544	MIDWAY PARK	63.1	60.8	23.8	24.1	1.9	2.2	10.6	12.7	15.9	5.9	4.3	6.6	27.1	26.9	10.2	2.9	0.2	71.3	23.2	50.1	49.9
28546	JACKSONVILLE	64.2	62.2	25.1	25.4	3.0	3.5	7.6	9.3	9.2	7.6	7.2	7.2	10.7	32.2	18.4	6.8	0.6	71.8	29.0	48.6	51.4
28547	CAMP LEJEUNE	69.8	67.4	17.3	17.3	1.8	2.1	11.6	14.3	4.5	5.0	4.5	13.9	50.1	20.8	1.2	0.0	0.0	84.3	22.2	82.8	17.2
28551	LA GRANGE	61.0	58.5	34.8	36.5	0.4	0.4	5.0	6.0	6.9	7.2	7.4	6.7	6.2	29.5	24.9	10.2	1.0	74.1	36.3	49.2	50.8
	NORTH CAROLINA	72.1	71.2	21.6	21.6	1.5	1.8	4.7	5.9	6.7	6.6	6.8	6.7	7.1	29.8	24.2	10.8	1.4	76.2	36.2	49.2	50.8
	UNITED STATES	75.1	73.6	12.3	12.5	3.8	4.2	12.5	14.1	6.9	6.7	7.2	7.0	7.3	28.6	23.8	10.8	1.7	75.1	36.0	49.1	50.9

ZIP CODE				2004 HOUSEHOLD INCOME DISTRIBUTION (%)					MEDIAN HOUSEHOLD INCOME					2004 HOME VALUE DISTRIBUTION (%)					
#	POST OFFICE NAME	2004 Per Capita Income	2004 HH Income Base	Less than $25,000	$25,000 to $49,999	$50,000 to $99,999	$100,000 to $149,999	$150,000 or More	2004	2009	2004 National Centile	2004 State Centile	2004 Home Value Base	Less than $50,000	$50,000 to $89,999	$90,000 to $174,999	$175,000 to $399,999	$400,000 or More	2004 Median Home Value
28386	SHANNON	14147	1954	41.8	30.2	21.3	4.8	1.9	31591	36025	17	17	1457	51.8	25.3	18.5	3.7	0.6	48511
28387	SOUTHERN PINES	29139	5789	26.6	28.6	29.0	8.3	7.4	44852	51715	61	74	3591	8.5	11.8	41.8	29.2	8.7	147259
28390	SPRING LAKE	15279	7736	36.9	38.1	21.2	3.2	0.7	32097	37026	18	18	3840	28.1	34.6	32.7	4.6	0.0	79753
28391	STEDMAN	20882	1916	25.0	28.9	37.0	7.2	2.0	46876	51483	66	81	1583	22.5	36.7	32.9	7.4	0.5	78833
28392	TAR HEEL	17699	849	32.2	31.7	31.6	3.3	1.3	38009	43694	39	44	706	39.8	29.5	28.5	1.6	0.7	62037
28393	TURKEY	14314	740	41.6	30.8	23.5	2.6	1.5	30181	34253	13	13	594	30.0	43.8	19.5	6.1	0.7	69863
28394	VASS	24452	2115	23.3	35.8	27.4	7.9	5.6	43708	50096	58	70	1627	21.3	19.7	35.1	17.6	6.4	107587
28395	WADE	20743	982	32.3	33.0	25.5	5.7	3.6	35988	40073	31	34	810	21.9	30.0	37.8	10.0	0.4	88171
28396	WAGRAM	18104	1194	32.7	22.8	36.0	7.0	1.6	43525	49633	57	69	977	29.3	29.1	26.6	15.1	0.0	76016
28398	WARSAW	15759	2707	42.5	32.0	19.8	4.0	1.8	29874	32866	12	11	1935	28.9	34.5	29.3	6.5	0.9	75837
28399	WHITE OAK	13501	749	42.7	35.9	18.7	2.3	0.4	28996	32906	10	9	599	43.6	36.9	17.2	2.0	0.3	55203
28401	WILMINGTON	16612	10223	49.9	29.9	16.4	2.7	1.2	25070	28573	5	2	4112	16.1	31.3	40.2	9.1	3.4	93171
28403	WILMINGTON	26481	14516	36.8	28.7	22.6	6.4	5.5	34438	39846	26	27	5885	2.9	10.6	43.4	33.7	9.4	159086
28405	WILMINGTON	28918	11404	21.7	29.2	34.0	9.2	5.8	49002	56409	70	84	8337	8.0	7.9	55.7	18.1	10.4	138198
28409	WILMINGTON	32844	11286	14.3	21.6	38.8	16.4	9.0	64531	75113	88	95	9877	5.2	4.0	36.5	44.4	9.9	183396
28411	WILMINGTON	29319	9481	14.7	26.3	40.2	13.5	5.4	58498	67515	83	92	8063	3.9	3.5	48.4	35.7	8.5	161912
28412	WILMINGTON	27208	11345	22.3	31.6	33.2	8.4	4.5	46640	54575	65	80	7356	7.7	5.2	53.5	30.4	3.2	147217
28420	ASH	17810	1760	42.0	24.9	25.2	5.2	2.7	30139	33751	13	12	1416	23.3	28.1	29.7	16.5	2.4	87143
28421	ATKINSON	21410	704	37.1	27.0	25.3	7.2	3.4	36444	41159	33	37	585	20.3	31.5	39.5	8.7	0.0	87000
28422	BOLIVIA	22705	2386	24.9	33.3	29.9	7.8	4.1	44099	51862	59	71	1957	21.5	27.2	21.1	19.0	11.3	92704
28423	BOLTON	17958	905	38.7	31.3	25.5	2.8	1.8	34574	39342	26	27	749	29.8	29.0	32.0	9.2	0.0	77090
28425	BURGAW	16484	3827	38.1	31.8	24.1	4.0	2.0	33815	37933	23	24	2977	20.3	24.5	42.4	11.9	0.9	95958
28428	CAROLINA BEACH	28780	2560	24.3	35.9	27.5	6.7	5.6	42355	49426	54	64	1845	3.7	5.5	39.8	43.1	7.9	177131
28429	CASTLE HAYNE	22156	2747	20.9	34.3	34.6	7.6	2.7	45668	52391	63	77	2233	13.9	14.2	52.3	18.5	1.0	114773
28430	CERRO GORDO	17084	829	46.6	24.6	21.2	4.5	3.1	27663	31216	8	7	665	31.7	31.6	29.2	7.1	0.5	69479
28431	CHADBOURN	14142	2498	48.4	28.5	19.2	3.1	0.8	26131	29638	6	3	1802	35.9	28.9	29.3	5.6	0.3	66476
28432	CLARENDON	15167	1149	40.6	34.1	21.3	3.1	0.9	30408	35211	13	13	929	22.2	29.5	33.7	13.2	1.4	88133
28433	CLARKTON	13792	1977	48.5	31.4	17.4	1.6	1.1	25831	28799	6	3	1553	29.5	39.2	25.9	4.6	0.8	67431
28434	COUNCIL	16503	709	41.3	34.0	19.8	4.2	0.7	29952	33807	12	11	593	28.3	35.8	29.5	6.4	0.0	75339
28435	CURRIE	18992	975	43.2	24.1	26.1	3.9	2.8	33133	36829	21	21	791	22.3	20.6	41.9	13.9	1.4	96647
28436	DELCO	17289	745	37.6	31.5	26.4	2.6	1.9	34353	39504	25	26	615	22.6	30.7	32.5	14.2	0.0	83788
28438	EVERGREEN	16278	829	45.1	31.5	15.7	4.5	3.3	28526	32555	10	8	652	42.0	23.0	26.4	8.3	0.3	65231
28439	FAIR BLUFF	13908	819	53.2	26.7	16.7	2.4	0.9	22698	25672	3	1	614	45.1	28.3	22.0	4.6	0.0	53704
28441	GARLAND	16338	1064	38.1	34.0	22.0	2.9	3.0	32339	36530	19	19	818	37.3	36.2	21.9	4.0	0.6	70377
28442	HALLSBORO	17920	776	40.6	27.6	26.7	4.3	0.9	34253	38852	25	26	607	32.3	29.5	30.8	6.9	0.5	73679
28443	HAMPSTEAD	26583	4990	22.3	29.5	34.9	8.7	4.5	48395	55814	69	83	4239	14.3	12.8	33.6	33.0	6.3	139063
28444	HARRELLS	14193	727	46.4	30.1	19.5	3.0	1.0	27979	31382	9	7	569	35.3	34.6	25.7	4.0	0.4	64306
28445	HOLLY RIDGE	25299	1981	26.9	31.0	30.5	6.4	5.2	42926	49395	56	66	1485	15.3	18.9	29.1	27.9	8.8	119763
28447	IVANHOE	13549	278	45.7	31.3	19.4	3.2	0.4	28881	32190	10	9	220	40.0	33.6	21.8	3.2	1.4	58800
28448	KELLY	20839	453	41.5	28.5	21.6	5.1	3.3	29510	33745	11	10	382	28.5	26.7	38.7	5.5	0.5	80000
28449	KURE BEACH	29315	771	26.3	28.8	30.9	9.2	4.8	44480	51469	60	73	584	0.2	8.2	28.1	55.3	8.2	196467
28450	LAKE WACCAMAW	24200	911	33.4	24.6	30.9	6.9	4.3	39806	45877	45	50	725	18.6	24.6	28.8	25.2	2.8	104038
28451	LELAND	18641	6872	29.9	33.6	29.2	5.2	2.1	38973	44907	43	47	5404	21.2	23.0	40.9	13.1	1.8	98280
28452	LONGWOOD	19089	79	40.5	24.1	25.3	5.1	5.1	31727	33893	17	17	67	25.4	25.4	19.4	25.4	4.5	87500
28453	MAGNOLIA	13586	1343	43.0	32.2	21.4	2.0	1.3	29908	32678	12	11	990	33.1	25.4	31.1	9.5	0.9	78352
28454	MAPLE HILL	15028	977	40.2	34.2	21.3	1.9	2.4	32203	36286	18	18	771	30.4	29.6	35.0	4.4	0.7	79746
28455	NAKINA	15702	697	41.2	29.6	26.5	2.2	0.6	35436	40274	29	31	570	37.0	33.0	20.0	10.0	0.0	57957
28456	RIEGELWOOD	17232	1297	37.2	29.6	26.2	4.8	2.2	35186	40162	28	30	1069	25.0	35.0	34.1	5.7	0.3	78836
28457	ROCKY POINT	16952	3236	33.9	32.2	27.0	6.1	0.9	36537	42416	34	37	2557	17.8	20.3	46.3	14.5	1.1	102905
28458	ROSE HILL	16992	2134	40.4	30.3	22.1	3.8	3.5	31624	35412	17	17	1658	28.0	33.8	30.2	7.1	0.8	75472
28460	SNEADS FERRY	21526	2693	27.5	36.4	27.4	7.1	1.6	39651	44238	45	50	2122	18.1	18.4	35.3	26.1	2.1	114315
28461	SOUTHPORT	26083	4957	28.7	30.8	28.0	7.4	5.1	41173	47137	50	59	3903	16.6	18.0	32.0	24.0	9.5	122739
28462	SUPPLY	21494	5295	36.1	30.1	25.3	5.5	3.1	35739	40218	31	33	4407	18.8	27.2	31.8	17.0	5.2	96136
28463	TABOR CITY	14721	2901	48.5	28.7	18.9	2.6	1.5	25872	29377	6	3	2183	33.9	35.2	25.1	5.5	0.3	66863
28464	TEACHEY	17845	722	35.3	37.8	19.5	4.6	2.8	32135	35714	18	18	566	25.1	31.5	33.6	8.3	1.6	80000
28465	OAK ISLAND	29213	3625	19.9	32.4	36.0	8.2	3.5	47869	54884	68	82	2952	3.4	12.6	50.6	27.5	5.9	141592
28466	WALLACE	16712	3355	41.5	30.1	21.8	4.3	2.4	31098	34796	15	15	2492	20.4	33.1	34.6	11.2	0.8	86228
28467	CALABASH	25880	2903	25.6	39.2	28.1	4.0	3.1	39113	43788	43	48	2537	6.0	12.3	52.9	25.3	3.6	137928
28468	SUNSET BEACH	35581	1938	24.9	26.1	32.3	8.7	8.1	48827	57309	70	84	1660	3.9	19.5	29.8	36.0	10.8	164648
28469	OCEAN ISLE BEACH	30639	2307	26.6	29.4	25.8	11.1	7.2	44689	50998	60	73	1922	8.7	16.7	27.3	35.2	12.1	164516
28470	SHALLOTTE	18960	3336	35.3	31.5	24.3	5.8	3.1	35749	40211	31	33	2725	17.5	22.4	39.4	18.4	2.4	105771
28472	WHITEVILLE	18234	8045	42.9	29.2	21.4	3.9	2.7	30041	34878	12	12	5951	27.8	27.3	32.6	11.4	0.9	82438
28478	WILLARD	17359	2406	35.8	35.4	22.8	4.1	1.9	34901	39136	27	29	1962	23.7	31.2	39.1	5.1	1.0	84809
28479	WINNABOW	16804	1137	32.3	35.4	26.5	4.5	1.3	36832	41171	35	39	937	31.0	17.1	39.9	9.7	2.4	93558
28480	WRIGHTSVILLE BEACH	46686	1368	14.9	25.7	34.1	13.6	11.6	63931	76234	88	94	784	0.0	1.3	4.7	23.2	70.8	574742
28501	KINSTON	16762	8837	48.3	29.3	17.3	2.9	2.2	26119	29562	6	3	4948	26.4	37.6	27.9	7.1	1.0	73025
28504	KINSTON	22816	8969	27.0	32.3	30.0	7.2	3.6	42173	47920	53	63	6623	20.4	23.7	42.4	12.3	1.2	100252
28508	ALBERTSON	13250	869	35.2	36.9	23.3	4.3	0.4	34662	40331	26	28	681	49.8	15.0	29.5	5.6	0.2	50417
28510	ARAPAHOE	22271	670	30.9	28.4	30.6	7.5	2.7	38183	45306	40	45	554	18.6	19.0	36.6	22.7	3.1	109593
28511	ATLANTIC	22090	360	38.6	34.4	17.5	5.8	3.6	32506	37514	19	19	303	25.1	23.1	41.3	9.2	1.3	92292
28512	ATLANTIC BEACH	37556	1916	19.7	31.0	32.1	10.5	6.7	49356	57778	71	85	1473	4.3	5.4	22.9	49.6	17.9	231130
28513	AYDEN	18847	3596	40.2	25.8	27.4	4.9	1.8	33685	39235	23	24	2381	19.2	36.7	36.9	6.6	0.6	83435
28515	BAYBORO	14335	1040	41.6	32.2	21.6	4.1	0.4	30691	33817	14	14	812	36.0	32.4	24.9	6.2	0.6	69615
28516	BEAUFORT	22328	5009	32.0	32.4	26.7	5.4	3.5	38010	43131	39	45	3783	18.9	21.9	31.1	21.9	6.2	113136
28518	BEULAVILLE	18755	2822	37.9	31.1	25.0	3.9	2.2	33745	37778	23	24	2267	32.7	28.0	32.1	7.0	0.2	74679
28520	CEDAR ISLAND	23177	135	23.7	25.2	40.0	9.6	1.5	50589	58947	73	86	115	21.7	23.5	40.9	13.0	0.9	99167
28521	CHINQUAPIN	18322	633	38.6	28.9	25.9	4.4	2.2	34493	38456	26	27	538	19.9	35.1	38.1	6.5	0.4	83250
28523	COVE CITY	17115	1032	35.8	31.8	26.6	4.9	1.0	34170	38512	25	26	850	32.5	30.4	29.9	6.9	0.4	74493
28525	DEEP RUN	19632	1278	34.7	27.0	33.5	2.8	2.0	37849	42715	39	44	1036	32.8	31.7	31.1	4.4	0.0	73958
28526	DOVER	15251	908	47.1	24.7	24.6	2.9	0.8	26807	29033	7	5	724	39.4	29.3	21.0	7.9	2.5	59747
28527	ERNUL	20521	207	27.5	33.3	34.8	3.4	1.0	41222	46934	50	59	174	25.9	28.7	32.2	13.2	0.0	83333
28528	GLOUCESTER	26242	206	25.2	34.5	34.0	4.9	1.5	42366	48920	54	64	176	21.0	9.1	32.4	33.5	4.0	147727
28529	GRANTSBORO	18937	780	29.2	33.5	31.7	4.7	0.9	39057	45301	43	48	645	34.7	25.3	31.2	8.4	0.5	77177
28530	GRIFTON	17623	2432	31.0	37.3	26.7	3.8	1.3	38592	45020	41	46	1909	23.9	34.9	33.3	6.8	1.2	79629
28531	HARKERS ISLAND	23321	652	33.3	29.0	28.8	3.8	5.1	36866	41920	35	39	553	11.9	16.3	50.1	21.7	0.0	120357
28532	HAVELOCK	15852	8542	26.6	39.4	28.4	4.4	1.2	38434	43749	41	46	4170	16.0	23.3	52.0	7.5	1.3	100816
28537	HOBUCKEN	16142	93	45.2	33.3	20.4	1.1	0.0	29432	30900	11	10	75	45.3	41.3	6.7	4.0	2.7	55833
28538	HOOKERTON	14589	1462	39.6	31.4	25.8	2.2	1.0	31999	35300	18	18	1141	26.4	37.8	29.9	6.0	0.0	73571
28539	HUBERT	16663	4969	26.0	36.7	31.8	4.1	1.4	39335	44260	44	49	3788	25.6	27.8	37.1	7.4	2.0	87331
28540	JACKSONVILLE	16538	17190	31.0	36.3	26.5	4.5	1.7	36159	40084	32	35	10045	17.1	34.2	42.3	5.6	0.8	88839
28543	TARAWA TERRACE	11099	1909	43.2	50.6	5.6	0.5	0.2	26734	30111	7	4	127	70.1	8.7	10.2	11.0	0.0	31196
28544	MIDWAY PARK	13576	2335	38.0	43.3	15.5	2.7	0.5	29606	33103	11	10	863	31.1	34.0	30.8	3.8	0.4	67782
28546	JACKSONVILLE	18202	13305	25.8	37.4	29.6	5.3	1.9	41120	45669	50	58	8161	8.5	36.0	44.8	10.2	0.5	94767
28547	CAMP LEJEUNE	12921	1492	9.1	49.4	34.9	5.1	1.5	46881	52202	66	81	9	0.0	0.0	100.0	0.0	0.0	112500
28551	LA GRANGE	19128	4827	32.3	31.8	28.6	5.3	1.9	37624	42700	38	42	3779	29.9	27.7	30.5	10.2	1.7	80288
	NORTH CAROLINA	23743		27.0	29.8	30.1	8.5	4.7	43794	50711				14.5	20.0	39.7	21.7	4.1	115673
	UNITED STATES	25866		24.7	27.1	30.8	10.9	6.5	48124	56710				10.9	15.0	33.7	30.1	10.4	145905

ZIP CODE #	POST OFFICE NAME	FINANCIAL SERVICES: Auto Loan	Home Loan	Investments	Retirement Plans	THE HOME: Home Improvements: Home Repair	Lawn & Garden	Furnishings: Computers & Hardware	Major Appliances	TV, Radio, Sound Equipment	Furniture	ENTERTAINMENT: Dine out/ Carry out	Sports Equipment	Fees & Tickets	Toys & Games	Travel	Cable TV	PERSONAL: Apparel & Services	Auto Repairs	Health Insurance	Pets & Supplies
28386	SHANNON	74	60	41	56	63	68	58	65	62	59	75	76	53	71	57	63	71	65	70	83
28387	SOUTHERN PINES	91	90	98	89	91	101	91	93	93	92	115	104	91	110	92	95	111	93	97	104
28390	SPRING LAKE	59	52	48	52	51	55	56	56	57	56	71	66	53	68	54	56	69	58	55	63
28391	STEDMAN	90	73	50	68	76	83	70	79	75	72	92	93	64	86	70	77	86	79	86	101
28392	TAR HEEL	70	63	49	61	65	69	60	65	62	61	76	76	57	73	60	62	73	64	67	79
28393	TURKEY	72	49	23	42	55	63	47	59	57	48	66	70	40	63	48	61	61	58	72	83
28394	VASS	91	85	72	83	85	90	82	87	82	84	102	100	78	97	81	81	98	87	86	102
28395	WADE	88	66	40	59	73	82	63	75	72	64	86	89	57	84	64	77	80	74	88	102
28396	WAGRAM	83	66	43	61	70	77	64	73	69	65	84	85	58	79	63	71	79	72	80	94
28398	WARSAW	64	50	39	46	52	60	53	57	59	52	71	67	48	68	52	61	67	58	65	72
28399	WHITE OAK	66	45	21	39	51	58	43	54	52	44	61	64	37	58	44	56	55	53	66	76
28401	WILMINGTON	50	42	50	42	41	48	50	48	53	49	65	56	48	62	48	53	63	51	50	54
28403	WILMINGTON	73	65	81	69	64	71	82	73	80	77	101	91	77	97	76	75	98	79	68	81
28405	WILMINGTON	95	95	98	95	95	101	95	96	94	96	118	110	95	115	95	93	115	96	94	108
28409	WILMINGTON	116	132	134	130	132	135	119	122	115	119	143	143	125	151	123	114	141	118	117	141
28411	WILMINGTON	97	112	114	114	108	107	102	102	95	104	120	119	106	123	102	91	119	99	90	112
28412	WILMINGTON	86	85	89	86	85	90	87	86	86	85	107	102	86	107	86	84	104	87	84	99
28420	ASH	76	65	46	61	66	72	62	69	65	63	79	80	57	75	61	66	75	68	72	85
28421	ATKINSON	95	64	29	55	72	83	61	77	74	62	87	92	52	82	62	80	79	76	95	109
28422	BOLIVIA	91	81	66	77	84	94	76	85	80	80	99	93	74	89	79	83	93	84	93	102
28423	BOLTON	88	59	27	51	67	77	57	71	69	58	81	85	49	77	58	74	74	71	88	101
28425	BURGAW	74	56	35	52	60	68	55	64	62	56	74	75	50	70	55	64	68	63	72	83
28428	CAROLINA BEACH	96	74	50	68	83	95	73	86	83	72	98	99	66	95	76	88	90	85	102	113
28429	CASTLE HAYNE	87	82	71	81	84	88	79	83	80	79	99	98	78	99	79	80	95	82	84	99
28430	CERRO GORDO	82	55	25	47	62	72	53	66	64	54	75	79	45	71	54	69	68	66	82	94
28431	CHADBOURN	60	45	30	40	49	56	44	52	51	45	61	60	40	58	45	55	57	51	61	68
28432	CLARENDON	71	47	22	41	54	62	46	57	55	47	65	68	39	61	47	60	59	57	70	81
28433	CLARKTON	59	44	26	40	48	55	44	51	50	44	60	60	39	56	44	53	55	51	61	67
28434	COUNCIL	74	49	22	43	56	64	48	60	57	48	67	71	40	64	48	62	61	59	73	85
28435	CURRIE	78	65	45	61	67	73	62	70	66	64	80	81	57	76	62	67	76	69	74	88
28436	DELCO	83	55	25	48	63	72	53	67	64	54	76	80	46	72	54	69	69	66	82	95
28438	EVERGREEN	77	52	24	45	59	68	50	63	60	51	71	75	43	67	51	65	64	62	77	89
28439	FAIR BLUFF	55	40	29	35	43	51	41	47	49	42	58	54	37	53	41	52	54	48	57	62
28441	GARLAND	81	54	25	47	61	70	52	65	63	53	74	78	45	70	53	68	67	65	80	92
28442	HALLSBORO	75	55	31	49	60	68	53	63	61	54	72	75	46	68	53	64	66	63	75	86
28443	HAMPSTEAD	101	87	69	81	93	105	81	94	88	84	107	104	77	98	86	92	100	92	107	117
28444	HARRELLS	70	47	21	40	53	61	45	57	55	46	64	68	39	61	46	59	58	56	70	80
28445	HOLLY RIDGE	95	80	59	75	85	93	76	87	82	77	99	101	70	95	78	84	93	86	94	110
28447	IVANHOE	65	44	20	38	49	57	42	53	51	43	60	63	36	56	43	55	54	52	65	75
28448	KELLY	86	59	29	51	67	77	57	71	68	58	80	84	49	76	58	73	73	70	86	100
28449	KURE BEACH	100	79	54	71	89	100	74	89	84	74	100	105	66	98	79	90	93	88	106	122
28450	LAKE WACCAMAW	107	80	48	71	89	101	76	92	87	76	103	109	67	100	79	93	95	91	110	127
28451	LELAND	77	72	58	70	71	74	68	72	68	70	84	83	65	80	67	67	81	72	70	85
28452	LONGWOOD	104	70	32	60	79	91	67	84	81	69	95	100	57	90	68	87	87	83	104	119
28453	MAGNOLIA	71	49	24	43	55	63	47	58	56	48	66	69	41	63	48	60	61	58	71	81
28454	MAPLE HILL	69	54	34	49	57	63	52	60	57	53	68	70	46	65	52	59	64	59	66	78
28455	NAKINA	70	52	30	47	56	63	50	59	57	51	68	70	44	64	50	59	63	59	68	79
28456	RIEGELWOOD	80	58	31	51	64	72	55	67	64	56	76	79	49	73	56	68	70	66	79	92
28457	ROCKY POINT	72	64	49	61	65	69	61	66	63	63	77	77	58	73	61	62	74	66	67	80
28458	ROSE HILL	84	57	27	49	64	74	55	68	66	56	78	82	47	73	56	71	71	68	84	97
28460	SNEADS FERRY	89	64	35	57	71	81	61	75	72	62	85	89	54	81	63	76	78	74	89	103
28461	SOUTHPORT	95	78	59	74	85	96	77	87	84	78	101	98	72	95	79	88	94	86	100	108
28462	SUPPLY	81	67	50	62	73	81	63	74	69	64	83	84	58	80	66	73	78	73	84	95
28463	TABOR CITY	64	46	31	41	50	59	48	55	56	48	66	63	42	61	47	60	61	55	67	73
28464	TEACHEY	86	58	27	51	65	76	57	70	68	57	80	83	48	75	57	73	72	69	86	98
28465	OAK ISLAND	102	82	60	75	91	104	77	92	86	78	103	105	71	99	83	92	96	90	109	122
28466	WALLACE	69	53	37	49	57	65	55	61	62	54	74	72	50	71	55	65	69	61	71	78
28467	CALABASH	80	74	70	71	78	90	70	78	73	73	91	80	70	79	74	77	85	76	89	91
28468	SUNSET BEACH	116	102	88	95	110	127	95	110	103	99	125	115	92	111	102	110	117	107	129	134
28469	OCEAN ISLE BEACH	110	91	69	83	100	113	85	100	94	86	113	113	79	107	91	100	106	99	117	131
28470	SHALLOTTE	75	67	53	63	69	76	63	70	66	65	81	79	60	75	64	67	77	69	75	86
28472	WHITEVILLE	75	57	38	53	62	71	58	66	65	58	77	77	52	74	58	68	72	66	76	85
28478	WILLARD	79	57	32	51	63	71	55	66	63	56	75	78	48	71	56	67	70	65	77	90
28479	WINNABOW	70	64	50	62	64	68	61	66	62	63	76	76	58	72	60	61	73	65	65	78
28480	WRIGHTSVILLE BEACH	133	123	152	126	126	141	127	130	132	128	164	151	126	163	130	135	158	132	137	156
28501	KINSTON	57	49	49	45	50	58	51	54	57	52	69	61	50	66	51	59	66	55	60	65
28504	KINSTON	85	79	67	76	81	87	77	81	79	77	97	93	74	95	77	80	92	80	85	96
28508	ALBERTSON	63	58	45	56	58	61	55	59	56	57	69	68	52	65	54	55	66	59	59	70
28510	ARAPAHOE	88	66	41	61	75	85	64	77	72	63	86	91	56	83	67	77	79	76	92	106
28511	ATLANTIC	73	55	36	53	60	72	61	67	68	58	80	75	54	76	60	72	73	67	80	81
28512	ATLANTIC BEACH	114	96	76	89	105	121	90	106	99	92	120	116	85	110	97	106	111	104	125	135
28513	AYDEN	71	60	50	57	62	70	62	66	67	62	81	75	58	76	61	69	76	66	73	79
28515	BAYBORO	70	47	22	41	53	61	45	56	55	46	64	67	39	61	46	59	58	56	69	80
28516	BEAUFORT	84	68	47	64	73	82	67	75	73	66	88	88	62	86	68	76	82	74	85	96
28518	BEULAVILLE	78	64	45	61	67	75	63	70	68	64	82	82	59	79	63	70	77	70	77	88
28520	CEDAR ISLAND	87	77	59	73	81	87	71	79	76	71	92	94	70	94	73	78	88	77	86	102
28521	CHINQUAPIN	82	55	25	48	63	72	53	67	64	54	76	80	45	71	54	69	69	66	82	95
28523	COVE CITY	79	56	29	49	62	70	54	66	63	55	75	78	47	70	54	67	68	65	78	91
28525	DEEP RUN	83	73	54	69	75	80	69	76	72	71	88	88	65	84	69	72	84	75	79	93
28526	DOVER	70	47	21	40	53	61	45	56	54	46	64	67	38	60	46	58	58	56	69	80
28527	ERNUL	82	61	35	55	66	74	58	69	66	60	79	82	52	75	59	69	73	69	80	93
28528	GLOUCESTER	109	76	40	72	89	99	75	93	86	74	101	112	64	99	78	91	92	91	110	129
28529	GRANTSBORO	82	59	33	56	68	76	58	70	66	58	78	85	51	77	60	69	72	69	83	97
28530	GRIFTON	75	60	41	57	64	71	59	67	64	60	78	77	55	75	59	66	73	66	74	84
28531	HARKERS ISLAND	89	70	47	63	78	88	66	79	74	65	88	92	59	87	70	79	82	78	93	108
28532	HAVELOCK	70	59	55	61	57	62	66	64	66	65	83	78	61	78	61	63	80	68	61	74
28537	HOBUCKEN	66	44	20	38	50	57	42	53	51	43	60	63	36	57	43	55	55	53	65	75
28538	HOOKERTON	66	53	36	50	56	61	51	58	55	52	67	68	47	63	51	57	63	58	63	74
28539	HUBERT	75	57	48	59	56	63	67	66	69	65	85	81	60	78	61	66	81	71	65	78
28540	JACKSONVILLE	67	59	56	60	58	63	64	63	65	63	80	76	61	77	61	62	78	66	61	72
28543	TARAWA TERRACE	48	30	29	35	28	33	45	39	46	42	58	52	39	52	37	42	55	46	36	45
28544	MIDWAY PARK	58	41	37	44	38	44	54	49	55	52	68	63	47	62	46	51	66	56	46	56
28546	JACKSONVILLE	72	66	65	68	64	68	71	69	71	70	88	84	68	85	67	67	85	72	65	78
28547	CAMP LEJEUNE	87	55	53	63	50	60	82	71	83	76	104	94	70	93	67	76	99	83	65	80
28551	LA GRANGE	78	67	50	64	70	75	65	71	68	66	83	83	61	80	65	69	79	71	75	88
	NORTH CAROLINA	90	81	73	80	83	90	81	85	84	82	103	100	79	101	81	84	99	85	88	102
	UNITED STATES	100	100	100	100	100	100	100	100	100	100	100	100	100	100	100	100	100	100	100	100

NORTH CAROLINA POPULATION CHANGE

A 28552-28705

#	POST OFFICE NAME	COUNTY FIPS CODE	POPULATION 2000	2004	2009	2000-2004 ANNUAL RATE % Rate	State Centile	HOUSEHOLDS 2000	2004	2009	% Annual Rate 2000-2004	2004 Average HH Size	FAMILIES 2000	2004	% Annual Rate 2000-2004
28552	LOWLAND	137	318	297	306	-1.6	0	143	136	142	-1.2	2.18	98	91	-1.7
28553	MARSHALLBERG	031	253	259	272	0.6	24	107	112	119	1.1	2.31	79	82	0.9
28555	MAYSVILLE	103	4601	4784	5066	0.9	34	1743	1847	1990	1.4	2.59	1291	1354	1.1
28556	MERRITT	137	1267	1404	1533	2.5	76	526	592	657	2.8	2.37	385	428	2.5
28557	MOREHEAD CITY	031	13155	13761	14650	1.1	38	5806	6197	6720	1.6	2.18	3705	3891	1.2
28560	NEW BERN	049	26705	27216	28264	0.5	20	11050	11432	12074	0.8	2.33	7514	7666	0.5
28562	NEW BERN	049	27732	29773	31557	1.7	57	11648	12721	13724	2.1	2.32	8234	8897	1.8
28570	NEWPORT	031	18350	20149	22043	2.2	71	6995	7821	8710	2.7	2.51	5189	5722	2.3
28571	ORIENTAL	137	2334	2483	2652	1.5	52	1105	1195	1296	1.9	2.07	787	839	1.5
28572	PINK HILL	061	5102	5916	6584	3.5	89	1909	2248	2534	3.9	2.58	1414	1641	3.6
28573	POLLOCKSVILLE	103	2292	2392	2454	1.0	36	887	946	991	1.5	2.44	630	663	1.2
28574	RICHLANDS	133	8965	10009	11207	2.6	80	3432	3900	4438	3.1	2.56	2549	2866	2.8
28577	SEALEVEL	031	461	452	470	-0.5	4	127	126	134	-0.2	3.11	86	84	-0.6
28578	SEVEN SPRINGS	191	4352	4590	4768	1.3	46	1495	1577	1648	1.3	2.91	1073	1116	0.9
28579	SMYRNA	031	923	942	993	0.5	21	399	416	446	1.0	2.26	293	301	0.6
28580	SNOW HILL	079	10549	10793	11278	0.5	23	3667	3805	4043	0.9	2.52	2651	2714	0.6
28581	STACY	031	206	200	209	-0.7	2	97	96	103	-0.2	2.08	70	68	-0.7
28582	STELLA	133	1034	1133	1244	2.2	70	414	461	515	2.6	2.46	304	334	2.2
28584	SWANSBORO	031	7735	8599	9517	2.5	77	3357	3791	4262	2.9	2.27	2366	2635	2.6
28585	TRENTON	103	5313	5288	5311	-0.1	8	2094	2124	2170	0.3	2.48	1539	1542	0.1
28586	VANCEBORO	049	6854	7215	7575	1.2	44	2483	2672	2866	1.7	2.52	1826	1939	1.4
28587	VANDEMERE	137	388	395	412	0.4	19	159	164	174	0.7	2.41	112	114	0.4
28590	WINTERVILLE	147	14296	16812	19222	3.9	92	5660	6782	7894	4.4	2.40	3846	4538	4.0
28594	EMERALD ISLE	031	3488	3782	4116	1.9	63	1644	1807	1997	2.3	2.09	1089	1174	1.8
28601	HICKORY	035	47844	50501	54206	1.3	47	19381	20618	22341	1.5	2.40	12884	13510	1.1
28602	HICKORY	035	27359	29012	31213	1.4	50	10707	11494	12496	1.7	2.51	7499	7935	1.3
28604	BANNER ELK	189	5389	5991	6720	2.5	77	2173	2478	2850	3.1	2.29	1425	1588	2.6
28605	BLOWING ROCK	011	3503	3913	4410	2.6	80	1581	1794	2056	3.0	2.12	928	1024	2.3
28606	BOOMER	193	1976	1965	1995	-0.1	7	772	781	804	0.3	2.52	583	582	0.0
28607	BOONE	189	27138	28919	31567	1.5	52	9898	10875	12287	2.2	2.18	4988	5362	1.7
28608	BOONE	189	155	152	164	-0.5	4	68	68	75	0.0	2.24	28	26	-1.7
28609	CATAWBA	035	5509	6012	6566	2.1	68	2150	2389	2643	2.5	2.52	1633	1785	2.1
28610	CLAREMONT	035	8375	9141	10047	2.1	68	3169	3510	3903	2.4	2.56	2341	2561	2.1
28611	COLLETTSVILLE	027	1040	1182	1291	3.1	85	421	488	542	3.5	2.42	326	373	3.2
28612	CONNELLYS SPRINGS	023	13392	13901	14416	0.9	33	5143	5406	5664	1.2	2.55	3809	3946	0.8
28613	CONOVER	035	20312	23072	25723	3.0	84	7606	8741	9840	3.3	2.61	5603	6342	3.0
28615	CRESTON	009	2216	2201	2298	-0.2	7	927	941	1003	0.4	2.34	689	691	0.1
28617	CRUMPLER	009	2252	2493	2719	2.4	75	928	1047	1162	2.9	2.37	689	770	2.7
28618	DEEP GAP	189	1728	1805	1958	1.0	37	703	749	828	1.5	2.37	508	533	1.1
28621	ELKIN	171	10445	10831	11268	0.9	32	4212	4405	4630	1.1	2.38	2933	3029	0.8
28622	ELK PARK	011	2979	3135	3388	1.2	44	1212	1304	1443	1.7	2.29	880	935	1.4
28623	ENNICE	005	1674	1794	1920	1.6	56	671	730	793	2.0	2.44	491	526	1.6
28624	FERGUSON	193	1677	1726	1772	0.7	26	707	744	777	1.2	2.25	519	538	0.9
28625	STATESVILLE	097	30398	33541	37974	2.3	73	11591	12971	14857	2.7	2.55	8746	9644	2.3
28626	FLEETWOOD	009	1638	1766	1892	1.8	59	685	754	825	2.3	2.34	505	549	2.0
28627	GLADE VALLEY	005	1257	1332	1415	1.4	49	547	592	641	1.9	2.24	396	423	1.6
28630	GRANITE FALLS	027	17709	18552	19524	1.1	39	6946	7364	7849	1.4	2.50	5143	5388	1.1
28631	GRASSY CREEK	009	635	714	782	2.8	82	274	315	352	3.3	2.27	194	220	3.0
28634	HARMONY	097	5217	5597	6242	1.7	57	1979	2150	2425	2.0	2.57	1477	1580	1.6
28635	HAYS	193	3578	3902	4152	2.1	67	1390	1547	1675	2.6	2.52	1058	1163	2.3
28636	HIDDENITE	003	5194	5522	5944	1.5	51	2001	2157	2353	1.8	2.56	1503	1600	1.5
28637	HILDEBRAN	023	1304	1471	1590	2.9	83	522	596	650	3.2	2.44	362	406	2.7
28638	HUDSON	027	10429	10757	11216	0.7	28	4156	4359	4612	1.1	2.45	3049	3149	0.8
28640	JEFFERSON	009	3885	4001	4207	0.7	27	1624	1712	1843	1.3	2.22	1112	1154	0.9
28642	JONESVILLE	197	5267	5514	5904	1.1	38	2257	2386	2576	1.3	2.31	1576	1641	1.0
28643	LANSING	009	3390	3505	3699	0.8	30	1452	1535	1657	1.3	2.26	1031	1076	1.0
28644	LAUREL SPRINGS	005	1733	1840	1956	1.4	50	752	813	881	1.9	2.24	525	559	1.5
28645	LENOIR	027	46059	47796	50263	0.9	32	18419	19404	20705	1.2	2.42	13216	13733	0.9
28649	MC GRADY	193	1010	1007	1023	-0.1	9	414	421	434	0.4	2.38	312	314	0.2
28650	MAIDEN	035	11016	11964	13106	2.0	63	4281	4719	5228	2.3	2.53	3263	3544	2.0
28651	MILLERS CREEK	193	6357	6585	6795	0.8	32	2601	2743	2876	1.3	2.40	1920	1997	0.9
28654	MORAVIAN FALLS	193	3189	3217	3289	0.2	14	1287	1317	1365	0.5	2.41	940	948	0.2
28655	MORGANTON	023	57058	58256	60106	0.5	22	21714	22387	23333	0.7	2.46	15193	15453	0.4
28657	NEWLAND	011	10634	11272	12256	1.4	49	4459	4853	5420	2.0	2.16	3130	3366	1.7
28658	NEWTON	035	24560	26407	28621	1.7	58	9427	10261	11239	2.0	2.53	6821	7310	1.6
28659	NORTH WILKESBORO	193	21483	22185	22924	0.8	29	8743	9177	9628	1.2	2.38	6163	6386	0.8
28660	OLIN	097	1616	1767	1991	2.1	69	638	707	805	2.5	2.49	483	527	2.1
28663	PINEY CREEK	005	624	661	703	1.4	49	266	287	311	1.8	2.30	192	204	1.4
28665	PURLEAR	193	2063	2185	2280	1.4	49	837	906	964	1.9	2.38	625	669	1.6
28668	ROARING GAP	005	121	132	142	2.1	68	63	70	77	2.5	1.89	44	48	2.1
28669	ROARING RIVER	193	2738	2763	2805	0.2	14	1086	1115	1149	0.6	2.48	793	801	0.2
28670	RONDA	193	2975	3066	3153	0.7	27	1186	1242	1297	1.1	2.47	900	931	0.8
28672	SCOTTVILLE	009	10	10	11	0.0	11	3	3	3	0.0	3.33	2	2	0.0
28673	SHERRILLS FORD	035	4619	5181	5749	2.7	81	1924	2191	2457	3.1	2.36	1405	1574	2.7
28675	SPARTA	005	5947	6145	6455	0.8	29	2592	2729	2923	1.2	2.18	1730	1793	0.9
28676	STATE ROAD	171	3594	3564	3652	-0.2	6	1488	1497	1553	0.1	2.37	1095	1085	-0.2
28677	STATESVILLE	097	32046	34170	38246	1.5	52	12656	13644	15444	1.8	2.46	8607	9145	1.4
28678	STONY POINT	097	4364	4735	5223	1.9	63	1678	1840	2048	2.2	2.57	1282	1388	1.9
28679	SUGAR GROVE	189	1462	1551	1699	1.4	50	603	651	725	1.8	2.38	444	472	1.5
28681	TAYLORSVILLE	003	23106	24459	26255	1.4	49	9049	9718	10583	1.7	2.49	6648	7047	1.4
28682	TERRELL	035	625	676	733	1.9	61	272	299	328	2.3	2.26	191	206	1.8
28683	THURMOND	171	1678	1651	1693	-0.4	4	685	682	707	-0.1	2.42	516	507	-0.4
28684	TODD	009	1619	1781	1962	2.3	72	650	727	814	2.7	2.45	492	542	2.3
28685	TRAPHILL	193	1856	2006	2119	1.9	61	755	827	885	2.2	2.43	562	607	1.8
28689	UNION GROVE	097	1833	1915	2084	1.0	37	713	754	827	1.3	2.54	539	561	1.0
28690	VALDESE	023	9343	9272	9456	-0.2	7	3944	3958	4073	0.1	2.31	2649	2610	-0.4
28692	VILAS	189	3794	4224	4753	2.6	78	1582	1802	2067	3.1	2.33	1055	1170	2.5
28693	WARRENSVILLE	009	1390	1418	1484	0.5	21	604	629	673	1.0	2.25	441	454	0.7
28694	WEST JEFFERSON	009	7336	7852	8388	1.6	55	3219	3514	3829	2.1	2.22	2247	2416	1.7
28697	WILKESBORO	193	11624	11760	12002	0.3	16	4757	4889	5067	0.7	2.32	3353	3398	0.3
28698	ZIONVILLE	189	1780	2162	2539	4.7	95	758	939	1123	5.2	2.30	539	655	4.7
28701	ALEXANDER	021	3653	3983	4368	2.1	67	1443	1603	1785	2.5	2.48	1082	1181	2.1
28702	ALMOND	075	673	683	715	0.4	18	294	306	328	1.0	2.23	215	221	0.7
28704	ARDEN	021	14796	16111	17535	2.1	65	6034	6680	7375	2.4	2.38	4197	4550	1.9
28705	BAKERSVILLE	121	7392	8018	8689	1.9	63	3092	3409	3754	2.3	2.34	2300	2505	2.0
	NORTH CAROLINA					1.9					2.2	2.46			1.8
	UNITED STATES					1.2					1.3	2.58			1.1

ZIP CODE #	POST OFFICE NAME	RACE (%) White 2000	White 2004	Black 2000	Black 2004	Asian/Pacific 2000	Asian/Pacific 2004	% Hispanic Origin 2000	% Hispanic Origin 2004	2004 AGE DISTRIBUTION (%) 0-4	5-9	10-14	15-19	20-24	25-44	45-64	65-84	85+	18+	MEDIAN AGE 2004	% 2004 Males	% 2004 Females
28552	LOWLAND	99.1	99.0	0.0	0.0	0.0	0.0	0.6	0.7	5.1	5.4	6.1	5.4	3.4	23.6	30.6	17.5	3.0	80.5	45.8	46.1	53.9
28553	MARSHALLBERG	99.2	98.8	0.0	0.0	0.4	0.4	0.0	0.0	4.3	4.6	7.0	5.8	3.5	25.9	33.2	13.9	1.9	80.3	44.4	49.0	51.0
28555	MAYSVILLE	67.3	66.6	28.8	28.9	0.5	0.7	2.6	3.3	6.9	7.0	7.6	6.3	5.8	29.0	25.4	10.9	1.0	74.6	37.5	49.7	50.3
28556	MERRITT	79.5	78.4	18.0	18.7	0.6	0.6	1.3	1.8	4.3	4.7	5.3	5.5	4.7	21.2	32.5	20.3	1.6	82.3	47.8	47.9	52.1
28557	MOREHEAD CITY	86.7	86.1	9.9	9.9	0.8	0.9	1.7	2.2	5.0	5.3	6.2	5.9	5.3	24.9	28.7	16.4	2.4	79.8	43.3	47.4	52.6
28560	NEW BERN	72.8	72.3	24.1	24.1	0.5	0.6	2.7	3.5	6.4	6.4	6.4	5.8	5.8	26.1	26.0	15.4	1.8	77.4	40.6	48.3	51.7
28562	NEW BERN	72.2	71.5	25.0	25.3	0.6	0.8	1.8	2.3	5.6	6.1	6.6	5.9	4.8	23.5	27.7	18.1	1.8	78.0	43.4	47.2	52.8
28570	NEWPORT	90.5	90.0	6.0	6.0	0.8	1.0	2.4	3.0	5.9	6.1	6.9	6.6	6.0	28.2	27.8	11.5	1.1	76.9	39.5	50.1	49.9
28571	ORIENTAL	78.3	77.3	19.7	20.4	0.3	0.4	1.3	1.6	2.9	3.4	4.1	3.9	3.5	14.7	35.9	29.0	2.6	87.0	55.4	48.1	51.9
28572	PINK HILL	81.7	79.5	10.5	11.1	0.2	0.2	9.9	12.2	7.2	7.1	7.0	6.0	6.2	30.0	23.9	11.1	1.5	74.9	35.6	51.3	48.7
28573	POLLOCKSVILLE	57.0	56.4	40.9	41.2	0.2	0.3	2.1	2.5	5.2	5.9	7.0	6.7	5.2	21.6	29.1	16.7	2.6	77.3	43.9	47.5	52.6
28574	RICHLANDS	84.1	83.2	11.3	11.2	0.4	0.4	4.2	5.4	7.0	6.8	6.7	6.5	7.2	30.4	24.5	9.9	1.1	75.5	35.7	49.4	50.6
28577	SEALEVEL	98.1	98.0	0.2	0.2	0.0	0.0	0.9	0.9	4.7	4.7	4.4	4.9	3.3	22.4	27.9	21.2	6.6	83.2	49.3	50.2	49.8
28578	SEVEN SPRINGS	68.2	63.9	8.4	8.3	0.2	0.2	27.2	32.7	8.5	7.6	7.0	6.0	8.3	33.5	20.3	8.2	0.8	73.5	31.3	52.7	47.3
28579	SMYRNA	99.0	98.8	0.1	0.1	0.2	0.2	0.4	0.4	4.8	5.1	6.6	5.5	4.1	26.4	31.9	13.9	1.7	79.9	43.4	49.3	50.7
28580	SNOW HILL	52.5	51.2	42.7	42.8	0.1	0.1	5.4	6.7	6.1	6.2	6.4	5.8	7.2	31.5	24.2	10.9	1.8	77.8	36.6	53.8	46.2
28581	STACY	99.0	99.0	0.5	0.5	0.0	0.0	0.0	0.0	4.5	4.5	5.0	4.0	4.0	26.0	32.5	17.0	2.5	83.0	46.2	50.5	49.5
28582	STELLA	93.7	93.3	3.4	3.4	0.7	0.8	2.0	2.6	5.7	6.0	7.2	6.0	5.0	28.0	28.6	12.4	1.0	77.3	40.8	50.0	50.0
28584	SWANSBORO	93.2	92.6	3.6	3.7	0.7	0.8	2.1	2.6	5.5	5.6	6.1	5.6	5.1	25.6	28.5	16.5	1.6	79.3	42.8	49.1	50.9
28585	TRENTON	66.4	65.2	29.8	30.2	0.1	0.2	3.2	4.0	6.1	6.5	7.0	6.8	5.3	26.6	26.9	13.1	1.7	75.9	40.0	48.8	51.2
28586	VANCEBORO	68.4	67.6	28.6	29.0	0.2	0.2	2.9	3.6	6.7	6.8	7.0	5.9	6.9	30.9	25.2	9.7	1.1	75.9	36.3	52.5	47.5
28587	VANDEMERE	34.3	33.2	64.2	64.8	0.5	0.5	1.3	1.8	4.8	5.1	6.8	7.6	6.1	21.5	30.4	16.0	1.8	78.2	43.7	46.8	53.2
28590	WINTERVILLE	69.9	68.1	26.4	27.5	1.3	1.5	2.2	2.8	7.7	6.8	7.5	7.8	8.8	33.5	20.6	6.5	0.8	73.8	31.6	47.4	52.7
28594	EMERALD ISLE	96.7	96.3	0.8	0.8	0.7	0.8	1.6	2.0	3.5	3.0	3.5	3.6	3.5	22.6	37.9	21.6	0.8	87.4	51.2	51.3	48.7
28601	HICKORY	88.0	86.6	4.9	5.0	2.9	3.4	6.8	8.5	6.5	6.4	6.6	6.3	6.7	30.0	24.3	11.7	1.6	77.1	36.8	49.1	50.9
28602	HICKORY	77.6	76.9	15.4	14.9	3.7	4.3	4.7	5.8	6.7	6.8	7.4	6.3	6.0	29.8	25.1	10.8	1.1	75.2	36.9	49.5	50.5
28604	BANNER ELK	97.0	96.6	1.0	1.0	0.3	0.4	1.1	1.4	4.8	5.3	5.4	6.7	6.6	27.5	29.3	12.8	1.5	81.5	40.8	50.3	49.7
28605	BLOWING ROCK	97.6	97.3	0.6	0.7	0.5	0.6	0.8	1.1	3.7	4.0	4.8	5.1	5.1	26.4	32.0	16.5	2.4	84.4	45.6	48.6	51.4
28606	BOOMER	86.6	85.5	11.8	12.6	0.2	0.2	1.5	2.0	6.2	6.3	6.7	5.9	6.1	28.4	27.5	11.8	1.2	77.2	39.1	50.2	49.8
28607	BOONE	95.6	95.1	2.2	2.3	0.8	1.0	1.7	2.1	3.3	3.4	4.0	15.7	23.3	20.4	20.1	8.6	1.2	86.5	25.2	49.6	50.4
28608	BOONE	92.9	92.1	2.6	2.6	3.2	4.6	1.3	1.3	4.0	2.0	3.3	6.6	28.3	27.0	19.1	9.9	0.0	87.5	27.8	52.0	48.0
28609	CATAWBA	89.7	88.8	8.3	8.8	0.7	0.8	1.9	2.5	6.1	6.5	7.2	6.0	5.3	31.0	26.9	9.9	1.2	76.4	38.3	50.9	49.1
28610	CLAREMONT	90.3	89.4	5.5	5.5	2.3	2.8	2.3	2.9	6.1	6.4	7.1	6.0	5.4	30.1	26.7	10.2	1.9	76.7	38.2	50.2	49.8
28611	COLLETTSVILLE	96.9	96.5	1.6	1.8	0.3	0.3	0.8	1.0	5.7	5.8	6.0	5.3	4.9	28.3	29.3	13.8	0.9	79.3	41.8	52.5	47.6
28612	CONNELLYS SPRINGS	93.9	92.9	0.9	1.0	3.6	4.3	1.0	1.3	6.3	6.6	7.3	6.5	5.6	30.5	25.0	10.9	1.3	75.6	37.5	49.8	50.2
28613	CONOVER	85.8	83.9	5.9	6.1	4.8	5.7	6.1	7.7	7.0	7.0	7.0	5.8	5.7	31.3	24.2	10.8	1.2	75.4	36.2	49.1	50.9
28615	CRESTON	98.6	98.4	0.1	0.1	0.3	0.3	1.2	1.5	5.6	5.6	5.3	5.0	5.5	25.8	30.0	15.1	2.0	80.5	43.0	50.2	49.8
28617	CRUMPLER	95.6	95.0	1.5	1.5	0.2	0.3	3.1	3.9	5.3	5.4	4.7	5.2	6.3	26.4	30.0	14.9	1.8	81.2	43.0	50.6	49.4
28618	DEEP GAP	97.0	96.6	0.8	0.8	0.5	0.6	1.0	1.4	4.9	5.3	7.5	6.4	6.5	29.3	28.5	10.5	1.1	78.1	39.0	51.7	48.3
28621	ELKIN	90.8	89.7	3.4	3.3	0.2	0.2	7.9	9.7	5.9	6.0	6.5	5.5	5.5	27.1	24.7	15.5	3.4	78.3	40.7	47.8	52.2
28622	ELK PARK	97.1	96.5	0.7	0.7	0.1	0.2	2.3	3.0	5.3	5.8	6.5	7.6	6.5	29.1	25.9	11.9	1.4	78.8	37.9	50.9	49.2
28623	ENNICE	95.0	94.0	1.0	1.1	0.1	0.1	5.7	7.3	6.7	6.8	5.8	5.0	5.2	28.1	26.5	14.3	1.6	77.7	39.7	49.8	50.2
28624	FERGUSON	94.6	94.2	4.5	4.8	0.0	0.0	0.6	0.8	5.5	5.7	4.7	4.8	4.6	27.0	32.0	13.9	1.9	81.3	43.6	51.2	48.8
28625	STATESVILLE	84.4	82.4	10.8	11.6	1.8	2.2	3.6	4.9	6.6	6.7	7.1	6.2	5.8	29.0	25.8	11.4	1.5	75.8	37.9	49.3	50.7
28626	FLEETWOOD	97.7	97.6	1.3	1.3	0.1	0.1	1.9	2.3	5.4	5.8	5.6	4.8	4.4	29.3	29.6	13.4	1.8	80.3	41.7	50.9	49.2
28627	GLADE VALLEY	95.7	95.2	1.6	1.6	0.2	0.2	3.3	4.1	4.7	4.7	4.9	4.3	4.4	23.7	32.2	19.0	2.2	83.1	47.5	50.2	49.8
28630	GRANITE FALLS	96.1	95.4	1.0	1.1	0.4	0.5	2.9	3.6	6.7	6.8	6.9	5.8	5.4	31.7	25.0	10.4	1.2	76.1	37.2	49.7	50.3
28631	GRASSY CREEK	95.1	94.3	0.6	0.7	0.0	0.0	4.3	5.2	4.8	5.2	5.7	4.8	4.3	24.4	30.8	18.4	1.7	81.4	45.6	53.1	46.9
28634	HARMONY	85.3	83.3	11.0	12.0	0.3	0.4	4.6	6.2	7.0	7.2	7.6	5.9	5.5	30.0	24.5	10.9	1.4	74.9	36.7	49.7	50.3
28635	HAYS	98.3	97.9	0.3	0.3	0.1	0.2	1.3	1.7	6.6	6.8	7.0	6.1	5.3	30.3	25.5	11.4	1.2	75.8	37.6	49.8	50.2
28636	HIDDENITE	93.3	92.4	3.1	3.2	0.3	0.4	4.0	4.9	7.4	7.3	6.6	5.9	6.1	31.2	24.6	9.6	1.3	75.2	36.3	50.9	49.2
28637	HILDEBRAN	93.4	92.3	0.9	1.0	3.8	4.6	0.9	1.2	6.2	6.1	5.9	5.6	5.4	29.4	26.2	13.3	1.9	78.4	39.8	48.3	51.7
28638	HUDSON	97.0	96.4	0.7	0.8	0.4	0.5	2.3	3.0	6.5	6.5	6.3	5.5	5.5	31.0	26.0	11.7	1.1	77.4	38.0	49.5	50.5
28640	JEFFERSON	95.9	95.1	1.1	1.1	0.4	0.4	3.2	4.2	5.1	5.3	5.2	4.7	5.0	26.4	27.5	17.2	3.7	81.7	43.9	48.5	51.5
28642	JONESVILLE	88.7	87.7	8.4	8.8	0.1	0.2	3.7	4.7	6.3	6.3	6.5	5.5	5.2	27.4	25.8	15.5	1.7	77.5	40.4	46.8	53.3
28643	LANSING	98.0	97.7	0.2	0.2	0.3	0.3	1.5	1.8	4.8	5.0	5.5	5.3	5.4	25.7	30.0	16.0	2.5	81.5	44.0	49.6	50.4
28644	LAUREL SPRINGS	97.4	97.0	0.5	0.4	0.1	0.1	2.9	3.6	4.9	5.6	5.5	4.0	4.4	27.3	29.4	16.7	2.3	81.6	43.8	51.6	48.4
28645	LENOIR	88.5	87.7	8.5	8.7	0.5	0.5	2.5	3.2	6.3	6.3	6.6	5.7	5.5	28.4	26.5	13.1	1.7	77.3	39.3	49.6	50.4
28649	MC GRADY	98.7	98.3	0.1	0.1	0.0	0.0	1.3	1.7	6.8	6.9	6.8	5.9	5.7	31.0	25.1	10.8	1.2	75.9	37.0	48.8	51.2
28650	MAIDEN	90.6	89.7	6.1	6.2	0.9	1.1	3.5	4.5	6.4	6.4	6.8	6.3	6.1	30.4	26.1	10.5	0.9	76.4	37.4	50.0	50.0
28651	MILLERS CREEK	97.3	96.6	0.1	0.1	0.1	0.2	2.7	3.6	6.2	6.1	6.4	5.5	5.4	31.2	27.0	11.0	1.2	78.0	38.7	49.8	50.2
28654	MORAVIAN FALLS	92.2	91.3	4.4	4.6	0.7	0.8	3.1	4.0	6.4	6.5	6.1	4.8	5.7	28.3	27.8	12.8	1.7	78.0	40.0	49.4	50.6
28655	MORGANTON	81.9	80.1	9.8	10.0	3.8	4.5	4.8	6.0	6.2	6.2	6.6	7.5	6.6	28.1	25.1	12.1	1.6	77.0	37.6	50.9	49.1
28657	NEWLAND	94.9	94.4	2.6	2.7	0.2	0.3	2.6	3.3	4.8	5.2	5.7	4.8	5.5	29.1	27.2	15.7	2.1	81.3	41.6	51.8	48.2
28658	NEWTON	83.8	82.0	8.9	9.2	3.0	3.6	6.0	7.7	6.5	6.6	7.0	6.0	6.0	30.3	25.1	11.1	1.4	76.3	37.3	50.2	49.9
28659	NORTH WILKESBORO	90.1	89.4	6.1	6.1	0.4	0.5	5.1	6.3	6.2	6.4	6.5	5.4	5.6	29.0	26.2	13.0	1.8	77.6	39.1	49.8	50.2
28660	OLIN	90.0	88.5	6.5	7.2	0.4	0.4	4.2	5.6	6.3	6.5	6.9	6.1	5.8	29.8	26.9	10.4	1.4	76.7	37.9	50.9	49.1
28663	PINEY CREEK	97.6	97.1	0.5	0.5	0.0	0.0	3.5	4.4	4.2	5.0	5.9	4.2	3.6	26.2	30.3	18.3	2.3	82.5	45.5	50.2	49.8
28665	PURLEAR	98.4	98.1	0.6	0.6	0.2	0.2	0.8	1.0	5.6	5.7	5.6	5.3	5.4	29.4	29.2	12.4	1.5	79.9	41.1	50.4	49.6
28668	ROARING GAP	97.5	97.7	0.0	0.0	0.8	0.8	1.7	1.5	2.3	3.8	4.6	4.6	3.0	21.2	36.4	22.0	2.3	84.9	52.7	51.5	48.5
28669	ROARING RIVER	90.8	89.8	6.9	7.3	0.1	0.1	3.2	4.1	5.9	6.1	6.8	6.1	6.1	30.2	26.3	11.5	1.0	77.6	38.0	50.2	49.8
28670	RONDA	95.7	95.1	2.2	2.3	0.1	0.1	2.6	3.5	6.1	6.4	6.6	5.7	5.3	29.1	26.7	12.9	1.3	77.6	39.1	49.8	50.2
28672	SCOTTVILLE	100.0	100.0	0.0	0.0	0.0	0.0	0.0	0.0	0.0	0.0	0.0	0.0	20.0	30.0	50.0	0.0	0.0	100.0	47.5	30.0	70.0
28673	SHERRILLS FORD	92.8	92.3	5.9	6.2	0.1	0.2	0.9	1.2	5.4	5.8	6.5	5.4	4.0	28.0	32.0	12.0	0.9	79.0	42.1	50.4	49.6
28675	SPARTA	95.5	94.8	1.4	1.4	0.3	0.4	5.5	7.0	5.2	5.5	5.5	4.5	5.2	25.7	27.9	17.6	2.8	81.1	43.8	49.2	50.8
28676	STATE ROAD	94.8	94.1	2.1	2.1	0.2	0.3	4.0	5.0	5.5	5.8	6.0	5.1	5.2	26.4	28.4	15.7	2.1	79.8	42.5	49.1	50.9
28677	STATESVILLE	68.7	67.8	25.3	25.3	1.5	1.7	5.8	7.0	7.1	6.9	7.2	6.2	6.2	29.1	23.3	12.4	1.7	75.0	36.5	48.1	51.9
28678	STONY POINT	89.9	88.7	6.1	6.5	1.4	1.8	2.5	3.2	7.1	7.2	7.3	6.4	5.8	30.1	25.3	9.7	1.2	74.6	36.1	50.5	49.6
28679	SUGAR GROVE	98.2	97.9	0.5	0.5	0.1	0.1	1.4	1.9	5.2	5.5	6.0	6.2	5.9	27.4	29.7	12.6	1.4	79.4	41.2	50.2	49.8
28681	TAYLORSVILLE	91.1	90.3	5.4	5.5	1.2	1.5	2.4	3.1	6.8	6.8	6.6	5.7	5.7	30.0	25.8	11.3	1.2	76.2	37.8	50.4	49.6
28682	TERRELL	98.2	97.9	0.3	0.4	0.2	0.3	0.3	0.4	3.9	3.6	5.2	4.7	3.0	25.6	41.4	12.3	0.4	84.6	47.3	50.4	49.6
28683	THURMOND	97.6	97.0	0.4	0.4	0.1	0.1	1.7	2.2	5.8	6.2	6.5	6.0	5.9	27.9	26.7	13.8	1.3	77.9	39.8	51.1	48.9
28684	TODD	98.7	98.5	0.4	0.3	0.1	0.2	1.2	1.6	5.7	6.1	6.5	5.3	4.9	28.0	29.3	12.4	1.6	78.2	40.7	50.7	49.4
28685	TRAPHILL	98.0	97.7	1.0	1.1	0.0	0.0	1.0	1.4	7.4	7.1	6.1	6.2	5.0	28.4	25.8	12.6	1.4	75.6	38.3	49.4	50.7
28689	UNION GROVE	95.5	94.5	1.0	1.2	0.2	0.2	3.6	4.7	5.9	6.2	6.8	5.9	5.2	29.1	27.9	11.4	1.5	77.5	39.7	51.0	49.0
28690	VALDESE	92.4	91.2	1.4	1.4	3.9	4.7	2.2	3.0	6.2	6.2	6.5	5.9	5.2	27.4	25.7	14.9	2.1	77.4	40.3	48.0	52.0
28692	VILAS	98.3	98.1	0.5	0.5	0.2	0.3	1.5	1.9	5.2	5.4	6.1	5.6	6.3	31.0	27.1	11.9	1.4	79.9	39.1	50.2	49.8
28693	WARRENSVILLE	98.1	97.9	0.4	0.4	0.4	0.4	1.7	2.1	5.6	5.9	5.5	4.9	5.0	27.8	29.0	14.5	1.9	80.1	42.0	50.3	49.7
28694	WEST JEFFERSON	97.0	96.6	0.6	0.6	0.3	0.3	3.0	3.6	5.4	5.5	5.4	4.9	5.1	26.7	28.4	16.7	2.1	80.8	43.2	48.9	51.1
28697	WILKESBORO	90.4	89.3	5.7	5.9	0.9	1.1	4.7	5.9	6.2	6.4	5.8	5.1	5.3	28.0	27.4	13.8	2.1	78.3	40.6	49.0	51.0
28698	ZIONVILLE	99.4	99.3	0.1	0.1	0.1	0.1	0.8	1.1	6.1	6.3	6.8	5.6	4.6	30.7	26.3	11.8	1.9	77.3	38.9	50.5	49.5
28701	ALEXANDER	96.9	96.3	0.3	0.3	0.3	0.4	2.5	3.5	6.3	7.5	7.4	5.7	4.8	30.9	25.9	10.4	1.2	75.0	37.6	49.5	50.5
28702	ALMOND	96.7	96.8	0.2	0.2	0.5	0.4	0.6	0.7	4.4	4.8	5.1	4.4	4.0	22.3	33.8	19.2	2.1	82.9	48.0	50.1	49.9
28704	ARDEN	90.6	89.5	6.3	6.8	0.9	1.1	2.1	2.8	6.1	6.3	7.0	6.2	5.8	28.4	28.0	10.7	1.6	76.8	39.0	48.2	51.9
28705	BAKERSVILLE	98.6	98.5	0.1	0.1	0.2	0.2	1.4	1.7	5.3	5.5	5.4	5.4	5.1	25.4	29.2	16.5	2.2	80.4	43.6	50.0	50.0
	NORTH CAROLINA	72.1	71.2	21.6	21.6	1.5	1.8	4.7	5.9	6.7	6.6	6.8	6.7	7.1	29.8	24.2	10.8	1.4	76.2	36.2	49.2	50.8
	UNITED STATES	75.1	73.6	12.3	12.5	3.8	4.2	12.5	14.1	6.9	6.7	7.2	7.0	7.3	28.6	23.8	10.8	1.7	75.1	36.0	49.1	50.9

#	POST OFFICE NAME	2004 Per Capita Income	2004 HH Income Base	2004 Household Income Distribution (%): Less than $25,000	$25,000 to $49,999	$50,000 to $99,999	$100,000 to $149,999	$150,000 or More	Median Household Income: 2004	2009	2004 National Centile	2004 State Centile	2004 Home Value Base	2004 Home Value Distribution (%): Less than $50,000	$50,000 to $89,999	$90,000 to $174,999	$175,000 to $399,999	$400,000 or More	2004 Median Home Value
28552	LOWLAND	15918	136	46.3	33.1	19.1	1.5	0.0	28423	33440	9	8	110	49.1	35.5	7.3	4.6	3.6	51250
28553	MARSHALLBERG	22307	112	25.0	34.8	33.0	5.4	1.8	42360	47791	54	64	96	20.8	9.4	33.3	32.3	4.2	145833
28555	MAYSVILLE	17333	1847	37.9	35.5	20.0	4.5	2.1	33800	36486	23	24	1456	30.2	33.9	28.7	6.0	1.2	69908
28556	MERRITT	23825	592	28.0	29.1	31.4	5.6	5.9	43425	49496	57	69	516	18.2	29.1	30.8	16.7	5.2	96087
28557	MOREHEAD CITY	24689	6197	32.6	26.2	29.5	7.8	3.9	40997	46890	50	58	4408	10.1	10.5	48.7	24.2	6.4	137024
28560	NEW BERN	20684	11432	33.9	29.3	28.6	5.7	2.5	36955	42521	35	40	7868	16.6	26.7	37.2	17.4	2.1	99478
28562	NEW BERN	27377	12721	24.0	29.4	32.4	9.4	4.8	46925	53336	66	81	9748	11.7	17.0	40.0	28.7	2.7	130034
28570	NEWPORT	21141	7821	25.9	33.1	32.1	6.9	2.0	43372	49892	57	68	6218	20.1	20.7	38.2	17.3	3.6	105844
28571	ORIENTAL	30191	1195	26.0	30.0	28.4	8.8	6.9	44375	51966	60	72	1006	12.0	15.7	25.8	38.1	8.4	160714
28572	PINK HILL	17748	2248	35.4	36.3	22.2	2.1	4.1	35814	40765	31	34	1777	39.8	23.4	33.2	3.2	0.5	68445
28573	POLLOCKSVILLE	21009	946	35.3	31.0	25.4	3.5	4.9	35592	39422	30	33	756	20.8	28.8	34.4	14.2	1.9	90536
28574	RICHLANDS	16319	3900	39.0	32.0	23.3	4.5	1.3	33118	35251	21	21	3050	22.8	34.8	35.7	6.1	0.7	82367
28577	SEALEVEL	14353	126	38.9	34.1	17.5	5.6	4.0	32594	37612	20	19	106	23.6	21.7	44.3	9.4	0.9	96250
28578	SEVEN SPRINGS	16268	1577	34.1	32.0	26.7	4.6	2.6	36799	42303	35	39	1184	38.0	20.3	30.5	10.8	0.4	74167
28579	SMYRNA	24289	416	26.9	33.9	32.5	5.3	1.4	40000	45923	46	51	351	25.1	13.7	32.5	25.6	3.1	115833
28580	SNOW HILL	17039	3805	37.5	30.4	26.3	4.1	1.7	34133	37869	24	25	2901	23.5	39.8	30.5	6.0	0.2	78697
28581	STACY	26036	96	24.0	25.0	40.6	9.4	1.0	50517	59272	73	86	82	20.7	23.2	41.5	13.4	1.2	100000
28582	STELLA	20432	461	30.2	34.5	26.0	6.9	2.4	41234	46221	51	59	374	21.1	22.7	36.6	15.5	4.0	100556
28584	SWANSBORO	23794	3791	29.7	30.7	28.8	7.0	3.8	41898	46856	53	62	2947	14.7	16.6	39.3	23.9	5.5	122145
28585	TRENTON	17646	2124	36.0	35.2	23.7	2.9	2.1	33549	37040	23	23	1745	30.5	29.9	32.7	4.5	2.3	77336
28586	VANCEBORO	15944	2672	35.1	35.2	25.6	3.2	0.8	34255	38634	25	26	2143	32.0	31.9	29.9	5.9	0.3	73128
28587	VANDEMERE	15216	164	41.5	33.5	21.3	3.1	0.6	29608	33504	11	11	130	38.5	31.5	22.3	6.2	1.5	60000
28590	WINTERVILLE	24697	6782	23.0	31.6	30.7	11.0	3.7	45152	53703	62	75	4778	15.6	25.0	42.4	16.3	0.6	103740
28594	EMERALD ISLE	40225	1807	16.4	22.1	38.6	15.4	7.5	62627	74958	87	94	1506	4.9	4.1	21.2	57.1	12.8	225219
28601	HICKORY	27821	20618	23.0	30.8	31.0	9.1	6.1	46497	52980	65	80	13920	8.7	15.3	43.7	26.3	6.0	131294
28602	HICKORY	20504	11494	27.8	33.7	29.9	6.2	2.5	40252	45877	47	54	7939	14.1	26.3	43.7	14.1	1.8	101346
28604	BANNER ELK	21422	2478	32.9	31.6	26.0	6.2	3.4	37443	42811	37	42	1946	12.4	13.4	35.3	30.3	8.6	140595
28605	BLOWING ROCK	31988	1794	23.9	27.4	31.9	9.1	7.8	48609	56532	69	84	1322	5.4	4.5	27.8	44.3	18.1	211714
28606	BOOMER	18663	781	37.8	30.6	24.8	4.0	2.8	34942	39059	27	29	662	23.3	27.2	34.6	14.1	0.9	89250
28607	BOONE	19743	10875	38.1	29.0	24.5	6.1	2.4	33976	38811	24	25	5623	9.1	9.7	36.4	37.8	7.0	160626
28608	BOONE	16426	68	51.5	29.4	11.8	2.9	4.4	24023	27707	4	2	23	0.0	0.0	65.2	30.4	4.4	157500
28609	CATAWBA	21112	2389	24.5	31.2	34.9	6.2	3.3	45851	51529	63	78	1994	16.7	24.3	43.2	14.1	1.6	102252
28610	CLAREMONT	22227	3510	19.9	33.9	35.3	7.6	3.4	46836	52805	66	81	2909	15.1	24.7	41.2	16.1	3.0	103889
28611	COLLETTSVILLE	18099	488	32.6	36.9	24.6	4.5	1.4	35935	40705	31	34	407	27.0	29.5	30.2	12.0	1.2	77791
28612	CONNELLYS SPRINGS	18145	5406	28.2	35.7	30.8	4.2	1.1	40134	44860	47	53	4328	26.1	27.2	37.7	8.0	1.0	85693
28613	CONOVER	20667	8741	21.5	35.4	34.3	6.1	2.8	44635	50454	60	73	6904	14.7	18.5	51.7	13.5	1.6	109175
28615	CRESTON	16765	941	46.9	30.8	17.8	2.7	1.9	27184	31027	7	6	794	34.3	19.9	33.5	9.5	2.9	80571
28617	CRUMPLER	18489	1047	32.5	37.0	24.3	4.6	1.7	34810	39435	27	29	869	20.5	18.4	38.3	19.0	3.8	106652
28618	DEEP GAP	20189	749	25.6	32.4	35.3	5.5	1.2	40219	47249	47	54	607	14.3	9.2	37.1	34.8	4.6	148415
28621	ELKIN	21345	4405	35.0	29.4	26.7	5.4	3.4	37503	42278	37	42	3300	18.6	28.9	36.7	15.3	0.5	94586
28622	ELK PARK	16467	1304	42.8	34.2	19.1	3.3	0.6	29442	33179	11	10	1064	26.8	25.5	32.4	13.4	2.0	84783
28623	ENNICE	18083	730	42.1	29.5	21.1	3.4	4.0	30603	33951	14	14	606	20.3	25.4	30.4	16.8	7.1	94194
28624	FERGUSON	19815	744	35.5	34.1	22.5	4.6	3.4	35294	39640	29	31	618	31.6	18.6	32.5	15.9	1.5	89524
28625	STATESVILLE	22683	12971	22.9	31.6	34.8	6.9	3.9	46719	53093	66	80	10139	9.8	17.8	48.6	21.7	2.0	117980
28626	FLEETWOOD	21572	754	32.9	33.2	26.5	4.0	3.5	35404	38804	29	31	627	12.3	23.9	40.2	20.4	3.2	110022
28627	GLADE VALLEY	25437	592	33.8	36.2	22.1	4.6	3.4	33423	38600	22	23	493	19.1	17.4	33.9	20.5	9.1	113702
28630	GRANITE FALLS	20420	7364	26.6	32.6	32.8	6.3	1.8	43412	48831	57	68	5765	16.7	25.6	44.2	12.2	1.3	102648
28631	GRASSY CREEK	18185	315	42.5	30.5	21.0	3.8	2.2	32814	36745	20	20	268	19.8	17.5	42.9	13.1	6.7	111224
28634	HARMONY	18108	2150	28.3	36.8	29.2	4.6	1.2	38538	43696	41	46	1751	21.1	25.6	41.7	9.9	1.7	94078
28635	HAYS	17455	1547	34.3	36.9	26.1	1.6	1.3	35805	40020	31	34	1275	24.9	30.1	33.6	9.5	2.0	84279
28636	HIDDENITE	19414	2157	25.8	36.4	31.9	4.9	1.1	40910	46189	49	57	1768	27.4	25.9	34.8	11.1	0.7	84685
28637	HILDEBRAN	19889	596	28.9	33.7	31.7	4.0	1.7	40470	45000	48	55	428	19.4	29.2	44.4	6.3	0.7	91538
28638	HUDSON	19540	4359	27.4	35.4	31.4	4.5	1.3	40717	45746	49	56	3314	18.7	23.8	46.7	10.1	0.7	99219
28640	JEFFERSON	18746	1712	41.1	30.3	22.8	3.7	2.1	31289	34781	16	16	1318	15.9	17.2	44.9	19.4	2.6	114689
28642	JONESVILLE	20890	2386	38.8	30.5	24.1	4.2	2.4	33168	37600	21	22	1728	19.2	37.8	35.7	6.9	0.5	83296
28643	LANSING	17559	1535	41.4	34.2	19.7	2.8	1.8	30287	34015	13	13	1279	21.6	27.1	35.0	13.5	2.8	92946
28644	LAUREL SPRINGS	22512	813	36.5	34.2	20.9	2.8	5.5	32754	37170	20	20	678	12.0	25.4	42.6	18.7	1.3	109773
28645	LENOIR	18760	19404	32.8	33.9	26.5	5.0	1.8	36636	41251	34	38	14406	19.8	30.0	39.1	10.0	1.2	90275
28649	MC GRADY	16485	421	30.6	41.6	26.4	1.0	0.5	37802	42329	39	43	350	29.4	25.4	30.6	10.3	4.3	82609
28650	MAIDEN	21621	4719	21.7	33.7	35.9	6.3	2.5	46295	52056	65	79	3831	14.0	23.8	48.8	12.1	1.4	105843
28651	MILLERS CREEK	21858	2743	24.7	39.3	28.0	4.2	3.9	41013	46014	50	58	2198	20.4	19.7	35.3	21.8	2.9	105573
28654	MORAVIAN FALLS	24862	1317	27.6	33.7	28.4	5.6	4.6	42333	47618	54	63	1047	23.1	21.5	33.0	19.0	3.4	101661
28655	MORGANTON	20460	22387	29.2	34.6	28.7	4.6	2.9	39587	44557	45	50	16322	19.4	27.2	40.1	12.1	1.2	94067
28657	NEWLAND	19947	4853	36.4	33.1	24.5	4.1	1.9	34734	38748	26	28	3961	22.4	26.3	33.3	14.8	3.3	91931
28658	NEWTON	21594	10261	24.5	32.9	33.1	7.1	2.5	43375	49136	57	68	7685	10.4	22.9	48.0	17.0	1.6	109268
28659	NORTH WILKESBORO	18195	9177	35.5	35.2	24.1	3.5	1.7	34522	38667	26	27	6895	19.7	27.9	39.8	11.4	1.1	93072
28660	OLIN	21846	707	22.1	34.4	36.5	5.7	1.4	45400	51233	62	76	576	17.0	22.4	40.5	18.1	2.1	105455
28663	PINEY CREEK	21611	287	31.4	34.2	26.8	3.5	4.2	37664	44272	38	43	237	16.9	19.8	44.7	16.9	1.7	108712
28665	PURLEAR	21148	906	30.1	35.8	26.5	5.0	2.7	39418	44469	44	49	752	22.6	23.7	30.3	20.2	3.2	97000
28668	ROARING GAP	41235	70	27.1	30.0	31.4	7.1	4.3	38210	42378	40	46	58	13.8	12.1	29.3	29.3	15.5	164286
28669	ROARING RIVER	21251	1115	33.8	34.2	26.2	3.5	2.3	35024	39363	28	29	902	30.5	25.5	34.5	9.5	0.0	79821
28670	RONDA	18878	1242	32.3	34.2	25.3	6.3	1.9	37657	42566	38	43	994	21.2	28.0	35.3	14.4	1.1	90909
28672	SCOTTVILLE	0	0	0.0	0.0	0.0	0.0	0.0	0	0	0	0	2	0.0	0.0	100.0	0.0	0.0	112500
28673	SHERRILLS FORD	28346	2191	20.8	26.4	34.3	12.4	6.1	52418	60096	76	88	1845	9.5	8.9	30.2	39.0	12.3	179056
28675	SPARTA	19534	2729	39.9	32.5	20.9	4.5	2.2	30944	34985	15	15	2083	15.5	24.2	39.7	15.0	5.6	104194
28676	STATE ROAD	21717	1497	34.6	29.2	27.8	5.0	3.4	40025	44570	46	52	1200	19.3	28.6	32.8	16.1	3.3	93611
28677	STATESVILLE	19811	13644	32.9	31.9	27.3	5.5	2.4	36919	42243	35	39	9035	14.4	25.6	44.0	14.1	1.8	102422
28678	STONY POINT	19957	1840	22.8	35.9	35.3	4.4	1.7	43593	49155	58	69	1458	16.5	23.9	43.0	14.5	2.2	104801
28679	SUGAR GROVE	19806	651	33.2	30.6	29.0	4.8	2.5	37779	43130	38	43	537	15.6	16.0	38.0	26.6	3.7	119342
28681	TAYLORSVILLE	20591	9718	26.0	33.6	33.2	5.3	2.0	42154	47533	53	62	7822	19.9	23.8	40.2	14.3	1.7	99515
28682	TERRELL	42106	299	15.7	16.7	33.8	20.1	13.7	69621	84396	91	96	251	3.2	7.2	18.7	48.2	22.7	249342
28683	THURMOND	19425	682	33.0	30.1	33.7	2.5	0.7	40724	46020	49	56	576	22.7	25.4	37.2	13.9	0.9	93333
28684	TODD	18897	727	32.9	36.0	24.2	3.6	3.3	35571	39816	30	32	602	17.1	20.1	38.5	21.3	3.0	110274
28685	TRAPHILL	17568	827	34.3	36.2	27.2	1.2	1.1	35573	39954	30	32	684	25.6	32.6	29.4	9.8	2.6	80345
28689	UNION GROVE	19706	754	26.3	35.8	32.2	3.7	2.0	39928	45423	46	51	622	24.9	21.5	36.5	15.3	1.8	95500
28690	VALDESE	20690	3958	32.7	33.1	26.4	5.3	2.5	36788	41033	35	39	2954	17.5	30.5	41.6	9.5	0.9	92332
28692	VILAS	19049	1802	33.8	31.7	29.0	3.8	1.7	36480	42275	33	37	1333	16.2	14.9	34.4	29.5	5.1	121935
28693	WARRENSVILLE	20105	629	43.6	33.6	18.1	2.7	2.1	28432	32160	9	8	522	27.4	21.5	35.4	11.3	4.4	92143
28694	WEST JEFFERSON	19347	3514	40.0	32.1	22.1	3.2	2.6	31407	35222	16	16	2675	14.1	22.5	42.7	17.9	2.9	110015
28697	WILKESBORO	24419	4889	31.3	26.7	28.8	7.5	5.8	42776	48319	55	66	3785	13.8	17.6	39.2	25.7	3.8	122622
28698	ZIONVILLE	20182	939	34.0	34.1	26.0	3.5	2.5	36415	41704	33	36	752	16.8	18.5	39.5	20.7	4.5	115169
28701	ALEXANDER	19798	1603	27.6	32.6	33.9	4.0	1.9	40519	46393	48	55	1334	24.2	14.2	35.0	25.1	1.4	118958
28702	ALMOND	19330	306	38.9	31.4	20.9	4.6	4.3	30291	35266	13	13	264	17.8	30.7	35.2	16.3	0.0	91481
28704	ARDEN	24284	6680	23.5	32.1	30.6	10.0	3.8	45583	52346	63	77	4996	17.1	8.8	37.9	31.9	4.4	141783
28705	BAKERSVILLE	16441	3409	40.6	34.0	21.3	3.0	1.1	30701	34341	14	14	2808	25.8	31.6	33.3	8.3	1.1	80929
	NORTH CAROLINA	23743		27.0	29.8	30.1	8.5	4.7	43794	50711				14.5	20.0	39.7	21.7	4.1	115673
	UNITED STATES	25866		24.7	27.1	30.8	10.9	6.5	48124	56710				10.9	15.0	33.7	30.1	10.4	145905

SPENDING POTENTIAL INDICES NORTH CAROLINA

28552-28705 D

ZIP CODE		FINANCIAL SERVICES				THE HOME						ENTERTAINMENT						PERSONAL			
						Home Improvements		Furnishings													
#	POST OFFICE NAME	Auto Loan	Home Loan	Investments	Retirement Plans	Home Repair	Lawn & Garden	Computers & Hardware	Major Appliances	TV, Radio, Sound Equipment	Furniture	Dine out/ Carry out	Sports Equipment	Fees & Tickets	Toys & Games	Travel	Cable TV	Apparel & Services	Auto Repairs	Health Insurance	Pets & Supplies
28552	LOWLAND	65	44	20	38	50	57	42	53	51	43	60	63	36	57	43	55	54	52	65	75
28553	MARSHALLBERG	93	65	34	62	76	85	64	80	74	64	87	96	55	85	67	78	79	78	95	111
28555	MAYSVILLE	77	61	40	56	65	71	59	67	64	60	77	79	53	73	59	66	73	67	74	87
28556	MERRITT	88	80	70	76	85	96	74	84	79	77	97	90	74	89	79	83	91	81	94	101
28557	MOREHEAD CITY	77	76	77	74	77	85	75	78	76	75	95	87	75	91	76	78	91	78	82	88
28560	NEW BERN	73	66	60	64	68	76	66	70	69	67	85	79	65	82	67	71	81	70	75	82
28562	NEW BERN	93	91	88	88	93	103	87	93	89	89	110	102	87	105	90	91	106	91	98	106
28570	NEWPORT	86	75	57	72	77	85	72	80	76	73	93	91	68	88	73	77	88	79	85	97
28571	ORIENTAL	96	88	83	84	94	110	82	94	87	87	108	93	82	91	89	93	101	91	109	109
28572	PINK HILL	79	63	41	58	66	73	60	69	66	62	80	81	55	75	60	68	75	69	76	89
28573	POLLOCKSVILLE	88	64	38	59	71	84	68	77	78	66	91	89	59	86	67	82	83	77	94	99
28574	RICHLANDS	69	58	42	55	60	65	56	62	60	57	73	72	52	68	56	60	69	62	66	77
28577	SEALEVEL	73	55	36	53	60	72	61	67	68	58	80	75	54	76	60	72	73	67	80	81
28578	SEVEN SPRINGS	75	69	54	66	69	73	66	70	66	67	82	81	62	77	65	65	79	70	70	83
28579	SMYRNA	95	73	45	69	81	89	71	84	78	71	93	100	63	91	72	81	87	82	95	112
28580	SNOW HILL	68	55	37	51	57	63	53	60	58	54	70	70	49	66	53	59	65	60	66	76
28581	STACY	87	77	59	73	82	88	71	79	76	71	92	94	70	94	74	78	88	77	86	102
28582	STELLA	75	72	68	72	72	76	71	73	70	72	87	85	69	83	70	68	84	73	72	84
28584	SWANSBORO	86	75	58	71	78	86	72	80	77	73	93	91	68	88	73	78	88	79	87	98
28585	TRENTON	81	57	29	50	63	71	55	66	64	56	76	79	47	71	55	68	69	66	79	92
28586	VANCEBORO	72	53	31	49	58	66	52	61	59	53	71	72	46	67	52	62	65	61	71	82
28587	VANDEMERE	69	46	21	40	52	60	45	56	54	45	63	67	38	60	45	58	57	55	69	79
28590	WINTERVILLE	88	87	85	90	85	88	86	86	84	88	105	101	85	103	84	81	102	86	80	97
28594	EMERALD ISLE	143	112	76	101	126	142	106	127	119	105	142	149	94	140	113	128	132	125	150	174
28601	HICKORY	101	92	88	92	95	103	93	97	96	93	118	114	91	117	93	96	113	97	99	115
28602	HICKORY	80	69	58	66	71	78	70	74	74	69	90	87	67	89	69	75	86	74	79	91
28604	BANNER ELK	84	67	46	61	74	84	64	75	71	63	85	88	57	84	67	76	79	74	88	101
28605	BLOWING ROCK	113	92	70	85	102	113	89	103	98	88	117	121	81	116	93	103	110	102	118	137
28606	BOOMER	88	59	28	52	67	77	57	71	69	58	81	85	49	77	58	74	74	71	87	101
28607	BOONE	69	52	52	54	54	61	69	63	70	63	86	79	61	81	62	67	82	69	64	75
28608	BOONE	52	32	40	36	31	38	61	45	60	52	74	63	50	67	49	52	70	55	42	51
28609	CATAWBA	89	72	49	67	78	86	69	79	76	69	91	93	65	91	70	79	85	77	89	103
28610	CLAREMONT	96	80	56	74	85	93	74	85	81	75	98	101	71	98	76	84	92	83	95	112
28611	COLLETTSVILLE	83	55	25	48	63	72	53	67	64	54	76	80	45	71	54	69	69	66	82	95
28612	CONNELLYS SPRINGS	79	63	42	58	68	75	60	69	66	60	80	82	56	78	61	69	74	68	78	91
28613	CONOVER	88	75	55	70	79	87	71	79	77	71	93	93	68	93	73	80	88	78	88	102
28615	CRESTON	74	49	22	43	56	64	48	60	58	49	68	71	41	64	49	62	61	59	74	85
28617	CRUMPLER	73	61	42	56	65	71	57	65	62	57	75	77	54	75	58	65	70	63	73	86
28618	DEEP GAP	78	68	51	64	73	78	63	71	68	63	82	84	61	83	65	70	78	69	78	92
28621	ELKIN	85	68	47	64	73	82	67	76	74	67	89	89	62	87	68	77	83	75	87	97
28622	ELK PARK	67	48	28	43	54	63	48	58	56	48	66	67	42	63	49	60	60	57	70	78
28623	ENNICE	83	56	25	48	63	73	54	67	65	55	76	80	46	72	55	70	69	67	83	96
28624	FERGUSON	85	57	26	49	64	74	55	69	66	56	78	82	47	74	56	71	71	68	85	98
28625	STATESVILLE	89	83	71	80	86	93	78	84	82	78	100	99	78	101	80	83	96	83	89	104
28626	FLEETWOOD	87	66	43	59	75	85	63	76	72	63	85	90	56	83	67	77	79	75	91	105
28627	GLADE VALLEY	102	74	42	65	84	95	71	87	83	71	97	103	62	94	74	89	90	86	105	121
28630	GRANITE FALLS	85	70	48	66	74	82	67	76	73	68	88	89	63	86	68	75	83	75	84	98
28631	GRASSY CREEK	70	55	37	49	62	69	52	62	59	51	69	73	46	68	55	63	64	61	74	85
28634	HARMONY	78	64	45	60	67	74	62	69	67	63	81	81	58	78	62	68	76	69	76	88
28635	HAYS	83	55	25	48	63	72	54	67	65	55	76	80	46	72	54	70	69	66	83	95
28636	HIDDENITE	88	66	39	60	72	80	64	75	72	65	86	88	57	82	64	75	80	74	86	100
28637	HILDEBRAN	89	63	32	55	70	80	60	74	71	61	84	88	53	80	61	76	77	73	89	103
28638	HUDSON	80	66	46	62	70	77	63	71	68	63	83	84	59	81	64	70	78	70	78	92
28640	JEFFERSON	77	53	27	48	60	69	53	64	62	53	73	76	45	70	54	66	66	64	78	89
28642	JONESVILLE	86	61	33	55	68	78	61	73	71	61	84	85	54	80	61	75	77	72	87	98
28643	LANSING	74	50	24	44	57	65	49	60	58	49	69	72	42	65	50	63	62	60	74	85
28644	LAUREL SPRINGS	92	65	35	58	74	84	63	77	73	63	86	92	54	83	65	78	79	76	93	108
28645	LENOIR	79	59	38	54	65	73	58	68	66	58	79	80	53	77	59	70	73	67	79	91
28649	MC GRADY	74	50	22	43	56	65	48	60	58	49	68	71	41	64	49	62	62	59	74	85
28650	MAIDEN	89	76	56	73	81	88	72	80	77	72	94	95	70	94	74	80	89	79	88	103
28651	MILLERS CREEK	89	72	49	67	77	84	68	78	75	69	90	92	64	88	69	77	84	77	87	102
28654	MORAVIAN FALLS	104	80	51	74	87	98	77	90	87	78	104	106	71	102	79	91	97	88	103	119
28655	MORGANTON	82	69	53	66	73	80	68	75	73	68	88	87	64	86	68	74	83	74	81	93
28657	NEWLAND	75	58	39	53	63	72	57	66	64	57	76	77	51	74	58	67	71	65	77	87
28658	NEWTON	89	75	55	71	80	88	72	81	79	72	95	95	69	95	74	82	89	79	90	103
28659	NORTH WILKESBORO	78	55	31	49	62	70	54	65	64	55	75	78	48	72	55	68	69	65	78	89
28660	OLIN	87	77	59	74	80	87	73	80	77	73	94	94	71	93	74	78	89	78	85	100
28663	PINEY CREEK	92	63	30	56	72	82	61	76	72	61	85	91	52	81	63	77	77	75	92	107
28665	PURLEAR	92	66	35	58	73	83	63	76	73	64	87	91	55	84	64	78	80	75	91	106
28668	ROARING GAP	132	103	71	93	116	131	98	118	110	97	131	138	87	129	104	118	122	116	139	161
28669	ROARING RIVER	99	66	30	57	75	87	64	80	77	65	91	96	55	86	65	83	83	79	99	114
28670	RONDA	85	60	31	53	67	76	58	70	68	59	81	84	51	77	59	73	74	70	85	97
28672	SCOTTVILLE	0	0	0	0	0	0	0	0	0	0	0	0	0	0	0	0	0	0	0	0
28673	SHERRILLS FORD	108	95	72	89	100	108	89	99	94	89	114	117	84	113	91	96	108	97	107	127
28675	SPARTA	74	54	33	50	60	70	55	65	63	55	75	75	49	72	56	67	69	64	77	85
28676	STATE ROAD	89	70	45	64	76	84	66	77	74	66	88	92	61	87	67	77	82	75	88	103
28677	STATESVILLE	76	65	55	62	68	75	66	71	71	65	86	82	63	85	66	72	81	71	77	86
28678	STONY POINT	86	71	49	67	75	82	68	76	73	69	88	90	63	86	68	75	83	75	83	98
28679	SUGAR GROVE	75	65	49	62	69	76	63	69	67	62	81	81	60	82	64	69	77	68	76	87
28681	TAYLORSVILLE	89	70	44	64	75	83	66	77	74	67	89	91	61	86	67	77	83	76	88	102
28682	TERRELL	161	127	86	114	143	160	119	144	135	118	160	168	107	158	127	144	149	142	170	197
28683	THURMOND	82	63	39	58	69	77	60	70	67	60	81	84	55	79	61	71	75	69	81	95
28684	TODD	82	61	36	54	67	76	58	70	67	59	79	83	51	76	60	71	73	69	82	96
28685	TRAPHILL	80	54	24	46	61	70	52	65	63	53	73	77	44	69	53	67	67	64	80	92
28689	UNION GROVE	84	69	46	64	74	81	64	74	71	65	86	88	61	85	66	74	80	72	84	98
28690	VALDESE	82	63	39	58	69	78	62	72	70	62	83	84	56	81	63	74	77	71	83	94
28692	VILAS	66	61	55	61	63	69	61	64	63	60	78	75	60	78	61	64	74	64	67	76
28693	WARRENSVILLE	85	57	26	49	65	75	55	69	67	56	78	82	47	74	56	72	71	68	85	98
28694	WEST JEFFERSON	78	54	28	48	61	70	54	65	63	54	75	77	47	71	55	68	68	65	79	89
28697	WILKESBORO	92	80	62	76	84	92	77	85	82	76	99	99	73	99	78	84	94	83	93	106
28698	ZIONVILLE	79	57	34	53	63	75	61	69	69	59	82	79	53	77	60	74	74	69	84	88
28701	ALEXANDER	83	67	45	63	71	78	65	73	70	66	85	86	59	81	65	72	80	73	81	94
28702	ALMOND	73	57	39	52	65	73	54	65	61	54	73	76	48	72	58	65	67	64	77	89
28704	ARDEN	86	85	77	84	86	90	81	84	81	81	100	99	80	101	81	80	97	83	84	100
28705	BAKERSVILLE	72	48	22	42	55	63	47	59	56	48	66	70	40	63	48	61	60	58	72	83
	NORTH CAROLINA	90	81	73	80	83	90	81	85	84	82	103	100	79	101	81	84	99	85	88	102
	UNITED STATES	100	100	100	100	100	100	100	100	100	100	100	100	100	100	100	100	100	100	100	100

POPULATION CHANGE

ZIP CODE			POPULATION			2000-2004 ANNUAL RATE		HOUSEHOLDS					FAMILIES		
#	POST OFFICE NAME	COUNTY FIPS CODE	2000	2004	2009	% Rate	State Centile	2000	2004	2009	% Annual Rate 2000-2004	2004 Average HH Size	2000	2004	% Annual Rate 2000-2004
28708	BALSAM GROVE	175	566	607	644	1.7	57	220	240	259	2.1	2.53	161	174	1.8
28709	BARNARDSVILLE	021	2245	2477	2711	2.3	73	887	989	1094	2.6	2.50	658	721	2.2
28711	BLACK MOUNTAIN	021	12591	13325	14285	1.3	48	5308	5734	6264	1.8	2.18	3396	3591	1.3
28712	BREVARD	175	16156	16715	17491	0.8	30	6840	7226	7727	1.3	2.17	4611	4803	1.0
28713	BRYSON CITY	173	8700	9352	10235	1.7	58	3663	4003	4455	2.1	2.28	2538	2734	1.8
28714	BURNSVILLE	199	15739	16557	17667	1.2	43	6632	7107	7722	1.6	2.31	4745	5016	1.3
28715	CANDLER	021	20605	21915	23557	1.5	51	8269	8931	9732	1.8	2.43	5994	6358	1.4
28716	CANTON	087	16380	17525	18807	1.6	54	6833	7407	8062	1.9	2.33	4843	5179	1.6
28717	CASHIERS	099	1418	1614	1867	3.1	85	656	761	896	3.6	2.12	459	524	3.2
28718	CEDAR MOUNTAIN	175	225	250	270	2.5	76	98	111	123	3.0	2.24	71	80	2.9
28719	CHEROKEE	173	5462	5892	6506	1.8	60	1842	2026	2281	2.3	2.81	1363	1480	2.0
28721	CLYDE	087	8377	9020	9668	1.8	59	3497	3833	4176	2.2	2.33	2494	2688	1.8
28722	COLUMBUS	149	7628	8275	8933	1.9	63	3291	3629	3968	2.3	2.25	2250	2441	1.9
28723	CULLOWHEE	099	8002	8645	9539	1.8	61	2537	2875	3345	3.0	2.17	1442	1602	2.5
28726	EAST FLAT ROCK	089	3207	3425	3783	1.6	54	1300	1389	1543	1.6	2.45	897	942	1.2
28729	ETOWAH	089	1762	2066	2363	3.8	91	812	968	1121	4.2	2.13	605	711	3.9
28730	FAIRVIEW	021	8299	9195	10104	2.4	75	3090	3477	3873	2.8	2.62	2392	2653	2.5
28731	FLAT ROCK	089	6535	7247	8072	2.5	76	2747	3094	3489	2.8	2.33	2020	2246	2.5
28732	FLETCHER	089	11218	12595	14041	2.8	81	4493	5121	5783	3.1	2.44	3271	3666	2.7
28733	FONTANA DAM	075	168	177	187	1.2	45	67	72	78	1.7	2.46	50	53	1.4
28734	FRANKLIN	113	24023	25462	27359	1.4	49	10251	10989	11942	1.7	2.28	7132	7538	1.3
28735	GERTON	089	159	174	193	2.1	70	70	78	87	2.6	2.23	52	56	1.8
28736	GLENVILLE	099	475	535	615	2.8	82	218	249	291	3.2	2.15	144	162	2.8
28739	HENDERSONVILLE	089	18660	19978	21966	1.6	55	8278	8951	9947	1.9	2.20	5720	6121	1.6
28740	GREEN MOUNTAIN	199	1759	1963	2179	2.6	79	719	814	918	3.0	2.39	542	605	2.6
28741	HIGHLANDS	113	2832	3118	3424	2.3	73	1290	1450	1619	2.8	2.10	841	929	2.4
28742	HORSE SHOE	089	6110	6669	7358	2.1	68	2449	2714	3031	2.5	2.46	1888	2067	2.2
28743	HOT SPRINGS	115	3076	3194	3396	0.9	33	1339	1418	1535	1.4	2.24	906	946	1.0
28745	LAKE JUNALUSKA	087	463	553	624	4.3	93	248	301	344	4.7	1.84	158	189	4.3
28746	LAKE LURE	161	2132	2437	2677	3.2	87	977	1139	1271	3.7	2.13	694	795	3.3
28747	LAKE TOXAWAY	175	2158	2319	2462	1.7	58	892	978	1059	2.2	2.37	630	678	1.7
28748	LEICESTER	021	9838	11050	12220	2.8	81	3817	4368	4907	3.2	2.51	2875	3241	2.9
28751	MAGGIE VALLEY	087	2767	3026	3267	2.1	69	1314	1462	1605	2.5	2.06	888	971	2.1
28752	MARION	111	29042	30155	31503	0.9	33	11489	12110	12838	1.3	2.39	8162	8493	0.9
28753	MARSHALL	115	9558	10066	10775	1.2	45	4004	4303	4699	1.7	2.29	2806	2973	1.4
28754	MARS HILL	115	7028	7507	8041	1.6	54	2683	2931	3212	2.1	2.33	1904	2049	1.7
28756	MILL SPRING	149	3912	4291	4656	2.2	71	1539	1708	1870	2.5	2.51	1111	1213	2.1
28761	NEBO	111	6705	7175	7597	1.6	55	2535	2771	2985	2.1	2.51	1912	2061	1.8
28762	OLD FORT	111	6831	7196	7556	1.2	45	2751	2955	3152	1.7	2.44	2011	2124	1.3
28763	OTTO	113	1621	1905	2162	3.9	92	698	832	954	4.2	2.29	513	601	3.8
28766	PENROSE	175	867	916	964	1.3	47	356	383	411	1.7	2.39	277	295	1.5
28768	PISGAH FOREST	175	6875	7062	7347	0.6	26	2888	3030	3216	1.1	2.33	2164	2242	0.8
28771	ROBBINSVILLE	075	7173	7475	7843	1.0	36	3000	3209	3458	1.6	2.29	2150	2268	1.3
28772	ROSMAN	175	2033	2144	2254	1.3	46	821	885	950	1.8	2.42	610	649	1.5
28773	SALUDA	149	2328	2373	2531	0.5	20	965	994	1071	0.7	2.33	664	676	0.4
28774	SAPPHIRE	175	854	971	1093	3.1	85	395	459	529	3.6	2.12	273	312	3.2
28775	SCALY MOUNTAIN	113	521	571	625	2.2	71	230	256	284	2.6	2.23	158	173	2.2
28777	SPRUCE PINE	121	9659	10004	10582	0.8	32	3532	3713	3994	1.2	2.48	2491	2579	0.8
28778	SWANNANOA	021	7873	8458	9116	1.7	57	3027	3312	3631	2.1	2.42	2089	2240	1.7
28779	SYLVA	099	14459	16139	18448	2.6	79	6282	7172	8402	3.2	2.20	4024	4512	2.7
28781	TOPTON	113	814	840	888	0.7	28	359	377	404	1.2	2.22	264	274	0.9
28782	TRYON	149	4567	4787	5099	1.1	40	2165	2289	2461	1.3	2.02	1359	1410	0.9
28783	TUCKASEGEE	099	1512	1655	1874	2.2	70	639	712	820	2.6	2.32	450	496	2.3
28785	WAYNESVILLE	087	6607	7108	7607	1.7	58	2798	3066	3336	2.2	2.28	2046	2208	1.8
28786	WAYNESVILLE	087	19407	19639	20505	0.3	16	8396	8642	9178	0.7	2.21	5604	5676	0.3
28787	WEAVERVILLE	021	17155	18668	20368	2.0	65	6861	7592	8404	2.4	2.43	5046	5500	2.1
28789	WHITTIER	099	5652	6216	7038	2.3	72	2302	2581	2980	2.7	2.40	1669	1846	2.4
28790	ZIRCONIA	089	2784	2892	3106	0.9	33	1085	1147	1249	1.3	2.52	829	866	1.0
28791	HENDERSONVILLE	089	13273	14038	15271	1.3	48	5784	6211	6847	1.7	2.19	4017	4241	1.3
28792	HENDERSONVILLE	089	27271	29823	33035	2.1	69	11013	12183	13661	2.4	2.37	7528	8193	2.0
28801	ASHEVILLE	021	13357	13409	14089	0.1	12	6063	6205	6661	0.6	1.89	2488	2442	-0.4
28803	ASHEVILLE	021	24111	25906	28084	1.7	57	10577	11485	12596	2.0	2.22	6559	6988	1.5
28804	ASHEVILLE	021	18513	19213	20407	0.9	33	7652	8086	8744	1.3	2.22	4739	4918	0.9
28805	ASHEVILLE	021	17258	17854	18959	0.8	30	7654	8037	8663	1.2	2.13	4465	4587	0.6
28806	ASHEVILLE	021	33943	35305	37703	0.9	35	14350	15154	16414	1.3	2.30	9110	9417	0.8
28901	ANDREWS	039	4870	4963	5261	0.5	20	2148	2235	2422	0.9	2.18	1449	1483	0.6
28902	BRASSTOWN	043	1005	1102	1234	2.2	71	432	487	559	2.9	2.26	306	340	2.5
28904	HAYESVILLE	043	7334	8100	9130	2.4	74	3236	3658	4223	2.9	2.18	2299	2565	2.6
28905	MARBLE	039	3336	3493	3755	1.1	38	1358	1452	1594	1.6	2.37	990	1046	1.3
28906	MURPHY	039	15909	17406	19117	2.1	70	6757	7562	8489	2.7	2.28	4880	5384	2.3
28909	WARNE	043	617	682	770	2.4	74	251	285	330	3.0	2.39	175	196	2.7
	NORTH CAROLINA					1.9					2.2	2.46			1.8
	UNITED STATES					1.2					1.3	2.58			1.1

#	POST OFFICE NAME	White 2000	White 2004	Black 2000	Black 2004	Asian/Pacific 2000	Asian/Pacific 2004	% Hispanic Origin 2000	% Hispanic Origin 2004	0-4	5-9	10-14	15-19	20-24	25-44	45-64	65-84	85+	18+	MEDIAN AGE 2004	% 2004 Males	% 2004 Females
28708	BALSAM GROVE	98.8	98.5	0.0	0.0	0.2	0.2	0.4	0.7	6.6	6.4	6.6	6.9	6.9	26.7	26.4	12.2	1.3	76.4	38.6	49.3	50.7
28709	BARNARDSVILLE	98.6	98.3	0.0	0.0	0.2	0.2	0.9	1.1	5.5	5.7	6.7	6.8	6.5	29.0	27.5	10.8	1.6	77.9	38.4	51.3	48.7
28711	BLACK MOUNTAIN	92.3	91.4	5.0	5.5	0.7	0.8	1.1	1.4	4.7	5.1	5.7	7.0	6.0	25.0	27.8	15.6	3.0	79.9	42.5	47.7	52.3
28712	BREVARD	91.6	91.1	5.8	5.9	0.6	0.7	1.1	1.4	4.8	4.7	5.2	6.1	6.2	21.3	26.5	21.7	3.6	82.0	46.4	47.2	52.9
28713	BRYSON CITY	87.3	86.1	1.0	1.0	0.2	0.2	1.1	1.4	5.3	5.7	5.8	5.0	4.6	25.4	29.4	16.3	2.4	80.0	43.7	48.6	51.4
28714	BURNSVILLE	97.9	97.7	0.6	0.7	0.1	0.2	2.9	3.7	5.4	5.7	6.0	5.4	5.1	25.6	28.7	15.9	2.3	79.6	42.8	49.1	50.9
28715	CANDLER	97.3	96.9	0.5	0.5	0.4	0.4	1.5	2.0	6.4	6.5	6.7	5.9	5.5	29.2	26.1	12.1	1.7	76.8	38.9	48.7	51.3
28716	CANTON	96.8	96.6	1.5	1.6	0.1	0.1	1.7	2.1	5.5	5.9	6.4	5.4	4.7	27.5	25.9	16.1	2.6	78.7	41.5	48.7	51.3
28717	CASHIERS	98.2	98.0	0.1	0.1	0.1	0.1	1.4	1.7	3.7	4.1	4.2	3.4	3.0	19.6	36.5	23.8	1.9	86.0	52.8	49.5	50.5
28718	CEDAR MOUNTAIN	97.3	96.8	0.0	0.0	0.9	1.2	0.9	0.8	4.4	4.8	4.8	4.4	4.0	24.0	33.2	18.4	2.0	83.6	46.8	48.0	52.0
28719	CHEROKEE	22.1	20.0	2.6	2.5	0.2	0.3	2.3	2.6	7.6	8.0	8.7	9.5	7.3	27.5	22.6	8.0	0.9	70.4	32.2	49.5	50.5
28721	CLYDE	96.8	96.5	0.9	1.0	0.4	0.5	1.4	1.8	6.2	6.2	6.1	5.6	5.6	27.1	27.4	14.2	1.6	78.2	40.5	48.5	51.5
28722	COLUMBUS	93.2	92.8	4.8	4.9	0.3	0.4	3.1	4.0	4.9	5.3	5.5	5.0	4.6	22.4	27.4	20.0	4.9	81.0	46.6	47.9	52.1
28723	CULLOWHEE	93.0	92.3	3.7	3.8	0.8	0.9	1.9	2.4	3.5	3.0	3.8	19.4	20.7	20.4	19.8	8.6	1.0	87.4	24.9	49.0	51.0
28726	EAST FLAT ROCK	86.4	84.9	2.7	2.7	0.4	0.5	16.0	18.8	6.9	6.9	6.5	5.7	6.2	31.4	22.7	12.2	1.5	76.3	35.9	50.0	50.0
28729	ETOWAH	97.2	97.0	1.4	1.5	0.6	0.7	0.7	1.0	4.3	4.3	4.7	4.9	4.2	20.7	30.2	24.7	2.1	83.9	50.3	48.6	51.4
28730	FAIRVIEW	97.4	97.1	0.4	0.4	0.5	0.6	0.9	1.2	5.9	6.6	7.6	6.5	4.9	26.8	29.6	10.7	1.5	75.9	40.5	48.7	51.3
28731	FLAT ROCK	96.2	95.6	1.0	1.1	0.3	0.4	4.5	5.7	5.9	6.0	5.6	4.6	4.4	23.8	28.7	19.5	1.6	79.8	44.9	49.5	50.5
28732	FLETCHER	92.8	91.9	4.1	4.4	1.0	1.2	2.0	2.6	6.4	6.7	6.6	5.4	4.5	29.1	27.7	11.5	2.1	76.8	39.8	48.8	51.2
28733	FONTANA DAM	98.2	98.3	0.0	0.0	0.0	0.0	1.2	1.1	4.5	4.5	5.1	6.2	4.5	24.3	28.8	19.8	2.3	81.9	45.6	48.0	52.0
28734	FRANKLIN	96.8	96.5	1.5	1.5	0.5	0.6	1.4	1.8	5.2	5.4	5.8	5.7	4.7	22.4	29.0	19.3	2.7	80.1	45.7	48.2	51.8
28735	GERTON	91.8	90.8	1.3	1.2	0.0	0.0	10.1	12.1	6.9	7.5	5.8	4.6	4.6	29.9	27.6	12.1	1.2	76.4	40.3	50.0	50.0
28736	GLENVILLE	96.4	95.9	0.2	0.2	0.2	0.2	4.4	5.4	4.7	5.1	5.6	5.2	3.9	25.8	32.3	16.3	1.1	81.7	44.8	50.5	49.5
28739	HENDERSONVILLE	93.7	93.2	3.2	3.1	0.6	0.7	3.8	4.8	4.7	4.9	5.3	4.9	4.4	21.4	28.5	23.1	3.0	82.1	48.2	48.3	51.7
28740	GREEN MOUNTAIN	98.2	98.0	0.1	0.2	0.1	0.1	1.4	1.9	6.1	6.2	6.2	5.3	4.6	26.1	28.1	15.4	2.0	78.1	42.1	49.9	50.1
28741	HIGHLANDS	98.8	98.6	0.0	0.0	0.1	0.1	2.4	3.1	3.7	3.9	5.0	4.8	3.0	19.4	34.0	22.1	4.2	84.2	51.8	47.5	52.5
28742	HORSE SHOE	98.2	98.0	0.6	0.6	0.3	0.3	1.3	1.7	5.9	6.3	6.4	5.4	4.1	26.0	29.2	15.2	1.7	78.1	42.6	49.4	50.7
28743	HOT SPRINGS	98.1	97.9	0.1	0.2	0.3	0.3	0.8	1.0	5.6	6.0	5.6	5.4	4.9	24.6	31.0	15.2	1.9	79.4	43.6	50.2	49.8
28745	LAKE JUNALUSKA	99.4	99.3	0.0	0.0	0.0	0.0	1.3	1.8	3.4	3.3	3.3	3.1	2.4	15.7	27.5	36.7	4.7	88.3	59.8	45.6	54.4
28746	LAKE LURE	88.0	87.1	10.5	11.2	0.1	0.2	1.0	1.2	4.2	4.4	4.4	4.4	4.0	21.6	32.1	23.4	1.6	84.4	50.0	51.1	48.9
28747	LAKE TOXAWAY	98.8	98.7	0.1	0.1	0.3	0.3	0.5	0.6	5.5	6.3	6.5	6.2	5.1	24.1	30.4	14.5	1.3	77.8	42.6	49.7	50.3
28748	LEICESTER	96.4	95.8	0.8	0.9	0.4	0.5	2.0	2.6	6.7	6.9	7.0	5.8	5.6	30.9	26.0	10.0	1.2	75.8	37.4	49.8	50.2
28751	MAGGIE VALLEY	97.5	97.2	0.4	0.5	0.3	0.4	0.2	0.3	3.2	3.7	4.4	3.4	2.9	19.8	37.0	23.6	2.0	86.5	52.2	47.4	52.6
28752	MARION	91.7	91.0	4.5	4.5	0.8	1.0	3.5	4.4	6.0	6.1	6.3	5.7	5.9	29.3	25.3	13.1	1.7	78.1	38.7	50.3	49.7
28753	MARSHALL	98.3	98.1	0.3	0.3	0.2	0.2	1.5	2.0	5.9	6.1	6.1	5.6	5.4	27.1	27.7	13.8	2.3	78.7	40.8	49.6	50.4
28754	MARS HILL	96.6	96.4	1.9	1.9	0.3	0.3	1.2	1.6	5.9	5.9	6.0	7.3	8.9	25.7	24.9	13.2	2.3	79.6	37.9	49.2	50.8
28756	MILL SPRING	93.3	92.8	4.6	4.8	0.3	0.3	3.8	5.0	6.4	6.7	7.3	6.1	5.7	29.4	26.3	11.1	1.1	75.9	37.5	49.6	50.4
28761	NEBO	93.0	92.0	3.3	3.6	2.0	2.4	1.2	1.6	6.0	6.3	6.7	5.8	5.4	29.6	26.7	11.9	1.6	77.4	39.0	50.0	50.0
28762	OLD FORT	93.2	92.2	4.0	4.4	0.4	0.4	1.7	2.2	6.3	6.3	6.1	5.8	5.5	27.5	27.2	14.0	1.3	77.9	40.0	50.0	50.0
28763	OTTO	98.2	98.0	0.3	0.4	0.3	0.3	1.5	1.9	5.0	5.3	5.3	4.8	4.4	23.3	31.9	18.5	1.6	81.5	46.1	49.7	50.3
28766	PENROSE	98.0	97.7	0.5	0.6	0.1	0.2	0.7	1.0	5.2	5.7	6.2	5.2	4.4	23.5	32.3	16.1	1.4	79.6	44.9	50.2	49.8
28768	PISGAH FOREST	94.2	93.6	4.2	4.5	0.1	0.2	1.3	1.7	4.7	4.9	5.5	5.2	4.9	23.0	31.3	19.2	1.4	81.6	46.2	49.8	50.2
28771	ROBBINSVILLE	91.3	90.7	0.2	0.2	0.2	0.2	0.8	1.0	6.0	6.3	6.2	5.4	5.3	25.4	27.3	16.0	2.1	78.2	41.7	49.4	50.7
28772	ROSMAN	98.2	97.9	0.4	0.5	0.2	0.2	0.5	0.8	6.1	6.3	6.9	5.9	5.0	27.0	26.5	15.2	1.2	77.0	40.4	49.5	50.5
28773	SALUDA	96.9	96.5	1.3	1.4	0.2	0.3	2.6	3.3	5.1	5.4	5.2	4.6	3.8	21.8	33.4	17.6	3.0	81.3	47.7	48.0	52.0
28774	SAPPHIRE	98.2	97.8	0.1	0.1	0.1	0.1	1.3	1.8	5.1	5.7	5.3	4.5	3.5	21.8	33.9	19.3	1.0	81.3	47.8	49.3	50.7
28775	SCALY MOUNTAIN	99.2	99.3	0.0	0.0	0.0	0.0	2.9	3.9	4.4	4.4	5.1	6.0	3.7	22.2	34.3	17.9	2.1	82.3	47.7	49.0	51.0
28777	SPRUCE PINE	94.3	93.5	3.1	3.3	0.2	0.2	2.7	3.4	4.6	5.0	6.2	5.5	5.7	29.4	26.4	15.2	1.9	80.7	41.1	52.0	48.1
28778	SWANNANOA	93.1	92.2	3.8	4.1	0.6	0.7	3.9	5.0	5.3	5.2	6.3	7.4	6.5	26.4	27.4	13.2	2.5	79.1	40.4	48.4	51.6
28779	SYLVA	94.5	93.7	1.6	1.6	0.6	0.7	1.3	1.6	5.2	5.2	5.3	5.6	6.7	27.0	28.0	14.9	2.0	81.1	41.3	48.4	51.6
28781	TOPTON	98.9	98.7	0.3	0.4	0.0	0.0	1.5	1.8	4.6	4.5	4.5	5.1	4.9	21.9	30.0	21.7	2.7	83.3	48.6	48.7	51.3
28782	TRYON	88.0	87.7	10.4	10.5	0.3	0.4	2.4	3.0	4.1	4.4	4.9	4.0	3.3	18.2	29.4	25.4	6.4	83.9	53.0	45.8	54.3
28783	TUCKASEGEE	96.8	96.2	0.5	0.5	0.1	0.2	2.2	2.8	6.2	6.0	5.9	5.0	5.9	28.2	29.7	12.0	1.2	78.9	40.4	50.8	49.2
28785	WAYNESVILLE	97.9	97.6	0.3	0.3	0.4	0.5	0.9	1.2	5.2	5.4	5.6	4.6	4.0	25.3	31.2	17.3	1.5	81.0	44.9	49.2	50.8
28786	WAYNESVILLE	96.3	95.9	1.7	1.7	0.3	0.3	1.5	2.0	4.9	5.1	5.7	5.4	4.6	24.6	28.7	18.3	2.5	80.7	44.7	47.7	52.3
28787	WEAVERVILLE	96.8	96.2	0.7	0.8	0.4	0.5	2.0	2.6	6.0	6.3	6.8	5.8	5.1	28.2	27.8	12.5	1.6	77.3	40.2	48.9	51.1
28789	WHITTIER	59.6	57.8	0.3	0.3	0.2	0.3	2.3	2.7	6.1	6.4	7.1	6.1	5.5	28.0	27.7	11.8	1.4	76.8	39.0	48.8	51.2
28790	ZIRCONIA	97.0	96.3	0.2	0.2	0.0	0.0	2.8	3.7	6.4	6.6	6.4	5.7	5.3	28.3	28.0	12.2	1.2	77.1	39.0	50.6	49.4
28791	HENDERSONVILLE	94.1	93.6	3.1	3.2	0.8	0.9	3.1	3.9	3.7	3.9	4.7	4.8	4.3	18.3	28.1	27.9	4.3	84.6	52.5	47.4	52.6
28792	HENDERSONVILLE	88.6	87.1	4.3	4.2	0.8	0.9	9.3	11.9	6.3	6.3	6.2	5.5	5.3	27.2	24.2	15.7	3.4	77.9	40.5	48.4	51.6
28801	ASHEVILLE	52.5	51.1	43.8	44.8	0.5	0.6	2.4	2.9	4.8	4.7	5.1	7.0	9.9	32.0	23.6	10.9	2.0	82.2	36.2	48.6	51.4
28803	ASHEVILLE	83.7	82.7	11.8	12.1	1.2	1.4	3.4	4.1	5.5	5.7	5.9	5.6	5.7	25.8	26.7	16.2	3.0	79.3	42.1	47.6	52.4
28804	ASHEVILLE	93.4	92.5	3.7	4.0	0.6	0.7	2.5	3.3	4.2	4.6	5.0	6.4	6.6	25.4	28.2	17.3	2.4	83.0	43.6	48.2	51.8
28805	ASHEVILLE	90.8	89.8	6.1	6.4	0.9	1.2	2.1	2.7	4.3	4.4	5.5	6.1	6.6	26.6	27.5	16.5	2.5	82.2	42.6	46.5	53.5
28806	ASHEVILLE	86.4	85.1	7.9	8.2	0.9	1.0	5.8	7.3	6.4	6.1	5.9	5.6	6.3	30.4	24.4	12.9	2.0	78.1	38.0	47.7	52.3
28901	ANDREWS	95.2	94.7	1.8	1.9	0.1	0.1	1.4	1.7	5.3	5.6	5.7	4.5	4.9	24.5	28.8	17.9	2.9	80.6	44.6	48.9	51.1
28902	BRASSTOWN	97.9	97.7	0.6	0.6	0.1	0.1	0.7	1.0	4.5	4.8	5.1	5.1	4.9	22.3	34.2	17.2	1.8	82.3	47.0	48.1	51.9
28904	HAYESVILLE	98.0	97.9	0.8	0.8	0.2	0.2	0.8	1.0	4.2	4.5	5.1	4.6	4.4	21.3	33.0	19.7	3.3	83.5	48.8	49.2	50.8
28905	MARBLE	95.0	94.4	1.1	1.2	0.3	0.3	1.9	2.4	6.1	6.3	5.8	5.4	5.5	24.8	27.5	16.2	2.6	78.4	42.2	49.6	50.4
28906	MURPHY	94.7	94.2	1.7	1.7	0.4	0.5	1.1	1.4	5.4	5.5	5.4	5.0	4.8	23.0	30.3	18.4	2.3	80.6	45.7	48.8	51.2
28909	WARNE	97.7	97.5	0.7	0.7	0.2	0.2	1.8	2.2	3.7	4.1	5.6	4.8	4.6	23.0	33.0	19.1	2.2	84.0	47.5	49.0	51.0
	NORTH CAROLINA	72.1	71.2	21.6	21.6	1.5	1.8	4.7	5.9	6.7	6.6	6.8	6.7	7.1	29.8	24.2	10.8	1.4	76.2	36.2	49.2	50.8
	UNITED STATES	75.1	73.6	12.3	12.5	3.8	4.2	12.5	14.1	6.9	6.7	7.2	7.0	7.3	28.6	23.8	10.8	1.7	75.1	36.0	49.1	50.9

#	POST OFFICE NAME	2004 Per Capita Income	2004 HH Income Base	Less than $25,000	$25,000 to $49,999	$50,000 to $99,999	$100,000 to $149,999	$150,000 or More	2004	2009	2004 National Centile	2004 State Centile	2004 Home Value Base	Less than $50,000	$50,000 to $89,999	$90,000 to $174,999	$175,000 to $399,999	$400,000 or More	2004 Median Home Value
28708	BALSAM GROVE	19714	240	37.9	32.5	22.9	4.6	2.1	32576	36902	20	19	191	28.8	26.7	32.5	11.0	1.1	82500
28709	BARNARDSVILLE	16858	989	35.2	35.8	23.2	4.8	1.1	33395	37871	22	22	789	20.9	25.0	35.7	16.4	2.0	96250
28711	BLACK MOUNTAIN	23179	5734	28.2	34.4	28.7	6.4	2.3	40867	46790	49	57	4267	14.1	16.2	39.2	26.6	4.0	124211
28712	BREVARD	23658	7226	28.7	31.7	30.0	6.9	2.8	41699	46964	52	61	5466	12.3	16.9	38.6	28.3	3.9	130448
28713	BRYSON CITY	18058	4003	37.6	34.7	22.4	3.5	1.8	33097	37609	21	21	3150	23.8	20.0	37.2	15.0	4.0	100161
28714	BURNSVILLE	18592	7107	39.1	32.6	23.0	3.3	1.9	31916	35691	18	17	5650	19.7	27.0	35.5	16.4	1.5	96678
28715	CANDLER	20852	8931	27.3	33.6	31.3	5.5	2.3	40797	46957	49	56	7148	21.4	11.7	41.5	23.6	1.9	118359
28716	CANTON	19842	7407	32.9	35.4	25.8	3.9	2.0	36334	40780	33	36	5864	16.0	26.8	43.6	12.5	1.2	98870
28717	CASHIERS	36571	761	17.0	32.6	30.4	10.1	10.0	50503	60501	73	86	642	13.1	7.0	17.9	29.0	33.0	251429
28718	CEDAR MOUNTAIN	23344	111	21.6	39.6	32.4	5.4	0.9	42928	48914	56	67	90	5.6	15.6	55.6	18.9	4.4	127381
28719	CHEROKEE	14280	2026	44.6	28.6	20.8	3.7	2.4	28759	32073	10	9	1608	28.8	27.1	31.8	9.6	2.7	80594
28721	CLYDE	22169	3833	28.6	33.7	30.2	5.3	2.3	40413	45339	48	54	2903	18.7	17.8	36.2	24.5	2.8	115153
28722	COLUMBUS	24128	3629	27.0	30.8	30.7	7.7	3.2	42557	48261	55	65	2780	14.6	21.1	32.5	25.0	6.9	119955
28723	CULLOWHEE	20272	2875	36.9	28.2	24.8	6.3	3.8	35309	40164	29	31	1744	12.9	14.0	36.4	31.6	5.2	137228
28726	EAST FLAT ROCK	16359	1389	36.9	38.1	21.1	2.7	1.2	32704	36070	20	20	1021	27.5	26.0	36.7	7.7	2.1	85069
28729	ETOWAH	24403	968	25.5	32.3	33.2	7.3	1.7	42367	47794	54	64	824	10.7	10.2	49.5	27.7	1.9	129128
28730	FAIRVIEW	23754	3477	21.3	30.5	32.1	11.4	4.8	48414	54983	69	84	2957	12.9	12.1	30.9	36.5	7.7	149958
28731	FLAT ROCK	28351	3094	20.9	34.3	30.4	7.6	6.7	46016	53435	64	78	2635	13.6	17.3	29.0	26.1	13.9	136941
28732	FLETCHER	24409	5121	23.0	30.5	32.9	8.9	4.8	46938	53376	66	81	4203	15.9	11.6	35.1	32.6	4.7	141810
28733	FONTANA DAM	17534	72	41.7	29.2	22.2	5.6	1.4	30000	34057	12	12	63	34.9	33.3	19.1	11.1	1.6	68750
28734	FRANKLIN	19855	10989	36.7	34.5	22.0	4.9	1.9	34217	37858	25	26	8720	11.6	22.0	43.2	21.3	2.0	113232
28735	GERTON	18914	78	35.9	26.9	30.8	5.1	1.3	36551	39443	34	37	63	23.8	15.9	36.5	22.2	1.6	106731
28736	GLENVILLE	25954	249	30.1	30.9	30.5	4.0	4.4	42351	48813	54	64	196	13.8	15.8	22.5	29.6	18.4	165000
28739	HENDERSONVILLE	28218	8951	24.0	32.5	29.7	7.9	5.9	44127	50922	59	71	6888	5.7	11.9	34.6	40.6	7.2	168781
28740	GREEN MOUNTAIN	19350	814	33.2	39.1	22.4	3.0	2.5	35698	39734	30	33	691	19.1	28.5	33.9	17.1	1.5	93837
28741	HIGHLANDS	34463	1450	24.3	29.1	28.6	8.5	9.5	46086	53849	64	79	1219	1.9	3.5	21.5	46.2	26.9	271573
28742	HORSE SHOE	24896	2714	16.8	31.3	38.6	9.9	3.4	51503	58557	75	87	2325	10.7	8.3	39.7	38.9	2.5	149206
28743	HOT SPRINGS	16407	1418	46.9	30.1	17.9	3.6	1.5	27252	31186	7	6	1118	27.7	24.5	23.9	16.5	7.4	85192
28745	LAKE JUNALUSKA	33988	301	21.6	23.9	37.5	12.6	4.3	54191	63910	79	89	241	4.2	7.1	28.2	48.6	12.0	207927
28746	LAKE LURE	22855	1139	32.6	31.3	25.9	7.4	2.8	38040	44282	39	45	950	12.1	16.5	26.3	35.4	9.7	147727
28747	LAKE TOXAWAY	25690	978	28.3	33.5	26.3	5.7	6.1	40954	46630	50	58	818	18.0	15.4	38.3	13.5	14.9	115141
28748	LEICESTER	19320	4368	28.3	34.1	31.6	4.2	1.8	40033	45600	46	52	3618	25.0	18.9	33.4	20.0	2.7	104027
28751	MAGGIE VALLEY	23793	1462	27.5	36.8	28.6	5.9	1.2	40989	46468	50	58	1199	10.0	11.6	49.2	23.3	5.9	134325
28752	MARION	18549	12110	34.1	36.1	23.4	4.5	1.9	35037	38904	28	29	9190	28.5	31.6	30.4	8.5	1.0	78423
28753	MARSHALL	18017	4303	39.3	31.9	23.1	4.4	1.5	32934	36775	21	20	3384	25.7	16.7	37.1	17.3	3.3	101711
28754	MARS HILL	19498	2931	31.3	32.7	28.7	5.3	2.1	37978	42696	39	44	2215	19.3	13.9	42.8	20.9	3.2	119615
28756	MILL SPRING	16782	1708	29.8	39.9	26.0	3.3	1.1	35117	39053	28	30	1356	21.3	28.7	32.3	13.2	4.5	90000
28761	NEBO	17781	2771	34.3	31.1	28.0	4.6	2.0	36561	40176	34	38	2281	26.6	32.1	27.5	11.3	2.5	78850
28762	OLD FORT	19528	2955	30.3	37.9	26.2	3.8	1.9	36975	41297	35	40	2326	25.8	35.6	30.7	7.4	0.4	78646
28763	OTTO	19545	832	27.9	40.4	26.0	4.3	1.4	37416	41529	37	41	700	12.6	27.3	36.4	22.9	0.9	105990
28766	PENROSE	23615	383	22.2	33.2	32.9	9.7	2.1	46334	51510	65	79	323	13.3	15.2	33.1	31.9	6.5	146759
28768	PISGAH FOREST	24641	3030	24.7	30.9	31.8	9.0	3.7	45921	51613	64	78	2552	12.1	16.7	34.5	31.8	4.9	135776
28771	ROBBINSVILLE	15960	3209	45.0	30.8	19.7	3.6	1.0	28548	32145	10	8	2600	31.2	29.2	26.4	11.7	1.5	74815
28772	ROSMAN	19939	885	29.8	34.9	29.5	4.4	1.4	38405	42952	41	46	714	23.7	20.6	31.9	20.3	3.5	103529
28773	SALUDA	23613	994	28.3	36.1	30.2	6.2	3.8	43888	49008	58	70	838	9.3	16.8	42.1	27.9	3.8	129464
28774	SAPPHIRE	29705	459	25.1	29.9	30.9	7.4	6.8	46358	53386	65	79	382	9.2	13.6	28.8	24.9	23.6	169643
28775	SCALY MOUNTAIN	24985	256	25.4	30.5	36.3	4.7	3.1	44075	49444	59	71	213	3.8	11.3	46.0	29.6	9.4	145500
28777	SPRUCE PINE	17737	3713	35.7	34.0	23.9	4.0	3.0	35703	39749	30	33	2918	21.6	29.9	35.3	12.6	0.6	87805
28778	SWANNANOA	20051	3312	32.4	30.8	29.1	6.0	1.7	37710	43237	38	43	2503	17.4	17.7	45.8	18.0	1.1	108814
28779	SYLVA	21135	7172	35.4	31.2	25.3	6.0	2.2	35466	40245	29	32	5011	16.9	19.9	38.2	22.7	2.4	113276
28781	TOPTON	16163	377	46.2	35.0	14.3	2.9	1.6	27049	31251	7	5	320	14.1	20.9	41.6	19.7	3.8	109444
28782	TRYON	28209	2289	26.5	34.4	25.7	7.9	5.5	41493	47857	51	60	1802	6.1	17.2	36.2	33.5	7.1	154490
28783	TUCKASEGEE	17743	712	37.2	35.0	24.0	2.0	1.8	32041	36804	18	18	551	28.5	21.2	26.3	20.5	3.5	90577
28785	WAYNESVILLE	22237	3066	27.4	35.3	29.2	5.1	3.0	40025	45418	46	52	2548	23.4	12.7	32.4	27.3	4.2	122212
28786	WAYNESVILLE	21434	8642	33.3	34.0	25.2	4.7	2.9	35586	40026	30	32	6380	17.2	21.5	36.8	21.1	3.3	108118
28787	WEAVERVILLE	22565	7592	24.5	32.1	32.7	7.6	3.1	44989	50827	61	74	6110	15.0	10.6	36.4	33.0	5.0	141713
28789	WHITTIER	19661	2581	34.3	32.8	25.9	4.8	2.2	36660	41628	34	38	2028	23.3	26.1	33.6	14.4	2.6	90902
28790	ZIRCONIA	23942	1147	25.1	38.0	26.8	5.2	4.9	40031	45088	46	52	957	20.8	10.0	45.1	21.7	2.3	116827
28791	HENDERSONVILLE	26841	6211	22.8	32.0	31.9	8.3	5.0	45667	52051	63	77	4955	5.2	10.6	39.1	42.4	2.8	166112
28792	HENDERSONVILLE	19791	12183	32.4	34.4	25.9	5.0	2.4	36612	41568	34	38	9088	19.2	17.1	41.0	20.9	1.9	114693
28801	ASHEVILLE	18563	6205	53.1	24.2	16.4	4.2	2.1	22811	25740	3	1	2144	6.6	19.6	42.4	26.0	5.3	133892
28803	ASHEVILLE	32807	11485	24.8	28.6	28.7	9.6	8.5	46574	53265	65	80	7586	6.9	15.0	32.2	33.9	12.0	162166
28804	ASHEVILLE	31371	8086	24.7	29.3	27.6	9.8	8.6	45567	51933	63	76	5893	8.0	9.5	24.4	46.7	11.4	195371
28805	ASHEVILLE	25584	8037	25.7	31.9	31.0	8.6	2.9	43401	49480	57	68	5238	7.0	10.2	47.0	32.6	3.3	144381
28806	ASHEVILLE	18826	15154	33.2	34.4	27.4	3.8	1.2	36232	41600	32	36	9984	19.4	19.7	46.8	13.4	0.6	104576
28901	ANDREWS	19283	2235	41.8	34.6	19.4	2.0	2.2	29984	33410	12	12	1750	27.5	30.8	31.5	9.9	0.3	81761
28902	BRASSTOWN	24004	487	33.1	30.4	27.5	6.2	2.9	37931	44049	39	44	410	16.3	29.5	35.6	15.4	3.2	97083
28904	HAYESVILLE	20525	3658	36.3	32.0	23.6	6.1	2.0	33823	37901	24	24	3030	12.2	19.0	39.3	21.8	7.7	116472
28905	MARBLE	16649	1452	38.5	36.8	21.2	2.8	0.7	32790	36370	20	20	1178	20.8	31.2	35.8	11.8	0.3	87931
28906	MURPHY	18304	7562	40.3	31.9	21.3	4.5	2.1	30638	34752	14	14	6166	20.5	25.6	38.6	14.1	1.2	96797
28909	WARNE	18084	285	37.5	35.1	21.1	4.9	1.4	31290	35726	16	16	240	12.5	24.6	40.0	21.7	1.3	105814
	NORTH CAROLINA	23743		27.0	29.8	30.1	8.5	4.7	43794	50711				14.5	20.0	39.7	21.7	4.1	115673
	UNITED STATES	25866		24.7	27.1	30.8	10.9	6.5	48124	56710				10.9	15.0	33.7	30.1	10.4	145905

SPENDING POTENTIAL INDICES

NORTH CAROLINA

#	ZIP CODE POST OFFICE NAME	FINANCIAL SERVICES				THE HOME						ENTERTAINMENT						PERSONAL			
		Auto Loan	Home Loan	Invest-ments	Retire-ment Plans	Home Repair	Lawn & Garden	Comput-ers & Hard-ware	Major Appli-ances	TV, Radio, Sound Equip-ment	Furni-ture	Dine out/ Carry out	Sports Equip-ment	Fees & Tickets	Toys & Games	Travel	Cable TV	Apparel & Services	Auto Repairs	Health Insur-ance	Pets & Supplies
28708	BALSAM GROVE	94	63	28	54	71	82	61	76	73	62	86	91	52	81	62	79	78	75	94	108
28709	BARNARDSVILLE	74	55	33	51	60	68	54	63	61	54	73	74	49	71	54	64	67	62	74	84
28711	BLACK MOUNTAIN	78	71	63	69	75	83	70	75	74	69	90	87	69	90	72	76	85	75	82	90
28712	BREVARD	85	71	56	66	76	88	69	79	76	70	91	86	65	85	72	80	85	77	92	97
28713	BRYSON CITY	69	53	35	49	59	68	54	62	61	52	72	71	48	69	55	64	66	62	73	80
28714	BURNSVILLE	78	54	28	48	61	70	54	65	63	54	75	77	47	71	55	68	68	64	79	89
28715	CANDLER	80	72	57	69	74	80	69	75	72	69	88	86	66	86	69	73	84	74	78	91
28716	CANTON	77	61	41	57	66	75	61	69	68	60	81	80	56	79	62	71	75	68	79	88
28717	CASHIERS	132	103	70	93	116	131	97	117	110	96	130	137	87	129	104	118	121	115	139	160
28718	CEDAR MOUNTAIN	89	70	48	63	79	88	66	79	75	65	88	93	59	87	70	80	82	78	94	108
28719	CHEROKEE	63	55	45	53	56	61	55	59	58	56	71	67	52	68	55	59	68	59	61	69
28721	CLYDE	85	68	47	65	74	83	69	77	75	67	90	89	64	88	69	78	84	76	87	97
28722	COLUMBUS	86	75	63	72	79	87	73	81	77	74	94	92	69	89	74	79	89	80	88	99
28723	CULLOWHEE	76	58	58	59	61	69	72	69	75	68	92	87	64	87	68	72	87	75	72	86
28726	EAST FLAT ROCK	70	54	33	49	58	64	52	60	58	53	69	71	46	65	52	60	64	60	68	80
28729	ETOWAH	81	69	57	66	74	88	69	77	75	70	91	81	66	80	72	80	84	76	91	91
28730	FAIRVIEW	99	89	70	85	94	101	83	91	87	83	106	109	81	109	85	89	101	89	98	117
28731	FLAT ROCK	108	91	72	85	98	110	86	99	94	89	114	109	82	104	90	98	107	97	113	123
28732	FLETCHER	92	88	75	86	89	94	82	87	83	83	102	102	81	101	82	83	98	86	89	106
28733	FONTANA DAM	73	57	39	52	65	73	54	65	61	54	73	76	48	72	58	65	67	64	77	89
28734	FRANKLIN	77	58	38	54	65	75	59	68	66	57	78	79	52	76	60	70	72	68	81	89
28735	GERTON	72	56	38	51	63	71	53	64	60	52	71	75	47	70	56	64	66	63	75	87
28736	GLENVILLE	95	74	50	67	83	94	70	84	79	69	94	99	62	93	74	85	87	83	100	115
28739	HENDERSONVILLE	94	84	76	81	88	102	84	91	90	85	109	98	82	101	87	94	103	90	103	105
28740	GREEN MOUNTAIN	85	59	30	52	66	76	58	70	68	58	80	83	50	77	58	73	73	69	85	97
28741	HIGHLANDS	125	98	67	88	110	124	92	111	104	91	124	130	82	122	98	111	115	109	131	152
28742	HORSE SHOE	98	87	68	83	92	100	81	90	86	81	104	105	79	105	83	88	99	87	98	114
28743	HOT SPRINGS	67	47	25	41	53	61	45	56	53	46	63	66	39	60	47	57	58	55	68	78
28745	LAKE JUNALUSKA	95	88	85	84	94	110	82	93	86	88	108	91	83	90	89	92	101	90	109	106
28746	LAKE LURE	84	65	42	58	73	82	61	74	70	61	82	87	54	81	65	74	76	73	88	101
28747	LAKE TOXAWAY	109	79	44	69	89	101	75	92	88	76	104	109	65	100	78	95	95	91	112	129
28748	LEICESTER	79	69	52	66	70	75	66	72	68	68	84	84	62	79	66	68	80	72	74	88
28751	MAGGIE VALLEY	83	65	45	59	74	83	62	74	70	61	83	87	55	82	66	74	77	73	88	101
28752	MARION	80	58	32	52	64	73	57	68	66	57	78	80	50	75	57	70	71	67	81	92
28753	MARSHALL	75	53	28	47	59	68	52	63	61	52	72	74	45	69	53	65	66	62	76	86
28754	MARS HILL	75	61	44	59	66	75	63	69	69	61	82	79	58	80	63	71	76	68	79	85
28756	MILL SPRING	78	54	26	47	60	69	52	64	62	53	73	76	45	69	53	66	66	63	78	90
28761	NEBO	77	62	41	57	66	73	59	68	65	59	78	80	54	75	59	67	73	67	76	89
28762	OLD FORT	87	61	32	54	69	78	59	72	69	60	82	86	52	78	60	74	75	71	87	100
28763	OTTO	76	60	41	54	67	75	56	68	64	56	75	79	50	74	60	68	70	67	80	92
28766	PENROSE	91	81	61	76	85	91	74	83	79	74	96	98	73	98	77	81	91	80	89	107
28768	PISGAH FOREST	98	77	52	70	84	96	73	86	82	75	99	98	67	92	76	87	91	84	102	113
28771	ROBBINSVILLE	68	47	23	41	53	61	45	56	54	46	63	66	39	60	46	58	58	55	68	79
28772	ROSMAN	89	62	30	54	69	79	59	73	71	60	83	87	51	79	60	76	76	72	89	103
28773	SALUDA	92	76	55	70	84	93	71	83	79	71	94	97	66	93	75	83	88	82	96	111
28774	SAPPHIRE	107	84	57	75	94	106	79	95	89	78	106	111	70	104	84	95	98	94	112	130
28775	SCALY MOUNTAIN	95	74	51	67	83	94	70	84	79	69	94	99	62	93	75	85	87	83	100	115
28777	SPRUCE PINE	82	57	29	51	64	74	56	68	66	57	78	81	49	74	57	70	71	67	82	94
28778	SWANNANOA	75	70	60	68	72	77	68	72	70	67	86	83	66	86	68	70	82	71	75	85
28779	SYLVA	76	59	44	57	65	74	63	69	69	61	82	81	57	79	63	71	76	69	79	87
28781	TOPTON	61	48	33	43	54	61	45	54	51	45	60	64	40	60	48	55	56	54	64	74
28782	TRYON	86	80	79	79	84	95	79	85	81	80	100	92	77	92	82	84	95	84	94	99
28783	TUCKASEGEE	74	53	30	47	60	69	51	63	60	51	70	74	44	68	53	64	65	62	76	87
28785	WAYNESVILLE	83	71	55	67	75	84	67	77	72	69	88	85	63	80	70	75	82	75	86	95
28786	WAYNESVILLE	78	62	44	58	67	78	63	71	70	62	84	80	58	79	64	74	77	70	83	89
28787	WEAVERVILLE	87	77	60	74	80	87	75	81	78	75	95	94	72	94	75	79	90	80	86	99
28789	WHITTIER	78	65	47	60	70	77	62	71	67	62	80	83	56	78	64	69	76	70	79	93
28790	ZIRCONIA	102	83	55	76	89	98	78	89	86	78	103	107	73	103	80	90	97	88	101	119
28791	HENDERSONVILLE	87	84	81	81	87	99	81	87	84	83	104	93	81	96	85	87	98	86	96	99
28792	HENDERSONVILLE	77	64	48	60	67	75	63	70	68	63	82	81	59	80	63	70	77	70	77	87
28801	ASHEVILLE	50	43	55	44	42	48	52	49	54	51	68	58	50	65	50	53	66	53	49	55
28803	ASHEVILLE	103	103	108	102	104	114	102	104	103	102	128	119	104	128	104	104	124	104	107	118
28804	ASHEVILLE	103	101	102	100	104	115	101	104	102	100	126	117	100	122	103	104	121	104	110	119
28805	ASHEVILLE	76	78	83	76	79	87	77	78	79	76	97	90	78	99	79	80	94	78	81	89
28806	ASHEVILLE	63	59	56	58	60	66	61	62	62	60	77	72	59	76	60	62	74	62	64	71
28901	ANDREWS	79	54	25	47	61	70	52	64	62	53	73	77	44	69	53	67	66	64	79	91
28902	BRASSTOWN	87	68	48	65	74	88	73	80	81	70	96	88	66	89	73	85	88	80	96	96
28904	HAYESVILLE	76	58	38	53	64	74	58	68	66	57	78	77	52	73	59	70	71	67	81	87
28905	MARBLE	72	51	26	45	57	65	49	60	58	50	68	71	43	65	50	61	62	59	72	83
28906	MURPHY	72	54	33	49	60	69	53	63	61	53	72	73	47	69	55	65	66	62	76	84
28909	WARNE	70	52	35	50	57	69	58	64	65	55	77	72	52	72	57	69	70	64	77	77
	NORTH CAROLINA	90	81	73	80	83	90	81	85	84	82	103	100	79	101	81	84	99	85	88	102
	UNITED STATES	100	100	100	100	100	100	100	100	100	100	100	100	100	100	100	100	100	100	100	100

ZIP CODE		POPULATION			2000-2004 ANNUAL RATE		HOUSEHOLDS					FAMILIES		
# POST OFFICE NAME	COUNTY FIPS CODE	2000	2004	2009	% Rate	State Centile	2000	2004	2009	% Annual Rate 2000-2004	2004 Average HH Size	2000	2004	% Annual Rate 2000-2004
58004 AMENIA	017	279	274	281	-0.4	69	106	108	114	0.4	2.51	80	79	-0.3
58005 ARGUSVILLE	017	548	534	545	-0.6	58	210	212	224	0.2	2.52	167	164	-0.4
58006 ARTHUR	017	506	497	509	-0.4	69	164	166	175	0.3	2.83	112	108	-0.9
58007 AYR	017	142	138	142	-0.7	55	62	62	65	0.0	2.18	45	43	-1.1
58008 BARNEY	077	293	318	325	2.0	97	101	113	118	2.7	2.80	75	82	2.1
58009 BLANCHARD	097	90	88	87	-0.5	63	36	36	37	0.0	2.44	27	27	0.0
58011 BUFFALO	017	429	422	433	-0.4	70	176	178	187	0.3	2.37	126	123	-0.6
58012 CASSELTON	017	2038	2014	2069	-0.3	74	777	790	833	0.4	2.55	558	543	-0.6
58013 CAYUGA	081	212	208	207	-0.5	67	85	86	88	0.3	2.42	60	59	-0.4
58015 CHRISTINE	077	362	377	377	1.0	93	131	139	142	1.4	2.71	104	107	0.7
58016 CLIFFORD	097	108	106	104	-0.4	69	46	46	47	0.0	2.30	35	34	-0.7
58017 COGSWELL	081	478	464	460	-0.7	53	198	198	202	0.0	2.34	146	142	-0.7
58018 COLFAX	077	380	384	380	0.3	85	137	141	142	0.7	2.72	102	102	0.0
58021 DAVENPORT	017	450	459	473	0.5	89	158	166	175	1.2	2.77	125	126	0.2
58027 ENDERLIN	073	1458	1485	1552	0.4	88	604	630	675	1.0	2.27	385	387	0.1
58029 ERIE	017	163	160	164	-0.4	69	62	63	66	0.4	2.40	43	41	-1.1
58030 FAIRMOUNT	077	748	714	686	-1.1	32	303	299	294	-0.3	2.39	209	199	-1.2
58031 FINGAL	017	504	462	449	-2.0	3	196	184	184	-1.5	2.51	148	135	-2.1
58032 FORMAN	081	756	746	742	-0.3	72	312	316	322	0.3	2.27	203	198	-0.6
58033 FORT RANSOM	073	470	464	481	-0.3	73	190	192	204	0.3	2.42	146	145	-0.2
58035 GALESBURG	097	377	370	366	-0.4	69	146	147	150	0.2	2.50	109	107	-0.4
58036 GARDNER	017	348	332	339	-1.1	32	135	134	141	-0.2	2.48	101	97	-1.0
58038 GRANDIN	017	252	241	246	-1.0	35	99	98	104	-0.2	2.45	74	71	-1.0
58040 GWINNER	081	899	908	913	0.2	85	371	386	398	0.9	2.35	262	264	0.2
58041 HANKINSON	077	1787	1733	1678	-0.7	52	707	704	698	-0.1	2.29	450	430	-1.1
58042 HARWOOD	017	1202	1229	1271	0.5	90	394	418	447	1.4	2.94	343	356	0.9
58043 HAVANA	081	232	226	225	-0.6	58	95	95	98	0.0	2.38	66	64	-0.7
58045 HILLSBORO	097	2401	2405	2390	0.0	82	984	1012	1029	0.7	2.33	655	649	-0.2
58046 HOPE	091	679	664	647	-0.5	64	273	271	269	-0.2	2.45	189	182	-0.9
58047 HORACE	017	2584	2749	2897	1.5	97	861	945	1024	2.2	2.91	743	804	1.9
58048 HUNTER	017	476	468	479	-0.4	70	200	202	213	0.2	2.18	136	132	-0.7
58049 KATHRYN	003	303	297	291	-0.5	65	124	125	125	0.2	2.38	96	95	-0.3
58051 KINDRED	017	1337	1409	1466	1.2	95	487	527	562	1.9	2.67	366	382	1.0
58052 LEONARD	017	672	656	660	-0.6	60	283	284	294	0.1	2.31	219	212	-0.8
58053 LIDGERWOOD	077	1348	1255	1197	-1.7	9	581	553	539	-1.2	2.27	381	350	-2.0
58054 LISBON	073	3384	3569	3788	1.3	95	1358	1476	1611	2.0	2.27	884	926	1.1
58056 LUVERNE	091	240	238	233	-0.2	76	94	95	95	0.3	2.51	65	64	-0.4
58057 MCLEOD	073	137	143	148	1.0	94	56	59	62	1.2	2.42	42	43	0.6
58058 MANTADOR	077	134	128	124	-1.1	33	57	56	56	-0.4	2.20	36	34	-1.3
58059 MAPLETON	017	1053	1105	1174	1.1	94	363	395	432	2.0	2.80	293	309	1.3
58060 MILNOR	081	1467	1503	1531	0.6	91	556	584	609	1.2	2.57	386	393	0.4
58061 MOORETON	077	433	462	468	1.5	97	175	193	201	2.3	2.37	121	129	1.5
58062 NOME	003	198	187	180	-1.3	20	79	76	75	-0.9	2.46	59	56	-1.2
58063 ORISKA	003	369	361	349	-0.5	64	133	134	133	0.2	2.69	105	103	-0.5
58064 PAGE	017	515	500	511	-0.7	54	209	208	218	-0.1	2.40	157	150	-1.1
58067 RUTLAND	081	308	300	298	-0.6	57	128	128	131	0.0	2.34	91	88	-0.8
58068 SHELDON	073	372	377	392	0.3	86	143	147	155	0.7	2.56	104	105	0.2
58069 STIRUM	081	141	137	136	-0.7	55	62	62	63	0.0	2.21	47	46	-0.5
58071 TOWER CITY	017	413	408	415	-0.3	73	169	171	179	0.3	2.39	123	120	-0.6
58072 VALLEY CITY	003	8323	8039	7746	-0.8	47	3532	3500	3450	-0.2	2.13	2101	1995	-1.2
58075 WAHPETON	077	9983	9674	9369	-0.7	51	3938	3933	3911	0.0	2.27	2384	2284	-1.0
58076 WAHPETON	077	487	480	477	-0.3	71	5	5	4	0.0	2.60	2	2	0.0
58077 WALCOTT	077	680	698	694	0.6	91	252	264	268	1.1	2.64	198	202	0.5
58078 WEST FARGO	017	15392	17035	18417	2.4	99	5918	6770	7527	3.2	2.52	4088	4469	2.1
58079 WHEATLAND	017	543	516	526	-1.2	28	203	200	210	-0.4	2.58	156	148	-1.2
58081 WYNDMERE	077	972	953	930	-0.5	66	371	371	370	0.0	2.57	262	253	-0.8
58102 FARGO	017	31919	31205	31963	-0.5	63	13196	13284	14039	0.2	2.12	6679	6372	-1.1
58103 FARGO	017	46791	48826	51781	1.0	94	21502	23226	25372	1.8	2.07	11092	11272	0.4
58104 FARGO	017	15182	18891	21622	5.3	100	5594	7258	8585	6.3	2.58	4012	4986	5.3
58201 GRAND FORKS	035	32317	32041	31875	-0.2	76	13717	13990	14181	0.5	2.25	7964	7797	-0.5
58203 GRAND FORKS	035	18599	18633	18617	0.0	82	6529	6733	6848	0.7	2.28	3548	3487	-0.4
58204 GRAND FORKS AFB	035	1384	1285	1242	-1.7	6	233	217	211	-1.7	5.29	224	208	-1.7
58205 GRAND FORKS AFB	035	3444	3199	3090	-1.7	6	1045	972	945	-1.7	2.94	1005	931	-1.8
58210 ADAMS	099	396	369	348	-1.7	9	162	156	152	-0.9	2.37	114	106	-1.7
58212 ANETA	063	546	528	512	-0.8	48	219	218	217	-0.1	2.31	139	134	-0.9
58214 ARVILLA	035	428	390	374	-2.2	2	172	163	159	-1.3	2.39	118	107	-2.3
58216 BATHGATE	067	165	163	158	-0.3	73	70	71	71	0.3	2.30	49	48	-0.5
58218 BUXTON	097	738	744	741	0.2	84	278	287	292	0.8	2.59	213	214	0.1
58219 CALEDONIA	097	132	130	128	-0.4	71	47	48	48	0.5	2.71	37	36	-0.6
58220 CAVALIER	067	2705	2629	2536	-0.7	55	1110	1114	1107	0.1	2.29	727	704	-0.8
58222 CRYSTAL	067	361	342	327	-1.3	25	147	144	141	-0.5	2.19	98	92	-1.5
58223 CUMMINGS	097	251	253	252	0.2	84	102	106	107	0.9	2.39	77	77	0.0
58224 DAHLEN	063	62	60	58	-0.8	49	27	27	27	0.0	2.22	19	18	-1.3
58225 DRAYTON	067	1167	1123	1079	-0.9	42	512	508	503	-0.2	2.21	328	314	-1.0
58227 EDINBURG	099	583	545	516	-1.6	12	263	254	248	-0.8	2.11	181	169	-1.6
58228 EMERADO	035	1185	1181	1176	-0.1	79	475	486	493	0.5	2.43	350	348	-0.1
58229 FAIRDALE	099	173	161	152	-1.7	8	76	73	71	-0.9	2.21	53	50	-1.1
58230 FINLEY	091	1297	1266	1234	-0.6	60	532	529	523	-0.1	2.39	370	356	-0.9
58231 FORDVILLE	099	550	518	494	-1.4	18	211	206	202	-0.6	2.51	144	135	-1.5
58233 FOREST RIVER	099	350	337	322	-0.9	43	131	131	130	0.0	2.57	90	87	-0.8
58235 GILBY	035	418	403	395	-0.9	45	163	161	161	-0.3	2.50	123	118	-1.0
58237 GRAFTON	099	5963	5747	5500	-0.9	45	2338	2319	2281	-0.2	2.36	1515	1449	-1.0
58238 HAMILTON	067	205	200	193	-0.6	60	86	86	86	0.0	2.33	60	59	-0.4
58239 HANNAH	019	73	67	61	-2.3	1	38	36	35	-1.3	1.83	26	24	-1.9
58240 HATTON	097	1087	1057	1038	-0.7	56	422	420	422	-0.1	2.40	295	284	-0.9
58241 HENSEL	067	168	161	155	-1.0	38	75	75	74	0.0	2.11	58	56	-0.8
58243 HOOPLE	099	623	591	561	-1.2	27	273	269	264	-0.4	2.19	185	176	-1.2
58244 INKSTER	035	461	458	456	-0.2	78	187	192	195	0.6	2.39	142	141	-0.2
58249 LANGDON	019	2998	2904	2785	-0.8	50	1258	1256	1239	0.0	2.24	818	789	-0.9
58250 LANKIN	099	388	363	342	-1.6	13	166	160	156	-0.9	2.27	121	114	-1.4
58251 LARIMORE	035	2200	2196	2192	0.0	80	867	890	905	0.6	2.43	601	596	-0.2
58254 MCVILLE	063	743	725	706	-0.6	60	330	331	331	0.1	2.03	183	175	-1.1
58255 MAIDA	019	78	75	72	-0.9	40	30	30	30	0.0	2.50	23	23	0.0
58256 MANVEL	035	1023	1031	1030	0.2	84	359	371	378	0.8	2.78	270	271	0.1
58257 MAYVILLE	097	2209	2193	2171	-0.2	77	846	861	872	0.4	2.17	486	474	-0.6
NORTH DAKOTA					0.1					0.8	2.33			-0.1
UNITED STATES					1.2					1.3	2.58			1.1

#	POST OFFICE NAME	RACE (%) White 2000	White 2004	Black 2000	Black 2004	Asian/Pacific 2000	Asian/Pacific 2004	% Hispanic Origin 2000	% Hispanic Origin 2004	2004 AGE DISTRIBUTION (%) 0-4	5-9	10-14	15-19	20-24	25-44	45-64	65-84	85+	18+	MEDIAN AGE 2004	% 2004 Males	% 2004 Females
58004	AMENIA	97.9	97.5	0.0	0.0	0.4	0.7	0.7	1.1	5.5	6.6	10.2	6.9	2.6	25.9	28.5	12.0	1.8	71.9	40.4	55.1	44.9
58005	ARGUSVILLE	99.5	99.3	0.0	0.0	0.0	0.0	0.6	0.8	6.2	6.7	7.7	6.9	5.2	25.7	30.2	10.5	0.9	75.1	40.4	51.7	48.3
58006	ARTHUR	97.6	97.4	0.0	0.0	0.0	0.0	2.2	2.4	5.6	6.4	9.5	6.6	4.0	23.3	23.7	16.1	4.6	72.8	41.5	49.9	50.1
58007	AYR	98.6	98.6	0.0	0.0	0.0	0.0	1.4	1.5	5.8	5.8	8.0	6.5	4.4	23.2	25.4	17.4	3.6	76.1	42.7	50.7	49.3
58008	BARNEY	99.0	99.1	0.0	0.0	0.0	0.0	0.0	0.0	5.7	7.2	9.4	8.8	4.1	24.5	24.2	13.5	2.5	71.7	40.0	52.8	47.2
58009	BLANCHARD	98.9	100.0	0.0	0.0	0.0	0.0	0.0	0.0	5.7	9.1	8.0	6.8	3.4	26.1	27.3	11.4	2.3	71.6	39.3	53.4	46.6
58011	BUFFALO	99.3	99.1	0.0	0.0	0.0	0.0	0.2	0.5	5.2	5.9	7.1	5.9	4.5	23.9	28.9	16.1	2.4	78.2	43.5	51.2	48.8
58012	CASSELTON	98.2	98.0	0.2	0.2	0.2	0.3	0.5	0.6	8.2	8.3	8.8	7.1	6.0	27.2	22.6	10.0	1.8	70.1	35.9	51.8	48.2
58013	CAYUGA	98.1	98.6	0.0	0.0	0.0	0.0	0.0	0.0	4.8	5.3	8.2	7.7	5.3	22.1	30.8	14.9	1.0	76.4	42.8	55.8	44.2
58015	CHRISTINE	99.2	99.7	0.0	0.0	0.0	0.0	0.6	0.5	8.0	7.2	8.8	7.4	3.5	28.7	26.3	8.8	1.6	70.3	37.8	52.8	47.2
58016	CLIFFORD	99.1	100.0	0.0	0.0	0.0	0.0	0.0	0.0	6.6	6.6	7.6	6.6	4.7	26.4	28.3	11.3	1.9	74.5	40.0	54.7	45.3
58017	COGSWELL	98.1	98.1	0.0	0.0	0.2	0.2	0.8	0.9	6.5	7.1	8.2	5.6	4.5	25.0	26.7	14.4	1.9	74.8	41.0	53.2	46.8
58018	COLFAX	98.7	98.4	0.3	0.3	0.0	0.0	0.3	0.3	7.3	7.6	7.6	7.3	5.2	26.0	24.7	12.5	1.8	72.7	39.1	52.9	47.1
58021	DAVENPORT	98.9	98.7	0.0	0.0	0.7	0.9	0.4	0.4	6.1	7.0	8.1	6.8	5.0	26.1	28.1	10.9	2.0	74.3	39.9	50.5	49.5
58027	ENDERLIN	96.9	96.4	0.3	0.3	0.3	0.4	1.8	2.1	5.9	6.0	6.4	5.9	5.7	22.2	26.3	17.2	4.4	77.7	43.7	51.0	49.0
58029	ERIE	97.6	97.5	0.0	0.0	0.0	0.0	1.8	2.5	5.6	6.3	7.5	6.9	3.8	24.4	25.0	16.3	4.4	74.4	42.3	51.3	48.8
58030	FAIRMOUNT	96.9	96.6	0.0	0.0	0.0	0.0	1.7	2.0	6.0	6.9	7.6	6.6	5.2	24.9	29.4	11.9	1.5	75.5	40.9	51.7	48.3
58031	FINGAL	99.0	98.9	0.0	0.0	0.0	0.0	0.4	0.7	6.7	7.1	6.7	6.1	5.0	21.2	29.0	15.8	2.4	75.5	43.2	52.6	47.4
58032	FORMAN	98.0	97.9	0.1	0.1	0.0	0.0	1.1	0.9	5.1	5.9	6.3	6.8	4.3	20.6	29.5	17.7	3.8	78.7	45.6	51.6	48.4
58033	FORT RANSOM	97.9	97.8	0.2	0.2	0.4	0.4	0.9	0.9	6.7	6.9	6.7	6.5	5.0	25.7	26.3	14.9	1.5	76.1	40.5	52.6	47.4
58035	GALESBURG	98.7	98.7	0.0	0.0	0.0	0.0	0.5	0.5	6.2	7.8	7.3	6.8	4.3	25.7	27.6	12.2	2.2	74.1	40.0	52.7	47.3
58036	GARDNER	99.7	100.0	0.0	0.0	0.0	0.0	0.9	0.9	5.4	5.7	6.9	6.6	5.4	24.4	30.1	13.6	1.8	78.3	42.4	50.9	49.1
58038	GRANDIN	99.6	100.0	0.0	0.0	0.0	0.0	0.8	0.8	5.4	5.8	7.1	6.2	5.4	25.3	30.7	12.5	1.7	77.2	42.2	51.0	49.0
58040	GWINNER	98.9	98.9	0.0	0.0	0.0	0.0	0.7	0.7	6.2	6.8	8.8	6.4	5.5	27.5	26.7	10.5	1.7	74.2	37.2	53.2	46.8
58041	HANKINSON	97.3	96.8	0.0	0.0	0.2	0.2	1.0	1.2	5.6	5.7	6.2	6.6	5.4	21.4	25.5	17.4	6.3	77.8	44.5	49.2	50.8
58042	HARWOOD	98.8	98.8	0.0	0.0	0.0	0.0	0.8	0.9	7.2	8.1	9.4	8.4	5.1	27.1	29.1	5.5	0.2	70.0	36.1	51.3	48.7
58043	HAVANA	97.4	97.4	0.0	0.0	0.0	0.0	0.0	0.0	3.5	5.3	9.3	6.6	3.5	23.0	27.0	19.0	2.7	77.9	44.2	55.8	44.3
58045	HILLSBORO	95.6	95.5	0.1	0.1	0.0	0.0	4.3	4.4	6.9	7.1	7.3	6.7	5.0	23.3	26.5	13.7	3.5	74.2	41.0	50.9	49.1
58046	HOPE	99.0	98.6	0.2	0.2	0.2	0.2	0.3	0.3	6.8	6.9	8.0	7.7	4.4	22.9	26.8	14.9	1.7	73.2	40.9	51.8	48.2
58047	HORACE	99.1	99.0	0.0	0.0	0.2	0.2	0.3	0.4	8.2	8.6	9.3	7.5	5.6	28.5	25.7	6.1	0.5	69.1	35.7	49.7	50.3
58048	HUNTER	97.7	97.4	0.0	0.0	0.0	0.0	2.1	2.4	5.8	6.4	8.6	6.6	4.3	23.1	23.9	16.9	4.5	73.7	42.0	50.4	49.6
58049	KATHRYN	98.7	98.7	0.0	0.0	0.0	0.0	0.0	0.3	6.1	6.4	7.1	6.7	4.4	22.2	30.0	15.2	2.0	75.8	43.3	52.5	47.5
58051	KINDRED	98.9	98.7	0.2	0.1	0.2	0.2	0.6	0.7	7.7	7.9	8.5	7.2	5.2	27.5	24.5	9.8	1.6	71.3	36.9	50.0	50.0
58052	LEONARD	99.0	98.6	0.2	0.2	0.5	0.6	0.6	0.6	6.7	7.2	7.6	6.6	4.9	25.6	27.6	11.9	2.0	74.4	40.3	51.7	48.3
58053	LIDGERWOOD	97.8	97.5	0.0	0.0	0.2	0.2	0.5	0.5	5.3	5.3	6.5	6.9	5.3	20.8	25.8	20.5	3.5	78.6	44.9	52.2	47.8
58054	LISBON	98.5	98.3	0.1	0.1	0.2	0.3	0.5	0.7	5.6	5.8	6.6	6.0	5.7	23.8	25.0	17.2	4.3	77.9	42.6	52.2	47.8
58056	LUVERNE	99.2	99.2	0.0	0.0	0.0	0.0	0.0	0.4	6.3	7.1	7.6	7.6	4.6	22.7	28.2	14.3	1.7	74.0	41.5	51.7	48.3
58057	MCLEOD	98.5	97.9	0.0	0.7	0.0	0.0	0.0	0.0	7.7	7.7	9.1	7.7	4.2	25.2	24.5	11.9	2.1	70.6	38.1	51.8	48.3
58058	MANTADOR	97.0	96.9	0.0	0.0	0.0	0.0	0.8	0.8	5.5	5.5	6.3	7.0	6.3	23.4	27.3	14.8	3.9	77.3	42.5	50.8	49.2
58059	MAPLETON	98.5	98.2	0.1	0.1	0.3	0.5	1.4	1.7	7.2	7.9	9.4	7.6	5.9	28.7	25.8	6.2	1.5	70.5	34.5	50.5	49.5
58060	MILNOR	98.1	98.1	0.1	0.1	0.0	0.0	0.8	0.8	6.5	6.8	8.3	6.7	4.7	24.2	27.0	14.2	1.9	74.3	40.6	52.2	47.8
58061	MOORETON	97.9	97.4	0.2	0.2	0.0	0.2	0.5	0.7	6.1	6.7	7.8	7.4	5.4	25.8	25.8	13.0	2.2	74.2	39.9	52.6	47.4
58062	NOME	98.5	98.4	0.0	0.0	0.0	0.0	0.0	0.0	7.0	7.0	6.4	6.4	5.4	21.4	27.3	16.6	2.7	75.4	42.5	52.9	47.1
58063	ORISKA	97.6	97.8	0.0	0.0	0.0	0.0	0.5	0.6	6.1	7.5	8.6	6.9	4.4	23.3	32.7	9.4	1.1	72.9	40.9	53.7	46.3
58064	PAGE	99.2	99.2	0.0	0.0	0.0	0.0	1.2	1.4	5.6	6.4	7.2	5.6	4.0	22.6	28.8	17.8	2.0	77.4	44.1	50.4	49.6
58067	RUTLAND	98.4	98.3	0.0	0.0	0.0	0.0	0.0	0.0	4.0	5.3	8.3	6.3	4.7	21.7	29.0	18.3	2.3	78.0	44.8	55.0	45.0
58068	SHELDON	98.1	98.1	0.5	0.5	0.0	0.0	0.0	0.0	8.2	8.2	10.1	7.2	4.5	24.9	22.6	12.5	1.9	68.7	36.4	51.2	48.8
58069	STIRUM	98.6	98.5	0.0	0.0	0.0	0.0	1.4	1.5	8.0	8.8	7.3	5.1	5.1	26.3	26.3	11.7	1.5	71.5	38.6	51.8	48.2
58071	TOWER CITY	99.0	98.8	0.0	0.0	0.0	0.0	0.2	0.5	5.4	6.1	7.4	6.4	4.2	23.8	29.7	15.2	2.0	77.0	43.1	52.0	48.0
58072	VALLEY CITY	97.6	97.2	0.6	0.7	0.2	0.3	0.7	0.9	5.0	4.8	5.5	7.5	9.4	22.3	24.8	16.0	4.8	81.1	41.4	48.5	51.5
58075	WAHPETON	96.2	95.6	0.4	0.5	0.4	0.6	0.7	0.8	6.3	6.1	5.9	9.8	12.9	25.7	21.5	9.7	2.2	77.9	31.3	52.2	47.8
58076	WAHPETON	91.6	90.6	3.3	3.5	0.2	0.2	0.8	1.0	0.4	0.6	1.5	38.8	33.8	5.8	4.2	6.0	9.0	97.3	21.3	66.5	33.5
58077	WALCOTT	99.1	99.3	0.2	0.1	0.0	0.0	0.4	0.4	7.7	7.5	8.5	7.3	3.9	27.5	26.1	9.9	1.7	71.1	38.2	52.4	47.6
58078	WEST FARGO	96.3	95.7	0.5	0.5	0.4	0.6	1.4	1.7	7.5	6.8	7.7	8.0	9.1	32.3	22.2	5.9	0.7	73.4	31.6	49.5	50.5
58079	WHEATLAND	98.5	98.3	0.0	0.0	0.4	0.6	0.7	0.8	6.0	6.8	8.3	6.6	3.3	25.2	29.8	12.6	1.4	73.8	41.4	54.7	45.4
58081	WYNDMERE	98.5	98.3	0.0	0.0	0.1	0.2	0.7	0.7	6.4	7.0	8.2	7.9	5.6	23.7	25.2	14.0	2.1	73.7	40.0	52.7	47.3
58102	FARGO	93.7	92.4	0.8	0.8	2.3	3.1	1.4	1.6	5.1	4.9	5.6	11.6	13.8	27.9	20.9	8.8	1.6	81.1	30.0	52.1	47.9
58103	FARGO	94.0	93.1	1.3	1.4	1.3	1.8	1.4	1.6	6.8	5.5	5.2	6.2	12.2	34.1	20.0	8.5	1.6	79.4	30.6	48.9	51.1
58104	FARGO	96.8	96.0	0.5	0.5	1.3	1.9	0.8	1.0	8.2	8.4	8.4	6.9	6.2	34.1	20.8	5.3	1.8	70.6	31.9	49.1	50.9
58201	GRAND FORKS	94.9	94.0	0.7	0.8	0.9	1.2	1.5	1.8	5.9	5.4	6.2	7.9	11.0	28.5	23.3	9.9	2.0	78.1	33.5	49.8	50.2
58203	GRAND FORKS	90.8	89.4	1.1	1.3	1.3	1.8	2.5	2.9	5.8	4.9	5.2	15.9	18.4	28.3	15.3	5.3	0.9	81.1	25.0	51.7	48.3
58204	GRAND FORKS AFB	80.9	78.4	8.4	9.3	2.8	3.7	5.9	6.9	13.6	11.0	9.9	9.3	13.2	41.1	1.9	0.1	0.0	61.6	22.4	53.5	46.5
58205	GRAND FORKS AFB	80.9	78.4	8.4	9.3	2.7	3.7	6.0	6.9	13.6	11.0	9.9	9.4	13.2	41.0	1.9	0.1	0.0	61.8	22.3	53.6	46.4
58210	ADAMS	97.0	97.0	0.3	0.3	0.0	0.0	2.0	2.4	5.2	5.7	6.0	6.0	4.6	21.1	29.0	19.0	3.5	79.4	46.0	51.8	48.2
58212	ANETA	98.5	98.5	0.2	0.2	0.4	0.4	0.2	0.0	4.7	5.1	5.7	6.8	4.7	18.6	29.4	20.8	4.2	79.4	47.6	52.1	47.9
58214	ARVILLA	96.0	95.4	1.6	1.8	0.2	0.5	1.9	2.6	4.6	4.9	5.9	8.2	8.0	28.7	26.9	11.8	1.0	79.5	39.0	56.7	43.3
58216	BATHGATE	97.6	97.6	0.0	0.0	0.0	0.0	3.0	3.7	4.9	4.9	6.1	6.8	6.8	22.1	31.3	14.7	2.5	79.8	43.8	50.9	49.1
58218	BUXTON	98.4	98.4	0.0	0.0	0.1	0.1	2.0	2.2	7.3	7.4	7.5	6.2	5.0	25.1	28.5	11.3	1.8	74.1	39.0	50.8	49.2
58219	CALEDONIA	97.0	96.9	0.0	0.0	0.0	0.0	3.8	3.9	5.4	6.2	9.2	7.7	3.1	23.9	33.1	10.8	0.8	73.9	42.1	54.6	45.4
58220	CAVALIER	95.6	94.9	0.3	0.3	0.4	0.7	2.8	3.3	5.1	5.3	6.7	7.4	6.1	22.5	27.3	15.8	3.9	78.4	43.1	49.5	50.6
58222	CRYSTAL	96.1	95.3	0.3	0.6	0.0	0.3	1.1	1.5	5.6	5.9	6.1	6.7	6.4	20.8	27.5	17.0	4.1	77.8	44.0	52.1	48.0
58223	CUMMINGS	98.4	98.4	0.0	0.0	0.0	0.0	1.6	2.0	7.1	7.5	7.5	5.9	4.7	25.7	28.1	11.5	2.0	73.5	39.0	51.0	49.0
58224	DAHLEN	98.4	98.3	0.0	0.0	0.0	0.0	0.0	0.0	5.0	5.0	6.7	6.7	5.0	21.7	25.0	23.3	1.7	83.3	45.0	53.3	46.7
58225	DRAYTON	97.3	97.1	0.0	0.0	0.0	0.0	3.6	4.2	5.0	5.3	6.7	7.6	6.2	24.7	26.5	14.6	3.3	78.3	41.5	51.4	48.6
58227	EDINBURG	96.6	96.2	0.3	0.4	0.2	0.2	2.1	2.2	5.0	5.5	6.1	5.9	5.3	20.7	28.6	18.9	4.0	79.6	45.9	50.8	49.2
58228	EMERADO	91.9	90.6	1.4	1.5	0.9	1.2	2.7	3.2	5.5	6.2	8.5	7.4	6.0	29.6	28.6	7.8	0.4	75.4	37.3	52.8	47.3
58229	FAIRDALE	97.1	96.9	0.6	0.6	0.0	0.0	2.3	1.9	5.0	5.0	5.6	5.6	5.0	20.5	30.4	19.3	3.7	80.1	47.1	52.2	47.8
58230	FINLEY	97.9	97.8	0.0	0.0	0.0	0.0	0.2	0.2	5.5	6.1	7.2	6.8	4.7	21.3	27.8	18.4	2.3	76.7	43.9	51.2	48.8
58231	FORDVILLE	97.3	97.1	0.2	0.2	0.2	0.2	0.9	1.0	5.8	6.0	6.6	6.4	5.2	23.2	27.4	17.4	2.1	77.8	43.3	52.1	47.9
58233	FOREST RIVER	98.3	98.2	0.0	0.0	0.3	0.3	4.0	4.8	6.5	6.5	7.1	7.1	5.6	23.2	28.2	14.0	1.8	74.8	40.9	52.2	47.8
58235	GILBY	97.4	97.0	0.2	0.3	0.7	1.0	1.0	1.2	5.7	5.7	6.5	7.4	6.5	26.8	26.3	13.7	1.5	77.4	40.2	51.6	48.4
58237	GRAFTON	93.0	92.0	0.4	0.5	0.4	0.5	8.4	9.7	5.9	5.9	7.0	7.2	6.3	24.5	26.0	13.9	3.3	76.4	40.7	49.1	50.9
58238	HAMILTON	96.6	96.0	0.0	0.0	0.0	0.0	6.8	8.0	4.5	5.5	6.5	6.5	6.0	22.5	31.0	15.5	2.0	79.5	43.9	54.0	46.0
58239	HANNAH	98.6	98.5	0.0	0.0	0.0	0.0	0.0	0.0	6.1	6.1	6.1	4.6	3.0	19.7	33.3	19.7	1.5	81.8	48.0	54.6	45.5
58240	HATTON	96.9	96.8	0.1	0.1	0.5	0.5	2.7	2.7	6.2	6.4	7.2	6.9	5.0	23.7	23.7	16.5	4.5	75.6	41.9	48.7	51.3
58241	HENSEL	97.0	96.9	0.0	0.0	0.6	0.6	1.2	1.2	5.0	5.6	7.5	8.1	5.0	24.8	32.3	10.6	1.2	77.0	41.8	53.4	46.6
58243	HOOPLE	97.8	97.3	0.2	0.2	0.2	0.2	3.5	4.1	5.8	6.1	6.4	6.6	6.6	22.5	30.3	13.0	2.7	78.0	42.5	51.4	48.6
58244	INKSTER	97.4	96.7	0.2	0.2	0.7	1.1	0.9	0.9	5.7	5.7	6.1	7.2	6.1	26.0	27.5	14.2	1.5	78.0	41.0	51.8	48.3
58249	LANGDON	98.4	98.2	0.1	0.2	0.1	0.1	0.7	0.8	4.0	4.8	6.8	7.3	4.4	18.4	29.1	20.5	4.7	79.3	47.6	49.0	51.0
58250	LANKIN	97.4	97.3	0.3	0.3	0.0	0.0	1.8	2.2	6.1	6.1	5.5	6.9	5.0	23.4	25.9	19.0	2.2	78.2	43.5	52.9	47.1
58251	LARIMORE	96.5	95.9	0.6	0.7	0.6	0.8	1.0	1.1	5.8	5.8	6.8	7.8	5.8	24.5	26.1	14.6	2.9	76.0	41.4	49.8	50.2
58254	MCVILLE	99.6	99.6	0.0	0.0	0.1	0.1	0.0	0.0	3.9	4.1	5.7	6.3	5.2	16.7	27.2	24.0	6.9	81.0	50.4	48.8	51.2
58255	MAIDA	98.7	98.7	0.0	0.0	0.0	0.0	0.0	0.0	4.0	5.3	6.7	8.0	1.3	20.0	40.0	13.3	1.3	76.0	47.2	54.7	45.3
58256	MANVEL	97.3	97.1	0.9	1.0	0.0	0.0	1.2	1.4	5.5	6.2	8.8	7.4	6.2	27.8	28.4	8.4	1.2	74.9	37.7	53.0	47.0
58257	MAYVILLE	97.7	97.5	0.2	0.2	0.3	0.3	0.6	0.6	4.5	4.5	5.3	9.6	14.0	20.8	20.2	15.2	6.1	82.4	36.4	49.1	50.9
	NORTH DAKOTA	92.4	91.7	0.6	0.7	0.6	0.8	1.2	1.4	6.3	6.1	6.8	7.9	8.5	26.2	23.9	12.0	2.4	76.5	36.5	50.0	50.0
	UNITED STATES	75.1	73.6	12.3	12.5	3.8	4.2	12.5	14.1	6.9	6.7	7.2	7.0	7.3	28.6	23.8	10.8	1.7	75.1	36.0	49.1	50.9

ZIP CODE #	POST OFFICE NAME	2004 Per Capita Income	2004 HH Income Base	2004 Household Income Distribution (%) Less than $25,000	$25,000 to $49,999	$50,000 to $99,999	$100,000 to $149,999	$150,000 or More	Median Household Income 2004	2009	2004 National Centile	2004 State Centile	2004 Home Value Base	2004 Home Value Distribution (%) Less than $50,000	$50,000 to $89,999	$90,000 to $174,999	$175,000 to $399,999	$400,000 or More	2004 Median Home Value
58004	AMENIA	23548	108	22.2	28.7	38.0	6.5	4.6	49090	58930	70	91	88	20.5	20.5	37.5	20.5	1.1	103571
58005	ARGUSVILLE	26006	212	12.3	25.5	47.2	11.3	3.8	58747	69034	83	99	189	15.3	23.3	47.1	14.3	0.0	108929
58006	ARTHUR	19173	166	22.9	33.7	35.5	5.4	2.4	46404	53595	65	87	132	36.4	34.1	20.5	8.3	0.8	63571
58007	AYR	21997	62	24.2	35.5	33.9	4.8	1.6	42346	51817	54	76	50	36.0	34.0	24.0	6.0	0.0	65000
58008	BARNEY	19945	113	21.2	37.2	31.0	6.2	4.4	44602	50631	60	83	100	29.0	28.0	33.0	8.0	2.0	78571
58009	BLANCHARD	28611	36	11.1	36.1	38.9	11.1	2.8	51084	57017	74	94	30	40.0	20.0	33.3	6.7	0.0	75000
58011	BUFFALO	20255	178	24.7	38.8	30.9	3.9	1.7	40975	47617	50	71	147	28.6	34.0	29.9	6.8	0.7	80263
58012	CASSELTON	22313	790	22.9	28.7	38.2	7.2	2.9	48300	58872	69	91	589	12.1	24.3	52.0	11.7	0.0	106686
58013	CAYUGA	22586	86	26.7	39.5	23.3	7.0	3.5	37936	45000	39	59	74	51.4	29.7	16.2	2.7	0.0	48333
58015	CHRISTINE	23353	139	15.1	28.1	42.5	10.1	4.3	55866	63252	81	98	123	24.4	13.8	46.3	14.6	0.8	103500
58016	CLIFFORD	26179	46	10.9	39.1	39.1	8.7	2.2	50000	55872	72	92	38	42.1	21.1	29.0	7.9	0.0	70000
58017	COGSWELL	22188	198	24.8	35.9	32.8	4.6	2.0	40372	46785	47	68	164	56.1	25.6	14.6	3.7	0.0	42857
58018	COLFAX	20336	141	20.6	33.3	36.9	7.1	2.1	46807	52290	66	87	118	27.1	21.2	38.1	12.7	0.9	92857
58021	DAVENPORT	22715	166	13.3	34.3	39.2	9.6	3.6	51772	62155	75	94	142	23.9	21.8	44.4	9.9	0.0	97500
58027	ENDERLIN	24641	630	29.4	33.2	27.1	6.0	4.3	40309	47297	47	68	477	49.9	29.4	17.2	3.1	0.4	50119
58029	ERIE	22366	63	23.8	33.3	34.9	4.8	3.2	46113	52835	64	86	50	36.0	32.0	22.0	10.0	0.0	64000
58030	FAIRMOUNT	20688	299	26.1	34.1	32.1	6.7	1.0	42061	47397	53	74	236	40.7	30.1	15.7	10.2	3.4	63529
58031	FINGAL	20562	184	26.6	36.4	28.8	4.9	3.3	41655	49335	52	73	161	52.2	17.4	23.6	6.2	0.6	47500
58032	FORMAN	24687	316	29.8	25.3	33.5	8.2	3.2	44416	52620	60	82	235	36.6	34.0	23.8	5.5	0.0	65667
58033	FORT RANSOM	21703	192	24.0	31.8	35.9	6.8	1.6	45967	52493	64	86	162	27.2	30.3	35.2	7.4	0.0	82500
58035	GALESBURG	23587	147	12.9	38.1	37.4	8.8	2.7	49350	55523	71	91	121	42.2	20.7	28.9	7.4	0.8	69167
58036	GARDNER	23347	134	16.4	29.9	44.0	7.5	2.2	52496	62078	76	96	116	24.1	31.0	35.3	9.5	0.0	82500
58038	GRANDIN	23596	98	17.4	31.6	39.8	8.2	3.1	50676	62614	73	93	84	25.0	31.0	34.5	9.5	0.0	81667
58040	GWINNER	23391	386	18.4	30.1	44.3	5.7	1.6	50697	60926	73	94	306	35.0	32.4	30.7	1.3	0.7	67826
58041	HANKINSON	18613	704	33.5	33.2	26.9	5.5	0.9	37022	42344	36	54	554	43.1	29.4	22.2	5.1	0.2	56667
58042	HARWOOD	25359	418	6.5	21.3	52.9	15.3	4.1	65341	79727	89	99	401	3.0	17.0	63.1	17.0	0.0	126293
58043	HAVANA	19303	95	30.5	37.9	24.2	6.3	1.1	36402	42697	33	51	80	63.8	22.5	11.3	2.5	0.0	37000
58045	HILLSBORO	21912	1012	25.7	32.3	32.8	8.4	0.8	42220	50039	54	75	773	30.3	27.8	38.8	3.1	0.0	78672
58046	HOPE	21103	271	24.0	36.2	29.9	7.8	2.2	42197	50740	53	75	217	54.8	24.9	15.7	4.6	0.0	44750
58047	HORACE	28400	945	6.6	23.3	47.6	16.7	5.8	66337	83001	89	100	865	5.1	13.2	49.7	29.9	2.1	141419
58048	HUNTER	24651	202	23.3	34.2	34.7	5.0	3.0	46109	54092	64	86	160	36.9	33.1	21.3	8.1	0.6	63750
58049	KATHRYN	22613	125	24.8	30.4	36.0	6.4	2.4	44687	52316	60	84	108	42.6	23.2	23.2	10.2	0.9	62857
58051	KINDRED	24185	527	15.8	27.5	44.2	9.1	3.4	54362	66589	79	97	431	19.3	23.2	42.5	14.4	0.7	100735
58052	LEONARD	24815	284	17.6	35.9	35.9	7.4	3.2	47079	55131	66	88	239	29.3	20.5	41.8	8.0	0.4	90385
58053	LIDGERWOOD	17636	553	34.2	40.9	20.8	3.1	1.1	32189	37673	18	24	460	59.1	23.5	14.6	2.0	0.9	40455
58054	LISBON	21946	1476	27.5	30.2	36.6	3.9	1.8	43724	50788	58	80	1096	27.1	34.6	33.3	4.3	0.7	78611
58056	LUVERNE	21557	95	26.3	31.6	31.6	8.4	2.1	44449	51257	60	82	77	53.3	23.4	16.9	6.5	0.0	45833
58057	MCLEOD	21084	59	23.7	37.3	28.8	8.5	1.7	42321	48892	54	75	50	34.0	28.0	26.0	8.0	4.0	75000
58058	MANTADOR	20665	56	33.9	32.1	26.8	5.4	1.8	36123	42337	32	50	46	47.8	21.7	21.7	8.7	0.0	53333
58059	MAPLETON	23410	395	13.7	31.9	39.5	11.1	3.8	53084	67209	77	96	351	11.1	25.6	49.0	14.3	0.0	104664
58060	MILNOR	20753	584	24.7	35.3	30.1	7.2	2.7	41774	48309	52	73	479	44.9	26.7	22.8	5.0	0.6	56282
58061	MOORETON	24257	193	19.2	31.6	39.4	8.3	1.6	49440	57328	71	92	166	27.7	26.5	34.9	10.8	0.0	81250
58062	NOME	20190	76	26.3	34.2	32.9	5.3	1.3	43416	49532	57	79	67	56.7	19.4	17.9	6.0	0.0	43571
58063	ORISKA	20060	134	26.9	26.1	35.8	10.5	0.8	47360	54785	67	89	112	24.1	30.4	36.6	8.9	0.0	82857
58064	PAGE	22570	208	26.4	33.2	32.7	3.9	3.9	41052	48301	50	71	169	36.7	32.0	26.0	5.3	0.0	66250
58067	RUTLAND	20413	128	28.9	37.5	25.8	5.5	2.3	38004	44162	39	60	106	59.4	22.6	14.2	3.8	0.0	38333
58068	SHELDON	20251	147	25.9	35.4	27.2	9.5	2.0	41781	48518	52	74	123	36.6	26.8	22.0	8.9	5.7	74091
58069	STIRUM	25534	62	21.0	33.9	38.7	4.8	1.6	45000	47988	61	84	51	51.0	25.5	17.7	5.9	0.0	48750
58071	TOWER CITY	20642	171	25.2	37.4	30.4	5.3	1.8	41254	48449	51	72	141	27.7	34.0	30.5	7.8	0.0	80294
58072	VALLEY CITY	20381	3500	36.6	29.3	27.2	4.7	2.3	35100	42410	28	43	2315	27.5	37.7	28.5	6.1	0.3	73786
58075	WAHPETON	20542	3933	29.2	32.6	30.2	6.1	1.9	41281	48117	51	72	2388	21.9	29.2	39.7	9.2	0.0	88555
58076	WAHPETON	8980	5	40.0	40.0	20.0	0.0	0.0	37166	50000	36	55	3	33.3	0.0	66.7	0.0	0.0	106250
58077	WALCOTT	23125	264	16.7	30.3	40.5	9.1	3.4	52274	59526	76	95	230	24.4	15.7	45.2	14.4	0.4	102604
58078	WEST FARGO	23908	6770	17.4	29.3	42.6	7.3	3.4	52118	63986	76	95	4358	10.1	17.2	60.4	12.1	0.3	116958
58079	WHEATLAND	22573	200	22.0	30.5	36.0	6.5	5.0	47102	54287	66	88	167	25.2	18.0	38.3	17.4	1.2	101339
58081	WYNDMERE	21910	371	19.7	38.5	35.0	5.1	1.6	46205	51345	64	87	304	34.5	35.2	25.7	4.0	0.7	68400
58102	FARGO	23490	13284	32.7	30.3	26.0	6.9	4.1	37379	46536	37	56	6712	9.0	21.9	53.6	14.5	1.0	111633
58103	FARGO	25736	23226	27.3	33.5	29.4	7.0	2.8	40528	48741	48	69	9979	9.3	21.8	52.5	15.9	0.5	113769
58104	FARGO	35541	7258	14.9	18.6	36.6	18.3	11.6	69664	85465	91	100	4948	2.0	2.4	42.4	48.1	5.2	180376
58201	GRAND FORKS	26431	13990	25.8	29.8	31.4	8.5	4.5	44448	53637	60	82	7694	7.0	20.2	54.9	17.0	1.0	115032
58203	GRAND FORKS	16885	6733	33.7	34.4	27.5	3.5	0.9	35193	42162	28	44	3272	22.0	34.6	41.3	2.1	0.0	83618
58204	GRAND FORKS AFB	8570	217	16.6	49.8	31.3	2.3	0.0	40768	46647	49	70	4	25.0	75.0	0.0	0.0	0.0	60000
58205	GRAND FORKS AFB	14621	972	16.8	50.0	31.2	1.9	0.2	40680	46426	48	69	18	50.0	38.9	0.0	11.1	0.0	50000
58210	ADAMS	17767	156	34.0	35.3	25.6	4.5	0.6	33288	38709	22	32	131	59.5	22.1	17.6	0.8	0.0	37500
58212	ANETA	16152	218	35.8	41.3	20.6	2.3	0.0	33945	38625	24	35	179	67.6	22.4	7.3	1.1	1.7	32955
58214	ARVILLA	23120	163	28.8	27.6	35.6	7.4	0.6	44242	52629	59	81	117	23.9	33.3	41.0	1.7	0.0	82273
58216	BATHGATE	26634	71	19.7	32.4	35.2	11.3	1.4	47996	53142	68	90	61	52.5	32.8	13.1	1.6	0.0	48333
58218	BUXTON	20933	287	18.8	34.2	38.3	7.3	1.4	47997	55383	68	90	240	22.1	40.4	33.8	3.3	0.4	77500
58219	CALEDONIA	21788	48	14.6	33.3	37.5	14.6	0.0	52181	60000	76	95	41	26.8	19.5	53.7	0.0	0.0	97500
58220	CAVALIER	22459	1114	27.2	30.9	33.2	5.7	3.1	42615	51019	55	77	853	27.3	34.9	28.0	9.3	0.5	78287
58222	CRYSTAL	19227	144	30.6	34.7	29.9	3.5	1.4	36373	41800	33	50	118	50.0	33.1	14.4	2.5	0.0	50000
58223	CUMMINGS	22059	106	19.8	35.9	35.9	7.6	0.9	46824	54090	66	88	89	24.7	41.6	28.1	4.5	1.1	75000
58224	DAHLEN	19742	27	33.3	37.0	25.9	3.7	0.0	36120	38616	32	49	23	47.8	39.1	13.0	0.0	0.0	55000
58225	DRAYTON	22966	508	26.4	32.3	34.3	5.3	1.8	44137	51891	59	81	379	37.5	37.7	23.0	1.9	0.0	62125
58227	EDINBURG	19845	254	32.7	35.0	26.8	4.7	0.8	34453	39714	26	38	211	59.2	25.1	15.2	0.5	0.0	38750
58228	EMERADO	22725	486	23.7	28.6	38.5	7.8	1.4	47970	55921	68	90	385	19.5	26.5	43.6	9.9	0.5	97381
58229	FAIRDALE	18990	73	32.9	35.6	27.4	4.1	0.0	33598	39524	23	34	61	62.3	23.0	14.8	0.0	0.0	34167
58230	FINLEY	21370	529	26.1	35.5	29.9	5.3	3.2	40663	47346	48	69	424	46.5	30.4	18.2	5.0	0.0	53947
58231	FORDVILLE	17751	206	35.4	32.5	26.7	3.9	1.5	35314	41046	29	45	175	56.0	25.7	17.1	1.1	0.0	45435
58233	FOREST RIVER	18356	131	30.5	34.4	28.2	3.8	3.1	38299	44308	40	62	111	47.8	32.4	17.1	2.7	0.0	51786
58235	GILBY	17532	161	26.7	45.3	23.6	3.7	0.6	36649	42800	34	52	132	43.9	34.9	15.2	3.8	2.3	54706
58237	GRAFTON	20365	2319	28.3	35.8	27.8	5.0	3.0	40405	46510	48	68	1678	28.3	37.5	26.8	6.9	0.5	71867
58238	HAMILTON	27395	86	20.9	31.4	31.4	11.6	4.7	47866	53964	68	90	73	49.3	32.9	13.7	4.1	0.0	50833
58239	HANNAH	20882	36	33.3	41.7	19.4	5.6	0.0	35000	41143	28	43	30	90.0	6.7	3.3	0.0	0.0	12500
58240	HATTON	19143	420	30.5	31.9	30.5	5.5	1.7	39145	46186	43	65	315	28.6	41.9	26.0	3.5	0.0	69324
58241	HENSEL	25206	75	25.3	24.0	42.7	6.7	1.3	50355	60000	73	92	67	26.9	40.3	19.4	11.9	1.5	76538
58243	HOOPLE	24034	269	26.8	37.6	27.1	5.6	3.0	39869	45180	45	66	222	46.4	28.8	19.8	3.6	1.4	55333
58244	INKSTER	18888	192	24.5	43.8	27.1	4.2	0.5	38274	44784	40	62	158	42.4	34.2	17.1	4.4	1.9	56316
58249	LANGDON	18720	1256	32.5	36.2	25.5	5.4	0.5	35569	41192	30	47	996	40.2	36.5	21.9	1.1	0.4	62955
58250	LANKIN	19431	160	31.9	35.0	27.5	3.1	2.5	35000	40000	28	43	137	54.0	24.1	17.5	4.4	0.0	45417
58251	LARIMORE	20293	890	24.4	37.3	31.7	4.8	1.8	41314	49210	51	72	680	31.8	42.1	23.2	2.8	0.2	69655
58254	MCVILLE	23526	331	38.7	32.0	22.1	3.9	3.3	32387	38144	19	27	254	57.5	31.5	10.6	0.0	0.4	40952
58255	MAIDA	20723	30	16.7	43.3	30.0	10.0	0.0	40000	45000	46	67	26	46.2	46.2	7.7	0.0	0.0	60000
58256	MANVEL	25756	371	13.5	29.9	47.7	5.9	3.0	53702	63080	78	97	329	21.3	39.5	35.9	3.3	0.0	78375
58257	MAYVILLE	21558	861	30.8	30.1	30.2	6.2	2.8	41054	48357	50	71	553	25.7	39.4	32.4	2.5	0.0	72910
	NORTH DAKOTA	22058		29.0	31.5	29.9	6.6	3.0	40503	48701				27.7	27.3	34.9	9.3	0.9	83011
	UNITED STATES	25866		24.7	27.1	30.8	10.9	6.5	48124	56710				10.9	15.0	33.7	30.1	10.4	145905

ZIP CODE	FINANCIAL SERVICES				THE HOME						ENTERTAINMENT						PERSONAL			
					Home Improvements		Furnishings													
# POST OFFICE NAME	Auto Loan	Home Loan	Investments	Retirement Plans	Home Repair	Lawn & Garden	Computers & Hardware	Major Appliances	TV, Radio, Sound Equipment	Furniture	Dine out/ Carry out	Sports Equipment	Fees & Tickets	Toys & Games	Travel	Cable TV	Apparel & Services	Auto Repairs	Health Insurance	Pets & Supplies
58004 AMENIA	108	75	39	71	88	98	74	92	86	73	100	111	63	98	77	90	91	91	109	128
58005 ARGUSVILLE	108	90	65	87	99	106	86	99	92	85	110	118	80	111	89	94	104	97	109	129
58006 ARTHUR	101	70	37	67	82	92	70	86	80	69	94	104	59	92	72	84	86	85	103	120
58007 AYR	88	61	32	58	71	80	60	75	70	60	82	90	52	80	63	73	74	74	89	104
58008 BARNEY	101	71	37	67	82	92	70	86	80	69	94	104	60	92	72	84	86	85	103	120
58009 BLANCHARD	127	88	46	83	103	115	87	108	101	86	118	130	75	116	91	106	108	106	129	150
58011 BUFFALO	87	61	32	57	71	79	60	74	69	59	81	89	51	79	62	72	74	73	88	103
58012 CASSELTON	103	72	38	68	84	94	71	88	82	70	96	106	61	94	74	86	87	87	104	122
58013 CAYUGA	99	69	36	65	80	90	68	84	79	67	92	102	58	90	71	82	84	83	100	117
58015 CHRISTINE	115	80	42	76	93	104	79	98	91	78	107	118	67	105	82	96	97	96	116	136
58016 CLIFFORD	109	76	40	72	89	99	75	93	87	74	102	112	64	100	78	91	93	92	111	130
58017 COGSWELL	88	71	48	67	78	85	67	78	74	67	88	93	62	89	69	76	82	76	88	104
58018 COLFAX	100	70	37	66	81	91	69	85	80	68	93	103	59	91	72	83	85	84	102	119
58021 DAVENPORT	111	81	47	77	93	103	79	96	90	78	106	116	69	104	82	94	97	95	113	132
58027 ENDERLIN	96	70	44	67	78	92	75	86	85	72	100	98	66	95	76	90	91	85	102	108
58029 ERIE	100	70	37	66	82	91	69	86	80	68	94	103	59	92	72	84	85	84	102	119
58030 FAIRMOUNT	89	63	34	60	73	81	62	76	71	61	83	91	53	82	64	74	76	75	90	105
58031 FINGAL	93	65	34	62	76	85	64	80	74	64	87	96	55	85	67	78	79	79	95	111
58032 FORMAN	91	76	58	75	81	91	78	84	83	76	100	97	74	100	77	85	94	83	92	102
58033 FORT RANSOM	92	69	41	65	78	86	66	80	75	66	89	96	59	88	69	78	82	78	93	109
58035 GALESBURG	107	75	39	71	87	98	74	91	85	73	100	110	63	98	77	89	91	90	109	127
58036 GARDNER	105	73	38	69	85	95	72	89	83	71	98	108	62	96	75	87	89	88	106	124
58038 GRANDIN	105	73	38	69	85	96	72	89	83	71	98	108	62	96	75	87	89	88	107	125
58040 GWINNER	88	78	60	75	83	89	73	80	77	73	94	96	71	96	75	79	89	78	87	104
58041 HANKINSON	76	55	33	53	62	72	57	67	65	55	76	78	50	74	58	68	70	66	79	87
58042 HARWOOD	99	119	123	119	117	115	107	107	100	107	126	126	112	132	109	97	125	104	97	119
58043 HAVANA	83	58	30	55	68	76	57	71	66	57	77	85	49	76	59	69	71	70	84	99
58045 HILLSBORO	89	64	37	61	73	84	67	78	76	65	89	92	58	86	68	80	81	78	93	103
58046 HOPE	94	65	34	62	76	85	65	80	74	64	87	96	55	85	67	78	79	79	95	111
58047 HORACE	113	129	131	130	126	125	119	119	112	120	141	141	123	145	119	107	139	117	106	132
58048 HUNTER	101	71	37	67	82	92	70	86	80	69	94	104	59	92	72	84	86	85	103	120
58049 KATHRYN	89	73	52	71	81	87	70	81	76	69	90	97	64	91	72	78	85	80	90	107
58051 KINDRED	95	96	88	96	97	99	91	95	89	91	110	113	89	112	91	87	107	93	91	111
58052 LEONARD	104	72	38	68	84	94	72	88	82	71	97	107	61	95	74	86	88	87	105	123
58053 LIDGERWOOD	68	49	30	47	55	65	52	60	59	50	69	69	46	67	53	62	63	60	72	77
58054 LISBON	89	65	39	62	74	84	67	78	75	65	89	92	59	86	68	79	81	77	92	103
58056 LUVERNE	98	68	36	64	79	89	67	83	78	67	91	100	58	89	70	81	83	82	99	116
58057 MCLEOD	92	65	34	61	75	84	64	79	73	63	86	95	54	84	66	77	79	78	94	110
58058 MANTADOR	84	59	31	55	68	76	58	72	67	57	78	86	49	77	60	70	71	71	85	100
58059 MAPLETON	100	96	84	96	97	100	91	96	90	92	112	115	89	112	91	88	108	95	94	115
58060 MILNOR	96	68	38	65	79	88	67	82	77	66	90	99	58	89	69	80	83	81	97	113
58061 MOORETON	105	73	38	69	85	95	72	89	83	71	97	107	62	96	75	87	89	88	106	124
58062 NOME	90	63	33	59	73	82	62	77	71	61	84	92	53	82	64	75	76	76	91	107
58063 ORISKA	98	68	36	64	80	89	67	83	78	67	91	101	58	89	70	82	83	82	99	116
58064 PAGE	98	69	36	65	80	89	68	84	78	67	91	101	58	90	70	82	83	83	100	117
58067 RUTLAND	86	61	32	57	70	79	60	74	69	59	81	89	51	79	62	72	74	73	88	102
58068 SHELDON	94	66	34	62	76	86	65	80	75	64	88	97	55	86	67	78	80	79	95	112
58069 STIRUM	90	80	61	76	85	91	74	82	79	74	96	98	73	98	77	81	91	80	89	106
58071 TOWER CITY	89	62	33	59	72	81	61	76	71	61	83	92	52	81	64	74	76	75	90	106
58072 VALLEY CITY	67	60	55	59	62	69	62	65	65	61	79	75	60	78	62	66	76	66	70	76
58075 WAHPETON	72	63	61	65	64	70	69	69	70	67	87	83	65	85	67	69	83	71	70	81
58076 WAHPETON	43	26	33	30	26	31	51	37	49	43	62	52	42	56	41	43	58	46	35	43
58077 WALCOTT	111	77	40	73	90	101	76	94	88	75	103	114	65	101	79	92	94	93	112	131
58078 WEST FARGO	86	88	88	91	87	88	87	86	83	87	104	102	86	104	85	79	102	86	79	96
58079 WHEATLAND	105	74	38	70	86	96	73	90	84	72	98	108	62	96	75	88	90	89	107	125
58081 WYNDMERE	102	71	37	67	83	93	70	87	81	69	95	105	60	93	73	85	87	86	103	121
58102 FARGO	71	67	81	71	66	71	79	71	76	75	96	88	76	94	74	72	94	76	67	79
58103 FARGO	74	70	82	75	68	72	79	74	77	78	97	90	76	93	74	72	95	78	68	82
58104 FARGO	129	137	147	144	133	135	134	131	126	136	160	155	136	157	131	120	157	132	117	144
58201 GRAND FORKS	81	78	92	82	77	81	89	82	86	85	108	101	86	106	84	81	106	87	76	91
58203 GRAND FORKS	59	51	57	53	50	55	63	57	62	59	77	71	58	74	58	58	75	62	54	64
58204 GRAND FORKS AFB	72	46	44	52	42	49	68	59	69	63	86	78	58	77	56	63	83	69	54	67
58205 GRAND FORKS AFB	72	46	44	52	42	50	68	59	69	64	86	78	58	77	56	63	83	69	54	67
58210 ADAMS	76	53	28	50	62	69	52	65	60	52	71	78	45	69	54	63	65	64	77	90
58212 ANETA	63	47	29	45	52	61	50	57	57	48	67	65	44	63	50	60	61	57	68	71
58214 ARVILLA	86	73	57	73	77	87	76	81	80	74	97	92	72	96	75	82	91	79	88	95
58216 BATHGATE	111	77	40	73	90	101	76	94	88	75	103	114	65	101	79	92	94	93	112	131
58218 BUXTON	98	69	36	65	80	89	68	84	78	67	91	101	58	90	70	82	83	83	100	117
58219 CALEDONIA	107	75	39	70	87	97	74	91	85	73	99	110	63	98	76	89	91	90	108	127
58220 CAVALIER	89	67	41	63	75	85	68	79	76	66	90	92	60	88	69	80	83	78	92	103
58222 CRYSTAL	79	56	29	52	65	72	55	68	63	54	74	82	47	73	57	66	68	67	80	94
58223 CUMMINGS	95	67	35	63	78	87	66	81	76	65	89	98	56	87	68	79	81	80	97	113
58224 DAHLEN	79	55	29	52	65	72	55	68	63	54	74	82	47	73	57	66	67	67	81	94
58225 DRAYTON	82	67	49	66	72	81	68	75	74	67	89	87	64	87	68	75	82	74	83	92
58227 EDINBURG	76	53	28	50	62	70	53	65	61	52	71	78	45	70	55	64	65	64	78	91
58228 EMERADO	82	80	73	81	81	84	78	80	77	78	95	94	77	96	77	75	92	79	78	93
58229 FAIRDALE	76	53	28	50	62	69	52	65	60	52	71	78	45	69	54	63	64	64	77	90
58230 FINLEY	89	67	42	61	76	85	64	78	73	63	86	92	56	85	68	77	79	77	92	107
58231 FORDVILLE	81	56	29	53	66	74	56	69	64	55	75	83	48	74	58	67	69	68	82	96
58233 FOREST RIVER	85	60	31	56	70	78	59	73	68	58	80	88	50	78	61	71	73	72	87	101
58235 GILBY	79	55	29	52	65	72	55	68	63	54	74	82	47	73	57	66	67	67	81	94
58237 GRAFTON	79	63	46	61	68	78	66	73	72	64	86	84	60	83	66	75	80	73	83	90
58238 HAMILTON	115	80	42	76	94	105	79	98	92	79	107	118	68	105	82	96	98	97	117	137
58239 HANNAH	69	48	25	46	56	63	48	59	55	47	65	71	41	63	50	58	59	58	70	82
58240 HATTON	78	58	36	55	64	75	62	70	70	59	82	80	55	78	62	74	75	70	84	88
58241 HENSEL	89	75	53	71	81	87	70	80	76	70	91	95	67	92	72	78	86	78	88	105
58243 HOOPLE	95	67	35	63	78	87	66	81	76	65	89	98	56	87	68	80	81	80	97	113
58244 INKSTER	82	57	30	54	66	74	56	70	65	56	76	84	48	74	58	68	69	69	83	97
58249 LANGDON	74	53	30	50	60	69	55	65	62	53	73	76	48	71	56	66	67	64	77	85
58250 LANKIN	80	56	29	53	65	73	55	68	63	54	74	82	47	73	57	67	68	67	81	95
58251 LARIMORE	83	61	38	59	68	80	65	74	74	63	87	85	58	83	66	78	79	74	88	94
58254 MCVILLE	81	61	40	58	67	80	67	74	75	64	88	83	60	83	66	79	81	74	89	90
58255 MAIDA	94	65	34	62	76	85	65	80	74	64	87	96	55	86	67	78	80	79	95	111
58256 MANVEL	105	107	98	106	107	109	101	104	99	101	123	123	100	124	100	96	119	102	99	121
58257 MAYVILLE	79	65	55	63	69	80	69	74	75	67	90	85	64	88	69	78	84	75	85	89
NORTH DAKOTA	80	69	63	69	72	79	73	76	75	71	92	90	69	90	72	75	88	77	79	90
UNITED STATES	100	100	100	100	100	100	100	100	100	100	100	100	100	100	100	100	100	100	100	100

POPULATION CHANGE

A 58258-58451

#	POST OFFICE NAME	COUNTY FIPS CODE	POPULATION 2000	2004	2009	2000-2004 ANNUAL RATE % Rate	State Centile	HOUSEHOLDS 2000	2004	2009	% Annual Rate 2000-2004	2004 Average HH Size	FAMILIES 2000	2004	% Annual Rate 2000-2004
58258	MEKINOCK	035	322	316	311	-0.4	69	119	119	119	0.0	2.66	92	90	-0.5
58259	MICHIGAN	063	488	475	461	-0.6	57	226	226	224	0.0	2.00	143	137	-1.0
58260	MILTON	019	183	175	167	-1.1	34	78	77	75	-0.3	2.19	56	53	-1.3
58261	MINTO	099	1282	1256	1209	-0.5	65	524	529	523	0.2	2.37	363	355	-0.5
58262	MOUNTAIN	067	177	168	161	-1.2	28	64	63	62	-0.4	2.46	43	40	-1.7
58265	NECHE	067	632	620	601	-0.5	67	236	239	238	0.3	2.59	169	166	-0.4
58266	NIAGARA	035	145	164	173	2.9	99	56	65	70	3.6	2.51	42	48	3.2
58267	NORTHWOOD	035	1445	1370	1336	-1.3	26	591	580	578	-0.4	2.23	391	369	-1.4
58269	OSNABROCK	019	505	483	461	-1.0	35	203	200	196	-0.4	2.33	145	139	-1.0
58270	PARK RIVER	099	2041	1937	1843	-1.2	28	848	829	811	-0.5	2.22	533	501	-1.5
58271	PEMBINA	067	797	775	747	-0.7	56	320	320	318	0.0	2.42	227	219	-0.8
58272	PETERSBURG	063	343	330	320	-0.9	41	142	141	140	-0.2	2.33	97	93	-1.0
58273	PISEK	099	261	245	231	-1.5	15	109	106	104	-0.7	2.31	71	67	-1.4
58274	PORTLAND	097	935	922	909	-0.3	72	379	383	388	0.3	2.39	254	249	-0.5
58275	REYNOLDS	035	840	894	917	1.5	97	293	319	333	2.0	2.80	241	257	1.5
58276	SAINT THOMAS	067	685	656	630	-1.0	37	271	267	264	-0.4	2.46	192	184	-1.0
58277	SHARON	091	153	150	147	-0.5	66	72	72	71	0.0	2.08	48	47	-0.5
58278	THOMPSON	035	1897	1938	1949	0.5	89	638	671	688	1.2	2.89	522	537	0.7
58281	WALES	019	84	76	71	-2.3	1	39	37	36	-1.2	2.05	26	24	-1.9
58282	WALHALLA	067	1541	1460	1395	-1.3	25	650	634	623	-0.6	2.22	426	401	-1.4
58301	DEVILS LAKE	071	9985	9657	9227	-0.8	49	4123	4086	3994	-0.2	2.26	2581	2464	-1.1
58311	ALSEN	019	148	140	133	-1.3	23	56	55	54	-0.4	2.55	40	38	-1.2
58316	BELCOURT	079	6312	6307	6264	0.0	81	1929	1967	1993	0.5	3.18	1487	1479	-0.1
58317	BISBEE	095	337	319	298	-1.3	24	142	139	134	-0.5	2.29	96	91	-1.3
58318	BOTTINEAU	009	3964	3825	3656	-0.8	46	1619	1600	1567	-0.3	2.21	1037	991	-1.1
58319	BREMEN	103	60	56	52	-1.6	10	23	22	21	-1.0	2.55	18	17	-1.3
58321	BROCKET	071	148	142	136	-1.0	38	66	65	64	-0.4	2.18	50	48	-1.0
58323	CALVIN	019	58	52	49	-2.5	0	24	23	22	-1.0	2.26	16	15	-1.5
58324	CANDO	095	1578	1508	1419	-1.1	34	692	680	658	-0.4	2.12	421	398	-1.3
58325	CHURCHS FERRY	071	58	177	168	-1.3	24	77	75	73	-0.6	2.36	59	56	-1.2
58327	CRARY	071	446	433	414	-0.7	54	166	166	163	0.0	2.61	129	125	-0.7
58329	DUNSEITH	079	3147	3098	3055	-0.4	70	996	1005	1013	0.2	3.04	769	759	-0.3
58330	EDMORE	071	459	413	384	-2.5	1	192	177	168	-1.9	2.19	124	109	-3.0
58331	EGELAND	095	197	182	168	-1.9	4	76	72	69	-1.3	2.53	55	51	-1.8
58332	ESMOND	005	387	377	372	-0.6	58	173	174	174	0.1	2.16	120	117	-0.6
58338	HAMPDEN	019	131	120	112	-2.0	3	59	55	53	-1.6	2.09	40	36	-2.5
58339	HANSBORO	095	73	69	64	-1.3	21	29	28	27	-0.8	2.46	20	19	-1.2
58341	HARVEY	103	2956	2751	2577	-1.7	8	1305	1251	1204	-1.0	2.11	826	762	-1.9
58343	KNOX	005	84	84	84	0.0	82	32	33	33	0.7	2.55	25	24	-1.0
58344	LAKOTA	063	1096	1070	1043	-0.6	61	473	475	475	0.1	2.13	298	287	-0.9
58345	LAWTON	071	215	197	184	-2.0	3	96	90	87	-1.5	2.10	65	59	-2.3
58346	LEEDS	005	760	707	685	-1.7	8	318	303	297	-1.1	2.33	212	194	-2.1
58348	MADDOCK	005	1021	998	984	-0.5	63	445	449	452	0.2	2.13	277	268	-0.8
58351	MINNEWAUKAN	005	532	522	517	-0.5	67	243	245	245	0.2	2.13	168	163	-0.7
58352	MUNICH	019	519	490	464	-1.3	20	207	202	197	-0.6	2.43	148	140	-1.3
58353	MYLO	079	264	253	246	-1.0	38	100	99	99	-0.2	2.56	77	74	-0.9
58356	NEW ROCKFORD	027	2047	1971	1910	-0.9	43	867	855	848	-0.3	2.25	549	523	-1.1
58357	OBERON	005	592	603	607	0.4	88	183	189	191	0.8	3.19	133	133	0.0
58361	PEKIN	063	177	172	167	-0.7	55	83	83	83	0.0	2.04	51	49	-0.9
58362	PENN	071	139	134	128	-0.9	45	49	49	48	0.0	2.73	39	38	-0.6
58363	PERTH	095	110	104	97	-1.3	22	38	37	36	-0.6	2.81	26	24	-1.9
58365	ROCKLAKE	095	394	366	339	-1.7	6	165	158	151	-1.0	2.32	118	110	-1.6
58366	ROLETTE	079	950	972	978	0.5	90	393	415	429	1.3	2.23	254	259	0.5
58367	ROLLA	079	1790	1755	1726	-0.5	66	734	735	738	0.0	2.36	463	446	-0.9
58368	RUGBY	069	4155	4018	3878	-0.8	48	1748	1738	1722	-0.1	2.23	1125	1078	-1.0
58369	SAINT JOHN	079	1294	1285	1271	-0.2	77	433	442	447	0.5	2.91	335	333	-0.1
58370	SAINT MICHAEL	005	3125	3175	3194	0.4	87	772	802	816	0.9	3.95	646	657	0.4
58372	SARLES	095	123	112	104	-2.2	2	56	53	51	-1.3	2.11	39	36	-1.9
58374	SHEYENNE	027	573	589	589	0.7	92	242	257	263	1.4	2.19	155	158	0.5
58377	STARKWEATHER	071	413	384	361	-1.7	7	158	151	145	-1.1	2.52	118	110	-1.6
58380	TOLNA	063	444	425	411	-1.0	36	204	200	198	-0.5	2.13	132	125	-1.3
58381	WARWICK	005	258	245	238	-1.2	28	89	86	84	-0.8	2.85	67	62	-1.8
58382	WEBSTER	071	158	147	139	-1.7	8	62	59	57	-1.2	2.49	47	44	-1.5
58384	WILLOW CITY	009	660	622	591	-1.4	18	278	270	263	-0.7	2.30	195	183	-1.5
58385	WOLFORD	069	223	231	229	0.8	92	87	93	96	1.6	2.48	58	60	0.8
58386	YORK	005	168	161	157	-1.0	38	72	71	71	-0.3	2.27	49	47	-1.0
58401	JAMESTOWN	093	17387	16977	16531	-0.6	61	7381	7439	7456	0.2	2.14	4504	4361	-0.8
58405	JAMESTOWN	093	740	773	785	1.0	94	54	63	68	3.7	4.67	26	29	2.6
58413	ASHLEY	051	1396	1345	1310	-0.9	44	628	622	618	-0.2	2.08	403	385	-1.1
58415	BERLIN	045	179	178	174	-0.1	79	67	69	69	0.7	2.58	52	53	0.5
58416	BINFORD	039	402	380	364	-1.3	21	174	170	168	-0.6	2.24	131	125	-1.1
58418	BOWDON	103	397	412	405	0.9	92	178	191	193	1.7	2.16	119	123	0.8
58420	BUCHANAN	093	296	286	277	-0.8	47	110	110	110	0.0	2.60	88	86	-0.5
58421	CARRINGTON	031	3137	2989	2832	-1.1	30	1277	1250	1215	-0.5	2.32	836	789	-1.4
58422	CATHAY	103	245	231	217	-1.4	19	94	91	88	-0.8	2.54	74	70	-1.3
58423	CHASELEY	103	84	83	79	-0.3	74	37	38	37	0.6	2.18	27	27	0.0
58424	CLEVELAND	093	371	358	347	-0.8	46	157	157	156	0.0	2.28	109	105	-0.9
58425	COOPERSTOWN	039	1777	1740	1696	-0.5	65	763	773	776	0.3	2.18	477	465	-0.6
58426	COURTENAY	093	258	241	230	-1.6	11	99	96	95	-0.7	2.51	76	71	-1.6
58428	DAWSON	043	283	288	286	0.4	87	116	123	127	1.4	2.34	85	87	0.6
58429	DAZEY	003	347	326	310	-1.5	16	140	135	132	-0.9	2.41	101	95	-1.4
58430	DENHOFF	083	134	133	131	-0.2	77	52	53	54	0.5	2.51	40	40	0.0
58431	DICKEY	045	166	165	160	-0.1	78	72	74	74	0.7	2.23	56	56	0.0
58433	EDGELEY	045	1308	1241	1189	-1.2	27	534	521	513	-0.6	2.32	338	317	-1.5
58436	ELLENDALE	021	2247	2197	2184	-0.5	63	854	857	875	0.1	2.24	543	526	-0.8
58438	FESSENDEN	103	878	830	780	-1.3	22	382	372	360	-0.6	2.22	253	237	-1.5
58439	FORBES	021	240	233	232	-0.7	54	102	102	104	0.0	2.28	73	71	-0.7
58440	FREDONIA	047	235	228	219	-0.7	53	97	98	97	0.2	2.33	73	72	-0.3
58441	FULLERTON	021	321	315	314	-0.4	69	122	123	126	0.2	2.56	97	95	-0.5
58442	GACKLE	047	563	525	492	-1.6	10	260	250	241	-0.9	1.96	167	155	-1.7
58443	GLENFIELD	031	356	337	317	-1.3	24	145	142	138	-0.5	2.37	108	103	-1.1
58444	GOODRICH	083	267	243	228	-2.2	2	123	116	112	-1.4	2.09	91	82	-2.4
58445	GRACE CITY	031	117	110	104	-1.4	17	48	47	45	-0.5	2.34	35	34	-0.7
58448	HANNAFORD	039	341	321	307	-1.4	18	150	147	145	-0.5	2.18	106	101	-1.1
58451	HURDSFIELD	103	230	218	205	-1.3	26	91	88	85	-0.8	2.48	71	68	-1.0
	NORTH DAKOTA					0.1					0.8	2.33			-0.1
	UNITED STATES					1.2					1.3	2.58			1.1

ZIP CODE #	POST OFFICE NAME	RACE (%) White 2000	White 2004	Black 2000	Black 2004	Asian/Pacific 2000	Asian/Pacific 2004	% Hispanic Origin 2000	% Hispanic Origin 2004	2004 AGE DISTRIBUTION (%) 0-4	5-9	10-14	15-19	20-24	25-44	45-64	65-84	85+	18+	MEDIAN AGE 2004	% 2004 Males	% 2004 Females
58258	MEKINOCK	97.5	97.2	0.9	1.0	0.0	0.0	0.6	1.0	6.3	6.3	8.5	8.2	6.3	26.6	27.5	9.5	0.6	73.1	37.9	51.6	48.4
58259	MICHIGAN	98.2	97.9	0.2	0.2	0.4	0.4	0.2	0.2	4.6	5.1	5.9	6.7	4.6	19.0	27.8	22.3	4.0	79.4	47.6	51.2	48.8
58260	MILTON	96.2	96.0	0.0	0.0	0.0	0.6	1.1	1.1	4.0	4.6	5.1	6.9	4.6	19.4	31.4	20.0	4.0	80.6	48.7	53.1	46.9
58261	MINTO	95.7	95.3	0.0	0.0	0.1	0.1	6.3	7.5	6.9	7.3	7.5	6.9	5.4	24.6	27.8	11.9	1.8	74.1	39.6	52.7	47.3
58262	MOUNTAIN	96.1	95.8	0.6	0.6	0.0	0.0	1.1	1.2	6.0	6.0	6.0	6.6	6.6	20.2	28.0	16.7	4.2	77.4	44.2	51.2	48.8
58265	NECHE	97.5	96.9	0.2	0.2	0.2	0.2	2.2	2.9	4.8	5.3	6.3	6.6	6.8	22.4	29.4	15.8	2.6	79.7	43.4	51.9	48.1
58266	NIAGARA	97.2	97.0	0.0	0.0	0.7	0.6	0.0	0.0	5.5	6.1	5.5	5.5	4.3	23.2	31.1	17.7	1.2	79.3	45.0	53.7	46.3
58267	NORTHWOOD	98.6	98.5	0.4	0.4	0.1	0.2	0.6	0.7	4.7	5.3	7.0	6.1	4.7	21.0	28.1	17.9	5.3	78.4	45.8	48.8	51.2
58269	OSNABROCK	96.4	95.7	0.2	0.2	0.2	0.4	1.2	1.7	4.1	4.6	5.6	6.6	4.6	19.3	31.3	20.1	3.9	80.3	48.6	52.8	47.2
58270	PARK RIVER	95.9	95.4	0.4	0.4	0.1	0.1	2.2	2.6	5.4	5.5	5.9	6.5	6.3	19.7	26.1	19.3	5.4	78.9	45.5	48.2	51.8
58271	PEMBINA	96.9	96.5	0.1	0.1	0.4	0.5	1.9	2.1	5.3	6.2	9.0	6.5	4.8	26.7	28.0	12.1	1.4	74.7	39.4	50.5	49.6
58272	PETERSBURG	98.0	97.3	0.3	0.3	0.3	0.3	0.6	0.3	4.6	4.9	7.0	6.4	4.9	20.9	26.7	22.4	2.4	79.7	46.0	52.4	47.6
58273	PISEK	97.3	97.1	0.4	0.4	0.0	0.0	1.2	0.8	5.3	5.7	6.9	6.1	4.9	22.5	28.2	18.4	2.0	77.6	44.2	52.2	47.8
58274	PORTLAND	99.3	99.2	0.0	0.0	0.1	0.1	0.9	0.9	6.4	6.6	6.8	6.7	6.1	22.9	24.8	17.4	2.3	76.3	41.9	51.4	48.6
58275	REYNOLDS	98.7	98.6	0.2	0.3	0.1	0.1	1.4	1.3	5.8	6.4	10.6	9.7	3.0	26.4	25.8	11.1	1.1	70.7	37.9	51.3	48.7
58276	SAINT THOMAS	95.0	94.4	0.0	0.0	0.0	0.0	12.0	14.3	5.2	5.8	7.2	6.6	4.9	22.4	30.3	16.3	1.4	77.6	43.7	53.8	46.2
58277	SHARON	97.4	98.0	0.0	0.0	0.0	0.0	0.0	0.0	4.7	4.7	6.0	6.0	6.0	19.3	29.3	21.3	2.7	80.7	47.5	50.7	49.3
58278	THOMPSON	98.0	97.7	0.3	0.3	0.5	0.6	0.7	1.0	6.0	6.6	8.7	9.2	6.8	26.4	27.7	7.8	0.8	72.9	37.0	53.2	46.9
58281	WALES	98.8	98.7	0.0	0.0	0.0	0.0	0.0	0.0	5.3	6.6	6.6	5.3	2.6	22.4	29.0	19.7	2.6	79.0	45.8	54.0	46.1
58282	WALHALLA	92.1	91.2	0.0	0.0	0.0	0.0	0.7	0.7	5.3	5.6	6.1	6.0	6.2	19.0	29.7	18.0	4.2	79.2	46.1	48.9	51.1
58301	DEVILS LAKE	91.2	90.1	0.2	0.2	0.3	0.4	0.5	0.6	6.1	5.9	7.1	7.7	7.8	24.0	24.0	13.8	3.7	76.3	39.4	49.1	50.9
58311	ALSEN	98.0	98.6	0.0	0.0	0.0	0.0	0.0	0.0	6.4	6.4	9.3	7.9	5.0	18.6	28.6	15.7	2.1	72.9	42.7	49.3	50.7
58316	BELCOURT	5.1	4.6	0.1	0.1	0.0	0.0	1.0	1.0	10.3	9.7	10.8	10.2	9.0	25.5	18.0	6.0	0.6	62.8	25.0	49.1	50.9
58317	BISBEE	96.7	96.6	0.0	0.0	0.0	0.0	0.3	0.3	5.0	4.4	10.7	7.5	2.8	22.9	28.2	16.0	2.5	74.9	42.8	50.8	49.2
58318	BOTTINEAU	96.3	95.8	0.3	0.3	0.3	0.3	0.7	0.8	3.8	5.0	6.4	9.4	5.9	19.6	28.9	16.4	4.4	80.5	44.8	50.1	49.9
58319	BREMEN	100.0	100.0	0.0	0.0	0.0	0.0	0.0	0.0	5.4	5.4	7.1	8.9	5.4	21.4	28.6	14.3	3.6	73.2	42.5	57.1	42.9
58321	BROCKET	97.3	97.9	0.0	0.0	0.0	0.0	0.0	0.0	6.3	5.6	7.0	7.0	4.2	22.5	29.6	16.2	1.4	76.1	43.3	54.2	45.8
58323	CALVIN	98.3	98.1	0.0	0.0	0.0	0.0	0.0	0.0	3.9	5.8	5.8	3.9	3.9	19.2	34.6	23.1	0.0	84.6	50.0	51.9	48.1
58324	CANDO	97.5	97.0	0.1	0.1	0.1	0.3	0.1	0.1	4.5	5.8	6.4	6.8	2.6	21.4	28.3	18.4	6.0	78.1	46.7	47.9	52.1
58325	CHURCHS FERRY	97.9	97.7	0.0	0.0	0.5	0.6	1.1	1.1	5.7	5.7	7.9	7.9	3.4	22.6	30.5	14.7	1.7	75.7	43.4	51.4	48.6
58327	CRARY	97.5	97.2	0.0	0.0	0.2	0.2	0.2	0.2	6.5	4.9	7.6	7.2	4.6	23.1	30.5	14.6	1.2	76.0	42.6	54.7	45.3
58329	DUNSEITH	18.8	17.3	0.1	0.1	0.0	0.0	1.0	0.9	9.8	9.4	10.5	10.2	7.9	25.0	18.7	7.6	1.0	64.1	27.0	49.1	50.9
58330	EDMORE	97.4	96.4	0.4	0.5	0.7	1.2	0.4	0.5	3.4	4.4	5.3	5.1	4.1	17.2	31.5	23.7	5.3	83.1	50.7	52.3	47.7
58331	EGELAND	98.0	97.3	0.0	0.0	0.0	0.0	0.0	0.0	5.5	5.5	5.5	8.2	5.5	19.8	28.0	19.8	2.2	78.6	45.0	50.6	49.5
58332	ESMOND	98.2	98.1	0.0	0.0	0.0	0.0	0.5	0.5	5.3	5.8	6.6	5.8	4.5	19.9	28.7	20.2	3.2	78.3	46.3	53.6	46.4
58338	HAMPDEN	97.7	98.3	0.0	0.0	0.0	0.0	0.0	0.0	4.2	5.0	6.7	5.8	4.2	19.2	30.8	20.0	4.2	79.2	47.5	51.7	48.3
58339	HANSBORO	97.3	97.1	0.0	0.0	0.0	0.0	0.0	0.0	4.4	4.4	13.0	8.7	2.9	24.6	27.5	13.0	1.5	71.0	39.6	49.3	50.7
58341	HARVEY	99.2	99.1	0.0	0.1	0.2	0.3	0.4	0.6	4.6	4.7	5.9	6.4	4.8	19.7	26.3	21.8	5.7	80.4	47.5	49.1	50.9
58343	KNOX	98.8	97.6	0.0	0.0	0.0	0.0	0.0	1.2	6.0	7.1	8.3	6.0	4.8	21.4	27.4	16.7	2.4	75.0	42.5	57.1	42.9
58344	LAKOTA	98.1	98.0	0.0	0.0	0.4	0.4	0.1	0.1	3.2	3.7	5.7	7.2	5.1	17.5	29.1	22.5	6.1	82.0	50.2	46.8	53.2
58345	LAWTON	97.2	96.5	0.5	0.5	0.5	1.0	0.9	0.5	4.6	4.6	5.6	6.1	4.6	19.3	28.9	22.3	4.1	81.2	48.3	52.3	47.7
58346	LEEDS	97.9	97.6	0.4	0.4	0.0	0.0	0.3	0.1	6.1	6.5	7.1	6.8	5.2	19.8	28.3	17.5	2.7	76.1	44.0	51.1	48.9
58348	MADDOCK	98.7	98.6	0.0	0.0	0.1	0.1	0.4	0.4	3.6	4.3	6.7	7.0	4.1	18.4	26.6	21.9	7.3	80.5	48.5	50.0	50.0
58351	MINNEWAUKAN	85.3	84.1	0.0	0.0	0.0	0.0	1.3	1.3	5.6	5.9	7.5	6.7	5.2	21.8	28.0	17.1	2.3	77.0	43.3	52.9	47.1
58352	MUNICH	98.3	98.2	0.2	0.2	0.0	0.0	0.4	0.4	5.7	6.5	9.2	7.8	4.9	19.0	29.0	15.7	2.2	73.9	43.1	49.8	50.2
58353	MYLO	92.1	91.7	0.0	0.0	0.0	0.0	0.0	0.0	5.5	6.3	8.7	7.1	4.0	23.3	28.9	14.6	1.6	74.7	42.4	53.4	46.6
58356	NEW ROCKFORD	96.5	96.4	0.1	0.1	0.2	0.2	0.6	0.7	4.7	5.2	7.4	6.4	5.3	20.8	26.0	19.8	4.4	78.7	45.2	48.3	51.7
58357	OBERON	41.2	39.1	0.3	0.3	0.0	0.0	2.0	2.0	11.3	9.0	9.5	10.1	8.6	22.1	19.7	9.0	0.8	63.9	26.5	48.8	51.2
58361	PEKIN	99.4	99.4	0.0	0.0	0.6	0.6	0.0	0.0	3.5	4.1	6.4	5.8	5.2	18.0	31.4	22.1	3.5	82.6	48.5	51.7	48.3
58362	PENN	98.6	99.3	0.0	0.0	0.0	0.0	0.0	0.0	4.5	6.7	7.5	7.5	3.7	24.6	34.3	10.5	0.8	76.1	42.7	52.2	47.8
58363	PERTH	96.4	96.2	0.0	0.0	0.0	0.0	0.0	0.0	4.8	4.8	11.5	7.7	2.9	22.1	27.9	15.4	2.9	74.0	42.1	50.0	50.0
58365	ROCKLAKE	97.5	97.3	0.0	0.0	0.0	0.0	0.0	0.0	5.5	5.5	6.6	7.9	4.6	21.6	27.6	18.6	2.2	77.6	44.0	49.7	50.3
58366	ROLETTE	78.3	76.7	0.1	0.1	0.0	0.0	0.0	0.0	7.0	6.6	6.5	6.8	5.9	22.2	23.6	17.3	4.2	75.8	42.0	50.1	49.9
58367	ROLLA	70.2	68.0	0.1	0.1	0.5	0.5	0.5	0.5	6.2	6.2	7.7	7.7	6.6	22.9	24.2	15.6	2.7	74.5	40.1	46.7	53.3
58368	RUGBY	98.5	98.2	0.1	0.1	0.3	0.4	0.6	0.7	5.3	5.5	6.4	6.5	6.1	21.4	24.4	19.4	5.2	78.6	44.3	49.3	50.8
58369	SAINT JOHN	29.9	27.6	0.0	0.0	0.0	0.0	0.9	0.9	8.6	8.4	9.5	8.7	8.8	26.1	22.1	7.2	0.7	68.3	29.5	52.1	47.9
58370	SAINT MICHAEL	11.3	10.4	0.0	0.0	0.0	0.0	0.8	0.8	12.7	11.7	12.5	10.8	8.2	24.3	15.3	4.1	0.4	56.2	21.4	49.5	50.5
58372	SARLES	98.4	98.2	0.0	0.0	0.0	0.0	0.0	0.0	5.4	5.4	5.4	6.3	3.6	22.3	31.3	18.8	1.8	78.6	46.1	52.7	47.3
58374	SHEYENNE	88.5	88.3	0.0	0.0	0.2	0.2	0.9	0.7	5.8	5.8	7.0	7.3	5.3	20.0	25.5	17.5	5.9	76.9	44.1	49.1	50.9
58377	STARKWEATHER	98.1	97.7	0.0	0.0	0.5	0.5	0.7	1.0	5.5	5.5	7.3	8.3	3.4	23.2	30.5	14.3	2.1	76.3	43.5	51.6	48.4
58380	TOLNA	98.0	97.9	0.0	0.0	0.5	0.5	0.0	0.0	4.5	4.5	6.4	6.4	4.9	19.8	30.1	21.2	2.4	80.7	47.3	51.5	48.5
58381	WARWICK	46.1	43.7	0.0	0.0	0.0	0.0	0.0	0.0	10.6	9.4	11.0	9.4	6.1	22.0	22.5	8.2	0.8	63.3	28.5	52.2	47.8
58382	WEBSTER	98.1	98.0	0.0	0.0	0.6	0.7	0.6	1.4	5.4	5.4	7.5	8.2	2.7	23.8	32.0	13.6	1.4	76.2	43.7	52.4	47.6
58384	WILLOW CITY	92.7	92.3	0.3	0.3	0.0	0.0	0.2	0.2	4.3	5.1	6.9	6.9	5.1	22.4	28.1	18.7	2.4	79.6	44.5	53.1	47.0
58385	WOLFORD	98.2	97.8	0.5	0.4	0.0	0.4	0.9	0.9	6.5	6.5	6.1	5.6	5.2	25.5	26.4	16.0	2.2	77.5	41.9	52.0	48.1
58386	YORK	98.2	98.1	0.6	0.6	0.0	0.0	0.0	0.0	6.2	6.2	7.5	6.8	5.6	20.5	28.0	16.8	2.5	75.8	43.1	51.6	48.5
58401	JAMESTOWN	97.3	96.8	0.3	0.3	0.5	0.6	1.1	1.3	5.7	5.6	6.2	6.9	7.3	24.4	26.1	14.6	3.2	78.4	41.0	48.7	51.3
58405	JAMESTOWN	95.8	95.1	1.2	1.3	1.1	1.4	0.8	1.2	3.4	0.9	1.4	26.3	48.0	9.4	7.6	2.5	0.5	93.0	21.9	47.4	52.7
58413	ASHLEY	98.7	98.6	0.0	0.0	0.6	0.7	0.6	0.7	4.4	4.2	4.2	5.3	4.5	15.3	24.0	30.9	7.2	84.3	55.0	47.7	52.3
58415	BERLIN	98.9	98.9	0.0	0.0	0.6	0.6	0.0	0.0	6.7	6.7	8.4	6.2	6.7	27.0	24.7	11.8	1.7	73.6	36.4	55.1	44.9
58416	BINFORD	99.8	99.7	0.0	0.0	0.3	0.3	0.0	0.0	4.5	4.7	5.0	6.8	6.6	17.4	32.9	18.4	3.7	81.3	48.0	50.5	49.5
58418	BOWDON	99.8	99.5	0.3	0.2	0.0	0.0	0.0	0.2	4.6	5.3	7.5	6.1	4.6	20.2	27.4	20.2	4.1	78.4	46.1	51.7	48.3
58420	BUCHANAN	99.0	98.3	0.0	0.4	0.0	0.4	0.3	0.0	3.9	6.6	8.4	7.7	4.2	24.8	32.5	10.1	1.8	75.9	42.2	55.6	44.4
58421	CARRINGTON	99.0	98.9	0.1	0.1	0.0	0.0	0.2	0.2	5.8	6.0	7.8	7.3	5.0	23.7	23.5	17.4	3.5	75.3	41.6	49.6	50.5
58422	CATHAY	99.6	99.6	0.0	0.0	0.0	0.0	0.0	0.0	5.2	5.6	6.9	6.9	5.2	22.1	29.0	16.9	2.2	77.5	44.0	52.0	48.1
58423	CHASELEY	100.0	100.0	0.0	0.0	0.0	0.0	0.0	0.0	4.8	4.8	7.2	6.0	4.8	22.9	28.9	16.9	3.6	77.1	44.7	54.2	45.8
58424	CLEVELAND	99.2	99.4	0.0	0.0	0.0	0.0	0.3	0.3	4.8	5.9	7.3	5.9	4.8	21.2	28.2	18.7	3.4	78.5	45.2	51.1	48.9
58425	COOPERSTOWN	99.1	99.1	0.0	0.0	0.2	0.2	0.6	0.6	4.9	5.5	6.3	5.9	5.1	19.4	27.6	19.5	5.8	79.5	46.9	49.5	50.5
58426	COURTENAY	99.2	99.6	0.0	0.0	0.0	0.0	0.0	0.0	5.0	5.8	7.1	7.5	5.8	19.5	31.5	16.2	1.7	77.2	44.6	51.9	48.1
58428	DAWSON	99.7	99.3	0.4	0.4	0.0	0.0	0.7	0.7	5.9	5.9	8.0	5.9	4.9	21.9	29.2	16.3	2.1	76.0	43.7	52.8	47.2
58429	DAZEY	99.4	99.4	0.0	0.0	0.0	0.0	0.0	0.0	6.1	6.8	7.7	6.8	5.8	22.7	26.4	16.0	1.8	75.8	41.4	50.0	50.0
58430	DENHOFF	99.3	100.0	0.0	0.0	0.0	0.0	0.0	0.0	3.0	4.5	6.8	6.8	4.5	17.3	33.1	22.6	1.5	81.2	49.0	53.4	46.6
58431	DICKEY	98.8	98.8	0.0	0.0	0.6	0.6	0.0	0.0	7.3	7.3	8.5	6.1	6.7	25.5	24.2	12.7	1.8	72.7	36.3	55.8	44.2
58433	EDGELEY	99.2	99.1	0.0	0.0	0.1	0.2	0.6	0.7	4.7	4.8	6.7	6.8	5.6	18.9	26.9	21.0	4.5	79.3	46.5	50.0	50.0
58436	ELLENDALE	97.7	97.7	0.1	0.1	0.2	0.2	0.9	0.9	4.8	5.2	6.0	8.5	11.9	18.8	23.4	16.2	5.3	80.3	40.2	48.8	51.2
58438	FESSENDEN	98.2	97.7	0.5	0.6	0.7	1.0	0.1	0.1	5.1	5.3	6.5	7.0	4.8	18.8	28.1	20.6	3.9	78.2	46.4	50.1	49.9
58439	FORBES	99.2	99.1	0.0	0.0	0.0	0.0	0.4	0.4	5.6	6.4	6.4	6.0	4.7	20.2	28.3	20.6	1.7	78.5	45.4	52.4	47.6
58440	FREDONIA	99.2	99.6	0.0	0.0	0.0	0.0	0.4	0.4	6.6	6.6	6.1	6.6	4.4	21.9	26.8	19.7	1.3	76.3	43.9	52.2	47.8
58441	FULLERTON	97.8	98.1	0.0	0.0	0.6	0.6	0.9	1.0	6.0	6.4	7.6	7.3	6.0	23.8	27.3	14.0	1.6	75.6	40.5	52.7	47.3
58442	GACKLE	99.3	99.4	0.0	0.0	0.0	0.0	1.1	1.3	3.6	4.0	4.0	3.8	4.4	17.1	30.7	24.6	7.8	85.9	52.9	49.0	51.1
58443	GLENFIELD	99.4	99.4	0.0	0.0	0.0	0.0	0.0	0.0	5.0	5.6	7.7	7.1	5.0	21.4	27.6	18.4	2.1	77.2	43.8	52.5	47.5
58444	GOODRICH	99.3	98.8	0.4	0.4	0.0	0.0	0.4	0.4	2.9	3.3	6.2	7.0	4.5	15.6	32.1	24.7	3.7	83.1	49.9	50.6	49.4
58445	GRACE CITY	99.2	99.1	0.0	0.0	0.0	0.0	0.0	0.0	5.5	5.5	8.2	6.4	5.5	20.9	25.5	20.0	2.7	75.5	43.9	51.8	48.2
58448	HANNAFORD	99.7	99.7	0.0	0.0	0.0	0.0	0.0	0.0	4.7	5.3	5.9	6.5	5.3	19.3	30.8	18.4	3.7	80.4	46.9	53.6	46.4
58451	HURDSFIELD	99.6	99.5	0.0	0.0	0.0	0.0	0.0	0.0	5.5	5.5	6.4	6.9	5.1	22.5	29.4	16.5	2.3	78.0	44.1	50.9	49.1
	NORTH DAKOTA	92.4	91.7	0.6	0.7	0.6	0.8	1.2	1.4	6.3	6.1	6.8	7.9	8.5	26.2	23.9	12.0	2.4	76.5	36.5	50.0	50.0
	UNITED STATES	75.1	73.6	12.3	12.5	3.8	4.2	12.5	14.1	6.9	6.7	7.2	7.0	7.3	28.6	23.8	10.8	1.7	75.1	36.0	49.1	50.9

ZIP CODE #	POST OFFICE NAME	2004 Per Capita Income	2004 HH Income Base	2004 HOUSEHOLD INCOME DISTRIBUTION (%) Less than $25,000	$25,000 to $49,999	$50,000 to $99,999	$100,000 to $149,999	$150,000 or More	MEDIAN HOUSEHOLD INCOME 2004	2009	2004 National Centile	2004 State Centile	2004 Home Value Base	2004 HOME VALUE DISTRIBUTION (%) Less than $50,000	$50,000 to $89,999	$90,000 to $174,999	$175,000 to $399,999	$400,000 or More	2004 Median Home Value
58258	MEKINOCK	21620	119	21.0	24.4	45.4	7.6	1.7	52730	60900	77	96	100	22.0	39.0	37.0	2.0	0.0	76667
58259	MICHIGAN	18894	226	36.3	39.8	20.8	3.1	0.0	33947	39205	24	35	185	66.0	24.3	8.1	0.5	1.1	33750
58260	MILTON	22450	77	19.5	41.6	31.2	6.5	1.3	42345	49445	54	76	64	65.6	21.9	12.5	0.0	0.0	38000
58261	MINTO	20142	529	28.4	34.2	31.0	4.5	1.9	40787	47982	49	70	442	30.1	44.6	22.0	3.2	0.2	64754
58262	MOUNTAIN	17058	63	30.2	36.5	30.2	3.2	0.0	36100	41136	32	49	51	49.0	37.3	13.7	0.0	0.0	51000
58265	NECHE	22737	239	20.9	34.3	31.8	10.5	2.5	45173	53059	62	84	207	51.2	30.4	15.0	2.9	0.5	49219
58266	NIAGARA	19687	65	18.5	38.5	38.5	4.6	0.0	43241	49191	57	78	54	38.9	33.3	24.1	3.7	0.0	62500
58267	NORTHWOOD	22269	580	25.2	34.7	31.4	6.7	2.1	42366	50630	54	76	448	29.5	44.2	22.3	3.8	0.2	70294
58269	OSNABROCK	21160	200	20.0	43.0	29.0	6.0	2.0	41639	48334	52	73	166	64.5	21.7	12.7	1.2	0.0	38333
58270	PARK RIVER	19090	829	31.1	38.5	26.3	2.9	1.2	35630	40973	30	47	632	34.5	44.3	19.9	0.8	0.5	63231
58271	PEMBINA	25943	320	13.1	26.9	47.8	10.3	1.9	57207	66599	82	98	269	26.4	42.0	26.4	5.2	0.0	74125
58272	PETERSBURG	18706	141	32.6	35.5	26.2	5.7	0.0	35745	40563	31	47	117	49.6	35.0	13.7	0.9	0.9	50625
58273	PISEK	19648	106	37.7	29.3	27.4	3.8	1.9	35000	40754	28	43	91	59.3	25.3	15.4	0.0	0.0	42273
58274	PORTLAND	21710	383	26.6	31.3	34.7	4.4	2.9	42698	49748	55	77	298	34.6	29.2	31.2	5.0	0.0	71667
58275	REYNOLDS	21135	319	14.7	28.2	49.5	5.3	2.2	54304	63346	79	97	283	18.4	30.7	44.5	6.0	0.4	91471
58276	SAINT THOMAS	27351	267	25.8	32.2	25.8	9.7	6.4	44258	52190	59	82	222	46.4	32.4	16.2	5.0	0.0	55714
58277	SHARON	24398	72	29.2	33.3	29.2	4.2	4.2	40000	46372	46	67	58	48.3	31.0	17.2	3.5	0.0	52000
58278	THOMPSON	26311	671	7.2	23.3	49.3	13.7	6.6	64197	79735	88	99	574	6.5	20.4	55.8	15.7	1.7	119444
58281	WALES	18611	37	32.4	43.2	18.9	5.4	0.0	36139	42357	32	50	31	90.3	6.5	3.2	0.0	0.0	11875
58282	WALHALLA	21617	634	27.0	38.2	27.6	5.8	1.4	37765	44815	38	58	474	38.4	41.6	15.4	4.2	0.4	59483
58301	DEVILS LAKE	22297	4086	30.1	32.3	28.8	6.0	2.9	40784	47764	49	70	2578	27.8	35.8	29.9	6.3	0.3	76608
58311	ALSEN	17355	55	38.2	32.7	20.0	7.3	1.8	35551	41541	30	47	46	52.2	30.4	17.4	0.0	0.0	45000
58316	BELCOURT	11586	1967	47.6	26.9	19.7	4.3	1.4	26904	33317	7	5	1174	44.6	29.6	22.5	3.4	0.0	60000
58317	BISBEE	20912	139	26.6	43.2	23.0	4.3	2.9	38733	43778	42	64	113	60.2	22.1	11.5	4.4	1.8	38500
58318	BOTTINEAU	19841	1600	35.0	31.2	25.5	6.6	1.7	35385	41853	29	45	1249	33.8	40.8	20.5	4.8	0.1	66445
58319	BREMEN	16696	22	27.3	40.9	31.8	0.0	0.0	40000	43604	46	67	19	47.4	21.1	21.1	5.3	5.3	55000
58321	BROCKET	25672	65	26.2	35.4	27.7	7.7	3.1	41359	47842	51	73	55	40.0	30.9	20.0	9.1	0.0	70625
58323	CALVIN	16739	23	39.1	39.1	17.4	4.4	0.0	31099	45000	15	19	19	89.5	10.5	0.0	0.0	0.0	12500
58324	CANDO	24530	680	34.6	29.9	25.4	5.4	4.7	38179	45631	40	61	522	36.8	44.1	17.6	1.3	0.2	63521
58325	CHURCHS FERRY	21526	75	24.0	34.7	32.0	6.7	2.7	42343	47349	54	75	61	54.1	26.2	13.1	6.6	0.0	43750
58327	CRARY	23939	166	22.9	34.9	27.7	8.4	6.0	44641	50782	60	83	141	31.9	29.1	24.1	13.5	1.4	79118
58329	DUNSEITH	11168	1005	43.4	31.3	22.9	2.4	0.0	28810	35892	10	10	697	49.4	31.7	13.5	4.9	0.6	50643
58330	EDMORE	18972	177	39.0	31.1	23.2	5.1	1.7	32584	38897	20	27	142	68.3	16.9	7.8	3.5	3.5	27727
58331	EGELAND	16810	72	31.9	40.3	23.6	2.8	1.4	33571	40362	23	33	58	75.9	19.0	5.2	0.0	0.0	34167
58332	ESMOND	22504	174	32.8	36.2	22.4	6.3	2.3	36031	41766	32	48	145	61.4	22.1	12.4	4.1	0.0	38438
58338	HAMPDEN	20767	55	36.4	32.7	23.6	5.5	1.8	35551	40553	30	47	44	63.6	20.5	9.1	4.6	2.3	32500
58339	HANSBORO	15761	28	32.1	42.9	21.4	3.6	0.0	33126	45721	21	29	23	69.6	21.7	8.7	0.0	0.0	28750
58341	HARVEY	24837	1251	33.4	30.2	27.5	5.2	3.7	38894	45963	42	65	939	41.3	37.4	16.6	3.7	1.0	60650
58343	KNOX	18348	33	33.3	27.3	33.3	6.1	0.0	42389	47396	54	77	28	57.1	17.9	17.9	7.1	0.0	35000
58344	LAKOTA	18978	475	36.2	33.5	24.8	4.6	0.8	32296	38392	19	25	363	41.9	39.7	15.4	2.5	0.6	58194
58345	LAWTON	21175	90	34.4	33.3	25.6	4.4	2.2	35000	39530	28	43	74	60.8	20.3	13.5	4.1	1.4	36250
58346	LEEDS	22300	303	32.0	28.4	31.4	5.0	3.3	39109	45529	43	65	247	51.4	28.3	16.2	4.1	0.0	48833
58348	MADDOCK	19155	449	38.8	37.0	18.7	4.2	1.3	32709	39380	20	28	347	66.6	22.2	7.5	3.5	0.3	36019
58351	MINNEWAUKAN	20370	245	30.6	38.0	26.9	4.5	0.0	34877	42747	27	42	193	65.3	22.3	9.8	2.6	0.0	38125
58352	MUNICH	18093	202	36.6	34.2	21.3	5.9	2.0	35959	40945	31	48	168	55.4	28.0	15.5	1.2	0.0	38571
58353	MYLO	16466	99	31.3	44.4	19.2	4.0	1.0	31223	38451	16	20	85	35.3	36.5	23.5	4.7	0.0	67500
58356	NEW ROCKFORD	20331	855	37.0	31.1	22.9	5.3	3.7	32697	40232	20	28	641	56.0	30.4	11.1	1.3	1.3	43889
58357	OBERON	12281	189	37.0	28.0	32.3	2.7	0.0	32118	38406	18	24	125	64.0	22.4	11.2	2.4	0.0	37083
58361	PEKIN	20384	83	36.1	37.4	19.3	4.8	2.4	34524	40268	26	38	68	55.9	25.0	17.7	0.0	1.5	42000
58362	PENN	19722	49	16.3	38.8	36.7	6.1	2.0	47307	56652	67	88	41	29.3	34.2	24.4	9.8	2.4	73750
58363	PERTH	14928	37	24.3	46.0	27.0	2.7	0.0	40332	46517	47	68	30	66.7	23.3	10.0	0.0	0.0	30000
58365	ROCKLAKE	18708	158	30.4	40.5	23.4	3.8	1.9	35000	39485	28	43	127	73.2	18.9	7.1	0.8	0.0	34318
58366	ROLETTE	18671	415	34.5	39.3	18.6	6.0	1.7	34269	40518	25	37	317	40.4	41.6	13.9	4.1	0.0	55865
58367	ROLLA	19586	735	35.8	28.4	29.0	4.4	2.5	37464	43966	37	57	516	37.6	38.2	21.7	2.1	0.4	62045
58368	RUGBY	17665	1738	39.3	35.8	19.0	4.3	1.6	30644	35772	14	17	1279	34.1	32.6	30.3	2.4	0.7	69844
58369	SAINT JOHN	14332	442	38.5	27.8	27.8	4.5	1.4	34595	40477	26	40	375	44.3	28.8	22.9	2.9	1.1	59773
58370	SAINT MICHAEL	8537	802	50.3	25.1	21.6	2.5	0.6	24816	29892	4	1	414	54.4	25.9	16.2	2.4	1.2	44375
58372	SARLES	18831	53	35.9	39.6	20.8	3.8	0.0	33317	42353	22	32	44	84.1	11.4	4.6	0.0	0.0	20000
58374	SHEYENNE	20431	257	38.1	29.6	23.0	5.8	3.5	33624	41241	23	34	190	60.0	27.9	10.5	0.5	1.1	40952
58377	STARKWEATHER	20381	151	23.2	37.1	29.8	6.6	3.3	40606	46891	48	69	120	54.2	28.3	12.5	5.0	0.0	43750
58380	TOLNA	19317	200	37.0	37.0	20.0	5.0	1.0	34563	41048	26	39	166	51.2	24.7	20.5	1.2	2.4	48333
58381	WARWICK	11928	86	48.8	22.1	26.7	2.3	0.0	25884	31543	6	3	64	60.9	20.3	17.2	1.6	0.0	35000
58382	WEBSTER	21154	59	20.3	37.3	32.2	6.8	3.4	42976	46354	56	78	48	52.1	29.2	12.5	6.3	0.0	47500
58384	WILLOW CITY	15847	270	39.3	38.5	19.3	2.6	0.4	29613	35390	11	13	213	68.5	22.5	5.6	1.9	1.4	31500
58385	WOLFORD	12998	93	45.2	39.8	12.9	2.2	0.0	26620	30474	7	4	72	62.5	25.0	6.9	4.2	1.4	32500
58386	YORK	20815	71	33.8	29.6	28.2	5.6	2.8	37329	42338	37	56	58	55.2	25.9	13.8	5.2	0.0	45714
58401	JAMESTOWN	21375	7439	30.9	32.4	29.5	5.4	1.8	38752	46101	42	64	4915	22.9	36.1	35.0	5.5	0.5	80504
58405	JAMESTOWN	9091	63	46.0	27.0	23.8	3.2	0.0	31712	38209	17	22	20	0.0	50.0	50.0	0.0	0.0	90000
58413	ASHLEY	15783	622	50.0	31.8	13.5	3.4	1.3	25000	29279	5	2	510	74.5	17.7	6.3	1.2	0.4	30179
58415	BERLIN	14326	69	42.0	29.0	23.2	5.8	0.0	29513	35439	11	13	58	55.2	24.1	15.5	5.2	0.0	42500
58416	BINFORD	19823	170	32.9	35.3	24.1	5.9	1.8	33251	38618	22	31	141	63.8	18.4	10.6	2.8	4.3	35250
58418	BOWDON	19541	191	39.8	34.6	19.4	4.2	2.1	31112	36552	15	20	156	65.4	23.1	9.0	1.3	1.3	30000
58420	BUCHANAN	26404	110	19.1	25.5	40.0	8.2	7.3	55560	64965	80	98	94	27.7	25.5	33.0	11.7	2.1	84000
58421	CARRINGTON	22193	1250	31.3	32.2	28.2	6.5	1.9	38234	46254	40	61	927	33.2	32.3	28.2	5.6	0.8	71587
58422	CATHAY	17032	91	38.5	36.3	18.7	4.4	2.2	32609	38853	20	28	76	51.3	23.7	17.1	4.0	4.0	48750
58423	CHASELEY	16175	38	44.7	34.2	15.8	5.3	0.0	28142	35733	9	9	31	64.5	22.6	12.9	0.0	0.0	32500
58424	CLEVELAND	23490	157	35.0	31.9	24.2	4.5	4.5	35502	41517	29	46	133	49.6	30.1	14.3	4.5	1.5	50455
58425	COOPERSTOWN	20256	773	34.4	35.1	23.5	5.1	1.9	33966	41118	24	36	597	49.1	28.5	19.6	2.2	0.7	51196
58426	COURTENAY	22081	96	29.2	25.0	32.3	9.4	4.2	45918	52413	64	86	81	46.9	18.5	27.2	4.9	2.5	56250
58428	DAWSON	14791	123	46.3	33.3	13.8	5.7	0.8	27038	31243	7	5	103	56.3	23.3	14.6	3.9	1.9	42778
58429	DAZEY	19166	135	27.4	35.6	30.4	5.2	1.5	36787	44216	35	53	111	64.0	20.7	11.7	2.7	0.9	39063
58430	DENHOFF	15127	53	43.4	34.0	18.9	3.8	0.0	28302	33606	9	9	45	53.3	22.2	15.6	6.7	2.2	42500
58431	DICKEY	20953	74	37.8	32.4	21.6	6.8	1.4	31256	36840	16	21	62	54.8	22.6	14.5	8.1	0.0	42500
58433	EDGELEY	21479	521	35.1	33.4	24.0	4.6	2.9	33292	39914	22	32	409	48.4	36.7	11.7	2.4	0.7	51250
58436	ELLENDALE	16525	857	43.4	31.9	19.4	4.3	1.1	29031	34529	10	12	620	52.9	29.8	13.9	2.4	1.0	47313
58438	FESSENDEN	21399	372	33.3	33.3	28.8	3.5	1.1	37534	43174	38	57	297	63.0	27.3	8.8	0.7	0.3	40833
58439	FORBES	20595	102	34.3	29.4	26.5	6.9	2.9	36862	45000	35	54	85	48.2	16.5	25.9	4.7	4.7	57500
58440	FREDONIA	21168	98	36.7	31.6	20.4	8.2	3.1	33417	41937	22	33	81	58.0	19.8	14.8	3.7	3.7	36875
58441	FULLERTON	21921	123	28.5	34.2	28.5	5.7	3.3	38724	44436	42	63	99	36.4	32.3	27.3	2.0	2.0	68077
58442	GACKLE	19486	250	44.8	32.4	17.2	4.0	1.6	27160	32936	7	6	205	58.1	30.7	7.8	2.0	1.5	41316
58443	GLENFIELD	19766	142	28.2	35.2	28.9	6.3	1.4	36500	42842	34	51	117	60.7	14.5	13.7	8.6	2.6	42188
58444	GOODRICH	16849	116	44.8	33.6	17.2	3.5	0.9	27257	30978	7	6	98	63.3	11.2	10.2	10.2	5.1	27222
58445	GRACE CITY	19364	47	27.7	36.2	27.7	6.4	2.1	36699	44078	34	52	38	71.1	13.2	5.3	7.9	2.6	36667
58448	HANNAFORD	18632	147	33.3	37.4	25.9	2.0	1.4	34714	40751	26	41	123	57.7	23.6	13.0	3.3	2.4	41364
58451	HURDSFIELD	16808	88	40.9	35.2	17.1	4.6	2.3	31095	37022	15	19	73	56.2	23.3	15.1	2.7	2.7	45000
	NORTH DAKOTA	22058		29.0	31.5	29.9	6.6	3.0	40503	48701				27.7	27.3	34.9	9.3	0.9	83011
	UNITED STATES	25866		24.7	27.1	30.8	10.9	6.5	48124	56710				10.9	15.0	33.7	30.1	10.4	145905

ZIP CODE #	POST OFFICE NAME	FINANCIAL SERVICES: Auto Loan	FINANCIAL SERVICES: Home Loan	FINANCIAL SERVICES: Invest-ments	FINANCIAL SERVICES: Retire-ment Plans	THE HOME: Home Improvements: Home Repair	THE HOME: Home Improvements: Lawn & Garden	THE HOME: Furnishings: Comput-ers & Hard-ware	THE HOME: Furnishings: Major Appli-ances	THE HOME: Furnishings: TV, Radio, Sound Equip-ment	THE HOME: Furnishings: Furni-ture	ENTERTAINMENT: Dine out/ Carry out	ENTERTAINMENT: Sports Equip-ment	ENTERTAINMENT: Fees & Tickets	ENTERTAINMENT: Toys & Games	ENTERTAINMENT: Travel	ENTERTAINMENT: Cable TV	PERSONAL: Apparel & Services	PERSONAL: Auto Repairs	PERSONAL: Health Insur-ance	PERSONAL: Pets & Supplies
58258	MEKINOCK	92	81	62	78	86	92	76	84	81	76	98	99	74	100	78	83	93	82	91	107
58259	MICHIGAN	64	47	30	45	53	62	51	58	58	49	68	66	45	65	51	61	62	58	69	72
58260	MILTON	91	63	33	60	74	83	63	78	72	62	85	93	54	83	65	76	77	76	92	108
58261	MINTO	86	61	32	57	70	79	60	74	69	59	81	89	51	79	62	72	74	73	87	102
58262	MOUNTAIN	79	55	29	52	64	72	54	67	63	54	73	81	46	72	56	66	67	66	80	93
58265	NECHE	107	75	39	70	87	97	74	91	85	73	99	110	63	97	76	89	91	90	108	127
58266	NIAGARA	89	63	33	59	73	82	62	76	72	61	84	92	53	82	64	75	76	75	91	105
58267	NORTHWOOD	86	63	39	60	71	83	67	77	76	65	90	88	59	85	68	80	82	77	92	98
58269	OSNABROCK	91	64	33	60	74	83	63	78	72	62	85	93	54	83	65	76	77	76	92	108
58270	PARK RIVER	71	53	34	51	59	70	58	65	65	55	76	73	51	72	58	69	70	64	77	80
58271	PEMBINA	102	88	65	84	94	102	82	92	88	82	107	110	79	109	85	91	101	90	101	121
58272	PETERSBURG	78	55	29	52	64	72	55	67	63	54	74	81	47	72	57	66	67	66	80	93
58273	PISEK	82	57	30	54	67	75	57	70	65	56	77	84	48	75	59	69	70	69	83	98
58274	PORTLAND	94	66	35	62	76	86	65	80	75	64	88	97	56	86	68	78	80	79	95	111
58275	REYNOLDS	97	82	59	78	89	96	77	88	83	77	100	105	73	102	80	86	95	86	97	115
58276	SAINT THOMAS	122	85	44	80	99	111	84	104	97	83	113	125	72	111	87	101	103	102	123	144
58277	SHARON	86	68	46	61	76	86	64	77	72	63	86	90	57	84	68	77	79	76	91	105
58278	THOMPSON	107	117	115	117	114	114	109	110	104	110	130	130	111	133	108	99	128	108	100	123
58281	WALES	69	48	25	46	56	63	48	59	55	47	64	71	41	63	49	58	59	58	70	82
58282	WALHALLA	82	60	37	57	67	79	65	73	73	62	86	84	57	82	65	77	78	73	88	93
58301	DEVILS LAKE	78	66	57	65	70	79	71	74	76	68	91	86	67	89	70	78	86	75	83	88
58311	ALSEN	80	56	29	53	65	73	55	68	64	54	74	82	47	73	57	67	68	67	81	95
58316	BELCOURT	53	48	52	46	47	53	51	51	53	52	66	58	50	64	50	54	64	52	52	59
58317	BISBEE	86	60	32	57	70	79	60	74	69	59	81	89	51	79	62	73	74	73	88	102
58318	BOTTINEAU	75	58	39	55	64	74	60	68	67	58	80	78	54	77	61	71	73	67	80	86
58319	BREMEN	77	54	28	51	63	70	53	66	61	52	72	79	45	70	55	64	65	65	78	91
58321	BROCKET	101	71	37	67	82	92	70	86	81	69	95	104	60	93	73	85	86	85	103	120
58323	CALVIN	68	48	25	45	56	62	47	58	54	47	64	70	40	63	49	57	58	58	70	81
58324	CANDO	91	66	39	63	75	87	69	81	79	67	93	94	61	89	70	83	84	80	96	105
58325	CHURCHS FERRY	92	64	34	61	75	84	63	78	73	63	86	94	54	84	66	77	78	77	93	109
58327	CRARY	113	79	42	75	92	103	78	96	90	77	105	116	67	103	81	94	96	95	115	134
58329	DUNSEITH	50	45	42	43	45	49	48	48	49	47	61	56	46	59	46	49	58	49	49	55
58330	EDMORE	69	52	34	50	57	68	58	63	65	55	76	71	51	72	57	68	69	63	76	76
58331	EGELAND	77	54	28	51	63	70	53	66	61	52	72	79	45	70	55	64	65	65	78	91
58332	ESMOND	87	61	33	58	71	80	61	75	70	60	82	90	52	80	63	74	75	74	89	103
58338	HAMPDEN	74	55	34	52	61	72	59	67	66	56	78	76	52	74	59	70	71	66	80	84
58339	HANSBORO	70	49	26	46	57	64	48	60	56	48	65	72	41	64	50	59	60	59	71	83
58341	HARVEY	90	66	41	63	73	86	71	80	80	68	94	92	62	89	71	84	86	80	96	101
58343	KNOX	85	59	31	56	69	77	58	72	67	58	79	87	50	77	60	70	72	71	86	100
58344	LAKOTA	69	51	32	49	57	67	55	62	62	53	73	71	48	69	55	65	66	62	74	78
58345	LAWTON	77	56	34	53	63	73	60	68	67	57	79	79	52	76	60	71	72	68	82	87
58346	LEEDS	94	66	35	62	76	86	65	80	75	64	88	97	56	86	67	79	80	79	96	111
58348	MADDOCK	70	51	31	49	58	67	55	63	62	52	73	72	48	69	55	65	66	62	75	80
58351	MINNEWAUKAN	76	55	32	52	63	70	55	66	63	54	74	79	48	72	57	65	68	65	78	90
58352	MUNICH	79	55	29	52	65	72	55	68	63	54	74	82	47	73	57	66	67	67	81	94
58353	MYLO	76	53	28	50	62	69	53	65	60	52	71	78	45	70	54	63	65	64	77	90
58356	NEW ROCKFORD	76	57	36	54	63	74	61	69	69	59	81	78	54	77	61	73	74	69	82	86
58357	OBERON	61	48	41	47	51	58	53	56	57	51	69	66	49	68	52	59	66	57	62	69
58361	PEKIN	75	53	29	50	61	69	53	64	61	52	71	77	46	69	55	64	65	64	77	88
58362	PENN	98	68	36	64	79	89	67	83	78	66	91	100	57	89	70	81	83	82	99	116
58363	PERTH	76	53	28	50	62	69	52	65	60	52	71	78	45	69	54	63	65	64	77	90
58365	ROCKLAKE	78	55	29	52	64	71	54	67	62	53	73	81	46	72	56	65	67	66	80	93
58366	ROLETTE	70	52	34	50	58	68	57	63	64	54	75	72	50	71	56	67	69	63	75	79
58367	ROLLA	80	58	34	55	65	75	60	70	68	58	80	82	53	77	61	72	73	70	84	92
58368	RUGBY	66	49	31	47	54	64	53	60	60	51	70	68	47	67	53	63	64	60	71	74
58369	SAINT JOHN	65	55	43	55	58	66	57	61	60	56	73	69	54	73	56	61	69	60	66	72
58370	SAINT MICHAEL	46	40	50	38	39	46	46	44	50	47	62	50	46	61	45	52	61	46	47	50
58372	SARLES	72	50	26	47	59	66	50	61	57	49	67	74	42	66	51	60	61	61	73	85
58374	SHEYENNE	75	56	37	54	62	73	61	68	68	58	81	77	54	77	61	72	74	68	80	84
58377	STARKWEATHER	93	65	34	62	76	85	64	80	74	64	87	96	55	85	67	78	79	79	95	111
58380	TOLNA	74	52	28	49	60	67	51	63	59	51	69	76	44	68	53	62	63	62	75	87
58381	WARWICK	49	42	41	40	43	49	47	47	50	45	61	55	44	60	46	51	59	49	51	55
58382	WEBSTER	95	67	35	63	78	87	66	81	76	65	89	98	56	87	68	80	81	80	97	113
58384	WILLOW CITY	59	44	30	43	49	58	49	54	55	47	64	61	44	61	48	57	59	54	64	66
58385	WOLFORD	52	39	26	38	43	51	43	48	49	41	57	53	39	54	43	51	52	48	57	58
58386	YORK	84	59	32	56	68	77	60	72	68	59	80	86	51	78	61	72	73	71	86	98
58401	JAMESTOWN	71	63	55	61	65	73	65	68	69	63	83	79	62	82	65	70	79	68	74	81
58405	JAMESTOWN	54	33	42	38	33	39	64	47	62	54	78	66	52	70	51	55	73	58	44	54
58413	ASHLEY	52	45	42	42	49	58	43	51	47	45	57	51	42	50	46	50	53	49	60	59
58415	BERLIN	67	47	24	44	54	61	46	57	53	46	62	69	39	61	48	56	57	56	68	79
58416	BINFORD	80	56	29	53	65	73	55	68	64	55	75	82	47	73	57	67	68	67	81	95
58418	BOWDON	69	51	33	49	57	67	56	63	63	53	74	71	50	70	56	67	68	62	75	77
58420	BUCHANAN	100	103	95	102	106	109	95	101	94	94	115	119	95	120	97	93	112	98	100	121
58421	CARRINGTON	87	64	40	61	71	84	69	78	78	66	92	89	61	87	69	82	84	78	94	98
58422	CATHAY	78	55	29	52	64	71	54	67	62	53	73	80	46	71	56	65	66	66	79	93
58423	CHASELEY	61	44	25	42	50	57	45	54	52	44	61	63	39	59	46	54	55	53	64	71
58424	CLEVELAND	84	68	50	66	73	85	73	79	79	69	94	89	67	90	72	83	87	78	91	94
58425	COOPERSTOWN	78	56	32	53	64	73	58	68	66	56	77	80	50	74	59	69	70	68	81	90
58426	COURTENAY	100	70	37	66	82	91	69	86	80	68	93	103	59	92	72	84	85	84	102	119
58428	DAWSON	59	46	30	42	52	58	43	52	49	43	58	62	39	57	46	52	54	52	62	72
58429	DAZEY	84	58	31	55	68	76	58	71	67	57	78	86	49	77	60	70	71	70	85	99
58430	DENHOFF	66	47	27	45	54	62	49	58	56	47	65	67	42	63	50	59	60	57	69	76
58431	DICKEY	84	59	31	56	68	77	58	72	67	58	79	86	50	77	61	71	72	71	86	100
58433	EDGELEY	84	62	39	59	69	81	67	76	75	64	88	86	59	84	67	79	81	75	90	95
58436	ELLENDALE	65	48	30	46	53	63	52	59	58	50	69	67	46	65	52	62	63	58	70	74
58438	FESSENDEN	86	60	31	57	70	78	59	73	68	59	80	89	51	79	62	72	73	72	88	102
58439	FORBES	85	59	31	56	69	78	59	73	68	58	79	87	50	78	61	71	72	72	86	101
58440	FREDONIA	89	62	33	59	72	81	61	76	71	61	83	92	52	81	64	74	76	75	90	106
58441	FULLERTON	102	71	37	67	83	93	70	87	81	69	95	104	60	93	73	85	86	85	103	121
58442	GACKLE	65	48	31	46	54	63	53	59	59	50	70	67	46	66	52	62	63	59	71	73
58443	GLENFIELD	85	59	31	56	69	77	59	72	67	58	79	87	50	78	61	71	72	71	86	101
58444	GOODRICH	57	43	28	41	47	56	47	52	53	45	62	58	42	59	47	56	57	52	62	63
58445	GRACE CITY	82	57	30	54	67	75	57	70	65	56	76	84	48	75	59	68	70	69	83	97
58448	HANNAFORD	74	51	27	49	60	67	51	63	58	50	69	76	43	67	53	61	63	62	75	87
58451	HURDSFIELD	75	53	28	50	61	69	52	64	60	51	70	77	44	69	54	63	64	63	77	89
	NORTH DAKOTA	80	69	63	69	72	79	73	76	75	71	92	90	69	90	72	75	88	77	79	90
	UNITED STATES	100	100	100	100	100	100	100	100	100	100	100	100	100	100	100	100	100	100	100	100

ZIP CODE #	POST OFFICE NAME	COUNTY FIPS CODE	POPULATION 2000	2004	2009	2000-2004 ANNUAL RATE % Rate	State Centile	HOUSEHOLDS 2000	2004	2009	% Annual Rate 2000-2004	2004 Average HH Size	FAMILIES 2000	2004	% Annual Rate 2000-2004
58454	JUD	045	404	367	345	-2.2	1	181	169	164	-1.6	2.17	124	112	-2.4
58455	KENSAL	093	360	337	321	-1.5	13	141	137	135	-0.7	2.46	108	102	-1.3
58456	KULM	045	634	587	556	-1.8	5	294	280	273	-1.1	2.10	198	183	-1.8
58458	LAMOURE	045	1466	1450	1409	-0.3	75	556	569	570	0.6	2.47	369	364	-0.3
58460	LEHR	047	295	285	274	-0.8	47	144	144	143	0.0	1.98	108	105	-0.7
58461	LITCHVILLE	003	532	584	597	2.2	98	229	260	273	3.0	2.25	170	187	2.3
58463	MCCLUSKY	083	806	743	704	-1.9	4	358	341	333	-1.1	2.12	229	209	-2.1
58464	MCHENRY	027	205	191	180	-1.7	9	89	85	83	-1.1	2.25	67	63	-1.4
58466	MARION	045	401	399	391	-0.1	79	170	174	175	0.6	2.29	120	119	-0.2
58467	MEDINA	093	626	605	585	-0.8	47	269	268	268	-0.1	2.26	183	176	-0.9
58472	MONTPELIER	093	480	479	472	-0.1	80	184	190	193	0.8	2.52	135	136	0.2
58474	OAKES	021	2794	2868	2903	0.6	91	1136	1196	1240	1.2	2.32	738	750	0.4
58475	PETTIBONE	043	186	173	165	-1.7	8	83	81	80	-0.6	2.14	62	59	-1.2
58476	PINGREE	093	317	299	286	-1.4	19	128	125	123	-0.6	2.39	96	91	-1.3
58477	REGAN	015	160	162	170	0.3	86	69	71	77	0.7	2.28	50	50	0.0
58478	ROBINSON	043	283	265	254	-1.5	13	127	125	125	-0.4	2.12	88	84	-1.1
58479	ROGERS	003	255	244	233	-1.0	36	94	92	91	-0.5	2.65	70	67	-1.0
58480	SANBORN	003	380	376	365	-0.3	75	145	146	146	0.2	2.58	111	110	-0.2
58481	SPIRITWOOD	003	266	264	258	-0.2	77	110	112	113	0.4	2.36	85	85	0.0
58482	STEELE	043	1151	1113	1082	-0.8	48	483	485	487	0.1	2.20	303	292	-0.9
58483	STREETER	093	360	346	333	-0.9	40	158	156	155	-0.3	2.21	110	105	-1.1
58484	SUTTON	039	91	86	83	-1.3	21	36	35	35	-0.7	2.46	28	26	-1.7
58486	SYKESTON	103	366	381	374	1.0	93	148	158	160	1.6	2.41	99	102	0.7
58487	TAPPEN	043	531	539	535	0.4	86	199	211	218	1.4	2.55	145	150	0.8
58488	TUTTLE	043	326	306	293	-1.5	15	152	150	149	-0.3	2.04	105	101	-0.9
58490	VERONA	045	311	338	346	2.0	98	120	136	144	3.0	2.49	90	99	2.3
58492	WIMBLEDON	003	515	488	465	-1.3	25	198	193	189	-0.6	2.53	145	137	-1.3
58494	WING	015	368	360	371	-0.5	64	167	169	179	0.3	2.13	119	116	-0.6
58495	WISHEK	051	1526	1517	1494	-0.1	78	611	623	628	0.5	2.24	402	397	-0.3
58496	WOODWORTH	093	251	237	228	-1.3	20	108	106	105	-0.4	2.24	82	78	-1.2
58497	YPSILANTI	093	355	390	401	2.2	99	134	152	161	3.0	2.57	102	112	2.2
58501	BISMARCK	015	27279	27815	29069	0.5	88	11889	12560	13560	1.3	2.14	6997	7040	0.1
58503	BISMARCK	015	16570	18155	19543	2.2	98	6287	7056	7791	2.8	2.56	4703	5116	2.0
58504	BISMARCK	015	22561	23537	24807	1.0	93	8335	9035	9855	1.9	2.44	5617	5901	1.2
58520	ALMONT	059	248	294	323	4.1	100	91	112	127	5.0	2.48	71	84	4.0
58521	BALDWIN	015	402	473	526	3.9	99	156	190	217	4.8	2.49	124	146	3.9
58523	BEULAH	057	4228	4192	4142	-0.2	76	1609	1643	1665	0.5	2.50	1153	1143	-0.2
58524	BRADDOCK	029	189	184	179	-0.6	57	80	80	81	0.0	2.21	55	53	-0.9
58529	CARSON	037	878	863	850	-0.4	70	341	350	355	0.6	2.41	244	242	-0.2
58530	CENTER	065	1824	1744	1656	-1.1	34	699	697	690	-0.1	2.50	528	513	-0.7
58531	COLEHARBOR	055	318	320	314	0.2	84	130	136	139	1.1	2.35	103	105	0.5
58532	DRISCOLL	015	223	214	219	-1.0	39	90	89	94	-0.3	2.39	68	65	-1.1
58533	ELGIN	037	1032	1010	993	-0.5	64	464	470	475	0.3	2.03	279	272	-0.6
58535	FLASHER	059	642	627	627	-0.6	61	255	258	266	0.3	2.43	184	181	-0.4
58538	FORT YATES	085	2301	2353	2407	0.5	90	598	628	655	1.2	3.66	474	487	0.6
58540	GARRISON	055	2020	1947	1875	-0.9	45	870	865	860	-0.1	2.15	577	556	-0.9
58541	GOLDEN VALLEY	057	183	173	168	-1.3	22	91	88	87	-0.8	1.97	64	60	-1.5
58542	HAGUE	029	227	220	213	-0.7	52	87	88	88	0.3	2.50	69	68	-0.3
58544	HAZELTON	029	451	439	427	-0.6	57	208	209	209	0.1	2.01	142	138	-0.7
58545	HAZEN	057	3643	3600	3548	-0.3	74	1375	1406	1427	0.5	2.54	1045	1042	-0.1
58549	KINTYRE	029	245	238	229	-0.7	54	87	88	87	0.3	2.64	61	60	-0.4
58552	LINTON	029	2135	2083	2026	-0.6	60	917	924	925	0.2	2.22	615	599	-0.6
58554	MANDAN	059	20273	20507	20838	0.3	85	7866	8224	8619	1.1	2.45	5551	5630	0.3
58558	MENOKEN	015	591	624	659	1.3	96	208	226	246	2.0	2.76	167	176	1.2
58559	MERCER	055	160	154	147	-0.9	42	84	84	83	0.0	1.83	58	56	-0.8
58560	MOFFIT	015	168	169	175	0.1	83	60	62	66	0.8	2.71	47	47	0.0
58561	NAPOLEON	047	1211	1151	1084	-1.2	28	496	487	472	-0.4	2.29	338	320	-1.3
58562	NEW LEIPZIG	037	586	564	550	-0.9	42	255	254	255	-0.1	2.22	180	173	-0.9
58563	NEW SALEM	059	1748	1839	1913	1.2	95	694	743	791	1.6	2.42	473	491	0.9
58564	RALEIGH	037	78	75	73	-0.9	40	32	32	32	0.0	2.19	24	23	-1.0
58565	RIVERDALE	055	284	269	257	-1.3	25	112	110	108	-0.4	2.45	85	81	-1.1
58566	SAINT ANTHONY	059	202	198	198	-0.5	65	74	75	77	0.3	2.64	57	56	-0.4
58568	SELFRIDGE	085	545	527	531	-0.8	48	196	194	199	-0.2	2.72	149	144	-0.8
58569	SHIELDS	037	124	119	116	-1.0	39	51	51	51	0.0	2.18	38	37	-0.6
58570	SOLEN	085	1440	1463	1495	0.4	87	376	390	406	0.9	3.73	303	309	0.5
58571	STANTON	057	590	553	533	-1.5	14	258	252	251	-0.6	2.17	178	168	-1.4
58572	STERLING	015	416	423	441	0.4	87	165	173	186	1.1	2.44	129	132	0.5
58573	STRASBURG	029	1187	1153	1119	-0.7	54	437	440	441	0.2	2.57	321	314	-0.5
58575	TURTLE LAKE	055	864	831	798	-0.9	41	405	405	404	0.0	2.03	257	246	-1.0
58576	UNDERWOOD	055	1097	1037	990	-1.3	22	432	422	416	-0.6	2.33	310	295	-1.2
58577	WASHBURN	055	1817	1763	1697	-0.7	53	721	724	719	0.1	2.43	529	516	-0.6
58579	WILTON	015	1451	1480	1500	0.5	89	560	591	618	1.3	2.48	409	418	0.5
58580	ZAP	057	231	222	217	-0.9	40	101	100	100	-0.2	2.22	78	76	-0.6
58581	ZEELAND	051	298	285	277	-1.0	35	133	131	131	-0.4	2.18	99	96	-0.7
58601	DICKINSON	089	19126	18857	18589	-0.3	72	7584	7722	7828	0.4	2.34	4893	4800	-0.5
58620	AMIDON	087	549	524	524	-1.1	32	215	213	213	-0.2	2.46	153	147	-0.9
58621	BEACH	033	1367	1316	1255	-0.9	43	565	557	542	-0.3	2.17	365	346	-1.3
58622	BELFIELD	089	1432	1387	1362	-0.8	50	558	558	561	0.0	2.48	384	370	-0.9
58623	BOWMAN	011	2222	2157	2079	-0.7	53	926	924	916	-0.1	2.24	584	561	-0.9
58625	DODGE	025	163	154	148	-1.3	20	65	64	63	-0.4	2.41	43	41	-1.1
58626	DUNN CENTER	025	226	215	206	-1.2	29	101	99	98	-0.5	2.16	78	75	-0.9
58627	FAIRFIELD	007	378	353	353	-1.6	11	151	148	148	-0.5	2.39	106	100	-1.4
58630	GLADSTONE	089	554	602	622	2.0	98	212	239	255	2.9	2.52	166	183	2.3
58631	GLEN ULLIN	059	1214	1212	1226	0.0	80	489	502	522	0.6	2.21	316	311	-0.4
58632	GOLVA	033	269	256	242	-1.2	29	103	101	99	-0.5	2.53	75	72	-1.0
58634	GRASSY BUTTE	053	213	210	209	-0.3	72	89	91	91	0.5	2.31	70	69	-0.3
58636	HALLIDAY	025	804	775	750	-0.9	45	316	313	312	-0.2	2.47	218	209	-1.0
58638	HEBRON	059	991	1003	1016	0.3	86	430	447	463	0.9	2.24	285	283	-0.2
58639	HETTINGER	001	2191	2096	1987	-1.0	35	943	933	914	-0.3	2.16	602	575	-1.1
58640	KILLDEER	025	1543	1520	1483	-0.4	71	591	600	601	0.4	2.45	415	409	-0.3
58641	LEFOR	089	105	100	97	-1.1	30	42	41	41	-0.6	2.39	33	31	-1.5
58642	MANNING	025	417	404	392	-0.7	51	147	148	148	0.2	2.73	113	111	-0.4
58643	MARMARTH	087	218	208	208	-1.1	32	98	97	97	-0.2	2.14	70	67	-1.0
58645	MEDORA	007	279	261	261	-1.6	12	128	126	126	-0.4	2.07	90	85	-1.3
58646	MOTT	041	1469	1398	1335	-1.2	29	603	592	584	-0.4	2.26	407	387	-1.2
	NORTH DAKOTA					0.1					0.8	2.33			-0.1
	UNITED STATES					1.2					1.3	2.58			1.1

ZIP CODE #	POST OFFICE NAME	RACE (%) White 2000	White 2004	Black 2000	Black 2004	Asian/Pacific 2000	Asian/Pacific 2004	% Hispanic Origin 2000	% Hispanic Origin 2004	2004 AGE DISTRIBUTION (%) 0-4	5-9	10-14	15-19	20-24	25-44	45-64	65-84	85+	18+	MEDIAN AGE 2004	% 2004 Males	% 2004 Females
58454	JUD	99.0	98.6	0.0	0.0	0.3	0.3	0.5	0.5	3.0	3.5	6.8	6.0	4.9	19.6	31.3	21.5	3.3	82.6	48.6	51.2	48.8
58455	KENSAL	99.4	99.4	0.3	0.3	0.0	0.0	0.0	0.0	4.8	5.6	7.4	7.7	5.3	19.6	32.1	16.0	1.5	77.2	44.7	53.1	46.9
58456	KULM	99.2	99.0	0.2	0.2	0.0	0.0	1.1	1.4	4.1	4.8	6.0	5.6	5.3	18.2	29.3	23.2	3.6	81.8	48.8	52.1	47.9
58458	LAMOURE	99.2	99.2	0.0	0.0	0.1	0.1	0.4	0.6	6.0	6.0	7.1	7.9	6.8	21.1	24.1	17.2	3.8	75.2	41.9	49.5	50.5
58460	LEHR	99.3	99.3	0.0	0.0	0.0	0.4	0.3	0.4	6.3	6.3	6.3	7.0	4.9	20.4	26.7	20.4	1.8	76.5	44.3	51.2	48.8
58461	LITCHVILLE	99.3	99.1	0.0	0.0	0.2	0.2	0.0	0.2	5.0	5.5	7.7	7.0	4.8	21.9	29.3	17.0	1.9	77.2	44.0	51.5	48.5
58463	MCCLUSKY	99.4	99.3	0.1	0.1	0.0	0.0	0.3	0.3	3.5	4.2	5.4	5.1	4.3	16.6	30.6	25.7	4.7	83.3	51.9	49.9	50.1
58464	MCHENRY	99.0	99.5	0.0	0.0	0.0	0.0	0.0	0.0	5.2	5.2	7.3	6.8	5.2	20.9	28.3	18.9	2.1	77.5	44.5	52.9	47.1
58466	MARION	99.3	99.0	0.0	0.0	0.3	0.3	0.3	0.3	4.0	4.3	7.3	6.3	4.8	21.1	30.3	19.6	2.5	80.2	46.3	51.6	48.4
58467	MEDINA	99.2	99.2	0.2	0.2	0.2	0.2	0.3	0.5	4.8	5.6	7.1	5.6	4.5	21.2	27.9	19.7	3.6	79.0	45.7	50.4	49.6
58472	MONTPELIER	99.2	98.8	0.0	0.0	0.0	0.2	0.4	0.6	4.4	5.0	7.5	7.1	4.2	23.8	31.5	14.6	1.9	78.5	43.8	52.6	47.4
58474	OAKES	97.6	97.7	0.1	0.1	0.8	0.8	1.9	2.0	6.7	6.8	7.2	6.0	5.3	22.8	24.9	16.0	4.3	75.5	41.2	50.2	49.8
58475	PETTIBONE	99.5	100.0	0.0	0.0	0.0	0.0	1.1	0.6	2.9	4.1	6.9	6.9	4.6	23.1	31.2	18.5	1.7	80.9	45.8	54.9	45.1
58476	PINGREE	99.1	98.7	0.3	0.3	0.3	0.3	0.3	0.7	5.0	6.0	6.7	6.4	4.7	24.1	31.4	14.1	1.7	78.3	43.2	54.5	45.5
58477	REGAN	98.1	97.5	0.0	0.0	0.6	0.6	0.0	0.0	6.2	6.2	6.2	5.6	4.9	22.8	29.0	17.3	1.9	77.8	43.5	51.9	48.2
58478	ROBINSON	99.3	99.6	0.0	0.0	0.0	0.0	1.1	1.1	2.3	3.4	5.7	6.0	4.9	18.5	34.0	21.9	3.4	85.3	50.5	52.8	47.2
58479	ROGERS	98.8	99.2	0.0	0.0	0.0	0.0	0.0	0.0	6.6	6.6	6.6	6.6	5.7	23.4	29.5	13.9	1.2	76.6	41.4	51.2	48.8
58480	SANBORN	98.4	97.9	0.3	0.3	0.0	0.3	0.0	0.0	6.9	6.9	6.1	6.1	5.6	23.4	30.9	12.8	1.3	76.9	41.5	52.1	47.9
58481	SPIRITWOOD	98.5	98.5	0.0	0.0	0.4	0.4	0.0	0.0	5.7	6.4	7.2	7.6	4.2	23.1	33.3	11.7	0.8	75.8	42.5	53.8	46.2
58482	STEELE	99.5	99.6	0.3	0.3	0.0	0.0	0.2	0.2	6.9	6.3	5.7	5.9	5.4	21.0	23.1	20.0	5.7	77.1	44.2	49.1	50.9
58483	STREETER	98.9	98.8	0.0	0.0	0.0	0.0	0.3	0.3	4.3	4.9	6.9	6.9	6.1	19.4	29.8	18.2	3.5	79.5	45.9	50.9	49.1
58484	SUTTON	100.0	100.0	0.0	0.0	0.0	0.0	0.0	0.0	4.7	4.7	4.7	7.0	7.0	15.1	36.1	17.4	3.5	80.2	48.8	48.8	51.2
58486	SYKESTON	99.7	99.5	0.3	0.3	0.0	0.0	0.0	0.3	4.5	5.5	7.6	6.0	4.5	20.5	27.0	20.2	4.2	78.5	46.0	51.7	48.3
58487	TAPPEN	99.6	99.6	0.2	0.2	0.0	0.0	0.8	0.7	5.6	6.1	7.8	5.8	4.8	21.7	30.2	16.1	1.9	76.6	44.0	53.4	46.6
58488	TUTTLE	99.4	99.7	0.0	0.0	0.0	0.0	1.2	1.3	2.3	3.3	5.6	5.9	5.2	18.6	33.0	22.9	3.3	85.3	50.4	52.9	47.1
58490	VERONA	99.4	99.4	0.0	0.0	0.0	0.0	0.6	0.3	4.7	5.0	7.4	6.8	4.4	22.8	29.3	17.2	2.4	78.1	44.4	53.6	46.5
58492	WIMBLEDON	99.2	99.2	0.2	0.2	0.0	0.0	0.2	0.2	6.2	6.6	7.6	7.0	5.5	22.8	28.1	14.8	1.6	75.4	41.5	51.0	49.0
58494	WING	98.1	98.1	0.0	0.0	0.3	0.3	0.5	0.3	6.4	6.7	6.4	5.3	5.0	23.3	27.5	17.5	1.9	77.2	42.6	51.4	48.6
58495	WISHEK	99.0	99.0	0.0	0.0	0.1	0.1	1.2	1.2	4.8	4.8	5.5	5.7	5.3	17.5	22.7	25.6	8.0	81.2	49.6	46.9	53.1
58496	WOODWORTH	99.2	99.2	0.0	0.0	0.0	0.0	0.4	0.4	4.6	6.3	6.8	6.3	4.6	24.1	32.1	13.5	1.7	78.1	43.2	54.9	45.2
58497	YPSILANTI	98.9	98.7	0.0	0.0	0.0	0.0	0.3	0.5	5.1	5.4	8.2	8.2	3.3	26.2	31.5	10.8	1.3	76.2	41.5	53.1	46.9
58501	BISMARCK	95.5	94.8	0.3	0.3	0.5	0.6	0.7	0.8	5.5	5.2	5.9	6.9	8.8	26.6	24.0	13.8	3.5	79.6	38.7	47.7	52.3
58503	BISMARCK	96.4	95.9	0.2	0.2	0.6	0.8	0.6	0.7	7.7	7.1	7.2	7.1	7.5	27.6	25.6	9.6	0.7	73.7	35.4	48.4	51.6
58504	BISMARCK	93.1	92.0	0.3	0.4	0.3	0.4	0.8	1.0	6.3	6.4	7.0	8.4	9.0	29.7	25.0	7.2	1.0	76.1	33.8	50.1	49.9
58520	ALMONT	98.8	98.6	0.0	0.0	0.4	0.3	0.0	0.0	6.5	6.8	9.2	6.8	5.1	22.8	22.8	16.0	4.1	72.5	41.0	50.7	49.3
58521	BALDWIN	97.8	97.3	0.0	0.0	1.0	1.5	0.3	0.4	6.1	5.9	5.9	6.3	5.5	24.5	30.7	14.0	1.1	78.2	42.3	53.5	46.5
58523	BEULAH	95.0	94.3	0.0	0.0	0.9	1.2	0.5	0.6	4.5	6.5	10.1	8.9	2.9	25.5	26.7	12.1	2.7	72.2	40.9	50.6	49.4
58524	BRADDOCK	98.9	98.9	0.0	0.0	0.5	0.5	1.6	1.6	4.9	5.4	7.1	6.0	3.8	19.0	27.2	22.3	4.4	77.7	47.3	51.6	48.4
58529	CARSON	96.5	96.3	0.0	0.0	0.1	0.1	0.7	0.8	5.2	5.8	6.7	7.3	4.8	21.0	29.4	16.9	2.9	77.1	44.4	52.8	47.2
58530	CENTER	97.4	97.3	0.2	0.2	0.1	0.1	0.6	0.6	4.5	5.9	7.2	8.4	4.4	21.8	33.9	12.3	1.5	76.0	43.7	52.1	47.9
58531	COLEHARBOR	98.4	98.1	0.0	0.0	0.3	0.3	0.0	0.0	4.4	5.0	6.3	6.9	3.4	21.3	33.8	17.5	1.6	79.7	46.4	52.5	47.5
58532	DRISCOLL	98.7	98.6	0.0	0.0	0.0	0.0	0.0	0.0	5.6	6.1	7.5	6.5	5.6	23.4	29.4	14.5	1.4	76.2	42.2	50.9	49.1
58533	ELGIN	96.8	96.6	0.0	0.0	0.8	0.8	0.7	0.7	4.0	4.6	5.4	5.6	4.5	15.8	28.2	24.3	7.7	82.0	52.3	49.2	50.8
58535	FLASHER	98.3	98.1	0.0	0.0	0.2	0.2	0.6	0.6	6.1	6.7	7.0	7.0	5.7	23.1	27.4	14.8	2.1	75.8	41.3	54.4	45.6
58538	FORT YATES	5.4	5.2	0.0	0.0	0.0	0.0	1.7	1.6	11.8	11.0	10.4	10.7	8.9	27.7	15.0	4.5	0.0	60.6	23.4	51.1	48.9
58540	GARRISON	94.1	92.9	0.0	0.0	0.2	0.3	0.9	1.0	4.2	4.5	5.3	5.6	5.1	18.2	28.2	22.4	6.6	82.3	49.8	46.3	53.7
58541	GOLDEN VALLEY	98.4	98.3	0.0	0.0	0.0	0.0	0.0	0.0	2.9	6.9	6.9	6.4	2.3	24.3	32.4	16.8	1.2	78.6	45.2	52.0	48.0
58542	HAGUE	99.6	100.0	0.0	0.0	0.0	0.0	0.4	0.5	8.2	7.3	7.3	6.8	5.5	21.4	25.5	16.4	1.8	72.7	40.9	52.7	47.3
58544	HAZELTON	98.7	98.4	0.0	0.0	0.4	0.7	2.0	2.3	5.0	5.7	7.5	5.5	3.9	18.9	26.4	22.8	4.3	77.5	47.3	51.0	49.0
58545	HAZEN	97.1	96.7	0.1	0.1	0.4	0.5	0.3	0.4	5.1	6.8	9.4	9.2	2.6	25.6	28.7	10.7	1.9	71.8	41.1	50.1	49.9
58549	KINTYRE	99.2	99.2	0.0	0.0	0.4	0.4	1.2	1.3	5.9	6.3	7.1	5.9	4.2	19.8	26.5	21.0	3.4	76.5	45.5	50.4	49.6
58552	LINTON	99.1	98.9	0.1	0.1	0.4	0.5	0.9	1.1	5.2	5.5	7.2	6.2	4.8	19.2	24.6	22.7	4.7	77.5	46.4	49.2	50.8
58554	MANDAN	95.3	94.7	0.2	0.2	0.3	0.4	0.7	0.9	6.8	6.8	7.3	7.4	7.4	27.1	25.4	10.3	1.6	74.5	36.6	49.9	50.1
58558	MENOKEN	99.0	98.9	0.2	0.2	0.2	0.2	0.3	0.3	5.3	6.1	7.1	6.4	5.3	24.5	32.2	12.0	1.1	77.7	42.5	53.4	46.6
58559	MERCER	99.4	99.4	0.0	0.0	0.0	0.0	0.0	0.7	4.6	5.2	7.1	5.8	4.6	20.1	38.3	12.3	2.0	79.2	46.4	52.6	47.4
58560	MOFFIT	98.8	98.8	0.0	0.0	0.0	0.0	0.0	0.0	5.3	6.5	7.7	6.5	5.3	24.3	29.6	13.6	1.2	76.3	41.8	53.3	46.8
58561	NAPOLEON	99.0	98.7	0.1	0.1	0.3	0.5	0.6	0.6	6.1	6.1	6.7	6.2	4.1	19.5	23.4	24.2	3.9	76.4	46.2	49.4	50.7
58562	NEW LEIPZIG	98.8	98.9	0.0	0.0	0.2	0.2	0.2	0.2	3.7	4.4	6.4	7.1	5.0	17.2	32.5	19.9	3.9	81.2	48.5	51.2	48.8
58563	NEW SALEM	97.7	97.5	0.0	0.0	0.2	0.3	0.0	0.0	6.2	6.6	7.6	6.9	4.6	21.3	24.4	18.6	3.9	74.7	43.0	49.3	50.7
58564	RALEIGH	93.6	93.3	0.0	0.0	0.0	0.0	0.0	0.0	5.3	6.7	8.0	9.3	4.0	20.0	30.7	13.3	2.7	72.0	42.5	56.0	44.0
58565	RIVERDALE	97.5	97.0	0.0	0.0	0.4	0.4	0.0	0.0	4.5	5.6	7.4	7.8	2.6	21.9	32.7	16.7	0.7	76.2	45.1	51.3	48.7
58566	SAINT ANTHONY	99.0	99.0	0.0	0.0	0.0	0.0	0.5	0.5	6.1	7.1	7.6	8.1	6.6	24.2	25.8	13.1	1.5	74.2	39.0	53.5	46.5
58568	SELFRIDGE	52.1	50.7	0.0	0.0	0.2	0.2	1.1	1.1	10.1	9.1	9.1	6.6	6.8	26.8	22.2	8.5	0.8	67.7	31.4	52.9	47.1
58569	SHIELDS	94.4	93.3	0.0	0.0	0.0	0.0	0.8	0.8	5.0	5.9	7.6	10.1	3.4	20.2	31.1	15.1	1.7	73.1	43.4	55.5	44.5
58570	SOLEN	28.5	27.1	0.0	0.0	0.1	0.1	1.6	1.6	9.8	10.1	11.8	9.8	8.2	24.5	19.1	6.3	0.4	61.7	25.3	49.4	50.7
58571	STANTON	96.6	96.2	0.0	0.0	0.7	0.9	0.2	0.2	3.3	4.3	6.9	7.4	4.2	21.7	36.0	14.8	1.5	79.8	46.0	52.4	47.6
58572	STERLING	98.8	98.8	0.0	0.0	0.2	0.2	0.0	0.2	5.4	6.2	7.3	6.4	5.4	24.1	30.5	13.5	1.2	77.1	42.3	52.5	47.5
58573	STRASBURG	99.2	99.0	0.1	0.1	0.3	0.4	1.2	1.4	6.3	6.5	7.5	6.3	4.6	20.6	25.9	19.3	3.0	75.3	43.9	52.0	48.0
58575	TURTLE LAKE	99.1	98.9	0.0	0.0	0.1	0.1	0.0	0.0	4.0	4.3	5.2	5.3	3.4	19.1	30.1	21.8	6.9	83.2	51.0	50.7	49.3
58576	UNDERWOOD	97.4	96.6	0.0	0.0	0.0	0.0	0.2	0.3	4.5	5.2	5.8	4.8	6.2	19.1	34.3	15.9	4.2	81.3	47.5	49.5	50.5
58577	WASHBURN	98.8	98.5	0.0	0.0	0.1	0.1	0.4	0.5	4.8	5.1	8.5	8.6	4.6	22.8	32.1	12.4	1.4	75.4	42.8	50.8	49.2
58579	WILTON	98.3	98.1	0.1	0.1	0.3	0.3	0.5	0.5	5.7	6.0	6.1	6.0	5.8	22.8	30.9	14.9	1.8	78.3	43.5	50.7	49.3
58580	ZAP	97.8	97.8	0.0	0.0	0.0	0.0	0.0	0.0	5.0	6.3	6.8	8.6	2.3	26.6	31.1	12.2	1.4	75.7	42.1	54.5	45.5
58581	ZEELAND	99.0	99.3	0.0	0.0	0.0	0.0	0.0	0.0	5.6	5.6	5.6	7.0	4.9	19.3	29.1	20.7	2.1	78.6	46.0	52.3	47.7
58601	DICKINSON	97.3	96.9	0.2	0.3	0.3	0.4	1.1	1.3	6.0	5.9	6.8	8.3	9.6	24.6	23.8	12.5	2.7	77.0	36.4	49.2	50.8
58620	AMIDON	99.8	99.6	0.0	0.0	0.0	0.0	0.2	0.2	4.8	5.2	6.7	8.6	3.1	23.7	30.9	15.8	1.3	76.2	44.0	54.4	45.6
58621	BEACH	97.4	97.3	0.0	0.0	0.2	0.2	1.4	1.4	5.6	6.3	7.4	9.7	5.5	18.8	24.9	16.8	5.0	73.3	42.4	46.7	53.3
58622	BELFIELD	98.0	97.8	0.2	0.2	0.4	0.5	1.0	1.2	6.1	6.6	8.7	7.4	5.2	24.8	26.2	12.4	2.5	73.1	39.6	51.8	48.2
58623	BOWMAN	99.0	98.8	0.0	0.0	0.0	0.0	0.7	0.9	4.7	5.2	6.6	6.5	5.3	21.6	27.4	18.0	4.7	79.1	45.1	48.6	51.4
58625	DODGE	96.3	95.5	0.0	0.0	0.0	0.0	1.2	1.3	3.9	5.2	6.5	5.8	4.6	18.2	33.1	19.5	3.3	80.5	48.8	50.7	49.4
58626	DUNN CENTER	97.4	96.3	0.0	0.0	0.0	0.0	0.0	0.5	4.2	4.7	7.0	8.4	4.2	21.9	31.6	15.8	2.3	78.1	44.9	53.5	46.5
58627	FAIRFIELD	98.7	99.2	0.0	0.0	0.0	0.0	0.3	0.3	3.7	5.1	7.9	8.8	2.8	24.9	30.9	14.2	1.7	76.2	43.5	53.3	46.7
58630	GLADSTONE	98.4	98.3	0.0	0.0	0.0	0.0	1.4	1.7	5.3	6.0	7.8	8.0	5.3	25.1	30.4	11.1	1.0	75.9	40.8	51.5	48.5
58631	GLEN ULLIN	98.9	98.9	0.0	0.0	0.2	0.3	0.0	0.0	4.9	4.7	6.2	6.4	3.9	18.9	23.3	24.4	7.3	79.5	48.6	48.3	51.7
58632	GOLVA	99.3	98.8	0.0	0.0	0.0	0.0	0.0	0.0	6.6	7.0	7.4	5.9	5.5	23.8	25.4	16.0	2.3	75.0	41.4	51.2	48.8
58634	GRASSY BUTTE	99.5	99.5	0.0	0.0	0.0	0.0	0.0	0.0	4.8	6.7	7.1	7.6	1.4	20.5	35.7	14.3	1.9	76.2	45.8	52.9	47.1
58636	HALLIDAY	69.2	66.3	0.0	0.0	0.1	0.1	1.0	1.0	6.5	6.7	7.2	7.0	6.5	20.3	27.9	15.6	2.5	74.8	41.9	51.6	48.4
58638	HEBRON	96.1	95.3	0.1	0.1	0.7	1.1	1.0	1.1	5.8	6.1	7.3	7.0	5.2	18.3	25.6	20.8	4.0	75.7	45.3	47.2	52.8
58639	HETTINGER	98.5	98.2	0.6	0.6	0.2	0.3	0.3	0.4	4.5	5.1	6.6	6.6	4.9	19.0	28.6	19.9	4.9	79.2	47.1	47.3	52.7
58640	KILLDEER	86.8	84.8	0.0	0.0	0.1	0.2	0.7	0.8	6.1	6.5	7.3	7.5	5.7	22.4	27.5	13.7	3.4	74.7	41.7	50.2	49.8
58641	LEFOR	99.1	99.0	0.0	0.0	0.0	1.0	0.0	1.0	6.0	8.0	7.0	8.0	4.0	24.0	26.0	15.0	2.0	73.0	40.0	50.0	50.0
58642	MANNING	98.1	98.0	0.0	0.0	0.0	0.0	0.7	0.7	5.5	6.7	7.2	8.2	5.2	23.8	28.7	13.4	1.5	75.3	41.5	54.5	45.5
58643	MARMARTH	99.5	100.0	0.0	0.0	0.0	0.0	0.0	0.0	4.8	4.8	7.2	8.7	2.9	23.6	29.8	16.8	1.4	76.0	44.0	53.9	46.2
58645	MEDORA	98.9	98.9	0.0	0.0	0.0	0.0	0.4	0.4	3.5	5.4	7.7	8.8	3.1	24.9	31.0	13.8	1.9	77.0	43.4	52.9	47.1
58646	MOTT	99.3	99.2	0.3	0.3	0.1	0.2	0.1	0.1	4.6	5.6	6.6	6.3	4.1	17.3	27.6	22.8	5.2	78.9	48.6	49.9	50.1
	NORTH DAKOTA	92.4	91.7	0.6	0.7	0.6	0.8	1.2	1.4	6.3	6.1	6.8	7.9	8.5	26.2	23.9	12.0	2.4	76.5	36.5	50.0	50.0
	UNITED STATES	75.1	73.6	12.3	12.5	3.8	4.2	12.5	14.1	6.9	6.7	7.2	7.0	7.3	28.6	23.8	10.8	1.7	75.1	36.0	49.1	50.9

ZIP CODE #	POST OFFICE NAME	2004 Per Capita Income	2004 HH Income Base	2004 Household Income Distribution (%): Less than $25,000	$25,000 to $49,999	$50,000 to $99,999	$100,000 to $149,999	$150,000 or More	Median Household Income: 2004	2009	2004 National Centile	2004 State Centile	2004 Home Value Base	2004 Home Value Distribution (%): Less than $50,000	$50,000 to $89,999	$90,000 to $174,999	$175,000 to $399,999	$400,000 or More	2004 Median Home Value
58454	JUD	21186	169	42.6	32.5	17.2	4.1	3.6	29378	33981	11	13	140	64.3	19.3	11.4	3.6	1.4	38333
58455	KENSAL	22132	137	29.2	27.7	31.4	8.8	2.9	43310	52552	57	79	116	45.7	19.8	26.7	6.0	1.7	60000
58456	KULM	23612	280	35.4	33.9	23.6	3.9	3.2	33342	39080	22	32	230	65.7	20.0	10.4	2.6	1.3	37308
58458	LAMOURE	19780	569	31.5	32.0	26.5	7.2	2.8	36702	45488	34	52	427	49.0	34.7	13.6	2.1	0.7	50900
58460	LEHR	23265	144	38.9	33.3	18.1	6.9	2.8	30798	38967	14	18	120	63.3	20.0	11.7	3.3	1.7	32000
58461	LITCHVILLE	21434	260	32.3	31.5	29.6	4.2	2.3	37055	44448	36	55	221	50.2	26.2	17.2	3.2	3.2	49583
58463	MCCLUSKY	16620	341	46.3	32.3	16.7	3.8	0.9	27196	31627	7	6	277	75.1	12.3	7.2	4.7	0.7	27841
58464	MCHENRY	20643	85	30.6	35.3	25.9	5.9	2.4	35309	41129	29	44	70	68.6	12.9	11.4	4.3	2.9	40000
58466	MARION	18377	174	37.9	33.3	22.4	4.6	1.7	32120	38108	18	24	146	58.9	23.3	13.7	2.7	1.4	40714
58467	MEDINA	22012	268	36.6	32.1	23.5	4.5	3.4	34402	40418	25	38	226	51.3	32.3	12.0	3.5	0.9	47857
58472	MONTPELIER	19696	190	27.9	39.5	25.8	4.7	2.1	38170	45648	40	61	161	44.7	23.6	26.7	4.4	0.6	56538
58474	OAKES	20740	1196	33.8	34.3	23.7	5.5	2.8	35390	41852	29	45	879	31.6	36.2	28.1	3.9	0.2	70966
58475	PETTIBONE	18264	81	45.7	29.6	22.2	2.5	0.0	27278	32831	8	7	68	51.5	19.1	17.7	7.4	4.4	47500
58476	PINGREE	27706	125	20.8	32.0	29.6	10.4	7.2	44604	53236	60	83	102	39.2	22.6	20.6	9.8	7.8	68571
58477	REGAN	20822	71	38.0	29.6	25.4	4.2	2.8	32967	39308	21	29	58	58.6	17.2	19.0	3.5	1.7	40000
58478	ROBINSON	18168	125	47.2	25.6	24.0	2.4	0.8	26998	31932	7	5	103	56.3	17.5	9.7	11.7	4.9	40714
58479	ROGERS	18557	92	25.0	38.0	29.4	5.4	2.2	37682	45453	38	58	75	56.0	24.0	17.3	2.7	0.0	45500
58480	SANBORN	20357	146	21.2	36.3	33.6	6.9	2.1	41145	47998	50	72	120	45.8	26.7	24.2	3.3	0.0	56250
58481	SPIRITWOOD	22936	112	21.4	33.0	39.3	4.5	1.8	45761	53293	63	85	94	37.2	22.3	36.2	4.3	0.0	72857
58482	STEELE	18911	485	37.9	33.6	21.2	4.7	2.5	32168	38727	18	24	373	41.8	35.1	20.1	2.1	0.8	61250
58483	STREETER	30184	156	41.0	28.9	21.8	2.6	5.8	34209	41136	25	36	131	58.0	19.1	17.6	1.5	3.8	39722
58484	SUTTON	18491	35	28.6	37.1	25.7	8.6	0.0	34268	39059	25	36	29	72.4	13.8	10.3	0.0	3.5	28750
58486	SYKESTON	17879	158	39.9	34.2	19.6	4.4	1.9	31109	36749	15	19	129	65.1	23.3	9.3	0.8	1.6	30417
58487	TAPPEN	13561	211	46.5	33.2	14.2	5.7	0.5	26996	31403	7	5	177	56.5	23.2	15.3	2.8	2.3	42333
58488	TUTTLE	18840	150	47.3	25.3	23.3	2.7	1.3	26813	33822	7	4	124	59.7	16.1	9.7	10.5	4.0	37857
58490	VERONA	23120	136	26.5	28.7	36.8	5.9	2.2	45000	53536	61	84	117	34.2	34.2	23.1	2.6	6.0	67353
58492	WIMBLEDON	18876	193	26.4	35.2	31.1	5.2	2.1	38116	45204	40	60	159	60.4	20.1	16.4	2.5	0.6	41750
58494	WING	21654	169	40.2	29.6	23.7	3.0	3.6	31261	36444	16	21	138	62.3	15.9	15.9	4.4	1.5	38636
58495	WISHEK	21148	623	33.9	38.7	19.6	3.2	4.7	34474	40758	26	38	474	52.7	33.3	12.2	1.5	0.2	47045
58496	WOODWORTH	29987	106	20.8	29.3	33.0	9.4	7.6	50000	55471	72	92	87	36.8	23.0	23.0	10.3	6.9	70833
58497	YPSILANTI	20024	152	19.1	40.8	32.9	4.6	2.6	42558	49164	55	77	129	37.2	27.9	29.5	4.7	0.8	65909
58501	BISMARCK	25498	12560	26.1	30.0	33.9	7.1	2.9	43570	52899	57	79	7244	4.1	28.0	62.8	4.6	0.5	104279
58503	BISMARCK	27521	7056	15.6	25.3	38.8	14.0	6.2	59763	71665	84	99	5479	14.5	9.4	49.5	25.2	1.4	134843
58504	BISMARCK	24316	9035	21.6	27.7	39.4	7.4	3.9	50448	60299	73	93	6559	24.8	18.7	42.0	12.9	1.7	98525
58520	ALMONT	19032	112	31.3	36.6	25.0	4.5	2.7	36505	42338	34	51	90	45.6	32.2	14.4	7.8	0.0	55714
58521	BALDWIN	23693	190	22.6	24.7	41.6	8.4	2.6	52024	59689	76	95	167	18.0	19.2	44.9	17.4	0.6	110096
58523	BEULAH	20934	1643	27.3	22.1	40.8	9.0	0.8	50457	60022	73	93	1325	27.0	36.5	32.7	3.1	0.7	77437
58524	BRADDOCK	17328	80	41.3	32.5	21.3	3.8	1.3	30616	36913	14	17	67	56.7	23.9	13.4	4.5	1.5	39375
58529	CARSON	16388	350	50.0	30.0	15.4	2.3	2.3	25000	29464	5	2	285	61.4	20.4	12.3	4.2	1.8	35893
58530	CENTER	20246	697	26.3	29.1	36.7	6.6	1.3	44450	54231	60	83	592	28.6	34.3	29.6	7.3	0.3	74211
58531	COLEHARBOR	20624	136	26.5	31.6	36.8	4.4	0.7	43019	50827	56	78	124	33.9	29.8	29.8	4.8	1.6	70000
58532	DRISCOLL	17760	89	30.3	37.1	30.3	2.3	0.0	35310	40000	29	44	73	46.6	34.3	15.1	4.1	0.0	56250
58533	ELGIN	19901	470	48.3	30.4	17.2	2.6	1.5	25839	30891	6	3	357	67.8	22.1	7.3	2.2	0.6	34875
58535	FLASHER	19279	258	37.6	29.8	24.4	5.0	3.1	37349	43749	37	56	216	43.5	29.2	13.9	7.9	5.6	60000
58538	FORT YATES	9738	628	44.4	29.1	23.6	2.4	0.5	28477	34047	10	10	235	48.1	23.4	26.8	1.7	0.0	54500
58540	GARRISON	19413	865	35.0	34.0	26.0	3.7	1.3	34788	41117	27	41	686	41.6	32.1	23.0	2.9	0.4	60000
58541	GOLDEN VALLEY	19963	88	46.6	26.1	21.6	4.6	1.1	27821	40449	8	8	75	53.3	18.7	25.3	1.3	1.3	45000
58542	HAGUE	21629	88	42.1	30.7	17.1	5.7	4.6	28718	35000	10	10	75	44.0	21.3	16.0	12.0	6.7	57500
58544	HAZELTON	18783	209	41.2	32.5	20.6	4.3	1.4	30639	35797	14	17	175	57.1	21.7	14.3	4.6	2.3	39167
58545	HAZEN	23598	1406	23.5	21.9	42.5	9.5	2.7	53680	62640	78	97	1162	22.7	37.7	33.5	5.1	1.0	80242
58549	KINTYRE	16625	88	39.8	30.7	22.7	5.7	1.1	31952	40449	18	23	73	56.2	21.9	13.7	5.5	2.7	39375
58552	LINTON	18085	924	42.0	31.0	20.9	4.8	1.4	30142	36614	13	16	723	50.4	30.7	14.5	2.6	1.8	49569
58554	MANDAN	21794	8224	25.3	29.5	34.9	7.5	2.8	45694	53897	63	85	6113	24.8	29.4	36.8	8.0	1.1	84485
58558	MENOKEN	23582	226	16.8	26.6	45.1	6.6	4.9	54441	61441	79	98	208	24.5	22.6	33.7	16.4	2.9	93529
58559	MERCER	25350	84	33.3	32.1	28.6	4.8	1.2	36850	42999	35	54	71	43.7	22.5	23.9	9.9	0.0	59000
58560	MOFFIT	19880	62	22.6	33.9	37.1	4.8	1.6	43633	52935	58	80	54	31.5	27.8	27.8	11.1	1.9	80000
58561	NAPOLEON	21796	487	37.8	30.6	23.0	4.7	3.9	33618	41546	23	34	400	60.3	26.5	10.3	2.3	0.8	40465
58562	NEW LEIPZIG	16960	254	40.6	35.4	18.9	3.9	1.2	30996	36059	15	18	210	68.6	14.8	12.4	3.3	1.0	32500
58563	NEW SALEM	20071	743	33.0	35.1	24.0	4.7	3.2	36037	42049	32	49	578	42.9	36.0	14.5	5.9	0.7	57069
58564	RALEIGH	22120	32	50.0	21.9	18.8	0.0	9.4	25000	35000	5	2	27	55.6	14.8	18.5	7.4	3.7	42500
58565	RIVERDALE	20245	110	25.5	30.0	37.3	6.4	0.9	44086	50755	59	81	101	38.6	31.7	27.7	2.0	0.0	59583
58566	SAINT ANTHONY	18459	75	32.0	36.0	22.7	5.3	4.0	38358	43369	41	62	64	37.5	29.7	20.3	7.8	4.7	72222
58568	SELFRIDGE	12518	194	49.0	32.0	14.4	2.6	2.1	25499	28186	5	2	124	58.9	16.1	18.6	0.8	5.7	40833
58569	SHIELDS	20201	51	49.0	23.5	19.6	0.0	7.8	26131	35748	6	3	43	55.8	18.6	16.3	4.7	4.7	43750
58570	SOLEN	8924	390	51.0	28.2	18.0	2.1	0.8	24371	29385	4	1	247	52.2	23.5	17.4	3.6	3.2	47708
58571	STANTON	23784	252	26.2	25.8	39.7	7.1	1.2	47794	57371	68	89	230	54.4	27.8	12.2	5.7	0.0	47826
58572	STERLING	23237	173	22.0	31.2	38.2	5.2	3.5	46457	54531	65	87	153	32.0	26.1	27.5	12.4	2.0	81071
58573	STRASBURG	17690	440	41.8	31.6	18.6	5.0	3.0	29549	35219	11	13	372	51.1	21.2	15.6	8.3	3.8	48261
58575	TURTLE LAKE	19728	405	37.0	34.8	23.7	3.2	1.2	32308	38060	19	25	314	58.6	27.7	9.9	3.2	0.6	43415
58576	UNDERWOOD	21950	422	27.0	27.3	37.7	6.6	1.4	43582	53641	58	80	363	45.5	38.3	14.6	1.7	0.0	53837
58577	WASHBURN	22057	724	26.1	26.2	38.5	7.3	1.8	45700	55050	63	85	600	30.3	30.2	34.7	4.7	0.2	75660
58579	WILTON	19710	591	29.4	30.1	33.7	5.3	1.5	39824	47142	45	66	501	29.9	33.3	28.9	6.2	1.6	72333
58580	ZAP	21671	100	35.0	24.0	36.0	3.0	2.0	37689	45919	38	58	84	58.3	19.1	16.7	3.6	2.4	44167
58581	ZEELAND	19346	131	40.5	35.1	16.0	5.3	3.1	29020	34221	10	11	109	66.1	20.2	9.2	2.8	1.8	31500
58601	DICKINSON	19875	7722	32.1	31.7	28.0	6.2	2.0	38113	45588	40	60	5220	12.5	37.7	42.0	7.5	0.4	89871
58620	AMIDON	17220	213	43.7	29.6	19.7	2.4	4.7	28364	35860	9	9	181	66.9	18.8	12.2	2.2	0.0	32045
58621	BEACH	17741	557	35.0	37.3	22.8	4.5	0.4	32958	37924	21	29	435	45.8	41.2	9.9	3.0	0.2	53190
58622	BELFIELD	15994	558	37.6	35.5	22.0	4.3	0.5	32410	38848	19	27	429	50.6	28.9	17.5	2.3	0.7	49265
58623	BOWMAN	21988	924	30.2	36.8	25.2	4.3	3.5	36746	42926	34	53	726	32.2	38.8	25.5	3.0	0.4	68052
58625	DODGE	17715	64	43.8	31.3	17.2	4.7	3.1	28861	35436	10	11	53	60.4	24.5	7.6	3.8	3.8	36250
58626	DUNN CENTER	16909	99	37.4	40.4	19.2	3.0	0.0	32290	36799	19	25	80	50.0	21.3	25.0	2.5	1.3	50000
58627	FAIRFIELD	20518	148	34.5	29.7	27.7	4.7	3.4	37982	47083	39	59	118	44.1	22.0	25.4	5.1	3.4	61667
58630	GLADSTONE	19089	239	25.1	31.4	38.9	4.6	0.0	43654	51361	58	80	211	24.6	21.8	44.1	8.5	1.0	95357
58631	GLEN ULLIN	18416	502	35.3	37.9	21.7	3.6	1.6	33205	39286	22	30	407	61.9	24.1	10.1	3.2	0.7	39609
58632	GOLVA	18423	101	35.6	37.6	21.8	3.0	2.0	34529	41760	26	39	81	50.6	28.4	19.8	1.2	0.0	49286
58634	GRASSY BUTTE	24961	91	23.1	40.7	24.2	8.8	3.3	38697	47772	42	63	82	40.2	22.0	35.4	1.2	1.2	72000
58636	HALLIDAY	16598	313	44.4	32.3	16.6	3.5	3.2	28477	34460	10	10	237	52.7	30.8	11.0	2.5	3.0	46579
58638	HEBRON	16033	447	45.9	32.0	17.9	2.7	1.6	27150	32168	7	6	370	71.4	20.3	6.8	1.6	0.0	29394
58639	HETTINGER	22022	933	38.3	35.1	18.8	4.4	3.5	31931	37215	18	23	681	50.1	33.3	14.4	1.3	0.9	49918
58640	KILLDEER	19480	600	36.0	30.7	25.8	4.2	3.3	36326	42202	33	50	474	45.2	35.9	14.4	3.2	1.5	55476
58641	LEFOR	17028	41	39.0	29.3	24.4	4.9	2.4	32312	39067	19	26	35	34.3	22.9	28.6	11.4	2.9	72500
58642	MANNING	17298	148	28.4	37.2	27.0	4.7	2.7	37919	44529	39	59	129	40.3	17.8	29.5	7.8	4.7	73125
58643	MARMARTH	19773	97	45.4	27.8	19.6	2.1	5.2	27598	33617	8	7	82	67.1	18.3	12.2	2.4	0.0	31000
58645	MEDORA	23515	126	33.3	30.2	27.8	5.6	3.2	38445	46142	41	63	100	47.0	22.0	22.0	5.0	4.0	56000
58646	MOTT	18818	592	39.0	33.6	19.4	4.6	3.4	31669	37208	17	21	495	67.3	20.8	10.5	1.4	0.0	37563
	NORTH DAKOTA	22058		29.0	31.5	29.9	6.6	3.0	40503	48701				27.7	27.3	34.9	9.3	0.9	83011
	UNITED STATES	25866		24.7	27.1	30.8	10.9	6.5	48124	56710				10.9	15.0	33.7	30.1	10.4	145905

ZIP CODE #	POST OFFICE NAME	FINANCIAL SERVICES: Auto Loan	FINANCIAL SERVICES: Home Loan	FINANCIAL SERVICES: Investments	FINANCIAL SERVICES: Retirement Plans	THE HOME: Home Improvements: Home Repair	THE HOME: Home Improvements: Lawn & Garden	THE HOME: Furnishings: Computers & Hardware	THE HOME: Furnishings: Major Appliances	THE HOME: Furnishings: TV, Radio, Sound Equipment	THE HOME: Furnishings: Furniture	ENTERTAINMENT: Dine out/Carry out	ENTERTAINMENT: Sports Equipment	ENTERTAINMENT: Fees & Tickets	ENTERTAINMENT: Toys & Games	ENTERTAINMENT: Travel	ENTERTAINMENT: Cable TV	PERSONAL: Apparel & Services	PERSONAL: Auto Repairs	PERSONAL: Health Insurance	PERSONAL: Pets & Supplies
58454	JUD	74	56	37	54	61	73	62	68	69	58	81	76	55	77	61	73	74	68	81	82
58455	KENSAL	99	69	36	65	80	90	68	84	78	67	92	101	58	90	70	82	84	83	100	117
58456	KULM	81	60	39	58	66	79	66	73	74	63	87	83	59	83	66	78	80	73	88	90
58458	LAMOURE	90	63	33	59	73	82	62	77	71	61	84	92	53	82	64	75	76	76	91	107
58460	LEHR	83	58	30	55	68	76	57	71	66	57	78	86	49	76	60	69	71	70	85	99
58461	LITCHVILLE	85	62	36	59	71	79	61	74	69	60	81	89	53	80	63	72	75	73	86	101
58463	MCCLUSKY	58	43	28	42	48	57	48	53	53	45	63	60	42	59	47	56	57	53	63	65
58464	MCHENRY	84	59	31	55	68	76	58	72	67	57	78	86	49	77	60	70	71	71	85	100
58466	MARION	72	52	31	50	59	68	55	63	62	53	73	74	48	70	55	65	66	63	76	83
58467	MEDINA	79	61	42	59	67	79	67	73	74	64	88	82	60	83	66	78	80	73	87	88
58472	MONTPELIER	82	66	45	63	71	80	65	74	72	64	86	86	61	84	66	75	80	72	84	94
58474	OAKES	81	62	41	61	69	79	65	73	72	63	85	85	59	83	65	74	78	72	84	92
58475	PETTIBONE	69	49	27	46	56	64	49	60	57	48	66	71	42	65	51	59	60	59	71	81
58476	PINGREE	115	87	55	84	99	108	85	101	94	84	112	121	76	111	88	98	103	99	116	136
58477	REGAN	86	60	31	57	70	78	59	73	68	59	80	88	51	79	61	72	73	72	87	102
58478	ROBINSON	65	47	29	45	53	62	50	58	57	49	67	66	44	64	51	60	61	57	69	74
58479	ROGERS	89	62	33	59	72	81	61	76	71	61	83	92	52	81	64	74	76	75	90	106
58480	SANBORN	93	67	38	64	78	86	66	81	75	65	88	97	57	87	68	78	81	79	95	111
58481	SPIRITWOOD	98	68	36	65	80	89	67	83	78	67	91	101	58	89	70	82	83	82	99	116
58482	STEELE	70	53	34	50	58	69	56	63	63	54	74	72	50	71	56	67	68	63	76	79
58483	STREETER	109	81	52	78	90	107	89	99	100	85	118	112	79	111	88	106	107	99	119	122
58484	SUTTON	82	57	30	54	67	75	57	70	65	56	77	85	48	75	59	69	70	69	83	98
58486	SYKESTON	71	53	34	50	58	69	57	64	64	55	76	73	51	72	57	68	69	64	77	79
58487	TAPPEN	59	46	30	42	52	58	43	52	49	43	58	62	39	57	46	53	54	52	62	72
58488	TUTTLE	64	47	29	45	53	62	50	58	57	48	67	66	44	64	51	60	61	57	69	73
58490	VERONA	103	74	41	70	85	95	72	88	82	71	97	106	63	96	75	86	89	87	104	122
58492	WIMBLEDON	86	60	32	57	70	79	60	74	69	59	80	89	51	79	62	72	73	73	88	103
58494	WING	83	58	30	55	68	76	58	71	66	57	78	86	49	76	60	70	71	70	85	99
58495	WISHEK	82	61	38	58	67	80	66	74	74	63	87	84	58	83	66	78	79	74	88	92
58496	WOODWORTH	112	91	64	88	101	109	87	101	94	86	113	121	80	113	90	97	106	99	113	134
58497	YPSILANTI	84	72	53	69	77	83	67	76	72	67	87	90	65	89	69	74	83	74	83	98
58501	BISMARCK	74	77	90	79	76	81	80	78	78	79	98	92	81	99	79	76	96	79	74	85
58503	BISMARCK	98	106	111	107	105	109	100	101	97	102	122	117	103	121	101	95	120	100	95	114
58504	BISMARCK	85	91	96	92	89	92	88	87	85	89	107	102	90	108	88	83	105	87	81	97
58520	ALMONT	88	62	33	58	72	80	61	75	70	60	82	90	52	80	63	73	75	74	89	104
58521	BALDWIN	101	80	53	78	88	95	77	90	83	77	100	107	70	98	78	85	93	88	99	118
58523	BEULAH	81	75	64	74	77	81	74	78	74	73	91	92	70	90	73	74	87	77	78	92
58524	BRADDOCK	63	47	31	45	52	62	52	58	59	50	69	65	46	65	52	62	63	58	69	70
58529	CARSON	69	52	33	48	59	67	50	61	57	49	67	72	44	66	53	60	62	60	72	84
58530	CENTER	92	64	33	60	75	83	63	78	73	62	85	94	54	84	66	76	78	77	93	109
58531	COLEHARBOR	88	61	32	58	71	80	61	75	70	60	82	90	52	80	63	73	75	74	89	104
58532	DRISCOLL	77	54	28	51	63	70	53	66	61	52	72	79	45	70	55	64	65	65	78	91
58533	ELGIN	69	51	33	49	57	67	55	62	62	53	73	71	49	69	55	65	66	62	74	78
58535	FLASHER	84	60	32	56	69	77	58	72	67	58	79	87	50	77	61	71	72	71	86	100
58538	FORT YATES	49	42	54	40	40	47	49	47	53	50	66	54	48	64	47	54	65	50	49	54
58540	GARRISON	71	52	33	50	58	69	56	64	63	54	75	73	50	71	56	67	68	64	76	80
58541	GOLDEN VALLEY	71	50	26	47	58	65	49	61	56	48	66	73	42	65	51	59	60	60	72	84
58542	HAGUE	98	68	36	65	80	89	67	83	78	67	91	101	58	89	70	82	83	82	99	116
58544	HAZELTON	62	47	31	45	51	61	52	57	58	49	68	64	46	64	51	61	62	57	68	69
58545	HAZEN	98	81	60	78	87	96	80	90	86	79	103	106	73	101	81	88	97	89	99	114
58549	KINTYRE	75	55	33	52	61	71	58	67	66	56	77	77	51	74	58	69	70	66	80	85
58552	LINTON	66	49	32	47	54	65	54	60	60	51	71	68	48	67	54	64	65	60	72	74
58554	MANDAN	79	78	71	77	78	82	76	78	76	75	93	91	74	93	75	75	90	78	78	90
58558	MENOKEN	90	102	101	101	102	103	92	95	88	91	109	111	95	115	94	86	108	91	89	109
58559	MERCER	83	59	33	56	69	77	58	71	67	57	78	86	50	77	61	70	72	70	85	99
58560	MOFFIT	86	77	61	75	82	87	72	81	75	71	91	96	69	93	74	77	86	79	86	103
58561	NAPOLEON	85	62	39	60	69	82	67	76	76	64	89	87	59	85	67	80	81	76	91	95
58562	NEW LEIPZIG	67	48	27	45	55	62	47	58	54	47	64	69	41	62	49	57	58	57	69	80
58563	NEW SALEM	82	62	39	59	69	79	65	74	72	62	85	85	57	82	65	76	78	73	87	94
58564	RALEIGH	91	64	33	60	74	83	63	78	72	62	85	94	54	83	65	76	77	77	93	108
58565	RIVERDALE	90	63	33	59	73	82	62	76	71	61	83	92	53	82	64	75	76	75	91	106
58566	SAINT ANTHONY	88	62	32	58	72	80	61	75	70	60	82	91	52	81	63	74	75	74	90	105
58568	SELFRIDGE	55	42	28	40	45	54	46	50	51	44	60	56	41	57	45	54	55	50	60	60
58569	SHIELDS	83	58	30	55	67	75	57	70	66	56	77	85	49	76	59	69	70	69	84	98
58570	SOLEN	49	39	43	37	40	46	45	46	50	45	61	53	42	58	44	51	58	48	50	55
58571	STANTON	94	66	34	62	77	86	65	80	75	64	88	97	55	86	67	78	80	79	95	112
58572	STERLING	87	82	70	81	87	91	77	84	78	76	95	100	75	98	79	79	91	82	87	105
58573	STRASBURG	78	57	34	54	64	74	60	69	68	58	79	80	52	76	60	71	72	69	83	89
58575	TURTLE LAKE	69	53	36	48	60	68	50	61	57	50	68	72	45	67	54	61	63	60	72	84
58576	UNDERWOOD	95	67	35	63	78	87	66	81	76	65	89	98	56	87	68	80	81	80	97	113
58577	WASHBURN	88	74	54	71	81	87	70	81	75	70	90	97	65	91	73	77	85	79	89	106
58579	WILTON	89	62	32	59	72	81	61	76	71	61	83	91	52	81	64	74	76	75	90	106
58580	ZAP	87	61	32	57	71	79	60	74	69	59	81	89	51	80	62	73	74	73	88	103
58581	ZEELAND	76	53	28	50	62	69	53	65	61	52	71	78	45	70	54	63	65	64	77	90
58601	DICKINSON	71	63	59	63	64	70	66	68	68	65	84	80	63	81	65	68	80	69	70	80
58620	AMIDON	77	54	28	51	62	70	53	65	61	52	71	79	45	70	55	64	65	64	78	91
58621	BEACH	69	50	29	47	56	65	52	61	59	50	69	71	45	67	52	62	63	60	72	79
58622	BELFIELD	66	49	30	47	54	64	52	59	59	50	69	68	46	66	52	62	63	59	71	75
58623	BOWMAN	91	64	33	60	74	83	63	78	72	62	85	94	54	83	65	76	77	77	93	108
58625	DODGE	69	52	34	50	57	68	57	63	64	54	75	71	51	71	57	68	69	63	75	76
58626	DUNN CENTER	66	46	24	44	54	60	46	57	53	45	62	68	39	61	47	55	56	56	67	79
58627	FAIRFIELD	89	62	32	58	72	81	61	76	70	60	83	91	52	81	63	74	75	74	90	105
58630	GLADSTONE	79	67	48	64	72	78	63	71	68	63	82	85	60	83	65	70	77	69	79	93
58631	GLEN ULLIN	71	52	33	50	58	68	56	63	63	54	74	73	49	71	56	67	68	63	76	80
58632	GOLVA	85	59	31	56	69	77	58	72	67	58	79	87	50	77	60	70	72	71	86	100
58634	GRASSY BUTTE	104	73	38	69	85	95	72	89	83	71	97	107	61	95	75	87	89	88	106	124
58636	HALLIDAY	68	51	33	48	57	66	54	61	61	52	71	70	48	68	54	64	65	61	73	78
58638	HEBRON	59	44	28	42	48	57	48	53	54	46	63	60	42	60	48	57	58	53	64	65
58639	HETTINGER	82	60	37	57	67	78	64	73	72	61	85	84	56	81	64	76	77	73	87	92
58640	KILLDEER	87	62	33	58	72	80	61	75	70	60	82	90	52	80	63	73	75	74	89	104
58641	LEFOR	74	52	27	49	61	68	51	63	59	51	69	77	44	68	53	62	63	63	76	88
58642	MANNING	85	60	31	56	70	78	59	73	68	58	80	88	50	78	61	71	73	72	87	101
58643	MARMARTH	77	54	28	51	62	70	53	65	61	52	71	79	45	70	55	64	65	64	78	91
58645	MEDORA	88	62	32	58	72	80	61	75	70	60	82	91	52	81	63	73	75	74	90	105
58646	MOTT	71	53	34	51	58	69	58	64	65	55	77	73	51	72	58	69	70	64	77	79
	NORTH DAKOTA	80	69	63	69	72	79	73	76	75	71	92	90	69	90	72	75	88	77	79	90
	UNITED STATES	100	100	100	100	100	100	100	100	100	100	100	100	100	100	100	100	100	100	100	100

A 58647-58856

#	POST OFFICE NAME	COUNTY FIPS CODE	POPULATION 2000	2004	2009	2000-2004 ANNUAL RATE % Rate	State Centile	HOUSEHOLDS 2000	2004	2009	% Annual Rate 2000-2004	2004 Average HH Size	FAMILIES 2000	2004	% Annual Rate 2000-2004
58647	NEW ENGLAND	041	977	955	922	-0.5	63	429	436	436	0.4	2.18	281	275	-0.5
58649	REEDER	001	364	347	328	-1.1	31	165	162	158	-0.4	2.14	113	108	-1.1
58650	REGENT	041	321	304	289	-1.3	25	138	136	134	-0.3	2.24	107	103	-0.9
58651	RHAME	011	424	411	396	-0.7	52	184	185	184	0.1	2.22	128	125	-0.6
58652	RICHARDTON	089	1159	1133	1112	-0.5	63	434	437	440	0.2	2.48	307	299	-0.6
58653	SCRANTON	011	596	572	548	-1.0	39	248	246	244	-0.2	2.33	179	172	-0.9
58654	SENTINEL BUTTE	033	286	273	258	-1.1	32	92	90	88	-0.5	2.93	66	63	-1.1
58655	SOUTH HEART	089	503	484	471	-0.9	42	171	170	170	-0.1	2.85	137	133	-0.7
58656	TAYLOR	089	353	336	326	-1.2	30	143	140	140	-0.5	2.33	109	105	-0.9
58701	MINOT	101	24518	24497	24367	0.0	81	10672	10963	11129	0.6	2.20	6418	6342	-0.3
58703	MINOT	101	17897	17763	17625	-0.2	77	7088	7210	7286	0.4	2.35	4644	4577	-0.3
58704	MINOT AFB	101	3827	3521	3383	-1.9	4	1068	996	969	-1.6	3.16	982	908	-1.8
58705	MINOT AFB	101	3235	2976	2860	-1.9	4	884	824	802	-1.6	3.23	813	752	-1.8
58707	MINOT	101	442	444	443	0.1	83	21	22	22	1.1	2.55	10	10	0.0
58710	ANAMOOSE	049	577	557	538	-0.8	46	245	243	242	-0.2	2.29	167	161	-0.9
58711	ANTLER	009	232	215	201	-1.8	5	102	98	95	-0.9	2.19	72	67	-1.7
58712	BALFOUR	049	110	112	111	0.4	88	48	51	52	1.4	2.18	35	36	0.7
58713	BANTRY	049	308	296	286	-0.9	40	128	128	128	0.0	2.31	88	85	-0.8
58716	BENEDICT	055	157	167	168	1.5	96	63	70	73	2.5	2.39	51	56	2.2
58718	BERTHOLD	101	953	912	888	-1.0	36	360	353	350	-0.5	2.57	271	259	-1.1
58721	BOWBELLS	013	588	563	530	-1.0	36	251	247	239	-0.4	2.28	174	166	-1.1
58722	BURLINGTON	101	1824	1836	1832	0.2	84	635	658	671	0.8	2.79	509	514	0.2
58723	BUTTE	055	166	152	142	-2.1	2	82	78	75	-1.2	1.95	55	50	-2.2
58725	CARPIO	101	323	302	291	-1.6	12	132	127	125	-0.9	2.38	95	89	-1.5
58727	COLUMBUS	013	335	315	293	-1.4	17	164	160	154	-0.6	1.97	113	106	-1.5
58730	CROSBY	023	1365	1290	1215	-1.3	21	601	585	566	-0.6	2.08	365	341	-1.6
58731	DEERING	049	312	299	289	-1.0	38	98	97	97	-0.2	3.03	66	63	-1.1
58733	DES LACS	101	426	437	441	0.6	91	150	158	163	1.2	2.77	121	124	0.6
58734	DONNYBROOK	101	301	282	272	-1.5	14	122	117	116	-1.0	2.41	88	83	-1.4
58735	DOUGLAS	101	289	270	259	-1.6	11	111	107	105	-0.9	2.52	77	72	-1.6
58736	DRAKE	049	534	515	498	-0.9	45	239	236	234	-0.3	2.18	159	152	-1.1
58737	FLAXTON	013	155	144	134	-1.7	6	78	75	72	-0.9	1.92	52	48	-1.9
58740	GLENBURN	075	1427	1365	1320	-1.0	35	529	522	518	-0.3	2.46	413	396	-1.0
58741	GRANVILLE	049	711	695	675	-0.5	63	274	277	278	0.3	2.47	197	193	-0.5
58744	KARLSRUHE	049	478	475	466	-0.2	78	194	200	202	0.7	2.37	142	142	0.0
58746	KENMARE	101	1648	1617	1591	-0.5	67	681	686	688	0.2	2.25	443	431	-0.6
58747	KIEF	083	137	142	141	0.9	92	59	63	65	1.6	2.24	45	46	0.5
58748	KRAMER	009	174	175	169	0.1	83	78	81	81	0.9	2.16	54	54	0.0
58750	LANSFORD	009	515	480	451	-1.6	10	204	197	191	-0.8	2.44	145	136	-1.5
58752	LIGNITE	013	256	240	224	-1.5	14	119	116	112	-0.6	2.07	82	77	-1.5
58755	MCGREGOR	105	99	93	89	-1.5	16	49	47	47	-1.0	1.96	33	31	-1.5
58756	MAKOTI	101	263	246	237	-1.6	12	124	118	116	-1.2	2.08	90	83	-1.9
58757	MANDAREE	053	1207	1235	1247	0.5	90	300	311	316	0.9	3.97	262	268	0.5
58758	MARTIN	083	235	248	248	1.3	95	95	104	107	2.2	2.38	74	79	1.6
58759	MAX	055	623	615	602	-0.3	73	260	265	267	0.5	2.32	194	193	-0.1
58760	MAXBASS	009	291	270	253	-1.8	5	125	120	116	-1.0	2.25	89	83	-1.6
58761	MOHALL	075	1292	1238	1187	-1.0	38	538	533	528	-0.2	2.22	352	336	-1.1
58762	NEWBURG	009	203	188	176	-1.8	5	96	92	89	-1.0	2.04	68	63	-1.8
58763	NEW TOWN	061	2248	2242	2208	-0.1	80	783	799	802	0.5	2.74	544	537	-0.3
58765	NOONAN	023	277	262	247	-1.3	23	132	129	124	-0.5	1.92	82	77	-1.5
58768	NORWICH	101	346	345	341	-0.1	79	122	125	126	0.6	2.74	93	93	0.0
58769	PALERMO	061	231	217	209	-1.5	16	97	95	93	-0.5	2.28	71	67	-1.4
58770	PARSHALL	061	1275	1265	1243	-0.2	76	191	186	184	-0.6	2.22	140	132	-1.4
58771	PLAZA	061	439	413	398	-1.4	17	191	186	184	-0.6	2.22	140	132	-1.4
58772	PORTAL	013	186	173	161	-1.7	8	86	83	80	-0.8	2.08	57	53	-1.7
58773	POWERS LAKE	013	640	620	585	-0.7	51	279	280	275	0.1	2.21	178	173	-0.7
58775	ROSEGLEN	055	695	661	632	-1.2	29	219	214	212	-0.5	3.09	173	165	-1.1
58776	ROSS	061	158	151	145	-1.1	34	68	67	67	-0.4	2.25	50	48	-1.0
58778	RUSO	055	142	133	127	-1.5	13	61	59	58	-0.8	2.25	42	40	-1.1
58779	RYDER	101	464	432	414	-1.7	9	183	175	172	-1.1	2.47	132	122	-1.8
58781	SAWYER	101	757	801	818	1.3	96	297	321	334	1.9	2.50	236	250	1.4
58782	SHERWOOD	075	458	431	409	-1.4	18	192	187	184	-0.6	2.30	131	123	-1.5
58783	SOURIS	009	416	417	403	0.1	82	184	191	191	0.9	2.18	127	127	0.0
58784	STANLEY	061	1953	1880	1824	-0.9	43	838	835	832	-0.1	2.18	530	508	-1.0
58785	SURREY	101	1042	1026	1013	-0.4	71	349	353	355	0.3	2.90	299	296	-0.2
58787	TOLLEY	075	151	142	135	-1.4	17	72	70	69	-0.7	2.03	49	46	-1.5
58788	TOWNER	049	1012	965	928	-1.1	31	461	458	455	-0.2	2.11	280	266	-1.2
58789	UPHAM	049	305	291	279	-1.1	32	144	143	141	-0.2	2.03	97	93	-1.0
58790	VELVA	049	1520	1518	1491	0.0	81	611	628	636	0.7	2.34	410	408	-0.1
58792	VOLTAIRE	049	252	239	229	-1.2	26	101	99	99	-0.5	2.41	78	75	-0.9
58793	WESTHOPE	009	749	699	657	-1.6	10	310	300	291	-0.8	2.18	191	177	-1.8
58794	WHITE EARTH	061	157	150	145	-1.1	33	60	59	59	-0.4	2.54	44	43	-0.5
58795	WILDROSE	105	262	246	235	-1.5	15	120	116	114	-0.8	2.10	83	78	-1.5
58801	WILLISTON	105	15862	15518	15116	-0.5	64	6434	6502	6529	0.3	2.32	4120	4011	-0.6
58830	ALAMO	105	181	170	162	-1.5	16	80	78	76	-0.6	2.17	55	52	-1.3
58831	ALEXANDER	053	457	442	435	-0.8	49	193	193	194	0.0	2.29	139	134	-0.9
58833	AMBROSE	023	215	204	192	-1.2	27	95	93	90	-0.5	2.16	69	65	-1.4
58835	ARNEGARD	053	162	156	154	-0.9	43	72	72	72	0.0	2.17	53	51	-0.9
58838	CARTWRIGHT	053	870	848	835	-0.6	58	366	368	369	0.1	2.30	256	250	-0.5
58843	EPPING	105	308	298	289	-0.8	49	131	132	132	0.2	2.26	97	95	-0.5
58844	FORTUNA	023	205	194	183	-1.3	23	87	85	82	-0.5	2.28	65	62	-1.1
58845	GRENORA	023	443	419	400	-1.3	23	196	192	189	-0.5	2.18	140	132	-1.4
58847	KEENE	053	272	265	262	-0.6	58	122	123	124	0.2	2.15	92	90	-0.5
58849	RAY	105	778	754	731	-0.7	52	332	333	333	0.1	2.26	225	218	-0.7
58852	TIOGA	105	1592	1543	1495	-0.7	52	679	686	688	0.2	2.20	451	439	-0.6
58853	TRENTON	105	413	403	392	-0.6	60	138	140	140	0.3	2.88	107	106	-0.2
58854	WATFORD CITY	053	2638	2575	2544	-0.6	60	1051	1059	1067	0.2	2.37	702	683	-0.6
58856	ZAHL	105	82	77	74	-1.5	15	39	38	38	-0.6	2.03	27	25	-1.8
	NORTH DAKOTA					0.1					0.8	2.33			-0.1
	UNITED STATES					1.2					1.3	2.58			1.1

ZIP CODE #	POST OFFICE NAME	RACE (%) White 2000	White 2004	Black 2000	Black 2004	Asian/Pacific 2000	Asian/Pacific 2004	% Hispanic Origin 2000	% Hispanic Origin 2004	2004 AGE DISTRIBUTION (%) 0-4	5-9	10-14	15-19	20-24	25-44	45-64	65-84	85+	18+	MEDIAN AGE 2004	% 2004 Males	% 2004 Females
58647	NEW ENGLAND	98.5	98.3	0.0	0.0	0.2	0.3	0.3	0.4	4.8	5.6	6.1	6.3	4.6	21.2	29.3	19.7	2.5	78.7	46.1	50.9	49.1
58649	REEDER	98.9	98.9	0.0	0.0	0.3	0.6	0.0	0.0	4.3	4.6	8.7	6.6	2.9	21.0	30.3	19.6	2.0	77.5	46.2	51.9	48.1
58650	REGENT	98.4	98.4	0.0	0.0	0.0	0.0	0.3	0.7	3.0	4.9	7.6	8.6	5.9	18.8	30.3	20.1	1.0	77.6	45.8	54.6	45.4
58651	RHAME	98.6	98.1	0.2	0.2	0.2	0.2	0.9	1.5	4.9	5.1	6.8	6.8	6.8	24.6	29.9	13.1	2.0	78.8	42.0	49.9	50.1
58652	RICHARDTON	98.8	98.7	0.1	0.1	0.1	0.1	0.7	0.7	4.8	4.9	5.8	6.9	5.5	21.0	29.6	17.8	3.8	79.4	45.7	50.8	49.3
58653	SCRANTON	99.3	99.1	0.0	0.0	0.0	0.0	0.3	0.4	5.1	5.2	6.5	6.6	5.4	20.3	31.6	16.3	3.0	79.4	45.5	47.7	52.3
58654	SENTINEL BUTTE	98.3	98.2	0.0	0.0	0.0	0.0	0.4	0.4	6.2	6.6	7.3	8.1	5.1	22.3	26.0	15.8	2.6	74.0	41.5	50.9	49.1
58655	SOUTH HEART	99.2	99.2	0.2	0.2	0.0	0.0	0.0	0.0	6.4	6.0	10.7	9.1	3.5	25.8	26.9	9.9	1.7	70.7	38.0	52.7	47.3
58656	TAYLOR	99.2	99.1	0.0	0.0	0.0	0.0	0.3	0.3	6.0	6.0	5.7	7.1	5.4	20.2	30.1	17.3	2.4	77.4	44.8	47.6	52.4
58701	MINOT	94.3	93.3	1.0	1.2	0.6	0.9	1.2	1.5	6.6	6.2	6.3	6.5	7.3	27.3	23.5	13.1	3.1	77.0	37.4	48.8	51.2
58703	MINOT	93.2	92.2	1.4	1.6	0.6	0.9	1.5	1.8	6.4	6.0	7.1	8.4	8.8	28.2	22.6	10.6	1.9	75.9	33.8	49.4	50.7
58704	MINOT AFB	79.2	76.1	10.2	11.4	3.0	4.1	6.2	7.2	13.9	11.0	7.9	8.5	18.4	38.6	1.7	0.1	0.0	64.1	22.4	54.7	45.3
58705	MINOT AFB	79.1	76.1	10.2	11.4	3.0	4.1	6.2	7.2	13.9	11.0	7.9	8.5	18.6	38.6	1.6	0.0	0.0	64.2	22.4	54.7	45.3
58707	MINOT	89.6	88.3	2.5	2.9	0.7	0.9	3.2	3.6	3.4	3.6	4.1	26.4	29.1	23.9	7.7	1.8	0.2	85.8	22.2	46.4	53.6
58710	ANAMOOSE	99.7	99.6	0.0	0.0	0.0	0.0	0.4	0.4	3.2	4.0	6.5	7.2	5.0	19.0	28.0	23.2	4.0	81.7	48.2	52.1	47.9
58711	ANTLER	98.7	99.1	0.0	0.0	0.0	0.0	0.0	0.0	5.1	5.6	7.0	6.5	5.1	23.3	29.8	15.4	2.3	78.1	43.6	51.6	48.4
58712	BALFOUR	100.0	100.0	0.0	0.0	0.0	0.0	0.0	0.9	7.1	7.1	6.3	6.3	4.5	21.4	29.5	16.1	1.8	75.0	43.3	54.5	45.5
58713	BANTRY	98.4	98.3	0.0	0.0	0.0	0.0	0.3	0.3	5.1	5.4	5.7	6.4	6.1	24.3	30.1	14.5	2.4	79.7	43.0	54.7	45.3
58716	BENEDICT	99.4	100.0	0.0	0.0	0.0	0.0	0.0	0.0	4.8	5.4	6.0	6.6	4.2	22.2	31.7	17.4	1.8	79.6	45.6	53.3	46.7
58718	BERTHOLD	98.0	97.8	0.3	0.3	0.2	0.3	0.9	1.2	7.5	7.5	7.1	6.4	4.8	25.3	26.2	13.3	2.0	73.8	39.2	53.0	47.0
58721	BOWBELLS	99.2	98.9	0.0	0.0	0.2	0.4	0.2	0.2	4.8	5.2	7.6	6.0	4.4	20.4	29.5	18.8	3.2	78.5	45.9	50.4	49.6
58722	BURLINGTON	97.5	97.1	0.3	0.4	0.2	0.2	0.9	1.1	7.4	7.7	9.0	8.4	6.8	27.6	24.7	7.5	0.9	70.6	34.7	50.6	49.4
58723	BUTTE	100.0	100.0	0.0	0.0	0.0	0.0	0.0	0.0	4.0	4.0	5.9	6.6	5.3	19.1	34.9	17.1	3.3	82.2	48.1	52.0	48.0
58725	CARPIO	98.1	97.7	0.3	0.3	0.3	0.3	1.6	1.7	6.3	6.6	7.3	5.3	4.6	24.2	26.5	16.9	2.3	76.2	42.5	53.3	46.7
58727	COLUMBUS	99.7	99.4	0.3	0.3	0.3	0.3	0.3	0.6	3.2	3.8	4.8	4.4	3.8	19.1	34.9	22.2	3.8	85.1	51.6	53.3	46.7
58730	CROSBY	98.7	98.3	0.0	0.0	0.7	1.0	0.7	0.9	3.4	3.9	5.4	6.4	5.0	16.6	27.8	23.7	7.8	82.6	51.3	49.0	51.0
58731	DEERING	97.1	97.0	0.0	0.0	0.3	0.3	1.0	0.7	5.7	5.7	7.0	8.0	6.0	26.8	25.8	12.7	2.3	76.3	38.8	53.9	46.2
58733	DES LACS	97.9	97.5	0.2	0.2	0.2	0.2	0.9	1.1	7.1	7.3	8.7	8.2	6.2	27.7	26.3	7.6	0.9	71.9	36.2	51.3	48.7
58734	DONNYBROOK	98.0	97.5	0.3	0.4	0.3	0.4	1.3	1.1	6.4	6.4	7.1	5.7	4.6	22.7	28.7	16.0	2.5	76.2	43.3	53.2	46.8
58735	DOUGLAS	97.6	96.7	0.0	0.0	0.4	0.7	0.7	1.1	5.2	5.9	7.0	6.3	4.8	21.5	31.1	15.9	2.2	77.4	44.5	50.7	49.3
58736	DRAKE	99.6	99.6	0.0	0.0	0.0	0.0	0.4	0.4	3.1	3.7	6.2	7.4	5.2	18.8	27.6	23.7	4.3	82.3	48.6	51.3	48.7
58737	FLAXTON	99.4	99.3	0.7	0.7	0.0	0.0	0.7	0.7	1.4	2.8	6.3	5.6	4.2	16.0	36.1	26.4	1.4	85.4	52.9	50.0	50.0
58740	GLENBURN	89.4	88.3	4.1	4.5	2.0	2.4	3.6	4.0	8.0	7.3	7.9	8.4	10.7	31.5	17.8	7.7	0.7	71.5	29.3	54.1	45.9
58741	GRANVILLE	97.3	97.0	0.3	0.3	0.0	0.0	0.3	0.3	6.0	6.6	6.5	6.8	5.5	24.6	27.9	13.1	3.0	76.3	41.2	53.7	46.3
58744	KARLSRUHE	99.4	99.6	0.0	0.0	0.0	0.0	0.4	0.4	6.1	6.3	5.5	6.5	5.7	22.5	29.3	16.4	1.7	77.7	43.4	54.1	45.9
58746	KENMARE	98.4	98.3	0.0	0.0	0.2	0.3	0.1	0.1	5.0	5.3	6.3	5.3	5.7	19.4	27.1	20.0	6.1	80.2	46.9	49.3	50.7
58747	KIEF	99.3	100.0	0.0	0.0	0.0	0.0	0.7	0.7	4.9	5.6	7.0	7.0	4.9	19.7	29.6	19.7	1.4	77.5	45.4	53.5	46.5
58748	KRAMER	98.9	99.4	0.0	0.0	0.0	0.0	0.6	0.6	5.1	5.7	6.9	6.3	5.1	22.3	29.1	17.1	2.3	78.3	44.2	53.7	46.3
58750	LANSFORD	98.5	98.5	0.2	0.2	0.2	0.2	0.4	0.4	5.2	5.6	6.9	6.5	5.2	23.1	30.6	14.8	2.1	78.3	43.5	52.7	47.3
58752	LIGNITE	99.6	99.6	0.4	0.4	0.0	0.0	0.4	0.4	2.9	3.8	5.0	4.6	3.8	17.9	35.8	22.9	3.3	85.4	52.1	52.9	47.1
58755	MCGREGOR	99.0	98.9	0.0	0.0	1.0	1.1	0.0	0.0	4.3	4.3	5.4	6.5	4.3	20.4	31.2	19.4	4.3	80.7	47.8	51.6	48.4
58756	MAKOTI	85.2	85.0	0.0	0.0	0.8	0.8	0.8	0.8	5.7	6.1	6.1	5.3	4.1	21.1	36.6	13.4	1.6	78.5	46.0	49.6	50.4
58757	MANDAREE	4.6	3.8	0.0	0.0	0.0	0.0	2.0	1.9	13.3	12.1	11.5	10.8	9.6	21.9	15.6	5.1	0.2	56.7	21.3	48.0	52.0
58758	MARTIN	99.2	99.2	0.0	0.0	0.0	0.0	0.4	0.4	3.2	4.8	7.7	6.9	4.4	19.4	33.1	19.4	1.2	79.0	47.1	54.0	46.0
58759	MAX	97.8	97.2	0.0	0.0	0.3	0.5	0.6	0.7	5.0	5.7	7.2	6.8	4.4	21.0	31.5	16.1	2.3	77.7	45.0	52.2	47.8
58760	MAXBASS	98.6	98.5	0.3	0.4	0.0	0.4	0.3	0.4	5.2	5.6	7.0	6.7	5.2	23.0	31.1	14.4	1.9	77.8	43.5	52.6	47.4
58761	MOHALL	98.4	98.4	0.1	0.1	0.2	0.2	0.2	0.2	4.4	4.8	6.1	6.1	5.3	19.5	27.1	20.3	6.4	80.7	47.4	49.0	51.0
58762	NEWBURG	98.5	98.9	0.0	0.0	0.0	0.0	0.0	0.0	4.8	5.9	6.9	6.9	4.8	23.9	29.8	14.9	2.1	78.2	43.2	52.1	47.9
58763	NEW TOWN	32.8	28.6	0.1	0.1	0.3	0.4	1.9	1.9	8.0	7.9	10.0	8.3	7.9	23.3	23.2	9.5	1.7	69.0	31.8	48.1	51.9
58765	NOONAN	98.9	98.5	0.0	0.0	0.7	0.8	0.7	0.8	3.4	3.8	5.3	6.5	5.0	17.2	28.6	23.3	6.9	82.4	51.0	50.0	50.0
58768	NORWICH	97.4	97.4	0.3	0.3	0.3	0.3	0.6	0.6	7.0	7.5	7.5	7.3	5.5	26.7	26.1	10.4	2.0	73.0	38.0	52.8	47.3
58769	PALERMO	97.4	97.2	0.0	0.0	0.4	0.5	0.0	0.0	4.6	4.6	5.1	6.9	5.1	18.9	35.0	17.5	2.3	81.1	47.4	53.0	47.0
58770	PARSHALL	47.1	42.6	0.2	0.3	0.0	0.0	2.6	2.8	8.6	7.6	7.8	7.4	8.0	21.7	21.3	14.6	3.1	70.4	35.8	49.1	50.9
58771	PLAZA	95.0	94.2	0.0	0.0	0.5	0.5	0.0	0.0	4.6	5.3	5.3	7.0	5.1	20.1	33.9	16.7	1.9	80.4	46.3	53.0	47.0
58772	PORTAL	99.5	99.4	0.5	0.6	0.0	0.0	0.5	0.6	2.3	2.3	5.8	4.6	4.1	16.8	37.0	26.0	1.2	86.1	53.0	50.9	49.1
58773	POWERS LAKE	98.8	98.9	0.0	0.0	0.2	0.2	0.5	0.5	4.8	5.3	6.6	5.2	4.8	21.1	27.3	20.5	4.4	79.8	46.4	49.2	50.8
58775	ROSEGLEN	42.0	37.1	0.0	0.0	0.3	0.3	5.5	5.6	7.6	8.5	10.6	7.6	6.1	21.8	26.2	10.6	1.2	68.5	34.4	49.2	50.8
58776	ROSS	98.1	98.0	0.0	0.0	0.0	0.7	0.0	0.0	4.6	6.0	6.0	6.6	5.3	18.5	37.1	13.3	2.7	78.8	46.5	54.3	45.7
58778	RUSO	100.0	100.0	0.0	0.0	0.0	0.0	0.0	0.0	3.8	3.8	5.3	6.8	4.5	21.1	32.3	18.8	3.8	82.7	48.0	50.4	49.6
58779	RYDER	83.0	80.6	0.0	0.0	0.2	0.5	1.9	2.1	6.5	7.2	8.3	6.3	4.6	22.2	30.8	12.7	1.4	73.8	41.7	50.7	49.3
58781	SAWYER	98.7	98.5	0.1	0.1	0.5	0.6	0.5	0.9	7.0	7.9	8.6	7.0	4.5	25.7	28.8	9.5	1.0	72.0	38.2	52.3	47.7
58782	SHERWOOD	98.3	98.1	0.2	0.2	0.0	0.0	0.0	0.0	4.9	5.1	6.5	6.0	5.1	20.9	29.9	19.0	2.6	80.1	45.8	50.8	49.2
58783	SOURIS	99.0	99.0	0.0	0.0	0.2	0.2	0.5	0.5	5.0	5.3	6.5	6.5	5.0	22.3	30.0	17.5	1.9	79.1	44.7	53.2	46.8
58784	STANLEY	98.7	98.4	0.0	0.0	0.3	0.5	0.4	0.5	5.0	5.3	6.1	6.5	5.7	19.0	27.8	18.9	5.7	79.3	46.6	49.3	50.7
58785	SURREY	97.1	96.5	0.0	0.0	0.3	0.4	1.5	2.0	7.4	7.6	8.9	9.2	6.4	28.3	23.6	7.9	0.8	70.6	34.1	49.7	50.3
58787	TOLLEY	98.0	98.6	0.0	0.0	0.0	0.0	0.0	0.0	4.9	4.9	6.3	6.3	4.9	19.7	32.4	18.3	2.1	79.6	46.5	52.1	47.9
58788	TOWNER	98.6	98.6	0.2	0.2	0.0	0.0	0.7	0.8	4.6	4.9	5.0	5.2	5.5	21.5	29.1	21.1	3.2	82.6	47.3	49.8	50.2
58789	UPHAM	98.0	97.9	0.0	0.0	0.0	0.0	0.3	0.3	5.5	5.8	6.5	6.9	5.8	25.4	27.8	13.8	2.4	78.0	41.2	53.3	46.7
58790	VELVA	99.1	99.0	0.1	0.1	0.1	0.2	0.3	0.4	5.3	5.5	7.0	7.3	6.6	20.4	25.6	16.7	5.7	77.3	43.5	48.2	51.8
58792	VOLTAIRE	98.4	97.9	0.0	0.0	0.0	0.4	0.0	0.0	5.0	5.4	4.2	8.4	6.7	19.7	34.3	14.6	1.7	80.3	45.3	52.3	47.7
58793	WESTHOPE	98.5	98.4	0.0	0.0	0.0	0.0	0.0	0.0	3.2	3.4	6.4	6.7	5.7	18.2	30.9	18.2	7.3	82.8	49.0	48.1	51.9
58794	WHITE EARTH	98.1	98.0	0.0	0.0	0.0	0.0	0.6	0.0	4.7	6.0	6.0	6.7	5.3	20.7	36.7	12.0	2.0	78.7	45.4	51.3	48.7
58795	WILDROSE	99.2	98.8	0.0	0.0	0.4	0.8	0.0	0.0	3.3	4.5	6.1	6.1	3.7	21.1	31.3	20.3	3.7	81.7	48.4	54.5	45.5
58801	WILLISTON	92.6	91.7	0.1	0.2	0.2	0.3	1.1	1.3	6.4	6.2	7.0	7.7	8.5	23.2	25.9	12.7	2.6	75.6	39.0	48.6	51.4
58830	ALAMO	98.9	98.8	0.0	0.0	0.6	0.6	0.0	0.0	3.5	4.1	5.9	5.9	4.1	20.0	31.8	20.6	4.1	81.8	48.9	53.5	46.5
58831	ALEXANDER	96.1	95.7	0.0	0.0	0.2	0.2	1.5	1.6	4.1	4.5	6.3	6.6	5.0	19.7	35.5	16.1	2.3	80.8	46.9	51.1	48.9
58833	AMBROSE	99.5	99.5	0.0	0.0	0.0	0.5	0.5	0.5	2.5	4.4	6.4	6.4	2.9	19.1	32.4	22.6	3.4	81.4	50.3	53.4	46.6
58835	ARNEGARD	97.5	96.8	0.0	0.0	0.0	0.0	0.0	0.0	5.1	6.4	7.7	7.7	4.5	18.0	34.6	13.5	2.6	75.6	45.4	50.6	49.4
58838	CARTWRIGHT	97.2	97.2	0.1	0.1	0.1	0.1	1.3	1.3	4.7	5.3	7.3	7.1	5.4	22.5	30.5	14.9	2.2	78.4	43.7	52.2	47.8
58843	EPPING	96.4	96.0	0.0	0.0	0.0	0.0	1.0	0.7	4.0	5.7	7.1	8.7	5.4	20.5	33.6	14.1	1.0	76.9	44.3	52.7	47.3
58844	FORTUNA	99.5	100.0	0.0	0.0	0.0	0.0	0.5	0.5	2.6	4.6	6.7	6.7	2.6	19.6	32.5	21.7	3.1	80.9	49.7	54.6	45.4
58845	GRENORA	98.2	98.1	0.0	0.0	0.0	0.0	0.0	0.2	3.3	4.3	5.5	6.2	4.3	20.1	33.2	19.6	3.6	82.6	48.5	54.9	45.1
58847	KEENE	97.1	97.0	0.0	0.0	0.0	0.0	0.0	0.0	4.9	6.0	7.6	8.3	3.0	20.4	34.0	13.6	2.3	75.1	44.9	50.6	49.4
58849	RAY	98.7	98.7	0.0	0.0	0.1	0.1	0.5	0.7	4.1	4.6	5.8	7.2	6.0	17.0	33.3	19.5	2.5	80.8	47.6	51.1	48.9
58852	TIOGA	97.7	97.5	0.1	0.1	0.1	0.1	0.3	0.3	4.3	4.8	6.1	7.1	5.8	18.8	29.6	19.3	4.2	79.6	46.6	48.2	51.9
58853	TRENTON	64.2	61.0	0.0	0.0	0.0	0.0	0.0	0.3	8.2	7.9	10.2	8.2	6.2	24.6	27.5	6.7	0.5	67.5	33.9	51.4	48.6
58854	WATFORD CITY	96.4	95.8	0.1	0.1	0.1	0.1	0.6	0.7	4.9	5.5	6.8	8.4	5.1	18.6	31.5	15.0	4.2	76.8	45.4	49.1	50.9
58856	ZAHL	97.6	97.4	0.0	0.0	0.0	0.0	0.0	0.0	3.9	5.2	5.2	5.2	5.2	20.8	31.2	19.5	3.9	81.8	47.5	54.6	45.5
	NORTH DAKOTA	92.4	91.7	0.6	0.7	0.6	0.8	1.2	1.4	6.3	6.1	6.8	7.9	8.5	26.2	23.9	12.0	2.4	76.5	36.5	50.0	50.0
	UNITED STATES	75.1	73.6	12.3	12.5	3.8	4.2	12.5	14.1	6.9	6.7	7.2	7.0	7.3	28.6	23.8	10.8	1.7	75.1	36.0	49.1	50.9

ZIP CODE #	POST OFFICE NAME	2004 Per Capita Income	2004 HH Income Base	2004 HOUSEHOLD INCOME DISTRIBUTION (%) Less than $25,000	$25,000 to $49,999	$50,000 to $99,999	$100,000 to $149,999	$150,000 or More	MEDIAN HOUSEHOLD INCOME 2004	2009	2004 National Centile	2004 State Centile	2004 Home Value Base	2004 HOME VALUE DISTRIBUTION (%) Less than $50,000	$50,000 to $89,999	$90,000 to $174,999	$175,000 to $399,999	$400,000 or More	2004 Median Home Value
58647	NEW ENGLAND	19239	436	34.9	36.5	22.7	5.3	0.7	34820	41050	27	41	359	54.6	27.3	15.3	2.8	0.0	46563
58649	REEDER	23310	162	34.0	40.1	19.8	2.5	3.7	35469	40286	29	46	131	62.6	22.1	11.5	1.5	2.3	34583
58650	REGENT	19241	136	39.0	34.6	21.3	2.9	2.2	32312	37612	19	26	114	54.4	28.1	14.0	3.5	0.0	43750
58651	RHAME	19601	185	35.1	34.6	25.4	2.2	2.7	35316	40587	29	45	149	40.9	28.9	24.8	2.7	2.7	59643
58652	RICHARDTON	17179	437	34.3	35.5	24.3	4.6	1.4	34578	40461	26	40	362	50.3	31.2	15.2	3.3	0.0	49762
58653	SCRANTON	19341	246	32.1	36.2	25.2	3.3	3.3	38071	45000	40	60	206	57.8	27.7	11.2	1.5	1.9	42000
58654	SENTINEL BUTTE	15678	90	33.3	38.9	22.2	3.3	2.2	35904	42370	31	48	73	50.7	26.0	21.9	1.4	0.0	49167
58655	SOUTH HEART	16438	170	25.9	38.8	28.2	7.1	0.0	38307	45000	40	62	152	31.6	28.3	36.2	2.6	1.3	79091
58656	TAYLOR	18027	140	31.4	37.9	24.3	4.3	2.1	34553	38981	26	39	115	44.4	23.5	21.7	9.6	0.9	58125
58701	MINOT	22582	10963	32.5	31.1	27.5	5.7	3.3	37171	44058	36	55	7110	23.3	25.3	38.6	11.7	1.1	91530
58703	MINOT	22392	7210	26.2	30.8	33.1	7.8	2.2	43489	52932	57	79	4786	9.6	32.0	48.0	10.0	0.4	97016
58704	MINOT AFB	13178	996	22.1	52.5	21.1	3.5	0.8	36783	41852	35	53	10	0.0	10.0	80.0	10.0	0.0	133333
58705	MINOT AFB	12925	824	22.1	52.3	21.2	3.6	0.7	36833	41878	35	53	8	0.0	12.5	87.5	0.0	0.0	118750
58707	MINOT	5930	22	40.9	40.9	18.2	0.0	0.0	28077	32290	9	8	8	0.0	75.0	25.0	0.0	0.0	70000
58710	ANAMOOSE	16315	243	41.6	35.0	19.3	3.7	0.4	30145	36644	13	16	200	65.5	19.5	10.5	3.5	1.0	34583
58711	ANTLER	21933	98	27.6	39.8	26.5	5.1	1.0	39292	45966	44	66	79	55.7	30.4	10.1	3.8	0.0	45500
58712	BALFOUR	17613	51	49.0	25.5	17.7	5.9	2.0	25535	28846	5	2	41	56.1	17.1	14.6	7.3	4.9	41667
58713	BANTRY	18460	128	39.8	32.8	21.9	4.7	0.8	30485	35995	13	16	107	49.5	28.0	19.6	2.8	0.0	50500
58716	BENEDICT	19980	70	28.6	32.9	32.9	4.3	1.4	41949	49444	53	74	63	30.2	30.2	30.2	7.9	1.6	75833
58718	BERTHOLD	19759	353	32.6	37.1	23.5	4.3	2.6	34669	40000	26	40	298	43.3	24.2	28.5	4.0	0.0	61053
58721	BOWBELLS	17894	247	34.0	40.1	21.1	3.6	1.2	33277	37947	22	31	207	56.0	22.7	17.9	2.4	1.0	43421
58722	BURLINGTON	19482	658	16.6	36.2	39.8	5.8	1.7	48051	58112	68	91	568	18.1	36.1	35.6	9.2	1.1	85862
58723	BUTTE	19960	78	41.0	37.2	16.7	3.9	1.3	30000	35939	12	15	64	43.8	18.8	17.2	17.2	3.1	64000
58725	CARPIO	22163	127	37.8	31.5	24.4	3.2	3.2	32315	37651	19	26	106	50.0	17.9	27.4	4.7	0.0	50000
58727	COLUMBUS	15619	160	53.1	24.4	21.3	1.3	0.0	22982	26482	3	0	135	63.0	31.1	5.9	0.0	0.0	27500
58730	CROSBY	19138	585	40.2	31.6	21.9	5.3	1.0	33152	39566	21	30	462	61.7	28.8	8.0	1.1	0.4	38226
58731	DEERING	12744	97	40.2	30.9	24.7	4.1	0.0	30365	35369	13	16	81	55.6	22.2	18.5	2.5	1.2	43571
58733	DES LACS	19861	158	18.4	34.8	38.6	5.7	2.5	47760	57369	68	89	137	19.7	34.3	35.0	10.2	0.7	85417
58734	DONNYBROOK	17562	117	39.3	33.3	22.2	2.6	2.6	31237	36717	16	20	98	54.1	18.4	23.5	4.1	0.0	45000
58735	DOUGLAS	15769	107	33.6	38.3	22.4	4.7	0.9	33944	39597	24	35	88	51.1	23.9	20.5	4.6	0.0	48571
58736	DRAKE	16985	236	42.0	34.3	19.9	3.8	0.0	30000	36780	12	15	193	70.0	18.1	8.3	2.6	1.0	30682
58737	FLAXTON	17213	75	48.0	30.7	18.7	2.7	0.0	26338	30000	6	4	64	82.8	9.4	3.1	4.7	0.0	14444
58740	GLENBURN	17965	522	25.3	43.9	26.1	2.9	1.9	38149	43834	40	61	297	33.0	33.3	28.3	4.7	0.7	69444
58741	GRANVILLE	18841	277	38.3	31.8	23.1	5.4	1.4	31870	37345	17	22	230	48.7	30.9	14.8	5.2	0.4	51667
58744	KARLSRUHE	18109	200	44.5	29.0	18.5	5.5	2.5	28032	33180	9	8	164	52.4	21.3	18.3	5.5	2.4	46364
58746	KENMARE	18231	686	34.0	37.6	22.9	4.7	0.9	34056	39712	24	36	543	49.2	22.8	23.9	3.9	0.2	51047
58747	KIEF	17413	63	44.4	31.8	19.1	4.8	0.0	28318	35557	9	9	53	52.8	22.6	15.1	7.6	1.9	46250
58748	KRAMER	18376	81	43.2	32.1	22.2	2.5	0.0	27813	31901	8	7	64	53.1	21.9	17.2	6.3	1.6	43333
58750	LANSFORD	19651	197	28.4	39.1	25.9	4.6	2.0	38778	45157	42	64	159	50.3	30.2	12.0	5.7	1.9	49667
58752	LIGNITE	15049	116	52.6	25.0	20.7	1.7	0.0	23288	26687	3	1	98	66.3	28.6	5.1	0.0	0.0	25833
58755	MCGREGOR	23904	47	42.6	34.0	17.0	4.3	2.1	29275	34066	11	12	39	69.2	15.4	15.4	0.0	0.0	22500
58756	MAKOTI	19929	118	33.1	38.1	23.7	4.2	0.9	34366	39299	25	37	99	42.4	27.3	25.3	5.1	0.0	58333
58757	MANDAREE	9267	311	39.6	30.6	28.3	1.6	0.0	30924	39028	15	18	127	52.8	32.3	12.6	2.4	0.0	47083
58758	MARTIN	16391	104	42.3	34.6	19.2	3.9	0.0	30000	36636	12	15	89	48.3	27.0	15.7	7.9	1.1	51500
58759	MAX	18920	265	31.3	38.1	25.3	4.2	1.1	36061	42196	32	49	227	41.0	22.5	26.9	9.3	0.4	67000
58760	MAXBASS	21403	120	27.5	39.2	25.8	5.0	2.5	39373	46000	44	66	97	52.6	30.9	11.3	5.2	0.0	47222
58761	MOHALL	20718	533	34.0	35.5	25.0	3.4	2.3	33712	39223	23	35	404	51.7	29.0	15.4	3.5	0.5	48409
58762	NEWBURG	23607	92	28.3	39.1	26.1	5.4	1.1	39196	45962	43	65	74	51.4	33.8	10.8	4.1	0.0	48571
58763	NEW TOWN	14632	799	36.4	34.2	25.0	3.4	1.0	33435	40194	22	33	509	47.9	36.0	15.1	0.8	0.2	51522
58765	NOONAN	20704	129	40.3	31.8	21.7	5.4	0.8	33286	40559	22	31	102	61.8	28.4	8.8	1.0	0.0	37500
58768	NORWICH	17758	125	28.8	33.6	31.2	5.6	0.8	41122	46530	50	71	107	32.7	32.7	28.0	5.6	0.9	71667
58769	PALERMO	17083	95	42.1	35.8	17.9	3.2	1.1	29034	34638	10	12	80	55.0	20.0	20.0	5.0	0.0	43333
58770	PARSHALL	15497	465	43.4	31.2	20.2	3.4	1.7	29124	33060	11	12	327	44.7	30.3	20.2	4.3	0.6	57292
58771	PLAZA	17637	186	39.3	35.0	20.4	4.3	1.1	30503	33593	14	17	156	49.4	22.4	22.4	5.8	0.0	51667
58772	PORTAL	15663	83	48.2	30.1	19.3	2.4	0.0	26100	28874	6	3	70	80.0	12.9	2.9	4.3	0.0	17500
58773	POWERS LAKE	17006	280	41.1	32.5	22.5	3.2	0.7	30000	35115	12	15	228	54.0	35.5	9.2	0.0	1.3	43571
58775	ROSEGLEN	11281	214	46.3	34.1	16.4	3.3	0.0	27895	35635	8	8	144	40.3	26.4	26.4	4.9	2.1	64444
58776	ROSS	21781	67	34.3	37.3	19.4	4.5	4.5	33224	37286	22	31	57	47.4	24.6	21.1	5.3	1.8	55000
58778	RUSO	18030	59	37.3	37.3	20.3	3.4	1.7	32298	37815	19	25	50	42.0	20.0	20.0	16.0	2.0	67500
58779	RYDER	15831	175	37.1	37.7	20.6	4.6	0.0	32953	39442	21	29	138	47.1	28.3	21.7	2.9	0.0	52667
58781	SAWYER	20913	321	26.2	33.6	32.1	6.2	1.9	42345	50000	54	76	284	21.8	25.7	41.9	8.5	2.1	93333
58782	SHERWOOD	18442	187	33.2	42.3	20.9	2.1	1.6	32908	37821	21	28	157	49.7	23.6	20.4	6.4	0.0	50500
58783	SOURIS	18362	191	40.8	33.0	20.9	3.7	1.6	29023	36029	10	11	152	50.7	23.7	17.8	5.9	2.0	48571
58784	STANLEY	18100	835	41.0	34.9	18.8	3.6	1.8	29667	33717	12	14	644	53.3	32.3	12.3	1.9	0.3	46613
58785	SURREY	19358	353	12.8	33.4	47.0	5.4	1.4	51631	62230	75	94	323	9.9	44.3	44.3	1.6	0.0	87589
58787	TOLLEY	18433	70	32.9	44.3	21.4	1.4	0.0	32523	37729	19	27	59	49.2	23.7	20.3	6.8	0.0	51250
58788	TOWNER	18984	458	38.9	31.7	26.0	1.8	1.8	31922	37987	18	23	346	63.6	24.9	10.7	0.9	0.0	38889
58789	UPHAM	19557	143	39.2	31.5	24.5	4.2	0.7	31251	36791	16	20	120	52.5	27.5	17.5	1.7	0.8	47000
58790	VELVA	18645	628	32.3	37.7	22.3	5.7	1.9	35446	42054	29	46	481	39.1	30.2	24.1	4.8	1.9	63472
58792	VOLTAIRE	21447	99	31.3	30.3	28.3	7.1	3.0	37542	43459	38	57	83	33.7	33.7	24.1	3.6	4.8	65000
58793	WESTHOPE	20973	300	36.3	38.3	20.7	3.0	1.7	31693	38057	17	22	250	68.8	24.0	6.0	1.2	0.0	32333
58794	WHITE EARTH	15958	59	37.3	40.7	18.6	1.7	1.7	31563	36094	17	21	49	53.1	28.6	18.4	0.0	0.0	46250
58795	WILDROSE	21884	116	42.2	32.8	19.0	4.3	1.7	30000	35913	12	15	95	66.3	17.9	14.7	1.1	0.0	25833
58801	WILLISTON	20788	6502	33.0	32.7	25.7	5.6	3.0	37032	43977	36	55	4399	28.8	39.8	27.4	4.0	0.0	71196
58830	ALAMO	21263	78	42.3	33.3	19.2	3.9	1.3	30000	36140	12	15	64	67.2	15.6	15.6	1.6	0.0	25000
58831	ALEXANDER	18207	193	36.8	34.7	21.2	5.2	2.1	33607	39075	23	34	160	32.5	38.8	23.8	1.3	3.8	67059
58833	AMBROSE	19620	93	36.6	32.3	24.7	5.4	1.1	36624	43430	34	51	74	58.1	27.0	12.2	2.7	0.0	36667
58835	ARNEGARD	19827	72	29.2	37.5	27.8	5.6	0.0	34269	39183	25	37	61	45.9	34.4	18.0	1.6	0.0	52500
58838	CARTWRIGHT	17274	368	38.0	36.7	19.8	4.6	0.8	32037	37339	18	23	301	40.5	31.9	22.3	3.7	1.7	59828
58843	EPPING	23627	132	27.3	34.9	31.1	4.6	2.3	38884	44308	42	64	121	36.4	33.9	22.3	5.8	1.7	68333
58844	FORTUNA	18984	85	36.5	30.6	25.9	5.9	1.2	37749	43423	38	58	68	54.4	27.9	13.2	4.4	0.0	42500
58845	GRENORA	21111	192	32.3	32.8	27.1	4.7	3.1	36973	41960	35	54	155	59.4	24.5	13.6	2.6	0.0	37917
58847	KEENE	23175	123	39.8	25.2	29.3	3.3	2.4	30832	36993	14	18	101	42.6	33.7	17.8	5.9	0.0	58333
58849	RAY	18827	333	34.5	34.5	27.3	2.4	1.2	35116	40454	28	43	290	53.5	36.9	8.3	1.0	0.3	46667
58852	TIOGA	20744	686	32.1	36.3	25.4	3.6	2.6	34714	40556	26	41	542	49.6	34.5	12.7	2.0	1.1	50370
58853	TRENTON	16452	140	29.3	37.9	25.7	5.0	2.1	37494	43498	37	57	110	32.7	36.4	23.6	7.3	0.0	70714
58854	WATFORD CITY	22351	1059	33.8	34.2	22.8	5.8	3.5	34565	41064	26	39	827	44.9	34.7	16.6	3.8	0.1	55822
58856	ZAHL	19675	38	36.8	34.2	23.7	5.3	0.0	33158	38170	21	30	31	61.3	19.4	19.4	0.0	0.0	37500
	NORTH DAKOTA	22058		29.0	31.5	29.9	6.6	3.0	40503	48701				27.7	27.3	34.9	9.3	0.9	83011
	UNITED STATES	25866		24.7	27.1	30.8	10.9	6.5	48124	56710				10.9	15.0	33.7	30.1	10.4	145905

SPENDING POTENTIAL INDICES

NORTH DAKOTA 58647-58856 D

ZIP CODE #	POST OFFICE NAME	FINANCIAL SERVICES Auto Loan	Home Loan	Invest-ments	Retire-ment Plans	THE HOME Home Improvements Home Repair	Furnishings Lawn & Garden	Comput-ers & Hard-ware	Major Appli-ances	TV, Radio, Sound Equip-ment	Furni-ture	ENTERTAINMENT Dine out/ Carry out	Sports Equip-ment	Fees & Tickets	Toys & Games	Travel	Cable TV	PERSONAL Apparel & Services	Auto Repairs	Health Insur-ance	Pets & Supplies
58647	NEW ENGLAND	71	52	32	49	58	68	55	63	62	53	73	72	49	70	55	66	67	63	75	80
58649	REEDER	90	63	33	60	73	82	62	77	72	62	84	93	53	83	65	75	77	76	92	107
58650	REGENT	78	54	28	51	63	71	54	66	62	53	73	80	46	71	56	65	66	65	79	92
58651	RHAME	79	55	29	52	64	72	54	67	63	54	73	81	46	72	56	66	67	66	80	94
58652	RICHARDTON	72	53	33	51	59	70	57	65	65	55	76	74	51	72	57	68	69	65	78	81
58653	SCRANTON	81	57	30	54	66	74	56	69	65	55	76	84	48	74	58	68	69	68	83	97
58654	SENTINEL BUTTE	84	59	31	56	69	77	58	72	67	57	79	87	50	77	60	70	72	71	86	100
58655	SOUTH HEART	85	59	31	56	69	77	58	72	67	58	79	87	50	77	61	71	72	71	86	101
58656	TAYLOR	76	54	30	51	62	70	54	65	61	53	72	78	46	71	55	64	66	64	77	90
58701	MINOT	72	68	68	68	70	76	70	72	71	69	88	83	68	87	70	72	84	72	74	83
58703	MINOT	73	74	82	76	74	78	78	76	77	76	95	90	77	95	76	74	93	78	72	84
58704	MINOT AFB	69	44	42	50	40	48	65	56	66	61	83	75	56	74	54	61	80	67	52	64
58705	MINOT AFB	69	44	42	50	40	48	65	56	67	61	83	75	56	74	54	61	80	67	52	64
58707	MINOT	46	36	47	41	36	40	51	44	50	47	63	57	46	58	45	46	61	50	41	49
58710	ANAMOOSE	63	46	28	44	52	60	49	56	55	47	65	65	43	62	49	58	59	56	67	72
58711	ANTLER	87	61	32	57	71	79	60	74	69	59	81	89	51	80	62	73	74	73	88	103
58712	BALFOUR	70	49	25	46	57	64	48	59	55	48	65	72	41	64	50	58	59	59	71	83
58713	BANTRY	73	53	31	50	59	69	56	64	63	54	74	75	49	71	56	66	67	64	77	83
58716	BENEDICT	86	60	32	57	70	79	59	73	68	59	80	88	51	79	62	72	73	72	87	102
58718	BERTHOLD	91	65	36	62	75	83	64	78	73	64	86	94	55	84	66	76	79	77	92	108
58721	BOWBELLS	72	51	28	48	59	67	51	62	59	50	69	74	44	67	53	62	63	62	74	85
58722	BURLINGTON	75	84	84	85	81	81	79	78	74	79	93	93	80	95	78	70	92	78	70	87
58723	BUTTE	66	52	35	47	58	65	49	59	55	48	65	69	44	65	52	59	61	58	69	80
58725	CARPIO	95	67	35	63	78	87	66	81	76	65	89	98	56	87	68	80	81	80	97	113
58727	COLUMBUS	50	37	25	36	41	49	41	45	46	39	54	51	37	51	41	49	50	45	54	55
58730	CROSBY	67	50	32	48	55	65	55	61	61	52	72	69	48	68	54	65	66	61	73	75
58731	DEERING	63	47	31	45	52	62	52	57	58	49	69	64	46	65	52	61	63	57	68	69
58733	DES LACS	76	85	85	86	83	82	79	79	75	80	94	94	80	96	79	71	92	78	71	88
58734	DONNYBROOK	77	53	28	51	62	70	53	65	61	52	71	79	45	70	55	64	65	64	78	91
58735	DOUGLAS	72	50	26	47	59	66	50	61	57	49	67	74	42	66	51	60	61	61	73	85
58736	DRAKE	62	45	28	43	51	60	49	55	55	47	65	63	43	62	49	58	59	55	66	70
58737	FLAXTON	53	40	26	38	44	53	44	49	50	42	59	55	40	55	44	53	53	49	58	59
58740	GLENBURN	77	57	40	56	60	67	62	66	66	61	80	81	55	76	59	66	76	69	71	84
58741	GRANVILLE	84	59	32	56	68	77	59	72	68	58	80	86	51	78	61	71	73	71	86	99
58744	KARLSRUHE	78	54	28	51	63	71	54	66	62	53	72	80	46	71	56	65	66	65	79	92
58746	KENMARE	69	51	33	49	56	67	56	62	63	53	74	70	50	70	56	66	66	65	79	92
58747	KIEF	71	49	26	47	57	64	49	60	56	48	66	73	42	65	51	59	60	60	72	84
58748	KRAMER	72	50	26	47	58	65	50	61	57	49	67	74	42	66	51	60	61	60	73	85
58750	LANSFORD	87	60	32	57	70	79	60	74	69	59	81	89	51	79	62	72	74	73	88	103
58752	LIGNITE	50	38	25	36	41	50	42	46	47	40	55	52	37	52	41	49	50	46	55	56
58755	MCGREGOR	76	57	38	55	62	75	63	70	71	60	83	78	56	79	63	75	76	70	83	84
58756	MAKOTI	73	54	32	51	62	68	53	64	59	52	70	77	46	69	55	62	64	63	74	87
58757	MANDAREE	50	45	52	44	44	51	51	49	54	51	68	56	51	67	50	55	66	51	51	55
58758	MARTIN	71	49	26	47	57	64	49	60	56	48	66	73	42	65	51	59	60	59	72	84
58759	MAX	79	55	29	52	65	72	55	68	63	54	74	82	47	73	57	66	67	67	81	94
58760	MAXBASS	87	61	32	57	71	79	60	74	69	59	81	90	51	80	62	73	74	73	88	103
58761	MOHALL	79	58	35	55	65	76	62	71	70	59	82	81	54	78	62	74	75	70	84	90
58762	NEWBURG	87	61	32	58	71	80	60	74	69	59	81	90	51	80	62	73	74	73	89	104
58763	NEW TOWN	57	55	55	55	56	59	57	58	57	56	71	69	56	71	56	56	68	58	56	66
58765	NOONAN	68	50	32	48	56	66	54	61	61	52	72	69	48	68	54	65	66	61	73	76
58768	NORWICH	85	64	40	61	72	79	62	74	69	62	82	89	55	81	64	72	76	73	85	100
58769	PALERMO	71	49	26	47	56	64	49	60	56	48	66	73	42	64	50	59	60	59	72	84
58770	PARSHALL	60	50	48	49	52	59	57	57	61	55	74	68	53	73	55	62	71	59	62	68
58771	PLAZA	71	49	26	47	58	65	49	60	56	48	66	73	42	65	51	59	60	60	72	84
58772	PORTAL	53	40	26	38	43	52	44	48	49	42	58	54	39	55	43	52	53	48	58	58
58773	POWERS LAKE	61	46	30	44	50	60	50	56	56	48	66	63	43	63	50	60	60	56	67	68
58775	ROSEGLEN	59	43	26	41	48	56	46	52	52	44	61	60	40	58	46	54	55	52	62	66
58776	ROSS	89	62	32	59	72	81	61	76	71	61	83	91	52	81	64	74	75	75	90	105
58778	RUSO	70	54	35	49	61	68	51	62	58	50	68	73	45	67	54	62	63	61	73	85
58779	RYDER	70	49	27	46	57	64	49	60	57	48	66	72	42	65	51	59	61	59	71	82
58781	SAWYER	94	66	34	62	77	86	65	81	75	64	88	97	56	86	68	79	80	79	96	112
58782	SHERWOOD	77	54	28	51	63	70	53	66	61	52	72	79	45	70	55	64	65	65	78	91
58783	SOURIS	72	51	27	48	59	66	50	62	58	49	68	74	43	66	52	60	62	61	74	86
58784	STANLEY	67	49	31	47	55	64	53	60	60	51	70	69	46	67	53	63	64	60	72	75
58785	SURREY	79	86	86	88	83	82	82	81	77	83	97	96	82	97	80	72	95	81	71	89
58787	TOLLEY	68	47	25	45	55	62	47	58	54	46	63	70	40	62	48	56	57	57	69	80
58788	TOWNER	67	49	30	47	55	64	53	60	59	51	70	68	46	67	53	63	64	60	72	75
58789	UPHAM	65	49	31	46	54	64	53	59	59	50	70	67	47	66	53	63	64	59	71	73
58790	VELVA	73	54	34	52	60	71	59	66	66	56	78	75	52	74	59	70	71	66	79	82
58792	VOLTAIRE	94	65	34	62	76	85	65	80	74	64	87	96	55	86	67	78	80	79	95	111
58793	WESTHOPE	78	58	36	55	64	76	63	71	71	60	83	81	55	79	63	75	76	70	85	88
58794	WHITE EARTH	73	51	27	48	60	67	51	63	58	50	68	75	43	67	53	61	62	62	75	87
58795	WILDROSE	77	57	36	54	63	74	61	69	69	59	81	79	54	77	61	73	74	69	82	86
58801	WILLISTON	77	65	52	64	69	77	66	72	71	65	85	83	62	83	66	72	80	72	79	87
58830	ALAMO	76	57	36	54	63	74	61	69	69	58	81	78	54	77	61	73	74	68	82	85
58831	ALEXANDER	75	53	28	50	61	69	52	66	60	51	70	78	44	69	54	63	64	63	77	90
58833	AMBROSE	76	54	29	51	62	70	54	66	62	53	73	78	46	71	56	65	66	65	78	89
58835	ARNEGARD	78	54	28	51	63	71	54	66	62	53	72	80	46	71	56	65	66	65	79	92
58838	CARTWRIGHT	71	50	27	47	58	65	50	61	58	49	67	73	43	66	52	60	62	60	73	84
58843	EPPING	96	67	36	64	78	88	67	82	77	66	90	99	57	88	69	81	82	81	98	114
58844	FORTUNA	78	55	29	52	64	71	54	67	62	53	73	81	46	72	56	65	67	66	80	93
58845	GRENORA	80	60	39	55	69	77	58	70	66	57	78	83	51	76	61	70	72	69	83	96
58847	KEENE	90	63	33	60	73	82	62	77	72	62	84	93	53	83	65	75	77	76	92	107
58849	RAY	70	52	33	50	58	68	57	63	64	54	75	72	50	71	56	67	68	63	76	79
58852	TIOGA	76	56	36	54	62	74	61	69	69	58	81	78	54	77	61	73	74	68	82	85
58853	TRENTON	66	72	73	74	70	69	69	68	65	70	82	81	69	82	67	61	80	68	60	75
58854	WATFORD CITY	91	66	40	63	74	87	70	81	80	68	94	93	62	90	71	84	85	80	96	103
58856	ZAHL	67	51	35	47	57	66	51	60	58	50	68	69	46	66	53	61	63	59	71	79
	NORTH DAKOTA	80	69	63	69	72	79	73	76	75	71	92	90	69	90	72	75	88	77	79	90
	UNITED STATES	100	100	100	100	100	100	100	100	100	100	100	100	100	100	100	100	100	100	100	100

POPULATION CHANGE

# POST OFFICE NAME	COUNTY FIPS CODE	POPULATION 2000	2004	2009	2000-2004 ANNUAL RATE % Rate	State Centile	HOUSEHOLDS 2000	2004	2009	% Annual Rate 2000-2004	2004 Average HH Size	FAMILIES 2000	2004	% Annual Rate 2000-2004
43001 ALEXANDRIA	089	1655	1862	2042	2.8	96	593	682	761	3.3	2.73	486	548	2.9
43002 AMLIN	049	17	21	24	5.1	99	6	8	9	7.0	2.63	4	4	0.0
43003 ASHLEY	117	3063	3435	4077	2.7	96	1123	1293	1569	3.4	2.65	847	946	2.6
43004 BLACKLICK	049	8608	10148	11287	4.0	98	3467	4219	4796	4.7	2.41	2431	2836	3.7
43006 BRINKHAVEN	075	625	623	629	-0.1	42	229	232	237	0.3	2.69	167	164	-0.4
43008 BUCKEYE LAKE	089	1204	1236	1293	0.6	71	482	506	540	1.2	2.44	307	309	0.2
43009 CABLE	021	1779	1868	1927	1.2	85	612	658	692	1.7	2.83	513	541	1.3
43011 CENTERBURG	083	5818	6559	7286	2.9	96	1995	2293	2587	3.3	2.80	1605	1808	2.8
43013 CROTON	089	1305	1385	1473	1.4	87	461	500	543	1.9	2.77	385	409	1.4
43014 DANVILLE	083	3391	3549	3758	1.1	83	1169	1240	1329	1.4	2.85	878	908	0.8
43015 DELAWARE	041	36133	43282	55484	4.3	98	13548	16722	22054	5.1	2.46	9555	11462	4.4
43016 DUBLIN	049	19850	22491	24625	3.0	97	8210	9501	10572	3.5	2.36	5030	5549	2.3
43017 DUBLIN	049	34145	37333	40987	2.1	94	12618	13883	15381	2.3	2.67	9160	9875	1.8
43019 FREDERICKTOWN	083	8928	9155	9581	0.6	70	3238	3388	3607	1.1	2.69	2486	2540	0.5
43021 GALENA	041	5978	7825	10466	6.5	100	2100	2806	3822	7.1	2.79	1802	2376	6.7
43022 GAMBIER	083	3454	3579	3728	0.8	78	819	878	948	1.7	2.49	563	584	0.9
43023 GRANVILLE	089	11504	12312	13107	1.6	90	3567	3922	4286	2.3	2.64	2779	2987	1.7
43025 HEBRON	089	6526	7034	7556	1.8	92	2625	2889	3159	2.3	2.43	1833	1955	1.5
43026 HILLIARD	049	47425	55568	61597	3.8	98	17680	20884	23388	4.0	2.65	12677	14449	3.1
43028 HOWARD	083	5540	6307	6984	3.1	97	2119	2454	2754	3.5	2.56	1678	1902	3.0
43029 IRWIN	097	495	497	517	0.1	49	116	120	128	0.8	3.95	91	93	0.5
43031 JOHNSTOWN	089	9886	10613	11396	1.7	91	3674	4037	4421	2.2	2.61	2864	3070	1.7
43035 LEWIS CENTER	041	10939	15608	21708	8.7	100	4211	6099	8612	9.1	2.56	3038	4294	8.5
43037 MARTINSBURG	083	216	248	276	3.3	97	72	84	94	3.7	2.95	58	67	3.5
43040 MARYSVILLE	159	25889	28649	31842	2.4	95	8953	10126	11478	2.9	2.61	6614	7318	2.4
43044 MECHANICSBURG	021	5317	5477	5577	0.7	73	1999	2104	2182	1.2	2.59	1544	1589	0.7
43045 MILFORD CENTER	159	1473	1526	1634	0.8	78	546	577	628	1.3	2.64	441	456	0.8
43046 MILLERSPORT	045	3206	3285	3470	0.6	69	1334	1408	1523	1.3	2.33	931	949	0.5
43050 MOUNT VERNON	083	27191	27985	29543	0.7	73	10522	11028	11843	1.1	2.37	7072	7163	0.3
43054 NEW ALBANY	049	8019	11499	14138	8.9	100	2821	4140	5180	9.5	2.75	2234	3175	8.6
43055 NEWARK	089	58028	59300	62378	0.5	66	23654	24714	26512	1.0	2.36	15594	15752	0.2
43056 HEATH	089	15518	16549	17670	1.5	89	5991	6517	7085	2.0	2.51	4419	4676	1.3
43060 NORTH LEWISBURG	021	2511	2613	2684	0.9	80	920	977	1022	1.4	2.66	700	726	0.9
43061 OSTRANDER	041	2990	3692	4733	5.1	99	1087	1382	1815	5.8	2.65	879	1098	5.4
43062 PATASKALA	089	20033	22161	24118	2.4	95	7278	8257	9174	3.0	2.67	5822	6469	2.5
43064 PLAIN CITY	097	10430	11721	12943	2.8	96	3776	4341	4884	3.3	2.68	2922	3292	2.9
43065 POWELL	041	25003	31364	39860	5.5	99	8566	10953	14177	6.0	2.85	6936	8693	5.5
43066 RADNOR	041	1046	1194	1497	3.2	97	387	454	582	3.8	2.63	329	382	3.6
43067 RAYMOND	159	1603	1805	2026	2.8	96	551	632	721	3.3	2.86	451	508	2.8
43068 REYNOLDSBURG	089	46530	49627	53076	1.5	89	18792	20292	21987	1.8	2.44	12725	13299	1.0
43071 SAINT LOUISVILLE	089	2230	2366	2516	1.4	87	780	845	916	1.9	2.80	633	672	1.4
43072 SAINT PARIS	021	5920	6122	6246	0.8	76	2264	2387	2478	1.3	2.56	1721	1773	0.7
43074 SUNBURY	041	9019	10985	14193	4.8	99	3218	4027	5318	5.4	2.71	2642	3242	4.9
43076 THORNVILLE	127	8335	8531	8790	0.6	68	3182	3335	3501	1.1	2.55	2406	2452	0.5
43078 URBANA	021	21081	21246	21591	0.2	52	8357	8620	8933	0.7	2.40	5755	5765	0.0
43080 UTICA	089	5343	5777	6227	1.9	92	1942	2134	2335	2.2	2.67	1473	1581	1.7
43081 WESTERVILLE	049	51231	54094	57455	1.3	86	19799	21355	23076	1.8	2.46	13608	14136	0.9
43082 WESTERVILLE	041	17908	23487	31362	6.6	100	5979	7983	10846	7.0	2.92	5099	6706	6.7
43084 WOODSTOCK	021	840	844	853	0.1	50	263	269	277	0.5	2.95	213	214	0.1
43085 COLUMBUS	049	23480	22995	23516	-0.5	22	9610	9545	9896	-0.2	2.37	6442	6169	-1.0
43102 AMANDA	045	3453	3629	3868	1.2	85	1231	1327	1445	1.8	2.73	1010	1066	1.3
43103 ASHVILLE	129	9550	9955	10329	1.0	81	3572	3809	4033	1.5	2.61	2715	2827	1.0
43105 BALTIMORE	045	8054	8407	8909	1.0	82	2964	3183	3449	1.7	2.63	2318	2429	1.1
43106 BLOOMINGBURG	047	1674	1698	1702	0.3	60	591	612	627	0.8	2.75	452	458	0.3
43107 BREMEN	045	3052	3124	3287	0.6	68	1109	1163	1248	1.1	2.68	870	890	0.5
43110 CANAL WINCHESTER	045	18999	23468	26826	5.1	99	7123	8972	10419	5.6	2.60	5203	6274	4.5
43112 CARROLL	045	4082	4414	4767	1.9	93	1420	1568	1725	2.4	2.79	1152	1246	1.9
43113 CIRCLEVILLE	129	23566	23728	24261	0.2	52	9052	9299	9689	0.6	2.47	6568	6582	0.1
43115 CLARKSBURG	141	1445	1397	1379	-0.8	13	517	511	513	-0.3	2.70	407	393	-0.8
43116 COMMERCIAL POINT	129	332	350	364	1.3	86	120	129	137	1.7	2.71	97	102	1.2
43119 GALLOWAY	049	22724	26079	28657	3.3	97	8331	9675	10754	3.6	2.69	6125	6922	2.9
43123 GROVE CITY	049	46332	50103	53476	1.9	93	17221	18887	20426	2.2	2.63	13081	14030	1.7
43125 GROVEPORT	049	9449	10668	11624	2.9	96	3829	4466	4978	3.7	2.39	2628	2914	2.5
43128 JEFFERSONVILLE	047	2297	2200	2171	-1.0	8	882	864	871	-0.5	2.54	651	623	-1.0
43130 LANCASTER	045	54921	56805	60364	0.8	77	21381	22684	24656	1.4	2.40	14944	15388	0.7
43135 LAURELVILLE	073	4987	5010	5070	0.1	50	1884	1929	1986	0.6	2.59	669	691	0.8
43137 LOCKBOURNE	049	2304	2391	2488	0.9	79	858	908	961	1.3	2.63	664	691	0.8
43138 LOGAN	073	17972	18171	18267	0.3	56	7088	7319	7510	0.8	2.44	5011	5039	0.1
43140 LONDON	097	22314	22883	23593	0.6	70	7009	7386	7827	1.2	2.55	5059	5193	0.6
43143 MOUNT STERLING	097	5497	5559	5688	0.3	56	2091	2156	2249	0.7	2.58	1566	1580	0.2
43145 NEW HOLLAND	129	1795	1771	1795	-0.3	31	690	696	721	0.2	2.52	518	510	-0.4
43146 ORIENT	129	13195	13654	14039	0.9	77	2679	2907	3107	1.9	2.72	2202	2343	1.5
43147 PICKERINGTON	045	28029	32345	36124	3.4	97	9315	10979	12492	3.9	2.93	7749	8972	3.5
43148 PLEASANTVILLE	045	2145	2150	2242	0.1	47	775	797	849	0.7	2.67	607	609	0.1
43149 ROCKBRIDGE	073	2704	2753	2769	0.4	62	1021	1065	1095	1.0	2.58	798	814	0.5
43150 RUSHVILLE	045	1832	1758	1794	-1.0	9	647	637	663	-0.4	2.70	521	501	-0.9
43152 SOUTH BLOOMINGVILLE	073	1208	1204	1204	-0.1	42	470	480	490	0.5	2.48	359	358	-0.1
43153 SOUTH SOLON	097	1170	1159	1182	-0.2	34	433	437	455	0.2	2.65	344	341	-0.2
43154 STOUTSVILLE	045	2969	3072	3232	0.8	77	1038	1100	1181	1.4	2.79	863	897	0.9
43155 SUGAR GROVE	045	1714	1797	1897	1.1	84	648	697	751	1.7	2.58	511	537	1.2
43160 WASHINGTON COURT HOU	047	22056	22192	22317	0.1	51	8690	8943	9187	0.7	2.41	6032	6037	0.0
43162 WEST JEFFERSON	097	7095	7142	7314	0.2	52	2658	2743	2874	0.7	2.52	2005	2024	0.2
43164 WILLIAMSPORT	129	2322	2409	2488	0.9	78	822	868	913	1.3	2.75	662	685	0.8
43201 COLUMBUS	049	32358	31523	32190	-0.6	18	14596	14394	14890	-0.3	2.13	3400	3129	-1.9
43202 COLUMBUS	049	20490	20378	20924	-0.1	38	10266	10382	10815	0.3	1.96	3515	3263	-1.7
43203 COLUMBUS	049	10664	10800	11145	0.3	58	4818	4907	5120	0.4	2.13	2180	2085	-1.0
43204 COLUMBUS	049	40072	39987	41259	-0.1	42	16361	16639	17433	0.4	2.38	10000	9658	-0.8
43205 COLUMBUS	049	14157	13637	13877	-0.9	11	5695	5585	5781	-0.5	2.37	3044	2832	-1.7
43206 COLUMBUS	049	25197	24656	25210	-0.5	22	10823	10774	11183	-0.1	2.27	5676	5369	-1.3
43207 COLUMBUS	049	43998	44184	45721	0.1	49	16946	17279	18135	0.5	2.53	11715	11583	-0.3
43209 COLUMBUS	049	30023	29675	30416	-0.3	33	12483	12483	12957	0.0	2.27	7470	7148	-1.0
43210 COLUMBUS	049	10009	10115	10207	0.3	55	612	663	708	1.9	2.44	361	378	1.1
43211 COLUMBUS	049	24959	23860	24266	-1.1	6	9204	8959	9246	-0.6	2.66	6339	5947	-1.5
43212 COLUMBUS	049	17739	18075	18814	0.4	63	9503	9868	10425	0.9	1.81	3643	3522	-0.8
43213 COLUMBUS	049	29298	30428	32054	0.9	79	13101	13862	14835	1.3	2.18	7550	7532	-0.1
OHIO					0.3					0.7	2.44			0.0
UNITED STATES					1.2					1.3	2.58			1.1

ZIP CODE #	POST OFFICE NAME	RACE (%) White 2000	White 2004	Black 2000	Black 2004	Asian/Pacific 2000	Asian/Pacific 2004	% Hispanic Origin 2000	% Hispanic Origin 2004	2004 AGE DISTRIBUTION (%) 0-4	5-9	10-14	15-19	20-24	25-44	45-64	65-84	85+	18+	MEDIAN AGE 2004	% 2004 Males	% 2004 Females
43001	ALEXANDRIA	98.2	98.0	0.4	0.5	0.2	0.3	0.4	0.4	6.2	6.7	7.3	6.2	4.8	26.4	30.2	11.1	1.1	75.9	40.9	51.5	48.6
43002	AMLIN	76.5	76.2	5.9	4.8	17.7	19.1	0.0	0.0	9.5	9.5	9.5	4.8	9.5	42.9	14.3	0.0	0.0	71.4	28.8	42.9	57.1
43003	ASHLEY	97.7	97.4	0.8	0.9	0.2	0.2	0.6	0.7	6.9	7.1	8.2	6.7	5.9	28.1	25.3	10.5	1.2	73.4	36.8	49.6	50.4
43004	BLACKLICK	80.9	77.2	14.4	17.2	2.0	2.4	1.6	1.8	10.2	9.2	6.6	5.2	5.6	38.0	19.7	5.1	0.4	70.8	31.8	48.0	52.0
43006	BRINKHAVEN	98.9	99.0	0.2	0.2	0.0	0.0	0.6	0.8	7.2	7.4	7.7	7.2	5.9	26.7	24.7	11.9	1.3	73.4	36.7	51.0	49.0
43008	BUCKEYE LAKE	97.3	97.2	0.7	0.7	0.0	0.0	0.5	0.5	5.2	5.6	7.8	6.4	6.7	26.1	27.6	13.8	0.9	77.8	40.2	49.1	50.9
43009	CABLE	98.0	97.8	0.8	1.0	0.1	0.2	0.5	0.4	6.4	6.9	8.2	7.1	5.8	28.1	27.9	8.9	0.8	74.1	37.9	50.1	49.9
43011	CENTERBURG	98.3	98.0	0.4	0.4	0.1	0.2	0.5	0.6	6.8	7.7	8.4	7.1	5.0	28.4	25.5	9.7	1.5	72.4	37.4	50.6	49.4
43013	CROTON	98.2	97.9	0.3	0.4	0.2	0.3	0.5	0.7	7.7	8.0	7.9	6.1	5.0	29.8	25.0	9.9	0.7	72.6	36.4	51.8	48.2
43014	DANVILLE	98.7	98.6	0.2	0.2	0.1	0.1	0.6	0.7	8.4	8.2	8.1	7.2	6.6	25.4	23.2	11.3	1.6	70.9	35.0	50.3	49.7
43015	DELAWARE	94.1	93.6	3.1	3.3	0.8	1.0	1.0	1.1	7.3	7.0	6.5	7.4	8.2	28.9	23.7	9.7	1.3	75.4	34.9	48.6	51.4
43016	DUBLIN	85.3	81.7	2.4	2.6	9.9	13.1	2.1	2.3	8.1	7.3	6.9	5.6	6.3	39.1	20.8	5.1	0.9	74.2	33.1	50.3	49.7
43017	DUBLIN	88.9	86.7	2.3	2.5	7.0	8.8	1.8	1.9	7.3	8.1	8.9	7.6	5.4	30.1	26.5	5.2	0.9	70.8	35.1	49.7	50.3
43019	FREDERICKTOWN	98.4	98.3	0.2	0.2	0.1	0.1	0.5	0.5	6.9	7.1	7.8	6.9	6.5	26.6	25.9	11.1	1.2	74.0	37.3	50.4	49.6
43021	GALENA	97.1	96.7	0.9	1.0	0.6	0.8	0.6	0.7	7.0	8.0	8.3	6.3	4.6	25.7	30.5	8.8	0.7	72.6	40.2	49.8	50.2
43022	GAMBIER	96.2	95.7	1.4	1.5	0.8	1.0	1.1	1.2	3.4	3.6	4.9	24.2	24.0	14.7	17.4	7.0	0.8	85.4	22.9	46.7	53.3
43023	GRANVILLE	95.7	95.2	1.1	1.2	1.4	1.8	1.0	1.1	4.8	5.9	6.6	12.3	14.0	19.5	26.2	9.6	1.0	78.3	35.2	48.4	51.6
43025	HEBRON	97.5	97.2	0.5	0.5	0.4	0.4	0.7	0.8	7.7	7.4	7.1	6.5	5.5	28.1	26.0	10.9	0.9	73.6	37.5	48.6	51.5
43026	HILLIARD	91.3	89.4	2.5	2.9	3.5	4.7	2.1	2.3	9.3	8.9	8.5	6.6	6.2	36.8	18.2	4.9	0.6	69.1	31.8	49.3	50.8
43028	HOWARD	98.4	98.1	0.4	0.5	0.3	0.4	0.6	0.7	6.5	6.9	7.4	5.8	4.6	26.5	27.6	13.8	0.9	75.3	40.1	50.5	49.5
43029	IRWIN	98.2	98.0	0.4	0.6	0.4	0.4	0.6	0.6	7.9	7.7	7.7	7.7	7.4	28.8	23.9	8.1	1.0	72.8	33.8	49.5	50.5
43031	JOHNSTOWN	98.0	97.8	0.3	0.3	0.3	0.5	0.4	0.4	6.7	6.9	7.1	6.4	5.5	26.9	28.5	10.5	1.3	75.3	39.5	49.5	50.5
43035	LEWIS CENTER	90.4	89.0	4.2	4.6	3.0	3.9	1.7	1.8	11.3	9.8	7.3	4.4	6.6	40.0	16.8	3.5	0.3	68.7	30.8	49.6	50.4
43037	MARTINSBURG	98.6	98.8	0.0	0.0	0.0	0.0	0.5	0.4	6.5	6.9	8.9	7.7	5.2	26.6	26.2	10.9	1.2	73.0	38.1	50.0	50.0
43040	MARYSVILLE	93.7	93.2	4.0	4.2	0.7	1.0	0.9	1.0	8.1	7.9	7.4	6.2	6.0	33.8	21.9	7.5	1.2	72.8	34.3	46.8	53.2
43044	MECHANICSBURG	97.5	97.2	0.9	1.0	0.3	0.4	0.7	0.8	6.8	7.0	7.5	6.7	6.0	28.4	25.7	10.8	1.2	74.5	37.5	50.4	49.6
43045	MILFORD CENTER	97.9	97.7	0.3	0.3	0.3	0.3	0.3	0.3	7.1	7.2	7.4	7.1	6.2	28.6	25.8	9.6	1.1	73.9	36.9	50.3	49.7
43046	MILLERSPORT	98.4	98.3	0.2	0.2	0.1	0.1	0.5	0.5	6.2	6.3	5.8	5.9	4.5	25.9	31.0	13.1	1.3	78.0	42.3	48.9	51.1
43050	MOUNT VERNON	97.1	96.8	0.9	1.0	0.5	0.7	0.8	0.8	6.0	5.9	6.5	7.4	8.2	24.9	25.3	13.4	2.4	77.9	38.6	47.5	52.5
43054	NEW ALBANY	92.5	90.5	3.1	3.6	3.1	4.4	0.8	1.0	9.0	9.8	8.9	5.9	3.5	29.7	25.5	6.8	1.0	67.9	36.6	49.0	51.0
43055	NEWARK	95.0	94.5	2.6	2.7	0.6	0.7	0.8	0.8	7.1	6.8	6.9	6.6	6.7	27.1	24.5	12.3	2.1	75.2	37.4	48.0	52.0
43056	HEATH	96.7	96.3	1.4	1.5	0.5	0.7	0.7	0.8	6.1	6.3	7.1	6.8	6.3	27.3	26.2	12.6	1.3	76.3	39.1	48.8	51.2
43060	NORTH LEWISBURG	97.7	97.4	0.7	0.9	0.1	0.1	0.6	0.6	8.2	8.2	8.9	6.9	6.2	31.5	21.9	7.5	0.8	70.5	32.9	50.7	49.3
43061	OSTRANDER	97.7	97.5	1.0	1.1	0.2	0.2	0.5	0.5	5.6	7.0	8.3	8.0	4.2	28.6	29.3	8.2	0.9	73.5	39.7	50.1	49.9
43062	PATASKALA	96.2	95.8	1.8	1.9	0.5	0.6	0.8	0.9	7.7	7.7	7.4	6.4	5.4	29.0	27.0	8.5	0.8	73.2	37.1	49.6	50.4
43064	PLAIN CITY	97.4	97.0	1.1	1.2	0.3	0.4	0.8	0.9	6.8	7.1	8.0	7.2	6.0	27.9	26.4	9.6	1.0	73.7	37.3	50.0	50.0
43065	POWELL	92.5	91.2	2.1	2.2	4.0	5.1	1.2	1.4	8.9	9.8	9.1	7.1	4.3	30.6	25.2	4.6	0.3	67.4	35.3	49.8	50.2
43066	RADNOR	98.1	98.0	0.9	0.9	0.2	0.3	0.4	0.3	5.5	6.6	7.9	6.7	4.7	26.3	31.8	9.6	0.9	75.7	41.5	51.3	48.7
43067	RAYMOND	97.8	97.3	0.5	0.6	0.9	1.1	0.6	0.7	7.9	8.1	7.8	7.2	5.2	30.6	25.3	7.2	0.8	71.8	35.9	51.6	48.4
43068	REYNOLDSBURG	83.3	81.0	11.9	13.3	2.0	2.6	1.9	2.1	7.7	7.3	7.4	6.4	6.5	32.0	23.2	8.7	0.8	73.7	34.6	48.0	52.0
43071	SAINT LOUISVILLE	98.3	98.1	0.4	0.4	0.1	0.1	0.5	0.6	6.7	7.0	8.0	7.1	5.7	26.8	27.6	10.2	0.9	73.8	38.2	51.4	48.6
43072	SAINT PARIS	98.4	98.2	0.2	0.3	0.2	0.3	0.5	0.5	6.4	7.0	7.7	6.4	5.8	27.5	27.1	10.9	1.1	74.8	37.9	49.2	50.8
43074	SUNBURY	98.2	97.9	0.3	0.4	0.3	0.5	0.6	0.7	5.7	6.9	8.3	6.9	5.0	27.3	29.1	9.6	1.3	74.5	39.8	49.8	50.2
43076	THORNVILLE	98.0	97.8	0.2	0.3	0.1	0.1	0.3	0.4	5.7	6.1	7.5	6.6	4.4	27.1	29.5	12.1	1.0	76.5	40.9	50.7	49.3
43078	URBANA	93.8	93.3	3.8	4.0	0.3	0.4	0.9	1.0	6.6	6.4	6.7	6.4	6.7	26.2	26.6	12.2	2.2	76.4	38.9	48.3	51.7
43080	UTICA	98.5	98.4	0.2	0.2	0.1	0.2	0.6	0.6	6.3	6.7	8.4	7.1	6.0	27.0	25.5	11.8	1.4	74.2	38.2	49.7	50.3
43081	WESTERVILLE	91.1	89.2	4.6	5.3	2.4	3.3	1.3	1.5	6.6	6.6	7.0	7.1	7.6	30.3	25.9	7.8	1.1	75.7	35.3	48.1	51.9
43082	WESTERVILLE	93.3	92.3	3.0	3.2	2.1	2.7	1.1	1.2	7.9	8.7	9.0	6.7	4.9	28.7	26.6	6.9	0.7	70.0	37.1	49.2	50.8
43084	WOODSTOCK	97.5	97.3	0.8	1.0	0.0	0.0	0.1	0.1	6.6	7.1	8.2	6.9	5.5	25.5	27.1	11.1	2.0	73.9	37.9	50.7	49.3
43085	COLUMBUS	90.8	89.0	3.3	3.7	3.7	4.8	1.4	1.5	5.8	6.1	6.8	6.8	5.8	26.6	28.2	12.4	1.7	77.1	39.9	47.4	52.6
43102	AMANDA	98.5	98.4	0.2	0.2	0.1	0.1	0.6	0.6	7.1	7.4	7.8	6.4	5.3	28.9	26.2	10.0	1.0	73.7	37.3	50.3	49.7
43103	ASHVILLE	97.9	97.7	0.2	0.3	0.2	0.2	0.8	0.9	7.1	7.0	7.8	7.1	6.6	28.6	25.7	9.5	0.8	73.8	36.2	49.8	50.2
43105	BALTIMORE	98.3	98.1	0.3	0.3	0.2	0.2	0.7	0.8	6.2	6.7	7.5	6.6	5.6	26.7	28.1	11.2	1.4	75.5	39.4	49.7	50.3
43106	BLOOMINGBURG	95.2	95.2	2.7	2.8	0.1	0.1	2.2	2.2	7.9	7.4	7.2	7.4	7.4	28.6	24.9	8.2	1.0	72.9	34.9	50.8	49.2
43107	BREMEN	98.0	97.9	0.1	0.1	0.1	0.1	0.5	0.6	6.6	6.9	7.8	7.4	5.9	26.8	26.4	10.9	1.4	74.2	38.3	50.1	49.9
43110	CANAL WINCHESTER	87.3	84.5	9.0	11.0	0.9	1.2	1.4	1.7	8.8	7.9	7.6	6.5	6.7	32.6	21.6	7.4	1.0	71.7	32.5	47.8	52.2
43112	CARROLL	98.1	97.8	0.2	0.3	0.4	0.5	0.4	0.5	5.9	6.5	7.1	6.7	5.2	26.4	29.9	11.1	1.2	76.1	40.7	50.0	50.0
43113	CIRCLEVILLE	96.5	96.0	1.8	2.0	0.4	0.5	0.7	0.8	6.6	6.6	7.0	7.5	5.9	25.9	25.5	13.1	1.9	74.8	38.2	49.2	50.8
43115	CLARKSBURG	96.5	96.2	2.0	2.2	0.1	0.1	0.1	0.1	7.8	8.0	7.6	6.2	6.1	27.0	25.8	10.3	1.2	72.7	36.4	51.0	49.0
43116	COMMERCIAL POINT	98.5	98.6	0.0	0.0	0.3	0.3	0.6	0.6	6.0	6.6	8.0	7.4	5.1	29.1	27.4	9.7	0.6	74.6	38.7	50.0	50.0
43119	GALLOWAY	90.2	88.5	5.0	5.7	1.5	2.0	2.8	3.2	9.7	8.7	7.9	6.9	7.7	35.5	19.1	4.3	0.3	69.4	30.4	49.2	50.8
43123	GROVE CITY	94.4	93.3	2.9	3.3	1.0	1.4	1.1	1.2	7.7	7.6	7.7	6.7	6.0	30.3	24.0	9.1	0.9	72.9	35.5	48.9	51.1
43125	GROVEPORT	91.9	90.5	4.8	5.6	1.1	1.4	1.6	1.8	6.3	6.1	6.5	6.1	6.1	30.2	26.1	11.2	1.4	77.3	37.8	48.9	51.1
43128	JEFFERSONVILLE	93.6	93.5	4.0	4.1	0.1	0.1	0.4	0.5	7.2	7.4	7.5	6.2	6.1	27.2	25.6	11.6	1.2	74.1	37.1	49.7	50.3
43130	LANCASTER	96.1	95.9	2.1	2.1	0.5	0.6	0.7	0.8	6.7	6.5	6.5	6.1	6.9	28.0	24.7	12.7	2.0	76.7	37.7	50.2	49.9
43135	LAURELVILLE	98.3	98.2	0.4	0.4	0.1	0.1	0.4	0.5	6.8	7.1	7.7	6.5	6.0	28.0	26.7	10.3	1.0	74.4	37.4	50.5	49.5
43137	LOCKBOURNE	97.6	97.2	0.4	0.6	0.3	0.4	0.4	0.5	7.3	7.2	7.9	7.0	6.7	29.0	25.6	8.6	0.8	73.3	35.7	51.3	48.7
43138	LOGAN	97.9	97.8	0.5	0.5	0.1	0.1	0.5	0.5	6.9	6.8	6.8	6.5	6.7	26.3	25.2	12.9	1.8	75.7	38.2	48.6	51.4
43140	LONDON	86.9	85.9	10.7	11.4	0.6	0.7	0.7	0.7	5.7	5.8	6.2	6.8	7.3	33.3	24.0	9.5	1.3	78.4	36.7	57.5	42.5
43143	MOUNT STERLING	97.8	97.6	0.4	0.5	0.2	0.3	1.1	1.1	7.0	6.9	7.3	7.0	6.4	27.8	25.7	10.6	1.4	74.5	37.0	48.6	51.4
43145	NEW HOLLAND	97.4	97.4	0.5	0.5	0.1	0.1	1.0	1.0	6.0	6.5	7.5	6.2	5.0	28.3	27.3	12.0	1.4	76.1	39.0	49.8	50.3
43146	ORIENT	76.5	75.5	22.2	23.1	0.2	0.2	0.5	0.5	3.6	3.9	4.7	5.5	10.3	41.1	23.8	6.6	0.5	85.2	36.4	71.0	29.0
43147	PICKERINGTON	91.6	90.9	5.2	5.3	1.7	2.1	1.2	1.3	7.8	8.5	9.1	7.5	5.5	29.8	25.6	5.6	0.6	69.7	35.0	49.7	50.3
43148	PLEASANTVILLE	98.7	98.5	0.1	0.1	0.2	0.3	0.5	0.5	6.3	6.8	7.9	7.0	5.4	27.4	26.2	11.4	1.7	74.5	38.5	49.2	50.8
43149	ROCKBRIDGE	98.3	98.3	0.2	0.2	0.2	0.2	0.3	0.3	6.6	6.8	7.2	6.3	4.6	28.3	30.0	9.7	0.6	75.7	39.0	50.7	49.3
43150	RUSHVILLE	98.4	98.3	0.2	0.2	0.1	0.1	0.4	0.5	6.1	6.7	8.0	6.5	5.9	27.3	27.5	10.2	1.8	75.0	39.0	49.6	50.4
43152	SOUTH BLOOMINGVILLE	98.4	98.4	0.2	0.2	0.0	0.0	0.3	0.3	6.9	7.1	7.5	7.0	6.3	28.6	25.8	10.0	0.9	74.3	36.5	51.1	48.9
43153	SOUTH SOLON	98.0	97.8	1.0	1.2	0.3	0.4	0.4	0.4	6.1	6.4	7.4	7.1	6.5	27.2	26.6	11.2	1.6	75.8	38.9	50.0	50.0
43154	STOUTSVILLE	98.8	98.7	0.2	0.2	0.1	0.1	0.4	0.5	6.6	7.0	8.0	6.7	5.6	28.8	27.0	9.4	0.9	74.3	37.4	50.0	50.0
43155	SUGAR GROVE	99.1	99.0	0.1	0.1	0.1	0.1	0.4	0.4	5.6	6.5	8.3	7.0	5.4	27.5	28.2	10.6	1.1	75.4	39.0	50.4	49.6
43160	WASHINGTON COURT HOU	95.6	95.5	2.0	2.0	0.6	0.6	1.3	1.3	6.6	6.4	6.8	6.3	6.1	26.9	25.3	13.5	2.1	76.2	38.8	49.0	51.0
43162	WEST JEFFERSON	97.8	97.6	0.9	1.0	0.3	0.4	0.6	0.6	6.6	6.5	7.2	6.8	6.1	27.8	25.9	11.5	1.6	75.3	38.1	49.9	50.1
43164	WILLIAMSPORT	98.1	97.8	0.8	1.0	0.1	0.2	0.7	0.8	6.1	6.7	8.1	7.3	5.4	28.9	26.6	9.9	1.0	74.4	38.0	49.8	50.2
43201	COLUMBUS	69.6	66.7	21.1	22.3	5.3	6.8	2.7	2.9	4.0	3.0	2.8	9.5	43.0	26.2	8.8	2.5	0.3	88.6	23.6	55.3	44.7
43202	COLUMBUS	80.8	77.6	4.3	4.7	10.6	13.2	2.6	2.7	4.9	3.6	3.3	5.2	21.3	41.2	14.8	4.8	0.9	86.4	28.8	52.5	47.5
43203	COLUMBUS	9.7	8.5	84.6	85.8	0.8	0.9	1.2	1.1	7.9	8.4	9.4	8.4	6.2	23.7	21.1	12.7	2.3	69.5	33.7	44.8	55.2
43204	COLUMBUS	83.5	81.3	9.8	10.7	2.9	3.9	2.1	2.4	7.7	7.2	7.2	6.7	7.5	31.0	22.2	9.3	1.2	74.1	34.1	48.8	51.2
43205	COLUMBUS	14.3	12.8	81.6	83.1	0.5	0.6	1.4	1.4	7.8	8.3	9.5	8.3	6.6	28.5	21.6	8.5	1.0	69.2	32.3	48.5	51.5
43206	COLUMBUS	49.3	47.5	46.1	47.6	1.2	1.5	1.7	1.8	6.8	6.7	7.3	6.5	7.5	32.8	23.0	8.6	0.9	75.3	33.7	49.4	50.6
43207	COLUMBUS	71.6	70.3	24.0	24.9	1.2	1.5	1.4	1.5	7.4	7.2	7.7	6.8	6.5	28.1	23.2	12.2	0.9	73.5	35.8	48.3	51.7
43209	COLUMBUS	68.9	66.8	26.0	27.7	1.1	1.5	2.5	2.5	6.4	6.4	6.8	8.3	8.1	25.4	24.6	11.6	2.5	76.6	36.6	46.8	53.2
43210	COLUMBUS	73.2	69.2	10.3	11.3	11.7	14.5	2.4	2.6	1.5	0.9	0.3	62.6	21.6	10.5	1.6	0.8	0.1	96.7	18.8	50.4	49.6
43211	COLUMBUS	29.3	27.3	65.8	67.6	0.6	0.8	1.5	1.6	8.3	8.7	10.0	8.8	6.9	27.0	20.9	8.8	0.7	67.6	30.9	46.4	53.6
43212	COLUMBUS	93.0	91.6	2.1	2.5	2.7	3.5	1.8	1.9	4.4	3.6	4.4	5.0	11.0	39.5	21.4	8.6	2.1	84.8	33.9	48.3	51.7
43213	COLUMBUS	69.3	65.9	23.9	26.2	2.5	3.4	3.3	3.4	7.0	6.4	6.7	6.4	8.2	30.1	22.7	11.3	1.2	76.2	34.7	48.1	51.9
	OHIO	85.0	84.1	11.5	11.8	1.2	1.6	1.9	2.1	6.7	6.6	7.1	7.0	7.1	27.5	24.7	11.6	1.8	75.6	37.0	48.6	51.4
	UNITED STATES	75.1	73.6	12.3	12.5	3.8	4.2	12.5	14.1	6.9	6.7	7.2	7.0	7.3	28.6	23.8	10.8	1.7	75.1	36.0	49.1	50.9

ZIP CODE # POST OFFICE NAME	2004 Per Capita Income	2004 HH Income Base	2004 HOUSEHOLD INCOME DISTRIBUTION (%) Less than $25,000	$25,000 to $49,999	$50,000 to $99,999	$100,000 to $149,999	$150,000 or More	MEDIAN HOUSEHOLD INCOME 2004	2009	2004 National Centile	2004 State Centile	2004 Home Value Base	2004 HOME VALUE DISTRIBUTION (%) Less than $50,000	$50,000 to $89,999	$90,000 to $174,999	$175,000 to $399,999	$400,000 or More	2004 Median Home Value
43001 ALEXANDRIA	27544	682	9.7	26.0	40.6	17.3	6.5	64563	75498	88	91	617	0.7	3.7	42.0	44.9	8.8	185045
43002 AMLIN	27213	8	0.0	0.0	75.0	25.0	0.0	75000	117154	93	96	4	0.0	0.0	0.0	100.0	0.0	250000
43003 ASHLEY	21880	1293	17.6	31.1	41.2	7.7	2.3	50792	61397	73	66	1035	14.9	13.8	51.1	17.8	2.4	114500
43004 BLACKLICK	38105	4219	14.7	22.9	34.0	17.1	11.4	64160	75471	88	90	2997	0.3	13.2	39.2	34.4	13.0	170859
43006 BRINKHAVEN	16866	232	28.9	37.5	28.9	3.0	1.7	38259	42933	40	26	193	21.2	24.4	30.6	18.7	5.2	97727
43008 BUCKEYE LAKE	17931	506	36.8	32.8	24.5	4.0	2.0	33254	38964	22	14	333	28.8	34.2	27.0	7.2	2.7	75256
43009 CABLE	23001	658	9.3	29.8	46.7	10.6	3.7	58177	65094	83	83	595	7.1	8.2	60.8	18.7	5.2	127995
43011 CENTERBURG	23043	2293	16.7	27.7	39.7	12.9	3.0	54278	63252	79	76	1960	5.0	9.4	51.5	31.5	2.6	147709
43013 CROTON	23193	500	15.0	26.2	44.0	13.2	1.6	58800	67492	83	84	422	4.0	12.1	40.8	41.5	1.7	164643
43014 DANVILLE	15372	1240	32.1	33.8	28.6	4.3	1.3	35984	40891	31	20	989	10.6	26.9	45.1	14.8	2.6	101594
43015 DELAWARE	28744	16722	16.9	24.1	38.5	14.7	6.0	60229	74850	85	86	11982	7.0	6.5	39.9	41.5	5.1	169095
43016 DUBLIN	39626	9501	9.7	19.4	38.0	20.7	12.3	72223	88159	92	95	5149	6.0	1.7	24.3	63.8	4.3	202449
43017 DUBLIN	47406	13883	8.1	14.5	30.8	22.4	24.1	92780	113078	97	99	10013	0.8	2.6	22.5	54.2	19.8	262688
43019 FREDERICKTOWN	21909	3388	21.4	30.6	36.6	8.4	3.0	48287	54956	69	58	2819	8.7	18.9	54.5	16.3	1.7	113704
43021 GALENA	39613	2806	7.6	14.2	37.7	22.1	18.5	85060	105473	96	98	2608	1.4	1.2	17.7	60.7	19.0	273978
43022 GAMBIER	20030	878	21.5	25.7	37.8	11.3	3.6	52588	61206	76	72	644	3.4	14.9	44.1	34.5	3.1	141327
43023 GRANVILLE	33039	3922	10.1	19.7	35.5	20.2	14.5	76535	87575	94	97	3408	1.6	2.0	30.2	50.4	15.9	215598
43025 HEBRON	24571	2889	26.8	30.6	29.8	8.6	4.2	42647	50015	55	38	2234	24.6	15.4	34.0	21.4	4.7	105935
43026 HILLIARD	31937	20884	9.4	19.5	43.4	20.0	7.7	70615	84514	91	95	15215	0.9	6.8	50.1	40.0	2.2	163817
43028 HOWARD	24459	2454	14.2	32.1	41.0	9.0	3.8	52674	60769	76	72	2158	2.8	13.3	60.4	20.6	3.0	124071
43029 IRWIN	16310	120	16.7	27.5	37.5	14.2	4.2	56627	62674	81	80	91	4.4	11.0	49.5	34.1	1.1	148864
43031 JOHNSTOWN	26707	4037	15.8	24.8	42.3	12.7	4.5	59045	67515	84	84	3320	3.6	9.4	47.4	36.8	2.8	157017
43035 LEWIS CENTER	38420	6099	7.5	17.8	38.1	23.1	13.5	79918	99976	95	98	4329	4.4	0.7	12.5	67.1	15.4	268491
43037 MARTINSBURG	18100	84	22.6	32.1	39.3	4.8	1.2	45912	54032	64	49	72	2.8	12.5	51.4	31.9	1.4	139286
43040 MARYSVILLE	24061	10126	17.1	23.0	42.5	14.1	3.2	59440	67551	84	85	7823	10.0	5.6	45.1	36.8	2.5	159074
43044 MECHANICSBURG	22471	2104	23.6	24.4	38.3	11.0	2.7	51321	57889	74	68	1706	9.6	18.0	51.2	19.5	1.8	121222
43045 MILFORD CENTER	26674	577	15.1	23.1	38.8	18.0	5.0	62238	71205	86	89	488	4.5	17.4	47.1	26.8	4.1	132083
43046 MILLERSPORT	28794	1408	21.4	26.2	37.2	11.9	3.3	52174	61396	76	70	1151	3.4	12.1	44.5	35.2	4.9	152810
43050 MOUNT VERNON	21303	11028	30.6	31.9	28.1	6.5	3.0	39375	45311	44	28	7637	9.3	20.7	49.2	19.7	1.1	111357
43054 NEW ALBANY	62194	4140	6.9	12.7	29.4	20.5	30.5	101614	122713	98	99	3615	0.0	0.6	14.0	48.9	36.6	321313
43055 NEWARK	21724	24714	28.5	31.0	31.0	7.0	2.6	41712	49250	52	35	16240	7.3	25.3	53.8	12.1	1.5	107693
43056 HEATH	23846	6517	21.1	31.8	35.2	8.7	3.3	47655	55792	68	56	5064	9.9	11.6	58.6	17.9	2.0	122461
43060 NORTH LEWISBURG	22644	977	17.8	27.0	43.0	8.6	3.6	53620	61358	78	75	770	10.3	18.6	57.4	10.7	3.1	111087
43061 OSTRANDER	31531	1382	10.3	25.0	40.2	19.1	5.4	64978	78771	89	92	1263	1.7	12.4	27.6	49.7	8.5	198103
43062 PATASKALA	27502	8257	13.9	22.6	42.5	16.8	4.3	63683	74707	88	90	6969	6.2	7.4	47.4	35.4	3.6	159880
43064 PLAIN CITY	26158	4341	15.0	26.6	40.0	12.6	5.8	58028	66008	83	82	3534	14.3	4.5	37.3	38.0	6.0	164906
43065 POWELL	47904	10953	4.3	12.4	32.7	24.7	26.0	100814	123377	98	99	9598	0.6	1.6	24.5	50.0	23.3	264788
43066 RADNOR	41448	454	9.5	22.0	44.1	15.6	8.8	67168	82179	90	93	411	1.5	6.8	35.8	45.7	10.2	198558
43067 RAYMOND	23169	632	11.7	19.9	53.2	13.1	2.1	60420	69245	85	86	571	4.0	7.0	51.0	36.6	1.4	153045
43068 REYNOLDSBURG	27989	20292	14.3	27.1	41.3	13.9	3.4	58534	68408	83	83	13375	3.5	4.9	65.8	25.2	0.6	143002
43071 SAINT LOUISVILLE	19150	845	18.8	35.3	39.1	5.1	1.8	47582	55303	67	55	739	10.4	12.5	62.0	12.5	2.7	119760
43072 SAINT PARIS	22434	2387	19.5	31.4	40.1	6.5	2.6	49311	54884	71	60	1997	8.0	17.9	50.5	21.8	1.9	118400
43074 SUNBURY	29429	4027	11.0	18.7	46.4	17.5	6.5	69729	83751	91	94	3500	2.4	4.6	36.8	48.1	8.0	189646
43076 THORNVILLE	24038	3335	17.2	29.2	40.9	9.3	3.4	52958	60754	77	73	2891	7.9	14.1	48.1	26.4	3.6	134630
43078 URBANA	22854	8620	23.8	29.9	35.2	8.6	2.5	46693	53514	65	52	6281	10.0	18.6	49.7	20.4	1.4	116772
43080 UTICA	20789	2134	23.6	30.8	34.7	8.6	2.3	46359	53559	65	50	1722	11.2	18.2	46.2	22.0	2.4	114343
43081 WESTERVILLE	33758	21355	11.2	21.8	38.6	18.9	9.5	68267	82502	90	94	14696	0.7	5.6	48.4	43.4	2.0	167242
43082 WESTERVILLE	45145	7983	6.0	10.1	29.5	28.6	25.8	105501	128103	99	100	7531	4.0	0.4	10.0	67.4	18.2	278739
43084 WOODSTOCK	24168	269	13.0	23.1	54.3	7.1	2.6	55057	62703	80	78	231	7.4	17.8	51.1	19.5	4.3	123476
43085 COLUMBUS	39423	9545	10.6	19.8	37.5	18.7	13.3	71326	86081	92	95	7375	0.7	8.5	36.2	50.1	4.5	183445
43102 AMANDA	20511	1327	18.3	34.4	37.2	8.4	1.7	47734	56188	68	56	1123	4.5	13.5	50.9	26.5	4.5	126239
43103 ASHVILLE	21904	3809	21.3	27.5	39.8	9.4	2.0	50933	58046	74	66	2919	22.5	9.8	40.2	25.7	1.9	128470
43105 BALTIMORE	26008	3183	17.9	25.4	38.6	13.9	4.2	57067	66997	82	81	2629	1.6	9.7	49.2	35.9	3.6	157847
43106 BLOOMINGBURG	16024	612	26.5	40.0	29.4	3.4	0.7	40302	45329	47	31	455	15.8	30.8	41.1	8.1	4.2	92719
43107 BREMEN	20714	1163	20.6	30.4	39.1	8.3	1.5	49048	57526	70	60	984	2.9	15.4	61.9	19.5	0.4	125000
43110 CANAL WINCHESTER	26307	8972	15.6	24.4	39.3	16.0	4.8	60054	69443	84	86	6063	0.4	3.1	56.6	36.5	3.5	163812
43112 CARROLL	28023	1568	9.6	23.7	43.6	16.1	7.0	65521	77888	89	92	1405	4.6	5.9	44.1	41.3	4.1	168601
43113 CIRCLEVILLE	22187	9299	26.1	28.1	33.2	9.8	2.8	46006	52648	64	49	6708	9.4	13.5	53.0	22.7	1.5	122740
43115 CLARKSBURG	18414	511	26.8	31.9	34.3	5.3	1.8	44470	50337	60	44	412	12.4	31.3	44.2	10.2	1.9	95000
43116 COMMERCIAL POINT	26027	129	14.0	22.5	45.7	12.4	5.4	64178	75737	88	91	113	14.2	6.2	38.1	37.2	4.4	162500
43119 GALLOWAY	25810	9675	12.9	27.6	40.3	14.8	4.4	59475	69437	84	85	6336	1.0	5.9	65.7	25.7	1.7	142471
43123 GROVE CITY	27223	18887	13.2	24.2	41.7	16.0	4.8	62106	74366	86	89	14897	4.0	6.2	59.5	28.2	2.1	143110
43125 GROVEPORT	24510	4466	19.8	27.7	39.3	11.8	1.4	51913	61271	75	70	3250	6.0	8.8	63.5	21.5	0.3	128867
43128 JEFFERSONVILLE	18847	864	28.2	30.6	34.6	5.9	0.7	42203	48974	54	36	625	8.8	29.6	50.7	7.4	3.5	98529
43130 LANCASTER	22596	22684	25.4	31.9	31.7	7.8	3.2	43349	51387	57	40	16229	6.9	15.7	53.9	21.3	2.2	124349
43135 LAURELVILLE	19134	1929	28.7	32.4	31.0	6.3	1.6	40294	46299	47	31	1566	12.5	23.4	46.6	16.2	1.4	106796
43137 LOCKBOURNE	24343	908	13.2	31.9	40.0	11.9	3.0	53907	62399	78	75	711	29.1	9.6	39.9	19.6	1.8	118981
43138 LOGAN	19698	7319	32.9	30.9	28.5	5.6	2.2	38153	43391	40	26	5433	17.0	23.5	46.3	11.8	1.4	98877
43140 LONDON	21904	7386	21.8	28.1	36.2	10.5	3.3	50022	57186	72	63	5408	9.2	13.7	48.6	25.6	2.9	123297
43143 MOUNT STERLING	21730	2156	18.5	33.9	37.2	8.4	2.1	48018	55671	68	57	1648	9.4	16.8	49.8	20.9	3.1	116000
43145 NEW HOLLAND	20858	696	21.4	34.5	35.9	6.5	1.7	45883	52333	64	48	580	13.6	25.3	45.2	12.2	3.6	104060
43146 ORIENT	20366	2907	14.2	27.1	38.9	14.8	5.0	58925	67538	83	84	2545	16.0	7.5	43.5	30.6	2.4	145375
43147 PICKERINGTON	32057	10979	5.6	16.5	39.8	27.4	10.8	82141	98273	96	98	9577	0.4	0.5	42.1	54.8	2.3	185444
43148 PLEASANTVILLE	20451	797	26.9	29.6	31.9	8.9	2.8	42710	50840	55	38	646	4.5	17.0	44.0	31.6	2.9	148182
43149 ROCKBRIDGE	21503	1065	24.6	35.1	32.1	5.5	2.6	44756	50078	61	45	913	12.9	14.8	54.3	15.8	2.2	115846
43150 RUSHVILLE	22118	637	16.0	32.7	38.2	10.5	2.7	51436	60071	75	69	555	5.1	15.3	52.8	25.1	1.8	137064
43152 SOUTH BLOOMINGVILLE	18620	480	29.0	34.4	30.6	5.0	1.0	38401	44052	41	26	399	23.1	22.6	38.4	13.3	2.8	96034
43153 SOUTH SOLON	22255	437	13.7	33.4	42.3	8.2	2.3	51503	58111	75	69	346	13.6	20.2	44.8	20.5	0.9	109231
43154 STOUTSVILLE	23855	1100	15.7	27.7	43.3	10.1	3.2	55307	63624	80	78	941	5.2	11.8	51.5	27.2	4.3	137286
43155 SUGAR GROVE	23420	697	22.4	31.7	34.0	8.5	3.4	47289	54895	67	54	590	8.8	13.2	55.8	19.8	2.4	116612
43160 WASHINGTON COURT HOU	22077	8943	26.2	34.9	30.5	5.4	3.1	40543	46465	48	31	6228	7.9	22.9	54.3	13.5	1.5	107013
43162 WEST JEFFERSON	25993	2743	16.9	31.0	37.8	9.1	5.2	51838	60000	75	70	2203	9.9	11.3	57.8	17.8	3.3	116447
43164 WILLIAMSPORT	20339	868	20.6	29.8	38.3	9.9	1.4	49467	55781	71	61	702	6.1	17.2	50.4	21.8	4.4	122692
43201 COLUMBUS	16178	14394	55.9	26.4	12.8	3.1	1.8	21404	24584	2	3	2130	9.9	26.2	36.9	24.9	2.2	114478
43202 COLUMBUS	23736	10382	35.2	30.8	24.9	7.2	2.0	36052	42572	32	20	3241	2.2	11.1	67.6	18.3	0.8	132822
43203 COLUMBUS	14364	4907	59.8	24.2	11.7	2.8	1.6	18662	22393	1	2	1444	21.5	37.5	31.5	8.7	0.9	80584
43204 COLUMBUS	21578	16639	26.6	32.1	32.6	6.6	2.2	42505	51063	55	37	9910	6.1	34.4	54.6	4.5	0.5	96973
43205 COLUMBUS	17240	5585	51.2	23.7	17.8	3.9	3.4	24143	28950	4	3	2115	9.3	38.2	37.2	13.4	2.0	92711
43206 COLUMBUS	25019	10774	29.7	33.0	26.1	6.5	4.8	39198	46635	43	27	5423	10.5	45.0	28.1	13.3	3.2	84563
43207 COLUMBUS	19131	17279	31.0	30.7	31.2	5.6	1.6	40058	48003	46	30	11606	10.6	40.4	45.8	2.9	0.2	89206
43209 COLUMBUS	34233	12483	24.7	24.3	28.9	11.9	10.3	51088	60911	74	67	7041	2.0	9.1	42.5	34.7	11.8	167916
43210 COLUMBUS	13452	663	43.9	26.2	25.0	3.8	1.1	28585	33612	10	6	118	0.0	0.0	74.6	25.4	0.0	159574
43211 COLUMBUS	14869	8959	42.6	34.6	18.6	2.8	1.3	29432	34331	11	7	4922	20.1	66.2	12.7	0.7	0.3	66972
43212 COLUMBUS	36166	9868	22.4	31.6	28.3	10.8	6.9	45931	55932	64	49	4041	0.3	6.4	44.8	41.0	7.5	172139
43213 COLUMBUS	24538	13862	27.4	33.9	28.7	6.2	3.7	40020	47830	46	30	6061	5.5	32.2	44.0	16.7	1.7	100553
OHIO	25510		24.6	28.1	32.2	10.1	5.0	47354	56168				9.2	18.6	47.0	22.1	3.1	121192
UNITED STATES	25866		24.7	27.1	30.8	10.9	6.5	48124	56710				10.9	15.0	33.7	30.1	10.4	145905

#	POST OFFICE NAME	FINANCIAL SERVICES: Auto Loan	Home Loan	Invest-ments	Retire-ment Plans	THE HOME: Home Improvements: Home Repair	Lawn & Garden	Furnishings: Comput-ers & Hard-ware	Major Appli-ances	TV, Radio, Sound Equip-ment	Furni-ture	ENTERTAINMENT: Dine out/ Carry out	Sports Equip-ment	Fees & Tickets	Toys & Games	Travel	Cable TV	PERSONAL: Apparel & Services	Auto Repairs	Health Insur-ance	Pets & Supplies
43001	ALEXANDRIA	98	121	128	121	119	118	108	108	100	108	126	126	115	134	111	98	126	104	97	119
43002	AMLIN	105	89	105	100	86	92	104	98	102	106	131	120	99	120	96	95	127	106	88	110
43003	ASHLEY	93	83	63	79	87	94	77	85	81	77	99	101	75	101	79	83	94	83	92	109
43004	BLACKLICK	130	131	146	140	126	130	133	128	127	136	162	153	134	156	128	119	159	132	114	142
43006	BRINKHAVEN	81	59	33	53	66	74	57	68	66	57	78	81	50	75	58	70	72	67	81	94
43008	BUCKEYE LAKE	57	60	63	57	61	67	61	60	63	58	78	67	63	83	62	65	75	59	64	66
43009	CABLE	105	93	71	88	98	105	86	95	91	86	111	114	84	113	89	94	106	93	103	123
43011	CENTERBURG	99	96	82	93	98	103	89	95	90	89	111	112	89	114	90	90	107	92	96	116
43013	CROTON	96	96	84	93	99	103	87	93	88	87	109	110	89	113	90	89	105	90	95	114
43014	DANVILLE	69	60	46	59	63	70	59	64	63	58	76	75	57	76	59	64	72	63	69	79
43015	DELAWARE	103	108	108	108	106	109	104	104	101	104	126	122	105	127	103	98	123	103	98	118
43016	DUBLIN	135	135	144	144	130	132	136	132	130	140	165	158	136	159	130	122	161	135	117	147
43017	DUBLIN	175	194	212	204	188	190	185	180	172	189	219	211	192	219	182	164	217	179	159	198
43019	FREDERICKTOWN	96	82	61	78	87	95	78	87	84	78	102	102	75	102	80	86	96	85	95	111
43021	GALENA	148	178	186	180	173	172	159	159	147	161	186	185	169	193	161	142	186	153	141	175
43022	GAMBIER	88	88	88	87	90	94	84	88	85	84	105	105	84	107	86	85	102	87	88	105
43023	GRANVILLE	129	153	164	154	151	154	139	139	131	139	164	161	147	170	142	128	163	135	129	155
43025	HEBRON	88	84	76	83	86	93	83	86	85	83	104	99	82	104	83	85	100	85	88	100
43026	HILLIARD	120	133	135	139	128	126	124	122	114	127	145	143	127	146	121	108	144	120	106	133
43028	HOWARD	101	89	68	85	94	101	83	92	88	83	107	109	81	109	85	90	102	89	100	118
43029	IRWIN	104	93	71	88	98	105	86	95	91	86	111	113	84	113	88	93	105	93	103	123
43031	JOHNSTOWN	100	104	99	103	106	109	98	101	97	97	119	119	98	123	99	96	116	99	100	119
43035	LEWIS CENTER	141	144	151	151	139	142	142	139	135	145	172	164	143	169	137	129	169	140	125	156
43037	MARTINSBURG	86	76	58	72	81	86	70	78	75	70	91	93	69	93	73	77	86	76	85	101
43040	MARYSVILLE	89	89	79	88	89	92	84	87	83	84	103	102	83	103	83	81	99	85	85	101
43044	MECHANICSBURG	93	82	63	79	87	94	77	85	82	77	100	101	76	101	79	84	95	83	92	108
43045	MILFORD CENTER	113	100	77	95	106	114	93	103	99	93	120	122	91	123	96	101	114	100	111	132
43046	MILLERSPORT	104	95	78	90	100	108	89	98	94	89	114	115	88	117	92	97	109	96	106	123
43050	MOUNT VERNON	76	71	65	68	73	81	71	74	74	69	91	85	70	91	72	76	86	73	80	88
43054	NEW ALBANY	224	264	318	268	261	274	247	245	233	248	293	283	263	298	253	229	291	241	229	268
43055	NEWARK	71	72	75	70	72	78	73	72	73	71	91	84	73	92	73	73	88	73	73	81
43056	HEATH	87	86	80	84	88	94	83	87	84	82	104	101	83	106	84	85	100	85	89	101
43060	NORTH LEWISBURG	95	82	64	81	86	96	82	88	87	81	105	102	79	105	82	88	99	87	95	107
43061	OSTRANDER	123	127	116	124	130	134	115	122	115	115	142	144	118	148	119	115	138	118	121	146
43062	PATASKALA	103	113	110	112	112	114	104	106	101	104	125	125	107	130	105	98	123	104	100	121
43064	PLAIN CITY	106	103	88	101	105	111	97	103	98	97	120	120	96	122	98	98	116	100	104	123
43065	POWELL	188	216	235	227	207	206	199	194	184	205	234	227	209	239	197	175	233	190	169	213
43066	RADNOR	142	176	187	176	173	170	157	156	145	156	183	183	167	195	161	141	183	151	140	173
43067	RAYMOND	105	95	74	91	100	106	88	97	92	88	113	115	86	115	90	94	107	94	103	123
43068	REYNOLDSBURG	94	102	109	105	99	101	99	97	94	100	119	114	101	120	97	90	117	97	88	107
43071	SAINT LOUISVILLE	86	77	59	73	80	86	71	78	75	71	91	93	69	93	73	77	87	77	84	100
43072	SAINT PARIS	92	81	62	77	85	92	76	84	81	76	99	99	75	100	78	83	93	82	91	106
43074	SUNBURY	104	127	135	126	125	125	115	114	108	114	135	133	122	145	117	106	135	110	105	126
43076	THORNVILLE	97	87	69	83	92	100	81	90	86	81	104	107	79	106	84	88	99	88	98	116
43078	URBANA	84	75	64	72	79	87	75	80	79	74	97	93	73	97	76	81	92	79	87	97
43080	UTICA	87	79	64	74	83	90	74	81	79	73	96	95	73	99	76	81	91	79	88	102
43081	WESTERVILLE	116	123	136	128	120	123	122	119	117	123	148	141	124	147	120	112	145	120	108	131
43082	WESTERVILLE	181	213	221	219	206	207	191	189	177	195	224	219	204	228	192	170	224	184	168	210
43084	WOODSTOCK	118	105	80	99	111	119	97	107	103	97	125	128	95	128	100	105	119	104	116	138
43085	COLUMBUS	128	139	158	144	136	141	136	133	129	138	164	156	140	163	135	125	162	134	122	147
43102	AMANDA	91	79	59	75	84	91	74	82	79	74	96	98	72	97	76	81	91	80	90	107
43103	ASHVILLE	88	82	68	79	84	89	78	84	80	78	98	99	76	98	79	80	94	83	86	102
43105	BALTIMORE	95	102	99	99	103	108	96	98	95	94	118	114	98	122	98	96	114	96	98	113
43106	BLOOMINGBURG	69	60	46	59	63	70	60	64	63	59	77	75	58	77	60	65	72	63	70	78
43107	BREMEN	90	79	59	75	84	90	73	81	78	73	95	97	71	96	75	80	90	79	89	106
43110	CANAL WINCHESTER	96	98	106	103	95	98	99	97	95	100	120	115	99	119	96	91	118	98	88	108
43112	CARROLL	113	120	112	118	121	124	109	114	107	109	133	134	112	138	112	106	130	111	111	135
43113	CIRCLEVILLE	83	76	66	73	79	87	76	80	80	74	97	92	74	97	76	82	92	79	87	95
43115	CLARKSBURG	80	71	54	68	75	80	66	73	70	66	85	87	64	87	68	71	81	71	79	94
43116	COMMERCIAL POINT	113	101	77	96	106	114	93	103	99	93	120	123	91	123	96	101	114	100	112	133
43119	GALLOWAY	100	100	105	105	96	98	101	98	96	103	122	118	100	119	97	91	120	100	88	110
43123	GROVE CITY	98	108	112	109	106	107	103	102	99	104	124	120	106	127	103	95	122	101	94	113
43125	GROVEPORT	79	87	92	87	86	88	84	83	81	83	101	98	85	103	84	78	99	83	78	92
43128	JEFFERSONVILLE	76	65	51	64	69	76	65	70	69	64	83	81	62	83	65	70	78	69	76	86
43130	LANCASTER	76	76	75	74	77	83	75	77	76	74	94	89	76	97	76	77	91	76	79	88
43135	LAURELVILLE	83	67	45	63	72	80	65	73	71	65	86	86	60	85	65	74	80	72	83	95
43137	LOCKBOURNE	101	93	76	90	95	100	88	94	89	89	110	110	85	108	88	89	106	93	96	114
43138	LOGAN	76	65	50	60	69	77	64	70	70	63	84	82	61	85	65	73	79	69	79	88
43140	LONDON	80	79	77	78	79	85	79	80	79	78	98	93	78	99	79	79	95	80	80	92
43143	MOUNT STERLING	86	78	64	76	82	89	76	81	79	75	97	95	75	98	77	81	92	80	86	99
43145	NEW HOLLAND	75	74	70	70	77	84	72	74	75	70	92	85	74	98	74	77	88	72	80	88
43146	ORIENT	93	90	77	87	93	98	83	89	85	82	104	105	83	107	85	86	100	86	92	110
43147	PICKERINGTON	128	153	158	158	148	146	137	135	125	140	159	158	145	164	137	120	159	131	118	149
43148	PLEASANTVILLE	88	74	54	70	79	88	73	80	79	71	95	94	69	94	74	82	89	79	91	101
43149	ROCKBRIDGE	91	78	57	73	83	90	73	82	78	73	95	97	70	96	75	81	90	80	90	107
43150	RUSHVILLE	97	86	65	82	91	97	79	88	84	79	103	105	78	105	82	86	98	86	95	114
43152	SOUTH BLOOMINGVILLE	82	62	37	56	68	76	58	69	67	59	80	83	53	78	60	70	74	68	81	95
43153	SOUTH SOLON	93	81	62	79	85	94	80	86	84	79	102	100	77	103	80	86	97	84	93	106
43154	STOUTSVILLE	104	96	77	92	101	107	89	97	93	89	113	115	88	116	91	95	108	94	103	123
43155	SUGAR GROVE	97	85	64	81	91	98	79	89	85	79	103	105	77	104	82	87	97	86	97	115
43160	WASHINGTON COURT HOU	81	73	62	69	76	84	73	77	78	71	94	89	71	96	74	80	90	76	85	93
43162	WEST JEFFERSON	92	93	88	90	95	103	89	92	92	88	113	107	91	118	91	93	109	90	96	108
43164	WILLIAMSPORT	88	79	63	76	83	90	75	82	79	75	96	96	74	98	77	81	92	80	87	102
43201	COLUMBUS	48	34	47	37	33	39	55	44	54	49	68	57	48	63	47	50	65	51	42	50
43202	COLUMBUS	63	53	69	58	52	57	72	61	70	66	88	78	66	83	64	64	85	68	56	68
43203	COLUMBUS	43	36	45	34	36	42	42	41	46	42	57	46	41	54	41	48	55	43	45	47
43204	COLUMBUS	69	70	80	71	69	74	74	71	73	72	92	83	74	94	73	72	90	72	69	78
43205	COLUMBUS	57	49	59	46	48	57	56	55	61	57	76	61	55	72	54	64	74	57	59	63
43206	COLUMBUS	76	71	95	72	69	78	80	75	83	80	105	88	81	104	78	84	102	79	76	85
43207	COLUMBUS	69	67	67	64	67	73	67	68	69	67	86	78	67	85	67	70	83	68	71	79
43209	COLUMBUS	105	110	135	111	108	116	115	110	113	114	142	129	117	142	114	111	140	113	105	121
43210	COLUMBUS	53	44	58	50	44	47	61	53	58	56	73	69	55	68	55	53	71	60	47	58
43211	COLUMBUS	54	49	58	47	48	55	54	53	58	55	73	60	55	71	53	60	70	54	56	60
43212	COLUMBUS	87	86	114	92	84	89	97	89	94	95	119	110	96	118	93	90	117	95	82	99
43213	COLUMBUS	73	72	81	73	71	77	77	74	76	75	96	87	77	96	75	75	93	76	72	82
	OHIO	89	88	90	87	88	95	88	89	89	87	110	103	88	111	88	89	107	89	90	102
	UNITED STATES	100	100	100	100	100	100	100	100	100	100	100	100	100	100	100	100	100	100	100	100

OHIO

POPULATION CHANGE

A 43214-43521

# POST OFFICE NAME	COUNTY FIPS CODE	POPULATION 2000	2004	2009	2000-2004 ANNUAL RATE % Rate	State Centile	HOUSEHOLDS 2000	2004	2009	% Annual Rate 2000-2004	2004 Average HH Size	FAMILIES 2000	2004	% Annual Rate 2000-2004
43214 COLUMBUS	049	25581	25541	26314	0.0	43	12405	12597	13184	0.4	1.97	6169	5906	-1.0
43215 COLUMBUS	049	10286	10321	10616	0.1	48	5863	6018	6308	0.6	1.49	1119	1041	-1.7
43217 COLUMBUS	049	2553	2517	2573	-0.3	30	797	803	835	0.2	3.13	594	580	-0.6
43219 COLUMBUS	049	20410	22974	25400	2.8	96	7935	9075	10182	3.2	2.46	5188	5774	2.6
43220 COLUMBUS	049	24129	23666	24206	-0.5	24	11657	11584	12007	-0.2	2.03	6047	5740	-1.2
43221 COLUMBUS	049	29798	30617	32065	0.6	71	12354	12808	13549	0.9	2.37	8093	8085	0.0
43222 COLUMBUS	049	5991	5893	6061	-0.4	27	2095	2106	2204	0.1	2.70	1197	1156	-0.8
43223 COLUMBUS	049	27465	27463	28272	0.0	45	10162	10312	10772	0.4	2.53	6563	6414	-0.5
43224 COLUMBUS	049	41150	41254	42453	0.1	47	17407	17639	18361	0.3	2.33	10274	9909	-0.9
43227 COLUMBUS	049	23001	22889	23612	-0.1	39	9743	9825	10261	0.2	2.33	6028	5810	-0.9
43228 COLUMBUS	049	45799	51129	55670	2.6	95	19003	21547	23777	3.0	2.36	11703	12689	1.9
43229 COLUMBUS	049	45791	47460	49789	0.9	78	20438	21497	22862	1.2	2.20	11286	11291	0.0
43230 COLUMBUS	049	48798	51181	53853	1.1	84	19096	20453	21892	1.6	2.49	12988	13343	0.6
43231 COLUMBUS	049	16764	18180	19525	1.9	93	7090	7761	8429	2.2	2.30	4207	4424	1.2
43232 COLUMBUS	049	40570	41404	43040	0.5	65	17125	17798	18777	0.9	2.31	10091	10018	-0.2
43235 COLUMBUS	049	37824	38738	40372	0.6	69	16508	17310	18361	1.1	2.22	9549	9495	-0.1
43240 COLUMBUS	041	1102	1429	1901	6.3	100	597	800	1091	7.1	1.79	311	396	5.9
43302 MARION	101	54700	54032	53341	-0.3	32	20285	20458	20592	0.2	2.42	13914	13638	-0.5
43310 BELLE CENTER	065	2945	3177	3348	1.8	92	1144	1266	1363	2.4	2.50	856	922	1.8
43311 BELLEFONTAINE	091	19122	19469	20185	0.4	62	7436	7713	8142	0.9	2.50	5149	5196	0.2
43314 CALEDONIA	101	2946	3062	3096	0.9	80	1123	1197	1237	1.5	2.53	847	880	0.9
43315 CARDINGTON	117	6275	6471	6603	0.7	74	2318	2450	2547	1.3	2.63	1732	1787	0.7
43316 CAREY	175	6212	6198	6238	-0.1	42	2354	2411	2487	0.6	2.53	1675	1667	-0.1
43318 DE GRAFF	091	3704	3749	3856	0.3	57	1338	1378	1442	0.7	2.72	1029	1036	0.2
43319 EAST LIBERTY	091	919	969	1017	1.3	86	341	368	393	1.8	2.63	276	292	1.3
43320 EDISON	117	1475	1446	1447	-0.5	23	550	552	563	0.1	2.61	401	392	-0.5
43321 FULTON	117	306	340	360	2.5	95	109	124	135	3.1	2.68	87	97	2.6
43323 HARPSTER	175	784	783	789	0.0	43	295	303	313	0.6	2.58	236	237	0.1
43324 HUNTSVILLE	091	2832	2927	3060	0.8	76	1138	1213	1298	1.5	2.38	840	868	0.8
43326 KENTON	065	13968	13736	13530	-0.4	27	5500	5528	5551	0.1	2.43	3760	3659	-0.6
43331 LAKEVIEW	091	5420	5759	6083	1.4	88	2410	2611	2810	1.9	2.20	1560	1634	1.1
43332 LA RUE	101	2161	2082	2032	-0.9	11	799	785	781	-0.4	2.65	606	580	-1.0
43333 LEWISTOWN	091	783	770	787	-0.4	27	280	282	295	0.2	2.60	212	208	-0.5
43334 MARENGO	117	5617	5793	5955	0.7	74	2015	2134	2239	1.4	2.70	1606	1667	0.9
43335 MARTEL	101	116	112	110	-0.8	12	49	49	49	0.0	2.29	37	36	-0.6
43337 MORRAL	101	1113	1086	1065	-0.6	19	408	409	412	0.1	2.66	326	321	-0.4
43338 MOUNT GILEAD	117	8838	8947	9108	0.3	57	3349	3459	3581	0.8	2.51	2496	2525	0.3
43340 MOUNT VICTORY	065	1496	1477	1465	-0.3	31	544	548	554	0.2	2.70	414	407	-0.4
43341 NEW BLOOMINGTON	101	1261	1221	1193	-0.8	13	432	427	425	-0.3	2.86	346	335	-0.8
43342 PROSPECT	101	3299	3375	3393	0.5	67	1218	1271	1302	1.0	2.66	963	983	0.5
43343 QUINCY	091	1523	1517	1552	-0.1	41	555	565	590	0.4	2.68	437	435	-0.1
43344 RICHWOOD	159	5365	5615	6071	1.1	83	1970	2093	2290	1.4	2.68	1498	1549	0.8
43345 RIDGEWAY	065	1069	1169	1230	2.1	94	339	379	408	2.7	3.08	287	316	2.3
43346 ROUNDHEAD	065	167	197	212	4.0	98	65	79	86	4.7	2.49	52	61	3.8
43347 RUSHSYLVANIA	091	1545	1697	1818	2.2	94	550	616	671	2.7	2.75	440	481	2.1
43348 RUSSELLS POINT	091	2160	2211	2310	0.6	68	943	985	1048	1.0	2.24	577	582	0.2
43351 UPPER SANDUSKY	175	10281	10445	10611	0.4	61	4058	4214	4374	0.9	2.40	2731	2754	0.2
43356 WALDO	101	997	969	968	-0.7	16	383	380	387	-0.2	2.55	304	294	-0.8
43357 WEST LIBERTY	091	4254	4374	4529	0.7	72	1511	1580	1667	1.1	2.60	1132	1155	0.5
43358 WEST MANSFIELD	159	2184	2274	2420	1.0	81	803	851	920	1.4	2.67	635	659	0.9
43359 WHARTON	175	886	915	935	0.8	75	323	341	356	1.3	2.68	261	270	0.8
43360 ZANESFIELD	091	1676	1894	2062	2.9	96	646	745	826	3.4	2.54	499	562	2.8
43402 BOWLING GREEN	173	36270	37519	38877	0.8	77	12601	13485	14416	1.6	2.27	6337	6534	0.7
43403 BOWLING GREEN	173	125	124	124	-0.2	36	48	45	46	-1.5	2.56	4	0	-100.0
43406 BRADNER	173	1931	1954	1996	0.3	57	723	750	785	0.9	2.60	533	538	0.2
43407 BURGOON	143	610	633	642	0.9	78	205	218	226	1.5	2.90	176	185	1.2
43410 CLYDE	143	9675	9613	9553	-0.2	37	3651	3726	3794	0.5	2.55	2687	2674	-0.1
43412 CURTICE	095	4525	4808	4925	1.4	88	1625	1763	1845	1.9	2.69	1299	1383	1.5
43413 CYGNET	173	1769	1825	1892	0.7	74	641	677	717	1.3	2.69	514	531	0.8
43416 ELMORE	123	2889	2920	2946	0.3	55	1131	1162	1193	0.6	2.51	869	874	0.1
43420 FREMONT	143	32100	31774	31440	-0.3	32	12593	12734	12912	0.3	2.44	8669	8516	-0.4
43430 GENOA	123	4879	4838	4876	-0.2	35	1843	1876	1937	0.4	2.53	1362	1354	-0.1
43431 GIBSONBURG	143	4504	4450	4408	-0.3	32	1670	1689	1711	0.3	2.58	1229	1211	-0.4
43432 GRAYTOWN	123	1263	1256	1260	-0.1	38	441	448	459	0.4	2.80	359	358	-0.1
43435 HELENA	143	1594	1618	1625	0.4	60	575	599	616	1.0	2.66	463	473	0.5
43436 ISLE SAINT GEORGE	123	32	32	33	0.0	45	13	13	14	0.0	2.46	8	8	0.2
43438 KELLEYS ISLAND	043	367	375	376	0.5	66	183	192	197	1.1	1.94	113	114	0.2
43440 LAKESIDE MARBLEHEAD	123	4338	4444	4521	0.6	69	1967	2063	2149	1.1	2.12	1322	1345	0.4
43442 LINDSEY	143	1184	1201	1204	0.3	60	444	463	476	1.0	2.57	346	353	0.5
43443 LUCKEY	173	1702	1764	1828	0.9	78	615	650	688	1.3	2.59	448	460	0.6
43445 MARTIN	123	1757	1770	1781	0.2	52	563	578	594	0.6	2.94	460	465	0.3
43447 MILLBURY	173	3415	3462	3545	0.3	58	1275	1322	1384	0.9	2.62	1014	1030	0.4
43449 OAK HARBOR	123	8697	8732	8788	0.1	49	3304	3391	3485	0.6	2.53	2425	2430	0.1
43450 PEMBERVILLE	173	3618	3705	3814	0.6	69	1349	1411	1485	1.1	2.59	1018	1038	0.5
43451 PORTAGE	173	1152	1188	1229	0.7	74	421	444	469	1.3	2.47	327	336	0.6
43452 PORT CLINTON	123	14095	14343	14569	0.4	62	6033	6307	6563	1.1	2.25	4036	4091	0.3
43456 PUT IN BAY	123	728	735	739	0.2	55	341	353	363	0.8	2.08	216	216	0.0
43457 RISINGSUN	173	1805	1833	1871	0.4	60	649	676	708	1.0	2.71	508	518	0.5
43460 ROSSFORD	173	6281	6337	6514	0.2	54	2536	2611	2739	0.7	2.42	1743	1735	-0.1
43462 RUDOLPH	173	1248	1296	1344	0.9	79	459	489	519	1.5	2.61	352	366	0.9
43464 VICKERY	143	1629	1742	1792	1.6	89	597	657	694	2.3	2.63	430	462	1.7
43465 WALBRIDGE	173	4563	4545	4657	-0.1	41	2016	2058	2157	0.5	2.20	1324	1307	-0.3
43466 WAYNE	173	2088	2156	2230	0.8	75	763	807	854	1.3	2.67	583	602	0.8
43469 WOODVILLE	143	3151	3221	3243	0.5	67	1177	1231	1268	1.1	2.57	873	889	0.4
43501 ALVORDTON	171	1018	1008	1003	-0.2	33	363	368	373	0.3	2.67	276	273	-0.3
43502 ARCHBOLD	051	7098	7297	7404	0.7	72	2654	2783	2870	1.1	2.58	1944	1990	0.6
43504 BERKEY	095	916	1000	1030	2.1	94	325	363	381	2.6	2.75	260	285	2.2
43506 BRYAN	171	15069	15424	15664	0.6	68	6157	6452	6670	1.1	2.35	4161	4235	0.4
43511 CUSTAR	173	1289	1318	1362	0.5	67	451	475	504	1.2	2.77	351	361	0.7
43512 DEFIANCE	039	29296	29026	28671	-0.2	34	11358	11553	11701	0.4	2.47	8158	8081	-0.2
43515 DELTA	051	8139	8224	8298	0.2	55	2978	3081	3168	0.8	2.66	2315	2346	0.3
43516 DESHLER	069	3041	3068	3103	0.2	54	1127	1166	1207	0.8	2.59	845	853	0.2
43517 EDGERTON	171	3784	3757	3742	-0.2	37	1410	1427	1444	0.3	2.58	1060	1047	-0.3
43518 EDON	171	2917	2965	2982	0.4	61	1074	1117	1144	0.9	2.65	818	832	0.4
43521 FAYETTE	051	2924	2924	2931	0.0	45	1104	1123	1144	0.4	2.60	803	795	-0.2
OHIO					0.3					0.7	2.44			0.0
UNITED STATES					1.2					1.3	2.58			1.1

229-A

# ZIP CODE	POST OFFICE NAME	RACE (%) White 2000	White 2004	Black 2000	Black 2004	Asian/Pacific 2000	Asian/Pacific 2004	% Hispanic Origin 2000	% Hispanic Origin 2004	2004 AGE DISTRIBUTION (%) 0-4	5-9	10-14	15-19	20-24	25-44	45-64	65-84	85+	18+	MEDIAN AGE 2004	% 2004 Males	% 2004 Females
43214	COLUMBUS	92.3	91.0	2.9	3.2	2.8	3.7	1.2	1.3	5.0	4.8	4.1	4.4	8.0	28.7	25.8	14.1	5.1	83.7	41.8	46.3	53.7
43215	COLUMBUS	69.1	66.1	24.7	26.8	2.3	2.9	2.7	2.9	3.6	2.6	2.0	3.7	12.4	42.1	19.5	10.7	3.5	90.7	34.6	55.5	44.5
43217	COLUMBUS	80.5	78.0	15.0	16.9	0.7	1.0	1.5	1.8	10.7	9.7	12.2	9.8	11.3	32.2	12.6	1.6	0.0	61.5	23.4	51.3	48.7
43219	COLUMBUS	18.4	16.0	77.0	79.2	0.6	0.7	1.5	1.4	8.4	8.2	8.7	8.0	6.6	23.5	21.7	12.5	2.4	69.9	33.9	43.7	56.3
43220	COLUMBUS	88.7	86.2	2.0	2.2	7.4	9.5	1.7	1.9	4.0	4.3	5.2	5.3	9.4	28.3	26.2	15.6	1.8	83.3	40.0	48.4	51.6
43221	COLUMBUS	93.5	92.0	1.1	1.2	3.8	5.1	1.2	1.3	6.3	6.8	7.4	6.6	5.1	27.2	26.6	11.7	2.3	75.4	39.6	47.7	52.3
43222	COLUMBUS	81.5	79.4	12.1	13.5	1.8	2.2	1.8	2.0	8.7	8.2	8.4	8.5	7.2	30.9	20.6	6.9	0.7	69.8	30.8	50.9	49.1
43223	COLUMBUS	77.5	75.9	16.1	17.1	1.7	2.2	1.5	1.6	7.7	7.4	7.6	7.1	6.8	29.9	22.8	9.5	1.2	73.2	34.4	48.1	51.9
43224	COLUMBUS	59.1	56.1	31.9	34.1	2.3	2.8	3.0	3.2	8.0	7.3	7.3	6.7	7.7	31.0	20.7	10.1	1.2	73.5	33.7	48.4	51.6
43227	COLUMBUS	42.7	39.4	50.3	52.9	2.5	3.1	2.3	2.4	6.7	6.6	7.3	6.9	6.7	27.7	24.3	12.5	1.2	75.1	37.2	46.7	53.3
43228	COLUMBUS	82.6	81.1	9.0	9.7	1.9	2.6	7.7	7.7	9.2	7.5	6.5	6.2	8.7	34.7	19.1	7.5	0.7	73.3	30.9	49.1	50.9
43229	COLUMBUS	67.7	64.7	23.6	25.4	3.0	3.8	4.4	4.7	7.2	6.4	6.0	5.6	8.7	35.1	20.4	9.5	1.1	77.1	32.8	47.9	52.1
43230	COLUMBUS	84.5	82.1	9.9	11.1	3.1	4.1	1.4	1.6	7.2	7.3	7.6	6.8	6.5	32.3	24.4	7.1	0.8	73.6	34.9	48.3	51.8
43231	COLUMBUS	73.2	69.2	19.8	22.5	2.7	3.6	2.4	2.6	8.4	7.3	6.2	6.0	8.1	34.8	19.7	7.4	2.2	74.7	32.5	47.6	52.5
43232	COLUMBUS	59.0	55.7	34.3	36.9	1.9	2.4	2.5	2.7	7.9	7.0	7.1	6.6	8.5	33.1	21.0	7.8	0.9	74.2	32.2	47.9	52.1
43235	COLUMBUS	87.1	84.1	3.0	3.4	7.1	9.3	2.3	2.6	5.8	5.5	6.0	6.2	7.8	35.3	23.4	8.6	1.4	78.9	34.3	48.8	51.3
43240	COLUMBUS	89.5	87.8	3.7	3.9	4.6	6.0	1.5	1.5	6.4	5.2	4.6	5.3	9.5	42.8	19.6	6.0	0.8	81.1	32.4	49.0	51.0
43302	MARION	90.7	89.9	6.9	7.4	0.6	0.8	1.2	1.3	6.2	6.1	6.6	6.4	7.0	29.2	24.9	12.0	1.7	77.2	37.6	52.2	47.8
43310	BELLE CENTER	98.5	98.4	0.3	0.3	0.1	0.2	0.9	0.9	6.7	7.0	7.1	5.8	5.0	27.2	26.0	14.0	1.3	75.6	39.2	50.7	49.4
43311	BELLEFONTAINE	93.1	92.4	3.7	3.9	0.8	1.0	0.9	1.0	7.9	7.1	7.4	6.7	7.2	27.6	23.5	11.0	1.5	73.3	35.4	48.8	51.2
43314	CALEDONIA	98.8	98.7	0.3	0.4	0.1	0.1	0.6	0.7	5.6	6.1	7.2	6.1	5.7	27.8	28.6	11.7	1.2	77.2	40.0	51.1	48.9
43315	CARDINGTON	98.4	98.3	0.2	0.2	0.1	0.2	0.5	0.5	6.8	7.2	7.8	6.9	6.1	28.8	25.4	9.9	1.1	74.0	36.5	49.5	50.5
43316	CAREY	97.0	96.4	0.1	0.2	1.1	1.5	1.3	1.5	7.4	7.2	7.2	7.2	6.8	27.6	23.3	11.8	1.7	73.9	35.6	49.7	50.3
43318	DE GRAFF	98.9	98.7	0.4	0.5	0.1	0.2	0.8	0.8	7.3	7.5	8.4	7.0	6.5	26.9	25.4	9.8	1.2	72.5	35.7	50.7	49.4
43319	EAST LIBERTY	98.0	97.6	0.5	0.6	0.1	0.2	0.4	0.5	7.2	7.7	8.5	6.8	5.1	29.4	25.6	8.9	0.8	72.2	36.8	50.0	50.1
43320	EDISON	98.7	98.6	0.2	0.2	0.1	0.2	0.4	0.4	5.4	5.9	7.8	6.9	5.9	25.6	26.9	13.6	2.1	76.7	40.3	48.9	51.1
43321	FULTON	99.4	99.1	0.0	0.0	0.0	0.3	0.7	0.6	7.9	7.4	7.7	7.1	6.5	30.6	22.7	9.4	0.9	72.7	34.8	50.3	49.7
43323	HARPSTER	99.0	98.9	0.1	0.3	0.0	0.0	0.6	0.8	5.8	6.1	7.3	6.6	5.5	26.2	28.9	12.4	1.3	76.6	40.6	50.2	49.8
43324	HUNTSVILLE	98.2	98.0	0.4	0.5	0.1	0.2	0.7	0.8	5.8	6.1	6.4	5.5	5.2	25.0	29.7	14.8	1.7	78.4	42.5	49.7	50.3
43326	KENTON	97.7	97.4	0.7	0.8	0.3	0.4	1.0	1.1	6.8	6.7	7.3	6.4	6.4	26.9	24.3	12.6	2.6	75.2	37.7	48.4	51.6
43331	LAKEVIEW	97.8	97.4	0.2	0.2	0.3	0.4	0.7	0.9	5.4	5.4	5.7	5.3	5.5	23.2	29.4	18.4	1.7	80.2	44.6	50.5	49.5
43332	LA RUE	98.8	98.8	0.1	0.2	0.1	0.1	0.5	0.5	6.5	6.6	7.6	7.8	6.1	27.5	24.2	12.3	1.5	73.8	37.9	50.0	50.0
43333	LEWISTOWN	99.0	98.6	0.3	0.3	0.3	0.5	0.5	0.5	5.5	6.0	7.5	6.9	5.8	26.0	27.0	13.0	2.3	76.9	40.4	49.6	50.4
43334	MARENGO	98.4	98.2	0.2	0.3	0.1	0.2	0.6	0.7	6.6	6.8	7.4	6.9	6.1	29.2	26.9	9.3	0.9	74.7	37.4	50.9	49.2
43335	MARTEL	98.3	99.1	0.0	0.0	0.0	0.0	0.9	0.9	5.4	6.3	6.3	6.3	5.4	27.7	30.4	11.6	0.9	78.6	40.6	55.4	44.6
43337	MORRAL	98.8	98.6	0.3	0.3	0.0	0.0	0.6	0.7	4.6	5.2	7.4	7.2	5.8	25.2	30.6	12.9	1.2	78.5	41.9	49.5	50.5
43338	MOUNT GILEAD	98.1	98.0	0.5	0.5	0.2	0.3	0.7	0.8	6.4	6.7	7.3	6.9	5.5	27.1	25.9	12.1	2.1	75.3	38.7	49.5	50.5
43340	MOUNT VICTORY	97.7	97.5	0.7	0.7	0.1	0.2	0.7	0.8	7.8	7.9	7.4	6.6	6.4	26.2	25.1	11.4	1.2	73.1	36.0	50.2	49.8
43341	NEW BLOOMINGTON	98.0	97.8	0.2	0.2	0.2	0.3	1.2	1.4	6.3	6.6	8.8	9.0	6.6	27.5	26.0	8.4	0.8	72.6	36.1	49.0	51.0
43342	PROSPECT	99.1	98.9	0.2	0.2	0.1	0.1	0.4	0.4	6.1	6.5	7.7	7.2	5.8	26.3	28.0	11.4	1.1	75.3	39.3	49.9	50.1
43343	QUINCY	98.8	98.7	0.2	0.2	0.1	0.3	0.5	0.6	6.8	7.3	8.5	6.9	6.1	27.2	26.4	9.9	1.0	73.2	36.6	50.2	49.8
43344	RICHWOOD	98.3	98.2	0.4	0.4	0.1	0.1	0.5	0.5	7.6	8.0	8.3	6.8	5.7	28.3	23.3	10.7	1.3	71.8	35.9	49.3	50.7
43345	RIDGEWAY	98.4	98.3	0.7	0.7	0.0	0.0	0.8	0.8	7.1	8.4	9.6	8.3	5.7	28.3	22.8	8.7	1.2	69.3	34.4	50.4	49.6
43346	ROUNDHEAD	98.8	99.0	0.6	0.5	0.0	0.0	0.0	0.0	7.6	7.6	7.1	5.6	4.6	29.4	24.9	12.2	1.0	74.1	37.2	50.8	49.2
43347	RUSHSYLVANIA	98.1	97.9	0.3	0.4	0.3	0.4	0.4	0.5	6.7	7.9	8.9	6.9	5.9	27.9	24.2	10.6	1.1	71.9	35.7	50.1	49.9
43348	RUSSELLS POINT	98.2	98.0	0.2	0.2	0.2	0.3	1.2	1.3	6.7	6.3	6.3	5.4	6.0	23.5	27.6	16.5	1.7	77.3	41.6	48.2	51.8
43351	UPPER SANDUSKY	97.8	97.6	0.2	0.2	0.4	0.5	2.0	2.2	6.4	6.2	6.6	6.4	6.4	26.1	24.6	14.5	2.9	76.7	39.4	48.2	51.8
43356	WALDO	99.0	98.9	0.1	0.1	0.4	0.4	0.5	0.5	4.6	5.8	6.9	7.2	5.5	23.0	33.1	12.6	1.2	78.0	43.2	48.4	51.6
43357	WEST LIBERTY	98.3	98.1	0.4	0.4	0.2	0.3	0.3	0.3	5.8	6.4	7.7	7.0	5.3	25.5	25.6	12.8	3.9	75.2	40.0	47.6	52.5
43358	WEST MANSFIELD	98.1	97.9	0.4	0.4	0.1	0.2	0.6	0.6	6.6	7.4	8.6	6.9	5.9	30.0	23.9	9.5	1.3	72.9	36.4	49.7	50.4
43359	WHARTON	98.7	98.7	0.0	0.0	0.2	0.2	0.6	0.4	7.0	7.4	8.5	7.2	5.9	27.4	23.4	11.5	1.6	72.6	36.1	52.8	47.2
43360	ZANESFIELD	98.6	98.4	0.4	0.4	0.1	0.2	0.3	0.4	6.9	7.4	8.1	6.3	5.5	29.1	26.4	9.5	1.0	73.8	37.0	51.2	48.8
43402	BOWLING GREEN	92.6	91.7	2.4	2.5	1.6	2.1	3.6	4.0	4.3	3.9	4.1	16.9	22.6	22.6	17.1	7.2	1.2	84.8	24.6	47.8	52.3
43403	BOWLING GREEN	91.2	91.1	5.6	5.7	0.8	0.8	2.4	2.4	0.0	0.0	0.0	66.1	33.9	0.0	0.0	0.0	0.0	100.0	18.8	40.3	59.7
43406	BRADNER	98.4	98.3	0.1	0.1	0.2	0.2	2.6	2.9	6.8	6.8	7.5	7.2	7.5	26.9	25.6	10.5	1.3	74.5	36.3	50.1	50.0
43407	BURGOON	96.1	95.4	1.0	1.1	0.7	1.0	3.6	3.8	4.7	5.7	9.2	7.7	6.0	26.5	26.9	12.3	1.0	75.4	39.4	48.8	51.2
43410	CLYDE	96.4	96.0	0.1	0.2	0.3	0.4	4.4	4.9	6.5	6.6	7.3	6.9	6.8	27.9	25.2	11.4	1.5	75.3	37.4	49.3	50.7
43412	CURTICE	96.7	96.2	0.1	0.2	0.2	0.2	3.9	4.5	5.6	6.1	7.6	7.2	5.8	26.8	29.3	10.8	0.9	76.2	39.9	50.8	49.2
43413	CYGNET	97.6	97.5	0.2	0.2	0.1	0.2	2.5	2.8	6.9	7.2	8.1	6.9	5.7	28.1	25.9	10.3	0.9	73.5	37.7	50.3	49.7
43416	ELMORE	97.4	97.1	0.1	0.1	0.1	0.1	3.9	4.4	6.4	6.7	7.4	7.1	5.5	25.2	27.1	12.6	2.0	74.9	39.8	48.8	51.2
43420	FREMONT	88.2	87.2	5.0	5.3	0.4	0.5	9.2	10.1	6.9	6.6	6.8	6.6	7.0	25.9	25.2	12.8	2.2	75.6	37.9	48.7	51.3
43430	GENOA	95.2	94.7	0.2	0.3	0.3	0.5	6.0	6.7	5.6	6.2	7.6	6.8	5.9	26.1	26.7	13.0	2.1	76.1	40.0	49.9	50.1
43431	GIBSONBURG	94.6	94.1	0.2	0.3	0.2	0.2	7.8	8.7	6.6	7.2	7.7	7.2	5.6	27.8	23.3	12.4	2.3	73.9	37.6	49.6	50.4
43432	GRAYTOWN	97.1	96.7	0.1	0.1	0.2	0.3	3.3	3.6	6.2	6.4	7.0	7.3	5.7	25.3	29.1	11.6	1.3	75.5	40.2	51.0	49.0
43435	HELENA	98.2	98.1	0.3	0.3	0.1	0.1	3.7	4.1	5.9	6.3	7.1	6.6	5.5	26.5	28.2	12.2	1.7	76.4	40.2	50.6	49.4
43436	ISLE SAINT GEORGE	100.0	100.0	0.0	0.0	0.0	0.0	0.0	0.0	3.1	6.3	6.3	3.1	6.3	25.0	31.3	18.8	0.0	84.4	45.0	53.1	46.9
43438	KELLEYS ISLAND	99.5	99.5	0.3	0.3	0.0	0.0	0.3	0.3	3.7	3.5	4.5	3.2	1.6	17.9	41.3	23.2	1.1	85.1	53.8	50.1	49.9
43440	LAKESIDE MARBLEHEAD	97.7	97.4	0.5	0.5	0.2	0.2	1.6	1.8	4.0	4.2	4.4	4.4	4.4	21.0	33.5	21.8	2.3	84.8	50.2	49.3	50.7
43442	LINDSEY	93.9	93.4	0.1	0.1	0.1	0.1	9.0	9.9	6.7	7.6	7.6	6.0	5.2	27.3	26.2	11.9	1.6	74.2	39.0	50.7	49.3
43443	LUCKEY	97.1	96.9	0.2	0.2	0.1	0.2	2.4	2.6	6.7	6.9	8.2	7.0	4.8	24.7	22.9	12.6	6.3	73.2	39.7	47.0	53.0
43445	MARTIN	95.7	95.2	0.2	0.2	0.3	0.3	5.2	5.7	5.7	6.2	7.2	7.0	5.5	26.6	29.1	11.5	1.3	76.4	40.2	50.4	49.6
43447	MILLBURY	98.0	97.8	0.1	0.1	0.2	0.3	2.5	2.7	5.4	6.1	7.3	6.5	6.0	26.6	29.6	11.5	1.0	77.2	40.3	48.9	51.1
43449	OAK HARBOR	98.1	97.8	0.2	0.2	0.4	0.5	2.2	2.5	5.5	6.1	7.2	6.8	6.2	26.4	27.5	12.1	2.2	76.9	40.2	49.3	50.7
43450	PEMBERVILLE	97.2	97.0	0.2	0.2	0.1	0.2	3.2	3.5	6.1	6.6	8.0	7.9	5.3	25.2	27.1	11.7	2.2	73.9	39.7	48.6	51.4
43451	PORTAGE	95.7	95.4	0.7	0.7	0.2	0.3	4.3	4.9	5.9	6.3	7.3	7.9	6.1	27.4	26.9	9.9	2.3	74.8	38.4	50.7	49.3
43452	PORT CLINTON	95.1	94.7	1.5	1.6	0.3	0.5	5.0	5.5	5.2	5.2	5.8	5.6	5.6	23.8	30.3	16.3	2.2	80.3	44.2	49.2	50.8
43456	PUT IN BAY	98.8	98.8	0.3	0.3	0.0	0.0	0.6	0.5	3.7	4.6	5.2	4.0	3.3	26.1	35.2	16.6	1.4	83.7	47.0	49.8	50.2
43457	RISINGSUN	98.1	97.9	0.1	0.1	0.1	0.1	2.1	2.4	6.3	6.4	7.3	7.1	6.2	28.6	26.5	10.7	0.9	75.6	37.9	49.2	50.9
43460	ROSSFORD	96.2	95.6	1.3	1.4	0.9	1.2	1.7	1.9	5.9	6.3	6.9	7.4	6.3	27.1	25.7	12.5	2.0	76.4	38.5	48.2	51.8
43462	RUDOLPH	95.1	94.5	0.1	0.1	0.2	0.2	6.1	6.9	6.9	7.3	8.0	7.3	5.9	27.9	28.1	7.9	0.8	73.1	37.6	51.2	48.8
43464	VICKERY	95.6	95.2	1.5	1.5	0.1	0.2	3.5	4.0	6.6	7.1	6.7	5.7	5.6	28.4	27.2	11.4	1.3	75.9	38.8	49.7	50.3
43465	WALBRIDGE	97.4	97.2	0.4	0.4	0.2	0.2	2.9	3.2	5.5	5.6	6.2	5.7	5.4	24.5	28.5	17.1	1.6	79.3	43.0	47.8	52.2
43466	WAYNE	96.8	96.4	0.1	0.1	0.3	0.4	2.7	3.1	6.2	6.6	7.8	6.4	6.1	28.9	26.5	10.3	1.2	75.5	37.8	49.7	50.3
43469	WOODVILLE	96.7	96.4	0.2	0.2	0.1	0.2	4.5	5.0	6.6	6.9	7.5	7.1	5.1	26.2	25.0	13.2	2.6	74.4	39.4	48.6	51.4
43501	ALVORDTON	97.2	97.1	0.4	0.4	0.0	0.0	2.4	2.6	5.7	6.3	7.8	6.9	6.2	28.0	26.0	12.0	1.2	75.9	38.9	51.8	48.2
43502	ARCHBOLD	93.4	92.8	0.3	0.3	0.6	0.8	9.5	10.4	7.0	6.9	7.8	7.0	6.4	24.8	23.5	13.4	3.4	74.0	38.3	48.7	51.3
43504	BERKEY	98.8	98.5	0.3	0.4	0.1	0.2	0.4	0.5	5.1	6.1	7.9	8.2	5.4	24.5	29.3	12.7	0.8	75.9	41.0	49.3	50.7
43506	BRYAN	96.6	96.1	0.4	0.4	0.7	1.0	3.2	3.5	6.2	6.2	6.8	6.7	6.3	26.2	26.8	12.5	2.2	76.6	39.4	49.1	50.9
43511	CUSTAR	96.0	95.7	0.1	0.1	0.2	0.3	5.4	5.8	5.8	6.3	8.0	7.1	6.4	27.9	25.4	11.5	1.6	75.6	38.7	49.7	50.3
43512	DEFIANCE	90.7	89.9	2.3	2.4	0.5	0.6	9.0	9.9	6.9	6.7	6.8	7.3	7.4	25.7	26.5	11.1	1.6	75.5	37.1	49.5	50.5
43515	DELTA	96.5	96.2	0.1	0.1	0.3	0.3	4.1	4.6	7.4	7.5	7.8	6.8	6.0	28.0	25.7	9.8	1.0	73.0	36.4	49.4	50.6
43516	DESHLER	95.1	94.5	0.1	0.1	0.6	0.8	5.6	6.2	6.7	7.1	8.0	6.4	5.8	26.9	23.9	13.0	2.2	74.0	37.3	50.7	49.4
43517	EDGERTON	97.8	97.6	0.1	0.1	0.2	0.2	1.5	1.7	7.5	7.6	7.7	6.7	5.7	27.3	23.8	11.4	2.3	73.0	36.7	49.4	50.6
43518	EDON	99.0	98.9	0.0	0.0	0.2	0.2	0.5	0.5	6.0	6.9	8.0	8.1	5.8	26.5	26.1	11.4	1.3	74.1	37.9	49.2	50.8
43521	FAYETTE	95.6	95.1	0.2	0.2	0.4	0.5	6.5	7.2	9.0	8.3	7.4	6.4	6.7	27.4	23.0	10.6	1.2	71.4	34.2	50.0	50.0
	OHIO	85.0	84.1	11.5	11.8	1.2	1.6	1.9	2.1	6.7	6.6	7.1	7.0	7.1	27.5	24.7	11.6	1.8	75.6	37.0	48.6	51.4
	UNITED STATES	75.1	73.6	12.3	12.5	3.8	4.2	12.5	14.1	6.9	6.7	7.2	7.0	7.3	28.6	23.8	10.8	1.7	75.1	36.0	49.1	50.9

#	ZIP CODE / POST OFFICE NAME	2004 Per Capita Income	2004 HH Income Base	2004 HOUSEHOLD INCOME DISTRIBUTION (%) Less than $25,000	$25,000 to $49,999	$50,000 to $99,999	$100,000 to $149,999	$150,000 or More	MEDIAN HOUSEHOLD INCOME 2004	2009	2004 National Centile	2004 State Centile	2004 Home Value Base	2004 HOME VALUE DISTRIBUTION (%) Less than $50,000	$50,000 to $89,999	$90,000 to $174,999	$175,000 to $399,999	$400,000 or More	2004 Median Home Value
43214	COLUMBUS	34007	12597	20.6	24.4	35.4	13.8	5.8	54775	65284	79	77	8065	1.1	3.5	54.6	39.7	1.2	162701
43215	COLUMBUS	26898	6018	47.6	25.2	18.4	5.7	3.2	27012	32942	7	5	864	6.4	9.5	30.2	44.1	9.8	185625
43217	COLUMBUS	18767	803	17.9	37.9	38.7	4.6	0.9	47238	54063	67	54	94	8.5	63.8	0.0	27.7	0.0	63333
43219	COLUMBUS	16753	9075	40.3	31.7	21.3	4.7	2.1	31942	37831	18	10	5170	14.6	47.2	32.4	5.3	0.5	80586
43220	COLUMBUS	44736	11584	17.1	24.3	32.1	13.3	13.3	60000	72028	84	86	6762	1.4	6.1	28.7	48.0	15.9	216101
43221	COLUMBUS	42661	12808	9.9	19.3	37.5	18.2	15.2	75345	90717	93	96	9992	0.3	2.5	35.9	51.3	10.1	198316
43222	COLUMBUS	11308	2106	52.0	30.0	15.8	1.9	0.5	23598	28634	4	3	686	39.4	54.5	6.1	0.0	0.0	56822
43223	COLUMBUS	16985	10312	34.0	31.8	28.6	4.4	1.1	35685	42781	30	20	6142	13.1	49.2	35.8	1.5	0.4	79894
43224	COLUMBUS	18877	17639	31.8	35.7	27.0	4.2	1.3	36089	43201	32	21	9448	6.5	41.9	50.0	1.3	0.3	90861
43227	COLUMBUS	21609	9825	26.1	33.7	31.8	6.8	1.6	40596	49209	48	32	5958	1.9	38.0	58.3	1.4	0.4	94462
43228	COLUMBUS	22490	21547	24.4	31.1	34.6	8.0	2.0	45241	53894	62	47	11064	4.2	15.5	67.5	12.8	0.1	117892
43229	COLUMBUS	24524	21497	22.0	35.7	32.3	7.9	2.1	43875	51801	58	42	9218	2.2	6.6	85.2	5.9	0.2	124699
43230	COLUMBUS	34957	20453	10.3	20.1	42.0	17.6	10.0	69290	83854	91	94	14504	0.2	3.1	56.8	36.8	3.1	161800
43231	COLUMBUS	26595	7761	17.1	30.6	38.0	10.9	3.5	51825	61460	75	69	4326	1.7	15.2	68.4	14.6	0.0	133225
43232	COLUMBUS	21911	17798	24.2	34.5	33.3	6.7	1.3	42828	50896	56	39	8499	4.1	23.5	66.8	5.6	0.1	103730
43235	COLUMBUS	41061	17310	11.7	22.9	36.8	15.7	13.0	65954	79277	89	92	9790	0.7	4.9	39.6	49.1	5.8	183734
43240	COLUMBUS	57224	800	9.5	26.3	35.0	12.0	17.3	63958	79651	88	90	377	0.0	0.0	21.8	53.9	24.4	230921
43302	MARION	21243	20458	27.8	32.2	31.3	6.5	2.2	41580	47617	52	34	14456	13.2	34.6	41.0	10.2	1.0	92105
43310	BELLE CENTER	22347	1266	21.6	26.8	40.8	8.5	2.4	51027	57965	74	67	1084	10.8	25.5	44.8	15.3	3.6	105622
43311	BELLEFONTAINE	22685	7713	23.4	30.5	34.0	9.0	3.1	46228	54194	64	50	5267	8.8	22.6	50.2	16.9	1.4	110915
43314	CALEDONIA	22102	1197	16.8	35.7	39.9	6.2	1.5	48452	54372	69	58	1009	22.2	20.8	43.2	11.2	2.6	97194
43315	CARDINGTON	19836	2450	25.3	29.8	37.7	5.6	1.7	45036	50764	61	46	1967	8.2	16.3	57.4	16.0	2.2	115699
43316	CAREY	18468	2411	27.4	34.1	33.2	4.2	1.1	40117	45221	46	30	1872	15.1	25.6	49.5	9.4	0.4	99202
43318	DE GRAFF	22683	1378	18.7	31.8	35.2	10.6	3.7	49487	56964	71	61	1143	11.1	25.4	44.4	18.1	1.1	105861
43319	EAST LIBERTY	27963	368	11.4	21.7	48.4	14.4	4.1	63106	74838	87	89	326	3.7	11.7	51.2	29.1	4.3	145833
43320	EDISON	19647	552	27.4	31.7	33.7	5.3	2.0	42428	47854	54	37	434	6.2	15.4	61.5	14.1	2.8	118466
43321	FULTON	21550	124	17.7	39.5	36.3	5.7	0.8	46111	52426	64	50	102	14.7	24.5	46.1	13.7	1.0	102941
43323	HARPSTER	22741	303	11.9	38.3	39.3	7.3	3.3	49853	54718	72	62	262	13.4	24.4	41.2	17.9	3.1	110185
43324	HUNTSVILLE	25031	1213	19.3	26.5	39.4	12.1	2.7	53003	60959	77	73	1035	9.9	17.9	44.5	23.4	4.4	119676
43326	KENTON	19867	5528	32.4	30.9	28.7	6.2	1.8	38127	43856	40	25	3909	15.5	35.7	38.3	9.6	0.8	88778
43331	LAKEVIEW	20980	2611	33.7	31.4	27.3	6.4	1.2	36696	41402	34	22	2075	29.5	28.8	28.4	11.1	2.2	77423
43332	LA RUE	21047	785	27.5	27.0	36.8	7.0	1.7	46886	52310	66	53	614	16.8	35.3	35.8	10.8	1.3	87593
43333	LEWISTOWN	21635	282	16.7	39.4	28.0	13.5	2.5	45673	52275	63	48	240	5.4	31.7	51.3	11.7	0.0	104730
43334	MARENGO	21302	2134	17.1	30.6	42.3	8.6	1.5	51808	59108	75	69	1827	5.0	17.5	55.2	21.3	1.0	124116
43335	MARTEL	24085	49	16.3	28.6	51.0	4.1	0.0	54518	60829	79	77	42	7.1	31.0	50.0	7.1	4.8	106250
43337	MORRAL	26454	409	15.2	29.8	42.5	7.6	4.9	53588	59581	78	75	357	14.6	21.6	51.5	9.5	2.8	104623
43338	MOUNT GILEAD	22367	3459	22.0	35.7	31.8	6.8	3.8	44301	50475	59	43	2779	9.8	14.7	50.9	23.5	1.2	123471
43340	MOUNT VICTORY	19385	548	25.7	27.9	36.9	8.2	1.3	45768	51384	63	48	456	15.8	24.3	44.5	15.4	0.0	98491
43341	NEW BLOOMINGTON	20529	427	16.4	33.5	41.9	5.4	2.8	50086	57100	72	63	379	27.4	30.6	33.5	8.4	0.0	80469
43342	PROSPECT	23696	1271	16.2	28.6	42.4	9.8	3.1	53660	60837	78	75	1087	3.8	18.5	55.0	22.5	0.3	121112
43343	QUINCY	21422	565	21.4	31.5	35.9	8.1	3.0	47681	54779	68	56	471	12.3	28.2	41.8	17.2	0.4	101264
43344	RICHWOOD	21743	2093	19.7	29.8	38.8	10.0	1.6	50303	57670	72	64	1660	6.7	19.0	52.3	21.3	0.7	120387
43345	RIDGEWAY	19453	379	15.6	31.9	43.3	7.4	1.9	51866	58412	75	70	332	10.8	27.1	43.7	17.5	0.9	105093
43346	ROUNDHEAD	19303	79	19.0	30.4	46.8	3.8	0.0	50267	51677	72	64	68	20.6	20.6	45.6	8.8	4.4	98571
43347	RUSHSYLVANIA	20706	616	18.7	31.2	38.5	10.2	1.5	50117	56762	72	63	538	9.3	32.3	36.4	20.6	1.3	101136
43348	RUSSELLS POINT	19941	985	35.5	28.9	27.4	6.3	1.8	37044	42362	36	23	681	20.6	33.5	27.5	14.4	4.1	84907
43351	UPPER SANDUSKY	20548	4214	22.3	37.1	34.2	5.0	1.4	43119	48240	56	39	3039	9.5	24.9	50.6	13.1	1.8	104556
43356	WALDO	27377	380	17.6	25.0	36.6	14.7	6.1	61082	69925	85	87	333	2.4	12.6	54.7	28.5	1.8	137897
43357	WEST LIBERTY	23555	1580	15.6	28.0	42.2	11.5	2.8	55558	63884	80	79	1315	4.0	13.5	59.1	21.9	1.5	130253
43358	WEST MANSFIELD	21701	851	15.3	30.2	44.1	10.2	0.2	53174	60258	77	74	725	7.3	22.2	53.7	16.4	0.4	113516
43359	WHARTON	19600	341	16.4	38.7	37.0	7.9	0.0	47493	52266	67	55	291	11.7	24.1	44.3	18.9	1.0	108769
43360	ZANESFIELD	25873	745	15.3	27.1	42.7	11.4	3.5	55349	64189	80	79	637	20.4	12.1	39.9	23.7	3.9	121208
43402	BOWLING GREEN	21327	13485	32.0	27.4	27.9	9.5	3.2	39502	47505	44	28	6796	11.2	5.4	48.3	32.4	2.6	149753
43403	BOWLING GREEN	19152	45	73.3	26.7	0.0	0.0	0.0	16796	18022	1	1	1	0.0	0.0	0.0	100.0	0.0	187500
43406	BRADNER	21703	750	21.1	34.0	35.1	7.5	2.4	45526	55390	63	47	579	15.2	28.0	49.2	7.1	0.5	95896
43407	BURGOON	24069	218	9.2	22.0	54.1	11.9	2.8	64504	76132	88	91	200	4.5	19.0	57.0	19.0	0.5	125806
43410	CLYDE	21431	3726	20.3	33.8	35.3	9.0	1.6	46098	52747	64	49	2946	11.3	23.3	54.1	10.5	0.8	106494
43412	CURTICE	24928	1763	19.4	24.5	34.8	16.9	4.5	60133	70686	84	86	1534	4.4	18.5	45.7	30.6	0.9	135303
43413	CYGNET	20555	677	14.0	35.3	43.7	6.4	0.6	50351	58142	73	64	589	13.9	27.3	44.3	13.1	1.4	102024
43416	ELMORE	24614	1162	20.7	26.2	37.8	12.7	2.7	52925	62345	77	73	972	3.6	9.5	50.6	35.8	0.5	140566
43420	FREMONT	22764	12734	25.2	32.4	31.9	7.0	3.5	43561	50462	57	41	9194	8.9	27.8	47.7	14.5	1.1	104947
43430	GENOA	25647	1876	17.6	28.5	38.0	12.7	3.2	52921	62420	77	73	1589	6.4	14.9	63.1	15.4	0.2	119479
43431	GIBSONBURG	22196	1689	20.4	30.3	38.2	8.6	2.4	49433	56112	71	61	1365	6.6	22.9	53.8	16.6	0.2	112727
43432	GRAYTOWN	24000	448	9.8	26.1	47.1	15.6	1.3	64253	76079	88	91	396	4.8	8.8	59.1	25.0	2.3	140805
43435	HELENA	23581	599	17.5	26.7	41.9	9.9	4.0	54337	61154	79	77	519	6.9	17.7	55.5	19.1	0.8	126125
43436	ISLE SAINT GEORGE	23672	13	7.7	38.5	46.2	7.7	0.0	54580	63927	79	77	11	0.0	0.0	9.1	72.7	18.2	312500
43438	KELLEYS ISLAND	25234	192	34.9	29.2	24.5	7.8	3.7	40000	45992	46	30	155	1.9	5.2	38.1	40.0	14.8	189423
43440	LAKESIDE MARBLEHEAD	35540	2063	19.8	31.9	34.3	9.0	4.9	48207	55731	69	58	1722	9.5	11.1	43.6	30.1	5.7	142668
43442	LINDSEY	25702	463	12.5	36.1	37.8	10.4	3.2	51035	57340	74	67	394	5.1	16.5	55.3	22.1	1.0	127632
43443	LUCKEY	23000	650	19.1	23.7	42.0	13.7	1.5	55274	65228	80	78	509	8.3	8.5	59.1	23.0	1.2	130907
43445	MARTIN	23446	578	14.0	21.8	41.2	20.4	2.6	66008	77888	89	93	520	2.3	9.4	53.1	34.2	1.0	147098
43447	MILLBURY	25708	1322	14.6	26.8	41.8	13.9	2.9	58329	68766	83	83	1151	8.3	11.1	56.7	23.0	1.0	130985
43449	OAK HARBOR	26299	3391	17.0	27.9	39.3	11.1	4.6	54505	64181	79	77	2820	7.3	13.4	52.6	24.6	2.1	127967
43450	PEMBERVILLE	26918	1411	13.8	24.7	43.6	15.0	3.0	60650	71387	85	87	1179	3.1	6.4	57.3	31.6	1.6	145036
43451	PORTAGE	23909	444	18.2	28.6	38.3	11.7	3.2	52241	61363	76	71	377	15.9	17.2	42.4	23.6	0.8	119420
43452	PORT CLINTON	24359	6307	25.1	31.1	31.3	9.9	2.7	44717	52168	60	44	4730	7.4	14.6	49.4	24.4	4.3	128200
43456	PUT IN BAY	32112	353	13.9	31.4	39.4	11.1	4.3	53978	61926	78	76	288	0.7	0.7	13.9	59.4	25.4	300000
43457	RISINGSUN	22104	676	16.9	31.5	39.2	9.5	3.0	51002	58617	74	67	573	15.0	25.8	48.9	9.6	0.7	99375
43460	ROSSFORD	33304	2611	17.5	29.0	35.6	11.2	6.6	52979	63578	77	73	1967	2.0	11.3	60.4	20.2	6.1	139787
43462	RUDOLPH	22335	489	20.9	29.9	39.1	6.3	3.9	49314	57531	71	60	414	24.6	21.5	38.9	14.3	0.7	94848
43464	VICKERY	22302	657	15.4	35.2	40.2	6.7	2.6	49365	54703	71	61	526	11.8	28.3	43.4	14.3	2.3	102750
43465	WALBRIDGE	23251	2058	27.4	30.0	32.9	8.3	1.5	43333	51415	57	40	1666	34.3	12.7	44.8	7.6	0.5	94386
43466	WAYNE	20583	807	20.1	30.5	40.4	7.9	1.1	49461	57757	71	61	686	16.6	24.9	46.7	10.5	1.3	99667
43469	WOODVILLE	24500	1231	17.7	29.1	39.2	11.3	2.8	53055	60427	77	73	1025	2.6	12.2	56.8	27.8	0.6	137811
43501	ALVORDTON	19321	368	21.5	34.0	37.8	4.6	2.2	46712	51241	66	52	305	20.7	27.2	38.4	11.5	2.3	94333
43502	ARCHBOLD	24640	2783	16.7	31.5	39.4	9.1	3.4	51315	58187	74	68	2193	8.4	11.0	55.5	24.4	0.8	126432
43504	BERKEY	28995	363	15.2	18.2	40.5	14.6	11.6	67192	80571	90	93	323	3.1	7.1	46.8	33.8	9.3	153365
43506	BRYAN	24405	6452	22.3	33.6	33.9	7.1	3.2	45613	51465	63	48	4767	10.4	21.7	51.9	15.0	1.1	110799
43511	CUSTAR	21308	475	20.0	33.7	33.9	9.1	3.4	47472	54976	67	55	411	12.7	21.7	50.1	14.6	1.0	108816
43512	DEFIANCE	23815	11553	20.2	28.3	39.5	9.6	2.4	51216	58382	74	68	8902	12.5	23.3	48.8	14.6	0.9	105669
43515	DELTA	22320	3081	17.3	31.9	38.8	9.2	2.8	50636	57477	73	65	2601	12.2	10.7	52.0	23.8	1.4	129093
43516	DESHLER	21005	1166	20.8	34.7	35.8	6.4	2.3	46238	52307	64	50	987	17.3	30.0	42.8	9.5	0.4	93232
43517	EDGERTON	21926	1427	20.0	32.1	37.6	7.9	2.5	48193	53511	69	58	1200	12.1	22.3	51.5	12.6	1.6	105694
43518	EDON	20480	1117	20.1	31.1	40.6	6.3	2.0	49128	54310	70	60	951	12.3	27.9	44.6	14.6	0.6	101907
43521	FAYETTE	19689	1123	24.5	38.5	30.5	5.1	1.5	40613	45894	48	32	803	11.5	33.6	40.0	13.2	1.7	97315
	OHIO	25510		24.6	28.1	32.2	10.1	5.0	47354	56168				9.2	18.6	47.0	22.1	3.1	121192
	UNITED STATES	25866		24.7	27.1	30.8	10.9	6.5	48124	56710				10.9	15.0	33.7	30.1	10.4	145905

ZIP CODE #	POST OFFICE NAME	FINANCIAL SERVICES: Auto Loan	FINANCIAL SERVICES: Home Loan	FINANCIAL SERVICES: Invest-ments	FINANCIAL SERVICES: Retire-ment Plans	THE HOME: Home Improvements: Home Repair	THE HOME: Home Improvements: Lawn & Garden	THE HOME: Furnishings: Comput-ers & Hard-ware	THE HOME: Furnishings: Major Appli-ances	THE HOME: Furnishings: TV, Radio, Sound Equip-ment	THE HOME: Furnishings: Furni-ture	ENTERTAINMENT: Dine out/ Carry out	ENTERTAINMENT: Sports Equip-ment	ENTERTAINMENT: Fees & Tickets	ENTERTAINMENT: Toys & Games	ENTERTAINMENT: Travel	ENTERTAINMENT: Cable TV	PERSONAL: Apparel & Services	PERSONAL: Auto Repairs	PERSONAL: Health Insur-ance	PERSONAL: Pets & Supplies
43214	COLUMBUS	88	93	115	96	92	98	100	94	96	97	121	113	100	121	98	93	119	97	87	103
43215	COLUMBUS	57	49	72	54	48	54	63	56	64	61	81	70	61	79	59	62	79	62	54	63
43217	COLUMBUS	87	74	86	82	71	76	86	81	84	87	108	99	82	99	79	78	104	87	72	90
43219	COLUMBUS	57	53	62	50	52	59	57	56	60	58	75	62	58	73	56	62	73	57	59	63
43220	COLUMBUS	119	124	156	128	122	132	133	125	129	130	162	150	134	160	130	124	159	130	118	138
43221	COLUMBUS	131	154	184	157	151	156	146	143	139	147	175	167	154	180	148	136	174	142	132	156
43222	COLUMBUS	41	36	42	36	35	41	43	40	45	41	56	48	41	55	41	45	54	43	42	45
43223	COLUMBUS	61	58	60	57	58	64	61	60	63	60	78	70	60	78	60	63	75	61	62	69
43224	COLUMBUS	59	59	66	59	58	63	63	61	63	62	79	71	63	79	62	62	77	62	60	67
43227	COLUMBUS	68	69	76	67	68	75	70	69	72	70	89	78	72	90	70	73	87	70	70	77
43228	COLUMBUS	74	73	80	76	71	75	77	74	75	77	95	87	76	93	74	72	93	76	69	82
43229	COLUMBUS	74	72	84	76	70	74	79	75	76	78	97	90	77	94	75	73	94	78	69	82
43230	COLUMBUS	121	130	138	136	126	128	127	123	120	128	152	146	129	151	124	114	149	124	110	136
43231	COLUMBUS	87	86	95	91	84	87	90	87	86	91	109	104	88	106	86	81	107	90	78	96
43232	COLUMBUS	69	69	79	71	67	71	73	70	72	73	91	84	73	89	71	69	89	73	66	77
43235	COLUMBUS	128	127	145	135	124	130	133	128	128	134	162	152	132	156	128	122	159	132	117	142
43240	COLUMBUS	150	128	150	143	123	132	149	140	146	152	187	171	142	172	137	136	181	151	126	157
43302	MARION	73	72	73	70	73	80	73	74	75	72	92	85	73	94	74	76	89	74	77	84
43310	BELLE CENTER	91	79	58	74	84	91	73	82	79	73	95	98	70	96	76	81	90	81	91	108
43311	BELLEFONTAINE	86	77	67	75	80	88	78	82	81	76	99	95	76	100	78	83	95	81	87	98
43314	CALEDONIA	89	77	60	75	81	90	76	82	80	75	97	96	73	98	76	82	92	80	89	101
43315	CARDINGTON	82	73	57	71	76	83	70	76	74	70	90	89	68	91	71	76	85	75	82	94
43316	CAREY	67	65	60	62	67	74	64	66	67	62	82	75	65	86	65	69	79	65	71	77
43318	DE GRAFF	95	88	71	83	92	99	82	89	87	81	106	105	82	109	84	89	101	87	96	112
43319	EAST LIBERTY	118	105	80	100	111	119	97	108	103	97	125	128	95	128	100	106	119	105	116	139
43320	EDISON	76	72	63	69	75	82	69	73	73	68	89	85	70	93	71	75	85	71	79	89
43321	FULTON	93	83	63	79	88	94	77	85	82	77	99	101	75	101	79	84	94	83	92	110
43323	HARPSTER	94	84	64	80	89	95	77	86	82	77	100	102	76	102	80	84	95	84	93	111
43324	HUNTSVILLE	98	83	61	78	90	98	78	89	84	77	102	105	74	103	81	88	96	87	99	117
43326	KENTON	78	65	49	61	70	78	64	71	70	63	85	82	61	85	65	73	79	70	81	90
43331	LAKEVIEW	80	61	38	55	68	77	58	70	66	58	78	82	51	77	61	71	72	69	83	96
43332	LA RUE	96	75	48	69	82	91	71	83	80	72	96	99	66	94	73	84	89	81	95	112
43333	LEWISTOWN	92	82	62	78	86	93	76	84	80	76	98	100	74	100	78	82	93	82	91	108
43334	MARENGO	92	82	64	78	87	93	76	84	81	76	98	100	75	100	78	82	93	82	91	108
43335	MARTEL	88	78	60	75	83	89	73	80	77	73	94	96	71	96	75	79	89	78	87	104
43337	MORRAL	111	101	79	96	106	113	93	102	98	93	120	122	92	122	96	100	114	100	110	131
43338	MOUNT GILEAD	86	79	67	76	83	91	76	82	81	75	98	95	76	100	78	83	94	80	89	100
43340	MOUNT VICTORY	82	71	55	70	75	83	71	76	75	70	91	88	68	91	71	76	86	75	83	93
43341	NEW BLOOMINGTON	94	84	63	79	88	95	77	86	82	77	100	102	76	102	80	84	95	84	93	111
43342	PROSPECT	101	90	69	85	95	102	83	92	88	83	107	110	81	109	85	90	102	89	99	118
43343	QUINCY	92	82	62	78	87	93	76	84	81	76	98	100	74	100	78	83	93	82	91	108
43344	RICHWOOD	92	80	62	78	84	93	79	85	83	78	101	99	76	102	79	85	95	83	92	105
43345	RIDGEWAY	96	86	65	81	90	97	79	88	84	79	102	104	78	104	81	86	97	85	95	113
43346	ROUNDHEAD	77	69	52	65	73	78	63	70	67	63	82	84	62	84	65	69	78	68	76	91
43347	RUSHSYLVANIA	91	81	62	77	86	92	75	83	80	75	97	99	74	99	77	82	92	81	90	108
43348	RUSSELLS POINT	80	58	34	51	66	74	55	68	65	56	76	80	48	74	58	69	70	67	82	94
43351	UPPER SANDUSKY	76	68	56	65	71	80	67	72	72	66	87	83	65	88	68	74	82	71	80	88
43356	WALDO	108	102	85	98	106	112	94	102	97	94	119	121	94	122	96	98	114	99	106	127
43357	WEST LIBERTY	101	87	65	83	93	102	83	92	90	83	108	109	80	109	85	93	102	90	102	118
43358	WEST MANSFIELD	93	83	63	79	87	94	76	85	81	76	99	101	75	101	79	83	94	82	92	109
43359	WHARTON	82	70	55	70	74	83	72	77	76	70	92	88	69	92	71	77	87	76	83	91
43360	ZANESFIELD	105	94	71	89	99	106	87	96	92	87	112	115	85	114	89	94	106	94	104	124
43402	BOWLING GREEN	73	64	74	67	63	69	80	71	78	75	98	89	75	94	73	73	94	77	66	80
43403	BOWLING GREEN	26	16	20	18	16	19	31	23	30	26	38	32	25	34	25	27	36	28	21	26
43406	BRADNER	89	76	59	75	80	89	77	82	81	75	99	95	74	98	77	83	93	81	89	100
43407	BURGOON	112	100	76	95	105	113	92	102	98	92	119	122	90	122	95	100	113	99	111	132
43410	CLYDE	86	77	62	73	80	87	74	80	78	73	95	93	72	95	75	79	90	78	86	99
43412	CURTICE	106	98	78	93	102	109	90	99	94	90	115	117	89	118	92	96	110	96	105	125
43413	CYGNET	89	79	60	75	83	90	73	81	78	73	94	96	72	96	75	80	90	79	88	104
43416	ELMORE	99	88	67	84	93	100	82	90	87	82	105	107	80	107	84	89	100	88	98	116
43420	FREMONT	79	78	76	76	79	86	78	79	79	76	98	92	78	100	78	80	94	79	82	92
43430	GENOA	89	95	96	93	96	102	92	93	92	90	114	106	95	119	93	92	111	91	93	104
43431	GIBSONBURG	86	81	70	77	84	92	78	83	82	77	100	96	78	104	80	84	96	81	89	100
43432	GRAYTOWN	99	101	91	98	103	107	92	97	92	92	114	115	94	118	94	92	110	94	98	118
43435	HELENA	101	90	69	86	95	102	83	92	89	83	108	110	82	110	86	91	102	90	100	119
43436	ISLE SAINT GEORGE	99	78	53	70	87	98	73	88	83	72	98	103	65	97	78	88	91	87	104	120
43438	KELLEYS ISLAND	83	65	45	59	74	83	62	74	70	61	83	87	55	82	66	74	77	73	88	101
43440	LAKESIDE MARBLEHEAD	129	101	69	91	114	128	96	115	108	95	128	135	85	126	102	115	119	113	136	157
43442	LINDSEY	106	95	72	90	100	107	87	97	93	87	113	115	86	115	90	95	107	94	105	125
43443	LUCKEY	86	86	90	88	87	92	86	87	84	86	105	103	85	103	86	83	102	87	86	100
43445	MARTIN	103	104	94	101	107	112	96	101	97	95	119	120	97	124	98	97	116	99	103	123
43447	MILLBURY	102	99	85	96	102	107	91	98	93	92	115	116	91	117	93	94	110	96	100	120
43449	OAK HARBOR	105	93	74	90	99	108	90	98	95	89	115	115	87	116	92	97	109	96	107	123
43450	PEMBERVILLE	99	105	102	103	106	110	97	101	97	97	120	119	100	124	100	96	117	98	100	118
43451	PORTAGE	98	87	67	83	92	99	81	90	86	81	104	107	79	107	83	88	99	87	97	116
43452	PORT CLINTON	83	74	65	69	79	88	73	80	78	72	95	91	70	95	76	82	90	79	89	98
43456	PUT IN BAY	113	89	61	80	100	113	84	101	95	83	112	118	75	111	89	101	105	100	119	138
43457	RISINGSUN	96	85	65	81	90	97	79	88	84	79	102	104	77	104	81	86	97	85	95	113
43460	ROSSFORD	104	120	134	119	119	123	115	113	111	114	139	132	121	146	117	110	138	112	108	124
43462	RUDOLPH	93	84	64	80	88	95	78	86	82	78	100	102	76	102	80	84	95	83	92	110
43464	VICKERY	91	84	70	81	88	94	79	86	82	79	101	102	78	102	81	83	96	84	90	107
43465	WALBRIDGE	75	72	71	69	74	83	70	75	72	71	89	81	70	84	72	73	85	74	81	85
43466	WAYNE	88	78	60	75	83	89	72	80	77	73	94	96	71	96	75	79	89	78	87	104
43469	WOODVILLE	95	91	79	87	95	102	85	92	89	85	109	107	86	112	88	91	104	89	97	113
43501	ALVORDTON	83	74	56	70	78	84	69	76	73	69	89	91	67	90	71	75	84	74	82	98
43502	ARCHBOLD	103	88	65	84	94	103	85	94	92	84	110	110	81	110	87	95	104	92	105	119
43504	BERKEY	104	129	137	129	127	125	115	115	107	115	134	134	122	143	118	103	134	111	103	127
43506	BRYAN	91	78	62	74	82	91	77	84	83	76	101	99	73	100	78	85	95	83	93	105
43511	CUSTAR	93	80	62	79	85	94	80	86	85	79	103	100	77	103	80	86	97	85	93	105
43512	DEFIANCE	91	82	68	79	86	94	80	86	84	79	103	100	78	104	81	86	97	84	92	105
43515	DELTA	94	83	66	81	88	95	80	87	84	79	102	102	78	104	81	86	97	85	93	108
43516	DESHLER	93	73	48	68	79	88	71	81	79	71	95	96	66	93	72	82	88	80	93	106
43517	EDGERTON	91	81	62	77	86	92	75	83	80	75	97	99	74	99	78	82	92	81	90	108
43518	EDON	89	77	56	72	81	88	71	80	77	71	93	95	69	94	73	79	88	78	88	104
43521	FAYETTE	81	70	54	69	74	82	69	75	73	68	89	87	67	89	70	75	84	73	81	92
	OHIO	89	88	90	87	88	95	88	89	89	87	110	103	88	111	88	89	107	89	90	102
	UNITED STATES	100	100	100	100	100	100	100	100	100	100	100	100	100	100	100	100	100	100	100	100

OHIO

POPULATION CHANGE

A 43522-43821

# ZIP CODE / POST OFFICE NAME	COUNTY FIPS CODE	POPULATION 2000	2004	2009	% Rate	State Centile	HOUSEHOLDS 2000	2004	2009	% Annual Rate 2000-2004	2004 Average HH Size	FAMILIES 2000	2004	% Annual Rate 2000-2004
43522 GRAND RAPIDS	173	3684	3915	4044	1.4	88	1379	1502	1588	2.0	2.59	1036	1097	1.4
43524 HAMLER	069	1422	1457	1478	0.6	69	512	539	559	1.2	2.70	398	410	0.7
43525 HASKINS	173	608	606	622	-0.1	42	230	235	246	0.5	2.58	172	171	-0.1
43526 HICKSVILLE	039	6162	6010	5887	-0.6	19	2331	2325	2329	-0.1	2.56	1663	1615	-0.7
43527 HOLGATE	069	2421	2352	2343	-0.7	15	874	872	889	-0.1	2.67	648	630	-0.7
43528 HOLLAND	095	14128	15193	15559	1.7	91	5274	5792	6050	2.2	2.56	3829	4091	1.6
43532 LIBERTY CENTER	069	4114	4133	4153	0.1	50	1422	1459	1497	0.6	2.70	1085	1087	0.0
43533 LYONS	051	1523	1524	1531	0.0	45	561	574	586	0.5	2.65	423	422	-0.1
43534 MC CLURE	069	1800	1942	2025	1.8	92	658	725	772	2.3	2.68	495	532	1.7
43535 MALINTA	069	782	767	770	-0.5	24	308	311	320	0.2	2.47	237	234	-0.3
43536 MARK CENTER	039	460	489	498	1.5	88	156	170	177	2.0	2.88	126	135	1.6
43537 MAUMEE	095	24581	25262	25361	0.7	72	9922	10480	10765	1.3	2.36	6665	6820	0.5
43540 METAMORA	051	1104	1156	1185	1.1	83	405	433	451	1.6	2.67	312	326	1.0
43542 MONCLOVA	095	2294	2535	2629	2.4	95	779	873	921	2.7	2.85	647	715	2.4
43543 MONTPELIER	171	8134	8085	8083	-0.1	38	3172	3218	3270	0.3	2.49	2256	2234	-0.2
43545 NAPOLEON	069	14734	14866	15057	0.2	54	5699	5877	6079	0.7	2.48	4006	4025	0.1
43548 NEW BAVARIA	069	740	725	724	-0.5	23	282	285	291	0.3	2.54	213	210	-0.3
43549 NEY	039	1348	1387	1388	0.7	73	501	531	546	1.4	2.61	391	406	0.9
43551 PERRYSBURG	173	33571	35092	36678	1.1	83	12899	13765	14691	1.5	2.52	9059	9389	0.9
43554 PIONEER	171	2744	2739	2739	0.0	43	1066	1090	1111	0.5	2.51	775	772	-0.1
43556 SHERWOOD	039	2001	2012	1995	0.1	50	733	756	768	0.7	2.66	577	583	0.2
43557 STRYKER	171	3378	3361	3352	-0.1	39	1037	1053	1068	0.4	2.63	789	782	-0.2
43558 SWANTON	051	13932	14525	14822	1.0	81	5031	5378	5600	1.6	2.66	3906	4089	1.1
43560 SYLVANIA	095	28123	28896	28995	0.6	71	10329	10791	11020	1.0	2.65	7668	7831	0.5
43566 WATERVILLE	095	6562	6780	6800	0.8	76	2361	2497	2557	1.3	2.65	1847	1911	0.8
43567 WAUSEON	051	12987	13160	13343	0.3	58	4787	4950	5102	0.8	2.64	3559	3595	0.2
43569 WESTON	173	2914	2998	3099	0.7	73	1097	1159	1227	1.3	2.59	807	830	0.7
43570 WEST UNITY	171	3456	3433	3429	-0.2	37	1300	1320	1342	0.4	2.55	927	917	-0.3
43571 WHITEHOUSE	095	5768	5993	6019	0.9	79	2031	2155	2208	1.4	2.74	1579	1639	0.9
43602 TOLEDO	095	4226	4015	3878	-1.2	5	1696	1646	1619	-0.7	2.38	1017	946	-1.7
43604 TOLEDO	095	5419	5188	5042	-1.0	8	2620	2576	2557	-0.4	1.86	1036	939	-2.3
43605 TOLEDO	095	31783	30046	28957	-1.3	4	11750	11285	11064	-1.0	2.59	7701	7139	-1.8
43606 TOLEDO	095	28524	27377	26584	-1.0	9	11190	10861	10697	-0.7	2.23	6132	5719	-1.6
43607 TOLEDO	095	25648	23773	22721	-1.8	1	10573	10022	9774	-1.3	2.35	6197	5628	-2.2
43608 TOLEDO	095	19203	17924	17188	-1.6	2	7051	6672	6500	-1.3	2.67	4714	4312	-2.1
43609 TOLEDO	095	27409	26899	26416	-0.4	24	10338	10372	10390	0.1	2.58	6526	6279	-0.9
43610 TOLEDO	095	6762	6254	5971	-1.8	1	2396	2270	2214	-1.3	2.71	1607	1475	-2.0
43611 TOLEDO	095	21153	20291	19674	-1.0	9	8415	8269	8190	-0.4	2.44	5757	5479	-1.2
43612 TOLEDO	095	31629	30849	30139	-0.6	19	13022	12948	12892	-0.1	2.37	8149	7792	-1.1
43613 TOLEDO	095	34409	33274	32377	-0.8	13	14685	14494	14389	-0.3	2.29	9046	8585	-1.2
43614 TOLEDO	095	30348	30894	30896	0.4	62	13759	14309	14601	0.9	2.12	7830	7840	0.0
43615 TOLEDO	095	39658	40393	40346	0.4	63	17579	18438	18864	1.1	2.17	10433	10487	0.1
43616 OREGON	095	16560	16278	15954	-0.4	27	6677	6677	6659	0.0	2.39	4537	4407	-0.7
43617 TOLEDO	095	7762	8143	8234	1.1	84	2829	3016	3104	1.5	2.70	2263	2355	0.9
43618 OREGON	095	3301	3309	3269	0.1	47	1207	1240	1252	0.6	2.65	944	949	0.1
43619 NORTHWOOD	173	7796	7770	7931	-0.1	42	2886	2943	3069	0.5	2.63	2150	2137	-0.1
43620 TOLEDO	095	7248	6748	6478	-1.7	2	3141	2975	2906	-1.3	2.14	1512	1370	-2.3
43623 TOLEDO	095	20596	20185	19773	-0.5	23	8850	8839	8822	0.0	2.28	5613	5410	-0.9
43624 TOLEDO	095	1389	1495	1538	1.8	91	577	636	665	2.3	1.84	109	106	-0.7
43701 ZANESVILLE	119	55818	55390	54934	-0.2	36	22207	22460	22676	0.3	2.41	15098	14833	-0.4
43713 BARNESVILLE	013	7167	7089	6919	-0.3	33	2847	2868	2853	0.2	2.42	1959	1919	-0.5
43716 BEALLSVILLE	111	2055	2043	2012	-0.1	38	793	810	818	0.5	2.52	590	588	-0.1
43718 BELMONT	013	3391	3335	3238	-0.4	27	1297	1305	1295	0.1	2.49	982	965	-0.4
43719 BETHESDA	013	2427	2346	2261	-0.8	13	973	963	949	-0.2	2.41	708	682	-0.9
43720 BLUE ROCK	119	1414	1354	1319	-1.0	8	534	523	520	-0.5	2.59	411	393	-1.1
43723 BYESVILLE	059	5054	5094	5176	0.2	53	2004	2063	2136	0.7	2.47	1395	1393	0.0
43724 CALDWELL	121	8743	8730	8902	0.0	43	2647	2707	2836	0.5	2.41	1831	1811	-0.3
43725 CAMBRIDGE	059	21140	21252	21575	0.1	50	8656	8857	9143	0.5	2.35	5748	5702	-0.2
43727 CHANDLERSVILLE	119	1342	1292	1263	-0.9	11	501	492	490	-0.4	2.62	392	377	-0.9
43728 CHESTERHILL	115	1335	1268	1227	-1.2	5	510	499	497	-0.5	2.54	380	364	-1.0
43730 CORNING	127	3072	3231	3300	1.2	85	1139	1221	1265	1.7	2.65	873	913	1.1
43731 CROOKSVILLE	115	4759	4583	4510	-0.9	11	1817	1782	1783	-0.5	2.57	1338	1281	-1.0
43732 CUMBERLAND	059	1785	1845	1892	0.8	76	665	700	730	1.2	2.64	525	541	0.7
43734 DUNCAN FALLS	119	1044	947	903	-2.3	0	426	394	383	-1.8	2.40	312	281	-2.4
43739 GLENFORD	127	2088	2192	2250	1.2	84	699	751	785	1.7	2.92	564	592	1.2
43746 HOPEWELL	119	1154	1198	1216	0.9	79	405	429	444	1.4	2.79	326	339	0.9
43747 JERUSALEM	111	1172	1328	1388	3.0	97	443	516	553	3.7	2.57	341	389	3.2
43748 JUNCTION CITY	127	2732	2932	3032	1.7	91	934	1019	1066	2.1	2.88	734	783	1.5
43749 KIMBOLTON	059	2452	2602	2741	1.4	87	929	1014	1091	2.1	2.54	704	751	1.5
43754 LEWISVILLE	111	1535	1522	1495	-0.2	35	578	588	591	0.4	2.53	427	423	-0.2
43755 LORE CITY	059	1791	1872	1937	1.1	83	698	745	786	1.6	2.51	530	552	1.0
43756 MC CONNELSVILLE	115	5366	5223	5121	-0.6	17	2194	2196	2213	0.0	2.30	1476	1435	-0.7
43758 MALTA	115	3442	3294	3198	-1.0	7	1323	1303	1300	-0.4	2.51	970	932	-0.9
43760 MOUNT PERRY	127	1841	1884	1898	0.5	67	627	657	675	1.1	2.87	504	518	0.7
43762 NEW CONCORD	119	5407	5407	5387	0.0	45	1662	1694	1715	0.5	2.51	1163	1149	-0.3
43764 NEW LEXINGTON	127	8301	8092	8022	-0.6	19	3082	3061	3081	-0.2	2.58	2230	2162	-0.7
43766 NEW STRAITSVILLE	127	1695	1745	1759	0.7	73	656	689	705	1.2	2.53	466	477	0.6
43767 NORWICH	119	1485	1496	1489	0.2	52	518	533	541	0.7	2.79	419	422	0.2
43771 PHILO	119	1686	1733	1743	0.7	72	614	644	661	1.1	2.69	469	480	0.6
43772 PLEASANT CITY	121	1838	1794	1811	-0.6	20	702	698	717	-0.1	2.57	524	510	-0.6
43773 QUAKER CITY	059	3142	3369	3537	1.7	90	1100	1194	1272	2.0	2.81	844	897	1.4
43777 ROSEVILLE	119	4820	4618	4512	-1.0	8	1784	1741	1731	-0.6	2.65	1342	1278	-1.1
43778 SALESVILLE	059	1368	1395	1423	0.5	64	442	458	474	0.8	3.02	343	347	0.3
43779 SARAHSVILLE	121	937	987	1029	1.2	86	331	354	375	1.6	2.79	267	280	1.1
43780 SENECAVILLE	121	2877	3046	3173	1.4	87	1142	1235	1311	1.9	2.47	822	867	1.3
43782 SHAWNEE	127	1027	988	970	-0.9	11	356	349	348	-0.5	2.83	276	264	-1.0
43783 SOMERSET	127	4200	4285	4352	0.5	64	1523	1581	1630	0.9	2.65	1117	1133	0.3
43787 STOCKPORT	115	2552	2908	3139	3.1	97	1003	1172	1299	3.7	2.48	721	818	3.0
43788 SUMMERFIELD	121	937	1003	1051	1.6	90	311	340	364	2.1	2.95	249	267	1.7
43793 WOODSFIELD	111	5042	4892	4764	-0.7	14	2030	2015	2008	-0.2	2.37	1436	1386	-0.8
43802 ADAMSVILLE	119	1100	1081	1064	-0.4	26	360	362	363	0.1	2.99	287	282	-0.4
43804 BALTIC	075	2725	2750	2749	0.2	54	756	778	788	0.7	3.43	624	630	0.2
43811 CONESVILLE	031	795	784	780	-0.3	30	316	320	325	0.3	2.44	241	238	-0.3
43812 COSHOCTON	031	20125	19842	19761	-0.3	30	8343	8390	8509	0.1	2.33	5572	5430	-0.6
43821 DRESDEN	119	4187	4288	4311	0.6	69	1604	1672	1709	1.0	2.55	1163	1181	0.4
OHIO					0.3					0.7	2.44			0.0
UNITED STATES					1.2					1.3	2.58			1.1

230-A

ZIP CODE #	POST OFFICE NAME	RACE (%) White 2000	White 2004	Black 2000	Black 2004	Asian/Pacific 2000	Asian/Pacific 2004	% Hispanic Origin 2000	% Hispanic Origin 2004	2004 AGE DISTRIBUTION (%) 0-4	5-9	10-14	15-19	20-24	25-44	45-64	65-84	85+	18+	MEDIAN AGE 2004	% 2004 Males	% 2004 Females
43522	GRAND RAPIDS	97.9	97.5	0.2	0.3	0.3	0.4	2.0	2.3	6.4	7.0	7.5	7.5	5.0	28.2	28.4	8.9	1.2	74.4	38.7	49.9	50.1
43524	HAMLER	93.4	92.9	0.4	0.4	0.1	0.1	10.4	11.4	7.1	7.5	9.0	7.3	5.8	25.0	24.1	12.6	1.6	71.9	36.2	49.8	50.2
43525	HASKINS	97.0	96.7	0.0	0.0	0.8	1.2	3.0	3.3	7.3	7.4	6.8	6.1	5.5	30.7	27.1	8.3	1.0	75.1	37.4	51.7	48.4
43526	HICKSVILLE	97.5	97.2	0.1	0.1	0.1	0.2	2.7	3.1	7.7	7.6	7.9	6.3	6.1	27.4	23.0	12.0	2.1	72.8	36.1	48.8	51.2
43527	HOLGATE	94.4	93.8	0.2	0.2	0.2	0.2	11.4	12.8	7.6	6.9	7.3	6.8	6.3	27.4	23.8	11.5	2.5	73.6	37.2	50.0	50.0
43528	HOLLAND	87.8	85.4	7.5	8.9	1.9	2.6	2.7	3.0	6.4	6.7	7.4	6.7	6.2	27.7	27.6	9.5	1.8	75.4	38.1	48.6	51.4
43532	LIBERTY CENTER	95.8	95.3	1.6	1.7	0.3	0.4	2.6	2.9	6.8	7.2	8.4	9.5	5.4	26.6	26.0	8.7	1.3	70.9	35.5	51.1	48.9
43533	LYONS	95.7	95.2	0.1	0.1	0.9	1.2	4.3	4.7	6.6	7.1	8.4	7.2	5.5	28.4	24.2	11.4	1.3	73.4	36.9	49.4	50.6
43534	MC CLURE	97.6	97.3	0.0	0.0	0.1	0.2	3.6	3.9	6.8	6.7	7.0	7.1	6.1	27.8	26.1	11.2	1.3	75.0	37.9	51.7	48.3
43535	MALINTA	96.6	96.2	0.0	0.0	0.3	0.4	5.5	6.0	5.9	6.4	8.3	7.4	4.8	25.0	28.7	11.9	1.6	74.7	39.7	50.5	49.5
43536	MARK CENTER	98.3	98.4	0.0	0.0	0.0	0.0	2.2	2.5	7.6	8.2	7.8	7.2	5.9	27.6	24.3	10.4	1.0	72.2	36.6	51.5	48.5
43537	MAUMEE	94.3	92.9	2.4	3.0	1.4	1.9	2.0	2.3	5.4	5.6	6.7	6.7	6.8	27.1	27.9	11.6	2.2	78.3	39.6	47.9	52.1
43540	METAMORA	98.0	97.9	0.3	0.3	0.2	0.2	2.2	2.3	6.8	7.5	7.6	7.8	5.1	26.2	27.5	9.7	1.7	73.3	38.4	50.5	49.5
43542	MONCLOVA	96.5	95.7	0.8	1.0	0.8	1.1	1.4	1.6	7.0	7.6	8.1	7.1	5.6	25.8	28.1	9.1	1.7	72.9	38.9	49.4	50.6
43543	MONTPELIER	97.1	96.7	0.2	0.2	0.9	1.2	1.6	1.9	7.0	7.1	7.6	6.9	6.7	26.6	23.9	12.3	1.9	74.0	36.6	49.2	50.8
43545	NAPOLEON	95.0	94.4	0.6	0.6	0.5	0.7	5.2	5.7	6.8	6.8	7.3	6.6	6.9	26.5	24.6	12.3	2.3	75.0	37.6	48.6	51.4
43548	NEW BAVARIA	98.5	98.5	0.4	0.4	0.1	0.1	1.8	2.1	5.8	6.1	7.0	6.2	5.9	26.5	27.0	13.1	2.3	77.1	40.5	50.6	49.4
43549	NEY	98.4	98.2	0.2	0.2	0.0	0.0	1.3	1.4	6.4	6.7	7.0	6.8	5.8	26.2	28.0	12.1	1.0	75.7	39.8	51.1	49.0
43551	PERRYSBURG	94.9	94.1	1.2	1.2	1.4	1.9	3.0	3.3	6.9	7.1	7.8	7.2	6.5	26.8	26.4	9.7	1.7	73.9	37.0	48.7	51.3
43554	PIONEER	97.6	97.3	0.2	0.3	0.1	0.2	2.2	2.5	6.3	6.7	7.4	6.1	6.4	28.2	26.5	11.0	1.5	75.8	37.3	50.6	49.4
43556	SHERWOOD	97.6	97.3	0.5	0.5	0.1	0.1	2.1	2.3	6.4	6.5	6.7	8.2	7.1	26.5	25.7	11.8	1.1	75.5	37.7	49.7	50.4
43557	STRYKER	90.1	89.4	5.7	6.0	0.2	0.2	6.0	6.6	5.8	5.8	6.5	7.3	8.6	32.4	22.8	9.2	1.6	77.6	35.4	54.8	45.2
43558	SWANTON	96.2	95.5	1.5	2.0	0.1	0.2	2.1	2.4	5.9	6.4	7.6	6.9	5.9	26.8	28.5	10.4	1.5	75.5	39.1	50.1	49.9
43560	SYLVANIA	94.4	93.1	1.4	1.7	2.4	3.2	1.8	2.1	6.2	7.0	8.6	7.8	5.8	24.1	27.9	10.8	2.0	73.3	39.4	47.9	52.1
43566	WATERVILLE	98.0	97.5	0.2	0.3	0.4	0.6	1.2	1.4	6.3	7.0	8.0	7.1	5.2	24.5	28.9	11.1	2.1	74.1	40.6	47.9	52.1
43567	WAUSEON	94.6	94.1	0.4	0.4	0.7	0.9	7.6	8.4	7.6	7.6	8.1	7.2	6.3	27.4	23.8	10.3	1.7	72.3	35.8	48.8	51.2
43569	WESTON	95.3	94.9	0.2	0.2	0.1	0.2	6.5	7.1	6.9	6.9	7.8	7.0	7.1	30.7	24.7	8.1	0.9	74.2	35.4	50.4	49.6
43570	WEST UNITY	97.3	97.0	0.3	0.4	0.2	0.2	2.7	2.9	7.0	6.7	8.2	7.4	7.2	27.2	23.8	10.0	2.6	73.1	36.0	50.0	50.0
43571	WHITEHOUSE	97.6	97.1	0.7	0.8	0.5	0.6	1.5	1.7	5.9	6.7	7.8	7.4	5.5	24.6	30.8	9.9	1.4	74.7	40.5	49.2	50.8
43602	TOLEDO	8.4	7.4	86.0	87.1	0.5	0.5	4.1	4.2	12.9	11.4	11.0	8.2	7.6	24.6	15.1	8.0	1.3	59.7	24.3	44.5	55.5
43604	TOLEDO	50.0	45.2	38.4	42.9	0.3	0.4	11.8	12.3	9.1	7.8	7.4	7.3	8.2	28.7	20.8	9.4	1.2	71.6	31.6	48.9	51.1
43605	TOLEDO	81.2	78.9	8.9	10.2	0.4	0.5	12.7	14.1	9.7	8.1	8.0	7.3	8.1	29.4	19.3	8.6	1.5	70.0	30.6	48.5	51.5
43606	TOLEDO	65.7	63.6	28.9	30.3	2.5	3.0	2.0	2.2	5.4	5.7	6.2	12.0	10.7	24.3	20.9	11.3	3.5	79.1	33.2	47.0	53.0
43607	TOLEDO	21.9	19.6	73.5	75.6	1.1	1.3	1.6	1.7	5.8	6.4	8.0	8.2	10.4	25.4	22.2	12.1	1.7	75.2	33.6	47.0	53.0
43608	TOLEDO	43.2	39.3	47.6	51.2	0.3	0.4	9.8	10.1	8.4	8.6	9.9	8.6	7.0	27.1	20.1	8.7	1.5	67.7	30.6	47.2	52.8
43609	TOLEDO	75.5	72.5	13.3	15.3	1.1	1.4	12.8	13.5	8.9	8.0	8.5	7.9	9.5	30.6	18.9	6.9	0.8	69.8	29.7	49.2	50.8
43610	TOLEDO	17.2	14.6	78.3	80.9	0.3	0.3	2.8	2.8	7.3	8.4	9.9	9.1	7.2	28.4	21.8	7.2	0.6	68.5	30.7	47.6	52.5
43611	TOLEDO	87.1	85.8	8.5	9.4	0.3	0.4	4.9	5.4	7.2	7.0	7.4	6.5	6.6	26.9	25.1	11.9	1.5	74.5	36.7	48.5	51.5
43612	TOLEDO	89.9	88.0	5.6	6.8	0.6	0.7	4.4	5.0	7.7	7.2	7.5	6.7	7.0	31.5	21.4	9.8	1.4	73.7	34.0	49.2	50.8
43613	TOLEDO	92.2	90.9	3.9	4.7	0.6	0.8	2.8	3.2	6.9	6.5	6.8	6.5	6.7	30.5	22.7	11.8	1.8	75.9	36.4	48.5	51.5
43614	TOLEDO	87.3	85.1	7.8	9.1	2.0	2.6	3.1	3.5	5.9	5.6	5.5	5.2	6.5	27.8	24.2	16.1	3.3	80.0	40.3	46.6	53.4
43615	TOLEDO	76.5	73.4	17.7	19.9	2.1	2.8	3.1	3.5	6.5	6.0	6.1	5.9	8.2	30.0	23.8	11.8	1.7	78.1	35.6	48.0	52.0
43616	OREGON	94.5	93.6	1.1	1.3	0.8	1.0	5.0	5.7	5.7	5.7	6.4	6.8	6.5	24.9	26.6	14.8	2.6	78.0	40.9	47.8	52.3
43617	TOLEDO	91.7	89.7	1.9	2.3	4.0	5.2	2.3	2.6	6.4	7.5	8.4	7.1	4.9	22.6	32.4	10.0	0.8	73.3	41.1	48.9	51.1
43618	OREGON	97.9	97.6	0.2	0.3	0.3	0.5	2.3	2.6	5.8	6.3	7.0	7.2	6.0	24.6	30.1	12.1	0.9	76.3	41.1	50.4	49.6
43619	NORTHWOOD	94.9	94.3	0.9	0.9	0.8	1.0	4.1	4.6	7.0	7.0	7.0	7.1	7.2	27.5	26.4	9.9	1.1	74.8	36.6	49.0	51.0
43620	TOLEDO	22.4	19.6	73.2	75.8	0.4	0.4	3.1	3.2	7.1	6.5	7.7	7.9	7.5	26.8	22.7	11.9	2.1	73.8	34.8	46.9	53.1
43623	TOLEDO	93.2	91.9	3.0	3.6	1.5	1.9	2.1	2.4	5.0	5.2	6.3	6.4	6.3	24.2	27.9	16.2	2.4	79.5	42.5	47.6	52.4
43624	TOLEDO	44.5	40.5	49.6	53.2	0.7	0.8	3.7	3.9	2.2	1.9	2.3	6.4	11.0	32.2	29.0	12.4	2.7	90.4	41.5	60.9	39.1
43701	ZANESVILLE	91.8	91.2	5.7	6.1	0.3	0.4	0.6	0.6	6.9	6.5	7.1	6.4	6.3	26.4	24.4	13.7	2.4	75.6	38.3	47.5	52.5
43713	BARNESVILLE	98.4	98.1	0.6	0.6	0.3	0.4	0.2	0.3	6.3	6.2	6.6	6.8	6.2	25.3	25.1	14.5	2.9	76.6	40.0	47.2	52.8
43716	BEALLSVILLE	98.2	97.9	0.2	0.2	0.4	0.5	0.3	0.3	5.2	5.5	6.6	6.5	6.7	25.3	30.1	12.7	1.4	78.8	41.1	50.4	49.6
43718	BELMONT	97.1	96.8	1.5	1.5	0.4	0.5	0.7	0.7	6.0	6.2	6.7	6.4	6.2	27.1	28.2	11.7	1.6	77.2	39.7	50.8	49.2
43719	BETHESDA	98.6	98.4	0.3	0.3	0.2	0.3	0.4	0.5	5.6	5.8	7.2	7.3	6.4	27.1	27.1	11.9	1.7	76.8	39.1	48.7	51.3
43720	BLUE ROCK	98.4	98.2	0.5	0.5	0.1	0.2	0.2	0.2	5.8	6.1	7.8	7.3	6.7	27.1	26.7	11.6	0.9	75.6	39.1	51.6	48.4
43723	BYESVILLE	98.1	97.9	0.3	0.3	0.2	0.2	0.8	0.9	8.1	7.2	7.9	6.7	7.8	27.2	23.1	10.7	1.2	72.8	34.1	47.9	52.1
43724	CALDWELL	88.6	87.5	10.6	11.7	0.1	0.2	0.4	0.4	4.3	4.4	5.1	6.1	11.6	34.0	21.0	11.4	2.0	83.1	35.7	61.2	38.9
43725	CAMBRIDGE	94.6	94.1	2.5	2.7	0.5	0.6	0.7	0.8	6.6	6.5	6.8	6.9	6.5	25.3	25.4	13.7	2.3	75.9	39.0	48.0	52.0
43727	CHANDLERSVILLE	98.5	98.3	0.3	0.3	0.2	0.2	0.2	0.2	5.6	6.1	7.7	7.0	6.0	27.7	27.9	11.0	1.2	76.1	39.5	50.8	49.2
43728	CHESTERHILL	75.7	75.1	15.7	16.4	0.0	0.0	0.4	0.4	6.6	6.9	7.3	7.1	6.1	26.3	25.5	12.9	1.3	75.0	38.3	49.5	50.6
43730	CORNING	98.4	98.3	0.4	0.4	0.1	0.1	0.1	0.1	6.9	6.9	7.2	6.6	6.8	28.2	25.4	10.7	1.3	75.0	36.5	50.6	49.4
43731	CROOKSVILLE	98.6	98.5	0.2	0.3	0.0	0.0	0.4	0.4	7.5	7.8	7.5	6.7	6.5	27.9	24.1	10.8	1.3	73.1	35.6	49.3	50.7
43732	CUMBERLAND	98.4	98.1	0.3	0.3	0.1	0.2	0.3	0.3	5.8	6.3	8.1	7.4	5.6	26.1	27.0	12.3	1.3	75.2	39.7	51.4	48.6
43734	DUNCAN FALLS	98.7	98.6	0.2	0.2	0.1	0.1	0.0	0.1	6.4	6.4	6.8	7.0	5.5	25.8	26.8	12.9	2.4	75.8	40.3	49.8	50.2
43739	GLENFORD	98.1	98.0	0.4	0.4	0.1	0.2	0.5	0.6	7.3	7.4	8.1	7.3	6.0	29.1	24.9	9.3	0.7	72.7	36.0	51.0	49.0
43746	HOPEWELL	96.2	96.0	1.3	1.4	0.0	0.0	0.1	0.2	7.1	7.4	8.5	7.6	6.2	27.5	25.1	9.8	0.9	72.4	36.3	49.4	50.6
43747	JERUSALEM	98.2	98.0	0.5	0.5	0.3	0.3	0.1	0.1	5.2	5.7	6.5	6.5	6.0	24.1	31.8	13.0	1.4	78.7	42.3	49.9	50.1
43748	JUNCTION CITY	99.0	98.8	0.1	0.1	0.1	0.2	0.7	0.8	8.2	8.4	9.1	6.8	6.6	27.1	24.4	8.4	1.1	70.1	33.7	51.7	48.3
43749	KIMBOLTON	97.8	97.6	0.5	0.5	0.1	0.2	0.2	0.2	6.5	6.5	6.6	6.1	5.6	24.7	28.7	14.0	1.3	76.6	41.1	51.5	48.5
43754	LEWISVILLE	98.6	98.4	0.1	0.1	0.1	0.1	0.7	0.7	5.9	6.1	7.4	7.8	6.4	22.8	26.7	14.4	2.6	75.6	40.3	49.8	50.2
43755	LORE CITY	97.8	97.5	0.5	0.6	0.3	0.4	0.6	0.7	6.1	6.5	7.2	7.1	6.0	25.1	27.9	12.9	1.2	75.5	40.1	48.9	51.1
43756	MC CONNELSVILLE	95.6	95.3	2.0	2.1	0.1	0.1	0.3	0.3	6.1	6.2	6.5	6.4	5.9	24.0	25.8	16.1	2.9	77.0	41.5	48.6	51.4
43758	MALTA	94.4	94.1	3.0	3.3	0.2	0.2	0.4	0.4	6.1	5.8	7.3	7.0	6.8	25.1	26.7	13.8	1.5	76.4	39.9	49.7	50.3
43760	MOUNT PERRY	98.0	97.8	0.7	0.7	0.1	0.2	0.4	0.5	7.3	7.4	7.8	7.4	5.6	28.7	25.5	9.7	0.7	72.8	36.5	50.7	49.3
43762	NEW CONCORD	97.4	96.9	0.9	1.0	0.9	1.2	0.6	0.7	5.0	5.1	6.0	11.7	16.7	24.1	20.3	9.0	2.2	80.6	28.7	48.6	51.4
43764	NEW LEXINGTON	98.8	98.7	0.2	0.3	0.2	0.2	0.4	0.4	7.8	7.3	7.6	6.7	7.2	26.9	23.4	11.4	1.7	73.3	35.4	49.7	50.3
43766	NEW STRAITSVILLE	98.2	98.2	0.3	0.3	0.1	0.1	1.3	1.3	7.3	7.3	7.9	7.1	6.8	27.3	23.8	11.3	1.3	73.2	36.0	49.6	50.4
43767	NORWICH	99.0	98.9	0.3	0.3	0.1	0.2	0.2	0.2	5.8	6.5	8.9	6.6	5.9	28.8	26.3	10.6	0.7	74.2	37.8	51.0	49.0
43771	PHILO	97.9	97.6	0.7	0.7	0.4	0.5	0.1	0.1	6.7	6.6	7.9	8.1	7.4	27.0	24.2	11.1	1.1	74.0	37.0	49.4	50.6
43772	PLEASANT CITY	98.8	98.8	0.3	0.3	0.0	0.0	0.4	0.5	6.1	6.4	7.1	6.6	6.0	24.4	27.8	14.3	1.5	76.4	40.6	48.8	51.2
43773	QUAKER CITY	98.3	98.1	0.6	0.6	0.1	0.1	0.3	0.3	8.3	8.2	8.5	6.7	6.3	25.5	23.3	11.8	1.5	70.9	35.3	49.7	50.3
43777	ROSEVILLE	98.2	98.1	0.5	0.5	0.0	0.1	0.6	0.6	8.3	8.1	8.1	6.8	6.8	28.2	22.4	10.3	1.1	71.4	34.0	49.5	50.5
43778	SALESVILLE	98.4	98.1	0.4	0.4	0.3	0.4	0.7	0.8	6.6	7.0	8.6	7.5	6.5	25.1	25.6	11.8	1.4	72.7	38.0	50.3	49.8
43779	SARAHSVILLE	98.9	99.0	0.2	0.2	0.0	0.0	0.8	0.7	6.7	6.9	8.4	7.4	6.6	26.8	24.9	11.6	0.8	73.3	36.8	50.2	49.9
43780	SENECAVILLE	98.3	98.2	0.5	0.6	0.1	0.1	0.4	0.5	6.3	6.5	7.5	6.5	5.6	25.7	27.2	13.4	1.4	75.5	40.1	48.8	51.2
43782	SHAWNEE	99.3	99.3	0.0	0.0	0.3	0.3	0.3	0.3	6.7	6.7	9.1	8.3	7.6	29.9	23.1	7.8	0.9	72.5	33.9	50.3	49.7
43783	SOMERSET	98.7	98.6	0.1	0.1	0.1	0.2	0.5	0.6	7.2	7.3	7.5	6.6	5.9	26.0	25.6	11.9	2.1	73.9	38.4	49.4	50.6
43787	STOCKPORT	94.2	94.5	3.2	3.1	0.1	0.1	0.6	0.7	6.7	6.8	7.0	6.3	6.9	26.1	26.1	12.6	1.4	75.7	38.6	50.3	49.7
43788	SUMMERFIELD	99.3	99.2	0.1	0.1	0.0	0.0	0.6	0.7	8.2	8.0	8.6	8.8	7.1	26.4	21.4	10.5	1.1	69.9	32.8	50.6	49.5
43793	WOODSFIELD	98.7	98.6	0.2	0.2	0.2	0.3	0.6	0.6	5.9	6.0	6.5	6.1	5.4	23.9	27.3	16.2	2.8	77.9	42.3	48.2	51.8
43802	ADAMSVILLE	98.8	98.6	0.4	0.4	0.1	0.2	0.2	0.2	6.9	7.6	9.3	7.1	6.2	27.6	24.3	10.2	0.8	71.7	35.2	51.1	48.9
43804	BALTIC	99.1	99.0	0.3	0.3	0.1	0.1	0.4	0.5	11.2	10.2	10.8	9.0	8.1	24.2	16.0	8.8	1.9	62.1	25.6	50.3	49.7
43811	CONESVILLE	99.0	99.0	0.1	0.1	0.0	0.0	0.4	0.4	6.1	6.6	7.5	6.6	6.4	26.5	28.3	11.0	0.9	75.5	37.6	50.1	49.9
43812	COSHOCTON	96.5	96.4	1.6	1.7	0.5	0.5	0.6	0.7	6.4	6.3	6.8	6.7	6.4	24.9	25.8	14.6	2.3	76.5	40.0	48.0	52.1
43821	DRESDEN	98.6	98.4	0.4	0.4	0.1	0.2	0.4	0.4	6.8	6.8	7.7	6.8	6.4	27.7	25.6	11.1	1.1	74.5	37.0	49.3	50.7
	OHIO	85.0	84.1	11.5	11.8	1.2	1.6	1.9	2.1	6.7	6.6	7.1	7.0	7.1	27.5	24.7	11.6	1.8	75.6	37.0	48.6	51.4
	UNITED STATES	75.1	73.6	12.3	12.5	3.8	4.2	12.5	14.1	6.9	6.7	7.2	7.0	7.3	28.6	23.8	10.8	1.7	75.1	36.0	49.1	50.9

ZIP CODE #	POST OFFICE NAME	2004 Per Capita Income	2004 HH Income Base	2004 Household Income Distribution (%) Less than $25,000	$25,000 to $49,999	$50,000 to $99,999	$100,000 to $149,999	$150,000 or More	Median Household Income 2004	2009	2004 National Centile	2004 State Centile	2004 Home Value Base	2004 Home Value Distribution (%) Less than $50,000	$50,000 to $89,999	$90,000 to $174,999	$175,000 to $399,999	$400,000 or More	2004 Median Home Value
43522	GRAND RAPIDS	26729	1502	14.3	26.0	41.6	12.7	5.5	58513	69374	83	83	1317	11.8	11.6	38.5	36.1	2.0	142534
43524	HAMLER	21060	539	18.4	33.0	40.3	6.9	1.5	49156	55665	70	60	461	10.6	29.9	47.3	11.9	0.2	98878
43525	HASKINS	30153	235	12.8	24.3	41.3	15.7	6.0	63561	75742	87	90	201	15.4	8.5	35.8	31.8	8.5	149405
43526	HICKSVILLE	21615	2325	20.4	35.3	34.8	6.6	2.9	46471	52459	65	51	1887	12.9	27.0	48.0	11.3	0.9	98473
43527	HOLGATE	20589	872	22.5	31.2	36.0	8.3	2.1	45827	52466	63	48	714	11.1	41.5	39.9	6.7	0.8	88125
43528	HOLLAND	35172	5792	17.9	23.3	30.6	14.2	14.0	61727	75493	86	88	4475	10.6	11.8	33.2	33.4	11.1	157570
43532	LIBERTY CENTER	22762	1459	20.2	30.6	37.7	9.0	2.5	49457	55988	71	61	1260	10.4	19.3	52.4	16.8	1.2	111583
43533	LYONS	20078	574	22.1	33.5	35.7	7.0	1.7	47006	52702	66	53	480	12.7	17.7	50.6	17.5	1.5	115561
43534	MC CLURE	21906	725	15.7	35.2	40.6	7.2	1.4	49330	55268	71	60	625	15.8	26.7	45.0	10.1	2.4	100521
43535	MALINTA	23166	311	22.5	26.7	40.8	8.0	1.9	50486	56494	73	65	269	7.1	29.0	53.2	10.0	0.7	107021
43536	MARK CENTER	20483	170	25.9	27.7	31.2	11.2	4.1	47532	53478	67	55	144	3.5	25.7	48.6	22.2	0.0	108333
43537	MAUMEE	32024	10480	16.0	26.1	35.3	14.1	8.6	59565	71688	84	85	7571	2.0	6.7	54.1	33.1	4.0	156085
43540	METAMORA	21843	433	18.9	27.7	40.9	10.4	2.1	52004	58497	75	70	362	4.1	10.2	60.8	23.5	1.4	131746
43542	MONCLOVA	31917	873	7.7	20.9	37.1	18.4	15.9	76526	91019	94	97	801	8.6	4.2	34.8	41.3	11.0	181086
43543	MONTPELIER	19337	3218	25.1	34.2	35.0	4.4	1.3	42257	47641	54	37	2459	14.0	29.2	46.6	9.7	0.5	97827
43545	NAPOLEON	22515	5877	21.5	32.1	36.4	7.1	2.9	47059	53211	66	53	4531	11.6	19.3	51.9	15.5	1.7	112277
43548	NEW BAVARIA	22407	285	18.6	33.7	36.1	9.5	2.1	47174	52862	67	54	249	15.7	27.7	49.0	7.2	0.4	94024
43549	NEY	22116	531	11.1	34.5	46.7	6.6	1.1	53307	60465	77	74	472	13.8	25.2	50.0	10.8	0.2	101374
43551	PERRYSBURG	33932	13765	14.9	22.6	35.4	17.0	10.0	64119	77039	88	90	10510	14.1	5.1	33.6	40.9	6.3	169344
43554	PIONEER	21622	1090	22.8	28.9	41.1	4.9	2.3	48650	53230	70	59	897	11.2	26.2	47.4	13.5	1.8	106174
43556	SHERWOOD	20410	756	19.4	33.3	38.9	7.5	0.8	48302	55281	69	58	652	14.7	31.8	40.5	12.4	0.6	93108
43557	STRYKER	19340	1053	18.0	33.4	42.0	5.3	1.3	48784	54242	70	59	873	10.8	28.4	47.3	12.8	0.7	99356
43558	SWANTON	24309	5378	16.3	28.3	38.0	13.8	3.7	55839	64396	81	79	4655	13.4	9.2	46.5	29.1	1.7	137652
43560	SYLVANIA	35719	10791	14.4	20.7	34.0	17.0	14.0	68260	82803	90	94	8551	1.9	7.1	39.3	45.1	6.7	178672
43566	WATERVILLE	29667	2497	10.0	22.5	39.3	20.9	7.4	70236	84722	91	95	2155	0.7	2.7	45.9	48.8	1.9	175962
43567	WAUSEON	21193	4950	18.3	33.8	39.0	7.0	1.8	47652	54352	68	56	3818	9.0	13.8	54.1	21.7	1.4	124111
43569	WESTON	23141	1159	17.3	31.1	37.5	12.3	2.0	51216	60823	74	68	964	22.1	22.9	39.6	14.5	0.8	95783
43570	WEST UNITY	19793	1320	23.6	34.5	35.5	4.7	1.7	43699	49316	58	41	1037	12.5	23.1	50.5	13.1	0.8	104841
43571	WHITEHOUSE	29619	2155	14.4	21.5	37.0	18.1	8.9	65459	79650	89	92	1869	4.2	7.0	38.7	43.5	6.6	175361
43602	TOLEDO	10752	1646	68.4	19.4	9.0	1.9	1.4	15055	17776	1	1	409	68.0	17.9	13.2	0.0	1.0	34219
43604	TOLEDO	14671	2576	67.7	18.3	10.6	1.9	1.5	13748	16178	1	1	471	66.7	21.7	5.5	5.1	1.1	41907
43605	TOLEDO	15372	11285	40.1	32.1	23.6	3.5	0.7	31668	37512	17	10	6298	42.0	50.7	6.8	0.4	0.1	54336
43606	TOLEDO	26595	10861	30.2	24.4	27.9	11.4	6.0	43608	52485	58	41	6421	10.9	16.2	46.1	23.2	3.6	132106
43607	TOLEDO	16914	10022	44.6	26.2	23.0	4.8	1.3	29186	34093	11	6	5513	36.3	42.1	18.6	2.7	0.3	61058
43608	TOLEDO	14308	6672	45.7	31.7	18.9	2.7	0.9	27800	32289	8	6	3950	48.2	45.5	5.9	0.4	0.0	51157
43609	TOLEDO	16250	10372	39.3	29.9	25.5	4.6	0.7	32400	39554	19	11	5602	33.9	49.3	15.8	1.0	0.1	63612
43610	TOLEDO	14837	2270	42.8	28.2	22.7	5.0	1.3	30078	34754	12	8	1293	36.2	37.1	23.8	2.9	0.0	65279
43611	TOLEDO	22417	8269	26.7	28.6	32.8	9.2	2.7	44062	53837	59	43	5965	14.2	28.7	50.1	6.3	0.7	96481
43612	TOLEDO	21854	12948	23.4	31.1	37.4	7.4	0.8	46127	55701	64	50	8811	11.3	46.8	40.6	1.1	0.2	85052
43613	TOLEDO	24269	14494	24.2	30.9	34.3	8.6	1.9	45491	54429	63	47	10121	6.1	29.5	60.3	4.0	0.1	101359
43614	TOLEDO	28713	14309	24.5	27.7	32.7	11.1	4.0	47806	57042	68	56	8746	1.5	11.6	67.5	18.8	0.6	133882
43615	TOLEDO	28736	18438	27.0	28.8	30.2	8.9	5.2	45480	53663	63	47	11409	15.6	20.3	46.6	14.4	3.2	106608
43616	OREGON	26438	6677	21.9	26.6	34.4	13.2	4.0	51707	62416	75	69	4821	3.2	13.5	55.6	26.6	1.2	138201
43617	TOLEDO	37056	3016	11.6	19.3	30.7	20.1	18.3	78183	93632	94	97	2820	9.5	5.8	24.6	54.9	5.2	196396
43618	OREGON	27822	1240	14.9	22.2	40.2	14.8	7.9	62241	75757	86	89	1133	2.5	15.5	49.6	30.2	2.3	137332
43619	NORTHWOOD	24708	2943	20.0	22.5	41.7	11.2	4.6	57627	67466	82	81	2376	11.8	14.9	53.3	17.0	3.0	124937
43620	TOLEDO	16642	2975	54.6	19.4	19.5	4.4	2.1	21451	25571	2	3	873	21.4	25.7	38.0	14.2	0.7	93072
43623	TOLEDO	32695	8839	23.4	25.5	32.4	10.2	8.5	51136	61523	74	67	6106	3.5	17.4	52.5	22.4	4.2	123593
43624	TOLEDO	14582	636	67.6	16.8	9.0	6.3	0.3	14536	17120	1	1	30	36.7	16.7	30.0	13.3	3.3	75000
43701	ZANESVILLE	20976	22460	33.0	31.4	27.8	4.8	3.1	37366	43108	37	23	15637	18.9	26.9	41.6	11.5	1.0	95086
43713	BARNESVILLE	17126	2868	42.2	29.0	24.0	3.1	1.8	30855	35069	14	9	2161	36.7	36.2	22.2	4.7	0.2	64471
43716	BEALLSVILLE	17951	810	38.3	30.4	27.4	3.0	1.0	32959	36609	21	13	673	32.4	37.4	25.0	5.1	0.2	71567
43718	BELMONT	19537	1305	30.3	31.7	31.1	4.3	2.5	39228	45126	44	28	1067	33.7	26.2	30.2	8.3	1.7	75282
43719	BETHESDA	17870	963	34.3	34.4	26.2	3.3	1.9	33676	38862	23	15	729	32.2	36.6	27.3	3.7	0.1	70915
43720	BLUE ROCK	18302	523	26.6	37.5	28.3	5.9	1.7	40164	45965	47	30	442	19.0	22.4	44.6	14.0	0.0	95758
43723	BYESVILLE	16930	2063	37.7	38.6	19.8	2.8	1.1	32405	36552	19	11	1423	30.2	40.9	24.4	4.5	0.0	66390
43724	CALDWELL	17251	2707	34.6	35.8	24.8	3.0	1.9	36121	40171	32	21	2106	25.6	30.9	34.0	8.6	1.0	82649
43725	CAMBRIDGE	19224	8857	38.6	31.0	23.7	4.7	2.0	32667	36998	20	12	5973	21.0	34.2	34.6	9.0	1.2	83665
43727	CHANDLERSVILLE	20295	492	17.5	39.0	35.6	7.5	0.4	46368	53093	65	51	431	11.8	20.4	50.1	17.2	0.5	110352
43728	CHESTERHILL	15367	499	38.7	30.7	25.9	4.0	0.8	32326	36305	19	11	411	34.6	28.7	32.1	4.4	0.2	70517
43730	CORNING	16258	1221	32.4	35.4	27.3	3.6	1.4	37241	41919	36	23	1024	32.7	31.5	30.2	5.6	0.0	69195
43731	CROOKSVILLE	17365	1782	35.5	34.5	25.6	2.7	1.7	34544	38773	26	16	1438	25.6	43.1	25.2	5.6	0.5	70068
43732	CUMBERLAND	22321	700	23.4	40.1	29.3	4.9	2.3	42277	47401	54	37	577	26.0	25.7	40.7	6.8	0.9	87683
43734	DUNCAN FALLS	20959	394	27.4	35.8	26.4	8.1	2.3	37855	43136	39	25	332	9.3	23.2	43.1	24.4	0.0	130769
43739	GLENFORD	22832	751	18.6	31.7	38.9	5.2	5.6	49685	56579	71	62	644	12.0	18.9	42.1	22.5	4.5	120050
43746	HOPEWELL	21093	429	15.9	32.9	41.7	6.5	3.0	50651	57611	73	65	369	16.3	16.8	36.0	30.4	0.5	116755
43747	JERUSALEM	16383	516	35.3	31.4	29.1	3.7	0.6	35597	39776	30	20	441	29.5	32.9	30.8	6.4	0.5	77558
43748	JUNCTION CITY	18723	1019	27.6	38.2	28.9	3.2	2.2	39800	44820	45	29	821	27.9	25.0	37.3	9.4	0.5	86594
43749	KIMBOLTON	17011	1014	34.1	32.8	27.7	4.4	0.9	34385	38515	25	16	862	22.0	19.4	43.4	13.9	1.3	102215
43754	LEWISVILLE	15199	588	36.2	39.3	22.1	1.4	1.0	31520	35636	16	9	488	27.3	34.8	26.8	10.5	0.6	77455
43755	LORE CITY	17458	745	34.0	34.6	26.6	3.5	1.3	35359	39130	29	19	622	23.0	27.8	37.5	11.6	0.2	89057
43756	MC CONNELSVILLE	17906	2196	37.8	32.2	25.1	4.0	0.9	34430	38716	25	16	1606	19.0	29.8	42.9	7.4	0.9	91227
43758	MALTA	14574	1303	41.7	32.9	22.0	3.0	0.4	30692	35134	14	8	1039	26.7	34.5	28.9	8.1	1.9	75808
43760	MOUNT PERRY	20934	657	21.2	38.8	31.4	4.4	4.3	41562	47929	52	34	564	17.7	19.7	38.7	19.7	4.3	108871
43762	NEW CONCORD	18996	1694	31.1	28.2	31.5	6.7	2.5	41986	47902	53	36	1249	9.6	23.2	48.8	17.3	1.1	107909
43764	NEW LEXINGTON	16380	3061	33.6	34.7	26.9	3.3	1.5	35804	40734	31	20	2260	21.9	33.9	37.3	5.8	1.2	83627
43766	NEW STRAITSVILLE	16641	689	34.7	36.9	24.4	3.1	1.0	32890	37435	21	13	551	51.7	25.8	19.1	3.5	0.0	48643
43767	NORWICH	20500	533	17.6	34.5	40.2	5.3	2.4	48127	54482	69	57	467	12.2	17.1	45.4	23.8	1.5	114347
43771	PHILO	19420	644	30.4	33.5	29.5	4.7	1.9	38142	44273	40	25	544	25.2	32.4	35.1	7.4	0.0	82931
43772	PLEASANT CITY	15547	698	35.4	35.5	25.9	2.9	0.3	35138	39034	28	18	586	30.4	37.9	26.1	5.3	0.3	65132
43773	QUAKER CITY	14841	1194	36.6	33.5	26.6	2.1	1.3	33545	37540	23	14	989	31.9	23.2	29.0	15.0	1.0	81161
43777	ROSEVILLE	15532	1741	37.7	35.8	22.5	2.8	1.3	32821	37084	20	13	1344	30.3	38.0	26.0	5.1	0.6	69225
43778	SALESVILLE	13993	458	33.2	35.2	27.3	3.5	0.9	36379	40778	33	21	385	27.0	27.8	32.2	13.0	0.0	83148
43779	SARAHSVILLE	16426	354	28.3	35.6	31.4	4.2	0.6	40144	43834	47	30	303	34.3	26.7	28.7	9.2	1.0	70313
43780	SENECAVILLE	17424	1235	38.6	29.6	24.9	4.9	1.9	32799	36882	20	12	1021	29.0	27.9	27.0	15.0	1.1	76636
43782	SHAWNEE	14907	349	28.7	39.3	28.7	3.4	0.0	36811	41666	35	22	296	48.0	30.4	19.9	1.4	0.3	51765
43783	SOMERSET	18403	1581	27.0	35.6	30.8	5.1	1.5	39881	45252	46	29	1258	13.3	18.4	47.1	18.7	2.5	114790
43787	STOCKPORT	15479	1172	41.6	30.9	23.6	2.7	1.4	29462	33738	11	7	956	38.5	24.0	29.0	8.2	0.4	69216
43788	SUMMERFIELD	14295	340	32.9	40.9	24.1	1.5	0.6	35331	39820	29	18	284	44.4	29.9	14.8	10.2	0.7	55714
43793	WOODSFIELD	16860	2015	39.8	32.8	23.6	2.5	1.3	31494	35187	16	9	1530	28.2	36.7	29.1	5.5	0.6	73172
43802	ADAMSVILLE	17319	362	24.3	32.0	37.0	5.3	1.4	44756	51250	61	45	308	22.1	24.7	40.3	13.0	0.0	95263
43804	BALTIC	12659	778	26.7	41.0	28.8	2.3	1.2	37740	42016	38	24	606	9.4	17.5	49.5	20.1	3.5	118277
43811	CONESVILLE	20025	320	29.4	32.8	30.9	5.0	1.9	39652	44414	45	28	270	31.9	21.9	37.0	9.3	0.0	84737
43812	COSHOCTON	19778	8390	32.4	32.8	27.4	5.4	2.0	36835	41837	35	22	5973	18.5	28.9	39.6	12.2	0.8	93553
43821	DRESDEN	22435	1672	23.0	30.0	36.1	7.7	3.2	47639	54080	67	55	1331	15.0	22.8	49.3	11.5	1.4	102669
	OHIO	25510		24.6	28.1	32.2	10.1	5.0	47354	56168				9.2	18.6	47.0	22.1	3.1	121192
	UNITED STATES	25866		24.7	27.1	30.8	10.9	6.5	48124	56710				10.9	15.0	33.7	30.1	10.4	145905

ZIP CODE #	POST OFFICE NAME	FINANCIAL SERVICES: Auto Loan	FINANCIAL SERVICES: Home Loan	FINANCIAL SERVICES: Invest-ments	FINANCIAL SERVICES: Retire-ment Plans	THE HOME: Home Improvements: Home Repair	THE HOME: Home Improvements: Lawn & Garden	THE HOME: Furnishings: Comput-ers & Hard-ware	THE HOME: Furnishings: Major Appli-ances	THE HOME: Furnishings: TV, Radio, Sound Equip-ment	THE HOME: Furnishings: Furni-ture	ENTERTAINMENT: Dine out/ Carry out	ENTERTAINMENT: Sports Equip-ment	ENTERTAINMENT: Fees & Tickets	ENTERTAINMENT: Toys & Games	ENTERTAINMENT: Travel	ENTERTAINMENT: Cable TV	PERSONAL: Apparel & Services	PERSONAL: Auto Repairs	PERSONAL: Health Insur-ance	PERSONAL: Pets & Supplies
43522	GRAND RAPIDS	100	103	97	103	102	106	99	100	96	98	120	117	99	121	98	94	116	99	96	113
43524	HAMLER	91	81	62	77	86	92	75	83	80	75	97	99	74	99	77	82	92	81	90	107
43525	HASKINS	118	115	97	111	119	125	105	113	108	105	132	134	105	136	108	109	127	110	117	141
43526	HICKSVILLE	89	77	58	72	82	90	73	81	79	72	95	96	70	97	75	82	90	79	90	104
43527	HOLGATE	87	76	58	74	80	88	74	80	79	73	96	94	72	96	75	80	90	79	87	99
43528	HOLLAND	132	136	131	137	135	141	129	131	126	130	157	152	131	157	129	124	153	129	127	150
43532	LIBERTY CENTER	101	90	68	85	95	101	83	92	88	83	107	109	81	109	85	90	102	89	99	118
43533	LYONS	85	76	58	72	80	86	70	78	74	70	91	93	69	93	72	76	86	76	84	100
43534	MC CLURE	94	84	64	79	88	95	77	86	82	77	100	102	76	102	80	84	95	83	93	111
43535	MALINTA	92	81	62	77	86	92	75	83	80	75	97	99	74	99	78	82	92	81	90	108
43536	MARK CENTER	94	84	64	80	89	95	78	86	82	78	100	103	76	102	80	85	95	84	93	111
43537	MAUMEE	102	113	125	115	112	115	110	108	105	110	132	127	113	134	110	102	130	108	101	119
43540	METAMORA	93	83	63	79	88	94	77	85	82	77	99	102	75	101	79	84	94	83	92	110
43542	MONCLOVA	123	146	150	146	143	142	132	132	124	132	155	156	138	163	134	120	154	128	120	148
43543	MONTPELIER	76	67	53	63	70	77	64	70	69	64	83	83	62	85	65	71	79	69	77	88
43545	NAPOLEON	87	78	65	75	81	89	76	82	80	76	97	95	74	97	77	81	93	81	87	100
43548	NEW BAVARIA	91	81	62	77	86	92	75	83	80	75	97	99	74	99	77	82	92	81	90	107
43549	NEY	93	82	63	78	87	93	76	84	81	76	98	101	75	100	78	83	93	82	91	109
43551	PERRYSBURG	119	129	133	128	127	133	122	123	119	122	148	142	125	151	123	117	146	121	117	138
43554	PIONEER	87	77	59	74	82	88	72	79	76	72	92	95	70	94	74	78	88	77	86	102
43556	SHERWOOD	87	77	59	74	82	88	72	79	76	72	92	95	70	94	74	78	88	77	86	102
43557	STRYKER	87	78	59	74	82	88	72	80	76	72	93	95	70	95	74	78	88	77	86	103
43558	SWANTON	101	95	79	91	98	103	88	95	91	88	111	113	87	113	90	91	107	93	98	118
43560	SYLVANIA	127	146	156	147	144	147	137	135	130	136	163	158	143	169	138	127	161	133	126	150
43566	WATERVILLE	102	125	137	124	123	123	114	113	108	114	135	132	121	143	117	105	135	110	103	124
43567	WAUSEON	85	79	66	77	82	88	76	81	79	75	97	95	75	98	77	80	92	80	85	99
43569	WESTON	93	85	69	82	89	96	81	87	84	80	103	102	79	104	82	86	98	85	93	108
43570	WEST UNITY	80	70	54	68	74	81	68	74	72	68	88	86	66	88	69	74	83	73	80	92
43571	WHITEHOUSE	109	130	135	130	128	127	117	118	110	117	138	138	123	145	119	106	137	114	106	131
43602	TOLEDO	35	29	37	26	28	34	34	33	39	35	48	38	33	45	33	40	46	36	37	38
43604	TOLEDO	37	31	43	30	30	36	38	36	41	38	51	41	37	50	37	43	50	39	39	40
43605	TOLEDO	54	50	55	49	50	56	56	54	59	55	73	63	55	73	55	59	70	56	57	60
43606	TOLEDO	83	85	104	85	84	91	91	87	90	89	113	102	92	113	90	89	111	89	84	96
43607	TOLEDO	56	49	54	46	48	57	55	54	59	55	73	60	54	68	53	61	70	56	58	62
43608	TOLEDO	52	48	54	46	47	54	53	51	56	52	70	59	53	69	52	57	67	53	54	58
43609	TOLEDO	56	53	59	53	52	58	60	57	61	58	76	68	59	76	58	60	74	60	57	63
43610	TOLEDO	55	51	60	49	50	57	55	54	59	56	73	61	56	72	55	60	71	55	56	61
43611	TOLEDO	74	77	81	74	77	83	76	76	78	75	96	88	78	100	77	78	94	76	78	86
43612	TOLEDO	69	71	76	70	72	77	74	72	74	71	92	84	75	95	73	73	89	72	72	80
43613	TOLEDO	73	78	85	77	78	83	79	78	79	77	98	90	81	101	79	78	96	78	76	85
43614	TOLEDO	82	85	98	86	84	90	88	85	87	87	109	100	89	108	87	85	106	87	82	94
43615	TOLEDO	86	86	95	87	85	91	90	87	89	89	111	103	89	110	88	87	108	89	84	98
43616	OREGON	83	92	101	90	91	98	90	89	89	88	111	102	93	116	92	89	109	88	88	99
43617	TOLEDO	138	157	160	157	154	159	142	143	135	144	170	164	150	172	145	132	168	140	135	161
43618	OREGON	104	112	109	111	113	117	104	107	102	103	126	125	107	131	106	101	123	104	104	123
43619	NORTHWOOD	89	100	100	98	98	100	92	93	89	92	111	109	95	116	93	87	109	91	88	105
43620	TOLEDO	50	44	53	42	44	51	49	49	54	50	66	55	49	63	49	55	64	51	53	55
43623	TOLEDO	98	106	119	106	106	113	106	104	104	104	130	121	109	133	107	104	127	104	103	115
43624	TOLEDO	36	31	45	32	31	37	39	36	41	37	51	42	38	50	38	42	50	39	39	40
43701	ZANESVILLE	73	69	67	67	71	78	70	72	73	69	90	83	69	90	71	74	86	72	76	84
43713	BARNESVILLE	67	53	36	50	57	67	55	61	62	53	73	70	50	71	55	65	67	61	72	76
43716	BEALLSVILLE	83	58	29	51	65	74	56	68	66	57	78	82	49	75	57	71	71	68	83	95
43718	BELMONT	78	63	45	61	68	76	63	71	68	62	82	83	58	81	64	70	76	69	79	90
43719	BETHESDA	69	58	44	57	61	69	58	63	62	58	75	73	56	75	58	64	71	62	69	77
43720	BLUE ROCK	87	61	32	54	68	78	59	72	69	59	82	85	51	78	60	74	75	71	86	100
43723	BYESVILLE	70	55	38	50	59	67	54	62	61	54	73	73	49	71	55	64	67	61	72	81
43724	CALDWELL	69	53	33	49	58	66	53	61	60	52	71	71	48	69	53	63	66	60	71	79
43725	CAMBRIDGE	69	60	52	57	63	70	61	65	66	60	80	76	59	79	62	68	75	65	72	79
43727	CHANDLERSVILLE	90	73	50	68	79	86	69	79	76	69	91	94	65	91	70	79	85	77	89	105
43728	CHESTERHILL	74	49	22	42	56	64	48	59	57	48	67	71	40	64	48	62	61	59	73	84
43730	CORNING	79	55	28	48	62	71	53	65	63	54	74	78	46	71	54	67	68	64	79	91
43731	CROOKSVILLE	75	59	39	54	64	72	58	66	65	58	78	77	53	76	58	68	72	65	76	86
43732	CUMBERLAND	96	83	60	78	88	95	77	86	83	77	100	103	74	102	79	85	95	84	95	113
43734	DUNCAN FALLS	69	73	73	70	74	81	69	72	70	69	87	82	71	90	72	72	84	70	74	83
43739	GLENFORD	107	95	72	90	100	108	88	97	93	88	113	116	86	116	90	96	108	95	105	126
43746	HOPEWELL	94	84	64	80	89	95	78	86	82	78	100	103	76	102	80	85	95	84	93	111
43747	JERUSALEM	71	58	40	54	62	68	54	62	60	55	72	74	51	72	56	62	68	61	70	82
43748	JUNCTION CITY	100	69	33	60	77	88	66	82	79	67	93	98	57	88	67	85	85	81	100	115
43749	KIMBOLTON	81	55	25	47	62	71	53	66	64	54	75	79	45	71	54	68	68	65	81	93
43754	LEWISVILLE	69	48	26	43	54	63	49	58	57	48	67	68	42	64	49	61	61	58	71	78
43755	LORE CITY	78	58	34	51	64	72	55	66	63	55	75	78	49	73	57	67	69	65	79	91
43756	MC CONNELSVILLE	70	53	33	49	58	67	54	62	61	53	72	72	48	69	55	65	66	62	74	80
43758	MALTA	61	46	31	42	50	58	47	54	54	47	64	63	42	61	48	57	59	54	64	70
43760	MOUNT PERRY	96	86	65	81	90	97	79	88	84	79	102	105	78	104	81	86	97	85	95	113
43762	NEW CONCORD	78	71	65	69	73	81	70	74	74	70	90	86	69	91	71	75	86	74	79	89
43764	NEW LEXINGTON	68	57	43	54	61	67	56	62	61	56	74	72	53	74	57	63	70	61	69	78
43766	NEW STRAITSVILLE	79	53	24	46	60	69	51	64	62	52	73	77	44	69	52	67	66	63	79	91
43767	NORWICH	92	82	62	78	86	93	76	84	80	76	98	100	74	100	78	82	93	82	91	108
43771	PHILO	84	69	50	67	73	83	70	77	76	69	92	88	66	90	70	78	85	76	85	94
43772	PLEASANT CITY	65	51	34	48	55	64	53	59	59	51	70	67	48	67	53	62	64	58	69	73
43773	QUAKER CITY	77	53	27	47	60	69	51	63	61	52	72	76	44	68	53	66	65	63	78	89
43777	ROSEVILLE	70	52	34	48	57	65	53	61	60	53	72	72	48	70	53	64	67	61	71	80
43778	SALESVILLE	78	54	28	47	61	70	52	64	62	52	72	76	45	69	54	66	66	64	78	90
43779	SARAHSVILLE	79	62	40	57	68	75	58	68	65	59	78	81	54	77	60	69	73	67	78	92
43780	SENECAVILLE	73	55	35	50	62	71	55	65	62	54	74	75	49	71	57	67	68	64	77	86
43782	SHAWNEE	79	53	24	46	60	69	51	64	62	52	73	77	44	69	52	67	66	64	79	91
43783	SOMERSET	79	67	49	63	71	79	65	72	70	64	85	84	62	84	66	73	79	71	81	91
43787	STOCKPORT	69	49	26	43	55	63	48	58	56	48	66	68	42	63	49	60	61	57	70	79
43788	SUMMERFIELD	79	53	25	46	60	69	51	64	62	52	73	77	44	69	52	67	66	63	79	91
43793	WOODSFIELD	67	52	34	47	57	65	52	60	59	51	70	69	47	68	53	62	65	59	70	77
43802	ADAMSVILLE	82	71	55	69	75	82	69	75	74	69	90	88	67	90	70	75	84	74	82	93
43804	BALTIC	75	59	37	54	64	71	55	65	62	56	74	77	51	73	57	65	69	63	74	87
43811	CONESVILLE	87	65	37	58	71	80	61	73	71	62	84	87	55	82	63	75	78	72	86	101
43812	COSHOCTON	70	63	56	59	66	73	62	66	66	62	81	76	61	81	63	69	77	66	73	80
43821	DRESDEN	91	79	61	74	84	92	75	83	82	75	99	98	73	101	77	85	93	82	93	107
	OHIO	89	88	90	87	88	95	88	89	89	87	110	103	88	111	88	89	107	89	90	102
	UNITED STATES	100	100	100	100	100	100	100	100	100	100	100	100	100	100	100	100	100	100	100	100

ZIP CODE		COUNTY FIPS CODE	POPULATION			2000-2004 ANNUAL RATE		HOUSEHOLDS					FAMILIES		
#	POST OFFICE NAME		2000	2004	2009	% Rate	State Centile	2000	2004	2009	% Annual Rate 2000-2004	2004 Average HH Size	2000	2004	% Annual Rate 2000-2004
43822	FRAZEYSBURG	119	4384	4754	5003	1.9	93	1664	1844	1978	2.5	2.57	1252	1360	2.0
43824	FRESNO	031	4116	4301	4375	1.0	82	1286	1374	1424	1.6	3.12	1059	1110	1.1
43830	NASHPORT	119	5321	5494	5580	0.8	75	1925	2035	2110	1.3	2.70	1534	1586	0.8
43832	NEWCOMERSTOWN	157	7581	7470	7444	-0.4	29	2983	3001	3039	0.1	2.46	2114	2066	-0.5
43837	PORT WASHINGTON	157	1930	1960	1972	0.4	60	711	735	749	0.8	2.67	563	570	0.3
43840	STONE CREEK	157	1104	1209	1265	2.2	94	406	457	488	2.8	2.60	324	358	2.4
43843	WALHONDING	031	895	1011	1098	2.9	96	337	387	425	3.3	2.59	261	293	2.8
43844	WARSAW	031	4036	4100	4146	0.4	61	1497	1556	1605	0.9	2.62	1132	1147	0.3
43845	WEST LAFAYETTE	031	4567	4556	4566	-0.1	42	1797	1830	1866	0.4	2.42	1290	1275	-0.3
43901	ADENA	081	2494	2518	2499	0.2	55	1028	1064	1080	0.8	2.34	734	740	0.2
43902	ALLEDONIA	013	292	278	266	-1.2	5	117	114	112	-0.6	2.44	84	80	-1.1
43903	AMSTERDAM	019	2196	2086	2015	-1.2	5	904	880	868	-0.6	2.37	653	618	-1.3
43906	BELLAIRE	013	10455	10040	9659	-1.0	10	4302	4221	4148	-0.5	2.36	2932	2795	-1.1
43907	CADIZ	067	5646	5544	5401	-0.4	25	2329	2341	2334	0.1	2.31	1601	1563	-0.6
43908	BERGHOLZ	081	1641	1557	1503	-1.2	4	633	615	607	-0.7	2.50	457	432	-1.3
43910	BLOOMINGDALE	081	3533	3357	3242	-1.2	5	1381	1352	1337	-0.5	2.48	1062	1014	-1.1
43912	BRIDGEPORT	013	7342	7016	6735	-1.1	6	3246	3177	3120	-0.5	2.17	2055	1939	-1.4
43913	BRILLIANT	081	1414	1468	1476	0.9	79	606	649	670	1.6	2.26	405	419	0.8
43915	CLARINGTON	111	2047	1958	1890	-1.0	7	831	816	808	-0.4	2.40	613	588	-1.0
43917	DILLONVALE	081	4287	4224	4142	-0.4	29	1721	1731	1732	0.1	2.40	1232	1205	-0.5
43920	EAST LIVERPOOL	029	25651	24941	24331	-0.7	16	10329	10231	10170	-0.2	2.40	7102	6835	-0.9
43930	HAMMONDSVILLE	081	1079	1079	1066	0.0	45	400	410	415	0.6	2.63	300	301	0.1
43932	IRONDALE	081	866	870	864	0.1	50	331	343	349	0.8	2.54	251	253	0.2
43933	JACOBSBURG	013	1649	1579	1516	-1.0	8	639	629	619	-0.4	2.51	498	480	-0.9
43935	MARTINS FERRY	013	9394	9005	8663	-1.0	8	4059	3966	3891	-0.5	2.25	2588	2457	-1.2
43938	MINGO JUNCTION	081	6562	6442	6310	-0.4	25	2718	2741	2748	0.2	2.35	1907	1866	-0.5
43942	POWHATAN POINT	013	2685	2602	2511	-0.7	14	1147	1142	1128	-0.1	2.28	803	775	-0.8
43943	RAYLAND	081	3999	4083	4078	0.5	65	1623	1703	1741	1.1	2.39	1182	1206	0.5
43944	RICHMOND	081	2492	2433	2376	-0.6	21	991	995	996	0.1	2.44	757	742	-0.5
43945	SALINEVILLE	029	3329	3257	3197	-0.5	22	1271	1272	1275	0.0	2.55	927	904	-0.6
43946	SARDIS	111	2279	2273	2244	-0.1	42	934	958	970	0.6	2.37	684	684	0.0
43947	SHADYSIDE	013	5255	5027	4827	-1.0	7	2278	2224	2178	-0.6	2.21	1482	1400	-1.3
43950	SAINT CLAIRSVILLE	013	15560	15391	15055	-0.3	33	5561	5637	5617	0.3	2.29	3856	3789	-0.4
43952	STEUBENVILLE	081	20557	19979	19553	-0.7	16	8427	8372	8366	-0.2	2.19	5038	4839	-0.9
43953	STEUBENVILLE	081	11822	11619	11387	-0.4	26	5040	5086	5098	0.2	2.22	3495	3420	-0.5
43963	TILTONSVILLE	081	1296	1240	1200	-1.0	7	596	583	575	-0.5	2.13	390	368	-1.4
43964	TORONTO	081	11098	11123	11049	0.1	47	4569	4687	4755	0.6	2.37	3179	3169	-0.1
43968	WELLSVILLE	029	7708	7558	7406	-0.5	24	3094	3101	3098	0.1	2.43	2200	2146	-0.6
43971	YORKVILLE	081	1442	1384	1339	-1.0	9	621	608	599	-0.5	2.24	399	376	-1.4
43973	FREEPORT	067	2027	2057	2068	0.4	60	790	817	836	0.8	2.52	576	582	0.2
43976	HOPEDALE	067	1767	1752	1713	-0.2	35	670	678	678	0.3	2.51	506	500	-0.3
43977	FLUSHING	013	2675	2681	2627	0.1	47	1084	1113	1114	0.6	2.41	774	773	0.0
43983	PIEDMONT	013	432	428	420	-0.2	34	174	176	177	0.3	2.43	128	126	-0.4
43986	JEWETT	067	2162	2096	2032	-0.7	14	809	801	793	-0.2	2.56	593	572	-0.8
43988	SCIO	067	2452	2381	2309	-0.7	15	1053	1051	1044	0.0	2.26	730	708	-0.7
44001	AMHERST	093	20535	21182	21859	0.7	74	7656	8104	8574	1.4	2.59	5845	6036	0.8
44003	ANDOVER	007	4363	4485	4537	0.7	72	1578	1656	1708	1.1	2.59	1149	1175	0.5
44004	ASHTABULA	007	35945	36112	36346	0.1	50	14563	14935	15321	0.6	2.39	9777	9708	-0.2
44010	AUSTINBURG	007	1778	1764	1764	-0.2	36	661	673	688	0.4	2.57	509	506	-0.1
44011	AVON	093	11075	13271	14722	4.4	99	3968	4930	5638	5.2	2.63	3050	3698	4.6
44012	AVON LAKE	093	18145	19023	19811	1.1	84	6711	7223	7715	1.7	2.63	5134	5380	1.1
44017	BEREA	035	19046	18182	17424	-1.1	6	7197	6958	6746	-0.8	2.31	4483	4181	-1.6
44021	BURTON	055	7727	7979	8271	0.8	75	2593	2734	2888	1.3	2.89	2013	2083	0.8
44022	CHAGRIN FALLS	035	17014	16688	16603	-0.5	24	6584	6541	6515	-0.2	2.54	4981	4846	-0.7
44023	CHAGRIN FALLS	055	14206	14788	15416	1.0	81	4974	5300	5636	1.5	2.78	4066	4265	1.1
44024	CHARDON	055	22600	23450	24308	0.9	78	8123	8637	9147	1.5	2.65	6183	6433	0.9
44026	CHESTERLAND	055	11888	12031	12389	0.3	57	4302	4466	4699	0.9	2.68	3493	3563	0.5
44028	COLUMBIA STATION	093	8497	8537	8658	0.1	50	2942	3046	3177	0.8	2.69	2412	2452	0.4
44030	CONNEAUT	007	16202	16079	16055	-0.2	36	6411	6501	6619	0.3	2.45	4489	4432	-0.3
44032	DORSET	007	1717	1753	1763	0.5	65	591	617	632	1.0	2.84	453	463	0.5
44035	ELYRIA	093	65376	65564	66833	0.1	48	26090	26963	28252	0.8	2.40	17613	17619	0.0
44039	NORTH RIDGEVILLE	093	22073	23216	24158	1.2	85	8244	8982	9628	2.1	2.57	6340	6761	1.6
44040	GATES MILLS	035	3345	3165	3010	-1.3	4	1239	1188	1147	-1.0	2.64	997	937	-1.5
44041	GENEVA	007	14986	14600	14480	-0.6	18	5799	5784	5857	-0.1	2.44	3922	3797	-0.8
44044	GRAFTON	093	15639	16040	16469	0.6	70	4179	4445	4722	1.5	2.85	3436	3590	1.0
44046	HUNTSBURG	055	2028	2160	2269	1.5	88	564	611	653	1.9	3.46	483	517	1.6
44047	JEFFERSON	007	9657	9680	9745	0.1	47	3523	3614	3713	0.6	2.62	2669	2676	0.1
44048	KINGSVILLE	007	2554	2712	2801	1.4	88	879	953	1004	1.9	2.71	688	734	1.5
44050	LAGRANGE	093	5965	6161	6342	0.8	75	2014	2138	2257	1.4	2.88	1688	1763	1.0
44052	LORAIN	093	33681	33226	33691	-0.3	31	13046	13207	13736	0.3	2.50	8770	8578	-0.5
44053	LORAIN	093	16726	17266	17851	0.8	75	7070	7506	7969	1.4	2.25	4566	4684	0.6
44054	SHEFFIELD LAKE	093	12233	12439	12723	0.4	61	4533	4748	4989	1.1	2.62	3396	3471	0.5
44055	LORAIN	093	22663	23083	23696	0.4	63	8049	8412	8857	1.0	2.73	5850	5953	0.4
44056	MACEDONIA	153	9259	9860	10140	1.5	88	3285	3593	3759	2.1	2.74	2659	2842	1.6
44057	MADISON	085	19315	19695	19843	0.5	64	7099	7448	7649	1.1	2.59	5295	5416	0.5
44060	MENTOR	085	63554	64471	65078	0.3	60	24033	25035	25766	1.0	2.55	17876	18131	0.3
44062	MIDDLEFIELD	055	13029	14019	14688	1.7	91	3622	4013	4316	2.4	3.45	2811	3046	1.9
44064	MONTVILLE	055	1771	1869	1953	1.3	86	641	693	740	1.9	2.67	526	559	1.4
44065	NEWBURY	055	4405	4422	4535	0.1	49	1589	1635	1712	0.7	2.67	1220	1229	0.2
44067	NORTHFIELD	153	17829	18550	18856	0.9	80	7179	7691	7962	1.6	2.37	5050	5243	0.9
44070	NORTH OLMSTED	035	34132	33360	32242	-0.5	21	13519	13463	13242	-0.1	2.45	9364	9087	-0.7
44072	NOVELTY	055	4564	4522	4614	-0.2	34	1710	1739	1813	0.4	2.59	1392	1391	0.0
44074	OBERLIN	093	12081	11866	11996	-0.4	26	4116	4138	4303	0.1	2.38	2537	2470	-0.6
44076	ORWELL	007	4417	4446	4463	0.2	51	1569	1600	1632	0.5	2.76	1171	1166	-0.1
44077	PAINESVILLE	085	50704	51174	51355	0.2	54	19326	19938	20342	0.7	2.52	13606	13691	0.2
44081	PERRY	085	6519	6738	6821	0.8	76	2242	2372	2442	1.3	2.83	1784	1848	0.8
44082	PIERPONT	007	1503	1538	1550	0.5	67	510	528	539	0.8	2.91	397	402	0.3
44084	ROCK CREEK	007	3558	3622	3640	0.4	62	1271	1324	1357	1.0	2.72	985	1004	0.5
44085	ROME	007	2837	2964	3034	1.0	82	1016	1081	1127	1.5	2.72	779	812	1.0
44086	THOMPSON	055	2821	2956	3068	1.1	84	1003	1078	1144	1.7	2.74	781	823	1.2
44087	TWINSBURG	153	18587	19252	19455	0.8	77	7206	7579	7733	1.2	2.52	5164	5277	0.5
44089	VERMILION	043	15959	15949	16024	0.0	44	6173	6348	6545	0.7	2.49	4587	4604	0.1
44090	WELLINGTON	093	10989	11491	11894	1.1	83	3938	4227	4487	1.7	2.68	3012	3168	1.2
44092	WICKLIFFE	085	17550	17058	16873	-0.7	16	7560	7536	7592	-0.1	2.22	4862	4682	-0.9
44093	WILLIAMSFIELD	007	1472	1520	1538	0.8	75	531	559	577	1.2	2.72	404	415	0.6
	OHIO					0.3					0.7	2.44			0.0
	UNITED STATES					1.2					1.3	2.58			1.1

ZIP CODE #	POST OFFICE NAME	RACE (%) White 2000	White 2004	Black 2000	Black 2004	Asian/Pacific 2000	Asian/Pacific 2004	% Hispanic Origin 2000	% Hispanic Origin 2004	2004 AGE DISTRIBUTION (%) 0-4	5-9	10-14	15-19	20-24	25-44	45-64	65-84	85+	18+	MEDIAN AGE 2004	% 2004 Males	% 2004 Females
43822	FRAZEYSBURG	97.9	97.7	0.7	0.8	0.2	0.2	0.4	0.5	6.8	6.9	7.8	7.1	6.5	29.2	25.8	9.0	0.9	74.0	36.1	50.2	49.9
43824	FRESNO	99.0	99.0	0.3	0.3	0.3	0.3	0.7	0.6	8.8	8.6	9.1	7.8	7.0	26.3	22.1	9.5	0.9	68.7	32.3	50.7	49.3
43830	NASHPORT	97.8	97.5	1.0	1.1	0.1	0.2	0.8	0.9	7.7	7.4	7.9	6.9	6.2	28.3	26.1	8.7	0.8	72.8	35.8	50.0	50.0
43832	NEWCOMERSTOWN	97.2	96.9	1.5	1.6	0.1	0.1	0.5	0.6	6.8	6.8	7.1	6.8	6.5	25.4	25.5	13.1	2.1	75.3	38.9	48.9	51.1
43837	PORT WASHINGTON	98.8	98.6	0.2	0.2	0.0	0.1	0.5	0.7	6.5	6.8	7.3	6.6	5.9	27.6	26.9	11.4	0.9	75.2	38.4	50.3	49.7
43840	STONE CREEK	99.5	99.4	0.1	0.1	0.0	0.0	0.5	0.6	6.6	7.0	7.2	5.5	5.3	27.1	27.5	11.5	2.3	75.5	39.3	49.3	50.7
43843	WALHONDING	98.2	98.1	0.6	0.6	0.1	0.1	0.3	0.3	6.5	6.8	8.4	7.2	6.6	27.1	26.8	9.6	0.9	73.7	37.0	52.2	47.8
43844	WARSAW	97.8	97.8	0.9	0.9	0.1	0.1	0.5	0.5	6.2	6.4	7.3	7.3	6.6	26.4	27.5	11.1	1.3	75.5	38.2	50.8	49.2
43845	WEST LAFAYETTE	98.4	98.3	0.2	0.2	0.0	0.0	0.6	0.6	6.2	6.2	6.8	6.4	6.4	26.4	25.6	14.1	2.0	77.1	39.9	48.6	51.5
43901	ADENA	98.4	98.3	0.6	0.7	0.2	0.3	0.2	0.2	4.9	5.1	5.7	5.6	5.5	24.5	29.0	16.8	2.8	80.9	44.1	48.8	51.2
43902	ALLEDONIA	96.2	95.7	0.3	0.4	1.4	1.8	0.7	0.4	5.0	5.4	6.5	6.1	5.8	25.2	31.7	13.3	1.1	78.8	42.5	51.4	48.6
43903	AMSTERDAM	99.0	98.9	0.1	0.1	0.1	0.2	0.4	0.3	6.4	6.7	6.9	6.5	5.6	25.9	26.0	14.2	1.8	76.0	39.7	49.8	50.2
43906	BELLAIRE	95.6	95.2	3.1	3.3	0.2	0.2	0.3	0.3	5.1	5.4	6.6	6.7	5.8	24.7	27.5	15.7	2.6	78.8	42.2	47.6	52.4
43907	CADIZ	91.9	91.4	5.7	6.0	0.3	0.3	0.3	0.4	5.8	5.9	6.2	5.8	5.3	24.4	27.6	16.0	3.1	78.5	42.7	47.4	52.6
43908	BERGHOLZ	98.7	98.5	0.2	0.3	0.3	0.4	0.1	0.1	5.7	5.9	6.6	6.5	6.4	26.0	27.6	13.8	1.5	78.0	40.3	50.2	49.8
43910	BLOOMINGDALE	97.9	97.6	1.1	1.2	0.3	0.5	0.4	0.4	4.5	5.4	6.4	6.4	5.4	24.6	32.3	13.6	1.5	79.7	43.3	49.9	50.1
43912	BRIDGEPORT	95.2	94.8	3.6	3.9	0.1	0.2	0.4	0.4	4.9	5.1	6.0	5.6	5.3	24.4	27.3	18.0	3.4	80.5	44.1	46.5	53.5
43913	BRILLIANT	98.4	98.4	0.3	0.3	0.0	0.0	0.2	0.3	5.5	5.5	5.8	5.7	6.1	26.7	26.1	16.8	2.0	79.8	41.6	46.7	53.3
43915	CLARINGTON	99.0	98.9	0.4	0.4	0.0	0.0	0.2	0.3	4.9	5.2	6.6	6.4	5.7	25.9	29.1	14.5	1.8	79.4	42.2	49.7	50.3
43917	DILLONVALE	96.4	95.9	2.2	2.4	0.1	0.1	0.2	0.2	5.1	5.4	6.2	5.6	5.5	23.9	27.8	17.4	3.0	79.8	43.8	48.7	51.4
43920	EAST LIVERPOOL	95.3	94.8	2.8	3.0	0.3	0.4	0.6	0.7	6.3	6.5	7.0	6.4	6.2	24.9	25.5	15.2	2.0	76.4	39.8	47.6	52.5
43930	HAMMONDSVILLE	96.8	96.4	2.1	2.4	0.1	0.1	0.7	0.9	5.4	5.6	6.7	7.2	6.7	26.1	27.0	13.9	1.5	78.0	40.3	50.9	49.1
43932	IRONDALE	97.6	97.5	1.2	1.4	0.1	0.1	0.4	0.5	5.6	6.1	6.8	6.4	6.1	25.9	28.1	13.6	1.5	77.7	40.7	50.7	49.3
43933	JACOBSBURG	99.2	99.0	0.1	0.1	0.1	0.2	0.4	0.5	5.9	6.1	5.8	6.0	5.8	26.5	29.1	13.6	1.2	78.7	41.2	50.2	49.8
43935	MARTINS FERRY	94.2	93.8	4.2	4.5	0.1	0.1	0.6	0.7	5.4	5.2	6.0	6.1	5.9	23.6	28.2	16.6	3.0	79.5	43.4	46.8	53.2
43938	MINGO JUNCTION	96.1	95.6	2.4	2.7	0.1	0.1	0.6	0.7	5.1	5.4	6.4	6.1	5.2	24.4	28.1	17.4	1.9	79.4	43.2	47.7	52.3
43942	POWHATAN POINT	98.4	98.3	0.5	0.5	0.0	0.0	0.2	0.2	5.8	5.9	5.9	5.2	5.1	26.4	27.5	16.0	2.2	79.3	42.2	49.0	51.0
43943	RAYLAND	97.4	97.2	1.4	1.5	0.1	0.1	0.3	0.3	4.3	4.8	6.6	5.8	5.6	24.4	30.2	16.4	2.0	80.9	44.0	49.3	50.7
43944	RICHMOND	98.4	98.1	0.6	0.6	0.4	0.6	0.4	0.5	4.8	5.4	6.1	5.8	4.9	24.7	31.1	15.7	1.4	80.2	43.9	49.7	50.3
43945	SALINEVILLE	98.4	98.3	0.6	0.7	0.0	0.0	0.7	0.7	6.4	6.9	8.2	6.9	5.9	27.3	25.7	11.5	1.1	74.0	37.2	50.4	49.6
43946	SARDIS	98.8	98.8	0.5	0.5	0.0	0.0	0.2	0.3	5.0	5.2	6.0	6.0	5.7	24.7	30.1	15.8	1.6	80.3	43.3	49.3	50.7
43947	SHADYSIDE	99.4	99.3	0.1	0.1	0.0	0.0	0.2	0.2	4.4	5.0	5.8	6.0	5.2	23.6	27.2	19.1	3.7	81.0	45.0	46.7	53.3
43950	SAINT CLAIRSVILLE	89.0	88.2	9.1	9.6	0.9	1.1	0.5	0.5	3.8	4.3	5.2	5.8	7.8	28.2	27.4	15.0	2.6	83.1	41.9	54.9	45.1
43952	STEUBENVILLE	81.2	80.0	15.8	16.7	0.5	0.7	1.1	1.1	5.3	5.3	5.7	7.1	8.1	23.7	25.1	16.7	3.1	80.2	41.2	46.6	53.4
43953	STEUBENVILLE	94.6	93.8	3.6	4.1	0.7	1.0	0.6	0.7	4.9	5.0	5.4	5.2	5.3	22.4	30.2	18.7	3.0	81.6	46.2	48.0	52.0
43963	TILTONSVILLE	98.8	98.7	0.2	0.2	0.1	0.1	0.2	0.2	4.5	4.8	5.7	5.0	5.7	22.4	27.7	20.0	4.2	81.9	46.3	45.0	55.0
43964	TORONTO	97.8	97.5	0.9	1.0	0.2	0.3	0.5	0.6	5.8	5.9	6.2	6.1	6.0	25.1	28.9	14.4	1.8	78.5	41.7	47.9	52.1
43968	WELLSVILLE	93.8	93.4	4.4	4.6	0.1	0.2	0.4	0.5	6.7	6.5	6.6	6.3	6.7	25.3	26.7	13.9	1.5	76.4	39.5	48.5	51.5
43971	YORKVILLE	98.0	97.8	1.3	1.4	0.1	0.1	0.5	0.5	4.4	4.8	6.2	6.8	6.7	23.8	24.9	18.8	3.5	80.3	43.0	48.7	51.3
43973	FREEPORT	98.1	97.9	0.3	0.3	0.1	0.1	0.5	0.6	6.2	6.4	7.1	7.1	5.7	24.9	27.4	14.0	1.2	76.0	40.3	49.3	50.7
43976	HOPEDALE	98.9	98.8	0.5	0.5	0.0	0.0	0.2	0.3	5.2	5.7	6.7	5.8	4.6	25.9	28.4	15.1	2.7	78.7	42.7	49.5	50.5
43977	FLUSHING	97.9	97.7	0.8	0.9	0.1	0.2	0.4	0.4	5.2	5.6	6.0	5.8	6.2	25.8	29.2	14.6	1.7	79.9	41.9	50.4	49.7
43983	PIEDMONT	97.9	97.9	0.7	0.7	0.0	0.0	0.5	0.5	5.4	5.6	5.6	5.8	6.3	23.6	31.1	15.0	1.6	79.9	43.3	50.7	49.3
43986	JEWETT	98.7	98.7	0.6	0.6	0.0	0.0	0.4	0.4	6.1	6.7	7.9	6.5	5.0	25.3	26.2	13.7	2.6	74.9	39.8	50.1	49.9
43988	SCIO	99.4	99.3	0.1	0.1	0.0	0.0	0.6	0.6	5.7	6.0	5.9	5.3	5.4	23.6	30.5	15.5	2.2	79.2	43.7	49.2	50.8
44001	AMHERST	96.5	96.0	0.8	0.8	0.6	0.8	3.1	3.7	5.8	6.4	7.7	6.7	5.2	25.3	28.6	12.6	1.7	75.7	40.8	48.7	51.3
44003	ANDOVER	97.0	96.7	2.0	2.1	0.1	0.2	0.5	0.6	5.9	6.1	7.1	6.6	6.0	25.8	27.1	13.9	1.6	76.7	40.2	49.8	50.2
44004	ASHTABULA	89.4	88.5	6.5	7.0	0.5	0.7	3.7	4.1	6.9	6.6	7.0	6.5	6.3	25.5	25.2	13.8	2.2	75.5	38.7	47.6	52.4
44010	AUSTINBURG	98.0	97.7	0.5	0.5	0.4	0.6	0.5	0.5	5.8	6.1	6.7	6.8	5.7	25.7	30.8	10.9	1.5	77.0	40.9	49.8	50.2
44011	AVON	97.0	96.4	0.7	0.8	1.0	1.4	1.3	1.5	8.3	8.9	7.4	5.5	3.8	27.9	25.8	10.8	1.6	71.5	38.9	48.5	51.5
44012	AVON LAKE	97.3	96.7	0.5	0.5	1.0	1.4	1.3	1.5	7.0	7.7	8.3	7.0	5.1	25.1	28.0	10.8	1.1	72.5	39.6	48.8	51.2
44017	BEREA	91.5	89.5	5.1	6.5	0.9	1.2	1.6	1.8	4.9	5.1	6.1	10.2	11.5	24.1	23.6	12.4	2.2	79.9	36.7	47.4	52.6
44021	BURTON	97.7	97.5	0.7	0.8	0.3	0.3	0.7	0.8	7.1	7.8	8.7	7.4	5.8	25.8	26.4	9.5	1.6	71.7	36.8	50.2	49.8
44022	CHAGRIN FALLS	94.3	93.0	3.2	3.9	1.7	2.2	0.7	0.8	5.5	6.8	8.2	7.2	4.2	19.1	33.0	14.3	1.9	74.6	44.5	48.6	51.4
44023	CHAGRIN FALLS	94.9	94.5	3.4	3.6	0.5	0.6	0.6	0.7	6.5	7.8	8.6	7.0	4.1	22.4	32.3	10.2	1.2	72.5	41.5	49.4	50.6
44024	CHARDON	98.0	97.7	0.6	0.7	0.4	0.6	0.4	0.5	6.2	6.7	7.3	6.6	5.2	25.0	29.5	11.4	2.1	75.7	40.9	48.8	51.2
44026	CHESTERLAND	98.1	97.8	0.6	0.7	0.6	0.8	0.8	0.9	4.8	5.9	7.9	6.5	4.0	22.7	31.6	14.9	1.6	76.9	43.9	49.3	50.7
44028	COLUMBIA STATION	96.3	95.9	2.2	2.4	0.4	0.5	1.3	1.5	5.3	6.4	7.1	6.6	5.6	28.4	29.4	10.0	1.3	77.0	40.0	52.3	47.7
44030	CONNEAUT	96.7	96.4	1.0	1.0	0.5	0.6	1.0	1.1	6.4	6.4	7.5	6.8	5.9	26.1	25.6	13.3	2.3	75.6	39.0	48.8	51.2
44032	DORSET	97.4	97.2	1.4	1.5	0.2	0.2	0.3	0.3	6.6	7.0	7.7	7.7	6.1	26.9	25.6	11.4	1.1	74.0	37.5	50.1	49.9
44035	ELYRIA	83.3	81.7	12.4	13.5	0.6	0.8	2.7	3.1	7.5	7.0	7.0	6.4	6.5	28.3	24.0	11.6	1.9	74.7	36.5	48.4	51.7
44039	NORTH RIDGEVILLE	96.4	95.7	0.9	1.0	0.9	1.2	2.0	2.3	6.4	6.6	6.7	6.0	5.4	28.2	28.8	10.7	1.2	76.6	39.5	49.2	50.8
44040	GATES MILLS	94.7	93.2	0.7	0.9	3.4	4.5	1.4	1.5	4.0	5.1	6.7	7.2	4.7	17.2	34.0	18.9	2.2	79.1	48.1	49.1	50.9
44041	GENEVA	95.9	95.5	0.9	1.0	0.3	0.4	3.9	4.3	6.0	5.9	6.7	7.0	6.7	26.9	26.1	12.8	1.8	77.0	39.1	49.2	50.8
44044	GRAFTON	85.6	84.6	12.8	13.5	0.3	0.5	1.5	1.7	4.6	5.0	6.1	6.3	6.8	34.4	27.8	8.3	0.8	80.6	38.4	60.5	39.5
44046	HUNTSBURG	98.8	98.7	0.6	0.7	0.0	0.0	0.4	0.4	11.7	10.8	9.6	9.2	6.3	24.3	19.0	6.9	2.3	62.2	27.3	48.5	51.5
44047	JEFFERSON	96.5	96.2	2.1	2.2	0.2	0.3	0.7	0.8	5.9	6.5	7.5	7.4	6.2	26.1	27.0	11.3	2.1	75.5	39.0	49.4	50.6
44048	KINGSVILLE	98.1	97.9	0.7	0.8	0.2	0.2	0.5	0.6	5.5	6.0	7.1	6.6	5.5	23.8	28.4	14.5	2.8	77.3	42.4	48.9	51.1
44050	LAGRANGE	98.4	98.1	0.3	0.3	0.2	0.3	0.9	1.1	7.3	7.6	8.3	6.9	5.7	29.2	26.1	8.3	0.7	72.5	36.7	49.8	50.2
44052	LORAIN	69.2	67.0	18.7	19.8	0.3	0.3	16.7	18.3	8.5	8.0	7.9	7.1	7.2	27.1	21.7	10.9	1.7	71.3	33.5	47.3	52.7
44053	LORAIN	82.6	80.8	9.0	9.7	0.7	0.9	10.5	11.8	6.6	6.4	6.4	5.4	6.1	26.7	25.3	14.7	2.4	77.5	39.4	46.9	53.1
44054	SHEFFIELD LAKE	95.3	94.5	1.7	2.0	0.5	0.6	3.7	4.3	6.7	6.9	7.2	6.6	6.2	28.7	27.1	9.9	0.7	75.1	37.6	48.6	51.4
44055	LORAIN	63.3	61.1	15.4	16.2	0.3	0.3	33.8	36.1	8.2	8.0	9.2	8.0	7.3	26.8	20.1	11.0	1.3	69.7	32.3	47.9	52.1
44056	MACEDONIA	90.2	87.9	6.9	8.3	1.8	2.5	0.8	0.8	6.2	6.7	7.7	6.7	5.2	27.5	29.5	9.9	0.7	75.0	39.8	49.3	50.7
44057	MADISON	98.1	97.9	0.4	0.4	0.3	0.4	1.1	1.3	6.5	6.7	7.5	6.8	5.5	28.8	26.1	10.8	1.3	74.9	38.0	49.6	50.4
44060	MENTOR	97.3	96.7	0.7	0.7	1.2	1.5	0.8	0.9	6.0	6.4	7.3	6.6	5.5	26.6	28.6	11.6	1.5	76.1	40.2	48.4	51.6
44062	MIDDLEFIELD	98.3	98.1	0.8	0.9	0.1	0.2	0.5	0.5	10.9	10.4	10.2	9.2	7.5	24.1	18.4	7.8	1.5	62.7	26.4	49.3	50.7
44064	MONTVILLE	97.8	97.5	1.1	1.2	0.5	0.6	0.2	0.3	6.7	7.4	7.6	6.2	4.9	29.0	26.7	10.1	1.4	74.3	38.5	50.6	49.4
44065	NEWBURY	97.7	97.3	1.0	1.0	0.5	0.6	0.5	0.6	6.9	7.4	7.2	6.2	4.8	25.9	29.2	10.8	1.7	74.6	40.6	49.3	50.7
44067	NORTHFIELD	95.0	93.9	2.6	3.1	1.2	1.6	0.8	0.9	6.2	6.3	6.0	4.7	4.6	29.5	27.5	13.7	1.4	78.5	40.9	48.4	51.6
44070	NORTH OLMSTED	94.0	92.5	1.0	1.3	2.8	3.6	1.7	1.9	5.5	5.9	6.8	6.5	6.1	25.4	28.3	13.8	1.9	77.9	41.2	48.4	51.7
44072	NOVELTY	96.8	96.3	1.2	1.4	0.9	1.2	0.9	1.1	4.9	5.9	6.7	6.5	4.1	19.1	35.6	15.6	1.6	78.4	46.5	48.7	51.4
44074	OBERLIN	78.5	76.4	14.1	15.1	2.6	3.3	2.7	3.0	4.2	4.3	5.0	11.9	18.1	20.2	22.4	11.5	2.5	83.7	30.7	46.2	53.8
44076	ORWELL	95.9	95.4	2.2	2.3	0.2	0.3	0.9	1.0	8.5	8.4	8.4	7.0	7.2	27.0	22.5	9.6	1.3	70.3	33.4	50.1	49.9
44077	PAINESVILLE	90.3	89.5	5.1	5.4	0.5	0.7	5.0	5.4	7.3	7.0	6.9	6.4	6.4	28.3	25.8	10.4	1.4	74.9	37.1	49.4	50.6
44081	PERRY	98.4	98.2	0.4	0.4	0.3	0.4	0.9	1.0	5.3	6.7	8.7	8.1	5.4	26.1	28.7	10.2	1.0	74.0	39.6	50.2	49.9
44082	PIERPONT	98.3	98.2	0.5	0.5	0.3	0.4	1.1	1.3	7.6	7.9	8.8	7.7	5.8	26.3	24.0	10.1	1.9	71.0	35.9	49.9	50.1
44084	ROCK CREEK	96.9	96.7	1.6	1.6	0.3	0.3	0.8	0.8	6.0	6.6	7.1	6.7	5.3	28.5	28.7	9.9	1.1	76.0	39.3	50.0	50.0
44085	ROME	97.7	97.4	1.3	1.4	0.1	0.2	0.5	0.6	6.9	7.3	7.4	6.4	5.5	29.4	26.2	9.8	1.2	74.4	37.2	51.3	48.7
44086	THOMPSON	98.3	98.2	0.5	0.5	0.2	0.2	0.5	0.5	6.6	7.2	7.6	5.5	5.2	28.7	27.8	10.3	1.2	75.2	38.6	50.6	49.4
44087	TWINSBURG	82.5	80.0	13.3	14.8	2.7	3.6	1.0	1.1	7.9	8.2	8.1	5.8	4.5	31.0	23.5	9.8	1.3	72.1	37.1	47.7	52.3
44089	VERMILION	98.3	98.0	0.2	0.2	0.2	0.3	1.7	1.9	5.8	6.0	6.9	6.6	5.9	25.3	30.0	12.0	1.6	77.2	40.9	49.0	51.1
44090	WELLINGTON	97.8	97.6	0.9	1.0	0.2	0.3	0.9	1.0	6.6	6.9	7.8	6.7	6.0	26.4	27.0	11.0	1.7	74.6	38.5	50.0	50.1
44092	WICKLIFFE	92.5	91.5	4.5	4.8	1.9	2.4	0.6	0.7	5.1	5.2	5.7	5.7	5.4	26.8	25.1	18.5	2.6	80.6	42.5	48.3	51.7
44093	WILLIAMSFIELD	97.4	97.2	1.4	1.5	0.0	0.0	0.1	0.1	7.0	7.0	7.8	8.0	6.8	27.0	23.0	12.0	1.3	73.2	36.2	51.5	48.6
	OHIO	85.0	84.1	11.5	11.8	1.2	1.6	1.9	2.1	6.7	6.6	7.1	7.0	7.1	27.5	24.7	11.6	1.8	75.6	37.0	48.6	51.4
	UNITED STATES	75.1	73.6	12.3	12.5	3.8	4.2	12.5	14.1	6.9	6.7	7.2	7.0	7.3	28.6	23.8	10.8	1.7	75.1	36.0	49.1	50.9

INCOME

ZIP CODE #	POST OFFICE NAME	2004 Per Capita Income	2004 HH Income Base	2004 HOUSEHOLD INCOME DISTRIBUTION (%) Less than $25,000	$25,000 to $49,999	$50,000 to $99,999	$100,000 to $149,999	$150,000 or More	MEDIAN HOUSEHOLD INCOME 2004	2009	2004 National Centile	2004 State Centile	2004 Home Value Base	2004 HOME VALUE DISTRIBUTION (%) Less than $50,000	$50,000 to $89,999	$90,000 to $174,999	$175,000 to $399,999	$400,000 or More	2004 Median Home Value
43822	FRAZEYSBURG	21189	1844	19.2	35.5	37.4	5.7	2.2	46937	53640	66	53	1518	15.6	19.1	45.7	17.9	1.8	109677
43824	FRESNO	16561	1374	26.6	32.9	30.0	8.5	2.0	42907	48833	56	39	1162	12.1	19.5	37.4	26.3	4.7	121207
43830	NASHPORT	26076	2035	16.8	29.3	37.4	10.3	6.2	52942	61421	77	73	1673	8.0	11.5	52.8	24.8	3.0	132546
43832	NEWCOMERSTOWN	17909	3001	36.6	31.8	26.4	3.6	1.6	35885	39590	31	20	2246	23.3	36.0	32.1	8.0	0.5	78167
43837	PORT WASHINGTON	16949	735	26.4	40.3	28.0	4.1	1.2	39133	43725	43	27	614	21.2	27.9	35.3	14.5	1.1	91277
43840	STONE CREEK	18148	457	22.1	42.2	30.4	4.2	1.1	43639	49636	58	41	386	9.6	23.6	43.3	19.7	3.9	111972
43843	WALHONDING	19399	387	24.0	35.7	33.6	4.7	2.1	43394	49691	57	40	326	18.4	22.4	36.8	18.4	4.0	106122
43844	WARSAW	18632	1556	24.3	37.1	32.7	4.4	1.5	41510	47212	51	34	1303	25.8	23.0	37.8	12.3	1.2	92171
43845	WEST LAFAYETTE	19647	1830	26.8	35.5	30.1	6.9	0.8	40313	46136	47	31	1467	25.0	31.1	38.4	5.6	0.0	84020
43901	ADENA	20336	1064	33.7	33.6	25.3	5.5	2.0	34321	39385	25	16	860	44.2	32.4	18.4	4.8	0.2	55952
43902	ALLEDONIA	15831	114	40.4	31.6	24.6	3.5	0.0	31974	35752	18	11	97	40.2	34.0	23.7	2.1	0.0	66875
43903	AMSTERDAM	16932	880	36.7	33.9	26.1	2.4	0.9	35062	39698	28	17	703	40.5	23.6	27.7	7.5	0.6	63936
43906	BELLAIRE	17209	4221	45.7	29.4	20.7	2.5	1.8	27510	31055	8	5	2900	37.0	37.2	21.6	3.7	0.5	63036
43907	CADIZ	20386	2341	36.9	32.5	22.8	4.5	3.3	33145	37842	21	14	1732	27.9	39.0	27.1	5.0	0.9	71557
43908	BERGHOLZ	17736	615	30.7	35.6	27.8	4.4	1.5	35527	40659	30	19	515	40.0	27.2	27.4	5.4	0.0	63241
43910	BLOOMINGDALE	19860	1352	26.6	32.8	34.3	4.7	1.6	42461	48503	54	37	1183	23.5	31.5	32.8	11.9	0.3	84439
43912	BRIDGEPORT	18858	3177	40.8	31.9	22.5	3.7	1.2	31603	36022	17	9	2302	40.8	40.1	17.4	1.7	0.0	58945
43913	BRILLIANT	15829	649	39.9	34.1	24.2	1.9	0.0	30589	35170	14	8	441	44.4	41.3	13.6	0.7	0.0	54537
43915	CLARINGTON	18754	816	35.9	32.4	28.1	2.8	0.9	35474	39103	29	19	682	33.0	32.0	30.9	3.1	1.0	67391
43917	DILLONVALE	18955	1731	36.5	30.9	25.1	5.4	2.1	34205	39664	25	16	1398	45.1	31.8	19.0	3.9	0.4	54759
43920	EAST LIVERPOOL	17500	10231	40.6	30.5	23.3	3.9	1.8	31123	35270	15	9	7121	32.7	30.7	29.3	6.7	0.5	70670
43930	HAMMONDSVILLE	18055	410	31.0	32.2	30.5	4.2	2.2	37381	42587	37	23	347	38.6	23.6	25.4	12.4	0.0	71042
43932	IRONDALE	19239	343	28.9	33.5	30.9	5.3	1.5	40739	46182	49	32	292	41.8	22.6	26.0	9.3	0.3	65500
43933	JACOBSBURG	17196	629	31.5	37.4	26.6	4.0	0.6	36095	40961	32	21	548	31.4	36.0	24.3	6.9	1.5	67414
43935	MARTINS FERRY	19371	3966	44.8	28.5	21.7	3.1	1.9	28403	32445	9	6	2659	36.4	44.1	16.6	2.9	0.0	60699
43938	MINGO JUNCTION	17812	2741	38.9	30.6	25.4	3.4	1.8	32210	37156	18	11	2020	34.3	39.5	23.1	3.2	0.0	63860
43942	POWHATAN POINT	17857	1142	39.7	29.3	25.7	4.5	0.8	31677	36190	17	10	878	34.9	43.2	19.7	2.2	0.1	64865
43943	RAYLAND	18768	1703	35.2	32.1	26.8	4.2	1.6	35132	40199	28	18	1421	38.4	35.9	21.3	4.2	0.4	63943
43944	RICHMOND	18321	995	30.5	31.9	32.2	4.8	0.7	40270	45439	47	31	868	19.5	32.6	34.9	12.8	0.2	88043
43945	SALINEVILLE	17627	1272	31.5	36.6	26.2	4.2	1.6	35344	40070	29	19	1025	37.1	28.3	26.3	8.1	0.2	65952
43946	SARDIS	21421	958	30.4	36.3	28.4	3.2	1.7	38253	42341	40	26	800	28.3	26.1	38.6	6.6	0.4	83750
43947	SHADYSIDE	19188	2224	35.2	34.0	25.7	3.7	1.4	35508	40462	30	19	1717	25.8	45.5	26.7	2.0	0.0	71747
43950	SAINT CLAIRSVILLE	22460	5637	28.3	31.2	30.4	6.5	3.7	41189	47611	50	33	4476	17.4	23.8	42.2	15.2	1.4	98914
43952	STEUBENVILLE	19679	8372	43.2	28.5	20.5	5.2	2.6	29700	34463	12	7	5255	26.0	37.0	30.7	5.8	0.6	74400
43953	STEUBENVILLE	24447	5086	26.9	31.9	29.7	7.9	3.6	41177	47332	50	33	3943	13.6	33.0	43.0	8.9	1.5	93185
43963	TILTONSVILLE	18634	583	39.6	35.2	19.7	4.3	1.2	31967	37138	18	11	437	33.0	48.5	18.1	0.2	0.2	65662
43964	TORONTO	18352	4687	34.8	32.7	26.8	5.3	0.4	37132	42618	36	23	3618	32.3	32.2	30.8	4.3	0.4	72491
43968	WELLSVILLE	17885	3101	35.4	34.2	25.1	4.0	1.3	35533	40191	30	19	2280	33.4	34.9	26.8	4.8	0.1	68866
43971	YORKVILLE	17705	608	38.2	31.7	25.2	4.1	0.8	33007	37802	21	13	409	33.0	50.1	14.7	2.2	0.0	62849
43973	FREEPORT	17906	817	37.6	34.3	22.0	3.7	2.5	32812	37362	20	12	661	27.4	28.4	33.7	10.3	0.2	79222
43976	HOPEDALE	22997	678	30.8	34.1	26.7	5.0	3.4	40108	45337	46	30	548	26.1	39.8	25.9	6.2	2.0	72456
43977	FLUSHING	18407	1113	36.9	36.4	20.9	3.5	2.3	31905	36574	18	10	907	39.3	35.9	19.6	3.1	2.1	60611
43983	PIEDMONT	17710	176	36.9	33.0	25.0	3.4	1.7	33409	38109	22	14	149	37.6	28.9	26.2	6.7	0.7	64091
43986	JEWETT	16264	801	34.2	37.5	23.1	3.4	1.9	34089	38652	24	15	624	33.2	35.9	23.6	5.8	1.6	64355
43988	SCIO	21442	1051	35.2	35.8	22.8	3.1	3.0	34665	39459	26	17	836	25.5	38.0	27.8	7.5	1.2	74744
44001	AMHERST	29646	8104	15.0	24.3	40.0	14.2	6.5	60428	69891	85	86	7081	10.1	5.7	46.3	35.8	2.0	157227
44003	ANDOVER	17808	1656	34.4	28.4	30.7	4.9	1.6	35561	40351	30	20	1331	18.2	32.2	39.5	9.5	0.6	89622
44004	ASHTABULA	19390	14935	33.9	31.4	27.0	5.9	1.9	36475	42157	33	22	10122	15.8	33.8	41.0	8.7	0.8	90392
44010	AUSTINBURG	24580	673	14.0	29.7	43.7	8.6	4.0	52900	59824	77	72	574	8.7	12.5	50.0	26.5	2.3	137640
44011	AVON	34879	4930	10.8	20.5	35.5	21.8	11.4	75523	88704	93	96	4379	0.7	1.5	37.2	55.7	4.9	203125
44012	AVON LAKE	38890	7223	10.3	19.9	35.9	17.4	16.6	75008	87780	93	96	6262	0.4	4.1	35.7	48.5	11.3	201834
44017	BEREA	27209	6958	18.8	28.2	34.6	13.0	5.5	52785	64749	77	72	4985	0.4	4.7	76.6	17.5	0.8	137066
44021	BURTON	25095	2734	16.1	22.4	40.4	15.0	6.3	61887	76193	86	88	2192	2.8	6.2	39.7	44.0	7.3	177768
44022	CHAGRIN FALLS	66445	6541	9.7	13.0	25.8	17.6	33.9	102993	129205	98	100	5770	0.4	2.0	9.5	53.4	34.7	323017
44023	CHAGRIN FALLS	45889	5300	8.4	14.9	28.2	23.9	24.6	96783	119188	98	99	4884	0.7	1.3	15.1	61.9	20.9	274347
44024	CHARDON	31722	8637	13.2	22.2	38.0	16.7	9.9	64919	79870	88	91	7351	8.8	1.7	28.3	51.8	9.4	208150
44026	CHESTERLAND	39794	4466	7.8	16.5	40.1	21.3	14.4	78274	97928	95	97	4167	2.0	1.2	23.0	60.7	13.2	222834
44028	COLUMBIA STATION	29197	3046	10.4	25.8	38.7	17.1	8.0	63855	75480	88	90	2752	0.3	4.7	43.5	45.5	6.1	178571
44030	CONNEAUT	18615	6501	31.9	34.3	28.2	4.6	1.1	37793	43833	39	25	4909	15.6	34.6	40.0	9.1	0.7	89799
44032	DORSET	18378	617	18.0	40.7	32.9	7.3	1.1	43977	49923	59	42	522	9.0	21.7	52.9	12.6	3.8	112216
44035	ELYRIA	24151	26963	24.4	31.1	32.8	8.4	3.3	45570	53437	63	48	18468	8.5	17.2	60.1	13.5	0.6	115270
44039	NORTH RIDGEVILLE	28255	8982	12.5	23.4	42.9	16.4	4.8	62504	74042	87	89	7896	3.7	3.8	63.4	28.2	0.8	153211
44040	GATES MILLS	80657	1188	5.1	11.7	21.6	17.8	43.9	129102	161578	100	100	1117	0.1	0.1	5.7	39.2	54.9	437847
44041	GENEVA	20957	5784	26.4	32.8	31.7	6.6	2.6	41824	47970	52	35	4219	14.7	19.1	48.6	16.5	1.1	110064
44044	GRAFTON	24330	4445	12.3	22.8	41.9	16.9	6.1	64921	76663	88	92	3961	1.0	5.7	51.5	38.1	3.8	163303
44046	HUNTSBURG	20182	611	14.1	27.7	40.8	13.4	4.1	58157	73642	83	82	504	3.2	2.8	46.6	43.1	4.4	170779
44047	JEFFERSON	21985	3614	21.7	32.1	33.5	10.0	2.6	46584	52568	65	51	2858	8.7	17.6	53.1	18.8	1.8	121799
44048	KINGSVILLE	21039	953	21.1	33.4	33.2	8.8	3.6	46547	52899	65	51	818	9.4	16.0	58.1	16.1	0.4	117956
44050	LAGRANGE	24752	2138	12.2	24.0	45.6	14.3	4.0	61693	72328	86	88	1859	1.1	9.7	51.6	35.9	1.8	159281
44052	LORAIN	19026	13207	34.6	29.3	28.1	5.7	2.3	37450	44888	37	24	7988	5.4	32.0	56.3	5.7	0.5	98165
44053	LORAIN	25096	7506	26.1	28.2	31.8	10.7	3.2	45662	54072	63	48	4792	3.6	7.1	64.6	23.8	0.9	140034
44054	SHEFFIELD LAKE	26012	4748	14.1	25.5	42.9	12.5	5.0	58655	68366	83	83	3854	0.8	8.8	66.0	22.7	1.7	132122
44055	LORAIN	16968	8412	34.1	31.1	28.6	4.7	1.5	36907	44497	35	23	5187	7.8	42.4	47.6	2.0	0.2	89903
44056	MACEDONIA	35074	3593	10.1	16.1	40.4	23.3	10.2	77200	92728	94	97	3431	1.1	1.6	37.9	57.7	1.8	187107
44057	MADISON	23652	7448	17.2	29.5	40.1	10.7	2.5	52560	61497	76	72	6188	11.0	9.5	57.8	20.4	1.3	128953
44060	MENTOR	29905	25035	12.3	24.1	40.4	16.9	6.3	63398	74612	87	90	21088	2.0	2.9	51.1	41.7	2.3	166807
44062	MIDDLEFIELD	16278	4013	21.9	33.4	32.8	8.9	3.1	46082	55371	64	49	2848	7.0	6.0	53.7	29.8	3.5	150052
44064	MONTVILLE	27896	693	12.1	19.5	50.1	13.0	5.3	64488	78205	88	91	618	1.9	1.8	49.0	41.6	5.7	172049
44065	NEWBURY	31879	1635	10.2	24.0	39.6	16.0	10.2	66711	82604	90	93	1394	2.6	4.7	33.8	49.6	9.3	195530
44067	NORTHFIELD	34099	7691	12.1	21.0	39.8	18.5	8.6	66564	80662	89	93	6517	0.3	4.9	41.5	51.3	2.0	181316
44070	NORTH OLMSTED	29464	13463	14.4	23.5	40.1	16.6	5.4	61546	75635	86	88	10873	1.3	5.7	57.1	35.6	0.3	161228
44072	NOVELTY	56630	1739	7.3	17.8	28.8	16.0	30.3	90355	112705	97	99	1600	0.0	0.9	20.7	49.4	28.9	270443
44074	OBERLIN	26180	4138	24.3	24.0	33.6	12.8	5.2	51751	60652	75	69	2738	1.5	9.8	48.4	37.7	2.7	158765
44076	ORWELL	18295	1600	27.0	31.6	33.7	5.9	1.8	42459	48203	54	37	1288	16.3	15.6	48.2	17.2	2.7	113780
44077	PAINESVILLE	26638	19938	19.2	26.4	36.9	12.5	5.0	54174	63674	79	76	14626	2.3	11.1	51.5	31.9	3.3	151454
44081	PERRY	25106	2372	15.6	22.3	42.0	15.5	4.7	61509	71819	86	88	2092	7.0	3.4	48.0	39.8	1.8	166002
44082	PIERPONT	16486	528	23.1	38.6	32.8	4.2	1.3	38879	44936	42	27	434	16.8	25.1	46.3	11.1	0.7	97609
44084	ROCK CREEK	22982	1324	18.8	30.1	35.2	12.4	3.6	51002	58089	74	67	1172	4.2	12.5	53.2	29.1	0.9	147857
44085	ROME	22330	1081	19.6	30.7	34.7	12.3	2.7	49765	57239	71	62	922	4.7	12.3	58.8	22.0	2.3	125800
44086	THOMPSON	25178	1078	12.8	26.7	46.0	12.8	1.7	58769	70261	83	84	981	16.3	5.6	41.0	33.9	3.2	157031
44087	TWINSBURG	33549	7579	14.4	19.2	37.9	18.4	10.2	69354	84053	91	94	5804	0.5	3.6	37.2	55.8	3.0	192852
44089	VERMILION	28216	6348	15.8	25.5	41.3	12.7	4.8	58199	67553	83	83	5092	6.6	7.8	52.1	30.2	3.2	145000
44090	WELLINGTON	25590	4227	16.3	27.8	39.5	12.2	4.2	54737	63923	79	77	3443	3.0	6.2	50.1	38.0	2.7	159418
44092	WICKLIFFE	27001	7536	20.0	29.1	37.2	10.8	3.0	50724	59558	73	66	5635	1.7	6.1	66.8	22.5	2.8	144084
44093	WILLIAMSFIELD	15878	559	35.4	25.6	34.9	3.9	0.2	37182	42407	36	23	465	14.0	30.5	48.6	6.9	0.0	96538
	OHIO	25510		24.6	28.1	32.2	10.1	5.0	47354	56168				9.2	18.6	47.0	22.1	3.1	121192
	UNITED STATES	25866		24.7	27.1	30.8	10.9	6.5	48124	56710				10.9	15.0	33.7	30.1	10.4	145905

ZIP CODE #	POST OFFICE NAME	FINANCIAL SERVICES: Auto Loan	Home Loan	Invest-ments	Retire-ment Plans	THE HOME: Home Improvements: Home Repair	Lawn & Garden	Furnishings: Comput-ers & Hard-ware	Major Appli-ances	TV, Radio, Sound Equip-ment	Furni-ture	ENTERTAINMENT: Dine out/ Carry out	Sports Equip-ment	Fees & Tickets	Toys & Games	Travel	Cable TV	PERSONAL: Apparel & Services	Auto Repairs	Health Insur-ance	Pets & Supplies
43822	FRAZEYSBURG	87	78	59	74	82	88	72	80	76	72	93	95	70	95	74	78	88	77	86	103
43824	FRESNO	84	73	54	69	78	84	68	76	73	68	88	90	66	90	70	75	84	74	83	99
43830	NASHPORT	105	103	90	101	106	112	96	102	98	96	120	120	97	124	98	98	116	99	105	124
43832	NEWCOMERSTOWN	67	60	51	56	63	70	59	63	64	58	77	73	58	79	60	66	73	62	70	77
43837	PORT WASHINGTON	77	62	41	57	67	73	58	67	64	58	77	80	54	77	59	67	72	66	76	90
43840	STONE CREEK	76	68	51	64	71	77	62	69	66	62	81	82	61	82	64	68	77	67	75	89
43843	WALHONDING	83	71	51	66	75	82	66	74	71	66	86	88	63	87	68	74	81	72	82	97
43844	WARSAW	80	67	48	63	71	79	64	72	70	64	84	85	61	84	65	72	79	71	80	93
43845	WEST LAFAYETTE	77	66	51	62	70	77	63	70	68	63	83	82	61	84	65	71	78	68	78	89
43901	ADENA	62	66	68	63	67	75	66	65	68	63	85	73	69	91	68	71	82	64	71	73
43902	ALLEDONIA	73	49	22	42	55	63	47	59	57	48	67	70	40	63	48	61	60	58	72	83
43903	AMSTERDAM	65	53	39	48	57	65	52	58	58	51	70	68	49	70	53	61	65	57	68	75
43906	BELLAIRE	60	52	48	49	54	62	55	58	60	54	72	64	53	70	55	63	68	58	66	68
43907	CADIZ	76	61	44	56	65	76	63	69	70	61	84	79	58	82	63	74	77	69	82	86
43908	BERGHOLZ	82	56	28	49	63	73	54	67	65	55	77	80	47	73	55	70	70	67	82	95
43910	BLOOMINGDALE	81	68	49	63	73	80	64	72	70	64	84	86	61	85	66	73	79	71	81	95
43912	BRIDGEPORT	57	54	53	52	56	64	57	57	60	54	73	64	56	75	57	62	70	57	64	65
43913	BRILLIANT	51	47	42	45	49	56	49	51	52	47	63	57	48	65	50	55	60	50	57	58
43915	CLARINGTON	82	56	28	50	63	73	56	68	66	56	78	80	48	74	57	71	71	67	83	93
43917	DILLONVALE	63	61	58	58	63	72	63	64	66	60	81	72	63	84	64	69	77	63	71	73
43920	EAST LIVERPOOL	61	56	52	53	58	65	58	59	61	56	75	68	57	76	58	63	71	59	65	70
43930	HAMMONDSVILLE	89	60	27	52	68	78	58	72	70	59	82	86	49	77	59	75	74	72	89	103
43932	IRONDALE	92	62	28	53	70	80	59	74	72	61	84	89	51	80	60	77	76	74	92	105
43933	JACOBSBURG	71	58	41	55	62	69	57	64	62	56	75	74	54	74	58	64	70	62	72	81
43935	MARTINS FERRY	58	58	62	56	59	67	61	60	63	58	78	68	61	80	62	65	75	61	65	67
43938	MINGO JUNCTION	57	58	57	55	59	66	57	58	60	56	74	65	59	77	59	62	71	57	64	66
43942	POWHATAN POINT	69	50	29	46	55	65	53	61	61	51	71	70	46	67	53	65	65	60	73	78
43943	RAYLAND	64	61	56	57	63	71	61	63	65	59	79	71	61	83	62	68	75	62	70	74
43944	RICHMOND	65	63	56	59	65	71	60	63	64	59	78	73	61	82	62	66	74	62	69	77
43945	SALINEVILLE	84	57	27	50	64	74	55	68	66	56	77	82	47	74	56	71	71	67	83	96
43946	SARDIS	96	64	29	55	73	84	62	77	75	63	88	92	53	83	63	80	80	77	95	110
43947	SHADYSIDE	65	56	45	53	59	68	58	62	63	55	75	70	55	75	58	65	70	61	70	73
43950	SAINT CLAIRSVILLE	68	73	76	70	74	81	71	72	72	69	89	81	73	92	73	74	86	71	75	81
43952	STEUBENVILLE	61	59	64	56	59	67	61	61	64	60	79	69	62	79	62	67	76	62	66	70
43953	STEUBENVILLE	75	79	81	76	80	87	76	78	77	75	95	89	78	99	78	79	93	76	81	89
43963	TILTONSVILLE	57	52	46	49	54	62	54	56	58	52	70	63	53	71	55	61	66	55	64	65
43964	TORONTO	69	58	44	53	61	69	57	63	63	56	76	73	54	76	58	66	71	62	72	80
43968	WELLSVILLE	66	58	51	54	60	67	58	62	63	57	76	72	57	77	59	65	73	62	69	76
43971	YORKVILLE	58	52	45	49	55	63	54	57	58	52	70	63	53	71	55	61	66	56	64	65
43973	FREEPORT	82	58	31	51	65	75	55	68	65	56	77	81	48	74	57	70	71	68	83	96
43976	HOPEDALE	94	76	54	73	82	94	78	86	86	76	102	99	72	99	78	89	95	85	99	107
43977	FLUSHING	62	62	59	58	64	71	60	63	63	58	77	71	60	81	62	66	74	61	69	74
43983	PIEDMONT	74	57	38	52	64	72	54	65	61	53	72	77	48	71	57	65	67	64	77	89
43986	JEWETT	72	53	33	49	59	68	54	62	61	53	73	72	48	70	54	65	67	62	74	81
43988	SCIO	81	64	44	57	69	78	62	71	70	62	84	83	58	84	63	75	78	70	83	93
44001	AMHERST	114	113	100	108	116	123	105	111	107	104	132	130	106	136	108	109	127	108	115	135
44003	ANDOVER	85	60	31	53	68	77	57	71	68	58	80	85	50	77	59	72	73	70	86	100
44004	ASHTABULA	68	62	59	59	64	71	63	66	67	62	82	76	62	83	64	69	78	66	71	78
44010	AUSTINBURG	102	91	69	86	96	103	84	93	89	84	109	111	82	111	87	92	103	91	101	120
44011	AVON	121	150	160	150	147	145	134	134	124	133	156	156	143	166	137	120	156	129	120	148
44012	AVON LAKE	132	160	179	161	156	160	147	144	138	147	174	166	158	182	150	135	174	140	132	158
44017	BEREA	86	99	113	98	97	102	96	94	93	95	116	109	100	121	97	92	115	94	90	103
44021	BURTON	113	106	88	102	111	117	98	106	101	98	124	126	97	127	100	103	119	103	111	133
44022	CHAGRIN FALLS	214	270	324	267	265	279	241	240	226	244	285	273	264	296	252	226	286	233	225	262
44023	CHAGRIN FALLS	170	205	219	209	201	203	184	182	171	185	216	210	198	223	187	166	215	176	166	202
44024	CHARDON	119	128	128	126	128	133	119	122	117	119	146	142	123	151	122	117	143	119	119	141
44026	CHESTERLAND	138	167	187	166	166	173	152	153	144	153	181	174	162	185	158	143	179	149	145	167
44028	COLUMBIA STATION	100	117	123	115	116	118	107	108	102	106	128	125	113	135	109	100	127	104	101	121
44030	CONNEAUT	68	62	54	58	65	72	62	65	66	60	80	75	61	83	63	68	76	64	72	78
44032	DORSET	88	72	49	67	78	85	67	77	74	68	89	92	64	89	69	77	84	76	87	103
44035	ELYRIA	81	81	83	80	82	89	81	82	82	80	102	94	82	104	82	83	99	82	83	93
44039	NORTH RIDGEVILLE	95	112	121	112	110	112	104	104	99	104	124	121	110	130	106	96	123	101	95	114
44040	GATES MILLS	264	345	453	340	339	363	305	303	285	310	360	341	341	375	323	287	363	292	284	330
44041	GENEVA	81	71	57	67	75	82	69	75	74	68	90	88	66	91	70	76	85	74	83	95
44044	GRAFTON	91	99	96	97	100	102	90	93	88	90	109	110	93	115	93	88	107	90	90	109
44046	HUNTSBURG	116	99	71	93	105	114	92	103	99	92	120	123	88	121	94	102	113	101	114	135
44047	JEFFERSON	92	82	63	77	86	94	77	85	82	76	99	100	75	101	79	84	94	83	93	108
44048	KINGSVILLE	88	83	71	79	87	94	78	84	81	77	100	98	77	102	80	84	95	82	90	104
44050	LAGRANGE	104	108	99	105	110	113	98	103	98	98	121	122	100	126	101	98	118	100	103	124
44052	LORAIN	64	63	69	61	63	70	67	65	69	65	85	75	67	87	67	70	83	66	68	72
44053	LORAIN	83	80	75	79	82	90	79	82	81	79	100	93	79	100	80	82	95	81	86	94
44054	SHEFFIELD LAKE	100	98	89	96	101	107	94	98	95	93	117	114	94	121	95	96	113	96	101	116
44055	LORAIN	61	61	68	59	61	68	64	63	67	63	84	72	65	86	64	69	81	64	66	70
44056	MACEDONIA	125	155	166	156	152	152	139	138	128	139	162	160	148	171	142	125	162	133	124	152
44057	MADISON	90	90	84	88	92	98	85	89	86	85	106	103	86	108	87	87	103	87	91	104
44060	MENTOR	102	116	125	116	115	118	109	109	105	109	131	127	114	136	111	103	130	107	102	121
44062	MIDDLEFIELD	92	76	56	72	81	89	75	83	81	75	98	97	70	96	75	83	92	82	91	105
44064	MONTVILLE	112	112	97	108	115	120	102	109	103	102	127	129	103	132	105	104	123	106	111	134
44065	NEWBURY	119	134	131	132	134	135	120	124	116	120	145	146	125	152	123	115	142	120	118	144
44067	NORTHFIELD	112	123	128	124	121	125	117	117	112	117	141	136	120	143	117	110	138	115	110	130
44070	NORTH OLMSTED	93	109	124	108	107	111	104	102	100	103	125	118	109	130	106	98	124	101	96	112
44072	NOVELTY	189	230	257	228	228	238	210	210	198	210	249	239	223	254	218	196	247	205	199	230
44074	OBERLIN	96	90	98	92	91	98	100	95	99	96	123	115	96	121	96	95	119	99	93	109
44076	ORWELL	89	66	40	60	73	82	64	76	73	65	87	89	58	85	65	77	81	74	88	101
44077	PAINESVILLE	91	99	103	99	99	103	96	96	94	95	117	112	99	121	97	92	115	95	92	107
44081	PERRY	95	112	115	111	111	112	101	102	96	100	120	120	106	127	103	94	119	99	95	116
44082	PIERPONT	90	61	27	52	69	79	58	73	71	60	83	87	50	78	59	76	75	72	90	104
44084	ROCK CREEK	100	89	68	85	94	101	83	91	88	83	107	109	81	109	85	90	101	89	99	118
44085	ROME	97	86	66	82	91	98	81	89	86	81	104	105	79	106	83	88	99	87	96	113
44086	THOMPSON	107	101	83	97	105	111	92	100	96	92	117	119	92	121	95	97	112	98	105	126
44087	TWINSBURG	111	129	147	132	126	127	123	120	116	123	146	141	128	151	123	112	145	119	108	132
44089	VERMILION	102	106	99	103	107	111	97	102	97	97	120	120	99	125	100	97	117	99	101	121
44090	WELLINGTON	104	99	85	96	102	110	94	100	97	93	119	117	94	122	96	98	114	97	105	121
44092	WICKLIFFE	78	87	99	85	86	94	85	84	85	84	106	95	89	109	87	86	104	84	85	92
44093	WILLIAMSFIELD	80	55	27	48	62	71	53	66	63	54	74	78	45	71	54	68	68	65	80	93
	OHIO	89	88	90	87	88	95	88	89	89	87	110	103	88	111	88	89	107	89	90	102
	UNITED STATES	100	100	100	100	100	100	100	100	100	100	100	100	100	100	100	100	100	100	100	100

# POST OFFICE NAME	COUNTY FIPS CODE	POPULATION 2000	POPULATION 2004	POPULATION 2009	2000-2004 ANNUAL RATE % Rate	2000-2004 ANNUAL RATE State Centile	HOUSEHOLDS 2000	HOUSEHOLDS 2004	HOUSEHOLDS 2009	% Annual Rate 2000-2004	2004 Average HH Size	FAMILIES 2000	FAMILIES 2004	% Annual Rate 2000-2004
44094 WILLOUGHBY	085	34186	34587	34805	0.3	56	14873	15357	15700	0.8	2.22	9173	9146	-0.1
44095 EASTLAKE	085	35556	34553	34173	-0.7	16	14531	14520	14645	0.0	2.38	9934	9626	-0.7
44099 WINDSOR	007	2049	2115	2145	0.8	75	589	615	632	1.0	3.34	454	463	0.5
44102 CLEVELAND	035	52176	49115	46722	-1.4	3	20422	19464	18774	-1.1	2.48	11410	10459	-2.0
44103 CLEVELAND	035	25370	23452	22168	-1.8	1	9603	8942	8540	-1.7	2.51	5581	5008	-2.5
44104 CLEVELAND	035	28651	26270	24701	-2.0	1	10683	9919	9461	-1.7	2.61	6850	6159	-2.5
44105 CLEVELAND	035	54190	51853	49636	-1.0	7	20440	19852	19304	-0.7	2.60	13541	12730	-1.4
44106 CLEVELAND	035	32320	31010	29863	-1.0	9	13620	13313	13015	-0.5	2.06	5857	5368	-2.0
44107 LAKEWOOD	035	56646	55667	53997	-0.4	26	26693	26725	26367	0.0	2.05	12556	12012	-1.0
44108 CLEVELAND	035	36752	34598	32920	-1.4	3	13657	13082	12658	-1.0	2.63	9107	8434	-1.8
44109 CLEVELAND	035	45876	44660	43154	-0.6	17	18406	18227	17900	-0.2	2.44	10946	10388	-1.2
44110 CLEVELAND	035	26765	25788	24941	-0.9	11	11297	10957	10708	-0.7	2.32	6298	5785	-2.0
44111 CLEVELAND	035	42536	41822	40581	-0.4	27	18051	18057	17812	0.0	2.30	10587	10167	-1.0
44112 CLEVELAND	035	33629	31634	30094	-1.4	3	13458	12875	12444	-1.0	2.41	8193	7548	-1.9
44113 CLEVELAND	035	19706	19183	18651	-0.6	17	7401	7454	7419	0.2	2.14	3321	3071	-1.8
44114 CLEVELAND	035	3984	4083	4047	0.6	70	2080	2197	2220	1.3	1.67	637	617	-0.8
44115 CLEVELAND	035	8215	7954	7713	-0.8	13	3099	2989	2904	-0.9	2.15	1660	1547	-1.7
44116 ROCKY RIVER	035	20346	19949	19343	-0.5	24	9483	9477	9351	0.0	2.08	5327	5096	-1.0
44117 EUCLID	035	11692	11420	11030	-0.6	21	5786	5727	5607	-0.2	1.94	2841	2677	-1.4
44118 CLEVELAND	035	44952	43769	42304	-0.6	17	17562	17416	17108	-0.2	2.40	10897	10415	-1.1
44119 CLEVELAND	035	13321	12954	12509	-0.7	16	6042	5948	5822	-0.4	2.13	3255	3066	-1.4
44120 CLEVELAND	035	47823	46601	45311	-0.6	18	20286	20080	19833	-0.2	2.30	12107	11527	-1.2
44121 CLEVELAND	035	34394	33992	33030	-0.3	32	14136	14237	14074	0.2	2.37	9289	9025	-0.7
44122 BEACHWOOD	035	34694	33860	32805	-0.6	20	14143	13990	13739	-0.3	2.25	9078	8716	-1.0
44123 EUCLID	035	18496	17766	17035	-0.9	10	8581	8317	8076	-0.7	2.13	4801	4487	-1.6
44124 CLEVELAND	035	41015	40019	38654	-0.6	19	18742	18584	18240	-0.2	2.12	11374	10941	-0.9
44125 CLEVELAND	035	29670	28615	27487	-0.9	12	12124	11902	11625	-0.4	2.37	8024	7619	-1.2
44126 CLEVELAND	035	17310	16713	16044	-0.8	12	7760	7615	7430	-0.4	2.19	4659	4416	-1.3
44127 CLEVELAND	035	9194	8652	8220	-1.4	3	3321	3124	2989	-1.4	2.73	2113	1921	-2.2
44128 CLEVELAND	035	32921	31423	30064	-1.1	6	13509	13141	12791	-0.7	2.36	8839	8313	-1.4
44129 CLEVELAND	035	30085	29098	28005	-0.8	13	12399	12217	11962	-0.4	2.34	7972	7560	-1.2
44130 CLEVELAND	035	52752	51250	49393	-0.7	15	23005	22786	22341	-0.2	2.21	14453	13811	-1.1
44131 INDEPENDENCE	035	20742	20017	19205	-0.8	12	8052	7927	7744	-0.4	2.51	6216	5980	-0.9
44132 EUCLID	035	15241	14886	14390	-0.6	21	6856	6793	6666	-0.2	2.19	3986	3814	-1.0
44133 NORTH ROYALTON	035	28672	29848	29634	1.0	81	11255	11939	12060	1.4	2.47	7700	7928	0.7
44134 CLEVELAND	035	40301	38809	37293	-0.9	11	16442	16137	15778	-0.4	2.36	11072	10522	-1.2
44135 CLEVELAND	035	29443	28663	27701	-0.6	17	12225	12146	11949	-0.2	2.32	7420	7075	-1.1
44136 STRONGSVILLE	035	25210	25572	25114	0.3	60	9312	9677	9693	0.9	2.61	6933	7027	0.3
44137 MAPLE HEIGHTS	035	26163	25241	24308	-0.8	12	10488	10307	10094	-0.4	2.43	6968	6629	-1.2
44138 OLMSTED FALLS	035	18416	18457	18008	0.1	47	7463	7634	7587	0.5	2.40	5091	5065	-0.1
44139 SOLON	035	22292	22781	22447	0.5	66	7769	8059	8065	0.9	2.83	6287	6408	0.5
44140 BAY VILLAGE	035	16087	15321	14633	-1.1	6	6239	6074	5911	-0.6	2.50	4683	4440	-1.3
44141 BRECKSVILLE	035	13704	13524	13137	-0.3	31	5158	5163	5088	0.0	2.51	3852	3782	-0.4
44142 BROOK PARK	035	21170	19816	18768	-1.5	2	8178	7848	7588	-1.0	2.51	5978	5589	-1.6
44143 CLEVELAND	035	23816	24106	23715	0.3	57	9649	9890	9872	0.6	2.41	6622	6631	0.0
44144 CLEVELAND	035	21828	21329	20582	-0.5	21	9997	9939	9755	-0.1	2.14	5893	5627	-1.1
44145 WESTLAKE	035	32104	32200	31573	0.1	48	12951	13183	13119	0.4	2.35	8290	8199	-0.3
44146 BEDFORD	035	31648	30433	29178	-0.9	10	14095	13823	13483	-0.5	2.17	8289	7817	-1.4
44147 BROADVIEW HEIGHTS	035	15916	16163	15862	0.4	60	6392	6587	6562	0.7	2.43	4361	4344	-0.1
44149 STRONGSVILLE	035	18648	19008	18704	0.5	63	6897	7170	7179	0.9	2.64	5456	5565	0.5
44201 ATWATER	133	7042	7188	7328	0.5	65	2490	2605	2719	1.1	2.76	2032	2084	0.6
44202 AURORA	133	16641	17594	18290	1.3	87	6223	6747	7175	1.9	2.57	4764	5040	1.3
44203 BARBERTON	153	42337	42149	41944	-0.1	40	17035	17335	17501	0.4	2.40	11681	11513	-0.3
44212 BRUNSWICK	103	38094	41068	44906	1.8	92	13536	15034	16855	2.5	2.71	10559	11481	2.0
44214 BURBANK	169	1871	2016	2127	1.8	92	655	723	779	2.4	2.78	529	573	1.9
44215 CHIPPEWA LAKE	103	2322	2493	2691	1.7	91	874	965	1067	2.4	2.56	613	659	1.7
44216 CLINTON	153	8891	8847	8761	-0.1	39	3177	3238	3258	0.5	2.73	2597	2599	0.0
44217 CRESTON	169	4063	4149	4282	0.5	65	1506	1564	1642	0.9	2.64	1177	1198	0.4
44221 CUYAHOGA FALLS	153	31029	30899	30846	-0.1	40	13764	14034	14225	0.5	2.19	8261	8084	-0.5
44223 CUYAHOGA FALLS	153	17266	17739	18002	0.6	71	7439	7766	7967	1.0	2.26	4700	4730	0.2
44224 STOW	153	36486	38976	40251	1.6	89	14176	15504	16255	2.1	2.47	10050	10684	1.5
44230 DOYLESTOWN	169	8429	8574	8766	0.4	62	3153	3276	3412	0.9	2.57	2329	2361	0.3
44231 GARRETTSVILLE	133	7599	7902	8163	0.9	80	2803	2989	3162	1.5	2.63	2071	2147	0.9
44233 HINCKLEY	103	6777	7106	7580	1.1	84	2341	2517	2745	1.7	2.82	1990	2110	1.4
44234 HIRAM	133	4112	4430	4661	1.8	92	1277	1428	1550	2.7	2.68	981	1071	2.1
44235 HOMERVILLE	103	1574	1842	2079	3.8	98	431	519	599	4.5	3.55	371	440	4.1
44236 HUDSON	153	24372	25277	25639	0.9	78	8069	8492	8703	1.2	2.94	6872	7109	0.8
44240 KENT	133	35369	35428	36175	0.0	46	14717	15139	15850	0.7	2.23	8244	8137	-0.3
44241 STREETSBORO	133	13189	13745	14199	1.0	81	5185	5583	5929	1.8	2.44	3643	3799	1.0
44243 KENT	133	5277	5354	5406	0.3	60	4	4	5	0.0	2.50	1	1	0.0
44253 LITCHFIELD	103	3398	3659	3948	1.8	92	1089	1205	1332	2.4	3.03	935	1020	2.1
44254 LODI	103	5292	5433	5731	0.6	71	2060	2167	2336	1.2	2.50	1440	1479	0.6
44255 MANTUA	133	8112	8513	8862	1.1	84	2931	3164	3377	1.8	2.64	2240	2358	1.2
44256 MEDINA	103	51310	56162	61445	2.2	94	18602	20836	23298	2.7	2.66	14282	15661	2.2
44260 MOGADORE	133	13823	14014	14193	0.3	58	5147	5354	5544	0.9	2.61	4004	4065	0.4
44262 MUNROE FALLS	153	5189	5061	4987	-0.6	19	1908	1909	1912	0.0	2.59	1496	1464	-0.5
44264 PENINSULA	153	2306	2358	2370	0.5	67	928	969	988	1.0	2.41	629	634	0.2
44266 RAVENNA	133	34109	34393	35037	0.2	53	13342	13757	14339	0.7	2.46	9289	9304	0.0
44270 RITTMAN	169	8557	8653	8832	0.2	54	3224	3330	3465	0.8	2.56	2370	2388	0.2
44272 ROOTSTOWN	133	4152	4272	4383	0.7	73	1504	1588	1669	1.3	2.68	1196	1237	0.8
44273 SEVILLE	103	7357	8061	8801	2.2	94	2634	2958	3302	2.8	2.69	2120	2337	2.3
44275 SPENCER	103	3118	3388	3684	2.0	93	1073	1197	1332	2.6	2.83	875	957	2.1
44276 STERLING	169	2033	2030	2068	0.0	43	704	720	748	0.5	2.77	554	556	0.1
44278 TALLMADGE	153	17090	17331	17387	0.3	59	6520	6760	6878	0.9	2.52	4876	4929	0.3
44280 VALLEY CITY	103	4485	4805	5177	1.6	90	1501	1653	1826	2.3	2.79	1282	1391	1.9
44281 WADSWORTH	103	25997	28225	30930	2.0	93	9934	11004	12306	2.4	2.54	7353	7949	1.9
44286 RICHFIELD	153	5433	5607	5659	0.7	74	1912	2018	2068	1.3	2.67	1532	1585	0.8
44287 WEST SALEM	169	7339	7676	7950	1.1	83	2530	2700	2847	1.5	2.84	1988	2076	1.0
44288 WINDHAM	133	4595	4498	4537	-0.5	22	1600	1612	1668	0.2	2.79	1243	1223	-0.4
44301 AKRON	153	17277	16751	16539	-0.7	14	6977	6883	6878	-0.3	2.41	4469	4248	-1.2
44302 AKRON	153	6752	6565	6516	-0.7	16	3265	3233	3253	-0.2	2.00	1394	1304	-1.6
44303 AKRON	153	7754	8009	8202	0.8	75	3500	3683	3819	1.2	2.12	1839	1872	0.4
44304 AKRON	153	7840	7301	7157	-1.7	2	2902	2714	2684	-1.6	2.05	981	848	-3.4
44305 AKRON	153	24111	23255	22993	-0.9	12	9687	9532	9557	-0.4	2.42	6350	6039	-1.2
44306 AKRON	153	25336	24431	24081	-0.9	12	10030	9821	9789	-0.5	2.47	6512	6163	-1.3
OHIO					0.3					0.7	2.44			0.0
UNITED STATES					1.2					1.3	2.58			1.1

232-A

ZIP CODE #	POST OFFICE NAME	RACE (%) White 2000	White 2004	Black 2000	Black 2004	Asian/Pacific 2000	Asian/Pacific 2004	% Hispanic Origin 2000	% Hispanic Origin 2004	2004 AGE DISTRIBUTION (%) 0-4	5-9	10-14	15-19	20-24	25-44	45-64	65-84	85+	18+	MEDIAN AGE 2004	% 2004 Males	% 2004 Females
44094	WILLOUGHBY	96.6	96.0	1.3	1.3	1.1	1.5	0.7	0.7	5.4	5.5	6.1	5.7	5.6	26.2	27.2	15.4	3.0	79.4	42.1	46.9	53.1
44095	EASTLAKE	97.7	97.2	0.6	0.7	0.8	1.1	0.7	0.8	5.5	5.7	6.5	6.1	5.6	28.0	26.2	14.7	1.7	78.5	40.5	48.3	51.7
44099	WINDSOR	94.8	94.5	2.5	2.7	0.1	0.1	0.7	0.7	9.9	9.7	8.9	7.1	5.2	26.3	21.7	9.1	2.0	66.9	33.0	50.2	49.8
44102	CLEVELAND	67.5	63.3	14.4	16.8	2.2	2.7	20.8	22.4	8.7	8.0	8.5	7.4	7.8	30.9	19.6	8.0	1.3	70.4	31.2	49.6	50.4
44103	CLEVELAND	14.6	12.8	79.2	80.6	1.5	1.9	4.3	4.4	7.9	8.3	9.6	8.2	6.4	25.4	20.9	11.6	1.9	69.0	33.5	47.6	52.4
44104	CLEVELAND	2.0	1.6	96.5	96.9	0.1	0.1	0.6	0.6	11.1	10.6	10.5	8.3	7.4	23.6	18.5	8.9	1.2	62.7	26.8	43.9	56.1
44105	CLEVELAND	36.1	34.0	61.4	63.4	0.2	0.2	1.9	2.0	7.9	8.2	9.2	7.7	6.4	27.2	22.0	10.3	1.1	69.9	33.6	46.9	53.1
44106	CLEVELAND	36.5	34.7	56.3	56.3	5.1	6.8	1.4	1.5	5.7	5.2	5.6	9.6	15.2	26.4	18.0	11.6	2.6	80.1	29.8	48.3	51.7
44107	LAKEWOOD	93.1	91.7	2.0	2.5	1.4	1.9	2.2	2.5	5.8	5.4	5.7	6.5	7.7	34.5	22.4	9.8	2.2	79.5	35.4	48.3	51.7
44108	CLEVELAND	3.7	3.6	95.0	95.2	0.1	0.1	0.7	0.6	7.8	8.1	9.5	8.1	6.5	23.8	21.4	13.1	1.8	69.5	34.2	45.1	55.0
44109	CLEVELAND	78.1	75.6	7.0	8.3	1.1	1.4	19.6	20.8	8.2	7.5	7.8	6.9	7.0	31.1	20.9	9.2	1.3	72.2	33.6	49.1	50.9
44110	CLEVELAND	23.7	20.1	73.7	77.3	0.2	0.2	1.0	1.0	8.1	8.2	9.0	7.4	6.3	27.7	21.5	10.3	1.6	70.2	33.9	45.8	54.3
44111	CLEVELAND	83.7	81.2	7.3	8.7	1.9	2.5	8.5	9.3	7.5	7.1	6.8	5.8	5.9	32.3	22.7	10.2	1.6	75.0	36.3	48.8	51.3
44112	CLEVELAND	5.2	4.4	92.8	93.7	0.2	0.2	0.8	0.8	7.1	7.5	8.7	7.7	6.8	24.4	24.6	11.7	1.5	71.9	35.4	44.5	55.6
44113	CLEVELAND	55.6	51.0	28.6	32.8	0.9	1.1	21.3	21.7	6.7	6.0	6.4	6.6	9.6	36.2	20.0	7.4	1.1	77.3	32.5	55.8	44.2
44114	CLEVELAND	37.3	31.8	34.0	37.8	22.8	24.6	7.1	6.7	5.5	3.4	2.9	3.7	8.5	32.1	27.7	14.1	2.0	86.5	41.1	53.6	46.4
44115	CLEVELAND	11.1	9.8	85.1	86.2	1.7	1.9	1.3	1.2	14.0	9.3	6.9	10.0	16.2	26.4	13.1	3.7	0.5	65.4	23.1	42.9	57.1
44116	ROCKY RIVER	96.9	96.1	0.4	0.6	1.4	1.8	1.2	1.3	5.2	5.5	6.4	5.7	4.2	22.3	26.5	19.6	4.7	79.1	45.5	45.0	55.0
44117	EUCLID	44.7	39.1	52.8	58.3	0.6	0.8	1.0	1.0	4.6	4.9	6.1	6.1	5.0	21.5	26.5	21.1	4.4	80.7	46.3	43.6	56.4
44118	CLEVELAND	58.5	54.1	36.7	40.6	1.9	2.3	1.5	1.6	6.7	6.8	6.8	8.8	8.1	27.6	23.7	10.2	1.5	75.8	34.8	46.9	53.1
44119	CLEVELAND	80.3	76.3	16.7	20.3	0.8	1.1	1.4	1.6	6.5	6.3	6.4	5.1	5.1	29.9	22.6	13.1	5.1	77.6	39.8	47.2	52.8
44120	CLEVELAND	19.9	18.3	76.0	77.3	1.8	2.2	1.1	1.1	7.2	7.3	8.1	7.1	6.4	26.8	23.3	12.0	1.9	73.1	36.2	44.6	55.4
44121	CLEVELAND	63.8	59.8	32.2	35.8	1.6	1.9	1.2	1.2	6.5	6.7	7.1	6.4	5.9	27.4	26.3	11.7	2.2	75.7	38.7	46.1	53.9
44122	BEACHWOOD	63.9	60.1	31.5	34.4	2.7	3.4	0.9	1.0	4.3	5.2	6.7	7.2	4.4	19.7	27.5	19.3	5.9	79.1	46.8	45.8	54.2
44123	EUCLID	77.0	73.4	19.9	23.2	1.0	1.3	1.1	1.2	6.8	6.5	6.3	5.7	6.0	30.5	22.9	12.6	2.7	76.9	38.1	46.9	53.1
44124	CLEVELAND	93.2	91.5	2.8	3.5	3.0	3.9	0.9	1.1	4.8	5.1	5.4	5.1	4.3	24.2	25.6	20.7	4.8	81.6	45.8	45.9	54.1
44125	CLEVELAND	91.6	90.2	6.0	6.9	1.0	1.4	1.3	1.4	6.1	6.1	6.6	6.1	5.9	27.3	23.8	15.1	3.0	77.4	40.0	47.4	52.6
44126	CLEVELAND	95.9	95.0	0.7	0.8	1.6	2.1	1.5	1.7	5.8	6.0	6.1	5.9	5.1	25.8	26.4	16.0	3.0	78.5	42.2	47.1	52.9
44127	CLEVELAND	53.4	47.6	39.3	44.8	0.4	0.5	7.0	7.3	9.4	9.8	10.0	8.1	7.3	26.8	18.6	9.0	1.1	65.6	29.4	47.8	52.2
44128	CLEVELAND	4.1	3.3	93.5	94.3	0.5	0.6	0.8	0.8	6.3	7.0	7.7	6.8	5.5	23.8	25.2	15.9	1.9	74.9	39.8	44.0	56.0
44129	CLEVELAND	96.2	95.3	0.9	1.2	1.2	1.7	1.8	2.0	6.2	6.1	6.6	6.0	5.7	29.1	22.7	14.7	3.1	77.4	39.1	47.4	52.6
44130	CLEVELAND	94.3	92.9	1.6	2.1	2.2	2.9	1.5	1.7	5.1	5.0	5.4	5.4	5.7	26.1	25.1	19.1	3.2	81.2	43.2	47.1	52.9
44131	INDEPENDENCE	97.3	96.5	0.3	0.5	1.7	2.3	0.8	0.9	4.5	5.0	6.4	5.8	4.3	21.2	28.6	21.2	3.0	80.4	46.7	47.8	52.2
44132	EUCLID	62.4	59.4	34.1	36.8	1.0	1.3	1.1	1.1	7.1	6.8	6.7	5.7	5.5	30.6	22.6	12.7	2.3	75.8	37.3	46.1	53.9
44133	NORTH ROYALTON	96.2	95.1	0.7	1.0	2.0	2.7	1.0	1.1	5.3	5.7	7.1	6.5	6.6	27.7	28.5	11.1	1.6	77.7	39.7	48.7	51.3
44134	CLEVELAND	96.2	95.2	0.5	0.7	1.8	2.4	1.4	1.6	5.7	5.8	6.3	6.1	5.3	26.9	23.9	16.9	3.1	78.4	41.2	47.9	52.1
44135	CLEVELAND	76.9	74.4	16.1	17.5	2.2	2.8	5.8	6.3	7.6	7.2	6.8	5.5	5.2	30.1	22.8	12.7	2.1	75.0	37.7	48.4	51.6
44136	STRONGSVILLE	93.6	91.8	1.5	1.9	3.5	4.6	1.3	1.5	5.7	6.4	7.7	6.7	6.0	25.6	29.4	10.9	1.5	75.9	40.4	48.8	51.2
44137	MAPLE HEIGHTS	51.6	46.4	44.4	49.2	1.8	2.1	1.2	1.3	6.4	6.5	7.6	6.8	6.0	28.1	23.4	13.2	2.1	75.4	38.3	47.0	53.0
44138	OLMSTED FALLS	96.4	95.4	1.2	1.6	1.1	1.5	1.5	1.8	5.7	6.1	6.7	6.3	5.5	26.4	27.2	14.1	2.1	77.5	41.1	47.7	52.4
44139	SOLON	88.0	84.8	6.1	7.7	4.8	6.3	0.7	0.8	5.7	7.3	9.2	8.1	4.5	22.7	31.2	10.2	1.3	72.6	41.0	49.0	51.0
44140	BAY VILLAGE	98.1	97.6	0.3	0.4	0.7	1.0	1.0	1.1	6.0	6.6	7.5	6.9	3.8	23.5	31.0	12.8	1.9	75.2	42.4	47.9	52.1
44141	BRECKSVILLE	94.9	93.3	1.9	2.6	2.6	3.4	1.0	1.1	4.6	6.0	7.5	6.1	3.9	20.1	33.3	16.1	2.6	77.9	45.9	50.2	49.8
44142	BROOK PARK	94.5	93.2	2.0	2.5	1.3	1.7	2.0	2.3	5.1	5.3	6.7	6.2	6.0	26.3	26.0	16.9	1.5	79.0	41.6	48.7	51.3
44143	CLEVELAND	79.7	76.0	14.4	16.7	4.4	5.6	1.1	1.2	5.1	5.7	6.6	6.1	5.6	24.0	28.1	16.2	2.7	78.9	43.1	47.7	52.3
44144	CLEVELAND	91.8	90.1	1.8	2.3	1.7	2.3	5.7	6.6	6.1	5.9	5.5	5.0	5.3	29.9	23.9	15.7	2.6	79.5	40.1	48.2	51.8
44145	WESTLAKE	93.0	91.1	0.9	1.2	4.2	5.5	1.3	1.4	5.1	5.8	6.8	6.1	4.8	24.1	29.1	14.4	3.8	78.2	43.3	47.3	52.7
44146	BEDFORD	57.5	52.9	38.8	43.2	1.3	1.5	1.3	1.3	5.2	5.2	6.1	5.9	6.3	27.1	26.5	15.1	2.6	80.0	41.3	46.9	53.1
44147	BROADVIEW HEIGHTS	95.0	93.6	0.8	1.1	3.0	4.0	0.9	1.1	6.1	6.4	7.2	6.2	5.3	26.7	26.8	13.4	1.9	76.5	40.4	47.9	52.1
44149	STRONGSVILLE	94.9	93.5	0.9	1.3	2.8	3.8	1.2	1.4	6.7	7.5	7.8	5.8	4.0	25.9	29.1	12.2	1.1	74.2	40.9	48.2	51.8
44201	ATWATER	98.5	98.3	0.4	0.4	0.1	0.2	0.7	0.7	6.3	6.8	7.5	6.6	5.7	27.5	27.7	10.8	1.1	75.2	39.2	50.6	49.4
44202	AURORA	95.6	94.9	2.2	2.5	1.1	1.5	0.6	0.7	6.7	7.3	7.5	6.2	4.2	25.9	27.8	12.3	2.1	74.5	40.5	48.5	51.5
44203	BARBERTON	94.2	93.4	3.9	4.5	0.4	0.5	0.6	0.6	6.9	6.3	6.5	6.3	6.2	26.3	25.0	14.4	2.2	76.4	39.4	47.8	52.2
44212	BRUNSWICK	97.2	96.7	0.7	0.7	0.9	1.2	1.4	1.5	7.2	7.3	7.7	6.6	6.5	30.7	25.2	8.1	0.8	73.7	35.8	49.1	50.9
44214	BURBANK	99.1	99.0	0.2	0.2	0.2	0.2	0.8	0.8	6.5	7.1	8.1	6.1	6.0	27.9	28.2	9.3	0.8	74.5	37.7	51.9	48.1
44215	CHIPPEWA LAKE	98.5	98.4	0.3	0.3	0.2	0.3	0.7	0.7	5.5	5.7	6.9	7.1	6.5	29.6	28.6	9.3	0.9	77.5	38.4	51.4	48.6
44216	CLINTON	97.7	97.1	0.5	0.6	0.8	1.1	0.5	0.6	5.8	6.4	7.4	6.7	5.5	25.4	30.7	11.2	0.9	76.0	40.7	50.2	49.8
44217	CRESTON	98.5	98.3	0.4	0.4	0.2	0.2	0.3	0.4	6.9	7.1	7.7	6.6	5.7	29.3	24.8	10.7	1.1	74.1	37.2	50.2	49.8
44221	CUYAHOGA FALLS	96.3	95.4	1.3	1.6	1.1	1.5	0.7	0.8	6.1	5.9	6.1	5.7	6.6	32.1	22.9	12.8	1.7	78.3	37.1	47.8	52.2
44223	CUYAHOGA FALLS	95.6	94.4	2.5	3.3	0.8	1.1	0.5	0.5	6.8	6.9	6.4	5.4	5.0	27.1	24.7	15.2	2.6	76.6	40.3	46.9	53.1
44224	STOW	95.1	94.0	1.6	2.0	1.9	2.5	0.9	1.0	6.4	6.6	7.2	6.7	6.0	27.6	26.2	11.4	2.0	75.7	38.5	48.4	51.6
44230	DOYLESTOWN	98.5	98.3	0.4	0.5	0.3	0.3	0.4	0.4	5.8	6.2	7.0	6.4	5.7	26.3	28.3	12.8	1.6	76.9	40.7	49.4	50.6
44231	GARRETTSVILLE	98.4	98.3	0.5	0.5	0.1	0.2	0.4	0.5	6.7	7.0	8.0	7.3	6.4	28.1	25.0	10.5	1.1	74.0	37.2	49.2	50.8
44233	HINCKLEY	98.3	98.0	0.1	0.1	0.8	1.1	0.7	0.8	5.3	6.4	7.2	6.8	4.6	23.4	33.9	11.3	1.1	76.8	43.0	50.5	49.5
44234	HIRAM	96.7	96.4	1.7	1.8	0.4	0.5	0.8	0.9	4.9	5.8	6.9	12.4	11.4	24.7	24.0	8.9	1.0	78.4	34.3	50.3	49.7
44235	HOMERVILLE	97.6	97.4	1.1	1.1	0.0	0.0	1.1	1.2	9.2	9.3	9.8	7.4	6.9	26.7	23.6	6.5	0.7	67.2	30.8	49.8	50.2
44236	HUDSON	94.4	92.9	1.8	2.3	2.8	3.7	0.8	1.0	6.4	8.3	10.3	8.7	4.3	21.8	30.7	8.1	1.5	68.9	39.9	49.5	50.5
44240	KENT	89.5	88.4	6.3	6.7	1.9	2.4	0.9	1.0	5.8	5.6	5.8	8.4	15.7	28.3	21.0	8.4	1.1	79.3	29.5	48.6	51.4
44241	STREETSBORO	95.6	94.7	1.8	2.0	1.3	1.9	0.7	0.8	6.9	6.8	7.0	5.9	6.6	32.7	23.7	9.6	0.9	75.8	35.6	49.1	50.9
44243	KENT	84.6	82.9	11.1	12.1	1.9	2.5	1.7	1.9	0.3	0.2	0.1	45.1	42.5	5.5	1.9	3.9	0.5	99.1	20.5	39.9	60.1
44253	LITCHFIELD	97.9	97.8	0.7	0.8	0.4	0.5	0.4	0.4	5.2	7.6	9.5	8.6	5.7	26.6	28.5	7.8	0.5	71.8	37.9	52.0	48.0
44254	LODI	98.5	98.4	0.1	0.2	0.2	0.2	0.6	0.7	6.3	6.5	7.0	6.9	6.5	26.9	26.9	11.8	1.4	76.0	39.2	48.9	51.2
44255	MANTUA	98.2	98.0	0.6	0.7	0.1	0.2	0.7	0.8	6.0	6.6	7.6	7.1	6.3	27.7	27.8	9.9	1.0	75.5	38.6	49.9	50.1
44256	MEDINA	96.2	95.7	1.6	1.7	0.8	1.0	0.9	1.0	7.6	7.8	7.8	6.4	5.6	28.7	25.9	8.9	1.5	72.7	37.0	48.9	51.1
44260	MOGADORE	98.8	98.6	0.3	0.3	0.2	0.2	0.3	0.4	5.6	6.1	7.0	6.5	5.7	25.9	29.7	12.4	1.2	77.4	41.0	49.8	50.2
44262	MUNROE FALLS	97.1	96.3	0.9	1.1	1.3	1.7	0.7	0.8	4.5	6.7	7.3	6.6	4.6	24.1	31.5	12.9	1.7	76.9	42.6	48.5	51.5
44264	PENINSULA	96.3	95.6	0.8	0.9	1.1	1.4	0.7	0.8	5.1	6.0	7.5	6.0	4.4	26.9	31.6	11.0	1.6	77.2	42.0	50.7	49.3
44266	RAVENNA	94.7	94.3	3.2	3.3	0.3	0.3	0.7	0.8	6.8	6.7	6.9	6.5	6.2	29.2	25.3	11.0	1.5	75.6	37.4	49.3	50.8
44270	RITTMAN	98.4	98.1	0.2	0.2	0.3	0.4	0.8	0.8	6.9	6.8	7.4	6.5	6.6	28.8	24.1	11.3	1.6	74.9	37.1	49.4	50.7
44272	ROOTSTOWN	98.1	97.9	0.3	0.3	0.4	0.5	0.5	0.5	5.9	6.4	7.3	6.4	5.8	27.1	28.4	11.5	1.3	76.3	40.2	50.2	49.8
44273	SEVILLE	98.7	98.6	0.3	0.3	0.3	0.3	0.6	0.6	6.5	7.0	7.4	6.3	4.9	27.0	28.6	10.9	1.3	75.0	39.6	49.3	50.8
44275	SPENCER	98.9	98.9	0.3	0.3	0.1	0.1	0.9	1.0	7.6	8.0	8.4	6.5	5.1	27.8	26.8	8.7	1.0	71.9	37.0	50.4	49.7
44276	STERLING	98.8	98.7	0.2	0.2	0.3	0.3	0.9	0.9	5.5	6.0	8.1	7.8	5.8	26.6	26.5	11.8	1.9	75.3	38.9	50.3	49.8
44278	TALLMADGE	95.7	94.8	2.1	2.5	0.9	1.2	0.6	0.7	5.3	5.7	7.1	6.6	5.5	23.4	27.6	16.8	2.0	77.7	42.8	48.3	51.8
44280	VALLEY CITY	97.4	97.1	1.3	1.4	0.3	0.4	1.0	1.2	5.2	6.0	7.0	6.2	5.1	24.9	32.1	11.7	2.0	77.8	42.7	50.0	50.0
44281	WADSWORTH	98.0	97.7	0.4	0.4	0.6	0.8	0.6	0.7	6.8	7.0	7.4	6.5	5.5	25.9	25.7	13.3	1.9	74.7	39.5	48.8	51.2
44286	RICHFIELD	97.6	97.1	0.6	0.7	0.9	1.2	0.4	0.4	5.1	6.3	7.3	5.9	3.9	21.4	32.4	15.0	2.8	77.4	45.1	48.7	51.3
44287	WEST SALEM	98.3	98.1	0.3	0.3	0.3	0.3	0.7	0.8	7.5	7.7	8.4	7.5	6.0	27.0	25.4	9.5	0.9	71.7	36.0	51.4	48.6
44288	WINDHAM	95.0	94.6	3.2	3.5	0.1	0.1	0.5	0.5	8.9	8.7	9.2	7.9	6.6	28.4	22.0	7.9	0.5	68.5	31.7	49.2	50.8
44301	AKRON	77.9	75.3	17.9	19.9	1.6	2.1	1.1	1.2	7.9	7.3	7.3	6.4	6.3	29.9	22.3	11.0	1.7	73.6	35.2	48.0	52.0
44302	AKRON	57.9	54.0	37.2	40.7	1.5	1.8	1.7	1.8	6.4	6.1	6.6	6.7	7.5	33.0	22.7	9.0	2.1	77.2	34.6	48.6	51.4
44303	AKRON	79.6	77.9	16.4	17.4	1.7	2.2	1.2	1.3	5.5	5.5	6.0	5.9	6.3	27.1	27.7	12.6	3.3	79.3	41.0	48.5	51.6
44304	AKRON	60.7	56.3	30.3	33.1	5.1	6.4	2.2	2.3	4.5	3.9	3.3	16.3	29.5	24.7	12.1	4.6	1.1	85.8	23.7	55.2	44.8
44305	AKRON	81.4	78.9	15.5	17.6	0.5	0.7	1.0	1.1	7.5	7.2	7.6	6.7	6.4	30.8	22.4	10.2	1.3	73.5	34.8	48.1	51.9
44306	AKRON	58.3	55.1	35.9	38.6	1.9	2.4	1.4	1.4	9.2	8.8	8.4	7.1	7.6	27.9	20.1	9.6	1.4	69.2	31.3	46.9	53.2
	OHIO	85.0	84.1	11.5	11.8	1.2	1.6	1.9	2.1	6.7	6.6	7.1	7.0	7.1	27.5	24.7	11.6	1.8	75.6	37.0	48.6	51.4
	UNITED STATES	75.1	73.6	12.3	12.5	3.8	4.2	12.5	14.1	6.9	6.7	7.2	7.0	7.3	28.6	23.8	10.8	1.7	75.1	36.0	49.1	50.9

INCOME

ZIP CODE #	POST OFFICE NAME	2004 Per Capita Income	2004 HH Income Base	2004 Household Income Distribution (%) Less than $25,000	$25,000 to $49,999	$50,000 to $99,999	$100,000 to $149,999	$150,000 or More	Median Household Income 2004	2009	2004 National Centile	2004 State Centile	2004 Home Value Base	2004 Home Value Distribution (%) Less than $50,000	$50,000 to $89,999	$90,000 to $174,999	$175,000 to $399,999	$400,000 or More	2004 Median Home Value
44094	WILLOUGHBY	31691	15357	18.1	28.1	34.9	12.5	6.5	53209	61572	77	74	10004	4.1	3.7	47.1	37.2	8.0	167962
44095	EASTLAKE	25347	14520	18.7	30.9	37.9	10.1	2.4	50360	59627	73	64	11504	1.2	6.6	79.1	12.7	0.4	133286
44099	WINDSOR	17424	615	26.3	26.7	39.2	5.7	2.1	48159	53923	69	57	525	3.6	13.5	55.2	23.2	4.4	124679
44102	CLEVELAND	16972	19464	42.6	31.7	20.1	3.8	1.9	30076	37192	12	8	7428	21.6	49.8	23.6	3.9	1.2	72940
44103	CLEVELAND	11641	8942	59.5	24.5	12.8	2.4	0.9	19788	23536	2	2	3008	38.4	40.4	14.9	6.0	0.3	61835
44104	CLEVELAND	10255	9919	63.1	22.8	11.5	2.1	0.6	17371	20588	1	1	3237	31.8	49.2	17.1	1.9	0.0	65355
44105	CLEVELAND	15847	19852	42.4	30.6	21.7	3.8	1.4	30231	35924	13	8	11239	20.1	57.9	20.5	1.3	0.2	71376
44106	CLEVELAND	21578	13313	50.0	22.7	16.9	5.3	5.1	24990	30054	5	4	4205	16.0	28.1	27.4	21.2	7.3	99485
44107	LAKEWOOD	29353	26725	23.4	30.0	31.7	10.7	4.2	46969	57173	66	53	12539	2.4	8.0	68.1	18.0	3.5	136585
44108	CLEVELAND	15898	13082	48.6	28.6	16.6	3.5	2.8	25888	30384	6	4	6695	20.1	49.2	23.7	4.7	2.3	74931
44109	CLEVELAND	18626	18227	35.6	31.4	26.7	5.0	1.4	35235	43816	28	18	9901	9.9	35.4	52.0	2.4	0.3	93192
44110	CLEVELAND	15991	10957	48.3	29.1	18.1	3.7	0.8	26142	31043	6	5	4769	15.5	58.8	23.3	1.9	0.5	75600
44111	CLEVELAND	24123	18057	24.2	32.5	33.1	7.8	2.5	44077	53881	59	43	11791	2.7	31.7	59.4	5.8	0.5	101907
44112	CLEVELAND	16565	12875	48.7	27.1	18.0	4.0	2.2	25869	30577	6	4	5980	7.7	54.7	32.8	4.4	0.5	82839
44113	CLEVELAND	19952	7454	46.9	25.6	19.6	4.7	3.2	27746	35759	8	5	1998	29.7	26.7	26.0	15.7	1.9	78173
44114	CLEVELAND	21859	2197	55.3	23.6	13.5	4.0	3.6	20926	26069	2	2	294	41.8	45.9	11.6	0.3	0.3	55217
44115	CLEVELAND	10580	2989	80.3	9.5	7.2	1.8	1.3	9519	11491	0	0	167	16.8	10.8	68.3	0.0	4.2	114688
44116	ROCKY RIVER	43344	9477	16.5	24.4	32.0	14.9	12.2	60399	74339	85	86	6756	1.0	8.4	28.0	54.0	8.7	205571
44117	EUCLID	23625	5727	42.1	26.1	23.0	7.3	1.6	32246	39963	18	11	2623	2.2	16.2	75.5	6.1	0.0	116760
44118	CLEVELAND	32159	17416	19.5	22.1	34.1	15.0	9.4	60446	74809	85	87	11587	1.0	7.7	63.3	24.9	3.1	141673
44119	CLEVELAND	24734	5948	26.8	29.1	33.9	7.8	2.4	44424	54457	60	44	3761	2.6	29.9	62.7	4.6	0.2	99683
44120	CLEVELAND	25420	20080	36.4	29.3	20.7	7.1	6.5	35273	42466	29	18	9943	9.3	33.4	35.2	16.4	5.7	98707
44121	CLEVELAND	27571	14237	19.6	25.1	38.3	12.6	4.4	55047	67247	80	78	11062	0.9	9.6	80.1	9.2	0.2	119371
44122	BEACHWOOD	46953	13990	16.6	21.0	27.8	15.1	19.6	69041	85881	91	94	9671	1.5	9.3	27.6	45.9	15.8	215315
44123	EUCLID	24195	8317	25.8	32.5	33.1	6.9	1.7	42815	52541	55	38	5244	4.0	23.1	69.0	3.7	0.2	103304
44124	CLEVELAND	39562	18584	20.3	25.8	31.4	11.9	10.5	54116	65588	79	76	13015	0.8	2.4	55.1	32.1	9.7	162942
44125	CLEVELAND	24252	11902	23.8	28.2	37.1	8.1	2.8	47815	58097	68	56	9680	0.6	16.9	75.7	6.7	0.2	108183
44126	CLEVELAND	33444	7615	19.3	23.7	38.2	13.4	5.4	58110	69936	83	82	5696	0.7	1.8	64.0	31.7	1.8	156462
44127	CLEVELAND	13052	3124	49.4	32.8	14.4	1.6	1.7	25256	30588	5	4	1403	53.5	37.4	7.8	0.8	0.6	47679
44128	CLEVELAND	21937	13141	28.9	33.1	28.9	6.8	2.3	39815	47534	45	29	8078	6.3	45.7	46.4	1.5	0.1	88856
44129	CLEVELAND	24986	12217	21.4	30.4	35.1	10.3	2.8	48518	58582	69	58	8789	0.4	3.3	85.3	10.8	0.2	127396
44130	CLEVELAND	26978	22786	21.3	29.3	35.0	11.0	3.4	49353	59149	71	61	15259	0.8	4.9	69.4	24.5	0.4	145472
44131	INDEPENDENCE	31022	7927	16.5	21.4	35.6	19.0	7.5	63560	78146	87	90	7564	0.4	0.7	37.1	58.3	3.5	190452
44132	EUCLID	23087	6793	25.8	35.0	30.4	6.5	2.3	41097	49514	50	33	3906	3.4	21.8	70.4	4.2	0.2	106082
44133	NORTH ROYALTON	32430	11939	12.9	23.4	37.7	18.2	7.9	65416	80104	89	92	8724	0.2	7.4	30.6	56.4	5.3	198084
44134	CLEVELAND	25605	16137	20.7	27.9	38.3	10.4	2.7	51072	61511	74	67	13172	0.6	4.7	82.7	12.0	0.1	128069
44135	CLEVELAND	23289	12146	26.5	30.3	33.7	7.7	2.0	44038	53312	59	42	8708	5.6	36.5	56.4	1.5	0.1	95790
44136	STRONGSVILLE	36287	9677	12.0	18.5	35.2	21.3	13.1	76733	91625	94	97	7547	0.3	0.7	31.4	65.3	2.3	200954
44137	MAPLE HEIGHTS	22726	10307	21.7	32.2	36.6	8.1	1.5	46956	56915	66	53	8258	1.9	28.0	69.3	0.7	0.1	98489
44138	OLMSTED FALLS	30261	7634	14.2	25.8	38.9	15.3	5.8	59844	71563	84	85	6288	11.5	7.8	44.1	35.3	1.3	156465
44139	SOLON	43206	8059	9.3	15.5	30.7	21.7	22.8	88937	110216	97	99	7149	0.8	0.8	15.3	65.6	17.4	246738
44140	BAY VILLAGE	44696	6074	10.3	15.6	35.7	22.0	16.4	81194	101061	95	98	5629	0.4	1.2	39.2	52.0	7.3	195293
44141	BRECKSVILLE	45849	5163	9.2	16.4	31.1	21.7	21.6	86956	108626	97	99	4678	0.3	2.2	17.2	67.3	13.0	240331
44142	BROOK PARK	25000	7848	16.7	29.0	40.2	11.7	2.4	53354	64417	77	74	6598	0.5	4.6	90.7	4.2	0.0	129165
44143	CLEVELAND	35556	9890	15.0	25.4	31.8	15.6	12.2	63350	79474	87	89	7538	0.7	1.9	40.0	49.1	8.3	191372
44144	CLEVELAND	24715	9939	25.8	33.2	31.3	7.7	2.0	42087	51238	53	36	6647	2.5	15.1	77.6	4.6	0.2	113388
44145	WESTLAKE	46469	13183	11.3	18.5	34.6	17.1	18.5	75411	94306	93	96	10115	1.0	3.6	32.2	48.9	14.4	213725
44146	BEDFORD	25983	13823	24.6	32.0	31.7	8.5	3.3	44452	53494	60	44	8452	6.1	13.2	66.6	13.7	0.5	118389
44147	BROADVIEW HEIGHTS	36130	6587	12.8	24.1	33.4	17.3	12.4	66593	82911	90	93	5156	0.3	3.4	33.7	52.1	10.6	198491
44149	STRONGSVILLE	37682	7170	8.0	16.6	40.1	20.6	14.8	78028	96149	94	97	6586	0.0	0.8	35.5	59.8	3.9	195676
44201	ATWATER	24431	2605	13.3	29.8	42.0	12.7	2.2	55629	64770	80	79	2266	9.8	8.7	48.0	32.2	1.3	145845
44202	AURORA	40697	6747	10.2	17.5	36.3	18.9	17.0	77118	91005	94	97	5590	1.7	2.4	26.5	58.8	10.7	220158
44203	BARBERTON	22435	17335	27.0	32.2	30.6	7.5	2.7	42384	51188	54	37	12572	7.7	27.2	55.3	9.4	0.5	103515
44212	BRUNSWICK	26674	15034	12.1	22.1	45.6	15.8	4.5	64351	75734	88	91	12016	0.7	2.7	57.3	38.5	0.9	164256
44214	BURBANK	22419	723	15.2	28.9	42.7	9.7	3.5	54027	60910	78	76	621	5.0	9.8	49.0	32.2	4.0	147049
44215	CHIPPEWA LAKE	23424	965	16.0	32.0	37.6	11.9	2.5	51408	61633	75	68	752	1.3	14.8	62.2	20.4	1.3	126008
44216	CLINTON	28600	3238	13.2	22.8	43.0	15.8	5.2	63328	76031	87	89	2922	1.6	9.6	60.1	26.5	2.3	144156
44217	CRESTON	20727	1564	18.4	32.7	40.2	7.4	1.3	48937	55144	70	59	1278	13.1	10.1	55.8	19.3	1.8	122650
44221	CUYAHOGA FALLS	24812	14034	23.2	30.8	36.5	7.8	1.7	46671	55287	65	52	8629	1.0	12.6	82.4	4.0	0.1	115122
44223	CUYAHOGA FALLS	30954	7766	20.8	24.1	34.9	14.5	5.8	55678	66146	80	79	5677	1.6	4.1	60.6	29.5	4.2	147261
44224	STOW	32196	15504	13.8	21.0	39.6	17.0	8.5	65411	78804	89	92	11254	1.3	3.7	50.6	42.5	2.0	168049
44230	DOYLESTOWN	24645	3276	17.3	28.3	38.4	12.8	3.3	53983	61878	78	76	2773	16.5	6.6	46.4	28.7	1.7	137997
44231	GARRETTSVILLE	22344	2989	19.7	28.5	38.2	11.7	1.8	51427	60348	75	68	2407	13.4	10.1	48.0	26.5	2.0	142445
44233	HINCKLEY	35671	2517	8.0	14.7	41.0	21.8	14.5	80618	94022	95	98	2394	0.4	0.2	21.4	60.8	17.1	256437
44234	HIRAM	23748	1428	16.0	22.8	42.7	14.8	3.7	59160	69746	84	84	1215	3.7	10.6	42.9	40.2	2.6	164117
44235	HOMERVILLE	16585	519	25.1	22.7	33.7	16.8	1.7	51437	60234	75	69	455	6.4	7.9	32.8	48.1	4.8	181750
44236	HUDSON	49447	8492	6.4	11.6	27.1	22.8	32.2	108259	131943	99	100	7551	1.2	1.4	11.5	66.7	19.2	271701
44240	KENT	24454	15139	32.3	28.1	26.2	9.4	4.0	39068	46466	43	27	7757	3.6	7.8	59.9	26.7	2.1	142139
44241	STREETSBORO	26354	5583	16.3	27.9	41.6	11.1	3.1	55199	64206	80	78	3866	12.9	6.4	57.0	21.7	1.9	135886
44243	KENT	9865	4	100.0	0.0	0.0	0.0	0.0	17500	13164	1	1	0	0.0	0.0	0.0	0.0	0.0	0
44253	LITCHFIELD	24647	1205	10.8	21.1	47.9	14.1	6.1	64474	75921	88	91	1137	0.8	2.8	37.9	55.2	3.3	188945
44254	LODI	21638	2167	24.3	29.8	35.4	8.4	2.0	45075	54263	61	46	1678	10.9	9.7	50.4	27.7	1.4	134774
44255	MANTUA	25796	3164	13.8	27.1	41.1	13.8	4.2	58985	68573	84	84	2699	10.2	4.7	42.9	38.5	3.7	162904
44256	MEDINA	31416	20836	12.4	22.2	39.2	17.9	8.2	66177	77529	89	93	16341	1.6	2.0	38.9	50.4	7.1	189688
44260	MOGADORE	24604	5354	16.8	26.4	40.6	13.4	2.8	56309	65630	81	80	4655	6.5	7.0	59.7	24.4	2.3	141407
44262	MUNROE FALLS	33776	1909	8.9	21.0	39.7	17.3	13.2	70841	86023	92	95	1678	0.7	0.7	59.2	37.5	2.0	162742
44264	PENINSULA	34312	969	16.1	23.3	34.6	15.9	10.1	64195	77833	88	91	825	23.4	4.2	21.8	36.9	13.7	176679
44266	RAVENNA	22399	13757	22.4	30.8	36.3	8.2	2.3	47386	55229	67	54	10235	18.7	12.7	49.7	17.8	1.1	114890
44270	RITTMAN	20799	3330	24.1	32.4	34.1	7.8	1.6	44726	51926	60	45	2484	3.7	15.9	63.5	16.3	0.7	117647
44272	ROOTSTOWN	24634	1588	13.5	27.6	41.3	14.3	3.3	56109	65873	81	80	1357	3.7	5.4	54.2	34.4	2.3	155798
44273	SEVILLE	28283	2958	12.3	24.1	42.0	15.0	6.6	61492	71581	86	87	2569	1.9	5.2	44.3	44.0	4.6	172514
44275	SPENCER	23122	1197	13.5	28.2	44.9	11.1	2.3	56484	65851	81	80	1057	1.8	6.6	45.0	43.1	3.5	169297
44276	STERLING	20984	720	17.8	27.6	45.6	7.5	1.5	52974	59205	77	73	607	3.8	9.4	61.5	23.9	1.5	139939
44278	TALLMADGE	25837	6760	18.5	24.6	38.8	13.6	4.5	56339	66504	81	80	5463	2.3	4.7	53.9	38.3	0.8	161081
44280	VALLEY CITY	33254	1653	12.3	19.0	39.6	18.4	10.7	69272	80956	91	94	1508	1.0	1.8	32.0	56.2	9.0	213774
44281	WADSWORTH	30972	11004	15.6	23.9	39.9	13.8	6.9	60891	70826	85	87	8701	1.2	5.6	50.4	37.9	4.9	164118
44286	RICHFIELD	46024	2018	9.7	18.2	32.4	19.4	20.3	82156	101840	96	98	1860	0.0	1.7	29.1	49.1	20.1	230496
44287	WEST SALEM	19430	2700	18.7	33.7	38.0	7.5	2.1	47928	53654	68	57	2306	9.8	11.5	54.1	22.3	2.3	129401
44288	WINDHAM	16539	1612	28.4	34.2	30.8	5.3	1.2	40347	47312	47	31	1092	15.3	23.7	49.2	10.7	1.1	101160
44301	AKRON	19662	6883	29.7	31.5	31.2	6.8	0.7	39504	47602	44	28	4658	9.3	38.3	51.7	0.6	0.2	91478
44302	AKRON	22135	3233	40.3	26.9	25.1	5.6	2.1	31703	38184	17	10	1193	12.8	32.3	50.0	4.7	0.2	93953
44303	AKRON	32679	3683	24.9	27.7	26.0	11.8	9.6	47422	57675	67	55	2258	3.7	12.9	46.4	31.1	5.9	147718
44304	AKRON	14837	2714	59.6	23.8	12.2	2.9	1.5	18717	21613	1	2	504	43.9	35.7	17.3	1.0	2.2	55741
44305	AKRON	20105	9532	24.7	35.6	34.2	4.6	1.0	41681	50999	52	35	6457	7.5	51.3	40.7	0.3	0.2	85265
44306	AKRON	15140	9821	42.2	31.2	23.4	2.7	0.6	30248	35892	13	8	5313	18.6	54.5	24.7	2.2	0.0	72828
	OHIO	25510		24.6	28.1	32.2	10.1	5.0	47354	56168				9.2	18.6	47.0	22.1	3.1	121192
	UNITED STATES	25866		24.7	27.1	30.8	10.9	6.5	48124	56710				10.9	15.0	33.7	30.1	10.4	145905

ZIP CODE #	POST OFFICE NAME	FINANCIAL SERVICES: Auto Loan	FINANCIAL SERVICES: Home Loan	FINANCIAL SERVICES: Invest-ments	FINANCIAL SERVICES: Retire-ment Plans	THE HOME: Home Improvements: Home Repair	THE HOME: Home Improvements: Lawn & Garden	THE HOME: Furnishings: Comput-ers & Hard-ware	THE HOME: Furnishings: Major Appli-ances	THE HOME: Furnishings: TV, Radio, Sound Equip-ment	THE HOME: Furnishings: Furni-ture	ENTERTAINMENT: Dine out/ Carry out	ENTERTAINMENT: Sports Equip-ment	ENTERTAINMENT: Fees & Tickets	ENTERTAINMENT: Toys & Games	ENTERTAINMENT: Travel	ENTERTAINMENT: Cable TV	PERSONAL: Apparel & Services	PERSONAL: Auto Repairs	PERSONAL: Health Insur-ance	PERSONAL: Pets & Supplies
44094	WILLOUGHBY	94	102	114	103	101	107	101	99	99	100	124	115	104	125	102	97	121	100	96	109
44095	EASTLAKE	79	87	94	84	87	94	84	84	84	83	105	96	88	110	87	86	103	83	85	93
44099	WINDSOR	98	81	55	75	87	95	76	87	83	76	100	103	72	100	78	87	94	85	97	115
44102	CLEVELAND	57	51	60	51	50	57	60	57	63	58	78	67	58	76	58	62	75	60	58	63
44103	CLEVELAND	40	34	41	32	33	40	39	39	44	40	54	43	39	51	38	46	52	41	43	44
44104	CLEVELAND	38	31	38	29	30	36	36	35	40	37	50	39	35	47	35	42	48	37	39	41
44105	CLEVELAND	57	52	57	49	51	59	57	56	61	57	75	63	57	73	56	63	73	57	60	63
44106	CLEVELAND	64	55	72	56	54	62	67	62	70	65	87	74	64	83	63	69	84	67	63	70
44107	LAKEWOOD	79	81	105	85	79	84	88	83	86	87	109	100	88	110	86	83	107	86	77	91
44108	CLEVELAND	59	51	58	47	50	60	56	57	62	58	77	62	56	72	55	65	74	58	63	65
44109	CLEVELAND	60	59	67	58	58	64	64	62	66	62	82	72	64	83	63	66	80	64	63	68
44110	CLEVELAND	51	46	55	44	45	52	51	49	55	51	68	56	51	66	50	56	66	51	53	56
44111	CLEVELAND	72	76	86	77	76	80	80	77	79	77	99	91	81	101	79	77	96	78	75	84
44112	CLEVELAND	56	50	58	46	48	57	54	54	59	55	73	59	54	70	54	62	71	55	59	62
44113	CLEVELAND	53	48	61	48	47	53	56	53	59	55	73	62	55	72	54	59	71	56	54	58
44114	CLEVELAND	48	46	65	49	47	51	55	51	55	52	68	62	53	67	54	54	66	55	51	56
44115	CLEVELAND	29	24	33	23	23	28	30	28	33	30	40	33	29	38	28	33	39	30	30	32
44116	ROCKY RIVER	117	131	158	132	130	138	130	127	126	129	158	147	134	160	132	125	156	128	122	139
44117	EUCLID	59	58	76	59	58	65	65	62	67	64	84	71	66	84	65	68	82	65	64	68
44118	CLEVELAND	102	111	139	112	109	117	113	109	111	113	140	127	117	142	114	110	138	111	104	120
44119	CLEVELAND	68	74	86	74	74	78	76	73	75	74	94	86	78	97	76	74	92	74	72	80
44120	CLEVELAND	79	76	94	74	74	84	81	79	85	82	106	89	83	104	81	87	104	81	82	89
44121	CLEVELAND	84	96	113	96	94	99	94	92	91	93	114	107	97	117	95	89	113	92	87	100
44122	BEACHWOOD	138	159	200	158	156	169	153	150	150	155	189	171	163	193	158	151	187	150	146	165
44123	EUCLID	67	70	79	69	70	77	73	71	74	70	92	81	75	96	73	74	89	71	72	78
44124	CLEVELAND	109	122	147	119	121	133	119	118	118	118	148	132	125	150	123	120	145	118	119	129
44125	CLEVELAND	75	82	89	79	82	89	81	80	82	79	102	91	84	106	83	83	99	80	82	88
44126	CLEVELAND	94	107	124	105	106	113	104	102	102	103	128	117	109	131	107	102	126	102	100	112
44127	CLEVELAND	49	42	49	40	42	49	49	48	54	49	66	55	48	63	48	55	64	50	51	54
44128	CLEVELAND	71	69	78	66	67	77	71	70	74	73	94	76	73	90	71	77	91	71	74	80
44129	CLEVELAND	76	83	93	81	82	89	83	81	83	81	104	93	86	108	85	84	102	81	82	89
44130	CLEVELAND	77	85	100	84	84	91	85	83	84	84	106	96	88	108	87	84	104	84	82	91
44131	INDEPENDENCE	101	117	131	113	117	126	110	111	107	110	134	123	116	137	114	109	132	108	111	121
44132	EUCLID	65	69	81	67	68	76	70	69	72	70	90	78	73	92	72	73	88	69	71	76
44133	NORTH ROYALTON	105	124	137	125	121	122	116	115	110	116	138	135	121	144	117	106	137	113	104	126
44134	CLEVELAND	78	88	98	85	88	96	85	85	85	84	106	95	90	111	88	87	104	84	87	93
44135	CLEVELAND	71	76	83	73	76	83	76	75	77	74	96	85	79	100	77	79	94	74	77	83
44136	STRONGSVILLE	126	146	164	150	142	146	138	134	129	138	164	157	145	168	138	126	163	133	122	148
44137	MAPLE HEIGHTS	71	78	86	76	78	84	78	77	78	76	97	88	81	102	79	78	95	76	77	84
44138	OLMSTED FALLS	100	113	119	113	111	114	104	105	99	106	125	119	108	124	105	97	122	103	99	115
44139	SOLON	160	196	214	200	191	195	176	173	162	177	206	199	190	213	179	159	206	167	157	191
44140	BAY VILLAGE	144	173	197	173	171	178	161	160	152	161	191	184	170	196	166	150	190	157	150	174
44141	BRECKSVILLE	156	185	206	189	183	188	170	169	159	171	201	194	182	205	174	156	200	165	156	185
44142	BROOK PARK	81	93	101	91	92	97	89	88	87	88	109	102	93	114	91	87	107	87	86	97
44143	CLEVELAND	114	127	143	128	124	132	123	121	119	124	150	140	128	151	124	117	148	121	115	133
44144	CLEVELAND	69	74	82	72	74	81	74	73	75	72	94	83	77	98	76	76	91	73	75	80
44145	WESTLAKE	148	166	194	169	164	173	161	158	154	161	194	183	167	194	163	151	191	158	149	174
44146	BEDFORD	75	79	90	78	78	85	80	78	80	79	100	90	82	102	81	81	98	79	79	87
44147	BROADVIEW HEIGHTS	113	132	157	134	130	134	127	124	121	127	152	146	132	156	129	118	151	124	115	136
44149	STRONGSVILLE	133	159	168	160	155	156	144	143	134	145	169	166	152	175	146	130	168	139	129	157
44201	ATWATER	108	96	73	91	102	109	89	98	94	89	115	117	87	117	91	97	109	96	107	127
44202	AURORA	141	168	179	171	164	165	152	150	141	154	179	175	162	184	154	137	178	147	136	166
44203	BARBERTON	72	76	80	73	76	83	75	75	77	74	95	86	77	99	77	78	93	75	78	85
44212	BRUNSWICK	100	109	112	111	107	109	104	104	100	105	125	122	107	127	104	96	123	103	95	115
44214	BURBANK	98	90	72	86	94	100	83	91	87	83	106	108	82	109	85	88	101	89	97	115
44215	CHIPPEWA LAKE	95	83	64	81	87	96	81	88	86	80	104	102	78	105	82	88	98	86	95	108
44216	CLINTON	110	119	114	116	120	123	108	112	107	108	132	132	112	139	111	107	130	109	110	132
44217	CRESTON	88	78	60	74	83	89	72	80	77	72	93	95	71	95	74	79	89	78	87	103
44221	CUYAHOGA FALLS	72	76	87	77	75	79	78	76	76	77	96	89	79	97	77	75	94	77	72	83
44223	CUYAHOGA FALLS	91	102	116	102	101	108	100	99	98	99	122	114	104	125	102	97	120	98	96	108
44224	STOW	106	122	134	123	120	122	116	114	110	116	138	133	120	142	117	106	137	113	105	125
44230	DOYLESTOWN	96	94	82	92	96	100	88	93	89	89	110	109	88	111	89	89	106	91	93	110
44231	GARRETTSVILLE	95	82	62	79	87	94	78	86	83	78	101	102	75	102	79	85	96	85	94	110
44233	HINCKLEY	131	164	175	165	160	159	145	144	134	146	169	168	156	179	148	130	169	138	128	159
44234	HIRAM	100	103	94	100	105	108	94	99	93	94	115	117	96	120	96	93	112	96	98	119
44235	HOMERVILLE	93	85	66	81	89	95	78	86	82	78	100	102	77	103	80	84	95	84	92	110
44236	HUDSON	192	234	260	239	228	232	212	208	196	213	248	240	228	255	215	190	248	202	188	229
44240	KENT	75	71	84	75	71	75	83	76	80	79	101	94	80	99	78	76	98	81	71	84
44241	STREETSBORO	96	93	88	94	93	96	91	93	90	92	112	111	89	111	89	87	109	93	89	109
44243	KENT	22	13	17	15	13	16	26	19	25	22	32	27	21	28	21	22	30	23	18	22
44253	LITCHFIELD	97	121	128	121	119	117	108	107	100	107	125	126	115	134	110	97	125	103	96	119
44254	LODI	79	79	71	77	80	85	75	78	76	75	93	90	75	95	76	76	90	76	79	91
44255	MANTUA	102	102	91	100	104	108	95	100	95	95	117	118	95	120	96	95	114	98	100	120
44256	MEDINA	114	129	137	131	126	126	121	120	115	122	144	141	125	148	121	110	143	118	109	133
44260	MOGADORE	85	98	103	95	97	100	91	91	88	90	110	106	95	116	93	88	109	89	88	102
44262	MUNROE FALLS	114	139	153	138	137	140	127	126	119	126	150	146	135	158	131	118	150	123	117	138
44264	PENINSULA	119	128	121	126	127	130	117	121	114	118	142	141	120	143	118	111	139	118	115	139
44266	RAVENNA	84	77	68	74	79	86	75	80	79	75	96	94	74	97	76	80	92	79	84	97
44270	RITTMAN	76	77	73	75	78	83	74	76	75	73	93	89	75	96	75	75	90	75	78	88
44272	ROOTSTOWN	106	95	73	90	100	107	87	97	92	87	113	115	86	115	90	95	107	94	104	124
44273	SEVILLE	113	114	104	111	117	123	105	111	106	105	130	131	106	134	108	106	126	108	113	134
44275	SPENCER	102	95	77	91	99	105	87	95	91	87	111	113	87	114	90	93	106	93	101	121
44276	STERLING	92	84	67	80	88	95	78	85	82	78	100	101	77	102	80	84	95	83	92	108
44278	TALLMADGE	91	96	95	94	97	104	92	94	92	90	113	107	94	116	94	93	110	92	96	107
44280	VALLEY CITY	121	151	160	151	148	146	135	134	125	134	157	157	143	167	138	121	157	129	120	148
44281	WADSWORTH	107	117	122	117	117	122	112	113	109	111	136	131	115	139	114	108	133	111	109	126
44286	RICHFIELD	163	199	220	198	197	203	181	181	170	181	214	207	192	220	187	168	212	176	169	198
44287	WEST SALEM	88	79	62	76	83	88	74	81	77	74	94	96	72	95	75	78	90	79	86	102
44288	WINDHAM	73	59	48	55	62	70	62	66	68	61	82	78	58	80	61	70	77	67	74	82
44301	AKRON	62	65	71	63	64	70	67	65	68	65	84	75	68	86	67	68	82	66	66	72
44302	AKRON	58	58	72	58	57	63	63	60	64	62	80	70	63	80	62	64	78	62	60	66
44303	AKRON	92	96	113	97	95	102	101	97	99	99	125	114	102	123	100	98	122	100	95	107
44304	AKRON	44	32	38	33	31	37	49	40	50	44	62	52	43	57	42	47	59	46	40	46
44305	AKRON	65	66	71	65	66	72	69	67	70	67	87	78	70	89	69	70	84	68	68	75
44306	AKRON	50	47	53	46	47	53	52	50	55	51	68	58	52	68	51	56	66	52	53	56
	OHIO	89	88	90	87	88	95	88	89	89	87	110	103	88	111	88	89	107	89	90	102
	UNITED STATES	100	100	100	100	100	100	100	100	100	100	100	100	100	100	100	100	100	100	100	100

OHIO

POPULATION CHANGE

A 44307-44637

# POST OFFICE NAME	COUNTY FIPS CODE	POPULATION			2000-2004 ANNUAL RATE		HOUSEHOLDS					FAMILIES		
		2000	2004	2009	% Rate	State Centile	2000	2004	2009	% Annual Rate 2000-2004	2004 Average HH Size	2000	2004	% Annual Rate 2000-2004
44307 AKRON	153	9463	9086	8926	-1.0	10	3965	3892	3873	-0.4	2.27	2422	2282	-1.4
44308 AKRON	153	789	857	890	2.0	93	515	583	619	3.0	1.11	33	34	0.7
44310 AKRON	153	24012	23387	23203	-0.6	17	10254	10184	10241	-0.2	2.26	5842	5567	-1.1
44311 AKRON	153	10352	10073	9953	-0.6	16	3332	3288	3284	-0.3	2.79	1813	1702	-1.5
44312 AKRON	153	33207	33278	33324	0.1	47	13792	14118	14343	0.6	2.35	9266	9175	-0.2
44313 AKRON	153	24550	25079	25410	0.5	66	11330	11815	12125	1.0	2.09	6461	6434	-0.1
44314 AKRON	153	20338	19853	19646	-0.6	20	8381	8356	8384	-0.1	2.37	5327	5110	-1.0
44319 AKRON	153	22034	22280	22494	0.3	56	9062	9383	9621	0.8	2.34	6254	6282	0.1
44320 AKRON	153	23639	22572	22197	-1.1	6	9562	9374	9372	-0.5	2.39	6305	5966	-1.3
44321 AKRON	153	11173	11912	12328	1.5	89	4029	4376	4588	2.0	2.65	2981	3140	1.2
44333 AKRON	153	18180	18318	18306	0.2	52	6990	7202	7299	0.7	2.45	5139	5148	0.0
44401 BERLIN CENTER	099	2606	2695	2681	0.8	76	959	1020	1039	1.5	2.64	773	805	1.0
44402 BRISTOLVILLE	155	3312	3306	3245	0.0	43	1186	1212	1216	0.5	2.73	946	947	0.0
44403 BROOKFIELD	155	4560	4440	4308	-0.6	17	1874	1875	1863	0.0	2.34	1347	1310	-0.7
44404 BURGHILL	155	1909	1852	1794	-0.7	14	722	720	716	-0.1	2.57	563	550	-0.6
44405 CAMPBELL	099	9428	9150	8845	-0.7	15	3717	3671	3619	-0.3	2.49	2596	2483	-1.0
44406 CANFIELD	099	21086	21210	20823	0.1	51	8118	8335	8361	0.6	2.54	6042	6043	0.0
44408 COLUMBIANA	029	10059	10259	10221	0.5	64	4070	4234	4303	0.9	2.38	2862	2897	0.3
44410 CORTLAND	155	17876	17873	17574	0.0	45	7117	7304	7352	0.6	2.43	5174	5165	0.0
44411 DEERFIELD	133	2582	2599	2627	0.2	51	929	956	988	0.7	2.72	725	727	0.1
44412 DIAMOND	133	2707	2889	3003	1.5	89	969	1065	1136	2.3	2.71	808	873	1.8
44413 EAST PALESTINE	029	7710	7516	7345	-0.6	19	3023	3007	2997	-0.1	2.49	2200	2133	-0.7
44417 FARMDALE	155	2026	2108	2108	0.9	80	728	776	794	1.5	2.72	583	608	1.0
44418 FOWLER	155	1397	1366	1330	-0.5	21	506	507	505	0.1	2.59	402	395	-0.4
44420 GIRARD	155	16843	16196	15652	-0.9	10	6903	6803	6728	-0.3	2.38	4695	4483	-1.1
44423 HANOVERTON	029	2417	2540	2569	1.2	85	908	977	1009	1.7	2.60	685	719	1.2
44425 HUBBARD	155	15715	15152	14643	-0.9	12	6291	6221	6153	-0.3	2.43	4422	4245	-1.0
44427 KENSINGTON	019	1592	1563	1537	-0.4	25	555	561	564	0.3	2.75	435	430	-0.3
44428 KINSMAN	155	3188	3112	3027	-0.6	20	1182	1182	1177	0.0	2.60	892	871	-0.6
44429 LAKE MILTON	099	3083	2989	2886	-0.7	14	1217	1214	1201	-0.1	2.44	850	820	-0.8
44430 LEAVITTSBURG	155	5625	5400	5233	-1.0	9	1567	1524	1497	-0.7	2.75	1169	1108	-1.3
44431 LEETONIA	029	4824	4726	4623	-0.5	23	1753	1758	1756	0.1	2.69	1335	1309	-0.5
44432 LISBON	029	14457	14543	14400	0.1	51	4526	4643	4693	0.6	2.63	3282	3283	0.0
44436 LOWELLVILLE	099	4168	4050	3914	-0.7	16	1597	1590	1572	-0.1	2.55	1163	1126	-0.8
44437 MC DONALD	155	4695	4578	4449	-0.6	19	1755	1763	1757	0.1	2.60	1358	1333	-0.4
44438 MASURY	155	5417	5211	5034	-0.9	11	2198	2172	2149	-0.3	2.31	1458	1393	-1.1
44440 MINERAL RIDGE	155	3951	3958	3893	0.0	46	1396	1433	1439	0.6	2.56	1028	1030	0.1
44441 NEGLEY	029	1757	1778	1766	0.3	57	668	693	703	0.9	2.57	507	514	0.3
44442 NEW MIDDLETOWN	099	3224	3316	3297	0.7	72	1316	1394	1422	1.4	2.38	955	984	0.7
44443 NEW SPRINGFIELD	099	1774	1755	1709	-0.3	33	676	686	684	0.4	2.56	505	500	-0.2
44444 NEWTON FALLS	155	10766	10524	10264	-0.5	21	4259	4263	4250	0.0	2.45	3013	2945	-0.5
44445 NEW WATERFORD	029	3330	3377	3350	0.3	59	1244	1283	1292	0.7	2.32	946	953	0.2
44446 NILES	155	23502	22935	22296	-0.6	20	9869	9859	9807	0.0	2.29	6217	5983	-0.9
44449 NORTH BENTON	099	1089	1086	1079	-0.1	42	434	442	449	0.4	2.46	325	323	-0.2
44450 NORTH BLOOMFIELD	155	2600	2692	2686	0.8	77	886	938	957	1.4	2.86	689	714	0.8
44451 NORTH JACKSON	099	3457	3484	3421	0.2	52	1274	1317	1325	0.8	2.62	995	1006	0.3
44452 NORTH LIMA	099	2147	2243	2244	1.0	82	746	802	822	1.7	2.64	570	598	1.1
44454 PETERSBURG	099	1386	1406	1385	0.3	60	460	476	479	0.8	2.93	373	378	0.3
44455 ROGERS	029	1555	1590	1584	0.5	67	557	581	591	1.0	2.48	431	440	0.5
44460 SALEM	029	26959	26576	26052	-0.3	29	10690	10761	10765	0.2	2.43	7577	7426	-0.5
44470 SOUTHINGTON	155	3812	3736	3634	-0.5	23	1407	1413	1405	0.1	2.64	1115	1097	-0.4
44471 STRUTHERS	099	11960	11709	11388	-0.5	22	4776	4768	4736	0.0	2.44	3312	3204	-0.8
44473 VIENNA	155	3633	3651	3596	0.1	50	1494	1542	1556	0.8	2.37	1062	1064	0.0
44481 WARREN	155	11066	10967	10733	-0.2	35	4339	4405	4425	0.3	2.47	3226	3208	-0.1
44483 WARREN	155	28849	28469	27905	-0.3	31	11848	11933	11931	0.2	2.32	7553	7357	-0.6
44484 WARREN	155	24126	24075	23608	-0.1	39	9647	9852	9917	0.5	2.39	6792	6765	-0.1
44485 WARREN	155	19906	19060	18391	-1.0	8	8136	7961	7845	-0.5	2.36	5354	5068	-1.3
44490 WASHINGTONVILLE	029	799	818	814	0.6	68	316	332	338	1.2	2.46	244	251	0.7
44491 WEST FARMINGTON	155	2567	2640	2649	0.7	72	862	904	927	1.1	2.92	714	735	0.7
44502 YOUNGSTOWN	099	12265	11422	10871	-1.7	2	4862	4608	4470	-1.3	2.32	2936	2678	-2.1
44503 YOUNGSTOWN	099	555	548	539	-0.3	31	416	412	407	-0.2	1.33	26	9	-22.1
44504 YOUNGSTOWN	099	5538	5245	5039	-1.3	4	1909	1825	1775	-1.1	2.32	990	905	-2.1
44505 YOUNGSTOWN	099	22481	21204	20331	-1.4	3	8486	8144	7949	-1.0	2.30	5322	4932	-1.7
44506 YOUNGSTOWN	099	3685	3307	3095	-2.5	0	1412	1302	1248	-1.9	2.54	930	828	-2.7
44507 YOUNGSTOWN	099	8939	8589	8295	-0.9	10	3246	3158	3103	-0.6	2.69	2063	1928	-1.6
44509 YOUNGSTOWN	099	13187	12622	12151	-1.0	7	5433	5323	5240	-0.5	2.31	3507	3307	-1.4
44510 YOUNGSTOWN	099	3089	2731	2542	-2.9	0	1262	1143	1087	-2.3	2.33	771	670	-3.3
44511 YOUNGSTOWN	099	23811	22863	21999	-1.0	10	9872	9725	9586	-0.4	2.34	6606	6306	-1.1
44512 YOUNGSTOWN	099	36388	36092	35288	-0.2	36	15673	15933	15943	0.4	2.23	9887	9678	-0.5
44514 YOUNGSTOWN	099	22898	22324	21621	-0.6	19	9045	9033	8950	0.0	2.43	6624	6441	-0.7
44515 YOUNGSTOWN	099	27876	27746	27119	-0.1	39	11646	11853	11864	0.4	2.29	7632	7559	-0.2
44555 YOUNGSTOWN	099	181	162	154	-2.6	0	1	1	1	0.0	3.00	0	0	0.0
44601 ALLIANCE	151	37112	36604	35949	-0.3	31	14072	14183	14213	0.2	2.44	9607	9397	-0.5
44606 APPLE CREEK	169	7247	7670	7993	1.3	87	2020	2161	2282	1.6	3.45	1662	1750	1.2
44608 BEACH CITY	151	3037	3105	3113	0.5	67	1113	1162	1186	1.0	2.60	833	848	0.4
44609 BELOIT	099	3853	3798	3707	-0.3	29	1495	1505	1499	0.2	2.51	1124	1104	-0.4
44611 BIG PRAIRIE	075	1951	1856	1823	-1.2	5	647	629	625	-0.7	2.95	500	476	-1.2
44612 BOLIVAR	157	5069	5293	5420	1.0	82	1947	2080	2166	1.6	2.54	1485	1550	1.0
44613 BREWSTER	151	2101	2107	2081	0.1	48	776	796	803	0.6	2.58	592	593	0.2
44614 CANAL FULTON	151	11037	11283	11250	0.5	67	3911	4103	4184	1.1	2.67	3088	3170	0.6
44615 CARROLLTON	019	11092	11118	11027	0.1	47	4333	4431	4487	0.5	2.46	3089	3085	0.1
44618 DALTON	169	7026	7170	7302	0.5	65	2271	2360	2443	1.0	3.00	1845	1883	0.5
44620 DELLROY	019	1702	1687	1659	-0.2	35	633	643	647	0.4	2.62	485	482	-0.2
44621 DENNISON	157	4894	4767	4727	-0.6	17	1849	1841	1857	-0.1	2.57	1363	1321	-0.7
44622 DOVER	157	18395	18582	18760	0.2	55	7295	7530	7729	0.8	2.41	5152	5160	0.0
44624 DUNDEE	075	5066	5892	6393	3.6	98	1448	1732	1911	4.3	3.35	1241	1455	3.8
44625 EAST ROCHESTER	029	1482	1436	1397	-0.7	14	515	511	509	-0.2	2.80	412	402	-0.6
44626 EAST SPARTA	151	3072	3084	3047	0.1	49	1168	1205	1219	0.7	2.56	909	916	0.2
44627 FREDERICKSBURG	075	5420	5655	5822	1.0	81	1241	1307	1358	1.2	4.32	1065	1107	0.9
44628 GLENMONT	075	1244	1229	1224	-0.3	32	467	470	473	0.2	2.61	346	339	-0.5
44629 GNADENHUTTEN	157	2979	2944	2931	-0.3	32	1169	1181	1196	0.2	2.49	867	854	-0.4
44632 HARTVILLE	151	9589	9742	9712	0.4	61	3362	3492	3556	0.9	2.76	2687	2736	0.4
44633 HOLMESVILLE	075	2365	2308	2283	-0.6	20	660	657	657	-0.1	3.39	557	546	-0.5
44634 HOMEWORTH	029	2383	2410	2398	0.3	56	837	866	880	0.8	2.72	665	674	0.3
44637 KILLBUCK	075	2265	2310	2318	0.5	64	901	938	953	1.0	2.46	648	656	0.3
OHIO					0.3					0.7	2.44			0.0
UNITED STATES					1.2					1.3	2.58			1.1

#	POST OFFICE NAME	White 2000	White 2004	Black 2000	Black 2004	Asian/Pacific 2000	Asian/Pacific 2004	% Hispanic Origin 2000	% Hispanic Origin 2004	0-4	5-9	10-14	15-19	20-24	25-44	45-64	65-84	85+	18+	MEDIAN AGE 2004	% 2004 Males	% 2004 Females
44307	AKRON	12.3	10.5	83.9	85.6	0.7	0.9	1.0	1.0	9.2	8.9	9.3	7.7	7.4	25.2	20.6	10.4	1.4	68.1	31.0	45.5	54.5
44308	AKRON	61.0	56.4	33.7	38.0	1.0	1.2	0.9	0.8	1.5	0.6	0.8	8.2	8.8	29.9	38.5	9.8	2.0	96.9	45.1	61.8	38.2
44310	AKRON	72.8	70.3	22.7	24.7	1.4	1.7	1.3	1.3	7.2	6.9	7.0	6.0	7.1	30.1	22.4	11.5	1.9	75.3	35.6	48.3	51.7
44311	AKRON	53.0	48.5	36.9	40.1	5.6	6.8	1.9	2.0	7.2	6.8	7.4	10.0	18.2	27.2	16.1	6.3	0.9	74.8	25.3	50.4	49.6
44312	AKRON	96.8	96.2	1.3	1.6	0.6	0.8	0.6	0.7	5.9	6.0	6.2	5.8	5.9	28.1	26.0	14.4	1.8	78.4	40.1	48.3	51.7
44313	AKRON	80.6	77.2	15.7	18.4	1.8	2.3	1.1	1.2	6.0	5.8	5.5	4.8	6.0	28.0	24.7	15.9	3.3	79.6	40.6	46.8	53.2
44314	AKRON	91.7	90.3	5.4	6.4	0.6	0.8	0.8	0.9	7.5	7.1	6.9	6.0	6.6	30.0	23.1	11.4	1.5	74.9	35.5	49.0	51.0
44319	AKRON	97.9	97.4	0.6	0.8	0.5	0.6	0.5	0.6	5.3	5.6	5.8	5.7	5.1	25.6	29.4	15.3	2.2	79.7	43.0	49.1	50.9
44320	AKRON	23.4	21.8	73.4	74.7	0.7	0.9	0.9	0.9	6.1	6.8	8.6	7.6	6.2	25.8	25.4	12.1	1.5	73.7	37.2	45.4	54.6
44321	AKRON	88.3	86.1	7.0	8.0	3.1	4.2	1.0	1.1	6.2	6.7	8.0	6.9	5.7	25.5	27.5	11.0	2.6	74.6	40.0	48.5	51.5
44333	AKRON	92.6	90.8	3.5	4.2	2.6	3.5	1.0	1.1	5.0	5.8	6.9	6.5	4.8	20.2	30.6	16.4	3.8	78.1	45.5	47.8	52.2
44401	BERLIN CENTER	98.8	98.6	0.1	0.2	0.0	0.1	0.6	0.8	4.8	5.6	7.2	6.4	5.7	25.1	33.2	11.2	0.9	78.5	41.9	51.4	48.6
44402	BRISTOLVILLE	98.6	98.3	0.5	0.5	0.2	0.3	0.3	0.4	6.0	6.7	7.5	6.6	5.9	26.6	29.5	10.2	1.0	75.8	39.2	50.6	49.4
44403	BROOKFIELD	98.1	97.7	0.9	1.0	0.3	0.4	0.7	0.7	4.8	5.3	6.4	5.9	4.9	23.4	30.5	16.6	2.2	79.7	44.5	48.5	51.6
44404	BURGHILL	98.7	98.5	0.5	0.5	0.1	0.2	0.4	0.4	6.5	7.1	6.6	6.6	4.6	26.8	28.4	12.0	1.4	75.5	40.0	50.4	49.6
44405	CAMPBELL	77.2	73.2	16.7	19.8	0.2	0.3	11.0	12.5	6.6	6.5	6.7	6.7	6.2	23.6	23.3	18.1	2.5	76.2	40.1	46.2	53.8
44406	CANFIELD	96.6	95.7	1.2	1.5	1.2	1.7	1.1	1.2	5.2	6.0	7.2	6.6	5.3	24.2	30.6	13.5	1.6	77.5	42.3	48.6	51.5
44408	COLUMBIANA	98.6	98.4	0.3	0.4	0.3	0.4	0.5	0.6	5.3	5.7	6.6	6.5	5.9	24.0	27.4	16.0	2.5	78.4	42.4	48.5	51.5
44410	CORTLAND	97.9	97.5	0.8	1.0	0.4	0.5	0.6	0.7	5.4	5.9	6.8	6.6	5.7	25.3	30.3	12.5	1.5	77.9	41.5	48.3	51.7
44411	DEERFIELD	98.2	98.0	0.6	0.7	0.1	0.2	0.3	0.4	6.8	7.1	7.5	6.4	5.0	29.6	26.8	9.9	0.9	74.6	37.3	50.5	49.5
44412	DIAMOND	98.2	98.0	1.1	1.2	0.0	0.0	0.5	0.6	5.5	6.2	7.3	6.8	5.8	27.2	30.7	9.6	1.0	76.8	40.1	51.0	49.0
44413	EAST PALESTINE	98.7	98.5	0.4	0.4	0.1	0.2	0.6	0.7	5.8	6.0	7.0	6.9	6.5	26.9	26.5	12.7	1.8	76.8	39.3	49.4	50.6
44417	FARMDALE	98.5	98.3	0.5	0.6	0.2	0.2	0.5	0.6	6.5	6.6	7.0	6.8	5.9	25.6	28.8	11.7	1.1	75.8	39.9	49.4	50.6
44418	FOWLER	98.8	98.5	0.6	0.7	0.1	0.2	0.4	0.4	5.3	6.2	7.0	5.8	4.5	24.5	30.5	13.6	2.6	78.0	43.1	49.1	50.9
44420	GIRARD	94.8	94.0	3.1	3.5	0.6	0.8	0.8	0.9	5.7	5.9	6.6	6.1	5.9	25.5	26.8	15.6	1.9	78.1	41.3	48.0	52.0
44423	HANOVERTON	98.8	98.6	0.3	0.3	0.1	0.1	0.5	0.6	6.3	6.5	6.7	7.3	5.5	26.8	27.4	12.2	1.3	76.0	39.0	49.9	50.1
44425	HUBBARD	96.2	95.9	2.4	2.6	0.3	0.4	0.7	0.7	5.0	5.4	6.7	6.6	5.8	24.5	28.8	15.3	2.0	78.9	42.3	48.5	51.5
44427	KENSINGTON	98.4	98.2	0.4	0.4	0.0	0.0	0.6	0.8	7.0	7.5	7.9	7.2	5.5	28.1	25.1	10.7	1.0	72.8	36.7	49.8	50.2
44428	KINSMAN	98.7	98.4	0.7	0.7	0.4	0.5	0.3	0.3	6.2	6.5	6.8	6.2	5.9	25.5	28.5	13.2	1.3	76.7	40.6	48.9	51.1
44429	LAKE MILTON	98.1	97.8	0.4	0.4	0.3	0.3	0.7	0.8	5.9	6.0	6.1	5.6	6.1	28.7	29.3	11.4	0.7	78.6	39.5	49.7	50.4
44430	LEAVITTSBURG	81.9	80.0	16.8	18.7	0.1	0.2	0.6	0.7	3.9	4.9	6.1	6.3	8.8	35.0	25.1	8.9	1.0	81.5	36.4	61.3	38.7
44431	LEETONIA	98.9	98.8	0.3	0.3	0.1	0.2	0.6	0.6	6.4	6.6	7.2	6.8	6.2	26.5	27.0	11.9	1.4	75.6	38.7	50.5	49.5
44432	LISBON	91.7	91.3	6.7	7.0	0.3	0.4	4.3	4.7	4.8	5.1	6.0	6.3	6.5	33.8	26.2	10.2	1.2	80.1	37.9	57.1	42.9
44436	LOWELLVILLE	96.4	95.6	2.0	2.5	0.1	0.1	2.0	2.4	4.7	5.3	6.6	6.6	6.0	24.2	28.2	16.5	2.0	79.4	42.8	49.5	50.5
44437	MC DONALD	97.3	96.9	1.4	1.6	0.1	0.1	1.1	1.3	5.7	6.2	7.5	6.6	6.1	26.1	28.2	12.2	1.4	76.5	39.5	48.0	52.0
44438	MASURY	92.3	91.3	6.0	6.7	0.3	0.4	0.7	0.7	5.8	6.0	6.2	6.2	5.4	25.9	26.3	15.2	3.1	78.2	41.2	48.1	51.9
44440	MINERAL RIDGE	97.1	96.5	1.6	2.0	0.1	0.2	1.1	1.3	5.2	5.8	6.6	5.8	5.4	25.4	29.1	12.7	4.0	78.8	42.0	47.9	52.1
44441	NEGLEY	98.2	98.0	0.3	0.3	0.2	0.2	0.9	1.0	5.7	6.8	7.8	6.5	6.0	26.8	28.9	10.4	1.2	75.7	39.0	51.6	48.4
44442	NEW MIDDLETOWN	99.3	99.2	0.0	0.0	0.0	0.1	0.9	1.0	4.3	4.7	6.9	6.4	5.9	23.4	29.8	16.7	2.1	80.2	44.0	46.1	53.9
44443	NEW SPRINGFIELD	98.9	98.6	0.0	0.1	0.2	0.2	1.0	1.1	5.5	5.6	5.9	6.6	6.1	26.8	27.8	14.3	1.5	79.0	40.8	48.2	51.8
44444	NEWTON FALLS	98.0	97.7	0.8	0.9	0.1	0.1	0.6	0.7	5.8	6.0	7.0	6.4	6.0	27.1	27.3	12.8	1.7	77.3	39.4	48.9	51.1
44445	NEW WATERFORD	93.3	93.0	5.4	5.6	0.2	0.3	3.8	4.0	5.5	6.0	6.4	5.9	5.9	31.7	27.1	10.6	1.1	78.4	38.5	55.8	44.2
44446	NILES	96.1	95.6	2.2	2.4	0.4	0.5	0.9	1.0	5.6	5.7	6.4	6.2	6.4	26.8	25.9	14.4	2.7	78.6	40.1	47.6	52.4
44449	NORTH BENTON	98.4	98.0	0.3	0.4	0.0	0.1	0.9	1.1	6.5	6.6	6.7	6.2	5.3	28.4	26.9	13.0	0.6	76.3	39.8	53.1	46.9
44450	NORTH BLOOMFIELD	96.8	96.4	1.9	2.2	0.1	0.1	0.7	0.8	8.5	8.3	8.4	7.4	6.5	26.1	24.1	9.6	1.1	70.1	34.0	50.2	49.8
44451	NORTH JACKSON	98.5	98.1	0.4	0.5	0.1	0.1	0.9	1.1	4.8	5.4	6.8	6.1	5.5	26.0	32.2	11.8	1.4	79.2	42.1	51.5	48.5
44452	NORTH LIMA	98.6	98.3	0.4	0.5	0.4	0.5	0.5	0.6	5.1	5.7	6.7	6.2	4.9	23.0	28.4	16.1	3.9	78.6	44.0	48.1	51.9
44454	PETERSBURG	97.6	97.2	0.1	0.2	0.0	0.0	1.3	1.7	7.3	7.3	7.1	7.5	6.7	26.7	26.7	9.5	1.1	73.2	36.8	48.8	51.2
44455	ROGERS	93.9	93.6	4.3	4.4	0.3	0.4	3.5	3.7	4.8	5.9	7.1	6.4	6.3	30.9	28.1	9.7	0.8	78.2	38.4	56.1	43.9
44460	SALEM	98.6	98.4	0.3	0.4	0.3	0.4	0.5	0.6	5.9	6.0	6.6	6.4	6.2	25.7	27.0	13.8	2.4	77.7	40.5	48.0	52.0
44470	SOUTHINGTON	97.9	97.6	1.2	1.4	0.1	0.2	0.8	0.9	5.7	6.2	6.5	5.5	5.9	27.7	29.0	12.6	0.9	78.3	40.4	50.9	49.1
44471	STRUTHERS	96.7	96.0	1.8	2.2	0.2	0.2	2.0	2.3	5.8	5.8	6.8	6.5	6.7	25.8	23.1	17.0	2.4	77.6	40.1	47.3	52.8
44473	VIENNA	98.7	98.4	0.6	0.7	0.1	0.2	0.6	0.7	5.1	5.5	6.1	6.2	5.5	24.0	30.6	15.3	1.8	79.5	43.5	50.4	49.6
44481	WARREN	95.4	95.0	3.4	3.7	0.2	0.3	0.5	0.6	5.4	6.1	7.1	6.4	5.4	25.7	30.8	12.0	1.2	77.6	41.1	50.0	50.0
44483	WARREN	86.3	85.4	11.6	12.2	0.4	0.4	1.0	1.1	7.1	6.3	6.4	6.2	6.2	26.0	23.7	15.4	2.8	76.5	39.2	47.0	53.1
44484	WARREN	86.7	85.8	10.4	10.7	1.4	1.8	1.0	1.1	5.9	6.0	6.9	6.4	5.7	24.2	28.0	14.9	2.1	77.3	41.6	47.7	52.3
44485	WARREN	62.0	59.4	35.1	37.5	0.4	0.5	0.8	0.8	7.7	7.1	7.6	6.8	6.9	25.4	23.4	13.5	1.7	73.6	36.1	47.4	52.6
44490	WASHINGTONVILLE	98.0	97.7	0.4	0.5	0.1	0.1	1.0	1.1	7.0	7.2	7.8	6.4	5.5	25.9	28.1	11.0	1.1	74.1	38.2	49.3	50.7
44491	WEST FARMINGTON	98.6	98.4	0.5	0.5	0.1	0.1	0.6	0.7	10.5	10.0	8.8	7.1	6.0	27.8	21.6	7.4	0.8	66.4	30.8	50.7	49.3
44502	YOUNGSTOWN	63.0	59.6	31.7	34.6	0.3	0.4	5.0	5.6	6.7	6.3	6.6	7.7	6.6	25.5	22.5	15.8	2.4	75.9	38.0	48.8	51.2
44503	YOUNGSTOWN	40.4	34.3	57.5	63.3	0.2	0.2	1.8	2.0	0.9	0.6	0.4	1.6	8.2	35.0	34.9	15.5	2.9	97.6	46.5	64.1	36.0
44504	YOUNGSTOWN	45.5	39.8	49.6	54.9	1.1	1.4	2.1	2.3	4.7	4.9	5.9	11.4	14.2	18.7	20.2	13.7	6.4	80.5	34.7	46.7	53.3
44505	YOUNGSTOWN	41.7	38.4	52.8	55.9	0.8	1.0	4.0	4.0	6.2	6.3	6.7	6.3	7.1	26.2	24.4	14.8	2.1	77.2	38.4	50.9	49.1
44506	YOUNGSTOWN	27.2	23.9	52.7	55.4	0.2	0.2	30.5	30.6	7.4	7.7	8.9	7.5	6.7	23.0	23.7	13.6	1.6	71.8	35.9	47.6	52.4
44507	YOUNGSTOWN	30.6	26.0	62.7	67.1	0.6	0.7	6.4	6.4	9.4	9.4	10.7	8.2	7.4	25.2	19.6	8.9	1.2	65.4	28.7	45.9	54.1
44509	YOUNGSTOWN	89.3	87.2	7.4	8.9	0.3	0.3	3.3	3.9	7.8	6.5	5.9	5.3	6.7	26.1	22.2	16.0	3.5	76.5	38.7	46.8	53.3
44510	YOUNGSTOWN	18.2	15.1	75.2	78.4	0.2	0.2	5.2	5.2	9.4	8.5	8.2	6.7	6.5	22.9	22.5	13.6	1.7	70.0	34.0	45.0	55.0
44511	YOUNGSTOWN	67.0	66.3	30.9	31.3	0.3	0.4	2.0	2.2	6.2	6.4	7.0	6.0	5.5	23.6	25.1	17.7	2.5	76.7	41.6	46.1	53.9
44512	YOUNGSTOWN	94.1	92.5	3.5	4.4	0.9	1.3	1.9	2.2	5.0	5.2	5.9	5.8	6.0	25.7	27.3	15.8	3.3	80.4	42.6	47.0	53.0
44514	YOUNGSTOWN	98.1	97.6	0.7	0.9	0.4	0.5	1.3	1.5	4.8	5.6	6.8	6.2	4.6	22.7	29.1	17.3	2.9	78.8	44.5	47.6	52.4
44515	YOUNGSTOWN	92.8	91.3	4.9	6.0	0.6	0.7	1.8	2.1	5.9	5.8	5.9	5.6	6.1	26.8	27.1	14.5	2.2	79.0	40.6	47.8	52.2
44555	YOUNGSTOWN	61.9	54.9	34.8	40.7	1.1	1.2	3.9	4.3	2.5	2.5	1.9	35.2	21.6	11.7	13.0	10.5	1.2	92.6	21.9	48.2	51.9
44601	ALLIANCE	89.5	88.4	7.9	8.6	0.7	0.9	0.9	1.0	6.3	6.1	6.7	7.9	8.3	24.8	23.8	13.9	2.3	77.2	37.6	47.6	52.4
44606	APPLE CREEK	98.3	98.1	0.5	0.5	0.4	0.5	0.9	1.0	11.6	10.2	9.6	8.7	7.6	25.8	18.8	7.0	0.7	63.2	26.7	50.5	49.5
44608	BEACH CITY	98.8	98.6	0.2	0.2	0.3	0.4	0.5	0.5	6.5	6.8	7.4	6.5	5.8	26.8	25.2	13.1	2.0	75.5	39.2	50.0	50.0
44609	BELOIT	98.8	98.5	0.2	0.2	0.1	0.2	0.3	0.4	5.1	5.7	7.2	5.8	5.8	25.8	28.5	14.1	2.1	78.4	41.9	49.1	51.0
44611	BIG PRAIRIE	98.4	98.2	0.6	0.6	0.3	0.3	0.8	1.0	8.8	8.8	8.7	7.1	6.2	26.8	23.4	9.3	1.0	69.3	33.8	49.9	50.1
44612	BOLIVAR	98.3	98.1	0.5	0.5	0.3	0.4	0.5	0.6	6.6	7.0	7.2	6.1	5.4	27.8	29.1	9.7	1.1	75.3	38.6	50.0	50.0
44613	BREWSTER	98.5	98.3	0.1	0.1	0.1	0.2	1.3	1.5	6.2	6.7	7.7	6.2	5.7	27.3	25.0	13.0	2.3	75.4	38.9	49.7	50.3
44614	CANAL FULTON	97.8	97.5	0.6	0.7	0.4	0.5	0.7	0.7	6.6	6.8	7.7	7.4	6.0	27.7	27.0	9.0	1.9	74.3	37.8	48.2	51.8
44615	CARROLLTON	98.6	98.4	0.3	0.3	0.1	0.2	0.5	0.6	6.0	6.2	6.8	6.6	5.8	26.2	27.0	13.4	2.1	77.0	40.2	49.2	50.9
44618	DALTON	98.3	98.1	0.3	0.3	0.4	0.5	0.7	0.8	7.9	7.9	8.4	7.6	6.6	26.0	24.0	10.0	1.5	71.1	34.7	49.3	50.7
44620	DELLROY	98.7	98.5	0.1	0.2	0.1	0.1	0.6	0.7	5.8	6.6	6.9	5.9	5.0	25.8	30.9	12.2	1.0	77.1	41.5	50.3	49.7
44621	DENNISON	97.0	96.8	1.5	1.6	0.2	0.2	0.7	0.7	7.2	6.7	7.2	7.0	7.0	26.6	24.7	12.2	1.4	74.7	36.8	50.2	49.8
44622	DOVER	97.6	97.3	1.0	1.1	0.4	0.5	0.6	0.7	5.8	6.0	6.5	6.7	6.2	24.6	27.0	14.3	2.9	77.5	41.2	48.1	51.9
44624	DUNDEE	99.2	99.1	0.2	0.2	0.1	0.2	0.3	0.4	11.0	10.0	10.0	8.8	8.8	25.2	17.7	7.3	1.3	63.9	26.0	51.2	48.9
44625	EAST ROCHESTER	98.7	98.6	0.1	0.1	0.0	0.1	0.4	0.5	7.2	7.6	7.5	7.0	5.6	28.0	25.8	10.2	1.0	73.3	36.6	50.1	49.9
44626	EAST SPARTA	98.4	98.3	0.6	0.7	0.0	0.0	0.3	0.3	5.0	6.0	7.0	6.2	5.5	24.6	30.4	13.8	1.5	78.2	42.2	50.1	49.9
44627	FREDERICKSBURG	99.2	99.1	0.2	0.2	0.0	0.1	0.6	0.6	12.7	11.0	10.8	9.4	9.2	24.4	15.8	6.1	0.7	59.8	23.4	50.8	49.3
44628	GLENMONT	99.3	99.2	0.2	0.2	0.2	0.2	0.6	0.8	7.7	7.9	8.2	6.8	5.5	27.0	24.9	11.0	1.1	72.0	36.2	50.8	49.2
44629	GNADENHUTTEN	99.0	98.9	0.1	0.1	0.1	0.1	0.2	0.3	6.9	6.7	6.6	6.2	6.6	27.2	25.4	13.2	1.4	76.2	38.2	49.5	50.5
44632	HARTVILLE	98.1	97.7	0.5	0.5	0.3	0.5	1.0	1.1	6.4	6.9	7.7	6.9	6.2	27.1	27.5	9.8	1.4	74.5	38.1	50.0	50.0
44633	HOLMESVILLE	99.0	98.9	0.2	0.3	0.0	0.0	1.0	1.1	10.3	9.8	9.2	7.9	7.1	27.4	18.7	8.2	1.4	65.9	28.9	50.7	49.3
44634	HOMEWORTH	99.0	98.8	0.2	0.2	0.3	0.4	0.3	0.4	6.0	6.4	7.3	6.8	5.7	25.9	27.5	12.6	1.8	76.0	40.2	49.6	50.4
44637	KILLBUCK	99.2	99.1	0.0	0.0	0.0	0.1	0.6	0.7	7.1	7.0	6.8	6.8	5.9	28.0	24.6	12.7	1.1	74.9	37.5	49.3	50.7
	OHIO	85.0	84.1	11.5	11.8	1.2	1.6	1.9	2.1	6.7	6.6	7.1	7.0	7.1	27.5	24.7	11.6	1.8	75.6	37.0	48.6	51.4
	UNITED STATES	75.1	73.6	12.3	12.5	3.8	4.2	12.5	14.1	6.9	6.7	7.2	7.0	7.3	28.6	23.8	10.8	1.7	75.1	36.0	49.1	50.9

INCOME

#	POST OFFICE NAME	2004 Per Capita Income	2004 HH Income Base	2004 Household Income Distribution (%): Less than $25,000	$25,000 to $49,999	$50,000 to $99,999	$100,000 to $149,999	$150,000 or More	Median Household Income: 2004	2009	2004 National Centile	2004 State Centile	2004 Home Value Base	2004 Home Value Distribution (%): Less than $50,000	$50,000 to $89,999	$90,000 to $174,999	$175,000 to $399,999	$400,000 or More	2004 Median Home Value
44307	AKRON	13188	3892	57.6	25.3	15.0	1.7	0.4	21029	24350	2	3	1561	39.9	46.9	12.8	0.5	0.0	58476
44308	AKRON	21054	583	77.5	11.8	6.0	1.2	3.4	10394	12708	1	0	7	0.0	0.0	100.0	0.0	0.0	117500
44310	AKRON	19611	10184	35.4	30.8	28.0	4.7	1.1	35575	42777	30	20	5820	10.6	48.1	39.6	1.5	0.1	84905
44311	AKRON	12756	3288	53.7	26.7	16.3	2.3	1.0	22795	26962	3	3	1097	34.9	46.6	17.2	1.0	0.3	59970
44312	AKRON	22593	14118	24.6	32.1	33.9	7.7	1.7	44504	53207	60	44	10715	8.6	22.9	55.7	12.1	0.7	106130
44313	AKRON	35155	11815	20.1	26.1	34.7	11.7	7.4	53561	63357	78	75	7344	1.6	6.4	56.4	30.8	4.7	155495
44314	AKRON	19865	8356	29.3	37.6	28.1	3.7	1.4	37598	45399	38	24	5670	10.6	61.0	28.0	0.4	0.1	78368
44319	AKRON	28582	9383	17.1	28.8	37.4	11.5	5.3	53877	64289	78	75	7691	3.5	12.3	58.8	22.7	2.7	136843
44320	AKRON	20610	9374	34.3	30.5	26.3	6.9	2.1	36651	43731	34	22	5912	10.7	43.4	41.4	3.8	0.7	87100
44321	AKRON	34904	4376	11.6	22.8	35.6	15.1	14.9	66838	81648	90	93	3324	0.3	5.4	38.9	47.8	7.7	186784
44333	AKRON	50794	7202	10.1	17.8	29.3	19.3	23.6	85299	104552	96	99	5812	0.3	0.6	20.4	58.9	19.9	240774
44401	BERLIN CENTER	26171	1020	11.4	23.3	47.9	13.4	3.9	60801	72311	85	87	904	6.0	12.0	51.4	29.2	1.4	146703
44402	BRISTOLVILLE	22475	1212	14.9	26.2	45.1	13.3	0.7	56467	66278	81	80	1057	6.8	14.8	62.4	15.0	1.0	122329
44403	BROOKFIELD	23677	1875	25.6	27.3	34.0	9.7	3.4	46365	53769	65	51	1644	25.2	16.1	40.7	14.4	3.7	103137
44404	BURGHILL	20935	720	23.2	26.9	42.2	6.1	1.5	49834	57928	72	62	612	6.4	25.5	50.7	15.4	2.1	106452
44405	CAMPBELL	20068	3671	39.0	27.8	26.7	4.2	2.3	33619	39302	23	15	2662	33.3	39.3	24.9	2.3	0.3	68102
44406	CANFIELD	34945	8335	14.4	24.7	33.9	16.8	10.3	63352	76281	87	90	6805	1.0	8.2	50.2	35.0	5.7	154761
44408	COLUMBIANA	22277	4234	27.0	31.7	31.0	7.3	3.1	42977	49533	56	39	3246	8.7	19.0	50.4	21.1	0.8	118325
44410	CORTLAND	26858	7304	18.3	25.6	37.4	13.9	4.8	55559	64593	80	79	5916	5.1	15.1	56.1	22.9	0.9	128337
44411	DEERFIELD	21372	956	16.1	30.3	43.8	8.6	1.2	53185	60845	77	74	824	21.4	16.3	42.2	17.5	2.7	114486
44412	DIAMOND	24664	1065	12.1	28.9	40.3	15.1	3.6	58833	68024	83	84	952	7.5	10.8	46.3	32.6	2.8	148413
44413	EAST PALESTINE	18951	3007	28.1	36.3	29.0	5.4	1.3	40234	46177	47	31	2397	13.8	35.5	39.6	10.8	0.3	90636
44417	FARMDALE	22382	776	20.1	27.3	40.3	10.6	1.7	51974	59729	75	70	668	3.7	24.7	47.2	21.3	3.1	125000
44418	FOWLER	22549	507	18.9	28.2	37.5	14.2	1.2	52700	61144	76	72	443	4.3	23.5	44.9	24.8	2.5	122575
44420	GIRARD	22966	6803	29.9	29.2	29.0	8.1	3.8	40981	47959	50	32	5169	11.1	34.4	44.1	9.3	1.0	93564
44423	HANOVERTON	18842	977	22.9	38.4	33.3	4.3	1.1	41927	48085	53	35	814	18.3	23.3	46.0	12.0	0.4	99189
44425	HUBBARD	23705	6221	27.6	32.7	28.7	7.9	3.1	41068	48546	50	33	4891	11.7	29.8	47.1	11.0	0.5	96669
44427	KENSINGTON	20502	561	30.1	31.9	30.0	5.2	2.9	41973	47428	53	36	471	16.6	26.1	38.4	18.3	0.6	98625
44428	KINSMAN	19967	1182	24.1	31.9	36.8	6.1	1.1	44387	52016	60	44	986	10.7	23.8	48.2	14.8	2.5	108040
44429	LAKE MILTON	22490	1214	23.6	28.7	34.4	11.6	1.8	47379	57355	67	54	956	9.7	27.7	39.0	20.2	3.4	106738
44430	LEAVITTSBURG	16627	1524	26.2	35.5	30.8	5.6	2.0	41205	48351	50	33	1244	27.2	36.3	32.5	3.8	0.3	75448
44431	LEETONIA	19804	1758	23.4	34.8	33.8	6.4	1.7	43631	50124	58	41	1468	14.1	31.7	40.2	12.4	1.6	95688
44432	LISBON	17515	4643	30.1	34.8	28.7	4.7	1.7	38573	44282	41	27	3669	18.6	29.4	43.0	8.2	0.8	92178
44436	LOWELLVILLE	21421	1590	26.3	28.4	33.0	10.3	2.1	43948	51712	58	42	1376	17.6	31.3	39.0	11.4	0.7	91172
44437	MC DONALD	22676	1763	21.5	28.3	37.7	10.3	2.3	50173	59323	72	63	1503	6.3	33.0	50.6	9.9	0.3	101063
44438	MASURY	22742	2172	32.5	30.5	29.5	5.3	2.2	37154	42413	36	23	1526	24.5	36.8	33.2	5.2	0.2	76014
44440	MINERAL RIDGE	22795	1433	16.6	31.1	36.5	14.0	1.7	51871	60768	75	70	1194	16.4	19.3	53.5	10.6	0.3	105142
44441	NEGLEY	21117	693	24.7	34.5	32.5	4.6	3.8	42032	48817	53	36	596	20.3	23.5	40.3	13.8	2.2	97255
44442	NEW MIDDLETOWN	24055	1394	26.5	30.4	31.6	8.2	3.3	43217	51283	57	40	1163	15.3	15.8	59.9	6.9	2.1	108320
44443	NEW SPRINGFIELD	21702	686	28.4	30.0	31.1	5.3	5.3	42574	50383	55	38	593	25.1	18.9	40.8	14.8	0.3	102404
44444	NEWTON FALLS	21269	4263	24.6	32.0	33.1	8.9	1.4	44189	52106	59	43	3178	9.6	25.9	52.1	11.3	1.1	105357
44445	NEW WATERFORD	22765	1283	24.1	35.7	31.8	5.6	2.8	43815	50269	58	42	1067	19.5	20.1	50.1	9.1	1.2	104223
44446	NILES	22485	9859	30.2	31.3	29.5	6.2	2.8	39387	46420	44	28	6631	14.5	33.5	43.9	7.4	0.7	91809
44449	NORTH BENTON	22132	442	19.9	33.7	36.4	8.8	1.1	47828	55264	68	57	383	14.6	21.2	42.3	20.9	1.0	118990
44450	NORTH BLOOMFIELD	19130	938	21.2	33.6	34.5	8.5	2.1	46199	52868	64	50	749	9.5	19.6	51.5	17.8	1.6	112424
44451	NORTH JACKSON	23463	1317	15.7	32.2	37.4	12.5	2.1	52249	61910	76	71	1140	4.0	18.5	45.9	29.9	1.7	136628
44452	NORTH LIMA	24216	802	21.3	30.7	30.9	12.0	5.1	48518	57344	69	58	685	8.0	13.1	51.4	24.2	3.2	131101
44454	PETERSBURG	21361	476	20.6	37.6	24.0	13.5	4.4	46854	54212	66	52	406	29.8	18.5	33.5	16.0	2.2	91892
44455	ROGERS	21445	581	23.9	34.9	33.2	4.8	3.1	44006	50391	59	42	496	22.6	23.8	37.1	14.9	1.6	96000
44460	SALEM	22198	10761	29.4	29.6	30.8	7.4	2.7	40773	47645	49	32	8122	10.5	27.2	46.0	14.5	1.8	102865
44470	SOUTHINGTON	24370	1413	16.5	27.1	39.5	13.7	3.3	56627	65319	81	80	1294	13.5	16.5	52.1	17.4	0.5	117907
44471	STRUTHERS	18578	4768	33.4	33.8	26.5	4.5	1.8	35301	41662	29	18	3575	25.3	49.9	22.0	2.9	0.1	71189
44473	VIENNA	24399	1542	22.1	27.6	37.0	11.5	1.9	50297	58661	72	64	1335	20.4	15.1	46.2	16.2	2.1	109340
44481	WARREN	25704	4402	19.0	27.3	38.4	11.2	4.2	53133	61807	77	74	3648	16.3	15.7	51.5	16.2	0.4	116588
44483	WARREN	22366	11933	31.0	31.6	28.6	6.5	2.2	38496	45405	41	27	7886	13.4	37.1	42.1	6.9	0.5	89538
44484	WARREN	26862	9852	22.7	26.6	33.7	12.6	4.4	50653	59586	73	65	7573	10.6	21.7	48.0	17.0	2.7	111923
44485	WARREN	18929	7961	37.3	33.5	22.5	5.0	1.8	33549	38587	23	14	4931	29.0	48.5	20.8	1.6	0.1	70558
44490	WASHINGTONVILLE	20818	332	26.2	36.5	30.4	5.4	1.5	42035	48578	53	36	263	17.1	36.1	34.6	9.9	2.3	87258
44491	WEST FARMINGTON	21690	904	16.3	28.0	40.9	12.2	2.7	55048	64927	80	78	775	3.0	12.1	57.4	26.2	1.3	137595
44502	YOUNGSTOWN	14628	4608	48.9	33.1	15.2	2.0	0.9	25674	29631	5	4	3158	69.7	27.1	2.5	0.4	0.3	41859
44503	YOUNGSTOWN	7541	412	92.7	6.8	0.5	0.0	0.0	7630	9292	0	0	9	66.7	0.0	33.3	0.0	0.0	17500
44504	YOUNGSTOWN	17940	1825	43.8	25.4	21.2	6.6	3.1	30201	34778	13	8	928	34.4	45.6	19.1	1.0	0.0	59119
44505	YOUNGSTOWN	18924	8144	43.8	28.2	19.6	4.6	3.9	29866	34367	12	7	4987	42.7	23.4	25.7	7.8	0.5	60658
44506	YOUNGSTOWN	11733	1302	60.1	25.4	11.8	1.7	1.0	18745	21147	1	2	818	92.2	4.4	3.4	0.0	0.0	19292
44507	YOUNGSTOWN	11468	3158	55.7	26.8	15.2	1.9	0.4	20931	23356	2	2	1591	83.7	13.8	2.5	0.0	0.0	34361
44509	YOUNGSTOWN	17547	5323	37.1	36.6	21.8	3.8	0.7	32756	38181	20	12	3745	42.2	48.0	9.5	0.1	0.2	55105
44510	YOUNGSTOWN	12903	1143	69.5	16.6	11.6	1.4	0.9	15159	16859	1	1	561	85.9	11.6	2.5	0.0	0.0	23929
44511	YOUNGSTOWN	20859	9725	33.2	30.7	26.4	7.6	2.1	37559	44149	38	24	7178	22.8	30.6	42.3	4.2	0.1	86729
44512	YOUNGSTOWN	28670	15933	24.4	28.0	33.2	9.7	4.7	47821	56773	68	57	11425	4.1	24.4	55.1	15.5	1.0	114986
44514	YOUNGSTOWN	26926	9033	20.4	28.2	34.8	11.2	5.4	51373	61361	75	68	7729	5.7	19.2	52.9	20.2	2.0	120390
44515	YOUNGSTOWN	22894	11853	27.2	29.0	33.9	8.2	1.7	44100	51831	59	43	8125	5.7	33.7	52.8	7.6	0.2	98398
44555	YOUNGSTOWN	7677	0	0.0	0.0	0.0	0.0	0.0	0	0	0	0	0	0.0	0.0	0.0	0.0	0.0	0
44601	ALLIANCE	20046	14183	31.5	32.6	27.2	6.3	2.4	38288	44734	40	26	9774	15.7	28.8	43.2	10.4	1.9	95872
44606	APPLE CREEK	15602	2161	21.9	34.6	35.1	6.1	2.2	44974	50785	61	45	1713	8.2	10.5	49.2	29.0	3.2	135318
44608	BEACH CITY	20261	1162	18.4	37.8	36.2	5.2	2.4	45343	52455	62	47	951	13.1	32.4	37.8	14.1	2.6	94830
44609	BELOIT	21711	1505	23.0	30.4	38.4	6.0	2.2	47061	54737	66	53	1230	18.1	26.0	42.7	12.6	0.7	96887
44611	BIG PRAIRIE	16712	629	23.7	39.3	30.8	4.5	1.8	39955	44433	46	29	531	13.4	21.9	40.9	19.6	4.3	116930
44612	BOLIVAR	24433	2080	18.5	30.3	35.1	12.9	3.2	51001	58054	74	66	1656	4.7	8.9	51.5	33.8	1.2	151058
44613	BREWSTER	21532	796	22.9	36.4	32.5	5.3	2.9	42758	49404	55	38	666	12.5	21.3	58.1	7.5	0.6	99818
44614	CANAL FULTON	25688	4103	15.2	25.2	44.0	12.4	3.2	58112	68424	83	82	3280	1.1	7.3	69.7	20.4	1.5	139250
44615	CARROLLTON	18312	4431	31.6	34.1	28.4	4.4	1.5	38268	43465	40	26	3512	12.2	21.6	47.8	16.7	1.6	109049
44618	DALTON	19983	2360	16.5	34.0	37.5	8.2	3.8	49383	55305	71	61	1984	12.6	10.2	46.1	28.6	2.5	139717
44620	DELLROY	19363	643	23.8	37.8	31.1	5.4	1.9	42742	47723	55	38	552	14.0	15.2	48.9	19.8	2.2	119444
44621	DENNISON	16488	1841	32.9	37.2	25.2	3.8	1.0	35266	39276	29	18	1386	20.3	37.4	35.1	6.8	0.4	79259
44622	DOVER	22932	7530	25.5	32.1	31.9	7.1	3.4	44153	50222	59	43	5733	6.2	13.5	59.2	20.0	1.1	121605
44624	DUNDEE	16374	1732	21.5	36.9	30.4	7.8	3.4	43171	49607	56	40	1375	9.5	9.3	42.3	31.8	7.2	150721
44625	EAST ROCHESTER	20592	511	20.6	33.9	37.2	5.7	2.7	44820	51794	61	45	433	11.1	26.8	44.1	17.3	0.7	104792
44626	EAST SPARTA	20422	1205	23.4	31.9	36.9	6.4	1.5	44795	51668	61	45	1020	11.1	22.2	48.8	17.1	0.9	108049
44627	FREDERICKSBURG	13225	1307	22.7	37.5	27.2	8.4	4.1	40898	47875	49	32	993	6.2	8.8	43.7	34.0	7.3	156828
44628	GLENMONT	18455	470	25.7	39.2	29.2	4.7	1.3	39205	43874	43	27	390	12.3	26.4	35.6	21.0	4.6	110377
44629	GNADENHUTTEN	18470	1181	29.3	36.8	28.6	3.6	1.7	36181	40983	32	21	965	14.6	28.7	48.8	7.4	0.5	95375
44632	HARTVILLE	25877	3492	14.3	23.0	42.9	14.7	5.1	61448	73056	86	87	2883	1.4	6.6	55.2	33.1	3.7	159354
44633	HOLMESVILLE	19362	657	21.8	36.8	29.8	4.6	7.0	41886	47296	53	35	485	5.4	14.9	43.5	28.9	7.4	145363
44634	HOMEWORTH	21463	866	19.1	28.8	41.8	7.7	2.7	51455	58419	75	69	747	8.4	17.9	49.7	22.2	1.7	128125
44637	KILLBUCK	18918	938	27.3	37.3	29.4	4.9	1.1	39517	43869	44	28	697	15.1	25.4	44.8	13.2	1.6	98867
	OHIO	25510		24.6	28.1	32.2	10.1	5.0	47354	56168				9.2	18.6	47.0	22.1	3.1	121192
	UNITED STATES	25866		24.7	27.1	30.8	10.9	6.5	48124	56710				10.9	15.0	33.7	30.1	10.4	145905

ZIP CODE #	POST OFFICE NAME	FINANCIAL SERVICES: Auto Loan	FINANCIAL SERVICES: Home Loan	FINANCIAL SERVICES: Invest-ments	FINANCIAL SERVICES: Retire-ment Plans	THE HOME: Home Improvements: Home Repair	THE HOME: Home Improvements: Lawn & Garden	THE HOME: Furnishings: Comput-ers & Hard-ware	THE HOME: Furnishings: Major Appli-ances	THE HOME: Furnishings: TV, Radio, Sound Equip-ment	THE HOME: Furnishings: Furni-ture	ENTERTAINMENT: Dine out/ Carry out	ENTERTAINMENT: Sports Equip-ment	ENTERTAINMENT: Fees & Tickets	ENTERTAINMENT: Toys & Games	ENTERTAINMENT: Travel	ENTERTAINMENT: Cable TV	PERSONAL: Apparel & Services	PERSONAL: Auto Repairs	PERSONAL: Health Insur-ance	PERSONAL: Pets & Supplies
44307	AKRON	41	35	43	33	34	41	40	40	45	41	55	44	40	53	40	47	53	42	44	45
44308	AKRON	33	29	43	31	29	35	37	34	39	35	49	40	36	48	36	40	47	37	37	38
44310	AKRON	59	59	68	58	59	65	62	61	64	61	80	69	64	82	62	65	78	62	63	67
44311	AKRON	48	39	50	41	39	45	52	46	54	49	67	57	49	64	48	52	64	51	47	52
44312	AKRON	77	74	68	70	76	84	72	76	76	71	93	87	72	95	74	78	89	74	81	90
44313	AKRON	99	105	122	106	104	112	105	104	103	105	130	119	108	129	106	103	127	105	101	114
44314	AKRON	61	65	72	64	66	71	66	65	67	64	83	74	69	88	67	67	81	65	66	71
44319	AKRON	87	101	109	97	100	106	95	95	93	94	116	108	100	122	98	94	114	93	93	105
44320	AKRON	66	66	77	64	65	73	68	67	71	69	89	75	70	87	69	72	86	68	70	76
44321	AKRON	122	142	162	143	141	146	135	133	128	134	161	154	141	164	137	126	159	131	126	146
44333	AKRON	163	198	237	198	194	205	183	181	173	184	218	207	196	223	189	171	217	177	170	197
44401	BERLIN CENTER	111	99	75	94	104	112	91	101	97	91	118	120	89	120	94	99	112	98	109	130
44402	BRISTOLVILLE	98	87	67	83	92	99	81	90	86	81	104	107	79	107	83	88	99	87	97	116
44403	BROOKFIELD	81	79	73	76	82	88	76	80	78	75	96	93	76	99	78	80	92	78	84	95
44404	BURGHILL	88	76	55	71	81	87	70	79	76	70	92	94	68	93	72	78	87	77	87	104
44405	CAMPBELL	65	69	77	64	68	76	69	69	72	68	89	76	72	91	70	74	87	68	72	76
44406	CANFIELD	117	136	147	134	135	139	126	127	121	125	151	147	132	157	129	120	149	124	120	141
44408	COLUMBIANA	75	75	73	72	77	84	73	75	75	72	92	86	74	95	75	77	89	74	79	88
44410	CORTLAND	94	98	91	95	100	104	90	94	90	89	112	110	92	117	93	91	108	92	95	112
44411	DEERFIELD	93	83	63	79	88	94	77	85	81	77	99	101	75	101	79	83	94	83	92	110
44412	DIAMOND	107	95	73	91	101	108	88	98	94	88	114	116	86	116	91	96	108	95	106	126
44413	EAST PALESTINE	73	64	52	60	68	75	62	68	68	62	82	80	60	83	64	71	78	67	77	85
44417	FARMDALE	98	86	64	82	91	98	80	89	85	80	104	106	78	105	82	88	98	87	97	115
44418	FOWLER	97	84	62	79	89	96	78	87	84	78	101	104	75	103	80	86	96	85	96	114
44420	GIRARD	74	77	78	74	78	86	75	76	77	74	96	87	78	100	78	79	92	75	81	87
44423	HANOVERTON	84	67	44	61	72	80	63	73	70	63	84	87	59	83	64	73	78	71	83	97
44425	HUBBARD	82	82	78	78	84	91	79	82	82	78	100	94	80	103	81	84	96	81	87	96
44427	KENSINGTON	101	75	44	68	83	93	71	85	82	72	97	101	64	95	73	86	90	84	100	116
44428	KINSMAN	83	72	56	67	77	84	68	76	74	68	90	89	67	92	70	77	85	74	84	97
44429	LAKE MILTON	87	75	58	74	79	88	74	80	79	73	96	94	72	96	75	80	90	79	87	99
44430	LEAVITTSBURG	68	59	47	53	62	70	57	63	63	56	77	72	56	79	59	67	72	62	72	78
44431	LEETONIA	80	74	64	71	78	85	72	76	75	71	92	88	72	96	73	78	88	74	82	93
44432	LISBON	75	61	44	56	66	74	59	67	66	59	79	78	56	79	61	69	74	66	77	86
44436	LOWELLVILLE	70	79	86	76	79	86	76	76	76	75	95	85	80	100	79	78	93	74	78	83
44437	MC DONALD	79	86	87	84	86	92	82	83	82	81	102	95	85	107	84	83	99	81	84	93
44438	MASURY	71	75	77	71	76	84	73	74	76	71	94	83	77	101	76	79	91	72	79	83
44440	MINERAL RIDGE	95	86	68	82	90	97	81	89	85	81	103	104	78	104	82	87	98	87	95	111
44441	NEGLEY	96	72	42	65	79	88	68	81	78	69	93	97	62	91	70	82	86	80	95	111
44442	NEW MIDDLETOWN	79	81	80	78	82	90	80	82	81	78	99	92	80	101	81	83	96	80	85	92
44443	NEW SPRINGFIELD	97	74	46	66	80	90	70	83	80	71	95	99	64	93	72	85	89	82	97	112
44444	NEWTON FALLS	78	74	65	70	76	83	71	75	74	70	90	87	71	93	72	76	86	74	80	91
44445	NEW WATERFORD	76	64	46	61	69	75	60	68	65	60	79	81	58	79	62	67	74	67	76	90
44446	NILES	72	70	68	67	72	81	71	73	75	69	92	83	72	94	72	77	88	72	79	83
44449	NORTH BENTON	88	76	57	72	82	89	71	80	76	71	92	95	68	94	74	79	87	78	88	105
44450	NORTH BLOOMFIELD	89	75	55	72	80	88	72	81	78	72	95	95	69	95	74	80	89	79	89	102
44451	NORTH JACKSON	91	91	82	87	93	98	84	89	86	84	105	105	86	110	87	86	102	87	91	108
44452	NORTH LIMA	93	94	90	91	96	104	91	95	92	89	113	108	91	115	93	94	109	93	99	109
44454	PETERSBURG	102	89	66	84	94	102	82	92	88	82	107	110	80	109	85	91	101	90	100	119
44455	ROGERS	86	63	36	57	70	79	60	72	70	61	83	87	54	80	62	74	76	71	86	100
44460	SALEM	82	74	64	71	78	86	73	78	78	72	95	90	72	96	75	80	90	77	85	94
44470	SOUTHINGTON	108	89	62	83	96	105	83	95	91	84	110	113	79	110	86	95	103	93	106	126
44471	STRUTHERS	60	64	68	60	65	73	62	63	65	61	80	69	66	83	65	67	77	62	69	69
44473	VIENNA	99	78	50	72	85	94	74	86	83	74	99	102	68	98	75	86	92	84	98	116
44481	WARREN	100	90	73	85	94	102	85	93	90	84	109	110	83	111	87	92	104	91	100	118
44483	WARREN	70	71	77	68	71	79	73	72	75	71	93	82	74	96	74	77	90	73	76	80
44484	WARREN	89	92	96	89	93	100	90	91	91	89	113	104	92	115	92	93	110	90	94	103
44485	WARREN	60	57	61	54	58	65	61	61	65	60	79	69	61	80	61	67	77	61	66	68
44490	WASHINGTONVILLE	75	69	61	68	72	81	70	73	74	69	90	83	70	93	71	76	86	72	79	85
44491	WEST FARMINGTON	105	88	63	83	94	103	82	93	90	83	108	111	79	109	85	93	102	91	104	123
44502	YOUNGSTOWN	47	45	46	42	46	52	47	47	50	46	61	52	47	62	47	52	59	47	52	53
44503	YOUNGSTOWN	13	11	16	12	11	13	14	13	15	13	19	15	14	18	14	15	18	14	14	14
44504	YOUNGSTOWN	61	52	62	51	51	60	64	58	67	62	83	69	61	78	60	66	80	63	61	66
44505	YOUNGSTOWN	59	55	61	52	54	63	58	59	63	59	77	65	58	74	58	65	74	60	63	67
44506	YOUNGSTOWN	44	35	36	31	35	43	39	41	45	40	55	44	38	48	38	49	52	42	48	48
44507	YOUNGSTOWN	43	36	42	34	36	43	41	41	46	42	57	46	41	53	40	48	55	43	46	47
44509	YOUNGSTOWN	53	55	60	52	55	61	57	56	59	55	73	63	58	76	57	60	71	56	59	61
44510	YOUNGSTOWN	44	35	38	31	35	43	40	41	46	41	55	44	38	50	39	49	53	42	48	48
44511	YOUNGSTOWN	65	67	77	65	66	74	68	67	69	68	86	76	70	86	69	71	84	68	70	75
44512	YOUNGSTOWN	83	92	107	91	92	99	91	90	90	90	113	102	95	117	93	91	111	89	89	98
44514	YOUNGSTOWN	86	98	106	95	97	103	93	93	91	92	114	106	97	119	96	92	112	91	92	102
44515	YOUNGSTOWN	69	76	85	74	75	81	74	73	74	73	93	84	77	96	76	75	91	73	73	81
44555	YOUNGSTOWN	0	0	0	0	0	0	0	0	0	0	0	0	0	0	0	0	0	0	0	0
44601	ALLIANCE	70	68	67	64	69	77	68	70	72	67	88	80	69	90	69	74	85	69	75	81
44606	APPLE CREEK	87	75	56	70	78	84	71	80	76	73	93	92	68	91	72	78	89	79	85	99
44608	BEACH CITY	87	72	52	66	78	86	69	78	76	69	92	92	66	92	71	80	86	76	89	101
44609	BELOIT	92	75	52	70	81	89	70	81	77	71	93	96	67	93	72	80	88	79	91	107
44611	BIG PRAIRIE	79	70	53	66	74	80	65	72	69	65	84	86	63	86	67	71	80	70	78	93
44612	BOLIVAR	89	91	84	89	92	98	86	89	87	85	107	103	87	111	88	88	103	87	91	104
44613	BREWSTER	82	79	71	75	82	89	76	79	79	74	97	92	77	102	78	82	93	78	86	96
44614	CANAL FULTON	91	109	115	108	106	106	100	99	94	100	119	116	105	124	101	91	118	97	90	109
44615	CARROLLTON	73	61	44	57	65	73	59	66	65	58	78	77	56	78	61	68	73	65	76	85
44618	DALTON	97	85	64	81	90	97	79	88	84	79	103	105	77	104	81	87	97	86	96	114
44620	DELLROY	82	72	54	68	76	83	66	75	71	66	86	89	64	88	69	74	82	73	82	97
44621	DENNISON	63	58	50	55	61	67	57	60	61	56	74	69	57	77	58	63	70	59	67	73
44622	DOVER	82	78	71	76	81	88	76	80	79	75	97	93	76	99	78	81	93	79	85	95
44624	DUNDEE	97	73	43	66	80	90	69	82	79	70	94	98	63	92	71	84	87	81	96	112
44625	EAST ROCHESTER	96	80	56	75	86	94	75	85	82	75	99	102	71	99	77	85	93	83	95	113
44626	EAST SPARTA	85	74	55	70	78	84	69	77	73	69	89	91	67	91	71	76	84	75	84	99
44627	FREDERICKSBURG	97	78	52	72	84	92	74	85	82	75	98	101	68	96	75	85	92	84	96	112
44628	GLENMONT	84	65	40	59	71	79	61	72	69	62	83	86	56	81	63	73	77	71	83	98
44629	GNADENHUTTEN	71	63	50	58	66	74	60	66	66	60	80	77	59	82	62	69	76	65	75	83
44632	HARTVILLE	98	110	110	108	109	113	101	103	98	100	122	120	105	128	103	97	120	100	99	117
44633	HOLMESVILLE	106	96	74	92	98	104	90	98	93	92	114	114	86	111	90	93	109	97	100	120
44634	HOMEWORTH	94	84	64	80	89	95	78	86	82	78	100	103	76	102	80	85	95	84	93	111
44637	KILLBUCK	83	61	35	55	68	76	58	70	67	59	80	83	52	78	60	71	74	69	83	96
	OHIO	89	88	90	87	88	95	88	89	89	87	110	103	88	111	88	89	107	89	90	102
	UNITED STATES	100	100	100	100	100	100	100	100	100	100	100	100	100	100	100	100	100	100	100	100

OHIO

POPULATION CHANGE

A 44638-44907

# POST OFFICE NAME	COUNTY FIPS CODE	POPULATION 2000	2004	2009	2000-2004 ANNUAL RATE % Rate	State Centile	HOUSEHOLDS 2000	2004	2009	% Annual Rate 2000-2004	2004 Average HH Size	FAMILIES 2000	2004	% Annual Rate 2000-2004
44638 LAKEVILLE	075	1602	1578	1570	-0.4	29	575	579	582	0.2	2.73	442	435	-0.4
44641 LOUISVILLE	151	20217	20364	20183	0.2	52	7311	7545	7641	0.7	2.62	5556	5599	0.2
44643 MAGNOLIA	019	3251	3202	3154	-0.4	28	1276	1287	1292	0.2	2.49	969	953	-0.4
44644 MALVERN	019	5091	5100	5048	0.0	46	2000	2059	2088	0.7	2.47	1481	1488	0.1
44645 MARSHALLVILLE	169	2504	2551	2626	0.4	63	863	897	940	0.9	2.83	696	709	0.4
44646 MASSILLON	151	46329	45624	44780	-0.4	28	18269	18430	18483	0.2	2.41	12697	12440	-0.5
44647 MASSILLON	151	17803	17594	17292	-0.3	32	7041	7125	7157	0.3	2.46	5055	4973	-0.4
44651 MECHANICSTOWN	019	732	728	720	-0.1	38	260	264	266	0.4	2.73	203	202	-0.1
44654 MILLERSBURG	075	18750	18809	18791	0.1	48	5489	5620	5676	0.6	3.24	4421	4438	0.1
44656 MINERAL CITY	157	3345	3385	3407	0.3	57	1290	1338	1370	0.9	2.53	960	970	0.2
44657 MINERVA	019	10688	10614	10465	-0.2	37	4062	4127	4158	0.4	2.54	3019	2991	-0.2
44662 NAVARRE	151	9931	9881	9750	-0.1	39	3772	3840	3867	0.4	2.53	2744	2721	-0.2
44663 NEW PHILADELPHIA	157	26298	26520	26759	0.2	53	10832	11148	11430	0.7	2.35	7261	7256	0.0
44666 NORTH LAWRENCE	151	2941	2994	2991	0.4	62	1040	1086	1110	1.0	2.76	842	862	0.6
44667 ORRVILLE	169	13712	13902	14204	0.3	58	5011	5175	5379	0.8	2.66	3746	3780	0.2
44669 PARIS	151	1402	1436	1433	0.6	69	513	540	551	1.2	2.63	403	415	0.7
44672 SEBRING	099	5509	5289	5090	-1.0	10	2332	2299	2266	-0.3	2.21	1434	1358	-1.3
44675 SHERRODSVILLE	019	1774	1753	1725	-0.3	32	743	756	761	0.4	2.32	537	532	-0.2
44676 SHREVE	169	4502	4562	4629	0.3	58	1656	1716	1774	0.8	2.66	1258	1274	0.3
44677 SMITHVILLE	169	2317	2301	2351	-0.2	37	879	890	926	0.3	2.57	692	684	-0.3
44680 STRASBURG	157	3642	3965	4145	2.0	93	1449	1604	1700	2.4	2.44	1047	1131	1.8
44681 SUGARCREEK	157	7077	7232	7343	0.5	66	2113	2191	2249	0.9	3.23	1701	1730	0.4
44683 UHRICHSVILLE	157	8707	8345	8245	-1.0	8	3364	3291	3306	-0.5	2.51	2346	2228	-1.2
44685 UNIONTOWN	153	23744	24684	24959	0.9	80	8682	9243	9521	1.5	2.67	6777	7039	0.9
44688 WAYNESBURG	151	3247	3207	3150	-0.3	32	1227	1243	1247	0.3	2.58	906	895	-0.3
44689 WILMOT	075	293	318	329	2.0	93	90	98	102	2.0	3.24	73	79	1.9
44691 WOOSTER	169	42893	43936	45175	0.6	69	16572	17359	18210	1.1	2.39	11127	11309	0.4
44695 BOWERSTON	019	1644	1614	1576	-0.4	25	618	623	624	0.2	2.52	454	446	-0.4
44699 TIPPECANOE	067	1135	1098	1068	-0.8	13	431	430	428	-0.1	2.55	312	303	-0.7
44702 CANTON	151	1042	986	955	-1.3	4	465	440	428	-1.3	1.59	119	105	-2.9
44703 CANTON	151	10856	10318	9967	-1.2	5	4357	4201	4125	-0.9	2.37	2433	2243	-1.9
44704 CANTON	151	5105	4671	4444	-2.1	0	2013	1883	1828	-1.6	2.40	1237	1114	-2.4
44705 CANTON	151	20815	19734	19039	-1.3	4	7888	7659	7551	-0.7	2.54	5520	5202	-1.4
44706 CANTON	151	18987	18276	17745	-0.9	11	7301	7191	7132	-0.4	2.53	5252	5040	-1.0
44707 CANTON	151	10045	9647	9359	-1.0	10	4054	3975	3935	-0.5	2.42	2657	2530	-1.2
44708 CANTON	151	25760	25072	24498	-0.6	17	11252	11234	11229	0.0	2.21	7099	6827	-0.9
44709 CANTON	151	19336	18992	18649	-0.4	26	8202	8201	8199	0.0	2.13	4776	4600	-0.9
44710 CANTON	151	9662	9379	9155	-0.7	15	4131	4102	4089	-0.2	2.27	2577	2460	-1.1
44714 CANTON	151	8891	8688	8491	-0.5	21	3874	3877	3873	0.0	2.22	2448	2365	-0.8
44718 CANTON	151	12331	13029	13301	1.3	86	5114	5560	5815	2.0	2.33	3403	3557	1.1
44720 CANTON	151	37332	37307	36845	0.0	43	14889	15239	15370	0.6	2.39	10370	10300	-0.2
44721 CANTON	151	12104	12122	11973	0.0	46	4511	4641	4694	0.7	2.60	3559	3583	0.2
44730 CANTON	151	6284	6163	6027	-0.5	24	2417	2431	2431	0.1	2.52	1850	1816	-0.4
44802 ALVADA	063	1222	1319	1378	1.8	92	426	473	507	2.5	2.79	345	375	2.0
44804 ARCADIA	063	1138	1179	1218	0.8	78	413	439	463	1.5	2.69	321	332	0.8
44805 ASHLAND	005	32793	33248	33849	0.3	58	12411	12858	13331	0.8	2.44	8559	8606	0.1
44807 ATTICA	147	2283	2206	2151	-0.8	13	878	868	865	-0.3	2.54	660	636	-0.9
44811 BELLEVUE	147	13349	13065	12896	-0.5	22	5153	5154	5195	0.0	2.53	3708	3613	-0.6
44813 BELLVILLE	139	7432	7629	7734	0.6	71	2794	2931	3022	1.1	2.59	2130	2181	0.6
44814 BERLIN HEIGHTS	043	2843	2881	2886	0.3	58	1012	1053	1081	0.9	2.73	844	863	0.5
44817 BLOOMDALE	173	1428	1456	1496	0.5	64	512	531	556	0.9	2.74	394	400	0.4
44818 BLOOMVILLE	033	3058	3095	3077	0.3	57	1106	1145	1163	0.8	2.68	868	878	0.3
44820 BUCYRUS	033	19162	18880	18572	-0.4	29	7772	7832	7871	0.2	2.36	5348	5237	-0.5
44822 BUTLER	139	3232	3497	3670	1.9	93	1119	1234	1314	2.3	2.83	896	968	1.8
44824 CASTALIA	043	4111	3983	3908	-0.7	14	1514	1507	1516	-0.1	2.64	1225	1198	-0.5
44826 COLLINS	077	1758	1872	1924	1.5	88	619	677	712	2.1	2.75	506	543	1.7
44827 CRESTLINE	033	7329	7320	7240	0.0	43	2907	2967	2995	0.5	2.45	2037	2018	-0.2
44830 FOSTORIA	147	20140	19664	19437	-0.6	21	7914	7908	7990	0.0	2.45	5416	5245	-0.8
44833 GALION	033	18384	18107	17912	-0.4	28	7515	7568	7643	0.2	2.37	5243	5145	-0.4
44836 GREEN SPRINGS	147	2774	2791	2775	0.1	51	981	1015	1034	0.8	2.68	751	759	0.3
44837 GREENWICH	077	4572	4570	4583	0.0	44	1593	1616	1646	0.3	2.82	1235	1230	-0.1
44839 HURON	043	12144	12150	12090	0.0	45	4957	5083	5180	0.6	2.34	3497	3483	-0.1
44840 JEROMESVILLE	005	3158	3225	3288	0.5	66	1174	1222	1265	1.0	2.63	915	931	0.4
44841 KANSAS	147	1262	1226	1202	-0.7	15	464	462	463	-0.1	2.65	360	351	-0.6
44842 LOUDONVILLE	005	6057	6011	6048	-0.2	36	2281	2296	2343	0.2	2.55	1594	1560	-0.5
44843 LUCAS	139	2078	2126	2148	0.5	67	763	799	823	1.1	2.65	630	648	0.7
44844 MC CUTCHENVILLE	175	799	834	851	1.0	82	295	315	329	1.6	2.55	233	244	1.1
44846 MILAN	043	3864	3957	3988	0.6	69	1381	1440	1481	1.0	2.70	1080	1102	0.5
44847 MONROEVILLE	077	3846	3890	3909	0.3	56	1362	1409	1446	0.8	2.76	1090	1107	0.4
44849 NEVADA	175	2454	2501	2535	0.5	63	943	985	1022	1.0	2.54	716	732	0.5
44851 NEW LONDON	077	5042	5149	5202	0.5	66	1854	1936	1996	1.0	2.64	1369	1396	0.5
44853 NEW RIEGEL	147	1679	1697	1687	0.3	55	583	605	615	0.9	2.78	450	456	0.3
44854 NEW WASHINGTON	033	1845	1843	1823	0.0	43	692	709	717	0.6	2.53	517	517	0.0
44855 NORTH FAIRFIELD	077	1274	1296	1302	0.4	62	444	462	474	0.9	2.76	357	364	0.5
44857 NORWALK	077	23074	23302	23376	0.2	55	8879	9156	9368	0.7	2.50	6209	6228	0.1
44859 NOVA	005	1712	1818	1886	1.4	88	618	672	711	2.0	2.71	512	547	1.6
44864 PERRYSVILLE	005	2973	3016	3055	0.3	60	1149	1196	1235	1.0	2.41	875	889	0.4
44865 PLYMOUTH	077	3710	3843	3899	0.8	77	1359	1439	1489	1.4	2.67	1066	1104	0.8
44866 POLK	005	1942	1975	2003	0.4	62	646	670	691	0.9	2.94	526	535	0.4
44867 REPUBLIC	147	2528	2518	2487	-0.1	41	893	908	917	0.4	2.76	716	714	-0.1
44870 SANDUSKY	043	43420	42962	42609	-0.3	33	17755	18033	18335	0.4	2.30	11282	11067	-0.5
44875 SHELBY	139	14946	14891	14837	-0.1	41	5826	5921	6001	0.4	2.44	4068	4012	-0.3
44878 SHILOH	139	3191	3211	3217	0.2	51	991	1011	1026	0.5	3.17	825	827	0.1
44880 SULLIVAN	005	2391	2625	2769	2.2	94	770	865	931	2.8	3.03	641	707	2.3
44882 SYCAMORE	175	2963	2988	3012	0.2	53	1144	1182	1220	0.8	2.52	840	846	0.2
44883 TIFFIN	147	30218	30114	29835	-0.1	42	11770	12037	12203	0.5	2.39	7980	7921	-0.2
44887 TIRO	033	1133	1197	1215	1.3	86	404	438	454	1.9	2.71	323	342	1.4
44889 WAKEMAN	077	6374	6581	6672	0.8	75	2314	2448	2538	1.3	2.69	1834	1902	0.9
44890 WILLARD	077	11768	11606	11500	-0.3	30	4318	4334	4373	0.1	2.65	3192	3129	-0.5
44902 MANSFIELD	139	6973	6809	6742	-0.6	21	2730	2703	2713	-0.2	2.30	1613	1538	-1.1
44903 MANSFIELD	139	27495	27277	27179	-0.2	36	10562	10716	10874	0.3	2.48	7396	7294	-0.3
44904 MANSFIELD	139	13758	13996	14135	0.4	62	5359	5586	5752	1.0	2.50	4049	4110	0.4
44905 MANSFIELD	139	17264	16982	16843	-0.4	27	5166	5184	5228	0.1	2.47	3640	3549	-0.6
44906 MANSFIELD	139	17684	17370	17225	-0.4	26	7458	7471	7535	0.0	2.30	4979	4847	-0.6
44907 MANSFIELD	139	14490	14600	14643	0.2	52	6637	6824	6960	0.7	2.10	3966	3916	-0.3
OHIO					0.3					0.7	2.44			0.0
UNITED STATES					1.2					1.3	2.58			1.1

ZIP CODE #	POST OFFICE NAME	RACE (%) White 2000	White 2004	Black 2000	Black 2004	Asian/Pacific 2000	Asian/Pacific 2004	% Hispanic Origin 2000	% Hispanic Origin 2004	2004 AGE DISTRIBUTION (%) 0-4	5-9	10-14	15-19	20-24	25-44	45-64	65-84	85+	18+	MEDIAN AGE 2004	% 2004 Males	% 2004 Females
44638	LAKEVILLE	98.8	98.7	0.4	0.4	0.3	0.3	1.1	1.2	8.5	8.7	8.7	7.0	6.0	27.1	24.0	9.1	1.1	69.7	34.3	50.8	49.2
44641	LOUISVILLE	96.1	95.6	2.5	2.8	0.2	0.3	0.6	0.7	6.6	6.8	7.4	6.7	5.8	26.2	25.2	13.2	2.0	75.0	39.0	48.4	51.6
44643	MAGNOLIA	97.6	97.3	1.1	1.3	0.1	0.1	1.0	1.1	5.9	6.4	7.6	6.7	5.5	26.0	27.4	13.1	1.6	76.0	40.0	49.6	50.4
44644	MALVERN	96.4	96.2	1.9	1.9	0.2	0.2	0.6	0.7	6.6	6.6	6.5	6.3	6.0	25.9	29.2	11.9	1.0	76.6	39.8	49.7	50.3
44645	MARSHALLVILLE	98.6	98.5	0.1	0.1	0.2	0.2	0.6	0.6	6.3	7.3	8.6	6.9	5.3	28.3	26.3	9.9	1.1	73.4	37.7	50.5	49.5
44646	MASSILLON	90.6	89.6	7.1	7.8	0.5	0.7	0.9	1.0	6.5	6.5	6.7	6.7	6.2	26.2	26.3	12.8	2.1	76.0	39.0	48.5	51.5
44647	MASSILLON	96.7	96.3	1.7	1.9	0.2	0.2	0.8	0.9	5.6	5.9	6.9	6.4	5.7	26.2	27.3	14.5	1.7	77.6	41.0	49.1	50.9
44651	MECHANICSTOWN	98.2	98.1	0.4	0.4	0.0	0.1	1.0	1.0	6.7	7.3	8.5	7.3	5.9	27.9	25.4	10.0	1.0	72.8	36.4	52.1	47.9
44654	MILLERSBURG	98.9	98.8	0.4	0.4	0.1	0.1	0.8	0.9	10.5	9.6	9.2	8.1	7.7	25.8	18.4	9.4	1.4	65.7	28.5	50.1	49.9
44656	MINERAL CITY	98.5	98.3	0.2	0.3	0.2	0.2	0.7	0.7	6.2	6.9	7.3	6.9	5.4	27.7	26.9	11.5	1.0	75.3	38.6	50.4	49.6
44657	MINERVA	98.5	98.3	0.3	0.3	0.2	0.3	0.5	0.6	6.1	6.6	7.0	6.7	5.9	26.7	26.3	13.2	1.5	76.2	39.2	49.4	50.6
44662	NAVARRE	98.6	98.3	0.4	0.4	0.2	0.3	0.5	0.6	5.9	6.2	6.7	6.0	5.7	24.7	27.2	15.4	2.2	77.4	41.5	49.0	51.0
44663	NEW PHILADELPHIA	97.6	97.3	0.7	0.7	0.4	0.6	1.0	1.1	6.3	6.3	6.4	6.0	6.2	27.0	26.4	13.5	2.0	77.3	39.5	48.6	51.4
44666	NORTH LAWRENCE	98.5	98.4	0.4	0.5	0.2	0.2	0.8	0.8	6.9	7.3	7.3	6.7	5.5	27.4	27.7	10.1	1.3	74.4	38.6	50.3	49.7
44667	ORRVILLE	93.2	92.5	4.1	4.3	1.0	1.4	1.1	1.2	7.4	7.2	7.4	7.5	6.9	27.1	24.4	10.6	1.7	73.3	35.9	49.4	50.6
44669	PARIS	97.5	97.2	1.4	1.5	0.4	0.4	0.3	0.4	5.9	6.2	6.6	5.9	6.0	24.7	29.1	14.0	1.7	77.8	41.8	50.2	49.8
44672	SEBRING	98.3	97.9	0.5	0.7	0.2	0.3	0.8	0.9	5.3	5.1	6.7	5.5	5.9	22.6	21.6	18.1	9.1	79.5	44.0	45.1	54.9
44675	SHERRODSVILLE	99.0	98.9	0.2	0.2	0.2	0.2	0.2	0.2	5.2	6.3	5.9	5.2	4.6	24.4	32.2	15.1	1.1	79.5	43.9	50.1	49.9
44676	SHREVE	98.8	98.7	0.3	0.4	0.1	0.2	0.4	0.4	7.8	8.2	8.3	7.0	6.0	27.2	25.0	9.8	0.9	71.3	35.4	50.4	49.7
44677	SMITHVILLE	98.6	98.4	0.2	0.3	0.5	0.7	0.4	0.4	7.0	7.2	7.5	7.9	6.2	27.2	24.9	11.2	1.0	73.0	36.2	49.3	50.7
44680	STRASBURG	98.6	98.5	0.1	0.1	0.4	0.5	1.3	1.3	7.2	7.2	7.2	6.1	5.7	27.9	24.4	12.4	1.9	74.6	37.6	49.2	50.8
44681	SUGARCREEK	99.2	99.1	0.1	0.1	0.2	0.2	0.4	0.5	9.9	9.1	8.8	7.5	7.3	25.5	19.2	10.5	2.2	67.6	30.6	49.7	50.3
44683	UHRICHSVILLE	97.8	97.5	0.9	1.0	0.1	0.1	0.6	0.6	7.4	6.9	7.2	7.4	7.1	26.4	22.9	12.7	2.0	73.9	36.2	48.8	51.3
44685	UNIONTOWN	97.7	97.1	0.7	0.8	0.7	1.0	0.7	0.8	6.3	6.9	7.9	6.8	5.5	25.4	29.1	11.0	1.0	74.5	39.7	49.0	51.0
44688	WAYNESBURG	95.4	94.7	3.5	4.0	0.2	0.2	1.1	1.2	6.7	6.7	7.5	7.1	5.9	26.2	25.5	12.6	1.7	74.7	38.5	49.9	50.1
44689	WILMOT	98.6	98.7	0.3	0.3	0.0	0.3	0.7	0.6	11.3	9.8	10.1	8.8	8.8	25.5	17.3	7.6	0.9	63.2	26.0	51.3	48.7
44691	WOOSTER	95.0	94.4	2.4	2.6	1.1	1.4	0.8	0.9	6.2	6.2	6.5	8.0	8.1	25.6	25.4	12.0	2.0	77.1	37.2	48.9	51.1
44695	BOWERSTON	99.0	98.8	0.2	0.3	0.1	0.1	0.2	0.3	6.1	6.4	6.5	5.7	5.2	24.4	28.2	15.4	2.2	77.2	42.2	49.3	50.7
44699	TIPPECANOE	98.9	98.6	0.0	0.0	0.0	0.1	0.4	0.5	5.7	5.8	6.2	6.8	5.7	24.9	28.1	15.1	1.6	78.3	41.9	50.2	49.8
44702	CANTON	60.9	57.6	34.0	36.8	0.6	0.7	1.4	1.4	4.0	3.8	4.9	5.0	4.6	25.8	26.5	19.5	6.2	84.1	46.2	49.1	50.9
44703	CANTON	77.6	75.2	16.2	18.0	0.3	0.3	2.2	2.3	8.3	7.4	7.4	7.4	8.2	31.8	21.1	7.5	1.1	72.5	32.1	49.3	50.7
44704	CANTON	33.1	31.3	61.3	63.1	0.2	0.2	1.4	1.4	7.9	8.3	7.7	7.0	6.2	22.6	24.3	14.0	2.1	71.5	37.4	45.9	54.1
44705	CANTON	71.7	69.3	23.8	25.8	0.4	0.5	1.1	1.1	7.5	7.2	8.1	7.5	6.7	25.9	24.2	11.8	1.2	72.7	36.0	47.6	52.4
44706	CANTON	91.9	91.0	5.6	6.3	0.2	0.3	0.9	1.0	6.4	6.4	7.1	7.0	6.4	26.8	26.7	11.9	1.2	75.7	38.3	49.3	50.7
44707	CANTON	64.3	63.0	31.8	33.1	0.2	0.2	1.0	1.0	9.3	7.6	7.6	7.1	7.5	24.0	23.5	11.9	1.5	71.5	34.5	46.9	53.2
44708	CANTON	93.8	92.9	3.3	3.7	0.9	1.2	1.1	1.2	5.8	5.8	6.1	5.7	5.4	24.5	26.5	17.0	3.3	78.9	42.8	46.6	53.4
44709	CANTON	91.4	90.3	5.6	6.4	0.7	0.9	1.0	1.1	5.8	5.4	5.4	6.7	8.0	26.3	23.6	14.8	4.0	80.3	39.4	45.7	54.3
44710	CANTON	91.8	90.6	5.9	6.9	0.3	0.4	0.7	0.8	7.5	7.1	6.6	5.8	6.3	27.6	22.5	14.1	2.6	75.2	37.3	46.1	53.9
44714	CANTON	80.0	78.4	17.2	18.6	0.3	0.4	0.9	1.0	5.7	5.8	6.4	6.2	5.7	26.2	25.5	16.0	2.5	78.0	41.0	46.6	53.5
44718	CANTON	94.6	93.8	2.2	2.4	2.1	2.7	1.1	1.2	5.0	5.5	6.5	6.2	5.7	23.8	30.2	15.0	2.1	79.2	43.2	48.5	51.5
44720	CANTON	96.6	96.0	1.1	1.3	1.2	1.5	0.9	1.0	5.5	5.9	6.7	6.6	6.0	25.2	27.8	13.9	2.3	78.0	41.1	48.2	51.8
44721	CANTON	95.5	94.8	2.5	2.8	0.5	0.7	1.0	1.2	6.2	6.9	7.5	6.8	4.9	25.9	29.5	11.2	1.2	75.1	40.3	49.2	50.8
44730	CANTON	93.0	92.2	4.9	5.5	0.3	0.4	0.6	0.7	5.1	5.7	7.0	6.3	5.9	26.4	28.6	13.7	1.2	78.3	41.0	50.1	49.9
44802	ALVADA	98.6	98.3	0.2	0.2	0.5	0.7	1.6	2.0	7.2	7.5	8.0	6.4	6.1	26.9	26.5	10.3	1.1	73.5	37.3	52.4	47.6
44804	ARCADIA	97.5	97.1	0.5	0.5	0.3	0.4	1.9	2.1	7.0	8.1	8.6	7.6	4.6	26.5	27.3	9.0	1.5	71.4	37.5	51.9	48.1
44805	ASHLAND	97.1	96.7	0.9	1.0	0.8	1.1	0.7	0.8	6.5	6.3	6.5	7.9	8.8	24.6	24.1	12.7	2.5	76.9	36.7	48.3	51.7
44807	ATTICA	98.9	98.7	0.0	0.1	0.0	0.1	0.9	1.0	6.8	6.7	6.8	5.8	6.2	27.5	25.6	13.2	1.6	76.2	38.8	50.1	49.9
44811	BELLEVUE	98.2	98.0	0.2	0.2	0.2	0.3	2.1	2.3	6.6	6.6	7.5	7.1	6.6	26.9	25.4	11.8	1.6	75.0	37.4	49.5	50.5
44813	BELLVILLE	98.8	98.8	0.2	0.2	0.3	0.3	0.6	0.6	6.5	6.8	7.5	7.0	5.6	25.2	27.6	12.5	1.4	75.0	39.4	48.9	51.2
44814	BERLIN HEIGHTS	98.3	98.1	0.4	0.4	0.1	0.1	1.8	2.1	5.8	6.5	7.5	6.5	5.5	25.6	31.4	10.3	0.9	76.0	40.8	51.5	48.5
44817	BLOOMDALE	97.6	97.4	0.2	0.3	0.2	0.3	2.2	2.5	7.4	7.6	8.4	6.6	5.9	29.3	23.9	9.9	1.1	72.5	36.2	50.6	49.4
44818	BLOOMVILLE	98.4	98.2	0.2	0.2	0.1	0.2	1.8	2.1	7.4	7.5	7.9	6.4	6.0	27.6	23.9	11.7	1.6	73.0	36.5	49.9	50.2
44820	BUCYRUS	97.8	97.5	0.7	0.8	0.4	0.5	0.8	0.9	6.7	6.4	6.6	6.3	6.4	25.8	26.3	13.4	2.1	76.6	39.2	48.7	51.3
44822	BUTLER	98.9	98.9	0.3	0.3	0.2	0.1	0.4	0.4	6.6	7.1	8.1	7.3	6.3	27.1	26.3	10.0	1.2	73.7	37.4	50.8	49.2
44824	CASTALIA	97.9	97.6	0.4	0.4	0.0	0.0	2.1	2.4	5.2	5.7	7.0	6.7	6.0	26.2	29.7	12.5	1.1	78.0	41.2	49.5	50.5
44826	COLLINS	98.4	98.3	0.3	0.4	0.1	0.1	1.1	1.1	6.5	6.9	7.8	6.6	5.3	27.4	28.2	10.1	1.2	74.7	38.4	51.1	48.9
44827	CRESTLINE	97.0	96.8	1.5	1.5	0.3	0.4	0.7	0.7	7.0	6.6	7.0	7.0	6.8	26.8	24.6	12.6	1.6	75.2	37.6	49.2	50.8
44830	FOSTORIA	90.0	89.2	4.2	4.5	0.4	0.5	6.9	7.5	6.8	6.7	7.5	7.1	6.8	26.2	24.6	12.4	2.0	74.7	36.8	48.8	51.2
44833	GALION	98.4	98.2	0.2	0.2	0.3	0.4	0.8	0.9	6.4	6.2	6.6	6.5	6.3	25.6	26.3	14.3	1.8	76.8	39.7	47.7	52.3
44836	GREEN SPRINGS	96.5	96.0	0.3	0.3	0.3	0.4	4.2	4.7	6.3	6.4	7.4	6.9	6.9	27.8	25.6	11.0	1.8	75.7	37.6	51.0	49.1
44837	GREENWICH	98.4	98.4	0.2	0.2	0.1	0.1	0.8	0.8	9.0	8.7	9.1	7.5	6.7	28.3	21.2	8.7	0.9	68.6	31.9	50.0	50.0
44839	HURON	97.4	97.0	0.8	0.9	0.6	0.7	1.6	1.8	5.7	6.3	7.0	6.1	4.6	24.9	28.7	14.5	2.1	76.9	42.0	48.3	51.7
44840	JEROMESVILLE	98.4	98.1	0.3	0.3	0.6	0.7	0.6	0.7	6.4	6.7	7.3	6.8	5.6	26.7	27.9	11.4	1.3	75.4	39.2	51.4	48.6
44841	KANSAS	96.2	95.8	0.3	0.3	0.2	0.3	4.4	4.9	5.8	6.0	7.6	7.5	6.9	28.0	26.0	11.2	1.0	76.0	37.8	49.8	50.2
44842	LOUDONVILLE	98.8	98.6	0.4	0.5	0.2	0.2	0.6	0.7	6.5	6.9	7.7	7.3	6.1	25.8	25.5	12.1	2.2	74.4	38.0	50.7	49.3
44843	LUCAS	98.0	98.0	1.1	1.1	0.1	0.1	0.4	0.4	5.2	5.9	7.2	6.6	6.0	25.3	30.1	12.8	0.9	77.6	41.4	50.8	49.2
44844	MC CUTCHENVILLE	99.1	99.2	0.0	0.0	0.0	0.0	1.1	1.3	5.4	6.0	7.8	7.1	6.4	25.3	27.3	11.9	2.9	76.4	40.4	49.6	50.4
44846	MILAN	98.1	97.9	0.3	0.4	0.2	0.3	1.4	1.5	6.2	7.1	7.5	7.5	5.5	25.4	27.1	12.4	1.2	74.2	39.4	49.5	50.5
44847	MONROEVILLE	98.3	98.2	0.2	0.2	0.2	0.2	1.2	1.3	6.6	6.8	7.5	7.6	6.2	27.6	26.5	10.4	0.9	74.4	37.3	50.3	49.7
44849	NEVADA	98.6	98.4	0.2	0.2	0.2	0.3	0.7	0.8	6.3	6.6	7.5	6.0	6.0	26.6	27.6	12.1	1.3	76.0	39.0	51.1	48.9
44851	NEW LONDON	97.1	97.1	1.5	1.5	0.3	0.3	0.7	0.7	7.0	7.2	7.8	7.0	6.5	27.3	25.1	10.7	1.5	73.8	36.5	50.0	50.1
44853	NEW RIEGEL	98.2	97.9	0.6	0.7	0.1	0.2	1.1	1.2	5.8	6.5	9.0	7.3	6.1	26.0	25.1	13.0	1.3	73.7	38.9	50.4	49.6
44854	NEW WASHINGTON	99.2	99.0	0.0	0.0	0.3	0.3	0.4	0.5	6.0	6.2	7.3	6.8	6.0	25.8	26.1	12.8	2.9	76.1	39.7	49.4	50.6
44855	NORTH FAIRFIELD	96.9	96.8	0.2	0.2	0.2	0.2	3.2	3.4	9.3	8.6	7.1	6.2	5.6	30.6	22.4	9.0	1.2	71.3	33.9	51.6	48.4
44857	NORWALK	95.4	95.4	1.5	1.5	0.3	0.3	3.2	3.2	7.5	7.3	7.8	6.9	6.6	27.6	23.3	11.3	1.8	73.1	35.5	48.6	51.5
44859	NOVA	98.8	98.7	0.1	0.1	0.0	0.1	0.4	0.6	6.1	6.6	7.4	6.4	5.6	27.5	27.3	12.0	1.1	75.9	39.3	51.9	48.1
44864	PERRYSVILLE	97.2	96.9	1.9	2.1	0.1	0.2	0.5	0.5	6.2	6.6	6.8	8.5	6.3	24.7	27.5	11.9	1.5	75.1	39.3	51.0	49.0
44865	PLYMOUTH	98.2	98.2	0.1	0.1	0.1	0.1	1.4	1.4	7.1	7.4	8.2	7.0	5.8	28.0	24.2	11.2	1.1	72.9	36.1	49.3	50.7
44866	POLK	98.3	98.1	0.3	0.4	0.2	0.3	0.8	1.0	8.1	8.1	7.9	7.1	6.6	26.3	25.4	9.7	0.8	71.5	35.0	50.3	49.7
44867	REPUBLIC	99.2	99.1	0.0	0.0	0.0	0.1	1.3	1.5	6.2	6.8	7.7	7.4	6.2	27.3	26.9	10.2	1.3	74.5	37.5	51.1	48.9
44870	SANDUSKY	80.8	79.5	15.5	16.5	0.5	0.6	2.5	2.7	6.4	6.2	6.8	6.6	6.6	24.9	25.3	14.8	2.4	76.6	39.9	48.4	51.6
44875	SHELBY	97.6	97.5	0.8	0.9	0.3	0.3	1.0	1.0	6.6	6.5	7.0	7.9	6.4	25.3	24.7	13.2	2.4	74.8	38.3	49.7	50.3
44878	SHILOH	98.1	98.1	0.8	0.8	0.1	0.1	0.4	0.4	8.8	9.0	9.2	8.6	7.2	25.7	22.3	8.4	0.8	67.7	31.4	50.1	50.0
44880	SULLIVAN	98.4	98.2	0.9	1.0	0.0	0.1	0.7	0.8	8.3	8.3	8.0	6.8	6.2	27.4	24.6	9.7	0.7	71.2	35.0	50.5	49.5
44882	SYCAMORE	99.4	99.3	0.0	0.0	0.0	0.0	0.5	0.7	6.4	6.6	7.7	6.9	6.6	26.1	26.1	12.2	1.6	75.2	37.9	49.4	50.6
44883	TIFFIN	96.7	96.2	1.0	1.1	0.5	0.7	2.0	2.3	6.0	5.9	6.6	7.3	8.6	25.7	25.2	12.9	1.9	77.6	37.8	49.4	50.6
44887	TIRO	98.8	98.5	0.0	0.0	0.2	0.3	0.8	1.0	6.4	6.8	7.5	6.6	5.6	26.2	27.1	11.8	2.1	75.2	39.3	50.7	49.3
44889	WAKEMAN	98.6	98.4	0.2	0.2	0.1	0.2	1.4	1.5	6.5	6.9	7.2	6.5	5.6	27.2	29.4	9.7	1.0	75.4	39.2	51.2	48.8
44890	WILLARD	93.2	93.0	1.0	1.0	0.3	0.3	8.5	8.6	7.9	7.6	7.9	7.5	7.0	26.5	23.4	10.8	1.5	72.2	34.7	48.5	51.5
44902	MANSFIELD	59.9	58.3	35.5	37.1	0.4	0.4	1.4	1.4	8.1	7.7	8.0	7.4	8.5	29.6	19.8	9.6	1.4	71.7	31.9	51.5	48.5
44903	MANSFIELD	82.0	81.5	15.1	15.6	0.5	0.5	0.9	1.0	6.7	6.8	7.4	6.8	6.5	26.1	26.7	11.8	1.3	75.1	38.0	49.5	50.5
44904	MANSFIELD	96.3	96.0	1.9	2.0	0.8	0.9	0.6	0.7	5.7	6.3	7.3	7.2	5.9	23.9	29.2	13.1	1.4	76.4	41.1	48.3	51.7
44905	MANSFIELD	80.8	80.1	16.8	17.5	0.4	0.4	0.9	0.9	4.8	4.9	5.0	5.1	8.6	35.7	23.8	11.0	1.2	82.5	36.9	61.1	38.9
44906	MANSFIELD	90.0	89.9	7.0	7.0	1.0	1.0	1.1	1.1	6.4	6.4	6.5	6.3	5.8	24.9	26.9	14.9	1.9	76.9	40.7	48.1	51.9
44907	MANSFIELD	91.1	90.7	6.3	6.7	0.7	0.7	1.1	1.1	6.7	6.3	6.0	5.5	5.7	25.3	24.1	16.9	3.5	77.6	40.7	46.1	53.9
	OHIO	85.0	84.1	11.5	11.8	1.2	1.6	1.9	2.1	6.7	6.6	7.1	7.0	7.1	27.5	24.7	11.6	1.8	75.6	37.0	48.6	51.4
	UNITED STATES	75.1	73.6	12.3	12.5	3.8	4.2	12.5	14.1	6.9	6.7	7.2	7.0	7.3	28.6	23.8	10.8	1.7	75.1	36.0	49.1	50.9

#	POST OFFICE NAME	2004 Per Capita Income	2004 HH Income Base	2004 Household Income Distribution (%): Less than $25,000	$25,000 to $49,999	$50,000 to $99,999	$100,000 to $149,999	$150,000 or More	Median Household Income: 2004	2009	2004 National Centile	2004 State Centile	2004 Home Value Base	2004 Home Value Distribution (%): Less than $50,000	$50,000 to $89,999	$90,000 to $174,999	$175,000 to $399,999	$400,000 or More	2004 Median Home Value
44638	LAKEVILLE	18719	579	23.8	35.1	33.0	6.2	1.9	42125	47284	53	36	469	11.9	17.1	41.8	24.1	5.1	128795
44641	LOUISVILLE	24593	7545	18.5	31.3	36.8	8.6	4.9	50219	59281	72	63	5888	3.2	10.7	62.2	22.2	1.8	133083
44643	MAGNOLIA	20506	1287	24.9	36.8	30.2	5.6	2.5	40776	46738	49	32	1074	20.8	19.7	45.6	13.2	0.7	102957
44644	MALVERN	22932	2059	28.4	28.5	33.0	6.6	3.5	42769	48518	55	38	1644	19.9	16.4	41.9	19.8	2.0	113347
44645	MARSHALLVILLE	20922	897	16.7	30.6	41.1	9.3	2.3	51866	58792	75	70	750	7.2	10.7	52.0	27.7	2.4	131931
44646	MASSILLON	25398	18430	23.8	29.1	32.7	9.7	4.8	47540	55811	67	55	13072	5.3	16.9	56.8	19.2	1.9	123711
44647	MASSILLON	22479	7125	23.4	34.4	32.7	7.3	2.1	42941	50429	56	39	5869	13.1	28.1	48.6	9.0	1.1	97649
44651	MECHANICSTOWN	19134	264	33.0	29.9	28.8	3.8	4.6	38474	43204	41	27	223	13.5	17.9	48.0	20.2	0.5	112772
44654	MILLERSBURG	18464	5620	23.8	37.2	27.4	6.0	5.5	41645	47570	52	34	4040	8.5	12.9	44.4	27.5	6.8	142764
44656	MINERAL CITY	21233	1338	21.9	39.5	30.9	5.8	1.9	41110	46624	50	33	1120	23.8	19.2	44.5	11.4	1.1	102577
44657	MINERVA	20171	4127	24.8	35.8	31.3	5.5	2.6	41455	47592	51	33	3334	11.9	24.6	47.8	14.6	1.1	101817
44662	NAVARRE	20138	3840	25.1	35.7	29.8	6.9	2.5	40925	47765	49	32	3208	17.1	15.7	52.1	13.6	1.6	109781
44663	NEW PHILADELPHIA	21342	11148	29.4	34.2	28.7	5.3	2.4	38333	43628	41	26	8280	13.7	21.1	51.7	12.2	1.4	105112
44666	NORTH LAWRENCE	26809	1086	18.6	29.3	35.5	12.0	4.6	51763	60388	75	69	946	6.6	17.2	44.5	27.7	4.0	135034
44667	ORRVILLE	20361	5175	20.9	35.0	33.2	8.6	2.3	45108	52056	61	46	3669	9.5	10.0	57.5	22.0	1.0	127193
44669	PARIS	22110	540	18.9	27.2	44.3	7.0	2.6	52382	60065	76	71	462	12.3	14.3	46.5	23.6	3.3	124405
44672	SEBRING	20372	2299	34.3	30.3	29.1	4.8	1.5	36115	43065	32	21	1332	19.9	42.6	33.1	4.4	0.0	79742
44675	SHERRODSVILLE	22794	756	24.7	40.3	26.3	5.8	2.8	37888	43078	39	25	637	14.9	28.9	38.6	15.9	1.7	98778
44676	SHREVE	20392	1716	25.2	28.9	37.5	6.2	2.3	46764	52670	66	52	1383	10.1	16.4	53.9	16.3	3.2	116100
44677	SMITHVILLE	21947	890	17.4	34.5	37.4	8.5	2.1	48646	55685	70	59	665	4.4	7.5	60.5	25.7	2.0	139857
44680	STRASBURG	21078	1604	26.3	32.0	32.4	7.4	1.9	42070	47848	53	36	1171	8.4	23.0	48.3	18.6	1.8	113762
44681	SUGARCREEK	16513	2191	23.3	38.1	30.9	4.8	3.0	41523	47187	51	34	1713	4.4	12.9	54.8	24.2	3.7	131152
44683	UHRICHSVILLE	15284	3291	37.1	38.7	20.6	2.5	1.1	32414	36510	19	12	2310	19.2	41.0	35.8	3.6	0.4	77617
44685	UNIONTOWN	29585	9243	14.3	21.9	38.8	17.7	7.3	64620	77715	88	91	7880	2.6	5.4	53.5	36.8	1.8	162395
44688	WAYNESBURG	18392	1243	33.2	32.3	27.6	5.7	1.2	38224	44801	40	26	982	15.3	25.9	47.9	10.5	0.5	97436
44689	WILMOT	16345	98	23.5	37.8	28.6	7.1	3.1	40000	47361	46	30	76	9.2	23.7	42.1	18.4	6.6	125000
44691	WOOSTER	24945	17359	24.3	29.9	32.9	8.5	4.4	46585	52699	65	52	12032	9.3	11.4	51.5	25.1	2.7	132139
44695	BOWERSTON	17805	623	30.7	38.2	26.3	2.4	2.4	36718	41905	34	22	520	23.9	31.4	32.1	12.3	0.4	81818
44699	TIPPECANOE	16658	430	37.0	34.7	22.8	3.5	2.1	33273	37430	22	14	349	22.4	32.1	37.3	8.3	0.0	83800
44702	CANTON	14580	440	75.7	17.7	5.9	0.0	0.7	11571	13940	1	0	47	34.0	57.5	8.5	0.0	0.0	59375
44703	CANTON	18561	4201	37.5	33.6	23.1	3.5	2.3	33209	40119	22	14	1844	21.0	41.6	33.1	3.6	0.7	79942
44704	CANTON	14717	1883	50.1	31.7	13.0	3.6	1.6	24904	28170	4	4	1026	38.9	38.3	21.1	1.7	0.1	56826
44705	CANTON	18512	7659	34.7	32.7	25.3	5.1	2.2	34841	39596	27	17	5442	21.7	41.2	29.1	7.6	0.3	74299
44706	CANTON	18899	7191	27.8	33.4	32.9	5.0	1.0	40077	46867	46	30	5479	16.9	28.6	47.8	6.2	0.5	94834
44707	CANTON	14875	3975	47.4	26.5	21.7	3.7	0.8	27139	31660	7	5	2352	22.5	33.5	37.0	6.9	0.2	82965
44708	CANTON	29936	11234	23.5	31.3	30.6	8.7	5.9	45443	53322	62	47	8025	3.3	17.9	59.0	15.5	4.4	121421
44709	CANTON	26836	8201	26.3	29.9	30.5	8.4	4.8	44562	52388	60	44	5150	2.4	19.1	61.4	15.5	1.6	114294
44710	CANTON	19291	4102	36.7	33.5	23.8	5.1	0.9	34079	39721	24	15	2781	8.3	47.4	41.6	2.6	0.1	85758
44714	CANTON	30163	3877	24.9	35.3	28.1	7.4	4.4	41932	49417	53	35	2675	7.9	33.6	42.1	15.6	0.8	96527
44718	CANTON	38376	5560	18.6	22.7	27.6	18.5	12.6	62054	73941	86	88	3895	0.0	1.5	37.7	51.9	8.9	196772
44720	CANTON	32043	15239	17.0	26.2	34.3	14.1	8.5	57023	67460	82	81	11413	2.0	3.1	54.5	37.1	3.3	162228
44721	CANTON	29502	4641	10.2	27.8	41.2	14.8	6.0	60651	71889	85	87	4014	1.4	2.3	63.4	30.0	2.9	153531
44730	CANTON	23674	2431	22.5	33.5	34.1	6.9	3.0	45773	52197	63	48	2035	11.0	22.1	54.4	11.9	0.5	105632
44802	ALVADA	22176	473	15.9	29.6	42.5	9.3	2.8	52861	59449	77	72	401	8.2	18.5	49.9	21.2	2.2	126434
44804	ARCADIA	26004	439	21.6	22.3	39.4	10.5	6.2	53504	60478	78	75	374	9.9	24.9	45.2	17.9	2.1	111301
44805	ASHLAND	21074	12858	27.1	31.7	30.6	7.8	2.7	42770	49114	55	38	9322	9.0	17.6	52.3	19.3	1.8	118461
44807	ATTICA	20291	868	22.5	34.0	37.7	5.0	0.9	45995	50764	64	49	723	11.5	25.9	49.2	12.3	1.1	103066
44811	BELLEVUE	23197	5154	19.0	32.3	37.4	8.5	3.0	48932	55544	70	59	4001	6.1	20.7	56.4	16.0	0.8	114291
44813	BELLVILLE	21258	2931	24.1	31.3	32.9	8.7	3.0	45519	52035	63	47	2478	12.7	13.5	51.5	21.2	1.2	117969
44814	BERLIN HEIGHTS	24355	1053	12.8	29.4	42.2	10.9	4.7	56806	65434	81	81	921	2.8	8.9	55.7	29.8	2.8	149909
44817	BLOOMDALE	19654	531	16.2	36.2	40.5	5.5	1.7	48636	56147	70	59	453	13.9	26.5	51.9	7.5	0.2	99255
44818	BLOOMVILLE	19224	1145	19.1	35.7	39.0	5.0	1.1	46762	52457	66	52	942	13.9	28.8	43.2	11.5	2.7	98214
44820	BUCYRUS	20799	7832	28.2	34.5	29.2	6.1	2.0	40487	45607	48	31	5640	12.9	28.2	47.3	10.7	0.9	99980
44822	BUTLER	20689	1234	23.3	29.5	36.8	7.5	2.9	47532	53907	67	55	1057	9.7	18.4	45.1	24.4	2.5	121940
44824	CASTALIA	25608	1507	17.3	19.8	45.1	14.0	3.8	61858	72594	86	88	1352	5.0	7.6	54.1	31.7	1.6	151059
44826	COLLINS	22497	677	19.2	29.8	39.4	8.6	3.0	50691	56172	73	66	581	5.5	8.6	58.9	23.9	3.1	141261
44827	CRESTLINE	21298	2967	27.8	31.6	31.9	7.1	1.7	40774	46474	49	32	2283	16.8	31.6	42.7	8.5	0.4	91362
44830	FOSTORIA	19783	7908	30.3	33.4	29.2	5.5	1.8	38269	44142	40	26	5765	23.1	34.0	35.2	7.3	0.3	81316
44833	GALION	20626	7568	30.2	32.2	30.4	5.1	2.1	39934	45234	46	29	5514	12.1	30.0	47.2	9.9	0.7	96911
44836	GREEN SPRINGS	21672	1015	22.1	32.9	34.8	8.8	1.5	46272	51797	64	50	823	9.6	23.7	54.8	10.9	1.0	108263
44837	GREENWICH	17890	1616	25.9	33.0	35.5	4.8	0.9	43169	48892	56	40	1332	17.8	21.3	42.9	15.6	2.3	105297
44839	HURON	32695	5083	16.5	25.0	35.4	14.8	8.3	60604	69771	85	87	4069	5.4	4.6	46.3	39.4	4.3	163867
44840	JEROMESVILLE	21677	1222	17.8	32.8	38.2	9.2	2.0	49518	56391	71	62	1040	6.8	11.4	54.4	23.7	3.8	135677
44841	KANSAS	20846	462	16.0	35.1	41.6	6.3	1.1	48913	54018	70	59	398	16.6	29.4	47.0	6.5	0.5	94103
44842	LOUDONVILLE	19678	2296	22.7	35.5	33.0	7.4	1.4	42929	49829	56	39	1722	11.6	22.0	44.0	18.8	3.7	108565
44843	LUCAS	25644	799	15.8	23.9	41.8	14.1	4.4	59928	69770	84	85	697	0.9	12.3	58.1	26.5	2.2	137242
44844	MC CUTCHENVILLE	20712	315	21.3	28.3	42.9	7.0	0.6	50373	54686	73	64	270	10.4	21.1	54.4	12.6	1.5	111818
44846	MILAN	26543	1440	14.5	28.2	39.7	11.3	6.3	59890	67459	84	85	1206	6.1	9.3	46.9	34.3	3.3	153343
44847	MONROEVILLE	22929	1409	15.9	29.9	42.4	8.5	3.3	52756	59178	77	72	1169	2.5	12.7	56.5	25.8	2.7	133203
44849	NEVADA	19967	985	22.0	37.0	34.2	5.1	1.7	44063	49097	59	43	825	16.1	22.8	39.0	19.2	2.9	101195
44851	NEW LONDON	19627	1936	22.6	35.2	32.8	8.1	1.3	44474	50932	60	44	1532	10.4	23.4	44.6	19.2	2.5	111799
44853	NEW RIEGEL	21336	605	19.7	29.1	40.7	7.9	2.6	50788	55504	73	66	527	6.1	20.3	51.0	20.3	2.3	120296
44854	NEW WASHINGTON	20743	709	18.2	34.3	40.5	5.9	1.1	48143	53551	69	57	590	12.7	29.0	45.9	10.9	1.5	99245
44855	NORTH FAIRFIELD	19620	462	15.8	35.7	43.1	4.6	0.9	49140	55173	70	60	393	10.4	25.2	50.9	11.7	1.8	108929
44857	NORWALK	22974	9156	23.4	31.2	34.6	7.9	3.0	46218	52221	64	50	6405	10.6	13.3	52.7	21.7	1.7	122257
44859	NOVA	20716	672	16.7	33.6	41.7	6.7	1.3	49289	53987	71	60	596	5.0	8.2	51.5	31.0	4.2	138720
44864	PERRYSVILLE	20612	1196	25.1	34.1	32.3	6.7	1.8	43171	49411	56	40	957	10.1	25.1	37.5	25.3	2.0	111357
44865	PLYMOUTH	19310	1439	22.2	36.2	33.8	6.6	1.3	44715	50881	60	44	1131	15.0	27.4	43.9	12.6	1.2	101953
44866	POLK	18862	670	19.7	34.5	35.5	7.5	2.8	47662	53828	68	56	572	7.5	16.6	47.9	23.6	4.4	132598
44867	REPUBLIC	21424	908	19.5	32.8	37.9	7.8	2.0	47120	52950	66	53	774	12.1	23.6	50.4	12.9	0.9	109124
44870	SANDUSKY	24003	18033	28.6	29.7	30.5	8.0	3.1	41519	49864	51	34	11969	8.7	26.1	47.0	15.7	2.4	108251
44875	SHELBY	20922	5921	25.4	32.7	32.9	7.1	1.9	43700	50566	58	41	4361	7.1	26.4	52.4	12.8	1.3	106160
44878	SHILOH	16600	1011	23.6	34.7	32.8	6.4	2.4	43149	50000	56	39	843	17.7	24.3	36.2	16.5	5.3	100091
44880	SULLIVAN	19383	865	23.1	25.7	38.7	9.9	2.5	50764	56108	73	66	768	5.7	8.2	51.8	29.6	4.7	146082
44882	SYCAMORE	20136	1182	23.3	35.0	34.8	5.4	1.5	44719	49748	60	45	971	16.3	29.4	41.3	10.5	2.6	94474
44883	TIFFIN	21116	12037	25.2	33.7	33.3	5.5	2.3	42733	48578	55	38	8902	11.4	25.5	47.7	14.5	0.9	104242
44887	TIRO	20498	438	16.4	36.8	37.4	7.3	2.1	47589	52364	67	55	378	17.7	23.3	43.1	13.2	2.7	104231
44889	WAKEMAN	22957	2448	15.4	27.0	44.6	11.1	1.9	55795	63557	80	79	2121	9.8	6.9	45.8	35.4	2.2	153402
44890	WILLARD	18841	4334	27.7	31.3	32.7	6.8	1.5	41601	47862	52	34	2978	10.8	24.5	50.2	13.9	0.7	107461
44902	MANSFIELD	15765	2703	46.9	31.3	17.0	3.6	1.2	27098	31443	7	5	1260	41.4	46.3	10.8	1.3	0.3	56089
44903	MANSFIELD	21430	10716	29.0	28.7	30.3	9.2	2.8	42559	49820	55	37	7541	12.7	22.2	46.7	17.2	1.2	110033
44904	MANSFIELD	28060	5586	18.8	26.5	36.2	12.9	5.6	54187	62775	79	76	4370	4.5	8.1	57.0	29.0	1.4	144337
44905	MANSFIELD	17941	5184	27.9	35.0	30.2	6.0	0.9	40070	46954	46	30	4016	17.7	31.4	46.9	3.8	0.3	90820
44906	MANSFIELD	24219	7471	28.7	30.4	29.5	7.1	4.3	40880	48433	49	32	5349	14.9	25.8	43.1	14.8	1.3	100805
44907	MANSFIELD	27579	6824	29.3	32.2	27.1	7.4	4.0	39744	46864	45	29	4341	7.3	25.5	52.3	13.6	1.3	109328
	OHIO	25510		24.6	28.1	32.2	10.1	5.0	47354	56168				9.2	18.6	47.0	22.1	3.1	121192
	UNITED STATES	25866		24.7	27.1	30.8	10.9	6.5	48124	56710				10.9	15.0	33.7	30.1	10.4	145905

ZIP CODE		FINANCIAL SERVICES				THE HOME						ENTERTAINMENT						PERSONAL			
						Home Improvements		Furnishings													
#	POST OFFICE NAME	Auto Loan	Home Loan	Invest-ments	Retire-ment Plans	Home Repair	Lawn & Garden	Comput-ers & Hard-ware	Major Appli-ances	TV, Radio, Sound Equip-ment	Furni-ture	Dine out/ Carry out	Sports Equip-ment	Fees & Tickets	Toys & Games	Travel	Cable TV	Apparel & Services	Auto Repairs	Health Insur-ance	Pets & Supplies
44638	LAKEVILLE	82	73	55	69	77	82	67	75	71	67	87	89	66	89	69	73	83	73	81	96
44641	LOUISVILLE	101	91	76	87	95	103	88	95	92	87	113	112	86	114	89	94	107	93	101	117
44643	MAGNOLIA	85	69	48	63	74	83	66	75	73	66	88	88	62	88	67	77	82	74	86	99
44644	MALVERN	92	78	57	72	83	92	74	83	81	74	98	98	71	99	76	84	92	81	93	107
44645	MARSHALLVILLE	95	85	64	80	89	96	78	87	83	78	101	103	77	103	81	85	96	84	94	112
44646	MASSILLON	83	89	94	87	88	94	87	87	87	86	108	100	90	112	88	87	106	86	86	97
44647	MASSILLON	78	79	74	75	81	87	76	78	78	74	96	90	77	101	78	80	93	76	83	92
44651	MECHANICSTOWN	91	71	44	64	77	85	67	78	75	67	90	93	61	88	68	79	84	77	90	106
44654	MILLERSBURG	102	81	54	76	87	97	79	90	87	79	104	105	73	103	80	90	97	88	102	117
44656	MINERAL CITY	95	71	42	64	78	88	68	80	77	68	92	96	61	90	69	82	85	79	94	110
44657	MINERVA	81	72	57	68	76	83	68	75	73	68	89	88	67	91	70	75	84	73	82	95
44662	NAVARRE	81	70	54	64	74	82	67	74	73	67	89	87	65	90	69	77	84	73	84	95
44663	NEW PHILADELPHIA	74	69	62	66	72	79	68	72	72	67	88	83	68	90	69	74	84	71	78	86
44666	NORTH LAWRENCE	115	107	86	102	111	119	98	107	103	98	126	128	98	129	101	105	120	105	114	136
44667	ORRVILLE	83	73	61	71	77	85	74	78	78	72	95	91	71	96	74	80	90	77	85	95
44669	PARIS	94	83	63	79	88	94	77	85	82	77	99	102	75	101	79	84	94	83	92	110
44672	SEBRING	64	63	63	59	65	75	61	65	65	61	80	69	63	80	64	68	76	63	73	74
44675	SHERRODSVILLE	91	71	45	64	78	87	67	79	76	67	90	94	61	89	69	80	84	78	92	108
44676	SHREVE	86	76	58	73	80	87	72	79	77	72	93	93	70	94	74	78	88	77	86	100
44677	SMITHVILLE	89	78	60	76	82	90	76	83	81	75	98	96	74	98	77	82	92	81	90	102
44680	STRASBURG	81	70	54	69	74	82	70	75	74	69	90	87	67	90	70	76	85	74	82	92
44681	SUGARCREEK	90	73	50	69	80	87	69	80	76	69	91	95	65	91	71	79	86	78	90	106
44683	UHRICHSVILLE	57	51	44	48	54	61	52	55	56	50	68	62	51	69	53	59	64	54	62	65
44685	UNIONTOWN	103	122	133	122	120	122	113	112	107	113	135	130	119	141	115	105	134	110	104	124
44688	WAYNESBURG	77	63	46	57	68	76	61	69	69	61	83	80	58	83	63	73	77	68	80	89
44689	WILMOT	100	67	31	58	76	87	65	81	78	66	91	96	55	86	66	84	83	80	99	114
44691	WOOSTER	89	85	81	83	87	94	85	87	87	83	107	102	84	108	85	87	103	87	90	103
44695	BOWERSTON	85	57	26	49	65	74	55	69	66	56	78	82	47	74	56	72	71	68	85	97
44699	TIPPECANOE	76	55	31	49	62	71	53	65	61	53	72	76	46	70	55	66	67	64	78	90
44702	CANTON	31	27	39	28	27	32	34	31	36	33	45	36	33	44	33	37	43	34	34	35
44703	CANTON	59	58	66	59	58	62	64	61	64	62	80	73	63	80	62	62	78	63	60	67
44704	CANTON	54	42	42	37	42	52	47	49	54	48	65	54	44	58	46	58	61	51	58	59
44705	CANTON	65	64	66	61	65	72	65	66	68	64	84	75	66	85	66	70	81	66	70	75
44706	CANTON	69	66	62	63	68	74	65	68	68	64	83	79	65	86	66	69	80	67	72	81
44707	CANTON	52	46	48	42	46	53	48	49	53	49	65	56	48	64	48	55	62	50	55	58
44708	CANTON	88	95	103	94	95	102	94	93	93	92	116	106	97	118	95	93	113	93	94	103
44709	CANTON	77	83	98	83	83	90	85	82	84	83	105	95	87	109	86	84	103	83	82	90
44710	CANTON	57	59	66	57	59	66	61	60	63	59	78	68	63	82	62	64	76	60	63	66
44714	CANTON	87	94	102	90	95	104	94	93	96	91	119	104	98	125	96	98	115	92	97	102
44718	CANTON	118	136	154	136	134	143	127	127	122	128	154	142	135	155	131	122	152	124	123	139
44720	CANTON	102	116	128	116	116	120	111	110	107	110	133	127	115	138	113	105	131	108	105	121
44721	CANTON	106	117	117	115	116	119	109	110	105	109	132	129	112	136	110	104	129	108	105	125
44730	CANTON	101	82	55	75	88	97	77	89	86	77	103	105	72	102	79	89	96	87	101	118
44802	ALVADA	99	88	67	84	93	100	82	90	87	82	105	108	80	108	84	89	100	88	98	117
44804	ARCADIA	110	95	74	93	100	111	94	102	100	93	121	118	91	122	95	102	114	100	111	125
44805	ASHLAND	79	73	63	70	75	82	71	76	75	70	91	88	70	92	72	76	87	75	81	92
44807	ATTICA	74	73	67	69	75	82	70	73	73	68	90	84	71	95	72	75	86	71	78	86
44811	BELLEVUE	90	82	67	80	85	93	80	85	83	79	102	99	78	103	80	85	96	83	91	103
44813	BELLVILLE	88	78	60	75	82	88	73	81	78	73	94	95	71	95	75	79	90	79	87	102
44814	BERLIN HEIGHTS	107	95	72	90	100	108	88	97	93	88	113	116	86	116	90	96	108	95	106	126
44817	BLOOMDALE	87	76	56	72	81	87	71	79	76	71	92	94	69	93	73	78	87	77	86	103
44818	BLOOMVILLE	82	72	55	69	76	83	69	75	73	69	89	88	67	90	70	75	84	74	82	94
44820	BUCYRUS	75	67	56	63	71	79	66	71	71	65	86	82	65	88	67	74	82	70	79	87
44822	BUTLER	94	83	64	79	88	95	77	86	82	77	100	102	76	102	79	84	95	83	93	110
44824	CASTALIA	103	99	83	95	102	108	91	98	94	91	115	116	91	119	94	95	111	96	103	122
44826	COLLINS	99	88	67	84	94	100	82	91	87	82	106	108	80	108	84	89	100	88	98	117
44827	CRESTLINE	79	71	61	67	74	82	70	75	75	69	92	87	69	93	71	77	87	74	81	91
44830	FOSTORIA	75	64	54	60	67	75	65	70	71	64	86	81	63	86	66	73	81	69	77	85
44833	GALION	73	67	59	64	69	77	66	70	70	65	86	81	65	87	67	72	82	69	76	84
44836	GREEN SPRINGS	93	82	63	79	86	94	78	86	83	78	101	100	76	102	80	85	96	84	93	107
44837	GREENWICH	86	67	45	63	73	81	66	75	73	66	87	88	61	86	66	76	81	74	85	98
44839	HURON	110	114	112	112	116	124	108	112	107	108	132	129	109	132	111	107	128	110	113	130
44840	JEROMESVILLE	91	81	62	77	86	92	75	83	80	75	97	99	74	99	78	82	92	81	90	108
44841	KANSAS	89	79	60	75	83	89	73	81	77	73	94	96	71	96	75	79	90	79	88	104
44842	LOUDONVILLE	77	71	59	66	74	81	67	73	72	66	88	85	67	91	69	74	83	71	80	90
44843	LUCAS	104	100	85	97	104	109	92	99	94	92	116	118	92	119	94	95	111	96	103	123
44844	MC CUTCHENVILLE	86	76	58	73	81	87	71	78	75	71	91	93	69	93	73	77	87	76	85	101
44846	MILAN	108	106	93	102	109	115	98	105	100	98	124	123	99	127	101	101	119	102	108	128
44847	MONROEVILLE	101	90	69	86	95	102	83	92	89	83	108	110	82	110	86	91	102	90	100	119
44849	NEVADA	80	70	54	68	74	81	68	74	72	67	87	87	66	88	69	73	83	72	80	93
44851	NEW LONDON	84	71	53	67	75	83	68	76	74	68	90	89	65	89	70	77	84	75	85	97
44853	NEW RIEGEL	95	85	65	81	90	96	78	87	83	79	101	104	77	104	81	85	96	85	94	112
44854	NEW WASHINGTON	84	74	57	71	78	85	71	77	75	70	91	91	69	92	72	77	86	76	84	97
44855	NORTH FAIRFIELD	87	78	59	74	82	88	72	80	76	72	93	95	70	95	74	78	88	78	86	103
44857	NORWALK	87	79	69	78	82	89	80	83	83	78	101	97	77	101	80	83	96	83	88	99
44859	NOVA	90	80	61	76	84	91	74	82	78	74	95	98	72	97	76	80	91	80	89	106
44864	PERRYSVILLE	85	69	48	64	75	82	65	75	72	66	86	89	61	86	67	75	81	73	84	99
44865	PLYMOUTH	88	69	45	64	74	83	67	76	74	67	89	90	62	88	68	78	83	75	87	100
44866	POLK	89	79	60	75	84	90	73	81	78	73	94	97	72	96	75	80	90	79	88	105
44867	REPUBLIC	95	84	64	80	89	96	78	87	83	78	101	103	77	103	80	85	96	84	94	112
44870	SANDUSKY	78	76	78	74	77	85	78	79	80	76	99	90	78	99	79	81	95	79	82	90
44875	SHELBY	75	72	66	69	74	81	70	74	73	69	90	85	71	92	72	75	86	72	79	87
44878	SHILOH	91	71	45	65	77	86	67	78	75	68	90	94	62	89	69	79	84	77	90	106
44880	SULLIVAN	94	84	64	80	89	95	78	86	82	78	100	102	76	102	80	84	95	84	93	111
44882	SYCAMORE	77	72	61	68	75	81	68	73	72	67	88	85	68	91	70	74	84	71	79	90
44883	TIFFIN	74	71	68	69	73	79	71	73	73	69	89	85	70	91	72	74	86	73	77	86
44887	TIRO	89	79	60	75	84	90	73	81	78	73	95	97	72	97	76	80	90	79	88	105
44889	WAKEMAN	99	88	68	84	93	100	81	90	86	81	105	107	80	107	84	88	100	88	97	116
44890	WILLARD	77	67	55	64	70	78	68	72	72	66	88	84	65	88	68	74	83	71	79	88
44902	MANSFIELD	47	42	47	41	42	48	49	47	51	47	63	54	47	61	47	52	61	49	50	52
44903	MANSFIELD	76	73	71	71	74	80	73	75	76	72	93	87	73	94	74	76	90	75	78	87
44904	MANSFIELD	97	104	106	102	104	110	98	100	97	98	121	116	101	125	100	97	118	98	99	115
44905	MANSFIELD	75	64	51	60	68	76	63	69	69	63	84	80	61	85	65	72	79	68	78	87
44906	MANSFIELD	79	77	74	74	79	88	76	79	80	75	98	90	77	100	78	82	94	78	85	92
44907	MANSFIELD	78	83	89	81	83	91	82	83	82	81	102	93	84	103	84	83	99	82	84	91
	OHIO	89	88	90	87	88	95	88	89	89	87	110	103	88	111	88	89	107	89	90	102
	UNITED STATES	100	100	100	100	100	100	100	100	100	100	100	100	100	100	100	100	100	100	100	100

POPULATION CHANGE

ZIP CODE			POPULATION			2000-2004 ANNUAL RATE		HOUSEHOLDS					FAMILIES		
#	POST OFFICE NAME	COUNTY FIPS CODE	2000	2004	2009	% Rate	State Centile	2000	2004	2009	% Annual Rate 2000-2004	2004 Average HH Size	2000	2004	% Annual Rate 2000-2004
45001	ADDYSTON	061	965	925	887	-1.0	8	342	330	319	-0.8	2.80	249	232	-1.7
45002	CLEVES	061	12572	12630	12372	0.1	50	4417	4484	4435	0.4	2.78	3384	3341	-0.3
45003	COLLEGE CORNER	135	918	954	980	0.9	80	393	422	446	1.7	2.26	287	300	1.1
45005	FRANKLIN	165	27899	30127	35368	1.8	92	10775	11970	14374	2.5	2.51	8022	8689	1.9
45011	HAMILTON	017	54723	58923	63172	1.8	92	18971	20820	22743	2.2	2.76	14411	15466	1.7
45013	HAMILTON	017	49673	50396	52341	0.3	60	19325	20100	21325	0.9	2.49	14071	14199	0.2
45014	FAIRFIELD	017	43408	43453	44916	0.0	45	17451	17920	18928	0.6	2.39	11751	11655	-0.2
45015	HAMILTON	017	12430	12286	12732	-0.3	33	5089	5137	5426	0.2	2.38	3364	3284	-0.6
45030	HARRISON	061	15424	15338	14938	-0.1	38	5678	5726	5642	0.2	2.68	4253	4168	-0.5
45034	KINGS MILLS	165	882	1002	1199	3.1	97	334	386	471	3.5	2.60	277	314	3.0
45036	LEBANON	165	30943	35905	42981	3.6	98	9549	11561	14467	4.6	2.63	7187	8523	4.1
45039	MAINEVILLE	165	13992	17388	21743	5.3	99	5339	6776	8633	5.8	2.56	4053	5048	5.3
45040	MASON	165	34190	43304	54598	5.7	100	11843	15316	19684	6.2	2.80	9260	11705	5.7
45042	MIDDLETOWN	017	28179	29008	30561	0.7	73	11315	11888	12773	1.2	2.43	8091	8316	0.7
45044	MIDDLETOWN	017	45168	47176	50065	1.0	82	17335	18447	19932	1.5	2.53	12046	12461	0.8
45050	MONROE	017	5130	6290	7168	4.9	99	2025	2538	2952	5.5	2.43	1515	1844	4.7
45052	NORTH BEND	061	3788	3856	3799	0.4	62	1317	1357	1352	0.7	2.83	1063	1070	0.2
45053	OKEANA	017	3168	3311	3467	1.0	82	1069	1151	1233	1.8	2.88	916	969	1.3
45054	OREGONIA	165	1472	1831	2278	5.3	99	534	660	879	6.1	2.54	441	556	5.6
45056	OXFORD	017	27335	28183	29366	0.7	73	7860	8421	9117	1.6	2.43	3659	3766	0.7
45064	SOMERVILLE	017	2401	2430	2490	0.3	57	810	840	879	0.9	2.85	682	695	0.5
45065	SOUTH LEBANON	165	3284	3667	4361	2.6	95	1277	1468	1786	3.3	2.50	906	1005	2.5
45066	SPRINGBORO	165	16458	19715	24220	4.3	98	5666	6910	8627	4.8	2.85	4808	5790	4.5
45067	TRENTON	017	10518	11769	12830	2.7	95	3793	4336	4818	3.2	2.71	2986	3332	2.6
45068	WAYNESVILLE	165	9302	10965	13324	4.0	98	3392	4105	5098	4.6	2.64	2695	3186	4.0
45069	WEST CHESTER	017	43497	48512	53060	2.6	95	15313	17624	19781	3.4	2.74	12342	13793	2.7
45101	ABERDEEN	015	2520	2574	2649	0.5	66	1033	1077	1128	1.0	2.38	690	697	0.2
45102	AMELIA	025	18674	19923	21429	1.5	89	6867	7510	8265	2.1	2.65	5209	5559	1.5
45103	BATAVIA	025	27544	28873	31013	1.1	84	9933	10666	11733	1.7	2.63	7393	7756	1.1
45106	BETHEL	025	12042	12678	13533	1.2	86	4297	4628	5048	1.8	2.73	3367	3555	1.3
45107	BLANCHESTER	027	8605	9050	9521	1.2	85	3169	3401	3634	1.7	2.62	2397	2525	1.2
45111	CAMP DENNISON	061	426	449	449	1.2	86	176	188	190	1.6	2.39	123	127	0.8
45113	CLARKSVILLE	027	3495	3810	4180	2.1	94	1243	1389	1555	2.7	2.74	1011	1112	2.3
45118	FAYETTEVILLE	015	3692	3757	3869	0.4	62	1308	1359	1426	0.9	2.76	1039	1059	0.5
45120	FELICITY	025	3443	3661	3920	1.5	88	1193	1300	1423	2.0	2.82	900	958	1.5
45121	GEORGETOWN	015	8466	8699	8981	0.6	71	3261	3423	3601	1.2	2.49	2351	2407	0.6
45122	GOSHEN	025	10977	11785	12836	1.7	91	3852	4248	4735	2.3	2.77	3095	3340	1.8
45123	GREENFIELD	071	7812	7856	8019	0.1	50	3012	3088	3206	0.6	2.50	2105	2094	-0.1
45130	HAMERSVILLE	015	3876	3963	4107	0.5	67	1361	1420	1499	1.0	2.79	1096	1124	0.6
45133	HILLSBORO	071	22898	23910	24927	1.0	82	8864	9432	9993	1.5	2.50	6458	6707	0.9
45135	LEESBURG	071	4338	4529	4704	1.0	82	1591	1693	1787	1.5	2.67	1202	1247	0.9
45140	LOVELAND	025	46784	52045	56960	2.5	95	16559	18749	20866	3.0	2.76	12959	14329	2.4
45142	LYNCHBURG	071	4491	4695	4884	1.1	83	1605	1712	1810	1.5	2.74	1244	1298	1.0
45144	MANCHESTER	001	4469	4363	4361	-0.6	21	1832	1834	1875	0.0	2.37	1272	1241	-0.6
45146	MARTINSVILLE	027	1335	1390	1430	1.0	81	484	512	534	1.3	2.71	396	411	0.9
45148	MIDLAND	027	1474	1516	1550	0.7	72	516	543	565	1.2	2.79	413	426	0.7
45150	MILFORD	025	28850	30630	33005	1.4	88	11220	12211	13467	2.0	2.48	7968	8452	1.4
45152	MORROW	165	7463	8944	10978	4.4	99	2710	3342	4199	5.1	2.65	2132	2577	4.6
45153	MOSCOW	025	2040	2255	2470	2.4	95	712	809	907	3.1	2.79	568	632	2.5
45154	MOUNT ORAB	015	8014	8623	9095	1.7	91	2851	3131	3362	2.2	2.74	2209	2371	1.7
45157	NEW RICHMOND	025	9310	9665	10281	0.9	79	3176	3387	3689	1.5	2.85	2522	2638	1.1
45159	NEW VIENNA	027	3176	3389	3543	1.5	89	1161	1263	1340	2.0	2.68	867	921	1.4
45160	OWENSVILLE	025	723	770	827	1.5	88	324	352	386	2.0	2.18	212	224	1.3
45162	PLEASANT PLAIN	165	2914	3445	4114	4.0	98	1004	1225	1499	4.8	2.81	842	1010	4.4
45167	RIPLEY	015	3723	3692	3758	-0.2	35	1430	1444	1495	0.2	2.51	996	978	-0.4
45168	RUSSELLVILLE	015	1476	1495	1533	0.3	58	567	586	612	0.8	2.49	445	449	0.2
45169	SABINA	027	5127	5101	5147	-0.1	39	1940	1964	2010	0.3	2.57	1449	1431	-0.3
45171	SARDINIA	015	5592	5968	6290	1.5	89	2074	2267	2435	2.1	2.62	1631	1750	1.7
45174	TERRACE PARK	061	2273	2170	2076	-1.1	6	760	724	696	-1.1	3.00	646	605	-1.5
45176	WILLIAMSBURG	025	8318	8667	9134	1.0	81	2945	3147	3394	1.6	2.72	2284	2388	1.1
45177	WILMINGTON	027	20896	21501	22028	0.7	73	8169	8576	8929	1.2	2.41	5580	5696	0.5
45202	CINCINNATI	061	15473	14953	14523	-0.8	13	7566	7414	7272	-0.5	1.70	2285	2034	-2.7
45203	CINCINNATI	061	3491	3285	3152	-1.4	3	1533	1454	1402	-1.2	1.84	618	539	-3.2
45204	CINCINNATI	061	7652	7240	6923	-1.3	4	2953	2823	2723	-1.1	2.38	1662	1510	-2.2
45205	CINCINNATI	061	23313	21835	20764	-1.5	2	9066	8577	8234	-1.3	2.51	5314	4789	-2.4
45206	CINCINNATI	061	12523	11918	11428	-1.2	5	6334	6083	5880	-1.0	1.87	2376	2132	-2.5
45207	CINCINNATI	061	8955	8262	7829	-1.9	1	2787	2563	2428	-2.0	2.74	1753	1546	-2.9
45208	CINCINNATI	061	19570	19104	18496	-0.6	20	9830	9727	9522	-0.3	1.92	4312	3996	-1.8
45209	CINCINNATI	061	9572	9331	9068	-0.6	19	5428	5367	5275	-0.3	1.72	1964	1807	-1.9
45211	CINCINNATI	061	36912	36617	35908	-0.2	36	16191	16176	15988	0.0	2.22	9059	8622	-1.2
45212	CINCINNATI	061	24729	23241	22130	-1.5	3	10799	10262	9874	-1.2	2.24	5890	5322	-2.4
45213	CINCINNATI	061	12798	12484	12086	-0.6	19	5722	5640	5513	-0.3	2.18	3294	3088	-1.5
45214	CINCINNATI	061	11043	10350	9918	-1.5	3	4743	4437	4263	-1.6	2.26	2245	1994	-2.8
45215	CINCINNATI	061	31440	30069	28829	-1.0	7	13125	12662	12249	-0.8	2.33	8109	7518	-1.8
45216	CINCINNATI	061	10033	9556	9151	-1.1	6	4350	4189	4055	-0.9	2.26	2491	2282	-2.0
45217	CINCINNATI	061	6259	6509	6597	0.9	80	2582	2715	2783	1.2	2.38	1554	1545	-0.1
45218	CINCINNATI	061	4338	4037	3822	-1.7	2	1725	1625	1554	-1.4	2.43	1197	1089	-2.2
45219	CINCINNATI	061	14889	13817	13116	-1.7	2	6855	6404	6126	-1.6	2.02	2135	1839	-3.5
45220	CINCINNATI	061	15376	14194	13461	-1.9	1	7833	7243	6902	-1.8	1.83	2652	2279	-3.5
45221	CINCINNATI	061	2626	2520	2465	-1.0	9	361	315	292	-3.2	2.04	116	93	-5.1
45223	CINCINNATI	061	14740	13900	13286	-1.4	3	6130	5824	5614	-1.2	2.38	3437	3132	-2.2
45224	CINCINNATI	061	22630	22372	21808	-0.3	33	9557	9517	9351	-0.1	2.29	5844	5616	-0.9
45225	CINCINNATI	061	14763	13778	13174	-1.6	2	5840	5493	5295	-1.4	2.43	3575	3221	-2.4
45226	CINCINNATI	061	5294	5214	5087	-0.4	28	2421	2412	2380	-0.1	2.16	1277	1208	-1.3
45227	CINCINNATI	061	20192	19094	18227	-1.3	4	8731	8345	8044	-1.1	2.27	5169	4720	-2.1
45228	CINCINNATI	061	472	464	448	-0.4	27	188	184	179	-0.5	2.52	145	138	-1.2
45229	CINCINNATI	061	17196	15933	15096	-1.8	1	7474	6981	6666	-1.6	2.16	3781	3336	-2.9
45230	CINCINNATI	061	27893	26630	25494	-1.1	6	11810	11384	11002	-0.9	2.32	7486	6953	-1.7
45231	CINCINNATI	061	42911	43020	42256	0.1	47	16461	16679	16547	0.3	2.55	11794	11612	-0.4
45232	CINCINNATI	061	7458	7836	7846	1.2	85	2803	2978	3015	1.4	2.63	1770	1804	0.5
45233	CINCINNATI	061	15195	14952	14544	-0.4	27	5226	5171	5065	-0.3	2.86	4139	4010	-0.7
45236	CINCINNATI	061	23898	22880	21952	-1.0	8	10884	10524	10193	-0.8	2.13	6361	5845	-2.0
45237	CINCINNATI	061	23514	22149	21095	-1.4	3	10459	9898	9494	-1.3	2.20	5995	5417	-2.4
45238	CINCINNATI	061	46649	45333	43854	-0.7	16	18806	18455	18026	-0.4	2.41	12163	11545	-1.2
45239	CINCINNATI	061	28972	28440	27587	-0.4	24	12098	11995	11748	-0.2	2.35	7753	7377	-1.2
	OHIO					0.3					0.7	2.44			0.0
	UNITED STATES					1.2					1.3	2.58			1.1

ZIP CODE #	POST OFFICE NAME	RACE (%) White 2000	White 2004	Black 2000	Black 2004	Asian/Pacific 2000	Asian/Pacific 2004	% Hispanic Origin 2000	% Hispanic Origin 2004	2004 AGE DISTRIBUTION (%) 0-4	5-9	10-14	15-19	20-24	25-44	45-64	65-84	85+	18+	MEDIAN AGE 2004	% 2004 Males	% 2004 Females
45001	ADDYSTON	94.0	93.1	3.5	4.2	0.1	0.1	1.0	1.2	8.1	7.9	8.2	7.8	7.6	27.2	22.9	9.4	0.9	71.2	33.0	50.0	50.1
45002	CLEVES	98.3	98.0	0.5	0.7	0.2	0.3	0.6	0.8	7.5	7.4	8.1	7.3	6.6	29.2	22.8	9.8	1.3	72.3	35.1	50.1	49.9
45003	COLLEGE CORNER	98.4	98.1	0.4	0.5	0.2	0.3	0.2	0.3	5.2	5.8	6.4	5.9	5.4	26.8	30.2	13.4	0.9	78.8	41.7	50.8	49.2
45005	FRANKLIN	97.7	97.3	0.8	1.0	0.4	0.5	0.6	0.7	6.8	6.7	7.0	6.4	6.6	29.1	25.0	11.5	0.8	75.7	36.8	48.9	51.1
45011	HAMILTON	87.9	87.4	8.2	8.2	1.1	1.4	2.6	2.7	8.9	8.3	7.9	7.1	6.5	31.0	21.7	7.7	0.9	70.4	33.3	49.7	50.3
45013	HAMILTON	96.3	95.8	1.7	1.9	0.5	0.6	0.9	1.0	6.4	6.3	6.9	6.8	6.3	26.6	25.7	13.4	1.7	76.2	38.9	48.2	51.8
45014	FAIRFIELD	90.3	89.1	5.8	6.3	2.2	2.8	1.5	1.6	6.2	6.0	6.6	6.7	7.7	30.7	24.7	10.3	1.2	77.2	35.7	48.5	51.5
45015	HAMILTON	93.4	92.6	4.5	5.0	0.4	0.5	1.6	1.7	7.5	6.9	6.8	6.4	7.0	30.3	22.0	11.4	1.6	75.0	35.6	47.7	52.3
45030	HARRISON	98.2	97.9	0.2	0.2	0.3	0.4	0.6	0.7	6.3	6.3	7.6	7.9	7.5	27.1	26.1	10.2	1.0	75.1	36.7	49.3	50.7
45034	KINGS MILLS	98.1	97.6	0.1	0.2	1.0	1.3	0.9	1.0	7.4	7.5	7.6	6.9	5.8	31.5	25.3	7.3	0.8	73.3	36.1	49.2	50.8
45036	LEBANON	88.8	88.3	9.0	9.2	0.6	0.7	1.1	1.2	7.0	6.9	6.6	5.9	7.7	34.4	21.1	8.6	2.1	76.0	35.0	55.3	44.8
45039	MAINEVILLE	96.3	95.8	0.9	1.0	1.6	2.0	1.3	1.5	7.7	7.7	7.4	6.3	5.4	32.5	24.8	7.6	0.7	73.3	35.7	48.8	51.2
45040	MASON	93.3	91.9	2.3	2.6	3.1	4.0	1.1	1.2	9.9	9.8	8.5	6.5	4.9	31.8	20.9	6.4	1.3	67.6	34.1	48.8	51.2
45042	MIDDLETOWN	96.4	96.1	1.9	2.1	0.4	0.5	0.5	0.6	5.9	6.1	6.8	6.6	5.9	26.2	27.3	13.5	1.7	77.2	40.5	48.9	51.1
45044	MIDDLETOWN	85.6	85.0	11.7	12.0	0.6	0.9	1.1	1.2	8.5	8.0	7.7	6.7	6.5	29.5	21.7	10.0	1.6	71.8	34.1	48.3	51.7
45050	MONROE	96.9	96.3	1.0	1.1	0.8	1.0	0.8	0.9	7.6	7.1	6.3	5.4	5.4	29.8	22.9	12.2	3.4	75.8	38.0	48.1	51.9
45052	NORTH BEND	97.5	97.1	0.8	1.0	0.2	0.3	0.6	0.8	6.5	7.1	8.9	8.6	6.2	24.6	26.8	10.4	1.1	72.2	37.9	49.6	50.4
45053	OKEANA	98.8	98.7	0.1	0.1	0.1	0.2	0.4	0.4	5.3	6.0	7.6	7.9	6.2	26.6	31.4	8.3	0.8	76.3	40.1	51.0	49.0
45054	OREGONIA	94.9	94.5	3.6	3.8	0.2	0.3	0.8	0.8	6.7	7.1	7.3	6.2	6.1	30.6	27.4	8.1	0.7	75.1	37.3	52.4	47.6
45056	OXFORD	92.5	91.4	3.6	4.0	2.0	2.6	1.3	1.4	2.8	2.8	3.3	21.8	34.8	14.2	13.9	5.5	1.0	89.0	22.8	47.8	52.2
45064	SOMERVILLE	98.6	98.4	0.3	0.3	0.3	0.3	0.4	0.5	6.2	6.7	7.3	6.8	5.4	27.1	29.1	10.0	1.4	75.6	39.7	50.3	49.7
45065	SOUTH LEBANON	98.5	98.3	0.4	0.5	0.2	0.2	0.9	1.0	7.9	7.9	7.4	5.8	6.5	30.8	23.4	9.3	1.0	73.3	34.8	49.4	50.6
45066	SPRINGBORO	96.6	96.0	0.8	0.9	1.4	1.8	0.9	1.0	8.7	9.3	8.7	6.3	4.4	28.8	26.4	7.0	0.5	69.2	36.5	49.7	50.3
45067	TRENTON	98.2	98.0	0.5	0.5	0.2	0.3	0.8	0.9	8.1	8.0	8.2	6.4	5.8	31.8	21.8	9.2	0.8	71.7	34.0	49.6	50.4
45068	WAYNESVILLE	98.1	97.9	0.3	0.4	0.3	0.3	0.9	1.1	6.5	7.1	7.5	6.7	5.1	27.2	27.9	10.8	1.3	74.7	39.7	49.1	51.0
45069	WEST CHESTER	88.5	86.3	4.4	5.0	4.9	6.2	2.0	2.2	7.7	8.1	8.3	7.1	5.9	29.9	25.8	6.8	0.5	71.4	35.5	49.5	50.5
45101	ABERDEEN	97.3	97.2	1.2	1.3	0.1	0.1	1.1	1.1	7.1	6.7	7.2	6.8	6.6	28.0	25.2	11.2	1.1	74.9	36.8	48.0	52.0
45102	AMELIA	97.4	97.0	0.6	0.7	0.4	0.6	0.9	1.1	8.9	8.2	7.7	6.8	7.0	32.1	21.7	6.9	0.7	71.1	32.5	48.7	51.3
45103	BATAVIA	96.7	96.3	1.1	1.1	0.8	1.1	0.8	0.9	8.5	7.6	7.4	6.8	7.2	30.8	22.9	7.7	1.0	72.5	33.8	49.4	50.6
45106	BETHEL	98.7	98.6	0.2	0.2	0.2	0.2	0.6	0.7	6.9	7.0	8.1	7.4	6.7	28.1	25.4	9.5	1.0	73.4	36.0	49.7	50.3
45107	BLANCHESTER	98.6	98.4	0.2	0.2	0.3	0.4	0.4	0.5	7.3	7.3	7.4	6.6	6.3	27.7	24.6	11.2	1.7	74.0	37.1	48.9	51.1
45111	CAMP DENNISON	77.2	74.4	18.5	21.6	0.0	0.0	1.9	1.8	3.1	4.0	6.9	6.5	5.8	25.6	34.3	12.0	1.8	82.0	44.0	51.5	48.6
45113	CLARKSVILLE	98.3	98.1	0.2	0.2	0.3	0.4	0.6	0.7	6.9	7.2	7.5	6.5	5.5	29.7	27.1	9.0	0.7	74.4	37.8	50.1	49.9
45118	FAYETTEVILLE	99.0	98.9	0.2	0.3	0.1	0.1	0.3	0.3	7.5	7.6	8.1	7.2	6.4	28.8	24.8	9.0	0.7	72.4	35.9	50.4	49.6
45120	FELICITY	98.1	97.9	0.6	0.6	0.1	0.1	0.6	0.7	7.9	7.7	7.9	7.2	6.8	28.5	24.0	9.2	0.9	72.2	34.8	49.7	50.3
45121	GEORGETOWN	97.8	97.6	1.2	1.2	0.3	0.3	0.3	0.4	6.9	6.9	7.6	6.5	6.2	28.1	24.4	11.2	2.1	74.7	36.8	48.1	52.0
45122	GOSHEN	98.2	98.1	0.5	0.6	0.2	0.3	0.5	0.6	7.2	7.2	7.9	7.0	6.3	28.7	25.8	9.3	0.7	73.3	36.3	49.7	50.4
45123	GREENFIELD	97.0	96.7	1.5	1.7	0.2	0.2	0.7	0.7	7.5	6.9	7.2	6.8	6.8	26.0	24.6	12.5	1.8	74.4	36.7	48.0	52.0
45130	HAMERSVILLE	99.1	98.9	0.2	0.3	0.1	0.1	0.5	0.6	6.8	6.9	8.1	7.2	6.3	29.1	25.1	9.8	0.8	73.9	36.4	50.1	49.9
45133	HILLSBORO	96.1	95.8	2.0	2.1	0.5	0.7	0.6	0.6	7.1	6.9	7.4	6.5	6.1	26.5	24.4	13.3	2.0	74.7	37.9	48.7	51.3
45135	LEESBURG	98.5	98.3	0.5	0.6	0.1	0.1	0.3	0.3	7.0	7.0	7.2	7.1	7.0	28.8	25.1	9.7	1.0	74.5	35.1	50.3	49.7
45140	LOVELAND	95.5	94.6	1.3	1.5	1.7	2.3	1.1	1.3	8.1	8.3	8.3	6.8	5.5	28.4	25.6	7.9	1.1	70.8	36.4	49.2	50.8
45142	LYNCHBURG	98.5	98.3	0.2	0.2	0.2	0.3	0.3	0.4	8.5	8.2	8.0	6.9	5.9	29.5	22.0	9.9	1.1	71.0	34.6	49.8	50.2
45144	MANCHESTER	97.6	97.4	0.2	0.2	0.1	0.2	0.6	0.6	6.1	6.2	7.0	6.6	6.2	27.7	26.6	12.0	1.7	76.7	38.8	49.9	50.1
45146	MARTINSVILLE	97.7	97.4	0.4	0.4	0.3	0.4	0.5	0.4	7.9	7.9	8.1	6.8	5.9	28.6	24.5	9.4	1.0	71.9	36.4	51.1	48.9
45148	MIDLAND	98.4	98.3	0.2	0.2	0.1	0.1	0.5	0.6	7.1	7.3	8.0	6.6	5.9	30.0	24.9	9.4	0.9	73.6	36.4	51.2	48.8
45150	MILFORD	96.4	96.0	1.7	1.8	0.6	0.8	0.9	1.0	7.0	7.1	7.1	6.4	6.2	28.1	25.2	10.9	2.1	74.9	37.6	48.0	52.1
45152	MORROW	98.9	98.8	0.2	0.3	0.3	0.3	1.1	1.1	6.2	6.7	7.2	6.2	5.2	27.6	29.1	10.7	1.1	76.1	39.8	49.3	50.7
45153	MOSCOW	97.9	97.7	0.4	0.4	0.3	0.3	0.5	0.5	6.6	6.8	8.3	8.3	7.3	27.8	26.0	8.3	0.6	73.2	35.6	49.5	50.5
45154	MOUNT ORAB	98.8	98.6	0.4	0.4	0.1	0.2	0.4	0.5	8.0	7.7	7.8	7.3	6.4	30.4	22.2	9.2	1.0	72.0	34.2	49.5	50.5
45157	NEW RICHMOND	97.6	97.4	1.0	1.0	0.1	0.2	0.8	0.9	6.7	7.0	8.1	7.8	7.2	27.6	26.4	8.5	0.8	73.3	35.9	49.9	50.1
45159	NEW VIENNA	97.8	97.5	0.4	0.4	0.3	0.4	0.6	0.7	7.9	7.8	8.4	7.1	6.5	29.4	23.3	8.7	1.0	71.6	34.7	48.3	51.7
45160	OWENSVILLE	97.2	96.9	0.6	0.7	0.3	0.4	2.1	2.5	9.6	6.8	6.9	6.8	7.3	24.8	23.4	12.5	2.1	72.5	36.4	46.9	53.1
45162	PLEASANT PLAIN	98.7	98.6	0.3	0.3	0.3	0.3	0.6	0.6	5.6	6.0	8.3	7.6	6.4	26.7	28.9	9.9	0.7	75.3	39.4	50.0	50.0
45167	RIPLEY	94.5	94.1	3.9	4.2	0.1	0.1	0.5	0.5	6.4	6.4	6.7	6.6	6.1	25.4	25.3	15.0	2.2	76.5	40.1	47.9	52.1
45168	RUSSELLVILLE	98.2	98.1	0.5	0.5	0.1	0.1	0.3	0.3	6.4	6.7	7.4	6.0	5.5	28.1	25.7	12.2	2.1	75.7	39.1	49.2	50.8
45169	SABINA	98.1	98.0	0.4	0.5	0.3	0.3	0.9	0.9	6.9	7.0	7.4	6.8	6.8	28.7	24.0	11.0	1.4	74.7	36.0	49.8	50.2
45171	SARDINIA	98.4	98.2	0.8	0.9	0.1	0.1	0.4	0.4	6.9	6.9	7.3	7.0	5.9	26.9	25.5	12.6	1.2	74.7	37.9	50.0	50.0
45174	TERRACE PARK	98.9	98.7	0.2	0.2	0.6	0.8	0.8	0.9	6.4	8.3	10.7	9.8	4.4	18.6	29.5	10.9	1.4	68.3	40.5	49.8	50.2
45176	WILLIAMSBURG	98.5	98.4	0.3	0.3	0.1	0.2	0.5	0.6	6.7	6.9	7.6	7.3	6.4	29.4	25.9	8.9	0.9	74.1	36.6	49.6	50.4
45177	WILMINGTON	93.9	93.4	4.0	4.3	0.5	0.7	0.7	0.8	7.2	6.5	6.5	7.4	8.6	27.3	24.2	10.8	1.7	76.1	35.7	49.0	51.0
45202	CINCINNATI	41.3	39.8	54.8	56.0	1.0	1.3	1.9	2.0	6.1	5.0	4.5	5.5	10.7	37.5	22.5	7.2	1.1	81.6	33.6	55.8	44.2
45203	CINCINNATI	16.7	15.5	81.0	82.0	0.6	0.7	1.0	1.0	7.4	5.9	5.9	9.4	10.9	33.1	19.8	6.7	1.0	76.3	30.5	52.8	47.2
45204	CINCINNATI	83.4	81.2	11.6	13.3	1.1	1.4	2.6	2.6	8.2	7.6	7.6	8.9	10.6	28.0	18.6	9.2	1.4	72.7	29.6	49.5	50.5
45205	CINCINNATI	77.9	75.2	18.1	20.3	1.1	1.4	1.2	1.3	8.8	7.8	8.3	8.0	8.3	30.0	19.3	8.4	1.2	70.4	30.7	48.4	51.6
45206	CINCINNATI	29.0	26.4	68.3	70.7	0.6	0.7	1.0	1.0	6.2	5.6	6.1	6.4	7.6	29.2	22.3	13.9	2.8	78.2	36.9	46.4	53.6
45207	CINCINNATI	18.7	18.3	78.7	79.0	0.5	0.7	0.8	0.8	6.0	7.1	8.0	16.1	13.5	20.9	16.2	10.4	1.7	74.2	24.7	44.1	55.9
45208	CINCINNATI	90.9	89.5	5.7	6.3	1.8	2.5	1.3	1.5	5.8	4.6	4.3	3.8	7.7	36.2	22.8	11.1	3.6	82.8	36.1	45.9	54.1
45209	CINCINNATI	86.7	84.3	8.8	10.4	1.5	2.0	2.3	2.5	5.1	3.8	3.6	3.6	10.4	41.5	20.3	9.8	2.1	85.5	33.7	46.9	53.1
45211	CINCINNATI	75.4	72.4	21.4	23.9	1.2	1.6	1.0	1.0	7.5	6.9	6.9	6.9	7.5	30.4	20.5	11.1	2.4	74.5	34.6	46.9	53.1
45212	CINCINNATI	87.7	86.3	8.8	9.7	0.9	1.2	1.8	2.0	6.2	5.7	6.2	6.9	9.0	31.9	21.9	10.6	1.8	78.0	35.2	48.6	51.4
45213	CINCINNATI	44.0	41.0	52.8	55.6	0.5	0.6	1.1	1.2	6.3	6.4	6.9	6.2	5.7	27.9	25.3	13.1	2.3	76.6	39.1	45.2	54.8
45214	CINCINNATI	31.8	29.8	63.9	65.4	1.0	1.3	2.1	2.1	7.9	7.9	8.9	9.0	9.6	28.1	19.0	8.7	1.0	69.8	29.5	49.0	51.0
45215	CINCINNATI	69.8	68.1	26.8	27.8	1.5	2.0	1.2	1.2	6.1	6.3	7.3	7.2	6.4	26.9	24.2	13.1	2.6	75.7	38.7	47.2	52.8
45216	CINCINNATI	80.3	78.2	16.8	18.5	0.7	0.8	1.2	1.3	7.8	7.1	6.4	6.2	6.7	28.8	24.2	11.2	1.8	75.0	36.6	49.2	50.8
45217	CINCINNATI	74.5	70.7	23.3	26.6	0.7	1.1	0.6	0.7	6.1	6.0	7.2	7.2	7.2	26.5	25.2	12.6	2.1	76.3	38.3	48.2	51.8
45218	CINCINNATI	94.6	93.6	2.9	3.4	0.4	0.5	1.2	1.4	7.1	6.8	7.1	7.2	6.8	28.4	21.0	13.8	1.9	74.2	36.1	47.6	52.4
45219	CINCINNATI	48.1	44.9	45.7	47.9	2.8	3.6	1.5	1.6	4.2	4.3	5.1	9.8	29.2	27.6	13.4	5.6	1.0	82.5	24.6	53.3	46.7
45220	CINCINNATI	60.5	57.3	28.8	29.8	8.0	10.1	1.9	2.0	3.8	3.2	4.2	6.9	17.4	34.2	18.0	9.7	2.5	85.9	30.9	49.6	50.4
45221	CINCINNATI	59.9	54.4	20.6	22.7	15.5	18.7	1.5	1.5	1.5	1.1	0.6	54.5	27.9	12.2	1.9	0.2	0.0	96.4	19.3	55.3	44.7
45223	CINCINNATI	44.4	39.3	51.6	56.3	0.9	1.1	1.3	1.3	8.8	8.1	8.7	7.9	8.6	29.5	20.0	7.5	0.9	69.5	30.3	46.7	53.3
45224	CINCINNATI	50.9	47.9	46.3	49.1	0.7	0.9	0.7	0.8	6.1	6.0	7.0	6.8	5.8	24.3	24.5	15.2	4.3	76.4	40.8	44.7	55.3
45225	CINCINNATI	23.2	21.5	73.5	75.0	0.8	1.0	1.0	1.0	13.2	9.9	9.3	8.6	11.5	26.4	15.3	5.1	0.6	62.6	23.9	45.5	54.5
45226	CINCINNATI	92.4	91.0	5.8	6.8	0.6	0.9	0.9	1.1	6.8	6.0	5.8	5.9	7.1	36.8	22.2	8.2	1.2	77.6	34.2	48.4	51.7
45227	CINCINNATI	61.9	59.6	34.9	36.7	1.0	1.3	0.9	1.0	6.1	6.3	7.6	7.5	6.7	27.4	23.8	12.3	2.5	75.5	37.2	46.1	53.9
45228	CINCINNATI	98.7	98.7	0.0	0.0	0.4	0.4	1.5	1.5	5.6	7.5	10.1	7.3	3.7	23.9	33.0	8.2	0.7	72.0	41.0	52.6	47.4
45229	CINCINNATI	16.5	15.2	81.0	82.3	0.6	0.7	0.9	0.9	6.8	6.9	7.6	8.2	9.9	24.1	22.4	12.1	2.1	74.2	34.8	45.6	54.4
45230	CINCINNATI	95.5	94.5	2.0	2.4	1.3	1.8	1.0	1.1	6.7	6.8	6.7	5.9	5.5	28.3	25.7	12.1	2.3	76.2	38.9	47.9	52.1
45231	CINCINNATI	70.3	67.0	26.7	29.6	0.9	1.2	0.9	1.0	6.6	6.7	7.9	7.3	6.3	26.6	24.2	12.7	1.8	74.3	37.4	47.1	52.9
45232	CINCINNATI	24.5	20.9	72.5	76.1	0.7	0.8	1.3	1.2	15.4	12.4	10.9	8.8	8.8	23.0	14.0	5.7	0.9	55.8	21.4	42.3	57.7
45233	CINCINNATI	97.4	97.1	1.4	1.5	0.4	0.5	0.4	0.4	6.4	7.2	8.6	8.0	6.0	23.3	26.6	11.8	2.1	72.8	39.1	49.0	51.0
45236	CINCINNATI	84.0	82.0	12.6	13.8	1.8	2.4	1.1	1.2	5.5	5.4	5.7	5.8	5.4	26.7	23.8	17.3	4.4	79.8	42.1	45.9	54.1
45237	CINCINNATI	25.7	23.8	71.1	72.9	0.7	0.9	0.8	0.8	6.0	6.2	7.1	6.9	6.5	24.9	26.6	13.9	1.8	76.3	39.8	45.0	55.0
45238	CINCINNATI	92.4	91.1	4.8	5.5	1.6	2.1	0.7	0.7	6.9	6.7	6.9	6.8	6.9	28.7	22.0	12.8	2.4	75.5	36.4	47.5	52.5
45239	CINCINNATI	84.5	82.3	12.5	14.2	0.9	1.2	1.2	1.3	7.2	6.7	7.0	6.3	6.7	29.3	20.8	13.8	2.2	75.2	36.4	47.6	52.4
	OHIO	85.0	84.1	11.5	11.8	1.2	1.6	1.9	2.1	6.7	6.6	7.1	7.0	7.1	27.5	24.7	11.6	1.8	75.6	37.0	48.6	51.4
	UNITED STATES	75.1	73.6	12.3	12.5	3.8	4.2	12.5	14.1	6.9	6.7	7.2	7.0	7.3	28.6	23.8	10.8	1.7	75.1	36.0	49.1	50.9

ZIP CODE				2004 HOUSEHOLD INCOME DISTRIBUTION (%)					MEDIAN HOUSEHOLD INCOME					2004 HOME VALUE DISTRIBUTION (%)					
#	POST OFFICE NAME	2004 Per Capita Income	2004 HH Income Base	Less than $25,000	$25,000 to $49,999	$50,000 to $99,999	$100,000 to $149,999	$150,000 or More	2004	2009	2004 National Centile	2004 State Centile	2004 Home Value Base	Less than $50,000	$50,000 to $89,999	$90,000 to $174,999	$175,000 to $399,999	$400,000 or More	2004 Median Home Value
45001	ADDYSTON	19320	330	27.3	33.6	28.5	7.6	3.0	40988	50586	50	33	192	20.8	33.9	27.1	14.1	4.2	84000
45002	CLEVES	24634	4484	16.2	29.1	37.7	12.1	5.0	53961	65887	78	75	3526	17.8	13.6	38.9	26.8	2.9	121498
45003	COLLEGE CORNER	27955	422	14.9	36.5	34.4	10.7	3.6	49045	55805	70	60	342	11.4	18.7	37.1	25.2	7.6	126744
45005	FRANKLIN	24437	11970	20.8	28.8	36.1	11.7	2.7	50365	60372	73	64	8556	1.9	13.7	65.4	18.0	1.1	129821
45011	HAMILTON	24039	20820	21.3	25.3	34.1	14.3	5.1	53845	64616	78	75	15259	12.1	17.9	33.2	33.6	3.2	149841
45013	HAMILTON	25319	20100	19.5	29.3	36.7	10.8	3.7	51147	61179	74	68	14942	5.2	15.3	55.8	21.4	2.3	124124
45014	FAIRFIELD	29405	17920	13.2	28.5	39.8	13.9	4.7	57506	67709	82	81	11712	3.8	10.2	61.1	23.7	1.3	142182
45015	HAMILTON	22148	5137	23.9	32.7	34.1	7.7	1.6	44724	53375	60	45	3569	6.8	28.9	56.0	7.7	0.6	99507
45030	HARRISON	23187	5726	18.2	27.9	40.2	10.5	3.2	52988	64232	77	73	4705	18.8	9.1	50.7	19.7	1.7	123770
45034	KINGS MILLS	42406	386	10.9	19.7	27.7	21.2	20.5	76170	97498	94	96	351	0.9	4.0	24.8	49.9	20.5	242130
45036	LEBANON	26216	11561	15.2	23.8	38.3	15.5	7.3	61627	74179	86	88	8204	1.3	3.4	44.5	43.3	7.5	176893
45039	MAINEVILLE	37570	6776	6.5	18.8	41.4	21.0	12.3	76175	89981	94	96	5474	0.8	1.8	45.9	46.7	4.8	177633
45040	MASON	34837	15316	8.0	16.3	39.3	22.8	13.6	80432	98812	95	98	13001	2.7	1.2	38.3	49.6	8.2	193503
45042	MIDDLETOWN	28323	11888	20.2	27.3	35.5	12.4	4.7	52586	62825	76	72	9177	7.7	13.2	50.0	26.5	2.7	131783
45044	MIDDLETOWN	22454	18447	25.9	29.3	32.0	9.5	3.3	45146	54318	62	46	11679	7.8	21.7	48.8	19.3	2.4	115544
45050	MONROE	29948	2538	7.5	24.7	47.9	14.3	5.6	65262	77841	89	92	2067	1.4	1.9	76.6	19.6	0.5	146228
45052	NORTH BEND	27325	1357	13.7	22.1	39.8	17.2	7.2	65653	79574	89	92	1167	6.9	18.2	26.1	41.7	7.1	171121
45053	OKEANA	28754	1151	9.6	19.8	45.6	17.1	7.8	67139	78504	90	93	1065	3.8	6.1	31.5	53.2	5.5	194935
45054	OREGONIA	29592	686	14.3	18.1	45.2	16.8	5.7	65810	78253	89	92	599	3.8	5.7	35.9	43.4	11.2	186270
45056	OXFORD	19793	8421	38.1	21.2	25.1	11.0	4.7	37517	44065	38	24	3879	6.2	5.4	46.9	37.6	3.8	158424
45064	SOMERVILLE	23372	840	14.5	25.7	42.5	14.6	2.6	59189	69310	84	84	732	5.1	10.4	45.2	35.5	3.8	154032
45065	SOUTH LEBANON	20889	1468	25.4	33.7	33.2	6.2	1.5	42431	51159	54	37	1113	31.2	19.7	37.6	10.0	1.6	88782
45066	SPRINGBORO	39018	6910	8.3	15.5	34.4	24.6	17.2	84760	102475	96	98	6235	0.2	1.7	31.9	56.0	10.3	219792
45067	TRENTON	23758	4336	14.9	25.6	44.4	12.8	2.3	58306	69323	83	83	3250	2.3	6.8	77.9	12.2	0.8	130057
45068	WAYNESVILLE	29607	4105	13.1	23.2	40.4	15.6	7.7	62898	75404	87	89	3497	4.6	5.3	41.9	41.2	7.1	171975
45069	WEST CHESTER	35730	17624	7.6	17.3	37.7	25.0	12.4	80915	95618	95	98	14273	2.9	6.3	35.9	50.5	4.4	184026
45101	ABERDEEN	19596	1077	35.2	31.9	26.5	3.9	2.5	35080	40513	28	17	789	38.0	19.9	34.4	6.7	1.0	75323
45102	AMELIA	24449	7510	20.9	24.1	39.8	11.4	3.8	54901	64767	80	78	5616	15.9	7.0	50.6	25.4	1.1	138617
45103	BATAVIA	24623	10666	18.1	25.5	39.3	12.7	4.4	55888	65950	81	80	7779	6.4	11.0	51.4	28.9	2.3	138592
45106	BETHEL	21918	4628	22.4	31.2	34.0	9.0	3.4	47494	55528	67	55	3676	10.2	16.1	52.8	18.6	2.4	117640
45107	BLANCHESTER	22723	3401	22.6	30.8	35.7	7.6	3.3	47218	54618	67	54	2691	6.0	17.2	55.3	18.5	3.1	115498
45111	CAMP DENNISON	31383	188	21.3	20.7	31.9	18.1	8.0	67901	85229	90	94	155	9.7	23.9	43.2	15.5	7.7	106500
45113	CLARKSVILLE	22593	1389	16.1	26.8	43.5	10.4	3.2	54734	64186	79	77	1199	6.8	13.5	47.5	27.7	4.4	138017
45118	FAYETTEVILLE	25386	1359	12.9	33.6	40.0	8.8	4.8	53171	60870	77	74	1205	7.6	13.4	53.0	24.5	1.4	123081
45120	FELICITY	16390	1300	33.1	30.0	30.3	5.4	1.2	38048	45368	39	25	958	23.5	22.8	39.3	11.4	3.1	94615
45121	GEORGETOWN	20075	3423	31.7	33.5	26.4	4.9	3.5	38111	43975	40	25	2620	12.5	25.5	46.8	14.2	1.1	104900
45122	GOSHEN	22511	4248	18.1	29.6	39.0	9.3	4.0	51897	60791	75	70	3537	16.1	14.5	48.5	18.7	2.2	113503
45123	GREENFIELD	18734	3088	31.6	33.2	29.1	4.2	1.9	39064	44304	43	27	2177	15.9	35.3	35.0	11.3	2.5	88684
45130	HAMERSVILLE	24981	1420	24.3	31.5	32.0	5.4	6.8	46022	52474	64	49	1193	13.8	21.0	46.8	16.4	1.9	108214
45133	HILLSBORO	19506	9432	32.5	32.3	26.9	5.8	2.5	37605	42761	38	24	7246	15.9	21.9	43.8	16.9	1.7	104234
45135	LEESBURG	19556	1693	21.9	32.4	39.1	5.2	1.4	46050	52155	64	49	1370	11.9	24.4	45.0	17.3	1.5	106442
45140	LOVELAND	36581	18749	9.5	19.8	34.7	19.5	16.5	76481	93005	94	96	15544	6.2	5.3	36.0	43.0	9.5	183206
45142	LYNCHBURG	19293	1712	23.3	35.0	32.7	6.7	2.3	44815	51211	61	45	1389	9.6	22.3	53.8	11.2	3.1	108455
45144	MANCHESTER	17118	1834	39.4	31.1	23.7	4.4	1.4	31934	36653	18	10	1418	31.1	31.3	29.6	7.1	0.9	74206
45146	MARTINSVILLE	21008	512	19.3	29.5	41.4	6.6	3.1	50760	57410	73	66	431	11.1	15.3	45.7	25.1	2.8	121558
45148	MIDLAND	19371	543	24.1	25.8	40.5	7.9	1.7	50059	56311	72	63	445	13.0	18.2	44.5	23.6	0.7	114224
45150	MILFORD	28212	12211	18.3	24.6	36.6	14.3	6.2	57634	67906	82	81	9223	7.5	7.1	53.0	30.1	2.4	142193
45152	MORROW	29127	3342	14.5	22.6	39.4	16.5	7.1	63308	76074	87	89	2832	4.2	4.9	44.9	37.1	8.9	167380
45153	MOSCOW	21165	809	25.7	30.2	32.3	7.2	4.7	45223	52987	62	47	674	18.6	18.3	43.9	15.6	3.7	106164
45154	MOUNT ORAB	20083	3131	23.9	30.6	36.5	6.5	2.5	46754	52678	66	52	2484	14.6	21.3	48.8	12.9	2.3	105755
45157	NEW RICHMOND	24275	3387	19.4	26.7	35.8	12.3	5.9	54217	64245	79	76	2766	19.5	12.0	36.4	27.3	4.9	125000
45159	NEW VIENNA	18302	1263	26.3	32.9	34.4	5.3	1.0	41980	48704	53	36	988	14.4	24.2	43.5	15.4	2.5	100599
45160	OWENSVILLE	24166	352	30.7	26.7	28.7	11.7	2.3	43726	51717	58	42	212	1.4	6.6	61.8	24.5	5.7	144595
45162	PLEASANT PLAIN	25442	1225	14.5	23.5	44.5	12.2	5.3	58711	69530	83	84	1081	4.8	13.4	45.8	32.2	3.8	140972
45167	RIPLEY	17315	1444	34.1	31.8	28.3	4.5	1.4	35862	41017	31	20	1079	20.6	30.0	39.6	8.5	1.3	89286
45168	RUSSELLVILLE	18528	586	28.2	32.9	32.1	6.5	0.3	37574	42627	38	24	484	15.3	30.6	37.6	13.0	3.5	95556
45169	SABINA	20214	1964	21.8	36.3	33.7	6.6	1.6	42898	49858	56	39	1493	13.3	27.1	46.3	12.0	1.4	97372
45171	SARDINIA	20041	2267	24.5	32.3	34.6	6.3	2.3	44246	50207	59	43	1904	11.5	24.1	47.8	15.7	1.1	108690
45174	TERRACE PARK	50536	724	7.5	9.8	24.9	24.3	33.6	112117	138269	99	100	688	0.0	0.0	11.8	48.8	39.4	344275
45176	WILLIAMSBURG	21805	3147	17.8	31.7	38.9	9.2	2.6	50419	58770	73	65	2558	7.4	18.3	51.9	18.9	3.5	117985
45177	WILMINGTON	22852	8576	24.3	29.9	34.7	8.1	3.0	45890	52625	64	49	5779	6.7	13.2	54.4	23.2	2.5	128887
45202	CINCINNATI	25809	7414	51.8	21.2	16.2	5.7	5.0	23271	29214	3	3	923	6.5	16.4	26.7	34.2	16.3	176815
45203	CINCINNATI	17028	1454	62.2	19.0	11.2	5.0	2.5	16479	20833	1	1	164	0.6	0.0	74.4	25.0	0.0	150595
45204	CINCINNATI	17042	2823	38.2	33.1	22.4	5.0	1.2	32524	40528	19	12	1099	23.9	51.2	19.6	4.6	0.7	66813
45205	CINCINNATI	17714	8577	38.0	30.7	25.0	4.9	1.5	33920	41748	24	15	3677	10.1	54.9	32.9	1.9	0.1	80806
45206	CINCINNATI	29073	6083	47.7	25.8	14.6	5.8	6.2	26501	32481	6	5	1687	8.7	27.3	38.5	14.4	11.2	108205
45207	CINCINNATI	14450	2563	47.2	27.3	19.5	3.9	2.2	26725	32049	7	5	1256	9.9	55.5	31.5	2.2	1.0	79592
45208	CINCINNATI	59339	9727	15.0	22.7	28.2	14.1	20.1	66708	87165	90	93	5308	1.7	6.2	24.8	46.4	21.0	238937
45209	CINCINNATI	34676	5367	26.2	28.8	28.5	11.9	4.6	45074	56450	61	46	2405	0.9	13.8	60.6	23.4	1.3	136697
45211	CINCINNATI	23910	16176	28.7	32.2	29.1	7.4	2.7	39697	48717	45	29	8381	1.7	16.9	72.0	9.1	0.4	113264
45212	CINCINNATI	22852	10262	30.6	32.9	27.0	7.3	2.2	38457	48028	41	27	5311	2.2	28.8	62.3	6.4	0.2	105567
45213	CINCINNATI	31049	5640	25.4	29.5	27.7	11.0	6.4	43940	55432	58	42	3459	1.7	14.9	62.4	18.3	2.8	125773
45214	CINCINNATI	14607	4437	57.8	25.3	13.4	2.1	1.4	19251	23444	2	2	1018	30.8	36.7	27.5	3.5	1.5	68125
45215	CINCINNATI	30850	12662	25.8	26.0	27.7	11.0	9.5	47869	59526	68	57	7332	4.3	21.9	45.9	21.3	6.6	123440
45216	CINCINNATI	21853	4189	32.3	33.3	27.0	5.2	2.2	36368	44498	33	21	2263	6.0	42.5	47.0	4.0	0.6	91149
45217	CINCINNATI	25148	2715	27.4	28.4	30.3	8.4	5.5	43984	55614	59	42	1740	6.4	19.0	57.3	14.3	3.0	112963
45218	CINCINNATI	31977	1625	14.7	32.9	32.3	13.2	7.0	53167	67356	77	74	1100	1.2	13.7	79.8	5.3	0.0	118766
45219	CINCINNATI	16762	6404	50.6	28.0	16.8	3.3	1.4	24652	28546	4	4	1411	8.4	37.6	44.6	9.3	0.2	93108
45220	CINCINNATI	27092	7243	44.2	25.3	16.8	7.0	6.6	29645	36728	12	7	2084	3.8	18.6	34.0	35.2	8.4	154193
45221	CINCINNATI	13080	315	63.5	21.3	13.0	0.6	1.6	17701	19813	1	1	11	0.0	0.0	100.0	0.0	0.0	112500
45223	CINCINNATI	18734	5824	37.7	33.3	21.7	4.7	2.6	32934	39501	21	13	2307	13.2	37.6	41.5	6.5	1.3	89394
45224	CINCINNATI	27848	9517	26.1	27.0	31.7	10.2	5.0	46494	57990	65	51	6132	2.5	17.5	63.7	15.3	1.1	117841
45225	CINCINNATI	11287	5493	60.9	26.9	9.2	2.5	0.4	17784	21076	1	2	1394	26.0	48.1	23.4	0.9	1.7	70543
45226	CINCINNATI	45065	2412	21.3	26.7	27.8	10.3	13.9	52772	67004	77	72	1412	7.2	12.5	34.1	27.9	18.3	167105
45227	CINCINNATI	32314	8345	24.1	29.7	29.9	8.2	8.1	46196	57088	64	50	5048	2.6	30.0	40.4	17.7	9.3	110598
45228	CINCINNATI	84173	184	8.2	15.8	20.7	14.7	40.8	116878	161292	99	100	165	1.8	17.6	16.4	16.4	47.9	361111
45229	CINCINNATI	19382	6981	49.5	24.1	17.2	5.1	4.1	25342	32242	5	4	2254	4.5	20.7	51.1	19.5	4.2	119500
45230	CINCINNATI	35142	11384	18.6	23.6	32.8	14.7	10.2	59395	74123	84	85	8093	0.4	5.9	61.7	26.7	5.3	143438
45231	CINCINNATI	26132	16679	17.5	27.7	37.8	11.7	5.3	54276	66815	79	76	12260	2.4	21.4	62.9	12.3	1.1	112280
45232	CINCINNATI	12627	2978	58.2	22.2	14.7	3.3	1.7	20130	24338	2	2	639	9.4	44.1	42.3	4.2	0.0	87115
45233	CINCINNATI	33916	5171	13.7	16.9	37.3	18.0	14.1	73144	89470	93	95	4441	1.5	7.0	36.8	47.2	7.5	187894
45236	CINCINNATI	30108	10524	21.0	30.6	32.4	10.0	6.0	48539	59518	69	59	7227	1.2	11.5	68.2	16.4	2.7	122708
45237	CINCINNATI	24952	9898	34.5	29.2	25.3	6.8	4.2	36434	44606	33	22	4986	2.8	26.9	55.8	11.0	3.6	106782
45238	CINCINNATI	26463	18455	20.0	29.3	35.5	10.9	4.4	50673	62385	73	66	12600	0.6	11.1	74.4	13.1	0.9	121424
45239	CINCINNATI	26223	11995	21.6	30.5	34.8	9.9	3.2	48266	59523	69	58	8175	2.6	17.4	71.8	7.9	0.4	115114
	OHIO	25510		24.6	28.1	32.2	10.1	5.0	47354	56168				9.2	18.6	47.0	22.1	3.1	121192
	UNITED STATES	25866		24.7	27.1	30.8	10.9	6.5	48124	56710				10.9	15.0	33.7	30.1	10.4	145905

# ZIP CODE	POST OFFICE NAME	FINANCIAL SERVICES: Auto Loan	FINANCIAL SERVICES: Home Loan	FINANCIAL SERVICES: Invest-ments	FINANCIAL SERVICES: Retire-ment Plans	THE HOME: Home Improvements: Home Repair	THE HOME: Home Improvements: Lawn & Garden	THE HOME: Furnishings: Comput-ers & Hard-ware	THE HOME: Furnishings: Major Appli-ances	THE HOME: Furnishings: TV, Radio, Sound Equip-ment	THE HOME: Furnishings: Furni-ture	ENTERTAINMENT: Dine out/ Carry out	ENTERTAINMENT: Sports Equip-ment	ENTERTAINMENT: Fees & Tickets	ENTERTAINMENT: Toys & Games	ENTERTAINMENT: Travel	ENTERTAINMENT: Cable TV	PERSONAL: Apparel & Services	PERSONAL: Auto Repairs	PERSONAL: Health Insur-ance	PERSONAL: Pets & Supplies
45001	ADDYSTON	78	68	66	67	69	78	76	75	80	73	98	87	73	96	74	81	93	77	80	85
45002	CLEVES	105	98	88	97	100	105	95	100	96	96	119	118	93	118	95	96	115	99	100	120
45003	COLLEGE CORNER	96	92	81	89	96	102	85	92	87	85	107	108	86	109	88	89	103	89	96	113
45005	FRANKLIN	88	86	82	84	87	94	85	87	87	84	107	101	85	109	86	87	103	86	89	101
45011	HAMILTON	93	96	97	96	95	99	95	94	93	95	117	110	96	118	93	92	114	94	90	105
45013	HAMILTON	87	90	91	88	91	98	88	89	89	87	110	104	90	113	90	89	107	88	91	102
45014	FAIRFIELD	98	100	109	104	99	103	102	100	99	102	124	118	102	123	100	95	122	101	93	111
45015	HAMILTON	71	74	77	72	74	79	74	73	75	73	93	84	76	96	75	75	91	73	74	82
45030	HARRISON	91	90	82	88	91	96	87	89	87	86	107	104	86	109	87	86	104	88	89	104
45034	KINGS MILLS	143	178	190	180	175	173	159	157	146	159	185	184	170	196	162	142	185	152	141	174
45036	LEBANON	104	109	107	110	108	112	104	105	101	104	126	122	105	127	104	99	123	104	101	119
45039	MAINEVILLE	141	152	141	157	148	146	138	140	130	143	164	164	141	165	136	124	161	136	125	158
45040	MASON	140	154	152	159	148	146	143	142	133	146	168	167	145	168	140	125	165	139	125	157
45042	MIDDLETOWN	96	99	100	97	100	107	96	98	96	95	120	113	98	122	98	97	116	97	98	111
45044	MIDDLETOWN	79	79	80	78	79	85	80	80	81	79	101	92	80	101	80	81	97	80	81	90
45050	MONROE	101	114	119	116	110	111	106	105	100	108	126	123	110	128	106	95	124	104	95	115
45052	NORTH BEND	116	113	100	110	116	122	106	113	108	106	132	132	106	136	108	109	128	110	115	136
45053	OKEANA	107	134	142	134	131	129	119	119	110	119	139	139	127	148	122	107	139	114	106	131
45054	OREGONIA	112	119	110	118	119	121	108	112	105	108	131	132	110	136	109	104	128	109	108	132
45056	OXFORD	74	65	76	69	64	70	84	72	81	77	101	92	77	97	76	75	98	79	67	81
45064	SOMERVILLE	108	95	71	90	101	109	88	98	94	88	114	117	85	116	91	97	108	96	108	128
45065	SOUTH LEBANON	94	68	37	61	75	85	66	79	76	67	90	94	58	85	66	80	83	78	93	108
45066	SPRINGBORO	151	177	182	180	172	171	161	159	149	163	189	186	169	195	161	144	187	155	142	176
45067	TRENTON	97	94	81	92	96	102	88	94	90	88	111	110	88	113	90	90	106	92	96	113
45068	WAYNESVILLE	117	118	105	115	121	125	108	114	108	108	133	135	109	138	110	108	129	111	115	139
45069	WEST CHESTER	135	154	161	159	149	148	143	140	132	145	168	164	148	170	141	126	167	138	123	155
45101	ABERDEEN	83	62	37	56	67	75	60	70	67	61	81	83	53	76	60	70	75	70	80	94
45102	AMELIA	95	97	90	97	96	99	92	94	89	93	111	110	91	111	91	87	108	93	89	108
45103	BATAVIA	96	96	92	97	95	98	93	94	91	94	114	112	92	113	91	88	111	94	90	109
45106	BETHEL	96	83	63	80	87	95	80	88	85	80	104	103	77	103	81	87	98	86	95	110
45107	BLANCHESTER	95	83	64	81	87	95	81	88	85	80	104	102	78	104	81	87	98	86	94	108
45111	CAMP DENNISON	95	115	127	113	113	116	107	106	102	106	128	122	114	137	110	101	128	103	98	115
45113	CLARKSVILLE	92	93	82	90	95	99	84	90	85	84	105	106	86	109	87	86	102	87	91	110
45118	FAYETTEVILLE	112	100	76	95	106	113	92	102	98	92	119	122	91	122	95	101	114	100	111	132
45120	FELICITY	79	63	41	58	67	74	60	69	66	61	79	81	55	77	61	68	74	68	77	90
45121	GEORGETOWN	78	68	54	65	71	80	68	73	72	67	88	84	65	88	68	75	83	72	80	88
45122	GOSHEN	100	89	69	85	93	100	83	91	87	84	107	108	81	107	85	89	102	90	97	116
45123	GREENFIELD	73	65	52	61	68	75	62	68	67	62	82	79	61	84	64	70	77	66	75	84
45130	HAMERSVILLE	128	90	46	79	101	114	86	105	102	88	120	126	75	115	88	108	110	104	127	147
45133	HILLSBORO	80	65	48	61	70	78	64	72	71	64	85	84	60	84	65	74	80	71	82	92
45135	LEESBURG	84	75	57	71	79	84	69	76	73	69	89	91	68	91	71	75	85	74	83	99
45140	LOVELAND	139	157	163	160	154	156	145	145	137	147	173	169	151	176	146	133	171	142	133	162
45142	LYNCHBURG	84	73	56	71	76	84	72	77	75	71	92	90	69	91	72	77	87	76	83	94
45144	MANCHESTER	76	52	24	45	58	66	50	62	59	51	70	74	43	66	50	64	64	61	75	87
45146	MARTINSVILLE	91	81	62	77	86	92	75	83	80	75	97	99	74	99	77	82	92	81	90	108
45148	MIDLAND	87	77	59	73	81	87	71	79	76	71	92	94	70	94	73	78	87	77	86	102
45150	MILFORD	97	106	109	106	104	107	101	101	97	101	121	118	103	122	101	94	119	100	94	112
45152	MORROW	112	115	106	112	118	123	106	111	107	106	132	131	109	138	109	108	128	108	113	134
45153	MOSCOW	107	77	42	68	85	97	73	89	86	74	101	106	65	98	75	91	93	88	106	123
45154	MOUNT ORAB	86	78	62	75	81	87	74	80	78	75	95	94	72	95	75	79	91	79	85	98
45157	NEW RICHMOND	107	100	84	97	103	109	94	101	97	95	119	118	93	118	95	97	114	99	104	123
45159	NEW VIENNA	78	71	55	68	72	77	67	72	69	68	84	85	64	82	67	69	81	71	75	89
45160	OWENSVILLE	85	66	45	63	72	84	71	78	79	68	93	88	64	89	70	83	85	78	92	95
45162	PLEASANT PLAIN	114	102	79	98	107	114	95	105	100	96	122	124	93	123	97	102	117	103	111	133
45167	RIPLEY	72	56	38	52	61	70	57	64	64	56	76	74	52	74	57	68	71	64	76	82
45168	RUSSELLVILLE	81	62	38	57	68	76	59	69	67	59	80	83	54	78	60	70	74	68	81	94
45169	SABINA	82	71	55	70	75	83	70	76	75	69	91	88	68	91	71	76	85	75	83	93
45171	SARDINIA	88	73	50	67	78	85	68	78	75	68	90	93	64	90	70	78	84	76	87	103
45174	TERRACE PARK	199	249	270	257	241	243	219	213	199	222	254	247	241	264	223	193	256	206	190	236
45176	WILLIAMSBURG	91	86	72	82	88	94	81	87	84	81	103	101	80	103	82	84	99	85	90	105
45177	WILMINGTON	81	78	73	78	80	86	78	80	79	76	97	95	77	99	78	79	94	80	82	94
45202	CINCINNATI	63	55	80	57	53	61	66	62	70	66	88	73	65	86	64	70	85	66	63	69
45203	CINCINNATI	44	37	51	37	36	42	46	43	50	46	62	50	45	59	44	50	60	47	45	48
45204	CINCINNATI	55	51	61	51	50	56	59	55	61	57	75	65	57	75	57	60	73	59	56	61
45205	CINCINNATI	59	56	66	57	56	61	64	61	65	62	81	71	63	81	62	64	79	63	61	66
45206	CINCINNATI	75	66	88	67	65	75	79	74	83	78	103	87	77	99	76	83	100	79	76	83
45207	CINCINNATI	56	50	58	46	48	57	54	54	60	56	74	60	55	70	54	62	72	56	59	62
45208	CINCINNATI	148	154	232	166	150	162	166	154	165	167	208	185	172	215	165	162	206	160	145	171
45209	CINCINNATI	78	76	109	82	75	81	87	80	86	86	109	98	87	110	85	84	107	85	75	89
45211	CINCINNATI	71	73	84	73	72	78	76	74	76	75	95	85	77	97	75	76	93	75	73	81
45212	CINCINNATI	67	70	79	69	70	75	73	71	73	71	92	83	74	95	73	73	89	72	70	77
45213	CINCINNATI	89	94	115	93	92	101	96	93	97	96	121	106	99	122	96	97	119	95	92	103
45214	CINCINNATI	46	38	47	37	38	44	46	44	50	46	61	51	44	58	44	50	59	47	47	50
45215	CINCINNATI	95	103	118	101	102	110	102	101	102	101	128	115	106	130	104	103	125	101	101	111
45216	CINCINNATI	66	65	71	63	65	72	70	68	72	68	89	78	70	91	69	73	87	69	70	75
45217	CINCINNATI	78	83	92	81	83	91	84	83	85	82	106	94	87	111	85	87	103	82	85	91
45218	CINCINNATI	102	112	127	114	112	116	114	110	109	111	137	130	116	141	114	106	135	111	103	120
45219	CINCINNATI	48	35	44	38	35	40	53	44	53	48	66	57	47	61	46	49	63	51	43	50
45220	CINCINNATI	70	56	79	61	54	63	77	66	78	73	98	83	71	93	70	74	94	74	64	75
45221	CINCINNATI	39	24	30	27	23	28	46	34	45	39	56	47	38	50	37	39	52	41	31	39
45223	CINCINNATI	60	56	67	54	54	61	62	60	66	62	81	70	62	80	61	66	79	63	62	67
45224	CINCINNATI	85	90	103	89	90	97	91	89	91	90	114	102	94	114	92	91	111	90	89	99
45225	CINCINNATI	38	32	40	30	30	36	37	36	41	38	51	41	37	49	36	42	50	38	38	41
45226	CINCINNATI	126	137	164	141	136	141	141	135	136	138	171	161	143	174	140	132	168	138	126	148
45227	CINCINNATI	96	102	123	102	100	108	105	101	104	104	130	119	108	132	105	102	128	103	98	111
45228	CINCINNATI	279	349	379	360	337	340	307	299	279	311	356	346	338	370	312	270	359	288	266	331
45229	CINCINNATI	58	52	64	50	51	60	59	57	63	59	78	65	58	75	58	65	76	60	62	65
45230	CINCINNATI	105	121	142	121	118	125	117	114	113	116	142	132	122	146	119	112	141	114	109	125
45231	CINCINNATI	89	97	106	96	96	102	95	94	93	94	117	108	98	120	96	93	115	93	92	104
45232	CINCINNATI	45	39	51	37	38	44	46	44	50	46	62	50	45	60	44	51	60	46	46	49
45233	CINCINNATI	128	147	163	148	145	151	140	138	133	139	168	159	147	171	142	131	165	136	130	151
45236	CINCINNATI	84	91	104	91	91	98	92	90	91	90	114	104	95	117	93	91	111	90	89	99
45237	CINCINNATI	74	70	88	69	69	79	77	74	80	77	101	84	78	99	76	82	98	77	77	83
45238	CINCINNATI	84	91	103	91	90	95	93	89	90	90	113	105	95	116	92	89	111	90	86	98
45239	CINCINNATI	83	87	93	86	87	93	87	86	87	86	109	99	90	112	88	87	106	86	86	95
	OHIO	89	88	90	87	88	95	88	89	89	87	110	103	88	111	88	89	107	89	90	102
	UNITED STATES	100	100	100	100	100	100	100	100	100	100	100	100	100	100	100	100	100	100	100	100

#	POST OFFICE NAME	COUNTY FIPS CODE	POPULATION 2000	POPULATION 2004	POPULATION 2009	2000-2004 ANNUAL RATE % Rate	2000-2004 ANNUAL RATE State Centile	HOUSEHOLDS 2000	HOUSEHOLDS 2004	HOUSEHOLDS 2009	% Annual Rate 2000-2004	2004 Average HH Size	FAMILIES 2000	FAMILIES 2004	% Annual Rate 2000-2004
45240	CINCINNATI	061	28654	27700	26658	-0.8	13	10623	10382	10097	-0.5	2.66	7825	7427	-1.2
45241	CINCINNATI	061	26532	26415	26269	-0.1	40	10679	10775	10843	0.2	2.41	7423	7269	-0.5
45242	CINCINNATI	061	21345	21337	20939	0.0	44	8140	8221	8148	0.2	2.55	5871	5758	-0.5
45243	CINCINNATI	061	15534	15330	14946	-0.3	31	5767	5724	5620	-0.2	2.63	4348	4195	-0.8
45244	CINCINNATI	061	25878	27246	28274	1.2	86	9175	9832	10400	1.6	2.77	7305	7661	1.1
45245	CINCINNATI	025	16357	17592	19245	1.7	91	6811	7521	8418	2.4	2.33	4455	4755	1.6
45246	CINCINNATI	061	14220	13851	13474	-0.6	17	6105	5990	5872	-0.5	2.27	3773	3541	-1.5
45247	CINCINNATI	061	20051	20306	20006	0.3	58	7442	7636	7609	0.6	2.66	5699	5673	-0.1
45248	CINCINNATI	061	23462	24095	23962	0.6	71	8953	9318	9374	0.9	2.58	6614	6686	0.3
45249	CINCINNATI	061	12145	12448	12433	0.6	70	4392	4534	4584	0.8	2.74	3349	3344	0.0
45251	CINCINNATI	061	23716	23584	23023	-0.1	38	8537	8584	8467	0.1	2.73	6499	6363	-0.5
45252	CINCINNATI	061	5178	5148	5017	-0.1	38	1989	2002	1973	0.2	2.57	1491	1457	-0.5
45255	CINCINNATI	061	22888	23702	24131	0.8	77	8968	9482	9855	1.3	2.49	6388	6536	0.5
45302	ANNA	149	3866	4141	4313	1.6	90	1300	1433	1529	2.3	2.89	1042	1123	1.8
45303	ANSONIA	037	2167	2115	2079	-0.6	20	816	816	821	0.0	2.59	633	620	-0.5
45304	ARCANUM	037	7819	7704	7605	-0.4	29	2919	2937	2959	0.1	2.62	2311	2279	-0.3
45305	BELLBROOK	057	9752	9947	10194	0.5	64	3579	3741	3926	1.1	2.63	2834	2906	0.6
45306	BOTKINS	149	2509	2531	2566	0.2	54	881	916	953	0.9	2.76	689	700	0.4
45308	BRADFORD	037	4900	4851	4802	-0.2	33	1771	1801	1820	0.4	2.69	1387	1381	-0.1
45309	BROOKVILLE	113	11989	12288	12311	0.6	70	4714	4886	4949	0.9	2.48	3456	3502	0.3
45311	CAMDEN	135	7468	7463	7493	0.0	43	2769	2844	2925	0.6	2.62	2151	2162	0.1
45312	CASSTOWN	109	1706	1695	1692	-0.2	37	628	640	649	0.5	2.65	501	501	0.0
45314	CEDARVILLE	057	5500	5703	5871	0.9	78	1239	1340	1432	1.9	2.69	895	942	1.2
45315	CLAYTON	113	4124	4183	4167	0.3	59	1492	1530	1541	0.6	2.72	1186	1190	0.1
45317	CONOVER	109	1074	1065	1063	-0.2	35	386	391	397	0.3	2.72	314	312	-0.2
45318	COVINGTON	109	5563	5554	5529	0.0	43	2096	2142	2164	0.5	2.55	1596	1594	0.0
45320	EATON	135	15412	15981	16372	0.9	78	5923	6275	6564	1.4	2.48	4364	4519	0.8
45321	ELDORADO	135	1074	1056	1055	-0.4	27	394	396	404	0.1	2.67	302	297	-0.4
45322	ENGLEWOOD	113	19883	20142	20055	0.3	58	7890	8111	8182	0.7	2.46	5718	5730	0.1
45323	ENON	023	5367	5144	4975	-1.0	8	2185	2152	2130	-0.4	2.34	1604	1535	-1.0
45324	FAIRBORN	057	39090	40044	41459	0.6	69	15771	16661	17750	1.3	2.25	9242	9360	0.3
45325	FARMERSVILLE	113	2630	2606	2565	-0.2	34	956	956	951	0.0	2.72	791	778	-0.4
45326	FLETCHER	109	1109	1091	1081	-0.4	27	406	410	413	0.2	2.66	328	324	-0.3
45327	GERMANTOWN	113	8081	8279	8296	0.6	69	3079	3200	3249	0.9	2.57	2398	2443	0.4
45331	GREENVILLE	037	23544	23650	23612	0.1	50	9548	9824	10036	0.7	2.33	6500	6500	0.0
45332	HOLLANSBURG	037	595	589	582	-0.2	33	227	230	232	0.3	2.56	185	184	-0.1
45333	HOUSTON	149	1402	1374	1372	-0.5	23	473	474	484	0.1	2.90	392	386	-0.4
45334	JACKSON CENTER	149	2099	2082	2085	-0.2	36	814	830	851	0.5	2.51	633	632	0.0
45335	JAMESTOWN	057	7228	7562	7850	1.1	83	2595	2780	2953	1.6	2.70	2074	2181	1.2
45337	LAURA	109	1707	1665	1650	-0.6	19	623	622	625	0.0	2.68	495	485	-0.5
45338	LEWISBURG	135	6158	6190	6228	0.1	50	2278	2347	2415	0.7	2.64	1767	1784	0.2
45339	LUDLOW FALLS	109	1623	1637	1641	0.2	53	606	627	639	0.8	2.61	485	492	0.3
45340	MAPLEWOOD	149	825	822	827	-0.1	41	293	299	308	0.5	2.75	241	242	0.1
45341	MEDWAY	023	3988	3970	3906	-0.1	39	1676	1721	1738	0.6	2.28	1151	1145	-0.1
45342	MIAMISBURG	113	31854	32955	33258	0.8	77	13143	13765	14057	1.1	2.36	8762	8853	0.2
45344	NEW CARLISLE	023	17839	17688	17402	-0.2	35	6570	6668	6693	0.4	2.63	5045	5002	-0.2
45345	NEW LEBANON	113	6751	6754	6690	0.0	45	2530	2563	2569	0.3	2.59	1930	1908	-0.3
45346	NEW MADISON	037	2239	2198	2167	-0.4	25	833	838	844	0.1	2.62	658	649	-0.3
45347	NEW PARIS	135	4201	4102	4088	-0.6	21	1616	1617	1648	0.0	2.50	1184	1156	-0.6
45348	NEW WESTON	037	1249	1228	1210	-0.4	27	394	398	401	0.2	3.09	315	312	-0.2
45356	PIQUA	109	25426	25192	25137	-0.2	34	10042	10201	10339	0.4	2.42	7015	6923	-0.3
45359	PLEASANT HILL	109	1874	1884	1885	0.1	50	690	708	718	0.6	2.66	563	567	0.2
45362	ROSSBURG	037	1202	1180	1163	-0.4	25	434	438	442	0.2	2.69	343	340	-0.2
45363	RUSSIA	149	1529	1555	1571	0.4	62	497	519	537	1.0	3.00	410	421	0.6
45365	SIDNEY	149	30520	30487	30680	0.0	43	11526	11796	12136	0.6	2.53	8238	8212	-0.1
45368	SOUTH CHARLESTON	023	4867	5039	5046	0.8	77	1832	1935	1976	1.3	2.58	1415	1461	0.8
45369	SOUTH VIENNA	023	3599	3632	3590	0.2	54	1329	1372	1385	0.8	2.64	1070	1082	0.3
45370	SPRING VALLEY	057	2304	2417	2513	1.1	84	867	929	988	1.6	2.60	677	712	1.2
45371	TIPP CITY	109	17364	17574	17643	0.3	57	6701	6930	7047	0.8	2.52	4988	5032	0.2
45373	TROY	109	32127	32468	32663	0.3	55	12613	13029	13277	0.8	2.44	8923	8987	0.2
45377	VANDALIA	113	15125	14703	14373	-0.7	16	6439	6334	6264	-0.4	2.29	4271	4069	-1.1
45380	VERSAILLES	037	5227	5258	5245	0.1	51	1895	1944	1978	0.6	2.66	1385	1386	0.0
45381	WEST ALEXANDRIA	135	5761	5716	5729	-0.2	36	2150	2184	2237	0.4	2.61	1688	1681	-0.1
45382	WEST MANCHESTER	135	1095	1076	1072	-0.4	26	410	414	423	0.2	2.60	311	308	-0.2
45383	WEST MILTON	109	7074	7080	7068	0.0	45	2835	2902	2935	0.6	2.44	2083	2080	0.0
45385	XENIA	057	36084	36671	37738	0.4	61	13437	13978	14735	0.9	2.50	9804	9979	0.4
45387	YELLOW SPRINGS	057	5743	5759	5847	0.1	48	2325	2384	2481	0.6	2.22	1452	1441	-0.2
45388	YORKSHIRE	037	1054	1027	1009	-0.6	18	358	359	362	0.1	2.86	288	284	-0.3
45390	UNION CITY	037	3934	3832	3764	-0.6	17	1489	1481	1486	-0.1	2.52	1088	1055	-0.7
45402	DAYTON	113	3205	3328	3394	0.9	79	1463	1567	1626	1.6	1.45	267	254	-1.2
45403	DAYTON	113	17859	16921	16387	-1.3	4	7381	7077	6933	-1.0	2.36	4168	3827	-2.0
45404	DAYTON	113	12424	12228	12089	-0.4	28	4944	4930	4934	-0.1	2.47	3177	3068	-0.8
45405	DAYTON	113	23601	23270	22968	-0.3	30	10552	10508	10482	-0.1	2.18	5483	5168	-1.4
45406	DAYTON	113	27251	26159	25481	-1.0	9	11229	10888	10721	-0.7	2.36	6782	6350	-1.5
45407	DAYTON	113	10560	9788	9388	-1.8	1	4146	3887	3774	-1.5	2.48	2441	2205	-2.4
45408	DAYTON	113	10735	9938	9538	-1.8	1	4277	4009	3897	-1.5	2.45	2744	2485	-2.3
45409	DAYTON	113	13987	13702	13513	-0.5	23	3281	3197	3151	-0.6	2.28	1586	1488	-1.5
45410	DAYTON	113	17871	17531	17269	-0.5	24	7861	7808	7784	-0.2	2.22	4139	3948	-1.1
45414	DAYTON	113	21547	21353	21095	-0.2	35	8862	8873	8866	0.0	2.40	6175	6010	-0.6
45415	DAYTON	113	12393	12229	12035	-0.3	31	5183	5188	5173	0.0	2.30	3396	3291	-0.7
45416	DAYTON	113	6641	6367	6192	-1.0	10	2472	2399	2360	-0.7	2.44	1680	1580	-1.4
45417	DAYTON	113	11171	10369	9952	-1.7	2	4556	4283	4158	-1.4	2.34	2768	2507	-2.3
45418	DAYTON	113	6973	6793	6659	-0.6	18	2254	2215	2188	-0.4	2.48	1556	1484	-1.1
45419	DAYTON	113	16673	17017	17087	0.5	65	7563	7853	8004	0.9	2.16	4298	4223	-0.4
45420	DAYTON	113	25715	24921	24344	-0.7	14	11956	11712	11569	-0.5	2.11	6584	6184	-1.5
45424	DAYTON	113	49220	49001	48598	-0.1	40	18477	18668	18771	0.2	2.61	13821	13635	-0.3
45426	DAYTON	113	16693	16754	16630	0.1	49	7161	7299	7346	0.5	2.27	4553	4470	-0.4
45427	DAYTON	113	11722	11349	11101	-0.8	13	4451	4349	4298	-0.5	2.53	3083	2931	-1.2
45429	DAYTON	113	26593	25927	25392	-0.6	19	11995	11826	11714	-0.3	2.17	7381	7024	-1.2
45430	DAYTON	057	6833	7140	7418	1.0	82	2507	2688	2863	1.7	2.58	1988	2086	1.1
45431	DAYTON	057	23255	23886	24448	0.6	71	9068	9455	9925	1.1	2.51	6390	6520	0.5
45432	DAYTON	057	15145	14892	14921	-0.4	27	6122	6131	6250	0.0	2.42	4400	4309	-0.5
45433	DAYTON	057	2836	2731	2756	-0.9	11	783	763	786	-0.6	3.21	777	757	-0.6
45434	DAYTON	057	9873	10146	10523	0.6	71	3531	3715	3948	1.2	2.67	2928	3033	0.8
45439	DAYTON	113	10046	9888	9725	-0.4	28	4400	4383	4361	-0.1	2.22	2733	2625	-0.9
	OHIO					0.3					0.7	2.44			0.0
	UNITED STATES					1.2					1.3	2.58			1.1

ZIP CODE #	POST OFFICE NAME	RACE (%) White 2000	White 2004	Black 2000	Black 2004	Asian/Pacific 2000	Asian/Pacific 2004	% Hispanic Origin 2000	% Hispanic Origin 2004	2004 AGE DISTRIBUTION (%) 0-4	5-9	10-14	15-19	20-24	25-44	45-64	65-84	85+	18+	MEDIAN AGE 2004	% 2004 Males	% 2004 Females
45240	CINCINNATI	45.9	41.9	48.0	51.4	3.0	3.6	1.4	1.4	6.9	7.1	7.8	7.4	7.1	28.8	25.0	9.4	0.7	73.7	34.8	47.8	52.2
45241	CINCINNATI	90.1	88.0	4.1	4.9	4.0	5.3	1.2	1.4	5.7	6.2	6.9	6.6	5.4	24.3	29.4	13.4	2.3	77.1	41.9	48.6	51.4
45242	CINCINNATI	90.2	87.6	3.3	4.0	5.1	7.0	1.0	1.1	5.4	6.3	7.9	7.1	5.4	22.4	29.2	14.3	2.1	75.8	42.3	47.5	52.5
45243	CINCINNATI	92.2	90.6	3.6	4.0	3.0	4.0	0.8	0.8	5.5	6.6	8.1	7.9	4.9	19.4	29.3	15.6	2.7	74.6	43.5	47.7	52.3
45244	CINCINNATI	96.8	96.2	0.8	0.9	1.1	1.5	1.0	1.1	7.4	8.0	8.9	7.0	5.1	27.0	27.7	8.3	0.6	71.2	37.1	49.3	50.7
45245	CINCINNATI	96.6	96.1	0.9	1.0	1.3	1.7	0.9	1.0	7.0	6.4	6.1	5.5	7.4	32.3	24.6	9.5	1.2	77.3	35.6	49.1	50.9
45246	CINCINNATI	70.3	66.7	22.7	25.1	3.2	4.1	4.0	4.4	6.2	5.8	6.1	6.3	6.2	27.1	24.0	14.5	3.8	78.1	39.4	46.6	53.4
45247	CINCINNATI	97.4	96.8	1.1	1.3	0.8	1.1	0.4	0.5	6.2	6.8	7.8	7.0	5.8	25.5	26.8	13.0	1.2	74.8	39.6	49.2	50.8
45248	CINCINNATI	98.4	98.1	0.4	0.5	0.4	0.5	0.5	0.6	5.6	6.1	7.7	7.3	5.8	25.0	25.0	15.7	1.9	76.1	40.5	48.1	51.9
45249	CINCINNATI	86.2	83.5	4.8	5.5	6.4	8.3	2.0	2.1	5.8	7.9	8.9	8.3	5.7	26.5	29.9	6.4	0.6	71.6	37.2	49.6	50.4
45251	CINCINNATI	86.2	84.1	10.4	12.1	1.1	1.5	1.3	1.4	7.1	7.2	8.0	7.2	6.6	28.7	23.7	10.4	1.2	73.3	35.7	48.5	51.5
45252	CINCINNATI	95.7	94.8	2.3	2.7	1.1	1.5	0.8	0.8	5.4	5.9	6.6	6.4	5.5	24.9	31.4	13.1	0.9	78.3	42.3	49.9	50.1
45255	CINCINNATI	95.8	94.8	0.9	1.1	2.0	2.7	1.1	1.3	6.6	6.7	7.5	6.7	6.1	25.8	27.0	11.7	1.9	74.9	39.1	47.7	52.3
45302	ANNA	98.4	98.0	0.2	0.2	0.7	0.9	0.4	0.5	7.9	8.3	9.4	7.0	5.5	29.4	22.7	8.6	1.1	69.9	34.5	50.9	49.1
45303	ANSONIA	98.9	98.8	0.1	0.1	0.1	0.1	1.0	1.0	6.4	6.7	7.9	7.3	6.3	27.3	26.3	10.5	1.3	74.6	36.9	49.6	50.5
45304	ARCANUM	98.4	98.3	0.2	0.3	0.2	0.3	0.4	0.5	6.5	6.8	7.5	6.8	5.9	27.7	26.6	10.8	1.4	75.1	37.8	50.1	49.9
45305	BELLBROOK	95.7	95.0	1.7	1.9	1.4	1.8	1.2	1.3	6.9	7.3	7.9	7.3	5.7	26.4	28.0	9.5	1.2	73.3	38.6	48.8	51.2
45306	BOTKINS	99.2	99.2	0.2	0.2	0.1	0.2	0.5	0.5	7.8	7.9	8.5	7.4	6.1	28.2	22.7	10.0	1.3	71.2	35.4	50.1	49.9
45308	BRADFORD	98.4	98.1	0.2	0.2	0.3	0.4	0.4	0.5	7.4	7.4	8.0	7.1	6.3	28.6	23.3	10.8	1.2	72.8	35.7	49.7	50.3
45309	BROOKVILLE	98.5	98.3	0.3	0.3	0.4	0.5	0.5	0.5	5.7	5.9	6.9	6.7	5.7	24.8	27.5	14.0	2.8	77.3	41.4	48.4	51.6
45311	CAMDEN	98.7	98.6	0.3	0.3	0.2	0.2	0.5	0.5	6.3	6.6	7.1	6.6	5.9	28.6	27.0	10.9	0.9	75.9	38.3	50.7	49.3
45312	CASSTOWN	99.2	99.0	0.1	0.1	0.2	0.2	0.5	0.5	4.8	5.4	7.1	7.4	5.9	24.3	31.7	12.3	1.0	78.2	41.8	50.7	49.3
45314	CEDARVILLE	95.4	94.8	2.0	2.2	0.7	0.9	0.7	0.8	3.6	3.8	4.4	20.9	27.7	17.0	15.5	6.6	0.6	85.6	23.1	47.6	52.4
45315	CLAYTON	91.2	89.4	6.1	7.4	1.1	1.4	0.6	0.6	5.6	7.5	8.4	7.6	4.1	24.9	29.0	11.5	1.5	73.4	40.5	49.1	50.9
45317	CONOVER	98.5	98.4	0.1	0.1	0.2	0.3	0.5	0.5	6.2	6.4	7.0	6.4	5.9	27.4	27.7	11.7	1.2	76.4	39.0	51.5	48.5
45318	COVINGTON	98.7	98.6	0.3	0.3	0.2	0.2	0.5	0.6	6.2	6.5	7.3	6.6	6.1	26.8	26.0	12.6	2.1	76.3	38.6	49.6	50.4
45320	EATON	98.3	98.1	0.5	0.5	0.4	0.5	0.5	0.5	6.8	6.6	6.9	6.4	6.3	26.8	25.0	13.1	2.1	75.9	38.5	49.2	50.8
45321	ELDORADO	97.5	97.4	0.8	0.9	0.0	0.0	1.0	1.0	8.1	8.1	7.5	6.3	5.4	27.9	24.9	10.5	1.4	72.5	36.7	49.7	50.3
45322	ENGLEWOOD	93.0	91.5	4.4	5.4	0.9	1.2	1.0	1.1	6.5	6.7	7.2	6.7	5.8	26.9	26.2	12.1	1.8	75.5	38.7	47.9	52.1
45323	ENON	97.0	96.4	0.8	0.9	0.6	0.8	1.0	1.2	5.6	5.9	6.1	5.9	5.8	25.5	29.1	14.7	1.6	79.0	42.0	48.7	51.3
45324	FAIRBORN	87.3	85.6	6.8	7.5	2.9	3.8	1.7	1.8	5.5	5.1	5.2	10.8	14.3	27.2	20.2	10.8	1.0	80.9	30.2	48.3	51.7
45325	FARMERSVILLE	97.6	97.2	1.5	1.8	0.3	0.4	0.4	0.5	6.0	6.6	7.6	6.9	5.5	26.7	28.5	11.2	1.1	75.6	39.8	49.4	50.6
45326	FLETCHER	98.4	98.3	0.5	0.5	0.1	0.1	0.3	0.4	6.8	7.0	7.3	6.3	6.3	26.8	27.2	11.2	1.1	75.0	38.0	50.2	49.8
45327	GERMANTOWN	97.3	96.9	1.9	2.1	0.2	0.3	0.6	0.7	5.8	6.3	7.3	6.9	5.4	26.8	28.8	11.4	1.5	76.3	40.3	49.8	50.2
45331	GREENVILLE	97.7	97.5	0.5	0.6	0.4	0.5	1.0	1.1	6.3	6.0	6.4	6.2	6.3	25.0	25.3	14.9	3.5	77.4	40.9	47.8	52.2
45332	HOLLANSBURG	98.0	98.0	0.7	0.7	0.0	0.0	0.3	0.3	6.6	7.3	7.3	5.9	5.8	27.0	27.5	11.4	1.2	75.2	38.1	52.8	47.2
45333	HOUSTON	98.3	98.0	0.4	0.4	0.1	0.2	0.4	0.5	7.5	7.8	8.1	7.0	6.3	28.8	24.4	9.2	1.0	72.4	35.9	51.0	49.1
45334	JACKSON CENTER	99.0	98.9	0.3	0.4	0.1	0.1	0.4	0.4	8.3	8.1	7.8	6.2	5.3	28.6	23.9	10.2	1.5	71.9	35.9	50.4	49.6
45335	JAMESTOWN	96.6	96.2	1.7	1.8	0.4	0.5	0.7	0.8	6.4	6.9	7.9	6.9	6.1	27.2	26.6	10.8	1.4	74.4	37.7	49.7	50.3
45337	LAURA	98.5	98.3	0.1	0.1	0.1	0.1	0.8	1.0	6.3	7.0	7.9	7.3	5.8	27.5	27.2	10.2	1.1	74.4	38.6	50.4	49.6
45338	LEWISBURG	98.7	98.5	0.1	0.1	0.4	0.5	0.6	0.7	6.3	6.6	7.7	7.0	6.0	27.2	26.3	11.7	1.2	75.1	38.6	50.0	50.1
45339	LUDLOW FALLS	99.2	99.1	0.1	0.1	0.1	0.1	0.4	0.5	5.8	6.1	6.4	6.6	5.5	24.1	30.1	14.0	1.5	77.7	42.2	50.3	49.7
45340	MAPLEWOOD	99.3	99.2	0.1	0.1	0.1	0.1	0.2	0.4	6.7	7.2	8.3	6.5	5.1	27.1	26.9	10.7	1.6	73.8	38.7	49.8	50.2
45341	MEDWAY	94.8	94.3	0.6	0.7	0.3	0.4	4.0	4.4	5.7	5.7	5.9	5.8	5.6	23.4	27.8	18.7	1.3	79.1	43.5	49.2	50.8
45342	MIAMISBURG	93.3	91.6	3.0	3.8	2.0	2.7	1.0	1.2	7.4	6.8	6.5	5.9	7.2	31.3	22.7	10.5	1.7	75.8	35.3	48.8	51.3
45344	NEW CARLISLE	96.7	96.2	0.3	0.4	0.3	0.4	2.1	2.3	6.4	6.4	7.5	7.1	6.8	26.6	26.1	11.8	1.3	75.3	38.0	49.1	50.9
45345	NEW LEBANON	94.6	93.8	4.1	4.7	0.1	0.2	0.6	0.7	6.7	6.8	7.3	6.5	5.7	26.1	25.9	13.2	1.9	75.1	39.6	48.8	51.2
45346	NEW MADISON	98.0	97.8	0.5	0.5	0.1	0.2	0.2	0.2	6.7	6.8	7.0	6.8	5.9	27.1	26.6	11.6	1.5	75.2	38.4	51.0	49.0
45347	NEW PARIS	98.7	98.6	0.4	0.4	0.2	0.2	0.2	0.2	5.8	6.0	6.8	6.8	5.7	26.2	27.0	14.3	1.5	77.3	40.4	50.2	49.8
45348	NEW WESTON	99.2	98.9	0.1	0.1	0.1	0.1	0.6	0.8	7.4	7.7	8.4	7.0	6.5	27.9	21.7	12.0	1.5	72.2	34.6	51.9	48.1
45356	PIQUA	95.0	94.5	2.9	3.1	0.4	0.5	0.7	0.8	6.8	6.6	6.9	6.8	6.9	27.1	24.3	12.4	2.1	75.4	37.2	48.5	51.5
45359	PLEASANT HILL	98.8	98.7	0.2	0.3	0.3	0.4	0.5	0.5	6.3	6.7	7.2	7.3	6.0	26.3	27.2	11.6	1.4	75.4	39.0	50.2	49.8
45362	ROSSBURG	98.8	98.6	0.1	0.1	0.1	0.1	0.9	1.1	8.1	7.8	8.0	6.8	6.5	27.7	22.5	11.3	1.4	72.0	34.6	50.9	49.1
45363	RUSSIA	99.2	99.1	0.1	0.1	0.1	0.1	0.5	0.6	10.4	9.9	8.7	6.5	5.9	28.5	19.9	9.1	1.2	67.0	31.8	50.2	49.8
45365	SIDNEY	94.4	93.6	2.2	2.4	1.5	2.0	1.0	1.1	7.4	7.2	7.6	6.6	6.6	27.6	24.2	10.7	2.1	73.7	36.2	49.3	50.7
45368	SOUTH CHARLESTON	97.0	96.5	1.4	1.7	0.3	0.5	0.3	0.3	6.8	6.7	7.5	6.8	6.2	26.6	27.5	10.7	1.2	74.7	38.0	49.4	50.6
45369	SOUTH VIENNA	97.4	97.0	0.7	0.8	0.2	0.2	0.7	0.9	7.1	7.4	7.3	6.1	5.2	28.9	27.8	9.4	0.9	74.6	37.7	49.7	50.3
45370	SPRING VALLEY	97.7	97.4	0.6	0.7	0.3	0.4	0.5	0.5	6.1	6.6	6.9	6.5	5.7	26.6	29.8	10.6	1.1	76.3	40.5	49.9	50.1
45371	TIPP CITY	97.9	97.6	0.2	0.2	0.6	0.8	1.0	1.1	6.2	6.4	7.4	6.6	6.0	25.3	28.5	12.2	1.5	75.8	40.4	49.2	50.9
45373	TROY	93.0	92.2	3.5	3.7	1.7	2.2	0.8	0.9	6.8	6.7	7.1	6.9	6.5	27.1	26.0	11.3	1.7	75.2	37.7	49.2	50.8
45377	VANDALIA	96.3	95.4	1.1	1.4	1.2	1.5	0.9	1.0	5.8	6.0	6.5	6.2	5.8	27.8	26.9	13.6	1.4	78.0	40.2	48.8	51.2
45380	VERSAILLES	99.4	99.3	0.0	0.0	0.1	0.2	0.2	0.2	7.5	7.6	8.1	6.9	5.7	26.8	22.8	12.2	2.5	72.5	36.6	49.6	50.4
45381	WEST ALEXANDRIA	98.5	98.4	0.2	0.3	0.2	0.3	0.2	0.3	6.1	6.4	7.4	6.7	5.9	26.8	27.8	11.5	1.3	75.7	39.1	50.4	49.6
45382	WEST MANCHESTER	98.8	98.8	0.0	0.0	0.1	0.1	0.6	0.7	6.3	6.7	6.9	6.5	6.2	28.8	27.0	10.0	1.5	76.2	38.2	50.7	49.4
45383	WEST MILTON	98.6	98.4	0.2	0.2	0.2	0.3	0.5	0.6	6.1	6.3	7.7	6.8	6.6	25.3	26.9	13.0	1.4	75.8	39.5	48.9	51.1
45385	XENIA	83.7	82.9	13.3	13.7	0.6	0.7	1.0	1.1	6.7	6.7	6.9	7.8	8.0	25.6	24.6	12.1	1.6	75.8	36.5	48.4	51.6
45387	YELLOW SPRINGS	82.5	81.0	10.8	11.7	1.2	1.6	1.5	1.6	4.1	4.7	5.9	8.1	9.3	20.7	29.9	15.0	2.4	81.6	43.0	45.7	54.3
45388	YORKSHIRE	98.8	98.5	0.2	0.2	0.4	0.5	0.5	0.5	8.6	8.3	8.5	8.1	6.3	26.0	20.7	12.1	1.5	69.6	33.7	51.4	48.6
45390	UNION CITY	96.6	96.2	0.9	0.9	0.3	0.4	3.0	3.3	8.3	7.8	7.0	6.5	6.3	26.4	23.6	12.7	1.5	73.2	36.3	49.2	50.8
45402	DAYTON	56.7	51.1	39.7	45.2	0.7	0.8	1.8	1.8	3.1	2.2	1.7	3.6	8.4	40.1	27.9	11.2	1.7	92.0	40.1	61.1	38.9
45403	DAYTON	89.7	88.0	5.5	6.6	1.2	1.4	2.3	2.6	7.8	6.9	6.8	6.4	8.6	32.2	21.5	8.9	1.0	74.8	32.9	50.9	49.1
45404	DAYTON	82.4	80.8	14.1	15.2	0.6	0.9	1.5	1.6	9.4	7.9	7.4	6.6	7.6	27.7	22.1	10.4	0.9	71.3	32.9	48.7	51.3
45405	DAYTON	47.0	42.5	48.5	53.0	0.5	0.6	1.7	1.7	7.1	6.7	7.5	7.2	7.9	30.0	22.9	9.3	1.4	74.5	34.5	47.9	52.1
45406	DAYTON	18.0	15.2	78.7	81.6	0.3	0.4	1.1	1.0	6.9	7.2	8.5	8.0	6.8	25.7	25.5	10.2	1.2	72.4	35.5	46.4	53.6
45407	DAYTON	4.7	3.9	92.9	93.8	0.2	0.3	1.0	1.0	7.0	7.5	9.3	8.8	6.9	23.9	22.8	12.6	1.4	70.8	34.7	45.4	54.6
45408	DAYTON	1.8	1.4	96.1	96.6	0.2	0.3	0.9	0.9	9.0	9.1	9.6	7.9	6.9	23.0	19.8	12.9	1.8	67.4	31.8	43.7	56.3
45409	DAYTON	93.6	92.4	3.4	4.1	0.9	1.2	2.0	2.3	2.7	2.6	2.7	19.6	40.7	13.3	11.6	5.6	1.2	90.3	22.7	49.6	50.4
45410	DAYTON	91.5	90.1	3.9	4.7	1.1	1.4	2.5	2.7	7.4	6.7	5.8	5.9	7.5	33.3	22.2	9.9	1.4	76.7	34.8	50.5	49.5
45414	DAYTON	87.9	86.4	9.5	10.6	0.7	0.9	0.9	1.0	7.2	6.1	6.4	6.7	7.0	24.2	27.8	13.2	1.4	76.5	39.9	47.7	52.3
45415	DAYTON	81.2	77.4	15.8	19.0	1.6	2.0	1.1	1.2	5.1	5.4	6.0	6.1	5.4	23.3	30.5	15.4	2.9	79.7	44.2	47.5	52.5
45416	DAYTON	38.6	33.6	58.8	63.7	0.2	0.2	0.7	0.7	5.5	6.5	7.2	6.4	5.3	23.1	24.6	16.5	4.9	76.7	41.9	42.9	57.1
45417	DAYTON	3.8	3.5	94.2	94.7	0.1	0.1	0.8	0.8	6.9	7.1	8.4	7.4	6.1	23.2	22.0	16.8	2.3	73.0	38.2	46.5	53.5
45418	DAYTON	41.3	38.3	57.0	59.9	0.4	0.5	0.8	0.8	5.5	5.6	5.9	6.6	10.7	29.2	22.0	13.2	1.3	79.6	35.6	55.4	44.6
45419	DAYTON	95.7	94.4	1.6	2.2	1.2	1.6	1.2	1.3	6.2	6.2	6.7	6.5	8.4	27.9	24.7	11.3	2.2	77.1	37.4	47.6	52.4
45420	DAYTON	95.7	94.9	1.7	2.1	0.9	1.2	1.2	1.3	6.2	5.9	5.5	5.2	6.2	31.2	23.6	13.9	2.4	79.4	38.7	47.6	52.4
45424	DAYTON	84.9	82.1	9.7	11.6	2.3	2.9	1.7	1.8	7.1	7.1	7.5	6.9	6.5	29.4	25.5	9.3	0.7	74.1	35.8	48.8	51.2
45426	DAYTON	32.9	28.8	63.9	68.1	0.3	0.4	0.9	0.9	6.2	6.1	7.3	7.0	6.7	24.7	26.4	13.1	2.6	76.1	39.4	45.7	54.3
45427	DAYTON	39.7	36.2	57.6	61.1	0.2	0.2	0.8	0.8	7.7	7.4	8.3	9.6	7.6	22.5	23.4	12.6	1.0	71.0	34.3	46.4	53.6
45429	DAYTON	95.5	94.5	1.1	1.3	1.9	2.5	1.0	1.2	5.4	5.5	6.0	5.8	5.5	24.0	26.1	18.2	3.4	79.6	43.4	47.2	52.8
45430	DAYTON	95.0	94.1	0.9	1.0	2.4	3.1	1.1	1.2	5.1	6.1	7.5	6.3	4.6	22.8	32.2	13.7	1.7	77.0	43.7	49.4	50.6
45431	DAYTON	88.3	86.0	5.4	6.2	3.4	4.7	2.3	2.4	7.5	7.1	7.4	6.6	8.8	29.2	21.7	11.0	0.8	74.2	33.5	49.0	51.0
45432	DAYTON	95.0	94.1	1.5	1.7	1.8	2.3	1.1	1.2	5.2	5.7	6.4	6.1	5.4	25.4	28.6	15.8	1.5	78.9	42.5	49.1	50.9
45433	DAYTON	80.1	78.2	12.6	13.7	2.2	2.8	3.4	3.7	13.6	12.1	9.5	7.5	8.2	41.0	7.8	0.3	0.0	60.8	24.4	53.2	46.8
45434	DAYTON	94.1	92.9	1.2	1.3	3.3	4.2	1.0	1.1	4.7	5.5	7.7	7.1	5.2	21.6	33.4	13.0	1.9	77.4	43.9	48.7	51.3
45439	DAYTON	90.9	88.9	4.2	5.2	2.5	3.2	1.4	1.5	7.5	7.1	6.4	5.7	6.3	32.4	21.4	11.5	1.7	75.5	35.1	48.5	51.5
	OHIO	85.0	84.1	11.5	11.8	1.2	1.6	1.9	2.1	6.7	6.6	7.1	7.0	7.1	27.5	24.7	11.6	1.8	75.6	37.0	48.6	51.4
	UNITED STATES	75.1	73.6	12.3	12.5	3.8	4.2	12.5	14.1	6.9	6.7	7.2	7.0	7.3	28.6	23.8	10.8	1.7	75.1	36.0	49.1	50.9

INCOME

#	POST OFFICE NAME	2004 Per Capita Income	2004 HH Income Base	2004 HOUSEHOLD INCOME DISTRIBUTION (%) Less than $25,000	$25,000 to $49,999	$50,000 to $99,999	$100,000 to $149,999	$150,000 or More	MEDIAN HOUSEHOLD INCOME 2004	2009	2004 National Centile	2004 State Centile	2004 Home Value Base	2004 HOME VALUE DISTRIBUTION (%) Less than $50,000	$50,000 to $89,999	$90,000 to $174,999	$175,000 to $399,999	$400,000 or More	2004 Median Home Value
45240	CINCINNATI	25670	10382	14.0	27.0	41.5	12.9	4.7	59414	71916	84	85	7369	0.6	12.6	73.3	12.9	0.7	123703
45241	CINCINNATI	40691	10775	12.8	20.2	31.5	18.7	16.7	73011	89772	92	95	8231	5.3	2.4	38.3	44.8	9.3	188608
45242	CINCINNATI	46016	8221	11.4	16.8	33.4	19.3	19.2	78936	99539	95	97	6677	0.8	4.6	34.4	50.0	10.2	203593
45243	CINCINNATI	60310	5724	11.8	16.5	28.3	16.1	27.4	83834	107513	96	98	5085	2.3	3.2	28.3	33.9	32.2	236776
45244	CINCINNATI	37423	9832	12.7	21.2	30.3	18.6	17.2	73332	88249	93	95	8049	0.4	5.3	41.3	45.1	7.9	183136
45245	CINCINNATI	29435	7521	17.1	26.8	38.4	12.1	5.7	55686	65789	80	79	4470	0.9	8.7	62.2	23.8	4.5	141522
45246	CINCINNATI	30821	5990	19.9	27.8	31.8	13.8	6.8	52332	64088	76	71	3565	1.5	8.8	67.7	15.6	6.3	125203
45247	CINCINNATI	33908	7636	11.7	22.3	35.5	18.2	12.3	68382	85467	91	94	6472	1.0	9.8	41.5	42.5	5.2	170694
45248	CINCINNATI	30606	9318	13.5	25.1	38.0	14.7	8.7	61676	75605	86	88	8023	1.6	7.8	60.5	26.5	3.6	140062
45249	CINCINNATI	51577	4534	8.2	15.1	29.4	19.6	27.7	93440	117559	97	99	3446	2.3	4.8	24.2	48.0	20.8	256886
45251	CINCINNATI	26021	8584	13.9	24.9	43.7	13.0	4.6	60359	73794	85	86	7003	2.0	22.2	63.5	11.9	0.4	112822
45252	CINCINNATI	37027	2002	11.9	19.7	33.5	22.2	12.6	73865	93824	93	95	1907	0.9	4.9	46.6	41.1	6.6	168229
45255	CINCINNATI	37412	9482	13.6	20.5	37.7	17.0	11.2	67371	81584	90	93	6966	0.6	5.0	50.0	36.7	7.7	167226
45302	ANNA	23608	1433	13.0	27.4	43.6	12.5	3.6	58476	66425	83	83	1233	3.0	13.7	57.1	25.0	1.2	129327
45303	ANSONIA	21867	816	21.5	33.5	36.5	5.2	3.4	45835	52708	63	48	659	13.2	27.8	44.8	12.3	2.0	98380
45304	ARCANUM	23935	2937	17.3	32.1	37.7	9.2	3.6	50502	58286	73	65	2418	2.9	13.2	57.2	24.4	2.3	132256
45305	BELLBROOK	34750	3741	11.5	17.5	38.5	22.2	10.3	75356	88163	93	96	3070	0.5	2.1	49.7	40.5	7.1	171990
45306	BOTKINS	23463	916	13.7	29.0	42.0	12.3	3.0	56809	64034	81	81	778	4.5	13.8	56.6	23.5	1.7	126606
45308	BRADFORD	20178	1801	18.4	35.7	36.9	7.2	1.8	46797	54348	66	52	1450	9.6	25.4	43.1	20.4	1.5	107920
45309	BROOKVILLE	24612	4886	20.9	28.2	34.7	12.9	3.4	50862	60319	74	66	3912	4.9	13.4	58.4	21.8	1.5	126413
45311	CAMDEN	21185	2844	21.0	33.4	36.3	7.6	1.7	46662	52291	65	52	2361	14.3	13.6	49.8	20.2	2.1	118223
45312	CASSTOWN	25089	640	13.4	27.8	41.4	13.8	3.6	58227	66159	83	83	555	2.7	12.4	48.3	33.5	3.1	149457
45314	CEDARVILLE	19053	1340	19.7	29.7	34.8	12.5	3.4	50445	60250	73	65	955	4.6	12.0	51.1	29.7	2.5	148467
45315	CLAYTON	31012	1530	11.3	18.6	42.0	19.0	9.2	70090	83113	91	95	1364	1.1	3.4	66.3	26.8	2.5	150771
45317	CONOVER	21359	391	15.4	37.1	37.6	7.4	2.6	48163	54161	69	58	327	11.3	21.7	44.0	20.2	2.8	118632
45318	COVINGTON	24217	2142	17.2	33.0	38.2	8.0	3.6	49810	57716	72	62	1715	5.4	14.2	59.9	18.5	2.0	121626
45320	EATON	21895	6275	20.9	31.8	38.7	6.8	1.8	47802	54534	68	56	4890	2.7	15.4	61.3	18.5	2.1	120079
45321	ELDORADO	18861	396	23.2	33.8	34.6	7.6	0.8	46491	52111	65	51	330	8.8	29.1	48.5	13.6	0.0	100431
45322	ENGLEWOOD	27581	8111	15.3	26.8	39.9	13.7	4.2	57578	68328	82	81	6515	1.1	9.5	76.4	12.3	0.7	123311
45323	ENON	28901	2152	13.1	30.4	38.7	14.5	3.4	57013	66799	82	81	1730	2.1	7.7	74.0	16.2	0.1	126053
45324	FAIRBORN	23137	16661	28.6	29.7	30.1	8.6	3.0	42823	51572	55	39	8943	4.7	24.2	57.7	12.4	1.0	111728
45325	FARMERSVILLE	25236	956	15.5	29.8	31.7	17.6	5.4	56695	67457	81	81	834	1.0	15.8	52.6	27.2	3.4	138859
45326	FLETCHER	25587	410	16.8	30.2	38.5	9.5	4.9	52404	60323	76	71	351	7.1	24.8	47.3	18.5	2.3	119133
45327	GERMANTOWN	28080	3200	14.7	27.2	38.3	14.0	5.8	59821	70555	84	85	2705	1.0	12.5	59.6	24.4	2.5	129585
45331	GREENVILLE	22698	9824	28.5	32.6	29.2	6.7	3.1	41582	47463	52	34	7209	8.4	21.9	53.3	14.6	1.8	112166
45332	HOLLANSBURG	21500	230	21.3	39.1	30.0	7.0	2.6	43645	49483	58	41	194	22.2	24.2	32.0	21.1	0.5	97000
45333	HOUSTON	21526	474	12.5	30.8	44.7	10.1	1.9	55805	62857	80	79	410	3.9	9.8	56.1	26.6	3.7	139167
45334	JACKSON CENTER	23090	830	21.1	26.3	41.0	9.2	2.5	51867	58469	75	70	675	8.7	18.5	53.0	17.8	1.9	115497
45335	JAMESTOWN	23697	2780	19.1	25.1	41.0	10.7	4.0	54341	64516	79	77	2338	4.0	17.4	60.2	15.7	2.7	120729
45337	LAURA	23363	622	12.4	34.2	40.0	10.9	2.4	52538	60190	76	71	533	4.7	18.2	55.2	20.6	1.3	123452
45338	LEWISBURG	22312	2347	18.6	30.5	39.2	10.1	1.7	50653	55499	73	65	1958	2.6	16.0	56.0	23.1	2.3	126087
45339	LUDLOW FALLS	23596	627	15.8	31.9	37.5	11.8	3.0	52206	60645	76	71	545	4.8	8.8	54.3	29.5	2.6	147068
45340	MAPLEWOOD	23451	299	15.1	26.1	44.2	11.4	3.3	59367	66403	84	84	269	7.1	14.1	53.5	23.8	1.5	124773
45341	MEDWAY	23180	1721	26.4	29.1	34.8	6.9	2.8	43364	49561	57	40	1433	33.4	27.2	33.4	6.1	0.0	78660
45342	MIAMISBURG	28349	13765	17.7	28.1	36.4	13.2	4.7	53941	64790	78	75	8907	6.9	15.6	57.4	19.2	1.0	129818
45344	NEW CARLISLE	22797	6668	18.3	32.4	35.6	10.7	3.1	49500	58188	71	61	5438	6.3	25.7	48.0	19.4	0.6	107350
45345	NEW LEBANON	23785	2563	18.8	30.8	39.1	8.0	3.4	50302	60045	72	64	2096	4.3	23.7	61.6	9.1	1.3	102737
45346	NEW MADISON	19897	838	25.2	31.5	35.3	6.0	2.0	44285	49910	59	43	709	9.0	26.5	46.1	16.6	1.7	106661
45347	NEW PARIS	19938	1617	25.1	33.6	34.8	5.7	0.9	41782	47651	52	35	1258	15.0	27.0	42.8	13.9	1.3	100000
45348	NEW WESTON	18965	398	23.9	32.9	36.2	5.0	2.0	43522	49640	57	40	333	9.3	19.2	46.9	16.2	8.4	120265
45356	PIQUA	22829	10201	27.1	30.9	32.1	6.8	3.1	43123	50920	56	39	7095	4.7	28.9	49.9	15.1	1.5	105170
45359	PLEASANT HILL	23598	708	12.9	31.2	43.6	10.0	2.3	54883	62584	80	78	595	1.0	8.9	64.7	22.4	3.0	140653
45362	ROSSBURG	20735	438	23.3	31.5	37.7	6.4	1.1	44793	50647	61	45	365	13.2	19.2	44.9	17.3	5.5	119612
45363	RUSSIA	25209	519	12.3	25.4	44.7	12.9	4.6	63009	73147	87	89	437	2.3	9.2	48.5	33.6	6.4	151359
45365	SIDNEY	23728	11796	21.7	32.0	34.8	8.1	3.5	47192	54068	67	54	8495	8.8	17.2	55.0	17.7	1.4	115372
45368	SOUTH CHARLESTON	24255	1935	18.8	28.3	39.3	11.0	2.6	52930	61225	77	73	1541	14.2	17.3	53.8	13.6	1.2	111352
45369	SOUTH VIENNA	25274	1372	15.2	26.9	40.6	14.0	3.3	56241	65210	81	80	1181	18.2	11.8	48.2	20.4	1.4	121304
45370	SPRING VALLEY	34353	929	14.8	23.6	33.3	16.4	12.1	64176	77069	88	90	825	18.1	8.5	29.3	35.3	8.9	146875
45371	TIPP CITY	30635	6930	15.5	25.7	37.1	13.6	8.1	58638	68543	83	83	5376	2.7	6.6	51.4	36.2	3.1	159493
45373	TROY	26785	13029	21.5	27.8	34.2	11.3	5.2	50657	59408	73	65	9237	1.9	11.3	58.0	26.1	2.7	134480
45377	VANDALIA	29756	6334	17.9	29.4	35.4	11.6	5.8	52458	63022	76	71	4563	0.4	9.8	63.8	23.5	2.5	135697
45380	VERSAILLES	23886	1944	21.3	27.9	37.8	9.9	3.2	50659	58096	73	65	1573	4.3	13.4	57.4	23.2	1.7	129441
45381	WEST ALEXANDRIA	23742	2184	18.6	31.2	38.0	9.2	3.0	50092	55300	72	63	1823	3.4	13.7	60.5	21.8	0.8	126241
45382	WEST MANCHESTER	20747	414	21.7	36.2	32.6	8.2	1.2	41622	47086	52	34	341	3.2	21.4	56.3	16.4	2.6	118223
45383	WEST MILTON	25503	2902	19.8	30.1	37.4	9.5	3.2	50104	57458	72	63	2198	4.5	10.8	62.1	20.9	1.7	124250
45385	XENIA	24056	13978	22.5	28.4	34.9	10.3	3.9	49068	59810	70	60	10277	3.5	25.8	48.6	19.6	2.4	112878
45387	YELLOW SPRINGS	33648	2384	17.4	23.5	33.2	16.1	9.8	61731	75340	86	88	1688	1.5	7.4	43.3	43.5	4.3	171523
45388	YORKSHIRE	20054	359	18.1	34.0	39.0	6.7	2.2	48531	54696	69	59	308	3.3	7.8	56.5	20.8	11.7	139286
45390	UNION CITY	19506	1481	31.8	34.7	28.3	2.7	2.5	37751	42776	38	25	1046	18.5	34.8	35.2	9.8	1.8	85584
45402	DAYTON	19338	1567	64.3	17.6	12.5	3.1	2.5	13362	16122	1	1	197	8.6	34.5	28.9	24.4	3.6	116964
45403	DAYTON	16847	7077	39.9	33.2	22.0	4.0	1.0	31366	37586	16	9	3606	20.2	60.6	18.8	0.5	0.0	70495
45404	DAYTON	17212	4930	43.6	29.9	22.4	3.0	1.1	29823	35653	12	7	2617	22.5	52.8	23.5	1.2	0.0	68015
45405	DAYTON	19655	10508	36.8	32.2	25.0	4.3	1.6	33530	39605	22	14	4867	10.7	59.6	27.1	2.6	0.1	76232
45406	DAYTON	19622	10888	36.6	29.6	24.7	7.4	1.7	35324	41600	29	18	6117	15.2	49.9	32.7	2.1	0.1	76248
45407	DAYTON	15557	3887	56.0	25.0	13.9	3.5	1.5	21388	24728	2	3	1848	37.9	43.8	16.5	1.7	0.2	57619
45408	DAYTON	12987	4009	57.1	23.6	15.3	3.0	1.0	20986	24024	2	2	1939	37.4	48.6	13.1	0.9	0.0	59294
45409	DAYTON	23472	3197	27.8	24.2	27.0	11.5	9.5	47014	56666	66	53	1846	1.1	10.7	54.0	28.1	6.1	139362
45410	DAYTON	19283	7808	37.6	29.2	27.4	5.1	0.7	34911	42074	27	17	4311	13.6	51.2	33.9	1.2	0.0	80566
45414	DAYTON	26245	8873	27.7	28.6	29.3	9.2	5.3	43618	52812	58	41	6246	12.2	25.1	40.7	19.2	2.9	108970
45415	DAYTON	31051	5188	17.2	24.5	36.1	15.1	7.0	59864	69502	84	85	3960	1.3	11.6	64.8	21.9	0.5	134426
45416	DAYTON	20888	2399	27.6	33.9	28.6	8.4	1.5	40490	47769	48	31	1775	10.0	56.1	33.1	0.9	0.0	76053
45417	DAYTON	16345	4283	51.4	29.7	15.0	2.4	1.6	24123	27735	4	3	2440	42.5	49.1	7.3	0.9	0.3	54191
45418	DAYTON	19385	2215	32.4	28.2	29.0	7.3	3.2	39467	47269	44	28	1599	12.3	38.9	40.1	7.7	1.1	88966
45419	DAYTON	40733	7853	20.8	23.6	31.5	12.7	11.4	56611	66863	81	80	5183	1.2	8.2	52.6	29.5	8.5	147598
45420	DAYTON	24364	11712	26.2	32.4	33.2	6.8	1.3	42617	51705	55	38	7569	2.0	40.0	56.8	1.2	0.1	93678
45424	DAYTON	25595	18668	14.8	26.6	41.1	13.6	3.8	57944	68421	83	82	14156	3.4	16.0	70.5	9.7	0.5	114217
45426	DAYTON	23262	7299	28.6	30.0	29.4	9.7	2.3	41880	49861	53	35	4328	4.1	27.8	63.0	4.9	0.4	103404
45427	DAYTON	15382	4349	45.6	29.6	18.1	5.3	1.5	27506	31758	8	5	2705	33.3	38.9	23.2	4.3	0.3	65485
45429	DAYTON	36473	11826	16.0	27.3	35.5	13.1	8.2	57649	67845	82	82	8469	0.6	6.7	66.0	23.1	3.6	141281
45430	DAYTON	34364	2688	8.2	19.1	39.6	23.9	9.2	77783	91760	94	97	2438	0.3	2.6	63.4	32.6	1.1	160538
45431	DAYTON	25190	9509	19.4	28.8	36.3	10.9	4.7	51538	62344	75	69	5492	4.9	21.1	50.1	22.5	1.4	116738
45432	DAYTON	28763	6131	16.4	26.4	36.8	14.5	5.9	57901	69204	83	82	5136	1.0	20.6	59.5	18.0	1.0	122179
45433	DAYTON	24871	763	4.7	29.8	52.7	9.6	3.3	58173	67134	83	82	11	0.0	9.1	45.5	45.5	0.0	170833
45434	DAYTON	39153	3715	7.2	12.3	40.4	25.6	14.5	85264	102932	96	99	3361	0.5	3.0	49.4	41.6	5.5	171887
45439	DAYTON	28902	4383	22.7	36.2	29.7	6.0	5.5	43586	52199	58	41	2804	15.8	33.6	43.3	3.7	3.6	90304
	OHIO	25510		24.6	28.1	32.2	10.1	5.0	47354	56168				9.2	18.6	47.0	22.1	3.1	121192
	UNITED STATES	25866		24.7	27.1	30.8	10.9	6.5	48124	56710				10.9	15.0	33.7	30.1	10.4	145905

ZIP CODE	FINANCIAL SERVICES				THE HOME						ENTERTAINMENT						PERSONAL			
					Home Improvements		Furnishings													
# POST OFFICE NAME	Auto Loan	Home Loan	Invest-ments	Retire-ment Plans	Home Repair	Lawn & Garden	Comput-ers & Hard-ware	Major Appli-ances	TV, Radio, Sound Equip-ment	Furni-ture	Dine out/ Carry out	Sports Equip-ment	Fees & Tickets	Toys & Games	Travel	Cable TV	Apparel & Services	Auto Repairs	Health Insur-ance	Pets & Supplies
45240 CINCINNATI	92	101	110	103	99	101	98	97	94	99	119	113	101	120	98	91	117	97	88	106
45241 CINCINNATI	132	150	166	152	149	154	142	141	135	142	170	163	148	174	144	133	168	138	132	156
45242 CINCINNATI	150	184	219	182	180	189	170	168	161	170	203	193	182	211	175	160	202	165	156	182
45243 CINCINNATI	202	250	308	248	246	261	229	227	217	231	273	259	248	283	239	216	273	222	214	247
45244 CINCINNATI	136	161	177	164	157	161	149	146	140	149	177	169	159	183	151	137	176	143	134	160
45245 CINCINNATI	95	98	107	101	97	100	99	97	95	99	120	116	99	120	97	92	118	98	90	109
45246 CINCINNATI	92	99	117	99	98	105	100	98	99	99	124	113	103	126	101	99	122	99	96	108
45247 CINCINNATI	116	139	153	138	137	141	129	128	122	128	154	147	136	160	132	121	153	125	120	140
45248 CINCINNATI	102	119	132	117	117	123	112	111	109	111	136	127	118	142	115	109	134	109	108	122
45249 CINCINNATI	191	214	245	223	208	214	204	198	193	206	244	232	214	249	203	187	242	196	181	220
45251 CINCINNATI	94	107	117	107	105	107	102	101	98	102	123	117	106	127	103	95	122	100	93	110
45252 CINCINNATI	129	149	152	148	149	150	135	138	128	134	160	161	141	169	138	126	158	133	129	157
45255 CINCINNATI	126	138	153	142	137	141	134	132	128	134	161	156	138	163	134	124	159	132	122	147
45302 ANNA	109	97	74	92	102	110	90	100	96	90	116	118	88	119	93	98	111	97	108	128
45303 ANSONIA	91	81	62	77	85	92	75	83	79	75	96	99	73	99	77	81	92	81	90	107
45304 ARCANUM	98	88	72	84	93	101	84	91	88	83	108	107	82	109	86	91	102	89	99	114
45305 BELLBROOK	123	145	152	147	141	142	133	131	124	134	156	153	140	161	134	119	155	128	118	145
45306 BOTKINS	104	92	70	88	98	105	85	95	91	85	110	113	84	113	88	93	105	92	103	122
45308 BRADFORD	87	76	58	73	80	87	72	79	77	72	93	94	70	94	74	78	88	77	86	100
45309 BROOKVILLE	87	87	85	85	89	95	85	88	86	84	106	102	86	109	86	87	103	86	90	102
45311 CAMDEN	93	76	52	70	82	91	71	82	79	72	95	98	67	94	74	82	89	81	93	110
45312 CASSTOWN	106	95	72	90	100	107	88	97	93	88	113	116	86	116	90	95	108	95	105	125
45314 CEDARVILLE	81	85	94	86	85	89	88	85	85	86	107	101	89	109	87	83	105	86	80	95
45315 CLAYTON	110	134	142	132	132	133	121	121	114	120	143	140	128	152	124	112	142	117	112	134
45317 CONOVER	93	83	63	79	87	94	77	85	82	77	99	101	75	101	79	84	94	83	92	109
45318 COVINGTON	98	86	67	84	91	99	83	91	88	83	107	106	81	108	85	90	102	89	98	113
45320 EATON	83	76	66	74	79	86	75	79	78	74	95	92	74	97	76	79	91	78	84	95
45321 ELDORADO	81	72	55	68	76	81	66	73	70	66	86	88	65	87	68	72	81	72	80	95
45322 ENGLEWOOD	93	102	103	101	101	105	97	98	94	96	118	113	99	122	98	93	115	96	94	109
45323 ENON	89	106	113	104	104	106	98	97	93	97	117	112	103	123	100	92	116	95	91	107
45324 FAIRBORN	71	70	81	71	69	75	79	73	77	75	97	87	77	96	76	75	94	76	70	80
45325 FARMERSVILLE	110	98	76	93	104	111	91	100	96	91	117	119	89	120	94	99	111	98	108	129
45326 FLETCHER	109	97	74	92	103	110	90	99	95	90	116	119	88	118	92	98	110	97	108	128
45327 GERMANTOWN	115	104	80	98	109	117	96	106	101	96	123	126	94	126	99	104	118	103	114	136
45331 GREENVILLE	79	73	67	71	76	83	73	77	77	72	94	89	72	95	74	78	89	76	82	91
45332 HOLLANSBURG	88	79	60	75	83	89	73	80	77	73	94	96	71	96	75	79	89	78	87	104
45333 HOUSTON	100	89	68	85	94	101	82	91	87	82	106	109	81	108	85	90	101	89	99	118
45334 JACKSON CENTER	93	83	63	78	87	94	76	85	81	76	99	101	75	101	79	83	94	82	92	109
45335 JAMESTOWN	91	94	89	93	96	101	89	92	89	88	110	107	91	114	91	89	107	90	93	107
45337 LAURA	100	89	68	85	94	101	82	91	88	82	106	109	81	109	85	90	101	89	99	118
45338 LEWISBURG	94	83	63	79	88	95	78	86	83	78	101	102	76	102	80	85	95	84	93	110
45339 LUDLOW FALLS	99	88	67	83	93	100	81	90	86	81	105	107	80	107	84	88	100	88	97	116
45340 MAPLEWOOD	103	92	70	87	97	104	85	94	90	85	110	112	83	112	88	93	104	92	102	122
45341 MEDWAY	77	77	72	74	78	84	73	76	74	73	92	88	74	93	75	75	89	75	79	89
45342 MIAMISBURG	95	92	100	95	91	97	96	94	95	96	120	112	96	118	94	92	116	96	91	106
45344 NEW CARLISLE	88	87	79	84	89	95	83	86	84	82	104	100	83	107	84	85	100	84	89	102
45345 NEW LEBANON	97	87	70	84	91	99	83	90	88	83	107	106	82	108	85	90	102	88	97	112
45346 NEW MADISON	84	74	55	70	79	84	69	77	73	69	89	91	67	90	71	75	84	75	83	99
45347 NEW PARIS	77	69	56	67	72	79	68	72	71	67	87	84	66	89	68	73	82	71	78	87
45348 NEW WESTON	100	80	52	73	86	95	75	87	83	75	100	104	70	99	77	87	94	85	99	117
45356 PIQUA	82	76	69	73	78	86	76	79	80	75	98	92	75	100	77	82	93	78	85	94
45359 PLEASANT HILL	100	89	69	85	95	101	83	92	88	83	107	109	81	109	85	90	102	89	99	118
45362 ROSSBURG	98	75	45	67	82	91	70	84	80	71	96	100	64	94	72	85	89	82	97	114
45363 RUSSIA	121	108	82	102	114	122	100	110	106	100	129	132	98	131	103	108	122	107	119	142
45365 SIDNEY	91	84	73	82	87	95	83	87	86	82	105	102	81	106	83	87	100	86	92	105
45368 SOUTH CHARLESTON	99	88	69	85	92	100	84	92	89	84	108	107	82	110	86	91	103	90	99	114
45369 SOUTH VIENNA	107	95	72	90	100	108	88	97	93	88	113	116	86	116	90	96	108	95	105	126
45370 SPRING VALLEY	127	138	135	138	136	141	127	129	121	129	152	149	131	151	128	119	150	126	122	147
45371 TIPP CITY	112	114	106	112	116	122	107	112	108	107	133	130	109	136	109	108	129	109	112	131
45373 TROY	92	95	96	94	95	102	93	94	92	92	115	109	94	117	93	92	111	93	94	106
45377 VANDALIA	91	101	108	101	101	105	98	97	95	97	119	113	101	123	99	93	117	96	93	108
45380 VERSAILLES	100	91	73	86	96	103	85	93	90	84	110	109	84	113	88	92	104	90	100	117
45381 WEST ALEXANDRIA	99	89	68	84	94	100	82	91	87	82	106	108	80	108	84	89	101	88	98	117
45382 WEST MANCHESTER	86	77	59	73	81	87	71	79	75	71	92	94	70	94	73	77	87	77	85	102
45383 WEST MILTON	101	85	63	82	91	100	82	91	89	82	107	107	79	107	84	91	101	89	101	116
45385 XENIA	84	88	92	87	88	95	86	87	86	85	107	99	89	109	87	87	104	86	87	97
45387 YELLOW SPRINGS	102	118	138	120	117	121	113	111	108	113	135	130	118	138	115	106	134	111	104	122
45388 YORKSHIRE	92	82	62	78	86	93	76	84	80	76	98	100	74	100	78	82	93	82	91	108
45390 UNION CITY	83	67	45	63	72	80	65	73	71	65	86	87	60	85	66	74	80	72	83	96
45402 DAYTON	33	31	42	32	31	36	37	34	38	35	47	40	36	47	36	38	46	37	36	38
45403 DAYTON	53	51	57	50	51	56	57	54	58	55	72	64	56	73	55	58	70	56	55	60
45404 DAYTON	59	54	57	52	54	61	59	58	63	57	77	67	58	77	58	64	74	60	62	66
45405 DAYTON	58	55	62	55	55	60	61	59	62	59	77	69	60	76	59	61	75	61	59	65
45406 DAYTON	63	60	70	57	58	66	64	62	68	65	84	70	65	83	64	69	82	64	66	71
45407 DAYTON	55	46	53	43	46	55	52	52	58	53	71	57	51	66	51	61	68	54	59	60
45408 DAYTON	45	38	44	35	37	45	43	43	48	44	59	47	42	54	42	50	56	44	48	49
45409 DAYTON	97	99	121	102	98	105	110	102	107	106	134	123	109	134	106	103	131	106	96	111
45410 DAYTON	57	55	63	56	54	60	62	58	62	59	77	69	60	78	60	61	75	61	58	64
45414 DAYTON	85	87	95	84	88	97	87	88	90	87	111	99	89	113	89	91	108	88	92	99
45415 DAYTON	93	108	122	107	107	111	103	102	100	102	125	118	108	129	105	98	123	101	97	111
45416 DAYTON	70	73	82	70	72	81	72	72	75	73	93	79	76	95	74	77	91	72	75	81
45417 DAYTON	56	46	49	41	46	56	51	53	58	52	71	56	50	64	50	62	67	54	61	61
45418 DAYTON	67	65	66	61	65	74	65	67	68	65	84	73	66	83	66	71	81	66	72	76
45419 DAYTON	115	122	148	127	121	127	129	122	123	126	155	146	130	156	126	119	153	126	114	134
45420 DAYTON	67	71	81	71	71	76	74	71	73	71	91	83	75	94	74	72	89	72	70	78
45424 DAYTON	90	100	106	101	99	101	96	95	92	96	116	111	99	119	96	89	114	94	88	105
45426 DAYTON	72	72	82	72	71	77	75	73	75	75	94	84	76	93	74	75	92	74	72	81
45427 DAYTON	55	49	52	45	48	57	53	54	58	53	71	59	52	67	52	61	68	55	61	61
45429 DAYTON	103	116	133	115	115	123	113	112	110	112	138	128	118	141	116	110	136	111	109	122
45430 DAYTON	118	140	153	140	139	141	129	129	122	129	153	150	136	159	132	120	152	126	120	142
45431 DAYTON	87	88	93	89	87	93	91	88	89	89	112	103	91	112	89	88	109	90	86	98
45432 DAYTON	90	105	116	103	104	109	99	98	96	98	120	112	104	125	102	96	118	96	95	107
45433 DAYTON	135	86	82	99	79	94	128	111	130	119	163	147	110	146	106	119	156	130	102	126
45434 DAYTON	137	168	185	169	166	170	152	152	142	152	179	174	163	185	157	140	178	147	141	166
45439 DAYTON	90	89	91	88	90	97	91	92	92	89	113	108	90	115	91	91	110	92	92	104
OHIO	89	88	90	87	88	95	88	89	89	87	110	103	88	111	88	89	107	89	90	102
UNITED STATES	100	100	100	100	100	100	100	100	100	100	100	100	100	100	100	100	100	100	100	100

OHIO

POPULATION CHANGE

A 45440-45776

# POST OFFICE NAME	COUNTY FIPS CODE	POPULATION 2000	2004	2009	2000-2004 ANNUAL RATE % Rate	State Centile	HOUSEHOLDS 2000	2004	2009	% Annual Rate 2000-2004	2004 Average HH Size	FAMILIES 2000	2004	% Annual Rate 2000-2004
45440 DAYTON	057	19839	20223	20422	0.5	63	8220	8510	8723	0.8	2.35	5584	5621	0.2
45449 DAYTON	113	20005	19972	19771	0.0	43	8788	8908	8937	0.3	2.21	5457	5331	-0.6
45458 DAYTON	113	25232	26049	26254	0.8	75	10177	10642	10869	1.1	2.43	7031	7130	0.3
45459 DAYTON	113	27341	27229	26941	-0.1	40	11607	11687	11693	0.2	2.25	7785	7591	-0.6
45502 SPRINGFIELD	023	17882	18220	18128	0.4	63	6819	7109	7225	1.0	2.53	5283	5401	0.5
45503 SPRINGFIELD	023	32498	32057	31428	-0.3	31	13498	13616	13624	0.2	2.29	8839	8591	-0.7
45504 SPRINGFIELD	023	19281	18925	18540	-0.4	24	7173	7149	7118	-0.1	2.42	4756	4612	-0.7
45505 SPRINGFIELD	023	21658	20628	19904	-1.1	6	8962	8711	8570	-0.7	2.35	5778	5428	-1.5
45506 SPRINGFIELD	023	16551	15627	15034	-1.3	4	6232	6003	5887	-0.9	2.52	4166	3887	-1.6
45601 CHILLICOTHE	141	55414	55434	55661	0.0	45	20442	20913	21380	0.5	2.40	14079	13998	-0.1
45612 BAINBRIDGE	141	5074	5281	5434	1.0	81	1833	1941	2029	1.4	2.70	1395	1444	0.8
45613 BEAVER	131	3627	3708	3831	0.5	67	1323	1386	1462	1.1	2.65	1009	1032	0.5
45614 BIDWELL	053	4478	4586	4622	0.6	69	1659	1750	1809	1.3	2.55	1220	1256	0.7
45616 BLUE CREEK	001	1740	1699	1684	-0.6	21	690	694	706	0.1	2.45	500	489	-0.5
45619 CHESAPEAKE	087	8200	8142	8123	-0.2	37	3291	3352	3427	0.4	2.42	2360	2335	-0.3
45620 CHESHIRE	053	1160	1144	1132	-0.3	30	456	460	465	0.2	2.49	339	334	-0.4
45622 CREOLA	163	559	548	545	-0.5	23	222	223	225	0.1	2.46	169	166	-0.4
45623 CROWN CITY	053	3589	3607	3609	0.1	50	1382	1425	1459	0.7	2.53	1070	1079	0.2
45628 FRANKFORT	141	4219	4285	4305	0.4	61	1595	1658	1694	0.9	2.55	1188	1203	0.3
45629 FRANKLIN FURNACE	145	3425	3355	3282	-0.5	23	1214	1224	1226	0.2	2.56	949	935	-0.4
45631 GALLIPOLIS	053	16028	15982	15906	-0.1	42	6467	6590	6701	0.4	2.33	4363	4317	-0.3
45634 HAMDEN	163	2041	2049	2081	0.1	49	753	773	799	0.6	2.59	564	565	0.1
45638 IRONTON	087	21606	21237	21154	-0.4	27	8864	8934	9121	0.2	2.33	6027	5910	-0.5
45640 JACKSON	079	14766	15065	15390	0.5	64	5792	6031	6284	1.0	2.47	4123	4184	0.4
45644 KINGSTON	141	3628	3755	3808	0.8	77	1351	1432	1478	1.4	2.59	1028	1064	0.8
45645 KITTS HILL	087	2841	2915	2949	0.6	70	1034	1088	1128	1.2	2.68	828	854	0.7
45646 LATHAM	131	347	354	365	0.5	64	131	137	144	1.1	2.58	101	103	0.5
45647 LONDONDERRY	163	1943	1959	1957	0.2	53	743	767	779	0.8	2.55	559	563	0.2
45648 LUCASVILLE	145	12884	12985	12923	0.2	52	4250	4399	4473	0.8	2.56	3246	3274	0.2
45650 LYNX	001	74	72	71	-0.6	16	31	31	32	0.0	2.32	22	22	0.0
45651 MC ARTHUR	163	5842	5978	6094	0.5	67	2220	2317	2399	1.0	2.55	1569	1594	0.4
45652 MC DERMOTT	145	3294	3315	3283	0.2	51	1211	1253	1271	0.8	2.58	923	931	0.2
45653 MINFORD	145	3874	3971	3964	0.6	70	1421	1493	1525	1.2	2.63	1100	1127	0.6
45654 NEW PLYMOUTH	163	859	846	842	-0.4	28	323	325	330	0.2	2.60	245	241	-0.4
45656 OAK HILL	079	6452	6512	6600	0.2	54	2511	2590	2677	0.7	2.47	1859	1870	0.1
45657 OTWAY	145	2612	2577	2529	-0.3	31	978	990	994	0.3	2.60	733	722	-0.4
45658 PATRIOT	053	2628	2654	2650	0.2	55	898	920	935	0.6	2.88	706	709	0.1
45659 PEDRO	087	3417	3517	3568	0.7	73	1220	1292	1345	1.4	2.72	949	984	0.9
45660 PEEBLES	001	8273	8588	8814	0.9	79	3007	3188	3336	1.4	2.66	2256	2337	0.8
45661 PIKETON	131	7329	7560	7830	0.7	74	2623	2766	2923	1.3	2.66	1963	2016	0.6
45662 PORTSMOUTH	145	31045	29968	29131	-0.8	12	13280	13075	12953	-0.4	2.21	8052	7651	-1.2
45663 WEST PORTSMOUTH	145	7065	6745	6510	-1.1	6	2762	2703	2667	-0.5	2.50	2066	1967	-1.2
45669 PROCTORVILLE	087	10256	10477	10598	0.5	66	4092	4297	4464	1.2	2.44	3079	3156	0.6
45671 RARDEN	145	455	462	459	0.4	60	184	192	196	1.0	2.41	131	133	0.4
45672 RAY	163	1888	2026	2134	1.7	90	721	792	849	2.2	2.56	547	585	1.6
45673 RICHMOND DALE	141	397	389	383	-0.5	23	166	168	169	0.3	2.32	125	122	-0.6
45675 ROCK CAMP	087	230	227	225	-0.3	31	82	83	85	0.3	2.73	66	66	0.1
45678 SCOTTOWN	087	1208	1248	1265	0.8	76	473	501	521	1.4	2.49	363	376	0.8
45679 SEAMAN	001	2729	2853	2934	1.1	83	1028	1100	1155	1.6	2.58	757	790	1.0
45680 SOUTH POINT	087	12696	12697	12714	0.0	45	4983	5134	5282	0.7	2.43	3626	3633	0.1
45681 SOUTH SALEM	141	1496	1626	1688	2.0	93	548	610	644	2.6	2.63	432	471	2.1
45682 SOUTH WEBSTER	145	2262	2221	2179	-0.4	25	849	855	858	0.2	2.60	637	624	-0.5
45684 STOUT	145	1556	1490	1448	-1.0	8	593	584	581	-0.4	2.55	429	409	-1.1
45685 THURMAN	079	1452	1489	1509	0.6	70	566	593	614	1.1	2.18	410	419	0.5
45686 VINTON	053	3027	2816	2724	-1.7	2	1128	1076	1064	-1.1	2.60	856	798	-1.6
45688 WATERLOO	087	450	509	541	2.9	96	177	206	225	3.6	2.47	126	143	3.0
45690 WAVERLY	131	14198	14568	15100	0.6	70	5586	5853	6187	1.1	2.45	3995	4085	0.5
45692 WELLSTON	079	9810	9999	10216	0.5	63	3726	3872	4032	0.9	2.55	2684	2718	0.3
45693 WEST UNION	001	8744	8744	8754	0.0	45	3401	3492	3578	0.6	2.45	2440	2441	0.0
45694 WHEELERSBURG	145	11759	11799	11691	0.1	48	4507	4634	4696	0.7	2.49	3384	3384	0.0
45695 WILKESVILLE	163	1042	1002	1001	-0.9	10	426	420	427	-0.3	2.38	316	304	-0.9
45696 WILLOW WOOD	087	1387	1447	1476	1.0	81	508	544	569	1.6	2.66	390	408	1.1
45697 WINCHESTER	001	4636	4746	4828	0.6	68	1686	1761	1824	1.0	2.68	1306	1332	0.5
45701 ATHENS	009	31496	31868	32329	0.3	57	10378	10760	11195	0.9	2.28	4707	4664	-0.2
45710 ALBANY	105	4567	4644	4718	0.4	61	1822	1900	1975	1.0	2.43	1298	1315	0.3
45711 AMESVILLE	009	1635	1629	1636	-0.1	41	639	652	670	0.5	2.50	457	452	-0.3
45714 BELPRE	167	9250	9218	9124	-0.1	42	4045	4119	4165	0.4	2.24	2697	2660	-0.3
45715 BEVERLY	115	2721	2635	2581	-0.8	14	1079	1073	1076	-0.1	2.42	744	718	-0.8
45723 COOLVILLE	009	4005	4044	4081	0.2	55	1566	1627	1684	0.9	2.45	1165	1178	0.3
45724 CUTLER	167	3055	3109	3108	0.4	62	1134	1184	1209	1.0	2.62	886	906	0.5
45727 DEXTER CITY	121	468	450	454	-0.9	10	181	179	184	-0.3	2.51	132	127	-0.9
45729 FLEMING	167	1232	1237	1227	0.1	49	456	468	473	0.6	2.64	363	365	0.1
45732 GLOUSTER	009	6425	6397	6406	-0.1	40	2535	2588	2651	0.5	2.45	1753	1733	-0.3
45734 GRAYSVILLE	111	1041	1001	971	-0.9	10	421	414	411	-0.4	2.41	324	312	-0.9
45735 GUYSVILLE	009	1218	1280	1316	1.2	85	469	506	532	1.8	2.53	346	362	1.1
45741 LANGSVILLE	105	1170	1188	1205	0.4	60	434	452	469	1.0	2.63	330	336	0.4
45742 LITTLE HOCKING	167	2818	2885	2899	0.6	68	1039	1092	1123	1.2	2.64	842	868	0.7
45743 LONG BOTTOM	105	1576	1669	1733	1.4	87	606	658	700	2.0	2.50	460	488	1.4
45744 LOWELL	167	1836	1804	1774	-0.4	26	723	726	728	0.1	2.48	527	515	-0.5
45745 LOWER SALEM	121	1653	1588	1561	-0.9	10	631	622	625	-0.3	2.53	462	444	-0.9
45746 MACKSBURG	167	439	433	428	-0.3	31	171	172	173	0.1	2.52	115	112	-0.6
45750 MARIETTA	167	26787	26485	26154	-0.3	33	10714	10820	10902	0.2	2.30	7080	6930	-0.5
45760 MIDDLEPORT	105	3701	3734	3790	0.2	54	1574	1621	1680	0.7	2.26	1003	1000	-0.1
45761 MILLFIELD	009	2638	2675	2707	0.3	59	1040	1077	1113	0.8	2.48	706	706	0.0
45764 NELSONVILLE	009	9943	9689	9656	-0.6	18	3706	3702	3780	0.0	2.34	2223	2130	-1.0
45766 NEW MARSHFIELD	009	1714	1813	1866	1.3	87	681	738	778	1.9	2.42	471	495	1.2
45767 NEW MATAMORAS	167	2728	2688	2647	-0.4	29	1099	1109	1116	0.2	2.42	797	782	-0.5
45768 NEWPORT	167	1661	1644	1622	-0.2	33	647	655	660	0.3	2.51	507	503	-0.2
45769 POMEROY	105	6166	6136	6228	-0.1	39	2479	2531	2632	0.5	2.37	1752	1743	-0.1
45770 PORTLAND	105	730	781	815	1.6	90	283	309	329	2.1	2.53	208	220	1.3
45771 RACINE	105	4089	4005	4034	-0.5	22	1639	1650	1705	0.2	2.43	1175	1151	-0.5
45772 REEDSVILLE	105	1854	1948	2016	1.2	85	738	794	838	1.7	2.45	541	567	1.1
45773 RENO	167	1554	1540	1520	-0.2	35	628	635	641	0.3	2.43	484	479	-0.2
45775 RUTLAND	105	1428	1536	1610	1.7	91	541	595	636	2.3	2.58	412	442	1.7
45776 SHADE	105	804	857	893	1.5	89	331	363	388	2.2	2.35	239	255	1.5
OHIO					0.3					0.7	2.44			0.0
UNITED STATES					1.2					1.3	2.58			1.1

POPULATION COMPOSITION

#	ZIP CODE POST OFFICE NAME	RACE (%) White 2000	White 2004	Black 2000	Black 2004	Asian/Pacific 2000	Asian/Pacific 2004	% Hispanic Origin 2000	% Hispanic Origin 2004	2004 AGE DISTRIBUTION (%) 0-4	5-9	10-14	15-19	20-24	25-44	45-64	65-84	85+	18+	MEDIAN AGE 2004	% 2004 Males	% 2004 Females
45440	DAYTON	93.6	92.4	2.5	2.9	2.3	3.0	1.1	1.2	5.3	5.6	6.6	6.4	6.6	24.6	27.1	15.7	2.2	78.6	41.7	48.3	51.8
45449	DAYTON	91.9	90.1	4.6	5.7	1.6	2.1	1.3	1.5	6.7	6.1	5.8	5.5	7.1	30.4	23.8	13.0	1.6	78.1	37.1	47.9	52.1
45458	DAYTON	90.5	88.4	3.7	4.5	4.1	5.3	1.3	1.4	6.4	6.9	7.6	6.4	5.4	27.3	29.1	9.6	1.3	75.1	39.1	47.9	52.1
45459	DAYTON	93.3	91.7	2.4	2.9	2.9	3.8	1.2	1.3	5.0	5.4	5.8	5.2	4.5	22.8	28.9	18.6	3.7	80.4	45.9	47.1	53.0
45502	SPRINGFIELD	96.2	95.6	2.1	2.4	0.4	0.5	0.6	0.7	5.3	5.8	6.8	6.8	5.8	24.6	31.0	12.5	1.4	78.0	41.8	49.6	50.4
45503	SPRINGFIELD	91.3	89.9	5.8	6.6	1.1	1.5	0.9	1.0	6.8	6.4	6.7	6.2	6.1	24.9	24.5	15.2	3.2	76.3	39.5	46.8	53.2
45504	SPRINGFIELD	93.3	92.4	3.6	4.2	0.8	1.0	1.0	1.1	5.7	5.7	6.2	9.5	11.8	22.8	24.1	12.1	2.1	78.7	35.7	48.1	51.9
45505	SPRINGFIELD	81.9	80.1	14.8	16.3	0.2	0.3	1.2	1.2	8.0	7.4	7.0	6.6	6.7	27.3	23.6	12.1	1.4	73.7	35.8	47.4	52.6
45506	SPRINGFIELD	56.7	54.7	39.5	41.4	0.2	0.3	1.1	1.1	6.8	6.6	7.7	7.7	6.6	24.6	24.2	13.3	2.6	74.0	37.9	47.7	52.3
45601	CHILLICOTHE	90.1	89.3	7.7	8.2	0.5	0.6	0.6	0.7	6.0	5.9	6.3	6.1	7.0	30.4	25.5	11.3	1.6	78.1	38.0	52.7	47.3
45612	BAINBRIDGE	98.3	98.1	0.5	0.6	0.1	0.1	0.6	0.6	7.1	7.1	7.8	7.0	6.8	28.4	24.6	10.2	1.0	73.6	35.7	50.2	49.8
45613	BEAVER	93.6	93.2	2.8	2.9	0.1	0.1	0.6	0.7	7.3	7.3	7.4	7.3	6.9	28.2	24.7	10.0	0.9	73.5	35.3	50.6	49.4
45614	BIDWELL	93.4	92.9	4.5	4.8	0.4	0.5	0.6	0.6	6.4	6.5	6.7	6.5	6.9	26.2	27.2	11.9	1.9	76.5	39.1	48.8	51.2
45616	BLUE CREEK	96.9	96.7	0.1	0.1	0.3	0.4	0.8	0.9	6.8	6.8	6.8	6.1	6.1	27.2	27.3	11.7	1.3	76.1	38.0	50.4	49.6
45619	CHESAPEAKE	97.9	97.7	0.9	1.0	0.2	0.3	0.6	0.6	6.2	6.4	6.5	6.3	6.1	28.5	26.3	12.3	1.4	77.1	38.6	48.8	51.2
45620	CHESHIRE	98.0	97.9	0.6	0.6	0.0	0.0	0.3	0.4	7.3	7.0	6.5	6.7	7.3	25.8	25.5	12.9	1.1	75.1	38.4	49.6	50.4
45622	CREOLA	98.9	98.7	0.2	0.2	0.0	0.0	0.4	0.4	6.4	6.4	7.5	8.2	6.8	27.6	25.6	10.6	1.1	74.8	37.1	51.3	48.7
45623	CROWN CITY	98.3	98.3	0.5	0.4	0.1	0.1	1.1	1.2	7.2	7.2	7.3	6.6	6.4	29.3	24.0	11.1	0.9	74.2	36.0	50.9	49.1
45628	FRANKFORT	93.6	93.2	4.3	4.5	0.1	0.2	0.4	0.4	6.3	6.5	7.0	7.1	6.4	26.8	26.7	11.4	1.6	75.5	38.3	50.2	49.9
45629	FRANKLIN FURNACE	95.6	95.1	2.7	3.0	0.1	0.1	0.5	0.6	6.2	6.0	7.2	10.8	6.1	24.7	26.6	11.4	1.0	73.1	36.3	51.9	48.1
45631	GALLIPOLIS	94.4	93.9	3.4	3.6	0.5	0.6	0.6	0.7	5.9	5.8	6.5	6.6	7.3	25.4	26.6	13.8	2.1	78.1	40.2	48.0	52.0
45634	HAMDEN	97.6	97.5	0.6	0.6	0.1	0.1	0.8	0.9	7.6	7.4	7.0	5.9	6.1	27.6	24.1	12.7	1.7	74.5	36.5	48.7	51.3
45638	IRONTON	95.8	95.4	3.0	3.2	0.2	0.2	0.5	0.6	5.9	6.0	6.7	6.6	6.2	25.4	26.1	15.0	2.2	77.5	40.1	47.4	52.6
45640	JACKSON	98.0	97.8	0.6	0.7	0.2	0.2	0.7	0.8	6.3	6.3	6.8	6.9	6.5	27.2	25.6	12.6	1.8	76.3	38.2	48.3	51.7
45644	KINGSTON	98.1	97.9	0.6	0.6	0.2	0.2	0.4	0.5	6.5	7.0	7.3	5.9	5.3	28.5	26.7	11.2	1.6	75.7	38.8	49.3	50.7
45645	KITTS HILL	98.9	98.8	0.1	0.1	0.1	0.1	0.6	0.8	6.7	6.6	7.4	7.0	7.1	29.8	25.0	9.7	0.9	75.2	35.9	50.0	50.0
45646	LATHAM	98.0	97.7	0.3	0.3	0.0	0.3	1.2	1.4	7.9	7.3	7.6	7.3	6.8	30.5	22.0	9.6	0.9	72.0	34.4	50.3	49.7
45647	LONDONDERRY	98.5	98.3	0.5	0.5	0.2	0.3	0.5	0.5	8.1	7.9	7.3	6.5	5.8	28.6	25.0	10.1	0.8	72.8	35.6	51.2	48.9
45648	LUCASVILLE	90.5	89.9	7.3	7.7	0.2	0.3	0.6	0.7	5.9	5.9	6.6	6.3	7.6	33.3	22.9	10.6	1.1	77.9	35.5	55.3	44.7
45650	LYNX	97.3	97.2	0.0	0.0	0.0	0.0	1.4	0.0	5.6	5.6	6.9	5.6	5.6	27.8	30.6	11.1	1.4	79.2	40.0	51.4	48.6
45651	MC ARTHUR	98.1	97.9	0.3	0.4	0.1	0.2	0.5	0.5	7.5	7.5	7.9	6.9	6.5	27.7	23.9	10.9	1.3	73.0	35.3	49.3	50.7
45652	MC DERMOTT	98.2	97.9	0.2	0.2	0.1	0.1	0.3	0.4	6.4	5.7	7.0	7.2	6.4	26.8	26.5	12.7	1.4	76.2	38.4	50.0	50.1
45653	MINFORD	98.7	98.5	0.0	0.1	0.1	0.1	0.5	0.5	6.5	6.6	6.9	6.6	6.4	27.8	26.5	11.2	1.5	76.0	37.8	50.2	49.8
45654	NEW PLYMOUTH	98.4	98.4	0.1	0.1	0.0	0.0	0.1	0.2	7.3	7.2	7.1	6.2	6.4	28.8	25.9	10.8	0.4	74.5	36.7	51.4	48.6
45656	OAK HILL	98.1	97.9	0.4	0.4	0.3	0.3	0.3	0.4	6.3	6.4	7.1	6.7	6.5	28.1	25.6	11.7	1.6	76.1	37.4	48.9	51.1
45657	OTWAY	97.0	96.7	0.0	0.0	0.2	0.2	0.7	0.8	6.7	6.7	7.5	6.8	6.8	29.6	23.3	11.6	1.0	75.0	35.6	50.6	49.4
45658	PATRIOT	97.9	97.7	0.6	0.6	0.1	0.1	0.5	0.5	7.8	7.7	8.2	7.2	7.3	27.5	23.3	9.9	1.1	71.9	34.6	51.2	48.8
45659	PEDRO	98.2	98.0	0.8	0.9	0.0	0.0	0.3	0.3	6.8	7.4	7.7	7.7	7.1	28.6	24.6	9.4	0.7	73.5	34.3	49.6	50.4
45660	PEEBLES	97.7	97.4	0.2	0.2	0.1	0.2	0.8	0.9	6.8	6.9	8.0	7.0	6.8	27.8	24.5	11.1	1.2	73.9	36.1	50.0	50.1
45661	PIKETON	97.6	97.3	0.5	0.5	0.2	0.3	0.5	0.5	7.1	6.9	7.5	7.1	7.0	28.9	23.5	10.9	1.3	74.3	35.5	49.0	51.0
45662	PORTSMOUTH	93.5	93.0	3.4	3.6	0.5	0.6	0.7	0.8	6.5	6.0	6.1	6.3	7.2	25.6	23.4	15.9	3.0	77.9	39.1	46.2	53.8
45663	WEST PORTSMOUTH	97.4	97.2	0.1	0.1	0.1	0.1	0.3	0.4	6.9	6.2	6.7	7.3	7.1	28.0	24.7	12.1	1.0	75.7	36.8	48.4	51.6
45669	PROCTORVILLE	98.2	97.9	0.5	0.5	0.4	0.6	0.5	0.6	5.5	5.9	6.8	6.3	5.5	27.1	27.9	13.7	1.3	77.9	40.5	48.9	51.1
45671	RARDEN	96.5	96.1	0.0	0.2	0.0	0.2	1.1	1.3	7.4	7.4	8.0	7.4	7.1	30.7	21.0	10.0	1.1	72.7	33.4	52.0	48.1
45672	RAY	97.0	96.8	1.1	1.0	0.2	0.3	0.6	0.8	6.7	6.9	7.6	7.6	6.3	29.2	24.9	10.0	0.9	74.1	36.0	52.3	47.7
45673	RICHMOND DALE	97.2	97.2	1.5	1.5	0.3	0.3	0.8	0.5	6.2	6.7	6.9	6.2	5.7	28.5	27.5	11.1	1.3	76.4	38.3	50.6	49.4
45675	ROCK CAMP	99.1	99.1	0.0	0.0	0.4	0.4	0.4	0.4	5.7	5.7	7.9	7.9	7.1	30.8	26.0	7.9	0.9	76.2	36.9	49.8	50.2
45678	SCOTTOWN	99.0	98.9	0.2	0.2	0.1	0.2	0.6	0.6	7.5	7.4	7.1	6.6	6.5	29.7	24.7	9.9	0.8	74.0	36.1	50.9	49.1
45679	SEAMAN	98.2	98.1	0.2	0.2	0.1	0.1	0.7	0.7	6.8	6.8	7.9	7.1	6.7	27.0	23.7	12.6	1.3	74.0	36.3	48.2	51.8
45680	SOUTH POINT	94.0	93.4	4.0	4.4	0.1	0.2	0.7	0.8	6.9	6.8	6.3	6.1	6.4	27.2	25.3	13.4	1.6	76.3	38.0	47.3	52.7
45681	SOUTH SALEM	98.0	97.8	1.1	1.2	0.1	0.1	1.1	1.2	6.1	6.4	7.7	7.4	7.0	28.0	26.5	10.1	0.9	75.1	37.0	51.5	48.5
45682	SOUTH WEBSTER	98.5	98.3	0.4	0.4	0.2	0.2	0.4	0.5	6.2	6.8	7.9	7.9	6.8	27.7	25.4	10.4	1.0	74.3	35.3	49.8	50.2
45684	STOUT	98.2	98.1	0.0	0.0	0.2	0.2	0.6	0.8	6.6	6.4	6.4	7.0	6.1	26.6	28.5	11.4	1.0	76.4	39.0	50.1	49.9
45685	THURMAN	95.8	95.4	1.6	1.7	0.7	0.9	0.6	0.5	6.5	5.8	6.3	10.7	15.7	23.9	20.6	9.5	1.1	77.7	29.2	50.0	50.0
45686	VINTON	96.9	96.6	1.2	1.3	0.1	0.1	0.5	0.5	6.6	6.8	6.9	6.6	6.5	28.5	26.6	10.6	1.0	75.7	37.3	50.8	49.3
45688	WATERLOO	97.8	97.8	0.9	1.0	0.0	0.0	0.9	1.0	6.1	6.1	6.3	7.5	6.9	27.7	26.1	11.8	1.6	76.8	38.4	48.7	51.3
45690	WAVERLY	97.0	96.7	0.8	0.8	0.3	0.4	0.5	0.6	6.9	6.7	7.3	6.6	6.5	27.1	23.0	13.4	2.6	75.1	37.2	48.2	51.8
45692	WELLSTON	97.8	97.6	0.5	0.5	0.2	0.2	0.7	0.7	7.3	7.1	7.4	6.8	6.7	27.7	23.6	11.7	1.7	74.1	35.8	48.3	51.7
45693	WEST UNION	97.7	97.5	0.3	0.3	0.2	0.2	0.6	0.7	6.5	6.6	6.9	6.6	6.1	27.6	25.1	12.6	2.0	75.9	37.8	48.3	51.7
45694	WHEELERSBURG	98.0	97.8	0.2	0.3	0.2	0.2	0.5	0.5	6.5	6.6	6.8	6.7	6.5	26.4	25.7	13.1	1.8	76.1	38.4	47.7	52.3
45695	WILKESVILLE	98.3	98.1	0.3	0.3	0.1	0.1	0.2	0.2	6.2	6.4	6.7	6.2	6.6	28.1	28.2	10.9	0.7	77.2	38.1	51.4	48.6
45696	WILLOW WOOD	99.3	99.2	0.1	0.1	0.1	0.2	0.5	0.6	7.5	7.3	7.3	6.7	6.4	28.7	25.0	10.2	0.9	73.8	36.5	50.3	49.7
45697	WINCHESTER	98.7	98.6	0.3	0.4	0.1	0.2	0.5	0.5	6.8	7.0	8.3	7.1	6.6	28.5	23.7	10.9	1.1	73.5	35.8	49.7	50.3
45701	ATHENS	91.0	89.6	3.1	3.3	3.4	4.5	1.3	1.4	3.4	3.0	3.2	17.1	33.6	18.6	14.6	5.8	0.8	88.3	23.5	48.1	51.9
45710	ALBANY	98.0	97.8	0.6	0.6	0.2	0.3	0.8	0.8	6.2	6.4	6.9	6.2	6.2	29.4	27.1	10.3	1.3	76.7	37.7	50.5	49.6
45711	AMESVILLE	89.5	89.2	6.0	6.1	0.1	0.1	0.6	0.6	6.0	6.9	6.9	7.2	6.6	29.1	26.7	9.8	0.9	75.6	37.4	49.4	50.6
45714	BELPRE	96.4	96.0	1.8	1.9	0.4	0.5	0.5	0.5	6.1	6.2	5.8	5.5	5.6	26.3	27.8	14.8	1.9	78.5	41.2	47.2	52.8
45715	BEVERLY	98.6	98.6	0.6	0.6	0.0	0.0	0.4	0.4	5.8	6.2	6.5	5.7	5.5	25.4	26.1	16.4	2.5	77.9	41.4	48.6	51.4
45723	COOLVILLE	98.4	98.2	0.5	0.5	0.1	0.2	0.4	0.5	4.9	5.5	7.3	6.6	5.3	27.0	28.7	13.2	1.5	78.1	40.9	50.6	49.4
45724	CUTLER	92.6	92.2	4.0	4.3	0.2	0.2	0.4	0.4	6.5	6.9	7.4	6.4	6.0	27.9	26.6	11.0	1.3	75.3	38.2	52.0	48.0
45727	DEXTER CITY	99.6	99.6	0.0	0.0	0.0	0.0	0.6	0.4	6.0	6.4	7.6	7.3	6.7	28.0	25.1	11.8	1.1	75.3	37.8	50.4	49.6
45729	FLEMING	98.1	98.0	0.4	0.4	0.1	0.2	0.3	0.4	6.9	7.1	7.0	6.5	5.7	25.6	28.9	11.2	1.1	75.0	39.3	50.4	49.6
45732	GLOUSTER	96.9	96.6	1.1	1.2	0.1	0.1	0.5	0.6	7.1	7.0	7.6	6.7	6.7	27.1	25.0	11.3	1.5	74.3	36.8	49.6	50.4
45734	GRAYSVILLE	99.3	99.3	0.1	0.1	0.0	0.0	0.5	0.6	5.3	5.7	6.5	6.3	5.9	25.0	29.6	14.1	1.7	78.6	41.8	52.1	48.0
45735	GUYSVILLE	95.6	95.2	1.5	1.6	0.4	0.6	0.6	0.6	6.2	6.9	7.8	7.0	5.7	27.5	28.0	9.8	1.2	74.8	37.8	50.6	49.5
45741	LANGSVILLE	98.0	97.7	0.3	0.3	0.1	0.1	0.9	0.9	6.1	6.0	6.4	6.4	6.7	26.9	28.6	11.9	1.0	77.7	39.5	50.2	49.8
45742	LITTLE HOCKING	97.0	96.7	1.3	1.4	0.3	0.4	0.6	0.6	5.5	6.0	6.9	6.5	5.5	26.9	29.6	12.1	0.9	77.6	40.7	50.2	49.8
45743	LONG BOTTOM	97.4	97.2	0.1	0.1	0.0	0.0	2.1	2.3	6.0	6.3	6.8	6.0	5.8	30.1	25.7	12.3	1.1	77.7	38.3	50.9	49.1
45744	LOWELL	99.2	99.1	0.1	0.1	0.4	0.5	0.5	0.6	6.3	6.8	8.0	5.5	5.8	25.7	25.8	14.5	1.6	75.4	39.7	49.8	50.2
45745	LOWER SALEM	98.8	98.7	0.1	0.1	0.1	0.1	0.4	0.4	6.1	6.4	6.8	6.6	6.2	26.5	27.2	12.7	1.6	76.8	39.5	51.2	48.8
45746	MACKSBURG	98.9	98.6	0.0	0.0	0.2	0.2	0.5	0.5	5.3	5.8	7.9	6.7	5.5	27.7	27.5	12.5	1.2	76.9	39.3	52.7	47.3
45750	MARIETTA	97.2	96.9	0.7	0.7	0.8	1.1	0.6	0.7	5.3	5.4	6.3	7.4	8.0	23.8	26.7	14.5	2.5	79.2	40.7	47.7	52.3
45760	MIDDLEPORT	96.4	96.0	1.8	1.9	0.1	0.1	0.7	0.8	6.0	5.8	6.8	6.5	6.9	24.8	24.9	16.0	2.4	77.5	40.3	46.8	53.2
45761	MILLFIELD	95.5	94.8	1.2	1.2	1.3	1.8	0.8	0.9	6.3	6.3	7.4	6.8	7.2	30.1	24.9	9.8	1.2	75.8	35.9	49.6	50.4
45764	NELSONVILLE	95.3	95.0	2.8	2.9	0.3	0.4	0.8	0.9	5.7	5.3	5.4	9.7	12.5	26.8	22.1	10.9	1.4	80.2	32.5	54.2	45.8
45766	NEW MARSHFIELD	98.3	98.1	0.2	0.2	0.1	0.2	0.2	0.2	7.0	6.9	5.9	6.4	7.7	29.3	26.6	9.3	0.8	77.2	35.8	49.8	50.3
45767	NEW MATAMORAS	99.0	99.0	0.2	0.2	0.1	0.1	0.3	0.3	5.7	5.7	6.5	6.4	6.0	25.3	27.4	15.3	1.6	78.1	40.9	49.1	50.9
45768	NEWPORT	99.8	99.8	0.0	0.0	0.0	0.0	0.3	0.4	6.0	6.3	6.5	5.8	5.4	29.3	27.7	11.9	1.1	77.6	39.3	49.5	50.5
45769	POMEROY	97.5	97.3	0.8	0.9	0.2	0.2	0.4	0.4	5.8	5.5	6.3	6.6	6.6	25.7	28.1	13.2	2.3	78.4	40.5	47.8	52.2
45770	PORTLAND	97.3	96.9	0.7	0.8	0.3	0.3	0.4	0.5	4.1	6.4	9.6	5.8	5.5	28.7	27.3	11.3	1.4	76.4	39.5	51.0	49.0
45771	RACINE	98.4	98.2	0.6	0.6	0.1	0.2	0.2	0.2	5.7	6.0	6.5	5.8	6.0	26.7	27.1	14.5	1.6	78.2	40.5	49.4	50.6
45772	REEDSVILLE	98.6	98.5	0.1	0.2	0.0	0.0	0.9	0.9	5.1	5.8	6.8	6.2	5.9	26.7	28.4	13.2	1.9	78.3	40.4	49.2	50.8
45773	RENO	98.8	98.6	0.3	0.3	0.3	0.4	0.4	0.5	6.2	6.4	6.5	5.7	5.1	28.1	28.2	12.8	1.1	77.4	40.5	49.0	51.0
45775	RUTLAND	98.4	98.4	0.2	0.2	0.1	0.1	0.8	0.9	6.0	5.7	7.8	6.7	6.4	26.6	28.0	11.7	1.1	76.8	38.7	49.9	50.1
45776	SHADE	97.8	97.4	0.6	0.7	0.1	0.2	0.6	0.5	6.3	6.3	7.0	7.5	6.8	28.6	26.7	9.5	1.4	75.7	37.1	50.4	49.6
	OHIO	85.0	84.1	11.5	11.8	1.2	1.6	1.9	2.1	6.7	6.6	7.1	7.0	7.1	27.5	24.7	11.6	1.8	75.6	37.0	48.6	51.4
	UNITED STATES	75.1	73.6	12.3	12.5	3.8	4.2	12.5	14.1	6.9	6.7	7.2	7.0	7.3	28.6	23.8	10.8	1.7	75.1	36.0	49.1	50.9

INCOME

#	POST OFFICE NAME	2004 Per Capita Income	2004 HH Income Base	2004 Household Income Distribution (%): Less than $25,000	$25,000 to $49,999	$50,000 to $99,999	$100,000 to $149,999	$150,000 or More	Median Household Income: 2004	2009	2004 National Centile	2004 State Centile	2004 Home Value Base	2004 Home Value Distribution (%): Less than $50,000	$50,000 to $89,999	$90,000 to $174,999	$175,000 to $399,999	$400,000 or More	2004 Median Home Value
45440	DAYTON	33376	8510	14.9	25.7	35.6	16.1	7.8	60831	72056	85	87	5939	0.5	5.2	58.5	31.7	4.2	161132
45449	DAYTON	27308	8908	19.8	30.3	35.6	10.6	3.8	49965	59453	72	62	5623	6.1	20.1	66.3	7.1	0.4	113714
45458	DAYTON	41236	10642	12.9	17.8	34.1	20.9	14.3	74799	89838	93	96	7938	0.5	6.5	38.1	47.5	7.4	185428
45459	DAYTON	40442	11687	11.5	22.5	34.8	17.9	13.2	67767	81259	90	94	8860	0.7	7.7	41.5	44.6	5.5	175214
45502	SPRINGFIELD	27671	7109	14.8	25.2	40.6	14.1	5.4	60534	69810	85	87	6105	12.3	8.4	53.2	24.9	1.3	135788
45503	SPRINGFIELD	24444	13616	24.8	30.7	32.0	9.5	3.0	45574	52476	63	48	9247	6.9	27.7	56.2	8.0	1.1	101681
45504	SPRINGFIELD	23826	7149	24.6	28.5	31.8	10.3	4.8	47272	54655	67	54	5037	11.8	21.6	47.9	16.5	2.2	109449
45505	SPRINGFIELD	18371	8711	36.8	31.2	25.8	4.8	1.5	33790	39811	23	15	5077	17.1	53.2	24.6	4.9	0.2	73348
45506	SPRINGFIELD	18490	6003	35.8	28.5	26.7	7.5	1.6	36443	42482	33	22	3846	16.7	47.8	28.9	5.8	0.8	75660
45601	CHILLICOTHE	21139	20913	29.2	30.6	29.9	7.4	2.9	41868	48150	53	35	15163	18.5	21.8	44.5	14.3	1.0	101234
45612	BAINBRIDGE	17016	1941	35.6	33.8	24.1	5.0	1.6	35421	40364	29	19	1521	33.1	24.0	32.4	8.8	1.7	77828
45613	BEAVER	18878	1386	32.5	30.7	31.0	4.6	1.3	37313	42442	37	23	1114	36.7	21.5	33.1	8.3	0.4	75789
45614	BIDWELL	17280	1750	40.2	28.6	23.4	5.4	2.3	33112	37825	21	14	1382	27.3	25.3	36.5	10.3	0.7	86602
45616	BLUE CREEK	15521	694	46.5	30.3	18.3	3.0	1.9	27901	31623	8	6	550	43.3	32.0	18.7	5.8	0.2	57115
45619	CHESAPEAKE	18750	3352	35.3	34.1	24.3	4.7	1.6	34542	39493	26	16	2572	24.7	31.7	37.1	6.0	0.6	82658
45620	CHESHIRE	17505	460	30.4	35.0	30.2	4.4	0.0	39719	45336	45	29	376	26.6	29.8	42.6	1.1	0.0	83684
45622	CREOLA	15995	223	39.9	34.1	20.6	3.6	1.8	30758	35362	14	9	186	26.3	31.2	34.4	7.0	1.1	83636
45623	CROWN CITY	15529	1425	40.3	35.8	20.1	2.8	1.1	29438	34097	11	7	1161	34.5	30.0	28.1	6.8	0.7	74069
45628	FRANKFORT	20857	1658	27.0	31.0	33.3	6.7	2.0	42315	48304	54	37	1297	13.0	23.8	49.2	12.9	1.2	103014
45629	FRANKLIN FURNACE	18022	1224	34.3	33.6	25.0	4.5	2.6	33745	38918	23	15	1005	18.5	35.3	36.9	7.8	1.5	84167
45631	GALLIPOLIS	20082	6590	36.7	30.5	23.9	6.2	2.7	35437	40443	29	19	4706	24.3	27.6	34.1	13.0	1.0	87568
45634	HAMDEN	14965	773	38.7	33.3	24.7	2.3	1.0	31788	35535	17	10	623	27.5	44.5	25.7	2.4	0.0	73141
45638	IRONTON	17124	8934	43.8	28.0	22.4	4.5	1.3	29759	33859	12	7	6375	26.6	42.8	26.7	3.7	0.3	71787
45640	JACKSON	17960	6031	36.2	31.1	26.8	4.5	1.4	34418	38939	25	16	4437	20.4	28.1	40.1	10.3	1.1	91903
45644	KINGSTON	24581	1432	21.1	28.5	35.2	11.5	3.7	50333	58101	73	64	1195	10.7	15.6	47.4	24.9	1.4	122897
45645	KITTS HILL	15639	1088	36.4	32.9	24.4	6.0	0.4	35000	39665	28	17	896	32.7	31.1	31.3	4.9	0.0	69224
45646	LATHAM	13898	137	46.0	33.6	17.5	2.9	0.0	28274	32968	9	6	109	51.4	25.7	17.4	5.5	0.0	49118
45647	LONDONDERRY	17508	767	29.5	31.9	33.6	4.4	0.5	39215	45326	43	28	632	30.4	24.8	38.9	4.6	1.3	77333
45648	LUCASVILLE	16809	4399	38.8	30.8	23.6	5.6	1.1	32984	38159	21	13	3584	30.5	27.2	31.7	9.9	0.7	77043
45650	LYNX	12604	31	51.6	32.3	16.1	0.0	0.0	23580	30000	4	3	24	54.2	33.3	12.5	0.0	0.0	45000
45651	MC ARTHUR	16072	2317	40.2	31.3	23.0	3.6	1.9	31888	35793	17	10	1734	25.8	34.5	31.5	7.7	0.5	77798
45652	MC DERMOTT	20144	1253	39.4	31.8	20.8	4.1	3.9	32329	37299	19	11	1010	36.3	31.6	24.8	5.9	1.4	66989
45653	MINFORD	17968	1493	32.2	29.3	30.8	6.7	0.9	39466	45307	44	28	1257	21.6	27.1	39.0	11.2	1.1	91618
45654	NEW PLYMOUTH	15741	325	34.5	35.1	26.2	3.1	1.2	35272	39743	29	18	265	34.7	25.7	30.2	7.6	1.9	73056
45656	OAK HILL	16573	2590	39.1	33.8	22.5	2.9	1.7	32082	36403	18	11	2041	33.0	30.9	26.5	9.1	0.5	68430
45657	OTWAY	16801	990	37.8	31.3	23.4	5.1	2.4	35000	40000	28	17	805	34.3	35.3	24.4	6.0	0.1	64104
45658	PATRIOT	15182	920	37.7	32.9	22.3	5.0	2.1	33062	37824	21	13	766	29.5	24.5	36.7	8.4	0.9	84464
45659	PEDRO	13065	1292	44.5	30.3	21.9	3.2	0.1	29065	33149	10	6	1044	42.3	33.1	21.9	2.0	0.6	61083
45660	PEEBLES	15730	3188	41.8	29.6	23.4	4.2	1.1	31058	35892	15	9	2475	32.1	30.4	27.7	8.9	0.9	74621
45661	PIKETON	18519	2766	37.8	29.9	24.9	5.0	2.4	35060	40012	28	17	2174	30.7	25.0	33.3	10.4	0.7	81338
45662	PORTSMOUTH	19125	13075	45.9	27.6	19.7	4.1	2.7	27773	31831	8	6	7822	30.8	37.0	26.2	5.7	0.3	68153
45663	WEST PORTSMOUTH	15993	2703	39.0	33.0	22.5	4.6	0.9	31769	36457	17	10	2037	45.2	33.5	16.0	5.0	0.3	54690
45669	PROCTORVILLE	19957	4297	31.3	33.9	26.7	5.2	2.9	37573	42761	38	24	3525	19.6	23.4	45.2	10.6	1.3	97360
45671	RARDEN	16330	192	40.1	31.3	25.5	2.1	1.0	31497	35957	16	9	151	37.8	33.1	23.8	5.3	0.0	61786
45672	RAY	16978	792	31.8	36.6	26.9	3.7	1.0	36431	40987	33	22	656	32.9	25.3	31.9	9.6	0.3	71463
45673	RICHMOND DALE	22490	168	27.4	39.3	20.8	7.1	5.4	41130	46904	50	33	135	20.7	23.7	38.5	17.0	0.0	93261
45675	ROCK CAMP	17153	83	34.9	25.3	32.5	6.0	1.2	38618	43627	41	27	68	30.9	39.7	27.9	1.5	0.0	65556
45678	SCOTTOWN	15856	501	41.3	30.5	23.8	3.4	1.0	32785	37261	20	12	409	37.7	19.1	31.5	10.5	1.2	75417
45679	SEAMAN	16835	1100	35.8	30.3	29.2	3.9	0.8	35397	40576	29	19	867	16.3	34.3	36.3	10.6	2.5	89444
45680	SOUTH POINT	16826	5134	39.6	32.1	23.2	3.8	1.3	32336	36823	19	11	3759	21.4	39.2	34.4	4.5	0.5	78903
45681	SOUTH SALEM	18625	610	27.5	31.8	33.6	5.1	2.0	41653	47784	52	35	513	21.4	26.5	37.0	12.9	2.1	94038
45682	SOUTH WEBSTER	14650	855	38.6	34.6	23.6	2.8	0.4	32876	37631	21	13	684	33.0	31.3	27.2	8.0	0.4	70385
45684	STOUT	17984	584	42.5	32.4	17.5	4.8	2.9	30544	35215	14	8	482	39.6	27.2	21.0	11.0	1.2	63548
45685	THURMAN	20157	593	40.1	30.2	22.8	5.2	1.7	32562	36928	19	12	434	29.7	24.4	29.3	14.3	2.3	81818
45686	VINTON	16149	1076	39.6	33.1	20.9	5.0	1.4	33398	38065	22	14	903	39.2	29.7	24.4	6.8	0.0	65667
45688	WATERLOO	12575	206	49.0	32.0	16.5	2.4	0.0	25733	29161	5	4	159	45.3	15.7	28.3	10.7	0.0	57500
45690	WAVERLY	20137	5853	33.3	30.2	27.2	7.1	2.2	38306	43972	40	26	4138	18.9	28.5	39.9	12.3	0.4	92494
45692	WELLSTON	15648	3872	36.8	34.6	25.0	3.2	0.4	34533	38850	26	16	2837	31.8	31.7	30.4	6.0	0.2	68503
45693	WEST UNION	17700	3492	36.9	31.1	25.1	5.3	1.6	33699	38572	23	15	2657	19.8	35.9	32.1	11.8	0.3	83900
45694	WHEELERSBURG	20726	4634	32.8	30.6	28.3	5.5	2.8	37456	43417	37	24	3555	19.6	28.8	40.1	10.5	1.0	91785
45695	WILKESVILLE	16676	420	35.5	36.0	24.3	3.8	0.5	32928	37362	21	13	351	29.9	34.5	25.6	10.0	0.0	74032
45696	WILLOW WOOD	13928	544	41.9	33.8	20.2	3.9	0.2	32771	36979	20	12	441	42.2	19.7	27.2	10.7	0.2	63036
45697	WINCHESTER	19235	1761	28.6	30.3	33.3	6.0	1.8	40993	47418	50	33	1400	15.4	28.6	38.8	15.3	1.9	96563
45701	ATHENS	18728	10760	45.7	22.9	19.2	8.2	4.1	29033	33906	10	6	5227	16.2	14.9	44.3	21.9	2.7	119902
45710	ALBANY	20016	1900	31.3	29.8	29.5	7.5	1.8	40185	47267	47	30	1505	20.8	24.1	39.5	13.6	2.1	100046
45711	AMESVILLE	18348	652	31.4	34.7	26.7	6.1	1.1	36282	42904	33	21	536	24.3	26.9	30.4	15.3	3.2	88462
45714	BELPRE	21812	4119	33.6	31.3	25.4	7.7	1.9	36028	42232	32	20	3050	17.0	33.3	41.2	7.9	0.7	89702
45715	BEVERLY	21418	1073	33.8	29.9	28.3	5.6	2.3	37746	43378	38	25	833	19.1	32.5	40.5	7.1	0.8	87545
45723	COOLVILLE	19805	1627	30.7	36.1	25.0	5.2	3.1	36831	43408	35	22	1386	30.8	30.2	32.5	5.8	0.7	77355
45724	CUTLER	18025	1184	31.3	29.4	32.5	4.6	2.2	37559	44045	38	24	1021	24.6	24.8	36.1	13.1	1.4	90644
45727	DEXTER CITY	15680	179	35.8	36.9	23.5	2.8	1.1	35378	39073	29	19	149	36.9	28.2	26.9	6.7	1.3	71154
45729	FLEMING	21805	468	22.7	26.7	40.2	6.6	3.9	50370	57769	73	64	408	16.4	20.3	33.1	27.2	2.9	121711
45732	GLOUSTER	15296	2588	43.2	31.2	22.2	2.7	0.7	30022	34518	12	7	1979	44.3	31.7	21.8	1.9	0.4	56202
45734	GRAYSVILLE	16212	414	34.5	38.7	24.9	1.7	0.2	35311	40068	29	18	344	39.2	29.4	25.6	4.4	1.5	61875
45735	GUYSVILLE	18497	506	36.8	30.0	25.5	4.4	3.4	35653	42830	30	20	430	23.5	27.4	30.9	15.6	2.6	88400
45741	LANGSVILLE	14634	452	44.5	26.8	23.7	4.9	0.2	28904	33081	10	6	375	35.2	30.7	28.5	5.1	0.5	73857
45742	LITTLE HOCKING	21663	1092	21.3	28.7	38.6	8.6	2.9	50060	57489	72	63	961	19.2	31.4	39.0	9.3	1.1	88472
45743	LONG BOTTOM	15356	658	38.6	34.7	23.0	2.6	1.2	31306	35923	16	9	552	29.9	33.5	29.7	6.9	0.0	68065
45744	LOWELL	22474	726	30.6	33.5	28.8	4.0	3.2	41175	47549	50	33	608	34.7	30.3	25.0	8.7	1.3	74576
45745	LOWER SALEM	16922	622	31.0	37.1	27.5	3.9	0.5	37109	42416	36	23	521	30.9	25.9	36.5	6.3	0.4	76351
45746	MACKSBURG	14817	172	36.6	38.4	23.3	1.7	0.0	33032	37458	21	13	138	54.4	17.4	26.1	2.2	0.0	48235
45750	MARIETTA	22723	10820	32.0	30.6	26.4	7.2	3.8	38074	44946	40	25	7541	17.6	29.5	41.6	10.1	1.3	92852
45760	MIDDLEPORT	14598	1621	49.9	27.3	19.4	3.3	0.2	25088	27727	5	4	1119	46.6	36.1	16.6	0.7	0.0	54140
45761	MILLFIELD	17108	1077	39.6	30.1	24.1	4.6	1.7	31848	37505	17	10	784	36.4	28.4	26.0	8.0	1.2	66456
45764	NELSONVILLE	15299	3702	46.4	29.7	18.7	4.2	1.0	26977	31507	7	5	2273	33.4	30.4	31.8	3.7	0.8	69627
45766	NEW MARSHFIELD	20380	738	24.8	34.3	33.2	6.8	1.0	45000	52855	61	46	601	33.8	21.1	34.8	10.2	0.2	75625
45767	NEW MATAMORAS	18456	1109	38.4	34.8	20.5	3.9	2.4	32412	36863	19	12	838	37.4	37.2	22.3	2.6	0.5	64146
45768	NEWPORT	20420	655	24.3	34.5	33.1	5.2	2.9	43189	50655	56	40	550	23.3	34.6	38.7	2.7	0.7	81731
45769	POMEROY	16143	2531	41.3	33.0	21.2	3.7	0.8	30528	34962	14	8	1920	35.6	31.0	26.9	6.4	0.1	69408
45770	PORTLAND	14924	309	40.5	34.3	23.0	0.7	1.6	30121	34383	13	8	254	44.1	23.2	25.2	7.5	0.0	67000
45771	RACINE	18278	1650	37.7	32.2	25.5	3.0	1.6	34144	38098	24	15	1299	30.9	29.3	32.8	6.5	0.6	76798
45772	REEDSVILLE	17578	794	37.5	32.5	24.4	3.0	2.5	34284	39040	25	16	676	40.1	26.5	29.4	2.4	1.6	66591
45773	RENO	22371	635	27.4	32.4	29.6	7.9	2.7	42026	49314	53	36	540	22.8	26.7	41.3	7.8	1.5	90882
45775	RUTLAND	14214	595	42.9	30.8	22.4	3.2	0.8	29801	33921	12	7	490	42.9	31.6	22.9	2.7	0.0	60930
45776	SHADE	17845	363	40.8	28.1	24.5	5.5	1.1	33058	38570	21	13	296	33.1	22.0	32.1	12.2	0.7	81176
	OHIO	25510		24.6	28.1	32.2	10.1	5.0	47354	56168				9.2	18.6	47.0	22.1	3.1	121192
	UNITED STATES	25866		24.7	27.1	30.8	10.9	6.5	48124	56710				10.9	15.0	33.7	30.1	10.4	145905

ZIP CODE #	POST OFFICE NAME	FINANCIAL SERVICES: Auto Loan	FINANCIAL SERVICES: Home Loan	FINANCIAL SERVICES: Invest-ments	FINANCIAL SERVICES: Retire-ment Plans	THE HOME: Home Improvements: Home Repair	THE HOME: Home Improvements: Lawn & Garden	THE HOME: Furnishings: Comput-ers & Hard-ware	THE HOME: Furnishings: Major Appli-ances	THE HOME: Furnishings: TV, Radio, Sound Equip-ment	THE HOME: Furnishings: Furni-ture	ENTERTAINMENT: Dine out/ Carry out	ENTERTAINMENT: Sports Equip-ment	ENTERTAINMENT: Fees & Tickets	ENTERTAINMENT: Toys & Games	ENTERTAINMENT: Travel	ENTERTAINMENT: Cable TV	PERSONAL: Apparel & Services	PERSONAL: Auto Repairs	PERSONAL: Health Insur-ance	PERSONAL: Pets & Supplies
45440	DAYTON	104	116	131	117	114	120	113	111	109	112	137	129	117	139	114	107	135	111	106	122
45449	DAYTON	80	86	96	87	85	89	87	84	85	86	107	99	89	110	86	83	105	85	80	93
45458	DAYTON	132	157	175	160	153	155	146	143	136	146	172	167	153	177	147	131	171	141	129	157
45459	DAYTON	119	139	163	138	137	145	133	131	128	132	161	150	139	165	136	127	159	130	125	143
45502	SPRINGFIELD	103	104	96	101	106	111	97	102	98	97	120	119	98	124	99	98	117	100	103	122
45503	SPRINGFIELD	76	78	86	77	78	85	80	79	80	78	100	91	81	102	80	81	97	79	80	88
45504	SPRINGFIELD	81	84	90	83	84	91	85	84	85	84	106	97	86	106	85	84	103	85	84	94
45505	SPRINGFIELD	57	57	63	55	57	63	60	59	63	59	78	68	61	79	60	64	75	60	62	66
45506	SPRINGFIELD	64	63	69	61	62	69	65	64	68	65	84	73	66	83	65	69	82	65	67	72
45601	CHILLICOTHE	80	72	61	68	75	83	70	76	75	70	91	88	68	91	71	77	87	75	82	92
45612	BAINBRIDGE	81	59	35	52	65	74	58	69	67	59	80	81	51	77	59	71	74	68	81	93
45613	BEAVER	93	64	31	56	72	82	62	76	73	63	87	91	53	82	63	79	79	75	93	107
45614	BIDWELL	82	56	27	49	63	73	55	67	65	55	77	80	47	73	56	70	70	67	82	94
45616	BLUE CREEK	71	48	22	41	54	62	46	58	56	47	65	69	39	62	47	60	59	57	71	82
45619	CHESAPEAKE	74	58	42	56	63	72	61	67	67	59	80	77	56	77	60	69	74	66	76	82
45620	CHESHIRE	82	55	25	47	62	72	53	66	64	54	75	79	45	71	54	69	68	66	82	94
45622	CREOLA	74	50	23	43	56	65	48	60	58	49	68	71	41	64	49	62	62	59	73	85
45623	CROWN CITY	74	50	23	43	56	65	48	60	58	49	68	71	41	64	49	62	62	59	74	85
45628	FRANKFORT	84	72	56	68	76	85	71	77	77	70	93	90	68	94	72	80	88	76	87	96
45629	FRANKLIN FURNACE	87	60	29	52	68	77	58	71	69	59	81	85	50	77	59	74	74	71	87	101
45631	GALLIPOLIS	79	62	43	58	67	76	62	70	69	62	83	81	57	80	63	72	77	70	81	90
45634	HAMDEN	73	49	22	42	56	64	47	59	57	48	67	71	40	63	48	62	61	59	73	84
45638	IRONTON	64	51	39	47	55	63	53	58	59	52	70	67	49	68	53	62	66	58	68	73
45640	JACKSON	72	58	42	54	62	71	58	65	65	57	78	75	54	77	59	68	72	64	75	83
45644	KINGSTON	98	91	76	86	95	102	85	92	90	85	110	108	85	114	88	93	105	90	99	115
45645	KITTS HILL	79	53	24	46	60	69	51	64	62	52	72	76	43	68	52	66	66	63	79	91
45646	LATHAM	68	45	21	39	51	59	44	55	53	45	62	65	37	59	44	57	56	54	67	78
45647	LONDONDERRY	84	56	26	49	64	74	54	68	66	55	77	81	46	73	55	71	70	67	84	97
45648	LUCASVILLE	71	54	34	49	58	66	52	61	59	53	71	72	47	68	53	62	66	61	71	81
45650	LYNX	55	37	17	32	42	48	36	45	43	36	50	53	30	48	36	46	46	44	55	63
45651	MC ARTHUR	77	52	23	45	59	67	50	62	60	51	71	75	42	67	51	65	64	62	77	89
45652	MC DERMOTT	88	67	44	63	72	83	69	78	77	68	92	90	62	87	69	80	85	78	90	98
45653	MINFORD	83	62	37	57	68	77	60	71	69	61	82	84	54	80	61	73	76	70	83	95
45654	NEW PLYMOUTH	77	52	24	45	59	67	50	62	60	51	71	74	43	67	51	64	64	62	76	88
45656	OAK HILL	75	52	27	46	59	67	51	62	60	52	71	74	44	68	52	64	65	61	75	86
45657	OTWAY	81	56	27	48	63	72	54	66	64	54	75	79	46	72	54	69	69	66	81	94
45658	PATRIOT	80	56	29	50	63	72	54	66	64	55	75	79	47	72	55	68	69	65	80	93
45659	PEDRO	67	45	20	39	51	58	43	54	52	44	61	65	37	58	44	56	56	54	67	77
45660	PEEBLES	79	53	24	46	60	69	51	64	62	52	72	76	44	68	52	66	66	63	78	90
45661	PIKETON	89	64	35	57	71	81	63	75	72	63	86	89	55	81	63	77	79	74	89	102
45662	PORTSMOUTH	61	55	54	53	56	64	59	60	63	57	76	68	57	75	59	65	73	61	66	69
45663	WEST PORTSMOUTH	62	52	42	50	55	62	54	58	58	52	70	66	51	69	54	60	66	57	65	70
45669	PROCTORVILLE	78	65	49	61	69	78	64	72	70	64	84	83	60	83	65	73	79	71	81	90
45671	RARDEN	74	50	22	43	56	65	48	60	58	49	68	71	41	64	49	62	62	59	74	85
45672	RAY	82	55	25	47	62	71	53	66	64	54	75	79	45	71	54	69	68	65	81	94
45673	RICHMOND DALE	98	66	30	57	74	86	63	79	76	65	90	95	54	85	64	82	82	78	98	113
45675	ROCK CAMP	88	59	27	51	67	77	57	71	69	58	81	85	49	76	58	74	74	71	88	101
45678	SCOTTOWN	74	50	23	43	56	65	48	60	58	49	68	72	41	64	49	62	62	60	74	85
45679	SEAMAN	73	56	37	53	61	70	57	64	64	56	76	75	52	73	57	67	70	64	75	83
45680	SOUTH POINT	65	54	42	51	57	65	55	60	60	54	72	69	51	70	55	62	67	60	68	74
45681	SOUTH SALEM	87	66	39	59	72	80	62	74	71	63	84	88	56	82	63	75	78	72	86	100
45682	SOUTH WEBSTER	72	48	22	41	54	63	46	58	56	47	66	69	39	62	47	60	60	57	71	82
45684	STOUT	83	59	32	52	66	75	57	69	67	58	79	82	50	76	58	72	73	68	84	96
45685	THURMAN	77	55	44	53	59	67	62	67	68	61	83	82	55	78	60	69	78	70	74	86
45686	VINTON	79	53	24	46	60	69	51	64	62	52	73	76	44	69	52	67	66	63	79	91
45688	WATERLOO	59	39	18	34	44	51	38	47	46	39	54	57	32	51	38	49	49	47	58	67
45690	WAVERLY	79	67	54	63	70	78	66	73	71	67	86	83	63	83	67	73	82	72	80	90
45692	WELLSTON	70	51	31	45	56	64	50	59	58	51	70	70	45	68	51	62	64	59	71	80
45693	WEST UNION	75	57	36	53	62	70	56	65	63	56	76	76	51	73	57	66	70	64	75	85
45694	WHEELERSBURG	85	69	48	64	74	84	68	77	75	67	90	89	63	89	69	79	84	76	88	98
45695	WILKESVILLE	75	50	23	43	57	65	48	60	58	49	68	72	41	65	49	63	62	60	74	86
45696	WILLOW WOOD	70	47	21	40	53	61	45	56	54	46	64	67	38	60	46	59	58	56	69	80
45697	WINCHESTER	83	72	55	70	76	82	69	76	73	69	89	89	67	89	70	74	84	74	81	94
45701	ATHENS	66	56	62	58	55	61	71	63	70	66	87	79	65	83	64	65	83	68	60	71
45710	ALBANY	81	66	45	62	70	78	64	72	70	64	84	85	59	83	64	72	79	71	81	93
45711	AMESVILLE	76	60	41	57	64	73	61	68	67	60	80	79	56	78	60	69	74	67	77	85
45714	BELPRE	74	66	54	63	69	77	66	71	70	65	85	81	64	84	67	73	80	70	78	84
45715	BEVERLY	90	66	40	61	73	84	67	78	76	66	90	91	60	87	68	81	83	77	93	102
45723	COOLVILLE	91	62	29	54	70	80	60	74	72	61	84	88	51	80	61	77	77	73	91	105
45724	CUTLER	80	65	43	60	70	77	61	70	67	61	81	83	57	80	62	70	76	68	79	93
45727	DEXTER CITY	73	50	23	44	57	65	48	60	57	49	67	72	41	64	49	61	61	59	73	85
45729	FLEMING	92	82	63	78	87	93	76	84	81	76	98	100	74	100	78	83	93	82	91	109
45732	GLOUSTER	61	48	36	44	51	59	49	55	55	48	66	63	45	65	50	58	62	55	63	69
45734	GRAYSVILLE	73	49	23	43	56	64	48	59	58	49	68	71	41	64	49	62	61	59	73	83
45735	GUYSVILLE	77	61	43	59	66	74	62	69	68	62	82	80	58	80	62	70	76	68	77	86
45741	LANGSVILLE	72	49	22	42	55	63	47	59	56	48	66	70	40	63	48	61	60	58	72	83
45742	LITTLE HOCKING	93	80	59	76	86	93	75	84	80	75	97	100	72	99	77	83	92	82	92	110
45743	LONG BOTTOM	72	49	22	42	55	63	47	59	57	48	66	70	40	63	48	61	60	58	72	83
45744	LOWELL	98	74	44	67	82	91	70	84	80	71	96	100	64	94	72	85	89	82	98	114
45745	LOWER SALEM	76	57	34	52	63	70	54	64	62	55	74	77	49	72	55	65	68	63	75	88
45746	MACKSBURG	70	47	22	41	54	61	46	57	55	46	64	68	39	61	46	59	58	56	70	80
45750	MARIETTA	80	72	62	69	75	84	73	77	78	71	94	88	71	94	74	80	89	76	84	91
45760	MIDDLEPORT	54	40	27	38	44	52	44	49	49	42	59	56	39	56	43	52	54	49	58	60
45761	MILLFIELD	65	55	47	53	56	63	58	61	62	57	76	70	55	74	57	63	72	61	65	72
45764	NELSONVILLE	57	45	38	44	47	53	50	52	54	49	65	62	46	62	48	54	61	54	57	63
45766	NEW MARSHFIELD	79	72	56	69	72	76	68	74	69	70	86	85	65	81	68	69	82	73	73	88
45767	NEW MATAMORAS	73	57	39	52	62	72	58	66	66	57	78	75	53	76	59	70	72	65	78	83
45768	NEWPORT	86	71	49	66	76	83	66	76	73	67	88	90	63	88	68	75	82	74	85	100
45769	POMEROY	65	50	33	46	54	61	50	57	56	50	67	67	45	64	50	58	62	57	65	74
45770	PORTLAND	71	48	22	41	54	62	46	57	55	47	65	69	39	61	47	60	59	57	71	82
45771	RACINE	79	55	29	50	62	72	56	67	66	56	77	78	49	73	56	70	70	66	81	90
45772	REEDSVILLE	81	54	25	47	62	71	52	66	63	53	74	78	45	70	53	68	67	65	81	93
45773	RENO	92	74	50	69	80	88	70	80	77	70	93	96	66	92	72	80	87	79	91	107
45775	RUTLAND	66	48	28	43	53	59	47	55	53	48	63	66	41	60	47	56	59	55	64	75
45776	SHADE	67	58	44	56	60	66	57	62	60	57	73	72	54	71	57	60	69	61	65	75
	OHIO	89	88	90	87	88	95	88	89	89	87	110	103	88	111	88	89	107	89	90	102
	UNITED STATES	100	100	100	100	100	100	100	100	100	100	100	100	100	100	100	100	100	100	100	100

OHIO

POPULATION CHANGE

A 45778-45898

# POST OFFICE NAME	COUNTY FIPS CODE	POPULATION			2000-2004 ANNUAL RATE		HOUSEHOLDS					FAMILIES		
		2000	2004	2009	% Rate	State Centile	2000	2004	2009	% Annual Rate 2000-2004	2004 Average HH Size	2000	2004	% Annual Rate 2000-2004
45778 STEWART	009	1052	1023	1018	-0.7	16	392	390	397	-0.1	2.62	288	279	-0.7
45780 THE PLAINS	009	2936	3104	3195	1.3	87	1225	1326	1396	1.9	2.20	716	739	0.8
45784 VINCENT	167	3140	3128	3093	-0.1	41	1184	1210	1224	0.5	2.59	952	954	0.1
45786 WATERFORD	167	3421	3425	3411	0.0	46	1251	1284	1308	0.6	2.67	956	958	0.1
45788 WHIPPLE	167	1984	1977	1957	-0.1	42	751	767	777	0.5	2.53	567	565	-0.1
45789 WINGETT RUN	167	445	437	430	-0.4	25	124	124	125	0.0	3.31	98	96	-0.5
45801 LIMA	003	26807	25946	25267	-0.8	13	9146	9022	8950	-0.3	2.46	6162	5906	-1.0
45804 LIMA	003	16844	16081	15543	-1.1	6	6786	6648	6582	-0.5	2.38	4305	4055	-1.4
45805 LIMA	003	24042	23620	23116	-0.4	26	9908	9952	9945	0.1	2.29	6457	6271	-0.7
45806 LIMA	003	11114	11382	11388	0.6	69	4231	4439	4529	1.1	2.52	3191	3269	0.6
45807 LIMA	003	11477	11632	11549	0.3	58	4201	4380	4458	1.0	2.64	3249	3309	0.4
45810 ADA	065	7889	7775	7680	-0.3	29	2658	2655	2661	0.0	2.32	1493	1436	-0.9
45812 ALGER	065	2370	2350	2322	-0.2	35	939	952	960	0.3	2.47	690	680	-0.3
45813 ANTWERP	125	3522	3531	3585	0.1	47	1396	1445	1511	0.8	2.44	1003	1012	0.2
45814 ARLINGTON	063	3028	3065	3120	0.3	57	1110	1152	1197	0.9	2.61	845	855	0.3
45817 BLUFFTON	003	6711	6716	6657	0.0	45	2279	2324	2348	0.5	2.53	1638	1623	-0.2
45821 CECIL	125	1475	1523	1568	0.8	75	545	580	614	1.5	2.62	418	437	1.1
45822 CELINA	107	19343	19399	19513	0.1	48	7542	7754	7990	0.7	2.48	5320	5321	0.0
45827 CLOVERDALE	137	2720	2709	2696	-0.1	40	894	914	934	0.5	2.93	710	711	0.0
45828 COLDWATER	107	6316	6282	6269	-0.1	38	2185	2227	2274	0.5	2.77	1667	1662	-0.1
45830 COLUMBUS GROVE	137	6406	6460	6460	0.2	53	2306	2388	2452	0.8	2.69	1786	1810	0.3
45831 CONTINENTAL	137	3360	3402	3415	0.3	57	1242	1290	1328	0.9	2.62	940	956	0.4
45832 CONVOY	161	2804	2748	2705	-0.5	23	1022	1024	1029	0.1	2.66	812	797	-0.4
45833 DELPHOS	003	11083	10926	10731	-0.3	29	4151	4201	4223	0.3	2.58	3026	2978	-0.4
45835 DOLA	065	361	370	372	0.6	70	151	158	162	1.1	2.34	118	121	0.6
45836 DUNKIRK	065	1734	1720	1700	-0.2	36	636	641	644	0.2	2.68	495	487	-0.4
45840 FINDLAY	063	52320	53682	55253	0.6	70	20791	21799	22885	1.1	2.39	13761	13996	0.4
45841 JENERA	063	700	700	711	0.0	45	255	262	273	0.6	2.67	195	195	0.0
45843 FOREST	065	3470	3446	3437	-0.2	37	1336	1359	1384	0.4	2.53	990	981	-0.2
45844 FORT JENNINGS	137	4343	4372	4372	0.2	52	1546	1601	1644	0.8	2.73	1216	1234	0.4
45845 FORT LORAMIE	149	3026	3334	3524	2.3	94	1025	1153	1244	2.8	2.89	795	875	2.3
45846 FORT RECOVERY	107	4359	4264	4237	-0.5	21	1433	1437	1462	0.1	2.97	1130	1111	-0.4
45849 GROVER HILL	125	1298	1272	1285	-0.5	23	483	486	504	0.2	2.62	374	369	-0.3
45850 HARROD	003	4115	4243	4248	0.7	73	1483	1567	1605	1.3	2.71	1196	1237	0.8
45851 HAVILAND	125	666	682	703	0.6	69	217	227	240	1.1	3.00	176	181	0.7
45856 LEIPSIC	137	5302	5224	5178	-0.4	29	1812	1829	1859	0.2	2.78	1365	1346	-0.3
45858 MC COMB	063	3146	3211	3278	0.5	65	1126	1173	1220	1.0	2.74	900	918	0.5
45860 MARIA STEIN	107	2223	2195	2183	-0.3	31	666	674	686	0.3	3.17	569	569	0.0
45862 MENDON	107	1457	1450	1447	-0.1	39	552	561	572	0.4	2.58	428	426	-0.1
45863 MIDDLE POINT	161	1335	1318	1301	-0.3	31	480	488	494	0.4	2.68	376	374	-0.1
45865 MINSTER	011	4679	4704	4716	0.1	50	1678	1726	1756	0.7	2.67	1279	1285	0.1
45867 MOUNT BLANCHARD	063	1058	1135	1191	1.7	90	394	434	466	2.3	2.62	299	320	1.6
45868 MOUNT CORY	063	767	799	828	1.0	81	275	295	312	1.7	2.71	227	239	1.2
45869 NEW BREMEN	011	4135	4108	4098	-0.2	37	1464	1484	1497	0.3	2.77	1130	1121	-0.2
45871 NEW KNOXVILLE	011	2120	2111	2102	-0.1	40	648	656	660	0.3	2.88	496	491	-0.2
45872 NORTH BALTIMORE	173	4073	4196	4362	0.7	73	1539	1618	1716	1.2	2.54	1098	1120	0.5
45873 OAKWOOD	125	2881	2928	2993	0.4	61	1100	1151	1211	1.1	2.54	828	847	0.5
45874 OHIO CITY	161	2616	2624	2609	0.1	48	996	1023	1038	0.6	2.57	745	744	0.0
45875 OTTAWA	137	11253	11158	11082	-0.2	35	3941	4019	4099	0.5	2.73	2932	2920	-0.1
45877 PANDORA	137	2113	2094	2076	-0.2	35	758	768	780	0.3	2.63	599	595	-0.2
45879 PAULDING	125	6555	6782	7003	0.8	77	2543	2699	2860	1.4	2.49	1814	1878	0.8
45880 PAYNE	125	2565	2556	2600	-0.1	42	989	1013	1060	0.6	2.47	718	716	-0.1
45881 RAWSON	063	1122	1127	1151	0.1	49	397	409	426	0.7	2.76	322	325	0.2
45882 ROCKFORD	107	3120	3248	3314	1.0	81	1124	1201	1255	1.6	2.57	864	903	1.0
45883 SAINT HENRY	107	3946	4063	4129	0.7	73	1203	1272	1325	1.3	3.19	1009	1050	0.9
45885 SAINT MARYS	011	13532	13441	13405	-0.2	37	5210	5302	5354	0.4	2.49	3719	3684	-0.2
45886 SCOTT	161	554	593	614	1.6	90	197	216	228	2.2	2.75	160	172	1.7
45887 SPENCERVILLE	003	4947	4958	4906	0.1	47	1828	1874	1893	0.6	2.59	1423	1425	0.0
45889 VAN BUREN	063	1212	1253	1289	0.8	76	418	444	467	1.4	2.82	347	361	0.9
45890 VANLUE	063	627	633	643	0.2	54	237	245	254	0.8	2.58	191	193	0.3
45891 VAN WERT	161	15687	15434	15246	-0.4	27	6350	6398	6449	0.2	2.35	4389	4299	-0.5
45894 VENEDOCIA	161	765	881	937	3.4	97	285	338	367	4.1	2.61	227	263	3.5
45895 WAPAKONETA	011	18343	18347	18337	0.0	45	6920	7089	7163	0.6	2.52	5095	5096	0.0
45896 WAYNESFIELD	011	2199	2320	2380	1.3	86	788	849	883	1.8	2.73	597	630	1.3
45898 WILLSHIRE	161	1315	1295	1280	-0.4	28	486	487	491	0.1	2.66	343	334	-0.6
OHIO					0.3					0.7	2.44			0.0
UNITED STATES					1.2					1.3	2.58			1.1

#	POST OFFICE NAME	RACE (%) White 2000	2004	Black 2000	2004	Asian/Pacific 2000	2004	% Hispanic Origin 2000	2004	2004 AGE DISTRIBUTION (%) 0-4	5-9	10-14	15-19	20-24	25-44	45-64	65-84	85+	18+	MEDIAN AGE 2004	% 2004 Males	% 2004 Females
45778	STEWART	89.6	89.2	5.8	6.1	0.2	0.3	0.7	0.7	5.9	6.9	7.6	7.9	6.7	28.1	26.4	9.7	0.9	74.5	36.9	49.7	50.3
45780	THE PLAINS	94.0	93.3	2.5	2.6	1.1	1.5	0.8	1.0	6.7	5.8	6.8	6.3	7.4	27.0	21.0	14.2	4.9	77.5	36.9	44.2	55.8
45784	VINCENT	96.8	96.5	1.5	1.6	0.2	0.4	0.5	0.5	6.5	7.0	7.2	6.2	5.1	26.4	30.8	10.2	0.8	75.5	40.3	50.8	49.2
45786	WATERFORD	99.0	98.9	0.2	0.2	0.2	0.2	0.4	0.5	7.0	7.2	7.5	6.7	5.7	28.2	24.9	11.7	1.2	74.2	37.8	50.6	49.4
45788	WHIPPLE	98.5	98.3	0.1	0.1	0.4	0.5	0.4	0.4	5.6	6.2	7.1	5.8	6.0	27.2	28.7	11.6	1.9	77.6	40.3	50.2	49.8
45789	WINGETT RUN	99.1	98.9	0.2	0.2	0.0	0.0	0.2	0.2	5.7	6.2	7.3	6.2	5.7	26.8	25.4	12.8	3.9	77.1	39.6	50.1	49.9
45801	LIMA	79.3	77.5	17.0	18.3	0.5	0.7	1.9	2.1	7.2	6.6	6.5	6.7	8.1	31.5	22.6	9.6	1.3	76.1	34.7	55.0	45.0
45804	LIMA	65.9	64.1	30.3	31.8	0.4	0.6	1.9	2.1	7.8	7.3	7.9	7.3	7.2	25.1	22.7	12.6	2.0	72.6	34.9	47.1	52.9
45805	LIMA	83.9	82.2	12.6	13.8	1.1	1.4	1.4	1.5	6.3	6.3	6.7	7.9	7.1	23.8	25.2	14.1	2.5	76.7	38.8	48.6	51.4
45806	LIMA	95.9	95.4	2.1	2.4	0.5	0.6	1.2	1.3	6.3	6.5	7.2	6.6	5.7	25.0	27.8	12.9	2.0	75.9	40.2	48.9	51.1
45807	LIMA	96.2	95.6	2.0	2.3	0.5	0.7	1.1	1.2	5.9	6.4	7.4	7.2	6.5	24.4	28.8	11.9	1.5	75.8	40.0	49.3	50.7
45810	ADA	96.2	95.7	1.2	1.3	1.1	1.4	0.6	0.7	4.5	4.4	4.7	16.1	21.8	21.8	17.3	8.5	1.0	83.5	24.7	49.8	50.2
45812	ALGER	99.0	98.9	0.1	0.1	0.0	0.0	0.3	0.3	6.7	6.9	7.5	6.9	6.1	28.3	24.5	12.0	1.1	74.7	36.4	48.2	51.8
45813	ANTWERP	97.8	97.5	0.5	0.6	0.1	0.1	1.8	2.0	6.5	6.6	7.3	7.0	6.1	27.7	26.2	11.3	1.3	75.3	38.0	49.4	50.6
45814	ARLINGTON	98.9	98.8	0.2	0.2	0.1	0.1	0.7	0.8	6.5	6.8	7.3	7.3	6.1	26.9	25.5	10.7	2.9	74.7	38.4	49.3	50.7
45817	BLUFFTON	98.2	98.0	0.6	0.7	0.4	0.5	0.9	1.0	5.6	6.0	7.1	10.2	10.7	22.9	21.2	12.7	3.5	76.9	35.9	46.6	53.4
45821	CECIL	96.2	95.8	0.5	0.6	0.1	0.1	2.6	2.9	7.6	7.5	7.6	6.3	6.2	28.9	26.7	8.7	0.6	73.2	36.2	50.8	49.2
45822	CELINA	97.7	97.4	0.1	0.1	0.5	0.7	1.6	1.8	6.7	6.8	7.4	7.0	6.8	24.8	25.7	13.0	1.8	74.8	38.1	49.6	50.5
45827	CLOVERDALE	98.9	98.8	0.2	0.2	0.0	0.0	1.0	1.1	7.2	7.3	8.9	8.2	7.1	27.0	23.0	10.0	1.4	71.5	34.7	50.4	49.6
45828	COLDWATER	98.9	98.7	0.1	0.1	0.1	0.1	1.0	1.1	8.3	8.3	8.7	7.6	6.1	25.3	21.8	12.0	2.0	69.8	35.5	49.8	50.2
45830	COLUMBUS GROVE	98.2	98.1	0.2	0.2	0.2	0.2	1.9	2.0	8.0	7.7	7.8	7.4	6.2	27.0	23.5	11.0	1.5	72.0	35.6	50.2	49.8
45831	CONTINENTAL	98.2	98.2	0.1	0.1	0.1	0.1	1.9	2.0	6.5	6.8	7.7	7.8	6.6	27.5	24.3	11.0	1.8	74.2	36.2	49.5	50.5
45832	CONVOY	97.8	97.6	0.1	0.2	0.2	0.3	1.3	1.5	6.7	7.4	8.5	7.1	5.9	26.5	25.1	11.2	1.6	72.8	36.8	50.5	49.5
45833	DELPHOS	98.8	98.6	0.2	0.2	0.1	0.2	0.7	0.8	6.9	6.7	7.8	7.1	6.7	26.6	23.4	12.8	2.0	74.2	36.9	50.2	49.8
45835	DOLA	98.1	97.6	0.3	0.3	0.3	0.5	0.3	0.3	6.2	6.8	7.6	6.5	6.0	26.0	27.6	12.2	1.4	75.4	39.4	51.6	48.4
45836	DUNKIRK	97.9	97.7	0.2	0.2	0.2	0.4	0.5	0.5	6.9	7.3	8.1	6.5	6.5	27.3	25.0	11.4	1.1	74.0	36.1	51.6	48.4
45840	FINDLAY	94.3	93.5	1.3	1.3	1.6	2.1	3.5	3.8	7.0	6.8	6.9	7.1	7.6	27.5	24.0	11.2	2.0	75.6	36.1	48.2	51.8
45841	JENERA	98.9	98.9	0.3	0.3	0.1	0.1	1.0	1.1	6.3	6.6	6.6	7.0	6.4	26.9	27.3	10.3	2.7	76.7	39.5	50.6	49.4
45843	FOREST	98.7	98.5	0.4	0.4	0.0	0.1	0.8	0.8	7.4	7.3	7.4	6.6	6.4	27.7	25.0	10.8	1.3	73.7	36.8	50.0	50.0
45844	FORT JENNINGS	99.1	99.1	0.1	0.1	0.2	0.2	0.6	0.6	7.5	7.6	8.7	7.9	6.2	27.3	23.6	10.0	1.3	71.0	35.4	50.6	49.4
45845	FORT LORAMIE	99.4	99.3	0.1	0.1	0.1	0.1	0.2	0.3	9.1	9.0	7.8	6.5	5.6	29.7	21.4	10.0	1.1	70.0	33.8	49.6	50.4
45846	FORT RECOVERY	99.2	99.0	0.0	0.0	0.3	0.3	0.3	0.4	8.2	8.2	8.9	8.1	6.9	26.1	21.6	10.7	1.4	69.7	33.0	51.1	48.9
45849	GROVER HILL	97.2	97.3	0.6	0.7	0.1	0.1	1.3	1.3	7.2	7.1	7.3	7.6	6.8	27.4	24.5	10.7	1.4	73.7	36.2	49.5	50.6
45850	HARROD	98.4	98.2	0.2	0.2	0.1	0.1	0.9	1.0	7.1	7.2	7.1	6.8	6.2	27.6	26.1	10.9	1.0	74.5	37.4	49.5	50.5
45851	HAVILAND	96.7	96.5	1.2	1.3	0.2	0.3	1.1	1.2	6.6	6.9	8.2	7.6	7.0	26.3	24.9	10.9	1.6	73.6	35.4	51.0	49.0
45856	LEIPSIC	88.0	87.8	0.2	0.2	0.2	0.2	14.8	15.1	8.3	7.9	8.0	7.3	6.5	25.9	21.6	11.9	2.7	71.2	35.5	49.3	50.8
45858	MC COMB	97.1	96.8	0.2	0.2	0.4	0.4	2.6	2.9	7.9	8.3	9.0	7.5	5.3	28.9	23.2	8.8	1.2	70.0	35.0	50.0	50.0
45860	MARIA STEIN	99.8	99.7	0.0	0.1	0.0	0.0	0.1	0.1	9.3	9.3	10.6	8.3	6.2	26.2	17.2	11.4	1.6	65.2	31.0	52.4	47.6
45862	MENDON	99.0	99.0	0.0	0.0	0.1	0.2	0.8	0.9	7.2	7.3	7.5	6.8	6.1	26.6	25.3	11.4	1.7	73.8	36.9	50.3	49.7
45863	MIDDLE POINT	98.2	98.1	0.5	0.5	0.1	0.2	1.1	1.2	6.9	7.4	7.6	6.8	5.8	26.5	26.6	10.9	1.5	73.8	38.0	50.0	50.0
45865	MINSTER	99.4	99.3	0.0	0.0	0.1	0.1	0.2	0.2	7.3	7.7	8.8	7.4	5.7	25.5	23.2	12.1	2.4	71.4	36.9	50.0	50.0
45867	MOUNT BLANCHARD	98.8	98.7	0.2	0.2	0.0	0.0	0.8	0.8	7.2	7.9	8.6	6.8	4.9	27.0	25.9	10.4	1.3	71.9	37.6	49.6	50.4
45868	MOUNT CORY	98.0	97.9	0.4	0.4	0.0	0.0	1.4	1.8	5.5	7.3	8.6	7.6	5.5	27.7	26.4	9.9	1.5	73.6	38.2	50.3	49.7
45869	NEW BREMEN	98.5	98.5	0.0	0.0	0.4	0.4	0.4	0.4	7.5	7.9	8.9	7.7	6.3	27.3	23.3	9.6	1.6	70.9	35.2	50.2	49.8
45871	NEW KNOXVILLE	98.1	98.0	0.7	0.7	0.3	0.3	1.0	1.1	7.3	7.3	7.3	7.3	5.9	28.8	25.3	9.7	1.4	73.7	37.3	48.9	51.1
45872	NORTH BALTIMORE	96.7	96.3	0.0	0.0	0.4	0.5	3.5	3.9	7.2	7.6	8.1	6.9	6.3	27.2	22.0	12.4	2.3	72.8	35.2	48.4	51.6
45873	OAKWOOD	97.4	97.2	0.4	0.4	0.2	0.2	1.8	1.9	6.6	6.9	7.6	6.8	6.2	27.3	26.9	10.6	1.2	74.8	37.3	49.6	50.4
45874	OHIO CITY	98.5	98.4	0.2	0.3	0.1	0.1	1.0	1.1	7.6	7.5	7.1	6.6	6.2	27.2	24.4	11.9	1.7	73.9	37.5	50.3	49.7
45875	OTTAWA	96.6	96.6	0.2	0.2	0.2	0.2	4.1	4.2	7.5	7.5	8.1	7.1	6.1	27.0	23.5	11.4	1.8	72.5	36.2	49.5	50.5
45877	PANDORA	97.7	97.6	0.3	0.3	0.1	0.1	1.7	1.8	7.3	7.4	7.5	6.7	6.0	25.0	24.2	12.8	3.2	73.9	37.7	49.0	51.0
45879	PAULDING	93.0	92.4	1.9	2.0	0.2	0.2	5.1	5.5	6.9	6.8	7.2	6.7	7.1	26.8	25.2	11.6	1.7	75.1	37.2	49.0	51.0
45880	PAYNE	97.0	96.7	0.5	0.5	0.2	0.2	2.6	2.9	6.2	6.2	6.7	6.7	6.0	26.6	24.5	14.4	2.6	77.1	39.3	47.8	52.2
45881	RAWSON	98.3	98.1	0.2	0.2	0.1	0.1	1.4	1.5	6.1	6.7	7.4	7.5	6.7	28.0	25.9	10.7	1.1	75.2	37.8	50.2	49.8
45882	ROCKFORD	99.0	99.0	0.1	0.1	0.0	0.1	0.9	0.9	6.2	6.6	7.2	6.7	5.6	24.5	26.2	13.5	3.5	75.8	40.3	48.9	51.1
45883	SAINT HENRY	99.2	99.1	0.1	0.1	0.0	0.1	0.9	1.0	9.5	9.4	9.9	8.7	6.2	26.3	18.9	9.9	1.3	65.6	30.8	52.0	48.0
45885	SAINT MARYS	97.7	97.7	0.3	0.3	0.8	0.8	0.5	0.5	6.6	6.7	7.6	7.0	6.2	26.1	24.8	12.7	2.3	74.7	38.0	49.6	50.4
45886	SCOTT	97.7	97.5	0.7	0.8	0.2	0.2	1.1	1.4	5.9	6.8	8.6	7.4	6.4	25.8	27.8	9.8	1.5	74.0	37.2	50.4	49.6
45887	SPENCERVILLE	98.2	98.1	0.4	0.5	0.2	0.2	0.6	0.6	6.2	6.6	8.0	7.3	5.9	25.7	25.5	12.9	2.0	74.7	38.6	49.8	50.2
45889	VAN BUREN	98.2	98.0	0.2	0.2	0.3	0.4	1.7	1.9	5.7	6.9	9.0	7.8	5.1	26.3	29.5	8.7	0.9	73.3	39.4	50.3	49.7
45890	VANLUE	98.1	98.0	0.2	0.2	0.0	0.0	1.0	1.1	5.4	7.7	9.5	7.0	4.4	27.0	27.7	10.1	1.3	71.9	37.9	49.5	50.6
45891	VAN WERT	96.5	96.1	1.2	1.3	0.3	0.4	2.1	2.4	6.1	6.3	7.0	6.6	6.3	25.3	25.4	14.2	2.7	76.4	39.6	48.1	51.9
45894	VENEDOCIA	99.1	98.9	0.1	0.1	0.1	0.1	0.4	0.5	5.5	5.9	7.8	7.4	5.9	25.8	27.9	12.0	1.8	76.3	40.2	49.6	50.4
45895	WAPAKONETA	98.3	98.3	0.2	0.2	0.3	0.3	0.8	0.8	6.9	6.8	7.1	6.7	6.7	26.9	24.8	11.9	2.2	75.1	37.7	49.1	51.0
45896	WAYNESFIELD	98.3	98.3	0.1	0.1	0.0	0.0	0.8	0.9	7.6	7.6	8.0	6.9	6.2	26.9	24.6	10.6	1.6	72.5	36.2	49.6	50.4
45898	WILLSHIRE	98.8	98.8	0.1	0.1	0.1	0.1	0.6	0.7	7.3	7.2	7.3	7.6	5.9	29.0	22.9	11.3	1.5	73.4	35.9	50.0	50.0
	OHIO	85.0	84.1	11.5	11.8	1.2	1.6	1.9	2.1	6.7	6.6	7.1	7.0	7.1	27.5	24.7	11.6	1.8	75.6	37.0	48.6	51.4
	UNITED STATES	75.1	73.6	12.3	12.5	3.8	4.2	12.5	14.1	6.9	6.7	7.2	7.0	7.3	28.6	23.8	10.8	1.7	75.1	36.0	49.1	50.9

C 45778-45898

# ZIP CODE / POST OFFICE NAME	2004 Per Capita Income	2004 HH Income Base	Less than $25,000	$25,000 to $49,999	$50,000 to $99,999	$100,000 to $149,999	$150,000 or More	2004	2009	2004 National Centile	2004 State Centile	2004 Home Value Base	Less than $50,000	$50,000 to $89,999	$90,000 to $174,999	$175,000 to $399,999	$400,000 or More	2004 Median Home Value
45778 STEWART	18221	390	37.7	31.5	22.6	5.1	3.1	34370	40446	25	16	323	26.9	26.0	29.4	13.9	3.7	84722
45780 THE PLAINS	20486	1326	38.5	28.7	24.0	6.5	2.4	34838	41555	27	17	743	21.4	21.1	44.6	12.1	0.8	99250
45784 VINCENT	22943	1210	17.9	31.0	36.9	12.2	2.1	51185	59690	74	68	1084	14.1	20.9	44.7	19.4	0.9	113624
45786 WATERFORD	18074	1284	25.0	35.3	34.6	4.4	0.7	40507	48071	48	31	1087	20.3	28.2	42.0	8.3	1.1	91260
45788 WHIPPLE	19347	767	30.3	31.0	31.6	4.4	2.7	39728	46679	45	29	635	26.8	33.7	31.7	6.5	1.4	73627
45789 WINGETT RUN	12302	124	34.7	32.3	30.7	1.6	0.8	33554	38580	23	15	103	42.7	29.1	22.3	5.8	0.0	62333
45801 LIMA	17388	9022	34.6	31.3	27.3	5.6	1.4	36412	42686	33	21	5771	22.6	38.4	32.1	6.5	0.4	76137
45804 LIMA	16778	6648	43.4	31.4	19.7	4.0	1.4	29215	33232	11	7	3996	49.7	27.2	17.9	4.4	0.5	50280
45805 LIMA	25196	9952	25.9	32.1	28.7	8.5	4.8	44324	51185	60	44	7086	9.2	31.8	42.8	14.1	2.0	98371
45806 LIMA	24000	4439	19.0	28.2	38.9	11.5	2.5	52217	60371	76	71	3707	11.6	20.9	54.8	11.6	1.1	107752
45807 LIMA	23608	4380	17.1	28.0	39.2	13.1	2.5	54082	62465	78	76	3650	4.3	18.0	59.0	17.9	0.9	118536
45810 ADA	18151	2655	36.8	30.9	24.5	5.8	2.0	34717	39165	26	17	1538	21.7	23.9	44.0	10.0	0.5	94107
45812 ALGER	17769	952	33.5	33.3	28.2	3.4	1.7	36107	40816	32	21	767	28.8	27.9	34.9	7.8	0.5	79906
45813 ANTWERP	22610	1445	23.9	32.3	34.0	7.4	2.4	45025	49446	61	46	1191	15.2	28.0	45.9	9.7	1.2	95780
45814 ARLINGTON	21915	1152	20.9	27.9	39.8	9.9	1.5	51142	58214	74	67	976	4.5	20.4	50.4	23.6	1.1	119505
45817 BLUFFTON	23523	2324	21.8	24.8	38.0	11.6	3.8	52354	60398	76	71	1878	8.7	15.2	53.8	20.4	1.9	125508
45821 CECIL	22545	580	16.9	36.0	36.6	7.9	2.6	47127	52396	66	54	530	25.7	18.5	45.7	9.3	0.9	96889
45822 CELINA	22139	7754	24.9	31.2	33.8	7.3	2.8	45190	51300	62	47	5943	10.5	19.0	47.9	20.2	2.4	113254
45827 CLOVERDALE	20336	914	19.6	30.7	37.6	9.4	2.6	49697	56310	71	62	804	14.9	19.3	50.0	15.4	0.4	110870
45828 COLDWATER	22491	2227	17.6	30.8	39.9	7.5	4.3	51039	58028	74	67	1849	5.1	20.8	50.0	22.9	1.2	117715
45830 COLUMBUS GROVE	22763	2388	17.9	27.4	41.8	10.0	3.0	53443	60882	78	74	2041	11.8	17.2	55.0	15.1	0.9	113476
45831 CONTINENTAL	20271	1290	23.4	28.9	41.1	5.2	1.4	48035	54654	68	57	1091	20.5	22.5	45.0	11.7	0.3	97083
45832 CONVOY	24364	1024	16.1	34.6	38.3	7.0	4.0	49429	54824	71	61	921	14.0	27.1	47.0	11.3	0.5	97546
45833 DELPHOS	20381	4201	24.7	32.7	34.2	6.6	1.9	43712	50202	58	41	3366	14.8	32.0	42.1	10.0	1.1	93183
45835 DOLA	26018	158	17.1	36.7	33.5	10.1	2.5	47684	54433	68	56	138	10.9	24.6	49.3	14.5	0.7	106667
45836 DUNKIRK	20900	641	22.6	29.2	40.7	6.4	1.1	48443	54971	69	58	532	19.6	32.7	40.0	7.5	0.2	86471
45840 FINDLAY	26202	21799	21.2	28.9	34.5	10.6	4.7	49839	57240	72	62	15185	9.2	15.3	48.6	24.6	2.4	124716
45841 JENERA	19561	262	21.4	36.3	33.2	8.4	0.8	46482	52955	65	51	226	8.0	19.5	46.9	22.1	3.5	121154
45843 FOREST	21147	1359	24.8	32.5	34.0	6.5	2.2	44284	50508	59	43	1134	15.8	32.6	42.8	8.0	0.8	91406
45844 FORT JENNINGS	22826	1601	17.1	27.2	43.0	10.3	2.5	54883	61631	80	78	1418	6.5	18.3	55.2	19.2	0.9	120263
45845 FORT LORAMIE	23770	1153	12.4	29.1	39.9	13.4	5.1	58140	66643	83	82	1001	3.8	8.2	50.6	35.0	2.5	151759
45846 FORT RECOVERY	20065	1437	18.8	29.4	39.1	9.4	3.3	51107	56638	74	67	1228	9.5	18.6	45.5	22.4	4.0	120276
45849 GROVER HILL	18890	486	24.5	32.7	37.0	5.1	0.6	43486	48786	57	40	418	25.1	32.1	34.2	7.9	0.7	77857
45850 HARROD	21921	1567	17.3	30.6	40.5	8.8	2.9	51339	57844	74	68	1352	11.0	20.2	50.4	15.8	2.5	111531
45851 HAVILAND	19518	227	17.2	37.4	33.0	7.5	4.9	46924	52441	66	53	194	18.6	32.5	40.7	8.3	0.0	87500
45856 LEIPSIC	19290	1829	22.6	30.2	39.3	6.1	1.9	47673	54185	68	56	1496	16.5	24.4	46.7	11.8	0.6	99577
45858 MC COMB	21588	1173	15.9	33.8	40.0	8.1	2.1	50135	56430	72	63	977	8.3	21.4	50.6	19.2	0.5	111402
45860 MARIA STEIN	19886	674	12.9	25.5	48.5	10.5	2.5	57964	64877	83	82	586	4.3	10.4	40.8	39.9	4.6	164744
45862 MENDON	19808	561	20.0	36.9	36.4	6.6	0.2	45270	51035	62	47	469	25.4	29.0	33.9	10.7	1.1	84306
45863 MIDDLE POINT	19467	488	16.2	38.5	38.9	5.9	0.4	46066	50799	64	49	442	18.8	38.5	35.3	6.1	1.4	82558
45865 MINSTER	26974	1726	16.0	24.3	38.7	13.9	7.1	60157	68891	84	86	1483	4.3	10.4	51.6	31.5	2.3	147638
45867 MOUNT BLANCHARD	23396	434	15.0	29.5	43.8	9.5	2.3	54976	61644	80	78	367	7.1	19.1	51.2	20.4	2.2	113375
45868 MOUNT CORY	21625	295	13.2	27.1	48.8	9.8	1.0	54289	61957	79	77	263	7.2	20.5	52.5	19.4	0.4	117500
45869 NEW BREMEN	24387	1484	14.0	28.6	41.2	11.3	5.0	60189	67514	85	86	1221	0.7	11.6	58.5	26.1	3.1	131812
45871 NEW KNOXVILLE	20472	656	17.1	31.6	37.7	9.9	3.8	51126	58793	74	67	548	2.7	22.6	57.1	15.0	2.6	115238
45872 NORTH BALTIMORE	20749	1618	23.5	32.2	34.8	7.7	1.8	45440	55213	62	47	1230	18.5	29.1	47.8	4.1	0.5	91801
45873 OAKWOOD	20165	1151	24.2	34.1	34.8	4.6	2.4	45023	50133	61	46	978	21.7	33.7	38.0	6.2	0.3	81587
45874 OHIO CITY	20432	1023	19.3	38.9	36.0	3.9	2.0	45126	50491	62	46	876	24.4	35.2	31.6	8.8	0.0	77667
45875 OTTAWA	23782	4019	19.6	26.6	39.1	10.3	4.5	53483	60928	78	74	3332	7.0	18.3	51.8	22.1	0.8	121154
45877 PANDORA	23010	768	15.0	30.3	44.7	7.6	2.5	52989	59325	77	73	658	6.2	19.0	59.6	15.2	0.0	113473
45879 PAULDING	21432	2699	22.2	36.6	32.8	5.8	2.6	43717	49485	58	42	2181	15.9	34.3	42.7	6.9	0.3	89770
45880 PAYNE	20987	1013	23.7	34.0	34.0	6.4	2.0	45028	50403	61	46	810	13.7	34.4	43.1	8.3	0.5	91456
45881 RAWSON	21755	409	13.5	28.6	46.5	10.0	1.5	54924	62276	80	78	355	9.6	22.8	42.3	23.4	2.0	116136
45882 ROCKFORD	21348	1201	20.6	34.6	36.1	7.7	1.1	46299	51935	65	50	1021	10.8	29.7	49.6	7.1	2.9	98705
45883 SAINT HENRY	22811	1272	13.3	29.1	42.7	11.2	3.8	56662	63632	81	80	1093	2.9	8.9	58.6	27.1	2.6	137345
45885 SAINT MARYS	22383	5302	21.6	33.6	34.2	8.4	2.2	46500	53218	65	51	4125	8.6	26.5	48.8	13.8	2.3	105818
45886 SCOTT	21984	216	17.1	32.9	36.6	9.3	4.2	50000	55785	72	62	188	11.7	28.9	49.5	13.3	1.6	105769
45887 SPENCERVILLE	22059	1874	22.0	31.4	36.3	7.8	2.4	47384	53842	67	54	1570	13.1	29.8	40.8	14.7	1.7	97687
45889 VAN BUREN	23122	444	14.6	27.9	40.5	13.5	3.4	55727	64545	80	79	401	8.0	12.0	46.4	30.2	3.5	142378
45890 VANLUE	23644	245	25.7	27.4	36.7	6.1	4.1	46987	53762	66	53	209	2.9	21.5	53.6	21.5	0.5	119167
45891 VAN WERT	22070	6398	24.4	36.0	31.1	6.2	2.3	41539	47352	51	34	4826	13.0	33.0	43.2	9.7	1.1	93946
45894 VENEDOCIA	22337	338	18.9	32.5	39.4	5.3	3.9	49228	54737	71	60	292	17.5	20.9	44.5	14.7	2.4	110106
45895 WAPAKONETA	24177	7089	20.4	31.0	36.0	8.7	3.9	48891	56184	70	59	5681	8.5	26.3	47.0	16.6	1.7	108422
45896 WAYNESFIELD	19928	849	22.3	29.9	38.4	7.4	2.0	47816	53803	68	57	705	13.5	30.6	43.3	11.8	0.9	95764
45898 WILLSHIRE	19454	487	20.9	34.1	39.2	5.5	0.2	46371	52961	65	51	395	26.8	33.7	34.7	3.8	1.0	78636
OHIO	25510		24.6	28.1	32.2	10.1	5.0	47354	56168				9.2	18.6	47.0	22.1	3.1	121192
UNITED STATES	25866		24.7	27.1	30.8	10.9	6.5	48124	56710				10.9	15.0	33.7	30.1	10.4	145905

#	POST OFFICE NAME	FINANCIAL SERVICES				THE HOME							ENTERTAINMENT						PERSONAL			
						Home Improvements		Furnishings														
		Auto Loan	Home Loan	Invest-ments	Retire-ment Plans	Home Repair	Lawn & Garden	Comput-ers & Hard-ware	Major Appli-ances	TV, Radio, Sound Equip-ment	Furni-ture	Dine out/ Carry out	Sports Equip-ment	Fees & Tickets	Toys & Games	Travel	Cable TV	Apparel & Services	Auto Repairs	Health Insur-ance	Pets & Supplies
45778	STEWART	82	62	38	58	68	77	62	71	70	62	83	83	56	81	62	73	77	70	83	93
45780	THE PLAINS	66	62	61	62	64	71	64	66	66	63	81	77	62	80	64	67	77	67	70	76
45784	VINCENT	95	85	64	80	89	96	78	87	83	78	101	103	77	103	81	85	96	84	94	112
45786	WATERFORD	78	68	51	65	72	78	63	71	68	63	82	84	62	84	65	69	78	69	77	91
45788	WHIPPLE	84	67	45	62	72	80	63	73	70	64	84	87	59	83	65	73	79	72	83	98
45789	WINGETT RUN	76	51	23	44	58	67	49	62	59	50	70	74	42	66	50	64	63	61	76	87
45801	LIMA	62	59	61	58	60	66	62	62	64	60	79	72	62	80	62	65	77	63	64	71
45804	LIMA	56	50	51	48	51	59	55	55	59	54	72	63	54	71	55	61	69	57	61	63
45805	LIMA	81	82	84	80	83	91	82	83	83	81	103	94	83	103	83	84	99	83	86	93
45806	LIMA	91	88	78	86	90	97	84	88	85	83	105	103	84	106	85	86	101	86	91	105
45807	LIMA	87	93	92	92	94	98	87	90	86	87	107	105	89	110	89	86	104	88	88	104
45810	ADA	67	56	54	58	58	64	64	63	66	62	81	77	60	79	61	64	78	66	65	75
45812	ALGER	81	56	27	49	63	72	54	66	64	55	76	79	47	72	55	69	69	66	81	94
45813	ANTWERP	87	76	58	74	80	88	74	81	79	74	96	94	72	96	75	80	90	79	87	99
45814	ARLINGTON	92	82	63	78	87	93	76	84	81	76	98	100	75	100	78	83	93	82	91	108
45817	BLUFFTON	90	91	87	89	93	100	88	91	89	86	109	105	88	111	89	90	105	90	94	106
45821	CECIL	95	84	64	80	89	96	78	86	83	78	101	103	76	103	80	85	96	84	94	111
45822	CELINA	86	75	61	72	79	87	74	80	79	73	95	93	71	96	75	81	90	79	87	99
45827	CLOVERDALE	102	82	54	75	88	97	77	89	85	77	102	106	72	102	79	89	96	87	101	119
45828	COLDWATER	100	88	68	85	93	101	83	92	89	83	108	108	81	109	85	91	102	90	99	116
45830	COLUMBUS GROVE	98	88	67	83	93	99	81	90	86	81	105	107	79	107	83	88	99	87	97	116
45831	CONTINENTAL	86	73	54	70	78	85	71	78	76	70	92	92	68	92	72	78	87	77	86	99
45832	CONVOY	104	93	71	88	98	105	86	95	91	86	111	113	84	113	88	93	105	93	103	123
45833	DELPHOS	82	71	58	69	75	83	71	77	76	70	92	90	68	91	72	77	86	76	84	94
45835	DOLA	98	87	66	83	92	98	80	89	85	80	104	106	79	106	83	87	99	87	96	115
45836	DUNKIRK	90	80	60	76	84	91	74	82	78	74	95	98	72	97	76	81	91	80	89	106
45840	FINDLAY	90	90	91	90	91	96	90	91	89	89	110	106	90	111	90	88	107	90	90	103
45841	JENERA	82	75	60	72	79	84	69	76	73	69	89	91	69	91	71	74	85	74	81	97
45843	FOREST	91	72	47	67	78	87	69	79	77	69	92	94	64	91	70	80	86	78	91	104
45844	FORT JENNINGS	100	89	68	84	94	101	82	91	87	82	106	108	81	108	85	89	101	89	99	117
45845	FORT LORAMIE	110	98	75	93	104	111	91	100	96	91	117	120	89	120	93	99	111	98	108	129
45846	FORT RECOVERY	95	85	65	81	90	96	78	87	83	78	101	104	77	103	81	85	96	85	94	112
45849	GROVER HILL	79	70	54	67	75	80	65	72	69	65	84	86	64	86	67	71	80	70	78	93
45850	HARROD	95	85	64	80	89	96	78	87	83	78	101	103	77	103	81	85	96	84	94	112
45851	HAVILAND	94	84	64	79	88	95	77	86	82	77	100	102	76	102	80	84	95	83	93	111
45856	LEIPSIC	79	77	71	74	79	85	74	77	76	73	93	91	74	96	75	77	90	76	81	93
45858	MC COMB	94	82	63	79	87	95	79	86	84	78	102	101	77	103	80	86	96	84	93	108
45860	MARIA STEIN	102	91	69	86	96	103	84	93	89	84	108	111	82	111	86	91	103	91	101	120
45862	MENDON	82	73	56	69	77	83	67	75	72	67	87	89	66	89	70	73	83	73	81	97
45863	MIDDLE POINT	84	75	57	71	79	85	69	77	73	69	89	91	68	91	71	75	85	74	83	99
45865	MINSTER	110	106	90	103	109	116	99	106	101	98	124	124	99	127	101	102	119	103	110	129
45867	MOUNT BLANCHARD	98	87	66	83	92	99	81	89	86	81	104	106	79	106	83	88	99	87	97	115
45868	MOUNT CORY	94	84	64	79	88	95	77	86	82	77	100	102	76	102	80	84	95	83	93	110
45869	NEW BREMEN	108	95	72	91	100	108	90	99	95	89	116	116	88	117	92	98	110	96	107	125
45871	NEW KNOXVILLE	99	88	67	83	93	99	81	90	86	81	105	107	79	107	83	88	100	87	97	116
45872	NORTH BALTIMORE	79	74	64	72	76	83	73	76	76	72	93	87	72	94	73	77	89	75	80	90
45873	OAKWOOD	86	71	48	66	76	83	66	76	73	67	88	90	63	88	68	76	82	74	85	101
45874	OHIO CITY	91	71	45	65	77	85	67	78	75	67	90	93	62	88	68	79	84	77	90	105
45875	OTTAWA	103	93	74	88	98	105	87	95	92	86	112	112	86	115	89	94	106	92	103	121
45877	PANDORA	99	88	67	83	93	99	81	90	86	81	105	107	79	107	84	88	100	87	97	116
45879	PAULDING	80	75	64	70	78	85	71	76	76	70	93	88	72	97	74	79	89	75	84	93
45880	PAYNE	75	74	68	70	76	83	71	74	74	69	91	85	72	96	73	76	87	72	79	88
45881	RAWSON	94	87	70	83	91	96	80	87	83	80	102	104	79	105	82	85	97	85	93	111
45882	ROCKFORD	89	78	60	75	82	90	75	82	79	74	96	96	73	97	76	81	91	80	89	103
45883	SAINT HENRY	117	104	79	99	110	118	96	106	102	96	124	127	94	127	99	105	118	104	115	137
45885	SAINT MARYS	84	78	68	76	81	89	77	81	80	75	98	93	76	100	77	82	93	79	86	96
45886	SCOTT	97	86	66	82	91	98	80	88	84	80	103	105	78	105	82	87	98	86	95	114
45887	SPENCERVILLE	88	82	68	77	85	92	77	83	81	76	99	97	77	103	79	83	94	81	90	103
45889	VAN BUREN	105	93	71	88	98	105	86	95	91	86	111	114	84	113	89	94	106	93	103	123
45890	VANLUE	98	87	66	83	92	99	81	89	86	81	104	106	79	106	83	88	99	87	97	115
45891	VAN WERT	76	72	65	69	75	83	71	75	75	69	91	85	71	94	73	77	87	73	81	89
45894	VENEDOCIA	93	83	63	79	88	94	77	85	82	77	99	101	75	101	79	84	94	83	92	110
45895	WAPAKONETA	90	87	78	85	90	97	84	88	87	83	107	102	85	110	86	88	102	87	93	105
45896	WAYNESFIELD	86	75	58	73	79	87	73	80	77	72	94	93	71	95	74	79	89	78	86	99
45898	WILLSHIRE	82	73	56	70	77	83	69	76	73	68	89	89	67	90	70	75	84	74	82	96
	OHIO	89	88	90	87	88	95	88	89	89	87	110	103	88	111	88	89	107	89	90	102
	UNITED STATES	100	100	100	100	100	100	100	100	100	100	100	100	100	100	100	100	100	100	100	100

OKLAHOMA

A 73002-73128

POPULATION CHANGE

ZIP CODE #	POST OFFICE NAME	COUNTY FIPS CODE	POPULATION 2000	2004	2009	2000-2004 ANNUAL RATE % Rate	State Centile	HOUSEHOLDS 2000	2004	2009	% Annual Rate 2000-2004	2004 Average HH Size	FAMILIES 2000	2004	% Annual Rate 2000-2004
73002	ALEX	051	1980	2034	2146	0.6	67	757	784	834	0.8	2.59	582	599	0.7
73003	EDMOND	109	37168	40923	43807	2.3	95	13126	14495	15580	2.4	2.82	10470	11591	2.4
73004	AMBER	051	2722	2944	3181	1.9	92	942	1025	1113	2.0	2.87	775	840	1.9
73005	ANADARKO	015	10469	10319	10217	-0.3	25	3669	3616	3590	-0.3	2.71	2646	2599	-0.4
73006	APACHE	015	3625	3736	3785	0.7	70	1366	1420	1449	0.9	2.63	1023	1060	0.8
73007	ARCADIA	109	1722	1876	1986	2.0	93	685	759	813	2.4	2.39	506	556	2.2
73008	BETHANY	109	21299	20975	21305	-0.4	24	8580	8509	8710	-0.2	2.31	5570	5480	-0.4
73009	BINGER	015	1862	1834	1815	-0.4	24	707	699	695	-0.3	2.57	539	531	-0.4
73010	BLANCHARD	087	6731	7416	8174	2.3	95	2462	2733	3032	2.5	2.71	1945	2150	2.4
73011	BRADLEY	051	435	449	474	0.8	72	162	169	180	1.0	2.66	132	137	0.9
73013	EDMOND	109	32194	35025	37266	2.0	93	11843	13047	14022	2.3	2.55	8731	9568	2.2
73014	CALUMET	017	2331	2363	2502	0.3	53	890	908	969	0.5	2.60	677	686	0.3
73015	CARNEGIE	015	3643	3715	3751	0.5	59	1420	1462	1487	0.7	2.50	991	1017	0.6
73016	CASHION	073	588	608	629	0.8	73	229	238	247	0.9	2.55	173	180	0.9
73017	CEMENT	015	1502	1443	1412	-0.9	5	594	573	563	-0.8	2.51	420	405	-0.9
73018	CHICKASHA	051	19816	20699	21996	1.0	80	7926	8360	8971	1.3	2.38	5291	5552	1.1
73020	CHOCTAW	109	17913	18906	19725	1.3	86	6590	7036	7405	1.6	2.60	5305	5644	1.5
73021	COLONY	149	257	246	243	-1.0	4	108	104	103	-0.9	2.37	83	80	-0.9
73024	CORN	149	1177	1193	1202	0.3	53	422	430	435	0.4	2.56	304	308	0.3
73026	NORMAN	027	10892	11532	12400	1.4	86	3950	4242	4615	1.7	2.72	3227	3445	1.6
73027	COYLE	083	2663	2678	2711	0.1	46	594	603	622	0.4	2.41	379	381	0.1
73028	CRESCENT	083	3209	3294	3392	0.6	65	1308	1358	1411	0.9	2.40	915	942	0.7
73029	CYRIL	015	1567	1556	1542	-0.2	32	586	586	583	0.0	2.58	428	426	-0.1
73030	DAVIS	099	4398	4467	4534	0.4	55	1746	1778	1809	0.4	2.48	1250	1268	0.3
73034	EDMOND	109	31096	33512	35447	1.8	91	11674	12718	13574	2.0	2.52	8162	8834	1.9
73036	EL RENO	017	18899	19205	20336	0.4	56	6725	6925	7451	0.7	2.50	4630	4725	0.5
73038	FORT COBB	015	1827	1776	1745	-0.7	12	707	691	682	-0.5	2.57	526	513	-0.6
73040	GEARY	011	1820	1828	1859	0.1	44	695	702	720	0.2	2.50	473	476	0.2
73041	GOTEBO	075	415	393	383	-1.3	1	181	173	170	-1.1	2.27	131	125	-1.1
73042	GRACEMONT	015	881	860	846	-0.6	15	343	338	336	-0.3	2.54	248	244	-0.4
73043	GREENFIELD	011	185	181	183	-0.5	16	74	73	75	-0.3	2.48	53	52	-0.5
73044	GUTHRIE	083	18451	18852	19459	0.5	62	6997	7203	7499	0.7	2.51	4904	5037	0.6
73045	HARRAH	109	9329	9729	10085	1.0	78	3358	3539	3697	1.2	2.71	2670	2806	1.2
73047	HINTON	015	3070	3153	3198	0.6	66	916	947	964	0.8	2.56	666	688	0.8
73048	HYDRO	015	2181	2145	2127	-0.4	23	836	829	826	-0.2	2.54	599	592	-0.3
73049	JONES	109	5006	5334	5609	1.5	89	1832	1972	2091	1.8	2.63	1387	1484	1.6
73051	LEXINGTON	027	8823	9341	9912	1.4	86	2333	2541	2775	2.0	2.65	1804	1953	1.9
73052	LINDSAY	049	5408	5572	5810	0.7	70	2199	2272	2376	0.8	2.43	1563	1603	0.6
73053	LOOKEBA	015	704	668	650	-1.2	1	257	245	240	-1.1	2.67	200	190	-1.2
73054	LUTHER	109	4123	4268	4425	0.8	75	1440	1509	1579	1.1	2.74	1117	1164	1.0
73055	MARLOW	137	8241	8147	8106	-0.3	27	3285	3264	3267	-0.2	2.45	2427	2405	-0.2
73056	MARSHALL	083	403	386	389	-1.0	4	169	164	167	-0.7	2.35	132	128	-0.7
73057	MAYSVILLE	049	2409	2409	2466	0.0	40	953	956	980	0.1	2.49	690	690	0.0
73058	MERIDIAN	083	221	228	234	0.7	71	97	101	104	1.0	2.23	71	72	0.3
73059	MINCO	051	2425	2572	2752	1.4	87	935	994	1068	1.5	2.59	697	737	1.3
73061	MORRISON	103	1302	1549	1701	4.2	99	499	601	666	4.5	2.58	373	448	4.4
73062	MOUNTAIN VIEW	075	1451	1395	1365	-0.9	5	606	590	583	-0.6	2.33	406	394	-0.7
73063	MULHALL	083	498	482	488	-0.8	9	188	183	187	-0.6	2.63	144	140	-0.7
73064	MUSTANG	017	15617	16994	18588	2.0	93	5563	6146	6809	2.4	2.74	4516	4963	2.3
73065	NEWCASTLE	087	5438	6057	6719	2.6	96	1993	2237	2496	2.8	2.70	1654	1850	2.7
73067	NINNEKAH	051	1283	1294	1361	0.2	49	491	501	531	0.5	2.58	381	387	0.4
73068	NOBLE	027	10566	11967	13267	3.0	97	3811	4322	4812	3.0	2.73	2946	3320	2.9
73069	NORMAN	027	22125	22825	24314	0.7	71	9945	10308	11082	0.9	2.11	4994	5160	0.8
73071	NORMAN	027	27584	28499	30478	0.8	73	11463	11970	12945	1.0	2.32	6650	6920	0.9
73072	NORMAN	027	37912	41926	46144	2.4	95	14470	16275	18228	2.8	2.31	8521	9545	2.7
73073	ORLANDO	083	364	353	357	-0.7	10	133	130	132	-0.5	2.72	102	99	-0.7
73074	PAOLI	049	1050	1055	1078	0.1	45	403	407	417	0.2	2.59	310	313	0.2
73075	PAULS VALLEY	049	9018	9148	9370	0.3	54	3535	3591	3687	0.4	2.44	2418	2449	0.3
73077	PERRY	103	7319	7194	7192	-0.4	23	3036	3005	3027	-0.2	2.35	2106	2073	-0.4
73078	PIEDMONT	017	4957	5412	5922	2.1	94	1656	1831	2026	2.4	2.96	1444	1591	2.3
73079	POCASSET	051	922	965	1026	1.1	81	346	366	391	1.3	2.64	276	291	1.3
73080	PURCELL	087	9950	10280	10950	0.8	73	3767	3907	4184	0.9	2.58	2799	2893	0.8
73082	RUSH SPRINGS	051	3740	3913	4157	1.1	81	1460	1539	1646	1.3	2.54	1096	1151	1.2
73084	SPENCER	109	6754	6614	6689	-0.5	17	2583	2557	2610	-0.2	2.56	1772	1742	-0.4
73086	SULPHUR	099	7987	8119	8220	0.4	56	3165	3239	3297	0.6	2.42	2266	2312	0.5
73089	TUTTLE	051	10575	11540	12579	2.1	94	3748	4125	4532	2.3	2.79	3118	3422	2.2
73090	UNION CITY	017	655	706	765	1.8	91	217	239	263	2.3	2.74	164	179	2.1
73092	VERDEN	051	790	825	876	1.0	80	296	311	332	1.2	2.65	224	235	1.1
73093	WASHINGTON	087	2171	2413	2671	2.5	96	779	872	971	2.7	2.76	631	703	2.6
73095	WAYNE	087	1589	1627	1726	0.6	63	591	607	646	0.6	2.68	445	454	0.5
73096	WEATHERFORD	039	11914	12119	12287	0.4	57	4706	4839	4957	0.7	2.34	2758	2828	0.6
73098	WYNNEWOOD	049	3755	3735	3794	-0.1	33	1526	1527	1559	0.0	2.39	1029	1026	-0.1
73099	YUKON	017	41564	45000	49242	1.9	93	15159	16583	18329	2.1	2.69	11990	13087	2.1
73102	OKLAHOMA CITY	109	1632	1611	1618	-0.3	25	767	746	760	-0.7	2.16	134	75	-12.8
73103	OKLAHOMA CITY	109	4337	4490	4695	0.8	75	2249	2347	2474	1.0	1.88	875	906	0.8
73104	OKLAHOMA CITY	109	1841	2366	2738	6.1	100	725	948	1111	6.5	2.44	412	546	6.9
73105	OKLAHOMA CITY	109	4899	4962	5174	0.3	52	2145	2218	2345	0.8	2.15	1297	1320	0.4
73106	OKLAHOMA CITY	109	15685	15737	16117	0.1	43	5030	5053	5217	0.1	2.61	2639	2612	-0.2
73107	OKLAHOMA CITY	109	24883	25084	25650	0.2	48	11010	11124	11425	0.2	2.23	5867	5864	0.0
73108	OKLAHOMA CITY	109	15255	15353	15699	0.2	47	5269	5281	5400	0.1	2.85	3504	3483	-0.1
73109	OKLAHOMA CITY	109	19415	19436	19846	0.0	41	7601	7591	7769	0.0	2.51	4446	4395	-0.3
73110	OKLAHOMA CITY	109	34475	34602	35561	0.1	43	14734	14936	15474	0.3	2.29	9125	9178	0.1
73111	OKLAHOMA CITY	109	12687	12598	12920	-0.2	32	5188	5222	5415	0.2	2.30	3195	3174	-0.2
73112	OKLAHOMA CITY	109	29674	29086	29467	-0.5	17	14751	14561	14847	-0.3	1.96	7226	7058	-0.6
73114	OKLAHOMA CITY	109	17253	17184	17583	-0.1	35	6759	6824	7048	0.2	2.51	4253	4237	-0.1
73115	OKLAHOMA CITY	109	21977	21642	22107	-0.4	24	8991	8953	9227	-0.1	2.41	6117	6050	-0.3
73116	OKLAHOMA CITY	109	9453	9435	9642	0.0	37	4429	4447	4575	0.1	2.07	2559	2548	-0.1
73117	OKLAHOMA CITY	109	5195	5192	5364	0.0	38	2292	2297	2387	0.1	2.18	1220	1210	-0.1
73118	OKLAHOMA CITY	109	14222	14108	14367	-0.2	31	6625	6626	6800	0.0	2.08	3267	3225	-0.3
73119	OKLAHOMA CITY	109	27307	27366	27877	0.1	42	10312	10333	10560	0.1	2.61	6698	6648	-0.1
73120	OKLAHOMA CITY	109	34928	36164	37692	0.8	75	17225	17943	18811	1.0	1.99	9114	9449	0.9
73121	OKLAHOMA CITY	109	3028	3057	3137	0.2	50	1188	1215	1260	0.5	2.46	841	857	0.4
73122	OKLAHOMA CITY	109	13442	13681	14133	0.4	58	5877	6012	6242	0.5	2.27	3635	3689	0.4
73127	OKLAHOMA CITY	109	25434	25965	26908	0.5	61	10197	10435	10855	0.5	2.45	6555	6672	0.4
73128	OKLAHOMA CITY	109	2230	2389	2545	1.6	91	930	999	1067	1.7	2.39	653	704	1.8
	OKLAHOMA					0.8					1.0	2.48			0.9
	UNITED STATES					1.2					1.3	2.58			1.1

ZIP CODE # POST OFFICE NAME	RACE (%) White 2000	White 2004	Black 2000	Black 2004	Asian/Pacific 2000	Asian/Pacific 2004	% Hispanic Origin 2000	% Hispanic Origin 2004	2004 AGE DISTRIBUTION (%) 0-4	5-9	10-14	15-19	20-24	25-44	45-64	65-84	85+	18+	MEDIAN AGE 2004	% 2004 Males	% 2004 Females
73002 ALEX	89.6	88.8	0.3	0.3	0.1	0.1	2.2	2.6	7.2	7.2	6.8	6.9	6.1	25.2	25.4	13.7	1.4	74.6	38.5	51.3	48.7
73003 EDMOND	87.8	86.4	4.6	4.9	1.8	2.3	2.8	3.3	8.9	8.8	8.5	7.0	6.3	31.7	22.7	5.6	0.5	69.4	32.8	48.6	51.4
73004 AMBER	89.6	88.7	0.2	0.1	0.5	0.5	2.7	3.1	8.0	7.9	8.3	7.4	6.7	28.4	24.5	8.3	0.4	71.2	33.8	50.4	49.6
73005 ANADARKO	47.4	46.0	4.3	4.4	0.3	0.3	7.6	8.0	8.0	8.0	8.6	10.0	7.4	23.8	21.7	10.8	1.8	68.6	32.4	48.1	51.9
73006 APACHE	66.5	66.1	0.4	0.4	0.3	0.3	3.6	3.8	6.8	7.5	7.7	7.8	6.3	25.8	25.3	11.4	1.4	73.1	36.7	49.1	50.9
73007 ARCADIA	80.4	78.5	11.2	12.2	0.3	0.4	2.2	2.6	5.4	5.5	6.1	7.8	5.0	25.0	31.9	11.8	1.4	77.2	42.3	51.3	48.7
73008 BETHANY	85.5	83.8	4.6	4.9	1.5	1.9	5.8	6.9	6.3	5.8	6.0	7.8	9.5	24.5	22.9	14.7	2.6	78.1	37.3	47.5	52.5
73009 BINGER	78.8	77.8	2.1	2.1	0.1	0.1	5.3	5.8	6.0	5.9	6.8	7.1	6.1	25.9	26.1	13.8	2.3	76.8	40.2	50.9	49.1
73010 BLANCHARD	89.9	88.9	0.2	0.2	0.2	0.2	2.9	3.4	7.3	7.2	7.3	7.3	6.7	28.2	24.9	10.2	1.0	73.7	36.5	49.5	50.5
73011 BRADLEY	88.1	87.3	0.2	0.2	0.0	0.0	2.3	2.5	7.1	7.1	6.7	6.5	6.2	24.9	27.0	13.6	0.9	75.1	39.2	51.7	48.3
73013 EDMOND	86.8	85.0	5.6	6.0	2.6	3.4	2.3	2.8	6.2	6.6	7.5	8.2	8.4	25.6	25.8	9.6	2.2	75.2	36.6	48.0	52.1
73014 CALUMET	84.6	83.5	0.6	0.6	0.1	0.1	3.7	4.3	7.2	7.1	7.1	6.9	6.6	25.7	27.3	11.3	0.9	74.5	37.9	50.5	49.5
73015 CARNEGIE	66.2	65.1	0.8	0.9	0.1	0.1	7.8	8.8	6.4	6.3	7.3	7.1	6.7	22.2	25.1	16.0	3.0	75.4	40.7	49.5	50.5
73016 CASHION	94.6	93.9	0.0	0.0	0.2	0.2	2.4	3.0	6.3	6.6	8.6	8.6	6.1	26.2	27.1	9.4	1.3	73.4	37.6	49.0	51.0
73017 CEMENT	87.0	86.6	1.3	1.4	0.2	0.2	1.6	1.7	6.3	6.3	7.1	6.8	6.4	23.5	27.4	14.1	2.1	76.1	40.1	47.4	52.6
73018 CHICKASHA	83.0	81.8	6.8	7.2	0.6	0.8	3.5	3.9	7.0	6.3	6.5	6.9	8.0	26.3	23.3	13.1	2.6	76.3	37.0	47.3	52.7
73020 CHOCTAW	87.4	86.0	2.8	3.0	0.7	0.8	2.7	3.2	5.8	6.2	7.3	6.9	6.3	26.8	29.2	10.8	0.8	76.4	39.5	49.6	50.4
73021 COLONY	89.9	90.2	0.4	0.4	0.0	0.0	3.1	3.3	5.3	5.3	4.9	5.3	5.3	25.6	29.3	17.1	2.0	82.1	44.1	50.4	49.6
73024 CORN	92.5	92.5	0.8	0.8	0.0	0.0	4.3	4.3	6.6	6.6	6.8	6.7	5.3	23.1	22.0	16.7	6.3	75.5	41.9	47.7	52.3
73026 NORMAN	88.3	87.2	1.2	1.3	0.6	0.8	2.1	2.4	5.7	6.1	7.1	7.3	6.1	26.1	31.7	9.6	0.5	76.7	40.4	50.6	49.4
73027 COYLE	32.2	31.2	62.6	63.4	0.1	0.1	1.7	1.9	3.0	3.7	4.1	17.9	35.6	14.7	13.3	6.9	0.8	86.5	23.0	49.4	50.6
73028 CRESCENT	90.6	89.4	2.9	3.3	0.1	0.1	1.7	2.0	6.2	6.3	6.7	6.1	5.7	24.1	25.2	16.8	2.8	77.1	41.4	50.1	49.9
73029 CYRIL	83.0	82.2	0.3	0.3	0.3	0.5	2.6	2.8	7.4	7.1	7.5	7.3	5.9	24.2	22.5	14.9	3.4	73.3	37.5	46.2	53.8
73030 DAVIS	80.5	79.5	3.7	3.9	0.3	0.4	1.3	1.5	7.1	6.7	7.0	5.9	6.5	24.8	24.8	14.9	2.5	75.6	39.7	49.2	50.8
73034 EDMOND	84.8	82.9	3.7	3.8	4.9	6.0	2.9	3.4	6.1	6.4	7.5	8.7	10.8	25.5	25.5	8.0	1.5	76.0	34.4	49.2	50.8
73036 EL RENO	78.7	77.3	6.8	7.2	0.6	0.7	7.2	8.1	6.6	6.2	6.3	6.8	7.9	29.7	23.5	11.4	1.7	76.8	36.0	53.4	46.6
73038 FORT COBB	70.2	69.4	1.4	1.5	0.1	0.1	3.7	3.7	5.6	6.5	7.4	8.3	5.6	23.9	24.5	16.1	2.2	75.3	39.9	49.3	50.7
73040 GEARY	75.6	75.6	3.2	2.8	0.1	0.1	4.7	5.0	6.7	6.5	7.7	7.2	5.4	24.0	22.9	15.3	4.3	74.5	39.7	48.1	51.9
73041 GOTEBO	74.2	73.0	0.5	0.5	0.2	0.3	3.4	3.8	3.8	4.3	5.9	5.9	5.6	21.4	32.1	18.1	3.1	82.2	47.0	52.2	47.8
73042 GRACEMONT	78.9	78.0	0.1	0.1	0.1	0.1	5.6	6.2	6.3	6.7	7.2	6.1	5.9	25.6	27.4	13.0	1.7	76.2	39.1	51.5	48.5
73043 GREENFIELD	88.7	88.4	1.6	1.1	0.0	0.0	0.5	0.6	3.9	5.0	7.2	7.7	6.6	20.4	34.8	12.7	1.7	78.5	44.3	51.9	48.1
73044 GUTHRIE	82.0	80.6	9.7	10.4	0.5	0.6	3.3	3.7	6.5	6.2	6.8	7.6	7.3	25.7	25.8	11.9	2.3	75.9	37.9	48.7	51.3
73045 HARRAH	87.9	86.7	0.6	0.7	0.4	0.5	2.4	2.9	6.7	6.7	7.5	7.5	7.0	27.3	25.5	10.1	1.6	74.3	37.0	49.1	50.9
73047 HINTON	78.6	77.4	9.5	9.6	0.2	0.3	6.6	7.4	5.5	5.6	5.9	5.9	7.6	34.5	22.9	10.3	1.8	79.8	36.7	60.0	40.0
73048 HYDRO	89.1	88.3	0.2	0.2	0.2	0.2	7.0	7.8	6.6	6.4	7.2	6.6	6.5	24.5	26.1	13.7	2.4	75.9	39.6	49.4	50.6
73049 JONES	82.3	80.9	8.8	9.2	0.3	0.4	2.5	3.0	6.5	6.4	6.5	7.1	6.8	25.4	28.5	11.4	1.5	76.3	39.6	49.8	50.2
73051 LEXINGTON	78.1	77.1	8.2	8.2	0.2	0.3	4.4	4.9	5.0	5.0	5.6	6.0	7.5	36.3	25.3	8.0	1.3	81.0	37.3	63.0	37.1
73052 LINDSAY	90.3	89.6	0.1	0.1	0.2	0.2	1.3	1.5	6.5	6.4	6.7	6.2	6.0	25.0	23.5	16.7	3.1	76.7	40.4	48.0	52.1
73053 LOOKEBA	79.8	78.1	1.0	1.1	0.1	0.2	12.6	14.2	5.7	6.6	7.5	7.8	6.3	25.5	24.3	15.1	1.4	75.9	39.5	50.6	49.4
73054 LUTHER	85.0	83.7	4.0	4.3	0.3	0.4	2.0	2.3	6.1	6.4	7.9	7.5	6.5	26.1	27.6	10.2	1.7	74.7	38.5	50.0	50.1
73055 MARLOW	91.3	91.3	0.1	0.1	0.2	0.2	1.8	1.8	6.4	6.4	6.5	6.6	6.1	24.4	25.8	15.0	2.9	76.6	40.9	49.0	51.0
73056 MARSHALL	93.1	92.2	1.5	1.8	0.0	0.0	2.2	2.6	6.0	6.2	6.2	5.7	6.2	25.9	27.5	14.0	2.3	77.7	41.3	52.3	47.7
73057 MAYSVILLE	87.3	86.3	0.3	0.3	0.1	0.1	2.1	2.5	7.1	7.1	7.1	6.2	6.5	24.4	23.9	15.2	2.5	74.8	39.0	49.0	51.0
73058 MERIDIAN	84.6	82.9	5.0	5.7	0.5	0.4	2.3	2.6	5.3	5.7	8.3	7.5	5.7	28.5	29.0	9.7	0.4	75.4	39.1	53.1	46.9
73059 MINCO	92.3	91.5	0.1	0.1	0.2	0.3	3.4	3.9	6.8	6.7	7.2	7.2	6.7	26.7	23.8	12.6	2.3	74.9	37.7	49.4	50.6
73061 MORRISON	88.5	87.4	0.2	0.2	0.4	0.5	2.5	2.8	7.0	7.3	7.7	7.4	6.7	28.3	26.0	8.8	0.8	73.5	35.7	50.0	50.0
73062 MOUNTAIN VIEW	79.6	78.9	0.3	0.4	0.1	0.1	2.8	3.2	5.4	5.5	6.5	6.7	5.6	21.4	26.0	18.4	4.7	78.7	44.3	47.1	52.9
73063 MULHALL	92.2	91.5	0.0	0.0	0.8	0.8	1.2	1.5	7.9	6.6	7.3	6.6	6.4	25.9	23.9	13.3	2.1	74.5	36.9	51.2	48.8
73064 MUSTANG	91.9	91.1	0.6	0.7	0.7	0.8	2.8	3.3	7.0	7.3	8.2	7.3	6.5	28.6	25.5	8.7	1.0	72.9	35.7	49.0	51.0
73065 NEWCASTLE	89.9	88.9	0.2	0.2	0.2	0.3	2.4	2.8	5.8	6.3	7.1	7.2	6.5	27.4	30.0	9.3	0.6	76.4	39.5	50.6	49.4
73067 NINNEKAH	89.6	88.3	0.6	0.6	0.0	0.0	2.4	2.9	6.3	6.3	6.5	7.1	6.4	25.4	28.6	12.4	1.1	76.7	39.9	51.2	48.8
73068 NOBLE	88.8	87.6	0.4	0.4	0.3	0.4	2.7	3.1	7.4	7.1	7.7	7.5	7.1	29.0	24.6	8.6	0.9	72.8	35.1	49.5	50.5
73069 NORMAN	83.7	82.0	3.2	3.4	2.9	3.5	4.9	5.6	5.4	4.9	5.4	8.0	14.0	29.6	20.0	10.6	2.0	80.4	31.6	50.2	49.8
73071 NORMAN	79.6	78.0	6.2	6.4	2.6	3.2	4.2	4.7	7.3	6.2	6.1	7.1	13.4	32.7	19.5	7.0	0.9	76.8	29.5	49.8	50.3
73072 NORMAN	82.3	80.3	4.2	4.3	5.2	6.6	3.6	4.0	5.5	4.8	5.0	12.6	15.4	28.3	20.0	7.4	1.0	81.4	28.4	50.0	50.0
73073 ORLANDO	92.3	91.2	0.0	0.0	0.6	0.9	1.4	1.4	6.8	6.8	7.4	6.8	6.5	26.1	24.1	13.6	2.0	74.8	37.3	51.0	49.0
73074 PAOLI	85.5	84.5	0.3	0.3	0.1	0.2	4.2	5.0	7.1	6.8	7.1	6.5	7.7	26.6	24.8	11.4	2.0	75.2	37.2	49.7	50.3
73075 PAULS VALLEY	81.4	80.0	3.7	3.9	0.5	0.7	6.7	7.7	6.7	6.4	6.5	6.4	6.9	26.1	24.3	13.7	2.9	76.4	38.5	48.2	51.8
73077 PERRY	91.1	90.2	2.3	2.4	0.4	0.5	1.5	1.7	6.6	6.5	6.6	6.0	6.0	26.3	25.2	14.4	2.5	76.7	39.6	49.3	50.7
73078 PIEDMONT	93.2	92.4	0.5	0.6	0.4	0.5	2.3	2.6	6.8	7.3	8.3	7.8	5.7	26.8	28.8	7.8	0.7	72.9	38.3	50.3	49.7
73079 POCASSET	92.2	91.6	0.2	0.2	0.2	0.2	2.5	3.0	6.8	6.5	6.0	8.0	6.3	25.4	28.6	11.0	1.4	75.7	39.8	50.8	49.2
73080 PURCELL	84.0	82.7	1.3	1.4	0.3	0.4	7.8	8.8	7.3	7.1	7.1	6.6	6.8	27.6	23.4	12.2	1.9	74.5	36.7	49.5	50.5
73082 RUSH SPRINGS	89.3	88.4	0.1	0.1	0.1	0.2	2.6	3.0	6.5	6.9	6.8	6.9	6.5	25.3	25.8	13.6	1.8	75.8	39.2	51.2	48.8
73084 SPENCER	32.5	30.9	60.3	61.3	0.4	0.4	2.4	2.7	6.2	7.0	8.0	8.5	6.4	22.4	26.3	14.0	1.4	73.5	39.1	49.4	50.7
73086 SULPHUR	81.0	80.0	0.9	1.0	0.4	0.5	4.1	4.6	6.7	5.9	5.8	5.9	6.5	23.9	25.9	16.9	2.5	78.1	41.6	49.6	50.4
73089 TUTTLE	91.4	90.6	0.1	0.1	0.2	0.2	2.1	2.4	7.1	7.1	7.5	7.3	6.8	27.0	27.7	8.7	0.8	73.9	37.2	49.6	50.4
73090 UNION CITY	89.5	88.4	2.4	2.7	0.5	0.4	1.7	1.7	6.2	6.0	6.4	13.6	8.6	23.7	25.6	8.8	1.1	71.7	33.8	52.8	47.2
73092 VERDEN	90.1	89.5	0.4	0.5	0.1	0.1	2.4	2.8	8.2	8.2	8.2	7.4	5.7	25.2	22.3	12.0	2.7	70.9	36.7	45.6	54.4
73093 WASHINGTON	88.5	87.3	0.3	0.3	0.5	0.6	4.5	5.2	6.1	6.7	7.7	7.0	6.6	26.8	28.1	10.2	0.8	75.0	38.0	50.6	49.4
73095 WAYNE	87.4	86.4	0.1	0.1	0.1	0.1	5.0	5.9	7.1	7.1	6.0	6.4	7.4	25.6	25.8	12.8	1.8	76.2	38.9	48.4	51.6
73096 WEATHERFORD	87.2	86.0	1.7	1.8	1.3	1.6	4.2	4.8	5.6	4.9	5.6	10.8	18.2	26.3	18.8	8.4	1.4	80.4	27.5	48.9	51.1
73098 WYNNEWOOD	81.7	80.4	6.9	7.4	0.1	0.2	2.4	2.9	5.8	5.9	6.8	6.5	6.1	24.2	25.5	16.1	3.2	77.4	41.3	47.8	52.2
73099 YUKON	88.4	86.7	1.0	1.0	4.4	5.5	3.0	3.4	6.9	7.0	7.6	7.4	6.8	28.3	26.7	8.3	1.0	73.9	36.4	48.4	51.6
73102 OKLAHOMA CITY	55.2	52.8	30.1	31.2	1.8	2.2	6.1	7.1	0.6	0.9	1.0	4.7	13.8	43.3	27.7	7.3	0.7	96.2	38.2	78.7	21.3
73103 OKLAHOMA CITY	63.6	60.3	20.6	21.7	5.8	6.9	5.4	6.3	5.8	5.4	5.9	6.3	9.1	34.7	25.1	6.6	1.1	79.1	34.2	50.4	49.6
73104 OKLAHOMA CITY	11.4	10.6	82.0	82.1	2.2	2.8	1.4	1.4	9.9	9.4	9.9	9.3	7.1	25.9	20.7	6.9	1.0	64.8	28.4	44.9	55.1
73105 OKLAHOMA CITY	13.8	13.4	80.8	80.4	0.9	1.3	1.4	1.7	6.3	6.0	6.0	6.5	7.2	24.9	26.0	14.7	2.3	77.6	39.8	45.5	54.5
73106 OKLAHOMA CITY	51.4	48.3	15.9	16.0	9.5	11.1	23.2	25.3	6.7	5.7	5.9	9.0	13.6	34.1	19.4	4.9	0.8	77.8	29.7	54.7	45.4
73107 OKLAHOMA CITY	71.3	68.5	8.0	8.2	4.4	5.3	14.8	16.9	7.9	6.9	6.1	5.3	7.1	32.8	21.8	9.7	2.3	76.0	34.8	49.6	50.4
73108 OKLAHOMA CITY	58.6	56.5	7.2	7.0	0.5	0.7	43.1	47.5	11.6	9.5	7.9	7.4	8.7	30.8	16.8	6.5	0.9	66.7	27.8	52.0	48.0
73109 OKLAHOMA CITY	61.8	59.0	5.3	5.4	1.1	1.3	32.1	35.2	8.9	7.6	7.2	6.6	7.5	28.2	19.4	12.5	2.1	72.2	33.1	48.8	51.2
73110 OKLAHOMA CITY	68.7	65.8	19.7	21.3	1.8	2.2	4.4	5.1	7.8	6.8	6.8	6.7	9.2	28.6	20.4	12.1	1.7	74.7	33.0	47.6	52.4
73111 OKLAHOMA CITY	6.5	5.9	89.4	89.6	0.2	0.2	1.9	2.0	6.1	6.3	7.1	7.3	6.5	22.4	24.5	17.5	2.4	76.0	40.9	43.5	56.5
73112 OKLAHOMA CITY	77.6	75.1	8.1	8.4	4.7	5.8	6.6	7.6	6.0	5.3	4.7	4.8	7.0	31.3	23.8	14.6	2.7	81.4	38.9	47.3	52.7
73114 OKLAHOMA CITY	33.4	32.0	55.5	55.7	1.8	2.2	6.7	7.6	9.3	8.8	8.8	7.8	9.6	29.9	18.9	6.2	0.7	68.4	28.2	47.2	52.8
73115 OKLAHOMA CITY	74.1	71.9	14.0	14.6	1.7	2.1	4.9	5.7	7.6	6.8	6.7	6.9	8.4	26.9	22.3	13.1	1.2	74.8	34.5	47.6	52.4
73116 OKLAHOMA CITY	87.0	85.3	3.5	3.7	3.8	4.7	2.9	3.4	5.3	5.4	5.5	5.5	5.5	25.2	26.6	16.8	4.1	80.4	43.3	46.6	53.4
73117 OKLAHOMA CITY	10.5	9.8	84.7	85.2	0.2	0.3	2.0	2.1	7.6	6.6	7.2	7.6	6.2	21.7	24.3	15.5	3.4	74.0	40.4	44.5	55.5
73118 OKLAHOMA CITY	69.1	66.7	14.0	14.3	6.2	7.4	6.3	7.1	6.7	5.9	5.5	5.8	6.8	33.4	24.4	9.1	2.4	78.3	35.9	49.3	50.7
73119 OKLAHOMA CITY	66.5	63.6	5.8	5.9	1.1	1.4	26.2	29.6	9.5	8.1	7.5	6.9	8.0	28.5	19.0	10.9	1.7	70.9	31.3	48.9	51.1
73120 OKLAHOMA CITY	76.3	74.2	15.2	16.3	2.4	3.0	3.3	3.7	5.8	5.2	4.8	4.8	9.2	29.6	23.1	15.2	2.5	81.9	37.7	46.7	53.3
73121 OKLAHOMA CITY	23.4	22.2	70.7	71.3	0.7	0.8	1.2	1.3	4.8	5.0	6.0	6.6	6.8	19.1	30.7	18.5	2.3	80.1	46.0	47.4	52.6
73122 OKLAHOMA CITY	81.6	79.7	7.9	8.3	1.6	2.0	7.5	8.9	6.9	6.3	6.5	6.5	7.8	27.5	22.7	14.2	1.6	76.6	36.6	48.0	52.0
73127 OKLAHOMA CITY	65.0	62.7	16.0	16.1	5.4	6.4	9.7	11.0	9.3	7.5	6.8	7.1	10.2	28.9	20.2	8.9	1.1	72.4	30.5	48.4	51.6
73128 OKLAHOMA CITY	86.3	84.1	1.4	1.6	4.9	6.3	3.5	3.9	6.0	6.1	6.2	6.3	6.3	26.3	29.9	11.9	1.1	77.8	40.7	48.6	51.4
OKLAHOMA	76.2	74.8	7.6	7.7	1.4	1.8	5.2	5.8	7.0	6.7	7.0	7.1	7.8	27.2	24.0	11.6	1.7	75.3	36.0	49.3	50.8
UNITED STATES	75.1	73.6	12.3	12.5	3.8	4.2	12.5	14.1	6.9	6.7	7.2	7.0	7.3	28.6	23.8	10.8	1.7	75.1	36.0	49.1	50.9

ZIP CODE #	POST OFFICE NAME	2004 Per Capita Income	2004 HH Income Base	2004 HOUSEHOLD INCOME DISTRIBUTION (%) Less than $25,000	$25,000 to $49,999	$50,000 to $99,999	$100,000 to $149,999	$150,000 or More	MEDIAN HOUSEHOLD INCOME 2004	2009	2004 National Centile	2004 State Centile	2004 Home Value Base	2004 HOME VALUE DISTRIBUTION (%) Less than $50,000	$50,000 to $89,999	$90,000 to $174,999	$175,000 to $399,999	$400,000 or More	2004 Median Home Value
73002	ALEX	16618	784	35.5	34.6	24.6	4.3	1.0	34221	40772	25	52	620	46.9	28.6	18.2	5.3	1.0	53958
73003	EDMOND	32191	14495	13.3	20.6	40.3	15.8	10.0	66239	82620	89	99	11733	4.3	14.0	53.6	21.2	7.0	131112
73004	AMBER	18025	1025	24.4	33.3	33.9	6.9	1.6	45135	51608	62	89	852	28.1	30.3	27.1	13.5	1.1	78108
73005	ANADARKO	14805	3616	42.0	32.5	21.1	3.0	1.5	30393	35161	13	25	2462	48.3	29.2	19.7	2.7	0.0	51872
73006	APACHE	15635	1420	36.7	34.9	23.2	4.6	0.6	32423	37580	19	40	1069	40.1	38.0	18.0	3.8	0.1	59505
73007	ARCADIA	29320	759	23.2	25.2	34.3	12.3	5.1	51916	64116	75	94	649	21.9	20.2	34.7	19.4	3.9	106753
73008	BETHANY	21731	8509	27.7	33.5	29.8	6.7	2.4	40088	47877	46	79	5210	13.4	46.3	34.6	5.0	0.7	82620
73009	BINGER	16018	699	37.3	33.8	24.2	4.0	0.7	34663	40155	26	55	569	49.0	28.3	19.5	3.0	0.2	50932
73010	BLANCHARD	20653	2733	26.6	29.9	32.6	7.7	3.2	44707	51811	60	88	2233	24.4	29.5	32.8	11.5	1.8	84272
73011	BRADLEY	15566	169	36.1	35.5	23.7	4.1	0.6	33987	41196	24	51	140	42.9	26.4	24.3	6.4	0.0	57692
73013	EDMOND	32738	13047	13.7	21.5	37.9	16.4	10.5	65496	80853	89	99	9749	1.6	14.8	51.0	27.4	5.2	135614
73014	CALUMET	19785	908	27.9	34.7	29.3	5.3	2.9	40571	47738	48	80	734	36.2	25.2	27.4	9.7	1.5	72800
73015	CARNEGIE	16654	1462	44.6	29.1	21.1	2.8	2.4	28455	33846	9	16	1081	48.4	32.5	14.6	4.2	0.4	51882
73016	CASHION	20120	238	31.1	27.3	34.5	4.2	2.9	41790	48874	52	83	193	30.6	30.1	33.2	6.2	0.0	76389
73017	CEMENT	15653	573	40.7	29.8	24.4	4.2	0.9	31118	36410	15	31	436	55.3	29.6	11.7	3.0	0.5	42333
73018	CHICKASHA	18241	8360	38.9	32.6	22.2	3.6	2.7	32276	38086	19	39	5423	37.3	33.3	23.2	5.8	0.4	62875
73020	CHOCTAW	24354	7036	17.1	26.9	40.0	12.5	3.6	55607	67082	80	96	5969	15.0	28.1	44.8	11.5	0.6	98246
73021	COLONY	19902	104	32.7	31.7	26.9	4.8	3.9	36980	42366	35	68	82	37.8	29.3	23.2	9.8	0.0	67000
73024	CORN	17614	430	34.2	38.4	21.9	3.7	1.9	33390	37717	22	47	335	45.1	30.2	16.4	8.4	0.0	53750
73026	NORMAN	24814	4242	17.7	26.9	38.8	11.4	5.3	55510	64426	80	95	3734	14.2	23.5	42.0	18.3	2.0	108731
73027	COYLE	15911	603	39.8	31.2	22.4	3.8	2.8	32714	39696	20	42	371	47.7	19.7	22.9	9.7	0.0	53036
73028	CRESCENT	18575	1358	34.4	37.3	21.5	5.0	1.8	34674	41470	26	55	1051	40.4	32.4	22.4	4.6	0.3	60942
73029	CYRIL	15690	586	37.4	31.6	26.6	3.4	1.0	33512	39495	22	47	437	39.4	37.8	20.6	2.1	0.2	61129
73030	DAVIS	17996	1778	39.9	29.7	24.1	4.6	1.8	33318	38487	22	46	1305	38.7	38.8	18.3	3.3	0.9	61863
73034	EDMOND	32018	12718	22.7	21.2	29.0	15.9	11.2	59352	73426	84	97	8680	7.1	11.9	36.7	40.3	4.0	163400
73036	EL RENO	17989	6925	33.2	31.9	26.9	6.1	1.9	36870	43551	35	67	4719	30.0	32.9	29.0	7.7	0.4	72573
73038	FORT COBB	16276	691	42.6	29.4	20.7	5.6	1.7	29263	34372	11	20	537	50.5	29.1	17.7	2.2	0.6	49627
73040	GEARY	15690	702	38.8	35.0	23.1	2.3	0.9	31237	36293	16	32	515	50.3	28.4	18.6	2.3	0.4	49694
73041	GOTEBO	18480	173	34.7	35.3	26.0	2.3	1.7	34806	40000	27	56	139	46.8	32.4	15.1	5.8	0.0	52647
73042	GRACEMONT	16751	338	39.1	31.4	26.0	2.1	1.5	33938	39705	24	51	270	41.9	35.2	18.5	4.1	0.4	55946
73043	GREENFIELD	18542	73	34.3	32.9	26.0	5.5	1.4	35560	42376	30	60	59	49.2	13.6	32.2	5.1	0.0	51667
73044	GUTHRIE	20586	7203	31.0	29.5	29.8	6.6	3.2	40317	47928	47	79	5389	26.8	31.2	32.6	8.7	0.6	77962
73045	HARRAH	21087	3539	21.1	31.2	36.7	8.4	2.6	47835	56378	68	92	2983	18.2	33.6	38.9	9.0	0.3	87843
73047	HINTON	16853	947	34.5	35.6	24.0	3.2	2.8	34266	40070	25	53	745	36.5	31.4	27.8	3.8	0.5	65833
73048	HYDRO	15146	829	36.9	39.3	20.3	2.3	1.2	32447	37729	19	40	610	44.9	25.4	22.8	5.4	1.5	55962
73049	JONES	24066	1972	24.8	30.6	31.5	8.2	5.0	45784	54615	63	90	1584	26.5	30.7	28.1	11.4	3.3	78043
73051	LEXINGTON	16798	2541	29.0	33.2	30.3	4.6	2.8	38491	46356	41	74	1985	38.6	29.1	23.8	7.9	0.5	67199
73052	LINDSAY	17957	2272	36.6	33.6	24.9	3.0	1.9	33384	38793	22	47	1708	48.9	29.2	18.2	3.6	0.1	51218
73053	LOOKEBA	17177	245	42.0	33.9	18.8	2.0	3.3	29337	33281	11	20	196	51.5	28.1	18.4	1.0	1.0	48500
73054	LUTHER	19455	1509	24.7	34.3	31.4	7.1	2.5	43739	51230	58	87	1282	35.8	28.9	25.7	7.9	1.6	69238
73055	MARLOW	16524	3264	39.0	32.8	23.2	3.4	1.7	32500	38238	19	41	2522	34.6	34.7	25.1	5.2	0.4	64078
73056	MARSHALL	18344	164	35.4	31.1	26.2	6.1	1.2	33293	39719	22	46	133	44.4	21.1	26.3	5.3	3.0	59375
73057	MAYSVILLE	16019	956	40.4	34.4	20.3	3.8	1.2	31099	36906	15	31	720	47.5	30.1	19.6	2.2	0.6	52195
73058	MERIDIAN	23013	101	32.7	30.7	26.7	6.9	3.0	41416	49303	51	82	84	39.3	23.8	26.2	10.7	0.0	66667
73059	MINCO	20610	994	30.5	33.9	28.9	4.4	2.3	37745	44820	38	72	760	38.7	30.5	23.4	6.7	0.7	64194
73061	MORRISON	18380	601	29.5	35.3	27.5	6.3	1.5	38044	43798	39	73	500	27.4	42.6	22.4	7.6	0.0	71875
73062	MOUNTAIN VIEW	18008	590	45.8	31.0	17.6	3.2	2.4	28112	33436	9	14	443	61.6	28.4	7.7	2.0	0.2	39338
73063	MULHALL	17226	183	27.3	38.3	27.9	6.0	0.6	38519	45476	41	75	150	40.7	26.7	23.3	8.7	0.7	64444
73064	MUSTANG	26486	6146	15.9	26.3	41.3	13.1	3.5	56151	64522	81	96	4733	3.2	33.5	46.2	15.9	1.1	105788
73065	NEWCASTLE	25232	2237	14.7	31.3	35.7	14.2	4.2	54869	65200	80	95	1908	6.2	26.7	48.6	16.3	2.3	109013
73067	NINNEKAH	20006	501	32.9	31.7	27.7	5.4	2.2	38987	45613	43	76	409	32.3	33.5	25.4	7.3	1.5	71071
73068	NOBLE	18323	4322	26.2	34.9	32.0	5.2	1.8	40439	48317	48	80	3308	28.8	35.5	29.1	6.5	0.1	73041
73069	NORMAN	22671	10308	35.9	29.1	24.7	7.7	2.7	36285	44245	33	63	4992	8.9	38.1	41.8	10.7	0.5	93432
73071	NORMAN	20559	11970	32.6	32.3	25.6	7.2	2.4	37812	45850	39	72	5835	10.9	31.8	50.2	6.4	0.6	95671
73072	NORMAN	30155	16275	26.7	20.2	31.3	13.2	8.6	53278	63461	77	95	8930	3.3	8.4	52.0	31.4	4.8	147022
73073	ORLANDO	16654	130	27.7	37.7	28.5	6.2	0.0	38155	45443	40	73	107	43.0	26.2	24.3	6.5	0.0	60833
73074	PAOLI	17983	407	28.5	37.6	27.8	4.2	2.0	40755	47128	49	80	315	38.4	39.7	16.5	5.1	0.3	61875
73075	PAULS VALLEY	18449	3591	39.6	30.8	21.9	4.9	2.8	32248	37818	18	39	2452	35.8	34.3	21.3	7.6	0.9	64622
73077	PERRY	21353	3005	29.6	32.7	27.1	7.8	2.9	38599	45638	41	75	2228	34.6	32.5	24.8	8.0	0.1	69362
73078	PIEDMONT	24739	1831	10.6	28.0	41.8	14.5	5.1	60885	69215	85	98	1660	4.2	19.7	48.9	24.2	3.0	125566
73079	POCASSET	19008	366	27.3	34.2	30.3	6.6	1.6	40370	46505	47	79	307	27.0	31.6	31.6	7.8	2.0	78167
73080	PURCELL	19361	3907	30.3	35.0	26.8	4.8	3.1	39135	45950	43	77	2876	29.7	31.3	27.3	9.7	2.0	74648
73082	RUSH SPRINGS	15543	1539	42.0	30.5	22.4	3.9	1.2	30020	35523	12	23	1200	42.3	30.3	20.6	6.2	0.6	57541
73084	SPENCER	18746	2557	38.7	29.0	26.0	4.9	1.5	34028	40997	24	51	1913	38.2	39.7	18.9	3.0	0.3	58509
73086	SULPHUR	18930	3239	34.7	33.0	26.0	4.6	1.7	35255	40924	28	58	2386	36.9	30.2	25.4	7.0	0.5	64947
73089	TUTTLE	20848	4125	19.3	27.5	41.3	9.9	2.0	52239	60294	76	94	3511	12.2	22.7	50.7	13.2	1.2	107864
73090	UNION CITY	18196	239	27.6	32.2	28.5	9.6	2.1	40621	48439	48	80	192	31.3	29.7	29.2	9.9	0.0	76667
73092	VERDEN	17431	311	41.2	31.8	19.3	4.5	3.2	30823	36380	14	28	241	55.2	22.0	18.3	2.9	1.7	47500
73093	WASHINGTON	28810	872	18.9	27.2	32.7	12.7	8.5	53650	63605	78	95	760	21.3	16.1	30.4	25.5	6.7	116136
73095	WAYNE	17290	607	35.1	33.9	23.9	5.3	1.8	34841	41659	27	56	478	42.3	31.4	17.8	6.3	2.3	57551
73096	WEATHERFORD	19989	4839	37.6	29.7	22.9	7.4	2.4	32833	39158	20	43	2696	17.4	25.6	45.2	10.9	0.9	97248
73098	WYNNEWOOD	17822	1527	37.1	34.3	22.0	4.4	2.2	33560	39914	23	48	1122	41.0	31.3	21.8	5.3	0.7	59528
73099	YUKON	24713	16583	14.6	28.0	40.5	13.2	3.7	56400	65237	81	96	13564	5.2	26.0	55.9	12.4	0.6	107530
73102	OKLAHOMA CITY	12661	746	61.4	20.2	16.4	2.0	0.0	18013	21597	1	1	42	59.5	9.5	31.0	0.0	0.0	39545
73103	OKLAHOMA CITY	28705	2347	44.7	25.9	18.2	5.8	5.5	29226	34743	11	20	739	21.1	19.8	32.5	19.5	7.2	111738
73104	OKLAHOMA CITY	11116	948	67.2	18.0	10.0	4.0	0.7	16134	20101	1	1	282	40.4	23.1	23.4	13.1	0.0	63462
73105	OKLAHOMA CITY	19974	2218	45.3	24.4	22.3	5.0	3.2	28662	34327	10	17	1265	29.7	31.5	28.7	9.9	0.2	76545
73106	OKLAHOMA CITY	14240	5053	50.4	26.6	17.3	3.1	2.6	24751	30519	4	6	1825	42.1	30.3	19.5	5.6	2.5	57646
73107	OKLAHOMA CITY	18042	11124	37.5	33.8	23.9	4.0	0.9	33121	39894	21	45	6133	35.4	47.7	15.4	1.5	0.0	58569
73108	OKLAHOMA CITY	11087	5281	54.1	31.5	11.5	2.0	1.0	22781	27534	3	3	2231	83.5	14.5	2.0	0.0	0.0	32575
73109	OKLAHOMA CITY	13367	7591	49.3	32.0	16.1	1.6	1.0	25368	30549	5	7	3884	53.2	39.3	6.8	0.5	0.2	48340
73110	OKLAHOMA CITY	19212	14936	31.8	36.9	25.7	4.4	1.3	36064	43038	32	62	7841	25.9	50.3	22.2	1.4	0.3	66136
73111	OKLAHOMA CITY	16571	5222	51.2	28.9	15.3	2.2	2.4	24241	28533	4	5	3145	42.5	39.6	16.0	1.4	0.5	54876
73112	OKLAHOMA CITY	25070	14561	30.7	33.4	27.4	5.7	2.9	37179	45132	36	69	7549	14.0	42.5	37.1	6.0	0.6	83276
73114	OKLAHOMA CITY	16926	6824	37.5	34.8	21.5	4.6	1.6	32923	39140	21	44	2958	38.0	49.3	8.0	4.1	0.5	56592
73115	OKLAHOMA CITY	18561	8953	31.3	36.2	27.2	3.6	1.7	36693	43800	34	67	5488	29.2	56.7	13.2	1.0	0.0	59896
73116	OKLAHOMA CITY	48364	4447	17.0	26.3	30.0	12.2	14.5	56983	71851	82	96	3024	4.0	19.7	36.9	24.1	15.3	143805
73117	OKLAHOMA CITY	12384	2297	62.6	23.3	11.2	2.5	0.5	16842	20087	1	1	1143	62.6	30.9	6.0	0.6	0.0	40682
73118	OKLAHOMA CITY	26812	6626	29.9	32.3	25.8	7.2	4.9	40412	49269	48	80	3537	19.2	35.1	29.4	14.1	2.3	84932
73119	OKLAHOMA CITY	13725	10333	42.8	36.5	18.0	1.7	1.0	28963	34094	10	18	5502	59.5	37.1	3.3	0.1	0.0	45815
73120	OKLAHOMA CITY	36165	17943	22.6	31.4	28.1	9.5	8.3	46562	56870	65	91	9763	4.4	28.7	39.9	23.2	3.9	114120
73121	OKLAHOMA CITY	25378	1215	26.5	27.9	28.6	10.0	7.0	46404	54840	65	91	1021	16.4	29.1	34.9	16.4	3.3	99490
73122	OKLAHOMA CITY	22654	6012	27.5	34.5	28.2	6.9	2.9	39934	48511	46	78	3454	9.3	45.2	41.7	3.8	0.1	85510
73127	OKLAHOMA CITY	18714	10435	36.6	32.5	23.2	5.0	2.8	33673	40193	23	48	4628	21.7	37.1	36.3	4.2	0.7	79281
73128	OKLAHOMA CITY	23313	999	23.1	31.0	34.8	8.5	2.5	45927	54844	64	90	883	36.7	26.1	31.3	5.9	0.1	70521
	OKLAHOMA	21077		31.9	30.4	27.2	7.1	3.4	38589	46268				26.7	29.5	32.0	10.2	1.6	81000
	UNITED STATES	25866		24.7	27.1	30.8	10.9	6.5	48124	56710				10.9	15.0	33.7	30.1	10.4	145905

ZIP CODE #	POST OFFICE NAME	FINANCIAL SERVICES: Auto Loan	Home Loan	Invest-ments	Retire-ment Plans	THE HOME: Home Improvements: Home Repair	Lawn & Garden	Furnishings: Comput-ers & Hard-ware	Major Appli-ances	TV, Radio, Sound Equip-ment	Furni-ture	ENTERTAINMENT: Dine out/ Carry out	Sports Equip-ment	Fees & Tickets	Toys & Games	Travel	Cable TV	PERSONAL: Apparel & Services	Auto Repairs	Health Insur-ance	Pets & Supplies
73002	ALEX	77	54	28	49	61	70	54	65	63	54	74	77	47	71	55	67	68	65	79	88
73003	EDMOND	126	142	146	147	136	136	132	130	123	135	156	152	137	157	130	117	154	127	114	142
73004	AMBER	83	73	56	70	77	83	69	76	73	69	89	89	67	90	70	75	84	74	82	96
73005	ANADARKO	61	52	45	49	55	62	55	58	59	53	72	67	52	71	55	61	68	58	65	70
73006	APACHE	67	54	37	51	58	66	54	61	60	54	72	70	51	70	55	62	67	60	69	76
73007	ARCADIA	114	102	81	99	107	113	97	106	100	97	122	125	92	120	98	100	116	105	111	132
73008	BETHANY	68	73	82	73	73	77	74	72	73	72	91	84	75	92	74	72	89	73	71	79
73009	BINGER	71	51	29	47	56	67	54	62	62	52	72	71	47	68	53	66	66	62	75	80
73010	BLANCHARD	89	79	61	76	82	88	76	82	79	76	97	96	73	95	76	80	92	81	86	101
73011	BRADLEY	78	52	24	45	59	68	50	63	61	51	71	75	43	67	51	65	65	62	78	89
73013	EDMOND	116	130	142	133	127	130	125	122	118	125	149	142	129	150	124	114	147	121	112	134
73014	CALUMET	85	70	50	66	75	82	68	77	73	68	88	89	63	86	69	75	83	76	84	97
73015	CARNEGIE	69	52	34	49	58	68	55	62	62	53	73	71	49	70	56	65	67	62	75	79
73016	CASHION	82	73	56	70	77	83	68	75	72	68	88	89	66	89	70	74	83	73	81	97
73017	CEMENT	73	49	24	43	56	64	48	60	58	49	68	71	41	64	49	62	62	59	73	83
73018	CHICKASHA	66	58	50	56	60	68	60	63	64	59	78	73	57	76	60	66	73	63	70	75
73020	CHOCTAW	91	98	97	97	98	101	92	94	90	91	111	109	94	115	93	89	109	92	91	107
73021	COLONY	85	59	31	56	69	78	59	73	68	58	79	88	50	78	61	71	72	72	87	101
73024	CORN	65	64	70	67	66	70	66	67	65	65	80	79	65	78	66	63	77	67	66	76
73026	NORMAN	100	102	91	100	102	105	94	98	93	95	115	115	94	115	95	91	112	97	95	116
73027	COYLE	71	56	52	57	56	61	71	64	70	67	87	80	63	81	63	66	83	70	62	75
73028	CRESCENT	77	55	33	53	63	72	58	68	66	56	77	79	51	74	59	69	71	67	81	88
73029	CYRIL	68	50	31	47	55	65	54	61	61	52	72	69	47	68	53	65	65	60	73	76
73030	DAVIS	72	58	42	55	63	72	59	66	65	58	78	76	55	77	60	69	73	65	76	83
73034	EDMOND	111	117	135	123	115	119	122	115	115	119	146	138	123	146	118	110	144	118	105	127
73036	EL RENO	62	57	52	55	58	64	58	60	61	57	74	70	57	74	58	62	71	60	64	70
73038	FORT COBB	68	51	33	49	56	67	56	62	63	53	74	69	50	70	56	66	68	62	74	75
73040	GEARY	65	49	32	47	54	63	53	59	59	51	69	67	47	66	53	62	64	59	70	73
73041	GOTEBO	56	61	63	58	61	67	58	60	59	57	72	67	60	75	60	60	70	58	62	67
73042	GRACEMONT	80	54	24	46	61	70	52	65	63	53	73	77	44	69	53	67	67	64	80	92
73043	GREENFIELD	87	58	26	50	66	76	56	70	68	57	79	84	48	75	57	73	72	69	86	99
73044	GUTHRIE	78	72	65	70	74	81	72	76	75	71	92	88	70	91	72	76	88	76	80	90
73045	HARRAH	91	80	62	78	84	91	78	84	82	77	100	98	75	99	78	83	94	83	90	103
73047	HINTON	77	58	38	55	63	76	63	70	71	60	83	79	56	79	63	75	76	70	84	86
73048	HYDRO	67	48	28	46	55	63	50	58	57	48	66	69	43	64	50	59	61	58	70	77
73049	JONES	98	90	76	88	92	101	88	94	91	88	111	107	86	109	88	92	106	92	98	111
73051	LEXINGTON	62	56	43	53	56	60	54	58	55	55	68	67	51	64	53	55	65	58	59	69
73052	LINDSAY	74	54	32	51	60	71	57	66	65	55	76	76	50	73	57	68	69	65	79	84
73053	LOOKEBA	75	56	37	54	61	74	62	68	70	59	82	77	55	77	61	74	75	68	82	82
73054	LUTHER	86	77	60	75	78	83	75	80	76	76	94	92	71	89	74	75	90	79	81	95
73055	MARLOW	68	52	34	49	57	66	53	61	60	52	71	70	48	68	54	63	65	60	71	78
73056	MARSHALL	78	55	29	52	63	71	54	67	62	53	73	80	46	71	56	65	67	66	79	92
73057	MAYSVILLE	69	50	29	46	56	65	51	60	59	50	69	70	45	66	52	62	63	60	72	79
73058	MERIDIAN	82	75	59	72	75	79	72	77	72	74	89	89	68	84	71	71	86	76	76	91
73059	MINCO	86	69	49	66	75	85	71	78	78	69	93	90	66	91	71	81	86	78	90	97
73061	MORRISON	74	63	49	63	66	75	65	69	69	63	83	79	62	82	64	70	78	68	75	82
73062	MOUNTAIN VIEW	64	54	43	52	57	67	57	61	62	55	74	69	54	72	57	65	69	61	71	72
73063	MULHALL	71	60	47	60	63	71	62	66	66	61	80	76	59	79	61	67	75	65	72	79
73064	MUSTANG	102	112	112	113	110	110	105	105	99	105	125	125	107	128	104	95	123	104	95	118
73065	NEWCASTLE	103	101	88	98	105	109	93	99	94	93	116	118	93	120	95	95	112	96	102	122
73067	NINNEKAH	91	67	39	63	76	85	65	79	74	65	87	95	58	86	68	77	80	77	92	108
73068	NOBLE	78	72	59	70	73	77	70	74	71	71	87	86	67	83	69	70	84	74	74	87
73069	NORMAN	66	62	73	65	62	68	72	67	71	68	89	81	69	87	69	68	86	71	65	74
73071	NORMAN	66	62	70	66	61	64	72	66	69	69	87	81	69	85	67	64	85	70	60	73
73072	NORMAN	104	97	112	104	95	101	111	102	107	108	135	125	107	129	104	100	131	108	94	113
73073	ORLANDO	71	60	47	60	63	71	62	66	66	61	80	75	59	79	61	67	75	65	72	78
73074	PAOLI	75	61	44	60	66	74	63	69	67	61	81	80	58	80	63	69	76	68	76	85
73075	PAULS VALLEY	73	58	42	56	62	72	61	67	67	59	80	77	56	78	61	70	74	67	77	82
73077	PERRY	77	68	57	66	72	80	68	73	73	67	88	84	66	88	69	75	83	72	81	88
73078	PIEDMONT	97	117	122	117	115	115	105	105	98	104	123	123	111	130	107	96	122	101	96	118
73079	POCASSET	80	71	54	68	75	81	66	73	70	66	85	87	65	87	68	72	81	71	79	94
73080	PURCELL	82	65	45	63	70	80	67	74	74	66	88	85	62	86	67	77	82	73	85	91
73082	RUSH SPRINGS	67	51	32	47	55	64	51	59	58	50	69	68	46	66	52	61	63	58	69	76
73084	SPENCER	71	62	59	58	63	74	65	67	70	65	86	73	64	81	65	74	82	68	76	79
73086	SULPHUR	76	58	40	55	64	74	61	69	68	59	81	79	55	78	62	72	74	69	81	87
73089	TUTTLE	86	86	78	85	88	91	81	85	81	81	100	99	81	101	82	80	96	83	84	100
73090	UNION CITY	82	73	56	69	77	83	68	75	72	68	87	89	66	89	70	74	83	73	81	97
73092	VERDEN	87	58	26	50	66	76	56	70	68	57	80	84	48	75	57	73	72	70	87	100
73093	WASHINGTON	115	120	111	118	122	126	110	115	109	110	135	136	113	140	113	109	131	112	114	137
73095	WAYNE	74	57	39	55	62	74	62	68	69	60	82	77	56	78	62	73	75	68	80	82
73096	WEATHERFORD	67	62	69	64	62	67	71	66	70	68	87	81	68	85	67	66	84	69	64	75
73098	WYNNEWOOD	72	53	33	50	59	69	57	64	64	54	75	74	50	72	57	67	69	64	77	81
73099	YUKON	92	103	105	105	101	101	96	96	91	97	114	113	99	117	96	87	113	95	87	106
73102	OKLAHOMA CITY	21	21	28	21	21	23	23	22	24	23	30	25	23	30	23	24	29	23	23	24
73103	OKLAHOMA CITY	73	63	83	70	63	69	81	73	80	77	101	91	76	96	75	75	98	80	68	81
73104	OKLAHOMA CITY	37	32	40	31	31	37	37	36	40	38	50	41	37	47	36	41	49	38	38	41
73105	OKLAHOMA CITY	62	53	59	51	53	63	60	59	65	60	80	66	59	74	58	67	77	62	65	68
73106	OKLAHOMA CITY	52	45	52	47	45	48	55	51	55	54	69	62	51	65	51	52	67	55	48	56
73107	OKLAHOMA CITY	54	53	60	54	53	58	58	56	58	56	72	66	57	73	57	57	70	57	55	61
73108	OKLAHOMA CITY	45	39	41	38	38	42	44	44	46	45	58	50	42	55	42	45	57	46	43	48
73109	OKLAHOMA CITY	47	42	44	41	42	48	47	46	49	46	61	52	45	59	46	50	59	48	49	51
73110	OKLAHOMA CITY	60	58	64	58	58	64	62	61	64	61	79	71	62	79	61	63	77	62	62	68
73111	OKLAHOMA CITY	55	48	52	44	47	57	52	53	57	53	70	57	51	65	51	61	67	54	60	61
73112	OKLAHOMA CITY	66	66	78	67	66	72	71	68	71	69	88	80	71	88	70	70	86	71	67	75
73114	OKLAHOMA CITY	58	54	62	55	53	58	60	58	62	60	77	68	60	76	58	61	75	60	57	64
73115	OKLAHOMA CITY	61	61	63	59	61	68	63	62	64	61	79	71	63	82	63	65	76	62	65	70
73116	OKLAHOMA CITY	130	148	182	148	146	158	145	142	141	144	177	163	152	181	148	141	175	142	138	155
73117	OKLAHOMA CITY	39	32	34	29	32	39	36	37	41	36	49	40	35	45	35	43	47	38	43	43
73118	OKLAHOMA CITY	75	75	89	78	75	81	81	78	80	80	101	92	81	99	80	78	98	81	76	86
73119	OKLAHOMA CITY	50	45	46	44	46	51	50	50	53	49	65	57	49	65	49	53	63	51	52	55
73120	OKLAHOMA CITY	95	99	120	102	98	105	105	100	102	103	129	119	106	128	103	99	126	104	95	110
73121	OKLAHOMA CITY	83	90	101	86	89	98	88	88	89	88	111	98	92	112	90	91	108	87	90	97
73122	OKLAHOMA CITY	67	72	82	72	72	76	73	72	72	72	90	83	75	92	74	71	88	72	70	79
73127	OKLAHOMA CITY	63	61	67	61	60	65	66	64	66	64	83	75	65	82	64	65	80	66	63	71
73128	OKLAHOMA CITY	85	83	70	81	83	87	77	82	77	79	95	96	76	94	77	76	92	80	80	97
	OKLAHOMA	79	71	65	70	73	80	73	76	76	72	93	88	70	91	72	76	88	76	79	89
	UNITED STATES	100	100	100	100	100	100	100	100	100	100	100	100	100	100	100	100	100	100	100	100

POPULATION CHANGE

#	POST OFFICE NAME	COUNTY FIPS CODE	POPULATION 2000	2004	2009	2000-2004 ANNUAL RATE % Rate	State Centile	HOUSEHOLDS 2000	2004	2009	% Annual Rate 2000-2004	2004 Average HH Size	FAMILIES 2000	2004	% Annual Rate 2000-2004
73129	OKLAHOMA CITY	109	19380	19362	19747	0.0	38	7065	7087	7260	0.1	2.72	4729	4706	-0.1
73130	OKLAHOMA CITY	109	17806	18236	18857	0.6	63	6684	6926	7225	0.8	2.63	5096	5259	0.7
73131	OKLAHOMA CITY	109	2300	2487	2625	1.9	92	894	980	1045	2.2	2.42	672	732	2.0
73132	OKLAHOMA CITY	109	24921	27969	30250	2.8	96	10208	11523	12543	2.9	2.42	6738	7564	2.8
73134	OKLAHOMA CITY	109	2094	2514	2844	4.4	99	896	1074	1220	4.4	2.22	478	573	4.4
73135	OKLAHOMA CITY	109	15136	15914	16867	1.2	84	5468	5807	6195	1.4	2.74	4147	4375	1.3
73139	OKLAHOMA CITY	109	16271	16252	16810	0.0	38	7311	7391	7717	0.3	2.17	4423	4429	0.0
73141	OKLAHOMA CITY	109	2727	2810	2904	0.7	70	1135	1181	1230	0.9	2.38	769	797	0.9
73142	OKLAHOMA CITY	109	8100	9884	11083	4.8	100	3687	4513	5063	4.9	2.17	2166	2622	4.6
73145	OKLAHOMA CITY	109	3026	2922	2942	-0.8	8	713	693	705	-0.7	3.51	685	665	-0.7
73149	OKLAHOMA CITY	109	5815	5615	5664	-0.8	8	2323	2256	2286	-0.7	2.49	1483	1423	-1.0
73150	OKLAHOMA CITY	109	4557	4651	4818	0.5	60	1701	1749	1828	0.7	2.66	1386	1422	0.6
73151	OKLAHOMA CITY	109	931	970	1002	1.0	78	321	337	351	1.2	2.88	271	284	1.1
73159	OKLAHOMA CITY	109	31040	32520	34051	1.1	82	12092	12680	13445	1.1	2.38	8298	8642	1.0
73160	OKLAHOMA CITY	027	40859	42598	45975	1.0	78	14838	15791	17306	1.5	2.68	11447	12031	1.2
73162	OKLAHOMA CITY	109	25666	27572	29131	1.7	91	10126	11031	11764	2.0	2.48	7166	7737	1.8
73165	OKLAHOMA CITY	027	4917	5154	5491	1.1	82	1716	1826	1969	1.5	2.81	1429	1513	1.4
73169	OKLAHOMA CITY	109	1670	1932	2112	3.5	98	592	694	767	3.8	2.73	477	557	3.7
73170	OKLAHOMA CITY	027	21881	25142	28043	3.3	98	7799	9050	10192	3.6	2.74	6435	7439	3.5
73173	OKLAHOMA CITY	027	554	584	623	1.3	85	213	228	246	1.6	2.56	167	177	1.4
73179	OKLAHOMA CITY	109	1655	1789	1887	1.9	92	616	668	710	1.9	2.58	442	477	1.8
73401	ARDMORE	019	32311	33362	34593	0.8	72	12829	13323	13897	0.9	2.44	8831	9148	0.8
73430	BURNEYVILLE	085	971	1010	1051	0.9	77	417	438	459	1.2	2.31	321	336	1.1
73432	COLEMAN	069	1058	1089	1116	0.7	68	419	433	446	0.8	2.52	308	317	0.7
73433	ELMORE CITY	049	2514	2941	3268	3.8	99	1044	1230	1375	3.9	2.39	749	879	3.8
73434	FOSTER	049	625	619	625	-0.2	29	242	241	245	-0.1	2.57	183	183	0.0
73437	GRAHAM	019	649	633	641	-0.6	14	248	244	249	-0.4	2.59	192	188	-0.5
73438	HEALDTON	019	3086	3115	3188	0.2	50	1247	1266	1304	0.4	2.40	865	872	0.2
73439	KINGSTON	095	5194	5975	6749	3.4	98	2247	2597	2945	3.5	2.29	1628	1874	3.4
73440	LEBANON	095	109	108	115	-0.2	30	49	49	52	0.0	2.20	36	35	-0.7
73441	LEON	085	888	900	928	0.3	53	354	362	375	0.5	2.49	273	279	0.5
73442	LOCO	137	326	325	324	-0.1	36	135	136	136	0.2	2.28	102	102	0.0
73443	LONE GROVE	019	3534	3665	3788	0.9	75	1289	1349	1404	1.1	2.71	1014	1056	1.0
73444	HENNEPIN	019	653	650	660	-0.1	34	262	261	266	-0.1	2.49	192	191	-0.1
73446	MADILL	095	7880	7998	8450	0.4	54	3075	3112	3288	0.3	2.49	2136	2151	0.2
73447	MANNSVILLE	069	1092	1152	1198	1.3	85	402	422	439	1.2	2.73	303	317	1.1
73448	MARIETTA	085	5101	5253	5451	0.7	68	1961	2021	2103	0.7	2.55	1422	1462	0.7
73449	MEAD	013	2412	2575	2775	1.6	90	1018	1094	1185	1.7	2.35	740	793	1.6
73450	MILBURN	069	292	296	301	0.3	53	116	118	121	0.4	2.51	87	88	0.3
73453	OVERBROOK	085	447	458	473	0.6	64	174	180	187	0.8	2.54	133	138	0.9
73456	RINGLING	067	2108	2086	2063	-0.3	28	846	836	827	-0.3	2.44	590	581	-0.4
73458	SPRINGER	019	1621	1664	1708	0.6	65	623	643	664	0.8	2.45	470	483	0.6
73459	THACKERVILLE	085	1424	1467	1516	0.7	69	536	558	581	1.0	2.63	406	421	0.9
73460	TISHOMINGO	069	5490	5522	5611	0.1	46	2117	2141	2186	0.3	2.46	1449	1461	0.2
73461	WAPANUCKA	069	780	805	826	0.8	72	316	327	338	0.8	2.46	231	238	0.7
73463	WILSON	019	3123	3130	3185	0.1	42	1226	1235	1264	0.2	2.49	872	874	0.1
73481	RATLIFF CITY	019	784	749	756	-1.1	3	319	307	313	-0.9	2.44	245	235	-1.0
73488	TUSSY	019	60	57	57	-1.2	2	25	24	24	-1.0	2.38	19	18	-1.3
73501	LAWTON	031	18819	18644	18694	-0.2	30	6697	6677	6756	-0.1	2.44	4351	4334	-0.1
73503	FORT SILL	031	11731	11511	11455	-0.4	20	1429	1387	1387	-0.7	3.63	1382	1340	-0.7
73505	LAWTON	031	45889	46132	46559	0.1	45	17195	17461	17786	0.4	2.59	12556	12689	0.3
73507	LAWTON	031	19385	19314	19427	-0.1	35	7582	7588	7685	0.0	2.51	5156	5151	0.0
73521	ALTUS	065	19940	19708	19386	-0.3	27	7615	7548	7450	-0.2	2.55	5278	5219	-0.3
73523	ALTUS AFB	065	2537	2443	2379	-0.9	6	659	636	621	-0.8	3.39	647	624	-0.9
73526	BLAIR	065	1110	1089	1067	-0.5	19	448	443	437	-0.3	2.46	327	322	-0.4
73527	CACHE	031	4889	5613	6032	3.3	98	1669	1932	2092	3.5	2.89	1385	1593	3.4
73528	CHATTANOOGA	031	487	472	467	-0.7	10	190	185	185	-0.6	2.55	133	128	-0.9
73529	COMANCHE	137	5072	5158	5212	0.4	57	1992	2037	2071	0.5	2.51	1492	1521	0.5
73530	DAVIDSON	141	633	594	565	-1.5	1	250	238	229	-1.2	2.50	173	164	-1.3
73531	DEVOL	033	287	289	294	0.2	47	117	119	122	0.4	2.43	89	90	0.3
73532	DUKE	065	699	691	694	-0.3	27	270	268	264	-0.2	2.58	189	186	-0.4
73533	DUNCAN	137	29310	29319	29379	0.0	41	11957	12034	12131	0.2	2.40	8499	8526	0.1
73537	ELDORADO	065	704	696	684	-0.3	27	306	304	299	-0.2	2.29	212	209	-0.3
73538	ELGIN	031	5740	5772	5781	0.1	46	2204	2240	2266	0.4	2.56	1693	1709	0.2
73539	ELMER	065	456	433	420	-1.2	2	178	170	166	-1.1	2.55	139	133	-1.0
73540	FAXON	031	353	343	340	-0.7	12	136	134	134	-0.4	2.56	102	99	-0.7
73541	FLETCHER	031	3889	3816	3791	-0.4	20	1462	1446	1447	-0.3	2.64	1143	1126	-0.4
73542	FREDERICK	141	5674	5508	5323	-0.7	11	2160	2114	2058	-0.5	2.47	1471	1436	-0.6
73543	GERONIMO	031	1302	1348	1371	0.8	75	467	488	501	1.0	2.76	364	376	0.8
73544	GOULD	057	514	504	497	-0.5	18	194	190	188	-0.5	2.65	144	140	-0.7
73546	GRANDFIELD	141	1320	1295	1256	-0.5	19	518	510	498	-0.4	2.49	376	368	-0.5
73547	GRANITE	055	2248	2201	2128	-0.5	16	611	594	565	-0.7	2.50	403	391	-0.7
73548	HASTINGS	067	209	212	212	0.3	54	94	96	96	0.5	2.21	72	73	0.3
73549	HEADRICK	065	2188	2156	2115	-0.4	24	821	815	805	-0.2	2.65	651	643	-0.3
73550	HOLLIS	057	2699	2660	2632	-0.3	25	1036	1020	1009	-0.4	2.46	693	680	-0.4
73551	HOLLISTER	141	106	102	99	-0.9	6	40	39	38	-0.6	2.10	29	28	-0.8
73552	INDIAHOMA	031	1165	1164	1163	0.0	38	443	447	451	0.2	2.60	349	349	0.0
73553	LOVELAND	141	284	279	270	-0.4	21	111	109	107	-0.4	2.51	80	79	-0.3
73554	MANGUM	055	3570	3407	3223	-1.1	2	1511	1436	1353	-1.2	2.27	961	909	-1.3
73559	MOUNTAIN PARK	075	523	509	500	-0.6	13	230	226	224	-0.4	2.25	152	149	-0.5
73560	OLUSTEE	065	805	798	785	-0.2	30	293	291	288	-0.2	2.74	224	221	-0.2
73561	OSCAR	067	27	26	25	-0.9	6	8	8	8	0.0	3.25	7	6	-3.6
73562	RANDLETT	033	966	993	1019	0.7	67	361	374	387	0.8	2.66	274	283	0.8
73564	ROOSEVELT	075	601	585	574	-0.6	14	275	271	268	-0.3	2.16	182	178	-0.5
73565	RYAN	067	1255	1229	1210	-0.5	17	518	510	504	-0.4	2.31	350	343	-0.5
73566	SNYDER	075	1710	1678	1652	-0.4	20	689	679	673	-0.3	2.40	454	446	-0.4
73568	TEMPLE	033	1442	1435	1455	-0.1	34	612	612	623	0.0	2.28	391	389	-0.1
73569	TERRAL	067	465	444	432	-1.1	3	210	202	197	-0.9	2.20	129	123	-1.1
73570	TIPTON	141	1270	1216	1169	-1.0	4	515	497	481	-0.8	2.33	356	342	-0.9
73571	VINSON	057	64	63	62	-0.4	23	35	34	34	-0.7	1.85	26	25	-0.9
73572	WALTERS	033	3919	3995	4086	0.5	59	1524	1563	1609	0.6	2.47	1086	1111	0.5
73573	WAURIKA	067	2754	2738	2713	-0.1	33	1040	1037	1031	-0.1	2.40	717	712	-0.2
73601	CLINTON	039	9797	9765	9813	-0.1	36	3711	3729	3784	0.1	2.53	2569	2572	0.0
73620	ARAPAHO	039	950	951	955	0.0	41	347	351	355	0.3	2.59	271	273	0.2
73622	BESSIE	149	207	201	199	-0.7	12	94	92	92	-0.5	2.18	66	65	-0.4
	OKLAHOMA					0.8					1.0	2.48			0.9
	UNITED STATES					1.2					1.3	2.58			1.1

ZIP CODE #	POST OFFICE NAME	RACE (%) White 2000	White 2004	Black 2000	Black 2004	Asian/Pacific 2000	Asian/Pacific 2004	% Hispanic Origin 2000	% Hispanic Origin 2004	2004 AGE DISTRIBUTION (%) 0-4	5-9	10-14	15-19	20-24	25-44	45-64	65-84	85+	18+	MEDIAN AGE 2004	% 2004 Males	% 2004 Females
73129	OKLAHOMA CITY	60.8	58.1	12.3	12.4	1.0	1.2	25.1	28.1	10.0	8.8	8.3	7.5	8.6	28.5	19.4	8.1	0.8	68.4	29.3	50.2	49.8
73130	OKLAHOMA CITY	72.2	70.2	17.5	18.2	1.9	2.4	3.6	4.2	6.5	6.7	7.9	7.3	6.7	26.4	26.7	11.1	0.7	74.4	37.3	48.6	51.4
73131	OKLAHOMA CITY	83.1	81.5	9.7	10.1	1.4	1.9	2.6	3.1	5.0	6.0	6.2	5.2	5.1	26.2	34.2	11.0	1.1	79.6	43.1	52.1	47.9
73132	OKLAHOMA CITY	74.0	71.2	13.8	14.6	3.9	4.8	5.7	6.7	7.8	7.1	7.0	6.9	8.4	30.2	22.6	9.2	0.7	74.1	32.9	48.0	52.0
73134	OKLAHOMA CITY	81.2	79.0	8.9	9.0	3.8	4.9	3.2	3.9	5.2	5.1	6.0	6.7	8.7	31.6	22.8	10.0	4.0	79.6	35.9	48.1	52.0
73135	OKLAHOMA CITY	54.5	53.0	29.3	28.6	6.6	8.1	5.2	5.9	8.0	7.6	8.0	7.6	8.7	29.6	23.9	6.2	0.4	71.8	31.9	48.6	51.4
73139	OKLAHOMA CITY	76.9	74.4	5.5	5.7	3.5	4.4	10.9	12.5	6.4	5.4	5.3	5.9	9.6	28.9	23.9	13.2	1.5	79.8	35.4	48.8	51.2
73141	OKLAHOMA CITY	56.5	53.7	34.5	36.3	0.7	0.9	3.5	4.0	8.4	7.8	7.5	6.8	7.4	25.7	23.7	11.5	1.3	72.0	34.7	48.2	51.8
73142	OKLAHOMA CITY	80.8	78.5	9.5	10.0	3.7	4.8	3.5	4.2	7.4	5.9	6.1	6.1	9.5	38.1	19.2	6.9	0.8	77.0	31.3	47.2	52.8
73145	OKLAHOMA CITY	68.3	65.5	18.5	19.2	3.0	3.7	8.5	10.0	14.2	11.8	7.7	8.8	18.4	36.0	2.6	0.5	0.0	63.4	22.0	55.7	44.3
73149	OKLAHOMA CITY	73.3	70.5	6.2	6.4	2.9	3.6	12.3	14.1	8.3	7.4	7.6	6.6	8.1	32.2	20.5	8.7	0.7	72.9	32.0	50.5	49.5
73150	OKLAHOMA CITY	84.6	82.5	4.1	4.6	2.4	3.2	3.2	3.8	5.7	6.6	7.7	6.8	5.0	26.4	30.5	10.8	0.6	75.6	40.8	50.7	49.3
73151	OKLAHOMA CITY	85.0	83.2	8.3	8.9	1.5	2.0	1.0	1.1	6.2	7.7	9.3	6.8	3.5	23.0	33.7	9.6	0.2	72.4	42.0	49.5	50.5
73159	OKLAHOMA CITY	77.2	74.4	6.9	7.5	4.4	5.5	6.5	7.3	6.6	5.9	6.1	5.9	8.1	31.5	23.2	11.6	1.1	78.1	35.3	50.5	49.5
73160	OKLAHOMA CITY	84.8	83.3	2.9	3.0	1.7	2.1	5.0	5.6	7.8	7.3	7.6	7.1	7.4	31.4	22.7	8.0	0.7	73.0	33.0	48.3	51.7
73162	OKLAHOMA CITY	83.2	80.8	6.5	7.0	4.6	6.0	2.5	3.0	5.5	6.0	7.1	7.6	6.4	26.9	29.1	9.9	1.6	76.7	39.3	47.5	52.5
73165	OKLAHOMA CITY	88.1	86.8	1.3	1.3	0.7	0.9	3.2	3.7	5.9	6.5	8.0	8.4	5.4	27.4	28.9	9.0	0.4	74.1	38.2	50.7	49.3
73169	OKLAHOMA CITY	91.6	90.5	0.5	0.6	0.5	0.6	3.7	4.4	7.6	7.7	8.2	6.3	6.6	28.5	25.3	9.2	0.7	72.1	35.2	50.9	49.1
73170	OKLAHOMA CITY	85.7	83.7	2.4	2.6	4.2	5.2	3.7	4.1	6.9	6.9	7.2	7.2	7.1	29.8	27.0	7.3	0.7	74.7	35.9	48.4	51.6
73173	OKLAHOMA CITY	92.4	91.6	0.5	0.7	0.4	0.5	2.0	2.2	4.1	4.5	6.9	6.2	6.2	23.5	33.2	14.9	0.7	80.7	44.2	52.4	47.6
73179	OKLAHOMA CITY	85.7	83.6	2.7	3.0	4.2	5.4	4.4	5.1	6.3	6.4	6.4	6.2	6.2	32.5	27.6	8.1	0.5	76.9	37.2	52.8	47.2
73401	ARDMORE	75.3	74.0	9.3	9.5	0.8	1.0	3.2	3.6	6.9	6.8	6.9	6.6	6.3	24.9	25.2	14.0	2.5	75.3	39.0	47.7	52.3
73430	BURNEYVILLE	87.2	86.2	0.8	0.8	0.5	0.6	3.4	3.9	4.4	4.9	5.5	4.9	5.3	21.4	30.0	21.4	2.4	82.2	48.1	50.8	49.2
73432	COLEMAN	79.0	77.8	1.1	1.2	0.1	0.3	2.8	3.2	6.4	6.6	6.8	6.0	5.9	25.7	27.1	13.8	1.7	76.5	39.6	52.5	47.5
73433	ELMORE CITY	89.6	89.1	1.8	1.7	0.2	0.3	1.2	1.3	6.9	6.8	6.4	5.6	6.3	24.5	26.5	14.5	2.6	76.6	40.5	50.0	50.0
73434	FOSTER	89.9	89.2	2.2	2.4	0.2	0.2	1.6	1.6	5.2	6.0	6.5	6.5	6.0	24.2	30.2	13.6	1.9	78.5	42.3	50.6	49.4
73437	GRAHAM	86.8	85.6	0.6	0.6	0.2	0.2	2.5	2.7	5.5	5.7	7.7	6.5	6.5	24.0	27.3	15.5	1.3	77.3	41.6	49.1	50.9
73438	HEALDTON	87.1	86.2	0.8	0.9	0.2	0.3	1.8	2.0	6.4	6.2	6.4	6.3	7.0	24.2	26.2	14.7	2.6	77.3	40.7	48.2	51.8
73439	KINGSTON	86.6	85.6	0.1	0.1	0.2	0.2	2.5	2.9	4.7	4.7	5.2	5.4	5.8	19.3	31.5	21.9	1.7	82.2	48.9	49.7	50.3
73440	LEBANON	82.6	81.5	0.0	0.0	0.0	0.0	0.9	0.9	5.6	5.6	6.5	5.6	4.6	23.2	27.8	19.4	1.9	79.6	44.4	50.9	49.1
73441	LEON	86.3	85.2	0.3	0.4	0.2	0.3	4.4	4.9	4.8	5.0	5.8	6.2	6.2	21.8	28.8	19.2	2.2	80.7	45.2	50.9	49.1
73442	LOCO	87.1	87.1	0.0	0.0	0.0	0.0	0.9	0.9	4.9	5.5	6.2	7.1	5.5	21.5	27.7	17.9	3.7	79.4	44.5	49.2	50.8
73443	LONE GROVE	84.9	83.6	2.0	2.2	0.2	0.3	1.4	1.6	8.5	8.4	8.2	7.5	6.9	27.9	23.3	8.7	0.6	70.3	33.1	50.2	49.8
73444	HENNEPIN	62.8	60.8	25.7	26.8	0.0	0.0	1.7	2.0	5.7	5.9	7.4	7.1	5.9	24.6	26.9	14.8	1.9	76.6	40.9	50.6	49.4
73446	MADILL	72.3	69.5	3.0	3.2	0.2	0.3	12.8	14.8	7.3	7.2	7.0	6.2	5.9	25.1	23.4	15.3	2.6	74.8	38.8	49.1	50.9
73447	MANNSVILLE	84.1	82.8	0.1	0.1	0.1	0.1	0.3	0.4	8.2	8.2	8.3	5.8	5.5	28.2	23.3	11.0	1.7	71.9	36.4	50.0	50.0
73448	MARIETTA	81.4	80.1	3.4	3.5	0.3	0.3	9.8	11.1	6.6	6.7	7.4	7.0	6.1	25.1	25.4	13.3	2.6	74.7	38.9	48.5	51.6
73449	MEAD	84.3	83.3	0.1	0.1	0.2	0.2	1.6	1.9	4.7	5.1	6.6	5.7	5.3	23.9	30.3	17.5	1.0	80.1	44.1	49.9	50.1
73450	MILBURN	81.9	80.7	0.0	0.0	0.0	0.0	2.4	3.0	5.4	6.1	7.4	7.1	5.4	22.3	29.7	14.9	1.7	77.0	42.1	48.7	51.4
73453	OVERBROOK	85.5	84.7	0.7	0.7	0.0	0.2	2.7	3.1	5.5	5.9	7.2	7.0	5.5	23.8	29.3	14.6	1.3	76.9	42.2	49.8	50.2
73456	RINGLING	84.9	84.8	0.0	0.0	0.2	0.2	3.6	3.6	7.1	7.1	7.4	5.9	6.0	25.1	22.9	15.7	2.8	74.4	38.9	47.1	52.9
73458	SPRINGER	75.7	73.9	11.3	12.0	0.3	0.3	2.7	3.1	5.2	5.6	6.4	6.4	5.1	29.3	27.2	13.4	1.5	78.7	40.3	53.7	46.3
73459	THACKERVILLE	90.2	89.4	0.3	0.3	0.3	0.3	2.6	3.1	7.3	7.2	6.9	7.3	6.6	25.1	26.7	11.5	1.4	74.2	37.1	52.8	47.2
73460	TISHOMINGO	73.9	72.7	2.7	2.8	0.4	0.4	3.1	3.4	6.4	6.5	6.3	7.5	8.2	22.8	25.3	14.4	2.7	77.0	39.0	48.1	51.9
73461	WAPANUCKA	78.5	77.1	1.3	1.4	0.1	0.3	3.0	3.5	6.6	6.7	6.8	6.1	5.8	25.6	26.8	13.7	1.9	75.9	39.3	52.6	47.5
73463	WILSON	89.7	88.9	0.4	0.5	0.2	0.3	1.5	1.7	6.9	6.7	7.6	6.2	5.8	24.3	25.8	15.0	1.8	74.7	39.5	49.1	50.9
73481	RATLIFF CITY	85.0	83.4	0.4	0.4	0.1	0.1	1.9	2.0	5.5	6.0	7.2	6.4	5.6	21.8	28.4	17.2	1.9	77.2	43.5	49.0	51.0
73488	TUSSY	85.0	82.5	0.0	0.0	0.0	0.0	1.7	1.8	5.3	5.3	7.0	7.0	5.3	21.1	28.1	19.3	1.8	79.0	44.5	47.4	52.6
73501	LAWTON	58.6	57.1	25.7	26.1	1.9	2.3	8.3	9.2	6.8	6.6	6.8	6.8	8.6	33.0	21.1	8.9	1.4	75.7	33.8	54.3	45.7
73503	FORT SILL	58.3	56.2	26.6	27.0	2.8	3.3	13.3	14.8	8.0	6.6	4.2	16.2	31.1	32.2	1.9	0.1	0.0	78.7	22.4	71.7	28.3
73505	LAWTON	62.5	60.3	22.4	22.9	3.4	4.2	8.4	9.3	8.9	7.7	7.7	7.4	8.7	29.3	19.5	9.7	1.2	71.3	31.1	48.0	52.0
73507	LAWTON	67.6	65.6	16.6	17.0	2.5	3.1	9.3	10.3	8.7	8.0	7.6	7.0	7.8	29.5	20.9	9.2	1.3	71.6	32.1	48.7	51.3
73521	ALTUS	72.3	70.4	10.0	10.1	1.4	1.7	18.2	20.1	7.9	7.5	7.6	7.4	7.8	26.9	22.2	11.0	1.9	72.6	34.4	49.4	50.6
73523	ALTUS AFB	79.5	77.2	10.3	10.9	2.5	3.2	7.8	9.1	15.8	10.7	7.9	6.6	18.4	38.4	2.1	0.1	0.0	62.8	22.4	55.2	44.8
73526	BLAIR	87.1	85.3	0.2	0.2	0.6	0.7	9.0	10.6	6.7	6.6	8.5	6.5	7.2	25.4	25.5	11.5	2.1	74.3	36.4	48.0	52.0
73527	CACHE	75.4	74.1	3.0	3.2	1.0	1.3	5.2	5.8	7.7	7.7	8.4	8.1	7.1	26.9	24.9	8.7	0.6	71.2	35.5	49.7	50.3
73528	CHATTANOOGA	82.3	80.7	0.6	0.6	0.8	1.1	9.9	11.4	7.0	8.3	8.3	6.6	5.1	27.3	24.2	11.7	1.7	71.8	35.2	48.5	51.5
73529	COMANCHE	88.2	88.2	0.1	0.1	0.2	0.2	1.7	1.6	6.4	6.5	6.3	6.5	6.0	22.7	26.7	17.0	1.9	76.8	41.9	50.0	50.0
73530	DAVIDSON	81.2	79.1	1.0	1.0	0.0	0.0	24.5	27.6	7.2	6.9	7.4	6.2	7.2	23.9	22.4	16.0	2.7	74.9	39.2	51.4	48.7
73531	DEVOL	89.6	89.6	1.4	1.4	0.0	0.0	7.3	6.9	4.8	5.9	8.7	5.9	4.8	29.4	27.0	11.8	1.7	76.8	38.1	53.3	46.7
73532	DUKE	86.8	85.1	0.1	0.1	0.4	0.6	12.3	14.3	7.4	7.0	6.5	7.1	6.5	23.6	23.3	16.1	2.6	74.8	38.5	49.1	50.9
73533	DUNCAN	87.6	87.5	3.2	3.2	0.4	0.4	5.0	5.1	6.4	6.3	6.7	6.5	5.9	23.7	26.0	15.8	2.6	76.6	41.1	48.1	51.9
73537	ELDORADO	87.6	85.8	0.1	0.1	0.4	0.6	11.4	13.1	7.3	6.8	6.3	6.9	6.8	23.4	23.0	16.8	2.7	75.3	39.0	49.3	50.7
73538	ELGIN	81.3	80.4	1.4	1.4	0.6	0.7	4.1	4.6	5.9	6.5	7.3	8.3	5.5	25.2	28.1	12.0	1.3	75.2	40.0	50.2	49.8
73539	ELMER	87.9	86.4	0.7	0.7	0.9	0.9	10.1	12.0	5.8	6.5	6.7	6.0	5.3	24.9	30.3	12.9	1.6	77.6	41.4	54.3	45.7
73540	FAXON	83.9	82.5	1.4	1.5	0.6	0.9	4.3	4.7	6.1	6.7	7.9	6.4	5.3	23.6	29.2	13.4	1.5	75.2	40.7	50.4	49.6
73541	FLETCHER	91.3	90.6	0.2	0.2	0.3	0.4	2.2	2.7	6.9	6.9	7.7	7.2	7.1	25.7	25.5	11.6	1.6	74.2	37.6	48.7	51.3
73542	FREDERICK	71.0	69.2	10.5	10.5	0.5	0.5	19.4	21.5	6.7	6.9	7.0	7.3	6.2	23.6	23.2	15.3	3.8	74.6	39.0	49.4	50.6
73543	GERONIMO	76.0	74.7	1.5	1.6	1.1	1.3	6.5	7.2	8.9	7.6	7.3	8.0	7.6	28.1	21.6	10.2	0.7	71.5	33.4	50.7	49.3
73544	GOULD	86.8	86.3	1.4	1.4	0.4	0.4	12.1	12.5	5.8	5.8	6.2	6.0	6.4	24.0	26.4	17.3	2.4	78.8	42.3	52.2	47.8
73546	GRANDFIELD	77.9	75.9	6.7	7.0	0.2	0.2	14.7	16.7	6.4	6.4	6.3	6.6	5.9	24.9	24.4	16.1	3.0	76.5	40.7	48.7	51.4
73547	GRANITE	76.3	74.9	12.1	12.3	0.4	0.6	6.8	7.6	3.0	3.2	4.2	5.8	8.7	38.1	22.1	12.6	2.2	86.3	38.2	66.1	33.9
73548	HASTINGS	92.8	92.5	0.5	0.5	0.0	0.0	4.8	4.7	6.6	5.7	4.7	3.3	5.2	19.8	31.1	20.3	3.3	80.2	48.9	45.8	54.3
73549	HEADRICK	91.0	90.0	0.9	1.0	0.6	0.8	5.5	6.3	6.3	6.5	7.1	7.1	6.6	25.9	28.6	10.7	1.3	75.9	38.9	50.5	49.5
73550	HOLLIS	69.6	69.2	11.6	11.8	0.2	0.2	25.1	25.4	6.7	6.4	6.6	7.4	7.1	22.4	23.4	15.6	4.5	75.4	39.9	48.6	51.4
73551	HOLLISTER	84.9	84.3	6.6	6.9	0.0	0.0	5.7	5.9	3.9	4.9	6.9	10.8	3.9	28.4	28.4	10.8	2.0	74.5	40.0	61.8	38.2
73552	INDIAHOMA	71.2	70.5	1.1	1.1	0.3	0.4	6.1	6.6	7.8	7.4	7.2	6.8	6.4	23.8	25.6	13.2	1.7	73.4	38.1	50.9	49.1
73553	LOVELAND	77.8	76.0	6.7	6.8	0.4	0.4	14.8	16.9	6.1	6.1	6.5	6.5	5.7	25.5	24.7	15.8	3.2	77.1	41.0	48.8	51.3
73554	MANGUM	85.8	84.7	5.9	6.1	0.1	0.2	7.8	9.0	6.1	5.9	6.1	6.3	6.4	21.6	25.1	18.1	4.3	78.0	42.9	48.1	51.9
73559	MOUNTAIN PARK	92.2	91.6	1.2	1.2	0.0	0.2	5.5	6.1	4.3	4.1	5.1	7.1	7.3	21.0	29.1	19.3	2.8	82.1	45.6	52.5	47.5
73560	OLUSTEE	78.6	76.2	0.5	0.5	0.5	0.5	22.5	25.9	7.9	7.8	8.9	9.4	5.6	23.6	24.6	11.2	1.1	68.8	34.3	48.9	51.1
73561	OSCAR	85.2	84.6	0.0	0.0	0.0	0.0	3.7	3.9	3.9	3.9	7.7	7.7	3.9	26.9	26.9	19.2	0.0	84.6	42.5	46.2	53.9
73562	RANDLETT	93.1	93.2	0.5	0.5	0.2	0.2	6.5	6.7	6.0	6.6	7.6	7.1	6.3	28.3	24.8	11.3	2.1	75.5	37.1	52.5	47.5
73564	ROOSEVELT	92.2	91.3	1.2	1.2	0.0	0.2	5.5	6.2	4.1	4.1	5.0	7.2	7.2	21.2	29.2	19.2	2.9	82.9	45.7	52.5	47.5
73565	RYAN	89.0	88.9	0.5	0.5	0.2	0.2	10.4	10.6	6.3	5.7	6.0	6.8	5.8	20.8	26.4	18.2	4.0	78.1	43.9	46.9	53.1
73566	SNYDER	85.2	84.4	6.6	6.8	0.1	0.1	9.4	10.6	6.5	6.3	7.5	7.0	7.2	22.8	24.0	15.9	3.0	75.4	40.2	47.3	52.7
73568	TEMPLE	78.7	78.3	9.3	9.6	0.2	0.2	6.7	6.8	6.8	6.6	7.0	5.9	5.7	23.6	22.9	17.1	4.3	76.1	40.1	49.3	50.7
73569	TERRAL	89.3	89.0	0.0	0.0	0.0	0.0	14.8	15.3	6.8	6.1	4.3	8.1	6.3	18.5	27.0	20.1	2.9	77.9	45.0	46.2	53.8
73570	TIPTON	79.8	78.0	9.6	10.0	0.3	0.4	11.2	12.9	5.6	6.3	7.4	8.2	6.9	21.0	23.7	17.6	3.3	75.3	41.3	48.3	51.7
73571	VINSON	87.5	87.3	1.6	1.6	0.0	0.0	12.5	12.7	4.8	4.8	6.4	6.4	6.4	23.8	28.6	15.9	3.2	84.1	43.1	50.8	49.2
73572	WALTERS	84.5	84.5	1.2	1.2	0.1	0.1	3.6	3.6	7.2	6.9	6.9	5.9	5.9	25.5	24.4	14.3	2.9	75.3	39.7	49.9	50.1
73573	WAURIKA	87.2	87.2	1.5	1.5	2.6	2.6	7.0	7.1	5.7	6.0	7.2	5.3	6.0	26.8	24.1	15.7	3.2	77.7	39.9	51.4	48.6
73601	CLINTON	70.9	68.6	5.4	5.5	0.7	0.9	17.3	19.4	7.6	6.9	7.0	7.1	7.5	24.4	22.5	14.0	2.9	74.0	36.9	48.9	51.1
73620	ARAPAHO	86.8	85.2	1.4	1.5	1.4	1.8	6.2	7.4	5.7	6.0	7.5	7.2	7.2	26.5	27.8	10.9	1.4	76.1	39.4	50.3	49.7
73622	BESSIE	91.3	91.5	0.0	0.0	0.5	0.5	4.4	4.5	6.5	6.0	6.5	6.5	7.5	23.4	29.9	12.9	1.0	77.6	41.1	54.2	45.8
	OKLAHOMA	76.2	74.8	7.6	7.7	1.4	1.8	5.2	5.8	7.0	6.7	7.0	7.1	7.8	27.2	24.0	11.6	1.7	75.3	36.0	49.3	50.8
	UNITED STATES	75.1	73.6	12.3	12.5	3.8	4.2	12.5	14.1	6.9	6.7	7.2	7.0	7.3	28.6	23.8	10.8	1.7	75.1	36.0	49.1	50.9

#	POST OFFICE NAME	2004 Per Capita Income	2004 HH Income Base	2004 HH Income: Less than $25,000	$25,000 to $49,999	$50,000 to $99,999	$100,000 to $149,999	$150,000 or More	Median HH Income 2004	Median HH Income 2009	2004 National Centile	2004 State Centile	2004 Home Value Base	2004 Home Value: Less than $50,000	$50,000 to $89,999	$90,000 to $174,999	$175,000 to $399,999	$400,000 or More	2004 Median Home Value
73129	OKLAHOMA CITY	13495	7087	49.4	33.8	14.0	1.8	1.1	25307	30000	5	6	3773	77.9	20.2	1.6	0.2	0.1	34858
73130	OKLAHOMA CITY	22605	6926	21.7	28.6	36.7	10.7	2.4	49783	60437	72	93	5386	17.8	32.2	43.8	5.9	0.4	90100
73131	OKLAHOMA CITY	46191	980	11.2	20.0	37.8	13.2	17.9	70723	89265	92	99	861	4.1	13.6	43.6	30.1	8.7	137763
73132	OKLAHOMA CITY	24406	11523	21.4	30.1	35.2	10.7	2.6	48411	58211	69	92	6345	1.2	20.8	66.8	10.8	0.5	113873
73134	OKLAHOMA CITY	32837	1074	20.1	27.5	29.0	13.8	9.7	53202	66552	77	94	399	2.8	12.3	11.5	61.7	11.8	212383
73135	OKLAHOMA CITY	20560	5807	23.9	31.5	32.4	9.0	3.3	46009	54183	64	90	3770	12.3	33.9	50.3	3.3	0.2	94414
73139	OKLAHOMA CITY	23168	7391	29.7	34.5	25.7	7.7	2.4	38066	45562	39	73	3395	3.6	37.8	49.3	9.0	0.4	98791
73141	OKLAHOMA CITY	16965	1181	39.0	34.7	20.2	5.4	0.7	32905	39373	21	44	723	40.7	46.1	10.5	1.9	0.8	57031
73142	OKLAHOMA CITY	33007	4513	19.3	31.1	31.1	10.5	8.0	49520	57736	71	93	2046	0.0	6.4	61.9	22.4	9.3	136364
73145	OKLAHOMA CITY	12116	693	23.2	49.1	24.2	3.0	0.4	38436	44305	41	74	41	65.9	12.2	22.0	0.0	0.0	37917
73149	OKLAHOMA CITY	16889	2256	35.2	36.9	23.2	3.4	1.2	33884	40535	24	50	1159	58.5	26.9	13.7	0.0	0.9	43920
73150	OKLAHOMA CITY	30159	1749	14.2	19.6	39.9	18.4	8.0	66340	82448	89	99	1499	18.6	16.1	32.2	31.1	1.9	130870
73151	OKLAHOMA CITY	44771	337	15.4	10.7	28.2	21.4	24.3	91204	110898	97	100	318	3.8	3.5	17.9	52.2	22.6	295455
73159	OKLAHOMA CITY	20153	12680	28.1	33.2	30.3	6.9	1.5	40846	48327	49	81	8306	6.9	53.8	37.3	1.6	0.4	81460
73160	OKLAHOMA CITY	21439	15791	18.4	31.5	38.8	9.4	1.8	50044	58524	72	93	11606	9.8	49.1	38.0	2.7	0.4	83181
73162	OKLAHOMA CITY	32198	11031	14.5	22.6	37.2	17.6	8.2	65092	80313	89	99	8091	1.1	9.0	64.5	23.5	1.9	133168
73165	OKLAHOMA CITY	24519	1826	13.0	28.6	39.4	14.5	4.4	57325	66767	82	96	1591	10.6	18.1	50.3	20.6	0.4	116402
73169	OKLAHOMA CITY	22105	694	23.9	25.5	35.9	9.5	5.2	50341	58892	73	93	587	21.0	31.7	30.3	15.7	1.4	86900
73170	OKLAHOMA CITY	30346	9050	8.3	18.4	46.6	18.6	8.0	70466	84318	91	99	7990	1.8	8.9	57.8	28.1	3.4	138770
73173	OKLAHOMA CITY	26041	228	14.9	19.7	48.3	13.6	3.5	63873	75000	88	98	196	3.6	18.4	28.6	49.5	0.0	174074
73179	OKLAHOMA CITY	22976	668	16.3	32.6	39.7	6.9	4.5	50692	59093	73	93	550	28.9	29.1	33.8	8.0	0.2	83125
73401	ARDMORE	18964	13323	36.4	29.3	26.2	5.6	2.5	34811	41613	27	56	9306	29.5	29.5	30.4	9.3	1.3	75980
73430	BURNEYVILLE	22695	438	30.8	29.5	31.5	5.5	2.7	41199	47653	50	82	370	38.9	20.3	31.9	7.8	1.1	73636
73432	COLEMAN	17463	433	43.2	30.7	20.1	3.7	2.3	29097	34789	10	19	360	51.1	26.7	16.7	5.0	0.6	49167
73433	ELMORE CITY	16329	1230	40.7	35.0	19.7	3.3	1.4	30422	35764	13	26	948	41.8	31.7	20.7	5.2	0.7	58764
73434	FOSTER	15148	241	38.6	33.6	24.5	2.1	1.2	31689	36873	17	35	201	39.8	22.4	26.4	9.0	2.5	68077
73437	GRAHAM	15748	244	33.2	39.8	22.1	4.5	0.4	36558	43692	34	66	199	48.2	27.1	15.6	7.0	2.0	53500
73438	HEALDTON	14401	1266	46.1	32.1	17.1	4.0	0.6	27344	32087	8	11	895	65.6	24.5	8.3	1.7	0.0	38764
73439	KINGSTON	19115	2597	40.3	32.4	21.0	3.8	2.5	31195	36044	15	32	2126	39.1	31.1	21.9	6.7	1.2	65926
73440	LEBANON	16806	49	44.9	30.6	20.4	4.1	0.0	27920	35000	9	13	41	31.7	36.6	24.4	7.3	0.0	67000
73441	LEON	18398	362	41.2	27.6	24.9	4.4	1.9	32519	40755	19	41	314	45.2	21.0	23.6	9.6	0.6	62105
73442	LOCO	16829	136	39.0	33.1	25.0	2.9	0.0	33877	40398	24	50	113	47.8	26.6	17.7	7.1	0.9	53125
73443	LONE GROVE	15739	1349	34.0	32.0	29.0	4.0	1.0	34806	41579	27	56	1053	33.7	35.4	22.6	7.8	0.5	66500
73444	HENNEPIN	16200	261	47.5	26.1	19.5	5.0	1.9	26623	31841	7	9	209	49.8	23.4	20.1	4.8	1.9	50500
73446	MADILL	16641	3112	43.6	30.9	20.2	3.4	1.9	28504	33371	10	16	2334	41.5	32.7	20.5	5.0	0.3	57500
73447	MANNSVILLE	14607	422	41.5	29.6	22.5	5.5	1.0	31670	37245	17	35	333	51.4	32.1	13.5	2.1	0.9	49262
73448	MARIETTA	19228	2021	34.1	30.8	27.5	5.3	2.3	36668	43320	34	66	1547	36.7	33.0	22.2	6.0	2.1	62040
73449	MEAD	16691	1094	39.0	33.3	23.4	3.7	0.6	32659	37489	20	42	898	39.4	29.6	26.5	4.5	0.0	63333
73450	MILBURN	12657	118	47.5	36.4	12.7	2.5	0.9	26319	29136	6	9	98	57.1	24.5	9.2	4.1	5.1	44167
73453	OVERBROOK	21131	180	30.0	29.4	31.7	6.1	2.8	43516	50526	57	86	153	31.4	30.1	27.5	8.5	2.6	75417
73456	RINGLING	15010	836	48.7	29.1	16.3	4.8	1.2	25798	30244	6	7	620	57.9	23.2	11.5	4.2	3.2	41695
73458	SPRINGER	19288	643	36.2	29.7	26.9	4.4	2.8	36511	44032	34	65	518	41.7	29.0	18.5	10.2	0.6	61967
73459	THACKERVILLE	21172	558	30.3	34.2	26.7	6.6	2.2	38980	46265	43	76	460	33.3	35.4	22.8	6.7	1.7	65319
73460	TISHOMINGO	16982	2141	47.1	29.7	17.4	3.5	2.3	26795	31768	7	10	1445	40.1	31.8	22.9	4.7	0.6	59441
73461	WAPANUCKA	17781	327	44.3	30.0	19.9	4.0	1.8	28379	33355	9	15	271	51.3	26.2	17.0	4.8	0.7	48939
73463	WILSON	15399	1235	40.5	34.5	20.2	3.2	1.7	29876	34886	12	22	987	50.2	28.8	15.7	3.2	2.1	49844
73481	RATLIFF CITY	19055	307	41.0	31.9	22.8	1.6	2.6	31641	37873	17	35	255	60.4	22.4	10.6	5.1	1.6	39643
73488	TUSSY	12368	24	54.2	25.0	20.8	0.0	0.0	22257	30000	3	2	20	70.0	20.0	10.0	0.0	0.0	37500
73501	LAWTON	16144	6677	43.2	28.5	22.2	4.8	1.3	30113	35120	13	23	3693	29.8	39.8	25.9	4.0	0.5	71647
73503	FORT SILL	12547	1387	15.6	45.6	31.5	7.1	0.3	41998	47713	53	84	18	0.0	50.0	50.0	0.0	0.0	102500
73505	LAWTON	19386	17461	27.6	32.8	31.0	6.4	2.2	40780	47753	49	80	10458	11.0	44.8	37.8	5.8	0.6	84958
73507	LAWTON	18865	7588	32.7	33.4	25.2	6.1	2.5	36361	42968	33	64	4472	22.8	42.7	28.0	6.3	0.2	73040
73521	ALTUS	18674	7548	36.3	29.0	26.3	5.7	2.6	34877	41909	27	57	4513	29.9	31.8	30.2	6.8	1.3	73715
73523	ALTUS AFB	14318	636	18.7	39.8	35.7	5.8	0.0	40789	46678	49	81	9	11.1	66.7	22.2	0.0	0.0	55833
73526	BLAIR	15900	443	36.3	36.1	24.4	2.7	0.5	35691	43489	30	60	305	42.3	37.7	16.1	3.9	0.0	55875
73527	CACHE	18598	1932	26.6	27.1	34.7	9.5	2.0	46426	53718	65	91	1594	21.5	28.0	36.7	13.2	0.6	90707
73528	CHATTANOOGA	17113	185	35.1	29.7	28.1	6.5	0.5	35755	41454	31	61	149	42.3	33.6	22.8	1.3	0.0	58846
73529	COMANCHE	17950	2037	37.8	33.7	23.8	3.2	1.6	33226	39154	22	46	1600	49.4	30.5	15.6	4.1	0.4	50542
73530	DAVIDSON	15427	238	41.2	31.5	22.3	3.8	1.3	32330	39308	19	39	174	61.5	25.3	7.5	3.5	2.3	37895
73531	DEVOL	19879	119	30.3	26.1	34.5	6.7	2.5	42783	50694	55	86	95	39.0	26.3	28.4	5.3	1.1	67500
73532	DUKE	16825	268	39.9	35.8	19.8	2.2	2.2	31421	38703	16	33	201	49.3	33.3	14.4	2.5	0.5	50789
73533	DUNCAN	20733	12034	35.1	30.5	25.3	6.0	3.2	36132	42655	32	63	8820	31.9	29.6	30.1	7.6	1.0	73393
73537	ELDORADO	19063	304	38.8	36.2	19.4	2.6	3.0	32005	38756	18	37	228	50.0	32.9	14.5	2.2	0.4	50000
73538	ELGIN	21574	2240	25.4	27.7	36.1	8.3	2.6	46527	54006	65	91	1810	26.4	24.7	35.3	12.8	0.8	87468
73539	ELMER	21162	170	30.6	28.8	34.7	2.9	2.9	41927	47580	53	84	136	39.0	29.4	20.6	7.4	3.7	57500
73540	FAXON	21033	134	28.4	33.6	28.4	5.2	4.5	41361	47728	51	82	109	36.7	22.0	36.7	4.6	0.0	81364
73541	FLETCHER	18666	1446	30.6	34.5	27.8	5.6	1.5	38802	45745	42	75	1131	33.2	29.1	30.9	5.0	1.9	71897
73542	FREDERICK	16759	2114	46.6	30.2	16.0	4.3	2.9	27104	32359	7	11	1581	66.5	17.9	12.4	2.3	0.9	33891
73543	GERONIMO	14692	488	34.6	36.9	25.0	2.5	1.0	34864	40523	27	57	381	32.0	52.2	15.0	0.8	0.0	64016
73544	GOULD	24769	190	35.3	33.7	22.1	4.7	4.2	34416	41199	25	54	154	66.9	18.2	7.8	7.1	0.0	39706
73546	GRANDFIELD	17795	510	43.7	31.8	17.8	4.1	2.6	28752	34252	10	17	410	51.7	27.1	16.6	2.4	2.2	48409
73547	GRANITE	14640	594	38.1	34.5	21.4	4.4	1.7	31494	36029	16	34	445	54.4	27.2	16.0	2.5	0.0	45761
73548	HASTINGS	15417	96	45.8	31.3	19.8	3.1	0.0	27282	33176	8	11	82	52.4	28.1	17.1	2.4	0.0	48000
73549	HEADRICK	19726	815	27.9	31.5	30.8	5.8	4.1	41703	49001	52	83	681	27.5	26.9	34.1	10.9	0.7	83980
73550	HOLLIS	14132	1020	52.8	29.0	14.1	2.7	1.5	23425	28115	3	4	745	68.5	17.9	12.2	1.5	0.0	35731
73551	HOLLISTER	23648	39	35.9	35.9	15.4	5.1	7.7	34057	40000	24	52	31	67.7	19.4	12.9	0.0	0.0	39167
73552	INDIAHOMA	17968	447	33.1	29.8	28.9	7.2	1.1	38914	45806	42	76	376	37.5	24.2	33.0	4.8	0.5	67407
73553	LOVELAND	17701	109	45.0	32.1	17.4	3.7	1.8	27847	33049	8	13	88	53.4	28.4	14.8	2.3	1.1	47273
73554	MANGUM	16069	1436	46.7	32.0	16.0	3.7	1.7	26681	30024	7	10	1050	64.9	20.7	11.3	2.5	0.7	39806
73559	MOUNTAIN PARK	15604	226	43.8	34.5	17.3	3.5	0.9	29283	34198	11	20	168	57.7	31.6	8.3	1.2	1.2	41333
73560	OLUSTEE	14531	291	39.5	32.0	25.1	2.1	1.4	31790	38775	17	36	217	43.8	38.7	16.1	1.4	0.0	54655
73561	OSCAR	22308	8	25.0	12.5	25.0	37.5	0.0	60000	100000	84	97	6	50.0	16.7	16.7	16.7	0.0	47500
73562	RANDLETT	16056	374	34.2	33.7	27.3	3.5	1.3	35279	42247	29	59	304	49.7	32.6	14.5	3.0	0.3	50476
73564	ROOSEVELT	16233	271	45.4	33.6	17.0	3.3	0.7	28106	33381	9	14	202	57.9	31.2	7.9	1.5	1.5	41111
73565	RYAN	14985	510	47.3	29.8	18.6	3.5	0.8	26439	30927	6	9	372	62.9	20.7	11.0	4.3	1.1	36053
73566	SNYDER	16283	679	45.4	28.4	20.5	4.0	1.8	28332	34113	9	15	477	54.3	28.3	13.8	3.4	0.2	46639
73568	TEMPLE	15485	612	52.6	23.7	18.1	3.8	1.8	23479	28190	4	4	442	61.8	23.5	10.6	3.6	0.5	37500
73569	TERRAL	12558	202	58.4	28.7	9.9	2.5	0.5	20228	23555	2	2	151	68.2	12.6	13.9	3.3	2.0	36731
73570	TIPTON	18573	497	41.1	30.0	22.3	3.8	2.8	30736	36927	14	28	355	57.2	29.6	8.7	4.5	0.0	43625
73571	VINSON	25595	34	35.3	35.3	23.5	2.9	2.9	33564	41505	23	48	28	71.4	17.9	3.6	7.1	0.0	38333
73572	WALTERS	18465	1563	37.1	28.1	27.2	6.1	1.5	35077	43095	28	58	1169	30.7	36.5	26.8	6.0	0.0	70381
73573	WAURIKA	15124	1037	43.5	31.8	20.5	2.7	1.5	30224	35504	13	24	764	55.0	27.4	14.0	3.7	0.0	46162
73601	CLINTON	16853	3729	39.2	32.2	23.4	3.3	1.8	30913	36338	15	29	2477	38.3	26.7	27.8	6.5	0.8	68297
73620	ARAPAHO	19141	351	26.5	35.0	29.9	6.3	2.3	41035	48747	50	81	284	57.8	25.7	12.7	2.8	1.1	44762
73622	BESSIE	21347	92	33.7	30.4	27.2	5.4	3.3	34283	40911	25	53	79	49.4	16.5	27.9	6.3	0.0	51250
	OKLAHOMA	21077		31.9	30.4	27.2	7.1	3.4	38589	46268				26.7	29.5	32.0	10.2	1.6	81000
	UNITED STATES	25866		24.7	27.1	30.8	10.9	6.5	48124	56710				10.9	15.0	33.7	30.1	10.4	145905

ZIP CODE #	POST OFFICE NAME	FINANCIAL SERVICES: Auto Loan	Home Loan	Invest-ments	Retire-ment Plans	THE HOME: Home Improvements: Home Repair	Lawn & Garden	Furnishings: Comput-ers & Hard-ware	Major Appli-ances	TV, Radio, Sound Equip-ment	Furni-ture	ENTERTAINMENT: Dine out/ Carry out	Sports Equip-ment	Fees & Tickets	Toys & Games	Travel	Cable TV	PERSONAL: Apparel & Services	Auto Repairs	Health Insur-ance	Pets & Supplies
73129	OKLAHOMA CITY	52	45	47	44	45	51	52	51	54	50	67	58	49	65	50	54	65	53	53	56
73130	OKLAHOMA CITY	81	89	92	88	89	92	84	85	82	84	102	98	87	106	85	81	101	83	81	95
73131	OKLAHOMA CITY	150	184	202	185	179	186	166	163	155	167	196	187	179	203	170	153	196	158	153	180
73132	OKLAHOMA CITY	83	82	90	86	81	85	85	83	83	85	104	99	85	102	83	79	102	85	77	93
73134	OKLAHOMA CITY	99	108	130	113	108	112	109	107	104	108	131	126	111	131	109	101	128	108	99	116
73135	OKLAHOMA CITY	80	83	85	85	80	82	81	80	78	83	98	94	82	97	79	74	96	80	72	89
73139	OKLAHOMA CITY	71	66	73	69	66	72	73	70	72	71	91	83	71	88	70	70	88	73	68	79
73141	OKLAHOMA CITY	57	52	53	50	52	58	56	56	59	55	73	64	55	71	55	60	70	57	59	63
73142	OKLAHOMA CITY	106	91	107	102	88	94	105	99	103	107	132	121	100	122	97	96	128	106	89	111
73145	OKLAHOMA CITY	69	44	42	50	40	47	65	56	66	61	83	75	56	74	54	60	79	66	52	64
73149	OKLAHOMA CITY	62	54	53	55	54	60	59	59	61	59	76	69	57	72	57	60	72	61	59	68
73150	OKLAHOMA CITY	112	125	123	123	124	126	113	116	109	113	136	136	117	140	115	107	133	113	111	134
73151	OKLAHOMA CITY	170	212	230	218	205	206	186	182	170	189	216	210	205	224	190	164	218	175	161	201
73159	OKLAHOMA CITY	68	70	74	70	69	74	71	70	70	70	87	81	71	88	70	69	85	70	68	77
73160	OKLAHOMA CITY	82	85	85	86	83	85	83	83	80	83	100	97	83	100	81	77	98	82	77	92
73162	OKLAHOMA CITY	108	121	134	123	119	123	115	114	109	116	138	132	119	138	116	107	136	113	106	126
73165	OKLAHOMA CITY	94	109	110	109	107	107	99	100	93	99	117	117	103	121	100	90	116	97	91	112
73169	OKLAHOMA CITY	96	87	70	83	92	98	81	89	85	81	103	105	80	106	83	87	99	86	95	113
73170	OKLAHOMA CITY	118	133	135	139	128	126	122	121	113	126	143	141	126	144	120	106	141	118	105	132
73173	OKLAHOMA CITY	86	104	117	103	103	108	95	95	90	95	113	108	101	115	99	89	112	93	91	104
73179	OKLAHOMA CITY	91	85	69	82	89	94	78	85	81	78	99	101	78	102	81	83	95	83	90	108
73401	ARDMORE	71	62	53	59	65	73	63	68	68	62	82	77	61	80	64	70	77	67	74	81
73430	BURNEYVILLE	95	66	34	62	77	86	65	81	75	65	88	97	56	86	67	79	81	80	96	113
73432	COLEMAN	83	55	25	48	63	72	53	67	65	54	76	80	45	72	54	69	69	66	82	95
73433	ELMORE CITY	66	50	31	46	55	63	51	58	57	50	68	67	46	65	51	61	63	57	69	75
73434	FOSTER	73	49	22	42	56	64	47	59	57	48	67	71	40	63	48	62	61	59	73	84
73437	GRAHAM	74	52	27	49	60	67	51	63	59	50	69	76	44	68	53	62	63	62	75	88
73438	HEALDTON	56	42	28	40	46	55	47	51	52	44	61	58	41	58	46	55	56	51	61	62
73439	KINGSTON	73	57	38	52	63	72	56	66	63	55	75	76	50	73	58	68	69	65	78	86
73440	LEBANON	69	47	23	41	53	61	45	56	54	46	64	67	39	61	46	58	58	56	69	80
73441	LEON	85	58	28	52	66	75	56	70	67	57	78	84	48	75	58	71	71	69	85	99
73442	LOCO	73	49	22	42	56	64	47	59	57	48	67	71	40	63	48	62	61	59	73	84
73443	LONE GROVE	72	58	39	54	61	68	56	64	61	57	74	74	52	71	56	63	69	63	70	81
73444	HENNEPIN	73	53	29	47	59	66	50	61	58	51	69	72	45	67	51	62	64	60	72	84
73446	MADILL	70	53	35	48	58	67	54	62	61	53	73	72	48	70	55	65	67	62	73	81
73447	MANNSVILLE	75	50	23	43	57	66	49	61	59	49	69	73	41	65	49	63	62	60	75	86
73448	MARIETTA	84	63	39	59	69	80	64	73	73	63	86	85	58	83	65	77	79	73	87	95
73449	MEAD	70	51	30	45	58	65	49	60	57	49	67	70	42	65	51	61	61	59	72	83
73450	MILBURN	60	40	18	35	45	52	39	48	47	39	55	58	33	52	39	50	50	48	60	69
73453	OVERBROOK	97	70	38	62	78	88	67	81	78	68	92	97	59	89	68	83	85	80	97	112
73456	RINGLING	62	45	27	43	51	59	48	55	55	46	64	64	42	61	48	58	59	55	66	71
73458	SPRINGER	89	61	30	55	70	80	60	74	70	60	82	89	51	79	61	75	75	73	90	104
73459	THACKERVILLE	105	70	32	61	80	92	68	85	82	69	96	101	58	91	69	88	87	84	104	120
73460	TISHOMINGO	68	53	38	51	57	67	57	63	63	55	75	71	52	71	57	66	69	63	73	76
73461	WAPANUCKA	82	55	25	48	63	72	53	67	64	54	75	80	45	71	54	69	69	66	82	95
73463	WILSON	64	49	32	46	53	62	51	57	57	50	68	65	46	65	51	60	62	57	67	71
73481	RATLIFF CITY	87	59	27	52	67	76	57	71	68	58	80	85	48	76	58	73	73	70	87	100
73488	TUSSY	55	37	17	32	42	48	36	45	43	36	51	53	30	48	36	46	46	44	55	63
73501	LAWTON	55	51	55	50	50	55	55	54	56	54	70	63	54	68	53	56	68	55	54	61
73503	FORT SILL	80	51	49	58	46	55	76	65	77	71	96	87	65	86	62	70	92	77	60	74
73505	LAWTON	70	70	76	71	69	73	73	71	72	72	90	84	73	89	71	69	87	72	67	78
73507	LAWTON	64	66	70	66	65	69	68	66	68	67	84	78	68	85	67	66	82	67	64	73
73521	ALTUS	68	64	64	63	64	70	68	67	69	66	85	79	66	84	66	69	82	69	69	76
73523	ALTUS AFB	80	51	49	58	47	55	76	65	77	70	96	87	65	86	62	70	92	77	60	74
73526	BLAIR	63	47	31	46	52	62	53	58	59	50	69	65	47	65	52	62	63	58	69	70
73527	CACHE	80	78	71	79	79	82	76	78	75	76	93	92	75	94	75	73	90	77	76	90
73528	CHATTANOOGA	68	58	45	58	61	69	60	64	63	59	77	73	57	76	59	64	72	63	69	75
73529	COMANCHE	81	56	29	50	63	74	57	68	67	57	79	80	49	74	57	72	72	68	83	92
73530	DAVIDSON	72	49	22	42	55	63	47	59	57	48	66	70	40	63	48	61	60	58	72	83
73531	DEVOL	87	61	32	58	71	80	60	74	69	60	81	90	51	80	62	73	74	73	89	104
73532	DUKE	70	54	37	52	58	69	59	64	65	56	77	72	53	73	58	68	70	64	75	77
73533	DUNCAN	75	67	58	64	70	79	68	72	72	66	87	83	65	87	69	75	83	72	80	87
73537	ELDORADO	70	54	37	52	58	69	59	64	65	56	77	72	53	73	58	69	71	64	76	77
73538	ELGIN	88	76	60	73	81	89	74	81	79	73	95	95	71	95	75	81	90	80	89	101
73539	ELMER	98	68	36	64	79	89	67	83	77	66	91	100	57	89	70	81	83	82	99	116
73540	FAXON	97	68	37	65	79	88	68	83	77	67	91	99	58	89	70	81	83	82	98	114
73541	FLETCHER	79	65	46	62	69	79	66	72	72	64	86	83	61	84	66	75	80	71	83	90
73542	FREDERICK	68	52	37	50	56	65	56	62	62	54	74	72	50	71	56	65	69	62	72	77
73543	GERONIMO	66	58	44	56	59	63	56	61	57	57	70	70	52	66	55	57	67	60	62	73
73544	GOULD	119	83	43	78	97	108	82	101	94	81	111	122	70	109	85	99	101	100	121	141
73546	GRANDFIELD	72	54	36	52	59	71	60	66	67	57	79	74	53	75	59	71	72	66	79	80
73547	GRANITE	41	31	20	30	34	41	34	38	38	32	45	42	30	43	34	41	41	38	45	45
73548	HASTINGS	55	41	27	40	45	54	46	50	51	43	60	56	41	57	45	54	55	50	60	61
73549	HEADRICK	94	66	34	62	77	86	65	81	75	64	88	97	56	86	68	79	80	79	96	112
73550	HOLLIS	57	43	28	41	47	56	47	52	53	45	62	59	42	59	47	56	56	52	62	64
73551	HOLLISTER	101	70	37	67	82	92	70	86	80	69	94	104	59	92	72	84	86	85	102	120
73552	INDIAHOMA	75	58	39	56	63	75	63	69	70	60	82	78	57	79	62	73	76	69	81	84
73553	LOVELAND	72	54	36	52	59	71	60	66	67	57	79	74	54	75	59	71	72	66	79	80
73554	MANGUM	60	45	30	43	49	59	50	55	56	47	65	61	44	62	49	59	60	55	65	66
73559	MOUNTAIN PARK	57	43	28	41	47	56	47	52	53	45	62	58	42	59	47	56	57	52	62	63
73560	OLUSTEE	62	53	41	53	55	63	54	58	58	53	70	66	52	69	54	59	66	57	63	69
73561	OSCAR	93	113	127	112	112	118	103	104	98	103	123	117	110	124	107	97	122	101	99	113
73562	RANDLETT	79	54	25	48	61	70	52	65	62	53	73	78	44	70	53	67	66	64	79	92
73564	ROOSEVELT	57	42	28	41	46	56	47	52	53	45	62	58	42	59	47	56	57	52	62	62
73565	RYAN	56	43	30	42	47	56	47	51	52	45	62	58	43	58	47	55	57	51	61	62
73566	SNYDER	64	48	32	46	52	63	53	58	59	50	70	65	47	66	52	63	64	58	70	70
73568	TEMPLE	57	43	28	41	47	57	48	53	54	45	63	59	43	59	47	57	57	53	63	63
73569	TERRAL	45	33	22	32	37	44	37	41	42	35	49	46	33	46	37	44	45	41	49	49
73570	TIPTON	71	53	35	51	58	70	59	65	66	56	78	73	53	74	59	70	71	65	78	79
73571	VINSON	86	60	31	57	70	78	59	73	68	58	80	88	51	78	61	72	73	72	87	102
73572	WALTERS	74	58	40	56	63	74	62	68	68	59	81	77	56	78	62	72	75	68	80	83
73573	WAURIKA	59	46	32	44	50	59	50	55	55	47	65	62	45	63	50	58	60	54	65	66
73601	CLINTON	63	56	50	54	58	66	59	61	63	57	76	70	57	76	59	64	72	61	67	72
73620	ARAPAHO	91	64	33	60	74	83	63	78	73	62	85	94	54	83	65	76	78	77	93	108
73622	BESSIE	84	59	31	56	69	77	58	72	67	57	79	87	50	77	60	70	72	71	86	100
	OKLAHOMA	79	71	65	70	73	80	73	76	76	72	93	88	70	91	72	76	88	76	79	89
	UNITED STATES	100	100	100	100	100	100	100	100	100	100	100	100	100	100	100	100	100	100	100	100

ZIP CODE		POPULATION			2000-2004 ANNUAL RATE		HOUSEHOLDS					FAMILIES		
# POST OFFICE NAME	COUNTY FIPS CODE	2000	2004	2009	% Rate	State Centile	2000	2004	2009	% Annual Rate 2000-2004	2004 Average HH Size	2000	2004	% Annual Rate 2000-2004
73624 BURNS FLAT	149	1881	1941	1970	0.7	71	660	686	701	0.9	2.83	513	532	0.9
73625 BUTLER	039	1119	1135	1148	0.3	53	441	452	462	0.6	2.48	331	338	0.5
73626 CANUTE	149	1183	1171	1167	-0.2	28	473	473	474	0.0	2.48	337	335	-0.1
73627 CARTER	009	555	532	532	-1.0	4	230	223	225	-0.7	2.39	159	154	-0.8
73628 CHEYENNE	129	1430	1402	1375	-0.5	18	613	613	612	0.0	2.23	391	389	-0.1
73632 CORDELL	149	4072	4090	4114	0.1	44	1649	1659	1672	0.1	2.38	1144	1147	0.1
73638 CRAWFORD	129	144	139	136	-0.8	7	55	54	54	-0.4	2.57	41	40	-0.6
73639 CUSTER CITY	039	654	647	648	-0.3	28	281	280	283	-0.1	2.31	198	197	-0.1
73641 DILL CITY	149	853	832	826	-0.6	15	343	337	337	-0.4	2.47	257	252	-0.5
73642 DURHAM	129	123	119	116	-0.8	9	60	59	59	-0.4	2.02	45	44	-0.5
73644 ELK CITY	009	12573	12788	13001	0.4	57	4917	5045	5169	0.6	2.49	3420	3497	0.5
73645 ERICK	009	1461	1434	1438	-0.4	20	619	607	612	-0.5	2.33	411	402	-0.5
73646 FAY	043	110	109	107	-0.2	30	52	52	52	0.0	2.10	38	38	0.0
73647 FOSS	149	411	399	396	-0.7	12	165	161	161	-0.6	2.48	117	113	-0.8
73650 HAMMON	129	696	678	662	-0.6	14	269	266	265	-0.3	2.55	194	191	-0.4
73651 HOBART	075	4436	4457	4438	0.1	45	1749	1768	1774	0.3	2.38	1166	1174	0.2
73654 LEEDEY	129	768	741	722	-0.8	7	307	299	295	-0.6	2.36	213	207	-0.7
73655 LONE WOLF	075	1112	1105	1094	-0.2	32	488	491	491	0.1	2.22	333	334	0.1
73658 OAKWOOD	043	262	259	254	-0.3	27	112	112	111	0.0	2.31	82	82	0.0
73659 PUTNAM	043	105	102	100	-0.7	12	47	46	45	-0.5	2.17	34	33	-0.7
73660 REYDON	129	420	407	397	-0.7	9	181	178	177	-0.4	2.28	134	132	-0.4
73661 ROCKY	149	249	244	242	-0.5	17	110	108	108	-0.4	2.26	82	81	-0.3
73662 SAYRE	009	5188	3737	3787	-7.4	0	1581	1613	1652	0.5	2.23	1010	1025	0.4
73663 SEILING	043	1613	1584	1553	-0.4	21	648	643	638	-0.2	2.43	441	437	-0.2
73664 SENTINEL	149	1197	1172	1165	-0.5	16	472	465	464	-0.4	2.52	353	347	-0.4
73666 SWEETWATER	129	314	304	299	-0.8	9	133	130	130	-0.5	2.34	96	94	-0.5
73667 TALOGA	043	681	660	644	-0.7	10	280	273	269	-0.6	2.35	200	195	-0.5
73668 TEXOLA	009	112	109	109	-0.6	13	39	38	38	-0.6	2.87	27	27	0.0
73669 THOMAS	039	1708	1690	1695	-0.3	28	650	646	652	-0.2	2.52	454	449	-0.3
73673 WILLOW	055	313	307	301	-0.5	19	148	143	137	-0.8	1.26	100	54	-13.5
73701 ENID	047	23205	22811	22577	-0.4	23	9123	8977	8907	-0.4	2.44	5868	5756	-0.5
73703 ENID	047	26048	26498	26705	0.4	57	10729	10967	11099	0.5	2.35	7450	7587	0.4
73705 ENID	047	220	224	225	0.4	58	0	0	0	0.0	0.00	0	0	0.0
73716 ALINE	003	408	391	377	-1.0	4	185	179	174	-0.8	2.15	124	119	-1.0
73717 ALVA	151	6745	6639	6480	-0.4	23	2650	2621	2567	-0.3	2.17	1584	1559	-0.4
73718 AMES	093	508	486	474	-1.0	3	215	208	206	-0.8	2.34	159	153	-0.9
73719 AMORITA	003	148	143	138	-0.8	8	70	68	66	-0.7	2.10	51	50	-0.5
73720 BISON	047	197	187	183	-1.2	2	86	83	81	-0.8	2.25	66	64	-0.7
73722 BURLINGTON	003	463	446	431	-0.9	6	184	179	174	-0.7	2.49	132	128	-0.7
73724 CANTON	011	1160	1158	1174	0.0	37	475	478	488	0.2	2.42	317	318	0.1
73726 CARMEN	003	552	531	513	-0.9	5	222	215	209	-0.8	2.43	148	143	-0.8
73727 CARRIER	047	644	645	646	0.0	42	229	231	232	0.2	2.79	183	184	0.1
73728 CHEROKEE	003	2012	1964	1909	-0.6	15	869	851	830	-0.5	2.28	583	568	-0.6
73729 CLEO SPRINGS	093	554	536	526	-0.8	9	226	222	220	-0.4	2.41	171	167	-0.6
73730 COVINGTON	047	939	886	861	-1.4	1	374	355	348	-1.2	2.50	281	267	-1.2
73731 DACOMA	151	306	284	270	-1.7	0	132	124	119	-1.5	2.29	90	84	-1.6
73733 DOUGLAS	047	213	201	195	-1.4	1	94	89	87	-1.3	2.26	71	67	-1.4
73734 DOVER	073	585	591	603	0.2	50	216	220	226	0.4	2.69	171	173	0.3
73735 DRUMMOND	047	791	759	743	-1.0	5	295	285	280	-0.8	2.66	236	227	-0.9
73736 FAIRMONT	047	651	613	595	-1.4	1	255	242	236	-1.2	2.53	198	188	-1.2
73737 FAIRVIEW	093	3785	3788	3774	0.0	41	1539	1555	1567	0.2	2.36	1064	1073	0.2
73738 GARBER	047	1145	1097	1073	-1.0	4	481	464	457	-0.8	2.36	334	319	-1.1
73739 GOLTRY	003	385	371	358	-0.9	7	170	165	161	-0.7	2.21	113	110	-0.6
73741 HELENA	003	1717	1696	1676	-0.3	26	291	283	275	-0.7	2.42	201	195	-0.7
73742 HENNESSEY	073	4138	4224	4379	0.5	61	1511	1547	1613	0.6	2.65	1155	1179	0.5
73744 HITCHCOCK	011	242	242	245	0.0	40	91	91	93	0.0	2.66	67	67	0.0
73747 ISABELLA	093	353	347	343	-0.4	23	136	135	135	-0.2	2.57	105	105	0.0
73749 JET	003	464	447	433	-0.9	7	226	220	214	-0.6	2.02	141	137	-0.7
73750 KINGFISHER	073	6663	6715	6897	0.2	48	2540	2572	2654	0.3	2.55	1834	1850	0.2
73753 KREMLIN	047	481	479	478	-0.1	35	187	187	187	0.0	2.56	148	148	0.0
73754 LAHOMA	047	1262	1236	1225	-0.5	17	499	494	493	-0.2	2.48	374	367	-0.4
73755 LONGDALE	011	668	672	682	0.1	46	279	283	289	0.3	2.37	190	192	0.3
73756 LOYAL	073	136	131	133	-0.9	6	56	54	56	-0.9	2.43	45	44	-0.5
73757 LUCIEN	103	109	107	107	-0.4	21	48	48	48	0.0	2.23	37	37	0.0
73758 MANCHESTER	053	200	194	190	-0.7	10	85	82	81	-0.8	2.23	57	55	-0.8
73759 MEDFORD	053	1842	1829	1809	-0.2	32	748	742	733	-0.2	2.39	509	503	-0.3
73760 MENO	093	518	513	508	-0.2	29	203	202	201	-0.1	2.54	158	157	-0.2
73761 NASH	053	537	514	500	-1.0	4	219	210	204	-1.0	2.45	159	152	-1.1
73762 OKARCHE	073	1950	2208	2406	3.0	97	761	867	950	3.1	2.55	558	635	3.1
73763 OKEENE	011	1644	1637	1656	-0.1	35	666	667	679	0.0	2.36	455	454	-0.1
73764 OMEGA	073	45	43	44	-1.1	3	16	16	16	0.0	2.69	13	12	-1.9
73766 POND CREEK	053	1065	1046	1029	-0.4	21	429	422	416	-0.4	2.48	312	306	-0.5
73768 RINGWOOD	093	1323	1303	1288	-0.4	24	509	505	503	-0.2	2.58	394	391	-0.2
73770 SOUTHARD	011	9	9	9	0.0	40	3	3	3	0.0	3.00	2	2	0.0
73771 WAKITA	053	572	554	543	-0.8	9	235	228	223	-0.7	2.30	158	153	-0.8
73772 WATONGA	011	6139	7170	7307	3.7	99	1843	1898	1956	0.7	2.55	1286	1320	0.6
73773 WAUKOMIS	047	1597	1536	1505	-0.9	5	649	629	621	-0.7	2.44	459	444	-0.8
73801 WOODWARD	153	13734	13689	13716	-0.1	36	5510	5549	5617	0.2	2.41	3828	3838	0.1
73832 ARNETT	045	1232	1199	1173	-0.6	13	531	524	520	-0.3	2.26	365	359	-0.4
73834 BUFFALO	059	1729	1713	1697	-0.2	30	714	713	713	0.0	2.34	509	507	-0.1
73835 CAMARGO	043	143	138	134	-0.8	7	69	67	66	-0.7	2.04	48	46	-1.0
73838 CHESTER	093	462	453	447	-0.5	18	199	197	197	-0.2	2.30	142	140	-0.3
73840 FARGO	045	653	642	631	-0.4	23	262	262	261	0.0	2.45	203	202	-0.1
73841 FORT SUPPLY	153	1211	1196	1193	-0.3	26	257	254	256	-0.3	2.94	201	198	-0.4
73842 FREEDOM	151	497	472	452	-1.2	2	212	203	196	-1.0	2.33	147	140	-1.1
73843 GAGE	045	536	530	522	-0.3	27	240	241	241	0.1	2.20	163	163	0.0
73844 GATE	007	248	246	241	-0.2	31	107	106	105	-0.2	2.32	81	80	-0.3
73847 KNOWLES	007	54	54	53	0.0	40	19	19	19	0.0	2.84	14	14	0.0
73848 LAVERNE	007	1932	1895	1863	-0.5	19	828	819	813	-0.3	2.31	560	552	-0.3
73851 MAY	059	72	70	69	-0.7	12	32	32	31	0.0	2.19	23	23	0.0
73852 MOORELAND	153	2111	2157	2180	0.5	62	815	835	848	0.6	2.52	602	615	0.5
73853 MUTUAL	153	230	231	232	0.1	44	101	102	103	0.2	2.26	81	81	0.0
73855 ROSSTON	059	222	216	213	-0.6	13	90	89	88	-0.3	2.43	65	64	-0.3
73857 SHARON	153	1200	1248	1275	0.9	77	458	480	494	1.1	2.59	367	383	1.0
73858 SHATTUCK	045	1654	1621	1590	-0.5	17	736	732	730	-0.1	2.15	489	484	-0.2
OKLAHOMA					0.8					1.0	2.48			0.9
UNITED STATES					1.2					1.3	2.58			1.1

ZIP CODE		RACE (%)						% Hispanic Origin		2004 AGE DISTRIBUTION (%)										MEDIAN AGE		
#	POST OFFICE NAME	White 2000	White 2004	Black 2000	Black 2004	Asian/Pacific 2000	Asian/Pacific 2004	2000	2004	0-4	5-9	10-14	15-19	20-24	25-44	45-64	65-84	85+	18+	2004	% 2004 Males	% 2004 Females
73624	BURNS FLAT	88.6	88.6	1.3	1.3	1.0	1.0	6.1	6.2	8.7	7.9	10.9	8.3	6.6	27.6	21.5	8.0	0.6	67.1	30.9	48.1	51.9
73625	BUTLER	86.5	85.4	0.5	0.4	0.1	0.1	6.0	7.1	4.9	5.5	6.3	5.8	5.7	23.9	29.7	16.7	1.5	79.1	43.7	49.2	50.8
73626	CANUTE	91.4	91.3	0.5	0.5	0.5	0.5	4.7	4.7	6.0	5.9	5.6	6.2	6.4	25.8	27.2	14.9	2.2	78.9	41.8	49.9	50.1
73627	CARTER	91.4	90.0	0.0	0.0	0.2	0.2	8.1	9.6	4.9	5.3	6.4	5.3	7.3	29.1	26.7	12.2	2.8	80.5	40.5	50.6	49.4
73628	CHEYENNE	96.6	96.7	0.4	0.4	0.1	0.1	2.2	2.1	6.4	6.1	5.4	5.1	5.9	22.9	27.9	16.6	3.9	78.9	43.9	50.8	49.2
73632	CORDELL	94.8	94.8	0.2	0.2	0.2	0.2	2.5	2.5	5.9	6.0	6.8	6.1	6.1	23.6	24.4	17.3	3.9	77.7	41.9	47.5	52.5
73638	CRAWFORD	95.8	95.7	0.0	0.0	0.0	0.0	1.4	2.2	4.3	5.0	6.5	6.5	5.8	22.3	28.1	18.0	3.6	79.9	44.8	50.4	49.6
73639	CUSTER CITY	93.7	93.2	0.2	0.2	0.0	0.0	2.3	2.8	5.9	6.2	6.7	6.0	6.0	23.2	28.6	15.5	2.0	77.6	42.3	48.7	51.3
73641	DILL CITY	92.4	92.6	0.0	0.0	0.0	0.0	4.9	4.9	5.9	6.0	6.7	7.1	6.6	22.6	23.3	19.1	2.6	77.2	41.3	50.2	49.8
73642	DURHAM	95.9	95.0	0.0	0.0	0.0	0.0	1.6	1.7	4.2	5.0	5.9	5.9	5.0	20.2	29.4	21.9	2.5	79.8	47.3	47.9	52.1
73644	ELK CITY	89.5	86.6	2.7	4.7	0.5	0.7	5.6	6.4	7.3	6.9	7.6	6.9	7.3	26.2	23.9	11.8	2.2	74.0	36.2	48.7	51.3
73645	ERICK	92.5	90.9	0.6	1.1	0.3	0.4	4.2	4.9	6.8	6.8	6.6	6.1	5.9	21.5	25.5	16.8	4.0	75.8	42.2	47.6	52.4
73646	FAY	91.8	90.8	0.0	0.0	0.0	0.0	1.8	1.8	5.5	5.5	6.4	4.6	4.6	22.0	31.2	17.4	2.8	79.8	46.1	51.4	48.6
73647	FOSS	91.5	91.5	0.0	0.0	0.2	0.3	4.1	4.3	6.3	6.0	6.3	6.5	7.3	24.6	29.3	12.8	1.0	77.7	41.2	54.6	45.4
73650	HAMMON	79.9	79.8	0.3	0.3	0.1	0.2	4.3	4.1	5.5	7.8	6.8	7.5	5.5	26.4	26.6	12.1	1.9	74.6	39.2	50.9	49.1
73651	HOBART	80.9	79.6	7.5	7.7	0.7	0.9	8.3	9.5	6.6	6.3	6.7	6.8	6.6	24.1	23.3	15.9	3.7	76.0	40.3	49.4	50.6
73654	LEEDEY	93.4	93.1	0.1	0.1	0.0	0.0	1.8	1.9	4.9	5.8	6.2	5.3	4.9	21.7	27.4	18.8	5.1	79.4	46.0	49.1	50.9
73655	LONE WOLF	91.8	91.2	1.0	1.0	0.0	0.0	3.8	4.2	5.2	5.3	5.4	6.4	5.4	21.6	32.0	16.3	2.4	79.9	45.4	51.8	48.2
73658	OAKWOOD	91.6	90.7	0.0	0.0	0.0	0.0	1.9	1.9	5.4	5.8	7.0	5.0	4.6	22.0	30.5	17.4	2.3	78.4	45.2	51.0	49.0
73659	PUTNAM	94.3	94.1	0.0	0.0	0.0	0.0	4.8	4.9	3.9	5.9	7.8	7.8	4.9	24.5	29.4	12.8	2.9	75.5	41.9	51.0	49.0
73660	REYDON	95.7	95.6	0.2	0.3	0.0	0.0	1.7	2.0	4.4	4.7	5.7	6.1	5.7	21.6	30.0	18.9	3.0	81.6	46.0	49.4	50.6
73661	ROCKY	91.2	91.0	0.0	0.0	0.0	0.0	8.0	8.2	5.7	6.2	6.6	7.0	6.2	24.2	25.8	16.0	2.5	77.1	41.1	49.2	50.8
73662	SAYRE	79.0	81.7	14.5	11.8	0.3	0.2	5.2	5.5	4.8	4.7	5.0	5.6	8.5	29.8	23.4	15.0	3.2	82.4	39.5	56.0	44.0
73663	SEILING	86.0	85.2	0.1	0.1	0.1	0.1	2.5	2.9	6.3	6.2	6.9	6.6	6.6	20.8	27.7	16.0	3.0	76.6	42.2	49.9	50.1
73664	SENTINEL	91.2	91.1	0.1	0.1	0.0	0.0	8.0	8.1	5.6	6.1	6.7	6.9	6.0	23.8	25.9	16.5	2.7	77.6	41.5	49.4	50.6
73666	SWEETWATER	94.0	93.1	0.6	1.3	0.3	0.3	2.6	3.0	5.9	5.9	5.3	4.9	4.9	20.4	29.3	20.7	2.6	79.3	46.7	51.6	48.4
73667	TALOGA	94.9	94.2	0.4	0.5	0.0	0.0	4.1	4.7	3.6	5.3	7.0	6.8	4.6	25.0	29.6	14.2	3.9	79.1	43.7	50.3	49.7
73668	TEXOLA	91.1	89.0	1.8	2.8	0.9	0.9	3.6	4.6	6.4	6.4	5.5	4.6	5.5	20.2	29.4	19.3	2.8	78.9	46.1	53.2	46.8
73669	THOMAS	90.5	89.8	0.1	0.1	0.0	0.0	1.8	2.0	6.2	6.1	6.7	7.0	6.2	22.4	25.2	16.4	3.9	76.3	41.6	47.8	52.3
73673	WILLOW	71.9	70.4	15.3	16.0	0.6	0.7	6.7	7.8	2.3	2.3	3.3	4.9	9.5	42.4	22.5	11.4	1.6	89.9	37.9	70.7	29.3
73701	ENID	84.5	83.1	5.1	5.3	1.2	1.4	6.9	7.9	7.6	7.0	6.9	6.8	7.5	27.5	22.5	11.8	2.4	74.2	35.6	48.9	51.1
73703	ENID	90.5	89.4	2.5	2.6	1.8	2.2	2.5	2.9	6.4	6.2	6.3	6.1	6.7	25.6	25.2	14.9	2.7	77.5	40.2	48.0	52.0
73705	ENID	79.1	76.8	7.7	8.0	2.3	2.7	6.4	7.6	17.0	9.8	5.4	4.0	25.0	38.4	0.5	0.0	0.0	66.5	22.8	58.9	41.1
73716	ALINE	95.8	95.1	0.3	0.3	0.3	0.3	1.2	1.3	5.6	5.6	5.6	6.1	5.1	22.0	26.6	19.2	4.1	79.3	44.9	50.1	49.9
73717	ALVA	92.9	92.3	2.9	3.0	0.7	0.9	1.9	2.2	4.7	4.3	4.9	7.8	12.3	26.7	20.6	15.0	3.7	83.1	35.7	52.4	47.6
73718	AMES	95.5	95.3	0.6	0.6	0.0	0.0	4.3	4.5	5.6	5.8	6.0	5.1	5.1	23.1	29.4	17.5	2.5	79.4	44.6	48.6	51.4
73719	AMORITA	96.6	95.8	0.7	0.7	0.0	0.0	1.4	2.1	4.9	4.9	5.6	6.3	6.3	19.6	30.1	20.3	2.1	80.4	46.3	49.0	51.1
73720	BISON	93.9	93.6	0.0	0.0	0.5	1.1	2.0	2.1	4.3	4.3	5.9	6.4	5.4	23.5	33.2	15.0	2.1	81.3	45.2	49.7	50.3
73722	BURLINGTON	96.1	95.7	0.7	0.7	0.0	0.0	1.7	1.8	5.2	5.6	5.6	6.1	6.1	19.7	28.7	20.4	2.7	80.3	46.1	49.1	50.9
73724	CANTON	82.0	81.5	0.0	0.0	0.1	0.1	2.8	3.1	6.0	6.4	6.7	7.0	7.1	21.2	28.2	15.4	2.1	76.7	41.1	49.3	50.7
73726	CARMEN	95.7	95.3	0.2	0.2	0.2	0.2	1.1	1.1	5.5	5.5	5.8	6.6	5.1	21.7	26.6	19.0	4.3	78.7	44.9	50.1	49.9
73727	CARRIER	96.6	96.1	0.5	0.5	0.3	0.3	1.4	1.4	6.8	7.8	7.9	6.8	4.7	23.6	29.3	11.6	1.6	73.0	40.3	50.2	49.8
73728	CHEROKEE	96.0	95.6	0.1	0.1	0.1	0.1	2.9	3.4	5.6	5.7	6.1	6.6	5.8	20.9	24.6	20.7	4.1	78.1	44.6	48.9	51.1
73729	CLEO SPRINGS	96.8	96.6	0.5	0.6	0.2	0.2	1.6	1.5	5.6	5.6	5.0	6.3	6.7	24.1	30.6	14.4	1.7	80.0	42.9	49.4	50.6
73730	COVINGTON	95.6	95.2	0.0	0.0	0.1	0.1	1.2	1.5	5.1	5.1	6.2	7.2	6.1	26.1	25.5	16.4	2.4	79.2	41.5	50.1	49.9
73731	DACOMA	97.7	97.2	0.0	0.0	0.3	0.4	1.6	2.1	3.9	4.2	7.0	4.9	5.3	23.9	27.8	19.7	3.2	81.7	45.5	51.1	48.9
73733	DOUGLAS	95.8	95.5	0.0	0.0	0.0	0.0	0.9	1.0	5.5	5.5	6.0	7.0	6.0	25.9	25.4	16.4	2.5	78.6	41.4	50.3	49.8
73734	DOVER	91.1	90.2	0.9	0.9	0.0	0.0	5.8	6.9	6.3	6.4	8.0	7.1	8.0	28.1	24.9	10.3	1.0	75.0	36.9	49.9	50.1
73735	DRUMMOND	92.9	92.4	1.1	1.2	0.1	0.3	3.0	3.7	7.1	7.3	7.3	7.3	5.8	27.5	25.4	11.6	0.8	73.9	38.0	50.1	49.9
73736	FAIRMONT	96.2	95.8	0.5	0.5	0.6	0.8	1.1	1.3	5.4	6.4	7.0	6.5	5.4	22.7	31.8	13.2	1.6	76.4	42.9	50.2	49.8
73737	FAIRVIEW	96.8	96.8	0.1	0.1	0.1	0.1	1.5	1.5	5.9	6.0	6.1	7.0	6.1	21.8	26.4	16.6	4.3	77.7	43.1	48.1	51.9
73738	GARBER	95.3	95.0	0.2	0.2	0.1	0.1	0.5	0.5	7.0	7.0	6.9	6.6	4.8	22.7	25.6	16.4	2.9	74.9	40.8	49.3	50.7
73739	GOLTRY	95.6	94.9	0.3	0.3	0.3	0.3	1.3	1.4	5.4	5.4	5.4	6.5	5.1	21.6	27.5	19.1	4.0	79.8	45.4	50.7	49.3
73741	HELENA	73.3	71.8	14.4	14.9	0.2	0.4	4.8	5.3	2.5	3.0	2.2	3.0	8.1	43.5	27.0	8.3	2.7	90.5	40.1	77.0	23.0
73742	HENNESSEY	85.3	83.7	2.2	2.2	0.1	0.2	12.3	14.0	6.9	6.9	7.6	6.7	6.7	24.6	25.2	13.5	2.0	74.4	38.8	48.8	51.2
73744	HITCHCOCK	93.0	93.0	0.8	0.8	0.0	0.0	1.2	1.2	6.2	6.2	6.6	7.4	6.2	22.7	26.0	16.5	2.1	76.5	41.8	49.6	50.4
73747	ISABELLA	95.5	95.1	0.3	0.3	0.0	0.0	5.1	5.2	5.8	6.3	8.1	6.6	5.8	21.9	25.1	19.0	1.4	75.5	42.0	52.5	47.6
73749	JET	94.4	93.5	0.2	0.2	0.2	0.5	2.6	3.1	5.4	5.6	5.4	5.8	4.7	21.3	28.6	19.7	3.6	79.9	46.3	49.2	50.8
73750	KINGFISHER	86.9	85.5	1.9	2.0	0.3	0.4	5.6	6.6	6.8	6.6	7.2	6.8	7.1	25.4	23.8	13.9	2.5	74.9	38.5	48.4	51.6
73753	KREMLIN	96.7	96.0	0.6	0.6	0.2	0.4	1.3	1.5	6.9	7.7	7.7	6.7	4.6	24.0	29.0	11.9	1.5	73.3	40.3	49.9	50.1
73754	LAHOMA	93.3	92.3	1.6	1.7	1.4	1.8	1.9	2.4	5.2	5.4	6.2	6.2	6.0	26.8	28.8	14.1	1.5	79.6	41.3	47.6	52.4
73755	LONGDALE	82.5	82.0	0.0	0.0	0.2	0.2	3.3	3.7	5.8	6.1	7.1	7.3	6.7	22.3	26.5	15.9	2.2	76.5	41.2	50.7	49.3
73756	LOYAL	91.9	91.6	1.5	1.5	0.0	0.0	2.9	3.1	4.6	6.1	6.1	6.1	6.1	24.4	30.5	14.5	1.5	78.6	43.0	50.4	49.6
73757	LUCIEN	95.4	94.4	0.0	0.0	0.9	0.9	0.0	0.9	5.6	5.6	6.5	4.7	5.6	26.2	29.0	15.0	1.9	79.4	42.2	51.4	48.6
73758	MANCHESTER	96.5	96.4	0.0	0.0	0.0	0.0	1.5	1.0	3.6	3.6	5.7	4.6	6.2	18.0	32.0	20.6	5.7	83.5	48.5	50.0	50.0
73759	MEDFORD	95.9	95.9	0.2	0.2	0.1	0.1	2.3	2.3	5.2	5.5	7.5	6.3	6.7	21.9	24.6	18.4	3.8	77.7	42.9	48.6	51.5
73760	MENO	87.8	88.1	0.2	0.2	0.2	0.2	12.7	13.1	6.2	6.8	8.2	5.7	5.1	23.4	26.1	16.0	2.5	75.1	41.7	49.9	50.1
73761	NASH	95.9	95.7	0.0	0.0	0.4	0.4	0.2	0.2	4.9	5.3	6.8	6.8	5.3	24.9	27.2	15.6	3.3	79.0	42.7	46.9	53.1
73762	OKARCHE	94.7	94.3	0.2	0.2	0.2	0.2	1.7	1.9	5.8	6.2	7.1	7.5	7.1	25.1	28.4	11.2	1.6	76.4	39.6	50.6	49.4
73763	OKEENE	97.6	97.5	0.4	0.3	0.1	0.1	3.2	3.5	6.6	7.0	7.3	6.2	5.1	22.3	24.2	17.5	3.9	75.4	42.1	49.4	50.6
73764	OMEGA	91.1	90.7	2.2	2.3	0.0	0.0	4.4	2.3	4.7	4.7	4.7	4.7	7.0	23.3	34.9	16.3	0.0	86.1	45.5	46.5	53.5
73766	POND CREEK	93.8	93.7	0.0	0.0	0.3	0.3	1.3	1.3	6.6	7.0	7.7	6.7	5.3	25.1	25.2	14.8	1.5	74.6	40.0	49.1	50.9
73768	RINGWOOD	90.3	90.3	0.3	0.3	0.2	0.2	9.7	9.8	6.1	6.5	7.3	6.0	5.6	23.6	27.2	15.4	2.3	76.4	41.8	49.7	50.4
73770	SOUTHARD	100.0	100.0	0.0	0.0	0.0	0.0	0.0	0.0	0.0	0.0	0.0	0.0	22.2	77.8	0.0	0.0	0.0	100.0	31.3	55.6	44.4
73771	WAKITA	96.7	96.6	0.2	0.2	0.2	0.2	1.1	1.3	3.1	3.6	6.0	4.7	6.1	19.5	29.2	22.2	5.6	83.8	48.9	48.4	51.6
73772	WATONGA	67.5	66.3	11.9	11.6	2.9	3.2	9.7	10.5	5.1	4.4	5.1	6.7	10.1	36.5	20.6	9.5	2.0	81.7	34.9	64.0	36.0
73773	WAUKOMIS	92.9	92.2	0.6	0.7	0.3	0.4	1.5	1.7	5.5	5.5	6.9	6.8	7.5	25.5	28.5	12.4	1.4	77.9	40.4	48.4	51.6
73801	WOODWARD	92.3	92.2	0.5	0.5	0.6	0.6	5.6	5.7	7.3	7.0	6.6	6.9	7.2	26.5	24.6	12.1	1.9	75.0	36.9	49.1	50.9
73832	ARNETT	97.1	97.0	0.2	0.2	0.0	0.0	1.8	1.8	5.1	5.9	6.5	4.9	4.7	22.3	28.9	18.6	3.1	79.5	45.5	51.2	48.8
73834	BUFFALO	94.9	94.8	0.1	0.1	0.1	0.1	7.5	7.6	4.3	4.8	5.9	6.1	5.6	22.5	28.6	19.5	2.9	81.0	45.5	49.2	50.8
73835	CAMARGO	95.8	94.9	0.0	0.0	0.0	0.0	1.4	2.2	4.4	4.4	5.8	7.3	6.5	21.7	31.2	15.9	2.9	80.4	45.0	50.0	50.0
73838	CHESTER	97.8	98.0	0.0	0.0	0.0	0.0	0.4	0.2	5.1	5.7	5.5	6.4	4.4	22.3	31.1	17.2	2.2	79.7	45.3	51.0	49.0
73840	FARGO	94.2	94.1	0.0	0.0	0.0	0.0	3.1	3.1	4.8	5.6	7.8	6.4	6.1	22.0	30.1	14.0	3.3	77.7	43.2	49.7	50.3
73841	FORT SUPPLY	81.6	81.3	11.5	11.8	0.2	0.2	2.6	2.6	3.8	3.8	4.4	8.5	11.6	33.9	24.4	8.9	0.8	85.5	36.8	66.8	33.2
73842	FREEDOM	96.0	95.3	0.0	0.0	0.6	0.6	4.2	4.9	3.2	3.6	7.0	7.2	6.8	21.8	28.8	18.6	3.0	81.4	45.3	47.5	52.5
73843	GAGE	97.8	97.7	0.0	0.0	0.6	0.6	1.5	1.5	4.3	5.3	6.0	4.9	4.7	19.6	33.6	18.3	3.2	81.5	48.1	49.6	50.4
73844	GATE	93.2	91.9	0.0	0.0	0.0	0.4	10.9	12.6	7.7	7.7	8.1	6.5	4.9	26.0	23.2	13.8	2.0	71.5	38.1	49.2	50.8
73847	KNOWLES	92.6	92.6	0.0	0.0	0.0	0.0	11.1	13.0	7.4	7.4	9.3	7.4	3.7	25.9	22.2	14.8	1.9	75.9	37.5	51.9	48.2
73848	LAVERNE	97.0	96.9	0.1	0.1	0.1	0.1	3.2	3.3	5.4	5.5	6.4	6.5	6.1	21.4	27.5	17.7	3.5	78.8	44.1	49.5	50.6
73851	MAY	95.8	95.7	0.0	0.0	0.0	0.0	5.6	5.7	4.3	4.3	7.1	5.7	5.7	21.4	32.9	15.7	2.9	84.3	45.7	52.9	47.1
73852	MOORELAND	95.8	95.8	0.1	0.1	0.1	0.1	2.9	3.0	6.0	6.6	7.8	7.4	5.6	23.6	25.4	13.7	3.9	74.2	40.5	48.0	52.0
73853	MUTUAL	94.4	94.4	0.0	0.0	0.4	0.4	3.9	3.9	6.1	6.5	6.9	4.8	5.2	23.4	30.7	14.7	1.7	77.5	43.2	48.5	51.5
73855	ROSSTON	96.4	96.8	0.0	0.0	0.0	0.0	5.9	5.1	4.2	5.1	7.4	5.1	5.6	19.0	33.8	17.1	2.8	80.1	47.0	54.6	45.4
73857	SHARON	96.2	96.2	0.1	0.1	0.2	0.2	2.4	2.3	5.7	6.1	6.6	6.2	5.5	23.9	31.2	13.4	1.6	77.6	42.6	49.0	51.0
73858	SHATTUCK	96.1	96.0	0.0	0.0	0.1	0.1	3.3	3.4	4.8	5.4	5.7	5.3	5.5	19.9	29.1	18.5	5.8	80.8	47.6	48.0	52.0
	OKLAHOMA	76.2	74.8	7.6	7.7	1.4	1.8	5.2	5.8	7.0	6.7	7.0	7.1	7.8	27.2	24.0	11.6	1.7	75.3	36.0	49.3	50.8
	UNITED STATES	75.1	73.6	12.3	12.5	3.8	4.2	12.5	14.1	6.9	6.7	7.2	7.0	7.3	28.6	23.8	10.8	1.7	75.1	36.0	49.1	50.9

ZIP CODE #	POST OFFICE NAME	2004 Per Capita Income	2004 HH Income Base	2004 Household Income Distribution (%) Less than $25,000	$25,000 to $49,999	$50,000 to $99,999	$100,000 to $149,999	$150,000 or More	Median Household Income 2004	2009	2004 National Centile	2004 State Centile	2004 Home Value Base	2004 Home Value Distribution (%) Less than $50,000	$50,000 to $89,999	$90,000 to $174,999	$175,000 to $399,999	$400,000 or More	2004 Median Home Value
73624	BURNS FLAT	17736	686	29.5	35.4	27.3	5.1	2.8	37522	44820	38	71	431	50.4	43.4	5.3	0.9	0.0	49789
73625	BUTLER	17887	452	31.6	37.2	24.3	4.2	2.7	35273	41671	29	58	370	45.7	23.2	16.0	13.5	1.6	56667
73626	CANUTE	21300	473	38.3	33.4	19.5	4.7	4.2	32397	37505	19	40	400	38.0	31.0	22.5	8.0	0.5	64545
73627	CARTER	18409	223	40.8	37.7	14.8	4.9	1.8	30681	35688	14	27	180	56.1	27.2	12.2	4.4	0.0	41538
73628	CHEYENNE	20617	613	38.0	29.4	24.6	5.9	2.1	33873	40968	24	50	452	41.8	28.3	22.4	6.0	1.6	64000
73632	CORDELL	18342	1659	38.5	34.4	19.6	4.9	2.7	32099	36990	18	38	1236	45.6	32.3	19.8	2.4	0.0	54508
73638	CRAWFORD	17644	54	37.0	31.5	24.1	3.7	3.7	33606	40000	23	48	43	41.9	25.6	27.9	4.7	0.0	66250
73639	CUSTER CITY	21463	280	32.1	28.6	29.6	7.9	1.8	40279	47551	47	79	225	41.8	24.9	25.8	6.7	0.9	59250
73641	DILL CITY	15345	337	41.8	33.8	19.9	4.2	0.3	29181	34206	11	19	255	66.3	22.0	9.8	2.0	0.0	33971
73642	DURHAM	25503	59	37.3	30.5	22.0	5.1	5.1	34293	41164	25	53	47	38.3	25.5	31.9	4.3	0.0	69000
73644	ELK CITY	18678	5045	38.3	30.1	22.9	5.8	2.9	33526	39083	22	47	3471	35.6	27.4	26.7	9.3	1.0	72691
73645	ERICK	17534	607	45.6	29.3	19.1	4.8	1.2	27675	32627	8	12	458	65.9	18.8	10.3	2.8	2.2	34200
73646	FAY	21445	52	36.5	30.8	23.1	7.7	1.9	33603	40000	23	48	43	44.2	23.3	27.9	4.7	0.0	58333
73647	FOSS	18876	161	32.9	31.1	27.3	6.2	2.5	34805	40755	27	56	137	48.9	17.5	27.0	6.6	0.0	51875
73650	HAMMON	19001	266	35.3	35.0	21.4	4.9	3.4	35463	40755	29	59	215	43.3	26.5	20.5	9.8	0.0	58056
73651	HOBART	16400	1768	42.3	29.8	21.7	5.2	1.1	31292	37296	16	33	1235	53.3	28.0	14.6	3.2	0.9	46860
73654	LEEDEY	18751	299	42.1	28.8	21.7	5.0	2.3	33132	38726	21	45	242	50.8	27.7	16.5	5.0	0.0	48750
73655	LONE WOLF	18030	491	41.6	30.8	20.6	5.7	1.4	31047	36739	15	30	397	51.6	27.7	17.1	2.5	1.0	47903
73658	OAKWOOD	22296	112	34.8	31.3	23.2	8.0	2.7	35000	40839	28	57	92	44.6	23.9	20.7	8.7	2.2	58333
73659	PUTNAM	24924	46	28.3	34.8	28.3	4.4	4.4	41115	49082	50	82	37	56.8	24.3	16.2	2.7	0.0	45000
73660	REYDON	22399	178	37.1	31.5	23.0	4.5	3.9	33710	39350	23	49	141	40.4	26.2	27.0	5.0	1.4	66071
73661	ROCKY	19963	108	34.3	35.2	24.1	5.6	0.9	35550	41304	30	60	86	53.5	27.9	15.1	3.5	0.0	45000
73662	SAYRE	16376	1613	44.7	32.1	19.4	2.6	1.2	28358	34207	9	15	1138	52.1	26.2	17.3	3.8	0.6	46962
73663	SEILING	17662	643	40.9	31.9	19.4	5.9	1.9	30308	36338	13	25	484	44.4	34.1	18.0	2.7	0.8	56000
73664	SENTINEL	17834	465	34.4	34.8	23.4	5.8	1.5	35823	40973	31	61	370	56.2	26.2	14.3	3.2	0.0	44524
73666	SWEETWATER	21105	130	38.5	34.6	19.2	4.6	3.1	33336	37827	22	46	105	44.8	26.7	18.1	7.6	2.9	55500
73667	TALOGA	22131	273	32.2	33.3	25.3	4.0	5.1	39611	45936	45	77	219	54.8	25.6	14.6	3.7	1.4	45435
73668	TEXOLA	13991	38	39.5	31.6	21.1	7.9	0.0	31496	40000	16	34	30	40.0	20.0	23.3	10.0	6.7	70000
73669	THOMAS	18461	646	37.3	28.6	27.2	4.5	2.3	36126	44008	32	62	482	48.3	33.0	14.9	2.5	1.2	51739
73673	WILLOW	24439	143	37.1	34.3	23.1	4.2	1.4	31543	36258	16	34	111	48.7	29.7	18.9	2.7	0.0	51875
73701	ENID	14863	8977	41.5	35.6	19.4	2.6	0.9	30237	35233	13	24	5734	58.6	28.2	10.7	2.1	0.4	44089
73703	ENID	25921	10967	24.8	32.1	30.5	8.3	4.3	43893	50984	58	87	7937	15.2	35.9	36.8	10.9	1.2	88791
73705	ENID	2419	0	0.0	0.0	0.0	0.0	0.0	0	0	0	0	0	0.0	0.0	0.0	0.0	0.0	0
73716	ALINE	20510	179	36.3	36.9	20.7	2.8	3.4	32700	36691	20	42	147	65.3	20.4	9.5	4.8	0.0	35278
73717	ALVA	21654	2621	38.5	28.3	24.4	5.2	3.6	34499	40636	26	54	1675	38.9	32.4	23.3	4.8	0.5	62964
73718	AMES	18176	208	35.6	28.4	31.3	3.9	1.0	35822	42096	31	61	172	48.8	31.4	15.1	4.7	0.0	51818
73719	AMORITA	26742	68	33.8	35.3	20.6	4.4	5.9	36496	41839	34	65	51	56.9	21.6	13.7	7.8	0.0	39375
73720	BISON	21778	83	26.5	34.9	32.5	4.8	1.2	41376	48379	51	82	68	26.5	29.4	36.8	5.9	1.5	82000
73722	BURLINGTON	21348	179	34.6	34.1	20.7	5.0	5.6	36251	41037	33	63	136	59.6	19.9	14.0	6.6	0.0	38333
73724	CANTON	17377	478	44.8	26.6	23.6	3.8	1.3	29217	34039	11	20	394	64.5	20.8	13.7	1.0	0.0	37879
73726	CARMEN	17605	215	36.7	37.7	20.5	2.3	2.8	32161	36449	18	39	176	66.5	19.9	9.1	4.6	0.0	34444
73727	CARRIER	20911	231	17.8	39.4	32.5	6.9	3.5	45582	52202	63	89	192	36.5	23.4	29.2	8.9	2.1	71667
73728	CHEROKEE	19527	851	35.7	33.8	22.7	5.5	2.2	34470	39791	26	54	646	57.4	28.3	12.5	1.7	0.0	42258
73729	CLEO SPRINGS	19931	222	32.9	33.8	23.9	5.4	4.1	37017	43740	35	68	184	31.5	26.6	36.4	5.4	0.0	75833
73730	COVINGTON	17583	355	32.7	33.8	29.6	3.1	0.9	36806	42340	35	67	288	55.6	23.3	18.1	3.1	0.0	44483
73731	DACOMA	26389	124	33.1	33.9	21.0	5.7	6.5	35884	40843	31	62	102	45.1	25.5	19.6	7.8	2.0	62222
73733	DOUGLAS	19480	89	31.5	34.8	31.5	2.3	0.0	37318	41929	37	70	72	52.8	23.6	19.4	4.2	0.0	45000
73734	DOVER	24595	220	17.3	39.6	29.6	9.1	4.6	44748	51766	61	88	182	36.3	19.8	26.4	16.5	1.1	77273
73735	DRUMMOND	18307	285	28.1	28.4	37.9	4.9	0.7	42201	48214	54	84	224	30.4	27.7	39.7	2.2	0.0	71538
73736	FAIRMONT	19175	242	23.6	36.8	32.2	7.0	0.4	41856	48456	52	83	205	26.3	28.8	33.7	9.8	1.5	80455
73737	FAIRVIEW	21910	1555	34.9	30.0	28.0	5.0	2.1	35073	41700	28	58	1178	38.5	30.5	25.5	4.6	1.0	62456
73738	GARBER	15583	464	41.6	36.4	19.2	2.4	0.4	29713	34739	12	22	352	64.8	24.4	9.4	1.1	0.3	35357
73739	GOLTRY	19017	165	36.4	37.6	20.6	1.8	3.6	32571	36340	20	41	135	67.4	19.3	8.9	4.4	0.0	34643
73741	HELENA	14275	283	29.7	41.3	25.1	2.1	1.8	36402	40420	33	65	229	64.2	22.3	12.2	1.3	0.0	38971
73742	HENNESSEY	18737	1547	31.7	33.2	24.1	7.5	3.5	37019	43865	36	68	1236	43.8	23.0	24.3	8.8	0.2	61798
73744	HITCHCOCK	18016	91	36.3	28.6	24.2	7.7	3.3	37375	45373	37	71	75	37.3	24.0	26.7	12.0	0.0	65000
73747	ISABELLA	18838	135	24.4	43.7	19.3	12.6	0.0	35974	43652	31	62	110	33.6	48.2	10.9	5.5	1.8	59000
73749	JET	17521	220	45.0	35.5	15.5	3.2	0.9	28041	31970	9	13	173	72.8	16.2	7.5	3.5	0.0	31912
73750	KINGFISHER	22473	2572	26.4	30.4	30.3	9.3	3.7	44307	51805	59	87	1999	28.2	27.6	33.9	10.1	0.3	80127
73753	KREMLIN	22004	187	19.3	40.6	31.0	6.4	2.7	43937	50183	58	87	155	38.7	23.2	27.7	8.4	1.9	68125
73754	LAHOMA	20178	494	22.9	37.7	33.8	4.1	1.6	41883	47534	53	83	397	22.7	33.3	35.5	7.6	1.0	84125
73755	LONGDALE	18960	283	45.9	26.5	22.3	3.2	2.1	27836	32522	8	12	234	70.9	17.1	9.8	2.1	0.0	34118
73756	LOYAL	21903	54	25.9	33.3	29.6	9.3	1.9	40000	51399	46	78	42	42.9	21.4	26.2	7.1	2.4	60000
73757	LUCIEN	24019	48	27.1	27.1	37.5	8.3	0.0	45000	54564	61	89	40	30.0	22.5	40.0	7.5	0.0	85000
73758	MANCHESTER	18659	82	37.8	35.4	20.7	3.7	2.4	32657	37745	20	42	66	84.9	10.6	4.6	0.0	0.0	26667
73759	MEDFORD	19318	742	36.4	31.9	25.6	4.2	1.9	33931	40590	24	50	555	40.4	30.8	23.4	5.1	0.4	63163
73760	MENO	18819	202	29.7	34.7	29.2	4.5	2.0	37921	44250	39	73	169	36.1	30.2	29.6	3.6	0.6	68750
73761	NASH	16849	210	39.5	31.0	23.3	5.2	1.0	31037	36198	15	30	165	36.4	35.8	21.8	4.9	1.2	65938
73762	OKARCHE	22242	867	23.3	33.1	32.9	7.6	3.1	43585	50388	58	86	717	17.6	26.1	44.4	11.6	0.4	97845
73763	OKEENE	21675	667	31.3	38.2	22.9	4.4	3.2	36268	42585	33	63	518	50.0	32.4	15.6	1.9	0.0	50000
73764	OMEGA	19065	16	25.0	31.3	37.5	6.3	0.0	42500	45000	55	85	13	53.9	15.4	30.8	0.0	0.0	47500
73766	POND CREEK	20712	422	33.2	31.8	24.6	5.5	5.0	36523	43052	34	65	338	52.4	20.4	23.1	3.3	0.9	48667
73768	RINGWOOD	18636	505	30.7	34.5	27.7	4.6	2.6	37406	43926	37	71	421	34.2	29.2	31.4	4.5	0.7	71364
73770	SOUTHARD	0	0	0.0	0.0	0.0	0.0	0.0	0	0	0	0	0	0.0	0.0	0.0	0.0	0.0	0
73771	WAKITA	18086	228	39.9	35.1	20.2	2.6	2.2	32031	37172	18	37	184	85.3	10.3	3.8	0.5	0.0	25556
73772	WATONGA	14741	1898	38.4	32.1	23.6	4.9	1.1	31999	37170	18	37	1368	44.0	31.7	19.9	4.4	0.0	56613
73773	WAUKOMIS	18596	629	30.7	34.7	30.7	3.2	0.8	39196	45715	43	77	478	36.2	40.6	19.0	2.9	1.3	58571
73801	WOODWARD	19984	5549	33.8	31.8	26.2	6.3	2.0	37306	43141	37	70	3929	31.7	35.0	27.7	5.1	0.4	72692
73832	ARNETT	18313	524	35.5	39.3	19.5	3.4	2.3	31424	35880	16	33	422	57.6	22.3	14.0	4.7	1.4	42195
73834	BUFFALO	20223	713	29.0	36.0	26.0	7.9	1.1	37513	42683	37	71	565	53.3	26.6	15.9	3.5	0.7	46917
73835	CAMARGO	17299	67	46.3	26.9	23.9	3.0	0.0	27946	33196	9	13	54	42.6	27.8	24.1	5.6	0.0	64000
73838	CHESTER	17383	197	41.6	28.9	23.9	5.1	0.5	30931	36618	15	29	163	38.0	23.9	26.4	6.1	5.5	65417
73840	FARGO	19262	262	36.3	31.3	25.2	5.3	1.9	32623	37813	20	41	206	47.1	35.0	13.6	3.4	1.0	55455
73841	FORT SUPPLY	15261	254	26.4	31.5	32.3	7.9	2.0	43063	49578	56	86	204	37.3	26.5	31.9	3.4	1.0	64545
73842	FREEDOM	22133	203	30.5	38.4	23.2	5.9	2.0	37608	43954	38	72	162	46.9	30.3	13.6	7.4	1.9	53846
73843	GAGE	19218	241	41.1	32.4	20.3	4.6	1.7	30988	35478	15	30	191	53.9	27.8	16.2	1.1	1.1	45588
73844	GATE	21318	106	33.0	34.9	20.8	7.6	3.8	36710	43640	34	67	86	53.5	22.1	18.6	1.2	4.7	45714
73847	KNOWLES	17244	19	36.8	26.3	26.3	10.5	0.0	37351	51328	37	70	15	53.3	26.7	20.0	0.0	0.0	45000
73848	LAVERNE	21225	819	32.5	34.4	23.9	6.7	2.4	38297	44460	40	74	625	48.3	27.4	18.4	5.4	0.5	52188
73851	MAY	22065	32	25.0	31.3	37.5	6.3	0.0	45000	43633	61	89	25	36.0	32.0	20.0	8.0	4.0	62500
73852	MOORELAND	20153	835	28.0	41.1	24.0	4.8	2.2	37629	44518	38	72	652	34.7	36.7	23.6	4.0	1.1	64390
73853	MUTUAL	26347	102	20.6	37.3	33.3	5.9	2.9	39424	46395	44	77	82	30.5	32.9	23.2	13.4	0.0	77000
73855	ROSSTON	20111	89	28.1	31.5	32.6	6.7	1.1	42763	47349	55	85	70	32.9	27.1	25.7	10.0	4.3	72500
73857	SHARON	20812	480	23.3	34.0	35.2	5.8	1.7	42670	49004	55	85	412	32.3	30.6	26.9	9.5	0.7	72813
73858	SHATTUCK	20168	732	39.3	30.1	23.6	4.6	2.3	31471	36977	16	34	562	54.6	27.6	15.1	2.1	0.5	45357
	OKLAHOMA	21077		31.9	30.4	27.2	7.1	3.4	38589	46268				26.7	29.5	32.0	10.2	1.6	81000
	UNITED STATES	25866		24.7	27.1	30.8	10.9	6.5	48124	56710				10.9	15.0	33.7	30.1	10.4	145905

ZIP CODE		FINANCIAL SERVICES				THE HOME						ENTERTAINMENT						PERSONAL			
						Home Improvements		Furnishings													
#	POST OFFICE NAME	Auto Loan	Home Loan	Invest-ments	Retire-ment Plans	Home Repair	Lawn & Garden	Comput-ers & Hard-ware	Major Appli-ances	TV, Radio, Sound Equip-ment	Furni-ture	Dine out/ Carry out	Sports Equip-ment	Fees & Tickets	Toys & Games	Travel	Cable TV	Apparel & Services	Auto Repairs	Health Insur-ance	Pets & Supplies
73624	BURNS FLAT	79	67	52	66	70	79	69	73	73	67	88	84	65	87	68	74	83	72	80	87
73625	BUTLER	81	56	29	53	66	74	56	69	64	55	75	83	48	74	58	67	69	68	82	96
73626	CANUTE	95	67	35	63	78	87	66	81	76	65	89	98	56	87	68	80	81	80	97	113
73627	CARTER	79	55	29	52	65	72	55	68	63	54	74	82	47	73	57	66	68	67	81	94
73628	CHEYENNE	77	57	36	54	63	74	62	69	69	59	82	79	54	77	61	73	74	69	83	86
73632	CORDELL	75	55	33	52	62	71	58	67	65	56	77	77	50	74	58	69	70	66	80	86
73638	CRAWFORD	82	57	30	54	67	75	57	70	65	56	77	84	48	75	59	69	70	69	83	98
73639	CUSTER CITY	90	63	33	59	73	82	62	77	71	61	84	92	53	82	64	75	76	75	91	107
73641	DILL CITY	63	46	29	44	52	61	50	57	56	48	66	64	44	63	50	60	61	56	68	71
73642	DURHAM	93	65	34	61	76	85	64	79	74	63	87	96	55	85	67	78	79	78	95	111
73644	ELK CITY	73	61	48	59	64	72	63	68	68	62	82	80	59	80	63	70	77	69	76	83
73645	ERICK	66	50	33	48	54	65	55	61	62	52	73	68	49	69	55	65	66	61	73	73
73646	FAY	81	57	30	54	66	74	56	69	65	55	76	84	48	74	58	68	69	68	83	97
73647	FOSS	85	59	31	56	69	77	58	72	67	58	79	87	50	77	61	71	72	71	86	101
73650	HAMMON	88	61	32	58	71	80	60	75	70	60	82	90	52	80	63	73	74	74	89	104
73651	HOBART	64	48	32	46	53	63	53	59	60	51	70	66	47	66	53	63	64	59	70	71
73654	LEEDEY	74	55	35	53	61	72	60	67	67	57	79	76	53	75	60	71	72	67	80	83
73655	LONE WOLF	65	49	32	47	53	64	54	59	60	51	71	66	48	67	53	64	65	59	71	72
73658	OAKWOOD	93	65	34	62	76	85	64	80	74	64	87	96	55	85	67	78	79	78	95	111
73659	PUTNAM	99	69	36	65	81	90	68	84	79	67	92	102	58	90	71	83	84	83	101	118
73660	REYDON	92	64	34	61	75	84	64	79	74	63	87	94	55	85	66	78	79	78	94	108
73661	ROCKY	82	57	30	54	66	74	56	70	65	56	76	84	48	75	58	68	69	69	83	97
73662	SAYRE	47	35	23	34	38	46	39	43	43	37	51	48	35	48	38	46	47	43	51	51
73663	SEILING	73	53	32	51	59	69	56	65	64	54	75	74	50	72	57	67	68	64	77	82
73664	SENTINEL	81	57	30	54	66	74	56	69	65	55	76	84	48	74	58	68	69	68	83	97
73666	SWEETWATER	80	60	39	57	66	79	66	73	74	63	87	82	59	82	66	78	80	73	87	88
73667	TALOGA	93	66	36	63	76	86	67	81	76	65	90	96	58	87	69	80	82	80	96	109
73668	TEXOLA	65	49	32	47	53	64	54	59	60	51	71	66	48	67	53	64	65	59	71	72
73669	THOMAS	79	58	36	55	64	76	62	71	70	60	83	81	55	79	62	74	75	70	84	89
73673	WILLOW	16	12	8	11	13	15	13	14	15	12	17	16	12	16	13	15	16	14	17	17
73701	ENID	53	47	44	46	48	54	51	51	54	49	66	59	49	65	50	54	62	52	55	59
73703	ENID	91	83	76	83	86	96	86	89	89	84	108	103	82	107	85	90	103	89	95	104
73705	ENID	0	0	0	0	0	0	0	0	0	0	0	0	0	0	0	0	0	0	0	0
73716	ALINE	73	54	35	52	60	71	59	66	66	56	78	75	52	74	59	70	71	66	79	81
73717	ALVA	81	61	46	60	67	78	68	74	75	65	90	86	61	86	67	78	83	75	85	91
73718	AMES	77	54	28	51	63	70	53	66	61	52	72	79	45	70	55	64	65	65	78	91
73719	AMORITA	102	71	37	67	83	93	70	87	81	69	95	105	60	93	73	85	86	86	103	121
73720	BISON	89	62	32	59	72	81	61	76	71	60	83	91	52	81	63	74	75	75	90	105
73722	BURLINGTON	95	67	36	63	77	87	67	82	77	66	90	97	58	88	69	81	82	81	97	112
73724	CANTON	72	52	30	48	57	68	55	63	63	53	74	72	48	70	55	67	67	63	76	80
73726	CARMEN	70	52	34	50	57	68	58	64	65	55	76	71	51	72	57	68	69	64	76	77
73727	CARRIER	97	79	56	77	88	95	76	88	82	75	98	106	70	99	78	85	92	87	98	116
73728	CHEROKEE	72	54	36	52	60	71	60	66	67	57	79	74	53	75	59	71	72	66	79	80
73729	CLEO SPRINGS	87	61	32	57	71	79	60	74	69	59	81	89	51	80	62	73	74	73	88	103
73730	COVINGTON	79	55	29	52	65	72	55	68	63	54	74	82	47	73	57	66	67	67	81	94
73731	DACOMA	109	76	40	72	89	100	76	93	87	75	102	112	65	100	78	91	93	92	111	129
73733	DOUGLAS	80	56	29	53	65	73	55	68	63	54	74	82	47	73	57	66	68	67	81	95
73734	DOVER	120	83	44	79	97	109	82	102	95	81	111	123	70	109	86	100	102	100	121	142
73735	DRUMMOND	88	62	32	58	72	80	61	75	70	60	82	91	52	81	63	74	75	74	90	105
73736	FAIRMONT	88	61	32	58	72	80	61	75	70	60	82	90	52	80	63	73	75	74	89	104
73737	FAIRVIEW	81	69	55	66	74	84	70	77	76	69	91	88	66	90	71	79	85	76	87	93
73738	GARBER	61	45	28	43	50	59	49	55	55	47	65	63	43	61	49	58	59	55	66	69
73739	GOLTRY	68	51	34	49	56	67	57	62	64	54	75	70	51	71	56	67	68	62	75	75
73741	HELENA	20	15	10	14	16	19	16	18	18	15	21	20	14	20	16	19	20	18	21	22
73742	HENNESSEY	87	63	40	60	71	80	64	76	73	63	86	91	56	84	66	76	80	75	88	102
73744	HITCHCOCK	87	61	32	57	71	79	60	74	69	59	81	89	51	79	62	72	74	73	88	103
73747	ISABELLA	88	61	32	58	71	80	60	75	70	60	82	90	52	80	63	73	74	74	89	104
73749	JET	57	43	28	41	47	56	48	52	53	45	63	59	42	59	47	56	57	52	63	63
73750	KINGFISHER	87	81	70	78	84	92	79	84	82	78	100	97	77	100	80	84	96	83	90	101
73753	KREMLIN	96	75	50	72	84	92	73	86	80	72	95	103	66	95	75	82	88	84	97	114
73754	LAHOMA	80	66	50	66	70	79	68	74	73	67	88	85	64	87	68	74	82	73	81	89
73755	LONGDALE	83	57	27	49	64	74	55	68	66	56	78	81	47	74	56	71	71	68	84	95
73756	LOYAL	96	67	35	63	78	88	66	82	76	65	90	99	57	88	69	80	82	81	98	114
73757	LUCIEN	72	75	87	79	76	80	77	76	74	76	93	90	77	91	77	72	90	77	73	84
73758	MANCHESTER	69	52	34	50	57	68	57	63	64	54	75	71	51	71	57	68	69	63	75	76
73759	MEDFORD	78	57	35	55	64	75	61	70	69	59	82	80	54	78	62	73	74	70	84	88
73760	MENO	87	60	32	57	70	79	60	74	69	59	81	89	51	79	62	72	73	73	88	103
73761	NASH	75	52	27	49	61	68	51	64	59	51	70	77	44	68	53	62	63	63	76	89
73762	OKARCHE	100	73	42	69	84	93	71	86	81	71	96	104	63	95	74	85	88	85	101	119
73763	OKEENE	90	65	38	62	73	85	67	79	76	65	90	92	59	87	68	81	82	78	94	104
73764	OMEGA	93	65	34	61	75	84	64	79	74	63	86	95	55	85	66	77	79	78	94	110
73766	POND CREEK	93	65	34	61	76	85	64	79	74	63	87	95	55	85	66	77	79	78	94	110
73768	RINGWOOD	87	61	32	57	71	79	60	74	69	59	81	89	51	79	62	73	74	73	88	103
73770	SOUTHARD	0	0	0	0	0	0	0	0	0	0	0	0	0	0	0	0	0	0	0	0
73771	WAKITA	68	51	34	49	56	67	57	63	64	54	75	70	51	71	56	67	68	63	75	76
73772	WATONGA	67	51	36	49	56	64	55	61	61	53	73	71	49	70	55	64	67	61	71	76
73773	WAUKOMIS	74	59	42	58	64	72	60	67	66	59	79	78	56	78	61	67	73	66	76	84
73801	WOODWARD	74	65	56	63	68	74	67	71	70	65	85	83	63	84	66	70	81	71	75	85
73832	ARNETT	71	52	30	49	58	67	54	63	61	52	72	73	47	69	55	64	65	62	75	82
73834	BUFFALO	80	59	36	56	66	77	63	72	71	60	83	82	55	80	63	75	76	71	86	91
73835	CAMARGO	64	45	24	42	52	58	44	55	51	44	60	66	38	59	46	54	55	54	65	76
73838	CHESTER	72	50	26	48	59	66	50	62	57	49	67	74	43	66	52	60	61	61	73	86
73840	FARGO	85	59	32	56	69	78	59	73	68	58	80	87	51	78	61	72	73	72	86	100
73841	FORT SUPPLY	93	65	34	61	75	85	64	79	74	63	86	95	55	85	66	77	79	78	94	110
73842	FREEDOM	93	65	34	61	76	85	64	79	74	63	87	96	55	85	67	78	79	78	95	111
73843	GAGE	69	51	34	49	56	67	57	63	63	54	75	70	50	71	56	67	68	62	75	76
73844	GATE	90	62	33	59	73	82	62	76	71	61	83	92	53	82	64	75	76	75	91	106
73847	KNOWLES	89	62	32	58	72	81	61	76	70	60	83	91	52	81	63	74	75	75	90	105
73848	LAVERNE	82	60	37	58	67	79	65	73	73	62	86	84	57	82	65	77	78	73	88	93
73851	MAY	87	61	32	58	71	80	60	74	69	60	81	90	51	80	62	73	74	73	89	104
73852	MOORELAND	90	64	36	61	73	84	66	78	75	64	88	92	57	85	67	79	80	77	93	104
73853	MUTUAL	108	75	39	71	88	98	74	92	86	74	101	111	64	99	77	90	92	91	110	128
73855	ROSSTON	88	62	32	58	72	80	61	75	70	60	82	91	52	81	63	74	75	74	90	105
73857	SHARON	98	68	36	64	80	89	67	83	78	67	91	100	58	89	70	82	83	82	99	116
73858	SHATTUCK	71	53	35	51	59	70	59	65	66	56	77	73	52	73	58	69	71	65	78	79
	OKLAHOMA	79	71	65	70	73	80	73	76	76	72	93	88	70	91	72	76	88	76	79	89
	UNITED STATES	100	100	100	100	100	100	100	100	100	100	100	100	100	100	100	100	100	100	100	100

# POST OFFICE NAME	COUNTY FIPS CODE	POPULATION 2000	2004	2009	2000-2004 ANNUAL RATE % Rate	State Centile	HOUSEHOLDS 2000	2004	2009	% Annual Rate 2000-2004	2004 Average HH Size	FAMILIES 2000	2004	% Annual Rate 2000-2004
73859 VICI	043	1210	1187	1164	-0.5	19	501	497	492	-0.2	2.28	318	315	-0.2
73860 WAYNOKA	151	1479	1417	1362	-1.0	4	667	642	620	-0.9	2.12	408	390	-1.1
73931 BALKO	007	657	634	613	-0.8	7	271	263	255	-0.7	2.41	212	205	-0.8
73932 BEAVER	007	2031	1972	1915	-0.7	12	795	772	749	-0.7	2.43	583	564	-0.8
73933 BOISE CITY	025	1962	1921	1898	-0.5	16	794	781	775	-0.4	2.41	534	523	-0.5
73937 FELT	025	219	215	213	-0.4	21	82	81	81	-0.3	2.65	61	60	-0.4
73938 FORGAN	007	749	743	728	-0.2	31	275	274	269	-0.1	2.71	207	206	-0.1
73939 GOODWELL	139	2020	2110	2257	1.0	80	687	719	769	1.1	2.59	451	470	1.0
73942 GUYMON	139	12429	13576	14994	2.1	94	4338	4672	5089	1.8	2.87	3190	3427	1.7
73944 HARDESTY	139	511	545	594	1.5	90	195	207	223	1.4	2.63	153	163	1.5
73945 HOOKER	139	2751	2815	2995	0.5	62	1054	1071	1127	0.4	2.62	791	801	0.3
73946 KENTON	025	129	127	125	-0.4	23	55	54	54	-0.4	2.35	41	40	-0.6
73947 KEYES	025	716	703	695	-0.4	21	278	274	272	-0.3	2.57	198	195	-0.4
73949 TEXHOMA	025	1616	1649	1724	0.5	60	607	615	636	0.3	2.68	460	465	0.3
73950 TURPIN	007	1725	1706	1667	-0.3	27	623	616	602	-0.3	2.77	482	475	-0.3
73951 TYRONE	139	1273	1298	1378	0.5	59	458	465	488	0.4	2.79	351	356	0.3
74002 BARNSDALL	113	3152	3170	3205	0.1	46	1186	1197	1217	0.2	2.62	873	877	0.1
74003 BARTLESVILLE	113	14936	14908	15017	0.0	37	6188	6193	6264	0.0	2.39	4029	4021	-0.1
74006 BARTLESVILLE	147	23995	24716	25305	0.7	69	10053	10460	10795	0.9	2.32	7118	7371	0.8
74008 BIXBY	143	16253	18276	19804	2.8	96	5913	6688	7269	2.9	2.72	4687	5290	2.9
74010 BRISTOW	037	8021	8257	8630	0.7	68	3185	3296	3464	0.8	2.48	2236	2302	0.7
74011 BROKEN ARROW	143	23000	24439	25819	1.4	88	8051	8627	9156	1.6	2.82	6659	7099	1.5
74012 BROKEN ARROW	143	47179	50930	54121	1.8	92	16554	17933	19096	1.9	2.81	13167	14243	1.9
74014 BROKEN ARROW	145	22967	26806	31606	3.7	99	8005	9447	11244	4.0	2.84	6812	8013	3.9
74015 CATOOSA	131	7798	8951	10393	3.3	98	2852	3297	3854	3.5	2.68	2211	2540	3.3
74016 CHELSEA	131	4549	4896	5469	1.7	91	1742	1880	2108	1.8	2.58	1261	1350	1.6
74017 CLAREMORE	131	25817	28647	32708	2.5	95	9823	10959	12590	2.6	2.57	7098	7902	2.6
74019 CLAREMORE	131	12591	14339	16575	3.1	97	4441	5103	5940	3.3	2.79	3721	4262	3.3
74020 CLEVELAND	117	9501	9915	10476	1.0	79	3679	3843	4066	1.0	2.56	2779	2896	1.0
74021 COLLINSVILLE	143	12517	13014	13622	0.9	76	4600	4817	5063	1.1	2.68	3594	3750	1.0
74022 COPAN	147	1611	1638	1654	0.4	56	670	690	703	0.7	2.37	486	499	0.6
74023 CUSHING	119	11116	11459	12017	0.7	70	4119	4266	4511	0.8	2.44	2837	2925	0.7
74026 DAVENPORT	081	986	969	985	-0.4	21	391	388	398	-0.2	2.50	300	297	-0.2
74027 DELAWARE	105	1226	1280	1352	1.0	79	478	499	525	1.0	2.57	368	383	0.9
74028 DEPEW	037	2266	2300	2383	0.4	54	842	863	900	0.6	2.67	634	647	0.5
74029 DEWEY	147	5212	5137	5144	-0.3	25	2104	2090	2107	-0.2	2.41	1502	1487	-0.2
74030 DRUMRIGHT	037	8093	8261	8609	0.5	60	3183	3264	3418	0.6	2.51	2294	2344	0.5
74032 GLENCOE	119	1173	1214	1270	0.8	74	459	477	502	0.9	2.55	347	359	0.8
74033 GLENPOOL	143	9455	9708	10025	0.6	65	3219	3333	3458	0.8	2.88	2628	2709	0.7
74035 HOMINY	113	3516	3414	3417	-0.7	12	1371	1339	1350	-0.6	2.30	919	891	-0.7
74036 INOLA	131	5566	6024	6763	1.9	92	1982	2159	2438	2.0	2.76	1588	1720	1.9
74037 JENKS	143	9555	10883	11806	3.1	97	3475	3979	4332	3.2	2.71	2758	3157	3.2
74038 JENNINGS	117	837	883	939	1.3	85	313	331	352	1.3	2.67	241	254	1.2
74039 KELLYVILLE	037	3154	3170	3303	0.1	45	1123	1136	1190	0.3	2.79	883	889	0.2
74042 LENAPAH	105	832	862	908	0.8	75	296	305	320	0.7	2.83	241	248	0.7
74044 MANNFORD	037	6676	6971	7329	1.0	79	2475	2608	2763	1.2	2.64	1915	2009	1.1
74045 MARAMEC	117	304	318	336	1.1	81	121	127	134	1.2	2.50	91	95	1.0
74047 MOUNDS	111	5081	5350	5638	1.2	84	1793	1895	2001	1.3	2.82	1422	1497	1.2
74048 NOWATA	105	6027	6340	6728	1.2	84	2421	2542	2694	1.2	2.41	1655	1731	1.1
74051 OCHELATA	147	1610	1673	1710	0.9	76	564	589	606	1.0	2.84	443	462	1.0
74053 OOLOGAH	131	3936	4175	4644	1.4	87	1423	1521	1701	1.6	2.74	1147	1220	1.5
74054 OSAGE	113	532	533	536	0.0	42	223	226	229	0.3	2.36	156	157	0.2
74055 OWASSO	131	27166	30838	34149	3.0	97	9531	10844	12033	3.1	2.82	7718	8754	3.0
74056 PAWHUSKA	113	5765	5658	5672	-0.4	20	2298	2263	2277	-0.4	2.43	1551	1518	-0.5
74058 PAWNEE	117	4341	4551	4825	1.1	82	1674	1759	1868	1.2	2.54	1169	1223	1.1
74059 PERKINS	119	3921	4126	4358	1.2	84	1546	1643	1748	1.4	2.50	1109	1173	1.3
74060 PRUE	113	2147	2297	2393	1.6	90	742	796	831	1.7	2.89	577	616	1.6
74061 RAMONA	147	1484	1519	1540	0.6	63	601	619	631	0.7	2.45	453	465	0.6
74062 RIPLEY	119	948	974	1016	0.6	67	342	351	367	0.6	2.77	266	272	0.5
74063 SAND SPRINGS	143	28710	29019	29616	0.3	51	10753	10962	11242	0.5	2.60	8204	8313	0.3
74066 SAPULPA	037	29684	31509	33499	1.4	87	11119	11858	12672	1.5	2.62	8404	8945	1.5
74070 SKIATOOK	113	10583	11320	11832	1.6	90	3797	4094	4303	1.8	2.76	3009	3233	1.7
74072 S COFFEYVILLE	105	1500	1530	1597	0.5	59	581	592	616	0.4	2.58	428	435	0.4
74073 SPERRY	143	3701	3825	3948	0.8	73	1326	1373	1421	0.8	2.76	1038	1069	0.7
74074 STILLWATER	119	26331	27430	29014	1.0	78	10667	11217	11992	1.2	2.26	5870	6159	1.1
74075 STILLWATER	119	18493	19442	20571	1.2	84	8499	9011	9605	1.4	2.12	4202	4442	1.3
74077 STILLWATER	119	142	142	143	0.0	40	0	0	0	0.0	0.00	0	0	0.0
74078 STILLWATER	119	4206	4354	4477	0.8	75	290	333	371	3.3	3.06	154	176	3.2
74079 STROUD	081	5048	5094	5203	0.2	49	1972	1999	2056	0.3	2.51	1391	1406	0.3
74080 TALALA	131	1541	1832	2143	4.2	99	557	664	779	4.2	2.76	442	525	4.1
74081 TERLTON	117	1065	1123	1192	1.3	85	369	391	417	1.4	2.87	301	318	1.3
74083 WANN	105	901	928	967	0.7	69	347	358	373	0.7	2.59	278	286	0.7
74084 WYNONA	113	2132	2117	2122	-0.2	32	386	385	389	-0.1	3.13	277	274	-0.3
74085 YALE	119	2390	2403	2484	0.1	46	951	963	1003	0.3	2.46	676	682	0.2
74103 TULSA	143	2173	2125	2124	-0.5	15	60	54	54	-2.5	2.56	15	13	-3.3
74104 TULSA	143	14078	13903	14170	-0.3	26	5959	5882	6015	-0.3	2.11	2742	2664	-0.7
74105 TULSA	143	29135	28890	29604	-0.2	30	14364	14299	14683	-0.1	2.01	7369	7278	-0.3
74106 TULSA	143	17929	17761	18066	-0.2	30	7035	6988	7123	-0.2	2.49	4501	4427	-0.4
74107 TULSA	143	20023	20005	20466	0.0	38	8155	8192	8403	0.1	2.43	5373	5365	0.0
74108 TULSA	143	7626	7594	7850	-0.1	35	2780	2793	2900	0.1	2.72	2110	2108	0.0
74110 TULSA	143	15663	15594	15847	-0.1	35	5759	5710	5795	-0.2	2.67	3748	3682	-0.4
74112 TULSA	143	22744	22396	22822	-0.4	24	10323	10194	10407	-0.3	2.20	5849	5718	-0.5
74114 TULSA	143	17131	16754	17048	-0.5	15	7769	7661	7828	-0.3	2.16	4668	4536	-0.7
74115 TULSA	143	23633	23458	23905	-0.2	32	9092	9045	9228	-0.1	2.59	6139	6057	-0.3
74116 TULSA	143	3667	3872	4113	1.3	86	1469	1564	1667	1.5	2.48	967	1016	1.2
74117 TULSA	143	108	113	117	1.1	81	40	42	43	1.2	2.64	30	32	1.5
74119 TULSA	143	3772	3671	3742	-0.6	13	2577	2506	2563	-0.7	1.36	634	610	-0.9
74120 TULSA	143	5801	5782	5885	-0.1	36	2872	2870	2933	0.0	1.90	1065	1050	-0.3
74126 TULSA	143	12267	12152	12440	-0.2	30	4133	4128	4240	0.0	2.94	3096	3071	-0.2
74127 TULSA	113	17989	17938	18340	-0.1	36	7108	7129	7322	0.1	2.47	4614	4580	-0.2
74128 TULSA	143	11637	11388	11562	-0.5	16	4689	4615	4700	-0.4	2.43	3190	3106	-0.6
74129 TULSA	143	17681	17875	18437	0.3	51	7252	7388	7652	0.4	2.38	4678	4716	0.2
74130 TULSA	143	2369	2378	2419	0.1	43	876	886	905	0.3	2.68	608	611	0.1
74131 TULSA	037	3297	3482	3686	1.3	86	1217	1293	1375	1.4	2.69	957	1015	1.4
74132 TULSA	143	6991	7347	7724	1.2	84	2511	2659	2810	1.4	2.76	1986	2094	1.3
OKLAHOMA					0.8					1.0	2.48			0.9
UNITED STATES					1.2					1.3	2.58			1.1

ZIP CODE #	POST OFFICE NAME	RACE (%) White 2000	White 2004	Black 2000	Black 2004	Asian/Pacific 2000	Asian/Pacific 2004	% Hispanic Origin 2000	% Hispanic Origin 2004	2004 AGE DISTRIBUTION (%) 0-4	5-9	10-14	15-19	20-24	25-44	45-64	65-84	85+	18+	MEDIAN AGE 2004	% 2004 Males	% 2004 Females
73859	VICI	96.1	95.6	0.0	0.0	0.2	0.3	3.1	3.5	5.3	4.9	5.3	6.6	7.3	20.8	26.9	16.9	6.2	80.9	44.9	48.0	52.0
73860	WAYNOKA	93.7	93.1	1.6	1.6	0.1	0.1	4.3	4.9	4.7	4.7	7.2	6.2	6.1	20.7	25.8	19.8	4.8	79.7	45.3	47.5	52.5
73931	BALKO	96.2	95.9	0.3	0.3	0.0	0.0	2.3	2.2	4.1	4.6	6.5	5.5	5.1	19.6	33.8	18.3	2.7	81.6	47.3	51.0	49.1
73932	BEAVER	93.4	92.8	0.5	0.5	0.2	0.2	7.9	9.0	5.9	6.0	7.1	5.9	5.7	24.5	24.0	16.8	4.1	77.2	41.8	50.1	50.0
73933	BOISE CITY	82.9	82.5	0.6	0.6	0.3	0.3	19.0	19.4	6.7	6.7	6.9	6.9	5.8	21.5	26.2	16.0	3.4	75.4	41.5	49.3	50.7
73937	FELT	84.5	84.7	1.8	1.9	0.0	0.0	14.2	14.4	4.7	5.6	8.4	7.4	5.1	22.8	29.3	14.4	2.3	75.8	42.3	53.0	47.0
73938	FORGAN	93.1	92.2	0.0	0.0	0.1	0.3	11.2	12.7	7.7	7.7	8.8	6.3	5.1	26.0	23.0	13.3	2.2	71.7	37.7	49.3	50.7
73939	GOODWELL	86.5	85.2	2.0	2.1	0.6	0.8	13.7	15.5	7.4	6.3	5.4	12.0	20.5	24.0	17.5	6.0	0.9	77.6	24.6	52.7	47.3
73942	GUYMON	72.3	70.0	0.8	0.7	0.9	1.1	36.6	39.8	9.2	8.3	7.2	6.7	8.5	30.7	20.0	8.3	1.2	71.3	30.8	51.5	48.5
73944	HARDESTY	84.3	82.9	0.6	0.6	0.2	0.2	24.1	26.8	8.3	8.1	8.4	7.3	7.9	28.4	22.2	8.4	0.9	70.8	31.7	52.3	47.7
73945	HOOKER	84.5	83.0	0.1	0.1	0.1	0.1	16.5	18.4	7.8	6.9	8.2	6.6	6.4	27.1	23.8	11.6	1.7	73.0	36.4	50.9	49.1
73946	KENTON	84.5	84.3	2.3	2.4	0.0	0.0	14.7	14.2	4.7	6.3	7.9	7.9	5.5	21.3	28.4	15.8	2.4	76.4	42.5	52.8	47.2
73947	KEYES	93.0	92.9	0.0	0.0	0.0	0.0	7.5	7.7	8.3	8.1	8.4	6.8	5.1	26.3	21.2	13.4	2.4	71.0	36.0	50.4	49.6
73949	TEXHOMA	82.9	81.7	0.3	0.2	0.1	0.1	26.6	29.0	8.7	8.5	8.1	7.3	5.9	28.6	20.6	11.0	1.5	70.3	33.6	52.1	47.9
73950	TURPIN	89.3	88.2	0.2	0.2	0.2	0.2	19.3	21.6	6.4	6.6	8.9	8.7	7.3	26.6	26.7	7.5	1.5	72.8	36.1	52.5	47.5
73951	TYRONE	80.0	78.0	0.2	0.2	0.1	0.1	20.9	23.2	8.1	7.8	8.4	6.9	8.0	27.6	23.2	9.4	0.6	71.7	33.1	50.6	49.4
74002	BARNSDALL	74.2	72.4	0.1	0.2	0.4	0.5	1.8	1.9	7.6	7.4	7.6	6.5	6.4	23.8	25.8	12.4	2.5	73.3	38.1	50.0	50.0
74003	BARTLESVILLE	74.8	73.2	5.6	5.7	0.5	0.6	3.8	4.3	7.1	6.7	7.1	7.3	7.4	26.1	24.6	11.7	1.9	74.6	36.1	48.5	51.5
74006	BARTLESVILLE	86.4	85.0	1.2	1.3	1.2	1.5	2.2	2.5	5.3	5.7	6.9	6.8	5.4	21.1	27.6	18.4	3.1	77.8	44.3	47.3	52.7
74008	BIXBY	86.0	84.7	1.2	1.4	0.5	0.7	3.8	4.3	7.3	7.3	7.8	7.1	6.5	28.5	25.1	9.5	1.0	73.1	35.9	49.8	50.2
74010	BRISTOW	77.9	76.5	6.5	6.9	0.1	0.2	1.6	1.7	7.2	7.0	7.3	7.1	7.2	24.6	24.0	13.2	2.3	74.3	37.2	48.3	51.7
74011	BROKEN ARROW	87.8	86.6	3.0	3.3	0.8	1.0	2.9	3.4	7.4	7.7	8.5	7.6	5.9	28.3	25.5	8.3	0.8	71.5	35.4	49.1	50.9
74012	BROKEN ARROW	83.9	82.0	4.1	4.5	2.6	3.4	4.0	4.6	8.2	8.2	8.3	7.1	6.6	30.8	23.1	6.7	1.0	70.8	33.6	48.5	51.5
74014	BROKEN ARROW	86.4	85.0	2.1	2.2	1.0	1.2	2.6	3.0	7.0	7.6	8.1	7.0	6.2	28.1	27.9	7.7	0.5	72.9	36.8	49.7	50.3
74015	CATOOSA	80.8	79.4	0.5	0.5	0.2	0.3	2.6	2.9	7.8	7.6	7.9	7.0	6.3	28.3	24.5	9.6	1.1	72.4	35.5	48.9	51.1
74016	CHELSEA	68.9	67.2	0.2	0.2	0.3	0.4	1.1	1.3	7.9	7.6	8.0	7.4	6.5	26.0	23.3	11.6	1.7	71.7	34.8	48.5	51.5
74017	CLAREMORE	77.3	75.9	1.2	1.2	0.4	0.5	2.1	2.4	7.1	6.9	7.4	7.0	6.8	26.1	24.7	12.2	1.8	74.3	37.3	48.7	51.3
74019	CLAREMORE	81.2	79.8	0.7	0.8	0.3	0.4	2.0	2.2	7.5	7.7	7.9	6.8	5.7	27.5	26.1	10.1	0.7	72.5	36.8	50.0	50.0
74020	CLEVELAND	85.4	84.4	0.2	0.3	0.4	0.5	1.3	1.4	6.5	6.6	7.1	6.6	6.1	24.9	27.5	13.0	1.8	75.8	39.5	49.5	50.5
74021	COLLINSVILLE	83.8	82.3	0.5	0.6	0.5	0.7	1.5	1.7	7.3	7.3	7.6	6.5	5.9	28.5	24.6	11.1	1.3	73.8	36.8	49.7	50.3
74022	COPAN	81.5	80.3	0.2	0.2	0.3	0.4	1.2	1.4	4.5	5.6	7.6	7.0	4.3	23.6	31.0	15.0	1.5	77.7	43.3	50.1	49.9
74023	CUSHING	81.9	80.8	5.5	5.6	0.1	0.2	2.3	2.6	6.0	6.0	6.4	6.8	6.8	28.0	23.7	13.8	2.5	77.4	38.1	52.1	47.9
74026	DAVENPORT	87.2	86.3	2.7	2.9	0.2	0.2	1.8	2.2	8.0	7.5	7.4	6.5	5.9	25.8	23.9	13.1	1.9	73.2	37.0	47.0	53.0
74027	DELAWARE	72.0	70.9	0.8	0.9	0.0	0.1	0.7	0.6	7.1	7.1	6.7	6.5	6.1	24.5	28.3	12.5	1.3	75.2	39.5	51.7	48.3
74028	DEPEW	76.4	75.0	6.4	6.7	0.3	0.4	1.9	2.1	5.9	6.2	8.6	8.6	6.0	26.6	25.9	11.5	0.8	73.7	37.5	49.6	50.4
74029	DEWEY	79.7	78.3	1.5	1.5	0.1	0.1	2.8	3.1	5.6	5.9	6.7	6.5	6.1	23.0	27.1	16.9	2.3	77.7	42.5	48.7	51.3
74030	DRUMRIGHT	84.7	83.7	1.0	1.0	0.1	0.1	1.3	1.5	7.0	7.1	7.8	6.2	6.0	25.3	24.8	13.9	2.1	74.4	38.5	48.8	51.2
74032	GLENCOE	90.7	89.8	0.3	0.3	0.8	0.8	0.9	1.2	7.0	6.8	6.9	6.3	6.5	27.7	26.1	11.5	1.2	75.4	38.1	49.6	50.4
74033	GLENPOOL	77.7	76.0	2.1	2.3	0.9	1.1	3.1	3.6	8.9	8.3	8.6	7.9	7.4	31.6	21.0	5.6	0.7	69.4	31.2	47.6	52.4
74035	HOMINY	68.1	66.2	4.7	5.4	0.1	0.2	3.0	3.3	6.6	6.4	6.9	7.0	7.3	27.0	23.9	12.9	2.2	76.1	37.3	52.6	47.4
74036	INOLA	82.5	81.1	0.6	0.7	0.2	0.3	1.1	1.3	7.0	7.3	8.1	7.6	6.3	27.3	25.8	9.5	1.1	72.8	36.5	49.7	50.3
74037	JENKS	86.9	85.5	1.5	1.7	0.8	1.0	4.1	4.8	7.4	7.7	7.9	7.5	6.4	28.5	24.9	8.7	1.0	72.3	35.7	49.2	50.8
74038	JENNINGS	85.1	84.5	0.6	0.6	0.1	0.1	0.8	1.0	6.9	7.3	8.4	6.5	5.1	27.2	25.4	11.9	1.5	73.5	36.8	48.2	51.8
74039	KELLYVILLE	83.1	82.0	2.2	2.4	0.2	0.2	1.0	1.2	6.9	6.9	8.2	7.1	7.4	27.0	26.1	9.7	0.8	73.7	36.2	50.2	49.8
74042	LENAPAH	66.4	65.1	4.6	4.5	0.0	0.0	1.1	1.4	6.8	7.1	7.9	8.1	7.2	25.5	22.7	13.1	1.5	73.3	35.9	52.8	47.2
74044	MANNFORD	87.2	86.2	0.5	0.5	0.5	0.6	1.3	1.5	7.1	7.2	7.5	7.2	6.0	26.2	26.7	10.8	1.1	73.3	37.4	50.1	49.9
74045	MARAMEC	87.2	86.8	0.3	0.3	0.0	0.0	1.3	1.6	6.6	6.3	6.3	6.6	7.6	23.3	29.9	11.3	2.2	76.4	41.0	50.9	49.1
74047	MOUNDS	80.5	79.1	1.5	1.6	0.2	0.2	2.5	2.8	7.7	7.6	8.0	7.7	7.6	26.7	25.3	9.0	0.6	72.1	34.8	50.2	49.8
74048	NOWATA	70.9	69.3	3.4	3.4	0.2	0.2	1.1	1.2	6.6	6.7	7.2	6.0	5.7	23.4	25.0	16.2	3.0	75.7	40.9	48.7	51.3
74051	OCHELATA	72.8	71.2	0.3	0.3	0.0	0.0	0.8	0.9	7.6	7.4	8.2	8.3	7.2	27.2	23.4	9.9	0.9	71.7	33.9	49.8	50.2
74053	OOLOGAH	78.7	76.9	0.1	0.1	0.2	0.2	0.7	0.8	7.4	7.6	8.8	7.7	6.5	27.0	24.8	9.5	0.7	71.4	35.8	49.7	50.3
74054	OSAGE	80.6	79.2	0.2	0.2	0.2	0.4	0.9	0.9	6.4	6.4	5.6	6.4	6.4	24.8	30.0	12.6	1.5	78.1	41.5	51.4	48.6
74055	OWASSO	87.6	86.3	1.2	1.4	0.8	1.0	3.2	3.7	7.9	7.8	8.7	7.8	6.4	28.6	23.6	8.0	1.1	70.6	34.7	48.8	51.2
74056	PAWHUSKA	64.0	62.3	2.6	2.9	0.2	0.3	1.8	2.0	6.2	6.3	7.6	6.9	6.7	22.2	25.7	15.8	2.6	75.3	40.8	48.6	51.4
74058	PAWNEE	74.3	73.4	2.0	2.0	0.0	0.0	1.1	1.2	6.3	6.4	7.6	7.4	6.6	22.9	26.0	14.4	2.6	75.1	39.7	48.6	51.4
74059	PERKINS	87.2	86.2	2.0	2.1	0.2	0.3	1.1	1.3	6.9	7.0	7.5	8.1	6.5	27.7	23.9	11.2	1.5	73.7	35.3	49.8	50.2
74060	PRUE	81.4	79.5	1.1	1.3	0.3	0.4	1.6	1.9	6.5	6.8	7.3	6.8	6.1	25.9	28.5	11.4	0.9	75.3	39.5	50.5	49.5
74061	RAMONA	75.4	73.6	0.4	0.4	0.3	0.4	1.4	1.5	5.9	6.1	7.2	6.0	6.1	24.6	26.7	15.7	1.7	77.2	41.2	49.2	50.8
74062	RIPLEY	86.5	85.1	1.1	1.1	0.4	0.5	0.8	1.0	7.0	7.0	8.4	7.8	7.4	25.5	24.3	11.3	1.3	72.7	36.0	50.0	50.0
74063	SAND SPRINGS	85.1	83.7	1.7	2.0	0.4	0.5	1.9	2.2	6.7	6.7	7.4	7.8	6.7	26.8	26.0	10.7	1.1	74.1	37.0	49.3	50.7
74066	SAPULPA	81.8	80.6	2.7	2.7	0.4	0.4	2.2	2.5	6.7	6.8	7.4	7.0	6.4	26.3	26.3	11.6	1.6	74.9	37.8	48.8	51.2
74070	SKIATOOK	74.7	72.9	0.5	0.6	0.1	0.2	1.9	2.2	7.8	7.6	8.2	7.6	6.7	27.6	23.5	9.8	1.2	71.8	35.1	49.2	50.8
74072	S COFFEYVILLE	81.9	80.8	0.3	0.3	0.2	0.3	1.9	2.2	6.2	6.1	7.0	7.8	7.4	25.2	25.7	12.7	1.9	76.0	39.0	48.6	51.4
74073	SPERRY	74.4	72.6	3.2	3.6	0.5	0.6	2.6	3.0	7.5	7.6	8.0	6.8	6.5	27.2	24.9	10.6	0.9	72.8	35.8	49.9	50.1
74074	STILLWATER	87.9	86.5	2.7	3.0	2.0	2.5	2.1	2.4	5.6	5.0	5.2	8.7	16.3	29.5	19.6	8.2	1.9	81.2	29.0	50.4	49.6
74075	STILLWATER	83.0	81.1	3.8	3.8	5.2	6.5	2.5	2.7	5.7	4.7	5.4	8.6	16.8	31.1	18.0	8.1	1.6	80.8	28.4	50.7	49.3
74077	STILLWATER	83.8	82.4	3.5	4.2	2.8	3.5	2.1	2.1	0.7	0.7	0.0	74.7	18.3	5.6	0.0	0.0	0.0	98.6	18.3	64.1	35.9
74078	STILLWATER	68.1	64.4	8.1	8.0	13.2	16.5	3.0	3.3	2.1	1.3	0.8	51.7	20.5	21.6	1.5	0.4	0.1	95.3	19.4	48.8	51.2
74079	STROUD	85.0	84.0	2.6	2.7	0.4	0.5	1.5	1.7	6.4	7.2	7.6	7.1	5.9	23.9	25.1	14.2	2.8	74.7	39.5	48.2	51.8
74080	TALALA	76.6	74.8	0.1	0.1	0.4	0.5	0.8	0.8	6.9	7.0	8.2	8.1	6.9	27.0	25.0	10.2	0.8	72.9	35.9	50.3	49.7
74081	TERLTON	81.8	80.6	0.0	0.0	0.3	0.5	0.9	0.9	6.1	6.5	8.5	8.1	6.2	25.5	28.9	9.6	0.5	73.8	38.1	51.4	48.6
74083	WANN	78.7	77.5	0.6	0.7	0.2	0.2	2.2	2.5	5.9	6.7	8.2	8.0	5.9	24.4	27.6	12.3	1.1	74.3	39.5	51.1	48.9
74084	WYNONA	56.0	53.4	13.2	14.9	0.1	0.2	3.6	3.9	4.0	3.9	3.8	5.2	8.2	40.9	25.7	7.7	0.7	85.5	37.3	71.7	28.3
74085	YALE	89.0	88.1	0.0	0.0	0.3	0.3	0.8	1.0	6.5	6.8	7.0	7.2	5.7	25.0	25.9	14.1	1.9	75.5	38.6	49.3	50.7
74103	TULSA	55.0	52.1	30.8	33.0	0.6	0.8	4.6	5.1	1.5	1.9	1.5	4.2	11.3	50.5	26.4	2.5	0.3	94.5	37.7	75.3	24.8
74104	TULSA	75.3	73.3	6.7	7.2	1.8	2.2	13.7	14.9	6.2	5.2	4.8	8.8	16.0	32.1	18.7	6.7	1.4	81.1	29.8	50.7	49.3
74105	TULSA	80.5	78.7	8.1	8.8	1.1	1.3	5.0	5.7	6.1	5.7	5.8	5.5	7.4	28.3	25.2	13.5	2.4	79.2	38.5	47.7	52.3
74106	TULSA	11.6	10.5	78.8	79.5	0.2	0.2	5.0	5.4	8.3	8.1	9.2	7.9	6.6	22.9	21.5	12.8	2.6	69.4	33.9	45.2	54.8
74107	TULSA	73.2	71.0	10.0	10.8	0.8	1.0	4.4	5.0	9.2	7.9	7.2	6.6	7.0	27.4	22.0	11.3	1.5	71.9	33.8	47.1	52.9
74108	TULSA	73.7	71.6	6.1	6.4	2.4	2.8	6.1	6.7	8.8	8.5	8.8	6.6	6.5	28.9	23.3	8.1	0.6	69.8	32.8	48.5	51.5
74110	TULSA	46.8	44.6	29.7	30.3	0.3	0.3	15.6	17.2	9.4	8.7	8.4	7.9	8.7	28.0	19.1	8.5	1.5	69.0	29.7	49.4	50.6
74112	TULSA	77.8	75.7	5.8	6.3	1.4	1.7	9.3	10.6	7.0	6.5	5.8	5.6	6.6	30.5	22.9	13.1	2.1	77.5	36.9	48.7	51.3
74114	TULSA	89.8	88.5	2.4	2.7	0.9	1.1	2.2	2.5	6.2	6.3	5.8	5.4	4.4	26.4	27.8	15.0	2.8	78.5	42.2	46.5	53.5
74115	TULSA	65.1	62.7	15.5	16.5	0.4	0.5	8.6	9.7	9.2	8.5	8.5	7.0	6.9	28.4	20.6	9.9	1.1	69.6	32.1	48.3	51.8
74116	TULSA	68.2	65.3	11.1	12.1	2.2	2.7	10.2	11.7	10.2	6.8	6.4	7.9	10.6	27.1	21.8	8.6	0.7	72.5	30.9	51.0	49.0
74117	TULSA	77.8	76.1	7.4	8.0	0.0	0.9	1.9	2.7	6.2	6.2	6.2	7.1	6.2	23.9	26.6	15.9	1.8	76.1	41.4	51.3	48.7
74119	TULSA	80.5	78.7	9.4	10.1	1.2	1.5	2.7	3.2	3.1	2.6	2.7	3.5	6.6	34.5	29.0	14.7	3.4	89.8	43.4	52.0	48.0
74120	TULSA	71.7	69.7	9.1	9.6	0.9	1.1	9.7	10.8	5.8	5.1	5.1	5.5	9.3	36.3	24.3	7.3	1.5	80.9	34.7	52.1	47.9
74126	TULSA	19.5	19.3	72.4	72.1	0.2	0.2	1.5	1.7	9.1	9.6	11.1	9.1	7.4	24.2	20.7	8.0	0.7	64.4	28.0	46.0	54.0
74127	TULSA	59.1	56.9	24.7	25.7	0.3	0.4	5.2	6.0	6.9	6.8	7.4	6.8	6.7	27.0	25.8	11.2	1.4	74.6	36.9	49.5	50.5
74128	TULSA	73.5	70.8	9.3	10.1	2.0	2.4	11.2	12.7	7.8	7.1	6.4	6.2	7.4	25.9	22.6	15.1	1.5	75.1	36.8	47.7	52.3
74129	TULSA	72.2	69.4	9.6	10.4	3.2	3.8	9.5	11.0	7.7	6.8	6.3	5.9	7.4	27.8	22.1	13.6	2.4	75.6	36.2	47.5	52.5
74130	TULSA	42.4	40.3	42.3	43.5	0.3	0.4	3.0	3.4	7.7	7.4	8.2	7.4	7.0	25.7	24.3	11.0	1.1	72.2	34.9	48.9	51.1
74131	TULSA	83.3	82.1	0.9	1.0	0.3	0.4	3.4	3.9	7.0	7.2	8.1	8.0	7.0	25.5	27.7	8.8	0.6	72.7	36.1	50.7	49.3
74132	TULSA	84.9	83.2	3.6	4.0	0.9	1.1	2.3	2.7	6.9	7.4	7.8	7.3	5.9	27.7	28.4	8.2	0.5	73.1	36.9	49.7	50.3
	OKLAHOMA	76.2	74.8	7.6	7.7	1.4	1.8	5.2	5.8	7.0	6.7	7.0	7.1	7.8	27.2	24.0	11.6	1.7	75.3	36.0	49.3	50.8
	UNITED STATES	75.1	73.6	12.3	12.5	3.8	4.2	12.5	14.1	6.9	6.7	7.2	7.0	7.3	28.6	23.8	10.8	1.7	75.1	36.0	49.1	50.9

INCOME

ZIP CODE #	POST OFFICE NAME	2004 Per Capita Income	2004 HH Income Base	2004 HOUSEHOLD INCOME DISTRIBUTION (%) Less than $25,000	$25,000 to $49,999	$50,000 to $99,999	$100,000 to $149,999	$150,000 or More	MEDIAN HOUSEHOLD INCOME 2004	2009	2004 National Centile	2004 State Centile	2004 Home Value Base	2004 HOME VALUE DISTRIBUTION (%) Less than $50,000	$50,000 to $89,999	$90,000 to $174,999	$175,000 to $399,999	$400,000 or More	2004 Median Home Value
73859	VICI	17042	497	41.5	29.2	24.6	3.8	1.0	30868	36368	14	29	371	53.1	29.1	15.4	1.9	0.5	46290
73860	WAYNOKA	17984	642	43.9	34.9	15.9	4.1	1.3	28507	34434	10	16	480	64.4	21.0	12.9	1.5	0.2	35625
73931	BALKO	21212	263	25.9	31.9	33.5	7.6	1.1	43377	49449	57	86	210	22.4	33.3	31.0	13.3	0.0	84286
73932	BEAVER	21329	772	29.0	28.0	34.2	6.7	2.1	42718	49788	55	85	604	33.3	34.6	26.2	6.0	0.0	70000
73933	BOISE CITY	19054	781	38.9	32.0	21.3	4.7	3.1	34460	40113	26	54	575	52.2	26.6	17.4	3.0	0.9	47951
73937	FELT	16947	81	32.1	39.5	21.0	4.9	2.5	35814	40310	31	61	58	39.7	22.4	27.6	5.2	5.2	65000
73938	FORGAN	18193	274	33.6	34.7	21.5	7.3	2.9	36355	43033	33	64	222	52.3	23.4	19.4	0.9	4.1	47059
73939	GOODWELL	18135	719	31.3	31.4	27.7	8.5	1.1	39069	46491	43	76	382	31.7	24.9	30.1	11.3	2.1	77500
73942	GUYMON	18419	4672	28.1	30.4	32.0	7.3	2.2	41566	48547	52	83	3232	25.2	34.3	29.6	9.6	1.3	79583
73944	HARDESTY	17495	207	29.0	37.2	28.5	4.4	1.0	38517	45390	41	75	146	43.2	21.2	28.1	6.2	1.4	58333
73945	HOOKER	20076	1071	28.5	34.7	27.0	6.7	3.1	39529	46417	44	77	827	33.9	33.5	25.0	6.5	1.1	70185
73946	KENTON	19244	54	31.5	38.9	20.4	5.6	3.7	35875	41819	31	61	39	43.6	23.1	23.1	5.1	5.1	61250
73947	KEYES	19011	274	38.0	31.4	24.1	3.7	2.9	34646	39686	26	55	213	51.2	20.7	21.1	7.0	0.0	48810
73949	TEXHOMA	18402	615	34.2	35.0	23.1	4.2	3.6	37006	43317	35	68	456	41.9	30.3	23.0	4.2	0.7	59024
73950	TURPIN	20975	616	20.5	36.2	35.1	6.2	2.1	44537	51428	60	88	481	40.1	20.4	29.3	7.5	2.7	67857
73951	TYRONE	16645	465	28.8	33.1	33.1	4.1	0.9	40221	47704	47	79	359	49.0	28.7	17.8	3.3	1.1	51591
74002	BARNSDALL	17123	1197	32.3	33.2	28.5	5.2	0.9	37101	43598	36	69	939	58.7	21.7	15.1	3.4	1.1	40944
74003	BARTLESVILLE	17906	6193	42.0	30.3	20.6	5.1	2.1	30561	37355	14	26	3853	54.7	24.8	13.9	5.7	0.9	46020
74006	BARTLESVILLE	31430	10460	22.0	27.2	29.4	12.7	8.8	50899	64039	74	94	8071	13.7	34.6	36.2	13.6	2.0	91996
74008	BIXBY	29006	6688	17.4	25.4	35.4	13.3	8.5	58464	70809	83	97	5363	15.3	16.8	41.4	19.0	7.5	116100
74010	BRISTOW	18013	3296	38.3	31.3	24.5	3.8	2.1	32742	37909	20	43	2312	39.4	27.7	25.6	6.7	0.7	63913
74011	BROKEN ARROW	27100	8627	12.4	22.8	42.5	15.4	6.9	64060	78167	88	98	7169	0.9	14.6	66.8	15.5	2.1	120175
74012	BROKEN ARROW	25332	17933	13.6	24.5	41.6	15.3	5.0	61641	75538	86	98	14169	2.6	22.7	56.6	17.7	0.4	116370
74014	BROKEN ARROW	25013	9447	12.3	25.8	42.9	14.3	4.7	60553	69919	85	97	8243	10.9	12.8	55.7	18.2	2.5	123765
74015	CATOOSA	20437	3297	23.0	29.4	36.9	8.8	2.0	48093	55807	69	92	2646	29.7	20.3	32.1	16.6	1.4	89929
74016	CHELSEA	16538	1880	35.3	32.9	26.2	4.2	1.4	35188	42065	28	58	1372	33.4	27.0	27.7	10.3	1.7	72911
74017	CLAREMORE	20523	10959	27.1	28.8	33.8	7.7	2.7	44447	52345	60	87	8025	18.6	26.5	41.4	12.1	1.4	96165
74019	CLAREMORE	24142	5103	15.1	23.5	46.4	11.5	3.5	59745	67766	84	97	4414	11.5	13.8	57.3	15.2	2.2	118167
74020	CLEVELAND	18906	3843	30.7	33.1	27.8	6.1	2.3	37699	43540	38	72	3041	35.5	28.4	27.4	7.9	0.8	70205
74021	COLLINSVILLE	22067	4817	22.6	30.1	35.1	8.8	3.5	47414	57611	67	92	3978	21.1	25.5	42.5	10.4	0.5	94512
74022	COPAN	21468	690	33.6	28.8	28.8	6.2	2.5	37040	45852	36	69	582	33.7	35.1	24.2	4.6	2.4	68163
74023	CUSHING	16722	4266	37.8	33.0	22.7	5.4	1.2	32660	39638	20	42	3040	38.5	33.6	20.4	5.9	1.7	65328
74026	DAVENPORT	15878	388	39.2	36.3	19.3	4.1	1.0	31447	36271	16	34	294	51.0	28.2	15.0	5.1	0.7	49250
74027	DELAWARE	16654	499	32.9	35.5	27.1	4.2	0.4	35171	40307	28	58	411	44.3	23.6	21.2	7.8	3.2	57121
74028	DEPEW	15226	863	32.7	38.7	24.3	3.4	0.9	33799	38831	23	49	706	46.7	23.8	23.2	6.0	0.3	55000
74029	DEWEY	20106	2090	33.7	29.1	28.5	6.5	2.2	37283	46410	36	70	1573	41.1	30.4	23.1	5.0	0.4	57881
74030	DRUMRIGHT	16994	3264	36.2	33.6	25.2	4.1	1.0	34120	39815	24	52	2486	45.1	30.8	18.0	5.4	0.8	55374
74032	GLENCOE	18044	477	28.7	40.0	23.7	6.3	1.3	36610	43726	34	66	392	39.3	25.8	25.8	7.7	1.5	66667
74033	GLENPOOL	21129	3333	17.9	31.0	40.3	7.9	3.0	50740	60939	73	94	2715	11.0	48.3	36.1	3.7	0.9	84068
74035	HOMINY	16831	1339	43.9	33.7	16.5	3.3	2.6	28462	33762	9	16	919	55.7	29.2	11.2	3.4	0.5	45732
74036	INOLA	20901	2159	19.9	33.1	32.5	11.4	3.2	47415	55087	67	92	1821	13.3	30.1	42.4	11.8	2.4	97774
74037	JENKS	28124	3979	13.4	26.0	40.1	14.8	5.8	62155	76944	86	98	3324	8.0	17.4	51.1	21.5	1.9	117969
74038	JENNINGS	16066	331	29.3	38.4	27.2	5.1	0.0	37548	43955	38	71	263	50.2	28.9	17.9	1.9	1.1	49868
74039	KELLYVILLE	15862	1136	26.9	37.9	29.8	5.0	0.3	39527	46048	44	77	941	33.1	32.6	27.6	6.1	0.6	72320
74042	LENAPAH	15887	305	31.8	30.5	31.8	4.3	1.6	37995	43800	39	73	251	37.1	30.3	19.9	7.6	5.2	65476
74044	MANNFORD	17422	2608	29.8	32.8	30.9	5.9	0.7	37925	44050	39	73	2133	29.1	33.8	31.0	5.8	0.3	76005
74045	MARAMEC	21226	127	25.2	34.7	33.1	5.5	1.6	41260	48199	51	82	109	46.8	21.1	20.2	11.9	0.0	53889
74047	MOUNDS	19180	1895	26.3	28.3	35.2	7.5	2.8	45730	53546	63	90	1547	26.7	29.7	29.5	11.5	2.5	79964
74048	NOWATA	16563	2542	40.4	32.5	21.4	4.1	1.6	30935	36081	15	30	1881	45.1	25.8	20.4	7.8	0.9	56444
74051	OCHELATA	17673	589	28.0	29.9	33.3	7.0	1.9	44499	52375	60	88	495	46.5	25.9	18.2	9.5	0.0	58333
74053	OOLOGAH	21254	1521	22.2	27.7	38.5	9.5	2.0	50024	57799	72	93	1255	16.0	26.5	40.0	13.6	3.8	98738
74054	OSAGE	17728	226	40.3	33.2	18.6	6.2	1.8	30000	35128	12	23	188	46.8	27.1	18.1	6.4	1.6	58571
74055	OWASSO	25525	10844	15.1	24.8	39.4	16.1	4.6	61521	74921	86	98	8534	5.2	16.0	52.9	23.9	2.1	126340
74056	PAWHUSKA	18177	2263	41.4	33.7	19.3	3.8	1.9	30238	35555	13	24	1609	61.3	18.8	14.4	4.3	1.2	41705
74058	PAWNEE	16293	1759	38.5	33.8	22.9	3.2	1.6	32080	37484	18	38	1324	47.2	26.6	19.6	6.3	0.4	53627
74059	PERKINS	19239	1643	30.9	32.3	28.6	6.5	1.8	37511	46809	37	71	1280	28.7	39.6	23.8	7.7	0.2	70604
74060	PRUE	19761	796	23.9	29.8	33.9	9.9	2.5	46584	54141	65	91	684	24.1	27.2	32.6	13.9	2.2	88269
74061	RAMONA	19667	619	28.4	32.6	31.8	4.5	2.6	40838	49726	49	81	513	38.2	25.2	24.0	11.7	1.0	66806
74062	RIPLEY	16468	351	31.3	35.0	28.8	4.0	0.9	35559	44277	30	60	293	37.5	37.5	16.7	7.5	0.7	62639
74063	SAND SPRINGS	21573	10962	23.3	31.0	34.6	8.6	2.6	46299	54772	65	90	8596	21.9	34.2	35.1	8.0	0.8	82758
74066	SAPULPA	19505	11858	29.2	33.1	28.4	6.1	3.2	38854	45817	42	76	8963	24.4	32.8	33.9	8.6	0.4	80498
74070	SKIATOOK	20140	4094	21.8	33.2	34.4	8.3	2.3	45938	53967	64	90	3346	21.3	33.7	28.0	15.7	1.3	84488
74072	S COFFEYVILLE	17413	592	33.3	35.0	26.5	3.7	1.5	36548	41904	34	66	482	43.4	31.5	21.6	2.7	0.8	55818
74073	SPERRY	17354	1373	31.5	32.9	27.4	6.0	2.3	37022	44269	36	69	1116	34.7	29.2	27.9	7.1	1.2	72614
74074	STILLWATER	21644	11217	39.9	25.1	22.6	7.9	4.5	33347	40849	22	47	6070	22.7	19.6	35.3	19.8	2.7	106258
74075	STILLWATER	21984	9011	39.8	26.3	23.2	7.8	2.9	33534	41654	23	48	3903	15.0	20.3	50.2	13.7	0.9	107820
74077	STILLWATER	9939	0	0.0	0.0	0.0	0.0	0.0	0	0	0	0	0	0.0	0.0	0.0	0.0	0.0	0
74078	STILLWATER	10774	333	65.5	28.5	1.2	4.8	0.0	16517	19155	1	1	29	0.0	0.0	100.0	0.0	0.0	112500
74079	STROUD	16117	1999	40.3	35.7	17.9	3.9	2.3	30646	35650	14	27	1484	39.0	32.6	20.6	6.9	0.9	62706
74080	TALALA	19941	664	23.3	31.2	35.7	6.8	3.0	46667	54798	65	92	565	22.0	31.7	34.3	9.0	3.0	86466
74081	TERLTON	15254	391	29.2	40.2	26.1	3.3	1.3	36619	42755	34	66	351	42.7	31.9	19.9	5.1	0.3	58793
74083	WANN	17943	358	30.5	34.4	28.5	4.5	2.2	38623	45539	42	75	310	32.3	25.8	32.6	6.5	2.9	74000
74084	WYNONA	13231	385	40.3	33.3	20.3	3.6	2.6	30867	36555	14	29	282	58.2	23.8	13.1	3.2	1.8	43030
74085	YALE	17224	963	35.9	33.8	26.1	3.6	0.6	32974	39789	21	45	707	51.6	27.4	15.1	4.4	1.4	48544
74103	TULSA	9800	54	61.1	29.6	9.3	0.0	0.0	16053	17228	1	1	10	20.0	40.0	40.0	0.0	0.0	80000
74104	TULSA	21458	5882	35.3	31.9	23.3	6.7	2.8	35334	43571	29	59	2803	14.2	29.6	48.4	7.7	0.1	100021
74105	TULSA	33444	14299	27.6	30.3	24.6	8.9	8.7	41658	50297	52	83	7574	4.4	23.3	41.0	24.0	7.3	118921
74106	TULSA	14217	6988	53.8	28.1	14.3	2.0	1.8	22621	26809	3	2	3718	53.0	32.4	12.8	1.4	0.4	48456
74107	TULSA	17572	8192	37.7	31.0	24.9	5.3	1.2	33006	40289	21	45	4754	28.9	46.8	21.0	2.8	0.5	65860
74108	TULSA	17287	2793	28.6	34.7	29.8	5.7	1.2	39987	47533	46	78	1828	18.3	56.9	22.2	2.6	0.1	72553
74110	TULSA	12525	5710	50.8	33.9	12.7	1.4	1.2	24528	29160	4	5	2880	68.6	25.0	5.6	0.8	0.0	42751
74112	TULSA	21301	10194	29.4	36.1	27.9	5.0	1.5	38423	46188	41	74	6129	10.4	55.1	33.3	1.0	0.3	77740
74114	TULSA	43597	7661	19.5	26.0	30.6	10.3	13.6	54756	67383	79	95	5852	3.5	28.3	35.3	20.1	12.8	111554
74115	TULSA	15618	9045	36.4	36.7	22.5	3.6	0.8	32829	39473	20	43	5693	51.8	44.0	3.4	0.7	0.1	49325
74116	TULSA	16233	1564	39.3	31.9	23.7	4.6	0.5	32009	37898	18	37	674	21.7	31.2	30.1	15.0	2.1	86275
74117	TULSA	19820	42	33.3	26.2	31.0	7.1	2.4	38178	46158	40	74	35	25.7	17.1	42.9	11.4	2.9	96250
74119	TULSA	38663	2506	39.0	27.0	21.1	6.0	6.9	33057	41146	21	45	721	8.3	21.6	42.6	21.2	6.2	118365
74120	TULSA	25343	2870	43.0	29.7	17.4	5.7	4.3	29454	36006	11	21	911	22.8	14.6	33.9	20.5	8.1	119459
74126	TULSA	12457	4128	46.9	31.7	17.1	2.7	1.7	26836	30899	7	10	2370	66.3	25.5	7.2	1.0	0.0	41921
74127	TULSA	18267	7129	35.0	33.6	24.2	5.2	2.0	35497	42784	29	59	4634	34.8	36.4	23.8	4.5	0.5	64987
74128	TULSA	19753	4615	24.6	39.9	29.5	4.6	1.5	40045	48002	46	79	3088	10.0	69.9	19.7	0.4	0.1	74354
74129	TULSA	22450	7388	27.5	30.6	31.2	8.7	2.1	42142	51176	53	84	4348	2.0	42.8	52.7	2.6	0.0	93620
74130	TULSA	16651	886	38.8	33.0	22.9	4.5	0.8	32734	39956	20	42	644	53.9	36.8	8.4	0.9	0.0	47748
74131	TULSA	23600	1293	25.4	34.3	26.6	9.1	4.5	39813	47503	45	78	1087	41.6	15.9	22.9	17.3	2.3	70897
74132	TULSA	27954	2659	18.5	24.2	36.4	14.1	6.7	57613	69986	82	96	2178	9.0	17.1	52.9	17.5	3.6	115045
	OKLAHOMA	21077		31.9	30.4	27.2	7.1	3.4	38589	46268				26.7	29.5	32.0	10.2	1.6	81000
	UNITED STATES	25866		24.7	27.1	30.8	10.9	6.5	48124	56710				10.9	15.0	33.7	30.1	10.4	145905

ZIP CODE #	POST OFFICE NAME	FINANCIAL SERVICES: Auto Loan	FINANCIAL SERVICES: Home Loan	FINANCIAL SERVICES: Investments	FINANCIAL SERVICES: Retirement Plans	THE HOME: Home Improvements: Home Repair	THE HOME: Home Improvements: Lawn & Garden	THE HOME: Furnishings: Computers & Hardware	THE HOME: Furnishings: Major Appliances	THE HOME: Furnishings: TV, Radio, Sound Equipment	THE HOME: Furnishings: Furniture	ENTERTAINMENT: Dine out/ Carry out	ENTERTAINMENT: Sports Equipment	ENTERTAINMENT: Fees & Tickets	ENTERTAINMENT: Toys & Games	ENTERTAINMENT: Travel	ENTERTAINMENT: Cable TV	PERSONAL: Apparel & Services	PERSONAL: Auto Repairs	PERSONAL: Health Insurance	PERSONAL: Pets & Supplies
73859	VICI	66	48	30	46	54	63	52	59	59	50	69	67	46	66	52	62	63	59	70	74
73860	WAYNOKA	63	47	30	45	52	62	52	57	58	49	68	65	46	65	51	61	62	57	69	71
73931	BALKO	93	65	34	61	75	84	64	79	74	63	86	95	54	85	66	77	79	78	94	110
73932	BEAVER	93	66	37	63	76	86	68	81	77	66	91	95	59	88	69	81	83	80	96	108
73933	BOISE CITY	76	57	36	54	63	74	61	69	69	59	81	78	54	77	61	73	74	69	82	86
73937	FELT	81	57	30	54	66	74	56	69	65	55	76	84	48	74	58	68	69	68	83	97
73938	FORGAN	89	62	33	59	73	81	62	76	71	61	83	92	53	82	64	74	76	75	90	106
73939	GOODWELL	75	58	57	60	60	67	70	69	72	67	89	86	63	84	66	70	84	74	71	84
73942	GUYMON	82	71	60	69	73	79	72	77	76	74	93	89	69	91	71	75	90	78	79	90
73944	HARDESTY	73	67	52	64	67	71	64	68	64	66	80	79	60	75	63	64	76	68	68	81
73945	HOOKER	92	70	43	66	77	85	68	80	75	68	90	96	60	87	69	77	83	79	91	107
73946	KENTON	82	57	30	54	67	75	56	70	65	56	76	84	48	75	59	68	70	69	83	97
73947	KEYES	88	62	32	58	72	80	61	75	70	60	82	91	52	81	63	74	75	74	90	105
73949	TEXHOMA	82	64	44	63	70	79	65	73	71	64	85	86	60	84	66	73	79	72	83	93
73950	TURPIN	93	83	64	80	86	92	78	85	81	79	100	101	75	98	79	82	95	84	90	107
73951	TYRONE	76	65	48	63	68	72	63	70	65	64	80	81	58	76	63	65	76	69	72	86
74002	BARNSDALL	72	60	43	57	62	70	61	67	65	61	79	76	56	74	61	67	74	66	73	80
74003	BARTLESVILLE	61	56	55	55	57	63	60	60	62	58	76	70	58	76	59	63	73	61	63	68
74006	BARTLESVILLE	105	103	104	104	106	116	103	106	104	102	128	121	103	126	104	104	123	105	109	120
74008	BIXBY	111	122	120	122	120	123	112	114	108	113	135	132	116	137	113	106	132	111	108	129
74010	BRISTOW	72	58	42	55	62	70	60	66	65	58	78	77	55	77	60	68	73	65	75	82
74011	BROKEN ARROW	104	120	125	122	117	117	111	110	103	112	131	129	115	133	111	99	129	108	98	121
74012	BROKEN ARROW	100	109	109	112	106	107	104	103	98	105	123	121	105	124	102	94	121	102	93	113
74014	BROKEN ARROW	99	112	110	112	110	110	101	103	96	102	120	120	105	124	102	93	119	100	94	116
74015	CATOOSA	84	81	69	79	81	84	77	81	77	79	95	95	75	92	76	75	92	80	78	95
74016	CHELSEA	71	57	38	53	61	69	56	63	62	56	74	74	52	72	57	64	69	63	72	81
74017	CLAREMORE	82	74	61	71	77	84	72	78	75	71	92	90	70	91	73	77	87	76	83	94
74019	CLAREMORE	98	103	94	100	104	107	93	98	93	93	114	115	95	118	96	92	112	95	97	117
74020	CLEVELAND	79	66	48	63	69	76	65	72	70	65	84	83	61	81	65	71	79	71	78	88
74021	COLLINSVILLE	89	87	77	86	88	92	82	86	82	83	102	101	81	102	82	82	98	85	86	102
74022	COPAN	90	68	40	61	74	83	64	76	73	65	87	91	58	85	65	78	81	75	90	105
74023	CUSHING	69	53	36	51	59	68	56	62	62	54	73	72	50	71	56	65	67	62	73	79
74026	DAVENPORT	75	50	23	43	57	65	48	60	58	49	68	72	41	65	49	63	62	60	74	86
74027	DELAWARE	76	55	31	50	62	70	54	64	62	54	73	77	48	71	55	66	68	63	76	88
74028	DEPEW	74	52	27	46	59	67	50	61	59	51	70	73	44	67	51	63	64	60	74	86
74029	DEWEY	78	63	45	61	68	78	65	72	72	63	85	82	61	83	65	75	79	71	82	88
74030	DRUMRIGHT	74	55	33	50	60	68	56	64	63	55	74	74	49	70	55	66	69	64	75	83
74032	GLENCOE	73	66	51	64	67	72	63	68	64	64	79	79	60	76	63	64	76	67	69	83
74033	GLENPOOL	87	93	91	94	90	90	88	88	84	89	106	104	89	106	87	80	104	88	79	98
74035	HOMINY	63	49	37	47	52	62	54	58	60	52	71	66	49	68	53	63	66	58	67	70
74036	INOLA	92	81	62	78	84	92	78	85	82	78	100	99	75	100	79	84	95	83	91	104
74037	JENKS	106	120	121	121	117	118	110	110	104	112	131	127	114	133	110	101	129	107	100	122
74038	JENNINGS	80	54	25	47	61	70	52	65	63	53	74	78	45	70	53	68	67	65	80	92
74039	KELLYVILLE	77	59	36	54	65	72	56	66	64	57	76	79	51	74	57	67	71	65	76	89
74042	LENAPAH	70	60	46	59	62	71	61	65	65	60	79	75	59	78	61	66	74	65	71	77
74044	MANNFORD	74	67	52	64	68	72	63	68	65	65	79	79	60	76	63	64	76	68	69	83
74045	MARAMEC	86	76	57	72	80	86	70	78	75	70	91	93	68	92	72	77	86	76	85	101
74047	MOUNDS	86	79	62	76	79	84	74	80	76	76	93	93	71	89	74	75	90	79	80	96
74048	NOWATA	70	50	29	47	56	65	52	61	60	51	70	70	46	67	52	63	64	60	73	79
74051	OCHELATA	80	73	56	70	74	78	69	74	70	70	86	86	65	83	68	70	83	73	75	90
74053	OOLOGAH	93	82	64	79	85	92	79	86	83	80	101	100	76	99	79	83	96	84	90	104
74054	OSAGE	79	53	24	45	60	69	51	64	61	52	72	76	43	68	52	66	66	63	78	90
74055	OWASSO	100	111	113	114	108	108	104	103	98	106	124	121	107	126	103	94	122	102	93	115
74056	PAWHUSKA	73	54	35	52	60	71	59	66	67	57	78	75	53	74	59	70	72	66	79	82
74058	PAWNEE	69	52	34	49	57	67	55	62	62	53	73	70	49	70	55	65	67	61	73	77
74059	PERKINS	76	65	51	65	68	75	66	71	69	65	84	81	63	83	65	70	80	70	75	83
74060	PRUE	93	79	57	75	83	91	75	84	81	76	98	99	72	97	76	83	93	82	92	107
74061	RAMONA	79	63	43	60	68	78	64	71	70	62	84	82	59	82	64	74	78	70	82	90
74062	RIPLEY	72	62	48	61	65	72	62	67	66	61	80	77	60	80	62	67	75	65	72	81
74063	SAND SPRINGS	83	81	73	79	82	88	78	81	80	78	98	94	78	100	79	80	95	80	83	96
74066	SAPULPA	78	71	61	68	73	80	70	74	73	69	89	86	68	89	70	75	85	73	79	89
74070	SKIATOOK	88	77	59	75	81	89	74	81	79	74	96	95	72	97	75	81	91	79	88	101
74072	S COFFEYVILLE	81	59	32	52	65	74	56	68	65	57	77	81	50	75	57	69	71	67	81	94
74073	SPERRY	82	65	42	60	70	78	62	71	69	62	83	85	57	81	63	72	77	70	82	95
74074	STILLWATER	71	64	72	67	63	68	75	69	74	72	92	86	71	89	70	69	89	74	65	78
74075	STILLWATER	66	55	64	59	54	60	71	63	70	67	87	80	65	82	64	65	84	69	60	71
74077	STILLWATER	0	0	0	0	0	0	0	0	0	0	0	0	0	0	0	0	0	0	0	0
74078	STILLWATER	34	21	26	24	21	25	41	30	39	34	49	41	33	44	32	35	46	36	28	34
74079	STROUD	70	50	29	47	56	66	53	61	60	51	71	71	46	67	53	64	65	61	74	79
74080	TALALA	90	77	56	73	82	89	72	81	78	72	94	96	69	95	74	80	89	79	89	106
74081	TERLTON	70	64	50	61	64	67	61	65	61	62	76	75	57	72	60	61	73	65	65	77
74083	WANN	75	66	51	63	70	75	61	68	65	61	79	81	60	81	63	67	75	66	74	88
74084	WYNONA	73	55	36	53	60	72	61	67	68	58	80	75	54	75	60	72	73	67	80	81
74085	YALE	68	55	39	53	59	68	57	63	62	55	74	72	52	72	57	65	69	62	72	77
74103	TULSA	13	11	13	12	11	13	14	13	15	14	18	16	13	17	13	14	17	14	13	14
74104	TULSA	64	62	73	64	61	65	70	65	68	68	86	79	68	85	67	65	84	69	61	72
74105	TULSA	88	91	113	93	90	97	97	92	95	95	120	109	98	120	96	94	118	96	89	102
74106	TULSA	51	43	47	39	42	51	48	48	53	49	65	53	47	60	47	56	62	50	54	55
74107	TULSA	59	56	59	55	57	63	60	59	62	58	76	68	60	78	59	63	74	60	62	67
74108	TULSA	66	68	69	67	66	69	67	67	66	67	82	78	67	83	66	64	80	67	64	75
74110	TULSA	46	41	46	40	40	46	47	45	50	46	61	53	46	59	45	50	59	47	48	51
74112	TULSA	62	64	71	64	64	69	66	65	67	65	83	75	67	85	66	66	81	66	65	71
74114	TULSA	120	140	168	137	139	150	134	133	132	133	164	151	142	172	138	133	162	131	130	145
74115	TULSA	56	53	55	52	53	59	57	56	59	55	72	65	56	73	56	59	70	57	58	63
74116	TULSA	57	52	52	51	53	58	56	56	58	54	72	66	54	72	55	59	69	57	58	65
74117	TULSA	85	72	52	68	76	85	70	78	76	69	92	91	67	91	71	79	86	76	87	98
74119	TULSA	71	71	100	75	69	76	79	74	79	78	100	88	80	100	78	78	98	78	71	81
74120	TULSA	64	59	72	62	58	63	70	65	70	67	87	79	67	85	66	66	85	69	62	71
74126	TULSA	52	46	51	44	45	52	50	50	54	51	67	56	50	65	49	55	65	51	53	58
74127	TULSA	60	60	64	59	60	66	63	62	64	61	79	72	63	81	62	64	77	62	63	69
74128	TULSA	67	66	65	65	66	73	68	68	69	66	85	78	67	87	67	69	82	68	70	76
74129	TULSA	73	77	83	77	76	80	77	76	75	76	94	88	78	95	76	74	92	76	73	84
74130	TULSA	70	62	48	60	63	69	61	66	64	62	78	75	58	75	61	64	74	65	69	78
74131	TULSA	97	94	80	91	95	99	88	93	88	89	109	109	86	108	88	88	105	92	93	112
74132	TULSA	113	119	111	119	118	120	109	112	105	111	131	132	110	132	109	103	128	110	106	130
	OKLAHOMA	79	71	65	70	73	80	73	76	76	72	93	88	70	91	72	76	88	76	79	89
	UNITED STATES	100	100	100	100	100	100	100	100	100	100	100	100	100	100	100	100	100	100	100	100

OKLAHOMA

POPULATION CHANGE

A 74133-74570

#	POST OFFICE NAME	COUNTY FIPS CODE	POPULATION 2000	2004	2009	% Rate	State Centile	HOUSEHOLDS 2000	2004	2009	% Annual Rate 2000-2004	2004 Average HH Size	FAMILIES 2000	2004	% Annual Rate 2000-2004
74133	TULSA	143	37532	42589	46313	3.0	97	15709	17726	19233	2.9	2.39	9982	11267	2.9
74134	TULSA	143	13014	13535	14065	0.9	77	5237	5498	5737	1.2	2.46	3338	3466	0.9
74135	TULSA	143	20920	20842	21269	-0.1	35	10082	10107	10354	0.1	2.00	5445	5390	-0.2
74136	TULSA	143	29823	30700	31842	0.7	68	14011	14547	15172	0.9	2.01	7243	7383	0.5
74137	TULSA	143	23599	25729	27460	2.1	93	8784	9649	10357	2.2	2.63	6592	7187	2.1
74145	TULSA	143	17827	18112	18678	0.4	55	8144	8312	8612	0.5	2.17	4819	4852	0.2
74146	TULSA	143	14357	15138	15911	1.3	85	5873	6289	6681	1.6	2.41	3488	3601	0.8
74171	TULSA	143	2202	2228	2248	0.3	51	3	3	3	0.0	2.67	2	2	0.0
74301	VINITA	035	10031	10292	10694	0.6	64	3721	3829	4000	0.7	2.40	2488	2551	0.6
74330	ADAIR	097	5691	5895	6217	0.8	75	2126	2223	2363	1.1	2.65	1707	1780	1.0
74331	AFTON	041	6200	6821	7466	2.3	94	2713	2977	3263	2.2	2.29	1933	2117	2.2
74332	BIG CABIN	035	2379	2488	2644	1.1	80	913	958	1018	1.1	2.59	714	746	1.0
74333	BLUEJACKET	035	1224	1266	1322	0.8	73	437	454	475	0.9	2.74	344	356	0.8
74337	CHOUTEAU	097	4496	4648	4897	0.8	73	1651	1710	1809	0.8	2.70	1264	1305	0.8
74338	COLCORD	041	4877	5059	5376	0.9	76	1790	1871	2003	1.1	2.65	1360	1419	1.0
74339	COMMERCE	115	2733	2715	2755	-0.2	32	995	980	988	-0.4	2.68	712	696	-0.5
74342	EUCHA	041	3666	3783	4010	0.7	71	1422	1479	1578	0.9	2.55	1026	1064	0.9
74343	FAIRLAND	115	2948	3059	3161	0.9	76	1179	1224	1262	0.9	2.48	881	913	0.8
74344	GROVE	041	13121	14434	15838	2.3	94	5606	6193	6833	2.4	2.29	3915	4311	2.3
74346	JAY	041	5923	6218	6649	1.2	83	2234	2353	2528	1.2	2.59	1631	1715	1.2
74347	KANSAS	041	2806	2972	3192	1.4	87	978	1040	1123	1.5	2.82	787	836	1.4
74352	LOCUST GROVE	097	6810	7272	7800	1.6	90	2564	2757	2977	1.7	2.62	1890	2026	1.7
74354	MIAMI	115	17792	18115	18589	0.4	58	7156	7267	7437	0.4	2.38	4816	4876	0.3
74358	NORTH MIAMI	115	326	374	407	3.3	98	121	138	149	3.1	2.71	92	105	3.2
74359	OAKS	041	300	302	315	0.2	47	92	93	98	0.3	3.13	73	74	0.3
74360	PICHER	115	2029	1995	2019	-0.4	23	771	753	760	-0.6	2.60	535	519	-0.7
74361	PRYOR	097	12811	13629	14602	1.5	88	5108	5470	5900	1.6	2.44	3562	3810	1.6
74363	QUAPAW	115	2899	2969	3046	0.6	63	1054	1079	1104	0.6	2.73	820	836	0.5
74364	ROSE	041	1504	1550	1636	0.7	70	552	574	610	0.9	2.70	435	451	0.9
74365	SALINA	097	4267	4462	4728	1.1	80	1623	1713	1831	1.3	2.56	1156	1215	1.2
74366	SPAVINAW	097	1248	1280	1350	0.6	64	476	489	517	0.6	2.61	335	343	0.6
74367	STRANG	097	2590	2649	2780	0.5	62	1097	1130	1195	0.7	2.25	754	773	0.6
74368	TWIN OAKS	041	555	559	585	0.2	47	185	188	198	0.4	2.88	148	150	0.3
74369	WELCH	035	1834	1908	2002	0.9	77	728	762	801	1.1	2.48	542	565	1.0
74370	WYANDOTTE	115	3075	3131	3204	0.4	58	1168	1190	1217	0.4	2.63	886	901	0.4
74401	MUSKOGEE	101	17979	18774	19461	1.0	79	6929	7273	7591	1.2	2.51	4620	4849	1.1
74403	MUSKOGEE	101	30155	30776	31614	0.5	60	12227	12585	13045	0.7	2.38	8285	8493	0.6
74421	BEGGS	111	5000	5311	5639	1.4	88	1865	1987	2112	1.5	2.66	1417	1506	1.4
74422	BOYNTON	101	788	772	780	-0.5	17	305	302	308	-0.2	2.56	228	226	-0.2
74423	BRAGGS	101	654	652	659	-0.1	36	256	259	264	0.3	2.52	196	197	0.1
74425	CANADIAN	121	1676	1744	1777	0.9	77	706	742	762	1.2	2.35	526	550	1.1
74426	CHECOTAH	091	11796	12400	13049	1.2	84	4874	5162	5473	1.4	2.37	3479	3670	1.3
74427	COOKSON	021	1649	1752	1890	1.4	88	746	800	870	1.7	2.19	513	550	1.7
74428	COUNCIL HILL	091	1029	1037	1066	0.2	48	403	410	426	0.4	2.53	312	317	0.4
74429	COWETA	145	10862	12315	14309	3.0	97	3936	4509	5289	3.3	2.72	3107	3545	3.2
74432	EUFAULA	091	5294	5375	5581	0.4	55	2240	2289	2394	0.5	2.28	1464	1491	0.4
74434	FORT GIBSON	101	7580	7789	8066	0.6	67	2726	2834	2964	0.9	2.72	2152	2231	0.9
74435	GORE	135	1380	1421	1488	0.7	68	559	583	618	1.0	2.40	416	433	1.0
74436	HASKELL	101	3575	3606	3671	0.2	49	1329	1356	1396	0.5	2.63	1002	1020	0.4
74437	HENRYETTA	111	11525	12263	13093	1.5	88	4508	4813	5153	1.6	2.50	3142	3339	1.4
74440	HOYT	061	161	164	167	0.4	58	60	61	63	0.4	2.69	45	46	0.5
74441	HULBERT	021	5613	5985	6493	1.5	89	2116	2281	2498	1.8	2.62	1634	1759	1.8
74442	INDIANOLA	121	2453	2507	2528	0.5	62	944	972	986	0.7	2.58	731	752	0.7
74445	MORRIS	111	3380	3494	3656	0.8	73	1220	1265	1325	0.9	2.76	952	985	0.9
74447	OKMULGEE	111	17564	18047	18901	0.6	67	6947	7153	7514	0.7	2.41	4573	4686	0.6
74450	OKTAHA	101	2147	2174	2207	0.3	52	763	782	801	0.6	2.78	612	624	0.5
74451	PARK HILL	021	3880	4204	4579	1.9	93	1546	1685	1848	2.1	2.45	1151	1253	2.0
74452	PEGGS	021	1531	1597	1706	1.0	79	563	593	639	1.2	2.69	433	455	1.2
74454	PORTER	145	3078	3282	3685	1.5	89	1161	1252	1421	1.8	2.60	876	940	1.7
74455	PORUM	101	3110	3148	3217	0.3	52	1260	1293	1335	0.6	2.43	938	959	0.5
74457	PROCTOR	001	920	958	1001	1.0	77	332	347	365	1.1	2.76	253	264	1.0
74461	STIDHAM	091	309	326	344	1.3	85	133	142	150	1.6	2.30	94	100	1.5
74462	STIGLER	061	5370	5482	5615	0.5	61	2117	2160	2214	0.5	2.47	1482	1507	0.4
74463	TAFT	101	2103	2093	2098	-0.1	34	217	216	220	-0.1	2.76	150	146	-0.6
74464	TAHLEQUAH	021	24806	26324	28363	1.4	87	9386	10055	10951	1.6	2.46	5946	6335	1.5
74467	WAGONER	145	15654	16930	19158	1.9	92	6172	6722	7666	2.0	2.50	4518	4890	1.9
74469	WARNER	101	2626	2617	2646	-0.1	36	917	924	945	0.2	2.56	666	669	0.1
74470	WEBBERS FALLS	101	1364	1369	1382	0.1	43	530	539	550	0.4	2.54	402	407	0.3
74471	WELLING	021	3199	3355	3594	1.1	83	1177	1243	1342	1.3	2.69	894	943	1.3
74472	WHITEFIELD	061	274	279	285	0.4	58	117	120	122	0.6	2.33	88	90	0.5
74501	MCALESTER	121	27970	28400	28874	0.4	55	10595	10809	11054	0.5	2.39	7202	7325	0.4
74523	ANTLERS	127	6144	6221	6286	0.3	52	2475	2519	2558	0.4	2.38	1719	1743	0.3
74525	ATOKA	005	9830	9975	10150	0.4	54	3386	3482	3593	0.7	2.58	2332	2392	0.6
74528	BLANCO	121	247	241	239	-0.6	15	101	99	99	-0.5	2.43	79	77	-0.6
74531	CALVIN	063	1031	1059	1097	0.6	66	410	422	439	0.7	2.51	297	306	0.7
74533	CANEY	005	1362	1366	1373	0.1	43	526	535	545	0.4	2.55	399	405	0.4
74534	CENTRAHOMA	029	422	438	454	0.9	76	168	174	180	0.8	2.52	126	131	0.9
74536	CLAYTON	127	1682	1722	1744	0.6	63	731	751	764	0.6	2.29	476	487	0.5
74538	COALGATE	029	4030	4110	4216	0.5	59	1624	1661	1708	0.5	2.43	1090	1110	0.4
74540	DAISY	005	164	165	166	0.1	46	68	70	72	0.7	1.03	49	10	-31.2
74543	FINLEY	127	217	217	217	0.0	40	95	96	96	0.3	2.26	66	66	0.0
74547	HARTSHORNE	121	5056	4909	4869	-0.7	12	2020	1975	1972	-0.5	2.40	1415	1378	-0.6
74549	HONOBIA	079	301	296	301	-0.4	23	123	122	125	-0.2	2.43	90	89	-0.3
74552	KINTA	061	2893	2935	2991	0.3	54	1172	1194	1219	0.4	2.46	884	899	0.4
74553	KIOWA	121	1311	1273	1262	-0.7	12	539	528	527	-0.5	2.41	399	389	-0.6
74555	LANE	005	1071	1082	1094	0.2	50	418	423	431	0.3	2.11	302	305	0.2
74557	MOYERS	127	161	163	164	0.3	52	64	65	66	0.4	2.51	47	47	0.0
74558	NASHOBA	127	597	602	604	0.2	49	242	246	248	0.4	2.45	172	174	0.3
74560	PITTSBURG	121	552	538	534	-0.6	14	209	205	205	-0.5	2.62	162	159	-0.4
74561	QUINTON	121	4685	4722	4729	0.2	48	2041	2075	2091	0.4	2.26	1428	1447	0.3
74562	RATTAN	127	1633	1623	1623	-0.1	33	655	657	661	0.1	2.47	474	474	0.0
74563	RED OAK	077	2187	2191	2193	0.0	42	856	866	875	0.3	2.53	642	648	0.2
74567	SNOW	127	312	312	313	0.0	40	134	135	136	0.2	2.31	93	93	0.0
74569	STRINGTOWN	005	591	593	597	0.1	43	229	233	237	0.2	2.45	170	172	0.3
74570	STUART	063	758	763	782	0.2	47	314	318	327	0.3	2.40	240	243	0.3
	OKLAHOMA					0.8					1.0	2.48			0.9
	UNITED STATES					1.2					1.3	2.58			1.1

#	POST OFFICE NAME	RACE (%) White 2000	White 2004	Black 2000	Black 2004	Asian/Pacific 2000	Asian/Pacific 2004	% Hispanic Origin 2000	% Hispanic Origin 2004	2004 AGE DISTRIBUTION (%) 0-4	5-9	10-14	15-19	20-24	25-44	45-64	65-84	85+	18+	MEDIAN AGE 2004	% 2004 Males	% 2004 Females
74133	TULSA	84.0	82.0	4.9	5.4	3.3	4.1	4.6	5.2	6.9	6.4	6.8	6.8	9.1	30.6	23.7	8.3	1.4	75.9	34.2	49.0	51.0
74134	TULSA	72.1	69.2	9.3	10.0	4.7	5.7	9.2	10.2	8.2	7.1	6.9	7.3	10.4	33.3	22.2	4.2	0.3	73.7	30.4	50.7	49.3
74135	TULSA	82.8	81.2	6.3	6.8	1.2	1.5	5.8	6.6	5.6	5.2	5.1	4.9	6.0	25.8	24.6	18.8	4.1	81.5	43.0	46.5	53.5
74136	TULSA	73.6	70.6	13.4	14.8	2.8	3.4	7.2	8.3	6.5	5.1	5.0	6.4	12.3	30.4	22.1	10.3	2.1	80.4	32.9	47.9	52.1
74137	TULSA	88.7	87.3	3.2	3.4	2.3	3.0	3.1	3.4	5.6	7.0	8.8	7.7	5.1	24.2	30.5	9.5	1.6	73.5	40.5	48.4	51.6
74145	TULSA	79.3	76.7	7.4	8.2	2.9	3.7	5.8	6.8	6.0	5.4	5.4	5.9	9.0	27.1	22.6	17.0	1.6	79.9	37.8	48.3	51.7
74146	TULSA	63.3	60.1	11.2	11.9	4.5	5.3	16.7	18.4	8.5	7.1	6.7	7.8	11.9	31.4	19.3	6.6	0.7	73.7	29.3	50.5	49.5
74171	TULSA	76.3	73.5	14.6	15.9	2.4	2.9	5.7	6.5	0.6	0.5	0.9	28.4	51.4	4.9	6.6	5.6	1.0	96.8	21.9	43.1	56.9
74301	VINITA	68.4	66.6	4.3	4.4	0.2	0.3	1.3	1.4	5.9	5.9	6.2	6.2	6.2	27.1	26.0	14.3	2.3	78.2	40.6	51.1	48.9
74330	ADAIR	76.0	74.5	0.2	0.2	0.1	0.2	1.5	1.6	6.7	6.7	6.6	6.8	6.3	25.2	27.6	13.0	1.2	75.9	39.9	49.8	50.2
74331	AFTON	82.1	80.7	0.1	0.1	0.2	0.2	1.0	1.1	5.4	5.5	5.5	5.0	4.5	20.7	32.1	19.8	1.6	80.5	47.3	50.0	50.0
74332	BIG CABIN	67.9	66.1	1.0	1.1	0.4	0.4	1.4	1.6	6.7	7.2	6.8	6.4	6.3	25.6	28.4	11.7	0.8	75.3	39.4	50.2	49.8
74333	BLUEJACKET	64.8	62.6	0.4	0.4	0.0	0.0	0.3	0.4	6.7	6.8	6.7	7.0	6.4	25.7	26.0	13.0	1.7	75.6	38.5	49.5	50.6
74337	CHOUTEAU	78.5	77.1	1.0	1.0	0.4	0.5	1.7	2.0	7.3	7.2	8.4	7.7	6.8	26.3	24.1	11.0	1.3	72.3	35.2	49.9	50.1
74338	COLCORD	72.2	70.5	0.1	0.1	0.1	0.2	1.9	2.2	7.3	7.3	7.9	7.0	6.0	27.2	24.5	10.8	2.0	73.1	36.5	50.1	49.9
74339	COMMERCE	68.6	66.6	0.6	0.6	0.3	0.3	17.7	20.0	8.8	7.7	7.6	7.3	7.9	26.6	18.8	12.5	3.0	71.5	32.6	47.3	52.7
74342	EUCHA	56.1	54.6	0.1	0.1	0.1	0.1	1.8	2.0	6.2	6.6	6.6	6.9	6.4	24.1	27.7	14.6	1.0	76.1	40.3	50.5	49.5
74343	FAIRLAND	74.7	73.5	0.1	0.1	0.2	0.3	0.8	0.9	6.0	6.0	6.4	6.2	6.0	24.5	26.7	16.3	1.9	77.5	41.6	49.5	50.5
74344	GROVE	80.5	79.1	0.1	0.1	0.4	0.5	1.6	1.8	5.1	5.0	5.4	5.4	5.2	19.3	29.5	22.3	2.9	81.1	48.5	48.3	51.7
74346	JAY	60.2	58.4	0.4	0.3	0.1	0.1	2.7	3.1	7.0	7.0	7.8	7.1	6.6	25.7	25.2	12.1	1.6	73.8	36.6	48.8	51.2
74347	KANSAS	55.1	53.4	0.0	0.0	0.1	0.2	1.4	1.6	9.1	8.5	8.1	7.9	6.7	27.9	21.1	9.8	0.9	69.4	32.5	49.6	50.4
74352	LOCUST GROVE	64.0	62.6	0.0	0.0	0.1	0.2	1.3	1.4	7.5	7.0	7.3	6.7	7.3	25.8	24.6	12.3	1.5	74.1	36.5	50.9	49.1
74354	MIAMI	75.1	73.8	0.9	1.0	0.6	0.8	2.2	2.5	6.5	6.3	6.7	7.4	7.5	24.1	23.2	16.0	2.4	76.5	38.2	48.0	52.0
74358	NORTH MIAMI	61.7	59.9	0.3	0.3	0.3	0.3	4.3	5.1	7.0	6.4	6.7	9.9	7.2	22.7	23.3	15.8	1.1	73.5	37.4	47.3	52.7
74359	OAKS	35.0	33.4	0.0	0.0	0.0	0.0	1.7	1.7	9.6	9.9	8.3	8.0	7.0	27.5	21.2	8.0	0.7	67.2	30.0	49.3	50.7
74360	PICHER	76.7	75.3	0.0	0.0	0.3	0.3	1.5	1.8	7.1	7.2	7.5	6.6	6.6	24.2	25.2	14.3	1.4	74.3	37.8	49.6	50.4
74361	PRYOR	77.8	76.4	0.2	0.2	0.5	0.7	2.4	2.7	6.8	6.6	7.1	7.4	6.2	26.4	23.4	13.7	2.4	74.7	37.2	49.0	51.1
74363	QUAPAW	71.4	70.2	0.0	0.0	0.2	0.3	1.6	1.8	7.4	7.4	7.4	6.6	6.6	26.1	26.3	11.3	1.0	73.5	36.4	50.8	49.2
74364	ROSE	48.7	47.7	0.0	0.0	0.0	0.0	1.8	1.9	7.5	8.2	7.8	7.7	7.6	26.5	24.4	9.6	0.8	71.7	33.4	51.6	48.4
74365	SALINA	57.0	55.8	0.2	0.2	0.1	0.1	1.2	1.3	7.5	7.2	7.1	6.8	7.3	25.3	23.7	13.6	1.6	74.0	36.7	50.0	50.0
74366	SPAVINAW	66.9	65.6	0.0	0.0	0.1	0.1	3.2	3.4	6.3	6.6	7.4	6.5	5.5	22.7	27.7	16.0	1.3	75.5	41.4	49.4	50.6
74367	STRANG	75.9	74.6	0.9	0.9	0.2	0.2	2.6	2.9	5.4	5.5	5.3	4.7	4.7	22.1	31.5	18.9	2.0	80.8	46.4	50.3	49.7
74368	TWIN OAKS	35.7	34.4	0.0	0.0	0.0	0.0	1.6	1.8	10.0	9.7	8.4	8.1	7.2	27.4	21.1	7.7	0.5	66.4	29.6	48.8	51.2
74369	WELCH	74.1	72.7	0.2	0.2	0.0	0.0	1.2	1.2	6.9	6.7	6.3	5.9	5.8	25.1	24.7	16.3	2.4	76.4	40.1	49.5	50.5
74370	WYANDOTTE	74.2	73.0	0.0	0.0	0.3	0.3	1.9	2.1	6.6	6.7	7.4	6.8	5.2	25.0	27.7	13.7	1.0	75.2	39.6	50.7	49.4
74401	MUSKOGEE	48.6	47.5	33.6	33.5	0.9	1.1	2.5	2.6	7.8	7.4	7.5	6.8	7.3	23.9	23.9	13.1	2.2	73.3	36.6	48.1	52.0
74403	MUSKOGEE	71.9	70.3	3.9	4.1	0.8	1.0	3.2	3.6	6.9	6.4	6.4	6.4	7.3	25.4	24.6	14.0	2.7	76.5	38.5	47.8	52.2
74421	BEGGS	73.1	71.5	8.7	9.0	0.2	0.3	2.1	2.2	7.5	7.4	7.7	7.4	7.1	26.2	26.0	9.8	0.9	72.8	35.9	49.8	50.2
74422	BOYNTON	59.4	57.8	22.0	22.7	0.0	0.0	1.1	1.2	6.0	6.2	8.0	8.2	7.6	22.2	25.5	14.4	1.9	74.9	38.4	51.3	48.7
74423	BRAGGS	70.0	68.6	0.8	0.9	0.0	0.0	0.9	1.1	6.1	6.6	7.5	5.8	6.6	26.5	28.4	11.2	1.2	76.4	38.5	51.2	48.8
74425	CANADIAN	85.7	84.9	0.3	0.3	0.1	0.1	0.6	0.7	4.0	4.1	5.2	6.4	6.1	18.5	33.8	20.6	1.4	82.9	49.0	49.1	50.9
74426	CHECOTAH	74.8	73.4	4.2	4.3	0.2	0.2	1.3	1.5	5.6	5.6	6.0	6.0	5.6	20.6	28.1	20.2	2.4	79.1	45.5	48.0	52.0
74427	COOKSON	68.0	66.9	0.1	0.1	0.2	0.2	0.4	0.5	3.5	3.8	4.9	4.8	4.2	18.8	35.5	22.7	1.9	85.0	50.9	50.2	49.8
74428	COUNCIL HILL	70.5	69.3	7.4	7.3	0.1	0.1	1.3	1.4	5.7	6.2	7.1	7.6	6.3	21.2	26.7	17.4	1.8	76.4	41.8	49.7	50.3
74429	COWETA	78.4	76.9	3.0	3.1	0.3	0.3	3.0	3.4	7.9	7.8	8.3	6.6	6.6	29.2	24.0	8.9	0.8	72.0	34.1	49.4	50.6
74432	EUFAULA	67.2	65.8	5.2	5.3	0.2	0.3	1.1	1.2	5.3	5.3	5.7	5.8	5.9	20.9	27.1	20.8	3.2	80.2	45.8	47.7	52.3
74434	FORT GIBSON	68.9	67.3	2.1	2.2	0.2	0.2	3.7	4.1	7.0	7.2	8.3	7.6	6.9	26.6	25.0	10.2	1.2	72.9	35.6	49.9	50.1
74435	GORE	66.2	64.7	2.3	2.4	0.1	0.1	1.3	1.3	6.0	6.1	7.3	7.1	5.5	23.7	27.5	15.1	1.8	76.4	41.2	49.6	50.4
74436	HASKELL	70.3	68.6	10.9	11.4	0.1	0.2	1.3	1.5	7.8	7.4	7.4	7.3	6.7	24.8	23.7	12.8	2.3	72.9	36.7	48.1	51.9
74437	HENRYETTA	77.3	76.1	1.8	1.8	0.2	0.3	2.0	2.2	6.5	6.3	7.3	7.2	6.5	23.1	25.8	14.7	2.6	75.6	39.8	48.0	52.0
74440	HOYT	77.0	75.6	0.6	0.6	0.0	0.6	0.0	0.0	5.5	6.1	6.7	5.5	5.5	22.6	29.3	17.1	1.8	78.1	43.5	51.8	48.2
74441	HULBERT	60.0	59.0	0.5	0.5	0.2	0.3	2.1	2.3	7.3	7.1	7.2	7.2	6.9	26.1	26.0	11.4	0.8	74.0	36.7	50.8	49.2
74442	INDIANOLA	83.5	82.6	0.4	0.4	0.2	0.2	1.2	1.4	5.7	6.5	7.3	8.0	5.5	24.1	27.8	13.9	1.2	75.2	40.4	50.4	49.6
74445	MORRIS	72.4	70.8	3.9	4.1	0.1	0.1	2.0	2.4	6.7	6.5	7.6	8.4	7.6	25.7	24.4	11.5	1.5	74.1	36.4	49.3	50.7
74447	OKMULGEE	62.0	60.3	18.4	19.2	0.3	0.3	1.8	2.0	7.2	6.6	6.9	7.7	8.3	23.3	23.6	14.1	2.5	75.4	36.8	49.0	51.0
74450	OKTAHA	65.9	64.2	10.8	11.4	0.5	0.6	1.6	1.9	7.2	7.2	8.0	7.3	6.9	25.1	26.2	11.0	1.2	73.2	37.1	49.5	50.5
74451	PARK HILL	58.4	57.0	0.4	0.4	0.2	0.3	2.6	2.8	7.1	6.9	6.9	6.4	5.9	25.1	26.7	14.0	1.0	75.1	39.0	49.9	50.1
74452	PEGGS	57.1	55.8	0.1	0.1	0.3	0.3	0.7	0.8	7.6	7.5	8.0	7.1	7.5	25.5	25.4	11.0	0.6	72.7	35.9	51.4	48.7
74454	PORTER	68.1	66.1	14.5	15.4	0.0	0.0	1.3	1.4	6.5	6.5	7.3	7.4	7.2	23.8	27.8	12.3	1.2	75.2	38.7	49.8	50.2
74455	PORUM	68.4	67.4	0.5	0.5	0.1	0.1	1.0	1.1	6.7	6.6	6.6	6.5	6.3	21.4	27.5	16.7	1.7	76.2	41.6	49.5	50.5
74457	PROCTOR	47.5	46.5	0.2	0.2	0.0	0.0	2.0	2.1	7.3	7.9	8.8	6.7	5.2	27.7	24.7	10.7	1.0	71.8	34.9	50.1	49.9
74461	STIDHAM	71.2	69.9	2.6	2.8	0.0	0.3	0.7	0.6	4.0	4.6	5.8	6.1	4.9	19.9	30.7	22.4	1.5	81.9	48.0	48.5	51.5
74462	STIGLER	78.7	77.6	0.0	0.0	0.3	0.4	1.9	2.2	7.8	7.3	6.7	6.2	6.4	24.6	23.2	14.8	3.1	74.6	37.9	48.2	51.8
74463	TAFT	42.6	40.6	41.2	42.6	0.3	0.4	2.1	2.3	2.9	2.7	2.3	3.2	8.6	56.4	19.5	3.9	0.6	90.5	36.6	54.2	45.8
74464	TAHLEQUAH	55.6	54.2	1.7	1.7	0.4	0.5	5.7	6.2	7.5	6.6	6.8	9.1	12.8	25.9	19.5	10.2	1.8	75.2	29.5	48.3	51.7
74467	WAGONER	74.0	72.6	5.5	5.7	0.3	0.4	2.0	2.2	6.9	6.6	6.7	6.3	6.8	23.9	26.3	14.7	1.8	76.0	39.8	48.5	51.5
74469	WARNER	65.1	63.7	2.9	3.1	0.0	0.0	1.8	2.0	7.7	6.5	5.9	7.6	10.4	24.0	22.4	13.2	2.3	77.0	34.2	48.8	51.2
74470	WEBBERS FALLS	68.8	67.6	0.5	0.6	0.0	0.0	1.8	1.9	6.9	7.2	6.9	6.7	5.6	24.8	25.8	14.8	1.5	75.0	39.2	48.5	51.5
74471	WELLING	46.4	45.2	0.4	0.4	0.1	0.1	2.3	2.4	7.1	7.3	8.3	8.0	5.7	28.0	24.5	10.2	1.1	72.4	35.7	50.4	49.6
74472	WHITEFIELD	77.0	76.0	0.4	0.4	0.4	0.4	0.0	0.4	5.4	6.1	7.2	5.7	5.4	22.2	28.3	17.9	1.8	77.8	43.4	52.0	48.0
74501	MCALESTER	76.4	75.0	5.9	6.0	0.4	0.5	2.6	2.9	5.8	5.9	6.5	6.3	6.9	27.7	24.6	13.8	2.6	77.9	39.0	51.2	48.8
74523	ANTLERS	79.8	78.7	1.1	1.1	0.2	0.2	1.7	2.0	6.7	6.6	6.9	6.7	5.7	24.1	24.3	16.0	3.1	75.8	40.0	47.9	52.2
74525	ATOKA	75.2	73.9	6.3	6.5	0.3	0.3	1.3	1.5	6.2	6.3	6.6	6.1	6.5	27.5	25.3	13.4	2.2	77.2	38.9	53.1	46.9
74528	BLANCO	69.2	67.6	0.4	0.4	0.0	0.0	3.2	4.2	5.8	5.8	6.2	6.6	6.2	24.5	29.9	13.3	1.7	78.0	41.3	50.2	49.8
74531	CALVIN	82.4	81.1	0.0	0.0	0.5	0.7	2.1	2.6	7.0	7.1	7.1	5.9	5.1	24.7	26.6	14.6	1.9	75.2	39.7	51.8	48.3
74533	CANEY	83.3	82.2	0.7	0.7	0.1	0.1	1.5	1.8	6.7	6.6	6.6	7.0	6.5	24.7	27.4	13.0	1.4	75.9	39.9	50.7	49.3
74534	CENTRAHOMA	73.7	72.4	0.2	0.2	0.2	0.5	1.9	2.3	7.3	7.3	6.4	7.3	6.9	22.8	26.0	13.7	2.3	74.0	38.5	50.7	49.3
74536	CLAYTON	73.6	72.4	1.3	1.4	0.0	0.0	1.3	1.5	7.2	6.7	6.6	7.0	6.2	22.1	24.3	17.7	2.1	75.2	40.8	49.4	50.6
74538	COALGATE	75.5	74.2	0.5	0.5	0.4	0.5	2.2	2.5	6.1	6.4	7.5	6.5	5.7	24.5	23.9	16.5	3.0	76.1	40.4	49.0	51.1
74540	DAISY	66.5	64.9	15.2	16.4	0.0	0.0	3.7	4.2	2.4	2.4	2.4	4.2	9.1	46.1	25.5	7.3	0.6	89.7	38.1	77.6	22.4
74543	FINLEY	80.7	80.7	0.0	0.0	0.0	0.0	1.4	1.4	4.6	5.1	6.0	7.8	5.1	20.3	30.9	18.4	1.8	78.8	45.7	50.2	49.8
74547	HARTSHORNE	70.7	69.6	2.1	2.2	0.2	0.2	1.6	1.8	6.2	6.9	7.7	6.8	5.8	22.7	26.4	14.8	2.7	75.1	40.4	48.6	51.4
74549	HONOBIA	76.7	75.7	0.7	0.7	0.0	0.0	1.0	1.0	6.4	6.4	7.4	6.8	5.7	21.0	29.1	15.5	1.7	75.7	42.5	49.0	51.0
74552	KINTA	75.6	74.2	2.3	2.4	0.1	0.2	0.5	0.6	5.8	6.2	7.3	5.7	5.4	22.9	28.0	17.2	1.7	77.3	42.7	51.1	48.9
74553	KIOWA	76.4	74.8	0.1	0.1	0.0	0.0	2.5	3.0	6.1	6.3	6.3	6.6	6.1	26.1	26.5	14.1	2.0	77.4	40.2	48.6	51.4
74555	LANE	74.5	72.6	5.2	5.5	0.4	0.6	1.6	1.9	5.4	5.6	6.1	5.8	5.8	32.4	25.8	11.9	1.2	79.4	38.9	59.0	41.0
74557	MOYERS	81.4	81.0	0.0	0.0	0.0	0.0	0.6	0.6	5.5	5.5	6.8	6.1	5.5	24.5	28.2	16.6	1.2	78.5	41.4	50.3	49.7
74558	NASHOBA	78.4	77.4	0.3	0.3	0.2	0.2	1.3	1.5	5.2	5.5	7.3	7.6	6.2	20.6	29.9	16.1	1.7	77.1	43.7	47.5	52.5
74560	PITTSBURG	70.1	69.0	0.2	0.2	0.0	0.0	3.3	3.4	5.8	6.0	6.5	6.7	6.1	24.7	28.8	13.6	1.9	77.7	40.9	49.8	50.2
74561	QUINTON	83.9	83.1	0.2	0.2	0.1	0.1	1.0	1.1	4.5	5.2	5.7	5.9	4.2	20.2	31.0	21.5	1.9	80.7	48.3	50.4	49.6
74562	RATTAN	76.1	75.0	0.1	0.1	0.3	0.4	1.8	2.0	6.5	6.7	6.9	6.7	5.6	21.7	29.1	15.0	1.8	75.9	42.2	49.6	50.4
74563	RED OAK	74.6	74.6	0.2	0.2	0.1	0.1	0.8	0.8	6.7	6.9	7.0	6.8	6.2	24.0	26.6	14.2	1.8	75.5	39.7	50.7	49.3
74567	SNOW	80.1	79.2	0.3	0.3	0.3	0.3	1.3	1.6	5.1	5.1	6.1	7.7	5.1	20.2	30.5	18.6	1.6	79.2	45.4	50.0	50.0
74569	STRINGTOWN	76.5	75.0	6.3	6.4	0.3	0.5	0.7	0.8	5.9	6.1	6.9	7.1	6.4	26.0	25.8	14.3	1.5	76.7	39.8	52.5	47.6
74570	STUART	86.8	86.2	0.1	0.1	0.0	0.0	1.9	2.0	4.5	4.9	7.2	5.4	5.2	23.7	27.9	19.0	2.2	80.5	44.4	50.3	49.7
	OKLAHOMA	76.2	74.8	7.6	7.7	1.4	1.8	5.2	5.8	7.0	6.7	7.0	7.1	7.8	27.2	24.0	11.6	1.7	75.3	36.0	49.3	50.8
	UNITED STATES	75.1	73.6	12.3	12.5	3.8	4.2	12.5	14.1	6.9	6.7	7.2	7.0	7.3	28.6	23.8	10.8	1.7	75.1	36.0	49.1	50.9

#	POST OFFICE NAME	2004 Per Capita Income	2004 HH Income Base	2004 Household Income Distribution (%) Less than $25,000	$25,000 to $49,999	$50,000 to $99,999	$100,000 to $149,999	$150,000 or More	Median Household Income 2004	2009	2004 National Centile	2004 State Centile	2004 Home Value Base	2004 Home Value Distribution (%) Less than $50,000	$50,000 to $89,999	$90,000 to $174,999	$175,000 to $399,999	$400,000 or More	2004 Median Home Value
74133	TULSA	31639	17726	16.2	25.8	34.0	16.0	8.2	59474	73970	84	97	10168	1.5	5.1	60.4	30.9	2.2	151540
74134	TULSA	22284	5498	22.9	32.0	35.4	7.8	2.0	46432	55260	65	91	2636	1.0	34.6	62.3	1.8	0.4	96667
74135	TULSA	28284	10107	26.9	29.1	29.4	9.8	4.8	43749	52377	58	87	5771	2.3	15.7	65.6	15.8	0.6	122232
74136	TULSA	32695	14547	29.0	29.1	24.6	9.0	8.3	40835	50567	49	81	5248	9.2	9.8	28.7	44.2	8.1	179670
74137	TULSA	49878	9649	11.4	16.8	28.2	18.1	25.6	87011	107850	97	100	7255	2.2	4.6	22.4	50.9	20.0	241883
74145	TULSA	25133	8312	23.2	32.5	33.4	9.0	1.9	45582	54725	63	89	4472	1.2	24.2	70.9	3.4	0.2	107402
74146	TULSA	19262	6289	35.9	34.2	22.8	5.0	2.1	34268	41073	25	53	2512	14.7	47.6	35.0	2.6	0.2	81676
74171	TULSA	9330	3	0.0	0.0	100.0	0.0	0.0	87500	81250	97	100	2	0.0	0.0	50.0	50.0	0.0	187500
74301	VINITA	18604	3829	36.1	35.2	23.0	3.0	2.6	33722	38596	23	49	2783	35.0	29.2	27.0	7.3	1.5	68147
74330	ADAIR	19655	2223	24.3	35.7	29.7	8.1	2.1	42882	49410	56	86	1886	22.4	25.0	38.3	12.8	1.5	95444
74331	AFTON	23586	2977	35.1	32.7	21.3	6.3	4.7	36221	43358	32	63	2408	28.4	23.6	26.7	14.8	6.5	85727
74332	BIG CABIN	21800	958	28.6	33.5	29.7	5.7	2.5	38401	44590	41	74	788	27.5	27.4	25.9	17.4	1.8	83276
74333	BLUEJACKET	16808	454	30.2	41.2	22.3	4.2	2.2	35000	40248	28	57	377	39.3	28.1	24.7	6.4	1.6	67414
74337	CHOUTEAU	16517	1710	35.2	27.7	30.0	5.6	1.5	36043	42474	32	62	1319	25.2	33.7	27.7	11.2	2.2	77695
74338	COLCORD	15070	1871	37.9	35.8	22.0	3.0	1.3	32129	37981	18	38	1482	36.9	28.2	23.7	7.9	3.3	69911
74339	COMMERCE	12910	980	40.4	39.0	18.9	1.7	0.0	30606	34819	14	27	597	59.5	31.2	9.2	0.2	0.0	43274
74342	EUCHA	15638	1479	46.6	29.4	18.1	3.3	2.6	26827	31176	7	10	1222	48.3	22.4	19.5	7.2	2.6	52442
74343	FAIRLAND	15984	1224	34.0	41.5	20.7	2.5	1.3	33301	38337	22	46	941	27.1	35.1	27.1	9.1	1.6	76359
74344	GROVE	19723	6193	38.0	31.6	23.1	4.7	2.6	32018	37517	18	37	4871	22.0	23.8	31.7	18.6	4.0	97545
74346	JAY	15677	2353	42.3	31.5	19.8	4.3	2.2	29514	35119	11	21	1707	36.1	29.9	24.7	5.5	3.8	70797
74347	KANSAS	14271	1040	33.1	39.8	23.0	2.5	1.6	33837	39665	24	49	857	37.5	31.3	22.5	7.2	1.5	66429
74352	LOCUST GROVE	14854	2757	38.0	33.5	24.8	3.3	0.4	31700	37081	17	36	2139	41.4	28.6	22.5	6.2	1.3	62279
74354	MIAMI	18935	7267	39.5	32.7	21.8	3.8	2.2	30907	35608	15	29	5032	35.8	31.8	25.0	6.5	0.9	66592
74358	NORTH MIAMI	13659	138	39.1	38.4	18.8	1.5	2.2	33439	35321	22	47	112	54.5	33.0	9.8	2.7	0.0	44444
74359	OAKS	12395	93	40.9	36.6	18.3	3.2	1.1	31217	37315	16	32	76	47.4	32.9	15.8	2.6	1.3	53333
74360	PICHER	12161	753	54.2	29.1	14.5	1.7	0.5	22527	25622	3	2	570	72.8	14.9	7.4	3.7	1.2	27564
74361	PRYOR	20810	5470	33.5	30.3	27.4	5.6	3.2	36842	43501	35	67	3886	19.5	33.4	36.5	9.8	1.0	86657
74363	QUAPAW	14466	1079	39.3	32.7	23.2	4.1	0.7	32965	37266	21	44	878	40.2	30.1	20.8	7.9	1.0	63563
74364	ROSE	15028	574	40.1	35.7	21.1	1.4	1.7	30519	35214	14	26	469	48.4	24.1	19.8	7.3	0.4	51744
74365	SALINA	16244	1713	38.7	30.8	26.4	3.2	0.9	32741	39064	20	43	1358	35.6	32.6	26.1	5.7	0.2	68190
74366	SPAVINAW	14521	489	46.4	29.9	19.2	2.5	2.0	27949	32872	9	13	384	46.9	30.5	15.9	4.4	2.3	53750
74367	STRANG	20175	1130	37.8	35.9	19.8	5.0	1.5	32140	38107	18	38	936	36.1	22.2	27.7	10.6	3.4	75660
74368	TWIN OAKS	13471	188	39.4	36.7	19.2	3.7	1.1	31741	36875	17	36	153	44.4	34.6	16.3	3.9	0.7	56538
74369	WELCH	17950	762	33.2	39.9	21.5	2.8	2.6	34736	38754	26	55	590	37.0	26.6	22.2	10.2	4.1	70588
74370	WYANDOTTE	15218	1190	35.8	38.5	21.1	3.5	1.1	34331	39449	25	53	989	35.4	26.5	25.8	10.5	1.8	72536
74401	MUSKOGEE	16981	7273	45.7	29.0	18.6	3.5	3.2	27943	33548	9	13	4480	38.2	31.1	21.8	7.4	1.5	64246
74403	MUSKOGEE	19788	12585	36.2	29.9	25.7	5.6	2.6	35296	42056	29	59	8361	29.0	34.2	30.4	5.9	0.5	75603
74421	BEGGS	17758	1987	31.7	31.9	29.1	5.8	1.4	38562	45537	41	75	1560	31.6	26.3	29.5	10.6	2.1	76727
74422	BOYNTON	17855	302	42.7	28.8	22.9	3.3	2.3	30229	35849	13	24	250	44.8	26.8	21.6	5.6	1.2	58667
74423	BRAGGS	15582	259	42.1	34.8	19.7	2.7	0.8	30291	35699	13	24	215	41.9	34.9	20.5	2.8	0.0	56731
74425	CANADIAN	17290	742	36.9	37.2	20.1	4.7	1.1	32145	36831	18	38	628	40.5	32.2	21.3	5.4	0.6	58824
74426	CHECOTAH	20620	5162	41.8	28.7	20.9	5.2	3.5	30665	37006	14	27	4025	34.5	29.7	26.5	8.2	1.1	68754
74427	COOKSON	18025	800	44.3	32.0	19.0	2.6	2.1	28985	33657	10	18	676	30.8	30.8	29.7	6.7	2.1	76308
74428	COUNCIL HILL	17718	410	40.7	28.8	26.1	3.4	1.0	31643	38517	17	35	340	39.1	29.7	27.1	1.8	2.4	57872
74429	COWETA	19204	4509	23.3	32.8	36.3	6.2	1.4	45356	51641	62	89	3445	15.3	30.7	41.8	11.2	1.0	94964
74432	EUFAULA	19202	2289	46.7	28.0	17.0	4.4	3.9	27175	32778	7	11	1766	43.0	24.0	27.2	4.5	1.3	61000
74434	FORT GIBSON	18654	2834	30.7	29.2	30.9	6.8	2.5	40965	49058	50	81	2209	19.5	33.1	35.7	10.9	0.8	86559
74435	GORE	18940	583	39.1	34.1	18.7	5.3	2.7	34237	40248	25	52	481	29.7	39.3	23.9	6.4	0.6	71357
74436	HASKELL	16455	1356	37.2	34.1	23.8	3.0	1.8	34248	40764	25	52	1067	44.3	29.0	19.6	4.5	2.6	56050
74437	HENRYETTA	14837	4813	44.4	29.9	20.7	4.6	0.5	28648	33820	10	17	3475	48.6	30.7	16.1	4.1	0.4	51746
74440	HOYT	14101	61	42.6	32.8	21.3	3.3	0.0	28568	32305	10	16	51	43.1	33.3	19.6	3.9	0.0	58750
74441	HULBERT	16014	2281	37.1	33.3	24.4	4.0	1.3	33945	39864	24	51	1848	32.9	32.6	26.9	7.1	0.5	70485
74442	INDIANOLA	18175	972	33.4	34.0	25.2	5.7	1.8	35970	42481	31	62	836	38.0	29.9	24.6	6.5	1.0	66567
74445	MORRIS	16818	1265	33.3	32.0	27.3	5.6	1.8	36882	44317	35	68	1005	30.3	33.6	28.7	6.8	0.7	72880
74447	OKMULGEE	16885	7153	43.4	29.9	20.6	4.2	1.9	30021	35432	12	23	4588	43.5	27.9	20.8	7.2	0.6	57673
74450	OKTAHA	17467	782	33.3	30.3	29.3	5.5	1.7	37195	44326	36	69	664	38.9	24.0	25.6	9.5	2.1	71176
74451	PARK HILL	16250	1685	40.4	28.8	26.5	2.8	1.6	31259	36846	16	32	1376	30.2	33.7	24.1	10.3	1.7	73103
74452	PEGGS	15061	593	37.3	35.8	22.3	3.0	1.7	33062	38637	21	45	490	42.5	23.3	24.5	6.9	2.9	60667
74454	PORTER	17063	1252	37.1	29.0	26.1	6.9	0.9	36343	42803	33	64	1002	44.4	26.1	18.8	10.6	0.2	56914
74455	PORUM	15569	1293	50.6	27.0	18.4	2.9	1.1	24674	29092	4	6	1059	51.7	22.1	20.2	5.4	0.7	48098
74457	PROCTOR	13386	347	43.5	32.0	21.0	2.6	0.9	29046	33443	10	19	285	36.8	33.0	19.3	5.6	5.3	60714
74461	STIDHAM	21393	142	46.5	26.1	17.6	4.9	4.9	27586	32337	8	12	120	48.3	20.8	28.3	2.5	0.0	54000
74462	STIGLER	16936	2160	49.4	27.9	17.0	2.5	3.2	25345	29632	5	6	1567	39.3	34.0	17.7	7.0	2.0	61260
74463	TAFT	13222	216	45.4	30.6	17.6	3.2	3.2	29062	33508	10	19	156	36.5	32.1	25.0	3.9	2.6	66429
74464	TAHLEQUAH	15770	10055	44.6	28.9	20.5	4.1	1.9	29021	34436	10	18	5715	22.7	33.6	34.3	8.2	1.2	82112
74467	WAGONER	18681	6722	35.0	30.0	27.6	4.7	2.7	37209	43852	36	70	4826	33.6	32.0	26.2	7.9	0.5	70458
74469	WARNER	14609	924	42.4	28.3	25.7	3.6	0.1	30671	36965	14	27	654	44.7	29.1	20.6	5.7	0.0	56604
74470	WEBBERS FALLS	15934	539	45.3	31.0	18.9	3.2	1.7	28485	33185	10	16	432	49.5	28.9	18.1	3.5	0.0	50476
74471	WELLING	15977	1243	38.7	36.8	19.9	3.5	1.2	30964	36518	15	30	1005	34.7	36.5	19.6	7.9	1.3	67114
74472	WHITEFIELD	16163	120	42.5	32.5	21.7	2.5	0.8	28951	34368	10	18	101	42.6	32.7	18.8	5.9	0.0	59375
74501	MCALESTER	18379	10809	38.8	30.1	23.5	5.2	2.4	33935	39889	24	50	7618	32.3	33.3	25.1	8.4	1.0	69069
74523	ANTLERS	15021	2519	50.8	29.5	15.4	2.4	2.0	24525	28443	4	5	1896	43.4	32.3	17.7	5.5	1.1	57241
74525	ATOKA	14021	3482	47.0	30.4	18.0	2.8	1.9	26624	30350	7	9	2599	41.1	35.1	17.0	6.0	0.8	61906
74528	BLANCO	15909	99	40.4	31.3	25.3	3.0	0.0	30720	36406	14	27	81	42.0	30.9	14.8	12.4	0.0	58125
74531	CALVIN	15163	422	43.1	29.6	23.5	3.6	0.2	30000	35356	12	23	343	47.2	23.6	23.3	5.5	0.3	54318
74533	CANEY	16872	535	39.4	34.8	20.0	3.0	2.8	30889	35916	15	29	449	48.6	30.3	17.4	3.6	0.2	51970
74534	CENTRAHOMA	15177	174	47.7	24.1	23.0	2.9	2.3	26642	30000	7	9	143	49.0	27.3	16.1	7.0	0.7	51667
74536	CLAYTON	15299	751	52.9	27.2	14.7	2.8	2.5	23123	26990	3	3	563	55.6	25.6	16.0	2.3	0.5	44569
74538	COALGATE	13196	1661	48.1	33.5	15.2	2.5	0.6	25961	29604	6	8	1180	54.7	31.2	9.0	3.0	2.2	46893
74540	DAISY	23676	70	37.1	32.9	24.3	5.7	0.0	31927	36502	18	36	60	36.7	28.3	23.3	11.7	0.0	65000
74543	FINLEY	19897	96	40.6	32.3	21.9	2.1	3.1	31960	37339	18	36	81	48.2	18.5	19.8	8.6	4.9	53750
74547	HARTSHORNE	16029	1975	42.5	32.3	21.1	3.3	0.7	30230	35660	13	24	1507	43.5	34.1	19.1	2.4	0.9	55636
74549	HONOBIA	13331	122	52.5	28.7	15.6	2.5	0.8	23548	28212	4	4	103	53.4	29.1	13.6	3.9	0.0	46500
74552	KINTA	16485	1194	40.1	34.4	20.6	2.9	2.0	30783	35904	14	28	999	40.5	31.1	20.7	7.1	0.5	62363
74553	KIOWA	18041	528	40.3	34.3	21.8	2.5	1.1	31192	36406	15	31	432	50.5	25.9	16.7	6.5	0.5	49535
74555	LANE	16064	423	47.5	30.3	17.7	3.3	1.2	26280	30077	6	8	344	37.8	33.4	20.9	6.1	1.7	69600
74557	MOYERS	13824	65	52.3	26.2	16.9	1.5	3.1	23554	29036	4	4	55	47.3	29.1	21.8	1.8	0.0	55000
74558	NASHOBA	13730	246	53.7	26.4	16.7	2.4	0.8	22951	27051	3	3	201	53.7	28.9	12.4	4.0	1.0	46875
74560	PITTSBURG	14942	205	39.0	31.7	25.4	2.9	1.0	31276	36557	16	33	167	41.9	32.3	14.4	11.4	0.0	58438
74561	QUINTON	17140	2075	45.2	28.3	21.8	3.1	1.5	28281	32952	9	14	1696	51.3	26.2	15.5	6.1	0.8	48878
74562	RATTAN	16269	657	41.4	34.9	18.4	4.1	1.2	29948	34936	12	22	545	43.9	27.9	18.2	7.5	2.6	57791
74563	RED OAK	15706	866	44.1	27.6	21.9	4.9	1.5	28847	35217	10	18	677	47.1	26.7	19.7	3.8	2.7	53611
74567	SNOW	19331	135	40.0	33.3	21.5	3.0	2.2	32064	35998	18	38	114	49.1	19.3	19.3	7.9	4.4	52000
74569	STRINGTOWN	15308	233	44.2	35.2	15.0	3.0	2.6	28178	31558	9	14	193	52.3	28.0	16.1	3.1	0.5	47000
74570	STUART	19178	318	46.9	25.5	20.4	4.1	3.1	27186	32935	7	11	268	35.1	27.6	23.1	12.7	1.5	72000
	OKLAHOMA	21077		31.9	30.4	27.2	7.1	3.4	38589	46268				26.7	29.5	32.0	10.2	1.6	81000
	UNITED STATES	25866		24.7	27.1	30.8	10.9	6.5	48124	56710				10.9	15.0	33.7	30.1	10.4	145905

# ZIP CODE POST OFFICE NAME	Auto Loan	Home Loan	Invest-ments	Retire-ment Plans	Home Repair	Lawn & Garden	Comput-ers & Hard-ware	Major Appli-ances	TV, Radio, Sound Equip-ment	Furni-ture	Dine out/ Carry out	Sports Equip-ment	Fees & Tickets	Toys & Games	Travel	Cable TV	Apparel & Services	Auto Repairs	Health Insur-ance	Pets & Supplies
74133 TULSA	106	109	121	116	106	110	110	107	105	112	133	126	111	130	107	100	130	108	97	118
74134 TULSA	79	75	82	81	72	74	80	77	77	82	98	92	78	93	75	72	96	80	68	85
74135 TULSA	76	78	93	80	77	83	83	79	81	81	102	94	83	101	82	80	100	82	77	87
74136 TULSA	92	91	110	95	89	96	98	94	96	98	121	112	97	117	95	92	118	98	89	104
74137 TULSA	172	204	242	208	200	208	191	186	179	192	226	217	204	231	194	175	226	184	171	205
74145 TULSA	74	76	86	77	75	81	78	76	77	78	96	89	79	96	77	76	94	77	74	85
74146 TULSA	65	59	66	63	58	62	68	64	67	66	84	78	65	81	64	63	81	68	60	71
74171 TULSA	133	124	119	118	131	155	115	131	121	123	151	128	116	125	125	130	141	127	153	149
74301 VINITA	79	58	35	55	65	75	61	70	69	59	81	81	53	78	61	73	74	70	84	90
74330 ADAIR	86	72	51	69	77	84	68	77	74	68	89	92	65	90	70	76	84	75	85	100
74331 AFTON	91	71	47	65	79	90	69	81	78	67	92	95	61	90	72	83	85	80	96	109
74332 BIG CABIN	96	76	50	72	84	91	73	85	80	73	96	102	67	95	75	83	90	84	96	113
74333 BLUEJACKET	87	59	28	51	67	76	57	71	68	58	80	84	48	76	58	73	73	70	86	100
74337 CHOUTEAU	73	60	44	58	64	71	59	66	64	59	78	77	56	77	60	66	73	65	73	83
74338 COLCORD	75	51	23	44	57	66	49	61	59	50	69	73	41	65	50	63	63	60	75	87
74339 COMMERCE	50	42	40	41	43	50	48	48	52	46	63	56	45	61	47	53	60	50	53	55
74342 EUCHA	69	52	34	47	59	66	50	60	57	50	68	71	45	66	53	61	63	59	71	82
74343 FAIRLAND	68	49	29	47	56	65	51	60	58	50	68	70	45	66	52	61	62	60	72	79
74344 GROVE	73	61	48	56	66	77	59	68	65	60	78	73	56	71	62	69	73	67	81	84
74346 JAY	66	52	40	49	56	63	54	59	60	53	72	69	50	70	54	62	67	60	67	75
74347 KANSAS	76	51	23	44	58	66	49	61	59	50	69	73	42	66	50	64	63	61	76	87
74352 LOCUST GROVE	73	49	22	42	56	64	47	59	57	48	67	71	40	64	48	62	61	59	73	84
74354 MIAMI	70	59	48	57	63	72	62	67	67	60	80	76	58	79	62	70	75	67	76	80
74358 NORTH MIAMI	58	49	38	49	52	58	51	54	54	50	65	62	48	64	50	55	61	53	59	64
74359 OAKS	73	49	22	42	56	64	47	59	57	48	67	71	40	63	48	62	61	59	73	84
74360 PICHER	58	40	21	36	45	52	39	48	46	40	55	57	34	52	40	50	50	47	58	66
74361 PRYOR	80	69	54	66	73	82	69	75	74	68	89	86	66	89	70	76	84	73	83	91
74363 QUAPAW	67	54	36	50	58	64	51	59	56	51	68	70	48	67	52	59	63	57	66	78
74364 ROSE	76	51	23	44	58	67	49	62	60	50	70	74	42	66	50	64	64	61	76	88
74365 SALINA	79	53	24	46	60	69	51	64	61	52	72	76	43	68	52	66	66	63	78	90
74366 SPAVINAW	70	48	24	42	55	63	46	58	55	47	65	69	40	62	48	59	59	57	70	81
74367 STRANG	82	60	35	53	68	77	57	70	67	57	79	83	50	76	60	71	72	69	84	97
74368 TWIN OAKS	73	49	22	42	56	64	47	59	57	48	67	71	40	63	48	62	61	59	73	84
74369 WELCH	77	55	32	53	63	73	57	68	65	56	77	79	50	74	58	69	70	67	81	89
74370 WYANDOTTE	69	54	34	49	59	66	51	60	57	51	68	71	46	67	53	60	63	59	70	81
74401 MUSKOGEE	65	52	48	50	55	64	58	61	63	57	77	69	54	73	57	66	72	62	69	73
74403 MUSKOGEE	69	64	60	63	66	73	66	68	68	64	84	78	64	84	66	70	80	68	72	79
74421 BEGGS	79	65	45	61	68	74	63	71	68	64	82	82	58	78	63	69	77	70	77	88
74422 BOYNTON	76	57	37	54	63	73	60	68	68	58	80	78	54	76	60	71	73	67	80	85
74423 BRAGGS	74	49	22	43	56	65	48	60	58	49	68	71	41	64	49	62	61	59	74	85
74425 CANADIAN	70	53	34	49	61	68	51	62	58	50	68	73	45	67	54	62	63	61	73	85
74426 CHECOTAH	83	62	40	58	70	81	63	74	72	62	85	85	56	82	65	76	78	73	88	96
74427 COOKSON	69	52	32	46	58	66	49	60	57	49	67	70	43	65	52	61	62	59	71	83
74428 COUNCIL HILL	81	56	28	50	63	73	56	68	66	56	78	80	48	73	56	71	71	67	83	93
74429 COWETA	78	74	66	73	75	80	72	75	74	72	91	89	71	92	72	74	87	74	77	90
74432 EUFAULA	72	55	40	52	60	70	58	65	65	56	77	75	52	75	59	69	71	65	77	82
74434 FORT GIBSON	82	70	52	67	73	81	68	75	73	68	88	87	65	87	68	74	83	74	81	93
74435 GORE	86	58	26	50	65	75	56	70	67	57	79	83	47	75	57	72	72	69	86	99
74436 HASKELL	76	54	31	50	60	70	56	65	64	55	76	76	49	72	56	68	69	65	78	86
74437 HENRYETTA	60	48	35	45	52	60	49	55	54	48	65	63	46	63	50	57	61	54	63	69
74440 HOYT	71	48	22	41	54	62	46	58	56	47	65	69	39	62	47	60	59	57	71	82
74441 HULBERT	75	54	30	49	60	68	53	63	61	54	73	75	47	69	54	65	67	63	75	85
74442 INDIANOLA	82	59	33	56	67	77	60	71	68	58	80	84	52	78	61	72	73	71	85	96
74445 MORRIS	74	64	48	62	67	73	63	68	66	63	80	79	59	79	63	67	76	68	73	84
74447 OKMULGEE	63	51	44	49	54	63	56	59	61	54	74	67	52	71	55	63	69	60	67	70
74450 OKTAHA	91	61	28	53	69	80	59	74	71	60	84	88	50	79	60	77	76	73	91	105
74451 PARK HILL	70	53	33	47	59	66	50	61	57	51	68	71	45	66	52	61	63	60	71	83
74452 PEGGS	76	51	23	44	58	67	49	62	60	50	70	74	42	66	50	64	64	61	76	88
74454 PORTER	79	59	34	53	65	73	56	67	64	56	76	80	50	74	58	68	71	66	79	92
74455 PORUM	70	48	24	42	55	63	46	58	55	47	65	69	40	62	48	60	59	57	71	81
74457 PROCTOR	70	47	21	40	53	61	45	56	54	46	64	67	38	60	46	58	58	56	69	80
74461 STIDHAM	83	65	45	59	74	83	62	74	70	61	83	87	55	82	66	74	77	73	88	102
74462 STIGLER	69	53	35	51	58	68	56	63	62	54	74	72	50	71	56	65	68	62	74	78
74463 TAFT	0	0	0	0	0	0	0	0	0	0	0	0	0	0	0	0	0	0	0	0
74464 TAHLEQUAH	59	49	47	50	51	56	56	56	58	54	71	66	52	68	53	57	67	58	57	65
74467 WAGONER	76	62	46	58	66	75	62	69	68	61	81	80	57	80	62	70	76	68	78	87
74469 WARNER	62	49	33	47	53	61	51	56	56	49	67	65	47	65	51	59	62	56	66	70
74470 WEBBERS FALLS	76	51	23	44	58	67	49	62	59	50	70	74	42	66	50	64	63	61	76	87
74471 WELLING	78	56	31	50	62	69	54	65	62	56	74	77	48	70	55	66	69	64	76	88
74472 WHITEFIELD	71	47	21	41	54	62	46	57	55	47	65	68	39	61	47	59	59	57	70	81
74501 MCALESTER	70	60	49	58	63	72	61	66	66	60	79	76	58	78	62	68	74	66	74	80
74523 ANTLERS	63	45	25	41	50	58	46	54	54	45	63	62	41	60	46	57	58	54	66	71
74525 ATOKA	61	46	31	43	50	58	48	54	54	47	64	63	43	61	48	57	59	54	64	68
74528 BLANCO	73	49	22	42	55	64	47	59	57	48	67	70	40	63	48	61	61	58	73	84
74531 CALVIN	65	47	28	45	53	61	50	57	56	48	66	66	43	63	50	59	60	57	68	74
74533 CANEY	81	54	25	47	62	71	52	66	63	53	74	78	45	70	53	68	68	65	81	93
74534 CENTRAHOMA	62	46	31	44	51	61	51	56	57	49	68	63	46	64	51	61	62	56	68	68
74536 CLAYTON	57	42	28	41	46	56	47	52	53	45	62	58	42	58	47	56	57	52	62	62
74538 COALGATE	55	39	23	37	44	52	42	48	48	41	56	55	37	53	42	51	51	48	58	61
74540 DAISY	0	0	0	0	0	0	0	0	0	0	0	0	0	0	0	0	0	0	0	0
74543 FINLEY	73	55	36	52	60	72	60	66	68	57	80	74	54	75	60	71	73	66	80	80
74547 HARTSHORNE	63	47	31	45	51	62	52	57	58	49	69	64	46	65	52	62	63	57	69	69
74549 HONOBIA	56	40	22	36	45	52	41	48	48	41	57	56	36	53	42	51	51	48	59	64
74552 KINTA	76	51	23	44	58	67	49	62	60	50	70	74	42	66	50	64	64	61	76	88
74553 KIOWA	71	53	34	50	58	69	58	64	65	55	77	73	52	73	57	69	70	64	77	79
74555 LANE	62	44	25	41	49	58	46	54	53	45	63	62	41	59	46	57	57	53	65	69
74557 MOYERS	65	44	20	38	50	57	42	53	51	43	60	63	36	56	43	55	54	52	65	75
74558 NASHOBA	54	41	27	39	45	53	45	50	51	43	59	56	40	56	44	53	54	50	59	60
74560 PITTSBURG	73	49	23	43	56	64	48	60	58	49	68	71	41	64	49	62	62	59	73	84
74561 QUINTON	67	50	31	45	56	64	49	58	56	48	66	68	43	64	51	60	61	58	70	79
74562 RATTAN	72	50	26	45	56	65	50	61	59	50	70	71	44	66	51	64	64	60	74	82
74563 RED OAK	69	49	28	45	55	64	51	60	59	50	70	69	45	66	51	63	63	59	72	78
74567 SNOW	72	54	36	52	59	71	60	66	67	57	79	74	53	75	59	71	72	66	79	80
74569 STRINGTOWN	67	45	20	38	51	58	43	54	52	44	61	64	37	58	44	56	55	53	66	76
74570 STUART	74	56	37	54	61	73	62	68	69	59	80	76	55	77	61	73	74	68	81	82
OKLAHOMA	79	71	65	70	73	80	73	76	76	72	93	88	70	91	72	76	88	76	79	89
UNITED STATES	100	100	100	100	100	100	100	100	100	100	100	100	100	100	100	100	100	100	100	100

# POST OFFICE NAME	COUNTY FIPS CODE	POPULATION 2000	2004	2009	2000-2004 ANNUAL RATE % Rate	State Centile	HOUSEHOLDS 2000	2004	2009	% Annual Rate 2000-2004	2004 Average HH Size	FAMILIES 2000	2004	% Annual Rate 2000-2004
74571 TALIHINA	079	2962	3014	3116	0.4	57	1095	1124	1172	0.6	2.63	772	792	0.6
74572 TUPELO	029	1509	1552	1599	0.7	67	556	572	590	0.7	2.71	418	429	0.6
74574 TUSKAHOMA	077	2828	2843	2851	0.1	45	1099	1117	1131	0.4	2.43	799	810	0.3
74576 WARDVILLE	005	362	365	367	0.2	48	145	149	153	0.6	1.06	105	27	-27.4
74577 WHITESBORO	079	173	174	179	0.1	46	68	69	71	0.3	2.52	49	50	0.5
74578 WILBURTON	077	6016	6005	6008	0.0	37	2174	2187	2207	0.1	2.52	1553	1558	0.1
74601 PONCA CITY	071	20467	20528	20729	0.1	43	8344	8386	8483	0.1	2.42	5384	5383	0.0
74604 PONCA CITY	113	13291	13932	14422	1.1	82	5195	5478	5698	1.3	2.48	3930	4120	1.1
74630 BILLINGS	103	848	837	837	-0.3	25	277	276	279	-0.1	2.51	204	202	-0.2
74631 BLACKWELL	071	8355	8102	8094	-0.7	10	3330	3233	3237	-0.7	2.47	2302	2225	-0.8
74632 BRAMAN	071	602	583	582	-0.8	9	251	245	246	-0.6	2.38	172	167	-0.7
74633 BURBANK	113	455	509	545	2.7	96	194	219	236	2.9	2.32	140	157	2.7
74636 DEER CREEK	053	256	255	252	-0.1	35	100	99	98	-0.2	2.58	70	69	-0.3
74637 FAIRFAX	113	2138	2052	2048	-1.0	5	876	844	846	-0.9	2.38	587	559	-1.1
74640 HUNTER	047	449	432	424	-0.9	6	186	180	177	-0.8	2.40	139	133	-1.0
74641 KAW CITY	071	553	677	756	4.9	100	236	291	326	5.1	2.33	177	217	4.9
74643 LAMONT	053	625	622	615	-0.1	34	253	252	249	-0.1	2.47	176	175	-0.1
74644 MARLAND	103	571	553	552	-0.8	9	201	198	199	-0.4	2.79	155	152	-0.5
74646 NARDIN	071	221	210	209	-1.2	2	85	81	81	-1.1	2.59	69	66	-1.0
74647 NEWKIRK	071	3728	4112	4361	2.3	95	1466	1628	1736	2.5	2.48	1045	1155	2.4
74650 RALSTON	117	685	682	706	-0.1	35	279	279	290	0.0	2.44	206	205	-0.1
74651 RED ROCK	103	717	695	693	-0.7	10	245	241	243	-0.4	2.88	188	185	-0.4
74652 SHIDLER	113	1057	1039	1046	-0.4	23	459	457	464	-0.1	2.27	323	320	-0.2
74653 TONKAWA	071	3950	3871	3877	-0.5	17	1440	1407	1411	-0.5	2.50	983	956	-0.7
74701 DURANT	013	18636	19873	21444	1.5	89	7364	7886	8552	1.6	2.42	4796	5123	1.6
74723 BENNINGTON	013	1676	1724	1819	0.7	67	634	656	697	0.8	2.63	504	520	0.7
74724 BETHEL	089	1663	1698	1720	0.5	61	618	640	656	0.8	2.65	470	486	0.8
74726 BOKCHITO	013	2223	2282	2407	0.6	65	896	922	976	0.7	2.48	642	659	0.6
74727 BOSWELL	023	2158	2158	2161	0.0	40	871	880	890	0.2	2.45	607	611	0.2
74728 BROKEN BOW	089	10775	10750	10756	-0.1	37	4097	4138	4187	0.2	2.56	2978	3000	0.2
74729 CADDO	013	2252	2319	2444	0.7	68	864	894	948	0.8	2.55	622	642	0.8
74730 CALERA	013	3323	3473	3696	1.0	80	1270	1335	1430	1.2	2.56	935	980	1.1
74731 CARTWRIGHT	013	1266	1330	1421	1.2	83	531	561	602	1.3	2.37	368	388	1.3
74733 COLBERT	013	3159	3314	3536	1.1	83	1228	1295	1388	1.3	2.53	874	919	1.2
74734 EAGLETOWN	089	1133	1118	1114	-0.3	25	454	454	458	0.0	2.46	328	327	-0.1
74735 FORT TOWSON	023	2376	2396	2410	0.2	49	943	958	971	0.4	2.50	694	703	0.3
74736 GARVIN	089	817	823	825	0.2	47	314	320	325	0.5	2.57	242	247	0.5
74738 GRANT	023	727	726	726	0.0	38	282	285	288	0.3	2.55	215	216	0.1
74740 HAWORTH	089	1729	1698	1691	-0.4	21	665	659	662	-0.2	2.58	469	462	-0.4
74741 HENDRIX	013	1708	1756	1854	0.7	67	662	684	726	0.8	2.57	498	513	0.7
74743 HUGO	023	8553	8544	8570	0.0	38	3487	3518	3566	0.2	2.36	2314	2326	0.1
74745 IDABEL	089	10413	10518	10614	0.2	50	4064	4146	4228	0.5	2.46	2786	2833	0.4
74748 KENEFIC	069	537	549	561	0.5	62	216	222	229	0.7	2.47	161	165	0.6
74754 RINGOLD	089	134	134	134	0.0	40	58	59	59	0.4	2.27	45	46	0.5
74755 RUFE	089	274	286	292	1.0	79	113	119	123	1.2	2.40	91	95	1.0
74756 SAWYER	023	447	461	469	0.7	70	180	187	192	0.9	2.47	137	142	1.0
74759 SOPER	023	950	952	954	0.1	42	397	403	407	0.4	2.36	273	276	0.3
74760 SPENCERVILLE	023	298	307	312	0.7	69	115	119	122	0.8	2.58	87	90	0.8
74764 VALLIANT	089	4326	4399	4445	0.4	56	1651	1692	1725	0.6	2.57	1234	1261	0.5
74766 WRIGHT CITY	089	1828	1811	1806	-0.2	30	667	670	677	0.1	2.70	513	515	0.1
74801 SHAWNEE	125	22009	22549	23218	0.6	64	8749	8999	9309	0.7	2.47	6005	6169	0.6
74804 SHAWNEE	125	19221	20405	21378	1.4	88	7131	7652	8087	1.7	2.46	5065	5402	1.5
74820 ADA	123	25768	26076	26539	0.3	51	10489	10649	10878	0.4	2.36	6772	6851	0.3
74824 AGRA	081	1525	1566	1612	0.6	66	554	573	594	0.8	2.73	448	462	0.7
74825 ALLEN	123	4998	5159	5290	0.8	72	1807	1884	1947	1.0	2.65	1381	1432	0.9
74826 ASHER	125	942	933	947	-0.2	29	366	364	372	-0.1	2.56	283	281	-0.2
74827 ATWOOD	063	688	707	732	0.6	67	289	298	310	0.7	2.37	207	214	0.8
74829 BOLEY	107	1505	1476	1471	-0.5	18	480	495	529	0.7	2.57	367	377	0.6
74831 BYARS	087	1244	1270	1345	0.5	61	269	279	290	0.9	2.55	200	207	0.8
74832 CARNEY	081	691	712	734	0.7	70	223	220	220	-0.3	2.62	171	168	-0.4
74833 CASTLE	107	592	581	578	-0.4	20	223	220	220	-0.3	2.62	171	168	-0.4
74834 CHANDLER	081	6091	6544	6940	1.7	91	2351	2538	2708	1.8	2.53	1718	1848	1.7
74839 DUSTIN	063	863	858	882	-0.1	33	337	337	347	0.0	2.54	250	250	0.0
74840 EARLSBORO	125	721	769	806	1.5	90	253	272	287	1.7	2.83	213	228	1.6
74842 FITTSTOWN	123	706	699	702	-0.2	29	276	274	276	-0.2	2.55	220	217	-0.3
74843 FITZHUGH	123	207	205	206	-0.2	29	76	75	76	-0.3	2.73	61	60	-0.4
74845 HANNA	091	520	507	520	-0.6	14	192	188	195	-0.5	2.70	148	144	-0.6
74848 HOLDENVILLE	063	8329	8600	8953	0.8	72	2974	3086	3235	0.9	2.40	2021	2089	0.8
74849 KONAWA	133	2977	3012	3035	0.3	51	1107	1124	1137	0.4	2.61	797	806	0.3
74850 LAMAR	063	277	280	287	0.3	51	110	112	115	0.4	2.50	87	88	0.3
74851 MCLOUD	125	7864	7989	8220	0.4	55	2520	2588	2690	0.6	2.74	2019	2069	0.6
74852 MACOMB	125	1029	1055	1081	0.6	64	369	381	393	0.8	2.77	300	310	0.8
74854 MAUD	125	4130	4163	4219	0.2	48	1601	1625	1657	0.4	2.54	1179	1194	0.3
74855 MEEKER	081	4915	5073	5235	0.8	72	1803	1882	1961	1.0	2.66	1414	1471	0.9
74856 MILL CREEK	069	1446	1480	1517	0.6	63	545	559	575	0.6	2.65	419	429	0.6
74857 NEWALLA	027	7555	8309	9004	2.3	94	2661	2969	3253	2.6	2.80	2181	2419	2.5
74859 OKEMAH	107	5763	5887	6000	0.5	61	2290	2355	2418	0.7	2.45	1558	1594	0.5
74860 PADEN	107	1567	1647	1691	1.2	84	591	628	651	1.4	2.54	451	477	1.3
74864 PRAGUE	081	4456	4419	4499	-0.2	30	1709	1706	1751	0.0	2.47	1250	1244	-0.1
74865 ROFF	123	1450	1432	1436	-0.3	26	548	543	546	-0.2	2.64	416	410	-0.3
74867 SASAKWA	133	730	705	700	-0.8	8	297	289	289	-0.6	2.44	211	205	-0.7
74868 SEMINOLE	133	11633	12007	12327	0.8	72	4530	4691	4834	0.8	2.53	3238	3343	0.8
74869 SPARKS	081	314	329	342	1.1	82	120	127	134	1.3	2.59	96	101	1.2
74871 STONEWALL	123	2322	2309	2320	-0.1	33	899	898	905	0.0	2.57	669	665	-0.1
74872 STRATFORD	049	3098	3183	3273	0.6	67	1223	1259	1299	0.7	2.50	867	889	0.6
74873 TECUMSEH	125	10898	11261	11602	0.8	73	4065	4226	4378	0.9	2.62	3036	3149	0.9
74875 TRYON	081	1553	1578	1616	0.4	56	600	616	635	0.6	2.56	433	443	0.5
74878 WANETTE	125	1431	1459	1491	0.5	59	553	565	579	0.5	2.58	435	443	0.4
74880 WELEETKA	107	2389	2326	2314	-0.6	14	901	883	884	-0.5	2.53	621	608	-0.5
74881 WELLSTON	081	3702	3861	4009	1.0	78	1394	1469	1539	1.2	2.63	1055	1110	1.2
74883 WETUMKA	063	2207	2293	2424	0.9	76	885	931	994	1.2	2.34	575	604	1.2
74884 WEWOKA	133	7475	7331	7305	-0.5	18	2816	2772	2771	-0.4	2.53	1945	1908	-0.5
74901 ARKOMA	079	2186	2316	2455	1.4	87	879	941	1005	1.6	2.41	599	640	1.6
74902 POCOLA	079	4491	4983	5420	2.5	95	1695	1900	2082	2.7	2.59	1311	1466	2.7
74930 BOKOSHE	079	3713	3750	3896	0.2	50	1401	1420	1483	0.2	2.64	1049	1060	0.3
OKLAHOMA					0.8					1.0	2.48			0.9
UNITED STATES					1.2					1.3	2.58			1.1

# ZIP CODE	POST OFFICE NAME	RACE (%) White 2000	White 2004	Black 2000	Black 2004	Asian/Pacific 2000	Asian/Pacific 2004	% Hispanic Origin 2000	% Hispanic Origin 2004	2004 AGE DISTRIBUTION (%) 0-4	5-9	10-14	15-19	20-24	25-44	45-64	65-84	85+	18+	MEDIAN AGE 2004	% 2004 Males	% 2004 Females
74571	TALIHINA	64.5	63.3	0.7	0.7	0.1	0.1	1.2	1.4	6.4	6.3	6.6	7.2	7.4	22.8	25.3	15.9	2.1	76.1	40.1	48.8	51.2
74572	TUPELO	74.9	73.7	0.1	0.1	0.2	0.2	2.1	2.2	8.1	7.9	7.6	6.8	5.9	24.8	24.3	12.8	1.8	71.8	36.3	49.5	50.5
74574	TUSKAHOMA	69.7	69.4	1.2	1.3	0.1	0.1	1.6	1.7	5.8	6.1	6.7	6.2	6.1	22.0	26.3	19.0	1.9	77.5	43.2	51.4	48.6
74576	WARDVILLE	66.3	64.7	15.5	16.2	0.0	0.0	3.6	4.4	2.5	2.5	2.5	4.4	9.3	46.0	25.5	6.9	0.6	90.4	37.7	78.1	21.9
74577	WHITESBORO	75.7	74.7	0.0	0.0	0.0	0.0	1.2	1.2	6.3	6.3	6.3	6.3	6.9	24.1	25.9	16.1	1.7	77.0	41.1	47.1	52.9
74578	WILBURTON	74.5	74.4	1.3	1.3	0.2	0.2	1.8	1.8	7.7	6.9	6.7	8.8	9.9	23.9	21.5	12.7	1.9	75.1	34.0	48.0	52.0
74601	PONCA CITY	79.4	78.2	3.3	3.4	0.5	0.7	5.0	5.7	8.2	7.1	7.1	6.9	8.0	25.9	22.5	12.2	2.1	73.5	35.4	48.3	51.7
74604	PONCA CITY	89.8	88.7	1.1	1.2	0.8	1.0	2.1	2.4	5.4	5.8	6.9	7.0	5.6	20.1	29.2	17.0	3.1	77.5	44.5	49.0	51.0
74630	BILLINGS	90.9	90.2	0.2	0.2	0.0	0.0	2.0	2.3	5.6	5.7	6.6	6.3	4.9	23.1	30.6	15.4	1.8	78.3	43.6	49.3	50.7
74631	BLACKWELL	87.4	86.0	0.1	0.1	0.5	0.6	5.5	6.3	7.5	7.3	7.2	6.8	6.9	23.3	23.2	15.0	2.8	73.8	37.9	48.2	51.8
74632	BRAMAN	90.7	89.7	0.2	0.2	0.0	0.0	2.3	2.6	5.8	5.5	5.3	7.2	5.8	23.0	28.1	17.2	2.1	79.4	43.4	48.7	51.3
74633	BURBANK	79.6	78.8	0.0	0.0	0.2	0.4	0.7	0.6	3.9	4.9	6.9	6.3	4.1	24.6	31.8	16.1	1.4	80.4	44.6	49.5	50.5
74636	DEER CREEK	94.5	94.5	0.0	0.0	0.0	0.0	3.1	3.1	7.1	7.1	7.5	7.1	6.3	21.6	23.9	16.9	2.8	73.7	40.4	50.6	49.4
74637	FAIRFAX	66.8	65.4	1.1	1.2	0.5	0.7	1.7	1.9	6.3	5.9	7.0	7.5	6.2	21.6	24.7	17.6	3.3	75.9	42.0	46.8	53.2
74640	HUNTER	97.3	97.0	0.0	0.0	0.0	0.0	1.3	1.6	5.6	6.0	6.3	6.7	4.2	22.2	30.1	15.7	3.2	78.0	44.4	50.5	49.5
74641	KAW CITY	87.5	87.0	0.0	0.0	0.0	0.2	1.5	1.6	5.6	5.8	7.2	5.2	5.2	20.2	31.8	17.6	1.5	78.3	45.4	49.2	50.8
74643	LAMONT	94.4	94.4	0.0	0.0	0.0	0.0	3.0	3.1	6.8	6.8	7.6	6.9	6.3	21.4	24.6	16.9	2.9	74.4	41.0	49.5	50.5
74644	MARLAND	52.9	51.0	0.5	0.5	0.2	0.2	3.2	3.3	6.9	7.4	9.4	8.0	6.7	23.0	26.4	11.2	1.1	71.6	36.4	48.5	51.5
74646	NARDIN	91.0	90.0	0.0	0.0	0.5	0.5	1.4	1.0	5.7	6.2	6.7	7.1	5.2	22.9	28.1	16.2	1.9	76.7	43.0	50.5	49.5
74647	NEWKIRK	83.7	82.5	0.7	0.7	0.1	0.1	1.9	2.2	6.1	6.2	7.3	6.6	6.9	24.2	26.3	14.6	2.0	76.2	40.2	50.3	49.7
74650	RALSTON	80.6	79.9	0.3	0.3	0.4	0.4	1.3	1.6	4.7	5.3	7.3	7.2	5.6	22.0	29.2	16.0	2.8	78.3	43.7	51.5	48.5
74651	RED ROCK	53.0	50.9	0.6	0.6	0.1	0.3	3.1	3.3	6.8	7.5	9.2	7.8	6.8	23.2	26.6	11.2	1.0	71.9	36.6	48.6	51.4
74652	SHIDLER	82.1	81.0	0.0	0.0	0.4	0.5	2.3	2.4	6.1	5.8	5.7	6.6	7.0	23.1	25.6	17.7	2.4	78.6	41.7	49.1	50.9
74653	TONKAWA	83.4	82.3	0.7	0.8	0.3	0.4	6.2	7.1	6.5	7.1	7.6	10.2	9.7	22.8	21.7	12.0	2.4	75.2	33.3	50.2	49.8
74701	DURANT	79.8	78.6	1.3	1.3	0.8	0.9	3.1	3.4	6.9	6.3	6.4	7.6	10.4	26.8	21.2	12.0	2.5	76.7	33.1	48.4	51.6
74723	BENNINGTON	73.9	73.1	0.2	0.2	0.1	0.1	2.0	2.2	7.0	7.1	6.9	6.0	5.9	23.3	27.2	14.8	1.8	75.3	40.5	49.4	50.6
74724	BETHEL	71.2	70.1	0.2	0.2	0.0	0.0	2.2	2.5	7.1	7.1	6.8	6.4	6.2	25.7	26.2	13.3	1.2	75.1	38.1	51.5	48.5
74726	BOKCHITO	79.9	78.7	0.1	0.1	0.2	0.2	2.3	2.6	6.3	6.6	7.3	6.6	5.8	25.0	25.9	14.5	2.1	75.9	39.7	49.3	50.7
74727	BOSWELL	68.3	68.3	5.3	5.4	0.2	0.2	2.2	2.2	6.9	6.3	7.7	7.3	5.3	23.9	25.3	15.2	2.2	74.5	38.9	49.0	51.0
74728	BROKEN BOW	72.3	70.9	4.9	5.1	0.3	0.3	3.8	4.2	8.0	7.4	7.4	7.3	6.7	25.4	23.8	12.3	1.6	72.7	36.1	48.3	51.7
74729	CADDO	79.4	78.2	0.4	0.4	0.2	0.2	1.7	1.9	6.2	6.3	7.3	6.8	5.7	25.6	24.8	14.7	2.7	75.9	39.4	49.6	50.4
74730	CALERA	81.9	80.8	0.3	0.3	0.2	0.2	2.9	3.3	7.4	7.3	6.8	6.2	5.6	26.3	24.5	13.5	2.3	74.6	37.7	48.4	51.6
74731	CARTWRIGHT	85.8	84.7	1.0	1.0	0.2	0.2	2.9	3.3	6.2	6.6	6.8	6.2	5.9	25.6	28.3	13.4	1.1	76.5	40.2	50.6	49.4
74733	COLBERT	79.5	78.1	6.7	6.9	0.1	0.2	2.6	3.0	6.3	6.4	7.2	6.4	6.4	26.3	25.2	13.6	2.1	76.3	38.8	48.5	51.5
74734	EAGLETOWN	77.9	76.9	5.5	5.9	0.2	0.2	2.5	2.6	6.2	6.2	6.8	6.8	6.6	24.8	27.6	14.0	1.2	76.7	39.2	49.6	50.5
74735	FORT TOWSON	82.7	82.6	2.4	2.5	0.2	0.3	1.3	1.3	5.6	5.9	6.4	6.2	6.1	24.6	28.4	15.2	1.6	78.3	41.7	49.1	50.9
74736	GARVIN	81.0	80.1	4.2	4.4	0.2	0.4	2.0	2.2	6.0	6.2	7.8	6.6	5.6	25.5	27.2	14.0	1.2	75.8	39.7	49.1	50.9
74738	GRANT	68.0	67.8	13.6	13.8	0.1	0.1	1.4	1.4	5.4	5.9	8.7	7.9	5.4	24.7	27.8	13.1	1.2	75.1	40.1	48.8	51.2
74740	HAWORTH	71.7	69.9	19.2	20.3	0.1	0.1	1.3	1.4	6.0	6.2	8.2	7.2	6.3	25.0	26.2	12.7	2.1	75.2	38.4	48.1	51.9
74741	HENDRIX	77.2	76.0	1.9	2.0	0.4	0.5	1.4	1.6	7.1	7.2	7.9	7.2	5.7	26.5	23.7	13.4	1.4	73.4	37.2	49.9	50.1
74743	HUGO	63.5	63.3	16.0	16.2	0.2	0.2	1.7	1.7	6.9	6.6	7.0	7.1	6.3	24.1	24.0	15.0	3.1	75.3	39.0	46.6	53.4
74745	IDABEL	63.2	62.0	19.3	19.7	0.4	0.5	4.0	4.4	7.8	7.5	7.7	6.8	6.7	25.3	23.9	12.2	2.1	72.8	36.2	47.4	52.6
74748	KENEFIC	80.8	79.6	0.6	0.6	0.2	0.2	2.4	2.9	6.0	6.4	7.1	6.4	6.0	24.6	27.9	14.0	1.6	76.3	40.3	51.0	49.0
74754	RINGOLD	80.6	79.1	0.0	0.0	0.0	0.0	2.2	3.0	6.0	6.0	7.5	7.5	7.5	26.1	26.1	11.9	1.5	76.1	38.6	50.8	49.3
74755	RUFE	86.5	85.7	1.1	1.4	0.0	0.0	1.1	1.1	5.9	6.6	7.7	5.6	5.9	25.5	28.0	13.6	1.1	75.9	40.2	50.7	49.3
74756	SAWYER	80.1	80.0	3.1	3.5	0.0	0.0	1.3	1.3	6.1	6.1	7.2	6.5	6.1	26.3	27.1	13.2	1.5	76.4	40.4	49.9	50.1
74759	SOPER	72.0	72.1	1.5	1.5	0.0	0.0	1.0	1.1	5.9	6.4	7.0	6.2	5.8	24.9	25.7	15.7	2.4	76.9	40.8	48.1	51.9
74760	SPENCERVILLE	79.9	79.8	3.4	3.6	0.0	0.0	1.3	1.3	6.2	6.2	7.2	6.5	6.2	25.4	27.4	13.4	1.6	75.9	40.1	50.5	49.5
74764	VALLIANT	81.4	80.3	3.3	3.5	0.1	0.1	1.3	1.6	6.8	6.9	7.9	6.7	6.1	25.8	26.3	11.7	1.8	74.4	37.5	49.3	50.7
74766	WRIGHT CITY	64.1	62.8	3.8	4.0	0.0	0.0	2.1	2.4	7.3	7.2	7.6	7.4	6.8	25.7	25.1	11.7	1.2	73.3	36.5	49.1	50.9
74801	SHAWNEE	77.2	76.1	3.9	4.0	0.6	0.7	2.6	2.9	7.9	7.2	7.1	6.6	7.4	27.1	22.8	12.2	1.8	73.9	35.4	48.7	51.3
74804	SHAWNEE	81.5	80.3	2.3	2.4	1.3	1.6	2.4	2.7	6.7	6.6	6.4	8.0	10.3	25.4	22.1	12.4	2.2	77.0	34.2	49.0	51.1
74820	ADA	75.8	74.6	2.5	2.6	0.6	0.8	2.5	2.8	6.4	6.1	6.4	7.3	9.9	25.7	22.4	13.4	2.4	77.3	35.5	48.3	51.7
74824	AGRA	91.6	90.8	0.0	0.0	0.1	0.1	1.3	1.4	8.4	7.9	6.9	6.6	6.8	25.5	24.1	12.7	1.0	72.9	35.7	51.0	49.0
74825	ALLEN	72.6	71.3	0.9	0.9	0.1	0.2	2.1	2.4	6.2	6.4	7.5	7.5	7.0	27.5	25.1	11.1	1.7	75.1	37.3	49.2	50.8
74826	ASHER	80.7	79.5	0.0	0.0	0.0	0.0	2.8	3.1	6.5	6.8	7.1	6.4	5.7	26.6	26.3	13.1	1.6	75.7	38.7	51.0	49.0
74827	ATWOOD	82.0	80.8	0.0	0.0	0.6	0.6	2.2	2.6	7.1	7.2	7.1	5.9	5.2	24.9	26.2	14.4	2.0	75.3	39.1	52.2	47.8
74829	BOLEY	36.5	34.4	52.5	54.5	0.1	0.1	2.7	2.9	3.3	3.3	3.9	4.4	8.3	43.0	24.1	8.3	1.6	87.0	38.1	72.7	27.3
74831	BYARS	85.7	84.7	2.1	2.2	0.2	0.3	3.2	3.6	7.3	6.9	5.8	6.5	6.1	23.5	26.9	15.5	1.7	76.3	40.5	50.6	49.5
74832	CARNEY	89.0	88.1	1.2	1.3	0.0	0.0	1.0	1.3	7.4	7.6	8.6	7.2	5.6	25.7	26.0	11.2	0.7	71.9	37.8	50.4	49.6
74833	CASTLE	72.5	71.4	6.9	7.2	0.0	0.0	1.2	1.2	6.2	6.5	7.9	6.5	6.5	24.4	26.5	13.8	1.6	75.4	39.5	51.3	48.7
74834	CHANDLER	84.4	83.6	5.5	5.5	0.4	0.5	1.5	1.7	6.7	6.9	7.3	7.3	6.1	24.8	26.0	13.0	2.0	74.8	38.9	49.3	50.7
74839	DUSTIN	61.8	60.1	1.7	1.8	0.1	0.1	1.7	2.0	4.9	5.5	8.3	6.8	5.1	23.7	27.4	17.1	1.3	77.2	41.8	51.1	49.0
74840	EARLSBORO	78.2	77.2	5.8	6.0	0.4	0.5	2.1	2.2	6.5	6.5	7.4	7.3	6.2	25.1	27.1	13.0	0.9	75.0	39.4	49.3	50.7
74842	FITTSTOWN	81.2	79.8	0.0	0.0	0.1	0.1	1.7	2.2	6.7	6.9	7.3	5.7	5.7	25.5	27.3	13.7	1.1	75.4	39.8	48.5	51.5
74843	FITZHUGH	81.2	80.0	0.0	0.0	0.0	0.0	1.5	2.0	6.8	6.8	7.3	5.9	5.9	25.9	26.8	13.7	1.0	75.6	39.4	48.8	51.2
74845	HANNA	61.7	60.4	0.8	0.8	0.0	0.0	2.3	2.4	7.5	6.9	7.9	9.7	5.7	24.3	23.5	13.2	1.4	71.8	36.6	49.9	50.1
74848	HOLDENVILLE	72.9	71.6	6.3	6.4	0.3	0.4	2.7	3.0	5.9	6.0	5.8	5.8	7.1	28.4	23.0	14.5	3.4	78.8	39.1	52.8	47.2
74849	KONAWA	69.8	68.3	1.4	1.6	0.2	0.3	2.0	2.4	6.7	7.3	7.5	6.5	7.0	25.0	23.8	13.8	2.4	74.4	37.6	49.9	50.1
74850	LAMAR	81.6	81.1	0.4	0.4	0.0	0.0	2.2	2.9	5.0	5.7	6.4	6.4	6.1	22.1	29.3	17.5	1.4	78.6	43.9	49.6	50.4
74851	MCLOUD	80.4	79.2	3.9	4.0	0.7	0.9	2.7	3.1	6.1	6.2	6.8	6.7	6.9	31.9	25.4	9.1	1.0	76.9	36.5	44.3	55.7
74852	MACOMB	85.5	84.3	0.7	0.7	0.2	0.2	1.7	1.9	6.0	6.1	6.7	7.2	5.8	23.8	30.6	13.1	0.8	76.9	41.5	50.4	49.6
74854	MAUD	80.1	78.8	0.5	0.6	0.2	0.2	1.7	2.0	7.1	6.7	6.3	6.3	7.1	23.9	26.4	14.5	1.8	76.1	40.0	49.7	50.3
74855	MEEKER	87.9	87.0	0.8	0.9	0.2	0.2	1.4	1.5	6.5	6.7	7.4	7.1	6.3	26.4	26.0	12.0	1.6	74.8	38.1	49.5	50.5
74856	MILL CREEK	73.2	71.8	0.0	0.0	0.6	0.7	1.0	1.2	6.2	6.4	7.4	6.5	7.1	24.5	27.7	12.6	1.6	76.2	40.1	48.2	51.8
74857	NEWALLA	87.2	86.2	0.9	1.0	0.4	0.5	2.0	2.3	5.6	7.1	8.1	8.5	5.3	28.4	29.5	7.3	0.3	73.8	37.4	51.0	49.0
74859	OKEMAH	70.3	68.8	2.8	3.0	0.1	0.1	1.6	1.8	7.0	6.5	6.9	7.1	6.6	23.8	24.1	15.1	2.9	75.3	38.9	47.8	52.2
74860	PADEN	78.8	77.8	3.7	3.9	0.1	0.1	0.8	1.0	6.4	6.5	6.5	6.8	6.1	24.4	27.4	14.6	1.3	76.6	40.8	49.9	50.2
74864	PRAGUE	85.0	84.1	2.4	2.5	0.2	0.3	1.2	1.4	5.6	6.0	6.8	8.3	6.1	23.7	26.4	14.3	2.8	75.8	40.7	48.9	51.1
74865	ROFF	83.2	82.1	0.2	0.2	0.1	0.2	1.5	1.8	7.3	6.9	6.6	6.0	7.5	25.5	24.7	13.7	1.9	75.7	38.5	49.3	50.7
74867	SASAKWA	70.8	68.9	2.5	2.6	0.0	0.0	2.6	3.0	6.4	7.0	8.1	6.4	5.3	22.3	28.5	14.5	1.7	74.5	41.3	49.7	50.4
74868	SEMINOLE	76.0	75.0	3.0	3.1	0.3	0.3	2.3	2.6	7.1	6.6	6.6	7.0	7.3	24.0	24.9	13.9	2.6	75.7	38.3	48.2	51.8
74869	SPARKS	88.2	87.5	1.9	2.1	0.3	0.3	0.3	0.3	4.9	7.3	7.0	9.4	4.3	24.9	29.5	11.9	0.9	74.8	40.9	50.8	49.2
74871	STONEWALL	76.1	75.1	1.9	1.9	0.0	0.0	1.9	2.1	5.7	6.2	8.8	6.9	6.0	24.2	27.3	13.4	1.5	75.0	39.2	48.1	51.9
74872	STRATFORD	84.1	83.0	0.7	0.7	0.1	0.2	1.4	1.6	7.3	7.2	6.5	6.3	6.6	23.7	25.1	14.7	2.7	75.1	39.0	48.4	51.7
74873	TECUMSEH	81.3	80.1	2.0	2.0	0.3	0.3	1.9	2.1	6.5	6.6	7.6	7.6	6.7	25.6	25.1	12.5	1.7	74.4	37.6	49.2	50.8
74875	TRYON	86.7	86.1	0.5	0.6	0.1	0.1	1.6	1.7	6.5	6.8	7.8	6.7	6.3	25.9	25.5	13.5	1.0	74.8	38.9	51.4	48.6
74878	WANETTE	85.9	84.6	0.1	0.1	0.2	0.3	0.8	0.9	5.9	6.3	7.7	6.9	5.6	23.2	29.1	13.8	1.5	75.8	40.5	51.5	48.5
74880	WELEETKA	61.5	59.9	7.4	8.1	0.0	0.1	1.6	1.9	6.8	6.5	6.3	7.3	6.7	22.4	26.4	15.1	2.5	75.8	41.0	49.5	50.5
74881	WELLSTON	87.8	86.7	3.0	3.1	0.1	0.1	2.2	2.6	7.1	7.3	7.6	7.2	6.5	24.8	27.1	11.4	1.0	73.6	37.9	50.3	49.7
74883	WETUMKA	63.3	62.4	4.3	4.5	0.1	0.0	2.5	2.6	6.5	6.2	6.5	7.4	6.1	22.8	25.5	15.7	3.4	75.7	40.9	47.3	52.7
74884	WEWOKA	60.8	59.0	12.9	13.6	0.3	0.4	2.2	2.3	6.9	6.2	7.4	7.4	6.7	23.1	24.4	15.3	2.6	74.8	39.3	48.4	51.6
74901	ARKOMA	89.2	88.3	0.4	0.4	0.3	0.4	1.8	2.0	6.8	6.2	6.2	6.0	7.7	24.4	27.0	13.6	2.0	77.2	39.0	48.8	51.2
74902	POCOLA	86.6	85.7	3.0	3.0	0.3	0.3	1.9	2.1	6.4	6.8	7.7	6.7	6.6	26.8	27.0	10.7	1.3	75.1	37.0	49.5	50.5
74930	BOKOSHE	81.8	80.5	0.1	0.1	0.3	0.4	1.5	1.8	7.5	7.6	8.0	7.1	5.9	26.7	24.1	11.9	1.4	72.6	35.7	49.6	50.4
	OKLAHOMA	76.2	74.8	7.6	7.7	1.4	1.8	5.2	5.8	7.0	6.7	7.0	7.1	7.8	27.2	24.0	11.6	1.7	75.3	36.0	49.3	50.8
	UNITED STATES	75.1	73.6	12.3	12.5	3.8	4.2	12.5	14.1	6.9	6.7	7.2	7.0	7.3	28.6	23.8	10.8	1.7	75.1	36.0	49.1	50.9

INCOME

ZIP CODE #	POST OFFICE NAME	2004 Per Capita Income	2004 HH Income Base	2004 Household Income Distribution (%): Less than $25,000	$25,000 to $49,999	$50,000 to $99,999	$100,000 to $149,999	$150,000 or More	Median Household Income: 2004	2009	2004 National Centile	2004 State Centile	2004 Home Value Base	2004 Home Value Distribution (%): Less than $50,000	$50,000 to $89,999	$90,000 to $174,999	$175,000 to $399,999	$400,000 or More	2004 Median Home Value
74571	TALIHINA	15179	1124	44.3	32.6	18.3	2.9	2.0	28706	33858	10	17	837	47.6	33.5	14.7	3.7	0.6	52887
74572	TUPELO	15488	572	44.4	27.3	22.4	3.7	2.3	29509	33821	11	21	475	45.5	25.1	22.1	5.9	1.5	56143
74574	TUSKAHOMA	15703	1117	45.2	31.7	17.2	4.2	1.7	28073	33392	9	14	905	39.6	33.9	19.7	4.6	2.2	60432
74576	WARDVILLE	23046	149	37.6	31.5	23.5	6.7	0.7	31810	37112	17	36	127	36.2	26.8	26.0	11.0	0.0	66111
74577	WHITESBORO	13311	69	53.6	29.0	14.5	1.5	1.5	22674	28582	3	2	57	52.6	31.6	15.8	0.0	0.0	48125
74578	WILBURTON	15598	2187	48.6	27.5	19.3	2.4	2.2	25901	30629	6	8	1558	40.2	41.7	15.9	2.1	0.2	57927
74601	PONCA CITY	16825	8386	42.0	30.3	22.1	3.8	1.8	30367	36205	13	25	5266	46.9	34.6	15.3	3.0	0.1	53151
74604	PONCA CITY	26995	5478	21.5	24.2	34.7	14.1	5.5	54525	65201	79	95	4527	12.2	27.8	41.9	16.4	1.7	101147
74630	BILLINGS	16879	276	26.8	39.1	29.0	5.1	0.0	42413	49632	54	85	200	47.5	31.5	13.0	3.5	4.5	52632
74631	BLACKWELL	15954	3233	40.9	35.0	18.8	3.8	1.5	30399	35757	13	25	2227	57.8	25.3	13.9	2.8	0.2	44541
74632	BRAMAN	20924	245	30.2	36.7	26.1	4.5	2.5	36470	43213	33	65	195	50.3	22.1	22.6	5.1	0.0	49737
74633	BURBANK	23401	219	33.3	32.0	24.7	5.9	4.1	34544	40490	26	54	183	39.3	23.5	27.9	6.6	2.7	67500
74636	DEER CREEK	14934	99	41.4	35.4	20.2	2.0	1.0	30310	35000	13	25	78	57.7	18.0	20.5	3.9	0.0	38750
74637	FAIRFAX	17818	844	44.9	34.6	15.8	3.2	1.5	28230	33171	9	14	611	69.2	20.3	7.4	1.2	2.0	32232
74640	HUNTER	19332	180	31.7	32.8	28.3	5.6	1.7	35000	39819	28	57	147	36.7	27.2	27.9	6.8	1.4	66250
74641	KAW CITY	22316	291	25.8	34.7	33.3	4.8	1.4	42379	50664	54	84	242	23.6	38.0	31.0	6.6	0.8	77692
74643	LAMONT	15490	252	41.3	35.3	20.2	2.4	0.8	30484	35984	13	26	199	56.8	19.1	20.6	3.5	0.0	39250
74644	MARLAND	13344	198	40.9	31.8	25.3	1.5	0.5	30401	36460	13	26	146	57.5	17.1	15.8	6.2	3.4	42143
74646	NARDIN	20273	81	24.7	37.0	28.4	8.6	1.2	42349	52106	54	84	65	26.2	20.0	40.0	9.2	4.6	100781
74647	NEWKIRK	18717	1628	32.8	32.5	28.9	4.6	1.2	36447	44107	33	65	1277	38.4	33.1	23.3	4.5	0.7	62480
74650	RALSTON	18130	279	34.4	35.8	23.7	2.9	3.2	32384	37868	19	40	234	39.7	24.4	26.1	6.0	3.9	71111
74651	RED ROCK	12942	241	40.3	32.0	24.9	2.1	0.8	30796	36969	14	28	178	57.3	16.9	15.7	6.7	3.4	42353
74652	SHIDLER	19427	457	39.2	30.0	26.7	2.2	2.0	32779	38521	20	43	340	72.4	17.1	5.6	3.2	1.8	30484
74653	TONKAWA	17903	1407	35.5	35.3	23.4	4.4	1.4	33844	40427	24	49	1028	48.9	32.4	16.1	2.3	0.3	51236
74701	DURANT	17037	7886	40.1	31.5	22.1	4.4	2.0	31645	36833	17	35	4811	30.2	29.2	32.1	8.1	0.4	76003
74723	BENNINGTON	15574	656	42.8	31.4	20.0	3.2	2.6	29345	34477	11	21	542	45.2	25.3	21.0	6.1	2.4	58667
74724	BETHEL	14214	640	46.1	26.9	22.8	2.3	1.9	28313	34134	9	15	516	44.6	30.4	16.7	7.0	1.4	57179
74726	BOKCHITO	16554	922	43.4	29.2	21.0	4.2	2.2	28813	34220	10	17	720	46.4	23.1	24.2	5.1	1.3	54815
74727	BOSWELL	12043	880	53.1	30.1	14.6	1.8	0.5	22946	26702	3	3	668	43.1	40.0	12.7	2.8	1.4	55542
74728	BROKEN BOW	14696	4138	45.8	30.6	18.0	4.0	1.7	27775	33561	8	12	2957	41.5	32.8	17.5	7.6	0.6	60188
74729	CADDO	16208	894	36.6	32.8	24.9	4.6	1.1	34291	39488	25	53	688	45.9	26.2	22.2	4.7	1.0	55600
74730	CALERA	17286	1335	35.6	36.9	21.3	4.0	2.3	34012	39489	24	51	1027	39.3	29.3	23.5	6.6	1.3	65779
74731	CARTWRIGHT	15163	561	45.5	29.2	21.9	2.0	1.4	29003	34258	10	18	459	53.8	23.3	21.1	1.7	0.0	47177
74733	COLBERT	15743	1295	41.7	32.7	19.6	4.3	1.7	31659	36970	17	35	1016	47.5	27.5	20.5	3.9	0.6	53623
74734	EAGLETOWN	14367	454	46.5	29.5	20.3	3.5	0.2	26691	31628	7	10	357	52.9	25.5	14.9	5.3	1.4	46719
74735	FORT TOWSON	15034	958	47.7	28.8	18.1	4.2	1.3	26276	30328	6	8	766	48.7	30.6	15.4	3.4	2.0	51449
74736	GARVIN	19221	320	39.1	25.3	26.6	6.9	2.2	35603	45111	30	60	259	45.6	27.0	19.3	7.0	1.2	60682
74738	GRANT	18288	285	37.9	26.7	28.1	4.6	2.8	33856	39629	24	50	239	41.0	28.9	22.2	8.0	0.0	56719
74740	HAWORTH	15421	659	52.4	30.2	11.7	3.8	2.0	23592	27922	4	4	534	60.1	21.0	12.6	5.2	1.1	41940
74741	HENDRIX	15419	684	42.4	34.4	18.4	3.2	1.6	30219	35485	13	23	564	49.8	27.0	15.6	6.0	1.6	50263
74743	HUGO	14041	3518	49.3	28.8	19.4	1.9	0.6	25407	29209	5	7	2301	46.7	32.1	17.2	3.9	0.0	53120
74745	IDABEL	16564	4146	48.3	26.1	18.5	5.1	2.0	26185	31728	6	8	2701	41.6	31.0	20.7	5.3	1.6	57362
74748	KENEFIC	15891	222	42.8	34.2	18.0	3.2	1.8	29089	33000	10	19	185	51.9	26.5	14.1	4.9	2.7	48478
74754	RINGOLD	16903	59	37.3	35.6	23.7	3.4	0.0	32298	39430	19	39	48	52.1	29.2	16.7	2.1	0.0	49000
74755	RUFE	27592	119	41.2	16.8	29.4	5.0	7.6	37774	47383	38	72	102	41.2	16.7	26.5	13.7	2.0	70000
74756	SAWYER	15612	187	44.4	31.0	21.4	2.7	0.5	29287	34440	11	20	157	49.7	28.0	15.9	5.7	0.6	50385
74759	SOPER	13580	403	50.6	29.3	17.1	2.7	0.3	24605	28335	4	6	331	46.2	32.6	16.9	3.9	0.3	53906
74760	SPENCERVILLE	14978	119	43.7	31.1	21.9	2.5	0.8	29639	34077	11	21	100	50.0	28.0	16.0	6.0	0.0	50000
74764	VALLIANT	18106	1692	41.1	25.3	27.3	4.0	2.3	33742	41079	23	49	1354	46.8	25.4	19.1	7.3	1.5	54490
74766	WRIGHT CITY	17827	670	39.0	31.8	24.8	2.7	1.8	32855	38675	20	44	537	59.4	24.4	13.2	1.7	1.3	42986
74801	SHAWNEE	17727	8999	39.9	31.0	22.4	4.6	2.1	32472	38313	19	40	5914	36.8	35.4	23.0	4.3	0.5	61935
74804	SHAWNEE	21880	7652	31.4	30.1	28.5	6.4	3.7	39750	46466	45	78	5415	18.1	31.1	40.1	10.3	0.5	90973
74820	ADA	17877	10649	41.4	30.4	21.0	4.9	2.4	31257	37156	16	32	6736	29.0	30.8	30.3	8.8	1.1	76290
74824	AGRA	17707	573	31.2	42.9	19.4	4.9	1.6	34738	40116	26	55	473	37.6	27.7	23.9	10.8	0.0	62027
74825	ALLEN	15729	1884	38.4	32.6	23.8	2.8	2.4	32631	38063	20	41	1524	40.8	29.0	24.5	5.0	0.7	64095
74826	ASHER	14708	364	42.6	31.6	20.3	5.0	0.6	28348	33633	9	15	299	56.5	31.1	10.0	2.3	0.0	45244
74827	ATWOOD	15592	298	43.0	29.5	23.8	3.7	0.0	30295	35647	13	25	241	49.0	23.2	22.4	5.4	0.0	51667
74829	BOLEY	12893	255	51.8	21.6	22.0	3.5	1.2	23499	27120	4	4	199	45.2	29.7	17.1	7.0	1.0	54750
74831	BYARS	17135	495	39.8	33.3	23.0	2.4	1.4	31211	36853	16	32	413	51.8	26.2	15.5	6.3	0.2	47656
74832	CARNEY	17178	279	31.5	37.6	25.5	3.2	2.2	36400	42340	33	64	227	31.7	37.9	26.4	4.0	0.0	70600
74833	CASTLE	16973	220	36.4	38.6	20.0	3.6	1.4	32865	37640	20	44	185	34.1	24.3	33.0	8.1	0.5	78214
74834	CHANDLER	19003	2538	33.7	32.0	24.6	7.3	2.4	35647	40625	30	60	1924	28.1	31.2	32.2	8.1	0.4	77669
74839	DUSTIN	11473	337	50.7	34.7	13.1	1.5	0.0	24556	28043	4	6	275	62.9	22.9	9.1	5.1	0.0	36827
74840	EARLSBORO	18050	272	24.6	34.6	33.8	5.5	1.5	42471	48767	55	85	232	27.6	31.5	33.2	6.9	0.9	76875
74842	FITTSTOWN	18345	274	29.9	33.9	27.4	6.6	2.2	37112	42527	36	69	221	33.9	24.0	27.2	12.7	2.3	75667
74843	FITZHUGH	17224	75	30.7	34.7	26.7	6.7	1.3	36378	42672	33	64	61	37.7	23.0	26.2	11.5	1.6	71250
74845	HANNA	12748	188	48.9	30.3	17.0	2.7	1.1	25668	31885	5	7	148	67.6	10.8	17.6	2.0	2.0	36944
74848	HOLDENVILLE	15268	3086	48.5	29.9	15.6	4.0	1.9	25864	30239	6	8	2281	54.1	25.9	15.1	4.7	0.2	45907
74849	KONAWA	12512	1124	48.6	30.3	19.0	1.6	0.4	25862	29412	6	7	777	49.8	32.7	13.8	2.7	1.0	50190
74850	LAMAR	16901	112	37.5	29.5	28.6	4.5	0.0	35000	41394	28	57	93	40.9	31.2	22.6	4.3	1.1	70500
74851	MCLOUD	19563	2588	24.2	30.8	35.2	7.7	2.1	44655	51786	60	88	2183	25.1	35.4	34.5	4.8	0.3	77354
74852	MACOMB	17268	381	29.1	36.0	27.6	5.5	1.8	37236	44464	36	70	322	35.1	31.4	28.0	5.3	0.3	67500
74854	MAUD	17203	1625	40.1	32.7	20.5	4.6	2.0	31151	36901	15	31	1298	54.1	25.3	15.0	3.9	1.9	45891
74855	MEEKER	17771	1882	31.2	35.2	27.2	4.9	1.4	38872	45048	42	76	1512	30.6	35.3	27.0	6.6	0.5	72810
74856	MILL CREEK	14604	559	42.8	34.5	18.4	2.7	1.6	29098	34451	10	19	442	56.1	23.8	15.6	3.2	1.4	43864
74857	NEWALLA	20472	2969	18.2	30.9	40.2	9.0	1.8	50709	59100	73	94	2643	19.0	34.6	38.6	7.6	0.2	85526
74859	OKEMAH	14751	2355	47.4	30.8	17.6	3.1	1.0	26393	30261	6	9	1654	45.5	26.2	22.7	5.3	0.4	55692
74860	PADEN	17340	628	34.7	36.0	23.4	3.5	2.4	33243	38025	22	46	528	43.4	32.6	16.9	5.3	1.9	56604
74864	PRAGUE	17489	1706	35.6	34.7	23.0	4.6	2.1	34669	39884	26	55	1301	35.4	37.0	20.0	6.8	0.9	65441
74865	ROFF	15650	543	41.1	27.6	26.0	4.4	0.9	32657	38934	20	42	408	56.1	20.1	13.7	8.1	2.0	44444
74867	SASAKWA	12966	289	54.7	28.7	12.8	2.8	1.0	22986	26965	3	3	241	55.6	25.3	15.8	3.3	0.0	43864
74868	SEMINOLE	18407	4691	40.1	33.3	21.1	3.3	2.3	30830	35866	14	28	3377	42.4	29.7	21.5	5.7	0.6	56943
74869	SPARKS	17838	127	33.9	29.1	29.1	7.1	0.8	35374	40000	29	59	111	32.4	36.0	27.0	4.5	0.0	69444
74871	STONEWALL	16343	898	41.7	26.7	25.4	5.1	1.1	30462	36090	13	26	731	48.8	25.2	19.7	4.2	2.1	51232
74872	STRATFORD	15380	1259	44.9	31.1	18.5	3.3	2.1	28330	32790	9	15	943	38.2	34.0	15.5	11.4	1.0	63476
74873	TECUMSEH	17256	4226	33.8	35.2	24.6	5.0	1.4	36206	42689	32	63	3227	36.0	33.9	24.3	5.1	0.7	61929
74875	TRYON	15079	616	38.8	33.0	25.0	2.6	0.7	31518	36332	16	34	504	38.3	35.3	19.3	6.4	0.8	60870
74878	WANETTE	17913	565	32.2	34.5	25.8	5.0	2.5	36379	43080	33	64	471	38.4	35.2	21.9	4.3	0.2	62647
74880	WELEETKA	15925	883	51.2	29.1	13.3	4.4	2.0	24196	28286	4	5	695	57.3	22.6	17.6	2.2	0.4	42109
74881	WELLSTON	17840	1469	29.7	37.6	26.4	4.8	1.5	36925	42405	35	68	1204	34.7	32.4	24.9	6.9	1.1	70093
74883	WETUMKA	13088	931	52.9	29.3	15.6	1.9	0.3	23200	27226	3	3	659	63.4	22.0	10.5	3.6	0.5	41729
74884	WEWOKA	14244	2772	47.0	30.3	18.2	3.2	1.2	26710	30600	7	10	1957	60.4	21.1	14.7	3.2	0.6	41450
74901	ARKOMA	16117	941	45.1	28.8	20.4	3.3	2.4	27811	32564	8	12	599	44.6	37.6	17.0	0.8	0.0	56500
74902	POCOLA	16816	1900	35.6	33.8	24.7	4.8	1.1	36589	42679	34	66	1509	32.5	34.1	28.6	3.5	1.3	70925
74930	BOKOSHE	15634	1420	42.0	31.1	21.6	4.3	1.1	31175	36801	15	31	1123	43.3	29.7	18.0	4.7	4.3	58389
	OKLAHOMA	21077		31.9	30.4	27.2	7.1	3.4	38589	46268				26.7	29.5	32.0	10.2	1.6	81000
	UNITED STATES	25866		24.7	27.1	30.8	10.9	6.5	48124	56710				10.9	15.0	33.7	30.1	10.4	145905

ZIP CODE #	POST OFFICE NAME	FINANCIAL SERVICES: Auto Loan	FINANCIAL SERVICES: Home Loan	FINANCIAL SERVICES: Invest-ments	FINANCIAL SERVICES: Retire-ment Plans	THE HOME: Home Improvements: Home Repair	THE HOME: Home Improvements: Lawn & Garden	THE HOME: Furnishings: Comput-ers & Hard-ware	THE HOME: Furnishings: Major Appli-ances	THE HOME: Furnishings: TV, Radio, Sound Equip-ment	THE HOME: Furnishings: Furni-ture	ENTERTAINMENT: Dine out/ Carry out	ENTERTAINMENT: Sports Equip-ment	ENTERTAINMENT: Fees & Tickets	ENTERTAINMENT: Toys & Games	ENTERTAINMENT: Travel	ENTERTAINMENT: Cable TV	PERSONAL: Apparel & Services	PERSONAL: Auto Repairs	PERSONAL: Health Insur-ance	PERSONAL: Pets & Supplies
74571	TALIHINA	66	49	31	46	54	64	53	59	60	51	71	67	47	67	53	64	65	59	71	73
74572	TUPELO	71	52	31	49	58	68	55	63	62	53	73	73	48	70	55	65	66	63	76	82
74574	TUSKAHOMA	62	47	31	45	51	61	52	57	58	49	68	64	46	64	51	61	62	57	68	69
74576	WARDVILLE	0	0	0	0	0	0	0	0	0	0	0	0	0	0	0	0	0	0	0	0
74577	WHITESBORO	54	41	27	39	45	53	45	50	50	43	59	56	40	56	45	53	54	50	59	60
74578	WILBURTON	67	50	34	47	55	63	53	59	59	51	70	70	47	68	53	62	65	60	69	76
74601	PONCA CITY	60	53	49	51	54	61	56	58	60	55	73	67	54	72	56	61	69	58	62	67
74604	PONCA CITY	98	96	93	95	99	107	94	98	95	93	117	114	94	117	95	95	112	97	101	115
74630	BILLINGS	73	55	36	53	60	72	61	67	68	58	80	75	54	75	60	72	73	67	80	80
74631	BLACKWELL	61	50	39	48	54	62	53	57	58	51	70	65	50	69	53	61	65	57	66	70
74632	BRAMAN	84	66	45	60	75	84	62	75	71	62	84	88	56	83	67	76	78	74	89	103
74633	BURBANK	98	69	36	65	80	90	68	84	78	67	92	101	58	90	70	82	84	83	100	117
74636	DEER CREEK	62	47	31	45	51	61	52	57	58	49	68	64	46	64	51	61	62	57	68	69
74637	FAIRFAX	71	52	33	50	58	69	57	64	64	54	75	73	50	71	57	67	68	64	76	79
74640	HUNTER	81	60	35	57	68	76	59	71	67	58	79	85	52	77	61	70	72	70	83	96
74641	KAW CITY	94	66	34	62	76	86	65	80	75	64	88	97	55	86	67	78	80	79	95	112
74643	LAMONT	62	46	31	45	51	61	51	56	58	49	68	63	46	64	51	61	62	56	68	68
74644	MARLAND	70	47	21	41	53	61	45	57	55	46	64	68	39	61	46	59	58	56	70	81
74646	NARDIN	95	66	35	63	77	87	66	81	76	65	89	98	56	87	68	79	81	80	97	113
74647	NEWKIRK	83	58	32	54	66	76	59	71	68	58	80	84	51	77	60	72	73	70	85	96
74650	RALSTON	73	54	34	52	60	71	59	66	66	56	78	75	52	74	59	70	71	66	79	82
74651	RED ROCK	70	47	21	41	53	61	45	57	55	46	64	68	39	61	46	59	58	56	70	81
74652	SHIDLER	72	54	35	52	59	70	59	65	66	56	78	74	52	74	59	70	71	65	78	80
74653	TONKAWA	74	61	46	61	65	73	63	68	67	62	81	78	59	80	63	69	76	67	75	82
74701	DURANT	61	55	53	55	56	61	58	59	60	57	74	70	56	73	57	60	71	60	61	69
74723	BENNINGTON	77	52	24	45	59	67	50	62	60	51	71	74	42	67	51	65	64	62	77	88
74724	BETHEL	71	48	22	41	54	62	46	57	55	47	65	69	39	61	47	60	59	57	71	81
74726	BOKCHITO	72	51	29	48	58	67	52	62	60	51	71	72	46	68	53	64	65	61	74	82
74727	BOSWELL	50	36	22	34	40	47	39	44	44	37	52	50	34	49	38	47	47	44	53	56
74728	BROKEN BOW	63	47	32	44	52	59	49	55	56	48	66	65	44	64	49	59	61	56	65	72
74729	CADDO	70	53	34	50	59	67	54	62	61	53	72	72	49	70	55	64	66	61	73	80
74730	CALERA	74	57	38	54	62	72	58	66	65	57	77	77	53	75	59	68	71	65	77	84
74731	CARTWRIGHT	68	45	21	39	51	59	44	55	53	45	62	65	37	59	44	57	56	54	67	78
74733	COLBERT	75	50	23	44	57	66	49	61	58	49	69	73	42	65	50	63	62	60	75	86
74734	EAGLETOWN	67	45	20	38	51	58	43	54	52	44	61	64	37	58	44	56	55	53	66	76
74735	FORT TOWSON	68	47	24	42	53	61	47	57	56	47	65	67	41	62	48	60	59	56	69	77
74736	GARVIN	77	66	51	65	69	78	68	72	72	66	87	82	65	86	67	73	81	71	78	85
74738	GRANT	88	59	27	51	67	77	57	71	68	58	80	85	48	76	58	74	73	70	87	101
74740	HAWORTH	75	50	23	43	57	65	48	60	58	49	69	72	41	65	49	63	62	60	75	86
74741	HENDRIX	75	50	23	43	57	65	48	60	58	49	68	72	41	65	49	63	62	60	74	86
74743	HUGO	54	40	29	38	44	52	44	49	50	43	59	56	39	56	44	53	54	49	58	61
74745	IDABEL	64	51	42	49	54	62	55	59	61	54	73	68	51	71	54	63	69	60	67	72
74748	KENEFIC	73	50	23	43	56	65	48	60	58	49	68	71	41	64	49	62	62	59	73	84
74754	RINGOLD	72	48	22	42	55	63	47	58	56	48	66	70	40	63	48	61	60	58	72	83
74755	RUFE	125	84	38	72	95	109	81	101	97	82	114	121	69	108	82	105	104	100	124	143
74756	SAWYER	72	49	22	42	55	63	47	59	57	48	66	70	40	63	48	61	60	58	72	83
74759	SOPER	52	39	26	37	43	51	43	47	48	41	57	53	38	54	43	51	52	47	57	57
74760	SPENCERVILLE	73	49	22	42	55	64	47	59	57	48	67	70	40	63	48	61	61	58	72	84
74764	VALLIANT	88	59	27	51	67	77	57	71	69	58	81	85	48	76	58	74	73	70	88	101
74766	WRIGHT CITY	91	61	28	52	69	79	59	73	71	60	83	88	50	79	60	76	76	73	90	104
74801	SHAWNEE	66	57	51	55	60	67	60	63	64	58	78	73	57	78	60	66	74	63	69	76
74804	SHAWNEE	84	75	66	74	79	87	77	81	80	75	98	94	74	97	77	82	93	80	87	96
74820	ADA	63	55	54	55	57	63	60	61	62	58	76	71	57	74	59	62	72	62	64	70
74824	AGRA	91	61	28	53	69	80	59	74	71	60	83	88	50	79	60	77	76	73	91	105
74825	ALLEN	69	54	37	53	59	67	56	62	61	54	73	72	51	71	56	63	68	62	71	78
74826	ASHER	71	48	22	41	54	62	46	57	55	47	65	69	39	61	47	60	59	57	71	81
74827	ATWOOD	63	46	27	44	51	60	48	56	55	46	64	65	42	61	49	57	58	55	67	72
74829	BOLEY	44	35	36	31	35	43	39	41	45	40	54	44	37	48	38	48	51	42	48	47
74831	BYARS	83	55	25	48	63	72	53	67	65	55	76	80	46	72	54	70	69	66	82	95
74832	CARNEY	83	55	25	48	63	72	53	67	64	54	76	80	45	71	54	69	69	66	82	95
74833	CASTLE	81	56	29	50	63	73	55	68	65	56	77	80	47	73	56	70	70	67	82	94
74834	CHANDLER	80	62	45	61	69	77	64	73	70	62	83	86	57	81	64	72	77	72	83	93
74839	DUSTIN	54	37	17	32	41	48	36	44	43	36	50	53	30	48	36	46	46	44	54	62
74840	EARLSBORO	82	73	55	69	77	82	67	75	71	67	87	89	66	89	69	73	83	73	81	96
74842	FITTSTOWN	85	59	31	56	69	77	58	72	67	58	79	87	50	77	61	71	72	71	86	101
74843	FITZHUGH	85	59	31	56	69	78	59	73	68	58	79	88	50	78	61	71	72	72	87	101
74845	HANNA	55	42	27	40	46	55	46	51	52	44	61	57	41	57	46	55	56	51	61	61
74848	HOLDENVILLE	56	41	25	39	46	54	44	50	50	42	58	58	39	56	44	52	53	50	60	64
74849	KONAWA	57	40	23	37	45	53	42	49	49	41	57	57	37	54	42	52	52	49	59	64
74850	LAMAR	76	53	28	50	62	70	53	65	61	52	71	79	45	70	55	64	65	64	78	91
74851	MCLOUD	90	80	62	77	82	89	76	83	80	77	97	97	73	96	77	80	93	82	87	101
74852	MACOMB	90	60	27	52	68	79	58	73	70	59	82	87	49	78	59	76	75	72	90	103
74854	MAUD	77	55	30	50	61	71	56	66	65	55	76	76	49	72	56	69	70	65	80	87
74855	MEEKER	76	66	50	64	69	76	63	70	67	63	82	82	61	82	64	69	77	68	75	87
74856	MILL CREEK	71	49	24	44	56	64	48	59	56	48	66	71	41	63	49	60	60	58	72	83
74857	NEWALLA	91	83	66	80	84	89	79	85	80	80	99	98	75	95	78	80	95	84	85	102
74859	OKEMAH	63	45	25	41	50	59	46	55	54	45	63	63	40	60	47	57	57	54	66	72
74860	PADEN	83	56	26	48	63	73	54	68	66	55	77	81	46	73	55	71	70	67	83	96
74864	PRAGUE	74	55	35	52	60	70	58	65	65	56	77	75	52	74	57	68	71	65	77	83
74865	ROFF	70	51	31	49	57	67	54	62	61	52	72	72	47	69	54	64	65	62	74	80
74867	SASAKWA	51	38	25	37	42	50	43	47	48	40	56	52	38	53	42	50	51	47	56	56
74868	SEMINOLE	75	59	43	56	64	73	62	68	69	61	82	79	57	80	62	71	77	68	78	85
74869	SPARKS	84	58	31	55	68	76	58	71	66	57	78	86	49	76	60	70	71	70	85	99
74871	STONEWALL	78	53	26	48	61	69	52	64	61	52	72	77	44	69	53	65	65	64	78	91
74872	STRATFORD	66	48	29	45	54	62	50	58	57	48	67	67	44	64	51	60	61	58	69	75
74873	TECUMSEH	77	58	36	55	64	73	59	68	67	58	79	79	53	76	60	70	73	67	80	87
74875	TRYON	73	49	22	42	55	64	47	59	57	48	67	70	40	63	48	61	61	58	72	83
74878	WANETTE	87	58	26	50	66	76	56	70	68	57	80	84	48	75	57	73	72	70	87	100
74880	WELEETKA	72	50	28	46	56	66	52	61	61	51	71	71	45	67	52	65	65	61	74	81
74881	WELLSTON	79	63	43	59	67	74	62	70	67	63	81	82	57	78	62	69	76	69	77	89
74883	WETUMKA	50	37	24	36	41	49	41	45	46	39	54	51	37	51	41	49	50	45	55	55
74884	WEWOKA	59	44	31	41	48	57	48	53	54	47	64	61	43	61	47	58	59	53	63	66
74901	ARKOMA	69	48	26	44	54	63	50	59	58	49	68	68	43	64	50	62	62	58	72	78
74902	POCOLA	78	58	33	52	64	71	55	65	63	55	75	78	49	73	56	67	69	64	77	90
74930	BOKOSHE	77	53	25	46	59	68	51	63	60	51	71	75	44	68	52	65	65	62	76	88
	OKLAHOMA	79	71	65	70	73	80	73	76	76	72	93	88	70	91	72	76	88	76	79	89
	UNITED STATES	100	100	100	100	100	100	100	100	100	100	100	100	100	100	100	100	100	100	100	100

ZIP CODE		COUNTY FIPS CODE	POPULATION			2000-2004 ANNUAL RATE		HOUSEHOLDS					FAMILIES		
#	POST OFFICE NAME		2000	2004	2009	% Rate	State Centile	2000	2004	2009	% Annual Rate 2000-2004	2004 Average HH Size	2000	2004	% Annual Rate 2000-2004
74931	BUNCH	001	1633	1634	1659	0.0	41	551	557	570	0.3	2.93	424	429	0.3
74932	CAMERON	079	1144	1208	1280	1.3	86	413	440	470	1.5	2.75	335	356	1.4
74937	HEAVENER	079	6389	6496	6742	0.4	56	2290	2318	2412	0.3	2.60	1710	1727	0.2
74939	HODGEN	079	936	938	957	0.1	42	97	98	101	0.2	6.28	77	77	0.0
74940	HOWE	079	1588	1653	1738	1.0	77	580	605	638	1.0	2.70	460	478	0.9
74941	KEOTA	061	1896	1904	1933	0.1	44	711	716	728	0.2	2.66	540	542	0.1
74944	MCCURTAIN	061	1199	1228	1257	0.6	63	448	457	467	0.5	2.69	340	346	0.4
74948	MULDROW	135	9716	10165	10711	1.1	81	3654	3863	4113	1.3	2.62	2795	2948	1.3
74949	MUSE	079	232	232	239	0.0	40	98	99	102	0.2	2.34	71	71	0.0
74953	POTEAU	079	11227	11997	12818	1.6	90	4230	4554	4900	1.8	2.53	3008	3227	1.7
74954	ROLAND	135	8381	8785	9280	1.1	82	3011	3187	3400	1.4	2.74	2369	2504	1.3
74955	SALLISAW	135	12754	13390	14132	1.2	83	4945	5231	5571	1.3	2.52	3516	3703	1.2
74956	SHADY POINT	079	1061	1080	1127	0.4	58	384	392	411	0.5	2.76	310	316	0.5
74957	SMITHVILLE	089	439	439	439	0.0	40	170	172	174	0.3	2.55	126	127	0.2
74959	SPIRO	079	8005	8117	8433	0.3	53	3037	3101	3241	0.5	2.59	2272	2314	0.4
74960	STILWELL	001	11548	11950	12393	0.8	74	4119	4307	4510	1.1	2.75	3033	3159	1.0
74962	VIAN	135	6741	6918	7225	0.6	64	2592	2695	2848	0.9	2.51	1893	1963	0.9
74963	WATSON	089	871	885	891	0.4	56	345	355	362	0.7	2.49	254	261	0.6
74964	WATTS	001	2569	2599	2657	0.3	51	875	894	922	0.5	2.69	665	678	0.5
74965	WESTVILLE	001	4654	4755	4871	0.5	62	1687	1725	1775	0.5	2.72	1261	1289	0.5
74966	WISTER	079	4318	4479	4699	0.9	76	1657	1724	1816	0.9	2.58	1222	1268	0.9
	OKLAHOMA					0.8					1.0	2.48			0.9
	UNITED STATES					1.2					1.3	2.58			1.1

#	POST OFFICE NAME	White 2000	White 2004	Black 2000	Black 2004	Asian/Pacific 2000	Asian/Pacific 2004	% Hispanic Origin 2000	% Hispanic Origin 2004	0-4	5-9	10-14	15-19	20-24	25-44	45-64	65-84	85+	18+	MEDIAN AGE 2004	% 2004 Males	% 2004 Females
74931	BUNCH	35.5	34.6	0.0	0.0	0.1	0.2	1.5	1.4	6.4	6.9	9.7	7.8	5.9	26.6	25.2	10.3	1.2	72.1	35.7	51.5	48.5
74932	CAMERON	87.2	86.0	0.1	0.1	0.3	0.3	2.0	2.4	7.2	7.2	8.0	7.5	6.0	26.2	26.2	10.6	1.1	73.2	36.8	51.2	48.8
74937	HEAVENER	75.2	73.6	1.9	2.0	0.1	0.2	12.1	13.7	7.2	6.5	6.3	7.0	8.9	28.2	22.8	11.1	2.0	76.2	34.8	53.5	46.5
74939	HODGEN	71.7	70.0	9.0	9.4	0.0	0.0	1.7	2.0	3.9	4.2	4.4	5.3	7.6	38.6	26.9	8.4	0.8	84.7	38.5	67.3	32.7
74940	HOWE	78.9	77.3	0.1	0.1	0.2	0.2	4.6	5.3	7.1	7.2	7.2	6.5	6.6	26.9	26.1	11.1	1.2	74.5	36.7	51.3	48.7
74941	KEOTA	82.1	81.3	0.0	0.0	0.3	0.3	2.4	2.7	8.0	6.9	7.6	6.4	7.0	24.3	25.6	12.6	1.5	73.4	37.0	48.3	51.7
74944	MCCURTAIN	76.9	75.8	0.2	0.2	0.6	0.7	0.9	1.2	6.7	6.8	8.6	7.3	6.0	24.9	26.1	11.9	1.7	73.5	37.5	51.3	48.7
74948	MULDROW	73.6	72.0	1.3	1.4	0.3	0.4	2.3	2.6	6.9	7.1	7.4	6.7	6.2	26.9	26.1	11.6	1.2	74.6	37.4	50.1	49.9
74949	MUSE	78.0	76.7	0.0	0.0	0.0	0.0	1.3	1.3	6.9	6.9	6.5	6.5	6.9	22.4	26.3	16.0	1.7	76.7	40.0	46.6	53.5
74953	POTEAU	83.5	82.5	1.6	1.6	0.4	0.4	4.6	5.3	7.7	7.0	6.9	6.9	7.6	27.1	22.4	12.1	2.3	74.7	35.1	48.3	51.7
74954	ROLAND	69.8	68.1	3.2	3.2	0.3	0.4	2.4	2.6	7.8	7.6	8.4	7.3	6.9	27.6	23.4	10.2	0.9	71.7	34.6	49.7	50.3
74955	SALLISAW	65.0	63.5	1.0	1.1	0.3	0.3	2.1	2.3	7.5	7.1	7.2	6.5	6.5	26.5	23.9	13.0	1.8	74.2	36.9	49.3	50.8
74956	SHADY POINT	85.8	84.8	0.1	0.1	0.4	0.4	1.6	1.9	7.7	7.6	7.7	6.3	5.9	25.3	26.3	12.2	1.0	73.2	36.9	47.7	52.3
74957	SMITHVILLE	64.7	63.3	0.9	0.9	0.0	0.0	2.1	2.1	7.1	7.3	8.0	7.1	5.9	24.4	26.2	12.8	1.4	73.1	37.1	50.6	49.4
74959	SPIRO	78.8	77.0	6.3	6.7	0.1	0.2	1.8	2.0	6.8	6.9	7.3	6.6	6.5	26.2	25.8	12.2	1.6	74.9	37.6	48.7	51.3
74960	STILWELL	40.9	40.1	0.2	0.2	0.1	0.1	3.7	4.0	7.9	7.7	8.8	7.5	7.3	27.5	21.5	10.4	1.4	71.0	32.9	49.2	50.8
74962	VIAN	64.5	62.9	2.6	2.6	0.1	0.1	1.4	1.6	6.4	6.4	6.9	6.8	5.8	23.6	26.7	15.4	2.1	76.1	40.7	49.7	50.3
74963	WATSON	69.1	67.6	0.8	0.9	0.1	0.1	2.0	2.3	6.6	6.8	7.8	7.3	5.7	24.8	26.2	13.5	1.5	74.2	38.2	50.5	49.5
74964	WATTS	65.8	64.6	0.2	0.3	0.3	0.4	1.5	1.7	7.8	8.0	8.1	8.2	6.4	25.7	24.0	11.0	0.9	70.0	34.2	50.7	49.3
74965	WESTVILLE	61.7	60.2	0.1	0.1	0.1	0.2	3.3	3.5	8.0	7.9	8.2	6.8	7.1	26.4	22.7	11.4	1.5	71.8	34.6	49.7	50.4
74966	WISTER	79.9	78.8	0.2	0.2	0.4	0.5	1.7	2.0	6.9	6.8	7.3	6.7	6.5	24.7	25.1	14.2	1.7	74.8	38.7	50.4	49.6
	OKLAHOMA	76.2	74.8	7.6	7.7	1.4	1.8	5.2	5.8	7.0	6.7	7.0	7.1	7.8	27.2	24.0	11.6	1.7	75.3	36.0	49.3	50.8
	UNITED STATES	75.1	73.6	12.3	12.5	3.8	4.2	12.5	14.1	6.9	6.7	7.2	7.0	7.3	28.6	23.8	10.8	1.7	75.1	36.0	49.1	50.9

OKLAHOMA
INCOME

C 74931-74966

#	POST OFFICE NAME	2004 Per Capita Income	2004 HH Income Base	2004 HOUSEHOLD INCOME DISTRIBUTION (%)					MEDIAN HOUSEHOLD INCOME				2004 Home Value Base	2004 HOME VALUE DISTRIBUTION (%)					2004 Median Home Value
				Less than $25,000	$25,000 to $49,999	$50,000 to $99,999	$100,000 to $149,999	$150,000 or More	2004	2009	2004 National Centile	2004 State Centile		Less than $50,000	$50,000 to $89,999	$90,000 to $174,999	$175,000 to $399,999	$400,000 or More	
74931	BUNCH	12848	557	41.5	35.6	18.1	3.6	1.3	29596	34241	11	21	464	43.1	29.5	16.8	9.3	1.3	56154
74932	CAMERON	15369	440	33.0	37.7	25.0	3.6	0.7	34347	40159	25	54	355	36.9	25.1	24.2	13.8	0.0	72321
74937	HEAVENER	14895	2318	44.0	31.1	19.8	3.7	1.5	28838	33980	10	17	1682	45.7	30.7	17.5	4.4	1.7	54645
74939	HODGEN	8663	98	42.9	29.6	21.4	3.1	3.1	30000	37763	12	23	83	36.1	31.3	20.5	7.2	4.8	65000
74940	HOWE	17750	605	34.7	33.4	24.6	5.6	1.7	33937	39871	24	51	493	40.2	29.2	22.1	7.1	1.4	63625
74941	KEOTA	14715	716	45.1	33.7	14.7	3.4	3.2	27603	32219	8	12	578	55.5	25.4	16.6	1.7	0.7	45362
74944	MCCURTAIN	15299	457	42.2	28.7	22.3	5.5	1.3	31964	37251	18	37	377	56.5	25.2	14.3	2.1	1.9	45545
74948	MULDROW	15197	3863	39.3	33.9	22.0	4.0	0.7	32797	38245	20	43	3080	38.1	32.4	24.0	4.9	0.7	63992
74949	MUSE	13490	99	55.6	28.3	12.1	2.0	2.0	21361	26679	2	2	83	53.0	30.1	16.9	0.0	0.0	47500
74953	POTEAU	17096	4554	39.5	30.8	23.5	3.7	2.5	32272	38010	18	39	3221	32.6	32.0	28.2	6.6	0.6	71237
74954	ROLAND	15979	3187	37.4	33.8	22.6	3.8	2.4	34090	39711	24	52	2410	33.8	38.0	23.4	3.9	1.0	67191
74955	SALLISAW	15367	5231	42.8	29.2	23.3	3.4	1.3	30176	35225	13	23	3516	33.2	35.6	23.2	7.3	0.7	67370
74956	SHADY POINT	19100	392	39.0	26.5	27.3	4.1	3.1	35715	41420	30	61	325	36.9	28.9	25.9	7.4	0.9	68125
74957	SMITHVILLE	13232	172	51.2	26.7	18.0	2.3	1.7	24163	28878	4	5	135	48.2	34.1	10.4	7.4	0.0	51923
74959	SPIRO	15095	3101	40.0	35.1	18.8	5.3	0.9	31284	36471	16	33	2379	40.4	35.6	20.6	3.1	0.3	58650
74960	STILWELL	12610	4307	49.3	30.4	16.8	2.3	1.2	25406	29051	5	7	3067	42.3	34.6	16.6	5.5	1.0	57524
74962	VIAN	16681	2695	42.6	30.5	20.1	4.4	2.4	30751	36294	14	28	2111	36.6	34.6	21.7	6.1	1.0	64613
74963	WATSON	13375	355	51.3	27.3	18.3	2.3	0.9	24093	28929	4	5	283	48.8	32.5	12.0	6.0	0.7	51250
74964	WATTS	13822	894	37.4	39.9	19.8	2.0	0.9	32388	37724	19	40	732	42.2	29.5	20.6	4.6	3.0	59048
74965	WESTVILLE	13289	1725	39.7	36.1	21.0	2.7	0.5	31178	35895	15	31	1248	42.6	27.7	17.1	9.1	3.5	58857
74966	WISTER	16003	1724	42.3	29.1	23.7	3.7	1.3	31011	36295	15	30	1358	39.4	28.8	25.2	5.2	1.5	66429
	OKLAHOMA	21077		31.9	30.4	27.2	7.1	3.4	38589	46268				26.7	29.5	32.0	10.2	1.6	81000
	UNITED STATES	25866		24.7	27.1	30.8	10.9	6.5	48124	56710				10.9	15.0	33.7	30.1	10.4	145905

SPENDING POTENTIAL INDICES

#	POST OFFICE NAME	Auto Loan	Home Loan	Invest-ments	Retire-ment Plans	Home Repair	Lawn & Garden	Comput-ers & Hard-ware	Major Appli-ances	TV, Radio, Sound Equip-ment	Furni-ture	Dine out/ Carry out	Sports Equip-ment	Fees & Tickets	Toys & Games	Travel	Cable TV	Apparel & Services	Auto Repairs	Health Insur-ance	Pets & Supplies
74931	BUNCH	71	48	22	41	54	62	46	57	55	47	65	69	39	61	47	60	59	57	71	81
74932	CAMERON	79	53	24	46	60	69	51	64	62	52	73	77	44	69	52	67	66	64	79	91
74937	HEAVENER	70	50	28	45	55	64	50	59	58	50	69	69	44	66	50	62	63	59	71	79
74939	HODGEN	84	56	25	48	63	73	54	68	65	55	77	81	46	72	55	70	70	67	83	96
74940	HOWE	82	63	40	59	68	77	63	72	70	62	84	83	57	82	63	73	78	71	82	92
74941	KEOTA	74	49	22	43	56	64	48	60	57	49	67	71	41	64	48	62	61	59	73	85
74944	MCCURTAIN	77	52	23	45	59	68	50	63	60	51	71	75	43	67	51	65	64	62	77	89
74948	MULDROW	69	52	33	47	56	63	51	59	58	52	69	70	46	66	51	61	64	59	68	78
74949	MUSE	51	38	25	37	42	50	42	47	48	40	56	52	38	53	42	50	51	47	56	56
74953	POTEAU	71	55	38	53	60	69	58	65	65	57	77	74	53	74	58	68	71	64	75	80
74954	ROLAND	76	58	36	53	63	71	56	65	64	57	76	77	52	74	57	67	70	64	76	86
74955	SALLISAW	62	49	38	45	52	60	52	56	57	51	69	65	48	66	51	60	64	57	64	69
74956	SHADY POINT	92	71	44	64	77	86	67	78	75	67	90	94	61	89	68	79	84	77	91	107
74957	SMITHVILLE	64	43	19	37	48	56	41	51	50	42	58	61	35	55	42	53	53	51	63	73
74959	SPIRO	71	49	27	43	55	63	49	59	58	49	68	70	43	65	49	62	63	59	71	81
74960	STILWELL	59	43	28	39	47	54	44	51	51	44	61	60	40	58	44	54	57	51	60	67
74962	VIAN	74	53	32	47	59	68	53	63	62	53	73	74	47	70	54	66	67	63	75	85
74963	WATSON	63	42	19	36	48	55	41	51	49	41	58	61	35	54	41	53	52	50	63	72
74964	WATTS	71	47	21	41	54	62	46	57	55	47	65	68	39	61	47	60	59	57	71	81
74965	WESTVILLE	67	47	24	41	52	59	45	55	53	45	62	65	39	60	46	56	57	54	66	77
74966	WISTER	73	53	31	49	58	67	53	62	60	53	72	73	47	69	53	64	66	61	73	82
	OKLAHOMA	79	71	65	70	73	80	73	76	76	72	93	88	70	91	72	76	88	76	79	89
	UNITED STATES	100	100	100	100	100	100	100	100	100	100	100	100	100	100	100	100	100	100	100	100

245-D   Copyright © 2004 ESRI BIS. All rights reserved. Reproduction by any method is prohibited.

OREGON

A 97001-97204

POPULATION CHANGE

#	POST OFFICE NAME	COUNTY FIPS CODE	POPULATION 2000	2004	2009	2000-2004 ANNUAL RATE % Rate	State Centile	HOUSEHOLDS 2000	2004	2009	% Annual Rate 2000-2004	2004 Average HH Size	FAMILIES 2000	2004	% Annual Rate 2000-2004
97001	ANTELOPE	065	185	171	164	-1.8	1	71	66	63	-1.7	2.55	50	45	-2.5
97002	AURORA	047	5627	5491	5641	-0.6	15	2106	2067	2131	-0.4	2.64	1601	1564	-0.6
97004	BEAVERCREEK	005	4280	4369	4542	0.5	52	1508	1567	1651	0.9	2.78	1238	1281	0.8
97005	BEAVERTON	067	22986	23462	24891	0.5	52	9480	9623	10192	0.4	2.39	5171	5188	0.1
97006	BEAVERTON	067	52732	58627	64607	2.5	95	20143	22518	24872	2.6	2.60	13261	14667	2.4
97007	BEAVERTON	067	56324	62734	69431	2.6	95	20362	22709	25138	2.6	2.75	14668	16246	2.4
97008	BEAVERTON	067	28580	29567	31565	0.8	65	11470	11934	12774	0.9	2.46	7382	7616	0.7
97009	BORING	005	12945	13164	13735	0.4	50	4599	4749	5015	0.8	2.76	3794	3896	0.6
97011	BRIGHTWOOD	005	1036	1084	1132	1.1	72	442	470	496	1.5	2.27	296	313	1.3
97013	CANBY	005	19714	21066	22400	1.6	83	6931	7482	8030	1.8	2.80	5311	5689	1.6
97014	CASCADE LOCKS	027	1298	1317	1384	0.3	48	495	501	523	0.3	2.63	363	366	0.2
97015	CLACKAMAS	005	23030	25211	27046	2.2	91	8657	9531	10296	2.3	2.64	6147	6746	2.2
97016	CLATSKANIE	009	6286	6458	6787	0.6	57	2418	2503	2645	0.8	2.57	1758	1813	0.7
97017	COLTON	005	2700	2754	2861	0.5	51	906	936	983	0.8	2.94	728	748	0.6
97018	COLUMBIA CITY	009	1547	1562	1625	0.2	43	584	590	615	0.2	2.64	450	453	0.2
97019	CORBETT	051	2868	2932	3037	0.5	53	1011	1030	1064	0.4	2.80	771	782	0.3
97021	DUFUR	065	1151	1114	1088	-0.8	9	467	454	445	-0.7	2.45	339	328	-0.8
97022	EAGLE CREEK	005	3384	3445	3582	0.4	50	1153	1185	1243	0.7	2.91	881	898	0.5
97023	ESTACADA	005	9596	9662	9968	0.2	40	3391	3456	3604	0.5	2.75	2568	2602	0.3
97024	FAIRVIEW	051	8144	9031	9663	2.5	94	3082	3388	3600	2.3	2.65	2078	2266	2.1
97026	GERVAIS	047	3268	3555	3793	2.0	89	820	888	945	1.9	3.95	682	735	1.8
97027	GLADSTONE	005	11959	12200	12670	0.5	51	4460	4604	4831	0.8	2.63	3177	3259	0.6
97028	GOVERNMENT CAMP	005	367	392	414	1.6	83	160	174	186	2.0	2.21	87	94	1.8
97029	GRASS VALLEY	055	414	414	419	0.0	35	171	172	175	0.1	2.41	118	118	0.0
97030	GRESHAM	051	30344	33513	35866	2.4	93	11704	12877	13734	2.3	2.56	7539	8260	2.2
97031	HOOD RIVER	027	16686	17700	19060	1.4	79	6015	6354	6810	1.3	2.69	4228	4443	1.2
97032	HUBBARD	047	4284	4145	4231	-0.8	9	1356	1312	1338	-0.8	3.16	1064	1023	-0.9
97033	KENT	055	46	46	47	0.0	35	18	18	18	0.0	2.56	12	12	0.0
97034	LAKE OSWEGO	005	18693	19419	20360	0.9	68	7423	7823	8294	1.2	2.48	5306	5557	1.1
97035	LAKE OSWEGO	005	22942	23767	24837	0.8	66	9920	10389	10947	1.1	2.28	6234	6452	0.8
97037	MAUPIN	065	1600	1558	1527	-0.6	13	579	563	552	-0.7	2.75	423	410	-0.7
97038	MOLALLA	005	12845	13356	14015	0.9	68	4469	4708	4993	1.2	2.81	3365	3516	1.0
97039	MORO	055	557	559	566	0.1	38	219	221	225	0.2	2.53	151	151	0.0
97040	MOSIER	065	982	1009	1013	0.6	57	388	400	403	0.7	2.50	258	264	0.5
97041	MOUNT HOOD PARKDALE	027	2597	2795	3025	1.7	86	802	861	930	1.7	2.91	629	673	1.6
97042	MULINO	005	2958	2828	2884	-1.1	6	1060	1027	1059	-0.7	2.75	844	813	-0.9
97045	OREGON CITY	005	45456	48366	51281	1.5	81	16428	17773	19092	1.9	2.67	12402	13388	1.8
97048	RAINIER	009	6563	6733	7125	0.6	55	2454	2536	2699	0.8	2.65	1838	1892	0.7
97049	RHODODENDRON	005	1854	1962	2062	1.3	78	784	845	901	1.8	2.28	463	495	1.6
97050	RUFUS	055	264	263	266	-0.1	28	130	130	132	0.0	2.02	87	86	-0.3
97051	SAINT HELENS	009	12940	13926	15004	1.7	86	4825	5193	5608	1.7	2.65	3405	3646	1.6
97053	WARREN	009	2966	3156	3379	1.5	81	1097	1170	1257	1.5	2.70	866	918	1.4
97054	DEER ISLAND	009	1713	1757	1845	0.6	55	633	653	689	0.7	2.69	500	514	0.7
97055	SANDY	005	13498	15081	16420	2.6	95	4858	5492	6039	2.9	2.74	3683	4127	2.7
97056	SCAPPOOSE	009	9292	10165	11048	2.1	90	3610	3977	4346	2.3	2.54	2627	2881	2.2
97057	SHANIKO	065	94	86	83	-2.1	0	45	41	40	-2.2	2.07	31	29	-1.6
97058	THE DALLES	065	18869	18864	18714	0.0	31	7441	7450	7411	0.0	2.46	5113	5091	-0.1
97060	TROUTDALE	051	17965	19634	20862	2.1	90	6157	6709	7105	2.0	2.87	4729	5128	1.9
97062	TUALATIN	067	24278	27739	30999	3.2	97	9100	10453	11719	3.3	2.64	6241	7101	3.1
97063	TYGH VALLEY	065	910	904	892	-0.2	26	410	409	405	-0.1	2.21	288	286	-0.2
97064	VERNONIA	009	3528	3667	3877	0.9	68	1248	1299	1377	1.0	2.82	945	979	0.8
97065	WASCO	055	653	661	674	0.3	45	259	262	268	0.3	2.52	178	179	0.1
97067	WELCHES	005	1295	1355	1414	1.1	72	491	522	551	1.5	2.55	327	346	1.3
97068	WEST LINN	005	25583	27674	29489	1.9	88	9361	10273	11069	2.2	2.68	7294	7953	2.1
97070	WILSONVILLE	005	15341	17042	18391	2.5	95	6401	7147	7761	2.6	2.37	4163	4600	2.4
97071	WOODBURN	047	25501	27542	29397	1.8	87	7868	8458	8996	1.7	3.17	5764	6156	1.6
97080	GRESHAM	051	37186	40935	43788	2.3	92	13516	14880	15911	2.3	2.74	10057	10993	2.1
97101	AMITY	071	3134	3224	3408	0.7	58	1036	1065	1125	0.7	3.02	834	854	0.6
97103	ASTORIA	007	17070	17020	17062	-0.1	29	6847	6880	6943	0.1	2.36	4418	4406	-0.1
97106	BANKS	067	4337	4756	5187	2.2	91	1469	1619	1770	2.3	2.93	1183	1299	2.2
97107	BAY CITY	057	1329	1400	1463	1.2	75	569	603	633	1.4	2.31	397	418	1.2
97108	BEAVER	057	568	595	620	1.1	73	229	242	253	1.3	2.46	170	179	1.2
97109	BUXTON	067	427	458	494	1.7	85	146	157	170	1.7	2.92	115	124	1.8
97111	CARLTON	071	2803	2840	2998	0.3	47	968	981	1036	0.3	2.89	768	776	0.2
97112	CLOVERDALE	057	2983	3013	3098	0.2	43	1256	1278	1324	0.4	2.36	890	899	0.2
97113	CORNELIUS	067	12101	12864	13848	1.5	81	3731	3945	4239	1.3	3.21	2844	2996	1.2
97114	DAYTON	071	4659	5079	5547	2.1	89	1517	1658	1815	2.1	3.04	1209	1316	2.0
97115	DUNDEE	071	3549	3794	4099	1.6	84	1239	1330	1440	1.7	2.83	993	1062	1.6
97116	FOREST GROVE	067	21434	22672	24339	1.3	77	7661	8150	8786	1.5	2.66	5223	5500	1.2
97117	GALES CREEK	067	535	553	598	0.8	64	203	210	226	0.8	2.63	157	161	0.6
97119	GASTON	067	4187	4172	4391	-0.1	29	1409	1410	1488	0.0	2.94	1161	1158	-0.1
97121	HAMMOND	007	945	971	976	0.6	57	384	400	406	1.0	2.41	269	278	0.8
97122	HEBO	057	261	276	288	1.3	77	106	113	119	1.5	2.44	76	81	1.5
97123	HILLSBORO	067	36229	38811	42023	1.6	84	11854	12702	13763	1.6	3.02	8935	9532	1.5
97124	HILLSBORO	067	38415	43716	48823	3.1	96	14452	16680	18736	3.4	2.59	9596	10835	2.9
97125	MANNING	067	89	108	124	4.7	100	29	35	41	4.5	3.09	21	26	5.2
97127	LAFAYETTE	071	2445	2735	3028	2.7	96	778	869	961	2.6	3.15	606	675	2.6
97128	MCMINNVILLE	071	30187	32531	35279	1.8	87	10680	11552	12575	1.9	2.67	7523	8092	1.7
97131	NEHALEM	057	2732	2805	2888	0.6	56	1281	1326	1374	0.8	2.07	819	843	0.7
97132	NEWBERG	071	24220	26071	28282	1.8	87	8278	8943	9740	1.8	2.78	6153	6629	1.8
97133	NORTH PLAINS	067	3554	3596	3800	0.3	45	1272	1291	1366	0.4	2.77	985	995	0.2
97136	ROCKAWAY BEACH	057	3409	3516	3629	0.7	61	1559	1622	1687	0.9	2.11	940	970	0.7
97137	SAINT PAUL	047	1498	1491	1533	-0.1	27	452	451	463	-0.1	3.12	333	331	-0.1
97138	SEASIDE	007	10089	10015	9967	-0.2	25	4454	4455	4461	0.0	2.21	2723	2705	-0.2
97140	SHERWOOD	067	16692	19617	22140	3.9	99	6013	7068	7974	3.9	2.77	4723	5523	3.8
97141	TILLAMOOK	057	12520	12882	13341	0.7	58	4979	5150	5369	0.8	2.44	3363	3463	0.7
97144	TIMBER	067	162	195	223	4.5	100	63	76	87	4.5	2.57	47	56	4.2
97145	TOLOVANA PARK	007	1301	1305	1303	0.1	37	586	591	594	0.2	2.14	355	355	0.0
97146	WARRENTON	007	5176	5421	5516	1.1	73	2028	2150	2201	1.4	2.46	1394	1467	1.2
97148	YAMHILL	071	3083	3089	3242	0.1	37	1039	1044	1098	0.1	2.95	865	867	0.1
97149	NESKOWIN	057	400	413	427	0.8	63	188	196	204	1.0	2.11	120	125	1.0
97201	PORTLAND	051	11411	12095	12737	1.4	79	6956	7407	7807	1.5	1.56	1817	1855	0.5
97202	PORTLAND	051	37005	36304	36784	-0.5	18	16630	16258	16417	-0.5	2.16	8052	7782	-0.8
97203	PORTLAND	051	27743	28109	28908	0.3	47	10004	10114	10374	0.3	2.65	6315	6334	0.1
97204	PORTLAND	051	1259	1328	1375	1.3	76	397	460	502	3.5	1.03	15	17	3.0
	OREGON					1.1					1.1	2.50			1.0
	UNITED STATES					1.2					1.3	2.58			1.1

ZIP CODE #	POST OFFICE NAME	RACE (%) White 2000	White 2004	Black 2000	Black 2004	Asian/Pacific 2000	Asian/Pacific 2004	% Hispanic Origin 2000	% Hispanic Origin 2004	2004 AGE DISTRIBUTION (%) 0-4	5-9	10-14	15-19	20-24	25-44	45-64	65-84	85+	18+	MEDIAN AGE 2004	% 2004 Males	% 2004 Females
97001	ANTELOPE	87.0	87.7	0.0	0.0	1.1	1.2	4.3	4.1	5.3	6.4	7.0	5.3	4.1	22.8	33.9	14.0	1.2	77.2	44.4	53.2	46.8
97002	AURORA	90.4	88.9	0.3	0.3	0.6	0.7	8.8	10.7	5.3	6.0	7.4	6.6	5.2	24.4	31.6	12.4	1.2	77.0	41.9	52.2	47.8
97004	BEAVERCREEK	95.4	95.0	0.4	0.4	0.7	0.8	1.9	2.4	4.9	6.0	7.6	6.9	5.2	23.9	35.3	9.5	0.8	77.3	42.5	51.0	49.0
97005	BEAVERTON	75.1	72.1	1.9	1.9	6.8	7.3	20.4	24.3	7.6	6.6	6.0	5.7	9.4	34.0	19.7	8.6	2.4	76.7	32.8	50.3	49.7
97006	BEAVERTON	75.5	73.2	1.8	1.9	13.1	14.2	10.6	12.6	8.5	7.3	7.0	6.7	9.0	35.9	19.7	5.3	0.7	73.2	30.6	50.4	49.6
97007	BEAVERTON	81.1	79.1	1.5	1.5	9.3	10.2	7.9	9.7	8.1	7.9	8.0	6.6	6.9	32.9	23.3	5.6	0.8	71.8	33.0	49.2	50.8
97008	BEAVERTON	83.3	81.7	1.6	1.6	6.4	7.1	9.9	11.5	6.6	6.6	7.2	6.3	7.4	30.4	25.0	8.9	1.6	75.8	35.6	48.7	51.3
97009	BORING	93.3	92.5	0.3	0.4	1.6	1.8	3.7	4.4	4.6	5.8	7.4	7.2	5.1	22.9	34.4	11.5	1.1	77.6	43.2	51.0	49.0
97011	BRIGHTWOOD	92.4	91.4	0.4	0.5	0.4	0.5	6.6	8.0	5.4	6.0	6.9	7.3	5.9	27.0	31.4	9.3	0.8	77.0	40.1	53.3	46.7
97013	CANBY	89.9	88.5	0.4	0.5	1.1	1.2	12.1	14.3	7.5	7.4	7.9	7.6	6.4	26.4	25.1	10.0	1.9	72.4	36.0	49.6	50.4
97014	CASCADE LOCKS	89.8	89.1	0.2	0.2	0.8	0.8	6.4	7.8	6.8	7.1	8.0	6.3	6.2	27.9	27.0	9.6	1.1	74.2	37.6	49.8	50.2
97015	CLACKAMAS	86.3	84.7	1.3	1.3	6.8	7.9	4.1	4.9	7.6	7.1	7.2	6.8	8.1	30.1	25.2	7.2	0.7	74.0	34.2	48.9	51.1
97016	CLATSKANIE	94.8	94.4	0.1	0.1	0.6	0.6	2.2	2.7	5.8	6.1	7.4	7.5	6.2	23.3	29.9	12.4	1.5	75.9	41.0	50.6	49.4
97017	COLTON	94.7	94.4	0.3	0.3	0.7	0.8	2.0	2.4	5.6	6.9	8.8	8.6	4.8	25.2	31.2	8.0	0.8	72.9	39.1	49.8	50.2
97018	COLUMBIA CITY	94.8	94.2	0.4	0.5	0.7	0.8	3.0	3.7	6.5	7.2	8.4	6.7	5.7	25.5	29.2	9.9	1.0	73.2	38.5	52.2	47.8
97019	CORBETT	94.1	93.8	0.2	0.2	1.5	1.6	2.3	2.8	5.1	6.7	7.2	7.0	5.3	25.9	33.6	8.6	0.8	76.6	40.7	50.8	49.3
97021	DUFUR	93.7	93.7	0.2	0.2	0.1	0.1	1.9	2.0	4.9	5.5	7.0	7.5	5.8	21.4	31.5	14.5	2.1	77.9	43.6	52.2	47.9
97022	EAGLE CREEK	94.0	93.4	0.4	0.4	0.4	0.5	3.6	4.4	5.4	6.2	7.7	7.4	5.1	24.4	32.8	10.0	1.0	76.1	41.4	50.9	49.1
97023	ESTACADA	90.9	89.7	0.5	0.6	0.9	1.0	6.8	8.2	5.5	5.8	7.5	8.9	6.5	25.5	29.7	9.2	1.4	75.8	39.0	51.1	48.9
97024	FAIRVIEW	78.6	76.1	2.8	3.0	3.4	3.9	13.6	16.0	8.2	7.7	7.6	6.0	6.6	32.2	23.0	7.9	0.8	73.0	33.0	50.7	49.3
97026	GERVAIS	53.7	49.8	0.3	0.4	0.5	0.5	48.4	53.2	10.0	9.4	9.8	8.3	8.1	31.4	16.4	5.9	0.7	66.2	27.5	53.1	47.0
97027	GLADSTONE	91.4	90.4	0.7	0.8	2.2	2.4	5.6	6.8	6.4	6.7	7.3	6.6	6.2	28.0	26.5	10.5	1.7	75.3	37.7	48.7	51.3
97028	GOVERNMENT CAMP	94.0	93.4	0.3	0.3	0.8	1.0	6.0	7.4	4.6	5.1	5.6	6.1	6.4	29.9	32.4	9.4	0.5	81.1	40.3	55.9	44.1
97029	GRASS VALLEY	94.7	94.9	0.5	0.5	0.2	0.2	4.1	4.1	3.9	5.3	11.6	8.9	3.4	19.6	28.3	17.2	1.9	73.0	43.3	49.8	50.2
97030	GRESHAM	84.2	82.2	1.9	2.0	3.3	3.7	10.7	12.9	7.7	7.1	7.0	7.0	8.8	28.9	21.8	9.4	2.3	74.3	32.9	48.7	51.4
97031	HOOD RIVER	78.5	75.7	0.7	0.8	1.6	1.8	25.2	29.2	7.5	7.2	7.5	7.0	6.4	28.0	23.8	10.4	2.3	73.3	35.9	49.3	50.8
97032	HUBBARD	78.4	74.8	0.2	0.2	0.7	0.8	22.3	26.7	8.4	8.1	8.8	7.8	6.8	29.0	22.5	7.8	0.9	69.9	32.4	51.0	49.1
97033	KENT	95.7	97.8	0.0	0.0	0.0	0.0	4.4	4.4	4.4	4.4	8.7	8.7	4.4	21.7	26.1	19.6	2.2	78.3	43.8	52.2	47.8
97034	LAKE OSWEGO	94.1	93.5	0.5	0.5	2.7	3.1	2.1	2.6	4.4	6.1	7.8	7.3	4.4	20.0	36.4	12.0	1.7	76.8	45.1	48.6	51.4
97035	LAKE OSWEGO	89.4	88.2	0.8	0.8	5.5	6.3	3.0	3.7	5.5	6.1	7.0	6.4	6.7	28.4	30.0	8.6	1.4	77.3	39.1	48.3	51.7
97037	MAUPIN	58.3	57.3	0.1	0.1	0.8	0.8	5.5	5.5	7.7	7.1	8.8	6.2	6.4	20.7	28.6	13.5	0.9	72.2	39.2	52.0	48.0
97038	MOLALLA	91.0	89.8	0.4	0.4	0.7	0.8	7.0	8.5	8.2	7.9	8.2	7.2	7.0	28.8	23.0	8.4	1.4	71.4	33.6	49.9	50.1
97039	MORO	94.1	94.1	0.4	0.4	0.4	0.4	4.5	4.5	4.7	5.7	10.4	8.2	3.8	20.4	28.3	16.5	2.2	73.7	43.0	49.9	50.1
97040	MOSIER	89.1	89.1	0.7	0.7	0.9	0.9	10.9	10.9	6.2	6.5	7.5	6.1	5.8	25.1	29.3	12.3	1.2	75.2	40.9	49.8	50.3
97041	MOUNT HOOD PARKDALE	76.5	73.7	0.0	0.0	1.8	1.9	31.7	36.4	7.3	7.6	8.5	6.7	6.7	27.1	25.8	9.1	1.3	72.5	35.1	52.6	47.4
97042	MULINO	96.2	95.8	0.2	0.2	0.6	0.7	2.1	2.6	5.1	5.7	8.6	7.0	5.0	24.9	31.9	11.2	0.8	76.2	41.7	51.4	48.6
97045	OREGON CITY	93.9	93.3	0.5	0.5	1.0	1.2	3.8	4.6	7.0	7.0	7.4	6.4	6.5	28.1	27.4	9.0	1.4	74.9	37.1	49.5	50.5
97048	RAINIER	94.5	94.2	0.1	0.1	0.6	0.7	1.7	2.1	5.5	5.8	7.3	7.3	6.2	23.2	32.0	11.5	1.3	76.8	41.5	49.4	50.6
97049	RHODODENDRON	93.2	92.3	0.3	0.3	0.7	0.8	6.3	7.7	5.1	5.4	6.1	6.6	6.2	29.0	31.2	9.6	0.8	79.4	40.1	54.3	45.7
97050	RUFUS	93.6	93.5	0.0	0.0	1.1	1.1	4.6	4.6	6.5	5.7	5.3	6.5	5.3	22.8	28.1	17.9	1.9	78.0	43.5	52.5	47.5
97051	SAINT HELENS	93.4	92.8	0.3	0.3	0.8	0.9	3.5	4.2	7.9	7.1	7.9	7.2	7.3	28.5	23.6	8.9	1.7	72.5	34.6	49.7	50.3
97053	WARREN	95.7	95.4	0.2	0.2	0.5	0.6	2.3	2.9	4.6	5.4	7.1	7.0	4.9	23.1	33.8	12.7	1.4	78.4	43.8	50.2	49.8
97054	DEER ISLAND	94.8	94.4	0.1	0.1	0.9	1.0	1.2	1.5	5.3	7.3	7.9	6.7	6.0	23.2	32.8	9.9	0.9	75.0	40.9	52.3	47.8
97055	SANDY	94.2	93.6	0.3	0.3	0.9	1.0	3.4	4.2	6.6	6.9	7.8	7.2	6.5	26.5	28.7	8.7	1.0	74.3	37.8	50.2	49.8
97056	SCAPPOOSE	94.5	94.1	0.3	0.3	0.8	0.9	2.4	2.9	5.9	6.1	7.0	6.3	6.0	26.3	30.1	10.8	1.4	76.8	40.6	49.5	50.5
97057	SHANIKO	90.4	90.7	0.0	0.0	1.1	1.2	4.3	3.5	5.8	5.8	7.0	5.8	4.7	23.3	30.2	15.1	2.3	76.7	43.6	55.8	44.2
97058	THE DALLES	88.1	88.0	0.3	0.3	1.5	1.5	10.3	10.4	6.7	6.5	6.6	6.9	6.8	23.8	26.1	13.9	2.7	75.8	39.8	48.8	51.2
97060	TROUTDALE	86.6	85.1	1.7	1.9	3.7	4.3	6.9	8.3	8.4	8.1	7.8	6.8	7.5	32.2	23.5	5.3	0.6	71.7	32.6	50.1	49.9
97062	TUALATIN	87.6	86.1	0.8	0.8	3.8	4.2	10.8	12.9	7.3	7.2	7.9	7.3	7.6	31.0	25.4	5.5	1.0	73.0	33.8	49.6	50.4
97063	TYGH VALLEY	93.4	93.3	0.2	0.2	0.9	0.9	4.0	3.9	4.0	4.0	4.7	5.3	3.8	14.4	35.3	27.3	1.3	84.3	54.6	51.3	48.7
97064	VERNONIA	95.9	95.7	0.4	0.4	0.5	0.6	1.9	2.2	7.7	7.8	8.3	7.9	6.6	26.6	24.6	9.5	1.1	71.4	35.8	50.1	49.9
97065	WASCO	92.5	92.4	0.0	0.0	0.3	0.3	5.8	5.8	5.9	6.5	7.7	7.1	4.8	21.9	29.1	15.0	2.0	75.3	42.6	50.4	49.6
97067	WELCHES	92.1	91.2	0.4	0.4	0.4	0.4	6.6	8.2	5.5	6.1	6.9	7.5	5.9	27.2	30.8	9.4	0.9	76.8	39.8	53.4	46.6
97068	WEST LINN	93.5	92.7	0.6	0.6	3.0	3.4	2.8	3.4	6.1	7.3	8.4	7.4	5.1	24.7	32.2	7.9	0.9	73.4	40.1	49.8	50.2
97070	WILSONVILLE	90.9	89.8	0.6	0.6	2.3	2.6	6.5	7.9	7.3	6.4	6.5	5.7	8.2	28.8	23.4	11.5	2.2	76.5	35.6	48.5	51.5
97071	WOODBURN	62.5	59.1	0.4	0.4	0.7	0.7	43.9	48.4	8.7	7.9	8.0	8.1	7.8	25.8	17.3	13.3	3.1	70.6	31.6	51.7	48.3
97080	GRESHAM	89.5	88.2	1.0	1.1	3.3	3.8	5.5	6.8	6.9	6.9	7.6	7.4	7.7	27.7	27.0	7.8	1.1	74.2	35.3	49.4	50.6
97101	AMITY	92.4	91.5	0.3	0.3	0.6	0.7	7.5	9.0	6.8	7.0	7.8	7.9	6.9	26.3	26.8	9.5	1.1	73.5	36.7	50.9	49.1
97103	ASTORIA	92.2	91.4	0.9	0.9	1.6	1.8	4.7	5.7	5.9	5.6	6.5	8.3	8.3	23.8	27.3	12.2	2.2	77.3	39.0	49.3	50.7
97106	BANKS	93.7	92.9	0.3	0.3	1.3	1.5	3.4	4.4	7.2	7.6	8.4	7.4	4.8	28.9	28.1	6.9	0.7	72.0	36.8	50.8	49.2
97107	BAY CITY	93.4	92.8	0.4	0.4	1.0	1.2	3.2	3.9	4.6	4.9	5.5	5.4	4.4	24.9	32.1	16.6	1.6	81.8	45.2	49.1	50.9
97108	BEAVER	96.3	95.6	0.2	0.2	0.2	0.2	5.5	6.7	6.1	6.7	8.2	6.7	4.9	21.9	30.1	14.1	1.3	74.6	42.0	48.1	51.9
97109	BUXTON	95.1	94.5	0.5	0.4	0.2	0.4	3.3	4.2	6.1	5.5	8.1	9.4	4.4	26.9	32.1	7.4	0.2	74.2	39.9	50.9	49.1
97111	CARLTON	93.0	92.2	0.1	0.1	0.4	0.4	4.7	5.7	7.0	7.6	8.4	7.2	5.9	25.0	28.1	9.8	1.1	72.4	37.6	50.5	49.5
97112	CLOVERDALE	93.6	93.0	0.2	0.2	0.6	0.7	2.7	3.3	4.0	5.2	5.9	6.7	3.8	19.8	33.5	19.1	2.1	80.7	48.0	49.6	50.4
97113	CORNELIUS	74.2	70.2	0.6	0.6	1.4	1.5	30.1	35.5	8.9	8.3	8.0	6.9	7.0	31.6	20.3	8.0	1.0	70.6	31.4	51.6	48.5
97114	DAYTON	85.7	83.9	0.9	1.1	0.7	0.8	19.6	22.9	7.4	7.6	8.8	7.9	6.4	25.8	24.7	10.2	1.2	71.3	34.8	50.5	49.5
97115	DUNDEE	92.7	91.7	0.2	0.2	1.1	1.2	6.9	8.3	7.1	7.7	8.3	6.7	4.9	28.9	26.2	9.2	0.9	72.3	37.4	50.8	49.2
97116	FOREST GROVE	83.2	80.3	0.4	0.4	2.1	2.3	15.9	19.6	8.3	7.6	7.7	7.2	8.3	29.2	20.5	8.6	2.8	72.8	32.4	48.6	51.4
97117	GALES CREEK	95.5	94.9	0.2	0.2	0.8	0.9	3.4	4.5	4.9	5.8	7.1	5.8	5.2	24.2	35.1	10.3	1.6	78.3	43.1	50.5	49.6
97119	GASTON	93.4	92.4	0.2	0.2	1.0	1.1	5.4	6.8	6.0	6.7	8.0	7.2	5.8	24.2	32.4	8.7	0.9	74.7	40.5	51.2	48.8
97121	HAMMOND	91.6	90.6	0.2	0.2	1.2	1.2	3.8	4.8	8.2	7.5	6.5	5.3	6.8	28.5	23.8	12.3	1.1	74.4	36.4	51.8	48.2
97122	HEBO	94.6	94.2	0.0	0.0	0.4	0.4	2.3	2.9	3.3	5.8	6.9	8.0	2.9	20.3	34.8	15.9	2.2	79.0	46.7	50.7	49.3
97123	HILLSBORO	77.5	75.1	0.8	0.9	4.5	5.3	23.3	25.8	9.2	8.4	7.7	6.6	7.5	32.2	20.9	6.5	1.0	70.8	31.9	51.5	48.5
97124	HILLSBORO	81.2	78.4	1.1	1.2	7.1	8.4	13.1	15.7	8.5	7.5	6.8	6.4	8.8	36.4	19.5	5.3	1.0	73.6	31.0	51.3	48.8
97125	MANNING	94.4	93.5	0.0	0.0	1.1	0.9	4.5	5.6	5.6	5.6	7.4	6.5	4.6	25.9	35.2	7.4	1.9	75.9	42.3	47.2	52.8
97127	LAFAYETTE	86.1	84.2	0.4	0.6	0.9	0.9	20.0	23.5	9.9	9.8	8.9	6.3	5.9	32.3	20.0	6.3	0.8	67.5	31.5	50.0	50.1
97128	MCMINNVILLE	87.3	85.7	0.6	0.7	1.4	1.5	13.4	15.8	7.3	6.8	7.1	8.4	9.5	26.2	21.1	11.5	2.3	74.7	33.2	48.7	51.3
97131	NEHALEM	95.9	95.5	0.3	0.4	1.0	1.1	2.8	3.4	3.7	3.9	4.1	3.8	4.1	17.4	34.1	25.6	3.4	85.9	53.7	49.0	51.0
97132	NEWBERG	91.5	90.4	0.3	0.4	1.2	1.3	8.9	10.6	7.4	6.9	7.3	7.7	9.2	27.8	23.2	8.9	1.8	74.2	33.5	49.0	51.0
97133	NORTH PLAINS	91.0	89.5	0.1	0.1	1.6	1.8	7.5	9.4	6.6	7.5	8.2	6.9	4.0	26.7	29.6	9.3	1.1	73.5	39.2	51.5	48.6
97136	ROCKAWAY BEACH	94.7	94.2	0.2	0.2	1.0	1.1	2.1	2.6	2.6	3.1	4.4	4.6	3.7	19.5	34.4	25.1	2.6	86.9	52.1	50.6	49.4
97137	SAINT PAUL	71.6	66.9	0.2	0.2	0.2	0.2	29.2	34.5	6.7	7.5	8.3	8.5	8.6	29.2	21.8	8.5	1.0	72.5	32.8	58.3	41.7
97138	SEASIDE	94.1	93.4	0.2	0.3	1.0	1.2	5.3	6.5	4.8	5.1	6.1	6.3	6.4	22.3	31.1	15.2	2.7	80.2	44.3	48.4	51.6
97140	SHERWOOD	92.6	91.6	0.4	0.4	2.1	2.3	4.6	5.8	9.5	9.2	8.0	5.9	4.8	33.1	22.4	6.5	0.7	69.6	34.5	49.2	50.8
97141	TILLAMOOK	93.2	92.4	0.2	0.2	0.9	1.0	7.4	8.9	5.9	6.4	7.3	7.2	5.9	24.2	27.6	13.6	1.9	75.6	40.3	50.9	49.1
97144	TIMBER	93.8	93.3	0.6	0.5	1.2	1.0	4.3	5.1	5.6	6.2	7.2	6.7	5.1	25.1	35.4	7.2	1.5	75.9	42.0	49.2	50.8
97145	TOLOVANA PARK	93.8	93.2	0.3	0.3	0.6	0.7	6.8	8.2	3.8	4.4	4.4	6.5	6.4	18.3	35.7	18.7	1.9	84.6	48.6	47.1	52.9
97146	WARRENTON	94.1	93.4	0.2	0.3	1.7	2.0	2.1	2.6	5.9	6.1	7.1	7.9	5.8	24.5	28.1	13.0	1.5	75.5	40.7	50.9	49.1
97148	YAMHILL	94.6	94.0	0.1	0.1	0.7	0.7	4.4	5.3	5.9	6.7	7.9	8.6	5.9	24.7	30.2	9.0	1.1	73.5	39.2	50.5	49.5
97149	NESKOWIN	95.3	94.9	0.3	0.2	1.3	1.5	3.0	3.9	3.2	4.1	5.6	5.8	2.2	17.2	37.3	21.6	3.2	84.0	51.9	48.2	51.8
97201	PORTLAND	83.0	80.8	2.0	2.2	9.5	11.0	3.6	4.4	2.2	2.0	2.0	5.9	16.0	36.1	22.1	11.5	2.3	92.5	33.7	51.2	48.8
97202	PORTLAND	86.5	85.0	1.9	2.1	5.5	6.3	4.4	5.3	5.1	4.7	4.9	5.6	8.7	35.6	24.1	9.1	2.2	82.6	35.7	48.9	51.1
97203	PORTLAND	68.9	66.8	9.5	9.6	6.4	7.1	13.7	16.0	8.2	7.3	6.8	8.6	9.3	30.1	20.5	7.9	1.3	74.1	31.1	49.8	50.2
97204	PORTLAND	64.6	62.3	21.4	22.3	2.1	2.4	7.6	8.8	0.3	0.5	0.2	4.2	11.5	52.2	25.2	5.7	0.3	98.3	37.5	77.0	23.0
	OREGON	86.6	85.2	1.6	1.7	3.2	3.6	8.1	9.5	6.5	6.4	6.8	6.9	7.4	27.7	25.6	11.0	1.9	76.3	36.9	49.6	50.4
	UNITED STATES	75.1	73.6	12.3	12.5	3.8	4.2	12.5	14.1	6.9	6.7	7.2	7.0	7.3	28.6	23.8	10.8	1.7	75.1	36.0	49.1	50.9

ZIP CODE #	POST OFFICE NAME	2004 Per Capita Income	2004 HH Income Base	2004 Household Income Distribution (%) Less than $25,000	$25,000 to $49,999	$50,000 to $99,999	$100,000 to $149,999	$150,000 or More	Median Household Income 2004	2009	2004 National Centile	2004 State Centile	2004 Home Value Base	2004 Home Value Distribution (%) Less than $50,000	$50,000 to $89,999	$90,000 to $174,999	$175,000 to $399,999	$400,000 or More	2004 Median Home Value
97001	ANTELOPE	17473	66	28.8	39.4	27.3	3.0	1.5	37303	43353	36	38	46	10.9	23.9	43.5	13.0	8.7	108333
97002	AURORA	25290	2067	16.6	29.3	37.0	10.0	7.1	52592	60317	76	84	1742	9.0	10.3	26.9	32.9	20.9	189865
97004	BEAVERCREEK	30005	1567	8.7	22.4	43.9	18.6	6.4	63768	74580	88	97	1398	1.4	2.2	11.0	66.2	19.2	280319
97005	BEAVERTON	22226	9623	25.2	34.9	29.5	7.8	2.6	40435	47678	48	49	3979	8.0	2.6	35.5	51.5	2.5	180859
97006	BEAVERTON	26175	22518	15.9	28.2	37.9	12.9	5.2	55253	63630	80	88	11843	5.3	6.7	21.9	61.9	4.4	202152
97007	BEAVERTON	29301	22709	11.6	24.5	38.8	16.7	8.4	63823	74391	88	97	15143	1.3	0.7	17.9	68.5	11.6	228198
97008	BEAVERTON	28519	11934	15.4	30.0	35.5	12.6	6.6	54381	62137	79	87	6935	1.5	0.6	19.5	75.6	2.9	216461
97009	BORING	29415	4749	10.9	21.8	40.0	18.5	8.9	68314	80306	90	98	4234	5.5	4.0	9.1	60.5	21.0	274364
97011	BRIGHTWOOD	28633	470	17.7	25.5	38.3	14.9	3.6	55672	64619	80	89	380	11.1	6.1	26.1	50.3	6.6	192568
97013	CANBY	23459	7482	18.0	27.6	36.2	13.5	4.8	53845	63089	78	86	5488	4.8	7.4	17.4	58.2	12.2	217566
97014	CASCADE LOCKS	18335	501	30.7	32.5	30.1	5.4	1.2	40610	45568	48	50	374	12.6	11.5	53.5	20.9	1.6	123641
97015	CLACKAMAS	28400	9531	14.6	26.4	36.5	15.7	6.8	60259	69593	85	94	6378	14.8	4.6	5.2	63.5	11.9	236055
97016	CLATSKANIE	21347	2503	27.3	28.0	35.0	6.9	2.8	44557	50082	60	66	1944	10.4	11.1	42.0	34.7	1.8	145229
97017	COLTON	24521	936	16.5	23.4	43.8	11.1	5.2	59290	68068	84	93	804	1.0	0.1	15.8	67.9	15.2	244903
97018	COLUMBIA CITY	27707	590	14.4	24.2	43.4	12.4	5.6	60594	66043	85	95	506	1.4	19.6	21.9	50.6	6.5	191071
97019	CORBETT	28387	1030	14.5	18.8	43.0	15.7	8.0	68702	77436	91	99	876	1.9	1.9	15.5	63.5	17.1	251969
97021	DUFUR	20437	454	27.1	31.9	32.8	5.5	2.6	41052	44257	50	53	340	6.5	18.2	50.0	17.1	8.2	120679
97022	EAGLE CREEK	22841	1185	16.5	31.7	37.0	11.3	3.5	51561	58805	75	82	1015	8.4	8.3	15.8	51.4	16.2	229028
97023	ESTACADA	22884	3456	21.0	27.6	33.9	14.0	3.5	51116	60214	74	81	2765	9.8	5.2	21.3	52.2	11.4	215056
97024	FAIRVIEW	22769	3388	20.9	32.9	32.5	9.8	3.9	47000	53190	66	73	2277	24.6	10.6	21.8	38.3	4.7	151951
97026	GERVAIS	14279	888	21.6	34.1	32.9	8.3	3.0	46410	51654	65	71	686	4.5	7.4	56.6	25.1	6.4	150388
97027	GLADSTONE	23044	4604	19.3	26.9	40.1	11.4	2.3	52996	62540	77	85	3330	6.5	2.7	27.6	60.5	2.8	198970
97028	GOVERNMENT CAMP	41748	174	25.3	17.8	32.8	14.4	9.8	62295	69793	86	96	123	0.0	4.9	22.0	61.8	11.4	217424
97029	GRASS VALLEY	20390	172	30.2	32.0	30.8	4.1	2.9	40819	45203	49	51	133	13.5	34.6	33.8	17.3	0.8	93571
97030	GRESHAM	21999	12877	24.7	30.5	33.0	9.0	2.8	45458	51378	62	68	6841	4.4	1.4	32.3	60.3	1.6	189655
97031	HOOD RIVER	20557	6354	24.5	34.2	30.8	6.9	3.6	42753	48010	55	59	4234	6.8	2.5	31.0	48.4	11.3	193773
97032	HUBBARD	18388	1312	20.4	33.4	34.3	9.0	3.0	46975	53093	66	73	1028	11.7	7.5	42.1	32.9	5.8	156529
97033	KENT	15435	18	33.3	27.8	38.9	0.0	0.0	40000	45000	46	48	14	0.0	35.7	42.9	21.4	0.0	106250
97034	LAKE OSWEGO	53827	7823	9.5	16.1	28.4	20.4	25.6	89705	103935	97	100	6207	0.4	0.3	4.2	49.0	46.1	383481
97035	LAKE OSWEGO	40390	10389	12.2	23.4	33.1	16.3	15.0	68039	78057	90	98	6772	0.4	0.1	11.2	63.2	25.1	286625
97037	MAUPIN	15196	563	32.0	38.0	25.9	2.5	1.6	35716	40322	30	30	428	14.0	19.9	44.6	17.3	4.2	110821
97038	MOLALLA	20832	4708	20.7	29.0	37.8	9.8	2.7	50225	58337	72	80	3448	7.0	4.3	28.4	48.7	11.7	196829
97039	MORO	19069	221	31.7	31.7	29.0	4.5	3.2	39400	45172	44	45	170	17.7	31.8	32.9	17.1	0.6	91111
97040	MOSIER	21197	400	25.0	34.0	31.5	5.8	3.8	43183	48955	56	61	312	13.1	18.3	18.3	41.7	8.7	176000
97041	MOUNT HOOD PARKDALE	18461	861	21.1	42.3	26.0	8.0	2.6	39795	45702	45	48	655	3.1	1.8	33.0	47.6	14.5	214648
97042	MULINO	28460	1027	14.8	23.7	39.4	14.3	7.8	63285	73665	87	96	899	4.6	2.0	9.3	60.2	23.9	286750
97045	OREGON CITY	26499	17773	15.5	25.7	39.1	14.8	5.0	58387	68148	83	91	13253	4.4	4.7	18.3	61.1	11.5	223650
97048	RAINIER	21562	2536	22.0	29.1	38.0	8.2	2.7	48948	54443	70	79	2051	12.1	6.1	34.6	43.3	3.9	169139
97049	RHODODENDRON	35956	845	21.9	20.7	35.3	14.8	7.3	60325	67438	85	94	629	4.9	5.4	24.3	56.4	8.9	206656
97050	RUFUS	21819	130	38.5	30.8	23.1	4.6	3.1	32043	37056	18	14	86	32.6	22.1	26.7	18.6	0.0	77500
97051	SAINT HELENS	20951	5193	25.1	27.3	37.3	7.9	2.4	47844	54303	68	76	3408	4.3	5.7	43.8	43.4	2.8	169192
97053	WARREN	27801	1170	18.6	23.8	37.0	13.7	7.0	56369	62841	81	90	1033	6.4	1.9	19.8	59.3	12.6	227376
97054	DEER ISLAND	24181	653	15.9	32.3	38.4	8.4	4.9	51294	58186	74	81	549	9.1	4.7	18.9	55.4	11.8	211090
97055	SANDY	24525	5492	20.0	26.8	37.2	11.1	4.9	52982	61570	77	84	4350	8.2	6.3	19.8	53.2	12.5	214341
97056	SCAPPOOSE	25335	3977	18.0	26.4	40.5	11.6	3.5	54702	61072	79	88	3161	6.6	5.4	27.3	51.0	9.6	196497
97057	SHANIKO	21960	41	31.7	39.0	22.0	4.9	2.4	35537	43183	30	29	29	6.9	20.7	51.7	13.8	6.9	121875
97058	THE DALLES	19830	7450	31.0	30.2	29.9	6.5	2.4	40088	45837	46	49	5076	8.1	13.0	51.6	24.9	2.4	127993
97060	TROUTDALE	24001	6709	14.0	25.0	42.9	15.0	3.3	58803	67110	83	92	4958	7.3	5.3	22.7	62.3	2.4	195419
97062	TUALATIN	31711	10453	12.0	25.0	36.2	16.2	10.5	62901	72731	87	96	6415	4.4	1.7	10.6	62.7	20.6	249264
97063	TYGH VALLEY	17863	409	36.2	40.3	19.6	2.0	2.0	32285	36341	19	16	349	16.3	16.9	36.7	25.2	4.9	123775
97064	VERNONIA	19875	1299	22.5	33.5	35.6	5.8	2.6	45789	52145	63	69	1055	4.4	8.3	43.3	40.6	3.5	163511
97065	WASCO	18614	262	32.1	30.2	28.6	7.3	1.9	39020	44630	43	43	204	22.6	25.0	36.8	13.7	2.0	95556
97067	WELCHES	25596	522	16.3	26.1	39.1	15.1	3.5	56203	64761	81	90	421	11.9	6.4	26.4	49.2	6.2	188393
97068	WEST LINN	42503	10273	9.8	17.8	30.7	21.5	20.1	83340	96424	96	100	8569	0.6	0.4	8.4	57.0	33.6	321668
97070	WILSONVILLE	35875	7147	15.4	25.8	32.7	16.6	9.4	61223	69070	86	95	4110	8.5	3.2	9.6	58.2	20.5	270584
97071	WOODBURN	15496	8458	28.6	35.6	28.0	5.8	2.0	38154	42520	40	42	5621	6.7	13.6	52.8	23.0	4.0	136450
97080	GRESHAM	26211	14880	16.2	24.1	39.7	14.5	5.5	59992	65802	84	94	10417	2.7	2.3	19.2	66.7	9.1	220675
97101	AMITY	19048	1065	17.3	31.2	39.4	10.7	1.4	51022	55659	74	80	855	3.3	5.5	40.4	41.3	9.6	178074
97103	ASTORIA	21163	6880	28.3	34.3	29.1	5.9	2.5	40871	46512	49	51	4402	5.1	5.6	46.1	39.0	4.3	163942
97106	BANKS	25926	1619	12.0	22.7	41.6	17.3	6.4	65626	76851	89	97	1395	3.7	1.0	17.8	54.5	23.0	247961
97107	BAY CITY	22394	603	30.0	32.8	28.7	6.0	2.5	38341	42542	41	42	476	3.2	11.6	53.2	30.7	1.5	137952
97108	BEAVER	20783	242	25.6	37.6	28.5	5.0	3.3	37334	40928	37	39	199	2.0	14.1	26.6	54.3	3.0	187946
97109	BUXTON	22508	157	21.0	21.7	37.6	14.0	5.7	55909	65185	81	89	137	13.1	0.0	13.1	52.6	21.2	239815
97111	CARLTON	18823	981	18.6	33.7	39.5	7.0	1.2	48322	53740	69	78	797	5.3	2.9	37.5	42.4	11.9	186655
97112	CLOVERDALE	23736	1278	29.1	29.3	32.3	6.7	2.6	39291	43875	44	44	1035	5.4	6.2	36.4	41.2	10.8	181327
97113	CORNELIUS	19649	3945	18.0	27.5	41.2	10.8	2.5	53066	61777	77	85	3157	13.1	7.0	37.8	35.5	6.7	165123
97114	DAYTON	19556	1658	19.7	32.5	35.3	9.2	3.3	48053	52485	68	76	1299	7.9	7.7	33.5	38.5	12.5	177520
97115	DUNDEE	25442	1330	15.5	23.7	40.1	14.6	6.2	59077	65789	84	93	1148	3.8	3.2	26.3	51.8	14.9	219149
97116	FOREST GROVE	20907	8150	24.9	27.0	36.1	9.3	2.8	48003	55010	68	76	5056	9.7	4.5	27.4	50.9	7.5	188625
97117	GALES CREEK	27240	210	16.2	17.6	44.3	16.7	5.2	62918	75000	87	96	177	4.5	2.8	17.0	54.2	21.5	247973
97119	GASTON	31346	1410	13.7	26.7	38.7	12.1	8.8	59497	66577	84	93	1195	2.4	2.3	16.5	47.6	31.1	290112
97121	HAMMOND	20048	400	33.5	26.3	33.8	2.8	3.8	41004	48425	50	52	266	0.0	3.4	57.5	37.6	1.5	160784
97122	HEBO	28649	113	31.0	22.1	40.7	3.5	2.7	39646	45780	45	47	91	8.8	5.5	47.3	29.7	8.8	156250
97123	HILLSBORO	23121	12702	16.4	25.1	39.4	14.1	5.0	57767	67190	82	91	8812	4.6	1.8	24.1	60.6	8.9	203165
97124	HILLSBORO	28307	16680	13.6	25.0	40.1	15.7	5.6	61214	70511	86	95	8364	0.5	1.0	22.1	68.0	8.3	218828
97125	MANNING	21922	35	20.0	20.0	40.0	11.4	8.6	60771	75704	85	95	30	6.7	0.0	13.3	56.7	23.3	275000
97127	LAFAYETTE	16499	869	25.2	33.3	35.0	5.1	1.5	42251	46913	54	57	698	8.2	20.1	48.9	20.5	2.4	128602
97128	MCMINNVILLE	20597	11552	24.0	32.3	32.9	7.8	3.0	45512	51672	63	68	7237	8.6	7.2	38.8	38.8	6.7	167629
97131	NEHALEM	24511	1326	30.6	37.0	21.7	5.3	5.4	36640	42039	34	35	1094	7.5	4.8	26.1	47.0	14.6	219792
97132	NEWBERG	24014	8943	17.7	27.5	39.2	10.2	5.5	54801	61038	79	88	6395	6.2	5.1	31.0	44.1	13.7	189758
97133	NORTH PLAINS	30273	1291	15.3	22.5	35.5	17.0	9.8	65915	76744	89	98	1089	3.5	6.2	17.5	37.3	35.6	279211
97136	ROCKAWAY BEACH	19593	1622	35.8	36.9	22.2	3.8	1.4	32853	36528	20	18	1262	8.5	8.2	41.1	34.2	8.1	157867
97137	SAINT PAUL	24084	451	23.3	30.8	29.3	10.2	6.4	47667	52909	68	75	281	5.7	5.0	27.1	42.4	19.9	211310
97138	SEASIDE	24484	4455	31.0	30.2	29.3	6.2	3.3	39220	44445	43	44	2852	6.3	5.3	26.4	50.6	11.5	203136
97140	SHERWOOD	32566	7068	11.0	18.5	39.1	21.3	10.1	72489	84701	92	99	5817	2.4	5.1	10.2	66.4	15.8	239034
97141	TILLAMOOK	20876	5150	30.6	35.4	27.2	3.7	3.1	38671	43416	42	43	3582	6.3	5.2	45.4	34.8	8.3	158770
97144	TIMBER	26128	76	21.1	21.1	36.8	13.2	7.9	60000	66695	84	94	65	7.7	0.0	12.3	55.4	24.6	269444
97145	TOLOVANA PARK	27194	591	30.5	25.4	31.6	5.8	6.8	42783	48218	55	59	428	0.9	0.0	6.5	57.5	35.1	308571
97146	WARRENTON	22566	2150	27.9	29.0	32.2	6.9	4.0	42650	47935	55	58	1623	10.3	7.1	41.5	32.9	8.3	159799
97148	YAMHILL	26285	1044	16.8	26.5	38.0	11.4	7.3	56450	61425	81	90	878	4.2	5.6	24.9	37.2	28.0	260959
97149	NESKOWIN	24820	196	23.0	32.1	34.2	10.7	0.0	44570	51920	60	66	167	0.0	5.4	10.2	50.9	33.5	290385
97201	PORTLAND	43601	7407	40.7	21.5	19.5	7.9	10.5	34875	37897	27	26	1801	0.0	0.2	4.4	40.1	55.3	434615
97202	PORTLAND	27021	16258	25.4	29.9	30.6	9.4	4.7	44873	51444	61	66	8226	0.1	0.5	26.7	63.0	9.6	212891
97203	PORTLAND	17375	10114	31.0	31.1	31.8	5.4	0.7	39861	45827	45	48	5646	1.7	5.1	67.1	25.2	1.0	148143
97204	PORTLAND	15442	460	88.0	8.9	2.8	0.2	0.0	10593	12026	1	1	0	0.0	0.0	0.0	0.0	0.0	0
	OREGON	24176		24.9	29.7	31.4	9.2	4.8	45702	52201				6.4	6.5	35.2	43.4	8.6	179540
	UNITED STATES	25866		24.7	27.1	30.8	10.9	6.5	48124	56710				10.9	15.0	33.7	30.1	10.4	145905

ZIP CODE		FINANCIAL SERVICES				THE HOME						ENTERTAINMENT						PERSONAL			
						Home Improvements		Furnishings													
#	POST OFFICE NAME	Auto Loan	Home Loan	Invest-ments	Retire-ment Plans	Home Repair	Lawn & Garden	Comput-ers & Hard-ware	Major Appli-ances	TV, Radio, Sound Equip-ment	Furni-ture	Dine out/ Carry out	Sports Equip-ment	Fees & Tickets	Toys & Games	Travel	Cable TV	Apparel & Services	Auto Repairs	Health Insur-ance	Pets & Supplies
97001	ANTELOPE	75	59	41	54	67	75	56	67	63	55	75	79	50	74	60	67	70	66	79	92
97002	AURORA	102	98	83	94	100	106	91	98	93	92	114	114	90	114	93	93	110	96	100	119
97004	BEAVERCREEK	113	132	133	131	131	131	118	120	113	118	141	142	124	149	121	111	139	116	112	137
97005	BEAVERTON	75	72	83	77	70	74	77	75	75	78	95	89	76	91	74	71	92	77	68	82
97006	BEAVERTON	97	97	104	103	93	95	99	96	95	101	120	115	98	117	94	89	118	98	85	106
97007	BEAVERTON	114	120	126	125	116	117	117	115	111	119	141	136	118	139	114	105	138	115	102	127
97008	BEAVERTON	96	104	113	107	101	103	101	100	97	102	122	117	103	123	100	93	120	100	91	109
97009	BORING	112	126	125	124	126	128	115	117	111	114	138	137	119	144	117	109	136	114	111	135
97011	BRIGHTWOOD	117	84	46	79	97	108	82	100	94	81	110	121	71	109	85	98	101	99	118	139
97013	CANBY	93	99	98	100	99	100	93	95	90	94	112	112	95	114	94	87	110	94	89	108
97014	CASCADE LOCKS	74	66	54	65	68	76	66	70	69	65	84	80	64	84	66	70	79	69	74	82
97015	CLACKAMAS	105	114	119	118	110	111	109	107	102	111	130	125	111	129	106	97	128	106	96	118
97016	CLATSKANIE	90	73	51	70	79	88	72	81	79	71	95	95	68	94	73	82	89	80	92	103
97017	COLTON	116	103	78	98	109	117	95	105	101	95	123	126	93	125	98	104	117	103	114	136
97018	COLUMBIA CITY	117	104	80	99	110	118	97	107	103	97	125	128	95	127	99	105	119	104	116	138
97019	CORBETT	104	129	137	129	127	125	115	115	107	115	134	134	122	143	118	104	134	111	103	127
97021	DUFUR	90	64	34	60	74	83	63	77	72	62	84	93	54	83	65	76	77	76	92	107
97022	EAGLE CREEK	101	98	84	95	100	105	91	97	92	91	113	114	90	114	92	92	109	95	98	118
97023	ESTACADA	97	90	77	88	93	100	86	92	88	86	108	108	84	109	87	89	104	90	96	112
97024	FAIRVIEW	86	89	89	91	88	89	87	87	83	87	105	102	87	104	85	80	103	87	80	98
97026	GERVAIS	87	72	61	70	74	79	77	81	81	79	101	93	72	98	73	79	98	83	81	93
97027	GLADSTONE	80	89	94	88	88	92	86	86	84	85	105	99	89	110	87	83	103	85	83	94
97028	GOVERNMENT CAMP	158	124	85	112	140	157	117	141	133	116	157	165	105	155	125	142	146	139	167	193
97029	GRASS VALLEY	89	62	32	59	72	81	61	76	71	60	83	91	52	81	64	74	75	75	90	105
97030	GRESHAM	80	78	82	81	78	82	81	80	80	81	100	95	80	98	79	77	97	82	76	90
97031	HOOD RIVER	83	77	71	76	80	85	77	81	79	76	96	96	74	96	77	79	92	81	84	97
97032	HUBBARD	85	87	80	87	86	88	83	85	80	84	100	99	82	99	82	77	97	84	79	97
97033	KENT	71	50	26	47	58	65	49	61	57	49	67	73	42	65	51	60	61	60	72	85
97034	LAKE OSWEGO	170	208	250	211	204	212	192	188	179	193	227	218	206	234	197	176	227	185	173	206
97035	LAKE OSWEGO	122	136	164	142	132	135	133	129	127	135	161	153	138	164	133	122	159	129	116	142
97037	MAUPIN	67	58	46	55	62	67	55	62	59	55	71	73	51	70	57	60	67	62	68	80
97038	MOLALLA	91	83	70	81	85	91	80	86	83	81	101	100	78	100	81	83	97	85	88	103
97039	MORO	86	61	32	57	70	79	61	74	70	60	82	89	52	80	63	73	74	73	88	102
97040	MOSIER	85	77	60	74	77	82	74	79	74	76	92	91	70	87	73	73	88	79	78	94
97041	MOUNT HOOD PARKDALE	90	72	54	68	78	87	70	81	78	71	93	96	64	93	72	80	88	81	91	106
97042	MULINO	109	122	120	121	122	123	110	113	106	110	132	133	114	139	113	105	130	109	107	131
97045	OREGON CITY	96	109	114	110	107	108	103	102	97	102	122	120	106	126	103	94	120	101	93	113
97048	RAINIER	91	81	62	78	85	92	76	84	81	76	98	99	74	99	78	82	93	82	90	106
97049	RHODODENDRON	144	108	67	99	123	138	104	126	118	103	139	149	91	137	109	125	129	124	150	174
97050	RUFUS	71	54	35	51	59	70	59	65	66	56	78	73	53	74	59	70	71	65	78	79
97051	SAINT HELENS	81	78	73	77	79	84	78	80	79	76	97	93	77	98	77	78	93	79	80	92
97053	WARREN	120	107	82	102	113	121	99	110	105	99	128	131	97	130	102	108	121	107	118	141
97054	DEER ISLAND	104	93	71	88	98	105	86	95	91	86	111	113	84	113	88	93	105	93	103	123
97055	SANDY	96	99	96	99	100	104	94	97	93	94	115	114	95	117	95	91	112	95	94	112
97056	SCAPPOOSE	94	96	88	94	97	101	89	93	89	89	110	111	90	113	91	88	107	91	92	111
97057	SHANIKO	77	60	41	55	68	76	57	69	64	56	76	80	51	75	61	69	71	68	81	94
97058	THE DALLES	74	66	57	64	69	76	67	71	70	66	86	83	64	85	67	71	81	71	76	85
97060	TROUTDALE	100	106	102	108	103	103	100	100	95	102	119	118	100	118	98	90	117	99	90	112
97062	TUALATIN	117	120	134	127	117	121	122	118	116	123	147	141	122	144	118	110	144	120	107	131
97063	TYGH VALLEY	67	53	36	47	59	66	50	60	56	49	66	70	44	66	53	60	62	59	71	82
97064	VERNONIA	89	78	60	76	83	90	75	82	79	74	96	96	73	98	76	81	91	80	89	103
97065	WASCO	83	59	32	56	68	77	59	72	68	58	80	86	51	78	61	71	73	71	86	98
97067	WELCHES	119	83	44	79	97	108	82	101	94	81	111	122	70	109	85	99	101	100	120	141
97068	WEST LINN	152	181	196	185	177	178	165	163	153	166	193	190	175	199	167	148	192	158	147	179
97070	WILSONVILLE	118	124	138	130	122	126	123	122	117	124	148	143	124	145	121	112	145	122	112	133
97071	WOODBURN	73	66	61	64	67	73	67	71	70	70	87	78	65	82	67	69	84	72	73	79
97080	GRESHAM	97	109	118	112	107	107	104	102	98	104	123	120	107	126	103	94	122	101	92	113
97101	AMITY	86	86	75	84	87	90	80	84	79	81	98	99	79	98	80	78	95	83	83	100
97103	ASTORIA	72	70	69	68	72	77	70	72	71	69	88	85	69	89	71	72	85	72	74	85
97106	BANKS	103	119	122	120	116	114	110	109	103	111	130	129	113	134	110	98	128	107	97	121
97107	BAY CITY	81	68	53	68	72	81	71	76	75	69	91	86	67	90	70	77	85	74	82	89
97108	BEAVER	96	64	29	56	73	84	62	78	75	63	88	93	53	83	63	81	80	77	96	110
97109	BUXTON	85	106	113	106	104	103	95	94	88	94	110	110	101	117	97	85	110	91	84	104
97111	CARLTON	87	78	59	74	82	88	72	80	76	72	93	95	70	95	74	78	88	77	86	102
97112	CLOVERDALE	92	75	55	68	83	93	71	84	80	71	95	97	66	94	75	85	89	82	97	111
97113	CORNELIUS	98	90	75	88	92	98	87	93	89	88	110	109	84	108	87	89	105	92	94	111
97114	DAYTON	90	86	76	86	88	92	83	88	82	83	102	104	80	101	83	81	98	87	87	105
97115	DUNDEE	100	111	111	112	108	107	105	104	98	105	124	123	106	125	103	94	122	103	93	115
97116	FOREST GROVE	77	82	88	84	82	84	81	81	77	81	97	95	81	97	80	75	95	80	75	89
97117	GALES CREEK	107	107	95	104	110	114	98	104	99	98	121	123	99	126	100	99	118	101	106	127
97119	GASTON	127	144	144	144	143	144	131	133	125	131	156	157	136	164	133	122	154	130	124	152
97121	HAMMOND	76	64	50	64	67	76	66	71	70	65	85	81	63	84	66	71	80	70	77	83
97122	HEBO	89	103	114	98	102	112	98	98	97	96	121	109	103	126	102	100	119	96	100	107
97123	HILLSBORO	99	104	103	106	102	103	100	100	96	102	121	117	101	122	98	92	120	100	91	111
97124	HILLSBORO	104	105	113	111	102	104	107	104	102	108	130	123	106	127	103	97	127	106	93	115
97125	MANNING	88	109	116	109	107	106	97	97	90	97	113	114	104	121	100	88	113	94	87	107
97127	LAFAYETTE	83	75	59	72	75	80	72	77	73	74	90	89	68	85	71	72	86	77	76	91
97128	MCMINNVILLE	81	77	73	77	79	84	78	80	79	77	97	94	76	96	77	78	93	80	81	93
97131	NEHALEM	85	66	44	61	74	84	66	77	74	64	87	88	59	85	68	79	81	76	91	101
97132	NEWBERG	93	97	104	100	97	100	97	96	94	97	118	114	98	118	96	91	115	97	90	107
97133	NORTH PLAINS	120	129	121	126	130	133	117	122	115	116	142	144	120	149	120	114	139	118	119	144
97136	ROCKAWAY BEACH	69	53	36	49	60	68	53	62	60	52	71	72	48	69	55	64	66	62	74	82
97137	SAINT PAUL	127	100	68	98	109	123	101	114	111	99	132	134	93	131	102	114	123	112	129	145
97138	SEASIDE	86	72	59	70	78	86	72	80	78	71	94	93	68	93	74	80	88	79	88	100
97140	SHERWOOD	128	142	142	148	136	134	132	130	122	136	155	152	135	155	128	114	153	128	112	143
97141	TILLAMOOK	82	67	52	65	72	81	68	75	74	67	89	88	64	88	69	76	83	75	84	95
97144	TIMBER	87	108	115	108	106	105	97	96	89	96	112	113	103	120	99	87	112	93	86	106
97145	TOLOVANA PARK	101	77	50	71	88	99	74	89	84	73	99	105	65	98	78	89	92	88	106	123
97146	WARRENTON	91	73	52	71	79	91	74	83	81	73	97	94	68	93	75	84	90	82	95	103
97148	YAMHILL	114	117	106	114	120	124	107	113	106	106	131	133	109	137	109	107	128	109	113	136
97149	NESKOWIN	89	70	47	63	78	88	66	79	74	65	88	93	59	87	70	79	82	78	93	108
97201	PORTLAND	93	81	120	89	78	88	105	91	104	100	131	115	101	128	97	98	128	101	85	101
97202	PORTLAND	78	79	99	83	78	83	86	81	83	85	105	98	86	104	83	80	103	85	75	89
97203	PORTLAND	62	62	67	62	61	66	66	64	66	64	82	75	65	83	65	65	80	66	63	70
97204	PORTLAND	7	6	9	6	6	7	7	7	8	7	10	8	7	9	7	8	9	7	7	7
	OREGON	87	85	86	85	86	91	86	87	86	85	106	102	85	106	85	84	103	87	86	100
	UNITED STATES	100	100	100	100	100	100	100	100	100	100	100	100	100	100	100	100	100	100	100	100

OREGON

POPULATION CHANGE

A 97205-97411

ZIP CODE #	POST OFFICE NAME	COUNTY FIPS CODE	POPULATION 2000	2004	2009	2000-2004 ANNUAL RATE % Rate	State Centile	HOUSEHOLDS 2000	2004	2009	% Annual Rate 2000-2004	2004 Average HH Size	FAMILIES 2000	2004	% Annual Rate 2000-2004
97205	PORTLAND	051	7044	7470	7809	1.4	79	4793	5121	5367	1.6	1.32	683	695	0.4
97206	PORTLAND	051	44646	44416	45315	-0.1	27	17690	17524	17808	-0.2	2.51	10403	10203	-0.5
97209	PORTLAND	051	8109	9193	9968	3.0	96	5226	6022	6577	3.4	1.31	670	761	3.0
97210	PORTLAND	051	9653	9784	10043	0.3	48	5576	5631	5753	0.2	1.72	1701	1696	-0.1
97211	PORTLAND	051	31287	30918	31374	-0.3	22	11825	11634	11761	-0.4	2.58	7024	6845	-0.6
97212	PORTLAND	051	23591	23268	23578	-0.3	20	10073	9913	10006	-0.4	2.34	5489	5339	-0.7
97213	PORTLAND	051	29315	29328	30020	0.0	35	12850	12797	13044	-0.1	2.26	6957	6849	-0.4
97214	PORTLAND	051	22906	22715	23075	-0.2	25	11504	11365	11509	-0.3	1.91	3784	3672	-0.7
97215	PORTLAND	051	16924	16919	17280	0.0	31	7189	7166	7295	-0.1	2.28	3878	3826	-0.3
97216	PORTLAND	051	13267	14145	14895	1.5	82	5102	5408	5666	1.4	2.60	3228	3406	1.3
97217	PORTLAND	051	29733	30134	30949	0.3	48	12302	12478	12792	0.3	2.40	6804	6819	0.1
97218	PORTLAND	051	14134	14157	14441	0.0	36	5163	5115	5180	-0.2	2.70	3191	3136	-0.4
97219	PORTLAND	051	37048	37252	38125	0.1	39	15350	15361	15664	0.0	2.36	9077	9025	-0.1
97220	PORTLAND	051	29771	30116	30795	0.3	44	10924	10968	11162	0.1	2.55	6611	6581	-0.1
97221	PORTLAND	051	11407	11673	12061	0.5	53	4802	4882	5017	0.4	2.35	3091	3124	0.3
97222	PORTLAND	005	35446	35952	37442	0.3	48	14773	15071	15822	0.5	2.35	9088	9218	0.3
97223	PORTLAND	067	41377	43562	46964	1.2	75	16536	17331	18640	1.1	2.50	10692	11193	1.1
97224	PORTLAND	067	27042	29051	31550	1.7	85	11783	12509	13507	1.4	2.30	7292	7704	1.3
97225	PORTLAND	067	21939	22696	24246	0.8	65	10098	10526	11283	1.0	2.15	5738	5894	0.6
97227	PORTLAND	051	3259	3322	3402	0.5	51	1292	1313	1339	0.4	2.47	632	637	0.2
97229	PORTLAND	067	42092	47504	52799	2.9	96	15564	17532	19464	2.8	2.71	11535	12986	2.8
97230	PORTLAND	051	34708	36531	38193	1.2	75	13850	14444	15001	1.0	2.51	9098	9416	0.8
97231	PORTLAND	051	4230	4358	4481	0.7	59	1693	1740	1782	0.7	2.45	1145	1167	0.5
97232	PORTLAND	051	10788	10848	11105	0.1	39	5803	5851	5982	0.2	1.81	2012	1983	-0.3
97233	PORTLAND	051	33916	35124	36305	0.8	66	12002	12294	12612	0.6	2.83	8082	8213	0.4
97236	PORTLAND	051	31609	34803	37198	2.3	92	10933	11987	12780	2.2	2.87	7968	8710	2.1
97239	PORTLAND	051	13356	13307	13567	-0.1	28	6661	6607	6706	-0.2	1.98	3103	3045	-0.4
97266	PORTLAND	051	37324	39407	41350	1.3	76	13978	14708	15404	1.2	2.65	8985	9340	0.9
97267	PORTLAND	005	29137	29376	30376	0.2	42	11578	11846	12390	0.5	2.47	7970	8094	0.4
97301	SALEM	047	53176	55650	58370	1.1	72	17649	18545	19523	1.2	2.60	11143	11658	1.1
97302	SALEM	047	37496	38015	39519	0.3	48	15507	15761	16378	0.4	2.37	9816	9901	0.2
97303	SALEM	047	53437	56295	59292	1.2	75	19441	20437	21479	1.2	2.73	13441	14031	1.0
97304	SALEM	053	22563	23554	24329	1.0	71	8775	9201	9543	1.1	2.50	6066	6332	1.0
97305	SALEM	047	35111	37355	39668	1.5	81	12719	13515	14311	1.4	2.75	8887	9387	1.3
97306	SALEM	047	21674	22610	23668	1.0	70	8305	8729	9157	1.2	2.58	6127	6397	1.0
97321	ALBANY	043	20404	21189	22063	0.9	67	7954	8291	8663	1.0	2.54	5683	5909	0.9
97322	ALBANY	043	28908	29873	30943	0.8	64	11370	11782	12243	0.8	2.49	7665	7888	0.7
97324	ALSEA	003	1156	1103	1112	-1.1	4	445	429	435	-0.9	2.55	323	309	-1.0
97325	AUMSVILLE	047	6057	6682	7213	2.3	93	2051	2280	2465	2.5	2.93	1692	1869	2.4
97326	BLODGETT	041	951	1004	1045	1.3	76	365	389	407	1.5	2.58	279	296	1.4
97327	BROWNSVILLE	043	2870	2981	3094	0.9	68	1058	1105	1151	1.0	2.70	817	849	0.9
97329	CASCADIA	043	38	42	44	2.4	93	13	14	15	1.8	3.00	10	11	2.3
97330	CORVALLIS	003	40491	41593	43073	0.6	56	16474	17030	17752	0.8	2.32	9178	9396	0.6
97331	CORVALLIS	003	2164	2190	2209	0.3	45	20	21	23	1.2	2.57	7	6	-3.6
97333	CORVALLIS	003	16708	17073	17716	0.5	52	6935	7137	7456	0.7	2.27	3727	3798	0.5
97338	DALLAS	053	17791	17972	18253	0.2	43	6597	6701	6828	0.4	2.61	4886	4939	0.3
97341	DEPOE BAY	041	3041	3184	3265	1.1	73	1536	1624	1683	1.3	1.96	932	978	1.1
97342	DETROIT	047	443	426	434	-0.9	7	185	178	182	-0.9	2.25	114	109	-1.1
97343	EDDYVILLE	041	575	575	575	0.0	35	216	218	220	0.2	2.64	160	161	0.2
97344	FALLS CITY	053	1175	1160	1168	-0.3	21	409	405	409	-0.2	2.85	319	316	-0.2
97345	FOSTER	043	536	564	587	1.2	75	216	229	239	1.4	2.46	167	176	1.2
97346	GATES	043	792	773	788	-0.6	15	332	326	333	-0.4	2.37	237	231	-0.6
97347	GRAND RONDE	071	1460	1572	1664	1.8	87	530	572	607	1.8	2.75	386	415	1.7
97348	HALSEY	043	1321	1343	1370	0.4	49	464	474	484	0.5	2.83	364	370	0.4
97350	IDANHA	047	255	246	250	-0.8	8	93	90	92	-0.8	2.60	61	59	-0.8
97351	INDEPENDENCE	053	7558	8245	8693	2.1	89	2526	2767	2926	2.2	2.92	1825	1989	2.1
97352	JEFFERSON	047	5238	5547	5849	1.4	78	1807	1926	2033	1.5	2.88	1452	1540	1.4
97355	LEBANON	043	26302	26770	27421	0.4	50	9887	10092	10367	0.5	2.63	7265	7380	0.4
97357	LOGSDEN	041	259	242	239	-1.6	2	105	99	99	-1.4	2.43	81	76	-1.5
97358	LYONS	047	2358	2311	2349	-0.5	17	880	868	885	-0.3	2.66	681	669	-0.4
97360	MILL CITY	043	2048	1997	2025	-0.6	14	770	755	767	-0.5	2.65	574	559	-0.6
97361	MONMOUTH	053	9916	10156	10408	0.6	54	3525	3622	3723	0.6	2.58	2142	2177	0.4
97362	MOUNT ANGEL	047	4216	4430	4634	1.2	74	1341	1421	1492	1.4	2.85	883	927	1.2
97364	NEOTSU	041	420	447	462	1.5	82	168	180	187	1.6	2.41	101	108	1.6
97365	NEWPORT	041	10162	10246	10341	0.2	42	4349	4418	4492	0.4	2.24	2651	2675	0.2
97366	SOUTH BEACH	041	1209	1308	1367	1.9	88	546	598	630	2.2	2.15	349	379	2.0
97367	LINCOLN CITY	041	9405	9438	9510	0.1	38	4316	4332	4382	0.1	2.16	2498	2491	-0.1
97368	OTIS	041	3215	3255	3278	0.3	45	1318	1337	1353	0.3	2.43	907	914	0.2
97370	PHILOMATH	003	8176	8429	8739	0.7	60	2938	3041	3168	0.8	2.77	2229	2292	0.7
97371	RICKREALL	053	543	537	542	-0.3	23	186	185	187	-0.1	2.90	148	147	-0.2
97374	SCIO	043	5126	5444	5710	1.4	80	1891	2022	2129	1.6	2.69	1496	1590	1.4
97375	SCOTTS MILLS	047	1375	1383	1429	0.1	40	447	452	469	0.3	3.03	361	363	0.1
97376	SEAL ROCK	041	1471	1516	1542	0.7	59	676	703	722	0.9	2.16	429	444	0.8
97377	SHEDD	043	836	878	913	1.2	74	312	329	343	1.3	2.67	236	248	1.2
97378	SHERIDAN	071	8110	8608	9043	1.4	79	2207	2303	2460	1.0	2.75	1629	1691	0.9
97380	SILETZ	041	2220	2144	2134	-0.8	9	833	814	818	-0.5	2.63	638	621	-0.6
97381	SILVERTON	047	13091	13514	14146	0.8	62	4574	4739	4959	0.8	2.83	3417	3508	0.6
97383	STAYTON	047	8721	9034	9425	0.8	66	3207	3338	3484	1.0	2.70	2394	2477	0.8
97385	SUBLIMITY	047	2703	2927	3130	1.9	88	889	979	1057	2.3	2.67	674	736	2.1
97386	SWEET HOME	043	12537	12563	12827	0.1	37	4731	4744	4852	0.1	2.63	3471	3462	-0.1
97389	TANGENT	043	1470	1696	1851	3.4	97	535	620	679	3.5	2.74	386	445	3.4
97390	TIDEWATER	041	702	713	721	0.4	49	321	330	336	0.7	2.09	200	204	0.5
97391	TOLEDO	041	5580	5475	5471	-0.5	18	2127	2103	2119	-0.3	2.60	1550	1525	-0.4
97392	TURNER	047	4302	4438	4655	0.7	61	1582	1640	1721	0.9	2.71	1242	1282	0.8
97394	WALDPORT	041	4353	4415	4452	0.3	48	1961	1999	2028	0.5	2.20	1240	1255	0.3
97396	WILLAMINA	071	2902	2918	3040	0.1	39	1067	1077	1124	0.2	2.71	785	791	0.2
97401	EUGENE	039	37177	39382	41272	1.4	78	17352	18474	19510	1.5	2.01	7121	7605	1.6
97402	EUGENE	039	44747	46124	47604	0.7	60	18433	19042	19743	0.8	2.39	10838	11153	0.7
97403	EUGENE	039	10393	10528	10749	0.3	46	3712	3803	3936	0.6	2.17	1653	1670	0.2
97404	EUGENE	039	28587	29534	30474	0.8	63	10842	11308	11767	1.0	2.60	7951	8246	0.9
97405	EUGENE	039	43806	44374	45480	0.3	46	18011	18390	18997	0.5	2.36	11204	11385	0.4
97406	AGNESS	015	133	132	134	-0.2	25	69	70	71	0.3	1.89	47	47	0.0
97408	EUGENE	039	9420	10447	11216	2.5	94	3820	4219	4536	2.4	2.47	2661	2922	2.2
97410	AZALEA	019	678	715	739	1.3	76	297	318	333	1.6	2.25	209	222	1.4
97411	BANDON	011	6543	6850	6990	1.1	72	2866	3037	3135	1.4	2.19	1857	1953	1.1
	OREGON					1.1					1.1	2.50			1.0
	UNITED STATES					1.2					1.3	2.58			1.1

#	POST OFFICE NAME	RACE (%) White 2000	White 2004	Black 2000	Black 2004	Asian/Pacific 2000	Asian/Pacific 2004	% Hispanic Origin 2000	% Hispanic Origin 2004	2004 AGE DISTRIBUTION (%) 0-4	5-9	10-14	15-19	20-24	25-44	45-64	65-84	85+	18+	MEDIAN AGE 2004	% 2004 Males	% 2004 Females
97205	PORTLAND	84.3	82.5	4.7	5.1	5.0	5.8	4.9	5.9	1.3	1.1	1.4	3.5	10.5	38.2	29.0	12.8	2.1	95.0	41.1	58.7	41.3
97206	PORTLAND	79.7	77.5	1.8	1.9	9.6	11.0	6.5	7.8	6.6	6.3	6.2	5.8	6.8	33.6	23.3	9.5	1.9	77.4	35.9	49.6	50.4
97209	PORTLAND	83.5	82.0	5.3	5.7	3.4	3.9	5.4	6.5	1.6	1.0	0.6	2.1	12.5	49.9	25.5	6.1	0.6	96.3	35.0	59.8	40.2
97210	PORTLAND	90.8	89.7	1.6	1.8	3.7	4.2	2.7	3.3	2.9	2.7	3.1	4.1	8.7	42.3	26.5	8.2	1.7	89.2	36.2	50.4	49.6
97211	PORTLAND	51.6	49.5	33.4	34.2	3.6	4.0	8.0	9.5	6.8	6.5	6.7	6.7	7.9	34.1	22.6	7.4	1.2	76.1	34.0	48.2	51.8
97212	PORTLAND	77.0	75.6	14.5	15.2	2.2	2.5	4.5	5.3	5.4	5.6	6.0	5.9	6.4	31.6	29.2	8.1	1.9	79.4	38.4	47.9	52.1
97213	PORTLAND	80.6	78.7	3.5	3.7	9.5	10.7	4.4	5.3	5.7	5.5	5.5	6.0	6.4	33.5	26.0	9.1	2.2	79.5	38.1	48.5	51.5
97214	PORTLAND	86.1	84.6	2.5	2.7	4.8	5.5	4.2	5.1	3.7	3.0	3.0	4.1	9.9	45.5	22.3	6.8	1.8	88.0	34.0	49.6	50.5
97215	PORTLAND	84.7	82.9	1.7	1.8	8.2	9.4	4.6	5.5	5.3	5.0	4.9	5.4	7.2	33.9	25.8	9.9	2.7	82.0	37.8	47.4	52.7
97216	PORTLAND	78.4	75.7	2.5	2.9	10.6	11.9	7.2	8.8	7.2	6.7	7.0	6.4	7.7	30.4	21.8	10.9	1.9	75.3	34.9	48.9	51.2
97217	PORTLAND	65.0	63.4	17.6	17.8	5.1	5.7	8.8	10.3	6.6	6.2	6.1	6.0	6.9	32.5	25.8	8.4	1.6	77.6	36.5	49.9	50.1
97218	PORTLAND	62.4	59.4	10.0	10.4	8.6	9.5	18.8	21.4	7.5	7.0	7.0	6.5	7.7	32.8	22.4	7.7	1.5	74.6	34.0	51.6	48.4
97219	PORTLAND	88.7	87.4	1.8	1.9	4.0	4.6	4.0	4.8	5.3	5.3	6.0	6.6	7.4	30.2	29.3	8.5	1.5	79.8	38.1	48.9	51.1
97220	PORTLAND	75.9	73.4	4.6	4.8	10.3	11.6	6.5	7.8	6.9	5.9	5.8	6.4	8.5	29.9	22.3	11.4	2.9	78.0	36.0	49.3	50.7
97221	PORTLAND	91.9	91.0	1.1	1.2	2.9	3.4	3.2	3.9	4.8	5.4	6.6	6.8	5.5	22.4	32.5	13.2	2.9	78.7	44.0	47.9	52.1
97222	PORTLAND	89.6	88.3	1.0	1.1	2.7	3.0	5.5	6.8	6.8	6.4	6.5	6.0	6.8	28.7	24.2	11.6	3.0	76.7	37.3	48.2	51.8
97223	PORTLAND	85.2	83.5	1.1	1.2	6.4	7.1	8.4	10.2	7.4	7.0	6.8	6.2	7.1	32.5	24.6	7.3	1.1	74.9	35.0	49.7	50.3
97224	PORTLAND	90.0	88.6	0.9	0.9	3.9	4.4	5.7	7.2	6.5	6.6	6.5	5.2	5.5	27.3	23.5	15.1	4.0	77.2	40.3	46.9	53.1
97225	PORTLAND	88.9	87.5	1.1	1.2	4.0	4.5	5.2	6.5	5.5	5.4	5.8	5.7	6.6	29.2	27.5	12.1	2.2	79.9	39.5	48.9	51.1
97227	PORTLAND	48.7	47.6	34.2	34.2	3.7	4.0	11.0	12.4	7.6	6.2	7.0	6.9	8.7	35.0	20.5	6.7	1.5	75.4	32.1	50.5	49.6
97229	PORTLAND	82.4	80.3	0.9	0.9	11.9	13.6	3.8	4.6	8.2	8.4	7.9	6.0	5.2	31.5	25.5	6.9	0.6	71.9	35.9	49.4	50.6
97230	PORTLAND	77.2	74.7	4.0	4.2	7.4	8.4	10.5	12.4	6.9	6.4	6.2	6.1	6.9	27.2	23.2	14.7	2.4	77.0	37.8	48.9	51.1
97231	PORTLAND	91.2	90.2	0.4	0.5	2.3	2.6	4.8	5.8	4.4	5.3	6.4	5.6	3.9	25.3	38.0	9.9	1.2	79.9	44.5	51.9	48.1
97232	PORTLAND	83.3	81.8	6.7	7.2	3.3	3.8	5.0	6.0	3.8	3.4	3.7	4.5	8.2	38.4	25.1	9.2	3.7	86.6	37.6	48.3	51.7
97233	PORTLAND	74.9	72.2	2.7	2.9	5.9	6.6	16.4	19.1	9.1	7.9	7.5	6.9	8.4	30.2	19.6	9.1	1.4	71.4	31.3	50.3	49.7
97236	PORTLAND	82.8	81.0	2.0	2.1	6.9	7.8	7.4	8.8	7.7	7.3	7.4	7.1	7.4	28.0	24.1	9.4	1.5	73.2	35.1	48.8	51.2
97239	PORTLAND	89.7	88.5	1.4	1.5	4.5	5.3	3.4	4.1	4.3	4.0	4.2	4.4	7.6	34.1	27.7	10.9	2.8	84.9	38.9	48.6	51.4
97266	PORTLAND	77.6	75.1	2.1	2.2	9.5	10.8	9.3	10.9	7.6	6.8	6.9	6.7	8.4	29.4	22.8	9.5	1.9	74.8	34.1	49.6	50.4
97267	PORTLAND	91.6	90.6	0.6	0.7	2.0	2.3	5.6	6.8	6.0	6.2	6.5	6.3	6.1	25.8	28.5	12.5	2.1	77.5	40.3	48.8	51.3
97301	SALEM	81.1	78.8	1.9	2.0	2.6	2.8	15.9	19.1	6.8	6.4	6.4	7.5	9.4	29.8	22.0	10.0	1.9	76.8	34.0	52.9	47.1
97302	SALEM	89.1	87.7	0.8	0.9	2.4	2.7	6.8	8.4	6.3	6.0	6.6	7.4	7.7	25.9	26.1	11.6	2.4	76.4	37.5	48.3	51.8
97303	SALEM	79.7	77.4	0.9	1.0	2.0	2.1	20.2	23.4	8.8	7.9	7.6	6.8	7.8	29.5	21.2	8.8	1.5	71.5	32.4	49.6	50.4
97304	SALEM	91.9	91.0	0.4	0.5	1.7	2.0	8.0	9.5	5.6	5.8	6.5	6.4	6.4	23.4	27.4	14.2	4.4	78.0	42.1	47.6	52.4
97305	SALEM	76.7	73.8	1.0	1.0	4.6	5.1	20.1	23.7	9.4	8.1	7.4	6.5	8.5	28.9	20.4	9.5	1.2	71.4	31.1	49.9	50.1
97306	SALEM	91.3	90.2	0.6	0.7	2.7	3.1	4.5	5.7	6.9	6.8	7.2	7.1	7.1	27.7	25.9	10.2	1.2	74.8	36.3	48.3	51.7
97321	ALBANY	93.4	92.8	0.4	0.5	1.4	1.6	3.9	4.6	6.3	6.5	7.0	6.8	6.2	26.0	28.9	10.8	1.6	76.0	39.2	49.4	50.6
97322	ALBANY	91.4	90.4	0.5	0.5	1.2	1.4	6.7	8.1	7.7	7.0	7.0	6.9	7.9	27.5	22.7	10.9	2.5	74.4	34.8	48.6	51.4
97324	ALSEA	96.0	95.7	0.3	0.3	0.4	0.5	2.3	3.0	4.3	5.4	7.2	7.4	6.0	22.6	33.4	12.5	1.3	78.8	43.2	48.5	51.5
97325	AUMSVILLE	90.8	89.7	0.2	0.2	0.8	0.9	7.2	8.8	7.7	7.8	8.1	7.2	6.6	25.7	25.6	10.4	1.0	71.8	35.8	49.0	51.0
97326	BLODGETT	92.7	92.6	0.3	0.4	0.5	0.6	2.7	3.5	4.6	5.4	6.6	6.4	6.2	22.7	35.2	11.9	1.2	79.5	43.8	50.2	49.8
97327	BROWNSVILLE	94.7	94.3	0.2	0.2	0.2	0.2	2.8	3.5	6.2	6.7	6.9	7.1	5.6	24.0	30.8	11.3	1.4	75.8	40.5	50.1	50.0
97329	CASCADIA	97.4	97.6	0.0	0.0	0.0	0.0	0.0	0.0	4.8	4.8	4.8	4.8	4.8	23.8	35.7	16.7	0.0	85.7	46.3	52.4	47.6
97330	CORVALLIS	87.7	86.3	1.0	1.0	6.0	6.9	4.9	5.9	4.9	4.6	5.6	8.7	13.8	27.8	22.9	9.6	2.1	81.1	31.9	49.5	50.5
97331	CORVALLIS	78.0	75.2	2.2	2.2	9.3	10.6	8.0	9.6	0.2	0.1	0.0	67.3	28.6	3.5	0.2	0.1	0.0	99.4	18.7	43.2	56.9
97333	CORVALLIS	88.0	86.7	1.1	1.1	4.8	5.6	5.5	6.5	5.4	4.9	5.0	10.1	14.9	30.2	20.0	8.3	1.4	81.6	29.6	50.1	50.0
97338	DALLAS	93.4	92.8	0.2	0.3	0.7	0.8	3.9	4.8	6.8	6.8	7.4	7.1	6.3	23.8	25.8	13.2	2.8	74.4	38.9	48.9	51.1
97341	DEPOE BAY	93.9	93.3	0.2	0.2	0.9	1.0	2.8	3.5	2.9	3.2	3.4	3.5	3.1	16.5	36.5	28.2	2.8	88.4	55.1	48.3	51.7
97342	DETROIT	93.7	92.7	0.2	0.2	0.0	0.0	5.4	6.8	6.6	6.1	5.4	5.9	4.0	25.6	32.6	12.9	0.9	78.2	43.1	50.5	49.5
97343	EDDYVILLE	95.8	95.7	0.2	0.2	0.4	0.5	2.3	3.0	4.5	5.0	5.7	5.7	5.9	23.1	34.8	13.9	1.2	81.4	44.9	50.4	49.6
97344	FALLS CITY	93.1	92.7	0.7	0.7	0.3	0.3	3.1	3.9	6.0	7.1	8.3	7.7	6.2	22.4	29.8	11.0	1.6	74.0	40.4	49.9	50.1
97345	FOSTER	95.2	94.9	0.2	0.2	1.1	1.2	1.7	2.0	6.4	6.7	6.9	5.9	5.1	23.6	30.5	13.3	1.6	76.4	41.8	52.1	47.9
97346	GATES	89.5	88.6	0.4	0.4	0.1	0.1	5.6	6.9	5.4	6.5	6.1	5.8	4.5	21.6	32.5	16.2	1.4	78.3	45.0	49.9	50.1
97347	GRAND RONDE	79.3	78.8	0.1	0.1	0.9	1.0	2.5	3.0	5.3	6.0	7.5	7.2	6.0	24.1	30.5	12.0	1.4	76.8	41.0	51.6	48.4
97348	HALSEY	93.0	92.4	0.2	0.2	0.3	0.3	4.0	4.9	6.7	7.4	7.2	7.0	8.1	26.5	26.1	9.5	1.6	74.7	34.6	52.9	47.1
97350	IDANHA	94.9	93.9	0.4	0.4	0.0	0.0	5.5	6.5	5.7	6.1	6.1	6.5	3.7	24.4	32.5	13.8	1.2	78.1	43.7	49.6	50.4
97351	INDEPENDENCE	76.5	73.7	0.4	0.5	1.0	1.0	26.5	30.5	8.0	7.5	7.9	8.0	9.4	28.1	22.1	8.1	1.1	72.0	30.0	49.5	50.5
97352	JEFFERSON	87.9	86.2	0.3	0.3	0.8	0.9	12.6	15.2	7.5	7.7	8.0	7.4	5.7	25.7	27.4	9.7	1.0	72.2	37.0	50.2	49.8
97355	LEBANON	94.5	94.0	0.2	0.2	0.8	1.0	2.9	3.6	6.7	6.7	7.2	6.7	6.3	24.5	25.8	13.8	2.4	75.3	39.2	49.3	50.7
97357	LOGSDEN	71.4	71.5	0.0	0.0	0.0	0.0	2.7	2.9	6.2	6.6	7.0	7.9	7.0	21.5	31.0	11.6	1.2	74.0	40.6	52.1	47.9
97358	LYONS	93.1	92.7	0.1	0.1	0.5	0.5	2.8	3.3	5.8	6.1	6.6	6.4	5.8	24.2	29.9	14.0	1.3	77.7	42.1	50.4	49.6
97360	MILL CITY	88.5	87.0	0.2	0.3	0.9	1.1	8.8	10.8	6.3	6.9	8.0	7.1	5.6	24.0	27.1	13.5	1.7	74.5	39.8	50.1	49.9
97361	MONMOUTH	87.0	85.5	0.7	0.8	2.3	2.6	8.7	10.5	5.8	5.1	5.5	13.1	18.7	22.4	19.8	8.6	1.2	80.2	26.3	47.8	52.2
97362	MOUNT ANGEL	76.4	72.7	0.4	0.4	0.7	0.7	26.9	32.0	7.5	7.2	8.8	7.9	7.4	26.0	19.4	11.3	4.5	71.7	33.4	51.0	49.0
97364	NEOTSU	92.6	92.0	0.5	0.9	1.0	1.1	3.6	4.0	4.9	5.4	5.8	5.2	4.9	17.7	31.3	19.9	4.9	80.8	49.3	47.7	52.4
97365	NEWPORT	88.8	87.6	0.4	0.5	1.8	2.1	8.4	10.0	5.3	5.5	5.9	6.1	6.2	23.2	29.0	16.2	2.7	79.4	43.4	48.9	51.1
97366	SOUTH BEACH	95.7	95.4	0.1	0.1	1.0	1.1	2.6	3.1	3.1	3.7	4.4	4.6	4.1	21.6	40.8	16.5	1.4	85.7	50.0	50.1	49.9
97367	LINCOLN CITY	89.8	88.8	0.4	0.4	1.3	1.5	6.9	8.2	5.0	5.1	5.7	5.5	5.6	21.3	30.7	18.4	2.7	80.9	46.2	47.2	52.8
97368	OTIS	93.1	92.6	0.2	0.2	0.4	0.5	2.8	3.4	4.5	5.0	5.9	5.4	5.0	21.5	33.9	17.0	1.9	81.4	46.5	50.0	50.1
97370	PHILOMATH	93.8	93.2	0.2	0.2	1.6	1.9	3.0	3.6	5.8	6.7	8.6	9.1	4.9	26.7	28.6	8.7	1.0	72.5	37.4	49.3	50.7
97371	RICKREALL	93.2	92.2	0.6	0.6	0.4	0.4	5.3	6.3	4.7	5.4	7.5	6.5	5.0	23.1	31.8	14.2	1.9	78.2	43.5	50.7	49.4
97374	SCIO	94.7	94.4	0.1	0.2	0.5	0.6	2.6	3.1	5.8	6.1	7.0	7.0	5.8	22.9	30.6	13.4	1.5	76.7	41.9	50.2	49.8
97375	SCOTTS MILLS	93.8	93.0	0.4	0.5	0.4	0.5	5.4	6.7	6.3	6.9	8.0	7.4	6.3	23.9	29.9	10.1	1.2	73.8	38.9	51.0	49.0
97376	SEAL ROCK	95.1	94.9	0.0	0.0	0.7	0.8	1.6	2.0	2.9	3.5	5.0	5.3	4.2	17.7	40.4	19.6	1.5	85.1	50.5	47.6	52.4
97377	SHEDD	96.4	96.0	0.1	0.1	0.5	0.5	2.4	3.1	6.2	6.5	7.1	7.4	5.8	24.2	29.6	11.6	1.7	75.9	40.6	50.5	49.5
97378	SHERIDAN	83.3	82.1	4.7	4.9	2.0	2.3	6.9	8.3	5.2	5.2	5.8	6.2	8.3	35.4	24.7	8.0	1.3	80.2	36.2	62.8	37.2
97380	SILETZ	76.8	76.4	0.2	0.2	0.4	0.5	2.3	2.7	6.4	6.7	7.2	7.0	6.6	23.6	29.2	11.9	1.3	74.7	40.1	50.4	49.6
97381	SILVERTON	91.3	89.7	0.2	0.2	0.5	0.6	8.9	11.3	7.8	7.7	8.4	7.9	6.9	23.9	24.4	11.1	2.0	71.0	35.6	48.3	51.7
97383	STAYTON	91.7	90.5	0.1	0.1	0.7	0.7	8.0	9.9	8.2	6.9	7.4	8.5	7.6	25.8	22.9	11.1	1.5	72.1	34.9	48.7	51.3
97385	SUBLIMITY	97.0	96.8	0.1	0.1	0.5	0.6	2.3	2.7	5.1	5.7	7.4	6.9	4.9	23.0	22.2	18.1	6.8	77.3	43.2	46.9	53.1
97386	SWEET HOME	94.1	93.7	0.2	0.2	0.6	0.7	2.8	3.4	6.7	6.5	6.7	6.9	6.5	22.9	26.9	14.7	2.2	75.9	40.5	49.6	50.4
97389	TANGENT	95.0	94.5	0.2	0.2	0.6	0.7	3.3	4.2	6.3	6.7	8.0	6.3	5.4	26.9	28.0	11.1	1.3	75.1	38.5	49.7	50.3
97390	TIDEWATER	94.7	94.4	0.4	0.4	0.7	0.8	2.1	2.7	2.8	3.2	3.5	5.5	4.2	14.6	38.4	25.4	2.4	87.1	54.3	49.7	50.4
97391	TOLEDO	91.9	91.5	0.2	0.2	0.7	0.8	2.3	2.8	6.2	6.2	7.1	8.2	6.6	25.3	28.3	11.0	1.2	75.4	39.0	49.8	50.2
97392	TURNER	93.9	93.2	0.1	0.1	0.8	0.9	3.9	4.8	5.0	6.0	7.6	7.3	5.3	22.1	31.5	13.3	1.9	76.8	42.9	49.5	50.5
97394	WALDPORT	93.5	93.1	0.1	0.1	0.9	1.0	2.6	3.1	3.9	4.9	6.3	5.6	3.3	19.4	32.5	21.9	2.2	80.8	49.3	47.7	52.3
97396	WILLAMINA	84.6	84.0	0.1	0.1	0.5	0.5	3.1	3.7	6.5	6.7	7.8	8.0	7.2	24.9	26.7	10.9	1.4	74.2	37.1	50.5	49.6
97401	EUGENE	86.9	85.5	1.5	1.5	5.8	6.6	3.9	4.7	4.1	3.6	3.9	8.9	19.3	26.5	20.4	10.3	3.0	85.4	30.3	48.8	51.2
97402	EUGENE	87.2	86.1	1.3	1.3	2.4	2.6	7.2	8.6	7.2	6.3	6.6	6.5	8.6	32.7	21.6	9.2	1.5	76.3	33.5	49.8	50.2
97403	EUGENE	88.6	87.4	0.9	0.9	5.1	5.8	3.8	4.6	2.5	2.7	3.4	21.7	19.1	21.3	20.5	7.5	1.4	88.9	25.4	50.1	49.9
97404	EUGENE	91.1	90.2	0.8	0.8	1.3	1.5	4.7	5.7	6.6	6.8	7.1	6.6	6.2	27.9	27.4	10.3	1.3	75.4	37.8	48.8	51.2
97405	EUGENE	90.9	90.0	1.0	1.1	3.0	3.5	3.2	3.9	4.3	4.7	6.0	6.9	8.6	24.6	31.2	11.3	2.5	80.8	41.3	48.4	51.6
97406	AGNESS	92.5	91.7	0.0	0.0	0.8	0.8	4.5	5.3	3.0	3.8	6.1	6.1	3.8	16.7	35.6	22.7	2.3	82.6	51.3	51.5	48.5
97408	EUGENE	93.0	92.2	0.5	0.5	1.9	2.2	2.6	3.2	5.3	5.9	7.1	6.8	5.6	22.3	29.5	15.1	2.3	77.3	42.9	47.8	52.2
97410	AZALEA	94.4	94.3	0.2	0.1	0.3	0.3	2.5	2.9	3.8	3.9	3.9	5.0	5.0	15.8	40.7	20.0	1.8	85.5	51.7	50.5	49.5
97411	BANDON	92.7	92.6	0.2	0.2	0.8	0.8	2.3	2.3	3.7	4.2	5.3	5.5	4.6	17.5	34.4	21.6	3.3	83.3	50.9	47.4	52.6
	OREGON	86.6	85.2	1.6	1.7	3.2	3.6	8.1	9.5	6.5	6.4	6.8	6.9	7.4	27.7	25.6	11.0	1.9	76.3	36.9	49.6	50.4
	UNITED STATES	75.1	73.6	12.3	12.5	3.8	4.2	12.5	14.1	6.9	6.7	7.2	7.0	7.3	28.6	23.8	10.8	1.7	75.1	36.0	49.1	50.9

#	POST OFFICE NAME	2004 Per Capita Income	2004 HH Income Base	2004 Household Income Distribution (%): Less than $25,000	$25,000 to $49,999	$50,000 to $99,999	$100,000 to $149,999	$150,000 or More	Median Household Income: 2004	2009	2004 National Centile	2004 State Centile	2004 Home Value Base	2004 Home Value Distribution (%): Less than $50,000	$50,000 to $89,999	$90,000 to $174,999	$175,000 to $399,999	$400,000 or More	2004 Median Home Value
97205	PORTLAND	29305	5121	53.8	24.7	12.9	3.7	4.9	21878	24977	3	2	552	0.0	0.5	10.3	40.9	48.2	389247
97206	PORTLAND	20562	17524	24.9	33.4	33.8	6.0	1.8	43109	50235	56	60	10659	1.8	3.9	61.5	32.7	0.1	156085
97209	PORTLAND	29665	6022	47.8	26.7	16.1	6.0	3.4	26224	31008	6	4	694	0.4	0.0	6.1	61.5	32.0	301575
97210	PORTLAND	47213	5631	26.3	25.4	23.8	10.3	14.1	47511	56013	67	74	1882	0.4	0.0	5.4	32.4	61.8	451869
97211	PORTLAND	21612	11634	23.2	31.6	34.2	8.5	2.6	46264	53668	64	70	7320	3.1	3.2	47.1	45.2	1.3	169996
97212	PORTLAND	33827	9913	20.3	22.7	31.7	15.3	10.1	58563	68810	83	92	6255	0.5	1.9	12.1	65.5	20.1	276962
97213	PORTLAND	26571	12797	23.0	28.0	34.9	10.5	3.6	48881	55676	70	78	7572	0.3	1.1	35.5	60.4	2.8	193675
97214	PORTLAND	28158	11365	27.1	32.7	28.5	7.9	3.8	41118	49817	50	54	4074	0.6	1.3	15.3	75.8	6.9	231453
97215	PORTLAND	28531	7166	21.0	25.6	35.9	12.4	5.2	52925	61267	77	84	4382	0.5	1.2	22.8	68.6	6.8	218364
97216	PORTLAND	19646	5408	22.4	35.7	34.6	5.6	1.7	43462	50515	57	63	3261	3.8	3.7	58.5	33.6	0.4	156241
97217	PORTLAND	21740	12478	26.4	31.4	32.9	7.5	1.9	43412	50078	57	63	7725	6.9	4.9	55.7	31.2	1.3	151925
97218	PORTLAND	18692	5115	27.0	31.7	33.3	6.3	1.8	43313	50785	57	62	3136	6.4	2.5	55.0	35.2	0.8	157903
97219	PORTLAND	37907	15361	14.2	23.4	34.0	15.4	12.9	65099	75089	89	97	10290	0.2	0.4	16.6	65.6	17.3	243509
97220	PORTLAND	20568	10968	24.2	33.1	33.9	6.3	2.5	43307	49803	57	62	6439	1.8	1.9	55.0	40.0	1.3	164475
97221	PORTLAND	46908	4882	14.3	20.4	28.3	16.1	20.9	75982	86494	94	99	3597	0.4	0.5	5.5	59.2	34.4	320663
97222	PORTLAND	24177	15071	20.7	32.6	34.8	9.3	2.7	46826	55598	66	73	8552	4.0	5.3	33.5	54.2	3.0	184689
97223	PORTLAND	28934	17331	16.8	25.8	35.5	14.2	7.6	58237	67180	83	91	10420	1.2	0.8	13.7	75.3	9.0	231985
97224	PORTLAND	32569	12509	18.6	26.7	31.8	13.8	9.1	54689	62426	79	87	8559	6.5	2.5	18.6	58.9	13.5	226020
97225	PORTLAND	41505	10526	16.3	26.0	32.2	13.5	12.0	58389	66582	83	91	6171	0.8	1.8	11.5	62.8	23.1	278802
97227	PORTLAND	17338	1313	35.6	32.3	26.0	4.7	1.5	35329	40206	29	28	595	1.9	2.2	54.8	39.8	1.3	162847
97229	PORTLAND	42072	17532	10.3	17.3	33.4	19.7	19.3	81102	92782	95	99	13811	0.8	0.9	6.4	62.3	29.7	307787
97230	PORTLAND	23361	14444	21.3	33.3	33.9	8.1	3.3	45844	52415	63	70	8493	2.3	1.5	29.4	65.0	1.7	198677
97231	PORTLAND	40390	1740	14.0	22.6	32.2	19.4	11.7	68308	77559	90	98	1462	2.3	2.1	14.9	42.3	38.3	330204
97232	PORTLAND	33532	5851	26.2	31.2	27.1	9.6	5.9	43710	52980	58	64	1990	0.8	0.8	17.9	65.6	14.9	258992
97233	PORTLAND	17379	12294	28.0	33.1	31.7	5.9	1.3	40490	46753	48	50	6597	7.0	1.9	54.6	36.4	0.2	163071
97236	PORTLAND	21926	11987	19.2	29.6	36.3	10.3	4.6	51092	59682	74	81	7853	3.3	6.3	29.6	51.2	9.6	193359
97239	PORTLAND	46613	6607	17.2	24.7	30.3	12.8	15.0	59012	69922	84	93	3416	0.5	1.8	7.5	59.4	30.8	308647
97266	PORTLAND	20791	14708	25.9	33.6	29.7	7.4	3.4	42736	49686	55	59	8075	3.7	2.2	48.2	39.6	6.3	168910
97267	PORTLAND	27241	11846	17.5	26.9	37.5	13.4	4.6	55753	65212	80	89	8605	7.5	2.4	20.3	65.8	4.0	206871
97301	SALEM	18982	18545	27.4	34.0	30.7	5.7	2.1	40882	46844	49	52	10733	9.2	7.5	57.9	21.5	3.9	131629
97302	SALEM	27670	15761	23.4	29.6	30.8	10.5	5.8	46889	52839	66	73	9379	4.1	3.4	48.0	39.2	5.2	166451
97303	SALEM	19780	20437	26.4	30.7	32.4	7.5	3.0	43252	49518	57	61	11882	4.3	6.9	60.4	26.6	1.9	142490
97304	SALEM	26328	9201	19.2	27.4	35.3	12.9	5.2	53695	60863	78	86	6677	1.9	2.0	38.8	51.3	5.9	185672
97305	SALEM	18757	13515	26.5	34.7	29.9	6.9	2.0	40397	45858	48	49	8013	11.2	7.2	57.5	22.5	1.7	140526
97306	SALEM	28906	8729	12.0	28.9	40.1	13.3	5.8	58708	65422	83	92	6081	2.3	4.8	41.0	45.9	6.1	178240
97321	ALBANY	25807	8291	20.4	27.7	34.6	12.3	5.1	52159	60656	76	83	6000	3.5	2.6	37.5	50.8	5.7	188405
97322	ALBANY	19972	11782	29.3	29.8	33.3	5.8	1.8	41757	47049	52	55	7017	10.0	7.7	48.9	31.5	1.9	150657
97324	ALSEA	18979	429	24.9	33.8	34.0	6.3	0.9	42549	48847	55	58	341	10.3	6.2	34.9	41.4	7.3	172794
97325	AUMSVILLE	20911	2280	19.9	28.0	41.7	6.1	4.3	51378	57902	75	82	1909	7.2	14.7	38.7	30.6	8.9	145696
97326	BLODGETT	22125	389	24.2	30.9	31.6	8.2	5.1	44443	50934	60	65	315	4.4	7.0	34.6	37.8	16.2	193382
97327	BROWNSVILLE	20664	1105	22.1	33.8	33.9	8.1	2.1	45826	50904	63	69	905	3.7	6.5	39.9	42.3	7.6	174901
97329	CASCADIA	16488	14	28.6	21.4	42.9	7.1	0.0	47500	54606	67	74	11	0.0	0.0	45.5	54.6	0.0	187500
97330	CORVALLIS	26937	17030	29.2	24.7	28.0	12.0	6.0	44987	53633	61	67	9013	6.5	2.1	31.2	53.1	7.2	195433
97331	CORVALLIS	15430	21	52.4	47.6	0.0	0.0	0.0	22301	21069	3	2	0	0.0	0.0	0.0	0.0	0.0	0
97333	CORVALLIS	23439	7137	33.2	25.9	29.4	8.4	3.1	39455	47097	44	46	3389	6.5	3.4	42.8	42.0	5.3	169602
97338	DALLAS	19974	6701	26.1	29.3	35.5	6.9	2.1	45055	50796	61	67	4953	7.6	7.9	44.3	35.2	5.1	156084
97341	DEPOE BAY	26694	1624	28.3	35.7	27.4	4.4	4.3	37912	44132	39	40	1290	8.1	6.6	27.8	39.5	18.0	193945
97342	DETROIT	19823	178	30.9	38.2	25.3	2.8	2.8	36529	41575	34	34	127	8.7	15.0	45.7	27.6	3.2	136458
97343	EDDYVILLE	17070	218	33.9	30.3	29.8	4.6	1.4	40519	41903	48	50	173	9.3	7.5	36.4	40.5	6.4	157813
97344	FALLS CITY	18371	405	21.5	37.0	32.8	7.7	1.0	44196	49909	59	64	334	4.5	12.6	43.4	31.7	7.8	145930
97345	FOSTER	21378	229	25.3	24.5	42.4	5.7	2.2	50118	52195	72	79	178	2.3	3.9	40.5	44.9	8.4	185714
97346	GATES	19434	326	30.1	38.0	27.3	3.1	1.5	37072	40375	36	37	265	12.8	13.6	41.9	29.8	1.9	131250
97347	GRAND RONDE	18252	572	23.3	36.7	34.1	5.1	0.9	42910	48508	56	59	467	8.1	8.4	26.3	49.5	7.7	194034
97348	HALSEY	22696	474	18.8	36.9	31.2	7.8	5.3	46224	50883	64	70	363	5.5	6.9	49.3	32.0	6.3	154167
97350	IDANHA	16913	90	28.9	43.3	23.3	3.3	1.1	37958	43864	39	41	66	1.5	12.1	54.6	30.3	1.5	142857
97351	INDEPENDENCE	17487	2767	27.8	31.1	31.8	6.3	2.9	44237	50169	59	64	1888	11.8	11.2	51.9	20.4	4.7	124392
97352	JEFFERSON	21908	1926	22.5	25.0	39.0	9.3	4.2	51748	58624	75	82	1554	5.0	9.3	38.4	37.1	10.3	167463
97355	LEBANON	18693	10092	29.6	32.4	30.0	5.9	2.1	39417	44397	44	45	7321	5.5	7.0	46.9	36.8	3.8	157066
97357	LOGSDEN	21558	99	30.3	26.3	32.3	8.1	3.0	43286	47371	57	61	80	2.5	11.3	41.3	40.0	5.0	165000
97358	LYONS	18438	868	27.9	30.8	33.5	7.1	0.7	42507	46441	55	58	712	1.7	6.9	47.8	40.2	3.5	164078
97360	MILL CITY	16183	755	29.7	40.5	25.6	3.8	0.4	36636	40581	34	35	587	2.2	13.1	56.4	26.9	1.4	137500
97361	MONMOUTH	19590	3622	31.4	26.0	33.5	6.2	2.8	42160	48023	53	56	1893	7.3	3.7	41.5	43.0	4.5	171568
97362	MOUNT ANGEL	17397	1421	30.1	29.2	32.5	5.9	2.3	42114	46299	53	56	878	8.2	4.9	47.3	31.2	8.4	154318
97364	NEOTSU	20604	180	37.2	22.8	30.6	5.6	3.9	41134	45252	50	54	121	0.0	0.8	24.0	66.1	9.1	243421
97365	NEWPORT	22788	4418	34.0	33.8	21.6	6.4	4.2	35935	41055	31	31	2516	7.9	4.8	40.8	38.2	8.4	166698
97366	SOUTH BEACH	25611	598	28.1	33.6	24.1	8.4	5.9	38319	43453	40	42	471	8.1	4.3	31.6	43.5	12.5	188702
97367	LINCOLN CITY	19348	4332	39.7	31.4	23.8	3.4	1.8	30765	34447	14	10	2622	7.7	4.7	38.6	42.9	6.1	172950
97368	OTIS	20716	1337	26.3	35.3	31.9	4.2	2.2	40758	45912	49	51	1082	10.3	11.6	40.8	33.1	4.3	146560
97370	PHILOMATH	25883	3041	16.6	29.1	35.3	12.5	6.5	53540	64540	78	85	2212	5.6	5.7	35.0	44.4	9.4	184606
97371	RICKREALL	22985	185	18.4	24.9	39.5	10.8	6.5	56137	61527	81	89	149	6.0	4.7	26.2	37.6	25.5	251923
97374	SCIO	23116	2022	19.1	28.9	37.7	9.8	4.5	51360	57378	74	82	1669	4.0	3.8	31.6	50.1	10.4	206835
97375	SCOTTS MILLS	21142	452	16.4	29.0	38.5	12.0	4.2	54419	59856	79	87	393	3.3	4.3	18.8	59.5	14.0	232143
97376	SEAL ROCK	21470	703	28.7	37.3	26.6	5.7	1.7	37103	42529	36	37	597	11.6	5.9	31.5	44.7	6.4	177462
97377	SHEDD	26348	329	21.6	37.7	23.7	10.0	7.0	43564	48246	57	63	269	8.9	4.5	25.3	47.6	13.8	210776
97378	SHERIDAN	17925	2303	27.1	31.2	33.2	6.0	2.5	43069	49446	56	60	1569	5.4	7.6	45.8	33.5	7.8	154660
97380	SILETZ	19272	814	27.5	28.8	35.9	6.0	1.8	43534	50318	57	63	667	11.4	9.8	43.9	31.6	3.3	141047
97381	SILVERTON	21402	4739	23.2	28.3	35.8	9.0	3.7	48503	54550	69	78	3316	3.2	4.4	29.3	52.2	11.0	197110
97383	STAYTON	18516	3338	31.2	29.2	30.5	6.3	2.9	40406	45237	48	49	2166	6.3	4.7	46.9	37.6	4.5	158301
97385	SUBLIMITY	22602	979	19.4	26.1	41.8	9.1	3.7	53676	60039	78	86	776	11.6	1.4	26.2	54.5	6.3	193103
97386	SWEET HOME	17129	4744	33.5	33.6	26.5	4.5	1.9	36580	41600	34	35	3460	8.5	11.7	45.4	29.7	4.7	137237
97389	TANGENT	20573	620	21.6	31.6	35.7	8.6	2.6	47950	53591	68	76	485	13.2	20.2	27.6	34.0	5.0	136397
97390	TIDEWATER	23456	330	27.9	36.7	27.0	5.5	3.0	39427	46189	44	46	278	3.6	4.3	24.5	57.2	10.4	213710
97391	TOLEDO	19411	2103	29.2	27.6	33.7	7.6	2.0	41610	47510	52	55	1576	0.6	9.3	49.1	38.6	2.4	158790
97392	TURNER	24015	1640	19.5	27.8	37.1	12.8	2.9	51967	58961	75	83	1350	6.4	6.8	27.8	48.4	10.6	190482
97394	WALDPORT	20452	1999	35.6	31.9	27.0	3.4	2.1	36505	41403	34	34	1603	8.7	6.6	36.5	43.6	4.6	170858
97396	WILLAMINA	17908	1077	25.3	35.3	34.1	4.2	1.2	40958	46974	50	52	816	3.9	10.9	46.8	31.4	7.0	145000
97401	EUGENE	24430	18474	39.5	27.5	22.0	6.6	4.4	33050	38059	21	19	6518	0.3	1.8	37.5	53.7	6.7	193518
97402	EUGENE	19431	19042	32.5	34.1	27.1	4.3	2.0	36440	41807	33	34	10063	12.1	11.2	57.3	17.0	2.3	131015
97403	EUGENE	25661	3803	39.0	23.9	21.1	8.3	7.6	36097	40953	32	32	1899	19.1	2.4	19.0	48.0	11.4	197438
97404	EUGENE	23294	11308	17.6	30.9	39.1	9.0	3.4	51153	58938	74	81	8593	1.5	1.9	57.8	37.8	1.0	162962
97405	EUGENE	30213	18390	22.9	27.3	29.5	11.9	8.4	49835	57365	72	79	12698	1.5	2.8	33.5	54.3	8.0	193923
97406	AGNESS	25061	70	35.7	34.3	22.9	5.7	1.4	32297	36732	19	16	58	8.6	3.5	29.3	39.7	19.0	200000
97408	EUGENE	33486	4219	18.7	25.4	34.4	13.6	8.0	55492	63224	80	88	3223	10.7	3.6	35.8	39.5	10.4	174866
97410	AZALEA	18294	318	37.7	28.9	28.3	4.7	0.3	34702	37353	26	25	264	6.1	6.1	42.1	37.5	8.3	164000
97411	BANDON	21010	3037	35.8	34.2	23.1	4.6	2.3	33888	38274	24	23	2252	8.1	9.1	42.4	34.6	5.9	151824
	OREGON	24176		24.9	29.7	31.4	9.2	4.8	45702	52201				6.4	6.5	35.2	43.4	8.6	179540
	UNITED STATES	25866		24.7	27.1	30.8	10.9	6.5	48124	56710				10.9	15.0	33.7	30.1	10.4	145905

ZIP CODE	FINANCIAL SERVICES				THE HOME						ENTERTAINMENT						PERSONAL			
					Home Improvements		Furnishings													
# POST OFFICE NAME	Auto Loan	Home Loan	Invest-ments	Retire-ment Plans	Home Repair	Lawn & Garden	Comput-ers & Hard-ware	Major Appli-ances	TV, Radio, Sound Equip-ment	Furni-ture	Dine out/ Carry out	Sports Equip-ment	Fees & Tickets	Toys & Games	Travel	Cable TV	Apparel & Services	Auto Repairs	Health Insur-ance	Pets & Supplies
97205 PORTLAND	52	47	76	52	45	51	58	52	60	57	75	64	58	75	56	59	74	57	51	58
97206 PORTLAND	68	71	81	72	70	74	75	72	73	73	91	86	75	93	74	71	90	74	68	78
97209 PORTLAND	56	47	72	54	46	51	62	54	62	60	78	69	59	76	57	58	76	60	50	61
97210 PORTLAND	104	103	175	115	99	109	117	106	118	118	149	129	122	154	116	116	148	112	99	118
97211 PORTLAND	73	78	92	79	77	80	81	78	79	79	99	92	82	101	80	77	97	79	73	85
97212 PORTLAND	102	112	138	115	110	115	116	110	111	113	139	132	118	142	114	107	138	113	101	120
97213 PORTLAND	77	84	105	87	83	87	87	83	85	86	107	100	89	110	87	82	105	85	77	91
97214 PORTLAND	73	66	91	73	65	71	81	73	80	78	101	91	78	98	76	75	99	80	68	81
97215 PORTLAND	85	95	117	98	94	97	95	92	92	95	115	109	98	118	95	89	114	93	85	100
97216 PORTLAND	69	70	76	71	70	75	73	72	72	71	90	85	73	90	72	71	87	73	71	79
97217 PORTLAND	69	72	81	73	71	74	75	73	74	73	92	86	75	94	74	71	90	74	69	80
97218 PORTLAND	65	67	76	69	67	69	71	69	70	70	87	82	71	88	70	66	86	71	64	75
97219 PORTLAND	119	134	162	139	131	135	131	127	125	132	158	150	136	160	131	120	156	128	115	139
97220 PORTLAND	69	74	84	75	73	77	76	74	74	75	93	87	77	95	75	72	91	75	70	80
97221 PORTLAND	142	170	209	172	167	174	160	157	151	161	191	183	170	196	164	148	190	156	145	171
97222 PORTLAND	77	80	91	83	79	82	82	80	80	82	100	95	83	100	81	76	98	82	74	88
97223 PORTLAND	101	106	115	112	103	104	106	103	100	107	127	122	106	125	102	94	125	104	91	113
97224 PORTLAND	105	113	118	113	111	117	106	109	103	109	130	122	109	126	107	102	127	107	105	120
97225 PORTLAND	117	129	154	133	128	133	129	126	123	128	155	149	132	156	129	119	152	127	117	138
97227 PORTLAND	57	56	67	56	54	60	61	58	62	60	78	68	61	77	59	61	76	60	57	65
97229 PORTLAND	156	179	189	186	173	173	165	162	153	169	194	190	173	197	164	146	193	159	143	179
97230 PORTLAND	79	82	91	82	82	88	83	83	82	83	103	95	84	102	83	81	100	83	81	91
97231 PORTLAND	138	154	158	155	155	157	142	145	136	141	169	170	146	176	145	134	167	141	137	166
97232 PORTLAND	82	79	102	85	78	83	90	84	88	88	111	102	89	109	86	83	108	89	77	92
97233 PORTLAND	68	65	69	67	65	70	70	69	70	69	88	81	69	87	68	69	85	70	67	76
97236 PORTLAND	84	93	101	95	92	94	91	89	87	90	109	105	93	112	91	84	108	89	82	98
97239 PORTLAND	121	126	172	134	123	133	135	127	131	134	166	152	138	167	133	128	164	132	118	140
97266 PORTLAND	75	78	84	79	77	81	79	78	77	78	97	92	80	98	78	75	94	78	74	86
97267 PORTLAND	89	99	107	99	98	102	96	95	93	95	116	111	99	120	97	91	114	94	90	105
97301 SALEM	68	68	71	68	68	73	70	70	69	69	86	81	69	85	69	68	83	70	69	78
97302 SALEM	88	94	105	96	94	99	95	94	92	94	115	109	96	115	95	90	112	94	90	103
97303 SALEM	75	75	78	76	74	78	77	76	76	77	96	89	77	96	75	74	94	77	73	84
97304 SALEM	89	99	108	100	98	101	95	95	91	95	114	110	98	115	96	89	112	94	89	104
97305 SALEM	73	73	76	74	71	74	74	73	72	74	91	86	73	89	72	69	89	74	68	81
97306 SALEM	100	115	122	116	111	113	108	106	102	108	128	124	111	131	108	98	127	105	97	117
97321 ALBANY	87	97	104	98	97	99	94	93	90	93	113	110	97	117	95	88	112	92	87	103
97322 ALBANY	72	69	67	69	70	75	70	71	71	69	87	83	69	87	70	70	84	71	72	82
97324 ALSEA	85	63	38	60	72	80	61	74	69	61	82	89	54	81	64	72	76	73	86	101
97325 AUMSVILLE	91	91	83	90	90	93	87	90	85	88	105	104	85	103	86	82	103	89	85	102
97326 BLODGETT	85	85	76	84	88	91	78	84	78	78	96	99	78	99	80	78	93	82	84	102
97327 BROWNSVILLE	89	79	61	75	84	90	73	81	78	73	95	97	72	97	76	80	90	79	88	105
97329 CASCADIA	79	71	54	67	75	80	65	72	69	65	84	86	64	86	67	71	80	70	78	93
97330 CORVALLIS	87	82	95	86	81	87	95	87	92	91	115	107	91	112	89	87	112	92	82	97
97331 CORVALLIS	32	20	25	22	19	23	38	28	37	32	46	39	31	41	30	32	43	34	26	32
97333 CORVALLIS	73	68	80	72	68	73	81	74	79	77	98	91	77	95	76	74	95	79	69	82
97338 DALLAS	74	73	72	72	74	80	73	74	74	72	92	87	73	93	73	74	88	74	76	86
97341 DEPOE BAY	80	74	70	70	78	92	68	78	73	73	90	77	69	75	74	78	84	76	91	90
97342 DETROIT	78	59	39	53	67	76	56	68	64	56	76	80	50	75	60	69	70	67	81	94
97343 EDDYVILLE	81	57	30	54	66	74	56	69	65	56	76	84	48	74	58	68	69	68	83	96
97344 FALLS CITY	84	75	57	71	79	85	69	77	73	69	89	91	68	91	71	75	85	75	83	99
97345 FOSTER	84	75	57	71	79	85	69	77	74	69	90	92	68	92	71	76	85	75	83	99
97346 GATES	86	58	28	52	66	76	57	70	67	57	79	84	48	75	58	72	72	70	86	99
97347 GRAND RONDE	80	72	56	69	74	78	68	74	70	70	86	86	65	83	68	70	83	73	76	90
97348 HALSEY	106	84	59	82	92	103	85	96	93	84	111	112	79	110	86	95	103	94	107	121
97350 IDANHA	76	58	37	53	66	74	55	67	63	55	74	79	49	73	58	67	69	66	79	92
97351 INDEPENDENCE	73	70	69	69	70	73	72	73	72	72	90	85	69	88	71	70	88	74	71	82
97352 JEFFERSON	95	92	79	90	94	99	87	92	88	88	108	107	86	108	88	88	104	90	93	110
97355 LEBANON	76	67	54	64	70	78	66	72	71	65	85	83	64	85	67	72	81	71	79	88
97357 LOGSDEN	84	76	59	73	76	81	73	78	74	75	91	90	68	86	72	73	87	78	78	93
97358 LYONS	81	68	48	64	73	80	64	73	69	64	83	87	61	84	66	71	78	71	81	95
97360 MILL CITY	69	56	40	54	60	68	57	63	62	56	75	72	53	73	57	65	69	62	72	78
97361 MONMOUTH	71	64	72	67	63	66	79	69	75	73	94	87	73	91	71	69	91	75	63	77
97362 MOUNT ANGEL	75	65	60	65	68	75	69	72	72	67	88	84	65	86	68	72	83	72	76	85
97364 NEOTSU	68	70	80	73	71	74	72	71	69	71	87	84	71	84	71	67	84	72	68	78
97365 NEWPORT	76	69	64	68	72	79	71	74	74	70	90	86	68	88	71	74	86	75	79	88
97366 SOUTH BEACH	97	72	44	66	82	92	69	85	79	69	93	100	61	92	73	84	86	83	100	117
97367 LINCOLN CITY	66	56	46	53	60	67	56	62	60	55	72	72	52	70	57	62	68	62	69	78
97368 OTIS	79	73	58	70	73	77	70	75	70	71	87	86	66	82	69	70	83	74	75	89
97370 PHILOMATH	96	108	113	109	107	108	103	102	98	102	123	121	105	127	103	95	121	101	95	114
97371 RICKREALL	108	92	71	89	100	109	88	100	94	87	113	118	83	113	91	96	106	98	110	128
97374 SCIO	97	89	72	86	93	100	84	91	87	83	106	108	82	108	85	89	101	89	97	114
97375 SCOTTS MILLS	93	98	90	95	99	102	89	93	88	88	109	110	91	113	91	88	106	90	92	112
97376 SEAL ROCK	80	61	39	56	69	77	58	70	66	58	78	83	51	76	61	70	72	69	83	96
97377 SHEDD	122	93	57	88	104	115	90	106	100	89	119	128	81	118	93	104	110	104	123	144
97378 SHERIDAN	81	69	53	68	72	80	69	75	73	68	89	86	66	88	69	74	83	73	81	90
97380 SILETZ	81	73	57	70	74	78	70	75	71	72	88	87	66	83	69	70	84	75	75	90
97381 SILVERTON	86	85	84	85	87	92	85	87	85	83	105	103	84	107	85	84	102	87	86	101
97383 STAYTON	77	69	55	67	71	78	69	73	72	68	87	84	66	86	69	73	82	72	78	87
97385 SUBLIMITY	110	81	47	77	92	102	79	95	89	78	105	114	69	104	82	93	97	94	111	130
97386 SWEET HOME	73	61	45	57	64	72	60	66	65	59	78	77	56	77	60	67	74	65	74	83
97389 TANGENT	87	83	69	81	82	85	79	83	78	81	97	96	76	93	78	77	94	83	80	97
97390 TIDEWATER	78	69	59	64	74	86	64	74	69	67	85	78	62	75	69	74	79	72	87	91
97391 TOLEDO	78	67	55	67	71	78	69	74	72	67	88	87	65	88	69	73	83	74	79	89
97392 TURNER	96	95	85	93	98	103	90	95	90	89	111	111	89	112	91	91	107	93	97	113
97394 WALDPORT	72	58	43	55	63	74	59	67	66	58	79	74	55	73	61	70	72	66	80	82
97396 WILLAMINA	76	66	52	65	69	76	66	71	69	66	85	82	63	84	66	70	80	70	76	86
97401 EUGENE	66	61	73	64	61	66	74	67	72	70	90	82	70	88	69	68	87	71	63	74
97402 EUGENE	66	61	67	63	61	65	67	65	66	66	83	77	65	80	64	64	81	68	63	73
97403 EUGENE	85	73	82	76	73	82	93	83	91	85	113	103	85	108	85	87	108	89	81	93
97404 EUGENE	80	91	97	91	90	91	87	86	83	86	104	101	90	108	87	81	103	85	80	94
97405 EUGENE	96	103	116	105	102	107	104	101	100	102	126	120	105	127	104	97	123	102	95	112
97406 AGNESS	75	59	42	56	64	77	63	70	70	61	83	77	58	77	64	74	76	70	83	84
97408 EUGENE	115	124	125	121	125	131	115	119	114	115	141	139	118	146	119	114	138	116	118	138
97410 AZALEA	77	52	23	45	59	68	50	63	60	51	71	75	43	67	51	65	64	62	77	89
97411 BANDON	69	62	55	60	65	74	63	67	67	62	81	75	61	78	64	69	76	67	75	78
OREGON	87	85	86	85	86	91	86	87	86	85	106	102	85	106	85	84	103	87	86	100
UNITED STATES	100	100	100	100	100	100	100	100	100	100	100	100	100	100	100	100	100	100	100	100

POPULATION CHANGE

ZIP CODE		COUNTY FIPS CODE	POPULATION			2000-2004 ANNUAL RATE		HOUSEHOLDS					FAMILIES		
#	POST OFFICE NAME		2000	2004	2009	% Rate	State Centile	2000	2004	2009	% Annual Rate 2000-2004	2004 Average HH Size	2000	2004	% Annual Rate 2000-2004
97412	BLACHLY	039	532	511	514	-0.9	7	195	189	192	-0.7	2.62	136	131	-0.9
97413	BLUE RIVER	039	841	817	824	-0.7	11	393	386	392	-0.4	2.11	257	248	-0.8
97414	BROADBENT	011	197	201	204	0.5	51	80	82	84	0.6	2.44	56	56	0.0
97415	BROOKINGS	015	13292	13628	13977	0.6	55	5947	6166	6396	0.9	2.18	3903	4022	0.7
97416	CAMAS VALLEY	019	765	750	750	-0.5	17	281	278	280	-0.3	2.70	206	202	-0.5
97417	CANYONVILLE	019	1750	1722	1724	-0.4	19	713	711	720	-0.1	2.41	468	463	-0.3
97419	CHESHIRE	039	1128	1098	1108	-0.6	12	449	442	450	-0.4	2.48	340	332	-0.6
97420	COOS BAY	011	27435	27654	27821	0.2	42	11471	11671	11859	0.4	2.32	7514	7603	0.3
97423	COQUILLE	011	6885	6796	6765	-0.3	21	2810	2803	2820	-0.1	2.35	1940	1923	-0.2
97424	COTTAGE GROVE	039	16238	16139	16379	-0.1	27	6204	6229	6375	0.1	2.56	4425	4410	-0.1
97426	CRESWELL	039	7901	8496	8940	1.7	86	2869	3106	3292	1.9	2.71	2149	2312	1.7
97427	CULP CREEK	039	279	275	279	-0.3	19	110	110	112	0.0	2.50	83	82	-0.3
97429	DAYS CREEK	019	701	686	687	-0.5	16	277	275	279	-0.2	2.48	202	199	-0.4
97430	DEADWOOD	039	571	546	550	-1.1	6	203	196	200	-0.8	2.71	139	133	-1.0
97431	DEXTER	039	2158	2157	2182	0.0	31	748	756	772	0.3	2.84	575	577	0.1
97434	DORENA	039	706	698	707	-0.3	23	264	263	269	-0.1	2.65	203	202	-0.1
97435	DRAIN	019	2050	1970	1963	-0.9	7	821	799	805	-0.6	2.47	581	562	-0.8
97436	ELKTON	019	840	807	803	-0.9	7	348	339	341	-0.6	2.38	248	241	-0.7
97437	ELMIRA	039	2216	2179	2218	-0.4	18	832	828	850	-0.1	2.63	655	648	-0.3
97438	FALL CREEK	039	1593	1579	1599	-0.2	24	579	581	594	0.1	2.71	441	439	-0.1
97439	FLORENCE	039	12902	13768	14444	1.5	83	6125	6623	7017	1.9	2.07	3967	4237	1.6
97441	GARDINER	019	12	11	11	-2.0	1	7	7	7	0.0	1.57	5	4	-5.1
97442	GLENDALE	019	2092	2074	2079	-0.2	25	811	808	816	-0.1	2.56	585	580	-0.2
97443	GLIDE	019	1840	1840	1854	0.0	35	637	643	655	0.2	2.71	467	469	0.1
97444	GOLD BEACH	015	4767	4822	4917	0.3	44	2142	2190	2259	0.5	2.17	1407	1429	0.4
97446	HARRISBURG	043	4258	4470	4641	1.2	74	1514	1596	1662	1.3	2.80	1173	1230	1.1
97447	IDLEYLD PARK	019	852	833	834	-0.5	15	333	329	332	-0.3	2.38	237	232	-0.5
97448	JUNCTION CITY	039	12126	12396	12769	0.5	53	4619	4748	4920	0.7	2.58	3282	3349	0.5
97449	LAKESIDE	011	1537	1499	1479	-0.6	14	718	709	707	-0.3	2.05	486	477	-0.4
97450	LANGLOIS	015	567	560	566	-0.3	22	257	257	263	0.0	2.18	172	171	-0.1
97451	LORANE	039	487	503	516	0.8	63	181	188	194	0.9	2.68	137	141	0.7
97452	LOWELL	039	1056	1041	1053	-0.3	19	405	404	412	-0.1	2.58	302	298	-0.3
97453	MAPLETON	039	1009	1055	1094	1.1	71	431	456	477	1.3	2.31	309	324	1.1
97454	MARCOLA	039	1451	1382	1389	-1.1	4	561	540	547	-0.9	2.56	428	409	-1.1
97455	PLEASANT HILL	039	3085	3094	3145	0.1	37	1103	1116	1144	0.3	2.76	866	871	0.1
97456	MONROE	003	2783	2748	2796	-0.3	21	1028	1021	1045	-0.2	2.69	788	777	-0.3
97457	MYRTLE CREEK	019	9722	9813	9917	0.2	43	3747	3825	3907	0.5	2.56	2735	2776	0.4
97458	MYRTLE POINT	011	4775	4754	4739	-0.1	28	1921	1933	1949	0.2	2.44	1354	1354	0.0
97459	NORTH BEND	011	14413	14108	13978	-0.5	16	5909	5840	5848	-0.3	2.35	3973	3907	-0.4
97461	NOTI	039	1014	1007	1021	-0.2	26	380	381	390	0.1	2.64	293	292	-0.1
97462	OAKLAND	019	3891	3845	3859	-0.3	22	1518	1517	1539	0.0	2.52	1148	1139	-0.2
97463	OAKRIDGE	039	3775	3663	3695	-0.7	10	1591	1560	1588	-0.5	2.35	1079	1049	-0.7
97465	PORT ORFORD	015	2074	2163	2234	1.0	70	1005	1061	1108	1.3	2.04	569	597	1.1
97466	POWERS	011	994	975	963	-0.5	18	438	433	431	-0.3	2.25	268	264	-0.4
97467	REEDSPORT	019	6164	5891	5864	-1.1	5	2758	2671	2689	-0.8	2.19	1809	1740	-0.9
97469	RIDDLE	019	2761	2682	2677	-0.7	11	1011	992	1001	-0.5	2.64	740	722	-0.6
97470	ROSEBURG	019	46373	47935	49255	0.8	64	18436	19234	19970	1.0	2.43	12884	13383	0.9
97473	SCOTTSBURG	019	224	206	203	-2.0	1	106	99	99	-1.6	2.08	76	70	-1.9
97476	SIXES	015	304	300	304	-0.3	21	123	123	126	0.0	2.44	82	82	0.0
97477	SPRINGFIELD	039	35720	35803	36644	0.1	37	14505	14610	15048	0.2	2.42	9092	9085	0.0
97478	SPRINGFIELD	039	31982	33078	34185	0.8	65	11800	12321	12838	1.0	2.67	8785	9112	0.9
97479	SUTHERLIN	019	8489	9014	9336	1.4	80	3406	3667	3848	1.8	2.45	2426	2592	1.6
97480	SWISSHOME	039	383	356	357	-1.7	2	150	141	142	-1.5	2.47	99	92	-1.7
97481	TENMILE	019	901	858	853	-1.1	4	317	306	307	-0.8	2.80	251	241	-1.0
97484	TILLER	019	273	265	264	-0.7	11	115	113	114	-0.4	2.32	82	80	-0.6
97486	UMPQUA	019	843	856	871	0.4	49	336	345	355	0.6	2.46	271	278	0.6
97487	VENETA	039	6798	7007	7199	0.7	60	2439	2531	2619	0.9	2.77	1878	1937	0.7
97488	VIDA	039	1055	1003	1007	-1.2	4	431	414	419	-0.9	2.42	300	284	-1.3
97489	WALTERVILLE	039	896	869	879	-0.7	10	372	364	371	-0.5	2.39	276	267	-0.8
97490	WALTON	039	275	284	293	0.8	63	100	104	108	0.9	2.73	76	78	0.6
97492	WESTFIR	039	620	600	605	-0.8	9	238	233	237	-0.5	2.58	177	172	-0.7
97493	WESTLAKE	039	183	179	181	-0.5	15	70	69	70	-0.3	2.59	52	51	-0.5
97496	WINSTON	019	6817	6868	6933	0.2	41	2613	2665	2721	0.5	2.56	1916	1941	0.3
97497	WOLF CREEK	033	1754	1808	1878	0.7	60	721	748	782	0.9	2.41	485	500	0.7
97498	YACHATS	041	1465	1461	1463	-0.1	30	666	670	676	0.1	2.00	392	391	-0.1
97499	YONCALLA	019	1943	1908	1908	-0.4	18	761	756	764	-0.2	2.52	551	543	-0.3
97501	MEDFORD	029	37167	38554	40708	0.9	67	14306	14862	15728	0.9	2.55	9457	9764	0.8
97502	CENTRAL POINT	029	23781	26115	28405	2.2	91	8717	9629	10519	2.4	2.70	6671	7309	2.2
97503	WHITE CITY	029	8894	9815	10721	2.4	93	2725	3019	3315	2.4	3.02	2156	2366	2.2
97504	MEDFORD	029	40846	43527	46503	1.5	82	16737	17930	19240	1.6	2.38	11237	11944	1.5
97520	ASHLAND	029	24016	24869	26167	0.8	65	10334	10778	11417	1.0	2.19	5738	5928	0.8
97522	BUTTE FALLS	029	645	664	694	0.7	58	239	248	261	0.9	2.68	179	185	0.8
97523	CAVE JUNCTION	033	6377	6534	6779	0.6	54	2697	2778	2896	0.7	2.34	1738	1775	0.5
97524	EAGLE POINT	029	10581	11705	12732	2.4	94	3851	4278	4671	2.5	2.73	2980	3288	2.3
97525	GOLD HILL	029	4818	4970	5245	0.7	61	1951	2030	2154	0.9	2.45	1366	1405	0.7
97526	GRANTS PASS	033	31896	33018	34524	0.8	65	13006	13569	14272	1.0	2.37	8723	9024	0.8
97527	GRANTS PASS	033	27299	28988	30637	1.4	80	11191	11950	12700	1.6	2.41	8023	8518	1.3
97530	JACKSONVILLE	029	6315	6907	7484	2.1	90	2617	2891	3151	2.4	2.38	1886	2067	2.2
97531	KERBY	033	277	285	296	0.7	58	114	118	123	0.8	2.42	70	72	0.7
97532	MERLIN	033	2112	2307	2473	2.1	90	837	924	998	2.4	2.50	648	711	2.2
97534	O BRIEN	033	327	338	352	0.8	64	139	145	152	1.0	2.33	88	91	0.8
97535	PHOENIX	029	3863	3984	4175	0.7	61	1634	1694	1782	0.9	2.33	988	1014	0.6
97536	PROSPECT	029	932	948	984	0.4	50	384	393	411	0.6	2.41	292	298	0.5
97537	ROGUE RIVER	029	6599	6920	7312	1.1	73	2784	2942	3126	1.3	2.35	1934	2025	1.1
97538	SELMA	033	2744	2832	2942	0.8	62	1090	1134	1186	0.9	2.50	760	785	0.8
97539	SHADY COVE	029	2935	3003	3131	0.5	53	1240	1280	1341	0.8	2.35	879	898	0.5
97540	TALENT	029	7542	7846	8342	0.9	69	3040	3171	3384	1.0	2.43	1955	2020	0.8
97541	TRAIL	029	1223	1262	1322	0.7	61	487	507	534	1.0	2.49	361	372	0.7
97543	WILDERVILLE	033	1477	1564	1648	1.4	78	594	634	673	1.6	2.46	440	466	1.4
97544	WILLIAMS	033	2581	2609	2702	0.3	44	1068	1089	1134	0.5	2.40	733	742	0.3
97601	KLAMATH FALLS	035	21632	21581	21883	-0.1	30	8684	8685	8847	0.0	2.42	5414	5374	-0.2
97603	KLAMATH FALLS	035	28806	29935	30839	0.9	68	11315	11839	12264	1.1	2.50	8021	8333	0.9
97620	ADEL	037	111	106	104	-1.1	5	51	50	49	-0.5	2.12	38	37	-0.6
97621	BEATTY	035	99	103	106	0.9	69	47	49	51	1.0	2.10	31	32	0.8
97623	BONANZA	035	2779	2901	2995	1.0	71	1053	1107	1149	1.2	2.62	815	854	1.1
	OREGON					1.1					1.1	2.50			1.0
	UNITED STATES					1.2					1.3	2.58			1.1

ZIP CODE #	POST OFFICE NAME	RACE (%) White 2000	White 2004	Black 2000	Black 2004	Asian/Pacific 2000	Asian/Pacific 2004	% Hispanic Origin 2000	% Hispanic Origin 2004	2004 AGE DISTRIBUTION (%) 0-4	5-9	10-14	15-19	20-24	25-44	45-64	65-84	85+	18+	MEDIAN AGE 2004	% 2004 Males	% 2004 Females
97412	BLACHLY	92.1	91.6	0.2	0.2	0.9	1.2	1.7	2.0	5.7	6.1	6.5	6.1	6.7	22.5	33.7	11.6	1.4	77.9	42.9	52.3	47.8
97413	BLUE RIVER	96.1	96.0	0.2	0.2	0.5	0.5	2.9	3.6	2.9	4.0	5.3	4.8	3.8	18.4	37.8	21.2	1.8	84.5	51.2	52.4	47.6
97414	BROADBENT	92.9	93.0	0.0	0.0	0.5	0.5	2.5	2.5	5.5	5.5	6.5	6.0	5.0	20.9	30.4	18.4	2.0	78.6	45.5	50.8	49.3
97415	BROOKINGS	92.4	91.8	0.2	0.2	0.9	1.0	3.9	4.7	4.4	4.5	5.3	5.3	4.6	18.1	29.5	24.8	3.5	82.2	50.5	48.9	51.1
97416	CAMAS VALLEY	93.6	93.3	0.0	0.0	0.4	0.4	2.2	2.5	5.2	5.6	6.5	7.5	6.1	23.1	30.3	14.3	1.5	78.3	42.4	51.5	48.5
97417	CANYONVILLE	91.7	91.2	0.2	0.2	0.9	1.1	3.8	4.4	5.4	5.5	7.0	6.9	6.2	21.0	28.2	17.3	2.7	77.6	43.5	49.0	51.1
97419	CHESHIRE	93.3	92.5	0.4	0.4	0.6	0.7	3.3	4.0	4.5	4.1	7.1	8.5	3.6	23.3	36.2	11.7	1.1	78.7	44.4	51.4	48.6
97420	COOS BAY	90.8	90.8	0.3	0.3	1.4	1.3	3.9	3.9	5.2	5.1	6.0	6.8	6.4	22.7	29.0	16.4	2.3	79.8	43.4	49.1	50.9
97423	COQUILLE	93.2	93.2	0.6	0.5	0.6	0.6	3.7	3.7	4.6	4.9	5.9	6.7	6.2	21.9	29.6	17.6	2.7	80.2	44.9	49.0	51.0
97424	COTTAGE GROVE	93.5	92.8	0.2	0.2	0.9	1.1	3.8	4.7	5.9	6.1	7.1	6.6	6.2	23.9	28.3	13.9	2.1	76.8	41.0	49.2	50.8
97426	CRESWELL	91.6	90.8	0.3	0.3	0.7	0.8	4.5	5.5	6.9	6.7	7.5	7.4	6.1	26.4	26.9	10.7	1.4	74.2	37.5	49.5	50.5
97427	CULP CREEK	93.9	92.7	0.4	0.4	0.7	1.1	2.9	3.6	3.6	4.7	7.3	7.3	5.5	21.8	33.8	15.6	0.4	80.0	44.9	52.7	47.3
97429	DAYS CREEK	92.9	92.4	0.1	0.2	0.6	0.6	2.7	3.4	4.4	5.4	7.4	7.7	3.6	18.7	35.4	16.0	1.3	77.7	46.6	49.4	50.6
97430	DEADWOOD	90.5	90.1	0.2	0.2	0.7	0.9	2.5	2.9	5.1	5.3	6.2	6.6	6.2	22.2	33.5	13.7	1.1	79.1	43.9	50.4	49.6
97431	DEXTER	94.3	94.0	0.3	0.3	0.4	0.5	3.4	4.0	5.2	6.0	8.2	7.9	5.8	23.9	32.4	9.5	1.1	75.6	40.8	51.3	48.7
97434	DORENA	92.8	92.3	0.1	0.1	0.7	0.9	3.3	3.7	4.4	5.4	7.2	8.0	2.9	25.5	31.7	14.2	0.7	77.2	43.0	52.2	47.9
97435	DRAIN	92.8	92.5	0.1	0.1	0.4	0.5	2.7	3.2	5.3	5.4	5.9	6.8	6.5	23.4	30.1	14.9	1.8	79.4	42.8	49.1	50.9
97436	ELKTON	95.0	94.8	0.2	0.3	0.2	0.4	1.2	1.4	4.0	4.5	6.4	6.3	5.0	20.5	31.9	20.0	1.6	81.2	47.2	49.6	50.4
97437	ELMIRA	95.6	95.3	0.1	0.1	0.5	0.6	2.4	2.9	4.0	4.7	5.6	7.0	6.1	22.0	35.3	13.9	1.4	81.6	45.4	50.2	49.8
97438	FALL CREEK	91.6	91.0	0.1	0.1	0.5	0.6	3.3	4.0	4.7	5.8	7.4	7.0	5.3	24.6	36.3	8.0	1.0	77.8	42.2	50.4	49.6
97439	FLORENCE	95.9	95.7	0.2	0.2	0.7	0.8	2.2	2.7	3.4	3.6	4.5	4.9	4.2	14.9	29.8	31.0	3.7	85.4	55.6	47.7	52.3
97441	GARDINER	91.7	100.0	0.0	0.0	0.0	0.0	0.0	0.0	0.0	0.0	0.0	0.0	18.2	36.4	45.5	0.0	0.0	100.0	33.8	27.3	72.7
97442	GLENDALE	91.5	91.1	0.1	0.1	1.0	1.1	6.8	8.0	6.1	6.2	7.8	7.5	7.0	21.7	28.7	13.9	1.2	75.4	40.4	49.7	50.3
97443	GLIDE	92.7	92.6	0.2	0.2	0.4	0.5	1.6	1.9	4.2	4.6	7.2	10.9	6.9	21.7	31.6	11.9	0.9	77.4	41.2	53.2	46.9
97444	GOLD BEACH	94.5	94.1	0.2	0.2	0.8	0.9	2.3	2.8	3.7	4.1	5.4	5.7	4.1	17.5	36.3	21.1	2.0	83.0	50.5	49.0	51.0
97446	HARRISBURG	93.3	92.5	0.2	0.2	0.5	0.7	5.2	6.4	9.1	8.6	7.2	6.7	6.3	28.3	23.6	9.2	1.0	71.1	34.1	51.3	48.7
97447	IDLEYLD PARK	90.7	90.3	0.4	0.4	0.6	0.7	2.8	3.4	5.0	5.6	7.3	10.4	6.8	22.0	30.7	11.0	1.0	75.9	40.0	53.4	46.6
97448	JUNCTION CITY	93.1	92.3	0.3	0.3	0.8	0.9	5.0	6.2	6.2	6.1	7.1	7.7	5.7	25.4	28.1	11.7	2.0	75.9	39.6	49.8	50.3
97449	LAKESIDE	92.9	92.8	0.4	0.4	0.3	0.3	3.2	3.2	3.0	3.3	3.7	4.8	3.9	16.6	36.2	26.0	2.5	87.3	53.5	51.0	49.0
97450	LANGLOIS	92.4	91.4	0.2	0.2	0.4	0.5	4.8	5.9	2.7	3.4	5.7	6.3	3.9	15.9	38.4	21.3	2.5	84.1	51.5	52.5	47.5
97451	LORANE	95.7	95.4	0.2	0.2	0.6	0.6	0.8	1.0	5.2	6.0	7.6	6.8	5.0	23.1	35.6	9.7	1.2	77.1	42.5	49.1	50.9
97452	LOWELL	92.2	91.9	0.2	0.2	0.5	0.5	4.6	5.4	6.1	6.9	7.7	8.7	6.2	27.5	28.6	7.6	0.9	74.3	36.8	50.0	50.1
97453	MAPLETON	90.8	90.4	0.1	0.1	0.5	0.6	3.4	4.0	3.9	4.1	4.8	6.6	4.9	18.5	35.5	20.4	1.3	83.2	49.0	50.0	50.1
97454	MARCOLA	93.7	93.3	0.1	0.1	0.5	0.5	2.9	3.6	4.3	5.3	6.3	5.6	5.1	23.6	37.1	11.9	0.9	80.3	44.9	51.5	48.6
97455	PLEASANT HILL	94.6	94.1	0.6	0.6	1.0	1.2	1.7	2.1	4.4	5.6	6.9	7.3	5.0	21.4	34.1	13.7	1.7	78.3	44.6	49.1	50.9
97456	MONROE	95.7	95.4	0.2	0.2	0.7	0.8	5.3	6.4	5.5	6.0	7.1	6.8	5.8	26.8	30.9	10.2	0.9	77.2	40.7	51.4	48.6
97457	MYRTLE CREEK	93.5	93.1	0.1	0.1	0.7	0.8	2.8	3.4	6.3	6.3	7.0	6.5	6.2	23.4	27.1	15.4	1.8	76.3	40.9	48.7	51.3
97458	MYRTLE POINT	93.1	93.0	0.2	0.2	0.3	0.3	3.1	3.2	5.0	5.5	6.7	6.9	5.9	20.2	29.9	17.4	2.5	78.4	44.9	48.8	51.2
97459	NORTH BEND	93.1	93.1	0.4	0.4	1.3	1.3	3.1	3.1	4.9	5.2	6.3	6.7	6.2	23.5	30.0	14.4	2.8	79.3	43.1	49.0	51.0
97461	NOTI	94.3	93.7	0.1	0.1	0.6	0.7	2.5	3.0	5.6	5.5	6.1	7.1	6.5	25.6	33.4	9.3	1.1	78.4	41.4	51.5	48.5
97462	OAKLAND	93.8	93.4	0.3	0.3	0.6	0.7	3.1	3.9	4.9	5.6	6.0	6.2	5.2	20.0	33.7	16.9	1.4	79.5	46.2	50.5	49.5
97463	OAKRIDGE	92.9	92.1	0.3	0.4	0.5	0.6	4.5	5.6	4.6	5.3	7.4	6.8	5.6	21.3	29.3	17.7	2.0	78.5	44.4	51.3	48.7
97465	PORT ORFORD	92.9	92.5	0.1	0.1	0.5	0.5	4.0	4.8	3.4	3.8	5.0	5.2	4.4	15.6	35.5	24.8	2.5	84.7	52.2	49.9	50.1
97466	POWERS	86.4	86.3	0.1	0.1	0.5	0.5	2.2	2.3	4.5	4.8	5.3	6.9	6.2	19.0	31.4	19.1	2.9	81.2	47.0	50.3	49.7
97467	REEDSPORT	94.1	93.6	0.0	0.0	0.5	0.5	4.0	4.8	4.7	4.9	5.4	5.6	5.3	18.1	30.3	22.9	2.9	81.7	49.2	49.5	50.6
97469	RIDDLE	92.8	92.4	0.1	0.1	0.4	0.4	2.5	3.0	6.1	6.3	6.7	6.3	7.0	21.2	28.2	16.0	2.3	76.7	42.2	49.1	50.9
97470	ROSEBURG	94.1	93.6	0.2	0.2	0.9	1.0	3.4	4.2	5.6	5.7	6.4	6.6	6.2	23.7	28.1	15.3	2.5	78.2	42.1	49.0	51.0
97473	SCOTTSBURG	94.6	93.7	0.0	0.0	0.5	0.5	3.6	4.4	4.9	5.3	4.9	4.9	4.9	20.9	31.1	21.4	1.9	81.6	47.5	51.9	48.1
97476	SIXES	92.4	91.3	0.0	0.0	0.3	0.7	4.6	6.0	2.7	3.7	6.0	6.3	3.7	15.7	38.0	21.7	2.3	83.7	51.5	52.3	47.7
97477	SPRINGFIELD	88.9	87.7	0.8	0.9	1.6	1.8	7.6	9.1	7.6	6.8	6.7	6.4	8.3	29.5	22.3	10.5	1.9	75.4	33.8	48.7	51.3
97478	SPRINGFIELD	93.1	92.4	0.4	0.4	0.9	1.1	4.1	4.9	6.9	6.9	7.5	7.0	6.4	28.2	26.1	9.7	1.4	74.3	36.5	49.6	50.4
97479	SUTHERLIN	94.2	93.7	0.1	0.1	0.5	0.7	3.8	4.6	5.9	6.1	7.1	6.8	5.2	22.9	26.2	17.3	2.6	76.6	42.0	48.3	51.7
97480	SWISSHOME	88.0	87.1	0.3	0.3	0.5	0.6	3.4	3.9	4.8	4.5	5.9	7.6	5.6	22.2	33.2	14.9	1.4	79.5	44.6	47.8	52.3
97481	TENMILE	94.1	93.8	0.2	0.2	0.4	0.5	2.6	3.2	4.7	5.2	6.8	7.3	6.1	23.8	32.2	12.9	1.1	78.4	42.6	51.5	48.5
97484	TILLER	91.2	91.3	0.0	0.0	0.4	0.4	2.2	1.9	4.2	7.6	7.2	6.4	2.3	19.3	38.1	14.7	0.4	76.6	46.7	48.3	51.7
97486	UMPQUA	95.0	94.7	0.1	0.1	0.8	0.9	2.3	2.8	3.3	4.1	5.0	5.5	4.7	17.5	38.9	19.4	1.6	84.0	51.5	51.6	48.4
97487	VENETA	93.8	93.4	0.2	0.2	0.7	0.8	2.7	3.3	6.2	6.7	7.5	7.5	6.2	25.7	29.6	9.6	1.1	75.0	39.3	49.7	50.3
97488	VIDA	95.9	95.4	0.5	0.5	0.8	1.0	2.7	3.3	3.8	5.0	6.4	6.1	4.1	21.5	37.7	13.9	1.6	80.7	46.8	50.1	50.0
97489	WALTERVILLE	97.3	97.1	0.1	0.1	0.8	0.9	2.0	2.3	3.6	4.3	5.4	5.5	4.4	20.3	37.5	17.3	1.8	83.2	48.6	50.4	49.6
97490	WALTON	94.9	94.7	0.4	0.4	0.4	0.7	1.1	1.4	6.0	6.3	6.0	6.3	7.4	23.2	34.5	8.8	1.4	77.5	41.7	51.4	48.6
97492	WESTFIR	95.5	95.0	0.5	0.5	0.8	1.0	1.8	2.2	5.0	5.3	6.2	6.8	6.5	20.0	32.8	15.7	1.7	79.5	45.1	52.0	48.0
97493	WESTLAKE	96.2	96.1	0.0	0.0	1.6	1.7	2.2	2.2	1.7	2.8	4.5	5.6	5.0	11.7	40.2	26.3	2.2	86.6	54.4	51.4	48.6
97496	WINSTON	94.6	94.2	0.2	0.2	0.5	0.5	2.7	3.2	7.3	6.4	6.8	7.0	7.2	24.1	25.5	13.9	1.8	75.2	38.3	49.1	50.9
97497	WOLF CREEK	93.8	93.5	0.3	0.3	0.5	0.6	3.1	3.8	4.2	5.0	6.6	5.9	5.1	17.9	37.0	17.0	1.3	79.9	47.9	51.3	48.7
97498	YACHATS	93.2	92.5	0.9	1.0	1.0	1.1	2.9	3.6	2.9	3.4	4.2	7.7	5.4	16.2	36.6	21.3	2.4	85.2	51.3	49.0	51.0
97499	YONCALLA	94.2	93.8	0.1	0.1	0.8	0.9	2.0	2.5	5.8	6.3	6.5	6.8	5.6	22.6	29.6	15.4	1.5	77.2	42.6	49.7	50.3
97501	MEDFORD	87.6	86.2	0.6	0.6	1.0	1.1	12.5	14.6	7.6	7.3	7.2	6.7	6.6	28.0	24.0	11.0	1.6	73.8	35.7	49.6	50.4
97502	CENTRAL POINT	93.8	93.0	0.2	0.2	0.8	0.9	4.6	5.6	6.6	6.9	7.7	6.7	5.6	25.4	27.1	12.3	1.8	74.6	38.9	48.9	51.1
97503	WHITE CITY	88.3	86.6	0.7	0.6	0.6	0.7	11.3	14.1	7.0	6.9	8.1	7.5	7.1	25.8	27.7	9.3	0.7	73.3	36.6	53.3	46.7
97504	MEDFORD	92.7	91.7	0.4	0.4	1.6	1.9	5.4	6.7	5.8	5.8	6.9	6.5	6.2	22.9	26.3	15.7	4.0	77.4	42.1	46.8	53.2
97520	ASHLAND	92.0	91.2	0.6	0.6	1.8	2.0	3.5	4.3	4.0	4.1	5.4	8.6	11.6	22.1	29.1	12.7	2.5	82.4	40.2	46.8	53.2
97522	BUTTE FALLS	94.6	94.3	0.0	0.0	0.3	0.3	2.3	2.6	5.3	5.9	6.8	7.4	5.9	21.8	31.6	14.0	1.4	77.6	43.0	51.1	49.0
97523	CAVE JUNCTION	92.3	91.8	0.3	0.3	0.8	0.9	4.4	5.3	4.6	5.1	6.9	6.9	5.6	19.5	32.6	16.7	2.1	79.0	45.8	50.5	49.5
97524	EAGLE POINT	93.6	92.9	0.2	0.3	0.6	0.6	4.0	5.0	6.9	7.0	7.6	7.4	6.4	25.4	27.5	10.8	1.1	74.0	37.4	49.6	50.4
97525	GOLD HILL	94.4	93.8	0.2	0.3	0.4	0.5	3.8	4.7	4.8	5.3	6.3	5.7	4.8	20.5	34.7	16.0	2.1	80.1	46.7	49.6	50.4
97526	GRANTS PASS	93.4	92.7	0.3	0.3	1.0	1.1	4.6	5.6	5.9	5.7	6.3	6.8	6.3	21.7	27.4	16.8	3.2	77.9	43.0	47.7	52.3
97527	GRANTS PASS	94.7	94.2	0.2	0.3	0.6	0.6	4.2	5.1	5.4	5.4	6.3	6.0	5.2	21.5	29.4	18.2	2.7	79.1	45.1	48.4	51.6
97530	JACKSONVILLE	95.2	94.7	0.2	0.2	0.6	0.7	2.9	3.6	4.0	5.2	7.0	6.5	3.7	19.7	36.3	15.7	2.0	79.4	47.1	49.8	50.2
97531	KERBY	91.3	90.5	0.4	0.4	0.7	1.1	5.1	5.6	4.2	4.9	6.7	7.0	5.3	20.0	33.7	16.1	2.1	80.0	46.1	51.6	48.4
97532	MERLIN	94.7	94.2	0.3	0.4	0.7	0.9	3.5	4.1	3.7	4.2	5.6	6.2	4.6	19.3	36.3	18.8	1.4	82.8	49.2	50.5	49.5
97534	O BRIEN	91.4	90.8	0.6	0.6	0.9	0.9	4.6	5.3	3.0	5.3	6.2	6.8	4.1	18.6	39.4	14.5	2.1	81.1	47.4	53.6	46.5
97535	PHOENIX	90.1	88.8	0.7	0.7	1.1	1.2	8.5	10.4	6.0	6.0	5.6	5.2	5.3	24.2	28.7	16.0	3.0	79.0	43.3	48.1	51.9
97536	PROSPECT	96.0	95.8	0.1	0.1	0.3	0.3	2.4	2.9	4.3	4.9	6.0	5.7	5.1	19.9	35.9	17.0	1.3	81.2	47.1	51.4	48.6
97537	ROGUE RIVER	94.8	94.3	0.2	0.1	0.6	0.7	3.7	4.5	4.5	4.8	5.7	6.0	4.8	19.1	32.7	19.9	2.5	81.2	48.2	49.4	50.6
97538	SELMA	93.5	93.0	0.3	0.3	0.4	0.4	3.2	3.9	4.4	4.8	6.2	6.8	5.0	20.5	34.9	16.5	1.0	80.4	46.4	50.9	49.2
97539	SHADY COVE	96.1	95.8	0.1	0.1	0.3	0.4	2.7	3.4	4.9	5.2	6.5	6.3	4.4	20.8	31.6	19.0	1.4	79.6	46.4	49.7	50.3
97540	TALENT	88.9	87.4	0.5	0.5	0.5	0.7	10.7	12.7	6.5	6.9	7.2	6.6	6.8	27.1	24.5	12.3	2.3	75.4	37.2	48.8	51.3
97541	TRAIL	95.3	95.0	0.2	0.2	0.4	0.4	3.2	3.9	4.8	5.2	7.0	6.7	4.8	21.3	35.4	13.6	1.1	78.8	45.1	51.0	49.1
97543	WILDERVILLE	95.7	95.3	0.1	0.1	0.4	0.5	2.7	3.4	4.1	4.7	5.5	5.2	4.5	19.6	37.2	17.7	1.5	82.4	48.8	50.8	49.2
97544	WILLIAMS	95.3	95.0	0.2	0.2	0.6	0.7	2.5	3.0	4.0	5.3	6.3	5.9	4.1	20.1	37.2	16.1	1.2	80.8	47.3	50.6	49.4
97601	KLAMATH FALLS	86.7	85.7	0.8	0.8	1.4	1.6	8.2	9.7	6.8	6.4	7.1	7.6	9.1	25.7	24.8	10.6	2.1	75.6	35.1	50.5	49.5
97603	KLAMATH FALLS	88.9	87.8	0.6	0.7	0.8	0.9	7.2	8.7	6.6	6.5	7.2	6.7	6.4	24.8	26.0	13.9	2.0	75.4	39.1	49.2	50.9
97620	ADEL	97.3	97.2	0.0	0.0	0.0	0.0	1.8	1.9	4.7	5.7	5.7	6.6	3.8	22.6	31.1	17.9	1.9	78.3	45.6	52.8	47.2
97621	BEATTY	85.9	85.4	1.0	1.0	0.0	0.0	3.0	4.9	3.9	4.9	4.9	6.8	3.9	20.4	36.9	17.5	1.0	80.6	48.1	50.5	49.5
97623	BONANZA	90.0	88.7	0.5	0.7	0.6	0.7	7.0	8.8	5.8	6.7	7.4	7.2	5.2	21.0	30.1	15.3	1.2	75.6	42.5	51.4	48.6
	OREGON	86.6	85.2	1.6	1.7	3.2	3.6	8.1	9.5	6.5	6.4	6.8	6.9	7.4	27.7	25.6	11.0	1.9	76.3	36.9	49.6	50.4
	UNITED STATES	75.1	73.6	12.3	12.5	3.8	4.2	12.5	14.1	6.9	6.7	7.2	7.0	7.3	28.6	23.8	10.8	1.7	75.1	36.0	49.1	50.9

#	POST OFFICE NAME	2004 Per Capita Income	2004 HH Income Base	2004 Household Income Distribution (%): Less than $25,000	$25,000 to $49,999	$50,000 to $99,999	$100,000 to $149,999	$150,000 or More	Median Household Income: 2004	2009	2004 National Centile	2004 State Centile	2004 Home Value Base	2004 Home Value Distribution (%): Less than $50,000	$50,000 to $89,999	$90,000 to $174,999	$175,000 to $399,999	$400,000 or More	2004 Median Home Value
97412	BLACHLY	18102	189	26.5	38.6	28.6	2.7	3.7	39520	43689	44	46	152	17.8	7.9	48.7	16.5	9.2	137500
97413	BLUE RIVER	24408	386	27.7	30.8	36.3	1.0	4.2	44470	50155	60	65	308	6.5	7.8	33.4	44.8	7.5	177365
97414	BROADBENT	13402	82	51.2	24.4	23.2	1.2	0.0	24160	27818	4	3	62	21.0	17.7	41.9	11.3	8.1	107692
97415	BROOKINGS	20508	6166	36.7	33.9	22.4	3.9	3.1	33120	37079	21	19	4542	17.5	7.3	31.7	34.9	8.6	158758
97416	CAMAS VALLEY	14669	278	34.5	37.4	24.5	2.9	0.7	34147	37642	25	24	210	3.3	19.5	40.5	30.5	6.2	144118
97417	CANYONVILLE	16193	711	38.5	37.4	20.3	2.5	1.3	30991	33762	15	11	447	14.5	21.0	45.0	17.5	2.0	111565
97419	CHESHIRE	24509	442	20.4	31.9	32.8	11.3	3.6	47600	53876	67	75	373	7.8	7.2	22.8	49.1	13.1	212755
97420	COOS BAY	20045	11671	37.7	30.0	24.8	5.1	2.5	35179	39694	28	28	7741	12.6	18.9	44.3	20.9	3.3	115238
97423	COQUILLE	19703	2803	35.1	33.4	25.3	3.1	3.1	33671	38465	23	22	2032	8.9	18.6	50.7	20.8	1.0	118062
97424	COTTAGE GROVE	18180	6229	31.2	31.9	30.0	5.4	1.6	37494	42153	37	39	4596	8.0	6.2	50.1	32.1	3.7	148606
97426	CRESWELL	20075	3106	27.1	29.4	33.8	6.6	3.1	45419	50903	62	67	2396	13.7	5.7	41.6	33.1	5.9	153239
97427	CULP CREEK	17558	110	24.6	36.4	37.3	0.9	0.9	39369	44302	44	45	92	7.6	8.7	56.5	27.2	0.0	147222
97429	DAYS CREEK	17221	275	37.1	33.8	23.6	3.3	2.2	33286	36925	22	20	197	11.2	16.8	38.1	25.9	8.1	136500
97430	DEADWOOD	15531	196	37.2	34.2	21.9	4.1	2.6	33231	36704	22	20	150	10.0	12.7	55.3	14.0	8.0	131250
97431	DEXTER	18720	756	34.4	24.9	30.3	7.4	3.0	41771	46290	52	55	633	17.4	5.2	29.9	40.4	7.1	170441
97434	DORENA	15034	263	27.0	47.2	23.2	2.3	0.4	35411	40056	29	29	218	19.7	2.8	43.6	33.9	0.0	143750
97435	DRAIN	16284	799	39.6	33.0	22.8	3.8	0.9	31088	33794	15	12	598	11.2	11.5	45.7	26.4	5.2	132377
97436	ELKTON	17649	339	33.3	39.5	22.7	3.2	1.2	34518	38409	26	24	271	9.2	10.3	34.3	36.5	9.6	166532
97437	ELMIRA	19187	828	20.7	40.0	30.7	7.3	1.5	40638	44839	48	51	708	2.8	1.1	35.0	54.4	6.6	194697
97438	FALL CREEK	21686	581	24.3	29.6	30.3	11.2	4.7	46657	52705	65	72	465	3.9	11.4	34.0	43.7	7.1	177652
97439	FLORENCE	21088	6623	35.2	39.1	20.1	3.1	2.6	35011	39148	28	28	5064	7.2	11.4	50.2	26.5	4.8	136411
97441	GARDINER	26669	7	28.6	42.9	28.6	0.0	0.0	30904	30904	15	10	5	0.0	0.0	40.0	60.0	0.0	208333
97442	GLENDALE	15900	808	39.0	34.5	21.5	3.2	1.7	31350	34232	16	13	591	12.0	22.5	42.1	18.6	4.7	108567
97443	GLIDE	20464	643	21.9	33.6	35.0	6.5	3.0	46771	52688	66	72	505	5.7	12.9	38.4	38.8	4.2	161553
97444	GOLD BEACH	21332	2190	34.6	32.1	26.4	5.3	1.6	36007	40626	32	32	1725	15.7	9.6	30.4	37.7	6.6	159893
97446	HARRISBURG	21169	1596	22.0	33.7	33.8	6.9	3.6	46360	51638	65	71	1259	12.7	9.0	44.0	28.8	5.6	148512
97447	IDLEYLD PARK	20753	329	28.0	31.6	33.1	5.2	2.1	42918	47359	56	60	245	15.5	10.6	33.5	37.6	2.9	150521
97448	JUNCTION CITY	21751	4748	23.5	33.4	32.0	8.2	2.9	44302	50884	59	65	3484	9.0	7.1	34.4	42.0	7.6	173507
97449	LAKESIDE	18036	709	41.8	35.8	18.8	3.2	0.4	30051	33424	12	8	560	8.4	26.8	45.7	18.6	0.5	107906
97450	LANGLOIS	20821	257	37.0	33.1	22.2	5.1	2.7	31159	34493	15	12	210	12.4	4.3	31.4	33.8	18.1	180263
97451	LORANE	21641	188	29.3	25.5	30.9	10.6	3.7	42026	47138	53	56	151	0.7	6.0	36.4	37.1	19.9	198864
97452	LOWELL	19108	404	26.0	33.9	32.9	5.7	1.5	43001	48589	56	60	331	4.5	13.3	50.8	28.7	2.7	135337
97453	MAPLETON	16673	456	37.9	34.7	23.3	3.7	0.4	31442	35754	16	13	344	9.3	20.1	33.7	27.9	9.0	129167
97454	MARCOLA	24253	540	19.3	29.3	37.2	10.9	3.3	50992	58023	74	80	468	6.0	8.1	29.5	48.7	7.7	189423
97455	PLEASANT HILL	26130	1116	18.3	26.3	35.0	12.7	7.6	57399	64504	82	90	959	8.9	2.7	23.3	49.8	15.3	217960
97456	MONROE	21356	1021	21.8	31.5	37.1	6.2	3.3	47121	55827	66	74	817	4.2	7.1	40.4	39.8	8.6	171165
97457	MYRTLE CREEK	17690	3825	34.7	33.5	25.4	4.6	1.9	36235	40212	32	33	2853	9.4	14.4	58.5	15.6	2.1	117176
97458	MYRTLE POINT	15272	1933	42.5	32.2	21.2	3.7	0.5	30469	33387	13	9	1460	14.7	22.6	48.0	12.8	1.9	105079
97459	NORTH BEND	21346	5840	32.3	30.9	28.2	6.2	2.3	38338	43731	41	42	4073	7.4	12.1	54.3	23.6	2.6	128401
97461	NOTI	21556	381	20.5	31.8	34.4	12.1	1.3	48096	53121	69	77	298	2.0	2.0	29.5	58.1	8.4	204310
97462	OAKLAND	17905	1517	31.3	36.4	26.1	4.6	1.6	36255	40268	33	33	1240	7.6	13.0	41.5	31.1	6.9	152006
97463	OAKRIDGE	16476	1560	40.6	38.0	16.9	3.5	1.0	30990	35048	15	11	1208	16.6	22.9	47.5	11.8	1.2	101176
97465	PORT ORFORD	18714	1061	45.5	31.2	17.7	3.4	2.2	27548	30441	8	5	819	9.8	19.3	40.4	23.1	7.5	119720
97466	POWERS	15755	433	46.2	34.6	15.9	2.3	0.9	27144	30074	7	5	318	29.3	34.9	24.8	8.2	2.8	77273
97467	REEDSPORT	17718	2671	42.5	31.5	20.7	3.6	1.8	28810	31645	10	7	1868	16.9	20.8	41.1	17.5	3.6	108210
97469	RIDDLE	17940	992	33.7	36.6	23.5	3.1	3.1	34855	37549	27	26	734	7.8	21.0	53.0	15.9	2.3	112817
97470	ROSEBURG	20619	19234	29.5	32.6	29.4	5.9	2.7	39737	45345	45	48	13904	9.4	11.6	46.0	28.5	4.5	134646
97473	SCOTTSBURG	21565	99	34.3	34.3	23.2	6.1	2.0	31994	34706	18	14	72	12.5	20.8	27.8	31.9	6.9	125000
97476	SIXES	18601	123	37.4	34.2	22.0	4.9	1.6	30214	34549	13	9	101	11.9	4.0	30.7	36.6	16.8	184722
97477	SPRINGFIELD	18402	14610	35.1	32.5	26.4	4.2	1.7	35749	41352	31	31	7585	5.7	7.6	64.3	21.2	1.2	136659
97478	SPRINGFIELD	21508	12321	24.2	30.4	34.3	8.5	2.5	46272	52697	64	71	8902	9.4	6.0	52.2	27.4	5.1	145544
97479	SUTHERLIN	16392	3667	35.9	35.6	24.2	3.0	1.3	33005	36250	21	18	2741	16.3	19.3	46.4	16.3	1.7	109085
97480	SWISSHOME	13839	141	52.5	29.1	11.4	5.7	1.4	23199	26334	3	2	100	5.0	19.0	59.0	11.0	6.0	118182
97481	TENMILE	16570	306	25.8	35.0	33.3	5.9	0.0	39294	44365	44	44	253	7.9	17.4	45.9	26.9	2.0	118160
97484	TILLER	19327	113	40.7	31.0	23.0	3.5	1.8	31628	37351	17	14	74	6.8	14.9	54.1	20.3	4.1	136842
97486	UMPQUA	20857	345	21.7	33.0	38.3	6.7	0.3	45796	51482	63	69	291	8.3	7.9	26.8	47.4	9.6	190530
97487	VENETA	20173	2531	20.0	32.5	37.5	7.6	2.5	47833	54060	68	75	2092	8.6	5.6	43.6	34.6	7.7	159601
97488	VIDA	24528	414	23.7	33.1	32.1	7.7	3.4	44586	50093	60	66	327	11.3	9.8	18.0	44.3	16.5	195170
97489	WALTERVILLE	28875	364	14.8	33.0	35.2	13.5	3.6	52521	59825	76	83	302	5.3	2.0	13.6	58.0	21.2	238462
97490	WALTON	20572	104	24.0	32.7	30.8	10.6	1.9	45000	47365	61	67	81	3.7	4.9	34.6	51.9	4.9	186458
97492	WESTFIR	20246	233	23.6	40.8	26.6	3.9	5.2	41942	47913	53	56	199	16.6	9.6	47.2	22.6	4.0	118750
97493	WESTLAKE	19469	69	29.0	31.9	30.4	7.3	1.5	39523	45000	44	47	57	7.0	0.0	36.8	40.4	15.8	187500
97496	WINSTON	15960	2665	35.6	33.7	27.1	2.7	0.8	34704	38542	26	25	1831	6.4	22.5	54.8	14.6	1.7	111500
97497	WOLF CREEK	19029	748	41.3	30.5	21.5	3.3	3.3	32499	36664	19	17	592	9.6	15.9	36.0	34.6	3.9	143617
97498	YACHATS	22726	670	34.0	36.9	21.6	4.2	3.3	35697	40317	30	30	543	2.6	5.3	27.1	49.9	15.1	215461
97499	YONCALLA	15812	756	39.2	36.5	20.4	2.7	1.3	30995	34381	15	11	602	12.0	20.9	41.5	21.4	4.2	119250
97501	MEDFORD	17039	14862	36.2	33.1	25.4	3.7	1.5	33999	39286	24	23	9215	12.6	8.4	47.5	28.1	3.5	143576
97502	CENTRAL POINT	21444	9629	21.5	34.2	32.8	8.1	3.4	45713	51935	63	68	7494	7.1	4.2	40.5	41.8	6.5	172118
97503	WHITE CITY	15340	3019	32.2	33.3	27.8	4.5	2.2	37948	43606	39	41	2374	23.6	8.2	40.7	22.0	5.6	122299
97504	MEDFORD	28970	17930	23.1	28.4	31.7	9.8	7.2	48516	56372	69	78	11267	1.7	1.3	29.3	58.4	9.3	209654
97520	ASHLAND	27324	10778	33.4	26.1	25.0	9.8	5.7	38986	45229	43	43	6275	4.2	1.8	10.7	59.0	24.3	266429
97522	BUTTE FALLS	17099	248	32.7	36.7	23.4	4.8	2.4	35000	39062	28	27	187	7.5	11.2	28.3	36.4	16.6	186458
97523	CAVE JUNCTION	14798	2778	52.7	25.4	17.0	4.1	0.8	23268	25281	3	3	1974	9.6	20.7	42.1	25.8	1.8	117877
97524	EAGLE POINT	19591	4278	25.2	34.2	31.4	5.8	3.3	42216	48172	54	57	3399	10.7	5.2	33.3	38.1	12.7	177076
97525	GOLD HILL	19513	2030	34.5	33.2	23.8	5.3	3.3	35488	39320	29	29	1574	11.4	2.9	39.9	40.3	5.4	166708
97526	GRANTS PASS	21122	13569	32.9	34.9	23.8	5.1	3.2	35927	40974	31	31	9200	8.1	8.1	47.9	31.6	4.4	145868
97527	GRANTS PASS	19307	11950	35.5	33.6	23.3	5.3	2.4	35255	39676	28	28	8906	8.4	7.3	45.1	35.2	4.0	157524
97530	JACKSONVILLE	27040	2891	25.1	29.2	30.3	9.1	6.3	46429	52276	65	72	2381	8.6	2.5	20.1	47.5	21.3	243389
97531	KERBY	13154	118	55.9	28.0	12.7	2.5	0.9	22034	24352	3	2	78	16.7	21.8	34.6	24.4	2.6	109615
97532	MERLIN	20025	924	31.2	30.2	29.9	6.3	2.5	41115	45760	50	53	776	3.4	3.6	42.7	44.2	6.2	175843
97534	O BRIEN	13710	145	56.6	29.0	11.0	2.8	0.7	21385	24621	2	1	98	13.3	19.4	39.8	25.5	2.0	118478
97535	PHOENIX	17529	1694	36.6	33.6	25.5	3.3	1.0	32588	36334	20	17	1280	34.5	16.3	30.2	16.6	2.5	87826
97536	PROSPECT	18849	393	31.0	38.2	22.4	6.9	1.5	34670	39772	26	25	314	10.8	6.4	33.8	37.9	11.2	171429
97537	ROGUE RIVER	21681	2942	33.3	28.6	27.4	8.1	2.7	37165	41581	36	38	2328	5.2	5.6	31.6	48.5	9.1	193830
97538	SELMA	16115	1134	40.0	35.4	18.3	4.7	1.6	31110	34282	15	12	902	3.2	19.1	36.5	34.8	6.4	152557
97539	SHADY COVE	20432	1280	32.2	33.4	27.1	4.7	2.6	37851	42314	39	40	992	8.8	13.6	29.2	39.0	9.4	171875
97540	TALENT	20111	3171	32.0	36.7	23.9	4.5	2.9	36007	42007	32	32	2056	14.6	8.4	39.2	28.1	9.8	148318
97541	TRAIL	20619	507	26.2	35.3	28.8	5.5	4.1	37710	42469	38	40	406	13.8	2.2	18.7	50.7	14.5	219333
97543	WILDERVILLE	20904	634	35.3	29.7	24.9	6.8	3.3	35000	38781	28	27	515	2.7	11.8	38.8	40.8	5.8	167325
97544	WILLIAMS	22168	1089	37.1	31.6	22.6	6.2	2.6	35712	39185	30	30	861	3.7	6.9	40.8	37.5	11.2	172209
97601	KLAMATH FALLS	18800	8685	38.8	32.1	21.0	5.2	2.9	32137	37205	18	15	4953	12.8	26.1	39.4	18.5	3.1	106606
97603	KLAMATH FALLS	19702	11839	32.1	31.0	29.6	4.9	2.3	38035	43057	39	41	8522	12.5	21.4	48.2	15.8	2.2	111481
97620	ADEL	18704	50	38.0	38.0	22.0	2.0	0.0	31106	35746	15	12	32	12.5	25.0	31.3	18.8	12.5	115000
97621	BEATTY	11675	49	57.1	32.7	10.2	0.0	0.0	20524	22900	2	1	41	17.1	26.8	41.5	14.6	0.0	101786
97623	BONANZA	15506	1107	39.2	35.7	19.0	3.6	2.5	32216	36061	18	15	886	10.1	24.9	37.0	20.1	7.9	113312
	OREGON	24176		24.9	29.7	31.4	9.2	4.8	45702	52201				6.4	6.5	35.2	43.4	8.6	179540
	UNITED STATES	25866		24.7	27.1	30.8	10.9	6.5	48124	56710				10.9	15.0	33.7	30.1	10.4	145905

ZIP CODE		FINANCIAL SERVICES				THE HOME						ENTERTAINMENT						PERSONAL			
						Home Improvements		Furnishings													
#	POST OFFICE NAME	Auto Loan	Home Loan	Investments	Retirement Plans	Home Repair	Lawn & Garden	Computers & Hardware	Major Appliances	TV, Radio, Sound Equipment	Furniture	Dine out/ Carry out	Sports Equipment	Fees & Tickets	Toys & Games	Travel	Cable TV	Apparel & Services	Auto Repairs	Health Insurance	Pets & Supplies
97412	BLACHLY	86	60	31	57	70	78	59	73	68	59	80	88	51	79	62	72	73	72	87	102
97413	BLUE RIVER	89	68	44	62	77	86	65	78	73	64	87	92	57	85	68	78	80	77	93	108
97414	BROADBENT	58	41	22	37	45	53	42	49	49	41	57	57	36	54	42	52	52	49	60	65
97415	BROOKINGS	69	61	56	57	65	77	59	67	64	61	78	68	58	68	62	68	72	65	79	77
97416	CAMAS VALLEY	75	50	23	43	57	65	48	60	58	49	68	72	41	64	49	63	62	60	74	86
97417	CANYONVILLE	65	48	29	45	52	62	51	58	58	49	69	66	45	65	51	62	63	58	70	72
97419	CHESHIRE	90	92	82	89	94	97	83	88	84	83	103	105	85	107	86	84	100	86	89	107
97420	COOS BAY	68	62	59	61	65	73	64	67	67	63	82	76	62	80	65	69	78	67	73	78
97423	COQUILLE	72	60	48	58	64	74	63	68	68	61	81	77	58	79	63	71	76	68	78	82
97424	COTTAGE GROVE	73	62	51	61	66	74	63	68	67	62	81	78	60	80	64	69	76	67	75	82
97426	CRESWELL	85	78	64	75	80	86	74	80	77	75	94	94	72	93	75	77	90	79	83	97
97427	CULP CREEK	71	62	47	59	66	71	58	64	61	58	75	77	56	76	60	63	71	63	70	83
97429	DAYS CREEK	79	54	26	49	62	70	53	65	62	53	73	79	45	70	54	66	66	65	79	92
97430	DEADWOOD	73	53	30	50	60	69	54	64	61	52	72	75	47	70	55	65	66	63	76	85
97431	DEXTER	83	78	64	75	79	83	73	78	74	74	91	91	71	90	73	74	88	77	78	94
97434	DORENA	64	58	45	55	59	62	54	59	56	55	69	69	52	67	54	56	66	58	60	72
97435	DRAIN	74	50	25	44	57	66	50	61	59	50	70	72	43	66	50	64	63	60	74	84
97436	ELKTON	68	51	34	49	56	67	56	62	63	53	74	69	50	70	56	67	68	62	74	75
97437	ELMIRA	81	72	55	68	76	82	67	74	71	67	86	88	65	88	69	72	82	72	80	95
97438	FALL CREEK	94	84	64	80	88	94	78	86	82	78	100	102	76	102	80	84	96	84	92	110
97439	FLORENCE	67	59	54	55	63	75	57	65	62	59	76	66	56	67	61	66	70	64	77	76
97441	GARDINER	68	51	34	49	56	67	56	62	63	53	74	69	50	70	56	67	68	62	74	75
97442	GLENDALE	72	52	30	48	58	66	52	61	60	52	71	72	46	68	52	63	65	60	72	82
97443	GLIDE	91	79	60	74	85	92	73	83	79	73	95	98	70	96	76	82	90	81	92	108
97444	GOLD BEACH	73	60	47	57	65	77	62	69	68	61	81	73	58	73	63	72	75	68	82	81
97446	HARRISBURG	97	83	61	80	88	94	79	88	83	80	101	104	75	99	80	84	96	87	94	111
97447	IDLEYLD PARK	82	70	51	65	74	81	66	75	71	66	85	87	61	84	68	73	81	74	82	96
97448	JUNCTION CITY	89	78	63	76	82	89	76	83	79	75	97	97	72	96	77	81	92	82	88	103
97449	LAKESIDE	55	52	52	47	55	66	48	56	52	51	64	54	48	55	52	56	60	54	66	63
97450	LANGLOIS	73	55	36	53	60	72	61	67	68	58	80	75	54	76	60	72	73	67	80	81
97451	LORANE	93	83	63	78	87	94	76	85	81	76	99	101	75	101	79	83	94	82	92	109
97452	LOWELL	79	71	55	68	72	77	67	73	69	68	85	85	64	82	67	69	81	72	74	89
97453	MAPLETON	63	48	32	45	52	62	51	57	57	49	68	64	46	64	51	61	62	57	68	70
97454	MARCOLA	102	87	63	82	93	101	81	92	87	81	105	109	78	107	84	90	99	89	101	120
97455	PLEASANT HILL	97	110	112	108	109	113	102	103	99	101	123	120	106	129	104	98	121	101	99	116
97456	MONROE	92	81	62	78	86	93	76	84	81	76	98	99	74	100	78	83	93	82	91	107
97457	MYRTLE CREEK	77	58	38	54	64	72	58	67	66	58	79	79	53	77	59	69	73	66	78	88
97458	MYRTLE POINT	59	47	34	44	51	59	50	55	55	48	65	62	46	63	50	58	60	54	64	66
97459	NORTH BEND	75	68	61	67	72	79	69	73	72	68	88	84	67	87	70	74	83	73	79	87
97461	NOTI	86	84	72	82	87	91	77	83	79	77	97	98	78	100	79	79	93	80	85	102
97462	OAKLAND	74	60	44	57	64	72	60	67	65	59	78	78	56	77	60	67	73	66	75	84
97463	OAKRIDGE	67	48	27	44	53	63	50	58	57	49	67	67	44	64	50	61	61	58	70	76
97465	PORT ORFORD	62	46	31	44	51	61	51	56	57	49	68	63	46	64	51	61	62	56	68	68
97466	POWERS	57	43	28	41	47	56	48	52	53	45	63	59	42	59	47	56	57	52	63	63
97467	REEDSPORT	59	50	42	48	54	64	52	57	57	51	68	61	49	63	53	60	63	56	67	66
97469	RIDDLE	77	58	43	54	63	73	63	69	71	61	84	80	57	81	62	74	79	70	80	86
97470	ROSEBURG	74	70	65	69	72	78	70	73	71	69	88	84	68	87	70	72	84	72	76	85
97473	SCOTTSBURG	72	54	36	52	60	71	60	66	67	57	79	74	54	75	60	71	72	66	79	80
97476	SIXES	73	55	36	53	60	72	61	67	68	58	80	75	54	76	60	72	73	67	80	81
97477	SPRINGFIELD	60	60	66	60	59	63	64	62	64	62	79	73	64	80	63	62	77	63	60	68
97478	SPRINGFIELD	84	81	77	81	83	87	81	83	81	80	100	98	79	100	80	79	96	83	82	97
97479	SUTHERLIN	69	51	31	47	56	65	52	60	59	51	70	70	46	67	52	63	64	60	72	79
97480	SWISSHOME	56	41	27	40	46	54	45	51	51	43	60	57	40	57	45	54	55	50	60	62
97481	TENMILE	87	58	26	50	66	76	56	71	68	57	80	84	48	76	57	73	73	70	87	100
97484	TILLER	81	57	30	54	66	74	56	69	65	55	76	84	48	74	58	68	69	68	83	97
97486	UMPQUA	76	72	64	66	74	83	68	74	73	68	89	85	68	89	71	76	85	73	81	90
97487	VENETA	88	80	63	77	83	89	75	82	78	75	96	96	73	96	76	79	91	80	86	102
97488	VIDA	95	80	62	76	87	97	78	88	84	77	101	103	73	102	81	88	95	87	99	113
97489	WALTERVILLE	88	103	115	99	102	111	97	97	95	96	119	109	103	123	101	97	117	95	97	106
97490	WALTON	90	80	61	76	85	91	74	82	79	74	96	98	72	98	76	81	91	80	89	106
97492	WESTFIR	94	66	35	62	76	86	65	80	75	64	88	96	56	86	68	79	80	79	96	111
97493	WESTLAKE	77	71	66	67	75	88	66	75	71	70	87	75	66	74	71	75	81	73	88	86
97496	WINSTON	68	53	36	49	57	65	53	60	60	53	72	70	49	69	53	62	67	60	69	77
97497	WOLF CREEK	80	60	38	55	66	76	58	69	67	59	80	79	53	75	60	71	73	68	82	91
97498	YACHATS	79	62	42	56	70	78	58	70	66	58	78	82	52	77	62	71	73	69	83	96
97499	YONCALLA	73	50	26	45	57	65	49	60	58	50	68	72	43	65	50	62	62	60	73	84
97501	MEDFORD	63	56	50	55	57	64	59	61	62	57	75	70	56	74	58	62	71	61	65	71
97502	CENTRAL POINT	88	82	71	80	85	91	79	85	82	79	100	99	77	100	80	82	95	83	88	102
97503	WHITE CITY	72	64	48	61	65	71	61	66	64	62	78	77	58	76	61	64	74	66	70	82
97504	MEDFORD	94	102	111	103	101	105	100	99	96	99	120	116	101	121	100	94	118	99	94	109
97520	ASHLAND	84	81	92	84	82	88	88	85	87	86	109	102	86	106	86	85	105	88	84	96
97522	BUTTE FALLS	83	58	30	54	67	75	57	71	66	56	77	85	49	76	59	69	70	70	84	98
97523	CAVE JUNCTION	57	42	27	40	46	55	46	51	52	44	61	58	41	58	46	55	56	51	62	63
97524	EAGLE POINT	86	72	54	70	77	85	72	79	77	71	93	91	68	92	72	78	87	77	86	97
97525	GOLD HILL	76	61	44	59	65	76	64	70	70	62	84	80	60	81	64	73	78	70	80	84
97526	GRANTS PASS	72	67	66	66	70	78	70	72	72	68	89	82	68	87	70	74	84	72	77	83
97527	GRANTS PASS	73	61	47	58	65	75	62	69	68	62	81	76	58	76	63	71	76	68	79	82
97530	JACKSONVILLE	100	89	74	85	95	105	85	95	91	85	110	111	82	110	89	94	104	94	105	120
97531	KERBY	55	39	22	36	44	51	41	48	47	40	56	55	36	53	41	50	51	47	58	62
97532	MERLIN	84	68	46	64	74	81	65	75	71	64	85	89	60	85	67	74	79	73	84	99
97534	O BRIEN	60	40	18	35	46	53	39	49	47	40	55	58	33	52	40	51	50	48	60	69
97535	PHOENIX	63	53	41	52	57	65	56	60	60	54	72	68	52	69	56	62	67	60	68	71
97536	PROSPECT	85	57	27	50	65	75	56	69	67	56	78	83	47	74	57	71	71	69	85	98
97537	ROGUE RIVER	84	67	47	63	73	84	66	76	74	66	88	87	61	84	68	77	81	75	89	96
97538	SELMA	73	50	25	45	57	66	50	61	59	50	70	72	43	66	51	64	64	60	74	83
97539	SHADY COVE	77	60	41	58	65	77	64	71	71	61	84	80	58	81	64	75	77	70	83	87
97540	TALENT	76	64	50	62	68	78	66	72	72	65	86	80	62	83	67	74	80	71	82	85
97541	TRAIL	90	69	42	62	75	84	65	77	74	66	88	91	59	86	66	78	82	75	89	104
97543	WILDERVILLE	87	71	48	66	76	83	66	76	73	67	88	91	62	88	68	76	82	74	86	101
97544	WILLIAMS	82	67	55	67	72	83	73	78	78	70	93	88	67	89	72	81	87	78	88	91
97601	KLAMATH FALLS	66	61	60	61	62	67	64	65	65	63	81	76	62	79	63	65	78	66	65	74
97603	KLAMATH FALLS	77	65	53	63	69	78	66	72	71	65	86	83	63	85	67	73	81	72	80	88
97620	ADEL	67	53	36	48	59	67	50	60	56	49	67	70	44	66	53	60	62	59	71	82
97621	BEATTY	46	31	14	27	35	40	30	37	36	30	42	45	25	40	30	39	38	37	46	53
97623	BONANZA	66	53	37	51	56	64	55	60	59	54	71	69	50	67	54	61	66	60	67	73
	OREGON	87	85	86	85	86	91	86	87	86	85	106	102	85	106	85	84	103	87	86	100
	UNITED STATES	100	100	100	100	100	100	100	100	100	100	100	100	100	100	100	100	100	100	100	100

OREGON

POPULATION CHANGE

A 97624-97909

ZIP CODE		COUNTY FIPS CODE	POPULATION			2000-2004 ANNUAL RATE		HOUSEHOLDS					FAMILIES		
#	POST OFFICE NAME		2000	2004	2009	% Rate	State Centile	2000	2004	2009	% Annual Rate 2000-2004	2004 Average HH Size	2000	2004	% Annual Rate 2000-2004
97624	CHILOQUIN	035	3883	3953	4013	0.4	50	1548	1591	1627	0.7	2.46	1099	1121	0.5
97625	DAIRY	035	211	234	248	2.5	94	67	75	80	2.7	3.12	55	61	2.5
97627	KENO	035	1039	1084	1115	1.0	70	411	433	448	1.2	2.50	311	325	1.0
97630	LAKEVIEW	037	4878	4865	4835	-0.1	30	2017	2044	2066	0.3	2.36	1405	1415	0.2
97632	MALIN	035	1274	1227	1228	-0.9	8	432	417	419	-0.8	2.88	340	326	-1.0
97633	MERRILL	035	1072	1070	1079	0.0	30	407	408	413	0.1	2.62	304	303	-0.1
97635	NEW PINE CREEK	037	182	183	181	0.1	39	78	80	81	0.6	2.29	54	55	0.4
97636	PAISLEY	037	498	477	467	-1.0	6	211	206	205	-0.6	2.31	157	152	-0.8
97637	PLUSH	037	155	149	145	-0.9	7	64	62	62	-0.7	2.39	48	46	-1.0
97638	SILVER LAKE	037	1571	1613	1624	0.6	56	651	676	690	0.9	2.38	442	458	0.8
97639	SPRAGUE RIVER	035	175	182	188	1.2	69	75	79	82	1.2	2.30	50	52	0.9
97640	SUMMER LAKE	037	1	1	1	0.0	35	1	1	1	0.0	1.00	1	0	-100.0
97701	BEND	017	45341	53251	63955	3.9	99	18162	21500	26014	4.1	2.44	11971	14106	3.9
97702	BEND	017	28715	33599	40323	3.8	98	11080	13035	15722	3.9	2.56	7923	9252	3.7
97707	BEND	017	5207	6115	7335	3.9	99	2244	2650	3193	4.0	2.31	1682	1972	3.8
97710	FIELDS	025	82	82	81	0.0	35	32	32	32	0.0	2.56	24	24	0.0
97711	ASHWOOD	031	140	148	157	1.3	77	52	55	58	1.3	2.69	40	41	0.6
97712	BROTHERS	017	46	48	53	1.0	71	15	16	18	1.5	3.00	12	13	1.9
97720	BURNS	025	4830	4762	4686	-0.3	20	1946	1933	1920	-0.2	2.39	1284	1267	-0.3
97721	PRINCETON	025	309	308	304	-0.1	29	124	125	125	0.2	2.46	91	91	0.0
97730	CAMP SHERMAN	031	359	396	431	2.3	92	143	158	172	2.4	2.51	118	130	2.3
97731	CHEMULT	035	298	290	290	-0.6	12	128	126	127	-0.4	2.19	88	85	-0.8
97733	CRESCENT	035	1254	1262	1284	0.2	40	512	521	533	0.4	2.42	371	374	0.2
97734	CULVER	031	2180	2274	2406	1.0	70	788	825	876	1.1	2.75	618	644	1.0
97735	FORT ROCK	037	26	27	27	0.9	67	11	11	12	0.0	2.45	7	8	3.2
97737	GILCHRIST	035	368	379	387	0.7	59	171	178	183	1.0	2.13	128	132	0.7
97738	HINES	025	2123	2096	2064	-0.3	21	823	820	813	-0.1	2.53	613	608	-0.2
97739	LA PINE	017	8446	9168	10466	2.0	89	3432	3747	4300	2.1	2.44	2528	2741	1.9
97741	MADRAS	031	10464	10836	11459	0.8	66	3760	3887	4114	0.8	2.77	2793	2869	0.6
97750	MITCHELL	069	488	487	489	-0.1	30	206	207	209	0.1	2.33	143	143	0.0
97751	PAULINA	013	127	148	164	3.7	98	60	70	77	3.7	2.11	42	48	3.2
97752	POST	013	254	296	328	3.7	98	96	112	124	3.7	2.64	66	77	3.7
97753	POWELL BUTTE	013	1678	1804	1914	1.7	86	660	710	753	1.7	2.54	534	571	1.6
97754	PRINEVILLE	013	16938	18185	19298	1.7	85	6471	6957	7390	1.7	2.57	4729	5060	1.6
97756	REDMOND	017	21493	25837	31408	4.4	99	8291	9989	12188	4.5	2.57	5995	7206	4.4
97758	RILEY	025	99	102	103	0.7	59	39	40	41	0.6	2.52	30	31	0.8
97759	SISTERS	017	4630	5354	6376	3.5	98	1860	2161	2583	3.6	2.48	1432	1653	3.4
97760	TERREBONNE	017	5912	6832	7826	3.5	97	2334	2717	3124	3.6	2.51	1821	2108	3.5
97761	WARM SPRINGS	031	2627	2792	2977	1.4	80	635	679	727	1.6	4.02	539	574	1.5
97801	PENDLETON	059	21955	21733	21945	-0.2	24	8002	7883	7936	-0.4	2.49	5314	5206	-0.5
97810	ADAMS	059	569	569	575	0.0	35	207	207	209	0.0	2.74	160	159	-0.2
97812	ARLINGTON	021	821	811	802	-0.3	22	342	343	346	0.1	2.36	231	230	-0.1
97813	ATHENA	059	1509	1499	1507	-0.2	26	545	542	543	-0.1	2.76	422	417	-0.3
97814	BAKER CITY	001	12474	12101	11688	-0.7	10	5052	4927	4792	-0.6	2.37	3427	3324	-0.7
97818	BOARDMAN	049	3771	4141	4560	2.2	91	1169	1270	1380	2.0	3.25	938	1014	1.9
97820	CANYON CITY	023	850	873	879	0.6	56	333	346	352	0.9	2.45	243	251	0.8
97823	CONDON	021	1087	1088	1081	0.0	36	475	482	485	0.3	2.21	312	314	0.2
97824	COVE	061	1409	1395	1387	-0.2	24	539	540	542	0.0	2.58	440	441	0.1
97825	DAYVILLE	023	138	132	128	-1.0	6	59	57	56	-0.8	2.28	41	39	-1.2
97826	ECHO	059	1021	969	967	-1.2	3	373	353	351	-1.3	2.62	265	248	-1.6
97827	ELGIN	061	2414	2349	2327	-0.6	12	963	949	950	-0.3	2.47	695	682	-0.4
97828	ENTERPRISE	063	3116	3073	3047	-0.3	20	1322	1318	1319	-0.1	2.28	886	878	-0.2
97830	FOSSIL	069	1040	1049	1060	0.2	42	441	447	455	0.2	2.29	297	300	0.2
97833	HAINES	001	982	972	945	-0.2	24	389	389	383	0.0	2.50	290	289	-0.1
97834	HALFWAY	001	1167	1132	1092	-0.7	10	505	495	481	-0.5	2.29	331	320	-0.8
97835	HELIX	059	427	416	417	-0.6	13	153	149	148	-0.6	2.77	117	113	-0.8
97836	HEPPNER	049	2120	2122	2235	0.0	36	866	860	897	-0.2	2.44	618	608	-0.4
97837	HEREFORD	001	220	220	216	0.0	35	87	88	87	0.3	2.50	61	61	0.0
97838	HERMISTON	059	21407	22884	23852	1.6	84	7740	8260	8575	1.5	2.75	5558	5890	1.4
97839	LEXINGTON	049	487	491	517	0.2	42	189	189	196	0.0	2.60	143	142	-0.1
97840	OXBOW	001	83	81	78	-0.6	15	35	34	34	-0.7	2.38	25	24	-1.0
97841	IMBLER	061	415	403	399	-0.7	11	152	149	149	-0.5	2.70	121	118	-0.6
97842	IMNAHA	063	175	175	174	0.0	35	74	75	75	0.3	2.33	53	53	0.0
97843	IONE	049	642	647	680	0.2	41	248	248	257	0.0	2.61	180	179	-0.1
97844	IRRIGON	049	3826	4404	4970	3.4	97	1262	1445	1616	3.2	3.04	1010	1149	3.1
97845	JOHN DAY	023	3516	3555	3548	0.3	44	1420	1452	1465	0.5	2.39	971	988	0.4
97846	JOSEPH	063	2006	1980	1963	-0.3	21	851	849	849	-0.1	2.28	577	572	-0.2
97848	KIMBERLY	023	20	19	18	-1.2	3	8	8	8	0.0	2.38	6	5	-4.2
97850	LA GRANDE	061	16229	16308	16368	0.1	38	6530	6621	6709	0.3	2.36	4081	4111	0.2
97856	LONG CREEK	023	494	458	440	-1.8	1	216	203	197	-1.5	2.26	145	135	-1.7
97857	LOSTINE	063	433	436	435	0.2	40	173	175	175	0.3	2.49	122	123	0.2
97862	MILTON FREEWATER	059	11215	11486	11769	0.6	54	4061	4155	4247	0.5	2.69	2893	2943	0.4
97864	MONUMENT	023	375	348	334	-1.7	2	170	160	155	-1.4	2.17	114	106	-1.7
97865	MOUNT VERNON	023	595	580	568	-0.6	13	248	244	242	-0.4	2.36	163	160	-0.4
97867	NORTH POWDER	061	786	806	812	0.6	55	285	293	296	0.7	2.75	209	213	0.5
97868	PILOT ROCK	059	2471	2377	2382	-0.9	8	937	902	902	-0.9	2.62	704	673	-1.1
97869	PRAIRIE CITY	023	1560	1481	1435	-1.2	3	628	603	590	-1.0	2.37	436	416	-1.1
97870	RICHLAND	001	615	658	668	1.6	84	295	317	324	1.7	2.08	195	209	1.6
97873	SENECA	023	358	342	331	-1.1	5	148	143	141	-0.8	2.36	103	99	-0.9
97874	SPRAY	069	26	26	26	0.0	35	8	8	8	0.0	3.25	6	6	0.0
97875	STANFIELD	059	2630	2585	2594	-0.4	18	909	894	894	-0.4	2.88	691	675	-0.6
97876	SUMMERVILLE	061	954	929	925	-0.6	13	359	354	356	-0.3	2.62	292	287	-0.4
97877	SUMPTER	001	111	111	108	0.0	35	60	60	60	0.0	1.83	41	41	0.0
97882	UMATILLA	059	6171	6583	6842	1.5	82	1817	1944	2020	1.6	3.04	1382	1469	1.5
97883	UNION	061	2416	2449	2461	0.3	48	942	961	974	0.5	2.55	697	708	0.4
97884	UNITY	001	237	239	234	0.2	42	100	102	101	0.5	2.34	70	71	0.3
97885	WALLOWA	063	1496	1497	1491	0.0	36	609	613	613	0.2	2.44	447	447	0.0
97886	WESTON	059	1322	1415	1474	1.6	84	493	525	544	1.5	2.69	371	394	1.4
97901	ADRIAN	045	588	588	584	0.0	35	205	205	204	0.0	2.86	161	161	0.0
97903	BROGAN	045	200	199	198	-0.1	27	71	68	67	-1.0	2.56	53	4	-45.6
97904	DREWSEY	025	149	148	145	-0.2	26	67	67	67	0.0	2.21	49	49	0.0
97906	HARPER	045	291	285	281	-0.5	16	109	104	102	-1.1	1.09	81	20	-28.0
97907	HUNTINGTON	001	808	786	760	-0.7	12	354	348	339	-0.4	2.21	237	231	-0.6
97908	IRONSIDE	045	57	57	56	0.0	35	24	23	22	-1.0	2.48	18	4	-29.8
97909	JAMIESON	045	73	79	82	1.9	88	24	26	27	1.9	3.04	19	21	2.4
	OREGON					1.1					1.1	2.50			1.0
	UNITED STATES					1.2					1.3	2.58			1.1

249-A

#	POST OFFICE NAME	RACE (%) White 2000	White 2004	Black 2000	Black 2004	Asian/Pacific 2000	Asian/Pacific 2004	% Hispanic Origin 2000	% Hispanic Origin 2004	2004 AGE DISTRIBUTION (%) 0-4	5-9	10-14	15-19	20-24	25-44	45-64	65-84	85+	18+	MEDIAN AGE 2004	% 2004 Males	% 2004 Females
97624	CHILOQUIN	77.1	76.5	0.2	0.2	0.5	0.5	4.0	4.8	5.3	5.7	6.6	6.8	4.5	18.6	34.1	17.3	1.2	77.9	46.7	51.3	48.7
97625	DAIRY	89.6	88.5	0.5	0.9	0.5	0.4	9.0	11.5	6.8	6.8	8.1	8.1	6.4	21.8	29.1	11.5	1.3	73.1	40.0	50.9	49.2
97627	KENO	89.9	89.3	0.2	0.2	0.8	0.9	3.8	4.6	4.3	5.4	7.7	5.4	4.4	23.0	34.8	14.1	0.8	79.2	44.8	50.0	50.0
97630	LAKEVIEW	90.2	90.1	0.0	0.0	1.1	1.1	6.7	6.7	4.6	5.5	7.5	7.3	5.0	21.2	29.7	16.5	2.8	77.3	44.3	49.3	50.7
97632	MALIN	76.1	73.5	0.7	0.7	0.5	0.5	33.5	38.1	6.5	6.9	8.1	8.4	6.7	25.8	23.5	12.8	1.5	73.4	35.8	53.4	46.6
97633	MERRILL	81.6	78.7	0.3	0.4	0.5	0.5	21.9	26.5	6.8	7.1	7.6	6.7	5.7	24.7	26.8	13.0	1.6	74.0	39.0	50.4	49.6
97635	NEW PINE CREEK	90.7	90.2	0.0	0.0	0.6	0.6	7.7	7.7	6.0	6.6	7.1	5.5	4.4	20.8	30.6	18.0	1.1	77.1	44.8	49.2	50.8
97636	PAISLEY	97.0	96.7	0.4	0.4	0.4	0.4	1.6	1.9	4.8	5.7	5.7	6.3	4.2	22.2	32.3	17.4	1.5	79.3	45.7	53.3	46.8
97637	PLUSH	96.8	96.0	0.7	0.7	0.7	0.7	1.9	2.0	5.4	5.4	6.0	6.0	4.0	22.2	30.9	18.8	1.3	78.5	45.6	52.4	47.7
97638	SILVER LAKE	90.5	90.6	0.3	0.3	0.3	0.3	3.3	3.4	6.0	6.2	6.9	6.0	5.0	23.2	30.5	15.4	0.9	76.6	42.8	51.5	48.5
97639	SPRAGUE RIVER	86.3	85.7	0.6	1.1	0.6	0.6	2.9	3.9	4.4	5.0	5.5	7.7	4.4	19.2	34.6	18.1	1.1	79.7	47.2	52.2	47.8
97640	SUMMER LAKE	100.0	100.0	0.0	0.0	0.0	0.0	0.0	0.0	0.0	0.0	0.0	0.0	100.0	0.0	0.0	0.0	0.0	100.0	22.5	100.0	0.0
97701	BEND	95.0	94.4	0.3	0.3	1.0	1.2	3.6	4.3	6.2	5.9	6.3	6.7	7.7	28.2	27.0	10.2	1.7	77.7	37.6	49.2	50.8
97702	BEND	94.2	93.5	0.2	0.2	0.9	1.0	4.5	5.4	6.5	6.6	7.5	7.1	5.9	27.1	27.1	10.6	1.6	75.0	38.4	49.9	50.1
97707	BEND	95.9	95.6	0.2	0.2	0.6	0.7	2.2	2.7	4.5	4.7	5.7	4.4	3.7	21.1	36.2	19.0	0.8	82.2	49.3	51.0	49.0
97710	FIELDS	93.9	95.1	0.0	0.0	0.0	0.0	6.1	4.9	6.1	6.1	12.2	4.9	4.9	25.6	28.1	11.0	1.2	70.7	39.2	52.4	47.6
97711	ASHWOOD	89.3	86.5	0.7	0.7	1.4	1.4	8.6	10.8	5.4	6.1	6.8	6.8	6.1	20.3	32.4	14.9	1.4	77.7	43.8	52.7	47.3
97712	BROTHERS	95.7	93.8	0.0	0.0	2.2	2.1	4.4	4.2	4.2	6.3	8.3	6.3	4.2	25.0	37.5	8.3	0.0	77.1	42.5	52.1	47.9
97720	BURNS	90.8	90.7	0.1	0.2	0.5	0.6	4.6	4.6	5.5	6.2	7.3	7.5	5.0	24.4	27.8	14.3	2.1	76.0	41.3	50.6	49.4
97721	PRINCETON	94.2	94.2	0.0	0.0	0.3	0.3	6.2	6.2	6.5	7.1	7.8	5.8	4.9	26.0	28.9	11.7	1.3	74.7	40.4	52.3	47.7
97730	CAMP SHERMAN	95.3	95.0	0.0	0.0	1.1	1.3	1.7	2.3	2.3	2.8	4.6	6.3	4.3	11.4	46.7	21.5	0.3	86.6	54.1	52.3	47.7
97731	CHEMULT	92.3	91.7	0.3	0.3	0.3	0.3	2.7	3.5	4.5	4.8	6.6	9.3	4.8	22.8	35.2	11.0	1.0	78.6	43.3	52.4	47.6
97733	CRESCENT	94.7	94.4	0.2	0.2	0.4	0.4	2.1	2.6	4.7	5.8	7.0	6.1	2.9	22.7	36.4	13.3	1.1	78.5	45.4	51.1	48.9
97734	CULVER	84.5	81.9	0.2	0.2	0.3	0.3	16.2	19.9	7.0	7.2	8.6	7.4	5.5	24.6	26.0	12.3	1.5	71.9	37.8	51.0	49.0
97735	FORT ROCK	88.5	92.6	0.0	0.0	0.0	0.0	3.9	0.0	7.4	7.4	7.4	7.4	7.4	29.6	29.6	3.7	0.0	77.8	33.8	48.2	51.9
97737	GILCHRIST	92.7	92.1	0.3	0.3	0.0	0.3	3.3	3.7	4.2	4.0	5.5	4.0	2.9	19.8	41.4	17.7	0.5	83.6	50.2	51.5	48.6
97738	HINES	94.1	94.0	0.1	0.1	0.7	0.7	2.9	2.9	6.1	6.7	8.0	7.0	4.8	23.9	29.2	12.9	1.4	74.7	41.1	51.7	48.3
97739	LA PINE	95.6	95.2	0.1	0.1	0.4	0.4	2.2	2.6	4.4	5.1	6.5	5.7	3.8	19.8	33.4	19.7	1.6	80.4	47.8	50.3	49.7
97741	MADRAS	73.2	69.5	0.4	0.4	0.6	0.7	26.4	31.7	8.8	8.4	8.5	7.0	6.6	27.6	21.8	9.8	1.5	69.8	32.8	50.0	50.0
97750	MITCHELL	93.4	93.2	0.2	0.2	0.4	0.4	5.3	5.1	4.5	4.5	4.9	7.6	4.5	17.3	32.4	22.2	2.1	79.5	49.1	51.1	48.9
97751	PAULINA	91.3	89.9	0.0	0.0	0.0	0.7	7.1	8.8	7.4	7.4	6.1	6.1	4.7	23.0	32.4	12.2	0.7	75.0	42.1	54.1	46.0
97752	POST	90.9	90.5	0.0	0.0	0.4	0.3	7.1	8.5	7.4	7.8	6.8	5.7	4.7	24.7	30.4	11.8	0.7	74.3	40.6	52.7	47.3
97753	POWELL BUTTE	94.0	93.0	0.1	0.1	0.7	0.9	3.9	4.8	4.8	5.7	6.1	5.7	4.1	23.6	35.6	13.4	1.1	79.9	45.0	50.0	50.0
97754	PRINEVILLE	92.9	91.9	0.0	0.0	0.4	0.5	5.8	7.0	6.8	6.5	7.2	7.2	6.3	24.3	26.3	13.7	1.8	74.7	38.8	49.8	50.2
97756	REDMOND	94.6	94.1	0.1	0.1	0.6	0.7	4.3	5.2	7.0	6.9	7.6	6.9	6.5	26.8	24.9	11.7	1.7	74.0	37.4	49.2	50.9
97758	RILEY	85.9	86.3	0.0	0.0	1.0	1.0	5.1	4.9	5.9	5.9	6.9	6.9	5.9	21.6	35.3	10.8	1.0	76.5	42.9	49.0	51.0
97759	SISTERS	96.5	96.3	0.1	0.1	0.5	0.5	2.2	2.6	4.0	5.2	7.2	6.4	3.4	20.1	35.6	16.8	1.3	79.2	47.0	49.4	50.7
97760	TERREBONNE	95.1	94.7	0.2	0.2	0.5	0.6	3.0	3.6	4.6	5.5	6.3	5.7	4.1	22.4	32.4	18.0	1.1	79.8	45.9	50.8	49.3
97761	WARM SPRINGS	2.5	2.6	0.1	0.1	0.1	0.1	6.2	6.8	10.0	9.0	11.0	12.3	9.2	27.7	16.3	4.2	0.3	61.9	24.2	51.2	48.9
97801	PENDLETON	84.6	83.5	1.2	1.2	0.9	1.0	5.0	6.1	6.5	6.4	6.6	7.0	8.2	28.4	24.2	11.0	1.8	76.4	36.3	52.1	47.9
97810	ADAMS	86.5	85.9	0.0	0.0	0.9	0.9	3.5	4.4	6.3	6.9	8.4	8.8	6.3	24.6	26.9	10.5	1.2	71.7	37.1	50.1	49.9
97812	ARLINGTON	96.0	96.1	0.0	0.0	0.0	0.0	2.6	2.6	4.7	5.7	7.9	5.8	4.8	25.8	31.1	13.3	1.0	77.3	42.0	50.7	49.3
97813	ATHENA	90.1	89.0	0.3	0.3	0.5	0.6	5.0	6.4	8.1	8.1	7.7	7.3	5.9	25.2	25.6	11.1	1.1	70.7	36.3	49.8	50.2
97814	BAKER CITY	95.4	95.0	0.3	0.3	0.5	0.6	2.5	3.0	5.7	5.9	6.9	6.8	5.5	22.4	28.0	15.9	3.1	77.2	42.9	49.2	50.8
97818	BOARDMAN	60.1	56.4	0.3	0.3	0.6	0.6	44.1	49.2	11.1	10.1	9.1	8.0	7.9	28.1	19.8	5.5	0.5	64.8	27.6	52.4	47.6
97820	CANYON CITY	95.4	95.2	0.0	0.0	0.2	0.2	2.5	3.0	6.2	6.6	7.6	6.8	7.0	22.0	28.9	12.8	2.2	74.8	40.8	49.7	50.3
97823	CONDON	97.3	97.2	0.3	0.3	0.3	0.3	1.3	1.3	4.6	4.9	5.2	6.0	4.9	21.2	29.7	20.2	3.3	81.1	46.7	51.2	48.8
97824	COVE	95.0	95.0	0.3	0.4	0.9	0.8	2.8	2.9	6.0	6.6	6.7	6.7	5.5	18.5	33.3	15.3	1.4	76.6	45.0	48.9	51.1
97825	DAYVILLE	95.7	94.7	0.7	0.8	0.7	0.8	2.2	2.3	5.3	6.1	6.8	6.1	3.8	21.2	34.9	14.4	1.5	77.3	45.4	52.3	47.7
97826	ECHO	90.4	88.9	0.4	0.4	0.3	0.3	7.4	9.0	6.9	7.1	6.9	6.3	6.9	25.4	26.1	12.8	1.6	75.1	37.8	52.0	48.0
97827	ELGIN	96.9	96.9	0.0	0.0	0.7	0.7	1.4	1.5	6.2	6.8	7.5	6.6	4.6	22.0	31.0	13.5	1.9	75.3	42.3	50.3	49.7
97828	ENTERPRISE	96.8	96.7	0.0	0.0	0.3	0.3	1.5	1.6	4.3	5.0	7.0	7.7	4.3	20.1	32.4	16.6	2.6	78.5	45.8	49.6	50.4
97830	FOSSIL	93.4	93.3	0.0	0.0	0.3	0.3	5.0	5.1	4.7	5.2	5.2	5.7	4.2	18.2	32.6	21.8	2.5	80.6	50.5	49.6	50.4
97833	HAINES	96.6	96.5	0.1	0.1	0.2	0.2	1.7	2.0	5.8	6.5	7.9	7.2	4.3	21.9	30.9	14.0	1.5	75.0	42.8	51.0	49.0
97834	HALFWAY	97.2	97.0	0.3	0.4	0.0	0.0	1.2	1.4	3.4	4.3	9.9	9.0	1.9	17.8	35.3	16.0	2.3	76.0	46.9	49.5	50.5
97835	HELIX	94.9	94.2	0.5	0.5	0.5	0.5	2.8	3.4	4.8	6.5	9.9	8.4	5.3	25.0	25.0	13.9	1.2	72.4	38.8	51.7	48.3
97836	HEPPNER	96.6	96.2	0.0	0.0	0.3	0.4	2.4	2.9	5.4	5.9	7.4	5.9	5.4	21.3	29.7	16.4	2.7	77.8	44.2	51.0	49.0
97837	HEREFORD	96.4	96.4	0.0	0.0	0.0	0.0	1.8	2.3	5.0	5.5	5.9	5.0	4.6	18.2	35.5	18.6	1.8	80.5	48.4	51.4	48.6
97838	HERMISTON	80.3	77.7	0.7	0.7	1.3	1.4	22.8	26.6	8.1	7.6	7.6	7.3	7.9	26.2	23.8	9.8	1.7	72.2	33.6	49.9	50.1
97839	LEXINGTON	93.2	92.7	0.0	0.0	0.4	0.4	3.9	4.9	6.7	7.5	7.9	6.1	5.1	23.0	29.3	13.0	1.2	73.9	41.3	53.4	46.6
97840	OXBOW	98.8	98.8	0.0	0.0	0.0	0.0	0.0	1.2	2.5	3.7	8.6	8.6	1.2	18.5	43.2	11.1	2.5	77.8	48.1	54.3	45.7
97841	IMBLER	97.4	97.0	0.2	0.3	1.7	1.7	0.7	0.7	4.2	5.0	8.7	8.7	6.0	21.6	32.0	11.4	2.5	76.7	42.7	50.6	49.4
97842	IMNAHA	96.0	96.0	0.0	0.0	0.0	0.0	2.9	2.9	3.4	4.0	5.7	5.7	3.4	18.9	37.7	18.9	2.3	82.9	50.7	53.1	46.9
97843	IONE	96.7	96.8	0.0	0.0	0.2	0.2	3.7	4.3	5.7	6.2	8.5	9.3	2.9	23.5	28.8	13.8	1.4	73.1	41.9	52.6	47.5
97844	IRRIGON	74.7	71.1	0.1	0.1	0.5	0.6	24.1	28.2	8.5	8.1	8.1	7.5	7.8	25.3	24.8	9.2	0.7	70.3	33.0	50.6	49.4
97845	JOHN DAY	96.1	95.8	0.1	0.1	0.3	0.4	2.3	2.8	6.3	6.6	7.3	6.8	6.3	22.0	28.2	14.0	2.4	75.1	41.3	49.2	50.8
97846	JOSEPH	95.8	95.7	0.0	0.0	0.2	0.2	1.4	1.4	4.8	5.3	6.2	6.4	4.6	19.1	33.8	16.9	2.9	79.3	47.1	51.6	48.4
97848	KIMBERLY	95.0	94.7	0.0	0.0	0.0	0.0	0.0	0.0	5.3	10.5	10.5	10.5	0.0	26.3	36.8	0.0	0.0	73.7	38.8	47.4	52.6
97850	LA GRANDE	93.3	93.3	0.7	0.7	1.9	1.9	2.8	2.8	6.1	5.8	6.3	7.9	10.5	24.3	24.9	11.6	2.7	77.8	35.4	48.2	51.8
97856	LONG CREEK	94.5	94.1	0.2	0.2	0.0	0.0	1.8	2.2	4.8	4.8	5.0	5.7	5.9	21.6	33.4	15.9	2.8	81.7	46.3	51.5	48.5
97857	LOSTINE	96.3	96.1	0.0	0.0	0.2	0.2	2.8	2.5	6.4	6.9	7.3	7.1	4.8	20.0	30.5	15.1	1.8	73.9	43.6	50.0	50.0
97862	MILTON FREEWATER	80.0	77.7	0.3	0.3	1.1	1.2	23.4	26.5	8.0	7.7	7.7	6.6	6.3	25.0	23.4	12.6	2.7	72.6	36.2	49.3	50.7
97864	MONUMENT	94.7	94.3	0.0	0.0	0.0	0.0	1.9	2.3	4.9	4.9	5.2	5.8	6.0	21.8	32.5	16.4	2.6	81.6	45.9	50.9	49.1
97865	MOUNT VERNON	95.3	94.8	0.2	0.2	0.2	0.2	1.9	2.1	5.7	6.2	6.6	6.9	5.5	22.2	30.3	14.8	1.7	77.4	42.9	48.8	51.2
97867	NORTH POWDER	96.1	96.0	0.4	0.4	0.5	0.6	4.5	4.5	5.6	6.0	8.1	7.9	6.7	23.3	27.7	12.8	2.0	75.3	40.4	51.4	48.6
97868	PILOT ROCK	93.1	92.4	0.2	0.2	0.5	0.5	2.1	2.6	6.1	6.4	7.8	7.4	5.4	24.0	28.4	13.1	1.5	74.9	40.6	49.5	50.5
97869	PRAIRIE CITY	95.7	95.4	0.0	0.0	0.1	0.1	1.5	1.9	5.3	5.8	7.5	6.5	4.7	20.1	29.8	16.6	3.8	77.0	45.1	50.4	49.6
97870	RICHLAND	94.6	94.2	0.0	0.0	0.5	0.5	2.6	3.2	4.0	4.3	5.0	5.2	4.1	14.9	35.1	24.8	2.7	83.6	52.4	52.1	47.9
97873	SENECA	95.3	95.0	0.6	0.6	0.3	0.3	2.2	2.6	5.0	5.9	7.3	6.1	4.1	21.1	34.2	14.6	1.8	77.5	45.3	51.2	48.8
97874	SPRAY	92.3	96.2	0.0	0.0	0.0	0.0	7.7	3.9	7.7	7.7	3.9	7.7	7.7	19.2	30.8	15.4	0.0	80.8	42.5	53.9	46.2
97875	STANFIELD	73.2	69.8	0.5	0.5	0.5	0.5	25.8	30.1	9.3	8.9	8.1	6.6	7.2	27.5	22.7	8.8	1.0	69.7	31.6	52.0	48.0
97876	SUMMERVILLE	95.3	95.1	0.4	0.4	0.9	1.0	1.9	1.9	4.6	5.7	7.6	6.8	2.9	22.2	37.1	11.4	1.6	77.5	45.1	51.5	48.6
97877	SUMPTER	96.4	96.4	0.0	0.0	0.0	0.0	1.8	1.8	4.5	4.5	5.4	5.4	4.5	18.9	36.9	18.0	1.8	81.1	48.8	51.4	48.7
97882	UMATILLA	75.9	73.1	2.2	2.2	0.5	0.6	28.0	31.9	9.4	8.2	7.5	7.5	8.5	31.6	20.0	6.7	0.6	70.8	30.4	56.4	43.6
97883	UNION	96.4	96.5	0.1	0.1	0.4	0.4	1.1	1.1	5.7	6.2	7.2	7.0	5.6	22.0	29.2	14.8	2.3	76.7	42.4	49.1	50.9
97884	UNITY	96.6	96.7	0.0	0.0	0.0	0.0	1.3	1.3	5.0	5.0	5.4	4.6	5.0	17.6	36.4	19.3	1.7	81.6	49.0	51.1	49.0
97885	WALLOWA	97.1	97.1	0.1	0.1	0.3	0.3	2.1	2.1	5.4	6.2	8.1	7.1	4.2	20.1	31.3	16.0	1.5	74.9	44.4	50.1	49.9
97886	WESTON	87.8	86.0	0.0	0.0	0.2	0.1	10.3	12.6	4.5	6.6	10.1	7.5	3.8	25.5	28.1	12.7	1.1	73.6	39.4	49.8	50.2
97901	ADRIAN	88.1	87.9	0.0	0.0	2.2	2.2	16.0	16.2	5.3	7.1	8.2	9.2	6.3	22.6	27.9	12.1	1.4	73.0	39.2	53.2	46.8
97903	BROGAN	78.5	78.4	8.0	8.0	1.0	1.0	10.5	11.1	1.5	1.5	1.0	3.5	16.6	50.8	21.6	3.5	0.0	95.5	35.1	92.5	7.5
97904	DREWSEY	94.6	95.3	0.0	0.0	0.0	0.0	3.4	2.7	3.4	6.1	6.8	6.8	3.4	23.7	35.8	13.5	0.7	78.4	45.0	50.7	49.3
97906	HARPER	81.4	81.1	5.8	6.0	0.7	0.7	8.6	8.8	3.2	3.2	2.8	4.2	13.3	43.9	22.8	6.0	0.7	88.4	35.5	81.4	18.6
97907	HUNTINGTON	96.4	96.2	0.5	0.5	0.1	0.1	3.3	3.9	3.7	4.8	7.1	5.7	4.6	20.4	32.4	20.0	1.3	80.8	48.0	53.8	46.2
97908	IRONSIDE	79.0	77.2	8.8	8.8	1.8	1.8	10.5	10.5	1.8	0.0	0.0	3.5	21.1	52.6	19.3	1.8	0.0	98.3	34.6	100.0	0.0
97909	JAMIESON	97.3	97.5	0.0	0.0	0.0	0.0	6.9	6.3	5.1	6.3	7.6	8.9	6.3	29.1	25.3	10.1	1.3	74.7	38.1	51.9	48.1
	OREGON	86.6	85.2	1.6	1.7	3.2	3.6	8.1	9.5	6.5	6.4	6.8	6.9	7.4	27.7	25.6	11.0	1.9	76.3	36.9	49.6	50.4
	UNITED STATES	75.1	73.6	12.3	12.5	3.8	4.2	12.5	14.1	6.9	6.7	7.2	7.0	7.3	28.6	23.8	10.8	1.7	75.1	36.0	49.1	50.9

#	POST OFFICE NAME	2004 Per Capita Income	2004 HH Income Base	2004 Household Income Distribution (%) Less than $25,000	$25,000 to $49,999	$50,000 to $99,999	$100,000 to $149,999	$150,000 or More	Median Household Income 2004	2009	2004 National Centile	2004 State Centile	2004 Home Value Base	2004 Home Value Distribution (%) Less than $50,000	$50,000 to $89,999	$90,000 to $174,999	$175,000 to $399,999	$400,000 or More	2004 Median Home Value
97624	CHILOQUIN	14924	1591	41.7	33.9	21.0	2.6	0.8	30021	32853	12	8	1279	14.9	23.7	39.6	18.7	3.2	110258
97625	DAIRY	14955	75	33.3	33.3	22.7	6.7	4.0	37598	42938	38	39	60	11.7	16.7	35.0	25.0	11.7	132143
97627	KENO	21382	433	38.1	24.3	29.6	5.5	2.5	37121	41976	36	37	361	11.9	12.7	50.4	19.1	5.8	128438
97630	LAKEVIEW	19080	2044	35.5	33.0	25.6	4.1	1.9	34166	39229	25	24	1479	21.6	37.1	26.8	12.8	1.7	82657
97632	MALIN	16207	417	32.4	35.0	24.9	5.0	2.6	37067	41267	36	37	298	11.1	27.2	35.6	19.8	6.4	117949
97633	MERRILL	21198	408	34.3	26.2	28.9	5.2	5.4	39098	40578	43	44	311	13.5	21.9	30.6	28.9	5.1	116987
97635	NEW PINE CREEK	19580	80	36.3	27.5	28.8	5.0	2.5	35000	36166	28	27	59	6.8	25.4	35.6	30.5	1.7	123611
97636	PAISLEY	17263	206	36.9	38.8	20.9	1.5	1.9	32307	35558	19	17	132	18.2	23.5	28.0	16.7	13.6	113462
97637	PLUSH	16971	62	37.1	38.7	21.0	1.6	1.6	31812	36129	17	14	40	15.0	22.5	30.0	17.5	15.0	120000
97638	SILVER LAKE	16258	676	48.1	32.0	16.1	1.9	1.9	26387	29078	6	5	546	35.7	23.1	25.3	9.9	6.0	77188
97639	SPRAGUE RIVER	12128	79	54.4	31.7	11.4	1.3	1.3	21858	23124	3	1	66	16.7	22.7	45.5	15.2	0.0	108333
97640	SUMMER LAKE	0	0	0.0	0.0	0.0	0.0	0.0	0	0	0	0	0	0.0	0.0	0.0	0.0	0.0	0
97701	BEND	26632	21500	21.5	30.1	33.0	9.8	5.5	48252	55590	69	77	14497	3.0	2.2	32.5	47.5	14.8	198434
97702	BEND	25423	13035	20.7	31.3	32.4	9.8	5.7	48199	55474	69	77	9867	8.2	7.9	36.3	38.7	9.0	170552
97707	BEND	32055	2650	20.8	28.9	28.3	10.1	11.9	50272	57324	72	80	2223	2.1	10.8	30.3	31.9	24.9	209375
97710	FIELDS	18753	32	34.4	31.3	28.1	3.1	3.1	33141	40000	21	19	21	9.5	9.5	33.3	28.6	19.1	162500
97711	ASHWOOD	19883	55	18.2	41.8	30.9	5.5	3.6	44302	48216	59	65	44	9.1	0.0	27.3	54.6	9.1	233333
97712	BROTHERS	23438	16	25.0	25.0	25.0	12.5	12.5	47500	60000	67	74	14	0.0	0.0	0.0	64.3	35.7	360000
97720	BURNS	17956	1933	37.8	35.9	19.2	4.3	2.7	30616	33593	14	9	1403	27.0	25.5	30.6	13.3	3.6	86450
97721	PRINCETON	19347	125	36.0	29.6	25.6	4.0	4.8	32555	35970	19	17	81	12.4	11.1	28.4	28.4	19.8	162500
97730	CAMP SHERMAN	24758	158	24.7	22.8	36.7	10.1	5.7	52004	54656	75	83	131	6.9	3.8	26.0	41.2	22.1	221000
97731	CHEMULT	19667	126	33.3	34.9	27.0	4.0	0.8	36994	40377	35	36	85	14.1	29.4	37.7	16.5	2.4	105833
97733	CRESCENT	16598	521	37.4	34.4	23.4	3.7	1.2	32899	35798	21	18	395	13.7	39.8	36.5	8.9	1.3	85781
97734	CULVER	18393	825	25.1	35.0	30.8	7.4	1.7	41018	45221	50	53	630	7.0	11.1	45.9	28.6	7.5	134701
97735	FORT ROCK	13611	11	36.4	45.5	18.2	0.0	0.0	32290	35000	19	16	9	11.1	44.4	44.4	0.0	0.0	87500
97737	GILCHRIST	19547	178	32.0	44.9	18.5	2.8	1.7	33591	37144	23	21	148	8.8	43.2	35.8	10.8	1.4	87692
97738	HINES	19659	820	23.7	36.2	32.9	5.9	1.3	43285	50202	57	61	666	12.2	21.3	52.1	12.3	2.1	103963
97739	LA PINE	17516	3747	33.1	40.4	21.6	3.2	1.6	33552	36781	23	21	3066	6.3	20.3	49.8	20.1	3.5	119853
97741	MADRAS	17578	3887	28.3	36.7	26.8	6.2	2.0	37812	41749	39	40	2711	12.8	13.3	45.7	24.1	4.0	123719
97750	MITCHELL	17382	207	42.0	35.3	16.9	2.4	3.4	29513	31947	11	7	151	12.6	17.2	33.1	22.5	14.6	121635
97751	PAULINA	18274	70	40.0	41.4	11.4	4.3	2.9	31272	35264	16	13	48	12.5	16.7	27.1	29.2	14.6	140000
97752	POST	14619	112	39.3	42.9	10.7	4.5	2.7	31329	35325	16	13	76	17.1	15.8	25.0	25.0	17.1	133333
97753	POWELL BUTTE	25753	710	8.9	33.4	44.1	8.3	5.4	54536	61191	79	87	612	3.9	3.3	21.9	44.4	26.5	241667
97754	PRINEVILLE	17986	6957	33.0	33.3	27.7	4.3	1.7	36649	40994	34	35	5122	11.3	12.1	51.5	21.1	4.1	121332
97756	REDMOND	22904	9989	23.6	34.3	32.3	6.5	3.3	43368	49488	57	62	7045	5.6	6.3	48.3	34.7	5.1	157080
97758	RILEY	22577	40	20.0	25.0	42.5	12.5	0.0	52804	63044	77	84	30	6.7	3.3	26.7	56.7	6.7	200000
97759	SISTERS	33006	2161	18.8	27.6	31.6	14.0	8.0	53930	61604	78	86	1796	2.8	3.2	14.6	50.2	29.2	253546
97760	TERREBONNE	21120	2717	19.9	39.3	31.4	7.2	2.2	42472	48014	55	57	2326	3.6	7.5	49.5	34.5	4.9	156512
97761	WARM SPRINGS	9684	679	37.4	38.6	19.7	3.8	0.4	33368	35920	22	20	392	18.9	33.7	41.3	4.1	2.0	86154
97801	PENDLETON	20412	7883	27.1	31.4	32.6	6.5	2.4	42386	48336	54	57	4990	9.5	13.8	48.9	25.6	2.2	129426
97810	ADAMS	19086	207	24.2	30.9	37.7	5.8	1.5	46370	51270	65	71	168	8.9	19.1	48.2	20.2	3.6	117308
97812	ARLINGTON	20314	343	25.4	39.7	27.4	5.3	2.3	39659	44433	45	47	233	16.7	24.5	43.4	8.2	7.3	103728
97813	ATHENA	18841	542	27.9	29.7	35.1	5.7	1.7	42541	46899	55	58	402	10.2	16.9	49.5	15.9	7.5	116176
97814	BAKER CITY	17632	4927	36.2	35.7	22.8	3.7	1.6	34016	37017	24	23	3508	10.5	24.0	42.6	17.8	5.1	110748
97818	BOARDMAN	15332	1270	25.3	34.7	33.7	4.8	1.5	41036	47300	50	53	857	30.0	11.7	41.4	15.8	1.2	104167
97820	CANYON CITY	20564	346	26.0	33.5	30.9	8.1	1.5	41678	47115	52	55	260	7.3	22.7	42.3	26.2	1.5	120833
97823	CONDON	19655	482	37.8	31.1	23.7	5.8	1.7	34533	38718	26	25	383	15.7	29.0	43.6	8.6	3.1	98913
97824	COVE	22319	540	24.6	30.2	33.3	8.3	3.5	45854	50772	63	70	439	3.6	8.4	37.8	40.8	9.3	175278
97825	DAYVILLE	16143	57	38.6	38.6	19.3	3.5	0.0	31082	33608	15	11	45	20.0	24.4	22.2	20.0	13.3	104167
97826	ECHO	18448	353	34.6	31.2	28.1	4.3	2.0	35665	37370	30	30	245	12.2	24.1	39.2	20.0	4.5	108438
97827	ELGIN	18505	949	31.8	37.5	24.2	4.1	2.3	36255	40177	33	33	732	18.0	20.5	35.4	21.7	4.4	108884
97828	ENTERPRISE	20157	1318	34.0	32.1	26.0	5.9	2.1	36225	41110	32	32	962	7.2	11.6	40.1	31.0	10.1	153922
97830	FOSSIL	18736	447	35.6	38.3	20.4	3.6	2.2	33524	37566	22	20	353	18.7	26.4	32.0	14.7	8.2	96481
97833	HAINES	19382	389	33.7	33.2	24.9	4.9	3.3	37030	39368	36	36	305	11.2	21.6	29.2	22.0	16.1	132738
97834	HALFWAY	16645	495	43.6	31.9	19.8	2.6	2.0	28485	31701	10	6	358	11.5	12.9	37.2	33.5	5.0	137931
97835	HELIX	19026	149	23.5	30.2	36.9	7.4	2.0	47543	50513	67	75	96	14.6	19.8	25.0	35.4	5.2	139286
97836	HEPPNER	21270	860	31.3	30.0	28.6	6.1	4.1	38485	42407	41	43	621	12.4	29.2	36.7	17.1	4.7	105307
97837	HEREFORD	16182	88	35.2	40.9	18.2	5.7	0.0	33590	38044	23	21	68	10.3	23.5	23.5	35.3	7.4	131250
97838	HERMISTON	19554	8260	27.1	32.2	30.7	7.0	3.0	41567	47070	52	54	5573	13.3	14.8	46.7	23.4	1.7	121005
97839	LEXINGTON	25130	189	18.0	31.8	34.4	10.1	5.8	50165	52602	72	79	150	23.3	20.7	29.3	20.0	6.7	103125
97840	OXBOW	19442	34	29.4	41.2	23.5	2.9	2.9	36496	41505	34	34	25	4.0	12.0	28.0	52.0	4.0	187500
97841	IMBLER	18885	149	26.2	33.6	31.5	6.7	2.0	43656	45462	58	64	119	8.4	16.8	38.7	26.9	9.2	144792
97842	IMNAHA	19563	75	32.0	40.0	13.3	10.7	4.0	32254	36604	18	15	60	5.0	3.3	23.3	43.3	25.0	235000
97843	IONE	20178	248	26.6	29.4	35.1	6.1	2.8	45526	50108	63	68	195	19.0	24.6	29.2	21.0	6.2	104167
97844	IRRIGON	16108	1445	25.4	34.7	33.6	5.2	1.0	40994	47304	50	52	1134	19.4	18.6	43.5	17.4	1.2	106751
97845	JOHN DAY	19488	1452	31.0	36.4	25.3	5.5	1.8	36903	41292	35	36	1115	17.6	23.1	35.9	20.5	3.1	103840
97846	JOSEPH	21534	849	32.0	38.4	19.3	6.2	4.0	35605	40277	30	29	643	3.4	10.3	39.4	36.6	10.4	161824
97848	KIMBERLY	11053	8	50.0	37.5	12.5	0.0	0.0	25000	25000	5	4	6	0.0	50.0	50.0	0.0	0.0	85000
97850	LA GRANDE	19875	6621	34.2	30.9	26.9	5.7	2.3	37167	42265	36	38	4111	11.4	12.7	53.2	20.5	2.3	118354
97856	LONG CREEK	18984	203	40.9	31.0	20.7	4.4	3.0	29844	31657	12	7	147	21.1	24.5	25.9	10.2	18.4	100781
97857	LOSTINE	16892	175	37.7	34.9	21.1	4.6	1.7	33219	36025	22	19	137	11.0	26.3	36.5	21.2	5.1	114583
97862	MILTON FREEWATER	15788	4155	37.4	33.6	22.7	5.2	1.2	32743	35805	20	18	2927	13.4	21.4	44.3	17.6	3.4	112500
97864	MONUMENT	19650	160	41.9	31.9	19.4	4.4	2.5	29223	32516	11	7	116	20.7	24.1	26.7	9.5	19.0	101786
97865	MOUNT VERNON	17490	244	29.9	41.8	24.6	3.3	0.4	36352	40327	33	33	194	28.4	22.7	28.4	18.6	2.1	88000
97867	NORTH POWDER	14947	293	42.0	35.5	16.0	3.8	2.7	30078	33222	12	8	211	14.7	33.2	31.3	15.2	5.7	92647
97868	PILOT ROCK	17015	902	29.3	37.8	28.4	3.2	1.3	38002	42070	39	41	702	16.0	23.8	45.2	12.0	3.1	102355
97869	PRAIRIE CITY	19519	603	36.0	35.7	22.7	3.3	2.3	34108	36521	24	24	478	13.6	27.0	41.4	14.0	4.0	103378
97870	RICHLAND	17394	317	49.2	28.1	16.4	4.7	1.6	25336	27674	5	4	259	18.5	19.7	25.9	27.0	8.9	117411
97873	SENECA	15926	143	39.9	39.2	17.5	3.5	0.0	30454	32306	13	9	114	17.5	29.0	23.7	19.3	10.5	98000
97874	SPRAY	8077	8	50.0	37.5	12.5	0.0	0.0	25000	25000	5	4	6	0.0	0.0	50.0	50.0	0.0	212500
97875	STANFIELD	16887	894	25.7	36.4	31.3	4.9	1.7	40526	45464	48	50	669	9.0	16.9	52.2	16.4	5.5	111769
97876	SUMMERVILLE	23055	354	20.3	34.5	29.4	11.9	4.0	46702	54742	66	72	311	2.3	4.5	25.1	53.1	15.1	219922
97877	SUMPTER	22112	60	33.3	40.0	21.7	5.0	0.0	35000	38623	28	27	49	6.1	24.5	30.6	30.6	8.2	123438
97882	UMATILLA	15051	1944	28.6	36.3	29.2	4.7	1.2	39707	45784	45	47	1253	20.0	19.3	44.7	14.8	1.1	101998
97883	UNION	16485	961	38.0	36.3	21.4	3.2	1.0	33676	36794	23	22	763	10.1	24.1	45.6	13.4	6.8	106449
97884	UNITY	17833	102	33.3	40.2	19.6	6.9	0.0	35000	39644	28	27	81	3.7	21.0	24.7	43.2	7.4	176389
97885	WALLOWA	17135	613	36.7	33.9	23.8	4.1	1.5	33863	36809	24	22	479	10.0	22.6	39.7	25.5	2.3	119500
97886	WESTON	16322	525	25.5	45.1	24.4	4.6	0.4	39421	44208	44	45	419	10.3	24.8	44.2	18.1	2.6	110505
97901	ADRIAN	16153	205	31.2	35.6	24.4	5.9	2.9	37022	41300	36	36	153	17.0	7.8	43.8	24.8	6.5	122917
97903	BROGAN	25216	68	45.6	30.9	20.6	2.9	0.0	27801	30434	8	6	47	29.8	19.2	25.5	12.8	12.8	95000
97904	DREWSEY	22341	67	34.3	37.3	17.9	7.5	3.0	32273	37323	19	16	56	10.7	8.9	35.7	33.9	10.7	160000
97906	HARPER	22976	104	45.2	33.7	18.3	2.9	0.0	27926	30542	9	6	72	25.0	23.6	25.0	12.5	13.9	93333
97907	HUNTINGTON	15180	348	43.7	37.4	15.5	2.6	0.9	27570	30281	8	5	255	31.0	37.3	20.4	6.3	5.1	71000
97908	IRONSIDE	14134	23	47.8	30.4	17.4	4.4	0.0	26087	32290	6	4	16	25.0	25.0	18.8	12.5	18.8	90000
97909	JAMIESON	14333	26	38.5	30.8	23.1	7.7	0.0	37321	43624	37	39	20	5.0	25.0	30.0	35.0	5.0	158333
	OREGON	24176		24.9	29.7	31.4	9.2	4.8	45702	52201				6.4	6.5	35.2	43.4	8.6	179540
	UNITED STATES	25866		24.7	27.1	30.8	10.9	6.5	48124	56710				10.9	15.0	33.7	30.1	10.4	145905

ZIP CODE #	POST OFFICE NAME	FINANCIAL SERVICES: Auto Loan	FINANCIAL SERVICES: Home Loan	FINANCIAL SERVICES: Invest-ments	FINANCIAL SERVICES: Retire-ment Plans	THE HOME: Home Improvements: Home Repair	THE HOME: Home Improvements: Lawn & Garden	THE HOME: Furnishings: Comput-ers & Hard-ware	THE HOME: Furnishings: Major Appli-ances	THE HOME: Furnishings: TV, Radio, Sound Equip-ment	THE HOME: Furnishings: Furni-ture	ENTERTAINMENT: Dine out/ Carry out	ENTERTAINMENT: Sports Equip-ment	ENTERTAINMENT: Fees & Tickets	ENTERTAINMENT: Toys & Games	ENTERTAINMENT: Travel	ENTERTAINMENT: Cable TV	PERSONAL: Apparel & Services	PERSONAL: Auto Repairs	PERSONAL: Health Insur-ance	PERSONAL: Pets & Supplies
97624	CHILOQUIN	66	46	23	41	51	60	46	55	54	46	64	65	40	60	46	58	58	55	68	76
97625	DAIRY	73	68	55	66	68	72	65	69	65	66	81	80	62	76	64	64	78	69	68	81
97627	KENO	86	76	58	72	80	85	71	79	75	72	91	93	68	91	73	76	87	78	84	100
97630	LAKEVIEW	74	57	42	56	63	71	59	67	65	58	78	79	54	76	60	67	72	67	76	86
97632	MALIN	77	61	43	57	64	69	61	70	67	64	81	79	55	75	61	67	78	71	74	85
97633	MERRILL	100	70	37	66	82	91	69	86	80	68	94	103	59	92	72	84	85	84	102	119
97635	NEW PINE CREEK	81	57	30	53	66	74	56	69	64	55	76	83	48	74	58	68	69	68	82	96
97636	PAISLEY	68	53	36	48	60	67	50	60	57	49	67	70	45	66	53	60	62	59	71	82
97637	PLUSH	69	54	37	49	61	68	51	61	58	50	68	72	46	67	54	62	64	60	73	84
97638	SILVER LAKE	73	49	22	42	55	64	47	59	57	48	67	70	40	63	48	61	61	58	73	84
97639	SPRAGUE RIVER	53	35	16	30	40	46	34	43	41	35	48	51	29	46	35	44	44	42	52	60
97640	SUMMER LAKE	0	0	0	0	0	0	0	0	0	0	0	0	0	0	0	0	0	0	0	0
97701	BEND	91	94	99	96	94	97	93	93	91	93	113	110	94	114	93	88	111	93	88	105
97702	BEND	95	95	90	95	96	100	92	95	91	92	113	110	91	111	92	89	109	94	93	109
97707	BEND	120	101	80	93	111	127	94	111	104	97	126	122	89	116	101	111	117	109	131	143
97710	FIELDS	87	61	32	57	71	79	60	74	69	59	81	89	51	79	62	73	74	73	88	103
97711	ASHWOOD	97	68	35	64	79	88	67	83	77	66	90	100	57	88	69	81	82	81	98	115
97712	BROTHERS	101	109	106	110	110	113	98	101	95	99	118	119	103	121	100	94	116	98	98	120
97720	BURNS	71	55	37	53	60	68	57	64	63	56	75	74	52	72	57	65	69	64	73	80
97721	PRINCETON	86	60	32	57	70	79	59	74	69	59	80	89	51	79	62	72	73	73	88	102
97730	CAMP SHERMAN	105	83	56	74	93	104	78	94	88	77	104	110	70	103	83	94	97	92	111	128
97731	CHEMULT	78	56	32	50	64	72	54	66	63	54	74	78	47	72	56	67	68	65	80	92
97733	CRESCENT	75	51	24	44	58	66	49	61	59	50	69	73	42	66	50	63	63	60	75	87
97734	CULVER	82	66	48	65	72	81	67	75	73	66	88	87	62	87	68	75	82	74	84	94
97735	FORT ROCK	63	42	19	36	48	55	41	51	49	41	58	61	35	54	41	53	52	50	63	72
97737	GILCHRIST	74	54	31	48	61	69	51	63	60	52	71	75	45	69	54	64	65	62	76	88
97738	HINES	81	70	52	67	74	80	66	73	70	66	85	87	63	85	67	72	81	72	80	94
97739	LA PINE	73	55	36	50	61	71	54	65	62	54	73	74	49	70	56	66	67	64	77	85
97741	MADRAS	77	66	51	64	69	75	66	71	70	66	85	83	62	83	66	70	80	71	76	87
97750	MITCHELL	65	49	32	47	54	65	55	60	61	52	72	67	49	68	54	65	66	60	72	72
97751	PAULINA	70	49	26	46	57	64	48	60	56	48	65	72	41	64	50	58	59	59	71	83
97752	POST	70	49	26	46	57	64	48	60	56	48	65	72	41	64	50	58	59	59	71	83
97753	POWELL BUTTE	105	93	71	89	99	106	86	96	92	86	111	114	85	114	89	94	106	93	104	123
97754	PRINEVILLE	75	61	46	58	65	73	61	68	67	61	81	80	57	80	62	69	76	67	76	86
97756	REDMOND	85	82	79	82	84	90	82	85	83	81	102	100	81	103	82	83	99	85	86	99
97758	RILEY	94	80	57	76	83	89	77	85	80	78	98	100	71	93	76	80	92	85	89	106
97759	SISTERS	119	120	112	117	124	132	112	119	113	111	139	138	112	141	116	115	134	116	122	142
97760	TERREBONNE	82	74	65	71	79	90	70	79	74	73	91	83	69	82	74	78	86	77	90	93
97761	WARM SPRINGS	51	50	59	50	49	54	54	52	55	54	69	61	55	70	53	55	68	53	51	58
97801	PENDLETON	72	71	70	70	72	76	71	72	71	70	88	85	70	88	71	70	85	72	72	83
97810	ADAMS	95	66	35	62	77	86	65	81	75	64	88	97	56	86	68	79	80	80	96	112
97812	ARLINGTON	86	60	32	57	70	79	60	74	69	59	81	89	51	79	62	72	74	73	88	102
97813	ATHENA	94	66	34	62	77	86	65	80	75	64	88	97	55	86	67	78	80	79	96	112
97814	BAKER CITY	68	53	38	51	58	67	56	62	61	54	73	72	50	70	56	64	67	62	72	78
97818	BOARDMAN	74	65	60	64	64	69	70	70	72	71	89	81	66	86	67	70	88	73	69	79
97820	CANYON CITY	92	64	33	60	75	84	63	78	73	62	85	94	54	84	66	76	78	77	93	109
97823	CONDON	75	54	31	51	61	71	56	66	64	55	75	77	49	72	57	67	68	65	79	87
97824	COVE	104	73	38	69	85	95	72	89	83	71	97	107	61	95	75	87	89	88	106	124
97825	DAYVILLE	50	52	60	54	52	55	53	53	51	53	64	62	53	63	53	50	62	53	50	58
97826	ECHO	76	62	46	61	66	75	64	69	68	62	82	80	60	81	63	70	77	68	77	85
97827	ELGIN	85	58	27	51	66	75	56	70	67	56	78	84	48	75	57	71	71	69	85	98
97828	ENTERPRISE	79	58	35	55	66	75	60	70	68	58	79	81	52	77	61	71	73	69	83	92
97830	FOSSIL	69	52	34	50	57	68	58	63	65	55	76	71	51	72	57	68	69	63	76	77
97833	HAINES	88	61	32	58	71	80	60	75	70	60	82	90	52	80	63	73	74	74	89	104
97834	HALFWAY	65	47	28	45	53	62	50	57	56	48	66	66	43	63	50	59	60	57	69	74
97835	HELIX	94	66	34	62	77	86	65	80	75	64	88	97	55	86	67	78	80	79	96	112
97836	HEPPNER	85	70	52	65	77	86	67	78	74	67	88	91	62	88	70	77	83	77	89	102
97837	HEREFORD	68	53	36	48	59	67	51	61	58	51	69	71	46	67	54	62	64	60	72	82
97838	HERMISTON	78	75	71	75	76	80	76	77	76	75	94	90	74	93	75	75	91	78	77	88
97839	LEXINGTON	118	82	43	78	96	108	81	101	94	80	110	121	70	108	84	98	100	99	120	140
97840	OXBOW	84	59	31	55	68	76	58	71	67	57	78	86	49	77	60	70	71	70	85	100
97841	IMBLER	92	65	34	61	75	84	64	79	73	63	86	95	54	84	66	77	79	78	94	110
97842	IMNAHA	77	61	41	55	68	77	57	69	65	57	77	81	51	76	61	69	71	68	82	94
97843	IONE	95	66	35	63	77	87	66	81	76	65	89	98	56	87	68	79	81	80	97	113
97844	IRRIGON	78	71	56	68	71	75	68	73	69	70	85	84	64	80	67	68	81	72	72	86
97845	JOHN DAY	78	63	45	61	68	74	62	70	67	62	80	83	57	78	63	68	75	70	76	89
97846	JOSEPH	85	62	37	59	71	81	63	75	72	62	85	88	55	82	65	76	77	74	89	100
97848	KIMBERLY	36	37	43	39	37	39	38	38	36	37	46	44	38	44	38	35	44	38	36	41
97850	LA GRANDE	68	64	63	65	66	71	66	68	67	65	83	80	65	83	66	66	80	68	68	78
97856	LONG CREEK	78	54	28	51	63	71	53	66	62	53	72	80	46	71	55	65	66	65	79	92
97857	LOSTINE	76	53	29	50	62	69	52	65	60	52	71	78	45	70	55	63	65	64	77	90
97862	MILTON FREEWATER	66	56	46	54	58	64	58	62	61	57	75	71	54	72	57	62	71	62	66	74
97864	MONUMENT	77	54	29	51	63	70	53	66	61	53	72	79	46	71	55	64	66	65	78	92
97865	MOUNT VERNON	66	60	47	58	60	63	57	61	58	59	71	71	54	67	56	57	69	61	61	73
97867	NORTH POWDER	74	52	27	49	61	68	51	63	59	51	69	76	44	68	53	62	63	63	76	88
97868	PILOT ROCK	78	58	35	55	65	73	57	68	64	56	76	81	50	75	59	67	70	67	79	91
97869	PRAIRIE CITY	82	60	35	56	69	77	58	71	67	58	78	85	51	77	61	70	72	70	85	98
97870	RICHLAND	56	50	46	45	54	63	46	55	51	49	62	56	45	55	50	54	58	53	64	65
97873	SENECA	52	53	59	55	53	56	54	54	52	53	65	63	53	64	53	51	63	54	52	60
97874	SPRAY	42	32	21	31	35	42	35	39	39	33	46	43	31	44	35	42	42	39	46	47
97875	STANFIELD	79	66	48	64	70	77	65	72	69	65	84	84	61	81	65	70	79	72	78	90
97876	SUMMERVILLE	98	84	64	82	92	98	80	91	85	79	102	109	75	103	82	86	96	89	99	117
97877	SUMPTER	69	54	37	49	61	69	51	62	58	51	69	72	46	68	55	62	64	61	73	84
97882	UMATILLA	70	62	52	61	63	68	63	66	65	63	80	76	60	77	62	65	76	66	67	77
97883	UNION	73	52	30	50	60	68	54	64	61	52	72	75	47	70	55	65	66	63	76	85
97884	UNITY	71	56	38	50	63	70	52	63	59	52	70	74	47	69	56	63	65	62	75	86
97885	WALLOWA	76	53	28	50	61	69	52	64	60	52	71	78	45	69	54	63	64	64	77	90
97886	WESTON	71	62	46	58	66	72	57	65	62	57	75	77	55	76	59	64	71	63	71	84
97901	ADRIAN	84	58	31	55	68	76	58	71	67	57	78	86	49	76	60	70	71	70	85	99
97903	BROGAN	0	0	0	0	0	0	0	0	0	0	0	0	0	0	0	0	0	0	0	0
97904	DREWSEY	89	62	33	59	73	81	62	76	71	61	83	92	53	82	64	74	76	75	91	106
97906	HARPER	18	12	6	12	14	16	12	15	14	12	16	18	10	16	13	15	15	15	18	21
97907	HUNTINGTON	52	41	29	39	44	53	44	49	49	42	58	53	40	54	44	52	53	48	58	58
97908	IRONSIDE	0	0	0	0	0	0	0	0	0	0	0	0	0	0	0	0	0	0	0	0
97909	JAMIESON	79	55	29	52	64	72	54	67	63	54	73	81	46	72	56	66	67	66	80	94
	OREGON	87	85	86	85	86	91	86	87	86	85	106	102	85	106	85	84	103	87	86	100
	UNITED STATES	100	100	100	100	100	100	100	100	100	100	100	100	100	100	100	100	100	100	100	100

OREGON

POPULATION CHANGE

#	POST OFFICE NAME	COUNTY FIPS CODE	POPULATION			2000-2004 ANNUAL RATE		HOUSEHOLDS					FAMILIES		
			2000	2004	2009	% Rate	State Centile	2000	2004	2009	% Annual Rate 2000-2004	2004 Average HH Size	2000	2004	% Annual Rate 2000-2004
97910	JORDAN VALLEY	045	634	590	569	-1.7	2	263	246	237	-1.6	2.37	181	168	-1.7
97911	JUNTURA	045	96	94	94	-0.5	16	38	36	35	-1.3	2.56	28	4	-36.7
97913	NYSSA	045	5770	5718	5656	-0.2	24	1910	1894	1872	-0.2	3.02	1460	1440	-0.3
97914	ONTARIO	045	19164	19106	18983	-0.1	29	5955	5919	5855	-0.1	2.78	4088	4041	-0.3
97917	RIVERSIDE	045	63	59	57	-1.5	3	22	21	20	-1.1	2.76	16	15	-1.5
97918	VALE	045	4638	4735	4759	0.5	52	1585	1610	1609	0.4	2.84	1229	1242	0.3
97920	WESTFALL	045	25	25	25	0.0	35	8	8	7	0.0	2.50	6	2	-22.8
	OREGON					1.1					1.1	2.50			1.0
	UNITED STATES					1.2					1.3	2.58			1.1

#	POST OFFICE NAME	RACE (%)						% Hispanic Origin		2004 AGE DISTRIBUTION (%)										MEDIAN AGE	% 2004 Males	% 2004 Females
		White		Black		Asian/Pacific																
		2000	2004	2000	2004	2000	2004	2000	2004	0-4	5-9	10-14	15-19	20-24	25-44	45-64	65-84	85+	18+	2004		
97910	JORDAN VALLEY	88.8	88.6	0.0	0.0	0.6	0.7	3.6	3.9	6.6	7.0	6.8	5.8	5.1	23.4	28.8	14.2	2.4	75.4	41.5	51.4	48.6
97911	JUNTURA	80.2	79.8	6.3	6.4	1.0	1.1	9.4	9.6	2.1	2.1	2.1	4.3	13.8	47.9	22.3	5.3	0.0	93.6	35.4	85.1	14.9
97913	NYSSA	68.2	68.0	0.4	0.4	1.2	1.2	42.1	42.4	9.7	9.2	8.7	7.9	7.2	25.0	19.4	11.3	1.6	67.4	31.0	49.6	50.4
97914	ONTARIO	73.9	73.5	1.6	1.6	2.6	2.6	25.1	25.5	7.7	7.1	7.0	6.6	8.9	28.0	21.4	11.0	2.4	74.5	33.7	54.5	45.5
97917	RIVERSIDE	88.9	89.8	0.0	0.0	0.0	0.0	3.2	5.1	6.8	8.5	8.5	5.1	5.1	25.4	25.4	13.6	1.7	72.9	36.9	52.5	47.5
97918	VALE	88.5	88.5	0.2	0.2	1.1	1.1	14.3	14.4	7.2	7.2	8.6	7.6	6.7	24.7	24.4	11.8	1.7	72.0	35.9	51.6	48.5
97920	WESTFALL	80.0	84.0	8.0	8.0	0.0	0.0	12.0	8.0	0.0	0.0	0.0	4.0	24.0	52.0	20.0	0.0	0.0	100.0	34.2	100.0	0.0
	OREGON	86.6	85.2	1.6	1.7	3.2	3.6	8.1	9.5	6.5	6.4	6.8	6.9	7.4	27.7	25.6	11.0	1.9	76.3	36.9	49.6	50.4
	UNITED STATES	75.1	73.6	12.3	12.5	3.8	4.2	12.5	14.1	6.9	6.7	7.2	7.0	7.3	28.6	23.8	10.8	1.7	75.1	36.0	49.1	50.9

ZIP CODE		2004 Per Capita Income	2004 HH Income Base	2004 HOUSEHOLD INCOME DISTRIBUTION (%)					MEDIAN HOUSEHOLD INCOME				2004 Home Value Base	2004 HOME VALUE DISTRIBUTION (%)					2004 Median Home Value
#	POST OFFICE NAME			Less than $25,000	$25,000 to $49,999	$50,000 to $99,999	$100,000 to $149,999	$150,000 or More	2004	2009	2004 National Centile	2004 State Centile		Less than $50,000	$50,000 to $89,999	$90,000 to $174,999	$175,000 to $399,999	$400,000 or More	
97910	JORDAN VALLEY	15839	246	39.4	35.4	21.1	2.9	1.2	30652	33388	14	10	180	18.9	38.3	26.7	8.9	7.2	82778
97911	JUNTURA	24970	36	44.4	33.3	19.4	2.8	0.0	28137	29040	9	6	25	24.0	28.0	24.0	12.0	12.0	85000
97913	NYSSA	12901	1894	39.4	36.6	20.3	2.2	1.4	30823	34129	14	10	1356	18.5	29.4	35.1	14.5	2.5	91918
97914	ONTARIO	17098	5919	36.2	31.5	24.2	5.4	2.7	33622	37656	23	22	3570	13.2	15.2	52.2	17.1	2.4	115222
97917	RIVERSIDE	14070	21	33.3	47.6	14.3	4.8	0.0	33586	35000	23	21	15	6.7	20.0	53.3	6.7	13.3	110417
97918	VALE	15089	1610	36.5	33.4	23.7	4.8	1.7	34891	38046	27	26	1198	11.6	25.3	40.6	20.4	2.2	110081
97920	WESTFALL	22273	8	50.0	25.0	25.0	0.0	0.0	25000	22183	5	4	6	33.3	33.3	33.3	0.0	0.0	55000
	OREGON	24176		24.9	29.7	31.4	9.2	4.8	45702	52201				6.4	6.5	35.2	43.4	8.6	179540
	UNITED STATES	25866		24.7	27.1	30.8	10.9	6.5	48124	56710				10.9	15.0	33.7	30.1	10.4	145905

#	POST OFFICE NAME	FINANCIAL SERVICES				THE HOME						ENTERTAINMENT						PERSONAL			
						Home Improvements		Furnishings													
		Auto Loan	Home Loan	Invest-ments	Retire-ment Plans	Home Repair	Lawn & Garden	Comput-ers & Hard-ware	Major Appli-ances	TV, Radio, Sound Equip-ment	Furni-ture	Dine out/ Carry out	Sports Equip-ment	Fees & Tickets	Toys & Games	Travel	Cable TV	Apparel & Services	Auto Repairs	Health Insur-ance	Pets & Supplies
97910	JORDAN VALLEY	68	47	25	45	55	62	47	58	54	46	63	70	40	62	48	57	58	57	69	80
97911	JUNTURA	15	10	5	10	12	13	10	12	12	10	14	15	9	13	10	12	12	12	15	17
97913	NYSSA	64	51	37	48	53	57	52	59	56	54	68	66	46	63	51	56	66	59	61	69
97914	ONTARIO	71	62	56	60	64	71	66	68	69	64	84	79	62	83	65	70	81	69	73	80
97917	RIVERSIDE	69	48	25	46	56	63	48	59	55	47	65	71	41	63	50	58	59	58	70	82
97918	VALE	70	55	36	53	60	67	55	63	61	55	73	74	50	70	56	63	67	62	71	80
97920	WESTFALL	0	0	0	0	0	0	0	0	0	0	0	0	0	0	0	0	0	0	0	0
	OREGON	87	85	86	85	86	91	86	87	86	85	106	102	85	106	85	84	103	87	86	100
	UNITED STATES	100	100	100	100	100	100	100	100	100	100	100	100	100	100	100	100	100	100	100	100

PENNSYLVANIA POPULATION CHANGE

A 15001-15212

#	POST OFFICE NAME	COUNTY FIPS CODE	POPULATION 2000	2004	2009	2000-2004 ANNUAL RATE % Rate	State Centile	HOUSEHOLDS 2000	2004	2009	% Annual Rate 2000-2004	2004 Average HH Size	FAMILIES 2000	2004	% Annual Rate 2000-2004
15001	ALIQUIPPA	007	35908	35258	34643	-0.4	19	14566	14593	14596	0.0	2.39	10241	10186	-0.1
15003	AMBRIDGE	007	12909	12483	12150	-0.8	8	5780	5696	5642	-0.3	2.17	3533	3443	-0.6
15005	BADEN	007	9343	9449	9393	0.3	53	3755	3869	3914	0.7	2.39	2741	2814	0.6
15007	BAKERSTOWN	003	229	245	248	1.6	89	85	93	95	2.1	2.63	60	65	1.9
15009	BEAVER	007	14980	14688	14395	-0.5	18	6005	5992	5970	-0.1	2.29	4082	4043	-0.2
15010	BEAVER FALLS	007	29728	29161	28616	-0.5	18	11591	11551	11512	-0.1	2.38	7982	7901	-0.2
15012	BELLE VERNON	129	17701	17832	17971	0.2	47	7348	7488	7638	0.5	2.36	5121	5183	0.3
15014	BRACKENRIDGE	003	3557	3403	3276	-1.0	4	1514	1468	1433	-0.7	2.24	937	899	-1.0
15015	BRADFORDWOODS	003	1182	1176	1149	-0.1	33	470	481	482	0.6	2.44	380	387	0.4
15017	BRIDGEVILLE	003	15744	16082	16003	0.5	64	6671	6957	7050	1.0	2.14	4056	4188	0.8
15018	BUENA VISTA	003	643	635	620	-0.3	25	271	274	273	0.3	2.24	211	212	0.1
15019	BULGER	125	1753	1825	1868	1.0	78	674	714	744	1.4	2.54	490	515	1.2
15021	BURGETTSTOWN	125	8249	8166	8177	-0.2	27	3253	3288	3358	0.3	2.44	2349	2355	0.1
15022	CHARLEROI	125	11808	11474	11414	-0.7	11	5142	5085	5150	-0.3	2.22	3240	3176	-0.5
15024	CHESWICK	003	8293	8188	7988	-0.3	25	3327	3345	3323	0.1	2.40	2293	2293	0.0
15025	CLAIRTON	003	17740	16997	16386	-1.0	4	7351	7165	7032	-0.6	2.33	4755	4606	-0.8
15026	CLINTON	007	3468	3488	3453	0.1	46	1271	1306	1318	0.6	2.67	972	992	0.5
15027	CONWAY	007	2295	2203	2139	-1.0	5	991	974	965	-0.4	2.24	659	641	-0.7
15030	CREIGHTON	003	1394	1336	1286	-1.0	5	613	599	588	-0.5	2.16	374	363	-0.7
15031	CUDDY	003	337	345	341	0.6	66	134	140	142	1.0	2.46	88	91	0.8
15033	DONORA	125	5769	5604	5569	-0.7	10	2515	2489	2519	-0.2	2.19	1470	1436	-0.6
15034	DRAVOSBURG	003	2015	1901	1819	-1.4	1	948	915	894	-0.8	2.08	563	537	-1.1
15035	EAST MC KEESPORT	003	2261	2154	2069	-1.1	3	1035	1012	994	-0.5	2.13	609	588	-0.8
15037	ELIZABETH	003	11788	11705	11453	-0.2	31	4620	4684	4675	0.3	2.46	3429	3457	0.2
15042	FREEDOM	007	8293	8470	8482	0.5	64	3100	3247	3319	1.1	2.61	2393	2486	0.9
15043	GEORGETOWN	007	2947	2974	2948	0.2	49	1059	1092	1101	0.7	2.72	841	861	0.6
15044	GIBSONIA	003	23205	24305	24516	1.1	82	8272	8799	9022	1.5	2.72	6462	6844	1.4
15045	GLASSPORT	003	4993	4806	4639	-0.9	6	2187	2155	2125	-0.4	2.21	1356	1323	-0.6
15049	HARWICK	003	982	998	985	0.4	58	473	495	500	1.1	2.02	280	290	0.8
15050	HOOKSTOWN	007	2242	2260	2242	0.2	48	796	820	828	0.7	2.74	619	632	0.5
15051	INDIANOLA	003	779	779	764	0.0	39	318	322	320	0.3	2.31	244	246	0.2
15052	INDUSTRY	007	4184	4088	3996	-0.5	14	1600	1603	1600	0.0	2.52	1238	1232	-0.1
15055	LAWRENCE	125	688	732	756	1.5	88	340	371	392	2.1	1.97	225	243	1.8
15056	LEETSDALE	003	1215	1157	1111	-1.1	3	570	553	541	-0.7	2.09	338	324	-1.0
15057	MC DONALD	125	12766	12866	12880	0.2	47	4943	5078	5179	0.6	2.53	3618	3687	0.5
15059	MIDLAND	007	4811	4798	4745	-0.1	36	2034	2070	2084	0.4	2.30	1304	1311	0.1
15060	MIDWAY	125	678	659	655	-0.7	11	277	274	277	-0.3	2.40	200	196	-0.5
15061	MONACA	007	13650	13400	13140	-0.4	19	5463	5472	5463	0.0	2.40	3868	3849	-0.1
15062	MONESSEN	129	8673	8442	8400	-0.6	12	3917	3840	3851	-0.5	2.17	2454	2382	-0.7
15063	MONONGAHELA	125	12776	12519	12426	-0.5	17	5333	5331	5394	0.0	2.31	3648	3616	-0.2
15064	MORGAN	003	480	456	437	-1.2	3	221	214	208	-0.8	2.13	150	143	-1.1
15065	NATRONA HEIGHTS	003	12024	11489	11059	-1.1	4	5216	5090	4996	-0.6	2.24	3453	3342	-0.8
15066	NEW BRIGHTON	007	13919	13571	13277	-0.6	13	5561	5506	5470	-0.2	2.42	3805	3742	-0.4
15067	NEW EAGLE	125	2292	2386	2435	1.0	78	978	1036	1075	1.4	2.30	662	693	1.1
15068	NEW KENSINGTON	129	41600	40915	40798	-0.4	21	17459	17300	17411	-0.2	2.33	11406	11231	-0.4
15071	OAKDALE	003	8576	9169	9287	1.6	89	3476	3789	3912	2.1	2.41	2323	2508	1.8
15074	ROCHESTER	007	9524	9351	9186	-0.4	19	3879	3874	3871	0.0	2.35	2533	2519	-0.1
15076	RUSSELLTON	003	960	977	965	0.4	60	415	432	436	1.0	2.26	306	317	0.8
15077	SHIPPINGPORT	007	138	140	139	0.3	56	52	54	54	0.9	2.57	40	41	0.6
15078	SLOVAN	125	1244	1218	1212	-0.5	16	506	504	511	-0.1	2.42	352	348	-0.3
15083	SUTERSVILLE	129	1120	1085	1080	-0.7	8	479	469	471	-0.5	2.31	337	326	-0.8
15084	TARENTUM	003	10834	10451	10102	-0.8	7	4543	4468	4402	-0.4	2.32	2998	2926	-0.6
15085	TRAFFORD	129	8084	7986	7972	-0.3	25	3350	3340	3364	-0.1	2.39	2372	2348	-0.2
15086	WARRENDALE	003	469	479	474	0.5	64	184	191	193	0.9	2.48	151	156	0.8
15089	WEST NEWTON	129	8951	8686	8627	-0.7	10	3611	3528	3532	-0.6	2.45	2578	2501	-0.7
15090	WEXFORD	003	19198	20485	20768	1.5	89	6597	7158	7379	1.9	2.83	5251	5666	1.8
15101	ALLISON PARK	003	24741	24402	23839	-0.3	24	8950	8975	8919	0.1	2.62	6870	6864	0.0
15102	BETHEL PARK	003	31356	31826	31513	0.4	57	12395	12827	12939	0.8	2.46	8907	9184	0.7
15104	BRADDOCK	003	11272	10566	10084	-1.5	1	4633	4395	4258	-1.2	2.39	2877	2701	-1.5
15106	CARNEGIE	003	18931	18724	18304	-0.3	27	8752	8825	8790	0.2	2.10	5123	5125	0.0
15108	CORAOPOLIS	003	39163	39531	39057	0.2	50	15399	15858	15962	0.7	2.36	10392	10631	0.5
15110	DUQUESNE	003	7262	6856	6562	-1.3	2	3148	3030	2953	-0.9	2.23	1834	1742	-1.2
15112	EAST PITTSBURGH	003	3774	3700	3599	-0.5	18	1762	1762	1749	0.0	2.09	966	953	-0.3
15116	GLENSHAW	003	14009	13759	13401	-0.4	20	5514	5541	5510	0.1	2.48	4142	4129	-0.1
15120	HOMESTEAD	003	20506	20055	19523	-0.5	15	8957	8920	8841	-0.1	2.22	5425	5339	-0.4
15122	WEST MIFFLIN	003	22053	21777	21292	-0.3	25	9317	9399	9373	0.2	2.30	6353	6342	0.0
15126	IMPERIAL	003	8227	8698	8767	1.3	85	3293	3538	3628	1.7	2.45	2293	2438	1.5
15129	SOUTH PARK	003	11433	11368	11142	-0.1	33	4316	4411	4423	0.5	2.55	3177	3217	0.3
15131	MC KEESPORT	003	8930	8798	8597	-0.4	23	3826	3849	3832	0.1	2.24	2529	2523	-0.1
15132	MC KEESPORT	003	26051	24752	23785	-1.2	3	10677	10281	10028	-0.9	2.28	6515	6205	-1.1
15133	MC KEESPORT	003	7025	6737	6501	-1.0	5	3004	2950	2908	-0.4	2.27	2002	1947	-0.7
15135	MC KEESPORT	003	5624	5413	5236	-0.9	6	2275	2236	2205	-0.4	2.42	1641	1600	-0.6
15136	MC KEES ROCKS	003	21757	20906	20202	-0.9	5	9093	8864	8704	-0.6	2.32	5826	5648	-0.7
15137	NORTH VERSAILLES	003	11155	10820	10502	-0.7	9	4955	4933	4895	-0.1	2.17	3113	3065	-0.4
15139	OAKMONT	003	6907	6700	6493	-0.7	9	3115	3082	3042	-0.3	2.04	1708	1668	-0.6
15140	PITCAIRN	003	3672	3469	3320	-1.3	2	1671	1612	1575	-0.8	2.15	910	866	-1.2
15142	PRESTO	003	610	728	778	4.3	99	219	268	293	4.9	2.72	152	184	4.6
15143	SEWICKLEY	003	16640	16675	16416	0.1	42	6631	6760	6775	0.5	2.42	4685	4754	0.3
15144	SPRINGDALE	003	4398	4231	4081	-0.9	6	1908	1866	1831	-0.5	2.26	1213	1178	-0.7
15145	TURTLE CREEK	003	7689	7458	7224	-0.7	9	3427	3393	3350	-0.2	2.13	1930	1889	-0.5
15146	MONROEVILLE	003	29366	29626	29285	0.2	49	12380	12806	12930	0.8	2.24	8046	8233	0.5
15147	VERONA	003	20407	20155	19726	-0.3	25	8561	8690	8701	0.4	2.29	5768	5809	0.2
15148	WILMERDING	003	2892	2704	2578	-1.6	0	1363	1301	1266	-1.1	2.06	714	673	-1.4
15201	PITTSBURGH	003	14367	13535	12951	-1.4	1	6568	6319	6163	-0.9	2.10	3535	3364	-1.2
15202	PITTSBURGH	003	21015	20149	19411	-1.0	5	9970	9764	9592	-0.5	2.03	5035	4864	-0.8
15203	PITTSBURGH	003	9382	9256	9057	-0.3	24	4839	4904	4907	0.3	1.84	1829	1807	-0.3
15204	PITTSBURGH	003	9634	8995	8571	-1.6	0	3870	3680	3571	-1.2	2.44	2564	2413	-1.4
15205	PITTSBURGH	003	23355	22911	22362	-0.5	18	10512	10543	10495	0.1	2.15	5956	5898	-0.2
15206	PITTSBURGH	003	32883	31929	31014	-0.7	10	15032	14930	14793	-0.2	2.05	7566	7378	-0.6
15207	PITTSBURGH	003	12968	12797	12517	-0.3	24	5545	5576	5554	0.1	2.25	3367	3349	-0.1
15208	PITTSBURGH	003	13494	12468	11833	-1.8	0	5618	5295	5124	-1.4	2.34	3385	3158	-1.6
15209	PITTSBURGH	003	13200	12978	12665	-0.4	21	5523	5531	5499	0.0	2.32	3558	3549	-0.1
15210	PITTSBURGH	003	31453	29648	28380	-1.4	1	12779	12273	11973	-1.0	2.41	8001	7607	-1.2
15211	PITTSBURGH	003	12420	11735	11236	-1.3	2	5917	5724	5596	-0.8	2.05	2792	2660	-1.1
15212	PITTSBURGH	003	31869	30181	28951	-1.3	2	14019	13531	13223	-0.8	2.18	7661	7305	-1.1
	PENNSYLVANIA					0.3					0.7	2.44			0.6
	UNITED STATES					1.2					1.3	2.58			1.1

ZIP CODE #	POST OFFICE NAME	RACE (%) White 2000	White 2004	Black 2000	Black 2004	Asian/Pacific 2000	Asian/Pacific 2004	% Hispanic Origin 2000	% Hispanic Origin 2004	2004 AGE DISTRIBUTION (%) 0-4	5-9	10-14	15-19	20-24	25-44	45-64	65-84	85+	18+	MEDIAN AGE 2004	% 2004 Males	% 2004 Females
15001	ALIQUIPPA	85.9	85.4	12.8	13.1	0.3	0.4	0.7	0.8	5.5	5.6	6.7	6.1	5.3	25.0	26.4	17.2	2.2	78.2	42.5	47.4	52.6
15003	AMBRIDGE	90.5	88.8	7.3	8.7	0.4	0.5	1.3	1.5	5.9	5.7	5.6	5.5	5.6	24.8	24.4	19.1	3.5	79.5	43.0	47.7	52.3
15005	BADEN	98.3	97.9	0.7	0.9	0.3	0.4	0.6	0.7	5.1	5.8	6.1	5.3	4.4	23.8	29.7	17.0	2.7	79.6	44.6	47.6	52.4
15007	BAKERSTOWN	97.4	97.1	1.8	2.5	0.0	0.0	1.3	1.2	8.2	7.8	6.9	7.8	7.4	23.7	25.7	11.4	1.2	72.2	37.1	49.0	51.0
15009	BEAVER	97.0	96.4	2.0	2.4	0.4	0.5	0.7	0.8	4.6	5.1	6.2	5.7	4.9	21.8	28.4	19.3	4.1	80.5	46.1	46.8	53.2
15010	BEAVER FALLS	90.8	89.6	7.1	8.1	0.5	0.6	0.6	0.7	5.3	5.5	6.6	7.1	7.5	23.6	26.1	15.8	2.7	78.7	41.4	47.3	52.7
15012	BELLE VERNON	96.9	96.4	2.0	2.3	0.3	0.4	0.5	0.6	5.3	5.7	6.2	5.6	4.8	24.8	27.3	17.4	2.9	79.3	43.4	47.6	52.4
15014	BRACKENRIDGE	95.0	93.9	3.5	4.4	0.3	0.3	0.5	0.6	5.0	5.1	5.9	5.4	5.9	26.9	24.8	16.8	4.3	80.4	42.3	45.1	54.9
15015	BRADFORDWOODS	98.4	98.0	0.1	0.1	1.0	1.4	0.8	0.9	4.1	5.4	5.9	4.7	3.8	19.4	39.1	16.6	1.1	81.7	48.8	49.2	50.9
15017	BRIDGEVILLE	93.6	92.0	4.1	5.2	1.3	1.7	0.8	0.9	5.7	5.6	5.3	5.1	4.6	27.6	26.0	15.2	4.9	80.1	42.7	46.5	53.5
15018	BUENA VISTA	97.1	96.2	2.3	2.8	0.2	0.3	0.2	0.2	5.0	5.7	6.1	6.0	4.9	23.2	30.1	16.1	3.0	79.4	44.4	48.8	51.2
15019	BULGER	97.3	97.0	1.7	1.9	0.1	0.1	0.2	0.3	6.0	6.3	7.3	6.1	5.2	26.8	27.7	12.6	2.0	76.4	40.4	49.7	50.3
15021	BURGETTSTOWN	97.7	97.4	1.2	1.4	0.2	0.2	1.0	1.1	5.5	5.8	6.7	5.7	4.8	25.6	28.0	15.5	2.3	78.5	42.6	49.7	50.3
15022	CHARLEROI	96.8	96.3	2.1	2.4	0.3	0.4	0.7	0.7	5.1	5.3	5.6	5.0	5.1	24.4	26.9	18.8	3.9	81.0	44.7	47.0	53.0
15024	CHESWICK	98.3	97.9	0.6	0.7	0.6	0.7	0.5	0.6	4.8	5.3	6.0	5.6	4.8	24.4	28.0	18.6	2.4	80.1	44.4	47.9	52.1
15025	CLAIRTON	83.5	81.7	14.2	15.8	0.7	0.8	0.7	0.8	5.3	5.7	6.7	6.4	5.3	24.8	26.8	15.9	3.1	78.0	42.2	46.8	53.2
15026	CLINTON	98.6	98.4	0.4	0.5	0.1	0.1	0.9	1.0	5.8	6.7	8.0	6.7	5.0	27.4	29.1	10.3	1.0	75.3	39.8	50.7	49.3
15027	CONWAY	98.3	97.9	1.3	1.5	0.0	0.0	0.5	0.5	5.0	5.3	5.5	5.0	4.8	23.9	27.3	20.5	2.8	81.5	45.3	47.5	52.5
15030	CREIGHTON	97.4	96.7	1.5	2.0	0.1	0.2	0.1	0.2	5.5	5.6	5.2	4.7	4.6	27.8	25.7	16.8	4.0	80.8	43.0	46.5	53.5
15031	CUDDY	95.0	93.9	3.6	4.6	0.3	0.3	0.3	0.0	5.5	5.8	6.7	5.5	5.8	23.5	31.0	13.0	3.2	78.6	43.1	47.0	53.0
15033	DONORA	82.4	80.4	14.6	16.3	0.3	0.3	2.0	2.2	5.8	5.9	6.8	5.3	5.2	24.2	23.9	18.6	4.3	78.2	42.7	45.5	54.5
15034	DRAVOSBURG	98.7	98.5	0.5	0.7	0.0	0.0	0.6	0.6	5.7	5.8	5.2	4.0	4.8	27.0	27.8	17.2	2.6	81.0	43.5	45.7	54.3
15035	EAST MC KEESPORT	95.7	94.6	2.8	3.6	0.1	0.2	0.7	0.9	5.5	5.4	5.2	5.1	5.0	27.8	25.7	17.1	3.2	80.8	42.5	48.3	51.7
15037	ELIZABETH	97.0	96.3	2.0	2.5	0.3	0.4	0.3	0.4	4.7	5.1	6.3	5.7	4.9	23.1	29.4	18.1	2.7	80.3	45.1	47.4	52.6
15042	FREEDOM	97.1	96.8	1.7	1.9	0.2	0.3	0.4	0.5	5.8	6.2	6.6	6.5	6.0	26.4	28.9	12.4	1.2	77.5	40.6	49.5	50.5
15043	GEORGETOWN	97.8	97.5	0.5	0.7	0.1	0.1	0.8	0.9	6.6	7.0	7.6	6.8	6.0	27.9	27.4	9.7	1.0	74.6	38.1	49.9	50.1
15044	GIBSONIA	98.0	97.4	0.5	0.7	1.0	1.3	0.5	0.6	7.1	8.0	8.5	6.9	4.7	25.0	28.0	10.0	2.0	71.7	39.8	48.7	51.3
15045	GLASSPORT	98.2	97.9	0.6	0.7	0.2	0.3	0.8	1.0	4.8	4.9	6.3	6.0	6.1	25.1	25.6	18.4	2.9	80.4	42.9	47.3	52.7
15049	HARWICK	99.8	99.8	0.0	0.0	0.0	0.0	0.1	0.1	3.8	4.2	4.9	4.7	3.5	26.2	28.4	21.8	2.5	84.1	46.7	46.7	53.3
15050	HOOKSTOWN	98.8	98.5	0.2	0.3	0.2	0.2	0.6	0.8	6.6	7.4	7.6	6.6	5.5	28.1	28.0	9.4	0.9	74.0	38.0	50.3	49.7
15051	INDIANOLA	95.9	94.7	1.4	1.8	2.2	2.7	0.6	0.8	4.5	7.3	10.5	8.1	3.3	23.9	27.9	11.3	3.2	71.6	41.7	48.9	51.1
15052	INDUSTRY	97.1	96.6	1.9	2.3	0.1	0.1	1.1	1.3	4.9	5.3	6.4	6.4	5.7	24.2	29.7	15.9	1.5	79.3	43.2	49.3	50.7
15055	LAWRENCE	93.9	93.0	3.9	4.5	1.2	1.4	0.9	1.2	5.2	5.5	5.7	5.1	4.4	29.8	28.4	14.1	1.9	80.5	41.6	45.1	54.9
15056	LEETSDALE	89.3	87.3	7.2	8.9	0.0	0.0	1.7	1.7	5.2	4.9	5.4	6.4	6.7	23.0	25.9	19.3	3.2	80.8	43.8	45.5	54.5
15057	MC DONALD	96.3	95.7	2.6	3.0	0.3	0.4	0.4	0.4	6.4	6.6	6.7	6.1	5.2	27.2	26.9	13.0	1.9	76.3	40.3	49.2	50.8
15059	MIDLAND	83.2	81.2	14.3	16.2	0.0	0.0	2.6	2.8	6.5	6.3	6.6	5.9	6.4	24.4	23.9	17.4	2.7	77.0	41.0	46.9	53.1
15060	MIDWAY	98.5	98.6	0.7	0.8	0.2	0.2	0.6	0.8	5.2	5.2	5.9	5.8	5.6	27.3	27.3	15.2	2.6	80.1	42.3	48.0	52.1
15061	MONACA	96.6	95.9	2.3	2.8	0.3	0.4	0.7	0.8	5.3	5.5	6.4	6.4	6.4	26.0	26.8	15.2	1.9	79.1	41.2	48.5	51.5
15062	MONESSEN	83.7	82.0	14.0	15.5	0.2	0.3	0.8	0.9	5.0	5.3	5.8	5.2	4.5	21.7	24.8	23.4	4.4	80.7	46.8	46.1	53.9
15063	MONONGAHELA	96.9	96.4	1.9	2.2	0.2	0.2	0.7	0.8	4.6	5.0	6.0	5.5	5.0	23.4	28.1	19.4	3.2	80.9	45.4	47.5	52.5
15064	MORGAN	97.1	96.3	2.3	3.1	0.2	0.4	0.2	0.2	7.7	7.5	7.2	5.3	5.3	29.2	24.1	11.8	2.0	74.3	38.8	50.7	49.3
15065	NATRONA HEIGHTS	95.2	94.1	3.4	4.3	0.4	0.5	0.5	0.6	5.5	5.5	5.8	5.8	5.5	24.0	27.2	17.7	3.1	79.7	43.6	46.8	53.2
15066	NEW BRIGHTON	91.9	90.7	6.0	7.0	0.2	0.2	0.4	0.5	6.1	6.1	6.7	6.6	6.7	26.5	26.2	13.4	1.8	77.0	39.6	48.0	52.0
15067	NEW EAGLE	97.0	96.7	1.1	1.3	0.6	0.7	0.1	0.1	4.8	5.2	6.8	5.2	5.3	25.9	27.1	17.4	2.3	79.9	42.8	47.7	52.3
15068	NEW KENSINGTON	92.4	91.6	5.9	6.5	0.3	0.4	0.6	0.7	5.3	5.6	6.5	5.9	5.4	24.7	26.6	17.1	3.0	78.9	42.9	47.5	52.5
15071	OAKDALE	93.7	92.3	2.3	2.9	3.1	3.8	0.9	1.0	6.3	6.1	6.3	5.8	5.4	31.1	26.0	11.7	1.3	77.5	39.3	49.0	51.0
15074	ROCHESTER	91.1	89.9	7.1	8.1	0.2	0.2	0.5	0.6	5.1	5.3	6.5	6.0	6.0	26.5	26.6	15.7	2.3	79.4	41.6	48.2	51.8
15076	RUSSELLTON	98.4	98.0	0.3	0.5	0.4	0.5	0.6	0.8	5.1	5.7	6.7	5.8	5.3	26.2	30.1	13.1	1.9	78.8	42.1	48.9	51.1
15077	SHIPPINGPORT	98.6	98.6	0.0	0.0	0.0	0.0	0.0	0.7	7.1	7.9	7.9	6.4	5.7	27.1	27.1	10.0	0.7	72.1	36.8	47.9	52.1
15078	SLOVAN	96.2	95.7	2.7	3.1	0.1	0.2	1.5	1.6	5.9	5.8	6.6	7.1	6.1	26.8	25.4	14.5	2.0	77.4	40.2	49.6	50.4
15083	SUTERSVILLE	99.4	99.2	0.2	0.3	0.1	0.1	0.2	0.2	3.9	4.2	5.8	5.8	5.2	26.9	26.5	19.1	2.7	82.5	44.0	48.2	51.8
15084	TARENTUM	96.5	95.8	1.8	2.3	0.5	0.7	0.7	0.7	5.2	5.3	6.1	6.0	6.1	27.2	27.6	14.6	2.0	79.7	41.6	48.0	52.0
15085	TRAFFORD	98.6	98.3	0.5	0.6	0.4	0.5	0.4	0.5	5.3	5.7	6.7	6.0	4.7	23.4	28.6	17.4	2.4	78.6	43.9	48.2	51.8
15086	WARRENDALE	97.9	97.3	0.6	0.6	1.3	1.7	0.4	0.4	6.7	7.7	7.7	7.3	5.2	27.1	27.4	9.8	1.0	72.4	38.7	51.4	48.6
15089	WEST NEWTON	98.0	97.7	1.0	1.2	0.2	0.3	0.4	0.5	5.0	5.4	6.5	5.7	5.4	25.9	28.8	14.9	2.3	79.5	42.4	48.2	51.8
15090	WEXFORD	94.5	93.2	1.5	1.9	3.2	3.9	0.8	0.9	7.0	8.5	9.2	7.2	4.6	24.1	29.7	8.3	1.3	70.4	39.0	49.0	51.0
15101	ALLISON PARK	96.6	95.7	1.0	1.3	1.7	2.2	0.6	0.6	5.8	6.5	7.4	7.2	5.4	23.9	28.2	13.8	1.9	75.9	41.4	48.4	51.6
15102	BETHEL PARK	97.1	96.4	1.1	1.3	1.1	1.4	0.5	0.5	5.2	5.9	7.0	6.5	4.6	23.0	29.5	16.2	2.3	77.7	43.7	48.0	52.0
15104	BRADDOCK	45.8	41.2	51.1	55.7	0.3	0.4	1.2	1.2	7.0	7.6	9.0	7.4	5.7	23.3	22.8	14.8	2.4	71.7	37.3	45.4	54.6
15106	CARNEGIE	94.2	93.1	3.3	4.1	1.2	1.5	0.8	0.9	5.2	5.2	5.4	5.2	5.0	26.9	26.2	18.0	3.0	81.1	43.3	47.1	52.9
15108	CORAOPOLIS	92.9	91.4	4.4	5.4	1.4	1.8	0.9	1.0	5.5	5.9	6.5	7.0	6.2	26.9	27.0	13.1	2.0	78.5	40.5	48.5	51.6
15110	DUQUESNE	48.8	43.1	47.9	53.5	0.2	0.2	0.7	0.8	8.8	7.7	7.4	6.9	7.4	22.6	21.0	15.0	3.2	72.2	36.2	44.7	55.3
15112	EAST PITTSBURGH	83.6	80.4	13.7	16.5	0.4	0.5	0.5	0.6	6.2	5.9	6.4	5.8	5.5	26.6	25.4	15.1	3.1	78.0	40.6	47.0	53.1
15116	GLENSHAW	97.4	96.8	0.4	0.6	1.5	1.9	0.6	0.6	5.1	5.7	6.9	6.1	4.5	23.9	28.7	17.3	2.0	78.3	43.8	48.0	52.0
15120	HOMESTEAD	84.8	82.8	12.6	14.3	0.9	1.1	0.7	0.8	5.2	5.5	6.4	5.9	5.2	25.0	26.0	17.7	3.2	79.3	43.0	46.5	53.5
15122	WEST MIFFLIN	89.4	87.6	9.1	10.7	0.3	0.4	0.6	0.6	5.2	5.3	6.4	5.9	5.3	24.0	26.4	18.6	3.0	79.5	43.6	47.1	52.9
15126	IMPERIAL	95.9	94.9	2.0	2.6	1.0	1.3	0.6	0.7	7.0	7.0	7.2	6.6	6.2	31.2	25.4	8.5	0.9	74.7	36.9	48.7	51.3
15129	SOUTH PARK	94.4	93.1	3.8	4.7	0.9	1.1	0.6	0.7	6.9	7.0	7.1	6.5	6.4	28.4	28.0	8.6	1.3	74.8	37.8	48.8	51.2
15131	MC KEESPORT	97.4	96.7	1.7	2.2	0.4	0.4	0.4	0.5	4.1	4.3	5.0	5.7	5.9	22.7	29.4	19.8	3.2	83.6	46.4	47.4	52.7
15132	MC KEESPORT	74.2	70.7	22.8	26.2	0.2	0.2	1.4	1.5	6.7	6.5	6.8	6.5	5.8	23.2	24.0	16.7	3.9	76.0	40.9	45.9	54.1
15133	MC KEESPORT	98.5	98.1	1.0	1.2	0.1	0.1	0.6	0.7	4.0	4.5	6.3	6.1	5.6	24.4	26.7	19.9	2.6	81.4	44.4	47.5	52.5
15135	MC KEESPORT	97.9	97.2	1.1	1.6	0.3	0.4	0.5	0.6	4.9	5.3	6.6	6.7	5.7	23.6	28.4	16.5	2.3	79.2	43.2	48.2	51.8
15136	MC KEES ROCKS	90.9	89.4	7.0	8.3	0.6	0.8	0.7	0.7	5.7	5.9	6.5	5.8	5.2	25.3	26.8	15.9	3.0	78.3	42.2	47.8	52.2
15137	NORTH VERSAILLES	87.8	85.9	9.8	11.4	0.8	1.0	0.5	0.5	5.2	5.3	5.7	5.6	5.1	25.9	26.4	17.9	3.0	80.4	43.2	47.1	52.9
15139	OAKMONT	97.8	97.3	0.9	1.2	0.5	0.6	0.6	0.7	4.5	4.8	5.6	5.5	4.1	23.8	26.4	19.0	6.3	81.5	46.0	44.3	55.8
15140	PITCAIRN	98.1	97.7	0.4	0.6	0.4	0.6	0.5	0.6	6.3	5.8	5.5	6.2	7.2	28.6	25.0	13.4	2.1	78.8	38.8	47.9	52.2
15142	PRESTO	96.7	95.9	1.0	1.4	1.0	1.4	0.5	0.7	5.1	5.9	6.6	5.4	3.9	24.5	33.1	13.5	2.2	78.7	44.3	49.0	51.0
15143	SEWICKLEY	94.4	93.2	3.4	4.2	1.2	1.5	0.6	0.7	5.3	6.1	7.1	6.4	4.2	22.5	30.5	15.3	2.5	77.1	44.0	47.2	52.9
15144	SPRINGDALE	99.1	98.9	0.3	0.3	0.1	0.1	0.2	0.3	4.4	4.7	6.6	6.6	5.7	25.2	27.3	17.0	2.7	80.0	43.1	47.7	52.3
15145	TURTLE CREEK	92.6	90.8	5.0	6.2	1.0	1.2	0.6	0.7	5.3	5.1	5.5	5.5	5.8	26.5	24.7	17.6	4.1	80.8	42.2	45.2	54.8
15146	MONROEVILLE	85.6	82.0	8.3	10.5	4.5	5.6	0.8	0.9	4.8	5.1	5.8	5.6	5.2	24.9	28.0	17.4	3.1	80.7	44.0	47.0	53.0
15147	VERONA	81.7	80.1	16.9	18.3	0.4	0.4	0.4	0.5	5.5	5.7	6.2	6.0	5.6	24.0	27.4	16.5	3.1	78.9	43.0	47.3	52.7
15148	WILMERDING	92.8	91.3	5.2	6.6	0.2	0.3	1.0	1.1	5.7	5.3	5.7	6.0	5.8	27.7	25.0	15.2	3.7	79.6	40.9	46.5	53.5
15201	PITTSBURGH	77.8	74.0	19.1	22.5	1.3	1.6	0.7	0.8	5.1	5.2	5.8	5.6	5.6	25.5	25.5	17.8	3.9	80.3	43.2	45.9	54.1
15202	PITTSBURGH	93.9	92.5	4.1	5.2	0.6	0.7	0.7	0.8	5.2	5.1	6.0	6.3	6.4	30.6	23.7	14.3	2.6	79.7	39.1	46.6	53.5
15203	PITTSBURGH	94.9	93.7	3.0	3.7	0.7	0.9	1.0	1.1	3.1	2.7	2.8	3.7	13.1	31.5	21.9	17.9	3.4	89.7	39.6	49.9	50.2
15204	PITTSBURGH	72.6	67.9	24.5	29.0	0.6	0.7	0.9	0.9	6.6	6.7	7.2	6.8	6.2	26.7	24.1	13.7	2.0	75.2	38.4	47.0	53.0
15205	PITTSBURGH	89.3	88.5	7.8	7.9	1.5	2.0	0.7	0.8	5.8	5.6	5.7	5.7	5.7	30.4	25.4	13.6	2.1	79.4	39.3	47.1	52.9
15206	PITTSBURGH	44.3	41.3	50.1	52.6	2.4	2.9	1.6	1.6	5.6	5.6	6.3	7.0	6.9	28.5	24.4	13.4	2.5	78.4	38.1	46.0	54.0
15207	PITTSBURGH	78.8	75.9	19.1	21.9	0.5	0.6	0.9	1.0	5.4	5.5	6.3	6.1	5.5	25.4	25.6	16.9	3.3	79.1	42.4	45.7	54.3
15208	PITTSBURGH	24.4	23.6	72.6	73.3	0.9	1.0	0.9	0.9	6.4	6.9	8.3	7.3	6.1	23.6	25.6	13.8	2.0	73.5	38.6	45.1	54.9
15209	PITTSBURGH	97.8	97.3	0.6	0.8	0.5	0.7	0.7	0.8	5.5	5.7	6.3	6.2	5.7	27.3	25.7	15.4	2.3	78.5	41.1	47.9	52.1
15210	PITTSBURGH	75.3	73.0	22.1	24.2	0.6	0.8	0.8	0.9	6.3	6.5	7.4	7.0	6.9	27.2	23.6	13.3	1.9	75.6	37.4	46.9	53.1
15211	PITTSBURGH	91.6	89.8	6.0	7.3	0.8	1.1	0.8	0.8	4.3	4.0	4.3	4.9	8.8	33.1	24.3	14.4	1.9	84.8	38.4	49.3	50.7
15212	PITTSBURGH	75.9	72.2	21.5	24.9	0.5	0.6	0.9	1.0	6.0	5.6	6.2	6.7	7.0	26.9	24.7	14.5	2.5	78.6	39.5	48.0	52.0
	PENNSYLVANIA	85.4	84.4	10.0	10.3	1.8	2.2	3.2	3.5	5.9	6.1	6.8	6.9	6.7	26.6	25.3	13.3	2.2	77.2	39.1	48.4	51.6
	UNITED STATES	75.1	73.6	12.3	12.5	3.8	4.2	12.5	14.1	6.9	6.7	7.2	7.0	7.3	28.6	23.8	10.8	1.7	75.1	36.0	49.1	50.9

#	POST OFFICE NAME	2004 Per Capita Income	2004 HH Income Base	2004 HOUSEHOLD INCOME DISTRIBUTION (%) Less than $25,000	$25,000 to $49,999	$50,000 to $99,999	$100,000 to $149,999	$150,000 or More	MEDIAN HOUSEHOLD INCOME 2004	2009	2004 National Centile	2004 State Centile	2004 Home Value Base	2004 HOME VALUE DISTRIBUTION (%) Less than $50,000	$50,000 to $89,999	$90,000 to $174,999	$175,000 to $399,999	$400,000 or More	2004 Median Home Value
15001	ALIQUIPPA	22032	14593	29.0	28.0	31.9	8.9	2.3	43100	51608	56	57	11226	14.0	22.2	48.9	14.0	0.9	107306
15003	AMBRIDGE	20925	5696	36.3	30.2	25.7	6.0	1.9	35649	42520	30	23	3697	15.0	41.9	34.7	7.3	1.1	83097
15005	BADEN	27794	3869	23.4	26.0	32.1	11.7	6.8	50581	61568	73	72	3295	4.2	21.6	45.6	25.9	2.9	123630
15007	BAKERSTOWN	21572	93	31.2	19.4	31.2	17.2	1.1	48680	64071	70	69	62	4.8	12.9	61.3	21.0	0.0	135714
15009	BEAVER	27056	5992	23.3	26.0	34.7	11.8	4.2	50662	60455	73	73	4389	5.0	13.0	53.6	26.8	1.7	134521
15010	BEAVER FALLS	22443	11551	26.7	30.4	32.5	7.4	3.0	43277	51459	57	57	8216	15.1	24.0	47.1	13.3	0.5	105591
15012	BELLE VERNON	22377	7488	30.9	30.7	28.6	7.0	2.8	38209	46207	40	36	5798	18.8	28.9	37.7	13.8	0.9	92854
15014	BRACKENRIDGE	23400	1468	35.6	28.9	28.3	5.3	2.0	35208	43537	28	21	1020	30.1	47.2	21.9	0.9	0.0	65462
15015	BRADFORDWOODS	67510	481	8.9	10.0	24.5	24.7	31.8	109670	139995	99	99	461	0.7	2.4	17.1	70.3	9.5	236739
15017	BRIDGEVILLE	30925	6957	19.1	26.5	34.8	13.4	6.3	54852	67904	79	80	4858	5.4	18.7	53.9	19.7	2.2	118016
15018	BUENA VISTA	28798	274	20.4	25.6	40.5	9.5	4.0	54819	67466	79	80	248	14.1	27.4	49.6	8.5	0.4	98400
15019	BULGER	19991	714	24.5	36.7	29.8	7.3	1.7	41017	49147	50	49	600	28.7	22.5	37.7	10.3	0.8	88333
15021	BURGETTSTOWN	21821	3288	25.8	29.4	34.4	7.9	2.5	45475	54956	63	63	2668	16.0	25.9	41.1	16.2	0.8	101049
15022	CHARLEROI	20462	5085	34.0	30.3	28.5	6.2	1.1	36051	43599	32	25	3633	23.3	38.8	32.3	5.3	0.3	73983
15024	CHESWICK	26710	3345	22.1	28.9	34.4	8.7	5.8	48958	61430	70	70	2712	12.6	22.5	49.1	13.9	2.0	105360
15025	CLAIRTON	23354	7165	31.5	25.7	29.2	9.1	4.4	42161	52748	53	54	5077	31.5	27.6	26.6	13.2	1.1	75453
15026	CLINTON	22313	1306	19.9	27.6	37.6	12.6	2.2	51853	61394	75	75	1130	21.4	13.7	36.8	26.3	1.8	118316
15027	CONWAY	22992	974	29.7	29.0	34.2	5.3	1.9	40688	49800	49	47	767	6.4	31.6	57.8	4.0	0.3	101850
15030	CREIGHTON	21539	599	29.9	32.7	31.1	5.3	1.0	38169	47572	40	36	444	32.7	38.1	25.5	3.6	0.2	70488
15031	CUDDY	18011	140	30.0	38.6	25.0	5.7	0.7	36162	47381	32	26	90	8.9	26.7	51.1	8.9	4.4	97647
15033	DONORA	20966	2489	39.4	30.7	25.8	3.5	0.7	32361	38577	19	11	1543	50.7	34.4	12.3	2.3	0.3	49580
15034	DRAVOSBURG	21210	915	35.4	31.9	27.5	3.3	1.9	35790	43436	31	24	630	32.1	56.0	11.9	0.0	0.0	59576
15035	EAST MC KEESPORT	19317	1012	37.1	32.8	25.4	3.2	1.6	33118	40259	21	14	674	24.9	56.5	17.4	1.2	0.0	65294
15037	ELIZABETH	24465	4684	22.7	31.5	33.4	8.7	3.8	45891	58039	64	64	3976	16.0	29.9	46.9	6.3	1.0	94397
15042	FREEDOM	23386	3247	20.4	25.0	41.8	10.4	2.4	53776	63015	78	78	2847	16.3	15.8	49.0	18.5	0.4	119376
15043	GEORGETOWN	20394	1092	23.1	29.4	35.1	10.7	1.7	47541	56214	67	67	947	18.5	26.3	36.6	16.5	2.1	100700
15044	GIBSONIA	36898	8799	12.7	17.7	35.8	19.3	14.5	72876	93106	92	94	7684	3.0	7.5	44.1	38.1	7.3	166721
15045	GLASSPORT	18394	2155	36.2	33.1	27.5	2.9	0.3	35569	42956	30	23	1463	44.8	41.7	12.0	1.2	0.3	54069
15049	HARWICK	26326	495	26.5	36.4	24.0	10.5	2.6	41061	50749	50	49	393	21.6	21.6	50.1	5.1	1.5	93897
15050	HOOKSTOWN	20466	820	23.5	28.8	35.0	10.4	2.3	48072	56066	68	68	715	19.4	21.5	37.5	20.7	0.8	105630
15051	INDIANOLA	45201	322	18.6	15.5	30.8	17.4	17.7	68800	94490	91	92	289	10.4	12.5	31.8	39.1	6.2	155147
15052	INDUSTRY	21773	1603	20.0	34.4	34.8	9.1	1.8	44222	54134	59	59	1377	9.2	28.8	52.1	9.6	0.4	104469
15055	LAWRENCE	36246	371	10.5	25.3	45.6	10.8	7.8	63106	76632	87	89	287	1.7	3.8	80.1	14.3	0.0	126136
15056	LEETSDALE	24451	553	36.2	33.1	19.4	7.4	4.0	34785	42809	27	19	336	24.1	43.2	23.8	7.4	1.5	70000
15057	MC DONALD	24125	5078	22.9	27.8	33.9	11.5	3.9	49277	60555	71	70	3980	15.2	22.4	38.7	22.5	1.2	108199
15059	MIDLAND	20265	2070	39.5	31.7	21.9	5.4	1.6	32285	37569	19	11	1290	30.9	30.7	32.0	6.1	0.4	73263
15060	MIDWAY	20696	274	25.9	33.6	33.2	5.1	2.2	41928	50442	53	53	216	9.7	38.9	47.2	4.2	0.0	91154
15061	MONACA	22889	5472	23.3	30.2	33.5	10.8	2.2	46918	56329	66	66	4067	9.3	22.3	50.5	17.5	0.5	111591
15062	MONESSEN	19695	3840	40.7	29.1	23.9	5.0	1.3	31120	37120	15	8	2938	32.5	37.7	26.7	3.1	0.0	65836
15063	MONONGAHELA	23035	5331	26.1	31.8	31.9	8.1	2.2	42984	52532	56	56	4356	17.9	27.1	43.3	11.2	0.5	95684
15064	MORGAN	26265	214	22.9	25.2	38.8	13.1	0.0	51927	64060	75	75	155	17.4	27.7	20.7	32.9	1.3	96250
15065	NATRONA HEIGHTS	22125	5090	30.0	30.9	30.3	6.9	1.9	39577	49273	45	42	3720	15.0	32.2	44.3	7.9	0.7	93569
15066	NEW BRIGHTON	17982	5506	33.6	33.5	27.7	4.5	0.7	35590	41959	30	23	3797	18.8	32.1	41.3	7.7	0.2	88977
15067	NEW EAGLE	18855	1036	31.2	40.1	23.7	4.2	1.0	34829	41122	27	20	785	33.8	35.0	25.0	6.2	0.0	67687
15068	NEW KENSINGTON	22138	17300	30.8	28.8	29.9	8.1	2.4	40689	49254	49	47	12301	13.0	28.3	44.6	13.5	0.6	102366
15071	OAKDALE	33607	3789	12.8	24.1	38.1	16.4	8.6	62798	79400	87	89	2603	8.0	19.4	54.0	15.9	2.7	115466
15074	ROCHESTER	20018	3874	28.6	34.6	31.0	4.4	1.4	38949	46615	43	40	2760	21.1	37.0	33.3	8.5	0.2	81808
15076	RUSSELLTON	28488	432	18.8	25.7	40.1	12.5	3.0	56934	73040	82	82	349	7.7	15.2	65.3	10.9	0.9	117578
15077	SHIPPINGPORT	21368	54	25.9	27.8	35.2	9.3	1.9	46547	56211	65	65	46	26.1	23.9	30.4	19.6	0.0	90000
15078	SLOVAN	19914	504	32.1	26.8	34.3	5.8	1.0	42196	51581	53	54	394	25.4	26.7	29.7	18.3	0.0	86800
15083	SUTERSVILLE	17971	469	32.4	40.7	21.5	4.9	0.4	32385	39202	19	11	389	19.0	26.7	42.7	10.8	0.8	93750
15084	TARENTUM	20688	4468	32.3	29.8	30.7	5.4	1.8	38295	47503	40	37	3164	25.5	35.1	32.6	6.0	0.8	76729
15085	TRAFFORD	27100	3340	27.1	27.7	30.0	9.3	5.8	46104	55800	64	64	2677	6.2	17.5	57.8	16.0	2.4	118281
15086	WARRENDALE	86554	191	12.0	14.1	23.6	18.9	31.4	100387	134062	98	98	170	0.0	11.8	26.5	56.5	5.3	221154
15089	WEST NEWTON	21607	3528	30.8	28.5	30.1	7.7	2.9	40543	48978	48	47	2802	18.1	27.2	38.0	15.2	1.4	95556
15090	WEXFORD	48015	7158	10.6	12.8	26.2	20.3	30.1	100677	130580	98	98	6138	0.5	4.3	24.8	58.3	12.2	231448
15101	ALLISON PARK	35752	8975	12.4	18.5	37.5	19.1	12.6	71649	90500	92	93	7701	1.2	4.8	54.1	35.9	4.0	160527
15102	BETHEL PARK	32179	12827	14.7	23.5	35.8	17.5	8.5	64091	80629	88	90	10620	1.2	8.4	63.0	26.8	0.7	143712
15104	BRADDOCK	15309	4395	53.2	24.1	18.9	2.8	1.1	23060	27483	3	2	2327	71.9	22.7	5.4	0.1	0.0	35104
15106	CARNEGIE	28360	8825	26.6	31.3	28.2	9.0	4.9	42843	53883	56	56	5901	10.8	31.9	44.4	11.7	1.1	97544
15108	CORAOPOLIS	30240	15858	17.3	23.5	36.2	15.5	7.6	60518	75307	85	87	11752	6.3	14.6	49.5	28.1	1.5	138476
15110	DUQUESNE	14234	3030	54.3	25.5	17.0	2.8	0.4	22349	26888	3	2	1479	62.1	32.7	4.7	0.1	0.3	41533
15112	EAST PITTSBURGH	19019	1762	40.4	30.5	24.2	4.0	0.9	32157	38881	18	11	938	32.0	49.7	17.6	0.8	0.0	61304
15116	GLENSHAW	32280	5541	14.4	22.3	40.5	15.2	7.7	62991	78432	87	89	4922	2.4	7.2	68.4	20.9	1.2	138057
15120	HOMESTEAD	21040	8920	36.1	30.1	26.8	5.3	1.7	35567	43839	30	23	6031	27.5	39.3	30.0	3.0	0.2	72545
15122	WEST MIFFLIN	22416	9399	28.8	27.7	33.6	8.5	1.6	43228	54237	57	57	7252	14.3	42.4	38.7	4.3	0.3	85254
15126	IMPERIAL	30486	3538	18.3	24.6	37.6	13.8	5.8	56328	68956	81	82	2825	28.0	13.1	38.7	19.5	0.7	110778
15129	SOUTH PARK	26588	4411	13.3	28.0	40.0	14.8	4.0	60468	74233	85	87	3291	1.2	12.7	66.9	18.8	0.4	130745
15131	MC KEESPORT	24839	3849	24.2	30.6	32.9	9.0	3.4	45789	56885	63	64	3055	14.2	30.4	45.8	9.0	0.5	95429
15132	MC KEESPORT	16061	10281	44.7	30.2	20.7	3.5	0.9	28164	33953	9	4	5885	54.8	33.6	10.3	1.1	0.2	47581
15133	MC KEESPORT	21671	2950	29.7	34.9	28.6	4.7	2.1	38330	47414	41	37	2396	24.4	58.4	16.0	1.3	0.0	66588
15135	MC KEESPORT	26581	2236	17.4	27.0	37.6	13.2	4.8	55160	68496	80	80	1717	8.9	30.2	45.5	15.4	0.0	104903
15136	MC KEES ROCKS	23819	8864	31.7	28.8	26.2	9.2	4.1	39135	49489	43	41	6037	25.8	27.4	32.0	14.2	0.7	85400
15137	NORTH VERSAILLES	20869	4933	33.1	33.4	26.3	5.6	1.6	36056	44527	32	26	3487	16.5	50.4	30.4	2.7	0.0	77243
15139	OAKMONT	33265	3082	21.6	27.8	31.8	11.1	7.7	50568	63481	73	72	1824	6.0	14.5	50.2	27.3	2.0	137421
15140	PITCAIRN	18184	1612	40.5	29.7	25.5	4.3	0.0	31043	38364	15	8	870	28.6	54.9	12.5	3.9	0.0	63720
15142	PRESTO	36217	268	13.1	26.9	34.3	10.8	14.9	60590	75593	85	87	231	7.4	22.9	35.1	14.7	19.9	114946
15143	SEWICKLEY	51937	6760	15.6	21.6	28.5	13.3	21.1	67906	88458	90	91	5538	4.7	10.7	34.7	30.8	19.1	174632
15144	SPRINGDALE	24369	1866	25.0	34.3	31.9	6.4	2.4	43109	52909	56	57	1288	10.3	40.8	43.3	5.4	0.3	89244
15145	TURTLE CREEK	23240	3393	34.7	29.1	26.8	5.8	3.7	36646	45522	34	28	1703	34.1	48.5	14.5	2.7	0.2	60112
15146	MONROEVILLE	30069	12806	21.2	26.0	33.2	12.5	7.1	52830	65809	77	76	9037	3.2	22.4	57.0	15.9	1.5	115878
15147	VERONA	23830	8690	25.7	29.9	33.4	8.8	2.1	44222	55712	59	59	6394	8.9	45.6	41.3	4.0	0.1	87120
15148	WILMERDING	17256	1301	41.1	38.4	17.5	2.4	0.5	29384	34841	11	5	606	46.2	44.9	7.9	0.2	0.8	52300
15201	PITTSBURGH	20904	6319	41.2	28.5	23.1	5.4	1.9	31717	38762	17	10	3599	40.3	38.6	19.3	1.8	0.1	58759
15202	PITTSBURGH	24983	9764	29.9	32.0	28.1	7.5	2.6	39617	48467	45	42	4947	9.5	34.0	47.5	8.3	0.8	95691
15203	PITTSBURGH	23305	4904	40.3	31.6	21.2	4.5	2.4	31498	37079	16	9	2320	29.9	33.9	30.3	5.7	0.2	72663
15204	PITTSBURGH	18888	3680	32.2	28.5	32.5	6.4	0.5	38685	48211	42	39	2601	25.5	52.1	21.5	0.9	0.0	68832
15205	PITTSBURGH	28806	10543	24.2	29.0	31.7	10.8	4.3	46967	59462	66	66	6666	8.9	33.9	43.0	13.0	1.2	97920
15206	PITTSBURGH	26581	14930	39.3	26.9	21.6	6.6	5.6	34197	41735	25	17	6432	21.7	34.0	28.6	12.8	2.9	82659
15207	PITTSBURGH	19417	5576	39.0	27.8	27.3	4.5	1.4	33881	41483	24	16	3668	33.1	41.5	24.4	1.0	0.1	64965
15208	PITTSBURGH	24856	5295	44.1	24.0	17.6	6.3	8.0	30023	36668	12	6	2754	33.4	25.0	20.4	17.7	3.5	71200
15209	PITTSBURGH	24134	5531	24.4	30.3	32.9	9.8	2.6	45359	56404	62	62	3985	13.7	23.6	51.4	11.4	0.0	107393
15210	PITTSBURGH	18296	12273	38.5	31.1	23.9	4.8	1.8	32144	38712	18	10	7616	41.5	46.0	11.9	0.5	0.0	55786
15211	PITTSBURGH	26625	5724	31.3	29.4	27.0	7.7	4.6	39377	49066	44	42	3078	31.1	35.8	23.8	7.0	2.3	67383
15212	PITTSBURGH	19190	13531	40.6	30.0	22.7	5.0	1.7	32053	39044	18	10	7510	33.2	36.7	27.4	2.5	0.3	68437
	PENNSYLVANIA	25764		25.8	27.2	31.2	10.2	5.7	46988	57000				11.9	18.4	40.7	25.1	4.1	123516
	UNITED STATES	25866		24.7	27.1	30.8	10.9	6.5	48124	56710				10.9	15.0	33.7	30.1	10.4	145905

ZIP CODE #	POST OFFICE NAME	FINANCIAL SERVICES: Auto Loan	Home Loan	Investments	Retirement Plans	THE HOME: Home Improvements: Home Repair	Lawn & Garden	Furnishings: Computers & Hardware	Major Appliances	TV, Radio, Sound Equipment	Furniture	ENTERTAINMENT: Dine out/Carry out	Sports Equipment	Fees & Tickets	Toys & Games	Travel	Cable TV	PERSONAL: Apparel & Services	Auto Repairs	Health Insurance	Pets & Supplies
15001	ALIQUIPPA	72	75	77	71	75	82	73	74	75	72	93	84	75	94	75	77	90	73	78	84
15003	AMBRIDGE	60	63	68	60	63	70	63	63	65	62	81	70	66	83	65	67	78	62	67	70
15005	BADEN	90	99	101	97	99	106	94	95	94	93	116	108	98	121	97	95	113	93	96	106
15007	BAKERSTOWN	89	75	59	75	79	89	78	83	82	76	100	95	74	99	77	84	94	82	90	98
15009	BEAVER	86	92	99	90	93	101	90	91	90	89	112	103	92	113	92	92	109	90	93	101
15010	BEAVER FALLS	73	78	84	75	78	85	76	76	77	75	96	87	79	99	78	79	94	76	78	86
15012	BELLE VERNON	77	72	66	69	74	83	72	75	76	71	93	86	71	94	73	78	89	75	81	88
15014	BRACKENRIDGE	69	75	81	73	76	83	74	74	75	72	94	83	78	99	76	77	91	73	77	81
15015	BRADFORDWOODS	212	257	289	256	255	268	235	236	222	236	280	267	251	284	244	221	277	229	224	257
15017	BRIDGEVILLE	91	99	112	99	99	106	98	97	97	97	121	112	101	123	100	96	118	97	96	107
15018	BUENA VISTA	83	100	110	96	98	103	93	93	90	92	113	105	99	119	96	90	112	90	89	101
15019	BULGER	73	72	67	69	73	79	70	72	72	70	89	82	71	91	71	73	86	72	75	83
15021	BURGETTSTOWN	74	76	73	72	77	85	73	75	76	72	94	86	76	99	76	78	90	74	80	87
15022	CHARLEROI	59	64	70	61	64	71	64	63	65	62	81	71	66	84	65	67	78	63	67	70
15024	CHESWICK	84	94	101	90	94	103	90	91	91	89	113	102	95	118	93	93	110	89	93	100
15025	CLAIRTON	73	77	84	74	77	84	76	76	78	76	96	85	79	98	78	80	94	75	79	85
15026	CLINTON	92	86	71	82	89	94	81	87	83	81	102	102	79	103	82	84	98	85	90	106
15027	CONWAY	66	77	85	73	76	83	72	72	72	72	90	81	77	93	75	74	88	71	74	79
15030	CREIGHTON	60	67	71	63	67	74	65	65	67	63	83	72	69	89	68	69	81	63	69	71
15031	CUDDY	57	63	67	59	63	70	61	61	63	59	78	68	65	84	64	65	76	60	65	67
15033	DONORA	59	62	71	59	62	70	64	62	67	62	83	71	67	88	66	69	81	63	67	69
15034	DRAVOSBURG	56	63	67	59	63	69	61	61	62	59	77	68	65	83	63	64	75	59	64	67
15035	EAST MC KEESPORT	53	57	60	54	58	64	57	56	59	55	73	63	60	79	59	61	70	55	60	62
15037	ELIZABETH	78	89	95	85	88	96	85	85	85	83	105	95	89	110	88	87	103	83	87	93
15042	FREEDOM	86	91	87	88	92	96	84	87	84	83	104	101	87	110	87	85	102	85	88	102
15043	GEORGETOWN	89	79	60	75	84	90	73	81	78	73	95	97	72	97	75	80	90	79	88	105
15044	GIBSONIA	134	159	170	160	156	158	145	145	137	146	172	168	154	179	148	133	171	141	133	160
15045	GLASSPORT	52	57	61	54	58	64	56	56	58	54	72	62	60	78	58	60	70	55	60	62
15049	HARWICK	68	74	78	70	75	83	73	72	76	70	94	81	77	102	76	79	91	71	78	80
15050	HOOKSTOWN	90	80	61	76	85	91	74	82	79	74	96	98	73	98	76	81	91	80	89	106
15051	INDIANOLA	142	165	180	164	165	175	153	155	147	153	184	175	161	186	158	147	181	151	150	170
15052	INDUSTRY	75	81	82	77	82	88	76	78	77	75	95	90	79	99	79	78	93	76	80	90
15055	LAWRENCE	91	105	129	108	103	106	104	100	98	103	124	120	107	127	104	95	123	101	91	109
15056	LEETSDALE	74	68	61	65	71	82	70	74	74	68	90	82	68	89	71	77	85	73	82	85
15057	MC DONALD	84	89	87	86	90	96	85	86	85	83	106	99	87	111	87	87	103	84	88	99
15059	MIDLAND	65	62	63	58	62	70	64	65	68	63	83	73	64	83	64	70	80	65	70	74
15060	MIDWAY	65	70	72	66	70	78	69	68	71	66	88	76	72	95	71	73	85	67	73	76
15061	MONACA	71	80	89	77	80	86	78	77	78	76	97	87	82	102	80	79	95	76	78	85
15062	MONESSEN	58	59	61	55	59	67	59	60	62	58	76	66	60	76	60	65	73	60	65	67
15063	MONONGAHELA	70	76	81	73	77	85	74	75	76	73	94	83	78	99	77	78	91	73	79	83
15064	MORGAN	71	86	95	84	84	86	80	79	76	79	96	91	85	102	82	75	95	77	74	86
15065	NATRONA HEIGHTS	67	69	73	67	70	77	69	69	71	68	87	79	71	90	70	72	85	69	72	78
15066	NEW BRIGHTON	59	61	61	58	62	68	60	61	62	59	77	69	62	81	62	64	74	60	64	69
15067	NEW EAGLE	69	58	44	52	62	70	56	63	63	56	76	73	54	77	58	67	71	62	73	80
15068	NEW KENSINGTON	71	72	74	69	73	80	72	73	74	70	91	83	73	93	73	76	88	72	77	83
15071	OAKDALE	105	122	139	123	120	123	116	115	111	116	140	134	121	144	118	109	138	114	106	126
15074	ROCHESTER	65	66	68	64	67	73	66	67	67	65	83	77	67	86	67	68	81	66	69	76
15076	RUSSELLTON	81	98	108	95	96	100	91	91	88	90	111	104	97	117	94	88	110	88	86	99
15077	SHIPPINGPORT	88	79	60	75	83	89	73	81	77	73	94	96	71	96	75	79	89	78	87	104
15078	SLOVAN	62	67	71	63	68	75	66	66	69	64	85	73	70	92	69	71	82	64	71	73
15083	SUTERSVILLE	53	58	61	55	59	65	57	57	59	55	74	63	61	80	59	62	71	56	61	63
15084	TARENTUM	65	67	67	64	68	75	66	67	69	65	85	76	68	89	68	71	82	66	71	76
15085	TRAFFORD	90	94	92	91	95	102	90	93	91	89	112	106	92	114	92	92	108	91	95	105
15086	WARRENDALE	285	356	387	367	344	347	313	305	285	318	363	353	345	377	319	276	366	294	271	338
15089	WEST NEWTON	77	73	70	69	75	83	72	75	76	71	93	87	72	94	73	78	89	75	81	90
15090	WEXFORD	183	216	237	224	209	213	198	193	183	201	233	224	212	238	199	177	233	189	173	213
15101	ALLISON PARK	124	148	166	148	146	151	137	136	130	137	164	156	145	169	141	128	163	133	127	149
15102	BETHEL PARK	103	121	135	120	120	126	113	113	108	113	136	129	119	139	116	108	134	111	108	124
15104	BRADDOCK	52	45	49	41	44	53	49	50	55	50	67	54	48	63	48	58	64	51	57	57
15106	CARNEGIE	76	84	97	82	83	91	84	82	85	82	106	93	88	110	86	86	103	82	84	90
15108	CORAOPOLIS	96	108	123	109	107	111	105	103	102	105	128	120	109	131	106	100	126	103	98	113
15110	DUQUESNE	46	38	42	35	38	45	43	43	48	43	59	48	41	55	42	51	56	45	49	50
15112	EAST PITTSBURGH	52	53	59	51	53	60	56	54	58	54	71	61	57	74	56	59	69	55	57	60
15116	GLENSHAW	102	120	136	116	119	127	113	113	110	112	138	127	120	143	117	111	136	111	111	123
15120	HOMESTEAD	63	63	66	60	64	72	65	65	68	63	84	72	66	86	66	70	80	64	70	72
15122	WEST MIFFLIN	68	73	79	70	73	80	72	72	73	71	91	81	75	93	74	75	88	71	75	80
15126	IMPERIAL	109	112	104	113	110	114	106	108	103	108	129	125	107	130	105	101	126	106	102	122
15129	SOUTH PARK	90	102	113	104	100	102	98	96	94	98	118	113	101	121	98	91	117	96	88	105
15131	MC KEESPORT	73	83	91	78	82	91	78	80	78	78	97	87	82	99	82	81	95	78	83	86
15132	MC KEESPORT	50	48	52	45	49	56	51	51	54	50	67	56	51	67	51	57	64	51	56	57
15133	MC KEESPORT	63	70	75	66	70	78	68	68	70	66	87	76	72	93	71	72	84	66	72	75
15135	MC KEESPORT	82	93	104	90	93	100	90	89	90	88	112	101	95	118	93	92	110	88	91	98
15136	MC KEES ROCKS	74	78	82	74	78	86	77	77	79	76	98	87	80	101	79	82	95	76	82	87
15137	NORTH VERSAILLES	59	62	70	60	62	69	63	62	65	62	81	70	65	82	64	67	78	63	65	69
15139	OAKMONT	93	98	115	99	98	106	100	98	100	98	124	113	102	127	101	100	121	99	98	109
15140	PITCAIRN	52	51	57	50	51	56	56	54	57	54	70	62	55	71	55	57	68	55	54	59
15142	PRESTO	126	153	172	152	152	160	140	141	132	140	167	159	149	169	146	132	165	137	134	153
15143	SEWICKLEY	165	191	226	192	189	201	181	179	174	182	219	204	192	224	186	174	217	177	172	197
15144	SPRINGDALE	70	79	86	75	79	87	77	76	78	75	97	85	81	103	79	80	94	75	80	84
15145	TURTLE CREEK	71	66	67	64	68	78	69	71	73	67	89	79	68	89	70	76	85	71	78	81
15146	MONROEVILLE	90	97	113	98	96	103	98	96	96	97	120	110	100	121	99	95	118	96	93	105
15147	VERONA	73	78	84	76	78	85	77	77	77	76	96	87	79	98	78	78	93	76	79	85
15148	WILMERDING	55	45	35	43	48	56	48	52	53	46	63	58	45	62	48	56	58	51	60	61
15201	PITTSBURGH	56	56	68	55	56	64	61	58	63	59	79	66	62	80	61	65	76	60	63	65
15202	PITTSBURGH	65	70	86	71	69	74	73	70	72	72	91	82	74	92	73	71	89	72	68	77
15203	PITTSBURGH	56	56	69	57	56	62	62	58	63	60	78	68	62	79	61	62	76	61	59	65
15204	PITTSBURGH	60	64	70	62	64	70	65	63	66	63	82	72	67	85	66	66	80	63	65	70
15205	PITTSBURGH	82	86	102	87	85	92	88	86	88	87	110	100	90	112	89	87	108	87	84	95
15206	PITTSBURGH	74	70	90	70	69	78	78	75	81	78	101	87	78	100	77	82	99	78	77	84
15207	PITTSBURGH	59	58	63	55	58	67	60	60	64	59	79	67	61	80	61	67	76	61	66	68
15208	PITTSBURGH	80	75	89	70	74	85	80	80	86	81	105	89	80	101	79	89	102	82	86	90
15209	PITTSBURGH	73	82	89	79	81	87	79	78	79	78	98	90	83	103	81	79	96	77	78	86
15210	PITTSBURGH	59	59	64	56	59	66	61	60	64	59	79	67	62	81	61	66	76	60	65	67
15211	PITTSBURGH	70	72	89	73	71	79	77	74	78	75	97	85	78	99	77	78	95	76	74	81
15212	PITTSBURGH	55	56	64	54	56	63	59	57	61	57	75	65	60	78	59	62	73	58	60	64
	PENNSYLVANIA	89	89	93	87	90	98	89	90	91	88	112	104	89	114	90	92	109	90	92	104
	UNITED STATES	100	100	100	100	100	100	100	100	100	100	100	100	100	100	100	100	100	100	100	100

# ZIP CODE / POST OFFICE NAME	COUNTY FIPS CODE	POPULATION 2000	POPULATION 2004	POPULATION 2009	2000-2004 ANNUAL RATE % Rate	2000-2004 ANNUAL RATE State Centile	HOUSEHOLDS 2000	HOUSEHOLDS 2004	HOUSEHOLDS 2009	% Annual Rate 2000-2004	2004 Average HH Size	FAMILIES 2000	FAMILIES 2004	% Annual Rate 2000-2004
15213 PITTSBURGH	003	28001	28121	27899	0.1	44	10314	10569	10639	0.6	1.81	2798	2825	0.2
15214 PITTSBURGH	003	17615	16423	15650	-1.6	0	6800	6439	6241	-1.3	2.51	4449	4173	-1.5
15215 PITTSBURGH	003	13214	12788	12368	-0.8	8	5611	5508	5416	-0.4	2.28	3451	3363	-0.6
15216 PITTSBURGH	003	25630	25766	25463	0.1	45	11244	11509	11578	0.6	2.21	6466	6551	0.3
15217 PITTSBURGH	003	25964	25350	24650	-0.6	13	11846	11754	11620	-0.2	2.10	6114	5980	-0.5
15218 PITTSBURGH	003	14834	14186	13653	-1.1	4	7132	6979	6857	-0.5	2.02	3722	3591	-0.8
15219 PITTSBURGH	003	19782	19430	19128	-0.4	20	7028	7027	7027	0.0	1.97	3236	3161	-0.6
15220 PITTSBURGH	003	18406	17776	17231	-0.8	7	8266	8135	8028	-0.4	2.15	4800	4646	-0.8
15221 PITTSBURGH	003	36280	34574	33256	-1.1	3	16797	16339	16022	-0.7	2.09	9145	8786	-0.9
15222 PITTSBURGH	003	1905	1887	1867	-0.2	28	771	780	780	0.3	2.42	135	100	-6.8
15223 PITTSBURGH	003	8203	7987	7762	-0.6	12	3648	3624	3591	-0.2	2.18	2209	2174	-0.4
15224 PITTSBURGH	003	12175	11495	11004	-1.3	2	5650	5454	5328	-0.8	2.08	2690	2551	-1.2
15225 PITTSBURGH	003	1232	1169	1121	-1.2	2	624	602	587	-0.8	1.94	314	299	-1.2
15226 PITTSBURGH	003	14715	14287	13827	-0.7	10	6252	6213	6138	-0.2	2.29	4001	3935	-0.4
15227 PITTSBURGH	003	30004	28898	27910	-0.9	6	13147	12923	12726	-0.4	2.22	8216	7997	-0.6
15228 PITTSBURGH	003	17080	16684	16206	-0.6	14	6995	6939	6855	-0.2	2.35	4499	4428	-0.4
15229 PITTSBURGH	003	14253	13950	13598	-0.5	16	6095	6094	6058	0.0	2.23	3881	3842	-0.2
15232 PITTSBURGH	003	11104	10875	10610	-0.5	16	6367	6323	6264	-0.2	1.63	1664	1622	-0.6
15233 PITTSBURGH	003	4866	4641	4499	-1.1	3	1436	1355	1311	-1.4	2.09	688	640	-1.7
15234 PITTSBURGH	003	14642	14145	13674	-0.8	7	6345	6268	6181	-0.3	2.23	4107	4016	-0.6
15235 PITTSBURGH	003	38508	36943	35662	-1.0	5	16345	16084	15868	-0.4	2.28	11093	10814	-0.6
15236 PITTSBURGH	003	30542	29778	28937	-0.6	13	12395	12336	12222	-0.1	2.37	8762	8646	-0.3
15237 PITTSBURGH	003	41806	42236	41801	0.2	51	16883	17450	17623	0.8	2.35	11553	11835	0.6
15238 PITTSBURGH	003	13324	13211	12933	-0.2	29	5227	5260	5234	0.2	2.45	3792	3790	0.0
15239 PITTSBURGH	003	20687	20117	19490	-0.7	11	7782	7754	7675	-0.1	2.59	6005	5948	-0.2
15241 PITTSBURGH	003	20930	20611	20108	-0.4	22	7397	7419	7370	0.1	2.71	6035	6028	0.1
15243 PITTSBURGH	003	12775	12672	12407	-0.2	30	4944	4996	4978	0.3	2.41	3595	3604	0.1
15282 PITTSBURGH	003	1	1	1	0.0	39	1	1	1	0.0	1.00	0	0	0.0
15301 WASHINGTON	125	49930	49638	49737	-0.1	32	20137	20446	20892	0.4	2.31	13235	13321	0.2
15310 ALEPPO	059	395	385	385	-0.6	12	151	150	154	-0.2	2.57	111	109	-0.4
15311 AMITY	125	1410	1395	1393	-0.3	27	526	533	544	0.3	2.59	414	417	0.2
15312 AVELLA	125	3858	3798	3791	-0.4	22	1447	1455	1481	0.1	2.60	1130	1130	0.0
15313 BEALLSVILLE	125	317	311	310	-0.5	18	126	126	128	0.0	2.47	94	94	0.0
15314 BENTLEYVILLE	125	3956	3903	3903	-0.3	24	1651	1660	1690	0.1	2.32	1117	1113	-0.1
15317 CANONSBURG	125	31318	32832	33735	1.1	82	12209	13081	13709	1.6	2.46	8925	9525	1.5
15320 CARMICHAELS	059	6432	6545	6657	0.4	60	2630	2727	2825	0.9	2.37	1791	1841	0.7
15321 CECIL	125	1537	1526	1522	-0.2	31	570	578	588	0.3	2.64	447	451	0.2
15322 CLARKSVILLE	059	3302	3232	3223	-0.5	16	1317	1313	1334	-0.1	2.42	915	903	-0.3
15323 CLAYSVILLE	125	5007	5058	5108	0.2	51	1818	1878	1935	0.8	2.63	1434	1472	0.6
15324 COKEBURG	125	543	528	524	-0.7	11	241	239	242	-0.2	2.21	161	158	-0.4
15327 DILLINER	059	2315	2284	2287	-0.3	24	950	962	985	0.3	2.37	665	668	0.1
15329 PROSPERITY	125	1970	2059	2111	1.1	81	674	721	755	1.6	2.74	536	570	1.5
15330 EIGHTY FOUR	125	4974	5155	5258	0.8	74	1910	2028	2113	1.4	2.54	1486	1568	1.3
15331 ELLSWORTH	125	952	931	926	-0.5	15	425	423	429	-0.1	2.18	256	252	-0.4
15332 FINLEYVILLE	125	7966	8037	8118	0.2	49	3289	3400	3507	0.8	2.36	2355	2412	0.6
15333 FREDERICKTOWN	125	2136	2083	2071	-0.6	13	878	871	883	-0.2	2.38	618	607	-0.4
15337 GRAYSVILLE	059	1040	1143	1205	2.3	94	386	435	468	2.9	2.51	294	328	2.6
15338 GREENSBORO	059	1973	1937	1937	-0.4	19	775	778	795	0.1	2.49	576	574	-0.1
15340 HICKORY	125	1550	1500	1489	-0.8	8	587	579	585	-0.3	2.59	468	459	-0.5
15341 HOLBROOK	059	837	833	839	-0.1	34	313	318	328	0.4	2.61	236	238	0.2
15342 HOUSTON	125	4688	4690	4724	0.0	39	1994	2039	2092	0.5	2.28	1331	1349	0.3
15344 JEFFERSON	059	1606	1597	1597	-0.1	33	641	652	666	0.4	2.43	469	473	0.2
15345 MARIANNA	125	1792	1761	1755	-0.4	20	711	713	724	0.1	2.47	497	493	-0.2
15346 MATHER	059	864	843	841	-0.6	13	351	351	358	0.0	2.39	237	234	-0.3
15349 MOUNT MORRIS	059	1767	1754	1758	-0.2	31	709	718	735	0.3	2.44	522	524	0.1
15352 NEW FREEPORT	059	877	851	850	-0.7	9	325	321	327	-0.3	2.65	240	235	-0.5
15353 NINEVEH	059	101	105	108	0.9	77	2	2	2	0.0	2.50	2	2	0.0
15357 RICES LANDING	059	2028	1985	1985	-0.5	16	814	817	835	0.1	2.41	592	590	-0.1
15359 ROGERSVILLE	059	190	188	188	-0.3	27	72	73	75	0.3	2.53	57	57	0.4
15360 SCENERY HILL	125	2256	2208	2197	-0.5	16	845	846	858	0.0	2.61	635	632	-0.1
15362 SPRAGGS	059	1389	1366	1367	-0.4	21	525	529	541	0.2	2.58	390	389	-0.1
15363 STRABANE	125	855	869	875	0.4	58	394	411	422	1.0	2.11	246	253	0.7
15364 SYCAMORE	059	812	831	843	0.6	66	296	310	321	1.1	2.54	232	242	1.0
15367 VENETIA	125	6892	7714	8177	2.7	97	2315	2625	2823	3.0	2.93	1913	2154	2.8
15370 WAYNESBURG	059	15018	15603	16181	0.9	77	4967	5320	5682	1.6	2.37	3322	3552	1.6
15376 WEST ALEXANDER	125	1687	1762	1809	1.0	80	638	681	712	1.6	2.56	487	516	1.4
15377 WEST FINLEY	125	924	966	993	1.1	81	317	340	356	1.7	2.82	251	267	1.5
15380 WIND RIDGE	059	804	896	955	2.6	96	309	351	381	3.0	2.55	230	260	2.9
15401 UNIONTOWN	051	36422	36067	35871	-0.2	28	15067	15209	15425	0.2	2.29	9790	9809	0.1
15410 ADAH	051	724	712	705	-0.4	21	279	279	281	0.0	2.54	193	192	-0.1
15411 ADDISON	111	639	640	640	0.0	41	280	288	294	0.7	2.17	195	198	0.4
15412 ALLENPORT	125	465	451	448	-0.7	9	204	202	204	-0.2	2.20	134	131	-0.5
15413 ALLISON	051	583	573	567	-0.4	20	237	238	240	0.1	2.39	165	165	0.0
15417 BROWNSVILLE	125	9404	9242	9179	-0.4	20	3947	3952	4003	0.0	2.32	2585	2563	-0.2
15419 CALIFORNIA	125	4094	4181	4222	0.5	64	1439	1503	1547	1.0	1.99	568	584	0.7
15423 COAL CENTER	125	1925	1950	1967	0.3	54	744	769	790	0.8	2.51	528	541	0.6
15424 CONFLUENCE	111	2588	2501	2484	-0.8	7	1071	1059	1075	-0.3	2.26	734	721	-0.4
15425 CONNELLSVILLE	051	21997	22023	21998	0.0	40	9054	9270	9458	0.6	2.35	6090	6190	0.4
15427 DAISYTOWN	125	2057	2017	2010	-0.5	18	854	854	867	0.0	2.36	600	594	-0.2
15428 DAWSON	051	2462	2440	2424	-0.2	29	997	1012	1028	0.4	2.40	730	736	0.2
15431 DUNBAR	051	5439	5135	5002	-1.3	2	2132	2058	2048	-0.8	2.48	1515	1452	-1.0
15432 DUNLEVY	125	149	144	143	-0.8	7	68	67	68	-0.4	2.09	46	44	-1.0
15433 EAST MILLSBORO	051	1020	1003	992	-0.4	21	399	401	405	0.1	2.49	285	283	-0.2
15434 ELCO	125	58	61	63	1.2	83	25	27	28	1.8	2.22	19	20	1.2
15436 FAIRCHANCE	051	3225	3235	3228	0.1	43	1288	1322	1347	0.6	2.43	901	917	0.4
15437 FARMINGTON	051	3862	3862	3849	0.0	39	1256	1286	1308	0.6	2.47	929	945	0.4
15438 FAYETTE CITY	051	2559	2562	2556	0.0	40	983	1002	1020	0.5	2.51	722	731	0.3
15440 GIBBON GLADE	051	293	294	293	0.1	43	108	111	113	0.7	2.12	82	84	0.6
15442 GRINDSTONE	051	3631	3565	3524	-0.4	19	1485	1493	1510	0.1	2.38	1017	1014	-0.1
15444 HILLER	051	537	521	513	-0.7	9	224	222	223	-0.2	2.35	153	151	-0.3
15445 HOPWOOD	051	3621	3755	3812	0.9	75	1523	1616	1674	1.4	2.31	1061	1114	1.2
15446 INDIAN HEAD	051	114	122	126	1.6	89	40	44	46	2.3	2.77	31	34	2.2
15450 LA BELLE	051	377	370	366	-0.4	19	154	155	157	0.2	2.39	108	107	-0.2
15451 LAKE LYNN	051	1294	1288	1280	-0.1	34	504	509	516	0.4	2.53	383	387	0.2
15456 LEMONT FURNACE	051	3256	3626	3819	2.6	96	1283	1453	1558	3.0	2.49	946	1067	2.9
PENNSYLVANIA					0.3					0.7	2.44			0.6
UNITED STATES					1.2					1.3	2.58			1.1

ZIP CODE #	POST OFFICE NAME	RACE (%) White 2000	White 2004	Black 2000	Black 2004	Asian/Pacific 2000	Asian/Pacific 2004	% Hispanic Origin 2000	% Hispanic Origin 2004	2004 AGE DISTRIBUTION (%) 0-4	5-9	10-14	15-19	20-24	25-44	45-64	65-84	85+	18+	MEDIAN AGE 2004	% 2004 Males	% 2004 Females
15213	PITTSBURGH	67.2	62.4	15.9	18.1	12.4	14.8	2.3	2.4	1.8	1.4	1.5	22.1	35.7	17.0	9.3	9.0	2.1	94.2	23.2	50.8	49.2
15214	PITTSBURGH	55.6	52.4	41.6	44.8	0.5	0.6	1.0	1.0	7.4	7.9	8.6	7.1	5.9	25.7	23.1	12.3	1.9	71.6	35.8	45.8	54.2
15215	PITTSBURGH	96.0	95.1	1.5	1.8	1.5	2.0	1.4	1.5	5.3	5.7	6.6	6.2	4.7	23.6	27.7	17.3	2.9	78.4	43.7	47.1	52.9
15216	PITTSBURGH	93.8	92.5	2.6	3.2	2.0	2.5	1.2	1.3	5.5	5.4	5.8	5.8	6.5	30.3	24.2	13.6	3.0	79.8	39.3	47.1	52.9
15217	PITTSBURGH	88.4	85.9	3.1	3.9	6.3	7.7	1.9	2.1	4.4	4.2	4.7	5.4	8.5	30.0	24.8	14.0	4.1	83.3	39.2	47.9	52.1
15218	PITTSBURGH	80.5	77.2	16.4	19.3	1.1	1.4	1.1	1.2	5.1	4.9	5.5	5.7	6.3	28.6	27.4	14.0	2.4	81.1	41.2	46.3	53.7
15219	PITTSBURGH	32.5	30.3	63.6	65.5	1.5	1.7	1.3	1.4	4.8	4.0	4.6	14.1	15.5	24.5	18.8	11.9	1.9	83.6	30.7	48.2	51.8
15220	PITTSBURGH	84.5	81.4	7.3	8.9	5.7	7.1	1.0	1.0	5.8	5.1	5.3	5.0	6.1	29.4	24.9	16.0	2.5	81.0	40.2	47.8	52.3
15221	PITTSBURGH	47.7	45.6	48.8	50.7	1.0	1.2	1.0	1.0	6.2	6.4	6.9	6.0	5.3	26.3	25.7	14.8	2.5	76.8	40.2	44.7	55.3
15222	PITTSBURGH	65.4	59.5	31.8	37.4	1.1	1.3	1.1	1.1	1.1	0.6	0.5	15.8	15.2	27.0	22.3	15.7	1.8	97.2	37.9	55.8	44.2
15223	PITTSBURGH	98.0	97.6	0.7	0.9	0.4	0.5	0.8	0.9	5.2	5.4	6.3	6.0	5.5	27.5	25.2	16.2	2.7	79.2	41.5	47.1	52.9
15224	PITTSBURGH	62.7	60.7	31.9	33.3	2.7	3.2	1.4	1.6	5.5	5.9	6.5	5.8	7.4	29.3	22.7	14.3	2.5	78.5	37.0	45.8	54.2
15225	PITTSBURGH	97.3	96.8	1.2	1.5	0.0	0.0	0.9	1.0	5.0	5.1	6.2	3.8	5.7	26.4	27.2	17.7	3.0	81.5	43.6	48.9	51.1
15226	PITTSBURGH	96.1	95.3	1.8	2.3	0.9	1.1	0.8	0.9	6.1	6.1	5.7	5.1	5.4	28.9	25.0	15.4	2.4	79.0	40.4	46.6	53.4
15227	PITTSBURGH	96.9	96.3	1.4	1.7	0.8	0.9	0.7	0.7	4.8	4.9	5.7	5.9	6.3	26.4	26.2	16.8	2.9	81.0	42.4	47.6	52.4
15228	PITTSBURGH	96.3	95.4	0.6	0.7	2.2	2.8	0.9	1.1	5.9	6.5	7.2	6.6	4.5	23.9	27.7	14.1	3.6	75.5	42.1	46.3	53.8
15229	PITTSBURGH	97.2	96.5	1.3	1.7	0.7	0.9	0.5	0.6	5.6	5.7	6.0	6.0	5.4	28.4	25.0	15.2	2.8	79.0	40.8	46.9	53.1
15232	PITTSBURGH	78.8	74.8	7.7	9.4	10.3	12.4	3.1	3.4	2.8	1.9	2.0	2.7	16.7	44.9	16.5	10.0	2.6	92.1	31.1	49.9	50.1
15233	PITTSBURGH	25.0	21.4	71.9	75.4	0.4	0.4	2.7	2.7	4.1	4.4	4.6	4.0	9.8	39.5	25.3	7.6	0.9	84.7	36.7	66.5	33.5
15234	PITTSBURGH	97.0	96.3	1.0	1.3	1.0	1.3	1.0	1.1	5.4	5.6	6.1	5.7	5.0	28.0	25.5	16.5	2.3	79.1	41.6	47.6	52.4
15235	PITTSBURGH	73.7	69.9	23.7	27.2	0.8	1.0	0.8	0.8	5.2	5.6	6.1	5.7	4.6	24.5	27.9	17.9	2.5	79.5	43.9	47.0	53.0
15236	PITTSBURGH	96.7	95.9	1.9	2.3	0.7	0.9	0.5	0.6	5.0	5.4	6.1	5.8	4.8	23.7	27.9	18.1	3.1	79.8	44.5	47.5	52.6
15237	PITTSBURGH	95.9	94.8	0.9	1.2	2.4	3.1	0.7	0.8	5.2	5.8	6.3	5.8	4.3	24.0	28.8	16.8	3.0	78.8	44.1	47.4	52.6
15238	PITTSBURGH	93.8	92.3	0.9	1.2	4.3	5.4	0.7	0.8	4.8	6.3	8.2	7.1	4.1	19.1	31.3	17.0	2.1	75.9	45.2	48.8	51.2
15239	PITTSBURGH	95.6	94.5	2.8	3.5	0.9	1.1	0.7	0.8	6.1	6.3	6.9	6.4	5.4	27.8	27.7	12.3	1.2	76.7	39.8	49.1	50.9
15241	PITTSBURGH	94.7	93.4	0.7	0.9	3.9	5.0	0.8	0.9	5.7	7.2	8.3	7.2	4.0	19.8	30.2	14.6	2.9	73.6	43.6	48.3	51.7
15243	PITTSBURGH	96.6	95.8	0.6	0.8	2.3	2.9	0.5	0.5	5.2	5.9	6.8	5.9	3.5	20.3	27.5	19.7	5.4	78.0	46.5	45.8	54.2
15282	PITTSBURGH	100.0	100.0	0.0	0.0	0.0	0.0	0.0	0.0	0.0	0.0	0.0	0.0	100.0	0.0	0.0	0.0	0.0	100.0	22.5	100.0	0.0
15301	WASHINGTON	92.3	91.5	5.8	6.4	0.4	0.4	0.6	0.6	5.4	5.5	6.1	6.5	6.5	24.8	27.0	15.3	2.8	79.3	41.8	47.3	52.7
15310	ALEPPO	99.2	99.2	0.0	0.0	0.0	0.0	0.0	0.0	5.7	6.5	7.5	6.2	6.2	24.9	29.1	12.0	1.8	76.4	39.9	51.7	48.3
15311	AMITY	98.8	98.7	0.3	0.3	0.1	0.1	0.1	0.2	5.5	6.0	6.0	6.6	5.0	25.8	32.0	11.8	1.4	78.3	42.1	50.3	49.7
15312	AVELLA	98.3	98.1	0.6	0.7	0.1	0.1	0.2	0.2	4.9	5.6	7.1	5.9	5.2	26.3	29.6	13.9	1.6	78.6	42.1	51.1	49.0
15313	BEALLSVILLE	99.1	99.0	0.6	1.0	0.0	0.0	0.0	0.0	6.4	7.1	7.4	5.8	5.8	23.8	30.2	12.2	1.3	75.2	41.1	49.8	50.2
15314	BENTLEYVILLE	97.1	96.9	1.3	1.5	0.1	0.1	0.5	0.5	6.5	6.1	6.1	5.8	5.7	25.4	25.8	16.2	2.4	77.9	41.1	48.2	51.8
15317	CANONSBURG	95.4	94.9	2.9	3.1	0.8	1.0	0.7	0.8	6.2	6.6	6.6	5.8	4.5	24.8	28.5	14.9	2.3	76.8	42.3	48.0	52.0
15320	CARMICHAELS	98.5	98.3	0.2	0.3	0.0	0.0	0.5	0.6	5.9	6.0	6.8	6.0	6.4	25.5	27.2	13.6	2.4	77.4	40.4	48.8	51.2
15321	CECIL	99.4	99.3	0.2	0.2	0.0	0.0	0.5	0.5	5.8	6.6	7.3	5.9	4.7	27.7	30.0	10.6	1.4	76.2	40.5	49.5	50.5
15322	CLARKSVILLE	96.8	96.4	2.2	2.4	0.2	0.3	0.2	0.3	5.1	5.2	6.0	5.7	6.2	24.3	27.2	17.3	3.0	80.3	43.1	48.1	51.9
15323	CLAYSVILLE	99.2	99.1	0.2	0.2	0.1	0.1	0.2	0.2	6.1	6.5	6.9	6.3	5.6	25.3	28.7	12.8	1.8	76.2	40.8	50.1	49.9
15324	COKEBURG	98.9	98.9	0.0	0.0	0.2	0.2	0.0	0.0	5.1	5.1	6.1	5.5	5.3	26.0	24.4	18.9	3.6	80.1	43.0	46.2	53.8
15327	DILLINER	98.9	98.6	0.3	0.4	0.2	0.3	0.7	0.7	5.7	6.0	6.9	5.8	5.2	26.7	27.4	14.2	2.2	78.0	40.5	50.4	49.7
15329	PROSPERITY	98.8	98.7	0.4	0.5	0.1	0.2	0.4	0.4	5.5	6.6	7.8	7.1	5.2	26.4	27.7	11.4	2.3	75.3	40.2	49.9	50.1
15330	EIGHTY FOUR	98.2	97.9	1.0	1.1	0.2	0.3	0.4	0.5	4.9	5.7	6.4	6.1	4.4	24.2	32.8	14.0	1.6	79.2	44.0	50.3	49.7
15331	ELLSWORTH	96.0	95.5	2.3	2.7	0.1	0.1	0.7	0.8	5.9	5.5	4.7	5.5	6.2	26.2	26.4	16.3	3.2	80.3	42.3	48.1	51.9
15332	FINLEYVILLE	97.9	97.6	1.0	1.2	0.3	0.3	0.5	0.6	5.0	5.6	6.7	5.7	4.3	25.8	28.7	16.1	2.0	79.1	43.2	49.0	51.0
15333	FREDERICKTOWN	97.4	97.2	1.3	1.5	0.1	0.1	0.5	0.5	5.4	5.6	6.8	6.2	5.5	26.4	25.9	15.7	2.5	78.4	40.7	47.9	52.1
15337	GRAYSVILLE	98.7	98.5	0.6	0.6	0.0	0.0	0.4	0.4	5.3	7.1	7.7	6.8	6.2	29.0	25.4	10.9	1.7	75.9	37.6	51.6	48.4
15338	GREENSBORO	99.0	98.9	0.2	0.3	0.2	0.2	0.5	0.6	5.6	6.0	6.9	5.6	5.7	25.6	28.0	14.6	2.0	78.0	40.9	49.4	50.6
15340	HICKORY	94.7	94.0	4.7	5.3	0.1	0.1	0.1	0.2	5.3	5.9	7.5	6.3	5.3	25.7	28.4	14.1	1.6	77.4	41.5	50.4	49.6
15341	HOLBROOK	99.0	99.0	0.1	0.1	0.0	0.0	0.2	0.2	5.2	6.2	7.3	6.6	6.0	25.6	29.5	11.9	1.7	77.2	40.2	51.3	48.7
15342	HOUSTON	95.0	94.5	3.9	4.4	0.3	0.3	0.4	0.5	4.7	5.0	5.8	5.6	4.9	24.8	27.4	19.3	2.5	81.1	44.5	47.9	52.1
15344	JEFFERSON	96.8	96.4	2.2	2.5	0.2	0.2	0.6	0.8	4.8	5.1	5.9	6.2	5.6	24.1	30.3	15.8	2.3	80.8	43.8	47.6	52.4
15345	MARIANNA	95.5	95.0	3.5	3.9	0.1	0.1	0.0	0.0	5.7	6.1	7.0	6.6	5.4	26.8	26.3	14.2	1.9	77.2	39.6	48.0	52.0
15346	MATHER	98.4	98.1	0.8	1.0	0.0	0.0	0.4	0.4	6.1	6.1	5.2	5.0	5.2	28.2	26.3	15.7	2.3	79.2	41.0	49.5	50.5
15349	MOUNT MORRIS	99.0	98.9	0.2	0.2	0.0	0.0	0.3	0.4	5.8	6.2	6.6	6.0	4.7	27.7	27.8	13.2	2.0	77.5	40.0	48.6	51.4
15352	NEW FREEPORT	99.2	99.2	0.0	0.0	0.0	0.0	0.0	0.0	6.0	7.8	8.7	6.7	5.2	27.3	25.7	11.1	1.7	73.0	37.0	49.6	50.4
15353	NINEVEH	99.0	98.1	1.0	1.9	0.0	0.0	0.0	0.0	3.8	7.6	7.6	6.7	6.7	28.6	27.6	9.5	1.9	76.2	38.8	54.3	45.7
15357	RICES LANDING	98.6	98.5	0.7	0.8	0.1	0.1	0.1	0.1	5.7	5.9	6.3	5.4	5.5	24.4	28.8	15.2	2.8	78.7	42.7	47.6	52.4
15359	ROGERSVILLE	99.0	98.9	0.0	0.0	0.0	0.0	0.5	0.5	4.3	6.4	7.5	7.5	5.3	27.1	29.3	11.2	1.6	76.6	40.0	48.4	51.6
15360	SCENERY HILL	99.3	99.1	0.2	0.2	0.2	0.2	0.1	0.2	5.4	5.9	6.1	5.7	5.3	27.0	29.3	13.7	1.7	79.1	41.8	49.5	50.5
15362	SPRAGGS	99.1	99.1	0.3	0.3	0.1	0.1	0.8	1.0	5.0	7.3	8.4	6.7	4.8	26.1	29.9	10.5	1.4	74.9	39.2	50.5	49.5
15363	STRABANE	96.0	95.6	3.0	3.5	0.1	0.1	0.8	0.8	4.7	4.8	5.6	5.3	4.3	26.5	25.1	20.3	3.5	81.6	44.3	46.8	53.2
15364	SYCAMORE	98.7	98.6	0.6	0.7	0.0	0.0	0.3	0.2	4.5	7.0	7.2	7.1	6.0	27.7	28.6	10.1	1.8	77.3	39.2	51.0	49.0
15367	VENETIA	97.7	97.3	0.4	0.5	1.3	1.7	0.7	0.8	7.1	8.5	10.1	7.2	4.4	23.9	28.6	9.3	1.1	69.5	39.7	48.5	51.5
15370	WAYNESBURG	89.2	88.3	9.6	10.4	0.5	0.6	1.7	1.8	4.5	4.9	5.4	6.8	9.9	30.8	24.3	11.0	2.4	82.1	36.9	55.6	44.5
15376	WEST ALEXANDER	99.0	98.9	0.2	0.3	0.2	0.2	0.3	0.3	6.1	6.6	7.4	6.4	5.3	27.4	27.1	12.5	1.4	75.4	39.3	50.6	49.4
15377	WEST FINLEY	99.1	99.0	0.1	0.1	0.1	0.1	0.2	0.1	6.6	7.1	7.7	6.4	5.5	26.6	27.9	11.2	1.0	74.2	38.3	52.0	48.0
15380	WIND RIDGE	98.9	99.0	0.0	0.0	0.0	0.0	0.3	0.3	6.1	6.3	7.8	6.3	6.1	27.6	26.3	12.2	1.3	75.9	38.0	50.9	49.1
15401	UNIONTOWN	91.5	90.7	6.7	7.3	0.5	0.6	0.4	0.4	5.8	5.8	6.0	5.7	5.8	24.7	26.5	16.4	3.4	79.0	42.4	46.8	53.2
15410	ADAH	92.3	91.4	6.5	7.3	0.1	0.1	0.4	0.3	5.3	5.6	7.6	6.7	6.2	26.8	24.4	15.2	2.1	77.3	39.2	49.3	50.7
15411	ADDISON	99.8	100.0	0.0	0.0	0.0	0.0	0.3	0.5	4.2	4.5	5.6	5.2	5.5	24.1	28.9	19.5	2.5	82.2	45.6	50.9	49.1
15412	ALLENPORT	98.9	99.1	0.7	0.7	0.0	0.0	0.2	0.2	4.4	4.4	4.9	4.9	4.2	24.4	29.5	19.7	3.6	83.6	46.8	47.9	52.1
15413	ALLISON	92.3	91.3	5.8	6.6	0.0	0.0	0.2	0.2	6.6	6.6	6.1	5.4	5.1	26.4	26.2	14.8	2.8	77.1	40.6	47.1	52.9
15417	BROWNSVILLE	92.5	91.6	5.8	6.6	0.1	0.2	0.5	0.6	5.5	5.6	6.1	5.4	6.4	24.7	26.6	17.0	2.7	79.5	42.2	47.0	53.0
15419	CALIFORNIA	93.0	92.1	4.9	5.5	0.9	1.1	0.5	0.5	2.1	1.9	2.3	18.3	33.6	14.4	13.9	11.2	2.2	92.0	23.8	48.3	51.7
15423	COAL CENTER	97.7	97.5	0.9	1.0	0.4	0.4	0.6	0.6	4.7	5.0	5.9	5.9	7.3	22.9	29.9	16.0	2.5	81.1	43.9	49.2	50.8
15424	CONFLUENCE	99.5	99.4	0.1	0.1	0.1	0.1	0.2	0.3	5.2	5.3	5.8	5.3	5.3	26.4	26.5	17.7	2.6	80.3	42.8	49.4	50.6
15425	CONNELLSVILLE	96.8	96.4	2.1	2.4	0.2	0.3	0.4	0.4	5.7	5.7	6.3	6.2	5.9	26.1	26.3	15.4	2.3	78.3	41.0	48.6	51.4
15427	DAISYTOWN	95.4	94.8	3.1	3.5	0.2	0.3	0.5	0.5	5.2	5.4	5.6	5.2	5.7	25.6	28.6	16.3	2.6	80.6	43.3	49.0	51.0
15428	DAWSON	98.2	98.0	1.3	1.4	0.0	0.1	0.1	0.1	5.0	5.5	6.3	6.0	5.7	26.7	28.9	14.1	1.8	79.4	41.7	50.3	49.7
15431	DUNBAR	98.4	98.1	0.9	1.1	0.2	0.3	0.3	0.3	5.4	5.7	6.7	6.4	6.0	27.4	27.4	13.4	1.7	78.3	40.5	49.3	50.7
15432	DUNLEVY	99.3	99.3	0.7	0.7	0.0	0.0	0.0	0.0	4.2	4.2	4.9	4.2	4.2	22.9	31.3	20.1	4.2	84.7	48.3	50.7	49.3
15433	EAST MILLSBORO	96.3	95.8	2.8	3.2	0.1	0.2	0.2	0.3	5.0	5.2	5.8	5.2	6.1	25.8	28.4	16.1	2.5	80.8	42.7	48.0	52.0
15434	ELCO	98.3	98.4	1.7	1.6	0.0	0.0	0.0	0.0	4.9	4.9	6.6	4.9	6.6	21.3	31.2	16.4	3.3	83.6	45.4	47.5	52.5
15436	FAIRCHANCE	97.0	96.6	1.8	2.1	0.1	0.1	0.5	0.5	5.4	5.6	6.0	6.3	6.0	27.5	26.0	15.0	2.2	79.2	40.6	48.0	52.0
15437	FARMINGTON	99.2	99.0	0.1	0.1	0.2	0.2	0.4	0.4	6.7	7.3	7.5	6.4	5.4	26.8	26.9	11.5	1.6	74.6	38.2	49.0	51.0
15438	FAYETTE CITY	99.3	99.2	0.3	0.3	0.1	0.1	0.4	0.4	5.4	5.4	6.2	5.8	5.8	24.9	26.7	16.6	3.4	79.5	42.8	48.6	51.4
15440	GIBBON GLADE	99.0	98.6	0.0	0.0	0.0	0.3	0.7	0.7	7.1	7.8	8.2	6.8	5.8	28.6	24.2	10.2	1.4	72.8	36.4	49.3	50.7
15442	GRINDSTONE	92.5	91.6	6.0	6.8	0.1	0.1	0.4	0.4	5.6	5.8	6.3	5.8	5.7	25.5	26.4	16.9	2.2	78.8	41.4	48.4	51.6
15444	HILLER	91.3	90.4	6.9	7.7	0.0	0.0	0.7	0.8	4.0	4.4	6.3	5.8	5.8	23.6	26.7	19.8	3.7	81.8	45.1	47.4	52.6
15445	HOPWOOD	98.2	98.0	1.0	1.2	0.3	0.4	0.4	0.5	4.9	5.0	5.7	5.8	5.0	25.2	29.0	16.9	2.5	80.9	43.9	49.1	50.9
15446	INDIAN HEAD	99.1	99.2	0.0	0.0	0.0	0.0	0.0	0.0	7.4	7.4	8.2	6.6	4.9	28.7	24.6	11.5	0.8	72.1	36.5	51.6	48.4
15450	LA BELLE	97.4	97.3	2.1	2.4	0.0	0.0	0.0	0.3	5.1	5.4	5.1	4.6	6.2	24.9	31.4	14.9	2.4	81.4	43.9	48.4	51.6
15451	LAKE LYNN	97.5	97.3	1.2	1.3	0.2	0.2	0.6	0.8	6.8	6.8	7.1	5.9	6.2	27.0	25.5	13.4	1.4	75.7	38.6	47.8	52.3
15456	LEMONT FURNACE	98.0	97.7	0.9	1.0	0.2	0.3	0.4	0.5	5.5	6.0	6.8	5.7	5.3	26.6	28.5	14.0	1.5	78.2	40.9	48.7	51.3
	PENNSYLVANIA	85.4	84.4	10.0	10.3	1.8	2.2	3.2	3.5	5.9	6.1	6.8	6.9	6.7	26.6	25.3	13.3	2.2	77.2	39.1	48.4	51.6
	UNITED STATES	75.1	73.6	12.3	12.5	3.8	4.2	12.5	14.1	6.9	6.7	7.2	7.0	7.3	28.6	23.8	10.8	1.7	75.1	36.0	49.1	50.9

ZIP CODE #	POST OFFICE NAME	2004 Per Capita Income	2004 HH Income Base	2004 HOUSEHOLD INCOME DISTRIBUTION (%) Less than $25,000	$25,000 to $49,999	$50,000 to $99,999	$100,000 to $149,999	$150,000 or More	MEDIAN HOUSEHOLD INCOME 2004	2009	2004 National Centile	2004 State Centile	2004 Home Value Base	2004 HOME VALUE DISTRIBUTION (%) Less than $50,000	$50,000 to $89,999	$90,000 to $174,999	$175,000 to $399,999	$400,000 or More	2004 Median Home Value
15213	PITTSBURGH	22434	10569	54.4	22.2	12.8	5.4	5.2	22014	26573	3	1	2625	21.3	32.9	21.1	14.4	10.3	83006
15214	PITTSBURGH	19426	6439	35.4	28.0	28.0	5.9	2.8	36195	44802	32	26	3915	21.2	37.2	37.6	3.9	0.1	80931
15215	PITTSBURGH	39698	5508	25.4	22.6	25.0	13.3	13.7	52878	68303	77	77	3707	8.6	16.4	35.4	28.6	11.1	146076
15216	PITTSBURGH	27791	11509	24.6	27.7	32.9	10.6	4.2	47506	59465	67	67	7163	8.2	33.1	44.9	13.2	0.6	99772
15217	PITTSBURGH	40776	11754	25.0	22.4	26.6	12.7	13.4	53078	68543	77	77	6196	2.9	13.3	41.9	29.9	11.9	154070
15218	PITTSBURGH	31697	6979	27.5	30.9	27.5	8.1	6.1	42440	52748	54	55	3996	18.6	33.1	36.2	10.9	1.1	87712
15219	PITTSBURGH	14429	7027	62.1	20.6	13.0	2.2	2.2	16950	20908	1	1	2100	48.9	26.2	20.4	3.9	0.6	51447
15220	PITTSBURGH	29792	8135	24.0	27.4	32.6	11.4	4.7	48631	60350	70	69	5140	11.5	24.3	49.8	13.8	0.6	106872
15221	PITTSBURGH	23958	16339	36.0	28.9	25.0	6.6	3.6	35805	43973	31	24	8600	19.2	38.5	33.7	8.3	0.3	82142
15222	PITTSBURGH	40661	780	54.2	15.6	13.0	8.3	8.9	21507	28825	2	1	174	11.5	28.2	27.6	25.9	6.9	125000
15223	PITTSBURGH	24560	3624	26.2	31.2	32.9	6.9	2.8	43604	54314	58	58	2543	11.1	29.6	53.8	5.4	0.1	98381
15224	PITTSBURGH	17887	5454	48.1	28.5	18.2	3.4	1.8	26290	31867	6	3	2168	41.8	38.7	17.1	2.2	0.2	55817
15225	PITTSBURGH	23366	602	33.7	33.7	26.9	4.5	1.2	36279	49904	33	27	276	16.7	45.7	34.4	2.2	1.1	78182
15226	PITTSBURGH	24718	6213	24.9	31.6	33.2	8.3	2.0	44796	55107	61	61	4816	8.3	50.7	39.1	1.8	0.2	84906
15227	PITTSBURGH	24522	12923	26.9	28.6	31.9	9.8	2.7	44279	55457	59	60	8906	5.5	34.0	53.7	6.8	0.0	98592
15228	PITTSBURGH	40118	6939	15.8	19.3	32.4	17.9	14.6	68789	88810	91	92	5021	1.5	5.5	46.6	40.9	5.5	169298
15229	PITTSBURGH	28239	6094	20.2	29.8	35.8	10.0	4.3	50013	62297	72	71	4447	3.1	22.6	64.4	9.9	0.1	109722
15232	PITTSBURGH	45361	6323	34.6	24.5	21.3	8.5	11.1	39298	50548	44	41	1561	1.7	10.0	33.0	36.3	19.0	194693
15233	PITTSBURGH	16829	1355	44.0	29.7	17.1	7.1	2.2	29188	35939	11	5	508	20.3	25.2	39.4	13.6	1.6	95000
15234	PITTSBURGH	29444	6268	21.9	27.8	33.6	11.6	5.0	50246	62684	72	72	4621	3.1	25.5	58.1	11.8	1.6	105142
15235	PITTSBURGH	28584	16084	21.9	28.5	34.1	10.6	4.9	49595	61277	71	71	12709	6.1	44.5	41.8	7.3	0.3	89545
15236	PITTSBURGH	29387	12336	17.6	25.4	38.2	13.3	5.6	57367	71343	82	83	10099	2.8	11.2	72.8	12.6	0.7	119887
15237	PITTSBURGH	37441	17450	15.6	21.5	35.1	16.3	11.5	64486	80813	88	90	13725	1.6	6.7	53.4	36.7	1.7	157898
15238	PITTSBURGH	59198	5260	16.4	18.9	24.9	13.2	26.6	75563	100329	93	95	4322	4.5	7.3	28.1	33.9	26.2	225368
15239	PITTSBURGH	25349	7754	14.3	27.9	40.4	14.1	3.3	57525	70718	82	83	6402	2.3	19.4	66.5	11.5	0.2	114997
15241	PITTSBURGH	53356	7419	6.9	14.4	28.2	21.2	29.2	100681	128497	98	98	6763	0.8	2.7	30.1	56.4	10.2	209328
15243	PITTSBURGH	40493	4996	11.6	19.6	35.3	17.8	15.6	71849	90975	92	93	4391	0.8	5.7	58.6	30.1	4.8	150498
15282	PITTSBURGH	0	0	0.0	0.0	0.0	0.0	0.0	0	0	0	0	0	0.0	0.0	0.0	0.0	0.0	0
15301	WASHINGTON	22825	20446	31.7	27.7	29.2	8.0	3.4	40157	48831	47	45	14192	16.7	22.8	41.7	17.1	1.7	106019
15310	ALEPPO	15359	150	44.0	25.3	26.7	4.0	0.0	31130	37006	15	8	123	33.3	24.4	31.7	8.9	1.6	75000
15311	AMITY	22225	533	21.6	26.1	42.6	7.1	2.6	51443	60905	75	74	452	12.8	20.4	44.5	20.8	1.6	117284
15312	AVELLA	20588	1455	25.8	31.4	32.0	8.4	2.5	43266	51983	57	57	1234	16.3	23.6	41.7	15.6	2.8	104881
15313	BEALLSVILLE	22549	126	27.8	32.5	30.2	6.4	3.2	41882	51814	53	52	113	28.3	24.8	31.9	15.0	0.0	85000
15314	BENTLEYVILLE	22859	1660	38.9	24.9	26.9	6.1	3.1	34270	41630	25	17	1126	21.4	32.7	36.0	9.5	0.4	84458
15317	CANONSBURG	34138	13081	17.9	23.5	33.1	14.2	11.3	61902	76336	86	88	10714	4.2	13.9	38.3	37.1	6.6	160269
15320	CARMICHAELS	17490	2727	41.3	25.4	28.4	3.9	1.1	31947	37798	18	10	1944	32.7	28.2	30.5	8.5	0.1	74133
15321	CECIL	25995	578	21.1	21.1	36.5	14.2	7.1	57731	68838	82	83	503	0.2	5.8	59.1	32.6	2.4	154920
15322	CLARKSVILLE	17104	1313	38.2	31.7	24.5	4.4	1.2	31173	37102	15	8	1022	43.1	33.9	17.7	4.8	0.6	55726
15323	CLAYSVILLE	19659	1878	25.7	31.4	34.5	6.9	1.6	44216	52533	59	59	1564	18.9	21.7	41.8	16.3	1.4	103351
15324	COKEBURG	18951	239	37.7	30.5	26.4	3.4	2.1	34831	42168	27	20	175	57.1	30.3	9.1	2.9	0.6	46711
15327	DILLINER	18101	962	42.3	31.2	19.0	4.7	2.8	29700	34391	12	5	752	53.1	24.1	18.6	4.3	0.0	47890
15329	PROSPERITY	19926	721	21.2	35.6	33.8	6.4	2.9	46525	54357	65	65	591	19.0	19.5	40.6	19.3	1.7	108995
15330	EIGHTY FOUR	30511	2028	17.9	22.8	37.9	12.8	8.6	60206	72991	85	86	1816	11.1	10.8	38.1	34.0	6.1	150676
15331	ELLSWORTH	20342	423	36.9	32.4	25.8	3.6	1.4	35994	43167	32	25	305	49.2	34.1	13.1	3.6	0.0	50781
15332	FINLEYVILLE	25334	3400	20.5	29.1	37.7	9.7	2.9	50295	60689	72	72	2916	17.2	17.3	45.6	18.0	1.9	111307
15333	FREDERICKTOWN	17874	871	39.2	30.2	24.3	4.9	1.4	32841	39936	20	13	662	34.1	32.9	26.1	6.3	0.5	66981
15337	GRAYSVILLE	18458	435	35.2	29.0	27.4	7.1	1.4	37155	43210	36	31	327	30.9	28.8	30.6	8.3	1.5	71842
15338	GREENSBORO	20261	778	34.7	31.5	23.8	7.1	3.0	35445	41747	29	22	637	41.1	27.9	26.2	4.1	0.6	60957
15340	HICKORY	23914	579	22.8	27.5	34.7	11.2	3.8	49733	59462	71	71	498	7.4	20.7	42.2	25.5	4.2	132721
15341	HOLBROOK	16145	318	37.7	28.9	28.0	5.0	0.3	35220	40803	28	21	258	28.3	27.1	34.5	8.9	1.2	82222
15342	HOUSTON	22699	2039	26.5	32.2	32.1	7.0	2.3	42270	51935	54	54	1536	4.4	16.0	60.1	18.8	0.8	117875
15344	JEFFERSON	18937	652	32.7	29.5	30.4	6.6	0.9	36472	42714	33	28	524	32.1	28.8	32.3	5.5	1.3	71795
15345	MARIANNA	16925	713	38.9	30.3	25.1	4.4	1.4	33384	40180	22	15	540	45.2	21.7	25.6	7.2	0.4	56667
15346	MATHER	18320	351	36.2	29.3	28.5	4.6	1.4	36671	44634	34	29	296	47.0	36.5	10.5	6.1	0.0	52308
15349	MOUNT MORRIS	19225	718	31.9	28.8	32.6	5.3	1.4	38917	48202	42	40	581	30.5	27.5	31.5	10.5	0.0	81545
15352	NEW FREEPORT	14101	321	47.4	27.7	20.6	3.4	0.9	26837	31065	7	3	259	43.2	23.2	23.6	9.7	0.4	60938
15353	NINEVEH	1292	0	0.0	0.0	0.0	0.0	0.0	0	0	0	0	0	0.0	0.0	0.0	0.0	0.0	0
15357	RICES LANDING	22409	817	31.7	28.4	31.3	6.7	1.8	37280	44631	36	31	679	33.0	34.0	28.3	4.6	0.2	66053
15359	ROGERSVILLE	17405	73	32.9	32.9	26.0	6.9	1.4	36113	41370	32	26	60	21.7	30.0	38.3	10.0	0.0	88333
15360	SCENERY HILL	21824	846	25.1	30.5	33.9	7.8	2.7	45792	54453	63	64	715	19.9	17.8	41.7	18.0	2.7	108770
15362	SPRAGGS	16536	529	37.4	32.0	25.0	4.7	1.0	33608	39352	23	15	422	43.4	29.9	22.0	4.0	0.7	57568
15363	STRABANE	18023	411	41.6	33.3	22.1	2.9	0.0	30548	37109	14	7	261	15.3	46.7	35.3	2.7	0.0	79844
15364	SYCAMORE	19528	310	28.7	31.6	30.7	6.8	2.3	41445	50116	51	51	247	20.2	27.5	38.1	12.2	2.0	93929
15367	VENETIA	39809	2625	8.9	18.6	33.6	18.7	20.2	79048	102020	95	96	2437	1.6	3.1	30.6	45.8	18.8	225347
15370	WAYNESBURG	18040	5320	35.4	30.2	25.5	7.0	1.9	36036	42740	32	25	3574	19.7	27.1	38.3	14.0	0.9	94935
15376	WEST ALEXANDER	19865	681	27.5	32.2	32.8	6.3	1.3	42153	50425	53	53	570	23.3	23.5	37.7	14.9	0.5	94615
15377	WEST FINLEY	16846	340	29.7	31.2	32.7	5.3	1.2	42226	50000	54	54	279	25.5	20.8	36.2	17.2	0.4	97500
15380	WIND RIDGE	17265	351	38.8	27.9	27.1	5.7	0.6	34300	40133	25	17	267	34.1	25.8	31.5	7.1	1.5	68864
15401	UNIONTOWN	19690	15209	43.8	24.9	21.9	6.4	3.1	29769	35215	12	6	10185	26.9	29.6	32.1	9.5	1.9	82145
15410	ADAH	16026	279	42.3	33.7	19.0	3.9	1.1	28516	33323	10	4	204	47.6	29.9	19.6	2.9	0.0	56250
15411	ADDISON	20538	288	38.9	33.0	22.9	3.5	1.7	31563	35441	17	9	239	37.2	33.1	25.1	4.2	0.4	66250
15412	ALLENPORT	21842	202	35.2	36.1	22.3	5.5	1.0	33360	40638	22	14	153	41.2	29.4	25.5	3.9	0.0	61923
15413	ALLISON	25309	238	44.1	25.6	22.7	2.1	5.5	29285	35572	11	5	168	48.8	18.5	24.4	6.0	2.4	51538
15417	BROWNSVILLE	19011	3952	42.2	28.7	21.3	4.8	3.0	31579	37888	17	9	2782	41.6	29.1	22.3	6.8	0.2	59957
15419	CALIFORNIA	17224	1503	50.3	24.0	20.8	3.1	1.8	24755	29019	4	2	602	25.9	31.6	33.6	9.0	0.0	84156
15423	COAL CENTER	23758	769	32.5	27.7	29.3	7.9	2.6	40719	49568	49	48	598	25.3	26.8	32.3	12.2	3.5	87073
15424	CONFLUENCE	16543	1059	42.0	34.7	19.6	2.6	1.1	30437	34315	13	7	836	34.7	34.1	25.2	5.5	0.5	70132
15425	CONNELLSVILLE	18524	9270	41.9	27.5	23.3	5.2	2.1	30851	36135	14	8	6232	28.0	30.9	32.0	8.7	0.4	80515
15427	DAISYTOWN	21329	854	32.1	30.1	27.6	8.9	1.3	38477	46337	41	38	700	40.6	28.9	18.7	10.9	1.0	61754
15428	DAWSON	17930	1012	36.4	32.9	25.2	3.7	1.9	34761	40665	27	19	804	31.0	28.9	28.7	10.1	1.4	75439
15431	DUNBAR	15966	2058	37.1	33.4	25.9	3.0	0.6	33567	39748	23	15	1618	44.1	25.7	26.1	3.4	0.7	58333
15432	DUNLEVY	19120	67	37.3	35.8	20.9	6.0	0.0	31343	37343	16	9	55	52.7	23.6	20.0	3.6	0.0	48333
15433	EAST MILLSBORO	21822	401	41.9	31.2	21.2	3.0	2.7	28592	33407	10	4	316	37.7	22.2	32.6	7.6	0.0	71429
15434	ELCO	19308	27	33.3	29.6	33.3	3.7	0.0	37370	45000	37	32	23	30.4	34.8	34.8	0.0	0.0	72500
15436	FAIRCHANCE	16018	1322	43.4	29.4	22.5	3.5	1.1	28767	33507	10	5	967	30.2	30.4	32.2	7.2	0.0	76337
15437	FARMINGTON	20154	1286	26.4	33.4	32.5	4.4	3.2	41709	49559	52	52	1045	17.9	17.6	48.0	12.9	3.5	109261
15438	FAYETTE CITY	19862	1002	29.0	31.4	31.2	6.7	1.6	40000	48751	46	44	825	29.6	30.3	29.6	9.7	0.9	74091
15440	GIBBON GLADE	22271	111	30.6	33.3	28.8	4.5	2.7	36384	44322	33	27	88	23.9	19.3	43.2	9.1	4.6	101000
15442	GRINDSTONE	16285	1493	43.0	30.1	21.0	4.6	1.3	30277	35419	13	6	1091	43.6	26.3	21.3	8.1	0.7	58081
15444	HILLER	17813	222	31.5	36.9	27.9	3.6	0.0	35986	44362	31	25	179	44.7	34.1	21.2	0.0	0.0	54524
15445	HOPWOOD	17856	1616	40.0	30.1	24.9	4.3	0.7	32926	39356	21	13	1243	18.7	26.7	46.3	7.6	0.6	95928
15446	INDIAN HEAD	16148	44	40.9	22.7	27.3	6.8	2.3	31507	35000	16	9	36	38.9	36.1	19.4	5.6	0.0	62500
15450	LA BELLE	24343	155	41.3	36.1	16.8	2.6	3.2	29087	33209	10	5	130	35.4	18.5	39.2	6.9	0.0	82857
15451	LAKE LYNN	14034	509	46.0	30.8	18.7	4.1	0.4	27165	31621	7	3	393	42.2	23.9	27.0	6.9	0.0	63056
15456	LEMONT FURNACE	16221	1453	42.5	28.8	22.7	4.9	1.2	30586	35619	14	7	1149	37.1	35.9	21.2	5.1	0.9	59281
	PENNSYLVANIA	25764		25.8	27.2	31.2	10.2	5.7	46988	57000				11.9	18.4	40.7	25.1	4.1	123516
	UNITED STATES	25866		24.7	27.1	30.8	10.9	6.5	48124	56710				10.9	15.0	33.7	30.1	10.4	145905

#	POST OFFICE NAME	FINANCIAL SERVICES: Auto Loan	FINANCIAL SERVICES: Home Loan	FINANCIAL SERVICES: Investments	FINANCIAL SERVICES: Retirement Plans	THE HOME: Home Improvements: Home Repair	THE HOME: Home Improvements: Lawn & Garden	THE HOME: Furnishings: Computers & Hardware	THE HOME: Furnishings: Major Appliances	THE HOME: Furnishings: TV, Radio, Sound Equipment	THE HOME: Furnishings: Furniture	ENTERTAINMENT: Dine out/Carry out	ENTERTAINMENT: Sports Equipment	ENTERTAINMENT: Fees & Tickets	ENTERTAINMENT: Toys & Games	ENTERTAINMENT: Travel	ENTERTAINMENT: Cable TV	PERSONAL: Apparel & Services	PERSONAL: Auto Repairs	PERSONAL: Health Insurance	PERSONAL: Pets & Supplies
15213	PITTSBURGH	69	47	59	52	46	55	80	62	78	70	98	83	68	89	66	71	93	74	59	71
15214	PITTSBURGH	65	65	74	63	64	72	68	67	71	68	88	76	69	88	68	72	85	68	70	75
15215	PITTSBURGH	116	132	160	130	131	142	129	127	128	128	160	144	136	164	133	129	157	127	126	139
15216	PITTSBURGH	79	88	104	87	87	94	88	85	87	86	109	99	91	113	89	87	107	86	84	94
15217	PITTSBURGH	109	121	170	126	118	127	125	118	123	125	155	140	130	160	126	121	153	121	111	129
15218	PITTSBURGH	83	88	109	89	87	94	91	88	91	90	114	103	93	116	92	90	112	90	86	97
15219	PITTSBURGH	42	36	43	34	35	42	41	40	45	41	56	45	40	52	40	47	54	42	44	46
15220	PITTSBURGH	84	87	111	88	86	94	92	88	92	91	116	102	94	118	92	92	113	90	87	97
15221	PITTSBURGH	66	65	81	65	64	72	71	68	73	70	91	78	71	90	70	73	89	70	69	76
15222	PITTSBURGH	85	76	111	79	76	89	95	87	100	90	124	101	93	123	93	102	120	95	94	96
15223	PITTSBURGH	69	77	86	74	77	84	75	74	76	73	94	83	79	99	78	78	92	73	77	81
15224	PITTSBURGH	50	47	58	48	46	52	53	50	54	52	68	59	52	66	52	54	66	53	51	56
15225	PITTSBURGH	58	63	67	60	64	71	63	62	65	60	80	69	66	87	65	67	78	61	67	68
15226	PITTSBURGH	72	81	90	77	81	88	79	78	80	77	100	88	83	105	82	82	97	77	81	86
15227	PITTSBURGH	71	77	86	75	77	84	77	76	77	75	96	86	80	98	78	78	94	76	77	83
15228	PITTSBURGH	120	143	176	142	139	148	137	133	132	136	166	154	144	172	140	131	165	133	126	145
15229	PITTSBURGH	84	91	100	90	91	98	90	90	90	89	112	103	93	115	92	90	109	89	90	99
15232	PITTSBURGH	100	91	149	103	87	98	112	99	113	111	143	124	112	143	107	109	141	109	93	111
15233	PITTSBURGH	56	49	59	48	48	55	56	54	60	57	75	62	56	72	54	61	73	57	57	62
15234	PITTSBURGH	85	95	109	93	95	102	93	92	92	92	115	104	97	119	96	93	113	91	92	100
15235	PITTSBURGH	85	95	105	91	94	103	91	91	91	91	114	102	96	116	94	93	112	90	94	101
15236	PITTSBURGH	90	103	117	100	102	111	99	99	98	98	122	111	104	126	102	99	120	97	98	107
15237	PITTSBURGH	115	133	154	133	132	139	128	126	123	127	155	144	134	159	131	123	153	125	121	138
15238	PITTSBURGH	188	225	273	221	222	240	209	208	201	210	253	234	224	259	218	203	251	204	203	227
15239	PITTSBURGH	86	99	107	97	97	101	93	93	90	93	113	107	98	118	95	89	112	91	88	102
15241	PITTSBURGH	187	231	274	230	227	237	211	209	198	212	250	239	227	259	218	197	250	204	195	228
15243	PITTSBURGH	132	152	173	149	152	164	142	144	138	143	173	161	150	173	148	139	170	141	143	157
15282	PITTSBURGH	0	0	0	0	0	0	0	0	0	0	0	0	0	0	0	0	0	0	0	0
15301	WASHINGTON	76	75	74	72	76	83	75	76	77	73	95	87	75	96	76	79	91	76	80	88
15310	ALEPPO	74	50	23	43	56	65	48	60	58	49	68	72	41	64	49	62	62	59	74	85
15311	AMITY	92	83	64	79	87	94	76	85	81	76	99	101	75	101	79	83	94	82	91	109
15312	AVELLA	79	74	66	71	77	85	73	76	76	71	94	88	73	97	74	79	89	75	82	91
15313	BEALLSVILLE	88	79	62	75	83	90	74	81	78	73	95	96	73	98	76	80	90	79	88	103
15314	BENTLEYVILLE	70	73	78	70	73	81	75	73	77	72	95	83	77	99	76	79	92	73	77	81
15317	CANONSBURG	111	126	137	123	126	134	119	120	117	118	147	136	125	153	123	119	144	117	119	133
15320	CARMICHAELS	64	53	42	50	57	66	56	60	61	54	73	68	52	72	56	64	68	60	70	73
15321	CECIL	87	106	117	103	103	106	98	97	93	97	117	112	104	125	100	92	117	94	90	105
15322	CLARKSVILLE	63	53	41	50	56	66	56	60	62	54	74	67	53	72	56	65	68	60	70	71
15323	CLAYSVILLE	83	73	56	68	77	84	69	76	74	68	89	90	67	91	70	76	85	74	84	97
15324	COKEBURG	54	58	62	55	59	66	58	57	60	56	74	64	61	80	60	62	72	56	61	63
15327	DILLINER	76	53	29	48	60	70	55	65	64	54	75	75	47	71	55	68	68	64	79	86
15329	PROSPERITY	90	79	60	75	83	89	74	82	78	74	95	97	71	95	75	79	90	80	87	104
15330	EIGHTY FOUR	108	118	117	115	119	124	108	112	106	108	131	130	112	136	111	106	129	108	110	129
15331	ELLSWORTH	57	62	66	59	63	70	61	61	64	59	79	68	65	86	64	66	76	60	65	67
15332	FINLEYVILLE	80	88	92	85	88	94	83	84	83	82	103	97	87	108	86	84	101	83	85	95
15333	FREDERICKTOWN	62	57	50	54	59	68	58	61	62	56	75	68	57	75	59	65	71	61	69	71
15337	GRAYSVILLE	89	59	27	51	67	77	57	72	69	58	81	86	49	77	58	74	74	71	88	102
15338	GREENSBORO	84	66	45	59	72	82	64	74	73	64	88	86	60	87	66	78	82	73	87	97
15340	HICKORY	105	83	55	78	92	101	80	93	88	79	105	111	73	106	82	92	98	91	106	124
15341	HOLBROOK	79	53	24	46	60	69	51	64	62	52	73	77	44	69	52	67	66	64	79	91
15342	HOUSTON	66	75	81	71	75	82	72	72	73	71	91	80	76	96	75	75	89	70	75	79
15344	JEFFERSON	74	61	47	55	66	74	60	67	67	59	81	77	57	82	61	71	76	66	78	85
15345	MARIANNA	62	55	46	52	58	66	57	60	61	54	73	68	55	74	57	64	69	59	68	71
15346	MATHER	58	61	62	57	62	69	60	60	63	58	78	68	63	83	62	65	75	59	66	68
15349	MOUNT MORRIS	81	58	33	53	64	76	60	70	70	59	82	81	53	77	60	74	75	70	85	91
15352	NEW FREEPORT	70	47	21	41	53	61	45	57	55	46	64	68	39	61	46	59	59	56	70	81
15353	NINEVEH	0	0	0	0	0	0	0	0	0	0	0	0	0	0	0	0	0	0	0	0
15357	RICES LANDING	70	77	82	73	78	86	75	75	77	73	95	84	79	101	78	79	93	73	79	83
15359	ROGERSVILLE	84	56	25	48	64	73	54	68	65	55	77	81	46	72	55	70	70	67	83	96
15360	SCENERY HILL	94	78	56	73	84	92	74	84	81	74	98	99	70	98	76	84	92	82	94	109
15362	SPRAGGS	80	54	24	46	61	70	52	65	63	53	74	78	44	70	53	68	67	64	80	92
15363	STRABANE	49	53	56	50	54	60	53	52	54	51	68	58	56	73	54	57	65	51	56	57
15364	SYCAMORE	91	67	38	60	74	83	63	76	73	64	87	91	57	84	65	78	80	75	90	105
15367	VENETIA	149	191	213	192	186	187	168	166	155	169	196	192	183	208	173	151	197	160	148	182
15370	WAYNESBURG	68	53	40	51	57	66	57	61	63	55	75	71	52	73	56	65	70	62	70	76
15376	WEST ALEXANDER	89	69	42	62	75	83	65	76	73	65	88	91	59	86	66	77	81	75	88	103
15377	WEST FINLEY	80	66	46	61	71	77	62	70	68	62	81	84	58	82	63	70	76	69	79	93
15380	WIND RIDGE	83	56	25	48	63	72	54	67	65	55	76	80	46	72	55	70	69	66	83	95
15401	UNIONTOWN	67	60	57	57	62	71	62	65	67	61	81	73	60	79	62	69	77	65	72	76
15410	ADAH	58	54	48	51	56	64	56	58	60	53	72	64	55	74	57	62	68	57	65	66
15411	ADDISON	76	60	41	54	67	76	56	68	64	56	76	80	50	75	60	68	70	67	80	93
15412	ALLENPORT	62	68	71	64	68	76	67	66	69	64	86	74	71	93	69	72	83	65	71	73
15413	ALLISON	84	82	77	77	84	96	83	85	88	80	108	95	84	112	85	92	102	84	95	96
15417	BROWNSVILLE	59	59	63	57	60	68	61	61	64	59	79	68	62	81	62	66	76	61	66	68
15419	CALIFORNIA	50	47	58	47	46	52	57	51	57	53	71	61	55	70	54	55	69	54	50	56
15423	COAL CENTER	77	85	92	80	85	94	83	82	85	81	106	92	88	113	86	88	103	81	87	90
15424	CONFLUENCE	64	48	30	44	54	62	49	57	55	48	65	66	43	63	50	59	60	56	68	75
15425	CONNELLSVILLE	66	57	50	53	60	68	58	62	63	57	77	71	56	77	59	66	73	62	70	76
15427	DAISYTOWN	65	71	76	67	72	79	70	69	72	67	89	77	74	95	72	74	86	68	73	76
15428	DAWSON	72	56	36	50	61	70	55	63	63	55	75	74	51	74	56	67	70	63	75	83
15431	DUNBAR	71	52	29	46	57	65	49	59	58	50	68	71	44	66	51	61	63	59	71	82
15432	DUNLEVY	52	56	59	53	57	63	56	55	58	54	72	61	59	78	58	60	69	54	59	61
15433	EAST MILLSBORO	78	72	65	68	75	86	74	77	80	71	96	86	73	99	75	83	91	76	87	88
15434	ELCO	55	60	63	57	61	67	59	59	61	57	76	65	63	82	61	64	74	57	63	65
15436	FAIRCHANCE	63	49	34	46	54	62	51	57	58	50	68	65	47	67	52	61	63	57	67	71
15437	FARMINGTON	97	70	39	65	79	89	68	82	78	68	92	99	60	90	70	82	85	81	97	113
15438	FAYETTE CITY	64	71	76	67	71	79	69	69	71	67	88	77	73	95	72	74	86	67	73	76
15440	GIBBON GLADE	92	71	43	64	77	86	67	79	76	67	90	94	61	89	68	80	84	77	91	107
15442	GRINDSTONE	53	52	52	49	53	60	53	54	56	52	69	60	54	70	54	59	66	53	60	61
15444	HILLER	54	58	61	55	59	65	58	57	60	55	74	64	61	80	60	62	72	56	61	63
15445	HOPWOOD	65	54	41	50	58	66	54	60	60	53	72	69	51	71	55	64	67	60	70	75
15446	INDIAN HEAD	84	56	26	49	64	74	54	68	66	56	77	81	46	73	55	71	70	67	84	97
15450	LA BELLE	75	81	85	77	82	91	80	79	83	77	103	88	85	112	83	86	100	78	85	88
15451	LAKE LYNN	67	45	20	39	51	58	43	54	52	44	61	65	37	58	44	56	56	53	67	77
15456	LEMONT FURNACE	64	54	42	49	58	65	53	59	58	52	70	68	50	71	54	61	66	58	67	74
	PENNSYLVANIA	89	89	93	87	90	98	89	90	91	88	112	104	89	114	90	92	109	90	92	104
	UNITED STATES	100	100	100	100	100	100	100	100	100	100	100	100	100	100	100	100	100	100	100	100

PENNSYLVANIA

POPULATION CHANGE

A 15458-15690

# POST OFFICE NAME	COUNTY FIPS CODE	POPULATION			2000-2004 ANNUAL RATE		HOUSEHOLDS					FAMILIES		
		2000	2004	2009	% Rate	State Centile	2000	2004	2009	% Annual Rate 2000-2004	2004 Average HH Size	2000	2004	% Annual Rate 2000-2004
15458 MC CLELLANDTOWN	051	3465	3433	3408	-0.2	28	1303	1314	1330	0.2	2.57	926	926	0.0
15459 MARKLEYSBURG	051	1818	1825	1823	0.1	44	637	654	667	0.6	2.65	474	483	0.4
15461 MASONTOWN	051	5050	4942	4880	-0.5	15	2095	2093	2108	0.0	2.34	1396	1383	-0.2
15462 MELCROFT	051	442	440	438	-0.1	34	170	173	176	0.4	2.54	128	130	0.4
15463 MERRITTSTOWN	051	987	971	961	-0.4	21	423	424	428	0.1	2.29	264	262	-0.2
15464 MILL RUN	051	1819	1838	1840	0.2	51	683	709	726	0.9	2.56	517	532	0.7
15468 NEW SALEM	051	3493	3422	3380	-0.5	17	1387	1384	1393	-0.1	2.47	984	974	-0.2
15469 NORMALVILLE	051	2973	3065	3101	0.7	72	1113	1176	1215	1.3	2.60	853	896	1.2
15470 OHIOPYLE	051	444	460	467	0.8	74	165	174	180	1.3	2.64	127	132	0.9
15473 PERRYOPOLIS	051	3261	3217	3187	-0.3	24	1384	1402	1422	0.3	2.28	934	939	0.1
15474 POINT MARION	051	2400	2385	2370	-0.2	32	999	1017	1034	0.4	2.33	699	706	0.2
15475 REPUBLIC	051	318	313	310	-0.4	22	128	128	130	0.0	2.43	94	93	-0.3
15477 ROSCOE	125	1074	1068	1072	-0.1	33	482	488	499	0.3	2.17	310	310	0.0
15478 SMITHFIELD	051	5492	5466	5439	-0.1	34	2100	2140	2175	0.4	2.55	1542	1561	0.3
15479 SMITHTON	129	1497	1488	1489	-0.1	32	620	620	623	0.0	2.40	462	458	-0.2
15480 SMOCK	051	2355	2343	2329	-0.1	33	924	940	954	0.4	2.48	681	689	0.3
15482 STAR JUNCTION	051	813	803	797	-0.3	25	356	363	369	0.5	2.15	234	236	0.2
15483 STOCKDALE	125	551	534	530	-0.7	9	249	247	250	-0.2	2.15	163	160	-0.4
15486 VANDERBILT	051	3194	3150	3121	-0.3	23	1221	1234	1248	0.3	2.53	886	889	0.1
15488 WALTERSBURG	051	140	138	137	-0.3	23	59	60	60	0.4	2.28	45	45	0.0
15490 WHITE	051	669	684	689	0.5	65	245	256	264	1.0	2.67	189	196	0.9
15501 SOMERSET	111	18761	19412	19920	0.8	74	6898	7250	7578	1.2	2.41	4570	4782	1.1
15521 ALUM BANK	009	2049	2134	2089	1.0	78	741	789	790	1.5	2.70	577	612	1.4
15522 BEDFORD	009	12099	11605	10941	-1.0	5	5075	4965	4782	-0.5	2.28	3466	3369	-0.7
15530 BERLIN	111	5581	5662	5724	0.3	56	2106	2233	2336	1.4	2.17	1560	1643	1.2
15531 BOSWELL	111	4785	4968	5110	0.9	76	1983	2106	2214	1.4	2.35	1391	1468	1.3
15533 BREEZEWOOD	009	1171	1111	1044	-1.2	2	475	460	442	-0.8	2.41	351	338	-0.9
15534 BUFFALO MILLS	009	765	728	683	-1.2	3	298	289	277	-0.7	2.48	232	224	-0.8
15535 CLEARVILLE	009	2289	2158	2018	-1.4	1	854	822	786	-0.9	2.63	669	641	-1.0
15536 CRYSTAL SPRING	057	461	484	531	1.2	83	188	202	227	1.7	2.38	135	144	1.5
15537 EVERETT	009	7995	7639	7183	-1.1	4	3241	3165	3046	-0.6	2.37	2323	2255	-0.7
15538 FAIRHOPE	111	740	737	737	-0.1	34	300	308	316	0.6	2.38	226	230	0.4
15539 FISHERTOWN	009	705	677	637	-1.0	5	292	286	276	-0.5	2.37	221	216	-0.5
15540 FORT HILL	111	431	431	430	0.0	39	166	170	174	0.6	2.49	119	121	0.4
15541 FRIEDENS	111	4698	4792	4860	0.5	62	1746	1821	1889	1.0	2.62	1337	1386	0.9
15542 GARRETT	111	1151	1134	1131	-0.4	23	412	415	423	0.2	2.73	327	328	0.1
15545 HYNDMAN	009	3017	2852	2694	-1.3	2	1215	1174	1135	-0.8	2.42	904	869	-0.9
15546 JENNERS	111	336	358	370	1.5	88	134	146	155	2.0	2.45	96	104	1.9
15550 MANNS CHOICE	009	1795	1711	1607	-1.1	3	704	684	656	-0.7	2.47	531	513	-0.8
15551 MARKLETON	111	884	889	890	0.1	45	324	334	341	0.7	2.61	253	259	0.6
15552 MEYERSDALE	111	6752	6696	6690	-0.2	29	2527	2567	2625	0.4	2.55	1869	1886	0.2
15554 NEW PARIS	009	2828	2851	2750	0.2	48	1062	1099	1087	0.8	2.59	806	829	0.7
15557 ROCKWOOD	111	3846	3881	3903	0.2	49	1565	1616	1662	0.8	2.37	1136	1164	0.6
15558 SALISBURY	111	2358	2371	2383	0.1	45	885	908	932	0.6	2.58	640	651	0.4
15559 SCHELLSBURG	009	1819	1731	1624	-1.2	3	708	689	663	-0.6	2.50	543	526	-0.8
15562 SPRINGS	111	54	53	53	-0.4	19	16	16	17	0.0	3.31	12	12	0.0
15563 STOYSTOWN	111	3525	3498	3507	-0.2	30	1390	1415	1451	0.4	2.47	1025	1036	0.3
15601 GREENSBURG	129	55641	56159	56739	0.2	50	22883	23268	23713	0.4	2.30	15065	15209	0.2
15610 ACME	051	3339	3654	3854	2.1	94	1268	1416	1523	2.6	2.57	958	1067	2.6
15611 ADAMSBURG	129	180	179	178	-0.1	33	62	62	63	0.0	2.87	48	48	0.0
15612 ALVERTON	129	527	517	515	-0.5	18	200	198	199	-0.2	2.61	143	141	-0.3
15613 APOLLO	129	16909	16935	17102	0.0	41	6638	6726	6876	0.3	2.48	4915	4949	-0.7
15615 ARDARA	129	247	239	238	-0.8	8	96	94	94	-0.5	2.54	73	71	-0.7
15616 ARMBRUST	129	450	447	447	-0.2	31	170	170	171	0.0	2.63	131	130	-0.2
15617 ARONA	129	407	419	424	0.7	71	166	169	172	0.4	2.47	122	123	0.2
15618 AVONMORE	005	2757	3125	3378	3.0	98	1084	1251	1371	3.4	2.49	810	921	3.1
15620 BRADENVILLE	129	88	88	88	0.0	39	39	39	40	0.0	2.05	28	28	0.0
15622 CHAMPION	051	679	687	689	0.3	53	278	289	297	0.9	2.37	199	205	0.7
15625 DARRAGH	129	162	177	185	2.1	93	65	72	76	2.4	2.46	48	52	1.9
15626 DELMONT	129	4941	5069	5142	0.6	68	2192	2285	2348	1.0	2.21	1471	1513	0.7
15627 DERRY	129	9202	9233	9307	0.1	43	3634	3673	3732	0.3	2.50	2630	2639	0.1
15628 DONEGAL	129	725	721	720	-0.1	33	288	289	291	0.1	2.49	203	202	-0.1
15631 EVERSON	051	678	658	647	-0.7	10	281	279	280	-0.2	2.35	189	186	-0.4
15632 EXPORT	129	8138	8119	8146	-0.1	36	3124	3144	3182	0.2	2.55	2293	2288	-0.1
15634 GRAPEVILLE	129	933	904	897	-0.7	8	360	352	353	-0.5	2.57	277	269	-0.7
15636 HARRISON CITY	129	2907	3123	3241	1.7	90	973	1046	1090	1.7	2.96	840	900	1.6
15637 HERMINIE	129	2733	2789	2823	0.5	62	1137	1170	1194	0.7	2.38	787	804	0.5
15639 HUNKER	129	1554	1609	1638	0.8	74	620	648	666	1.0	2.47	455	471	0.8
15641 HYDE PARK	129	513	493	489	-0.9	5	212	206	206	-0.7	2.38	156	150	-0.9
15642 IRWIN	129	44851	46752	48018	1.0	79	17312	18190	18833	1.2	2.54	13012	13573	1.0
15644 JEANNETTE	129	22474	22444	22608	0.0	37	9231	9272	9403	0.1	2.40	6402	6397	0.0
15646 JONES MILLS	129	329	327	327	-0.1	32	147	148	149	0.2	2.21	103	103	0.0
15647 LARIMER	129	106	107	108	0.2	50	38	39	40	0.6	2.72	28	29	0.8
15650 LATROBE	129	30231	30232	30476	0.0	39	12159	12248	12451	0.2	2.33	8219	8218	0.0
15655 LAUGHLINTOWN	129	627	617	615	-0.4	21	282	280	282	-0.2	2.20	202	199	-0.4
15656 LEECHBURG	129	10445	10409	10519	-0.1	35	4304	4359	4473	0.3	2.37	3086	3092	0.1
15658 LIGONIER	129	8645	8611	8641	-0.1	34	3665	3675	3714	0.1	2.31	2532	2522	-0.1
15661 LOYALHANNA	129	295	337	363	3.2	98	130	151	165	3.6	2.22	93	107	3.4
15663 MADISON	129	360	393	411	2.1	93	157	173	183	2.2	2.27	115	126	2.2
15665 MANOR	129	1182	1213	1230	0.6	68	462	477	487	0.8	2.53	332	339	0.5
15666 MOUNT PLEASANT	129	17828	17688	17765	-0.2	30	7285	7290	7389	0.0	2.39	5090	5058	-0.2
15668 MURRYSVILLE	129	12886	13304	13581	0.8	72	4909	5117	5269	1.0	2.57	3878	4019	0.8
15670 NEW ALEXANDRIA	129	3118	3143	3172	0.2	48	1223	1244	1266	0.4	2.50	898	908	0.3
15672 NEW STANTON	129	3116	3364	3502	1.8	91	1366	1490	1566	2.1	2.21	896	970	1.9
15675 PENN	129	1199	1244	1273	0.9	75	485	508	524	1.1	2.45	351	366	1.0
15677 RECTOR	129	440	434	433	-0.3	24	183	182	183	-0.1	2.38	127	125	-0.4
15678 RILLTON	129	207	214	217	0.8	74	85	88	90	0.8	2.43	55	57	0.8
15679 RUFFS DALE	129	5675	5557	5531	-0.5	16	2234	2207	2217	-0.3	2.51	1638	1607	-0.5
15681 SALTSBURG	063	4246	4578	4823	1.8	91	1686	1852	1991	2.2	2.47	1199	1313	2.2
15683 SCOTTDALE	129	8045	8162	8267	0.3	56	3316	3414	3501	0.7	2.36	2275	2318	0.4
15684 SLICKVILLE	129	491	485	483	-0.3	25	200	199	200	-0.1	2.44	139	137	-0.3
15686 SPRING CHURCH	005	901	911	931	0.3	52	356	368	383	0.8	2.48	273	281	0.7
15687 STAHLSTOWN	129	2640	2611	2605	-0.3	27	1005	1003	1008	-0.1	2.50	754	748	-0.2
15688 TARRS	129	202	196	195	-0.7	9	80	79	79	-0.3	2.48	59	57	-0.8
15690 VANDERGRIFT	005	9298	9211	9244	-0.2	28	3993	3985	4036	-0.1	2.31	2596	2570	-0.2
PENNSYLVANIA					0.3					0.7	2.44			0.6
UNITED STATES					1.2					1.3	2.58			1.1

#	POST OFFICE NAME	RACE (%) White 2000	White 2004	Black 2000	Black 2004	Asian/Pacific 2000	Asian/Pacific 2004	% Hispanic Origin 2000	% Hispanic Origin 2004	2004 AGE DISTRIBUTION (%) 0-4	5-9	10-14	15-19	20-24	25-44	45-64	65-84	85+	18+	MEDIAN AGE 2004	% 2004 Males	% 2004 Females
15458	MC CLELLANDTOWN	90.4	89.2	8.5	9.6	0.1	0.1	0.4	0.4	5.3	5.9	7.7	6.3	5.3	26.2	27.3	13.8	2.2	77.0	40.6	48.1	51.9
15459	MARKLEYSBURG	99.2	99.0	0.3	0.3	0.1	0.1	0.4	0.4	6.0	6.0	6.0	6.0	5.8	28.3	24.8	14.3	2.9	78.2	40.0	49.9	50.1
15461	MASONTOWN	93.7	92.9	5.2	5.9	0.1	0.1	0.4	0.5	5.7	6.1	7.1	6.5	5.8	24.3	25.9	15.8	2.9	77.1	41.1	46.4	53.6
15462	MELCROFT	99.6	99.6	0.0	0.0	0.0	0.0	0.9	0.9	6.4	6.6	7.3	7.5	6.6	28.9	25.9	9.8	1.1	75.0	36.4	51.6	48.4
15463	MERRITTSTOWN	92.5	91.6	5.7	6.4	0.0	0.0	0.4	0.4	5.5	5.8	6.7	5.4	5.6	25.2	25.9	17.4	2.7	78.6	41.8	45.5	54.5
15464	MILL RUN	99.0	98.9	0.0	0.0	0.1	0.1	0.7	0.8	6.3	6.9	6.7	6.4	6.0	29.0	26.3	11.0	1.5	75.9	37.5	50.5	49.5
15468	NEW SALEM	91.5	90.4	7.1	8.1	0.3	0.3	0.3	0.4	6.1	5.6	6.9	6.8	5.3	26.6	25.3	15.1	2.4	77.2	40.8	46.9	53.1
15469	NORMALVILLE	99.2	99.1	0.0	0.0	0.0	0.1	0.3	0.4	6.5	7.2	7.0	6.3	5.3	29.8	25.6	10.9	1.3	75.1	37.2	51.0	49.0
15470	OHIOPYLE	99.6	99.4	0.2	0.2	0.0	0.0	0.7	0.7	4.8	5.2	7.4	6.5	6.3	27.0	29.1	12.2	1.5	78.5	41.1	50.9	49.1
15473	PERRYOPOLIS	97.7	97.5	1.4	1.6	0.3	0.3	0.3	0.3	4.5	4.8	5.7	5.1	5.2	24.3	28.3	19.2	3.0	81.9	45.3	47.7	52.4
15474	POINT MARION	98.8	98.7	0.2	0.3	0.0	0.0	0.5	0.6	5.9	5.7	6.2	6.1	6.3	26.3	27.0	14.4	2.1	78.5	40.4	50.5	49.5
15475	REPUBLIC	95.0	93.9	3.5	4.2	0.3	0.3	0.3	0.0	4.8	5.1	6.7	6.1	6.1	27.2	24.3	17.3	2.6	79.2	40.8	47.9	52.1
15477	ROSCOE	98.2	98.0	0.9	1.1	0.1	0.2	0.3	0.3	4.9	5.0	5.4	4.7	5.0	23.2	27.8	20.8	3.3	81.7	46.1	46.4	53.7
15478	SMITHFIELD	98.5	98.3	0.5	0.6	0.1	0.2	0.5	0.5	5.6	6.0	6.4	6.4	6.3	27.9	27.0	13.0	1.5	78.0	39.5	48.6	51.5
15479	SMITHTON	97.3	97.0	1.1	1.2	0.1	0.2	0.5	0.5	5.1	5.4	6.6	5.7	4.8	26.8	29.1	14.6	1.9	79.3	42.2	48.9	51.1
15480	SMOCK	98.2	98.0	1.1	1.3	0.0	0.0	0.1	0.1	5.8	6.2	6.8	5.8	4.9	26.7	27.7	14.5	1.6	77.6	40.8	48.7	51.3
15482	STAR JUNCTION	98.0	97.8	1.0	1.1	0.3	0.4	0.1	0.3	4.1	4.5	5.5	5.5	5.4	25.5	27.3	18.8	3.5	82.3	44.7	45.8	54.2
15483	STOCKDALE	99.1	98.9	0.5	0.6	0.2	0.2	0.2	0.2	4.1	4.3	4.5	5.1	3.8	25.7	29.4	19.7	3.6	84.6	46.7	46.6	53.4
15486	VANDERBILT	98.1	97.8	1.2	1.3	0.1	0.1	0.1	0.1	4.8	5.6	6.7	6.1	5.4	26.7	28.6	14.5	1.7	79.0	41.7	49.5	50.5
15488	WALTERSBURG	98.6	99.3	0.7	0.7	0.0	0.0	0.0	0.0	5.1	5.8	8.0	5.8	5.8	26.8	27.5	13.0	2.2	76.1	40.5	50.7	49.3
15490	WHITE	99.3	99.1	0.0	0.0	0.0	0.0	0.2	0.3	6.1	6.1	6.7	6.6	6.4	28.5	27.2	11.3	1.0	77.1	38.3	51.5	48.5
15501	SOMERSET	93.5	92.9	4.5	4.9	0.6	0.7	1.3	1.4	5.2	5.2	5.7	5.9	6.8	28.6	25.9	14.1	2.7	80.2	40.3	52.3	47.7
15521	ALUM BANK	98.2	97.8	0.3	0.4	0.2	0.2	1.0	1.0	6.9	6.9	7.6	6.8	6.3	27.7	23.9	12.8	1.1	74.4	37.3	49.8	50.2
15522	BEDFORD	97.8	97.5	0.8	0.9	0.6	0.7	0.6	0.6	5.2	5.4	6.0	5.6	5.3	25.5	27.3	17.0	2.8	79.9	43.2	48.9	51.1
15530	BERLIN	91.1	90.1	6.8	7.5	0.3	0.4	1.8	1.9	5.5	5.5	5.7	5.4	7.4	31.0	24.5	12.6	2.4	80.0	38.4	54.7	45.4
15531	BOSWELL	99.4	99.3	0.0	0.0	0.1	0.1	0.2	0.1	5.7	6.1	5.9	5.7	5.4	26.0	27.9	15.0	2.3	78.8	41.8	48.8	51.2
15533	BREEZEWOOD	99.0	98.9	0.1	0.1	0.2	0.3	0.6	0.5	5.9	6.4	7.0	6.0	5.1	27.7	28.2	12.2	1.4	76.6	39.2	50.3	49.7
15534	BUFFALO MILLS	98.6	98.4	0.1	0.1	0.1	0.1	0.5	0.7	6.5	6.5	5.9	5.9	4.7	25.3	28.3	15.4	1.7	77.6	41.7	51.4	48.6
15535	CLEARVILLE	98.5	98.4	0.3	0.3	0.1	0.1	0.4	0.5	5.6	5.8	6.6	6.7	5.6	26.1	28.4	14.1	1.2	77.9	41.1	51.7	48.3
15536	CRYSTAL SPRING	98.3	98.1	0.0	0.0	0.0	0.0	0.4	0.6	7.2	7.2	6.6	5.4	4.8	24.4	26.2	16.1	2.1	75.4	41.0	48.8	51.2
15537	EVERETT	98.7	98.6	0.3	0.3	0.2	0.3	0.4	0.5	5.8	5.8	6.0	5.3	5.4	26.0	26.5	16.6	2.6	79.0	42.1	48.4	51.6
15538	FAIRHOPE	98.2	97.8	0.1	0.1	0.5	0.7	1.0	1.1	5.0	5.2	6.2	6.2	5.7	24.7	30.7	15.1	1.2	79.8	43.2	51.7	48.3
15539	FISHERTOWN	98.4	97.9	0.6	0.6	0.7	0.9	0.7	0.7	6.9	6.8	7.1	6.8	5.8	29.5	23.3	12.9	0.9	75.0	37.2	51.0	49.0
15540	FORT HILL	99.8	100.0	0.0	0.0	0.0	0.0	0.2	0.5	5.1	5.3	6.0	5.6	5.6	24.8	27.2	18.1	2.3	80.1	43.3	50.4	49.7
15541	FRIEDENS	99.4	99.3	0.1	0.1	0.2	0.2	0.2	0.2	6.7	6.8	7.1	6.6	5.8	27.7	25.4	12.7	1.4	75.4	38.5	50.3	49.8
15542	GARRETT	99.1	99.0	0.2	0.2	0.1	0.1	0.0	0.1	6.4	6.4	7.2	6.4	6.4	28.5	24.7	12.4	1.6	76.1	37.9	51.2	48.9
15545	HYNDMAN	98.6	98.5	0.1	0.1	0.0	0.0	0.5	0.5	6.3	6.4	6.4	6.1	5.2	25.5	26.2	16.1	1.9	77.1	41.1	49.9	50.1
15546	JENNERS	99.1	99.2	0.0	0.0	0.0	0.0	0.0	0.0	4.2	4.5	6.2	6.2	5.9	26.0	30.5	14.5	2.2	81.6	43.3	50.8	49.2
15550	MANNS CHOICE	99.0	98.9	0.1	0.1	0.3	0.4	0.6	0.6	5.6	6.2	6.8	6.0	4.6	25.8	27.0	15.8	2.1	77.1	41.9	50.5	49.5
15551	MARKLETON	99.1	99.0	0.1	0.1	0.0	0.0	0.2	0.2	5.5	5.9	7.3	7.0	5.2	26.4	27.7	13.5	1.6	76.9	40.9	51.6	48.4
15552	MEYERSDALE	99.2	99.0	0.2	0.2	0.1	0.1	0.4	0.5	5.6	5.7	6.6	6.6	6.0	26.0	25.7	15.4	2.5	77.9	40.7	48.7	51.3
15554	NEW PARIS	98.4	98.1	0.6	0.6	0.5	0.6	0.5	0.6	6.8	6.8	6.9	6.8	5.4	28.8	25.3	12.0	1.1	75.2	38.0	50.4	49.6
15557	ROCKWOOD	99.4	99.4	0.2	0.2	0.1	0.1	0.2	0.3	5.3	5.5	6.8	5.6	5.1	26.7	27.2	15.8	2.0	78.7	41.8	49.2	50.8
15558	SALISBURY	99.5	99.4	0.0	0.0	0.0	0.0	0.6	0.7	6.2	6.3	7.1	6.3	6.1	25.3	24.4	15.9	2.4	76.3	40.1	48.9	51.1
15559	SCHELLSBURG	98.7	98.6	0.4	0.4	0.2	0.3	0.7	0.8	5.4	5.8	6.4	6.4	4.0	26.6	29.6	14.3	1.6	78.3	42.2	50.5	49.5
15562	SPRINGS	100.0	100.0	0.0	0.0	0.0	0.0	0.0	0.0	7.6	7.6	7.6	7.6	7.6	26.4	18.9	15.1	1.9	73.6	33.1	52.8	47.2
15563	STOYSTOWN	99.5	99.4	0.0	0.0	0.1	0.1	0.5	0.5	5.3	5.8	6.8	6.0	5.4	26.0	29.1	14.1	1.6	78.5	41.7	50.0	50.0
15601	GREENSBURG	96.2	95.6	1.9	2.2	0.9	1.1	0.6	0.6	4.7	5.1	5.9	6.5	5.7	25.3	28.3	15.4	3.1	80.5	42.9	47.3	52.7
15610	ACME	99.4	99.3	0.0	0.0	0.2	0.2	0.5	0.6	6.3	6.5	6.3	5.5	5.3	28.5	29.0	11.3	1.3	77.5	39.9	50.1	49.9
15611	ADAMSBURG	97.8	97.8	1.1	1.1	0.6	0.6	0.0	0.6	5.0	6.2	6.7	6.2	5.0	26.8	30.7	11.7	1.7	78.2	42.1	49.7	50.3
15612	ALVERTON	98.9	98.8	0.2	0.2	0.4	0.4	0.4	0.6	6.4	6.0	6.0	6.0	5.4	30.0	23.6	15.1	1.6	78.1	38.6	48.6	51.5
15613	APOLLO	98.1	97.9	1.1	1.2	0.1	0.2	0.4	0.4	5.3	5.7	6.6	6.1	5.3	24.8	28.8	15.3	2.1	78.5	42.8	49.1	51.0
15615	ARDARA	99.2	99.6	0.0	0.0	0.4	0.4	0.4	0.4	5.9	6.3	7.1	5.4	4.6	25.9	29.3	14.2	1.3	77.0	42.0	49.4	50.6
15616	ARMBRUST	99.1	98.9	0.0	0.0	0.9	1.1	0.4	0.7	4.9	5.6	6.0	5.2	4.9	25.3	32.0	14.8	1.3	80.1	43.9	49.2	50.8
15617	ARONA	98.5	98.3	0.3	0.2	0.3	0.2	0.5	0.5	5.0	5.3	6.7	6.0	5.0	27.0	29.8	13.4	1.9	79.2	42.2	49.6	50.4
15618	AVONMORE	98.1	97.9	1.1	1.3	0.2	0.2	0.3	0.3	5.8	6.1	6.4	5.4	5.3	26.0	27.2	15.3	2.5	78.2	42.0	48.5	51.5
15620	BRADENVILLE	98.9	100.0	0.0	0.0	0.0	0.0	0.0	0.0	3.4	4.6	4.6	4.6	5.7	20.5	28.4	23.9	4.6	85.2	49.3	50.0	50.0
15622	CHAMPION	99.1	99.0	0.0	0.0	0.2	0.3	0.6	0.6	5.4	5.7	6.6	5.8	5.1	29.0	27.7	13.4	1.5	78.6	40.4	51.1	48.9
15625	DARRAGH	98.8	98.9	0.6	0.6	0.6	0.6	0.0	0.0	4.5	4.5	5.1	5.1	6.2	25.4	32.2	15.3	1.7	82.5	44.5	49.2	50.9
15626	DELMONT	97.7	97.3	0.8	1.0	0.6	0.8	0.4	0.5	5.9	6.1	5.8	5.8	4.5	24.0	28.7	17.0	2.2	78.5	43.8	48.0	52.0
15627	DERRY	98.7	98.6	0.8	0.9	0.1	0.1	0.5	0.6	5.6	5.8	6.9	6.0	5.7	26.9	27.4	13.8	1.9	78.1	40.7	48.9	51.1
15628	DONEGAL	99.3	99.5	0.0	0.0	0.0	0.0	0.7	0.8	6.4	6.4	5.8	5.7	4.9	27.1	28.7	13.5	1.7	78.0	40.8	49.9	50.1
15631	EVERSON	96.5	95.9	3.1	3.5	0.3	0.3	0.0	0.0	6.5	6.7	6.7	4.7	5.2	28.3	22.5	16.7	2.7	76.8	40.0	51.2	48.8
15632	EXPORT	96.9	96.2	0.6	0.7	1.9	2.4	0.5	0.5	5.3	6.3	7.3	7.0	4.9	24.5	29.3	13.5	1.9	76.6	42.2	49.5	50.5
15634	GRAPEVILLE	99.3	99.1	0.1	0.1	0.2	0.2	0.1	0.3	6.0	6.0	5.2	5.8	6.0	23.2	30.2	16.4	1.3	79.4	43.6	47.1	52.9
15636	HARRISON CITY	98.6	98.3	0.2	0.3	0.7	0.9	0.5	0.5	7.0	7.9	9.1	7.2	5.1	25.9	29.0	7.6	1.3	71.0	38.8	49.6	50.4
15637	HERMINIE	98.8	98.8	0.2	0.2	0.2	0.3	0.7	0.7	5.2	5.5	6.1	5.8	5.2	26.7	27.9	15.2	2.4	79.6	42.1	48.9	51.1
15639	HUNKER	98.0	97.7	0.5	0.6	0.5	0.7	0.3	0.3	5.3	5.9	5.4	4.9	5.1	27.0	32.3	12.7	1.5	80.4	42.8	50.0	50.0
15641	HYDE PARK	97.3	97.0	1.6	1.8	0.0	0.0	0.4	0.6	7.7	7.5	6.9	5.9	5.7	22.3	26.2	16.2	1.6	74.2	40.4	47.7	52.3
15642	IRWIN	98.5	98.2	0.5	0.5	0.5	0.6	0.4	0.5	5.5	5.9	6.7	5.9	5.2	25.7	28.7	14.6	1.9	78.1	42.1	48.4	51.6
15644	JEANNETTE	96.0	95.5	2.4	2.7	0.4	0.5	0.5	0.6	5.4	5.7	6.6	6.1	5.4	26.0	27.2	15.2	2.5	78.5	41.8	47.9	52.1
15646	JONES MILLS	99.4	99.4	0.0	0.0	0.0	0.0	0.6	0.9	6.4	6.4	5.8	5.8	4.9	26.9	28.4	13.8	1.5	77.7	40.7	50.8	49.2
15647	LARIMER	99.1	100.0	0.0	0.0	0.0	0.0	0.0	0.9	5.6	6.5	6.5	5.6	5.6	25.2	28.0	15.0	1.9	75.7	42.3	49.5	50.5
15650	LATROBE	98.6	98.4	0.4	0.4	0.5	0.6	0.4	0.4	4.9	5.2	6.0	6.4	6.4	25.3	26.3	16.9	2.7	80.2	42.3	48.5	51.5
15655	LAUGHLINTOWN	99.4	99.2	0.2	0.2	0.2	0.2	0.5	0.5	4.5	5.0	6.2	5.4	4.4	20.8	32.9	19.0	1.9	81.0	47.0	48.5	51.5
15656	LEECHBURG	98.1	97.8	0.9	1.0	0.2	0.2	0.4	0.5	5.3	5.5	6.2	5.8	5.4	24.1	28.1	16.8	2.8	79.4	43.6	48.8	51.2
15658	LIGONIER	99.4	99.3	0.1	0.1	0.1	0.2	0.3	0.4	4.4	4.7	5.7	5.7	4.8	22.8	30.6	18.5	2.9	81.8	46.1	48.7	51.3
15661	LOYALHANNA	99.3	99.4	0.3	0.3	0.0	0.0	0.0	0.6	5.9	5.9	6.2	5.9	5.6	24.0	24.9	19.3	2.1	78.0	42.3	48.4	51.6
15663	MADISON	98.9	98.7	0.6	0.5	0.3	0.3	0.0	0.0	4.1	4.3	5.1	5.3	5.9	25.2	33.3	14.8	2.0	83.2	45.1	49.9	50.1
15665	MANOR	99.3	99.3	0.1	0.1	0.3	0.4	0.9	1.1	6.8	6.6	6.7	6.6	6.4	29.4	23.3	12.6	1.7	76.0	38.0	49.6	50.4
15666	MOUNT PLEASANT	98.6	98.4	0.7	0.8	0.1	0.2	0.4	0.4	5.0	5.2	5.9	5.8	5.3	26.1	27.7	16.5	2.6	80.3	42.9	48.1	51.9
15668	MURRYSVILLE	95.0	93.9	0.7	0.8	3.5	4.4	0.5	0.6	4.9	6.0	7.1	6.3	4.0	20.4	33.4	16.3	1.6	77.6	45.7	49.3	50.7
15670	NEW ALEXANDRIA	98.8	98.6	0.4	0.4	0.1	0.1	0.3	0.4	4.7	5.3	6.6	6.0	5.4	26.5	30.0	14.0	1.5	79.6	42.5	50.2	49.8
15672	NEW STANTON	97.7	97.3	1.1	1.2	0.5	0.5	0.8	0.9	4.5	4.7	4.7	4.9	5.3	28.1	31.4	14.5	1.9	83.0	43.7	49.4	50.6
15675	PENN	91.5	90.9	6.3	6.7	0.3	0.4	0.3	0.2	6.0	6.2	6.3	6.2	6.0	27.6	26.5	13.7	1.7	77.6	39.4	47.5	52.5
15677	RECTOR	99.6	99.5	0.2	0.2	0.0	0.0	0.0	0.0	4.4	5.3	6.5	5.3	3.7	21.9	33.4	17.5	2.1	80.7	46.6	50.5	49.5
15678	RILLTON	98.6	98.1	0.0	0.0	0.5	0.5	1.0	1.4	5.6	5.6	5.6	5.6	5.1	28.0	25.2	15.9	3.3	79.4	41.0	49.1	50.9
15679	RUFFS DALE	98.7	98.5	0.4	0.4	0.1	0.2	0.3	0.3	5.6	5.8	6.6	5.8	5.3	28.4	27.2	13.9	1.6	78.4	40.7	49.1	50.9
15681	SALTSBURG	98.8	98.7	0.4	0.4	0.2	0.2	0.7	0.7	5.8	6.3	7.0	6.8	4.9	26.5	27.2	13.9	1.8	76.7	40.6	49.9	50.2
15683	SCOTTDALE	98.3	98.1	1.0	1.2	0.2	0.2	0.3	0.3	5.0	5.3	6.2	5.8	5.6	26.0	26.8	16.8	2.6	79.8	42.4	47.3	52.7
15684	SLICKVILLE	98.0	97.5	1.4	1.7	0.0	0.0	0.4	0.4	5.2	6.2	8.5	7.6	3.9	26.2	27.2	13.6	1.7	75.7	40.6	51.3	48.7
15686	SPRING CHURCH	98.6	98.4	0.3	0.4	0.1	0.2	0.4	0.4	6.0	6.3	6.4	5.8	5.9	28.0	28.2	12.2	1.2	77.9	40.2	49.2	50.8
15687	STAHLSTOWN	99.4	99.4	0.1	0.1	0.0	0.0	0.5	0.6	4.9	5.4	6.9	5.6	4.6	26.0	29.4	15.2	2.1	79.4	42.8	50.9	49.1
15688	TARRS	98.5	98.5	0.5	0.5	0.0	0.0	0.0	0.0	5.6	5.6	6.1	5.6	4.6	28.1	26.5	16.3	1.5	79.1	41.6	48.5	51.5
15690	VANDERGRIFT	95.3	94.7	3.0	3.4	0.2	0.2	0.4	0.5	5.4	5.4	6.5	5.9	5.3	26.6	25.1	16.7	3.1	78.9	41.8	47.7	52.3
	PENNSYLVANIA	85.4	84.4	10.0	10.3	1.8	2.2	3.2	3.5	5.9	6.1	6.8	6.9	6.7	26.6	25.3	13.3	2.2	77.2	39.1	48.4	51.6
	UNITED STATES	75.1	73.6	12.3	12.5	3.8	4.2	12.5	14.1	6.9	6.7	7.2	7.0	7.3	28.6	23.8	10.8	1.7	75.1	36.0	49.1	50.9

#	POST OFFICE NAME	2004 Per Capita Income	2004 HH Income Base	2004 Household Income Distribution (%): Less than $25,000	$25,000 to $49,999	$50,000 to $99,999	$100,000 to $149,999	$150,000 or More	Median Household Income: 2004	2009	2004 National Centile	2004 State Centile	2004 Home Value Base	2004 Home Value Distribution (%): Less than $50,000	$50,000 to $89,999	$90,000 to $174,999	$175,000 to $399,999	$400,000 or More	2004 Median Home Value
15458	MC CLELLANDTOWN	19827	1314	37.8	29.5	24.7	4.7	3.4	32645	39190	20	12	1014	40.7	30.1	24.1	5.1	0.0	63421
15459	MARKLEYSBURG	14578	654	40.5	33.3	21.7	2.9	1.5	30584	35410	14	7	537	27.6	25.3	39.7	6.7	0.7	85441
15461	MASONTOWN	17573	2093	45.1	28.9	19.0	5.1	1.9	27343	31689	8	3	1457	28.0	37.3	31.2	3.4	0.1	71076
15462	MELCROFT	18276	173	28.3	31.8	35.8	4.1	0.0	44782	51717	61	61	144	37.5	14.6	34.0	11.8	2.1	87000
15463	MERRITTSTOWN	16898	424	47.2	26.4	19.8	4.3	2.4	26743	31455	7	3	290	40.7	30.3	22.1	6.9	0.0	58710
15464	MILL RUN	14957	709	37.5	36.7	22.1	2.4	1.3	32693	37774	20	12	578	34.6	29.1	28.2	7.3	0.9	68750
15468	NEW SALEM	16468	1384	44.9	26.9	21.1	5.6	1.5	28325	33284	9	4	1031	44.5	28.4	22.5	4.6	0.0	57338
15469	NORMALVILLE	17964	1176	37.4	26.8	29.2	4.3	2.3	34927	41454	27	20	970	30.8	27.5	29.9	10.7	1.0	78333
15470	OHIOPYLE	16580	174	31.6	40.2	21.8	3.5	2.9	36545	42164	34	28	146	28.1	31.5	29.5	8.2	2.7	77273
15473	PERRYOPOLIS	20642	1402	31.9	31.5	29.0	6.1	1.6	37554	46004	38	33	1107	23.4	22.8	39.8	13.3	0.7	95449
15474	POINT MARION	15883	1017	44.3	29.3	21.6	4.4	0.4	29764	33720	12	6	715	42.8	26.0	25.5	4.9	0.8	63152
15475	REPUBLIC	17287	128	42.2	25.8	26.6	3.9	1.6	28099	33270	9	4	92	42.4	27.2	21.7	8.7	0.0	62857
15477	ROSCOE	21482	488	33.2	33.8	25.6	6.6	0.8	36023	43213	32	25	369	32.8	36.6	27.6	2.4	0.5	68333
15478	SMITHFIELD	15855	2140	42.1	29.5	22.4	4.5	1.5	30584	35586	14	7	1632	35.7	27.9	28.2	8.2	0.1	72281
15479	SMITHTON	21543	620	25.2	35.0	30.0	8.1	1.8	42225	50944	54	54	506	20.8	26.5	37.0	13.4	2.4	95833
15480	SMOCK	18181	940	29.9	32.8	30.4	6.1	0.9	37467	44390	37	33	762	39.5	27.2	25.7	7.0	0.7	64032
15482	STAR JUNCTION	18785	363	39.9	30.3	25.1	4.1	0.6	33377	40112	22	14	268	47.8	23.5	21.3	6.3	1.1	55455
15483	STOCKDALE	24160	247	32.8	38.5	23.5	2.8	2.4	34160	41063	25	17	173	26.6	32.4	32.4	7.5	1.2	81389
15486	VANDERBILT	16982	1234	33.7	33.7	26.7	4.5	1.3	35714	42317	30	24	977	33.2	32.5	25.2	8.1	1.1	69943
15488	WALTERSBURG	19975	60	30.0	38.3	25.0	5.0	1.7	37333	45000	37	32	48	35.4	25.0	27.1	10.4	2.1	70000
15490	WHITE	20395	256	39.1	20.3	32.4	4.7	3.5	36390	45000	33	27	218	28.0	21.1	42.7	7.8	0.5	90833
15501	SOMERSET	19604	7250	32.7	33.6	26.6	4.1	3.0	36062	41357	32	26	5211	20.4	30.2	39.1	9.1	1.3	89473
15521	ALUM BANK	16301	789	32.2	38.8	24.0	3.7	1.4	34959	38917	27	20	667	20.5	23.7	40.0	15.3	0.5	95746
15522	BEDFORD	22126	4965	29.5	34.8	27.1	5.8	2.8	38078	44613	40	35	3771	11.7	14.6	50.6	21.0	2.2	121866
15530	BERLIN	19987	2233	30.0	35.3	29.1	3.5	2.1	38267	43778	40	37	1751	25.4	33.7	32.0	8.7	0.3	81658
15531	BOSWELL	18267	2106	32.9	35.7	25.6	4.6	1.1	35437	40516	29	22	1603	26.8	34.8	31.0	6.9	0.5	72398
15533	BREEZEWOOD	18208	460	35.0	36.5	22.8	3.5	2.2	34381	38711	25	18	386	30.3	17.4	36.3	14.3	1.8	92813
15534	BUFFALO MILLS	16492	289	30.1	39.5	28.0	2.4	0.0	37204	42633	36	31	244	16.0	25.4	43.4	14.3	0.8	101163
15535	CLEARVILLE	17132	822	27.5	40.3	26.6	3.7	2.0	36079	40769	32	26	704	12.9	18.0	45.5	21.3	2.3	113830
15536	CRYSTAL SPRING	16524	202	34.7	39.1	22.3	4.0	0.0	33998	38712	24	16	171	18.1	25.2	40.4	14.0	2.3	99583
15537	EVERETT	19610	3165	33.7	35.1	24.8	3.7	2.6	34094	38985	24	17	2424	16.4	24.0	43.5	14.0	2.1	100525
15538	FAIRHOPE	17923	308	34.7	33.1	26.6	3.9	1.6	34571	38792	26	18	257	30.7	33.1	26.9	8.2	1.2	71786
15539	FISHERTOWN	20581	286	28.3	33.2	30.8	6.6	1.1	39650	44577	45	43	240	24.2	17.5	42.9	14.6	0.8	102604
15540	FORT HILL	18181	170	37.7	32.9	22.9	4.1	2.4	32894	37112	21	13	140	32.1	34.3	26.4	6.4	0.7	71667
15541	FRIEDENS	17155	1821	27.6	41.0	25.9	3.5	2.0	37746	42961	38	34	1523	26.5	28.4	33.6	10.8	0.7	84102
15542	GARRETT	15069	415	36.6	33.7	25.5	2.9	1.2	36233	41206	32	26	347	41.2	33.1	19.6	4.9	1.2	59839
15545	HYNDMAN	16777	1174	37.9	33.8	24.3	3.3	0.7	32321	36671	19	11	954	23.6	31.5	36.0	8.5	0.5	83924
15546	JENNERS	15554	146	37.7	37.0	19.2	6.2	0.0	30581	33409	14	7	120	44.2	37.5	10.0	8.3	0.0	53889
15550	MANNS CHOICE	17478	684	27.5	41.5	26.8	3.7	0.6	37947	43448	39	35	574	17.4	20.9	44.1	15.2	2.4	104854
15551	MARKLETON	15583	334	33.2	41.6	21.3	3.3	0.6	35000	39268	28	21	284	34.2	33.5	24.7	7.4	0.4	72000
15552	MEYERSDALE	15982	2567	40.2	32.5	22.2	4.1	1.1	31153	35196	15	8	1997	32.9	37.1	24.0	5.5	0.5	66514
15554	NEW PARIS	18489	1099	30.9	34.2	27.2	5.6	2.1	37231	42511	36	31	925	22.7	17.6	42.5	16.0	1.2	103372
15557	ROCKWOOD	17986	1616	36.5	35.0	22.6	3.9	2.0	34950	39705	27	20	1323	28.9	38.3	26.0	5.9	0.9	73423
15558	SALISBURY	16646	908	39.8	30.8	22.6	4.6	2.2	32465	36675	19	11	707	27.9	39.2	25.7	6.2	1.0	71190
15559	SCHELLSBURG	17906	689	31.6	34.3	29.2	3.6	1.3	37836	43516	39	34	586	17.4	18.1	47.6	15.2	1.7	111111
15562	SPRINGS	11698	16	43.8	31.3	18.8	6.3	0.0	30000	42353	12	6	13	15.4	30.8	53.9	0.0	0.0	95000
15563	STOYSTOWN	17519	1415	32.2	35.3	27.6	3.6	1.3	36503	41572	34	28	1166	33.2	30.6	27.7	7.7	0.8	69688
15601	GREENSBURG	26491	23268	26.9	27.6	30.1	9.9	5.5	45714	55390	63	64	16808	8.2	16.0	48.9	23.4	3.5	124084
15610	ACME	19351	1416	24.6	31.9	36.5	6.2	0.9	45048	52300	61	62	1232	21.4	16.8	44.5	15.3	2.1	106410
15611	ADAMSBURG	24584	62	16.1	24.2	33.9	19.4	6.5	58314	71624	83	84	58	1.7	12.1	50.0	32.8	3.5	140625
15612	ALVERTON	17129	198	28.8	33.3	34.3	3.5	0.0	44254	51368	59	60	161	36.7	24.8	31.7	6.8	0.0	71667
15613	APOLLO	20586	6726	28.9	30.8	30.6	7.6	2.0	41559	48596	52	51	5513	16.8	22.3	44.4	15.7	0.9	104929
15615	ARDARA	20778	94	33.0	24.5	30.9	7.5	4.3	38223	50000	40	36	86	22.1	23.3	40.7	12.8	1.2	98000
15616	ARMBRUST	22900	170	22.4	25.3	36.5	12.9	2.9	52324	62029	76	76	147	9.5	21.8	45.6	21.1	2.0	109375
15617	ARONA	30013	169	18.9	30.2	33.7	8.9	8.3	50785	62098	73	73	149	18.1	18.1	45.6	18.1	0.0	115341
15618	AVONMORE	21544	1251	27.5	29.8	33.4	7.0	2.3	41885	49764	53	52	1055	20.1	32.3	32.8	14.0	0.8	87398
15620	BRADENVILLE	20953	39	33.3	30.8	30.8	5.1	0.0	37321	47372	37	32	32	3.1	37.5	37.5	18.8	3.1	104167
15622	CHAMPION	24652	289	29.4	25.3	35.6	5.2	4.5	45711	52472	63	64	241	19.1	24.9	30.7	20.8	4.6	100962
15625	DARRAGH	22805	72	27.8	30.6	29.2	11.1	1.4	42357	51211	54	54	62	12.9	19.4	50.0	14.5	3.2	112500
15626	DELMONT	29002	2285	26.5	25.5	31.5	11.8	4.7	46564	57975	65	65	1854	18.2	9.9	48.9	22.0	1.0	122337
15627	DERRY	18450	3673	31.6	34.3	27.5	4.9	1.7	36768	44228	35	29	2911	24.7	28.9	39.6	5.6	1.3	86300
15628	DONEGAL	17455	289	32.2	36.0	26.0	4.5	1.4	34665	40131	26	19	229	26.2	21.4	31.4	15.3	5.7	94231
15631	EVERSON	15646	279	41.9	32.3	22.6	2.9	0.4	30745	36260	14	8	200	36.0	44.0	20.0	0.0	0.0	59655
15632	EXPORT	32269	3144	21.0	23.5	30.2	14.2	11.1	56748	69609	81	82	2662	11.9	11.3	32.2	38.2	6.4	157976
15634	GRAPEVILLE	24128	352	22.7	32.1	34.4	8.0	2.8	47381	55207	67	67	292	9.9	30.5	48.0	11.6	0.0	100000
15636	HARRISON CITY	26828	1046	11.6	18.9	40.4	22.4	6.7	70848	85507	92	93	979	1.4	7.3	44.3	45.7	1.3	169806
15637	HERMINIE	18815	1170	34.5	30.5	28.5	4.8	1.7	35575	43451	30	23	881	19.0	31.9	37.5	11.2	0.5	89157
15639	HUNKER	24134	648	21.6	30.1	35.7	11.1	1.5	47921	58640	68	68	542	10.9	19.2	50.7	18.5	0.7	120570
15641	HYDE PARK	18360	206	35.0	30.1	26.7	6.8	1.5	34419	41689	25	18	145	19.3	19.3	52.4	9.0	0.0	98684
15642	IRWIN	24825	18190	20.6	28.2	35.3	12.0	4.0	51162	62437	74	74	15136	5.8	12.6	58.3	21.9	1.4	126466
15644	JEANNETTE	21936	9272	30.8	28.0	31.0	7.1	3.1	40419	49343	48	46	7170	15.7	28.2	40.2	15.0	0.9	97866
15646	JONES MILLS	19596	148	33.1	35.8	25.0	4.1	2.0	34121	39741	24	17	117	27.4	21.4	30.8	15.4	5.1	92143
15647	LARIMER	20432	39	28.2	28.2	33.3	7.7	2.6	43645	56292	58	58	35	14.3	17.1	54.3	14.3	0.0	110938
15650	LATROBE	22604	12248	28.3	31.1	30.0	7.9	2.8	41335	50214	51	50	9244	10.6	24.5	46.8	15.6	2.5	108685
15655	LAUGHLINTOWN	34443	280	27.1	33.6	20.7	12.1	6.4	41071	50000	50	49	233	8.2	13.3	42.9	29.6	6.0	144271
15656	LEECHBURG	22694	4359	28.5	29.7	30.2	8.0	3.6	42616	50486	55	55	3483	13.3	25.1	43.1	17.2	1.4	104121
15658	LIGONIER	27109	3675	28.1	30.7	28.0	8.5	4.7	41617	50178	52	52	2889	9.3	16.6	46.0	24.1	4.1	127538
15661	LOYALHANNA	19225	151	29.8	37.1	28.5	4.6	0.0	38739	47351	42	39	118	11.9	22.9	59.3	5.9	0.0	100833
15663	MADISON	24808	173	27.8	30.1	29.5	10.4	2.3	42605	51890	55	55	150	14.7	20.0	48.7	14.0	2.7	110417
15665	MANOR	19762	477	25.2	35.6	33.1	4.0	2.1	43846	52344	58	58	350	6.3	36.6	48.0	6.9	2.3	94310
15666	MOUNT PLEASANT	19202	7290	32.6	29.7	31.3	5.1	1.3	38429	46210	41	38	5698	20.3	26.4	43.1	9.5	0.6	93624
15668	MURRYSVILLE	41365	5117	10.8	17.5	36.0	18.4	17.4	76461	95036	94	95	4624	2.5	7.3	36.0	46.3	7.9	184639
15670	NEW ALEXANDRIA	21011	1244	30.6	28.0	31.2	8.1	2.1	41671	49837	52	52	1018	19.8	16.0	48.5	13.9	1.8	104098
15672	NEW STANTON	22501	1490	28.8	34.6	27.1	8.1	1.4	38688	47251	42	39	1017	15.0	18.1	50.4	15.0	1.5	113851
15675	PENN	18790	508	27.0	35.4	33.3	3.5	0.8	41676	50487	52	52	428	40.0	24.1	27.1	7.9	0.9	66154
15677	RECTOR	35616	182	24.2	34.1	23.1	6.6	12.1	43379	52989	57	57	144	9.0	20.1	32.6	25.0	13.2	144231
15678	RILLTON	16845	88	40.9	26.1	29.6	2.3	1.1	31507	38900	16	9	59	17.0	42.4	32.2	8.5	0.0	83125
15679	RUFFS DALE	18552	2207	31.9	34.5	26.5	6.0	1.2	36385	42922	33	27	1730	23.8	26.5	36.3	11.6	1.7	89641
15681	SALTSBURG	17891	1852	34.0	33.8	25.8	5.4	1.0	36469	42793	33	28	1443	23.9	27.6	36.2	11.4	0.9	88320
15683	SCOTTDALE	20012	3414	33.2	30.4	28.7	5.6	2.1	37523	45963	38	33	2576	18.3	30.7	43.3	7.5	0.2	91135
15684	SLICKVILLE	17099	199	30.7	37.7	28.1	3.0	0.5	37161	43183	36	31	166	30.7	33.1	28.9	7.2	0.0	76429
15686	SPRING CHURCH	19429	368	30.4	27.5	34.8	6.3	1.1	42923	49198	56	56	311	22.5	21.9	36.3	19.3	0.0	101645
15687	STAHLSTOWN	19322	1003	30.1	33.9	28.2	5.0	2.8	37540	44091	38	33	853	22.9	28.5	29.4	14.2	5.0	88309
15688	TARRS	18204	79	31.7	35.4	26.6	5.1	1.3	36739	45570	34	29	63	27.0	25.4	38.1	9.5	0.0	88636
15690	VANDERGRIFT	18574	3985	38.4	30.9	25.7	4.1	1.0	32460	38580	19	11	2714	26.3	45.1	22.6	5.6	0.3	69236
	PENNSYLVANIA	25764		25.8	27.2	31.2	10.2	5.7	46988	57000				11.9	18.4	40.7	25.1	4.1	123516
	UNITED STATES	25866		24.7	27.1	30.8	10.9	6.5	48124	56710				10.9	15.0	33.7	30.1	10.4	145905

#	POST OFFICE NAME	Financial Services: Auto Loan	Financial Services: Home Loan	Financial Services: Invest-ments	Financial Services: Retire-ment Plans	The Home: Home Improvements: Home Repair	The Home: Home Improvements: Lawn & Garden	The Home: Furnishings: Comput-ers & Hard-ware	The Home: Furnishings: Major Appli-ances	The Home: Furnishings: TV, Radio, Sound Equip-ment	The Home: Furnishings: Furni-ture	Entertainment: Dine out/Carry out	Entertainment: Sports Equip-ment	Entertainment: Fees & Tickets	Entertainment: Toys & Games	Entertainment: Travel	Entertainment: Cable TV	Personal: Apparel & Services	Personal: Auto Repairs	Personal: Health Insur-ance	Personal: Pets & Supplies
15458	MC CLELLANDTOWN	81	67	51	62	72	82	67	74	75	66	90	85	64	90	68	79	84	73	86	93
15459	MARKLEYSBURG	72	50	26	44	56	65	48	59	57	48	67	70	41	64	49	61	61	59	72	83
15461	MASONTOWN	66	50	38	46	53	64	54	60	62	53	74	66	50	68	54	66	68	60	71	72
15462	MELCROFT	87	59	27	51	66	76	57	70	68	58	80	84	48	76	58	73	73	70	86	100
15463	MERRITTSTOWN	58	49	41	47	52	61	52	55	57	50	69	62	50	68	52	60	64	55	64	65
15464	MILL RUN	72	48	22	42	55	63	47	58	56	48	66	70	40	63	48	61	60	58	72	83
15468	NEW SALEM	61	53	43	50	56	65	55	58	60	53	72	66	52	72	55	63	67	58	67	70
15469	NORMALVILLE	86	60	31	53	67	77	58	71	68	59	81	84	51	77	59	73	74	70	85	99
15470	OHIOPYLE	83	55	25	48	63	72	53	67	64	54	76	80	45	71	54	69	69	66	82	95
15473	PERRYOPOLIS	64	66	67	63	67	75	65	66	67	63	83	74	67	86	67	70	80	65	71	74
15474	POINT MARION	60	48	34	44	52	60	48	54	54	47	65	62	45	64	49	58	60	54	64	68
15475	REPUBLIC	68	51	34	49	56	67	57	62	63	54	74	70	50	70	56	67	68	62	74	75
15477	ROSCOE	60	65	69	62	66	73	65	64	67	62	83	71	68	90	67	69	80	63	69	71
15478	SMITHFIELD	68	53	35	47	57	65	51	59	59	51	70	70	47	70	52	63	65	59	70	79
15479	SMITHTON	70	72	72	68	74	82	71	72	74	69	91	81	73	96	73	77	88	71	78	82
15480	SMOCK	81	58	33	51	65	74	56	68	66	57	78	80	50	75	58	70	72	67	82	93
15482	STAR JUNCTION	59	55	49	51	58	65	55	58	59	53	72	65	55	75	56	62	68	57	65	69
15483	STOCKDALE	67	73	77	69	73	82	72	71	74	69	92	79	76	100	74	77	89	70	76	78
15486	VANDERBILT	71	57	40	51	61	69	55	63	63	55	75	73	52	75	57	66	70	62	74	82
15488	WALTERSBURG	86	58	26	50	65	75	56	69	67	57	79	83	47	74	56	72	72	69	86	99
15490	WHITE	103	69	31	59	78	90	66	83	80	68	94	99	56	89	67	86	85	82	102	118
15501	SOMERSET	76	65	55	61	68	77	65	71	71	65	86	82	62	86	66	74	81	71	79	88
15521	ALUM BANK	83	56	26	48	63	72	54	67	65	55	76	80	46	72	55	70	69	66	82	95
15522	BEDFORD	77	69	62	66	73	81	68	74	73	67	88	86	66	89	70	75	84	73	81	91
15530	BERLIN	61	49	33	46	53	60	49	55	54	48	64	64	45	63	49	57	60	54	64	71
15531	BOSWELL	63	59	52	56	61	67	58	61	61	57	75	71	57	77	59	63	71	60	67	74
15533	BREEZEWOOD	83	55	25	48	63	72	53	67	65	55	76	80	46	72	54	70	69	66	82	95
15534	BUFFALO MILLS	75	53	28	46	60	68	51	62	60	51	70	74	44	67	52	64	64	62	76	88
15535	CLEARVILLE	80	58	33	51	66	75	56	68	65	56	77	81	49	74	58	70	70	67	82	95
15536	CRYSTAL SPRING	74	50	22	43	56	65	48	60	58	49	68	72	41	64	49	62	62	59	74	85
15537	EVERETT	82	60	35	54	67	77	59	70	68	59	81	83	52	78	60	73	74	70	84	96
15538	FAIRHOPE	75	56	35	50	63	71	53	65	61	53	72	76	47	71	56	66	67	64	77	89
15539	FISHERTOWN	78	69	53	66	73	79	64	71	68	64	83	85	63	85	66	70	79	69	77	92
15540	FORT HILL	79	60	37	54	68	76	57	69	65	56	77	82	50	75	60	69	71	68	82	95
15541	FRIEDENS	76	60	40	54	65	73	57	66	65	57	78	78	53	77	59	69	73	65	78	88
15542	GARRETT	74	53	29	48	60	68	51	62	60	52	70	75	45	68	53	63	65	61	74	87
15545	HYNDMAN	68	53	35	47	58	66	52	60	59	52	71	70	48	70	53	63	66	59	71	79
15546	JENNERS	49	53	56	50	54	60	53	52	54	51	68	58	56	73	54	57	65	51	56	57
15550	MANNS CHOICE	80	55	28	48	63	72	53	66	63	54	74	78	46	71	55	68	68	65	80	93
15551	MARKLETON	77	52	23	45	58	67	50	62	60	51	71	74	42	67	51	65	64	62	77	88
15552	MEYERSDALE	70	52	32	47	58	66	52	61	60	52	71	71	47	69	53	64	66	60	73	80
15554	NEW PARIS	86	63	35	56	70	78	60	72	69	61	82	86	54	80	61	74	76	71	85	99
15557	ROCKWOOD	72	56	39	51	62	70	54	63	62	54	74	74	50	74	56	66	69	62	75	84
15558	SALISBURY	68	57	44	53	62	69	56	63	62	55	75	73	54	76	58	65	70	62	72	80
15559	SCHELLSBURG	83	57	29	50	65	74	55	68	65	56	77	81	47	73	56	70	70	67	83	96
15562	SPRINGS	70	49	26	46	57	64	48	60	56	48	65	72	41	64	50	58	60	59	71	83
15563	STOYSTOWN	72	57	39	51	62	70	55	64	63	55	75	75	51	75	57	67	70	63	75	84
15601	GREENSBURG	84	89	96	88	90	96	88	88	88	86	109	102	90	111	89	88	106	88	89	99
15610	ACME	82	69	49	65	74	81	65	73	70	65	85	87	62	85	66	73	80	72	82	96
15611	ADAMSBURG	92	114	122	115	112	111	102	102	95	102	119	119	109	127	104	92	119	98	91	112
15612	ALVERTON	78	59	37	52	64	73	56	67	65	57	77	79	51	75	58	69	71	66	79	90
15613	APOLLO	76	72	63	68	75	82	69	73	73	68	89	85	69	92	71	76	85	72	80	89
15615	ARDARA	85	75	57	72	80	85	70	77	74	70	90	92	68	92	72	76	85	75	84	100
15616	ARMBRUST	76	93	102	90	91	93	86	85	82	85	103	98	91	110	88	81	103	83	79	92
15617	ARONA	115	106	86	100	111	119	99	107	104	98	127	126	98	132	102	107	122	105	116	135
15618	AVONMORE	80	76	66	72	79	86	72	76	76	71	93	89	73	97	74	78	89	75	83	93
15620	BRADENVILLE	73	54	35	52	60	71	60	66	67	57	79	75	53	75	59	71	72	66	80	82
15622	CHAMPION	95	82	61	77	88	96	76	86	82	76	99	102	73	101	79	85	94	84	96	113
15625	DARRAGH	72	78	82	74	79	88	77	76	80	74	99	85	82	108	80	83	96	75	82	84
15626	DELMONT	89	91	89	88	93	101	89	92	91	87	111	104	90	113	91	92	107	90	95	104
15627	DERRY	74	62	47	58	66	74	61	67	66	60	80	78	58	80	62	69	75	66	76	85
15628	DONEGAL	70	53	35	51	58	69	58	64	65	55	77	72	52	73	58	69	70	64	77	78
15631	EVERSON	47	51	54	49	52	58	51	50	53	49	65	56	54	71	53	55	63	49	54	56
15632	EXPORT	117	123	119	119	125	132	114	119	115	113	142	138	117	147	118	116	138	116	121	139
15634	GRAPEVILLE	80	87	91	82	87	97	85	85	89	82	110	94	90	119	88	92	106	83	91	93
15636	HARRISON CITY	107	128	132	130	125	122	115	115	107	117	135	134	121	141	116	102	134	111	101	126
15637	HERMINIE	70	57	43	54	62	71	60	65	66	58	79	74	56	78	60	70	73	65	76	79
15639	HUNKER	88	83	76	79	86	94	80	85	85	79	104	99	81	107	83	87	99	83	92	103
15641	HYDE PARK	56	61	64	58	62	69	60	60	63	58	78	67	64	84	63	65	75	59	64	66
15642	IRWIN	84	94	100	92	94	99	89	89	88	88	110	102	93	114	91	88	107	88	88	100
15644	JEANNETTE	71	74	75	71	75	82	73	74	75	71	93	84	75	97	75	77	90	73	77	83
15646	JONES MILLS	70	53	35	50	57	69	58	64	65	55	77	72	52	72	58	69	70	64	77	77
15647	LARIMER	89	79	61	75	84	90	73	81	78	73	95	97	72	97	76	80	90	79	88	105
15650	LATROBE	75	75	74	72	76	85	74	76	77	73	95	86	76	98	76	80	91	75	81	87
15655	LAUGHLINTOWN	103	110	113	104	111	122	104	108	106	103	131	122	107	135	109	109	127	106	113	124
15656	LEECHBURG	77	77	72	73	79	86	73	76	76	72	94	88	75	98	76	78	90	75	81	90
15658	LIGONIER	92	87	79	82	90	101	86	91	90	84	110	103	85	110	88	94	104	90	100	107
15661	LOYALHANNA	55	60	63	56	60	67	59	58	61	57	76	65	62	82	61	63	73	57	63	64
15663	MADISON	72	79	83	74	80	88	78	77	81	75	100	86	82	108	80	84	97	75	83	85
15665	MANOR	64	70	74	66	71	78	69	68	72	67	89	76	73	96	71	74	86	67	73	76
15666	MOUNT PLEASANT	71	62	51	58	66	74	61	67	66	60	80	77	59	81	63	69	76	66	75	82
15668	MURRYSVILLE	138	169	188	168	167	172	153	153	144	153	181	175	163	187	158	142	180	149	143	168
15670	NEW ALEXANDRIA	83	74	60	70	78	85	70	77	74	70	91	90	69	92	72	77	86	75	84	97
15672	NEW STANTON	65	69	80	67	69	76	70	68	72	68	89	78	73	93	72	73	87	69	71	76
15675	PENN	69	64	55	61	67	73	62	66	65	61	80	76	62	83	63	68	76	64	72	80
15677	RECTOR	137	114	91	107	126	139	110	127	120	109	144	148	101	142	115	125	135	125	144	166
15678	RILLTON	66	50	33	48	54	65	55	60	62	52	73	68	49	68	54	65	66	60	72	73
15679	RUFFS DALE	83	60	35	54	67	76	59	70	68	59	81	82	53	78	60	72	74	69	83	94
15681	SALTSBURG	80	55	28	49	62	72	55	67	65	55	77	79	48	73	56	70	70	66	81	91
15683	SCOTTDALE	69	65	58	60	68	76	64	67	68	62	83	77	64	86	65	71	79	66	75	81
15684	SLICKVILLE	78	53	24	45	60	69	51	63	61	52	72	76	43	68	52	66	65	63	78	90
15686	SPRING CHURCH	86	64	37	57	70	79	60	72	69	61	83	86	54	80	62	74	76	71	85	99
15687	STAHLSTOWN	81	64	47	61	69	78	65	73	71	64	85	85	59	82	65	74	79	72	82	92
15688	TARRS	85	57	26	49	65	74	55	69	66	56	78	82	47	74	56	71	71	68	85	98
15690	VANDERGRIFT	62	57	50	54	60	68	58	61	62	56	76	69	57	78	59	65	71	60	68	72
	PENNSYLVANIA	89	89	93	87	90	98	89	90	91	88	112	104	89	114	90	92	109	90	92	104
	UNITED STATES	100	100	100	100	100	100	100	100	100	100	100	100	100	100	100	100	100	100	100	100

# POST OFFICE NAME	COUNTY FIPS CODE	POPULATION 2000	POPULATION 2004	POPULATION 2009	2000-2004 ANNUAL RATE % Rate	State Centile	HOUSEHOLDS 2000	HOUSEHOLDS 2004	HOUSEHOLDS 2009	% Annual Rate 2000-2004	2004 Average HH Size	FAMILIES 2000	FAMILIES 2004	% Annual Rate 2000-2004
15692 WESTMORELAND CITY	129	1051	1174	1245	2.6	97	421	471	502	2.7	2.49	305	338	2.5
15697 YOUNGWOOD	129	4173	4108	4096	-0.4	22	1517	1501	1509	-0.3	2.13	900	881	-0.5
15698 YUKON	129	551	538	535	-0.6	13	244	241	242	-0.3	2.23	159	156	-0.5
15701 INDIANA	063	31645	31940	32375	0.2	50	12706	13162	13683	0.8	2.23	6939	7144	0.7
15705 INDIANA	063	2554	2541	2543	-0.1	33	146	147	151	0.2	4.39	4	4	0.0
15711 ANITA	065	302	306	310	0.3	54	119	122	126	0.6	2.43	90	92	0.5
15713 AULTMAN	063	337	369	388	2.2	94	117	132	143	2.9	2.80	92	103	2.7
15714 NORTHERN CAMBRIA	021	6637	6596	6475	-0.2	32	2681	2730	2740	0.4	2.41	1890	1913	0.3
15716 BLACK LICK	063	434	424	424	-0.6	14	161	161	166	0.0	2.46	112	111	-0.2
15717 BLAIRSVILLE	063	10718	10793	10933	0.2	46	4282	4404	4557	0.7	2.35	2946	2996	0.4
15720 BRUSH VALLEY	063	109	107	107	-0.4	19	32	32	33	0.0	3.34	25	24	-1.0
15721 BURNSIDE	033	283	284	288	0.1	43	102	105	109	0.7	2.69	80	81	0.3
15722 CARROLLTOWN	021	2912	2791	2680	-1.0	5	1099	1082	1063	-0.4	2.54	833	814	-0.5
15724 CHERRY TREE	063	2378	2406	2439	0.3	53	836	869	903	0.9	2.65	657	677	0.7
15725 CLARKSBURG	063	1975	1988	2038	0.2	46	810	840	884	0.9	2.36	561	575	0.6
15728 CLYMER	063	4643	4678	4751	0.2	47	1825	1886	1963	0.8	2.45	1308	1340	0.6
15729 COMMODORE	063	1307	1317	1337	0.2	47	476	493	513	0.8	2.62	383	394	0.7
15730 COOLSPRING	065	85	90	94	1.4	86	38	41	44	1.8	2.20	29	31	1.6
15732 CREEKSIDE	063	1497	1465	1467	-0.5	15	578	585	602	0.3	2.50	441	442	0.1
15739 ERNEST	063	404	397	398	-0.4	20	134	136	140	0.4	2.82	106	107	0.2
15742 GLEN CAMPBELL	063	1267	1237	1238	-0.6	13	471	472	484	0.1	2.53	349	346	-0.2
15744 HAMILTON	065	49	49	50	0.0	39	18	19	19	1.3	2.58	13	14	1.8
15747 HOME	063	2936	2921	2941	-0.1	33	1079	1102	1138	0.5	2.63	833	844	0.3
15748 HOMER CITY	063	8221	8457	8667	0.7	70	3406	3592	3771	1.3	2.35	2404	2512	1.0
15753 LA JOSE	033	1042	1045	1063	0.1	43	384	394	409	0.6	2.64	292	299	0.6
15757 MAHAFFEY	033	1914	1919	1952	0.1	42	711	728	756	0.6	2.63	534	543	0.4
15758 MARCHAND	063	487	519	539	1.5	89	173	188	200	2.0	2.73	138	148	1.7
15759 MARION CENTER	063	2799	2769	2781	-0.3	27	967	979	1007	0.3	2.80	733	736	0.1
15760 MARSTELLER	021	155	155	151	0.0	39	56	58	57	0.8	2.67	43	44	0.5
15762 NICKTOWN	021	1155	1125	1087	-0.6	12	399	398	393	-0.1	2.80	320	317	-0.2
15763 NORTHPOINT	063	46	50	53	2.0	92	19	21	23	2.4	2.38	16	18	2.8
15764 OLIVEBURG	065	65	66	67	0.4	58	23	24	25	1.0	2.75	17	18	1.4
15765 PENN RUN	063	2094	2165	2225	0.8	74	747	792	835	1.4	2.63	586	617	1.2
15767 PUNXSUTAWNEY	065	14738	15048	15403	0.5	63	5939	6176	6437	0.9	2.38	4017	4155	0.8
15770 RINGGOLD	065	164	164	166	0.0	39	64	65	67	0.4	2.52	49	49	0.0
15771 ROCHESTER MILLS	063	1047	1063	1082	0.4	58	404	419	436	0.9	2.51	306	315	0.7
15772 ROSSITER	063	1735	1684	1683	-0.7	10	611	607	622	-0.2	2.51	442	433	-0.5
15773 SAINT BENEDICT	021	554	533	513	-0.9	6	209	206	203	-0.3	2.49	160	157	-0.4
15774 SHELOCTA	005	4929	5106	5266	0.8	74	1895	2017	2131	1.5	2.49	1437	1517	1.3
15775 SPANGLER	021	496	481	464	-0.7	9	192	191	189	-0.1	2.51	140	138	-0.3
15776 SPRANKLE MILLS	065	211	214	217	0.3	56	81	84	87	0.9	2.55	62	63	0.4
15777 STARFORD	063	420	410	410	-0.6	13	136	136	139	0.0	2.88	109	109	0.0
15778 TIMBLIN	065	230	230	232	0.0	39	87	89	92	0.5	2.58	66	67	0.4
15780 VALIER	065	180	182	184	0.3	52	73	75	78	0.6	2.43	54	56	0.9
15784 WORTHVILLE	065	134	135	136	0.2	47	54	56	57	0.9	2.41	41	42	0.6
15801 DU BOIS	033	19531	20289	21079	0.9	77	7940	8415	8924	1.4	2.34	5349	5633	1.2
15821 BENEZETT	047	222	222	222	0.0	39	101	103	105	0.5	2.16	73	74	0.3
15823 BROCKPORT	047	2081	2059	2064	-0.3	27	863	877	899	0.4	2.35	600	605	0.2
15824 BROCKWAY	065	4563	4524	4568	-0.2	29	1828	1852	1908	0.3	2.39	1279	1291	0.2
15825 BROOKVILLE	065	10547	10942	11280	0.9	75	4196	4453	4686	1.4	2.37	2905	3062	1.3
15827 BYRNEDALE	047	1895	1883	1882	-0.2	32	777	791	809	0.4	2.38	519	525	0.3
15828 CLARINGTON	065	314	315	319	0.1	43	145	149	154	0.6	2.11	98	100	0.5
15829 CORSICA	065	1644	1680	1725	0.5	65	643	670	699	1.0	2.50	470	485	0.7
15832 DRIFTWOOD	023	519	519	520	0.0	39	217	220	224	0.3	2.36	153	154	0.2
15834 EMPORIUM	023	5331	5355	5402	0.1	44	2194	2240	2294	0.5	2.35	1434	1453	0.3
15840 FALLS CREEK	065	2123	2122	2149	0.0	37	850	871	901	0.6	2.40	611	622	0.4
15845 JOHNSONBURG	047	3003	3022	3038	0.2	46	1292	1334	1374	0.8	2.27	811	831	0.6
15846 KERSEY	047	3698	3785	3835	0.6	66	1403	1474	1530	1.2	2.57	1042	1088	1.0
15848 LUTHERSBURG	033	2234	2316	2399	0.9	75	824	877	930	1.5	2.64	642	679	1.3
15849 PENFIELD	033	1542	1567	1606	0.4	58	639	665	696	0.9	2.36	442	456	0.7
15851 REYNOLDSVILLE	065	7351	7719	8050	1.2	83	2875	3090	3295	1.7	2.48	2106	2240	1.5
15853 RIDGWAY	047	7426	7568	7686	0.5	62	3012	3134	3257	0.9	2.37	2048	2114	0.8
15856 ROCKTON	033	921	960	998	1.0	79	356	378	401	1.4	2.54	269	284	1.3
15857 SAINT MARYS	047	14568	14476	14508	-0.2	32	5750	5860	6017	0.5	2.42	4021	4074	0.3
15860 SIGEL	047	1030	1041	1054	0.3	51	446	462	478	0.8	2.25	320	329	0.7
15861 SINNAMAHONING	023	129	129	129	0.0	39	57	58	59	0.4	2.22	40	40	0.0
15864 SUMMERVILLE	065	1164	1138	1145	-0.5	14	445	444	454	-0.1	2.54	344	341	-0.2
15865 SYKESVILLE	065	1246	1215	1224	-0.6	13	548	547	563	0.0	2.22	341	337	-0.3
15868 WEEDVILLE	047	199	198	198	-0.1	33	96	98	100	0.5	2.02	66	67	0.4
15870 WILCOX	047	1722	1708	1708	-0.2	30	688	702	720	0.5	2.43	481	488	0.3
15901 JOHNSTOWN	021	5554	5221	4982	-1.4	1	2763	2670	2606	-0.8	1.85	1164	1090	-1.5
15902 JOHNSTOWN	021	13493	12696	12104	-1.4	1	5943	5714	5564	-0.9	2.21	3679	3506	-1.1
15904 JOHNSTOWN	021	16977	16735	16307	-0.3	23	6665	6684	6623	0.1	2.24	4430	4406	-0.1
15905 JOHNSTOWN	021	22679	21931	21203	-0.8	8	9404	9275	9149	-0.3	2.26	6356	6222	-0.5
15906 JOHNSTOWN	021	12047	11618	11207	-0.9	7	5396	5341	5276	-0.2	2.17	3408	3335	-0.5
15909 JOHNSTOWN	021	6391	6089	5831	-1.1	3	2636	2577	2527	-0.5	2.36	1888	1836	-0.7
15920 ARMAGH	063	577	564	565	-0.5	14	225	226	232	0.1	2.50	165	165	0.0
15923 BOLIVAR	129	2016	1973	1962	-0.5	15	756	746	747	-0.3	2.58	578	567	-0.5
15924 CAIRNBROOK	111	1014	995	991	-0.4	19	424	426	433	0.1	2.33	296	295	-0.1
15926 CENTRAL CITY	111	3046	2998	2995	-0.4	22	1265	1272	1299	0.1	2.36	887	886	0.0
15927 COLVER	021	1204	1170	1130	-0.7	11	472	470	463	-0.1	2.35	336	332	-0.3
15928 DAVIDSVILLE	111	1617	1613	1612	-0.1	36	631	646	662	0.6	2.41	467	475	0.4
15931 EBENSBURG	021	9501	9254	8969	-0.6	12	3340	3317	3272	-0.2	2.45	2319	2288	-0.3
15935 HOLLSOPPLE	111	3969	3922	3915	-0.3	26	1565	1583	1616	0.3	2.46	1183	1190	0.1
15936 HOOVERSVILLE	111	1615	1594	1589	-0.3	24	661	669	683	0.3	2.38	443	445	0.1
15938 LILLY	021	4552	4445	4330	-0.6	13	1230	1226	1213	-0.1	2.63	880	871	-0.2
15940 LORETTO	021	3467	3748	3756	1.9	92	590	626	638	1.4	3.27	437	461	1.3
15942 MINERAL POINT	021	2265	2236	2173	-0.3	25	880	891	888	0.3	2.49	666	671	0.2
15943 NANTY GLO	021	4403	4199	4024	-1.1	3	1793	1759	1727	-0.5	2.38	1243	1209	-0.7
15944 NEW FLORENCE	129	3896	4141	4319	1.5	87	1529	1657	1757	1.9	2.48	1139	1220	1.6
15945 PARKHILL	021	58	55	53	-1.2	2	21	21	20	0.0	2.62	16	16	0.0
15946 PORTAGE	021	7075	7023	6854	-0.2	31	2789	2833	2823	0.4	2.42	1911	1931	0.3
15949 ROBINSON	063	596	622	639	1.0	80	234	249	262	1.5	2.50	183	194	1.4
15951 SAINT MICHAEL	021	341	324	311	-1.2	3	131	128	125	-0.5	2.47	92	89	-0.8
15952 SALIX	021	1664	1603	1539	-0.9	7	642	636	625	-0.2	2.52	495	487	-0.4
PENNSYLVANIA					0.3					0.7	2.44			0.6
UNITED STATES					1.2					1.3	2.58			1.1

ZIP CODE #	POST OFFICE NAME	RACE (%) White 2000	White 2004	Black 2000	Black 2004	Asian/Pacific 2000	Asian/Pacific 2004	% Hispanic Origin 2000	% Hispanic Origin 2004	2004 AGE DISTRIBUTION (%) 0-4	5-9	10-14	15-19	20-24	25-44	45-64	65-84	85+	18+	MEDIAN AGE 2004	% 2004 Males	% 2004 Females
15692	WESTMORELAND CITY	97.2	96.9	0.8	0.9	0.5	0.6	0.8	0.8	7.1	7.0	6.7	6.5	5.6	29.5	23.9	12.0	1.8	75.2	38.5	49.2	50.8
15697	YOUNGWOOD	87.8	86.4	11.6	12.8	0.2	0.2	2.4	2.6	3.6	3.6	4.3	4.9	6.6	36.6	24.0	13.4	3.1	85.8	39.8	57.9	42.1
15698	YUKON	99.5	99.3	0.0	0.0	0.2	0.2	0.4	0.4	6.1	6.3	6.0	4.1	4.3	28.6	21.4	20.3	3.0	79.4	41.4	46.8	53.2
15701	INDIANA	94.5	93.6	2.7	3.0	1.7	2.2	0.8	0.9	3.7	3.9	4.8	9.9	17.7	21.3	23.4	12.6	2.8	84.5	34.2	47.5	52.5
15705	INDIANA	84.4	82.4	11.6	12.9	2.4	3.0	1.5	1.6	0.0	0.0	0.1	50.7	44.6	3.4	0.8	0.3	0.0	99.7	19.9	42.7	57.3
15711	ANITA	98.7	98.4	0.3	0.3	0.0	0.0	0.7	0.3	6.5	6.5	6.5	6.5	5.2	25.8	27.1	14.4	1.3	75.8	40.6	49.7	50.3
15713	AULTMAN	98.8	98.6	0.6	0.5	0.3	0.3	0.3	0.3	5.4	5.7	5.7	6.0	5.2	26.0	31.2	13.6	1.4	79.4	42.4	51.5	48.5
15714	NORTHERN CAMBRIA	99.4	99.2	0.1	0.1	0.2	0.2	0.3	0.4	5.6	5.6	6.3	5.8	6.4	25.6	26.4	15.3	3.0	78.8	41.1	48.8	51.2
15716	BLACK LICK	98.4	98.1	0.7	0.7	0.0	0.0	0.9	1.2	5.7	5.7	5.9	5.2	5.7	24.8	26.7	16.8	3.8	79.5	42.7	47.9	52.1
15717	BLAIRSVILLE	96.7	96.3	2.4	2.7	0.3	0.3	0.4	0.4	5.3	5.6	6.3	6.1	5.2	25.6	27.9	15.7	2.3	79.0	42.4	49.5	50.5
15720	BRUSH VALLEY	100.0	100.0	0.0	0.0	0.0	0.0	0.0	0.0	6.5	6.5	6.5	7.5	4.7	28.0	28.0	11.2	0.9	74.8	39.7	51.4	48.6
15721	BURNSIDE	99.3	99.7	0.0	0.0	0.0	0.0	0.4	0.4	6.0	6.0	6.3	6.0	5.6	27.5	26.4	14.1	2.1	77.8	40.6	50.0	50.0
15722	CARROLLTOWN	99.6	99.5	0.1	0.1	0.0	0.0	0.0	0.0	5.3	5.6	6.0	6.8	6.0	25.0	27.9	14.6	2.7	79.0	41.8	50.2	49.8
15724	CHERRY TREE	99.0	98.9	0.2	0.2	0.0	0.0	0.5	0.5	5.9	6.0	6.7	6.3	6.1	25.6	27.9	13.1	2.5	77.6	40.7	49.5	50.5
15725	CLARKSBURG	99.2	99.1	0.2	0.2	0.1	0.1	0.0	0.0	5.8	6.0	6.8	5.7	5.1	27.0	27.9	13.9	1.8	77.9	41.1	50.0	50.1
15728	CLYMER	99.2	99.1	0.2	0.2	0.0	0.1	0.3	0.4	5.8	5.9	6.7	6.2	6.2	26.2	26.3	14.2	2.5	77.9	40.1	48.5	51.5
15729	COMMODORE	98.9	98.9	0.2	0.2	0.0	0.0	0.5	0.5	6.0	6.4	6.8	6.1	6.5	26.0	27.7	12.2	2.3	77.1	39.2	50.3	49.7
15730	COOLSPRING	98.8	100.0	0.0	0.0	0.0	0.0	0.0	0.0	4.4	4.4	5.6	6.7	5.6	22.2	32.2	16.7	2.2	82.2	45.4	51.1	48.9
15732	CREEKSIDE	99.0	98.8	0.3	0.3	0.1	0.1	0.1	0.1	7.0	6.8	6.0	5.7	6.8	28.8	28.2	9.7	1.0	76.7	37.9	51.9	48.1
15739	ERNEST	99.5	99.2	0.3	0.3	0.3	0.3	0.0	0.0	4.5	5.0	6.8	8.3	4.3	26.2	31.2	11.1	2.5	78.3	41.7	50.1	49.9
15742	GLEN CAMPBELL	98.9	98.7	0.0	0.0	0.2	0.2	0.3	0.4	5.0	5.5	6.6	6.2	5.5	26.3	28.1	14.6	2.1	78.8	41.8	51.0	49.0
15744	HAMILTON	100.0	100.0	0.0	0.0	0.0	0.0	0.0	0.0	4.1	6.1	8.2	4.1	6.1	26.5	26.5	16.3	2.0	81.6	41.9	51.0	49.0
15747	HOME	99.3	99.1	0.2	0.2	0.1	0.2	0.1	0.1	7.1	7.3	7.8	7.1	5.0	27.3	26.0	11.1	1.5	73.4	37.3	51.0	49.0
15748	HOMER CITY	99.2	99.0	0.4	0.4	0.1	0.1	0.4	0.5	5.2	5.5	6.4	5.6	5.7	26.2	28.1	15.1	2.3	79.4	42.1	49.4	50.6
15753	LA JOSE	98.9	98.8	0.2	0.2	0.3	0.3	0.6	0.8	6.3	7.3	6.9	7.2	5.2	26.8	26.8	12.1	1.5	75.0	38.6	51.5	48.5
15757	MAHAFFEY	99.3	99.3	0.0	0.0	0.2	0.2	0.3	0.3	6.5	6.8	6.7	6.6	5.2	25.6	26.7	14.3	1.6	75.9	40.1	50.8	49.2
15758	MARCHAND	98.6	98.5	0.2	0.4	0.0	0.0	0.0	0.0	6.7	6.9	7.7	7.9	7.1	25.4	24.7	12.3	1.2	73.2	37.0	51.3	48.8
15759	MARION CENTER	99.0	98.9	0.2	0.2	0.4	0.5	0.1	0.1	6.9	6.9	7.4	7.1	6.0	26.6	26.3	11.2	1.6	74.5	37.7	49.7	50.3
15760	MARSTELLER	100.0	100.0	0.0	0.0	0.0	0.0	0.0	0.0	5.8	5.8	6.5	5.8	6.5	24.5	29.0	14.8	1.3	78.1	41.6	50.3	49.7
15762	NICKTOWN	99.8	99.7	0.0	0.0	0.0	0.0	0.2	0.2	6.1	6.8	7.6	7.0	6.5	23.6	29.0	11.3	2.1	75.0	39.4	49.0	51.0
15763	NORTHPOINT	100.0	100.0	0.0	0.0	0.0	0.0	0.0	0.0	10.0	12.0	12.0	8.0	10.0	22.0	16.0	10.0	0.0	66.0	24.0	50.0	50.0
15764	OLIVEBURG	98.5	98.5	0.0	0.0	0.0	0.0	0.0	0.0	4.6	6.1	6.1	6.1	4.6	28.8	27.3	15.2	1.5	83.3	41.7	50.0	50.0
15765	PENN RUN	99.0	99.0	0.3	0.3	0.1	0.1	0.1	0.1	5.8	6.1	6.5	6.3	5.8	26.4	30.2	11.5	1.4	77.9	40.7	51.6	48.4
15767	PUNXSUTAWNEY	99.0	98.9	0.1	0.1	0.2	0.3	0.5	0.5	5.8	5.8	6.4	6.5	6.7	25.0	25.6	15.5	2.8	78.2	41.0	48.0	52.0
15770	RINGGOLD	99.4	99.4	0.0	0.0	0.0	0.0	0.6	0.6	4.9	6.1	7.3	5.5	4.3	26.2	29.3	14.0	2.4	78.1	42.3	50.0	50.0
15771	ROCHESTER MILLS	98.9	98.7	0.2	0.2	0.2	0.2	0.2	0.2	6.2	6.5	7.3	7.1	6.5	26.0	26.5	12.5	1.4	75.4	38.7	50.6	49.4
15772	ROSSITER	99.7	99.4	0.0	0.0	0.1	0.1	0.4	0.5	4.3	4.7	6.4	6.7	5.6	25.7	26.3	18.3	2.0	80.2	43.0	49.9	50.1
15773	SAINT BENEDICT	99.6	99.4	0.0	0.0	0.0	0.0	0.0	0.0	4.3	4.7	6.0	6.9	5.4	23.8	26.3	18.4	4.1	81.1	44.3	49.9	50.1
15774	SHELOCTA	99.1	98.9	0.2	0.3	0.1	0.1	0.3	0.4	5.7	5.8	6.2	6.2	6.2	27.6	28.3	12.2	1.8	78.2	40.3	49.5	50.5
15775	SPANGLER	99.4	99.4	0.0	0.0	0.2	0.2	0.2	0.4	4.8	5.0	6.7	5.8	6.7	25.2	27.4	15.8	2.7	80.0	42.2	48.0	52.0
15776	SPRANKLE MILLS	98.1	97.7	0.5	0.5	0.5	0.5	0.5	0.5	5.6	6.1	6.1	5.1	4.7	28.0	29.4	13.6	1.4	79.0	41.5	52.3	47.7
15777	STARFORD	99.3	99.0	0.5	0.5	0.0	0.0	0.0	0.0	5.6	6.1	7.1	6.3	6.1	26.1	23.4	15.1	4.2	77.3	40.2	49.0	51.0
15778	TIMBLIN	99.6	99.1	0.0	0.0	0.0	0.0	0.4	0.9	5.2	6.1	7.4	5.2	4.8	27.0	27.4	15.2	1.7	77.8	41.6	50.4	49.6
15780	VALIER	99.4	99.5	0.0	0.0	0.0	0.0	0.0	0.0	4.4	6.6	7.7	5.5	6.0	26.9	28.0	12.6	2.2	78.0	40.7	51.1	48.9
15784	WORTHVILLE	97.8	98.5	0.0	0.0	0.0	0.0	0.0	0.0	6.7	6.7	7.4	6.7	6.7	27.4	25.9	11.1	1.5	74.8	37.8	53.3	46.7
15801	DU BOIS	98.4	98.1	0.2	0.3	0.6	0.8	0.4	0.5	5.5	5.7	6.5	6.4	5.8	25.0	25.6	16.0	3.4	78.4	41.8	47.8	52.2
15821	BENEZETT	99.1	99.1	0.0	0.0	0.9	0.9	0.0	0.0	5.9	5.4	5.4	5.4	5.0	25.7	28.8	17.1	1.4	80.2	43.2	50.9	49.1
15823	BROCKPORT	99.1	99.1	0.1	0.1	0.2	0.2	0.2	0.2	5.2	5.6	6.2	5.8	6.3	26.0	28.3	15.5	1.1	79.4	41.9	51.7	48.3
15824	BROCKWAY	99.4	99.3	0.0	0.0	0.1	0.2	0.2	0.3	6.0	6.0	6.5	6.5	6.0	25.5	24.8	16.3	3.0	77.5	41.3	49.7	50.3
15825	BROOKVILLE	98.6	98.5	0.2	0.2	0.4	0.5	0.4	0.4	5.2	5.3	6.2	6.3	6.3	25.4	26.7	15.6	3.1	79.5	41.9	48.8	51.2
15827	BYRNEDALE	99.3	99.3	0.1	0.1	0.3	0.4	0.7	0.9	5.9	5.9	6.2	5.7	5.0	26.1	25.5	17.3	2.4	78.7	41.9	49.4	50.6
15828	CLARINGTON	97.8	97.8	0.3	0.3	0.3	0.3	1.0	1.0	3.8	3.8	5.1	6.7	4.8	21.3	33.0	19.7	1.9	82.9	47.6	50.2	49.8
15829	CORSICA	99.0	98.9	0.2	0.2	0.2	0.2	0.2	0.2	5.7	5.8	6.5	5.3	6.0	27.3	27.0	14.8	1.6	78.8	40.7	51.1	48.9
15832	DRIFTWOOD	98.3	98.3	0.2	0.2	0.2	0.2	0.6	0.6	4.4	4.8	7.1	7.1	6.2	22.4	28.5	17.9	1.5	79.6	43.8	49.5	50.5
15834	EMPORIUM	98.9	98.9	0.4	0.4	0.2	0.2	0.6	0.6	5.0	5.2	7.2	6.7	6.2	23.2	26.9	16.6	3.0	78.1	42.4	48.9	51.1
15840	FALLS CREEK	99.1	98.9	0.1	0.1	0.1	0.1	0.4	0.5	5.0	5.0	6.1	6.6	5.6	26.3	27.0	15.9	2.4	79.8	42.1	49.4	50.6
15845	JOHNSONBURG	98.8	98.6	0.0	0.0	0.4	0.5	1.3	1.5	5.9	5.3	6.9	7.2	6.4	26.0	22.1	17.8	2.5	77.8	39.7	49.1	50.9
15846	KERSEY	99.5	99.5	0.1	0.1	0.1	0.1	0.1	0.2	6.5	6.8	7.4	6.7	5.2	29.4	24.9	12.1	1.0	75.2	37.9	51.2	48.9
15848	LUTHERSBURG	99.1	99.0	0.0	0.0	0.0	0.0	0.3	0.3	6.5	6.3	6.4	7.3	7.6	25.3	27.3	11.9	1.3	76.5	38.9	50.7	49.3
15849	PENFIELD	99.7	99.7	0.0	0.0	0.1	0.1	0.0	0.0	6.2	6.4	6.8	5.1	5.0	28.9	25.3	14.9	1.4	77.6	40.0	50.9	49.1
15851	REYNOLDSVILLE	99.1	98.9	0.2	0.2	0.1	0.2	0.5	0.6	6.4	6.5	7.0	6.7	6.2	26.1	25.8	13.6	1.7	75.7	38.7	49.8	50.2
15853	RIDGWAY	98.8	98.7	0.2	0.2	0.5	0.6	0.4	0.5	6.1	6.0	6.2	6.7	6.4	25.5	26.3	14.6	2.3	77.5	40.8	48.8	51.2
15856	ROCKTON	99.5	99.5	0.0	0.0	0.0	0.0	0.2	0.2	5.5	6.3	6.7	7.1	4.8	25.5	30.3	12.0	1.9	77.2	41.8	50.5	49.5
15857	SAINT MARYS	98.8	98.5	0.2	0.3	0.5	0.6	0.3	0.3	5.6	5.9	6.8	6.6	5.4	26.8	25.0	15.0	2.9	77.2	40.7	49.0	51.0
15860	SIGEL	98.8	98.8	0.2	0.2	0.1	0.2	0.5	0.4	5.4	5.8	6.1	6.1	4.5	25.7	28.4	16.2	1.9	79.2	43.0	51.6	48.4
15861	SINNAMAHONING	98.5	98.5	0.0	0.0	0.0	0.0	0.0	0.8	4.7	4.7	7.0	7.0	6.2	22.5	28.7	17.8	1.6	79.1	43.9	48.8	51.2
15864	SUMMERVILLE	98.5	98.5	0.1	0.1	0.1	0.1	0.2	0.2	5.3	5.4	6.2	6.5	7.3	27.1	26.2	14.2	1.9	78.9	40.8	51.7	48.3
15865	SYKESVILLE	99.4	99.3	0.2	0.3	0.0	0.0	0.2	0.3	5.2	5.4	7.0	6.5	6.1	26.0	23.0	17.6	3.2	78.4	41.1	48.9	51.1
15868	WEEDVILLE	99.0	99.5	0.0	0.0	0.5	0.5	0.5	0.5	5.6	6.1	6.1	5.6	5.1	25.8	26.8	17.2	2.0	78.8	42.3	50.0	50.0
15870	WILCOX	99.5	99.4	0.1	0.1	0.0	0.0	0.3	0.3	4.5	5.1	6.6	6.0	5.8	25.9	30.3	13.9	1.9	79.7	42.8	52.7	47.3
15901	JOHNSTOWN	75.0	74.0	21.0	21.8	0.2	0.3	2.1	2.2	5.1	5.3	4.9	4.5	4.8	21.9	25.7	22.3	5.5	81.9	47.6	45.1	54.9
15902	JOHNSTOWN	91.6	90.5	6.2	7.0	0.2	0.3	1.2	1.3	5.8	5.8	6.3	5.6	5.9	26.0	25.6	16.5	2.5	78.7	41.2	46.9	53.1
15904	JOHNSTOWN	97.4	96.9	0.8	0.9	1.2	1.6	0.5	0.5	4.1	4.5	5.3	8.8	9.7	19.7	25.5	19.1	3.4	82.9	43.4	46.4	53.6
15905	JOHNSTOWN	97.9	97.6	0.7	0.8	0.7	0.9	0.6	0.7	4.4	5.0	5.8	5.9	4.9	22.2	28.9	18.8	4.2	81.2	46.1	46.8	53.2
15906	JOHNSTOWN	92.9	92.1	5.4	6.0	0.2	0.3	1.1	1.2	5.8	5.8	6.0	5.1	5.2	24.4	26.6	18.3	2.9	79.3	43.3	46.8	53.3
15909	JOHNSTOWN	97.3	97.0	2.1	2.3	0.1	0.1	0.5	0.6	4.4	4.8	6.0	5.5	5.1	24.4	29.4	18.2	2.1	81.3	44.8	48.4	51.6
15920	ARMAGH	99.1	99.1	0.0	0.0	0.2	0.2	0.0	0.0	4.3	4.8	5.9	5.9	6.9	25.9	31.2	14.4	0.9	81.9	42.6	49.8	50.2
15923	BOLIVAR	98.1	97.9	0.5	0.6	0.1	0.1	0.1	0.1	4.8	5.6	6.8	7.6	5.0	25.3	28.7	14.9	1.4	77.9	41.7	51.3	48.7
15924	CAIRNBROOK	99.3	99.3	0.2	0.2	0.0	0.0	0.1	0.1	5.0	5.1	5.9	5.3	5.7	26.6	26.0	18.0	2.2	80.6	42.2	50.7	49.4
15926	CENTRAL CITY	99.4	99.3	0.0	0.0	0.1	0.1	0.3	0.4	5.4	5.7	6.1	5.7	4.9	25.6	27.9	16.4	2.2	79.3	42.7	49.5	50.5
15927	COLVER	98.7	98.6	0.8	0.9	0.3	0.4	0.3	0.3	6.2	6.2	6.3	5.1	6.2	27.6	24.4	14.4	3.6	77.9	39.9	51.0	49.0
15928	DAVIDSVILLE	99.4	99.3	0.1	0.1	0.3	0.4	0.4	0.6	4.7	5.0	5.6	6.0	5.5	22.4	28.5	18.0	4.4	81.2	45.5	46.9	53.1
15931	EBENSBURG	97.1	96.7	1.9	2.2	0.4	0.5	0.5	0.6	4.7	5.1	5.6	6.6	6.2	24.9	28.4	15.0	3.5	80.4	43.0	49.8	50.2
15935	HOLLSOPPLE	99.5	99.3	0.0	0.0	0.2	0.2	0.6	0.6	4.7	5.2	6.5	6.3	5.2	23.5	28.5	18.1	2.1	79.6	44.1	48.0	52.0
15936	HOOVERSVILLE	99.1	99.2	0.1	0.1	0.0	0.0	0.5	0.6	4.8	5.5	7.3	5.7	5.0	26.4	26.6	15.9	2.8	78.7	42.2	49.6	50.4
15938	LILLY	86.9	85.6	10.2	11.3	0.2	0.2	2.6	2.9	4.1	4.1	4.3	6.4	8.9	33.9	24.7	11.5	2.2	84.5	38.5	60.4	39.6
15940	LORETTO	89.2	87.1	9.2	10.9	0.8	1.0	5.9	6.6	3.9	3.4	3.9	10.8	17.2	35.2	18.7	6.3	0.7	86.4	30.3	58.8	41.2
15942	MINERAL POINT	99.1	98.8	0.2	0.3	0.1	0.1	0.1	0.1	5.0	5.4	6.4	6.3	5.6	25.1	28.7	15.8	1.7	79.0	42.5	49.6	50.4
15943	NANTY GLO	99.4	99.4	0.2	0.2	0.0	0.0	0.3	0.3	5.5	5.7	6.1	5.5	5.5	24.2	27.1	17.8	2.7	79.4	43.1	48.3	51.7
15944	NEW FLORENCE	99.0	98.9	0.1	0.1	0.1	0.1	0.6	0.6	6.0	5.9	6.3	5.9	5.3	26.0	27.9	15.3	1.4	78.1	41.4	50.0	50.0
15945	PARKHILL	98.3	98.2	1.7	1.8	0.0	0.0	0.0	0.0	3.6	3.6	7.3	7.3	3.6	25.5	30.9	16.4	1.8	85.5	44.5	49.1	50.9
15946	PORTAGE	99.2	99.1	0.2	0.2	0.1	0.2	0.4	0.4	5.3	5.4	6.0	6.1	5.8	25.3	27.5	16.3	2.3	79.6	42.3	49.0	51.1
15949	ROBINSON	99.2	99.0	0.2	0.2	0.3	0.3	0.5	0.6	6.6	6.9	6.6	5.3	5.5	27.3	27.0	13.3	1.5	76.9	39.6	51.3	48.7
15951	SAINT MICHAEL	98.8	98.8	0.3	0.3	0.0	0.0	0.3	0.3	4.6	4.3	5.6	6.8	6.5	25.3	25.3	18.5	3.1	81.5	42.7	47.2	52.8
15952	SALIX	98.6	98.5	0.0	0.1	0.3	0.4	0.8	0.9	5.4	5.9	6.9	5.9	5.5	27.1	29.1	13.1	1.3	78.4	40.9	49.8	50.2
	PENNSYLVANIA	85.4	84.4	10.0	10.3	1.8	2.2	3.2	3.5	5.9	6.1	6.8	6.9	6.7	26.6	25.3	13.3	2.2	77.2	39.1	48.4	51.6
	UNITED STATES	75.1	73.6	12.3	12.5	3.8	4.2	12.5	14.1	6.9	6.7	7.2	7.0	7.3	28.6	23.8	10.8	1.7	75.1	36.0	49.1	50.9

ZIP CODE #	POST OFFICE NAME	2004 Per Capita Income	2004 HH Income Base	2004 Household Income Distribution (%): Less than $25,000	$25,000 to $49,999	$50,000 to $99,999	$100,000 to $149,999	$150,000 or More	Median Household Income: 2004	2009	2004 National Centile	2004 State Centile	2004 Home Value Base	2004 Home Value Distribution (%): Less than $50,000	$50,000 to $89,999	$90,000 to $174,999	$175,000 to $399,999	$400,000 or More	2004 Median Home Value
15692	WESTMORELAND CITY	25019	471	23.8	20.2	37.8	15.3	3.0	55469	66138	80	81	383	5.7	33.2	34.5	25.6	1.0	104449
15697	YOUNGWOOD	20319	1501	29.7	32.0	33.1	3.6	1.7	37967	46262	39	35	919	8.5	31.9	49.6	10.0	0.0	98850
15698	YUKON	19115	241	31.1	41.5	18.3	9.1	0.0	35814	42034	31	24	176	42.6	37.5	19.9	0.0	0.0	57647
15701	INDIANA	22322	13162	39.6	25.0	23.6	7.9	3.9	33766	40669	23	15	7609	13.2	16.7	46.6	20.9	2.6	118487
15705	INDIANA	10504	147	83.7	5.4	0.0	5.4	5.4	10758	11761	1	0	2	0.0	0.0	100.0	0.0	0.0	162500
15711	ANITA	18351	122	27.1	41.8	25.4	4.1	1.6	37871	43012	39	35	100	34.0	32.0	28.0	5.0	1.0	65455
15713	AULTMAN	16460	132	27.3	45.5	19.7	6.1	1.5	37541	44237	38	33	110	19.1	30.9	40.9	9.1	0.0	90000
15714	NORTHERN CAMBRIA	15418	2730	43.0	33.4	19.9	3.2	0.6	29357	33533	11	5	2074	49.0	30.3	17.5	2.7	0.5	51088
15716	BLACK LICK	15434	161	44.7	26.1	23.6	5.0	0.6	27821	32549	8	4	121	28.9	29.8	38.8	2.5	0.0	80455
15717	BLAIRSVILLE	19173	4404	33.7	31.1	28.3	5.6	1.4	37179	43830	36	31	3289	17.3	31.7	40.0	9.8	1.2	91559
15720	BRUSH VALLEY	12499	32	31.3	40.6	25.0	3.1	0.0	36490	42313	34	28	27	25.9	29.6	37.0	7.4	0.0	82500
15721	BURNSIDE	14716	105	40.0	33.3	23.8	1.9	1.0	31400	37336	16	9	88	40.9	28.4	27.3	3.4	0.0	58000
15722	CARROLLTOWN	18504	1082	32.4	34.0	27.3	4.9	1.5	36988	43485	35	30	892	39.1	36.2	22.0	2.5	0.2	60690
15724	CHERRY TREE	14446	869	39.0	35.8	21.5	2.9	0.8	31625	36597	17	9	712	38.3	29.4	24.9	6.0	1.4	63830
15725	CLARKSBURG	17526	840	35.7	35.5	24.3	3.2	1.3	34353	39908	25	18	694	31.7	27.2	30.6	8.7	1.9	77674
15728	CLYMER	16671	1886	38.7	32.6	24.0	4.2	0.5	32665	38199	20	12	1479	36.4	26.5	31.2	4.5	1.4	66462
15729	COMMODORE	14176	493	38.7	38.7	18.9	3.5	0.2	31149	35639	15	8	412	45.4	25.5	20.4	8.0	0.7	54872
15730	COOLSPRING	22556	41	26.8	36.6	26.8	7.3	2.4	40743	52167	49	48	34	11.8	29.4	44.1	14.7	0.0	104167
15732	CREEKSIDE	17560	585	30.9	36.6	26.2	5.3	1.0	36039	42154	32	25	474	24.3	31.7	38.0	5.7	0.4	81765
15739	ERNEST	17744	136	27.9	31.6	33.1	5.2	2.2	41553	50548	52	51	113	10.6	24.8	48.7	15.0	0.9	105729
15742	GLEN CAMPBELL	15462	472	42.0	36.2	18.4	2.1	1.3	30339	34664	13	6	389	40.4	30.6	25.5	3.6	0.0	61833
15744	HAMILTON	18168	19	26.3	36.8	31.6	5.3	0.0	37351	36091	37	32	16	12.5	37.5	43.8	6.3	0.0	90000
15747	HOME	17495	1102	31.9	34.7	28.2	3.9	1.4	36637	42679	34	28	909	22.7	28.3	38.8	9.7	0.6	88836
15748	HOMER CITY	19751	3592	32.9	33.2	27.0	5.5	1.5	36412	42846	33	27	2766	19.4	33.7	39.6	7.2	0.1	86945
15753	LA JOSE	14938	394	39.1	37.1	19.0	3.1	1.8	30996	35599	15	8	332	43.7	28.9	22.0	5.1	0.3	57778
15757	MAHAFFEY	14934	728	39.0	37.1	19.2	3.6	1.1	31413	36228	16	9	610	37.2	31.2	26.1	4.8	0.8	62778
15758	MARCHAND	15025	188	33.5	38.3	25.0	1.6	1.6	35269	40637	29	21	153	26.1	26.1	37.9	8.5	1.3	86500
15759	MARION CENTER	15117	979	36.5	33.8	25.2	3.4	1.1	33514	38903	22	15	795	27.4	26.8	36.1	9.1	0.6	84224
15760	MARSTELLER	15013	58	37.9	32.8	24.1	5.2	0.0	32318	35752	19	11	45	48.9	26.7	24.4	0.0	0.0	51667
15762	NICKTOWN	16101	398	28.9	34.9	30.4	5.3	0.5	40293	46173	47	46	329	29.2	30.4	32.2	8.2	0.0	78654
15763	NORTHPOINT	14846	21	38.1	47.6	14.3	0.0	0.0	27793	32829	8	4	18	27.8	27.8	33.3	11.1	0.0	80000
15764	OLIVEBURG	16579	24	25.0	41.7	33.3	0.0	0.0	37313	43618	37	32	21	23.8	28.6	42.9	4.8	0.0	87500
15765	PENN RUN	17784	792	26.6	36.6	30.3	5.7	0.8	39443	46382	44	42	664	22.4	23.8	45.5	7.2	1.1	95556
15767	PUNXSUTAWNEY	18644	6176	35.8	36.0	21.4	4.3	2.6	33539	38232	23	15	4456	23.3	36.0	31.5	8.6	0.6	78997
15770	RINGGOLD	16162	65	29.2	46.2	20.0	4.6	0.0	34627	38782	26	18	54	31.5	31.5	31.5	5.6	0.0	72500
15771	ROCHESTER MILLS	15896	419	37.0	36.0	23.6	2.4	1.0	32824	37878	20	13	342	30.4	27.8	33.0	7.9	0.9	77917
15772	ROSSITER	15213	607	39.2	34.6	23.4	2.0	0.8	31785	36771	17	10	498	42.6	27.9	25.1	4.4	0.0	58222
15773	SAINT BENEDICT	16144	206	36.4	39.3	21.4	2.4	0.5	32420	37324	19	11	178	57.3	30.9	10.7	1.1	0.0	44800
15774	SHELOCTA	18473	2017	31.2	31.5	31.5	4.9	0.9	38381	44174	41	37	1672	23.9	24.1	40.0	11.2	0.8	93063
15775	SPANGLER	16719	191	38.7	33.0	22.5	5.8	0.0	31655	37344	17	9	143	46.2	36.4	17.5	0.0	0.0	54583
15776	SPRANKLE MILLS	18007	84	26.2	41.7	27.4	3.6	1.2	36960	42761	35	30	73	21.9	32.9	39.7	5.5	0.0	85000
15777	STARFORD	13888	136	38.2	33.8	25.0	2.9	0.0	32964	38079	21	13	118	36.4	28.8	33.1	1.7	0.0	64545
15778	TIMBLIN	15666	89	29.2	48.3	19.1	3.4	0.0	34728	39419	26	19	74	32.4	33.8	29.7	4.1	0.0	70000
15780	VALIER	17816	75	29.3	40.0	25.3	4.0	1.3	35362	41853	29	22	65	18.5	27.7	47.7	6.2	0.0	94167
15784	WORTHVILLE	18441	56	30.4	41.1	21.4	5.4	1.8	34036	39429	24	17	48	22.9	37.5	31.3	8.3	0.0	80000
15801	DU BOIS	23306	8415	31.9	29.4	27.7	7.0	4.0	39722	46507	45	43	6248	12.8	29.3	42.9	13.8	1.3	103260
15821	BENEZETT	21307	103	26.2	36.9	34.0	2.9	0.0	38709	44713	42	39	89	18.0	32.6	40.5	9.0	0.0	89375
15823	BROCKPORT	22104	877	28.5	39.0	26.2	4.6	1.7	39122	45182	43	41	733	22.2	31.4	42.0	4.1	0.3	85508
15824	BROCKWAY	21421	1852	25.4	37.9	30.2	4.6	1.9	41086	47422	50	49	1435	13.9	38.1	39.8	7.9	0.3	88293
15825	BROOKVILLE	20192	4453	32.6	33.8	26.1	5.1	2.5	36053	41290	32	25	3439	19.5	32.6	38.6	8.7	0.7	87878
15827	BYRNEDALE	18566	791	32.5	32.9	30.2	3.5	0.9	36860	42861	35	29	646	24.5	33.0	31.9	10.1	0.6	80000
15828	CLARINGTON	18348	149	40.3	32.9	22.2	4.7	0.0	32328	37985	19	11	125	22.4	32.8	35.2	8.8	0.8	79545
15829	CORSICA	18697	670	29.4	37.0	28.7	3.7	1.2	36929	41777	35	30	555	23.1	33.9	33.9	9.0	0.2	81444
15832	DRIFTWOOD	17100	220	36.8	33.2	25.9	3.6	0.5	33946	37698	24	16	186	29.6	30.1	32.3	5.9	2.2	75556
15834	EMPORIUM	18870	2240	32.3	34.1	28.2	4.0	1.4	36453	41745	33	27	1620	18.4	37.5	37.4	5.9	0.8	84483
15840	FALLS CREEK	19907	871	29.3	36.5	28.0	4.7	1.5	38735	44833	42	39	713	18.7	39.4	33.8	7.7	0.4	81786
15845	JOHNSONBURG	17968	1334	40.7	26.9	27.1	4.9	0.4	31457	35932	16	9	923	34.2	46.2	16.7	2.9	0.0	60636
15846	KERSEY	18459	1474	23.9	35.4	37.2	2.8	0.8	45648	51827	63	63	1261	11.7	16.7	52.9	17.9	0.7	117701
15848	LUTHERSBURG	18234	877	28.2	40.1	24.9	4.8	2.1	37860	43011	39	34	743	24.6	29.9	37.7	6.3	1.5	85282
15849	PENFIELD	19593	665	31.1	34.4	29.5	4.1	0.9	38126	43324	40	36	569	27.4	33.9	30.6	7.6	0.5	74459
15851	REYNOLDSVILLE	18270	3090	35.2	32.1	26.2	4.7	1.8	35309	40069	29	22	2367	23.5	33.6	35.7	6.5	0.8	82099
15853	RIDGWAY	21907	3134	28.5	28.4	35.5	5.6	2.0	41726	48881	52	52	2363	14.0	35.4	39.0	11.0	0.6	91051
15856	ROCKTON	19063	378	20.1	42.1	33.3	3.2	1.3	42815	49491	55	56	326	17.2	32.2	40.2	10.4	0.0	90667
15857	SAINT MARYS	24394	5860	23.8	27.7	38.1	8.4	2.0	48451	55905	69	69	4678	3.9	17.4	59.1	18.6	1.1	118931
15860	SIGEL	21163	462	31.4	37.0	25.1	4.8	1.7	36797	42115	35	29	395	21.8	33.2	35.4	9.1	0.5	82778
15861	SINNAMAHONING	18034	58	34.5	32.8	31.0	1.7	0.0	35880	37966	31	25	49	32.7	30.6	32.7	4.1	0.0	68750
15864	SUMMERVILLE	17682	444	30.2	39.0	25.0	4.5	1.4	35690	40537	30	24	372	31.7	40.9	21.8	5.7	0.0	63846
15865	SYKESVILLE	17021	547	43.7	31.4	21.0	2.9	0.9	29759	34304	12	5	361	29.4	51.0	19.7	0.0	0.0	63302
15868	WEEDVILLE	22125	98	29.6	34.7	32.7	3.1	0.0	37581	43618	38	33	82	22.0	34.2	32.9	11.0	0.0	82857
15870	WILCOX	23066	702	24.5	31.8	35.9	5.7	2.1	45284	51855	62	62	600	15.2	26.3	47.0	10.8	0.7	99107
15901	JOHNSTOWN	13513	2670	69.6	20.3	8.3	1.1	0.7	15828	17640	1	1	926	82.8	11.1	4.4	0.7	1.0	26544
15902	JOHNSTOWN	17001	5714	43.2	33.9	19.4	2.6	0.9	29027	32798	10	5	3514	50.8	34.8	11.3	2.7	0.4	49507
15904	JOHNSTOWN	23072	6684	30.0	31.4	27.6	7.0	4.0	39840	47199	45	43	5038	11.3	32.7	43.9	11.2	0.9	94327
15905	JOHNSTOWN	28916	9275	26.2	29.5	29.7	8.8	5.9	44197	52613	59	59	7332	20.6	36.2	32.7	9.2	1.3	83225
15906	JOHNSTOWN	16504	5341	48.2	33.3	15.0	2.6	0.9	26167	29923	6	3	3496	58.8	32.0	8.8	0.3	0.0	45472
15909	JOHNSTOWN	19141	2577	32.0	35.5	27.2	3.5	1.8	36614	43203	34	28	2141	39.9	29.2	28.7	1.9	0.4	65863
15920	ARMAGH	17131	226	35.0	33.2	27.0	4.4	0.4	35000	40000	28	21	186	29.6	24.2	40.9	5.4	0.0	85000
15923	BOLIVAR	18763	746	35.4	34.5	24.1	3.1	3.0	33845	40291	24	16	623	30.8	31.6	26.7	8.4	2.6	74605
15924	CAIRNBROOK	15300	426	44.4	32.4	19.7	2.1	1.4	29365	33453	11	5	341	55.1	33.1	10.9	0.9	0.0	47083
15926	CENTRAL CITY	17185	1272	37.3	34.6	23.7	3.0	1.4	32960	37783	21	13	1029	39.9	33.3	19.7	6.3	0.7	60152
15927	COLVER	14650	470	42.8	39.2	16.6	1.1	0.4	27669	31939	8	4	390	51.8	34.4	10.3	3.6	0.0	49293
15928	DAVIDSVILLE	19423	646	29.4	34.2	27.9	7.0	1.6	38196	44256	40	36	515	27.0	19.8	44.3	8.7	0.2	93173
15931	EBENSBURG	20211	3317	26.9	34.3	30.8	5.6	2.5	40177	48242	47	45	2515	18.3	30.9	39.6	10.1	1.0	90762
15935	HOLLSOPPLE	18075	1583	32.3	34.6	28.7	3.4	1.0	34903	40532	27	20	1322	36.2	28.2	29.4	5.2	1.0	68901
15936	HOOVERSVILLE	16071	669	40.5	32.6	22.9	3.3	0.8	31506	35845	16	9	521	44.9	37.0	15.7	2.3	0.0	54569
15938	LILLY	17169	1226	30.3	33.4	27.5	6.3	2.5	38503	45952	41	38	1010	33.2	36.4	25.8	4.5	0.1	65164
15940	LORETTO	14331	626	26.8	29.7	34.4	7.4	1.8	44483	51896	60	60	519	18.5	28.3	44.3	8.5	0.4	92661
15942	MINERAL POINT	18407	891	29.7	39.2	24.2	4.9	1.9	37623	44257	38	33	770	29.0	27.9	40.1	2.5	0.5	84301
15943	NANTY GLO	17064	1759	40.5	29.6	24.8	3.9	1.1	31854	36875	17	10	1334	49.5	31.4	14.8	4.3	0.0	50378
15944	NEW FLORENCE	18608	1657	34.2	32.1	26.3	4.9	2.6	35509	41594	30	23	1324	27.6	28.9	35.7	7.6	0.4	83359
15945	PARKHILL	17455	21	23.8	38.1	33.3	4.8	0.0	41107	47309	50	49	20	25.0	50.0	25.0	0.0	0.0	80000
15946	PORTAGE	18895	2833	36.2	31.3	25.7	4.8	1.9	34052	40164	24	17	2294	34.0	38.2	24.3	3.5	0.0	63930
15949	ROBINSON	16951	249	35.3	34.1	26.9	2.8	0.8	33790	38770	23	16	213	31.5	37.6	26.3	4.7	0.0	65870
15951	SAINT MICHAEL	15334	128	39.1	31.3	25.8	1.6	2.3	32813	38961	20	13	93	47.3	30.1	19.4	3.2	0.0	54167
15952	SALIX	19371	636	27.0	37.1	28.1	6.3	1.4	37766	43912	38	34	518	25.1	21.8	41.9	11.2	0.0	92712
	PENNSYLVANIA	25764		25.8	27.2	31.2	10.2	5.7	46988	57000				11.9	18.4	40.7	25.1	4.1	123516
	UNITED STATES	25866		24.7	27.1	30.8	10.9	6.5	48124	56710				10.9	15.0	33.7	30.1	10.4	145905

Copyright © 2004 ESRI BIS. All rights reserved. Reproduction by any method is prohibited.

#	POST OFFICE NAME	FINANCIAL SERVICES: Auto Loan	Home Loan	Invest-ments	Retire-ment Plans	THE HOME: Home Improvements: Home Repair	Lawn & Garden	Furnishings: Comput-ers & Hard-ware	Major Appli-ances	TV, Radio, Sound Equip-ment	Furni-ture	ENTERTAINMENT: Dine out/ Carry out	Sports Equip-ment	Fees & Tickets	Toys & Games	Travel	Cable TV	PERSONAL: Apparel & Services	Auto Repairs	Health Insur-ance	Pets & Supplies
15692	WESTMORELAND CITY	81	94	100	92	94	98	88	87	86	86	107	100	93	115	90	86	106	85	86	96
15697	YOUNGWOOD	48	52	55	49	52	58	51	51	53	49	66	56	54	71	53	55	64	50	54	56
15698	YUKON	55	60	63	56	60	67	59	58	61	57	76	65	62	82	61	63	73	57	63	64
15701	INDIANA	73	64	69	65	65	73	75	71	76	71	94	85	71	91	71	75	90	75	73	82
15705	INDIANA	37	23	29	26	22	27	44	32	43	37	53	45	36	48	35	38	50	40	30	37
15711	ANITA	85	57	26	49	65	74	55	69	66	56	78	82	47	74	56	71	71	68	85	98
15713	AULTMAN	74	66	50	62	69	74	61	67	64	61	78	80	59	80	62	66	74	65	73	87
15714	NORTHERN CAMBRIA	55	49	42	46	51	59	50	53	54	48	65	60	49	66	51	57	62	52	60	62
15716	BLACK LICK	73	49	22	42	55	63	47	59	57	48	66	70	40	63	48	61	60	58	72	83
15717	BLAIRSVILLE	72	59	44	56	64	73	61	67	67	59	80	76	57	79	61	70	75	66	77	82
15720	BRUSH VALLEY	76	53	28	50	62	69	52	64	60	52	70	78	45	69	54	63	64	64	77	90
15721	BURNSIDE	75	50	23	43	57	65	48	60	58	49	68	72	41	65	49	63	62	60	74	86
15722	CARROLLTOWN	65	66	64	62	68	75	64	66	67	62	83	75	66	88	66	70	80	64	71	76
15724	CHERRY TREE	67	49	28	44	54	62	49	57	57	49	67	67	44	64	50	61	62	57	69	76
15725	CLARKSBURG	74	53	31	48	59	67	52	62	60	53	72	74	46	68	53	64	66	62	74	85
15728	CLYMER	62	55	46	52	58	65	55	59	59	53	72	67	54	73	56	62	68	58	66	71
15729	COMMODORE	64	46	27	42	51	60	48	55	55	47	65	64	42	62	48	59	59	55	67	72
15730	COOLSPRING	70	70	68	67	73	80	67	71	69	66	85	81	68	87	70	72	82	70	76	84
15732	CREEKSIDE	82	56	26	48	63	72	54	67	65	55	76	80	46	72	55	69	69	66	82	95
15739	ERNEST	81	72	55	69	76	82	67	74	71	67	86	88	65	88	69	73	82	72	80	96
15742	GLEN CAMPBELL	74	50	23	43	56	65	48	60	58	49	68	72	41	64	49	62	62	59	74	85
15744	HAMILTON	88	59	27	51	67	77	57	71	69	58	81	85	48	76	58	74	73	71	88	101
15747	HOME	81	61	37	55	67	75	58	69	67	59	79	82	53	78	59	71	73	68	81	93
15748	HOMER CITY	68	63	56	60	66	74	63	66	67	61	81	75	62	84	64	69	77	65	73	79
15753	LA JOSE	74	50	23	43	56	65	48	60	58	49	68	72	41	64	49	63	62	60	74	85
15757	MAHAFFEY	74	50	22	43	56	65	48	60	58	49	68	72	41	64	49	62	62	59	74	85
15758	MARCHAND	77	52	23	45	59	68	50	63	60	51	71	75	43	67	51	65	64	62	77	89
15759	MARION CENTER	71	56	38	53	60	68	56	63	62	55	74	73	52	72	56	64	69	62	71	80
15760	MARSTELLER	76	51	23	44	57	66	49	61	59	50	69	73	42	65	50	63	63	60	75	87
15762	NICKTOWN	77	62	40	57	67	73	58	67	64	58	77	80	54	77	59	67	72	66	76	90
15763	NORTHPOINT	67	45	20	38	50	58	43	54	52	44	61	64	37	58	44	56	55	53	66	76
15764	OLIVEBURG	71	60	47	60	63	72	62	67	66	61	80	76	60	79	62	67	75	66	72	79
15765	PENN RUN	80	65	44	61	70	77	61	70	67	61	81	84	57	81	63	70	76	69	79	93
15767	PUNXSUTAWNEY	69	59	49	55	62	70	59	64	65	58	78	74	57	79	60	68	74	64	73	79
15770	RINGGOLD	77	51	23	44	58	67	50	62	60	51	70	74	42	66	50	65	64	61	76	88
15771	ROCHESTER MILLS	73	51	26	45	57	65	50	60	59	50	69	72	43	66	50	63	63	60	73	84
15772	ROSSITER	73	49	22	42	56	64	47	59	57	48	67	71	40	64	48	62	61	59	73	84
15773	SAINT BENEDICT	52	57	60	54	57	64	56	55	58	54	72	62	59	78	58	60	70	54	60	61
15774	SHELOCTA	82	61	36	55	67	75	59	70	67	60	80	83	52	76	59	70	74	69	81	94
15775	SPANGLER	62	57	49	52	60	67	56	60	61	55	74	68	55	77	57	64	70	59	67	72
15776	SPRANKLE MILLS	72	61	47	61	64	72	63	67	67	62	81	76	60	80	62	68	76	66	73	79
15777	STARFORD	76	51	23	44	57	66	49	61	59	50	69	73	42	66	50	64	63	61	75	87
15778	TIMBLIN	76	51	23	44	58	67	49	62	59	50	70	74	42	66	50	64	63	61	76	87
15780	VALIER	81	55	25	47	62	71	53	66	64	54	75	79	45	70	54	68	68	65	81	93
15784	WORTHVILLE	78	57	34	53	63	72	57	66	65	57	77	78	51	75	57	68	71	66	78	88
15801	DU BOIS	78	76	75	73	78	86	75	78	79	74	97	89	76	100	77	81	93	77	83	91
15821	BENEZETT	78	61	42	55	69	77	58	69	65	57	77	81	52	76	61	70	72	68	82	95
15823	BROCKPORT	94	67	36	60	75	85	64	78	75	65	89	93	57	86	66	80	82	77	94	109
15824	BROCKWAY	79	70	57	67	74	83	69	75	74	68	90	86	67	91	71	77	85	73	83	91
15825	BROOKVILLE	76	65	52	61	69	77	65	71	70	64	85	82	61	84	66	73	79	70	79	88
15827	BYRNEDALE	80	57	31	50	64	73	54	67	64	55	76	80	47	73	56	69	69	66	81	94
15828	CLARINGTON	66	52	35	47	58	65	49	59	55	48	65	69	43	64	52	59	61	58	69	80
15829	CORSICA	74	62	48	60	66	75	63	68	68	62	82	79	60	81	63	70	76	67	76	84
15832	DRIFTWOOD	68	54	37	48	60	68	51	61	57	50	68	71	45	67	54	61	63	60	72	83
15834	EMPORIUM	69	60	49	55	64	72	58	64	64	57	78	74	57	80	61	68	73	63	74	81
15840	FALLS CREEK	70	68	60	64	70	77	65	68	68	63	83	79	66	87	67	70	80	67	74	82
15845	JOHNSONBURG	52	57	60	54	57	64	56	56	58	54	72	62	59	78	58	60	70	54	60	61
15846	KERSEY	76	68	51	64	71	77	62	69	66	62	81	83	61	82	64	68	77	67	75	89
15848	LUTHERSBURG	91	61	28	52	69	79	59	73	71	60	83	88	50	78	60	76	75	73	90	104
15849	PENFIELD	78	62	42	56	69	78	58	70	65	58	78	82	52	77	62	70	72	69	82	95
15851	REYNOLDSVILLE	71	60	48	56	64	71	60	65	66	59	79	76	57	80	61	68	75	65	73	82
15853	RIDGWAY	75	74	69	70	76	83	71	74	74	70	91	85	72	95	73	76	87	72	79	88
15856	ROCKTON	66	68	78	71	69	72	70	69	67	69	84	81	70	82	69	65	82	70	66	76
15857	SAINT MARYS	84	85	80	80	87	95	81	84	84	79	104	96	83	109	84	87	100	82	90	99
15860	SIGEL	81	63	43	57	71	80	60	72	68	59	80	84	54	79	64	72	75	71	85	98
15861	SINNAMAHONING	68	53	36	48	60	68	50	61	57	50	67	71	45	67	54	61	63	60	72	83
15864	SUMMERVILLE	68	61	51	56	64	72	59	64	65	58	79	73	59	82	61	68	75	63	73	79
15865	SYKESVILLE	49	53	56	50	53	59	52	52	54	50	67	57	55	73	54	56	65	51	56	57
15868	WEEDVILLE	79	58	34	52	66	75	55	68	64	55	76	80	49	74	58	69	70	67	82	94
15870	WILCOX	95	75	51	67	84	94	70	85	80	70	94	99	63	93	75	85	88	83	100	116
15901	JOHNSTOWN	34	30	37	29	30	36	34	34	37	34	46	38	34	45	34	39	44	35	38	38
15902	JOHNSTOWN	51	50	50	48	51	58	52	52	55	50	67	59	52	69	53	56	64	52	57	59
15904	JOHNSTOWN	73	76	81	73	77	87	75	77	77	74	95	85	77	96	78	80	92	76	82	85
15905	JOHNSTOWN	87	97	107	93	97	106	94	94	94	92	117	105	98	121	97	96	114	92	96	103
15906	JOHNSTOWN	49	47	48	44	48	55	49	49	52	48	64	55	49	65	49	55	61	50	55	56
15909	JOHNSTOWN	61	64	64	60	65	72	62	63	64	60	79	71	64	84	64	66	76	62	68	72
15920	ARMAGH	80	54	24	47	61	70	52	65	63	53	74	78	44	70	53	68	67	64	80	92
15923	BOLIVAR	84	64	40	56	70	79	62	72	71	62	85	85	56	83	63	76	79	71	86	97
15924	CAIRNBROOK	46	50	52	47	50	56	49	49	51	47	63	54	52	68	51	53	61	48	52	54
15926	CENTRAL CITY	57	56	52	52	58	65	54	57	58	53	71	65	55	75	56	61	68	56	63	68
15927	COLVER	46	49	49	46	50	55	48	48	50	46	61	54	50	66	49	51	59	47	52	54
15928	DAVIDSVILLE	74	64	55	63	68	74	64	70	67	63	81	83	60	80	65	68	77	70	76	87
15931	EBENSBURG	72	74	74	70	75	82	72	73	74	70	91	84	73	95	74	76	88	72	78	85
15935	HOLLSOPPLE	63	62	57	58	64	71	60	63	64	59	78	72	61	82	62	66	74	62	69	74
15936	HOOVERSVILLE	55	51	46	48	53	61	52	54	56	50	68	61	51	70	53	58	64	53	61	64
15938	LILLY	55	57	57	54	58	64	56	57	58	54	72	64	58	77	58	60	69	55	61	64
15940	LORETTO	84	73	56	71	77	85	71	78	76	71	92	90	69	92	72	77	87	76	84	96
15942	MINERAL POINT	74	62	47	56	66	74	60	67	66	60	80	78	57	79	61	70	75	66	77	86
15943	NANTY GLO	57	54	50	51	56	64	56	57	59	53	72	64	56	74	57	62	68	56	64	65
15944	NEW FLORENCE	79	59	36	54	65	75	60	69	68	59	81	80	54	77	60	72	74	68	82	90
15945	PARKHILL	59	64	67	60	65	72	63	62	65	61	81	70	67	88	65	68	78	61	67	69
15946	PORTAGE	65	63	59	60	65	73	63	65	67	61	81	73	64	84	65	69	77	64	72	75
15949	ROBINSON	80	53	24	46	60	70	52	64	62	53	73	77	44	69	52	67	66	64	79	92
15951	SAINT MICHAEL	49	53	56	50	54	60	53	52	54	51	67	58	56	73	54	56	65	51	56	57
15952	SALIX	68	72	71	70	73	76	68	70	67	67	83	82	69	87	69	67	81	69	70	82
	PENNSYLVANIA	89	89	93	87	90	98	89	90	91	88	112	104	89	114	90	92	109	90	92	104
	UNITED STATES	100	100	100	100	100	100	100	100	100	100	100	100	100	100	100	100	100	100	100	100

POPULATION CHANGE

ZIP CODE			POPULATION			2000-2004 ANNUAL RATE		HOUSEHOLDS					FAMILIES		
# POST OFFICE NAME	COUNTY FIPS CODE		2000	2004	2009	% Rate	State Centile	2000	2004	2009	% Annual Rate 2000-2004	2004 Average HH Size	2000	2004	% Annual Rate 2000-2004
15953 SEANOR	111		166	165	165	-0.1	32	73	75	77	0.6	2.20	53	54	0.4
15954 SEWARD	063		3003	2918	2911	-0.7	11	1219	1207	1227	-0.2	2.41	895	881	-0.4
15955 SIDMAN	021		3183	3058	2937	-0.9	5	1247	1226	1204	-0.4	2.48	904	882	-0.6
15956 SOUTH FORK	021		3130	3110	3037	-0.2	32	1245	1270	1269	0.5	2.43	909	922	0.3
15957 STRONGSTOWN	063		565	552	543	-0.6	14	225	225	226	0.0	2.45	178	177	-0.1
15958 SUMMERHILL	021		2384	2406	2372	0.2	50	834	860	866	0.7	2.76	629	645	0.6
15960 TWIN ROCKS	021		5	5	5	0.0	39	1	1	1	0.0	5.00	1	1	0.0
15961 VINTONDALE	063		1572	1518	1478	-0.8	7	598	591	589	-0.3	2.57	443	436	-0.4
15963 WINDBER	111		11960	11727	11593	-0.5	18	4958	4987	5048	0.1	2.30	3336	3331	0.0
16001 BUTLER	019		42041	42676	44297	0.4	57	17751	18476	19605	1.0	2.26	11340	11697	0.7
16002 BUTLER	019		16884	17111	17658	0.3	54	6059	6313	6668	1.0	2.59	4588	4739	0.8
16020 BOYERS	019		1146	1199	1254	1.1	81	437	467	498	1.6	2.55	330	350	1.4
16022 BRUIN	019		385	371	379	-0.9	7	145	143	149	-0.3	2.59	108	106	-0.4
16023 CABOT	019		4235	4495	4727	1.4	87	1430	1569	1695	2.2	2.58	1065	1158	2.0
16025 CHICORA	019		5494	5538	5722	0.2	48	1953	2025	2143	0.9	2.66	1465	1505	0.6
16028 EAST BRADY	005		2136	2153	2199	0.2	48	912	939	979	0.7	2.21	617	632	0.6
16030 EAU CLAIRE	019		295	338	371	3.3	98	113	133	149	3.9	2.52	88	102	3.5
16033 EVANS CITY	019		6717	6874	7155	0.6	66	2573	2690	2857	1.1	2.54	1919	1992	0.9
16034 FENELTON	019		1900	2006	2106	1.3	85	645	705	760	2.1	2.68	489	528	1.8
16036 FOXBURG	031		1177	1222	1274	0.9	76	456	478	506	1.1	2.56	342	357	1.0
16037 HARMONY	019		4338	4565	4778	1.2	84	1587	1716	1837	1.9	2.61	1230	1322	1.7
16038 HARRISVILLE	019		3741	3755	3802	0.1	44	1424	1461	1510	0.6	2.50	1054	1072	0.4
16040 HILLIARDS	019		1063	1131	1193	1.5	88	390	423	455	1.9	2.66	302	325	1.7
16041 KARNS CITY	019		2435	2384	2433	-0.5	16	941	945	985	0.1	2.52	708	706	-0.1
16045 LYNDORA	019		1149	1175	1222	0.5	65	548	578	616	1.3	2.03	342	356	1.0
16046 MARS	019		9126	10472	11471	3.3	98	3268	3810	4247	3.7	2.66	2453	2841	3.5
16049 PARKER	019		3151	3191	3288	0.3	54	1203	1244	1307	0.8	2.56	888	913	0.7
16050 PETROLIA	019		1426	1388	1421	-0.6	12	513	509	531	-0.2	2.73	391	384	-0.4
16051 PORTERSVILLE	019		4143	4268	4368	0.7	71	1609	1697	1770	1.3	2.51	1210	1266	1.1
16052 PROSPECT	019		2181	2256	2344	0.8	74	855	907	963	1.4	2.49	632	665	1.2
16053 RENFREW	019		3738	3790	3923	0.3	56	1400	1452	1534	0.9	2.61	1060	1090	0.7
16055 SARVER	019		8240	8304	8559	0.2	47	3016	3114	3278	0.8	2.63	2375	2435	0.6
16056 SAXONBURG	019		5027	5060	5211	0.2	46	1942	2006	2116	0.8	2.40	1377	1410	0.6
16057 SLIPPERY ROCK	019		13201	13394	13732	0.3	56	4103	4252	4460	0.8	2.53	2526	2587	0.6
16059 VALENCIA	019		7155	7217	7464	0.2	48	2589	2673	2822	0.8	2.63	2001	2047	0.5
16061 WEST SUNBURY	019		2304	2352	2433	0.5	63	843	880	928	1.0	2.65	639	660	0.5
16063 ZELIENOPLE	019		6861	6927	7113	0.2	50	3044	3148	3304	0.8	2.18	1872	1917	0.6
16066 CRANBERRY TWP	019		23498	27371	30474	3.7	99	8296	9744	10987	3.9	2.79	6525	7624	3.7
16101 NEW CASTLE	073		37156	36852	36634	-0.2	30	14641	14798	14931	0.3	2.40	9970	10013	0.1
16102 NEW CASTLE	073		6092	6067	6041	-0.1	34	2378	2410	2434	0.3	2.50	1694	1707	0.2
16105 NEW CASTLE	073		14528	14562	14576	0.1	42	6066	6203	6303	0.5	2.31	4202	4264	0.4
16110 ADAMSVILLE	039		315	329	343	1.0	80	126	134	142	1.5	2.46	102	108	1.4
16111 ATLANTIC	039		2064	2102	2158	0.4	61	680	704	735	0.8	2.99	526	542	0.7
16112 BESSEMER	073		1637	1661	1666	0.3	56	668	693	708	0.9	2.39	494	509	0.7
16114 CLARKS MILLS	085		722	758	775	1.2	83	265	284	295	1.6	2.66	201	214	1.5
16115 DARLINGTON	007		3320	3133	3022	-1.4	1	1234	1188	1167	-0.9	2.56	892	851	-1.1
16116 EDINBURG	073		3246	3195	3161	-0.4	22	1292	1300	1308	0.2	2.43	912	909	-0.1
16117 ELLWOOD CITY	073		17691	17671	17591	0.0	37	7180	7295	7371	0.4	2.41	5002	5047	0.2
16120 ENON VALLEY	073		2572	2603	2604	0.3	53	906	937	953	0.8	2.78	707	726	0.6
16121 FARRELL	085		6766	6437	6286	-1.2	3	2833	2753	2730	-0.7	2.30	1810	1739	-0.9
16123 FOMBELL	007		2085	2283	2372	2.2	94	762	852	902	2.7	2.65	571	634	2.5
16124 FREDONIA	085		2004	2023	2028	0.2	50	717	738	750	0.7	2.70	562	575	0.5
16125 GREENVILLE	085		19246	18849	18621	-0.5	16	7482	7470	7483	0.0	2.36	5204	5156	-0.2
16127 GROVE CITY	085		15485	15533	15536	0.1	43	5237	5334	5400	0.4	2.38	3594	3624	0.3
16130 HADLEY	085		2014	1971	1947	-0.5	15	786	789	793	0.1	2.47	596	594	-0.1
16131 HARTSTOWN	039		913	1033	1122	3.0	97	337	389	431	3.4	2.66	261	299	3.3
16133 JACKSON CENTER	085		1388	1383	1376	-0.1	35	514	524	529	0.5	2.61	401	406	0.3
16134 JAMESTOWN	039		4090	4498	4795	2.3	94	1673	1881	2041	2.8	2.38	1187	1321	2.6
16137 MERCER	085		12689	12660	12621	-0.1	36	4497	4580	4632	0.4	2.50	3269	3309	0.3
16141 NEW GALILEE	073		1926	1819	1763	-1.3	2	754	728	719	-0.8	2.49	553	530	-1.0
16142 NEW WILMINGTON	085		6384	6381	6371	0.0	39	2176	2205	2225	0.3	2.75	1606	1627	0.3
16143 PULASKI	073		4019	3942	3895	-0.5	18	1472	1469	1471	-0.1	2.61	1118	1108	-0.2
16145 SANDY LAKE	085		2729	2832	2881	0.9	76	1069	1129	1164	1.3	2.49	805	844	1.1
16146 SHARON	085		16433	16139	15981	-0.4	20	6844	6842	6864	0.0	2.29	4219	4186	-0.2
16148 HERMITAGE	085		16351	17019	17330	1.0	78	6879	7290	7521	1.4	2.29	4674	4920	1.2
16150 SHARPSVILLE	085		8660	8516	8440	-0.4	21	3530	3543	3563	0.1	2.40	2516	2511	-0.1
16153 STONEBORO	085		2601	2639	2651	0.3	56	1037	1066	1082	0.7	2.47	748	763	0.5
16154 TRANSFER	085		2943	2831	2775	-0.9	6	1146	1125	1120	-0.4	2.52	854	833	-0.6
16156 VOLANT	073		2732	2756	2761	0.2	49	975	1003	1020	0.7	2.75	757	776	0.6
16157 WAMPUM	073		4820	4684	4600	-0.7	11	1991	1977	1975	-0.2	2.33	1391	1370	-0.4
16159 WEST MIDDLESEX	085		4480	4390	4337	-0.5	17	1798	1800	1808	0.0	2.43	1349	1341	-0.1
16172 NEW WILMINGTON	073		840	836	835	-0.1	34	11	10	10	-2.2	2.10	3	3	0.0
16201 KITTANNING	005		18981	19726	20473	0.9	77	7599	8059	8525	1.4	2.38	5255	5542	1.3
16210 ADRIAN	005		742	749	762	0.2	50	271	279	288	0.7	2.68	206	211	0.6
16212 CADOGAN	005		378	379	383	0.1	42	169	173	179	0.6	2.18	122	124	0.4
16213 CALLENSBURG	031		700	713	736	0.4	61	278	288	303	0.8	2.48	189	195	0.7
16214 CLARION	031		8707	9209	9697	1.3	86	3049	3345	3643	2.2	2.19	1415	1548	2.1
16217 COOKSBURG	053		45	44	45	-0.5	14	16	16	17	0.0	2.75	11	11	0.0
16218 COWANSVILLE	005		1245	1263	1288	0.3	56	476	493	513	0.8	2.40	365	376	0.7
16222 DAYTON	005		2125	2136	2170	0.1	45	800	815	840	0.4	2.61	596	604	0.3
16224 FAIRMOUNT CITY	031		1681	1706	1757	0.4	57	641	662	695	0.8	2.58	495	510	0.7
16225 FISHER	031		393	403	418	0.6	68	166	173	183	1.0	2.33	120	126	1.2
16226 FORD CITY	005		9982	10121	10377	0.3	56	4206	4339	4527	0.7	2.32	2856	2931	0.6
16229 FREEPORT	005		5385	5489	5621	0.5	62	2154	2234	2327	0.9	2.45	1546	1594	0.7
16232 KNOX	031		7219	7339	7568	0.3	59	2844	2951	3104	0.9	2.47	2100	2170	0.8
16233 LEEPER	031		458	463	475	0.3	52	184	191	200	0.9	2.42	129	133	0.7
16234 LIMESTONE	031		1272	1301	1347	0.5	65	479	502	530	1.1	2.59	372	388	1.0
16235 LUCINDA	031		991	990	1021	0.0	37	367	375	395	0.5	2.64	273	278	0.4
16238 MANORVILLE	005		401	493	555	5.0	100	180	225	259	5.4	2.18	122	152	5.3
16239 MARIENVILLE	053		1356	1345	1358	-0.2	30	556	564	582	0.3	1.96	362	364	0.1
16240 MAYPORT	005		1865	1875	1905	0.1	45	657	674	698	0.6	2.66	504	514	0.5
16242 NEW BETHLEHEM	031		5200	5209	5317	0.0	41	2134	2179	2269	0.5	2.35	1491	1515	0.4
16248 RIMERSBURG	031		3666	3691	3786	0.2	46	1455	1492	1558	0.6	2.47	1043	1065	0.5
16249 RURAL VALLEY	005		3485	3490	3540	0.0	40	1348	1374	1419	0.5	2.50	988	1001	0.3
16254 SHIPPENVILLE	031		2620	2651	2723	0.3	53	1005	1042	1095	0.9	2.35	698	718	0.7
PENNSYLVANIA						0.3					0.7	2.44			0.6
UNITED STATES						1.2					1.3	2.58			1.1

ZIP CODE #	POST OFFICE NAME	RACE (%) White 2000	White 2004	Black 2000	Black 2004	Asian/Pacific 2000	Asian/Pacific 2004	% Hispanic Origin 2000	% Hispanic Origin 2004	2004 AGE DISTRIBUTION (%) 0-4	5-9	10-14	15-19	20-24	25-44	45-64	65-84	85+	18+	MEDIAN AGE 2004	% 2004 Males	% 2004 Females
15953	SEANOR	100.0	100.0	0.0	0.0	0.0	0.0	0.6	0.6	4.2	4.9	6.7	6.1	5.5	23.0	30.3	17.0	2.4	80.0	44.8	49.7	50.3
15954	SEWARD	99.0	98.9	0.1	0.1	0.0	0.0	0.5	0.6	5.0	5.4	6.3	6.1	5.9	24.3	28.9	16.3	1.8	79.8	43.1	49.6	50.5
15955	SIDMAN	99.2	99.2	0.1	0.1	0.1	0.1	0.3	0.4	5.5	5.7	7.1	6.4	5.8	26.7	26.1	14.6	2.0	77.6	40.1	48.2	51.8
15956	SOUTH FORK	99.7	99.6	0.1	0.1	0.0	0.0	0.5	0.6	5.8	6.1	7.1	5.9	5.6	26.8	25.4	15.3	2.1	77.5	40.4	49.9	50.1
15957	STRONGSTOWN	99.1	99.1	0.0	0.0	0.0	0.0	0.2	0.2	6.2	6.2	6.3	6.2	6.5	28.6	27.7	11.1	1.3	77.5	39.3	50.2	49.8
15958	SUMMERHILL	99.2	99.0	0.3	0.3	0.1	0.1	0.2	0.3	5.9	6.2	7.2	7.3	6.0	25.9	26.5	13.4	1.6	76.2	39.7	50.5	49.5
15960	TWIN ROCKS	100.0	100.0	0.0	0.0	0.0	0.0	0.0	0.0	0.0	0.0	0.0	0.0	40.0	60.0	0.0	0.0	0.0	100.0	26.3	60.0	40.0
15961	VINTONDALE	99.6	99.5	0.1	0.1	0.0	0.0	0.5	0.5	4.8	5.0	6.0	6.7	6.2	26.0	28.5	14.7	2.2	80.2	41.8	51.1	49.0
15963	WINDBER	99.2	99.0	0.1	0.1	0.2	0.2	0.6	0.6	4.7	5.0	6.5	6.1	5.8	23.6	27.0	18.2	3.2	80.1	43.9	47.6	52.4
16001	BUTLER	97.4	97.2	1.1	1.2	0.5	0.6	0.7	0.8	5.9	5.9	6.1	6.0	5.8	26.3	26.7	14.8	2.6	78.4	41.0	48.3	51.7
16002	BUTLER	97.9	97.7	1.3	1.4	0.3	0.4	0.5	0.6	5.7	6.3	7.4	7.9	4.9	25.4	26.9	13.1	2.4	75.2	40.5	50.5	49.5
16020	BOYERS	98.6	98.5	0.4	0.5	0.4	0.5	0.4	0.3	6.7	6.8	6.8	6.3	4.8	29.1	27.4	11.1	1.0	75.6	38.6	51.8	48.2
16022	BRUIN	98.7	98.7	0.0	0.0	0.0	0.0	0.5	0.5	5.7	5.7	7.6	7.8	7.3	25.3	26.4	12.9	1.4	76.3	39.6	50.4	49.6
16023	CABOT	99.2	99.1	0.1	0.2	0.1	0.2	0.3	0.3	5.7	6.0	6.6	5.8	4.1	23.5	23.7	16.4	8.1	78.0	43.9	46.7	53.3
16025	CHICORA	99.3	99.3	0.3	0.3	0.0	0.0	0.2	0.3	6.1	6.6	7.6	6.3	5.0	27.3	25.5	13.5	2.1	75.5	39.7	49.4	50.6
16028	EAST BRADY	99.0	98.9	0.5	0.5	0.1	0.1	0.3	0.3	5.5	5.4	5.2	5.9	5.3	23.8	27.2	17.7	4.2	80.3	44.3	49.6	50.4
16030	EAU CLAIRE	99.3	99.7	0.0	0.0	0.0	0.0	0.3	0.0	7.1	6.5	5.6	7.1	5.6	28.1	26.9	12.1	0.9	76.3	38.1	53.3	46.8
16033	EVANS CITY	98.9	98.7	0.2	0.2	0.4	0.5	0.3	0.4	6.3	6.8	7.3	6.2	5.4	28.2	26.6	11.6	1.4	75.6	39.0	50.1	49.9
16034	FENELTON	98.9	98.7	0.2	0.3	0.1	0.1	0.6	0.8	6.8	6.8	6.8	6.3	5.6	28.1	25.4	12.0	2.1	75.2	38.8	50.2	49.8
16036	FOXBURG	99.4	99.3	0.2	0.2	0.1	0.1	0.9	1.0	5.9	6.4	7.6	6.3	5.2	26.7	27.1	13.6	1.2	76.2	39.8	51.5	48.5
16037	HARMONY	98.9	98.8	0.2	0.2	0.2	0.3	0.4	0.5	5.5	6.0	6.9	6.1	5.6	26.7	29.6	11.8	1.8	77.9	41.3	50.4	49.6
16038	HARRISVILLE	98.3	98.1	0.4	0.5	0.3	0.5	0.3	0.4	6.0	6.4	6.6	5.7	5.2	27.5	27.4	13.1	2.1	77.3	40.4	50.3	49.7
16040	HILLIARDS	99.0	98.9	0.1	0.1	0.2	0.2	0.6	0.6	6.6	6.6	7.5	7.2	5.9	28.6	25.0	11.5	1.1	74.5	37.9	50.2	49.8
16041	KARNS CITY	99.3	99.2	0.3	0.3	0.1	0.2	0.1	0.1	6.0	6.3	7.2	6.0	5.4	28.4	26.9	12.6	1.4	76.8	39.5	50.0	50.0
16045	LYNDORA	98.3	98.2	0.5	0.5	0.1	0.1	0.6	0.6	5.3	5.4	5.5	4.6	4.9	26.4	28.1	16.6	3.4	81.2	43.7	49.5	50.6
16046	MARS	97.6	97.1	0.6	0.7	1.2	1.5	0.7	0.8	8.0	8.4	7.5	6.0	3.9	30.5	24.2	9.2	2.3	71.9	37.7	47.9	52.1
16049	PARKER	98.5	98.4	0.7	0.8	0.2	0.2	0.2	0.2	6.0	6.0	6.8	6.4	6.2	25.6	27.2	14.3	1.5	77.1	40.3	50.1	49.9
16050	PETROLIA	99.0	98.9	0.2	0.2	0.2	0.2	0.4	0.4	6.3	6.6	7.9	6.5	6.0	27.8	25.4	12.3	1.3	75.1	38.6	49.4	50.6
16051	PORTERSVILLE	98.9	98.8	0.1	0.1	0.3	0.3	0.3	0.3	6.2	6.4	6.9	6.4	6.2	26.7	28.1	12.1	1.2	76.4	39.6	50.1	49.9
16052	PROSPECT	99.2	99.1	0.1	0.0	0.2	0.3	0.4	0.4	6.1	6.6	6.4	6.5	6.0	28.6	28.3	10.6	1.0	77.0	39.1	50.5	49.5
16053	RENFREW	98.9	98.8	0.3	0.3	0.4	0.4	0.5	0.6	6.5	7.0	7.2	6.2	5.2	27.2	27.8	11.4	1.4	75.4	39.5	50.1	49.9
16055	SARVER	99.0	98.9	0.2	0.2	0.3	0.3	0.3	0.3	5.8	6.3	6.9	6.3	5.4	25.6	28.9	13.2	1.8	76.8	41.3	49.7	50.3
16056	SAXONBURG	99.1	98.9	0.2	0.2	0.0	0.1	0.7	0.8	5.6	6.1	6.6	5.9	4.7	25.4	27.5	15.0	3.2	77.8	42.3	47.2	52.8
16057	SLIPPERY ROCK	95.8	95.2	1.7	1.9	1.3	1.6	0.7	0.8	3.7	4.2	5.0	15.0	23.9	20.4	18.6	8.1	1.0	84.4	24.6	48.1	51.9
16059	VALENCIA	98.5	98.3	0.5	0.5	0.3	0.3	0.8	0.9	6.0	6.9	7.7	6.9	4.7	25.2	28.5	12.1	2.0	74.6	41.0	48.8	51.2
16061	WEST SUNBURY	98.9	98.7	0.3	0.3	0.3	0.3	0.5	0.6	6.5	6.8	7.4	6.4	5.8	29.6	27.2	9.4	0.9	75.0	37.9	51.1	48.9
16063	ZELIENOPLE	98.0	97.7	0.7	0.8	0.5	0.6	0.4	0.5	5.2	5.4	6.1	5.8	5.4	26.0	25.4	16.3	4.4	79.7	42.7	47.5	52.5
16066	CRANBERRY TWP	96.8	96.3	0.9	1.0	1.4	1.7	0.7	0.8	9.2	9.4	8.4	6.1	4.8	31.4	22.8	6.5	1.5	69.1	35.3	49.2	50.8
16101	NEW CASTLE	90.1	89.2	8.0	8.7	0.2	0.2	0.7	0.8	5.9	6.1	6.6	6.5	5.8	24.4	25.2	16.7	2.8	77.4	41.3	47.9	52.1
16102	NEW CASTLE	97.1	96.6	1.4	1.7	0.3	0.3	0.4	0.5	5.7	5.9	7.0	6.4	5.3	24.8	26.8	15.7	2.5	77.4	41.5	48.1	51.9
16105	NEW CASTLE	97.4	97.0	1.2	1.3	0.8	1.0	0.4	0.5	4.9	5.2	5.9	5.8	4.5	21.8	28.1	19.9	3.9	80.1	46.2	46.4	53.6
16110	ADAMSVILLE	97.1	96.7	1.0	1.2	0.3	0.3	1.0	1.2	9.7	9.7	10.0	7.6	6.1	25.2	21.0	9.7	0.9	66.0	31.3	50.8	49.2
16111	ATLANTIC	98.3	98.1	0.6	0.6	0.2	0.3	0.5	0.7	8.1	8.2	8.5	7.4	6.2	26.7	24.2	9.4	1.3	70.5	34.8	50.7	49.3
16112	BESSEMER	98.6	98.3	0.4	0.4	0.4	0.5	0.9	1.1	5.4	5.7	6.9	5.5	4.7	27.0	26.7	15.7	2.4	78.3	41.8	49.0	51.1
16114	CLARKS MILLS	99.2	99.1	0.1	0.1	0.1	0.1	0.1	0.0	5.7	6.5	6.5	6.9	5.2	25.9	28.8	13.5	1.3	76.8	40.9	50.4	49.6
16115	DARLINGTON	98.5	98.3	0.7	0.8	0.2	0.2	0.3	0.4	4.4	4.9	7.0	6.4	5.4	24.6	29.3	16.0	2.1	79.7	43.5	48.4	51.6
16116	EDINBURG	98.8	98.7	0.3	0.3	0.2	0.2	0.3	0.3	5.4	5.7	6.9	6.5	5.5	25.7	27.3	15.0	1.9	77.8	41.5	49.2	50.8
16117	ELLWOOD CITY	98.6	98.3	0.6	0.7	0.2	0.3	0.5	0.6	5.7	5.8	6.5	6.3	5.9	25.6	25.8	15.9	2.5	78.0	41.2	48.0	52.0
16120	ENON VALLEY	99.3	99.2	0.2	0.2	0.1	0.1	0.7	0.9	6.1	6.4	7.7	7.3	5.7	27.2	26.8	12.0	0.9	75.4	38.4	49.4	50.6
16121	FARRELL	54.2	51.3	42.9	45.8	0.2	0.2	0.7	0.7	6.5	6.5	6.9	6.1	5.6	22.9	23.2	19.2	3.2	76.4	41.6	44.9	55.1
16123	FOMBELL	99.2	99.1	0.2	0.2	0.1	0.1	0.8	0.9	6.0	6.3	7.1	6.8	5.6	28.1	27.4	11.2	1.6	76.2	40.1	50.0	50.0
16124	FREDONIA	99.3	99.2	0.1	0.1	0.1	0.1	0.2	0.3	6.9	7.0	7.1	6.8	7.0	24.8	25.9	12.9	1.7	74.9	38.7	50.5	49.5
16125	GREENVILLE	97.9	97.5	0.8	1.0	0.5	0.6	0.5	0.5	5.5	5.7	6.1	7.3	7.1	23.7	25.6	16.0	2.9	78.6	41.2	48.3	51.7
16127	GROVE CITY	96.2	95.4	2.1	2.5	0.9	1.1	0.7	0.7	4.6	5.0	5.8	12.3	14.1	21.3	21.4	13.2	2.3	79.3	33.7	50.4	49.6
16130	HADLEY	99.1	99.0	0.2	0.2	0.1	0.2	0.2	0.2	5.1	6.0	6.3	6.8	5.0	25.7	29.6	13.7	1.8	78.2	41.9	50.6	49.4
16131	HARTSTOWN	97.5	97.3	0.2	0.2	0.1	0.1	0.3	0.5	6.4	6.7	8.6	7.2	6.6	26.4	25.2	12.0	1.0	73.9	37.2	51.5	48.5
16133	JACKSON CENTER	99.0	98.8	0.3	0.4	0.1	0.1	0.7	0.7	6.0	6.3	6.4	6.6	5.9	26.5	29.3	11.4	1.6	77.2	40.1	49.8	50.3
16134	JAMESTOWN	98.9	98.7	0.1	0.1	0.2	0.3	0.1	0.1	4.9	5.3	6.5	5.8	5.1	22.8	30.2	17.7	1.8	79.6	44.8	49.1	50.9
16137	MERCER	95.7	95.0	3.2	3.8	0.3	0.3	1.2	1.4	5.9	6.2	6.2	5.8	5.5	28.2	27.5	12.9	1.8	78.0	40.4	53.2	46.8
16141	NEW GALILEE	98.6	98.5	0.5	0.6	0.1	0.1	0.6	0.6	4.8	5.1	6.4	6.3	6.3	25.6	30.1	14.1	1.4	79.8	42.3	49.1	50.9
16142	NEW WILMINGTON	98.5	98.3	0.4	0.5	0.2	0.3	0.7	0.8	6.8	7.1	7.6	7.9	9.3	21.3	23.8	13.3	3.1	74.3	36.6	45.9	54.1
16143	PULASKI	98.8	98.6	0.5	0.6	0.1	0.2	0.3	0.3	5.6	5.9	7.1	6.7	5.9	25.0	26.9	15.0	2.0	77.3	40.9	48.1	51.9
16145	SANDY LAKE	99.3	99.1	0.2	0.2	0.2	0.2	0.2	0.3	6.4	6.5	6.5	6.2	6.1	25.9	27.5	13.1	1.9	76.6	39.8	49.1	50.9
16146	SHARON	86.4	84.6	10.9	12.5	0.2	0.3	0.9	1.0	6.8	6.4	6.7	6.2	6.4	25.9	24.1	14.5	3.2	76.3	39.0	47.0	53.0
16148	HERMITAGE	95.1	94.3	3.0	3.5	0.8	1.0	0.7	0.8	4.9	5.3	6.3	6.1	4.9	21.7	27.7	19.9	3.4	79.6	45.5	46.9	53.1
16150	SHARPSVILLE	97.3	96.9	1.5	1.8	0.3	0.4	0.7	0.7	5.7	5.9	6.6	6.4	5.3	24.7	26.7	16.6	2.3	78.0	42.2	48.1	51.9
16153	STONEBORO	99.0	98.8	0.1	0.2	0.2	0.2	0.4	0.4	6.9	7.0	7.0	6.0	5.7	25.5	26.1	13.7	2.2	75.4	39.2	49.3	50.7
16154	TRANSFER	98.4	98.2	0.5	0.6	0.2	0.3	0.5	0.6	6.4	6.5	7.0	6.5	5.2	26.0	27.5	13.5	1.4	76.1	40.4	51.2	48.8
16156	VOLANT	99.5	99.4	0.1	0.1	0.2	0.2	0.6	0.6	6.8	7.2	7.7	6.1	6.0	25.4	27.7	11.5	1.6	74.7	38.8	49.5	50.5
16157	WAMPUM	97.6	97.2	1.3	1.6	0.2	0.2	0.5	0.6	4.9	5.1	5.7	5.6	5.3	24.7	28.2	17.7	2.7	80.8	44.1	49.0	51.0
16159	WEST MIDDLESEX	97.5	97.0	1.5	1.8	0.3	0.4	0.4	0.5	5.3	5.7	6.7	6.5	5.0	25.2	28.3	15.6	1.7	78.3	42.5	48.8	51.3
16172	NEW WILMINGTON	97.4	97.0	1.0	1.1	0.6	0.7	0.5	0.5	0.1	0.0	0.0	45.3	52.6	1.3	0.4	0.2	0.0	99.8	20.4	37.4	62.6
16201	KITTANNING	98.7	98.5	0.5	0.5	0.2	0.3	0.5	0.6	5.4	5.5	6.2	6.4	6.2	25.5	26.9	15.5	2.5	78.9	41.8	48.0	52.0
16210	ADRIAN	99.5	99.3	0.1	0.1	0.3	0.3	0.3	0.3	6.4	6.7	7.6	5.5	5.5	25.0	28.0	13.9	1.5	75.8	40.9	50.5	49.5
16212	CADOGAN	99.5	99.5	0.0	0.0	0.3	0.3	0.0	0.0	4.5	5.0	6.9	5.8	6.1	25.1	28.5	15.8	2.4	79.4	42.9	51.7	48.3
16213	CALLENSBURG	99.3	99.3	0.1	0.1	0.0	0.0	0.3	0.3	6.3	6.6	6.5	6.3	5.8	27.9	25.3	13.7	1.7	76.9	38.7	50.1	49.9
16214	CLARION	95.3	94.9	2.9	3.1	0.8	1.0	0.7	0.7	3.9	3.6	3.5	17.7	22.7	19.1	17.2	10.6	1.7	87.0	24.7	45.0	55.0
16217	COOKSBURG	97.8	97.7	0.0	0.0	0.0	0.0	0.0	0.0	4.6	4.6	4.6	6.8	4.6	20.5	34.1	20.5	0.0	86.4	47.5	52.3	47.7
16218	COWANSVILLE	98.7	98.5	0.9	1.0	0.1	0.1	0.4	0.3	5.6	5.9	7.0	5.6	5.0	24.6	27.7	15.4	3.2	77.9	42.8	50.0	50.0
16222	DAYTON	99.5	99.4	0.0	0.0	0.1	0.1	0.1	0.1	6.3	6.3	7.0	6.7	5.9	25.3	26.0	14.7	1.9	76.4	39.8	50.1	49.9
16224	FAIRMOUNT CITY	98.6	98.5	0.5	0.5	0.2	0.3	0.3	0.4	6.1	6.0	7.6	7.4	5.2	26.7	26.0	13.7	1.3	75.7	38.9	50.2	49.8
16225	FISHER	99.2	99.3	0.3	0.3	0.0	0.0	0.3	0.3	4.0	4.5	6.5	5.5	6.0	27.8	27.8	16.9	1.2	82.1	42.6	51.6	48.4
16226	FORD CITY	97.4	97.1	1.6	1.7	0.1	0.2	0.5	0.5	5.5	5.6	6.3	5.8	5.4	24.5	26.8	17.5	2.8	78.9	43.1	48.4	51.6
16229	FREEPORT	98.9	98.8	0.2	0.2	0.2	0.2	0.3	0.3	5.4	5.8	6.5	6.0	5.6	27.2	28.1	13.5	2.0	78.4	41.0	49.3	50.7
16232	KNOX	99.0	98.9	0.0	0.0	0.2	0.3	0.4	0.4	5.6	6.1	6.8	6.3	5.5	26.8	27.4	13.7	1.7	77.6	40.5	49.2	50.9
16233	LEEPER	99.3	99.4	0.2	0.2	0.0	0.0	0.0	0.2	5.2	5.6	6.5	6.3	5.4	25.3	30.9	13.4	1.5	79.1	42.0	50.3	49.7
16234	LIMESTONE	99.6	99.5	0.1	0.1	0.2	0.2	0.0	0.0	5.4	6.1	7.0	6.1	5.7	28.7	28.3	12.0	0.9	77.8	40.0	51.1	48.9
16235	LUCINDA	99.0	98.9	0.1	0.2	0.0	0.1	0.1	0.1	5.9	6.0	6.1	6.0	5.9	26.0	28.7	14.0	1.6	78.5	41.3	49.3	50.7
16238	MANORVILLE	98.8	98.8	0.5	0.6	0.0	0.0	0.3	0.2	5.1	5.1	6.3	6.3	6.9	26.0	27.6	14.8	2.0	79.1	41.7	49.5	50.5
16239	MARIENVILLE	92.3	91.8	4.9	5.4	0.2	0.2	2.3	2.4	2.9	3.2	5.2	17.5	3.4	17.9	28.3	19.4	2.2	76.0	45.0	55.2	44.8
16240	MAYPORT	99.0	98.8	0.1	0.1	0.2	0.3	0.4	0.5	5.2	5.4	7.3	6.7	5.4	26.5	26.3	14.7	2.6	77.9	41.2	49.5	50.5
16242	NEW BETHLEHEM	99.0	99.0	0.3	0.4	0.1	0.1	0.3	0.3	5.7	5.8	6.6	6.0	5.6	25.0	26.0	16.5	2.9	78.3	42.0	48.1	51.9
16248	RIMERSBURG	99.4	99.4	0.2	0.2	0.0	0.0	0.3	0.4	6.0	6.1	7.2	6.6	6.6	26.0	25.4	14.0	2.0	76.6	39.1	48.5	51.5
16249	RURAL VALLEY	99.1	98.9	0.2	0.3	0.1	0.1	0.4	0.5	5.7	6.1	7.8	6.7	5.6	25.9	25.2	15.0	2.1	76.3	40.3	50.1	49.9
16254	SHIPPENVILLE	98.1	97.8	0.5	0.5	1.0	1.3	0.7	0.7	5.6	5.9	5.9	5.0	4.9	24.3	27.6	17.4	3.5	79.4	43.9	48.1	51.9
	PENNSYLVANIA	85.4	84.4	10.0	10.3	1.8	2.2	3.2	3.5	5.9	6.1	6.8	6.9	6.7	26.6	25.3	13.3	2.2	77.2	39.1	48.4	51.6
	UNITED STATES	75.1	73.6	12.3	12.5	3.8	4.2	12.5	14.1	6.9	6.7	7.2	7.0	7.3	28.6	23.8	10.8	1.7	75.1	36.0	49.1	50.9

INCOME

ZIP CODE #	POST OFFICE NAME	2004 Per Capita Income	2004 HH Income Base	2004 HOUSEHOLD INCOME DISTRIBUTION (%) Less than $25,000	$25,000 to $49,999	$50,000 to $99,999	$100,000 to $149,999	$150,000 or More	MEDIAN HOUSEHOLD INCOME 2004	2009	2004 National Centile	2004 State Centile	2004 Home Value Base	2004 HOME VALUE DISTRIBUTION (%) Less than $50,000	$50,000 to $89,999	$90,000 to $174,999	$175,000 to $399,999	$400,000 or More	2004 Median Home Value
15953	SEANOR	18942	75	40.0	29.3	26.7	2.7	1.3	34302	40366	25	17	63	28.6	41.3	25.4	4.8	0.0	69286
15954	SEWARD	17882	1207	35.8	33.1	25.2	4.7	1.2	34047	40662	24	17	1000	27.5	33.2	34.6	4.6	0.1	79000
15955	SIDMAN	16610	1226	37.4	33.9	24.6	2.9	1.4	32657	37864	20	12	952	47.0	28.8	18.9	5.0	0.3	53718
15956	SOUTH FORK	17535	1270	33.9	35.6	25.2	4.4	0.9	35667	41242	30	24	1058	45.5	30.1	20.0	4.1	0.4	56761
15957	STRONGSTOWN	17288	225	32.4	39.1	23.1	4.0	1.3	35487	41179	29	23	182	37.9	17.6	35.2	9.3	0.0	81667
15958	SUMMERHILL	16711	860	32.0	33.1	28.4	5.2	1.3	37284	43391	36	32	738	30.5	29.0	34.6	5.6	0.4	78000
15960	TWIN ROCKS	0	0	0.0	0.0	0.0	0.0	0.0	0	0	0	0	0	0.0	0.0	0.0	0.0	0.0	0
15961	VINTONDALE	15855	591	36.6	34.9	24.5	3.4	0.7	33589	39134	23	15	482	45.0	25.3	24.3	5.4	0.0	58000
15963	WINDBER	18035	4987	38.7	34.9	21.3	3.6	1.5	32477	37302	19	11	3695	30.1	40.4	24.6	4.6	0.3	68333
16001	BUTLER	23248	18476	30.8	27.9	31.5	7.1	2.7	41066	50231	50	49	12469	10.4	19.7	49.4	19.1	1.4	117707
16002	BUTLER	23516	6313	19.7	28.0	38.6	9.8	3.9	52114	62890	76	75	5401	12.8	9.9	47.9	26.6	2.7	134677
16020	BOYERS	18033	467	28.9	33.0	32.6	4.7	0.9	40248	47562	47	45	396	26.0	28.8	31.8	12.4	1.0	84063
16022	BRUIN	16232	143	28.7	45.5	19.6	6.3	0.0	33866	39423	24	16	112	36.6	34.8	25.0	3.6	0.0	58824
16023	CABOT	19975	1569	23.1	29.9	36.8	8.6	1.5	46718	56840	66	66	1301	14.9	12.1	45.7	26.2	1.2	128347
16025	CHICORA	20050	2025	25.7	29.5	34.7	8.7	1.3	44930	54092	61	61	1699	15.5	20.6	49.3	13.6	1.0	110241
16028	EAST BRADY	20618	939	38.1	31.5	24.0	4.7	1.7	33566	38798	23	15	681	24.5	35.1	34.5	5.4	0.4	78265
16030	EAU CLAIRE	17094	133	31.6	35.3	28.6	3.8	0.8	37940	44297	39	35	108	26.9	26.9	36.1	10.2	0.0	85556
16033	EVANS CITY	24511	2690	18.3	31.3	35.9	11.1	3.5	50414	61403	73	72	2163	9.4	10.6	48.3	28.1	3.6	136542
16034	FENELTON	18210	705	26.8	32.6	32.1	7.0	1.6	41566	50223	52	51	603	24.4	18.7	41.5	15.3	0.2	104167
16036	FOXBURG	16915	478	32.0	39.1	23.0	4.0	1.9	35000	39857	28	21	392	32.1	31.9	28.6	6.4	1.0	69394
16037	HARMONY	24736	1716	19.8	27.5	36.0	13.0	3.7	52106	62326	76	75	1459	14.5	8.5	37.3	33.7	6.1	152485
16038	HARRISVILLE	18600	1461	29.6	33.6	30.6	4.7	1.5	39215	46252	43	41	1168	20.9	28.5	39.1	10.1	1.4	90787
16040	HILLIARDS	16472	423	33.1	33.3	27.7	5.0	1.0	37165	43845	36	31	353	32.9	23.5	34.8	7.9	0.9	79250
16041	KARNS CITY	21113	945	28.5	31.3	30.8	7.6	1.8	40500	49513	48	47	797	21.3	29.0	37.9	11.2	0.6	89576
16045	LYNDORA	20949	578	38.6	31.5	23.4	5.5	1.0	33880	41011	24	16	426	12.2	30.1	47.0	10.1	0.7	100926
16046	MARS	38686	3810	13.5	20.3	32.5	19.4	14.3	70880	88200	92	93	3129	4.6	5.5	36.8	41.8	11.4	185218
16049	PARKER	16942	1244	32.7	36.4	25.1	4.7	1.1	36348	42145	33	27	999	27.8	31.7	33.3	6.5	0.6	79236
16050	PETROLIA	17188	509	29.7	34.4	28.1	6.5	1.4	38318	45390	40	37	423	29.1	30.5	33.1	6.6	0.7	79483
16051	PORTERSVILLE	19961	1697	29.1	32.1	30.8	5.7	2.5	40839	48553	49	48	1442	28.2	13.1	40.0	17.1	1.6	104258
16052	PROSPECT	21236	907	25.5	34.1	31.2	6.6	2.7	41968	50816	53	53	759	22.3	14.0	41.4	19.6	2.8	112300
16053	RENFREW	25503	1452	19.6	31.6	34.2	9.6	5.0	48872	59830	70	70	1221	12.5	10.2	44.0	30.6	2.9	144288
16055	SARVER	24648	3114	20.0	27.2	34.7	12.9	5.2	52876	64604	77	77	2787	17.8	8.8	37.0	34.3	2.1	146968
16056	SAXONBURG	24825	2006	25.8	27.7	31.0	11.4	4.1	47104	57663	66	66	1621	20.6	9.2	41.8	27.3	1.1	127514
16057	SLIPPERY ROCK	17821	4252	35.3	28.9	25.9	7.3	2.7	38110	45144	40	36	2777	18.3	15.7	42.4	21.4	2.2	117115
16059	VALENCIA	29231	2673	18.1	25.3	35.8	13.8	7.0	55105	66788	80	80	2383	13.3	7.3	42.1	32.0	5.3	145216
16061	WEST SUNBURY	20811	880	26.7	32.6	32.4	5.8	2.5	43423	51547	57	58	746	23.5	18.8	39.5	16.9	1.3	103913
16063	ZELIENOPLE	29269	3148	26.1	26.8	30.0	11.2	6.0	47819	57558	68	68	2006	4.1	6.2	52.1	34.5	3.1	154181
16066	CRANBERRY TWP	33511	9744	8.6	16.1	40.6	22.0	12.6	78539	95043	95	96	8387	7.5	2.3	36.5	48.6	5.0	184585
16101	NEW CASTLE	18404	14798	36.8	30.8	25.8	5.0	1.7	35000	41241	28	21	10766	29.5	29.1	31.8	9.1	0.6	76262
16102	NEW CASTLE	19406	2410	32.5	29.3	29.3	6.9	2.1	38893	46168	42	40	1846	25.3	31.1	31.7	11.2	0.7	79008
16105	NEW CASTLE	29241	6203	26.5	26.1	29.5	11.3	6.6	46337	56584	65	65	4848	5.9	23.7	42.9	24.5	3.0	121142
16110	ADAMSVILLE	18136	134	29.1	40.3	26.1	3.7	0.8	35727	41117	30	24	114	23.7	24.6	37.7	11.4	2.6	92500
16111	ATLANTIC	14991	704	26.7	40.5	28.0	3.7	1.1	38338	44274	41	37	595	25.4	29.6	36.1	7.7	1.2	84100
16112	BESSEMER	19268	693	30.9	33.2	28.4	6.1	1.4	37281	45000	36	32	555	18.2	27.0	45.1	9.4	0.4	96023
16114	CLARKS MILLS	17858	284	24.3	40.9	28.9	4.2	1.8	40000	46498	46	44	249	26.5	22.1	34.9	15.3	1.2	92188
16115	DARLINGTON	20224	1188	24.1	34.1	33.8	5.6	2.4	44322	51651	59	60	997	20.5	24.5	44.8	9.9	0.3	96645
16116	EDINBURG	18576	1300	34.2	30.5	28.5	5.7	1.2	36643	43371	34	28	1061	32.4	22.9	31.3	13.4	0.0	82756
16117	ELLWOOD CITY	20589	7295	31.6	31.0	28.8	6.4	2.3	39200	46752	43	41	5546	11.0	25.9	51.6	11.1	0.4	105217
16120	ENON VALLEY	20109	937	26.9	32.7	31.7	5.9	2.9	41301	48367	51	50	784	24.7	19.8	37.2	16.1	2.2	100676
16121	FARRELL	17071	2753	47.3	29.9	19.3	2.1	1.4	26670	30887	7	3	1871	43.8	34.1	22.0	0.2	0.0	56508
16123	FOMBELL	23720	852	22.7	27.9	36.3	9.5	3.6	49542	58069	71	71	703	10.7	12.4	50.9	24.0	2.0	131956
16124	FREDONIA	18391	738	27.2	28.7	36.5	5.4	2.2	44408	51292	60	60	610	18.2	29.0	36.7	14.4	1.6	94722
16125	GREENVILLE	20502	7470	29.1	31.2	32.3	5.2	2.2	40369	47367	47	46	5741	17.5	28.4	41.5	11.6	1.1	94948
16127	GROVE CITY	22135	5334	26.7	30.9	31.0	7.7	3.8	43397	51277	57	58	3999	12.9	18.3	48.9	18.6	1.3	113063
16130	HADLEY	19513	789	26.4	38.3	28.9	4.2	2.3	40217	46629	47	45	681	23.6	21.9	39.7	14.2	0.6	96932
16131	HARTSTOWN	16633	389	31.4	37.3	25.7	4.9	0.8	36649	42342	34	29	327	16.2	31.2	41.3	10.1	1.2	93269
16133	JACKSON CENTER	21474	524	20.8	33.4	36.8	6.1	2.9	47155	54308	66	67	453	13.7	20.8	40.0	23.0	2.7	115709
16134	JAMESTOWN	19550	1881	32.0	33.3	28.1	5.1	1.5	36682	42643	34	29	1590	16.9	29.6	40.0	12.8	0.8	94590
16137	MERCER	21001	4580	25.9	32.7	31.9	6.9	2.5	42172	49427	53	54	3664	19.3	19.2	42.4	18.0	1.0	105509
16141	NEW GALILEE	20310	728	26.8	33.7	32.3	6.0	1.2	41558	49002	52	51	604	30.1	23.3	38.1	7.8	0.7	84324
16142	NEW WILMINGTON	20939	2205	27.4	28.4	30.4	9.5	4.4	44156	52589	59	59	1707	5.7	14.2	47.0	28.9	4.1	140759
16143	PULASKI	19330	1469	28.8	30.4	32.1	6.2	2.5	40846	48763	49	48	1282	24.7	16.9	42.0	15.4	1.1	101310
16145	SANDY LAKE	19672	1129	26.2	36.1	29.6	5.7	2.5	40510	47327	48	47	926	18.9	24.5	40.8	14.6	1.2	98026
16146	SHARON	19051	6842	41.4	30.6	21.5	4.3	2.2	30591	34988	14	7	4242	36.5	37.7	20.6	4.7	0.6	62238
16148	HERMITAGE	27924	7290	24.3	32.1	30.1	7.9	5.6	45165	52636	62	62	5540	9.0	17.2	47.0	23.6	3.2	126391
16150	SHARPSVILLE	23331	3543	25.9	32.8	31.0	6.8	3.6	43190	50843	56	57	2807	12.1	24.2	49.2	13.8	0.7	105992
16153	STONEBORO	19047	1066	30.4	33.6	29.4	4.3	2.4	39351	45756	44	42	850	20.9	26.1	37.5	13.8	1.7	94545
16154	TRANSFER	18972	1125	26.8	35.9	30.5	5.3	1.5	38444	45066	41	38	930	20.7	25.7	40.8	12.5	0.4	94304
16156	VOLANT	20560	1003	24.5	32.5	32.4	6.9	3.7	44443	51952	60	60	842	14.6	18.5	43.9	18.7	4.3	114933
16157	WAMPUM	20728	1977	30.9	32.4	29.9	5.0	1.8	38893	46084	42	40	1506	21.8	34.1	37.1	7.1	0.0	82605
16159	WEST MIDDLESEX	20653	1800	24.8	37.1	29.7	6.4	2.1	42283	49378	54	54	1541	17.5	17.9	45.6	18.8	0.3	112270
16172	NEW WILMINGTON	12032	10	50.0	30.0	20.0	0.0	0.0	20000	30000	2	1	2	0.0	0.0	0.0	100.0	0.0	300000
16201	KITTANNING	18831	8059	36.1	31.4	24.7	5.7	2.0	35432	41048	29	22	5870	19.7	30.1	38.0	11.7	0.5	90315
16210	ADRIAN	16402	279	40.9	33.7	21.9	2.5	1.1	30730	35000	14	7	237	32.9	31.7	29.1	5.1	1.3	70625
16212	CADOGAN	20288	173	33.5	30.1	28.9	7.5	0.0	38490	45865	41	38	146	19.2	32.9	40.4	6.2	1.4	88421
16213	CALLENSBURG	18856	288	40.3	33.3	18.8	3.1	4.5	31427	36316	16	9	230	23.5	26.5	39.1	10.4	0.4	90000
16214	CLARION	16718	3345	48.1	22.8	22.8	4.8	1.4	26582	30918	7	3	1596	11.1	17.5	52.4	18.1	0.9	115339
16217	COOKSBURG	12614	16	43.8	31.3	25.0	0.0	0.0	30000	32330	12	6	13	15.4	30.8	53.9	0.0	0.0	95000
16218	COWANSVILLE	20552	493	34.1	35.7	24.3	3.7	2.2	35171	40183	28	21	416	22.8	33.2	35.6	7.7	0.7	80741
16222	DAYTON	16267	815	33.1	39.1	21.2	4.9	1.6	34504	39905	26	18	654	25.5	33.2	31.8	8.9	0.6	77551
16224	FAIRMOUNT CITY	16746	662	35.4	37.5	22.4	3.8	1.1	33671	39369	23	15	503	27.8	37.6	28.8	4.8	1.0	67754
16225	FISHER	22593	173	22.5	34.7	34.7	4.6	3.5	44329	51038	60	60	162	24.7	27.2	35.8	12.4	0.0	87857
16226	FORD CITY	19639	4339	34.3	35.5	24.3	4.2	1.8	35375	41146	29	22	3227	19.4	35.2	34.4	10.5	0.4	83882
16229	FREEPORT	20974	2234	31.2	28.5	29.1	8.8	2.4	41148	48367	50	49	1708	16.2	26.0	38.3	17.3	2.2	104388
16232	KNOX	20443	2951	29.1	34.6	28.1	5.4	2.8	39571	46573	45	42	2392	15.7	27.9	42.1	12.9	1.5	98902
16233	LEEPER	19347	191	29.3	34.0	29.3	6.3	1.1	37469	44149	37	33	166	15.7	32.5	39.8	11.5	0.6	92308
16234	LIMESTONE	22747	502	24.9	32.7	32.9	6.0	3.6	44640	51939	60	61	427	13.1	21.6	48.2	16.4	0.7	109626
16235	LUCINDA	18591	375	23.7	33.3	37.3	4.3	1.3	44042	50801	59	59	328	10.7	24.7	47.9	16.5	0.3	108333
16238	MANORVILLE	21393	225	30.2	34.2	31.6	2.2	1.8	37004	43245	35	30	162	24.7	31.5	27.8	16.1	0.0	83333
16239	MARIENVILLE	17901	564	41.7	32.1	22.2	3.7	0.4	30595	35753	14	7	431	21.4	32.0	40.4	6.3	0.0	85000
16240	MAYPORT	15961	674	30.7	42.3	21.7	4.2	1.2	35549	40421	30	23	552	28.4	32.8	31.7	6.3	0.7	75405
16242	NEW BETHLEHEM	18017	2179	36.0	33.9	24.9	4.0	1.2	33588	38999	23	15	1659	25.9	34.7	32.9	6.2	0.4	79390
16248	RIMERSBURG	15756	1492	39.7	34.9	21.2	3.6	0.7	30933	35678	15	8	1108	32.2	34.8	29.5	3.2	0.3	68889
16249	RURAL VALLEY	16322	1374	38.1	33.6	22.4	4.7	1.2	32706	37537	20	12	1076	25.5	34.5	33.1	5.7	1.3	76042
16254	SHIPPENVILLE	23398	1042	24.7	34.4	28.3	8.5	4.2	42611	50474	55	55	849	25.3	20.4	34.0	18.9	1.4	99359
	PENNSYLVANIA	25764		25.8	27.2	31.2	10.2	5.7	46988	57000				11.9	18.4	40.7	25.1	4.1	123516
	UNITED STATES	25866		24.7	27.1	30.8	10.9	6.5	48124	56710				10.9	15.0	33.7	30.1	10.4	145905

ZIP CODE		FINANCIAL SERVICES				THE HOME						ENTERTAINMENT						PERSONAL			
						Home Improvements		Furnishings													
#	POST OFFICE NAME	Auto Loan	Home Loan	Invest-ments	Retire-ment Plans	Home Repair	Lawn & Garden	Comput-ers & Hard-ware	Major Appli-ances	TV, Radio, Sound Equip-ment	Furni-ture	Dine out/ Carry out	Sports Equip-ment	Fees & Tickets	Toys & Games	Travel	Cable TV	Apparel & Services	Auto Repairs	Health Insur-ance	Pets & Supplies
15953	SEANOR	60	55	49	52	57	66	57	59	61	54	74	66	56	75	58	64	70	58	67	68
15954	SEWARD	74	55	33	49	60	70	55	64	63	54	75	75	49	73	56	68	69	63	77	85
15955	SIDMAN	53	58	62	56	59	64	57	57	59	55	73	63	61	79	59	60	71	55	60	62
15956	SOUTH FORK	62	59	53	56	61	68	57	60	61	56	74	69	58	78	59	63	71	59	66	72
15957	STRONGSTOWN	79	54	25	46	61	70	52	64	62	53	73	77	44	69	53	67	67	64	79	91
15958	SUMMERHILL	71	62	50	57	65	74	61	67	67	60	81	76	59	82	63	70	76	66	76	82
15960	TWIN ROCKS	0	0	0	0	0	0	0	0	0	0	0	0	0	0	0	0	0	0	0	0
15961	VINTONDALE	61	55	47	50	58	65	54	58	59	53	71	66	53	74	55	62	68	57	65	70
15963	WINDBER	59	55	52	53	57	65	57	59	60	55	74	67	56	75	58	63	70	59	65	68
16001	BUTLER	74	73	75	71	74	81	73	75	75	72	93	86	74	94	75	76	90	75	78	86
16002	BUTLER	93	90	79	86	92	99	85	90	87	84	107	105	84	108	86	88	103	88	94	109
16020	BOYERS	72	62	48	61	66	73	62	67	66	61	80	78	60	80	62	67	75	66	73	82
16022	BRUIN	79	53	24	46	60	69	51	64	62	52	73	77	44	69	52	67	66	63	79	91
16023	CABOT	92	71	45	65	77	87	69	80	78	69	93	94	63	91	70	82	86	79	93	106
16025	CHICORA	84	75	60	70	79	87	71	78	77	71	93	92	70	95	73	79	88	76	86	99
16028	EAST BRADY	81	57	32	52	64	75	59	69	69	58	81	80	52	76	59	73	74	69	84	91
16030	EAU CLAIRE	67	57	45	57	60	68	59	63	63	58	76	72	56	75	59	64	71	62	68	74
16033	EVANS CITY	95	88	74	84	92	100	84	90	88	83	107	105	83	111	86	90	103	88	97	111
16034	FENELTON	84	69	47	64	72	79	66	74	71	67	86	87	61	82	66	73	81	74	81	95
16036	FOXBURG	81	54	25	47	62	71	53	66	64	54	75	78	45	71	54	68	68	65	81	93
16037	HARMONY	102	94	76	89	98	105	87	95	91	87	111	112	86	114	89	93	106	93	101	119
16038	HARRISVILLE	80	61	38	57	66	76	61	70	69	60	82	81	55	79	61	72	75	69	82	91
16040	HILLIARDS	77	57	33	52	62	71	56	66	64	56	76	77	50	73	56	68	70	65	77	88
16041	KARNS CITY	88	72	50	65	77	86	68	78	76	68	92	92	64	92	70	80	86	77	90	103
16045	LYNDORA	55	60	64	57	61	67	59	58	61	57	75	65	62	81	61	62	73	57	62	64
16046	MARS	150	161	156	163	159	162	150	152	144	152	180	177	153	182	149	140	176	148	143	172
16049	PARKER	77	55	30	49	61	71	55	65	64	55	76	76	48	72	55	68	69	65	79	88
16050	PETROLIA	83	62	36	55	68	76	59	70	68	59	81	83	53	79	60	72	75	69	83	96
16051	PORTERSVILLE	82	71	52	67	74	80	66	74	71	67	86	87	63	85	67	72	81	73	80	94
16052	PROSPECT	85	75	57	72	79	85	70	77	74	70	90	92	68	92	72	76	86	75	83	99
16053	RENFREW	102	95	82	92	98	105	90	96	93	90	114	113	89	116	92	94	110	95	101	119
16055	SARVER	103	94	75	90	98	105	87	96	91	88	111	113	85	112	89	93	106	94	102	120
16056	SAXONBURG	98	83	61	79	88	97	82	90	88	81	106	104	77	104	82	90	99	89	99	112
16057	SLIPPERY ROCK	76	58	50	57	60	67	71	67	73	66	89	84	63	85	65	70	84	72	69	82
16059	VALENCIA	114	115	106	112	117	124	107	113	108	107	133	132	109	137	110	109	129	110	114	134
16061	WEST SUNBURY	97	74	45	67	81	90	70	83	80	71	95	98	64	93	72	84	88	81	96	112
16063	ZELIENOPLE	90	90	92	90	92	98	90	92	90	88	111	107	90	112	90	90	107	91	93	105
16066	CRANBERRY TWP	131	150	150	155	144	141	137	135	126	141	160	158	142	161	134	119	158	132	117	148
16101	NEW CASTLE	63	60	59	58	62	69	61	63	64	60	79	72	61	81	62	66	76	63	68	73
16102	NEW CASTLE	72	67	57	63	70	77	66	69	70	64	85	80	65	87	67	72	81	68	77	83
16105	NEW CASTLE	87	99	109	95	99	108	95	95	95	94	118	106	100	124	99	98	116	93	98	104
16110	ADAMSVILLE	84	56	25	48	64	73	54	68	65	55	77	81	46	73	55	70	70	67	84	96
16111	ATLANTIC	79	59	35	53	65	73	56	67	65	57	77	80	51	75	58	68	71	66	79	92
16112	BESSEMER	60	65	67	61	65	72	64	63	66	61	82	71	67	88	66	68	79	62	68	71
16114	CLARKS MILLS	86	62	34	55	69	78	59	72	69	60	82	85	53	79	61	73	75	70	85	99
16115	DARLINGTON	72	74	72	70	76	83	71	73	74	70	92	83	74	98	74	77	88	71	78	85
16116	EDINBURG	79	59	35	52	65	74	57	67	66	57	79	79	51	77	58	71	73	67	81	91
16117	ELLWOOD CITY	69	69	67	66	71	79	68	70	71	66	87	79	69	91	70	73	84	68	76	81
16120	ENON VALLEY	97	74	46	66	81	91	71	83	81	71	96	98	65	95	72	86	89	82	98	112
16121	FARRELL	55	51	52	47	51	59	53	55	58	53	71	60	53	70	54	61	68	55	61	62
16123	FOMBELL	101	90	69	86	95	102	83	92	89	83	108	110	82	110	86	91	102	90	100	119
16124	FREDONIA	75	71	60	67	74	80	67	71	70	66	86	83	67	90	69	73	82	70	77	88
16125	GREENVILLE	70	69	67	66	71	78	68	70	71	67	87	80	69	89	69	73	84	69	75	82
16127	GROVE CITY	88	80	71	77	83	92	78	84	82	77	100	98	76	101	80	85	96	83	91	103
16130	HADLEY	85	64	39	58	70	79	61	73	70	62	83	86	55	81	62	74	77	72	85	99
16131	HARTSTOWN	83	56	25	48	63	73	54	67	65	55	76	80	46	72	55	70	69	67	83	95
16133	JACKSON CENTER	90	80	61	76	85	91	74	82	79	74	96	98	73	98	77	81	91	80	89	106
16134	JAMESTOWN	75	63	50	58	68	76	61	69	66	60	80	80	57	79	63	69	75	68	78	89
16137	MERCER	89	75	55	70	80	88	72	81	78	72	95	95	69	94	74	81	89	79	90	103
16141	NEW GALILEE	79	68	53	61	72	81	66	73	73	65	89	84	64	90	68	77	83	72	84	92
16142	NEW WILMINGTON	96	77	60	74	84	94	77	87	84	76	101	103	71	101	79	87	95	86	98	113
16143	PULASKI	82	71	53	66	75	82	67	74	72	66	87	88	64	89	68	75	83	73	83	96
16145	SANDY LAKE	79	67	51	62	71	79	64	72	70	64	85	84	61	85	66	73	80	71	81	92
16146	SHARON	57	59	66	57	59	66	61	60	63	60	79	68	63	82	62	65	76	60	63	66
16148	HERMITAGE	87	93	97	89	93	101	90	91	91	89	112	103	92	115	92	92	109	90	94	103
16150	SHARPSVILLE	77	79	80	76	80	88	77	79	79	76	98	90	79	101	79	81	95	78	83	91
16153	STONEBORO	69	66	58	62	69	75	63	67	67	62	82	77	64	86	65	69	78	65	73	81
16154	TRANSFER	80	64	44	59	69	77	62	71	69	62	83	83	58	81	63	72	77	69	81	92
16156	VOLANT	94	78	54	74	85	92	73	84	80	73	96	100	69	97	76	82	90	82	94	111
16157	WAMPUM	67	68	65	63	69	77	66	68	69	64	85	77	68	91	68	72	82	66	74	79
16159	WEST MIDDLESEX	74	70	63	67	73	80	68	72	71	67	87	83	68	89	70	73	84	71	77	86
16172	NEW WILMINGTON	36	22	28	25	21	26	42	31	41	36	51	43	34	46	34	36	48	38	29	35
16201	KITTANNING	70	61	50	56	64	72	60	65	65	59	79	75	58	80	61	68	75	64	73	81
16210	ADRIAN	75	58	39	52	66	74	55	67	63	55	74	78	49	73	59	67	69	66	79	91
16212	CADOGAN	57	62	65	58	63	69	61	60	63	59	79	67	65	85	63	66	76	59	65	67
16213	CALLENSBURG	88	59	27	51	67	77	57	71	69	58	81	85	48	76	58	74	73	70	88	101
16214	CLARION	59	45	44	45	46	53	58	53	59	53	73	67	51	69	53	58	69	58	56	65
16217	COOKSBURG	59	46	31	42	52	58	44	52	49	43	58	61	39	58	46	53	54	52	62	72
16218	COWANSVILLE	93	65	34	57	73	84	62	77	74	63	87	91	54	83	64	79	79	76	94	108
16222	DAYTON	71	56	37	50	61	69	54	62	62	54	74	73	50	73	55	66	69	62	74	83
16224	FAIRMOUNT CITY	77	56	31	50	62	70	54	65	63	55	75	77	48	72	55	67	69	64	77	88
16225	FISHER	89	70	48	63	79	89	66	80	75	65	89	93	59	87	70	80	82	78	94	109
16226	FORD CITY	66	63	58	60	65	73	62	65	65	60	80	74	62	82	64	68	76	64	71	76
16229	FREEPORT	79	71	58	68	75	82	69	74	73	68	89	86	68	91	70	76	84	73	82	92
16232	KNOX	84	67	46	63	73	82	66	75	73	66	88	87	62	86	67	76	82	74	85	96
16233	LEEPER	80	62	43	56	70	79	59	71	67	58	79	83	53	78	63	71	73	70	84	97
16234	LIMESTONE	94	84	64	80	89	95	78	86	83	78	100	103	76	102	80	85	95	84	93	111
16235	LUCINDA	79	70	53	66	74	79	65	72	69	65	84	86	63	85	67	71	79	70	78	93
16238	MANORVILLE	60	65	69	62	66	73	65	64	67	62	83	71	68	90	67	69	80	63	69	70
16239	MARIENVILLE	64	50	34	45	56	63	47	57	53	47	63	67	42	62	50	57	59	56	67	78
16240	MAYPORT	77	55	30	49	61	70	54	65	63	54	74	76	48	71	54	67	68	64	77	88
16242	NEW BETHLEHEM	70	54	36	50	59	68	55	63	63	54	75	72	51	73	56	66	69	62	74	80
16248	RIMERSBURG	70	49	25	43	54	63	49	59	58	49	68	69	42	64	49	62	62	58	72	80
16249	RURAL VALLEY	68	52	35	48	57	66	53	60	60	52	72	70	48	70	54	64	66	60	72	78
16254	SHIPPENVILLE	98	75	48	66	82	93	72	84	83	72	99	99	66	98	74	89	92	83	100	113
	PENNSYLVANIA	89	89	93	87	90	98	89	90	91	88	112	104	89	114	90	92	109	90	92	104
	UNITED STATES	100	100	100	100	100	100	100	100	100	100	100	100	100	100	100	100	100	100	100	100

#	POST OFFICE NAME	COUNTY FIPS CODE	POPULATION			2000-2004 ANNUAL RATE		HOUSEHOLDS					FAMILIES		
			2000	2004	2009	% Rate	State Centile	2000	2004	2009	% Annual Rate 2000-2004	2004 Average HH Size	2000	2004	% Annual Rate 2000-2004
16255	SLIGO	031	1242	1266	1305	0.5	62	421	436	458	0.8	2.61	322	332	0.7
16256	SMICKSBURG	063	1853	2021	2124	2.1	93	483	536	574	2.5	3.76	399	441	2.4
16258	STRATTANVILLE	031	2157	2350	2518	2.0	93	903	1006	1101	2.6	2.32	578	642	2.5
16259	TEMPLETON	005	1587	1581	1599	-0.1	34	615	625	645	0.4	2.53	446	450	0.2
16260	VOWINCKEL	031	1580	1595	1638	0.2	50	662	685	720	0.8	2.33	452	466	0.7
16262	WORTHINGTON	005	2979	2979	3016	0.0	39	1158	1185	1226	0.5	2.48	863	878	0.4
16301	OIL CITY	121	19147	18666	18249	-0.6	12	7827	7773	7740	-0.2	2.36	5212	5140	-0.3
16311	CARLTON	085	482	462	452	-1.0	5	174	170	170	-0.6	2.59	134	131	-0.5
16313	CLARENDON	123	599	645	667	1.8	91	244	269	284	2.3	2.40	172	188	2.1
16314	COCHRANTON	039	4435	4413	4506	-0.1	33	1691	1719	1792	0.4	2.56	1282	1297	0.3
16316	CONNEAUT LAKE	039	4922	5038	5186	0.6	66	2150	2244	2353	1.0	2.25	1420	1469	0.8
16317	COOPERSTOWN	121	460	443	430	-0.9	6	187	184	182	-0.4	2.41	147	145	-0.3
16319	CRANBERRY	121	356	360	358	0.3	52	149	153	155	0.6	2.34	116	118	0.4
16321	EAST HICKORY	053	261	262	265	0.1	44	113	115	119	0.4	2.28	80	82	0.6
16323	FRANKLIN	121	17736	17575	17340	-0.2	29	6998	7087	7134	0.3	2.33	4796	4821	0.1
16326	FRYBURG	031	1912	1965	2039	0.7	70	689	725	769	1.2	2.71	515	540	1.1
16327	GUYS MILLS	039	2464	2489	2544	0.2	51	876	906	945	0.8	2.71	686	706	0.7
16329	IRVINE	123	286	285	284	-0.1	35	108	110	111	0.4	2.09	70	71	0.3
16331	KOSSUTH	031	49	52	54	1.4	87	21	23	24	2.2	2.26	17	18	1.4
16332	LICKINGVILLE	031	64	66	68	0.7	72	28	29	31	0.8	2.28	21	22	1.1
16333	LUDLOW	083	534	527	518	-0.3	24	236	239	240	0.3	2.21	155	156	0.2
16334	MARBLE	031	61	63	65	0.8	73	27	28	30	0.9	2.25	20	21	1.2
16335	MEADVILLE	039	30205	30901	31904	0.5	66	12125	12651	13319	1.0	2.29	7662	7942	0.9
16340	PITTSFIELD	123	3253	3246	3233	-0.1	36	1287	1317	1338	0.5	2.40	958	973	0.4
16341	PLEASANTVILLE	121	2311	2234	2181	-0.8	8	934	924	922	-0.3	2.42	694	683	-0.4
16342	POLK	121	2799	2929	2962	1.1	81	905	972	1005	1.7	2.63	675	722	1.6
16345	RUSSELL	123	3788	4028	4148	1.5	88	1485	1622	1702	2.1	2.48	1140	1237	1.9
16346	SENECA	121	3519	3525	3497	0.0	41	1425	1464	1485	0.6	2.40	1043	1064	0.5
16347	SHEFFIELD	123	2346	2354	2352	0.1	43	955	975	988	0.5	2.39	665	673	0.3
16350	SUGAR GROVE	123	3803	3795	3780	-0.1	36	1360	1380	1395	0.3	2.75	1044	1052	0.2
16351	TIDIOUTE	123	2576	2577	2573	0.0	39	1099	1124	1143	0.5	2.25	755	765	0.3
16353	TIONESTA	053	2575	2673	2760	0.9	76	997	1062	1122	1.5	2.39	665	703	1.3
16354	TITUSVILLE	123	13698	13574	13695	-0.2	29	5431	5506	5670	0.3	2.39	3713	3732	0.1
16360	TOWNVILLE	039	1185	1200	1229	0.3	54	429	443	461	0.8	2.70	334	343	0.6
16362	UTICA	121	2010	1994	1963	-0.2	30	753	765	769	0.4	2.61	581	587	0.2
16364	VENUS	121	512	503	492	-0.4	20	187	187	187	0.0	2.69	142	142	0.0
16365	WARREN	123	20758	20374	20177	-0.4	19	8789	8800	8858	0.0	2.23	5580	5543	-0.2
16371	YOUNGSVILLE	123	2124	2102	2087	-0.2	27	805	812	819	0.2	2.51	557	557	0.0
16372	CLINTONVILLE	121	530	520	509	-0.5	18	216	216	216	0.0	2.41	160	159	-0.2
16373	EMLENTON	121	3233	3167	3113	-0.5	17	1284	1285	1290	0.0	2.43	914	908	-0.2
16374	KENNERDELL	121	1315	1279	1248	-0.7	11	545	543	541	-0.1	2.36	391	388	-0.2
16401	ALBION	049	6362	6292	6261	-0.3	27	1719	1715	1724	-0.1	2.57	1243	1234	-0.2
16402	BEAR LAKE	123	1079	1080	1077	0.0	40	342	348	352	0.4	3.10	272	275	0.3
16403	CAMBRIDGE SPRINGS	039	6683	7187	7590	1.7	90	2306	2548	2755	2.4	2.54	1655	1812	2.2
16404	CENTERVILLE	039	2813	2861	2938	0.4	59	990	1024	1069	0.8	2.78	751	772	0.7
16405	COLUMBUS	123	1719	1697	1682	-0.3	25	654	659	663	0.2	2.58	483	482	-0.1
16406	CONNEAUTVILLE	039	3309	3276	3335	-0.2	27	1184	1193	1236	0.2	2.58	872	872	0.0
16407	CORRY	049	10278	10140	10095	-0.3	24	3905	3908	3941	0.0	2.54	2761	2736	-0.2
16410	CRANESVILLE	049	1687	1703	1702	0.2	50	590	605	611	0.6	2.81	469	478	0.5
16411	EAST SPRINGFIELD	049	1463	1463	1452	0.0	39	534	544	548	0.4	2.69	402	407	0.3
16412	EDINBORO	049	12525	12841	12993	0.6	68	4090	4224	4311	0.8	2.56	2419	2467	0.5
16415	FAIRVIEW	049	7717	7891	7955	0.5	65	2675	2779	2841	0.9	2.72	2153	2225	0.8
16417	GIRARD	049	8612	8563	8509	-0.1	33	3231	3249	3265	0.1	2.62	2387	2385	0.0
16420	GRAND VALLEY	123	66	66	65	0.0	39	27	28	28	0.9	2.36	20	21	1.2
16421	HARBORCREEK	049	3045	3097	3118	0.4	59	1116	1153	1175	0.8	2.59	833	855	0.6
16423	LAKE CITY	049	4268	4283	4270	0.1	43	1617	1642	1656	0.4	2.59	1197	1210	0.3
16424	LINESVILLE	039	5148	5342	5554	0.9	75	2106	2230	2363	1.4	2.39	1475	1550	1.2
16426	MC KEAN	049	4146	4093	4076	-0.3	25	1501	1505	1519	0.1	2.71	1199	1196	-0.1
16428	NORTH EAST	049	13995	14157	14247	0.3	53	4809	4938	5035	0.6	2.59	3503	3583	0.5
16433	SAEGERTOWN	039	5772	5826	5956	0.2	50	2051	2110	2198	0.7	2.61	1529	1562	0.5
16434	SPARTANSBURG	039	2931	3157	3340	1.8	91	850	936	1010	2.3	3.37	692	758	2.2
16435	SPRINGBORO	039	2089	2103	2149	0.2	46	753	771	801	0.6	2.72	557	566	0.4
16436	SPRING CREEK	123	142	144	144	0.3	56	54	56	58	0.9	2.50	40	41	0.6
16438	UNION CITY	049	8875	8742	8726	-0.4	23	3244	3240	3277	0.0	2.69	2412	2393	-0.2
16440	VENANGO	039	1007	1032	1071	0.6	68	364	382	405	1.1	2.67	267	278	1.0
16441	WATERFORD	049	9504	9651	9712	0.4	58	3378	3476	3541	0.7	2.78	2657	2717	0.5
16442	WATTSBURG	049	2812	2788	2773	-0.2	29	950	957	965	0.2	2.91	761	762	0.0
16443	WEST SPRINGFIELD	049	1554	1568	1565	0.2	49	579	591	597	0.5	2.65	438	444	0.3
16444	EDINBORO	049	108	108	107	0.0	39	48	48	48	0.0	2.25	17	18	1.4
16501	ERIE	049	3045	3110	3146	0.5	64	1367	1445	1493	1.3	1.33	191	196	0.6
16502	ERIE	049	17470	16947	16780	-0.7	9	7219	7070	7076	-0.5	2.30	3857	3729	-0.8
16503	ERIE	049	18580	17896	17651	-0.9	6	6581	6354	6312	-0.8	2.69	4186	4001	-1.1
16504	ERIE	049	18023	17656	17516	-0.5	17	6639	6558	6578	-0.3	2.39	4207	4121	-0.5
16505	ERIE	049	18176	18111	18062	-0.1	35	7822	7885	7958	0.2	2.26	4830	4826	0.0
16506	ERIE	049	22554	23696	24331	1.2	83	9029	9590	9961	1.4	2.45	6269	6610	1.3
16507	ERIE	049	9824	9564	9518	-0.6	12	3851	3787	3814	-0.4	2.32	2020	1963	-0.7
16508	ERIE	049	15654	15484	15455	-0.3	27	6602	6622	6694	0.1	2.29	4292	4270	-0.1
16509	ERIE	049	25996	26629	26923	0.6	67	10636	11051	11323	0.9	2.35	7068	7281	0.7
16510	ERIE	049	25574	25654	25752	0.1	43	9306	9472	9641	0.4	2.66	6900	6982	0.3
16511	ERIE	049	11477	11348	11313	-0.3	26	4377	4376	4410	0.0	2.46	3034	3009	-0.2
16565	ERIE	049	2	2	2	0.0	39	1	1	1	0.0	2.00	1	1	0.0
16601	ALTOONA	013	31962	32379	32744	0.3	54	12592	13012	13296	0.8	2.38	8026	8219	0.6
16602	ALTOONA	013	31793	30475	29800	-1.0	5	13193	12900	12753	-0.5	2.30	8589	8339	-0.7
16611	ALEXANDRIA	061	2762	2763	2790	0.0	39	1069	1095	1129	0.6	2.51	787	801	0.4
16613	ASHVILLE	021	1640	1770	1797	1.8	91	595	655	682	2.3	2.60	441	481	2.1
16616	BECCARIA	033	1379	1383	1410	0.1	43	559	574	598	0.6	2.41	394	401	0.4
16617	BELLWOOD	013	6490	6307	6201	-0.7	11	2539	2520	2504	-0.2	2.48	1888	1862	-0.3
16620	BRISBIN	033	413	422	433	0.5	65	166	174	182	1.1	2.43	118	122	0.8
16621	BROAD TOP	061	384	386	389	0.1	45	162	166	171	0.6	2.33	117	119	0.4
16622	CALVIN	061	1306	1314	1331	0.1	46	508	526	545	0.8	2.50	399	410	0.6
16623	CASSVILLE	061	116	116	117	0.0	39	51	52	54	0.5	2.23	40	41	0.6
16625	CLAYSBURG	013	2878	2781	2711	-0.8	7	1104	1092	1080	-0.3	2.54	804	788	-0.5
16627	COALPORT	021	1142	1127	1139	-0.3	24	470	474	490	0.2	2.34	321	322	0.1
16630	CRESSON	021	4382	4253	4111	-0.7	10	1801	1783	1755	-0.2	2.22	1133	1113	-0.4
16634	DUDLEY	061	598	601	606	0.1	45	236	242	249	0.6	2.48	170	173	0.4
	PENNSYLVANIA					0.3					0.7	2.44			0.6
	UNITED STATES					1.2					1.3	2.58			1.1

ZIP CODE #	POST OFFICE NAME	RACE (%) White 2000	White 2004	Black 2000	Black 2004	Asian/Pacific 2000	Asian/Pacific 2004	% Hispanic Origin 2000	% Hispanic Origin 2004	2004 AGE DISTRIBUTION (%) 0-4	5-9	10-14	15-19	20-24	25-44	45-64	65-84	85+	18+	MEDIAN AGE 2004	% 2004 Males	% 2004 Females
16255	SLIGO	97.6	97.2	0.0	0.0	0.6	0.7	0.8	1.0	5.2	5.5	7.5	6.8	5.9	24.1	21.0	18.6	5.4	77.5	41.7	46.9	53.1
16256	SMICKSBURG	99.2	99.2	0.2	0.3	0.2	0.2	0.0	0.0	11.9	10.8	10.3	8.6	8.2	23.5	17.0	9.0	0.8	61.7	25.2	51.8	48.2
16258	STRATTANVILLE	97.6	97.2	1.3	1.4	0.2	0.3	0.2	0.2	6.9	6.8	6.5	4.8	5.2	31.8	23.2	13.5	1.3	77.1	37.0	49.1	50.9
16259	TEMPLETON	99.1	99.1	0.3	0.3	0.0	0.0	0.5	0.6	6.3	6.2	7.0	6.4	6.1	27.3	25.6	13.4	1.8	76.6	39.1	51.4	48.6
16260	VOWINCKEL	99.4	99.3	0.2	0.2	0.1	0.1	0.1	0.1	5.1	5.6	6.1	5.8	4.9	24.9	30.9	15.2	1.5	79.8	43.3	50.5	49.5
16262	WORTHINGTON	99.2	99.2	0.1	0.2	0.1	0.1	0.6	0.6	5.4	5.8	6.6	5.9	5.4	27.2	28.4	13.3	2.0	78.5	41.5	49.1	50.9
16301	OIL CITY	98.2	98.0	0.7	0.7	0.3	0.4	0.6	0.7	6.0	6.1	7.0	6.9	6.2	24.4	26.0	15.1	2.4	76.5	40.5	48.0	52.1
16311	CARLTON	99.4	99.1	0.2	0.2	0.4	0.4	0.6	0.9	6.3	6.1	6.1	6.1	5.8	25.5	27.5	14.5	2.2	77.1	41.1	49.1	50.9
16313	CLARENDON	98.8	98.9	0.0	0.0	0.2	0.2	0.5	0.5	4.8	5.4	7.4	5.9	4.8	25.0	30.4	15.2	1.1	78.5	43.1	50.5	49.5
16314	COCHRANTON	99.3	99.1	0.2	0.2	0.2	0.3	0.2	0.3	6.1	6.5	6.9	6.3	5.4	27.1	27.9	12.3	1.4	76.4	39.7	49.4	50.6
16316	CONNEAUT LAKE	99.0	98.8	0.1	0.1	0.4	0.4	0.3	0.4	4.7	5.1	6.4	5.8	4.9	24.9	30.8	15.8	1.5	80.3	43.8	49.9	50.1
16317	COOPERSTOWN	99.4	99.3	0.2	0.2	0.2	0.2	0.9	1.1	4.1	5.0	7.0	6.1	5.4	24.4	32.1	15.4	0.7	79.9	43.7	48.1	51.9
16319	CRANBERRY	98.6	98.1	0.3	0.3	0.0	0.3	0.6	0.8	4.2	4.7	5.8	7.8	4.7	22.8	30.0	18.6	1.4	80.3	45.0	48.1	51.9
16321	EAST HICKORY	98.5	98.5	0.0	0.4	0.0	0.0	0.4	0.4	3.8	4.2	6.1	6.1	4.6	22.5	30.5	20.2	1.9	81.7	46.8	50.4	49.6
16323	FRANKLIN	95.9	95.4	2.4	2.6	0.2	0.3	0.7	0.7	5.6	5.6	6.1	7.7	6.0	23.9	27.1	15.6	2.4	77.7	41.7	48.6	51.4
16326	FRYBURG	99.4	99.3	0.1	0.1	0.1	0.1	0.2	0.2	8.1	8.4	8.2	6.9	5.4	25.0	24.7	12.1	1.2	70.9	36.3	50.7	49.3
16327	GUYS MILLS	99.0	98.9	0.3	0.4	0.2	0.3	0.4	0.5	6.8	7.0	7.4	7.3	5.8	26.2	26.9	11.1	1.5	74.4	38.3	51.7	48.3
16329	IRVINE	99.0	98.6	0.0	0.0	0.4	0.4	0.0	0.0	4.9	4.2	4.2	4.6	4.9	19.7	24.2	23.2	10.2	83.5	51.1	45.6	54.4
16331	KOSSUTH	98.0	96.2	0.0	0.0	0.0	1.9	0.0	0.0	7.7	7.7	7.7	5.8	5.8	25.0	25.0	13.5	1.9	76.9	38.8	51.9	48.1
16332	LICKINGVILLE	100.0	100.0	0.0	0.0	0.0	0.0	0.0	0.0	9.1	9.1	9.1	7.6	7.6	24.2	22.7	10.6	0.0	68.2	32.5	54.6	45.5
16333	LUDLOW	99.4	99.2	0.0	0.0	0.0	0.0	0.2	0.2	5.7	6.5	7.4	5.1	4.4	24.5	28.1	16.5	1.9	77.2	42.9	51.6	48.4
16334	MARBLE	100.0	100.0	0.0	0.0	0.0	0.0	0.0	0.0	6.4	6.4	7.9	6.4	4.8	25.4	27.0	14.3	1.6	76.2	39.5	52.4	47.6
16335	MEADVILLE	95.1	94.5	2.9	3.2	0.5	0.6	0.8	0.8	5.5	5.5	5.9	7.9	8.9	23.9	25.5	13.8	3.1	79.5	39.4	47.4	52.6
16340	PITTSFIELD	99.3	99.2	0.1	0.2	0.1	0.1	0.2	0.2	5.7	6.3	8.0	6.8	5.5	24.6	27.5	13.6	2.0	75.7	40.6	50.7	49.3
16341	PLEASANTVILLE	98.6	98.5	0.1	0.2	0.1	0.1	0.3	0.3	4.3	4.7	6.3	6.7	5.7	23.4	29.7	17.7	1.6	80.5	44.3	50.5	49.5
16342	POLK	97.9	97.6	0.9	1.1	0.3	0.3	0.0	0.0	4.4	5.0	5.7	5.6	4.7	25.1	34.0	14.2	1.2	81.1	44.7	50.4	49.6
16345	RUSSELL	98.6	98.4	0.2	0.2	0.5	0.6	0.3	0.4	4.8	5.4	6.5	6.8	5.6	23.4	32.8	13.4	1.3	79.1	43.6	50.7	49.3
16346	SENECA	99.0	98.9	0.3	0.3	0.2	0.2	0.5	0.5	6.1	6.2	6.6	6.7	6.0	24.5	28.4	14.2	1.4	77.0	41.3	49.1	50.9
16347	SHEFFIELD	98.8	98.8	0.3	0.3	0.2	0.2	0.7	0.7	5.7	5.9	6.9	6.3	5.5	25.2	26.9	15.3	2.2	77.6	41.3	49.6	50.4
16350	SUGAR GROVE	99.0	98.8	0.2	0.3	0.1	0.1	0.2	0.3	7.3	7.3	7.9	7.8	7.0	24.6	25.7	11.3	1.2	72.7	37.2	50.7	49.3
16351	TIDIOUTE	99.2	99.1	0.2	0.2	0.1	0.1	0.2	0.3	4.4	4.8	6.1	5.6	4.7	22.5	30.9	18.7	2.2	81.3	46.1	50.3	49.7
16353	TIONESTA	96.9	96.9	1.6	1.7	0.2	0.2	1.1	1.1	4.2	4.4	5.8	9.2	4.6	20.8	29.4	19.2	2.4	79.6	45.8	51.6	48.4
16354	TITUSVILLE	98.4	98.2	0.6	0.7	0.2	0.3	0.5	0.6	5.6	5.7	7.2	8.4	6.5	23.4	26.0	15.2	2.2	77.0	40.4	48.6	51.4
16360	TOWNVILLE	98.6	98.3	0.3	0.3	0.3	0.5	0.8	1.0	6.4	6.8	8.3	7.8	5.7	26.3	26.0	11.7	1.2	73.6	37.9	52.1	47.9
16362	UTICA	99.0	98.9	0.2	0.2	0.1	0.1	0.4	0.4	5.3	5.8	7.7	7.2	5.6	25.5	29.4	12.4	1.1	76.8	40.5	50.1	49.9
16364	VENUS	99.2	99.2	0.0	0.0	0.6	0.6	0.6	0.6	5.6	5.8	7.2	6.4	4.6	25.7	29.0	14.5	1.4	77.9	41.9	49.7	50.3
16365	WARREN	98.4	98.2	0.2	0.3	0.4	0.6	0.4	0.5	5.6	5.7	6.1	6.1	5.6	24.8	28.0	15.7	2.6	78.8	42.5	48.3	51.7
16371	YOUNGSVILLE	99.1	98.9	0.0	0.0	0.1	0.1	0.5	0.6	6.1	5.9	6.4	6.4	6.4	23.0	25.5	17.3	3.1	77.9	42.0	46.2	53.8
16372	CLINTONVILLE	97.4	97.3	1.3	1.5	0.2	0.2	0.0	0.2	6.4	6.4	6.7	6.9	6.4	26.7	26.5	12.5	1.5	76.5	38.3	50.6	49.4
16373	EMLENTON	98.3	98.1	0.5	0.6	0.3	0.4	0.2	0.3	5.5	5.5	6.5	6.1	6.3	24.9	27.3	15.0	3.0	78.7	41.7	48.9	51.2
16374	KENNERDELL	98.9	98.8	0.1	0.1	0.4	0.6	0.6	0.7	4.6	5.0	5.8	6.4	4.8	22.2	32.8	17.2	1.2	80.7	45.6	51.6	48.4
16401	ALBION	83.0	82.0	15.7	16.7	0.3	0.3	3.5	3.6	4.0	4.6	5.7	5.7	10.8	38.3	21.8	8.3	0.9	82.4	34.8	64.6	35.4
16402	BEAR LAKE	99.0	98.7	0.1	0.3	0.1	0.2	0.1	0.1	8.2	8.2	10.2	8.7	6.7	24.4	23.2	9.5	0.9	68.2	34.4	49.0	51.0
16403	CAMBRIDGE SPRINGS	94.1	93.7	4.6	4.8	0.2	0.3	1.3	1.4	5.6	6.0	7.3	6.7	5.9	31.1	25.8	10.2	1.5	76.9	37.8	46.5	53.5
16404	CENTERVILLE	98.8	98.7	0.4	0.4	0.1	0.1	0.3	0.4	8.1	7.3	8.5	7.7	6.4	25.0	24.3	11.3	1.4	71.0	36.0	51.3	48.7
16405	COLUMBUS	98.4	98.2	0.1	0.1	0.0	0.0	0.4	0.4	5.4	5.8	7.0	7.2	5.8	25.8	29.2	12.3	1.5	77.4	40.2	49.3	50.7
16406	CONNEAUTVILLE	98.7	98.4	0.5	0.5	0.1	0.2	0.2	0.3	6.1	6.2	7.0	6.6	6.4	24.9	25.1	13.8	3.9	76.3	40.2	49.9	50.2
16407	CORRY	98.3	98.2	0.2	0.2	0.3	0.3	0.7	0.7	6.7	6.8	7.7	7.2	6.8	24.6	25.0	12.9	2.4	74.1	37.7	48.1	51.9
16410	CRANESVILLE	98.4	98.4	0.1	0.1	0.2	0.2	0.7	0.7	7.1	7.1	7.5	7.4	6.2	28.1	25.3	10.6	0.9	73.9	37.1	50.2	49.9
16411	EAST SPRINGFIELD	97.2	97.1	0.9	1.0	0.3	0.3	0.8	0.8	6.0	6.6	8.0	7.5	6.0	25.9	28.4	10.5	1.0	74.8	38.5	50.2	49.8
16412	EDINBORO	95.0	94.6	2.6	2.9	1.0	1.0	0.9	0.9	4.1	4.0	5.1	15.2	24.3	20.2	19.7	6.6	0.9	83.3	24.5	49.0	51.1
16415	FAIRVIEW	98.4	98.3	0.4	0.4	0.5	0.5	0.7	0.8	5.0	6.3	7.9	6.9	4.8	22.0	30.8	14.0	2.4	76.4	43.3	48.5	51.5
16417	GIRARD	98.6	98.5	0.3	0.4	0.2	0.2	0.4	0.4	6.3	7.0	8.2	7.8	5.9	27.1	26.0	10.3	1.4	73.4	37.6	49.0	51.0
16420	GRAND VALLEY	98.5	98.5	1.5	1.5	0.0	0.0	0.0	0.0	4.6	6.1	9.1	9.1	6.1	24.2	27.3	13.6	0.0	71.2	38.8	50.0	50.0
16421	HARBORCREEK	98.7	98.7	0.3	0.3	0.1	0.1	0.6	0.6	4.3	4.4	7.4	9.0	6.5	22.8	29.3	14.1	2.0	78.0	42.3	48.0	52.0
16423	LAKE CITY	99.3	99.2	0.1	0.1	0.2	0.2	0.6	0.6	7.1	7.3	7.6	6.8	6.5	27.6	25.0	10.9	1.3	73.7	37.3	48.5	51.6
16424	LINESVILLE	98.2	98.0	0.4	0.4	0.1	0.2	0.5	0.7	4.7	5.2	6.9	6.4	4.9	23.1	29.5	17.4	2.0	78.9	44.2	50.7	49.3
16426	MC KEAN	98.3	98.2	0.5	0.6	0.1	0.1	0.7	0.7	6.3	6.7	7.5	8.0	6.2	26.4	29.2	9.0	0.8	74.2	38.2	50.6	49.5
16428	NORTH EAST	97.8	97.6	0.9	1.0	0.3	0.3	1.1	1.2	5.7	5.8	7.6	11.8	9.8	23.5	24.0	10.2	1.7	76.2	34.5	50.3	49.8
16433	SAEGERTOWN	97.9	97.6	0.8	0.9	0.2	0.2	0.4	0.4	5.9	6.4	7.3	6.4	5.8	27.7	26.3	12.4	1.9	76.3	39.1	50.5	49.6
16434	SPARTANSBURG	99.3	99.2	0.2	0.2	0.0	0.0	0.2	0.2	11.2	10.3	10.0	8.5	7.5	23.9	19.6	8.2	0.8	62.8	27.0	52.5	47.5
16435	SPRINGBORO	97.5	97.1	1.1	1.2	0.2	0.4	0.5	0.7	6.8	7.0	7.7	7.2	7.1	26.9	25.3	10.8	1.3	74.1	36.3	51.2	48.8
16436	SPRING CREEK	99.3	99.3	0.0	0.0	0.0	0.0	0.0	0.0	4.9	5.6	6.3	6.3	6.3	22.2	32.6	14.6	1.4	79.2	44.1	52.1	47.9
16438	UNION CITY	98.7	98.7	0.2	0.2	0.3	0.3	0.5	0.5	6.9	6.8	7.8	7.3	6.7	27.2	25.1	10.9	1.3	73.6	36.6	49.9	50.1
16440	VENANGO	97.6	97.3	0.7	0.8	0.4	0.5	0.5	0.5	6.5	7.0	7.6	6.1	5.9	28.0	26.8	10.6	1.6	75.1	38.2	50.5	49.5
16441	WATERFORD	98.6	98.5	0.3	0.4	0.1	0.1	0.5	0.6	6.7	7.0	7.8	7.4	6.2	27.5	27.1	9.6	0.8	73.9	37.0	50.6	49.4
16442	WATTSBURG	99.0	99.0	0.1	0.1	0.3	0.3	0.3	0.3	6.4	6.9	7.9	7.1	6.4	27.9	28.7	8.0	0.8	74.5	37.3	50.3	49.7
16443	WEST SPRINGFIELD	98.5	98.5	0.4	0.4	0.1	0.1	0.5	0.4	7.0	7.5	7.5	7.0	6.0	27.7	24.7	11.7	1.0	73.8	36.8	50.6	49.4
16444	EDINBORO	95.4	95.4	1.9	1.9	1.9	1.9	1.9	1.9	2.8	2.8	3.7	5.6	41.7	20.4	13.0	9.3	0.9	90.7	24.2	49.1	50.9
16501	ERIE	86.4	85.3	10.2	11.3	0.9	0.8	1.7	1.7	2.3	1.1	1.2	19.2	23.7	16.0	15.9	17.4	3.3	94.7	27.7	44.3	55.7
16502	ERIE	84.5	83.5	9.8	10.7	0.7	0.8	5.1	5.3	7.3	6.6	7.0	7.3	9.3	30.3	19.7	9.7	3.1	74.9	33.0	48.3	51.7
16503	ERIE	57.4	55.4	33.6	35.5	0.8	0.7	8.7	8.8	9.7	8.9	9.2	8.4	8.4	28.2	18.6	7.6	1.0	67.3	28.6	49.5	50.5
16504	ERIE	90.5	89.6	6.9	7.7	0.7	0.8	1.8	1.9	5.8	5.7	6.3	8.9	9.7	25.4	20.4	14.5	3.4	78.8	36.0	46.2	53.8
16505	ERIE	96.8	96.4	1.2	1.4	0.7	0.8	1.5	1.6	5.4	5.9	6.8	6.3	5.1	23.1	28.3	15.8	3.5	77.8	43.3	46.9	53.1
16506	ERIE	96.4	96.1	0.9	1.1	1.7	1.8	0.9	1.0	6.0	6.4	7.2	6.5	5.4	25.9	27.6	13.4	1.7	76.2	40.5	48.6	51.5
16507	ERIE	72.9	71.5	21.2	22.6	1.0	1.0	4.6	4.7	7.5	6.7	7.2	7.3	9.8	28.4	20.2	10.8	2.1	74.2	32.2	50.8	49.2
16508	ERIE	94.5	94.1	2.8	3.1	0.5	0.5	1.9	2.1	6.7	6.6	6.5	5.4	5.3	28.7	22.9	15.3	2.6	76.9	39.0	47.1	52.9
16509	ERIE	96.5	96.3	1.6	1.7	0.9	0.9	0.8	0.8	5.1	5.5	6.4	6.1	5.9	25.3	27.0	16.0	2.7	79.2	42.1	48.2	51.8
16510	ERIE	87.7	87.4	8.5	8.8	0.9	0.9	2.6	2.6	6.2	6.5	7.5	7.3	7.6	26.1	26.7	11.2	1.0	75.6	37.1	49.9	50.1
16511	ERIE	91.9	91.4	4.9	5.3	0.4	0.4	2.6	2.7	6.2	5.8	6.6	6.9	6.7	22.9	25.4	15.9	3.7	76.9	41.3	46.7	53.3
16565	ERIE	100.0	100.0	0.0	0.0	0.0	0.0	0.0	0.0	0.0	0.0	0.0	0.0	100.0	0.0	0.0	0.0	0.0	100.0	22.5	50.0	50.0
16601	ALTOONA	95.7	95.3	2.7	2.9	0.3	0.4	0.7	0.8	5.8	5.7	6.2	9.1	8.3	24.9	25.0	13.3	1.9	78.8	37.8	47.9	52.1
16602	ALTOONA	97.4	97.0	1.4	1.6	0.4	0.5	0.6	0.7	6.0	6.0	6.1	5.7	5.9	26.0	25.7	15.8	2.8	78.5	41.0	47.2	52.8
16611	ALEXANDRIA	98.8	98.5	0.1	0.2	0.4	0.6	0.9	1.1	5.1	5.9	7.0	6.6	5.5	25.3	30.9	12.1	1.7	77.7	41.7	49.4	50.6
16613	ASHVILLE	97.9	97.5	1.3	1.6	0.1	0.2	1.0	1.2	5.4	5.9	6.6	7.3	5.5	29.4	25.6	12.8	1.6	77.5	39.1	53.0	47.0
16616	BECCARIA	99.2	99.2	0.1	0.1	0.1	0.1	0.2	0.2	5.7	5.8	6.7	5.6	5.9	26.6	26.8	14.8	2.0	78.4	41.0	49.5	50.5
16617	BELLWOOD	99.0	98.8	0.1	0.1	0.2	0.2	0.5	0.6	5.7	5.8	6.4	6.1	6.0	26.8	27.1	14.4	1.6	78.4	40.7	49.0	51.0
16620	BRISBIN	99.3	99.3	0.0	0.0	0.0	0.0	0.0	0.2	5.7	5.9	6.6	6.4	4.7	28.2	26.5	14.0	1.9	77.7	40.3	47.2	52.8
16621	BROAD TOP	99.2	99.0	0.3	0.5	0.3	0.3	0.0	0.3	6.2	6.5	5.7	6.2	5.7	28.2	26.7	13.2	1.6	77.7	39.3	51.0	49.0
16622	CALVIN	99.5	99.2	0.0	0.1	0.0	0.0	0.2	0.3	6.2	6.6	7.0	5.5	5.1	26.9	26.7	14.7	1.2	76.6	39.0	49.0	51.0
16623	CASSVILLE	100.0	100.0	0.0	0.0	0.0	0.0	0.0	0.0	6.9	6.9	6.9	6.0	5.2	26.7	25.9	13.8	1.7	74.1	37.5	49.1	50.9
16625	CLAYSBURG	99.1	99.0	0.1	0.1	0.0	0.0	0.3	0.3	6.3	6.2	6.5	6.1	6.2	28.2	26.8	12.4	1.2	77.2	38.5	48.9	51.1
16627	COALPORT	99.3	99.2	0.1	0.1	0.2	0.3	0.1	0.2	5.1	5.2	6.2	5.8	6.4	27.0	27.3	14.8	2.2	79.9	41.2	48.6	51.4
16630	CRESSON	96.4	96.0	2.2	2.5	0.3	0.4	0.9	1.0	5.4	5.4	6.0	5.9	6.8	29.5	25.2	13.7	2.1	79.7	39.1	49.8	50.2
16634	DUDLEY	99.2	98.7	0.3	0.5	0.2	0.3	0.2	0.3	6.3	6.3	5.7	6.0	5.5	28.6	26.8	13.3	1.5	78.2	39.5	51.1	48.9
	PENNSYLVANIA	85.4	84.4	10.0	10.3	1.8	2.2	3.2	3.5	5.9	6.1	6.8	6.9	6.7	26.6	25.3	13.3	2.2	77.2	39.1	48.4	51.6
	UNITED STATES	75.1	73.6	12.3	12.5	3.8	4.2	12.5	14.1	6.9	6.7	7.2	7.0	7.3	28.6	23.8	10.8	1.7	75.1	36.0	49.1	50.9

ZIP CODE #	POST OFFICE NAME	2004 Per Capita Income	2004 HH Income Base	2004 Household Income Distribution (%): Less than $25,000	$25,000 to $49,999	$50,000 to $99,999	$100,000 to $149,999	$150,000 or More	Median Household Income: 2004	2009	2004 National Centile	2004 State Centile	2004 Home Value Base	2004 Home Value Distribution (%): Less than $50,000	$50,000 to $89,999	$90,000 to $174,999	$175,000 to $399,999	$400,000 or More	2004 Median Home Value
16255	SLIGO	18961	436	37.2	34.2	22.5	3.4	2.8	34809	40642	27	20	312	23.7	36.5	34.0	5.8	0.0	81351
16256	SMICKSBURG	9825	536	40.5	38.4	17.7	2.1	1.3	29287	33487	11	5	448	27.2	28.1	31.3	12.7	0.7	82500
16258	STRATTANVILLE	19145	1006	39.0	32.3	23.3	3.4	2.1	32271	36807	18	11	682	28.9	19.8	39.6	10.7	1.0	91957
16259	TEMPLETON	16731	625	38.4	33.1	24.2	3.4	1.0	32823	37567	20	13	506	41.5	38.9	16.2	2.2	1.2	55244
16260	VOWINCKEL	19153	685	30.8	36.5	26.6	5.1	1.0	36254	41847	33	26	588	16.8	34.7	35.7	11.4	1.4	88448
16262	WORTHINGTON	18698	1185	31.6	33.0	27.8	6.5	1.2	37642	43652	38	34	958	15.9	23.8	45.8	13.1	1.5	104388
16301	OIL CITY	18533	7773	37.2	31.0	25.5	4.5	1.9	34916	40775	27	20	5517	34.5	34.0	25.4	5.8	0.3	65456
16311	CARLTON	19524	170	27.1	34.7	28.8	5.9	3.5	39563	47375	45	42	145	20.7	21.4	43.5	14.5	0.0	102604
16313	CLARENDON	23515	269	28.3	33.8	30.1	4.5	3.4	38714	44321	42	39	233	31.3	27.9	33.1	6.0	1.7	75313
16314	COCHRANTON	21139	1719	27.9	29.9	33.0	6.9	2.4	42648	50758	55	55	1461	17.3	23.5	41.8	16.4	1.2	104779
16316	CONNEAUT LAKE	23167	2244	27.0	34.3	29.3	6.6	2.9	41533	49084	51	51	1791	12.1	20.2	44.2	20.0	3.5	114570
16317	COOPERSTOWN	20332	184	23.9	32.6	36.4	7.1	0.0	44568	51909	60	61	165	15.8	47.9	33.3	3.0	0.0	80217
16319	CRANBERRY	20033	153	28.1	30.1	36.0	4.6	1.3	42797	50680	55	56	130	21.5	33.1	34.6	10.8	0.0	85385
16321	EAST HICKORY	18004	115	36.5	35.7	22.6	4.4	0.9	33278	36942	22	14	97	19.6	36.1	36.1	7.2	1.0	83889
16323	FRANKLIN	20481	7087	34.4	29.1	27.6	6.6	2.4	37146	43517	36	31	5152	26.1	34.1	30.9	8.4	0.5	75500
16326	FRYBURG	15818	725	35.6	33.1	25.1	4.8	1.4	35210	41015	28	21	593	15.9	23.4	48.7	12.0	0.0	104733
16327	GUYS MILLS	19486	906	24.7	34.7	32.8	5.0	2.9	41715	49108	52	52	798	18.6	29.7	41.1	9.7	1.0	92692
16329	IRVINE	21784	110	31.8	31.8	29.1	4.6	2.7	37348	42779	37	32	84	21.4	36.9	36.9	4.8	0.0	81250
16331	KOSSUTH	21537	23	26.1	39.1	30.4	4.4	0.0	41115	47330	50	49	20	10.0	30.0	45.0	15.0	0.0	104167
16332	LICKINGVILLE	14280	29	48.3	31.0	17.2	3.5	0.0	26103	33615	6	2	23	21.7	30.4	43.5	4.4	0.0	88750
16333	LUDLOW	21188	239	31.8	30.5	30.1	5.0	2.5	37185	43301	36	31	209	30.1	27.3	35.4	6.2	1.0	76765
16334	MARBLE	18968	28	32.1	32.1	32.1	3.6	0.0	37327	42343	37	32	23	4.4	21.7	65.2	8.7	0.0	114583
16335	MEADVILLE	23038	12651	33.4	28.9	26.6	7.7	3.5	37705	45051	38	34	8449	17.1	23.8	45.5	12.4	1.3	102731
16340	PITTSFIELD	19152	1317	30.1	34.0	29.7	5.1	1.1	39331	44928	44	41	1100	26.4	34.2	32.6	6.7	0.2	78193
16341	PLEASANTVILLE	18451	924	33.0	31.5	30.0	4.4	1.1	36944	43222	35	30	773	23.7	37.1	33.8	4.9	0.5	78897
16342	POLK	17828	972	27.8	34.4	29.3	6.9	1.7	40264	46242	47	46	817	25.2	32.8	33.1	8.5	0.5	81027
16345	RUSSELL	23403	1622	19.7	31.1	37.6	8.5	3.1	49334	55827	71	70	1421	12.0	22.1	47.3	17.4	1.2	111658
16346	SENECA	19804	1464	30.3	32.5	28.8	6.9	1.6	39550	46608	45	42	1181	21.1	29.7	41.1	8.0	0.2	89112
16347	SHEFFIELD	19082	975	33.1	27.9	33.2	4.5	1.2	40358	45770	47	46	763	33.6	40.4	20.8	3.2	2.1	63941
16350	SUGAR GROVE	17801	1380	26.1	34.6	33.6	4.6	1.1	42717	49044	55	55	1157	23.5	30.1	36.5	8.7	1.2	85389
16351	TIDIOUTE	20448	1124	34.5	32.4	25.4	5.8	2.0	35320	40717	29	22	903	25.1	36.8	29.9	7.0	1.2	76645
16353	TIONESTA	16796	1062	40.0	32.0	22.3	4.2	1.4	31704	36846	17	10	794	22.2	35.8	34.6	6.6	0.9	81000
16354	TITUSVILLE	21023	5506	35.7	32.4	24.1	5.1	2.6	35147	41165	28	21	3930	28.3	33.3	31.2	6.0	1.2	75925
16360	TOWNVILLE	17527	443	27.8	36.6	29.4	4.5	1.8	38534	45283	41	38	375	21.9	32.8	33.3	10.9	1.1	85000
16362	UTICA	17770	765	29.4	32.3	31.9	5.6	0.8	40152	46615	47	45	653	30.9	28.5	32.5	7.8	0.3	78021
16364	VENUS	19349	187	29.4	34.8	29.4	4.3	2.1	40439	46132	48	47	153	21.6	29.4	41.8	6.5	0.7	88333
16365	WARREN	23193	8800	28.3	32.9	29.8	6.0	3.0	40936	47435	49	48	6349	17.8	34.9	38.8	7.9	0.6	86850
16371	YOUNGSVILLE	18179	812	29.7	35.0	29.9	3.9	1.5	36988	43393	35	30	613	13.4	46.0	35.1	5.6	0.0	82628
16372	CLINTONVILLE	19890	216	38.4	28.7	26.9	4.6	1.4	33050	38044	21	14	174	31.6	31.0	30.5	6.9	0.0	73571
16373	EMLENTON	19587	1285	33.1	31.9	26.9	5.6	2.6	36570	42496	34	28	1003	24.5	28.3	35.6	10.2	1.4	86149
16374	KENNERDELL	18243	543	30.6	43.8	19.5	4.4	1.7	34660	39812	26	19	486	23.3	36.2	33.7	6.0	0.8	80213
16401	ALBION	16436	1715	29.7	32.9	31.1	5.0	1.3	40287	47562	47	46	1345	17.6	30.4	44.1	7.7	0.3	91964
16402	BEAR LAKE	14418	348	28.7	39.4	27.0	3.5	1.4	37427	42576	37	33	296	27.4	35.8	31.8	5.1	0.0	73000
16403	CAMBRIDGE SPRINGS	19577	2548	25.8	32.7	32.7	6.7	2.2	44004	51398	59	59	2072	16.1	25.4	42.0	15.4	1.0	101177
16404	CENTERVILLE	16056	1024	31.9	35.7	26.5	4.0	1.9	36278	42624	33	27	861	27.1	28.3	33.1	11.0	0.5	83162
16405	COLUMBUS	21570	659	28.2	30.8	31.9	7.0	2.1	41562	47591	52	51	559	14.1	29.7	47.1	8.8	0.4	97340
16406	CONNEAUTVILLE	17831	1193	29.9	36.7	27.2	4.6	1.5	37705	43775	38	34	999	26.0	25.3	38.8	9.1	0.7	88354
16407	CORRY	17959	3908	32.5	34.2	27.9	4.1	1.3	37429	43998	37	33	2755	28.4	44.7	21.8	4.7	0.4	68858
16410	CRANESVILLE	19098	605	22.2	34.1	36.9	5.1	1.8	45746	52848	63	64	513	19.3	28.7	40.7	10.3	1.0	92234
16411	EAST SPRINGFIELD	21081	544	23.5	37.7	28.1	6.8	3.9	45542	52212	63	63	471	20.6	27.6	39.9	10.2	1.7	91809
16412	EDINBORO	21163	4224	30.9	25.0	29.9	9.4	4.8	45071	52193	61	62	2554	11.0	13.5	48.2	24.9	2.3	127787
16415	FAIRVIEW	30508	2779	14.5	22.5	37.6	15.7	9.8	63533	76812	87	89	2493	3.4	10.9	45.1	34.9	5.7	161001
16417	GIRARD	19851	3249	22.6	38.0	31.7	5.8	2.0	44020	51267	59	59	2648	17.4	18.9	52.0	10.7	1.0	103453
16420	GRAND VALLEY	17790	28	28.6	39.3	28.6	3.6	0.0	40000	45000	46	44	25	36.0	32.0	24.0	8.0	0.0	67500
16421	HARBORCREEK	23285	1153	19.4	28.9	43.9	6.0	1.8	51248	60525	74	74	929	4.8	10.6	67.1	15.6	1.9	123397
16423	LAKE CITY	19882	1642	24.0	38.8	28.1	6.0	3.1	37689	45282	38	34	1324	22.1	23.9	46.8	6.3	0.9	93313
16424	LINESVILLE	19162	2230	32.7	34.4	26.8	4.4	1.7	35989	41906	31	25	1819	18.1	31.3	41.1	8.6	0.9	90833
16426	MC KEAN	22313	1505	16.7	32.2	38.0	10.4	2.7	50769	58803	73	73	1367	22.1	13.5	40.8	21.2	2.5	115310
16428	NORTH EAST	20549	4938	24.1	29.9	34.1	9.4	2.5	46808	54887	66	66	3869	15.6	14.9	51.6	16.3	1.6	114493
16433	SAEGERTOWN	20730	2110	24.1	31.8	34.1	7.4	2.7	43937	52271	58	58	1780	19.3	21.3	43.3	15.2	1.0	104417
16434	SPARTANSBURG	13851	936	32.6	36.2	23.3	5.6	2.4	34420	40080	25	18	786	27.1	29.6	34.1	8.1	1.0	81846
16435	SPRINGBORO	17050	771	33.3	33.5	27.1	4.9	1.2	36199	41981	32	26	626	27.2	23.2	39.5	9.9	0.3	89545
16436	SPRING CREEK	21945	56	19.6	35.7	35.7	7.1	1.8	45000	52908	61	62	47	21.3	25.5	44.7	8.5	0.0	93750
16438	UNION CITY	17771	3240	30.6	33.3	28.7	5.4	1.9	39329	45796	44	41	2441	24.9	31.3	32.9	10.2	0.8	80939
16440	VENANGO	21138	382	25.1	31.9	31.4	8.1	3.4	42960	51094	56	56	322	13.0	22.7	45.7	18.0	0.6	110776
16441	WATERFORD	20631	3476	19.3	31.8	37.8	9.1	2.1	49239	57657	71	70	2949	19.0	16.3	41.4	21.9	1.4	113430
16442	WATTSBURG	20874	957	18.5	27.1	38.4	13.6	2.5	53209	62379	77	78	825	11.2	18.4	48.5	21.2	0.7	119184
16443	WEST SPRINGFIELD	19929	591	26.2	29.4	34.5	8.0	1.9	45192	52843	62	62	493	18.1	27.0	48.9	6.1	0.0	95444
16444	EDINBORO	16642	48	56.3	16.7	18.8	8.3	0.0	21745	23822	2	1	13	7.7	15.4	69.2	7.7	0.0	118750
16501	ERIE	14039	1445	81.4	12.8	4.4	0.5	0.9	11097	12485	1	0	64	17.2	29.7	37.5	14.1	1.6	96667
16502	ERIE	16388	7070	42.9	32.4	21.5	2.5	0.7	29612	34343	11	5	2974	25.3	53.4	19.9	1.5	0.0	68818
16503	ERIE	12117	6354	51.6	32.6	13.9	1.0	0.9	24018	27353	4	2	2510	69.1	28.1	2.4	0.4	0.0	42056
16504	ERIE	19931	6558	28.9	30.7	32.2	6.4	1.8	41637	49423	52	52	4515	11.7	55.2	30.2	3.0	0.0	78868
16505	ERIE	34248	7885	23.7	28.0	29.3	9.4	9.6	47939	58188	68	68	5947	13.5	16.6	45.9	18.9	5.1	115248
16506	ERIE	29139	9590	18.1	26.9	35.7	12.9	6.5	54817	65942	79	80	7052	8.3	10.6	50.0	28.3	2.9	137529
16507	ERIE	14798	3787	50.9	29.6	15.9	2.1	1.5	24437	27949	4	2	1458	53.9	33.3	8.6	2.1	2.1	48564
16508	ERIE	20310	6622	26.1	37.0	31.6	4.2	1.2	40533	48100	48	47	4866	8.4	49.9	38.5	3.2	0.0	85301
16509	ERIE	26718	11051	20.8	30.2	33.7	10.1	5.1	49077	58452	70	70	8355	10.2	15.3	54.2	18.9	1.3	118422
16510	ERIE	20665	9472	23.5	27.7	38.8	8.1	1.9	48880	57524	70	70	7491	11.2	32.5	45.0	11.2	0.0	96645
16511	ERIE	21248	4376	28.6	27.7	32.6	9.1	2.2	43671	52087	58	58	3165	12.5	29.3	46.1	11.1	0.9	100361
16565	ERIE	0	0	0.0	0.0	0.0	0.0	0.0	0	0	0	0	0	0.0	0.0	0.0	0.0	0.0	0
16601	ALTOONA	17819	13012	38.6	30.5	24.4	4.9	1.6	33426	39306	22	15	8687	27.2	38.1	29.8	4.7	0.2	73483
16602	ALTOONA	20226	12900	35.2	31.2	25.7	6.0	1.9	35796	41621	31	24	9161	28.1	33.9	32.1	5.5	0.4	76246
16611	ALEXANDRIA	19241	1095	28.6	30.7	33.9	5.9	0.9	42754	49020	55	56	915	16.7	22.4	45.0	14.6	1.2	105997
16613	ASHVILLE	17665	655	35.0	34.4	25.5	3.5	1.7	34942	40201	27	20	540	26.5	37.6	29.6	5.7	0.6	76500
16616	BECCARIA	16180	574	39.6	36.1	22.1	1.7	0.5	30973	35000	15	8	486	48.2	28.6	20.2	3.1	0.0	52250
16617	BELLWOOD	20045	2520	26.4	30.9	34.4	6.8	1.6	44246	50986	59	60	2011	13.3	30.7	50.0	5.8	0.2	96495
16620	BRISBIN	17425	174	34.5	35.6	24.1	4.6	1.2	36031	40773	32	25	140	31.4	33.6	32.1	2.9	0.0	69000
16621	BROAD TOP	18463	166	36.8	31.9	27.1	4.2	0.0	35000	41215	28	21	137	22.6	37.2	35.8	4.4	0.0	81563
16622	CALVIN	18434	526	27.6	35.6	32.3	3.4	1.1	38207	43586	40	36	437	17.6	22.4	45.5	13.5	0.9	102527
16623	CASSVILLE	21019	52	26.9	36.5	34.6	1.9	0.0	38613	43877	41	38	43	16.3	23.3	46.5	14.0	0.0	104167
16625	CLAYSBURG	16845	1092	38.0	34.5	22.1	3.9	1.6	32643	37190	20	12	870	24.3	31.2	38.6	5.2	0.8	84125
16627	COALPORT	16522	474	37.8	34.4	24.9	3.0	0.0	32105	36583	18	10	358	47.8	32.1	17.3	2.8	0.0	52286
16630	CRESSON	19305	1783	35.4	32.2	26.2	4.9	1.3	35495	41578	29	23	1219	29.0	39.3	28.1	3.5	0.3	73555
16634	DUDLEY	17274	242	35.5	31.8	26.9	5.0	0.8	35737	41560	31	24	199	22.6	37.2	35.7	4.5	0.0	81522
	PENNSYLVANIA	25764		25.8	27.2	31.2	10.2	5.7	46988	57000				11.9	18.4	40.7	25.1	4.1	123516
	UNITED STATES	25866		24.7	27.1	30.8	10.9	6.5	48124	56710				10.9	15.0	33.7	30.1	10.4	145905

#	POST OFFICE NAME	FINANCIAL SERVICES: Auto Loan	FINANCIAL SERVICES: Home Loan	FINANCIAL SERVICES: Invest-ments	FINANCIAL SERVICES: Retire-ment Plans	THE HOME: Home Improvements: Home Repair	THE HOME: Home Improvements: Lawn & Garden	THE HOME: Furnishings: Comput-ers & Hard-ware	THE HOME: Furnishings: Major Appli-ances	THE HOME: Furnishings: TV, Radio, Sound Equip-ment	THE HOME: Furnishings: Furni-ture	ENTERTAINMENT: Dine out/ Carry out	ENTERTAINMENT: Sports Equip-ment	ENTERTAINMENT: Fees & Tickets	ENTERTAINMENT: Toys & Games	ENTERTAINMENT: Travel	ENTERTAINMENT: Cable TV	PERSONAL: Apparel & Services	PERSONAL: Auto Repairs	PERSONAL: Health Insur-ance	PERSONAL: Pets & Supplies
16255	SLIGO	83	62	41	60	68	82	69	76	78	66	91	85	62	86	68	82	83	76	91	92
16256	SMICKSBURG	70	47	21	40	53	61	45	56	54	46	64	67	38	60	46	58	58	56	69	80
16258	STRATTANVILLE	82	57	29	50	64	73	55	68	65	55	77	81	47	73	56	70	70	67	82	95
16259	TEMPLETON	71	55	37	49	60	68	54	62	62	54	74	73	50	73	55	66	68	61	74	82
16260	VOWINCKEL	76	59	40	54	67	75	56	67	63	55	75	79	50	74	60	68	70	66	80	92
16262	WORTHINGTON	82	60	35	55	66	75	59	70	68	59	81	82	53	78	60	72	74	69	82	93
16301	OIL CITY	64	58	53	55	61	69	60	63	64	58	78	71	59	78	61	66	74	62	70	73
16311	CARLTON	70	73	84	76	73	77	74	74	72	74	90	86	74	87	74	69	87	74	70	81
16313	CLARENDON	94	77	54	71	84	93	72	84	80	72	96	99	67	95	75	84	89	82	96	113
16314	COCHRANTON	86	75	59	73	79	87	72	79	77	72	93	93	70	94	74	78	88	77	85	99
16316	CONNEAUT LAKE	92	67	39	61	77	86	65	79	75	65	88	94	57	86	68	80	81	78	95	110
16317	COOPERSTOWN	78	70	53	66	74	79	65	72	69	65	83	85	63	85	66	70	79	70	77	92
16319	CRANBERRY	64	65	64	61	66	74	64	65	67	62	83	73	66	88	66	70	80	64	72	75
16321	EAST HICKORY	70	55	37	49	61	69	51	62	58	51	69	73	46	68	55	62	64	61	73	85
16323	FRANKLIN	72	66	59	62	69	77	66	69	70	64	86	80	65	88	67	73	82	69	77	83
16326	FRYBURG	69	57	42	55	61	69	57	63	62	56	74	73	53	73	58	64	69	62	71	80
16327	GUYS MILLS	86	75	56	71	80	86	70	78	74	70	90	93	68	92	72	76	86	76	85	101
16329	IRVINE	83	61	39	58	68	81	67	75	76	64	89	85	59	84	66	80	81	75	90	92
16331	KOSSUTH	78	69	53	66	73	79	64	71	68	64	83	85	63	85	66	70	79	69	77	92
16332	LICKINGVILLE	55	43	29	39	49	55	41	49	46	40	55	58	36	54	43	49	51	48	58	67
16333	LUDLOW	77	62	45	57	70	78	59	70	66	58	79	81	54	79	63	71	74	69	82	94
16334	MARBLE	67	57	44	57	59	67	58	62	62	57	75	71	56	74	58	63	70	61	68	74
16335	MEADVILLE	79	73	71	70	75	83	74	76	78	73	96	89	73	96	75	80	92	77	82	90
16340	PITTSFIELD	83	60	34	54	67	76	58	70	68	58	80	83	51	77	60	72	73	69	84	96
16341	PLEASANTVILLE	72	59	43	56	64	72	59	66	64	58	77	76	55	76	60	67	72	65	75	83
16342	POLK	74	67	58	62	71	80	65	71	70	63	85	81	63	88	68	74	81	69	80	88
16345	RUSSELL	100	78	50	73	86	95	74	88	83	74	98	105	67	98	77	86	91	86	101	118
16346	SENECA	75	65	50	62	68	76	64	69	68	63	83	81	61	83	64	70	78	68	76	86
16347	SHEFFIELD	70	62	51	57	66	74	60	66	66	59	80	76	59	82	62	69	75	65	75	82
16350	SUGAR GROVE	80	68	48	64	72	79	64	72	69	64	84	85	61	84	65	72	79	70	80	93
16351	TIDIOUTE	81	60	37	54	68	77	58	70	67	58	79	82	51	77	61	71	73	69	84	96
16353	TIONESTA	68	53	36	48	59	67	52	61	59	51	70	71	47	68	54	63	64	60	73	81
16354	TITUSVILLE	85	66	44	60	72	82	66	75	75	65	89	87	60	86	67	79	82	75	89	98
16360	TOWNVILLE	86	62	33	55	69	78	59	71	69	60	82	85	52	79	60	73	75	70	86	99
16362	UTICA	86	59	28	51	66	76	57	70	68	58	80	84	49	76	58	73	73	70	86	99
16364	VENUS	98	66	30	57	74	86	63	79	76	65	90	95	54	85	64	82	82	78	98	112
16365	WARREN	75	73	70	70	75	83	72	75	75	70	92	86	72	95	74	77	88	74	80	88
16371	YOUNGSVILLE	60	64	66	60	65	72	63	63	66	61	82	70	67	88	65	69	79	62	68	70
16372	CLINTONVILLE	90	60	27	52	68	79	58	73	70	59	83	87	50	78	59	76	75	72	90	103
16373	EMLENTON	85	61	34	54	68	78	60	72	70	60	83	85	53	79	61	75	76	72	87	98
16374	KENNERDELL	73	57	39	52	64	72	54	65	61	53	72	76	48	71	58	65	67	64	77	89
16401	ALBION	75	63	47	58	67	75	61	68	67	60	81	79	58	83	62	71	77	67	78	87
16402	BEAR LAKE	72	64	49	61	67	72	59	65	63	59	76	78	58	78	61	64	72	64	71	84
16403	CAMBRIDGE SPRINGS	83	71	53	68	75	83	69	76	74	68	90	89	66	90	70	76	84	74	84	95
16404	CENTERVILLE	83	57	27	49	64	74	55	68	65	56	77	81	47	73	56	70	70	67	83	96
16405	COLUMBUS	89	79	60	75	84	90	73	81	78	73	95	97	72	97	75	80	90	79	88	105
16406	CONNEAUTVILLE	83	60	35	53	67	77	59	70	69	59	81	83	52	79	60	73	75	69	85	96
16407	CORRY	73	60	47	56	64	72	61	66	67	60	81	77	58	80	61	69	76	66	75	83
16410	CRANESVILLE	87	76	57	72	81	87	70	79	76	71	92	94	69	93	73	78	87	77	86	102
16411	EAST SPRINGFIELD	91	81	62	77	85	92	75	83	79	75	97	99	73	99	77	81	92	81	90	107
16412	EDINBORO	83	75	80	77	75	81	86	80	85	82	106	99	82	103	81	81	102	85	77	93
16415	FAIRVIEW	119	129	129	127	130	136	119	122	116	119	145	142	124	149	122	116	142	119	120	142
16417	GIRARD	80	74	60	71	76	82	71	76	74	71	90	88	69	90	71	75	86	75	80	92
16420	GRAND VALLEY	71	56	38	50	63	71	53	63	60	52	71	74	47	70	56	64	66	62	75	87
16421	HARBORCREEK	87	88	83	83	90	98	83	87	86	82	106	100	86	111	86	89	103	85	92	102
16423	LAKE CITY	85	68	49	66	73	82	69	76	75	68	90	88	64	89	69	77	84	75	85	95
16424	LINESVILLE	77	61	42	55	67	76	58	68	66	58	79	80	53	78	61	70	73	67	80	91
16426	MC KEAN	95	88	71	85	91	96	82	89	84	82	103	105	80	104	83	85	99	87	92	110
16428	NORTH EAST	83	77	67	74	79	87	76	80	79	75	97	93	74	97	76	81	93	79	85	96
16433	SAEGERTOWN	87	79	63	75	83	89	74	80	78	73	95	95	73	98	76	80	90	78	87	102
16434	SPARTANSBURG	88	59	27	51	67	77	57	71	69	58	80	85	48	76	58	74	73	70	87	101
16435	SPRINGBORO	87	59	27	51	66	76	57	71	68	58	80	84	49	76	58	73	73	70	87	100
16436	SPRING CREEK	94	74	50	67	83	94	70	84	79	69	94	98	62	92	74	84	87	83	99	115
16438	UNION CITY	75	65	53	62	69	76	63	69	68	63	83	82	61	83	65	70	78	69	77	88
16440	VENANGO	91	81	62	77	85	92	75	83	79	75	97	99	73	99	77	81	92	81	90	107
16441	WATERFORD	89	82	67	78	85	91	77	83	80	77	99	97	76	100	79	82	94	81	88	103
16442	WATTSBURG	97	85	65	82	90	98	81	89	86	81	104	105	79	106	83	88	99	87	96	112
16443	WEST SPRINGFIELD	88	73	51	68	79	86	68	78	75	69	90	93	65	91	70	78	85	76	87	103
16444	EDINBORO	53	32	41	37	32	38	63	46	61	53	76	64	51	68	50	53	71	56	43	52
16501	ERIE	26	22	31	23	22	26	29	26	30	28	38	31	28	37	28	30	37	29	27	29
16502	ERIE	51	48	56	49	48	52	55	52	55	52	69	62	54	69	53	54	67	54	51	57
16503	ERIE	45	39	45	38	39	45	45	44	49	45	60	50	44	58	44	50	58	46	46	49
16504	ERIE	64	69	80	68	69	74	71	69	71	69	88	79	73	92	71	71	86	69	69	75
16505	ERIE	105	112	121	111	112	121	110	110	109	109	136	126	113	139	112	110	133	109	111	122
16506	ERIE	97	107	113	106	106	111	101	102	99	101	124	117	105	127	103	99	121	100	99	114
16507	ERIE	47	43	48	43	43	48	50	47	51	48	64	56	49	63	48	51	62	49	48	52
16508	ERIE	60	66	73	64	66	72	66	65	66	64	82	74	68	86	67	67	80	65	66	71
16509	ERIE	88	91	95	89	91	98	89	90	89	89	111	105	90	112	90	89	108	90	90	102
16510	ERIE	80	79	76	76	80	86	76	79	78	76	96	91	77	99	77	79	93	77	81	93
16511	ERIE	69	75	86	73	74	80	75	74	76	74	95	84	78	98	76	76	93	74	74	81
16565	ERIE	0	0	0	0	0	0	0	0	0	0	0	0	0	0	0	0	0	0	0	0
16601	ALTOONA	56	58	65	56	58	65	60	59	62	58	77	67	62	79	61	63	74	59	61	65
16602	ALTOONA	63	64	68	62	65	72	65	65	67	64	83	73	67	86	66	69	80	65	69	73
16611	ALEXANDRIA	72	68	59	65	71	77	65	69	68	64	84	80	65	87	67	70	80	67	75	85
16613	ASHVILLE	81	60	35	54	66	75	59	70	68	59	80	82	53	77	60	72	74	69	83	93
16616	BECCARIA	71	50	25	43	56	64	48	59	57	49	67	70	42	64	49	61	62	58	72	82
16617	BELLWOOD	73	70	61	66	73	80	67	71	71	66	87	82	67	91	69	73	83	69	78	86
16620	BRISBIN	80	53	24	46	60	69	51	64	62	52	73	77	44	69	52	67	66	64	79	91
16621	BROAD TOP	81	54	25	47	61	71	52	65	63	53	74	78	44	70	53	68	67	65	81	93
16622	CALVIN	78	61	42	55	69	77	58	70	65	57	77	81	52	76	62	70	72	69	82	95
16623	CASSVILLE	80	62	43	56	70	79	59	71	67	58	79	83	53	78	63	71	73	70	84	97
16625	CLAYSBURG	76	55	32	48	61	70	53	64	63	54	74	75	48	72	55	67	68	63	77	87
16627	COALPORT	62	52	40	47	55	62	50	56	56	50	68	65	48	69	52	59	64	55	65	71
16630	CRESSON	61	52	41	49	55	64	55	58	60	52	72	65	52	71	55	63	67	58	68	69
16634	DUDLEY	81	54	25	47	61	71	52	65	63	53	74	78	44	70	53	68	67	65	80	93
	PENNSYLVANIA	89	89	93	87	90	98	89	90	91	88	112	104	89	114	90	92	109	90	92	104
	UNITED STATES	100	100	100	100	100	100	100	100	100	100	100	100	100	100	100	100	100	100	100	100

A 16635-16878

# ZIP CODE / POST OFFICE NAME	COUNTY FIPS CODE	POPULATION 2000	2004	2009	2000-2004 ANNUAL RATE % Rate	State Centile	HOUSEHOLDS 2000	2004	2009	% Annual Rate 2000-2004	2004 Average HH Size	FAMILIES 2000	2004	% Annual Rate 2000-2004
16635 DUNCANSVILLE	013	15331	15501	15535	0.3	52	5872	6067	6154	0.8	2.46	4253	4360	0.6
16636 DYSART	021	791	756	725	-1.1	4	307	302	297	-0.4	2.48	233	228	-0.5
16637 EAST FREEDOM	013	2620	2540	2494	-0.7	9	1067	1056	1048	-0.2	2.39	778	763	-0.5
16639 FALLENTIMBER	021	1723	1695	1646	-0.4	21	621	623	615	0.1	2.52	457	455	-0.1
16640 FLINTON	021	685	679	661	-0.2	29	266	270	268	0.4	2.39	193	194	0.1
16641 GALLITZIN	021	2748	2852	2841	0.9	76	1075	1134	1156	1.3	2.41	756	792	1.1
16645 GLEN HOPE	033	149	149	152	0.0	39	55	56	58	0.4	2.66	39	40	0.6
16646 HASTINGS	021	2792	2709	2617	-0.7	9	1064	1060	1048	-0.1	2.48	773	767	-0.2
16647 HESSTON	061	1055	1072	1088	0.4	58	400	416	433	0.9	2.53	308	319	0.8
16648 HOLLIDAYSBURG	013	13672	13873	13943	0.3	56	5406	5583	5662	0.8	2.36	3728	3834	0.7
16650 HOPEWELL	009	1775	1699	1598	-1.0	4	709	695	669	-0.5	2.44	516	502	-0.7
16651 HOUTZDALE	033	4498	4644	4792	0.8	72	1137	1229	1321	1.9	2.31	787	841	1.6
16652 HUNTINGDON	061	17131	17349	17590	0.3	54	5517	5721	5940	0.9	2.27	3600	3711	0.7
16655 IMLER	009	2362	2211	2060	-1.5	0	910	877	840	-0.9	2.52	689	660	-1.0
16656 IRVONA	033	1203	1216	1243	0.3	51	435	450	470	0.8	2.70	328	337	0.6
16657 JAMES CREEK	061	534	542	551	0.4	57	231	241	250	1.0	2.21	178	184	0.8
16659 LOYSBURG	009	662	637	601	-0.9	6	243	239	230	-0.4	2.66	198	194	-0.6
16661 MADERA	033	1384	1382	1410	0.0	37	555	565	588	0.4	2.45	398	401	0.2
16662 MARTINSBURG	013	5171	5071	4985	-0.5	18	1982	1986	1978	0.1	2.41	1363	1353	-0.2
16664 NEW ENTERPRISE	009	2003	1939	1831	-0.8	8	699	690	667	-0.3	2.80	573	564	-0.4
16666 OSCEOLA MILLS	033	4145	4321	4493	1.0	79	1707	1826	1945	1.6	2.36	1189	1263	1.4
16667 OSTERBURG	009	546	566	554	0.9	75	208	223	224	1.7	2.54	155	164	1.3
16668 PATTON	021	4099	3997	3861	-0.6	13	1596	1595	1582	0.0	2.41	1090	1081	-0.2
16669 PETERSBURG	061	2168	2167	2185	0.0	37	840	861	888	0.6	2.52	628	640	0.5
16671 RAMEY	033	528	537	551	0.4	59	209	217	227	0.9	2.47	148	153	0.8
16673 ROARING SPRING	013	5035	4939	4860	-0.5	18	2011	2021	2017	0.1	2.44	1509	1506	-0.1
16674 ROBERTSDALE	061	634	634	638	0.0	39	246	252	260	0.6	2.52	184	187	0.4
16678 SAXTON	009	3310	3187	3046	-0.9	6	1362	1339	1309	-0.4	2.37	964	943	-0.5
16679 SIX MILE RUN	009	1684	1578	1474	-1.5	1	650	620	591	-1.1	2.53	482	457	-1.3
16680 SMITHMILL	033	1244	1266	1298	0.4	60	515	535	560	0.9	2.37	365	377	0.8
16683 SPRUCE CREEK	061	365	362	365	-0.2	30	162	164	169	0.3	2.21	123	124	0.2
16685 TODD	061	1004	1048	1080	1.0	80	343	367	387	1.6	2.67	271	288	1.4
16686 TYRONE	013	11028	11741	12176	1.5	88	4521	4908	5149	2.0	2.36	3102	3360	1.9
16689 WATERFALL	057	606	636	698	1.1	82	240	258	289	1.7	2.47	175	187	1.6
16691 WELLS TANNERY	057	440	462	507	1.2	83	187	201	225	1.7	2.28	134	143	1.5
16692 WESTOVER	033	1401	1404	1428	0.1	42	523	536	557	0.6	2.61	405	413	0.5
16693 WILLIAMSBURG	013	5002	4951	4907	-0.2	27	1878	1900	1904	0.3	2.55	1373	1378	0.1
16695 WOODBURY	009	663	627	587	-1.3	2	239	230	220	-0.9	2.73	199	191	-1.0
16701 BRADFORD	083	18639	18249	17811	-0.5	16	7556	7519	7508	-0.1	2.29	4841	4783	-0.3
16720 AUSTIN	105	1233	1336	1485	1.9	92	507	560	633	2.4	2.39	359	394	2.2
16724 CROSBY	083	633	678	698	1.6	90	248	270	283	2.0	2.49	170	183	1.8
16726 CYCLONE	083	299	335	347	2.7	97	116	131	139	2.9	2.04	85	95	2.7
16727 DERRICK CITY	083	326	309	299	-1.3	2	125	121	119	-0.8	2.55	87	83	-1.1
16729 DUKE CENTER	083	885	858	838	-0.7	9	349	346	345	-0.2	2.47	254	250	-0.4
16731 ELDRED	083	2628	2560	2505	-0.6	12	1077	1074	1074	-0.1	2.38	755	747	-0.3
16732 GIFFORD	083	604	666	681	2.3	95	233	251	261	1.8	2.00	170	182	1.6
16734 JAMES CITY	047	509	511	511	0.1	44	210	216	222	0.7	2.37	145	148	0.5
16735 KANE	083	7220	6938	6759	-0.9	5	3056	3004	2985	-0.4	2.27	2008	1959	-0.6
16738 LEWIS RUN	083	2629	2806	2776	1.5	89	544	547	549	0.1	2.81	373	372	-0.1
16740 MOUNT JEWETT	083	471	462	453	-0.5	18	198	199	200	0.1	2.32	138	138	0.0
16743 PORT ALLEGANY	083	4464	4360	4281	-0.6	14	1771	1762	1763	-0.1	2.47	1241	1226	-0.3
16744 REW	083	271	279	281	0.7	71	103	109	112	1.3	2.52	80	84	1.2
16745 RIXFORD	083	757	735	719	-0.7	10	296	294	293	-0.2	2.49	217	214	-0.3
16746 ROULETTE	105	1455	1574	1749	1.9	92	585	646	731	2.4	2.44	416	457	2.2
16748 SHINGLEHOUSE	105	3433	3580	3842	1.0	79	1323	1405	1534	1.4	2.55	930	981	1.3
16749 SMETHPORT	083	4121	4563	4766	2.4	95	1568	1782	1903	3.1	2.44	1120	1260	2.8
16750 TURTLEPOINT	083	649	637	624	-0.4	19	249	250	250	0.1	2.55	186	185	-0.1
16801 STATE COLLEGE	027	44074	45672	47855	0.8	74	15805	16748	17981	1.4	2.31	6071	6431	1.4
16802 UNIVERSITY PARK	027	683	678	681	-0.2	31	157	150	154	-1.1	2.56	0	0	0.0
16803 STATE COLLEGE	027	23992	26461	28726	2.3	95	8108	9315	10464	3.3	2.38	4221	4828	3.2
16820 AARONSBURG	027	1089	1096	1126	0.2	46	364	374	391	0.6	2.93	275	280	0.4
16821 ALLPORT	033	356	364	374	0.5	65	130	136	143	1.1	2.68	90	93	0.8
16822 BEECH CREEK	035	1933	2044	2156	1.3	85	778	839	902	1.8	2.44	573	615	1.7
16823 BELLEFONTE	027	24178	24778	25759	0.6	68	8960	9399	9997	1.1	2.38	6110	6351	0.9
16827 BOALSBURG	027	4566	4616	4770	0.3	52	1719	1764	1851	0.6	2.61	1283	1305	0.4
16828 CENTRE HALL	027	4207	4253	4390	0.3	52	1682	1736	1826	0.8	2.38	1226	1254	0.5
16829 CLARENCE	027	734	718	738	-0.5	15	284	283	297	-0.1	2.54	214	212	-0.2
16830 CLEARFIELD	033	14506	14485	14768	0.0	37	6197	6331	6598	0.5	2.21	3974	4030	0.3
16832 COBURN	027	481	478	492	-0.2	32	177	180	189	0.4	2.53	142	143	0.2
16833 CURWENSVILLE	033	3897	4044	4199	0.9	76	1605	1703	1807	1.4	2.34	1123	1183	1.2
16836 FRENCHVILLE	033	1292	1251	1267	-0.8	8	481	475	492	-0.3	2.41	349	343	-0.4
16837 GLEN RICHEY	033	334	336	342	0.1	46	134	139	144	0.9	2.42	103	105	0.5
16838 GRAMPIAN	033	3331	3376	3455	0.3	55	1278	1325	1386	0.9	2.54	968	999	0.7
16839 GRASSFLAT	033	2311	2347	2403	0.4	58	905	938	981	0.9	2.50	673	690	0.6
16840 HAWK RUN	033	2512	2567	2638	0.5	65	1023	1069	1123	1.0	2.40	710	733	0.8
16841 HOWARD	027	5536	5521	5701	-0.1	36	2102	2142	2253	0.4	2.57	1607	1624	0.3
16844 JULIAN	027	2752	2917	3083	1.4	86	1040	1124	1209	1.8	2.60	801	860	1.7
16845 KARTHAUS	027	1140	1137	1161	-0.1	36	358	364	380	0.4	2.76	255	257	0.2
16852 MADISONBURG	027	332	342	355	0.7	71	114	119	126	1.0	2.85	91	95	1.0
16854 MILLHEIM	027	954	933	959	-0.5	15	394	392	409	-0.1	2.38	269	265	-0.4
16858 MORRISDALE	033	1259	1629	1893	6.3	100	471	625	743	6.9	2.61	382	503	6.7
16859 MOSHANNON	027	462	486	513	1.2	84	182	196	211	1.8	2.48	142	152	1.6
16860 MUNSON	033	419	427	439	0.5	62	157	164	172	1.0	2.53	109	113	0.9
16861 NEW MILLPORT	033	660	668	683	0.3	53	273	283	296	0.9	2.36	203	210	0.8
16863 OLANTA	033	40	40	41	0.0	39	19	20	21	1.2	2.00	14	15	1.6
16864 ORVISTON	027	40	39	40	-0.6	13	15	15	16	0.0	2.60	11	11	0.0
16865 PENNSYLVANIA FURNACE	027	2002	2202	2377	2.3	95	751	841	924	2.7	2.62	586	652	2.5
16866 PHILIPSBURG	027	7835	8005	8372	0.5	65	3283	3425	3653	1.0	2.28	2139	2206	0.7
16870 PORT MATILDA	027	5637	5794	6047	0.7	70	2001	2090	2217	1.0	2.77	1569	1632	0.9
16871 POTTERSDALE	035	74	76	78	0.6	69	33	35	36	1.4	2.00	22	23	1.1
16872 REBERSBURG	027	1180	1215	1263	0.7	71	394	413	436	1.1	2.92	315	327	0.9
16874 SNOW SHOE	027	1392	1399	1443	0.1	45	528	543	571	0.7	2.58	403	411	0.5
16875 SPRING MILLS	027	3204	3260	3374	0.4	60	1162	1206	1269	0.9	2.68	899	925	0.7
16877 WARRIORS MARK	061	2313	2385	2454	0.7	72	859	900	943	1.1	2.65	670	698	1.0
16878 WEST DECATUR	033	2176	2188	2229	0.1	45	863	890	927	0.7	2.46	644	660	0.6
PENNSYLVANIA					0.3					0.7	2.44			0.6
UNITED STATES					1.2					1.3	2.58			1.1

ZIP CODE #	POST OFFICE NAME	RACE (%) White 2000	White 2004	Black 2000	Black 2004	Asian/Pacific 2000	Asian/Pacific 2004	% Hispanic Origin 2000	% Hispanic Origin 2004	2004 AGE DISTRIBUTION (%) 0-4	5-9	10-14	15-19	20-24	25-44	45-64	65-84	85+	18+	MEDIAN AGE 2004	% 2004 Males	% 2004 Females
16635	DUNCANSVILLE	98.8	98.5	0.4	0.5	0.3	0.5	0.3	0.3	5.2	5.6	6.4	5.6	5.3	25.8	28.4	15.7	2.1	79.4	42.6	49.8	50.2
16636	DYSART	99.2	99.1	0.1	0.1	0.1	0.1	0.4	0.4	5.8	6.0	5.8	7.1	6.8	27.4	26.9	13.1	1.2	77.9	39.7	51.2	48.8
16637	EAST FREEDOM	98.8	98.7	0.2	0.2	0.0	0.0	0.4	0.5	7.2	7.0	6.7	5.8	5.9	28.2	24.9	12.9	1.5	75.7	37.4	47.6	52.4
16639	FALLENTIMBER	98.2	97.9	0.4	0.4	0.6	0.9	0.4	0.4	4.6	5.1	6.3	7.3	5.6	27.0	25.8	15.6	2.8	79.1	41.3	51.3	48.7
16640	FLINTON	98.0	97.6	0.4	0.4	0.9	1.2	0.3	0.3	4.6	5.3	6.5	7.5	5.5	27.5	26.5	14.7	1.9	78.5	40.6	52.4	47.6
16641	GALLITZIN	97.4	96.8	1.6	1.9	0.2	0.2	1.6	1.7	5.4	5.5	5.8	7.2	6.5	30.2	24.8	12.5	2.1	78.9	38.5	50.8	49.2
16645	GLEN HOPE	99.3	99.3	0.0	0.0	0.0	0.0	0.0	0.0	5.4	5.4	6.0	7.4	5.4	25.5	26.2	16.1	2.7	78.5	42.1	47.7	52.4
16646	HASTINGS	99.5	99.4	0.1	0.1	0.1	0.1	0.4	0.4	5.2	5.4	6.1	5.8	6.2	25.1	25.7	17.4	3.0	79.7	42.3	48.9	51.1
16647	HESSTON	99.2	99.0	0.1	0.2	0.0	0.0	0.6	0.8	5.0	5.4	6.1	6.4	4.5	26.3	30.1	14.3	1.9	79.4	42.4	50.8	49.3
16648	HOLLIDAYSBURG	97.6	97.1	0.6	0.6	1.1	1.5	0.5	0.6	4.5	4.9	6.7	6.5	5.8	23.9	28.5	15.7	3.7	79.9	43.7	48.4	51.6
16650	HOPEWELL	99.3	99.2	0.1	0.1	0.0	0.0	0.5	0.5	5.9	6.2	6.9	6.1	5.7	27.7	26.6	13.4	1.5	77.3	39.4	49.6	50.4
16651	HOUTZDALE	74.6	72.1	21.3	23.3	0.3	0.3	3.8	4.1	3.1	3.3	4.2	7.9	6.7	40.8	22.6	9.8	1.5	85.9	37.6	68.2	31.8
16652	HUNTINGDON	85.8	84.6	11.6	12.5	0.4	0.5	2.1	2.2	4.3	4.3	4.8	7.1	11.5	30.7	23.6	11.8	2.0	83.7	37.2	57.2	42.8
16655	IMLER	99.4	99.2	0.1	0.1	0.0	0.0	0.3	0.3	5.7	5.7	6.6	6.5	6.3	29.1	26.4	12.5	1.1	78.0	38.5	50.3	49.7
16656	IRVONA	99.5	99.6	0.0	0.0	0.1	0.2	0.0	0.0	5.8	6.2	7.8	6.3	6.0	28.0	26.6	12.1	1.2	76.3	38.8	50.0	50.0
16657	JAMES CREEK	99.3	99.1	0.2	0.2	0.0	0.0	0.8	0.7	5.0	5.4	5.9	6.5	4.2	26.0	31.2	14.2	1.7	79.5	43.0	50.9	49.1
16659	LOYSBURG	99.4	99.4	0.0	0.0	0.0	0.2	0.3	0.3	7.5	7.7	7.2	6.1	5.8	28.6	25.3	10.7	1.1	74.1	36.7	50.6	49.5
16661	MADERA	99.1	99.0	0.1	0.1	0.1	0.1	0.1	0.2	5.7	5.6	6.2	7.0	5.6	25.3	25.9	15.8	2.9	78.3	41.8	48.0	52.0
16662	MARTINSBURG	99.2	99.1	0.1	0.1	0.2	0.2	0.4	0.5	5.7	5.7	6.3	6.1	5.3	25.2	23.5	16.3	6.0	78.4	42.0	47.3	52.8
16664	NEW ENTERPRISE	99.3	99.2	0.1	0.1	0.1	0.2	0.4	0.5	7.8	7.8	7.4	6.4	5.7	28.4	25.3	10.4	0.9	73.3	36.4	50.1	49.9
16666	OSCEOLA MILLS	99.0	98.8	0.1	0.1	0.1	0.2	0.7	0.8	5.7	6.1	6.1	5.2	5.1	28.2	27.2	14.6	1.9	78.9	40.9	49.7	50.3
16667	OSTERBURG	98.9	98.4	0.4	0.4	0.4	0.5	0.0	0.2	7.2	6.9	6.5	6.7	6.0	29.3	25.6	10.4	1.2	75.3	36.9	50.5	49.5
16668	PATTON	98.3	97.8	1.2	1.6	0.1	0.2	0.9	1.1	5.7	5.8	6.3	6.3	6.4	26.7	27.1	13.7	2.1	78.5	40.4	50.2	49.8
16669	PETERSBURG	98.8	98.6	0.6	0.7	0.1	0.1	0.2	0.3	6.3	6.4	6.1	5.9	5.7	28.8	27.2	12.3	1.4	77.6	39.2	49.8	50.2
16671	RAMEY	99.2	99.1	0.0	0.0	0.0	0.2	0.2	0.4	4.5	4.8	6.7	6.9	5.4	25.0	25.7	17.5	3.5	79.5	42.6	49.5	50.5
16673	ROARING SPRING	98.9	98.8	0.2	0.2	0.4	0.4	0.2	0.2	5.3	5.7	6.8	5.9	6.1	27.0	27.6	14.1	1.6	78.5	40.4	49.9	50.1
16674	ROBERTSDALE	99.4	99.1	0.0	0.0	0.0	0.0	0.8	1.1	6.2	5.8	6.8	6.8	7.9	24.6	26.0	15.1	0.8	77.4	38.7	51.3	48.7
16678	SAXTON	98.9	98.8	0.2	0.2	0.1	0.1	0.5	0.6	6.2	6.4	6.4	5.6	5.0	26.5	27.1	15.0	2.0	77.4	40.5	48.2	51.8
16679	SIX MILE RUN	99.1	99.0	0.2	0.3	0.2	0.3	0.5	0.6	6.7	6.6	6.7	6.5	6.3	26.0	25.5	14.1	1.6	76.3	38.7	50.8	49.2
16680	SMITHMILL	99.4	99.2	0.0	0.0	0.1	0.1	0.3	0.3	4.5	4.8	6.6	7.0	5.4	25.0	26.0	17.2	3.6	79.7	42.6	49.7	50.3
16683	SPRUCE CREEK	98.6	98.6	0.0	0.0	0.0	0.0	1.4	1.4	5.8	6.6	7.5	7.5	4.4	27.6	29.0	10.8	0.8	74.6	39.4	51.4	48.6
16685	TODD	98.0	97.5	1.4	1.7	0.0	0.0	2.0	2.5	6.9	6.8	6.4	12.1	6.8	25.7	22.0	12.8	0.7	70.6	34.9	55.1	44.9
16686	TYRONE	99.1	99.0	0.2	0.2	0.2	0.2	0.4	0.5	5.6	5.8	6.8	6.2	6.1	25.7	25.9	15.5	2.5	78.1	41.0	47.7	52.3
16689	WATERFALL	99.0	99.1	0.0	0.0	0.0	0.0	0.3	0.2	7.2	7.1	6.8	6.1	5.8	26.1	25.5	13.8	1.6	75.0	39.8	50.8	49.2
16691	WELLS TANNERY	98.4	98.3	0.0	0.0	0.0	0.0	0.5	0.7	7.1	7.1	6.7	5.4	4.6	24.0	27.1	16.0	2.0	75.8	41.4	49.4	50.7
16692	WESTOVER	99.1	99.1	0.1	0.1	0.1	0.2	0.4	0.6	5.7	6.4	6.5	7.0	5.6	26.9	26.7	13.5	1.9	76.9	39.9	50.6	49.4
16693	WILLIAMSBURG	98.6	98.4	0.7	0.8	0.1	0.1	0.3	0.4	6.3	6.4	6.8	6.2	5.6	27.6	26.4	12.7	1.9	76.7	38.7	49.8	50.2
16695	WOODBURY	97.4	97.0	0.0	0.0	0.9	1.3	1.4	1.6	9.1	9.4	8.6	7.0	5.1	25.4	23.0	11.2	1.3	68.6	35.2	48.6	51.4
16701	BRADFORD	97.4	97.1	0.9	1.0	0.5	0.7	0.9	0.9	5.9	6.0	6.8	6.8	6.8	26.2	24.4	14.5	2.6	77.5	39.1	48.4	51.6
16720	AUSTIN	98.3	98.1	0.2	0.2	0.2	0.3	0.7	0.7	7.0	7.0	7.2	7.1	5.4	26.4	25.9	13.0	1.1	74.2	37.7	49.3	50.8
16724	CROSBY	98.4	98.4	0.2	0.3	0.5	0.4	0.6	0.6	5.8	6.2	7.4	6.6	6.2	25.5	26.0	13.4	3.0	76.4	40.2	50.3	49.7
16726	CYCLONE	90.6	90.8	6.7	6.6	0.3	0.3	2.7	3.0	4.5	4.8	6.0	6.3	5.4	31.0	24.8	13.7	3.6	80.6	40.6	56.1	43.9
16727	DERRICK CITY	99.4	99.7	0.0	0.0	0.3	0.3	0.6	0.3	5.2	5.5	6.5	7.1	6.2	25.9	26.5	15.2	1.9	79.0	41.1	50.2	49.8
16729	DUKE CENTER	98.5	98.3	0.3	0.4	0.2	0.4	0.3	0.4	6.3	6.5	7.1	7.3	6.3	26.5	25.9	12.4	1.8	74.9	38.2	49.3	50.7
16731	ELDRED	99.1	99.0	0.1	0.1	0.0	0.0	0.2	0.2	6.3	6.3	6.8	6.9	6.1	26.2	27.4	12.6	1.5	76.4	39.3	49.5	50.6
16732	GIFFORD	83.9	83.8	11.8	11.7	0.5	0.6	4.0	4.1	3.8	4.2	5.0	5.1	6.2	36.8	25.4	12.0	1.7	83.8	39.5	61.0	39.0
16734	JAMES CITY	99.0	98.8	0.2	0.2	0.0	0.0	0.0	0.0	6.3	6.5	6.9	5.3	3.7	26.6	26.0	17.0	1.8	77.1	41.8	52.5	47.6
16735	KANE	99.1	99.0	0.1	0.1	0.1	0.2	0.6	0.7	5.9	6.0	6.5	5.7	5.5	25.7	26.1	15.6	3.1	77.9	41.2	48.8	51.2
16738	LEWIS RUN	71.2	69.9	21.7	22.4	0.8	1.0	7.2	7.6	3.0	3.2	3.2	3.9	7.4	45.8	24.5	8.1	0.9	88.0	37.2	71.9	28.1
16740	MOUNT JEWETT	99.4	99.6	0.0	0.0	0.0	0.0	0.4	0.4	5.4	6.1	6.3	5.2	5.8	24.7	29.9	15.2	1.5	79.0	42.5	50.7	49.4
16743	PORT ALLEGANY	98.7	98.6	0.1	0.1	0.1	0.1	0.4	0.5	6.6	6.7	8.1	7.1	6.1	25.8	24.7	13.4	1.6	73.7	38.1	49.8	50.2
16744	REW	98.9	98.9	0.0	0.0	0.0	0.0	0.0	0.0	5.4	5.4	6.1	6.8	5.0	25.8	27.6	15.8	2.2	78.9	42.7	48.8	51.3
16745	RIXFORD	98.6	98.4	0.3	0.3	0.3	0.3	0.1	0.3	6.3	6.4	7.5	7.2	6.3	26.1	26.0	12.5	1.8	75.0	38.5	49.0	51.0
16746	ROULETTE	98.8	98.5	0.1	0.1	0.3	0.4	1.0	1.2	8.5	6.5	6.0	6.9	7.4	24.1	26.1	12.9	1.5	75.1	38.2	48.4	51.6
16748	SHINGLEHOUSE	98.6	98.4	0.1	0.1	0.2	0.2	0.4	0.5	6.2	6.4	7.5	7.2	5.6	24.5	26.1	14.6	1.9	75.5	39.6	49.4	50.6
16749	SMETHPORT	98.9	98.8	0.2	0.3	0.2	0.2	0.6	0.7	5.6	5.8	6.8	6.7	5.7	25.0	26.1	14.9	3.5	77.2	41.5	49.0	51.0
16750	TURTLEPOINT	98.3	98.3	0.3	0.3	0.2	0.2	0.2	0.2	6.8	6.4	6.8	7.1	6.3	25.9	26.4	13.2	1.3	75.8	39.0	51.3	48.7
16801	STATE COLLEGE	86.5	84.3	3.0	3.3	7.9	9.6	2.4	2.6	2.9	2.6	3.0	11.5	40.3	19.5	11.9	7.0	1.4	89.6	23.7	51.1	48.9
16802	UNIVERSITY PARK	78.8	76.1	10.0	10.9	6.2	7.7	3.7	4.1	0.0	0.0	0.0	37.5	58.0	4.6	0.0	0.0	0.0	100.0	21.1	43.7	56.3
16803	STATE COLLEGE	86.8	84.4	3.6	4.0	6.6	8.5	2.7	2.9	4.1	3.8	4.1	16.3	24.5	23.4	16.6	6.5	0.7	85.5	24.4	52.3	47.7
16820	AARONSBURG	99.0	98.7	0.1	0.1	0.7	0.9	0.7	0.7	6.8	7.4	8.6	7.0	5.7	26.4	23.8	12.7	1.6	72.8	37.4	49.4	50.6
16821	ALLPORT	99.4	99.5	0.0	0.0	0.3	0.3	0.6	0.8	6.3	6.3	6.6	6.3	5.0	27.5	26.1	14.3	1.7	76.7	39.7	49.5	50.6
16822	BEECH CREEK	98.8	98.6	0.1	0.1	0.4	0.4	0.7	0.7	4.4	4.9	6.9	6.2	5.5	27.0	28.9	15.0	1.2	80.0	41.9	49.8	50.2
16823	BELLEFONTE	93.5	93.0	4.6	4.9	0.4	0.5	1.2	1.2	5.5	5.5	6.1	5.8	6.6	32.2	25.2	11.6	1.7	79.4	38.4	52.5	47.5
16827	BOALSBURG	95.2	94.3	1.3	1.5	1.8	2.4	1.2	1.3	5.2	6.1	7.9	7.5	4.9	24.5	30.2	12.4	1.2	75.4	41.6	48.4	51.6
16828	CENTRE HALL	98.8	98.6	0.4	0.5	0.2	0.3	0.4	0.5	5.8	6.8	6.8	6.3	4.7	26.4	28.8	13.0	1.4	76.5	40.8	49.2	50.8
16829	CLARENCE	99.2	99.3	0.0	0.0	0.1	0.1	0.4	0.4	6.4	6.4	6.3	5.3	5.9	26.2	27.4	14.4	1.8	77.6	40.7	51.7	48.3
16830	CLEARFIELD	98.6	98.4	0.5	0.6	0.3	0.4	0.4	0.4	5.3	5.4	5.9	6.0	5.5	25.9	26.4	16.6	3.1	79.9	42.2	48.0	52.0
16832	COBURN	98.1	98.1	0.6	0.6	0.8	1.1	0.6	0.4	7.5	7.3	5.9	7.3	5.7	27.8	25.1	10.7	2.7	74.3	37.4	51.1	49.0
16833	CURWENSVILLE	99.1	99.0	0.3	0.3	0.1	0.2	0.3	0.3	5.8	5.7	6.6	5.7	5.6	25.9	27.1	14.7	2.8	78.4	41.5	47.2	52.8
16836	FRENCHVILLE	94.4	93.5	4.2	4.9	0.1	0.2	1.1	1.2	5.7	5.8	6.5	5.9	7.0	32.5	23.4	11.6	1.5	78.7	36.0	53.8	46.2
16837	GLEN RICHEY	99.1	98.8	0.3	0.3	0.6	0.6	0.3	0.3	5.7	6.3	6.6	6.3	6.0	25.0	30.1	12.8	1.5	78.0	40.7	48.5	51.5
16838	GRAMPIAN	99.5	99.4	0.0	0.0	0.1	0.1	0.2	0.3	5.7	6.3	7.2	5.9	5.0	27.3	28.0	13.0	1.6	77.2	40.7	50.9	49.1
16839	GRASSFLAT	99.7	99.7	0.0	0.0	0.1	0.1	0.2	0.3	6.3	7.3	6.8	6.4	4.6	29.2	25.0	12.4	2.1	75.3	38.5	48.9	51.1
16840	HAWK RUN	99.4	99.3	0.1	0.1	0.2	0.2	0.7	0.8	6.2	6.3	6.5	6.3	5.1	27.6	25.9	14.3	1.7	76.7	39.5	49.5	50.5
16841	HOWARD	99.1	99.1	0.1	0.1	0.1	0.1	0.4	0.4	6.2	6.5	6.7	6.0	5.1	28.4	27.2	12.6	1.1	76.9	39.8	51.0	49.0
16844	JULIAN	98.1	97.8	0.3	0.3	0.3	0.4	1.1	1.3	5.8	6.2	6.5	6.5	5.1	29.1	29.2	10.8	0.9	77.5	39.5	51.2	48.8
16845	KARTHAUS	91.9	91.0	6.0	6.7	0.2	0.3	1.7	1.9	5.4	5.5	6.0	4.9	6.9	32.7	23.8	13.2	1.6	80.4	37.2	56.1	43.9
16852	MADISONBURG	98.8	98.3	0.6	0.9	0.0	0.3	0.0	0.3	10.8	9.7	9.1	6.1	5.0	24.3	22.2	11.7	1.2	67.0	32.9	48.0	52.1
16854	MILLHEIM	99.2	99.1	0.1	0.1	0.2	0.2	0.2	0.1	6.8	6.4	6.5	7.0	6.8	27.1	23.8	13.7	1.9	76.1	38.3	48.9	51.1
16858	MORRISDALE	98.5	98.3	0.0	0.0	0.0	0.0	0.2	0.2	5.3	6.1	6.6	5.2	4.9	28.3	31.2	11.4	1.0	78.7	41.2	51.0	49.1
16859	MOSHANNON	99.8	99.8	0.0	0.0	0.0	0.0	0.4	0.6	5.1	5.6	6.2	5.8	5.6	27.8	30.9	11.9	1.2	79.4	41.2	51.7	48.4
16860	MUNSON	99.5	99.5	0.0	0.0	0.2	0.2	0.5	0.7	6.1	5.9	6.3	6.1	5.2	27.2	24.8	15.5	3.0	77.5	40.7	48.2	51.8
16861	NEW MILLPORT	99.7	99.6	0.2	0.2	0.0	0.0	0.2	0.2	5.7	6.0	7.2	5.7	6.0	27.5	27.5	12.9	1.5	77.7	39.9	51.7	48.4
16863	OLANTA	100.0	100.0	0.0	0.0	0.0	0.0	0.0	0.0	5.0	5.0	7.5	5.0	5.0	30.0	25.0	17.5	0.0	82.5	42.0	50.0	50.0
16864	ORVISTON	100.0	100.0	0.0	0.0	0.0	0.0	0.0	0.0	5.1	5.1	5.1	5.1	5.1	25.6	30.8	18.0	0.0	84.6	44.4	48.7	51.3
16865	PENNSYLVANIA FURNACE	96.7	96.0	0.5	0.5	1.8	2.3	0.5	0.5	5.7	7.0	7.8	6.5	4.1	26.7	30.7	11.0	0.7	75.2	40.5	50.1	49.9
16866	PHILIPSBURG	98.9	98.8	0.1	0.1	0.3	0.4	0.2	0.2	5.7	5.8	6.5	5.4	5.3	27.1	25.1	16.1	3.1	78.8	41.1	47.2	52.8
16870	PORT MATILDA	97.6	97.1	0.4	0.4	0.9	1.2	0.8	0.9	6.8	7.6	8.5	7.1	5.5	29.6	26.9	7.1	0.9	72.6	36.8	51.6	48.4
16871	POTTERSDALE	94.6	94.7	4.1	4.0	0.0	0.0	1.4	1.3	4.0	4.0	5.3	5.3	4.0	29.0	32.9	14.5	1.3	82.9	44.2	55.3	44.7
16872	REBERSBURG	98.6	98.4	0.7	0.8	0.2	0.2	0.2	0.3	10.0	9.7	9.1	6.3	5.0	24.9	22.0	11.8	1.3	67.4	33.4	48.2	51.8
16874	SNOW SHOE	99.6	99.5	0.0	0.0	0.2	0.3	0.4	0.4	5.9	6.5	7.2	5.6	5.3	26.5	28.6	12.8	1.7	77.0	40.0	52.0	48.0
16875	SPRING MILLS	99.0	98.9	0.1	0.2	0.5	0.6	0.4	0.5	6.8	7.2	7.2	6.3	5.1	27.3	27.2	11.5	1.5	74.9	39.0	51.0	49.0
16877	WARRIORS MARK	98.7	98.3	0.3	0.3	0.6	0.8	0.4	0.4	7.0	7.3	6.8	6.4	4.6	29.1	27.8	9.8	1.1	74.7	39.0	49.8	50.2
16878	WEST DECATUR	98.9	98.8	0.1	0.1	0.3	0.4	0.1	0.1	5.6	5.7	6.8	7.0	6.4	28.7	26.4	12.5	1.0	77.5	39.0	48.9	51.1
	PENNSYLVANIA	85.4	84.4	10.0	10.3	1.8	2.2	3.2	3.5	5.9	6.1	6.8	6.9	6.7	26.6	25.3	13.3	2.2	77.2	39.1	48.4	51.6
	UNITED STATES	75.1	73.6	12.3	12.5	3.8	4.2	12.5	14.1	6.9	6.7	7.2	7.0	7.3	28.6	23.8	10.8	1.7	75.1	36.0	49.1	50.9

ZIP CODE #	POST OFFICE NAME	2004 Per Capita Income	2004 HH Income Base	2004 HOUSEHOLD INCOME DISTRIBUTION (%) Less than $25,000	$25,000 to $49,999	$50,000 to $99,999	$100,000 to $149,999	$150,000 or More	MEDIAN HOUSEHOLD INCOME 2004	2009	2004 National Centile	2004 State Centile	2004 Home Value Base	2004 HOME VALUE DISTRIBUTION (%) Less than $50,000	$50,000 to $89,999	$90,000 to $174,999	$175,000 to $399,999	$400,000 or More	2004 Median Home Value
16635	DUNCANSVILLE	21026	6067	27.0	34.5	29.9	5.7	3.0	41331	47393	51	50	5011	23.5	23.9	38.4	13.8	0.6	93688
16636	DYSART	18803	302	30.5	34.1	30.8	3.3	1.3	38359	45150	41	37	263	25.5	34.6	32.3	7.2	0.4	78810
16637	EAST FREEDOM	15875	1056	39.2	34.7	22.9	2.8	0.4	31803	36258	17	10	810	25.6	39.0	32.1	3.0	0.4	77573
16639	FALLENTIMBER	14414	623	40.9	36.1	19.6	2.7	0.6	30726	34700	14	7	525	47.4	32.2	15.8	4.0	0.6	53000
16640	FLINTON	16034	270	37.4	37.0	21.9	3.0	0.7	33235	38085	22	14	230	47.0	31.7	16.5	4.4	0.4	53333
16641	GALLITZIN	18307	1134	33.7	35.9	25.8	3.4	1.2	36170	41985	32	26	908	43.4	36.6	16.7	3.0	0.3	55714
16645	GLEN HOPE	11997	56	50.0	32.1	16.1	1.8	0.0	25000	31116	5	2	48	31.3	43.8	20.8	4.2	0.0	68000
16646	HASTINGS	16015	1060	41.0	30.9	24.1	2.9	1.1	31733	36770	17	10	835	40.5	37.7	18.7	3.0	0.1	59138
16647	HESSTON	19973	416	25.2	34.1	31.7	6.7	2.2	43957	50363	59	59	362	11.1	20.4	47.0	19.1	2.5	114474
16648	HOLLIDAYSBURG	26752	5583	22.5	31.4	30.7	9.1	6.3	46352	54599	65	65	4182	7.6	22.5	47.9	18.0	4.0	123629
16650	HOPEWELL	18578	695	33.5	36.7	23.5	4.3	2.0	36201	41343	32	26	568	21.0	26.1	42.6	9.3	1.1	94359
16651	HOUTZDALE	15267	1229	37.8	34.0	23.4	4.5	0.3	33211	38578	22	14	891	25.6	35.6	34.5	3.9	0.5	78934
16652	HUNTINGDON	19634	5721	30.2	31.5	29.4	6.8	2.2	39930	46274	46	44	4128	10.2	26.6	47.8	14.2	1.2	107885
16655	IMLER	19066	877	32.5	33.3	27.3	4.5	2.5	37091	42055	36	30	732	21.5	24.2	44.1	8.9	1.4	95517
16656	IRVONA	14003	450	35.8	40.0	22.0	2.2	0.0	32696	37180	20	12	366	46.7	29.8	19.4	3.8	0.3	53871
16657	JAMES CREEK	22782	241	25.3	33.6	32.8	6.2	2.1	44224	50757	59	60	210	11.0	20.0	47.6	19.5	1.9	114444
16659	LOYSBURG	20583	239	21.8	41.0	29.3	5.9	2.1	41759	48090	52	52	202	12.9	17.8	51.5	15.8	2.0	113636
16661	MADERA	14794	565	45.5	32.7	17.9	2.8	1.1	27437	31544	8	3	479	30.9	43.6	22.3	3.1	0.0	68333
16662	MARTINSBURG	18230	1986	32.7	34.7	26.0	5.1	1.4	36875	42414	35	29	1513	23.3	23.7	44.0	7.5	1.5	93182
16664	NEW ENTERPRISE	19202	690	22.2	39.7	30.1	5.8	2.2	41899	48208	53	53	585	12.0	15.6	54.2	16.2	2.1	116951
16666	OSCEOLA MILLS	19715	1826	34.2	33.7	25.5	4.4	2.2	35622	41020	30	23	1460	30.3	34.1	29.8	5.8	0.0	72542
16667	OSTERBURG	19159	223	33.2	32.3	25.6	5.8	3.1	36935	42777	35	30	184	26.6	17.9	39.7	15.2	0.5	97692
16668	PATTON	17557	1595	38.5	29.8	26.4	4.1	1.1	34145	40131	25	17	1224	38.4	33.3	23.7	4.3	0.3	62703
16669	PETERSBURG	19858	861	25.9	37.5	28.7	6.5	1.4	41432	47264	51	51	700	14.1	24.1	41.0	17.9	2.9	110000
16671	RAMEY	16460	217	37.8	32.7	24.9	3.7	0.9	33344	38530	22	14	185	28.1	38.9	29.2	3.8	0.0	72500
16673	ROARING SPRING	21356	2021	23.8	35.1	33.6	4.7	2.9	43905	50580	58	58	1600	12.3	36.1	41.5	8.8	1.4	91862
16674	ROBERTSDALE	15626	252	37.3	31.8	27.4	3.6	0.0	34252	39086	25	17	207	51.2	26.1	19.3	1.9	1.5	48958
16678	SAXTON	21446	1339	32.4	35.3	25.8	3.9	2.6	34561	39620	26	18	1029	20.5	31.2	41.1	5.8	1.4	88284
16679	SIX MILE RUN	16724	620	37.1	38.2	21.3	2.3	1.1	33020	36917	21	13	492	42.7	32.9	20.9	3.1	0.4	57660
16680	SMITHMILL	17187	535	38.9	32.5	24.5	3.4	0.8	32589	38192	20	12	457	27.1	38.1	31.1	3.7	0.0	73837
16683	SPRUCE CREEK	23000	164	26.8	31.7	31.7	9.2	0.6	42365	47368	54	54	136	13.2	16.9	40.4	23.5	5.9	121739
16685	TODD	16748	367	34.1	32.2	25.9	6.3	1.6	36579	42739	34	28	324	15.7	20.1	46.9	16.7	0.6	111250
16686	TYRONE	18548	4908	34.5	32.5	27.7	3.7	1.7	36752	42701	35	29	3575	20.5	34.1	36.9	7.6	0.9	84954
16689	WATERFALL	17796	258	29.8	34.5	30.6	4.3	0.8	37723	42099	38	34	214	12.6	23.8	44.9	17.3	1.4	106111
16691	WELLS TANNERY	17215	201	35.8	38.8	21.9	3.5	0.0	33433	38358	22	15	171	18.1	25.2	40.4	14.0	2.3	99583
16692	WESTOVER	16050	536	40.5	35.1	21.3	1.9	1.3	30710	35281	14	7	440	43.2	29.1	24.6	3.2	0.0	56522
16693	WILLIAMSBURG	18421	1900	30.2	34.5	28.6	4.5	2.2	38318	43718	40	37	1489	23.1	32.6	31.4	10.5	2.5	83500
16695	WOODBURY	18321	230	26.1	34.8	34.4	3.5	1.3	41417	45834	51	51	194	13.9	17.5	46.9	13.9	7.7	111486
16701	BRADFORD	21612	7519	33.5	30.8	27.9	5.6	2.3	36551	42924	34	28	5258	29.0	34.7	29.0	6.7	0.7	73368
16720	AUSTIN	18127	560	32.3	35.2	28.2	3.6	0.7	36676	42111	34	29	464	20.5	25.7	35.6	17.7	0.7	96667
16724	CROSBY	18447	270	31.1	38.2	23.3	5.6	1.9	37924	44189	39	35	215	40.5	27.9	24.7	7.0	0.0	63000
16726	CYCLONE	21917	131	27.5	35.1	30.5	5.3	1.5	40278	45855	47	46	108	23.2	32.4	38.0	6.5	0.0	82500
16727	DERRICK CITY	19446	121	25.6	33.1	32.2	6.6	2.5	39684	46402	45	43	101	16.8	48.5	28.7	5.0	1.0	79545
16729	DUKE CENTER	19225	346	31.5	33.8	29.5	2.9	2.3	36756	42365	35	29	290	35.5	37.2	24.8	2.4	0.0	62000
16731	ELDRED	18410	1074	32.2	34.2	28.5	4.3	0.8	36620	42396	34	28	846	28.5	35.0	31.1	5.1	0.4	72941
16732	GIFFORD	24936	251	23.9	31.9	33.5	8.8	2.0	45420	52736	62	63	217	22.1	35.5	35.5	6.9	0.0	79773
16734	JAMES CITY	17021	216	37.0	36.1	22.7	2.8	1.4	33880	38326	24	16	183	32.2	33.3	29.5	4.9	0.0	68684
16735	KANE	19700	3004	33.0	32.1	28.2	5.3	1.4	37132	43592	36	31	2259	24.1	38.7	31.8	5.3	0.1	74263
16738	LEWIS RUN	15697	547	28.5	34.6	30.0	4.6	2.4	40397	46511	48	46	449	25.8	35.2	33.0	5.8	0.2	75000
16740	MOUNT JEWETT	20704	199	28.6	35.2	30.2	3.5	2.5	39797	45000	45	43	164	29.9	33.5	31.7	4.9	0.0	72500
16743	PORT ALLEGANY	19709	1762	31.0	30.8	31.2	4.1	2.9	40148	46713	47	45	1341	22.9	37.1	31.9	7.2	0.9	76516
16744	REW	20143	109	26.6	33.0	33.0	6.4	0.9	44539	51924	60	60	95	25.3	36.8	32.6	5.3	0.0	75500
16745	RIXFORD	18902	294	31.0	34.0	30.6	2.7	1.7	37340	44027	37	32	247	34.0	37.7	26.3	2.0	0.0	63400
16746	ROULETTE	16482	646	32.7	42.7	20.9	2.9	0.8	34026	38956	24	16	514	25.9	35.0	30.5	8.0	0.6	73902
16748	SHINGLEHOUSE	16788	1405	35.9	32.9	26.8	2.8	1.7	34970	40588	27	20	1092	24.4	37.5	29.8	7.2	1.2	75283
16749	SMETHPORT	18561	1782	30.5	35.5	27.2	5.4	1.4	38521	44972	41	38	1415	32.4	29.7	31.7	6.1	0.2	73239
16750	TURTLEPOINT	18815	250	31.2	32.4	30.0	4.4	2.0	39209	45850	43	41	199	21.6	35.7	34.2	7.0	1.5	80333
16801	STATE COLLEGE	20460	16748	41.9	23.5	22.0	9.0	3.7	31939	39344	18	10	6365	3.9	5.5	42.6	43.3	4.7	171800
16802	UNIVERSITY PARK	17398	150	43.3	34.0	19.3	3.3	0.0	27692	32274	8	4	0	0.0	0.0	0.0	0.0	0.0	0
16803	STATE COLLEGE	25961	9315	25.7	24.7	30.1	11.8	7.7	49457	61303	71	71	4684	6.2	3.3	41.0	45.8	3.8	174206
16820	AARONSBURG	18054	374	23.3	36.1	30.5	7.2	2.9	43123	52065	56	57	322	8.7	18.9	53.4	16.2	2.8	114103
16821	ALLPORT	14548	136	35.3	40.4	21.3	2.2	0.7	34478	40926	26	18	111	18.9	35.1	41.4	4.5	0.0	86538
16822	BEECH CREEK	19586	839	30.9	34.0	29.6	4.4	1.2	38841	45317	42	40	699	17.7	26.5	46.4	8.4	1.0	96136
16823	BELLEFONTE	21597	9399	23.0	33.9	34.4	7.0	1.8	45044	53753	61	62	6772	13.3	12.4	57.3	16.3	0.8	116808
16827	BOALSBURG	39875	1764	14.9	20.3	36.9	15.0	12.9	66503	82683	89	91	1470	3.3	2.2	36.5	46.5	11.6	189033
16828	CENTRE HALL	27719	1736	23.8	25.9	34.7	10.5	5.2	50291	61837	72	72	1465	13.5	7.6	46.9	26.7	5.3	135417
16829	CLARENCE	21143	283	31.8	32.5	30.4	3.2	2.1	36562	44537	34	28	255	20.4	28.2	44.7	5.1	1.6	91522
16830	CLEARFIELD	19659	6331	39.2	29.3	24.3	5.1	2.0	32822	38376	20	13	4432	23.5	36.6	33.1	6.6	0.2	79667
16832	COBURN	20355	180	22.2	30.6	37.8	8.9	0.6	47771	56265	68	68	152	9.9	19.7	46.1	19.7	4.6	117143
16833	CURWENSVILLE	17527	1703	38.6	29.4	27.7	3.1	1.2	33601	38515	23	15	1229	24.8	32.7	33.0	9.0	0.6	80160
16836	FRENCHVILLE	18967	475	35.2	35.8	23.4	3.6	2.1	34772	39489	27	19	400	27.0	34.5	34.5	3.5	0.5	77059
16837	GLEN RICHEY	22742	139	33.8	21.6	31.7	7.9	5.0	38012	50000	39	35	113	9.7	32.7	35.4	22.1	0.0	103906
16838	GRAMPIAN	17825	1325	30.3	36.8	27.0	4.5	1.4	38250	43957	40	37	1153	25.8	32.1	35.3	6.1	0.8	82458
16839	GRASSFLAT	19189	938	32.4	32.9	28.4	3.8	2.5	38410	44759	41	38	795	21.3	34.1	39.1	4.9	0.6	85278
16840	HAWK RUN	16255	1069	34.6	40.7	22.0	2.2	0.6	35267	40399	29	21	869	19.8	35.3	40.4	4.5	0.0	85637
16841	HOWARD	18960	2142	26.0	33.7	33.9	5.5	1.0	42810	51197	55	56	1803	19.8	21.2	47.5	10.5	1.0	101684
16844	JULIAN	20854	1124	25.0	31.1	33.7	7.2	2.9	45801	54035	63	64	969	14.1	16.4	47.1	19.6	2.8	115983
16845	KARTHAUS	18227	364	33.0	33.5	28.0	3.3	2.2	36454	42245	33	27	315	22.2	34.9	37.1	5.1	0.6	81964
16852	MADISONBURG	15327	119	27.7	39.5	29.4	3.4	0.0	36854	41835	35	29	96	12.5	17.7	53.1	9.4	7.3	111538
16854	MILLHEIM	23519	392	26.3	33.2	31.4	4.9	4.3	42735	52266	55	55	299	8.0	19.1	60.2	11.7	1.0	111433
16858	MORRISDALE	18453	625	27.2	33.0	35.0	4.2	0.6	41931	47877	53	53	555	16.9	27.2	45.4	10.5	0.0	96771
16859	MOSHANNON	17733	196	36.2	30.6	27.6	4.6	1.0	35685	43132	30	24	161	26.1	35.4	32.3	5.0	1.2	81591
16860	MUNSON	15919	164	32.9	39.6	24.4	3.1	0.0	36385	42525	33	27	134	25.4	32.8	38.1	3.7	0.0	82143
16861	NEW MILLPORT	15739	283	38.5	39.9	17.7	3.2	0.7	31388	35362	16	9	226	46.0	25.7	22.6	5.3	0.4	55625
16863	OLANTA	18244	20	40.0	40.0	20.0	0.0	0.0	30000	33586	12	6	16	50.0	25.0	25.0	0.0	0.0	50000
16864	ORVISTON	16388	15	40.0	33.3	26.7	0.0	0.0	32320	45000	19	11	12	25.0	33.3	33.3	8.3	0.0	80000
16865	PENNSYLVANIA FURNACE	29881	841	9.3	20.9	45.5	19.7	4.5	71611	87792	92	93	746	2.8	3.4	57.2	32.3	4.3	155315
16866	PHILIPSBURG	18838	3425	34.4	34.0	25.5	5.4	0.7	35560	42607	30	23	2481	27.7	28.0	36.7	7.3	0.3	82433
16870	PORT MATILDA	28262	2090	14.7	24.7	37.4	15.0	8.1	60179	74259	85	86	1777	5.8	11.0	39.5	38.2	5.5	158980
16871	POTTERSDALE	19587	35	31.4	37.1	28.6	2.9	0.0	35730	36502	30	24	29	27.6	37.9	31.0	3.5	0.0	75000
16872	REBERSBURG	14913	413	28.6	39.5	27.6	3.9	0.5	36225	42183	32	26	335	12.2	16.7	54.9	9.9	6.3	111510
16874	SNOW SHOE	20283	543	26.7	34.1	31.1	6.6	1.5	42441	51738	54	55	461	15.4	29.7	48.8	5.4	0.7	94327
16875	SPRING MILLS	22186	1206	20.8	31.7	35.3	9.5	2.7	48191	58104	69	68	1015	11.9	14.9	43.4	24.1	5.7	123643
16877	WARRIORS MARK	24324	900	19.4	28.1	36.8	10.9	4.8	51905	60696	75	75	764	6.0	10.1	46.7	32.2	5.0	151887
16878	WEST DECATUR	16801	890	33.9	37.4	24.0	4.3	0.3	34771	39699	27	19	776	32.1	33.6	28.1	5.3	0.9	70508
	PENNSYLVANIA	25764		25.8	27.2	31.2	10.2	5.7	46988	57000				11.9	18.4	40.7	25.1	4.1	123516
	UNITED STATES	25866		24.7	27.1	30.8	10.9	6.5	48124	56710				10.9	15.0	33.7	30.1	10.4	145905

ZIP CODE #	POST OFFICE NAME	FINANCIAL SERVICES: Auto Loan	Home Loan	Investments	Retirement Plans	THE HOME: Home Improvements: Home Repair	Lawn & Garden	Furnishings: Computers & Hardware	Major Appliances	TV, Radio, Sound Equipment	Furniture	ENTERTAINMENT: Dine out/ Carry out	Sports Equipment	Fees & Tickets	Toys & Games	Travel	Cable TV	PERSONAL: Apparel & Services	Auto Repairs	Health Insurance	Pets & Supplies
16635	DUNCANSVILLE	79	75	66	71	77	84	71	76	74	71	91	87	71	92	73	76	87	75	81	91
16636	DYSART	76	63	45	59	67	75	62	69	67	61	81	80	58	80	63	70	75	68	78	87
16637	EAST FREEDOM	63	50	35	45	54	61	49	56	55	48	66	65	46	66	50	59	62	55	65	72
16639	FALLENTIMBER	69	47	21	40	53	61	45	56	54	46	63	67	38	60	46	58	58	55	69	79
16640	FLINTON	72	49	24	43	55	64	48	59	57	48	67	70	41	64	48	61	61	58	72	82
16641	GALLITZIN	67	61	52	56	64	71	59	64	64	58	78	73	59	81	61	67	74	63	72	78
16645	GLEN HOPE	60	40	18	35	46	52	39	49	47	40	55	58	33	52	40	51	50	48	60	69
16646	HASTINGS	58	52	45	50	55	63	55	57	59	52	71	64	53	71	55	61	66	56	65	66
16647	HESSTON	86	68	46	61	76	86	64	77	72	63	86	90	57	85	68	77	80	76	91	105
16648	HOLLIDAYSBURG	92	92	89	88	94	103	89	93	92	88	113	106	90	114	92	94	108	92	98	107
16650	HOPEWELL	86	57	26	49	65	75	55	69	67	56	78	83	47	74	56	72	71	68	85	98
16651	HOUTZDALE	38	32	25	29	34	38	31	35	35	31	42	40	30	43	32	37	39	34	40	44
16652	HUNTINGDON	74	67	61	64	70	78	68	72	72	66	88	83	66	88	69	74	83	72	78	86
16655	IMLER	91	61	27	52	69	79	58	73	71	60	83	87	50	78	59	76	75	72	90	104
16656	IRVONA	71	48	22	41	54	62	46	58	56	47	65	69	39	62	47	60	59	57	71	82
16657	JAMES CREEK	86	67	46	61	76	85	64	77	72	63	85	90	57	84	68	77	79	76	91	105
16659	LOYSBURG	88	78	59	74	82	88	72	80	77	72	93	95	71	95	74	79	89	78	87	103
16661	MADERA	68	46	21	39	52	59	44	55	53	45	62	66	38	59	45	57	57	54	68	78
16662	MARTINSBURG	72	58	40	56	62	71	60	66	66	58	78	76	55	76	60	68	73	66	76	81
16664	NEW ENTERPRISE	86	77	58	73	81	87	71	79	75	71	92	94	69	94	73	77	87	77	85	102
16666	OSCEOLA MILLS	78	61	42	55	66	75	59	68	68	59	81	80	55	81	61	72	75	67	80	90
16667	OSTERBURG	92	61	28	53	69	80	59	74	71	60	84	88	50	79	60	77	76	73	91	105
16668	PATTON	66	56	43	53	59	68	58	62	63	55	75	71	54	74	58	66	70	61	71	75
16669	PETERSBURG	82	67	48	65	72	80	66	74	72	65	86	86	62	86	67	74	81	73	82	93
16671	RAMEY	66	49	33	47	54	65	55	60	61	52	72	67	49	68	54	65	66	60	72	73
16673	ROARING SPRING	75	74	67	70	76	83	70	74	74	69	91	85	72	95	73	76	87	72	80	88
16674	ROBERTSDALE	74	50	22	43	56	65	48	60	58	49	68	71	41	64	49	62	62	59	74	85
16678	SAXTON	80	68	52	64	72	81	67	74	74	66	89	85	65	90	68	77	84	73	83	91
16679	SIX MILE RUN	80	53	24	46	61	70	52	65	62	53	73	77	44	69	52	67	66	64	80	92
16680	SMITHMILL	66	49	32	47	54	65	55	60	61	52	72	67	49	68	54	65	66	60	72	73
16683	SPRUCE CREEK	84	70	49	67	76	82	66	75	72	66	86	90	62	87	68	74	81	74	84	99
16685	TODD	77	61	41	55	68	77	57	69	65	57	77	81	51	76	61	69	71	68	81	94
16686	TYRONE	68	58	49	54	61	69	58	63	64	57	77	73	56	78	59	67	73	62	71	78
16689	WATERFALL	83	55	25	48	63	72	53	67	64	54	76	80	45	71	54	69	69	66	82	95
16691	WELLS TANNERY	74	50	22	43	56	65	48	60	58	49	68	72	41	64	49	62	62	59	74	85
16692	WESTOVER	79	53	24	46	60	69	51	64	62	52	72	76	43	68	52	66	66	63	79	91
16693	WILLIAMSBURG	75	65	49	60	69	76	62	69	68	61	82	80	60	83	63	71	77	67	77	88
16695	WOODBURY	90	63	33	60	74	82	62	77	72	62	84	93	53	83	65	75	77	76	92	107
16701	BRADFORD	70	69	71	67	70	77	71	71	73	69	90	81	71	91	71	74	86	71	74	80
16720	AUSTIN	73	58	39	52	65	73	54	65	61	54	73	77	48	72	58	66	68	64	77	89
16724	CROSBY	82	57	30	51	64	75	58	69	68	58	80	81	50	76	58	73	73	69	85	93
16726	CYCLONE	81	65	47	63	70	79	67	73	73	66	87	85	62	86	66	75	81	72	82	91
16727	DERRICK CITY	65	69	71	65	70	78	68	68	71	66	88	76	71	94	70	73	84	67	74	77
16729	DUKE CENTER	89	60	27	52	68	78	58	72	70	59	82	86	49	78	59	75	75	72	89	103
16731	ELDRED	68	58	46	55	62	70	58	63	64	57	77	73	56	78	59	66	72	62	72	78
16732	GIFFORD	100	79	50	72	86	95	74	87	83	75	100	103	69	99	76	87	93	85	100	117
16734	JAMES CITY	68	54	37	48	60	68	51	61	57	50	68	71	45	67	54	61	63	60	72	83
16735	KANE	62	62	60	58	64	72	61	63	64	59	79	71	62	84	63	67	75	62	69	74
16738	LEWIS RUN	94	68	38	60	77	87	65	80	76	66	90	94	57	87	67	82	83	79	96	111
16740	MOUNT JEWETT	82	64	44	58	72	81	60	73	68	60	81	85	54	80	64	73	75	72	86	99
16743	PORT ALLEGANY	85	63	37	58	69	79	62	73	71	62	85	86	56	82	63	75	78	72	86	97
16744	REW	88	69	44	63	75	83	65	76	73	66	88	91	60	87	67	77	82	75	88	103
16745	RIXFORD	88	60	28	52	68	77	58	72	69	59	81	85	49	77	59	74	74	71	87	101
16746	ROULETTE	75	51	24	44	58	66	49	61	59	50	69	73	42	66	50	63	63	60	75	86
16748	SHINGLEHOUSE	72	54	36	51	61	70	55	64	62	54	74	74	49	71	57	66	68	64	76	84
16749	SMETHPORT	77	59	38	56	64	74	61	68	68	59	81	79	55	78	61	71	74	68	80	87
16750	TURTLEPOINT	90	60	27	52	68	79	58	73	70	59	83	87	50	78	59	76	75	72	90	104
16801	STATE COLLEGE	69	58	70	62	57	63	80	66	76	72	96	86	72	91	70	70	92	74	61	74
16802	UNIVERSITY PARK	48	29	37	33	29	35	57	42	55	48	69	58	46	62	45	48	65	51	39	47
16803	STATE COLLEGE	92	84	104	90	82	88	104	91	100	97	126	114	98	122	95	93	122	98	83	101
16820	AARONSBURG	96	67	35	63	78	87	66	82	76	65	89	98	56	87	68	80	81	80	97	113
16821	ALLPORT	73	49	22	42	56	64	47	59	57	48	67	71	40	63	48	62	61	59	73	84
16822	BEECH CREEK	76	64	50	58	70	78	62	70	68	61	82	81	58	83	65	72	77	69	81	90
16823	BELLEFONTE	76	74	69	72	75	81	73	75	75	72	92	87	73	94	73	75	89	74	77	87
16827	BOALSBURG	134	162	181	161	160	164	149	148	141	149	177	171	158	184	153	138	176	145	138	162
16828	CENTRE HALL	97	99	92	95	101	107	92	96	93	91	114	112	94	118	95	94	111	94	99	115
16829	CLARENCE	101	68	31	58	77	88	65	82	79	67	93	98	56	87	66	85	84	81	101	116
16830	CLEARFIELD	63	59	56	56	61	69	60	62	64	58	78	71	59	79	61	66	74	62	69	73
16832	COBURN	85	75	56	71	79	85	69	77	74	69	90	92	67	91	71	76	85	75	84	100
16833	CURWENSVILLE	64	54	43	50	57	66	55	59	60	53	72	68	52	73	56	63	68	59	69	73
16836	FRENCHVILLE	80	63	43	57	71	80	59	71	67	59	80	84	53	78	63	72	74	70	84	98
16837	GLEN RICHEY	88	78	60	74	83	89	72	80	77	72	94	96	71	96	75	79	89	78	87	104
16838	GRAMPIAN	82	60	33	53	66	74	57	68	66	57	78	81	51	75	58	70	72	67	81	94
16839	GRASSFLAT	76	64	48	58	68	77	62	69	70	61	84	80	60	85	64	74	79	68	80	88
16840	HAWK RUN	73	49	22	42	56	64	47	59	57	48	67	71	40	64	48	62	61	59	73	84
16841	HOWARD	79	69	52	64	72	78	64	72	69	65	84	85	62	83	66	71	79	70	78	92
16844	JULIAN	87	77	59	73	82	87	71	79	76	71	92	94	70	94	73	78	88	77	86	102
16845	KARTHAUS	93	69	41	61	77	88	65	80	75	65	89	94	57	87	68	81	82	79	96	110
16852	MADISONBURG	68	58	45	58	61	69	60	64	63	59	77	73	57	76	59	64	72	63	69	75
16854	MILLHEIM	78	77	73	73	80	89	76	78	80	73	98	89	77	104	78	83	94	77	86	91
16858	MORRISDALE	77	68	52	65	72	78	63	70	67	63	82	84	62	84	65	69	78	68	76	91
16859	MOSHANNON	83	55	25	48	63	72	53	67	65	55	76	80	46	72	54	70	69	66	82	95
16860	MUNSON	71	53	32	46	58	66	51	60	59	51	70	71	46	69	52	63	65	60	72	81
16861	NEW MILLPORT	70	47	21	40	53	61	45	57	55	46	64	68	38	61	46	59	58	56	70	80
16863	OLANTA	69	46	21	40	52	60	44	56	54	45	63	66	38	59	45	58	57	55	68	79
16864	ORVISTON	80	54	24	46	61	70	52	65	63	53	73	77	44	69	53	67	67	64	80	92
16865	PENNSYLVANIA FURNACE	105	123	129	124	122	123	111	112	105	112	132	132	117	138	114	103	131	109	104	127
16866	PHILIPSBURG	64	57	53	54	60	68	58	61	63	57	76	70	57	77	60	66	72	61	69	74
16870	PORT MATILDA	114	119	112	121	119	122	110	113	107	112	134	132	113	135	110	105	130	110	108	131
16871	POTTERSDALE	69	54	37	49	61	68	51	61	58	51	68	72	46	67	54	62	64	60	73	84
16872	REBERSBURG	68	58	45	58	61	68	60	64	63	58	77	73	57	76	59	64	72	63	69	75
16874	SNOW SHOE	89	68	43	64	74	84	68	78	76	68	91	91	62	88	68	80	84	77	90	100
16875	SPRING MILLS	94	86	68	82	90	96	79	87	83	79	102	104	79	104	82	85	97	85	93	111
16877	WARRIORS MARK	101	94	77	92	98	103	87	94	89	87	109	112	86	111	89	90	105	92	98	118
16878	WEST DECATUR	78	52	24	45	59	68	50	63	61	51	71	75	43	67	51	65	65	62	77	89
	PENNSYLVANIA	89	89	93	87	90	98	89	90	91	88	112	104	89	114	90	92	109	90	92	104
	UNITED STATES	100	100	100	100	100	100	100	100	100	100	100	100	100	100	100	100	100	100	100	100

#	POST OFFICE NAME	COUNTY FIPS CODE	POPULATION			2000-2004 ANNUAL RATE		HOUSEHOLDS					FAMILIES		
			2000	2004	2009	% Rate	State Centile	2000	2004	2009	% Annual Rate 2000-2004	2004 Average HH Size	2000	2004	% Annual Rate 2000-2004
16879	WINBURNE	033	308	312	319	0.3	54	112	116	121	0.8	2.68	84	86	0.6
16881	WOODLAND	033	3300	3387	3488	0.6	68	1202	1258	1321	1.1	2.69	961	1000	0.9
16882	WOODWARD	027	216	217	223	0.1	44	93	95	100	0.5	2.28	70	71	0.3
16901	WELLSBORO	117	9898	10131	10285	0.6	66	3957	4139	4271	1.1	2.36	2719	2820	0.9
16912	BLOSSBURG	117	1995	1971	1973	-0.3	26	848	857	871	0.3	2.26	543	544	0.0
16914	COLUMBIA CROSS ROADS	015	2542	2570	2596	0.3	52	929	960	989	0.8	2.67	741	762	0.7
16915	COUDERSPORT	105	5864	6440	7195	2.2	94	2271	2552	2914	2.8	2.44	1594	1779	2.6
16917	COVINGTON	117	1478	1510	1531	0.5	65	578	601	618	0.9	2.51	415	429	0.8
16920	ELKLAND	117	1809	1800	1803	-0.1	33	762	772	783	0.3	2.33	499	502	0.1
16921	GAINES	117	502	498	499	-0.2	30	228	231	236	0.3	2.16	154	155	0.2
16922	GALETON	105	2210	2355	2591	1.5	89	873	945	1058	1.9	2.43	616	664	1.8
16923	GENESEE	105	1414	1522	1685	1.8	91	538	590	664	2.2	2.58	390	425	2.0
16925	GILLETT	015	4516	4602	4671	0.4	61	1703	1784	1855	1.1	2.55	1286	1339	1.0
16926	GRANVILLE SUMMIT	015	1492	1519	1541	0.4	60	546	569	590	1.0	2.67	431	446	0.8
16927	HARRISON VALLEY	105	1371	1455	1598	1.4	87	492	533	597	1.9	2.68	365	393	1.8
16928	KNOXVILLE	117	900	936	958	0.9	77	352	372	386	1.3	2.51	252	265	1.2
16929	LAWRENCEVILLE	117	2258	2345	2396	0.9	76	887	940	978	1.4	2.48	656	691	1.2
16930	LIBERTY	117	1121	1123	1126	0.0	41	419	431	441	0.7	2.60	308	316	0.6
16932	MAINESBURG	117	933	937	940	0.1	44	348	357	364	0.6	2.58	279	286	0.6
16933	MANSFIELD	117	7685	7793	7865	0.3	56	2584	2682	2752	0.9	2.41	1683	1735	0.7
16935	MIDDLEBURY CENTER	117	2566	2579	2589	0.1	45	964	993	1013	0.7	2.60	723	741	0.6
16936	MILLERTON	117	2060	2066	2072	0.1	43	779	801	818	0.7	2.52	601	616	0.6
16937	MILLS	105	126	133	145	1.3	85	45	49	54	2.0	2.63	33	36	2.1
16938	MORRIS	117	678	671	671	-0.2	27	275	279	284	0.3	2.37	199	200	0.1
16939	MORRIS RUN	117	462	472	478	0.5	65	176	184	189	1.1	2.51	120	124	0.8
16940	NELSON	117	563	569	573	0.3	51	222	230	235	0.8	2.47	169	174	0.7
16941	GENESEE	105	99	107	119	1.9	92	34	37	42	2.0	2.89	25	28	2.7
16942	OSCEOLA	117	544	545	546	0.0	41	211	216	220	0.6	2.52	152	154	0.3
16943	SABINSVILLE	117	554	555	556	0.0	41	218	224	229	0.6	2.48	164	168	0.6
16946	TIOGA	117	1772	1775	1780	0.0	41	682	696	707	0.5	2.54	481	488	0.3
16947	TROY	015	3930	3932	3959	0.0	39	1403	1429	1467	0.4	2.53	928	937	0.2
16948	ULYSSES	105	1603	1740	1935	2.0	92	595	656	742	2.3	2.65	458	502	2.2
16950	WESTFIELD	117	2738	2781	2818	0.4	58	1110	1150	1184	0.8	2.40	809	834	0.7
17002	ALLENSVILLE	061	1019	1011	1011	-0.2	30	319	322	327	0.2	3.14	260	261	0.1
17003	ANNVILLE	075	11278	11526	11850	0.5	65	3923	4111	4322	1.1	2.51	2831	2948	1.0
17004	BELLEVILLE	087	4562	4585	4598	0.1	45	1507	1545	1577	0.6	2.86	1148	1171	0.5
17005	BERRYSBURG	043	294	320	335	2.0	93	121	135	144	2.6	2.36	93	102	2.2
17006	BLAIN	099	777	793	822	0.5	62	278	290	307	1.0	2.73	207	214	0.8
17007	BOILING SPRINGS	041	5230	5369	5533	0.6	69	1928	2030	2136	1.2	2.63	1572	1644	1.1
17009	BURNHAM	087	1920	1877	1864	-0.5	14	815	809	816	-0.2	2.32	537	529	-0.4
17011	CAMP HILL	041	33839	34061	34988	0.2	46	13379	13771	14472	0.7	2.19	8581	8719	0.4
17013	CARLISLE	041	52036	53361	55586	0.6	68	20430	21409	22693	1.1	2.33	13711	14284	1.0
17014	COCOLAMUS	067	1021	1033	1058	0.3	53	360	370	385	0.7	2.77	291	298	0.6
17017	DALMATIA	097	1869	1858	1857	-0.1	32	743	756	771	0.4	2.46	567	573	0.3
17018	DAUPHIN	043	4017	4068	4104	0.3	54	1581	1639	1685	0.9	2.48	1204	1239	0.7
17019	DILLSBURG	133	15245	16023	16871	1.2	83	5768	6162	6587	1.6	2.59	4439	4710	1.4
17020	DUNCANNON	099	9160	9468	9883	0.8	73	3526	3726	3974	1.3	2.50	2533	2659	1.2
17021	EAST WATERFORD	067	965	976	1000	0.3	53	382	393	409	0.7	2.48	288	295	0.6
17022	ELIZABETHTOWN	071	27116	28354	29546	1.1	81	9993	10668	11330	1.6	2.46	7108	7570	1.5
17023	ELIZABETHVILLE	043	3179	3182	3210	0.0	40	1231	1259	1292	0.5	2.49	872	885	0.4
17024	ELLIOTTSBURG	099	2203	2272	2369	0.7	72	822	867	924	1.3	2.61	624	655	1.2
17025	ENOLA	041	15133	15953	16736	1.3	84	6210	6693	7162	1.8	2.35	4197	4483	1.6
17026	FREDERICKSBURG	075	2759	2861	2961	0.9	75	994	1047	1101	1.2	2.73	757	792	1.1
17028	GRANTVILLE	043	3274	3425	3523	1.1	81	1253	1336	1396	1.5	2.49	954	1010	1.4
17029	GRANVILLE	087	526	520	517	-0.3	26	186	188	190	0.3	2.59	146	146	0.0
17030	GRATZ	043	731	703	700	-0.9	6	285	280	284	-0.4	2.51	210	204	-0.7
17032	HALIFAX	043	7796	8102	8302	0.9	77	2980	3171	3311	1.5	2.55	2304	2435	1.3
17033	HERSHEY	043	15180	15302	15504	0.2	48	6383	6506	6674	0.5	2.28	4028	4080	0.3
17034	HIGHSPIRE	043	2412	2399	2406	-0.1	33	1111	1131	1156	0.4	2.12	609	611	0.1
17035	HONEY GROVE	067	942	966	996	0.6	68	354	370	388	1.1	2.61	267	278	1.0
17036	HUMMELSTOWN	043	18687	19045	19343	0.5	62	7222	7492	7731	0.9	2.50	5173	5310	0.6
17037	ICKESBURG	099	1207	1254	1312	0.9	77	433	460	492	1.4	2.71	332	351	1.3
17038	JONESTOWN	075	5857	6140	6434	1.1	82	2238	2395	2554	1.6	2.56	1652	1753	1.4
17040	LANDISBURG	099	2294	2360	2458	0.7	70	871	916	975	1.2	2.58	688	720	1.1
17042	LEBANON	075	35125	35959	37066	0.6	66	13714	14302	15017	1.0	2.36	9479	9812	0.8
17043	LEMOYNE	041	5689	5627	5747	-0.3	27	2771	2797	2910	0.2	2.01	1431	1417	-0.2
17044	LEWISTOWN	087	21123	21017	21034	-0.1	33	8973	9086	9243	0.3	2.27	5845	5867	0.1
17045	LIVERPOOL	099	3832	3928	4071	0.6	68	1435	1504	1593	1.1	2.54	1055	1100	1.0
17046	LEBANON	075	29287	29910	30795	0.5	64	11488	11924	12476	0.9	2.50	7913	8169	0.8
17047	LOYSVILLE	099	2228	2303	2402	0.8	73	772	817	872	1.3	2.69	595	627	1.2
17048	LYKENS	043	4451	4312	4305	-0.7	8	1795	1770	1793	-0.3	2.44	1239	1211	-0.5
17049	MC ALISTERVILLE	067	3158	3200	3281	0.3	54	1202	1235	1284	0.6	2.57	931	952	0.5
17050	MECHANICSBURG	041	26597	28444	30027	1.6	89	10177	11161	12044	2.2	2.52	7557	8231	2.0
17051	MC VEYTOWN	087	5051	5157	5231	0.5	63	1932	2016	2085	1.0	2.54	1447	1502	0.9
17052	MAPLETON DEPOT	061	1270	1301	1331	0.6	67	499	524	549	1.2	2.48	373	389	1.0
17053	MARYSVILLE	099	4548	4651	4827	0.5	65	1857	1941	2057	1.1	2.39	1299	1348	0.9
17055	MECHANICSBURG	041	32973	34117	35470	0.8	74	12456	13203	14040	1.4	2.34	8383	8818	1.2
17057	MIDDLETOWN	043	21918	22041	22238	0.1	45	8860	9079	9315	0.6	2.34	5856	5951	0.4
17058	MIFFLIN	067	1671	1755	1832	1.2	83	675	721	765	1.6	2.36	491	522	1.5
17059	MIFFLINTOWN	067	6178	6485	6782	1.2	83	2330	2491	2648	1.6	2.53	1718	1827	1.5
17060	MILL CREEK	061	982	981	990	0.0	37	362	369	380	0.5	2.66	281	285	0.3
17061	MILLERSBURG	043	6812	6868	6968	0.2	48	2762	2838	2932	0.6	2.35	1862	1904	0.5
17062	MILLERSTOWN	099	1689	1738	1810	0.7	70	656	689	732	1.2	2.52	493	515	1.0
17063	MILROY	087	3543	3487	3465	-0.4	22	1381	1385	1399	0.1	2.52	1006	1001	-0.1
17065	MOUNT HOLLY SPRINGS	041	3556	3664	3787	0.7	71	1446	1524	1606	1.2	2.38	1050	1096	1.0
17066	MOUNT UNION	061	5049	5223	5355	0.8	74	2212	2338	2447	1.3	2.22	1436	1511	1.2
17067	MYERSTOWN	075	13921	14520	15097	1.0	79	5133	5478	5803	1.5	2.59	3819	4050	1.4
17068	NEW BLOOMFIELD	099	3632	3741	3893	0.7	71	1365	1444	1540	1.3	2.46	1006	1058	1.2
17070	NEW CUMBERLAND	133	14872	15420	16147	0.9	75	6481	6851	7295	1.3	2.24	4209	4406	1.1
17071	NEW GERMANTOWN	099	494	504	523	0.5	62	195	203	215	0.8	2.48	145	150	0.8
17073	NEWMANSTOWN	075	3870	3954	4054	0.5	65	1432	1492	1557	1.0	2.64	1064	1101	0.8
17074	NEWPORT	099	7346	7448	7716	0.3	55	2887	2990	3164	0.8	2.48	2105	2167	0.7
17076	OAKLAND MILLS	067	490	498	511	0.4	58	163	168	175	0.7	2.88	119	122	0.6
17078	PALMYRA	075	18721	19286	19923	0.7	71	7801	8166	8574	1.1	2.32	5381	5603	1.0
17080	PILLOW	043	304	331	347	2.0	93	131	146	156	2.6	2.25	100	111	2.5
	PENNSYLVANIA					0.3					0.7	2.44			0.6
	UNITED STATES					1.2					1.3	2.58			1.1

ZIP CODE #	POST OFFICE NAME	RACE (%) White 2000	White 2004	Black 2000	Black 2004	Asian/Pacific 2000	Asian/Pacific 2004	% Hispanic Origin 2000	% Hispanic Origin 2004	2004 AGE DISTRIBUTION (%) 0-4	5-9	10-14	15-19	20-24	25-44	45-64	65-84	85+	18+	MEDIAN AGE 2004	% 2004 Males	% 2004 Females
16879	WINBURNE	99.7	99.7	0.0	0.0	0.3	0.3	0.3	0.6	7.1	7.1	7.4	6.7	5.5	26.6	24.0	13.1	2.6	73.7	38.7	49.4	50.6
16881	WOODLAND	98.9	98.7	0.2	0.2	0.1	0.2	0.2	0.3	6.1	6.3	7.4	6.8	6.7	27.0	27.2	11.6	0.9	76.0	38.2	50.0	50.0
16882	WOODWARD	99.1	99.1	0.0	0.0	0.9	0.9	0.9	0.5	6.9	7.4	8.3	6.9	5.5	24.9	25.8	12.9	1.4	72.8	38.4	50.7	49.3
16901	WELLSBORO	98.3	98.0	0.3	0.4	0.6	0.7	0.6	0.7	5.2	5.5	6.5	6.4	6.0	23.1	28.0	16.1	3.2	78.5	43.1	48.1	51.9
16912	BLOSSBURG	99.3	99.3	0.2	0.2	0.1	0.1	0.4	0.4	6.1	6.1	5.8	7.7	5.8	23.1	26.1	16.6	2.7	77.0	41.2	48.3	51.7
16914	COLUMBIA CROSS ROADS	98.8	98.8	0.1	0.1	0.1	0.1	0.2	0.2	6.0	6.2	7.6	7.0	5.5	25.1	27.2	13.7	1.6	75.5	40.8	49.5	50.5
16915	COUDERSPORT	97.3	96.9	0.4	0.5	1.1	1.4	0.5	0.6	5.6	6.2	7.3	6.4	5.2	24.4	27.8	14.2	3.0	76.7	41.3	49.6	50.4
16917	COVINGTON	98.0	97.9	0.1	0.1	0.2	0.3	0.5	0.7	6.2	6.4	7.6	6.2	5.8	27.7	26.0	12.8	1.3	75.9	38.8	49.3	50.7
16920	ELKLAND	98.3	98.2	0.9	1.1	0.0	0.0	0.8	0.9	6.1	5.9	6.9	6.8	5.7	25.7	23.3	16.4	3.1	76.9	40.1	47.9	52.1
16921	GAINES	98.2	98.4	0.2	0.2	0.0	0.0	0.0	0.0	4.2	4.8	5.8	5.4	5.4	22.7	31.5	18.3	1.8	81.5	46.2	50.0	50.0
16922	GALETON	97.8	97.5	0.6	0.6	0.5	0.7	0.5	0.6	5.7	5.4	5.9	6.4	5.6	23.0	27.2	17.6	3.3	79.1	43.8	48.1	51.9
16923	GENESEE	98.4	98.2	0.5	0.6	0.0	0.1	0.4	0.4	6.2	6.5	7.0	7.2	5.7	23.7	27.8	14.1	1.8	75.8	40.5	50.9	49.1
16925	GILLETT	98.7	98.5	0.4	0.5	0.1	0.1	0.6	0.6	6.3	6.4	7.3	7.2	5.4	25.2	27.8	13.1	1.5	75.2	40.0	50.0	50.0
16926	GRANVILLE SUMMIT	98.5	98.4	0.4	0.5	0.1	0.1	0.6	0.6	5.7	6.6	8.6	7.2	5.6	25.1	29.0	10.9	1.3	74.6	39.1	52.1	47.9
16927	HARRISON VALLEY	98.5	98.5	0.2	0.1	0.1	0.1	0.5	0.6	6.7	6.9	8.0	8.5	7.0	25.8	24.3	12.2	0.7	72.7	36.4	50.0	50.0
16928	KNOXVILLE	99.4	99.5	0.2	0.2	0.0	0.0	0.3	0.4	6.5	6.7	7.5	7.1	6.2	25.1	23.0	15.4	2.6	74.9	38.4	50.5	49.5
16929	LAWRENCEVILLE	99.3	99.1	0.2	0.3	0.1	0.1	0.4	0.4	6.4	6.6	7.6	6.6	5.7	27.0	25.1	13.7	1.3	75.1	38.6	49.6	50.4
16930	LIBERTY	99.5	99.5	0.0	0.0	0.0	0.0	0.3	0.3	6.1	6.2	5.9	6.7	6.1	24.0	28.4	15.0	1.8	77.7	41.6	51.0	49.0
16932	MAINESBURG	97.9	97.3	0.2	0.2	0.3	0.4	0.3	0.5	6.2	6.8	7.4	6.1	4.9	26.3	28.2	12.9	1.3	75.7	40.4	50.2	49.8
16933	MANSFIELD	95.9	95.4	2.0	2.2	0.6	0.7	0.8	0.8	4.7	4.7	5.4	12.6	17.4	21.6	21.8	10.5	1.3	81.7	29.3	48.5	51.5
16935	MIDDLEBURY CENTER	98.6	98.5	0.1	0.2	0.1	0.2	0.6	0.7	5.5	6.1	7.6	8.0	4.8	25.5	27.9	13.3	1.5	76.0	40.3	50.5	49.5
16936	MILLERTON	98.6	98.5	0.3	0.3	0.1	0.2	0.3	0.3	4.7	5.9	7.8	6.7	5.6	25.6	29.5	12.4	1.7	77.4	41.1	50.3	49.7
16937	MILLS	98.4	99.3	0.0	0.0	0.0	0.0	0.0	0.8	6.0	6.8	8.3	9.0	6.8	26.3	24.1	12.0	0.8	72.2	37.2	48.1	51.9
16938	MORRIS	98.5	98.5	0.2	0.2	0.4	0.5	0.6	0.5	5.4	5.8	6.0	6.4	5.1	23.4	27.3	18.8	1.9	78.8	43.8	51.6	48.4
16939	MORRIS RUN	99.1	98.9	0.0	0.0	0.4	0.4	0.2	0.2	5.7	5.9	6.4	6.4	4.9	26.1	25.2	17.0	2.5	77.3	41.9	49.8	50.2
16940	NELSON	99.1	99.0	0.2	0.2	0.0	0.0	0.2	0.4	5.6	6.2	8.1	6.9	4.9	26.0	27.4	13.7	1.2	75.8	40.0	49.7	50.3
16941	GENESEE	98.0	98.1	0.0	0.0	0.0	0.0	0.0	0.0	10.3	7.5	8.4	7.5	7.5	24.3	22.4	11.2	0.9	68.2	32.9	48.6	51.4
16942	OSCEOLA	97.8	97.6	0.6	0.6	0.2	0.2	0.2	0.2	6.6	6.8	7.0	7.9	7.0	26.4	24.4	11.9	2.0	74.7	37.4	48.4	51.6
16943	SABINSVILLE	98.7	98.7	0.0	0.0	0.2	0.4	0.4	0.4	6.0	6.1	6.1	5.6	5.6	21.8	32.6	14.4	1.8	78.6	44.1	51.5	48.5
16946	TIOGA	99.1	99.2	0.1	0.1	0.1	0.1	0.2	0.2	6.8	6.9	6.9	6.9	6.4	26.1	25.1	13.4	1.6	75.5	38.2	50.8	49.2
16947	TROY	98.7	98.6	0.3	0.3	0.4	0.4	0.5	0.6	5.2	5.7	6.4	6.0	5.8	25.6	27.5	14.5	3.5	79.2	41.8	46.9	53.1
16948	ULYSSES	98.8	98.6	0.1	0.1	0.1	0.2	0.7	0.7	7.0	7.0	7.9	7.2	6.8	23.9	25.5	13.3	1.4	73.7	38.0	50.5	49.5
16950	WESTFIELD	98.4	98.2	0.4	0.5	0.2	0.2	0.5	0.6	5.6	5.4	7.0	7.3	5.5	24.3	26.7	15.9	2.3	77.1	41.7	49.1	50.9
17002	ALLENSVILLE	98.0	97.7	1.1	1.2	0.0	0.1	0.5	0.4	10.5	9.8	9.0	7.9	6.3	25.4	20.2	9.9	1.0	65.9	29.7	49.9	50.2
17003	ANNVILLE	97.0	96.5	0.6	0.7	0.9	1.2	1.5	1.7	5.1	5.2	5.7	9.6	10.4	25.0	25.6	11.5	1.9	80.5	37.1	48.7	51.3
17004	BELLEVILLE	98.8	98.7	0.6	0.7	0.1	0.1	0.3	0.4	8.9	8.6	8.4	6.9	5.7	22.8	20.5	14.7	3.7	69.8	35.9	47.2	52.8
17005	BERRYSBURG	99.0	98.4	0.7	0.9	0.0	0.0	0.0	0.0	7.2	7.2	5.9	5.9	5.6	26.9	26.6	12.8	1.9	75.3	39.6	50.9	49.1
17006	BLAIN	98.6	98.4	0.8	0.9	0.0	0.0	0.1	0.3	6.4	6.4	7.8	7.2	6.2	24.6	24.8	15.0	1.5	74.8	39.2	51.7	48.3
17007	BOILING SPRINGS	98.2	97.8	0.6	0.7	0.7	0.9	0.6	0.7	5.8	6.5	7.0	7.0	4.8	24.6	31.7	11.7	0.9	75.7	41.8	49.5	50.5
17009	BURNHAM	99.3	99.3	0.3	0.3	0.1	0.1	0.4	0.3	4.8	5.2	6.4	6.3	5.5	26.8	28.1	14.6	2.3	79.8	41.7	48.4	51.6
17011	CAMP HILL	89.5	88.1	6.1	6.6	2.8	3.6	2.6	2.8	4.7	5.0	5.6	5.3	6.4	27.7	25.9	16.4	3.0	81.6	42.0	51.7	48.3
17013	CARLISLE	93.5	92.7	3.4	3.8	1.3	1.6	1.4	1.5	5.4	5.5	6.3	6.8	7.2	26.0	26.6	13.7	2.5	79.1	40.4	48.1	51.9
17014	COCOLAMUS	99.5	99.5	0.2	0.2	0.0	0.0	0.2	0.2	7.4	7.5	7.3	6.8	6.9	30.5	22.6	10.2	1.1	73.9	35.0	52.6	47.4
17017	DALMATIA	99.4	99.1	0.4	0.5	0.1	0.1	0.2	0.3	5.3	5.3	5.4	5.9	6.0	28.5	26.9	15.3	1.5	80.4	41.3	51.0	49.0
17018	DAUPHIN	98.4	97.9	0.2	0.3	0.4	0.6	0.6	0.8	4.3	4.8	6.7	6.4	5.0	26.0	32.9	12.7	1.1	80.1	43.2	49.5	50.5
17019	DILLSBURG	98.1	97.6	0.3	0.4	0.6	0.8	0.7	0.9	6.3	6.9	7.9	6.4	4.8	28.8	28.4	9.5	1.1	74.9	39.0	49.8	50.2
17020	DUNCANNON	98.7	98.6	0.3	0.3	0.2	0.2	0.8	0.9	6.0	6.2	7.2	6.5	5.5	28.3	27.6	11.1	1.5	76.3	39.0	49.3	50.8
17021	EAST WATERFORD	99.1	99.0	0.1	0.1	0.1	0.1	0.4	0.4	5.0	5.3	7.5	5.7	6.2	24.5	28.6	15.6	1.6	78.5	41.6	51.3	48.7
17022	ELIZABETHTOWN	97.1	96.5	0.6	0.7	1.0	1.3	1.2	1.4	6.0	6.3	6.8	7.9	7.9	27.4	22.5	11.7	3.6	77.3	37.1	47.8	52.2
17023	ELIZABETHVILLE	98.2	97.8	0.5	0.6	0.4	0.6	0.9	1.1	6.5	6.8	7.2	5.8	5.6	28.1	24.6	13.3	2.2	75.9	38.2	49.9	50.1
17024	ELLIOTTSBURG	98.5	98.2	0.5	0.5	0.2	0.2	0.7	0.8	6.8	7.4	7.9	6.7	5.1	27.7	26.3	10.9	1.2	73.6	37.8	50.0	50.0
17025	ENOLA	96.0	95.3	0.8	0.9	1.3	1.7	1.2	1.4	5.9	6.0	6.7	6.9	6.1	30.5	26.4	10.8	0.9	77.9	38.0	48.1	51.9
17026	FREDERICKSBURG	97.8	97.4	0.3	0.3	0.2	0.2	1.9	2.2	7.2	7.4	7.3	6.2	5.6	29.2	25.2	11.0	1.0	74.3	37.5	51.1	48.9
17028	GRANTVILLE	95.8	94.8	1.0	1.2	0.5	0.6	2.7	3.4	5.8	6.4	7.8	7.0	6.1	29.1	28.4	8.7	0.9	75.6	38.1	50.3	49.8
17029	GRANVILLE	98.7	98.7	0.6	0.6	0.0	0.0	0.2	0.2	7.1	6.9	6.2	6.2	5.2	24.4	25.2	15.6	3.3	76.2	39.9	51.9	48.1
17030	GRATZ	99.2	99.0	0.1	0.3	0.0	0.0	0.4	0.6	7.7	7.3	6.5	6.3	6.8	26.6	22.8	14.7	1.4	75.0	36.9	52.4	47.7
17032	HALIFAX	98.4	98.0	0.2	0.3	0.4	0.5	0.8	1.0	6.1	6.5	6.9	6.2	5.4	27.7	28.8	11.4	1.2	76.7	40.1	50.1	49.9
17033	HERSHEY	92.8	91.1	1.8	2.3	3.6	4.6	1.4	1.7	5.2	5.6	6.8	6.5	5.2	25.2	24.8	17.0	3.7	78.3	42.1	47.4	52.6
17034	HIGHSPIRE	87.7	85.1	7.4	9.0	0.9	1.2	4.7	5.6	6.0	5.7	5.6	5.1	6.0	31.7	25.3	13.0	1.8	79.6	38.7	48.1	51.9
17035	HONEY GROVE	98.8	98.8	0.2	0.2	0.2	0.3	1.0	1.1	6.5	6.3	6.0	6.5	6.4	26.9	26.8	13.4	1.1	77.2	38.8	51.7	48.3
17036	HUMMELSTOWN	94.5	93.1	1.4	1.8	2.3	3.1	1.5	1.8	5.7	6.3	7.6	6.8	5.9	27.2	28.1	10.9	1.5	75.9	39.4	48.6	51.5
17037	ICKESBURG	98.3	98.2	0.7	0.7	0.2	0.2	0.7	0.7	7.3	7.8	7.8	6.7	5.1	27.5	26.6	10.2	0.9	72.7	37.1	51.4	48.6
17038	JONESTOWN	97.9	97.6	0.6	0.7	0.4	0.5	1.0	1.2	5.4	5.8	6.8	6.4	5.4	29.2	28.4	11.7	1.1	78.0	39.8	51.5	48.5
17040	LANDISBURG	98.6	98.4	0.3	0.3	0.1	0.2	0.6	0.7	6.3	6.7	7.1	6.3	5.3	28.1	28.3	10.9	0.9	75.9	39.2	50.4	49.6
17042	LEBANON	94.4	93.6	1.5	1.7	1.3	1.6	4.1	4.7	5.4	5.6	6.2	5.8	5.2	25.3	26.6	16.4	3.6	79.2	42.8	49.0	51.0
17043	LEMOYNE	95.7	95.0	0.8	1.0	1.8	2.2	1.1	1.3	5.8	5.6	6.0	5.7	5.8	31.7	25.4	12.3	1.7	79.2	38.5	47.8	52.2
17044	LEWISTOWN	98.1	97.9	0.6	0.7	0.4	0.5	0.8	0.9	5.8	5.8	6.3	6.0	5.5	26.5	25.7	15.8	2.7	78.3	41.1	47.7	52.3
17045	LIVERPOOL	98.7	98.5	0.4	0.5	0.2	0.3	0.5	0.5	6.0	6.2	7.0	6.3	5.4	27.3	27.6	12.1	2.2	76.9	40.1	49.1	50.9
17046	LEBANON	88.4	87.2	2.4	2.5	1.0	1.3	13.3	14.6	7.3	6.8	7.5	6.7	6.2	27.8	24.8	11.7	1.4	74.2	37.0	48.9	51.1
17047	LOYSVILLE	96.0	95.6	2.2	2.3	0.1	0.3	1.5	1.5	6.4	7.0	7.4	9.8	6.2	25.5	25.4	11.0	1.4	72.3	36.1	52.8	47.2
17048	LYKENS	98.3	97.8	0.3	0.4	0.5	0.6	0.4	0.5	6.3	6.3	6.9	5.9	5.7	26.2	24.6	16.0	2.1	77.0	40.1	49.7	50.4
17049	MC ALISTERVILLE	98.8	98.5	0.4	0.4	0.3	0.4	0.7	0.9	7.4	7.5	7.5	6.3	5.4	26.7	24.8	12.8	1.6	73.7	37.8	50.2	49.8
17050	MECHANICSBURG	94.3	93.1	0.8	0.9	3.5	4.4	1.1	1.2	5.9	6.6	7.3	6.4	4.6	25.9	29.8	11.8	1.7	76.0	41.2	48.7	51.3
17051	MC VEYTOWN	99.3	99.2	0.2	0.2	0.1	0.1	0.3	0.4	5.8	6.1	7.0	6.3	5.5	26.8	26.6	14.0	2.0	77.2	40.4	49.0	51.0
17052	MAPLETON DEPOT	98.4	98.2	0.3	0.3	0.0	0.0	0.4	0.6	5.3	5.6	5.7	6.2	5.9	25.3	29.1	15.8	1.1	79.6	42.4	48.4	51.6
17053	MARYSVILLE	98.7	98.5	0.2	0.3	0.2	0.3	0.4	0.5	5.1	5.4	6.8	6.2	5.9	26.5	29.8	12.9	1.5	79.1	41.5	48.1	51.9
17055	MECHANICSBURG	96.2	95.4	0.9	1.0	1.6	2.0	1.1	1.3	4.8	5.2	6.0	8.4	9.0	23.9	25.8	14.2	2.8	80.5	40.2	47.0	53.0
17057	MIDDLETOWN	92.2	90.6	4.5	5.4	0.9	1.2	2.4	2.8	5.5	5.8	6.8	6.1	7.2	27.7	26.0	12.7	2.2	78.2	39.1	47.6	52.4
17058	MIFFLIN	94.7	94.0	0.1	0.2	0.7	0.7	6.0	6.7	5.5	5.8	6.5	5.8	4.8	30.0	26.2	12.9	2.5	78.4	39.5	49.6	50.4
17059	MIFFLINTOWN	97.9	97.8	0.3	0.4	0.9	1.1	2.0	2.2	6.7	6.8	6.9	5.8	5.0	26.7	25.3	14.4	2.4	75.9	39.7	49.2	50.8
17060	MILL CREEK	98.9	98.5	0.1	0.2	0.0	0.0	0.5	0.6	8.0	7.1	7.1	8.5	5.9	26.9	24.3	11.5	0.7	72.6	35.2	50.9	49.1
17061	MILLERSBURG	98.7	98.5	0.4	0.5	0.3	0.5	0.7	0.8	5.5	5.7	6.3	5.8	5.4	27.1	25.0	16.1	3.1	78.7	41.3	48.0	52.0
17062	MILLERSTOWN	99.4	99.4	0.2	0.2	0.1	0.1	1.0	1.0	5.7	7.0	7.0	6.6	5.4	26.9	27.8	12.4	1.4	76.5	39.6	48.6	51.4
17063	MILROY	98.8	98.6	0.1	0.1	0.4	0.5	0.7	0.7	6.3	6.7	7.5	6.2	5.5	27.4	26.0	13.0	1.3	75.6	38.7	50.7	49.4
17065	MOUNT HOLLY SPRINGS	97.6	97.2	0.8	1.0	0.5	0.7	0.7	0.9	6.1	6.4	7.2	6.9	5.4	29.6	26.0	11.4	1.1	75.8	38.6	50.3	49.7
17066	MOUNT UNION	92.7	91.6	5.7	6.7	0.1	0.1	0.9	1.1	6.5	6.2	6.9	6.5	5.5	25.4	25.5	15.4	2.1	76.4	40.1	47.0	53.0
17067	MYERSTOWN	98.2	97.8	0.7	0.7	0.4	0.5	1.0	1.3	6.5	6.7	6.9	6.2	5.8	25.7	25.1	14.4	2.8	76.1	39.6	48.7	51.3
17068	NEW BLOOMFIELD	98.9	98.8	0.3	0.4	0.2	0.2	0.6	0.6	5.5	5.9	7.0	6.8	5.7	28.0	27.2	11.4	2.5	77.3	39.6	49.2	50.8
17070	NEW CUMBERLAND	96.1	95.5	1.0	1.2	1.1	1.4	1.6	1.8	5.5	5.7	6.3	5.7	5.1	27.7	28.2	14.3	1.5	78.8	41.6	48.7	51.3
17071	NEW GERMANTOWN	98.6	98.6	0.8	0.8	0.0	0.0	0.2	0.0	6.6	6.6	7.7	7.3	6.2	24.4	25.0	14.7	1.6	75.0	39.2	51.6	48.4
17073	NEWMANSTOWN	98.6	98.4	0.4	0.5	0.2	0.2	1.0	1.2	7.0	7.3	7.4	6.7	6.0	26.6	26.5	11.3	1.4	74.1	38.0	50.0	50.1
17074	NEWPORT	98.2	98.0	0.4	0.5	0.2	0.3	0.8	0.9	6.1	6.2	7.0	6.8	6.0	27.5	27.2	11.7	1.4	76.4	39.0	49.5	50.5
17076	OAKLAND MILLS	98.6	98.4	0.4	0.4	0.2	0.4	0.4	0.6	8.2	8.0	7.8	6.8	5.0	26.9	22.3	12.3	2.6	71.7	35.8	48.6	51.4
17078	PALMYRA	97.2	96.7	0.7	0.8	1.0	1.3	1.1	1.3	6.0	6.2	6.4	5.7	4.9	27.0	26.5	14.6	2.7	77.7	41.2	47.5	52.5
17080	PILLOW	99.0	98.5	0.7	0.9	0.0	0.0	0.0	0.0	7.3	7.0	6.3	5.7	6.0	26.3	26.6	13.0	1.8	75.2	39.5	50.8	49.2
	PENNSYLVANIA	85.4	84.4	10.0	10.3	1.8	2.2	3.2	3.5	5.9	6.1	6.8	6.9	6.7	26.6	25.3	13.3	2.2	77.2	39.1	48.4	51.6
	UNITED STATES	75.1	73.6	12.3	12.5	3.8	4.2	12.5	14.1	6.9	6.7	7.2	7.0	7.3	28.6	23.8	10.8	1.7	75.1	36.0	49.1	50.9

#	POST OFFICE NAME	2004 Per Capita Income	2004 HH Income Base	2004 Household Income Distribution (%): Less than $25,000	$25,000 to $49,999	$50,000 to $99,999	$100,000 to $149,999	$150,000 or More	Median Household Income: 2004	2009	2004 National Centile	2004 State Centile	2004 Home Value Base	2004 Home Value Distribution (%): Less than $50,000	$50,000 to $89,999	$90,000 to $174,999	$175,000 to $399,999	$400,000 or More	2004 Median Home Value
16879	WINBURNE	16358	116	31.9	32.8	31.0	3.5	0.9	38875	45746	42	40	101	17.8	40.6	39.6	2.0	0.0	83462
16881	WOODLAND	18078	1258	32.0	36.8	25.4	3.4	2.4	36397	41543	33	27	1061	28.6	33.3	27.1	9.6	1.4	74296
16882	WOODWARD	23291	95	24.2	36.8	28.4	7.4	3.2	41936	52113	53	53	82	9.8	18.3	53.7	15.9	2.4	113095
16901	WELLSBORO	20239	4139	34.1	30.4	26.9	5.4	3.2	37093	43735	36	30	3079	11.4	20.4	45.2	21.5	1.5	114229
16912	BLOSSBURG	19347	857	37.5	28.4	28.7	3.5	2.0	33313	39235	22	14	617	13.3	40.4	40.0	5.5	0.8	86918
16914	COLUMBIA CROSS ROADS	18703	960	28.8	32.9	29.9	6.3	2.2	40905	47086	49	48	810	15.9	23.2	43.3	14.8	2.7	103503
16915	COUDERSPORT	24271	2552	27.0	30.0	31.9	7.0	4.2	43560	51343	57	58	1927	10.7	18.3	44.6	24.0	2.4	123255
16917	COVINGTON	18860	601	32.6	38.8	22.5	3.5	2.7	35859	41189	31	25	491	19.1	26.5	43.0	10.8	0.6	95658
16920	ELKLAND	16880	772	42.1	28.5	24.1	4.2	1.2	29814	33868	12	6	530	28.9	34.3	34.2	2.6	0.0	72955
16921	GAINES	18883	231	39.4	33.8	21.7	3.5	1.7	30460	33917	13	7	191	16.2	28.8	38.7	14.7	1.6	97308
16922	GALETON	16553	945	38.2	32.8	24.2	3.3	1.5	32045	37194	18	10	715	22.9	32.5	34.7	8.8	1.1	81047
16923	GENESEE	19438	590	33.4	32.4	27.5	4.2	2.5	36399	41809	33	27	482	22.2	25.7	34.2	16.2	1.7	93333
16925	GILLETT	19120	1784	29.9	33.6	29.8	4.4	2.4	38820	44530	42	39	1469	21.4	25.9	38.1	13.4	1.2	93657
16926	GRANVILLE SUMMIT	16953	569	31.5	30.4	31.1	6.7	0.4	40190	45568	47	45	468	20.3	26.3	41.9	10.7	0.9	93810
16927	HARRISON VALLEY	14163	533	37.7	35.1	24.2	2.6	0.4	32513	37134	19	12	429	24.2	30.1	36.1	7.2	2.3	85488
16928	KNOXVILLE	18072	372	32.0	36.8	25.3	3.2	2.7	35183	41534	28	21	276	23.6	47.1	23.6	5.4	0.4	66818
16929	LAWRENCEVILLE	19380	940	28.0	39.5	27.5	3.9	1.2	38559	44391	41	38	760	30.5	20.7	38.4	9.6	0.8	88163
16930	LIBERTY	18809	431	27.8	33.2	31.8	5.8	1.4	41877	48594	53	52	361	10.8	24.1	47.4	15.8	1.9	106656
16932	MAINESBURG	17995	357	25.2	35.6	33.9	3.9	1.4	41036	47772	50	49	309	8.7	29.5	42.7	18.1	1.0	104427
16933	MANSFIELD	18256	2682	32.7	32.0	26.9	6.8	1.8	37292	43147	36	32	1800	13.9	19.7	42.8	22.2	1.3	115265
16935	MIDDLEBURY CENTER	18530	993	32.0	34.1	27.0	4.6	2.2	37391	43643	37	33	811	17.5	24.2	42.5	14.8	1.0	101990
16936	MILLERTON	18980	801	30.7	33.8	30.5	3.4	1.6	37918	43657	39	35	673	20.4	24.1	45.2	9.4	1.0	97979
16937	MILLS	13947	49	36.7	36.7	24.5	2.0	0.0	32937	36532	21	13	40	30.0	30.0	32.5	5.0	2.5	80000
16938	MORRIS	21115	279	34.1	38.0	21.2	3.6	3.2	33041	37834	21	13	237	27.0	25.3	38.0	8.4	1.3	87105
16939	MORRIS RUN	15742	184	40.8	34.8	20.1	3.3	1.1	30286	35509	13	6	155	40.7	21.9	24.5	11.6	1.3	65000
16940	NELSON	18286	230	33.0	33.9	27.8	3.9	1.3	35691	41977	30	24	186	15.6	27.4	41.4	14.5	1.1	99286
16941	GENESEE	12453	37	40.5	32.4	24.3	2.7	0.0	30726	37357	14	7	28	17.9	32.1	35.7	14.3	0.0	90000
16942	OSCEOLA	19140	216	33.8	31.0	25.0	7.4	2.8	37808	43542	39	34	174	32.2	31.0	26.4	10.3	0.0	66471
16943	SABINSVILLE	17300	224	34.4	35.3	24.1	4.0	2.2	34695	40158	26	19	188	21.3	24.5	35.1	18.1	1.1	98000
16946	TIOGA	18634	696	35.5	31.3	25.6	5.8	1.9	35673	41776	30	24	549	33.9	25.3	31.3	9.3	0.2	76310
16947	TROY	19386	1429	31.9	33.5	26.9	4.9	2.7	37206	42836	36	31	1031	15.6	22.7	46.0	13.4	2.3	104041
16948	ULYSSES	16320	656	36.0	32.9	24.5	4.3	2.3	34875	40397	27	20	535	20.6	26.2	37.8	14.2	1.3	93977
16950	WESTFIELD	16256	1150	37.2	36.7	22.1	3.1	0.9	34219	39837	25	17	867	24.3	35.5	30.0	8.9	1.3	76458
17002	ALLENSVILLE	13553	322	35.1	36.3	22.7	4.7	1.2	33950	38912	24	16	257	15.2	24.1	42.4	14.4	3.9	106105
17003	ANNVILLE	24486	4111	16.8	31.1	36.6	11.9	3.6	51934	61220	75	75	3129	12.1	12.2	53.8	20.1	1.9	125078
17004	BELLEVILLE	15338	1545	33.5	35.8	24.5	3.9	2.3	35987	40668	31	25	1243	9.3	27.0	45.7	15.0	3.1	108240
17005	BERRYSBURG	21344	135	23.0	36.3	33.3	5.9	1.5	43387	50511	57	57	112	19.6	35.7	33.9	7.1	3.6	84000
17006	BLAIN	18655	290	30.3	33.5	27.9	4.1	4.1	38166	43915	40	36	240	19.2	27.1	32.1	18.3	3.3	97500
17007	BOILING SPRINGS	30006	2030	13.4	21.0	39.3	18.5	7.8	69206	81808	91	92	1724	1.4	2.2	54.4	41.4	0.7	162121
17009	BURNHAM	18693	809	29.8	38.7	26.7	4.1	0.7	38026	43633	39	35	599	18.4	34.4	43.4	3.8	0.0	86887
17011	CAMP HILL	31920	13771	17.7	24.9	35.2	14.4	7.8	58065	69484	83	83	10178	0.8	5.1	60.9	31.3	2.0	145996
17013	CARLISLE	28110	21409	21.6	27.3	34.5	11.7	4.9	51113	62061	74	74	15286	12.2	10.5	50.4	24.7	2.3	129841
17014	COCOLAMUS	18356	370	25.4	34.9	32.4	4.1	3.2	43120	49047	56	57	307	11.1	18.9	49.2	19.2	1.6	113787
17017	DALMATIA	20218	756	22.0	36.1	36.6	4.1	1.2	44334	50912	60	60	632	16.0	26.0	38.6	16.3	3.2	104481
17018	DAUPHIN	31461	1639	13.0	23.3	44.4	12.1	7.3	61238	73165	86	88	1411	6.1	12.4	56.5	23.3	1.7	132095
17019	DILLSBURG	27396	6162	14.6	25.9	40.7	12.8	6.0	57397	65600	82	83	4929	7.1	7.9	46.1	35.5	3.4	156241
17020	DUNCANNON	21715	3726	23.8	29.9	34.4	10.4	1.5	47003	54049	66	66	2811	15.2	16.6	54.4	13.0	0.9	113416
17021	EAST WATERFORD	16594	393	34.6	37.9	23.2	3.8	0.5	32800	37027	20	12	340	18.8	25.6	35.9	17.4	2.4	98636
17022	ELIZABETHTOWN	25567	10668	16.7	26.6	39.8	13.1	3.8	55564	65224	80	81	7715	6.4	4.8	60.1	27.4	1.2	142950
17023	ELIZABETHVILLE	22020	1259	26.3	28.6	36.1	7.4	1.7	45243	55244	62	62	972	10.5	30.3	44.3	13.3	1.7	99890
17024	ELLIOTTSBURG	20977	867	23.4	30.2	36.8	7.3	2.3	47223	53844	67	67	714	8.4	17.4	53.9	17.2	3.1	120599
17025	ENOLA	27930	6693	16.5	29.6	38.6	11.7	3.6	53477	64694	78	78	4755	2.7	13.5	58.6	23.1	2.2	128313
17026	FREDERICKSBURG	20689	1047	21.8	31.2	36.4	8.0	2.6	48248	55632	69	68	867	11.0	13.8	55.6	16.6	3.0	123166
17028	GRANTVILLE	28463	1336	13.3	27.0	39.4	11.5	8.9	58631	68709	83	84	1174	22.9	8.5	41.7	24.9	2.0	128435
17029	GRANVILLE	17406	188	24.5	37.2	33.0	5.3	0.0	41328	46417	51	50	154	8.4	36.4	37.7	17.5	0.0	101136
17030	GRATZ	20116	280	26.4	30.4	35.0	5.4	2.9	42669	51647	55	55	224	14.3	33.5	39.3	10.3	2.7	92941
17032	HALIFAX	24808	3171	21.7	25.2	41.2	8.9	3.1	52383	62815	76	76	2669	14.5	16.8	53.2	14.7	0.8	113600
17033	HERSHEY	34747	6506	19.4	26.2	32.1	12.0	10.3	55968	67911	81	81	4185	5.0	5.1	46.0	39.5	4.4	166276
17034	HIGHSPIRE	22688	1131	23.5	40.9	29.7	4.9	1.0	38393	45844	41	37	671	14.6	37.0	45.3	3.1	0.0	88704
17035	HONEY GROVE	18774	370	33.2	31.9	29.5	3.5	1.9	35424	39550	29	22	316	18.7	22.8	40.2	13.9	4.4	104018
17036	HUMMELSTOWN	36649	7492	12.6	22.6	36.5	15.9	12.3	66437	80841	89	91	5399	2.8	7.5	49.4	34.6	5.7	158381
17037	ICKESBURG	19036	460	22.6	32.8	38.0	5.0	1.5	45482	51770	63	63	394	9.9	21.1	48.5	17.3	3.3	113110
17038	JONESTOWN	23412	2395	19.7	32.4	36.5	9.0	2.5	48308	55950	69	68	1951	8.4	12.3	61.8	16.1	1.4	124668
17040	LANDISBURG	22119	916	20.6	30.1	38.1	8.7	2.4	49392	56122	71	71	785	9.2	18.6	53.1	16.7	2.4	120807
17042	LEBANON	25704	14302	21.7	29.3	34.3	10.8	3.9	49053	57953	70	70	10611	4.1	19.5	53.6	20.5	2.3	119783
17043	LEMOYNE	33805	2797	17.8	38.4	30.1	7.8	5.9	45533	54476	63	63	1560	0.6	24.5	56.9	12.4	5.5	113663
17044	LEWISTOWN	19526	9086	38.4	32.5	22.4	4.9	1.8	33191	37944	21	14	6178	16.8	32.0	41.6	8.9	0.8	91563
17045	LIVERPOOL	21327	1504	22.5	33.8	34.2	7.3	2.3	45786	52278	63	64	1180	8.7	20.6	53.4	15.7	1.6	113587
17046	LEBANON	18804	11924	31.8	32.3	28.9	5.6	1.4	37980	44271	39	35	7649	15.5	29.4	44.7	9.5	1.1	97057
17047	LOYSVILLE	17773	817	28.9	32.0	31.0	7.1	1.1	40472	46481	48	47	659	9.1	25.5	44.8	16.1	4.6	109637
17048	LYKENS	20303	1770	29.0	32.3	32.3	4.9	1.5	40418	48701	48	46	1374	28.2	40.5	25.7	4.9	0.7	71240
17049	MC ALISTERVILLE	19621	1235	30.6	38.1	23.9	5.1	2.4	34747	39310	26	19	984	8.0	16.0	56.4	19.4	0.2	123794
17050	MECHANICSBURG	36327	11161	10.7	21.7	37.7	19.3	10.6	69116	83153	91	92	9363	8.9	3.4	38.9	44.9	3.9	172673
17051	MC VEYTOWN	18024	2016	32.1	34.7	27.6	3.7	1.8	37486	42633	37	33	1691	16.3	26.1	44.8	11.8	1.0	102077
17052	MAPLETON DEPOT	17082	524	32.3	35.1	28.8	3.8	0.0	35987	41609	31	25	438	34.3	32.7	29.0	3.7	0.5	68333
17053	MARYSVILLE	25821	1941	21.4	24.9	40.3	10.5	2.9	52588	61176	76	76	1524	8.5	14.2	57.0	18.6	1.8	118830
17055	MECHANICSBURG	29458	13203	15.9	24.7	38.1	14.9	6.4	59244	71023	84	85	9510	2.6	7.4	57.8	29.0	3.2	149798
17057	MIDDLETOWN	24120	9079	20.5	33.2	34.3	9.5	2.5	46744	56756	66	66	6282	16.4	18.5	52.2	11.9	1.0	105979
17058	MIFFLIN	19259	721	30.9	31.2	32.0	4.4	1.4	37914	43375	39	35	533	12.6	21.6	46.3	16.9	2.6	113295
17059	MIFFLINTOWN	19393	2491	27.5	36.2	29.1	4.7	2.6	38918	44511	42	40	2012	9.1	17.7	51.0	19.9	2.3	125515
17060	MILL CREEK	15603	369	37.9	32.3	23.6	5.2	1.1	32129	36858	18	10	305	26.6	27.9	37.1	7.9	0.7	82059
17061	MILLERSBURG	21534	2838	26.4	30.8	36.6	4.9	1.3	43681	52066	58	58	2112	13.4	27.1	48.1	9.9	1.5	99136
17062	MILLERSTOWN	23864	689	21.2	26.6	40.5	8.7	3.1	51512	60187	75	75	583	4.3	20.4	59.9	13.7	1.7	115685
17063	MILROY	16327	1385	30.7	36.9	30.5	1.7	0.2	38937	44039	43	40	1140	13.1	23.7	51.1	11.5	0.6	103559
17065	MOUNT HOLLY SPRINGS	24645	1524	18.4	27.8	41.9	10.5	1.3	52555	63658	76	76	1176	10.5	14.5	62.0	11.4	1.6	116581
17066	MOUNT UNION	16858	2338	44.5	29.7	21.6	3.4	0.8	29370	33491	11	5	1609	28.2	38.5	28.7	4.4	0.3	68439
17067	MYERSTOWN	22152	5478	20.2	34.8	33.6	8.9	2.6	46631	54541	65	66	4302	10.8	13.5	54.8	18.4	2.5	123533
17068	NEW BLOOMFIELD	22439	1444	20.8	30.5	37.8	9.1	1.7	48904	55943	70	70	1161	10.9	12.8	58.8	16.2	1.3	120249
17070	NEW CUMBERLAND	31289	6851	15.3	28.3	37.0	13.2	6.2	56596	67379	81	82	5225	5.8	9.1	59.1	24.3	1.7	136725
17071	NEW GERMANTOWN	20589	203	30.1	32.5	29.6	4.4	3.5	38780	44473	42	39	168	20.2	26.2	32.1	18.5	3.0	96667
17073	NEWMANSTOWN	23073	1492	18.6	29.6	39.3	8.5	4.1	51322	60950	74	74	1211	2.9	14.2	56.4	21.8	4.7	127825
17074	NEWPORT	21693	2990	24.1	30.6	36.7	6.4	2.1	46137	52390	64	65	2251	12.6	19.4	53.1	13.4	1.5	111493
17076	OAKLAND MILLS	16144	168	29.8	35.7	28.0	4.2	2.4	38028	42683	39	35	124	7.3	15.3	51.6	25.0	0.8	135714
17078	PALMYRA	29264	8166	15.9	28.5	38.0	13.3	4.4	54711	65290	79	79	6143	3.8	12.1	58.4	24.6	1.2	135099
17080	PILLOW	22337	146	24.0	36.3	32.9	5.5	1.4	42901	51388	56	56	121	19.0	35.5	34.7	7.4	3.3	85000
	PENNSYLVANIA	25764		25.8	27.2	31.2	10.2	5.7	46988	57000				11.9	18.4	40.7	25.1	4.1	123516
	UNITED STATES	25866		24.7	27.1	30.8	10.9	6.5	48124	56710				10.9	15.0	33.7	30.1	10.4	145905

ZIP CODE		FINANCIAL SERVICES				THE HOME						ENTERTAINMENT						PERSONAL			
						Home Improvements		Furnishings													
#	POST OFFICE NAME	Auto Loan	Home Loan	Investments	Retirement Plans	Home Repair	Lawn & Garden	Computers & Hardware	Major Appliances	TV, Radio, Sound Equipment	Furniture	Dine out/ Carry out	Sports Equipment	Fees & Tickets	Toys & Games	Travel	Cable TV	Apparel & Services	Auto Repairs	Health Insurance	Pets & Supplies
16879	WINBURNE	56	61	65	58	62	69	61	60	63	58	78	67	64	84	63	65	75	59	64	66
16881	WOODLAND	92	61	28	53	70	80	59	74	71	60	84	88	50	79	60	77	76	73	91	105
16882	WOODWARD	96	67	35	63	78	88	66	82	76	66	90	99	57	88	69	80	82	81	98	114
16901	WELLSBORO	80	64	45	60	70	79	63	72	70	62	83	84	58	82	65	73	78	71	83	93
16912	BLOSSBURG	67	56	45	54	60	70	59	64	65	57	78	72	56	77	60	68	72	63	74	76
16914	COLUMBIA CROSS ROADS	85	68	44	64	74	81	64	75	71	64	85	90	59	85	66	73	79	73	85	100
16915	COUDERSPORT	99	79	57	75	87	98	79	90	87	77	104	103	72	102	81	91	96	88	103	115
16917	COVINGTON	89	60	28	52	68	78	58	72	69	59	82	86	49	77	59	75	74	71	88	102
16920	ELKLAND	68	48	28	44	54	63	51	59	59	49	69	68	44	65	51	62	63	58	71	76
16921	GAINES	69	54	37	49	61	69	51	62	58	51	68	72	46	68	54	62	64	61	73	84
16922	GALETON	63	53	42	50	58	66	53	59	59	52	70	67	50	70	55	62	66	58	69	74
16923	GENESEE	86	66	44	60	75	84	63	76	71	62	85	89	56	83	67	76	78	75	90	104
16925	GILLETT	85	64	39	59	70	79	63	73	71	63	85	86	57	82	63	75	78	72	85	97
16926	GRANVILLE SUMMIT	82	57	30	54	67	75	56	70	65	56	76	84	48	75	59	68	70	69	83	97
16927	HARRISON VALLEY	72	48	22	41	54	63	46	58	56	47	66	69	39	62	47	60	60	57	71	82
16928	KNOXVILLE	66	62	55	58	65	72	61	64	65	59	79	74	61	83	63	68	75	63	72	77
16929	LAWRENCEVILLE	91	61	28	52	69	79	59	73	71	60	83	88	50	78	60	76	75	73	90	104
16930	LIBERTY	87	63	35	58	72	81	61	75	70	60	82	90	53	81	64	74	75	74	89	104
16932	MAINESBURG	75	67	51	63	70	76	62	68	65	62	80	81	60	81	63	67	76	67	74	88
16933	MANSFIELD	72	61	54	59	64	70	65	66	68	63	83	81	61	82	64	68	79	68	71	83
16935	MIDDLEBURY CENTER	89	61	30	54	69	79	59	73	70	60	82	87	51	79	61	75	75	72	89	103
16936	MILLERTON	77	69	52	65	73	78	64	71	68	64	82	84	62	84	66	69	78	69	76	91
16937	MILLS	70	47	21	40	53	61	45	56	54	46	64	67	38	60	46	59	58	56	69	80
16938	MORRIS	86	67	45	60	75	85	63	76	71	62	85	89	56	83	67	76	79	75	90	104
16939	MORRIS RUN	67	53	36	48	60	67	50	60	56	49	67	70	45	66	53	60	62	59	71	82
16940	NELSON	85	57	26	49	65	74	55	69	66	56	78	82	47	74	56	72	71	68	85	98
16941	GENESEE	68	45	21	39	51	59	44	55	53	45	62	66	37	59	45	57	56	54	68	78
16942	OSCEOLA	91	61	28	52	69	79	59	73	71	60	83	88	50	79	60	76	76	73	90	104
16943	SABINSVILLE	73	57	39	51	64	72	54	65	61	53	72	76	48	71	57	65	67	64	77	89
16946	TIOGA	89	60	27	52	68	78	58	72	70	59	82	86	49	77	59	75	74	71	89	102
16947	TROY	89	63	35	58	71	82	65	76	75	63	88	89	56	84	65	80	80	76	92	102
16948	ULYSSES	77	56	33	50	63	72	54	66	62	54	74	78	47	71	56	67	68	65	79	91
16950	WESTFIELD	62	52	40	47	56	63	51	57	56	50	68	66	48	69	52	60	64	56	66	72
17002	ALLENSVILLE	80	54	24	46	61	70	52	65	63	53	73	77	44	69	53	67	67	64	80	92
17003	ANNVILLE	97	91	81	90	93	99	91	93	92	89	113	111	89	114	90	91	109	93	95	112
17004	BELLEVILLE	80	57	30	50	64	72	55	67	64	56	76	79	48	73	56	69	70	66	80	93
17005	BERRYSBURG	79	67	52	67	70	79	69	74	73	68	89	84	66	88	68	74	83	73	80	87
17006	BLAIN	87	68	46	61	76	86	64	77	72	63	86	90	57	85	68	77	80	76	91	105
17007	BOILING SPRINGS	106	126	130	125	125	124	113	114	106	112	133	134	119	141	115	104	132	110	105	128
17009	BURNHAM	57	61	63	57	61	68	60	59	62	58	77	66	63	83	62	64	74	58	64	66
17011	CAMP HILL	93	105	121	103	104	113	102	101	100	101	126	114	107	129	105	101	123	100	100	110
17013	CARLISLE	98	96	94	94	98	105	95	97	96	94	118	113	94	119	95	96	114	97	99	114
17014	COCOLAMUS	94	66	34	58	74	84	63	77	74	64	88	92	55	84	64	79	80	76	93	108
17017	DALMATIA	80	70	53	67	74	80	66	73	70	66	85	86	64	86	67	72	81	71	79	93
17018	DAUPHIN	99	121	133	119	119	121	111	110	106	111	133	128	119	142	114	104	133	107	102	121
17019	DILLSBURG	99	108	106	107	108	110	101	103	97	101	121	120	103	125	102	95	119	100	97	117
17020	DUNCANNON	83	77	66	74	81	87	73	79	77	73	94	93	73	97	75	78	90	77	84	97
17021	EAST WATERFORD	72	54	34	48	61	69	51	62	59	51	70	73	45	68	54	63	64	62	75	86
17022	ELIZABETHTOWN	92	95	97	96	95	99	93	94	91	92	113	111	93	114	93	89	110	94	90	107
17023	ELIZABETHVILLE	83	77	66	74	81	88	74	79	78	73	96	92	74	99	76	80	91	77	86	96
17024	ELLIOTTSBURG	88	76	57	73	81	88	73	80	78	72	94	95	70	95	74	80	89	79	89	103
17025	ENOLA	87	100	108	102	98	98	96	94	90	95	114	111	99	118	96	87	113	93	85	103
17026	FREDERICKSBURG	89	76	59	75	80	89	77	82	81	75	99	95	74	98	77	83	93	81	89	100
17028	GRANTVILLE	108	108	96	106	109	112	100	106	99	102	123	123	100	123	101	98	120	104	103	124
17029	GRANVILLE	87	58	26	50	66	76	56	70	68	57	79	84	48	75	57	73	72	69	86	99
17030	GRATZ	95	64	29	55	72	83	61	77	74	63	87	92	52	82	63	80	79	76	95	109
17032	HALIFAX	97	89	74	87	93	100	86	92	89	85	109	108	85	111	87	90	104	90	97	112
17033	HERSHEY	109	114	129	115	114	122	114	113	113	114	142	132	117	142	115	112	138	114	111	126
17034	HIGHSPIRE	62	66	75	65	66	72	68	66	68	66	85	76	70	89	69	69	83	66	67	72
17035	HONEY GROVE	92	62	28	53	70	81	60	75	72	61	85	89	51	80	61	78	77	74	92	106
17036	HUMMELSTOWN	123	141	154	143	138	142	133	131	126	133	159	152	139	164	134	123	158	129	121	144
17037	ICKESBURG	83	74	56	70	78	84	68	76	72	68	88	90	67	90	70	74	84	74	82	98
17038	JONESTOWN	96	85	65	81	90	97	79	88	84	79	102	104	77	104	81	86	97	85	95	113
17040	LANDISBURG	91	81	62	77	86	92	75	83	80	75	97	99	74	99	77	82	92	81	90	107
17042	LEBANON	86	88	88	86	89	97	85	87	86	84	107	100	87	109	87	88	103	86	90	100
17043	LEMOYNE	88	96	111	98	96	99	98	95	94	96	119	113	100	121	98	91	117	96	89	103
17044	LEWISTOWN	68	59	52	56	62	69	60	63	65	59	79	74	58	79	61	67	74	64	71	78
17045	LIVERPOOL	83	78	66	74	81	88	73	79	77	72	94	92	73	98	76	79	90	77	85	97
17046	LEBANON	69	62	57	60	64	71	64	66	68	63	83	77	63	83	64	69	79	67	71	79
17047	LOYSVILLE	85	62	36	59	71	79	62	74	70	61	83	88	54	81	64	74	76	73	87	100
17048	LYKENS	71	68	62	63	70	78	66	69	71	65	87	79	67	91	68	74	83	68	77	83
17049	MC ALISTERVILLE	88	66	40	61	72	82	65	76	74	65	88	89	59	85	65	77	81	75	88	99
17050	MECHANICSBURG	126	142	147	143	141	144	131	132	125	132	157	155	136	161	133	122	154	129	124	149
17051	MC VEYTOWN	82	61	34	54	67	75	57	69	66	58	79	82	52	77	59	70	73	68	81	95
17052	MAPLETON DEPOT	66	57	47	53	62	70	55	62	60	54	73	71	53	74	58	64	69	61	71	79
17053	MARYSVILLE	80	92	97	90	92	97	87	86	86	85	107	99	92	115	89	87	105	84	86	95
17055	MECHANICSBURG	94	107	124	107	106	111	104	102	101	103	127	119	109	131	106	100	125	102	97	112
17057	MIDDLETOWN	81	82	80	80	82	88	80	81	81	79	100	95	80	102	81	81	97	81	82	94
17058	MIFFLIN	72	61	48	61	64	72	63	67	67	62	81	77	60	80	62	68	76	66	73	79
17059	MIFFLINTOWN	79	68	50	63	72	80	65	72	71	65	86	85	63	86	67	74	81	71	81	92
17060	MILL CREEK	78	52	24	45	59	68	50	63	61	51	72	75	43	68	51	66	65	62	78	90
17061	MILLERSBURG	75	72	64	68	74	81	69	73	73	68	89	84	70	93	71	75	85	71	79	87
17062	MILLERSTOWN	88	87	79	83	90	97	81	86	84	81	103	100	82	106	84	86	99	84	91	104
17063	MILROY	75	53	27	46	60	68	50	62	60	51	70	74	44	67	52	64	64	62	76	88
17065	MOUNT HOLLY SPRINGS	93	79	62	78	84	93	80	86	85	79	103	99	77	103	80	86	97	84	93	104
17066	MOUNT UNION	65	46	28	42	51	60	48	56	56	48	66	64	42	62	48	60	60	56	68	73
17067	MYERSTOWN	89	82	69	79	85	92	78	84	82	78	100	98	77	102	80	83	95	82	89	103
17068	NEW BLOOMFIELD	91	77	57	73	82	91	75	83	81	74	97	97	71	97	76	84	91	81	93	105
17070	NEW CUMBERLAND	93	104	112	103	103	108	100	99	97	99	121	115	103	125	102	96	119	98	96	110
17071	NEW GERMANTOWN	87	68	46	61	77	86	64	77	73	64	86	90	57	85	68	78	80	76	91	106
17073	NEWMANSTOWN	97	85	65	82	89	98	82	89	87	81	105	104	79	106	83	89	100	87	97	111
17074	NEWPORT	82	76	63	71	79	86	72	77	76	71	93	90	72	97	74	79	89	76	85	96
17076	OAKLAND MILLS	74	61	46	60	65	74	64	69	69	62	83	78	60	81	63	70	77	68	76	81
17078	PALMYRA	99	99	92	98	101	107	96	99	96	95	119	115	96	121	96	96	114	97	100	114
17080	PILLOW	79	67	52	67	70	79	69	74	73	68	89	84	66	88	68	74	83	73	80	87
	PENNSYLVANIA	89	89	93	87	90	98	89	90	91	88	112	104	89	114	90	92	109	90	92	104
	UNITED STATES	100	100	100	100	100	100	100	100	100	100	100	100	100	100	100	100	100	100	100	100

PENNSYLVANIA

A 17082-17401

POPULATION CHANGE

# POST OFFICE NAME	COUNTY FIPS CODE	POPULATION 2000	2004	2009	2000-2004 ANNUAL RATE % Rate	State Centile	HOUSEHOLDS 2000	2004	2009	% Annual Rate 2000-2004	2004 Average HH Size	FAMILIES 2000	2004	% Annual Rate 2000-2004
17082 PORT ROYAL	067	3622	3678	3776	0.4	58	1343	1381	1436	0.7	2.64	1017	1042	0.6
17084 REEDSVILLE	087	4195	4264	4291	0.4	58	1514	1564	1598	0.8	2.69	1162	1194	0.6
17086 RICHFIELD	109	1810	1830	1858	0.3	52	644	659	678	0.5	2.73	518	528	0.5
17087 RICHLAND	011	2942	2997	3094	0.4	61	1041	1074	1121	0.7	2.77	808	830	0.6
17090 SHERMANS DALE	099	5356	5936	6435	2.5	95	1980	2248	2492	3.0	2.64	1541	1741	2.9
17094 THOMPSONTOWN	067	2741	2809	2898	0.6	68	1105	1152	1206	1.0	2.39	801	832	0.9
17097 WICONISCO	043	67	65	65	-0.7	9	28	28	28	0.0	2.32	20	19	-1.2
17098 WILLIAMSTOWN	043	2568	2550	2560	-0.2	31	1065	1074	1094	0.2	2.37	745	745	0.0
17099 YEAGERTOWN	087	1185	1170	1163	-0.3	25	486	490	496	0.2	2.39	356	357	0.1
17101 HARRISBURG	043	1793	1762	1778	-0.4	20	1388	1397	1439	0.2	1.18	191	183	-1.0
17102 HARRISBURG	043	8427	8123	8104	-0.9	7	4286	4194	4253	-0.5	1.80	1392	1339	-0.9
17103 HARRISBURG	043	11085	10943	11007	-0.3	25	4361	4383	4480	0.1	2.46	2728	2712	-0.1
17104 HARRISBURG	043	21305	21069	21276	-0.3	27	7957	8038	8257	0.2	2.54	5095	5062	-0.2
17109 HARRISBURG	043	22959	23255	23700	0.3	54	10299	10563	10913	0.6	2.14	5864	5935	0.3
17110 HARRISBURG	043	22525	22779	23100	0.3	52	9043	9303	9580	0.7	2.37	5667	5777	0.5
17111 HARRISBURG	043	26072	27123	27931	0.9	77	10495	11083	11579	1.3	2.30	6855	7155	1.0
17112 HARRISBURG	043	30938	32149	33105	0.9	77	12032	12774	13391	1.4	2.50	9005	9493	1.3
17113 HARRISBURG	043	11207	11315	11441	0.2	50	4514	4602	4709	0.5	2.43	2944	2970	0.2
17201 CHAMBERSBURG	055	48510	50012	52178	0.7	72	19427	20411	21696	1.2	2.37	13275	13859	1.0
17211 ARTEMAS	009	338	321	302	-1.2	2	137	133	127	-0.7	2.41	106	102	-0.9
17212 BIG COVE TANNERY	057	986	1033	1132	1.1	82	377	406	455	1.8	2.54	284	303	1.5
17213 BLAIRS MILLS	061	648	664	678	0.6	68	238	248	258	1.0	2.66	180	187	0.9
17214 BLUE RIDGE SUMMIT	055	1057	1093	1140	0.8	74	466	494	526	1.4	2.21	296	310	1.1
17215 BURNT CABINS	057	181	189	207	1.0	80	81	87	98	1.7	2.11	60	64	1.5
17217 CONCORD	055	9	10	10	2.5	96	4	4	5	0.0	2.25	3	3	0.0
17219 DOYLESBURG	055	320	344	367	1.7	90	114	125	136	2.2	2.67	87	94	1.8
17220 DRY RUN	055	418	450	479	1.8	91	131	144	156	2.3	3.03	99	108	2.1
17221 FANNETTSBURG	055	550	578	609	1.2	83	218	233	250	1.6	2.48	160	170	1.4
17222 FAYETTEVILLE	055	8751	8956	9336	0.6	66	3441	3611	3848	1.1	2.37	2600	2713	1.0
17223 FORT LITTLETON	057	522	546	596	1.1	81	200	215	241	1.7	2.47	148	159	1.7
17224 FORT LOUDON	055	1700	1810	1918	1.5	88	683	740	798	1.9	2.45	516	554	1.7
17225 GREENCASTLE	055	16339	17130	18000	1.1	82	6188	6617	7079	1.6	2.58	4711	5002	1.4
17228 HARRISONVILLE	057	1068	1136	1255	1.5	88	398	435	492	2.1	2.61	297	323	2.0
17229 HUSTONTOWN	057	1115	1168	1279	1.1	82	432	464	521	1.7	2.49	318	340	1.6
17232 LURGAN	055	45	48	51	1.5	89	19	21	22	2.4	2.29	15	17	3.0
17233 MC CONNELLSBURG	057	4300	4957	5726	3.4	99	1793	2112	2495	3.9	2.32	1217	1427	3.8
17236 MERCERSBURG	055	7913	8182	8542	0.8	74	3055	3223	3426	1.3	2.54	2329	2441	1.1
17237 MONT ALTO	055	1008	1051	1100	1.0	79	410	436	464	1.5	2.40	316	333	1.2
17238 NEEDMORE	057	1770	1864	2046	1.2	84	679	732	823	1.8	2.55	512	550	1.7
17239 NEELYTON	061	939	955	971	0.4	59	344	359	373	1.0	2.65	259	269	0.9
17240 NEWBURG	041	2967	3073	3202	0.8	74	973	1021	1080	1.1	3.01	816	851	1.0
17241 NEWVILLE	041	11776	12521	13171	1.5	87	4339	4714	5057	2.0	2.62	3401	3672	1.8
17243 ORBISONIA	061	2470	2494	2526	0.2	50	951	983	1019	0.8	2.39	664	682	0.6
17244 ORRSTOWN	055	2679	2854	3025	1.5	88	985	1071	1157	2.0	2.66	780	844	1.9
17246 PLEASANT HALL	055	13	14	14	1.8	91	6	6	7	0.0	2.33	5	5	0.0
17252 SAINT THOMAS	055	3419	3551	3715	0.9	77	1292	1372	1463	1.4	2.58	1001	1056	1.3
17255 SHADE GAP	061	438	446	453	0.4	61	172	179	186	0.9	2.48	130	134	0.7
17257 SHIPPENSBURG	041	23247	24367	25469	1.1	82	7918	8432	8979	1.5	2.60	5210	5533	1.4
17260 SHIRLEYSBURG	061	1383	1391	1406	0.1	46	530	548	569	0.8	2.46	395	406	0.7
17262 SPRING RUN	055	1842	1981	2109	1.7	90	670	736	799	2.2	2.66	508	554	2.1
17264 THREE SPRINGS	061	2323	2382	2431	0.6	68	947	994	1038	1.2	2.40	692	722	1.0
17265 UPPERSTRASBURG	055	169	178	188	1.2	84	67	72	78	1.7	2.47	53	57	1.7
17266 WALNUT BOTTOM	041	418	419	426	0.1	42	156	160	166	0.6	2.55	122	124	0.4
17267 WARFORDSBURG	057	2591	2789	3099	1.8	91	1003	1106	1260	2.3	2.52	757	832	2.3
17268 WAYNESBORO	055	26718	27622	28808	0.8	74	10511	11082	11776	1.3	2.42	7433	7795	1.1
17271 WILLOW HILL	055	478	504	531	1.3	84	164	176	189	1.7	2.85	121	129	1.5
17301 ABBOTTSTOWN	001	3435	3918	4334	3.1	98	1216	1409	1580	3.5	2.76	958	1102	3.4
17302 AIRVILLE	133	2754	2816	2918	0.5	65	974	1011	1064	0.9	2.78	768	792	0.7
17304 ASPERS	001	3249	3395	3585	1.0	80	1138	1207	1293	1.4	2.79	877	925	1.3
17307 BIGLERVILLE	001	5359	5635	5973	1.2	83	2004	2138	2300	1.5	2.61	1522	1614	1.4
17309 BROGUE	133	2261	2414	2564	1.6	89	858	932	1005	2.0	2.59	683	737	1.8
17313 DALLASTOWN	133	9764	9996	10457	0.6	66	3950	4109	4369	0.9	2.37	2732	2832	0.9
17314 DELTA	133	5595	5783	6044	0.8	73	1970	2066	2192	1.1	2.79	1522	1586	1.0
17315 DOVER	133	22366	23797	25257	1.5	88	8663	9415	10178	2.0	2.50	6421	6919	1.8
17316 EAST BERLIN	001	7265	7663	8120	1.3	85	2646	2835	3050	1.6	2.70	2075	2208	1.5
17319 ETTERS	133	9540	10007	10532	1.1	82	3506	3745	4005	1.6	2.67	2704	2871	1.4
17320 FAIRFIELD	001	6908	7493	8076	1.9	92	2583	2855	3128	2.4	2.60	1997	2191	2.2
17321 FAWN GROVE	133	2143	2331	2496	2.0	93	759	841	915	2.4	2.77	612	673	2.3
17322 FELTON	133	5600	5822	6094	0.9	77	1991	2111	2248	1.4	2.76	1607	1694	1.3
17324 GARDNERS	041	4321	4398	4560	0.4	60	1600	1664	1757	0.9	2.63	1229	1269	0.8
17325 GETTYSBURG	001	25218	26155	27493	0.9	75	9237	9787	10509	1.4	2.39	6226	6567	1.3
17327 GLEN ROCK	133	7293	7595	7970	1.0	78	2750	2913	3105	1.4	2.60	2149	2263	1.2
17329 GLENVILLE	133	2168	2260	2372	1.0	79	767	817	873	1.5	2.77	651	690	1.4
17331 HANOVER	133	44068	46481	49262	1.3	85	17510	18755	20193	1.6	2.44	12288	13122	1.6
17339 LEWISBERRY	133	5597	5904	6247	1.3	85	2068	2229	2404	1.8	2.60	1626	1739	1.6
17340 LITTLESTOWN	001	9895	10465	11131	1.3	86	3664	3933	4241	1.7	2.65	2835	3028	1.6
17344 MC SHERRYSTOWN	001	3117	3279	3477	1.2	84	1264	1364	1476	1.8	2.39	832	890	1.6
17345 MANCHESTER	133	7804	8144	8582	1.0	80	3103	3291	3520	1.4	2.47	2275	2400	1.3
17347 MOUNT WOLF	133	3337	3658	3947	2.2	94	1304	1450	1587	2.5	2.52	962	1062	2.4
17349 NEW FREEDOM	133	7459	7847	8271	1.2	84	2685	2893	3109	1.8	2.68	2118	2266	1.6
17350 NEW OXFORD	001	12101	12796	13598	1.3	85	4401	4743	5131	1.8	2.61	3253	3479	1.6
17352 NEW PARK	133	1171	1289	1390	2.3	95	432	484	530	2.7	2.66	354	394	2.6
17353 ORRTANNA	001	3149	3329	3538	1.3	85	1193	1288	1394	1.8	2.51	902	968	1.7
17356 RED LION	133	18129	19028	20087	1.2	83	7037	7507	8050	1.5	2.53	5155	5473	1.4
17360 SEVEN VALLEYS	133	4801	4838	5028	0.2	47	1785	1838	1946	0.7	2.63	1385	1415	0.5
17361 SHREWSBURY	133	4579	4859	5139	1.4	87	1788	1929	2071	1.8	2.51	1328	1423	1.6
17362 SPRING GROVE	133	12599	13130	13780	1.0	79	4619	4917	5255	1.5	2.66	3697	3912	1.3
17363 STEWARTSTOWN	133	8136	9082	9865	2.6	96	2912	3291	3624	2.9	2.75	2357	2649	2.8
17364 THOMASVILLE	133	2993	3342	3630	2.6	97	1118	1276	1410	3.2	2.60	872	989	3.0
17365 WELLSVILLE	133	2403	2475	2601	0.7	71	954	1005	1075	1.2	2.45	734	769	1.1
17366 WINDSOR	133	4945	5078	5303	0.6	69	1804	1886	2003	1.1	2.69	1368	1419	0.9
17368 WRIGHTSVILLE	133	7716	7824	8111	0.3	56	3071	3186	3365	0.9	2.45	2194	2254	0.6
17370 YORK HAVEN	133	5614	5899	6209	1.2	83	2112	2256	2412	1.6	2.61	1611	1710	1.4
17372 YORK SPRINGS	001	3356	3432	3584	0.5	65	1222	1273	1351	1.0	2.67	945	978	0.6
17401 YORK	133	888	908	947	0.5	65	456	474	504	0.9	1.76	146	145	-0.2
PENNSYLVANIA					0.3					0.7	2.44			0.6
UNITED STATES					1.2					1.3	2.58			1.1

ZIP CODE #	POST OFFICE NAME	RACE (%) White 2000	White 2004	Black 2000	Black 2004	Asian/Pacific 2000	Asian/Pacific 2004	% Hispanic Origin 2000	% Hispanic Origin 2004	2004 AGE DISTRIBUTION (%) 0-4	5-9	10-14	15-19	20-24	25-44	45-64	65-84	85+	18+	MEDIAN AGE 2004	% 2004 Males	% 2004 Females
17082	PORT ROYAL	97.0	96.7	0.9	1.0	0.3	0.4	2.5	2.8	6.3	6.5	7.2	6.4	5.8	28.4	25.7	12.4	1.4	76.1	38.3	50.1	49.9
17084	REEDSVILLE	98.7	98.5	0.3	0.4	0.5	0.6	0.3	0.4	7.2	7.3	7.5	6.6	5.1	25.9	25.2	13.4	1.8	73.8	38.6	49.4	50.6
17086	RICHFIELD	99.2	99.2	0.3	0.3	0.1	0.1	0.3	0.3	6.4	6.6	7.7	7.1	5.3	28.5	21.7	15.1	1.8	74.8	38.1	50.3	49.7
17087	RICHLAND	97.8	97.3	0.7	0.8	0.3	0.3	1.2	1.5	7.1	7.4	7.6	6.5	5.6	27.7	24.0	12.2	1.9	73.9	37.6	50.2	49.8
17090	SHERMANS DALE	98.9	98.8	0.2	0.3	0.1	0.1	0.6	0.7	6.9	7.2	7.4	6.0	5.8	31.1	27.5	7.6	0.6	74.8	36.6	49.7	50.3
17094	THOMPSONTOWN	99.2	99.2	0.1	0.1	0.2	0.2	0.3	0.3	6.5	6.4	5.7	5.4	5.6	27.6	25.4	15.3	2.1	77.9	40.3	48.5	51.5
17097	WICONISCO	98.5	100.0	0.0	0.0	0.0	0.0	0.0	0.0	6.2	6.2	6.2	6.2	6.2	24.6	24.6	18.5	1.5	81.5	40.6	47.7	52.3
17098	WILLIAMSTOWN	98.8	98.5	0.2	0.2	0.1	0.2	0.6	0.7	5.3	5.8	6.7	5.8	5.4	27.4	25.8	15.8	1.8	78.5	40.8	49.8	50.2
17099	YEAGERTOWN	98.1	97.9	0.4	0.4	0.5	0.6	0.6	0.7	6.5	6.3	6.5	5.7	5.9	26.7	26.1	14.5	1.8	77.3	39.6	48.1	51.9
17101	HARRISBURG	61.3	56.3	30.6	34.6	2.3	2.8	4.9	5.5	2.7	2.1	1.7	1.9	5.6	32.6	29.0	20.0	4.5	93.1	47.2	51.8	48.2
17102	HARRISBURG	44.8	40.6	46.4	49.8	1.7	2.0	6.0	6.5	5.3	4.7	5.1	4.7	6.2	34.1	25.6	11.5	2.9	82.3	38.9	50.1	49.9
17103	HARRISBURG	29.7	27.5	61.2	63.0	1.3	1.4	7.4	7.6	7.8	7.7	8.5	7.9	7.1	28.2	22.1	9.7	1.1	71.3	33.8	46.4	53.6
17104	HARRISBURG	32.3	28.7	48.4	50.9	4.7	5.3	18.1	18.5	9.6	8.5	8.5	7.5	7.3	27.8	21.8	7.8	1.2	68.7	31.2	46.5	53.5
17109	HARRISBURG	77.8	74.2	15.6	18.1	2.9	3.6	3.1	3.6	5.4	5.3	5.7	5.5	6.2	28.8	24.4	15.6	3.1	80.3	40.3	46.7	53.3
17110	HARRISBURG	57.7	54.5	36.1	38.6	1.9	2.3	3.8	4.1	6.3	6.4	7.1	7.1	6.0	27.8	27.6	10.2	1.5	75.6	38.3	47.2	52.9
17111	HARRISBURG	81.0	78.0	13.4	15.3	2.2	2.8	3.5	4.1	5.8	6.0	6.4	6.2	6.1	29.8	26.0	12.0	1.7	78.0	39.0	48.7	51.3
17112	HARRISBURG	93.3	91.7	3.3	4.1	1.9	2.5	1.3	1.7	5.3	6.0	7.3	6.4	4.9	25.9	30.4	12.5	1.3	77.2	41.8	48.8	51.2
17113	HARRISBURG	67.7	63.3	26.1	29.8	0.8	1.0	7.2	8.2	6.5	6.4	7.7	7.7	6.5	25.3	23.8	13.8	2.2	74.6	38.1	46.6	53.4
17201	CHAMBERSBURG	92.5	91.7	3.9	4.3	0.8	1.0	3.2	3.5	6.1	6.2	6.3	5.9	5.8	26.2	25.0	15.4	3.1	77.9	40.5	47.7	52.3
17211	ARTEMAS	99.1	99.1	0.3	0.3	0.0	0.0	0.3	0.3	5.9	6.2	6.9	6.5	5.0	26.5	28.0	14.0	0.9	77.3	40.5	52.0	48.0
17212	BIG COVE TANNERY	98.1	98.0	0.8	0.8	0.2	0.3	0.5	0.5	6.2	6.3	6.5	6.6	6.6	27.7	27.6	11.7	0.9	77.2	38.7	51.2	48.8
17213	BLAIRS MILLS	100.0	100.0	0.0	0.0	0.0	0.0	0.0	0.0	8.1	8.0	6.2	5.6	6.2	29.2	22.9	12.8	1.1	73.6	36.5	49.9	50.2
17214	BLUE RIDGE SUMMIT	94.5	93.9	2.4	2.7	1.1	1.4	1.9	2.1	5.7	5.7	5.8	5.7	5.8	28.5	27.5	13.6	1.9	79.3	41.1	49.2	50.8
17215	BURNT CABINS	99.5	99.5	0.6	0.5	0.0	0.0	0.0	0.0	5.3	5.3	6.9	6.9	5.8	27.0	27.5	13.8	1.6	78.3	40.8	47.1	52.9
17217	CONCORD	100.0	100.0	0.0	0.0	0.0	0.0	0.0	0.0	0.0	0.0	0.0	0.0	20.0	80.0	0.0	0.0	0.0	100.0	32.5	50.0	50.0
17219	DOYLESBURG	98.1	98.0	1.3	1.2	0.3	0.3	0.3	0.3	8.4	8.4	8.4	6.4	5.2	26.5	23.0	11.6	2.0	70.4	35.4	48.6	51.5
17220	DRY RUN	98.3	98.0	1.0	1.1	0.2	0.4	0.2	0.2	8.2	8.7	8.4	6.7	5.3	26.4	22.9	11.6	1.8	70.0	35.0	48.9	51.1
17221	FANNETTSBURG	99.1	99.0	0.4	0.4	0.2	0.2	0.4	0.5	6.1	6.4	7.6	6.2	5.4	28.7	25.4	13.0	1.2	75.8	39.2	51.0	49.0
17222	FAYETTEVILLE	95.9	95.4	2.0	2.2	0.5	0.6	1.2	1.4	5.5	5.9	6.1	6.6	4.4	24.9	26.4	18.0	2.1	78.0	42.5	49.6	50.4
17223	FORT LITTLETON	99.4	99.6	0.4	0.4	0.0	0.0	0.2	0.2	5.0	5.1	7.0	7.0	5.9	27.5	27.3	13.7	1.7	78.2	40.7	47.4	52.6
17224	FORT LOUDON	98.5	98.3	1.0	1.1	0.1	0.1	0.9	1.1	6.7	6.7	6.9	6.1	5.3	28.0	26.1	13.1	1.1	76.0	39.1	50.7	49.3
17225	GREENCASTLE	97.8	97.5	0.8	0.9	0.4	0.5	0.8	0.9	6.3	6.6	7.5	6.4	5.6	28.6	26.6	11.3	1.2	75.5	38.3	49.8	50.2
17228	HARRISONVILLE	98.9	98.7	0.0	0.0	0.2	0.3	0.1	0.2	6.3	6.7	7.7	6.4	5.6	27.9	25.3	12.9	1.2	75.4	38.1	51.2	48.8
17229	HUSTONTOWN	99.3	99.4	0.3	0.3	0.0	0.0	0.2	0.2	6.2	6.3	6.9	6.7	5.8	26.8	26.1	13.8	1.5	76.5	40.1	49.6	50.4
17232	LURGAN	97.8	100.0	0.0	0.0	0.0	0.0	0.0	0.0	8.3	8.3	8.3	6.3	4.2	31.3	20.8	12.5	0.0	75.0	33.8	54.2	45.8
17233	MC CONNELLSBURG	96.7	96.5	1.7	1.9	0.2	0.2	0.5	0.6	5.7	5.8	6.6	6.6	5.9	27.6	25.6	14.4	1.8	77.7	39.7	49.4	50.6
17236	MERCERSBURG	97.3	97.0	1.7	1.9	0.2	0.2	0.9	1.0	6.2	6.3	6.5	6.5	5.7	27.8	27.3	12.3	1.3	76.9	39.4	49.9	50.1
17237	MONT ALTO	97.6	97.2	1.0	1.1	0.8	1.1	0.2	0.2	6.8	6.8	7.0	5.7	5.9	30.9	24.2	11.7	1.1	76.2	37.0	48.5	51.5
17238	NEEDMORE	99.5	99.5	0.1	0.1	0.1	0.1	0.2	0.1	7.2	7.5	7.1	5.8	5.0	28.2	25.9	12.1	1.3	74.6	37.7	51.5	48.6
17239	NEELYTON	98.7	98.4	0.4	0.5	0.0	0.0	0.6	0.8	6.4	6.4	6.5	5.7	7.8	28.3	25.5	12.3	1.4	77.0	37.5	52.2	47.9
17240	NEWBURG	98.3	98.0	0.5	0.7	0.2	0.2	0.5	0.6	7.9	8.1	8.4	6.7	5.6	27.3	24.4	10.8	0.9	71.4	35.9	50.2	49.8
17241	NEWVILLE	98.3	98.1	0.4	0.5	0.3	0.4	0.6	0.7	7.1	7.2	7.4	6.1	5.9	27.8	26.2	10.6	1.7	74.5	37.9	50.1	49.9
17243	ORBISONIA	99.2	98.9	0.3	0.4	0.0	0.1	0.5	0.6	5.9	5.9	5.8	6.6	5.4	25.1	23.9	17.6	3.9	78.3	41.7	47.6	52.4
17244	ORRSTOWN	98.3	98.0	0.9	1.0	0.1	0.2	0.5	0.6	7.0	7.1	6.9	6.1	6.0	28.4	26.0	11.5	1.1	75.1	37.4	51.0	49.1
17246	PLEASANT HALL	100.0	100.0	0.0	0.0	0.0	0.0	0.0	0.0	0.0	0.0	0.0	0.0	0.0	57.1	42.9	0.0	0.0	100.0	42.5	57.1	42.9
17252	SAINT THOMAS	98.0	97.8	0.6	0.7	0.3	0.3	0.8	1.0	6.1	6.4	6.9	6.5	5.8	27.8	27.3	12.0	1.1	76.5	39.3	50.3	49.7
17255	SHADE GAP	98.6	98.7	0.5	0.5	0.0	0.0	0.7	0.7	6.3	6.5	6.5	5.8	7.6	28.3	25.6	12.3	1.1	76.9	37.5	51.6	48.4
17257	SHIPPENSBURG	95.9	95.3	2.1	2.3	0.8	0.9	0.9	1.0	5.7	5.6	6.2	12.2	15.4	22.9	20.2	10.5	1.3	78.9	29.2	48.3	51.7
17260	SHIRLEYSBURG	98.3	98.0	0.6	0.8	0.2	0.3	0.7	0.7	5.5	5.8	6.5	6.6	5.4	24.8	28.4	15.1	1.9	78.4	41.9	50.5	49.5
17262	SPRING RUN	99.0	98.8	0.4	0.5	0.1	0.2	0.5	0.6	8.3	8.3	8.0	6.4	5.7	27.1	23.9	11.0	1.3	71.2	34.7	49.8	50.2
17264	THREE SPRINGS	99.2	99.1	0.1	0.2	0.0	0.0	0.2	0.2	6.1	6.1	6.7	6.0	5.0	26.5	26.1	15.8	1.8	77.5	40.3	51.4	48.6
17265	UPPERSTRASBURG	98.2	97.8	1.2	1.7	0.0	0.0	0.6	1.1	6.2	6.2	6.7	5.6	6.2	29.2	28.1	10.7	1.1	77.5	38.3	52.3	47.8
17266	WALNUT BOTTOM	98.3	98.1	0.5	0.5	0.2	0.2	0.5	0.5	6.9	7.2	8.1	7.2	6.4	26.3	26.5	10.0	1.4	73.5	37.0	49.6	50.4
17267	WARFORDSBURG	98.6	98.5	0.2	0.2	0.1	0.1	0.4	0.4	6.7	6.8	6.5	6.2	5.5	27.7	27.3	12.0	1.4	76.3	38.2	51.3	48.7
17268	WAYNESBORO	96.5	95.9	1.7	1.9	0.7	0.9	1.0	1.2	6.2	5.9	6.4	7.0	6.6	26.6	24.8	14.3	2.4	77.7	39.2	48.4	51.6
17271	WILLOW HILL	99.0	98.8	0.4	0.6	0.2	0.2	0.4	0.4	6.4	6.6	7.7	6.4	5.4	28.8	25.0	12.5	1.4	75.4	38.9	50.4	49.6
17301	ABBOTTSTOWN	97.5	97.1	0.3	0.4	0.4	0.5	2.4	2.8	6.8	7.2	7.2	6.4	5.1	30.1	27.0	9.4	0.7	74.6	37.8	50.4	49.6
17302	AIRVILLE	97.8	97.2	0.5	0.7	0.6	0.8	0.5	0.7	6.7	7.7	9.5	7.7	5.0	29.5	24.9	8.0	1.1	71.1	36.2	51.1	48.9
17304	ASPERS	93.1	92.3	1.2	1.4	0.2	0.2	9.2	10.3	6.9	7.4	7.8	6.1	6.1	29.0	25.6	10.0	1.1	74.3	36.9	50.7	49.3
17307	BIGLERVILLE	93.2	92.4	1.0	1.1	0.1	0.1	8.9	10.0	5.9	6.4	7.7	6.8	5.7	27.4	26.6	12.0	1.5	75.8	38.9	50.4	49.6
17309	BROGUE	97.5	97.1	0.6	0.8	0.4	0.6	0.8	0.9	6.5	6.8	7.7	6.7	5.0	30.9	25.8	9.4	1.2	74.7	37.3	51.2	48.8
17313	DALLASTOWN	97.1	96.6	0.8	0.9	0.7	0.8	1.4	1.6	5.9	6.0	6.9	6.8	6.1	29.0	24.9	12.2	2.2	77.0	38.4	49.1	50.9
17314	DELTA	96.9	96.2	1.7	2.1	0.3	0.4	0.5	0.6	7.1	7.4	8.6	7.1	5.2	30.1	24.5	8.8	1.1	72.4	36.6	51.3	48.7
17315	DOVER	97.2	96.6	1.0	1.2	0.4	0.6	1.0	1.2	6.0	6.4	6.9	6.4	5.6	29.2	27.4	10.9	1.3	76.7	39.0	49.7	50.3
17316	EAST BERLIN	98.1	97.8	0.3	0.3	0.2	0.3	1.5	1.7	7.5	7.8	7.9	6.5	5.0	30.7	24.7	9.2	0.8	72.6	36.7	49.5	50.5
17319	ETTERS	97.2	96.6	0.9	1.0	0.7	1.0	1.3	1.6	6.9	7.2	8.1	6.8	5.9	32.1	26.3	6.2	0.5	73.5	36.4	49.6	50.4
17320	FAIRFIELD	97.2	96.9	0.4	0.5	0.4	0.5	0.9	1.0	6.5	6.8	7.7	6.5	4.7	28.8	26.8	11.0	1.2	74.7	38.9	49.5	50.5
17321	FAWN GROVE	98.3	97.9	0.7	0.9	0.3	0.3	0.4	0.6	6.6	7.0	7.6	6.2	4.8	29.9	26.8	9.8	1.3	74.8	39.0	49.4	50.6
17322	FELTON	98.2	97.8	0.7	0.9	0.3	0.5	0.5	0.6	6.3	6.9	7.7	6.4	4.9	29.4	29.2	8.4	1.0	75.0	38.6	50.9	49.1
17324	GARDNERS	96.9	96.4	0.7	0.8	0.5	0.6	3.7	4.2	5.7	6.4	6.5	6.9	5.6	28.8	27.5	11.6	1.1	77.3	39.5	50.5	49.5
17325	GETTYSBURG	92.3	91.5	2.9	3.1	1.0	1.2	4.5	5.0	4.8	5.2	6.2	8.8	11.1	22.8	25.0	13.7	2.4	80.1	38.2	48.3	51.8
17327	GLEN ROCK	98.5	98.2	0.5	0.5	0.3	0.4	0.4	0.5	5.0	5.8	7.7	6.9	5.7	25.5	29.6	12.4	1.3	77.1	41.4	50.2	49.8
17329	GLENVILLE	98.6	98.4	0.1	0.0	0.3	0.4	0.3	0.3	5.5	6.5	7.8	7.2	5.1	26.5	31.1	9.7	0.7	75.5	40.6	50.8	49.2
17331	HANOVER	97.5	97.0	0.5	0.6	0.7	0.9	1.4	1.7	5.8	6.0	6.9	6.4	5.6	27.7	26.1	13.4	2.2	77.3	40.1	49.0	51.0
17339	LEWISBERRY	97.8	97.3	0.5	0.6	0.7	1.0	0.7	0.9	5.3	6.1	6.9	5.9	5.1	27.0	32.5	9.9	1.4	78.0	41.6	49.8	50.2
17340	LITTLESTOWN	97.8	97.5	0.5	0.6	0.5	0.6	1.1	1.2	6.1	6.6	8.0	7.3	5.9	27.9	25.0	11.8	1.4	74.5	38.1	48.8	51.2
17344	MC SHERRYSTOWN	98.0	97.7	0.5	0.6	0.3	0.3	1.4	1.6	6.5	6.2	6.6	6.1	5.7	29.8	23.1	13.8	2.2	76.9	38.2	47.4	52.6
17345	MANCHESTER	97.3	96.8	0.9	1.1	0.4	0.6	1.3	1.6	6.3	6.5	6.9	6.1	5.5	30.4	26.8	10.7	1.0	76.5	38.2	49.8	50.2
17347	MOUNT WOLF	97.3	96.7	1.0	1.3	0.6	0.8	1.1	1.3	6.3	6.6	6.9	5.4	4.9	30.5	25.9	11.9	1.5	76.7	38.8	50.0	50.0
17349	NEW FREEDOM	97.4	96.8	0.5	0.7	0.9	1.2	0.8	1.0	5.6	6.4	7.3	6.6	5.1	24.5	31.6	10.7	2.2	76.5	41.9	48.9	51.1
17350	NEW OXFORD	95.9	95.3	0.6	0.7	0.5	0.6	4.1	4.7	6.2	6.6	7.4	6.9	5.8	27.7	22.8	13.0	3.8	75.5	38.5	48.9	51.1
17352	NEW PARK	97.5	97.1	0.9	1.1	0.5	0.7	0.3	0.5	6.0	6.8	8.6	6.4	5.0	28.5	29.0	8.8	0.9	74.6	39.3	49.3	50.7
17353	ORRTANNA	95.5	95.0	1.5	1.7	0.2	0.2	2.8	3.1	5.1	5.6	6.6	6.6	5.3	26.1	30.2	12.6	2.1	78.6	41.9	50.1	49.9
17356	RED LION	97.7	97.2	0.5	0.6	0.5	0.7	1.0	1.2	6.7	6.9	7.3	6.4	5.5	29.8	25.7	10.5	1.3	75.1	37.9	49.4	50.6
17360	SEVEN VALLEYS	98.2	97.9	0.3	0.4	0.3	0.4	0.6	0.7	5.0	5.6	7.1	6.2	5.6	27.6	29.9	12.1	1.0	78.6	41.3	50.1	49.9
17361	SHREWSBURY	98.0	97.4	0.6	0.8	0.7	1.0	0.9	1.1	6.1	6.6	7.5	6.6	5.0	24.8	30.4	11.6	1.5	75.6	41.5	49.2	50.8
17362	SPRING GROVE	98.3	97.9	0.3	0.3	0.3	0.4	0.8	1.0	5.5	6.1	7.6	7.0	5.3	28.0	28.9	10.7	1.0	76.3	39.7	50.8	49.2
17363	STEWARTSTOWN	97.7	97.2	0.9	1.1	0.4	0.6	1.0	1.2	6.9	7.5	8.4	6.8	4.7	28.8	27.4	8.7	0.9	72.9	38.4	50.1	49.9
17364	THOMASVILLE	98.8	98.5	0.3	0.4	0.3	0.4	0.5	0.7	6.1	6.6	6.7	6.8	4.8	28.9	28.4	10.9	0.8	76.0	39.8	51.1	49.0
17365	WELLSVILLE	98.3	97.9	0.3	0.4	0.4	0.6	0.8	1.0	5.3	5.9	6.7	6.1	5.0	28.2	31.9	9.9	0.9	78.2	41.0	50.1	49.9
17366	WINDSOR	98.6	98.3	0.4	0.5	0.1	0.2	1.0	1.2	7.0	7.2	8.0	7.4	6.2	30.7	23.9	8.7	0.9	73.3	35.9	49.7	50.3
17368	WRIGHTSVILLE	98.0	97.6	0.4	0.5	0.2	0.3	1.4	1.8	5.9	6.1	6.9	6.4	5.5	30.3	27.3	10.5	1.2	77.1	39.1	49.8	50.2
17370	YORK HAVEN	97.5	97.0	0.5	0.5	0.4	0.6	1.4	1.7	7.4	7.4	7.9	6.7	6.1	31.6	24.7	7.7	0.6	73.1	36.1	50.5	49.5
17372	YORK SPRINGS	96.8	96.3	0.2	0.3	0.6	0.8	5.0	5.5	6.6	7.0	7.2	6.1	5.2	29.8	26.0	11.0	1.2	75.2	38.5	51.0	49.0
17401	YORK	64.0	59.1	23.3	26.3	1.6	1.9	16.1	18.4	5.8	5.0	4.5	4.9	9.7	37.9	23.8	7.7	0.8	82.6	35.7	55.4	44.6
	PENNSYLVANIA	85.4	84.4	10.0	10.3	1.8	2.2	3.2	3.5	5.9	6.1	6.8	6.9	6.7	26.6	25.3	13.3	2.2	77.2	39.1	48.4	51.6
	UNITED STATES	75.1	73.6	12.3	12.5	3.8	4.2	12.5	14.1	6.9	6.7	7.2	7.0	7.3	28.6	23.8	10.8	1.7	75.1	36.0	49.1	50.9

#	POST OFFICE NAME	2004 Per Capita Income	2004 HH Income Base	2004 Household Income Distribution (%): Less than $25,000	$25,000 to $49,999	$50,000 to $99,999	$100,000 to $149,999	$150,000 or More	Median Household Income: 2004	2009	2004 National Centile	2004 State Centile	2004 Home Value Base	2004 Home Value Distribution (%): Less than $50,000	$50,000 to $89,999	$90,000 to $174,999	$175,000 to $399,999	$400,000 or More	2004 Median Home Value
17082	PORT ROYAL	18314	1381	25.4	38.1	29.3	5.7	1.5	41047	47151	50	49	1116	8.4	22.0	49.3	17.9	2.3	114228
17084	REEDSVILLE	19565	1564	27.3	32.2	29.3	8.2	3.0	42049	48079	53	53	1297	4.7	20.4	54.2	19.4	1.3	119974
17086	RICHFIELD	19037	659	24.3	34.1	33.5	5.0	3.0	43134	50341	56	57	551	8.5	14.5	53.7	21.4	1.8	121221
17087	RICHLAND	22004	1074	16.7	31.8	39.8	8.6	3.3	51145	60178	74	74	881	3.8	15.9	64.5	13.6	2.3	119853
17090	SHERMANS DALE	23651	2248	17.5	31.6	37.9	10.5	2.6	50581	57329	73	72	1915	24.9	12.4	44.2	17.3	1.3	111036
17094	THOMPSONTOWN	20352	1152	26.7	39.6	27.8	3.8	2.2	38535	44002	41	38	873	10.7	17.9	53.8	15.8	1.8	115892
17097	WICONISCO	19671	28	28.6	28.6	39.3	3.6	0.0	42337	50000	54	54	23	34.8	43.5	21.7	0.0	0.0	61667
17098	WILLIAMSTOWN	19705	1074	27.7	33.9	33.2	4.1	1.1	41127	48753	50	49	839	30.6	41.6	24.9	2.3	0.6	65105
17099	YEAGERTOWN	23146	490	15.9	40.2	32.2	11.0	0.6	46289	53774	65	65	374	5.6	27.3	56.2	10.7	0.3	107207
17101	HARRISBURG	30496	1397	51.8	23.1	20.1	3.4	1.7	23903	28207	4	2	88	5.7	26.1	59.1	9.1	0.0	122727
17102	HARRISBURG	21533	4194	45.7	29.3	20.0	3.6	1.5	27959	33357	9	4	1130	17.4	45.3	35.4	1.9	0.0	82577
17103	HARRISBURG	17440	4383	35.2	34.9	24.4	4.0	1.5	34636	40672	26	19	2515	20.3	49.5	27.1	2.5	0.6	72563
17104	HARRISBURG	17423	8038	41.4	29.1	21.9	5.4	2.3	30551	35945	14	7	3751	24.6	55.0	16.1	3.7	0.5	65162
17109	HARRISBURG	26529	10563	19.1	34.5	34.3	9.5	2.6	46854	56445	66	66	6029	1.9	12.0	75.1	10.6	0.4	121306
17110	HARRISBURG	30636	9303	20.7	26.6	31.9	14.0	6.8	52957	64652	77	77	6255	7.6	21.5	49.5	19.8	1.6	120508
17111	HARRISBURG	28797	11083	16.7	27.8	37.8	13.0	4.8	55824	67722	80	81	7848	1.7	12.4	67.8	16.7	1.4	125949
17112	HARRISBURG	33426	12774	12.2	21.3	41.4	15.8	9.3	65334	78668	89	90	10802	1.9	6.9	57.6	30.6	3.0	148691
17113	HARRISBURG	20739	4602	29.6	34.4	28.3	5.2	2.6	39492	47490	44	42	3013	14.7	35.9	46.3	3.1	0.0	89548
17201	CHAMBERSBURG	24757	20411	24.3	31.3	32.2	8.6	3.7	45589	52479	63	63	14444	7.9	10.5	57.8	22.1	1.7	132640
17211	ARTEMAS	18295	133	26.3	43.6	24.8	3.0	2.3	35836	40745	31	24	114	9.7	21.1	48.3	20.2	0.9	110577
17212	BIG COVE TANNERY	21131	406	26.4	34.0	31.3	5.7	2.7	41352	46812	51	50	329	12.2	13.1	56.5	14.6	3.7	122243
17213	BLAIRS MILLS	17436	248	31.9	35.9	26.2	4.4	1.6	37822	43176	39	34	211	18.0	18.5	41.2	19.9	2.4	115074
17214	BLUE RIDGE SUMMIT	26294	494	17.4	35.6	37.7	5.7	3.6	48520	57127	69	69	335	7.5	12.8	46.6	31.0	2.1	137500
17215	BURNT CABINS	22007	87	31.0	33.3	28.7	4.6	2.3	39530	45000	44	42	70	18.6	24.3	48.6	8.6	0.0	98333
17217	CONCORD	425	0	0.0	0.0	0.0	0.0	0.0	0	79167	0	0	3	0.0	0.0	100.0	0.0	0.0	112500
17219	DOYLESBURG	18103	125	30.4	32.8	28.8	6.4	1.6	40320	46745	47	46	102	11.8	20.6	39.2	24.5	3.9	114706
17220	DRY RUN	15940	144	31.3	32.6	28.5	6.3	1.4	40000	47086	46	44	118	11.0	20.3	40.7	23.7	4.2	115476
17221	FANNETTSBURG	20176	233	27.9	34.3	30.9	4.7	2.2	39862	46543	45	44	194	15.0	20.6	47.9	12.4	4.1	106875
17222	FAYETTEVILLE	24706	3611	16.6	31.5	39.1	10.0	2.8	51262	59816	74	74	3065	9.0	13.7	50.7	24.3	2.2	129074
17223	FORT LITTLETON	18855	215	29.3	33.0	31.2	4.2	2.3	40746	45160	49	48	174	16.7	23.6	50.0	8.6	1.2	101250
17224	FORT LOUDON	20246	740	29.5	35.7	26.4	5.4	3.1	38911	45000	42	40	596	9.7	19.8	50.0	16.6	3.9	113321
17225	GREENCASTLE	23029	6617	18.9	29.7	40.6	8.2	2.6	50944	58735	74	74	5163	5.4	6.4	55.6	30.2	2.4	143438
17228	HARRISONVILLE	18254	435	26.4	36.1	30.6	4.8	2.1	40076	44728	46	45	356	15.5	19.9	41.3	20.2	3.1	112698
17229	HUSTONTOWN	18318	464	29.5	33.6	31.0	4.3	1.5	39014	43735	43	40	380	14.2	24.0	46.6	14.0	1.3	103797
17232	LURGAN	23998	21	19.1	23.8	47.6	9.5	0.0	57143	60000	82	83	18	0.0	11.1	61.1	27.8	0.0	140000
17233	MC CONNELLSBURG	20034	2112	31.8	33.8	27.6	5.1	1.8	37674	42960	38	34	1514	18.7	15.3	49.3	14.1	2.5	110757
17236	MERCERSBURG	23582	3223	21.4	30.0	34.9	9.8	3.8	48485	55512	69	69	2480	7.9	9.9	51.8	28.2	2.2	136629
17237	MONT ALTO	21344	436	19.5	38.1	34.6	6.7	1.2	44862	53157	61	61	346	4.9	18.5	66.8	9.8	0.0	113514
17238	NEEDMORE	20878	732	24.5	38.4	29.6	5.5	2.1	41404	46926	51	50	619	12.6	15.4	49.4	20.0	2.6	118989
17239	NEELYTON	21715	359	29.0	35.9	26.2	5.6	3.3	38355	44462	41	37	302	18.9	21.2	43.4	15.2	1.3	103070
17240	NEWBURG	21339	1021	20.0	31.8	39.3	6.4	2.6	48614	56734	69	69	869	6.8	13.8	56.5	20.4	2.5	128328
17241	NEWVILLE	21050	4714	19.8	31.0	40.4	7.4	1.4	49362	58309	71	70	3845	11.9	13.7	52.6	19.0	2.8	121545
17243	ORBISONIA	18886	983	32.2	32.7	29.6	3.8	1.8	37818	44023	39	34	780	22.7	28.9	39.9	7.4	1.2	88378
17244	ORRSTOWN	21232	1071	18.2	35.6	35.5	7.8	2.9	47531	54585	67	67	905	9.1	10.1	54.1	24.1	2.7	138203
17246	PLEASANT HALL	25648	6	0.0	33.3	66.7	0.0	0.0	60000	79274	84	85	5	0.0	0.0	60.0	40.0	0.0	162500
17252	SAINT THOMAS	20836	1372	20.8	34.7	35.6	6.7	2.2	46134	52819	64	64	1158	16.8	10.6	53.0	18.1	1.4	116327
17255	SHADE GAP	19569	179	28.5	36.3	27.4	5.0	2.8	38846	44145	42	40	150	18.0	22.0	42.7	16.0	1.3	102778
17257	SHIPPENSBURG	18552	8432	29.1	29.3	33.5	6.2	1.9	42476	50128	55	55	5719	14.7	14.9	50.3	17.3	2.9	119504
17260	SHIRLEYSBURG	18215	548	31.6	34.9	30.1	2.7	0.7	35566	41307	30	23	472	28.4	29.9	32.0	7.2	2.5	80930
17262	SPRING RUN	19062	736	27.6	35.3	28.7	6.4	2.0	40864	47516	49	48	604	12.4	16.7	49.3	18.2	3.3	113542
17264	THREE SPRINGS	17905	994	34.8	35.6	23.6	4.4	1.5	34853	40438	27	20	802	23.9	29.4	37.4	8.7	0.5	85781
17265	UPPERSTRASBURG	22491	72	18.1	37.5	34.7	8.3	1.4	46517	52547	65	65	61	13.1	11.5	54.1	21.3	0.0	131250
17266	WALNUT BOTTOM	22241	160	16.3	31.3	44.4	5.6	2.5	51486	60000	75	74	136	6.6	16.9	52.9	19.1	4.4	123077
17267	WARFORDSBURG	18571	1106	25.2	40.1	29.1	4.5	1.0	40229	45229	47	45	907	15.1	16.5	47.3	20.0	1.1	117336
17268	WAYNESBORO	22385	11082	24.1	31.6	34.2	7.9	2.3	45070	52457	61	62	8072	6.3	12.2	59.5	20.2	1.8	126414
17271	WILLOW HILL	17445	176	28.4	33.5	31.3	4.6	2.3	40000	46472	46	44	146	14.4	21.2	46.6	13.7	4.1	107143
17301	ABBOTTSTOWN	22983	1409	15.7	25.8	45.4	9.7	3.4	55378	62897	80	80	1214	8.7	6.3	52.4	30.2	2.4	145455
17302	AIRVILLE	21095	1011	17.8	31.4	40.1	8.7	2.1	50670	58376	73	73	844	5.9	11.0	55.5	23.3	4.3	139773
17304	ASPERS	19447	1207	22.3	31.7	34.0	10.6	1.5	47385	53980	67	67	975	4.6	10.1	58.5	24.9	2.0	136662
17307	BIGLERVILLE	20775	2138	20.9	32.4	37.2	7.5	2.0	47149	53842	66	66	1701	5.7	7.1	50.1	35.2	1.9	151042
17309	BROGUE	25389	932	18.6	22.4	43.7	11.5	3.9	58747	65838	83	84	799	9.9	10.6	58.8	18.8	1.9	127854
17313	DALLASTOWN	25807	4109	20.0	27.4	37.8	12.1	2.8	52527	61654	76	76	2826	2.4	13.4	70.3	12.4	1.5	127786
17314	DELTA	19890	2066	18.4	33.9	38.3	7.4	1.9	48239	55719	69	68	1708	3.7	12.4	62.4	19.7	1.8	132133
17315	DOVER	23934	9415	16.3	29.5	42.9	9.6	1.8	52991	61322	77	77	7635	11.0	9.3	61.3	17.3	1.1	127483
17316	EAST BERLIN	23308	2835	15.6	28.6	41.9	11.3	2.7	54268	62045	79	79	2364	4.1	5.8	52.8	35.0	2.4	152836
17319	ETTERS	26059	3745	12.8	27.0	41.3	13.0	5.9	60363	68405	85	86	3319	11.2	10.0	56.0	19.7	3.0	129160
17320	FAIRFIELD	24445	2855	14.9	26.7	44.1	10.7	3.7	55730	63878	80	81	2475	2.8	5.3	50.6	38.5	2.8	161531
17321	FAWN GROVE	23960	841	12.6	24.1	46.0	14.6	2.6	61141	68546	85	88	716	2.0	6.0	51.4	38.7	2.0	162684
17322	FELTON	25076	2111	14.2	24.7	44.1	12.2	4.8	60074	67281	84	85	1876	4.2	8.2	56.9	27.7	3.0	147602
17324	GARDNERS	24321	1664	17.4	27.9	42.4	7.2	5.1	52976	61591	77	77	1396	9.5	14.2	56.3	17.6	2.5	125794
17325	GETTYSBURG	22627	9787	25.2	29.3	32.4	9.5	3.6	45482	52317	63	63	6988	8.1	6.4	45.6	35.2	4.8	156721
17327	GLEN ROCK	24287	2913	15.1	28.5	41.8	10.7	3.9	55689	64154	80	81	2366	2.3	5.8	52.9	33.5	5.5	154351
17329	GLENVILLE	26713	817	13.1	22.6	44.4	13.5	6.4	62186	70126	86	88	738	0.8	4.1	40.9	50.7	3.5	182381
17331	HANOVER	24092	18755	20.0	29.2	39.6	8.3	2.9	50573	58855	73	72	14051	1.7	11.1	63.8	22.4	1.0	133806
17339	LEWISBERRY	30874	2229	10.9	25.0	39.2	15.1	9.8	63159	73305	87	89	1929	2.6	5.8	51.7	34.9	4.9	156129
17340	LITTLESTOWN	21589	3933	20.2	31.6	37.1	8.8	2.3	48493	55782	69	69	3083	0.8	4.6	53.7	37.7	3.3	161485
17344	MC SHERRYSTOWN	23506	1364	27.8	35.1	26.7	8.2	2.2	39758	46716	45	43	847	2.7	5.6	78.8	13.0	0.0	122942
17345	MANCHESTER	22834	3291	16.2	34.2	38.7	9.3	1.7	49621	57840	71	71	2533	7.5	18.8	62.8	10.7	0.1	114852
17347	MOUNT WOLF	23144	1450	18.2	31.2	38.4	9.5	2.6	50459	58830	73	72	1293	22.0	12.8	51.9	13.1	0.2	116524
17349	NEW FREEDOM	29487	2893	11.3	18.8	42.2	20.0	7.7	69873	83592	91	92	2494	2.7	2.7	41.3	51.2	2.1	181050
17350	NEW OXFORD	21093	4743	20.4	31.9	37.9	7.9	1.9	48309	55474	69	69	3655	9.2	6.9	57.9	23.3	2.7	137858
17352	NEW PARK	25441	484	12.0	25.0	43.4	16.1	3.5	60278	68092	85	86	421	3.3	4.8	42.8	45.8	3.3	173694
17353	ORRTANNA	22884	1288	18.5	28.0	42.9	7.5	3.1	51664	58866	75	75	1075	5.5	11.7	54.1	27.0	1.7	139710
17356	RED LION	24367	7507	17.8	31.1	37.9	9.4	3.8	50804	59511	73	73	5847	3.6	12.3	62.3	20.7	1.2	128511
17360	SEVEN VALLEYS	25187	1838	15.3	27.2	42.7	11.1	3.8	56103	64359	81	82	1559	4.0	5.3	57.7	30.0	3.1	147799
17361	SHREWSBURY	27066	1929	16.7	19.7	44.8	13.4	5.3	60318	69750	85	86	1552	0.8	2.1	55.8	40.0	1.4	167002
17362	SPRING GROVE	24092	4917	13.3	27.8	46.3	10.0	2.7	56332	64281	81	82	4069	2.5	8.4	59.2	27.5	2.4	144139
17363	STEWARTSTOWN	25723	3291	15.3	22.2	40.2	18.8	3.4	63348	72729	87	89	2795	4.9	2.9	45.6	42.3	4.2	169867
17364	THOMASVILLE	22353	1276	17.6	27.7	45.4	7.4	1.9	53523	61667	78	78	1096	12.1	5.5	53.9	26.4	2.1	138083
17365	WELLSVILLE	25361	1005	14.8	30.0	42.4	8.8	4.1	53786	61970	78	78	848	2.8	10.0	53.2	31.7	2.2	147314
17366	WINDSOR	21027	1886	18.3	30.9	41.2	6.8	2.8	50425	58612	73	72	1524	12.5	20.5	51.1	15.3	0.7	111986
17368	WRIGHTSVILLE	23374	3186	18.3	30.3	40.9	8.1	2.4	50937	59212	74	73	2517	7.4	16.0	57.9	16.8	2.0	117693
17370	YORK HAVEN	23764	2256	16.0	29.6	39.9	10.9	3.6	53312	61369	77	78	1875	22.5	14.6	43.8	16.9	2.2	114638
17372	YORK SPRINGS	21997	1273	17.8	28.2	42.7	8.6	2.8	52599	60186	76	76	1055	3.6	8.0	55.4	29.4	3.7	147229
17401	YORK	16104	474	49.6	35.4	13.7	1.3	0.0	25168	28648	5	2	77	28.6	49.4	9.1	13.0	0.0	63056
	PENNSYLVANIA	25764		25.8	27.2	31.2	10.2	5.7	46988	57000				11.9	18.4	40.7	25.1	4.1	123516
	UNITED STATES	25866		24.7	27.1	30.8	10.9	6.5	48124	56710				10.9	15.0	33.7	30.1	10.4	145905

ZIP CODE #	POST OFFICE NAME	FINANCIAL SERVICES: Auto Loan	Home Loan	Invest-ments	Retire-ment Plans	THE HOME: Home Improvements: Home Repair	Lawn & Garden	Furnishings: Comput-ers & Hard-ware	Major Appli-ances	TV, Radio, Sound Equip-ment	Furni-ture	ENTERTAINMENT: Dine out/ Carry out	Sports Equip-ment	Fees & Tickets	Toys & Games	Travel	Cable TV	PERSONAL: Apparel & Services	Auto Repairs	Health Insur-ance	Pets & Supplies
17082	PORT ROYAL	73	68	58	65	71	78	65	70	69	64	84	81	65	87	67	71	80	68	75	85
17084	REEDSVILLE	81	74	61	70	78	85	70	76	75	70	91	89	70	94	72	77	87	74	83	95
17086	RICHFIELD	92	70	41	63	76	85	66	78	75	67	90	93	60	88	67	80	83	77	92	107
17087	RICHLAND	97	87	69	83	92	98	81	89	85	81	104	106	80	106	83	87	99	87	95	113
17090	SHERMANS DALE	100	90	69	86	92	98	85	92	87	86	107	108	81	105	85	88	102	91	95	114
17094	THOMPSONTOWN	79	67	49	63	71	79	65	72	70	64	84	84	62	84	66	73	79	71	80	91
17097	WICONISCO	59	64	67	60	64	72	63	62	65	61	81	69	67	88	65	68	78	61	67	69
17098	WILLIAMSTOWN	60	65	69	62	66	73	65	64	67	62	83	71	68	90	67	69	80	63	69	70
17099	YEAGERTOWN	86	79	65	76	83	89	74	80	77	74	94	95	73	96	76	79	90	78	86	101
17101	HARRISBURG	49	46	62	47	45	51	53	50	55	52	69	58	53	67	52	55	67	53	51	55
17102	HARRISBURG	53	45	61	48	45	51	58	52	59	55	74	64	55	71	55	58	72	58	53	59
17103	HARRISBURG	58	55	64	53	54	61	59	58	63	60	78	66	60	77	59	64	76	60	60	65
17104	HARRISBURG	60	56	68	54	54	61	61	59	65	62	81	68	62	80	60	65	79	61	60	67
17109	HARRISBURG	75	80	95	80	79	86	82	79	81	81	102	92	84	103	82	81	100	81	78	87
17110	HARRISBURG	96	104	123	104	102	108	104	102	103	104	129	118	108	131	105	102	127	103	97	113
17111	HARRISBURG	90	99	108	99	97	101	96	95	93	96	116	110	99	119	96	91	114	94	89	104
17112	HARRISBURG	109	130	142	129	128	131	120	119	114	119	143	137	127	150	122	112	142	116	111	130
17113	HARRISBURG	68	68	68	64	69	78	69	70	73	67	89	78	70	93	70	75	85	69	76	78
17201	CHAMBERSBURG	86	84	81	81	86	93	82	85	84	81	104	98	82	105	83	85	100	84	89	100
17211	ARTEMAS	75	59	40	53	66	74	55	67	63	55	74	78	50	73	59	67	69	66	79	91
17212	BIG COVE TANNERY	97	70	39	63	78	88	67	81	78	68	92	97	60	89	68	83	85	80	96	112
17213	BLAIRS MILLS	87	59	27	51	66	76	57	71	68	58	80	84	48	76	57	73	73	70	87	100
17214	BLUE RIDGE SUMMIT	91	77	60	77	81	91	80	85	84	78	102	97	76	101	79	86	96	84	92	100
17215	BURNT CABINS	89	59	27	51	67	77	57	72	69	58	81	86	49	77	58	75	74	71	88	102
17217	CONCORD	0	0	0	0	0	0	0	0	0	0	0	0	0	0	0	0	0	0	0	0
17219	DOYLESBURG	92	61	28	53	70	80	59	74	72	60	84	89	50	79	60	77	76	73	91	105
17220	DRY RUN	92	61	28	53	70	80	59	74	72	60	84	89	50	79	60	77	76	73	91	105
17221	FANNETTSBURG	94	63	29	54	71	82	61	76	74	62	86	91	52	82	62	79	78	75	94	108
17222	FAYETTEVILLE	87	86	80	81	88	96	81	86	84	81	103	99	82	106	84	87	100	84	92	103
17223	FORT LITTLETON	89	59	27	51	67	77	57	72	69	58	81	86	49	77	58	74	74	71	88	102
17224	FORT LOUDON	87	66	39	59	72	81	62	74	71	63	85	88	57	83	64	75	79	73	87	101
17225	GREENCASTLE	94	84	66	81	88	96	79	87	84	79	102	102	78	104	81	86	97	85	94	109
17228	HARRISONVILLE	90	60	27	52	68	78	58	73	70	59	82	87	49	78	59	75	75	72	89	103
17229	HUSTONTOWN	86	58	26	50	65	75	56	70	67	57	79	83	47	75	57	72	72	69	86	99
17232	LURGAN	88	78	60	74	83	89	72	80	77	72	93	96	71	95	74	79	89	78	87	103
17233	MC CONNELLSBURG	85	58	29	52	65	76	58	71	69	58	81	83	50	77	59	74	74	70	86	96
17236	MERCERSBURG	97	83	61	79	88	96	79	88	85	78	103	103	76	103	81	88	97	86	97	112
17237	MONT ALTO	82	73	56	69	77	83	68	75	72	68	87	89	66	89	70	74	83	73	81	97
17238	NEEDMORE	96	70	39	62	77	87	66	80	77	67	91	95	59	88	68	82	84	79	95	110
17239	NEELYTON	109	73	33	63	82	95	70	88	85	71	99	105	60	94	71	91	90	87	108	125
17240	NEWBURG	103	92	70	87	97	104	85	94	90	85	109	112	83	112	87	92	104	91	102	121
17241	NEWVILLE	86	79	64	76	83	89	74	80	78	74	95	96	73	97	76	79	91	79	86	101
17243	ORBISONIA	76	61	42	54	66	75	59	68	67	59	81	79	55	80	61	71	75	67	79	88
17244	ORRSTOWN	91	81	61	77	85	91	74	83	79	74	96	98	73	98	77	81	91	80	89	107
17246	PLEASANT HALL	96	85	65	81	90	97	79	88	84	79	102	104	77	104	81	86	97	85	95	113
17252	SAINT THOMAS	84	77	63	73	81	87	71	78	75	71	92	92	71	94	74	77	88	76	84	99
17255	SHADE GAP	92	61	28	53	69	80	59	74	71	60	84	88	50	79	60	77	76	73	91	105
17257	SHIPPENSBURG	76	64	57	64	66	74	71	70	73	68	90	85	66	88	68	72	85	72	74	85
17260	SHIRLEYSBURG	85	57	26	49	65	75	55	69	67	56	78	82	47	74	56	72	71	68	85	98
17262	SPRING RUN	94	66	33	58	73	84	63	77	74	64	88	92	55	84	64	79	80	76	93	108
17264	THREE SPRINGS	79	55	28	48	62	71	53	65	62	53	74	77	45	70	54	67	67	64	79	92
17265	UPPERSTRASBURG	89	79	60	75	84	90	73	81	78	73	95	97	72	97	75	80	90	79	88	105
17266	WALNUT BOTTOM	92	82	62	78	87	93	76	84	80	76	98	100	74	100	78	82	93	82	91	108
17267	WARFORDSBURG	88	59	27	51	67	77	57	71	69	58	81	85	48	76	58	74	73	71	88	101
17268	WAYNESBORO	84	76	63	72	79	87	74	79	78	73	95	93	72	97	75	80	90	78	86	98
17271	WILLOW HILL	94	63	28	54	71	82	61	76	73	62	86	91	52	81	62	79	78	75	93	108
17301	ABBOTTSTOWN	102	91	69	86	96	103	84	93	89	84	108	111	82	111	86	91	103	91	101	120
17302	AIRVILLE	91	84	69	82	87	93	80	86	83	80	101	101	78	102	81	83	96	84	89	105
17304	ASPERS	86	75	58	73	80	87	73	80	77	72	94	93	71	95	74	79	89	78	86	99
17307	BIGLERVILLE	87	77	59	74	81	88	72	80	77	72	93	94	71	95	74	79	88	78	86	101
17309	BROGUE	105	93	71	89	99	106	87	96	92	87	112	114	85	114	89	95	107	94	104	123
17313	DALLASTOWN	84	90	93	90	91	95	88	88	86	86	107	103	90	111	89	85	104	87	86	99
17314	DELTA	82	80	71	78	81	86	77	80	78	76	96	94	76	98	77	78	92	79	81	94
17315	DOVER	94	85	68	82	89	96	80	87	85	80	103	103	79	105	82	86	98	86	93	110
17316	EAST BERLIN	100	88	68	85	93	101	84	92	89	83	108	108	82	110	85	91	102	90	100	116
17319	ETTERS	100	104	102	106	102	104	99	100	96	101	120	118	100	120	98	92	118	99	92	114
17320	FAIRFIELD	88	96	95	95	95	98	90	91	88	90	110	106	93	115	91	87	108	89	87	103
17321	FAWN GROVE	106	95	72	90	100	107	88	97	93	88	113	116	86	115	90	95	107	94	105	125
17322	FELTON	106	102	85	98	105	111	93	101	96	93	117	119	93	121	96	97	113	98	105	126
17324	GARDNERS	103	91	69	87	96	103	85	94	90	85	109	111	83	112	87	92	104	91	101	120
17325	GETTYSBURG	84	78	72	76	80	89	78	81	81	77	100	95	77	100	79	83	95	81	86	97
17327	GLEN ROCK	95	93	81	90	95	100	86	91	88	86	108	108	86	112	88	89	104	89	94	112
17329	GLENVILLE	103	115	112	113	115	117	104	107	100	103	125	126	108	131	106	99	123	103	102	124
17331	HANOVER	84	83	81	81	85	92	82	84	84	80	103	97	83	106	83	85	99	83	87	98
17339	LEWISBERRY	112	127	126	126	127	128	114	117	110	114	137	138	119	144	117	108	135	113	111	135
17340	LITTLESTOWN	88	80	66	77	84	91	77	83	81	76	99	96	76	102	78	83	94	81	89	102
17344	MC SHERRYSTOWN	84	77	66	75	80	89	77	81	81	75	99	92	76	101	77	83	94	79	87	95
17345	MANCHESTER	88	80	64	76	83	89	76	82	80	76	97	96	74	98	77	81	93	81	87	101
17347	MOUNT WOLF	95	80	59	75	85	92	77	86	83	77	101	102	72	100	78	85	95	85	94	110
17349	NEW FREEDOM	108	124	127	124	123	123	113	115	107	114	135	135	118	140	115	105	133	112	105	129
17350	NEW OXFORD	89	75	57	73	79	88	75	82	80	74	97	94	72	96	75	82	91	81	90	100
17352	NEW PARK	104	100	85	97	103	108	92	99	94	92	115	117	92	118	94	94	111	96	101	122
17353	ORRTANNA	93	83	63	79	88	94	77	85	82	77	99	101	75	101	79	84	94	83	92	110
17356	RED LION	94	87	73	83	91	98	83	89	87	82	106	105	82	109	85	89	101	87	95	110
17360	SEVEN VALLEYS	101	96	81	93	100	106	89	96	92	89	113	114	89	116	92	93	108	94	100	119
17361	SHREWSBURY	97	100	94	99	101	107	96	99	95	94	117	114	96	119	97	95	113	96	99	113
17362	SPRING GROVE	102	90	69	87	95	103	85	94	90	85	110	111	83	112	87	93	104	91	102	119
17363	STEWARTSTOWN	102	110	104	110	108	109	101	103	96	102	121	121	103	124	101	93	118	100	95	118
17364	THOMASVILLE	93	83	63	79	88	94	77	85	82	77	99	102	75	101	79	84	94	83	92	110
17365	WELLSVILLE	100	89	68	84	94	101	82	91	87	82	106	109	81	108	85	89	101	89	99	118
17366	WINDSOR	90	79	61	76	84	91	75	83	80	75	97	97	73	98	77	82	92	81	90	104
17368	WRIGHTSVILLE	87	82	69	79	84	90	78	83	81	78	99	97	77	101	79	82	95	81	87	101
17370	YORK HAVEN	95	89	76	87	91	96	85	90	87	85	107	107	83	107	86	86	103	89	92	110
17372	YORK SPRINGS	95	84	64	80	89	95	78	86	83	78	101	103	76	103	80	85	96	84	93	111
17401	YORK	40	33	40	35	33	37	43	39	43	40	54	48	40	51	39	41	52	43	38	43
	PENNSYLVANIA	89	89	93	87	90	98	89	90	91	88	112	104	89	114	90	92	109	90	92	104
	UNITED STATES	100	100	100	100	100	100	100	100	100	100	100	100	100	100	100	100	100	100	100	100

# POST OFFICE NAME	COUNTY FIPS CODE	POPULATION 2000	2004	2009	2000-2004 ANNUAL RATE % Rate	State Centile	HOUSEHOLDS 2000	2004	2009	% Annual Rate 2000-2004	2004 Average HH Size	FAMILIES 2000	2004	% Annual Rate 2000-2004
17402 YORK	133	42457	44365	46748	1.0	80	17042	18187	19542	1.5	2.31	11694	12379	1.4
17403 YORK	133	43218	43935	45795	0.4	59	16758	17379	18462	0.9	2.37	10360	10608	0.6
17404 YORK	133	57793	60473	64164	1.1	81	23156	24621	26553	1.5	2.41	15399	16271	1.3
17406 YORK	133	6553	6910	7301	1.3	85	2620	2822	3037	1.8	2.44	1903	2028	1.5
17407 YORK	133	1659	1710	1796	0.7	71	633	666	711	1.2	2.56	514	537	1.0
17501 AKRON	071	4618	4626	4732	0.0	41	1856	1891	1967	0.4	2.37	1318	1334	0.3
17502 BAINBRIDGE	071	2353	2494	2618	1.4	86	842	906	965	1.7	2.75	661	707	1.6
17505 BIRD IN HAND	071	1695	1747	1817	0.7	71	483	508	537	1.2	3.44	375	392	1.1
17509 CHRISTIANA	071	4306	4364	4499	0.3	55	1249	1282	1340	0.6	3.33	1044	1067	0.5
17512 COLUMBIA	071	17373	17747	18384	0.5	64	6823	7076	7442	0.9	2.46	4581	4741	0.8
17516 CONESTOGA	071	4377	4421	4538	0.2	51	1572	1615	1683	0.6	2.74	1229	1255	0.5
17517 DENVER	071	14228	14880	15562	1.1	81	4954	5257	5577	1.4	2.81	3967	4186	1.3
17518 DRUMORE	071	1350	1364	1395	0.2	51	433	444	461	0.6	3.07	352	359	0.5
17519 EAST EARL	071	5610	5772	5995	0.7	70	1718	1791	1884	1.0	3.20	1451	1506	0.9
17520 EAST PETERSBURG	071	4612	4553	4644	-0.3	25	1759	1768	1832	0.1	2.55	1372	1371	0.0
17522 EPHRATA	071	28028	28517	29434	0.4	60	10336	10687	11203	0.8	2.62	7430	7646	0.7
17527 GAP	071	5761	5868	6077	0.4	61	1836	1895	1989	0.8	3.05	1487	1527	0.6
17529 GORDONVILLE	071	3649	3815	3977	1.1	81	1111	1181	1249	1.5	3.23	898	950	1.3
17532 HOLTWOOD	071	3258	3319	3421	0.4	61	1109	1149	1203	0.8	2.89	899	926	0.7
17535 KINZERS	071	2598	2655	2752	0.5	65	733	759	796	0.8	3.47	611	630	0.7
17536 KIRKWOOD	071	2599	2643	2735	0.4	59	798	826	868	0.8	3.20	691	713	0.7
17538 LANDISVILLE	071	6111	6087	6209	-0.1	34	2210	2244	2328	0.4	2.69	1776	1794	0.2
17540 LEOLA	071	10137	10295	10628	0.4	58	3509	3620	3792	0.7	2.83	2745	2818	0.6
17543 LITITZ	071	37834	40425	42672	1.6	89	13800	15066	16199	2.1	2.61	10397	11288	2.0
17545 MANHEIM	071	18916	19220	19800	0.4	58	6996	7234	7568	0.8	2.62	5358	5512	0.7
17547 MARIETTA	071	6150	6395	6682	0.9	77	2357	2493	2646	1.3	2.56	1716	1810	1.3
17551 MILLERSVILLE	071	9519	10240	10869	1.7	90	2928	3232	3515	2.4	2.43	1822	1972	1.9
17552 MOUNT JOY	071	14263	14961	15667	1.1	82	5530	5919	6309	1.6	2.52	3977	4228	1.5
17554 MOUNTVILLE	071	5269	5335	5481	0.3	53	2127	2191	2288	0.7	2.33	1543	1578	0.5
17555 NARVON	071	6993	7449	7837	1.5	88	2082	2247	2396	1.8	3.28	1775	1909	1.7
17557 NEW HOLLAND	071	12794	13160	13625	0.7	70	4550	4760	5003	1.1	2.75	3458	3595	0.9
17560 NEW PROVIDENCE	071	4557	4799	5016	1.2	84	1663	1782	1891	1.6	2.68	1253	1334	1.5
17562 PARADISE	071	3925	3923	4037	0.0	37	1203	1219	1272	0.3	3.19	970	979	0.2
17563 PEACH BOTTOM	071	3332	3654	3904	2.2	94	1087	1208	1308	2.5	3.02	872	964	2.4
17565 PEQUEA	071	2413	2429	2488	0.2	46	855	875	911	0.6	2.75	673	685	0.4
17566 QUARRYVILLE	071	11239	11581	11966	0.7	71	3630	3802	3989	1.1	2.95	2912	3034	1.0
17569 REINHOLDS	071	5386	5461	5624	0.3	56	1931	1985	2070	0.7	2.72	1564	1599	0.5
17572 RONKS	071	3991	4010	4117	0.1	44	1271	1294	1347	0.4	3.08	982	994	0.3
17576 SMOKETOWN	071	239	229	232	-1.0	4	84	82	84	-0.6	2.79	65	63	-0.7
17578 STEVENS	071	6647	7060	7432	1.4	87	2199	2369	2530	1.8	2.91	1720	1844	1.7
17579 STRASBURG	071	5711	5938	6165	0.9	77	2033	2147	2260	1.3	2.77	1585	1664	1.2
17581 TERRE HILL	071	863	945	1010	2.2	94	316	352	381	2.6	2.68	269	298	2.4
17582 WASHINGTON BORO	071	2372	2437	2530	0.6	69	819	858	906	1.1	2.80	668	696	1.0
17584 WILLOW STREET	071	8410	8653	8971	0.7	70	3278	3445	3635	1.2	2.46	2405	2498	0.9
17601 LANCASTER	071	45421	47433	49637	1.0	80	17934	19149	20415	1.6	2.41	12756	13485	1.3
17602 LANCASTER	071	46994	48312	50259	0.7	70	17395	18153	19171	1.0	2.54	11386	11821	0.9
17603 LANCASTER	071	57245	58829	61107	0.6	69	23166	24148	25449	1.0	2.34	13977	14463	0.8
17701 WILLIAMSPORT	081	45962	45448	45351	-0.3	27	18567	18751	19094	0.2	2.25	11006	11011	0.0
17702 WILLIAMSPORT	081	10911	10755	10682	-0.3	23	4466	4497	4559	0.2	2.38	3063	3058	0.0
17723 CAMMAL	081	256	246	243	-0.9	5	135	134	136	-0.2	1.84	88	87	-0.3
17724 CANTON	117	5163	5123	5161	-0.2	30	2012	2041	2098	0.3	2.49	1438	1448	0.2
17728 COGAN STATION	081	5372	5327	5299	-0.2	29	2029	2063	2096	0.4	2.58	1577	1594	0.3
17729 CROSS FORK	105	193	202	215	1.1	81	105	112	122	1.5	1.80	73	78	1.6
17737 HUGHESVILLE	081	6833	6866	6893	0.1	44	2774	2854	2924	0.7	2.41	1954	1993	0.5
17740 JERSEY SHORE	081	11664	11729	11747	0.1	45	4437	4562	4664	0.7	2.53	3227	3290	0.5
17742 LAIRDSVILLE	081	300	307	309	0.5	66	113	119	123	1.2	2.58	89	93	1.0
17744 LINDEN	081	2650	2788	2854	1.2	84	1027	1106	1157	1.8	2.52	758	811	1.6
17745 LOCK HAVEN	035	17921	18487	19161	0.7	72	6820	7204	7648	1.3	2.28	4233	4441	1.1
17747 LOGANTON	035	2672	2718	2799	0.4	59	915	948	994	0.8	2.87	731	754	0.7
17751 MILL HALL	035	7419	7593	7846	0.6	66	2866	2994	3155	1.0	2.52	2137	2216	0.9
17752 MONTGOMERY	081	4893	5027	5361	0.6	69	1554	1767	1920	3.1	2.59	1160	1314	3.0
17754 MONTOURSVILLE	081	12438	12464	12489	0.1	42	4938	5051	5162	0.5	2.43	3601	3658	0.4
17756 MUNCY	081	10792	11028	11145	0.5	65	3930	4105	4234	1.0	2.44	2890	2995	0.7
17758 MUNCY VALLEY	113	1748	1761	1757	0.2	47	726	754	773	0.9	2.11	499	515	0.8
17763 RALSTON	081	519	504	499	-0.7	10	203	202	205	-0.1	2.43	155	153	-0.3
17764 RENOVO	035	3394	3450	3570	0.4	59	1476	1535	1620	0.9	2.22	917	946	0.7
17765 ROARING BRANCH	081	445	440	438	-0.3	26	171	173	176	0.3	2.51	133	134	0.2
17768 SHUNK	113	332	326	322	-0.4	19	135	137	138	0.4	2.32	90	91	0.3
17771 TROUT RUN	081	3698	3693	3687	0.0	37	1422	1457	1488	0.6	2.53	1041	1058	0.4
17772 TURBOTVILLE	097	4018	3964	3964	-0.3	24	1428	1440	1469	0.2	2.74	1156	1162	0.1
17774 UNITYVILLE	081	1135	1125	1120	-0.2	29	446	456	465	0.5	2.47	332	338	0.4
17776 WATERVILLE	081	496	491	489	-0.2	27	218	222	227	0.4	2.19	153	155	0.3
17777 WATSONTOWN	097	6858	6946	6985	0.3	54	2739	2832	2904	0.8	2.40	1900	1952	0.6
17778 WESTPORT	035	27	28	29	0.9	75	15	16	17	1.5	1.75	10	11	2.3
17779 WOOLRICH	035	4549	4606	4730	0.3	53	1877	1944	2040	0.8	2.37	1323	1362	0.7
17801 SUNBURY	097	16472	16164	16067	-0.4	19	6803	6802	6893	0.0	2.30	4426	4404	-0.1
17810 ALLENWOOD	081	6300	6755	6828	1.7	90	884	952	1001	1.8	2.73	712	758	1.5
17812 BEAVER SPRINGS	109	1560	1582	1598	0.3	56	594	614	631	0.8	2.58	449	462	0.7
17813 BEAVERTOWN	109	2235	2302	2347	0.7	71	871	916	949	1.2	2.51	659	689	1.1
17814 BENTON	037	5733	5642	5618	-0.4	21	2305	2321	2359	0.2	2.42	1676	1679	0.0
17815 BLOOMSBURG	037	27834	28280	28740	0.4	60	10148	10493	10865	0.8	2.39	6299	6471	0.6
17820 CATAWISSA	037	5968	6026	6124	0.2	50	2455	2532	2623	0.7	2.38	1774	1823	0.6
17821 DANVILLE	093	19206	19623	20130	0.5	65	7537	7857	8216	1.0	2.37	5111	5292	0.8
17823 DORNSIFE	097	435	431	429	-0.2	28	151	153	155	0.3	2.82	114	114	0.0
17824 ELYSBURG	097	3765	3893	3951	0.8	74	1498	1586	1644	1.4	2.42	1122	1180	1.2
17827 FREEBURG	109	641	640	643	0.0	36	265	270	276	0.4	2.37	189	192	0.4
17830 HERNDON	097	2029	1997	1984	-0.4	22	800	806	817	0.2	2.44	596	597	0.0
17832 MARION HEIGHTS	097	735	716	710	-0.6	12	314	313	317	-0.1	2.29	213	211	-0.2
17834 KULPMONT	097	3303	3290	3289	-0.1	34	1462	1489	1522	0.4	2.18	922	931	0.2
17835 LAURELTON	119	222	216	215	-0.6	11	86	86	87	0.0	2.33	66	66	0.0
17836 LECK KILL	097	600	597	595	-0.1	33	224	229	233	0.5	2.61	171	173	0.3
17837 LEWISBURG	119	19229	19389	19431	0.2	48	6193	6261	6393	0.3	2.31	3961	3979	0.1
17841 MC CLURE	087	4604	4673	4709	0.4	57	1700	1764	1812	0.9	2.65	1315	1358	0.8
17842 MIDDLEBURG	109	8157	8230	8313	0.2	49	3088	3175	3264	0.7	2.57	2318	2372	0.7
17843 BEAVER SPRINGS	109	944	956	965	0.3	54	337	349	358	0.8	2.74	274	282	0.7
PENNSYLVANIA					0.3					0.7	2.44			0.6
UNITED STATES					1.2					1.3	2.58			1.1

ZIP CODE #	POST OFFICE NAME	RACE (%) White 2000	White 2004	Black 2000	Black 2004	Asian/Pacific 2000	Asian/Pacific 2004	% Hispanic Origin 2000	% Hispanic Origin 2004	2004 AGE DISTRIBUTION (%) 0-4	5-9	10-14	15-19	20-24	25-44	45-64	65-84	85+	18+	MEDIAN AGE 2004	% 2004 Males	% 2004 Females
17402	YORK	93.1	91.7	3.1	3.6	2.0	2.5	2.3	2.6	4.9	5.2	6.3	5.9	5.8	26.4	26.8	16.3	2.6	80.1	42.3	49.2	50.8
17403	YORK	76.0	74.0	15.5	16.7	1.3	1.6	9.4	10.1	6.2	6.0	6.9	8.5	8.8	24.6	23.2	12.8	3.0	76.9	36.8	47.5	52.5
17404	YORK	85.5	84.1	7.6	8.2	1.1	1.4	6.5	7.1	6.7	6.6	7.0	6.3	5.8	28.3	24.6	12.5	2.4	75.8	38.3	48.1	51.9
17406	YORK	97.8	97.3	0.7	0.8	0.4	0.5	1.0	1.2	5.5	6.0	6.8	5.7	5.0	28.1	29.4	12.2	1.3	77.9	41.2	50.2	49.8
17407	YORK	99.3	99.1	0.1	0.1	0.4	0.5	0.5	0.6	5.1	6.0	6.7	6.0	4.5	24.0	32.2	14.0	1.5	78.4	43.6	50.2	49.8
17501	AKRON	96.5	95.7	0.5	0.7	1.4	1.8	2.1	2.5	6.0	6.0	6.2	5.9	5.3	26.9	25.1	16.2	2.5	77.8	40.9	47.8	52.2
17502	BAINBRIDGE	98.9	98.7	0.0	0.0	0.2	0.3	0.9	1.1	6.2	7.2	8.4	7.6	5.2	30.8	25.2	8.6	0.9	73.4	37.9	51.2	48.8
17505	BIRD IN HAND	95.3	94.2	1.2	1.4	1.9	2.5	2.6	3.2	9.9	8.8	8.8	8.4	8.0	25.0	20.3	9.6	1.1	67.1	29.2	49.5	50.5
17509	CHRISTIANA	98.2	97.9	0.8	0.9	0.2	0.3	1.1	1.3	9.1	9.4	9.4	7.7	6.2	24.6	22.7	9.1	1.8	67.4	32.1	49.4	50.6
17512	COLUMBIA	91.5	90.0	3.5	4.0	0.7	0.8	5.3	6.5	7.0	7.0	7.5	6.6	6.3	28.4	23.6	11.7	2.1	74.5	36.9	47.9	52.1
17516	CONESTOGA	98.4	98.2	0.4	0.4	0.4	0.4	1.1	1.2	5.5	6.7	8.2	7.0	5.6	26.4	29.3	10.3	1.1	75.1	40.0	50.8	49.2
17517	DENVER	96.9	96.2	0.5	0.6	1.3	1.7	1.4	1.7	7.9	8.1	8.4	6.8	5.6	28.5	23.4	10.2	1.2	71.5	35.8	49.6	50.4
17518	DRUMORE	98.7	98.6	0.2	0.3	0.1	0.1	0.7	1.0	8.2	8.5	8.7	7.5	6.4	25.1	26.2	8.6	1.0	69.9	35.2	50.9	49.1
17519	EAST EARL	98.2	97.9	0.5	0.6	0.4	0.6	0.8	1.0	9.1	9.0	9.1	7.6	6.5	26.0	21.2	10.3	1.3	68.2	31.8	49.7	50.4
17520	EAST PETERSBURG	95.2	94.3	1.3	1.5	1.2	1.5	2.7	3.3	5.7	6.3	7.3	6.7	5.4	26.5	27.3	13.5	1.2	76.2	40.0	48.5	51.5
17522	EPHRATA	96.5	95.7	0.5	0.6	1.4	1.8	2.0	2.5	7.5	7.3	7.6	7.0	6.3	27.7	23.1	11.5	2.1	73.3	36.0	49.3	50.7
17527	GAP	97.1	96.4	1.0	1.2	0.6	0.8	1.4	1.8	9.1	9.1	8.9	7.1	5.6	27.3	22.5	9.3	1.3	68.3	33.0	50.2	49.8
17529	GORDONVILLE	98.0	97.5	0.5	0.6	0.7	0.9	0.7	0.9	11.2	10.3	9.7	7.1	7.5	23.7	18.6	10.8	1.3	64.5	27.7	50.5	49.5
17532	HOLTWOOD	98.3	98.0	0.5	0.5	0.2	0.2	1.1	1.4	7.2	7.8	9.0	7.2	5.4	28.7	26.1	7.9	0.7	71.5	37.1	51.2	48.8
17535	KINZERS	97.7	97.1	0.7	0.9	0.4	0.5	0.9	1.1	10.3	10.1	9.4	7.3	5.8	26.2	20.9	9.0	0.9	65.6	30.2	51.1	48.9
17536	KIRKWOOD	97.9	97.4	0.8	1.0	0.1	0.2	1.0	1.3	10.0	9.8	9.0	8.4	6.6	24.3	22.8	8.4	0.9	66.0	30.3	50.5	49.5
17538	LANDISVILLE	96.6	95.8	0.9	1.1	1.6	2.1	1.3	1.6	5.1	6.4	7.8	7.3	4.6	25.2	30.4	11.9	1.5	75.8	41.7	50.1	49.9
17540	LEOLA	93.3	91.8	0.9	1.0	3.5	4.5	2.8	3.4	8.2	8.2	8.1	7.1	6.5	26.1	24.1	10.5	1.3	70.9	34.3	49.4	50.6
17543	LITITZ	96.8	96.1	0.7	0.8	1.1	1.4	1.6	2.0	6.6	7.1	7.8	6.5	5.2	26.3	25.7	11.5	3.4	74.3	39.3	48.5	51.5
17545	MANHEIM	97.4	96.9	0.5	0.7	0.8	1.0	1.0	1.3	6.5	6.7	7.4	6.7	6.0	25.8	26.4	12.6	1.9	75.2	39.2	49.8	50.3
17547	MARIETTA	96.6	96.0	1.5	1.8	0.4	0.5	1.8	2.3	7.7	7.5	7.3	5.9	6.0	32.5	23.5	8.7	0.8	74.0	35.0	50.1	50.0
17551	MILLERSVILLE	93.6	92.5	3.6	4.1	1.2	1.5	2.0	2.3	3.4	3.5	4.0	17.4	20.8	18.6	18.6	12.3	1.5	86.4	25.9	47.0	53.0
17552	MOUNT JOY	96.2	95.4	1.1	1.4	0.7	0.9	2.4	2.9	6.6	6.7	7.3	6.4	5.9	31.0	24.2	10.6	1.2	75.3	37.1	49.7	50.3
17554	MOUNTVILLE	94.7	93.5	1.7	2.0	1.4	1.7	3.1	3.7	5.8	6.1	6.7	6.6	5.4	27.6	27.2	12.6	2.1	77.2	40.7	47.4	52.6
17555	NARVON	98.4	98.0	0.5	0.7	0.4	0.5	0.7	0.8	9.5	9.5	9.5	7.4	6.2	26.8	21.6	8.3	1.2	67.0	31.6	50.3	49.7
17557	NEW HOLLAND	94.5	93.4	0.8	1.0	2.3	2.8	3.2	3.9	7.5	7.3	7.5	7.0	6.2	24.3	24.0	14.1	2.0	73.3	37.3	49.1	50.9
17560	NEW PROVIDENCE	97.9	97.4	0.6	0.7	0.3	0.4	0.8	1.1	6.3	6.7	7.8	6.9	6.2	26.1	27.2	11.7	1.3	75.0	38.5	49.6	50.4
17562	PARADISE	98.5	98.2	0.5	0.6	0.2	0.2	0.5	0.7	8.8	8.8	9.5	7.3	6.3	25.3	22.1	11.0	1.0	68.5	32.2	50.7	49.3
17563	PEACH BOTTOM	97.6	97.2	1.1	1.4	0.2	0.3	1.1	1.4	9.0	9.2	9.1	7.6	5.7	27.7	22.7	8.2	0.9	67.9	33.0	49.7	50.3
17565	PEQUEA	98.2	97.9	0.6	0.7	0.2	0.2	1.7	2.0	6.2	7.1	8.0	8.2	5.7	28.1	27.3	8.6	0.8	73.2	38.3	52.2	47.8
17566	QUARRYVILLE	98.1	97.7	0.6	0.7	0.2	0.2	1.0	1.4	8.0	8.0	8.6	7.6	6.7	24.9	22.7	11.1	2.5	70.8	34.6	49.0	51.0
17569	REINHOLDS	97.8	97.3	0.5	0.7	0.7	0.8	1.2	1.4	7.5	8.0	8.7	6.5	4.7	29.7	25.1	9.1	0.8	71.7	36.9	50.4	49.6
17572	RONKS	97.4	96.9	0.6	0.7	0.8	1.0	1.2	1.5	9.2	8.7	8.8	7.2	6.9	24.4	21.0	12.3	1.4	68.9	31.7	49.9	50.1
17576	SMOKETOWN	96.2	95.6	0.8	0.9	1.3	1.8	3.4	3.9	8.3	7.9	6.1	7.4	6.1	27.1	21.0	14.9	1.3	72.9	34.8	48.9	51.1
17578	STEVENS	96.7	96.0	0.3	0.3	1.6	2.0	1.3	1.7	7.8	8.0	8.2	6.6	5.2	27.5	24.1	11.3	1.5	72.0	36.9	49.8	50.2
17579	STRASBURG	98.3	98.0	0.4	0.4	0.5	0.6	0.4	0.5	8.0	8.0	8.5	6.9	5.9	26.4	25.0	10.2	1.2	71.3	35.4	49.5	50.5
17581	TERRE HILL	98.5	98.2	0.4	0.4	0.2	0.3	0.9	1.2	9.2	8.9	9.6	8.4	6.5	25.3	20.3	10.6	1.3	67.1	30.8	50.3	49.7
17582	WASHINGTON BORO	98.3	97.8	0.4	0.5	0.5	0.7	1.2	1.4	5.8	6.3	7.6	7.6	6.7	25.0	29.3	10.2	1.6	75.7	39.7	50.1	49.9
17584	WILLOW STREET	98.0	97.5	0.5	0.6	0.5	0.6	1.1	1.4	5.3	6.0	6.8	5.9	4.6	21.2	24.1	20.3	5.7	78.2	45.1	47.6	52.4
17601	LANCASTER	93.2	91.9	1.4	1.7	3.1	3.9	2.8	3.3	5.5	6.0	6.7	6.2	5.4	23.5	27.9	16.1	2.8	77.9	42.9	47.8	52.2
17602	LANCASTER	67.7	66.1	11.7	12.0	2.6	3.2	25.0	26.1	7.5	7.1	7.7	7.5	7.6	28.5	21.2	11.0	2.0	73.3	34.2	49.2	50.8
17603	LANCASTER	81.0	78.6	6.9	7.6	2.0	2.5	14.1	15.8	6.6	6.2	6.5	7.3	8.1	27.9	22.4	12.7	2.4	77.1	36.1	47.8	52.2
17701	WILLIAMSPORT	88.0	86.6	9.2	10.2	0.7	0.9	0.9	1.0	5.7	5.5	6.2	8.5	10.3	24.2	23.2	13.6	3.0	78.9	37.1	48.8	51.2
17702	WILLIAMSPORT	98.8	98.7	0.3	0.4	0.2	0.3	0.5	0.6	5.4	5.5	6.8	6.8	6.3	26.3	25.9	15.1	2.0	78.2	40.6	49.3	50.7
17723	CAMMAL	99.2	99.6	0.0	0.0	0.0	0.0	0.8	0.4	4.1	4.1	5.3	3.7	3.7	19.5	32.5	24.8	2.4	84.6	51.5	52.0	48.0
17724	CANTON	98.5	98.3	0.5	0.6	0.1	0.1	0.4	0.4	6.5	6.7	7.3	7.1	5.7	25.6	24.9	13.9	2.2	74.9	38.7	49.7	50.3
17728	COGAN STATION	98.5	98.3	0.3	0.4	0.4	0.5	0.2	0.2	5.1	5.9	8.1	6.9	5.1	25.7	30.5	11.8	1.0	76.7	40.9	50.5	49.5
17729	CROSS FORK	98.5	98.5	0.0	0.0	0.5	0.5	0.0	0.0	3.0	3.5	5.9	6.4	4.0	22.3	36.6	16.3	2.0	83.2	47.8	52.0	48.0
17737	HUGHESVILLE	98.8	98.7	0.2	0.2	0.2	0.2	0.4	0.4	5.8	6.0	6.8	6.8	5.6	26.8	27.3	13.2	1.8	77.2	40.2	49.8	50.2
17740	JERSEY SHORE	98.8	98.7	0.3	0.3	0.3	0.4	0.2	0.3	6.5	6.6	7.3	6.9	6.4	27.8	24.6	12.2	1.8	75.5	37.7	48.7	51.3
17742	LAIRDSVILLE	99.7	99.7	0.0	0.0	0.0	0.0	0.0	0.0	6.2	6.2	5.5	5.2	6.5	29.3	28.7	11.1	1.3	79.2	39.2	51.5	48.5
17744	LINDEN	98.4	98.0	0.7	0.8	0.2	0.3	0.2	0.3	5.5	6.1	7.3	5.6	6.1	27.5	28.6	12.3	1.0	77.7	39.7	50.2	49.8
17745	LOCK HAVEN	97.5	97.1	0.9	1.0	0.6	0.8	0.8	0.9	5.2	4.8	5.2	9.6	13.5	23.0	21.9	14.0	2.7	81.8	35.1	47.4	52.6
17747	LOGANTON	98.9	98.7	0.2	0.2	0.2	0.3	0.8	0.9	9.2	8.0	8.0	6.7	6.1	25.9	23.3	11.9	1.1	70.8	35.4	50.8	49.2
17751	MILL HALL	99.0	98.8	0.2	0.3	0.3	0.3	0.3	0.3	5.7	5.9	6.8	6.1	5.7	27.0	26.9	14.7	1.3	77.8	40.4	50.0	50.0
17752	MONTGOMERY	92.1	91.0	6.9	7.8	0.4	0.5	1.1	1.2	5.2	5.3	6.1	6.3	6.3	33.6	25.8	10.2	1.3	79.3	37.9	56.4	43.6
17754	MONTOURSVILLE	98.5	98.2	0.3	0.4	0.5	0.6	0.5	0.5	4.9	5.3	6.9	7.0	5.2	23.5	27.6	17.0	2.6	78.3	43.3	48.1	51.9
17756	MUNCY	94.1	93.7	4.2	4.4	0.3	0.4	1.0	1.1	5.1	5.3	6.2	6.1	6.2	28.7	27.2	13.1	2.1	79.6	40.3	44.8	55.2
17758	MUNCY VALLEY	93.6	93.4	3.7	3.9	0.1	0.1	1.5	1.6	3.5	3.6	4.3	8.8	6.5	21.8	27.9	20.6	3.0	83.3	46.0	51.7	48.3
17763	RALSTON	96.9	96.6	1.5	1.8	0.0	0.0	0.2	0.2	4.6	5.4	6.8	5.0	5.0	27.8	28.4	15.9	1.4	79.8	42.6	49.0	51.0
17764	RENOVO	99.2	99.2	0.1	0.1	0.1	0.1	0.2	0.3	4.9	5.0	6.1	6.3	6.1	20.8	29.2	18.2	3.5	79.8	45.5	49.1	50.9
17765	ROARING BRANCH	98.2	98.0	0.9	0.9	0.0	0.0	0.2	0.2	5.0	5.7	6.6	5.9	5.5	26.6	28.4	15.0	1.4	78.9	41.9	50.0	50.0
17768	SHUNK	99.1	98.8	0.0	0.0	0.6	0.6	0.3	0.3	4.9	4.9	4.3	5.5	4.9	24.9	32.2	15.6	2.8	82.8	45.3	50.3	49.7
17771	TROUT RUN	99.1	98.9	0.2	0.2	0.1	0.1	0.5	0.6	5.1	5.4	6.8	6.5	5.2	26.4	29.7	13.8	1.2	78.6	42.0	50.9	49.1
17772	TURBOTVILLE	99.2	99.1	0.1	0.2	0.2	0.2	0.3	0.3	7.0	7.0	6.9	6.7	6.1	26.4	27.2	11.6	1.1	74.8	38.7	50.2	49.8
17774	UNITYVILLE	99.7	99.6	0.3	0.3	0.0	0.0	0.0	0.0	6.1	6.2	6.1	6.0	5.9	27.9	26.2	14.1	1.4	77.8	40.1	51.2	48.8
17776	WATERVILLE	99.4	99.2	0.2	0.2	0.0	0.0	0.6	0.6	4.7	5.1	5.7	5.5	4.3	22.8	30.1	20.0	1.8	81.3	46.3	51.5	48.5
17777	WATSONTOWN	98.8	98.7	0.4	0.4	0.3	0.2	0.5	0.5	5.9	5.9	6.7	6.4	5.8	27.2	25.9	14.3	2.0	77.3	39.9	47.8	52.2
17778	WESTPORT	100.0	100.0	0.0	0.0	0.0	0.0	0.0	0.0	3.6	3.6	7.1	7.1	0.0	28.6	35.7	14.3	0.0	85.7	45.0	53.6	46.4
17779	WOOLRICH	99.1	99.0	0.3	0.3	0.3	0.4	0.1	0.1	4.9	5.4	6.7	6.3	5.5	25.6	27.8	16.0	1.7	78.9	42.2	49.2	50.9
17801	SUNBURY	96.5	96.4	0.9	1.0	0.3	0.3	2.2	2.2	5.5	5.4	6.2	6.6	6.5	27.5	25.8	13.8	2.7	78.9	40.3	48.2	51.8
17810	ALLENWOOD	66.3	64.7	27.3	28.2	1.5	1.9	15.4	16.0	2.8	2.8	2.8	3.3	7.7	53.7	22.0	4.5	0.3	89.7	35.6	80.2	19.8
17812	BEAVER SPRINGS	98.5	98.4	0.1	0.1	0.1	0.2	0.3	0.4	6.1	6.4	7.7	6.8	6.0	26.7	25.9	12.6	1.9	75.7	38.2	48.4	51.6
17813	BEAVERTOWN	99.2	99.2	0.1	0.1	0.0	0.0	0.4	0.4	5.8	6.0	7.0	6.6	6.2	28.5	25.5	12.9	1.5	77.2	39.1	48.8	51.2
17814	BENTON	98.6	98.5	0.2	0.3	0.1	0.1	0.5	0.6	5.3	5.5	6.8	6.2	5.5	26.5	27.4	15.2	1.6	78.6	41.6	50.2	49.8
17815	BLOOMSBURG	96.5	96.1	1.4	1.5	0.9	1.1	1.1	1.3	4.4	4.5	5.1	11.9	15.6	22.7	22.5	11.4	1.9	83.0	32.8	46.8	53.3
17820	CATAWISSA	98.8	98.8	0.3	0.3	0.2	0.2	0.5	0.6	5.4	5.6	6.1	6.2	5.3	25.2	28.9	15.4	1.8	79.0	42.6	49.3	50.7
17821	DANVILLE	96.8	96.3	1.0	1.1	1.3	1.6	0.9	1.0	5.6	6.0	6.9	6.9	5.0	25.6	26.8	14.5	2.9	77.1	41.4	47.7	52.3
17823	DORNSIFE	99.5	99.8	0.0	0.0	0.0	0.0	0.0	0.0	5.8	6.5	8.8	7.0	5.1	27.4	24.4	13.7	1.4	74.3	39.4	51.0	49.0
17824	ELYSBURG	99.3	99.3	0.1	0.1	0.3	0.3	0.4	0.4	4.7	5.4	6.6	6.3	4.8	22.3	30.5	17.5	2.1	79.1	45.1	48.8	51.2
17827	FREEBURG	99.2	99.2	0.3	0.3	0.2	0.2	0.0	0.0	5.3	5.6	6.9	6.9	5.6	26.1	26.1	15.9	1.6	78.4	41.3	49.8	50.2
17830	HERNDON	98.8	98.7	0.4	0.4	0.3	0.3	0.4	0.6	5.3	5.6	5.6	6.4	5.8	26.4	27.7	15.8	1.5	79.4	42.0	49.1	50.9
17832	MARION HEIGHTS	99.3	99.3	0.0	0.0	0.0	0.0	0.4	0.4	4.1	4.5	5.2	6.2	5.3	25.3	29.1	16.9	3.6	82.5	44.8	48.6	51.4
17834	KULPMONT	99.0	98.9	0.4	0.5	0.0	0.0	0.5	0.5	4.6	4.8	5.4	6.0	4.8	23.4	26.2	21.3	3.7	81.5	45.8	47.8	52.2
17835	LAURELTON	99.1	98.6	0.0	0.0	0.0	0.5	0.5	0.5	7.4	7.4	6.9	6.9	6.0	25.9	23.6	13.0	2.8	74.5	37.9	49.1	50.9
17836	LECK KILL	99.7	99.8	0.0	0.0	0.0	0.0	0.3	0.3	4.7	5.2	6.7	7.2	5.7	25.1	29.3	13.7	2.4	79.2	42.0	51.1	48.9
17837	LEWISBURG	91.1	89.9	5.7	6.3	1.6	2.1	2.9	3.2	4.3	4.4	4.9	10.0	14.1	25.3	21.1	12.7	3.3	83.3	35.1	52.8	47.2
17841	MC CLURE	99.2	99.1	0.4	0.4	0.1	0.1	0.3	0.3	6.4	6.5	7.0	6.8	5.8	28.5	25.3	12.5	1.2	75.8	38.3	51.0	49.0
17842	MIDDLEBURG	99.0	98.9	0.3	0.3	0.1	0.1	0.5	0.5	6.4	6.5	7.2	6.9	6.2	29.0	25.5	11.1	1.3	75.8	37.5	49.7	50.3
17843	BEAVER SPRINGS	99.2	99.2	0.1	0.1	0.1	0.1	0.5	0.7	6.2	6.5	7.3	6.5	5.4	30.0	27.4	9.8	0.8	76.2	38.0	50.5	49.5
	PENNSYLVANIA	85.4	84.4	10.0	10.3	1.8	2.2	3.2	3.5	5.9	6.1	6.8	6.9	6.7	26.6	25.3	13.3	2.2	77.2	39.1	48.4	51.6
	UNITED STATES	75.1	73.6	12.3	12.5	3.8	4.2	12.5	14.1	6.9	6.7	7.2	7.0	7.3	28.6	23.8	10.8	1.7	75.1	36.0	49.1	50.9

#	POST OFFICE NAME	2004 Per Capita Income	2004 HH Income Base	2004 Household Income Distribution (%): Less than $25,000	$25,000 to $49,999	$50,000 to $99,999	$100,000 to $149,999	$150,000 or More	Median Household Income: 2004	2009	2004 National Centile	2004 State Centile	2004 Home Value Base	2004 Home Value Distribution (%): Less than $50,000	$50,000 to $89,999	$90,000 to $174,999	$175,000 to $399,999	$400,000 or More	2004 Median Home Value
17402	YORK	29007	18187	16.6	27.1	39.2	11.2	6.0	55454	64537	80	80	13359	4.8	3.9	62.7	26.2	2.3	142418
17403	YORK	23929	17379	30.7	29.8	27.6	6.5	5.3	39905	46602	46	44	10477	11.4	24.3	42.7	17.9	3.8	114560
17404	YORK	23801	24621	23.4	30.7	34.2	8.6	3.2	46594	54448	65	66	17112	7.7	21.0	52.2	17.9	1.2	115071
17406	YORK	25112	2822	17.4	30.0	40.7	8.9	3.0	51848	60415	75	75	2300	11.5	8.4	59.0	19.5	1.6	127022
17407	YORK	33194	666	13.5	23.9	35.3	17.1	10.2	62708	75469	87	89	593	0.8	4.4	62.9	31.0	0.8	147721
17501	AKRON	24770	1891	15.3	31.5	42.0	8.7	2.5	52447	61687	76	76	1314	5.5	3.0	72.8	18.1	0.6	134722
17502	BAINBRIDGE	23947	906	13.0	29.4	42.9	12.1	2.5	55473	64159	80	81	752	6.0	6.5	59.7	27.0	0.8	141544
17505	BIRD IN HAND	19569	508	22.4	28.9	32.5	10.4	5.7	48601	58101	69	69	343	0.6	0.9	46.1	42.0	10.5	179722
17509	CHRISTIANA	19965	1282	17.2	24.3	40.4	13.6	4.6	57030	66159	82	83	1053	4.6	2.1	52.0	34.6	6.8	164175
17512	COLUMBIA	21423	7076	26.2	30.9	32.6	8.2	2.2	44135	51512	59	59	4807	4.6	25.7	52.0	17.0	0.8	112398
17516	CONESTOGA	25456	1615	16.6	24.5	45.5	10.0	3.5	58016	66110	83	83	1371	6.4	3.4	56.8	27.9	5.6	151011
17517	DENVER	25103	5257	13.9	25.4	43.9	11.8	5.0	58892	67550	83	84	4309	4.4	4.3	58.8	30.1	2.5	148503
17518	DRUMORE	20309	444	16.4	29.7	41.4	9.5	2.9	53509	61964	78	78	376	9.6	2.9	48.7	29.3	9.6	156250
17519	EAST EARL	20189	1791	14.7	28.1	44.8	9.1	3.2	54375	62700	79	79	1435	4.6	4.4	57.4	25.8	7.9	149646
17520	EAST PETERSBURG	27479	1768	11.4	22.9	47.2	15.3	3.3	61931	73541	86	88	1500	0.5	1.6	82.5	14.3	1.1	135612
17522	EPHRATA	23720	10687	19.2	29.8	38.5	8.9	3.6	50702	59488	73	73	7725	7.7	5.9	61.1	23.4	1.9	134178
17527	GAP	19867	1895	17.9	30.1	37.9	10.7	3.4	51464	60240	75	74	1536	14.5	4.8	43.2	32.0	5.5	152465
17529	GORDONVILLE	16242	1181	25.2	32.1	31.6	8.8	2.4	43657	50680	58	58	808	10.4	2.6	34.4	41.5	11.1	180469
17532	HOLTWOOD	23010	1149	16.0	21.8	46.4	11.1	4.7	58398	66741	83	84	997	7.1	5.0	53.0	32.2	2.7	153980
17535	KINZERS	17380	759	17.7	32.2	35.4	11.1	3.7	50169	58040	72	71	588	1.5	3.2	50.2	36.1	9.0	168696
17536	KIRKWOOD	19539	826	20.9	24.5	39.8	10.5	4.2	53598	62460	78	78	685	3.1	2.6	42.2	42.5	9.6	178180
17538	LANDISVILLE	29240	2244	9.8	21.8	41.4	20.4	6.6	68106	81194	90	91	1945	3.0	0.9	48.7	46.0	1.4	171127
17540	LEOLA	28204	3620	14.9	28.0	37.5	12.9	6.7	55483	64933	80	81	2691	3.5	1.9	55.1	35.2	4.4	162803
17543	LITITZ	28285	15066	13.6	26.0	39.6	14.1	6.8	59508	69503	84	85	11895	4.5	2.5	54.4	34.2	4.4	155468
17545	MANHEIM	23965	7234	15.8	28.2	42.5	10.3	3.2	54191	63245	79	79	5588	6.0	3.2	60.4	26.9	3.6	146948
17547	MARIETTA	23796	2493	13.7	29.8	45.3	9.4	1.8	54351	63682	79	79	1931	2.9	14.4	64.2	17.3	1.2	122481
17551	MILLERSVILLE	22329	3232	24.2	26.3	34.0	10.6	4.9	49435	58508	71	71	2175	1.3	2.6	65.4	28.3	2.4	145868
17552	MOUNT JOY	25474	5919	14.8	28.6	43.1	10.5	3.1	54833	63798	79	80	4305	5.3	5.6	65.4	22.7	1.1	138887
17554	MOUNTVILLE	27082	2191	13.8	28.4	43.5	9.5	4.8	55101	64662	80	80	1637	3.7	5.7	64.3	24.8	1.5	141021
17555	NARVON	20130	2247	15.5	28.7	42.2	9.4	4.3	55268	63430	80	80	1911	4.3	6.9	46.9	36.5	5.3	160864
17557	NEW HOLLAND	23026	4760	18.2	31.0	36.0	10.8	4.1	50674	59607	73	73	3462	5.1	3.2	54.3	33.0	4.4	154991
17560	NEW PROVIDENCE	21331	1782	18.5	30.5	39.5	9.8	1.7	50808	59200	73	73	1510	30.0	8.5	39.1	21.8	0.6	121311
17562	PARADISE	18801	1219	19.3	32.4	36.0	8.4	3.9	48820	56354	70	70	962	1.6	5.7	53.7	31.7	7.3	159503
17563	PEACH BOTTOM	18923	1208	20.5	32.8	37.5	6.7	2.6	47767	55403	68	68	974	6.9	10.8	54.0	23.0	5.3	141779
17565	PEQUEA	24760	875	16.2	19.5	49.7	9.1	5.4	60595	68847	85	87	768	4.8	4.7	57.2	31.1	2.2	154618
17566	QUARRYVILLE	20299	3802	20.7	28.3	36.3	11.2	3.6	50841	59590	74	73	2939	2.8	4.9	53.7	34.0	4.6	159841
17569	REINHOLDS	25519	1985	11.3	27.2	44.0	12.5	4.9	59187	68227	84	85	1729	3.5	2.8	55.9	33.3	4.5	154018
17572	RONKS	18701	1294	23.7	30.1	34.2	8.9	3.1	47495	55259	67	67	894	4.4	5.9	46.4	33.5	9.8	161726
17576	SMOKETOWN	19556	82	28.1	29.3	26.8	13.4	2.4	46487	54006	65	65	53	0.0	1.9	47.2	37.7	13.2	179167
17578	STEVENS	24449	2369	15.0	27.4	41.9	10.8	4.9	56557	64990	81	82	1982	8.1	6.4	55.7	27.9	2.0	145823
17579	STRASBURG	26171	2147	13.4	25.3	43.7	13.3	4.3	60485	68880	85	87	1714	0.9	2.7	52.3	36.6	7.6	166349
17581	TERRE HILL	26486	352	14.5	31.3	40.6	8.8	4.8	53477	62203	78	78	290	1.4	3.1	62.8	23.5	9.3	148944
17582	WASHINGTON BORO	24735	858	13.1	28.7	39.9	12.7	5.7	58814	67328	83	84	726	1.1	3.6	47.8	42.8	4.7	171371
17584	WILLOW STREET	27324	3445	14.2	30.5	37.5	13.6	4.2	55512	63962	80	81	2499	4.0	2.1	57.7	32.9	3.3	154237
17601	LANCASTER	34579	19149	13.8	23.5	37.5	14.9	10.3	62469	74244	87	89	14143	2.2	2.7	53.3	37.4	4.4	163628
17602	LANCASTER	20333	18153	28.2	31.7	29.9	7.1	3.2	41330	48312	51	50	9965	3.2	25.4	49.7	20.1	1.6	119606
17603	LANCASTER	24353	24148	25.5	32.3	29.9	8.0	4.3	43875	51162	58	58	14357	4.9	22.0	54.0	16.8	2.4	116744
17701	WILLIAMSPORT	20712	18751	37.5	31.0	22.3	6.1	3.1	34031	39953	24	17	10854	11.4	34.6	43.7	9.4	0.9	94268
17702	WILLIAMSPORT	21720	4497	28.3	34.0	28.8	6.6	2.2	40823	48085	49	48	3455	7.6	37.6	47.3	7.1	0.5	93937
17723	CAMMAL	25919	134	31.3	29.1	31.3	7.5	0.8	41140	47361	50	49	111	5.4	27.9	57.7	9.0	0.0	102917
17724	CANTON	17180	2041	33.8	35.9	25.2	3.9	1.2	35013	40514	28	21	1520	18.0	30.2	42.7	7.8	1.3	92177
17728	COGAN STATION	21678	2063	24.7	32.0	31.8	8.4	3.1	45047	51799	61	62	1773	16.5	19.9	47.4	14.8	1.4	104514
17729	CROSS FORK	25385	112	34.8	33.9	25.0	3.6	2.7	34364	38624	25	18	92	20.7	30.4	33.7	12.0	3.3	88571
17737	HUGHESVILLE	20914	2854	30.0	30.8	31.9	5.5	1.8	40063	46954	46	45	2246	15.0	22.9	51.3	9.8	1.0	101382
17740	JERSEY SHORE	19232	4562	28.7	34.0	29.8	5.2	2.3	39585	46317	45	42	3417	13.6	31.3	44.8	9.3	1.0	94359
17742	LAIRDSVILLE	19571	119	22.7	36.1	33.6	5.9	1.7	44072	50267	59	59	98	12.2	33.7	41.8	12.2	0.0	94000
17744	LINDEN	18347	1106	25.0	39.8	30.0	4.5	0.7	39945	46048	46	44	943	30.2	21.4	37.7	10.1	0.6	88133
17745	LOCK HAVEN	18910	7204	39.1	30.0	23.2	5.6	2.1	32644	38011	20	12	4563	10.7	22.8	53.7	11.6	1.3	107963
17747	LOGANTON	16970	948	27.4	35.3	33.0	3.1	1.2	38763	44765	42	39	795	10.8	25.3	48.1	13.8	2.0	108594
17751	MILL HALL	19386	2994	31.0	33.4	27.7	5.6	2.2	38019	44095	39	35	2466	15.3	20.4	49.6	13.1	1.8	106570
17752	MONTGOMERY	17402	1767	27.4	34.8	31.7	5.8	0.3	40721	47171	49	48	1356	10.3	35.8	47.5	5.6	0.7	93171
17754	MONTOURSVILLE	25284	5051	22.4	30.2	32.3	10.7	4.4	47638	56179	67	67	4143	8.5	15.7	56.6	17.9	1.3	119582
17756	MUNCY	20243	4105	29.0	32.0	29.3	8.1	1.7	40882	47579	49	48	3168	14.2	23.8	48.4	12.3	1.3	103396
17758	MUNCY VALLEY	22001	754	32.0	33.0	25.1	7.8	2.1	37420	44376	37	33	641	10.1	20.9	36.2	28.2	4.5	119922
17763	RALSTON	16610	202	39.1	32.7	22.3	4.5	1.5	32847	37923	20	13	163	31.9	37.4	27.6	2.5	0.6	71000
17764	RENOVO	16246	1535	46.6	30.4	19.4	2.9	0.7	27462	31563	8	3	1056	51.5	30.1	16.3	1.5	0.6	49111
17765	ROARING BRANCH	18461	173	33.0	34.1	26.6	4.6	1.7	37123	44077	36	31	143	19.6	32.9	37.1	9.1	1.4	87500
17768	SHUNK	18999	137	37.2	27.0	27.7	6.6	1.5	34599	42009	26	18	114	15.8	18.4	39.5	22.8	3.5	119118
17771	TROUT RUN	20469	1457	25.4	36.2	30.5	5.5	2.4	41524	48335	51	51	1244	16.6	26.6	44.4	10.9	1.5	96855
17772	TURBOTVILLE	20299	1440	19.5	34.9	35.4	7.4	2.9	46306	53158	65	65	1218	5.0	15.4	54.7	22.8	2.1	129831
17774	UNITYVILLE	20345	456	31.1	36.4	25.4	4.4	2.6	38791	44586	42	39	378	20.1	25.7	40.5	12.4	1.3	94848
17776	WATERVILLE	21842	222	26.6	35.6	29.7	6.8	1.4	41306	47363	51	50	191	12.6	25.1	49.7	11.5	1.1	100938
17777	WATSONTOWN	20279	2832	31.5	30.2	31.1	5.5	1.7	40138	46039	47	45	2103	13.4	20.2	47.7	17.4	1.3	112015
17778	WESTPORT	19107	16	50.0	31.3	18.8	0.0	0.0	25000	37343	5	2	13	15.4	30.8	53.9	0.0	0.0	92500
17779	WOOLRICH	23142	1944	27.9	34.7	26.8	6.3	4.3	41821	48695	52	52	1578	17.2	17.5	48.0	15.7	1.6	107724
17801	SUNBURY	18548	6802	35.7	32.5	27.3	3.1	1.3	35491	40844	29	23	4198	9.1	27.9	47.5	14.2	1.3	105910
17810	ALLENWOOD	15090	952	20.7	34.9	36.9	4.9	2.6	45590	52600	63	63	790	7.1	20.6	56.2	15.1	1.0	112568
17812	BEAVER SPRINGS	17398	614	30.8	37.3	28.3	2.8	0.8	37978	43713	39	35	496	8.5	26.0	47.4	17.1	1.0	109459
17813	BEAVERTOWN	20113	916	26.2	38.0	29.9	3.6	2.3	38616	44658	41	38	734	6.0	26.7	52.6	12.1	2.6	110090
17814	BENTON	19587	2321	27.9	35.4	30.3	5.3	1.1	39985	46446	46	44	1885	12.2	21.3	47.7	17.5	1.3	108692
17815	BLOOMSBURG	21922	10493	31.3	30.1	27.4	7.4	3.8	39886	46747	46	44	6912	12.6	16.3	51.1	18.7	1.3	113661
17820	CATAWISSA	21042	2532	26.9	34.2	31.1	5.9	1.8	41442	48147	51	51	2012	11.7	21.9	47.2	15.9	3.3	109897
17821	DANVILLE	24750	7857	25.9	30.8	29.4	8.8	5.1	44454	52391	60	60	5826	8.7	15.0	49.6	24.0	2.8	125847
17823	DORNSIFE	16213	153	32.0	32.7	28.1	6.5	0.7	38098	44170	40	36	133	11.3	27.8	47.4	13.5	0.0	102016
17824	ELYSBURG	24849	1586	25.7	23.1	35.9	11.9	3.3	51100	60245	74	74	1362	4.3	10.4	50.7	32.7	1.9	148834
17827	FREEBURG	17873	270	31.9	34.1	31.9	2.2	0.0	34775	40603	27	19	218	9.2	16.1	68.8	6.0	0.0	111728
17830	HERNDON	22022	806	27.7	32.8	33.1	3.4	3.1	43707	50320	58	58	693	11.0	24.5	47.6	15.3	1.6	106397
17832	MARION HEIGHTS	18804	313	40.3	28.1	26.2	2.6	2.9	32813	38270	20	13	247	34.8	32.4	28.7	3.6	0.4	66053
17834	KULPMONT	19236	1489	37.7	35.1	21.4	4.4	1.4	33557	38652	23	15	1153	45.6	25.3	23.0	6.0	0.1	54509
17835	LAURELTON	19625	86	25.6	36.1	31.4	4.7	2.3	42685	48635	55	55	70	11.4	22.9	47.1	15.7	2.9	108824
17836	LECK KILL	17529	229	28.4	30.6	36.2	4.8	0.0	41601	48002	52	51	194	10.3	26.3	38.7	22.2	2.6	111207
17837	LEWISBURG	24861	6261	26.6	25.4	31.4	10.4	6.3	48061	56775	68	68	4209	3.7	7.8	47.9	36.0	4.6	154761
17841	MC CLURE	17646	1764	26.1	37.6	30.7	4.9	0.7	41435	47309	51	51	1441	16.7	22.7	46.5	11.9	2.2	102390
17842	MIDDLEBURG	18663	3175	28.1	35.9	29.6	4.7	1.7	39397	45568	44	42	2513	9.2	19.3	54.1	15.9	1.5	114517
17843	BEAVER SPRINGS	19183	349	20.1	38.7	34.7	4.3	2.3	44226	50859	59	60	297	7.1	15.8	63.0	14.1	0.0	117835
	PENNSYLVANIA	25764		25.8	27.2	31.2	10.2	5.7	46988	57000				11.9	18.4	40.7	25.1	4.1	123516
	UNITED STATES	25866		24.7	27.1	30.8	10.9	6.5	48124	56710				10.9	15.0	33.7	30.1	10.4	145905

ZIP CODE #	POST OFFICE NAME	FINANCIAL SERVICES: Auto Loan	Home Loan	Investments	Retirement Plans	THE HOME: Home Improvements: Home Repair	Lawn & Garden	Furnishings: Computers & Hardware	Major Appliances	TV, Radio, Sound Equipment	Furniture	ENTERTAINMENT: Dine out/ Carry out	Sports Equipment	Fees & Tickets	Toys & Games	Travel	Cable TV	PERSONAL: Apparel & Services	Auto Repairs	Health Insurance	Pets & Supplies
17402	YORK	93	98	101	96	98	105	94	96	94	94	117	111	96	119	96	94	114	95	95	109
17403	YORK	77	80	91	79	79	87	83	81	84	81	104	94	84	106	83	84	101	82	81	90
17404	YORK	80	81	82	79	81	88	81	81	82	79	102	94	81	104	81	83	98	81	83	93
17406	YORK	99	85	65	82	90	98	82	90	87	81	106	106	79	106	83	89	100	88	98	113
17407	YORK	109	134	145	132	131	132	122	121	115	121	145	140	130	154	125	113	144	117	111	132
17501	AKRON	87	83	77	82	85	93	82	85	85	81	104	98	82	105	83	86	100	85	89	99
17502	BAINBRIDGE	105	94	72	89	99	106	87	96	92	87	112	115	85	115	90	95	107	94	104	124
17505	BIRD IN HAND	109	90	66	88	96	107	90	99	97	89	117	116	85	116	90	99	109	97	110	124
17509	CHRISTIANA	107	96	73	91	101	108	88	98	94	88	114	117	87	117	91	96	109	95	106	126
17512	COLUMBIA	74	73	73	72	74	81	74	75	76	72	94	86	75	96	74	77	90	74	78	85
17516	CONESTOGA	111	100	77	95	105	113	92	102	97	92	119	121	90	121	95	100	113	99	110	131
17517	DENVER	113	100	76	95	105	114	94	103	100	94	121	122	92	123	96	102	115	101	112	131
17518	DRUMORE	100	89	68	84	94	101	82	91	87	82	106	109	81	108	85	90	101	89	99	118
17519	EAST EARL	105	92	69	87	97	105	85	95	91	85	110	113	83	112	87	93	105	92	103	123
17520	EAST PETERSBURG	94	109	115	109	107	107	102	101	96	102	120	118	106	125	102	92	119	99	91	111
17522	EPHRATA	94	88	77	85	91	99	85	90	89	84	109	105	84	111	86	90	104	89	96	109
17527	GAP	97	87	68	83	90	96	82	90	85	83	105	106	79	103	83	86	100	88	93	111
17529	GORDONVILLE	91	68	41	64	76	85	67	79	76	67	90	94	60	88	68	79	83	78	92	105
17532	HOLTWOOD	107	95	72	90	100	107	88	97	93	88	113	116	86	116	90	95	108	95	105	125
17535	KINZERS	99	85	62	80	90	97	80	89	85	80	104	107	76	103	81	88	98	88	97	116
17536	KIRKWOOD	100	89	68	85	94	101	82	91	88	82	106	109	81	109	85	90	101	89	99	118
17538	LANDISVILLE	102	125	134	124	123	124	113	113	107	112	134	130	120	142	116	105	133	109	104	124
17540	LEOLA	126	112	88	109	118	128	107	117	113	107	138	137	105	139	109	115	131	114	126	146
17543	LITITZ	107	110	106	108	111	117	104	108	104	104	129	126	106	132	106	104	125	106	107	126
17545	MANHEIM	95	90	78	87	93	100	86	91	89	85	109	106	86	112	88	90	105	89	96	110
17547	MARIETTA	89	88	82	87	89	93	85	88	85	85	105	105	85	107	85	83	102	87	86	104
17551	MILLERSVILLE	82	84	98	86	84	89	90	85	88	87	110	102	90	110	88	85	107	88	81	95
17552	MOUNT JOY	96	90	80	89	93	100	89	93	91	88	112	108	88	113	89	91	107	91	95	109
17554	MOUNTVILLE	94	95	87	93	97	102	89	93	90	88	111	108	91	115	91	90	107	91	94	110
17555	NARVON	106	95	72	90	100	107	87	97	93	87	113	115	86	115	90	95	107	94	105	125
17557	NEW HOLLAND	104	86	62	80	92	102	83	93	91	83	110	109	78	110	84	95	103	92	105	120
17560	NEW PROVIDENCE	90	83	67	80	84	89	79	84	80	80	99	99	76	96	78	79	95	83	85	102
17562	PARADISE	97	86	65	81	91	97	79	88	84	79	102	105	78	105	82	86	97	86	95	114
17563	PEACH BOTTOM	92	82	62	78	86	92	75	84	80	75	97	100	74	100	78	82	93	81	91	108
17565	PEQUEA	103	101	87	98	105	109	93	99	94	93	116	118	93	120	95	95	112	96	102	123
17566	QUARRYVILLE	96	86	67	82	90	97	81	89	86	81	104	105	79	106	83	87	99	87	95	111
17569	REINHOLDS	109	102	83	97	106	112	93	102	97	93	119	121	93	122	96	99	114	99	107	128
17572	RONKS	94	79	58	76	84	93	76	85	82	76	100	100	73	100	78	85	94	83	93	108
17576	SMOKETOWN	85	72	57	72	76	86	75	80	79	73	96	91	71	95	74	80	90	78	86	94
17578	STEVENS	115	101	77	97	107	116	96	105	102	95	123	124	93	125	98	104	117	103	114	133
17579	STRASBURG	109	105	91	103	107	113	100	105	101	100	124	124	99	126	100	101	120	103	106	126
17581	TERRE HILL	114	101	77	96	107	115	94	104	100	94	121	124	92	124	97	102	115	101	112	134
17582	WASHINGTON BORO	106	103	88	100	107	112	94	101	96	94	118	120	95	122	97	97	114	99	105	126
17584	WILLOW STREET	100	98	94	98	100	105	94	98	94	95	117	116	94	117	95	93	113	97	98	116
17601	LANCASTER	113	127	137	127	126	132	121	120	117	120	146	139	126	150	123	115	143	118	115	133
17602	LANCASTER	71	71	83	70	70	75	74	72	75	73	94	84	73	95	73	75	92	74	72	81
17603	LANCASTER	82	77	82	76	77	85	81	81	83	80	104	95	80	103	80	84	100	83	83	93
17701	WILLIAMSPORT	65	64	69	63	65	71	68	67	69	66	86	77	68	87	67	70	83	68	69	75
17702	WILLIAMSPORT	72	74	72	70	75	82	71	73	73	70	90	84	73	95	73	75	87	72	77	85
17723	CAMMAL	81	63	43	57	71	80	60	72	68	59	80	84	53	79	64	72	74	71	85	98
17724	CANTON	69	57	42	52	62	69	55	62	62	55	75	73	53	75	57	65	70	61	72	81
17728	COGAN STATION	92	77	58	73	82	90	73	82	79	74	96	98	70	95	75	82	90	81	91	107
17729	CROSS FORK	78	61	42	55	69	77	57	69	65	57	77	81	51	76	61	69	72	68	82	95
17737	HUGHESVILLE	78	69	56	65	73	81	66	73	72	66	87	85	65	89	68	75	82	71	81	91
17740	JERSEY SHORE	74	67	57	63	70	77	66	70	70	65	85	82	64	87	67	72	81	69	77	86
17742	LAIRDSVILLE	81	72	55	68	76	82	67	74	71	67	86	88	65	88	69	72	82	72	80	95
17744	LINDEN	74	66	51	63	68	73	62	68	65	63	79	80	60	78	63	65	76	67	71	84
17745	LOCK HAVEN	64	58	61	57	60	67	62	62	65	60	80	73	61	80	62	66	77	64	67	73
17747	LOGANTON	88	63	34	56	70	80	60	73	71	61	84	88	53	81	62	75	77	72	88	102
17751	MILL HALL	81	66	47	60	71	79	63	72	70	63	85	84	60	85	65	74	79	71	83	94
17752	MONTGOMERY	75	63	47	59	67	73	61	68	66	61	80	80	58	80	62	69	76	67	75	87
17754	MONTOURSVILLE	87	89	87	86	91	98	85	88	87	84	107	101	87	110	87	88	104	86	91	102
17756	MUNCY	80	71	57	67	75	82	69	75	73	68	89	87	67	90	70	76	84	73	82	92
17758	MUNCY VALLEY	82	65	44	58	73	82	61	73	69	60	82	86	55	81	65	74	76	72	87	100
17763	RALSTON	69	54	37	49	61	68	51	61	58	51	68	72	46	68	54	62	64	61	73	84
17764	RENOVO	58	46	35	43	50	57	48	53	53	46	63	61	43	61	48	56	59	53	61	67
17765	ROARING BRANCH	79	63	43	58	70	77	59	70	66	59	79	83	54	78	62	69	73	69	81	94
17768	SHUNK	75	59	40	53	67	75	56	67	63	55	75	79	50	74	59	67	70	66	79	92
17771	TROUT RUN	89	69	45	63	77	86	65	78	74	65	88	92	59	87	68	78	82	76	91	106
17772	TURBOTVILLE	89	78	60	75	83	89	74	81	78	74	95	96	72	97	76	80	90	79	88	103
17774	UNITYVILLE	91	65	35	58	73	82	62	76	73	63	86	90	55	83	64	77	79	75	90	105
17776	WATERVILLE	82	64	44	58	72	81	60	73	68	60	81	85	54	80	64	73	75	72	86	99
17777	WATSONTOWN	74	67	56	64	70	78	66	70	71	65	86	81	65	88	67	73	81	69	77	84
17778	WESTPORT	57	44	30	40	50	56	42	51	47	42	56	59	37	56	45	51	52	50	60	69
17779	WOOLRICH	88	74	55	67	79	88	71	80	79	71	95	93	68	96	73	83	89	78	91	103
17801	SUNBURY	59	58	61	57	59	65	60	60	62	58	76	69	61	79	61	63	74	60	63	68
17810	ALLENWOOD	50	45	34	43	47	51	41	46	44	41	54	55	41	55	43	45	51	45	50	59
17812	BEAVER SPRINGS	84	57	26	49	64	74	55	68	66	56	77	82	46	73	55	71	70	68	84	97
17813	BEAVERTOWN	95	64	29	55	72	83	61	77	74	63	87	92	52	82	63	80	79	76	95	109
17814	BENTON	76	65	49	60	70	77	62	70	67	61	81	82	58	82	64	70	76	68	79	91
17815	BLOOMSBURG	81	72	69	71	74	81	78	77	80	75	99	92	75	99	76	80	95	79	81	92
17820	CATAWISSA	77	70	57	66	74	80	66	72	71	66	86	85	66	89	69	73	82	71	79	91
17821	DANVILLE	85	87	86	85	88	94	84	86	84	83	104	99	85	106	85	85	101	85	87	99
17823	DORNSIFE	86	58	26	50	65	75	56	70	67	57	79	83	47	74	57	72	72	69	86	99
17824	ELYSBURG	94	84	69	80	90	98	80	89	85	79	103	104	78	105	83	88	98	87	98	112
17827	FREEBURG	56	59	61	56	60	67	58	58	60	56	75	65	61	81	60	63	72	57	63	65
17830	HERNDON	96	72	41	64	79	88	68	81	78	69	93	97	61	90	69	83	86	80	96	112
17832	MARION HEIGHTS	55	60	63	57	61	67	59	59	61	57	76	65	63	83	61	64	74	58	63	65
17834	KULPMONT	60	56	50	53	58	66	57	59	61	55	75	66	57	77	58	64	70	59	67	68
17835	LAURELTON	89	59	27	51	67	77	57	72	69	58	81	86	49	77	58	74	74	71	88	102
17836	LECK KILL	73	65	50	62	69	74	60	67	64	60	78	80	59	79	62	66	74	65	72	86
17837	LEWISBURG	94	87	83	86	90	100	90	92	92	87	112	106	87	111	90	93	107	92	97	107
17841	MC CLURE	77	63	45	58	68	76	60	68	67	60	81	80	57	81	62	71	76	67	79	89
17842	MIDDLEBURG	78	66	49	61	70	78	63	70	69	63	83	83	61	84	64	72	78	69	79	90
17843	BEAVER SPRINGS	84	75	57	71	79	85	69	77	74	69	89	91	68	91	71	75	85	75	83	99
	PENNSYLVANIA	89	89	93	87	90	98	89	90	91	88	112	104	89	114	90	92	109	90	92	104
	UNITED STATES	100	100	100	100	100	100	100	100	100	100	100	100	100	100	100	100	100	100	100	100

PENNSYLVANIA

POPULATION CHANGE

17844-18088

#	POST OFFICE NAME	COUNTY FIPS CODE	POPULATION			2000-2004 ANNUAL RATE		HOUSEHOLDS					FAMILIES		
			2000	2004	2009	% Rate	State Centile	2000	2004	2009	% Annual Rate 2000-2004	2004 Average HH Size	2000	2004	% Annual Rate 2000-2004
17844	MIFFLINBURG	119	9355	9851	10196	1.2	84	3482	3766	3983	1.9	2.62	2587	2764	1.6
17845	MILLMONT	119	2244	2195	2184	-0.5	15	816	820	834	0.1	2.61	601	598	-0.1
17846	MILLVILLE	037	4213	4128	4124	-0.5	17	1573	1570	1598	0.0	2.54	1175	1168	-0.1
17847	MILTON	097	11126	11510	11791	0.8	74	4600	4871	5098	1.4	2.30	3079	3228	1.1
17850	MONTANDON	097	710	703	699	-0.2	28	308	313	318	0.4	2.24	215	217	0.2
17851	MOUNT CARMEL	097	8773	8754	8774	-0.1	36	3997	4073	4163	0.4	2.12	2323	2339	0.2
17853	MOUNT PLEASANT MILLS	109	2012	2027	2041	0.2	47	700	718	734	0.6	2.82	550	562	0.5
17855	NEW BERLIN	119	798	763	756	-1.1	4	322	315	318	-0.5	2.42	235	228	-0.7
17856	NEW COLUMBIA	119	3412	3483	3538	0.5	63	1310	1375	1428	1.2	2.52	1008	1052	1.0
17857	NORTHUMBERLAND	097	7436	7453	7449	0.1	42	3100	3177	3242	0.6	2.27	2101	2136	0.4
17859	ORANGEVILLE	037	2502	2532	2562	0.3	53	999	1033	1065	0.8	2.35	749	770	0.7
17860	PAXINOS	097	2159	2191	2201	0.4	57	851	882	903	0.9	2.48	648	669	0.8
17864	PORT TREVORTON	109	2906	2873	2878	-0.3	26	925	931	948	0.2	3.09	732	733	0.0
17866	COAL TOWNSHIP	097	10638	10652	10665	0.0	40	3739	3822	3904	0.5	2.21	2374	2404	0.3
17867	REBUCK	097	659	656	653	-0.1	34	262	267	272	0.5	2.46	199	202	0.4
17868	RIVERSIDE	097	832	836	839	0.1	44	325	335	344	0.7	2.48	250	256	0.6
17870	SELINSGROVE	109	15310	15480	15658	0.3	52	5476	5657	5835	0.8	2.34	3723	3820	0.6
17872	SHAMOKIN	097	8685	8594	8579	-0.3	27	4002	4022	4088	0.1	2.13	2235	2225	-0.1
17877	SNYDERTOWN	097	357	357	356	0.0	39	136	140	143	0.7	2.54	99	101	0.5
17878	STILLWATER	037	717	696	694	-0.7	10	289	288	293	-0.1	2.42	217	215	-0.2
17881	TREVORTON	097	2538	2486	2469	-0.5	16	1063	1065	1080	0.0	2.33	707	703	-0.1
17888	WILBURTON	037	539	508	504	-1.4	1	228	220	223	-0.8	2.31	159	152	-1.1
17889	WINFIELD	119	2321	2313	2320	-0.1	35	868	887	907	0.5	2.46	689	699	0.3
17901	POTTSVILLE	107	27256	28556	29623	1.1	82	10484	11155	11828	1.5	2.35	6793	7182	1.3
17921	ASHLAND	107	7592	7618	7745	0.1	43	3131	3209	3326	0.6	2.34	2090	2123	0.4
17922	AUBURN	107	4737	4865	5018	0.6	69	1785	1870	1966	1.1	2.60	1401	1460	1.0
17923	BRANCHDALE	107	530	539	550	0.4	59	223	232	241	0.9	2.32	146	150	0.6
17925	BROCKTON	107	1123	1126	1141	0.1	42	503	515	532	0.6	2.19	345	350	0.3
17929	CRESSONA	107	1988	2021	2065	0.4	59	799	827	861	0.8	2.44	570	585	0.6
17931	FRACKVILLE	107	8653	8725	8847	0.2	48	2465	2554	2663	0.8	2.18	1547	1587	0.6
17935	GIRARDVILLE	107	1814	1798	1824	-0.2	29	798	807	834	0.3	2.22	508	509	0.1
17938	HEGINS	107	2567	2644	2719	0.7	71	1016	1070	1124	1.2	2.44	727	760	1.1
17941	KLINGERSTOWN	107	542	555	568	0.6	67	207	216	225	1.0	2.57	160	166	0.9
17948	MAHANOY CITY	107	5341	5348	5447	0.0	40	2388	2428	2515	0.4	2.19	1399	1405	0.1
17954	MINERSVILLE	107	4668	4680	4762	0.1	42	2089	2130	2205	0.5	2.19	1264	1275	0.1
17957	MUIR	107	478	479	492	0.1	42	197	202	211	0.6	2.37	148	151	0.5
17959	NEW PHILADELPHIA	107	2512	2519	2552	0.1	43	1089	1113	1149	0.5	2.26	685	693	0.3
17960	NEW RINGGOLD	107	3677	3754	3842	0.5	63	1417	1480	1545	1.0	2.54	1079	1120	0.9
17961	ORWIGSBURG	107	6566	6934	7234	1.3	85	2503	2703	2879	1.8	2.43	1803	1936	1.7
17963	PINE GROVE	107	9328	9550	9789	0.6	66	3642	3811	3987	1.1	2.48	2670	2777	0.9
17964	PITMAN	107	901	932	960	0.8	74	343	361	379	1.2	2.58	263	275	1.1
17965	PORT CARBON	107	2197	2201	2259	0.0	41	928	949	993	0.5	2.31	632	641	0.3
17967	RINGTOWN	107	2228	2249	2291	0.2	50	888	914	949	0.7	2.46	620	632	0.5
17968	SACRAMENTO	107	294	301	309	0.6	67	112	118	123	1.2	2.55	84	88	1.1
17970	SAINT CLAIR	107	3591	3571	3635	-0.1	33	1651	1678	1742	0.4	2.13	985	991	0.1
17972	SCHUYLKILL HAVEN	107	9836	10030	10290	0.5	62	4096	4262	4454	0.9	2.32	2794	2888	0.8
17976	SHENANDOAH	107	9170	9087	9228	-0.2	29	4111	4144	4285	0.2	2.14	2328	2319	-0.1
17978	SPRING GLEN	107	344	353	362	0.6	68	132	139	145	1.2	2.54	99	104	1.2
17980	TOWER CITY	107	2950	3035	3127	0.7	70	1262	1326	1393	1.2	2.29	856	893	1.0
17981	TREMONT	107	2722	2941	3059	1.8	91	1055	1142	1220	1.9	2.18	694	744	1.7
17983	VALLEY VIEW	107	1876	1891	1922	0.2	48	789	811	841	0.7	2.33	565	577	0.5
17985	ZION GROVE	037	1818	1829	1859	0.1	46	732	754	782	0.7	2.43	504	514	0.5
18011	ALBURTIS	011	4755	4859	5009	0.5	65	1791	1846	1913	0.7	2.62	1347	1377	0.5
18013	BANGOR	095	16979	17104	17626	0.2	47	6585	6762	7093	0.6	2.51	4712	4794	0.4
18014	BATH	095	11670	11955	12402	0.6	67	4573	4795	5072	1.1	2.48	3397	3537	1.0
18015	BETHLEHEM	095	30931	32778	34515	1.4	86	10478	11318	12140	1.8	2.58	6732	7203	1.6
18017	BETHLEHEM	095	35493	36158	37540	0.4	61	14076	14651	15510	1.0	2.39	9923	10248	0.8
18018	BETHLEHEM	077	30918	31812	33123	0.7	70	13315	13861	14604	1.0	2.17	7615	7821	0.6
18020	BETHLEHEM	095	18807	20196	21471	1.7	90	6692	7376	8015	2.3	2.65	5187	5677	2.2
18031	BREINIGSVILLE	077	3536	4007	4347	3.0	98	1478	1695	1852	3.3	2.34	1059	1200	3.0
18032	CATASAUQUA	077	9274	9277	9493	0.0	39	3699	3742	3866	0.3	2.46	2499	2503	0.0
18034	CENTER VALLEY	077	6035	6310	6569	1.1	81	1906	2016	2117	1.3	2.91	1559	1639	1.3
18035	CHERRYVILLE	095	229	224	230	-0.5	15	81	81	85	0.0	2.73	63	63	0.0
18036	COOPERSBURG	077	12401	12627	12968	0.4	61	4442	4557	4714	0.6	2.66	3522	3594	0.5
18037	COPLAY	077	7232	7503	7807	0.9	75	2816	2930	3059	0.9	2.55	2064	2137	0.8
18038	DANIELSVILLE	095	2555	2675	2799	1.1	81	909	976	1043	1.7	2.73	721	769	1.5
18040	EASTON	095	10071	12707	14698	5.6	100	3702	4720	5531	5.9	2.68	2893	3676	5.8
18041	EAST GREENVILLE	091	5822	5882	5974	0.2	51	2084	2143	2203	0.7	2.74	1591	1630	0.6
18042	EASTON	095	39468	39667	40876	0.1	45	14788	15112	15866	0.5	2.44	9233	9340	0.3
18045	EASTON	095	22147	22783	23800	0.7	70	8729	9186	9792	1.2	2.45	6478	6777	1.1
18049	EMMAUS	077	17024	17172	17957	0.5	62	7073	7258	7530	0.6	2.38	4839	4931	0.4
18051	FOGELSVILLE	077	3111	3533	3840	3.0	98	1142	1307	1429	3.2	2.69	887	1005	3.0
18052	WHITEHALL	077	25098	25774	26607	0.6	69	10454	10779	11168	0.7	2.36	6871	7012	0.5
18053	GERMANSVILLE	077	2316	2346	2402	0.3	54	833	851	875	0.5	2.75	659	669	0.4
18054	GREEN LANE	091	4766	4924	5043	0.8	73	1834	1936	2012	1.3	2.51	1405	1476	1.2
18055	HELLERTOWN	095	10743	11116	11618	0.8	74	4469	4716	5021	1.3	2.35	3114	3264	1.1
18056	HEREFORD	011	1173	1190	1228	0.3	56	453	464	482	0.6	2.56	338	344	0.4
18058	KUNKLETOWN	089	8525	9524	10917	2.6	97	3080	3494	4048	3.0	2.69	2368	2667	2.8
18059	LAURYS STATION	077	1251	1304	1352	1.0	79	429	446	462	0.9	2.92	338	350	0.8
18062	MACUNGIE	077	14663	16117	17325	2.3	94	5649	6239	6732	2.4	2.56	4176	4596	2.3
18064	NAZARETH	095	21747	22672	23682	1.0	79	7778	8259	8787	1.4	2.61	5813	6145	1.3
18066	NEW TRIPOLI	077	5031	5261	5469	1.1	81	1798	1892	1977	1.2	2.77	1407	1470	1.0
18067	NORTHAMPTON	095	15611	16266	17019	1.0	78	6242	6644	7082	1.5	2.42	4538	4796	1.3
18069	OREFIELD	077	6641	7001	7320	1.3	84	2223	2349	2462	1.3	2.88	1740	1823	1.1
18070	PALM	011	765	796	821	0.9	78	281	297	310	1.3	2.68	225	237	1.2
18071	PALMERTON	025	9998	10205	10367	0.5	62	4034	4198	4334	0.9	2.42	2792	2885	0.8
18072	PEN ARGYL	095	6074	6176	6385	0.4	59	2329	2416	2543	0.9	2.52	1692	1742	0.7
18073	PENNSBURG	091	6525	7127	7525	2.1	93	2374	2644	2830	2.6	2.65	1806	1992	2.3
18074	PERKIOMENVILLE	091	5357	5669	5859	1.3	86	1829	1972	2064	1.8	2.79	1441	1544	1.6
18076	RED HILL	091	2422	2557	2639	1.3	85	967	1039	1084	1.7	2.46	636	676	1.5
18077	RIEGELSVILLE	017	2476	2470	2509	-0.1	36	977	994	1027	0.4	2.48	720	726	0.2
18078	SCHNECKSVILLE	077	6200	6682	7064	1.8	91	2319	2525	2687	2.0	2.60	1861	2011	1.8
18080	SLATINGTON	077	11988	12322	12750	0.7	70	4590	4745	4929	0.8	2.59	3392	3482	0.6
18087	TREXLERTOWN	077	466	497	522	1.5	89	210	225	237	1.6	2.20	176	187	1.4
18088	WALNUTPORT	095	8114	8209	8480	0.3	53	3148	3265	3444	0.9	2.49	2341	2409	0.7
	PENNSYLVANIA					0.3					0.7	2.44			0.6
	UNITED STATES					1.2					1.3	2.58			1.1

Copyright © 2004 ESRI BIS. All rights reserved. Reproduction by any method is prohibited. 261-A

ZIP CODE #	POST OFFICE NAME	RACE (%) White 2000	White 2004	Black 2000	Black 2004	Asian/Pacific 2000	Asian/Pacific 2004	% Hispanic Origin 2000	% Hispanic Origin 2004	2004 AGE DISTRIBUTION (%) 0-4	5-9	10-14	15-19	20-24	25-44	45-64	65-84	85+	18+	MEDIAN AGE 2004	% 2004 Males	% 2004 Females
17844	MIFFLINBURG	98.2	98.0	0.5	0.5	0.2	0.3	0.7	0.8	6.9	7.0	8.1	7.4	6.3	27.1	24.1	11.7	1.3	73.5	36.5	49.4	50.7
17845	MILLMONT	98.8	98.7	0.2	0.2	0.3	0.3	0.3	0.3	7.0	7.3	7.7	6.6	4.9	26.5	25.3	12.8	1.9	73.9	38.4	49.9	50.1
17846	MILLVILLE	98.9	98.7	0.1	0.2	0.3	0.3	0.3	0.3	5.7	5.9	6.2	5.9	5.7	27.1	26.4	14.5	2.5	78.7	40.8	48.7	51.3
17847	MILTON	96.1	96.0	1.8	1.8	0.2	0.3	1.6	1.6	5.7	5.7	6.2	6.4	6.5	25.9	25.8	15.3	2.6	78.3	40.9	48.7	51.3
17850	MONTANDON	98.5	98.4	0.6	0.6	0.1	0.1	0.6	0.3	4.8	5.3	6.1	5.8	5.4	26.5	29.6	15.1	1.4	80.1	42.8	50.6	49.4
17851	MOUNT CARMEL	98.8	98.8	0.1	0.1	0.3	0.3	0.7	0.7	4.6	4.6	5.5	5.9	5.5	22.7	26.2	20.6	4.4	81.7	45.8	47.5	52.5
17853	MOUNT PLEASANT MILLS	99.3	99.1	0.1	0.1	0.1	0.2	0.4	0.4	8.0	7.7	8.0	7.7	5.7	27.6	24.4	10.0	0.9	71.5	34.9	52.1	48.0
17855	NEW BERLIN	98.5	98.3	0.3	0.3	0.0	0.0	1.0	1.1	6.3	6.6	8.1	7.0	5.9	28.6	24.1	12.5	1.1	74.7	37.5	48.9	51.1
17856	NEW COLUMBIA	98.3	98.0	0.6	0.6	0.2	0.3	0.6	0.7	5.6	6.0	6.3	6.1	5.5	26.9	29.7	12.6	1.2	78.0	41.2	50.3	49.7
17857	NORTHUMBERLAND	98.5	98.4	0.5	0.6	0.3	0.3	0.7	0.7	4.8	5.0	5.6	6.1	5.0	25.3	28.4	16.5	3.4	80.5	43.9	48.1	51.9
17859	ORANGEVILLE	99.1	99.0	0.2	0.2	0.1	0.2	0.6	0.7	4.9	5.6	6.8	6.0	4.8	25.2	29.8	14.5	2.5	78.9	43.1	49.2	50.8
17860	PAXINOS	99.4	99.3	0.2	0.2	0.2	0.2	0.2	0.3	5.6	5.9	5.7	5.8	5.2	27.8	28.6	14.1	1.3	79.2	41.9	51.4	48.6
17864	PORT TREVORTON	99.4	99.3	0.1	0.1	0.1	0.1	0.6	0.7	8.8	8.7	8.7	8.0	6.7	26.1	22.2	9.7	1.1	68.9	32.5	51.0	49.0
17866	COAL TOWNSHIP	89.5	89.0	9.0	9.4	0.3	0.3	2.1	2.1	3.5	3.6	4.7	6.6	7.0	30.2	23.2	17.5	3.8	83.9	41.4	56.3	43.7
17867	REBUCK	99.7	99.5	0.2	0.2	0.0	0.0	0.5	0.5	4.7	5.3	6.7	7.3	5.6	25.0	28.7	14.2	2.4	78.7	41.9	50.8	49.2
17868	RIVERSIDE	99.0	99.0	0.0	0.0	0.2	0.2	0.8	0.7	6.1	6.3	6.0	6.1	4.9	24.3	30.0	14.2	2.0	77.4	42.8	48.4	51.6
17870	SELINSGROVE	96.2	95.7	1.8	2.0	0.9	1.1	1.8	2.0	4.4	4.6	5.6	8.6	9.8	25.6	25.4	13.5	2.5	81.9	38.9	48.0	52.0
17872	SHAMOKIN	98.8	98.8	0.2	0.2	0.3	0.3	0.7	0.7	5.7	5.3	6.0	6.4	6.5	24.9	24.6	17.5	3.3	79.1	41.7	47.1	52.9
17877	SNYDERTOWN	99.2	99.2	0.0	0.0	0.6	0.6	0.0	0.0	6.2	6.4	5.3	5.3	5.6	26.6	30.3	12.9	1.4	79.3	41.5	50.1	49.9
17878	STILLWATER	99.3	99.3	0.0	0.0	0.1	0.1	0.7	0.9	5.0	5.5	6.0	5.6	4.9	26.2	31.6	13.7	1.6	80.0	42.9	49.9	50.1
17881	TREVORTON	98.9	98.8	0.2	0.2	0.2	0.2	0.4	0.4	5.1	5.2	6.1	6.4	6.0	25.7	26.2	17.0	2.3	79.8	42.3	50.4	49.6
17888	WILBURTON	99.6	99.6	0.0	0.0	0.0	0.0	0.7	0.8	4.5	4.9	6.3	5.1	5.1	24.4	28.7	18.5	2.4	80.7	44.7	48.2	51.8
17889	WINFIELD	97.1	96.7	0.3	0.4	1.1	1.4	0.3	0.3	4.9	5.5	6.6	7.4	6.1	23.8	31.2	12.3	2.2	79.3	42.5	50.6	49.4
17901	POTTSVILLE	94.9	94.1	3.6	4.1	0.5	0.6	1.7	1.9	5.0	5.1	5.9	6.0	5.8	27.0	26.3	15.8	3.1	80.3	41.8	50.2	49.8
17921	ASHLAND	99.2	99.1	0.3	0.3	0.2	0.2	0.2	0.2	5.1	5.2	5.4	5.8	5.8	25.4	28.1	16.8	2.4	80.7	43.1	49.0	51.0
17922	AUBURN	98.3	97.9	0.5	0.6	0.4	0.5	0.5	0.7	6.0	6.5	7.3	6.3	4.8	27.3	28.7	12.2	0.9	76.3	40.3	49.8	50.2
17923	BRANCHDALE	99.6	99.6	0.0	0.0	0.0	0.0	0.4	0.2	6.7	6.3	6.5	6.1	5.9	28.2	22.8	15.8	1.7	77.2	39.6	48.4	51.6
17925	BROCKTON	99.4	99.4	0.1	0.1	0.1	0.1	0.1	0.1	4.2	4.4	4.4	4.3	3.8	23.5	30.1	21.9	3.5	84.5	48.5	48.2	51.8
17929	CRESSONA	98.5	98.3	0.1	0.1	0.9	1.1	0.2	0.2	5.4	5.6	6.9	6.0	6.4	29.0	25.4	13.5	1.8	78.3	39.3	50.3	49.7
17931	FRACKVILLE	77.4	76.1	19.4	20.5	0.8	1.0	3.9	4.1	3.3	3.3	3.4	3.8	9.8	38.9	21.4	13.5	2.7	87.9	38.0	65.8	34.3
17935	GIRARDVILLE	99.4	99.4	0.1	0.1	0.0	0.0	0.2	0.2	4.2	4.6	6.8	6.5	5.3	25.1	27.4	17.5	2.7	80.5	43.5	48.4	51.6
17938	HEGINS	99.4	99.3	0.0	0.0	0.2	0.2	0.4	0.4	4.5	5.8	6.6	5.9	5.4	26.7	26.8	15.8	2.5	78.8	41.9	49.2	50.8
17941	KLINGERSTOWN	100.0	100.0	0.0	0.0	0.0	0.0	0.6	0.7	5.2	5.4	6.0	6.0	6.1	28.8	24.5	15.0	3.1	80.2	40.5	49.6	50.5
17948	MAHANOY CITY	98.9	98.7	0.2	0.2	0.2	0.2	1.1	1.3	5.1	5.2	6.2	6.2	5.1	24.2	23.8	19.9	4.5	79.7	43.6	48.1	51.9
17954	MINERSVILLE	98.5	98.3	0.4	0.5	0.2	0.3	0.6	0.7	5.6	5.6	6.5	5.5	5.0	26.5	23.0	18.4	3.8	78.8	41.4	46.7	53.4
17957	MUIR	99.6	99.6	0.0	0.0	0.2	0.2	0.2	0.2	4.8	5.2	5.6	5.9	5.9	27.4	29.0	14.8	1.5	80.8	41.7	50.9	49.1
17959	NEW PHILADELPHIA	99.4	99.3	0.0	0.0	0.4	0.5	0.3	0.3	4.6	4.8	6.8	4.8	5.0	26.7	25.6	18.4	3.3	80.4	43.2	50.1	49.9
17960	NEW RINGGOLD	98.8	98.5	0.1	0.2	0.3	0.4	0.5	0.6	4.9	5.5	6.2	5.8	4.8	27.9	29.9	13.2	1.7	79.9	42.2	51.0	49.0
17961	ORWIGSBURG	97.2	96.6	0.3	0.3	1.8	2.3	0.4	0.5	5.1	5.5	6.2	6.2	5.0	24.3	27.9	16.0	3.9	79.1	43.4	47.7	52.3
17963	PINE GROVE	99.1	98.9	0.1	0.1	0.3	0.4	0.2	0.3	5.6	5.8	6.7	6.0	5.7	27.3	26.9	14.1	1.9	78.2	40.8	50.0	50.0
17964	PITMAN	99.5	99.4	0.1	0.1	0.4	0.5	0.4	0.4	5.0	5.4	5.6	5.4	5.9	27.3	28.8	14.1	2.7	80.8	42.2	52.4	47.6
17965	PORT CARBON	99.1	99.0	0.6	0.6	0.1	0.1	0.5	0.6	5.0	5.0	5.5	5.6	5.9	26.1	26.3	18.0	2.6	81.1	42.7	47.7	52.3
17967	RINGTOWN	99.3	99.1	0.3	0.3	0.2	0.2	0.8	1.0	4.7	5.2	7.2	6.0	5.3	24.3	30.0	15.6	1.9	79.2	43.5	49.4	50.6
17968	SACRAMENTO	99.3	99.3	0.3	0.3	0.3	0.3	1.0	1.0	4.3	5.3	6.3	6.0	5.0	27.9	25.9	17.6	1.7	80.1	42.0	53.5	46.5
17970	SAINT CLAIR	98.8	98.6	0.6	0.8	0.1	0.1	0.7	0.8	4.5	4.8	6.0	4.7	4.3	26.2	24.2	21.5	4.0	81.9	44.7	47.5	52.5
17972	SCHUYLKILL HAVEN	97.8	97.6	0.6	0.7	0.6	0.8	0.9	1.0	5.8	5.9	6.6	5.8	5.5	27.0	25.9	15.3	2.3	78.0	41.0	48.5	51.5
17976	SHENANDOAH	98.0	97.7	0.3	0.3	0.4	0.5	1.9	2.1	5.0	5.0	5.8	5.5	5.5	24.2	24.6	19.8	4.7	80.9	44.3	47.0	53.0
17978	SPRING GLEN	99.1	99.4	0.3	0.3	0.3	0.3	1.2	0.9	4.3	5.1	6.2	6.0	4.8	27.2	27.2	17.9	1.4	80.7	42.7	52.4	47.6
17980	TOWER CITY	99.2	99.1	0.1	0.1	0.1	0.1	0.7	0.8	4.9	5.1	6.5	6.7	5.5	27.7	25.5	16.2	2.0	79.5	41.0	48.3	51.7
17981	TREMONT	94.0	92.9	5.1	6.1	0.3	0.4	2.1	2.3	4.6	4.7	5.3	5.9	6.0	30.3	23.8	16.0	3.6	81.9	40.5	53.4	46.7
17983	VALLEY VIEW	98.9	98.7	0.2	0.2	0.4	0.5	0.8	0.8	4.9	5.3	5.9	4.9	5.6	25.9	26.8	18.3	2.4	80.9	43.4	49.6	50.5
17985	ZION GROVE	98.5	98.2	0.0	0.0	0.4	0.6	0.4	0.4	5.0	5.9	6.5	4.7	4.7	26.6	29.6	14.8	2.2	79.8	42.7	50.3	49.7
18011	ALBURTIS	97.8	97.3	0.4	0.4	0.9	1.2	0.9	1.0	6.5	7.0	7.7	6.2	5.0	31.4	25.6	9.2	1.3	74.9	37.6	49.6	50.4
18013	BANGOR	98.4	98.2	0.4	0.5	0.3	0.4	1.2	1.4	6.0	6.2	7.3	6.8	5.8	26.3	26.1	13.1	2.5	76.3	40.3	49.0	51.0
18014	BATH	98.0	97.7	0.7	0.7	0.4	0.5	1.3	1.6	5.1	5.6	6.7	6.0	5.1	26.8	29.9	13.3	1.6	78.9	41.9	49.7	50.3
18015	BETHLEHEM	77.4	75.0	4.2	4.5	2.6	3.1	24.0	26.3	5.7	5.6	6.3	11.5	14.4	24.6	20.3	10.0	1.6	78.1	30.6	50.6	49.4
18017	BETHLEHEM	86.8	85.5	2.7	2.8	2.4	3.0	11.5	12.3	5.9	6.0	6.4	6.0	5.1	23.2	26.7	17.3	3.5	77.8	43.3	46.9	53.1
18018	BETHLEHEM	90.0	88.6	2.5	2.8	1.5	1.9	9.0	10.3	5.1	5.0	5.5	6.2	7.5	28.4	23.9	15.5	3.0	81.2	40.0	47.2	52.8
18020	BETHLEHEM	93.8	92.7	2.1	2.4	1.9	2.4	4.0	4.7	5.3	6.1	7.5	7.5	5.1	24.5	28.9	11.9	3.2	76.5	41.7	48.2	51.8
18031	BREINIGSVILLE	96.3	95.5	0.9	1.1	1.5	1.9	1.4	1.6	4.9	5.4	6.0	4.9	4.4	24.6	31.2	16.6	2.0	80.4	44.9	48.3	51.7
18032	CATASAUQUA	96.2	95.6	1.0	1.1	0.6	0.7	3.0	3.6	5.6	5.6	7.1	6.9	6.6	28.8	25.8	12.1	1.7	77.3	38.7	48.3	51.7
18034	CENTER VALLEY	97.1	96.4	0.7	0.8	1.2	1.5	1.1	1.4	5.2	6.0	7.1	9.2	7.3	23.4	28.5	11.7	1.4	77.8	40.5	49.7	50.4
18035	CHERRYVILLE	98.3	97.8	0.4	0.9	0.0	0.0	1.8	2.2	3.6	4.5	5.4	7.6	5.4	25.5	32.1	14.7	1.3	81.3	44.0	52.2	47.8
18036	COOPERSBURG	97.4	96.9	0.6	0.7	0.9	1.2	1.1	1.3	5.2	6.1	7.2	7.3	5.6	24.5	30.2	12.2	1.8	77.4	41.9	49.9	50.1
18037	COPLAY	97.2	96.8	1.0	1.1	0.5	0.6	1.7	2.0	6.2	7.0	7.5	6.4	4.9	29.0	25.4	12.3	1.3	74.9	39.0	49.3	50.7
18038	DANIELSVILLE	98.7	98.4	0.2	0.3	0.2	0.3	0.7	0.9	5.2	5.9	7.6	6.7	4.9	27.4	30.8	10.4	1.1	77.1	40.8	51.8	48.2
18040	EASTON	95.6	94.7	1.9	2.2	1.2	1.6	1.9	2.2	6.8	7.5	7.8	6.2	4.2	26.4	27.7	12.0	1.4	73.8	40.4	48.5	51.5
18041	EAST GREENVILLE	97.2	96.7	0.8	0.9	0.5	0.7	1.8	2.1	7.1	7.2	7.7	6.9	5.9	29.9	25.3	8.9	1.1	73.6	36.6	49.9	50.1
18042	EASTON	84.0	82.3	9.0	9.8	1.6	2.0	7.5	8.5	6.0	5.7	6.8	8.8	10.1	28.0	22.4	10.4	1.9	77.4	34.6	49.2	50.8
18045	EASTON	94.1	93.0	2.3	2.6	2.1	2.6	2.3	2.7	5.5	6.1	6.6	5.8	4.2	24.8	27.9	16.6	2.5	77.9	43.2	48.2	51.8
18049	EMMAUS	96.2	95.4	0.6	0.7	1.8	2.3	1.5	1.8	5.0	5.6	6.8	6.2	5.1	27.7	26.9	14.5	2.3	78.6	41.3	48.6	51.4
18051	FOGELSVILLE	96.5	95.8	0.8	1.0	1.3	1.7	1.5	1.8	6.5	7.2	6.8	5.6	4.2	26.5	31.0	11.0	1.2	75.9	41.7	49.3	50.8
18052	WHITEHALL	90.6	89.1	2.7	3.0	3.7	4.5	4.4	5.0	5.5	5.4	6.0	5.8	5.8	28.2	25.1	15.8	2.5	79.5	40.9	47.9	52.1
18053	GERMANSVILLE	98.7	98.5	0.3	0.3	0.3	0.4	0.9	1.0	6.4	6.8	7.0	6.2	5.0	29.9	29.4	8.4	0.9	75.8	38.9	51.4	48.6
18054	GREEN LANE	97.6	97.3	0.8	0.9	0.3	0.3	0.9	1.1	5.8	6.2	7.0	7.0	5.2	27.0	28.7	11.4	1.7	76.4	40.7	49.9	50.1
18055	HELLERTOWN	97.7	97.3	0.4	0.4	0.5	0.6	2.4	2.7	5.0	5.4	6.3	5.8	5.1	25.9	28.3	16.0	2.4	79.8	43.0	48.6	51.4
18056	HEREFORD	97.0	96.5	0.3	0.4	0.5	0.8	1.9	2.3	4.8	5.5	7.6	6.3	6.2	27.6	29.4	11.5	1.2	78.2	40.1	51.4	48.6
18058	KUNKLETOWN	97.1	96.7	1.2	1.3	0.4	0.6	2.4	2.8	5.7	6.4	7.9	6.6	5.1	27.0	27.2	12.5	1.6	75.9	40.1	49.7	50.3
18059	LAURYS STATION	97.1	96.7	0.9	1.0	0.6	0.7	1.5	1.8	8.4	8.6	10.3	7.1	5.8	29.2	24.2	6.0	0.4	68.3	35.4	49.9	50.2
18062	MACUNGIE	95.2	93.9	0.8	1.0	2.8	3.7	1.5	1.9	5.8	6.5	7.1	6.1	5.1	25.8	28.9	13.1	1.6	76.6	41.3	49.1	51.0
18064	NAZARETH	98.2	97.9	0.5	0.5	0.5	0.6	1.1	1.3	4.9	5.6	7.1	6.7	4.9	24.4	27.7	14.4	4.3	78.3	42.9	47.9	52.1
18066	NEW TRIPOLI	98.1	97.8	0.3	0.3	0.3	0.4	1.0	1.2	5.8	6.4	7.1	6.4	5.5	27.9	29.7	10.1	1.2	76.6	40.3	50.7	49.3
18067	NORTHAMPTON	98.4	98.0	0.4	0.4	0.4	0.5	1.4	1.7	5.1	5.6	6.5	5.9	4.8	27.9	28.1	14.1	2.1	78.9	41.7	48.6	51.4
18069	OREFIELD	94.6	93.4	1.1	1.2	2.3	2.9	2.1	2.5	5.8	7.1	8.6	8.6	4.3	24.7	28.5	11.2	1.2	72.0	40.2	48.7	51.3
18070	PALM	97.8	97.4	0.7	0.8	0.4	0.5	1.2	1.3	5.0	5.7	6.8	6.4	5.9	25.9	31.0	12.1	1.3	78.3	41.7	50.6	49.4
18071	PALMERTON	98.5	98.3	0.2	0.2	0.2	0.2	1.8	2.0	5.8	6.0	6.5	6.2	5.4	28.8	25.9	13.0	2.4	77.7	39.9	48.8	51.2
18072	PEN ARGYL	98.4	98.1	0.4	0.5	0.4	0.5	1.0	1.2	5.3	5.6	7.5	6.7	5.9	26.6	26.1	13.8	2.4	77.0	40.3	48.2	51.8
18073	PENNSBURG	97.6	97.3	0.7	0.8	0.4	0.5	1.2	1.4	6.4	6.6	7.2	6.7	5.7	27.7	26.8	11.0	2.0	75.4	39.2	49.3	50.7
18074	PERKIOMENVILLE	97.5	97.1	0.9	1.0	0.5	0.6	0.7	0.8	6.8	7.3	7.4	5.8	4.5	28.6	26.7	10.7	2.1	74.7	39.7	49.6	50.4
18076	RED HILL	98.0	97.7	0.3	0.4	0.2	0.2	1.5	1.6	6.0	6.1	7.4	6.4	5.8	26.4	24.4	15.3	2.2	76.5	39.8	48.4	51.6
18077	RIEGELSVILLE	98.8	98.5	0.2	0.2	0.4	0.5	0.7	0.9	5.2	6.1	6.9	6.4	4.5	26.5	31.0	12.0	1.4	77.9	41.9	51.3	48.7
18078	SCHNECKSVILLE	97.6	97.1	0.6	0.7	0.7	0.9	1.4	1.6	5.1	6.3	8.1	7.7	4.5	25.1	31.5	10.5	1.2	74.7	41.4	49.2	50.8
18080	SLATINGTON	97.7	97.4	0.7	0.8	0.4	0.5	1.4	1.7	5.6	6.1	7.3	6.4	5.6	28.6	28.2	10.8	1.4	76.9	39.9	50.2	49.8
18087	TREXLERTOWN	92.5	90.5	0.6	0.8	5.8	7.4	1.3	1.6	6.6	8.3	9.9	7.0	3.6	26.0	29.0	8.9	0.8	70.2	39.3	48.7	51.3
18088	WALNUTPORT	98.4	98.1	0.4	0.4	0.4	0.6	1.0	1.1	4.8	5.2	6.1	5.9	5.1	26.7	30.5	14.0	1.7	80.1	42.8	50.0	50.0
	PENNSYLVANIA	85.4	84.4	10.0	10.3	1.8	2.2	3.2	3.5	5.9	6.1	6.8	6.9	6.7	26.6	25.3	13.3	2.2	77.2	39.1	48.4	51.6
	UNITED STATES	75.1	73.6	12.3	12.5	3.8	4.2	12.5	14.1	6.9	6.7	7.2	7.0	7.3	28.6	23.8	10.8	1.7	75.1	36.0	49.1	50.9

#	POST OFFICE NAME	2004 Per Capita Income	2004 HH Income Base	2004 Household Income Distribution (%) Less than $25,000	$25,000 to $49,999	$50,000 to $99,999	$100,000 to $149,999	$150,000 or More	Median Household Income 2004	2009	2004 National Centile	2004 State Centile	2004 Home Value Base	2004 Home Value Distribution (%) Less than $50,000	$50,000 to $89,999	$90,000 to $174,999	$175,000 to $399,999	$400,000 or More	2004 Median Home Value
17844	MIFFLINBURG	20951	3766	25.9	31.0	33.2	7.4	2.5	43304	50736	57	57	2961	12.1	8.5	56.3	19.8	3.3	125128
17845	MILLMONT	18109	820	25.5	37.9	30.6	4.6	1.3	40670	47179	48	47	677	9.6	22.2	51.7	14.8	1.8	111953
17846	MILLVILLE	21062	1570	26.6	34.1	29.8	7.3	2.2	41587	48439	52	51	1251	13.2	22.0	48.3	14.6	1.9	109728
17847	MILTON	20656	4871	31.0	33.2	29.9	4.0	1.9	37755	43691	38	34	3306	12.8	19.5	53.0	13.8	0.9	110131
17850	MONTANDON	21806	313	29.1	35.8	29.7	3.5	1.9	40646	45862	48	47	262	35.9	14.9	39.7	9.2	0.4	88571
17851	MOUNT CARMEL	17469	4073	47.0	29.5	18.9	3.5	1.1	27023	31180	7	3	2976	57.0	25.0	13.2	4.5	0.3	44914
17853	MOUNT PLEASANT MILLS	17226	718	27.7	33.8	32.0	4.3	2.1	39799	46124	45	43	592	8.8	17.1	57.6	15.2	1.4	115268
17855	NEW BERLIN	21119	315	28.6	34.6	27.0	7.6	2.2	39787	47229	45	43	236	3.0	14.0	74.6	8.1	0.4	117308
17856	NEW COLUMBIA	22590	1375	22.7	31.8	35.6	6.8	3.2	47451	55059	67	67	1179	8.4	13.3	61.2	16.0	1.1	122777
17857	NORTHUMBERLAND	23244	3177	25.5	34.8	31.6	5.2	2.8	41002	47594	50	48	2382	7.7	18.0	57.1	16.5	0.8	116938
17859	ORANGEVILLE	25551	1033	22.0	29.6	35.5	9.6	3.3	48658	57682	70	69	874	13.3	12.9	48.1	23.7	2.1	123276
17860	PAXINOS	21694	882	21.7	34.5	32.4	10.1	1.4	45447	51730	62	63	766	7.1	13.3	52.6	24.2	2.9	130425
17864	PORT TREVORTON	16116	931	29.3	33.5	30.3	4.7	2.2	39703	45638	45	43	769	10.9	18.9	49.4	17.7	3.1	122140
17866	COAL TOWNSHIP	17803	3822	41.3	32.6	20.8	3.9	1.5	30166	34861	13	6	2863	45.5	27.8	21.0	5.3	0.4	55039
17867	REBUCK	18659	267	28.5	31.1	35.6	4.9	0.0	41381	47016	51	50	227	11.5	26.0	37.4	21.6	3.5	111250
17868	RIVERSIDE	30797	335	16.7	25.7	34.9	14.9	7.8	59351	69958	84	85	301	5.0	6.6	62.1	24.9	1.3	144965
17870	SELINSGROVE	24138	5657	27.9	30.1	30.5	7.1	4.4	42342	50174	54	54	4134	7.6	12.0	56.3	21.8	2.3	126989
17872	SHAMOKIN	14504	4022	51.9	29.7	16.7	1.2	0.5	23701	27000	4	2	2404	61.5	22.6	14.3	1.6	0.0	41948
17877	SNYDERTOWN	18301	140	26.4	39.3	27.9	5.7	0.7	42740	48748	55	56	115	6.1	19.1	54.8	17.4	2.6	125595
17878	STILLWATER	21815	288	23.6	34.0	33.7	6.9	1.7	45000	51993	61	62	247	8.5	16.2	47.8	25.1	2.4	122045
17881	TREVORTON	17867	1065	33.7	36.7	26.4	2.4	0.8	36462	41819	33	27	818	22.6	37.4	34.1	5.8	0.1	77463
17888	WILBURTON	16227	220	38.2	37.3	22.3	0.9	1.4	32302	36865	19	11	191	43.5	27.8	24.1	4.2	0.5	58333
17889	WINFIELD	30339	887	14.4	25.4	38.0	13.4	8.8	59433	70868	84	85	775	5.0	9.0	47.6	33.6	4.8	145445
17901	POTTSVILLE	21685	11155	34.6	27.8	28.1	5.9	3.5	38716	45798	42	39	7982	20.1	31.2	34.3	13.5	1.0	88015
17921	ASHLAND	20762	3209	34.2	28.6	29.4	6.2	1.7	36108	42443	32	26	2499	30.2	27.9	31.2	10.7	0.0	76635
17922	AUBURN	23762	1870	17.9	30.9	40.1	7.9	3.2	50806	58661	73	73	1691	4.5	11.8	54.2	28.0	1.5	137210
17923	BRANCHDALE	17643	232	37.9	31.5	28.5	1.3	0.9	32803	38457	20	12	195	38.5	30.8	26.7	4.1	0.0	66250
17925	BROCKTON	20133	515	32.8	35.3	27.4	3.9	0.6	36236	42152	32	26	441	33.3	36.7	24.0	5.9	0.0	63700
17929	CRESSONA	24265	827	20.3	35.6	34.1	7.3	2.8	46436	54139	65	65	619	9.7	31.7	46.7	10.5	1.5	102035
17931	FRACKVILLE	18457	2554	33.6	30.8	26.8	5.9	3.0	35945	42421	31	25	1926	14.6	43.9	34.2	7.3	0.0	78942
17935	GIRARDVILLE	15733	807	47.3	34.2	15.9	1.9	0.7	26395	30850	6	3	578	71.1	22.7	4.7	1.6	0.0	38889
17938	HEGINS	20218	1070	35.1	28.3	28.3	5.6	2.6	39886	46287	46	44	887	11.6	27.7	46.9	13.1	0.7	101898
17941	KLINGERSTOWN	17985	216	29.2	35.7	31.0	2.8	1.4	40215	45774	47	45	181	15.5	23.2	37.6	23.2	0.6	105515
17948	MAHANOY CITY	16726	2428	44.6	33.5	18.5	2.4	1.0	28224	32808	9	4	1777	72.7	20.7	5.4	1.3	0.0	38489
17954	MINERSVILLE	18526	2130	43.6	28.4	24.0	3.1	1.0	31983	38017	18	10	1380	33.6	40.7	21.7	4.1	0.0	60112
17957	MUIR	21526	202	26.7	31.7	33.7	5.9	2.0	42029	50186	53	53	169	25.4	32.0	36.1	5.3	1.2	79583
17959	NEW PHILADELPHIA	19590	1113	39.3	28.8	27.3	3.4	1.3	33801	39669	23	16	804	37.8	34.7	22.0	5.5	0.0	59245
17960	NEW RINGGOLD	22370	1480	26.6	30.2	32.8	7.3	3.2	43024	50089	56	57	1250	7.1	13.2	48.3	27.7	3.7	136126
17961	ORWIGSBURG	30236	2703	21.7	25.1	34.8	9.7	8.8	52545	61669	76	76	2149	4.6	15.9	47.3	29.4	2.8	132652
17963	PINE GROVE	21410	3811	23.9	32.1	35.5	6.8	1.7	45570	52401	63	63	3116	8.7	21.6	49.0	19.3	1.4	121291
17964	PITMAN	21498	361	24.4	39.1	27.7	5.8	3.1	39222	44621	43	41	299	12.7	18.4	48.8	19.1	1.0	113068
17965	PORT CARBON	19899	949	32.2	36.5	25.0	3.5	2.9	35914	41754	31	25	711	16.3	45.3	32.9	5.5	0.0	75189
17967	RINGTOWN	22127	914	29.7	30.7	31.3	5.7	2.6	40509	47479	48	47	777	15.1	18.8	47.5	17.8	0.9	113387
17968	SACRAMENTO	20343	118	29.7	25.4	34.8	6.8	3.4	46525	53814	65	65	96	17.7	26.0	41.7	12.5	2.1	100000
17970	SAINT CLAIR	17978	1678	40.2	33.0	23.5	2.4	0.9	31176	36023	15	8	1206	29.2	47.3	21.2	2.3	0.0	63188
17972	SCHUYLKILL HAVEN	21331	4262	28.2	32.1	31.7	6.1	1.9	41171	48392	50	50	3178	14.2	26.2	41.6	17.3	0.8	103145
17976	SHENANDOAH	17901	4144	47.2	31.0	18.8	1.7	1.4	27106	31493	7	3	3131	69.0	18.0	9.6	3.4	0.0	38870
17978	SPRING GLEN	20444	139	29.5	25.9	34.5	7.2	2.9	46449	53121	65	65	113	17.7	24.8	44.3	10.6	2.7	101442
17980	TOWER CITY	20366	1326	30.1	34.8	28.3	5.1	1.8	38105	45219	40	36	1017	25.7	40.4	30.6	3.1	0.3	71467
17981	TREMONT	17535	1142	35.2	34.8	27.6	1.8	0.6	34546	40153	26	18	868	32.5	40.6	24.9	2.0	0.1	62300
17983	VALLEY VIEW	23034	811	27.1	29.6	32.7	8.1	2.5	44954	52675	61	61	658	8.8	22.8	59.0	8.8	0.6	107661
17985	ZION GROVE	20054	754	29.2	35.3	27.6	6.2	1.7	39789	46186	45	43	615	9.9	17.4	53.7	17.4	1.6	114681
18011	ALBURTIS	25797	1846	13.1	25.6	43.9	14.1	3.3	60370	71863	85	86	1558	5.7	4.1	59.4	28.5	2.4	146161
18013	BANGOR	24084	6762	23.6	25.9	37.1	10.2	3.2	50414	61002	73	72	4979	2.1	9.0	53.7	33.0	2.3	150682
18014	BATH	26039	4795	17.0	27.7	38.1	13.0	4.2	54573	64875	79	79	3984	13.0	10.1	35.9	38.9	2.1	157740
18015	BETHLEHEM	20916	11318	31.9	27.1	28.0	8.3	4.7	41092	50202	50	49	6641	6.2	21.2	46.9	20.9	4.8	118531
18017	BETHLEHEM	29201	14651	20.2	25.2	34.7	12.9	7.0	55265	66441	80	80	10487	1.3	3.5	51.9	40.5	2.8	164990
18018	BETHLEHEM	25924	13861	25.1	29.6	32.3	10.0	3.0	45781	56018	63	64	8306	1.1	13.3	71.0	13.4	1.2	121169
18020	BETHLEHEM	30029	7376	10.9	22.2	38.9	20.6	7.4	69553	83438	91	92	6346	1.8	1.6	45.2	49.7	1.6	177344
18031	BREINIGSVILLE	31319	1695	17.8	23.2	37.6	14.5	7.0	58918	69102	83	85	1459	30.0	9.1	26.6	30.6	3.7	136558
18032	CATASAUQUA	23148	3742	19.7	32.6	36.2	8.8	2.7	48401	59065	69	69	2629	0.2	16.6	69.1	14.1	0.0	117783
18034	CENTER VALLEY	33697	2016	8.1	19.7	34.9	23.1	14.1	77218	99830	94	95	1852	4.6	2.9	26.6	51.8	14.1	200324
18035	CHERRYVILLE	26987	81	9.9	28.4	38.3	14.8	8.6	62969	75544	87	89	73	2.7	5.5	37.0	46.6	8.2	185938
18036	COOPERSBURG	34192	4557	9.4	21.4	37.6	19.9	11.7	72057	89711	92	93	4016	1.0	0.6	29.9	58.2	10.3	205914
18037	COPLAY	27037	2930	18.4	23.0	41.7	13.0	4.0	57354	68515	82	83	2397	4.1	6.3	55.8	31.3	2.6	150904
18038	DANIELSVILLE	23151	976	12.7	29.4	44.1	11.1	2.8	56101	66224	81	81	899	1.9	9.7	47.1	39.0	2.3	159981
18040	EASTON	31123	4720	9.6	18.0	43.2	22.4	6.7	73747	86593	93	94	4164	0.7	2.4	37.6	57.8	1.5	194654
18041	EAST GREENVILLE	27174	2143	14.9	22.6	43.4	13.7	5.4	62505	76582	87	89	1704	0.7	1.2	48.2	45.7	4.2	174776
18042	EASTON	21544	15112	27.5	31.3	30.7	7.7	2.8	42430	51472	54	55	8607	3.8	24.4	55.1	14.4	2.2	109150
18045	EASTON	33030	9186	14.6	20.9	39.5	16.1	8.9	65340	78382	89	90	7968	0.7	1.3	51.3	44.6	2.1	171253
18049	EMMAUS	31678	7258	17.4	23.4	36.9	14.4	8.0	60201	73394	85	86	5287	1.1	3.4	52.9	38.3	4.3	163417
18051	FOGELSVILLE	35816	1307	11.7	19.2	35.6	16.8	16.7	73126	88672	92	94	1153	10.3	4.0	29.1	48.2	8.4	193568
18052	WHITEHALL	26056	10779	20.6	28.5	36.2	11.7	3.1	50773	62325	73	73	7207	1.7	4.7	62.9	29.7	1.0	149840
18053	GERMANSVILLE	27489	851	16.7	18.8	43.5	13.8	7.3	60721	71304	85	87	755	5.3	7.3	39.9	42.8	4.8	170510
18054	GREEN LANE	32561	1936	12.2	18.3	44.3	17.2	8.1	67553	82552	90	91	1654	2.5	4.7	22.1	62.8	7.8	212411
18055	HELLERTOWN	30601	4716	17.9	27.3	36.1	12.1	6.7	54980	66302	80	80	3742	0.9	3.1	54.1	34.4	7.5	163765
18056	HEREFORD	23129	464	20.9	27.8	37.7	10.3	3.2	51069	61218	74	74	398	42.2	9.1	19.4	25.1	4.3	85000
18058	KUNKLETOWN	21737	3494	23.0	30.4	34.1	9.5	3.0	47390	55817	67	67	2991	6.9	7.5	47.5	36.4	1.8	157269
18059	LAURYS STATION	26639	446	15.5	22.7	37.9	17.9	6.1	65024	78081	89	90	420	29.5	1.7	10.7	51.7	6.4	207090
18062	MACUNGIE	33816	6239	10.8	20.4	37.1	20.5	11.3	71661	87942	92	93	5135	4.1	2.8	44.7	43.7	4.7	172549
18064	NAZARETH	27436	8259	15.6	23.4	40.0	14.9	6.0	61845	73205	86	88	6642	1.9	3.9	45.5	46.2	2.6	173179
18066	NEW TRIPOLI	28493	1892	12.7	21.4	40.1	19.0	6.8	65272	77516	89	90	1643	2.7	4.3	41.4	47.1	4.6	177989
18067	NORTHAMPTON	25665	6644	17.7	28.0	39.2	11.9	3.3	53884	65194	78	78	5404	4.4	8.7	56.9	28.7	1.3	141538
18069	OREFIELD	32413	2349	12.8	19.5	35.4	16.4	15.8	69024	84676	91	92	2034	10.0	6.1	25.0	45.9	13.0	199727
18070	PALM	30129	297	14.8	21.2	39.7	16.5	7.7	65466	78954	89	90	259	13.5	3.9	24.7	51.0	7.0	190074
18071	PALMERTON	20991	4198	25.2	35.2	31.3	6.3	2.0	41252	48000	51	50	3188	7.0	26.4	50.6	15.6	0.4	111914
18072	PEN ARGYL	23046	2416	21.9	27.3	39.1	8.1	3.6	50524	60730	73	72	1812	1.8	11.5	59.1	26.4	1.2	139966
18073	PENNSBURG	27872	2644	13.7	20.8	44.3	15.9	5.3	64546	78855	88	90	2118	0.3	1.3	34.4	59.3	4.7	196154
18074	PERKIOMENVILLE	28573	1972	10.9	20.9	42.0	18.2	8.1	69020	83512	91	92	1771	1.0	0.6	26.8	62.6	9.0	220527
18076	RED HILL	26596	1039	22.5	21.1	39.4	14.2	2.8	57420	72509	82	83	725	0.0	8.1	55.6	35.6	0.7	160105
18077	RIEGELSVILLE	35127	994	12.1	19.8	39.1	18.7	10.3	69733	86723	91	92	807	0.6	1.1	18.8	59.0	20.5	235694
18078	SCHNECKSVILLE	34970	2525	10.1	16.3	39.5	22.5	11.6	76079	93576	94	95	2229	5.2	3.8	31.3	56.0	3.8	194351
18080	SLATINGTON	22817	4745	20.1	26.2	39.9	11.9	1.9	53190	64209	77	77	3815	8.4	15.2	46.3	28.2	2.0	137474
18087	TREXLERTOWN	57040	225	6.2	12.9	31.6	22.2	27.1	98298	117150	98	98	211	7.1	4.7	12.3	56.9	19.0	262097
18088	WALNUTPORT	24576	3265	20.4	28.6	37.6	9.3	4.1	50753	60900	73	73	2900	12.9	9.0	48.5	28.0	1.6	140569
	PENNSYLVANIA	25764		25.8	27.2	31.2	10.2	5.7	46988	57000				11.9	18.4	40.7	25.1	4.1	123516
	UNITED STATES	25866		24.7	27.1	30.8	10.9	6.5	48124	56710				10.9	15.0	33.7	30.1	10.4	145905

# ZIP CODE	POST OFFICE NAME	FINANCIAL SERVICES: Auto Loan	Home Loan	Invest-ments	Retire-ment Plans	THE HOME: Home Improvements: Home Repair	Lawn & Garden	Furnishings: Comput-ers & Hard-ware	Major Appli-ances	TV, Radio, Sound Equip-ment	Furni-ture	ENTERTAINMENT: Dine out/ Carry out	Sports Equip-ment	Fees & Tickets	Toys & Games	Travel	Cable TV	PERSONAL: Apparel & Services	Auto Repairs	Health Insur-ance	Pets & Supplies
17844	MIFFLINBURG	89	74	54	71	79	88	72	80	79	72	95	94	69	94	74	81	89	79	90	102
17845	MILLMONT	85	62	35	55	70	79	59	72	69	59	81	86	51	79	61	74	75	71	87	101
17846	MILLVILLE	87	75	55	71	80	87	72	80	77	71	93	93	69	94	73	80	88	78	88	101
17847	MILTON	76	64	50	60	68	76	64	69	69	63	84	81	61	84	65	72	79	69	78	86
17850	MONTANDON	89	64	34	56	71	80	61	74	71	62	84	88	54	81	62	76	77	73	88	103
17851	MOUNT CARMEL	53	48	45	46	50	58	51	52	54	49	66	59	50	67	51	57	62	52	59	60
17853	MOUNT PLEASANT MILLS	92	61	28	53	69	80	59	74	71	60	84	88	50	79	60	77	76	73	91	105
17855	NEW BERLIN	80	68	53	68	71	80	70	75	74	69	90	85	67	89	69	75	84	74	81	88
17856	NEW COLUMBIA	91	79	61	77	83	91	76	83	81	76	99	98	74	99	77	83	93	82	90	104
17857	NORTHUMBERLAND	79	75	66	71	78	86	72	77	76	71	93	88	73	96	74	79	89	75	83	92
17859	ORANGEVILLE	98	88	67	83	92	99	81	90	86	81	104	107	79	107	83	88	99	87	97	116
17860	PAXINOS	86	77	58	73	81	87	71	79	75	71	92	94	70	94	73	77	87	77	85	102
17864	PORT TREVORTON	86	67	42	61	73	81	63	74	71	64	85	88	58	84	65	75	79	73	85	100
17866	COAL TOWNSHIP	52	51	50	49	53	59	52	53	54	50	66	59	52	69	53	56	63	52	58	60
17867	REBUCK	73	65	50	62	69	74	60	67	64	60	78	80	59	80	62	66	74	65	73	86
17868	RIVERSIDE	98	118	132	116	117	124	109	109	104	109	131	123	116	133	113	104	129	106	106	119
17870	SELINSGROVE	89	83	79	81	85	93	85	87	88	83	108	102	83	108	85	88	103	88	91	103
17872	SHAMOKIN	45	38	36	37	40	46	42	43	46	41	55	49	40	54	42	48	52	44	49	51
17877	SNYDERTOWN	75	66	51	63	70	75	61	68	65	61	79	81	60	81	63	67	75	66	74	88
17878	STILLWATER	84	75	57	71	79	85	69	77	74	69	90	92	68	92	72	76	85	75	83	99
17881	TREVORTON	58	57	54	53	59	66	56	58	60	55	74	66	58	78	58	63	70	57	64	68
17888	WILBURTON	71	47	21	41	54	62	46	57	55	46	65	68	39	61	46	59	59	56	70	81
17889	WINFIELD	117	114	99	110	118	124	105	112	107	105	131	133	106	135	108	108	127	109	116	139
17901	POTTSVILLE	72	71	73	68	73	81	72	73	75	70	92	83	73	95	74	78	89	73	79	83
17921	ASHLAND	65	68	69	65	69	77	67	68	70	65	86	76	70	90	69	72	83	67	73	76
17922	AUBURN	92	90	79	87	93	99	84	89	86	83	106	104	85	110	86	87	102	86	93	109
17923	BRANCHDALE	53	57	60	54	58	64	57	56	59	54	73	62	60	79	58	61	70	55	60	62
17925	BROCKTON	57	61	65	58	62	69	61	60	63	58	78	67	64	85	63	65	75	59	65	66
17929	CRESSONA	87	81	71	79	84	94	81	84	85	79	104	96	81	107	82	87	99	83	91	99
17931	FRACKVILLE	55	57	58	54	58	65	57	58	59	55	73	64	59	77	59	62	70	57	62	64
17935	GIRARDVILLE	45	49	52	46	49	55	48	48	50	46	62	53	51	67	50	52	60	47	51	53
17938	HEGINS	67	68	67	65	70	78	68	69	71	66	88	77	70	93	70	73	84	68	74	77
17941	KLINGERSTOWN	84	59	30	51	66	76	57	70	68	58	80	83	50	77	58	73	73	69	85	97
17948	MAHANOY CITY	48	50	54	47	50	56	51	50	53	49	65	56	53	70	52	55	63	50	54	56
17954	MINERSVILLE	57	54	50	51	56	64	56	57	59	53	72	64	56	74	57	62	68	56	64	65
17957	MUIR	96	64	29	55	73	84	62	78	75	63	88	93	53	83	63	81	80	77	96	110
17959	NEW PHILADELPHIA	57	62	65	58	63	69	61	60	63	59	79	67	65	85	63	66	76	59	65	67
17960	NEW RINGGOLD	95	79	55	73	84	92	73	84	80	74	97	100	70	97	75	83	91	82	94	111
17961	ORWIGSBURG	121	106	81	100	113	123	100	112	107	99	129	132	96	131	103	110	122	109	123	143
17963	PINE GROVE	82	74	60	69	78	86	71	77	76	70	93	89	70	95	73	79	88	75	85	96
17964	PITMAN	77	76	73	71	79	88	75	77	80	73	98	88	77	103	77	83	94	76	85	90
17965	PORT CARBON	59	64	68	61	65	72	64	63	66	61	82	70	67	88	66	68	79	62	68	69
17967	RINGTOWN	88	72	52	65	77	88	70	79	79	70	95	92	66	96	72	84	89	78	92	102
17968	SACRAMENTO	83	74	56	70	78	84	68	76	73	68	88	90	67	90	70	74	84	74	82	98
17970	SAINT CLAIR	54	51	47	48	53	60	52	54	56	50	68	60	52	70	53	58	64	53	60	61
17972	SCHUYLKILL HAVEN	76	68	56	64	71	79	67	72	71	65	87	83	66	89	68	74	82	70	79	87
17976	SHENANDOAH	50	50	58	49	51	58	53	52	56	51	69	59	55	73	54	58	67	53	56	58
17978	SPRING GLEN	83	74	56	70	78	84	68	76	73	68	88	90	67	90	70	75	84	74	82	98
17980	TOWER CITY	75	62	46	56	66	75	60	67	68	60	81	78	58	82	62	72	76	67	78	86
17981	TREMONT	46	47	47	44	48	54	46	47	49	45	60	53	48	64	48	51	58	46	51	53
17983	VALLEY VIEW	71	75	76	71	76	84	74	74	77	71	95	83	77	102	76	79	91	72	80	84
17985	ZION GROVE	77	66	50	64	69	77	66	71	70	65	85	82	63	85	66	71	80	70	77	87
18011	ALBURTIS	102	100	87	98	101	105	94	99	94	94	116	117	93	117	94	93	112	97	97	118
18013	BANGOR	87	85	78	82	88	96	83	86	86	81	106	99	84	110	85	89	101	84	92	102
18014	BATH	106	89	64	84	95	104	85	95	92	85	111	112	81	111	86	95	104	93	105	122
18015	BETHLEHEM	74	74	93	74	73	80	81	77	81	79	103	90	80	103	79	81	101	80	76	85
18017	BETHLEHEM	94	103	116	102	101	108	100	99	99	100	124	114	103	127	102	99	122	99	97	109
18018	BETHLEHEM	75	78	93	78	78	85	82	79	83	80	103	92	84	106	83	83	101	81	80	87
18020	BETHLEHEM	107	126	134	126	124	127	116	116	110	115	138	134	122	144	118	108	137	113	108	128
18031	BREINIGSVILLE	115	108	87	104	109	115	101	109	103	103	126	127	98	124	101	102	122	107	109	131
18032	CATASAUQUA	75	83	88	80	82	88	81	80	80	79	100	91	84	106	82	81	98	78	79	87
18034	CENTER VALLEY	133	165	177	165	162	161	148	148	137	147	173	172	157	183	152	134	172	142	133	163
18035	CHERRYVILLE	94	114	126	111	112	114	106	105	101	105	127	121	113	135	109	100	127	102	97	114
18036	COOPERSBURG	124	146	151	144	145	146	132	133	126	132	158	155	140	168	136	125	157	129	125	150
18037	COPLAY	91	106	112	105	104	108	98	98	95	98	119	112	104	124	100	94	117	95	93	107
18038	DANIELSVILLE	102	90	68	85	95	102	83	93	89	83	108	110	82	110	86	91	102	90	100	120
18040	EASTON	113	128	131	127	128	132	118	120	115	117	143	138	124	150	121	114	140	116	115	134
18041	EAST GREENVILLE	110	109	101	108	110	114	104	108	103	104	128	128	104	130	104	101	124	106	105	127
18042	EASTON	74	71	77	71	72	78	77	75	78	74	97	88	76	99	76	78	94	76	76	84
18045	EASTON	108	123	131	120	122	129	115	116	112	114	140	132	120	145	118	112	137	113	113	128
18049	EMMAUS	101	110	118	108	110	117	106	106	105	105	131	123	110	136	108	106	129	105	106	120
18051	FOGELSVILLE	133	153	155	154	150	152	138	139	130	139	163	162	145	168	140	127	162	135	128	157
18052	WHITEHALL	83	88	99	87	88	95	87	87	87	87	108	99	90	109	88	87	106	87	86	96
18053	GERMANSVILLE	107	117	111	115	118	120	105	109	103	105	128	129	109	134	108	102	125	106	106	129
18054	GREEN LANE	116	126	121	125	126	129	116	119	113	115	140	140	119	145	118	111	137	116	115	138
18055	HELLERTOWN	97	106	109	102	107	115	100	102	100	99	124	116	104	129	103	102	121	100	104	116
18056	HEREFORD	112	75	34	65	85	98	72	90	87	74	102	108	61	97	73	94	93	89	111	128
18058	KUNKLETOWN	97	82	58	77	88	95	76	87	83	77	100	103	73	101	79	86	94	85	96	114
18059	LAURYS STATION	112	126	122	132	120	116	114	113	104	118	133	132	117	133	111	97	131	110	96	123
18062	MACUNGIE	117	134	142	135	133	136	124	124	118	124	148	145	130	153	126	115	147	122	116	139
18064	NAZARETH	100	105	102	103	107	113	99	101	99	98	122	118	102	128	101	99	119	99	103	119
18066	NEW TRIPOLI	116	119	108	116	122	126	109	115	108	108	134	135	111	139	111	108	130	111	114	138
18067	NORTHAMPTON	88	90	85	87	92	99	86	89	88	84	108	102	88	114	88	89	105	87	92	104
18069	OREFIELD	138	143	135	142	145	153	133	137	131	133	163	160	137	166	135	131	158	134	137	161
18070	PALM	137	111	74	102	120	131	104	120	115	104	138	143	97	137	106	120	129	117	136	160
18071	PALMERTON	72	72	68	68	74	81	69	72	72	68	89	82	71	94	71	75	85	70	77	84
18072	PEN ARGYL	82	83	80	79	85	93	80	83	82	78	102	94	82	106	82	85	98	81	88	96
18073	PENNSBURG	109	107	99	106	110	115	103	107	104	102	128	127	103	131	104	103	124	106	108	127
18074	PERKIOMENVILLE	111	127	127	126	127	128	115	117	109	114	137	138	120	144	117	108	135	113	110	134
18076	RED HILL	93	90	93	90	91	97	91	92	92	90	115	109	90	115	91	92	111	93	93	107
18077	RIEGELSVILLE	112	138	149	137	136	136	125	124	117	125	148	145	133	157	128	115	147	120	113	137
18078	SCHNECKSVILLE	124	143	146	144	143	144	131	132	125	130	156	154	137	164	133	122	154	128	124	148
18080	SLATINGTON	85	85	79	82	87	92	81	84	83	80	102	98	82	106	83	84	99	83	87	100
18087	TREXLERTOWN	166	207	225	213	200	202	182	177	166	185	211	205	200	219	185	160	213	171	158	196
18088	WALNUTPORT	95	87	71	82	91	99	82	90	87	82	105	105	80	106	84	89	100	88	97	112
	PENNSYLVANIA	89	89	93	87	90	98	89	90	91	88	112	104	89	114	90	92	109	90	92	104
	UNITED STATES	100	100	100	100	100	100	100	100	100	100	100	100	100	100	100	100	100	100	100	100

#	POST OFFICE NAME	COUNTY FIPS CODE	POPULATION 2000	2004	2009	2000-2004 ANNUAL RATE % Rate	State Centile	HOUSEHOLDS 2000	2004	2009	% Annual Rate 2000-2004	2004 Average HH Size	FAMILIES 2000	2004	% Annual Rate 2000-2004
18091	WIND GAP	095	5578	5785	6036	0.9	75	2180	2304	2447	1.3	2.47	1550	1631	1.2
18092	ZIONSVILLE	077	2835	2833	2889	0.0	37	1030	1037	1062	0.2	2.73	824	825	0.0
18101	ALLENTOWN	077	3898	3794	3838	-0.6	12	1144	1104	1120	-0.8	2.76	576	551	-1.0
18102	ALLENTOWN	077	43402	43994	45599	0.3	55	16749	16787	17329	0.1	2.56	9717	9636	-0.2
18103	ALLENTOWN	077	43160	44233	45947	0.6	68	17307	17848	18637	0.7	2.42	11524	11760	0.5
18104	ALLENTOWN	077	38694	39976	41541	0.8	73	15046	15682	16424	1.0	2.33	9960	10279	0.7
18106	ALLENTOWN	077	6180	6934	7480	2.8	97	2337	2647	2873	3.0	2.58	1790	2012	2.8
18109	ALLENTOWN	077	16955	16968	17418	0.0	40	6916	6947	7154	0.1	2.39	4435	4408	-0.1
18201	HAZLETON	079	25503	25433	25333	-0.1	36	11187	11363	11533	0.4	2.21	6632	6670	0.1
18202	HAZLETON	079	11052	11131	11133	0.2	47	4610	4742	4840	0.7	2.23	2895	2958	0.5
18210	ALBRIGHTSVILLE	025	3974	4578	5074	3.4	99	1448	1680	1877	3.6	2.71	1110	1281	3.4
18211	ANDREAS	107	1186	1211	1238	0.5	63	456	475	495	1.0	2.55	354	367	0.9
18214	BARNESVILLE	107	2473	2517	2571	0.4	60	976	1011	1050	0.8	2.48	728	748	0.6
18216	BEAVER MEADOWS	025	2234	2210	2214	-0.3	27	930	942	960	0.3	2.31	632	635	0.1
18218	COALDALE	107	2295	2335	2400	0.4	60	1046	1085	1138	0.9	2.10	607	624	0.7
18219	CONYNGHAM	079	1619	1568	1538	-0.8	8	658	649	649	-0.3	2.37	479	470	-0.5
18220	DELANO	107	269	271	275	0.2	47	103	106	110	0.7	2.56	74	76	0.6
18222	DRUMS	079	6692	7078	7242	1.3	86	2347	2564	2691	2.1	2.47	1763	1914	2.0
18224	FREELAND	079	5899	5756	5666	-0.6	13	2532	2520	2531	-0.1	2.28	1605	1585	-0.3
18229	JIM THORPE	025	6945	7082	7181	0.5	62	2795	2909	2999	1.0	2.42	1982	2049	0.8
18232	LANSFORD	025	4230	4148	4140	-0.5	18	1878	1870	1891	-0.1	2.20	1099	1082	-0.4
18235	LEHIGHTON	025	18559	19019	19381	0.6	68	7406	7763	8051	1.1	2.41	5285	5510	1.0
18237	MCADOO	107	3904	4048	4186	0.9	75	1741	1844	1945	1.4	2.19	1095	1153	1.2
18240	NESQUEHONING	025	3890	3997	4076	0.6	69	1596	1681	1747	1.2	2.21	1044	1090	1.0
18245	QUAKAKE	107	968	978	993	0.2	51	269	279	290	0.9	2.88	201	208	0.8
18246	ROCK GLEN	079	1720	1714	1701	-0.1	35	670	682	691	0.4	2.47	479	484	0.2
18248	SHEPPTON	107	1231	1253	1280	0.4	60	549	570	593	0.9	2.20	349	358	0.6
18249	SUGARLOAF	079	3846	3816	3782	-0.2	30	1467	1491	1512	0.4	2.43	1133	1146	0.3
18250	SUMMIT HILL	025	2974	2829	2809	-1.2	3	1291	1257	1271	-0.6	2.24	844	815	-0.8
18252	TAMAQUA	107	10693	10833	11081	0.3	54	4528	4692	4899	0.8	2.27	2927	3007	0.6
18255	WEATHERLY	025	4350	4339	4359	-0.1	36	1588	1617	1652	0.4	2.53	1155	1167	0.2
18301	EAST STROUDSBURG	089	37207	42660	50019	3.3	98	12690	14777	17583	3.7	2.72	9164	10621	3.5
18321	BARTONSVILLE	089	1398	1602	1883	3.3	98	486	565	671	3.6	2.82	368	425	3.5
18322	BRODHEADSVILLE	089	1758	1962	2275	2.6	96	628	712	835	3.0	2.71	490	552	2.8
18324	BUSHKILL	103	5892	7705	10050	6.5	100	2047	2706	3562	6.8	2.84	1614	2121	6.6
18325	CANADENSIS	089	2581	2787	3246	1.8	91	1026	1127	1331	2.2	2.42	720	784	2.0
18326	CRESCO	089	3972	4428	5138	2.6	96	1585	1789	2095	2.9	2.47	1097	1229	2.7
18327	DELAWARE WATER GAP	089	1069	1164	1334	2.0	93	486	538	624	2.4	2.13	289	315	2.1
18328	DINGMANS FERRY	103	6694	7864	9762	3.9	99	2410	2871	3604	4.2	2.73	1867	2212	4.1
18330	EFFORT	089	8626	9740	11360	2.9	97	2862	3266	3844	3.2	2.94	2284	2588	3.0
18331	GILBERT	089	37	41	47	2.4	95	12	13	16	1.9	3.15	9	10	2.5
18332	HENRYVILLE	089	2633	2993	3500	3.1	98	991	1146	1359	3.5	2.55	715	819	3.3
18333	KRESGEVILLE	089	1111	1247	1450	2.8	97	405	461	542	3.1	2.67	320	361	2.9
18334	LONG POND	089	1888	2169	2553	3.3	98	658	763	906	3.5	2.84	512	589	3.4
18336	MATAMORAS	103	3951	4410	5322	2.6	96	1553	1766	2163	3.1	2.47	1081	1219	2.9
18337	MILFORD	103	11543	13887	17404	4.5	99	4185	5055	6370	4.5	2.74	3190	3830	4.4
18340	MILLRIFT	103	236	264	318	2.7	97	87	99	122	3.1	2.61	62	70	2.9
18343	MOUNT BETHEL	095	4054	4179	4355	0.7	72	1597	1674	1774	1.1	2.49	1149	1194	0.9
18344	MOUNT POCONO	089	3361	3697	4254	2.3	95	1248	1395	1624	2.7	2.61	854	943	2.4
18346	POCONO SUMMIT	089	1808	1995	2302	2.3	95	640	717	837	2.7	2.78	475	527	2.5
18347	POCONO LAKE	089	2588	2845	3276	2.3	94	1067	1195	1392	2.7	2.37	755	836	2.4
18350	POCONO PINES	089	998	1092	1254	2.1	94	429	477	555	2.5	2.29	304	334	2.2
18352	REEDERS	089	477	544	637	3.1	98	200	232	276	3.6	2.31	152	175	3.4
18353	SAYLORSBURG	089	9713	11413	13597	3.9	99	3380	4027	4845	4.2	2.82	2716	3215	4.1
18354	SCIOTA	089	439	483	557	2.3	95	168	188	219	2.7	2.56	117	130	2.5
18355	SCOTRUN	089	1753	1899	2169	1.9	92	666	733	847	2.3	2.56	484	527	2.0
18360	STROUDSBURG	089	26713	29767	34480	2.6	96	10092	11411	13378	2.9	2.55	6954	7817	2.8
18370	SWIFTWATER	089	678	734	839	1.9	92	259	285	330	2.3	2.55	188	205	2.1
18371	TAMIMENT	103	1613	2075	2687	6.1	100	552	719	941	6.4	2.89	440	569	6.2
18372	TANNERSVILLE	089	2582	2978	3515	3.4	99	956	1118	1332	3.8	2.66	722	838	3.6
18403	ARCHBALD	069	6670	6663	6624	0.0	37	2593	2643	2677	0.5	2.52	1867	1890	0.3
18405	BEACH LAKE	127	1188	1233	1304	0.9	76	451	478	515	1.4	2.58	336	352	1.1
18407	CARBONDALE	069	14658	14346	14121	-0.5	16	6030	6041	6065	0.0	2.30	3927	3898	-0.2
18411	CLARKS SUMMIT	069	23275	24147	24448	0.9	75	8666	9182	9478	1.4	2.53	6365	6707	1.2
18414	DALTON	069	6035	6014	6022	-0.1	35	2286	2338	2394	0.5	2.54	1708	1734	0.4
18415	DAMASCUS	127	1505	1571	1665	1.0	80	604	647	702	1.6	2.42	421	448	1.5
18417	EQUINUNK	127	901	942	998	1.1	81	350	376	409	1.7	2.50	255	273	1.6
18419	FACTORYVILLE	069	4418	4411	4440	0.0	36	1561	1591	1635	0.5	2.58	1157	1170	0.3
18421	FOREST CITY	127	5107	5130	5218	0.1	44	2066	2109	2183	0.5	2.36	1377	1399	0.4
18424	GOULDSBORO	069	4506	4627	4729	0.6	69	1750	1834	1911	1.1	2.52	1291	1343	0.9
18425	GREELEY	103	1241	1380	1666	2.5	96	484	550	672	3.1	2.51	343	386	2.8
18426	GREENTOWN	103	3297	3760	4636	3.1	98	1372	1593	1993	3.6	2.33	973	1121	3.4
18427	HAMLIN	127	2066	2152	2279	1.0	78	810	863	933	1.5	2.49	599	634	1.4
18428	HAWLEY	127	3052	3219	3474	1.3	85	1290	1379	1516	1.6	2.33	846	900	1.5
18430	HERRICK CENTER	115	237	243	247	0.6	68	102	107	112	1.1	2.27	71	75	1.3
18431	HONESDALE	127	13499	14465	15703	1.6	90	5442	5975	6648	2.2	2.37	3610	3949	2.1
18433	JERMYN	069	6233	6100	6002	-0.5	15	2512	2514	2522	0.0	2.39	1751	1738	-0.2
18434	JESSUP	069	4238	4250	4234	0.1	43	1828	1870	1897	0.5	2.27	1199	1213	0.3
18435	LACKAWAXEN	103	2919	3305	4022	3.0	98	1212	1401	1728	3.5	2.36	857	982	3.3
18436	LAKE ARIEL	127	9406	9829	10271	1.0	80	3483	3727	3981	1.6	2.59	2660	2833	1.5
18437	LAKE COMO	127	361	364	381	0.2	48	155	162	174	1.0	2.23	106	109	0.7
18438	LAKEVILLE	127	2059	2210	2377	1.7	90	825	898	983	2.0	2.44	620	670	1.8
18439	LAKEWOOD	127	786	787	824	0.0	40	316	327	351	0.8	2.40	221	227	0.6
18441	LENOXVILLE	115	733	738	741	0.2	46	271	279	286	0.7	2.64	190	193	0.4
18443	MILANVILLE	127	1059	1098	1160	0.9	75	429	456	492	1.5	2.41	314	332	1.3
18444	MOSCOW	069	11490	11672	11721	0.4	58	4233	4400	4508	0.9	2.61	3253	3357	0.7
18445	NEWFOUNDLAND	127	1220	1357	1500	2.5	96	471	536	606	3.1	2.45	327	370	3.0
18446	NICHOLSON	115	3699	3727	3789	0.2	47	1422	1463	1518	0.7	2.54	1045	1069	0.5
18447	OLYPHANT	069	8829	8617	8476	-0.6	13	3785	3791	3812	0.0	2.27	2445	2426	-0.2
18451	PAUPACK	103	479	535	647	2.6	97	200	227	278	3.0	2.36	137	155	3.0
18452	PECKVILLE	069	5570	5436	5344	-0.6	13	2209	2205	2210	0.0	2.29	1461	1445	-0.3
18453	PLEASANT MOUNT	127	1283	1303	1369	0.4	58	516	541	584	1.1	2.41	358	373	0.8
18455	PRESTON PARK	127	294	298	312	0.3	55	121	126	136	1.0	2.37	89	92	0.8
18456	PROMPTON	127	706	719	750	0.4	61	295	309	331	1.1	2.05	209	217	0.8
18458	SHOHOLA	103	2302	2781	3484	4.6	100	921	1135	1442	5.0	2.43	650	793	4.8
	PENNSYLVANIA					0.3					0.7	2.44			0.6
	UNITED STATES					1.2					1.3	2.58			1.1

#	POST OFFICE NAME	White 2000	White 2004	Black 2000	Black 2004	Asian/Pacific 2000	Asian/Pacific 2004	% Hispanic Origin 2000	% Hispanic Origin 2004	0-4	5-9	10-14	15-19	20-24	25-44	45-64	65-84	85+	18+	MEDIAN AGE 2004	% 2004 Males	% 2004 Females
18091	WIND GAP	97.9	97.5	0.4	0.4	0.5	0.6	1.3	1.5	5.6	6.0	7.0	5.8	4.9	27.4	27.5	13.6	2.3	77.7	41.1	48.6	51.4
18092	ZIONSVILLE	98.2	97.9	0.1	0.1	0.5	0.7	0.7	0.8	4.4	5.8	7.2	7.3	4.6	25.8	33.0	10.6	1.4	77.9	42.5	51.1	48.9
18101	ALLENTOWN	53.6	50.4	17.4	18.0	1.4	1.6	43.8	47.3	7.1	6.9	6.4	6.8	10.8	36.3	18.0	6.9	1.0	76.2	31.0	56.8	43.2
18102	ALLENTOWN	62.5	59.2	10.5	11.0	1.9	2.3	35.6	39.0	8.1	7.6	8.5	7.9	7.8	28.5	19.5	10.2	2.0	71.1	32.4	48.5	51.5
18103	ALLENTOWN	83.7	81.2	4.4	4.9	3.3	4.0	11.8	13.6	6.0	6.3	6.7	6.2	5.7	27.1	25.5	14.0	2.5	77.2	39.8	48.1	51.9
18104	ALLENTOWN	93.7	92.5	1.6	1.8	2.5	3.2	2.6	3.0	4.8	5.1	6.0	7.6	7.1	22.5	25.8	15.9	5.2	80.5	42.9	45.9	54.1
18106	ALLENTOWN	93.7	92.4	0.7	0.8	3.9	4.9	1.6	1.9	5.5	6.2	7.6	7.1	5.5	24.8	29.8	11.4	2.1	75.9	41.0	48.0	52.0
18109	ALLENTOWN	76.2	73.4	7.0	7.7	2.5	2.9	20.6	23.0	7.3	6.4	6.6	6.1	6.9	28.3	22.6	13.8	2.1	76.2	37.2	48.1	51.9
18201	HAZLETON	95.1	94.6	0.8	0.8	0.6	0.8	4.5	4.9	5.1	5.1	6.0	6.0	5.9	25.9	24.4	18.2	3.6	80.2	42.3	47.2	52.8
18202	HAZLETON	98.0	97.6	0.4	0.5	0.4	0.5	1.6	1.8	5.0	5.0	5.6	7.1	5.5	23.6	25.3	19.3	3.7	81.2	43.7	48.1	51.9
18210	ALBRIGHTSVILLE	89.1	88.1	5.1	5.6	0.7	0.8	8.0	8.8	7.0	7.4	7.8	6.7	4.7	24.7	27.9	13.1	0.7	73.1	40.2	50.4	49.7
18211	ANDREAS	98.8	98.6	0.2	0.2	0.3	0.3	0.9	1.0	5.2	5.7	6.1	6.0	5.1	25.1	31.5	13.6	1.6	79.4	43.2	50.4	49.6
18214	BARNESVILLE	99.6	99.5	0.1	0.1	0.1	0.1	0.5	0.6	4.4	4.9	6.0	6.3	6.4	24.2	32.1	14.2	1.7	81.0	43.6	50.2	49.8
18216	BEAVER MEADOWS	99.2	99.2	0.2	0.2	0.1	0.1	0.9	1.0	4.6	5.4	7.3	5.2	5.1	25.4	24.9	19.4	2.8	79.0	43.1	49.3	50.7
18218	COALDALE	98.3	98.2	0.3	0.3	0.3	0.3	1.1	1.2	4.5	4.3	5.5	6.1	5.7	25.0	23.1	20.3	5.4	82.2	44.2	47.4	52.6
18219	CONYNGHAM	97.5	96.8	0.1	0.1	2.2	2.7	0.7	1.0	4.8	5.3	5.9	8.9	5.2	21.6	29.8	15.9	2.6	79.3	43.9	47.2	52.8
18220	DELANO	99.3	99.3	0.0	0.0	0.7	0.7	0.0	0.0	4.1	3.7	4.8	4.4	7.4	23.6	30.6	18.8	2.6	86.0	46.0	54.2	45.8
18222	DRUMS	92.4	91.7	5.9	6.4	0.5	0.7	1.9	1.9	4.8	5.4	6.0	9.4	6.2	26.0	27.8	11.9	2.5	78.1	40.3	50.0	50.0
18224	FREELAND	98.7	98.4	0.2	0.2	0.6	0.7	0.6	0.8	5.2	5.2	6.1	6.2	5.2	25.0	25.5	18.6	3.1	79.8	43.1	47.8	52.2
18229	JIM THORPE	97.9	97.6	0.8	0.9	0.4	0.5	1.2	1.3	5.0	5.2	6.0	6.3	5.2	27.4	28.7	14.5	1.9	79.9	41.9	49.4	50.7
18232	LANSFORD	98.2	98.1	0.4	0.4	0.4	0.5	1.4	1.5	5.6	5.4	6.2	6.7	6.3	24.6	21.9	19.3	4.0	78.6	41.6	45.9	54.1
18235	LEHIGHTON	98.4	98.2	0.3	0.3	0.5	0.6	0.6	0.7	5.1	5.3	5.9	6.0	5.4	26.7	27.9	15.4	2.4	79.9	42.3	49.0	51.0
18237	MCADOO	99.4	99.3	0.1	0.1	0.1	0.2	0.4	0.5	4.9	5.0	5.9	5.1	4.7	26.2	25.1	19.7	3.2	80.9	43.7	48.1	52.0
18240	NESQUEHONING	97.0	96.7	1.3	1.4	0.4	0.6	1.6	1.7	4.3	4.5	5.8	5.4	6.5	27.4	25.0	18.2	2.9	82.7	42.5	49.3	50.7
18245	QUAKAKE	93.2	92.2	5.2	5.6	0.5	0.6	2.2	2.3	3.8	3.4	5.0	7.7	10.5	21.2	26.7	18.0	3.8	86.1	43.6	47.8	52.3
18246	ROCK GLEN	99.2	99.1	0.5	0.6	0.1	0.1	0.4	0.5	4.1	4.6	6.1	6.9	5.5	23.8	29.8	17.2	2.0	80.4	44.3	51.9	48.1
18248	SHEPPTON	99.2	99.0	0.0	0.0	0.1	0.1	0.9	1.0	3.5	4.2	5.7	5.8	4.2	26.0	30.9	16.7	3.1	83.1	45.4	49.9	50.1
18249	SUGARLOAF	98.3	97.9	0.2	0.2	1.0	1.3	0.6	0.8	4.3	5.1	6.6	9.8	5.3	23.1	30.9	13.3	1.6	79.7	42.4	50.5	49.5
18250	SUMMIT HILL	99.0	98.8	0.1	0.1	0.2	0.2	0.4	0.5	4.5	4.7	5.9	5.4	5.3	26.1	26.6	18.7	2.8	81.2	43.6	48.3	51.7
18252	TAMAQUA	98.7	98.4	0.3	0.3	0.3	0.4	1.1	1.2	4.9	4.9	5.9	6.3	5.8	25.4	25.5	18.0	3.3	80.3	42.8	48.2	51.8
18255	WEATHERLY	98.7	98.6	0.2	0.2	0.2	0.2	0.6	0.6	4.8	4.9	6.5	6.3	5.8	23.9	26.3	18.0	3.5	79.3	43.6	47.0	53.0
18301	EAST STROUDSBURG	85.7	84.1	7.3	8.0	1.4	1.8	7.8	8.6	6.1	6.3	7.5	9.1	8.7	26.1	24.7	10.2	1.2	75.5	36.1	49.1	50.9
18321	BARTONSVILLE	90.3	89.1	2.9	3.1	1.9	2.4	5.2	5.7	6.3	6.9	7.4	7.1	4.7	27.2	29.3	10.0	1.1	74.8	40.0	49.0	51.0
18322	BRODHEADSVILLE	94.7	94.0	2.5	2.8	1.0	1.3	3.1	3.4	6.1	6.7	7.7	6.8	5.7	25.7	28.1	11.9	1.4	75.3	40.1	49.0	51.0
18324	BUSHKILL	79.8	78.8	12.3	12.6	1.2	1.5	11.6	12.4	6.0	6.8	9.2	8.1	5.3	25.3	27.8	10.7	0.7	72.8	38.9	49.3	50.7
18325	CANADENSIS	96.4	96.1	1.2	1.2	0.4	0.5	1.8	1.9	4.7	5.2	7.1	6.4	4.9	24.2	29.8	16.0	1.7	79.2	43.5	50.0	50.0
18326	CRESCO	94.1	93.4	2.9	3.3	0.9	1.1	2.3	2.6	5.0	5.4	7.1	7.0	5.6	25.4	29.2	13.8	1.5	78.3	41.9	49.2	50.8
18327	DELAWARE WATER GAP	92.1	91.2	3.9	4.3	1.2	1.5	4.8	5.2	5.1	4.7	5.8	7.8	8.6	29.3	27.5	9.9	1.3	79.6	38.0	49.9	50.1
18328	DINGMANS FERRY	95.3	95.0	2.1	2.2	0.4	0.5	4.7	5.1	7.0	7.5	9.0	8.0	4.9	27.0	25.2	10.6	0.7	71.4	38.1	49.7	50.3
18330	EFFORT	91.6	90.7	4.5	4.9	1.0	1.2	5.7	6.2	6.8	7.5	9.2	7.5	5.3	26.9	25.4	10.1	1.3	71.5	38.1	50.4	49.6
18331	GILBERT	94.6	97.6	2.7	2.4	0.0	0.0	5.4	2.4	4.9	4.9	9.8	9.8	4.9	26.8	26.8	12.2	0.0	78.1	40.5	46.3	53.7
18332	HENRYVILLE	92.0	91.2	3.7	4.0	1.2	1.5	3.9	4.3	5.3	5.7	7.1	6.4	5.4	26.6	28.8	13.2	1.5	77.8	41.3	49.3	50.7
18333	KRESGEVILLE	97.7	97.5	1.0	1.0	0.2	0.3	2.1	2.3	6.7	6.8	6.7	7.5	4.8	25.7	26.1	14.0	1.7	75.3	40.3	48.8	51.2
18334	LONG POND	87.7	86.5	6.7	7.2	0.8	1.0	8.3	9.1	6.5	6.9	8.7	7.5	6.0	27.0	26.3	10.8	0.5	73.2	38.2	50.8	49.2
18336	MATAMORAS	96.5	96.1	0.5	0.5	1.0	1.3	2.9	3.2	5.5	5.9	7.3	6.7	5.7	22.8	27.7	15.9	2.7	76.8	42.6	47.1	52.9
18337	MILFORD	94.7	94.3	2.0	2.2	0.6	0.7	4.5	4.9	6.6	7.2	8.8	7.2	4.7	26.3	27.0	11.2	1.0	72.6	39.2	49.9	50.1
18340	MILLRIFT	96.2	95.8	0.4	0.4	1.3	1.5	2.5	2.7	5.3	6.1	6.8	5.3	4.6	21.6	32.2	15.5	2.7	78.0	45.2	48.9	51.1
18343	MOUNT BETHEL	97.9	97.4	0.7	0.7	0.5	0.7	1.7	2.0	5.1	5.7	7.0	6.1	4.8	26.0	29.2	14.4	1.8	78.4	42.6	50.2	49.8
18344	MOUNT POCONO	83.6	82.3	9.6	10.3	0.9	1.1	9.2	9.9	6.5	6.2	7.3	7.7	7.5	26.5	24.4	12.4	1.7	75.0	37.5	48.0	52.0
18346	POCONO SUMMIT	90.7	89.8	4.8	5.2	0.7	0.8	6.5	7.1	5.5	6.6	7.2	6.4	5.4	26.5	27.7	13.6	1.1	76.7	40.3	49.4	50.6
18347	POCONO LAKE	93.9	93.3	3.2	3.4	0.6	0.8	3.8	4.3	5.5	5.7	6.8	6.6	4.6	24.7	29.2	15.7	1.1	77.6	42.6	49.0	51.0
18350	POCONO PINES	93.7	93.0	3.3	3.6	0.8	1.0	4.2	4.6	5.2	5.9	6.9	5.9	4.5	25.0	29.4	16.1	1.2	78.3	43.0	49.1	50.9
18352	REEDERS	92.7	92.1	2.7	2.9	1.3	1.7	4.2	4.4	5.7	6.8	8.3	6.8	4.4	26.3	30.0	10.5	1.3	74.3	40.8	48.9	51.1
18353	SAYLORSBURG	95.3	94.7	2.2	2.3	0.7	0.9	2.9	3.2	6.2	7.0	8.4	7.4	5.2	26.6	28.7	9.8	0.8	73.5	39.5	50.4	49.6
18354	SCIOTA	95.2	94.8	2.3	2.5	0.7	1.0	2.1	2.3	5.8	6.6	7.5	5.0	4.1	27.5	30.0	12.2	1.2	76.6	41.3	50.3	49.7
18355	SCOTRUN	93.6	92.9	2.5	2.7	1.0	1.3	4.2	4.6	4.7	6.0	7.3	6.2	5.1	26.7	30.0	12.9	1.2	78.0	41.5	50.2	49.8
18360	STROUDSBURG	91.4	90.5	4.0	4.3	1.5	1.8	4.6	5.0	5.6	6.0	7.1	6.3	6.5	25.9	27.5	13.0	2.1	77.1	40.6	49.1	50.9
18370	SWIFTWATER	93.7	92.9	2.4	2.6	1.2	1.4	4.0	4.5	4.8	6.0	7.4	6.1	4.9	26.8	29.8	12.9	1.2	77.9	41.5	50.1	49.9
18371	TAMIMENT	85.4	84.3	8.0	8.5	0.5	0.6	12.2	13.0	6.9	7.5	10.5	8.4	5.8	27.3	24.4	8.6	0.5	69.7	35.8	50.3	49.7
18372	TANNERSVILLE	91.4	90.3	3.7	4.1	1.2	1.5	5.3	5.8	5.2	5.8	8.3	6.8	6.1	26.7	30.0	10.3	0.8	76.3	39.7	49.6	50.4
18403	ARCHBALD	98.6	98.4	0.3	0.4	0.2	0.3	0.4	0.5	6.0	6.3	6.8	6.1	4.9	26.7	26.6	14.7	2.0	77.2	40.8	48.2	51.8
18405	BEACH LAKE	98.0	97.7	0.8	0.8	0.3	0.3	1.8	1.9	5.6	6.0	7.4	6.9	5.9	23.9	27.7	14.7	2.0	76.7	41.5	51.0	49.0
18407	CARBONDALE	98.7	98.5	0.3	0.3	0.2	0.3	1.0	1.2	5.8	5.7	6.1	6.2	5.7	25.0	24.1	17.8	3.7	78.6	41.8	46.6	53.4
18411	CLARKS SUMMIT	97.4	96.8	0.4	0.5	1.5	2.0	0.8	0.9	5.3	6.0	7.2	7.0	5.9	23.4	29.6	13.6	2.0	77.2	42.0	48.6	51.5
18414	DALTON	98.2	97.9	0.4	0.4	0.7	0.8	0.6	0.7	5.1	5.9	7.6	6.4	5.2	24.7	30.6	13.0	1.6	77.3	42.1	50.3	49.7
18415	DAMASCUS	98.0	97.8	0.7	0.9	0.2	0.3	1.3	1.5	5.2	5.4	7.3	6.8	3.6	21.5	32.0	16.4	1.9	77.3	45.1	50.7	49.3
18417	EQUINUNK	99.0	98.9	0.2	0.2	0.0	0.0	0.2	0.2	5.9	6.1	6.8	6.5	6.8	23.5	27.2	16.0	1.3	77.4	41.8	51.6	48.4
18419	FACTORYVILLE	97.3	96.9	1.2	1.3	0.7	0.9	0.8	0.9	5.3	6.1	7.4	9.5	8.6	25.8	26.0	9.7	1.5	77.2	36.9	49.0	51.0
18421	FOREST CITY	99.2	99.0	0.2	0.2	0.2	0.3	0.5	0.5	5.7	5.9	6.5	6.1	4.9	24.5	24.5	17.5	4.4	78.0	42.7	48.5	51.5
18424	GOULDSBORO	96.8	96.3	1.2	1.4	0.6	0.8	2.3	2.6	6.2	6.5	6.5	6.5	4.9	25.9	28.4	14.0	1.2	76.4	41.0	50.4	49.6
18425	GREELEY	95.3	95.0	2.5	2.6	0.6	0.7	2.4	2.6	5.7	6.2	7.8	6.4	4.3	22.4	30.7	14.9	1.8	76.3	43.5	50.6	49.4
18426	GREENTOWN	97.1	96.8	0.6	0.6	0.4	0.5	2.5	2.7	5.2	5.6	6.4	5.5	3.7	21.9	29.4	20.7	1.7	79.5	46.1	51.6	48.4
18427	HAMLIN	96.4	95.9	1.0	1.1	0.2	0.3	1.8	2.0	6.6	6.6	6.9	5.8	4.9	22.4	28.4	16.4	1.9	76.2	42.9	50.0	50.1
18428	HAWLEY	97.8	97.5	0.5	0.6	0.4	0.5	2.2	2.5	5.7	5.9	7.4	6.8	5.7	21.0	28.0	16.6	2.8	76.8	43.2	46.4	53.6
18430	HERRICK CENTER	98.3	97.9	0.4	0.4	0.4	0.8	0.8	0.8	5.8	5.8	5.4	4.9	5.4	23.5	31.3	16.9	1.2	79.8	44.5	53.1	46.9
18431	HONESDALE	97.9	97.7	0.5	0.6	0.6	0.8	1.3	1.5	5.8	6.1	7.1	6.2	5.3	24.8	26.8	15.2	2.8	77.1	41.6	48.3	51.7
18433	JERMYN	98.6	98.4	0.7	0.8	0.3	0.3	0.5	0.5	5.6	5.8	6.4	6.3	5.0	26.5	26.1	15.9	2.4	78.1	41.6	49.1	50.9
18434	JESSUP	98.8	98.6	0.3	0.3	0.3	0.4	0.3	0.3	5.0	5.3	5.9	5.5	4.6	26.7	25.3	18.3	3.4	80.2	43.0	46.5	53.5
18435	LACKAWAXEN	94.7	94.3	2.6	2.7	0.4	0.5	2.9	3.1	4.8	5.4	7.2	5.7	4.1	20.2	30.3	20.5	1.9	79.0	46.7	50.1	49.9
18436	LAKE ARIEL	97.9	97.6	1.0	1.1	0.2	0.3	1.1	1.2	5.7	6.3	6.7	5.9	5.4	25.5	29.1	13.8	1.7	77.5	41.5	49.7	50.3
18437	LAKE COMO	98.9	98.9	0.0	0.0	0.6	0.8	1.4	1.4	4.1	4.4	4.7	5.0	5.0	21.4	34.3	19.5	1.7	83.5	48.5	50.3	49.7
18438	LAKEVILLE	97.1	96.5	1.2	1.4	0.6	0.7	2.7	3.2	4.3	4.8	7.0	6.9	4.3	22.1	29.6	19.6	1.5	78.6	45.4	49.3	50.7
18439	LAKEWOOD	99.1	98.9	0.0	0.0	0.4	0.5	1.4	1.7	5.1	5.3	5.3	4.6	4.6	23.1	33.0	17.4	1.5	80.9	46.2	50.4	49.6
18441	LENOXVILLE	98.8	98.8	0.3	0.4	0.0	0.0	0.7	0.8	6.0	6.5	7.6	7.2	5.8	27.9	27.0	11.0	1.1	75.5	38.7	51.5	48.5
18443	MILANVILLE	98.8	98.6	0.4	0.5	0.5	0.6	0.9	1.1	6.0	6.3	6.7	6.7	4.9	22.6	29.8	15.2	1.8	76.3	42.9	50.2	49.8
18444	MOSCOW	98.7	98.4	0.5	0.5	0.3	0.4	0.6	0.7	5.4	6.0	7.5	6.4	5.4	26.3	28.2	12.7	2.2	77.0	40.8	49.2	50.8
18445	NEWFOUNDLAND	96.6	96.0	1.5	1.8	0.2	0.2	1.4	1.6	5.6	6.0	7.7	6.3	4.1	22.3	30.1	15.6	2.3	76.5	43.6	48.9	51.1
18446	NICHOLSON	98.7	98.4	0.4	0.4	0.2	0.2	0.5	0.5	5.9	6.0	7.8	6.5	6.0	26.5	28.3	11.6	1.5	76.1	39.7	49.7	50.3
18447	OLYPHANT	98.7	98.4	0.4	0.5	0.4	0.4	0.6	0.6	5.0	5.3	5.8	5.6	5.3	27.1	26.3	16.7	2.9	80.5	42.4	47.6	52.4
18451	PAUPACK	97.9	97.6	0.6	0.8	0.4	0.6	2.3	2.4	3.0	4.5	6.9	6.9	4.3	23.9	29.2	20.2	1.1	79.6	45.3	50.7	49.4
18452	PECKVILLE	98.2	97.9	0.2	0.3	0.5	0.6	0.8	0.9	4.8	4.8	5.4	5.7	5.5	21.7	24.9	20.3	7.1	81.4	46.6	44.2	55.8
18453	PLEASANT MOUNT	99.1	99.1	0.2	0.2	0.2	0.3	1.5	1.6	5.5	6.0	6.1	5.8	4.5	24.3	32.4	14.0	1.5	78.4	43.6	51.0	49.0
18455	PRESTON PARK	99.0	98.3	0.0	0.0	0.3	0.3	0.7	1.0	5.4	6.0	5.7	5.0	5.0	23.8	31.2	16.4	1.3	79.2	44.3	50.0	50.0
18456	PROMPTON	95.3	95.0	2.6	2.8	0.4	0.4	1.1	1.3	5.2	5.6	6.0	5.2	4.2	24.6	27.7	17.0	4.7	79.8	44.6	51.2	48.8
18458	SHOHOLA	97.7	97.6	0.3	0.3	0.4	0.4	3.7	3.9	5.5	6.2	7.9	5.3	3.7	23.3	31.3	14.9	1.9	76.5	43.9	49.5	50.5
	PENNSYLVANIA	85.4	84.4	10.0	10.3	1.8	2.2	3.2	3.5	5.9	6.1	6.8	6.9	6.7	26.6	25.3	13.3	2.2	77.2	39.1	48.4	51.6
	UNITED STATES	75.1	73.6	12.3	12.5	3.8	4.2	12.5	14.1	6.9	6.7	7.2	7.0	7.3	28.6	23.8	10.8	1.7	75.1	36.0	49.1	50.9

ZIP CODE #	POST OFFICE NAME	2004 Per Capita Income	2004 HH Income Base	2004 HOUSEHOLD INCOME DISTRIBUTION (%) Less than $25,000	$25,000 to $49,999	$50,000 to $99,999	$100,000 to $149,999	$150,000 or More	MEDIAN HOUSEHOLD INCOME 2004	2009	2004 National Centile	2004 State Centile	2004 Home Value Base	2004 HOME VALUE DISTRIBUTION (%) Less than $50,000	$50,000 to $89,999	$90,000 to $174,999	$175,000 to $399,999	$400,000 or More	2004 Median Home Value
18091	WIND GAP	24895	2304	21.7	28.1	35.8	10.7	3.7	50163	61053	72	71	1696	4.1	6.6	52.9	34.7	1.7	158114
18092	ZIONSVILLE	38778	1037	10.0	17.7	37.6	18.9	15.7	75816	93672	94	95	929	2.2	2.3	28.6	52.1	14.9	210462
18101	ALLENTOWN	12269	1104	52.1	31.1	12.6	3.1	1.2	23803	27701	4	2	256	17.2	55.9	21.9	5.1	0.0	69318
18102	ALLENTOWN	15202	16787	42.5	30.9	21.5	4.2	0.9	30019	35418	12	6	6912	12.8	55.9	28.7	2.5	0.2	76203
18103	ALLENTOWN	26768	17848	22.2	30.0	31.5	10.5	5.9	47939	58904	68	68	12054	1.6	17.7	53.5	23.8	3.5	130130
18104	ALLENTOWN	32860	15682	17.4	23.3	34.3	16.0	9.1	61480	75156	86	88	11560	1.0	3.9	52.9	38.8	3.4	162500
18106	ALLENTOWN	35195	2647	9.6	19.3	34.6	23.7	12.8	76609	95384	94	95	2196	11.4	6.7	25.6	52.7	3.5	190814
18109	ALLENTOWN	19985	6947	29.6	34.4	28.8	5.7	1.6	38412	46606	41	38	3993	7.6	34.0	51.4	6.9	0.2	99956
18201	HAZLETON	21224	11363	38.9	30.8	23.3	3.9	3.3	33220	39623	22	14	7049	23.1	33.2	35.8	7.8	0.1	82302
18202	HAZLETON	21301	4742	35.3	28.5	27.8	5.3	3.1	36976	43998	35	30	3253	26.6	23.3	39.0	10.7	0.4	90142
18210	ALBRIGHTSVILLE	19128	1680	23.0	33.8	34.6	7.5	1.1	42069	49696	53	53	1393	1.4	9.6	63.0	25.3	0.7	133547
18211	ANDREAS	23493	475	24.0	24.4	38.1	9.1	4.4	50963	57178	74	74	404	3.5	11.9	46.0	34.7	4.0	152000
18214	BARNESVILLE	21986	1011	25.2	32.2	32.6	7.5	2.5	45353	52142	62	62	891	13.0	22.5	45.1	19.3	0.1	112164
18216	BEAVER MEADOWS	20488	942	31.7	33.6	27.5	5.0	2.2	38387	44760	41	37	744	20.6	34.3	41.5	3.6	0.0	82800
18218	COALDALE	15896	1085	48.0	34.0	15.4	1.9	0.7	26153	30408	6	3	771	39.6	40.3	19.5	0.7	0.0	56440
18219	CONYNGHAM	34374	649	15.3	26.4	35.6	12.5	10.3	58424	69316	83	84	548	1.5	8.9	61.0	25.6	3.1	143805
18220	DELANO	16902	106	35.9	29.3	29.3	5.7	0.0	37346	44086	37	32	91	51.7	30.8	16.5	1.1	0.0	49348
18222	DRUMS	26311	2564	17.9	27.7	36.8	12.5	5.1	54132	65848	79	79	2255	4.2	10.8	62.4	19.8	2.8	131354
18224	FREELAND	19223	2520	33.1	33.9	27.4	4.3	1.3	37007	43666	35	30	1895	24.2	36.8	31.8	7.0	0.2	75690
18229	JIM THORPE	20396	2909	27.8	34.1	28.2	8.3	1.6	41258	47822	51	50	2429	4.6	23.9	57.4	13.5	0.7	112862
18232	LANSFORD	16419	1870	44.1	28.9	23.9	3.0	0.2	30109	33595	13	6	1282	60.2	26.7	12.4	0.7	0.0	45148
18235	LEHIGHTON	20014	7763	29.1	30.5	33.0	5.9	1.6	39889	46352	46	44	5855	9.7	19.9	49.2	20.5	0.8	119070
18237	MCADOO	17908	1844	39.3	31.5	25.2	3.4	0.8	31221	36666	16	8	1325	18.2	35.9	40.5	5.2	0.2	85709
18240	NESQUEHONING	20110	1681	28.5	34.3	31.8	4.0	1.4	41858	48893	52	52	1332	19.9	31.7	37.8	10.3	0.3	87789
18245	QUAKAKE	19504	279	14.0	28.0	44.8	9.7	3.6	53561	62662	78	78	246	2.9	8.9	60.2	26.4	1.6	143103
18246	ROCK GLEN	22828	682	25.5	34.8	29.5	6.7	3.5	41058	48952	50	49	567	16.1	25.9	38.5	18.3	1.2	97000
18248	SHEPPTON	21864	570	33.0	33.2	27.7	3.3	2.8	36732	42752	34	29	455	22.4	26.2	34.1	15.8	1.5	92241
18249	SUGARLOAF	31081	1491	18.4	25.0	32.6	15.0	9.1	59602	73293	84	85	1311	5.9	9.5	55.2	25.5	4.0	139709
18250	SUMMIT HILL	26255	1257	25.7	32.2	31.6	8.0	2.6	43083	50766	56	57	1030	13.8	48.8	30.0	7.4	0.0	80441
18252	TAMAQUA	19595	4692	34.4	32.3	26.6	5.4	1.4	35321	41419	29	22	3236	20.6	31.1	36.4	11.2	0.8	87317
18255	WEATHERLY	19305	1617	27.6	34.0	30.9	5.1	2.5	42005	48671	53	53	1360	14.3	27.0	48.8	9.3	0.6	99008
18301	EAST STROUDSBURG	24440	14777	19.2	23.8	38.7	13.7	4.6	56718	67595	81	82	11184	4.0	4.0	41.7	47.6	2.7	175578
18321	BARTONSVILLE	28958	565	15.2	29.2	34.9	14.3	6.4	55617	65712	80	81	488	10.7	2.3	29.9	53.7	3.5	190909
18322	BRODHEADSVILLE	25234	712	23.0	19.5	37.8	13.5	6.2	56868	67542	82	82	589	0.2	3.6	36.0	57.2	3.1	191440
18324	BUSHKILL	24622	2706	14.8	26.1	39.6	13.1	6.4	58911	71164	83	84	2300	0.6	4.8	50.2	41.4	3.0	166794
18325	CANADENSIS	23468	1127	27.0	28.3	30.9	10.7	3.2	46077	53695	64	64	871	8.3	4.6	38.2	42.0	6.9	172552
18326	CRESCO	27854	1789	19.6	25.8	37.0	12.4	5.3	54245	64681	79	79	1407	0.7	5.1	48.3	41.2	4.7	167394
18327	DELAWARE WATER GAP	28907	538	25.7	27.7	31.4	10.2	5.0	46666	56266	65	66	270	1.9	1.1	39.3	54.8	3.0	184906
18328	DINGMANS FERRY	23119	2871	19.2	26.5	41.1	10.0	3.2	53069	62469	77	77	2454	0.5	3.3	56.5	37.5	2.2	157507
18330	EFFORT	22896	3266	15.8	26.2	39.7	14.0	4.3	56622	66420	81	82	2865	1.2	6.5	42.1	48.8	1.5	157431
18331	GILBERT	14878	13	23.1	38.5	30.8	7.7	0.0	42330	50000	54	54	11	0.0	0.0	63.6	36.4	0.0	165625
18332	HENRYVILLE	25150	1146	21.0	23.8	38.2	12.7	4.2	54747	65191	79	79	911	1.5	3.8	41.4	47.4	5.8	181303
18333	KRESGEVILLE	27107	461	16.5	28.9	43.2	7.4	4.1	53081	62227	77	77	391	0.3	4.1	50.1	38.4	7.2	168371
18334	LONG POND	23160	763	17.7	29.9	34.3	13.6	4.5	52538	63316	76	76	651	4.8	7.5	47.9	39.5	0.3	158540
18336	MATAMORAS	23494	1766	24.1	30.4	34.2	8.7	2.7	45961	54769	64	64	1352	7.0	3.0	42.4	44.0	3.7	171509
18337	MILFORD	25651	5055	15.3	25.2	39.6	14.8	5.1	58451	68097	83	84	4280	1.3	0.5	27.8	63.4	7.0	215608
18340	MILLRIFT	23703	99	19.2	31.3	37.4	8.1	4.0	49539	58062	71	71	82	13.4	3.7	26.8	50.0	6.1	188889
18343	MOUNT BETHEL	24595	1674	21.0	25.8	37.4	11.8	4.1	52842	63604	77	76	1364	3.2	12.8	36.2	42.8	5.1	170199
18344	MOUNT POCONO	22944	1395	23.3	28.3	35.1	10.4	2.9	48367	59333	69	69	926	1.6	3.5	48.6	43.6	2.7	169516
18346	POCONO SUMMIT	20569	717	28.7	24.1	31.9	12.7	2.5	47841	57749	68	68	603	0.5	3.7	56.2	38.3	1.3	157244
18347	POCONO LAKE	26789	1195	25.5	24.2	35.5	10.7	4.1	50321	61611	73	72	980	0.5	5.5	55.5	34.7	3.8	155651
18350	POCONO PINES	25358	477	30.2	22.4	37.1	8.0	2.3	47462	57166	67	67	392	0.3	5.6	52.0	37.0	5.1	159500
18352	REEDERS	30810	232	15.1	24.6	40.5	14.7	5.2	60313	70753	85	86	202	3.5	2.5	31.7	58.9	3.5	195161
18353	SAYLORSBURG	24547	4027	17.7	25.2	38.3	13.8	5.0	56709	66560	81	82	3505	3.2	4.1	37.6	52.8	2.3	182584
18354	SCIOTA	24947	188	17.6	33.5	33.5	10.1	5.3	48660	57776	70	69	150	8.7	8.7	36.7	41.3	4.7	166176
18355	SCOTRUN	22787	733	23.7	28.7	30.4	13.2	4.0	47303	56616	67	67	611	7.5	7.9	34.2	47.3	3.1	175631
18360	STROUDSBURG	26609	11411	21.7	25.7	33.0	13.6	6.0	52923	63638	77	77	8579	4.8	3.7	37.6	48.9	5.1	181980
18370	SWIFTWATER	22958	285	23.9	28.1	31.2	13.0	3.9	47914	57251	68	68	237	6.3	7.2	35.4	47.7	3.4	176736
18371	TAMIMENT	23744	719	17.8	23.4	43.1	10.3	5.4	58473	70984	83	84	599	0.5	3.5	54.3	38.9	2.8	162985
18372	TANNERSVILLE	25342	1118	18.3	26.7	35.3	15.7	4.0	54095	63716	78	79	945	2.1	2.8	35.1	54.5	5.5	191996
18403	ARCHBALD	24275	2643	25.2	25.1	34.4	9.5	5.8	49559	61832	71	71	2199	3.8	20.0	50.4	25.0	0.9	118522
18405	BEACH LAKE	19662	478	29.9	30.3	31.2	5.2	3.4	41978	48652	53	53	412	7.0	6.6	45.2	35.9	5.3	154070
18407	CARBONDALE	19393	6041	35.5	32.1	25.2	5.1	2.1	35035	41790	28	21	4227	12.2	37.1	40.3	9.8	0.6	90624
18411	CLARKS SUMMIT	34219	9182	16.8	22.9	34.2	15.2	10.9	62249	76342	86	88	7576	2.8	5.8	45.7	39.4	6.3	167421
18414	DALTON	28620	2338	20.9	27.9	33.5	10.1	7.6	51004	61522	74	74	2003	7.7	11.7	47.0	28.1	5.4	140718
18415	DAMASCUS	23722	647	30.8	30.3	28.6	6.2	4.2	39225	45700	44	41	543	7.9	8.7	40.3	38.9	4.2	159631
18417	EQUINUNK	19010	376	29.5	37.2	27.7	4.3	1.3	40122	45501	46	45	316	13.3	13.9	42.7	26.6	3.5	117434
18419	FACTORYVILLE	22525	1591	24.2	26.8	35.3	8.2	5.5	49008	58890	70	70	1309	12.4	10.8	50.0	25.1	1.8	124864
18421	FOREST CITY	19640	2109	34.6	31.0	26.3	5.6	2.5	35558	42356	30	23	1671	8.4	28.7	39.7	21.1	2.1	111504
18424	GOULDSBORO	23804	1834	23.3	32.0	32.9	7.9	3.8	45701	53636	63	63	1559	10.4	14.4	48.0	24.6	2.5	125915
18425	GREELEY	19747	550	29.6	33.6	30.0	5.6	1.1	38706	45197	42	39	458	2.4	5.2	38.7	49.8	3.9	184444
18426	GREENTOWN	23766	1593	27.4	33.3	29.4	6.2	3.8	41745	48981	52	52	1333	7.5	8.8	37.1	40.7	5.9	166697
18427	HAMLIN	20506	863	30.9	32.7	27.4	6.1	2.9	38140	44663	40	36	720	6.8	6.4	49.6	33.5	3.8	150269
18428	HAWLEY	21662	1379	38.4	28.5	24.4	5.8	2.9	34408	40775	25	18	958	3.4	10.3	50.6	32.2	3.4	143322
18430	HERRICK CENTER	18948	107	36.5	29.9	27.1	4.7	1.9	34641	38198	26	19	91	14.3	13.2	36.3	31.9	4.4	143750
18431	HONESDALE	20386	5975	33.3	32.4	25.8	5.3	3.2	37055	43600	36	30	4449	8.3	9.3	48.0	31.6	2.9	140949
18433	JERMYN	22505	2514	29.9	31.4	28.3	7.0	3.4	39969	47875	46	44	2017	6.8	23.0	54.1	15.0	1.1	109646
18434	JESSUP	20902	1870	37.8	27.4	25.5	7.2	2.1	36755	45227	35	29	1477	4.9	24.7	58.5	11.9	0.0	106332
18435	LACKAWAXEN	24273	1401	25.9	27.8	34.3	9.3	2.8	46223	53640	64	65	1194	1.3	4.4	45.1	38.2	10.9	173154
18436	LAKE ARIEL	21466	3727	25.0	32.6	30.8	8.1	3.6	44364	51562	60	60	3237	7.2	10.5	47.5	32.0	2.9	143043
18437	LAKE COMO	26635	162	33.3	29.6	29.0	3.7	4.3	37988	44389	39	35	136	7.4	17.7	42.7	27.9	4.4	131667
18438	LAKEVILLE	21444	898	27.1	33.5	28.2	9.0	2.2	41920	48644	53	53	772	1.2	6.1	48.6	39.3	4.9	164078
18439	LAKEWOOD	23318	327	30.9	30.9	28.8	5.2	4.3	39510	45357	44	42	275	7.3	14.6	44.0	28.7	5.5	132661
18441	LENOXVILLE	21230	279	28.3	32.3	29.0	6.8	3.6	40757	47732	49	48	226	15.9	8.4	41.2	31.4	3.1	133333
18443	MILANVILLE	22435	456	29.6	33.3	27.9	4.4	4.8	39805	46489	45	43	403	7.0	4.2	47.4	36.7	4.7	151689
18444	MOSCOW	24503	4400	19.2	28.7	36.7	11.3	4.2	51866	62222	75	75	3795	9.9	8.5	49.9	29.0	2.7	144170
18445	NEWFOUNDLAND	20349	536	30.4	32.5	27.1	7.1	3.0	39360	45714	44	42	449	3.8	9.4	48.6	36.1	2.2	152371
18446	NICHOLSON	20858	1463	28.4	32.7	29.4	6.1	3.4	40249	47636	47	46	1219	14.1	14.3	46.5	22.6	2.5	118724
18447	OLYPHANT	22236	3791	32.0	27.7	29.9	8.1	2.3	40692	50126	49	47	2770	6.3	19.7	57.9	15.3	0.8	113289
18451	PAUPACK	26991	227	21.6	24.7	39.7	8.8	5.3	52702	61242	76	76	192	0.0	2.1	35.4	54.2	8.3	209211
18452	PECKVILLE	23204	2205	31.2	25.2	32.3	7.8	3.6	44431	53416	60	60	1606	0.9	16.8	64.9	16.4	0.9	117949
18453	PLEASANT MOUNT	22924	541	24.8	29.2	35.5	7.6	3.0	45298	52080	62	62	458	7.6	8.1	45.9	33.0	5.5	147768
18455	PRESTON PARK	23143	126	31.0	34.1	25.4	5.6	4.0	38626	45498	42	38	106	11.3	20.8	44.3	20.8	2.8	116667
18456	PROMPTON	21402	309	33.7	34.3	24.3	5.5	2.3	38281	43961	40	37	253	9.1	8.7	48.6	29.6	4.0	146284
18458	SHOHOLA	25463	1135	21.7	30.0	37.4	8.4	2.5	48739	56731	70	69	969	2.8	4.9	35.5	44.7	12.2	193680
	PENNSYLVANIA	25764		25.8	27.2	31.2	10.2	5.7	46988	57000				11.9	18.4	40.7	25.1	4.1	123516
	UNITED STATES	25866		24.7	27.1	30.8	10.9	6.5	48124	56710				10.9	15.0	33.7	30.1	10.4	145905

ZIP CODE #	POST OFFICE NAME	FINANCIAL SERVICES: Auto Loan	FINANCIAL SERVICES: Home Loan	FINANCIAL SERVICES: Invest-ments	FINANCIAL SERVICES: Retire-ment Plans	THE HOME: Home Improvements: Home Repair	THE HOME: Home Improvements: Lawn & Garden	THE HOME: Furnishings: Comput-ers & Hard-ware	THE HOME: Furnishings: Major Appli-ances	THE HOME: Furnishings: TV, Radio, Sound Equip-ment	THE HOME: Furnishings: Furni-ture	ENTERTAINMENT: Dine out/ Carry out	ENTERTAINMENT: Sports Equip-ment	ENTERTAINMENT: Fees & Tickets	ENTERTAINMENT: Toys & Games	ENTERTAINMENT: Travel	ENTERTAINMENT: Cable TV	PERSONAL: Apparel & Services	PERSONAL: Auto Repairs	PERSONAL: Health Insur-ance	PERSONAL: Pets & Supplies
18091	WIND GAP	95	85	71	83	89	97	85	90	88	83	108	105	82	108	85	90	102	89	96	109
18092	ZIONSVILLE	147	165	163	163	166	167	149	153	143	149	178	180	155	188	153	141	176	148	145	177
18101	ALLENTOWN	45	40	53	39	39	45	48	45	51	47	63	52	46	63	46	51	62	48	46	49
18102	ALLENTOWN	50	47	65	46	46	52	55	52	58	54	73	60	53	73	53	59	71	55	53	57
18103	ALLENTOWN	87	92	102	92	92	98	93	91	92	92	115	106	95	117	93	91	113	92	89	101
18104	ALLENTOWN	105	117	136	117	116	124	115	113	113	114	141	130	120	143	117	112	139	113	111	124
18106	ALLENTOWN	129	140	140	140	141	144	129	132	125	129	155	155	134	160	131	123	153	128	126	153
18109	ALLENTOWN	64	64	74	63	64	70	67	66	69	66	86	76	68	88	68	70	84	67	67	73
18201	HAZLETON	62	64	68	61	64	72	65	64	68	63	84	73	67	88	66	70	81	64	69	72
18202	HAZLETON	70	66	59	63	69	77	66	69	70	64	85	78	65	87	67	73	81	68	76	81
18210	ALBRIGHTSVILLE	88	69	47	62	78	87	65	79	74	65	87	92	58	86	69	79	81	77	93	107
18211	ANDREAS	96	85	65	81	89	96	79	87	84	79	102	104	78	104	81	86	97	85	95	112
18214	BARNESVILLE	80	77	68	73	80	87	74	78	77	72	95	90	75	99	76	80	91	76	84	94
18216	BEAVER MEADOWS	61	67	70	63	67	75	66	65	68	63	84	72	70	92	68	71	82	64	70	72
18218	COALDALE	54	41	27	39	45	53	45	50	51	43	59	56	40	56	45	53	54	50	59	60
18219	CONYNGHAM	105	122	135	116	121	132	115	115	115	114	143	129	122	149	120	118	140	113	117	126
18220	DELANO	56	60	64	57	61	68	60	59	62	57	77	66	63	83	62	64	74	58	63	65
18222	DRUMS	100	104	97	102	105	109	96	100	95	96	118	116	98	121	98	95	115	97	99	118
18224	FREELAND	60	60	58	57	62	69	60	61	63	58	77	69	61	82	62	65	74	60	67	70
18229	JIM THORPE	73	68	61	64	72	80	66	71	70	64	86	81	66	89	69	73	82	69	79	86
18232	LANSFORD	47	51	53	48	51	57	50	49	52	48	64	55	53	69	52	54	62	48	53	55
18235	LEHIGHTON	70	68	62	64	70	77	66	69	69	64	85	79	67	89	68	71	81	67	75	82
18237	MCADOO	50	55	58	52	55	62	54	54	56	52	70	60	57	75	56	58	67	53	58	59
18240	NESQUEHONING	59	65	70	62	65	72	63	63	65	62	81	70	67	86	66	67	78	62	67	69
18245	QUAKAKE	77	90	100	85	89	97	85	85	85	84	105	95	90	110	89	87	104	83	87	93
18246	ROCK GLEN	79	78	74	73	81	90	77	80	81	74	100	91	78	106	80	85	95	78	88	94
18248	SHEPPTON	62	67	71	63	68	75	66	66	69	64	85	73	70	92	69	71	82	64	71	72
18249	SUGARLOAF	113	116	107	112	118	124	107	113	108	106	132	132	108	137	110	109	128	110	115	135
18250	SUMMIT HILL	76	82	87	78	83	92	81	80	84	78	105	90	86	113	84	88	101	79	87	89
18252	TAMAQUA	61	62	62	59	63	70	62	62	64	60	79	70	63	83	63	66	76	61	67	71
18255	WEATHERLY	73	67	58	64	70	79	68	71	72	65	88	80	67	90	69	76	83	70	80	83
18301	EAST STROUDSBURG	98	99	96	98	100	105	96	98	95	95	118	115	96	120	97	95	115	98	97	114
18321	BARTONSVILLE	126	120	100	115	125	131	110	119	114	110	139	142	110	143	113	115	134	116	125	149
18322	BRODHEADSVILLE	111	97	73	92	103	111	91	101	97	91	118	120	89	120	94	100	112	99	110	130
18324	BUSHKILL	109	99	83	95	104	111	94	104	98	94	119	122	89	118	96	99	114	103	109	129
18325	CANADENSIS	100	75	46	69	85	96	72	88	82	71	97	104	63	95	76	87	89	86	104	121
18326	CRESCO	106	100	85	96	104	110	93	101	95	93	117	119	91	119	95	97	112	99	105	126
18327	DELAWARE WATER GAP	88	88	94	88	91	96	86	89	86	86	107	106	85	108	88	86	104	89	89	106
18328	DINGMANS FERRY	94	94	85	93	94	97	88	92	87	89	108	109	88	109	88	85	105	91	89	108
18330	EFFORT	100	101	92	101	100	103	96	98	94	97	117	116	95	117	95	91	113	97	94	114
18331	GILBERT	75	67	51	64	71	76	62	69	66	62	80	82	61	82	64	67	76	67	74	89
18332	HENRYVILLE	102	93	76	91	98	103	87	96	90	87	110	114	85	112	89	91	105	94	101	121
18333	KRESGEVILLE	117	104	78	98	110	118	96	107	102	96	124	127	94	127	99	105	118	104	116	138
18334	LONG POND	108	91	67	85	99	108	85	97	93	85	112	115	81	112	89	97	105	95	109	129
18336	MATAMORAS	87	80	70	76	85	94	78	85	83	76	101	98	76	103	81	86	96	83	93	103
18337	MILFORD	114	97	73	91	105	115	92	105	99	91	119	123	86	119	96	104	112	103	118	136
18340	MILLRIFT	113	79	41	75	92	103	78	96	90	77	105	116	67	103	81	94	96	95	115	134
18343	MOUNT BETHEL	93	88	75	84	92	99	82	89	86	82	105	104	82	108	85	88	101	86	94	110
18344	MOUNT POCONO	96	80	60	79	85	96	82	89	87	80	105	102	77	104	81	89	99	87	97	107
18346	POCONO SUMMIT	97	76	52	69	86	96	72	86	81	71	96	101	64	95	77	87	90	85	102	118
18347	POCONO LAKE	110	83	53	76	95	106	80	97	91	79	107	114	70	106	84	96	99	95	115	133
18350	POCONO PINES	98	77	53	70	87	98	73	88	82	72	98	103	65	96	78	88	91	86	104	120
18352	REEDERS	100	112	110	111	112	114	101	104	97	101	121	122	105	128	103	96	119	100	99	120
18353	SAYLORSBURG	101	105	96	103	107	110	96	101	95	96	117	119	98	122	98	95	114	98	100	121
18354	SCIOTA	95	96	84	93	98	102	87	93	88	87	108	110	88	112	90	88	105	90	94	114
18355	SCOTRUN	96	82	60	76	88	96	76	87	83	76	100	103	72	100	79	86	94	85	97	115
18360	STROUDSBURG	96	99	99	98	100	106	96	98	96	95	118	114	97	121	97	96	115	97	97	113
18370	SWIFTWATER	96	82	61	77	89	96	77	87	83	76	100	103	74	101	80	86	94	85	96	114
18371	TAMIMENT	108	97	80	92	102	109	92	102	96	92	116	120	87	116	94	97	111	101	108	128
18372	TANNERSVILLE	99	101	92	98	104	108	92	99	93	92	114	116	92	118	95	93	110	96	100	120
18403	ARCHBALD	81	87	89	83	88	97	85	86	86	83	107	96	88	112	87	89	103	84	90	96
18405	BEACH LAKE	89	65	39	61	75	84	63	78	73	63	85	92	55	84	67	77	79	76	92	107
18407	CARBONDALE	63	61	60	58	63	70	62	63	65	60	80	71	63	83	63	68	76	62	69	72
18411	CLARKS SUMMIT	119	134	142	132	134	141	124	127	121	124	152	146	130	156	129	122	149	124	124	143
18414	DALTON	114	103	86	99	110	118	98	108	102	97	124	127	95	126	101	105	118	106	116	135
18415	DAMASCUS	98	76	52	69	86	97	72	87	82	71	97	102	64	95	77	87	90	86	103	119
18417	EQUINUNK	81	63	43	57	71	80	60	72	68	59	80	84	53	79	64	72	74	71	85	98
18419	FACTORYVILLE	93	85	73	82	89	96	81	88	84	80	103	104	79	104	83	86	98	86	93	109
18421	FOREST CITY	75	61	44	58	67	76	62	69	68	60	81	80	58	81	63	71	76	68	80	87
18424	GOULDSBORO	99	82	59	75	90	100	77	90	85	76	101	105	71	101	81	90	95	88	103	120
18425	GREELEY	84	66	45	59	74	83	62	75	70	62	83	88	56	82	66	75	77	74	89	102
18426	GREENTOWN	94	74	51	67	83	94	70	84	79	69	94	99	62	92	74	84	87	83	100	115
18427	HAMLIN	86	69	47	62	76	85	65	77	72	64	86	90	58	85	69	77	80	76	90	104
18428	HAWLEY	86	63	39	60	71	82	65	76	74	63	87	89	57	84	66	78	80	75	91	100
18430	HERRICK CENTER	73	57	39	52	64	72	54	65	61	53	72	76	48	71	58	65	67	64	77	89
18431	HONESDALE	76	63	51	60	68	78	65	71	71	63	85	82	61	84	66	74	79	71	82	89
18433	JERMYN	78	75	68	71	78	86	73	77	77	71	95	87	74	99	75	80	90	75	84	91
18434	JESSUP	65	67	69	65	68	74	66	67	67	64	83	76	67	86	67	68	80	66	69	76
18435	LACKAWAXEN	97	76	52	69	86	96	72	87	81	71	96	101	64	95	77	87	90	85	102	118
18436	LAKE ARIEL	91	79	60	74	84	91	74	83	79	74	95	98	70	95	76	81	90	82	91	107
18437	LAKE COMO	101	79	54	72	89	100	75	90	85	74	100	105	67	99	80	90	93	89	106	123
18438	LAKEVILLE	89	70	48	63	79	88	66	79	75	65	88	93	59	87	70	80	82	78	94	108
18439	LAKEWOOD	95	74	51	67	84	94	70	85	79	70	94	99	63	93	75	85	88	83	100	116
18441	LENOXVILLE	90	80	61	76	84	91	74	82	78	74	95	98	72	97	76	80	91	80	89	106
18443	MILANVILLE	93	71	45	65	80	90	68	82	77	67	91	97	60	90	71	82	84	81	97	113
18444	MOSCOW	94	96	88	93	98	103	88	93	89	88	110	109	90	113	91	90	107	91	94	112
18445	NEWFOUNDLAND	85	68	47	62	76	85	64	76	72	63	85	89	58	84	68	76	79	75	89	103
18446	NICHOLSON	83	74	59	69	79	86	70	77	75	69	91	91	68	93	72	78	86	76	86	99
18447	OLYPHANT	65	70	78	67	70	78	70	69	72	68	89	78	73	94	72	74	87	69	73	76
18451	PAUPACK	108	85	58	76	95	107	80	96	90	79	107	113	71	106	85	96	99	95	114	131
18452	PECKVILLE	76	76	74	73	78	88	76	78	79	74	96	88	76	97	78	82	92	77	85	89
18453	PLEASANT MOUNT	98	71	41	66	82	92	69	84	79	68	93	101	60	91	72	83	85	83	100	117
18455	PRESTON PARK	93	73	50	66	82	92	69	83	78	68	92	97	61	91	73	83	86	81	98	113
18456	PROMPTON	70	54	37	50	61	70	54	63	61	53	73	73	49	70	56	65	67	63	75	83
18458	SHOHOLA	104	84	60	77	93	104	79	94	88	78	105	110	72	104	84	93	98	92	109	126
	PENNSYLVANIA	89	89	93	87	90	98	89	90	91	88	112	104	89	114	90	92	109	90	92	104
	UNITED STATES	100	100	100	100	100	100	100	100	100	100	100	100	100	100	100	100	100	100	100	100

A 18460-18915

#	POST OFFICE NAME	COUNTY FIPS CODE	POPULATION			2000-2004 ANNUAL RATE		HOUSEHOLDS					FAMILIES		
			2000	2004	2009	% Rate	State Centile	2000	2004	2009	% Annual Rate 2000-2004	2004 Average HH Size	2000	2004	% Annual Rate 2000-2004
18460	SOUTH STERLING	127	367	404	440	2.3	95	155	173	193	2.6	2.27	107	118	2.3
18461	STARLIGHT	127	327	334	350	0.5	64	150	158	170	1.2	2.09	102	107	1.1
18462	STARRUCCA	127	372	379	397	0.4	61	157	165	177	1.2	2.30	116	121	1.0
18463	STERLING	127	832	883	944	1.4	87	318	346	379	2.0	2.55	251	273	2.0
18464	TAFTON	103	4875	5562	6763	3.2	98	1907	2225	2756	3.7	2.41	1445	1675	3.5
18465	THOMPSON	115	1518	1541	1555	0.4	57	583	606	625	0.9	2.52	421	434	0.7
18466	TOBYHANNA	089	15159	17507	20671	3.5	99	5077	5858	6928	3.4	2.99	4033	4622	3.3
18469	TYLER HILL	127	614	634	669	0.8	73	234	249	269	1.5	2.53	167	177	1.4
18470	UNION DALE	115	1557	1576	1586	0.3	53	607	630	648	0.9	2.50	428	441	0.7
18472	WAYMART	127	4949	5268	5624	1.5	88	1414	1573	1749	2.5	2.55	1033	1142	2.4
18503	SCRANTON	069	814	812	808	-0.1	36	483	488	493	0.2	1.66	79	58	-7.0
18504	SCRANTON	069	22119	21607	21258	-0.6	14	9433	9404	9424	-0.1	2.29	5795	5719	-0.3
18505	SCRANTON	069	20271	20013	19786	-0.3	25	8831	8905	8970	0.2	2.18	5199	5186	-0.1
18507	MOOSIC	069	5349	5358	5331	0.0	41	1993	2037	2062	0.5	2.42	1407	1426	0.3
18508	SCRANTON	069	11530	11296	11120	-0.5	17	4864	4868	4885	0.0	2.31	3055	3022	-0.3
18509	SCRANTON	069	14176	13783	13537	-0.7	11	5571	5518	5514	-0.2	2.19	3083	3015	-0.5
18510	SCRANTON	069	13981	13807	13660	-0.3	25	4915	4907	4918	0.0	2.37	2548	2516	-0.3
18512	SCRANTON	069	12651	12389	12195	-0.5	16	5563	5582	5610	0.1	2.21	3542	3517	-0.2
18517	TAYLOR	069	5323	5232	5158	-0.4	21	2140	2155	2168	0.2	2.35	1459	1455	-0.1
18518	OLD FORGE	069	8803	8646	8516	-0.4	20	3747	3759	3775	0.1	2.27	2457	2440	-0.2
18519	DICKSON CITY	069	4964	4869	4794	-0.5	18	2174	2169	2173	-0.1	2.24	1363	1347	-0.3
18603	BERWICK	037	19756	20379	20963	0.7	72	8171	8621	9052	1.3	2.32	5403	5649	1.1
18610	BLAKESLEE	089	3330	4216	5219	5.7	100	1090	1389	1729	5.9	3.03	874	1106	5.7
18612	DALLAS	079	12246	12534	12657	0.6	66	4530	4749	4903	1.1	2.44	3201	3331	0.9
18614	DUSHORE	113	1868	1839	1815	-0.4	22	824	830	839	0.2	2.20	487	487	0.0
18615	FALLS	131	2343	2437	2528	0.9	77	872	930	989	1.5	2.52	637	675	1.4
18616	FORKSVILLE	113	1161	1140	1125	-0.4	19	452	457	464	0.3	2.36	327	329	0.1
18617	GLEN LYON	079	2717	2648	2609	-0.6	12	830	817	816	-0.4	2.23	496	484	-0.6
18618	HARVEYS LAKE	079	3482	3412	3364	-0.5	17	1418	1418	1426	0.0	2.40	963	956	-0.2
18619	HILLSGROVE	113	265	261	257	-0.4	22	113	114	116	0.2	2.23	76	76	0.0
18621	HUNLOCK CREEK	079	3977	3888	3829	-0.5	14	1466	1464	1471	0.0	2.66	1136	1129	-0.2
18622	HUNTINGTON MILLS	079	130	142	148	2.1	93	50	57	61	3.1	2.42	39	43	2.3
18623	LACEYVILLE	015	3407	3453	3512	0.3	55	1295	1344	1398	0.9	2.56	953	982	0.7
18624	LAKE HARMONY	025	1066	1076	1083	0.2	50	450	463	473	0.7	2.30	312	317	0.4
18628	LOPEZ	113	640	652	655	0.4	61	176	184	190	1.1	2.57	112	116	0.8
18629	MEHOOPANY	131	1735	1824	1903	1.2	83	680	731	780	1.7	2.49	481	514	1.6
18630	MESHOPPEN	115	3111	3172	3235	0.5	62	1168	1217	1268	1.0	2.60	862	893	0.8
18631	MIFFLINVILLE	037	1353	1310	1307	-0.8	8	564	560	571	-0.2	2.34	421	416	-0.3
18632	MILDRED	113	564	560	555	-0.2	31	243	247	251	0.4	2.26	170	171	0.1
18634	NANTICOKE	079	13898	13763	13653	-0.2	28	6080	6144	6216	0.3	2.18	3717	3719	0.0
18635	NESCOPECK	079	3443	3382	3347	-0.4	20	1392	1398	1411	0.1	2.42	986	986	0.0
18636	NOXEN	131	1734	1771	1820	0.5	64	665	696	732	1.1	2.53	454	473	1.0
18640	PITTSTON	079	17465	17081	16840	-0.5	15	7168	7158	7199	0.0	2.33	4765	4727	-0.2
18641	PITTSTON	079	6374	6256	6184	-0.4	19	2732	2757	2791	0.2	2.26	1812	1814	0.0
18642	DURYEA	079	4151	4120	4088	-0.2	30	1787	1812	1835	0.3	2.26	1159	1165	0.1
18643	PITTSTON	079	13736	13648	13540	-0.2	32	5723	5820	5899	0.4	2.32	3810	3842	0.2
18644	WYOMING	079	7756	7635	7550	-0.4	22	3316	3321	3345	0.0	2.28	2191	2184	-0.1
18651	PLYMOUTH	079	10110	9873	9721	-0.6	13	4206	4179	4193	-0.2	2.35	2692	2655	-0.3
18655	SHICKSHINNY	079	5975	6342	6514	1.4	87	2356	2565	2693	2.0	2.43	1677	1810	1.8
18656	SWEET VALLEY	079	3391	3522	3573	0.9	77	1267	1350	1402	1.5	2.58	939	994	1.4
18657	TUNKHANNOCK	131	12564	12864	13248	0.6	67	4925	5177	5465	1.2	2.43	3494	3649	1.0
18660	WAPWALLOPEN	079	1867	1825	1797	-0.6	14	687	685	688	-0.1	2.64	527	523	-0.2
18661	WHITE HAVEN	079	5131	5061	5012	-0.3	24	1985	1992	2007	0.1	2.38	1396	1391	-0.1
18701	WILKES BARRE	079	3955	4048	4096	0.6	66	1403	1474	1523	1.2	1.61	255	271	1.4
18702	WILKES BARRE	079	42840	42908	42864	0.0	41	17747	18193	18566	0.6	2.20	10437	10589	0.3
18704	KINGSTON	079	32774	32054	31608	-0.5	15	14302	14295	14386	0.0	2.18	8593	8508	-0.2
18705	WILKES BARRE	079	14623	14337	14145	-0.5	18	6336	6364	6416	0.1	2.25	4055	4038	-0.1
18706	WILKES BARRE	079	17034	16791	16635	-0.3	23	7307	7359	7438	0.2	2.26	4669	4657	-0.1
18707	MOUNTAIN TOP	079	15972	16303	16381	0.5	62	5830	6072	6222	1.0	2.65	4602	4767	0.8
18708	SHAVERTOWN	079	11951	12084	12109	0.3	52	3875	4012	4105	0.8	2.54	2957	3040	0.7
18709	LUZERNE	079	2949	2854	2799	-0.8	8	1409	1394	1397	-0.3	2.05	766	749	-0.5
18801	MONTROSE	115	6706	6756	6814	0.2	47	2695	2784	2875	0.8	2.39	1876	1923	0.6
18810	ATHENS	015	7801	7870	7965	0.2	49	3062	3148	3251	0.7	2.45	2126	2174	0.5
18812	BRACKNEY	115	1944	1936	1938	-0.1	34	704	717	733	0.4	2.70	558	565	0.3
18817	EAST SMITHFIELD	015	1543	1544	1551	0.0	40	569	580	593	0.5	2.66	435	441	0.3
18818	FRIENDSVILLE	115	1706	1680	1677	-0.4	22	659	668	683	0.3	2.51	492	495	0.1
18821	GREAT BEND	115	1574	1548	1546	-0.4	21	696	703	720	0.2	2.20	447	449	0.1
18822	HALLSTEAD	115	2836	2787	2782	-0.4	20	1143	1152	1178	0.2	2.42	786	786	0.0
18823	HARFORD	115	1275	1286	1293	0.2	48	509	526	541	0.8	2.41	375	385	0.6
18824	HOP BOTTOM	115	1138	1131	1131	-0.2	32	447	455	466	0.4	2.49	327	331	0.3
18825	JACKSON	115	709	699	698	-0.3	23	286	290	297	0.3	2.41	213	215	0.2
18826	KINGSLEY	115	1262	1263	1266	0.0	40	484	497	510	0.6	2.54	353	359	0.4
18828	LAWTON	115	1429	1450	1462	0.3	56	538	561	579	1.0	2.57	408	423	0.9
18829	LE RAYSVILLE	015	975	966	970	-0.2	28	344	350	359	0.4	2.76	273	276	0.3
18830	LITTLE MEADOWS	115	709	697	695	-0.4	21	271	275	281	0.4	2.53	203	205	0.2
18831	MILAN	015	368	367	369	-0.1	36	143	146	150	0.5	2.47	106	108	0.4
18832	MONROETON	015	2466	2503	2538	0.4	57	920	956	991	0.9	2.62	686	708	0.8
18833	NEW ALBANY	015	1425	1433	1447	0.1	45	569	589	609	0.8	2.43	418	429	0.7
18834	NEW MILFORD	115	2737	3150	3441	3.4	99	1072	1257	1402	3.8	2.51	768	897	3.7
18837	ROME	015	2005	1991	2003	-0.2	31	763	778	801	0.5	2.56	569	577	0.3
18840	SAYRE	015	10553	10748	10944	0.4	61	4463	4640	4826	0.9	2.30	2898	2992	0.8
18842	SOUTH GIBSON	115	434	439	442	0.3	53	161	167	172	0.9	2.50	120	124	0.8
18844	SPRINGVILLE	115	2192	2195	2197	0.0	40	805	823	842	0.5	2.66	609	619	0.4
18845	STEVENSVILLE	015	409	412	416	0.2	47	162	168	174	0.9	2.45	120	124	0.8
18846	SUGAR RUN	015	1177	1201	1220	0.5	62	454	476	495	1.1	2.52	339	353	1.0
18847	SUSQUEHANNA	115	5256	5204	5230	-0.2	28	2005	2027	2083	0.3	2.52	1401	1406	0.1
18848	TOWANDA	015	7202	7221	7294	0.1	42	2901	2971	3064	0.6	2.33	1967	2000	0.4
18850	ULSTER	015	2136	2165	2193	0.3	55	802	831	860	0.8	2.58	607	625	0.7
18851	WARREN CENTER	015	1019	1072	1106	1.2	84	360	387	408	1.7	2.75	288	308	1.6
18853	WYALUSING	015	3528	3568	3611	0.3	53	1375	1428	1481	0.9	2.44	958	988	0.7
18854	WYSOX	015	2359	2416	2458	0.6	67	920	960	996	1.0	2.52	668	692	0.8
18901	DOYLESTOWN	017	46856	49792	52234	1.4	87	16977	18440	19737	2.0	2.54	12122	13046	1.7
18913	CARVERSVILLE	017	175	186	194	1.4	87	58	63	67	2.0	2.95	44	48	2.1
18914	CHALFONT	017	17708	18704	19618	1.3	85	6269	6704	7132	1.6	2.78	4922	5253	1.5
18915	COLMAR	091	1600	1541	1538	-0.9	6	654	645	654	-0.3	2.38	494	484	-0.5
	PENNSYLVANIA					0.3					0.7	2.44			0.6
	UNITED STATES					1.2					1.3	2.58			1.1

#	POST OFFICE NAME	RACE (%) White 2000	White 2004	Black 2000	Black 2004	Asian/Pacific 2000	Asian/Pacific 2004	% Hispanic Origin 2000	% Hispanic Origin 2004	2004 AGE DISTRIBUTION (%) 0-4	5-9	10-14	15-19	20-24	25-44	45-64	65-84	85+	18+	MEDIAN AGE 2004	% 2004 Males	% 2004 Females
18460	SOUTH STERLING	94.8	94.3	2.7	3.0	0.3	0.3	2.7	2.7	6.2	6.4	7.7	6.4	4.2	22.0	29.2	15.4	2.5	74.8	42.9	49.3	50.7
18461	STARLIGHT	98.8	98.2	0.0	0.0	0.9	0.9	0.6	0.9	3.6	3.9	4.8	5.4	5.1	20.7	34.7	20.4	1.5	84.4	49.2	51.2	48.8
18462	STARRUCCA	98.9	98.4	0.0	0.0	0.3	0.3	0.5	0.8	5.5	5.8	6.1	5.3	5.0	23.5	31.4	16.4	1.1	79.4	44.1	50.7	49.3
18463	STERLING	96.4	95.6	1.8	2.0	0.4	0.6	1.9	2.2	5.3	6.1	6.6	6.9	4.6	27.4	29.7	12.3	1.0	77.7	40.5	51.9	48.1
18464	TAFTON	94.0	93.6	2.7	2.8	0.6	0.7	3.4	3.7	4.8	5.0	5.5	5.4	4.7	22.1	29.7	21.7	1.1	81.3	46.6	51.7	48.3
18465	THOMPSON	98.1	97.9	0.3	0.3	0.2	0.3	0.9	1.0	5.5	5.7	6.4	6.3	5.7	23.8	29.0	15.6	2.1	78.7	42.8	51.1	48.9
18466	TOBYHANNA	71.6	69.6	15.7	16.6	1.1	1.3	15.3	16.4	6.7	7.0	9.0	8.5	7.0	25.2	25.3	10.6	0.7	71.9	36.3	49.1	50.9
18469	TYLER HILL	98.1	97.6	1.1	1.3	0.3	0.5	0.5	0.3	4.4	5.1	6.5	6.9	5.8	23.5	30.6	15.6	1.6	78.1	43.4	49.7	50.3
18470	UNION DALE	98.3	98.2	0.4	0.4	0.3	0.3	1.6	1.7	6.4	6.7	6.9	6.9	5.2	26.4	26.5	13.5	1.7	75.9	39.9	51.1	48.9
18472	WAYMART	88.5	87.8	8.0	8.3	0.3	0.4	3.2	3.5	4.8	5.0	5.5	5.6	4.8	31.9	27.4	11.9	3.3	81.1	41.2	59.2	40.8
18503	SCRANTON	85.3	83.5	8.7	9.6	2.6	3.1	3.3	3.6	1.7	1.1	1.6	6.4	13.4	27.7	20.9	21.9	5.2	93.8	43.6	51.9	48.2
18504	SCRANTON	97.6	97.3	0.8	0.9	0.5	0.7	1.1	1.2	5.4	5.4	6.4	6.2	6.3	25.8	24.9	16.5	3.1	79.0	41.3	47.1	52.9
18505	SCRANTON	93.6	92.8	3.0	3.3	0.9	1.1	3.0	3.3	5.4	5.1	5.6	6.4	6.2	24.7	24.4	18.3	3.9	80.2	42.6	46.3	53.7
18507	MOOSIC	98.7	98.5	0.3	0.4	0.5	0.6	0.5	0.6	4.5	4.9	5.7	5.0	4.7	24.5	27.8	19.1	3.9	81.7	45.5	47.6	52.4
18508	SCRANTON	93.7	93.1	2.5	2.6	0.8	1.0	3.7	4.1	6.3	6.2	6.8	6.3	6.1	26.6	24.2	15.1	2.4	76.9	39.1	47.1	52.9
18509	SCRANTON	94.4	93.6	3.1	3.5	0.9	1.1	2.0	2.2	4.9	4.7	5.4	7.7	8.6	25.6	22.7	16.5	3.8	81.3	39.9	46.6	53.4
18510	SCRANTON	88.6	87.3	5.6	6.1	2.6	3.1	3.6	3.9	5.0	4.5	4.9	13.0	14.9	21.9	18.9	13.5	3.5	82.4	32.0	46.4	53.6
18512	SCRANTON	98.9	98.7	0.3	0.4	0.3	0.4	0.8	0.8	4.9	5.2	6.0	5.7	5.1	26.5	24.6	18.8	3.2	80.4	42.7	47.1	52.9
18517	TAYLOR	98.6	98.4	0.2	0.2	0.7	0.9	0.5	0.6	4.5	4.8	6.0	5.8	5.6	24.8	27.9	17.0	3.6	80.8	43.9	46.8	53.2
18518	OLD FORGE	99.0	98.8	0.2	0.2	0.4	0.5	0.3	0.4	5.1	5.2	5.7	5.0	5.1	25.2	26.4	18.2	4.1	80.9	44.0	46.3	53.7
18519	DICKSON CITY	98.7	98.4	0.3	0.3	0.3	0.4	0.9	1.1	5.0	5.1	5.7	5.5	5.3	27.9	24.6	17.7	3.2	80.8	42.1	46.8	53.2
18603	BERWICK	97.9	97.6	0.7	0.7	0.4	0.5	1.2	1.3	5.2	5.4	6.7	6.2	5.8	25.8	26.1	16.0	3.0	78.9	41.7	48.0	52.0
18610	BLAKESLEE	86.8	85.5	6.9	7.5	1.0	1.2	9.3	10.2	7.0	7.5	9.7	7.9	5.8	26.7	25.2	9.8	0.5	70.7	36.8	50.6	49.4
18612	DALLAS	98.4	98.1	0.3	0.4	0.7	0.8	0.6	0.7	5.2	5.3	6.0	6.8	7.1	23.5	26.7	15.9	3.6	79.9	42.4	46.3	53.7
18614	DUSHORE	98.2	98.2	0.3	0.3	0.1	0.1	0.6	0.6	5.6	5.2	5.7	7.0	5.8	23.4	26.6	18.1	2.8	79.4	43.6	48.0	52.0
18615	FALLS	97.4	97.1	1.6	1.7	0.4	0.6	1.2	1.2	5.3	6.0	8.5	7.5	5.2	26.4	28.3	11.5	1.3	74.8	39.2	53.7	46.3
18616	FORKSVILLE	97.2	97.2	0.5	0.5	0.3	0.3	0.3	0.4	4.7	5.0	5.7	4.7	4.3	23.3	28.1	20.4	4.0	81.1	46.9	50.6	49.4
18617	GLEN LYON	82.7	81.4	15.7	16.9	0.4	0.5	3.8	4.1	4.3	4.2	4.5	5.0	11.3	40.5	18.6	9.3	2.4	84.5	34.9	65.0	35.1
18618	HARVEYS LAKE	98.3	98.0	0.1	0.1	0.4	0.5	0.6	0.7	5.1	5.5	6.6	6.4	5.5	28.6	28.9	11.9	1.7	78.7	40.6	49.4	50.6
18619	HILLSGROVE	98.9	99.2	0.0	0.0	0.4	0.4	0.0	0.0	5.0	5.0	4.6	5.4	4.6	24.5	32.6	16.1	2.3	82.0	45.5	50.6	49.4
18621	HUNLOCK CREEK	98.8	98.6	0.1	0.1	0.5	0.6	0.1	0.1	5.4	5.9	6.3	6.7	5.7	27.5	29.4	11.9	1.2	78.3	40.4	51.5	48.5
18622	HUNTINGTON MILLS	98.5	99.3	0.0	0.0	0.0	0.0	0.0	0.0	4.9	4.9	6.3	7.0	5.6	24.7	28.9	15.5	2.1	78.9	42.7	50.0	50.0
18623	LACEYVILLE	98.6	98.5	0.3	0.3	0.2	0.3	0.6	0.7	6.5	6.8	7.3	6.4	5.9	25.9	27.3	12.4	1.5	75.4	38.8	49.3	50.7
18624	LAKE HARMONY	95.1	94.8	1.3	1.4	0.1	0.1	3.7	4.1	3.4	4.0	6.1	5.2	2.9	23.5	33.8	19.6	1.4	82.8	48.7	50.8	49.2
18628	LOPEZ	84.4	84.1	10.3	10.7	0.0	0.0	3.8	3.8	2.9	2.9	3.8	16.6	9.4	17.6	21.8	20.3	4.8	80.7	41.8	54.8	45.3
18629	MEHOOPANY	98.1	97.8	0.2	0.3	0.1	0.1	0.7	0.8	6.4	6.5	7.0	6.3	6.4	25.7	28.8	11.8	1.2	76.4	39.4	51.2	48.8
18630	MESHOPPEN	99.0	98.9	0.1	0.1	0.2	0.3	0.5	0.5	6.4	7.0	8.8	7.0	5.9	27.4	25.7	10.4	1.3	73.2	36.6	49.7	50.4
18631	MIFFLINVILLE	99.0	98.7	0.0	0.0	0.7	0.9	0.4	0.4	4.7	5.0	6.3	6.3	4.5	25.5	30.8	15.6	1.4	80.0	43.5	48.5	51.5
18632	MILDRED	98.8	98.9	0.2	0.2	0.2	0.2	0.7	0.9	5.4	5.5	6.6	6.4	5.2	23.9	28.0	17.1	1.8	78.2	43.3	50.2	49.8
18634	NANTICOKE	98.9	98.8	0.2	0.3	0.2	0.3	0.5	0.5	4.6	4.6	5.8	5.6	5.5	25.1	25.5	19.2	4.1	81.7	44.1	47.3	52.7
18635	NESCOPECK	98.3	98.2	0.2	0.3	0.4	0.5	0.7	0.7	6.0	6.0	6.2	5.8	5.8	27.7	27.3	13.5	1.7	78.4	40.6	49.3	50.7
18636	NOXEN	98.6	98.5	0.4	0.4	0.1	0.1	0.2	0.2	6.9	6.7	7.1	6.4	6.1	28.0	24.8	12.7	1.4	75.7	37.8	50.7	49.4
18640	PITTSTON	98.8	98.6	0.5	0.5	0.2	0.3	0.5	0.6	5.0	5.1	6.1	6.0	5.5	26.0	25.9	16.8	3.7	80.3	42.6	47.1	53.0
18641	PITTSTON	99.2	99.2	0.3	0.4	0.2	0.2	0.2	0.2	4.5	4.9	5.4	5.0	4.9	26.8	26.7	18.8	3.0	82.1	44.0	48.1	52.0
18642	DURYEA	98.9	98.8	0.2	0.2	0.4	0.5	0.3	0.2	4.3	4.3	5.5	5.8	5.1	25.8	28.0	18.1	3.1	82.3	44.5	47.0	53.0
18643	PITTSTON	99.1	98.9	0.3	0.3	0.1	0.1	0.4	0.5	5.2	5.3	5.9	5.8	5.1	26.7	26.3	16.7	2.9	79.9	42.4	46.7	53.3
18644	WYOMING	99.3	99.2	0.2	0.2	0.1	0.2	0.3	0.4	5.2	5.7	6.3	5.6	4.5	25.4	26.6	17.6	3.3	79.5	43.5	47.5	52.5
18651	PLYMOUTH	98.6	98.4	0.6	0.6	0.1	0.2	0.8	0.9	5.8	5.7	6.6	6.3	6.5	26.3	24.6	15.3	2.9	78.1	40.2	47.5	52.6
18655	SHICKSHINNY	98.9	98.8	0.2	0.2	0.2	0.3	0.5	0.6	5.2	5.8	6.8	5.9	4.9	27.1	26.9	15.0	2.4	78.2	41.2	49.5	50.5
18656	SWEET VALLEY	99.2	99.1	0.0	0.1	0.1	0.1	0.3	0.5	5.4	6.0	7.2	5.7	5.2	27.7	29.6	11.9	1.5	77.8	40.6	50.8	49.2
18657	TUNKHANNOCK	98.7	98.5	0.3	0.3	0.3	0.3	0.6	0.7	5.7	6.2	7.0	6.4	5.5	26.2	28.3	12.7	2.0	76.8	40.6	49.4	50.6
18660	WAPWALLOPEN	98.2	97.9	0.5	0.6	0.3	0.4	0.6	0.9	5.4	5.7	6.9	6.3	6.0	27.3	27.3	13.5	1.6	77.5	41.0	50.9	49.1
18661	WHITE HAVEN	97.7	97.4	1.0	1.1	0.4	0.5	1.3	1.4	4.2	4.8	6.9	7.2	4.7	26.3	30.2	14.1	1.6	79.8	42.7	50.5	49.5
18701	WILKES BARRE	91.3	90.1	5.1	5.7	1.3	1.8	2.0	2.2	3.7	2.9	2.6	16.8	21.6	12.0	11.0	19.5	9.9	89.4	28.2	48.0	52.0
18702	WILKES BARRE	92.6	91.7	4.5	5.0	1.2	1.5	1.4	1.6	5.0	4.9	5.7	6.2	7.2	26.3	24.6	16.8	3.4	80.9	41.4	48.9	51.1
18704	KINGSTON	97.6	97.2	0.8	0.9	0.8	1.0	0.7	0.8	4.7	4.8	5.7	6.2	5.8	25.0	25.9	17.8	4.1	81.0	43.4	46.3	53.7
18705	WILKES BARRE	98.1	97.8	1.1	1.3	0.3	0.4	0.6	0.7	4.6	4.7	5.6	5.7	5.4	25.8	26.6	18.6	3.0	81.5	43.7	47.7	52.3
18706	WILKES BARRE	98.1	97.9	0.9	1.0	0.2	0.3	0.6	0.6	5.6	5.2	5.8	6.2	6.3	26.2	25.1	17.0	2.7	79.8	41.6	46.9	53.1
18707	MOUNTAIN TOP	97.1	96.5	0.5	0.6	1.6	2.0	1.1	1.2	5.9	6.5	7.6	6.5	5.0	25.9	28.4	12.7	1.6	75.8	41.0	49.0	51.0
18708	SHAVERTOWN	89.2	88.6	9.4	9.8	0.5	0.7	1.8	1.8	4.4	5.0	6.0	5.7	5.6	30.7	30.3	10.9	1.3	81.1	41.1	57.0	43.0
18709	LUZERNE	98.9	98.8	0.3	0.4	0.1	0.1	0.4	0.5	5.3	4.7	4.1	5.0	6.1	26.7	25.9	18.2	4.0	83.0	43.8	47.3	52.7
18801	MONTROSE	98.4	98.3	0.5	0.5	0.2	0.2	0.5	0.5	6.0	6.2	6.9	6.3	5.5	24.9	26.6	15.3	2.4	76.8	41.2	48.9	51.1
18810	ATHENS	98.0	97.8	0.6	0.6	0.3	0.4	0.7	0.8	6.5	6.5	7.1	6.8	6.0	25.2	26.3	13.3	2.3	75.6	39.9	47.7	52.3
18812	BRACKNEY	98.3	98.0	0.2	0.3	0.1	0.1	0.8	0.9	5.4	6.0	8.3	7.4	5.8	23.9	30.9	11.5	0.8	75.7	41.4	50.5	49.5
18817	EAST SMITHFIELD	98.8	98.7	0.9	1.0	0.1	0.2	0.7	0.7	5.4	6.0	8.1	6.4	5.2	23.6	29.8	13.9	1.6	75.9	42.0	50.1	49.9
18818	FRIENDSVILLE	98.8	98.6	0.0	0.1	0.1	0.1	1.1	1.3	5.1	5.8	7.4	6.9	5.8	23.4	31.9	12.7	1.0	77.5	42.2	51.0	49.1
18821	GREAT BEND	98.6	98.4	0.2	0.2	0.6	0.8	0.2	0.2	5.0	5.1	6.1	6.5	6.3	23.8	29.7	15.6	2.0	79.9	43.2	48.6	51.4
18822	HALLSTEAD	98.3	98.1	0.4	0.4	0.2	0.3	0.4	0.4	6.4	6.3	6.6	6.7	6.3	24.9	28.3	12.8	1.7	76.8	40.7	49.6	50.4
18823	HARFORD	99.0	98.8	0.2	0.2	0.1	0.1	0.6	0.5	5.1	5.8	7.5	6.8	5.1	25.4	28.2	13.8	2.6	77.4	42.0	50.4	49.6
18824	HOP BOTTOM	98.3	98.1	0.7	0.8	0.1	0.1	0.3	0.4	5.2	5.8	7.4	6.6	5.7	25.5	30.2	11.9	1.7	77.4	40.9	51.4	48.6
18825	JACKSON	98.0	97.7	0.6	0.6	0.1	0.1	0.6	0.6	4.3	4.6	4.6	5.7	4.7	21.9	35.1	17.3	1.9	83.1	47.6	48.9	51.1
18826	KINGSLEY	98.7	98.6	0.1	0.1	0.1	0.1	0.3	0.4	5.9	6.4	7.6	6.8	5.1	24.2	27.9	14.3	1.8	75.7	41.8	49.9	50.1
18828	LAWTON	98.6	98.4	0.3	0.3	0.1	0.1	0.5	0.6	5.7	6.2	8.1	6.3	5.3	26.5	28.1	12.6	1.3	75.8	40.3	51.6	48.4
18829	LE RAYSVILLE	98.4	98.2	0.6	0.7	0.0	0.0	1.2	1.4	8.9	8.1	7.5	6.6	6.6	27.0	23.0	11.1	1.2	71.5	34.6	51.5	48.6
18830	LITTLE MEADOWS	97.9	97.6	0.3	0.3	0.4	0.6	0.9	0.9	6.0	6.5	7.3	6.7	3.2	29.1	30.9	9.8	0.6	75.8	40.2	52.2	47.8
18831	MILAN	97.6	96.7	0.5	0.5	0.3	0.3	0.8	0.8	6.5	7.1	7.9	6.0	5.7	26.2	26.7	12.5	1.4	74.1	39.2	48.5	51.5
18832	MONROETON	98.3	98.1	0.1	0.1	0.0	0.0	0.3	0.3	6.0	6.4	8.3	6.6	6.2	27.1	26.8	11.6	1.1	75.3	38.5	50.9	49.1
18833	NEW ALBANY	98.0	97.8	0.0	0.0	0.1	0.1	0.4	0.5	5.9	6.1	6.6	7.5	6.8	25.5	28.1	12.1	1.5	76.9	40.1	52.4	47.6
18834	NEW MILFORD	98.3	98.1	0.7	0.7	0.2	0.2	0.9	1.1	6.6	6.8	7.6	6.9	5.8	26.2	26.6	12.2	1.4	74.9	39.2	50.6	49.4
18837	ROME	98.9	98.8	0.2	0.2	0.1	0.1	0.7	0.7	7.3	7.3	7.0	6.6	6.1	27.1	25.3	12.1	1.2	74.4	37.3	49.3	50.7
18840	SAYRE	96.8	96.2	0.5	0.6	1.5	1.9	0.6	0.7	6.5	6.5	6.7	6.1	5.8	24.7	26.5	14.8	2.6	76.5	40.9	47.2	52.8
18842	SOUTH GIBSON	99.3	99.3	0.2	0.2	0.0	0.0	0.9	1.1	4.8	5.7	6.8	6.4	5.9	24.2	28.5	13.9	3.9	78.6	42.7	50.8	49.2
18844	SPRINGVILLE	98.9	98.5	0.3	0.4	0.1	0.3	0.6	0.7	6.6	7.0	8.1	6.5	5.5	25.8	26.7	12.1	1.6	73.9	38.9	50.2	49.8
18845	STEVENSVILLE	97.3	96.8	0.5	0.5	0.5	0.5	1.0	1.0	5.1	5.3	6.6	6.3	6.8	22.8	30.6	15.1	1.5	79.1	42.9	50.0	50.0
18846	SUGAR RUN	98.2	97.8	0.3	0.4	0.3	0.4	0.5	0.8	6.1	6.4	6.6	6.7	4.7	25.7	28.7	13.8	1.3	76.8	40.9	51.3	48.7
18847	SUSQUEHANNA	98.3	98.1	0.1	0.1	0.7	0.9	1.1	1.2	5.8	6.1	7.7	7.2	6.4	24.5	26.3	13.9	2.2	75.8	39.7	49.2	50.8
18848	TOWANDA	97.6	97.3	0.5	0.5	0.7	0.8	0.9	0.9	5.4	5.7	7.1	6.7	5.9	25.0	25.9	15.1	3.3	77.5	41.1	48.6	51.4
18850	ULSTER	97.9	97.6	0.3	0.4	0.1	0.2	0.3	0.4	6.8	7.3	7.6	6.3	5.5	26.7	26.7	11.9	1.2	74.1	38.7	50.2	49.8
18851	WARREN CENTER	98.9	98.8	0.2	0.2	0.2	0.3	0.8	0.8	6.7	7.2	7.7	7.1	5.4	25.9	26.8	12.1	1.1	73.9	38.5	51.8	48.2
18853	WYALUSING	97.3	97.0	0.2	0.2	0.2	0.3	1.2	1.3	5.5	5.9	6.8	6.2	5.8	25.5	27.9	14.2	2.2	77.9	41.4	48.9	51.1
18854	WYSOX	97.4	97.0	0.3	0.3	0.5	0.6	0.8	1.1	5.5	6.0	7.9	6.8	5.6	26.3	26.3	14.2	1.6	76.5	40.5	50.9	49.1
18901	DOYLESTOWN	95.8	95.1	1.7	2.0	1.3	1.6	1.5	1.7	6.7	7.3	7.3	6.6	5.3	26.2	26.2	11.5	3.1	74.8	39.9	48.2	51.8
18913	CARVERSVILLE	97.7	97.9	0.6	0.5	0.6	0.5	1.1	1.1	4.3	5.4	6.5	7.0	4.3	18.8	41.4	10.8	1.6	79.6	46.8	47.9	52.2
18914	CHALFONT	96.0	95.1	1.3	1.5	1.6	2.2	1.1	1.3	8.2	8.7	8.3	5.9	4.1	29.1	25.0	9.9	0.8	70.8	38.0	49.2	50.8
18915	COLMAR	89.9	87.8	2.1	2.3	6.2	7.9	2.0	2.3	5.5	6.0	7.4	7.1	6.0	24.3	29.9	12.2	1.8	76.5	41.3	49.5	50.5
	PENNSYLVANIA	85.4	84.4	10.0	10.3	1.8	2.2	3.2	3.5	5.9	6.1	6.8	6.9	6.7	26.6	25.3	13.3	2.2	77.2	39.1	48.4	51.6
	UNITED STATES	75.1	73.6	12.3	12.5	3.8	4.2	12.5	14.1	6.9	6.7	7.2	7.0	7.3	28.6	23.8	10.8	1.7	75.1	36.0	49.1	50.9

#	POST OFFICE NAME	2004 Per Capita Income	2004 HH Income Base	2004 Household Income Distribution (%): Less than $25,000	$25,000 to $49,999	$50,000 to $99,999	$100,000 to $149,999	$150,000 or More	Median Household Income: 2004	2009	2004 National Centile	2004 State Centile	2004 Home Value Base	2004 Home Value Distribution (%): Less than $50,000	$50,000 to $89,999	$90,000 to $174,999	$175,000 to $399,999	$400,000 or More	2004 Median Home Value
18460	SOUTH STERLING	20687	173	33.0	31.8	27.8	5.2	2.3	38107	43760	40	36	146	6.2	13.0	47.3	31.5	2.1	140000
18461	STARLIGHT	29489	158	35.4	29.1	27.2	3.8	4.4	36531	42085	34	28	131	7.6	22.9	42.0	23.7	3.8	122794
18462	STARRUCCA	23796	165	32.1	33.9	24.9	5.5	3.6	38104	45185	40	36	138	10.9	23.2	44.2	18.8	2.9	113636
18463	STERLING	21721	346	22.0	35.6	34.1	5.8	2.6	44790	51193	61	61	298	4.4	9.1	46.0	37.3	3.4	157051
18464	TAFTON	24481	2225	25.1	27.9	33.0	9.1	4.9	46964	54194	66	66	1911	1.1	2.0	34.3	54.3	8.3	207500
18465	THOMPSON	18520	606	36.3	31.2	24.3	5.6	2.6	35381	41886	29	22	505	10.9	15.5	40.2	28.9	4.6	130585
18466	TOBYHANNA	20522	5858	21.0	24.0	41.1	11.6	2.3	54608	66202	79	79	4791	2.2	11.9	57.1	27.3	1.4	138702
18469	TYLER HILL	21654	249	32.1	28.9	32.5	2.4	4.0	38289	44359	40	37	205	6.3	5.4	43.9	41.5	2.9	157031
18470	UNION DALE	20842	630	31.6	31.3	27.0	7.1	3.0	37110	43355	36	30	521	11.9	14.4	41.3	28.4	4.0	133686
18472	WAYMART	17676	1573	29.8	33.7	27.4	6.6	2.5	39786	45998	45	43	1237	6.1	10.7	51.3	28.8	3.2	137119
18503	SCRANTON	12383	488	72.1	19.3	8.0	0.6	0.0	13240	15283	1	1	32	0.0	56.3	15.6	28.1	0.0	85000
18504	SCRANTON	19771	9404	37.9	31.3	22.4	6.3	2.1	33315	40141	22	14	5816	8.7	34.0	48.7	7.8	0.7	95294
18505	SCRANTON	21285	8905	37.8	28.4	26.1	5.8	1.9	34891	42155	27	20	5400	7.1	30.1	53.7	8.6	0.4	100192
18507	MOOSIC	27356	2037	26.1	29.0	27.6	9.7	7.6	45343	55454	62	62	1686	14.6	18.2	48.8	14.8	3.7	113604
18508	SCRANTON	18684	4868	36.3	32.6	25.6	3.6	1.9	34708	41217	26	19	3040	6.4	41.5	47.6	4.5	0.0	91407
18509	SCRANTON	21550	5518	36.3	29.2	24.5	6.4	3.7	35463	42409	29	22	2921	6.6	27.3	49.6	15.4	1.2	106758
18510	SCRANTON	19026	4907	39.2	27.8	24.7	6.0	2.4	32888	39855	21	13	2366	7.4	30.9	50.4	10.8	0.5	97803
18512	SCRANTON	22851	5582	33.7	29.0	28.8	6.4	2.2	38234	46836	40	37	3935	3.3	20.4	60.5	15.5	0.2	114759
18517	TAYLOR	20271	2155	33.0	25.5	33.8	6.9	0.7	40710	50841	49	48	1643	20.2	16.8	53.7	9.0	0.4	103181
18518	OLD FORGE	23613	3759	29.2	29.6	30.5	7.9	2.8	41262	50878	51	50	2817	3.0	25.5	51.3	19.5	0.8	115322
18519	DICKSON CITY	20112	2169	36.0	30.7	27.9	4.2	1.2	34769	42361	27	19	1539	4.0	33.7	54.8	7.4	0.1	98767
18603	BERWICK	19168	8621	33.2	34.5	25.7	4.7	1.9	35435	41295	29	22	6266	15.2	30.1	46.0	8.2	0.5	94383
18610	BLAKESLEE	18959	1389	22.2	27.9	38.5	9.2	2.2	49960	59052	72	71	1187	6.2	9.6	47.2	36.7	0.3	151304
18612	DALLAS	30843	4749	21.4	21.3	35.8	12.9	8.6	58674	70694	83	84	3772	7.8	8.1	48.3	31.2	4.6	147233
18614	DUSHORE	20759	830	37.1	29.5	25.8	5.7	1.9	34350	40635	25	18	567	14.5	26.1	43.9	14.3	1.2	102808
18615	FALLS	20498	930	25.6	33.2	31.9	7.4	1.8	41923	49950	53	53	776	10.2	17.8	53.9	17.5	0.6	117222
18616	FORKSVILLE	21268	457	35.7	34.1	23.0	4.4	2.8	33482	40000	22	15	377	12.5	20.7	42.4	22.3	2.1	113949
18617	GLEN LYON	15233	817	45.5	30.7	18.2	4.9	0.6	28273	33185	9	4	505	28.9	44.8	26.3	0.0	0.0	66919
18618	HARVEYS LAKE	26904	1418	23.3	32.9	30.3	8.7	4.8	44855	53587	61	61	1123	8.1	18.4	49.1	19.9	4.5	120774
18619	HILLSGROVE	19848	114	38.6	27.2	27.2	6.1	0.9	33187	36869	21	14	94	13.8	19.2	39.4	23.4	4.3	121154
18621	HUNLOCK CREEK	18452	1464	25.3	34.2	32.7	7.0	0.9	42166	49350	53	54	1262	17.6	18.8	50.3	12.8	0.6	104911
18622	HUNTINGTON MILLS	20390	57	26.3	31.6	35.1	5.3	1.8	44088	51805	59	59	50	6.0	22.0	52.0	20.0	0.0	115909
18623	LACEYVILLE	20378	1344	33.0	32.2	25.6	6.4	2.8	37172	43477	36	31	1106	18.2	20.2	45.8	15.6	0.4	105970
18624	LAKE HARMONY	23708	463	31.5	31.5	22.7	8.2	6.1	37360	43278	37	32	374	3.7	14.7	54.0	24.3	3.2	128125
18628	LOPEZ	17015	184	37.5	25.0	27.2	8.2	2.2	33987	42026	24	16	158	6.3	24.1	43.7	24.1	1.9	118750
18629	MEHOOPANY	21759	731	25.4	31.2	31.7	8.6	3.0	44717	52441	60	61	610	16.7	18.5	49.3	13.0	2.5	109856
18630	MESHOPPEN	18328	1217	30.1	33.0	29.1	6.2	1.6	39186	46099	43	41	960	12.8	19.6	47.5	18.2	1.9	113889
18631	MIFFLINVILLE	23163	560	22.5	37.7	28.8	8.2	2.9	42267	50774	54	54	465	9.5	14.4	66.9	8.8	0.4	111257
18632	MILDRED	21687	247	34.4	32.4	25.1	5.3	2.8	35414	41481	29	22	211	17.1	24.6	39.8	16.6	1.9	103869
18634	NANTICOKE	18954	6144	37.4	31.4	25.2	5.2	0.7	33063	39430	21	14	4013	16.2	42.8	35.5	5.5	0.0	82652
18635	NESCOPECK	20282	1398	29.3	30.8	32.7	5.3	1.9	41170	49107	50	50	1090	10.3	18.4	57.7	12.3	1.3	108136
18636	NOXEN	18675	696	32.0	33.6	26.6	5.3	2.4	36420	42882	33	27	531	23.0	20.2	44.4	10.4	2.1	95703
18640	PITTSTON	21436	7158	32.6	30.3	27.2	7.2	2.8	38202	46000	40	36	5177	12.6	27.8	45.3	12.9	1.4	98689
18641	PITTSTON	21551	2757	30.6	33.2	27.8	6.4	2.0	39062	46734	43	40	2196	7.1	29.3	55.7	7.3	0.6	100167
18642	DURYEA	22292	1812	31.4	31.7	27.4	6.7	2.9	38454	46655	41	38	1340	5.8	32.6	52.8	8.4	0.5	98764
18643	PITTSTON	21460	5820	30.0	32.3	29.4	6.4	1.8	38715	46062	42	39	4286	13.7	21.1	50.8	13.2	1.2	104620
18644	WYOMING	23537	3321	26.0	31.7	30.0	9.9	2.5	44190	53134	59	59	2496	4.1	17.7	54.8	21.4	2.1	121248
18651	PLYMOUTH	17785	4179	37.8	31.7	25.6	4.4	0.6	33875	40325	24	16	2768	20.5	38.6	35.3	5.3	0.3	79204
18655	SHICKSHINNY	20916	2565	29.1	28.6	33.7	6.3	2.3	42306	50454	54	54	2050	12.7	27.5	44.4	14.6	0.7	102410
18656	SWEET VALLEY	22155	1350	27.2	27.4	35.5	6.6	3.3	46692	54705	65	66	1198	14.7	15.7	47.0	20.9	1.8	118128
18657	TUNKHANNOCK	22043	5177	27.7	30.0	30.6	8.4	3.3	42890	51453	56	56	4166	11.2	15.3	51.2	20.2	2.1	118507
18660	WAPWALLOPEN	19389	685	24.8	32.7	33.9	8.0	0.6	45203	52809	62	62	593	9.4	19.1	51.6	18.6	1.4	116557
18661	WHITE HAVEN	21849	1992	24.5	33.3	31.9	7.3	3.0	44053	51981	59	59	1703	12.1	21.5	48.2	17.3	0.9	109188
18701	WILKES BARRE	14667	1474	63.2	24.3	9.2	2.9	0.3	18607	21664	1	1	162	13.0	29.6	50.6	6.8	0.0	102976
18702	WILKES BARRE	20448	18193	38.1	30.3	23.7	5.5	2.5	33998	40272	24	16	10951	15.1	39.1	35.7	9.4	0.7	85975
18704	KINGSTON	22665	14295	33.8	29.1	27.2	6.9	3.0	37583	45322	38	33	9237	5.2	24.3	57.1	12.8	0.7	107728
18705	WILKES BARRE	22687	6364	30.8	30.3	29.4	7.6	2.0	38952	47792	43	40	4786	9.7	34.7	48.3	6.9	0.4	94658
18706	WILKES BARRE	19742	7359	35.8	31.7	25.3	5.9	1.3	35500	42406	29	23	5075	17.1	34.9	39.5	8.1	0.4	88134
18707	MOUNTAIN TOP	27557	6072	16.0	24.2	39.0	13.4	7.4	60298	72306	85	86	5449	5.0	9.6	51.6	31.3	2.5	147307
18708	SHAVERTOWN	28844	4012	19.5	21.5	34.5	15.5	9.0	60923	75594	85	87	3497	4.8	7.9	54.3	26.9	6.2	142454
18709	LUZERNE	19522	1394	39.5	33.8	21.2	4.2	1.3	33069	40204	21	14	853	14.0	43.1	41.9	1.1	0.0	84739
18801	MONTROSE	21494	2784	31.1	32.0	28.3	5.6	3.0	39263	45530	44	41	2157	10.8	16.6	50.2	20.9	1.6	118861
18810	ATHENS	22111	3148	29.7	32.2	27.8	6.5	3.8	39622	46510	45	43	2341	17.0	26.1	42.8	12.9	1.3	98240
18812	BRACKNEY	24617	717	19.1	26.4	38.9	9.5	6.1	53117	62320	77	77	631	8.1	10.5	51.8	26.9	2.7	133604
18817	EAST SMITHFIELD	19029	580	23.8	36.7	30.9	5.9	2.8	41437	49097	51	51	502	14.9	19.5	43.4	18.9	3.2	114096
18818	FRIENDSVILLE	20491	668	26.7	30.8	34.0	5.8	2.7	42620	50201	55	55	574	8.9	16.2	52.4	21.4	1.1	120144
18821	GREAT BEND	19586	703	34.7	33.9	25.5	4.8	1.1	34850	40598	27	20	502	14.5	32.1	41.8	11.2	0.4	94474
18822	HALLSTEAD	17740	1152	34.5	34.1	26.2	4.5	0.7	35471	41681	29	22	869	14.2	31.2	44.1	10.1	0.5	95704
18823	HARFORD	20437	526	26.6	35.9	30.8	4.9	1.7	40369	46614	47	46	448	8.7	16.1	44.9	27.7	2.7	133654
18824	HOP BOTTOM	19009	455	31.9	34.5	25.3	6.8	1.5	36878	42655	35	30	373	13.7	26.0	42.4	16.6	1.3	104356
18825	JACKSON	20849	290	31.7	29.3	28.3	7.6	3.1	39410	46499	44	42	249	6.0	16.1	53.0	21.7	3.2	123958
18826	KINGSLEY	18115	497	28.6	37.8	27.0	5.2	1.4	38870	45246	42	40	421	9.3	14.3	50.4	22.8	3.3	124038
18828	LAWTON	19054	561	26.2	34.8	31.7	5.0	2.3	40069	46889	46	45	473	9.7	15.2	46.7	23.9	4.4	124059
18829	LE RAYSVILLE	21451	350	26.9	24.9	37.7	8.0	2.6	47391	54916	67	67	291	12.7	24.4	47.4	13.8	1.7	106117
18830	LITTLE MEADOWS	19989	275	26.6	28.7	37.5	5.1	2.2	46813	53804	66	66	235	15.3	24.7	44.3	12.8	3.0	102344
18831	MILAN	19609	146	24.0	34.3	37.0	4.1	0.7	42846	50000	56	56	118	9.3	29.7	48.3	11.9	0.9	102679
18832	MONROETON	18365	956	28.6	37.0	26.9	5.4	2.1	38649	44774	42	39	793	19.3	25.6	43.5	10.8	0.8	97642
18833	NEW ALBANY	19189	589	26.7	37.7	29.0	5.8	0.9	40149	46177	47	45	486	18.7	32.1	38.7	9.9	0.6	89000
18834	NEW MILFORD	18711	1257	32.9	33.7	26.7	4.9	1.9	37161	43463	36	31	1023	10.2	22.3	49.1	16.3	2.2	111328
18837	ROME	18634	778	31.6	33.0	27.9	5.1	2.3	37186	43702	36	31	655	23.5	26.3	37.4	12.2	0.6	90395
18840	SAYRE	23487	4640	29.6	32.6	27.0	6.9	3.9	39093	46282	43	40	3348	16.1	25.2	44.2	13.4	1.1	99668
18842	SOUTH GIBSON	23094	167	26.4	29.9	31.7	9.6	2.4	42921	50604	56	56	145	9.0	13.1	40.0	33.8	4.1	141346
18844	SPRINGVILLE	18312	823	28.8	32.9	30.5	5.7	2.1	40370	47108	47	46	690	10.9	16.2	48.6	22.3	2.0	120956
18845	STEVENSVILLE	18853	168	33.3	35.1	23.2	5.4	3.0	35309	40000	29	22	143	13.3	23.8	42.0	18.9	2.1	109500
18846	SUGAR RUN	20369	476	28.6	34.7	25.2	8.8	2.7	39102	46455	43	41	403	16.1	15.9	48.6	15.1	4.2	116952
18847	SUSQUEHANNA	17614	2027	37.2	31.8	24.5	4.6	1.9	34157	40157	25	17	1533	19.7	29.4	39.0	11.4	0.6	91142
18848	TOWANDA	21855	2971	28.6	33.4	27.6	7.1	3.4	40582	47651	48	47	2115	13.1	20.9	48.8	15.6	1.7	108118
18850	ULSTER	18999	831	24.6	34.9	34.3	4.9	1.3	41881	48781	53	52	692	16.3	25.4	41.9	14.9	1.5	100680
18851	WARREN CENTER	19783	387	21.2	29.5	39.8	8.3	1.3	49245	56149	71	70	322	12.1	22.7	48.8	14.0	2.5	112500
18853	WYALUSING	22021	1428	30.3	30.1	29.8	6.8	2.9	39759	46632	45	43	1131	14.2	24.3	44.6	15.7	1.2	105472
18854	WYSOX	22115	960	24.9	33.3	29.0	9.1	3.8	42882	50476	56	56	793	18.9	18.5	37.2	22.8	2.5	112688
18901	DOYLESTOWN	43306	18440	11.7	15.5	30.6	21.2	21.1	84922	105473	96	97	14499	1.9	0.9	8.8	59.9	28.5	322914
18913	CARVERSVILLE	62314	63	7.9	7.9	27.0	23.8	33.3	110913	134769	99	99	56	0.0	0.0	0.0	25.0	75.0	600000
18914	CHALFONT	35003	6704	6.7	14.7	40.8	24.1	13.7	82819	103855	96	96	5888	1.0	1.0	10.6	77.2	10.2	260018
18915	COLMAR	35123	645	10.9	20.3	39.4	19.8	9.6	75311	89356	93	95	518	0.0	0.4	18.7	79.5	1.4	220096
	PENNSYLVANIA	25764		25.8	27.2	31.2	10.2	5.7	46988	57000				11.9	18.4	40.7	25.1	4.1	123516
	UNITED STATES	25866		24.7	27.1	30.8	10.9	6.5	48124	56710				10.9	15.0	33.7	30.1	10.4	145905

SPENDING POTENTIAL INDICES PENNSYLVANIA
18460-18915 D

#	POST OFFICE NAME	FINANCIAL SERVICES: Auto Loan	FINANCIAL SERVICES: Home Loan	FINANCIAL SERVICES: Invest-ments	FINANCIAL SERVICES: Retire-ment Plans	THE HOME: Home Improvements: Home Repair	THE HOME: Home Improvements: Lawn & Garden	THE HOME: Furnishings: Comput-ers & Hard-ware	THE HOME: Furnishings: Major Appli-ances	THE HOME: Furnishings: TV, Radio, Sound Equip-ment	THE HOME: Furnishings: Furni-ture	ENTERTAINMENT: Dine out/ Carry out	ENTERTAINMENT: Sports Equip-ment	ENTERTAINMENT: Fees & Tickets	ENTERTAINMENT: Toys & Games	ENTERTAINMENT: Travel	ENTERTAINMENT: Cable TV	PERSONAL: Apparel & Services	PERSONAL: Auto Repairs	PERSONAL: Health Insur-ance	PERSONAL: Pets & Supplies
18460	SOUTH STERLING	81	63	43	57	71	80	60	72	67	59	80	84	53	79	64	72	74	71	85	98
18461	STARLIGHT	105	83	56	74	93	104	78	94	88	77	104	110	70	103	83	94	97	92	111	128
18462	STARRUCCA	93	73	50	66	82	92	69	83	78	68	92	97	61	91	73	83	85	81	98	113
18463	STERLING	89	79	60	75	84	90	73	81	78	73	94	97	71	96	75	80	90	79	88	105
18464	TAFTON	102	80	55	72	90	101	75	91	85	75	101	106	67	100	80	91	94	89	107	124
18465	THOMPSON	79	63	44	57	70	78	59	70	66	59	79	83	54	78	63	70	74	69	82	95
18466	TOBYHANNA	90	91	85	91	91	93	86	89	84	87	105	106	85	106	86	82	102	88	85	104
18469	TYLER HILL	100	69	36	66	81	91	69	85	79	68	93	102	59	91	71	83	85	84	101	118
18470	UNION DALE	88	70	48	65	78	86	66	78	74	66	88	92	61	88	70	78	82	77	90	105
18472	WAYMART	69	51	32	48	57	66	53	61	60	51	70	71	47	68	54	63	64	61	73	79
18503	SCRANTON	26	23	34	24	23	27	29	26	31	28	38	31	28	38	29	31	37	29	29	29
18504	SCRANTON	61	62	64	59	63	70	63	63	65	60	80	71	64	84	64	67	77	62	68	70
18505	SCRANTON	62	64	67	61	64	72	65	65	68	63	84	73	67	87	66	70	81	65	69	72
18507	MOOSIC	105	95	81	87	100	112	92	100	100	91	121	115	90	123	94	105	115	98	112	123
18508	SCRANTON	57	59	62	56	59	66	60	59	62	58	77	66	62	81	61	64	74	59	64	66
18509	SCRANTON	67	67	74	65	68	76	70	69	72	68	89	79	71	91	71	74	86	70	73	77
18510	SCRANTON	63	62	73	62	62	68	69	65	70	66	87	76	69	89	68	70	85	67	66	71
18512	SCRANTON	68	69	69	66	71	80	70	71	73	67	89	79	71	93	71	75	85	70	77	79
18517	TAYLOR	71	66	58	61	68	77	65	69	69	63	85	78	64	86	66	73	80	68	77	83
18518	OLD FORGE	71	76	79	72	77	85	75	75	77	72	95	83	78	101	77	80	92	73	80	83
18519	DICKSON CITY	62	61	59	58	63	71	62	63	65	60	80	71	63	83	63	68	76	62	70	72
18603	BERWICK	64	62	57	58	64	71	61	63	64	59	79	72	61	82	62	66	75	62	69	75
18610	BLAKESLEE	94	80	60	75	86	94	75	85	81	75	98	101	71	98	78	84	92	83	95	112
18612	DALLAS	109	114	115	111	116	126	110	113	110	108	136	128	112	138	113	112	132	111	117	128
18614	DUSHORE	76	59	40	54	65	75	59	69	67	58	79	79	53	76	61	71	73	68	82	89
18615	FALLS	87	73	51	69	79	85	68	78	74	68	89	93	65	90	70	76	84	76	87	103
18616	FORKSVILLE	87	68	47	62	77	87	64	78	73	64	87	91	58	85	69	78	80	77	92	106
18617	GLEN LYON	54	49	42	46	51	59	51	53	54	48	66	59	49	67	51	57	62	52	60	61
18618	HARVEYS LAKE	111	86	55	80	96	107	82	98	92	81	109	116	73	108	86	97	101	96	114	133
18619	HILLSGROVE	76	60	41	54	67	75	56	68	64	56	75	79	50	74	60	68	70	67	80	92
18621	HUNLOCK CREEK	76	67	53	62	71	79	64	71	70	64	85	82	63	87	66	73	80	69	80	89
18622	HUNTINGTON MILLS	87	67	41	60	73	81	63	74	72	64	85	89	58	84	64	75	79	73	87	101
18623	LACEYVILLE	98	66	30	57	75	86	64	79	77	65	90	95	54	85	65	82	82	79	98	112
18624	LAKE HARMONY	93	72	49	66	81	92	69	83	78	68	92	97	62	91	73	83	86	81	98	112
18628	LOPEZ	82	65	44	58	73	82	61	73	69	60	82	86	55	81	65	74	76	72	87	100
18629	MEHOOPANY	87	71	52	70	76	86	73	80	79	72	95	92	69	94	73	81	89	78	88	97
18630	MESHOPPEN	83	64	39	58	70	78	60	71	68	61	82	85	55	80	62	72	76	70	83	97
18631	MIFFLINVILLE	85	73	56	72	76	86	74	79	78	73	95	91	71	94	73	80	89	78	86	95
18632	MILDRED	83	65	45	59	74	83	62	74	70	61	83	87	55	81	66	74	77	73	88	101
18634	NANTICOKE	55	56	59	54	57	65	58	57	60	55	74	64	59	78	59	62	71	57	63	64
18635	NESCOPECK	71	69	62	66	72	78	66	69	69	65	85	80	67	90	68	72	82	68	75	84
18636	NOXEN	89	60	27	52	68	78	58	72	70	59	82	86	49	77	59	75	74	71	89	102
18640	PITTSTON	70	69	70	66	70	78	70	71	72	68	89	81	70	91	71	74	86	71	76	81
18641	PITTSTON	65	69	71	65	70	77	67	67	69	65	86	76	70	92	69	72	83	66	72	76
18642	DURYEA	68	71	72	67	72	80	70	71	72	68	88	79	72	92	72	74	85	70	76	79
18643	PITTSTON	76	67	56	63	71	80	67	72	72	65	88	82	65	89	68	76	83	71	81	88
18644	WYOMING	70	79	83	75	79	85	75	75	75	73	94	85	79	99	78	77	91	73	77	84
18651	PLYMOUTH	57	58	56	54	59	66	57	58	60	55	74	65	59	78	59	63	71	57	64	66
18655	SHICKSHINNY	79	71	58	67	75	82	68	74	73	67	89	86	67	91	70	76	84	72	82	93
18656	SWEET VALLEY	92	82	62	78	87	93	76	84	81	76	98	100	74	100	78	83	93	82	91	108
18657	TUNKHANNOCK	90	73	50	68	79	88	70	80	77	70	93	95	66	92	72	81	87	79	91	105
18660	WAPWALLOPEN	77	73	63	69	76	82	69	73	72	68	89	85	69	93	71	75	85	72	79	90
18661	WHITE HAVEN	83	73	60	68	79	87	71	78	76	69	92	90	68	94	73	80	87	77	88	99
18701	WILKES BARRE	35	28	39	30	28	33	40	34	40	37	50	43	37	48	36	39	48	39	35	38
18702	WILKES BARRE	60	62	70	60	62	68	64	63	66	62	82	72	66	85	65	67	79	63	65	69
18704	KINGSTON	64	69	79	67	69	76	70	69	71	68	89	78	73	92	72	73	86	69	71	75
18705	WILKES BARRE	65	72	77	69	73	80	71	70	72	69	90	78	75	96	73	75	87	69	74	77
18706	WILKES BARRE	62	61	58	58	62	70	62	63	65	60	79	71	62	81	63	66	75	63	68	72
18707	MOUNTAIN TOP	102	113	110	110	113	117	103	106	100	102	125	124	107	131	106	100	122	103	103	123
18708	SHAVERTOWN	102	120	130	117	119	125	111	111	107	110	134	127	117	140	115	107	132	109	108	123
18709	LUZERNE	51	53	61	51	53	60	55	54	58	53	72	61	57	76	56	60	69	54	58	59
18801	MONTROSE	88	67	43	62	74	84	66	77	75	65	89	91	60	88	68	79	82	76	91	102
18810	ATHENS	87	72	55	68	76	86	73	80	79	72	96	92	69	94	73	82	90	79	89	99
18812	BRACKNEY	112	89	62	81	100	111	84	100	94	83	112	117	76	111	89	100	105	98	117	135
18817	EAST SMITHFIELD	86	69	46	65	76	83	65	76	72	65	86	91	60	86	67	74	80	74	86	101
18818	FRIENDSVILLE	83	73	55	69	78	83	68	75	72	68	88	90	66	89	70	74	83	73	82	98
18821	GREAT BEND	64	57	52	57	59	67	60	62	62	58	76	72	57	73	59	63	71	63	68	72
18822	HALLSTEAD	62	61	56	58	62	68	58	61	61	57	75	70	59	78	60	62	72	60	65	72
18823	HARFORD	79	71	54	67	75	80	65	72	69	65	84	86	64	86	67	71	80	70	78	93
18824	HOP BOTTOM	89	60	27	52	68	78	58	72	69	59	81	86	49	77	59	74	74	71	88	102
18825	JACKSON	85	67	46	60	75	85	63	76	71	62	85	89	56	83	67	76	79	75	90	104
18826	KINGSLEY	80	61	37	57	68	75	59	70	66	58	78	84	53	77	61	68	72	68	81	95
18828	LAWTON	82	67	46	64	73	80	63	73	69	63	83	87	60	84	66	72	78	71	82	97
18829	LE RAYSVILLE	95	84	64	80	89	96	78	87	83	78	101	103	77	103	80	85	96	84	94	112
18830	LITTLE MEADOWS	81	72	55	69	76	82	67	74	71	67	86	88	65	88	69	73	82	72	80	96
18831	MILAN	78	70	53	66	73	79	64	71	68	64	83	85	63	85	66	70	79	69	77	92
18832	MONROETON	84	64	39	57	71	79	60	72	69	61	82	86	54	80	62	73	76	71	85	99
18833	NEW ALBANY	87	59	29	52	67	77	57	71	68	58	80	85	49	76	58	73	73	70	87	100
18834	NEW MILFORD	78	62	43	56	68	77	60	69	68	59	81	81	55	81	62	72	75	68	81	92
18837	ROME	83	64	40	59	70	78	61	71	68	61	82	85	56	80	62	72	76	70	82	96
18840	SAYRE	76	75	71	71	77	86	74	76	78	72	95	86	75	99	76	80	91	75	83	88
18842	SOUTH GIBSON	95	84	64	80	89	96	78	86	83	78	101	103	76	103	80	85	96	84	94	111
18844	SPRINGVILLE	85	65	40	61	72	80	62	74	70	62	83	88	56	82	64	72	77	72	85	100
18845	STEVENSVILLE	87	58	26	50	66	76	56	70	68	57	80	84	48	75	57	73	72	70	87	100
18846	SUGAR RUN	87	68	47	62	77	86	64	78	73	64	86	91	58	85	69	78	80	76	92	106
18847	SUSQUEHANNA	74	58	42	53	63	71	58	65	65	58	78	77	53	76	59	68	73	65	75	85
18848	TOWANDA	82	68	52	62	73	83	68	75	76	67	91	86	65	91	69	80	85	74	87	95
18850	ULSTER	80	69	51	65	74	80	64	72	69	65	84	86	62	85	66	71	79	70	79	94
18851	WARREN CENTER	93	73	49	66	82	92	68	82	77	68	92	97	61	91	73	83	85	81	98	113
18853	WYALUSING	94	71	43	65	78	88	69	81	79	69	94	96	63	91	70	83	87	80	95	108
18854	WYSOX	97	75	47	68	82	91	71	83	80	71	95	99	65	94	72	84	89	81	96	112
18901	DOYLESTOWN	149	178	206	181	173	179	165	162	155	166	196	187	176	202	168	152	196	159	149	177
18913	CARVERSVILLE	223	300	411	294	292	315	261	259	243	267	308	291	297	324	278	246	313	249	240	281
18914	CHALFONT	131	155	164	159	150	149	141	139	131	143	166	163	148	170	141	125	165	136	123	153
18915	COLMAR	109	135	144	135	133	131	121	120	112	120	141	141	128	150	123	109	140	116	108	133
	PENNSYLVANIA	89	89	93	87	90	98	89	90	91	88	112	104	89	114	90	92	109	90	92	104
	UNITED STATES	100	100	100	100	100	100	100	100	100	100	100	100	100	100	100	100	100	100	100	100

POPULATION CHANGE

#	POST OFFICE NAME	COUNTY FIPS CODE	POPULATION 2000	2004	2009	2000-2004 ANNUAL RATE % Rate	State Centile	HOUSEHOLDS 2000	2004	2009	% Annual Rate 2000-2004	2004 Average HH Size	FAMILIES 2000	2004	% Annual Rate 2000-2004
18917	DUBLIN	017	2083	2213	2316	1.4	87	851	920	979	1.9	2.41	521	557	1.6
18920	ERWINNA	017	788	788	804	0.0	39	313	319	331	0.5	2.47	219	221	0.2
18923	FOUNTAINVILLE	017	312	349	375	2.7	97	123	140	152	3.1	2.47	102	115	2.9
18925	FURLONG	017	2715	3022	3250	2.6	96	958	1092	1199	3.1	2.76	795	900	3.0
18927	HILLTOWN	017	91	98	103	1.8	91	38	42	45	2.4	2.33	29	32	2.3
18929	JAMISON	017	7444	9093	10220	4.8	100	2338	2912	3331	5.3	3.12	1946	2414	5.2
18930	KINTNERSVILLE	017	2682	2762	2843	0.7	71	1004	1058	1110	1.2	2.61	765	800	1.1
18932	LINE LEXINGTON	017	550	547	554	-0.1	33	204	208	215	0.5	2.55	160	162	0.3
18933	LUMBERVILLE	017	193	205	214	1.4	87	73	79	84	1.9	2.59	56	60	1.6
18934	MECHANICSVILLE	017	109	122	132	2.7	97	50	57	63	3.1	2.14	43	49	3.1
18936	MONTGOMERYVILLE	091	54	59	62	2.1	93	4	4	4	0.0	2.50	3	3	0.0
18938	NEW HOPE	017	12876	13642	14258	1.4	86	5484	5921	6302	1.8	2.27	3582	3847	1.7
18940	NEWTOWN	017	27711	29524	31068	1.5	88	9995	10784	11516	1.8	2.71	7614	8183	1.7
18942	OTTSVILLE	017	2977	3058	3142	0.6	69	1121	1178	1235	1.2	2.59	829	864	1.0
18944	PERKASIE	017	21561	22173	22875	0.7	70	7757	8117	8516	1.1	2.73	5914	6153	0.9
18947	PIPERSVILLE	017	6452	6741	7008	1.0	80	2163	2294	2423	1.4	2.91	1645	1736	1.3
18951	QUAKERTOWN	017	31277	33258	34953	1.5	88	11579	12520	13386	1.9	2.61	8378	9015	1.7
18954	RICHBORO	017	10381	10540	10785	0.4	58	3135	3268	3417	1.0	3.18	2863	2977	0.9
18955	RICHLANDTOWN	017	1503	1502	1522	0.0	37	511	524	543	0.6	2.63	384	391	0.4
18960	SELLERSVILLE	017	11266	11730	12204	1.0	78	4158	4419	4685	1.4	2.61	3024	3198	1.3
18964	SOUDERTON	091	12413	12681	12920	0.5	64	4801	4976	5129	0.9	2.50	3411	3513	0.7
18966	SOUTHAMPTON	017	38361	39009	40245	0.4	59	13893	14372	15087	0.8	2.69	10832	11178	0.7
18969	TELFORD	091	15032	15522	15902	0.8	73	5562	5844	6077	1.2	2.60	4044	4225	1.0
18972	UPPER BLACK EDDY	017	3684	3763	3862	0.5	64	1467	1529	1597	1.0	2.46	1049	1085	0.8
18974	WARMINSTER	017	37865	38582	39889	0.4	61	13609	14257	15069	1.1	2.68	10517	10947	1.0
18976	WARRINGTON	017	16346	18044	19279	2.4	95	5598	6273	6809	2.7	2.85	4366	4872	2.6
18977	WASHINGTON CROSSING	017	3706	3870	4012	1.0	80	1371	1468	1553	1.6	2.63	1164	1240	1.5
19001	ABINGTON	091	18711	18421	18503	-0.4	22	7019	7008	7114	0.0	2.58	4915	4869	-0.2
19002	AMBLER	091	30753	31380	31979	0.5	62	11508	11892	12241	0.8	2.57	8212	8433	0.6
19003	ARDMORE	045	13024	13116	13285	0.2	47	5785	5969	6166	0.7	2.15	3221	3291	0.5
19004	BALA CYNWYD	091	9431	9367	9465	-0.2	31	3798	3856	3949	0.4	2.41	2640	2655	0.1
19006	HUNTINGDON VALLEY	091	20462	20677	21056	0.3	51	7761	7968	8216	0.6	2.52	5849	5978	0.5
19007	BRISTOL	017	21727	21912	22562	0.2	48	8361	8587	8999	0.6	2.53	5455	5559	0.5
19008	BROOMALL	045	20407	20243	20157	-0.2	30	7226	7291	7373	0.2	2.66	5517	5527	0.0
19010	BRYN MAWR	045	21605	21692	21864	0.1	44	8074	8200	8363	0.4	2.28	4673	4735	0.3
19012	CHELTENHAM	091	6623	6577	6605	-0.2	31	2294	2297	2323	0.0	2.83	1778	1770	-0.1
19013	CHESTER	045	38939	38287	38120	-0.4	21	13635	13630	13781	0.0	2.59	8674	8580	-0.3
19014	ASTON	045	20780	20840	20840	0.1	43	7495	7691	7832	0.6	2.62	5506	5606	0.4
19015	BROOKHAVEN	045	15872	15471	15314	-0.6	12	6328	6292	6330	-0.1	2.45	4244	4179	-0.4
19018	CLIFTON HEIGHTS	045	23056	22852	22795	-0.2	29	9695	9792	9927	0.2	2.33	6004	6005	0.0
19020	BENSALEM	017	53604	54882	56938	0.6	67	20711	21624	22843	1.0	2.52	13782	14260	0.8
19021	CROYDON	017	10129	10216	10463	0.2	48	3788	3896	4058	0.7	2.62	2612	2665	0.5
19022	CRUM LYNNE	045	3807	3696	3654	-0.7	10	1565	1543	1547	-0.3	2.39	940	918	-0.6
19023	DARBY	045	21292	21038	21037	-0.3	26	7420	7448	7560	0.1	2.75	5154	5134	-0.1
19025	DRESHER	091	5692	5744	5798	0.2	49	1839	1885	1924	0.6	3.00	1575	1608	0.5
19026	DREXEL HILL	045	31847	31736	31731	-0.1	35	12778	12960	13164	0.3	2.44	8206	8231	0.1
19027	ELKINS PARK	091	19726	19993	20301	0.3	55	8008	8216	8420	0.6	2.42	5309	5409	0.4
19029	ESSINGTON	045	4570	4444	4402	-0.7	11	1833	1814	1825	-0.2	2.45	1202	1178	-0.5
19030	FAIRLESS HILLS	017	13455	13890	14364	0.8	72	5057	5334	5621	1.3	2.58	3603	3774	1.1
19031	FLOURTOWN	091	4039	4054	4106	0.1	44	1531	1569	1612	0.6	2.43	1065	1084	0.4
19032	FOLCROFT	045	6930	6916	6913	-0.1	36	2501	2551	2594	0.5	2.71	1848	1868	0.3
19033	FOLSOM	045	7081	7085	7114	0.0	39	2689	2744	2799	0.5	2.58	1882	1903	0.3
19034	FORT WASHINGTON	091	6073	6039	6065	-0.1	33	2121	2143	2179	0.2	2.73	1573	1579	0.1
19035	GLADWYNE	091	4046	3959	3963	-0.5	15	1474	1459	1476	-0.2	2.50	1088	1070	-0.4
19036	GLENOLDEN	045	13545	13309	13201	-0.4	20	5420	5433	5482	0.1	2.44	3546	3524	-0.2
19038	GLENSIDE	091	31785	31186	31283	-0.5	18	11768	11700	11862	-0.1	2.56	8160	8050	-0.3
19040	HATBORO	091	21440	21362	21573	-0.1	34	8505	8618	8810	0.3	2.47	5748	5782	0.1
19041	HAVERFORD	045	6983	7262	7508	0.9	77	2601	2748	2876	1.3	2.28	1477	1523	0.7
19043	HOLMES	045	3267	3198	3169	-0.5	16	1266	1262	1271	-0.1	2.53	884	872	-0.3
19044	HORSHAM	091	15266	15192	15270	-0.1	34	5836	5880	5974	0.2	2.55	3932	3931	0.0
19046	JENKINTOWN	091	18015	18339	18711	0.4	60	7492	7742	7987	0.8	2.33	4802	4934	0.6
19047	LANGHORNE	017	33309	34629	36180	0.9	77	11353	12067	12862	1.5	2.72	8478	8946	1.3
19050	LANSDOWNE	045	29343	28582	28297	-0.6	12	11900	11768	11819	-0.3	2.39	7323	7165	-0.5
19053	FEASTERVILLE TREVOSE	017	26111	26422	27184	0.3	53	9698	10023	10504	0.8	2.62	7289	7485	0.6
19054	LEVITTOWN	017	17623	17503	17826	-0.2	31	6377	6482	6736	0.4	2.69	4773	4822	0.2
19055	LEVITTOWN	017	14067	13779	13993	-0.5	16	4848	4861	5036	0.1	2.83	3751	3737	-0.1
19056	LEVITTOWN	017	16152	16475	17033	0.5	62	5947	6182	6504	0.9	2.64	4238	4380	0.8
19057	LEVITTOWN	017	16365	16138	16450	-0.3	23	5603	5657	5885	0.2	2.84	4354	4371	0.1
19061	MARCUS HOOK	045	26678	28125	29029	1.3	84	9708	10348	10810	1.5	2.70	6967	7441	1.6
19063	MEDIA	045	38389	38847	39085	0.3	53	14891	15319	15647	0.7	2.34	9458	9643	0.5
19064	SPRINGFIELD	045	23807	24043	24245	0.2	50	8677	8935	9158	0.7	2.66	6777	6932	0.5
19066	MERION STATION	091	6071	5985	6004	-0.3	23	2008	1998	2024	-0.1	2.73	1529	1511	-0.3
19067	MORRISVILLE	017	53274	54064	55482	0.4	57	20350	21022	21946	0.8	2.56	14819	15237	0.7
19070	MORTON	045	7197	7075	7028	-0.4	21	2779	2775	2797	0.0	2.54	1917	1903	-0.2
19072	NARBERTH	091	9510	9322	9337	-0.5	17	4082	4055	4107	-0.2	2.30	2506	2469	-0.4
19073	NEWTOWN SQUARE	045	16756	17132	17390	0.5	65	6642	6916	7136	1.0	2.40	4666	4826	0.6
19074	NORWOOD	045	5791	5775	5782	-0.1	35	2215	2259	2303	0.5	2.56	1480	1493	0.2
19075	ORELAND	091	7129	6990	7001	-0.5	18	2736	2728	2765	-0.1	2.56	2054	2036	-0.2
19076	PROSPECT PARK	045	6577	6443	6383	-0.5	17	2566	2550	2563	-0.2	2.46	1595	1568	-0.4
19078	RIDLEY PARK	045	11672	11508	11465	-0.3	23	4783	4793	4848	0.1	2.39	3064	3045	-0.2
19079	SHARON HILL	045	9228	8964	8865	-0.7	10	3472	3441	3462	-0.2	2.60	2386	2345	-0.4
19081	SWARTHMORE	045	10761	10609	10543	-0.3	23	3836	3827	3853	-0.1	2.45	2620	2590	-0.3
19082	UPPER DARBY	045	37836	38492	38769	0.4	60	14550	14901	15163	0.6	2.57	9138	9271	0.3
19083	HAVERTOWN	045	36533	36472	36570	0.0	36	13440	13649	13898	0.4	2.66	10026	10098	0.2
19085	VILLANOVA	045	9238	9287	9349	0.1	45	1912	1957	2004	0.6	2.96	1575	1600	0.4
19086	WALLINGFORD	045	11452	11699	11808	0.5	64	4274	4454	4571	1.0	2.57	3184	3293	0.8
19087	WAYNE	029	31793	33080	34707	0.9	78	12573	13345	14245	1.4	2.33	7965	8360	1.2
19090	WILLOW GROVE	091	19672	19147	19156	-0.6	12	7603	7518	7609	-0.3	2.47	5262	5168	-0.4
19094	WOODLYN	045	4765	4746	4735	-0.1	34	1880	1902	1927	0.3	2.49	1253	1255	0.0
19095	WYNCOTE	091	6598	6732	6884	0.5	62	2780	2957	3101	1.5	1.96	1695	1782	1.2
19096	WYNNEWOOD	091	12793	12749	12877	-0.1	35	4978	4993	5083	0.1	2.47	3525	3518	-0.1
19102	PHILADELPHIA	101	4247	4263	4243	0.1	44	2521	2580	2613	0.6	1.39	531	533	0.1
19103	PHILADELPHIA	101	18042	18223	17986	0.2	51	12424	12809	12867	0.7	1.35	2543	2589	0.4
19104	PHILADELPHIA	101	50360	49867	49019	-0.2	28	17131	17289	17252	0.2	2.16	6123	5986	-0.5
19106	PHILADELPHIA	101	7638	7877	7828	0.7	72	4922	5187	5255	1.2	1.46	1348	1391	0.2
	PENNSYLVANIA					0.3					0.7	2.44			0.6
	UNITED STATES					1.2					1.3	2.58			1.1

ZIP CODE #	POST OFFICE NAME	RACE (%) White 2000	White 2004	Black 2000	Black 2004	Asian/Pacific 2000	Asian/Pacific 2004	% Hispanic Origin 2000	% Hispanic Origin 2004	2004 AGE DISTRIBUTION (%) 0-4	5-9	10-14	15-19	20-24	25-44	45-64	65-84	85+	18+	MEDIAN AGE 2004	% 2004 Males	% 2004 Females
18917	DUBLIN	95.1	94.2	1.5	1.7	1.3	1.6	1.9	2.2	8.4	7.3	7.0	6.7	8.3	36.5	17.6	7.3	1.0	73.4	31.8	49.0	51.0
18920	ERWINNA	98.2	98.0	0.3	0.3	0.4	0.5	1.1	1.1	4.8	5.8	5.8	5.7	3.6	25.1	33.4	14.2	1.5	79.8	44.6	52.9	47.1
18923	FOUNTAINVILLE	96.2	95.4	0.6	0.9	1.6	2.3	1.3	1.4	8.0	8.6	9.2	6.9	4.3	31.2	23.8	7.2	0.9	69.6	35.8	49.6	50.4
18925	FURLONG	97.2	96.6	0.6	0.7	1.4	1.8	0.9	1.0	5.3	6.3	6.7	6.1	3.9	22.0	33.3	15.0	1.4	77.9	44.8	48.7	51.3
18927	HILLTOWN	97.8	99.0	1.1	1.0	0.0	0.0	0.0	0.0	6.1	6.1	6.1	6.1	5.1	25.5	31.6	12.2	1.0	75.5	41.9	49.0	51.0
18929	JAMISON	95.8	94.9	1.0	1.2	2.3	2.9	1.0	1.1	9.3	9.5	8.9	6.7	4.8	31.8	22.8	5.7	0.5	67.7	34.2	49.0	51.0
18930	KINTNERSVILLE	98.7	98.5	0.2	0.3	0.4	0.5	0.8	0.9	4.8	5.9	7.3	6.2	5.0	26.5	32.8	10.6	0.9	78.1	41.9	51.5	48.6
18932	LINE LEXINGTON	96.7	96.2	0.9	1.1	1.5	1.8	1.3	1.5	5.7	6.2	7.5	6.6	3.7	23.8	30.0	12.6	4.0	75.7	42.9	49.7	50.3
18933	LUMBERVILLE	97.9	97.6	0.5	1.0	0.5	0.5	1.0	1.0	4.4	5.4	6.8	6.8	3.9	19.0	41.0	11.2	1.5	79.0	46.8	48.8	51.2
18934	MECHANICSVILLE	98.2	98.4	0.9	0.8	0.9	0.8	1.8	0.8	6.6	7.4	8.2	6.6	4.1	23.0	32.8	9.8	1.6	73.0	42.1	51.6	48.4
18936	MONTGOMERYVILLE	83.3	79.7	3.7	5.1	11.1	13.6	0.0	1.7	10.2	10.2	10.2	6.8	3.4	18.6	20.3	17.0	3.4	69.5	38.5	50.9	49.2
18938	NEW HOPE	96.9	96.4	0.7	0.8	0.9	1.1	2.1	2.3	4.3	5.1	5.5	4.9	3.5	22.4	34.8	17.6	2.0	81.8	47.4	49.6	50.4
18940	NEWTOWN	94.5	93.2	1.1	1.2	3.3	4.3	1.2	1.4	7.1	7.9	7.9	6.7	4.4	28.0	28.6	8.2	1.2	72.5	39.0	48.3	51.7
18942	OTTSVILLE	97.8	97.5	0.3	0.4	0.3	0.4	1.3	1.5	5.4	6.2	6.6	5.2	4.6	26.9	31.8	12.0	1.4	78.6	42.5	50.7	49.3
18944	PERKASIE	97.9	97.5	0.6	0.7	0.5	0.7	1.0	1.2	7.1	7.4	8.0	6.8	5.4	29.4	25.4	9.4	1.2	73.1	37.5	49.8	50.2
18947	PIPERSVILLE	96.5	95.9	1.0	1.2	0.9	1.2	1.7	2.0	7.9	8.4	7.9	5.9	4.1	30.2	26.3	8.5	0.8	71.9	37.8	50.8	49.2
18951	QUAKERTOWN	96.4	95.8	0.9	1.0	1.1	1.4	1.6	1.9	6.8	6.8	7.1	6.4	5.7	29.4	25.4	10.6	1.9	75.2	38.2	49.6	50.4
18954	RICHBORO	97.1	96.4	0.5	0.6	1.8	2.3	0.7	0.8	5.8	7.0	9.1	7.4	4.8	23.3	31.7	9.2	1.7	73.2	40.9	49.0	51.0
18955	RICHLANDTOWN	98.2	97.8	0.5	0.5	0.5	0.7	1.2	1.4	6.6	6.7	7.8	6.3	6.6	28.7	20.7	11.8	4.9	74.4	37.6	47.0	53.0
18960	SELLERSVILLE	97.6	97.3	0.6	0.7	0.4	0.5	1.3	1.5	6.5	6.9	7.8	6.7	5.2	28.7	25.5	11.0	1.7	74.6	38.6	50.2	49.8
18964	SOUDERTON	93.4	92.1	1.2	1.4	3.2	4.0	2.9	3.2	6.7	6.5	6.6	6.1	5.7	27.9	22.1	15.3	3.1	76.3	39.1	48.0	52.0
18966	SOUTHAMPTON	97.0	96.3	0.5	0.6	1.6	2.1	0.9	1.0	5.4	6.1	7.5	6.7	5.2	24.7	29.0	13.3	2.2	76.7	41.8	48.1	51.9
18969	TELFORD	94.0	92.8	1.5	1.8	2.6	3.3	2.3	2.6	7.5	7.5	7.1	6.4	5.1	28.7	23.4	11.3	3.1	73.8	37.8	48.0	52.0
18972	UPPER BLACK EDDY	98.4	98.1	0.5	0.6	0.2	0.3	0.7	0.9	5.0	5.8	6.3	5.7	4.6	27.1	33.2	11.0	1.3	79.3	42.8	51.2	48.8
18974	WARMINSTER	92.0	91.0	2.9	3.1	2.0	2.6	4.0	4.3	6.6	6.7	7.3	6.5	5.9	27.5	24.5	13.6	1.5	75.2	38.6	48.7	51.3
18976	WARRINGTON	94.5	93.4	2.0	2.3	2.3	2.9	1.6	1.8	7.3	7.9	8.2	6.5	5.1	30.3	25.2	8.7	0.8	72.5	36.9	49.8	50.2
18977	WASHINGTON CROSSING	97.1	96.5	0.8	0.9	1.4	1.8	1.0	1.1	5.2	6.6	7.8	7.0	4.4	20.8	36.1	11.1	1.0	75.9	43.9	49.0	51.0
19001	ABINGTON	82.2	79.9	12.4	13.7	3.3	4.1	1.9	2.0	6.4	6.5	7.0	6.5	5.5	26.6	24.2	14.1	3.3	75.9	40.0	47.5	52.5
19002	AMBLER	87.8	85.9	6.2	6.8	4.8	6.1	1.3	1.4	6.2	6.8	7.4	6.4	4.6	24.4	27.6	13.5	3.1	75.2	41.5	47.6	52.5
19003	ARDMORE	83.7	81.3	11.0	12.4	2.9	3.7	2.1	2.3	5.1	5.1	5.6	7.5	8.8	28.5	23.5	13.4	2.6	80.3	37.7	46.5	53.5
19004	BALA CYNWYD	92.6	91.1	2.1	2.5	3.9	5.0	1.4	1.5	5.5	6.3	6.9	5.8	3.7	23.7	27.3	17.3	3.5	77.3	43.7	47.5	52.5
19006	HUNTINGDON VALLEY	95.0	93.8	0.7	0.8	3.6	4.6	1.1	1.2	4.2	4.9	6.3	6.6	4.8	20.2	29.4	20.0	3.6	80.3	46.9	47.8	52.2
19007	BRISTOL	76.3	74.2	14.3	15.4	3.1	3.5	8.8	9.8	6.5	6.3	6.9	7.0	7.0	28.9	23.5	12.0	1.8	76.0	36.7	48.6	51.4
19008	BROOMALL	92.7	90.6	1.0	1.3	5.6	7.3	0.6	0.7	5.0	5.5	6.3	6.1	5.1	23.1	26.7	18.7	3.5	79.4	44.3	47.8	52.2
19010	BRYN MAWR	85.9	83.1	5.5	6.4	6.6	8.3	1.7	1.9	4.4	4.9	5.5	10.2	13.0	20.8	22.0	14.2	5.0	81.4	37.6	42.0	58.0
19012	CHELTENHAM	74.1	71.0	13.8	14.9	9.0	10.9	2.6	2.8	5.6	6.3	7.7	7.5	5.6	24.9	27.9	12.4	2.3	75.3	40.6	47.6	52.4
19013	CHESTER	19.5	16.8	75.3	78.0	0.6	0.7	5.2	5.0	8.4	8.2	8.5	8.9	9.3	25.2	20.1	10.0	1.5	70.4	30.5	47.0	53.0
19014	ASTON	91.4	90.0	6.2	7.1	1.1	1.4	1.1	1.4	6.4	6.4	6.8	6.6	6.6	27.8	25.8	12.2	1.4	76.7	38.4	47.7	52.3
19015	BROOKHAVEN	79.9	77.7	17.2	19.0	1.0	1.2	1.6	1.8	6.6	6.6	7.1	6.2	5.8	29.1	24.2	12.9	1.5	75.8	38.0	47.2	52.8
19018	CLIFTON HEIGHTS	90.6	88.5	4.3	5.3	3.8	4.7	1.1	1.2	6.3	6.1	6.5	6.1	6.4	30.1	23.1	13.5	2.0	77.3	38.0	48.3	51.8
19020	BENSALEM	83.3	80.9	6.0	6.7	7.1	8.6	4.5	4.9	5.7	5.7	6.3	6.6	6.9	31.4	26.1	9.9	1.4	78.2	37.2	49.7	50.3
19021	CROYDON	93.3	92.4	2.9	3.2	1.3	1.6	3.7	4.2	6.3	6.1	6.9	6.7	6.6	31.1	25.1	10.3	1.0	76.6	36.9	50.9	49.1
19022	CRUM LYNNE	87.4	85.0	8.8	10.6	1.1	1.4	2.3	2.7	7.2	6.9	7.8	7.3	6.6	29.4	22.7	10.7	1.5	73.5	35.7	50.1	50.0
19023	DARBY	59.0	56.2	37.3	39.7	1.2	1.5	1.0	1.0	7.6	7.9	9.1	7.9	7.0	27.2	20.4	10.1	2.9	70.5	34.0	47.2	52.8
19025	DRESHER	85.8	82.9	5.2	5.9	8.2	10.3	1.0	1.0	5.7	7.4	9.2	7.9	4.1	21.1	31.2	12.3	1.2	71.7	41.8	49.0	51.0
19026	DREXEL HILL	93.4	91.9	1.9	2.4	3.6	4.5	1.0	1.1	6.7	6.6	6.9	6.4	5.8	29.9	23.1	12.5	2.1	75.8	37.5	47.6	52.4
19027	ELKINS PARK	60.8	58.5	28.8	29.5	7.7	9.3	2.1	2.2	5.0	5.3	6.7	7.3	6.2	25.5	27.1	14.6	2.2	78.2	40.9	47.0	53.0
19029	ESSINGTON	97.2	96.5	0.8	1.0	0.5	0.6	1.3	1.5	5.8	5.7	6.6	6.4	6.1	29.3	25.1	13.3	1.6	77.9	39.3	49.8	50.2
19030	FAIRLESS HILLS	91.2	89.7	3.4	3.8	3.2	4.0	2.7	3.1	6.2	6.2	6.8	6.7	6.4	28.5	26.2	11.6	1.4	76.7	38.3	47.7	52.3
19031	FLOURTOWN	92.9	91.5	3.2	3.9	2.7	3.5	1.0	1.2	5.7	6.4	6.5	5.7	4.2	25.1	26.9	16.3	3.3	77.6	42.9	47.9	52.1
19032	FOLCROFT	94.0	92.3	3.9	5.0	1.0	1.3	1.1	1.3	7.2	6.9	7.1	7.1	6.6	28.7	22.5	13.1	0.8	74.2	36.0	48.9	51.1
19033	FOLSOM	96.0	94.9	2.2	2.7	1.2	1.7	0.7	0.8	5.1	5.6	6.9	6.7	5.5	26.9	25.0	16.5	2.0	78.4	41.2	48.1	51.9
19034	FORT WASHINGTON	89.1	86.9	3.7	4.2	6.2	7.9	1.0	1.1	5.4	6.4	7.4	6.6	5.0	23.3	31.5	12.3	2.2	76.1	42.5	49.0	51.0
19035	GLADWYNE	96.3	95.4	0.6	0.8	2.2	2.9	1.0	1.1	4.7	6.2	7.6	6.3	2.8	17.1	28.3	18.7	8.3	76.9	48.6	46.4	53.6
19036	GLENOLDEN	93.1	91.5	4.2	5.2	1.7	2.2	0.9	1.0	6.3	6.3	6.8	6.1	6.2	29.5	23.1	14.2	1.6	77.0	38.1	47.3	52.7
19038	GLENSIDE	84.4	82.3	12.0	13.3	2.3	2.9	1.3	1.5	5.6	6.0	6.7	6.6	5.3	25.0	25.8	15.3	3.7	77.6	41.7	46.7	53.3
19040	HATBORO	93.3	92.2	2.6	2.9	2.7	3.4	1.5	1.8	5.7	5.8	6.6	6.5	5.9	28.4	24.6	14.3	2.2	77.8	39.9	48.6	51.4
19041	HAVERFORD	89.8	87.1	4.9	6.2	3.6	4.8	1.9	2.2	3.5	4.3	4.9	12.1	15.0	17.5	23.0	15.1	4.6	84.0	38.2	46.4	53.6
19043	HOLMES	96.5	95.7	1.4	1.8	1.0	1.4	0.6	0.7	6.1	6.1	6.8	7.0	6.8	28.7	23.5	13.2	1.9	76.8	38.0	48.1	51.9
19044	HORSHAM	88.9	86.9	4.5	5.1	4.8	6.0	1.7	1.9	6.8	7.0	7.6	7.2	6.5	32.5	23.7	8.0	0.7	73.8	35.8	49.4	50.6
19046	JENKINTOWN	93.4	92.0	2.3	2.7	3.1	4.0	1.1	1.3	4.7	5.1	6.3	6.2	5.4	22.3	27.4	18.7	4.0	80.1	45.1	46.0	54.0
19047	LANGHORNE	93.1	91.8	2.7	3.1	2.7	3.5	1.6	1.8	5.6	6.2	7.3	7.5	7.0	27.3	27.4	9.5	2.1	76.3	38.4	49.0	51.0
19050	LANSDOWNE	51.0	46.7	43.6	47.3	2.6	3.2	1.3	1.3	6.3	6.4	7.1	6.6	6.1	28.2	25.7	11.4	2.3	76.0	38.4	46.4	53.6
19053	FEASTERVILLE TREVOSE	93.1	92.1	4.0	4.3	1.6	2.1	1.5	1.7	5.5	5.9	6.5	6.2	5.6	27.9	28.0	12.8	1.6	78.2	40.6	49.3	50.8
19054	LEVITTOWN	94.3	93.5	2.3	2.6	1.4	1.8	1.7	1.9	6.1	6.4	7.4	7.2	6.8	28.8	24.3	12.0	1.1	75.7	37.8	48.8	51.2
19055	LEVITTOWN	94.5	93.7	2.4	2.8	0.8	1.0	2.4	2.8	6.5	6.7	7.5	6.9	5.8	29.2	23.4	12.8	1.2	75.1	37.7	48.7	51.3
19056	LEVITTOWN	90.0	88.5	4.9	5.5	2.1	2.7	3.0	3.3	6.3	6.3	7.0	7.1	6.9	28.6	23.8	12.7	1.2	76.0	37.4	49.3	50.7
19057	LEVITTOWN	89.2	88.3	7.9	8.4	0.9	1.1	2.4	2.8	6.1	6.5	7.6	7.1	6.0	27.7	24.3	13.7	1.1	75.4	38.5	48.5	51.5
19061	MARCUS HOOK	92.3	90.6	4.6	5.6	1.7	2.2	1.4	1.6	7.0	7.0	7.6	6.7	6.0	29.3	24.8	10.3	1.3	74.1	37.2	48.7	51.4
19063	MEDIA	90.4	88.3	5.8	7.0	2.4	3.2	1.1	1.3	4.7	5.3	6.3	6.3	5.5	23.1	27.7	16.2	5.0	79.6	44.3	46.8	53.2
19064	SPRINGFIELD	96.3	95.4	0.8	1.0	2.2	2.8	0.7	0.8	5.3	5.7	6.9	6.7	5.4	23.1	27.0	17.3	2.6	77.9	43.0	47.4	52.6
19066	MERION STATION	93.7	92.5	2.0	2.4	2.7	3.5	1.4	1.6	5.6	6.3	8.0	9.4	7.1	19.7	29.7	12.5	1.7	75.6	40.8	46.9	53.1
19067	MORRISVILLE	88.2	86.5	6.8	7.4	3.1	4.0	2.4	2.7	7.0	7.5	7.3	5.9	4.7	28.5	27.7	10.3	1.2	74.4	39.2	48.6	51.4
19070	MORTON	86.9	85.6	9.9	10.4	2.2	2.8	0.9	1.0	5.7	6.2	7.3	7.1	6.0	26.9	25.1	14.0	1.9	76.3	39.7	47.9	52.1
19072	NARBERTH	94.5	93.3	1.4	1.6	2.9	3.7	1.3	1.4	5.0	5.9	7.0	6.8	4.5	25.4	30.4	13.4	1.7	77.6	42.1	47.0	53.0
19073	NEWTOWN SQUARE	95.2	93.8	1.2	1.5	2.7	3.6	0.8	1.0	5.4	6.2	6.5	6.3	4.1	21.6	28.2	17.4	4.4	77.5	45.0	47.2	52.8
19074	NORWOOD	97.5	96.9	1.1	1.4	0.7	0.9	0.7	0.9	6.2	6.0	7.1	7.5	7.1	29.7	24.2	10.9	1.2	76.0	37.3	48.2	51.8
19075	ORELAND	90.8	89.5	6.1	6.8	1.9	2.3	1.1	1.2	6.2	6.4	7.0	6.6	5.3	24.8	27.7	14.2	2.0	76.2	41.1	48.6	51.4
19076	PROSPECT PARK	95.4	94.2	1.4	1.8	1.8	2.3	0.9	1.2	6.3	6.1	7.0	7.0	7.2	29.9	23.2	10.9	2.5	76.4	36.9	48.2	51.9
19078	RIDLEY PARK	96.9	96.2	0.8	1.0	1.3	1.7	0.6	0.7	5.7	5.8	6.5	6.2	5.7	28.0	24.8	15.0	2.3	78.0	40.2	47.7	52.3
19079	SHARON HILL	46.4	43.1	50.3	53.3	1.0	1.2	1.3	1.4	6.5	7.0	8.6	8.1	7.1	26.1	23.4	12.0	1.3	72.8	36.1	46.2	53.8
19081	SWARTHMORE	89.4	87.0	4.1	5.1	3.9	5.0	2.2	2.5	4.8	5.3	6.4	10.9	11.8	20.6	24.0	14.4	1.9	79.6	37.3	47.3	52.7
19082	UPPER DARBY	60.2	55.1	20.2	23.1	15.5	17.7	2.4	2.6	7.0	6.7	7.5	7.2	7.7	30.8	22.1	9.3	1.6	74.5	34.5	48.2	51.9
19083	HAVERTOWN	95.1	93.8	1.0	1.2	2.9	3.8	0.8	0.9	6.6	7.1	7.4	6.6	5.0	26.4	25.3	13.5	2.2	74.7	39.5	48.0	52.0
19085	VILLANOVA	92.3	90.2	2.1	2.6	3.8	5.1	2.5	2.8	4.1	4.9	5.6	25.7	15.3	14.4	20.3	8.7	1.0	82.6	23.2	48.9	51.2
19086	WALLINGFORD	93.5	91.9	2.9	3.6	2.3	3.0	1.3	1.4	5.2	6.2	7.7	7.1	4.6	23.0	28.7	15.1	2.5	75.8	42.9	47.7	52.3
19087	WAYNE	91.4	89.6	3.2	3.7	4.2	5.3	1.6	1.8	5.6	6.0	6.1	8.2	7.0	25.0	27.3	13.1	1.7	78.7	40.2	46.7	53.3
19090	WILLOW GROVE	80.0	78.2	15.1	16.1	2.7	3.4	1.7	1.8	6.3	6.3	6.6	6.0	5.8	27.0	24.1	15.1	2.8	76.9	40.1	46.9	53.1
19094	WOODLYN	87.2	84.5	9.9	12.1	1.1	1.4	1.2	1.4	6.1	6.2	7.7	7.4	6.5	26.6	23.5	14.0	2.0	75.4	38.5	47.9	52.2
19095	WYNCOTE	72.3	70.3	23.7	25.0	2.4	3.0	1.2	1.3	3.5	4.3	4.9	8.6	8.4	15.7	23.1	23.3	8.2	84.2	48.7	42.0	58.0
19096	WYNNEWOOD	92.9	91.5	2.4	2.8	3.3	4.1	1.3	1.5	5.7	6.8	7.0	6.5	3.8	21.9	28.7	15.4	4.2	76.0	43.9	46.9	53.1
19102	PHILADELPHIA	78.9	72.5	7.7	10.5	10.1	13.1	3.1	3.7	1.3	0.5	0.4	2.6	13.7	48.6	18.1	10.7	4.1	97.2	33.0	47.7	52.3
19103	PHILADELPHIA	81.5	76.5	7.2	9.3	8.5	10.9	3.6	4.2	1.8	1.0	0.9	4.3	9.4	41.7	19.1	16.0	5.9	95.7	37.1	46.0	54.0
19104	PHILADELPHIA	32.2	28.7	51.7	52.6	12.1	14.6	3.0	3.2	4.2	3.9	4.5	19.4	25.8	22.1	12.4	6.4	1.2	84.9	23.5	49.8	50.3
19106	PHILADELPHIA	85.9	81.5	6.7	8.9	5.2	6.9	3.0	3.6	1.7	1.5	1.2	1.6	5.3	46.1	27.6	13.3	1.7	94.8	40.2	51.2	48.9
	PENNSYLVANIA	85.4	84.4	10.0	10.3	1.8	2.2	3.2	3.5	5.9	6.1	6.8	6.9	6.7	26.6	25.3	13.3	2.2	77.2	39.1	48.4	51.6
	UNITED STATES	75.1	73.6	12.3	12.5	3.8	4.2	12.5	14.1	6.9	6.7	7.2	7.0	7.3	28.6	23.8	10.8	1.7	75.1	36.0	49.1	50.9

INCOME

ZIP CODE #	POST OFFICE NAME	2004 Per Capita Income	2004 HH Income Base	2004 Household Income Distribution (%) Less than $25,000	$25,000 to $49,999	$50,000 to $99,999	$100,000 to $149,999	$150,000 or More	Median Household Income 2004	2009	2004 National Centile	2004 State Centile	2004 Home Value Base	2004 Home Value Distribution (%) Less than $50,000	$50,000 to $89,999	$90,000 to $174,999	$175,000 to $399,999	$400,000 or More	2004 Median Home Value
18917	DUBLIN	27090	920	15.3	27.6	40.5	12.9	3.6	56260	68204	81	82	409	0.0	5.4	19.8	73.4	1.5	218275
18920	ERWINNA	38898	319	14.1	16.0	35.4	17.9	16.6	72241	91612	92	93	277	2.5	1.4	7.9	44.4	43.7	370339
18923	FOUNTAINVILLE	41608	140	5.0	15.0	42.1	26.4	11.4	83245	101374	96	97	128	3.1	0.0	9.4	73.4	14.1	276000
18925	FURLONG	46542	1092	7.8	12.0	29.9	22.2	28.2	100551	121547	98	98	1005	2.2	0.0	3.2	60.3	34.3	352128
18927	HILLTOWN	41397	42	14.3	14.3	45.2	11.9	14.3	71951	84004	92	93	39	0.0	0.0	5.1	79.5	15.4	248214
18929	JAMISON	36182	2912	4.6	10.8	35.5	30.2	19.0	98573	117566	98	98	2782	0.0	0.0	11.6	71.1	17.2	285326
18930	KINTNERSVILLE	33537	1058	11.9	18.5	38.3	20.4	10.9	71475	88385	92	93	912	0.6	0.2	11.7	62.6	24.9	276389
18932	LINE LEXINGTON	34442	208	13.9	13.0	42.3	19.2	11.5	75418	93519	93	95	176	0.0	1.1	7.4	79.0	12.5	277143
18933	LUMBERVILLE	71160	79	7.6	7.6	27.9	22.8	34.2	112271	136039	99	100	71	0.0	0.0	1.4	26.8	71.8	576389
18934	MECHANICSVILLE	71742	57	10.5	8.8	24.6	24.6	31.6	111038	129527	99	100	53	0.0	0.0	0.0	41.5	58.5	450000
18936	MONTGOMERYVILLE	9147	4	0.0	0.0	0.0	50.0	50.0	137500	175000	100	100	4	0.0	0.0	0.0	25.0	75.0	500000
18938	NEW HOPE	58295	5921	12.2	15.7	29.6	18.8	23.7	84077	104250	96	97	4921	0.6	0.0	8.8	46.1	44.5	369989
18940	NEWTOWN	46599	10784	6.3	13.6	31.6	24.3	24.2	96873	118861	98	98	9383	0.3	0.3	12.3	62.7	24.4	287874
18942	OTTSVILLE	39723	1178	9.8	24.8	35.0	15.2	15.3	66527	82820	89	91	968	0.1	1.1	9.4	56.2	33.2	313298
18944	PERKASIE	31298	8117	11.9	18.7	42.5	18.2	8.7	68642	83476	91	91	6739	0.3	0.4	18.9	69.3	11.1	226321
18947	PIPERSVILLE	35605	2294	9.0	17.6	35.8	23.0	14.6	80047	98878	95	96	2013	2.5	1.4	9.2	52.6	34.3	331046
18951	QUAKERTOWN	26006	12520	15.9	24.4	41.4	14.5	3.7	58909	71101	83	84	9977	6.6	2.7	31.7	54.5	4.5	191249
18954	RICHBORO	40609	3268	4.3	11.8	28.6	27.0	28.4	106923	128435	99	99	3175	0.0	0.5	1.6	71.8	26.2	332964
18955	RICHLANDTOWN	24004	524	15.1	28.6	42.8	9.5	4.0	53952	66148	78	79	361	0.0	0.3	49.9	47.7	2.2	174734
18960	SELLERSVILLE	27898	4419	14.4	24.2	39.8	15.3	6.3	60821	75118	85	87	3456	3.5	0.8	29.2	60.3	6.2	203530
18964	SOUDERTON	28803	4976	15.5	23.2	38.7	17.2	5.4	61948	76312	86	88	3458	0.5	0.7	31.9	64.0	3.0	199746
18966	SOUTHAMPTON	37595	14372	9.4	16.7	36.5	21.9	15.5	79695	99185	95	96	12478	0.2	0.9	13.0	75.5	10.4	263240
18969	TELFORD	28812	5844	16.5	19.0	42.5	15.7	6.3	64072	77903	88	89	4198	0.9	0.4	29.0	64.0	5.7	202471
18972	UPPER BLACK EDDY	32401	1529	13.5	21.9	39.2	16.0	9.4	64887	79048	88	90	1318	1.8	1.7	11.9	66.2	18.4	274551
18974	WARMINSTER	30306	14257	12.7	21.2	39.7	18.7	7.8	67090	81810	90	91	10957	0.5	1.7	11.7	80.3	5.8	223693
18976	WARRINGTON	31630	6273	8.2	16.3	41.5	22.6	11.5	78183	95354	94	95	5214	0.2	0.4	12.0	79.8	7.6	273035
18977	WASHINGTON CROSSING	67974	1468	6.1	9.1	23.4	22.6	38.9	122486	146979	99	100	1376	0.0	0.1	2.7	38.1	59.2	449219
19001	ABINGTON	31278	7008	12.9	20.5	39.6	17.9	9.1	67506	83702	90	91	5486	0.4	0.2	44.3	51.7	3.4	181656
19002	AMBLER	46337	11892	10.4	17.1	30.6	17.7	24.3	83597	107024	96	97	9195	0.9	1.0	14.5	54.3	29.3	306425
19003	ARDMORE	45565	5969	14.3	19.0	34.7	16.8	15.2	70618	87865	91	93	3576	0.8	1.1	28.1	56.6	13.5	213539
19004	BALA CYNWYD	56663	3856	11.1	13.6	27.0	18.9	29.5	95525	122597	98	98	3170	0.3	1.3	10.4	51.7	36.4	343455
19006	HUNTINGDON VALLEY	48193	7968	12.5	14.4	29.7	18.9	24.4	86144	108687	96	97	6473	0.6	0.3	8.0	72.1	19.0	293419
19007	BRISTOL	20863	8587	26.8	29.5	32.0	9.4	2.3	44900	54926	61	61	5236	1.3	6.3	68.3	22.5	1.6	140840
19008	BROOMALL	33027	7291	13.0	20.8	34.8	18.0	13.5	69279	86311	91	92	6129	0.1	0.9	7.7	84.5	6.8	243194
19010	BRYN MAWR	63002	8200	16.1	14.8	24.4	13.5	31.2	84551	110980	96	97	5115	0.6	1.7	12.7	31.9	53.1	434845
19012	CHELTENHAM	31914	2297	12.0	18.9	37.3	17.8	14.0	73804	91326	93	94	1983	1.3	0.3	33.0	62.9	2.5	196157
19013	CHESTER	15456	13630	44.1	28.5	20.9	5.0	1.6	29628	35873	11	5	6595	35.8	42.4	19.6	2.2	0.0	61013
19014	ASTON	29279	7691	12.6	19.6	42.5	18.8	6.5	67942	83893	90	91	6532	3.8	1.9	42.7	50.8	0.8	177447
19015	BROOKHAVEN	25762	6292	18.0	28.6	37.9	12.7	2.8	52937	65280	77	77	4708	2.5	21.5	53.9	21.9	0.2	131474
19018	CLIFTON HEIGHTS	26494	9792	19.9	27.4	37.8	12.0	2.9	52312	64781	76	75	6192	0.7	4.4	76.7	18.0	0.3	137878
19020	BENSALEM	27499	21624	17.0	24.5	37.9	15.6	5.0	59146	72620	84	85	12500	4.5	1.4	39.9	53.3	0.9	182360
19021	CROYDON	24172	3896	16.3	26.8	42.9	11.6	2.5	54805	67105	79	80	2850	1.9	3.9	71.7	21.8	0.8	150894
19022	CRUM LYNNE	20056	1543	28.8	33.6	29.2	7.3	1.1	40882	51162	49	48	870	3.3	26.3	62.4	7.5	0.5	104202
19023	DARBY	18050	7448	28.0	29.6	33.4	7.8	1.2	42706	52984	55	55	4865	6.2	54.3	37.0	2.3	0.2	82953
19025	DRESHER	46387	1885	8.8	9.4	26.1	21.9	33.7	109827	137183	99	99	1787	0.7	0.2	2.6	66.5	29.9	333856
19026	DREXEL HILL	31867	12960	16.2	24.7	34.9	16.0	8.3	60131	74840	84	86	8636	0.3	1.2	49.7	48.2	0.6	172797
19027	ELKINS PARK	41311	8216	14.3	21.9	31.8	16.9	15.2	68619	85949	91	91	5308	0.2	1.3	23.6	66.7	8.3	223523
19029	ESSINGTON	23262	1814	18.0	30.2	42.4	8.3	1.1	51587	64151	75	75	1314	0.6	6.3	79.9	12.3	0.8	127768
19030	FAIRLESS HILLS	28004	5334	17.5	21.9	38.5	15.4	6.7	62652	77541	87	89	4171	6.8	0.8	37.8	54.4	0.1	179484
19031	FLOURTOWN	48239	1569	6.1	19.4	30.9	24.7	18.9	87627	110380	97	97	1255	0.3	0.2	8.0	81.0	10.6	243839
19032	FOLCROFT	22129	2551	18.1	27.9	42.6	9.5	2.0	53248	65351	77	78	1891	0.0	21.4	74.6	3.0	1.1	105417
19033	FOLSOM	28882	2744	18.1	21.0	38.2	17.9	4.8	60312	75283	85	86	2290	0.4	0.6	63.9	33.7	1.4	161098
19034	FORT WASHINGTON	49678	2143	8.6	15.3	30.5	19.7	25.9	90201	115146	97	97	1691	1.0	1.0	5.3	63.9	28.8	321895
19035	GLADWYNE	128604	1459	5.8	7.6	13.8	11.4	61.5	205298	268240	100	100	1260	0.0	0.6	3.8	13.0	82.6	834112
19036	GLENOLDEN	24261	5433	20.3	27.9	37.4	12.2	2.3	51432	64084	75	74	4010	1.9	7.9	81.7	8.5	0.0	118040
19038	GLENSIDE	35428	11700	11.6	17.9	38.5	18.9	13.0	73969	91868	93	94	9507	0.6	0.7	26.8	66.4	5.6	208086
19040	HATBORO	29368	8618	14.6	25.8	38.3	15.9	5.4	62001	76370	86	88	5955	1.3	0.6	22.8	72.5	2.8	204232
19041	HAVERFORD	70327	2748	9.4	12.5	26.3	19.0	32.8	103482	129210	98	99	1843	0.6	0.4	11.5	37.7	49.9	399088
19043	HOLMES	24422	1262	15.7	29.2	39.4	13.0	2.7	53941	65860	78	78	904	0.0	3.4	71.2	25.3	0.0	144136
19044	HORSHAM	31459	5880	10.8	22.0	40.5	18.5	8.3	67860	83778	90	91	4150	1.3	0.4	28.5	64.3	5.5	197861
19046	JENKINTOWN	49487	7742	11.9	20.2	32.0	16.2	19.8	74062	93452	93	94	5651	0.2	2.3	22.7	54.8	20.1	241195
19047	LANGHORNE	32361	12067	10.0	16.9	38.2	23.2	11.7	77474	94387	94	95	9401	0.4	0.3	15.4	78.0	5.9	239353
19050	LANSDOWNE	28299	11768	18.0	27.0	36.9	13.0	5.1	54737	67706	79	79	7599	1.3	12.8	67.6	18.0	0.3	122180
19053	FEASTERVILLE TREVOSE	29991	10023	13.0	20.2	42.2	16.5	8.2	65514	80689	89	90	8364	5.5	2.4	23.3	66.1	2.8	198316
19054	LEVITTOWN	26208	6482	13.4	24.0	42.6	15.2	4.8	61983	76249	86	88	4904	1.4	0.4	65.5	32.2	0.5	163248
19055	LEVITTOWN	23622	4861	13.6	23.8	45.8	14.1	2.8	60898	74333	85	87	4237	0.8	0.0	88.3	11.0	0.0	150583
19056	LEVITTOWN	26071	6182	13.5	25.1	41.0	16.4	3.9	60571	74464	85	87	4261	1.3	0.5	38.1	59.6	0.5	184144
19057	LEVITTOWN	23025	5657	14.3	24.9	44.7	13.0	3.1	60231	73393	85	86	4742	1.6	2.8	68.8	26.4	0.4	156650
19061	MARCUS HOOK	28562	10348	18.2	19.8	36.7	17.1	8.3	63678	79265	88	89	7662	1.6	9.7	38.2	46.1	4.4	176302
19063	MEDIA	42718	15319	12.3	19.5	32.4	18.3	17.4	73322	92084	93	94	10817	0.8	1.4	19.6	60.0	18.2	246223
19064	SPRINGFIELD	33639	8935	10.2	18.6	38.2	22.3	10.8	76139	92855	94	95	8175	0.5	0.9	13.2	83.7	1.7	223233
19066	MERION STATION	63960	1998	5.3	8.6	26.1	20.2	39.9	123154	153192	99	100	1692	0.3	0.3	5.1	39.5	54.7	436697
19067	MORRISVILLE	45152	21022	10.2	17.6	31.4	19.4	21.4	82229	102708	96	96	16531	6.1	1.3	14.4	61.9	16.3	252151
19070	MORTON	29673	2775	16.0	23.5	38.6	16.2	5.8	61358	75791	86	88	2122	0.4	2.5	48.1	48.6	0.4	173768
19072	NARBERTH	63795	4055	9.5	14.3	29.9	16.6	29.7	91258	118488	97	98	2976	0.4	0.5	13.6	43.2	42.3	356929
19073	NEWTOWN SQUARE	57523	6916	10.0	15.6	29.9	17.6	27.0	87612	110639	97	97	5729	0.7	0.8	11.7	53.9	32.9	293984
19074	NORWOOD	26037	2259	18.0	27.1	37.5	13.5	3.9	54776	67947	79	79	1679	0.0	1.2	79.5	18.6	0.7	141326
19075	ORELAND	35442	2728	10.6	19.2	38.0	21.9	10.4	75249	92208	93	94	2358	0.2	0.3	14.8	81.1	3.6	218934
19076	PROSPECT PARK	24170	2550	18.2	27.7	40.2	11.3	2.6	53199	65388	77	78	1620	0.4	1.1	84.3	14.1	0.0	139773
19078	RIDLEY PARK	27180	4793	18.1	25.4	39.4	13.4	3.7	57126	69972	82	83	3397	0.5	1.8	67.6	29.9	0.2	152958
19079	SHARON HILL	20377	3441	29.9	27.9	31.8	8.0	2.4	43370	53493	57	57	2310	7.6	33.4	56.0	2.2	0.8	95897
19081	SWARTHMORE	42513	3827	15.2	16.7	30.9	19.9	17.3	76102	97451	94	95	2857	0.0	1.8	32.7	49.8	15.7	219139
19082	UPPER DARBY	20121	14901	28.2	31.5	29.5	9.0	2.0	41096	51136	50	49	8593	5.5	38.7	50.0	5.8	0.1	95435
19083	HAVERTOWN	33605	13649	11.6	18.5	36.7	21.3	11.9	74995	92248	93	94	11822	0.6	1.6	18.1	77.9	1.8	217428
19085	VILLANOVA	64774	1957	5.1	4.2	17.6	16.4	56.7	174619	219532	100	100	1777	0.0	0.1	1.0	16.7	82.3	695794
19086	WALLINGFORD	41033	4454	10.8	17.2	32.3	19.6	20.0	79610	102061	95	96	3837	0.2	4.5	24.5	60.3	10.6	232391
19087	WAYNE	59635	13345	9.3	13.7	26.1	21.1	29.8	101416	126808	98	98	10011	0.3	0.5	11.5	49.8	38.0	343184
19090	WILLOW GROVE	29707	7518	13.8	24.2	39.0	16.6	6.3	61999	77073	86	88	5349	0.7	1.5	34.7	61.5	1.7	188009
19094	WOODLYN	26683	1902	26.0	23.4	34.4	11.6	4.6	50506	63424	73	72	1279	0.3	2.7	67.8	28.5	0.7	150232
19095	WYNCOTE	43803	2957	14.2	18.1	32.7	19.3	15.7	76244	93218	94	95	1603	2.3	2.1	11.5	73.4	10.8	244157
19096	WYNNEWOOD	64018	4993	8.8	13.4	23.1	18.7	36.0	109341	139441	99	99	4116	0.2	0.8	5.0	54.2	39.8	347421
19102	PHILADELPHIA	45883	2580	24.6	30.2	22.4	12.5	10.3	45603	55223	63	63	414	0.0	8.7	38.2	31.2	22.0	189773
19103	PHILADELPHIA	57936	12809	30.8	25.0	23.3	8.5	12.4	43911	54919	58	58	3886	20.6	13.1	16.8	25.4	24.2	172612
19104	PHILADELPHIA	13438	17289	59.7	22.7	13.5	2.7	1.4	18092	21539	1	1	4264	46.2	26.8	17.7	8.8	0.6	53839
19106	PHILADELPHIA	74972	5187	14.1	20.7	30.6	15.9	18.6	69801	87307	91	92	2117	0.0	3.7	21.0	42.6	32.7	288130
	PENNSYLVANIA	25764		25.8	27.2	31.2	10.2	5.7	46988	57000				11.9	18.4	40.7	25.1	4.1	123516
	UNITED STATES	25866		24.7	27.1	30.8	10.9	6.5	48124	56710				10.9	15.0	33.7	30.1	10.4	145905

ZIP CODE #	POST OFFICE NAME	FINANCIAL SERVICES: Auto Loan	FINANCIAL SERVICES: Home Loan	FINANCIAL SERVICES: Invest-ments	FINANCIAL SERVICES: Retire-ment Plans	THE HOME: Home Improvements: Home Repair	THE HOME: Home Improvements: Lawn & Garden	THE HOME: Furnishings: Comput-ers & Hard-ware	THE HOME: Furnishings: Major Appli-ances	THE HOME: Furnishings: TV, Radio, Sound Equip-ment	THE HOME: Furnishings: Furni-ture	ENTERTAINMENT: Dine out/ Carry out	ENTERTAINMENT: Sports Equip-ment	ENTERTAINMENT: Fees & Tickets	ENTERTAINMENT: Toys & Games	ENTERTAINMENT: Travel	ENTERTAINMENT: Cable TV	PERSONAL: Apparel & Services	PERSONAL: Auto Repairs	PERSONAL: Health Insur-ance	PERSONAL: Pets & Supplies
18917	DUBLIN	96	81	96	91	78	84	95	89	93	97	119	109	90	110	88	87	116	96	80	100
18920	ERWINNA	123	149	168	148	148	156	137	137	129	137	163	155	145	165	142	129	161	134	131	150
18923	FOUNTAINVILLE	139	169	179	175	163	162	150	147	137	153	174	171	162	180	151	131	175	142	129	162
18925	FURLONG	166	203	236	201	201	212	183	183	172	185	217	206	198	221	191	172	216	178	175	201
18927	HILLTOWN	125	156	166	156	153	151	139	139	129	139	162	162	148	173	142	125	162	134	124	153
18929	JAMISON	155	184	189	191	177	175	164	161	150	169	191	188	175	195	164	142	190	156	140	178
18930	KINTNERSVILLE	114	141	150	141	139	137	126	126	117	126	147	147	134	157	129	113	147	121	112	139
18932	LINE LEXINGTON	119	136	150	139	135	137	129	128	122	128	153	151	133	156	130	118	151	127	119	141
18933	LUMBERVILLE	223	301	413	295	293	317	262	260	244	268	309	292	298	325	280	246	314	250	241	282
18934	MECHANICSVILLE	202	252	274	260	244	246	222	216	202	225	257	250	244	267	226	196	259	209	192	240
18936	MONTGOMERYVILLE	171	207	233	205	206	216	189	190	179	190	226	215	202	229	197	179	223	185	182	207
18938	NEW HOPE	174	207	248	204	206	221	188	191	181	192	227	212	202	227	197	183	225	186	186	210
18940	NEWTOWN	168	206	227	210	199	201	184	180	169	187	215	209	199	222	187	164	215	175	161	198
18942	OTTSVILLE	144	159	156	156	160	164	144	149	140	144	174	174	150	182	148	139	171	144	144	173
18944	PERKASIE	115	133	136	134	131	131	123	123	116	123	145	144	128	151	124	112	144	120	112	136
18947	PIPERSVILLE	141	168	176	171	163	165	150	149	139	152	176	172	160	181	152	134	175	144	134	165
18951	QUAKERTOWN	99	100	94	99	101	106	95	98	95	95	118	115	96	121	96	95	114	97	98	115
18954	RICHBORO	171	207	229	212	203	208	188	185	174	189	220	213	202	225	191	169	220	180	169	203
18955	RICHLANDTOWN	102	89	71	89	93	104	90	96	95	89	115	110	87	115	90	96	109	94	103	114
18960	SELLERSVILLE	101	111	113	111	110	112	105	105	101	105	126	124	107	129	105	98	124	104	99	118
18964	SOUDERTON	102	106	110	105	106	114	102	105	101	103	126	118	104	123	104	101	122	104	105	117
18966	SOUTHAMPTON	133	158	178	159	155	161	146	145	137	147	173	166	155	177	149	135	172	142	135	158
18969	TELFORD	106	113	113	114	113	116	108	109	104	108	130	128	109	132	108	102	127	108	104	124
18972	UPPER BLACK EDDY	112	122	118	120	123	127	111	115	109	111	135	135	115	140	114	108	132	112	113	135
18974	WARMINSTER	107	124	136	123	122	127	116	116	112	117	140	132	122	143	119	110	139	114	110	127
18976	WARRINGTON	122	144	153	148	140	138	131	130	122	133	154	153	138	159	132	116	153	127	114	143
18977	WASHINGTON CROSSING	222	288	369	284	282	301	255	253	238	259	301	286	283	313	269	239	303	245	237	276
19001	ABINGTON	103	124	147	123	122	126	117	115	112	116	140	133	123	147	120	110	139	114	107	125
19002	AMBLER	157	182	217	185	180	189	174	172	166	174	209	199	183	212	177	163	206	170	161	187
19003	ARDMORE	126	139	192	144	135	145	143	135	139	143	176	161	149	181	144	137	174	139	126	148
19004	BALA CYNWYD	173	215	271	208	212	229	193	196	185	197	233	216	210	238	204	189	232	190	190	213
19006	HUNTINGDON VALLEY	157	185	226	183	184	197	176	174	170	175	213	197	187	218	182	171	211	172	170	190
19007	BRISTOL	69	73	82	72	73	78	75	73	75	73	94	84	77	98	75	75	92	73	73	80
19008	BROOMALL	115	135	156	132	134	143	127	127	124	127	156	143	135	160	132	125	154	125	125	138
19010	BRYN MAWR	205	229	326	237	223	242	235	220	227	234	286	261	247	293	236	223	284	225	205	242
19012	CHELTENHAM	114	140	167	140	138	143	130	129	123	130	155	149	138	161	134	122	154	127	119	140
19013	CHESTER	56	50	60	48	49	57	55	54	60	56	74	61	56	72	55	61	72	56	58	62
19014	ASTON	101	119	131	117	117	121	111	110	107	111	134	127	117	140	114	106	133	108	105	121
19015	BROOKHAVEN	82	89	101	86	88	96	88	87	89	88	111	99	92	115	90	91	109	87	88	96
19018	CLIFTON HEIGHTS	80	86	100	86	85	92	87	85	87	86	109	98	90	112	88	87	107	86	84	93
19020	BENSALEM	91	99	120	101	97	102	99	96	97	99	122	113	102	126	99	96	121	97	91	106
19021	CROYDON	85	91	99	91	90	95	90	89	88	89	111	103	93	114	90	87	109	88	85	98
19022	CRUM LYNNE	63	64	68	61	64	72	67	65	70	64	86	74	69	90	67	71	83	66	69	72
19023	DARBY	66	67	75	65	66	73	70	68	72	69	90	77	72	93	70	73	88	69	70	76
19025	DRESHER	182	224	251	226	219	226	202	200	188	204	238	229	218	245	208	185	238	194	184	219
19026	DREXEL HILL	98	114	143	114	111	118	111	108	108	111	136	125	117	142	113	108	135	108	102	117
19027	ELKINS PARK	128	144	175	144	141	151	144	139	140	142	176	162	149	178	145	138	174	141	132	152
19029	ESSINGTON	73	80	84	75	80	89	79	78	81	76	101	87	83	109	81	84	98	76	84	86
19030	FAIRLESS HILLS	100	107	107	105	107	113	102	104	101	100	125	120	104	129	104	101	122	102	103	118
19031	FLOURTOWN	145	195	251	188	189	196	176	173	166	176	208	200	191	226	184	165	211	169	156	185
19032	FOLCROFT	76	89	97	86	88	93	85	84	83	83	104	95	90	111	87	83	102	82	82	91
19033	FOLSOM	95	110	123	106	109	117	105	104	103	104	129	118	111	134	108	105	127	102	104	114
19034	FORT WASHINGTON	180	206	247	210	204	213	200	197	190	199	239	230	207	242	202	186	236	196	184	214
19035	GLADWYNE	419	564	774	553	550	594	492	487	458	503	579	548	559	610	524	462	588	468	453	529
19036	GLENOLDEN	76	84	93	82	84	90	84	82	84	82	104	94	87	110	85	84	102	82	82	90
19038	GLENSIDE	117	140	169	140	138	143	133	131	127	133	160	152	140	167	136	126	159	130	122	142
19040	HATBORO	95	105	122	106	104	110	104	102	100	103	127	117	107	128	104	99	125	102	97	112
19041	HAVERFORD	232	263	353	271	259	277	261	252	250	262	315	295	275	320	264	245	313	254	235	276
19043	HOLMES	79	89	100	87	88	94	88	86	86	86	108	99	91	112	90	86	106	86	85	94
19044	HORSHAM	111	123	128	128	119	118	118	115	110	119	139	136	120	141	115	104	138	114	101	126
19046	JENKINTOWN	149	173	212	173	171	182	166	164	160	166	202	188	175	206	171	160	200	163	156	179
19047	LANGHORNE	120	137	154	141	135	138	131	128	124	131	157	151	137	160	132	120	155	127	117	141
19050	LANSDOWNE	90	95	111	97	93	99	98	94	96	97	121	111	99	121	97	94	118	96	90	104
19053	FEASTERVILLE TREVOSE	104	119	131	117	117	123	111	111	108	111	136	128	117	140	114	108	134	109	107	124
19054	LEVITTOWN	91	106	117	105	104	107	101	99	97	100	122	115	106	128	102	95	121	98	93	109
19055	LEVITTOWN	88	100	107	97	100	104	94	94	92	93	115	109	99	121	97	92	114	92	91	105
19056	LEVITTOWN	89	101	116	100	100	105	99	97	96	97	120	112	103	125	100	95	119	96	92	105
19057	LEVITTOWN	85	98	106	94	96	102	92	92	91	91	113	104	97	119	95	91	112	90	90	101
19061	MARCUS HOOK	102	114	125	114	112	117	110	108	107	109	135	125	115	139	111	106	133	107	104	119
19063	MEDIA	135	156	192	157	153	162	152	148	146	151	183	173	159	187	154	143	181	149	140	162
19064	SPRINGFIELD	115	137	155	134	136	144	128	128	123	127	154	144	135	158	133	124	152	125	124	139
19066	MERION STATION	228	307	420	301	299	322	268	265	249	274	315	298	303	332	285	251	320	255	246	288
19067	MORRISVILLE	151	176	204	178	172	179	166	163	158	167	199	190	176	205	168	155	198	161	150	179
19070	MORTON	98	111	126	111	109	115	107	106	104	107	131	122	112	135	109	103	129	105	101	116
19072	NARBERTH	179	217	318	221	209	224	209	200	202	212	255	233	227	271	216	201	257	200	184	218
19073	NEWTOWN SQUARE	178	221	277	218	217	233	201	200	191	203	240	226	219	248	210	191	240	195	190	218
19074	NORWOOD	84	98	111	96	96	102	94	92	92	93	116	106	99	122	96	92	114	91	90	101
19075	ORELAND	112	139	167	134	136	144	128	127	124	128	156	145	138	166	134	126	155	124	121	138
19076	PROSPECT PARK	77	86	98	86	86	90	86	84	84	84	105	98	89	110	87	83	104	84	80	91
19078	RIDLEY PARK	83	91	109	90	90	98	92	89	92	90	115	102	95	118	94	92	113	90	89	98
19079	SHARON HILL	71	71	77	69	71	79	74	73	76	73	95	82	75	95	74	77	92	73	76	81
19081	SWARTHMORE	146	168	198	166	166	179	161	159	157	160	197	182	170	202	166	158	194	158	156	175
19082	UPPER DARBY	67	70	87	73	70	73	75	72	73	74	92	86	75	92	74	70	90	74	67	78
19083	HAVERTOWN	109	140	171	134	136	143	128	126	122	127	153	144	137	164	133	122	153	123	118	136
19085	VILLANOVA	346	466	639	457	454	490	406	402	378	415	478	452	461	503	433	382	486	386	374	437
19086	WALLINGFORD	137	163	188	163	161	168	153	151	146	153	183	174	162	188	157	144	182	149	143	165
19087	WAYNE	182	220	292	224	215	228	209	203	199	211	251	235	225	262	215	197	251	201	188	221
19090	WILLOW GROVE	96	109	128	108	107	114	106	104	104	106	130	120	111	134	108	103	129	104	100	114
19094	WOODLYN	91	93	91	89	94	105	92	94	95	89	116	106	93	119	94	98	112	93	101	106
19095	WYNCOTE	122	138	170	138	135	146	136	132	133	136	168	151	143	171	139	133	166	133	128	145
19096	WYNNEWOOD	201	262	336	252	256	276	229	231	217	234	273	255	254	284	244	221	275	222	220	251
19102	PHILADELPHIA	75	73	133	83	69	77	85	76	87	86	110	93	88	115	84	86	109	81	71	85
19103	PHILADELPHIA	104	98	166	109	95	107	116	105	119	116	150	127	119	154	114	118	148	112	102	117
19104	PHILADELPHIA	42	31	38	32	30	36	45	39	47	42	58	48	40	53	40	45	55	44	39	44
19106	PHILADELPHIA	142	138	255	157	131	146	161	143	165	164	209	176	168	219	159	163	208	153	134	160
	PENNSYLVANIA	89	89	93	87	90	98	89	90	91	88	112	104	89	114	90	92	109	90	92	104
	UNITED STATES	100	100	100	100	100	100	100	100	100	100	100	100	100	100	100	100	100	100	100	100

PENNSYLVANIA
A 19107-19492

POPULATION CHANGE

# POST OFFICE NAME	COUNTY FIPS CODE	POPULATION 2000	2004	2009	% Rate	State Centile	HOUSEHOLDS 2000	2004	2009	% Annual Rate 2000-2004	2004 Average HH Size	FAMILIES 2000	2004	% Annual Rate 2000-2004
19107 PHILADELPHIA	101	11287	11854	11874	1.2	83	6029	6372	6479	1.3	1.48	1127	1205	1.6
19111 PHILADELPHIA	101	58563	58246	56911	-0.1	33	23908	24166	24014	0.3	2.36	14884	14948	0.1
19114 PHILADELPHIA	101	31043	30621	29777	-0.3	24	13356	13620	13582	0.5	2.22	8170	8221	0.2
19115 PHILADELPHIA	101	30795	30000	28968	-0.6	12	13209	13106	12880	-0.2	2.23	8458	8336	-0.3
19116 PHILADELPHIA	101	33617	32901	31858	-0.5	15	13059	13043	12873	0.0	2.46	9067	9014	-0.1
19118 PHILADELPHIA	101	9746	9486	9190	-0.6	12	4360	4317	4253	-0.2	2.03	2307	2277	-0.3
19119 PHILADELPHIA	101	28749	27759	26796	-0.8	7	11879	11706	11516	-0.3	2.26	7056	6905	-0.5
19120 PHILADELPHIA	101	67719	66735	64800	-0.3	23	21954	21758	21382	-0.2	3.06	16447	16246	-0.3
19121 PHILADELPHIA	101	35086	33790	32566	-0.9	6	12698	12510	12313	-0.4	2.63	7730	7561	-0.5
19122 PHILADELPHIA	101	19495	19329	18958	-0.2	29	5652	5801	5833	0.6	2.78	3736	3802	0.4
19123 PHILADELPHIA	101	9917	9270	8849	-1.6	0	4220	4041	3932	-1.0	2.11	1997	1874	-1.5
19124 PHILADELPHIA	101	63305	62784	61192	-0.2	30	22403	22363	22063	0.0	2.78	15151	15061	-0.1
19125 PHILADELPHIA	101	23710	22849	21982	-0.9	7	8544	8401	8239	-0.4	2.67	5521	5400	-0.5
19126 PHILADELPHIA	101	16699	16322	15815	-0.5	14	6007	5984	5903	-0.1	2.59	3945	3915	-0.2
19127 PHILADELPHIA	101	5789	6008	6017	0.9	76	2676	2869	2951	1.7	2.08	1100	1162	1.3
19128 PHILADELPHIA	101	35650	35160	34250	-0.3	23	15637	15773	15684	0.2	2.19	8490	8511	0.1
19129 PHILADELPHIA	101	12436	11894	11438	-1.0	4	5085	4991	4897	-0.4	2.15	2486	2414	-0.7
19130 PHILADELPHIA	101	22238	22492	22203	0.3	53	11321	11671	11734	0.7	1.83	3984	4099	0.7
19131 PHILADELPHIA	101	46797	46258	45100	-0.3	26	19027	19194	19051	0.2	2.24	10050	10050	0.0
19132 PHILADELPHIA	101	41027	38600	36747	-1.4	1	15355	14816	14418	-0.8	2.57	9712	9328	-0.9
19133 PHILADELPHIA	101	27045	24849	23448	-2.0	0	8349	7861	7576	-1.4	3.13	6101	5720	-1.5
19134 PHILADELPHIA	101	59382	57083	54811	-0.9	5	20336	19693	19153	-0.8	2.87	13969	13463	-0.9
19135 PHILADELPHIA	101	30490	29390	28249	-0.9	7	12038	11810	11563	-0.5	2.47	7717	7533	-0.6
19136 PHILADELPHIA	101	40614	39122	37758	-0.9	6	13627	13296	12988	-0.6	2.41	8659	8407	-0.7
19137 PHILADELPHIA	101	8023	7842	7612	-0.5	14	3170	3164	3131	0.0	2.47	2058	2045	-0.2
19138 PHILADELPHIA	101	34718	33124	31710	-1.1	3	12425	12172	11910	-0.5	2.69	8952	8736	-0.6
19139 PHILADELPHIA	101	42835	40611	38821	-1.3	2	17023	16475	16056	-0.8	2.41	10030	9648	-0.9
19140 PHILADELPHIA	101	57258	54673	52523	-1.1	3	19028	18508	18111	-0.7	2.89	13106	12729	-0.7
19141 PHILADELPHIA	101	35662	33919	32494	-1.2	3	12362	12017	11734	-0.7	2.63	7989	7717	-0.8
19142 PHILADELPHIA	101	28946	28551	27742	-0.3	24	9856	9783	9623	-0.2	2.90	6965	6884	-0.3
19143 PHILADELPHIA	101	72111	68124	64988	-1.3	2	26965	26104	25440	-0.8	2.56	17098	16466	-0.9
19144 PHILADELPHIA	101	45429	43690	41997	-0.9	6	18794	18445	18061	-0.4	2.28	10013	9760	-0.6
19145 PHILADELPHIA	101	45859	44239	42580	-0.8	7	18175	17826	17464	-0.5	2.47	11712	11449	-0.5
19146 PHILADELPHIA	101	37603	37028	35955	-0.4	22	16037	16055	15870	0.0	2.28	8025	7994	-0.1
19147 PHILADELPHIA	101	33046	32584	31656	-0.3	23	16341	16499	16376	0.2	1.96	6709	6725	0.1
19148 PHILADELPHIA	101	49671	48787	47276	-0.4	20	19581	19579	19323	0.0	2.48	12510	12447	0.1
19149 PHILADELPHIA	101	48683	48598	47518	0.0	36	19068	19231	19076	0.2	2.52	12750	12798	0.1
19150 PHILADELPHIA	101	25097	24021	23017	-1.0	4	9923	9781	9605	-0.3	2.45	6914	6785	-0.4
19151 PHILADELPHIA	101	31184	30397	29385	-0.6	12	11958	11783	11555	-0.4	2.54	7809	7649	-0.5
19152 PHILADELPHIA	101	31586	30755	29711	-0.6	12	13365	13196	12947	-0.3	2.24	8228	8077	-0.4
19153 PHILADELPHIA	101	12483	12389	12105	-0.2	30	5295	5356	5334	0.3	2.31	3302	3326	0.2
19154 PHILADELPHIA	101	35606	34479	33247	-0.8	8	12868	12837	12683	-0.1	2.66	9669	9612	-0.1
19301 PAOLI	029	6692	6742	7095	0.2	47	2757	2821	3012	0.5	2.34	1827	1857	0.4
19310 ATGLEN	029	2813	2935	3135	1.0	79	930	982	1061	1.3	2.99	735	770	1.1
19311 AVONDALE	029	6062	6686	7308	2.3	95	1781	1968	2168	2.4	3.21	1413	1552	2.2
19312 BERWYN	029	11644	11860	12506	0.4	61	4373	4515	4823	0.8	2.58	3293	3379	0.6
19317 CHADDS FORD	029	8943	9388	9858	1.2	83	3362	3581	3811	1.5	2.59	2629	2796	1.5
19319 CHEYNEY	045	203	219	230	1.8	91	68	78	85	3.3	1.63	57	51	-2.6
19320 COATESVILLE	029	42528	45498	49068	1.6	89	15045	16348	17883	2.0	2.70	11079	11972	1.8
19330 COCHRANVILLE	029	4535	4904	5313	1.9	92	1532	1683	1848	2.2	2.84	1216	1324	2.0
19333 DEVON	029	6685	6972	7459	1.0	79	2911	3131	3426	1.7	2.18	1781	1864	1.1
19335 DOWNINGTOWN	029	40766	43587	47088	1.6	89	14223	15426	16877	1.9	2.80	10939	11813	1.8
19341 EXTON	029	14150	15380	16743	2.0	92	5907	6553	7244	2.5	2.34	3876	4259	2.2
19342 GLEN MILLS	045	13435	14833	15657	2.4	95	4372	4929	5296	2.9	2.69	3487	3926	2.8
19343 GLENMOORE	029	8349	8577	9073	0.6	69	2626	2741	2941	1.0	3.02	2208	2289	0.9
19344 HONEY BROOK	029	9728	10349	11104	1.5	88	3299	3556	3864	1.8	2.82	2523	2697	1.6
19348 KENNETT SQUARE	029	18521	19900	21505	1.7	90	6641	7232	7919	2.0	2.67	4736	5109	1.8
19350 LANDENBERG	029	9404	10505	11587	2.6	97	3040	3418	3800	2.8	3.04	2617	2926	2.7
19352 LINCOLN UNIVERSITY	029	7720	8568	9372	2.5	96	1982	2257	2527	3.1	3.23	1696	1919	3.0
19355 MALVERN	029	23271	24799	26672	1.5	89	8381	9074	9903	1.9	2.61	6024	6471	1.7
19362 NOTTINGHAM	029	5290	5819	6315	2.3	95	1837	2046	2246	2.6	2.84	1468	1626	2.4
19363 OXFORD	029	13207	15388	17340	3.7	99	4606	5385	6111	3.8	2.82	3413	3988	3.7
19365 PARKESBURG	029	6298	6571	7016	1.0	79	2256	2385	2576	1.3	2.75	1664	1745	1.1
19372 THORNDALE	029	2453	2655	2882	1.9	92	938	1025	1125	2.1	2.58	693	754	2.0
19373 THORNTON	045	3912	4064	4138	0.9	77	771	821	852	1.5	3.43	676	716	1.4
19374 TOUGHKENAMON	029	849	982	1099	3.5	99	228	263	296	3.4	3.54	178	204	3.3
19380 WEST CHESTER	029	44971	47504	50945	1.3	85	17191	18397	19978	1.6	2.53	11746	12508	1.5
19382 WEST CHESTER	029	51349	53572	57012	1.0	79	18010	19141	20762	1.4	2.53	12006	12670	1.3
19383 WEST CHESTER	029	870	904	957	0.9	77	182	191	206	1.1	4.06	140	147	1.2
19390 WEST GROVE	029	10309	11430	12552	2.5	96	3412	3830	4258	2.8	2.92	2701	3003	2.5
19401 NORRISTOWN	091	37975	38973	39885	0.6	68	14913	15458	15954	0.9	2.43	8887	9107	0.6
19403 NORRISTOWN	091	41333	41759	42315	0.2	51	15657	16081	16507	0.6	2.46	10707	10923	0.5
19405 BRIDGEPORT	091	4988	4995	5058	0.0	40	2180	2223	2279	0.5	2.24	1224	1234	0.2
19406 KING OF PRUSSIA	091	21478	22397	23100	1.0	79	9504	10134	10604	1.5	2.19	5567	5873	1.3
19422 BLUE BELL	091	18333	18679	18970	0.4	61	7001	7261	7465	0.9	2.54	5136	5286	0.7
19425 CHESTER SPRINGS	029	7974	8651	9388	1.9	92	2833	3113	3419	2.2	2.75	2241	2445	2.1
19426 COLLEGEVILLE	091	30218	33375	35405	2.4	95	9312	10547	11382	3.0	2.72	7142	8048	2.9
19428 CONSHOHOCKEN	091	16508	16854	17187	0.5	63	7015	7275	7504	0.9	2.31	4119	4232	0.6
19435 FREDERICK	091	361	367	372	0.4	59	133	139	142	1.0	2.63	106	110	0.9
19436 GWYNEDD	091	497	516	528	0.9	76	295	314	327	1.5	1.57	211	201	-1.1
19438 HARLEYSVILLE	091	21316	22618	23463	1.4	86	7557	8154	8558	1.8	2.76	5929	6362	1.7
19440 HATFIELD	091	17482	18299	18873	1.1	81	6524	6947	7257	1.5	2.60	4521	4745	1.1
19444 LAFAYETTE HILL	091	10462	10617	10754	0.4	57	3834	3963	4067	0.8	2.56	2828	2901	0.6
19446 LANSDALE	091	50857	52595	54082	0.8	74	19579	20611	21473	1.2	2.51	13531	14136	1.0
19453 MONT CLARE	091	1134	1249	1318	2.3	95	549	612	651	2.6	2.04	379	418	2.3
19454 NORTH WALES	091	24400	25457	26180	1.0	79	9556	10036	10392	1.2	2.52	6861	7148	1.0
19460 PHOENIXVILLE	029	34083	36240	39017	1.5	87	13358	14401	15729	1.8	2.45	8821	9471	1.7
19462 PLYMOUTH MEETING	091	13625	14221	14747	1.0	80	5417	5765	6063	1.5	2.42	3839	4051	1.3
19464 POTTSTOWN	091	42303	44256	45723	1.1	81	16600	17585	18352	1.4	2.49	11205	11814	1.3
19465 POTTSTOWN	029	14131	14984	16067	1.4	86	5426	5855	6370	1.8	2.53	3962	4240	1.7
19468 ROYERSFORD	091	21665	24243	25892	2.7	97	8260	9391	10152	3.1	2.55	5747	6528	3.0
19473 SCHWENKSVILLE	091	13462	14544	15200	1.8	91	4785	5235	5525	2.1	2.70	3563	3881	2.0
19475 SPRING CITY	029	9578	10463	11442	2.1	93	3639	4020	4452	2.4	2.50	2528	2786	2.3
19477 SPRING HOUSE	091	30	35	38	3.7	99	10	12	13	4.4	2.75	6	7	3.7
19492 ZIEGLERVILLE	091	295	322	338	2.1	93	127	141	150	2.5	2.27	99	109	2.3
PENNSYLVANIA					0.3					0.7	2.44			0.6
UNITED STATES					1.2					1.3	2.58			1.1

# ZIP CODE	POST OFFICE NAME	RACE (%) White 2000	White 2004	Black 2000	Black 2004	Asian/Pacific 2000	Asian/Pacific 2004	% Hispanic Origin 2000	% Hispanic Origin 2004	2004 AGE DISTRIBUTION (%) 0-4	5-9	10-14	15-19	20-24	25-44	45-64	65-84	85+	18+	MEDIAN AGE 2004	% 2004 Males	% 2004 Females
19107	PHILADELPHIA	61.7	55.1	12.1	14.6	22.3	26.2	3.9	4.3	1.6	1.1	1.1	5.6	20.7	46.2	15.1	7.1	1.5	95.4	30.2	54.7	45.3
19111	PHILADELPHIA	83.9	80.0	6.1	7.7	4.9	6.3	6.3	7.5	6.1	5.8	6.4	6.3	6.2	27.3	22.7	15.3	4.0	77.8	39.5	46.8	53.2
19114	PHILADELPHIA	88.0	84.5	6.8	8.9	2.6	3.5	3.4	4.1	5.6	5.2	5.1	4.9	5.8	27.9	24.2	18.1	3.2	81.1	41.7	46.8	53.2
19115	PHILADELPHIA	87.0	83.2	3.5	4.7	7.1	9.3	3.3	3.9	4.2	4.3	4.8	4.9	5.1	22.6	26.3	22.9	4.9	83.8	48.0	45.7	54.3
19116	PHILADELPHIA	84.6	80.7	4.0	5.2	8.4	10.6	3.2	3.8	5.3	5.2	5.7	5.9	6.3	27.1	26.2	15.6	2.8	80.2	41.0	47.3	52.7
19118	PHILADELPHIA	79.4	76.3	15.3	17.6	2.4	3.0	2.3	2.6	5.2	5.0	4.9	5.9	5.8	26.5	28.3	14.9	3.5	82.1	42.7	42.2	57.8
19119	PHILADELPHIA	27.4	23.2	67.8	71.9	1.0	1.2	1.9	1.9	5.3	5.7	6.6	6.4	5.5	26.3	27.4	14.2	2.6	78.3	41.4	43.5	56.5
19120	PHILADELPHIA	25.9	22.0	40.9	43.5	14.2	15.2	23.6	23.8	8.4	8.4	10.0	9.1	7.9	29.2	19.7	6.5	0.8	67.5	29.7	46.8	53.2
19121	PHILADELPHIA	2.0	1.7	95.7	96.1	0.6	0.6	1.5	1.5	7.8	8.3	9.8	8.9	7.2	25.8	19.8	10.6	1.8	68.7	32.0	44.6	55.5
19122	PHILADELPHIA	22.7	19.8	49.6	52.5	2.1	2.3	32.7	31.9	7.0	7.1	8.4	15.9	12.4	22.2	16.8	9.1	1.1	73.0	24.7	44.7	55.3
19123	PHILADELPHIA	28.2	25.8	62.5	64.2	1.8	2.1	10.8	11.5	6.0	6.3	7.2	6.3	7.1	32.2	22.1	10.9	1.9	76.7	35.3	48.6	51.5
19124	PHILADELPHIA	54.9	49.2	25.9	29.3	4.4	5.1	18.8	20.8	8.3	8.1	9.2	8.2	7.4	28.5	19.5	9.3	1.4	69.3	31.4	47.4	52.6
19125	PHILADELPHIA	80.6	78.0	4.4	5.2	5.3	6.1	11.5	12.6	7.6	7.4	8.1	7.9	7.2	29.2	22.3	9.3	1.2	72.1	33.3	49.2	50.8
19126	PHILADELPHIA	11.7	9.2	80.5	82.8	3.8	4.2	2.8	2.8	5.9	6.1	7.6	7.4	6.9	25.9	25.1	12.9	2.2	75.9	38.0	45.2	54.8
19127	PHILADELPHIA	93.6	91.9	3.4	4.2	1.4	2.0	1.1	1.4	3.8	3.6	4.2	4.3	13.8	40.0	18.9	10.1	1.4	86.3	32.1	50.4	49.6
19128	PHILADELPHIA	88.9	85.9	6.6	8.5	2.5	3.2	1.9	2.2	4.9	4.8	5.2	5.2	7.1	32.9	24.4	12.8	2.7	82.0	38.4	47.1	52.9
19129	PHILADELPHIA	53.8	50.5	40.3	42.5	3.2	4.1	2.2	2.5	4.5	4.6	5.8	10.9	11.3	30.6	21.1	10.0	1.2	81.8	31.8	45.0	55.0
19130	PHILADELPHIA	59.3	54.9	30.6	33.9	3.5	4.3	7.6	8.1	4.2	3.5	4.3	4.6	9.4	39.7	21.4	10.8	2.1	85.3	34.9	48.3	51.7
19131	PHILADELPHIA	17.9	15.5	76.8	78.9	2.4	2.9	1.7	1.7	5.4	5.6	6.6	8.7	8.7	25.9	21.6	13.9	3.7	78.7	36.3	43.5	56.5
19132	PHILADELPHIA	1.0	0.7	97.0	97.3	0.3	0.3	1.3	1.2	7.5	7.7	9.3	7.9	6.6	25.7	21.8	12.0	1.5	70.7	34.6	43.9	56.1
19133	PHILADELPHIA	14.8	13.8	43.8	44.7	0.6	0.6	55.9	55.2	9.3	9.4	11.0	9.5	7.6	26.0	19.7	6.9	0.6	64.4	27.5	46.5	53.5
19134	PHILADELPHIA	58.3	54.6	14.1	15.8	2.1	2.4	33.2	34.9	9.9	9.3	9.8	8.3	7.6	27.7	18.4	7.9	1.2	65.9	28.6	47.3	52.7
19135	PHILADELPHIA	92.3	90.2	3.5	4.6	0.9	1.3	3.8	4.7	6.7	6.5	7.2	7.0	6.7	28.7	22.5	12.7	2.0	75.3	36.6	48.2	51.8
19136	PHILADELPHIA	76.7	73.5	18.0	20.3	1.3	1.6	5.0	5.6	5.4	5.3	5.8	6.7	9.4	32.0	20.8	12.2	2.3	80.0	35.9	53.8	46.2
19137	PHILADELPHIA	95.5	94.4	1.1	1.4	0.5	0.6	2.8	3.4	5.8	5.9	7.3	7.2	6.6	27.4	23.8	13.6	2.4	76.5	38.3	47.7	52.3
19138	PHILADELPHIA	1.6	1.2	95.6	96.2	0.3	0.3	1.2	1.1	6.5	7.2	8.8	7.9	6.4	24.9	25.9	11.4	1.1	72.5	36.4	43.8	56.2
19139	PHILADELPHIA	3.1	2.5	93.4	94.1	1.1	1.2	1.2	1.2	7.1	7.3	8.7	8.0	6.6	25.9	21.2	12.8	2.4	72.0	35.2	43.7	56.3
19140	PHILADELPHIA	12.8	11.8	61.4	61.9	1.3	1.3	34.0	34.3	8.6	8.5	9.8	8.9	7.7	25.8	20.9	8.7	1.0	67.7	30.2	46.1	54.0
19141	PHILADELPHIA	9.4	8.1	83.3	84.7	3.8	3.9	2.9	2.7	6.3	6.5	7.9	10.1	10.0	24.5	22.3	10.3	2.1	74.6	32.7	44.7	55.3
19142	PHILADELPHIA	31.9	26.3	54.7	59.3	10.3	11.3	2.3	2.3	8.8	8.8	10.4	8.9	7.2	28.6	18.5	7.8	1.1	66.4	29.6	46.4	53.6
19143	PHILADELPHIA	5.8	4.6	90.4	91.6	1.2	1.3	1.4	1.4	7.3	7.3	8.6	7.9	7.3	26.5	22.4	11.6	1.3	72.2	34.2	44.3	55.7
19144	PHILADELPHIA	14.1	11.4	81.6	84.3	1.0	1.2	1.7	1.7	7.2	7.0	7.7	7.5	7.6	28.7	22.4	10.0	1.8	73.7	34.0	45.1	54.9
19145	PHILADELPHIA	50.6	47.7	38.4	40.2	8.6	9.5	1.8	2.0	6.4	6.6	7.8	7.0	6.2	26.6	23.0	14.3	2.2	74.9	37.5	45.3	54.7
19146	PHILADELPHIA	25.9	22.9	67.7	70.3	3.5	3.9	2.5	2.5	6.8	6.5	7.5	7.0	7.8	31.2	21.2	10.3	1.8	75.1	33.7	47.1	52.9
19147	PHILADELPHIA	67.9	63.0	16.4	18.6	11.4	13.7	4.8	5.3	4.1	3.7	4.3	4.8	7.6	38.1	24.1	11.5	1.9	85.3	37.4	49.7	50.4
19148	PHILADELPHIA	73.1	69.1	10.9	12.4	11.2	13.3	4.9	5.4	6.0	6.1	7.1	6.4	6.4	27.9	23.8	14.1	2.3	76.9	38.0	46.7	53.3
19149	PHILADELPHIA	81.5	77.3	6.8	8.5	5.7	7.1	7.6	8.9	7.1	6.9	7.4	6.7	6.3	29.6	21.1	12.7	2.3	74.6	36.2	47.2	52.8
19150	PHILADELPHIA	2.2	1.6	95.3	96.1	0.2	0.2	1.1	1.0	5.6	6.4	7.2	6.8	5.8	25.0	31.1	11.3	0.8	76.7	40.0	43.7	56.3
19151	PHILADELPHIA	23.0	19.1	71.9	75.7	1.8	2.0	1.9	1.9	7.1	7.0	8.1	8.3	7.5	27.7	21.7	10.9	1.8	73.0	34.9	45.0	55.0
19152	PHILADELPHIA	87.3	83.9	4.1	5.3	5.0	6.5	4.7	5.7	5.1	4.8	5.0	4.9	4.9	24.4	23.3	21.6	6.0	82.1	45.6	45.7	54.3
19153	PHILADELPHIA	36.1	30.3	59.1	64.7	1.9	2.1	1.9	2.0	6.1	6.1	6.7	6.5	6.7	27.6	26.5	12.5	1.4	77.2	38.2	45.9	54.1
19154	PHILADELPHIA	89.5	86.5	5.6	7.4	2.3	3.1	3.2	3.9	6.7	6.5	6.6	6.0	6.4	29.9	24.5	12.4	1.0	76.5	37.1	48.7	51.3
19301	PAOLI	91.5	90.0	4.4	4.9	3.1	3.9	0.9	1.1	5.7	6.3	6.6	5.7	4.2	24.6	28.4	16.0	2.6	77.6	43.2	47.8	52.2
19310	ATGLEN	92.0	90.7	5.4	6.3	0.2	0.3	3.0	3.5	8.2	8.5	8.8	7.3	6.5	28.8	22.5	8.7	0.8	69.7	33.6	49.5	50.5
19311	AVONDALE	83.8	82.3	5.7	6.1	0.8	1.0	24.0	25.9	8.5	8.3	8.1	6.8	6.7	32.6	21.2	7.2	0.6	70.7	33.3	54.2	45.8
19312	BERWYN	93.2	91.9	2.7	3.1	3.1	4.0	1.0	1.2	6.1	7.1	7.8	6.3	3.9	21.5	30.0	15.6	1.7	74.7	43.4	48.3	51.8
19317	CHADDS FORD	95.0	93.7	1.2	1.5	2.4	3.2	2.8	3.3	5.6	6.7	7.6	6.4	4.2	22.9	32.1	13.3	1.3	75.9	43.1	49.3	50.7
19319	CHEYNEY	55.2	51.1	38.9	42.5	2.0	2.3	3.5	3.2	5.5	5.5	5.5	27.9	12.3	21.9	15.5	5.0	0.9	67.6	22.3	59.4	40.6
19320	COATESVILLE	73.4	72.1	22.3	23.4	0.5	0.6	4.5	4.7	7.3	7.4	7.9	7.2	5.5	27.3	25.1	10.8	1.5	72.5	37.3	49.5	50.5
19330	COCHRANVILLE	95.0	94.1	1.8	2.1	0.4	0.5	5.2	6.0	7.0	7.5	8.5	6.7	5.1	27.8	26.6	9.9	1.0	72.7	37.8	50.5	49.5
19333	DEVON	90.2	88.7	2.4	2.7	6.2	7.4	1.3	1.5	6.0	6.5	6.7	6.0	4.3	28.1	27.1	13.3	2.0	76.5	40.4	47.7	52.3
19335	DOWNINGTOWN	91.1	89.8	4.9	5.5	2.2	2.8	1.8	2.0	7.6	8.0	8.5	7.2	5.5	28.7	26.4	7.1	1.0	70.9	36.6	49.2	50.8
19341	EXTON	91.2	89.5	2.9	3.3	4.3	5.5	1.5	1.7	6.6	6.5	7.0	5.5	5.0	33.4	25.9	9.1	0.9	76.3	37.0	48.6	51.4
19342	GLEN MILLS	86.8	85.1	9.4	10.3	2.1	2.7	1.4	1.6	6.5	7.3	7.5	11.3	5.4	22.6	25.7	11.9	1.8	71.3	38.3	51.0	49.0
19343	GLENMOORE	96.8	96.1	1.6	1.9	0.8	1.1	1.1	1.3	7.2	8.8	8.9	7.8	4.6	26.1	29.2	6.7	0.7	69.7	38.0	50.6	49.5
19344	HONEY BROOK	97.2	96.7	1.2	1.4	0.3	0.3	1.0	1.2	7.6	7.8	8.3	7.1	6.2	27.4	22.4	10.0	3.3	71.9	36.2	48.8	51.2
19348	KENNETT SQUARE	86.5	85.1	4.4	4.7	1.7	2.1	14.9	16.2	6.6	7.1	7.5	6.5	5.4	26.3	25.4	11.5	3.7	74.5	39.3	49.6	50.4
19350	LANDENBERG	95.1	94.1	1.5	1.8	1.3	1.7	4.6	5.4	6.5	8.0	10.0	7.9	4.6	24.6	30.6	7.2	0.5	69.9	39.1	51.0	49.0
19352	LINCOLN UNIVERSITY	78.5	78.5	18.7	18.2	0.5	0.6	3.0	3.4	7.1	7.6	8.8	13.3	13.7	23.3	21.1	4.7	0.4	71.5	24.9	49.0	51.0
19355	MALVERN	92.8	91.3	2.6	2.9	3.3	4.2	1.5	1.7	6.0	7.0	7.2	6.7	4.9	25.5	28.2	12.6	1.9	75.5	41.0	47.4	52.6
19362	NOTTINGHAM	95.7	95.0	1.5	1.8	0.3	0.3	3.4	3.9	7.8	7.9	8.4	7.1	6.0	29.3	24.2	8.4	0.9	71.5	35.0	50.5	49.5
19363	OXFORD	87.8	86.8	6.1	6.6	0.5	0.6	8.9	9.5	8.6	8.1	8.1	7.1	6.2	28.3	22.0	9.9	1.8	70.7	34.8	49.8	50.2
19365	PARKESBURG	92.1	91.0	5.9	6.8	0.3	0.4	2.5	2.8	6.9	7.1	8.5	7.4	6.0	28.5	23.7	10.8	1.2	72.6	36.5	49.0	51.0
19372	THORNDALE	87.0	84.9	8.3	9.5	2.5	3.1	3.0	3.5	7.4	7.6	7.0	5.5	4.6	33.2	24.7	9.1	0.9	74.2	36.8	47.9	52.1
19373	THORNTON	77.6	73.3	19.4	23.2	1.1	1.4	1.7	1.9	4.9	5.7	6.6	7.3	8.7	35.6	23.8	6.6	0.7	78.8	35.9	61.6	38.4
19374	TOUGHKENAMON	74.2	72.0	5.2	5.6	0.9	1.0	39.6	43.0	10.4	9.5	7.4	6.6	7.2	35.1	17.5	5.5	0.7	69.0	30.6	55.6	44.4
19380	WEST CHESTER	88.7	87.2	6.5	7.2	2.5	3.1	3.3	3.6	6.7	7.0	7.0	6.3	5.3	29.1	25.2	11.7	1.5	74.9	38.1	49.1	50.9
19382	WEST CHESTER	88.5	86.9	7.0	7.8	2.6	3.3	2.7	2.9	5.2	5.6	6.2	10.0	11.6	26.4	24.9	8.9	1.4	79.1	34.7	48.7	51.3
19383	WEST CHESTER	93.2	91.7	4.3	5.0	1.8	2.3	1.2	1.3	5.9	6.9	7.7	7.0	7.1	28.5	24.7	9.6	2.7	75.2	36.2	45.2	54.8
19390	WEST GROVE	89.2	88.1	3.8	4.3	0.3	0.4	11.1	12.1	7.4	7.9	8.5	6.8	5.5	29.1	23.5	9.8	1.5	71.5	36.8	50.4	49.6
19401	NORRISTOWN	60.0	56.9	29.9	32.0	3.3	4.0	8.9	9.4	6.5	6.3	6.7	6.2	7.3	30.6	22.3	11.9	2.1	76.7	36.2	48.4	51.6
19403	NORRISTOWN	87.8	85.7	6.8	7.7	3.8	4.8	1.7	2.0	5.8	6.2	6.2	5.9	5.0	30.6	26.1	12.8	1.4	78.0	39.7	50.4	49.6
19405	BRIDGEPORT	92.2	90.9	2.5	2.8	2.3	3.0	3.6	4.0	5.2	5.0	5.6	5.3	6.4	33.7	24.0	12.9	1.9	81.2	38.3	49.3	50.7
19406	KING OF PRUSSIA	83.5	80.4	4.4	4.9	9.8	12.3	1.9	2.1	5.2	5.2	4.9	4.8	5.3	35.5	22.9	14.6	1.6	81.7	38.3	49.5	50.5
19422	BLUE BELL	86.1	83.6	5.0	5.5	7.8	9.7	1.4	1.6	5.7	6.2	7.3	6.7	4.9	23.5	29.9	13.5	2.4	76.4	42.5	47.9	52.1
19425	CHESTER SPRINGS	96.1	95.3	1.3	1.5	1.6	2.0	1.0	1.1	7.8	8.9	8.7	6.0	3.5	26.7	29.7	7.9	0.8	70.6	39.5	49.6	50.5
19426	COLLEGEVILLE	85.3	84.5	10.2	10.2	2.3	2.9	2.3	2.4	7.9	7.8	6.7	5.5	5.9	35.9	22.5	6.8	1.1	74.7	35.7	54.2	45.8
19428	CONSHOHOCKEN	89.3	88.0	5.8	6.4	3.4	4.2	1.3	1.5	5.5	5.3	5.9	5.6	6.9	34.0	22.7	12.3	1.7	79.8	36.9	49.0	51.0
19435	FREDERICK	98.3	98.4	0.3	0.3	0.6	0.8	0.3	0.3	5.2	5.7	5.7	6.3	4.9	27.0	30.8	12.8	1.6	80.1	42.5	50.7	49.3
19436	GWYNEDD	89.9	88.0	2.8	3.1	6.0	7.8	1.2	1.2	5.0	6.0	7.2	6.8	5.4	21.7	31.2	13.2	3.5	77.5	43.7	46.1	53.9
19438	HARLEYSVILLE	93.3	91.9	2.7	3.2	2.7	3.4	1.3	1.5	7.9	8.1	8.2	6.8	5.3	29.4	24.7	8.4	1.2	71.2	36.5	48.5	51.5
19440	HATFIELD	82.9	79.7	3.3	3.7	10.6	13.2	2.5	2.7	6.6	6.5	6.9	6.4	6.1	29.4	25.1	10.9	2.1	75.7	37.7	49.9	50.2
19444	LAFAYETTE HILL	94.0	92.7	2.6	3.0	2.8	3.6	0.9	1.0	6.9	7.4	6.8	5.3	3.8	26.9	26.0	13.6	3.3	75.3	40.6	47.3	52.7
19446	LANSDALE	87.3	85.0	3.5	3.9	7.3	9.0	2.0	2.2	6.3	6.7	7.0	6.1	5.2	28.6	26.2	11.4	2.5	76.0	39.2	48.1	51.9
19453	MONT CLARE	93.1	91.8	2.7	3.0	3.3	4.2	1.8	1.9	7.5	7.8	7.5	5.7	4.8	32.4	25.3	8.1	1.0	73.7	37.9	48.9	51.1
19454	NORTH WALES	85.4	82.6	4.5	5.1	8.6	10.8	1.3	1.4	7.6	7.9	7.7	6.1	4.6	29.1	25.0	10.7	1.4	72.8	38.3	48.4	51.6
19460	PHOENIXVILLE	91.3	89.9	4.4	5.0	2.5	3.1	2.0	2.2	6.6	6.8	6.8	6.3	5.7	30.2	25.0	11.1	1.5	75.9	38.3	49.0	51.0
19462	PLYMOUTH MEETING	90.8	88.8	3.7	4.2	4.4	5.8	1.1	1.3	4.5	5.2	6.1	5.4	4.9	25.7	27.4	18.9	2.0	80.7	43.9	48.3	51.7
19464	POTTSTOWN	84.9	83.3	10.9	12.1	0.8	1.0	3.0	3.2	7.3	7.3	7.4	6.5	5.7	28.6	23.4	12.0	1.9	73.8	37.2	48.2	51.8
19465	POTTSTOWN	97.2	96.8	1.3	1.5	0.6	0.7	0.8	1.0	5.2	5.8	6.5	6.2	5.1	26.1	30.2	13.2	1.9	78.6	42.4	49.4	50.6
19468	ROYERSFORD	95.0	94.1	2.2	2.6	1.4	1.8	1.3	1.4	8.6	8.3	7.1	5.6	4.7	33.8	22.0	8.6	1.3	72.4	35.9	48.6	51.4
19473	SCHWENKSVILLE	95.1	94.1	2.0	2.3	1.2	1.6	1.5	1.7	8.4	8.5	7.5	6.8	5.7	32.0	22.6	7.6	0.9	71.8	35.5	49.0	51.0
19475	SPRING CITY	94.0	93.0	3.5	4.1	0.9	1.1	1.1	1.3	7.3	7.0	7.2	6.3	5.0	27.7	25.3	11.7	2.3	74.2	38.9	50.3	49.7
19477	SPRING HOUSE	93.3	94.3	3.3	2.9	3.3	2.9	0.0	0.0	5.7	5.7	8.6	5.7	5.7	20.0	25.7	20.0	2.9	80.0	44.2	48.6	51.4
19492	ZIEGLERVILLE	97.3	96.9	0.7	0.6	0.7	0.6	0.7	0.9	7.8	8.1	8.1	6.2	4.4	29.8	26.4	8.4	0.9	72.4	37.8	49.7	50.3
	PENNSYLVANIA	85.4	84.4	10.0	10.3	1.8	2.2	3.2	3.5	5.9	6.1	6.8	6.9	6.7	26.6	25.3	13.3	2.2	77.2	39.1	48.4	51.6
	UNITED STATES	75.1	73.6	12.3	12.5	3.8	4.2	12.5	14.1	6.9	6.7	7.2	7.0	7.3	28.6	23.8	10.8	1.7	75.1	36.0	49.1	50.9

#	POST OFFICE NAME	2004 Per Capita Income	2004 HH Income Base	2004 Household Income Distribution (%) Less than $25,000	$25,000 to $49,999	$50,000 to $99,999	$100,000 to $149,999	$150,000 or More	Median Household Income 2004	2009	2004 National Centile	2004 State Centile	2004 Home Value Base	2004 Home Value Distribution (%) Less than $50,000	$50,000 to $89,999	$90,000 to $174,999	$175,000 to $399,999	$400,000 or More	2004 Median Home Value
19107	PHILADELPHIA	27651	6372	45.8	24.6	19.0	6.2	4.4	28495	34918	10	4	723	2.9	8.9	24.3	50.1	13.8	209250
19111	PHILADELPHIA	23063	24166	26.9	28.7	32.4	9.3	2.7	44770	54752	61	61	15035	1.4	18.1	72.2	8.0	0.3	118188
19114	PHILADELPHIA	26690	13620	23.3	28.1	35.9	9.7	3.1	48713	59912	70	69	8396	0.9	7.0	81.7	9.7	0.6	125999
19115	PHILADELPHIA	26526	13106	27.9	25.3	30.4	12.2	4.2	45737	57022	63	64	7934	2.1	4.2	55.7	37.3	0.7	159436
19116	PHILADELPHIA	24719	13043	24.8	23.1	35.3	12.5	4.3	51783	63367	75	75	7969	0.9	4.5	63.7	30.6	0.3	156457
19118	PHILADELPHIA	56642	4317	13.2	20.1	31.4	15.8	19.5	72349	90810	92	94	2177	0.6	1.2	16.6	49.3	32.3	284360
19119	PHILADELPHIA	34884	11706	21.1	24.6	31.7	13.2	9.4	54880	68099	80	80	7317	5.0	16.8	45.6	27.2	5.4	138697
19120	PHILADELPHIA	14745	21758	35.0	32.0	26.0	5.2	1.8	36110	42663	32	26	14035	11.4	63.2	24.1	1.1	0.2	73535
19121	PHILADELPHIA	11475	12510	60.9	22.4	13.6	2.1	1.0	18055	21456	1	1	5588	74.7	17.9	5.4	2.0	0.0	31119
19122	PHILADELPHIA	12367	5801	55.7	23.6	16.3	3.5	1.0	20739	25020	2	1	2561	44.7	33.7	20.2	1.4	0.0	56013
19123	PHILADELPHIA	22685	4041	47.5	22.8	19.6	5.1	5.1	27216	33644	7	3	1315	10.7	20.6	47.4	16.4	5.0	113320
19124	PHILADELPHIA	15694	22363	39.8	29.6	24.2	5.1	1.4	32745	39412	20	12	14627	18.4	63.9	16.4	1.1	0.2	66928
19125	PHILADELPHIA	15409	8401	39.7	28.3	26.2	4.3	1.5	32460	38457	19	11	5565	36.8	44.7	17.8	0.6	0.2	60294
19126	PHILADELPHIA	19267	5984	29.4	31.2	28.5	7.7	3.2	39329	47612	44	41	3766	7.1	40.0	40.9	11.7	0.2	92571
19127	PHILADELPHIA	29034	2869	24.3	24.8	34.4	12.0	4.5	50924	63162	74	73	1359	2.4	22.5	68.7	6.4	0.0	107899
19128	PHILADELPHIA	29086	15773	20.4	27.5	35.2	12.5	4.5	52124	64705	76	75	9543	0.9	10.2	66.8	21.3	0.8	135080
19129	PHILADELPHIA	24849	4991	33.9	25.3	27.0	8.5	5.3	40611	49800	48	47	2339	18.8	27.5	35.4	14.6	3.7	94943
19130	PHILADELPHIA	34755	11671	29.1	24.5	28.9	10.4	7.1	45632	57281	63	63	4215	9.7	14.2	37.8	33.0	5.4	138190
19131	PHILADELPHIA	20528	19194	38.9	27.1	25.0	6.3	2.7	34415	41397	25	18	9821	24.2	34.6	36.1	5.1	0.1	80535
19132	PHILADELPHIA	12657	14816	55.9	25.6	14.4	2.5	1.7	20932	24944	2	1	8721	75.0	21.2	3.5	0.1	0.3	33697
19133	PHILADELPHIA	8643	7861	64.2	20.7	12.2	2.0	1.0	15942	18532	1	1	3963	81.1	13.4	5.1	0.2	0.1	26628
19134	PHILADELPHIA	11568	19693	51.8	26.7	18.0	2.9	0.7	23750	28192	4	2	12246	49.4	40.5	9.5	0.4	0.2	50374
19135	PHILADELPHIA	19866	11810	30.1	30.6	30.1	7.8	1.5	40432	50040	48	46	8287	5.2	56.6	36.9	1.1	0.2	84070
19136	PHILADELPHIA	19741	13296	28.5	29.0	33.1	7.2	2.2	42621	52727	55	55	8723	5.0	35.5	54.9	4.6	0.1	96063
19137	PHILADELPHIA	18756	3164	32.6	32.5	27.0	5.8	2.1	37342	45165	37	32	2405	15.8	52.9	30.2	0.9	0.3	77374
19138	PHILADELPHIA	17323	12172	31.5	32.4	28.8	6.0	1.4	37785	44720	38	34	8859	16.4	45.7	35.9	1.9	0.2	81325
19139	PHILADELPHIA	14766	16475	51.2	27.4	17.4	2.8	1.3	24137	28580	4	2	8416	48.8	40.5	9.5	0.8	0.3	50753
19140	PHILADELPHIA	11348	18508	53.8	26.5	15.8	3.1	0.8	22235	26350	3	1	10515	66.7	29.1	3.6	0.5	0.1	42288
19141	PHILADELPHIA	15795	12017	39.0	31.1	23.7	4.7	1.5	32727	38783	20	12	6756	16.2	57.2	23.8	2.5	0.3	73382
19142	PHILADELPHIA	13590	9783	43.5	30.2	21.5	3.4	1.4	29827	35123	12	6	6298	30.0	57.9	11.5	0.6	0.0	60298
19143	PHILADELPHIA	16117	26104	44.0	28.5	21.3	4.5	1.7	29119	34679	11	5	15260	37.6	43.6	15.3	3.0	0.4	57120
19144	PHILADELPHIA	20712	18445	41.3	27.3	22.4	5.9	3.2	31664	38380	17	9	7814	23.1	39.0	31.7	5.3	1.0	76283
19145	PHILADELPHIA	17792	17826	43.1	26.9	21.9	5.8	2.2	30853	37392	14	8	11495	25.6	38.3	28.9	7.0	0.3	72720
19146	PHILADELPHIA	19222	16055	44.1	26.9	20.3	5.6	3.2	30056	35939	12	6	7636	47.9	20.9	16.0	11.3	3.9	52724
19147	PHILADELPHIA	30373	16499	32.5	27.6	24.5	9.2	6.2	40304	49301	47	46	7713	9.1	26.8	34.1	24.0	6.1	112091
19148	PHILADELPHIA	17419	19579	41.6	27.8	24.2	4.8	1.6	31103	37344	15	8	13353	20.2	44.1	33.8	1.8	0.0	77839
19149	PHILADELPHIA	20883	19231	25.9	30.3	34.0	8.1	1.8	43806	54183	58	58	14381	1.6	46.7	50.7	1.0	0.1	90754
19150	PHILADELPHIA	25184	9781	19.2	31.4	36.4	10.0	3.0	49395	59763	71	71	7300	2.0	21.9	71.6	4.5	0.1	106983
19151	PHILADELPHIA	19352	11783	30.7	30.4	29.8	6.9	2.3	39758	47727	45	43	7669	9.9	40.2	44.5	4.9	0.5	89931
19152	PHILADELPHIA	24378	13196	27.1	27.5	32.5	10.1	2.8	44991	56478	61	61	8634	1.3	5.0	87.4	6.2	0.1	129310
19153	PHILADELPHIA	22625	5356	28.5	28.7	31.4	8.9	2.5	41931	51119	53	53	3217	4.3	28.4	64.3	2.9	0.2	105847
19154	PHILADELPHIA	26988	12837	14.2	24.8	42.0	14.3	4.7	61406	75475	86	88	10260	0.5	4.5	89.1	5.5	0.4	126202
19301	PAOLI	48056	2821	12.2	16.8	31.5	20.0	19.5	79138	102251	95	96	2149	0.1	0.9	6.6	66.5	25.9	279313
19310	ATGLEN	23241	982	18.5	21.5	39.3	15.9	4.8	60158	75238	84	86	741	3.6	2.8	38.3	49.7	5.5	184167
19311	AVONDALE	31190	1968	10.3	17.1	35.8	21.3	15.5	79285	101829	95	96	1528	3.3	1.4	17.2	62.0	16.1	253535
19312	BERWYN	64214	4515	8.0	10.6	25.2	21.4	34.9	111484	137358	99	100	3799	0.3	0.3	3.2	43.9	52.4	413602
19317	CHADDS FORD	60420	3581	7.5	11.1	28.0	23.1	30.4	105232	130902	99	99	3205	0.3	1.1	11.6	49.8	37.1	339956
19319	CHEYNEY	50471	78	9.0	9.0	25.6	29.5	26.9	106136	127507	99	99	65	0.0	0.0	1.5	49.2	49.2	397222
19320	COATESVILLE	25674	16348	19.1	21.9	37.9	15.9	5.2	60079	74399	84	86	12289	5.2	6.4	36.2	48.0	4.2	178801
19330	COCHRANVILLE	27833	1683	16.6	20.2	38.0	17.4	7.8	64525	80772	88	90	1441	7.4	2.9	21.7	57.3	10.7	210574
19333	DEVON	62192	3131	10.2	14.4	28.2	18.8	28.3	93239	117933	97	98	2133	0.2	0.0	14.5	40.2	45.1	375635
19335	DOWNINGTOWN	37500	15426	8.3	15.2	35.4	24.6	16.5	85307	107557	96	97	12490	1.4	1.9	20.5	63.5	12.8	239602
19341	EXTON	45260	6553	6.8	14.7	37.4	23.8	17.3	86416	109239	97	97	4187	0.8	0.4	16.4	72.8	9.6	249457
19342	GLEN MILLS	43227	4929	8.0	12.7	29.3	25.1	24.9	100066	121991	98	98	4458	0.2	1.1	7.0	62.3	29.4	333695
19343	GLENMOORE	38202	2741	9.1	13.3	31.2	24.9	21.6	92936	115378	97	98	2533	5.4	2.1	8.7	60.8	22.9	295356
19344	HONEY BROOK	23704	3556	17.6	21.0	42.2	14.7	4.5	60319	73755	85	86	2904	16.8	6.2	19.0	52.1	5.9	191314
19348	KENNETT SQUARE	42441	7232	9.8	17.6	31.1	21.1	20.5	83704	107601	96	97	5313	0.6	1.4	18.8	52.0	27.1	298295
19350	LANDENBERG	43121	3418	4.8	11.8	29.3	26.5	27.7	105722	129311	99	99	3139	1.5	0.3	6.7	63.6	28.0	319428
19352	LINCOLN UNIVERSITY	26946	2257	7.8	12.5	41.2	27.6	11.0	82603	104550	96	96	2017	0.9	1.0	16.2	70.9	11.0	244180
19355	MALVERN	49125	9074	8.5	15.0	31.0	19.3	26.2	90000	114516	97	97	7131	2.6	0.7	10.3	56.3	30.2	307604
19362	NOTTINGHAM	23302	2046	15.6	27.5	41.5	11.6	3.8	55431	66778	80	80	1742	16.0	5.7	31.1	43.0	4.3	169635
19363	OXFORD	23519	5385	18.9	23.5	39.5	14.2	3.9	56016	69158	81	81	3884	2.4	2.8	30.5	58.5	5.8	199429
19365	PARKESBURG	24443	2385	15.9	25.7	40.0	13.9	4.4	57796	72193	82	83	1762	4.5	3.4	46.1	42.5	3.6	169262
19372	THORNDALE	35598	1025	4.8	16.7	44.7	24.4	9.5	77838	99167	94	95	785	1.2	0.3	40.0	57.7	0.9	188500
19373	THORNTON	30852	821	5.6	9.3	31.1	29.0	25.1	105087	128556	99	99	777	0.0	0.6	2.7	60.1	36.6	346684
19374	TOUGHKENAMON	25096	263	12.9	17.1	37.3	19.8	12.9	79848	104911	95	96	179	8.4	3.9	22.4	57.0	8.4	238793
19380	WEST CHESTER	43202	18397	9.0	17.7	33.6	21.1	18.6	81566	104025	95	96	13763	1.0	0.5	13.2	65.1	20.2	274558
19382	WEST CHESTER	42117	19141	11.0	17.1	30.5	21.0	20.5	82963	104952	96	97	13497	0.8	2.1	12.3	59.9	25.0	289269
19383	WEST CHESTER	31566	191	4.2	12.6	28.3	25.1	29.8	107721	130949	99	99	168	0.0	0.6	2.4	63.1	33.9	325000
19390	WEST GROVE	30784	3830	9.9	17.5	41.5	21.2	9.9	74663	92247	93	94	3201	6.3	2.6	22.7	59.4	9.0	219358
19401	NORRISTOWN	24544	15458	26.1	27.6	33.2	9.0	4.1	46259	57354	64	65	8258	2.7	13.2	62.3	20.8	1.0	132985
19403	NORRISTOWN	34320	16081	11.0	18.7	38.5	20.7	11.1	73552	91183	93	94	12614	2.3	1.9	27.3	62.4	6.1	211994
19405	BRIDGEPORT	24388	2223	20.7	31.5	38.0	8.5	1.3	47663	60282	68	68	1311	0.5	3.4	68.4	25.8	1.8	145354
19406	KING OF PRUSSIA	40332	10134	10.5	19.6	39.3	19.6	11.0	72683	89126	92	94	6142	0.5	1.0	20.4	74.3	3.8	214453
19422	BLUE BELL	52621	7261	7.0	13.8	27.4	22.3	29.5	102789	129074	98	99	5644	0.0	0.6	9.6	56.4	33.4	335024
19425	CHESTER SPRINGS	57028	3113	5.3	9.3	29.6	22.8	33.0	109165	134044	99	99	2779	0.0	0.1	11.3	45.3	43.2	368719
19426	COLLEGEVILLE	35076	10547	6.1	14.1	36.4	25.9	17.4	89222	110770	97	97	9077	0.3	0.6	18.3	70.6	10.3	241667
19428	CONSHOHOCKEN	34098	7275	17.1	23.1	36.3	13.2	10.4	60564	75525	85	87	4414	0.7	2.3	45.5	44.3	7.3	177706
19435	FREDERICK	30997	139	13.0	25.9	32.4	20.9	7.9	65284	83322	89	90	127	3.2	0.8	22.8	59.1	14.2	232895
19436	GWYNEDD	92683	314	4.5	13.7	27.1	18.2	36.6	110030	138604	99	99	230	1.3	0.4	3.5	35.7	59.1	484000
19438	HARLEYSVILLE	36068	8154	9.3	14.2	39.0	23.9	13.7	81877	103153	96	96	6523	0.4	0.8	18.5	69.4	11.0	238980
19440	HATFIELD	29076	6947	13.7	22.3	40.7	16.1	7.2	63650	78667	88	89	4464	2.1	2.4	23.0	71.4	1.1	208535
19444	LAFAYETTE HILL	50678	3963	7.5	13.7	29.1	22.4	27.3	99218	125112	98	98	3460	0.8	0.6	6.0	71.1	21.6	276004
19446	LANSDALE	36103	20611	11.2	19.1	36.8	19.5	13.4	73167	91147	93	94	14854	0.7	1.4	28.1	63.5	6.5	220108
19453	MONT CLARE	43374	612	9.0	20.4	41.7	16.8	12.1	71381	87725	92	93	492	0.0	6.5	29.9	51.2	12.4	195938
19454	NORTH WALES	42722	10036	9.6	18.0	33.4	20.5	18.6	81050	103134	95	96	8398	1.3	6.1	20.5	56.2	16.0	235003
19460	PHOENIXVILLE	38488	14401	13.6	21.6	32.4	19.3	13.2	68751	88965	91	92	10320	2.3	2.9	31.4	49.6	13.8	211999
19462	PLYMOUTH MEETING	40003	5765	12.5	21.0	35.0	18.5	13.1	70040	87174	91	92	4549	0.0	0.8	21.8	69.8	7.6	223292
19464	POTTSTOWN	25979	17585	21.2	26.2	36.6	11.7	4.4	52558	65915	76	76	12006	1.9	5.8	60.4	30.5	1.4	145337
19465	POTTSTOWN	33717	5855	12.5	22.7	35.5	19.5	9.9	67676	87417	90	91	4712	1.9	1.1	22.5	65.3	9.2	219368
19468	ROYERSFORD	32709	9391	9.1	20.2	42.3	19.5	9.0	72081	87903	92	93	7061	1.4	1.3	34.1	59.8	3.5	200813
19473	SCHWENKSVILLE	32811	5235	9.6	18.6	40.8	20.1	10.8	75094	90815	93	94	4381	0.5	2.0	35.1	55.8	6.6	200748
19475	SPRING CITY	32354	4020	19.2	19.6	33.9	19.2	8.2	64184	83621	88	90	2807	5.1	2.5	33.1	50.4	8.9	193010
19477	SPRING HOUSE	49630	12	16.7	8.3	25.0	16.7	33.3	100000	188958	98	98	10	0.0	0.0	0.0	50.0	50.0	450000
19492	ZIEGLERVILLE	37580	141	9.9	21.3	41.8	14.9	12.1	69640	83668	91	92	122	0.0	0.8	17.2	72.1	9.8	243103
	PENNSYLVANIA	25764		25.8	27.2	31.2	10.2	5.7	46988	57000				11.9	18.4	40.7	25.1	4.1	123516
	UNITED STATES	25866		24.7	27.1	30.8	10.9	6.5	48124	56710				10.9	15.0	33.7	30.1	10.4	145905

ZIP CODE		FINANCIAL SERVICES				THE HOME						ENTERTAINMENT						PERSONAL			
						Home Improvements		Furnishings													
#	POST OFFICE NAME	Auto Loan	Home Loan	Invest-ments	Retire-ment Plans	Home Repair	Lawn & Garden	Comput-ers & Hard-ware	Major Appli-ances	TV, Radio, Sound Equip-ment	Furni-ture	Dine out/ Carry out	Sports Equip-ment	Fees & Tickets	Toys & Games	Travel	Cable TV	Apparel & Services	Auto Repairs	Health Insur-ance	Pets & Supplies
19107	PHILADELPHIA	61	51	84	58	50	56	70	59	70	66	88	76	66	87	64	66	85	66	55	66
19111	PHILADELPHIA	71	75	90	74	74	81	77	75	78	76	98	86	79	100	78	79	95	76	76	82
19114	PHILADELPHIA	78	84	97	82	83	92	83	83	84	84	105	93	86	104	85	84	102	84	85	91
19115	PHILADELPHIA	79	81	99	82	81	90	84	83	85	84	106	94	86	105	85	85	104	85	84	91
19116	PHILADELPHIA	78	88	108	85	86	94	86	85	86	87	109	95	90	111	88	88	107	85	85	93
19118	PHILADELPHIA	154	175	232	178	172	184	175	168	170	175	214	197	183	221	178	169	213	171	160	184
19119	PHILADELPHIA	107	113	138	111	111	122	113	111	115	115	144	126	118	143	115	116	141	113	112	124
19120	PHILADELPHIA	57	56	81	53	53	61	62	59	66	63	84	67	62	86	62	69	83	61	60	65
19121	PHILADELPHIA	43	35	40	32	34	42	40	41	46	41	56	44	39	51	39	48	53	42	46	47
19122	PHILADELPHIA	45	40	58	38	39	46	47	45	52	48	65	50	46	63	46	54	64	48	48	50
19123	PHILADELPHIA	65	59	88	60	57	67	69	65	74	69	92	75	69	92	68	75	90	69	67	73
19124	PHILADELPHIA	59	56	64	54	55	62	61	59	64	60	79	68	61	79	60	65	77	61	61	66
19125	PHILADELPHIA	55	52	60	51	52	59	58	56	61	56	75	64	57	76	57	62	73	57	59	62
19126	PHILADELPHIA	68	69	81	67	67	76	70	69	72	71	91	76	73	90	71	74	89	70	71	78
19127	PHILADELPHIA	77	80	115	85	78	85	86	81	86	86	109	96	89	112	86	86	107	84	78	89
19128	PHILADELPHIA	83	89	109	90	88	95	92	89	91	91	114	104	94	115	92	90	112	91	86	97
19129	PHILADELPHIA	76	68	87	72	67	75	82	75	82	80	103	91	79	99	77	79	101	81	73	84
19130	PHILADELPHIA	84	78	128	85	75	85	92	83	95	93	120	101	94	122	90	94	118	89	81	93
19131	PHILADELPHIA	65	58	70	57	57	67	66	64	70	66	87	72	65	82	65	71	84	67	67	72
19132	PHILADELPHIA	48	38	41	34	38	47	43	45	50	44	60	48	41	54	42	53	57	46	52	52
19133	PHILADELPHIA	34	31	51	28	29	35	35	34	41	37	52	38	35	51	35	44	51	37	37	38
19134	PHILADELPHIA	43	41	55	38	40	46	45	44	49	45	62	49	45	63	45	51	60	45	46	48
19135	PHILADELPHIA	65	67	70	64	67	75	68	67	70	66	87	77	70	92	69	72	84	67	71	75
19136	PHILADELPHIA	67	71	80	68	71	78	72	70	74	70	92	80	75	97	73	76	89	71	74	78
19137	PHILADELPHIA	60	63	67	60	64	71	64	63	67	62	83	71	67	88	66	69	80	63	66	70
19138	PHILADELPHIA	65	61	67	57	60	70	63	63	68	65	84	68	65	80	64	71	82	64	69	73
19139	PHILADELPHIA	51	43	48	39	42	51	48	49	54	49	66	53	47	60	47	57	63	50	55	56
19140	PHILADELPHIA	43	38	57	35	37	44	43	42	49	45	62	47	43	60	43	52	61	45	46	48
19141	PHILADELPHIA	58	53	62	51	52	61	57	57	62	59	77	62	58	74	57	64	75	58	61	65
19142	PHILADELPHIA	54	49	59	46	47	55	54	52	58	55	73	59	54	71	53	60	71	54	55	60
19143	PHILADELPHIA	58	52	60	50	51	60	56	56	61	58	76	62	57	72	56	63	73	58	60	64
19144	PHILADELPHIA	65	59	74	58	57	66	66	63	70	67	88	72	66	86	65	72	86	66	66	72
19145	PHILADELPHIA	59	57	67	54	56	64	60	60	64	60	79	66	61	79	61	67	77	61	64	67
19146	PHILADELPHIA	61	52	68	52	51	60	61	59	66	61	81	67	60	78	59	67	79	62	63	67
19147	PHILADELPHIA	76	75	119	80	72	81	85	78	87	85	109	94	86	112	84	87	108	83	76	87
19148	PHILADELPHIA	56	56	69	54	56	63	60	58	63	59	78	66	61	80	61	65	76	59	62	65
19149	PHILADELPHIA	68	73	81	70	73	79	74	72	75	71	94	82	76	99	75	76	91	72	74	79
19150	PHILADELPHIA	85	83	92	79	82	94	83	83	88	86	111	89	88	106	85	92	108	84	90	95
19151	PHILADELPHIA	67	64	73	63	63	71	69	67	71	69	89	76	69	87	68	72	87	69	69	75
19152	PHILADELPHIA	72	77	93	76	76	84	78	77	79	77	98	87	81	100	80	80	96	78	78	84
19153	PHILADELPHIA	73	68	73	66	68	78	72	72	76	72	94	79	72	90	72	78	90	73	77	82
19154	PHILADELPHIA	93	107	120	106	105	110	103	101	99	102	125	116	107	129	104	98	124	100	96	110
19301	PAOLI	145	173	213	174	171	180	164	162	155	164	195	187	173	200	168	153	194	160	152	176
19310	ATGLEN	110	96	74	93	101	111	93	101	99	92	120	118	90	121	94	101	113	99	110	126
19311	AVONDALE	140	160	173	160	153	155	148	147	141	153	180	168	154	183	148	137	179	145	131	160
19312	BERWYN	206	267	345	261	261	279	239	237	225	242	284	267	264	297	252	227	286	230	222	257
19317	CHADDS FORD	199	253	311	252	247	261	225	223	211	229	266	253	249	276	235	210	267	216	208	244
19319	CHEYNEY	168	209	227	216	202	204	184	180	168	187	214	208	203	222	188	162	215	173	160	199
19320	COATESVILLE	95	103	108	100	102	108	98	99	98	98	122	113	102	126	100	98	119	97	98	112
19330	COCHRANVILLE	114	123	116	120	124	127	111	116	110	111	136	136	115	142	114	109	133	112	114	137
19333	DEVON	169	198	305	205	190	206	196	185	192	200	243	217	213	258	202	192	244	187	172	203
19335	DOWNINGTOWN	140	164	179	168	160	162	152	149	143	153	180	174	161	186	153	138	180	147	135	164
19341	EXTON	137	153	206	163	148	154	153	144	147	154	186	172	161	194	153	143	186	146	131	159
19342	GLEN MILLS	164	200	223	202	196	202	181	179	169	182	213	205	195	219	186	166	213	174	165	197
19343	GLENMOORE	159	191	202	196	185	187	171	168	157	173	199	195	184	206	172	152	200	163	150	187
19344	HONEY BROOK	103	97	85	95	99	106	93	99	95	93	117	116	92	116	94	95	112	98	101	118
19348	KENNETT SQUARE	153	173	199	176	170	178	166	163	158	167	200	188	173	202	167	155	198	162	153	179
19350	LANDENBERG	174	216	235	223	209	211	191	186	174	194	222	215	210	230	194	169	224	180	166	206
19352	LINCOLN UNIVERSITY	134	150	149	154	145	144	139	137	129	141	163	161	143	165	137	122	161	134	121	152
19355	MALVERN	170	205	246	209	201	208	191	187	179	192	226	218	204	233	195	175	226	184	171	205
19362	NOTTINGHAM	105	96	75	92	98	104	90	97	93	91	114	114	87	112	90	93	109	96	100	120
19363	OXFORD	97	95	89	94	96	101	93	96	94	92	116	112	92	117	93	93	112	95	96	111
19365	PARKESBURG	103	95	78	91	100	108	89	97	95	89	115	114	89	119	92	97	110	94	105	121
19372	THORNDALE	119	142	162	145	140	140	133	131	125	132	157	154	139	164	135	121	156	129	118	144
19373	THORNTON	175	216	238	219	211	217	193	191	179	195	226	219	210	233	198	175	227	185	175	210
19374	TOUGHKENAMON	122	135	152	132	129	134	129	127	126	134	161	144	133	165	128	124	161	128	117	138
19380	WEST CHESTER	150	167	188	172	163	168	160	157	151	162	191	182	166	191	160	146	189	156	144	172
19382	WEST CHESTER	151	170	198	175	165	172	167	159	157	166	199	188	174	201	165	151	198	160	144	176
19383	WEST CHESTER	185	227	248	230	221	226	203	199	188	205	239	228	221	248	207	185	239	192	182	219
19390	WEST GROVE	122	141	147	140	137	140	131	130	124	131	156	151	136	161	132	121	154	127	120	142
19401	NORRISTOWN	80	80	95	80	79	87	85	83	87	84	109	95	86	109	85	87	106	85	83	91
19403	NORRISTOWN	113	131	152	132	129	133	125	123	120	125	151	143	131	156	127	117	150	122	114	135
19405	BRIDGEPORT	71	73	85	72	73	80	77	74	78	75	98	86	79	101	77	79	95	76	76	82
19406	KING OF PRUSSIA	111	124	180	129	120	130	127	120	125	128	158	141	134	165	129	124	157	122	113	131
19422	BLUE BELL	173	207	252	209	204	214	193	191	183	194	230	220	206	235	198	180	229	188	179	209
19425	CHESTER SPRINGS	211	259	276	268	250	250	229	224	209	233	266	259	249	274	231	201	267	216	197	247
19426	COLLEGEVILLE	141	164	168	169	157	155	149	147	137	153	174	172	155	177	147	130	173	144	128	161
19428	CONSHOHOCKEN	101	112	137	114	110	117	113	109	110	112	138	128	116	141	114	108	136	111	104	119
19435	FREDERICK	127	119	96	114	124	131	109	119	113	109	139	141	108	142	112	116	133	116	126	150
19436	GWYNEDD	205	213	246	222	214	225	218	216	210	216	263	254	218	257	216	203	255	218	207	236
19438	HARLEYSVILLE	140	159	159	163	154	153	144	144	134	148	170	167	150	172	143	128	168	140	128	159
19440	HATFIELD	105	109	119	113	107	110	110	108	106	110	133	128	110	132	108	101	131	109	98	118
19444	LAFAYETTE HILL	174	213	242	216	209	216	193	190	179	194	227	218	208	233	198	176	227	185	176	209
19446	LANSDALE	121	136	154	138	134	139	131	129	126	131	158	151	136	161	132	123	156	129	121	142
19453	MONT CLARE	122	143	143	147	138	134	129	128	118	132	150	150	134	154	128	112	149	124	111	140
19454	NORTH WALES	146	167	180	171	164	165	156	155	146	158	185	180	162	187	157	141	183	152	140	170
19460	PHOENIXVILLE	127	142	159	144	139	146	138	134	132	137	166	156	143	170	138	129	164	134	126	148
19462	PLYMOUTH MEETING	128	146	166	145	146	155	139	139	134	139	169	157	145	169	143	135	166	137	136	153
19464	POTTSTOWN	87	92	98	91	92	98	92	91	91	90	114	105	94	118	92	91	111	91	90	101
19465	POTTSTOWN	110	130	148	130	128	133	122	121	117	122	147	139	129	153	126	116	146	119	114	133
19468	ROYERSFORD	117	128	131	132	124	125	122	120	115	123	145	141	124	146	120	110	143	119	108	133
19473	SCHWENKSVILLE	124	143	145	148	138	136	131	130	121	134	154	152	136	157	130	115	152	127	113	142
19475	SPRING CITY	114	122	125	122	121	126	118	118	115	117	144	138	120	147	118	112	141	117	113	133
19477	SPRING HOUSE	194	201	232	210	202	213	206	204	198	204	248	240	206	242	204	192	241	206	195	223
19492	ZIEGLERVILLE	111	138	147	138	136	134	123	123	114	123	144	144	131	153	126	111	144	119	110	136
	PENNSYLVANIA	89	89	93	87	90	98	89	90	91	88	112	104	89	114	90	92	109	90	92	104
	UNITED STATES	100	100	100	100	100	100	100	100	100	100	100	100	100	100	100	100	100	100	100	100

POPULATION CHANGE

ZIP CODE			POPULATION			2000-2004 ANNUAL RATE		HOUSEHOLDS					FAMILIES		
#	POST OFFICE NAME	COUNTY FIPS CODE	2000	2004	2009	% Rate	State Centile	2000	2004	2009	% Annual Rate 2000-2004	2004 Average HH Size	2000	2004	% Annual Rate 2000-2004
19501	ADAMSTOWN	071	1000	1012	1036	0.3	53	407	419	435	0.7	2.42	285	291	0.5
19503	BALLY	011	1027	1015	1046	-0.3	26	402	401	416	-0.1	2.53	297	293	-0.3
19504	BARTO	011	4650	4958	5211	1.5	89	1651	1782	1890	1.8	2.78	1330	1427	1.7
19505	BECHTELSVILLE	011	3540	3723	3918	1.2	83	1289	1367	1448	1.4	2.72	1021	1076	1.2
19506	BERNVILLE	011	6761	7320	7833	1.9	92	2487	2718	2928	2.1	2.66	1887	2044	1.9
19507	BETHEL	011	4327	4594	4860	1.4	87	1473	1584	1690	1.7	2.80	1132	1210	1.6
19508	BIRDSBORO	011	15558	16680	17744	1.7	90	5791	6253	6682	1.8	2.66	4360	4674	1.7
19510	BLANDON	011	5535	6616	7441	4.3	99	1915	2295	2588	4.4	2.88	1570	1866	4.2
19512	BOYERTOWN	011	17071	18438	19720	1.8	91	6685	7265	7807	2.0	2.51	4785	5179	1.9
19518	DOUGLASSVILLE	011	10490	11568	12494	2.3	95	3826	4241	4598	2.5	2.72	2970	3268	2.3
19520	ELVERSON	029	5291	5661	6084	1.6	89	2020	2202	2402	2.1	2.55	1573	1702	1.9
19522	FLEETWOOD	011	13627	14475	15343	1.4	87	5137	5491	5848	1.6	2.62	3888	4130	1.4
19525	GILBERTSVILLE	091	10241	11142	11700	2.0	93	3494	3843	4072	2.3	2.89	2878	3159	2.2
19526	HAMBURG	011	11157	11458	11933	0.6	69	4340	4488	4701	0.8	2.48	3095	3178	0.6
19529	KEMPTON	011	2922	3094	3255	1.4	86	1061	1133	1200	1.6	2.72	821	871	1.4
19530	KUTZTOWN	011	14973	15129	15563	0.2	51	4724	4822	5020	0.5	2.56	2980	3009	0.2
19533	LEESPORT	011	7263	7488	7765	0.7	72	2069	2170	2287	1.1	2.61	1572	1635	0.9
19534	LENHARTSVILLE	011	1786	1844	1920	0.8	72	682	711	746	1.0	2.54	512	530	0.8
19539	MERTZTOWN	011	4457	4669	4915	1.1	82	1650	1741	1843	1.3	2.61	1274	1335	1.1
19540	MOHNTON	011	10583	10871	11311	0.6	69	3941	4078	4266	0.8	2.66	3048	3132	0.6
19541	MOHRSVILLE	011	4094	4361	4622	1.5	88	1495	1606	1712	1.7	2.71	1141	1217	1.5
19543	MORGANTOWN	011	3838	4262	4611	2.5	96	1324	1496	1638	2.9	2.84	1026	1147	2.7
19547	OLEY	011	4468	4583	4802	0.6	68	1717	1775	1869	0.8	2.58	1285	1319	0.6
19549	PORT CLINTON	107	288	285	290	-0.3	27	132	134	139	0.4	2.13	91	91	0.0
19551	ROBESONIA	011	5180	5340	5568	0.7	72	1925	2007	2108	1.0	2.59	1460	1508	0.8
19555	SHOEMAKERSVILLE	011	4354	4448	4619	0.5	64	1473	1520	1598	0.7	2.45	1059	1085	0.6
19560	TEMPLE	011	6504	6648	6919	0.5	65	2778	2861	2994	0.7	2.27	1874	1909	0.4
19562	TOPTON	011	2430	2390	2454	-0.4	21	895	886	917	-0.2	2.44	641	628	-0.5
19565	WERNERSVILLE	011	7305	7829	8326	1.6	90	2844	3076	3296	1.9	2.41	1994	2138	1.7
19567	WOMELSDORF	011	4577	4640	4783	0.3	55	1723	1761	1826	0.5	2.56	1218	1231	0.3
19601	READING	011	30791	31324	32700	0.4	59	11491	11670	12191	0.4	2.66	7012	7020	0.0
19602	READING	011	17104	17532	18367	0.6	68	6717	6874	7206	0.6	2.51	3689	3708	0.1
19604	READING	011	24273	24919	25975	0.6	69	8467	8584	8912	0.3	2.79	5602	5611	0.0
19605	READING	011	17064	17512	18298	0.6	68	6859	7074	7424	0.7	2.44	4879	4999	0.6
19606	READING	011	30382	32214	34273	1.4	86	11948	12718	13577	1.5	2.52	8604	9121	1.4
19607	READING	011	20722	20946	21694	0.3	51	9152	9349	9749	0.5	2.17	5691	5748	0.2
19608	READING	011	16497	18034	19401	2.1	93	6037	6633	7163	2.2	2.69	4528	4935	2.1
19609	READING	011	9999	10020	10398	0.1	42	4271	4310	4495	0.2	2.32	2939	2942	0.0
19610	READING	011	14622	15100	15841	0.8	73	5940	6243	6634	1.2	2.24	3896	4052	0.9
19611	READING	011	10056	10274	10728	0.5	65	3957	4046	4244	0.5	2.35	2334	2369	0.4
PENNSYLVANIA						0.3					0.7	2.44			0.6
UNITED STATES						1.2					1.3	2.58			1.1

#	POST OFFICE NAME	White 2000	White 2004	Black 2000	Black 2004	Asian/Pacific 2000	Asian/Pacific 2004	% Hispanic Origin 2000	% Hispanic Origin 2004	0-4	5-9	10-14	15-19	20-24	25-44	45-64	65-84	85+	18+	MEDIAN AGE 2004	% 2004 Males	% 2004 Females
19501	ADAMSTOWN	99.2	99.0	0.1	0.1	0.2	0.3	0.9	1.1	7.3	6.8	6.0	5.4	5.4	30.9	24.2	12.7	1.2	76.4	38.1	48.4	51.6
19503	BALLY	98.7	98.5	0.5	0.6	0.5	0.6	0.3	0.4	5.2	5.8	7.4	5.8	4.3	28.8	24.4	16.2	2.1	77.9	40.2	50.6	49.4
19504	BARTO	98.7	98.5	0.4	0.4	0.3	0.4	0.5	0.7	6.5	7.0	7.2	6.5	4.9	28.4	28.1	10.4	1.1	75.3	39.7	50.7	49.3
19505	BECHTELSVILLE	98.3	97.9	0.5	0.6	0.3	0.4	0.7	0.9	6.7	7.2	7.4	6.2	4.9	29.5	26.5	10.7	0.9	74.8	38.8	50.8	49.2
19506	BERNVILLE	97.3	96.8	0.9	1.0	0.4	0.5	1.8	2.2	5.9	6.4	7.7	6.5	5.1	28.7	27.3	11.2	1.3	75.9	39.5	51.0	49.0
19507	BETHEL	95.7	94.8	1.7	2.0	0.6	0.7	2.3	2.9	6.6	7.0	7.7	6.2	5.7	30.2	25.8	9.9	1.0	75.0	37.3	52.9	47.1
19508	BIRDSBORO	96.5	95.7	1.5	1.8	0.4	0.6	1.3	1.6	6.7	7.0	7.5	6.3	4.9	28.9	26.5	11.0	1.3	74.8	38.8	50.0	50.0
19510	BLANDON	96.6	95.7	0.8	1.0	1.3	1.7	2.4	3.0	8.4	8.4	7.7	6.3	4.9	33.0	23.0	7.6	0.7	71.6	35.7	50.0	50.0
19512	BOYERTOWN	97.0	96.2	1.9	2.5	0.4	0.5	0.6	0.7	5.4	5.9	6.8	6.9	5.3	27.7	28.1	12.3	1.6	77.4	40.5	49.8	50.2
19518	DOUGLASSVILLE	96.0	95.1	1.9	2.3	0.6	0.8	0.8	1.1	6.7	7.1	7.6	6.3	4.8	28.4	27.2	10.9	1.2	74.6	38.9	49.5	50.5
19520	ELVERSON	97.8	97.4	0.5	0.6	0.6	0.8	0.7	0.8	5.6	6.4	7.1	6.1	4.4	25.0	30.0	14.3	1.2	77.0	42.3	50.0	50.0
19522	FLEETWOOD	98.3	97.9	0.3	0.3	0.4	0.5	1.3	1.7	5.9	6.3	7.4	6.4	5.2	27.8	27.8	11.9	1.3	76.4	40.2	49.6	50.4
19525	GILBERTSVILLE	97.8	97.4	0.7	0.8	0.9	1.2	0.6	0.7	7.1	8.0	9.0	7.0	4.5	28.8	25.4	9.4	0.9	71.1	37.6	49.5	50.5
19526	HAMBURG	97.9	97.5	0.4	0.4	0.2	0.3	1.1	1.4	5.9	6.1	6.2	5.6	5.1	28.2	26.9	13.7	2.3	78.3	40.7	49.4	50.6
19529	KEMPTON	98.6	98.3	0.2	0.3	0.4	0.5	0.7	0.8	5.6	6.5	8.1	6.6	5.5	26.7	30.3	9.6	1.2	75.6	40.3	51.2	48.8
19530	KUTZTOWN	97.0	96.4	1.2	1.5	0.7	0.8	1.1	1.5	3.9	3.9	4.8	15.7	20.4	20.7	19.4	9.5	1.7	84.8	26.2	47.1	52.9
19533	LEESPORT	93.6	92.6	4.1	4.6	1.1	1.4	7.4	8.7	4.2	4.5	5.2	5.9	7.3	29.6	25.3	12.9	5.0	82.7	41.2	54.6	45.4
19534	LENHARTSVILLE	98.3	98.1	0.3	0.4	0.1	0.1	0.8	1.0	5.5	6.1	6.5	6.2	5.5	28.7	30.2	10.4	0.9	78.1	40.5	51.5	48.5
19539	MERTZTOWN	98.6	98.3	0.3	0.4	0.3	0.4	0.9	1.1	5.6	6.2	7.1	6.3	6.0	27.2	28.4	11.3	1.8	77.3	40.4	49.4	50.6
19540	MOHNTON	97.2	96.6	0.8	1.0	0.5	0.7	1.4	1.7	5.6	6.3	7.7	6.6	5.4	26.6	29.7	10.9	1.3	76.3	40.7	49.6	50.4
19541	MOHRSVILLE	97.8	97.3	0.6	0.7	0.4	0.5	1.6	2.0	5.6	6.3	7.1	6.0	5.3	29.6	28.9	10.4	0.8	77.3	39.7	50.6	49.4
19543	MORGANTOWN	98.2	97.7	0.4	0.5	0.6	0.8	0.7	0.9	6.9	7.3	8.3	7.3	6.1	26.6	25.1	11.1	1.5	73.1	37.5	50.0	50.0
19547	OLEY	98.8	98.6	0.2	0.2	0.3	0.4	0.8	1.1	5.0	5.9	6.8	6.5	5.0	28.1	28.9	12.4	1.4	78.0	41.0	50.4	49.6
19549	PORT CLINTON	98.3	97.5	0.4	0.4	0.0	0.0	1.7	1.8	3.5	5.3	7.0	5.3	3.2	26.3	34.7	13.7	1.1	80.7	44.7	51.2	48.8
19551	ROBESONIA	96.7	96.0	1.2	1.5	0.4	0.6	1.7	2.2	5.5	6.2	7.7	7.3	4.7	26.7	29.7	11.1	1.3	75.8	40.7	49.9	50.1
19555	SHOEMAKERSVILLE	95.5	94.6	1.7	1.9	0.4	0.6	4.0	4.9	4.7	4.8	5.2	5.4	5.5	28.7	26.3	16.1	3.4	82.1	42.3	51.3	48.7
19560	TEMPLE	96.8	96.1	0.8	1.0	0.4	0.5	4.1	5.1	4.5	4.8	5.8	5.5	4.7	25.0	26.1	20.1	3.6	81.6	44.9	48.1	51.9
19562	TOPTON	99.1	98.7	0.1	0.1	0.2	0.3	1.2	1.5	5.2	5.3	5.9	5.9	4.9	24.4	24.2	16.7	7.4	79.6	43.9	46.1	53.9
19565	WERNERSVILLE	97.0	96.2	1.3	1.7	0.5	0.7	1.4	1.7	5.2	5.9	7.1	5.9	4.0	26.9	26.6	14.6	3.8	77.8	42.3	49.4	50.6
19567	WOMELSDORF	95.8	94.9	1.4	1.7	1.0	1.3	2.2	2.7	6.5	6.8	7.1	6.5	5.7	29.1	24.9	11.9	1.5	75.5	38.0	51.1	48.9
19601	READING	50.5	47.1	17.6	18.0	1.4	1.7	42.6	46.2	9.4	8.0	8.4	7.9	8.4	27.7	19.3	9.5	1.4	69.4	30.5	48.4	51.6
19602	READING	57.1	53.4	11.4	11.9	1.8	2.0	42.4	46.3	8.7	7.7	8.3	7.6	7.8	29.0	18.5	10.2	2.1	70.9	31.7	49.4	50.7
19604	READING	68.9	65.1	7.7	8.4	1.8	2.2	29.3	33.1	8.2	7.6	8.2	9.2	9.5	27.8	18.0	9.8	1.7	71.5	30.1	48.9	51.1
19605	READING	94.5	93.3	1.5	1.7	0.8	1.1	4.7	5.7	4.9	5.3	6.2	6.0	4.9	25.3	26.7	18.0	2.6	79.8	43.4	48.4	51.6
19606	READING	94.6	93.6	1.9	2.2	1.1	1.5	3.3	3.9	6.1	6.5	7.2	6.1	5.2	27.7	26.6	12.8	1.8	76.4	39.8	48.8	51.2
19607	READING	93.9	92.6	1.9	2.3	1.7	2.1	3.1	3.8	4.6	4.7	5.5	5.7	5.7	26.4	25.9	17.9	3.6	81.9	43.2	47.3	52.7
19608	READING	94.1	92.7	2.1	2.5	1.7	2.2	2.8	3.4	6.1	6.6	7.7	6.7	5.3	27.3	26.6	12.0	1.8	75.4	39.6	48.5	51.5
19609	READING	95.9	95.0	1.1	1.3	1.3	1.6	2.1	2.7	5.2	5.7	6.3	5.3	4.2	26.9	25.9	18.0	2.5	79.4	42.8	47.9	52.1
19610	READING	94.2	92.7	1.4	1.7	2.7	3.5	1.9	2.4	3.6	4.3	5.8	9.3	5.4	17.6	28.2	19.9	5.9	82.8	47.9	46.4	53.6
19611	READING	73.4	70.0	6.2	6.8	1.6	2.0	24.9	28.2	8.1	7.1	7.0	6.6	6.9	27.0	18.2	14.6	4.5	74.1	35.2	45.6	54.4
	PENNSYLVANIA	85.4	84.4	10.0	10.3	1.8	2.2	3.2	3.5	5.9	6.1	6.8	6.9	6.7	26.6	25.3	13.3	2.2	77.2	39.1	48.4	51.6
	UNITED STATES	75.1	73.6	12.3	12.5	3.8	4.2	12.5	14.1	6.9	6.7	7.2	7.0	7.3	28.6	23.8	10.8	1.7	75.1	36.0	49.1	50.9

#	POST OFFICE NAME	2004 Per Capita Income	2004 HH Income Base	2004 HOUSEHOLD INCOME DISTRIBUTION (%) Less than $25,000	$25,000 to $49,999	$50,000 to $99,999	$100,000 to $149,999	$150,000 or More	MEDIAN HOUSEHOLD INCOME 2004	2009	2004 National Centile	2004 State Centile	2004 Home Value Base	2004 HOME VALUE DISTRIBUTION (%) Less than $50,000	$50,000 to $89,999	$90,000 to $174,999	$175,000 to $399,999	$400,000 or More	2004 Median Home Value
19501	ADAMSTOWN	25017	419	15.8	34.1	39.6	7.9	2.6	50063	59360	72	71	278	1.8	8.3	70.1	19.1	0.7	131356
19503	BALLY	29508	401	20.5	22.9	41.7	9.0	6.0	56192	66184	81	82	333	1.5	2.1	81.4	15.0	0.0	138125
19504	BARTO	25377	1782	15.0	23.3	41.9	13.8	6.0	60918	72392	85	87	1563	5.8	3.9	31.7	52.9	5.8	191444
19505	BECHTELSVILLE	24456	1367	14.5	23.9	45.7	12.6	3.4	60024	70012	84	85	1139	2.7	4.7	52.9	37.2	2.6	161065
19506	BERNVILLE	25322	2718	16.3	25.4	42.0	11.6	4.8	56672	66382	81	82	2285	3.5	8.5	52.7	31.7	3.7	148737
19507	BETHEL	20890	1584	17.4	27.8	44.3	7.6	2.9	52957	62131	77	77	1318	5.5	10.8	53.7	27.7	2.4	141012
19508	BIRDSBORO	25249	6253	15.9	22.9	43.9	13.8	3.6	59330	70410	84	85	5247	6.6	12.7	54.4	24.7	1.7	137766
19510	BLANDON	30446	2295	10.0	17.0	47.0	19.0	7.0	70576	81937	91	92	2019	4.2	3.1	62.6	30.1	0.0	152393
19512	BOYERTOWN	27206	7265	15.7	25.6	41.6	11.6	5.5	57692	67899	82	83	5706	2.1	4.3	60.3	31.2	2.0	152344
19518	DOUGLASSVILLE	30680	4241	13.5	19.6	40.4	18.3	8.2	67808	81663	90	91	3419	3.3	5.3	44.9	43.6	3.0	169857
19520	ELVERSON	32144	2202	12.3	21.6	38.1	19.6	8.4	66699	83961	90	91	1893	2.8	2.3	21.3	61.8	11.8	230057
19522	FLEETWOOD	28189	5491	14.8	24.6	39.8	15.5	5.3	60704	72030	85	87	4652	3.6	7.2	51.3	35.3	2.6	152800
19525	GILBERTSVILLE	29624	3843	10.3	16.7	42.2	22.5	8.3	76124	92081	94	95	3372	0.5	0.9	25.7	70.3	2.6	210206
19526	HAMBURG	24861	4488	19.1	28.0	40.0	10.3	2.6	52378	62459	76	76	3522	8.4	16.6	53.0	19.9	2.1	119684
19529	KEMPTON	27019	1133	14.0	25.5	39.1	14.8	6.5	58469	68945	83	84	982	2.7	6.8	40.1	43.5	6.9	175885
19530	KUTZTOWN	23825	4822	23.9	25.6	33.7	10.9	6.0	50428	59875	73	72	3240	10.6	6.9	50.4	28.6	3.5	139741
19533	LEESPORT	24865	2170	12.5	23.6	43.3	15.9	4.7	62594	75645	87	89	1826	2.9	10.0	56.1	28.0	3.0	142491
19534	LENHARTSVILLE	28266	711	14.5	28.6	38.7	12.5	5.8	56251	66138	81	82	598	8.5	9.2	40.6	34.6	7.0	157877
19539	MERTZTOWN	27978	1741	15.7	23.2	40.8	15.2	5.1	60823	71549	85	87	1460	6.0	7.3	50.5	33.1	3.2	153708
19540	MOHNTON	30398	4078	13.5	24.7	39.4	14.7	7.8	62437	75146	87	88	3428	1.3	8.8	48.5	37.7	3.7	159355
19541	MOHRSVILLE	24694	1606	13.1	26.2	45.0	13.3	2.5	58652	67819	83	84	1391	8.6	9.1	52.7	28.0	1.7	143285
19543	MORGANTOWN	23731	1496	15.6	23.3	43.7	13.4	3.9	57784	68740	82	83	1138	3.8	2.7	45.1	43.3	5.1	172887
19547	OLEY	26233	1775	14.0	22.8	45.4	14.6	3.3	59819	69932	84	85	1436	1.1	7.0	49.6	38.0	4.3	160622
19549	PORT CLINTON	25497	134	21.6	36.6	27.6	14.2	0.0	45363	51132	62	63	96	5.2	30.2	41.7	22.9	0.0	102632
19551	ROBESONIA	28244	2007	16.0	24.6	42.0	12.3	5.0	57793	68939	82	83	1639	2.6	12.5	54.7	26.2	4.0	135408
19555	SHOEMAKERSVILLE	21941	1520	19.2	28.2	41.0	9.5	2.0	51719	62418	75	75	1219	5.1	16.0	59.6	18.3	1.1	119958
19560	TEMPLE	25093	2861	20.0	30.8	36.8	9.7	2.7	49000	59112	70	70	2380	3.2	16.3	67.2	12.5	0.8	113122
19562	TOPTON	25600	886	17.5	28.4	37.9	13.0	3.2	52963	63897	77	77	623	6.3	8.0	61.8	23.3	0.6	124280
19565	WERNERSVILLE	28524	3076	16.5	23.8	40.8	13.5	5.4	59727	72532	84	85	2550	7.5	8.8	56.6	24.4	2.7	134404
19567	WOMELSDORF	25292	1761	17.2	28.5	42.4	8.7	3.2	53347	63877	77	78	1362	1.5	21.5	58.4	16.1	2.6	118012
19601	READING	14618	11670	44.8	29.4	19.7	4.5	1.5	28318	33448	9	4	5042	40.3	37.4	16.8	4.9	0.7	57026
19602	READING	13300	6874	50.7	30.1	16.0	2.3	1.0	24515	28880	4	2	2802	58.4	31.9	7.8	1.5	0.5	46047
19604	READING	16993	8584	32.5	33.4	26.7	5.5	1.9	36747	43274	34	29	5087	41.3	39.6	14.8	3.9	0.5	55052
19605	READING	26809	7074	18.0	26.1	38.9	13.3	3.7	55828	67247	81	81	6089	5.6	15.3	60.8	17.5	0.8	123288
19606	READING	28995	12718	14.8	25.9	38.9	14.6	5.7	59599	71042	84	85	10357	6.2	13.7	57.8	20.8	1.6	133171
19607	READING	31099	9349	18.9	27.3	36.3	11.4	6.0	53190	64581	77	77	6648	1.9	12.6	66.8	16.6	2.1	120975
19608	READING	29420	6633	13.0	22.1	40.7	16.7	7.5	64965	78595	88	90	5177	2.0	4.3	54.2	36.3	3.1	156512
19609	READING	29154	4310	14.6	27.8	41.4	10.5	5.7	55742	66970	80	81	3531	1.1	8.2	77.7	12.8	0.3	122439
19610	READING	45545	6243	14.3	19.7	33.2	15.4	17.5	71250	85586	92	93	4716	0.8	5.7	44.8	41.0	7.8	172564
19611	READING	19026	4046	32.7	32.8	27.5	5.0	2.0	37350	44879	37	32	2167	4.5	47.5	43.7	4.0	0.3	88832
	PENNSYLVANIA	25764		25.8	27.2	31.2	10.2	5.7	46988	57000				11.9	18.4	40.7	25.1	4.1	123516
	UNITED STATES	25866		24.7	27.1	30.8	10.9	6.5	48124	56710				10.9	15.0	33.7	30.1	10.4	145905

#	POST OFFICE NAME	Auto Loan	Home Loan	Invest-ments	Retire-ment Plans	Home Repair	Lawn & Garden	Comput-ers & Hard-ware	Major Appli-ances	TV, Radio, Sound Equip-ment	Furni-ture	Dine out/ Carry out	Sports Equip-ment	Fees & Tickets	Toys & Games	Travel	Cable TV	Apparel & Services	Auto Repairs	Health Insur-ance	Pets & Supplies
19501	ADAMSTOWN	97	86	66	82	91	98	80	88	85	80	103	105	78	105	82	87	98	86	96	114
19503	BALLY	120	107	81	101	113	121	98	109	105	98	127	130	97	130	101	107	121	106	118	141
19504	BARTO	113	101	76	95	106	114	93	103	99	93	120	123	91	123	96	101	114	101	112	133
19505	BECHTELSVILLE	107	95	72	90	100	108	88	97	93	88	113	116	86	116	90	96	108	95	105	126
19506	BERNVILLE	105	98	79	94	102	108	90	98	94	90	114	117	89	118	92	95	109	95	104	124
19507	BETHEL	95	85	65	80	90	96	78	87	83	78	101	103	77	103	81	85	96	85	94	112
19508	BIRDSBORO	105	96	78	92	101	108	90	98	94	90	115	117	88	117	92	96	110	96	105	124
19510	BLANDON	133	134	116	134	134	136	122	128	120	125	149	151	123	151	122	118	145	124	123	152
19512	BOYERTOWN	104	98	84	94	102	110	92	99	97	92	118	116	93	122	95	99	113	97	105	122
19518	DOUGLASSVILLE	117	129	126	128	129	130	118	120	114	118	142	141	122	148	120	112	139	117	114	138
19520	ELVERSON	120	124	117	121	127	134	113	120	113	114	140	136	116	139	117	114	135	116	122	141
19522	FLEETWOOD	107	111	103	108	113	117	102	106	102	102	127	125	105	132	105	103	123	103	107	126
19525	GILBERTSVILLE	119	135	134	136	132	133	122	123	116	124	146	144	128	151	123	113	144	120	113	139
19526	HAMBURG	92	88	76	83	91	100	84	89	89	83	108	103	84	112	87	92	103	87	97	108
19529	KEMPTON	111	109	94	106	113	118	100	107	102	100	125	127	101	129	103	103	121	104	110	132
19530	KUTZTOWN	98	89	87	89	90	97	98	94	98	93	121	114	93	121	94	95	117	97	94	111
19533	LEESPORT	99	103	96	100	105	109	95	99	95	94	117	116	97	123	97	95	114	96	99	118
19534	LENHARTSVILLE	116	104	80	99	109	117	97	107	102	97	124	126	94	125	99	104	118	104	114	136
19539	MERTZTOWN	111	109	94	106	112	118	101	108	103	101	126	127	102	130	103	104	122	105	110	131
19540	MOHNTON	112	123	122	121	123	127	113	116	111	113	138	136	118	144	116	110	135	113	112	134
19541	MOHRSVILLE	106	96	75	92	101	108	89	98	94	89	114	117	87	117	91	96	109	95	105	125
19543	MORGANTOWN	104	99	82	95	103	108	91	98	93	91	114	117	91	118	93	95	110	95	102	123
19547	OLEY	102	98	85	93	101	109	91	98	95	90	116	114	91	119	94	97	111	95	104	120
19549	PORT CLINTON	87	77	59	73	82	88	71	79	76	71	92	94	70	94	74	78	88	77	86	102
19551	ROBESONIA	115	104	85	102	109	118	101	108	105	100	128	126	99	130	102	107	122	106	115	132
19555	SHOEMAKERSVILLE	86	83	74	79	86	93	79	83	82	78	101	97	80	106	81	84	97	81	89	100
19560	TEMPLE	81	82	77	78	84	92	78	81	81	77	100	93	80	106	81	84	97	79	87	96
19562	TOPTON	100	88	74	87	92	104	90	95	95	88	116	108	88	117	90	97	110	94	103	111
19565	WERNERSVILLE	100	103	106	104	105	110	99	102	98	99	122	120	100	122	101	97	118	101	100	118
19567	WOMELSDORF	93	92	89	89	94	101	91	93	93	89	115	109	92	119	92	93	111	92	96	109
19601	READING	50	48	63	46	47	53	54	52	57	53	72	59	53	72	53	59	70	54	54	57
19602	READING	43	40	56	39	39	45	46	44	49	46	62	51	45	62	46	51	61	46	46	48
19604	READING	64	61	68	60	61	68	68	65	70	66	87	76	67	87	66	70	84	67	67	72
19605	READING	89	95	96	91	96	105	91	93	93	89	115	105	95	121	94	95	111	90	97	106
19606	READING	99	108	112	106	107	113	103	104	102	102	127	120	106	131	105	101	124	102	101	116
19607	READING	90	98	110	96	98	106	97	96	96	95	120	110	100	124	99	97	117	96	97	107
19608	READING	108	121	126	121	120	124	113	113	108	113	136	131	118	140	115	107	134	111	107	127
19609	READING	87	100	110	96	100	108	95	95	94	94	117	106	100	122	99	96	115	93	96	104
19610	READING	142	161	183	159	161	173	152	154	148	153	186	171	159	183	157	149	182	151	153	169
19611	READING	59	60	77	58	59	66	64	61	66	63	84	70	65	86	64	68	82	63	64	68
	PENNSYLVANIA	89	89	93	87	90	98	89	90	91	88	112	104	89	114	90	92	109	90	92	104
	UNITED STATES	100	100	100	100	100	100	100	100	100	100	100	100	100	100	100	100	100	100	100	100

RHODE ISLAND

POPULATION CHANGE

A 02804-02921

# POST OFFICE NAME	COUNTY FIPS CODE	POPULATION 2000	2004	2009	2000-2004 ANNUAL RATE % Rate	State Centile	HOUSEHOLDS 2000	2004	2009	% Annual Rate 2000-2004	2004 Average HH Size	FAMILIES 2000	2004	% Annual Rate 2000-2004
02804 ASHAWAY	009	2920	3084	3257	1.3	84	1080	1158	1239	1.7	2.66	809	863	1.5
02806 BARRINGTON	001	16825	16929	17003	0.2	23	6014	6107	6186	0.4	2.70	4718	4768	0.3
02807 BLOCK ISLAND	009	1010	1042	1087	0.7	55	472	495	524	1.1	2.10	250	259	0.8
02808 BRADFORD	009	2009	2052	2128	0.5	39	675	697	731	0.8	2.94	542	557	0.6
02809 BRISTOL	001	22452	22842	23112	0.4	32	8308	8587	8800	0.8	2.42	5645	5812	0.7
02812 CAROLINA	009	1279	1334	1400	1.0	78	449	476	506	1.4	2.80	358	377	1.2
02813 CHARLESTOWN	009	7901	8373	8862	1.4	86	3197	3448	3704	1.8	2.42	2294	2461	1.7
02814 CHEPACHET	007	7753	8236	8585	1.4	88	2791	2987	3130	1.6	2.76	2202	2346	1.5
02815 CLAYVILLE	007	176	183	190	0.9	72	65	68	71	1.1	2.69	53	56	1.3
02816 COVENTRY	003	31680	32655	33682	0.7	54	11957	12507	13081	1.1	2.57	8761	9121	1.0
02817 WEST GREENWICH	003	5074	5633	5997	2.5	99	1742	1936	2075	2.5	2.90	1447	1602	2.4
02818 EAST GREENWICH	003	18306	18723	19105	0.5	43	7354	7611	7861	0.8	2.44	5008	5162	0.7
02822 EXETER	009	5503	5719	5981	0.9	70	1926	2030	2153	1.3	2.70	1476	1547	1.1
02825 FOSTER	007	5053	5268	5449	1.0	77	1799	1888	1961	1.1	2.78	1425	1489	1.0
02827 GREENE	003	2092	2270	2393	1.9	96	688	759	812	2.3	2.93	568	624	2.2
02828 GREENVILLE	007	7132	7410	7631	0.9	69	2765	2891	2992	1.1	2.47	1969	2042	0.9
02830 HARRISVILLE	007	6585	6806	6994	0.8	58	2408	2506	2589	0.9	2.70	1846	1909	0.8
02831 HOPE	007	3883	4039	4165	0.9	73	1331	1391	1438	1.0	2.89	1084	1129	1.0
02832 HOPE VALLEY	009	4715	4914	5154	1.0	76	1794	1899	2021	1.4	2.58	1330	1401	1.2
02833 HOPKINTON	009	334	356	377	1.5	92	115	124	134	1.8	2.87	73	78	1.6
02835 JAMESTOWN	005	5622	5815	5929	0.8	59	2359	2473	2561	1.1	2.35	1625	1691	0.9
02836 KENYON	009	27	28	29	0.9	66	11	12	12	2.1	2.33	9	9	0.0
02837 LITTLE COMPTON	005	3599	3694	3751	0.6	50	1477	1542	1593	1.0	2.40	1043	1081	0.9
02838 MANVILLE	007	3573	3574	3621	0.0	20	1465	1475	1502	0.2	2.39	942	941	0.0
02839 MAPLEVILLE	007	916	966	1002	1.3	82	348	369	385	1.4	2.62	277	293	1.3
02840 NEWPORT	005	25663	25034	25019	-0.6	4	11549	11466	11674	-0.2	2.04	5635	5515	-0.5
02841 NEWPORT	005	1009	954	946	-1.3	3	62	54	53	-3.2	2.56	58	50	-3.4
02842 MIDDLETOWN	005	17129	17352	17594	0.3	31	6943	7191	7430	0.8	2.37	4596	4709	0.6
02852 NORTH KINGSTOWN	009	23456	23993	25024	0.5	43	9091	9410	9939	0.8	2.52	6482	6677	0.7
02857 NORTH SCITUATE	007	8788	9266	9630	1.3	81	3250	3447	3599	1.4	2.67	2491	2628	1.3
02858 OAKLAND	007	484	495	505	0.5	43	168	173	177	0.7	2.86	135	138	0.5
02859 PASCOAG	007	7649	7534	7605	-0.4	5	2569	2543	2578	-0.2	2.79	1943	1919	-0.3
02860 PAWTUCKET	007	46495	46921	47807	0.2	26	19049	19273	19686	0.3	2.41	11326	11381	0.1
02861 PAWTUCKET	007	26642	26910	27461	0.2	28	11062	11250	11530	0.4	2.37	7232	7298	0.2
02863 CENTRAL FALLS	007	18724	19189	19677	0.6	49	6625	6782	6964	0.6	2.74	4315	4391	0.4
02864 CUMBERLAND	007	31831	33157	34387	1.0	74	12217	12776	13297	1.1	2.58	9047	9414	0.9
02865 LINCOLN	007	17184	17802	18357	0.8	64	6688	6930	7158	0.8	2.55	4765	4917	0.7
02871 PORTSMOUTH	005	17069	17427	17749	0.5	38	6710	6956	7207	0.9	2.50	4849	4994	0.7
02872 PRUDENCE ISLAND	005	88	78	77	-2.8	1	53	48	48	-2.3	1.63	21	19	-2.3
02874 SAUNDERSTOWN	009	4722	5017	5356	1.4	89	1758	1876	2020	1.5	2.67	1300	1384	1.5
02877 SLOCUM	009	105	109	113	0.9	68	34	36	38	1.4	2.89	25	26	0.9
02878 TIVERTON	005	15258	15718	16005	0.7	53	6077	6371	6602	1.1	2.46	4408	4589	1.0
02879 WAKEFIELD	009	19424	20535	21806	1.3	85	7692	8245	8871	1.7	2.47	5234	5568	1.5
02881 KINGSTON	009	6458	6682	6892	0.8	61	912	1005	1095	2.3	2.79	637	686	1.8
02882 NARRAGANSETT	009	14691	15460	16331	1.2	80	6177	6575	7026	1.5	2.34	3410	3602	1.3
02885 WARREN	001	11377	11366	11427	0.0	16	4714	4773	4849	0.3	2.33	3000	3019	0.2
02886 WARWICK	003	30325	30247	30608	-0.1	15	13159	13321	13670	0.3	2.23	8025	8046	0.1
02888 WARWICK	003	20769	20663	20867	-0.1	11	8617	8696	8902	0.2	2.35	5554	5562	0.0
02889 WARWICK	003	29337	29936	30580	0.5	36	11348	11754	12172	0.8	2.53	7923	8150	0.7
02891 WESTERLY	009	21384	22096	23208	0.8	57	8891	9290	9874	1.0	2.34	5711	5956	1.0
02892 WEST KINGSTON	009	4781	5138	5473	1.7	93	1682	1836	1984	2.1	2.72	1325	1442	2.0
02893 WEST WARWICK	003	29511	30395	31369	0.7	53	12464	12969	13523	0.9	2.33	7681	7936	0.8
02894 WOOD RIVER JUNCTION	009	984	1066	1141	1.9	95	331	363	394	2.2	2.94	259	283	2.1
02895 WOONSOCKET	007	43234	43016	43631	-0.1	11	17756	17784	18131	0.0	2.36	10771	10707	-0.1
02896 NORTH SMITHFIELD	007	10526	10779	11004	0.6	45	3927	4052	4159	0.7	2.59	2934	3013	0.6
02898 WYOMING	009	1841	2008	2156	2.1	97	615	678	737	2.3	2.95	493	541	2.2
02903 PROVIDENCE	007	9389	9505	9804	0.3	30	4466	4604	4836	0.7	1.69	1233	1214	-0.4
02904 PROVIDENCE	007	29183	29782	30620	0.5	36	13309	13631	14074	0.6	2.16	7399	7518	0.4
02905 PROVIDENCE	007	25277	25460	25912	0.2	24	8607	8715	8911	0.3	2.77	5830	5857	0.1
02906 PROVIDENCE	007	30787	31554	32358	0.6	49	12085	12520	12954	0.8	2.07	5093	5203	0.5
02907 PROVIDENCE	007	26602	28352	29696	1.5	92	8288	8844	9277	1.5	3.14	5918	6279	1.4
02908 PROVIDENCE	007	35550	36441	37489	0.6	49	13008	13307	13698	0.5	2.62	8209	8334	0.4
02909 PROVIDENCE	007	41398	42871	44240	0.8	64	14782	15164	15596	0.6	2.81	9370	9538	0.4
02910 CRANSTON	007	20784	20719	20983	-0.1	12	8581	8597	8734	0.0	2.41	5501	5473	-0.1
02911 NORTH PROVIDENCE	007	14734	14662	14875	-0.1	11	6322	6330	6451	0.0	2.28	3772	3747	-0.2
02912 PROVIDENCE	007	400	399	399	-0.1	15	3	3	3	0.0	2.67	0	0	0.0
02914 EAST PROVIDENCE	007	22015	21760	21981	-0.3	7	9069	9017	9149	-0.1	2.38	5786	5709	-0.3
02915 RIVERSIDE	007	18470	18476	18796	0.0	20	7936	7989	8157	0.2	2.26	4867	4857	-0.1
02916 RUMFORD	007	8213	8249	8389	0.1	22	3528	3560	3634	0.2	2.32	2197	2201	0.0
02917 SMITHFIELD	007	13503	13780	14127	0.5	36	4438	4568	4725	0.7	2.45	3026	3099	0.6
02918 PROVIDENCE	007	3160	3274	3357	0.8	65	154	181	200	3.9	5.75	83	98	4.0
02919 JOHNSTON	007	28133	28413	28871	0.2	27	11166	11355	11588	0.4	2.46	7708	7783	0.2
02920 CRANSTON	007	37830	37825	38327	0.0	18	14681	14746	15021	0.1	2.28	9377	9348	-0.1
02921 CRANSTON	007	9599	11071	12074	3.4	100	3255	3735	4086	3.3	2.95	2709	3134	3.5
RHODE ISLAND					0.5					0.7	2.46			0.5
UNITED STATES					1.2					1.3	2.58			1.1

ZIP CODE #	POST OFFICE NAME	RACE (%) White 2000	White 2004	Black 2000	Black 2004	Asian/Pacific 2000	Asian/Pacific 2004	% Hispanic Origin 2000	% Hispanic Origin 2004	2004 AGE DISTRIBUTION (%) 0-4	5-9	10-14	15-19	20-24	25-44	45-64	65-84	85+	18+	MEDIAN AGE 2004	% 2004 Males	% 2004 Females
02804	ASHAWAY	96.5	96.0	0.7	0.8	0.7	0.8	1.1	1.3	6.0	6.6	7.4	6.2	4.8	29.5	27.4	10.9	1.3	76.2	39.4	50.2	49.8
02806	BARRINGTON	96.4	95.7	0.7	0.8	1.8	2.2	1.1	1.3	5.7	7.2	8.8	7.7	4.9	21.8	29.0	13.1	1.9	73.2	41.8	48.7	51.3
02807	BLOCK ISLAND	97.8	97.4	0.6	0.7	0.8	1.0	1.2	1.4	6.1	5.7	5.0	4.0	4.2	26.9	31.3	15.8	1.1	80.8	44.0	48.2	51.8
02808	BRADFORD	96.4	95.9	0.6	0.7	0.5	0.6	1.5	1.9	8.6	8.4	9.1	8.3	6.9	29.3	21.4	7.2	0.9	68.1	32.6	50.3	49.7
02809	BRISTOL	97.1	96.8	0.6	0.7	0.7	0.9	1.3	1.6	5.2	5.2	5.6	9.5	7.9	25.2	24.0	14.9	2.7	80.8	39.2	48.2	51.8
02812	CAROLINA	96.6	96.0	0.2	0.2	0.7	0.9	2.0	2.6	6.5	7.1	7.0	6.6	5.6	29.5	30.0	7.1	0.8	75.5	39.1	50.4	49.6
02813	CHARLESTOWN	96.3	95.8	0.4	0.4	0.6	0.8	1.1	1.4	5.5	5.8	6.0	5.3	4.8	26.5	30.7	13.8	1.6	79.3	42.8	49.2	50.8
02814	CHEPACHET	98.4	98.0	0.3	0.4	0.3	0.4	0.7	0.9	5.8	6.5	7.7	6.9	5.3	27.7	30.5	8.5	1.0	75.7	40.1	50.1	49.9
02815	CLAYVILLE	98.3	97.8	0.0	0.0	0.6	1.1	1.1	1.1	6.6	7.7	8.2	6.0	4.9	25.7	32.2	7.7	1.1	73.8	39.8	49.2	50.8
02816	COVENTRY	97.6	97.2	0.4	0.4	0.6	0.8	1.2	1.5	6.2	6.5	7.1	6.2	5.4	28.5	26.4	11.9	1.8	76.2	39.4	48.3	51.7
02817	WEST GREENWICH	97.7	97.4	0.3	0.3	0.6	0.7	0.7	0.8	6.8	7.5	7.9	6.8	5.0	28.4	29.8	7.2	0.6	73.4	39.0	49.8	50.2
02818	EAST GREENWICH	95.9	95.2	0.7	0.7	2.3	2.8	1.0	1.2	5.4	6.5	7.9	6.4	4.2	23.0	30.6	13.6	2.5	75.9	43.1	48.1	51.9
02822	EXETER	96.4	95.9	0.7	0.8	0.8	0.9	1.3	1.6	5.7	6.6	7.8	6.6	5.1	28.4	29.4	8.6	1.9	75.5	40.1	49.2	50.9
02825	FOSTER	97.4	96.8	0.2	0.3	0.7	0.9	0.8	1.1	5.4	7.0	8.4	6.7	3.8	27.0	31.9	8.5	1.4	74.8	40.7	49.8	50.2
02827	GREENE	97.7	97.3	0.6	0.7	0.3	0.5	0.7	0.8	7.1	7.6	7.7	6.7	4.8	28.9	28.1	7.8	1.4	73.4	38.4	51.0	49.0
02828	GREENVILLE	98.5	98.0	0.2	0.3	0.6	0.8	0.5	0.7	4.5	5.2	6.5	6.4	4.3	23.0	29.2	16.5	4.5	79.4	45.1	47.2	52.8
02830	HARRISVILLE	98.9	98.6	0.1	0.1	0.2	0.2	0.6	0.8	5.7	6.1	7.1	7.2	6.4	29.6	27.7	9.0	1.3	76.6	39.0	49.1	50.9
02831	HOPE	97.8	97.3	0.4	0.5	0.8	1.1	0.8	1.0	6.8	7.5	8.2	6.3	4.5	27.9	28.3	9.4	1.1	73.5	39.3	49.8	50.2
02832	HOPE VALLEY	97.0	96.6	0.6	0.7	0.3	0.4	1.2	1.4	6.4	6.9	7.4	6.3	5.2	29.3	28.2	9.3	1.0	75.2	39.0	49.9	50.1
02833	HOPKINTON	97.9	97.5	0.3	0.3	0.3	0.3	0.9	1.1	5.1	5.6	7.0	7.0	5.9	24.4	29.5	13.2	2.3	78.1	41.8	48.0	52.0
02835	JAMESTOWN	97.6	97.2	0.8	0.9	0.4	0.5	0.9	1.1	3.7	5.4	7.2	6.0	3.6	22.0	36.9	13.6	1.7	79.7	46.0	48.4	51.6
02836	KENYON	96.3	96.4	0.0	0.0	0.0	0.0	0.0	0.0	7.1	7.1	7.1	7.1	7.1	32.1	32.1	0.0	0.0	78.6	35.0	50.0	50.0
02837	LITTLE COMPTON	98.8	98.5	0.1	0.1	0.3	0.4	0.9	1.1	4.8	5.6	6.3	5.4	3.7	23.0	33.1	15.9	2.3	80.1	45.7	49.3	50.7
02838	MANVILLE	94.3	93.0	1.7	2.0	1.5	2.1	2.4	3.1	5.8	6.0	7.7	7.0	6.0	27.8	23.5	13.5	2.6	76.1	38.3	47.1	52.9
02839	MAPLEVILLE	98.7	98.1	0.1	0.2	0.3	0.4	1.0	1.2	5.2	5.8	6.0	6.7	5.6	28.8	32.2	9.2	0.5	78.9	40.9	49.7	50.3
02840	NEWPORT	84.9	83.1	7.3	8.1	1.3	1.6	5.4	6.4	5.7	5.2	5.5	7.6	8.4	31.0	23.5	11.0	2.1	80.4	36.3	47.5	52.5
02841	NEWPORT	64.5	60.4	20.1	22.0	5.9	6.8	9.2	10.9	4.8	3.7	5.5	13.4	22.6	40.6	8.3	1.1	0.1	83.4	25.0	68.5	31.6
02842	MIDDLETOWN	89.2	87.6	4.7	5.2	2.2	2.7	2.9	3.5	6.8	6.9	6.8	5.8	6.0	27.8	24.9	12.4	2.9	75.8	39.1	48.8	51.2
02852	NORTH KINGSTOWN	95.6	95.0	1.0	1.1	1.0	1.2	1.9	2.3	6.5	7.0	7.2	6.3	5.1	26.5	29.0	10.8	1.6	75.1	40.1	48.4	51.6
02857	NORTH SCITUATE	98.3	97.9	0.3	0.4	0.4	0.5	0.7	1.0	5.5	6.3	7.2	6.3	4.8	25.1	31.6	11.8	1.5	76.9	42.2	49.0	51.0
02858	OAKLAND	99.2	99.0	0.0	0.0	0.0	0.2	0.8	1.0	5.5	5.9	6.9	6.7	6.1	28.9	30.1	9.3	0.8	77.6	40.1	50.1	49.9
02859	PASCOAG	98.2	97.9	0.4	0.4	0.3	0.4	1.1	1.4	5.6	6.2	7.4	7.6	5.8	28.8	26.0	9.7	2.8	75.7	38.8	49.1	50.9
02860	PAWTUCKET	66.3	63.0	10.3	11.2	1.0	1.2	18.7	22.5	7.4	7.0	7.4	7.0	7.6	30.3	20.8	10.5	1.9	74.0	34.1	47.9	52.1
02861	PAWTUCKET	91.1	89.5	2.1	2.4	0.8	1.0	5.8	7.4	5.6	5.7	6.5	6.0	5.8	28.9	24.3	14.6	2.6	78.5	39.8	47.3	52.7
02863	CENTRAL FALLS	57.2	53.4	5.8	5.8	0.7	0.8	47.7	53.7	8.8	7.8	7.9	7.8	8.7	31.0	17.3	9.1	1.8	71.0	30.5	50.1	49.9
02864	CUMBERLAND	96.7	95.9	0.6	0.7	0.9	1.1	2.1	2.8	6.1	6.6	7.0	6.1	4.8	27.2	26.2	14.0	2.2	76.5	40.8	47.7	52.3
02865	LINCOLN	95.8	94.7	0.7	0.8	1.8	2.4	1.5	2.0	5.4	6.0	7.3	6.7	5.1	25.3	27.4	14.3	2.6	76.9	41.8	47.8	52.2
02871	PORTSMOUTH	95.8	95.0	1.2	1.3	1.4	1.8	1.5	1.8	5.9	6.3	7.5	6.1	4.3	25.9	30.0	12.4	1.7	76.3	41.8	49.1	50.9
02872	PRUDENCE ISLAND	98.9	98.7	1.1	1.3	0.0	0.0	0.0	0.0	1.3	1.3	6.4	2.6	0.0	12.8	41.0	30.8	3.9	89.7	58.8	47.4	52.6
02874	SAUNDERSTOWN	96.6	96.0	0.6	0.6	1.1	1.4	0.8	1.0	7.2	7.8	7.7	5.7	5.2	28.9	28.1	8.3	1.1	73.8	38.3	49.5	50.5
02877	SLOCUM	96.2	94.5	1.0	0.9	1.0	0.9	1.0	0.9	5.5	6.4	9.2	7.3	5.5	30.3	27.5	7.3	0.9	74.3	38.4	48.6	51.4
02878	TIVERTON	98.0	97.6	0.4	0.5	0.4	0.5	0.7	0.9	5.0	5.6	6.6	5.9	4.6	26.8	28.6	14.6	2.4	79.2	42.6	48.7	51.3
02879	WAKEFIELD	92.7	91.8	1.2	1.3	2.2	2.8	1.1	1.3	6.0	6.5	7.5	6.7	5.6	25.0	28.2	12.2	2.2	75.5	40.7	47.9	52.1
02881	KINGSTON	85.6	83.5	3.0	3.2	6.3	7.6	3.9	4.6	2.3	2.7	3.2	41.5	24.1	11.2	10.8	3.6	0.6	89.8	20.1	46.3	53.7
02882	NARRAGANSETT	95.7	95.2	0.8	0.8	0.8	1.0	1.3	1.6	3.9	4.2	4.8	5.8	16.8	24.5	26.2	12.3	1.6	84.2	37.2	48.7	51.3
02885	WARREN	96.8	96.5	0.8	0.9	0.5	0.7	0.9	1.1	4.9	5.1	6.5	6.3	5.9	27.2	26.1	14.9	3.3	79.7	41.6	47.5	52.5
02886	WARWICK	95.3	94.6	1.0	1.1	2.0	2.4	1.5	1.7	4.9	5.1	5.7	5.7	5.2	27.0	26.8	16.5	3.1	80.8	42.8	47.2	52.8
02888	WARWICK	95.3	94.7	1.2	1.3	1.2	1.4	1.9	2.3	5.3	5.6	6.2	5.9	5.4	27.4	26.9	14.2	3.1	79.1	41.6	47.3	52.7
02889	WARWICK	94.7	94.0	1.4	1.5	1.3	1.6	1.6	2.0	5.9	6.2	6.9	6.6	5.6	29.2	26.4	11.9	1.4	76.9	39.4	48.3	51.7
02891	WESTERLY	95.1	94.3	0.7	0.8	2.1	2.6	1.1	1.4	6.0	6.1	6.5	5.8	5.6	26.9	25.9	14.2	3.1	77.8	40.9	48.3	51.7
02892	WEST KINGSTON	95.5	95.0	0.5	0.6	0.8	0.9	1.0	1.2	6.3	7.0	7.7	7.5	5.2	28.8	28.0	8.3	1.3	74.2	38.5	49.6	50.5
02893	WEST WARWICK	93.8	92.9	1.1	1.2	1.5	1.8	3.1	3.7	6.5	6.1	6.2	6.0	6.8	30.8	24.2	11.8	1.7	77.7	37.2	48.3	51.7
02894	WOOD RIVER JUNCTION	97.0	96.5	0.3	0.4	0.7	0.8	1.4	2.0	8.5	8.8	7.5	5.6	3.8	31.5	26.1	7.2	0.9	71.5	36.8	49.1	50.9
02895	WOONSOCKET	83.1	80.2	4.4	5.0	4.1	5.0	9.3	11.4	7.7	6.8	7.1	6.7	7.1	28.5	21.5	12.2	2.5	74.4	35.4	48.0	52.0
02896	NORTH SMITHFIELD	98.3	97.9	0.4	0.5	0.5	0.7	0.5	0.7	5.2	5.8	6.6	5.6	4.6	24.8	29.3	14.6	3.6	78.9	43.5	47.6	52.4
02898	WYOMING	97.1	96.8	0.5	0.6	0.3	0.4	0.9	1.2	7.7	8.2	7.7	6.1	4.3	31.7	26.7	7.0	0.7	72.5	37.6	50.0	50.1
02903	PROVIDENCE	62.6	58.6	14.9	15.6	6.0	7.5	18.7	21.3	3.6	3.2	3.1	13.8	15.6	27.3	17.0	12.9	3.5	88.2	29.7	49.3	50.7
02904	PROVIDENCE	83.0	80.2	7.2	8.0	2.1	2.6	8.3	10.4	5.3	5.2	5.6	5.4	5.8	28.9	24.3	16.3	3.4	80.6	40.9	46.7	53.3
02905	PROVIDENCE	53.3	50.8	18.3	18.5	3.4	3.9	26.5	29.0	7.3	7.0	8.3	11.2	9.0	27.4	20.6	7.8	1.4	72.4	30.1	47.7	52.3
02906	PROVIDENCE	77.8	74.1	7.4	8.5	7.0	8.7	5.0	6.2	3.9	3.5	3.6	12.1	20.9	28.1	18.0	7.9	2.0	86.7	28.0	47.8	52.2
02907	PROVIDENCE	26.8	24.7	23.4	22.4	9.7	10.4	50.4	53.6	9.4	8.7	10.0	9.9	9.6	27.3	18.4	5.9	0.9	66.0	26.7	49.2	50.8
02908	PROVIDENCE	62.0	58.7	13.0	13.4	4.7	5.4	25.6	29.0	7.5	7.1	7.8	9.2	11.4	28.9	17.4	8.8	2.0	73.4	29.7	47.6	52.4
02909	PROVIDENCE	48.4	44.8	11.9	11.9	6.7	7.3	44.1	48.7	9.4	8.5	8.9	8.4	9.1	30.5	16.5	7.4	1.3	68.3	28.3	49.0	51.0
02910	CRANSTON	88.3	85.8	2.5	2.9	4.6	5.9	4.0	5.1	5.7	5.7	6.7	6.7	6.3	29.5	24.7	12.3	2.5	77.9	38.9	47.1	52.9
02911	NORTH PROVIDENCE	93.2	91.7	1.9	2.2	1.7	2.2	3.8	4.9	4.5	4.7	5.9	5.8	5.8	28.9	25.6	15.6	3.2	81.4	41.5	46.1	53.9
02912	PROVIDENCE	76.8	72.7	3.0	3.3	14.5	17.8	5.0	6.0	0.0	0.0	0.0	61.2	34.3	3.3	1.3	0.0	0.0	100.0	19.1	43.1	56.9
02914	EAST PROVIDENCE	80.2	77.5	7.0	8.1	1.3	1.6	2.4	3.0	5.7	5.5	6.2	6.2	6.9	28.8	22.9	14.8	3.1	78.9	38.9	47.0	53.0
02915	RIVERSIDE	91.5	89.9	3.5	4.2	1.3	1.7	1.6	2.0	5.1	5.2	5.9	5.9	5.3	27.0	26.2	15.8	3.6	80.0	42.4	46.0	54.0
02916	RUMFORD	92.2	90.9	3.1	3.7	0.8	1.0	1.4	1.8	5.3	5.6	6.4	5.6	5.1	25.1	27.5	16.2	3.3	79.1	43.1	46.5	53.5
02917	SMITHFIELD	96.8	96.0	1.1	1.3	1.1	1.4	1.1	1.5	4.0	4.6	5.5	12.8	11.9	23.0	23.8	10.9	3.6	82.6	37.0	50.0	50.0
02918	PROVIDENCE	88.0	85.4	4.3	5.0	1.5	2.0	7.0	9.2	1.6	1.5	2.5	39.7	39.0	8.2	4.8	2.5	0.3	93.2	20.6	42.5	57.5
02919	JOHNSTON	96.5	95.7	0.7	0.8	1.1	1.5	2.0	2.6	5.4	5.7	6.3	5.4	4.7	27.7	26.1	15.6	3.2	79.4	42.0	46.8	53.2
02920	CRANSTON	88.5	86.3	4.9	5.4	3.2	4.0	5.5	6.8	4.5	4.7	5.4	5.7	6.2	29.0	24.2	17.0	3.3	81.9	41.7	50.7	49.3
02921	CRANSTON	96.6	95.7	0.5	0.6	1.9	2.5	1.2	1.5	6.8	7.8	8.7	6.7	4.8	26.4	28.4	9.0	1.5	72.1	39.2	49.2	50.8
	RHODE ISLAND	85.0	83.4	4.5	4.7	2.3	2.8	8.7	10.0	6.1	6.1	6.8	7.4	7.3	27.6	24.4	12.1	2.3	77.1	37.7	48.2	51.8
	UNITED STATES	75.1	73.6	12.3	12.5	3.8	4.2	12.5	14.1	6.9	6.7	7.2	7.0	7.3	28.6	23.8	10.8	1.7	75.1	36.0	49.1	50.9

# ZIP CODE	POST OFFICE NAME	2004 Per Capita Income	2004 HH Income Base	2004 Household Income Distribution (%) Less than $25,000	$25,000 to $49,999	$50,000 to $99,999	$100,000 to $149,999	$150,000 or More	Median Household Income 2004	2009	2004 National Centile	2004 State Centile	2004 Home Value Base	2004 Home Value Distribution (%) Less than $50,000	$50,000 to $89,999	$90,000 to $174,999	$175,000 to $399,999	$400,000 or More	2004 Median Home Value
02804	ASHAWAY	28280	1158	12.3	21.4	45.0	13.6	7.7	59368	71688	84	54	974	0.0	0.0	20.0	71.4	8.6	220117
02806	BARRINGTON	44813	6107	11.1	15.3	29.3	22.0	22.3	87443	112644	97	100	5358	0.2	0.0	5.5	58.1	36.2	334394
02807	BLOCK ISLAND	36600	495	22.6	23.2	31.1	14.3	8.7	54977	71356	80	45	328	0.0	0.0	0.6	8.2	91.2	853333
02808	BRADFORD	20659	697	14.6	30.3	41.5	11.3	2.3	53170	61510	77	43	483	0.0	0.0	31.1	65.0	3.9	195424
02809	BRISTOL	26642	8587	24.4	24.5	31.5	13.6	6.0	51262	64672	74	36	5520	0.5	0.4	7.0	77.6	14.5	258764
02812	CAROLINA	27459	476	5.5	27.7	44.5	15.1	7.1	67785	80128	90	80	411	2.4	3.9	13.4	67.2	13.1	232143
02813	CHARLESTOWN	30745	3448	15.7	22.6	40.6	15.0	6.1	58987	70387	84	51	2800	1.8	2.6	11.9	62.2	21.5	248852
02814	CHEPACHET	27041	2987	13.2	18.3	46.9	16.2	5.3	65157	78252	89	69	2563	2.6	2.3	14.4	71.6	9.1	242255
02815	CLAYVILLE	31456	68	8.8	13.2	48.5	22.1	7.4	78834	94824	95	96	62	0.0	0.0	6.5	69.4	24.2	305882
02816	COVENTRY	26250	12507	19.1	22.6	40.8	13.6	3.9	58316	67799	83	50	9838	3.1	4.2	24.4	64.0	4.3	203667
02817	WEST GREENWICH	31393	1936	11.0	16.7	43.9	18.6	9.8	75079	87222	93	92	1732	0.4	1.9	15.7	64.7	17.4	277006
02818	EAST GREENWICH	43098	7611	15.6	18.8	30.4	15.6	19.6	75166	87619	91	84	5529	0.5	0.8	8.3	48.2	42.2	352698
02822	EXETER	29867	2030	11.3	17.4	41.2	21.4	8.7	75166	87609	93	93	1765	4.1	2.3	12.1	54.9	26.7	273214
02825	FOSTER	27591	1888	11.0	20.0	43.3	19.2	6.5	70263	85909	91	82	1666	0.0	1.0	8.8	75.6	14.6	270216
02827	GREENE	26862	759	6.9	21.3	48.5	17.9	5.4	69101	81665	91	81	692	0.0	0.0	12.6	76.5	11.0	252395
02828	GREENVILLE	29739	2891	16.5	23.1	34.4	18.1	8.0	63894	79356	88	65	2332	0.5	1.2	11.2	80.2	7.0	237204
02830	HARRISVILLE	25307	2506	16.8	23.7	40.1	14.3	5.3	59524	70297	84	55	1982	1.2	1.3	17.5	75.4	4.7	225971
02831	HOPE	32707	1391	9.1	20.1	40.1	17.7	13.0	72976	91156	92	86	1195	0.0	0.0	16.1	57.1	26.9	283275
02832	HOPE VALLEY	26464	1899	19.0	22.0	39.5	14.1	5.5	59201	69034	84	53	1518	0.0	1.3	14.8	75.1	8.8	238996
02833	HOPKINTON	22842	124	32.3	16.9	30.7	11.3	8.9	50766	58209	73	32	83	0.0	0.0	8.4	74.7	16.9	251250
02835	JAMESTOWN	49300	2473	11.7	20.1	32.5	18.7	17.0	72986	93970	92	88	1991	0.0	0.0	4.7	51.9	43.4	362958
02836	KENYON	32401	12	0.0	25.0	50.0	16.7	8.3	75000	89441	93	91	10	0.0	0.0	10.0	80.0	10.0	237500
02837	LITTLE COMPTON	40443	1542	16.3	18.0	36.5	14.9	14.3	64331	80667	88	68	1296	0.5	0.2	4.4	50.1	44.8	374340
02838	MANVILLE	21949	1475	28.1	34.1	26.0	9.2	2.7	41275	49069	51	19	547	0.0	0.0	14.3	72.2	13.5	232040
02839	MAPLEVILLE	27149	369	13.0	24.9	39.3	16.3	6.5	59603	72073	84	57	313	18.5	11.2	14.3	48.2	8.6	207622
02840	NEWPORT	31410	11466	27.6	23.9	30.3	11.5	7.4	48087	57973	68	28	4958	0.3	0.2	10.9	61.4	27.3	275779
02841	NEWPORT	9925	54	13.0	11.1	48.2	20.4	7.4	80697	98459	95	97	0	0.0	0.0	0.0	0.0	0.0	0
02842	MIDDLETOWN	31341	7191	16.1	27.6	34.7	15.0	6.6	56131	65864	81	47	4190	1.9	2.0	7.2	73.8	15.2	261345
02852	NORTH KINGSTOWN	34104	9410	17.9	18.1	35.5	18.5	10.1	66962	82009	90	76	6929	3.2	0.0	9.9	65.6	21.3	259596
02857	NORTH SCITUATE	32767	3447	12.9	21.0	39.4	17.2	9.5	67701	84548	90	78	2978	1.4	1.1	8.6	68.6	20.4	282353
02858	OAKLAND	25717	173	13.9	20.2	42.8	17.9	5.2	65952	78462	89	73	144	0.7	1.4	13.9	79.2	4.9	241892
02859	PASCOAG	24205	2543	15.6	23.4	43.9	12.4	4.7	59893	71016	84	58	1885	1.3	1.1	20.0	73.5	4.2	219184
02860	PAWTUCKET	18159	19273	41.4	28.5	22.8	5.2	2.0	31327	36177	16	11	6389	0.9	2.2	50.8	44.5	1.6	170569
02861	PAWTUCKET	21978	11250	27.5	29.8	33.4	7.0	2.4	43782	51050	58	22	7168	2.6	1.9	50.0	45.0	0.6	171201
02863	CENTRAL FALLS	12049	6782	49.5	29.1	17.6	3.3	0.5	25244	28459	5	5	1580	1.3	3.9	60.4	33.7	0.7	155081
02864	CUMBERLAND	30821	12776	17.2	22.3	35.5	16.4	8.6	61967	76316	86	61	9803	0.6	0.5	13.4	74.0	11.5	237124
02865	LINCOLN	33981	6930	19.0	22.7	32.5	16.9	8.9	61267	76557	86	59	4972	0.7	0.9	9.6	67.7	21.1	258438
02871	PORTSMOUTH	34160	6956	12.8	20.4	39.1	16.9	10.8	66540	81070	89	74	5336	3.6	1.1	8.6	63.9	22.8	274102
02872	PRUDENCE ISLAND	21859	48	58.3	16.7	25.0	0.0	0.0	22407	27566	3	3	44	0.0	0.0	27.3	56.8	15.9	241667
02874	SAUNDERSTOWN	33309	1876	7.3	17.1	42.7	23.9	9.0	78722	95022	95	95	1614	0.7	0.7	6.6	64.4	27.6	288525
02877	SLOCUM	28147	36	13.9	22.2	30.6	25.0	8.3	75000	94737	93	91	29	0.0	0.0	13.8	69.0	17.2	305000
02878	TIVERTON	27448	6371	20.8	21.2	38.3	14.9	4.8	58464	68212	82	49	5152	1.3	2.3	15.6	68.6	12.3	236952
02879	WAKEFIELD	33495	8245	14.9	21.9	36.9	16.4	9.8	63700	77389	88	64	6163	0.4	0.3	11.3	63.1	24.9	285570
02881	KINGSTON	20179	1005	16.3	21.0	32.1	16.6	13.9	67400	82226	90	77	695	0.1	0.0	4.3	62.7	32.8	341990
02882	NARRAGANSETT	34081	6575	23.6	22.1	30.8	15.0	8.6	55889	68051	81	46	4119	0.3	0.3	6.6	64.7	28.1	283685
02885	WARREN	27250	4773	25.4	25.8	31.6	12.0	5.2	48495	61501	69	30	2752	0.4	0.8	17.6	72.0	9.2	230764
02886	WARWICK	28067	13321	22.9	26.1	35.9	9.6	4.2	50901	60027	74	34	8617	1.2	1.1	35.1	55.9	6.8	190639
02888	WARWICK	27679	8696	20.0	27.5	36.4	11.6	4.5	51895	60575	75	38	6407	0.5	1.4	44.8	51.3	2.0	179426
02889	WARWICK	26008	11754	20.0	26.2	39.1	10.9	3.9	53032	62113	77	42	8887	0.3	2.5	46.5	47.3	3.5	175961
02891	WESTERLY	29624	9290	21.9	26.6	33.6	12.2	5.6	51184	60075	74	35	5806	0.7	0.3	11.0	70.3	17.7	247603
02892	WEST KINGSTON	29129	1836	7.0	21.8	46.7	18.0	6.4	70879	83402	92	85	1637	0.5	3.0	13.4	69.9	13.3	248634
02893	WEST WARWICK	23485	12969	26.6	29.7	32.5	7.8	3.4	44354	50644	60	23	6743	1.0	1.6	45.5	51.1	0.8	177541
02894	WOOD RIVER JUNCTION	22974	363	15.7	19.6	47.4	13.0	4.4	62269	75000	86	62	311	0.0	0.0	17.4	73.6	9.0	225538
02895	WOONSOCKET	18499	17784	37.8	29.8	25.3	5.2	1.8	34237	39938	25	14	6070	0.9	0.9	35.8	61.7	0.7	189280
02896	NORTH SMITHFIELD	29663	4052	16.9	19.7	38.3	16.7	8.4	65446	80669	89	72	3244	0.0	0.0	12.2	76.5	11.3	246063
02898	WYOMING	24084	678	9.4	20.9	51.0	15.0	3.5	65254	77490	89	70	611	0.0	3.6	17.2	72.8	6.4	232774
02903	PROVIDENCE	20334	4604	61.8	18.3	12.9	3.6	3.5	15835	18884	1	1	565	0.0	0.7	49.6	34.2	15.6	174747
02904	PROVIDENCE	24236	13631	34.9	27.9	27.1	7.0	3.2	37720	44276	38	15	6630	0.6	2.4	37.6	56.8	2.6	189172
02905	PROVIDENCE	18820	8715	33.5	27.6	27.9	6.9	4.2	37991	44955	39	16	4286	0.6	4.0	45.5	44.2	5.7	174941
02906	PROVIDENCE	37145	12520	26.8	21.5	25.3	12.6	13.8	52326	67013	76	39	5111	0.0	0.1	11.6	49.5	38.7	336117
02907	PROVIDENCE	12006	8844	49.0	26.8	19.0	3.7	1.6	25561	28529	5	7	2470	2.4	6.5	61.7	27.8	1.6	146384
02908	PROVIDENCE	16847	13307	38.5	29.1	24.6	5.7	2.1	33768	39546	23	12	5607	0.0	1.7	54.9	42.4	1.1	167766
02909	PROVIDENCE	12307	15164	50.8	26.7	17.9	3.1	1.4	24396	27831	4	4	4152	1.5	2.8	67.2	27.5	1.1	148812
02910	CRANSTON	24434	8597	22.1	31.4	33.2	9.8	3.5	46455	54986	65	27	5585	0.3	0.8	46.1	52.2	0.7	178049
02911	NORTH PROVIDENCE	27433	6330	26.5	30.8	29.5	9.2	3.9	42956	50950	56	20	3696	0.7	2.0	31.0	65.1	1.2	195317
02912	PROVIDENCE	9600	3	33.3	66.7	0.0	0.0	0.0	31250	36250	16	9	0	0.0	0.0	0.0	0.0	0.0	0
02914	EAST PROVIDENCE	19358	9017	33.4	28.3	31.1	6.0	1.2	38869	45614	42	18	4763	0.6	0.1	33.2	64.6	1.6	193019
02915	RIVERSIDE	23434	7989	26.7	28.0	34.9	8.4	2.0	45805	53402	63	24	4965	0.4	0.5	31.8	65.9	1.5	194155
02916	RUMFORD	30541	3560	20.4	26.3	33.7	11.6	8.0	52415	63012	76	41	2383	2.6	0.7	21.5	67.6	7.6	220023
02917	SMITHFIELD	27452	4568	18.5	18.5	37.1	18.2	7.7	64238	80100	88	66	3450	0.1	0.2	21.3	70.0	8.4	232470
02918	PROVIDENCE	9617	181	44.2	27.1	23.2	1.7	3.9	28314	32676	9	8	59	0.0	0.0	71.2	28.8	0.0	149375
02919	JOHNSTON	25177	11355	27.4	22.4	31.9	13.2	5.1	50212	60912	72	31	8145	0.2	1.2	23.2	70.9	4.5	215213
02920	CRANSTON	24789	14746	26.3	27.5	32.0	10.1	4.1	45929	54936	64	26	9473	0.4	0.6	26.4	68.8	3.9	207842
02921	CRANSTON	33102	3735	9.1	13.3	40.0	24.5	13.1	81867	102373	96	99	3374	0.1	0.3	6.0	68.6	25.0	311611
	RHODE ISLAND	25865		26.5	25.0	31.6	11.2	5.7	48328	57374				1.0	1.3	25.3	60.5	11.9	218642
	UNITED STATES	25866		24.7	27.1	30.8	10.9	6.5	48124	56710				10.9	15.0	33.7	30.1	10.4	145905

#	POST OFFICE NAME	FINANCIAL SERVICES				THE HOME						ENTERTAINMENT						PERSONAL			
						Home Improvements		Furnishings													
		Auto Loan	Home Loan	Invest-ments	Retire-ment Plans	Home Repair	Lawn & Garden	Comput-ers & Hard-ware	Major Appli-ances	TV, Radio, Sound Equip-ment	Furni-ture	Dine out/ Carry out	Sports Equip-ment	Fees & Tickets	Toys & Games	Travel	Cable TV	Apparel & Services	Auto Repairs	Health Insur-ance	Pets & Supplies
02804	ASHAWAY	96	117	128	115	115	117	108	107	102	107	128	123	115	137	110	101	128	104	99	117
02806	BARRINGTON	157	195	228	194	192	200	176	175	166	177	209	200	191	217	183	164	208	170	164	192
02807	BLOCK ISLAND	131	102	70	92	115	130	97	116	109	96	129	136	86	128	103	117	120	115	138	159
02808	BRADFORD	83	94	96	96	92	91	88	88	82	89	104	104	90	106	87	78	103	86	77	96
02809	BRISTOL	91	97	105	96	97	104	97	96	96	95	119	111	99	122	98	96	116	96	95	106
02812	CAROLINA	101	124	131	124	121	120	111	111	103	111	129	130	117	137	113	100	129	107	99	122
02813	CHARLESTOWN	111	110	98	107	113	117	102	109	103	102	127	129	101	129	104	103	122	107	110	132
02814	CHEPACHET	97	119	126	119	117	116	107	107	100	106	125	125	114	134	109	97	125	103	97	118
02815	CLAYVILLE	110	137	145	137	134	132	122	122	113	121	142	142	130	151	125	110	142	117	109	134
02816	COVENTRY	93	102	105	101	102	105	96	97	94	96	117	113	99	121	97	92	115	95	93	110
02817	WEST GREENWICH	129	143	138	144	142	141	129	132	123	131	154	155	134	159	130	120	152	128	122	151
02818	EAST GREENWICH	136	159	186	161	155	163	151	147	144	151	182	170	161	188	154	143	181	146	139	162
02822	EXETER	113	131	132	130	129	129	118	120	112	119	140	140	123	146	120	109	139	116	110	134
02825	FOSTER	100	124	132	124	122	120	111	110	103	110	129	129	118	137	113	100	129	106	99	122
02827	GREENE	103	129	137	129	126	125	115	114	106	114	134	134	122	142	117	103	134	110	102	126
02828	GREENVILLE	98	110	127	111	110	117	107	106	104	107	130	122	111	131	109	103	128	106	103	116
02830	HARRISVILLE	91	104	110	105	103	103	99	98	94	98	117	116	102	122	99	90	116	96	89	108
02831	HOPE	126	151	161	153	147	148	137	136	127	138	161	157	145	165	138	123	160	131	122	149
02832	HOPE VALLEY	97	103	99	99	104	108	95	98	94	94	117	114	97	121	97	95	114	96	98	115
02833	HOPKINTON	83	97	108	93	96	105	92	92	91	91	113	103	97	118	96	93	111	90	93	100
02835	JAMESTOWN	149	181	201	179	179	185	165	165	156	165	197	189	176	203	171	155	195	161	156	180
02836	KENYON	98	122	130	122	120	118	109	109	101	108	127	127	116	135	111	98	127	105	97	120
02837	LITTLE COMPTON	134	145	149	141	149	159	134	141	132	134	164	160	137	165	140	134	160	137	142	163
02838	MANVILLE	68	74	84	74	74	78	75	73	74	73	93	86	77	97	76	74	91	74	72	80
02839	MAPLEVILLE	113	102	78	97	107	115	94	104	99	94	121	124	92	124	97	102	115	101	112	133
02840	NEWPORT	88	90	113	92	88	95	97	92	95	95	120	109	97	120	95	93	118	95	87	101
02841	NEWPORT	132	84	80	96	77	91	125	108	127	117	159	144	107	142	103	116	152	128	100	123
02842	MIDDLETOWN	99	107	121	109	106	111	108	105	105	107	131	124	110	133	108	102	129	107	99	115
02852	NORTH KINGSTOWN	115	128	141	130	127	132	124	122	119	124	150	142	128	152	125	117	147	122	116	135
02857	NORTH SCITUATE	114	141	151	140	138	138	126	126	118	126	148	147	134	157	129	115	148	122	114	139
02858	OAKLAND	98	117	122	117	116	115	105	106	99	105	124	124	111	131	108	96	123	102	96	118
02859	PASCOAG	92	106	112	106	105	106	100	99	96	99	120	116	104	126	101	93	118	97	92	109
02860	PAWTUCKET	58	56	67	55	55	61	62	59	64	61	80	69	61	80	61	64	78	62	60	65
02861	PAWTUCKET	68	73	79	71	73	80	74	72	74	71	92	82	76	97	75	75	90	72	74	79
02863	CENTRAL FALLS	40	38	64	36	36	43	44	42	50	46	63	47	44	64	44	52	63	45	44	46
02864	CUMBERLAND	104	119	131	118	117	123	114	112	110	112	138	129	119	143	116	109	136	111	107	123
02865	LINCOLN	115	128	140	127	128	136	123	123	120	122	150	142	128	155	126	120	147	121	121	136
02871	PORTSMOUTH	110	131	145	130	129	134	122	121	116	121	146	139	129	151	125	115	145	119	115	133
02872	PRUDENCE ISLAND	60	47	32	43	53	60	45	54	50	44	60	63	40	59	48	54	56	53	63	73
02874	SAUNDERSTOWN	119	141	150	143	137	137	129	128	120	130	151	149	135	156	130	115	150	124	114	140
02877	SLOCUM	109	136	144	136	133	131	121	120	112	120	141	141	129	150	124	109	141	116	108	133
02878	TIVERTON	88	101	113	101	100	104	97	96	93	96	116	111	101	120	98	91	115	94	91	105
02879	WAKEFIELD	113	124	134	125	124	128	118	119	114	118	143	139	121	145	119	112	140	118	113	134
02881	KINGSTON	124	132	150	139	129	134	140	127	130	135	165	154	141	164	133	123	162	130	114	141
02882	NARRAGANSETT	113	112	117	111	114	122	113	114	112	112	140	132	111	137	113	112	135	115	114	132
02885	WARREN	87	89	93	87	89	97	91	90	92	88	113	104	91	115	91	92	110	91	92	100
02886	WARWICK	82	91	104	89	90	97	89	88	88	88	110	101	93	114	91	89	108	88	87	97
02888	WARWICK	84	96	108	94	95	100	93	92	91	91	114	105	97	118	95	91	112	91	89	100
02889	WARWICK	85	99	111	97	97	100	94	93	91	93	114	107	99	120	96	90	113	92	87	101
02891	WESTERLY	98	98	100	97	99	107	98	100	99	96	122	115	98	123	99	99	118	99	102	113
02892	WEST KINGSTON	105	129	137	129	127	125	116	116	108	116	136	136	123	144	119	105	135	112	104	128
02893	WEST WARWICK	71	77	90	78	77	81	79	76	77	77	96	89	80	99	79	76	95	77	73	83
02894	WOOD RIVER JUNCTION	94	104	105	105	100	99	98	97	92	99	116	115	99	117	96	87	114	97	86	107
02895	WOONSOCKET	58	56	65	56	56	62	62	60	64	60	80	69	62	80	61	64	77	62	62	66
02896	NORTH SMITHFIELD	104	118	123	116	118	123	111	112	108	109	134	128	115	139	113	108	131	109	109	124
02898	WYOMING	95	113	117	113	110	109	103	102	96	103	120	120	107	126	104	92	120	100	92	114
02903	PROVIDENCE	51	41	57	44	41	47	56	49	57	53	72	61	52	68	52	55	69	55	49	55
02904	PROVIDENCE	68	70	84	69	69	77	74	71	75	72	94	82	76	96	75	76	92	73	73	79
02905	PROVIDENCE	69	68	92	68	67	73	75	71	77	75	97	83	75	98	74	77	96	74	70	78
02906	PROVIDENCE	117	110	150	118	108	118	132	118	129	127	163	146	128	160	124	123	159	127	110	131
02907	PROVIDENCE	45	45	79	41	42	49	50	48	56	53	72	53	50	75	51	60	73	51	49	52
02908	PROVIDENCE	58	56	73	55	55	62	63	60	66	62	82	70	62	83	62	66	81	63	60	66
02909	PROVIDENCE	42	41	66	38	39	45	47	44	51	48	66	50	46	67	47	54	65	47	45	48
02910	CRANSTON	75	83	94	82	83	88	84	82	83	82	103	94	86	108	85	82	101	82	80	89
02911	NORTH PROVIDENCE	80	88	105	87	87	94	89	87	89	88	111	100	92	114	91	89	109	88	86	95
02912	PROVIDENCE	34	20	26	23	20	24	40	29	39	34	48	41	32	43	32	34	45	36	27	33
02914	EAST PROVIDENCE	60	62	71	61	62	69	65	63	66	63	83	72	67	86	66	67	80	64	65	69
02915	RIVERSIDE	69	76	88	74	75	81	76	74	75	75	94	85	79	97	77	76	93	74	74	81
02916	RUMFORD	93	100	115	99	100	108	99	98	99	98	123	113	102	126	102	100	121	99	99	110
02917	SMITHFIELD	102	112	122	113	112	116	110	109	106	108	132	128	112	136	110	104	130	108	104	121
02918	PROVIDENCE	60	39	48	43	38	45	70	53	68	60	85	72	58	77	57	60	80	63	49	60
02919	JOHNSTON	84	90	95	89	91	97	88	89	87	87	108	102	90	111	90	88	105	88	89	99
02920	CRANSTON	79	86	97	83	85	93	85	84	85	84	106	95	88	109	87	86	104	84	86	92
02921	CRANSTON	130	157	171	161	151	153	141	138	131	143	166	160	152	171	143	127	166	134	124	152
	RHODE ISLAND	85	91	106	90	90	96	92	90	92	91	115	104	94	117	92	91	113	91	88	99
	UNITED STATES	100	100	100	100	100	100	100	100	100	100	100	100	100	100	100	100	100	100	100	100

# POST OFFICE NAME	COUNTY FIPS CODE	POPULATION 2000	2004	2009	2000-2004 ANNUAL RATE % Rate	State Centile	HOUSEHOLDS 2000	2004	2009	% Annual Rate 2000-2004	2004 Average HH Size	FAMILIES 2000	2004	% Annual Rate 2000-2004
29001 ALCOLU	027	2472	2499	2584	0.3	28	863	897	957	0.9	2.77	655	665	0.4
29003 BAMBERG	009	7757	7645	7569	-0.3	10	2797	2845	2891	0.4	2.51	1992	1973	-0.2
29006 BATESBURG	081	10997	11517	12331	1.1	56	4287	4616	5057	1.8	2.48	3120	3270	1.1
29009 BETHUNE	055	2120	2314	2480	2.1	83	844	946	1037	2.7	2.45	596	648	2.0
29010 BISHOPVILLE	061	14536	14525	14646	0.0	19	4904	5079	5311	0.8	2.53	3466	3492	0.2
29014 BLACKSTOCK	039	1617	1590	1582	-0.4	9	613	621	630	0.3	2.56	462	457	-0.3
29015 BLAIR	039	1701	1677	1705	-0.3	10	565	575	605	0.4	2.89	406	402	-0.2
29016 BLYTHEWOOD	079	10002	11586	12753	3.5	96	3579	4235	4757	4.0	2.70	2852	3297	3.5
29018 BOWMAN	075	4135	4023	4047	-0.6	4	1520	1531	1585	0.2	2.62	1106	1084	-0.5
29020 CAMDEN	055	21509	21775	22549	0.3	29	8608	8924	9441	0.9	2.39	6029	6070	0.2
29030 CAMERON	017	3653	3894	4126	1.5	70	1490	1644	1799	2.3	2.37	1063	1140	1.7
29031 CARLISLE	023	1482	1442	1420	-0.6	4	586	589	595	0.1	2.44	408	396	-0.7
29032 CASSATT	055	3700	3949	4191	1.5	72	1316	1443	1566	2.2	2.74	997	1063	1.5
29033 CAYCE	063	11441	11232	11527	-0.4	8	4943	4992	5242	0.2	2.24	3100	3007	-0.7
29036 CHAPIN	063	12294	13469	14396	2.2	84	4657	5250	5745	2.9	2.49	3730	4107	2.3
29037 CHAPPELLS	071	620	653	679	1.2	60	248	269	285	1.9	2.43	188	199	1.4
29038 COPE	075	2637	2659	2681	0.2	27	969	1008	1044	0.9	2.64	729	739	0.3
29039 CORDOVA	075	4069	3931	3920	-0.8	1	1499	1491	1527	-0.1	2.64	1140	1105	-0.7
29040 DALZELL	085	6788	7257	7529	1.6	73	2483	2742	2931	2.4	2.65	1891	2036	1.8
29042 DENMARK	009	5903	6045	6127	0.6	39	2120	2246	2343	1.4	2.45	1432	1473	0.7
29044 EASTOVER	079	5812	5834	5977	0.1	23	2108	2185	2299	0.9	2.64	1575	1574	0.0
29045 ELGIN	055	13261	15288	16845	3.4	95	4744	5595	6294	4.0	2.73	3807	4404	3.5
29046 ELLIOTT	061	112	108	107	-0.9	1	34	34	36	0.0	3.18	25	25	0.0
29047 ELLOREE	075	2787	2845	2892	0.5	37	1166	1233	1291	1.3	2.31	783	799	0.5
29048 EUTAWVILLE	075	4870	4965	5018	0.5	35	1845	1947	2028	1.3	2.54	1333	1367	0.6
29051 GABLE	027	2381	2373	2399	-0.1	16	448	460	485	0.6	2.68	348	349	0.1
29052 GADSDEN	079	2247	2299	2331	0.3	31	746	785	827	1.2	2.90	590	602	0.5
29053 GASTON	063	15091	16607	17851	2.3	85	5376	6047	6623	2.8	2.74	3998	4372	2.1
29054 GILBERT	063	7597	8075	8519	1.5	69	2866	3119	3358	2.0	2.56	2242	2383	1.5
29055 GREAT FALLS	039	4781	4863	4921	0.4	33	1846	1928	1982	1.0	2.52	1324	1343	0.3
29056 GREELEYVILLE	089	2622	2553	2581	-0.6	4	990	1005	1056	0.4	2.52	702	693	-0.3
29058 HEATH SPRINGS	057	4805	4937	5125	0.6	42	1891	2011	2152	1.5	2.31	1386	1431	0.8
29059 HOLLY HILL	075	6266	6111	6118	-0.6	5	2333	2356	2432	0.2	2.55	1719	1689	-0.4
29061 HOPKINS	079	13267	13833	14445	1.0	53	4697	5058	5426	1.8	2.73	3623	3773	1.0
29063 IRMO	079	24162	27176	29598	2.8	91	8556	9839	10937	3.3	2.75	6920	7757	2.7
29065 JENKINSVILLE	039	733	732	747	0.0	18	289	299	316	0.8	2.45	210	212	0.2
29067 KERSHAW	057	10060	10665	11216	1.4	67	3500	3833	4150	2.2	2.49	2538	2699	1.5
29069 LAMAR	031	4671	4795	4861	0.6	41	1755	1855	1925	1.3	2.58	1294	1331	0.7
29070 LEESVILLE	063	11500	12039	12612	1.1	56	4421	4742	5069	1.7	2.53	3286	3427	1.0
29072 LEXINGTON	063	31063	35218	38324	3.0	92	11245	13049	14482	3.6	2.61	8675	9815	3.0
29073 LEXINGTON	063	29971	32396	34536	1.9	79	11234	12445	13535	2.4	2.60	8454	9118	1.8
29075 LITTLE MOUNTAIN	071	2767	2946	3091	1.5	69	1077	1175	1260	2.1	2.51	826	881	1.5
29078 LUGOFF	055	12419	13160	13875	1.4	66	4606	5008	5397	2.0	2.62	3572	3796	1.4
29080 LYNCHBURG	061	3800	4082	4268	1.7	75	1322	1474	1595	2.6	2.77	971	1051	1.9
29081 EHRHARDT	009	1508	1486	1469	-0.4	10	599	613	624	0.6	2.41	411	408	-0.2
29082 LODGE	029	734	852	943	3.6	96	283	339	387	4.3	2.40	197	229	3.6
29101 MC BEE	025	2967	3072	3246	0.8	48	1072	1142	1238	1.5	2.63	810	843	0.9
29102 MANNING	027	16043	16778	17741	1.1	55	6125	6646	7289	1.9	2.50	4401	4651	1.3
29104 MAYESVILLE	061	2267	2236	2235	-0.3	11	782	798	824	0.5	2.80	589	586	-0.1
29105 MONETTA	003	1267	1338	1415	1.3	62	459	498	540	1.9	2.67	350	371	1.4
29107 NEESES	075	2958	3174	3322	1.7	74	1181	1297	1390	2.2	2.45	872	932	1.6
29108 NEWBERRY	071	19606	19987	20510	0.5	34	7338	7629	7985	0.9	2.49	4991	5027	0.2
29111 NEW ZION	027	1189	1211	1257	0.4	34	413	435	467	1.2	2.78	326	337	0.8
29112 NORTH	075	4663	4712	4766	0.3	28	1797	1884	1963	1.1	2.50	1262	1282	0.4
29113 NORWAY	075	1734	1731	1740	0.0	17	631	652	675	0.8	2.65	466	469	0.2
29114 OLANTA	041	2106	2336	2461	2.5	88	729	837	907	3.3	2.69	548	615	2.8
29115 ORANGEBURG	075	29515	29898	30436	0.3	30	11527	11956	12485	0.9	2.39	7418	7451	0.1
29117 ORANGEBURG	075	2437	2361	2348	-0.7	3	37	31	31	-4.1	2.55	21	17	-4.9
29118 ORANGEBURG	075	14264	15239	15884	1.6	72	5313	5835	6251	2.2	2.55	3943	4228	1.7
29123 PELION	063	5670	6283	6754	2.4	88	2037	2315	2541	3.1	2.69	1534	1694	2.4
29125 PINEWOOD	085	4374	4579	4796	1.1	56	1540	1656	1785	1.7	2.72	1139	1199	1.2
29126 POMARIA	071	2448	2454	2488	0.1	22	960	989	1027	0.7	2.48	693	695	0.1
29127 PROSPERITY	071	6888	7314	7648	1.4	68	2790	3049	3265	2.1	2.39	2063	2196	1.5
29128 REMBERT	085	6952	7139	7317	0.6	42	2260	2397	2537	1.4	2.67	1632	1686	0.8
29129 RIDGE SPRING	081	3780	4121	4519	2.1	82	1382	1540	1721	2.6	2.67	998	1084	2.0
29130 RIDGEWAY	039	5684	6169	6563	2.0	81	2127	2398	2639	2.9	2.47	1570	1725	2.2
29133 ROWESVILLE	075	904	1037	1122	3.3	94	345	410	457	4.2	2.52	248	286	3.4
29135 SAINT MATTHEWS	017	11401	11765	12227	0.7	45	4362	4649	4986	1.5	2.50	3165	3287	0.9
29137 SALLEY	003	2788	2836	2957	0.4	33	1077	1126	1204	1.1	2.52	780	793	0.4
29138 SALUDA	081	11282	12238	13563	1.9	80	4067	4495	5077	2.4	2.66	3037	3276	1.8
29142 SANTEE	075	4619	4772	4872	0.8	47	1747	1861	1953	1.5	2.56	1286	1332	0.8
29145 SILVERSTREET	071	1009	1031	1055	0.5	37	375	394	413	1.2	2.60	274	281	0.6
29146 SPRINGFIELD	075	1782	1752	1759	-0.4	9	685	696	719	0.4	2.42	478	471	-0.4
29148 SUMMERTON	027	5923	6324	6766	1.6	72	2361	2630	2928	2.6	2.37	1677	1819	1.9
29150 SUMTER	085	38267	38316	38760	0.0	20	14633	15065	15665	0.7	2.46	9907	9896	0.0
29152 SHAW A F B	085	6216	5997	5967	-0.8	1	1616	1591	1624	-0.4	3.25	1500	1468	-0.5
29153 SUMTER	085	14207	14507	14778	0.5	37	5078	5338	5597	1.2	2.66	3824	3922	0.6
29154 SUMTER	085	24070	24107	24290	0.0	21	8770	9028	9347	0.7	2.64	6679	6720	0.1
29160 SWANSEA	063	5404	5958	6429	2.3	86	2080	2344	2578	2.9	2.54	1519	1663	2.2
29161 TIMMONSVILLE	041	11593	11878	12105	0.6	39	4245	4492	4699	1.3	2.63	3211	3320	0.8
29162 TURBEVILLE	027	2613	2858	3114	2.1	83	953	1063	1191	2.6	2.66	726	793	2.1
29163 VANCE	075	2048	2116	2165	0.8	47	727	778	819	1.6	2.72	525	546	0.9
29164 WAGENER	003	4344	4556	4806	1.1	57	1697	1824	1967	1.7	2.50	1220	1274	1.0
29166 WARD	081	1086	1157	1274	1.5	69	414	450	504	2.0	2.57	297	315	1.4
29168 WEDGEFIELD	085	3521	3806	3975	1.9	79	1282	1425	1530	2.5	2.67	938	1017	1.9
29169 WEST COLUMBIA	063	21228	21502	22257	0.3	30	9363	9728	10297	0.9	2.10	4950	4899	-0.2
29170 WEST COLUMBIA	063	18209	18579	19271	0.5	36	7142	7494	7949	1.1	2.48	5269	5363	0.4
29172 WEST COLUMBIA	063	9229	9247	9567	0.1	22	3432	3550	3761	0.8	2.60	2521	2534	0.1
29175 WESTVILLE	055	457	472	490	0.8	46	176	186	197	1.3	2.54	130	134	0.7
29178 WHITMIRE	071	3657	3620	3667	-0.2	12	1539	1558	1612	0.3	2.31	1022	1000	-0.5
29180 WINNSBORO	039	14439	14840	15390	0.7	43	5488	5825	6244	1.4	2.52	3956	4085	0.8
29201 COLUMBIA	079	15800	15614	15918	-0.3	12	5699	5771	6091	0.3	1.83	1905	1743	-2.1
29203 COLUMBIA	079	43510	42665	43842	-0.5	6	15052	15174	16025	0.2	2.58	10320	9970	-0.8
29204 COLUMBIA	079	21423	20701	21067	-0.8	2	8604	8555	8962	-0.1	2.13	4827	4509	-1.6
29205 COLUMBIA	079	25416	24562	25007	-0.8	2	12017	11889	12388	-0.3	1.97	5253	4807	-2.1
SOUTH CAROLINA					1.2					1.8	2.47			1.1
UNITED STATES					1.2					1.3	2.58			1.1

ZIP CODE #	POST OFFICE NAME	RACE (%) White 2000	White 2004	Black 2000	Black 2004	Asian/Pacific 2000	Asian/Pacific 2004	% Hispanic Origin 2000	% Hispanic Origin 2004	2004 AGE DISTRIBUTION (%) 0-4	5-9	10-14	15-19	20-24	25-44	45-64	65-84	85+	18+	MEDIAN AGE 2004	% 2004 Males	% 2004 Females
29001	ALCOLU	41.5	39.9	57.2	58.5	0.0	0.0	1.2	1.4	5.5	5.9	8.0	8.2	7.9	25.4	26.9	11.2	0.9	75.4	37.4	48.9	51.1
29003	BAMBERG	41.9	42.0	57.2	57.1	0.2	0.2	0.6	0.6	6.1	6.4	7.1	8.8	8.0	25.2	24.0	12.4	2.0	75.7	36.4	47.0	53.1
29006	BATESBURG	72.3	71.9	25.4	25.5	0.1	0.1	2.2	2.7	6.6	6.7	6.8	6.0	6.0	26.6	26.6	13.2	1.7	76.3	39.3	49.2	50.8
29009	BETHUNE	67.2	65.9	31.7	32.8	0.1	0.2	0.9	1.2	6.8	6.9	6.6	5.5	6.2	26.8	26.6	13.0	1.6	76.4	38.9	49.2	50.8
29010	BISHOPVILLE	37.8	37.7	61.1	61.1	0.2	0.3	1.1	1.3	6.4	6.5	6.8	6.4	8.1	29.0	24.5	10.8	1.6	76.6	36.1	52.2	47.8
29014	BLACKSTOCK	61.7	60.3	37.0	38.2	0.3	0.3	0.3	0.4	6.0	6.5	7.6	6.7	5.7	28.4	26.8	11.3	0.9	75.7	38.3	50.1	49.9
29015	BLAIR	14.9	14.3	84.1	84.6	0.1	0.1	0.9	1.0	5.7	6.0	8.2	7.2	6.1	26.1	27.3	11.5	1.9	75.4	39.1	45.9	54.1
29016	BLYTHEWOOD	60.2	57.4	37.0	39.2	0.7	0.9	1.8	2.2	7.4	7.7	8.1	6.8	5.7	30.6	26.0	7.1	0.7	72.4	36.2	48.5	51.5
29018	BOWMAN	34.5	33.2	64.5	65.7	0.2	0.2	1.0	1.1	6.2	6.8	7.1	7.8	7.4	25.8	26.5	11.0	1.4	75.2	38.0	48.0	52.1
29020	CAMDEN	61.9	61.1	36.4	36.9	0.4	0.5	1.6	2.0	5.8	6.1	6.6	6.4	6.0	24.2	27.0	15.5	2.4	77.6	41.5	47.2	52.8
29030	CAMERON	49.0	48.2	50.4	51.2	0.1	0.1	0.9	1.0	5.5	5.9	6.7	6.2	5.3	23.7	30.0	14.8	1.9	78.0	43.0	48.1	51.9
29031	CARLISLE	25.6	24.6	73.6	74.5	0.1	0.1	0.4	0.5	5.2	5.6	6.7	6.8	6.8	27.5	27.5	12.7	1.2	78.4	39.6	47.4	52.6
29032	CASSATT	64.9	64.2	33.4	34.0	0.1	0.1	1.6	1.9	6.4	6.6	8.4	7.4	7.7	27.9	26.3	8.6	0.7	74.1	35.3	50.0	50.0
29033	CAYCE	73.1	71.7	24.1	25.0	1.0	1.3	1.3	1.6	5.9	5.8	6.2	6.0	6.6	29.1	25.1	13.5	1.8	78.5	38.8	47.2	52.8
29036	CHAPIN	95.2	94.8	3.7	3.8	0.3	0.4	0.8	1.0	4.8	5.8	6.7	6.2	3.8	22.5	33.5	13.8	2.9	78.6	45.1	49.1	51.0
29037	CHAPPELLS	69.2	68.2	30.2	31.1	0.0	0.0	1.3	1.7	5.2	5.4	6.3	6.7	5.8	26.7	29.6	13.2	1.2	79.3	41.3	51.8	48.2
29038	COPE	62.8	61.6	36.2	37.3	0.2	0.2	0.5	0.5	6.3	6.7	8.2	7.7	6.6	28.0	26.0	9.6	0.9	74.1	36.8	48.8	51.2
29039	CORDOVA	55.3	53.9	43.2	44.4	0.2	0.2	1.0	1.2	7.2	7.6	7.9	8.0	7.5	28.0	25.3	7.8	0.7	72.1	33.8	47.6	52.5
29040	DALZELL	52.5	51.4	43.2	43.6	1.4	1.8	2.0	2.4	7.5	7.3	7.7	8.0	7.5	30.2	23.4	7.9	0.5	72.8	33.5	49.3	50.7
29042	DENMARK	18.4	18.5	80.5	80.5	0.3	0.3	0.5	0.5	6.9	6.8	6.9	8.1	10.1	25.1	24.2	10.6	1.3	75.7	33.1	47.7	52.3
29044	EASTOVER	33.1	31.4	65.0	66.3	0.2	0.3	1.1	1.4	7.1	7.8	8.2	7.5	5.8	26.0	27.0	9.4	1.2	72.1	36.8	47.7	52.3
29045	ELGIN	76.5	74.0	19.9	21.6	0.9	1.2	2.5	3.1	7.9	8.0	8.2	7.3	6.0	31.4	24.7	6.2	0.4	71.2	34.9	49.0	51.0
29046	ELLIOTT	13.4	13.0	85.7	86.1	0.0	0.9	0.9	0.9	5.6	5.6	6.5	8.3	9.3	25.9	25.9	12.0	0.9	76.9	37.5	47.2	52.8
29047	ELLOREE	44.9	43.3	53.7	55.0	0.0	0.0	1.5	1.7	5.8	6.1	7.0	6.1	5.8	23.2	27.5	17.1	1.5	77.4	42.4	46.9	53.1
29048	EUTAWVILLE	36.1	35.3	62.2	62.6	0.1	0.1	0.8	1.1	5.8	6.0	7.7	7.5	6.6	22.1	28.3	14.7	1.3	75.7	41.1	48.0	52.0
29051	GABLE	35.2	34.0	62.8	63.8	0.1	0.1	1.2	1.4	3.3	3.4	3.6	13.2	29.1	24.8	15.2	6.6	0.7	85.9	24.5	73.7	26.3
29052	GADSDEN	6.7	6.2	92.5	93.0	0.0	0.0	0.9	0.8	7.2	8.0	8.8	7.6	7.2	24.7	27.7	7.9	0.9	71.6	34.6	44.9	55.1
29053	GASTON	82.7	81.4	14.2	15.0	0.3	0.4	1.8	2.3	8.3	7.8	8.4	7.7	8.0	31.4	22.2	5.7	0.5	70.6	31.6	49.6	50.4
29054	GILBERT	92.6	91.8	4.1	4.1	0.2	0.3	3.5	4.3	6.1	6.4	7.0	6.7	6.0	29.6	27.7	9.8	0.8	76.2	38.1	51.5	48.5
29055	GREAT FALLS	65.6	63.4	33.3	35.4	0.2	0.2	0.7	0.8	6.7	6.3	7.2	7.3	6.9	26.4	24.9	12.8	1.5	75.4	37.7	49.0	51.0
29056	GREELEYVILLE	23.4	23.6	75.7	75.4	0.2	0.2	1.2	1.4	7.0	7.1	6.9	8.0	6.6	24.1	26.1	12.5	1.6	74.0	37.5	47.0	53.0
29058	HEATH SPRINGS	68.6	67.5	30.6	31.6	0.1	0.1	0.5	0.6	5.5	5.7	6.4	6.3	6.9	28.2	26.7	12.9	1.5	78.8	39.1	51.6	48.4
29059	HOLLY HILL	28.1	27.2	69.3	70.1	0.0	0.0	0.8	0.9	6.8	6.8	7.5	7.4	7.4	25.7	26.1	11.1	1.2	74.5	36.6	47.2	52.8
29061	HOPKINS	35.3	33.4	61.0	62.1	0.7	0.8	2.7	3.2	6.6	6.9	8.1	7.6	6.9	28.4	27.2	7.8	0.6	73.8	35.9	48.2	51.8
29063	IRMO	77.5	76.1	19.4	20.3	1.4	1.8	1.4	1.8	8.4	8.5	8.6	7.0	5.2	34.0	22.9	4.8	0.6	69.7	33.9	48.7	51.3
29065	JENKINSVILLE	15.4	14.8	83.9	84.6	0.1	0.1	0.6	0.4	6.7	6.7	7.9	7.5	5.9	27.2	25.7	10.7	1.8	74.0	37.2	47.1	52.9
29067	KERSHAW	73.8	72.8	24.6	25.3	0.2	0.2	1.0	1.3	5.4	5.6	6.4	6.2	7.7	30.3	24.9	12.3	1.4	79.0	37.6	54.5	45.5
29069	LAMAR	50.4	49.2	48.6	49.6	0.1	0.1	0.6	0.7	7.0	6.9	7.6	7.2	6.3	27.0	26.2	10.5	1.3	74.2	36.7	48.5	51.6
29070	LEESVILLE	84.0	83.1	13.7	14.1	0.2	0.3	2.0	2.5	6.8	6.7	7.2	6.6	6.3	28.6	26.3	10.4	1.2	75.3	37.2	50.3	49.7
29072	LEXINGTON	91.3	90.6	5.9	5.9	1.1	1.4	2.0	2.5	7.7	7.8	7.6	6.0	5.2	31.0	25.6	8.1	1.1	73.1	36.8	49.4	50.6
29073	LEXINGTON	90.6	89.9	6.7	6.9	0.6	0.8	1.6	2.1	7.7	7.6	7.9	6.7	6.3	33.0	24.0	6.5	0.5	72.8	34.2	49.2	50.8
29075	LITTLE MOUNTAIN	78.9	78.0	19.8	20.3	0.1	0.2	1.0	1.2	5.5	6.2	7.3	5.9	4.7	27.7	30.0	11.3	1.4	77.2	41.0	49.5	50.5
29078	LUGOFF	79.9	78.8	17.7	18.3	0.5	0.6	1.8	2.3	7.5	7.6	7.7	6.7	6.0	29.2	25.7	9.0	0.7	73.0	36.2	48.6	51.4
29080	LYNCHBURG	20.6	19.7	77.0	77.4	0.0	0.0	2.8	3.3	6.2	6.5	8.0	7.4	7.3	24.9	26.8	11.4	1.6	74.8	37.4	48.2	51.8
29081	EHRHARDT	57.8	57.7	40.9	41.1	0.0	0.0	1.5	1.6	5.2	5.9	7.7	6.3	5.6	25.5	27.2	14.6	2.1	77.3	41.0	47.0	53.0
29082	LODGE	64.4	62.1	27.8	28.6	0.0	0.0	9.5	11.2	5.1	5.3	5.9	7.8	6.9	27.8	26.3	13.4	1.6	79.7	38.7	52.1	47.9
29101	MC BEE	63.9	63.0	33.7	34.1	0.2	0.3	3.9	4.8	6.3	6.4	7.7	7.2	7.7	28.6	26.3	9.2	0.7	74.9	35.8	49.9	50.1
29102	MANNING	47.0	46.5	51.0	51.1	0.3	0.4	1.9	2.3	6.4	6.3	7.4	7.1	6.3	24.0	27.6	13.4	1.4	75.3	39.4	47.7	52.3
29104	MAYESVILLE	19.0	18.5	79.5	79.7	0.3	0.4	1.0	1.2	6.6	6.9	8.7	8.5	7.9	24.2	26.4	9.5	1.2	72.6	35.4	45.8	54.2
29105	MONETTA	62.1	61.4	35.0	35.4	0.1	0.1	3.4	4.3	6.7	7.0	8.2	6.7	6.2	30.7	24.2	9.6	0.8	73.8	35.8	49.9	50.2
29107	NEESES	63.4	61.8	33.2	34.3	0.1	0.1	0.8	1.0	7.2	7.2	7.7	6.8	6.5	27.9	24.8	11.0	1.0	73.8	36.3	49.1	51.0
29108	NEWBERRY	56.6	55.8	39.2	39.2	0.5	0.6	7.0	8.7	7.1	6.7	6.6	7.5	8.5	27.0	22.8	11.5	2.3	75.9	35.0	48.3	51.7
29111	NEW ZION	51.5	49.8	47.4	48.9	0.2	0.3	0.9	1.1	6.5	6.5	6.6	7.2	7.6	24.8	26.8	12.8	1.2	76.0	38.0	50.2	49.8
29112	NORTH	52.1	50.6	46.0	47.2	0.2	0.3	0.4	0.4	6.6	6.6	7.2	6.5	6.5	26.3	26.6	12.2	1.5	75.7	38.8	47.5	52.5
29113	NORWAY	47.3	45.6	49.3	50.7	0.1	0.1	0.5	0.6	7.3	7.5	7.3	6.6	6.8	27.0	24.3	12.1	1.2	73.8	36.1	48.6	51.4
29114	OLANTA	45.9	44.3	52.7	54.1	0.0	0.0	1.8	2.1	6.1	6.3	7.6	7.2	7.0	27.0	24.5	12.7	1.6	75.5	38.0	48.2	51.8
29115	ORANGEBURG	28.9	29.1	69.4	69.0	0.4	0.4	1.0	1.2	6.8	6.4	6.9	7.7	9.3	25.8	22.1	12.4	2.6	75.7	35.0	45.8	54.2
29117	ORANGEBURG	0.9	0.8	96.5	96.2	0.2	0.3	1.6	1.7	1.4	1.0	1.8	36.1	42.8	7.8	5.1	3.3	0.8	94.6	21.1	42.8	57.2
29118	ORANGEBURG	43.7	43.0	53.6	53.7	1.7	2.1	0.8	1.0	7.0	7.1	7.6	6.9	6.8	27.0	25.9	10.6	1.0	74.0	36.6	47.8	52.2
29123	PELION	91.9	91.0	5.5	5.8	0.3	0.3	1.2	1.5	7.6	7.3	8.5	7.8	7.6	29.7	23.4	7.5	0.6	71.8	33.3	49.6	50.4
29125	PINEWOOD	41.4	41.7	57.0	56.5	0.2	0.2	1.2	1.4	7.0	6.7	8.1	7.6	7.1	26.5	23.6	11.7	1.8	73.6	36.2	47.5	52.5
29126	POMARIA	71.9	71.0	26.9	27.8	0.2	0.2	0.8	1.0	6.3	6.6	6.3	5.5	6.0	29.0	27.3	11.5	1.6	77.4	39.0	50.8	49.2
29127	PROSPERITY	74.7	74.2	23.8	24.1	0.4	0.5	1.1	1.4	5.9	6.1	6.4	6.0	4.8	27.1	29.0	13.4	1.4	77.8	41.4	49.2	50.8
29128	REMBERT	26.7	25.8	71.7	72.3	0.3	0.4	1.2	1.4	5.7	6.3	7.2	8.1	8.1	29.7	24.6	9.6	0.8	76.2	35.7	53.5	46.5
29129	RIDGE SPRING	55.6	55.1	41.9	41.9	0.3	0.3	4.5	5.4	6.7	6.8	7.9	6.3	6.8	27.8	24.7	11.8	1.3	74.8	36.6	48.9	51.1
29130	RIDGEWAY	52.4	52.0	46.0	46.1	0.2	0.3	1.0	1.2	5.5	5.6	5.9	5.6	5.3	25.9	30.5	13.5	2.2	79.6	42.6	48.3	51.7
29133	ROWESVILLE	38.9	37.4	60.3	61.7	0.0	0.0	0.9	1.2	7.6	7.5	6.8	5.9	6.8	26.2	28.0	9.8	1.5	74.4	36.8	48.2	51.8
29135	SAINT MATTHEWS	49.2	48.6	49.3	49.7	0.2	0.2	1.5	1.8	6.4	6.7	7.1	6.3	5.9	26.3	28.2	11.3	1.7	75.8	38.9	47.5	52.5
29137	SALLEY	57.8	57.1	40.2	40.7	0.2	0.3	1.0	1.1	7.2	7.1	7.0	6.5	6.1	27.1	25.6	11.8	1.7	74.9	37.6	48.6	51.5
29138	SALUDA	61.4	60.5	33.2	33.0	0.1	0.1	9.7	12.0	6.9	6.9	7.3	6.4	7.1	27.5	23.8	12.2	2.1	75.3	36.3	50.2	49.8
29142	SANTEE	32.8	31.2	65.2	66.3	0.1	0.2	1.5	1.9	6.3	6.2	6.4	6.9	6.5	23.7	25.5	17.0	1.6	77.0	41.1	46.3	53.8
29145	SILVERSTREET	58.7	57.6	40.1	40.8	0.0	0.2	1.8	2.0	6.2	6.3	6.7	7.0	6.5	27.6	27.8	10.6	1.3	76.4	38.6	50.6	49.4
29146	SPRINGFIELD	41.9	40.6	56.6	57.8	0.1	0.1	1.5	1.7	6.1	6.2	7.0	6.2	5.7	27.2	26.6	13.0	2.1	76.8	40.0	48.2	51.8
29148	SUMMERTON	35.9	35.5	61.8	61.7	0.4	0.5	1.7	2.0	5.9	5.9	6.4	6.5	5.7	20.7	28.8	18.2	1.9	78.0	44.2	46.7	53.3
29150	SUMTER	46.1	45.9	51.5	51.2	0.9	1.1	1.5	1.8	7.2	7.0	7.5	7.4	7.2	26.1	23.0	12.6	2.0	74.0	36.0	46.3	53.7
29152	SHAW A F B	65.7	63.9	23.0	23.0	3.3	4.0	5.7	7.0	13.8	10.8	7.4	7.5	21.3	35.3	3.3	0.5	0.1	65.3	22.5	55.0	45.0
29153	SUMTER	45.1	44.0	52.5	53.2	0.4	0.5	1.9	2.3	7.2	7.3	7.8	7.2	6.7	28.5	23.6	10.7	1.0	73.3	35.3	49.2	50.8
29154	SUMTER	66.4	65.3	30.5	30.9	1.1	1.4	1.6	1.9	7.3	7.3	7.7	7.1	6.4	29.4	24.5	9.2	1.2	73.1	35.8	49.1	50.9
29160	SWANSEA	74.7	73.8	23.0	23.7	0.3	0.4	1.0	1.3	7.4	7.5	8.0	7.0	6.5	28.4	25.5	9.0	0.8	72.9	35.3	49.4	50.7
29161	TIMMONSVILLE	50.5	49.6	48.2	48.9	0.2	0.2	1.0	1.2	6.8	7.0	7.3	6.9	7.0	28.7	25.6	9.5	1.2	74.8	35.7	48.4	51.6
29162	TURBEVILLE	68.4	66.0	29.5	31.4	0.2	0.2	2.5	3.3	7.0	7.6	6.9	7.7	7.0	27.5	24.8	10.2	1.2	73.8	35.2	47.4	52.6
29163	VANCE	21.2	20.2	77.8	78.7	0.1	0.1	0.9	0.9	6.0	7.3	7.7	9.0	6.3	22.8	27.5	12.2	1.3	73.7	38.2	46.7	53.3
29164	WAGENER	64.8	64.0	33.0	33.4	0.2	0.2	2.0	2.5	6.3	6.5	7.8	7.2	6.4	27.9	25.6	11.0	1.2	75.0	36.9	49.5	50.5
29166	WARD	66.3	65.1	29.7	30.1	0.1	0.1	5.2	6.1	7.9	7.6	7.4	7.6	7.0	27.7	23.9	9.7	1.2	72.4	34.6	49.5	50.5
29168	WEDGEFIELD	40.5	40.3	57.0	56.8	0.5	0.6	1.0	1.3	8.2	7.5	7.4	8.2	8.4	28.8	23.5	7.4	0.6	72.0	32.3	49.8	50.2
29169	WEST COLUMBIA	78.4	77.1	16.5	16.9	1.9	2.3	3.5	4.3	5.2	4.8	4.5	5.4	10.1	27.6	22.2	15.7	4.7	83.1	39.2	45.7	54.3
29170	WEST COLUMBIA	89.4	88.4	7.4	7.8	1.1	1.4	1.8	2.3	6.9	7.0	7.2	6.3	5.6	31.2	25.5	9.5	0.8	75.1	36.8	48.3	51.7
29172	WEST COLUMBIA	68.9	68.3	27.9	28.0	0.8	0.9	2.3	2.9	6.8	6.7	7.9	7.5	7.8	28.7	26.5	7.6	0.5	74.1	34.8	48.9	51.1
29175	WESTVILLE	79.2	78.2	18.8	19.5	0.2	0.4	1.3	1.5	5.9	6.1	7.6	7.2	5.7	24.8	30.3	10.6	1.7	76.3	40.3	49.2	50.9
29178	WHITMIRE	71.3	70.6	27.4	28.0	0.3	0.3	0.7	0.8	5.7	6.2	6.4	5.9	5.9	24.9	27.0	15.7	2.4	77.9	41.6	47.9	52.2
29180	WINNSBORO	40.7	40.0	58.0	58.3	0.2	0.2	1.2	1.4	7.4	7.5	7.6	6.8	6.2	27.1	25.2	10.9	1.3	73.2	36.1	48.0	52.0
29201	COLUMBIA	57.2	55.1	37.5	38.6	2.7	3.3	2.4	2.9	2.7	2.5	3.1	18.9	23.7	25.1	14.9	7.6	1.6	89.7	24.8	49.5	50.5
29203	COLUMBIA	15.5	15.2	82.3	82.3	0.7	0.8	1.6	1.8	7.1	7.0	7.9	8.5	7.5	26.8	23.2	10.6	1.4	73.1	34.1	46.5	53.5
29204	COLUMBIA	38.4	37.9	59.4	59.4	0.5	0.6	1.7	1.9	5.5	5.6	5.9	9.3	10.1	23.8	22.9	14.0	2.9	79.3	37.0	45.3	54.7
29205	COLUMBIA	72.5	71.1	22.9	23.4	2.2	2.6	2.3	2.9	4.9	4.5	4.6	7.1	13.4	34.2	21.3	8.7	1.5	83.1	32.5	48.6	51.4
	SOUTH CAROLINA	67.2	66.6	29.5	29.5	0.9	1.2	2.4	2.9	6.6	6.6	7.0	7.1	7.3	28.4	24.7	11.0	1.4	75.9	36.3	48.8	51.2
	UNITED STATES	75.1	73.6	12.3	12.5	3.8	4.2	12.5	14.1	6.9	6.7	7.2	7.0	7.3	28.6	23.8	10.8	1.7	75.1	36.0	49.1	50.9

ZIP CODE #	POST OFFICE NAME	2004 Per Capita Income	2004 HH Income Base	2004 HOUSEHOLD INCOME DISTRIBUTION (%) Less than $25,000	$25,000 to $49,999	$50,000 to $99,999	$100,000 to $149,999	$150,000 or More	MEDIAN HOUSEHOLD INCOME 2004	2009	2004 National Centile	2004 State Centile	2004 Home Value Base	2004 HOME VALUE DISTRIBUTION (%) Less than $50,000	$50,000 to $89,999	$90,000 to $174,999	$175,000 to $399,999	$400,000 or More	2004 Median Home Value
29001	ALCOLU	15067	897	34.2	32.3	28.1	4.9	0.5	36089	41036	32	44	728	34.8	34.6	23.6	7.0	0.0	72644
29003	BAMBERG	14997	2845	46.6	26.1	21.8	4.2	1.4	27580	31401	8	7	2095	37.0	33.3	22.4	6.4	0.8	67469
29006	BATESBURG	20039	4616	29.0	32.9	29.7	6.0	2.4	40394	46364	47	63	3651	26.4	28.5	31.5	12.2	1.3	84183
29009	BETHUNE	17208	946	31.6	39.6	23.5	5.0	0.3	35790	40809	31	42	802	31.9	30.8	33.0	3.5	0.8	73382
29010	BISHOPVILLE	17162	5079	42.8	28.1	22.4	4.5	2.3	30784	35344	14	19	3883	38.2	35.9	21.8	3.7	0.5	60738
29014	BLACKSTOCK	17744	621	31.7	38.3	22.9	5.0	2.1	37268	41826	36	49	536	28.5	33.8	28.7	6.0	3.0	75366
29015	BLAIR	12451	575	41.0	31.8	25.2	1.9	0.0	30557	35366	14	18	485	29.1	38.6	24.1	6.6	1.7	70854
29016	BLYTHEWOOD	27678	4235	14.8	27.3	35.7	14.7	7.5	59293	69619	84	94	3724	9.2	18.8	39.4	26.8	5.8	123092
29018	BOWMAN	15907	1531	42.1	29.6	23.1	3.3	1.9	30635	35330	14	19	1224	37.8	31.2	26.0	4.3	0.7	65976
29020	CAMDEN	22307	8924	31.8	28.3	29.8	6.6	3.5	40054	45497	46	61	6949	16.5	28.1	35.5	17.0	3.0	96437
29030	CAMERON	22907	1644	35.4	27.7	24.9	8.1	3.9	36910	42816	35	47	1388	29.8	28.2	29.0	11.6	1.4	77778
29031	CARLISLE	16696	589	38.5	31.1	24.6	4.4	1.4	33148	36955	21	29	473	31.7	39.5	22.2	5.9	0.6	65588
29032	CASSATT	18316	1443	30.6	31.9	31.5	4.4	1.6	41659	47338	52	69	1197	30.0	27.7	35.3	5.5	1.5	79050
29033	CAYCE	21733	4992	28.9	32.9	29.2	7.7	1.4	40768	47173	49	65	3449	12.9	33.8	46.5	6.8	0.0	92959
29036	CHAPIN	36169	5250	12.3	17.9	39.1	19.0	11.8	71737	82660	92	98	4829	4.8	10.1	27.3	42.6	15.2	204073
29037	CHAPPELLS	22233	269	24.9	31.2	33.1	8.6	2.2	45372	50663	62	81	226	22.6	20.4	37.2	14.2	5.8	105469
29038	COPE	18180	1008	31.9	30.7	29.8	5.5	2.3	39017	44119	43	58	848	35.0	34.7	22.8	6.5	1.1	65974
29039	CORDOVA	17835	1491	32.0	33.6	28.4	4.2	1.8	37582	43134	38	51	1169	34.1	39.9	22.3	3.2	0.6	66893
29040	DALZELL	18344	2742	28.3	29.9	35.1	5.1	1.5	42371	48290	54	71	2173	25.1	35.2	34.2	5.1	0.5	80723
29042	DENMARK	14165	2246	50.9	27.3	16.9	3.9	1.1	24330	27349	4	2	1560	43.0	34.7	18.2	4.2	0.0	55978
29044	EASTOVER	17188	2185	33.4	31.6	26.6	5.9	2.5	36071	41406	32	44	1726	26.0	36.7	30.9	5.6	0.9	77386
29045	ELGIN	23759	5595	17.2	28.4	40.2	10.8	3.4	53931	62633	78	91	4845	13.2	19.5	47.0	18.7	1.6	111715
29046	ELLIOTT	11445	34	41.2	32.4	23.5	2.9	0.0	30000	31491	12	15	28	57.1	28.6	14.3	0.0	0.0	45000
29047	ELLOREE	18910	1233	45.7	29.4	17.6	4.9	2.4	27554	31973	8	6	976	38.7	28.7	25.2	5.7	1.6	64353
29048	EUTAWVILLE	17160	1947	41.4	29.2	24.2	3.5	1.8	32090	36776	18	25	1659	32.9	27.5	27.4	11.0	1.2	76389
29051	GABLE	12651	460	36.5	30.2	29.8	3.3	0.2	38001	42919	39	53	378	38.9	28.6	27.3	4.8	0.5	68000
29052	GADSDEN	16408	785	30.7	32.6	28.4	6.5	1.8	41532	49349	51	69	597	25.1	41.4	26.6	5.2	1.7	74900
29053	GASTON	16039	6047	30.6	37.9	26.5	4.2	0.8	37209	43251	36	49	4717	35.4	34.6	27.0	2.8	0.2	67657
29054	GILBERT	26717	3119	21.4	25.0	36.9	12.7	4.1	53656	61901	78	91	2693	17.3	18.9	34.8	22.2	6.8	112104
29055	GREAT FALLS	16869	1928	39.6	31.6	22.6	3.9	2.3	32806	37037	20	28	1474	47.2	32.2	16.6	3.4	0.6	54200
29056	GREELEYVILLE	17824	1005	47.8	29.7	14.9	2.1	5.6	26370	30613	6	4	820	44.5	31.3	20.4	3.2	0.6	56716
29058	HEATH SPRINGS	19384	2011	31.8	33.3	28.5	4.7	1.6	37638	42532	38	52	1693	20.6	40.7	29.7	8.3	0.8	79633
29059	HOLLY HILL	15598	2356	45.2	27.4	21.9	4.2	1.4	28829	33225	10	10	1825	41.0	27.4	25.4	5.5	0.7	59850
29061	HOPKINS	19917	5058	24.9	33.2	30.7	8.2	3.2	43475	50800	57	75	4101	19.2	37.3	32.6	10.0	0.9	84616
29063	IRMO	29918	9839	8.3	19.3	47.2	18.1	7.2	68171	80862	90	97	8863	1.1	11.6	57.4	25.3	4.6	125213
29065	JENKINSVILLE	15847	299	39.5	28.4	27.8	4.4	0.0	34474	40000	26	36	250	30.4	32.8	26.4	7.6	2.8	73158
29067	KERSHAW	18484	3833	32.5	33.8	28.0	4.5	1.2	38788	43753	42	56	3137	28.2	38.7	27.6	4.8	0.8	73589
29069	LAMAR	16502	1855	42.3	29.4	21.6	4.5	2.2	30081	35155	12	15	1495	36.9	28.8	27.3	6.1	0.9	71623
29070	LEESVILLE	22395	4742	23.1	30.9	34.8	8.3	2.8	46308	53591	65	82	3934	22.2	29.1	32.5	13.8	2.4	88468
29072	LEXINGTON	31256	13049	13.2	18.1	41.7	19.2	7.8	69318	80064	91	98	11102	7.7	7.3	38.7	40.3	5.9	165664
29073	LEXINGTON	22260	12445	18.8	32.6	38.3	7.9	2.3	48687	56072	70	85	10280	18.5	20.9	51.2	8.7	0.7	100233
29075	LITTLE MOUNTAIN	25289	1175	20.3	28.8	35.8	11.1	4.1	50775	58478	73	88	1025	15.5	21.0	36.0	23.8	3.7	112193
29078	LUGOFF	21581	5008	21.5	30.2	37.5	7.9	3.0	48297	54422	69	85	4212	18.0	21.2	44.2	15.5	1.1	104129
29080	LYNCHBURG	16171	1474	44.6	27.1	21.4	3.7	3.2	30000	34609	12	15	1172	48.1	29.6	17.2	4.4	0.8	52500
29081	EHRHARDT	17038	613	37.9	34.9	20.4	4.9	2.0	31104	35541	15	20	508	30.3	33.1	29.9	6.7	0.0	74048
29082	LODGE	15702	339	42.2	31.9	20.7	5.3	0.0	29891	34388	12	14	271	46.9	23.6	24.0	5.5	0.0	54474
29101	MC BEE	16756	1142	38.7	28.1	25.0	5.7	2.5	34584	38670	26	36	967	41.0	33.3	18.9	6.6	0.2	58495
29102	MANNING	18140	6646	42.0	25.5	24.9	4.9	2.8	31286	36545	16	22	5133	28.0	29.7	29.3	12.0	1.1	78488
29104	MAYESVILLE	17357	798	45.7	27.6	19.2	3.9	3.6	28305	32841	9	8	648	42.6	33.3	15.6	6.8	1.7	56486
29105	MONETTA	16666	498	30.3	33.7	31.3	3.8	0.8	38994	45102	43	57	412	52.4	24.5	17.2	3.9	1.9	48333
29107	NEESES	20182	1297	36.9	30.2	25.5	4.0	3.5	34315	39642	25	35	1046	38.3	34.4	22.8	4.4	0.1	63689
29108	NEWBERRY	17503	7629	37.2	32.0	23.5	5.5	1.9	34176	39074	25	34	5311	25.9	32.2	32.3	8.9	0.7	78901
29111	NEW ZION	15686	435	33.8	32.4	27.8	4.8	1.2	40219	45481	47	62	358	38.0	30.7	24.3	7.0	0.0	68125
29112	NORTH	16435	1884	42.3	31.0	22.3	3.1	1.3	30455	35269	13	17	1512	38.6	31.0	24.9	4.8	0.7	64615
29113	NORWAY	16492	652	39.7	29.3	24.5	4.3	2.2	31606	36347	17	23	528	40.0	28.6	25.6	5.9	0.0	65111
29114	OLANTA	15443	837	41.8	30.9	22.7	3.1	1.4	30882	35858	15	20	675	41.2	36.4	15.4	5.0	1.9	58041
29115	ORANGEBURG	17860	11956	41.4	28.7	23.8	4.3	1.8	31634	36722	17	23	7959	30.2	36.7	26.5	6.1	0.6	73289
29117	ORANGEBURG	8346	31	41.9	25.8	25.8	6.5	0.0	27185	37376	7	5	11	27.3	36.4	36.4	0.0	0.0	75000
29118	ORANGEBURG	24478	5835	28.8	25.6	31.5	9.0	5.2	45027	53041	61	80	4459	14.3	25.6	42.4	15.8	1.9	101271
29123	PELION	17700	2315	28.3	34.4	30.6	4.5	2.2	39653	46252	45	60	1939	35.5	29.0	30.9	3.9	0.7	71098
29125	PINEWOOD	14204	1656	43.1	32.3	19.5	3.9	1.2	30173	34853	13	16	1318	41.4	31.6	24.2	2.4	0.4	59262
29126	POMARIA	19374	989	30.6	27.0	35.8	5.3	1.3	42108	47544	53	71	853	19.2	28.4	37.4	13.8	1.2	93868
29127	PROSPERITY	22111	3049	24.3	32.8	32.2	9.0	1.6	43539	50070	57	75	2607	20.2	21.8	31.9	24.2	1.9	105377
29128	REMBERT	14841	2397	41.5	29.8	23.5	3.2	2.0	31599	36203	17	23	2028	40.1	32.6	20.8	4.7	1.8	60417
29129	RIDGE SPRING	16786	1540	35.1	32.1	26.6	4.6	1.7	35705	41161	30	42	1250	31.8	26.1	28.0	10.5	3.7	78551
29130	RIDGEWAY	20668	2398	31.0	24.6	34.0	7.5	3.0	43208	51212	57	74	2032	18.8	29.2	27.7	22.9	1.5	93529
29133	ROWESVILLE	14983	410	43.7	29.0	23.2	2.4	1.7	29588	33961	11	13	331	39.9	33.8	21.5	4.8	0.0	63571
29135	SAINT MATTHEWS	19986	4649	34.6	29.0	27.5	6.5	2.5	37279	43283	36	49	3837	29.9	33.2	26.7	9.3	1.0	72845
29137	SALLEY	16172	1126	36.9	34.6	23.8	4.1	0.7	32249	37679	18	25	923	45.4	29.8	21.5	2.5	0.9	57203
29138	SALUDA	18494	4495	32.6	30.9	29.7	4.8	2.0	38703	43480	42	55	3569	23.5	31.4	33.3	10.3	1.5	84478
29142	SANTEE	17862	1861	43.4	27.7	21.3	3.9	3.7	29796	34746	12	13	1524	32.7	23.6	23.9	17.4	2.4	78202
29145	SILVERSTREET	18047	394	32.0	33.5	26.4	6.9	1.3	37399	42252	37	51	327	27.8	23.9	34.6	11.9	1.8	87250
29146	SPRINGFIELD	17179	696	42.5	30.3	20.4	4.5	2.3	29227	34086	11	11	578	46.2	31.0	20.1	2.3	0.5	55789
29148	SUMMERTON	16978	2630	47.2	28.8	17.1	3.8	3.2	26535	30621	6	4	2048	33.8	23.8	30.8	10.4	1.2	75500
29150	SUMTER	19377	15065	36.3	29.8	24.6	6.1	3.3	34985	40099	27	38	9812	24.8	32.9	32.1	9.5	0.7	80170
29152	SHAW A F B	12470	1591	26.6	48.8	20.5	2.5	1.6	34111	38836	24	33	143	51.8	24.5	23.8	0.0	0.0	38438
29153	SUMTER	15421	5338	38.4	32.2	26.0	2.3	1.1	31926	36358	18	24	4229	31.0	35.7	26.1	6.6	0.6	69881
29154	SUMTER	23595	9028	21.9	31.4	34.4	8.2	4.2	47471	54140	67	84	7038	17.1	25.8	46.3	9.9	1.0	96825
29160	SWANSEA	18538	2344	34.4	27.4	30.5	6.6	1.2	38969	45096	43	56	1959	29.7	33.1	30.4	6.2	0.6	73125
29161	TIMMONSVILLE	17089	4492	35.8	28.6	28.1	6.0	1.6	35310	40764	29	40	3557	34.7	32.0	26.0	6.8	0.5	68160
29162	TURBEVILLE	15817	1063	36.2	34.6	23.2	4.8	1.1	33281	38161	22	30	825	41.9	31.2	21.3	4.0	1.6	66325
29163	VANCE	13730	778	48.2	28.7	18.6	2.6	1.9	26123	29842	6	3	639	49.8	27.5	16.7	5.2	0.8	50211
29164	WAGENER	16901	1824	36.0	32.4	25.7	5.2	0.7	33788	39762	23	32	1493	36.4	31.4	27.9	3.9	0.5	68826
29166	WARD	18868	450	34.2	29.1	27.8	5.6	3.3	36542	41412	34	46	368	37.0	30.2	28.0	2.7	2.2	64167
29168	WEDGEFIELD	15252	1425	38.4	32.9	23.9	3.2	1.6	31222	36382	16	21	1105	38.4	39.2	17.0	5.0	0.5	61639
29169	WEST COLUMBIA	22860	9728	33.4	29.9	26.7	7.3	2.7	37337	43524	37	51	5445	13.1	26.3	46.4	12.9	1.3	100517
29170	WEST COLUMBIA	23739	7494	17.9	31.5	38.5	9.9	2.1	50399	57980	73	87	6029	13.1	19.7	55.9	11.0	0.4	106101
29172	WEST COLUMBIA	19272	3550	29.6	30.4	32.3	6.7	1.0	41231	47920	51	67	2789	25.2	30.9	39.0	4.7	0.1	84506
29175	WESTVILLE	17839	186	32.8	24.2	40.3	1.6	1.1	41772	49696	52	70	164	35.4	41.5	20.7	2.4	0.0	58889
29178	WHITMIRE	16406	1558	44.5	27.7	23.2	4.0	0.6	28314	31678	9	8	1191	51.6	26.2	19.1	2.8	0.4	48978
29180	WINNSBORO	17862	5825	39.9	28.1	23.7	5.8	2.5	32414	37776	19	26	4213	29.3	31.5	28.1	9.2	2.0	75142
29201	COLUMBIA	18122	5771	49.3	26.4	17.0	4.8	2.5	25465	29921	5	3	1877	11.3	37.5	35.2	13.8	2.2	91619
29203	COLUMBIA	15409	15174	42.3	29.8	21.5	4.6	1.8	30427	35602	13	17	8753	18.1	46.9	31.3	2.8	0.9	78748
29204	COLUMBIA	24257	8555	36.6	26.4	23.6	7.1	6.2	36701	43374	34	47	4766	6.2	29.5	47.4	13.3	3.7	104700
29205	COLUMBIA	31447	11889	32.2	28.5	24.2	8.4	6.9	38254	45318	40	54	5715	3.8	19.4	37.7	31.1	8.1	143338
	SOUTH CAROLINA	22607		28.8	29.3	29.6	8.3	4.0	42042	49103				19.3	24.1	35.5	17.1	3.9	100170
	UNITED STATES	25866		24.7	27.1	30.8	10.9	6.5	48124	56710				10.9	15.0	33.7	30.1	10.4	145905

SPENDING POTENTIAL INDICES SOUTH CAROLINA
29001-29205 D

#	POST OFFICE NAME	FINANCIAL SERVICES: Auto Loan	FINANCIAL SERVICES: Home Loan	FINANCIAL SERVICES: Investments	FINANCIAL SERVICES: Retirement Plans	THE HOME: Home Improvements: Home Repair	THE HOME: Home Improvements: Lawn & Garden	THE HOME: Furnishings: Computers & Hardware	THE HOME: Furnishings: Major Appliances	THE HOME: Furnishings: TV, Radio, Sound Equipment	THE HOME: Furnishings: Furniture	ENTERTAINMENT: Dine out/Carry out	ENTERTAINMENT: Sports Equipment	ENTERTAINMENT: Fees & Tickets	ENTERTAINMENT: Toys & Games	ENTERTAINMENT: Travel	ENTERTAINMENT: Cable TV	PERSONAL: Apparel & Services	PERSONAL: Auto Repairs	PERSONAL: Health Insurance	PERSONAL: Pets & Supplies
29001	ALCOLU	79	53	24	46	60	69	51	64	61	52	72	76	43	68	52	66	66	63	78	90
29003	BAMBERG	63	48	37	44	52	60	50	56	57	50	68	64	46	64	50	61	63	56	66	71
29006	BATESBURG	83	66	46	61	71	79	65	73	72	65	86	86	60	84	66	75	81	73	83	95
29009	BETHUNE	79	53	24	46	60	69	51	64	62	52	73	76	44	69	52	66	66	63	79	91
29010	BISHOPVILLE	79	57	38	50	62	73	58	67	68	59	81	78	52	76	58	73	75	67	81	89
29014	BLACKSTOCK	86	57	26	49	65	75	55	69	67	56	78	83	47	74	56	72	71	68	85	98
29015	BLAIR	68	45	21	39	51	59	44	55	53	45	62	65	37	59	45	57	56	54	68	78
29016	BLYTHEWOOD	113	115	101	114	114	116	106	110	103	108	129	129	106	128	105	101	125	108	105	128
29018	BOWMAN	74	52	31	45	57	66	52	62	62	53	73	72	46	68	52	67	67	62	76	84
29020	CAMDEN	85	74	61	69	77	86	72	79	77	72	94	91	69	91	73	80	89	78	87	97
29030	CAMERON	93	72	46	64	78	88	69	81	79	69	94	95	62	91	70	83	87	80	95	108
29031	CARLISLE	77	51	23	44	58	67	50	62	60	51	70	74	42	67	51	65	64	62	77	88
29032	CASSATT	85	69	47	64	72	79	66	75	71	68	87	88	61	82	66	73	82	74	81	95
29033	CAYCE	64	69	75	68	69	74	69	68	69	68	86	78	71	88	70	69	84	68	68	75
29036	CHAPIN	121	144	154	143	143	147	131	132	124	131	155	152	138	161	135	122	154	128	124	147
29037	CHAPPELLS	101	68	32	59	77	89	66	82	79	67	93	98	56	88	67	85	85	81	101	116
29038	COPE	84	65	39	59	69	76	62	72	69	63	83	85	55	78	62	72	77	72	81	95
29039	CORDOVA	75	68	52	65	68	72	65	70	66	67	81	81	61	77	64	65	78	70	70	84
29040	DALZELL	76	71	58	69	71	74	68	72	68	69	84	83	65	80	67	66	81	71	70	84
29042	DENMARK	55	43	39	39	44	53	47	50	54	48	65	55	44	59	46	57	61	51	59	61
29044	EASTOVER	70	63	56	60	63	68	62	65	65	64	80	75	60	77	62	65	77	66	67	78
29045	ELGIN	97	94	86	93	95	99	91	95	90	92	112	110	88	108	90	88	108	94	93	110
29046	ELLIOTT	68	46	21	40	52	60	44	55	53	45	63	66	38	59	45	58	57	55	68	79
29047	ELLOREE	82	55	25	47	62	72	53	66	64	54	75	79	45	71	54	69	68	66	82	94
29048	EUTAWVILLE	79	56	30	49	64	72	54	66	63	54	75	79	47	72	56	68	68	66	81	93
29051	GABLE	77	51	23	44	58	67	49	62	60	50	70	74	42	66	50	64	64	61	76	88
29052	GADSDEN	73	63	57	58	65	75	62	67	68	64	84	74	62	80	64	72	80	67	76	83
29053	GASTON	70	64	50	61	64	67	61	65	62	63	76	75	58	72	60	61	73	65	65	77
29054	GILBERT	104	101	89	98	102	108	95	101	95	97	118	117	94	115	96	95	114	99	101	119
29055	GREAT FALLS	80	54	24	46	61	70	52	65	62	53	73	77	44	69	53	67	67	64	80	92
29056	GREELEYVILLE	85	57	26	49	64	74	55	69	66	56	78	82	47	74	56	71	71	68	85	98
29058	HEATH SPRINGS	84	60	31	53	67	76	57	70	67	58	79	83	50	76	58	72	73	69	84	97
29059	HOLLY HILL	71	50	29	43	55	64	50	59	59	51	70	69	44	65	50	64	65	59	73	81
29061	HOPKINS	81	79	72	77	78	83	76	79	76	77	94	90	75	92	75	75	92	78	77	91
29063	IRMO	116	133	131	137	127	124	120	119	111	124	140	139	124	142	118	104	139	116	103	130
29065	JENKINSVILLE	73	49	22	42	55	64	47	59	57	48	67	71	40	63	48	61	61	58	73	84
29067	KERSHAW	86	63	36	56	69	79	61	73	71	61	84	86	54	81	62	75	77	72	87	99
29069	LAMAR	79	55	27	48	61	70	53	65	62	54	74	77	45	70	53	67	67	64	78	90
29070	LEESVILLE	91	79	60	75	82	89	77	84	80	77	98	97	72	95	77	82	93	83	89	103
29072	LEXINGTON	117	129	129	131	126	127	120	120	114	121	143	141	122	145	119	109	140	118	110	135
29073	LEXINGTON	86	88	79	88	86	87	83	85	80	84	100	99	81	98	81	77	97	84	78	96
29075	LITTLE MOUNTAIN	100	91	73	87	96	102	84	93	88	84	108	110	83	110	87	90	103	90	99	118
29078	LUGOFF	87	82	68	80	84	89	78	83	79	78	97	96	76	98	78	80	93	81	85	99
29080	LYNCHBURG	84	56	26	49	64	74	54	68	66	56	77	81	46	73	55	71	70	67	84	97
29081	EHRHARDT	78	52	24	45	59	68	50	63	60	51	71	75	43	67	51	65	65	62	77	89
29082	LODGE	72	48	22	42	55	63	47	58	56	48	66	70	40	63	47	61	60	58	72	83
29101	MC BEE	82	57	29	50	64	73	55	67	65	56	77	80	48	73	56	69	70	66	81	94
29102	MANNING	77	58	39	52	63	73	58	67	66	58	79	78	52	76	59	71	73	67	80	89
29104	MAYESVILLE	82	59	43	52	64	75	61	71	73	63	86	81	56	79	61	78	80	71	86	92
29105	MONETTA	72	64	48	61	65	69	61	66	63	63	77	77	57	73	60	62	74	66	67	80
29107	NEESES	91	64	33	56	71	80	61	75	72	63	85	89	53	81	62	76	78	74	89	103
29108	NEWBERRY	69	58	49	55	61	68	60	64	65	59	79	75	57	77	60	67	74	64	71	78
29111	NEW ZION	82	55	25	48	62	72	53	66	64	54	75	79	45	71	54	69	68	66	82	94
29112	NORTH	74	54	31	49	59	66	52	62	59	53	71	73	46	67	52	62	66	62	72	84
29113	NORWAY	82	55	25	48	62	72	53	67	64	54	76	79	46	71	54	69	69	66	82	94
29114	OLANTA	79	53	24	46	60	69	51	64	62	52	73	77	44	69	52	67	66	63	79	91
29115	ORANGEBURG	67	56	50	52	57	65	59	62	64	59	78	71	55	73	58	66	74	63	68	75
29117	ORANGEBURG	62	38	48	43	37	45	73	54	71	62	88	75	60	80	58	62	83	66	50	61
29118	ORANGEBURG	91	92	91	89	91	97	88	91	88	90	110	103	88	107	89	89	107	90	91	104
29123	PELION	76	69	54	67	69	73	66	71	67	68	83	82	63	78	65	66	79	71	70	84
29125	PINEWOOD	69	52	31	47	56	62	50	58	56	51	67	69	44	63	50	59	62	58	67	78
29126	POMARIA	86	63	35	56	70	79	60	72	70	61	83	86	53	80	61	74	76	71	86	100
29127	PROSPERITY	92	70	43	63	78	88	66	80	76	67	90	94	59	88	69	81	83	78	94	109
29128	REMBERT	73	53	31	47	58	66	52	61	60	53	71	72	46	67	52	64	66	61	73	83
29129	RIDGE SPRING	81	59	32	52	64	73	56	68	65	58	78	80	50	74	57	69	71	67	80	92
29130	RIDGEWAY	94	68	37	60	76	86	65	79	76	65	89	94	56	86	66	81	82	78	95	110
29133	ROWESVILLE	71	48	22	41	54	62	46	58	56	47	65	69	39	62	47	60	59	57	71	82
29135	SAINT MATTHEWS	86	69	45	63	73	80	66	75	72	67	87	88	60	83	66	74	81	74	83	98
29137	SALLEY	75	52	26	46	58	66	50	62	59	52	70	73	44	66	51	63	64	61	74	86
29138	SALUDA	90	64	35	57	72	82	62	75	72	63	86	89	55	82	63	77	79	74	90	103
29142	SANTEE	86	58	26	50	65	75	56	70	67	57	79	83	47	75	57	72	72	69	86	99
29145	SILVERSTREET	89	59	27	51	67	77	57	72	69	58	81	86	49	77	58	75	74	71	88	102
29146	SPRINGFIELD	80	53	24	46	60	70	51	64	62	52	73	77	44	69	52	67	66	64	79	91
29148	SUMMERTON	71	51	32	45	57	66	50	61	59	51	70	71	45	66	52	64	65	60	73	83
29150	SUMTER	66	62	66	60	63	70	64	65	67	64	83	74	64	81	64	69	80	66	69	75
29152	SHAW A F B	67	43	41	49	39	46	64	55	65	59	81	73	54	72	52	59	77	65	51	62
29153	SUMTER	73	53	32	48	58	66	52	61	60	53	72	73	46	68	53	63	66	61	72	83
29154	SUMTER	89	94	93	94	92	94	90	90	86	90	108	106	90	108	89	84	106	90	84	101
29160	SWANSEA	77	67	50	64	68	73	64	70	66	66	81	81	60	77	63	66	78	70	72	86
29161	TIMMONSVILLE	79	59	37	53	64	72	58	67	65	59	78	79	52	74	58	68	73	67	77	90
29162	TURBEVILLE	80	53	24	46	60	70	51	64	62	52	73	77	44	69	52	67	66	64	79	91
29163	VANCE	70	47	22	41	53	61	45	57	55	46	64	68	39	61	46	59	59	56	70	81
29164	WAGENER	75	56	32	50	61	68	54	64	61	55	73	75	48	69	54	64	67	63	73	86
29166	WARD	91	61	28	53	69	80	59	74	71	60	84	88	50	79	60	77	76	73	91	105
29168	WEDGEFIELD	70	56	36	51	59	65	53	61	58	55	70	72	48	66	53	60	66	61	68	79
29169	WEST COLUMBIA	70	63	66	64	64	71	71	69	72	68	89	82	68	86	69	71	85	71	70	78
29170	WEST COLUMBIA	86	87	80	85	86	90	82	85	82	83	101	100	82	101	82	80	98	85	83	99
29172	WEST COLUMBIA	78	73	61	71	74	78	69	74	70	70	86	86	67	84	69	70	83	73	74	88
29175	WESTVILLE	85	57	26	49	65	74	55	69	66	56	78	82	47	74	56	72	71	68	85	98
29178	WHITMIRE	64	47	32	43	51	59	49	56	56	49	67	65	44	64	49	59	62	56	65	72
29180	WINNSBORO	75	58	43	52	62	71	58	66	66	59	79	76	54	75	59	70	74	66	77	85
29201	COLUMBIA	55	45	58	49	45	50	61	53	60	57	75	66	56	71	55	56	73	59	51	59
29203	COLUMBIA	58	53	59	50	52	59	56	56	60	57	74	62	56	71	55	61	72	57	59	64
29204	COLUMBIA	74	75	89	73	74	83	77	76	80	78	99	86	79	98	78	81	97	77	79	85
29205	COLUMBIA	85	81	104	85	79	86	94	86	92	91	116	106	92	114	89	88	114	92	81	96
	SOUTH CAROLINA	87	78	69	75	80	87	77	82	81	78	99	95	74	96	77	82	95	82	86	99
	UNITED STATES	100	100	100	100	100	100	100	100	100	100	100	100	100	100	100	100	100	100	100	100

SOUTH CAROLINA

POPULATION CHANGE

A 29206-29512

ZIP CODE #	POST OFFICE NAME	COUNTY FIPS CODE	POPULATION			2000-2004 ANNUAL RATE		HOUSEHOLDS					FAMILIES		
			2000	2004	2009	% Rate	State Centile	2000	2004	2009	% Annual Rate 2000-2004	2004 Average HH Size	2000	2004	% Annual Rate 2000-2004
29206 COLUMBIA	079		21565	21864	22591	0.3	31	8571	8924	9483	1.0	2.09	5711	5672	-0.2
29207 COLUMBIA	079		6407	6337	6382	-0.3	12	42	41	43	-0.6	2.56	29	27	-1.7
29208 COLUMBIA	079		747	747	747	0.0	19	2	2	2	0.0	1.00	1	0	-100.0
29209 COLUMBIA	079		27925	29650	31340	1.4	68	10935	12033	13085	2.3	2.39	7414	7779	1.1
29210 COLUMBIA	079		34920	35915	37617	0.7	43	16631	17656	18967	1.4	2.00	8167	8044	-0.4
29212 COLUMBIA	063		31953	33132	34590	0.9	49	10493	11259	12111	1.7	2.55	7743	8088	1.0
29223 COLUMBIA	079		43663	46066	48496	1.3	62	16620	18073	19531	2.0	2.48	11776	12349	1.1
29229 COLUMBIA	079		18930	23535	26941	5.3	98	6446	8216	9619	5.9	2.86	5394	6738	5.4
29301 SPARTANBURG	083		28874	30761	32694	1.5	69	11231	12215	13228	2.0	2.48	7631	8028	1.2
29302 SPARTANBURG	083		17043	16727	17071	-0.4	7	6908	6916	7198	0.0	2.32	4576	4430	-0.8
29303 SPARTANBURG	083		25135	24997	25669	-0.1	14	9260	9372	9820	0.3	2.35	5667	5513	-0.7
29306 SPARTANBURG	083		16396	16308	16807	-0.1	14	6595	6728	7081	0.5	2.40	4217	4143	-0.4
29307 SPARTANBURG	083		19784	19877	20480	0.1	24	8195	8427	8856	0.7	2.28	5395	5356	-0.2
29316 BOILING SPRINGS	083		14462	15700	16693	2.0	81	5403	6007	6516	2.5	2.59	4241	4600	1.9
29321 BUFFALO	087		2525	2638	2672	1.0	54	1020	1096	1141	1.7	2.40	735	765	1.0
29322 CAMPOBELLO	083		7548	7990	8403	1.4	64	2906	3145	3370	1.9	2.53	2226	2348	1.3
29323 CHESNEE	083		13654	14401	15078	1.3	62	5208	5621	6000	1.8	2.55	3919	4112	1.1
29325 CLINTON	059		15960	15761	15799	-0.3	11	5685	5750	5872	0.3	2.41	3878	3795	-0.5
29330 COWPENS	021		8693	9139	9568	1.2	59	3378	3618	3853	1.6	2.52	2478	2578	0.9
29332 CROSS HILL	059		1967	2074	2124	1.3	61	809	883	924	2.1	2.35	595	634	1.5
29334 DUNCAN	083		8358	8919	9418	1.5	72	3158	3439	3697	2.0	2.59	2410	2559	1.4
29335 ENOREE	083		5776	5723	5810	-0.2	13	1731	1748	1806	0.2	2.89	1310	1286	-0.4
29340 GAFFNEY	021		21284	20901	21008	-0.4	8	8289	8342	8567	0.2	2.44	5804	5671	-0.5
29341 GAFFNEY	021		16846	17504	17987	0.9	50	6553	6976	7317	1.5	2.49	4701	4870	0.8
29349 INMAN	083		23892	25736	27334	1.8	77	9078	9986	10806	2.3	2.54	6896	7400	1.7
29351 JOANNA	059		2305	2209	2184	-1.0	1	953	936	942	-0.4	2.36	676	644	-1.1
29353 JONESVILLE	087		4273	4375	4396	0.6	39	1702	1795	1854	1.3	2.42	1220	1251	0.6
29355 KINARDS	071		417	425	434	0.5	34	170	178	186	1.1	2.39	126	129	0.6
29356 LANDRUM	045		7861	8285	8645	1.2	61	3235	3470	3671	1.7	2.38	2336	2429	0.9
29360 LAURENS	059		22031	21760	21767	-0.3	11	8522	8618	8770	0.3	2.44	5968	5850	-0.5
29365 LYMAN	083		7169	7943	8566	2.4	88	2886	3254	3568	2.9	2.43	2147	2363	2.3
29369 MOORE	083		10931	12469	13598	3.2	93	3959	4629	5151	3.8	2.68	3209	3670	3.2
29370 MOUNTVILLE	059		1438	1462	1471	0.4	33	522	546	561	1.1	2.64	392	400	0.5
29372 PACOLET	021		5206	5324	5479	0.5	38	2068	2164	2272	1.1	2.40	1445	1466	0.3
29374 PAULINE	083		3439	3543	3673	0.7	45	1319	1385	1469	1.2	2.11	1025	1049	0.6
29376 ROEBUCK	083		4837	5295	5661	2.2	84	1869	2099	2291	2.8	2.52	1427	1558	2.1
29379 UNION	087		20815	20474	20191	-0.4	9	8481	8574	8688	0.3	2.34	5910	5810	-0.4
29384 WATERLOO	059		4330	4756	5032	2.2	85	1818	2048	2207	2.8	2.32	1296	1420	2.2
29385 WELLFORD	083		6738	6936	7249	0.7	44	2571	2690	2857	1.1	2.57	1878	1908	0.4
29388 WOODRUFF	083		13161	14117	14981	1.7	74	5026	5497	5937	2.1	2.54	3737	3983	1.5
29401 CHARLESTON	019		10115	10268	10681	0.4	32	4690	4887	5237	1.0	1.85	1786	1733	-0.7
29403 CHARLESTON	019		23635	24177	25574	0.5	38	8984	9551	10509	1.5	2.20	4351	4347	0.0
29404 CHARLESTON AFB	019		4384	4182	4305	-1.1	0	1208	1184	1260	-0.5	3.13	1140	1106	-0.7
29405 NORTH CHARLESTON	019		31038	30474	31715	-0.4	8	11113	11193	12019	0.2	2.45	7062	6827	-0.8
29406 CHARLESTON	019		36640	37073	38741	0.3	29	14706	15317	16486	1.0	2.29	8744	8683	-0.2
29407 CHARLESTON	019		36689	37438	39653	0.5	36	16175	17060	18625	1.3	2.14	9162	9157	0.0
29412 CHARLESTON	019		33871	36102	38818	1.5	70	14299	15734	17420	2.3	2.28	9073	9581	1.3
29414 CHARLESTON	019		23710	26887	29737	3.0	92	9675	11320	12886	3.8	2.35	6336	7107	2.7
29418 NORTH CHARLESTON	019		21624	22271	23646	0.7	45	8754	9261	10086	1.3	2.39	5599	5693	0.4
29420 NORTH CHARLESTON	035		15414	17198	19148	2.6	89	5179	5881	6678	3.0	2.92	4087	4534	2.5
29426 ADAMS RUN	019		1812	1904	2019	1.2	59	658	716	783	2.0	2.66	495	523	1.3
29429 AWENDAW	019		2989	3987	4788	7.0	99	1027	1416	1752	7.9	2.81	819	1104	7.3
29431 BONNEAU	015		5597	5743	5998	0.6	41	2137	2270	2448	1.4	2.53	1590	1646	0.8
29432 BRANCHVILLE	075		2648	2647	2682	0.0	19	1063	1095	1142	0.7	2.40	741	740	0.0
29434 CORDESVILLE	015		705	689	713	-0.5	5	247	250	267	0.3	2.72	183	180	-0.4
29435 COTTAGEVILLE	029		3795	4049	4299	1.5	72	1423	1563	1707	2.2	2.59	1053	1128	1.6
29436 CROSS	015		4448	4435	4572	-0.1	16	1635	1694	1805	0.8	2.62	1220	1231	0.2
29437 DORCHESTER	035		2332	2326	2485	-0.1	17	864	884	968	0.5	2.63	645	642	-0.1
29438 EDISTO ISLAND	019		2301	2497	2684	1.9	81	989	1121	1248	3.0	2.23	687	753	2.2
29440 GEORGETOWN	043		29576	31172	33745	1.2	61	10725	11637	12997	1.9	2.64	8018	8502	1.4
29445 GOOSE CREEK	015		48714	52525	56815	1.8	78	16013	17907	20053	2.7	2.77	12459	13576	2.0
29446 GREEN POND	029		2052	2148	2276	1.1	56	750	813	888	1.9	2.64	541	572	1.3
29448 HARLEYVILLE	035		2224	2265	2421	0.4	34	864	906	993	1.1	2.50	639	651	0.4
29449 HOLLYWOOD	019		7338	7950	8567	1.9	80	2628	2957	3290	2.8	2.69	1968	2146	2.1
29450 HUGER	015		2865	3071	3282	1.7	74	979	1088	1201	2.5	2.82	741	797	1.7
29451 ISLE OF PALMS	019		4584	4575	4770	-0.1	17	1944	1994	2135	0.6	2.29	1385	1372	-0.2
29453 JAMESTOWN	015		1441	1458	1510	0.3	29	532	558	596	1.1	2.61	384	392	0.5
29455 JOHNS ISLAND	019		13725	15185	16573	2.4	87	5366	6096	6831	3.1	2.49	3962	4354	2.2
29456 LADSON	019		17577	18426	19703	1.1	56	6089	6572	7229	1.8	2.77	4676	4929	1.3
29458 MC CLELLANVILLE	019		3087	3229	3462	1.1	55	1091	1188	1316	2.0	2.71	790	825	1.0
29461 MONCKS CORNER	015		23939	24731	26036	0.8	47	8768	9335	10132	1.5	2.59	6596	6858	0.9
29464 MOUNT PLEASANT	019		39614	42236	45358	1.5	71	16140	17677	19502	2.2	2.35	10426	10999	1.3
29466 MOUNT PLEASANT	019		12370	18133	22719	9.4	100	4492	6791	8759	10.2	2.67	3540	5294	9.9
29468 PINEVILLE	015		2091	2117	2216	0.3	29	780	820	887	1.2	2.58	551	562	0.5
29469 PINOPOLIS	015		661	680	710	0.7	43	240	254	273	1.3	2.67	187	194	0.9
29470 RAVENEL	019		4061	4388	4718	1.8	78	1478	1649	1824	2.6	2.66	1134	1231	2.0
29471 REEVESVILLE	035		1338	1577	1811	3.9	96	528	643	760	4.8	2.45	383	453	4.0
29472 RIDGEVILLE	035		9075	9496	10083	1.1	55	2472	2692	2979	2.0	2.71	1877	1994	1.4
29474 ROUND O	029		1785	1937	2077	1.9	81	680	759	837	2.6	2.55	510	556	2.1
29475 RUFFIN	029		2306	2337	2455	0.3	30	900	940	1015	1.0	2.49	659	671	0.4
29477 SAINT GEORGE	035		7011	7240	7783	0.8	46	2712	2884	3185	1.5	2.44	1892	1949	0.7
29479 SAINT STEPHEN	015		7312	7282	7534	-0.1	15	2607	2681	2860	0.7	2.68	1920	1924	0.1
29481 SMOAKS	029		1875	1869	1940	-0.1	16	671	688	734	0.6	2.72	504	504	0.0
29482 SULLIVANS ISLAND	019		1911	1914	1986	0.0	21	797	821	876	0.7	2.33	484	475	-0.4
29483 SUMMERVILLE	015		48121	52082	56876	1.9	79	17404	19359	21708	2.5	2.67	13363	14531	2.0
29485 SUMMERVILLE	035		28714	30943	34151	1.8	77	10411	11522	13029	2.4	2.66	8027	8697	1.9
29487 WADMALAW ISLAND	019		2611	2677	2817	0.6	40	960	1024	1115	1.5	2.55	718	742	0.8
29488 WALTERBORO	029		22009	23102	24570	1.2	58	8293	8925	9740	1.7	2.56	5991	6285	1.1
29492 CHARLESTON	015		2092	3342	4322	11.7	100	723	1201	1607	12.7	2.78	597	968	12.0
29501 FLORENCE	041		38285	39119	39816	0.5	37	15441	16172	16842	1.1	2.35	10209	10376	0.4
29505 FLORENCE	041		18741	19370	19761	0.8	47	7106	7567	7915	1.5	2.51	5385	5593	0.9
29506 FLORENCE	041		21402	21505	21865	0.1	24	7456	7680	7998	0.7	2.60	5271	5276	0.0
29510 ANDREWS	089		8816	9166	9760	0.9	51	3232	3478	3829	1.7	2.62	2417	2537	1.2
29511 AYNOR	051		4299	4541	4988	1.3	63	1641	1781	2006	2.0	2.53	1211	1278	1.3
29512 BENNETTSVILLE	069		19289	18920	18514	-0.5	7	6857	6890	6913	0.1	2.51	4773	4661	-0.6
SOUTH CAROLINA						1.2					1.8	2.47			1.1
UNITED STATES						1.2					1.3	2.58			1.1

ZIP CODE #	POST OFFICE NAME	RACE (%) White 2000	White 2004	Black 2000	Black 2004	Asian/Pacific 2000	Asian/Pacific 2004	% Hispanic Origin 2000	% Hispanic Origin 2004	2004 AGE DISTRIBUTION (%) 0-4	5-9	10-14	15-19	20-24	25-44	45-64	65-84	85+	18+	MEDIAN AGE 2004	% 2004 Males	% 2004 Females
29206	COLUMBIA	74.1	73.3	19.9	19.7	1.8	2.1	4.8	5.7	5.5	5.8	5.9	10.8	10.6	23.9	21.6	13.7	2.1	79.2	34.5	48.6	51.4
29207	COLUMBIA	48.8	46.1	35.7	36.0	3.3	3.8	13.1	15.4	5.6	5.5	4.2	27.2	29.3	26.1	1.7	0.3	0.0	81.4	21.3	58.1	41.9
29208	COLUMBIA	73.2	71.0	22.1	23.4	2.5	3.1	1.9	2.3	0.0	0.0	0.0	62.7	36.6	0.7	0.1	0.0	0.0	99.7	19.0	31.5	68.5
29209	COLUMBIA	53.7	52.9	41.8	41.8	1.9	2.3	2.1	2.6	6.6	6.7	6.9	6.5	7.2	29.9	24.8	10.8	0.8	75.9	36.1	48.0	52.0
29210	COLUMBIA	53.6	51.6	41.6	42.7	2.5	3.1	1.9	2.2	6.0	4.9	5.2	6.0	13.4	34.8	20.5	8.4	0.9	80.8	31.2	47.5	52.5
29212	COLUMBIA	72.3	71.0	24.4	25.0	1.8	2.2	1.3	1.6	5.9	6.0	7.1	8.7	7.4	31.4	26.4	6.5	0.8	75.1	35.3	52.8	47.2
29223	COLUMBIA	49.0	46.8	43.7	44.6	3.4	4.1	4.4	5.2	6.1	6.3	7.2	7.1	6.8	29.2	26.8	9.7	1.0	75.9	36.8	46.9	53.1
29229	COLUMBIA	59.9	57.5	34.2	35.6	3.0	3.4	3.1	3.7	8.4	8.5	8.6	7.5	6.2	31.9	24.3	4.3	0.2	69.8	33.7	47.9	52.1
29301	SPARTANBURG	62.1	60.1	30.2	30.8	3.1	3.7	5.7	6.8	6.4	6.5	7.2	7.3	7.1	29.1	24.5	10.6	1.3	75.8	35.8	48.4	51.6
29302	SPARTANBURG	76.8	75.3	18.0	18.6	3.8	4.4	1.2	1.5	5.9	6.2	6.4	7.0	7.2	27.1	26.2	12.2	1.7	77.7	38.5	46.7	53.3
29303	SPARTANBURG	64.7	63.0	28.5	28.7	1.9	2.4	5.8	7.2	6.3	5.9	5.9	7.9	10.2	29.6	21.0	11.1	2.0	78.8	33.9	49.3	50.7
29306	SPARTANBURG	32.5	32.1	65.4	65.3	0.7	0.9	1.4	1.7	7.2	7.6	7.9	7.4	6.6	26.0	23.8	11.9	1.7	72.8	36.0	45.2	54.8
29307	SPARTANBURG	83.6	82.8	13.4	13.7	1.1	1.4	1.8	2.2	5.6	5.7	6.2	6.1	5.7	24.9	26.0	15.9	3.9	78.8	41.9	46.5	53.5
29316	BOILING SPRINGS	88.6	87.5	7.7	8.0	2.2	2.7	1.4	1.8	7.1	7.1	7.0	6.1	5.7	32.0	24.5	9.5	1.0	75.0	36.0	49.7	50.3
29321	BUFFALO	83.2	82.4	15.9	16.6	0.3	0.3	0.6	0.8	6.4	6.6	6.9	5.7	5.7	27.8	26.7	13.2	1.1	76.6	38.9	47.7	52.4
29322	CAMPOBELLO	91.8	90.9	6.0	6.5	0.8	1.0	1.5	1.9	6.3	6.7	7.0	5.9	5.6	27.9	28.8	11.0	1.1	76.6	39.3	50.9	49.2
29323	CHESNEE	86.7	85.7	10.5	10.9	1.1	1.4	1.6	2.1	6.9	7.0	7.3	6.3	6.0	30.0	25.3	10.1	1.0	74.9	36.6	50.2	49.8
29325	CLINTON	65.8	64.9	32.7	33.3	0.3	0.3	0.8	1.0	5.5	5.9	6.9	9.2	8.7	24.9	23.4	13.0	2.5	77.3	36.7	47.3	52.7
29330	COWPENS	88.1	87.4	9.6	9.8	0.2	0.3	1.7	2.2	6.8	6.9	7.5	6.5	6.1	28.6	25.2	11.3	1.2	74.8	37.1	49.5	50.5
29332	CROSS HILL	64.4	63.6	34.2	34.9	0.2	0.2	0.5	0.6	5.7	6.2	5.7	6.7	5.4	23.1	30.8	15.4	1.1	78.4	43.1	49.6	50.4
29334	DUNCAN	77.6	76.3	19.2	19.7	1.0	1.2	2.6	3.2	8.6	8.0	7.1	6.5	5.9	29.6	23.4	10.0	0.9	72.4	34.8	49.3	50.7
29335	ENOREE	79.1	77.9	19.1	19.9	0.5	0.6	1.0	1.4	6.1	6.2	6.4	6.0	6.6	34.0	24.9	9.1	0.9	77.8	36.7	55.5	44.5
29340	GAFFNEY	77.5	76.2	20.8	21.8	0.2	0.3	1.7	2.1	7.2	7.2	7.1	6.8	6.8	28.2	23.8	11.2	1.8	74.9	35.5	48.2	51.8
29341	GAFFNEY	66.0	65.7	30.6	30.3	0.6	0.8	2.8	3.4	7.3	7.2	7.4	6.6	6.0	28.9	24.7	10.7	1.3	74.1	36.4	48.5	51.5
29349	INMAN	85.9	84.8	11.2	11.6	1.1	1.3	1.7	2.3	6.6	6.9	7.1	5.7	5.4	29.7	26.5	10.7	1.5	75.9	37.9	48.8	51.3
29351	JOANNA	85.0	84.1	13.1	13.7	0.2	0.3	1.5	1.8	6.1	6.0	6.2	6.4	5.8	26.0	26.8	14.8	1.8	77.6	40.7	48.4	51.7
29353	JONESVILLE	70.7	70.1	28.3	28.7	0.1	0.1	0.8	1.0	6.0	6.3	6.9	6.5	5.7	28.6	26.1	12.6	1.3	76.6	38.8	49.0	51.0
29355	KINARDS	69.1	68.5	30.2	31.1	0.0	0.0	0.7	1.2	4.9	5.4	6.1	6.6	6.4	27.5	29.4	12.0	1.7	80.0	40.8	51.5	48.5
29356	LANDRUM	92.4	91.9	6.0	6.2	0.3	0.3	1.2	1.5	5.6	5.8	6.8	5.9	5.0	25.4	29.6	14.2	1.9	78.2	42.2	49.5	50.6
29360	LAURENS	63.9	63.1	33.1	33.3	0.2	0.3	2.8	3.5	6.7	6.5	6.9	6.7	6.3	27.1	24.8	12.6	2.4	75.8	37.7	48.1	51.9
29365	LYMAN	88.0	87.4	9.5	9.6	0.5	0.7	1.6	2.1	6.4	6.7	6.7	5.7	5.2	30.2	26.4	11.2	1.5	76.7	38.5	49.0	51.0
29369	MOORE	79.1	77.4	17.8	18.8	1.8	2.3	1.4	1.8	6.7	7.4	8.4	6.8	5.2	28.8	27.6	8.5	0.6	72.9	37.5	49.0	51.0
29370	MOUNTVILLE	65.0	63.9	33.6	34.4	0.1	0.1	1.0	1.2	7.0	7.2	7.4	6.8	5.8	26.0	27.4	11.5	1.1	74.2	38.0	50.3	49.7
29372	PACOLET	77.5	76.4	20.7	21.5	0.5	0.6	1.0	1.4	5.9	6.1	6.7	5.9	5.6	26.8	25.7	15.7	1.7	77.8	40.4	48.1	51.9
29374	PAULINE	80.9	80.2	17.3	17.8	0.5	0.6	0.6	0.7	5.2	5.8	6.1	5.6	6.7	36.8	25.1	7.8	0.9	79.6	36.7	59.0	41.0
29376	ROEBUCK	86.0	85.0	12.0	12.5	1.0	1.2	1.3	1.7	6.4	6.9	7.5	5.9	5.2	29.4	27.6	10.2	1.0	75.6	38.5	49.2	50.8
29379	UNION	67.7	66.9	31.0	31.6	0.3	0.3	0.7	0.8	6.4	6.5	6.7	5.9	5.6	26.6	25.8	14.5	2.1	76.8	39.9	47.1	52.9
29384	WATERLOO	82.2	79.2	16.8	19.6	0.1	0.2	0.8	1.0	6.4	6.6	6.2	5.6	5.5	27.2	28.1	13.7	0.8	77.4	40.4	49.9	50.1
29385	WELLFORD	71.6	70.2	24.0	24.5	1.5	1.9	2.7	3.4	7.1	7.2	7.5	6.5	5.8	30.5	24.4	10.1	1.0	74.3	36.2	48.4	51.6
29388	WOODRUFF	81.7	80.8	15.4	15.6	0.3	0.4	2.6	3.3	7.1	7.0	7.3	6.1	5.8	28.5	25.6	11.2	1.4	74.8	37.5	49.1	50.9
29401	CHARLESTON	89.5	88.4	8.6	9.3	0.9	1.1	1.0	1.3	2.8	2.5	3.0	14.2	16.9	22.3	22.0	13.4	2.9	89.7	31.8	44.9	55.1
29403	CHARLESTON	32.5	31.5	65.3	65.9	0.7	0.8	1.6	1.9	4.8	5.0	5.7	14.1	15.9	23.0	18.8	11.0	1.7	80.9	28.3	49.3	50.7
29404	CHARLESTON AFB	74.5	72.2	17.3	18.0	1.6	2.0	6.5	8.2	15.5	9.8	7.1	5.3	18.4	39.2	3.4	1.2	0.1	65.2	23.3	53.1	46.9
29405	NORTH CHARLESTON	28.5	27.9	68.4	68.6	0.8	1.0	2.5	2.9	6.9	7.1	7.9	8.3	8.3	28.4	20.9	10.7	1.4	73.2	33.0	50.1	49.9
29406	CHARLESTON	63.2	61.5	30.1	30.6	1.8	2.2	4.6	5.5	7.5	6.3	6.5	7.1	10.9	31.8	19.7	9.2	1.0	76.4	31.1	50.1	49.9
29407	CHARLESTON	66.2	64.5	30.6	31.5	1.6	2.0	1.6	2.0	5.2	5.0	5.5	7.1	8.5	29.2	24.1	13.4	2.0	80.7	37.1	47.1	52.9
29412	CHARLESTON	79.1	77.1	18.8	20.4	0.7	0.8	1.2	1.5	5.2	5.4	5.7	5.9	6.1	29.9	26.7	13.4	1.8	80.2	40.0	48.2	51.8
29414	CHARLESTON	76.1	74.5	20.2	20.9	1.8	2.3	1.6	2.1	6.6	6.4	6.2	6.1	7.1	33.8	24.2	8.6	1.1	77.1	35.3	47.8	52.2
29418	NORTH CHARLESTON	52.0	50.7	40.4	40.5	3.0	3.6	3.9	4.7	7.9	7.2	7.6	7.1	8.4	33.6	21.2	6.6	0.4	73.2	31.7	48.7	51.3
29420	NORTH CHARLESTON	56.3	55.1	36.1	36.0	2.8	3.4	4.3	5.3	8.4	8.1	9.0	8.1	7.7	32.6	20.7	5.2	0.2	69.5	30.6	48.6	51.4
29426	ADAMS RUN	32.0	30.4	66.8	68.0	0.2	0.2	1.0	1.3	6.8	7.0	8.7	7.7	6.7	25.6	26.0	10.1	1.4	72.7	36.7	48.0	52.0
29429	AWENDAW	47.1	47.7	51.4	50.5	0.3	0.5	0.9	1.2	7.1	7.4	8.0	6.8	5.2	28.5	26.7	9.6	0.8	73.1	37.6	48.4	51.6
29431	BONNEAU	79.0	78.4	19.5	20.0	0.1	0.1	1.3	1.6	6.7	6.9	7.8	6.8	6.1	25.9	26.5	12.3	1.0	74.5	37.7	49.1	50.9
29432	BRANCHVILLE	54.5	52.8	44.0	45.5	0.1	0.1	0.8	1.0	6.8	6.9	7.4	6.7	6.4	24.7	26.8	12.8	1.6	75.0	38.9	47.3	52.7
29434	CORDESVILLE	67.5	66.5	31.4	32.2	0.1	0.3	1.0	1.2	5.8	6.0	7.4	7.8	7.4	26.3	26.7	11.6	1.0	75.6	38.1	49.5	50.5
29435	COTTAGEVILLE	70.8	68.9	25.0	26.5	0.4	0.6	1.0	1.1	6.8	6.9	7.3	6.2	6.6	26.9	28.1	10.4	0.8	75.3	38.2	49.4	50.6
29436	CROSS	36.0	35.2	62.4	62.9	0.1	0.1	1.2	1.4	6.1	6.5	7.7	8.1	6.5	24.3	27.9	11.7	1.2	74.8	39.0	48.1	51.9
29437	DORCHESTER	53.3	52.0	44.0	44.9	0.1	0.1	0.6	0.7	5.8	6.1	7.9	7.3	6.1	26.4	27.5	11.5	1.4	75.8	39.4	48.5	51.6
29438	EDISTO ISLAND	59.6	59.6	39.1	38.9	0.1	0.1	1.4	1.4	3.8	4.1	5.4	5.6	4.9	19.7	37.1	17.9	1.5	83.3	49.1	47.9	52.1
29440	GEORGETOWN	48.4	46.9	49.4	50.6	0.3	0.4	2.2	2.6	7.1	7.1	7.7	7.3	6.6	25.8	25.5	11.6	1.4	73.6	36.4	48.0	52.0
29445	GOOSE CREEK	72.4	70.9	18.7	18.7	4.0	4.9	4.2	5.1	8.4	7.3	7.2	10.1	11.0	31.1	19.3	5.4	0.3	72.9	28.4	52.0	48.0
29446	GREEN POND	26.0	24.5	73.2	74.5	0.0	0.0	0.8	0.7	6.5	6.9	8.4	7.7	6.6	23.7	26.2	12.5	1.6	73.4	37.4	48.5	51.5
29448	HARLEYVILLE	50.8	49.7	47.3	48.2	0.1	0.1	0.4	0.4	5.8	6.4	8.2	7.4	6.4	26.2	26.8	11.5	1.4	75.1	38.3	48.2	51.8
29449	HOLLYWOOD	37.5	35.6	60.4	61.7	0.2	0.3	2.3	2.9	5.7	6.5	8.4	7.7	6.0	24.7	29.0	11.0	1.1	74.5	39.4	48.2	51.9
29450	HUGER	26.6	26.1	72.3	72.6	0.3	0.4	0.8	0.9	7.1	7.2	8.2	8.3	7.6	26.3	26.7	7.8	0.9	72.6	35.3	48.8	51.2
29451	ISLE OF PALMS	98.1	97.7	0.5	0.5	0.6	0.7	1.2	1.6	4.7	5.4	5.6	4.7	3.6	24.0	34.7	16.3	1.0	81.4	46.2	49.4	50.6
29453	JAMESTOWN	48.3	47.1	50.3	51.4	0.1	0.1	0.6	0.5	5.8	5.9	6.5	7.1	7.5	26.4	28.5	11.0	1.2	77.4	39.2	49.3	50.7
29455	JOHNS ISLAND	62.5	59.4	33.0	35.1	0.5	0.6	5.6	6.8	5.3	5.5	6.2	5.8	5.4	25.0	30.3	15.4	1.2	79.4	42.9	48.6	51.4
29456	LADSON	74.4	73.1	19.9	20.3	1.9	2.3	2.8	3.3	7.3	7.2	8.3	7.7	7.2	32.0	23.2	6.7	0.6	72.2	33.3	49.7	50.3
29458	MC CLELLANVILLE	34.1	33.2	64.9	65.6	0.1	0.1	1.0	1.2	5.5	6.0	7.5	8.0	6.5	23.3	29.8	11.9	1.6	75.8	40.5	49.3	50.7
29461	MONCKS CORNER	65.8	65.3	30.7	30.7	0.4	0.5	2.1	2.5	6.6	6.8	7.5	7.1	6.4	27.7	25.9	10.8	1.2	74.6	37.1	48.9	51.1
29464	MOUNT PLEASANT	87.7	86.6	9.8	10.4	1.1	1.4	1.3	1.7	6.6	6.6	6.5	6.0	5.9	31.6	25.1	9.9	1.7	76.3	37.2	47.7	52.3
29466	MOUNT PLEASANT	76.7	75.9	20.7	21.0	1.3	1.7	1.6	2.0	9.1	9.2	7.7	5.6	4.3	33.5	23.7	6.4	0.5	70.5	35.4	48.4	51.6
29468	PINEVILLE	16.0	15.5	83.3	83.7	0.0	0.0	0.8	0.9	5.2	6.8	7.9	7.8	6.2	24.0	28.4	12.2	1.5	75.5	39.4	48.8	51.2
29469	PINOPOLIS	54.5	53.2	44.0	45.0	0.0	0.0	0.9	1.0	7.2	7.5	7.9	7.4	6.6	28.1	25.0	9.6	0.7	72.5	35.6	51.3	48.7
29470	RAVENEL	53.5	52.0	45.3	46.6	0.1	0.2	1.1	1.4	6.0	6.7	8.0	7.3	6.2	26.0	28.7	9.9	1.2	74.6	38.8	48.3	51.7
29471	REEVESVILLE	50.5	50.0	48.2	48.7	0.1	0.1	1.3	1.3	6.3	6.3	7.5	7.6	6.3	24.8	27.1	12.3	1.8	75.4	38.7	50.0	50.0
29472	RIDGEVILLE	48.5	47.4	47.4	48.0	0.2	0.2	1.2	1.3	4.8	5.0	5.9	6.2	8.4	35.8	24.9	8.3	0.8	80.6	36.5	60.7	39.4
29474	ROUND O	62.1	59.8	32.6	34.2	0.5	0.5	1.2	1.4	7.1	7.1	7.3	6.5	6.6	25.8	27.5	10.7	1.3	74.6	38.0	49.0	51.0
29475	RUFFIN	60.4	59.4	37.9	38.7	0.4	0.5	1.0	1.1	6.1	6.2	7.4	6.7	6.7	26.4	27.2	12.0	1.3	76.3	38.7	49.2	50.8
29477	SAINT GEORGE	45.6	44.4	53.1	54.0	0.4	0.5	0.8	0.9	5.8	6.0	7.4	6.6	6.5	25.4	26.4	13.9	2.0	76.8	39.8	49.0	51.0
29479	SAINT STEPHEN	38.8	38.0	59.7	60.4	0.1	0.1	1.2	1.4	7.2	7.4	8.4	8.1	6.6	24.5	25.4	10.6	1.8	71.9	35.7	47.7	52.3
29481	SMOAKS	37.7	36.0	60.9	62.4	0.2	0.2	0.8	0.8	7.4	7.7	8.7	7.2	6.5	24.0	26.0	11.3	1.2	71.8	35.9	47.8	52.2
29482	SULLIVANS ISLAND	98.7	98.6	0.6	0.7	0.2	0.2	0.8	1.1	4.2	5.1	7.8	7.4	5.1	25.2	33.7	9.8	1.8	78.2	42.0	50.4	49.6
29483	SUMMERVILLE	76.7	75.8	19.3	19.6	0.9	1.1	2.1	2.6	7.1	7.0	8.0	7.7	7.2	29.6	24.6	7.9	0.8	72.9	34.5	48.7	51.3
29485	SUMMERVILLE	81.5	80.7	15.0	15.1	1.2	1.5	1.9	2.3	6.8	7.1	8.4	7.8	6.2	28.6	25.4	8.8	0.9	72.7	36.1	48.3	51.8
29487	WADMALAW ISLAND	37.7	36.2	60.9	62.2	0.1	0.1	4.1	5.1	4.6	4.8	6.2	6.9	7.0	23.4	31.9	13.5	1.8	80.1	43.1	49.2	50.8
29488	WALTERBORO	55.3	54.8	42.8	42.9	0.3	0.4	1.4	1.7	7.4	7.3	7.7	7.2	6.9	26.0	24.6	11.4	1.5	73.2	36.1	47.4	52.6
29492	CHARLESTON	57.6	56.7	41.5	42.3	0.5	0.6	0.7	0.8	9.8	8.8	7.3	6.6	7.1	31.5	23.6	4.8	0.4	70.1	32.9	47.5	52.5
29501	FLORENCE	69.6	68.9	28.0	28.2	1.2	1.5	1.0	1.2	6.4	6.5	6.8	6.4	6.2	29.5	25.4	10.9	2.0	76.4	37.5	46.9	53.1
29505	FLORENCE	73.0	71.6	24.4	25.3	1.5	1.8	0.8	0.9	6.6	6.6	7.1	6.7	6.2	28.7	26.0	11.2	1.0	75.6	37.4	47.2	52.8
29506	FLORENCE	33.8	34.1	64.4	63.8	0.3	0.4	1.2	1.5	6.6	6.6	7.4	9.0	10.1	25.8	23.4	9.6	1.5	75.0	32.9	46.1	53.9
29510	ANDREWS	49.1	48.0	49.6	50.4	0.1	0.1	1.8	2.1	6.7	7.1	9.0	7.7	6.7	25.9	24.9	10.8	1.2	72.4	35.6	47.2	52.8
29511	AYNOR	85.3	84.6	13.3	13.7	0.1	0.1	1.5	1.8	7.1	7.0	7.3	6.4	6.8	29.6	25.1	9.8	0.9	74.8	35.7	49.2	50.8
29512	BENNETTSVILLE	39.7	39.1	57.5	57.7	0.4	0.4	0.7	0.7	6.5	6.7	7.0	6.9	7.2	29.1	24.1	11.0	1.5	75.6	36.1	50.4	49.6
	SOUTH CAROLINA	67.2	66.6	29.5	29.5	0.9	1.2	2.4	2.9	6.6	6.6	7.0	7.1	7.3	28.4	24.7	11.0	1.4	75.9	36.3	48.8	51.2
	UNITED STATES	75.1	73.6	12.3	12.5	3.8	4.2	12.5	14.1	6.9	6.7	7.2	7.0	7.3	28.6	23.8	10.8	1.7	75.1	36.0	49.1	50.9

#	ZIP CODE / POST OFFICE NAME	2004 Per Capita Income	2004 HH Income Base	2004 HOUSEHOLD INCOME DISTRIBUTION (%)					MEDIAN HOUSEHOLD INCOME				2004 Home Value Base	2004 HOME VALUE DISTRIBUTION (%)					2004 Median Home Value
				Less than $25,000	$25,000 to $49,999	$50,000 to $99,999	$100,000 to $149,999	$150,000 or More	2004	2009	2004 National Centile	2004 State Centile		Less than $50,000	$50,000 to $89,999	$90,000 to $174,999	$175,000 to $399,999	$400,000 or More	
29206	COLUMBIA	35448	8924	16.4	31.2	30.6	11.6	10.2	52543	62246	76	89	5534	2.3	7.8	48.6	32.4	9.0	160602
29207	COLUMBIA	7217	41	4.9	24.4	22.0	7.3	41.5	92818	105530	97	100	22	0.0	0.0	4.6	54.6	40.9	366667
29208	COLUMBIA	9961	2	100.0	0.0	0.0	0.0	0.0	20000	20000	2	0	0	0.0	0.0	0.0	0.0	0.0	0
29209	COLUMBIA	27766	12033	22.2	30.1	31.2	10.3	6.3	47291	55258	67	83	7822	4.7	20.9	51.1	19.2	4.1	117676
29210	COLUMBIA	24540	17656	26.6	35.8	28.4	7.5	1.7	39624	44833	45	60	6694	4.6	26.1	58.7	10.4	0.2	109680
29212	COLUMBIA	28878	11259	13.5	20.2	40.3	18.0	8.1	66001	75959	89	96	8518	0.5	10.5	56.0	29.2	3.8	142244
29223	COLUMBIA	31021	18073	18.2	27.4	33.1	12.2	9.2	54060	64099	78	91	11954	7.2	21.8	44.3	20.7	6.1	117619
29229	COLUMBIA	30710	8216	9.3	21.0	41.6	19.6	8.5	69123	83043	91	97	7279	4.3	8.0	51.4	32.6	3.8	145667
29301	SPARTANBURG	23461	12215	28.4	29.9	29.1	8.0	4.6	42407	49506	54	72	7884	15.6	23.5	43.3	14.4	3.2	105858
29302	SPARTANBURG	31724	6916	22.2	26.9	31.5	11.8	7.7	50826	58888	74	88	5019	8.3	23.8	37.6	22.5	7.8	118438
29303	SPARTANBURG	17065	9372	38.7	31.1	23.9	4.5	1.7	32411	37705	19	26	5442	22.8	35.9	34.4	6.4	0.4	82184
29306	SPARTANBURG	16185	6728	47.5	27.9	18.5	3.5	2.5	26639	30553	7	5	3481	22.3	42.2	27.3	5.4	2.9	75780
29307	SPARTANBURG	28197	8427	27.1	29.1	28.1	9.6	6.1	43730	50271	58	76	5935	12.9	19.8	44.7	20.9	1.8	115263
29316	BOILING SPRINGS	24439	6007	17.2	28.7	39.8	11.5	2.8	53335	62038	77	90	5065	7.6	17.1	63.9	11.0	0.4	113114
29321	BUFFALO	18310	1096	25.2	38.1	33.4	2.7	0.7	40327	44329	47	63	883	36.0	38.3	22.1	3.6	0.0	64295
29322	CAMPOBELLO	21643	3145	25.3	33.0	29.7	9.1	2.8	43638	50198	58	76	2675	22.1	25.4	30.4	16.8	5.4	94066
29323	CHESNEE	19652	5621	28.5	31.6	31.5	6.4	2.1	41129	46765	50	67	4530	23.7	26.3	38.9	10.1	1.0	90027
29325	CLINTON	16839	5750	36.7	33.5	23.0	5.3	1.6	34167	38589	25	34	3922	30.7	31.5	28.9	8.3	0.6	76293
29330	COWPENS	18438	3618	32.1	31.7	28.1	6.5	1.6	38317	43879	40	55	2865	28.2	32.7	30.1	8.2	0.8	77675
29332	CROSS HILL	19477	883	34.0	37.0	19.8	7.0	2.2	37320	41718	37	50	787	31.8	21.7	34.6	10.2	1.8	85089
29334	DUNCAN	20960	3439	28.0	29.7	31.8	7.4	3.1	43293	49714	57	74	2587	17.6	25.9	37.9	15.7	2.9	99686
29335	ENOREE	16200	1748	30.2	28.7	33.6	5.7	1.8	40252	45749	47	62	1479	32.6	32.4	25.7	7.8	1.5	73804
29340	GAFFNEY	18829	8342	33.9	32.0	27.0	4.8	2.4	36472	41204	33	45	6169	27.9	38.3	28.2	5.0	0.7	74792
29341	GAFFNEY	20172	6976	30.9	29.7	30.8	6.4	2.2	41036	46205	50	66	4979	18.4	31.8	37.7	11.0	1.1	89809
29349	INMAN	22257	9986	21.5	31.5	33.8	10.2	3.0	47293	53947	67	83	8223	15.0	24.8	42.9	15.8	1.5	104004
29351	JOANNA	19632	936	37.0	33.8	23.5	3.7	2.0	36580	40769	34	46	722	37.8	35.9	18.4	6.1	1.8	60968
29353	JONESVILLE	18155	1795	32.9	34.8	26.6	4.4	1.3	36629	40790	34	46	1452	36.6	31.1	25.6	6.0	0.8	66600
29355	KINARDS	18797	178	29.2	38.2	25.8	5.6	1.1	35000	39420	28	38	147	31.3	30.6	26.5	8.8	2.7	76563
29356	LANDRUM	22898	3470	28.4	32.0	29.3	6.8	3.5	41862	49099	52	70	2782	18.6	20.3	36.1	20.2	4.9	108267
29360	LAURENS	18169	8618	35.0	31.6	26.5	5.3	1.6	35932	40128	31	43	6142	24.6	32.1	30.9	11.4	1.0	82772
29365	LYMAN	22603	3254	24.9	27.5	37.0	8.7	2.0	47527	54430	67	84	2676	13.1	31.5	40.7	13.6	1.1	97059
29369	MOORE	27233	4629	14.7	26.0	37.0	14.9	7.5	57361	66077	82	93	3999	7.4	14.9	36.9	38.5	2.3	148149
29370	MOUNTVILLE	17070	546	29.1	39.0	24.5	5.1	2.2	37728	41936	38	53	458	35.6	23.1	26.0	12.7	2.6	80476
29372	PACOLET	18668	2164	36.3	31.9	26.7	4.3	0.9	35680	41089	30	42	1689	35.2	36.5	23.3	4.7	0.2	69519
29374	PAULINE	26387	1385	21.3	29.2	36.9	8.3	4.3	49611	55940	71	86	1217	20.4	28.5	33.2	16.1	1.8	91901
29376	ROEBUCK	23055	2099	21.9	28.0	38.5	8.8	2.9	50080	56422	72	87	1742	15.6	16.8	46.7	18.5	2.4	111862
29379	UNION	18700	8574	37.1	33.1	23.6	4.5	1.7	33984	37801	24	33	6446	33.5	32.4	26.5	6.8	0.8	71335
29384	WATERLOO	19445	2048	30.9	30.3	35.2	2.6	1.0	38956	43653	43	56	1664	29.9	26.6	33.5	9.4	0.7	83669
29385	WELLFORD	18992	2690	28.6	31.8	32.7	5.1	1.8	41548	47625	51	69	2142	16.2	42.0	31.5	9.8	0.7	80745
29388	WOODRUFF	20898	5497	30.3	28.3	32.1	6.3	3.0	41744	48027	52	70	4322	19.5	29.2	37.2	12.0	2.2	91791
29401	CHARLESTON	47057	4887	32.4	21.2	19.7	8.9	17.7	43367	57635	57	75	2146	0.1	0.7	5.0	20.2	74.0	664352
29403	CHARLESTON	16065	9551	57.1	21.2	14.4	4.6	2.7	20416	23670	2	1	3500	6.3	21.9	39.5	24.7	7.6	126863
29404	CHARLESTON AFB	14743	1184	18.6	52.3	25.2	3.0	1.0	39007	44159	43	58	107	48.6	17.8	15.0	9.4	9.4	61875
29405	NORTH CHARLESTON	13951	11193	48.5	29.6	18.6	2.6	0.8	26005	30399	6	3	5176	18.9	48.9	27.9	3.4	0.9	75817
29406	CHARLESTON	19938	15317	32.9	33.4	25.8	6.2	1.7	35862	41193	31	43	7394	25.2	22.4	38.9	12.4	1.2	94808
29407	CHARLESTON	27160	17060	27.5	31.1	27.5	9.2	4.8	41778	49674	52	70	10059	4.0	16.3	46.7	27.1	6.0	138819
29412	CHARLESTON	30127	15734	20.5	26.9	34.6	12.0	6.0	52413	62638	76	89	11457	2.2	8.6	44.5	35.3	9.5	163880
29414	CHARLESTON	27873	11320	16.9	28.5	37.5	12.7	4.5	54161	64200	79	92	7440	2.4	9.1	47.3	37.6	3.7	161331
29418	NORTH CHARLESTON	20006	9261	26.6	36.0	30.1	6.1	1.2	39007	45171	43	58	5099	23.5	22.9	39.8	13.0	0.7	95259
29420	NORTH CHARLESTON	21933	5881	19.2	26.5	39.9	11.1	3.3	53501	62938	78	90	4262	12.7	21.2	48.2	13.4	4.6	111449
29426	ADAMS RUN	16195	716	39.8	27.7	24.9	6.6	1.1	32739	38837	20	28	609	25.8	33.0	31.9	7.1	2.3	77128
29429	AWENDAW	26788	1416	26.2	22.3	30.1	11.4	10.0	51737	63342	75	88	1283	17.1	15.0	23.9	29.8	14.3	141267
29431	BONNEAU	18909	2270	27.7	32.7	32.5	5.9	1.3	41055	45697	50	67	1924	27.6	31.1	26.6	14.1	0.6	78716
29432	BRANCHVILLE	18772	1095	39.5	32.2	22.4	3.3	2.6	31280	36216	16	21	880	40.0	29.4	25.2	5.2	0.1	64079
29434	CORDESVILLE	16288	250	36.0	28.8	28.0	4.8	2.4	35340	39834	29	40	199	35.7	30.7	27.1	3.0	3.5	62647
29435	COTTAGEVILLE	17110	1563	34.9	31.8	27.9	3.2	2.2	33740	38345	23	32	1330	31.7	28.0	32.1	7.8	0.5	75432
29436	CROSS	12988	1694	42.0	34.8	21.3	1.8	0.2	30514	34479	14	17	1413	31.8	28.0	32.9	4.3	3.1	74919
29437	DORCHESTER	16949	884	35.8	30.4	28.3	4.2	1.4	33827	38985	24	33	757	32.6	31.2	27.3	8.9	0.0	70306
29438	EDISTO ISLAND	36628	1121	35.0	21.6	23.3	11.8	8.4	40766	48701	49	64	943	15.9	7.7	18.1	30.0	28.2	224254
29440	GEORGETOWN	19914	11637	34.8	29.9	25.9	5.8	3.6	35617	41744	30	41	9141	28.9	26.3	31.1	10.3	3.4	83880
29445	GOOSE CREEK	20102	17907	19.6	31.5	37.9	8.9	2.2	48919	55194	70	86	11726	7.9	25.2	49.4	16.9	0.7	111729
29446	GREEN POND	18214	813	46.1	32.4	14.5	4.1	3.0	27842	31623	8	7	666	35.3	34.1	26.0	4.2	0.5	61228
29448	HARLEYVILLE	20375	906	35.4	27.3	31.0	4.0	2.3	35720	40758	30	42	743	34.3	27.3	26.8	11.6	0.0	73370
29449	HOLLYWOOD	21207	2957	36.1	27.2	23.7	8.3	4.8	36136	42289	32	44	2488	22.1	28.9	24.6	17.0	7.5	88750
29450	HUGER	14898	1088	30.2	37.5	27.6	3.8	0.9	37231	41845	36	49	965	25.2	27.3	29.8	14.9	2.8	87299
29451	ISLE OF PALMS	57224	1994	6.6	16.9	30.4	21.1	25.1	91564	117675	97	100	1669	0.2	0.5	2.0	28.0	69.2	546210
29453	JAMESTOWN	14347	558	42.3	31.0	21.7	5.0	0.0	30249	33971	13	16	489	44.2	17.0	29.5	9.2	0.2	59194
29455	JOHNS ISLAND	28364	6096	26.5	27.8	26.7	11.7	7.3	44423	53233	60	79	5113	15.5	19.4	23.3	17.5	24.3	121994
29456	LADSON	20552	6572	19.5	33.6	36.6	8.2	2.1	47769	54584	68	84	5018	15.5	26.6	51.3	6.0	0.5	99356
29458	MC CLELLANVILLE	17092	1188	39.0	26.3	26.4	5.0	3.4	33328	39357	22	30	991	25.1	22.3	31.7	14.9	6.0	94250
29461	MONCKS CORNER	19887	9335	28.0	31.1	30.3	8.3	2.3	40900	45514	49	65	7385	20.3	22.0	39.3	16.3	2.1	101380
29464	MOUNT PLEASANT	36169	17677	13.2	22.0	37.9	16.0	10.9	65758	79401	89	96	12740	1.2	2.9	28.4	53.9	13.6	216170
29466	MOUNT PLEASANT	38313	6791	11.2	16.1	37.3	20.0	15.5	77216	95028	94	99	6034	6.1	4.9	16.1	53.3	19.5	246279
29468	PINEVILLE	14139	820	47.8	31.6	14.4	4.3	2.0	25978	29074	6	3	742	58.9	20.6	11.3	5.7	3.5	44962
29469	PINOPOLIS	18935	254	29.1	27.6	35.4	7.5	0.4	45246	50393	62	80	226	40.7	21.7	25.7	11.1	0.9	62000
29470	RAVENEL	19714	1649	34.0	27.0	28.3	7.5	3.3	38796	45411	42	56	1407	27.3	25.2	27.5	13.8	6.3	86920
29471	REEVESVILLE	18820	643	37.2	38.9	16.3	4.4	3.3	35513	40297	30	40	545	35.4	25.1	25.9	12.3	1.3	71800
29472	RIDGEVILLE	15298	2692	34.0	27.0	32.1	5.9	1.0	38016	42940	39	53	2307	34.5	23.4	30.3	11.4	0.4	74205
29474	ROUND O	15953	759	38.7	33.1	22.9	3.3	2.0	32136	36798	18	25	634	33.3	25.4	32.7	7.6	1.1	73947
29475	RUFFIN	16293	940	39.5	33.4	21.6	3.9	1.6	32996	37887	21	29	768	29.6	31.3	26.4	10.3	2.5	74848
29477	SAINT GEORGE	16517	2884	42.3	31.6	19.8	4.5	1.8	30545	35149	14	18	2324	35.6	28.1	27.9	8.4	0.0	68118
29479	SAINT STEPHEN	14827	2681	44.0	27.3	22.5	4.7	1.5	29809	33274	12	14	2137	34.0	29.6	28.7	7.4	0.4	73563
29481	SMOAKS	14605	688	51.7	22.5	21.8	2.0	1.9	23800	26803	4	2	570	35.4	24.9	31.2	8.1	0.4	69310
29482	SULLIVANS ISLAND	65631	821	11.8	15.7	30.2	17.1	25.2	84128	106270	96	99	575	0.0	0.2	2.4	15.8	81.6	761842
29483	SUMMERVILLE	21008	19359	22.7	31.1	34.8	8.7	2.7	46707	52796	66	83	14911	17.5	22.7	41.2	15.5	3.2	103495
29485	SUMMERVILLE	25355	11522	15.2	27.4	40.0	13.5	4.0	56605	64260	81	93	8849	7.3	14.2	43.4	33.5	1.6	145738
29487	WADMALAW ISLAND	22405	1024	38.3	24.5	23.9	7.2	6.1	35178	41683	28	39	866	19.9	23.8	25.4	14.0	17.0	99649
29488	WALTERBORO	16969	8925	38.0	31.4	24.4	4.6	1.6	33664	38714	23	31	6740	27.2	33.1	29.9	9.2	0.6	76751
29492	CHARLESTON	27307	1201	15.3	23.2	37.2	17.4	6.8	63140	68498	87	96	1097	9.6	10.3	20.9	42.3	17.0	238592
29501	FLORENCE	28375	16172	25.8	28.3	30.0	9.4	6.6	45470	53622	63	81	11053	11.8	24.6	37.8	21.3	4.4	110731
29505	FLORENCE	25299	7567	21.6	28.3	35.3	10.8	4.0	50027	57748	72	87	6135	11.8	23.2	48.1	15.5	1.5	106873
29506	FLORENCE	16202	7680	42.0	30.3	21.7	3.9	2.0	30103	35335	12	16	5088	35.2	34.6	24.3	4.2	1.8	66065
29510	ANDREWS	14613	3478	46.1	27.4	21.8	3.6	1.1	27376	31418	8	6	2806	41.6	28.5	23.9	5.5	0.6	62150
29511	AYNOR	18576	1781	34.6	31.0	26.3	6.1	2.0	34978	39118	27	38	1426	37.4	21.0	31.4	9.4	0.9	70545
29512	BENNETTSVILLE	15792	6890	44.6	28.8	21.7	3.0	1.9	28499	32046	10	9	4916	36.2	39.2	21.3	2.9	0.4	63580
	SOUTH CAROLINA	22607		28.8	29.3	29.6	8.3	4.0	42042	49103				19.3	24.1	35.5	17.1	3.9	100170
	UNITED STATES	25866		24.7	27.1	30.8	10.9	6.5	48124	56710				10.9	15.0	33.7	30.1	10.4	145905

SPENDING POTENTIAL INDICES SOUTH CAROLINA
29206-29512 D

ZIP CODE #	POST OFFICE NAME	FINANCIAL SERVICES: Auto Loan	Home Loan	Invest-ments	Retire-ment Plans	THE HOME: Home Improvements: Home Repair	Lawn & Garden	Furnishings: Computers & Hardware	Major Appliances	TV, Radio, Sound Equipment	Furniture	ENTERTAINMENT: Dine out/ Carry out	Sports Equipment	Fees & Tickets	Toys & Games	Travel	Cable TV	PERSONAL: Apparel & Services	Auto Repairs	Health Insurance	Pets & Supplies
29206	COLUMBIA	110	118	135	119	116	125	119	116	116	118	146	135	122	146	119	115	144	118	112	127
29207	COLUMBIA	199	255	345	252	248	269	230	225	215	233	272	256	256	283	240	216	275	220	209	245
29208	COLUMBIA	28	17	22	20	17	21	33	25	32	28	41	34	27	36	27	29	38	30	23	28
29209	COLUMBIA	90	96	110	97	94	100	97	94	94	96	119	110	99	119	96	93	117	95	90	104
29210	COLUMBIA	68	62	75	67	61	66	73	67	71	71	90	82	70	86	68	68	88	72	63	75
29212	COLUMBIA	110	124	134	128	121	122	117	115	110	119	140	135	122	141	117	105	138	114	103	126
29223	COLUMBIA	107	115	126	118	112	117	112	110	108	114	137	128	115	136	111	105	134	111	102	122
29229	COLUMBIA	123	134	140	139	130	131	128	126	120	130	151	148	130	150	125	114	148	125	114	138
29301	SPARTANBURG	83	82	83	81	82	88	82	83	83	82	103	97	82	103	82	83	100	83	83	95
29302	SPARTANBURG	103	108	115	108	109	115	107	107	106	105	132	125	109	135	108	104	128	107	105	121
29303	SPARTANBURG	65	54	45	51	57	64	56	60	61	55	74	70	53	72	56	62	69	60	66	74
29306	SPARTANBURG	57	47	47	43	47	56	51	53	57	52	69	60	49	66	50	59	66	54	59	63
29307	SPARTANBURG	94	92	93	91	93	102	91	94	93	91	114	109	91	113	92	93	110	94	96	109
29316	BOILING SPRINGS	93	96	88	94	96	99	88	92	88	89	109	108	90	111	89	87	106	90	90	109
29321	BUFFALO	81	56	28	49	63	72	54	67	64	55	76	80	47	72	55	69	69	66	81	94
29322	CAMPOBELLO	94	75	48	68	80	89	71	82	78	72	94	97	65	92	72	82	88	81	93	109
29323	CHESNEE	87	68	43	62	73	81	65	75	72	66	87	89	59	83	66	75	81	74	85	99
29325	CLINTON	69	55	44	51	58	66	57	62	63	57	76	72	53	72	56	65	71	63	71	78
29330	COWPENS	81	62	39	57	67	74	60	70	67	61	80	82	54	76	60	69	75	69	79	92
29332	CROSS HILL	81	60	35	53	67	76	57	69	66	57	78	82	50	75	59	71	72	68	83	96
29334	DUNCAN	82	74	65	71	77	84	73	78	77	73	95	92	72	95	74	79	90	77	83	95
29335	ENOREE	91	63	32	55	71	81	61	74	72	62	85	89	53	81	62	77	77	74	90	104
29340	GAFFNEY	77	61	44	56	65	74	60	68	67	60	81	80	56	79	61	71	76	68	78	89
29341	GAFFNEY	79	68	55	64	71	78	68	73	72	68	88	85	64	86	68	74	83	73	80	90
29349	INMAN	91	79	60	75	83	91	76	83	81	76	98	98	73	97	77	83	93	82	91	105
29351	JOANNA	87	58	26	50	66	76	56	70	68	57	80	84	48	75	57	73	73	70	87	100
29353	JONESVILLE	83	56	25	48	63	73	54	67	65	55	76	80	46	72	55	70	69	66	83	95
29355	KINARDS	85	57	26	49	64	74	55	68	66	56	77	82	46	73	56	71	70	68	84	97
29356	LANDRUM	94	72	48	66	79	91	69	82	79	71	94	93	64	88	72	84	87	80	97	107
29360	LAURENS	71	59	48	55	62	70	60	65	66	59	79	75	56	77	60	68	75	65	73	81
29365	LYMAN	84	78	65	74	81	88	74	79	77	74	95	93	73	97	76	79	91	78	85	98
29369	MOORE	104	111	106	109	112	115	102	106	100	101	124	125	104	129	104	100	121	103	103	125
29370	MOUNTVILLE	84	58	29	50	66	75	56	69	66	56	78	82	48	74	57	71	71	68	84	97
29372	PACOLET	84	58	28	51	65	74	56	69	66	57	78	82	48	74	57	71	72	68	83	96
29374	PAULINE	104	88	63	82	94	102	82	93	89	83	108	111	78	107	84	93	101	91	104	122
29376	ROEBUCK	91	83	68	79	87	93	78	85	82	78	99	101	76	101	79	83	95	83	90	107
29379	UNION	77	56	34	50	61	71	56	66	65	56	77	76	50	74	57	69	71	65	79	87
29384	WATERLOO	82	58	32	51	66	75	56	68	65	56	77	81	49	74	58	70	71	68	83	96
29385	WELLFORD	81	68	48	63	71	78	64	72	69	65	84	85	60	82	65	71	79	71	79	93
29388	WOODRUFF	91	72	47	66	78	87	69	79	77	69	92	94	64	91	70	81	86	78	91	105
29401	CHARLESTON	126	117	174	127	114	127	144	126	141	138	178	157	141	176	135	135	174	137	117	140
29403	CHARLESTON	53	42	49	41	42	50	53	50	57	52	70	57	50	64	49	58	67	53	54	57
29404	CHARLESTON AFB	77	49	47	56	45	53	73	63	74	68	93	84	63	83	60	68	89	74	58	72
29405	NORTH CHARLESTON	49	43	49	40	43	50	47	47	52	48	64	52	47	61	47	54	61	49	52	54
29406	CHARLESTON	66	61	69	62	59	65	67	65	68	67	85	77	65	82	64	66	83	68	62	72
29407	CHARLESTON	79	78	93	79	77	85	84	81	84	83	106	94	84	104	83	84	103	84	80	90
29412	CHARLESTON	91	100	114	102	99	104	99	97	95	99	120	113	101	121	99	93	118	97	92	107
29414	CHARLESTON	93	93	102	99	90	92	96	92	92	98	117	111	95	113	92	86	114	95	82	102
29418	NORTH CHARLESTON	70	67	68	69	65	68	69	68	67	70	85	80	67	81	66	65	83	69	63	77
29420	NORTH CHARLESTON	91	100	97	102	97	96	93	93	87	95	110	108	94	110	91	83	108	91	83	103
29426	ADAMS RUN	77	57	33	52	62	69	55	65	62	56	74	77	49	70	55	65	69	64	75	87
29429	AWENDAW	118	111	91	108	113	117	103	111	105	106	129	130	100	127	103	104	124	109	112	135
29431	BONNEAU	85	63	37	57	69	77	61	72	69	62	83	85	54	78	61	72	76	72	83	97
29432	BRANCHVILLE	85	57	26	49	65	74	55	69	66	56	78	82	47	74	56	72	71	68	85	98
29434	CORDESVILLE	84	56	25	48	64	73	54	68	65	55	77	81	46	73	55	70	70	67	84	96
29435	COTTAGEVILLE	77	60	38	55	64	70	58	67	63	59	77	78	52	72	58	65	72	66	74	86
29436	CROSS	59	44	29	39	47	54	44	50	50	45	59	58	39	55	44	52	55	50	58	66
29437	DORCHESTER	84	56	25	49	64	73	54	68	66	55	77	81	46	73	55	71	70	67	84	96
29438	EDISTO ISLAND	147	105	58	92	119	135	101	124	118	101	139	147	87	134	104	127	128	122	150	173
29440	GEORGETOWN	85	71	56	66	75	84	70	77	76	71	92	89	66	89	70	79	87	77	86	97
29445	GOOSE CREEK	84	81	82	85	79	81	83	81	80	84	101	97	82	98	79	76	99	83	74	91
29446	GREEN POND	91	61	27	52	69	79	59	73	71	60	83	88	50	78	60	76	75	72	90	104
29448	HARLEYVILLE	96	64	29	55	73	84	62	78	75	63	88	93	53	83	63	81	80	77	96	110
29449	HOLLYWOOD	104	74	39	66	82	92	71	86	83	73	98	102	62	93	72	88	90	86	102	118
29450	HUGER	68	60	45	58	61	65	57	63	59	59	73	73	54	69	57	59	69	62	64	76
29451	ISLE OF PALMS	161	212	279	208	207	222	187	185	174	190	220	209	209	230	198	175	222	179	173	202
29453	JAMESTOWN	71	47	21	41	54	62	46	57	55	46	65	68	39	61	46	59	59	56	70	81
29455	JOHNS ISLAND	110	98	81	95	102	113	95	104	100	97	123	116	92	116	97	102	116	102	112	124
29456	LADSON	83	86	81	86	84	86	82	83	79	83	99	97	81	98	81	76	96	83	77	94
29458	MC CLELLANVILLE	87	58	26	50	66	76	56	71	68	57	80	84	48	76	57	73	73	70	87	100
29461	MONCKS CORNER	82	72	58	68	74	81	71	76	74	71	91	89	67	88	70	75	86	76	81	93
29464	MOUNT PLEASANT	114	129	147	133	126	129	124	122	118	125	148	144	128	150	124	113	146	122	111	134
29466	MOUNT PLEASANT	141	162	168	168	156	153	149	147	138	152	174	173	154	178	147	130	173	144	128	161
29468	PINEVILLE	69	46	21	40	52	60	44	56	54	45	63	66	38	59	45	58	57	55	68	79
29469	PINOPOLIS	79	74	59	71	74	78	70	75	71	72	88	86	67	83	69	70	84	74	74	88
29470	RAVENEL	86	74	55	70	76	81	71	78	74	73	91	91	66	86	70	74	86	78	81	96
29471	REEVESVILLE	87	58	26	50	66	76	56	70	68	57	80	84	48	75	57	73	72	69	86	100
29472	RIDGEVILLE	68	52	31	47	56	62	50	58	56	51	67	69	45	63	50	58	62	58	66	77
29474	ROUND O	69	56	38	52	59	64	54	61	58	55	70	71	49	66	54	59	66	61	66	78
29475	RUFFIN	73	53	29	47	58	65	51	61	59	52	70	73	45	66	51	62	64	61	72	83
29477	SAINT GEORGE	75	51	25	45	58	67	50	62	60	51	71	73	43	67	51	65	64	61	76	86
29479	SAINT STEPHEN	71	51	30	45	55	64	50	60	59	51	70	70	44	65	50	63	64	59	71	80
29481	SMOAKS	75	50	23	43	57	65	48	60	58	49	68	72	41	65	49	63	62	60	74	86
29482	SULLIVANS ISLAND	185	249	342	244	243	262	217	215	202	222	256	242	247	269	232	204	260	207	200	234
29483	SUMMERVILLE	83	83	76	82	83	86	79	82	78	80	97	96	78	96	79	76	94	81	79	94
29485	SUMMERVILLE	95	102	102	102	101	104	97	98	93	97	116	115	98	118	97	91	114	96	92	110
29487	WADMALAW ISLAND	94	76	61	69	80	92	74	83	84	76	102	94	71	97	76	89	96	83	96	107
29488	WALTERBORO	69	59	49	56	61	67	59	64	63	60	76	73	56	72	58	64	72	64	68	77
29492	CHARLESTON	109	123	118	128	117	113	111	110	102	116	129	129	114	130	108	95	128	107	93	120
29501	FLORENCE	95	96	102	97	95	101	96	96	95	97	119	112	96	117	95	93	116	97	93	108
29505	FLORENCE	91	94	92	92	94	98	90	92	89	91	111	107	90	111	91	88	108	92	90	105
29506	FLORENCE	65	58	55	55	58	65	59	61	63	60	77	69	57	72	58	64	74	62	65	72
29510	ANDREWS	66	49	32	43	52	60	49	57	57	50	67	66	44	63	49	60	63	57	67	75
29511	AYNOR	75	67	52	65	68	73	65	70	67	66	82	81	61	78	64	66	78	69	71	83
29512	BENNETTSVILLE	71	52	34	46	56	65	52	60	61	53	72	70	47	68	52	65	67	60	72	80
	SOUTH CAROLINA	87	78	69	75	80	87	77	82	81	78	99	95	74	96	77	82	95	82	86	99
	UNITED STATES	100	100	100	100	100	100	100	100	100	100	100	100	100	100	100	100	100	100	100	100

# POST OFFICE NAME	COUNTY FIPS CODE	POPULATION			2000-2004 ANNUAL RATE		HOUSEHOLDS					FAMILIES		
		2000	2004	2009	% Rate	State Centile	2000	2004	2009	% Annual Rate 2000-2004	2004 Average HH Size	2000	2004	% Annual Rate 2000-2004
29516 BLENHEIM	069	650	700	712	1.8	77	278	309	325	2.5	2.27	180	193	1.7
29518 CADES	089	1384	1356	1378	-0.5	6	500	509	537	0.4	2.58	381	379	-0.1
29520 CHERAW	025	14159	15308	16695	1.9	79	5545	6166	6914	2.5	2.42	3875	4188	1.8
29525 CLIO	069	2036	1976	1922	-0.7	3	756	766	772	0.3	2.58	535	528	-0.3
29526 CONWAY	051	30270	33955	38569	2.7	90	11393	13146	15347	3.4	2.48	8293	9300	2.7
29527 CONWAY	051	18297	19794	22020	1.9	79	6679	7416	8460	2.5	2.60	4949	5348	1.8
29530 COWARD	041	2266	2377	2425	1.1	57	866	933	974	1.8	2.55	652	685	1.2
29532 DARLINGTON	031	20017	20273	20524	0.3	30	7706	8004	8283	0.9	2.47	5305	5351	0.2
29536 DILLON	033	17142	17266	17380	0.2	26	6249	6474	6654	0.8	2.63	4416	4445	0.2
29540 DARLINGTON	031	5700	5932	6084	0.9	52	2038	2191	2304	1.7	2.70	1529	1603	1.1
29541 EFFINGHAM	041	8486	8573	8647	0.2	27	2945	3054	3153	0.9	2.68	2263	2291	0.3
29543 FORK	033	711	723	724	0.4	33	238	252	258	1.4	2.43	173	178	0.7
29544 GALIVANTS FERRY	051	4438	4743	5263	1.6	73	1676	1843	2096	2.3	2.57	1233	1317	1.6
29545 GREEN SEA	051	1468	1522	1664	0.9	49	581	618	693	1.5	2.46	417	430	0.7
29546 GRESHAM	067	2548	2559	2561	0.1	24	875	903	928	0.7	2.83	650	654	0.1
29547 HAMER	033	2940	3217	3353	2.1	84	969	1090	1161	2.8	2.94	758	838	2.4
29550 HARTSVILLE	031	31448	31432	31706	0.0	19	12257	12600	13012	0.7	2.44	8747	8748	0.0
29554 HEMINGWAY	043	9202	9669	10268	1.2	59	3436	3747	4121	2.1	2.58	2559	2726	1.5
29555 JOHNSONVILLE	041	6338	6321	6372	-0.1	17	2291	2344	2419	0.5	2.69	1770	1769	0.0
29556 KINGSTREE	089	16645	17875	19225	1.7	75	6159	6818	7580	2.4	2.59	4442	4797	1.8
29560 LAKE CITY	041	13640	13418	13453	-0.4	9	5020	5080	5226	0.3	2.62	3697	3642	-0.4
29563 LAKE VIEW	033	2580	2529	2497	-0.5	6	996	1005	1013	0.2	2.46	698	685	-0.4
29564 LANE	089	1650	1653	1687	0.0	21	619	640	676	0.8	2.58	445	447	0.1
29565 LATTA	033	6195	6068	6009	-0.5	6	2334	2345	2367	0.1	2.59	1719	1683	-0.5
29566 LITTLE RIVER	051	11475	14459	17377	5.6	98	5049	6489	7958	6.1	2.23	3560	4434	5.3
29567 LITTLE ROCK	033	443	431	427	-0.6	4	136	135	136	-0.2	3.04	105	103	-0.5
29568 LONGS	051	7813	8754	9907	2.7	90	2935	3386	3931	3.4	2.58	2155	2416	2.7
29569 LORIS	051	13803	15341	17326	2.5	89	5175	5900	6824	3.1	2.58	3812	4225	2.5
29570 MC COLL	069	4239	4129	4022	-0.6	4	1598	1603	1605	0.1	2.58	1129	1099	-0.6
29571 MARION	067	18571	18850	18999	0.4	32	6919	7225	7477	1.0	2.59	4984	5065	0.4
29572 MYRTLE BEACH	051	8045	8370	9153	0.9	52	4109	4383	4911	1.5	1.87	2128	2156	0.3
29574 MULLINS	067	12531	12426	12474	-0.2	13	4809	4903	5052	0.5	2.50	3378	3347	-0.2
29575 MYRTLE BEACH	051	15430	16350	18265	1.4	66	7148	7790	8927	2.0	2.09	4679	4901	1.1
29576 MURRELLS INLET	043	16189	18440	21023	3.1	92	7746	9026	10538	3.7	2.04	5081	5763	3.0
29577 MYRTLE BEACH	051	23326	24393	26999	1.1	55	10425	11177	12669	1.7	2.17	5575	5697	0.5
29579 MYRTLE BEACH	051	9168	11952	14579	6.4	99	3786	5082	6357	7.2	2.35	2389	3064	6.0
29580 NESMITH	089	3664	3684	3750	0.1	25	1271	1332	1409	1.1	2.77	977	1001	0.6
29581 NICHOLS	051	4729	4932	5276	1.0	53	1854	1981	2167	1.6	2.49	1308	1354	0.8
29582 NORTH MYRTLE BEACH	051	12185	13824	15829	3.0	92	5866	6811	7975	3.6	2.03	3448	3839	2.6
29583 PAMPLICO	041	5364	5407	5472	0.2	26	2009	2079	2152	0.8	2.58	1539	1554	0.2
29584 PATRICK	025	2988	3232	3525	1.9	79	1160	1293	1449	2.6	2.47	834	905	1.9
29585 PAWLEYS ISLAND	043	10261	11792	13363	3.3	94	4514	5353	6260	4.1	2.19	3312	3832	3.5
29588 MYRTLE BEACH	051	23480	26886	30938	3.2	94	9241	10915	12896	4.0	2.46	6559	7525	3.3
29590 SALTERS	089	2092	2057	2089	-0.4	9	734	745	783	0.4	2.76	546	541	-0.2
29591 SCRANTON	041	5305	5479	5587	0.8	46	1957	2086	2184	1.5	2.55	1462	1517	0.9
29592 SELLERS	033	678	683	683	0.2	26	252	262	267	0.9	2.60	188	190	0.3
29593 SOCIETY HILL	031	1846	1922	1960	1.0	52	678	726	758	1.6	2.65	500	522	1.0
29596 WALLACE	069	2467	2470	2432	0.0	20	936	966	979	0.8	2.56	688	692	0.1
29601 GREENVILLE	045	9733	9510	9673	-0.5	5	4279	4250	4390	-0.2	1.94	1904	1766	-1.8
29605 GREENVILLE	045	31295	31098	32012	-0.2	14	13170	13208	13709	0.1	2.35	8341	8057	-0.8
29607 GREENVILLE	045	29476	30296	31390	0.7	43	12834	13388	14020	1.0	2.20	7577	7533	-0.1
29609 GREENVILLE	045	29141	29302	30240	0.1	25	11012	11188	11677	0.4	2.39	7019	6885	-0.5
29611 GREENVILLE	045	28132	27883	28593	-0.2	13	10977	11026	11423	0.1	2.50	7457	7226	-0.7
29613 GREENVILLE	045	2315	2309	2310	-0.1	17	9	8	8	-2.7	2.50	7	6	-3.6
29615 GREENVILLE	045	31538	33955	36024	1.8	76	14355	15511	16543	1.8	2.17	8224	8558	0.9
29617 GREENVILLE	045	23787	23878	24492	0.1	23	9629	9734	10055	0.3	2.41	6452	6269	-0.7
29620 ABBEVILLE	001	13107	13004	13304	-0.2	13	5161	5226	5457	0.3	2.45	3684	3628	-0.4
29621 ANDERSON	007	32164	33620	34912	1.1	54	12638	13557	14373	1.7	2.38	8903	9242	0.9
29624 ANDERSON	007	15748	15222	15403	-0.8	2	6273	6183	6373	-0.3	2.38	4035	3855	-1.1
29625 ANDERSON	007	23566	24339	25269	0.8	46	9699	10249	10847	1.3	2.33	6615	6782	0.6
29626 ANDERSON	007	11773	12416	12992	1.3	62	4658	5032	5368	1.8	2.47	3491	3663	1.1
29627 BELTON	007	17712	18113	18693	0.5	38	7033	7338	7707	1.0	2.44	5229	5312	0.4
29628 CALHOUN FALLS	001	3154	3166	3243	0.1	23	1242	1279	1339	0.7	2.47	904	906	0.1
29630 CENTRAL	077	11786	13023	14029	2.4	87	4808	5434	5962	2.9	2.33	2762	2945	1.5
29631 CLEMSON	077	11677	11702	12076	0.1	22	4877	4986	5235	0.5	2.31	2254	2176	-0.8
29632 CLEMSON	077	6091	6087	6087	0.0	19	28	27	27	-0.9	2.22	14	13	-1.7
29635 CLEVELAND	045	1396	1449	1509	0.9	50	597	632	667	1.4	2.27	425	434	0.5
29638 DONALDS	001	3263	3678	4012	2.9	91	1276	1457	1618	3.2	2.36	915	1019	2.6
29639 DUE WEST	001	1763	1767	1815	0.1	22	504	520	550	0.7	2.88	359	359	0.0
29640 EASLEY	077	29657	31200	32832	1.2	59	11611	12428	13286	1.6	2.50	8554	8938	1.0
29642 EASLEY	007	24037	26600	28628	2.4	87	9039	10192	11153	2.9	2.58	7000	7752	2.4
29643 FAIR PLAY	073	2497	2763	2969	2.4	87	1051	1194	1312	3.1	2.30	786	870	2.4
29644 FOUNTAIN INN	059	15739	17387	18427	2.4	86	5878	6604	7092	2.8	2.58	4428	4838	2.1
29645 GRAY COURT	059	11027	11839	12250	1.7	75	4057	4455	4685	2.2	2.66	3101	3320	1.6
29646 GREENWOOD	047	28077	28125	28463	0.0	21	10758	10961	11249	0.4	2.49	7387	7309	-0.3
29649 GREENWOOD	047	23500	24536	25223	1.0	53	9210	9799	10222	1.5	2.37	6163	6362	0.8
29650 GREER	045	22446	26231	28937	3.7	96	8385	9919	11047	4.0	2.62	6250	7208	3.4
29651 GREER	045	34775	37333	39426	1.7	75	13353	14499	15469	2.0	2.56	9798	10347	1.3
29653 HODGES	047	4272	4332	4390	0.3	31	1630	1684	1730	0.8	2.55	1227	1236	0.2
29654 HONEA PATH	007	9228	9436	9786	0.5	38	3755	3916	4132	1.0	2.39	2735	2777	0.4
29655 IVA	007	7515	7958	8332	1.4	65	3011	3260	3479	1.9	2.43	2187	2302	1.2
29657 LIBERTY	077	14495	15127	15842	1.0	53	5485	5839	6219	1.5	2.57	4161	4323	0.9
29658 LONG CREEK	073	293	295	302	0.2	26	137	142	149	0.9	2.08	93	94	0.3
29659 LOWNDESVILLE	001	166	170	175	0.6	39	76	80	84	1.2	2.13	51	51	0.0
29661 MARIETTA	045	6019	6261	6511	0.9	51	2301	2426	2551	1.3	2.54	1684	1722	0.5
29662 MAULDIN	045	11870	12565	13159	1.4	64	4736	5079	5364	1.7	2.46	3352	3473	0.8
29664 MOUNTAIN REST	073	1488	1492	1527	0.1	22	666	688	722	0.8	2.17	473	474	0.1
29666 NINETY SIX	047	6224	6295	6384	0.3	28	2505	2587	2664	0.8	2.43	1826	1836	0.1
29667 NORRIS	077	388	401	416	0.8	47	157	165	174	1.2	2.43	119	122	0.6
29669 PELZER	045	11690	12181	12676	1.0	52	4591	4873	5147	1.4	2.44	3396	3506	0.8
29670 PENDLETON	007	7663	7958	8225	0.9	50	3299	3513	3705	1.5	2.26	2213	2282	0.7
29671 PICKENS	077	17920	18161	18774	0.3	30	7060	7297	7672	0.8	2.46	5153	5182	0.1
29672 SENECA	073	9443	10158	10778	1.7	76	3926	4345	4725	2.4	2.29	2868	3088	1.8
29673 PIEDMONT	045	21516	23312	24713	1.9	80	8178	9022	9705	2.3	2.57	6234	6684	1.7
29676 SALEM	073	4878	5012	5186	0.6	42	2267	2399	2543	1.3	2.06	1763	1824	0.8
SOUTH CAROLINA					1.2					1.8	2.47			1.1
UNITED STATES					1.2					1.3	2.58			1.1

ZIP CODE #	POST OFFICE NAME	RACE (%) White 2000	White 2004	Black 2000	Black 2004	Asian/Pacific 2000	Asian/Pacific 2004	% Hispanic Origin 2000	% Hispanic Origin 2004	2004 AGE DISTRIBUTION (%) 0-4	5-9	10-14	15-19	20-24	25-44	45-64	65-84	85+	18+	MEDIAN AGE 2004	% 2004 Males	% 2004 Females
29516	BLENHEIM	66.3	65.1	30.9	31.6	0.0	0.0	0.5	0.6	5.7	6.0	7.4	5.9	5.1	25.9	29.7	12.9	1.4	77.0	41.1	46.1	53.9
29518	CADES	49.9	49.9	49.4	49.3	0.0	0.0	1.2	1.3	5.6	6.4	7.5	7.5	6.1	25.7	27.8	11.5	1.8	75.7	38.3	48.6	51.4
29520	CHERAW	54.9	53.9	43.3	44.0	0.6	0.7	0.7	0.7	6.3	6.5	7.6	7.0	6.1	26.2	26.8	11.8	1.9	75.2	38.6	46.8	53.2
29525	CLIO	33.0	32.2	61.0	61.1	0.1	0.1	0.7	0.8	7.0	8.6	8.3	6.9	5.7	26.3	25.2	10.4	1.8	71.7	35.6	46.1	53.9
29526	CONWAY	80.1	79.1	16.7	16.9	0.6	0.8	2.6	3.4	6.6	6.2	6.5	6.9	8.3	28.8	23.6	12.2	1.0	77.1	36.2	48.9	51.1
29527	CONWAY	64.1	63.9	33.8	33.7	0.3	0.3	1.4	1.8	6.9	6.9	7.6	7.1	7.1	29.3	23.8	9.9	1.3	74.3	35.1	48.8	51.2
29530	COWARD	78.5	77.0	20.1	21.3	0.3	0.3	1.2	1.5	7.2	7.1	6.9	5.7	6.7	28.8	26.8	10.3	0.6	75.5	36.6	49.4	50.6
29532	DARLINGTON	51.2	50.8	47.6	47.8	0.2	0.2	1.0	1.1	6.6	6.8	7.6	6.5	6.4	27.1	25.3	11.8	1.9	74.9	36.9	47.3	52.7
29536	DILLON	48.4	47.3	47.2	47.5	0.5	0.7	1.9	2.2	7.8	7.7	8.4	7.7	7.0	26.7	23.1	10.3	1.3	71.2	33.7	46.8	53.3
29540	DARLINGTON	40.0	38.8	59.1	60.2	0.1	0.1	0.6	0.7	7.2	7.3	8.0	6.8	6.9	29.0	24.9	9.1	0.9	73.3	34.6	48.3	51.7
29541	EFFINGHAM	64.1	62.2	34.6	36.3	0.3	0.3	0.8	0.9	6.1	6.2	6.7	7.0	7.2	29.9	26.9	8.6	1.3	76.9	36.8	50.3	49.7
29543	FORK	67.0	66.5	31.5	32.0	0.0	0.0	0.3	0.4	2.9	3.3	5.5	5.8	6.1	22.5	27.5	20.6	5.7	84.8	47.6	44.4	55.6
29544	GALIVANTS FERRY	88.2	87.5	9.7	10.0	0.0	0.0	2.3	2.9	6.8	6.8	6.9	6.4	6.7	30.9	24.3	10.4	0.9	75.6	35.5	50.0	50.0
29545	GREEN SEA	74.9	74.2	22.8	23.1	0.0	0.0	1.4	1.7	5.8	6.5	7.1	7.0	6.5	26.7	25.4	13.3	1.6	76.3	38.0	48.6	51.4
29546	GRESHAM	39.0	38.4	55.0	54.2	0.2	0.3	10.1	12.1	6.5	6.1	6.5	7.2	8.5	29.9	25.0	9.3	1.1	76.8	34.6	50.3	49.8
29547	HAMER	46.8	45.2	46.1	46.8	0.1	0.1	2.9	3.5	8.4	8.4	8.7	7.4	7.1	30.8	21.7	6.9	0.6	69.9	31.7	48.4	51.6
29550	HARTSVILLE	67.4	67.3	31.2	31.0	0.3	0.4	1.2	1.5	6.8	7.0	7.5	6.3	6.2	27.1	26.3	11.4	1.3	74.9	37.4	47.7	52.3
29554	HEMINGWAY	47.8	47.5	50.8	50.9	0.1	0.2	1.1	1.2	7.2	7.2	7.7	6.8	6.3	26.5	26.0	11.1	1.3	73.8	36.7	48.4	51.7
29555	JOHNSONVILLE	65.9	64.6	32.5	33.6	0.2	0.2	1.0	1.0	7.2	7.1	7.9	7.6	6.8	27.5	25.1	9.7	1.1	73.1	35.6	48.3	51.7
29556	KINGSTREE	28.3	26.8	70.7	72.1	0.3	0.3	0.5	0.5	7.1	7.3	8.4	7.7	6.8	24.9	24.9	11.6	1.3	72.5	35.5	46.5	53.5
29560	LAKE CITY	40.3	38.7	58.3	59.7	0.4	0.4	1.3	1.6	7.1	7.1	7.8	7.9	7.0	26.4	24.6	10.7	1.4	73.2	35.3	46.2	53.8
29563	LAKE VIEW	55.5	54.9	42.2	42.5	0.2	0.3	1.5	1.7	6.5	6.6	7.0	6.9	6.6	25.8	26.3	12.5	1.7	75.7	38.4	46.3	53.7
29564	LANE	8.9	9.1	90.8	90.6	0.0	0.0	0.5	0.5	6.8	7.1	8.1	7.9	7.3	22.8	25.8	12.6	1.6	73.1	36.2	46.6	53.4
29565	LATTA	52.3	52.1	44.9	44.6	0.2	0.2	1.2	1.5	7.2	7.3	7.8	7.0	7.2	27.1	25.7	9.8	1.0	73.2	35.0	46.9	53.1
29566	LITTLE RIVER	81.5	80.1	16.8	18.0	0.3	0.4	1.1	1.4	5.0	5.2	5.3	4.3	3.9	23.9	30.6	20.7	1.2	81.9	46.8	48.4	51.6
29567	LITTLE ROCK	25.5	24.8	56.4	55.9	0.2	0.2	1.1	1.4	6.5	6.7	8.8	8.6	9.1	27.4	23.2	9.1	0.7	72.9	32.5	49.9	50.1
29568	LONGS	54.2	52.7	41.7	42.4	0.4	0.5	4.0	4.9	7.2	7.0	7.2	6.3	6.9	28.5	24.8	11.4	0.8	74.8	35.8	49.2	50.9
29569	LORIS	65.5	64.7	32.0	32.2	0.3	0.4	2.3	2.8	6.9	7.2	7.2	6.5	6.7	28.0	25.4	10.8	1.3	74.7	36.4	48.5	51.5
29570	MC COLL	58.0	56.0	27.3	27.7	0.1	0.1	1.0	1.3	7.4	7.2	7.3	7.1	6.9	27.7	25.0	10.0	1.4	73.7	35.8	47.9	52.1
29571	MARION	39.1	38.8	59.4	59.4	0.3	0.3	1.0	1.2	7.2	7.2	7.9	7.3	7.3	26.8	25.0	10.2	1.3	73.2	34.6	46.6	53.4
29572	MYRTLE BEACH	95.2	94.6	1.8	1.8	1.2	1.5	1.7	2.2	3.6	3.2	3.3	2.7	5.0	26.2	29.9	23.3	2.8	88.3	49.4	48.5	51.5
29574	MULLINS	45.0	43.9	53.2	54.0	0.4	0.4	1.3	1.5	6.7	6.8	7.4	6.8	6.7	24.9	27.3	11.6	1.7	74.9	37.6	46.0	54.0
29575	MYRTLE BEACH	95.7	95.1	1.5	1.6	1.2	1.5	1.5	1.9	3.7	3.6	4.0	4.0	4.6	23.9	30.3	24.4	1.4	86.2	49.7	48.7	51.3
29576	MURRELLS INLET	94.3	93.8	4.0	4.2	0.4	0.5	0.9	1.1	3.6	3.7	4.0	3.7	3.4	23.0	30.6	26.5	1.5	86.3	51.2	48.8	51.2
29577	MYRTLE BEACH	78.9	78.1	14.7	14.4	1.6	1.9	4.7	5.7	5.4	4.9	5.4	5.5	7.4	33.6	23.8	12.5	1.4	81.1	37.4	50.7	49.3
29579	MYRTLE BEACH	88.3	87.3	7.9	8.0	1.1	1.4	2.5	3.2	7.1	6.5	6.0	6.6	12.7	32.8	20.4	7.6	0.4	77.1	31.5	48.9	51.1
29580	NESMITH	36.2	36.5	62.4	62.0	0.5	0.6	0.7	0.7	7.1	7.0	8.2	7.7	7.6	24.9	25.4	11.1	1.1	73.2	35.4	49.0	51.0
29581	NICHOLS	64.0	63.3	33.8	34.0	0.1	0.1	2.1	2.6	6.2	6.2	6.6	6.6	6.9	25.7	27.7	12.9	1.3	77.0	39.1	48.0	52.0
29582	NORTH MYRTLE BEACH	90.3	89.6	6.1	6.2	0.7	0.9	2.6	3.2	3.9	3.9	4.0	3.7	4.1	24.7	33.5	20.7	1.5	86.0	49.1	49.8	50.2
29583	PAMPLICO	59.3	58.5	38.7	39.0	0.1	0.2	1.5	1.9	6.1	6.5	7.3	6.3	5.9	26.2	27.8	12.6	1.4	76.4	39.1	48.0	52.0
29584	PATRICK	83.1	82.8	15.5	15.6	0.0	0.0	2.1	2.5	6.3	6.2	7.2	7.9	5.4	28.6	27.7	10.1	0.8	75.4	37.8	50.5	49.5
29585	PAWLEYS ISLAND	84.8	84.0	14.3	14.8	0.3	0.3	0.6	0.8	4.3	4.8	5.0	4.1	2.9	20.1	35.5	21.8	1.4	82.9	50.8	47.8	52.2
29588	MYRTLE BEACH	86.4	85.2	8.6	9.0	1.6	1.9	3.7	4.5	6.4	6.3	6.4	5.7	6.4	31.8	24.8	11.7	0.6	77.4	37.2	49.7	50.3
29590	SALTERS	10.4	10.4	89.4	89.3	0.0	0.0	0.2	0.2	6.7	6.9	8.4	8.6	7.9	23.5	25.2	11.0	1.9	72.9	34.7	45.7	54.3
29591	SCRANTON	72.1	70.0	26.1	27.9	0.1	0.1	2.1	2.5	6.2	6.3	7.1	6.2	6.4	28.4	25.9	12.3	1.2	76.6	38.1	48.4	51.6
29592	SELLERS	61.5	61.2	35.3	35.0	0.0	0.0	2.5	3.1	7.9	7.2	6.7	7.6	7.9	28.7	26.2	7.2	0.6	72.9	33.7	48.8	51.2
29593	SOCIETY HILL	33.5	32.6	65.6	66.5	0.0	0.0	0.4	0.4	6.5	7.0	7.1	6.5	6.7	27.5	27.1	10.4	1.2	75.3	36.5	48.0	52.0
29596	WALLACE	61.3	59.7	36.0	37.3	0.0	0.0	0.6	0.7	6.0	6.3	7.2	6.6	6.4	27.9	27.9	11.0	0.8	76.6	38.4	47.7	52.3
29601	GREENVILLE	48.0	46.8	49.7	50.6	0.6	0.8	2.0	2.4	4.4	4.3	5.1	5.9	6.5	31.5	26.1	13.5	2.7	82.8	40.6	51.2	48.8
29605	GREENVILLE	51.8	50.3	45.4	46.6	0.4	0.5	2.6	3.2	6.8	6.7	7.1	6.5	6.3	28.0	24.7	12.0	1.9	75.4	37.4	46.7	53.3
29607	GREENVILLE	62.9	62.6	32.7	32.2	1.8	2.2	3.3	4.1	6.4	6.3	6.2	6.4	8.4	30.9	22.8	10.7	1.8	77.5	35.0	47.9	52.1
29609	GREENVILLE	80.6	79.1	14.7	15.1	1.7	2.1	4.4	5.6	6.2	6.0	5.9	8.3	10.0	27.7	22.8	11.1	1.9	78.5	34.8	48.0	52.0
29611	GREENVILLE	65.0	63.4	30.2	30.9	0.3	0.4	6.0	7.4	7.1	7.0	7.4	6.6	6.4	28.4	23.6	11.9	1.6	74.5	36.3	48.2	51.8
29613	GREENVILLE	93.2	92.4	4.7	5.1	1.3	1.6	1.1	1.5	0.1	0.0	0.5	43.4	52.5	1.8	1.3	0.1	0.1	98.6	20.6	43.7	56.3
29615	GREENVILLE	84.5	83.4	8.9	9.0	3.2	3.9	5.2	6.2	5.4	5.3	5.6	5.5	7.4	30.7	24.5	13.2	2.4	80.4	38.2	49.5	50.5
29617	GREENVILLE	80.7	78.9	11.8	12.2	1.4	1.7	10.5	13.0	7.0	6.5	6.2	6.1	7.1	30.2	22.3	13.2	1.6	77.0	36.1	47.8	52.2
29620	ABBEVILLE	63.8	62.6	35.0	36.0	0.3	0.4	0.6	0.8	7.1	7.2	7.1	6.5	6.2	26.0	25.4	12.6	2.0	74.6	37.8	47.5	52.5
29621	ANDERSON	79.0	78.0	18.5	19.0	1.0	1.2	1.2	1.4	6.9	6.7	6.7	6.5	6.7	26.8	24.5	13.0	2.2	76.0	37.7	47.3	52.7
29624	ANDERSON	57.2	56.7	41.1	41.2	0.2	0.2	1.0	1.3	7.1	6.6	7.0	6.3	6.1	26.4	24.2	13.9	2.4	75.7	38.3	47.7	52.4
29625	ANDERSON	81.9	81.0	16.1	16.6	0.7	0.8	0.9	1.1	6.3	6.3	6.5	5.7	5.7	29.6	25.4	12.8	1.7	77.4	38.5	48.5	51.5
29626	ANDERSON	79.5	78.4	18.9	19.8	0.3	0.4	0.9	1.1	6.8	6.6	6.6	6.2	5.8	27.9	26.5	12.7	1.0	76.3	38.4	48.5	51.5
29627	BELTON	83.8	82.7	14.7	15.5	0.2	0.2	1.1	1.4	6.9	7.0	6.7	5.9	5.8	27.7	25.9	12.9	1.3	75.9	38.4	48.8	51.2
29628	CALHOUN FALLS	51.3	50.9	46.8	47.0	0.2	0.3	1.5	1.8	6.4	6.3	7.1	8.1	5.8	25.5	25.8	13.3	1.7	75.1	38.9	48.9	51.1
29630	CENTRAL	86.4	84.9	9.4	10.0	1.9	2.4	2.3	3.0	5.4	5.2	5.6	7.2	19.6	27.1	19.8	8.7	1.3	80.7	29.2	52.0	48.1
29631	CLEMSON	80.2	77.9	11.1	11.5	6.7	8.3	1.8	2.2	3.7	3.9	4.4	6.0	30.7	21.6	16.5	10.4	2.9	85.5	25.8	52.1	47.9
29632	CLEMSON	86.0	85.1	11.0	11.2	1.7	2.2	1.1	1.4	0.0	0.0	0.0	57.3	40.9	1.3	0.3	0.1	0.0	99.7	19.4	53.2	46.9
29635	CLEVELAND	96.9	96.6	1.8	1.9	0.1	0.1	1.0	1.3	4.6	6.1	6.5	5.2	5.0	26.9	31.5	13.4	0.9	79.5	42.4	51.2	48.8
29638	DONALDS	77.9	76.7	20.4	21.4	0.2	0.3	1.0	1.2	6.4	6.6	6.8	7.7	9.0	25.8	24.5	11.7	1.6	76.9	35.7	49.1	51.0
29639	DUE WEST	78.5	77.4	20.4	21.3	0.4	0.5	1.0	1.3	4.7	4.9	6.1	9.2	11.2	20.9	24.1	15.3	3.7	81.0	39.0	46.8	53.3
29640	EASLEY	89.8	89.5	8.0	7.9	0.2	0.3	2.1	2.6	7.2	7.1	6.9	6.3	6.0	29.9	25.1	10.4	1.2	75.0	36.8	49.6	50.4
29642	EASLEY	93.2	92.6	4.9	5.1	0.6	0.7	1.6	2.0	6.9	7.0	7.1	6.3	5.6	29.5	26.6	9.7	1.3	74.9	37.5	48.6	51.4
29643	FAIR PLAY	96.4	95.8	2.0	2.2	0.3	0.4	1.3	1.8	6.1	6.1	5.6	4.5	4.7	25.7	30.4	16.0	0.9	79.4	43.2	51.0	49.0
29644	FOUNTAIN INN	79.5	78.0	18.6	19.7	0.2	0.3	1.9	2.5	7.9	7.6	7.7	6.9	6.1	31.9	23.0	8.2	0.9	72.6	34.9	49.2	50.8
29645	GRAY COURT	80.3	79.3	17.1	17.4	0.1	0.2	3.0	3.6	6.9	6.9	7.3	7.0	6.3	30.3	25.3	9.2	0.8	74.6	36.1	50.4	49.6
29646	GREENWOOD	54.1	53.9	42.7	42.3	0.4	0.5	5.0	6.0	7.3	7.1	7.4	7.0	7.6	26.9	22.7	12.0	1.9	74.1	35.0	47.5	52.5
29649	GREENWOOD	72.9	71.7	24.1	24.6	1.5	1.9	1.9	2.5	6.8	6.5	6.6	7.7	8.4	28.4	22.9	11.2	1.6	76.4	34.9	46.2	53.8
29650	GREER	86.5	85.1	7.4	7.4	3.4	4.1	3.9	5.1	6.5	6.9	7.6	7.2	6.1	28.5	28.0	8.1	1.2	74.4	37.1	48.8	51.2
29651	GREER	84.7	84.0	11.1	11.0	0.7	0.9	4.0	4.9	7.2	7.2	7.1	6.0	5.7	30.6	24.4	10.6	1.4	74.9	36.9	49.4	50.6
29653	HODGES	75.8	74.2	23.0	24.3	0.3	0.4	0.4	0.5	6.2	6.5	7.2	6.4	5.8	26.9	27.7	12.0	1.5	76.1	39.3	48.5	51.6
29654	HONEA PATH	86.3	85.2	12.3	13.1	0.2	0.2	1.0	1.2	6.5	6.7	6.6	6.2	5.7	26.7	26.4	13.6	1.7	76.4	39.3	49.2	50.8
29655	IVA	85.5	84.6	13.4	14.1	0.1	0.1	0.4	0.5	6.5	6.7	7.1	5.9	5.2	27.3	26.6	13.1	1.7	76.1	39.1	49.1	50.9
29657	LIBERTY	93.1	92.7	5.5	5.6	0.1	0.2	1.0	1.2	7.4	7.5	7.5	6.3	5.7	30.4	24.0	9.9	1.3	73.7	35.9	49.9	50.1
29658	LONG CREEK	98.3	98.3	0.0	0.0	0.0	0.0	0.7	0.7	5.8	6.4	6.4	5.8	3.7	28.8	30.2	11.9	1.0	77.6	40.5	52.5	47.5
29659	LOWNDESVILLE	90.4	88.8	7.2	7.7	0.0	0.6	1.2	1.8	7.7	7.1	7.1	5.9	6.5	25.9	27.1	11.8	1.2	74.7	38.3	52.9	47.1
29661	MARIETTA	94.2	93.5	3.6	3.7	0.2	0.2	3.7	4.7	6.6	6.7	6.6	6.1	6.2	30.0	25.5	11.0	1.5	76.4	37.5	51.2	48.8
29662	MAULDIN	74.1	72.0	21.4	22.7	2.0	2.3	2.8	3.6	7.4	7.1	6.6	6.2	6.2	31.4	24.6	9.7	0.9	75.1	35.9	48.2	51.8
29664	MOUNTAIN REST	98.5	98.1	0.3	0.3	0.2	0.3	0.9	1.1	4.9	5.2	5.4	5.0	4.5	23.7	32.6	17.5	1.3	81.6	45.8	50.8	49.2
29666	NINETY SIX	77.8	75.7	21.2	23.2	0.1	0.1	0.6	0.9	6.4	6.5	6.9	6.3	6.1	26.4	26.9	13.0	1.6	76.5	39.3	48.1	51.9
29667	NORRIS	93.6	93.3	4.6	4.7	0.0	0.0	0.8	1.0	7.2	6.7	6.7	6.0	5.7	28.4	25.7	12.2	1.3	75.8	37.7	48.9	51.1
29669	PELZER	86.5	85.2	11.7	12.7	0.2	0.3	1.0	1.4	6.5	6.6	6.6	6.1	6.0	29.9	26.2	10.9	1.2	76.5	37.6	51.3	48.7
29670	PENDLETON	74.1	73.2	24.1	24.8	0.4	0.5	0.9	1.0	6.1	6.0	6.2	5.8	6.0	29.4	25.9	13.1	1.5	78.1	38.4	48.6	51.5
29671	PICKENS	94.7	94.4	4.0	4.0	0.2	0.2	1.3	1.6	6.3	6.5	7.1	6.2	5.5	28.1	25.9	12.9	1.6	76.4	38.7	49.5	50.5
29672	SENECA	93.3	92.5	4.4	4.7	0.9	1.1	1.4	1.8	4.9	5.3	5.6	5.2	4.8	24.4	31.1	16.9	1.9	81.1	44.9	49.5	50.5
29673	PIEDMONT	80.9	79.9	16.9	17.6	0.4	0.5	1.5	1.9	6.8	7.0	7.4	6.4	5.9	29.3	26.6	9.8	1.0	74.8	37.1	49.0	51.0
29676	SALEM	98.4	98.0	0.6	0.6	0.2	0.2	0.7	1.0	3.1	3.6	3.9	3.5	3.2	16.5	29.1	35.8	1.4	87.2	58.0	49.9	50.1
	SOUTH CAROLINA	67.2	66.6	29.5	29.5	0.9	1.2	2.4	2.9	6.6	6.6	7.0	7.1	7.3	28.4	24.7	11.0	1.4	75.9	36.3	48.8	51.2
	UNITED STATES	75.1	73.6	12.3	12.5	3.8	4.2	12.5	14.1	6.9	6.7	7.2	7.0	7.3	28.6	23.8	10.8	1.7	75.1	36.0	49.1	50.9

#	POST OFFICE NAME	2004 Per Capita Income	2004 HH Income Base	2004 Household Income Distribution (%): Less than $25,000	$25,000 to $49,999	$50,000 to $99,999	$100,000 to $149,999	$150,000 or More	Median Household Income: 2004	2009	2004 National Centile	2004 State Centile	2004 Home Value Base	2004 Home Value Distribution (%): Less than $50,000	$50,000 to $89,999	$90,000 to $174,999	$175,000 to $399,999	$400,000 or More	2004 Median Home Value
29516	BLENHEIM	19131	309	40.8	34.3	21.0	1.9	1.9	30666	34328	14	19	248	55.2	27.4	8.9	6.9	1.6	46667
29518	CADES	15029	509	40.7	28.1	26.7	3.5	1.0	32652	37802	20	27	416	36.3	42.3	15.9	4.6	1.0	66087
29520	CHERAW	17220	6166	39.4	29.1	24.7	5.6	1.3	33268	37842	22	30	4432	25.0	35.7	31.6	6.9	0.8	79469
29525	CLIO	15202	766	44.7	29.4	20.2	3.3	2.5	28170	31478	9	8	571	41.9	37.7	15.1	3.9	1.6	57750
29526	CONWAY	21647	13146	29.4	30.7	29.5	7.0	3.5	40304	45247	47	62	9997	17.6	21.0	37.3	22.3	1.8	111559
29527	CONWAY	17202	7416	35.4	32.2	25.9	4.5	2.0	34926	39111	27	37	5534	27.1	26.2	36.4	9.4	0.9	85501
29530	COWARD	15226	933	37.9	36.8	21.9	1.5	1.9	29528	34100	11	13	782	41.6	40.7	14.5	3.3	0.0	56600
29532	DARLINGTON	18296	8004	38.4	29.2	24.4	5.4	2.7	33473	39106	22	31	5930	35.2	32.9	24.2	7.2	0.5	68585
29536	DILLON	15461	6474	44.2	27.8	22.6	3.6	1.8	29364	33366	11	12	4465	39.4	34.6	19.6	6.1	0.2	63420
29540	DARLINGTON	16513	2191	42.0	28.9	21.1	5.5	2.6	31159	36510	15	21	1809	37.1	31.8	22.8	7.0	1.3	65392
29541	EFFINGHAM	19248	3054	27.2	31.3	32.0	5.9	3.6	42461	49159	54	72	2548	32.5	31.6	28.6	5.9	1.3	74329
29543	FORK	16168	252	34.9	31.0	30.6	3.2	0.4	36642	41287	34	47	210	32.9	45.2	19.5	2.4	0.0	63600
29544	GALIVANTS FERRY	17539	1843	33.7	32.0	28.5	4.5	1.3	36922	40956	35	48	1492	30.9	24.8	30.0	13.7	0.7	81237
29545	GREEN SEA	15212	618	43.9	29.1	21.4	5.5	0.2	28329	31694	9	9	480	45.8	28.8	22.1	1.9	1.5	54167
29546	GRESHAM	15798	903	39.4	34.6	22.0	2.7	1.3	31983	37062	18	25	716	46.1	32.5	17.7	3.6	0.0	54375
29547	HAMER	13626	1090	36.4	37.3	21.6	3.9	0.8	32794	37183	20	28	890	47.9	33.9	16.3	1.7	0.2	53725
29550	HARTSVILLE	21363	12600	35.5	27.6	26.4	7.0	3.6	37332	43257	37	50	9610	31.2	27.6	29.7	10.6	0.9	78446
29554	HEMINGWAY	15846	3747	39.6	33.2	21.5	4.5	1.3	31527	36619	16	22	3020	39.6	31.8	22.3	5.4	0.8	60428
29555	JOHNSONVILLE	17528	2344	37.8	31.6	25.6	2.8	2.2	33726	39013	23	32	1892	40.4	35.8	19.9	3.7	0.2	57126
29556	KINGSTREE	15758	6818	48.1	26.6	19.5	3.4	2.4	26417	29923	6	4	5056	36.6	35.0	21.5	6.8	0.1	64581
29560	LAKE CITY	15905	5080	43.7	26.7	23.8	3.6	2.2	30449	35528	13	17	3665	37.7	34.5	21.0	6.1	0.7	60853
29563	LAKE VIEW	16672	1005	44.3	28.6	21.0	4.5	1.7	29419	33601	11	13	791	39.1	34.6	22.6	3.3	0.4	64077
29564	LANE	13091	640	55.6	27.2	13.9	1.6	1.7	20610	24053	2	1	524	50.2	31.9	11.6	5.9	0.4	49714
29565	LATTA	16263	2345	42.9	31.0	20.4	4.1	1.6	29255	33536	11	11	1788	43.9	33.2	17.6	4.5	0.8	57143
29566	LITTLE RIVER	26695	6489	21.6	35.2	30.8	8.4	4.1	44689	52393	60	79	5317	6.9	17.2	46.1	26.2	3.5	128649
29567	LITTLE ROCK	15274	135	37.0	29.6	27.4	3.7	2.2	39540	45498	44	59	110	40.0	29.1	25.5	5.5	0.0	60000
29568	LONGS	18505	3386	34.3	30.2	28.7	5.3	1.5	36412	40992	33	44	2792	23.7	21.4	34.3	18.5	2.1	98896
29569	LORIS	15776	5900	39.5	31.5	23.1	4.7	1.2	31920	35611	18	24	4575	27.8	29.5	31.9	10.5	0.3	81086
29570	MC COLL	13744	1603	43.7	32.8	20.4	2.8	0.3	29326	32842	11	12	1188	37.2	43.4	17.9	1.5	0.0	60993
29571	MARION	16743	7225	43.0	27.7	22.8	4.4	2.2	30119	35051	13	16	5174	35.1	33.7	24.8	6.0	0.4	67577
29572	MYRTLE BEACH	40919	4383	20.2	30.7	28.1	12.1	9.0	48913	57386	70	86	2836	4.5	10.7	30.8	35.3	18.7	194828
29574	MULLINS	16017	4903	44.8	29.0	20.6	3.7	1.9	28509	32655	10	9	3633	32.6	34.7	23.0	9.5	0.2	72543
29575	MYRTLE BEACH	33188	7790	17.8	34.7	31.3	10.7	5.6	47794	54713	68	84	6082	6.1	15.4	39.2	36.2	3.1	156009
29576	MURRELLS INLET	30988	9026	20.9	35.0	31.5	7.6	5.0	44226	51521	59	78	7644	17.9	14.3	36.9	22.7	8.3	119979
29577	MYRTLE BEACH	25391	11177	29.3	32.4	27.2	7.0	4.1	39123	44220	43	58	5965	13.3	17.2	41.7	20.8	7.1	118614
29579	MYRTLE BEACH	21675	5082	23.5	38.2	30.1	5.6	2.7	40287	44409	47	62	2982	9.6	12.2	52.4	24.7	1.0	120437
29580	NESMITH	13368	1332	46.0	27.3	23.2	2.6	0.9	27499	31810	8	6	1116	47.4	26.9	21.8	3.9	0.0	53333
29581	NICHOLS	17075	1981	39.7	30.8	21.5	6.2	1.8	31892	36060	18	24	1557	36.8	32.1	24.5	6.5	0.1	65038
29582	NORTH MYRTLE BEACH	32504	6811	23.5	33.3	29.8	9.2	4.3	44135	52009	59	78	5003	10.0	11.6	38.2	34.1	6.2	149764
29583	PAMPLICO	16714	2079	37.3	31.6	24.8	4.1	2.2	35987	41027	31	43	1694	31.2	38.6	24.9	5.0	0.3	65177
29584	PATRICK	15045	1293	42.7	33.4	19.0	3.6	1.3	29323	33518	11	12	1100	46.1	32.0	18.7	2.6	0.6	53707
29585	PAWLEYS ISLAND	38549	5353	17.7	21.2	36.4	14.5	10.4	61559	76306	86	95	4525	6.3	5.7	24.0	47.3	16.7	225032
29588	MYRTLE BEACH	21248	10915	20.8	36.1	34.0	7.7	1.4	44350	50784	60	79	8237	14.4	14.6	52.6	17.1	1.3	116080
29590	SALTERS	10625	745	53.3	27.9	17.7	1.1	0.0	22820	25924	3	2	612	60.3	20.3	13.7	5.7	0.0	37188
29591	SCRANTON	16160	2086	35.7	32.1	27.3	3.8	1.1	33726	38791	23	32	1676	41.9	34.7	19.2	4.1	0.2	57432
29592	SELLERS	15174	262	40.1	34.0	21.4	4.2	0.4	31494	36308	16	22	205	47.8	33.2	13.7	4.4	1.0	52500
29593	SOCIETY HILL	15845	726	44.4	24.2	25.5	3.3	2.6	29379	34844	11	12	578	42.4	30.6	21.1	5.5	0.4	56471
29596	WALLACE	15962	966	34.7	37.5	20.8	6.0	1.0	34134	38541	24	34	796	41.1	39.7	19.0	0.3	0.0	56961
29601	GREENVILLE	23777	4250	47.0	25.4	15.4	6.1	6.0	27066	31912	7	5	1708	13.1	24.4	23.1	23.9	15.5	128125
29605	GREENVILLE	25851	13208	32.3	29.5	24.1	7.9	6.2	37634	44318	38	52	8707	18.3	29.0	28.8	18.0	5.9	93922
29607	GREENVILLE	29532	13388	27.4	28.7	27.4	10.9	5.5	43601	51314	58	76	6618	4.6	18.0	47.3	24.1	6.1	126946
29609	GREENVILLE	23319	11188	29.9	29.2	26.2	9.5	5.3	40807	48577	49	65	7236	10.4	22.6	42.0	21.5	3.5	119752
29611	GREENVILLE	17341	11026	38.3	32.1	22.6	5.5	1.5	32873	38230	21	29	7193	28.6	39.8	25.7	5.1	0.9	71099
29613	GREENVILLE	9724	8	12.5	25.0	25.0	25.0	12.5	75000	50000	93	99	6	0.0	16.7	66.7	16.7	0.0	137500
29615	GREENVILLE	36229	15511	17.9	27.7	30.6	13.8	9.9	54289	65011	79	92	8627	1.5	5.7	38.2	45.7	8.9	184874
29617	GREENVILLE	19658	9734	33.2	33.6	26.1	5.1	2.0	35664	41499	30	41	6196	16.8	32.0	42.3	8.0	0.9	91174
29620	ABBEVILLE	17493	5226	34.5	33.1	26.4	4.6	1.4	35517	39806	30	41	4057	28.8	26.9	31.2	12.4	0.7	81335
29621	ANDERSON	26628	13557	25.0	27.2	31.8	10.6	5.3	47213	54233	67	83	9726	8.1	17.8	44.3	26.7	3.2	122371
29624	ANDERSON	14858	6183	47.3	28.9	19.9	3.2	0.7	26628	30615	7	4	3674	43.7	38.1	15.4	2.8	0.0	56784
29625	ANDERSON	22851	10249	28.1	30.2	31.7	7.2	2.7	42970	50230	56	73	7488	13.5	25.5	48.2	11.3	1.6	102217
29626	ANDERSON	19318	5032	30.7	32.2	28.6	6.6	1.9	37123	42257	36	48	4153	19.5	29.4	35.0	14.1	2.1	91303
29627	BELTON	20035	7338	31.1	30.9	29.9	6.4	1.8	38987	44247	43	57	5964	23.1	35.0	30.5	9.6	1.9	81693
29628	CALHOUN FALLS	14467	1279	41.4	33.7	21.8	2.6	0.5	30549	34414	14	18	1006	42.1	33.5	19.1	3.5	1.9	57921
29630	CENTRAL	18650	5434	38.1	30.4	24.4	5.6	1.6	34215	38412	25	35	3071	20.1	26.9	35.9	15.1	2.0	93894
29631	CLEMSON	23291	4986	42.4	22.6	19.2	10.1	5.7	31498	36063	16	22	2359	7.1	8.3	48.4	31.3	4.8	151272
29632	CLEMSON	10057	27	25.9	44.4	14.8	11.1	3.7	41127	43624	50	67	14	14.3	0.0	42.9	35.7	7.1	162500
29635	CLEVELAND	28601	632	25.0	27.4	36.1	7.8	3.8	48157	55627	69	85	529	19.3	23.6	27.8	22.7	6.6	105664
29638	DONALDS	18592	1457	32.5	32.5	28.7	5.2	1.1	38298	42476	40	54	1200	24.2	33.6	33.1	8.7	0.5	81143
29639	DUE WEST	15876	520	29.0	31.0	31.9	6.5	1.5	42100	47375	53	71	418	21.1	30.1	31.3	17.2	0.2	88611
29640	EASLEY	21148	12428	27.4	33.2	30.6	6.2	2.6	41363	47220	51	68	9723	21.2	28.6	36.2	13.0	1.0	90229
29642	EASLEY	25341	10192	20.1	25.0	37.9	12.6	4.4	54802	62826	79	92	8421	10.1	12.6	48.9	25.6	2.9	128397
29643	FAIR PLAY	22699	1194	25.9	37.3	26.7	6.9	3.3	40046	46354	46	61	1038	23.7	21.6	28.7	23.7	2.3	96533
29644	FOUNTAIN INN	21709	6604	24.5	30.4	34.9	7.8	2.5	45253	52074	62	80	5279	16.3	21.2	47.5	12.5	2.6	105413
29645	GRAY COURT	19228	4455	27.0	31.6	33.6	5.9	2.0	42259	47752	54	71	3766	23.3	27.5	37.6	10.5	1.1	89088
29646	GREENWOOD	19278	10961	36.7	31.2	24.5	4.3	3.4	34744	39969	26	37	7065	20.2	36.4	30.5	11.0	1.9	83184
29649	GREENWOOD	22800	9799	26.1	30.8	30.7	8.2	4.2	43264	49989	57	74	6571	12.8	20.7	44.9	19.3	2.3	113140
29650	GREER	34959	9919	16.1	18.8	33.6	19.3	12.3	68860	83541	91	97	7523	2.7	9.0	40.0	40.7	7.6	171634
29651	GREER	22559	14499	26.2	29.9	30.6	9.7	3.7	43645	51097	58	76	11291	16.6	18.9	41.0	21.3	2.2	110341
29653	HODGES	19634	1684	25.6	33.9	32.2	6.5	1.7	40957	46558	50	66	1422	27.4	25.4	32.2	13.9	1.1	86460
29654	HONEA PATH	19118	3916	33.6	30.6	29.5	4.8	1.5	37673	42671	38	52	3190	25.8	35.7	29.9	7.6	1.0	75326
29655	IVA	17680	3260	36.5	29.5	29.5	2.9	1.6	36445	41215	33	45	2690	32.7	30.1	28.7	7.4	1.2	73349
29657	LIBERTY	18648	5839	26.7	34.5	32.4	5.1	1.3	40558	45724	48	64	4855	26.4	29.7	34.3	9.0	0.5	81927
29658	LONG CREEK	19745	142	38.7	39.4	12.0	6.3	3.5	31641	35219	17	24	119	24.4	26.1	36.1	13.5	0.0	89444
29659	LOWNDESVILLE	21611	80	36.3	22.5	33.8	5.0	2.5	35000	38897	28	38	62	46.8	22.6	21.0	9.7	0.0	53333
29661	MARIETTA	19062	2426	29.3	34.8	28.9	5.0	2.1	39060	45318	43	58	1965	28.6	28.9	29.9	10.3	2.3	80487
29662	MAULDIN	28649	5079	16.1	23.2	39.1	18.0	3.7	60637	72122	85	94	3658	1.8	8.5	68.5	20.6	0.7	136969
29664	MOUNTAIN REST	21249	688	32.3	33.4	25.2	7.4	1.7	34641	40584	26	36	584	21.2	28.1	32.0	16.3	2.4	90714
29666	NINETY SIX	21100	2587	30.0	32.2	30.7	5.0	2.1	40397	45793	48	63	2116	21.9	36.8	30.5	9.4	1.4	80707
29667	NORRIS	17615	165	27.9	38.8	30.9	2.4	0.0	38226	43171	40	54	138	41.3	33.3	21.0	4.4	0.0	58571
29669	PELZER	20573	4873	27.0	32.3	32.5	6.1	2.1	41479	47939	51	68	3957	26.0	29.1	33.3	10.4	1.2	83723
29670	PENDLETON	20980	3513	34.2	30.4	26.3	6.7	2.4	37009	43022	35	48	2488	19.6	32.9	32.3	12.9	2.3	87265
29671	PICKENS	19940	7297	30.1	34.6	28.5	5.3	1.5	38979	44097	43	57	5919	24.5	28.5	32.1	12.9	2.0	86473
29672	SENECA	28591	4345	18.7	27.5	35.5	11.8	6.5	52908	62097	77	89	3600	15.0	13.3	33.7	26.4	11.6	135847
29673	PIEDMONT	20669	9022	24.9	30.9	35.1	7.3	1.8	45591	52455	63	81	7430	21.0	26.3	38.3	13.5	0.9	93862
29676	SALEM	38278	2399	19.2	25.2	33.7	11.3	10.6	55923	65696	81	93	2098	15.3	14.6	18.5	32.0	19.5	182783
	SOUTH CAROLINA	22607		28.8	29.3	29.6	8.3	4.0	42042	49103				19.3	24.1	35.5	17.1	3.9	100170
	UNITED STATES	25866		24.7	27.1	30.8	10.9	6.5	48124	56710				10.9	15.0	33.7	30.1	10.4	145905

ZIP CODE		FINANCIAL SERVICES				THE HOME						ENTERTAINMENT						PERSONAL			
						Home Improvements		Furnishings													
#	POST OFFICE NAME	Auto Loan	Home Loan	Invest-ments	Retire-ment Plans	Home Repair	Lawn & Garden	Comput-ers & Hard-ware	Major Appli-ances	TV, Radio, Sound Equip-ment	Furni-ture	Dine out/ Carry out	Sports Equip-ment	Fees & Tickets	Toys & Games	Travel	Cable TV	Apparel & Services	Auto Repairs	Health Insur-ance	Pets & Supplies
29516	BLENHEIM	82	55	25	47	62	71	53	66	64	54	75	79	45	71	54	69	68	65	81	94
29518	CADES	74	49	22	43	56	64	48	60	58	49	68	71	41	64	48	62	61	59	73	85
29520	CHERAW	68	54	41	50	57	66	55	61	62	56	74	70	51	70	55	65	69	61	70	77
29525	CLIO	74	49	22	43	56	64	48	60	58	49	68	71	41	64	49	62	61	59	74	85
29526	CONWAY	84	78	68	75	79	85	75	81	77	77	95	92	73	90	76	77	91	80	83	95
29527	CONWAY	70	63	54	60	63	69	62	65	64	63	79	75	60	76	61	65	76	65	68	78
29530	COWARD	73	49	22	42	55	64	47	59	57	48	67	71	40	63	48	61	61	58	73	84
29532	DARLINGTON	73	61	48	57	63	71	61	67	66	62	80	77	57	76	61	68	76	67	73	82
29536	DILLON	63	54	47	50	55	62	55	59	59	56	72	66	52	68	54	62	69	59	65	71
29540	DARLINGTON	79	59	35	53	64	72	57	67	64	58	77	79	51	73	57	67	71	67	77	90
29541	EFFINGHAM	87	74	54	70	77	83	70	78	75	72	91	92	66	88	71	76	86	77	83	98
29543	FORK	79	53	24	46	60	69	51	64	62	52	72	76	43	68	52	66	66	63	79	91
29544	GALIVANTS FERRY	72	65	50	62	65	69	62	67	63	64	78	77	59	74	61	63	75	67	67	80
29545	GREEN SEA	70	47	22	41	53	61	46	57	55	47	65	68	39	61	47	59	59	56	70	80
29546	GRESHAM	76	62	41	57	65	71	59	67	64	60	77	79	54	73	59	65	73	67	73	86
29547	HAMER	65	57	43	54	58	62	55	60	57	56	69	69	51	66	54	57	66	60	61	73
29550	HARTSVILLE	83	72	59	68	74	82	71	77	75	71	92	89	67	89	71	77	87	76	83	94
29554	HEMINGWAY	71	52	32	46	56	65	52	61	60	53	71	71	46	67	52	64	66	61	72	80
29555	JOHNSONVILLE	85	61	34	55	68	77	59	71	69	60	81	85	52	78	60	73	75	70	85	98
29556	KINGSTREE	68	52	39	47	55	64	53	60	61	54	72	68	49	67	53	64	67	60	70	76
29560	LAKE CITY	68	52	41	47	55	64	55	60	62	55	74	69	50	69	54	65	70	61	70	76
29563	LAKE VIEW	78	52	24	45	59	68	50	63	61	51	71	75	43	67	51	65	65	62	78	89
29564	LANE	59	42	27	36	45	53	42	50	50	43	60	58	38	55	42	54	55	50	61	67
29565	LATTA	71	54	36	49	58	66	55	62	62	55	74	72	49	69	54	65	69	62	72	80
29566	LITTLE RIVER	91	85	78	80	89	102	79	89	83	83	103	90	79	88	84	87	96	86	101	102
29567	LITTLE ROCK	88	60	29	53	68	77	58	72	69	59	81	85	50	77	59	74	74	71	87	100
29568	LONGS	76	69	54	66	70	74	66	71	67	67	82	82	62	79	65	67	79	70	71	85
29569	LORIS	68	56	40	51	58	64	54	61	59	55	71	70	50	67	54	60	67	60	67	76
29570	MC COLL	67	45	20	39	51	58	43	54	52	44	61	64	37	58	44	56	55	53	66	77
29571	MARION	72	56	41	51	59	68	56	63	63	57	76	74	52	73	56	67	72	63	73	82
29572	MYRTLE BEACH	112	102	109	102	106	120	106	110	108	107	135	122	104	123	108	110	129	112	118	127
29574	MULLINS	71	50	30	44	55	64	50	60	60	51	70	70	44	66	51	64	65	60	72	81
29575	MYRTLE BEACH	105	98	94	93	103	119	92	103	97	96	120	106	92	105	98	102	113	101	118	120
29576	MURRELLS INLET	94	89	88	85	94	109	83	94	88	88	109	96	84	96	90	93	103	92	107	108
29577	MYRTLE BEACH	76	71	78	73	71	77	76	75	76	76	96	90	74	93	74	74	93	78	73	86
29579	MYRTLE BEACH	75	69	72	72	68	72	73	72	72	74	90	86	70	87	70	69	88	75	68	83
29580	NESMITH	70	47	21	40	53	61	45	56	54	46	64	67	38	60	46	58	58	56	69	80
29581	NICHOLS	79	53	26	47	60	70	52	64	63	53	73	77	45	70	53	67	67	64	79	90
29582	NORTH MYRTLE BEACH	107	89	71	82	98	112	84	99	93	86	112	109	79	105	90	99	105	97	116	127
29583	PAMPLICO	77	56	32	51	62	70	55	65	63	55	75	77	48	72	55	67	69	64	77	88
29584	PATRICK	69	48	24	42	53	61	46	57	55	47	64	67	40	61	47	58	59	56	68	79
29585	PAWLEYS ISLAND	123	120	124	118	125	141	115	124	118	120	147	131	116	130	121	121	139	123	136	140
29588	MYRTLE BEACH	80	74	68	73	74	81	72	76	73	75	91	86	70	84	72	73	87	77	77	88
29590	SALTERS	43	34	36	30	34	42	39	40	45	40	54	43	37	48	38	48	51	41	48	47
29591	SCRANTON	75	55	31	49	60	67	53	63	60	54	72	74	47	68	53	64	66	62	73	85
29592	SELLERS	67	54	36	50	57	62	52	59	56	53	68	69	47	64	52	58	64	59	64	76
29593	SOCIETY HILL	79	53	24	46	60	69	51	64	62	52	72	76	43	68	52	66	66	63	79	91
29596	WALLACE	77	51	23	44	58	67	50	62	60	51	70	74	42	67	51	65	64	61	77	88
29601	GREENVILLE	66	62	74	60	62	70	68	67	72	68	89	76	67	85	67	74	86	69	71	75
29605	GREENVILLE	86	83	87	80	83	92	84	85	87	84	107	97	84	105	84	88	104	86	89	98
29607	GREENVILLE	92	90	101	92	88	95	94	92	93	95	117	107	93	113	91	92	114	94	89	102
29609	GREENVILLE	81	81	87	81	80	86	83	82	83	82	104	96	83	104	82	83	101	83	81	92
29611	GREENVILLE	68	56	48	53	58	66	58	62	64	58	77	72	55	75	58	66	73	63	69	76
29613	GREENVILLE	131	80	101	90	78	95	154	113	150	130	187	158	126	168	123	132	176	138	105	129
29615	GREENVILLE	109	109	127	115	107	114	114	110	110	115	140	131	114	136	111	106	137	114	103	122
29617	GREENVILLE	76	62	49	60	66	74	64	69	70	63	84	80	61	83	64	72	79	69	77	85
29620	ABBEVILLE	72	57	39	52	61	69	56	64	63	56	75	75	51	73	57	66	70	63	74	83
29621	ANDERSON	93	90	93	89	91	99	90	92	92	90	113	107	90	113	90	92	110	92	93	107
29624	ANDERSON	59	44	34	39	47	55	46	52	53	47	64	59	42	58	46	57	59	52	61	66
29625	ANDERSON	83	74	62	70	77	85	72	77	77	71	94	90	71	94	73	79	89	76	85	95
29626	ANDERSON	82	64	43	59	70	79	61	71	68	62	82	83	57	78	63	72	76	70	83	94
29627	BELTON	84	66	44	61	71	79	64	73	71	64	85	86	59	82	64	74	79	72	83	96
29628	CALHOUN FALLS	67	45	20	39	51	59	43	54	52	44	62	65	37	58	44	57	56	54	67	77
29630	CENTRAL	66	50	49	52	52	58	65	60	66	60	82	76	58	77	59	63	77	65	60	72
29631	CLEMSON	75	59	73	64	58	66	86	70	83	77	104	91	76	97	75	76	99	80	66	79
29632	CLEMSON	67	57	73	60	56	64	77	65	76	71	95	82	71	91	70	72	92	73	63	73
29635	CLEVELAND	111	88	60	81	97	108	83	98	93	83	111	116	76	110	87	98	103	96	113	132
29638	DONALDS	81	58	32	52	64	74	57	68	66	58	79	80	51	75	58	70	72	67	81	92
29639	DUE WEST	74	67	58	64	70	78	66	71	70	65	85	81	64	85	67	72	81	70	77	85
29640	EASLEY	86	72	52	69	76	84	71	78	76	71	92	91	66	90	71	78	87	77	85	97
29642	EASLEY	93	100	96	99	101	103	92	95	90	92	112	112	94	115	94	89	109	93	92	110
29643	FAIR PLAY	87	71	51	66	78	86	68	79	74	68	89	92	62	87	70	77	83	78	89	104
29644	FOUNTAIN INN	88	81	67	79	83	88	78	83	80	79	98	98	75	96	78	79	94	82	85	101
29645	GRAY COURT	85	72	50	67	74	80	68	76	72	70	88	89	63	84	68	74	83	75	81	96
29646	GREENWOOD	73	63	58	60	65	74	66	69	71	65	86	79	63	83	66	73	82	70	76	83
29649	GREENWOOD	82	76	71	76	78	84	78	80	79	76	98	94	76	98	77	79	94	80	82	94
29650	GREER	126	141	151	145	137	141	132	130	126	133	158	151	139	162	132	123	157	128	120	145
29651	GREER	90	80	66	77	82	90	78	84	83	78	101	98	76	99	79	84	96	83	90	102
29653	HODGES	88	67	41	61	73	82	64	75	72	64	86	89	58	84	65	76	80	74	87	101
29654	HONEA PATH	81	60	35	53	66	75	58	69	67	58	79	81	52	76	59	71	73	68	82	93
29655	IVA	80	54	26	47	62	71	52	65	63	53	74	78	45	70	54	68	67	65	80	93
29657	LIBERTY	80	66	46	62	69	76	64	72	69	65	83	84	59	80	64	70	78	71	77	90
29658	LONG CREEK	77	52	23	45	59	67	50	62	60	51	71	75	42	67	51	65	64	62	77	89
29659	LOWNDESVILLE	86	58	26	50	66	76	56	70	67	57	79	84	48	75	57	73	72	69	86	99
29661	MARIETTA	87	64	37	58	70	79	62	74	71	63	84	87	55	80	62	74	78	73	86	100
29662	MAULDIN	96	107	113	110	104	104	103	101	97	103	122	120	105	124	102	92	120	100	90	110
29664	MOUNTAIN REST	80	61	38	54	68	77	57	70	66	57	78	82	51	76	61	71	72	69	83	96
29666	NINETY SIX	87	68	45	61	74	83	65	76	74	66	89	89	61	87	67	78	83	75	89	101
29667	NORRIS	80	54	26	47	61	70	52	65	63	54	74	78	45	70	53	67	67	64	79	92
29669	PELZER	88	68	43	62	74	82	65	76	73	66	87	90	59	85	66	77	81	75	87	102
29670	PENDLETON	73	65	54	63	67	74	65	69	68	64	83	79	63	83	65	70	79	68	74	82
29671	PICKENS	85	65	42	60	71	79	63	73	71	64	85	86	58	83	64	75	79	72	85	97
29672	SENECA	105	93	76	89	99	110	88	98	93	89	114	111	86	109	91	96	107	96	109	121
29673	PIEDMONT	87	75	56	71	78	84	71	79	75	72	92	93	67	90	72	77	87	78	84	99
29676	SALEM	129	109	90	101	118	138	102	120	112	107	137	126	98	120	109	120	127	117	142	148
	SOUTH CAROLINA	87	78	69	75	80	87	77	82	81	78	99	95	74	96	77	82	95	82	86	99
	UNITED STATES	100	100	100	100	100	100	100	100	100	100	100	100	100	100	100	100	100	100	100	100

#	POST OFFICE NAME	COUNTY FIPS CODE	POPULATION 2000	2004	2009	2000-2004 ANNUAL RATE % Rate	State Centile	HOUSEHOLDS 2000	2004	2009	% Annual Rate 2000-2004	2004 Average HH Size	FAMILIES 2000	2004	% Annual Rate 2000-2004
29678	SENECA	073	19026	20153	21433	1.4	65	7827	8483	9221	1.9	2.35	5314	5604	1.3
29680	SIMPSONVILLE	045	20153	22369	24052	2.5	88	6925	7807	8492	2.9	2.79	5452	6004	2.3
29681	SIMPSONVILLE	045	29800	32717	34934	2.2	85	10784	11894	12764	2.3	2.73	8706	9420	1.9
29682	SIX MILE	077	3451	3570	3702	0.8	48	1277	1348	1422	1.3	2.62	993	1025	0.8
29684	STARR	007	4365	4346	4427	-0.1	15	1649	1679	1741	0.4	2.59	1248	1238	-0.2
29685	SUNSET	077	809	857	904	1.4	66	346	375	403	1.9	2.26	255	269	1.3
29686	TAMASSEE	073	962	1021	1076	1.4	67	366	399	431	2.1	2.53	270	287	1.5
29687	TAYLORS	045	35814	37966	39900	1.4	67	14282	15337	16275	1.7	2.47	10253	10663	0.9
29688	TIGERVILLE	045	101	122	136	4.5	97	38	47	52	5.1	2.60	28	34	4.7
29689	TOWNVILLE	007	3836	4065	4242	1.4	66	1604	1743	1857	2.0	2.33	1169	1234	1.3
29690	TRAVELERS REST	045	17596	18616	19515	1.3	63	6341	6809	7221	1.7	2.63	4808	5015	1.0
29691	WALHALLA	073	11328	11555	12068	0.5	36	4503	4682	4989	0.9	2.45	3240	3286	0.3
29692	WARE SHOALS	059	4912	5376	5765	2.2	84	2006	2254	2466	2.8	2.37	1390	1512	2.0
29693	WESTMINSTER	073	13166	14050	14979	1.5	72	5336	5843	6376	2.2	2.39	3857	4110	1.5
29696	WEST UNION	073	3360	3484	3678	0.9	49	1321	1405	1517	1.5	2.48	1003	1041	0.9
29697	WILLIAMSTON	007	10650	11264	11774	1.3	63	4055	4348	4608	1.7	2.59	3109	3259	1.1
29702	BLACKSBURG	021	9815	10227	10577	1.0	52	3883	4139	4362	1.5	2.47	2773	2874	0.9
29704	CATAWBA	091	2938	3321	3816	2.9	91	1042	1211	1424	3.6	2.70	832	946	3.1
29706	CHESTER	023	20943	20697	20572	-0.3	12	7926	8031	8082	0.3	2.54	5691	5620	-0.3
29708	FORT MILL	091	10614	13224	16039	5.3	98	3808	4824	5952	5.7	2.74	2939	3633	5.1
29709	CHESTERFIELD	025	6563	6883	7389	1.1	57	2657	2855	3140	1.7	2.39	1838	1918	1.0
29710	CLOVER	091	21946	24551	28237	2.7	90	8434	9651	11318	3.2	2.54	6446	7183	2.6
29712	EDGEMOOR	023	2003	2314	2495	3.5	95	753	894	975	4.1	2.59	574	664	3.5
29714	FORT LAWN	023	3009	3098	3111	0.7	44	1091	1153	1171	1.3	2.66	810	832	0.6
29715	FORT MILL	091	19944	22957	26383	3.4	95	7720	9026	10554	3.8	2.54	5843	6672	3.2
29717	HICKORY GROVE	091	1170	1243	1390	1.4	68	431	468	534	2.0	2.66	340	361	1.4
29718	JEFFERSON	025	3865	4094	4411	1.4	65	1470	1590	1751	1.9	2.57	1070	1127	1.2
29720	LANCASTER	057	44028	44873	46422	0.5	34	16923	17700	18778	1.1	2.50	12223	12455	0.4
29726	MC CONNELLS	091	1571	1799	2093	3.2	94	544	638	758	3.8	2.81	422	482	3.2
29727	MOUNT CROGHAN	025	1914	2084	2284	2.0	82	750	840	945	2.7	2.48	549	598	2.0
29728	PAGELAND	025	8780	9363	10140	1.5	71	3223	3525	3914	2.1	2.64	2270	2415	1.5
29729	RICHBURG	023	2582	2549	2522	-0.3	11	954	970	975	0.4	2.62	730	724	-0.2
29730	ROCK HILL	091	46067	50348	57453	2.1	83	16809	18910	22162	2.8	2.54	11788	12875	2.1
29732	ROCK HILL	091	39574	45491	53055	3.3	94	15037	17638	20996	3.8	2.51	10734	12295	3.3
29741	RUBY	025	534	548	582	0.6	41	235	248	270	1.3	2.19	164	167	0.4
29742	SHARON	091	2024	2177	2442	1.7	76	722	794	907	2.3	2.74	560	602	1.7
29743	SMYRNA	091	1200	1265	1391	1.3	61	458	492	551	1.7	2.57	360	378	1.2
29745	YORK	091	22802	25345	29052	2.5	89	8045	9139	10699	3.1	2.71	6161	6843	2.5
29801	AIKEN	003	26907	27711	29004	0.7	45	10472	11068	11877	1.3	2.39	6959	7116	0.5
29803	AIKEN	003	30045	32124	34324	1.6	73	11783	12907	14101	2.2	2.47	8746	9320	1.5
29805	AIKEN	003	4773	5055	5339	1.4	65	1784	1938	2094	2.0	2.61	1354	1434	1.4
29808	AIKEN	011	76	81	83	1.5	70	26	28	29	1.8	2.89	20	21	1.2
29809	NEW ELLENTON	003	2479	2433	2505	-0.4	7	969	976	1027	0.2	2.46	675	655	-0.7
29810	ALLENDALE	005	5400	5445	5534	0.2	27	2041	2119	2215	0.9	2.55	1352	1360	0.1
29812	BARNWELL	011	12254	12320	12317	0.1	25	4725	4887	4972	0.8	2.50	3364	3385	0.2
29817	BLACKVILLE	011	5171	5098	5082	-0.3	10	1932	1971	2005	0.5	2.53	1388	1379	-0.2
29819	BRADLEY	047	1599	1683	1727	1.2	60	586	628	654	1.6	2.61	444	465	1.1
29821	CLARKS HILL	065	897	941	983	1.1	57	333	357	383	1.7	2.64	255	268	1.2
29824	EDGEFIELD	037	8491	8538	8774	0.1	25	2583	2575	2729	-0.1	2.48	1880	1821	-0.8
29827	FAIRFAX	005	4241	4224	4233	-0.1	15	1232	1267	1312	0.7	2.45	832	830	-0.1
29828	GLOVERVILLE	003	1026	994	1021	-0.7	3	433	430	453	-0.2	2.31	299	288	-0.9
29829	GRANITEVILLE	003	7017	7009	7275	0.0	18	2672	2736	2908	0.6	2.54	1960	1957	0.0
29831	JACKSON	003	3134	3462	3764	2.4	86	1251	1407	1560	2.8	2.46	889	970	2.1
29832	JOHNSTON	037	4993	5093	5403	0.5	36	1906	2002	2178	1.2	2.53	1359	1385	0.5
29835	MC CORMICK	065	6950	7104	7314	0.5	37	2383	2550	2736	1.6	2.28	1729	1803	1.0
29836	MARTIN	005	488	490	494	0.1	24	197	204	212	0.8	2.39	130	131	0.2
29838	MODOC	065	355	362	370	0.5	35	162	170	178	1.1	2.13	119	121	0.4
29840	MOUNT CARMEL	065	1042	1163	1248	2.6	89	352	418	471	4.1	2.50	282	328	3.6
29841	NORTH AUGUSTA	003	29821	30848	32529	0.8	48	12124	12824	13819	1.3	2.39	8227	8445	0.6
29842	BEECH ISLAND	003	9034	9551	10104	1.3	63	3375	3654	3950	1.9	2.61	2450	2582	1.2
29843	OLAR	009	1610	1564	1539	-0.7	3	649	653	662	0.1	2.40	453	444	-0.5
29845	PLUM BRANCH	065	1222	1268	1310	0.9	49	503	541	578	1.7	2.34	361	376	1.0
29847	TRENTON	037	3723	4456	5118	4.3	97	1166	1487	1795	5.9	2.56	873	1085	5.3
29848	TROY	065	400	428	445	1.6	73	131	145	155	2.4	2.69	101	109	1.8
29849	ULMER	005	1188	1221	1241	0.7	43	480	506	531	1.3	2.40	328	337	0.6
29851	WARRENVILLE	003	8467	8479	8794	0.0	20	3447	3536	3751	0.6	2.40	2356	2337	-0.2
29853	WILLISTON	011	6813	7154	7399	1.2	58	2647	2860	3012	1.8	2.48	1882	1978	1.2
29856	WINDSOR	003	2637	3246	3704	5.0	98	940	1184	1380	5.6	2.74	710	872	5.0
29860	NORTH AUGUSTA	037	11403	12792	13973	2.7	90	3938	4527	5059	3.3	2.79	3227	3640	2.9
29902	BEAUFORT	013	18495	19225	21344	0.9	51	5803	6234	7248	1.7	2.41	3883	4030	0.9
29906	BEAUFORT	013	21728	23691	27190	2.1	83	6590	7315	8596	2.5	3.00	5329	5837	2.2
29907	LADYS ISLAND	013	9321	10658	12590	3.2	93	3521	4063	4858	3.4	2.62	2690	3032	2.9
29909	OKATIE	013	4458	5632	6970	5.7	99	2129	2758	3484	6.3	2.04	1700	2155	5.7
29910	BLUFFTON	013	13387	16387	20045	4.9	97	5171	6457	8039	5.4	2.54	3817	4659	4.8
29911	BRUNSON	049	1554	1595	1638	0.6	41	587	620	655	1.3	2.57	425	438	0.7
29916	EARLY BRANCH	049	1578	1657	1752	1.2	58	604	653	710	1.9	2.54	452	477	1.3
29918	ESTILL	049	7904	8110	8336	0.6	41	2262	2429	2588	1.7	2.68	1626	1698	1.0
29920	SAINT HELENA ISLAND	013	9486	10854	12874	3.2	93	3761	4471	5452	4.2	2.41	2755	3190	3.5
29922	GARNETT	049	106	112	117	1.3	63	31	34	36	2.2	3.29	22	24	2.1
29924	HAMPTON	049	4278	4347	4453	0.4	32	1748	1824	1919	1.0	2.38	1191	1205	0.3
29926	HILTON HEAD ISLAND	013	18763	23649	29475	5.6	99	7633	9711	12247	5.8	2.42	5722	7062	5.1
29927	HARDEEVILLE	053	6555	7191	7943	2.2	85	2317	2590	2916	2.7	2.77	1645	1788	2.0
29928	HILTON HEAD ISLAND	013	17162	20308	25027	4.0	97	7796	9332	11671	4.3	2.14	5011	5791	3.5
29929	ISLANDTON	029	1297	1341	1419	0.8	48	477	501	542	1.2	2.64	331	338	0.5
29932	LURAY	049	505	549	581	2.0	82	176	197	215	2.7	2.79	135	147	2.0
29934	PINELAND	053	1256	1290	1376	0.6	42	474	501	546	1.3	2.57	341	351	0.7
29935	PORT ROYAL	013	2947	3103	3502	1.2	60	1280	1385	1603	1.9	2.14	810	844	1.0
29936	RIDGELAND	053	9812	10392	11201	1.4	65	3108	3392	3770	2.1	2.67	2257	2400	1.5
29940	SEABROOK	013	3917	4199	4800	1.7	74	1354	1487	1735	2.2	2.82	1013	1086	1.7
29941	SHELDON	013	183	197	226	1.8	76	85	94	110	2.4	2.10	60	65	1.9
29943	TILLMAN	053	2026	2197	2412	1.9	80	754	841	945	2.6	2.61	560	609	2.0
29944	VARNVILLE	049	4617	4610	4724	0.0	17	1730	1770	1860	0.5	2.59	1251	1247	-0.1
29945	YEMASSEE	013	4163	4413	4828	1.4	67	1531	1672	1877	2.1	2.63	1075	1138	1.4
	SOUTH CAROLINA					1.2					1.8	2.47			1.1
	UNITED STATES					1.2					1.3	2.58			1.1

ZIP CODE #	POST OFFICE NAME	RACE (%) White 2000	White 2004	Black 2000	Black 2004	Asian/Pacific 2000	Asian/Pacific 2004	% Hispanic Origin 2000	% Hispanic Origin 2004	2004 AGE DISTRIBUTION (%) 0-4	5-9	10-14	15-19	20-24	25-44	45-64	65-84	85+	18+	MEDIAN AGE 2004	% 2004 Males	% 2004 Females
29678	SENECA	77.1	76.7	20.8	20.8	0.4	0.5	1.3	1.7	7.0	6.7	6.5	6.1	6.3	29.0	24.9	12.0	1.6	76.1	37.0	48.4	51.6
29680	SIMPSONVILLE	83.3	82.0	13.3	14.0	1.1	1.3	2.8	3.6	8.7	8.3	7.5	6.3	6.2	36.0	21.8	4.9	0.3	71.5	33.4	51.1	48.9
29681	SIMPSONVILLE	88.1	87.1	8.7	9.1	1.4	1.8	2.4	3.1	8.2	8.6	8.3	6.2	4.7	30.3	25.4	7.5	0.9	71.0	36.5	48.9	51.1
29682	SIX MILE	98.4	98.2	0.4	0.5	0.2	0.2	0.7	0.9	6.2	6.5	7.0	6.5	6.0	28.0	26.9	11.4	1.6	76.3	39.1	50.6	49.4
29684	STARR	84.9	83.7	13.8	14.8	0.1	0.1	1.1	1.4	6.5	6.6	7.0	6.7	6.1	28.5	26.7	11.1	0.8	75.8	37.5	49.4	50.6
29685	SUNSET	97.5	97.6	0.9	0.8	0.1	0.2	0.4	0.5	5.5	6.0	6.4	6.7	5.4	28.0	29.5	11.2	1.4	78.2	40.3	51.3	48.7
29686	TAMASSEE	98.0	97.7	0.7	0.8	0.1	0.1	0.7	1.1	5.2	5.6	6.3	5.5	5.0	26.6	31.4	13.3	1.1	79.5	42.3	50.7	49.3
29687	TAYLORS	83.5	82.1	11.9	12.5	2.1	2.4	3.5	4.3	6.8	6.9	7.1	6.2	6.0	29.7	25.6	10.7	1.0	75.4	37.0	48.8	51.3
29688	TIGERVILLE	99.0	98.4	1.0	0.8	0.0	0.0	1.0	0.8	6.6	6.6	6.6	5.7	5.7	29.5	27.9	10.7	0.8	75.4	39.0	49.2	50.8
29689	TOWNVILLE	93.2	92.6	5.6	6.0	0.3	0.4	1.0	1.4	5.7	5.8	5.6	4.8	4.6	26.5	32.4	13.7	1.1	80.0	43.2	51.1	48.9
29690	TRAVELERS REST	89.5	88.6	8.3	8.9	0.5	0.5	1.7	2.2	6.6	6.7	7.0	7.9	8.0	27.0	26.0	9.8	1.0	75.9	36.0	50.3	49.7
29691	WALHALLA	91.7	90.6	3.3	3.3	0.3	0.3	7.2	9.0	6.5	6.6	7.0	6.4	6.1	27.4	26.1	12.5	1.5	76.1	38.4	49.7	50.3
29692	WARE SHOALS	81.1	79.5	17.5	18.9	0.2	0.2	0.9	1.1	7.0	6.9	7.1	6.3	5.7	26.0	25.7	13.4	1.9	74.8	38.7	47.8	52.2
29693	WESTMINSTER	93.3	92.8	4.9	5.2	0.2	0.2	1.3	1.7	6.4	6.6	6.8	5.9	5.6	28.2	26.6	12.6	1.3	76.6	38.6	49.6	50.4
29696	WEST UNION	95.3	94.9	2.3	2.3	0.2	0.2	3.5	4.3	5.2	5.6	6.8	6.1	5.2	27.2	29.1	13.8	1.1	78.7	41.3	49.5	50.6
29697	WILLIAMSTON	89.1	88.4	8.5	8.8	0.2	0.2	2.4	2.9	7.2	7.3	7.4	6.0	5.9	29.9	24.6	10.7	1.0	74.3	36.6	49.8	50.2
29702	BLACKSBURG	87.5	86.5	9.7	10.1	0.1	0.1	2.0	2.7	6.9	6.9	7.0	6.4	6.1	29.7	25.4	10.7	1.1	75.5	36.6	50.1	49.9
29704	CATAWBA	82.1	79.8	14.3	16.1	0.3	0.3	0.9	1.1	7.0	7.1	7.4	6.7	5.5	30.7	26.5	8.6	0.5	74.3	37.1	50.8	49.2
29706	CHESTER	53.9	53.4	44.8	45.1	0.3	0.4	0.7	0.8	6.9	7.0	7.6	7.1	6.6	26.6	25.5	11.3	1.5	74.1	36.5	48.0	52.0
29708	FORT MILL	91.6	90.2	5.1	5.9	1.5	1.8	1.4	1.8	6.5	7.0	8.7	7.1	4.7	29.2	28.2	8.0	0.6	73.1	37.9	48.8	51.2
29709	CHESTERFIELD	68.2	67.6	30.7	31.2	0.2	0.2	0.7	0.8	6.1	6.4	7.2	6.2	5.8	28.8	26.2	12.1	1.3	76.6	38.5	48.8	51.2
29710	CLOVER	87.7	86.5	9.5	10.2	0.8	1.0	1.4	1.7	6.2	6.4	7.2	6.3	5.7	27.9	28.1	11.5	0.8	76.3	39.1	50.2	49.8
29712	EDGEMOOR	77.4	76.2	20.7	21.5	0.1	0.0	1.5	1.9	6.8	6.9	6.8	6.7	5.9	30.2	26.2	9.5	1.0	75.5	37.1	50.4	49.6
29714	FORT LAWN	67.7	66.3	30.5	31.6	0.1	0.1	0.7	0.9	7.0	7.1	7.5	7.4	5.9	29.5	25.8	8.7	1.1	74.1	36.1	48.6	51.4
29715	FORT MILL	90.1	89.2	7.5	7.9	0.7	0.8	1.4	1.8	6.9	7.2	7.9	6.8	5.5	28.7	26.4	9.6	1.1	73.8	37.7	49.2	50.8
29717	HICKORY GROVE	83.0	81.2	15.7	17.5	0.1	0.1	0.9	1.2	6.4	6.7	7.2	6.3	6.3	29.4	25.9	10.9	1.1	76.0	37.2	52.1	48.0
29718	JEFFERSON	71.2	70.6	27.0	27.2	0.1	0.1	3.2	3.4	7.8	7.7	7.3	6.7	5.9	28.9	24.6	10.2	1.1	73.2	36.2	50.1	49.9
29720	LANCASTER	68.6	67.6	29.1	29.7	0.3	0.4	1.9	2.3	6.8	6.9	7.5	6.6	6.1	28.7	25.0	10.9	1.4	74.7	36.7	48.6	51.5
29726	MC CONNELLS	78.6	76.9	19.5	20.8	0.1	0.1	1.1	1.5	6.8	6.8	7.0	6.7	7.7	29.9	26.4	8.1	0.6	75.3	36.0	48.6	51.4
29727	MOUNT CROGHAN	73.7	72.9	24.8	25.4	0.1	0.1	1.2	1.3	6.8	6.7	6.8	6.1	6.3	27.3	26.8	11.9	1.3	76.0	37.8	50.3	49.7
29728	PAGELAND	60.0	59.1	34.4	34.1	0.4	0.4	5.2	6.4	8.0	7.7	8.3	7.0	6.8	30.1	21.6	9.5	1.1	71.9	33.4	49.2	50.9
29729	RICHBURG	69.3	68.1	28.9	29.9	0.7	0.9	1.0	1.2	6.0	6.2	7.1	7.1	6.3	29.0	25.9	11.2	1.1	76.3	38.3	50.0	50.0
29730	ROCK HILL	59.0	58.2	36.5	36.5	0.8	1.0	2.1	2.6	6.9	6.6	7.0	8.6	9.6	29.1	22.3	8.9	1.0	75.4	32.7	47.2	52.8
29732	ROCK HILL	83.0	81.8	13.2	13.8	1.5	1.8	2.3	2.8	6.9	6.9	7.1	6.3	6.0	30.4	24.8	9.8	1.8	75.0	36.6	48.3	51.7
29741	RUBY	83.5	82.9	15.4	15.7	0.2	0.2	1.1	1.5	6.6	6.2	5.5	5.7	5.8	28.5	24.6	15.7	1.5	78.7	39.5	49.6	50.4
29742	SHARON	79.5	78.0	18.9	20.2	0.1	0.1	0.9	1.1	6.9	6.8	6.5	6.7	6.6	29.1	25.6	10.8	1.0	75.7	37.1	50.8	49.2
29743	SMYRNA	89.3	88.1	8.8	9.8	0.0	0.1	1.0	1.3	6.5	6.6	7.2	6.3	6.2	29.8	26.1	10.3	1.0	75.7	37.2	51.7	48.3
29745	YORK	77.6	76.5	18.8	19.4	0.3	0.4	2.8	3.3	7.1	7.2	7.8	7.0	6.3	30.5	24.1	8.8	1.0	73.4	35.7	49.7	50.3
29801	AIKEN	55.2	54.3	42.4	42.8	0.4	0.5	1.5	1.8	6.2	6.6	7.2	7.3	7.3	25.9	23.9	13.2	2.4	76.0	37.4	47.2	52.8
29803	AIKEN	81.0	80.2	15.3	15.5	1.2	1.5	2.1	2.7	6.0	6.3	7.0	6.6	6.1	25.8	28.1	12.7	1.3	76.5	40.3	48.4	51.6
29805	AIKEN	79.7	78.9	18.1	18.5	0.3	0.4	1.1	1.4	7.3	7.4	7.9	6.6	6.3	29.9	24.8	9.0	0.7	73.3	35.6	49.6	50.5
29808	AIKEN	60.5	60.5	36.8	37.0	0.0	0.0	2.6	1.2	7.4	7.4	9.9	8.6	7.4	27.2	24.7	7.4	0.0	67.9	34.4	48.2	51.9
29809	NEW ELLENTON	62.5	61.3	33.7	34.3	0.4	0.5	2.5	3.0	5.7	5.9	6.9	6.8	6.6	28.1	25.8	13.4	1.0	77.0	38.7	48.0	52.0
29810	ALLENDALE	22.4	22.3	75.4	75.6	0.3	0.3	2.5	2.4	8.1	7.9	8.6	7.7	7.1	23.6	24.5	10.9	1.7	70.5	34.5	47.8	52.2
29812	BARNWELL	59.5	59.2	37.5	37.8	0.7	0.7	2.0	2.0	7.5	7.1	7.8	7.6	6.5	27.4	24.7	10.1	1.3	72.8	35.4	48.9	51.1
29817	BLACKVILLE	40.1	39.9	58.8	58.9	0.2	0.2	0.7	0.7	6.9	6.9	7.0	7.7	6.7	26.1	25.6	11.5	1.5	74.2	37.1	48.2	51.8
29819	BRADLEY	67.8	65.8	31.0	32.6	0.1	0.1	0.5	0.7	6.8	7.1	7.2	6.0	5.2	29.1	24.6	12.1	1.8	74.9	37.7	51.0	49.0
29821	CLARKS HILL	69.2	68.7	29.2	29.5	0.2	0.2	0.8	1.0	5.5	6.1	7.0	5.8	5.5	26.1	31.2	11.6	1.1	77.8	41.2	48.0	52.0
29824	EDGEFIELD	48.9	47.7	49.9	50.9	0.2	0.3	2.6	3.4	4.7	4.6	5.3	5.2	7.3	35.9	24.8	10.5	1.7	82.3	37.6	59.0	41.1
29827	FAIRFAX	27.1	26.7	71.9	72.3	0.1	0.1	0.5	0.5	5.5	5.5	5.8	5.9	8.9	34.2	22.9	9.4	1.9	79.7	35.5	61.1	38.9
29828	GLOVERVILLE	84.9	84.0	12.7	13.2	0.2	0.2	1.0	1.2	8.5	8.3	7.0	5.4	5.6	29.0	23.7	11.3	1.2	73.0	35.6	48.4	51.6
29829	GRANITEVILLE	67.8	67.1	28.4	28.5	0.4	0.5	2.3	2.8	8.2	7.4	7.2	7.0	7.0	26.8	24.5	10.9	1.1	73.1	35.5	48.3	51.7
29831	JACKSON	76.2	74.6	21.4	22.7	0.3	0.4	2.1	2.7	6.0	6.4	8.4	7.7	5.8	28.5	24.5	11.9	0.9	74.5	37.4	48.3	51.7
29832	JOHNSTON	46.4	45.4	51.9	52.7	0.2	0.2	2.5	3.0	7.2	7.3	6.6	7.0	7.6	26.0	25.7	11.2	1.5	74.9	36.9	48.7	51.3
29835	MC CORMICK	39.8	39.1	58.7	59.2	0.3	0.4	0.9	1.0	4.3	4.5	5.3	6.0	7.2	29.2	27.1	14.7	1.8	82.3	40.7	55.9	44.1
29836	MARTIN	22.8	22.5	75.4	75.7	0.0	0.0	1.8	1.8	5.9	6.3	6.1	7.8	5.5	23.5	29.8	12.7	2.5	77.4	41.6	48.8	51.2
29838	MODOC	61.7	60.8	37.5	38.1	0.0	0.0	0.6	0.6	4.4	5.0	6.4	5.3	5.3	24.6	32.6	14.9	1.7	80.9	44.5	47.2	52.8
29840	MOUNT CARMEL	61.6	60.5	37.0	37.8	0.6	0.8	0.9	1.0	3.1	3.5	3.4	5.6	3.0	13.0	33.1	32.2	3.2	85.6	59.2	47.7	52.3
29841	NORTH AUGUSTA	74.8	73.7	21.8	22.3	0.9	1.1	2.8	3.4	7.1	6.9	7.1	6.4	6.7	28.8	24.3	11.4	1.4	75.0	36.7	47.9	52.1
29842	BEECH ISLAND	63.4	62.4	33.9	34.5	0.4	0.5	2.6	3.1	6.5	6.6	8.5	7.7	7.0	27.8	25.2	9.7	1.0	73.7	35.7	48.9	51.1
29843	OLAR	64.7	64.4	34.1	34.3	0.3	0.3	1.1	1.0	6.5	6.5	6.1	6.1	6.1	24.7	28.6	14.0	1.5	77.2	40.8	51.3	48.7
29845	PLUM BRANCH	39.9	38.9	59.5	60.5	0.2	0.2	1.1	1.1	5.1	5.5	7.7	5.5	5.1	26.9	28.9	14.5	0.8	77.7	41.2	47.1	52.9
29847	TRENTON	49.0	47.2	48.4	49.9	0.2	0.2	2.9	3.2	5.0	5.1	5.8	9.9	13.9	28.8	23.1	7.6	1.0	80.3	32.4	59.2	40.8
29848	TROY	64.8	63.3	34.0	35.3	0.3	0.2	0.5	0.5	5.4	5.8	5.8	5.6	4.9	26.2	26.4	17.5	2.3	79.2	42.2	52.6	47.4
29849	ULMER	54.7	54.2	43.9	44.4	0.1	0.1	1.9	2.0	6.6	6.7	7.4	6.6	6.0	25.6	26.9	12.8	1.5	75.4	39.8	49.0	51.0
29851	WARRENVILLE	85.2	84.4	12.5	12.9	0.3	0.3	1.2	1.4	7.3	7.2	7.0	5.9	6.0	28.8	24.7	12.0	1.2	75.0	37.2	49.6	50.4
29853	WILLISTON	57.7	57.1	40.2	40.6	0.1	0.1	1.0	1.1	6.7	7.2	7.8	6.9	6.4	26.8	25.1	11.6	1.6	74.1	37.0	48.1	51.9
29856	WINDSOR	79.1	78.0	15.3	15.6	0.2	0.2	6.2	7.6	8.3	8.0	9.4	7.9	7.5	30.2	22.6	5.9	0.4	69.6	31.7	50.5	49.5
29860	NORTH AUGUSTA	81.3	80.9	16.6	16.6	0.7	0.8	0.9	1.2	7.1	7.5	8.1	6.9	6.1	28.4	26.7	8.3	1.0	73.0	36.9	49.0	51.0
29902	BEAUFORT	68.5	66.1	24.3	25.5	1.5	1.8	6.1	7.0	6.6	5.8	5.2	14.5	14.7	26.6	16.6	8.6	1.4	79.0	26.8	54.8	45.2
29906	BEAUFORT	59.2	56.8	33.9	35.0	1.2	1.5	6.5	7.6	11.5	8.8	7.8	7.1	14.3	32.1	13.6	4.3	0.5	68.0	25.2	52.6	47.4
29907	LADYS ISLAND	75.7	73.8	20.7	21.8	1.2	1.5	3.1	3.6	8.0	7.5	7.4	6.7	5.8	28.9	24.4	10.3	1.0	73.0	35.7	48.3	51.7
29909	OKATIE	85.2	84.5	13.0	13.3	0.3	0.4	1.8	2.2	4.1	4.3	4.4	3.4	2.8	17.1	30.3	32.4	1.2	85.0	56.7	49.0	51.0
29910	BLUFFTON	82.1	80.8	13.6	14.2	0.5	0.6	6.2	7.1	7.1	6.4	6.7	5.3	5.4	28.9	22.8	16.5	1.0	76.7	38.9	48.9	51.1
29911	BRUNSON	50.3	49.2	47.6	48.4	0.1	0.1	1.6	1.9	6.7	6.8	8.3	7.5	6.9	25.5	24.5	12.1	1.7	73.6	35.8	48.1	51.9
29916	EARLY BRANCH	45.1	44.2	53.7	54.4	0.1	0.1	1.2	1.5	7.2	7.4	7.8	7.5	6.0	25.2	25.8	11.7	1.3	72.9	36.4	47.0	53.0
29918	ESTILL	30.5	30.8	68.2	67.6	0.1	0.1	5.2	6.3	6.1	6.3	7.6	6.6	7.0	33.8	22.9	8.3	1.4	75.6	34.4	57.6	42.4
29920	SAINT HELENA ISLAND	42.0	44.5	56.0	53.3	0.3	0.4	3.6	3.7	5.0	5.4	6.7	6.4	4.9	20.4	28.1	21.8	1.3	78.7	45.8	48.1	51.9
29922	GARNETT	13.2	12.5	85.9	86.6	0.0	0.0	0.0	0.0	7.1	7.1	14.3	8.0	8.0	25.0	22.3	7.1	0.9	66.1	30.0	49.1	50.9
29924	HAMPTON	58.2	57.3	40.1	40.8	0.3	0.4	0.8	0.9	6.5	6.5	7.4	7.6	6.5	24.7	25.4	13.9	1.5	74.7	38.3	47.3	52.7
29926	HILTON HEAD ISLAND	81.3	79.3	12.1	12.5	0.6	0.7	11.5	14.6	5.0	5.1	5.5	4.8	5.5	22.1	27.6	22.3	2.2	81.5	46.6	50.4	49.6
29927	HARDEEVILLE	41.1	40.3	50.3	49.4	0.9	1.0	11.3	13.7	8.1	7.7	7.9	7.9	7.7	30.4	21.0	8.6	0.8	71.7	31.9	51.8	48.2
29928	HILTON HEAD ISLAND	91.3	89.7	3.2	3.5	0.5	0.7	10.2	12.8	3.5	3.3	3.8	3.9	5.6	23.4	30.3	23.3	2.9	87.3	50.4	50.3	49.7
29929	ISLANDTON	60.5	58.4	36.7	38.0	0.0	0.0	3.1	4.2	6.3	6.6	6.3	7.1	5.5	25.4	28.1	12.5	2.2	76.7	39.4	49.2	50.8
29932	LURAY	45.0	44.1	53.1	53.9	0.0	0.0	2.0	2.4	8.4	8.6	8.2	7.1	6.4	25.0	25.5	9.8	1.1	70.3	35.6	47.5	52.5
29934	PINELAND	17.1	17.0	82.0	82.1	0.1	0.1	0.9	0.9	6.8	7.4	8.5	7.0	5.6	24.7	26.5	11.5	2.2	73.0	37.5	47.9	52.1
29935	PORT ROYAL	64.0	61.3	30.0	31.7	1.6	1.9	3.9	4.6	7.8	6.9	6.4	6.3	9.4	33.8	18.5	9.4	1.6	75.7	31.3	47.3	52.7
29936	RIDGELAND	44.6	43.6	51.7	51.9	0.4	0.4	3.8	4.6	6.9	6.8	6.9	6.4	7.8	31.8	22.4	9.8	1.4	76.0	34.8	55.3	44.7
29940	SEABROOK	31.3	29.0	66.6	68.6	0.2	0.2	2.2	2.3	7.1	7.0	9.0	8.4	7.9	25.1	23.9	10.7	1.1	71.9	33.6	48.6	51.4
29941	SHELDON	36.1	33.5	62.3	64.5	0.0	0.0	1.1	1.5	5.6	6.1	7.6	6.6	5.6	23.9	25.9	17.3	1.5	76.7	41.0	49.2	50.8
29943	TILLMAN	47.2	46.8	50.0	49.8	0.4	0.5	2.7	3.2	7.6	7.7	7.6	6.6	6.4	27.5	25.2	10.3	1.1	73.2	36.0	50.0	50.0
29944	VARNVILLE	51.1	50.8	47.7	47.9	0.2	0.2	0.8	1.1	7.4	7.4	8.2	7.4	6.8	26.3	25.2	10.3	1.1	72.5	35.4	47.7	52.3
29945	YEMASSEE	25.6	23.5	73.3	75.2	0.2	0.2	1.0	1.1	7.1	7.1	7.8	8.6	7.0	24.8	24.2	11.9	1.5	72.4	36.0	47.5	52.5
	SOUTH CAROLINA	67.2	66.6	29.5	29.5	0.9	1.2	2.4	2.9	6.6	6.6	7.0	7.1	7.3	28.4	24.7	11.0	1.4	75.9	36.3	48.8	51.2
	UNITED STATES	75.1	73.6	12.3	12.5	3.8	4.2	12.5	14.1	6.9	6.7	7.2	7.0	7.3	28.6	23.8	10.8	1.7	75.1	36.0	49.1	50.9

#	POST OFFICE NAME	2004 Per Capita Income	2004 HH Income Base	2004 HOUSEHOLD INCOME DISTRIBUTION (%) Less than $25,000	$25,000 to $49,999	$50,000 to $99,999	$100,000 to $149,999	$150,000 or More	MEDIAN HOUSEHOLD INCOME 2004	2009	2004 National Centile	2004 State Centile	2004 Home Value Base	2004 HOME VALUE DISTRIBUTION (%) Less than $50,000	$50,000 to $89,999	$90,000 to $174,999	$175,000 to $399,999	$400,000 or More	2004 Median Home Value
29678	SENECA	19731	8483	32.2	31.0	29.3	5.6	2.0	38413	43869	41	55	6263	20.2	28.1	36.1	14.0	1.7	92477
29680	SIMPSONVILLE	26174	7807	11.9	24.4	42.2	16.8	4.7	63119	76037	87	95	6572	6.5	8.4	56.7	26.5	2.0	133994
29681	SIMPSONVILLE	34494	11894	10.8	19.4	37.6	19.9	12.5	73100	87878	92	99	10567	4.4	6.5	40.2	41.0	7.9	172260
29682	SIX MILE	20235	1348	24.0	34.6	33.8	5.0	2.7	44171	50310	59	78	1156	22.2	23.6	32.2	19.0	2.9	97619
29684	STARR	17771	1679	30.0	34.4	30.0	3.8	1.9	37337	42494	37	51	1438	28.8	34.1	28.5	7.4	1.2	75688
29685	SUNSET	21920	375	24.3	38.1	29.6	6.9	1.1	39511	44516	44	59	328	22.3	33.5	28.1	11.9	4.3	84063
29686	TAMASSEE	19482	399	31.8	31.8	29.1	4.5	2.8	38143	44166	40	53	332	26.5	23.5	29.8	19.3	0.9	90000
29687	TAYLORS	25507	15337	19.9	28.7	34.8	12.1	4.5	51100	60467	74	88	11236	8.3	14.4	55.8	20.2	1.3	122295
29688	TIGERVILLE	17213	47	25.5	40.4	29.8	4.3	0.0	44080	50000	59	77	41	19.5	12.2	39.0	22.0	7.3	122917
29689	TOWNVILLE	24860	1743	27.5	27.9	30.4	10.2	4.0	43891	52521	58	77	1478	24.6	21.2	27.5	22.4	4.3	98378
29690	TRAVELERS REST	21663	6809	26.5	30.8	31.7	7.4	3.6	42625	50293	55	73	5452	20.0	26.0	35.3	13.7	5.0	96197
29691	WALHALLA	19099	4682	34.6	31.7	27.0	5.2	1.5	36909	41966	35	47	3639	27.0	25.6	33.6	12.4	1.4	86054
29692	WARE SHOALS	18307	2254	38.2	28.0	28.0	4.6	1.2	32682	37377	20	28	1766	32.5	36.4	26.9	3.5	0.8	69586
29693	WESTMINSTER	18915	5843	30.3	36.4	26.6	5.2	1.5	36955	41801	35	48	4732	29.4	25.5	32.8	11.1	1.3	83123
29696	WEST UNION	21739	1405	23.1	29.5	38.1	7.8	1.6	45881	52317	64	82	1203	19.5	22.6	34.1	19.0	4.8	101243
29697	WILLIAMSTON	19320	4348	27.2	33.5	31.3	6.1	1.8	42504	48843	55	72	3540	23.8	30.4	33.6	10.4	1.8	85630
29702	BLACKSBURG	18896	4139	35.6	33.9	23.8	4.8	2.0	35226	40380	28	39	3270	34.0	31.4	27.2	6.8	0.7	71544
29704	CATAWBA	23081	1211	20.6	25.8	41.1	8.5	4.0	52409	60385	76	89	1018	17.4	22.2	49.0	11.2	0.2	104733
29706	CHESTER	16686	8031	34.8	32.7	26.4	5.3	0.9	34722	38718	26	37	5976	26.6	36.0	29.9	6.6	1.0	76811
29708	FORT MILL	33382	4824	11.6	21.4	37.7	18.9	10.5	71074	82484	92	98	4069	6.1	6.7	32.0	46.3	8.9	190616
29709	CHESTERFIELD	18284	2855	35.6	31.8	26.4	4.8	1.4	36507	41098	34	46	2307	37.9	30.5	25.0	6.3	0.4	65184
29710	CLOVER	26155	9651	20.5	24.8	37.8	11.4	5.5	53567	62038	78	90	7941	16.2	16.9	33.8	26.2	6.8	122869
29712	EDGEMOOR	21529	894	20.4	34.6	34.5	7.9	2.7	46218	52329	64	82	768	17.6	28.1	36.7	16.3	1.3	96875
29714	FORT LAWN	17039	1153	30.3	33.7	31.2	3.6	1.2	39240	43823	44	59	965	28.7	33.8	30.7	6.8	0.0	73688
29715	FORT MILL	25864	9026	20.7	25.6	36.5	13.3	4.0	53648	61825	78	90	7319	9.8	12.1	40.4	34.7	2.9	145862
29717	HICKORY GROVE	20087	468	27.1	30.1	33.8	7.3	1.7	44133	50754	59	77	396	28.3	33.1	27.5	10.4	0.8	78065
29718	JEFFERSON	14245	1590	43.6	29.9	23.3	2.3	0.8	29834	33842	12	14	1274	40.0	29.8	23.1	5.7	1.5	62162
29720	LANCASTER	18957	17700	31.1	32.5	28.8	5.6	2.0	38150	43168	40	54	13055	19.9	33.2	36.1	10.1	0.7	86812
29726	MC CONNELLS	23936	638	22.6	26.7	41.7	6.3	2.8	50567	57677	73	87	541	23.3	24.0	37.9	10.7	4.1	94394
29727	MOUNT CROGHAN	14326	840	39.5	40.5	17.3	2.3	0.5	31051	35468	15	20	676	53.4	28.1	9.5	7.0	2.1	47579
29728	PAGELAND	15875	3525	38.6	30.0	25.8	4.2	1.4	32324	36695	19	26	2561	36.4	32.1	25.3	5.8	0.3	68810
29729	RICHBURG	18644	970	26.4	33.7	32.1	7.0	0.8	41568	46692	52	69	826	24.7	30.0	29.1	15.6	0.6	82041
29730	ROCK HILL	20261	18910	28.2	31.6	30.8	7.3	2.2	40772	47439	49	65	11921	15.9	28.3	41.8	12.7	1.3	100356
29732	ROCK HILL	28414	17638	15.7	26.8	38.3	12.0	7.1	56259	64961	81	93	12852	6.7	12.8	46.4	30.5	3.6	142121
29741	RUBY	19230	248	38.3	31.9	22.6	6.5	0.8	33433	37711	22	31	207	34.8	33.3	16.4	15.5	0.0	68600
29742	SHARON	17755	794	27.7	32.8	32.8	4.7	2.1	40909	47430	49	66	677	30.3	29.4	30.6	7.8	1.9	79479
29743	SMYRNA	20506	492	30.5	30.9	29.9	6.3	2.4	40000	46239	46	61	417	26.1	29.7	33.8	8.9	1.4	84302
29745	YORK	19466	9139	26.7	29.0	33.9	8.4	2.0	44156	51383	59	78	7091	19.1	24.0	36.1	17.2	3.6	100621
29801	AIKEN	19737	11068	35.8	27.8	26.9	6.8	2.8	36485	42815	33	45	7841	21.5	32.1	35.0	10.0	1.4	86429
29803	AIKEN	29999	12907	18.0	22.7	35.2	16.0	8.1	60289	71341	85	94	10260	11.6	17.5	37.5	29.2	4.2	125412
29805	AIKEN	20149	1938	29.1	30.4	31.1	6.8	2.6	42695	50205	55	73	1612	30.1	27.2	30.9	9.6	2.3	81583
29808	AIKEN	17903	28	32.1	28.6	32.1	7.1	0.0	40000	46137	46	61	24	45.8	20.8	20.8	12.5	0.0	60000
29809	NEW ELLENTON	19525	976	29.8	32.5	30.2	6.1	1.4	40943	47475	49	66	784	30.7	41.8	25.1	2.2	0.1	68396
29810	ALLENDALE	12605	2119	54.5	25.7	14.8	4.2	0.9	21401	24350	2	1	1431	44.4	31.6	21.3	2.2	0.5	54939
29812	BARNWELL	19989	4887	37.0	25.6	27.4	6.9	3.2	35475	42338	29	40	3747	36.0	28.9	27.9	6.8	0.4	69330
29817	BLACKVILLE	15760	1971	46.8	27.4	18.8	5.8	1.2	27414	32217	8	6	1524	44.7	29.5	20.6	5.3	0.0	56429
29819	BRADLEY	18831	628	30.3	29.9	31.7	6.2	1.9	43465	49297	57	75	535	25.6	29.2	34.2	11.0	0.0	84574
29821	CLARKS HILL	18080	357	31.7	31.7	30.5	5.0	1.1	41471	46856	51	68	303	31.7	22.8	29.7	12.2	3.6	81000
29824	EDGEFIELD	16971	2575	34.6	30.6	25.5	6.6	2.6	35855	41191	31	43	1941	22.1	32.4	33.3	10.9	1.2	85219
29827	FAIRFAX	15554	1267	53.9	25.7	13.5	4.3	2.6	22137	25704	3	1	957	44.3	36.2	15.7	3.9	0.0	54291
29828	GLOVERVILLE	15420	430	46.1	29.5	20.9	3.3	0.2	27848	32779	8	7	312	57.4	26.6	14.1	1.9	0.0	44524
29829	GRANITEVILLE	18838	2736	32.9	30.7	27.3	7.4	1.7	40000	46625	46	61	1976	27.7	29.0	32.7	10.3	0.3	82048
29831	JACKSON	20508	1407	32.5	27.3	29.7	9.0	1.6	40761	47546	49	64	1156	29.0	39.9	25.4	5.4	0.4	73871
29832	JOHNSTON	16878	2002	38.2	30.6	24.4	5.2	1.6	32599	37731	20	27	1452	26.7	34.9	24.5	12.4	1.5	78984
29835	MC CORMICK	18795	2550	38.5	29.8	23.1	5.1	3.6	35258	40131	28	39	1982	30.3	31.8	18.4	15.3	4.2	69122
29836	MARTIN	15427	204	45.1	23.5	29.4	2.0	0.0	34216	38002	25	35	159	60.4	37.7	1.3	0.6	0.0	45000
29838	MODOC	17506	170	41.2	31.8	25.3	1.8	0.0	32345	36538	19	26	140	40.0	26.4	21.4	7.9	4.3	57000
29840	MOUNT CARMEL	23867	418	23.0	28.7	32.3	9.6	6.5	48485	58027	69	85	369	21.7	11.1	12.7	42.8	11.7	194643
29841	NORTH AUGUSTA	23464	12824	26.3	28.0	32.8	10.3	2.6	45376	54101	62	81	9082	11.1	36.0	44.5	7.6	0.9	93103
29842	BEECH ISLAND	18647	3654	33.8	27.7	28.9	7.6	2.1	37512	43896	37	51	2881	28.4	36.2	28.1	6.9	0.5	73017
29843	OLAR	17921	653	44.9	29.3	21.6	3.4	0.9	29200	33760	11	11	541	49.4	29.0	13.9	7.8	0.0	51094
29845	PLUM BRANCH	18736	541	46.8	23.3	25.1	3.9	0.9	28078	32348	9	7	466	52.4	26.2	17.0	3.7	0.9	48590
29847	TRENTON	19098	1487	29.3	30.9	28.9	8.7	2.3	40541	46310	48	63	1218	29.2	31.0	26.2	11.7	2.0	76636
29848	TROY	19080	145	29.7	28.3	31.7	6.9	3.5	44606	51148	60	79	125	25.6	24.8	26.4	19.2	4.0	89375
29849	ULMER	20723	506	42.5	31.4	19.8	2.6	3.8	29210	33477	11	11	415	39.5	35.7	13.7	8.7	2.4	61889
29851	WARRENVILLE	17409	3536	40.5	32.5	22.1	4.1	0.8	30787	36207	14	20	2752	49.4	30.5	17.6	2.4	0.1	50667
29853	WILLISTON	17627	2860	42.3	27.5	24.2	4.6	1.5	31140	36748	15	21	2247	40.8	33.3	22.3	3.4	0.3	59305
29856	WINDSOR	15908	1184	33.5	36.0	25.3	3.6	1.6	34162	40896	25	34	982	49.3	30.5	15.9	3.8	0.6	50921
29860	NORTH AUGUSTA	24315	4527	20.3	23.5	38.4	12.7	5.1	55880	63683	81	92	3968	16.1	18.4	43.9	19.9	1.8	115370
29902	BEAUFORT	21436	6234	27.7	29.2	30.4	8.1	4.6	43072	50817	56	74	3728	7.7	15.1	47.2	20.6	9.5	121474
29906	BEAUFORT	16195	7315	22.8	39.1	30.7	6.0	1.4	42440	49350	54	72	4298	26.3	23.7	37.8	11.1	1.2	90094
29907	LADYS ISLAND	31849	4063	19.4	22.7	35.9	12.6	9.4	58436	69029	83	94	3277	7.5	10.3	28.6	37.6	16.1	184221
29909	OKATIE	44972	2758	11.5	23.4	36.8	14.8	13.5	66041	81018	89	96	2439	6.8	4.3	16.2	50.9	21.8	240935
29910	BLUFFTON	30018	6457	15.4	24.3	38.7	14.0	7.7	61012	74504	85	95	4477	7.3	9.2	19.8	48.9	14.9	208832
29911	BRUNSON	15361	620	41.3	31.3	22.9	3.2	1.3	30636	35146	14	19	510	41.8	28.2	24.7	4.3	1.0	58235
29916	EARLY BRANCH	15596	653	39.1	36.0	19.6	3.8	1.5	32468	36852	19	27	544	47.1	20.0	24.8	5.3	2.8	58421
29918	ESTILL	15024	2429	45.5	27.8	20.7	3.6	2.5	28286	32136	9	8	1895	47.3	31.1	16.6	4.1	0.8	52799
29920	SAINT HELENA ISLAND	27774	4471	28.1	26.2	29.8	9.3	6.6	45275	54083	62	80	3779	18.8	14.6	21.0	26.5	19.1	153224
29922	GARNETT	9643	34	50.0	29.4	17.7	2.9	0.0	25000	32334	5	2	28	53.6	35.7	7.1	3.6	0.0	47500
29924	HAMPTON	19966	1824	36.5	30.4	25.3	5.1	2.7	35111	40563	28	39	1341	31.6	30.9	29.2	7.6	0.7	74903
29926	HILTON HEAD ISLAND	40557	9711	10.8	23.0	34.9	17.4	13.9	68878	82609	91	97	7506	3.6	4.1	11.5	44.3	36.5	341839
29927	HARDEEVILLE	19577	2590	37.4	24.3	27.2	7.4	3.8	37602	43301	38	52	1864	25.2	28.8	32.4	11.9	1.8	84859
29928	HILTON HEAD ISLAND	49651	9332	11.5	21.2	32.8	16.3	18.4	71401	86043	92	98	7076	1.7	3.0	13.3	35.6	46.4	374573
29929	ISLANDTON	15049	501	46.3	26.8	23.0	2.0	2.0	29111	33209	11	10	409	40.6	31.5	21.8	6.1	0.0	63305
29932	LURAY	15380	197	37.1	34.5	22.3	3.1	3.1	32894	36561	21	29	167	39.5	37.1	18.6	4.8	0.0	62250
29934	PINELAND	15618	501	32.7	45.3	15.6	4.8	1.6	34286	38949	25	35	417	38.9	32.9	21.8	5.8	0.7	57750
29935	PORT ROYAL	23237	1385	23.5	39.3	27.7	7.6	2.0	39915	47308	46	60	697	11.6	22.0	54.7	9.5	2.3	103096
29936	RIDGELAND	15998	3392	38.3	30.6	24.4	4.5	2.2	33366	38271	22	30	2633	29.4	24.8	31.6	9.8	4.4	84907
29940	SEABROOK	18487	1487	46.2	26.0	18.7	4.4	4.7	28526	33038	10	10	1185	30.3	32.3	20.8	12.4	4.1	76217
29941	SHELDON	30713	94	45.7	22.3	21.3	5.3	5.3	30000	36866	12	15	78	20.5	33.3	24.4	11.5	10.3	86250
29943	TILLMAN	19711	841	37.6	25.8	27.6	4.6	4.4	34093	39243	24	33	693	41.1	26.4	21.4	8.7	2.5	65351
29944	VARNVILLE	17117	1770	35.6	30.4	27.2	5.0	1.9	34789	39761	27	37	1407	32.8	32.7	29.1	4.6	0.9	73423
29945	YEMASSEE	16345	1672	44.9	26.6	20.7	5.6	2.2	28772	33022	10	10	1349	38.9	30.4	22.7	5.2	2.8	67181
	SOUTH CAROLINA	22607		28.8	29.3	29.6	8.3	4.0	42042	49103				19.3	24.1	35.5	17.1	3.9	100170
	UNITED STATES	25866		24.7	27.1	30.8	10.9	6.5	48124	56710				10.9	15.0	33.7	30.1	10.4	145905

ZIP CODE #	POST OFFICE NAME	FINANCIAL SERVICES: Auto Loan	Home Loan	Invest-ments	Retire-ment Plans	THE HOME: Home Improvements: Home Repair	Lawn & Garden	Furnishings: Comput-ers & Hard-ware	Major Appli-ances	TV, Radio, Sound Equip-ment	Furni-ture	ENTERTAINMENT: Dine out/ Carry out	Sports Equip-ment	Fees & Tickets	Toys & Games	Travel	Cable TV	PERSONAL: Apparel & Services	Auto Repairs	Health Insur-ance	Pets & Supplies
29678	SENECA	76	62	46	59	66	74	61	68	67	61	81	79	58	80	62	70	76	67	77	86
29680	SIMPSONVILLE	109	115	106	117	112	112	106	108	101	109	127	126	107	127	104	97	124	106	98	122
29681	SIMPSONVILLE	133	148	148	151	145	145	136	136	128	138	161	160	140	164	135	123	159	133	124	153
29682	SIX MILE	91	73	48	67	79	87	68	79	76	69	91	94	64	91	70	79	85	77	90	106
29684	STARR	84	59	30	52	66	75	57	69	67	58	79	83	50	76	58	72	72	69	84	97
29685	SUNSET	94	63	28	54	71	82	61	76	73	62	86	91	52	81	62	79	78	75	93	108
29686	TAMASSEE	84	67	46	61	74	83	63	74	70	62	84	88	57	83	66	75	78	73	87	101
29687	TAYLORS	90	91	91	91	91	95	89	90	88	89	109	106	89	111	89	86	106	90	87	104
29688	TIGERVILLE	72	64	49	61	67	72	59	65	63	59	76	78	58	78	61	64	72	64	71	84
29689	TOWNVILLE	98	78	54	71	87	97	74	87	82	73	98	102	66	96	78	87	91	86	102	118
29690	TRAVELERS REST	93	82	64	78	84	90	78	85	82	79	100	101	75	98	78	83	96	85	89	106
29691	WALHALLA	84	62	35	55	68	77	59	71	68	60	81	84	52	78	60	72	74	70	83	97
29692	WARE SHOALS	82	55	25	47	62	71	53	66	64	54	75	79	45	71	54	69	68	65	82	94
29693	WESTMINSTER	79	60	38	54	65	73	58	68	65	59	78	81	52	75	59	69	72	67	79	91
29696	WEST UNION	88	76	56	72	81	87	71	79	76	71	92	94	69	93	73	78	87	77	87	103
29697	WILLIAMSTON	82	69	49	64	72	80	66	74	71	67	87	86	62	85	67	74	82	73	81	94
29702	BLACKSBURG	84	61	34	55	67	75	59	71	68	60	81	83	52	76	59	71	74	70	82	96
29704	CATAWBA	101	90	69	86	92	98	86	93	88	87	108	108	81	104	85	88	104	92	95	114
29706	CHESTER	69	55	42	50	58	66	56	62	62	56	75	72	52	73	56	65	71	62	71	78
29708	FORT MILL	125	148	150	151	143	140	133	132	122	135	155	154	139	160	133	116	154	128	115	145
29709	CHESTERFIELD	80	56	29	50	62	72	55	66	64	55	76	78	48	72	55	69	69	65	80	91
29710	CLOVER	105	96	78	92	97	105	91	98	93	93	115	112	87	108	91	94	110	97	101	117
29712	EDGEMOOR	91	79	58	75	81	87	75	83	79	77	96	97	70	92	75	79	91	82	86	102
29714	FORT LAWN	78	63	41	58	66	72	60	68	65	61	79	80	54	74	60	67	74	68	75	88
29715	FORT MILL	95	100	92	99	98	101	93	95	90	94	113	110	94	114	92	89	110	93	90	108
29717	HICKORY GROVE	100	67	30	58	76	88	65	81	78	66	92	97	55	87	66	84	84	80	100	115
29718	JEFFERSON	69	46	21	40	52	60	45	56	54	45	63	67	38	60	45	58	57	55	69	79
29720	LANCASTER	77	65	50	60	68	75	63	70	69	63	83	81	60	81	64	71	78	69	77	88
29726	MC CONNELLS	108	97	74	92	100	107	90	99	94	91	115	117	87	115	92	95	110	97	104	124
29727	MOUNT CROGHAN	67	45	20	39	51	58	43	54	52	44	61	65	37	58	44	56	56	53	67	77
29728	PAGELAND	73	55	35	49	59	66	54	62	61	55	73	74	48	70	54	64	68	62	72	82
29729	RICHBURG	89	63	33	56	70	80	61	74	72	62	85	88	54	81	62	76	78	73	88	101
29730	ROCK HILL	77	72	70	70	72	78	73	75	75	73	93	87	72	91	72	75	90	75	76	87
29732	ROCK HILL	100	107	113	110	106	109	104	103	100	104	126	121	106	127	103	97	123	103	97	116
29741	RUBY	80	53	24	46	60	70	51	64	62	52	73	77	44	69	52	67	66	64	79	91
29742	SHARON	86	65	39	59	70	78	62	73	70	64	84	86	56	79	63	73	78	73	83	97
29743	SMYRNA	93	70	42	64	76	84	68	79	76	69	91	94	60	86	68	79	85	79	90	105
29745	YORK	83	75	62	72	76	82	73	78	76	74	93	90	70	90	73	76	89	77	80	93
29801	AIKEN	74	65	57	61	67	74	65	70	69	66	85	80	62	81	65	71	81	70	75	83
29803	AIKEN	103	111	113	110	111	115	105	107	102	106	128	124	107	128	106	101	125	106	103	121
29805	AIKEN	84	76	59	73	76	81	73	78	74	75	91	90	69	86	72	73	87	78	77	93
29808	AIKEN	82	75	59	72	75	79	72	77	73	74	90	89	68	85	71	72	86	77	76	91
29809	NEW ELLENTON	81	67	46	62	71	78	63	72	69	63	83	85	59	82	64	71	78	70	80	94
29810	ALLENDALE	51	39	34	35	40	48	42	46	48	43	58	51	39	53	41	52	54	46	54	56
29812	BARNWELL	85	66	45	61	70	79	65	74	73	66	88	87	60	84	65	76	82	74	84	96
29817	BLACKVILLE	73	50	28	43	55	65	50	60	60	51	70	70	43	66	50	64	64	60	73	82
29819	BRADLEY	80	72	55	68	72	77	68	74	70	70	86	86	64	82	68	70	82	74	75	89
29821	CLARKS HILL	85	63	36	57	68	77	61	72	69	62	82	85	54	78	61	72	76	71	83	97
29824	EDGEFIELD	68	54	40	50	57	65	54	60	60	54	72	70	50	69	54	63	68	60	69	77
29827	FAIRFAX	55	37	17	32	41	48	35	44	43	36	50	53	30	47	36	46	46	44	54	63
29828	GLOVERVILLE	67	45	20	39	51	59	43	54	52	44	61	65	37	58	44	56	56	54	67	77
29829	GRANITEVILLE	78	63	51	58	67	75	63	70	69	64	84	82	59	82	63	72	79	70	78	89
29831	JACKSON	81	70	53	67	72	78	69	75	72	70	88	86	65	83	68	72	83	75	78	89
29832	JOHNSTON	74	57	35	51	62	69	54	64	62	55	74	76	50	72	55	65	69	63	74	86
29835	MC CORMICK	73	55	38	49	60	70	54	63	62	55	74	71	49	67	55	67	68	63	76	83
29836	MARTIN	69	47	21	40	53	61	45	56	54	46	64	67	38	60	46	58	58	56	69	80
29838	MODOC	70	47	21	41	53	61	45	57	55	46	64	68	39	61	46	59	58	56	70	81
29840	MOUNT CARMEL	96	90	86	85	95	112	83	95	88	89	110	93	84	91	91	94	103	92	111	108
29841	NORTH AUGUSTA	79	80	81	80	80	86	79	80	79	79	98	93	79	98	79	79	95	80	80	91
29842	BEECH ISLAND	77	68	55	65	68	74	67	71	69	68	85	83	63	81	66	69	82	72	73	85
29843	OLAR	80	55	26	48	61	70	53	65	63	54	74	78	45	70	54	67	68	65	79	92
29845	PLUM BRANCH	83	55	25	48	63	72	53	67	65	54	76	80	45	72	54	69	69	66	82	95
29847	TRENTON	91	70	43	63	74	82	67	78	74	68	89	92	60	84	67	77	83	77	88	102
29848	TROY	77	70	59	67	72	79	66	73	68	69	84	80	64	77	68	69	80	72	76	85
29849	ULMER	93	62	28	54	71	81	60	75	73	61	85	90	51	81	61	78	78	75	93	107
29851	WARRENVILLE	77	53	26	47	60	68	51	63	61	53	72	75	44	68	52	65	66	63	77	88
29853	WILLISTON	82	56	26	48	63	72	54	67	64	55	76	80	46	72	54	69	69	66	82	95
29856	WINDSOR	70	63	49	60	63	67	60	65	61	62	75	75	57	71	59	60	72	64	65	77
29860	NORTH AUGUSTA	101	103	94	101	104	107	95	100	94	96	116	117	95	117	96	93	113	98	97	117
29902	BEAUFORT	85	79	79	80	79	86	84	84	85	83	105	99	82	103	82	84	101	86	84	95
29906	BEAUFORT	77	67	59	68	66	70	72	71	72	71	89	86	67	85	68	69	86	74	68	82
29907	LADYS ISLAND	113	130	139	133	127	126	121	120	113	123	143	140	125	145	121	108	141	118	107	131
29909	OKATIE	138	131	127	125	138	160	121	136	127	129	158	136	123	135	131	134	149	133	156	155
29910	BLUFFTON	113	115	107	113	115	122	106	112	104	110	131	124	107	123	108	104	126	109	112	127
29911	BRUNSON	74	50	23	43	56	65	48	60	58	49	68	72	41	64	49	62	62	60	74	85
29916	EARLY BRANCH	74	50	23	43	57	65	48	60	58	49	68	72	41	64	49	63	62	60	74	85
29918	ESTILL	59	47	37	44	49	56	49	53	54	49	66	63	45	63	49	56	62	54	59	67
29920	SAINT HELENA ISLAND	105	96	80	92	98	108	91	100	94	94	116	110	88	107	93	96	110	98	106	117
29922	GARNETT	60	40	18	35	45	52	39	48	47	39	55	58	33	52	39	50	50	48	60	69
29924	HAMPTON	82	62	38	57	67	77	61	71	69	61	83	83	55	80	62	73	76	70	82	93
29926	HILTON HEAD ISLAND	145	138	143	138	141	158	136	143	137	141	172	154	136	154	139	139	164	143	151	161
29927	HARDEEVILLE	83	74	62	72	75	82	75	79	78	75	96	91	72	92	74	78	91	79	81	92
29928	HILTON HEAD ISLAND	157	150	158	145	156	177	145	156	151	149	187	168	145	172	152	157	178	155	172	181
29929	ISLANDTON	75	50	23	43	57	66	49	61	59	49	69	73	41	65	49	63	63	60	75	86
29932	LURAY	81	54	24	47	61	70	52	65	63	53	74	78	44	70	53	68	67	65	80	93
29934	PINELAND	67	57	41	53	58	63	54	60	57	56	69	70	50	66	54	57	66	60	63	74
29935	PORT ROYAL	77	61	62	66	58	64	76	69	75	73	94	87	69	89	68	70	91	76	64	78
29936	RIDGELAND	74	60	43	56	63	70	60	66	65	60	79	78	55	76	59	67	74	66	73	83
29940	SEABROOK	88	73	50	68	75	82	70	78	74	71	90	91	64	85	69	75	85	78	83	98
29941	SHELDON	121	81	37	70	92	106	78	98	95	80	111	117	67	105	80	102	101	97	121	139
29943	TILLMAN	79	68	60	64	68	77	70	74	75	72	91	83	66	84	68	77	87	75	79	87
29944	VARNVILLE	81	58	31	51	64	72	55	67	64	56	76	80	49	73	56	68	70	66	80	93
29945	YEMASSEE	72	56	40	51	59	67	56	63	63	57	75	73	51	70	56	66	71	63	72	81
	SOUTH CAROLINA	87	78	69	75	80	87	77	82	81	78	99	95	74	96	77	82	95	82	86	99
	UNITED STATES	100	100	100	100	100	100	100	100	100	100	100	100	100	100	100	100	100	100	100	100

ZIP CODE		COUNTY FIPS CODE	POPULATION			2000-2004 ANNUAL RATE		HOUSEHOLDS					FAMILIES		
#	POST OFFICE NAME		2000	2004	2009	% Rate	State Centile	2000	2004	2009	% Annual Rate 2000-2004	2004 Average HH Size	2000	2004	% Annual Rate 2000-2004
57001	ALCESTER	127	2070	2163	2343	1.0	78	807	854	940	1.3	2.45	570	605	1.4
57002	AURORA	011	888	851	864	-1.0	5	353	345	357	-0.5	2.46	256	252	-0.4
57003	BALTIC	099	1654	1951	2228	4.0	98	606	728	844	4.4	2.68	484	579	4.3
57004	BERESFORD	083	3170	3290	3622	0.9	74	1272	1339	1493	1.2	2.42	879	923	1.2
57005	BRANDON	099	6985	8047	9084	3.4	96	2340	2759	3167	4.0	2.90	1955	2302	3.9
57006	BROOKINGS	011	19134	19840	20639	0.9	73	7926	8379	8885	1.3	2.23	4160	4436	1.5
57007	BROOKINGS	011	1904	1902	1907	0.0	47	4	4	4	0.0	2.50	3	3	0.0
57010	BURBANK	027	454	481	498	1.4	84	176	190	198	1.8	2.53	134	145	1.9
57012	CANISTOTA	087	1319	1377	1437	1.0	78	474	497	522	1.1	2.67	348	366	1.2
57013	CANTON	083	4258	4232	5093	-0.1	41	1615	1619	1975	0.1	2.55	1155	1151	-0.1
57014	CENTERVILLE	125	1482	1488	1554	0.1	52	615	627	664	0.5	2.32	420	430	0.6
57015	CHANCELLOR	125	873	918	969	1.2	82	323	343	367	1.4	2.64	239	255	1.5
57016	CHESTER	079	956	995	1062	1.0	76	349	370	401	1.4	2.69	274	290	1.3
57017	COLMAN	101	1263	1389	1453	2.3	92	470	528	561	2.8	2.63	349	392	2.8
57018	COLTON	099	1384	1466	1584	1.4	84	509	546	597	1.7	2.66	383	409	1.6
57020	CROOKS	099	1222	1422	1610	3.6	97	410	490	566	4.3	2.80	338	402	4.2
57021	DAVIS	125	294	292	302	-0.2	40	123	123	128	0.0	2.37	88	88	0.0
57022	DELL RAPIDS	099	4107	4501	4933	2.2	91	1499	1672	1859	2.6	2.62	1095	1217	2.5
57024	EGAN	101	654	649	649	-0.2	38	240	242	245	0.2	2.67	165	167	0.3
57025	ELK POINT	127	3027	3280	3590	1.9	89	1166	1285	1428	2.3	2.51	837	924	2.4
57026	ELKTON	011	1298	1408	1504	1.9	89	472	518	560	2.2	2.71	345	380	2.3
57027	FAIRVIEW	083	194	212	256	2.1	91	58	64	78	2.3	3.22	40	44	2.3
57028	FLANDREAU	101	3538	3430	3379	-0.7	16	1395	1376	1372	-0.3	2.45	929	917	-0.3
57029	FREEMAN	067	2161	2149	2147	-0.1	42	899	906	913	0.2	2.29	603	611	0.3
57030	GARRETSON	099	2692	2750	2904	0.5	63	909	943	1013	0.9	2.67	698	722	0.8
57031	GAYVILLE	135	664	650	650	-0.5	24	261	260	263	-0.1	2.50	185	184	-0.1
57032	HARRISBURG	083	2747	3479	4569	5.7	99	962	1256	1682	6.5	2.77	778	1007	6.3
57033	HARTFORD	099	3829	4250	4707	2.5	94	1308	1480	1664	3.0	2.84	1086	1225	2.9
57034	HUDSON	083	784	854	1031	2.0	90	291	320	391	2.3	2.59	201	220	2.2
57035	HUMBOLDT	099	1101	1127	1197	0.6	65	397	415	447	1.1	2.71	312	325	1.0
57036	HURLEY	125	899	898	928	0.0	46	357	360	376	0.2	2.49	263	266	0.3
57037	IRENE	135	1058	1068	1085	0.2	57	396	405	418	0.5	2.53	283	291	0.7
57038	JEFFERSON	127	1352	1494	1652	2.4	93	506	570	641	2.8	2.62	370	418	2.9
57039	LENNOX	083	3156	3241	3798	0.6	68	1224	1279	1522	1.0	2.48	864	892	0.8
57040	LESTERVILLE	135	429	432	435	0.2	55	160	164	168	0.6	2.63	127	130	0.6
57042	MADISON	079	8006	8360	8910	1.0	78	3143	3350	3647	1.5	2.29	1911	2044	1.5
57043	MARION	125	1543	1636	1733	1.4	85	581	625	671	1.7	2.52	417	450	1.8
57044	MECKLING	027	222	227	227	0.5	64	96	100	101	1.0	2.27	73	76	1.0
57045	MENNO	067	1327	1318	1313	-0.2	40	519	525	528	0.3	2.39	362	367	0.3
57046	MISSION HILL	135	840	862	881	0.6	67	313	326	337	1.0	2.63	227	236	0.9
57047	MONROE	125	219	225	234	0.6	69	94	98	103	1.0	2.27	75	78	0.9
57048	MONTROSE	087	1105	1138	1181	0.7	71	404	422	442	1.0	2.70	309	324	1.1
57049	NORTH SIOUX CITY	127	4263	4771	5311	2.7	94	1668	1906	2157	3.2	2.50	1206	1380	3.2
57050	NUNDA	079	314	315	330	0.1	51	123	126	135	0.6	2.37	88	90	0.5
57051	OLDHAM	077	403	432	448	1.7	87	171	188	198	2.3	2.27	114	125	2.2
57052	OLIVET	067	466	458	454	-0.4	28	158	157	158	-0.2	2.92	124	123	-0.2
57053	PARKER	125	1789	1874	1973	1.1	80	706	749	798	1.4	2.47	518	550	1.4
57054	RAMONA	079	577	584	613	0.3	59	237	245	262	0.8	2.32	174	179	0.7
57055	RENNER	099	933	1029	1136	2.3	93	337	378	424	2.7	2.72	266	297	2.6
57056	ROWENA	099	69	79	89	3.2	96	27	31	36	3.3	2.55	24	28	3.7
57057	RUTLAND	079	107	108	112	0.2	57	39	40	43	0.6	2.55	28	28	0.0
57058	SALEM	087	2059	2109	2182	0.6	66	806	838	876	0.9	2.44	539	563	1.0
57059	SCOTLAND	009	1497	1499	1499	0.0	50	593	602	609	0.4	2.23	385	391	0.4
57062	SPRINGFIELD	009	2069	2043	2037	-0.3	33	543	543	549	0.0	2.42	381	383	0.1
57063	TABOR	009	913	935	945	0.6	66	352	366	376	0.9	2.55	257	268	1.0
57064	TEA	083	2825	3509	4517	5.2	99	929	1178	1540	5.8	2.98	768	974	5.8
57065	TRENT	101	709	698	692	-0.4	30	263	264	266	0.1	2.60	199	200	0.1
57066	TYNDALL	009	1791	1809	1817	0.2	58	721	738	750	0.6	2.35	467	479	0.6
57067	UTICA	135	633	627	629	-0.2	36	214	217	220	0.3	2.89	164	166	0.3
57068	VALLEY SPRINGS	099	1524	1621	1756	1.5	85	525	567	622	1.8	2.86	420	452	1.7
57069	VERMILLION	027	11349	11300	11275	-0.1	43	4061	4108	4128	0.3	2.24	2118	2147	0.3
57070	VIBORG	125	1412	1489	1573	1.3	83	580	625	672	1.8	2.29	370	399	1.8
57071	VOLGA	011	2456	2515	2599	0.6	66	950	988	1037	0.9	2.54	713	744	1.0
57072	VOLIN	135	673	706	724	1.1	80	254	271	282	1.5	2.61	196	210	1.6
57073	WAKONDA	027	745	752	753	0.2	57	266	273	275	0.6	2.49	188	193	0.6
57075	WENTWORTH	079	847	956	1064	2.9	95	339	393	447	3.5	2.42	247	287	3.6
57076	WINFRED	079	404	493	571	4.8	99	128	159	188	5.2	3.10	99	123	5.2
57077	WORTHING	083	1008	1174	1471	3.7	97	367	432	546	3.9	2.72	290	338	3.7
57078	YANKTON	135	17859	18283	18584	0.6	65	6787	7015	7239	0.8	2.34	4354	4519	0.9
57103	SIOUX FALLS	099	32847	35013	38156	1.5	86	12643	13698	15127	1.9	2.54	8675	9373	1.8
57104	SIOUX FALLS	099	26022	26413	28001	0.4	60	11258	11597	12502	0.7	2.09	5368	5509	0.6
57105	SIOUX FALLS	099	24194	24312	25757	0.1	53	10214	10520	11373	0.7	2.19	6261	6390	0.5
57106	SIOUX FALLS	099	27526	31185	35283	3.0	95	10988	12654	14499	3.4	2.44	7058	8142	3.4
57107	SIOUX FALLS	099	5125	6351	7433	5.2	99	1922	2443	2910	5.8	2.59	1430	1811	5.7
57108	SIOUX FALLS	083	6070	9462	13482	11.0	100	2213	3525	5099	11.6	2.68	1703	2712	11.6
57110	SIOUX FALLS	099	8446	10230	11852	4.6	98	2853	3506	4112	5.0	2.90	2334	2856	4.9
57197	SIOUX FALLS	099	773	814	850	1.2	82	5	6	8	4.4	2.50	4	5	5.4
57201	WATERTOWN	029	23494	23469	23445	0.0	46	9492	9632	9771	0.4	2.39	6187	6296	0.4
57212	ARLINGTON	077	2173	2144	2151	-0.3	32	872	873	888	0.0	2.39	597	599	0.1
57213	ASTORIA	039	491	471	455	-1.0	6	206	202	199	-0.5	2.33	137	135	-0.4
57216	BIG STONE CITY	051	890	861	843	-0.8	14	361	358	357	-0.2	2.37	249	248	-0.1
57217	BRADLEY	025	394	381	368	-0.8	12	145	142	139	-0.5	2.61	103	101	-0.5
57218	BRANDT	039	609	588	571	-0.8	10	238	235	233	-0.3	2.50	166	164	-0.3
57219	BRISTOL	037	625	641	650	0.6	67	265	279	287	1.2	2.16	167	175	1.1
57220	BRUCE	011	854	825	839	-0.8	10	333	326	337	-0.5	2.53	258	254	-0.4
57221	BRYANT	057	696	694	725	-0.1	44	266	266	279	0.2	2.52	180	181	0.1
57223	CASTLEWOOD	057	1183	1362	1522	3.4	96	420	492	556	3.8	2.73	321	375	3.7
57224	CLAIRE CITY	109	324	322	343	-0.2	41	128	130	141	0.4	2.48	101	103	0.5
57225	CLARK	025	2060	2010	1950	-0.6	22	807	794	776	-0.4	2.45	532	525	-0.3
57226	CLEAR LAKE	039	1939	1898	1857	-0.5	24	795	789	784	-0.2	2.32	525	524	-0.1
57227	CORONA	109	772	826	899	1.6	87	313	342	378	2.1	2.42	217	237	2.1
57231	DE SMET	077	1827	1820	1815	-0.1	44	784	799	813	0.5	2.19	497	507	0.5
57232	EDEN	091	296	297	299	0.1	52	121	123	126	0.4	2.41	87	88	0.4
57233	ERWIN	077	179	177	176	-0.3	34	70	71	72	0.3	2.49	53	54	0.4
57234	ESTELLINE	057	1388	1419	1484	0.5	64	554	573	605	0.8	2.39	379	393	0.9
	SOUTH DAKOTA					0.9					1.3	2.47			1.4
	UNITED STATES					1.2					1.3	2.58			1.1

ZIP CODE #	POST OFFICE NAME	RACE (%) White 2000	White 2004	Black 2000	Black 2004	Asian/Pacific 2000	Asian/Pacific 2004	% Hispanic Origin 2000	% Hispanic Origin 2004	2004 AGE DISTRIBUTION (%) 0-4	5-9	10-14	15-19	20-24	25-44	45-64	65-84	85+	18+	MEDIAN AGE 2004	% 2004 Males	% 2004 Females
57001	ALCESTER	98.7	98.5	0.0	0.0	0.6	0.8	0.2	0.2	4.7	5.5	7.8	7.3	4.7	23.4	26.0	16.4	4.4	76.8	43.0	48.4	51.6
57002	AURORA	98.0	97.8	0.0	0.0	0.1	0.2	1.0	0.9	6.8	6.6	6.5	6.4	7.1	29.0	27.0	9.8	0.9	76.4	37.1	52.3	47.7
57003	BALTIC	98.9	98.8	0.0	0.0	0.2	0.2	0.1	0.1	7.6	8.1	8.8	6.9	5.4	31.2	23.2	7.8	1.0	71.3	34.5	51.6	48.4
57004	BERESFORD	98.9	98.8	0.1	0.1	0.3	0.3	0.5	0.6	6.3	6.4	7.2	7.0	6.6	23.8	25.2	14.1	3.5	75.8	39.6	49.4	50.6
57005	BRANDON	98.3	97.9	0.3	0.4	0.3	0.4	0.4	0.6	9.4	8.7	8.9	7.8	5.8	30.6	22.1	6.1	0.8	68.0	32.5	49.3	50.7
57006	BROOKINGS	95.4	94.4	0.4	0.5	1.9	2.6	0.9	1.0	5.9	5.0	5.0	7.6	23.4	24.9	18.0	8.1	2.1	81.0	26.7	50.3	49.7
57007	BROOKINGS	99.0	98.6	0.1	0.1	0.4	0.5	0.2	0.3	0.4	0.3	1.2	55.3	37.1	2.9	2.5	0.4	0.0	97.7	19.4	49.1	51.0
57010	BURBANK	97.1	96.7	0.2	0.2	0.7	0.8	0.4	0.6	7.3	7.3	7.1	5.8	5.0	26.0	29.9	10.6	1.0	74.6	39.5	52.2	47.8
57012	CANISTOTA	98.4	98.2	0.1	0.2	0.2	0.2	1.0	1.0	7.3	7.1	8.9	7.9	4.9	23.6	22.9	13.3	4.1	71.7	39.1	50.8	49.2
57013	CANTON	97.8	97.4	0.3	0.3	0.5	0.6	0.4	0.5	7.4	7.2	7.4	7.5	6.2	26.1	23.6	11.8	2.9	73.0	36.9	49.6	50.4
57014	CENTERVILLE	99.2	99.1	0.1	0.1	0.1	0.2	0.5	0.5	5.0	5.2	6.7	7.7	6.1	22.7	25.6	17.3	3.8	78.0	42.9	49.4	50.6
57015	CHANCELLOR	98.2	98.0	0.3	0.3	0.1	0.2	0.5	0.5	6.2	7.0	7.2	6.6	5.7	26.6	25.2	13.0	2.6	75.0	39.0	50.7	49.4
57016	CHESTER	98.3	98.2	0.0	0.0	0.3	0.4	0.2	0.2	6.2	6.3	7.0	7.0	6.4	23.9	28.4	13.7	0.9	76.1	40.7	50.4	49.7
57017	COLMAN	97.0	96.9	0.3	0.4	0.5	0.5	0.7	0.7	6.4	6.8	8.4	8.4	6.8	26.7	25.3	9.7	1.5	72.6	36.3	51.1	48.9
57018	COLTON	99.2	99.2	0.0	0.0	0.1	0.1	0.7	0.8	7.6	7.0	7.5	7.2	5.5	27.2	23.3	12.6	2.2	73.6	37.8	51.2	48.8
57020	CROOKS	96.6	96.1	0.7	0.8	0.2	0.2	1.0	1.2	7.0	7.9	9.1	9.6	7.1	29.8	23.8	4.9	0.9	69.3	32.1	52.5	47.5
57021	DAVIS	99.7	99.3	0.0	0.0	0.3	0.3	0.0	0.0	7.5	7.9	6.9	5.5	4.5	25.7	27.1	12.7	2.4	73.6	39.7	50.3	49.7
57022	DELL RAPIDS	98.5	98.2	0.1	0.2	0.2	0.3	0.6	0.7	7.3	7.4	8.2	7.5	6.3	26.1	22.3	11.6	3.2	72.0	36.4	49.0	51.0
57024	EGAN	80.3	79.4	0.2	0.2	0.2	0.2	0.8	0.8	6.9	7.2	7.7	8.0	6.8	25.4	25.1	10.8	2.0	72.9	36.4	49.9	50.1
57025	ELK POINT	98.4	98.1	0.3	0.3	0.3	0.5	0.8	1.0	7.6	7.9	8.1	6.3	5.1	26.8	24.8	11.2	2.1	72.5	37.4	49.7	50.3
57026	ELKTON	98.3	98.3	0.1	0.1	0.1	0.1	1.0	1.0	5.8	6.2	7.6	9.2	7.1	24.4	25.6	11.4	2.8	74.1	38.4	50.6	49.4
57027	FAIRVIEW	99.0	98.6	0.0	0.0	0.0	0.0	1.0	0.9	6.6	7.1	8.5	8.0	5.7	26.4	23.1	11.3	3.3	71.7	38.3	51.9	48.1
57028	FLANDREAU	77.3	75.5	0.3	0.4	0.8	0.8	0.9	0.9	6.6	6.4	7.1	9.0	7.1	23.1	23.9	13.5	3.4	74.0	38.0	49.1	50.9
57029	FREEMAN	99.4	99.3	0.1	0.1	0.1	0.1	0.2	0.2	5.4	5.4	6.3	6.3	5.4	20.1	25.0	20.2	5.9	78.6	45.7	47.7	52.3
57030	GARRETSON	98.0	97.7	0.1	0.2	0.2	0.3	0.3	0.5	6.7	6.9	7.4	7.4	6.3	26.6	24.4	11.7	2.7	74.0	38.7	49.8	50.2
57031	GAYVILLE	97.4	97.2	0.0	0.0	0.3	0.3	0.5	0.5	7.2	7.7	7.7	6.6	4.8	25.7	27.9	10.8	1.7	73.2	39.2	52.2	47.9
57032	HARRISBURG	98.1	97.6	0.3	0.3	0.5	0.7	0.6	0.7	7.9	8.0	7.8	7.4	6.4	30.6	24.8	6.5	0.6	71.6	34.6	50.7	49.4
57033	HARTFORD	98.4	98.1	0.1	0.1	0.1	0.1	0.4	0.4	7.1	8.1	9.6	8.6	5.2	29.2	23.6	7.4	1.3	69.3	34.9	50.2	49.8
57034	HUDSON	98.7	98.7	0.0	0.0	0.0	0.0	0.5	0.6	6.8	7.0	8.4	7.7	5.7	25.9	23.3	11.6	3.5	71.9	38.2	50.9	49.1
57035	HUMBOLDT	98.0	97.5	0.0	0.0	0.6	0.8	0.1	0.1	7.9	8.0	9.1	6.9	5.2	28.7	23.1	10.2	1.0	70.5	35.9	50.1	49.9
57036	HURLEY	99.6	99.4	0.0	0.0	0.2	0.3	0.1	0.1	7.2	7.5	7.5	5.8	4.7	24.6	27.4	13.4	2.0	74.1	40.2	50.9	49.1
57037	IRENE	98.9	98.9	0.0	0.0	0.0	0.0	0.8	0.8	5.8	5.9	8.2	7.5	5.2	24.2	24.3	14.8	4.1	75.0	40.9	50.9	49.1
57038	JEFFERSON	96.2	95.5	0.7	0.9	1.2	1.6	1.6	1.7	6.6	7.1	8.2	7.0	5.5	28.5	27.0	9.5	0.7	73.7	36.9	50.8	49.2
57039	LENNOX	98.7	98.7	0.2	0.2	0.1	0.1	0.7	0.7	6.8	7.0	7.4	6.4	6.0	26.5	24.5	12.3	3.3	74.5	38.5	48.4	51.6
57040	LESTERVILLE	98.1	98.2	0.0	0.0	0.2	0.2	0.9	0.9	6.7	7.6	9.3	6.3	4.4	25.0	27.1	12.3	1.4	72.5	39.8	52.6	47.5
57042	MADISON	97.4	96.9	0.2	0.3	0.7	1.0	0.9	1.0	5.7	5.5	6.1	10.7	11.6	22.1	21.6	13.4	3.3	78.5	35.1	49.3	50.7
57043	MARION	98.6	98.3	0.2	0.2	0.2	0.3	1.0	1.2	5.0	5.6	8.2	7.3	5.8	20.1	26.3	17.5	4.3	76.0	43.7	50.0	50.0
57044	MECKLING	98.7	98.2	0.0	0.0	0.0	0.0	0.0	0.0	7.1	7.5	6.2	5.7	5.3	23.4	28.2	15.4	1.3	75.8	41.2	52.0	48.0
57045	MENNO	98.9	98.9	0.1	0.1	0.1	0.1	0.2	0.2	5.2	6.5	6.2	5.9	4.9	18.8	24.1	22.5	5.8	78.1	46.8	49.6	50.4
57046	MISSION HILL	97.0	96.6	0.1	0.1	0.2	0.4	1.0	1.0	7.3	7.4	8.5	7.0	5.7	26.3	26.3	9.9	1.6	72.3	37.2	52.4	47.6
57047	MONROE	98.2	98.2	0.5	0.4	0.5	0.4	0.5	0.4	4.9	6.2	8.0	7.1	7.1	25.8	27.1	12.0	1.8	76.0	39.1	53.8	46.2
57048	MONTROSE	99.3	99.1	0.0	0.1	0.1	0.1	0.6	0.7	8.0	7.7	9.1	7.5	5.9	25.2	22.4	12.4	1.9	70.5	36.4	50.4	49.6
57049	NORTH SIOUX CITY	94.0	92.8	0.5	0.6	3.0	4.0	2.3	2.5	7.8	7.6	7.7	6.4	6.5	29.6	25.0	8.7	0.6	72.9	35.4	50.8	49.2
57050	NUNDA	98.4	98.4	0.3	0.3	0.3	0.3	0.3	0.3	5.7	5.7	5.7	6.4	6.0	23.8	27.9	16.2	2.5	77.5	43.0	51.8	48.3
57051	OLDHAM	98.3	98.6	0.3	0.2	0.3	0.2	1.0	0.9	6.0	6.7	7.6	6.9	4.6	18.5	25.5	20.8	3.2	75.0	44.7	49.1	50.9
57052	OLIVET	99.1	99.1	0.0	0.0	0.2	0.2	0.2	0.2	7.9	7.9	7.9	7.0	6.1	23.1	26.4	12.7	1.1	72.1	38.0	53.1	46.9
57053	PARKER	98.2	97.9	0.3	0.3	0.2	0.3	0.4	0.4	6.6	7.0	7.1	6.2	5.3	26.2	25.6	13.5	2.6	75.0	39.6	50.8	49.3
57054	RAMONA	99.1	99.1	0.2	0.2	0.2	0.2	0.4	0.2	6.0	6.7	7.2	8.1	4.5	23.8	29.3	13.2	1.4	74.0	41.4	53.1	46.9
57055	RENNER	97.8	97.6	0.2	0.2	0.2	0.2	1.1	1.1	6.5	6.9	7.1	6.3	5.3	30.2	28.3	8.4	1.0	75.5	38.5	50.8	49.2
57056	ROWENA	98.6	98.7	0.0	0.0	0.0	0.0	0.0	0.0	7.6	8.9	8.9	7.6	5.1	26.6	30.4	5.1	0.0	67.1	39.5	51.9	48.1
57057	RUTLAND	98.1	97.2	0.0	0.0	0.0	0.9	0.0	0.0	5.6	5.6	5.6	6.5	6.5	23.2	28.7	16.7	1.9	77.8	43.3	50.9	49.1
57058	SALEM	98.9	98.7	0.1	0.1	0.2	0.4	0.4	0.5	6.8	6.7	7.3	6.1	5.8	23.2	23.4	16.4	4.4	75.3	40.8	49.3	50.7
57059	SCOTLAND	95.7	95.6	0.7	0.7	0.3	0.3	1.2	1.2	4.5	5.1	5.5	10.0	5.5	17.0	24.3	21.3	6.9	77.1	46.7	50.4	49.6
57062	SPRINGFIELD	90.5	90.0	1.1	1.1	0.0	0.0	0.5	0.5	3.7	4.1	4.9	5.8	10.0	36.3	23.4	10.7	1.0	84.0	37.3	68.0	32.0
57063	TABOR	98.6	98.6	0.3	0.3	0.0	0.0	0.4	0.4	6.7	7.0	7.3	6.1	5.4	24.9	26.4	13.5	2.8	75.2	40.1	50.4	49.6
57064	TEA	96.2	95.7	0.5	0.6	0.7	0.9	1.0	1.0	11.0	9.6	8.0	6.4	6.5	38.6	16.3	3.5	0.3	67.7	30.1	50.9	49.1
57065	TRENT	98.5	98.4	0.1	0.1	0.0	0.0	0.6	0.4	6.0	6.9	7.3	8.5	5.2	25.5	28.7	10.5	1.6	73.9	39.3	52.9	47.1
57066	TYNDALL	98.4	98.4	0.5	0.4	0.0	0.0	0.5	0.5	5.6	6.0	7.2	6.8	5.5	22.0	24.7	17.5	4.9	76.5	43.2	50.1	49.9
57067	UTICA	98.3	98.1	0.2	0.2	0.0	0.0	0.5	0.5	8.1	8.6	9.3	6.7	5.3	26.3	23.8	11.0	1.0	69.9	36.4	53.3	46.7
57068	VALLEY SPRINGS	98.0	97.8	0.5	0.6	0.4	0.5	0.7	0.8	8.0	7.9	7.7	7.4	6.7	29.6	24.2	7.6	0.9	71.9	35.1	50.5	49.5
57069	VERMILLION	91.6	91.4	1.2	1.2	2.3	2.3	1.0	1.0	5.1	4.7	5.3	15.7	18.7	25.8	16.0	7.3	1.4	81.7	25.2	47.8	52.2
57070	VIBORG	99.5	99.6	0.0	0.0	0.1	0.1	0.1	0.1	5.4	5.8	6.9	6.4	5.4	21.2	24.4	18.7	5.8	77.4	44.2	47.6	52.4
57071	VOLGA	98.1	97.9	0.0	0.0	0.3	0.4	0.6	0.7	6.8	7.0	6.9	6.1	6.2	27.9	26.1	11.5	1.4	75.5	37.5	50.4	49.6
57072	VOLIN	97.6	97.3	0.0	0.0	0.2	0.1	0.3	0.3	7.1	6.9	8.8	7.1	6.0	24.9	27.1	10.6	1.6	72.8	38.3	52.3	47.7
57073	WAKONDA	99.3	99.3	0.0	0.0	0.1	0.1	0.1	0.1	6.1	6.3	7.5	6.4	4.9	20.9	24.3	17.4	6.3	76.1	43.3	47.9	52.1
57075	WENTWORTH	98.4	98.0	0.4	0.3	0.2	0.2	0.5	0.6	4.4	5.9	5.9	8.4	5.5	23.2	34.6	11.6	0.5	77.6	43.2	53.6	46.4
57076	WINFRED	99.0	99.0	0.0	0.0	0.3	0.2	1.2	1.4	7.5	7.5	7.5	6.9	6.3	22.9	29.6	11.2	0.6	73.0	39.9	51.7	48.3
57077	WORTHING	98.9	99.0	0.1	0.1	0.2	0.3	0.3	0.3	8.0	7.7	7.7	6.9	6.8	32.5	22.4	7.2	0.8	72.3	33.9	52.6	47.4
57078	YANKTON	94.6	93.8	1.4	1.6	0.5	0.7	2.1	2.3	6.4	6.2	6.9	6.6	7.3	28.2	24.4	11.5	2.5	76.7	37.3	50.7	49.3
57103	SIOUX FALLS	91.1	89.6	2.0	2.3	1.6	2.3	2.9	3.2	7.5	7.5	8.0	7.2	6.8	30.0	23.7	8.3	1.1	72.5	34.6	49.5	50.5
57104	SIOUX FALLS	85.3	83.1	3.5	4.0	1.3	1.8	4.6	5.1	6.9	5.9	5.8	6.1	10.4	34.8	19.6	8.5	2.2	78.3	32.8	53.1	46.9
57105	SIOUX FALLS	95.2	94.3	1.0	1.1	0.8	1.1	1.4	1.6	5.7	5.4	5.5	7.0	8.1	26.3	23.8	15.5	2.7	79.7	39.1	47.2	52.8
57106	SIOUX FALLS	95.3	94.3	0.9	1.0	1.2	1.6	1.3	1.5	8.0	7.2	6.8	6.5	8.9	34.1	20.0	7.0	1.5	74.4	31.5	48.0	52.0
57107	SIOUX FALLS	95.2	94.5	1.0	1.1	0.4	0.5	1.7	1.9	8.1	8.0	7.7	6.3	6.1	33.6	21.8	7.8	0.6	72.2	33.2	50.6	49.4
57108	SIOUX FALLS	97.1	96.7	0.5	0.6	0.7	0.9	0.9	0.9	8.1	8.3	7.6	6.8	6.2	29.7	26.4	6.4	0.8	71.6	35.1	49.6	50.5
57110	SIOUX FALLS	94.0	92.8	1.6	1.9	1.2	1.7	1.8	2.1	10.4	9.4	8.7	6.9	6.1	31.4	21.0	5.5	0.7	66.9	31.7	49.1	50.9
57197	SIOUX FALLS	96.5	95.6	0.8	0.9	1.8	2.5	0.8	0.9	2.1	1.6	1.2	29.2	53.7	6.0	3.2	2.8	0.1	94.6	21.5	39.1	60.9
57201	WATERTOWN	96.6	96.5	0.1	0.1	0.3	0.3	1.1	1.1	7.4	6.8	7.1	7.2	7.9	27.2	22.5	11.8	2.2	74.3	35.4	49.5	50.5
57212	ARLINGTON	98.6	98.5	0.0	0.0	0.4	0.5	0.6	0.6	6.0	6.2	6.7	6.5	5.6	23.1	24.7	17.0	4.2	77.0	42.4	50.0	50.0
57213	ASTORIA	98.4	98.3	0.2	0.2	0.2	0.2	0.6	0.4	7.2	6.8	6.6	6.6	5.7	22.7	24.6	17.2	2.6	75.4	41.3	51.8	48.2
57216	BIG STONE CITY	98.9	99.0	0.0	0.0	0.0	0.0	0.5	0.4	5.5	5.8	6.5	7.2	5.8	23.1	30.0	14.1	2.1	76.9	42.9	51.2	48.8
57217	BRADLEY	99.0	98.7	0.0	0.0	0.3	0.3	0.0	0.3	4.2	4.7	7.4	6.6	6.6	21.8	25.2	19.7	3.9	79.3	44.2	51.2	48.8
57218	BRANDT	98.7	98.6	0.2	0.2	0.2	0.2	0.8	0.9	6.1	6.1	7.1	7.0	5.4	23.6	26.2	16.2	2.2	76.2	41.7	50.7	49.3
57219	BRISTOL	99.7	99.7	0.3	0.3	0.0	0.0	0.0	0.0	5.5	5.8	5.9	5.5	5.0	19.3	25.0	22.6	5.5	78.5	46.9	50.1	49.9
57220	BRUCE	97.8	97.5	0.0	0.0	0.4	0.5	1.9	2.1	6.4	7.0	7.4	7.3	5.2	27.4	27.3	10.9	1.1	74.8	38.7	53.5	46.6
57221	BRYANT	99.3	99.3	0.1	0.1	0.1	0.1	0.1	0.1	8.1	7.6	7.6	7.5	6.9	21.6	20.0	16.9	3.8	71.2	38.0	49.9	50.1
57223	CASTLEWOOD	98.8	98.6	0.2	0.2	0.3	0.4	0.6	0.6	6.6	7.3	9.2	8.7	5.7	25.9	23.8	10.5	2.4	70.9	36.7	50.7	49.3
57224	CLAIRE CITY	87.0	85.1	0.0	0.0	0.0	0.0	0.0	0.0	4.4	6.2	7.1	9.0	5.9	22.7	30.8	13.0	0.9	75.2	41.0	53.4	46.6
57225	CLARK	98.9	98.7	0.2	0.2	0.2	0.3	0.4	0.5	5.5	5.6	6.8	7.2	5.6	20.5	25.1	19.6	4.3	77.1	44.3	47.9	52.1
57226	CLEAR LAKE	98.7	98.7	0.0	0.0	0.3	0.3	0.4	0.4	5.7	5.8	7.1	6.7	5.2	22.7	23.8	17.7	5.2	77.4	42.7	48.7	51.3
57227	CORONA	97.7	97.1	0.0	0.0	0.4	0.6	0.0	0.0	6.2	6.9	7.8	5.9	4.4	19.3	30.3	17.9	1.5	75.5	44.7	50.7	49.3
57231	DE SMET	98.4	98.4	0.1	0.1	0.2	0.2	0.8	0.8	5.9	5.3	6.2	6.5	4.7	20.8	25.3	19.7	5.6	78.9	45.4	47.9	52.1
57232	EDEN	83.8	82.8	0.3	0.3	0.0	0.0	0.7	0.3	6.4	5.7	9.1	7.7	4.4	21.2	27.3	15.8	2.4	73.4	41.8	52.9	47.1
57233	ERWIN	99.4	99.4	0.0	0.0	0.0	0.0	0.0	0.0	5.7	5.7	7.3	7.3	5.7	19.8	29.9	16.4	2.3	76.3	44.2	52.0	48.0
57234	ESTELLINE	97.6	97.3	0.2	0.3	0.3	0.4	1.2	1.3	4.2	4.7	6.9	5.9	5.4	22.3	27.8	18.5	4.2	79.9	45.5	50.0	50.0
	SOUTH DAKOTA	88.7	87.8	0.6	0.7	0.6	0.8	1.4	1.6	7.0	6.8	7.3	7.7	7.9	26.1	23.4	11.7	2.2	74.5	35.9	49.7	50.3
	UNITED STATES	75.1	73.6	12.3	12.5	3.8	4.2	12.5	14.1	6.9	6.7	7.2	7.0	7.3	28.6	23.8	10.8	1.7	75.1	36.0	49.1	50.9

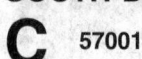

#	POST OFFICE NAME	2004 Per Capita Income	2004 HH Income Base	2004 HOUSEHOLD INCOME DISTRIBUTION (%) Less than $25,000	$25,000 to $49,999	$50,000 to $99,999	$100,000 to $149,999	$150,000 or More	MEDIAN HOUSEHOLD INCOME 2004	2009	2004 National Centile	2004 State Centile	2004 Home Value Base	2004 HOME VALUE DISTRIBUTION (%) Less than $50,000	$50,000 to $89,999	$90,000 to $174,999	$175,000 to $399,999	$400,000 or More	2004 Median Home Value
57001	ALCESTER	19893	854	25.1	33.3	35.7	4.7	1.3	42167	53094	53	76	638	24.5	32.3	32.9	8.5	1.9	81224
57002	AURORA	20996	345	20.6	35.4	38.6	2.9	2.6	45106	56246	61	85	282	18.1	30.5	41.5	9.6	0.4	91600
57003	BALTIC	24317	728	14.4	25.7	49.3	7.6	3.0	57074	67556	82	96	630	14.9	16.2	46.7	20.5	1.8	117708
57004	BERESFORD	21288	1339	24.1	34.8	33.4	4.9	2.8	42683	53308	55	80	981	17.6	28.6	42.9	9.9	0.9	94101
57005	BRANDON	25530	2759	9.4	19.2	50.3	17.3	3.9	68693	83039	91	99	2343	2.2	6.0	64.6	25.7	1.5	140607
57006	BROOKINGS	23637	8379	30.3	28.9	30.4	7.1	3.4	40999	52317	50	70	4142	16.4	16.6	49.7	16.4	0.9	109623
57007	BROOKINGS	9057	4	0.0	0.0	100.0	0.0	0.0	75000	75000	93	100	2	0.0	0.0	100.0	0.0	0.0	137500
57010	BURBANK	23689	190	22.6	27.9	35.8	10.5	3.2	49322	62841	71	89	149	18.1	27.5	32.9	19.5	2.0	95417
57012	CANISTOTA	17384	497	27.6	35.0	31.2	4.4	1.8	39548	47799	44	61	386	27.2	29.8	35.0	7.5	0.5	79677
57013	CANTON	22592	1619	19.8	35.9	31.9	10.1	2.4	46035	57636	64	86	1213	15.3	31.7	41.7	10.5	0.8	93802
57014	CENTERVILLE	20570	627	27.0	37.5	28.6	5.4	1.6	39640	48540	45	62	468	30.1	33.6	29.3	6.6	0.4	72273
57015	CHANCELLOR	21124	343	23.6	31.2	35.9	5.8	3.5	46432	54815	65	87	276	19.9	30.4	36.6	12.0	1.1	89500
57016	CHESTER	23485	370	18.4	36.2	32.7	6.5	6.2	47387	56161	67	88	306	21.9	23.2	34.6	18.3	2.0	97500
57017	COLMAN	21423	528	21.6	33.9	36.0	5.9	2.7	44557	52722	60	84	421	20.2	30.2	39.2	7.8	2.6	89531
57018	COLTON	22898	546	15.6	31.0	42.9	7.5	3.1	52251	63838	76	94	432	17.1	28.2	42.8	11.1	0.7	95000
57020	CROOKS	25247	490	11.6	22.5	53.1	9.4	3.5	62224	76969	86	98	412	3.9	11.7	66.8	17.0	0.7	120697
57021	DAVIS	20723	123	26.8	31.7	35.0	4.1	2.4	38469	47889	41	58	100	24.0	39.0	26.0	11.0	0.0	75000
57022	DELL RAPIDS	22231	1672	20.0	26.0	42.3	8.7	2.9	52554	64357	76	94	1234	9.2	21.2	52.4	16.4	0.9	112768
57024	EGAN	18086	242	28.9	36.0	28.1	4.1	2.9	38824	46587	42	58	166	32.5	34.3	27.1	4.8	1.2	72778
57025	ELK POINT	23312	1285	21.4	27.7	39.5	9.0	2.4	50723	63330	73	91	993	17.0	24.4	44.8	12.4	1.4	98143
57026	ELKTON	20840	518	27.2	29.0	36.5	3.3	4.1	44847	54800	61	84	402	30.9	36.3	25.6	6.5	0.8	71190
57027	FAIRVIEW	15072	64	21.9	37.5	34.4	4.7	1.6	42348	50000	54	78	53	49.1	24.5	18.9	3.8	3.8	51250
57028	FLANDREAU	19991	1376	29.1	33.7	28.6	6.1	2.5	39813	48527	45	63	954	27.2	43.3	25.0	3.9	0.7	69063
57029	FREEMAN	19535	906	31.6	38.5	25.1	2.1	2.8	35699	42614	30	41	670	33.0	33.1	25.2	8.4	0.3	70345
57030	GARRETSON	21307	943	15.5	31.4	42.3	8.3	2.6	51762	62298	75	93	780	12.3	25.5	42.8	15.9	3.5	110556
57031	GAYVILLE	18414	260	26.5	33.5	34.6	5.0	0.4	41538	49261	51	72	206	22.8	49.0	25.7	1.9	0.5	72667
57032	HARRISBURG	29632	1256	13.1	21.3	43.6	13.8	8.3	63818	79407	88	98	1058	6.6	11.6	45.0	30.1	6.7	146875
57033	HARTFORD	25247	1480	11.4	24.8	49.1	11.4	3.5	60707	75044	85	98	1251	9.8	13.2	55.5	21.1	0.4	121328
57034	HUDSON	18664	320	21.9	40.0	32.5	4.1	1.6	40777	50291	49	70	261	42.5	26.4	20.7	5.8	4.6	59286
57035	HUMBOLDT	21203	415	21.0	27.0	42.4	7.0	2.7	51209	61315	74	92	341	11.4	30.8	38.1	18.2	1.5	102163
57036	HURLEY	20828	360	26.4	31.9	33.9	4.4	3.3	40000	49659	46	65	291	24.4	38.5	26.5	10.7	0.0	75167
57037	IRENE	18836	405	29.4	33.3	28.6	6.9	1.7	39542	48210	44	61	309	31.4	34.3	26.5	7.8	0.0	73857
57038	JEFFERSON	29492	570	16.5	24.0	42.8	10.7	6.0	58817	72399	83	97	449	20.0	23.2	35.9	16.3	4.7	96630
57039	LENNOX	21522	1279	20.0	30.1	42.0	6.3	1.6	49883	61435	72	89	1024	15.7	24.8	46.7	12.3	0.5	101316
57040	LESTERVILLE	19752	164	25.0	37.8	29.3	5.5	2.4	42335	50599	54	77	133	27.1	27.1	26.3	15.0	4.5	82143
57042	MADISON	19187	3350	31.5	33.6	29.1	4.0	1.9	37704	46214	38	55	2161	15.2	35.4	40.1	9.0	0.4	89468
57043	MARION	22002	625	25.6	32.8	32.0	6.2	3.4	43995	52939	59	83	472	36.4	31.4	25.0	6.8	0.4	65758
57044	MECKLING	25405	100	24.0	29.0	33.0	9.0	5.0	45000	60412	61	85	80	15.0	33.8	36.3	12.5	2.5	91429
57045	MENNO	18625	525	35.2	33.1	26.3	2.7	2.7	34462	40681	26	32	420	53.1	23.6	17.6	5.5	0.2	46667
57046	MISSION HILL	17873	326	26.4	35.6	31.9	5.2	0.9	40609	48397	48	69	255	29.4	42.0	22.0	5.5	1.2	69828
57047	MONROE	25974	98	22.5	33.7	31.6	8.2	4.1	46125	56041	64	86	78	19.2	23.1	37.2	19.2	1.3	103571
57048	MONTROSE	19565	422	26.1	32.7	32.0	7.8	1.4	43927	51990	58	83	339	25.1	23.9	39.8	10.9	0.3	91346
57049	NORTH SIOUX CITY	45655	1906	13.8	20.5	32.3	18.7	14.7	70020	93596	91	99	1348	19.0	9.4	26.3	31.7	13.7	151154
57050	NUNDA	20101	126	30.2	34.9	26.2	7.1	1.6	35000	40849	28	37	102	32.4	32.4	23.5	10.8	1.0	73000
57051	OLDHAM	20525	188	37.8	32.5	20.7	5.9	3.2	31121	37858	15	19	147	50.3	16.3	23.8	7.5	2.0	49500
57052	OLIVET	18280	157	30.6	36.9	22.9	5.1	4.5	35781	41518	31	42	122	50.8	16.4	19.7	11.5	1.6	49375
57053	PARKER	22392	749	24.4	32.2	35.1	5.1	3.2	45130	53341	62	85	600	21.3	33.0	35.8	9.3	0.5	84468
57054	RAMONA	23877	245	24.5	32.7	34.7	5.7	2.5	41580	49163	52	72	199	23.1	31.7	33.7	11.1	0.5	84063
57055	RENNER	24118	378	9.8	23.0	55.8	8.5	2.9	58774	70433	83	97	329	17.6	11.3	49.2	21.0	0.9	119007
57056	ROWENA	36304	31	9.7	19.4	38.7	22.6	9.7	69624	85566	91	99	30	0.0	6.7	33.3	56.7	3.3	190000
57057	RUTLAND	16730	40	30.0	37.5	25.0	7.5	0.0	33835	41153	24	30	32	34.4	31.3	28.1	6.3	0.0	70000
57058	SALEM	22692	838	27.5	31.4	32.3	6.1	2.7	42625	51836	55	79	628	26.0	35.5	32.6	5.7	0.2	76418
57059	SCOTLAND	16725	602	35.2	37.0	25.1	2.5	0.2	34093	40244	24	31	444	51.8	30.4	12.6	5.2	0.0	48462
57062	SPRINGFIELD	15118	543	31.9	35.5	26.5	6.1	0.0	36454	41902	33	47	418	29.7	37.8	26.6	6.0	0.0	75510
57063	TABOR	17349	366	30.9	37.2	26.5	4.4	1.1	37342	43420	37	54	288	31.9	39.9	23.6	3.8	0.7	69333
57064	TEA	22357	1178	7.9	27.6	53.7	9.0	1.8	58652	71657	83	96	1103	3.5	13.0	75.7	7.8	0.1	116639
57065	TRENT	21000	264	21.2	43.6	24.6	4.9	5.7	42120	49753	53	76	209	20.1	34.5	31.6	12.4	1.4	85682
57066	TYNDALL	18404	738	34.4	36.6	23.2	3.5	2.3	34567	40888	26	33	534	35.2	35.8	25.5	3.6	0.0	66333
57067	UTICA	17047	217	32.3	35.5	24.0	5.5	2.8	38838	46263	42	59	170	23.5	34.7	23.5	15.9	2.4	77500
57068	VALLEY SPRINGS	23096	567	13.2	23.8	49.6	10.4	3.0	60349	72390	85	98	481	10.8	23.9	39.9	23.7	1.7	111815
57069	VERMILLION	18634	4108	40.9	23.2	26.7	6.3	3.0	32702	45558	20	24	1939	22.4	26.4	37.9	12.0	1.2	91278
57070	VIBORG	21077	625	31.2	36.0	23.7	6.1	3.0	35883	44259	31	43	443	27.8	41.3	26.6	3.4	0.9	74508
57071	VOLGA	22265	988	20.2	28.3	42.2	7.8	1.4	51101	63526	74	91	806	19.7	25.8	39.7	14.3	0.5	96102
57072	VOLIN	20525	271	25.8	33.2	29.9	8.1	3.0	41134	50306	50	71	214	26.2	37.4	22.9	11.2	2.3	76154
57073	WAKONDA	19039	273	32.2	28.9	28.9	7.3	2.6	40586	52850	48	68	206	42.2	26.2	24.8	6.3	0.5	60667
57075	WENTWORTH	28934	393	15.5	29.8	37.9	7.6	9.2	52735	63640	77	95	325	17.5	25.9	32.3	19.1	5.2	101645
57076	WINFRED	16407	159	27.0	21.4	47.2	2.5	1.9	50782	60278	73	91	128	7.8	33.6	50.8	7.8	0.0	97333
57077	WORTHING	20606	432	13.4	34.7	43.8	6.7	1.4	51394	63321	75	93	363	11.9	29.2	53.4	4.1	1.4	99559
57078	YANKTON	22053	7015	28.1	31.4	31.5	5.1	4.0	41828	51381	52	74	4787	17.7	29.5	40.3	11.5	1.1	92915
57103	SIOUX FALLS	27950	13698	17.1	26.8	37.9	12.1	6.2	55380	69204	80	95	9232	5.2	15.2	56.8	20.7	2.2	124211
57104	SIOUX FALLS	20506	11597	31.5	35.2	27.2	4.5	1.6	36547	46177	34	48	4873	12.4	40.5	40.7	5.4	1.1	87379
57105	SIOUX FALLS	31117	10520	18.6	31.5	34.6	9.3	6.0	49991	60862	72	90	7194	3.4	18.1	59.7	15.9	3.0	117580
57106	SIOUX FALLS	26062	12654	17.1	29.2	38.5	10.9	4.4	53011	65292	77	95	7691	11.8	7.1	62.2	18.2	0.7	128973
57107	SIOUX FALLS	22392	2443	14.0	32.8	42.2	9.5	1.4	52178	66189	76	94	2165	46.5	14.2	30.2	9.0	0.2	57217
57108	SIOUX FALLS	37078	3525	12.9	17.5	37.2	18.8	13.7	73081	87549	92	100	2836	2.6	6.0	28.4	50.4	12.7	199344
57110	SIOUX FALLS	26567	3506	10.2	20.1	45.9	18.6	5.1	68468	83332	91	99	2840	7.6	2.6	47.3	41.1	1.4	163193
57197	SIOUX FALLS	8302	6	0.0	33.3	50.0	16.7	0.0	60000	100000	84	97	5	0.0	0.0	100.0	0.0	0.0	118750
57201	WATERTOWN	23268	9632	27.8	30.7	30.9	7.9	2.8	42423	52330	54	78	6588	16.1	27.6	43.2	11.9	1.2	97885
57212	ARLINGTON	22538	873	26.4	34.0	30.4	6.5	2.8	42257	51543	54	76	658	36.2	32.5	21.6	9.1	0.6	68060
57213	ASTORIA	17982	202	39.6	30.7	23.8	4.5	1.5	32564	40185	19	24	166	52.4	21.7	17.5	8.4	0.0	46667
57216	BIG STONE CITY	20114	358	32.4	35.2	27.7	3.4	1.4	35705	42626	30	41	300	40.7	28.3	24.0	6.0	1.0	63636
57217	BRADLEY	22810	142	38.7	27.5	26.8	4.2	2.8	33152	41402	21	26	117	52.1	33.3	8.6	3.4	2.6	45000
57218	BRANDT	17783	235	34.9	32.8	26.4	4.3	1.7	35146	42174	28	38	193	42.0	23.8	22.8	11.4	0.0	63462
57219	BRISTOL	19301	279	31.5	35.5	27.6	4.7	0.7	36049	42495	32	44	221	65.6	16.7	14.9	2.3	0.5	34821
57220	BRUCE	27824	326	17.8	33.7	35.0	8.0	5.5	48895	60318	70	89	263	23.2	25.1	31.9	17.5	2.3	93214
57221	BRYANT	26536	266	35.3	30.1	24.1	6.4	4.1	35230	42828	28	38	211	54.0	27.5	14.7	3.8	0.0	47424
57223	CASTLEWOOD	21022	492	21.8	35.0	35.6	3.7	4.1	44082	53446	59	83	402	19.9	41.5	30.6	5.7	2.2	78372
57224	CLAIRE CITY	20628	130	18.5	50.0	23.1	4.6	3.9	39609	46568	45	62	103	64.1	17.5	12.6	5.8	0.0	41471
57225	CLARK	17895	794	32.9	33.9	27.7	4.2	1.4	35545	42897	30	40	614	43.7	35.7	17.8	1.1	1.8	57800
57226	CLEAR LAKE	19517	789	29.7	37.4	27.6	4.1	1.3	38037	45458	39	57	584	37.3	35.3	23.6	3.3	0.5	64211
57227	CORONA	21757	342	32.2	31.3	26.3	7.0	3.2	36743	45285	34	50	287	37.6	21.6	23.3	13.2	4.2	71944
57231	DE SMET	20239	799	35.2	30.7	27.5	4.5	2.1	36016	44340	32	44	608	42.9	29.1	22.2	4.6	1.2	57167
57232	EDEN	17617	123	35.0	31.7	26.8	4.9	1.6	34711	39302	26	35	99	43.4	26.3	22.2	7.1	1.0	59286
57233	ERWIN	19195	71	28.2	36.6	25.4	8.5	1.4	37732	46854	38	55	59	45.8	22.0	17.0	15.3	0.0	56250
57234	ESTELLINE	21527	573	27.2	34.4	29.8	5.8	2.8	39805	49157	45	63	479	31.1	36.3	27.4	5.0	0.2	72300
	SOUTH DAKOTA	22046		27.6	30.9	31.1	7.0	3.4	42239	52729				25.5	24.3	36.2	12.2	1.8	90416
	UNITED STATES	25866		24.7	27.1	30.8	10.9	6.5	48124	56710				10.9	15.0	33.7	30.1	10.4	145905

ZIP CODE	FINANCIAL SERVICES				THE HOME						ENTERTAINMENT						PERSONAL			
					Home Improvements		Furnishings													
# POST OFFICE NAME	Auto Loan	Home Loan	Invest-ments	Retire-ment Plans	Home Repair	Lawn & Garden	Comput-ers & Hard-ware	Major Appli-ances	TV, Radio, Sound Equip-ment	Furni-ture	Dine out/ Carry out	Sports Equip-ment	Fees & Tickets	Toys & Games	Travel	Cable TV	Apparel & Services	Auto Repairs	Health Insur-ance	Pets & Supplies
57001 ALCESTER	85	61	36	58	69	80	64	75	73	62	86	87	56	82	65	77	78	74	89	97
57002 AURORA	84	73	55	70	78	84	68	76	73	68	88	90	66	90	70	74	83	74	83	98
57003 BALTIC	91	100	100	102	96	95	95	94	89	96	112	112	95	113	93	84	111	94	83	103
57004 BERESFORD	94	66	34	62	76	86	65	80	75	64	88	97	55	86	67	78	80	79	95	112
57005 BRANDON	105	120	118	125	115	111	108	107	99	112	126	126	112	128	106	93	125	104	92	118
57006 BROOKINGS	77	66	76	70	65	71	82	73	81	77	101	92	76	96	75	76	97	80	70	83
57007 BROOKINGS	94	57	72	65	56	68	111	82	108	94	134	113	91	121	89	95	126	100	76	93
57010 BURBANK	86	91	86	90	93	95	83	88	82	83	101	104	84	105	85	81	98	85	86	104
57012 CANISTOTA	79	58	35	55	65	76	62	71	70	59	82	81	54	78	62	73	75	70	84	90
57013 CANTON	98	76	50	74	84	94	76	88	84	75	101	103	70	99	77	87	93	86	100	113
57014 CENTERVILLE	80	59	37	57	66	77	64	72	72	61	84	82	56	80	64	76	77	72	86	90
57015 CHANCELLOR	100	72	40	68	83	92	71	86	80	70	95	104	61	93	73	84	87	85	102	119
57016 CHESTER	107	84	57	76	95	106	79	95	90	78	106	112	71	105	84	96	99	94	113	131
57017 COLMAN	102	71	37	67	83	93	70	87	81	69	95	105	60	93	73	85	87	86	104	121
57018 COLTON	91	87	78	88	88	93	86	89	86	86	107	103	84	106	85	85	102	88	88	101
57020 CROOKS	102	110	108	111	107	106	105	104	99	105	124	124	105	125	103	94	122	104	93	116
57021 DAVIS	89	62	33	59	72	81	61	76	71	61	83	91	52	81	64	74	76	75	90	106
57022 DELL RAPIDS	93	79	62	79	83	93	81	87	85	79	103	100	77	102	80	86	97	85	93	104
57024 EGAN	82	60	36	57	67	78	63	73	72	61	84	84	55	80	64	75	77	72	87	93
57025 ELK POINT	97	77	54	76	84	95	78	88	85	77	102	103	72	101	79	88	95	87	99	111
57026 ELKTON	90	76	58	75	80	90	76	83	81	75	99	96	73	98	76	83	92	81	90	101
57027 FAIRVIEW	89	62	32	59	72	81	61	76	71	60	83	91	52	81	63	74	75	75	90	105
57028 FLANDREAU	82	60	38	58	67	79	65	74	74	63	87	84	58	82	65	78	79	73	88	92
57029 FREEMAN	76	56	34	53	62	73	60	68	67	57	79	78	53	76	60	71	72	68	81	86
57030 GARRETSON	104	78	47	74	88	97	76	91	85	75	101	110	67	99	78	88	93	90	105	124
57031 GAYVILLE	83	58	30	55	68	76	57	71	66	57	78	86	49	76	60	69	71	70	85	99
57032 HARRISBURG	121	127	117	130	124	123	118	120	112	120	140	141	118	140	115	106	137	118	109	136
57033 HARTFORD	99	112	115	114	109	108	105	104	98	105	123	123	107	126	104	93	122	102	92	115
57034 HUDSON	89	62	32	59	72	81	61	76	70	60	83	91	52	81	63	74	75	75	90	105
57035 HUMBOLDT	100	75	46	72	85	94	74	88	82	73	97	106	65	96	76	85	90	87	101	119
57036 HURLEY	94	66	34	62	76	86	65	80	75	64	88	96	55	86	67	78	80	79	95	111
57037 IRENE	83	60	36	57	68	79	63	73	72	61	84	85	55	81	64	75	77	73	88	95
57038 JEFFERSON	119	116	98	114	117	121	106	113	106	108	132	133	106	133	107	105	127	110	112	137
57039 LENNOX	82	75	62	73	79	86	73	79	77	72	93	91	71	93	74	79	88	77	85	95
57040 LESTERVILLE	94	66	34	62	77	86	65	80	75	64	88	97	55	86	67	78	80	79	96	112
57042 MADISON	67	61	57	60	63	70	63	65	66	61	80	76	61	81	63	67	77	65	70	77
57043 MARION	95	70	43	67	78	91	74	85	84	71	99	98	65	94	75	88	90	84	102	108
57044 MECKLING	103	74	41	70	85	95	72	89	83	72	97	107	63	96	75	87	89	87	105	123
57045 MENNO	77	56	34	53	63	73	60	68	68	57	79	79	52	76	60	71	72	68	82	87
57046 MISSION HILL	84	61	34	58	69	77	60	72	68	59	80	87	52	78	62	70	73	71	84	99
57047 MONROE	107	75	39	71	87	98	74	91	85	73	100	110	63	98	77	89	91	90	109	127
57048 MONTROSE	95	67	37	64	78	87	66	81	76	66	89	98	57	87	69	79	81	80	96	112
57049 NORTH SIOUX CITY	164	185	178	193	176	170	167	166	153	174	195	194	172	195	163	142	192	161	140	181
57050 NUNDA	88	62	32	58	72	81	61	75	70	60	82	91	52	81	63	74	75	74	90	105
57051 OLDHAM	76	57	37	55	62	75	63	69	70	60	83	78	56	78	62	74	76	69	83	84
57052 OLIVET	96	67	35	64	78	88	67	82	77	66	90	99	57	88	69	80	82	81	98	114
57053 PARKER	101	70	37	67	82	92	70	86	80	69	94	104	59	92	72	84	86	85	102	120
57054 RAMONA	97	75	48	71	84	92	72	85	80	72	95	102	66	95	74	83	89	83	97	114
57055 RENNER	101	96	80	93	98	103	89	96	91	90	112	114	88	114	90	91	108	94	98	118
57056 ROWENA	120	149	159	150	147	145	133	133	123	133	155	156	142	165	136	120	155	128	119	147
57057 RUTLAND	79	55	29	52	64	72	55	67	63	54	74	81	47	72	57	66	67	66	80	94
57058 SALEM	94	69	43	66	77	90	74	84	84	71	99	96	66	94	74	89	90	84	101	105
57059 SCOTLAND	63	47	31	46	52	62	52	58	59	50	69	65	46	65	52	62	63	58	69	70
57062 SPRINGFIELD	70	52	34	50	58	69	58	64	65	55	76	72	51	72	57	68	69	64	77	78
57063 TABOR	80	56	30	53	65	73	55	68	64	55	75	82	47	73	57	67	68	67	81	94
57064 TEA	96	108	103	112	103	99	97	97	89	101	113	113	100	114	95	83	112	94	83	106
57065 TRENT	100	70	36	66	81	91	69	85	79	68	93	102	59	91	71	83	85	84	101	118
57066 TYNDALL	72	54	34	51	59	70	59	65	66	56	77	74	52	73	58	70	71	65	78	81
57067 UTICA	89	62	33	59	73	81	61	76	71	61	83	92	52	81	64	74	76	75	91	106
57068 VALLEY SPRINGS	92	101	101	103	98	97	96	95	90	97	114	113	97	114	94	85	112	95	84	105
57069 VERMILLION	65	55	63	59	55	60	69	62	67	65	84	78	64	80	63	63	82	68	59	71
57070 VIBORG	81	60	38	58	67	79	65	73	73	62	86	83	58	82	65	78	79	73	88	91
57071 VOLGA	92	80	59	76	85	92	74	83	80	74	96	99	72	98	77	82	91	81	91	108
57072 VOLIN	97	68	35	64	79	88	67	82	77	66	90	99	57	88	69	81	82	81	98	115
57073 WAKONDA	82	62	40	59	69	80	66	74	73	63	87	85	58	83	66	77	79	74	88	93
57075 WENTWORTH	120	93	63	84	105	118	88	106	100	87	118	125	79	117	94	107	110	105	126	146
57076 WINFRED	91	65	35	61	75	84	64	78	73	63	86	94	55	84	66	76	79	77	92	108
57077 WORTHING	91	79	58	75	84	91	73	83	79	73	95	99	71	97	76	81	90	81	90	107
57078 YANKTON	79	77	72	77	78	83	77	79	77	76	95	92	76	95	77	76	92	79	79	90
57103 SIOUX FALLS	99	102	107	105	100	104	103	101	99	102	125	119	103	124	100	96	122	102	94	112
57104 SIOUX FALLS	58	56	65	58	56	59	63	59	62	61	77	72	61	77	60	59	75	62	57	66
57105 SIOUX FALLS	91	100	116	100	99	105	101	98	99	99	124	115	104	126	102	97	122	99	94	107
57106 SIOUX FALLS	91	90	95	93	88	91	93	90	90	93	113	107	91	110	89	85	110	92	83	101
57107 SIOUX FALLS	89	85	72	84	85	88	82	86	81	83	100	100	79	97	80	79	97	85	82	100
57108 SIOUX FALLS	143	161	155	168	153	148	146	144	133	152	169	169	150	170	142	124	168	140	122	158
57110 SIOUX FALLS	108	123	122	126	118	116	113	112	104	115	132	131	116	134	111	98	130	109	97	122
57197 SIOUX FALLS	94	57	72	65	56	68	111	81	107	93	134	113	90	121	88	94	126	99	75	93
57201 WATERTOWN	80	79	79	79	80	85	79	80	79	79	98	93	79	98	79	78	95	80	79	91
57212 ARLINGTON	92	68	42	65	76	88	72	82	81	69	95	95	63	91	72	85	87	81	97	105
57213 ASTORIA	76	53	28	50	62	69	52	65	60	52	71	78	45	69	54	63	64	64	77	90
57216 BIG STONE CITY	87	61	32	57	71	79	60	74	69	59	81	89	51	79	62	72	74	73	88	103
57217 BRADLEY	99	74	47	71	81	97	80	90	90	77	106	102	71	101	80	95	97	90	108	111
57218 BRANDT	81	56	29	53	66	73	56	69	64	55	75	83	47	74	58	67	68	68	82	96
57219 BRISTOL	69	52	34	50	57	68	58	63	65	55	76	71	51	72	57	68	69	63	76	77
57220 BRUCE	122	93	58	88	105	115	90	106	100	89	119	128	81	119	93	104	110	104	122	144
57221 BRYANT	124	86	45	81	100	113	85	105	98	84	115	127	73	113	88	103	105	104	125	147
57223 CASTLEWOOD	104	73	39	69	85	95	72	89	83	71	97	107	62	96	75	87	89	88	106	124
57224 CLAIRE CITY	92	65	34	61	75	84	64	79	73	63	86	95	54	84	66	77	79	78	94	110
57225 CLARK	77	55	32	52	63	72	57	67	65	56	77	79	50	74	58	69	70	67	80	89
57226 CLEAR LAKE	76	56	35	54	63	74	61	69	69	58	81	78	54	77	61	72	74	68	82	86
57227 CORONA	89	70	47	63	79	88	66	79	75	65	88	93	59	87	70	80	82	78	94	108
57231 DE SMET	73	57	40	56	62	72	60	67	66	59	79	77	55	77	60	69	73	66	77	82
57232 EDEN	75	55	32	51	63	71	53	65	61	53	72	78	46	70	56	64	66	64	77	90
57233 ERWIN	87	60	32	57	70	79	60	74	69	59	81	89	51	79	62	72	74	73	88	103
57234 ESTELLINE	90	69	45	63	78	88	66	80	75	65	88	94	58	87	70	79	82	78	94	109
SOUTH DAKOTA	84	74	67	74	77	84	76	80	79	75	97	94	73	95	76	79	92	81	84	95
UNITED STATES	100	100	100	100	100	100	100	100	100	100	100	100	100	100	100	100	100	100	100	100

SOUTH DAKOTA — POPULATION CHANGE

A 57235-57401

# ZIP CODE / POST OFFICE NAME	COUNTY FIPS CODE	POP 2000	POP 2004	POP 2009	% Rate	State Centile	HH 2000	HH 2004	HH 2009	% Annual Rate 2000-2004	2004 Average HH Size	FAM 2000	FAM 2004	% Annual Rate 2000-2004
57235 FLORENCE	029	809	806	796	-0.1	44	284	290	292	0.5	2.77	221	225	0.4
57236 GARDEN CITY	025	156	155	151	-0.2	41	62	62	61	0.0	2.50	47	47	0.0
57237 GARY	039	567	568	561	0.0	50	259	264	266	0.5	2.15	186	190	0.5
57238 GOODWIN	039	568	596	603	1.1	81	211	227	234	1.7	2.62	155	167	1.8
57239 GRENVILLE	037	311	308	308	-0.2	36	139	141	143	0.3	2.18	103	105	0.5
57241 HAYTI	057	841	844	878	0.1	52	296	300	314	0.3	2.81	226	229	0.3
57242 HAZEL	057	453	452	468	-0.1	45	158	159	166	0.2	2.79	114	115	0.2
57243 HENRY	029	573	565	556	-0.3	32	212	215	216	0.3	2.62	166	168	0.3
57245 KRANZBURG	029	180	182	182	0.3	58	62	64	65	0.8	2.83	52	54	0.9
57246 LABOLT	051	206	199	194	-0.8	10	77	75	75	-0.6	2.65	54	53	-0.4
57247 LAKE CITY	091	390	387	389	-0.2	38	145	146	149	0.2	2.65	108	109	0.2
57248 LAKE NORDEN	057	1067	1125	1198	1.3	83	388	412	443	1.4	2.59	261	278	1.5
57249 LAKE PRESTON	077	1122	1110	1109	-0.3	35	469	469	476	0.0	2.25	295	296	0.1
57251 MARVIN	051	147	154	157	1.1	80	52	56	58	1.8	2.68	39	42	1.8
57252 MILBANK	051	5051	4970	4904	-0.4	30	2021	2032	2045	0.1	2.34	1360	1371	0.2
57255 NEW EFFINGTON	109	398	412	441	0.8	72	162	171	185	1.3	2.41	111	114	0.6
57256 ORTLEY	051	223	218	224	-0.5	23	77	76	80	-0.3	2.87	61	61	0.0
57257 PEEVER	109	998	1025	1094	0.6	68	302	315	340	1.0	3.23	235	245	1.0
57258 RAYMOND	025	345	338	328	-0.5	24	116	115	113	-0.2	2.93	90	89	-0.3
57259 REVILLO	051	488	479	471	-0.4	26	199	198	198	-0.1	2.42	144	144	0.0
57260 ROSHOLT	109	857	876	933	0.5	64	317	329	356	0.9	2.50	222	224	0.2
57261 ROSLYN	037	413	401	396	-0.7	17	161	159	159	-0.3	2.45	113	112	-0.2
57262 SISSETON	109	5034	5611	6342	2.6	94	1805	2028	2313	2.8	2.70	1284	1457	3.0
57263 SOUTH SHORE	029	566	617	642	2.1	90	211	236	251	2.7	2.56	168	188	2.7
57264 STOCKHOLM	051	212	228	235	1.7	88	92	102	107	2.5	2.24	69	76	2.3
57265 STRANDBURG	051	220	214	210	-0.7	19	84	83	83	-0.3	2.58	58	57	-0.4
57266 SUMMIT	109	633	648	682	0.6	65	238	247	263	0.9	2.62	178	185	0.9
57268 TORONTO	039	268	259	252	-0.8	12	105	104	103	-0.2	2.49	74	73	-0.3
57269 TWIN BROOKS	051	416	451	465	1.9	89	154	171	180	2.5	2.61	117	130	2.5
57270 VEBLEN	091	632	622	622	-0.4	30	272	272	276	0.0	2.29	179	180	0.1
57271 VIENNA	025	435	422	413	-0.7	17	145	143	140	-0.3	2.94	103	101	-0.5
57272 WALLACE	029	165	165	163	0.0	49	68	70	70	0.7	2.34	53	54	0.4
57273 WAUBAY	037	1249	1247	1248	0.0	46	464	473	478	0.5	2.62	310	317	0.5
57274 WEBSTER	037	3061	3022	3009	-0.3	33	1294	1300	1304	0.1	2.26	823	828	0.1
57276 WHITE	011	1430	1417	1447	-0.2	37	528	530	550	0.1	2.60	408	411	0.1
57278 WILLOW LAKE	025	625	605	584	-0.8	15	251	247	241	-0.4	2.45	181	178	-0.4
57279 WILMOT	109	1042	1062	1126	0.5	62	433	454	492	1.1	2.29	285	300	1.2
57301 MITCHELL	035	17476	17740	18072	0.4	60	7098	7306	7543	0.7	2.34	4402	4550	0.8
57311 ALEXANDRIA	061	1357	1435	1529	1.3	83	475	506	543	1.5	2.84	350	374	1.6
57312 ALPENA	005	582	578	568	-0.2	40	237	241	242	0.4	2.40	175	179	0.5
57313 ARMOUR	043	1303	1277	1257	-0.5	25	526	525	524	0.0	2.35	361	362	0.1
57314 ARTESIAN	111	630	588	565	-1.6	1	252	239	233	-1.2	2.46	189	180	-1.1
57315 AVON	009	1046	1018	1011	-0.6	20	447	441	446	-0.3	2.23	316	313	-0.2
57317 BONESTEEL	053	655	628	607	-1.0	5	252	246	243	-0.6	2.52	174	170	-0.6
57319 BRIDGEWATER	087	1189	1232	1278	0.8	73	433	453	474	1.1	2.62	300	315	1.2
57321 CANOVA	097	493	485	476	-0.4	30	192	193	194	0.1	2.51	144	146	0.3
57322 CARPENTER	005	187	180	173	-0.9	7	78	77	75	-0.3	2.34	63	62	-0.4
57323 CARTHAGE	097	334	323	314	-0.8	14	167	166	166	-0.1	1.95	103	103	0.0
57324 CAVOUR	005	414	395	379	-1.1	4	170	165	161	-0.7	2.39	130	127	-0.6
57325 CHAMBERLAIN	015	3078	3093	3111	0.1	53	1152	1176	1202	0.5	2.32	726	745	0.6
57328 CORSICA	043	1262	1245	1226	-0.3	32	461	464	466	0.2	2.54	329	332	0.2
57329 DANTE	023	339	332	330	-0.5	24	111	110	110	-0.2	3.02	90	89	-0.3
57330 DELMONT	043	687	677	669	-0.3	31	244	245	246	0.1	2.76	183	184	0.1
57331 DIMOCK	067	454	483	497	1.5	86	170	184	191	1.9	2.63	136	146	1.7
57332 EMERY	061	864	874	904	0.3	59	343	350	366	0.5	2.48	256	262	0.6
57334 ETHAN	035	948	975	1000	0.7	70	331	345	359	1.0	2.81	258	270	1.1
57335 FAIRFAX	053	342	328	317	-1.0	6	145	142	140	-0.5	2.28	100	98	-0.5
57337 FEDORA	097	204	197	192	-0.8	10	85	85	84	0.0	2.32	52	52	0.0
57339 FORT THOMPSON	017	1833	1896	1969	0.8	72	444	466	490	1.1	4.04	367	386	1.2
57340 FULTON	061	335	361	389	1.8	88	123	134	146	2.0	2.69	103	113	2.2
57341 GANN VALLEY	017	199	192	195	-0.8	8	82	81	83	-0.3	2.37	55	54	-0.4
57342 GEDDES	023	625	613	611	-0.5	26	259	257	259	-0.2	2.39	172	171	-0.1
57344 HARRISON	043	270	263	258	-0.6	20	99	99	99	0.0	2.66	77	77	0.0
57345 HIGHMORE	069	1524	1473	1411	-0.8	12	623	608	588	-0.6	2.36	409	401	-0.5
57348 HITCHCOCK	005	704	697	681	-0.2	36	250	253	252	0.3	2.75	183	185	0.3
57349 HOWARD	097	1882	1838	1792	-0.6	23	782	779	776	-0.1	2.29	500	499	-0.1
57350 HURON	005	13987	13508	13064	-0.8	10	6008	5919	5834	-0.4	2.21	3621	3574	-0.3
57353 IROQUOIS	077	895	890	881	-0.1	42	325	330	333	0.4	2.70	252	256	0.4
57354 KAYLOR	067	104	102	101	-0.5	26	39	39	39	0.0	2.62	31	30	-0.8
57355 KIMBALL	015	1460	1445	1444	-0.2	35	531	533	540	0.1	2.70	363	366	0.2
57356 LAKE ANDES	023	2448	2426	2424	-0.2	37	790	788	792	-0.1	3.01	551	551	0.0
57358 LANE	073	4	4	4	0.0	49	1	1	1	0.0	4.00	1	1	0.0
57359 LETCHER	111	850	876	882	0.7	71	288	305	314	1.4	2.85	209	222	1.4
57361 MARTY	023	1	1	1	0.0	49	1	1	1	0.0	1.00	1	0	-100.0
57362 MILLER	059	2283	2206	2127	-0.8	12	987	974	959	-0.3	2.20	629	623	-0.2
57363 MOUNT VERNON	035	1015	1010	1018	-0.1	43	364	368	375	0.3	2.74	281	285	0.3
57364 NEW HOLLAND	043	50	49	48	-0.5	25	25	25	25	0.0	1.96	19	19	0.0
57366 PARKSTON	067	2498	2498	2495	0.0	49	961	974	982	0.3	2.45	661	671	0.3
57368 PLANKINTON	003	1218	1183	1175	-0.7	18	465	458	463	-0.4	2.32	317	314	-0.2
57369 PLATTE	023	2527	2509	2504	-0.2	39	981	993	1003	0.3	2.47	687	697	0.3
57370 PUKWANA	015	662	661	661	0.0	46	259	263	268	0.4	2.46	191	195	0.5
57371 REE HEIGHTS	059	278	268	259	-0.9	8	100	99	98	-0.2	2.71	79	79	0.0
57373 SAINT LAWRENCE	059	456	441	425	-0.8	14	182	180	177	-0.3	2.39	123	122	-0.2
57374 SPENCER	087	467	459	470	-0.3	28	177	175	181	-0.3	2.62	133	132	-0.2
57375 STICKNEY	003	830	845	851	0.4	61	342	355	363	0.9	2.34	238	248	1.0
57376 TRIPP	067	1208	1174	1160	-0.7	18	521	511	508	-0.5	2.17	337	331	-0.4
57379 VIRGIL	005	110	121	125	2.3	92	45	51	53	3.0	2.37	35	39	2.6
57380 WAGNER	023	3318	3351	3372	0.2	57	1173	1192	1209	0.4	2.75	810	826	0.5
57381 WESSINGTON	059	642	635	618	-0.3	34	268	271	269	0.3	2.34	202	204	0.2
57382 WESSINGTON SPRINGS	073	1664	1624	1587	-0.6	22	724	723	722	0.0	2.19	459	461	0.1
57383 WHITE LAKE	003	855	869	874	0.4	61	309	319	326	0.8	2.54	224	232	0.8
57384 WOLSEY	005	878	952	970	1.9	89	355	394	410	2.5	2.42	271	300	2.4
57385 WOONSOCKET	111	1551	1524	1500	-0.4	28	634	633	633	0.0	2.35	431	433	0.1
57386 YALE	005	246	236	226	-1.0	6	87	85	83	-0.6	2.78	67	66	-0.5
57401 ABERDEEN	013	28944	28804	28683	-0.1	43	12102	12290	12440	0.4	2.23	7425	7570	0.5
SOUTH DAKOTA					0.9					1.3	2.47			1.4
UNITED STATES					1.2					1.3	2.58			1.1

273-A

ZIP CODE		RACE (%)						% Hispanic Origin		2004 AGE DISTRIBUTION (%)										MEDIAN AGE		
#	POST OFFICE NAME	White 2000	White 2004	Black 2000	Black 2004	Asian/Pacific 2000	Asian/Pacific 2004	2000	2004	0-4	5-9	10-14	15-19	20-24	25-44	45-64	65-84	85+	18+	2004	% 2004 Males	% 2004 Females
57235	FLORENCE	98.4	98.3	0.1	0.1	0.1	0.1	0.1	0.3	7.2	8.4	9.9	5.8	5.3	27.5	23.6	11.2	1.0	70.6	35.6	50.4	49.6
57236	GARDEN CITY	98.7	98.7	0.0	0.0	0.0	0.0	1.3	1.3	8.4	7.7	7.7	8.4	5.8	25.8	23.9	11.6	0.7	71.0	35.7	49.7	50.3
57237	GARY	98.4	98.4	0.2	0.2	0.0	0.0	1.2	1.2	5.5	5.8	7.0	6.9	5.3	24.3	27.8	15.5	1.9	77.3	42.1	51.2	48.8
57238	GOODWIN	97.7	97.7	0.0	0.0	0.2	0.2	1.2	1.2	6.4	6.7	7.1	6.9	5.2	24.7	27.0	14.6	1.5	75.3	40.6	52.9	47.2
57239	GRENVILLE	76.9	75.7	0.0	0.0	0.0	0.0	0.3	0.3	6.2	6.8	7.5	9.1	5.5	20.5	28.6	14.9	1.0	73.7	41.7	52.6	47.4
57241	HAYTI	98.9	98.8	0.0	0.0	0.0	0.0	0.0	0.0	9.7	8.9	8.1	7.9	6.8	26.2	20.4	10.7	1.4	68.4	32.7	51.3	48.7
57242	HAZEL	99.1	99.1	0.0	0.0	0.0	0.0	0.2	0.2	8.6	8.2	7.7	7.5	6.6	24.3	21.2	13.3	2.4	70.4	35.9	51.1	48.9
57243	HENRY	98.6	98.4	0.2	0.2	0.0	0.0	0.5	0.5	7.4	7.6	7.4	6.2	5.5	28.7	26.7	9.6	0.9	73.8	38.2	52.2	47.8
57245	KRANZBURG	98.3	98.4	0.0	0.0	0.6	0.6	0.0	0.6	8.8	8.8	8.8	7.7	6.6	25.8	24.7	8.2	0.6	68.7	34.1	52.8	47.3
57246	LABOLT	98.5	98.5	0.0	0.0	0.0	0.0	1.0	0.5	6.0	8.0	9.1	7.5	5.0	24.1	24.1	14.1	2.0	71.4	38.7	51.8	48.2
57247	LAKE CITY	68.5	66.7	0.5	0.5	0.0	0.0	0.5	0.5	7.8	5.7	8.5	9.8	3.4	20.2	27.9	14.5	2.3	70.8	40.9	51.7	48.3
57248	LAKE NORDEN	98.1	97.7	0.1	0.2	0.2	0.3	1.0	1.1	7.8	7.6	8.4	6.8	5.6	22.5	20.9	16.0	4.4	71.4	38.3	49.2	50.8
57249	LAKE PRESTON	98.9	99.0	0.0	0.0	0.1	0.1	0.8	0.7	4.8	5.4	7.5	6.0	5.3	21.6	24.9	20.0	4.6	78.5	44.7	49.2	50.8
57251	MARVIN	98.6	98.7	0.0	0.0	0.0	0.0	0.0	0.0	5.2	5.8	7.1	9.1	5.8	21.4	30.5	12.3	2.6	74.7	42.5	55.2	44.8
57252	MILBANK	98.7	98.7	0.0	0.0	0.3	0.3	0.6	0.6	6.1	6.0	6.9	7.0	6.3	21.4	25.7	16.1	4.4	75.9	42.5	48.2	51.8
57255	NEW EFFINGTON	80.7	78.2	0.0	0.0	0.0	0.0	0.0	0.0	7.3	5.8	7.5	6.1	4.4	21.8	24.3	20.4	2.4	76.2	41.8	51.5	48.5
57256	ORTLEY	90.1	89.0	0.0	0.0	0.0	0.0	0.0	0.0	5.5	6.0	9.6	8.7	4.6	21.6	27.1	14.2	2.8	73.9	40.7	54.1	45.9
57257	PEEVER	50.9	47.7	0.0	0.1	0.2	0.2	0.8	0.8	8.0	7.9	9.5	10.0	7.9	21.7	23.3	10.2	1.6	68.3	32.1	50.1	50.0
57258	RAYMOND	99.4	99.1	0.0	0.0	0.0	0.0	0.9	0.9	6.2	6.2	7.7	8.6	6.2	22.5	26.3	14.8	1.5	74.3	40.2	50.6	49.4
57259	REVILLO	97.8	97.7	0.0	0.0	0.0	0.0	1.4	1.5	6.3	7.5	7.9	7.3	5.4	24.0	26.5	13.4	1.7	73.3	39.8	51.8	48.2
57260	ROSHOLT	95.7	95.1	0.6	0.6	0.1	0.1	0.5	0.5	7.2	7.4	7.0	4.0	4.3	22.6	24.2	17.1	6.2	75.7	43.3	48.5	51.5
57261	ROSLYN	98.1	98.0	0.5	0.5	0.2	0.3	0.5	0.5	4.2	5.0	6.0	7.0	5.5	19.7	30.7	18.2	3.7	80.6	46.5	50.6	49.4
57262	SISSETON	55.7	53.3	0.1	0.1	0.2	0.3	0.9	0.9	7.3	7.6	9.4	7.9	7.3	22.8	22.8	12.5	2.4	70.8	34.7	49.4	50.6
57263	SOUTH SHORE	98.9	98.9	0.2	0.2	0.0	0.0	0.2	0.2	7.3	7.8	7.6	5.8	4.7	25.1	27.4	12.3	1.9	73.3	39.7	51.4	48.6
57264	STOCKHOLM	98.6	98.3	0.0	0.0	0.0	0.0	0.5	0.4	5.3	6.1	7.9	6.6	4.8	25.4	25.9	15.8	2.2	75.9	41.5	52.2	47.8
57265	STRANDBURG	98.6	99.1	0.0	0.0	0.0	0.0	0.5	0.0	6.1	7.5	7.9	7.9	4.7	25.2	23.4	15.0	2.3	73.4	39.6	50.5	49.5
57266	SUMMIT	68.4	64.8	0.0	0.0	0.0	0.0	0.2	0.2	6.5	6.5	10.3	8.2	6.6	22.7	23.6	13.0	2.6	71.3	36.4	51.5	48.5
57268	TORONTO	98.9	98.8	0.0	0.0	0.0	0.0	1.1	1.2	5.8	6.2	7.3	7.0	5.4	23.9	27.0	15.4	1.9	76.1	41.7	50.2	49.8
57269	TWIN BROOKS	98.3	98.2	0.0	0.0	0.2	0.2	0.5	0.7	5.1	5.8	7.8	7.3	4.9	24.4	28.2	14.4	2.2	76.3	42.0	53.2	46.8
57270	VEBLEN	81.2	79.9	0.0	0.0	0.2	0.2	1.4	1.5	7.7	6.4	6.4	7.4	5.3	18.3	24.9	20.3	3.2	74.4	43.3	50.8	49.2
57271	VIENNA	97.7	97.4	0.0	0.0	0.0	0.0	0.5	0.7	7.1	7.1	8.3	7.8	6.2	20.6	23.9	16.4	2.6	72.5	40.3	50.7	49.3
57272	WALLACE	98.2	98.8	0.0	0.0	0.0	0.0	0.0	0.0	7.3	8.5	8.5	6.1	5.5	27.3	23.6	12.1	1.2	71.5	36.8	51.5	48.5
57273	WAUBAY	69.4	68.0	0.0	0.0	0.1	0.1	0.7	0.7	7.1	7.1	7.7	8.6	6.5	18.9	25.2	16.8	2.1	72.4	41.1	48.9	51.1
57274	WEBSTER	97.6	97.6	0.1	0.1	0.1	0.1	0.2	0.2	5.7	5.9	6.7	6.3	5.2	21.3	25.8	18.6	4.5	77.5	44.3	49.0	51.0
57276	WHITE	98.2	98.0	0.1	0.1	0.1	0.1	1.3	1.4	7.1	7.5	8.0	5.3	5.2	26.0	24.8	13.8	2.3	74.1	39.4	50.7	49.3
57278	WILLOW LAKE	97.8	97.5	0.0	0.0	0.0	0.0	0.5	0.7	6.6	6.9	8.9	7.9	6.0	20.5	25.0	16.0	2.2	72.4	40.5	51.6	48.4
57279	WILMOT	93.7	92.7	0.0	0.0	0.5	0.8	0.7	0.6	6.2	6.4	6.3	6.5	5.7	21.9	25.5	17.4	4.1	76.2	43.1	51.2	48.8
57301	MITCHELL	96.1	95.5	0.3	0.3	0.5	0.7	0.7	0.8	6.8	6.4	6.7	7.5	8.8	25.7	22.3	13.0	2.9	76.1	35.5	48.7	51.4
57311	ALEXANDRIA	99.2	99.0	0.0	0.0	0.3	0.4	0.2	0.1	7.4	7.7	8.4	6.6	6.4	26.4	24.5	10.9	1.6	72.4	35.8	51.1	48.9
57312	ALPENA	98.8	98.6	0.0	0.0	0.2	0.2	0.3	0.4	4.0	5.2	6.8	7.1	5.9	25.3	29.8	14.7	1.4	79.1	42.7	54.0	46.0
57313	ARMOUR	96.5	96.4	0.0	0.0	0.1	0.1	0.5	0.6	5.1	5.3	7.1	7.4	5.6	19.6	27.5	18.3	4.2	77.3	45.0	48.9	51.1
57314	ARTESIAN	99.4	99.5	0.0	0.0	0.0	0.0	1.0	0.9	7.0	7.1	7.8	7.7	6.5	22.6	25.5	15.1	0.7	73.6	39.2	53.7	46.3
57315	AVON	97.6	97.5	0.1	0.1	0.1	0.1	0.2	0.2	6.0	6.4	6.8	6.0	5.3	23.6	25.3	17.8	2.9	77.2	42.6	53.1	46.9
57317	BONESTEEL	85.2	83.3	0.0	0.0	0.2	0.3	0.9	1.0	6.7	6.9	6.7	7.2	5.6	20.2	24.2	18.6	4.0	74.4	43.1	50.5	49.5
57319	BRIDGEWATER	98.7	98.6	0.1	0.1	0.3	0.4	1.4	1.5	6.1	6.5	9.3	7.2	5.1	21.7	24.5	14.9	4.8	73.4	40.9	50.1	49.9
57321	CANOVA	98.6	98.6	1.0	1.0	0.0	0.0	0.0	0.0	6.4	6.6	6.6	8.3	6.0	23.1	26.8	14.9	1.4	75.1	41.0	52.6	47.4
57322	CARPENTER	99.5	99.4	0.0	0.0	0.0	0.0	0.0	0.0	6.1	7.2	10.0	9.4	5.0	21.7	25.6	14.4	0.6	70.0	38.6	52.2	47.8
57323	CARTHAGE	99.1	99.1	0.3	0.3	0.0	0.0	0.6	0.6	4.3	5.3	6.2	6.2	5.0	19.5	29.1	21.1	3.4	80.5	47.1	53.3	46.8
57324	CAVOUR	98.8	98.5	0.2	0.3	0.0	0.0	0.2	0.3	6.8	6.3	7.9	7.9	4.3	26.3	27.6	12.2	0.8	73.7	39.7	51.9	48.1
57325	CHAMBERLAIN	84.1	83.5	0.5	0.5	0.5	0.5	0.6	0.6	5.6	7.5	9.4	9.9	6.7	22.0	22.7	13.2	3.0	70.6	36.5	46.8	53.2
57328	CORSICA	99.1	99.1	0.2	0.2	0.0	0.0	0.2	0.2	6.7	6.4	6.8	7.8	5.5	19.5	23.5	18.3	5.5	75.3	42.8	48.8	51.2
57329	DANTE	79.4	78.0	0.3	0.3	0.3	0.3	0.6	0.9	8.4	8.1	8.1	8.4	7.5	22.9	23.5	12.7	0.3	70.2	34.4	53.0	47.0
57330	DELMONT	95.5	95.3	0.0	0.0	0.4	0.4	0.2	0.3	7.1	7.5	8.4	7.5	5.8	19.9	27.8	14.3	1.6	72.2	40.1	49.8	50.2
57331	DIMOCK	99.1	99.2	0.0	0.0	0.2	0.2	1.3	1.0	8.5	8.3	6.8	7.5	5.4	25.9	22.6	13.9	1.2	71.8	36.3	53.2	46.8
57332	EMERY	99.7	99.8	0.0	0.0	0.0	0.0	0.2	0.1	7.8	7.7	7.2	6.5	4.9	22.8	25.2	15.5	2.5	73.2	40.4	49.9	50.1
57334	ETHAN	98.5	98.4	0.1	0.1	0.3	0.5	0.5	0.5	7.1	7.5	9.3	7.3	4.9	27.3	25.1	10.3	1.2	71.3	36.1	51.2	48.8
57335	FAIRFAX	84.5	82.3	0.0	0.0	0.0	0.3	0.6	0.9	7.0	7.0	6.7	7.0	5.2	19.5	23.5	19.5	4.6	73.8	43.5	50.0	50.0
57337	FEDORA	99.0	99.0	0.5	0.5	0.0	0.0	1.0	0.5	4.1	5.1	6.1	5.6	5.1	18.3	30.5	21.8	3.6	81.2	48.6	53.3	46.7
57339	FORT THOMPSON	7.3	7.1	0.1	0.1	0.0	0.0	1.0	1.0	12.2	10.2	11.1	10.8	10.0	23.5	16.0	5.8	0.4	59.8	22.8	50.6	49.4
57340	FULTON	100.0	99.7	0.0	0.0	0.0	0.3	0.0	0.0	8.0	8.9	8.6	6.7	5.0	26.0	22.4	13.6	0.8	70.4	35.8	49.6	50.4
57341	GANN VALLEY	99.5	99.5	0.0	0.0	0.0	0.0	0.0	0.0	5.7	6.3	7.3	5.7	4.7	20.8	32.3	15.1	2.1	77.6	44.5	53.7	46.4
57342	GEDDES	96.6	96.4	0.0	0.0	0.2	0.2	1.4	1.3	6.2	6.2	7.5	7.0	6.4	23.0	24.6	15.8	3.3	75.7	41.1	51.7	48.3
57344	HARRISON	98.9	98.9	0.0	0.0	0.0	0.0	0.7	0.8	7.6	7.6	8.8	8.4	5.3	22.1	23.2	14.8	2.3	70.7	38.1	51.0	49.1
57345	HIGHMORE	90.4	89.9	0.1	0.1	0.1	0.1	0.5	0.5	7.5	7.0	5.9	6.5	6.0	21.0	23.6	18.2	4.3	75.1	42.3	50.6	49.4
57348	HITCHCOCK	99.3	99.3	0.1	0.1	0.0	0.0	0.3	0.1	6.2	6.9	7.9	7.5	5.5	22.2	27.6	14.9	1.4	74.3	41.1	52.1	47.9
57349	HOWARD	98.7	98.6	0.4	0.4	0.2	0.2	0.7	0.8	5.7	5.7	7.0	6.8	6.1	21.5	24.1	17.6	5.7	77.2	43.2	49.0	51.0
57350	HURON	96.4	95.9	0.8	1.0	0.4	0.6	1.1	1.2	5.8	5.7	6.7	7.2	6.9	23.3	25.0	15.8	3.7	77.5	41.2	48.6	51.4
57353	IROQUOIS	97.7	97.5	0.2	0.2	0.5	0.5	1.1	1.1	5.8	6.1	7.4	8.0	6.2	23.3	27.0	14.9	1.4	75.8	40.7	50.6	49.4
57354	KAYLOR	99.0	100.0	0.0	0.0	0.0	0.0	0.0	0.0	7.8	7.8	8.8	6.9	5.9	23.5	25.5	12.8	1.0	69.6	37.5	52.9	47.1
57355	KIMBALL	98.5	98.4	0.0	0.0	0.5	0.5	0.3	0.2	6.9	7.0	7.7	7.1	6.6	23.3	23.5	14.5	3.3	74.3	39.2	49.5	50.5
57356	LAKE ANDES	46.7	45.0	0.3	0.3	0.1	0.1	2.0	2.1	11.1	9.5	9.4	7.9	7.2	21.6	20.7	11.0	1.7	65.0	29.0	49.0	51.0
57358	LANE	100.0	100.0	0.0	0.0	0.0	0.0	0.0	0.0	0.0	0.0	0.0	0.0	50.0	50.0	0.0	0.0	0.0	100.0	25.0	50.0	50.0
57359	LETCHER	98.7	98.7	0.0	0.0	0.1	0.1	1.4	1.5	6.3	6.6	7.3	6.4	5.9	23.3	27.1	14.8	2.3	75.7	41.4	54.1	45.9
57361	MARTY	0.0	0.0	0.0	0.0	0.0	0.0	0.0	0.0	0.0	0.0	0.0	0.0	100.0	0.0	0.0	0.0	0.0	100.0	22.5	100.0	0.0
57362	MILLER	99.2	99.1	0.0	0.1	0.1	0.1	0.4	0.4	5.3	5.7	6.4	6.2	5.2	19.7	25.3	21.6	4.7	78.5	46.1	48.4	51.6
57363	MOUNT VERNON	98.5	98.5	0.2	0.2	0.0	0.0	0.8	0.9	7.3	7.4	8.5	7.0	6.6	26.8	24.2	11.0	1.1	72.3	37.4	53.2	46.8
57364	NEW HOLLAND	98.0	100.0	0.0	0.0	0.0	0.0	0.0	0.0	8.2	8.2	8.2	8.2	4.1	22.5	22.5	16.3	2.0	75.5	39.2	46.9	53.1
57366	PARKSTON	98.2	98.2	0.1	0.1	0.0	0.0	0.6	0.6	6.1	6.5	7.0	7.3	5.2	21.5	21.4	20.1	4.9	75.1	42.4	48.8	51.2
57368	PLANKINTON	91.5	91.0	0.6	0.6	0.2	0.2	4.2	4.2	5.1	5.8	7.0	12.5	6.0	21.1	24.0	15.4	3.1	72.5	39.2	53.1	46.9
57369	PLATTE	99.1	99.0	0.0	0.0	0.2	0.2	0.6	0.6	5.9	6.8	7.9	7.3	5.5	21.6	23.4	17.0	4.6	74.1	41.5	48.9	51.1
57370	PUKWANA	95.9	95.8	0.0	0.0	0.5	0.5	0.6	0.6	6.2	6.8	8.3	6.7	5.8	24.2	26.8	12.9	2.4	74.4	39.9	50.7	49.3
57371	REE HEIGHTS	99.3	99.3	0.0	0.0	0.0	0.0	0.0	0.0	5.2	6.3	9.0	8.6	5.6	21.3	27.6	15.7	0.8	73.1	41.5	52.2	47.8
57373	SAINT LAWRENCE	99.3	99.1	0.0	0.0	0.0	0.0	0.2	0.5	5.2	5.7	6.8	6.6	5.2	19.7	26.1	20.6	4.1	77.8	45.5	49.0	51.0
57374	SPENCER	99.6	99.4	0.0	0.0	0.2	0.4	0.0	0.0	8.5	8.5	9.2	6.8	5.0	23.8	23.1	13.9	1.3	69.9	37.5	51.4	48.6
57375	STICKNEY	99.6	99.6	0.0	0.0	0.0	0.0	0.1	0.1	6.8	7.0	7.7	6.4	4.7	20.8	25.3	17.8	3.6	74.0	42.7	50.5	49.5
57376	TRIPP	98.8	98.8	0.0	0.0	0.3	0.3	0.9	0.9	7.1	4.6	5.7	5.5	4.9	20.5	23.6	22.8	5.3	78.7	46.3	47.6	52.4
57379	VIRGIL	100.0	100.0	0.0	0.0	0.0	0.0	0.0	0.0	5.8	5.8	5.8	5.8	5.0	24.0	28.9	17.4	1.7	77.7	43.9	52.1	47.9
57380	WAGNER	58.0	56.3	0.2	0.2	0.1	0.1	3.0	3.0	10.0	8.8	8.7	6.8	6.5	22.1	20.9	13.1	3.0	68.0	33.8	47.8	52.2
57381	WESSINGTON	99.4	99.5	0.0	0.0	0.0	0.0	0.3	0.3	5.4	6.1	8.0	7.9	5.2	21.1	29.0	15.9	1.4	75.3	42.7	52.9	47.1
57382	WESSINGTON SPRINGS	99.2	99.2	0.0	0.0	0.1	0.1	0.2	0.3	3.9	4.4	5.5	6.0	5.9	19.2	26.2	22.4	6.5	82.1	49.2	48.2	51.9
57383	WHITE LAKE	97.9	97.8	0.2	0.2	0.1	0.1	0.8	0.8	6.7	6.8	7.0	6.3	5.2	20.5	22.2	19.8	5.5	75.4	43.2	50.4	49.6
57384	WOLSEY	99.5	99.5	0.0	0.0	0.0	0.0	0.2	0.3	5.5	5.9	6.5	6.1	5.2	23.2	29.5	16.8	1.4	78.4	43.7	52.4	47.6
57385	WOONSOCKET	98.4	98.4	0.0	0.0	0.6	0.6	1.1	1.1	5.3	5.3	5.7	6.3	7.2	22.4	27.0	17.7	3.1	79.8	43.5	51.3	48.7
57386	YALE	98.8	98.3	0.4	0.4	0.0	0.0	0.0	0.0	7.6	7.2	8.1	8.9	3.4	25.9	26.3	12.3	0.4	71.2	38.2	50.0	50.0
57401	ABERDEEN	94.7	94.0	0.3	0.4	0.6	0.8	0.7	0.8	6.3	6.1	6.0	7.3	8.6	26.5	23.6	12.9	2.8	78.0	37.2	47.8	52.2
	SOUTH DAKOTA	88.7	87.8	0.6	0.7	0.6	0.8	1.4	1.6	7.0	6.8	7.3	7.7	7.9	26.1	23.4	11.7	2.2	74.5	35.9	49.7	50.3
	UNITED STATES	75.1	73.6	12.3	12.5	3.8	4.2	12.5	14.1	6.9	6.7	7.2	7.0	7.3	28.6	23.8	10.8	1.7	75.1	36.0	49.1	50.9

ZIP CODE #	POST OFFICE NAME	2004 Per Capita Income	2004 HH Income Base	2004 HOUSEHOLD INCOME DISTRIBUTION (%) Less than $25,000	$25,000 to $49,999	$50,000 to $99,999	$100,000 to $149,999	$150,000 or More	MEDIAN HOUSEHOLD INCOME 2004	2009	2004 National Centile	2004 State Centile	2004 Home Value Base	2004 HOME VALUE DISTRIBUTION (%) Less than $50,000	$50,000 to $89,999	$90,000 to $174,999	$175,000 to $399,999	$400,000 or More	2004 Median Home Value
57235	FLORENCE	19823	290	23.5	34.5	33.1	3.5	5.5	43744	51293	58	82	242	31.0	29.8	28.5	9.1	1.7	79630
57236	GARDEN CITY	21340	62	30.7	33.9	25.8	4.8	4.8	40890	49309	49	70	52	55.8	15.4	13.5	5.8	9.6	42500
57237	GARY	22412	264	32.6	34.1	27.7	4.2	1.5	36617	43400	34	50	215	37.2	24.2	24.7	12.1	1.9	70357
57238	GOODWIN	17340	227	30.4	34.4	29.5	4.4	1.3	40365	46315	47	67	186	33.9	21.5	29.0	12.4	3.2	77778
57239	GRENVILLE	21706	141	30.5	28.4	34.8	4.3	2.1	41267	51065	51	71	112	37.5	31.3	21.4	8.9	0.9	67273
57241	HAYTI	19608	300	25.0	38.7	29.7	4.0	2.7	41810	49514	52	73	241	31.5	36.5	26.1	5.8	0.0	72708
57242	HAZEL	21969	159	28.9	32.7	28.9	5.7	3.8	40553	47864	48	68	127	42.5	31.5	21.3	4.7	0.0	60625
57243	HENRY	19651	215	19.1	33.5	40.9	6.1	0.5	48024	56298	68	88	178	28.1	30.3	31.5	10.1	0.0	80000
57245	KRANZBURG	21678	64	17.2	32.8	35.9	7.8	6.3	50000	61760	72	90	53	7.6	17.0	54.7	17.0	3.8	116346
57246	LABOLT	19537	75	26.7	37.3	26.7	6.7	2.7	39588	50513	45	61	61	54.1	23.0	16.4	6.6	0.0	45833
57247	LAKE CITY	15536	146	42.5	26.7	26.0	3.4	1.4	29515	34739	11	14	117	34.2	25.6	27.4	12.8	0.0	75625
57248	LAKE NORDEN	17791	412	29.6	36.9	26.9	4.4	2.2	37634	46053	38	55	318	52.8	28.9	15.1	2.2	0.9	48085
57249	LAKE PRESTON	20920	469	35.2	28.8	27.9	6.4	1.7	36502	45763	34	48	347	51.3	25.4	16.7	4.0	2.6	48784
57251	MARVIN	17987	56	26.8	32.1	35.7	3.6	1.8	41823	52908	52	74	48	29.2	33.3	33.3	2.1	2.1	75000
57252	MILBANK	19937	2032	32.4	32.1	27.4	5.4	2.8	36920	45483	35	52	1492	26.7	33.0	34.3	5.4	0.5	78800
57255	NEW EFFINGTON	22756	171	38.6	32.2	21.1	2.9	5.3	36571	42811	34	49	130	57.7	27.7	6.9	7.7	0.0	40000
57256	ORTLEY	14401	76	36.8	30.3	26.3	4.0	2.6	33883	38895	24	31	61	54.1	19.7	13.1	8.2	4.9	41667
57257	PEEVER	11319	315	46.0	28.9	21.6	2.2	1.3	28312	35234	9	11	207	48.8	22.7	20.3	7.3	1.0	51389
57258	RAYMOND	16142	115	31.3	33.9	27.8	4.4	2.6	37771	46955	38	56	96	52.1	21.9	16.7	3.1	6.3	48000
57259	REVILLO	20508	198	27.8	36.4	27.8	6.1	2.0	39365	46542	44	61	161	51.6	21.7	17.4	8.7	0.6	48333
57260	ROSHOLT	15602	329	36.2	36.2	23.4	2.7	1.5	35068	40657	28	37	248	40.3	29.4	22.6	6.5	1.2	63462
57261	ROSLYN	18879	159	37.1	32.1	23.9	5.0	1.9	33830	40674	24	30	131	62.6	17.6	11.5	5.3	3.1	38438
57262	SISSETON	15657	2028	37.1	31.2	25.4	4.9	1.4	33598	41527	23	28	1317	36.9	31.6	23.7	7.3	0.5	62815
57263	SOUTH SHORE	24216	236	21.6	32.6	33.5	6.4	5.9	46908	54748	66	87	199	26.1	30.2	32.7	7.5	3.5	81667
57264	STOCKHOLM	22991	102	23.5	40.2	28.4	2.9	4.9	43760	52822	58	82	84	42.9	28.6	21.4	7.1	0.0	67500
57265	STRANDBURG	20852	83	27.7	33.7	26.5	8.4	3.6	40448	50455	48	68	68	58.8	20.6	14.7	5.9	0.0	44545
57266	SUMMIT	16624	247	40.1	29.2	22.3	5.3	3.2	32938	39842	21	25	177	48.0	27.7	13.0	10.2	1.1	52188
57268	TORONTO	18361	104	33.7	32.7	26.9	3.9	2.9	36294	42774	33	46	85	42.4	23.5	22.4	11.8	0.0	62500
57269	TWIN BROOKS	19154	171	24.6	37.4	31.6	2.9	3.5	43345	51898	57	81	142	36.6	31.7	25.4	5.6	0.7	72143
57270	VEBLEN	14973	272	48.5	28.3	21.3	1.8	0.0	26042	31511	6	7	197	51.3	26.9	16.8	5.1	0.0	48077
57271	VIENNA	13746	143	37.8	35.7	22.4	2.8	1.4	31912	38186	18	21	113	58.4	26.6	12.4	1.8	0.9	42083
57272	WALLACE	23285	70	24.3	35.7	32.9	2.9	4.3	42319	50901	54	77	58	31.0	29.3	27.6	10.3	1.7	80000
57273	WAUBAY	17190	473	37.0	34.7	24.1	2.8	1.5	32854	39473	20	25	347	55.0	22.2	15.6	6.3	0.9	39896
57274	WEBSTER	19432	1300	34.9	29.9	29.3	4.9	1.1	36674	45160	34	50	958	51.6	29.3	16.2	2.5	0.4	48295
57276	WHITE	19790	530	21.1	37.2	34.5	3.2	4.0	44160	53819	59	83	438	25.1	29.7	30.8	12.3	2.1	82222
57278	WILLOW LAKE	18347	247	36.8	36.4	22.3	2.8	1.6	32179	38363	18	23	196	57.7	26.5	13.3	1.5	1.0	42857
57279	WILMOT	19519	454	35.2	35.0	22.5	5.1	2.2	32883	39828	21	25	363	49.6	28.7	16.5	4.7	0.6	50484
57301	MITCHELL	22925	7306	30.2	29.1	31.1	5.7	3.8	40365	52067	47	67	4589	18.9	35.4	33.6	11.2	1.0	85977
57311	ALEXANDRIA	17217	506	31.6	30.4	29.6	6.3	2.0	38991	49317	43	60	397	37.0	32.0	24.9	5.3	0.8	64792
57312	ALPENA	18068	241	31.5	34.0	28.6	4.2	1.7	38255	45348	40	57	195	43.6	31.3	20.0	4.6	0.5	56944
57313	ARMOUR	16895	525	36.0	34.9	24.8	2.7	1.7	33172	38992	21	26	404	49.0	30.0	17.1	2.5	1.5	51143
57314	ARTESIAN	24066	239	28.5	33.1	25.1	8.0	5.4	41748	49698	52	73	192	47.9	25.5	21.9	4.7	0.0	53333
57315	AVON	19195	441	32.4	37.6	25.6	3.0	1.4	34645	40000	26	34	353	35.1	39.9	19.6	4.8	0.6	65288
57317	BONESTEEL	12861	246	49.2	32.1	17.1	1.6	0.0	25477	30384	5	6	188	67.6	22.3	7.5	2.7	0.0	29286
57319	BRIDGEWATER	18304	453	28.9	33.3	31.8	3.1	2.9	39604	47924	45	62	338	38.2	29.0	25.7	6.8	0.3	58696
57321	CANOVA	21511	193	27.5	33.7	31.6	4.7	2.6	39003	45918	43	60	158	63.9	16.5	12.7	4.4	2.5	35500
57322	CARPENTER	20768	77	35.1	26.0	33.8	3.9	1.3	39092	45568	43	60	59	33.9	27.1	30.5	6.8	1.7	75833
57323	CARTHAGE	18157	166	46.4	31.9	18.1	3.0	0.6	27817	31837	8	10	131	64.1	16.0	16.8	3.1	0.0	35313
57324	CAVOUR	23327	165	25.5	31.5	31.5	7.9	3.6	45511	55337	63	86	138	37.7	29.0	24.6	8.0	0.7	70833
57325	CHAMBERLAIN	20453	1176	27.5	34.6	29.4	5.6	2.9	39659	48056	45	63	746	22.7	34.1	34.5	6.4	2.4	83976
57328	CORSICA	17151	464	32.3	39.7	21.6	3.5	3.0	33628	39845	23	29	353	45.3	28.3	23.2	2.6	0.6	56600
57329	DANTE	14474	110	32.7	33.6	26.4	5.5	1.8	35751	46168	31	42	91	41.8	24.2	24.2	7.7	2.2	68750
57330	DELMONT	12471	245	42.5	35.5	20.4	1.6	0.0	29309	32876	11	13	200	57.5	24.0	14.0	2.5	2.0	44231
57331	DIMOCK	26106	184	28.3	29.9	30.4	7.6	3.8	43279	51564	57	80	149	28.2	36.9	30.9	4.0	0.0	67708
57332	EMERY	19357	350	30.6	35.7	27.4	4.9	1.4	36686	45000	34	50	282	42.9	28.0	24.5	4.3	0.4	56897
57334	ETHAN	22684	345	20.3	30.7	38.6	6.7	3.8	48997	59216	70	89	277	17.7	35.0	37.2	9.4	0.7	86739
57335	FAIRFAX	13788	142	49.3	33.1	16.2	1.4	0.0	25430	30435	5	6	108	69.4	22.2	6.5	1.9	0.0	28889
57337	FEDORA	14947	85	48.2	31.8	16.5	2.4	1.2	26346	33888	6	9	67	61.2	16.4	17.9	4.5	0.0	36875
57339	FORT THOMPSON	4990	466	67.6	23.4	8.8	0.2	0.0	12070	13841	1	1	167	65.9	15.0	15.0	4.2	0.0	35357
57340	FULTON	22917	134	25.4	27.6	33.6	6.7	6.7	47360	56947	67	88	107	27.1	29.0	32.7	8.4	2.8	79444
57341	GANN VALLEY	20633	81	39.5	34.6	12.4	8.6	4.9	31600	41129	17	20	62	59.7	14.5	11.3	9.7	4.8	38333
57342	GEDDES	16020	257	42.8	28.8	23.4	5.1	0.0	29083	34011	10	13	202	51.5	18.8	15.4	8.9	5.5	48125
57344	HARRISON	18377	99	34.3	35.4	22.2	4.0	4.0	33939	38629	24	31	82	61.0	11.0	24.4	2.4	1.2	40000
57345	HIGHMORE	20648	608	32.7	33.2	26.0	5.6	2.5	36613	45712	34	49	438	52.5	25.6	17.6	3.4	0.9	45600
57348	HITCHCOCK	16923	253	35.2	34.0	24.5	4.4	2.0	34848	43343	27	35	201	52.7	22.4	15.9	7.5	1.5	46071
57349	HOWARD	18746	779	34.2	33.8	26.4	4.0	1.7	34957	41711	27	36	577	56.3	25.5	14.2	3.0	1.0	41512
57350	HURON	22382	5919	34.8	30.2	28.6	3.9	2.6	35702	45033	30	41	3808	30.9	37.1	26.6	5.1	0.3	71611
57353	IROQUOIS	18940	330	27.9	36.4	27.9	5.2	2.7	40161	48009	47	66	267	46.8	24.3	20.2	7.5	1.1	55667
57354	KAYLOR	16936	39	30.8	41.0	20.5	5.1	2.6	35414	39065	29	40	30	53.3	16.7	16.7	13.3	0.0	48000
57355	KIMBALL	16106	533	32.5	40.2	22.1	4.7	0.6	34220	39556	25	32	419	46.3	29.6	17.2	3.3	3.6	53229
57356	LAKE ANDES	10954	788	47.7	29.2	20.6	2.5	0.0	26280	31264	6	9	512	50.6	25.2	16.6	3.5	4.1	49388
57358	LANE	0	0	0.0	0.0	0.0	0.0	0.0	0	0	0	0	0	0.0	0.0	0.0	0.0	0.0	0
57359	LETCHER	18596	305	30.2	38.0	23.6	4.6	3.6	38182	44579	40	57	242	47.1	25.2	21.5	5.4	0.8	55833
57361	MARTY	0	0	0.0	0.0	0.0	0.0	0.0	0	0	0	0	0	0.0	0.0	0.0	0.0	0.0	0
57362	MILLER	23933	974	33.6	32.9	25.6	4.2	3.8	36764	45699	35	51	708	42.9	37.0	15.3	4.1	0.7	57813
57363	MOUNT VERNON	17144	368	28.8	34.0	29.6	6.8	0.8	40000	49567	46	65	300	44.0	30.7	22.7	1.3	1.3	54737
57364	NEW HOLLAND	24908	25	40.0	32.0	20.0	4.0	4.0	31106	41122	15	18	21	61.9	14.3	23.8	0.0	0.0	37500
57366	PARKSTON	18743	974	33.9	31.8	27.9	4.9	1.4	36536	44404	34	48	725	37.7	33.1	24.1	4.1	1.0	65282
57368	PLANKINTON	17726	458	32.3	36.5	27.1	3.3	0.9	36514	44143	34	48	338	44.7	37.3	14.2	3.3	0.6	55000
57369	PLATTE	18157	993	31.9	35.5	28.0	2.7	1.9	35668	43212	30	40	741	28.2	34.8	30.1	3.8	3.1	76039
57370	PUKWANA	17537	263	29.3	39.9	26.2	4.6	0.0	36878	42175	35	52	208	34.1	27.4	26.0	8.2	4.3	75000
57371	REE HEIGHTS	25335	99	26.3	36.4	20.2	10.1	7.1	39643	50000	45	63	76	46.1	23.7	18.4	10.5	1.3	60000
57373	SAINT LAWRENCE	23765	180	31.1	33.3	26.1	5.0	4.4	37679	46286	38	55	133	44.4	34.6	15.0	4.5	1.5	57500
57374	SPENCER	21411	175	26.9	34.3	32.0	4.0	2.9	42348	50173	54	78	142	32.4	26.8	25.4	15.5	0.0	78000
57375	STICKNEY	18749	355	31.6	34.7	28.5	4.5	0.9	37065	44486	36	53	287	56.5	26.5	14.3	1.7	1.1	43148
57376	TRIPP	21018	511	38.6	36.0	20.2	2.5	2.7	31730	37717	17	21	404	65.8	20.5	8.4	4.7	0.5	35000
57379	VIRGIL	20054	51	27.5	37.3	31.4	3.9	0.0	40431	49089	48	67	41	39.0	29.3	19.5	9.8	2.4	65000
57380	WAGNER	12546	1192	45.6	30.3	20.5	3.0	0.7	27488	31999	8	10	746	38.1	33.2	23.9	3.0	1.9	65397
57381	WESSINGTON	22764	271	33.2	32.8	24.7	5.5	3.7	36281	45174	33	46	213	47.9	22.5	17.4	10.3	1.9	54091
57382	WESSINGTON SPRINGS	23595	723	36.2	31.5	24.5	4.8	2.9	34673	42293	26	35	515	42.9	37.3	19.0	0.8	0.0	57449
57383	WHITE LAKE	14457	319	40.4	35.1	20.1	4.4	0.0	30583	36297	14	16	251	59.0	28.3	10.0	2.0	0.8	38611
57384	WOLSEY	19611	394	28.4	34.0	32.0	3.8	1.8	40646	49540	48	69	319	41.7	26.7	20.7	8.8	2.2	62708
57385	WOONSOCKET	24393	633	34.6	33.7	24.3	4.0	3.5	37070	44303	36	53	479	58.3	23.4	15.7	2.5	0.2	42685
57386	YALE	18511	85	30.6	28.2	34.1	4.7	2.4	41927	51597	53	75	69	37.7	31.9	24.6	5.8	0.0	68750
57401	ABERDEEN	23477	12290	28.5	30.4	32.1	6.1	2.9	42068	52085	53	75	7876	21.1	32.0	37.2	9.2	0.6	87090
	SOUTH DAKOTA	22046		27.6	30.9	31.1	7.0	3.4	42239	52729				25.5	24.3	36.2	12.2	1.8	90416
	UNITED STATES	25866		24.7	27.1	30.8	10.9	6.5	48124	56710				10.9	15.0	33.7	30.1	10.4	145905

ZIP CODE #	POST OFFICE NAME	FINANCIAL SERVICES: Auto Loan	Home Loan	Invest-ments	Retire-ment Plans	THE HOME: Home Improvements: Home Repair	Lawn & Garden	Furnishings: Comput-ers & Hard-ware	Major Appli-ances	TV, Radio, Sound Equip-ment	Furni-ture	ENTERTAINMENT: Dine out/ Carry out	Sports Equip-ment	Fees & Tickets	Toys & Games	Travel	Cable TV	PERSONAL: Apparel & Services	Auto Repairs	Health Insur-ance	Pets & Supplies
57235	FLORENCE	88	78	60	75	83	89	73	80	77	73	94	96	71	96	75	79	89	78	87	104
57236	GARDEN CITY	97	67	35	64	79	88	67	82	77	66	90	99	57	88	69	80	82	81	98	115
57237	GARY	87	61	32	58	71	79	60	74	69	59	81	90	51	80	62	73	74	73	89	104
57238	GOODWIN	79	59	37	57	67	74	58	69	65	58	77	83	51	76	60	67	71	69	79	94
57239	GRENVILLE	83	61	37	57	70	79	59	72	68	59	80	86	52	79	62	72	73	71	86	100
57241	HAYTI	100	70	36	66	81	91	69	85	79	68	93	103	59	91	71	83	85	84	101	118
57242	HAZEL	110	80	44	75	91	102	78	95	89	77	105	114	68	103	81	93	96	93	112	131
57243	HENRY	83	74	56	70	78	83	68	75	72	68	88	90	67	90	70	74	84	73	82	97
57245	KRANZBURG	86	94	94	96	91	90	90	89	84	90	106	105	90	107	88	79	104	88	78	97
57246	LABOLT	94	65	34	62	76	85	65	80	75	64	87	96	55	86	67	78	80	79	95	111
57247	LAKE CITY	71	54	35	49	61	69	52	63	59	51	69	74	46	68	55	62	64	62	74	86
57248	LAKE NORDEN	76	62	46	61	67	76	63	70	68	62	82	80	59	81	63	70	76	69	78	87
57249	LAKE PRESTON	79	59	38	56	65	77	64	72	72	61	85	81	57	81	64	76	78	72	86	88
57251	MARVIN	88	62	32	58	72	80	61	75	70	60	82	91	52	80	63	73	75	74	89	105
57252	MILBANK	78	60	43	59	67	76	63	71	70	61	83	83	57	80	64	72	76	71	82	89
57255	NEW EFFINGTON	89	67	44	64	73	87	74	81	82	70	97	91	65	92	73	87	88	81	97	98
57256	ORTLEY	69	51	31	49	57	67	54	62	61	52	72	71	48	69	54	64	66	62	74	79
57257	PEEVER	56	45	37	43	47	55	50	52	54	48	65	60	46	63	49	56	61	53	59	63
57258	RAYMOND	84	59	32	56	69	78	60	73	69	59	80	87	51	78	61	72	73	72	87	99
57259	REVILLO	90	63	33	59	73	82	62	77	71	61	84	92	53	82	64	75	76	75	91	107
57260	ROSHOLT	66	49	31	47	54	64	53	59	59	50	70	68	46	66	53	63	64	59	71	74
57261	ROSLYN	80	58	35	55	65	76	61	71	69	59	81	82	54	78	62	73	74	70	84	91
57262	SISSETON	70	52	35	50	58	67	57	63	63	54	75	73	50	72	56	66	69	63	74	79
57263	SOUTH SHORE	102	88	65	84	94	102	82	92	88	82	107	110	79	109	85	91	101	90	101	121
57264	STOCKHOLM	93	65	34	61	76	85	64	79	74	63	87	96	55	85	67	78	79	78	94	110
57265	STRANDBURG	97	68	36	64	79	89	67	83	77	66	91	100	57	89	70	81	83	82	99	116
57266	SUMMIT	72	53	33	51	59	70	58	65	65	55	76	74	51	73	58	68	70	65	78	82
57268	TORONTO	82	58	31	55	67	75	57	70	66	56	77	85	49	76	59	69	70	69	84	98
57269	TWIN BROOKS	91	63	33	60	74	83	63	78	72	62	85	93	54	83	65	76	77	76	92	108
57270	VEBLEN	58	42	26	40	48	55	45	52	50	43	59	60	39	57	45	53	54	51	62	66
57271	VIENNA	73	51	27	48	59	67	50	62	58	50	68	75	43	67	52	61	62	61	74	87
57272	WALLACE	88	78	60	74	83	89	72	80	77	72	93	95	71	95	74	79	89	78	87	103
57273	WAUBAY	75	57	38	54	63	73	59	67	66	57	78	77	53	75	60	70	72	67	80	86
57274	WEBSTER	72	55	39	54	61	71	60	66	66	57	78	75	54	74	59	69	72	66	77	81
57276	WHITE	93	67	37	63	77	86	66	80	75	65	88	96	57	87	68	78	81	79	94	110
57278	WILLOW LAKE	81	57	30	54	66	74	56	69	65	55	76	84	48	74	58	68	69	68	83	97
57279	WILMOT	73	55	36	53	60	72	61	67	68	57	80	75	54	75	60	72	73	67	80	81
57301	MITCHELL	81	72	67	72	74	82	76	78	79	74	97	91	73	95	75	79	92	79	82	91
57311	ALEXANDRIA	88	62	32	58	72	80	61	75	70	60	82	91	52	81	63	74	75	74	90	105
57312	ALPENA	78	55	29	52	64	71	54	67	62	53	73	81	46	72	56	65	67	66	80	93
57313	ARMOUR	68	50	30	47	56	65	53	61	59	51	70	70	46	67	53	63	64	60	72	78
57314	ARTESIAN	107	75	39	71	87	98	74	91	85	73	100	110	63	98	77	89	91	90	109	127
57315	AVON	78	55	29	52	64	72	55	67	63	54	74	80	47	72	56	66	67	66	80	92
57317	BONESTEEL	53	40	26	38	44	52	43	48	49	41	57	54	39	54	43	52	52	48	58	59
57319	BRIDGEWATER	82	60	37	57	67	78	64	73	72	61	85	84	56	81	64	76	78	73	87	92
57321	CANOVA	98	68	36	65	80	89	67	83	78	67	91	101	58	89	70	82	83	82	99	116
57322	CARPENTER	85	63	39	58	72	81	61	74	69	60	82	88	53	80	64	73	75	73	88	102
57323	CARTHAGE	57	43	28	41	47	56	47	52	53	45	62	59	42	59	47	56	57	52	63	63
57324	CAVOUR	101	71	37	67	82	92	70	86	80	69	94	104	59	92	72	84	86	85	103	120
57325	CHAMBERLAIN	82	68	54	65	72	79	67	75	72	67	87	88	62	85	68	74	82	75	82	95
57328	CORSICA	75	55	33	52	61	72	58	67	66	56	78	77	51	74	59	70	71	67	80	85
57329	DANTE	79	55	29	52	64	72	55	67	63	54	74	81	47	72	57	66	67	66	80	94
57330	DELMONT	62	44	23	41	51	57	43	53	50	42	58	64	37	57	45	52	53	52	63	74
57331	DIMOCK	124	87	45	82	101	113	86	106	99	84	116	127	73	113	89	103	105	104	126	147
57332	EMERY	87	61	32	58	71	79	60	74	69	59	81	90	51	80	62	73	74	73	89	103
57334	ETHAN	107	87	59	83	96	104	83	95	90	82	109	114	77	109	85	94	102	93	107	127
57335	FAIRFAX	51	38	25	37	42	50	42	47	47	40	56	52	38	53	42	50	51	47	56	56
57337	FEDORA	56	42	28	40	46	55	47	51	52	44	61	57	41	58	46	55	56	51	61	62
57339	FORT THOMPSON	27	22	31	20	21	26	27	26	30	28	38	30	26	36	26	32	37	28	28	30
57340	FULTON	112	78	41	74	91	102	77	95	89	76	104	115	66	102	80	93	95	94	113	133
57341	GANN VALLEY	89	62	32	58	72	81	61	75	70	60	82	91	52	81	63	74	75	74	90	105
57342	GEDDES	69	48	25	46	56	63	48	59	55	47	64	71	41	63	49	58	59	58	70	82
57344	HARRISON	88	62	32	58	72	80	61	75	70	60	82	91	52	81	63	74	75	74	90	105
57345	HIGHMORE	82	62	39	59	68	79	65	74	73	63	86	85	58	82	65	77	79	74	87	93
57348	HITCHCOCK	84	59	31	56	69	77	58	72	67	57	79	87	50	77	60	70	72	71	86	100
57349	HOWARD	73	53	33	51	60	70	57	65	65	55	76	75	50	72	57	68	69	65	78	82
57350	HURON	75	66	57	64	69	79	68	72	73	66	89	83	66	89	69	76	83	72	81	86
57353	IROQUOIS	92	65	34	61	75	84	64	79	73	63	86	95	54	84	66	77	79	78	94	110
57354	KAYLOR	80	56	29	53	65	73	55	68	64	55	75	82	47	73	57	67	68	67	81	95
57355	KIMBALL	73	54	33	51	60	70	57	65	65	55	76	75	50	73	57	68	69	65	78	83
57356	LAKE ANDES	53	42	32	41	46	52	44	49	48	43	57	57	40	56	44	50	53	49	55	61
57358	LANE	0	0	0	0	0	0	0	0	0	0	0	0	0	0	0	0	0	0	0	0
57359	LETCHER	96	67	35	63	78	88	66	82	76	66	90	99	57	88	69	80	82	81	98	114
57361	MARTY	0	0	0	0	0	0	0	0	0	0	0	0	0	0	0	0	0	0	0	0
57362	MILLER	89	66	41	63	73	86	71	80	80	68	94	91	63	89	71	84	86	80	96	100
57363	MOUNT VERNON	85	59	31	56	69	77	59	73	68	58	79	87	50	78	61	71	72	72	86	101
57364	NEW HOLLAND	88	62	32	58	72	80	61	75	70	60	82	91	52	81	63	74	75	74	90	105
57366	PARKSTON	78	57	36	55	64	75	62	70	70	59	82	80	55	78	62	74	75	70	84	88
57368	PLANKINTON	72	53	33	51	59	69	57	65	64	54	75	74	50	72	57	67	69	64	77	82
57369	PLATTE	76	56	34	53	62	73	59	68	67	57	79	78	52	75	60	71	72	67	81	86
57370	PUKWANA	79	55	29	52	64	72	54	67	63	54	74	81	46	72	56	66	67	66	80	94
57371	REE HEIGHTS	124	87	45	82	101	113	86	106	99	85	116	128	73	113	89	103	105	104	126	147
57373	SAINT LAWRENCE	98	71	43	68	80	93	75	87	85	72	100	100	66	96	76	90	91	86	104	112
57374	SPENCER	102	71	37	67	83	93	70	87	81	69	95	104	60	93	73	85	86	85	103	121
57375	STICKNEY	79	55	30	53	64	72	56	68	64	55	75	81	48	73	57	67	69	67	81	92
57376	TRIPP	79	58	35	55	65	76	62	71	70	59	82	81	54	78	62	73	75	70	84	90
57379	VIRGIL	86	60	31	57	70	78	59	73	68	59	80	88	51	79	62	72	73	72	87	102
57380	WAGNER	54	43	35	42	46	52	47	50	51	45	61	58	43	60	46	53	58	51	56	60
57381	WESSINGTON	97	67	35	64	79	88	67	82	77	66	90	99	57	88	69	80	82	81	98	115
57382	WESSINGTON SPRINGS	88	64	40	62	72	84	69	78	78	66	91	90	61	87	69	82	83	78	94	99
57383	WHITE LAKE	62	46	29	44	51	60	50	56	56	47	66	64	44	63	50	59	60	56	67	69
57384	WOLSEY	86	60	31	57	70	78	59	73	68	58	80	88	50	78	61	71	73	72	87	102
57385	WOONSOCKET	100	72	42	69	82	94	75	88	85	73	100	102	66	97	76	90	91	87	105	115
57386	YALE	91	66	38	61	76	85	64	79	74	63	87	94	56	85	67	78	79	78	94	109
57401	ABERDEEN	75	74	79	75	75	80	76	76	76	75	94	90	76	95	76	75	92	77	75	86
	SOUTH DAKOTA	84	74	67	74	77	84	76	80	79	75	97	94	73	95	76	79	92	81	84	95
	UNITED STATES	100	100	100	100	100	100	100	100	100	100	100	100	100	100	100	100	100	100	100	100

#	POST OFFICE NAME	COUNTY FIPS CODE	POPULATION			2000-2004 ANNUAL RATE		HOUSEHOLDS					FAMILIES		
			2000	2004	2009	% Rate	State Centile	2000	2004	2009	% Annual Rate 2000-2004	2004 Average HH Size	2000	2004	% Annual Rate 2000-2004
57420	AKASKA	129	31	31	31	0.0	49	16	16	17	0.0	1.94	12	12	0.0
57421	AMHERST	091	191	193	195	0.3	58	55	56	58	0.4	3.45	38	39	0.6
57422	ANDOVER	037	332	335	338	0.2	56	140	145	148	0.8	2.23	91	94	0.8
57424	ASHTON	115	394	398	394	0.2	58	158	162	163	0.6	2.46	118	121	0.6
57426	BARNARD	013	11	10	10	-2.2	0	3	3	3	0.0	3.33	2	2	0.0
57427	BATH	013	523	526	525	0.1	54	204	209	212	0.6	2.52	164	168	0.6
57428	BOWDLE	045	843	814	804	-0.8	10	340	332	331	-0.6	2.33	233	228	-0.5
57429	BRENTFORD	115	39	38	37	-0.6	21	13	13	13	0.0	2.92	9	9	0.0
57430	BRITTON	091	2429	2452	2478	0.2	57	980	1002	1026	0.5	2.36	653	670	0.6
57432	CLAREMONT	013	426	416	411	-0.6	23	173	173	173	0.0	2.40	125	125	0.0
57433	COLUMBIA	013	415	407	402	-0.5	26	176	176	177	0.0	2.31	135	135	0.0
57434	CONDE	115	600	590	579	-0.4	29	268	269	268	0.1	2.18	191	192	0.1
57435	CRESBARD	049	287	282	282	-0.4	28	118	116	117	-0.4	2.42	91	90	-0.3
57436	DOLAND	115	828	822	807	-0.2	39	286	289	289	0.3	2.84	211	214	0.3
57437	EUREKA	089	1638	1596	1564	-0.6	21	736	730	725	-0.2	2.09	459	456	-0.2
57438	FAULKTON	049	1631	1623	1626	-0.1	43	610	615	622	0.2	2.56	396	400	0.2
57440	FRANKFORT	115	427	424	416	-0.2	39	159	161	161	0.3	2.63	117	119	0.4
57441	FREDERICK	013	656	619	602	-1.4	1	276	266	263	-0.9	2.33	201	193	-1.0
57442	GETTYSBURG	107	1729	1709	1696	-0.3	33	749	760	769	0.3	2.17	479	488	0.4
57445	GROTON	013	1949	1951	1945	0.0	50	753	764	771	0.3	2.46	548	557	0.4
57446	HECLA	013	617	586	571	-1.2	2	267	260	259	-0.6	2.25	181	176	-0.7
57448	HOSMER	045	451	438	433	-0.7	17	179	176	175	-0.4	2.36	126	124	-0.4
57449	HOUGHTON	013	183	175	171	-1.1	4	78	76	76	-0.6	2.30	53	51	-0.9
57450	HOVEN	107	822	810	800	-0.4	31	326	330	333	0.3	2.43	236	240	0.4
57451	IPSWICH	045	2454	2550	2601	0.9	75	905	954	983	1.3	2.61	680	717	1.3
57452	JAVA	129	373	363	352	-0.6	20	166	165	163	-0.1	2.19	118	118	0.0
57454	LANGFORD	091	561	567	572	0.3	58	241	247	253	0.6	2.30	167	171	0.6
57455	LEBANON	107	172	170	168	-0.3	33	69	70	71	0.3	2.40	50	51	0.5
57456	LEOLA	089	938	936	929	-0.1	45	391	396	398	0.3	2.36	282	286	0.3
57457	LONGLAKE	089	154	153	152	-0.2	41	71	72	72	0.3	2.13	59	59	0.0
57460	MANSFIELD	013	407	424	430	1.0	76	140	149	153	1.5	2.83	111	118	1.5
57461	MELLETTE	115	540	543	537	0.1	54	207	211	212	0.5	2.57	154	157	0.5
57465	NORTHVILLE	115	299	300	298	0.1	52	114	116	116	0.4	2.59	87	89	0.5
57466	ONAKA	049	124	119	118	-1.0	6	54	52	52	-0.9	2.29	41	40	-0.6
57467	ORIENT	059	359	360	356	0.1	51	136	139	140	0.5	2.59	108	111	0.7
57468	PIERPONT	037	271	264	262	-0.6	21	122	122	123	0.0	2.16	82	82	0.0
57469	REDFIELD	115	3799	3656	3559	-0.9	7	1457	1413	1387	-0.7	2.24	914	889	-0.7
57470	ROCKHAM	049	264	271	273	0.6	68	98	102	103	1.0	2.66	77	80	0.9
57471	ROSCOE	045	634	591	580	-1.6	1	272	258	257	-1.2	2.27	184	175	-1.2
57472	SELBY	129	1225	1234	1222	0.2	55	491	502	505	0.5	2.32	344	353	0.6
57473	SENECA	049	204	210	214	0.7	70	82	84	86	0.6	2.50	64	65	0.4
57474	STRATFORD	013	338	339	339	0.1	51	105	108	109	0.7	3.14	82	84	0.6
57475	TOLSTOY	107	181	176	174	-0.7	19	77	77	77	0.0	2.26	55	55	0.0
57476	TULARE	115	539	533	522	-0.3	34	217	219	218	0.2	2.43	162	164	0.3
57477	TURTON	115	114	112	109	-0.4	27	56	56	56	0.0	2.00	39	39	0.0
57479	WARNER	013	603	633	646	1.2	81	207	222	230	1.7	2.85	165	177	1.7
57481	WESTPORT	013	698	704	704	0.2	55	219	225	229	0.6	3.12	172	176	0.5
57501	PIERRE	065	15591	16097	16758	0.8	71	6195	6528	6933	1.2	2.35	4064	4298	1.3
57520	AGAR	119	125	131	137	1.1	80	59	63	67	1.6	2.08	43	46	1.6
57521	BELVIDERE	071	177	181	188	0.5	64	72	75	78	1.0	2.41	47	49	1.0
57522	BLUNT	065	490	515	538	1.2	81	200	213	225	1.5	2.42	156	166	1.5
57523	BURKE	053	1170	1133	1100	-0.8	15	517	511	507	-0.3	2.19	310	308	-0.2
57528	COLOME	123	691	684	680	-0.2	35	278	282	284	0.3	2.42	206	209	0.3
57529	DALLAS	123	299	292	287	-0.6	23	125	125	125	0.0	2.31	91	92	0.3
57531	DRAPER	075	275	266	258	-0.8	14	117	116	116	-0.2	2.29	75	75	0.0
57532	FORT PIERRE	117	2643	2747	2881	0.9	75	1060	1127	1208	1.5	2.43	736	784	1.5
57533	GREGORY	053	2140	2096	2043	-0.5	24	907	908	902	0.0	2.24	567	569	0.1
57534	HAMILL	123	119	118	117	-0.2	38	43	44	44	0.5	2.68	33	33	0.0
57536	HARROLD	065	605	629	654	0.9	75	197	205	214	0.9	3.07	148	154	0.9
57537	HAYES	117	129	132	137	0.5	65	51	53	57	0.9	2.49	39	41	1.2
57538	HERRICK	053	264	250	240	-1.3	2	105	102	100	-0.7	2.45	72	70	-0.7
57540	HOLABIRD	069	135	129	123	-1.1	4	53	52	50	-0.5	2.48	44	43	-0.5
57541	IDEAL	123	378	374	372	-0.3	35	125	127	128	0.4	2.94	95	97	0.5
57542	IONA	085	145	147	150	0.3	60	63	65	67	0.7	2.26	46	48	1.0
57543	KADOKA	071	989	1005	1038	0.4	61	399	410	428	0.6	2.40	248	256	0.8
57544	KENNEBEC	085	509	516	527	0.3	60	196	202	209	0.7	2.55	142	147	0.8
57547	LONG VALLEY	071	219	223	229	0.4	62	68	69	71	0.3	3.23	57	58	0.4
57548	LOWER BRULE	085	1358	1413	1464	0.9	76	358	381	402	1.5	3.70	278	297	1.6
57551	MARTIN	007	2351	2278	2184	-0.7	16	793	771	742	-0.7	2.89	551	537	-0.6
57552	MIDLAND	055	688	665	637	-0.8	12	264	263	260	-0.1	2.53	204	203	-0.1
57553	MILESVILLE	055	147	140	133	-1.1	3	53	52	51	-0.5	2.69	44	44	0.0
57555	MISSION	121	3550	3680	3837	0.9	73	1107	1168	1238	1.3	3.10	829	877	1.3
57559	MURDO	075	750	726	703	-0.8	15	325	323	322	-0.2	2.25	209	209	0.0
57560	NORRIS	095	369	357	347	-0.8	14	123	121	120	-0.4	2.95	88	87	-0.3
57562	OKATON	075	166	161	156	-0.7	16	65	65	64	0.0	2.48	42	42	0.0
57564	ONIDA	119	1223	1248	1287	0.5	63	488	505	529	0.8	2.47	341	353	0.8
57566	PARMELEE	121	1426	1494	1568	1.1	80	339	361	385	1.5	4.12	271	289	1.5
57567	PHILIP	055	1361	1288	1223	-1.3	1	553	541	531	-0.5	2.29	372	366	-0.4
57568	PRESHO	085	801	797	812	-0.1	43	334	338	349	0.3	2.34	238	241	0.3
57569	RELIANCE	085	875	909	942	0.9	74	365	387	408	1.4	2.35	246	261	1.4
57571	SAINT CHARLES	053	57	54	53	-1.3	2	26	25	25	-0.9	2.16	18	17	-1.3
57572	SAINT FRANCIS	121	4074	4193	4369	0.7	70	1016	1060	1122	1.0	3.90	817	854	1.1
57574	TUTHILL	007	254	242	230	-1.1	4	100	97	93	-0.7	2.49	75	73	-0.6
57576	VIVIAN	085	202	201	205	-0.1	43	82	83	86	0.3	2.40	58	59	0.4
57577	WANBLEE	071	1383	1421	1478	0.6	69	330	344	362	1.0	4.13	274	286	1.0
57579	WHITE RIVER	095	1411	1399	1375	-0.2	38	455	458	456	0.2	2.96	325	328	0.2
57580	WINNER	123	5006	4993	4984	-0.1	45	2005	2042	2070	0.4	2.40	1311	1339	0.5
57584	WITTEN	123	101	100	99	-0.2	36	44	45	45	0.5	2.22	34	34	0.0
57585	WOOD	095	306	293	284	-1.0	5	119	117	116	-0.4	2.50	88	86	-0.5
57601	MOBRIDGE	129	3968	3866	3773	-0.6	21	1692	1678	1666	-0.2	2.24	1063	1058	-0.1
57620	BISON	105	626	601	579	-1.0	7	272	266	261	-0.5	2.26	190	187	-0.4
57622	CHERRY CREEK	137	652	664	689	0.4	62	155	162	171	1.0	4.10	123	129	1.1
57623	DUPREE	137	1801	1904	2030	1.3	83	562	601	650	1.6	3.17	452	484	1.6
57625	EAGLE BUTTE	041	1070	1140	1222	1.5	86	316	341	370	1.8	3.34	262	283	1.8
57626	FAITH	093	739	727	753	-0.4	30	290	292	311	0.2	2.49	210	212	0.2
	SOUTH DAKOTA					0.9					1.3	2.47			1.4
	UNITED STATES					1.2					1.3	2.58			1.1

ZIP CODE #	POST OFFICE NAME	RACE (%) White 2000	White 2004	Black 2000	Black 2004	Asian/Pacific 2000	Asian/Pacific 2004	% Hispanic Origin 2000	% Hispanic Origin 2004	2004 AGE DISTRIBUTION (%) 0-4	5-9	10-14	15-19	20-24	25-44	45-64	65-84	85+	18+	MEDIAN AGE 2004	% 2004 Males	% 2004 Females
57420	AKASKA	96.8	96.8	0.0	0.0	0.0	0.0	0.0	0.0	6.5	6.5	6.5	6.5	6.5	25.8	25.8	16.1	0.0	80.7	38.8	51.6	48.4
57421	AMHERST	99.0	99.0	0.0	0.0	0.0	0.0	0.5	0.0	5.7	6.2	9.8	6.2	4.7	22.8	25.4	16.6	2.6	74.1	41.5	52.9	47.2
57422	ANDOVER	98.8	99.1	0.0	0.0	0.0	0.0	0.6	0.6	5.4	5.7	6.0	6.0	5.1	21.2	26.3	20.0	4.5	78.8	45.5	50.2	49.9
57424	ASHTON	98.7	98.7	0.0	0.0	0.0	0.0	0.3	0.5	6.3	7.0	8.3	6.8	4.8	21.9	28.4	15.3	1.3	74.1	41.8	51.3	48.7
57426	BARNARD	100.0	100.0	0.0	0.0	0.0	0.0	0.0	0.0	0.0	0.0	0.0	0.0	20.0	80.0	0.0	0.0	0.0	100.0	32.5	50.0	50.0
57427	BATH	98.5	98.5	0.2	0.2	0.0	0.0	0.2	0.0	6.8	7.8	8.4	5.9	4.8	25.1	30.0	10.5	0.8	73.2	39.7	52.1	47.9
57428	BOWDLE	99.3	99.1	0.1	0.1	0.1	0.1	0.5	0.5	5.2	5.7	7.3	5.5	4.7	19.5	23.6	22.9	5.8	78.3	46.7	48.4	51.6
57429	BRENTFORD	100.0	100.0	0.0	0.0	0.0	0.0	0.0	0.0	5.3	5.3	5.3	7.9	5.3	21.1	26.3	21.1	2.6	84.2	45.0	55.3	44.7
57430	BRITTON	98.4	98.4	0.0	0.0	0.1	0.1	0.7	0.7	5.5	6.0	7.8	6.4	5.5	21.0	26.4	16.5	5.0	76.1	43.4	48.9	51.1
57432	CLAREMONT	99.3	99.3	0.0	0.0	0.0	0.0	0.2	0.2	5.5	6.3	7.9	5.8	4.3	22.4	29.3	16.8	1.7	76.4	43.6	52.4	47.6
57433	COLUMBIA	99.0	99.0	0.0	0.0	0.0	0.0	0.0	0.0	6.1	6.9	7.9	5.7	4.4	23.3	31.2	13.5	1.0	75.4	42.3	53.1	46.9
57434	CONDE	98.8	98.8	0.0	0.0	0.0	0.0	0.0	0.0	5.1	5.4	6.3	6.6	5.8	22.0	28.8	17.3	2.7	79.0	44.2	52.9	47.1
57435	CRESBARD	99.3	99.3	0.0	0.0	0.0	0.0	0.0	0.4	6.7	7.1	8.2	8.2	6.4	22.7	23.8	14.9	2.1	73.8	38.5	51.4	48.6
57436	DOLAND	99.3	99.0	0.1	0.2	0.0	0.0	0.2	0.2	7.5	7.7	7.4	7.2	5.8	23.8	25.7	13.8	1.1	73.2	38.2	49.9	50.1
57437	EUREKA	99.2	99.1	0.0	0.0	0.2	0.2	0.1	0.1	4.5	5.4	5.6	4.7	4.0	15.7	22.7	30.4	7.0	81.5	53.5	47.3	52.7
57438	FAULKTON	99.5	99.5	0.1	0.1	0.0	0.0	0.2	0.2	5.5	5.7	6.4	7.0	5.4	20.3	24.5	21.3	4.0	77.8	44.8	49.1	50.9
57440	FRANKFORT	99.1	98.8	0.2	0.2	0.0	0.0	0.5	0.5	7.8	7.6	7.6	7.1	5.7	23.6	25.9	13.7	1.2	72.9	38.3	49.5	50.5
57441	FREDERICK	97.6	97.6	0.0	0.0	0.0	0.0	1.1	1.1	7.3	7.4	6.8	5.2	5.0	22.1	28.3	16.0	1.9	75.3	41.8	50.7	49.3
57442	GETTYSBURG	98.0	98.0	0.0	0.0	0.1	0.1	0.2	0.2	5.0	5.4	7.0	6.4	5.0	18.4	27.4	20.1	5.2	78.1	46.8	48.8	51.2
57445	GROTON	99.0	98.9	0.0	0.0	0.0	0.0	0.4	0.5	7.3	7.1	7.6	7.4	5.9	23.3	22.5	14.9	4.1	72.6	38.8	48.9	51.1
57446	HECLA	99.0	99.0	0.0	0.0	0.0	0.0	0.5	0.3	4.8	5.5	5.3	6.0	5.1	20.3	30.2	20.1	2.7	80.9	46.8	52.1	48.0
57448	HOSMER	99.3	99.1	0.0	0.0	0.2	0.2	0.7	0.7	5.5	5.9	7.3	5.5	4.6	19.4	23.7	22.4	5.7	77.6	46.4	48.4	51.6
57449	HOUGHTON	99.5	99.4	0.0	0.0	0.0	0.0	0.0	0.0	4.6	5.1	5.1	5.7	5.1	20.0	31.4	20.0	2.9	81.1	47.5	51.4	48.6
57450	HOVEN	98.3	98.3	0.0	0.0	0.2	0.3	0.2	0.3	4.1	4.7	6.1	6.1	4.8	20.4	29.8	21.4	2.8	81.0	47.6	50.9	49.1
57451	IPSWICH	98.9	98.9	0.1	0.1	0.1	0.1	0.5	0.5	6.2	7.0	8.1	7.4	5.5	22.4	25.8	14.6	2.9	73.6	40.9	50.0	50.0
57452	JAVA	98.4	98.4	0.3	0.3	0.0	0.0	0.3	0.3	4.1	5.2	6.6	5.8	4.7	18.7	30.3	22.0	2.5	80.7	47.9	52.6	47.4
57454	LANGFORD	98.8	98.8	0.0	0.0	0.0	0.0	0.5	0.4	5.1	6.0	8.6	6.7	4.6	22.8	26.8	16.8	2.7	76.2	42.5	52.2	47.8
57455	LEBANON	98.3	98.2	0.0	0.0	0.6	0.6	0.0	0.0	4.1	4.7	5.9	5.9	4.7	20.0	30.0	21.8	2.9	81.2	48.1	50.0	50.0
57456	LEOLA	99.6	99.6	0.0	0.0	0.0	0.0	0.3	0.3	7.1	7.3	6.7	5.8	4.9	22.3	25.3	18.1	2.6	75.4	41.8	50.3	49.7
57457	LONGLAKE	99.4	100.0	0.0	0.0	0.0	0.0	0.7	0.7	7.8	7.8	7.8	5.9	3.9	20.9	26.8	17.7	1.3	72.6	41.8	51.6	48.4
57460	MANSFIELD	98.8	98.6	0.0	0.0	0.0	0.0	0.3	0.5	6.8	7.8	9.2	7.1	5.0	24.5	27.6	10.9	1.2	71.5	38.8	51.2	48.8
57461	MELLETTE	98.7	98.7	0.0	0.0	0.0	0.0	0.4	0.4	6.3	7.0	8.3	6.6	5.0	22.1	28.2	15.3	1.3	74.4	41.7	50.6	49.4
57465	NORTHVILLE	98.7	98.7	0.0	0.0	0.0	0.0	0.3	0.3	7.3	7.7	8.3	6.7	5.0	23.0	26.0	14.7	1.3	72.7	40.2	50.3	49.7
57466	ONAKA	99.2	100.0	0.0	0.0	0.0	0.0	0.0	0.0	6.7	7.6	8.4	8.4	5.9	23.5	21.9	15.1	2.5	72.3	38.2	51.3	48.7
57467	ORIENT	99.7	100.0	0.0	0.0	0.0	0.0	0.3	0.3	5.8	6.1	7.8	7.5	5.8	22.2	26.1	17.5	1.1	75.3	42.0	51.4	48.6
57468	PIERPONT	97.4	96.6	0.0	0.0	0.7	0.8	1.9	1.9	3.8	4.6	5.7	7.2	4.9	22.4	30.7	17.8	3.0	81.1	46.0	50.8	49.2
57469	REDFIELD	96.3	95.8	0.3	0.4	0.1	0.2	0.5	0.6	4.9	5.1	6.4	7.1	6.8	25.2	23.5	16.9	4.1	78.9	41.6	52.7	47.4
57470	ROCKHAM	99.6	100.0	0.0	0.0	0.0	0.0	0.4	0.4	5.9	6.3	7.8	7.8	5.5	22.1	26.6	16.6	1.5	74.9	41.9	52.8	47.2
57471	ROSCOE	99.8	99.8	0.0	0.0	0.0	0.0	0.2	0.2	6.4	6.9	7.1	6.4	4.4	22.3	23.7	19.3	3.4	75.5	42.7	50.8	49.2
57472	SELBY	98.0	97.8	0.0	0.0	0.0	0.0	0.2	0.2	4.9	5.3	6.2	6.7	5.6	18.3	27.7	20.8	4.5	79.0	47.0	49.7	50.3
57473	SENECA	99.5	100.0	0.0	0.0	0.0	0.0	0.0	0.5	6.7	6.7	7.6	7.6	5.7	24.3	24.3	15.7	1.4	73.8	40.5	52.9	47.1
57474	STRATFORD	98.5	98.5	0.0	0.0	0.0	0.0	0.3	0.3	9.4	8.9	7.1	6.2	5.0	27.7	23.0	11.5	1.2	70.2	35.8	52.8	47.2
57475	TOLSTOY	98.9	98.9	0.0	0.0	0.0	0.0	0.0	0.0	4.6	5.1	6.3	6.3	4.6	21.6	27.8	21.0	2.8	80.1	46.3	50.0	50.0
57476	TULARE	98.7	98.5	0.2	0.2	0.2	0.4	0.0	0.0	6.4	6.8	8.3	6.9	6.0	23.6	26.6	14.1	1.3	74.1	40.3	54.6	45.4
57477	TURTON	99.1	99.1	0.0	0.0	0.0	0.0	0.0	0.0	3.6	4.5	5.4	7.1	5.4	19.6	33.9	17.9	2.7	81.3	47.3	52.7	47.3
57479	WARNER	98.7	98.6	0.0	0.0	0.0	0.0	0.2	0.3	7.1	8.1	8.7	7.3	5.2	25.9	27.8	9.0	1.0	71.7	37.8	52.0	48.0
57481	WESTPORT	98.7	98.6	0.1	0.1	0.0	0.0	0.1	0.1	6.5	7.2	7.4	6.0	4.6	24.6	28.6	13.6	1.6	74.9	40.9	51.0	49.0
57501	PIERRE	89.6	88.4	0.2	0.2	0.4	0.6	1.2	1.3	6.6	6.9	7.6	7.2	6.4	25.3	26.3	11.3	2.5	74.3	38.5	47.9	52.1
57520	AGAR	96.8	97.7	0.0	0.0	0.0	0.0	1.6	0.8	4.6	4.6	6.9	6.9	5.3	22.1	27.5	20.6	1.5	79.4	44.8	53.4	46.6
57521	BELVIDERE	87.0	85.6	0.0	0.0	0.0	0.0	0.6	1.1	6.1	6.6	7.2	6.6	5.5	23.8	27.6	14.4	2.2	75.7	41.3	49.7	50.3
57522	BLUNT	95.7	95.2	0.2	0.2	0.2	0.2	0.8	1.2	6.8	7.4	8.7	7.4	5.4	24.7	28.0	10.7	1.0	72.4	39.1	50.9	49.1
57523	BURKE	96.5	96.0	0.0	0.0	0.3	0.4	0.3	0.4	5.1	5.4	6.9	6.4	5.2	19.6	27.3	19.3	4.9	78.2	46.0	47.5	52.5
57528	COLOME	96.7	96.6	0.0	0.0	0.1	0.2	0.4	0.4	5.6	6.7	7.0	8.2	6.3	22.7	27.3	13.7	2.5	74.3	41.1	51.5	48.5
57529	DALLAS	96.0	94.9	0.0	0.0	0.7	1.0	0.7	0.7	4.5	5.5	7.5	6.5	5.1	21.6	29.1	17.5	2.7	78.4	44.6	53.4	46.6
57531	DRAPER	95.6	95.9	0.0	0.0	0.0	0.0	0.4	0.0	5.3	5.6	6.4	7.1	6.4	22.6	28.2	16.2	2.3	78.2	42.8	50.4	49.6
57532	FORT PIERRE	92.9	92.0	0.2	0.2	0.3	0.4	0.5	0.5	5.9	6.2	8.0	7.1	6.4	26.5	28.3	10.6	1.1	75.3	38.9	50.2	49.8
57533	GREGORY	95.4	94.8	0.1	0.1	0.2	0.2	1.0	1.2	4.4	4.6	6.5	7.5	6.2	19.0	25.9	20.0	5.9	79.6	46.2	48.0	52.1
57534	HAMILL	83.2	83.1	0.0	0.0	0.0	0.0	0.0	0.0	7.6	7.6	7.6	6.8	5.9	23.7	26.3	11.9	2.5	72.0	39.3	50.0	50.0
57536	HARROLD	67.8	65.3	0.0	0.0	0.0	0.0	1.2	1.3	7.8	8.6	9.4	7.6	8.3	22.1	23.5	11.3	1.4	70.0	34.9	51.7	48.3
57537	HAYES	96.9	97.0	0.0	0.0	0.0	0.8	0.0	0.8	4.6	6.1	8.3	5.3	4.6	29.6	30.3	9.9	1.5	76.5	40.0	50.8	49.2
57538	HERRICK	92.1	91.6	0.4	0.4	0.0	0.0	1.5	1.2	4.8	4.0	7.6	9.2	9.2	22.4	28.0	13.2	1.6	77.2	41.5	54.4	45.6
57540	HOLABIRD	98.5	97.7	0.0	0.0	0.0	0.0	0.0	0.0	6.2	7.8	7.0	6.2	3.9	20.9	25.6	20.9	1.6	74.4	43.8	55.8	44.2
57541	IDEAL	82.3	81.3	0.0	0.0	0.0	0.0	0.0	0.0	8.0	8.3	9.6	6.4	5.4	23.3	26.2	10.4	2.4	69.8	37.8	48.9	51.1
57542	IONA	93.1	92.5	0.0	0.0	0.7	0.7	0.0	0.0	6.8	6.8	6.8	6.1	4.8	25.2	24.5	16.3	2.7	75.5	41.6	52.4	47.6
57543	KADOKA	85.2	83.9	0.1	0.1	0.1	0.1	0.4	0.4	6.2	6.3	6.8	7.7	6.7	20.3	25.8	16.7	3.7	75.6	42.0	47.9	52.1
57544	KENNEBEC	93.7	93.0	0.0	0.0	0.6	0.6	0.4	0.4	6.4	6.6	6.4	6.2	4.5	25.2	25.6	16.5	2.7	77.1	42.2	52.3	47.7
57547	LONG VALLEY	64.4	61.4	0.0	0.0	0.0	0.0	0.0	0.0	7.6	7.2	8.1	10.8	4.5	20.6	29.2	12.1	0.0	69.5	39.3	53.4	46.6
57548	LOWER BRULE	9.2	7.9	0.1	0.1	0.0	0.0	0.5	0.5	14.5	12.2	11.6	8.8	8.6	24.5	15.4	4.2	0.4	55.8	21.7	48.4	51.6
57551	MARTIN	47.4	44.4	0.4	0.4	0.2	0.3	2.3	2.5	9.1	10.1	8.7	8.2	6.2	23.9	20.6	10.9	2.3	66.9	32.1	48.6	51.4
57552	MIDLAND	97.0	96.5	0.0	0.0	0.0	0.0	0.0	0.0	6.8	7.1	7.7	5.6	6.8	23.5	27.4	13.5	1.8	75.0	40.2	50.7	49.3
57553	MILESVILLE	96.6	96.4	0.0	0.0	0.0	0.0	0.0	0.0	5.7	5.7	6.4	7.1	5.7	23.6	30.0	14.3	1.4	77.1	42.3	52.9	47.1
57555	MISSION	22.8	20.9	0.1	0.2	0.0	0.0	1.8	1.6	11.0	11.1	11.1	8.8	7.9	24.5	18.5	6.7	0.5	61.1	25.1	49.2	50.8
57559	MURDO	95.7	95.6	0.0	0.0	0.1	0.1	0.4	0.3	5.4	5.4	6.6	7.0	6.5	22.3	28.5	16.1	2.2	78.5	42.8	50.4	49.6
57560	NORRIS	36.0	35.0	0.0	0.0	0.0	0.0	1.6	1.7	11.2	10.4	10.1	9.0	7.0	25.2	17.7	8.7	0.8	61.9	28.0	51.8	48.2
57562	OKATON	95.8	95.7	0.0	0.0	0.0	0.0	0.0	0.0	5.0	5.0	6.2	7.5	6.2	22.4	29.8	15.5	2.5	79.5	43.4	49.7	50.3
57564	ONIDA	98.0	98.0	0.0	0.0	0.1	0.1	0.7	0.6	6.5	6.6	7.1	6.4	5.4	25.4	26.0	14.3	2.3	76.0	41.0	51.8	48.2
57566	PARMELEE	4.4	3.9	0.1	0.1	0.0	0.0	0.6	0.5	14.0	11.7	12.4	11.1	8.4	23.7	13.5	4.9	0.3	55.2	20.5	49.1	50.9
57567	PHILIP	96.1	95.6	0.0	0.0	0.2	0.2	1.0	1.1	5.1	5.2	5.8	6.6	7.8	20.7	29.0	15.6	4.4	80.1	44.3	48.5	51.5
57568	PRESHO	97.0	96.7	0.3	0.3	0.5	0.5	0.8	0.9	5.7	5.9	6.5	6.4	5.0	21.7	27.4	18.1	3.4	77.3	44.3	54.0	46.1
57569	RELIANCE	92.7	91.9	0.0	0.0	0.1	0.1	0.1	0.1	6.8	7.0	7.4	6.2	5.4	25.3	28.2	12.2	1.5	75.0	39.6	51.7	48.3
57571	SAINT CHARLES	87.7	85.2	0.0	0.0	0.0	0.0	0.0	0.0	5.6	5.6	7.4	7.4	7.4	20.4	25.9	18.5	1.9	74.1	43.0	51.9	48.2
57572	SAINT FRANCIS	6.5	5.7	0.1	0.1	0.3	0.4	1.7	1.5	13.3	11.9	12.7	11.0	8.4	23.3	14.9	4.3	0.3	55.0	20.7	49.0	51.0
57574	TUTHILL	76.8	74.0	0.0	0.0	0.8	1.2	0.4	0.4	6.6	8.7	8.7	5.0	3.3	25.2	26.5	14.9	1.2	72.7	40.5	50.8	49.2
57576	VIVIAN	97.0	97.0	0.0	0.0	0.5	0.5	1.0	0.5	5.5	6.0	6.5	6.0	5.0	21.4	29.4	16.9	3.5	77.6	44.9	54.7	45.3
57577	WANBLEE	13.7	12.7	0.0	0.0	0.0	0.0	0.4	0.4	11.3	11.3	12.2	12.0	10.7	21.8	15.6	4.9	0.4	57.4	21.5	51.2	48.8
57579	WHITE RIVER	40.0	38.7	0.0	0.0	0.1	0.1	2.1	2.1	9.2	10.1	10.2	7.9	5.4	22.8	21.6	10.7	2.1	65.6	31.7	50.1	49.9
57580	WINNER	86.5	85.9	0.0	0.0	0.1	0.1	1.0	1.0	7.0	6.8	7.5	7.1	5.9	22.3	23.3	16.6	3.5	74.0	40.7	49.1	51.0
57584	WITTEN	82.2	81.0	0.0	0.0	0.0	0.0	0.0	0.0	8.0	9.0	11.0	6.0	5.0	23.0	27.0	9.0	2.0	66.0	37.0	47.0	53.0
57585	WOOD	77.5	76.8	0.0	0.0	0.0	0.0	0.0	0.0	6.8	9.9	7.9	4.8	3.8	21.2	30.0	14.3	1.4	72.0	41.1	51.5	48.5
57601	MOBRIDGE	80.8	78.6	0.0	0.0	0.3	0.4	0.8	0.9	7.0	6.6	6.2	6.2	6.2	21.2	25.5	18.0	3.2	76.3	42.1	47.2	52.8
57620	BISON	97.8	97.5	0.3	0.3	0.0	0.0	1.0	1.3	6.8	7.3	6.5	5.7	5.0	20.1	29.0	16.6	3.0	75.7	44.0	51.8	48.3
57622	CHERRY CREEK	7.8	7.2	0.0	0.0	0.0	0.0	1.1	1.1	15.7	11.9	10.4	12.1	10.4	21.5	14.5	3.5	0.2	55.0	20.0	50.0	50.0
57623	DUPREE	32.5	29.5	0.0	0.0	0.1	0.2	1.0	1.0	10.8	9.1	10.1	8.4	8.7	24.4	20.2	7.7	0.5	65.0	27.0	48.8	51.2
57625	EAGLE BUTTE	15.6	14.0	0.0	0.0	0.0	0.0	0.2	0.3	9.8	9.9	11.4	10.0	7.5	26.2	17.1	7.4	0.7	62.3	26.3	50.1	49.9
57626	FAITH	94.1	93.3	0.1	0.1	0.0	0.0	0.4	0.4	5.9	6.3	7.4	6.6	5.0	21.1	29.7	15.1	2.9	76.2	43.4	52.5	47.5
	SOUTH DAKOTA	88.7	87.8	0.6	0.7	0.6	0.8	1.4	1.6	7.0	6.8	7.3	7.7	7.9	26.1	23.4	11.7	2.2	74.5	35.9	49.7	50.3
	UNITED STATES	75.1	73.6	12.3	12.5	3.8	4.2	12.5	14.1	6.9	6.7	7.2	7.0	7.3	28.6	23.8	10.8	1.7	75.1	36.0	49.1	50.9

ZIP CODE #	POST OFFICE NAME	2004 Per Capita Income	2004 HH Income Base	2004 HOUSEHOLD INCOME DISTRIBUTION (%) Less than $25,000	$25,000 to $49,999	$50,000 to $99,999	$100,000 to $149,999	$150,000 or More	MEDIAN HOUSEHOLD INCOME 2004	2009	2004 National Centile	2004 State Centile	2004 Home Value Base	2004 HOME VALUE DISTRIBUTION (%) Less than $50,000	$50,000 to $89,999	$90,000 to $174,999	$175,000 to $399,999	$400,000 or More	2004 Median Home Value
57420	AKASKA	27146	16	31.3	25.0	37.5	6.3	0.0	42500	47361	55	79	13	46.2	30.8	23.1	0.0	0.0	52500
57421	AMHERST	12776	56	30.4	37.5	25.0	7.1	0.0	36123	43209	32	45	45	51.1	28.9	17.8	0.0	2.2	48333
57422	ANDOVER	20999	145	31.0	36.6	26.9	4.1	1.4	35945	42669	31	43	117	59.0	19.7	17.1	3.4	0.9	39643
57424	ASHTON	21787	162	26.5	33.3	30.9	6.2	3.1	40403	50986	48	67	134	53.7	23.1	15.7	4.5	3.0	45455
57426	BARNARD	0	0	0.0	0.0	0.0	0.0	0.0	0	0	0	0	0	0.0	0.0	0.0	0.0	0.0	0
57427	BATH	24819	209	14.4	34.0	41.6	6.2	3.8	51209	60000	74	92	175	21.7	28.6	38.9	10.9	0.0	89500
57428	BOWDLE	16587	332	38.0	37.1	20.5	3.6	0.9	31962	38144	18	22	273	72.2	19.8	7.0	1.1	0.0	29300
57429	BRENTFORD	18010	13	30.8	30.8	30.8	7.7	0.0	37321	37321	37	54	11	63.6	36.4	0.0	0.0	0.0	42500
57430	BRITTON	20655	1002	30.5	31.4	31.1	4.9	2.0	38477	47155	41	58	758	42.5	35.9	18.2	2.6	0.8	58143
57432	CLAREMONT	20698	173	33.5	32.4	24.9	6.4	2.9	35753	44692	31	42	141	50.4	25.5	17.0	6.4	0.7	49500
57433	COLUMBIA	24108	176	25.0	34.1	30.1	6.3	4.6	41828	50260	52	74	146	36.3	26.0	28.1	8.9	0.7	68182
57434	CONDE	24751	269	31.6	30.9	27.1	7.1	3.4	36127	44309	32	45	220	50.9	27.3	15.5	4.1	2.3	48667
57435	CRESBARD	17719	116	35.3	34.5	24.1	4.3	1.7	32851	38233	20	25	96	56.3	15.6	19.8	4.2	4.2	41429
57436	DOLAND	17312	283	31.8	37.0	20.8	6.6	3.8	38372	45560	41	57	227	59.9	21.2	15.9	2.2	0.9	34773
57437	EUREKA	16319	730	49.2	29.5	16.4	3.6	1.4	25568	31126	5	7	578	65.1	22.5	8.8	2.6	1.0	30385
57438	FAULKTON	17708	615	35.0	31.7	27.0	5.2	1.1	34941	42676	27	36	474	55.1	28.9	12.7	2.3	1.1	45000
57440	FRANKFORT	18617	161	31.7	37.9	20.5	6.2	3.7	38840	45202	42	59	127	61.4	20.5	15.8	1.6	0.8	32917
57441	FREDERICK	19694	266	28.6	39.5	25.2	5.3	1.5	38830	45961	42	59	217	50.2	27.7	15.2	4.6	2.3	49800
57442	GETTYSBURG	21311	760	34.1	32.6	26.2	4.5	2.6	36396	44709	33	47	563	47.3	35.5	14.9	2.1	0.2	52981
57445	GROTON	21892	764	29.3	27.1	33.1	6.3	4.2	43083	53701	56	80	559	29.2	32.2	32.9	4.8	0.9	75595
57446	HECLA	25409	260	34.2	36.2	24.6	3.5	1.5	34534	42194	26	33	204	57.8	25.0	12.8	3.4	1.0	41111
57448	HOSMER	16069	176	39.8	36.4	19.3	4.0	0.6	31489	36890	16	20	145	70.3	19.3	9.0	1.4	0.0	29423
57449	HOUGHTON	17543	76	34.2	34.2	27.6	4.0	0.0	35000	42361	28	37	59	59.3	25.4	11.9	3.4	0.0	39167
57450	HOVEN	22085	330	32.7	34.6	23.0	5.8	3.9	35000	42498	28	37	273	49.1	27.8	18.3	3.7	1.1	51563
57451	IPSWICH	21584	954	28.4	30.0	31.5	7.2	2.9	42303	52896	54	76	748	32.0	30.4	27.3	9.0	1.5	75152
57452	JAVA	19755	165	31.5	32.1	29.7	6.1	0.6	34510	42679	26	32	136	64.7	15.4	11.8	2.9	5.2	31429
57454	LANGFORD	19056	247	30.4	36.0	27.9	5.7	0.0	35921	43267	31	43	199	52.8	28.1	15.6	2.5	1.0	46071
57455	LEBANON	23141	70	30.0	35.7	22.9	5.7	5.7	37345	41741	37	54	58	48.3	29.3	19.0	3.5	0.0	52500
57456	LEOLA	16125	396	42.9	32.6	18.7	4.0	1.8	28852	33940	10	12	315	63.5	16.2	14.0	3.5	2.9	34306
57457	LONGLAKE	18198	72	45.8	29.2	19.4	4.2	1.4	30000	35000	12	14	59	42.4	18.6	28.8	6.8	3.4	67500
57460	MANSFIELD	20828	149	19.5	28.9	42.3	7.4	2.0	51143	60790	74	92	124	30.7	30.7	25.8	11.3	1.6	77000
57461	MELLETTE	20875	211	25.1	32.7	33.2	6.6	2.4	41229	50497	51	71	174	54.6	24.1	14.9	4.0	2.3	44286
57465	NORTHVILLE	19867	116	25.9	34.5	31.9	5.2	2.6	40000	47884	46	65	96	53.1	22.9	16.7	4.2	3.1	46250
57466	ONAKA	18166	52	38.5	34.6	23.1	3.9	0.0	31455	35000	16	20	43	60.5	16.3	18.6	2.3	2.3	36250
57467	ORIENT	24619	139	28.1	30.2	30.9	7.2	3.6	40981	51429	50	70	111	57.7	19.8	15.3	3.6	3.6	38929
57468	PIERPONT	22026	122	30.3	36.9	26.2	4.1	2.5	36485	42576	33	47	103	55.3	20.4	16.5	5.8	1.9	43125
57469	REDFIELD	18944	1413	35.6	32.8	23.4	6.2	2.0	34663	42053	26	34	977	53.2	31.7	13.9	1.1	0.0	47308
57470	ROCKHAM	21523	102	29.4	30.4	30.4	6.9	2.9	40000	49453	46	65	82	57.3	17.1	18.3	4.9	2.4	38750
57471	ROSCOE	19135	258	31.8	40.7	20.5	4.7	2.3	33769	40130	23	29	209	64.6	24.9	5.7	2.9	1.9	34808
57472	SELBY	18671	502	31.5	34.9	26.3	6.6	0.8	35354	43223	29	39	387	56.9	26.1	16.0	1.0	0.0	42639
57473	SENECA	17990	84	35.7	31.0	26.2	4.8	2.4	35000	42368	28	37	69	60.9	13.0	21.7	2.9	1.5	35833
57474	STRATFORD	17662	108	29.6	34.3	26.9	4.6	4.6	37038	44684	36	52	89	32.6	27.0	30.3	6.7	3.4	75000
57475	TOLSTOY	23360	77	35.1	35.1	20.8	5.2	3.9	33602	40446	23	28	63	50.8	30.2	15.9	3.2	0.0	49167
57476	TULARE	21449	219	24.7	44.3	21.9	7.3	1.8	37869	45376	39	56	174	52.9	26.4	17.2	2.9	0.6	45455
57477	TURTON	26323	56	30.4	32.1	23.2	10.7	3.6	36123	47390	32	45	46	54.4	28.3	13.0	4.4	0.0	43333
57479	WARNER	21548	222	14.9	27.9	47.3	8.1	1.8	55409	64941	80	96	184	20.7	35.9	28.8	13.6	1.1	83684
57481	WESTPORT	18603	225	23.1	33.8	32.4	5.8	4.9	43234	52572	57	80	185	32.4	22.2	31.9	12.4	1.1	79583
57501	PIERRE	25740	6528	20.5	28.8	38.0	8.0	4.7	50531	61614	73	91	4463	15.5	18.7	50.4	14.8	0.6	107925
57520	AGAR	21944	63	34.9	38.1	19.1	6.4	1.6	35299	40562	29	39	49	40.8	20.4	24.5	8.2	6.1	71667
57521	BELVIDERE	17863	75	38.7	33.3	21.3	4.0	2.7	30260	31940	13	15	60	53.3	15.0	15.0	8.3	8.3	30000
57522	BLUNT	25282	213	20.2	27.7	41.8	8.0	2.4	51832	62219	75	93	179	27.4	19.6	38.0	14.5	0.6	93667
57523	BURKE	17760	511	45.8	29.4	21.5	1.6	1.8	27976	34161	9	11	377	48.0	34.2	13.8	3.2	0.8	51875
57528	COLOME	17166	282	33.7	33.7	28.7	2.1	1.8	36857	43208	35	51	232	47.8	24.6	18.5	6.0	3.0	52273
57529	DALLAS	16496	125	43.2	30.4	21.6	2.4	2.4	30214	36252	13	15	102	48.0	28.4	13.7	7.8	2.0	51818
57531	DRAPER	19648	116	35.3	31.9	25.0	6.0	1.7	35989	43448	31	43	88	54.6	25.0	13.6	5.7	1.1	45000
57532	FORT PIERRE	25378	1127	20.9	28.9	38.5	6.7	4.9	50098	60415	72	90	893	28.1	23.9	31.7	13.9	2.5	86635
57533	GREGORY	18133	908	44.8	29.7	19.5	4.3	1.7	28332	35000	9	12	667	52.2	26.4	17.2	3.5	0.8	46184
57534	HAMILL	13208	44	45.5	34.1	18.2	2.3	0.0	30000	38182	12	14	35	62.9	14.3	17.1	5.7	0.0	41000
57536	HARROLD	27448	205	31.7	33.7	23.9	5.4	5.4	36450	46055	33	47	150	43.3	27.3	16.7	12.0	0.7	57692
57537	HAYES	21685	53	17.0	39.6	32.1	7.6	3.8	43338	53693	57	81	41	19.5	17.1	22.0	31.7	9.8	117500
57538	HERRICK	14380	102	51.0	23.5	21.6	2.9	1.0	24267	27311	4	5	81	58.0	21.0	14.8	3.7	2.5	31250
57540	HOLABIRD	23469	52	26.9	36.5	25.0	7.7	3.9	41815	50000	52	73	42	42.9	31.0	16.7	7.1	2.4	57500
57541	IDEAL	11834	127	42.5	36.2	18.1	2.4	0.8	31107	37972	15	19	100	59.0	16.0	19.0	5.0	1.0	41818
57542	IONA	24274	65	29.2	27.7	32.3	4.6	6.2	42369	52659	54	78	55	32.7	34.6	23.6	9.1	0.0	67857
57543	KADOKA	16830	410	39.3	34.4	23.7	1.0	1.7	30876	35942	15	17	309	64.1	20.4	11.0	1.9	2.6	39028
57544	KENNEBEC	21783	202	30.7	28.2	31.2	4.5	5.5	40506	52049	48	68	169	37.3	33.1	19.5	8.9	1.2	63947
57547	LONG VALLEY	12410	69	34.8	31.9	30.4	2.9	0.0	27687	32337	8	10	58	69.0	17.2	13.8	0.0	0.0	38846
57548	LOWER BRULE	8796	381	49.3	32.3	16.0	2.4	0.0	25330	31115	5	6	156	35.3	42.3	19.2	3.2	0.0	68750
57551	MARTIN	13698	771	41.0	30.1	24.0	4.7	0.3	31031	37287	15	18	477	49.3	30.2	17.2	2.9	0.4	50795
57552	MIDLAND	20827	263	30.0	42.2	19.4	3.8	4.6	33475	40278	22	27	203	50.7	26.1	14.8	4.4	3.9	48846
57553	MILESVILLE	21236	52	30.8	32.7	21.2	11.5	3.9	33858	43657	24	30	40	27.5	27.5	22.5	12.5	10.0	80000
57555	MISSION	11919	1168	45.0	31.5	17.5	5.1	0.9	26982	32201	7	9	660	59.1	20.8	16.8	2.4	0.9	38103
57559	MURDO	19996	323	36.2	31.6	24.2	5.6	2.5	35272	43111	29	39	246	52.4	26.8	13.0	6.5	1.2	47273
57560	NORRIS	11120	121	49.6	29.8	16.5	4.1	0.0	25268	30634	5	6	75	64.0	14.7	17.3	4.0	0.0	21875
57562	OKATON	18034	65	38.5	32.3	23.1	4.6	1.5	33336	42348	22	27	50	50.0	28.0	12.0	8.0	2.0	50000
57564	ONIDA	22224	505	25.4	37.0	28.9	5.5	3.2	38725	48189	42	58	394	37.6	28.9	27.2	3.3	3.1	64231
57566	PARMELEE	5073	361	76.5	14.7	6.9	1.4	0.6	12458	13288	1	1	177	55.9	17.5	15.8	4.0	6.8	36563
57567	PHILIP	22666	541	29.0	33.1	25.9	7.0	5.0	37896	50656	39	56	434	41.0	34.3	21.2	1.8	1.6	58125
57568	PRESHO	18568	338	36.1	33.1	25.4	3.9	1.5	35210	43066	28	38	277	58.8	27.1	11.6	0.7	1.8	44024
57569	RELIANCE	33525	387	32.3	27.1	30.0	4.7	5.9	39887	51622	46	64	320	47.2	27.2	19.7	3.4	2.5	56000
57571	SAINT CHARLES	12778	25	56.0	28.0	16.0	0.0	0.0	21076	26093	2	3	19	73.7	21.1	5.3	0.0	0.0	22500
57572	SAINT FRANCIS	8904	1060	54.2	24.2	16.6	3.3	1.8	22479	27453	3	3	417	59.5	14.9	16.3	3.4	6.0	29821
57574	TUTHILL	15290	97	40.2	28.9	29.9	1.0	0.0	31084	37756	15	18	75	52.0	28.0	18.7	1.3	0.0	47500
57576	VIVIAN	18078	83	36.1	33.7	25.3	3.6	1.2	34524	43905	26	32	68	58.8	26.5	11.8	1.5	1.5	44000
57577	WANBLEE	6764	344	57.9	29.1	9.3	1.2	2.6	18595	21098	1	2	163	46.6	23.9	16.0	3.7	9.8	61154
57579	WHITE RIVER	12407	458	46.9	27.3	20.7	4.2	0.9	27310	35203	8	9	289	66.1	18.7	11.4	2.4	1.4	33654
57580	WINNER	18060	2042	39.0	29.9	24.5	3.2	3.4	33668	41165	23	29	1495	45.0	25.1	24.2	4.6	1.2	58297
57584	WITTEN	15331	45	46.7	33.3	17.8	2.2	0.0	28620	39072	10	12	36	63.9	13.9	16.7	5.6	0.0	37500
57585	WOOD	17710	117	41.9	24.8	25.6	6.8	0.9	31929	42362	18	22	96	59.4	11.5	15.6	7.3	6.3	40000
57601	MOBRIDGE	18677	1678	40.5	30.9	23.2	4.1	1.3	31189	38084	15	19	1094	45.6	30.5	18.5	5.4	0.0	55053
57620	BISON	19527	266	39.9	31.6	21.1	4.9	2.6	31926	39017	18	21	212	52.8	23.6	6.6	5.7	11.3	46842
57622	CHERRY CREEK	4929	162	71.0	22.8	5.6	0.6	0.0	15000	16488	1	2	53	64.2	24.5	11.3	0.0	0.0	44643
57623	DUPREE	10354	601	53.1	30.3	12.7	2.0	2.0	22671	26422	3	4	400	47.5	25.5	17.3	6.5	3.3	52857
57625	EAGLE BUTTE	10420	341	44.3	37.8	12.9	4.1	0.9	28165	31919	9	11	242	50.8	23.6	18.2	4.1	3.3	49259
57626	FAITH	18053	292	36.6	35.6	19.9	3.1	4.8	32644	38725	20	24	235	48.9	20.0	13.6	5.5	11.9	51563
	SOUTH DAKOTA	22046		27.6	30.9	31.1	7.0	3.4	42239	52729				25.5	24.3	36.2	12.2	1.8	90416
	UNITED STATES	25866		24.7	27.1	30.8	10.9	6.5	48124	56710				10.9	15.0	33.7	30.1	10.4	145905

ZIP CODE #	POST OFFICE NAME	FINANCIAL SERVICES: Auto Loan	Home Loan	Invest-ments	Retire-ment Plans	THE HOME: Home Improvements: Home Repair	Lawn & Garden	Furnishings: Comput-ers & Hard-ware	Major Appli-ances	TV, Radio, Sound Equip-ment	Furni-ture	ENTERTAINMENT: Dine out/ Carry out	Sports Equip-ment	Fees & Tickets	Toys & Games	Travel	Cable TV	PERSONAL: Apparel & Services	Auto Repairs	Health Insur-ance	Pets & Supplies
57420	AKASKA	89	70	48	63	79	89	66	79	75	65	88	93	59	87	70	80	82	78	94	109
57421	AMHERST	80	56	29	53	65	73	55	68	63	54	74	82	47	73	57	66	68	67	81	95
57422	ANDOVER	80	59	36	56	66	77	62	72	70	60	83	83	55	79	63	74	75	71	85	91
57424	ASHTON	97	68	35	64	79	88	67	83	77	66	90	100	57	88	69	81	82	81	98	115
57426	BARNARD	0	0	0	0	0	0	0	0	0	0	0	0	0	0	0	0	0	0	0	0
57427	BATH	97	91	75	88	94	99	84	91	87	85	107	108	83	109	86	87	102	89	94	113
57428	BOWDLE	64	48	31	46	53	63	52	58	59	50	69	66	46	66	52	62	63	58	70	72
57429	BRENTFORD	95	67	35	63	77	87	66	81	76	65	89	98	56	87	68	79	81	80	97	113
57430	BRITTON	83	61	38	58	68	80	65	74	74	63	87	85	57	83	65	78	79	74	89	94
57432	CLAREMONT	90	63	33	59	73	82	62	77	72	61	84	93	53	82	64	75	77	76	91	107
57433	COLUMBIA	96	74	47	70	83	91	71	84	79	71	94	101	65	94	74	82	88	82	96	113
57434	CONDE	96	68	37	64	78	89	69	83	79	67	92	98	59	90	70	83	84	82	99	112
57435	CRESBARD	78	54	28	51	63	71	54	66	62	53	72	80	46	71	56	65	66	65	79	92
57436	DOLAND	89	62	33	59	72	81	61	76	71	61	83	92	52	81	64	74	76	75	90	106
57437	EUREKA	58	43	27	41	47	56	46	52	52	44	61	59	40	58	46	54	55	52	62	65
57438	FAULKTON	77	56	35	54	63	74	60	69	68	58	80	79	53	76	60	72	73	69	82	88
57440	FRANKFORT	89	62	32	59	72	81	61	76	70	60	83	91	52	81	63	74	75	75	90	105
57441	FREDERICK	82	58	32	55	68	75	57	70	66	57	77	85	50	76	60	69	71	69	83	98
57442	GETTYSBURG	77	58	39	55	64	76	62	70	70	60	83	79	56	79	63	74	76	70	84	87
57445	GROTON	99	70	38	66	81	90	69	85	79	68	93	102	59	91	71	82	85	83	100	117
57446	HECLA	104	72	38	68	84	94	71	88	82	71	97	106	61	95	74	86	88	87	105	123
57448	HOSMER	63	47	30	45	52	62	51	57	58	49	68	65	46	64	51	61	62	57	69	71
57449	HOUGHTON	73	51	27	48	59	67	50	62	58	50	68	75	43	67	52	61	62	61	74	87
57450	HOVEN	93	71	47	65	81	91	68	82	77	67	91	96	60	90	72	82	84	81	97	112
57451	IPSWICH	98	71	41	67	80	93	74	86	84	71	98	101	64	95	75	88	90	86	103	114
57452	JAVA	79	55	29	52	64	72	54	67	62	54	73	81	46	72	56	65	67	66	80	93
57454	LANGFORD	79	55	29	52	64	72	55	67	63	54	74	81	47	72	57	66	67	67	80	94
57455	LEBANON	95	74	51	67	84	94	70	85	79	70	94	99	63	93	75	85	87	83	100	116
57456	LEOLA	64	47	29	45	52	61	50	57	57	48	67	65	44	63	50	60	61	57	68	72
57457	LONGLAKE	70	49	26	46	57	64	48	60	56	48	65	72	41	64	50	58	59	59	71	83
57460	MANSFIELD	93	84	68	83	87	91	81	88	83	81	101	105	76	100	81	82	96	87	90	108
57461	MELLETTE	97	68	36	64	79	89	67	83	77	66	91	100	57	89	70	81	83	82	99	115
57465	NORTHVILLE	93	65	34	61	76	85	64	79	74	63	87	96	55	85	66	78	79	78	94	110
57466	ONAKA	75	53	27	50	61	69	52	64	60	51	70	77	44	69	54	63	64	63	76	89
57467	ORIENT	115	81	42	76	94	105	80	98	92	79	108	119	68	105	83	96	98	97	117	137
57468	PIERPONT	85	60	32	57	69	78	60	73	69	59	80	88	51	79	62	72	73	72	87	101
57469	REDFIELD	75	56	35	53	61	73	60	68	68	58	80	77	53	76	60	72	73	68	81	84
57470	ROCKHAM	104	72	38	68	84	94	71	88	82	70	96	106	61	95	74	86	88	87	105	123
57471	ROSCOE	78	55	30	52	64	72	55	67	63	54	74	80	47	72	57	66	67	66	80	92
57472	SELBY	73	55	37	52	61	72	59	66	66	56	78	75	52	74	59	70	71	66	79	83
57473	SENECA	81	57	30	54	66	74	56	69	65	55	76	84	48	74	58	68	69	68	83	97
57474	STRATFORD	100	70	38	67	82	91	69	85	80	69	94	103	59	92	72	83	85	84	101	119
57475	TOLSTOY	92	70	45	64	79	89	67	81	76	66	90	95	59	88	71	81	83	80	96	111
57476	TULARE	94	66	34	62	77	86	65	81	75	64	88	97	56	86	68	79	80	79	96	112
57477	TURTON	95	67	35	63	77	87	66	81	76	65	89	98	56	87	68	79	81	80	97	113
57479	WARNER	87	93	91	94	91	91	89	89	84	89	106	106	88	106	87	80	104	89	80	100
57481	WESTPORT	97	77	52	73	84	94	76	87	84	75	100	102	70	99	77	87	93	85	99	112
57501	PIERRE	88	89	92	89	90	95	87	89	87	87	107	105	87	108	88	86	104	89	88	103
57520	AGAR	83	58	30	54	67	75	57	70	66	56	77	85	49	75	59	69	70	69	84	98
57521	BELVIDERE	78	54	28	51	63	71	54	67	62	53	73	80	46	71	56	65	66	66	79	93
57522	BLUNT	111	77	40	73	90	101	76	94	88	75	103	114	65	101	79	92	94	93	112	131
57523	BURKE	65	48	30	46	53	63	52	58	58	49	68	67	45	65	52	61	62	58	70	73
57528	COLOME	75	53	28	50	61	69	52	64	60	51	70	77	44	69	54	63	64	63	76	89
57529	DALLAS	69	48	25	46	56	63	48	59	55	47	65	71	41	63	50	58	59	58	70	82
57531	DRAPER	82	57	30	54	66	74	56	70	65	56	76	84	48	74	58	68	69	69	83	97
57532	FORT PIERRE	100	88	66	84	90	96	84	92	87	86	106	107	78	101	84	87	101	92	94	112
57533	GREGORY	68	50	32	48	56	66	54	61	61	52	72	70	48	69	54	65	66	61	73	77
57534	HAMILL	64	45	23	42	52	58	44	55	51	44	60	66	38	59	46	53	54	54	65	76
57536	HARROLD	147	111	67	105	123	136	108	129	120	108	143	153	96	139	111	124	132	127	146	172
57537	HAYES	98	68	36	64	80	89	67	83	78	67	91	100	58	89	70	81	83	82	99	116
57538	HERRICK	64	44	23	42	52	58	44	54	51	43	59	65	38	58	46	53	54	54	65	75
57540	HOLABIRD	105	74	38	69	86	96	73	90	84	72	98	108	62	96	75	88	90	89	107	125
57541	IDEAL	63	44	23	42	51	57	43	54	50	43	59	65	37	58	45	53	54	53	64	75
57542	IONA	99	69	36	66	81	90	68	85	79	68	93	102	58	91	71	83	84	83	101	118
57543	KADOKA	67	50	31	48	55	65	54	61	61	51	71	69	47	68	54	64	65	60	73	76
57544	KENNEBEC	100	71	39	67	82	91	70	86	80	69	94	103	60	92	72	83	86	84	101	118
57547	LONG VALLEY	68	54	36	52	60	65	52	61	57	51	68	73	47	68	54	59	63	60	69	81
57548	LOWER BRULE	46	37	47	34	36	43	44	43	49	45	61	49	42	58	42	51	59	46	46	50
57551	MARTIN	66	49	31	47	55	64	53	59	59	51	70	68	47	66	53	62	64	59	70	75
57552	MIDLAND	95	67	35	63	78	87	66	81	76	65	89	98	56	87	68	79	81	80	97	113
57553	MILESVILLE	103	72	38	68	84	94	71	88	82	70	96	106	61	95	74	86	88	87	105	123
57555	MISSION	54	46	49	45	47	52	51	52	54	50	66	61	48	65	50	54	64	53	54	61
57559	MURDO	81	57	30	54	66	74	56	69	65	55	76	84	48	74	58	68	69	68	83	97
57560	NORRIS	45	40	43	39	39	45	47	44	49	45	60	52	45	59	45	49	58	46	46	49
57562	OKATON	81	56	30	53	66	74	56	69	64	55	75	83	48	74	58	67	69	68	82	96
57564	ONIDA	99	69	36	66	81	91	69	85	79	68	93	102	59	91	71	83	84	84	101	118
57566	PARMELEE	28	23	32	22	22	27	28	27	32	29	39	31	28	37	27	33	38	29	29	31
57567	PHILIP	96	67	35	63	78	87	66	82	76	65	89	99	56	88	69	80	82	81	97	114
57568	PRESHO	79	55	29	52	64	72	54	67	63	54	73	81	46	72	56	66	67	66	80	94
57569	RELIANCE	127	113	85	108	114	122	108	117	111	110	136	136	101	129	107	110	130	117	119	142
57571	SAINT CHARLES	47	34	21	32	38	45	36	41	41	35	48	48	32	46	36	43	44	41	50	53
57572	SAINT FRANCIS	48	38	53	36	37	44	47	45	53	48	66	51	46	62	45	55	64	48	48	51
57574	TUTHILL	69	48	25	46	56	63	48	59	55	47	64	71	41	63	49	58	59	58	70	82
57576	VIVIAN	79	55	29	52	64	72	54	67	63	54	73	81	46	72	56	66	67	66	80	94
57577	WANBLEE	41	32	37	30	33	38	37	38	42	38	51	44	36	49	37	43	49	40	42	45
57579	WHITE RIVER	53	45	44	44	46	52	51	51	55	49	67	60	48	65	50	55	64	53	55	59
57580	WINNER	73	53	33	51	59	70	58	65	65	55	76	74	51	73	58	69	70	65	78	82
57584	WITTEN	62	43	23	41	50	56	43	53	49	42	57	63	36	56	44	51	52	52	63	73
57585	WOOD	80	56	29	53	65	73	55	68	64	55	75	82	47	73	57	67	68	67	81	95
57601	MOBRIDGE	63	54	49	53	56	64	59	61	62	57	75	69	55	73	58	64	71	61	66	70
57620	BISON	80	56	29	53	65	73	55	68	63	54	74	82	47	73	57	67	68	67	81	95
57622	CHERRY CREEK	28	22	31	21	21	26	27	26	31	28	38	30	27	36	26	32	37	28	28	30
57623	DUPREE	56	40	28	38	45	51	42	48	48	42	57	57	37	55	42	50	53	49	56	64
57625	EAGLE BUTTE	53	51	44	50	51	53	49	51	48	50	60	60	47	58	48	47	58	51	49	59
57626	FAITH	81	57	30	54	66	74	56	69	65	55	76	84	48	74	58	68	69	68	83	97
	SOUTH DAKOTA	84	74	67	74	77	84	76	80	79	75	97	94	73	95	76	79	92	81	84	95
	UNITED STATES	100	100	100	100	100	100	100	100	100	100	100	100	100	100	100	100	100	100	100	100

POPULATION CHANGE

#	POST OFFICE NAME	COUNTY FIPS CODE	POPULATION			2000-2004 ANNUAL RATE		HOUSEHOLDS					FAMILIES		
			2000	2004	2009	% Rate	State Centile	2000	2004	2009	% Annual Rate 2000-2004	2004 Average HH Size	2000	2004	% Annual Rate 2000-2004
57630	GLENCROSS	041	44	44	46	0.0	49	15	15	16	0.0	2.93	11	11	0.0
57631	GLENHAM	129	293	292	287	-0.1	44	114	116	116	0.4	2.52	85	87	0.6
57632	HERREID	021	756	718	678	-1.2	2	293	283	271	-0.8	2.51	205	199	-0.7
57633	ISABEL	041	3869	4040	4282	1.0	78	1189	1263	1360	1.4	3.11	859	915	1.5
57634	KELDRON	031	116	112	116	-0.8	10	46	45	47	-0.5	2.49	32	32	0.0
57638	LEMMON	105	1944	1892	1836	-0.6	20	831	825	816	-0.2	2.21	514	513	-0.1
57640	LODGEPOLE	105	194	191	185	-0.4	30	87	88	87	0.3	2.17	64	65	0.4
57641	MC INTOSH	031	409	402	415	-0.4	28	170	170	177	0.0	2.35	121	121	0.0
57642	MC LAUGHLIN	031	2591	2701	2836	1.0	77	732	766	807	1.1	3.53	558	585	1.1
57644	MEADOW	105	387	374	368	-0.8	12	155	153	153	-0.3	2.44	111	110	-0.2
57645	MORRISTOWN	031	154	149	153	-0.8	14	54	53	55	-0.4	2.81	38	37	-0.6
57646	MOUND CITY	021	324	308	290	-1.2	3	126	122	117	-0.8	2.49	88	86	-0.5
57648	POLLOCK	021	446	424	400	-1.2	3	204	197	189	-0.8	2.13	143	138	-0.8
57649	PRAIRIE CITY	105	165	160	155	-0.7	16	68	67	66	-0.4	2.39	49	48	-0.5
57650	RALPH	063	68	66	64	-0.7	17	31	31	30	0.0	2.13	22	22	0.0
57651	REVA	063	250	242	233	-0.8	15	82	81	80	-0.3	2.90	55	55	0.0
57656	TIMBER LAKE	041	909	933	981	0.6	68	315	326	345	0.8	2.86	233	242	0.9
57657	TRAIL CITY	041	80	83	88	0.9	74	28	30	31	1.6	2.77	21	23	2.2
57658	WAKPALA	031	739	804	865	2.0	90	206	228	248	2.4	3.53	156	173	2.5
57660	WATAUGA	031	91	88	91	-0.8	12	29	29	30	0.0	3.03	20	20	0.0
57701	RAPID CITY	103	39844	40965	42915	0.7	69	15710	16461	17595	1.1	2.37	9569	10047	1.2
57702	RAPID CITY	103	29483	31262	33252	1.4	85	11807	12793	13883	1.9	2.41	8489	9225	2.0
57703	RAPID CITY	103	10544	11657	12633	2.4	93	3879	4374	4831	2.9	2.67	2889	3258	2.9
57706	ELLSWORTH AFB	093	4292	4172	4385	-0.7	18	1083	1097	1202	0.3	3.28	1016	1025	0.2
57714	ALLEN	007	969	945	909	-0.6	21	230	226	219	-0.4	4.18	194	192	-0.2
57716	BATESLAND	113	551	541	569	-0.4	27	144	144	155	0.0	3.65	122	123	0.2
57717	BELLE FOURCHE	019	7146	7426	7798	0.9	75	2760	2898	3073	1.2	2.52	1906	2007	1.2
57718	BLACK HAWK	093	4621	5070	5544	2.2	91	1637	1845	2072	2.9	2.75	1320	1490	2.9
57719	BOX ELDER	103	4320	4635	5018	1.7	88	1553	1703	1886	2.2	2.72	1189	1298	2.1
57720	BUFFALO	063	728	704	680	-0.8	12	310	308	306	-0.2	2.18	204	202	-0.2
57722	BUFFALO GAP	033	336	369	411	2.2	91	147	166	189	2.9	2.20	108	122	2.9
57724	CAMP CROOK	063	230	221	212	-0.9	7	85	83	82	-0.6	2.61	61	60	-0.4
57725	CAPUTA	103	269	304	333	2.9	95	104	120	133	3.4	2.53	80	92	3.3
57730	CUSTER	033	5551	5950	6539	1.7	87	2292	2523	2849	2.3	2.25	1568	1732	2.4
57732	DEADWOOD	081	2357	2313	2369	-0.4	26	1044	1049	1100	0.1	2.07	653	657	0.1
57735	EDGEMONT	047	1275	1276	1305	0.0	50	578	591	617	0.5	2.14	387	398	0.7
57736	ELM SPRINGS	093	93	123	147	6.8	100	35	48	59	7.7	2.56	28	38	7.5
57737	ENNING	093	162	192	220	4.1	98	61	74	87	4.7	2.59	48	58	4.6
57738	FAIRBURN	033	200	221	247	2.4	93	83	94	108	3.0	2.32	61	69	2.9
57741	FORT MEADE	093	236	243	255	0.7	71	58	62	67	1.6	3.44	45	49	2.0
57744	HERMOSA	033	1382	1529	1708	2.4	94	530	602	689	3.0	2.51	391	445	3.1
57745	HILL CITY	103	1936	1960	2023	0.3	59	760	783	823	0.7	2.50	537	553	0.7
57747	HOT SPRINGS	047	5617	5768	5945	0.6	68	2317	2426	2550	1.1	2.19	1421	1494	1.2
57748	HOWES	093	117	116	122	-0.2	38	51	52	56	0.5	2.23	37	38	0.6
57750	INTERIOR	071	152	155	161	0.5	63	70	73	76	1.0	2.12	46	48	1.0
57751	KEYSTONE	103	656	771	861	3.9	98	269	325	372	4.6	2.31	190	229	4.5
57752	KYLE	113	1757	1817	1937	0.8	72	409	432	468	1.3	4.11	332	351	1.3
57754	LEAD	081	3645	3670	3774	0.2	55	1569	1615	1698	0.7	2.24	1011	1044	0.8
57755	LUDLOW	063	139	134	130	-0.9	8	48	48	47	0.0	2.79	34	34	0.0
57756	MANDERSON	113	1270	1329	1427	1.1	79	271	291	319	1.7	4.49	230	248	1.8
57758	MUD BUTTE	093	249	245	254	-0.4	30	95	96	102	0.3	2.55	72	73	0.3
57759	NEMO	081	467	484	502	0.8	73	110	117	125	1.5	3.53	80	86	1.7
57760	NEWELL	019	1244	1310	1385	1.2	82	492	527	564	1.6	2.48	350	376	1.7
57761	NEW UNDERWOOD	093	1153	1269	1376	2.3	92	412	464	516	2.8	2.64	311	351	2.9
57762	NISLAND	019	354	363	378	0.6	66	134	140	147	1.0	2.54	107	112	1.1
57763	OELRICHS	047	257	258	263	0.1	52	111	114	119	0.6	2.25	79	81	0.6
57766	ORAL	047	263	265	270	0.2	55	103	106	111	0.7	2.50	76	78	0.6
57767	OWANKA	103	84	97	108	3.4	97	30	35	40	3.7	2.77	22	26	4.0
57769	PIEDMONT	093	3193	3404	3666	1.5	86	1192	1303	1441	2.1	2.60	958	1049	2.2
57770	PINE RIDGE	113	7620	8232	8936	1.8	88	1664	1821	2002	2.1	4.41	1418	1552	2.2
57772	PORCUPINE	113	463	491	529	1.4	85	123	134	146	2.0	3.60	105	114	2.0
57775	QUINN	103	101	101	104	0.0	49	31	31	33	0.0	3.26	23	24	1.0
57777	RED OWL	093	69	69	72	0.0	49	28	29	31	0.8	2.38	22	23	1.1
57779	SAINT ONGE	081	347	362	378	1.0	77	131	140	149	1.6	2.59	105	112	1.5
57780	SCENIC	103	134	142	150	1.4	84	57	62	66	2.0	2.29	41	44	1.7
57782	SMITHWICK	047	20	20	21	0.0	49	8	8	9	0.0	2.50	6	6	0.0
57783	SPEARFISH	081	12120	12709	13293	1.1	80	5108	5491	5881	1.7	2.19	3052	3295	1.8
57785	STURGIS	093	8873	9257	9854	1.0	77	3642	3881	4233	1.5	2.33	2416	2590	1.7
57787	UNION CENTER	093	153	156	167	0.5	63	58	61	67	1.2	2.56	46	49	1.5
57788	VALE	093	446	448	464	0.1	53	166	170	179	0.6	2.58	133	137	0.7
57790	WALL	103	1273	1281	1326	0.2	54	526	538	566	0.5	2.36	340	347	0.5
57791	WASTA	093	165	189	209	3.3	96	64	73	82	3.1	2.59	46	53	3.4
57792	WHITE OWL	093	143	141	149	-0.3	32	52	53	57	0.5	2.66	38	38	0.0
57793	WHITEWOOD	081	1813	1905	2000	1.2	81	692	746	803	1.8	2.49	523	564	1.8
57794	WOUNDED KNEE	113	805	838	904	1.0	76	174	183	199	1.2	4.50	146	154	1.3
57799	SPEARFISH	081	888	918	950	0.8	71	151	162	173	1.7	4.42	92	99	1.7
	SOUTH DAKOTA					0.9					1.3	2.47			1.4
	UNITED STATES					1.2					1.3	2.58			1.1

ZIP CODE #	POST OFFICE NAME	RACE (%) White 2000	White 2004	Black 2000	Black 2004	Asian/Pacific 2000	Asian/Pacific 2004	% Hispanic Origin 2000	% Hispanic Origin 2004	2004 AGE DISTRIBUTION (%) 0-4	5-9	10-14	15-19	20-24	25-44	45-64	65-84	85+	18+	MEDIAN AGE 2004	% 2004 Males	% 2004 Females
57630	GLENCROSS	68.2	68.2	0.0	0.0	0.0	0.0	0.0	0.0	6.8	6.8	9.1	6.8	6.8	20.5	29.6	13.6	0.0	72.7	40.0	47.7	52.3
57631	GLENHAM	97.3	97.3	0.0	0.0	0.0	0.0	0.3	0.3	5.5	6.2	6.5	6.9	6.5	20.2	30.8	15.8	1.7	77.1	43.8	52.4	47.6
57632	HERREID	99.3	99.3	0.0	0.0	0.0	0.0	0.1	0.3	5.7	6.0	7.5	6.6	4.9	21.0	25.8	19.8	2.8	75.8	44.0	50.1	49.9
57633	ISABEL	18.5	16.9	0.1	0.1	0.1	0.2	1.2	1.2	10.5	9.4	10.5	10.4	9.0	25.8	17.4	6.1	0.8	62.6	25.1	47.9	52.1
57634	KELDRON	87.1	86.6	0.0	0.0	0.0	0.0	0.9	0.9	6.3	7.1	8.0	6.3	6.3	22.3	24.1	17.0	2.7	74.1	41.1	53.6	46.4
57638	LEMMON	95.8	95.2	0.1	0.2	0.4	0.5	0.6	0.6	5.3	5.5	6.5	6.4	6.0	21.3	25.3	19.5	4.3	78.6	44.3	47.6	52.4
57640	LODGEPOLE	96.4	96.3	0.0	0.0	0.5	0.5	1.0	1.1	5.8	5.8	5.8	5.8	5.8	17.3	30.9	19.9	3.1	79.1	47.7	50.3	49.7
57641	MC INTOSH	80.2	78.1	0.2	0.3	0.2	0.3	0.7	0.8	6.2	7.5	8.2	7.0	6.0	21.4	25.1	16.2	2.5	73.4	40.7	52.5	47.5
57642	MC LAUGHLIN	28.3	26.2	0.1	0.2	0.0	0.0	2.6	2.5	10.4	10.4	10.1	9.0	8.3	24.4	18.8	8.1	0.6	63.5	26.4	50.1	49.9
57644	MEADOW	87.6	86.9	0.3	0.3	0.0	0.0	1.0	1.3	7.0	7.5	7.2	6.2	5.4	20.6	27.5	16.0	2.7	74.6	42.4	50.8	49.2
57645	MORRISTOWN	87.7	85.9	0.0	0.0	0.0	0.7	0.7	0.7	6.0	7.4	8.7	6.0	6.0	20.8	24.8	17.5	2.7	73.8	41.6	54.4	45.6
57646	MOUND CITY	99.4	99.4	0.0	0.0	0.0	0.0	0.3	0.3	5.5	6.2	7.5	6.5	4.9	21.8	25.0	19.8	2.9	75.3	43.8	50.7	49.4
57648	POLLOCK	99.3	99.3	0.0	0.0	0.0	0.0	0.2	0.2	5.7	6.1	7.3	6.6	5.0	20.8	25.9	19.8	2.8	75.9	44.1	49.8	50.2
57649	PRAIRIE CITY	97.0	97.5	0.0	0.0	0.0	0.0	1.2	0.6	6.3	6.3	6.3	5.6	5.6	18.8	30.6	18.1	2.5	77.5	45.6	51.9	48.1
57650	RALPH	98.5	98.5	0.0	0.0	1.5	1.5	1.5	1.5	4.6	10.6	12.1	7.6	4.6	22.7	27.3	9.1	1.5	65.2	36.0	47.0	53.0
57651	REVA	97.6	97.5	0.4	0.4	0.4	0.4	1.6	1.2	4.6	7.9	9.1	11.2	3.3	24.0	27.3	11.2	1.7	69.4	38.8	51.7	48.4
57656	TIMBER LAKE	55.1	51.8	0.0	0.0	0.6	0.6	0.2	0.2	7.5	8.3	10.6	8.3	6.2	25.1	21.9	11.2	1.1	68.2	33.0	49.0	51.0
57657	TRAIL CITY	32.5	31.3	0.0	0.0	0.0	0.0	0.0	0.0	7.2	8.4	10.8	8.4	9.6	26.5	19.3	9.6	0.0	66.3	30.6	50.6	49.4
57658	WAKPALA	14.8	13.4	0.0	0.0	0.0	0.0	2.2	2.0	10.7	10.1	11.2	9.6	9.0	25.4	16.7	7.3	0.1	61.7	24.7	50.6	49.4
57660	WATAUGA	87.9	85.2	0.0	0.0	0.0	0.0	0.0	1.1	5.7	6.8	8.0	6.8	5.7	19.3	27.3	18.2	2.3	73.9	43.6	54.6	45.5
57701	RAPID CITY	80.1	77.9	1.2	1.4	1.2	1.7	3.5	3.8	7.7	6.5	6.5	8.2	10.7	28.7	20.7	9.4	1.9	75.0	31.5	49.7	50.3
57702	RAPID CITY	93.5	92.6	0.4	0.5	0.6	0.9	1.5	1.7	5.7	6.2	7.1	7.0	5.3	24.8	29.1	13.2	1.6	76.5	41.2	49.1	50.9
57703	RAPID CITY	90.2	88.7	0.6	0.7	0.7	1.0	2.2	2.4	8.4	8.0	7.8	7.0	7.1	30.8	22.8	7.7	0.5	71.6	33.1	50.1	49.9
57706	ELLSWORTH AFB	81.8	79.1	6.8	7.9	2.5	3.4	6.5	7.1	14.7	9.6	7.1	7.9	20.9	35.0	3.9	0.7	0.1	65.4	22.6	53.9	46.1
57714	ALLEN	15.7	14.0	0.1	0.1	0.0	0.0	1.7	1.7	9.6	11.8	11.9	12.2	8.7	23.8	16.9	4.9	0.3	59.1	22.7	51.9	48.2
57716	BATESLAND	13.8	12.6	0.5	0.6	0.0	0.0	0.4	0.6	10.5	10.5	10.7	9.2	8.7	26.4	18.1	5.2	0.6	61.6	25.2	48.8	51.2
57717	BELLE FOURCHE	95.3	94.7	0.1	0.1	0.3	0.4	3.4	3.8	6.7	6.5	7.9	8.0	6.8	24.3	24.7	13.2	2.1	73.5	38.4	49.0	51.1
57718	BLACK HAWK	94.9	94.2	0.3	0.4	0.3	0.5	1.2	1.4	7.0	7.2	8.0	7.8	6.8	29.5	27.1	6.2	0.5	72.5	35.5	49.0	51.0
57719	BOX ELDER	86.3	84.6	2.0	2.4	1.7	2.2	3.1	3.3	9.7	8.1	8.4	8.1	9.8	29.6	20.7	5.2	0.4	69.0	28.4	50.7	49.3
57720	BUFFALO	97.4	97.2	0.4	0.4	0.4	0.4	1.5	1.7	4.1	7.2	8.8	12.6	2.8	23.4	27.7	11.5	1.7	68.9	39.4	52.7	47.3
57722	BUFFALO GAP	94.4	93.8	0.3	0.5	0.3	0.3	1.5	1.6	4.3	4.9	7.3	7.9	3.8	22.5	35.5	11.9	1.9	77.8	44.6	50.7	49.3
57724	CAMP CROOK	97.8	97.7	0.0	0.0	0.9	0.9	1.3	1.4	4.5	8.1	9.5	8.6	3.6	24.0	28.1	11.8	1.8	71.0	39.5	49.8	50.2
57725	CAPUTA	93.3	92.4	0.0	0.0	0.4	0.7	0.4	0.7	5.9	6.6	6.6	6.3	5.6	24.7	32.6	10.9	1.0	77.0	41.6	51.3	48.7
57730	CUSTER	94.1	93.5	0.3	0.3	0.2	0.2	1.5	1.7	4.8	4.8	6.4	9.5	4.1	20.6	33.6	14.0	2.3	77.3	44.9	51.6	48.5
57732	DEADWOOD	94.8	94.0	0.1	0.1	0.3	0.4	1.9	2.0	3.9	4.0	5.2	10.3	6.4	23.6	31.6	13.8	1.4	80.6	43.0	51.0	49.0
57735	EDGEMONT	93.7	93.0	0.1	0.1	0.1	0.1	1.5	1.8	4.4	4.9	6.0	4.9	3.8	19.3	33.3	21.0	2.5	81.4	49.0	52.0	48.0
57736	ELM SPRINGS	89.3	87.8	3.2	3.3	1.1	1.6	2.2	2.4	10.6	6.5	7.3	8.9	10.6	30.1	20.3	5.7	0.0	69.9	28.1	52.0	48.0
57737	ENNING	92.0	90.6	1.9	2.1	0.6	1.0	1.2	2.1	8.3	6.8	7.8	7.8	9.4	27.1	22.9	8.9	1.0	71.4	31.7	52.1	47.9
57738	FAIRBURN	94.5	94.1	0.5	0.5	0.0	0.5	1.5	1.4	4.5	5.0	7.7	7.7	4.1	22.6	35.3	11.3	1.8	77.4	44.0	50.2	49.8
57741	FORT MEADE	95.3	95.1	0.4	0.4	0.4	0.8	0.9	1.2	3.7	5.4	7.0	7.8	2.5	18.9	31.7	20.6	2.5	77.8	47.7	56.8	43.2
57744	HERMOSA	94.5	93.9	0.3	0.4	0.2	0.3	1.5	1.6	4.5	5.0	7.5	7.7	3.8	22.8	35.8	11.4	1.6	77.4	44.3	50.2	49.8
57745	HILL CITY	93.3	92.5	0.1	0.1	0.1	0.2	5.0	5.6	4.1	5.0	8.2	7.9	5.1	24.3	31.2	13.6	0.7	77.6	42.4	49.5	50.5
57747	HOT SPRINGS	89.7	88.6	0.3	0.4	0.4	0.5	1.8	2.0	5.1	5.3	6.3	7.1	5.7	18.1	29.6	19.7	3.1	78.5	46.6	53.1	46.9
57748	HOWES	93.2	92.2	0.0	0.0	0.0	0.0	0.0	0.0	6.0	6.0	7.8	7.8	5.2	22.4	26.7	14.7	3.5	75.0	41.3	54.3	45.7
57750	INTERIOR	86.8	85.2	0.0	0.0	0.0	0.0	0.7	1.3	5.8	7.1	8.4	6.5	5.2	23.9	27.1	13.6	2.6	74.8	40.6	51.0	49.0
57751	KEYSTONE	95.3	94.6	0.3	0.3	0.0	0.0	1.8	2.1	5.1	6.2	7.4	6.5	4.2	23.4	35.0	11.5	0.8	76.8	43.4	50.5	49.6
57752	KYLE	4.8	4.4	0.1	0.1	0.0	0.0	1.5	1.3	11.2	10.0	12.1	11.6	9.7	25.7	14.5	5.1	0.2	59.2	22.7	49.3	50.7
57754	LEAD	95.8	95.4	0.2	0.2	0.2	0.3	2.5	2.7	5.6	5.6	6.7	7.4	7.2	27.3	27.6	11.4	1.4	77.5	39.0	51.0	49.0
57755	LUDLOW	98.6	98.5	0.0	0.0	1.4	1.5	2.2	2.2	5.2	8.2	10.5	7.5	3.0	23.9	27.6	12.7	1.5	70.2	39.4	47.0	53.0
57756	MANDERSON	2.8	2.4	0.0	0.0	0.0	0.0	1.7	1.4	11.0	10.1	12.9	12.4	9.5	24.1	15.1	4.7	0.3	57.6	21.9	51.2	48.8
57758	MUD BUTTE	96.0	95.9	0.0	0.0	0.0	0.0	0.4	0.4	6.1	6.5	7.8	6.1	4.5	22.9	28.2	15.9	2.0	75.1	42.2	52.2	47.8
57759	NEMO	91.7	90.5	0.2	0.2	0.4	0.6	1.5	1.7	3.7	4.1	4.8	15.3	3.9	23.1	30.8	12.8	1.5	77.5	41.8	54.1	45.9
57760	NEWELL	96.9	96.6	0.1	0.1	0.1	0.1	1.1	1.2	5.0	5.3	7.8	8.5	6.2	22.0	27.8	15.3	2.1	76.6	41.8	48.8	51.2
57761	NEW UNDERWOOD	92.8	91.7	0.5	0.8	0.3	0.5	1.1	1.3	7.6	7.2	8.4	7.6	6.5	26.0	22.8	11.0	3.1	71.9	35.9	49.2	50.8
57762	NISLAND	94.4	93.7	0.0	0.0	0.3	0.3	2.0	2.2	5.8	5.8	10.2	8.8	4.4	25.3	27.8	11.0	0.8	72.2	39.7	52.9	47.1
57763	OELRICHS	92.2	91.5	0.8	0.8	0.0	0.0	2.0	1.9	3.1	3.9	6.2	5.8	3.9	19.8	34.5	20.2	2.7	83.0	49.1	52.3	47.7
57766	ORAL	91.6	90.2	0.8	1.1	0.0	0.0	1.9	1.9	2.3	3.0	6.0	6.4	3.8	20.0	36.6	19.3	2.6	84.9	49.7	52.1	47.9
57767	OWANKA	91.7	90.7	1.2	1.0	0.0	1.0	1.2	0.0	8.3	7.2	7.2	7.2	6.2	28.9	24.7	10.3	0.0	72.2	36.3	50.5	49.5
57769	PIEDMONT	95.3	94.7	0.4	0.5	0.3	0.4	0.9	1.0	6.2	6.5	7.3	7.7	6.4	27.0	30.4	8.2	0.5	75.2	38.7	50.4	49.6
57770	PINE RIDGE	4.0	3.7	0.1	0.1	0.1	0.1	1.4	1.3	12.0	11.3	12.9	12.1	8.9	24.6	13.8	4.2	0.3	55.8	21.0	49.0	51.0
57772	PORCUPINE	1.7	1.6	0.0	0.0	0.0	0.0	1.5	1.4	11.2	10.4	13.0	12.4	9.4	24.2	14.5	4.7	0.2	56.6	21.6	51.3	48.7
57775	QUINN	96.0	96.0	0.0	0.0	0.0	0.0	0.0	0.0	5.9	5.9	7.9	8.9	5.9	20.8	29.7	12.9	2.0	74.3	41.1	53.5	46.5
57777	RED OWL	95.7	95.7	0.0	0.0	0.0	0.0	0.0	0.0	5.8	5.8	8.7	5.8	2.9	24.6	27.5	18.8	0.0	76.8	42.5	52.2	47.8
57779	SAINT ONGE	97.7	97.2	0.0	0.0	0.9	1.1	0.9	1.1	5.5	5.8	7.7	8.8	5.0	23.8	31.8	11.1	0.6	74.9	41.3	51.4	48.6
57780	SCENIC	94.0	93.7	0.0	0.0	0.0	0.0	0.8	0.0	6.3	7.8	7.8	6.3	4.9	22.5	28.9	14.1	1.4	73.9	41.7	52.1	47.9
57782	SMITHWICK	90.0	95.0	0.0	0.0	0.0	0.0	0.0	0.0	0.0	0.0	10.0	5.0	0.0	15.0	50.0	20.0	0.0	90.0	55.0	45.0	55.0
57783	SPEARFISH	95.9	95.3	0.3	0.3	0.5	0.6	1.7	1.9	5.1	5.1	6.4	8.5	10.4	25.7	23.0	12.5	3.3	79.3	35.4	47.8	52.2
57785	STURGIS	95.3	94.6	0.2	0.3	0.3	0.4	1.6	1.8	6.1	6.0	6.6	7.1	6.3	23.5	27.3	14.2	2.9	76.6	41.3	48.7	51.3
57787	UNION CENTER	95.4	94.2	0.0	0.6	0.0	0.6	0.7	0.6	5.8	5.8	8.3	5.8	5.1	26.3	26.9	14.7	1.3	76.3	40.0	53.2	46.8
57788	VALE	96.9	96.7	0.2	0.2	0.2	0.2	1.4	1.3	4.9	5.8	7.6	7.8	4.9	23.2	30.4	14.3	1.1	76.3	42.5	52.7	47.3
57790	WALL	92.6	91.7	0.2	0.2	0.4	0.5	0.6	0.6	5.8	6.0	6.8	8.4	6.3	21.0	28.4	15.3	2.0	76.2	41.2	49.4	50.6
57791	WASTA	92.1	91.0	1.2	1.1	0.6	0.5	1.2	1.6	7.9	7.4	7.4	6.4	6.4	25.9	27.0	10.6	1.1	73.0	37.5	51.3	48.7
57792	WHITE OWL	93.0	92.9	0.0	0.0	0.0	0.0	0.0	0.0	5.7	6.4	7.8	7.1	5.0	20.6	29.1	15.6	2.8	75.2	43.3	53.2	46.8
57793	WHITEWOOD	96.7	96.2	0.2	0.2	0.4	0.4	1.7	1.8	5.2	5.7	7.0	7.5	5.1	23.2	31.6	13.3	1.5	76.8	42.7	51.6	48.5
57794	WOUNDED KNEE	6.6	5.6	0.0	0.0	0.0	0.0	1.4	1.2	11.2	10.3	12.1	11.5	9.2	25.4	14.7	5.5	0.2	58.7	22.7	50.4	49.6
57799	SPEARFISH	95.7	95.0	0.5	0.7	0.3	0.4	0.9	1.1	3.9	3.8	5.7	18.2	19.8	20.3	21.2	6.3	0.8	82.8	24.6	49.8	50.2
	SOUTH DAKOTA	88.7	87.8	0.6	0.7	0.6	0.8	1.4	1.6	7.0	6.8	7.3	7.7	7.9	26.1	23.4	11.7	2.2	74.5	35.9	49.7	50.3
	UNITED STATES	75.1	73.6	12.3	12.5	3.8	4.2	12.5	14.1	6.9	6.7	7.2	7.0	7.3	28.6	23.8	10.8	1.7	75.1	36.0	49.1	50.9

SOUTH DAKOTA

INCOME

C 57630-57799

#	POST OFFICE NAME	2004 Per Capita Income	2004 HH Income Base	2004 HOUSEHOLD INCOME DISTRIBUTION (%) Less than $25,000	$25,000 to $49,999	$50,000 to $99,999	$100,000 to $149,999	$150,000 or More	MEDIAN HOUSEHOLD INCOME 2004	2009	2004 National Centile	2004 State Centile	2004 Home Value Base	2004 HOME VALUE DISTRIBUTION (%) Less than $50,000	$50,000 to $89,999	$90,000 to $174,999	$175,000 to $399,999	$400,000 or More	2004 Median Home Value
57630	GLENCROSS	11932	15	33.3	46.7	20.0	0.0	0.0	32153	35000	18	22	12	83.3	16.7	0.0	0.0	0.0	35000
57631	GLENHAM	19771	116	32.8	29.3	28.5	7.8	1.7	37045	44211	36	52	96	52.1	26.0	18.8	3.1	0.0	47143
57632	HERREID	16796	283	36.8	32.9	24.4	5.0	1.1	34528	41207	26	33	230	62.2	23.9	9.6	3.0	1.3	38077
57633	ISABEL	11231	1263	48.1	32.5	16.6	2.2	0.6	25993	30551	6	7	556	63.3	21.6	12.8	2.0	0.4	37619
57634	KELDRON	14844	45	42.2	31.1	22.2	2.2	2.2	30736	31140	14	17	37	78.4	13.5	5.4	2.7	0.0	17500
57638	LEMMON	20442	825	37.9	33.3	21.5	3.9	3.4	32467	40657	19	23	605	63.0	23.1	8.4	3.5	2.0	38663
57640	LODGEPOLE	19078	88	36.4	37.5	18.2	4.6	3.4	32664	39443	20	24	72	45.8	18.1	18.1	8.3	9.7	60000
57641	MC INTOSH	15071	170	46.5	28.2	21.2	2.4	1.8	27819	32902	8	11	133	75.9	12.8	8.3	3.0	0.0	19750
57642	MC LAUGHLIN	9211	766	53.5	27.4	16.6	1.6	0.9	22931	27614	3	4	411	68.4	20.2	8.3	3.2	0.0	32083
57644	MEADOW	17782	153	39.9	33.3	20.3	4.6	2.0	31432	37905	16	19	121	52.9	22.3	9.9	5.8	9.1	46500
57645	MORRISTOWN	12785	53	45.3	26.4	24.5	1.9	1.9	29061	32336	10	13	44	77.3	13.6	6.8	2.3	0.0	16667
57646	MOUND CITY	16837	122	37.7	32.8	24.6	4.9	0.0	33614	40973	23	29	99	62.6	24.2	9.1	3.0	1.0	37917
57648	POLLOCK	19782	197	36.0	33.0	24.4	5.1	1.5	34780	41333	27	35	160	61.9	24.4	9.4	3.1	1.3	38333
57649	PRAIRIE CITY	18117	67	38.8	32.8	20.9	4.5	3.0	32311	40000	19	23	54	48.2	22.2	11.1	7.4	11.1	52500
57650	RALPH	15644	31	48.4	32.3	12.9	6.5	0.0	26108	32320	6	8	24	37.5	29.2	12.5	4.2	16.7	57500
57651	REVA	14354	81	42.0	33.3	18.5	3.7	2.5	30305	36846	13	16	62	43.6	30.7	16.1	1.6	8.1	56667
57656	TIMBER LAKE	14571	326	38.3	37.4	18.7	3.4	2.2	31958	36155	18	22	246	63.4	20.7	11.8	3.3	0.8	41538
57657	TRAIL CITY	11583	30	53.3	30.0	13.3	3.3	0.0	23094	29032	3	4	23	43.5	17.4	4.4	21.7	13.0	65000
57658	WAKPALA	7685	228	56.1	30.7	12.7	0.4	0.0	20530	24314	2	3	130	60.0	13.9	21.5	4.6	0.0	32500
57660	WATAUGA	10057	29	48.3	27.6	24.1	0.0	0.0	26103	30000	6	8	24	79.2	12.5	8.3	0.0	0.0	17500
57701	RAPID CITY	20251	16461	31.2	33.2	27.5	5.5	2.6	37107	46605	36	53	8826	19.8	34.0	36.6	8.3	1.4	86636
57702	RAPID CITY	31654	12793	15.4	27.9	36.9	12.7	7.2	55899	70510	81	96	9636	4.8	9.3	51.9	29.2	4.8	144836
57703	RAPID CITY	20943	4374	20.8	34.9	34.9	5.9	3.4	45776	57190	63	86	3617	27.5	21.5	45.8	4.9	0.4	90772
57706	ELLSWORTH AFB	13144	1097	20.9	53.7	21.6	1.9	1.9	36815	41620	35	51	96	43.8	18.8	21.9	13.5	2.1	67500
57714	ALLEN	6036	226	51.3	40.7	6.6	0.4	0.9	24075	25849	4	5	114	61.4	14.0	22.8	1.8	0.0	41333
57716	BATESLAND	7815	144	66.0	19.4	8.3	6.3	0.0	19304	22224	2	2	81	72.8	24.7	2.5	0.0	0.0	23438
57717	BELLE FOURCHE	17008	2898	36.1	33.4	23.8	5.1	1.6	34639	41681	26	34	2127	37.9	26.6	27.0	7.5	1.0	67723
57718	BLACK HAWK	23041	1845	14.8	33.1	40.2	9.1	2.8	51470	63708	75	93	1640	17.7	22.7	46.9	11.8	0.9	101450
57719	BOX ELDER	17930	1703	24.0	41.1	28.9	3.5	2.6	40183	49839	47	66	1075	45.0	27.9	20.5	5.9	0.7	61797
57720	BUFFALO	19104	308	42.9	30.2	20.8	4.2	0.0	30187	36737	13	15	235	40.9	33.2	17.0	1.7	7.2	59348
57722	BUFFALO GAP	22161	166	27.1	33.7	33.1	5.4	0.6	42118	50585	53	75	140	32.1	22.1	23.6	18.6	3.6	84000
57724	CAMP CROOK	13204	83	44.6	34.9	15.7	3.6	1.2	28593	35000	10	12	64	40.6	18.8	15.6	4.7	20.3	63333
57725	CAPUTA	21639	120	19.2	37.5	34.2	5.8	3.3	46222	53875	64	87	98	32.7	13.3	36.7	15.3	2.0	95000
57730	CUSTER	22644	2523	26.2	30.6	33.6	7.1	2.5	43836	53575	58	82	1945	20.5	24.2	32.0	19.9	3.4	98991
57732	DEADWOOD	25576	1049	22.5	38.6	31.6	5.4	1.9	41787	51377	52	73	697	21.1	23.8	37.3	16.8	1.0	97100
57735	EDGEMONT	22509	591	37.4	29.1	25.7	6.4	1.4	35592	44474	30	40	474	59.7	17.5	12.7	5.3	4.9	37581
57736	ELM SPRINGS	22671	48	18.8	45.8	27.1	2.1	6.3	40000	50691	46	65	24	33.3	20.8	29.2	16.7	0.0	80000
57737	ENNING	20252	74	27.0	41.9	23.0	2.7	5.4	36266	43628	33	46	46	39.1	21.7	21.7	8.7	8.7	66667
57738	FAIRBURN	21114	94	28.7	34.0	30.9	5.3	1.1	41294	50684	51	71	80	32.5	22.5	22.5	18.8	3.8	83333
57741	FORT MEADE	14912	62	22.6	33.9	37.1	1.6	4.8	44179	53860	59	84	45	15.6	8.9	40.0	26.7	8.9	141071
57744	HERMOSA	19716	602	26.6	34.2	32.4	5.3	1.5	42578	51115	55	79	510	30.4	21.8	25.9	18.8	3.1	87105
57745	HILL CITY	24135	783	24.1	32.2	32.1	6.9	4.7	44377	54207	60	84	630	21.3	14.8	37.0	21.8	5.2	113918
57747	HOT SPRINGS	21180	2426	34.3	30.7	26.6	6.2	2.3	35411	45086	29	39	1668	35.4	33.1	24.0	5.2	2.3	71595
57748	HOWES	20046	52	34.6	34.6	21.2	3.9	5.8	33858	40000	24	30	42	47.6	21.4	14.3	7.1	9.5	53333
57750	INTERIOR	20280	73	37.0	32.9	23.3	4.1	2.7	30929	33396	15	17	58	56.9	13.8	13.8	6.9	8.6	28000
57751	KEYSTONE	27644	325	20.6	31.7	30.8	9.5	7.4	47529	60000	67	88	252	21.4	6.4	42.1	23.4	6.8	140972
57752	KYLE	9553	432	36.1	31.3	28.9	2.6	1.2	34594	41998	26	34	270	71.5	12.6	8.5	4.4	3.0	32200
57754	LEAD	21328	1615	29.4	38.5	27.4	3.5	1.2	36568	45393	34	49	1109	41.5	33.7	16.1	7.9	0.7	58591
57755	LUDLOW	11250	48	47.9	35.4	12.5	4.2	0.0	26090	32933	6	8	38	39.5	23.7	21.1	2.6	13.2	58000
57756	MANDERSON	7324	291	50.9	25.8	19.6	2.4	1.4	24049	28751	4	5	161	66.5	18.0	11.2	1.9	2.5	31250
57758	MUD BUTTE	16816	96	39.6	30.2	21.9	5.2	3.1	31479	36116	16	20	77	42.9	24.7	16.9	3.9	11.7	56875
57759	NEMO	14790	117	21.4	37.6	33.3	6.8	0.9	43395	52778	57	81	100	19.0	16.0	44.0	21.0	0.0	111765
57760	NEWELL	15530	527	40.0	36.1	21.1	1.9	1.0	30355	36376	13	16	395	53.2	26.8	9.6	6.8	0.0	47159
57761	NEW UNDERWOOD	18822	464	24.4	39.9	27.6	5.0	3.2	40364	47533	47	66	334	42.2	29.9	21.0	6.0	0.9	59286
57762	NISLAND	17904	140	34.3	31.4	30.0	2.9	1.4	33595	40199	23	28	115	38.3	18.3	26.1	12.2	5.2	59643
57763	OELRICHS	20524	114	32.5	37.7	22.8	6.1	0.9	33576	40974	23	27	92	54.4	18.5	18.5	2.2	6.5	42000
57766	ORAL	18551	106	30.2	42.5	21.7	4.7	0.9	33355	40839	22	27	86	47.7	19.8	23.3	2.3	7.0	56667
57767	OWANKA	19744	35	22.9	40.0	25.7	8.6	2.9	40735	50000	49	69	25	36.0	16.0	32.0	12.0	4.0	85000
57769	PIEDMONT	26559	1303	16.5	30.5	39.2	10.0	3.8	52132	64571	76	94	1122	14.1	18.6	39.0	24.1	4.2	112394
57770	PINE RIDGE	8008	1821	49.3	28.0	17.6	4.5	0.7	25520	32405	5	7	895	68.2	22.1	6.9	2.8	0.0	25625
57772	PORCUPINE	8345	134	52.2	26.1	20.9	0.8	0.0	22655	29072	3	4	74	70.3	14.9	10.8	1.4	2.7	28333
57775	QUINN	13983	31	32.3	35.5	25.8	6.5	0.0	35722	47396	30	42	25	40.0	28.0	16.0	8.0	8.0	71250
57777	RED OWL	17197	29	41.4	27.6	24.1	6.9	0.0	30711	31120	14	17	23	39.1	26.1	21.7	0.0	13.0	56250
57779	SAINT ONGE	21500	140	26.4	32.1	29.3	9.3	2.9	41531	49547	51	72	114	30.7	19.3	40.4	6.1	3.5	90000
57780	SCENIC	22344	62	24.2	32.3	33.9	8.1	1.6	43633	48642	58	81	50	44.0	18.0	24.0	10.0	4.0	66667
57782	SMITHWICK	12250	8	37.5	50.0	12.5	0.0	0.0	30000	37278	12	14	6	50.0	16.7	33.3	0.0	0.0	55000
57783	SPEARFISH	22600	5491	36.4	27.2	25.7	6.2	4.4	36197	45768	32	45	3248	18.8	18.8	44.0	15.6	2.8	108482
57785	STURGIS	22622	3881	30.7	33.5	28.3	4.9	2.7	38927	47586	42	60	2756	20.8	31.2	39.4	8.0	0.6	87669
57787	UNION CENTER	16951	61	42.6	27.9	23.0	4.9	1.6	30352	36894	13	16	47	34.0	27.7	25.5	2.1	10.6	61250
57788	VALE	17137	170	32.9	37.7	24.7	2.4	2.4	36235	42108	32	45	136	29.4	22.1	21.3	18.4	8.8	87143
57790	WALL	21900	538	30.7	31.4	28.4	7.1	2.4	40000	48258	46	65	402	46.5	27.6	17.4	6.2	2.2	55833
57791	WASTA	20924	73	23.3	35.6	27.4	8.2	5.5	42341	50000	54	77	54	40.7	16.7	31.5	9.3	1.9	75000
57792	WHITE OWL	16815	53	35.9	34.0	20.8	3.8	5.7	33317	40435	22	26	43	46.5	20.9	14.0	7.0	11.6	55000
57793	WHITEWOOD	22557	746	25.7	34.7	29.0	4.4	6.2	42054	51351	53	75	599	20.9	21.0	35.4	18.5	4.2	104066
57794	WOUNDED KNEE	5537	183	67.2	18.6	12.6	1.6	0.0	15293	18836	1	2	100	64.0	29.0	6.0	1.0	0.0	22500
57799	SPEARFISH	11428	162	35.8	24.7	26.5	9.9	3.1	37072	46169	36	53	100	13.0	20.0	48.0	17.0	2.0	114474
	SOUTH DAKOTA	22046		27.6	30.9	31.1	7.0	3.4	42239	52729				25.5	24.3	36.2	12.2	1.8	90416
	UNITED STATES	25866		24.7	27.1	30.8	10.9	6.5	48124	56710				10.9	15.0	33.7	30.1	10.4	145905

ZIP CODE		FINANCIAL SERVICES				THE HOME						ENTERTAINMENT						PERSONAL			
						Home Improvements		Furnishings													
#	POST OFFICE NAME	Auto Loan	Home Loan	Invest-ments	Retire-ment Plans	Home Repair	Lawn & Garden	Comput-ers & Hard-ware	Major Appli-ances	TV, Radio, Sound Equip-ment	Furni-ture	Dine out/ Carry out	Sports Equip-ment	Fees & Tickets	Toys & Games	Travel	Cable TV	Apparel & Services	Auto Repairs	Health Insur-ance	Pets & Supplies
57630	GLENCROSS	56	43	30	42	47	56	47	52	52	45	62	58	43	59	47	55	57	51	61	62
57631	GLENHAM	85	66	43	60	74	83	62	75	71	62	84	89	55	83	66	75	78	74	89	103
57632	HERREID	77	53	28	51	62	70	53	65	61	52	71	79	45	70	55	64	65	64	78	91
57633	ISABEL	51	43	46	41	43	49	48	48	52	48	64	56	46	61	47	53	61	50	51	57
57634	KELDRON	67	47	24	44	54	61	46	57	53	46	62	69	39	61	48	56	57	56	68	79
57638	LEMMON	76	56	35	54	63	74	61	69	69	58	81	78	54	77	61	72	74	68	82	86
57640	LODGEPOLE	75	52	27	49	61	68	52	64	60	51	70	77	44	68	54	62	64	63	76	89
57641	MC INTOSH	62	45	26	42	51	57	45	54	51	44	61	65	39	59	46	54	56	54	63	74
57642	MC LAUGHLIN	44	39	43	39	39	44	46	44	48	44	60	51	44	58	44	49	57	46	46	48
57644	MEADOW	79	55	29	52	64	72	54	67	62	54	73	81	46	72	56	66	67	66	80	93
57645	MORRISTOWN	65	45	24	43	53	59	45	55	52	44	61	67	38	59	47	54	55	55	66	77
57646	MOUND CITY	76	53	28	50	62	70	53	65	61	52	71	79	45	70	55	64	65	64	78	91
57648	POLLOCK	77	53	28	51	62	70	53	65	61	52	71	79	45	70	55	64	65	64	78	91
57649	PRAIRIE CITY	78	55	29	52	64	71	54	67	62	53	73	80	46	72	56	65	67	66	79	93
57650	RALPH	60	42	22	40	49	55	42	51	48	41	56	62	35	55	43	50	51	51	61	72
57651	REVA	76	53	28	50	62	69	52	65	60	52	71	78	45	69	54	63	65	64	77	90
57656	TIMBER LAKE	66	54	40	52	57	65	57	61	61	55	73	70	52	70	56	63	68	61	69	73
57657	TRAIL CITY	51	46	36	44	47	50	44	48	45	44	55	55	41	53	44	45	53	47	49	58
57658	WAKPALA	37	33	36	32	33	37	38	37	40	37	50	43	37	49	37	40	48	38	38	40
57660	WATAUGA	55	39	20	36	45	50	38	47	44	38	51	57	33	50	39	46	47	46	56	66
57701	RAPID CITY	69	64	70	66	64	69	71	68	71	69	88	82	69	86	68	68	85	71	66	77
57702	RAPID CITY	104	115	121	114	115	120	109	110	106	109	132	126	113	135	111	105	130	108	106	123
57703	RAPID CITY	83	83	75	83	82	84	79	82	77	81	96	96	78	94	78	74	94	81	76	93
57706	ELLSWORTH AFB	72	46	44	52	42	49	68	59	69	63	86	78	58	77	56	63	83	69	54	67
57714	ALLEN	38	30	30	29	31	36	34	35	38	34	46	40	32	43	33	39	44	36	39	42
57716	BATESLAND	38	35	43	33	33	39	38	37	42	39	52	42	39	51	38	43	51	38	39	42
57717	BELLE FOURCHE	69	58	44	57	61	67	59	64	62	58	75	74	55	72	58	63	71	63	68	77
57718	BLACK HAWK	88	97	97	99	94	93	92	91	86	93	109	108	93	110	90	81	107	91	80	100
57719	BOX ELDER	78	65	54	65	63	69	70	70	70	69	87	84	64	81	65	68	84	73	68	82
57720	BUFFALO	77	54	28	51	63	70	53	66	61	53	72	79	45	70	55	64	66	65	78	92
57722	BUFFALO GAP	88	62	33	59	72	81	61	76	70	60	83	91	52	81	64	74	75	74	90	105
57724	CAMP CROOK	63	44	23	41	51	57	43	54	50	43	59	65	37	57	45	52	53	53	64	75
57725	CAPUTA	86	79	64	77	79	84	76	81	77	78	95	94	72	90	75	76	91	81	80	96
57730	CUSTER	91	66	40	63	76	86	67	80	76	66	89	93	59	85	69	80	82	79	95	106
57732	DEADWOOD	83	74	63	69	79	89	73	80	79	72	95	91	70	94	76	83	90	79	91	98
57735	EDGEMONT	80	59	37	57	66	78	64	72	72	61	85	82	57	81	64	76	77	72	86	90
57736	ELM SPRINGS	93	59	57	68	54	64	88	76	90	82	112	101	76	100	73	82	107	90	71	87
57737	ENNING	89	58	45	62	60	69	74	74	79	71	97	94	64	89	67	76	91	81	76	91
57738	FAIRBURN	89	62	33	59	73	81	62	76	71	61	83	92	53	82	64	74	76	75	91	106
57741	FORT MEADE	97	68	35	64	79	88	67	83	77	66	90	100	57	89	69	81	82	81	98	115
57744	HERMOSA	89	64	35	60	73	82	63	77	71	62	84	92	54	82	65	75	77	76	90	106
57745	HILL CITY	106	78	48	72	90	101	76	92	86	75	102	110	66	100	80	91	94	91	109	127
57747	HOT SPRINGS	73	54	35	52	60	71	59	66	66	56	78	75	52	74	59	70	71	66	79	82
57748	HOWES	81	56	30	53	66	74	56	69	64	55	75	83	48	74	58	67	69	68	82	96
57750	INTERIOR	78	54	28	51	63	71	54	66	62	53	73	80	46	71	56	65	66	65	79	93
57751	KEYSTONE	103	92	73	86	99	107	85	97	91	84	109	113	80	110	89	95	104	95	107	126
57752	KYLE	58	52	52	49	51	56	54	55	57	55	70	63	52	67	53	57	68	56	56	64
57754	LEAD	70	64	62	63	67	72	67	69	69	65	84	82	64	84	67	69	81	70	72	81
57755	LUDLOW	57	40	21	37	46	52	39	48	45	39	53	58	33	52	41	47	48	48	58	67
57756	MANDERSON	46	37	49	35	36	43	44	43	49	46	61	49	43	58	43	51	60	46	46	49
57758	MUD BUTTE	78	54	28	51	63	71	54	66	62	53	72	80	46	71	56	65	66	65	79	92
57759	NEMO	93	73	50	66	82	93	69	83	78	68	92	97	62	91	74	83	86	82	98	114
57760	NEWELL	65	48	29	45	53	62	50	58	57	48	67	67	44	64	51	60	61	58	68	74
57761	NEW UNDERWOOD	79	68	59	68	67	72	72	72	72	72	90	87	67	84	68	70	86	75	70	84
57762	NISLAND	83	58	30	55	68	76	57	71	66	57	77	85	49	76	59	69	71	70	84	99
57763	OELRICHS	77	60	41	55	67	77	59	70	67	58	79	80	53	77	62	71	73	69	83	92
57766	ORAL	79	62	42	56	69	78	58	70	66	58	78	82	52	77	62	70	73	69	83	96
57767	OWANKA	78	70	78	75	69	75	80	76	79	78	98	93	76	93	75	75	95	81	72	84
57769	PIEDMONT	102	103	95	103	103	105	98	100	96	98	119	119	97	121	97	93	116	99	96	117
57770	PINE RIDGE	49	41	52	39	40	47	47	46	52	49	65	52	47	63	46	54	63	49	49	53
57772	PORCUPINE	41	33	46	31	32	39	40	39	45	42	56	44	40	54	39	47	55	42	42	44
57775	QUINN	82	58	30	54	67	75	57	70	65	56	77	85	49	75	59	69	70	69	84	98
57777	RED OWL	74	52	27	49	60	67	51	63	59	50	69	76	44	68	53	62	63	62	75	88
57779	SAINT ONGE	89	79	60	75	84	90	73	81	78	73	95	97	72	97	75	80	90	79	88	105
57780	SCENIC	73	71	74	73	73	78	72	74	71	71	88	87	70	86	72	70	85	74	74	85
57782	SMITHWICK	52	41	28	37	46	52	38	46	43	38	52	54	34	51	41	46	48	46	55	63
57783	SPEARFISH	73	63	71	66	63	70	73	70	74	71	93	85	69	88	69	72	89	75	70	81
57785	STURGIS	85	70	52	68	74	84	73	79	78	71	93	90	67	90	72	80	87	78	88	95
57787	UNION CENTER	77	54	30	52	61	69	55	66	63	54	74	80	47	72	56	65	68	66	77	90
57788	VALE	81	56	29	53	66	73	56	69	64	55	75	83	47	74	58	67	68	68	82	96
57790	WALL	85	65	44	63	72	83	69	77	76	66	90	89	62	87	69	80	83	77	91	97
57791	WASTA	76	72	81	76	71	76	79	76	77	77	96	92	76	92	75	73	93	79	72	84
57792	WHITE OWL	81	57	30	53	66	74	56	69	64	55	75	83	48	74	58	67	69	68	82	96
57793	WHITEWOOD	102	73	41	69	84	94	72	87	82	71	96	105	62	95	74	85	88	86	103	120
57794	WOUNDED KNEE	34	27	38	25	26	31	33	32	37	34	46	36	32	44	32	39	45	34	34	36
57799	SPEARFISH	71	57	74	64	56	62	79	69	77	73	97	88	72	91	70	71	94	78	64	77
	SOUTH DAKOTA	84	74	67	74	77	84	76	80	79	75	97	94	73	95	76	79	92	81	84	95
	UNITED STATES	100	100	100	100	100	100	100	100	100	100	100	100	100	100	100	100	100	100	100	100

ZIP CODE #	POST OFFICE NAME	COUNTY FIPS CODE	POPULATION 2000	2004	2009	2000-2004 ANNUAL RATE % Rate	State Centile	HOUSEHOLDS 2000	2004	2009	% Annual Rate 2000-2004	2004 Average HH Size	FAMILIES 2000	2004	% Annual Rate 2000-2004
37010	ADAMS	147	3312	3799	4308	3.3	96	1170	1363	1566	3.7	2.75	952	1092	3.3
37012	ALEXANDRIA	041	1949	2053	2125	1.2	66	785	839	879	1.6	2.44	576	604	1.1
37013	ANTIOCH	037	49947	51120	52566	0.6	43	20968	21498	22130	0.6	2.37	12436	12367	-0.1
37014	ARRINGTON	187	1278	1379	1556	1.8	81	472	517	592	2.2	2.67	380	408	1.7
37015	ASHLAND CITY	021	16721	17782	19076	1.5	72	6078	6553	7122	1.8	2.67	4634	4915	1.4
37016	AUBURNTOWN	189	972	1034	1103	1.5	73	364	394	426	1.9	2.61	284	302	1.5
37018	BEECHGROVE	031	1645	1809	1935	2.3	89	686	773	841	2.9	2.34	508	561	2.4
37019	BELFAST	117	643	686	738	1.5	75	228	247	268	1.9	2.77	175	186	1.4
37020	BELL BUCKLE	003	3521	4128	4741	3.8	97	1338	1590	1842	4.1	2.58	1021	1190	3.7
37022	BETHPAGE	165	4725	4999	5334	1.3	69	1762	1903	2066	1.8	2.62	1375	1457	1.4
37023	BIG ROCK	161	1923	1967	2008	0.5	42	723	748	770	0.8	2.63	544	552	0.3
37025	BON AQUA	081	5087	5556	5916	2.1	86	1860	2062	2220	2.5	2.69	1419	1546	2.0
37026	BRADYVILLE	015	2094	2221	2306	1.4	71	769	825	865	1.7	2.69	597	629	1.2
37027	BRENTWOOD	187	36382	40448	45426	2.5	92	13083	14820	16845	3.0	2.71	10290	11453	2.6
37028	BUMPUS MILLS	161	626	635	643	0.3	36	252	257	262	0.5	2.47	189	189	0.0
37029	BURNS	043	4392	4650	5008	1.4	69	1651	1784	1953	1.8	2.60	1311	1394	1.5
37030	CARTHAGE	159	6138	6067	6144	-0.3	10	2482	2487	2545	0.1	2.38	1683	1644	-0.6
37031	CASTALIAN SPRINGS	165	2502	2714	2932	1.9	83	948	1052	1158	2.5	2.58	763	832	2.1
37032	CEDAR HILL	147	3543	3887	4350	2.2	88	1251	1392	1579	2.5	2.78	1016	1113	2.2
37033	CENTERVILLE	081	8094	8130	8306	0.1	25	3194	3255	3362	0.5	2.43	2245	2238	-0.1
37034	CHAPEL HILL	117	5062	5645	6217	2.6	92	1852	2088	2318	2.9	2.70	1451	1607	2.4
37035	CHAPMANSBORO	021	2783	2923	3107	1.2	64	961	1022	1100	1.5	2.85	780	818	1.1
37036	CHARLOTTE	043	5313	5640	6034	1.4	72	1975	2129	2311	1.8	2.57	1493	1579	1.3
37037	CHRISTIANA	149	3877	4455	5293	3.3	97	1356	1579	1898	3.7	2.82	1089	1245	3.2
37040	CLARKSVILLE	125	31120	33787	37355	2.0	83	11931	13117	14694	2.3	2.48	8039	8688	1.8
37042	CLARKSVILLE	125	53902	59042	65510	2.2	88	18737	20721	23204	2.4	2.84	14588	15850	2.0
37043	CLARKSVILLE	125	31576	34201	37689	1.9	83	12259	13484	15072	2.3	2.48	8851	9564	1.8
37046	COLLEGE GROVE	187	3332	3650	4113	2.2	88	1200	1337	1528	2.6	2.73	964	1056	2.2
37047	CORNERSVILLE	117	2352	2541	2744	1.8	81	878	963	1053	2.2	2.63	655	703	1.7
37048	COTTONTOWN	165	5184	5595	6102	1.8	81	1888	2069	2292	2.2	2.70	1538	1667	1.9
37049	CROSS PLAINS	147	2748	3118	3551	3.0	95	1015	1170	1352	3.4	2.66	831	945	3.1
37050	CUMBERLAND CITY	161	1488	1473	1496	-0.2	10	588	587	602	0.0	2.49	437	429	-0.4
37051	CUMBERLAND FURNACE	043	3204	3521	3853	2.2	89	1205	1345	1492	2.6	2.61	940	1029	2.2
37052	CUNNINGHAM	125	2636	2773	2985	1.2	65	983	1050	1144	1.6	2.64	793	832	1.1
37055	DICKSON	043	24008	25454	27387	1.4	70	9264	9962	10868	1.7	2.51	6655	7024	1.3
37057	DIXON SPRINGS	169	979	1044	1096	1.5	75	361	390	414	1.8	2.67	275	292	1.4
37058	DOVER	161	6454	6745	6973	1.0	61	2606	2764	2889	1.4	2.40	1903	1985	1.0
37059	DOWELLTOWN	041	1650	1666	1676	0.2	31	653	670	683	0.6	2.46	478	482	0.2
37060	EAGLEVILLE	149	1971	2213	2575	2.8	93	739	843	995	3.2	2.60	582	650	2.6
37061	ERIN	083	5540	5570	5630	0.1	27	2184	2233	2293	0.5	2.41	1557	1560	0.1
37062	FAIRVIEW	187	9314	10118	11348	2.0	84	3422	3809	4348	2.6	2.65	2670	2918	2.1
37064	FRANKLIN	187	37184	41308	47019	2.5	92	13469	15203	17571	2.9	2.67	10435	11617	2.6
37066	GALLATIN	165	33849	36700	39983	1.9	83	12836	14216	15798	2.4	2.52	9423	10277	2.1
37067	FRANKLIN	187	15249	17801	20748	3.7	97	5989	7096	8383	4.1	2.51	4332	5057	3.7
37069	FRANKLIN	187	16287	19329	22687	4.1	98	5427	6538	7772	4.5	2.96	4674	5551	4.1
37072	GOODLETTSVILLE	037	27377	28719	30392	1.1	63	10778	11368	12117	1.3	2.51	7782	8091	0.9
37073	GREENBRIER	147	11414	12482	13960	2.1	87	4197	4674	5309	2.6	2.67	3374	3700	2.2
37074	HARTSVILLE	169	6592	6876	7265	1.0	59	2502	2638	2816	1.3	2.54	1807	1869	0.8
37075	HENDERSONVILLE	165	47787	50502	54227	1.3	68	18219	19716	21598	1.9	2.55	13604	14443	1.4
37076	HERMITAGE	037	30589	33685	36182	2.3	90	12910	14183	15216	2.2	2.34	8095	8693	1.7
37078	HURRICANE MILLS	085	912	885	877	-0.7	4	360	357	359	-0.2	2.44	250	242	-0.8
37079	INDIAN MOUND	161	2143	2162	2209	0.2	30	839	858	886	0.5	2.52	637	640	0.1
37080	JOELTON	037	6806	7227	7642	1.4	72	2560	2741	2922	1.6	2.63	1980	2089	1.3
37082	KINGSTON SPRINGS	021	5833	6448	7055	2.4	91	2110	2375	2634	2.8	2.71	1719	1908	2.5
37083	LAFAYETTE	111	11733	12194	12645	0.9	56	4688	4934	5164	1.2	2.45	3420	3534	0.8
37085	LASCASSAS	149	2792	3332	4008	4.3	99	1012	1223	1492	4.6	2.68	815	968	4.1
37086	LA VERGNE	149	18712	24144	30283	6.2	100	6548	8579	10895	6.6	2.81	5196	6669	6.1
37087	LEBANON	189	31501	34689	38535	2.3	90	12078	13560	15353	2.8	2.48	8606	9486	2.3
37090	LEBANON	189	12007	12736	13882	1.4	71	4462	4820	5341	1.8	2.64	3533	3749	1.4
37091	LEWISBURG	117	19100	20025	21344	1.1	62	7444	7895	8504	1.4	2.49	5272	5476	0.9
37095	LIBERTY	041	2129	2145	2169	0.2	29	843	862	882	0.5	2.48	637	640	0.1
37096	LINDEN	135	4632	4693	4776	0.3	33	1841	1894	1957	0.7	2.40	1309	1320	0.2
37097	LOBELVILLE	135	2915	2956	3008	0.3	35	1151	1193	1237	0.9	2.48	830	843	0.4
37098	LYLES	081	5110	5494	5776	1.7	79	1889	2061	2189	2.1	2.67	1451	1556	1.7
37101	MC EWEN	085	5732	5824	5876	0.4	37	2257	2337	2390	0.8	2.49	1639	1662	0.3
37110	MC MINNVILLE	177	30646	30970	31420	0.3	31	12300	12645	13015	0.7	2.40	8626	8689	0.2
37115	MADISON	037	34301	34942	35815	0.4	39	15123	15420	15845	0.5	2.24	8536	8464	-0.2
37118	MILTON	149	1305	1344	1478	0.7	48	403	424	476	1.2	2.93	323	334	0.8
37122	MOUNT JULIET	189	32176	36358	40987	2.9	94	11402	13162	15114	3.4	2.75	9508	10824	3.1
37127	MURFREESBORO	149	10873	12940	15621	4.2	98	3801	4576	5590	4.5	2.79	3021	3581	4.1
37128	MURFREESBORO	149	18471	23373	29091	5.7	100	6586	8482	10708	6.1	2.74	5134	6470	5.6
37129	MURFREESBORO	149	38090	42085	48931	2.4	90	13743	15485	18303	2.9	2.66	10399	11507	2.4
37130	MURFREESBORO	149	41414	47527	56411	3.3	96	17143	19889	23915	3.6	2.33	9244	10390	2.8
37132	MURFREESBORO	149	2983	2988	2999	0.0	23	34	37	43	2.0	2.00	22	24	2.1
37134	NEW JOHNSONVILLE	085	3018	3201	3306	1.4	70	1210	1314	1378	2.0	2.44	912	972	1.5
37135	NOLENSVILLE	187	4300	4903	5642	3.1	95	1435	1648	1913	3.3	2.98	1215	1378	3.0
37137	NUNNELLY	081	1897	2041	2142	1.7	79	756	841	902	2.5	1.95	552	601	2.0
37138	OLD HICKORY	037	21566	22845	24295	1.4	69	8473	9047	9693	1.6	2.52	6168	6500	1.2
37140	ONLY	081	1281	1331	1367	0.9	56	76	84	90	2.4	2.56	55	60	2.1
37141	ORLINDA	147	745	809	901	2.0	84	292	323	365	2.4	2.50	227	247	2.0
37142	PALMYRA	125	1550	1651	1788	1.5	74	531	573	628	1.8	2.82	424	449	1.4
37143	PEGRAM	021	3843	4064	4369	1.3	68	1411	1518	1655	1.7	2.61	1111	1175	1.3
37144	PETERSBURG	103	2945	3126	3267	1.4	71	1141	1231	1300	1.8	2.53	867	916	1.3
37145	PLEASANT SHADE	159	3049	3295	3463	1.8	81	1173	1291	1373	2.3	2.55	911	984	1.8
37146	PLEASANT VIEW	021	5110	5483	5939	1.7	78	1778	1934	2123	2.0	2.83	1478	1588	1.7
37148	PORTLAND	165	17362	19346	21310	2.6	92	6482	7344	8226	3.0	2.62	4973	5535	2.6
37149	READYVILLE	149	2238	2391	2631	1.6	76	827	903	1010	2.1	2.62	647	692	1.6
37150	RED BOILING SPRINGS	111	4877	4949	5064	0.4	36	1907	1968	2042	0.7	2.46	1376	1391	0.3
37151	RIDDLETON	159	318	377	414	4.1	98	123	148	165	4.5	2.55	95	113	4.2
37153	ROCKVALE	149	4516	5100	5979	2.9	94	1558	1787	2121	3.3	2.85	1274	1435	2.8
37160	SHELBYVILLE	003	27224	28839	31053	1.4	70	10107	10742	11598	1.4	2.64	7395	7720	1.0
37166	SMITHVILLE	041	12622	12833	13009	0.4	37	4988	5145	5278	0.7	2.44	3540	3581	0.3
37167	SMYRNA	149	34906	40859	49063	3.8	97	12717	15205	18553	4.3	2.67	9704	11330	3.7
37171	SOUTHSIDE	125	1020	1062	1137	1.0	58	384	407	442	1.4	2.61	301	313	0.9
37172	SPRINGFIELD	147	24895	27289	30527	2.2	88	9242	10275	11660	2.5	2.62	6834	7469	2.1
	TENNESSEE					1.0					1.3	2.45			0.9
	UNITED STATES					1.2					1.3	2.58			1.1

ZIP CODE #	POST OFFICE NAME	RACE (%) White 2000	White 2004	Black 2000	Black 2004	Asian/Pacific 2000	Asian/Pacific 2004	% Hispanic Origin 2000	% Hispanic Origin 2004	2004 AGE DISTRIBUTION (%) 0-4	5-9	10-14	15-19	20-24	25-44	45-64	65-84	85+	18+	MEDIAN AGE 2004	% 2004 Males	% 2004 Females
37010	ADAMS	92.1	91.2	5.2	5.5	0.7	0.8	2.1	2.6	6.4	7.0	7.8	6.8	5.2	29.0	26.9	9.7	1.3	74.4	38.6	50.6	49.4
37012	ALEXANDRIA	94.6	94.2	3.7	3.9	0.1	0.1	0.8	0.9	6.6	6.7	6.8	6.2	5.7	30.2	24.3	11.6	2.0	75.9	37.8	49.5	50.5
37013	ANTIOCH	65.6	62.6	25.1	26.7	4.0	4.8	5.6	6.5	7.5	6.7	6.3	6.2	9.1	38.8	20.3	4.8	0.5	76.1	31.8	49.0	51.0
37014	ARRINGTON	92.2	91.5	6.6	7.0	0.3	0.4	1.2	1.4	5.8	6.5	7.3	6.6	4.7	25.3	31.7	10.9	1.2	76.3	41.7	51.3	48.7
37015	ASHLAND CITY	96.1	95.7	1.9	2.0	0.2	0.3	1.4	1.7	6.7	6.9	7.3	6.6	6.2	30.8	25.3	8.9	1.2	74.8	36.6	50.2	49.8
37016	AUBURNTOWN	97.3	96.9	1.4	1.6	0.0	0.2	1.1	1.3	6.1	6.4	7.5	6.7	5.7	29.2	26.6	10.6	1.3	75.9	38.5	50.6	49.4
37018	BEECHGROVE	97.2	96.9	1.2	1.2	0.6	0.8	1.1	1.3	6.0	6.3	6.7	6.1	5.8	28.0	26.8	13.3	1.0	77.2	39.9	51.4	48.7
37019	BELFAST	94.3	93.6	3.4	3.8	0.3	0.3	2.0	2.2	6.4	6.6	7.1	6.9	5.5	28.6	28.6	9.2	1.2	75.4	38.2	49.1	50.9
37020	BELL BUCKLE	94.6	94.0	3.5	3.7	0.6	0.7	1.4	1.7	6.6	6.9	7.8	6.4	5.5	31.0	24.9	10.0	1.0	74.6	36.5	50.5	49.5
37022	BETHPAGE	96.4	95.9	1.9	2.1	0.2	0.2	0.9	1.1	5.5	6.2	7.1	6.7	6.5	28.9	27.6	10.6	1.0	76.9	38.5	50.5	49.5
37023	BIG ROCK	97.3	97.0	0.3	0.4	0.3	0.3	1.2	1.4	6.9	7.0	7.6	6.8	6.1	28.4	24.8	11.2	1.2	74.4	37.0	50.0	50.0
37025	BON AQUA	96.7	96.3	1.4	1.5	0.1	0.2	1.1	1.3	7.7	7.8	8.0	6.6	5.8	31.0	23.5	9.0	0.7	72.5	35.0	51.5	48.5
37026	BRADYVILLE	97.2	96.9	1.4	1.5	0.1	0.1	1.1	1.4	7.5	7.6	8.1	6.4	6.0	29.9	23.3	10.3	1.0	72.9	35.6	50.6	49.4
37027	BRENTWOOD	93.4	92.3	2.7	3.0	2.6	3.2	1.4	1.7	5.4	7.1	8.5	7.3	4.3	24.7	33.1	8.9	0.8	74.0	41.1	48.7	51.4
37028	BUMPUS MILLS	96.7	96.2	0.6	0.8	0.5	0.5	1.3	1.3	6.9	6.9	7.7	6.5	6.1	28.4	24.9	11.3	1.3	74.5	37.5	51.0	49.0
37029	BURNS	93.1	92.5	4.9	5.1	0.3	0.4	1.1	1.4	7.0	7.1	7.6	6.2	5.3	31.0	25.5	9.6	0.8	74.4	37.2	49.2	50.8
37030	CARTHAGE	94.4	93.9	3.5	3.7	0.3	0.4	1.2	1.5	6.8	6.7	6.6	6.2	6.2	26.5	24.8	13.4	2.7	76.2	39.3	47.9	52.1
37031	CASTALIAN SPRINGS	92.8	92.2	4.5	4.8	0.6	0.7	1.5	1.8	5.7	6.2	7.4	7.0	6.3	28.2	28.3	10.1	0.9	76.5	38.9	50.3	49.7
37032	CEDAR HILL	94.6	93.7	3.4	3.9	0.3	0.3	1.3	1.7	6.4	7.2	8.4	7.2	5.7	29.0	25.7	9.3	1.2	73.4	37.0	51.5	48.5
37033	CENTERVILLE	95.5	95.2	3.0	3.2	0.1	0.1	0.8	1.0	6.3	6.3	6.4	6.4	5.7	25.7	26.0	14.9	2.5	77.3	40.7	49.6	50.4
37034	CHAPEL HILL	95.8	95.3	2.5	2.7	0.1	0.1	1.7	2.1	7.1	7.2	7.5	6.5	6.6	29.9	25.2	9.0	0.9	74.2	35.7	49.8	50.2
37035	CHAPMANSBORO	96.4	96.1	1.7	1.8	0.3	0.3	1.1	1.4	7.5	7.5	7.7	7.0	5.8	31.5	23.6	8.8	0.8	72.7	35.7	50.7	49.3
37036	CHARLOTTE	92.8	92.3	5.8	6.2	0.1	0.1	0.8	0.9	6.2	6.4	7.5	6.5	6.1	30.5	25.1	10.4	1.3	75.9	37.1	51.6	48.4
37037	CHRISTIANA	92.5	91.7	5.0	5.3	0.8	1.0	0.9	1.0	7.6	7.5	7.7	6.4	6.1	32.7	23.9	7.4	0.7	73.2	34.3	49.8	50.2
37040	CLARKSVILLE	69.7	68.4	25.1	25.6	1.0	1.3	3.4	4.1	8.0	7.3	7.1	8.0	9.1	32.3	19.5	7.7	0.9	73.4	31.1	49.5	50.6
37042	CLARKSVILLE	63.1	61.2	25.3	25.7	3.1	3.7	8.1	9.3	10.5	8.9	8.2	7.0	8.8	37.0	14.9	4.5	0.2	68.3	28.1	50.2	49.8
37043	CLARKSVILLE	86.9	85.8	8.7	9.2	1.6	2.0	2.4	2.9	6.7	6.8	6.9	6.3	5.9	30.2	24.4	10.9	1.8	75.7	37.0	48.9	51.1
37046	COLLEGE GROVE	92.0	91.1	6.7	7.2	0.2	0.3	1.1	1.3	5.4	6.0	7.5	6.8	5.7	26.6	29.7	10.9	1.4	76.9	40.4	50.3	49.7
37047	CORNERSVILLE	97.0	96.6	1.8	2.1	0.2	0.2	0.7	0.8	6.2	6.7	8.0	6.1	5.4	29.2	25.5	11.3	1.6	75.3	38.1	48.9	51.1
37048	COTTONTOWN	97.0	96.6	1.2	1.4	0.2	0.3	1.0	1.3	6.6	7.0	6.9	6.1	5.7	28.5	28.3	10.0	0.9	75.6	38.8	50.9	49.1
37049	CROSS PLAINS	94.3	93.5	4.0	4.4	0.2	0.2	1.2	1.6	6.8	7.2	7.8	6.7	5.8	29.3	27.0	8.7	0.7	74.1	37.4	49.9	50.1
37050	CUMBERLAND CITY	93.4	92.8	4.2	4.5	0.3	0.3	1.1	1.2	6.6	7.1	7.5	5.8	5.6	26.9	27.2	12.0	1.5	75.2	38.9	50.2	49.8
37051	CUMBERLAND FURNACE	96.0	95.6	1.8	1.9	0.3	0.4	0.8	0.9	6.0	6.3	7.4	7.1	5.8	28.3	26.3	11.3	1.5	75.8	38.4	50.7	49.3
37052	CUNNINGHAM	96.1	95.9	2.0	2.1	0.2	0.2	1.1	1.4	5.5	6.1	7.5	7.9	5.6	27.6	27.6	11.0	1.2	76.0	39.4	51.0	49.0
37055	DICKSON	91.6	90.9	5.9	6.2	0.3	0.4	1.4	1.7	7.4	7.1	7.3	6.8	6.6	28.1	24.0	11.0	1.7	74.0	36.3	48.4	51.6
37057	DIXON SPRINGS	95.3	94.7	2.5	2.7	0.2	0.2	1.5	1.8	7.0	7.1	7.6	6.7	5.8	28.5	25.3	10.6	1.5	74.1	37.0	50.2	49.8
37058	DOVER	94.6	93.9	1.6	1.6	2.1	2.5	0.9	1.1	5.4	5.7	6.5	6.0	5.5	26.0	27.5	15.5	2.0	78.8	41.8	49.2	50.8
37059	DOWELLTOWN	95.8	95.1	1.1	1.1	0.1	0.1	3.2	3.9	5.2	5.8	7.0	6.5	5.7	30.6	26.4	11.5	1.4	78.0	39.1	50.8	49.2
37060	EAGLEVILLE	93.6	93.0	5.1	5.4	0.3	0.3	1.2	1.5	6.0	6.4	7.4	6.9	5.6	27.3	26.7	12.5	1.3	75.9	39.7	49.3	50.7
37061	ERIN	93.9	93.8	4.4	4.5	0.2	0.2	0.8	0.8	6.7	7.0	6.8	6.0	5.3	25.6	25.2	14.8	2.5	75.7	39.5	49.6	50.4
37062	FAIRVIEW	97.4	97.1	0.6	0.6	0.2	0.3	1.3	1.6	7.3	7.3	7.8	7.1	6.7	29.5	25.3	8.3	0.7	73.2	35.3	49.0	51.0
37064	FRANKLIN	86.0	85.3	10.5	10.6	0.8	1.0	3.4	4.0	7.8	8.1	7.8	6.5	5.5	30.0	25.5	7.7	1.2	72.3	36.3	48.7	51.3
37066	GALLATIN	82.7	82.0	13.8	14.1	0.5	0.6	2.7	3.2	6.9	6.8	6.8	6.3	6.3	28.1	26.1	11.2	1.7	75.7	37.8	48.4	51.6
37067	FRANKLIN	89.3	88.1	5.0	5.4	2.3	2.8	5.5	6.0	7.3	7.4	7.4	6.4	6.4	35.0	25.0	4.4	0.7	73.9	34.1	49.9	50.1
37069	FRANKLIN	96.5	95.9	1.4	1.5	1.1	1.4	1.6	2.0	7.6	9.1	9.8	7.8	4.0	26.7	28.0	6.6	0.5	68.4	37.2	48.9	51.1
37072	GOODLETTSVILLE	89.7	88.8	7.4	7.7	1.1	1.4	1.3	1.5	6.7	6.8	6.9	6.1	6.0	29.6	26.6	10.3	1.2	76.0	37.8	48.9	51.1
37073	GREENBRIER	97.3	96.8	0.9	1.1	0.3	0.4	0.9	1.2	6.9	7.1	7.6	6.5	5.9	30.7	25.0	9.5	0.8	74.4	36.2	49.9	50.1
37074	HARTSVILLE	87.0	86.3	11.0	11.3	0.2	0.2	1.4	1.7	6.2	6.4	7.2	6.2	6.2	27.5	26.0	12.4	1.9	76.4	38.7	49.4	50.6
37075	HENDERSONVILLE	93.5	92.7	3.8	4.1	1.0	1.3	1.6	2.0	6.3	6.6	7.1	6.9	6.5	28.9	26.7	9.6	1.3	75.6	37.7	48.8	51.2
37076	HERMITAGE	83.8	82.1	11.2	12.1	1.3	1.6	3.7	4.4	7.3	6.8	6.5	5.5	7.3	34.6	22.0	8.2	1.8	76.1	34.7	48.0	52.0
37078	HURRICANE MILLS	96.5	96.1	1.9	2.2	0.3	0.5	1.1	1.4	5.8	5.9	6.7	8.4	6.0	26.4	28.6	11.2	1.1	75.8	39.6	52.5	47.5
37079	INDIAN MOUND	96.2	95.7	1.2	1.3	0.5	0.7	1.2	1.4	6.9	7.0	7.4	6.2	5.7	29.8	25.4	10.5	1.1	74.9	37.6	52.6	47.4
37080	JOELTON	97.2	96.9	1.5	1.7	0.2	0.2	1.0	1.3	6.3	6.7	6.7	5.9	5.3	28.6	28.6	11.2	0.8	76.7	39.8	50.1	49.9
37082	KINGSTON SPRINGS	97.8	97.5	0.9	1.0	0.4	0.5	0.8	1.0	7.1	7.4	7.7	6.9	5.6	30.9	27.8	6.3	0.4	73.6	36.9	49.6	50.4
37083	LAFAYETTE	97.9	97.6	0.2	0.2	0.3	0.4	1.6	2.0	6.8	6.8	6.7	6.2	6.1	29.2	24.6	11.9	1.8	75.9	37.1	49.6	50.4
37085	LASCASSAS	91.8	91.0	6.8	7.3	0.1	0.2	1.0	1.3	8.2	7.7	7.6	6.4	6.7	34.6	21.6	6.5	0.7	72.9	32.8	49.3	50.7
37086	LA VERGNE	85.2	83.8	10.5	11.1	1.3	1.6	3.4	4.2	9.9	9.0	7.8	6.3	6.0	36.8	19.1	4.8	0.3	69.4	31.7	49.2	50.8
37087	LEBANON	86.8	86.0	10.4	10.8	0.6	0.7	1.8	2.2	7.2	6.8	6.8	6.4	6.9	29.4	23.9	10.8	1.8	75.5	36.4	48.7	51.3
37090	LEBANON	94.0	93.5	4.1	4.4	0.3	0.3	1.1	1.3	6.2	6.5	7.0	6.5	5.7	29.7	27.5	9.8	1.0	76.3	38.2	49.8	50.2
37091	LEWISBURG	86.7	85.6	10.0	10.5	0.4	0.5	3.5	4.2	6.6	6.6	6.9	6.2	6.7	28.6	25.4	11.3	1.7	76.2	37.3	48.8	51.2
37095	LIBERTY	96.7	96.3	1.0	1.1	0.2	0.2	1.9	2.3	6.8	6.9	6.9	6.8	5.9	28.4	26.7	10.4	1.3	75.3	37.9	50.1	49.9
37096	LINDEN	95.8	95.6	2.6	2.7	0.2	0.2	0.8	0.9	5.5	6.0	6.4	6.5	5.4	24.9	26.7	16.1	2.5	77.8	41.4	49.5	50.5
37097	LOBELVILLE	97.7	97.4	0.3	0.3	0.3	0.4	0.9	1.0	6.7	7.1	7.3	6.3	5.6	24.6	28.0	13.1	1.2	74.9	39.4	50.8	49.2
37098	LYLES	95.9	95.4	2.1	2.2	0.1	0.2	1.0	1.2	7.4	7.5	7.7	6.8	6.2	30.2	24.3	9.3	0.6	73.3	35.1	51.5	48.5
37101	MC EWEN	98.0	97.7	0.4	0.5	0.2	0.3	0.6	0.8	6.5	6.8	7.4	6.4	5.8	28.2	25.6	12.0	1.3	75.4	37.5	49.7	50.3
37110	MC MINNVILLE	91.3	90.2	3.3	3.4	0.5	0.6	5.1	6.2	6.6	6.3	6.5	6.2	6.6	28.5	24.6	12.8	1.8	76.8	37.8	49.2	50.8
37115	MADISON	73.1	70.5	19.7	21.3	1.2	1.4	6.1	7.3	6.6	6.0	5.8	6.3	8.7	29.8	22.4	12.1	2.2	78.1	35.9	47.9	52.1
37118	MILTON	92.3	91.7	6.2	6.6	0.4	0.5	0.5	0.6	7.0	6.6	7.0	8.0	8.7	29.1	24.4	8.3	0.9	75.7	34.8	47.1	52.9
37122	MOUNT JULIET	94.1	93.6	4.0	4.2	0.5	0.6	1.0	1.2	6.9	7.3	7.6	6.5	5.1	30.6	27.7	7.6	0.7	74.0	37.6	49.7	50.3
37127	MURFREESBORO	83.7	82.3	8.8	8.9	5.4	6.5	1.3	1.5	8.3	7.9	7.2	6.1	6.7	32.8	23.0	7.1	0.9	72.9	34.1	49.4	50.6
37128	MURFREESBORO	87.5	86.4	7.5	7.7	3.1	3.9	1.5	1.7	8.7	7.9	7.7	6.4	7.0	37.4	19.8	4.7	0.3	71.8	31.5	49.3	50.7
37129	MURFREESBORO	88.9	87.9	6.6	6.8	1.9	2.4	2.6	3.0	7.0	7.0	7.5	6.6	6.9	31.5	25.0	7.7	1.0	74.7	35.1	49.8	50.2
37130	MURFREESBORO	78.5	77.2	15.7	16.1	2.0	2.4	3.8	4.5	6.6	5.8	5.8	7.1	14.6	31.6	18.1	8.9	1.5	78.6	29.5	50.0	50.0
37132	MURFREESBORO	70.2	68.4	27.2	28.5	1.3	1.6	1.1	1.4	0.1	0.0	0.0	49.4	46.3	3.5	0.7	0.0	0.0	99.4	20.1	53.8	46.2
37134	NEW JOHNSONVILLE	97.8	97.6	1.2	1.2	0.2	0.2	0.6	0.7	6.1	6.4	6.9	6.2	5.6	26.0	28.4	13.2	1.2	76.7	40.1	49.6	50.4
37135	NOLENSVILLE	93.4	92.5	5.1	5.6	0.3	0.3	1.3	1.7	6.5	7.4	8.4	7.4	5.0	26.5	30.1	8.1	0.8	73.1	39.6	49.8	50.2
37137	NUNNELLY	87.2	86.9	10.9	11.1	0.1	0.2	1.1	1.3	5.0	5.3	5.9	6.1	7.0	35.1	24.9	9.7	1.2	80.1	37.6	60.0	40.0
37138	OLD HICKORY	92.2	91.1	5.1	5.7	0.9	1.1	1.4	1.8	6.5	6.8	7.1	6.0	5.2	29.2	27.7	10.2	1.3	75.9	39.0	48.6	51.5
37140	ONLY	73.1	71.6	25.6	26.8	0.2	0.3	1.6	1.9	2.4	3.0	3.4	5.9	9.1	46.1	24.6	5.0	0.6	87.4	36.5	76.5	23.5
37141	ORLINDA	94.4	93.8	4.4	4.9	0.1	0.1	0.7	0.7	6.7	6.8	6.7	6.4	5.9	30.4	26.2	9.9	1.0	76.1	37.4	48.7	51.3
37142	PALMYRA	95.8	95.3	2.0	2.2	0.3	0.4	0.9	1.1	6.3	6.7	7.5	7.0	6.2	27.6	27.0	10.5	1.2	75.0	38.6	50.6	49.4
37143	PEGRAM	95.7	95.4	2.6	2.7	0.5	0.6	1.3	1.6	7.6	7.6	6.3	5.4	4.9	31.0	26.9	9.0	1.4	74.9	38.5	50.7	49.3
37144	PETERSBURG	94.8	94.2	3.0	3.4	0.2	0.3	1.5	1.8	5.7	6.0	6.7	6.8	5.5	27.3	28.3	12.2	1.6	77.4	40.3	50.0	50.0
37145	PLEASANT SHADE	97.3	96.9	1.0	1.1	0.0	0.0	1.1	1.4	6.5	6.5	6.6	6.7	6.5	28.8	25.6	11.2	1.6	76.1	37.9	50.4	49.6
37146	PLEASANT VIEW	97.5	97.2	1.0	1.0	0.2	0.2	1.1	1.3	7.9	7.9	8.2	6.7	5.8	32.3	23.5	7.2	0.7	71.7	34.9	50.4	49.6
37148	PORTLAND	95.5	94.9	2.3	2.5	0.2	0.2	1.5	1.9	7.5	7.4	7.5	6.6	6.5	30.2	22.9	10.0	1.3	73.4	34.8	49.3	50.7
37149	READYVILLE	96.9	96.5	1.6	1.7	0.3	0.4	0.9	1.0	6.6	6.7	6.9	6.1	6.6	29.0	26.6	10.4	1.1	76.1	37.7	50.8	49.2
37150	RED BOILING SPRINGS	97.4	97.0	0.1	0.1	0.3	0.3	2.5	3.1	6.7	6.7	6.7	5.9	6.2	27.8	25.6	12.5	2.0	76.2	38.4	49.3	50.7
37151	RIDDLETON	91.8	91.0	5.0	5.3	0.0	0.0	2.8	3.2	7.2	7.2	7.2	6.6	5.8	28.9	23.3	11.4	2.4	74.0	37.0	48.5	51.5
37153	ROCKVALE	94.9	94.4	3.1	3.3	0.7	0.9	1.0	1.2	7.8	7.7	8.2	6.7	6.0	32.7	23.0	7.2	0.7	72.1	34.4	49.5	50.5
37160	SHELBYVILLE	83.8	82.5	10.4	10.8	0.6	0.7	9.7	11.6	7.7	7.1	6.6	6.1	6.9	29.4	23.1	11.4	1.7	75.0	35.4	49.4	50.6
37166	SMITHVILLE	95.2	94.5	1.3	1.3	0.2	0.2	4.7	5.7	6.2	6.2	6.3	5.9	6.1	29.4	25.4	12.8	1.8	77.8	38.5	49.9	50.2
37167	SMYRNA	88.5	87.2	7.0	7.4	1.3	1.6	3.6	4.4	8.3	7.6	7.5	7.1	8.1	32.3	22.5	6.1	0.5	72.5	32.4	49.1	50.9
37171	SOUTHSIDE	94.7	94.2	3.9	4.1	0.1	0.1	1.3	1.6	6.1	6.7	6.9	6.2	5.1	30.2	26.7	10.9	1.2	76.5	38.4	51.1	48.9
37172	SPRINGFIELD	80.8	79.9	16.4	16.9	0.4	0.5	4.6	5.4	6.9	6.7	6.8	6.6	6.8	29.5	24.1	11.1	1.6	75.7	36.7	49.2	50.8
	TENNESSEE	80.2	79.4	16.4	16.7	1.0	1.3	2.2	2.6	6.6	6.5	6.8	6.6	7.0	29.0	24.8	11.1	1.5	76.3	36.8	48.9	51.1
	UNITED STATES	75.1	73.6	12.3	12.5	3.8	4.2	12.5	14.1	6.9	6.7	7.2	7.0	7.3	28.6	23.8	10.8	1.7	75.1	36.0	49.1	50.9

ZIP CODE #	POST OFFICE NAME	2004 Per Capita Income	2004 HH Income Base	2004 Household Income Distribution (%): Less than $25,000	$25,000 to $49,999	$50,000 to $99,999	$100,000 to $149,999	$150,000 or More	Median Household Income: 2004	2009	2004 National Centile	2004 State Centile	2004 Home Value Base	2004 Home Value Distribution (%): Less than $50,000	$50,000 to $89,999	$90,000 to $174,999	$175,000 to $399,999	$400,000 or More	2004 Median Home Value
37010	ADAMS	27136	1363	17.2	27.5	35.4	12.0	7.8	53843	60988	78	92	1155	9.8	13.9	44.4	28.7	3.2	135019
37012	ALEXANDRIA	19514	839	29.8	33.1	30.3	5.8	1.0	39366	44405	44	66	691	13.2	28.2	45.4	11.1	2.0	99754
37013	ANTIOCH	25658	21498	15.3	33.6	38.7	9.7	2.7	50723	57488	73	89	11108	4.0	7.4	71.9	15.5	1.2	130033
37014	ARRINGTON	31578	517	16.4	20.9	36.8	17.8	8.1	62794	72881	87	96	454	3.1	11.5	31.1	38.8	15.6	191129
37015	ASHLAND CITY	20076	6553	21.0	34.4	36.0	6.4	2.3	45326	50726	62	81	5321	11.5	21.1	49.6	16.1	1.7	111036
37016	AUBURNTOWN	22958	394	24.9	30.5	33.8	7.6	3.3	44392	50201	60	79	329	17.0	26.8	31.0	22.5	2.7	100284
37018	BEECHGROVE	20884	773	33.9	31.1	26.9	5.1	3.1	36236	41004	32	54	643	28.3	19.9	35.9	12.9	3.0	92447
37019	BELFAST	18481	247	25.1	30.8	34.8	8.5	0.8	44172	50545	59	79	206	19.4	21.4	40.3	17.5	1.5	108571
37020	BELL BUCKLE	23223	1590	21.2	29.4	36.7	8.6	4.2	49432	54610	71	87	1346	11.3	19.0	42.2	21.1	6.4	117105
37022	BETHPAGE	22549	1903	25.2	30.7	34.5	5.8	3.8	46066	52130	64	82	1592	14.3	25.9	38.1	17.2	4.4	109018
37023	BIG ROCK	17228	748	29.1	35.4	29.8	4.7	0.9	37674	41052	38	59	598	21.6	29.1	37.0	11.9	0.5	89355
37025	BON AQUA	17277	2062	30.1	34.2	29.2	4.9	1.6	38290	42512	40	61	1711	17.0	30.1	39.4	11.6	1.9	93741
37026	BRADYVILLE	16544	825	30.1	33.0	32.1	3.8	1.1	37674	41924	38	59	681	23.8	17.6	43.0	14.5	1.0	98478
37027	BRENTWOOD	51898	14820	5.7	13.6	28.5	23.5	28.8	103479	118758	98	100	12514	0.2	0.5	8.9	55.9	34.5	327949
37028	BUMPUS MILLS	19916	257	29.6	31.5	31.5	5.1	2.3	42373	45840	54	76	214	19.2	28.0	39.3	13.6	0.0	92000
37029	BURNS	22911	1784	20.4	31.2	37.5	7.9	3.0	48629	54110	70	86	1497	7.0	19.8	49.2	22.3	1.7	121896
37030	CARTHAGE	20307	2487	37.1	31.3	23.2	5.0	3.5	34704	37924	26	46	1801	14.7	22.7	43.3	16.6	2.8	108983
37031	CASTALIAN SPRINGS	20920	1052	25.8	28.4	36.1	6.9	2.8	46676	52029	65	83	898	12.4	22.2	49.3	15.5	0.7	110691
37032	CEDAR HILL	20033	1392	21.7	31.0	38.1	7.0	2.3	47229	52629	67	84	1173	7.6	17.3	53.1	18.9	3.1	128660
37033	CENTERVILLE	16114	3255	41.8	30.5	23.0	2.8	1.9	30729	33932	14	22	2484	21.0	24.6	41.6	11.8	1.0	95870
37034	CHAPEL HILL	21808	2088	23.3	28.5	36.8	8.1	3.4	47962	53078	68	85	1740	11.7	23.6	49.3	12.4	3.0	105290
37035	CHAPMANSBORO	18329	1022	19.5	32.2	42.7	3.7	2.0	48936	54486	70	86	871	5.3	16.3	57.3	19.6	1.5	118140
37036	CHARLOTTE	20781	2129	26.1	34.1	31.6	5.3	3.0	40859	45854	49	70	1757	14.7	26.2	45.0	11.2	2.9	101203
37037	CHRISTIANA	21738	1579	14.5	30.8	43.4	9.1	2.3	52816	59588	77	91	1368	6.9	13.8	54.7	22.3	2.3	125397
37040	CLARKSVILLE	17924	13117	32.5	34.5	26.2	5.4	1.5	36293	40373	33	55	8145	12.4	37.7	42.7	6.6	0.7	89955
37042	CLARKSVILLE	17127	20721	22.7	39.8	31.3	5.2	1.1	41515	46007	51	73	12168	9.1	35.6	52.4	2.7	0.2	92983
37043	CLARKSVILLE	25902	13484	21.3	29.9	33.3	10.0	5.5	48938	54006	70	86	9659	4.4	22.5	48.1	22.3	2.7	116355
37046	COLLEGE GROVE	27427	1337	20.6	25.0	33.6	13.7	7.2	53904	64496	78	92	1144	4.8	11.5	31.7	38.1	13.8	181471
37047	CORNERSVILLE	21034	963	25.4	27.9	33.9	9.8	3.0	46132	51560	64	83	796	13.6	23.6	43.8	14.8	4.2	107124
37048	COTTONTOWN	23299	2069	18.6	25.2	43.2	10.2	2.9	55369	62198	80	93	1799	5.0	16.4	45.8	30.3	2.6	141686
37049	CROSS PLAINS	23331	1170	19.2	30.3	39.3	8.5	2.7	50389	56308	73	88	989	8.3	18.8	46.6	21.9	4.4	127648
37050	CUMBERLAND CITY	18588	587	32.7	33.1	27.8	4.6	1.9	38524	42690	41	62	474	22.6	34.6	31.7	10.8	0.4	83200
37051	CUMBERLAND FURNACE	18927	1345	27.7	32.4	33.0	4.8	2.2	41330	46414	51	73	1127	19.2	30.4	36.4	12.3	1.8	90632
37052	CUNNINGHAM	18567	1050	27.5	33.1	32.2	5.2	2.0	40693	45000	49	70	894	19.4	29.5	39.3	10.0	1.9	90870
37055	DICKSON	20358	9962	28.8	30.2	31.9	6.9	2.2	42300	47463	54	75	7047	9.4	23.2	46.8	18.4	2.2	112925
37057	DIXON SPRINGS	18853	390	35.4	31.0	25.1	5.9	2.6	34795	38300	27	46	323	27.9	21.1	38.7	11.5	0.9	91667
37058	DOVER	19438	2764	34.6	34.0	25.8	3.5	2.1	35047	38403	28	48	2204	26.1	28.1	34.9	10.3	0.6	85079
37059	DOWELLTOWN	18012	670	37.9	33.7	22.7	2.8	2.8	32066	36172	18	31	534	17.6	32.0	37.6	11.6	1.1	90385
37060	EAGLEVILLE	25851	843	21.2	28.2	34.6	10.1	5.8	50426	56697	73	89	697	5.9	16.2	42.2	31.1	4.6	130833
37061	ERIN	17767	2233	40.2	31.4	22.8	3.5	2.0	32707	36504	20	36	1702	28.0	36.1	27.7	8.0	0.3	73456
37062	FAIRVIEW	25495	3809	17.5	32.3	35.0	9.3	5.9	50144	60240	72	88	3000	7.0	11.7	55.5	23.4	2.4	132242
37064	FRANKLIN	33185	15203	15.0	21.2	32.9	19.6	11.3	68743	81275	91	97	12471	4.7	5.7	24.0	55.9	9.7	222978
37066	GALLATIN	23453	14216	26.9	27.2	32.5	9.2	4.2	46085	52476	64	82	10517	9.4	13.9	44.0	27.9	4.9	139527
37067	FRANKLIN	43992	7096	8.7	20.5	32.5	21.7	16.5	79934	94241	95	99	4722	0.6	1.8	12.8	59.9	24.8	282228
37069	FRANKLIN	41416	6538	5.0	11.7	33.4	29.2	20.7	99938	112184	98	100	6213	0.2	0.3	12.2	65.5	21.8	277450
37072	GOODLETTSVILLE	24980	11368	19.7	27.8	37.3	10.7	4.6	51849	59211	75	91	8232	6.0	8.5	51.8	30.8	2.9	148696
37073	GREENBRIER	22004	4674	18.4	33.1	37.3	8.7	2.5	48886	55149	70	86	3874	5.7	12.5	59.3	20.8	1.8	127083
37074	HARTSVILLE	18159	2638	35.6	32.3	26.2	3.8	2.0	34425	38328	25	45	2033	18.6	31.4	39.1	9.5	1.4	89971
37075	HENDERSONVILLE	28452	19716	16.1	26.5	36.5	13.9	7.1	56772	63482	81	94	14365	1.1	5.2	50.1	37.9	5.8	163339
37076	HERMITAGE	26025	14183	17.1	31.3	37.2	10.7	3.7	51255	58991	74	90	7910	0.7	12.0	66.1	20.0	1.2	133634
37078	HURRICANE MILLS	18936	357	30.5	31.7	32.5	3.1	2.2	37422	42117	37	58	290	17.9	38.6	31.7	11.4	0.3	83667
37079	INDIAN MOUND	19405	858	25.5	37.4	31.4	3.0	2.7	39001	44003	43	65	704	24.6	21.6	38.5	14.6	0.7	94355
37080	JOELTON	23956	2741	19.5	31.5	35.0	11.2	2.9	49267	55523	71	87	2332	7.9	14.6	57.3	18.7	1.5	124606
37082	KINGSTON SPRINGS	25216	2375	14.9	25.6	42.6	11.8	5.2	57717	61441	82	95	2095	3.9	10.0	39.9	42.6	3.7	168886
37083	LAFAYETTE	17362	4934	38.3	31.4	25.3	3.3	1.8	33004	36776	21	38	3862	26.0	29.7	35.0	7.7	1.6	83432
37085	LASCASSAS	23578	1223	17.7	26.4	43.9	8.6	3.4	54744	60799	79	93	1087	3.5	10.8	54.7	25.6	5.5	137071
37086	LA VERGNE	22347	8579	12.0	32.1	43.1	10.4	2.4	55181	61108	80	93	7325	11.4	8.5	67.9	11.6	0.6	120631
37087	LEBANON	23439	13560	26.3	29.1	32.7	8.2	3.7	45185	52112	62	80	9359	8.1	12.8	49.3	25.4	4.3	136206
37090	LEBANON	23946	4820	18.6	29.1	40.2	9.2	2.8	51709	59708	75	90	4030	7.2	12.1	45.0	30.4	5.3	146089
37091	LEWISBURG	19464	7895	30.3	30.8	30.6	6.4	2.0	40503	45721	48	70	5645	14.8	29.1	42.1	11.6	2.4	98876
37095	LIBERTY	17833	862	33.4	34.9	27.6	2.3	1.7	36332	41129	33	55	702	18.2	28.8	36.8	13.7	2.6	94118
37096	LINDEN	21333	1894	40.9	30.6	22.4	3.7	2.4	31343	35260	16	26	1571	36.4	32.8	23.7	6.4	0.7	66065
37097	LOBELVILLE	16922	1193	40.9	32.1	20.5	4.4	2.1	31421	35320	16	26	1010	38.3	28.4	25.0	7.8	0.5	62211
37098	LYLES	16412	2061	32.7	35.9	26.3	3.7	1.5	35893	39722	31	53	1709	18.6	31.3	40.4	8.3	1.5	90185
37101	MC EWEN	18966	2337	30.8	33.8	29.6	3.9	2.0	38989	43844	43	64	1887	19.5	29.8	38.8	9.7	2.1	90702
37110	MC MINNVILLE	18099	12645	39.2	30.1	24.1	4.6	2.1	33096	37390	21	39	8928	19.8	33.6	33.6	11.6	1.5	86548
37115	MADISON	21121	15420	32.7	33.4	26.3	5.7	1.9	35892	41089	31	53	7608	7.8	23.0	57.6	10.9	0.8	107378
37118	MILTON	19992	424	28.5	21.9	33.7	10.9	5.0	49427	53854	71	87	367	10.9	18.8	23.4	38.2	8.7	160625
37122	MOUNT JULIET	28706	13162	11.2	23.1	42.5	17.0	6.2	65073	72265	89	97	11870	5.6	4.5	43.2	42.5	4.1	169771
37127	MURFREESBORO	24691	4576	14.1	24.9	44.0	11.8	5.2	58176	64502	83	95	3907	4.2	9.9	54.5	28.8	2.6	142300
37128	MURFREESBORO	23790	8482	12.7	27.4	46.4	10.7	2.8	56419	62829	81	94	6823	0.7	3.3	72.2	22.9	0.9	142239
37129	MURFREESBORO	25104	15485	15.6	26.6	41.8	11.7	4.3	56027	62801	81	93	11878	3.4	7.8	58.8	27.8	2.2	141504
37130	MURFREESBORO	21119	19889	36.5	28.6	25.6	6.1	3.2	34951	39320	27	47	9197	6.8	14.7	53.5	21.8	3.1	121094
37132	MURFREESBORO	11953	37	27.0	13.5	56.8	2.7	0.0	63110	72775	87	96	21	0.0	0.0	52.4	47.6	0.0	148214
37134	NEW JOHNSONVILLE	24782	1314	24.4	26.9	38.8	6.6	3.3	48407	53271	69	86	1098	16.8	36.5	35.7	10.2	0.8	86211
37135	NOLENSVILLE	28515	1648	12.6	20.3	38.2	20.1	8.9	70917	81265	92	98	1502	0.7	5.0	23.5	59.1	11.7	216308
37137	NUNNELLY	20131	841	37.2	36.4	20.8	3.8	1.8	34443	37851	26	45	676	27.1	28.9	30.0	11.4	2.7	83548
37138	OLD HICKORY	28628	9047	18.1	24.9	37.0	13.2	6.8	57081	64712	82	94	7498	4.5	12.5	51.5	26.9	4.7	146390
37140	ONLY	9067	84	36.9	36.9	16.7	6.0	3.6	35000	38184	28	48	67	37.3	22.4	28.4	7.5	4.5	80714
37141	ORLINDA	20946	323	22.6	31.0	37.5	8.4	0.6	47846	53215	68	85	274	12.8	24.8	45.3	11.7	5.5	109375
37142	PALMYRA	17785	573	22.7	35.1	33.9	7.5	0.9	43674	48951	58	79	484	20.3	38.4	31.4	9.9	0.0	82364
37143	PEGRAM	26066	1518	17.5	24.2	40.8	11.8	5.6	57524	62010	82	94	1323	3.4	12.6	46.3	33.9	3.9	155469
37144	PETERSBURG	22650	1231	28.4	31.4	29.0	7.4	3.7	41146	47013	50	72	1039	22.8	22.0	36.8	15.3	3.1	101035
37145	PLEASANT SHADE	18854	1291	35.8	32.8	26.7	2.4	2.3	35646	39155	30	52	1078	20.0	25.3	39.0	12.9	2.8	97813
37146	PLEASANT VIEW	22968	1934	14.6	27.2	44.9	9.8	3.6	55179	60853	80	93	1691	3.3	11.5	57.5	26.7	1.0	132982
37148	PORTLAND	18595	7344	26.3	32.3	35.5	5.1	0.8	42539	48474	55	76	5659	10.2	26.0	50.1	12.6	1.1	104870
37149	READYVILLE	20201	903	23.9	33.1	36.8	4.3	1.9	43349	49457	57	78	754	15.5	21.8	39.4	22.6	0.8	108800
37150	RED BOILING SPRINGS	17060	1968	42.2	34.0	18.7	2.4	2.7	29887	33188	12	19	1566	39.1	30.2	20.4	8.1	2.3	63788
37151	RIDDLETON	18999	148	35.8	26.4	26.4	8.8	2.7	36171	40508	32	54	122	24.6	7.4	48.4	19.7	0.0	109286
37153	ROCKVALE	22605	1787	15.0	29.6	41.5	10.1	3.9	54196	60455	79	92	1563	5.2	10.5	55.5	25.9	3.0	133490
37160	SHELBYVILLE	18524	10742	30.7	33.8	27.5	5.9	2.2	38960	43159	43	64	7701	15.5	33.0	37.4	11.9	2.2	91852
37166	SMITHVILLE	19821	5145	40.7	28.9	23.0	4.2	3.3	31718	35632	17	28	3943	14.0	31.7	40.3	11.6	2.4	96232
37167	SMYRNA	22747	15205	17.9	29.9	38.4	10.9	2.9	51773	58137	75	90	10310	5.6	7.3	63.7	22.0	1.5	136788
37171	SOUTHSIDE	21193	407	14.7	40.8	33.7	8.4	2.5	45606	51303	63	81	347	19.6	15.0	47.6	13.0	4.9	107885
37172	SPRINGFIELD	21651	10275	27.3	28.2	33.0	7.8	3.7	44716	51045	60	80	7271	8.0	21.3	47.9	20.6	2.1	117777
	TENNESSEE	22498		30.2	30.2	28.1	7.5	4.1	40531	46137				15.0	25.0	39.4	17.3	3.3	104905
	UNITED STATES	25866		24.7	27.1	30.8	10.9	6.5	48124	56710				10.9	15.0	33.7	30.1	10.4	145905

ZIP CODE #	POST OFFICE NAME	FINANCIAL SERVICES: Auto Loan	Home Loan	Invest-ments	Retire-ment Plans	THE HOME: Home Improvements: Home Repair	Lawn & Garden	Furnishings: Comput-ers & Hard-ware	Major Appli-ances	TV, Radio, Sound Equip-ment	Furni-ture	ENTERTAINMENT: Dine out/ Carry out	Sports Equip-ment	Fees & Tickets	Toys & Games	Travel	Cable TV	PERSONAL: Apparel & Services	Auto Repairs	Health Insur-ance	Pets & Supplies
37010	ADAMS	108	113	106	112	114	118	105	109	104	105	128	127	107	133	107	103	125	106	107	127
37012	ALEXANDRIA	86	62	34	56	69	78	59	72	69	60	82	86	53	79	61	73	75	71	85	99
37013	ANTIOCH	87	85	93	92	82	84	89	86	85	91	108	103	88	104	84	79	106	88	76	95
37014	ARRINGTON	120	128	124	126	130	135	117	122	115	117	143	142	121	147	120	115	139	118	120	143
37015	ASHLAND CITY	85	76	60	74	79	85	73	79	76	73	93	92	71	93	74	77	88	78	83	97
37016	AUBURNTOWN	96	86	65	81	91	97	79	88	84	79	102	105	78	105	82	86	97	86	95	113
37018	BEECHGROVE	92	62	28	53	70	80	60	74	72	61	84	89	51	80	61	77	77	74	91	105
37019	BELFAST	85	72	51	67	76	83	67	75	72	67	87	90	64	88	68	75	82	74	84	99
37020	BELL BUCKLE	96	86	65	81	91	97	79	88	84	79	102	105	78	105	82	86	97	86	95	113
37022	BETHPAGE	98	82	57	77	88	96	77	87	84	77	101	104	73	101	79	87	95	85	97	115
37023	BIG ROCK	77	60	39	56	65	73	59	67	65	59	78	79	54	77	59	68	73	66	77	88
37025	BON AQUA	78	63	43	59	67	74	61	69	67	62	80	81	57	78	61	69	75	68	76	88
37026	BRADYVILLE	80	59	33	52	65	73	56	67	64	56	77	80	50	74	57	68	71	66	79	92
37027	BRENTWOOD	184	227	261	232	221	225	204	200	188	207	239	231	222	247	208	183	240	194	180	220
37028	BUMPUS MILLS	79	70	53	67	74	80	65	72	69	65	84	86	64	86	67	71	80	70	78	93
37029	BURNS	95	84	64	80	89	96	79	87	84	79	102	103	77	104	81	86	97	85	94	111
37030	CARTHAGE	85	63	38	58	69	79	63	73	71	62	85	86	56	82	63	75	78	72	86	97
37031	CASTALIAN SPRINGS	88	76	56	71	81	87	71	80	76	71	92	95	68	93	72	78	87	78	87	103
37032	CEDAR HILL	89	79	61	76	84	90	74	81	78	74	95	97	72	97	76	80	90	79	88	104
37033	CENTERVILLE	68	49	29	45	54	64	51	59	58	50	69	68	45	65	51	62	63	59	71	77
37034	CHAPEL HILL	94	84	64	80	89	95	78	86	83	78	100	103	76	103	80	85	95	84	93	111
37035	CHAPMANSBORO	84	74	57	71	78	84	69	76	74	69	89	91	68	91	71	75	85	75	83	98
37036	CHARLOTTE	90	74	52	70	79	87	71	80	77	71	93	94	67	93	72	80	87	78	90	104
37037	CHRISTIANA	94	90	76	88	92	96	84	89	85	84	105	106	83	106	85	85	101	87	91	110
37040	CLARKSVILLE	65	59	59	60	59	63	64	63	65	63	81	75	62	79	62	63	78	65	62	71
37042	CLARKSVILLE	73	63	60	66	60	65	71	68	71	69	88	83	67	84	66	67	85	72	63	76
37043	CLARKSVILLE	92	96	94	96	95	98	92	93	90	92	112	109	93	113	92	88	109	93	90	106
37046	COLLEGE GROVE	119	107	83	102	113	121	99	109	105	99	127	130	97	130	102	107	121	106	118	140
37047	CORNERSVILLE	89	79	60	75	83	89	73	81	78	73	94	96	71	96	75	80	90	79	88	105
37048	COTTONTOWN	93	94	84	92	97	100	86	91	86	86	107	108	87	111	88	87	103	89	92	111
37049	CROSS PLAINS	100	89	68	84	94	100	82	91	87	82	106	108	80	108	84	89	101	88	98	117
37050	CUMBERLAND CITY	86	60	30	52	67	76	57	70	68	58	80	84	50	76	58	73	73	70	85	99
37051	CUMBERLAND FURNACE	89	64	35	57	72	81	61	74	72	62	85	89	55	82	63	76	78	73	89	103
37052	CUNNINGHAM	84	67	43	61	72	80	63	73	70	63	84	87	58	83	64	73	78	71	84	98
37055	DICKSON	78	70	60	67	72	79	70	74	73	69	89	86	68	89	70	75	85	73	79	89
37057	DIXON SPRINGS	91	66	37	59	73	82	63	76	73	64	87	91	56	84	64	78	80	75	90	105
37058	DOVER	82	60	36	55	67	77	60	71	69	59	81	83	53	78	61	73	75	70	84	95
37059	DOWELLTOWN	83	56	27	49	64	73	55	68	65	55	77	80	47	73	56	70	70	67	83	95
37060	EAGLEVILLE	108	96	73	92	102	109	89	99	95	89	115	118	87	117	92	97	109	96	107	127
37061	ERIN	80	54	26	48	61	71	54	66	64	54	75	78	46	71	54	69	68	65	81	91
37062	FAIRVIEW	104	99	83	96	101	106	92	99	94	93	116	117	91	117	93	94	111	97	100	121
37064	FRANKLIN	129	138	132	140	135	137	128	129	122	130	154	151	130	154	127	118	150	127	120	146
37066	GALLATIN	83	84	85	83	85	91	84	85	85	83	105	98	85	107	84	85	101	84	85	96
37067	FRANKLIN	156	166	173	174	161	162	160	157	151	163	191	186	162	188	156	143	187	157	141	174
37069	FRANKLIN	168	200	205	207	192	189	178	175	162	183	207	203	190	211	177	154	207	169	152	192
37072	GOODLETTSVILLE	88	92	96	93	91	94	89	90	87	90	109	105	91	110	89	85	107	89	84	101
37073	GREENBRIER	92	85	69	82	88	93	79	86	82	79	100	102	78	102	81	82	96	84	89	107
37074	HARTSVILLE	83	59	33	53	66	75	59	70	68	59	81	83	52	77	59	73	74	69	84	95
37075	HENDERSONVILLE	98	110	120	112	107	109	105	103	99	105	125	121	108	127	105	95	124	103	93	114
37076	HERMITAGE	86	86	95	91	83	86	89	86	86	90	109	103	88	106	86	81	106	89	78	95
37078	HURRICANE MILLS	84	60	32	53	67	76	57	70	67	58	80	83	51	77	59	72	73	69	84	97
37079	INDIAN MOUND	90	63	32	56	70	80	61	74	71	62	84	88	53	80	61	76	77	73	89	103
37080	JOELTON	100	90	71	86	94	101	84	93	88	84	107	110	81	108	86	90	102	91	99	117
37082	KINGSTON SPRINGS	99	108	101	109	106	105	97	99	93	99	116	117	100	119	97	89	114	96	91	114
37083	LAFAYETTE	75	55	32	50	61	69	54	64	62	54	74	75	48	71	55	66	68	63	76	86
37085	LASCASSAS	93	95	89	95	95	96	90	92	88	91	110	110	90	111	90	85	107	91	87	106
37086	LA VERGNE	90	101	98	104	96	93	92	91	85	95	107	107	94	108	90	79	106	89	78	100
37087	LEBANON	88	83	72	81	85	92	81	85	84	80	102	99	80	103	82	85	98	84	89	102
37090	LEBANON	99	91	73	88	95	101	85	92	88	86	108	109	84	109	87	89	103	90	97	115
37091	LEWISBURG	78	66	51	63	70	77	65	71	70	64	85	84	62	85	66	72	80	70	79	90
37095	LIBERTY	83	56	26	48	63	73	54	67	65	55	76	81	46	72	55	70	70	67	83	96
37096	LINDEN	95	65	32	57	73	85	65	79	77	65	90	93	55	85	65	82	82	78	96	108
37097	LOBELVILLE	76	54	29	48	60	68	53	63	61	53	73	75	46	69	53	65	67	62	76	86
37098	LYLES	79	57	31	51	63	71	55	66	64	56	76	78	49	72	56	67	70	65	78	90
37101	MC EWEN	87	60	30	53	68	77	58	72	69	59	81	85	50	77	59	74	74	71	87	101
37110	MC MINNVILLE	71	57	42	53	61	68	57	64	64	57	77	75	53	75	58	66	72	64	72	82
37115	MADISON	64	63	72	64	62	67	68	65	68	67	85	77	67	84	66	67	83	68	64	72
37118	MILTON	96	87	67	83	91	97	80	88	85	80	103	105	79	105	82	86	98	86	95	113
37122	MOUNT JULIET	110	126	125	127	123	122	114	114	107	115	134	134	118	139	114	103	133	111	103	128
37127	MURFREESBORO	102	105	97	107	103	104	99	101	95	101	119	118	99	119	97	92	116	99	93	114
37128	MURFREESBORO	94	103	101	108	99	96	95	94	88	99	112	111	97	112	93	82	111	93	81	104
37129	MURFREESBORO	94	98	102	100	97	100	97	96	94	97	117	114	97	117	96	90	115	97	90	108
37130	MURFREESBORO	70	61	70	65	60	66	73	68	72	71	91	83	69	87	68	69	88	73	64	76
37132	MURFREESBORO	80	56	72	63	55	64	91	73	89	81	111	97	78	102	77	80	106	86	68	82
37134	NEW JOHNSONVILLE	105	81	50	74	89	98	77	90	87	77	103	107	70	102	78	91	96	88	104	122
37135	NOLENSVILLE	110	137	145	137	134	133	122	122	113	122	142	143	130	152	125	110	142	117	109	135
37137	NUNNELLY	51	34	16	30	39	45	33	41	40	34	47	49	28	44	34	43	43	41	51	59
37138	OLD HICKORY	99	109	113	108	108	112	102	103	99	102	124	119	106	127	103	98	122	101	98	116
37140	ONLY	0	0	0	0	0	0	0	0	0	0	0	0	0	0	0	0	0	0	0	0
37141	ORLINDA	84	75	57	71	79	85	69	77	73	69	89	91	68	91	71	75	85	75	83	99
37142	PALMYRA	88	68	43	62	74	82	64	75	72	65	87	90	59	85	66	76	81	74	87	102
37143	PEGRAM	100	105	99	105	104	106	98	100	94	98	118	118	98	120	97	92	115	98	94	116
37144	PETERSBURG	99	78	49	71	85	94	73	86	82	74	98	102	67	97	75	86	92	84	99	116
37145	PLEASANT SHADE	84	64	39	58	70	78	61	72	69	61	82	86	55	81	62	73	76	71	84	98
37146	PLEASANT VIEW	99	99	85	98	99	101	90	95	89	92	111	112	90	112	90	88	107	92	92	114
37148	PORTLAND	79	67	49	64	72	78	64	72	69	64	84	84	62	84	66	71	79	70	79	91
37149	READYVILLE	88	73	52	69	78	86	69	78	75	69	91	93	66	91	71	78	86	77	87	102
37150	RED BOILING SPRINGS	79	53	24	46	60	69	51	64	62	52	73	77	44	69	52	67	66	64	79	91
37151	RIDDLETON	91	61	28	53	69	80	59	74	71	60	83	88	50	79	60	77	76	73	91	105
37153	ROCKVALE	97	99	88	100	98	99	90	94	88	93	110	110	91	111	90	85	107	91	89	110
37160	SHELBYVILLE	78	66	53	62	69	77	66	71	71	65	86	84	63	86	66	73	81	71	79	89
37166	SMITHVILLE	87	62	34	56	69	80	61	73	71	62	84	86	54	81	62	76	77	73	88	99
37167	SMYRNA	88	91	88	93	89	90	87	88	84	89	105	103	88	105	86	80	103	87	80	99
37171	SOUTHSIDE	89	79	60	75	83	89	73	81	77	73	94	96	71	96	75	79	89	79	87	104
37172	SPRINGFIELD	89	77	62	74	81	89	77	82	82	76	99	97	74	99	77	83	94	82	89	102
	TENNESSEE	85	76	68	73	78	85	76	80	79	76	97	94	73	96	75	81	93	80	85	97
	UNITED STATES	100	100	100	100	100	100	100	100	100	100	100	100	100	100	100	100	100	100	100	100

#	POST OFFICE NAME	COUNTY FIPS CODE	POPULATION			2000-2004 ANNUAL RATE		HOUSEHOLDS					FAMILIES		
			2000	2004	2009	% Rate	State Centile	2000	2004	2009	% Annual Rate 2000-2004	2004 Average HH Size	2000	2004	% Annual Rate 2000-2004
37174	SPRING HILL	119	8050	10571	12838	6.6	100	2889	3861	4752	7.1	2.72	2266	2972	6.6
37175	STEWART	083	1482	1542	1584	0.9	57	625	663	693	1.4	2.32	436	453	0.9
37178	TENNESSEE RIDGE	161	1316	1334	1350	0.3	34	513	529	545	0.7	2.50	392	398	0.4
37179	THOMPSONS STATION	187	6457	8592	10661	7.0	100	2170	2905	3636	7.1	2.96	1816	2399	6.8
37180	UNIONVILLE	003	2289	2458	2659	1.7	79	791	856	931	1.9	2.87	633	674	1.5
37181	VANLEER	043	1202	1356	1499	2.9	94	443	508	570	3.3	2.67	341	383	2.8
37183	WARTRACE	003	2603	2812	3045	1.8	81	986	1074	1170	2.0	2.60	763	817	1.6
37184	WATERTOWN	189	4749	4930	5304	0.9	55	1823	1923	2101	1.3	2.56	1389	1436	0.8
37185	WAVERLY	085	8307	8366	8444	0.2	28	3429	3516	3601	0.6	2.32	2358	2365	0.1
37186	WESTMORELAND	165	9122	9783	10424	1.7	78	3321	3613	3903	2.0	2.68	2530	2703	1.6
37187	WHITE BLUFF	043	5692	6070	6580	1.5	75	2170	2361	2601	2.0	2.56	1623	1730	1.5
37188	WHITE HOUSE	147	10252	11526	12900	2.8	94	3548	4053	4605	3.2	2.84	2901	3266	2.8
37189	WHITES CREEK	037	2909	2849	2864	-0.5	6	1070	1048	1056	-0.5	2.68	776	745	-1.0
37190	WOODBURY	015	7923	8007	8141	0.3	31	3160	3249	3345	0.7	2.42	2233	2248	0.2
37191	WOODLAWN	125	3968	4172	4490	1.2	65	1420	1515	1649	1.5	2.75	1104	1154	1.1
37201	NASHVILLE	037	1438	1435	1443	-0.1	17	324	313	315	-0.8	1.84	35	28	-5.1
37203	NASHVILLE	037	10837	10768	10959	-0.2	13	4826	4817	4929	0.0	1.96	1850	1777	-0.9
37204	NASHVILLE	037	10905	10511	10553	-0.9	3	5152	4996	5038	-0.7	2.09	2711	2534	-1.6
37205	NASHVILLE	037	25569	25932	26495	0.3	35	12222	12441	12760	0.4	2.05	6599	6477	-0.4
37206	NASHVILLE	037	27589	27286	27591	-0.3	10	10929	10822	10978	-0.2	2.46	6554	6312	-0.9
37207	NASHVILLE	037	35943	36162	36855	0.1	27	13166	13288	13593	0.2	2.70	9450	9352	-0.2
37208	NASHVILLE	037	15723	15568	15840	-0.2	10	5910	5857	5983	-0.2	2.40	3296	3129	-1.2
37209	NASHVILLE	037	34904	34933	35610	0.0	22	12936	12989	13325	0.1	2.30	7382	7190	-0.6
37210	NASHVILLE	037	16192	16168	16511	0.0	18	6650	6609	6748	-0.2	2.36	3620	3501	-0.8
37211	NASHVILLE	037	63469	66972	70176	1.3	67	27845	29405	30896	1.3	2.27	15295	15635	0.5
37212	NASHVILLE	037	17006	16770	16969	-0.3	8	7272	7168	7298	-0.3	1.87	2475	2327	-1.4
37213	NASHVILLE	037	180	186	190	0.8	50	11	11	11	0.0	2.55	10	10	0.0
37214	NASHVILLE	037	26421	26352	26685	-0.1	16	11816	11853	12058	0.1	2.16	6741	6548	-0.7
37215	NASHVILLE	037	22711	22989	23497	0.3	32	10149	10294	10557	0.3	2.10	5571	5483	-0.4
37216	NASHVILLE	037	19755	19635	19953	-0.1	14	8276	8251	8409	-0.1	2.37	5272	5114	-0.7
37217	NASHVILLE	037	30892	32213	33361	1.0	59	12508	12882	13294	0.7	2.36	6843	6830	0.0
37218	NASHVILLE	037	14874	14443	14488	-0.7	4	5011	4876	4914	-0.6	2.67	3635	3464	-1.1
37219	NASHVILLE	037	580	658	708	3.0	95	463	528	570	3.1	1.25	54	44	-4.7
37220	NASHVILLE	037	5776	6129	6430	1.4	71	2324	2471	2599	1.5	2.48	1747	1816	0.9
37221	NASHVILLE	037	31282	33177	34677	1.4	70	13342	14274	15000	1.6	2.31	8506	8827	0.9
37228	NASHVILLE	037	226	235	241	0.9	57	213	223	230	1.1	1.05	67	45	-8.9
37240	NASHVILLE	037	2811	2883	2930	0.6	44	159	204	233	6.0	1.56	28	31	2.4
37301	ALTAMONT	061	1197	1294	1350	1.9	82	411	457	489	2.5	2.77	314	344	2.2
37302	APISON	065	2570	2767	2885	1.8	80	992	1092	1162	2.3	2.53	758	818	1.8
37303	ATHENS	107	24164	24847	25467	0.7	47	9833	10290	10686	1.1	2.37	6950	7144	0.7
37305	BEERSHEBA SPRINGS	061	1114	1118	1124	0.1	25	438	449	461	0.6	2.48	334	337	0.2
37306	BELVIDERE	051	2576	2647	2762	0.6	46	936	983	1046	1.2	2.69	760	786	0.8
37307	BENTON	139	4028	4074	4109	0.3	32	1576	1638	1688	0.9	2.45	1172	1196	0.5
37308	BIRCHWOOD	121	3072	3193	3300	0.9	56	1157	1226	1289	1.4	2.60	927	969	1.1
37309	CALHOUN	107	1865	1959	2000	1.2	64	691	742	769	1.7	2.62	542	571	1.2
37310	CHARLESTON	011	3331	3632	3857	2.1	85	1291	1438	1554	2.6	2.53	989	1079	2.1
37311	CLEVELAND	011	24545	24924	25617	0.4	36	10013	10371	10852	0.8	2.26	6088	6125	0.1
37312	CLEVELAND	011	28018	29081	30086	0.9	55	10752	11394	12000	1.4	2.50	8029	8347	0.9
37313	COALMONT	061	902	923	934	0.5	42	353	370	383	1.1	2.49	269	278	0.8
37317	COPPERHILL	139	3559	3561	3580	0.0	21	1480	1515	1553	0.6	2.26	1017	1019	0.1
37318	COWAN	051	2233	2233	2310	0.0	20	921	943	996	0.6	2.36	653	653	0.0
37321	DAYTON	143	18780	19602	20625	1.0	60	7190	7653	8210	1.5	2.47	5269	5505	1.0
37322	DECATUR	121	4979	5374	5713	1.8	81	1935	2127	2296	2.3	2.47	1448	1567	1.9
37323	CLEVELAND	011	25811	27186	28496	1.2	66	9748	10463	11152	1.7	2.59	7659	8080	1.3
37324	DECHERD	051	5118	5459	5803	1.5	75	2105	2290	2479	2.0	2.38	1480	1575	1.5
37325	DELANO	139	1911	1939	1958	0.3	36	739	768	792	0.9	2.51	572	586	0.6
37327	DUNLAP	153	8899	9359	9788	1.2	65	3477	3738	3980	1.7	2.47	2566	2709	1.3
37328	ELORA	103	1343	1353	1360	0.2	28	554	573	585	0.8	2.36	411	415	0.2
37329	ENGLEWOOD	107	4856	5015	5101	0.8	50	1937	2040	2104	1.2	2.43	1444	1487	0.7
37330	ESTILL SPRINGS	051	6978	7551	8056	1.9	82	2646	2922	3176	2.4	2.57	2110	2293	2.0
37331	ETOWAH	107	7810	7668	7622	-0.4	7	3255	3265	3293	0.1	2.30	2234	2181	-0.6
37332	EVENSVILLE	143	1007	1147	1253	3.1	95	386	448	499	3.6	2.56	299	342	3.2
37333	FARNER	139	836	847	855	0.3	33	325	338	349	0.9	2.51	256	261	0.5
37334	FAYETTEVILLE	103	20583	20508	20587	-0.1	15	8331	8448	8601	0.3	2.37	5906	5879	-0.1
37335	FLINTVILLE	103	2469	2542	2574	0.7	47	930	979	1007	1.2	2.60	703	725	0.7
37336	GEORGETOWN	121	4171	4234	4350	0.4	36	1558	1615	1689	0.9	2.61	1259	1286	0.5
37337	GRANDVIEW	143	1350	1338	1383	-0.2	11	575	584	617	0.4	2.29	406	405	-0.1
37338	GRAYSVILLE	007	860	879	906	0.5	42	322	337	353	1.1	2.58	249	256	0.7
37339	GRUETLI LAAGER	061	2173	2194	2207	0.2	31	835	866	890	0.9	2.53	631	642	0.4
37340	GUILD	115	1313	1370	1443	1.0	59	534	570	614	1.6	2.40	402	422	1.2
37341	HARRISON	065	12140	12162	12341	0.0	23	4441	4539	4691	0.5	2.67	3600	3629	0.2
37342	HILLSBORO	031	3129	3293	3438	1.2	65	1139	1220	1292	1.6	2.70	911	961	1.3
37343	HIXSON	065	36456	37628	38688	0.8	49	14068	14862	15596	1.3	2.52	10702	11118	0.9
37345	HUNTLAND	051	2240	2211	2271	-0.3	9	861	870	912	0.2	2.52	643	638	-0.2
37347	JASPER	115	7792	8077	8472	0.9	54	3121	3316	3563	1.4	2.41	2292	2388	1.0
37348	KELSO	103	1085	1177	1224	1.9	83	406	448	472	2.3	2.63	320	346	1.9
37350	LOOKOUT MOUNTAIN	065	1998	1952	1953	-0.6	5	790	780	791	-0.3	2.50	585	566	-0.8
37352	LYNCHBURG	127	3062	3255	3434	1.5	72	1205	1311	1410	2.0	2.45	889	951	1.6
37353	MC DONALD	011	4487	4497	4598	0.1	24	1782	1817	1888	0.5	2.47	1323	1323	0.0
37354	MADISONVILLE	123	14015	14819	15473	1.3	68	5546	5982	6349	1.8	2.44	4010	4239	1.3
37355	MANCHESTER	031	22133	23400	24504	1.3	68	8528	9168	9738	1.7	2.50	6203	6542	1.3
37356	MONTEAGLE	115	2492	2538	2605	0.4	39	990	1031	1081	1.0	2.35	710	726	0.5
37357	MORRISON	177	5458	5934	6212	2.0	84	2073	2302	2451	2.5	2.55	1589	1731	2.0
37359	MULBERRY	103	505	496	495	-0.4	7	199	201	203	0.2	2.47	158	157	-0.2
37360	NORMANDY	003	1635	1706	1796	1.0	60	621	659	702	1.4	2.52	480	500	1.0
37361	OCOEE	139	719	754	775	1.1	62	298	321	337	1.8	2.35	223	237	1.4
37362	OLDFORT	139	3292	3403	3496	0.8	51	1270	1345	1410	1.4	2.53	963	1001	0.9
37363	OOLTEWAH	065	23489	25046	26058	1.5	75	8100	8852	9406	2.1	2.67	6558	7057	1.7
37365	PALMER	061	1802	1791	1792	-0.1	14	706	722	740	0.5	2.48	510	510	0.0
37366	PELHAM	061	683	681	681	-0.1	16	275	282	289	0.6	2.41	202	203	0.1
37367	PIKEVILLE	007	9132	9325	9549	0.5	41	3188	3326	3474	1.0	2.47	2357	2414	0.6
37369	RELIANCE	139	1753	1764	1777	0.2	27	736	760	782	0.8	2.32	556	565	0.4
37370	RICEVILLE	107	4457	4520	4535	0.3	35	1698	1759	1790	0.8	2.56	1344	1367	0.4
37373	SALE CREEK	065	2716	2818	2907	0.9	54	1095	1164	1227	1.5	2.42	867	906	1.0
37374	SEQUATCHIE	115	1230	1282	1349	1.0	58	461	493	532	1.6	2.60	357	376	1.2
	TENNESSEE					1.0					1.3	2.45			0.9
	UNITED STATES					1.2					1.3	2.58			1.1

#	POST OFFICE NAME	White 2000	White 2004	Black 2000	Black 2004	Asian/Pacific 2000	Asian/Pacific 2004	% Hispanic Origin 2000	% Hispanic Origin 2004	0-4	5-9	10-14	15-19	20-24	25-44	45-64	65-84	85+	18+	MEDIAN AGE 2004	% 2004 Males	% 2004 Females
37174	SPRING HILL	89.2	87.9	7.2	8.0	0.5	0.6	3.4	4.1	8.1	7.9	7.3	6.3	5.9	33.0	24.7	6.1	0.6	72.6	34.4	50.4	49.6
37175	STEWART	93.2	92.5	0.5	0.5	2.1	2.6	3.3	3.2	4.3	4.5	5.5	5.3	5.3	23.0	32.1	18.5	1.5	82.4	46.4	51.1	48.9
37178	TENNESSEE RIDGE	98.0	97.8	0.8	0.9	0.4	0.4	0.8	0.8	6.7	6.8	7.1	6.2	5.5	26.0	26.4	13.9	1.4	75.2	38.9	48.7	51.4
37179	THOMPSONS STATION	92.4	91.2	5.0	5.5	0.5	0.6	2.7	3.5	9.7	9.2	8.0	5.8	5.4	34.2	21.7	5.4	0.6	69.4	33.2	50.2	49.8
37180	UNIONVILLE	95.3	94.6	2.7	2.9	0.0	0.0	1.7	2.2	8.3	8.2	7.8	6.0	5.6	31.4	23.0	8.7	1.1	72.1	33.8	50.3	49.7
37181	VANLEER	96.5	96.1	1.1	1.2	0.3	0.4	0.5	0.7	6.0	6.3	7.2	7.2	5.9	28.5	26.3	11.4	1.4	76.1	38.4	51.0	49.0
37183	WARTRACE	93.9	93.3	4.2	4.5	0.3	0.4	1.4	1.8	6.4	6.6	7.3	6.6	6.1	28.6	26.2	11.0	1.2	75.5	38.0	51.0	49.0
37184	WATERTOWN	93.7	93.3	4.5	4.7	0.1	0.1	1.0	1.2	6.5	6.6	6.9	6.5	5.9	28.4	26.5	11.1	1.7	76.1	38.7	50.1	49.9
37185	WAVERLY	92.9	92.4	5.4	5.7	0.3	0.4	1.1	1.2	5.5	5.7	6.2	5.7	5.5	26.1	27.7	15.7	2.0	79.0	41.9	49.2	50.8
37186	WESTMORELAND	98.4	98.1	0.1	0.1	0.2	0.2	1.0	1.3	8.0	7.8	7.4	6.7	6.5	28.6	23.8	10.0	1.2	72.7	35.3	49.9	50.1
37187	WHITE BLUFF	98.5	98.2	0.4	0.4	0.2	0.2	0.6	0.8	6.6	7.1	7.6	6.1	5.9	30.1	25.9	10.0	0.7	74.7	36.4	50.1	50.0
37188	WHITE HOUSE	96.9	96.4	1.6	1.7	0.4	0.5	1.1	1.4	8.2	8.0	8.4	6.9	6.1	33.4	21.8	6.8	0.6	71.3	33.8	50.2	49.8
37189	WHITES CREEK	70.9	68.7	27.2	29.2	0.3	0.4	0.7	0.8	5.6	6.0	6.6	5.6	5.4	27.0	29.7	12.5	1.8	78.2	41.4	49.0	51.0
37190	WOODBURY	96.5	96.2	1.7	1.8	0.2	0.2	1.3	1.5	6.5	6.4	6.8	6.2	6.4	27.1	25.1	13.4	2.1	76.5	38.8	48.8	51.2
37191	WOODLAWN	89.3	88.2	5.2	5.5	1.2	1.4	3.1	3.6	8.2	7.7	8.0	6.6	6.1	35.9	19.9	6.9	0.7	72.0	33.1	50.7	49.3
37201	NASHVILLE	54.6	51.9	41.5	43.8	0.9	1.0	5.2	5.9	0.1	0.1	0.0	5.0	16.8	61.0	14.7	2.2	0.1	99.2	33.1	85.0	15.1
37203	NASHVILLE	38.7	36.7	54.7	55.7	3.7	4.4	3.3	3.8	7.4	6.2	6.2	5.9	10.9	31.7	19.1	10.1	2.6	76.9	32.1	49.6	50.4
37204	NASHVILLE	65.3	63.9	31.5	32.3	1.6	1.9	1.3	1.5	4.9	4.8	5.3	6.3	6.6	30.8	26.7	12.5	2.3	81.2	39.7	47.4	52.6
37205	NASHVILLE	93.2	92.1	2.9	3.3	2.3	2.9	1.2	1.5	5.4	5.4	5.3	4.9	6.2	29.7	26.3	13.9	3.0	81.0	40.6	47.0	53.0
37206	NASHVILLE	49.5	46.6	44.4	46.7	1.2	1.4	3.2	3.7	8.0	7.4	7.8	7.7	6.9	29.9	22.0	9.1	1.3	72.7	33.9	48.1	51.9
37207	NASHVILLE	26.2	24.8	69.8	70.8	0.7	0.9	2.6	3.0	8.1	8.4	8.9	7.9	7.2	26.9	22.7	9.0	1.0	69.8	32.4	46.2	53.8
37208	NASHVILLE	5.1	4.6	92.3	92.7	0.6	0.6	0.9	0.9	6.4	6.4	7.3	8.7	11.2	24.5	21.1	12.4	1.9	75.7	33.5	45.0	55.0
37209	NASHVILLE	60.8	59.2	31.2	31.5	3.5	4.2	4.1	4.8	6.1	5.6	5.3	9.3	10.2	32.9	20.7	8.8	1.1	79.9	32.7	51.9	48.1
37210	NASHVILLE	50.6	49.2	34.1	33.4	3.5	3.9	12.8	14.9	8.2	6.9	6.2	7.8	10.0	29.5	19.6	9.8	2.0	75.3	31.8	49.8	50.3
37211	NASHVILLE	69.2	66.9	17.6	18.3	3.6	4.3	10.1	11.5	7.1	6.1	5.7	6.0	9.3	35.6	20.5	8.6	1.2	77.8	33.1	49.1	50.9
37212	NASHVILLE	74.2	71.4	17.2	18.4	5.9	7.2	2.1	2.5	3.5	3.2	3.6	10.5	21.1	32.8	17.4	6.3	1.6	87.6	29.0	48.6	51.4
37213	NASHVILLE	33.3	30.7	62.2	64.0	0.0	0.0	3.3	4.3	8.1	9.7	8.6	29.0	3.8	18.3	22.0	0.5	0.0	48.4	19.1	69.4	30.7
37214	NASHVILLE	86.4	84.7	9.1	10.0	1.6	2.0	2.8	3.3	5.9	5.6	5.5	5.2	6.6	33.7	24.3	11.6	1.7	79.9	38.0	48.4	51.7
37215	NASHVILLE	95.6	94.9	1.6	1.8	1.6	2.0	1.0	1.3	3.9	4.6	5.1	7.2	7.3	24.7	28.6	15.1	3.5	83.4	43.0	45.7	54.3
37216	NASHVILLE	66.7	64.5	29.4	31.0	0.9	1.1	1.9	2.2	6.5	6.0	6.4	6.1	6.8	28.2	25.7	12.5	1.9	77.6	39.1	47.9	52.1
37217	NASHVILLE	62.4	59.3	23.2	24.1	3.2	3.7	13.2	15.5	6.5	5.6	5.1	5.5	10.1	39.1	20.8	6.8	0.6	79.9	33.1	53.8	46.2
37218	NASHVILLE	25.8	24.6	71.7	72.6	0.4	0.5	1.1	1.3	5.4	5.5	6.2	7.0	6.7	25.0	27.2	14.1	2.9	78.5	40.8	44.8	55.2
37219	NASHVILLE	68.6	67.6	26.0	26.0	2.1	2.9	3.6	4.0	0.3	0.2	0.3	2.7	14.3	55.3	21.4	5.2	0.3	98.9	34.8	72.3	27.7
37220	NASHVILLE	96.8	96.1	1.2	1.4	1.1	1.4	0.9	1.2	5.7	6.6	6.7	5.7	3.3	23.5	30.2	16.6	1.9	77.5	44.3	48.7	51.4
37221	NASHVILLE	90.3	88.6	4.2	4.7	3.4	4.3	1.8	2.3	6.7	6.9	6.2	5.3	5.8	31.9	26.0	10.0	1.4	77.0	37.8	46.6	53.4
37228	NASHVILLE	25.2	23.0	72.6	74.9	0.4	0.4	0.9	0.4	0.9	2.6	1.7	3.8	4.7	24.7	23.8	31.5	6.4	93.2	55.5	36.2	63.8
37240	NASHVILLE	82.4	79.4	4.5	4.8	9.4	11.5	4.3	5.2	0.3	0.4	0.1	59.1	35.3	4.1	0.6	0.1	0.0	98.7	19.2	46.7	53.3
37301	ALTAMONT	97.5	97.0	0.1	0.1	0.1	0.2	3.0	3.6	8.5	8.3	7.7	5.5	6.6	28.8	23.4	10.3	0.9	71.8	34.0	51.2	48.8
37302	APISON	93.9	92.6	1.3	1.5	1.4	1.7	3.1	3.9	5.2	5.6	6.5	5.9	5.6	29.2	28.3	12.1	1.6	79.0	40.0	50.4	49.6
37303	ATHENS	91.0	90.3	5.6	5.7	1.1	1.3	2.3	2.7	6.4	6.4	6.8	6.2	6.3	27.6	25.7	12.8	1.8	76.8	38.6	47.9	52.1
37305	BEERSHEBA SPRINGS	99.5	99.5	0.0	0.0	0.0	0.0	0.8	0.9	6.4	6.6	7.0	5.8	6.0	27.6	25.7	13.5	1.3	76.3	37.4	49.3	50.7
37306	BELVIDERE	94.1	93.5	3.8	4.0	0.2	0.2	2.1	2.5	6.3	6.5	7.0	6.5	5.9	27.7	26.8	12.2	1.2	76.4	38.5	50.1	49.9
37307	BENTON	98.8	98.6	0.1	0.2	0.1	0.1	1.0	1.2	7.0	7.0	6.4	5.8	5.5	30.5	25.7	11.2	1.1	76.1	37.3	49.7	50.3
37308	BIRCHWOOD	97.5	97.3	1.1	1.2	0.1	0.1	0.6	0.7	6.5	6.8	6.8	5.8	5.3	28.7	28.3	10.9	1.0	76.3	38.8	50.2	49.8
37309	CALHOUN	95.0	94.2	2.5	2.8	0.4	0.5	2.7	3.4	5.9	6.2	6.8	6.2	6.6	27.9	27.5	12.0	1.0	77.0	39.0	51.3	48.8
37310	CHARLESTON	90.6	89.7	6.9	7.5	0.2	0.3	1.3	1.6	6.9	7.1	6.8	5.2	5.0	29.2	28.0	10.6	1.2	75.9	38.6	48.9	51.1
37311	CLEVELAND	88.6	87.7	7.3	7.6	0.7	0.9	3.0	3.6	6.8	6.0	5.9	8.1	10.5	28.5	21.7	11.1	1.5	78.0	33.1	48.0	52.0
37312	CLEVELAND	93.3	92.6	3.7	3.8	0.9	1.1	2.1	2.5	6.2	6.4	6.5	5.9	5.9	28.9	25.9	12.5	1.8	77.2	38.7	48.5	51.5
37313	COALMONT	98.6	98.4	0.0	0.0	0.1	0.2	0.8	1.0	7.0	6.9	7.4	7.6	6.9	29.0	23.4	10.5	1.2	74.0	35.2	49.8	50.2
37317	COPPERHILL	97.6	97.3	0.3	0.3	0.4	0.4	0.9	1.1	5.3	5.3	5.5	5.0	4.8	23.6	28.0	19.0	3.6	81.0	45.5	47.8	52.2
37318	COWAN	89.6	88.4	7.7	8.4	0.1	0.1	1.2	1.4	7.1	6.9	6.8	6.8	6.8	24.8	24.8	14.5	1.6	75.0	38.2	46.4	53.6
37321	DAYTON	94.7	94.2	2.2	2.3	0.4	0.5	2.0	2.4	6.7	6.7	6.7	7.2	7.4	28.0	24.7	11.0	1.6	76.0	36.0	48.7	51.4
37322	DECATUR	98.7	98.6	0.4	0.5	0.1	0.2	0.5	0.6	6.5	6.6	6.7	6.3	6.2	28.4	26.3	11.7	1.4	76.2	38.2	50.5	49.5
37323	CLEVELAND	96.1	95.6	1.7	1.8	0.3	0.4	1.5	1.8	6.8	6.9	7.0	6.1	6.0	31.4	25.1	10.0	0.7	75.7	36.5	49.7	50.3
37324	DECHERD	90.0	89.6	8.2	8.4	0.2	0.2	1.4	1.6	6.5	6.5	6.2	5.5	5.3	27.7	26.4	14.1	1.8	77.3	39.3	49.4	50.6
37325	DELANO	97.8	97.5	0.5	0.5	0.2	0.2	0.7	0.9	6.2	6.6	6.5	5.9	5.3	29.9	27.0	11.5	1.2	76.8	38.6	50.8	49.3
37327	DUNLAP	98.7	98.6	0.2	0.2	0.2	0.2	0.7	0.8	7.1	7.1	6.9	5.9	5.7	29.3	25.0	11.6	1.6	75.5	37.1	50.1	49.9
37328	ELORA	96.6	96.2	0.9	1.0	0.2	0.2	1.7	2.0	6.3	6.5	7.4	6.4	6.2	27.9	26.8	11.5	1.0	75.8	38.1	50.9	49.1
37329	ENGLEWOOD	97.0	96.6	0.9	0.9	0.2	0.2	1.1	1.4	6.7	6.7	7.1	6.2	5.7	27.3	26.0	12.8	1.6	75.9	38.4	50.0	50.0
37330	ESTILL SPRINGS	96.5	96.0	1.5	1.6	0.7	0.9	1.3	1.6	6.0	6.4	6.9	6.1	5.8	27.5	26.9	13.1	1.3	76.7	40.0	50.6	49.4
37331	ETOWAH	91.7	90.7	6.0	6.7	0.2	0.3	1.4	1.7	5.5	5.7	6.6	5.2	5.5	25.5	26.4	16.9	2.7	79.0	42.1	47.8	52.2
37332	EVENSVILLE	97.3	97.0	0.3	0.4	0.1	0.2	1.1	1.4	7.1	7.1	7.0	6.3	6.5	29.1	26.1	9.8	1.1	75.0	36.4	49.4	50.7
37333	FARNER	97.4	97.2	0.0	0.0	0.0	0.0	0.1	0.1	7.3	7.4	7.2	5.9	5.9	26.8	25.6	12.8	1.1	74.3	37.2	50.9	49.1
37334	FAYETTEVILLE	87.2	86.4	10.5	11.0	0.4	0.5	0.9	1.1	6.2	6.3	6.4	5.9	5.7	26.3	25.5	15.1	2.5	77.5	40.5	47.8	52.2
37335	FLINTVILLE	96.6	96.2	0.8	0.9	0.2	0.3	1.4	1.7	6.4	6.6	7.2	6.5	6.1	28.5	26.6	11.1	1.0	75.8	37.9	50.6	49.5
37336	GEORGETOWN	97.1	96.8	1.8	2.0	0.2	0.2	0.5	0.6	6.1	6.5	6.9	5.8	5.2	29.6	27.9	10.8	1.0	76.8	38.8	50.1	49.9
37337	GRANDVIEW	97.8	97.5	0.4	0.4	0.3	0.4	0.8	1.1	4.5	4.9	6.4	6.4	5.5	27.1	30.0	13.4	1.7	80.4	42.1	51.6	48.4
37338	GRAYSVILLE	97.1	96.8	0.2	0.2	0.1	0.2	1.7	2.2	6.3	6.1	6.4	6.0	6.1	28.8	27.4	11.5	1.4	77.6	39.1	51.2	48.8
37339	GRUETLI LAAGER	98.8	98.6	0.0	0.0	0.1	0.2	0.8	1.0	7.1	7.1	7.1	6.8	6.4	28.9	24.3	11.0	1.3	74.5	35.8	49.7	50.3
37340	GUILD	95.4	94.8	1.6	1.8	0.5	0.7	1.1	1.2	5.0	4.9	5.7	6.1	5.6	26.1	31.8	13.7	1.2	80.9	42.9	49.9	50.1
37341	HARRISON	93.6	92.8	4.4	4.9	0.4	0.6	0.8	1.0	5.9	6.5	7.2	6.3	5.1	29.9	28.6	9.6	0.9	76.5	39.0	49.4	50.6
37342	HILLSBORO	98.1	97.8	0.0	0.0	0.2	0.2	1.9	2.3	7.0	7.1	7.5	6.9	6.1	28.1	25.4	11.0	0.9	74.1	37.0	50.1	49.9
37343	HIXSON	93.3	92.1	3.0	3.4	2.1	2.6	1.4	1.7	5.9	6.1	6.7	6.4	6.0	27.3	29.3	11.4	1.0	77.5	39.8	48.3	51.7
37345	HUNTLAND	94.6	94.0	2.8	3.0	0.1	0.1	2.5	3.2	6.0	6.0	6.7	6.7	6.9	28.0	24.3	13.6	1.8	77.0	38.5	49.1	50.9
37347	JASPER	93.1	92.4	4.9	5.4	0.4	0.5	0.8	1.0	5.7	5.9	6.2	6.2	6.1	28.8	28.2	11.7	1.2	78.4	39.5	49.4	50.6
37348	KELSO	97.0	96.6	0.9	1.0	0.3	0.3	0.7	0.8	7.1	6.7	6.4	7.1	6.2	29.6	25.7	10.5	0.9	75.5	37.3	49.9	50.1
37350	LOOKOUT MOUNTAIN	96.9	96.3	2.1	2.5	0.6	0.8	0.4	0.5	7.0	8.0	7.9	7.0	3.7	19.2	28.7	15.7	2.8	72.6	43.2	48.0	52.0
37352	LYNCHBURG	94.7	94.4	3.8	4.0	0.2	0.2	0.7	0.8	5.5	5.8	6.5	5.8	5.6	25.4	28.1	15.2	2.2	78.5	41.8	49.7	50.3
37353	MC DONALD	96.8	96.5	0.6	0.6	0.2	0.2	1.6	1.9	6.1	6.2	6.1	5.9	5.6	29.0	28.9	11.2	1.1	78.1	39.8	51.6	48.4
37354	MADISONVILLE	96.0	95.5	1.5	1.6	0.2	0.3	1.8	2.2	6.6	6.7	7.0	6.1	6.2	29.4	25.0	11.6	1.5	76.1	36.8	49.9	50.1
37355	MANCHESTER	95.1	94.5	2.2	2.3	0.7	0.9	2.7	3.2	6.6	6.4	6.8	6.3	6.4	27.8	24.5	13.6	1.7	76.4	38.3	49.3	50.7
37356	MONTEAGLE	97.4	97.2	0.6	0.6	0.3	0.4	0.7	0.9	5.5	5.8	5.9	5.9	5.5	25.0	27.9	15.8	2.8	79.0	42.7	49.1	51.0
37357	MORRISON	94.1	93.3	2.6	2.7	0.4	0.5	2.9	3.5	6.8	7.0	7.4	6.3	6.2	29.3	25.1	11.0	1.0	75.0	36.6	50.5	49.5
37359	MULBERRY	94.9	94.6	3.8	4.2	0.2	0.2	0.6	0.4	5.0	5.2	5.7	6.1	6.1	25.8	30.0	14.7	1.4	80.4	42.4	50.4	49.6
37360	NORMANDY	93.9	93.3	3.5	3.7	0.6	0.7	1.4	1.8	5.9	6.1	6.2	6.3	5.7	26.1	28.8	13.3	1.6	78.0	40.6	50.8	49.2
37361	OCOEE	98.3	98.0	0.0	0.0	0.1	0.1	0.8	1.1	6.9	6.6	5.7	5.6	5.4	29.8	27.3	11.4	1.2	77.2	38.5	51.1	48.9
37362	OLDFORT	98.8	98.6	0.1	0.1	0.2	0.2	0.6	0.7	7.5	7.2	6.5	6.2	5.9	30.9	25.7	9.2	0.9	75.0	36.3	51.3	48.8
37363	OOLTEWAH	90.0	88.5	5.6	6.2	1.3	1.6	3.1	3.8	6.1	6.5	6.8	8.2	8.2	28.0	25.6	9.4	1.2	76.6	36.2	48.5	51.5
37365	PALMER	99.0	98.9	0.0	0.0	0.1	0.2	0.4	0.5	6.9	7.0	7.0	6.0	5.3	28.0	24.8	13.3	1.7	75.3	38.2	49.5	50.5
37366	PELHAM	99.3	99.1	0.0	0.0	0.2	0.2	1.3	1.5	6.3	6.5	7.6	6.0	5.9	26.7	26.4	12.5	2.1	75.9	38.8	51.3	48.8
37367	PIKEVILLE	93.7	93.2	4.7	4.9	0.2	0.2	1.0	1.2	5.6	5.8	6.3	6.9	5.7	31.0	26.3	11.3	1.1	77.9	38.3	56.0	44.0
37369	RELIANCE	99.0	98.8	0.1	0.1	0.1	0.1	0.7	0.8	5.5	5.8	6.1	5.4	5.4	28.4	29.0	13.1	1.3	79.3	40.9	49.4	50.6
37370	RICEVILLE	95.4	94.8	2.1	2.3	0.7	0.9	1.7	2.1	6.5	6.6	6.7	6.1	6.1	27.9	28.1	11.0	1.0	76.6	38.8	49.9	50.1
37373	SALE CREEK	97.6	97.2	1.3	1.5	0.3	0.3	0.6	0.7	5.3	5.7	6.5	5.5	5.1	28.1	30.1	12.4	1.4	79.2	41.7	49.8	50.3
37374	SEQUATCHIE	97.2	96.8	1.1	1.3	0.2	0.4	0.7	0.9	6.3	6.4	6.9	7.0	6.0	31.0	25.0	10.5	0.9	76.1	36.2	49.9	50.1
	TENNESSEE	80.2	79.4	16.4	16.7	1.0	1.3	2.2	2.6	6.6	6.5	6.8	6.6	7.0	29.0	24.8	11.1	1.5	76.3	36.8	48.9	51.1
	UNITED STATES	75.1	73.6	12.3	12.5	3.8	4.2	12.5	14.1	6.9	6.7	7.2	7.0	7.3	28.6	23.8	10.8	1.7	75.1	36.0	49.1	50.9

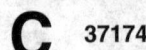

#	POST OFFICE NAME	2004 Per Capita Income	2004 HH Income Base	2004 HOUSEHOLD INCOME DISTRIBUTION (%) Less than $25,000	$25,000 to $49,999	$50,000 to $99,999	$100,000 to $149,999	$150,000 or More	MEDIAN HOUSEHOLD INCOME 2004	2009	2004 National Centile	2004 State Centile	2004 Home Value Base	2004 HOME VALUE DISTRIBUTION (%) Less than $50,000	$50,000 to $89,999	$90,000 to $174,999	$175,000 to $399,999	$400,000 or More	2004 Median Home Value
37174	SPRING HILL	25503	3861	12.5	23.7	46.2	14.2	3.4	62030	70549	86	95	3239	4.2	9.7	47.0	36.0	3.1	160139
37175	STEWART	19090	663	43.9	27.5	21.3	4.7	2.7	28830	32214	10	17	554	31.1	31.4	27.8	9.6	0.2	76600
37178	TENNESSEE RIDGE	17669	529	32.5	35.7	27.4	4.0	0.4	36374	40338	33	55	431	25.1	38.3	32.5	3.9	0.2	75270
37179	THOMPSONS STATION	25163	2905	12.2	20.6	49.0	13.9	4.4	64386	76286	88	96	2669	5.9	4.5	33.4	47.2	9.1	184561
37180	UNIONVILLE	18072	856	25.1	32.7	33.4	6.7	2.1	43600	48902	58	78	722	17.9	30.2	42.1	6.8	3.1	91687
37181	VANLEER	18353	508	28.2	32.9	32.9	3.9	2.2	41205	47060	50	72	422	20.6	30.8	33.9	12.6	2.1	88286
37183	WARTRACE	19357	1074	27.8	34.0	30.3	6.1	1.9	40914	45086	49	71	891	19.6	22.6	34.9	18.2	4.7	105546
37184	WATERTOWN	21264	1923	27.7	27.8	34.8	7.3	2.4	44928	51700	61	80	1597	12.7	24.0	37.3	20.7	5.3	111701
37185	WAVERLY	20214	3516	33.2	31.0	29.1	4.9	1.9	37281	41606	36	57	2679	21.4	28.6	35.5	12.5	2.0	90029
37186	WESTMORELAND	16711	3613	33.6	33.4	27.9	3.5	1.6	36927	42388	35	57	2908	25.6	34.8	30.2	8.7	0.8	80590
37187	WHITE BLUFF	20340	2361	25.7	30.4	33.8	8.2	1.9	44491	49395	60	79	1930	11.9	23.4	49.9	12.9	1.9	108551
37188	WHITE HOUSE	21774	4053	15.8	28.0	44.5	9.3	2.4	53901	60574	78	92	3433	2.0	7.9	71.0	17.7	1.5	134486
37189	WHITES CREEK	22668	1048	18.1	33.0	33.5	11.0	4.4	49344	56796	71	87	837	5.9	17.3	52.7	21.5	2.6	131722
37190	WOODBURY	18834	3249	36.5	30.4	27.5	3.8	1.8	35560	39069	30	51	2426	16.5	28.7	39.8	14.0	1.0	96609
37191	WOODLAWN	20079	1515	21.5	28.3	42.0	5.6	2.6	50130	53847	72	88	1213	16.0	19.9	54.6	7.9	1.7	101269
37201	NASHVILLE	17651	313	27.5	39.0	27.8	3.5	2.2	34045	40095	24	43	53	0.0	5.7	90.6	0.0	3.8	133750
37203	NASHVILLE	16212	4817	55.0	27.3	13.9	1.7	2.1	21683	25089	2	4	1100	11.6	35.4	42.0	8.7	2.4	93208
37204	NASHVILLE	33153	4996	24.1	29.9	28.1	10.8	7.1	46160	54156	64	83	2824	1.6	9.0	30.8	50.1	8.5	201727
37205	NASHVILLE	58912	12441	15.6	20.6	27.8	15.3	20.6	70093	82203	91	98	7830	0.5	2.6	16.5	50.2	30.2	280297
37206	NASHVILLE	17107	10822	39.8	31.3	22.5	4.2	2.3	31870	36801	17	30	5345	7.2	35.1	48.6	8.4	0.7	98496
37207	NASHVILLE	16792	13288	39.2	31.9	22.1	4.6	2.3	32037	35622	18	30	7848	12.4	37.7	44.3	5.2	0.5	89930
37208	NASHVILLE	13032	5857	56.8	25.8	13.3	2.9	1.2	20712	23369	2	3	2063	25.6	55.1	15.5	2.9	0.9	67865
37209	NASHVILLE	20312	12989	30.2	34.5	26.7	6.1	2.5	37486	43127	37	58	6475	4.1	25.5	51.2	17.5	1.7	116436
37210	NASHVILLE	15969	6609	47.4	28.3	19.8	3.0	1.5	26503	30624	6	11	2530	9.3	40.1	49.1	0.9	0.6	90423
37211	NASHVILLE	22894	29405	25.6	34.3	30.5	7.0	2.5	41300	47727	51	73	13202	2.7	13.9	65.8	17.0	0.7	125229
37212	NASHVILLE	28735	7168	35.1	26.8	23.8	8.8	5.5	37402	44341	37	58	2539	2.8	8.9	30.4	51.5	6.4	197389
37213	NASHVILLE	8727	11	0.0	72.7	27.3	0.0	0.0	42313	51158	54	75	0	0.0	0.0	0.0	0.0	0.0	0
37214	NASHVILLE	27074	11853	17.4	35.2	35.6	8.4	3.5	47954	54885	68	85	7646	0.5	18.6	65.9	14.6	0.4	118097
37215	NASHVILLE	60572	10294	13.0	19.4	27.3	15.0	25.3	77422	90158	94	99	7261	0.2	2.6	14.2	47.4	35.6	330268
37216	NASHVILLE	21497	8251	27.6	33.5	30.3	6.6	2.0	39824	45427	45	68	5722	3.0	32.5	59.8	4.3	0.4	100093
37217	NASHVILLE	21825	12882	23.9	34.3	31.6	8.2	2.1	42966	49230	56	78	5473	2.1	14.8	72.0	10.6	0.5	128057
37218	NASHVILLE	18800	4876	30.0	28.4	31.4	7.4	2.8	41973	48170	53	75	3689	5.4	33.9	48.0	11.9	0.9	99487
37219	NASHVILLE	30202	528	44.7	32.4	15.7	5.3	1.9	26964	32109	7	12	24	0.0	54.2	25.0	0.0	20.8	88000
37220	NASHVILLE	47007	2471	7.5	22.0	34.5	17.5	18.5	75236	85415	93	98	2261	0.0	1.0	29.1	51.9	18.0	227704
37221	NASHVILLE	36176	14274	11.8	25.3	35.2	17.3	10.4	63527	73154	87	96	9736	0.7	5.0	38.7	50.5	5.2	187365
37228	NASHVILLE	23493	223	67.3	22.9	8.1	0.0	1.8	13960	17749	1	2	57	31.6	36.8	31.6	0.0	0.0	61923
37240	NASHVILLE	11814	204	51.0	49.0	0.0	0.0	0.0	24171	25675	4	6	0	0.0	0.0	0.0	0.0	0.0	0
37301	ALTAMONT	12036	457	48.4	31.5	15.5	4.4	0.2	25905	27761	6	10	387	48.6	30.8	16.3	3.1	1.3	52391
37302	APISON	24115	1092	21.7	28.2	36.3	9.6	4.2	50077	57430	72	88	889	11.5	21.2	30.4	31.5	5.5	133686
37303	ATHENS	19245	10290	36.2	30.9	25.6	5.0	2.3	35572	40031	30	52	7417	16.6	29.7	37.6	13.7	2.4	94481
37305	BEERSHEBA SPRINGS	16412	449	48.8	27.8	16.0	3.8	3.6	25584	27781	5	9	360	51.7	33.9	13.1	0.8	0.6	48667
37306	BELVIDERE	19476	983	28.0	34.6	28.8	5.4	3.3	41726	46996	52	74	837	17.7	27.7	32.9	17.0	4.8	96525
37307	BENTON	18424	1638	33.9	35.7	23.4	4.3	2.7	34166	38910	25	44	1286	31.0	32.4	26.8	6.8	3.0	73670
37308	BIRCHWOOD	19720	1226	29.7	32.8	31.6	4.1	1.9	39773	44738	45	68	1045	19.3	27.5	32.7	17.1	3.4	97614
37309	CALHOUN	19145	742	28.2	32.2	32.6	4.9	2.2	40865	45763	49	71	615	21.1	31.7	32.7	12.5	2.0	86698
37310	CHARLESTON	24814	1438	25.0	28.0	34.0	9.4	3.6	47781	53770	68	85	1228	15.6	18.8	39.5	20.6	5.5	116803
37311	CLEVELAND	17456	10371	47.6	28.5	17.8	3.9	2.2	26359	29732	6	11	5483	17.8	30.8	33.7	13.7	4.0	91932
37312	CLEVELAND	25302	11394	23.8	29.2	32.6	9.7	4.7	47339	52938	67	84	8259	5.4	11.1	53.9	26.9	2.7	131824
37313	COALMONT	13706	370	49.7	31.1	16.2	2.2	0.8	25145	27706	5	8	306	38.9	34.0	23.9	3.3	0.0	63600
37317	COPPERHILL	16247	1515	47.1	30.8	17.4	3.2	1.5	26697	28958	7	12	1208	24.8	34.5	33.4	6.4	0.9	78189
37318	COWAN	18972	943	38.8	31.8	23.9	4.1	1.4	32192	36312	18	31	683	27.8	32.9	29.1	8.6	1.5	77982
37321	DAYTON	17573	7653	37.7	32.5	23.7	4.4	1.7	33192	37144	21	39	5825	25.8	31.3	32.6	9.2	1.3	81657
37322	DECATUR	18514	2127	36.9	32.1	26.0	3.2	1.9	34325	38154	25	44	1721	26.6	26.8	35.1	10.3	1.2	85667
37323	CLEVELAND	18685	10463	25.5	37.8	30.9	3.7	2.1	40572	46166	48	70	8574	12.7	32.7	43.2	10.7	0.6	93809
37324	DECHERD	18012	2290	38.0	34.2	22.9	3.3	1.7	32383	36739	19	33	1725	25.2	32.6	33.5	6.9	1.7	80719
37325	DELANO	20482	768	29.8	35.3	26.4	5.5	3.0	37500	42144	37	59	645	27.0	25.4	32.4	12.9	2.3	85156
37327	DUNLAP	19043	3738	37.0	32.6	23.6	4.5	2.3	35380	38746	29	49	2925	21.9	28.3	32.8	14.2	2.8	89715
37328	ELORA	22047	573	37.4	32.1	19.7	7.3	3.5	32594	37451	20	35	461	27.1	33.4	29.1	9.1	1.3	74091
37329	ENGLEWOOD	18062	2040	38.7	32.1	23.9	4.2	1.2	31658	35406	17	27	1628	25.7	33.4	29.4	9.9	1.6	78714
37330	ESTILL SPRINGS	22450	2922	24.1	31.2	34.4	7.6	2.7	45321	51050	62	81	2461	15.8	23.9	42.9	14.1	3.3	103481
37331	ETOWAH	18796	3265	39.9	32.4	21.7	4.8	1.3	31633	35231	17	27	2472	24.5	35.8	29.9	7.9	2.1	78068
37332	EVENSVILLE	18802	448	30.1	31.7	31.0	5.8	1.3	38662	43732	42	63	374	30.8	28.9	34.5	5.4	0.5	72174
37333	FARNER	14544	338	51.5	30.8	12.7	3.6	1.5	24260	27431	4	7	278	53.6	25.9	18.0	2.5	0.0	47674
37334	FAYETTEVILLE	22459	8448	33.4	30.1	25.7	7.9	2.9	37740	42999	38	60	6382	18.2	32.1	35.0	13.6	1.2	89692
37335	FLINTVILLE	21394	979	33.3	32.9	23.9	6.1	3.8	35438	40616	29	50	793	24.3	36.6	31.7	6.6	0.9	76864
37336	GEORGETOWN	22422	1615	28.4	29.1	31.6	7.6	3.3	42882	48753	56	77	1397	14.8	20.8	35.2	24.1	5.2	113304
37337	GRANDVIEW	19365	584	39.2	30.0	23.8	5.7	1.4	31755	35190	17	28	486	33.1	29.8	26.8	8.4	1.9	76341
37338	GRAYSVILLE	18261	337	33.5	31.8	28.2	5.3	1.2	36701	40990	34	56	300	36.3	19.7	29.0	15.0	0.0	80526
37339	GRUETLI LAAGER	13867	866	48.5	32.0	16.3	2.4	0.8	25732	28179	5	9	712	42.3	34.1	18.8	3.8	1.0	59016
37340	GUILD	26961	570	39.5	27.9	18.6	6.7	7.4	31770	35656	17	29	468	44.0	16.9	19.9	12.0	7.3	55385
37341	HARRISON	27535	4539	16.5	26.7	40.1	12.0	4.7	56087	64198	81	94	3930	5.7	15.8	53.9	20.3	4.4	122694
37342	HILLSBORO	17745	1220	26.6	34.5	31.5	6.5	0.9	41279	46978	51	72	1002	24.3	25.1	36.9	11.7	2.1	90946
37343	HIXSON	27963	14862	18.2	27.1	35.8	12.6	6.4	54414	62727	79	93	11757	3.7	14.7	59.4	19.7	2.6	123404
37345	HUNTLAND	19558	870	34.7	29.0	28.1	5.4	2.9	39019	43391	43	65	708	21.1	39.4	27.1	10.3	2.1	79733
37347	JASPER	19543	3316	29.6	35.8	25.9	7.2	1.5	38056	42342	39	61	2693	21.4	31.3	39.2	7.2	0.9	86674
37348	KELSO	20404	448	28.1	32.1	32.4	4.7	2.7	39705	46380	45	67	365	14.3	44.1	37.3	4.4	0.0	84020
37350	LOOKOUT MOUNTAIN	73505	780	10.3	15.0	20.5	18.7	35.5	109300	127054	99	100	707	0.9	1.6	9.8	37.9	49.9	399612
37352	LYNCHBURG	21148	1311	30.1	34.2	24.6	7.0	4.2	39504	44138	44	66	1070	15.1	21.3	35.7	22.2	5.7	108725
37353	MC DONALD	22514	1817	29.8	30.1	30.5	4.8	4.8	40118	45545	46	69	1465	18.0	22.7	37.3	18.6	3.5	103467
37354	MADISONVILLE	17336	5982	37.0	35.2	22.8	3.5	1.6	32640	36145	20	36	4614	25.4	26.3	36.5	9.9	1.9	88102
37355	MANCHESTER	19832	9168	31.4	30.1	30.8	5.4	2.4	39319	44255	44	65	6765	18.1	25.8	41.8	12.4	2.0	97690
37356	MONTEAGLE	17488	1031	44.7	30.9	16.5	5.3	2.5	28467	31358	9	16	817	26.6	31.7	26.6	12.0	3.2	79416
37357	MORRISON	18671	2302	31.8	31.2	28.8	6.1	2.0	38891	43218	42	64	1892	21.7	28.5	33.4	14.1	2.3	89714
37359	MULBERRY	19618	201	32.3	29.9	33.3	3.5	1.0	42395	48672	54	76	169	10.7	32.5	32.5	21.9	2.4	98214
37360	NORMANDY	20563	659	29.9	29.0	31.0	8.0	2.1	41711	46401	52	74	550	20.4	20.2	33.8	22.2	3.5	109091
37361	OCOEE	19857	321	24.3	37.1	33.0	5.6	0.0	41144	45401	50	72	248	21.4	21.0	50.0	6.9	0.8	95938
37362	OLDFORT	18529	1345	32.4	33.5	26.8	3.9	3.4	38156	42467	40	61	1096	27.7	36.2	28.0	7.9	0.1	71205
37363	OOLTEWAH	26771	8852	17.9	24.1	38.5	12.4	7.1	57832	65662	82	95	7521	12.4	10.1	44.6	27.0	6.0	139945
37365	PALMER	12900	722	51.3	31.6	14.0	2.2	1.0	24215	26245	4	6	618	50.3	31.7	14.4	2.8	0.8	49792
37366	PELHAM	15648	282	37.9	35.8	22.0	4.3	0.0	31006	35353	15	23	239	29.7	46.9	12.6	10.0	0.8	65119
37367	PIKEVILLE	17706	3326	40.7	32.1	21.8	3.3	2.1	31135	34612	15	25	2639	31.0	30.2	25.6	11.2	2.1	76330
37369	RELIANCE	21713	760	31.1	35.1	24.9	5.4	3.6	36490	41184	34	56	642	28.7	32.1	24.8	10.8	3.7	76364
37370	RICEVILLE	20828	1759	27.3	34.6	30.6	5.6	1.9	39794	44325	45	68	1475	15.8	22.9	38.9	17.6	4.8	104919
37373	SALE CREEK	21436	1164	24.7	38.3	26.6	9.0	1.5	42622	49966	55	77	998	17.9	27.4	38.3	12.1	4.3	94747
37374	SEQUATCHIE	15058	493	34.3	43.2	19.3	2.2	1.0	32895	36733	21	38	413	27.6	37.8	29.3	3.9	1.5	73929
	TENNESSEE	22498		30.2	30.2	28.1	7.5	4.1	40531	46137				15.0	25.0	39.4	17.3	3.3	104905
	UNITED STATES	25866		24.7	27.1	30.8	10.9	6.5	48124	56710				10.9	15.0	33.7	30.1	10.4	145905

#	POST OFFICE NAME	FINANCIAL SERVICES: Auto Loan	Home Loan	Invest-ments	Retire-ment Plans	THE HOME: Home Improvements: Home Repair	Lawn & Garden	Furnishings: Comput-ers & Hard-ware	Major Appli-ances	TV, Radio, Sound Equip-ment	Furni-ture	ENTERTAINMENT: Dine out/ Carry out	Sports Equip-ment	Fees & Tickets	Toys & Games	Travel	Cable TV	PERSONAL: Apparel & Services	Auto Repairs	Health Insur-ance	Pets & Supplies
37174	SPRING HILL	106	102	87	101	104	109	96	101	97	97	119	119	95	121	96	96	115	99	102	122
37175	STEWART	77	58	36	52	66	74	55	67	63	55	75	79	49	73	58	68	69	66	80	93
37178	TENNESSEE RIDGE	83	56	25	48	63	73	54	67	65	55	76	81	46	72	55	70	69	67	83	96
37179	THOMPSONS STATION	111	116	104	117	114	114	105	108	101	108	127	127	106	128	104	98	124	105	101	126
37180	UNIONVILLE	83	74	56	70	78	84	68	76	73	68	88	90	67	90	70	74	84	74	82	98
37181	VANLEER	92	62	28	53	70	81	60	75	72	61	84	89	51	80	61	78	77	74	92	106
37183	WARTRACE	82	71	52	67	76	82	66	74	71	66	86	88	64	87	68	73	81	72	81	96
37184	WATERTOWN	89	75	54	71	80	88	72	80	78	72	94	94	68	94	73	80	88	79	89	103
37185	WAVERLY	84	62	35	55	68	78	59	71	69	60	81	85	53	79	61	73	75	70	85	98
37186	WESTMORELAND	84	57	27	49	64	74	55	68	66	56	78	82	47	73	56	71	71	68	84	97
37187	WHITE BLUFF	83	73	56	70	78	84	69	76	74	69	89	90	68	91	71	75	85	74	83	97
37188	WHITE HOUSE	89	98	93	100	95	94	89	90	84	91	105	105	91	107	88	80	104	87	80	101
37189	WHITES CREEK	81	92	98	89	91	95	86	87	84	86	105	99	90	109	88	84	104	85	83	96
37190	WOODBURY	78	60	37	55	65	74	59	68	67	59	79	80	54	77	60	70	73	67	80	90
37191	WOODLAWN	79	84	80	84	81	82	80	80	76	81	95	95	79	95	78	72	93	80	72	90
37201	NASHVILLE	55	46	63	52	45	49	58	52	58	57	73	66	55	70	54	54	71	58	48	59
37203	NASHVILLE	44	37	49	38	36	41	46	42	48	45	60	51	44	57	43	47	58	46	43	48
37204	NASHVILLE	91	96	117	97	95	102	99	96	98	99	123	111	101	122	99	97	120	98	93	106
37205	NASHVILLE	156	175	237	182	171	183	175	168	170	176	214	198	184	220	178	168	212	170	158	185
37206	NASHVILLE	56	55	65	54	55	61	59	58	61	59	76	66	60	77	59	62	74	59	59	64
37207	NASHVILLE	63	59	67	57	58	66	62	62	66	64	82	69	63	81	62	67	80	63	64	70
37208	NASHVILLE	46	37	41	34	36	44	43	43	48	43	58	47	41	53	41	50	56	45	49	50
37209	NASHVILLE	68	66	77	68	65	71	71	69	72	71	90	81	71	89	70	70	88	71	67	76
37210	NASHVILLE	52	48	55	47	48	54	53	52	56	53	69	60	52	68	52	56	67	54	54	58
37211	NASHVILLE	72	71	81	75	69	73	75	72	73	75	93	86	75	91	73	70	90	75	67	80
37212	NASHVILLE	80	73	114	80	71	80	90	80	91	88	115	98	89	115	86	89	113	87	77	89
37213	NASHVILLE	59	55	66	52	52	61	59	57	64	61	80	64	61	79	58	66	78	59	60	66
37214	NASHVILLE	82	81	93	85	79	84	86	82	84	86	106	98	85	104	83	81	103	85	77	91
37215	NASHVILLE	170	194	260	199	191	205	191	185	184	192	233	215	202	238	195	182	231	186	174	202
37216	NASHVILLE	66	70	79	69	70	76	72	70	72	70	90	80	74	93	72	73	88	71	71	77
37217	NASHVILLE	71	69	78	73	67	70	74	71	72	74	91	85	72	88	71	68	89	74	64	78
37218	NASHVILLE	71	69	75	66	68	78	70	70	73	71	91	76	72	88	71	76	89	70	75	80
37219	NASHVILLE	35	28	36	31	27	30	38	34	38	36	48	43	35	44	34	35	46	38	31	37
37220	NASHVILLE	147	181	217	179	179	189	166	165	157	167	198	188	179	203	173	157	197	161	157	180
37221	NASHVILLE	113	122	142	128	119	123	121	117	116	122	147	138	124	147	120	112	145	118	107	129
37228	NASHVILLE	31	28	41	29	28	33	35	32	37	33	46	37	34	45	34	37	44	35	35	35
37240	NASHVILLE	31	19	24	21	19	23	37	27	36	31	44	38	30	40	29	31	42	33	25	31
37301	ALTAMONT	63	42	19	36	48	55	41	51	49	41	58	61	35	54	41	53	52	50	63	72
37302	APISON	97	85	65	82	89	98	82	89	87	81	105	105	79	106	83	89	100	87	97	111
37303	ATHENS	73	60	47	56	64	72	61	67	67	60	80	78	57	79	61	69	76	66	75	84
37305	BEERSHEBA SPRINGS	77	51	23	44	58	67	50	62	60	51	70	74	42	66	50	65	64	61	76	88
37306	BELVIDERE	90	71	46	65	77	85	67	78	75	67	90	93	62	89	69	78	84	76	89	105
37307	BENTON	85	58	27	50	65	75	55	69	67	56	78	83	47	74	56	72	71	68	85	98
37308	BIRCHWOOD	91	68	40	62	75	84	65	77	74	65	88	92	59	86	66	78	82	76	90	105
37309	CALHOUN	94	64	29	55	72	83	61	77	74	62	87	91	52	82	62	79	79	76	94	108
37310	CHARLESTON	100	89	68	85	94	101	83	92	88	83	107	109	81	109	85	90	101	89	99	118
37311	CLEVELAND	59	51	52	51	52	58	56	56	59	55	72	66	54	70	55	59	69	58	59	66
37312	CLEVELAND	95	91	83	90	93	99	89	92	90	88	111	108	88	112	89	90	106	91	94	109
37313	COALMONT	64	43	20	37	49	56	42	52	50	42	59	62	35	56	42	54	54	52	64	74
37317	COPPERHILL	68	47	23	41	52	61	46	56	55	46	64	66	40	61	47	59	59	56	69	78
37318	COWAN	72	59	45	54	64	72	58	65	65	57	78	75	55	79	60	69	73	64	76	83
37321	DAYTON	77	57	34	52	62	71	56	66	64	56	76	77	50	73	57	67	70	65	77	88
37322	DECATUR	87	58	26	50	66	76	56	70	68	57	80	84	48	75	57	73	72	70	87	100
37323	CLEVELAND	78	67	50	64	72	78	64	71	69	64	83	84	62	84	65	71	79	69	78	91
37324	DECHERD	76	55	31	50	61	70	54	64	63	55	74	76	48	71	55	66	68	64	76	87
37325	DELANO	97	65	29	56	74	85	63	78	76	64	89	94	53	84	64	82	81	78	97	111
37327	DUNLAP	86	60	31	54	67	77	59	71	69	60	82	85	52	78	60	74	75	71	86	98
37328	ELORA	98	66	30	57	74	86	63	79	76	65	90	95	54	85	64	82	82	78	98	113
37329	ENGLEWOOD	81	57	29	50	64	72	54	67	64	55	76	80	47	73	55	69	69	66	80	93
37330	ESTILL SPRINGS	95	81	59	76	87	94	76	85	82	76	99	101	73	100	78	84	93	83	94	111
37331	ETOWAH	76	56	33	51	62	71	55	65	64	55	76	76	50	73	56	67	70	64	77	87
37332	EVENSVILLE	91	61	27	52	69	79	59	73	71	60	83	88	50	78	60	76	75	73	90	104
37333	FARNER	69	46	21	40	52	60	44	55	54	45	63	66	38	59	45	58	57	55	68	79
37334	FAYETTEVILLE	86	73	56	68	77	86	71	79	77	71	93	91	68	92	72	80	88	77	88	99
37335	FLINTVILLE	104	70	32	61	79	91	68	84	82	69	96	101	58	91	69	88	87	84	104	120
37336	GEORGETOWN	100	80	53	74	87	95	75	87	84	76	100	104	71	100	77	87	94	85	99	116
37337	GRANDVIEW	84	56	25	48	63	73	54	68	65	55	77	81	46	72	55	70	70	67	83	96
37338	GRAYSVILLE	89	60	27	51	68	78	58	72	69	59	82	86	49	77	59	75	74	71	89	102
37339	GRUETLI LAAGER	66	44	20	38	50	58	43	53	52	44	61	64	36	57	43	56	55	53	66	76
37340	GUILD	120	82	39	73	94	107	80	99	94	80	111	119	68	106	81	101	101	98	121	140
37341	HARRISON	100	114	117	113	112	113	105	106	100	105	126	124	109	131	106	97	124	103	97	118
37342	HILLSBORO	85	63	37	57	70	78	60	72	69	61	82	86	54	80	62	73	76	71	84	98
37343	HIXSON	95	107	113	106	106	110	100	101	97	100	121	117	104	125	102	95	119	99	96	113
37345	HUNTLAND	93	62	28	54	71	81	60	75	73	61	85	90	51	81	61	78	78	75	93	107
37347	JASPER	84	61	36	56	68	77	60	71	69	60	82	84	54	79	61	73	75	70	83	95
37348	KELSO	100	68	33	60	77	88	66	81	78	67	92	97	57	88	67	84	84	80	99	114
37350	LOOKOUT MOUNTAIN	223	300	411	294	292	315	261	259	243	267	308	291	297	324	278	246	313	249	240	281
37352	LYNCHBURG	84	71	52	68	76	84	69	76	75	68	90	89	66	90	70	77	84	75	85	97
37353	MC DONALD	96	75	48	68	81	90	71	83	80	72	96	98	66	94	73	84	89	81	95	111
37354	MADISONVILLE	78	54	28	48	60	69	53	64	62	53	74	76	46	70	53	67	67	64	78	89
37355	MANCHESTER	80	68	52	64	72	79	66	73	72	66	87	85	63	86	67	74	82	72	81	92
37356	MONTEAGLE	76	53	28	47	60	69	51	63	61	52	71	75	44	68	53	65	65	63	77	89
37357	MORRISON	83	65	41	59	70	78	61	71	68	62	82	85	56	80	62	72	76	70	81	96
37359	MULBERRY	78	69	53	66	73	78	64	71	68	64	82	84	63	84	66	69	78	69	77	91
37360	NORMANDY	84	74	57	71	79	85	69	77	74	69	90	91	68	91	71	76	85	75	83	98
37361	OCOEE	75	67	51	63	70	75	61	68	65	61	79	81	60	81	63	67	75	66	74	88
37362	OLDFORT	87	60	30	52	67	77	58	71	68	59	81	85	50	77	59	73	74	70	86	100
37363	OOLTEWAH	108	110	103	110	111	115	103	107	102	104	127	126	104	128	104	101	123	105	104	125
37365	PALMER	60	40	18	35	46	53	39	49	47	40	55	58	33	52	40	51	50	48	60	69
37366	PELHAM	71	48	22	41	54	62	46	58	56	47	65	69	39	62	47	60	59	57	71	82
37367	PIKEVILLE	84	57	28	50	65	75	57	69	68	57	79	82	49	75	57	73	72	69	85	96
37369	RELIANCE	95	64	29	55	72	83	61	77	74	62	87	92	52	82	62	80	79	76	95	109
37370	RICEVILLE	90	73	50	68	79	87	69	79	76	69	91	94	65	91	71	79	86	77	89	105
37373	SALE CREEK	87	72	49	67	77	84	67	77	74	67	89	91	64	89	69	76	83	75	86	102
37374	SEQUATCHIE	74	49	22	43	56	64	48	60	58	49	68	71	41	64	48	62	61	59	73	85
	TENNESSEE	85	76	68	73	78	85	76	80	79	76	97	94	73	96	75	81	93	80	85	97
	UNITED STATES	100	100	100	100	100	100	100	100	100	100	100	100	100	100	100	100	100	100	100	100

#	POST OFFICE NAME	COUNTY FIPS CODE	POPULATION 2000	2004	2009	% Rate	State Centile	HOUSEHOLDS 2000	2004	2009	% Annual Rate 2000-2004	2004 Average HH Size	FAMILIES 2000	2004	% Annual Rate 2000-2004
37375	SEWANEE	051	3681	3685	3769	0.0	22	1046	1072	1132	0.6	2.23	681	681	0.0
37376	SHERWOOD	051	502	526	550	1.1	62	211	227	242	1.7	2.32	154	163	1.4
37377	SIGNAL MOUNTAIN	065	15840	16122	16428	0.4	38	6331	6583	6836	0.9	2.43	4485	4572	0.5
37379	SODDY DAISY	065	23415	24587	25437	1.2	64	8910	9559	10087	1.7	2.56	6980	7355	1.2
37380	SOUTH PITTSBURG	115	6130	6318	6670	0.7	48	2429	2554	2756	1.2	2.41	1695	1746	0.7
37381	SPRING CITY	143	8273	8551	8877	0.8	51	3462	3652	3865	1.3	2.30	2463	2547	0.8
37383	SEWANEE	051	10	10	10	0.0	20	5	5	5	0.0	2.00	3	1	-22.8
37385	TELLICO PLAINS	123	7947	8017	8158	0.2	30	3114	3223	3345	0.8	2.49	2338	2377	0.4
37387	TRACY CITY	061	4417	4389	4397	-0.2	13	1744	1782	1825	0.5	2.45	1241	1242	0.0
37388	TULLAHOMA	031	24699	25361	26336	0.6	45	9869	10295	10850	1.0	2.43	7064	7242	0.6
37391	TURTLETOWN	139	757	724	720	-1.0	2	333	329	335	-0.3	2.20	239	232	-0.7
37396	WHITESIDE	115	38	39	41	0.6	45	21	22	24	1.1	1.77	15	16	1.5
37397	WHITWELL	115	10232	10879	11562	1.5	72	4053	4419	4806	2.1	2.46	3036	3252	1.6
37398	WINCHESTER	051	12699	13216	13863	0.9	57	5065	5384	5760	1.5	2.40	3680	3836	1.0
37402	CHATTANOOGA	065	4185	4328	4504	0.8	52	2377	2503	2658	1.2	1.51	607	575	-1.3
37403	CHATTANOOGA	065	3963	4240	4421	1.6	76	1268	1485	1641	3.8	1.63	414	444	1.7
37404	CHATTANOOGA	065	14762	14342	14357	-0.7	5	5434	5322	5403	-0.5	2.52	3370	3204	-1.2
37405	CHATTANOOGA	115	13317	13241	13360	-0.1	14	6347	6434	6618	0.3	2.00	3151	3066	-0.6
37406	CHATTANOOGA	065	14064	14124	14373	0.1	25	5412	5548	5756	0.6	2.52	3738	3745	0.0
37407	CHATTANOOGA	065	7812	7572	7574	-0.7	4	3185	3120	3166	-0.5	2.43	1993	1895	-1.2
37408	CHATTANOOGA	065	1935	1897	1903	-0.5	6	708	693	700	-0.5	2.61	388	365	-1.4
37409	CHATTANOOGA	065	3158	2974	2954	-1.4	1	1252	1195	1206	-1.1	2.48	776	719	-1.8
37410	CHATTANOOGA	065	4473	4167	4132	-1.7	1	1667	1582	1597	-1.2	2.59	1122	1037	-1.8
37411	CHATTANOOGA	065	17530	17326	17481	-0.3	9	7465	7531	7749	0.2	2.29	4782	4690	-0.5
37412	CHATTANOOGA	065	20556	20363	20570	-0.2	11	9236	9355	9642	0.3	2.15	5713	5615	-0.4
37415	CHATTANOOGA	065	22499	22763	23224	0.3	32	10426	10773	11208	0.8	2.10	6169	6162	0.0
37416	CHATTANOOGA	065	14577	14321	14342	-0.4	7	5987	6002	6128	0.1	2.38	4234	4151	-0.5
37419	CHATTANOOGA	065	5412	5382	5448	-0.1	14	2285	2335	2416	0.5	2.30	1590	1584	-0.1
37421	CHATTANOOGA	065	40746	43178	45004	1.4	70	16650	18140	19342	2.0	2.29	11041	11771	1.5
37601	JOHNSON CITY	179	33567	34248	35037	0.5	40	14511	15123	15746	1.0	2.20	9141	9269	0.3
37604	JOHNSON CITY	179	33175	32928	33205	-0.2	12	13774	13943	14311	0.3	2.15	7960	7805	-0.5
37615	JOHNSON CITY	179	15122	15734	16172	0.9	57	6145	6533	6831	1.5	2.38	4444	4613	0.9
37616	AFTON	059	4874	5162	5413	1.4	69	1825	1980	2120	1.9	2.49	1323	1403	1.4
37617	BLOUNTVILLE	163	13047	13549	13853	0.9	56	5027	5354	5596	1.5	2.45	3805	3975	1.0
37618	BLUFF CITY	163	12150	12377	12480	0.4	39	4839	5027	5166	0.9	2.46	3669	3745	0.5
37620	BRISTOL	163	38555	38461	38772	-0.1	16	16187	16479	16943	0.4	2.26	10969	10926	-0.1
37640	BUTLER	019	3740	3964	4138	1.4	70	1570	1713	1833	2.1	2.26	1139	1218	1.6
37641	CHUCKEY	059	7519	8179	8656	2.0	84	2998	3340	3605	2.6	2.42	2219	2418	2.0
37642	CHURCH HILL	073	14585	14222	14221	-0.6	5	5917	5902	6008	-0.1	2.39	4398	4303	-0.5
37643	ELIZABETHTON	019	33405	33202	33306	-0.1	14	13963	14172	14449	0.4	2.29	9736	9669	-0.2
37645	MOUNT CARMEL	073	5964	5957	5978	0.0	18	2436	2487	2538	0.5	2.37	1811	1814	0.0
37650	ERWIN	171	12400	12419	12520	0.0	23	5316	5447	5606	0.6	2.23	3633	3640	0.1
37656	FALL BRANCH	179	3463	3557	3646	0.6	46	1433	1499	1563	1.1	2.37	1104	1134	0.6
37657	FLAG POND	171	976	973	976	-0.1	16	424	435	446	0.6	2.23	301	303	0.2
37658	HAMPTON	019	4620	5077	5368	2.2	89	1953	2199	2366	2.8	2.31	1395	1538	2.3
37659	JONESBOROUGH	179	23236	24352	25122	1.1	62	9120	9780	10275	1.7	2.45	6950	7297	1.2
37660	KINGSPORT	163	40508	40819	41199	0.2	29	17340	17858	18385	0.7	2.24	11706	11780	0.2
37663	KINGSPORT	163	14872	14986	15084	0.2	29	5882	6054	6217	0.7	2.45	4533	4583	0.3
37664	KINGSPORT	163	26384	26442	26520	0.1	24	11099	11341	11588	0.5	2.30	7794	7800	0.0
37665	KINGSPORT	163	4841	4629	4582	-1.1	2	2118	2068	2087	-0.6	2.23	1444	1376	-1.1
37680	LAUREL BLOOMERY	091	852	874	906	0.6	44	352	369	391	1.1	2.37	255	262	0.6
37681	LIMESTONE	179	5639	6098	6396	1.9	82	2194	2429	2595	2.4	2.47	1634	1768	1.9
37683	MOUNTAIN CITY	091	12358	12923	13630	1.1	61	4670	5023	5453	1.7	2.29	3205	3376	1.2
37686	PINEY FLATS	163	6996	7343	7512	1.2	63	2788	2972	3091	1.5	2.47	2108	2205	1.1
37687	ROAN MOUNTAIN	019	4722	5057	5244	1.6	77	1827	2014	2132	2.3	2.37	1332	1438	1.8
37688	SHADY VALLEY	091	1123	1142	1177	0.4	37	477	500	529	1.1	2.28	349	359	0.7
37690	TELFORD	179	3429	3647	3791	1.5	72	1320	1433	1515	2.0	2.55	1027	1094	1.5
37691	TRADE	091	885	889	911	0.1	26	366	377	396	0.7	2.36	255	257	0.2
37692	UNICOI	171	4373	4520	4612	0.8	51	1802	1903	1983	1.3	2.37	1313	1360	0.8
37694	WATAUGA	019	1752	2016	2168	3.4	97	697	818	893	3.8	2.46	524	605	3.4
37701	ALCOA	009	6239	6118	6199	-0.5	6	2780	2781	2860	0.0	2.20	1768	1718	-0.7
37705	ANDERSONVILLE	001	5454	5565	5751	0.5	40	2130	2200	2306	0.8	2.51	1587	1610	0.3
37708	BEAN STATION	057	6237	6493	6748	1.0	58	2503	2669	2832	1.5	2.43	1876	1966	1.1
37709	BLAINE	057	3060	3166	3280	0.8	52	1205	1278	1353	1.4	2.48	909	947	1.0
37710	BRICEVILLE	001	1580	1497	1473	-1.3	2	602	584	586	-0.7	2.56	458	436	-1.2
37711	BULLS GAP	073	4611	4815	4970	1.0	58	1817	1939	2037	1.5	2.48	1347	1411	1.1
37713	BYBEE	029	1584	1662	1714	1.1	63	645	692	727	1.7	2.40	483	509	1.2
37714	CARYVILLE	013	4421	4420	4428	0.0	19	1775	1821	1864	0.6	2.43	1287	1293	0.1
37715	CLAIRFIELD	025	1102	1060	1090	-0.9	3	416	413	436	-0.2	2.57	328	321	-0.5
37716	CLINTON	001	24469	25511	26261	1.0	59	10086	10744	11279	1.5	2.35	7165	7470	1.0
37721	CORRYTON	093	9949	10647	11380	1.6	77	3829	4151	4487	1.9	2.56	3026	3224	1.5
37722	COSBY	029	4787	5100	5316	1.5	74	1937	2115	2248	2.1	2.41	1408	1510	1.7
37723	CRAB ORCHARD	035	813	929	1024	3.2	96	326	383	432	3.9	2.43	248	286	3.4
37724	CUMBERLAND GAP	025	3455	3527	3702	0.5	41	1253	1314	1418	1.1	2.47	954	983	0.7
37725	DANDRIDGE	089	12595	13819	15059	2.2	89	4986	5562	6154	2.6	2.42	3760	4122	2.2
37726	DEER LODGE	129	1614	1761	1871	2.1	86	610	680	739	2.6	2.53	452	495	2.2
37727	DEL RIO	029	1989	1994	2004	0.1	24	809	834	857	0.7	2.39	577	582	0.2
37729	DUFF	013	1727	1804	1860	1.0	60	665	718	759	1.8	2.51	495	524	1.4
37731	EIDSON	073	999	946	940	-1.3	2	424	413	419	-0.6	2.29	288	272	-1.3
37737	FRIENDSVILLE	009	5687	6209	6597	2.1	86	2181	2422	2610	2.5	2.56	1723	1880	2.1
37738	GATLINBURG	155	4729	5171	5612	2.1	86	2120	2359	2602	2.6	2.17	1401	1522	2.0
37742	GREENBACK	105	4496	4787	5034	1.5	73	1726	1865	1988	1.8	2.57	1368	1455	1.5
37743	GREENEVILLE	059	23737	24608	25533	0.9	54	9747	10329	10938	1.4	2.32	6812	7083	0.9
37745	GREENEVILLE	059	16372	16562	17007	0.3	32	7078	7329	7685	0.8	2.18	4715	4769	0.3
37748	HARRIMAN	145	19161	18976	19113	-0.2	10	7786	7874	8089	0.3	2.38	5496	5443	-0.2
37752	HARROGATE	025	4974	5182	5480	1.0	58	1939	2073	2246	1.6	2.45	1449	1521	1.2
37753	HARTFORD	029	798	787	788	-0.3	8	328	332	340	0.3	2.37	231	229	-0.2
37754	HEISKELL	001	4745	4911	5069	0.8	52	1765	1859	1948	1.2	2.61	1401	1452	0.8
37755	HELENWOOD	151	3603	3714	3823	0.7	48	1385	1469	1549	1.4	2.48	1028	1069	0.9
37756	HUNTSVILLE	151	2643	2635	2666	-0.1	16	986	1018	1060	0.8	2.51	742	753	0.4
37757	JACKSBORO	013	8849	9079	9202	0.6	45	3455	3639	3771	1.2	2.45	2590	2678	0.8
37760	JEFFERSON CITY	089	12337	12798	13579	0.9	54	4655	4911	5307	1.3	2.36	3160	3262	0.8
37762	JELLICO	013	3673	3621	3666	0.0	23	1476	1514	1548	0.6	2.32	992	992	0.0
37763	KINGSTON	145	13921	14247	14507	0.6	43	5757	6004	6227	1.0	2.34	4177	4272	0.5
37764	KODAK	155	8205	9202	10107	2.7	93	3106	3523	3915	3.0	2.61	2439	2724	2.6
	TENNESSEE					1.0					1.3	2.45			0.9
	UNITED STATES					1.2					1.3	2.58			1.1

ZIP CODE #	POST OFFICE NAME	RACE (%) White 2000	White 2004	Black 2000	Black 2004	Asian/Pacific 2000	Asian/Pacific 2004	% Hispanic Origin 2000	% Hispanic Origin 2004	2004 AGE DISTRIBUTION (%) 0-4	5-9	10-14	15-19	20-24	25-44	45-64	65-84	85+	18+	MEDIAN AGE 2004	% 2004 Males	% 2004 Females
37375	SEWANEE	94.5	93.9	3.7	4.0	0.7	0.8	1.4	1.7	3.5	3.5	3.5	16.9	24.3	16.5	20.1	10.1	1.6	87.2	24.6	47.7	52.4
37376	SHERWOOD	98.0	97.9	0.0	0.0	0.0	0.0	1.0	1.1	5.5	5.5	5.1	4.6	6.3	23.6	31.9	14.8	2.7	81.0	44.6	48.5	51.5
37377	SIGNAL MOUNTAIN	97.5	97.0	0.9	1.0	0.5	0.7	0.9	1.1	5.3	6.1	7.3	6.5	5.1	24.4	28.9	13.3	3.0	77.2	41.9	48.6	51.4
37379	SODDY DAISY	97.4	97.1	1.3	1.5	0.3	0.3	0.7	0.8	6.4	6.5	6.5	5.7	5.6	29.1	27.8	11.3	1.1	77.1	38.9	48.9	51.1
37380	SOUTH PITTSBURG	88.5	88.0	10.0	10.4	0.2	0.2	0.6	0.7	5.9	6.3	6.8	6.5	5.4	26.4	26.6	13.9	2.2	77.1	40.2	48.2	51.8
37381	SPRING CITY	96.7	96.4	1.8	1.9	0.2	0.2	1.0	1.2	5.2	5.5	6.0	5.3	5.1	24.9	30.1	15.8	2.2	80.1	43.6	49.1	50.9
37383	SEWANEE	90.0	90.0	10.0	10.0	0.0	0.0	0.0	0.0	0.0	0.0	0.0	40.0	60.0	0.0	0.0	0.0	0.0	100.0	20.8	50.0	50.0
37385	TELLICO PLAINS	98.1	98.0	0.2	0.2	0.2	0.2	0.9	1.0	6.0	6.3	6.9	6.3	5.8	27.5	27.9	11.9	1.3	76.9	38.7	50.7	49.3
37387	TRACY CITY	98.1	97.9	0.1	0.1	0.2	0.3	0.6	0.7	6.7	6.7	6.9	6.2	6.1	28.0	25.7	12.4	1.4	75.9	37.5	49.4	50.6
37388	TULLAHOMA	91.6	90.9	5.3	5.6	0.9	1.1	1.5	1.8	6.7	6.7	7.2	6.4	6.2	26.5	25.1	13.4	1.7	75.4	38.6	48.4	51.6
37391	TURTLETOWN	98.3	98.2	0.0	0.0	0.0	0.0	0.1	0.1	5.5	5.7	5.0	3.9	4.0	25.0	31.6	17.5	1.8	81.8	45.7	49.9	50.1
37396	WHITESIDE	97.4	100.0	0.0	0.0	0.0	0.0	0.0	0.0	5.1	5.1	5.1	5.1	5.1	23.1	35.9	15.4	0.0	84.6	45.8	51.3	48.7
37397	WHITWELL	98.0	97.8	1.1	1.1	0.1	0.1	0.7	1.0	6.3	6.4	6.7	5.9	6.1	28.4	27.8	11.3	1.0	77.0	38.3	49.6	50.5
37398	WINCHESTER	88.6	87.8	8.6	8.9	0.5	0.5	1.9	2.3	6.1	6.1	6.1	6.1	5.7	25.4	26.9	15.1	2.5	78.0	41.3	48.1	51.9
37402	CHATTANOOGA	37.0	36.3	59.8	60.0	1.0	1.2	2.6	3.0	5.9	4.4	2.9	4.4	9.6	28.4	21.8	16.9	5.8	85.4	40.7	48.2	51.8
37403	CHATTANOOGA	43.8	39.8	51.8	55.4	1.8	2.1	1.7	1.9	2.6	2.3	2.8	18.7	24.3	21.1	17.1	8.8	2.4	90.5	24.9	48.0	52.0
37404	CHATTANOOGA	30.6	28.4	63.0	64.7	1.3	1.4	6.0	6.6	6.4	6.6	7.5	8.6	8.4	26.2	22.4	11.1	2.9	75.1	34.4	47.9	52.1
37405	CHATTANOOGA	84.9	82.8	11.3	12.8	1.5	1.9	1.5	1.8	4.9	4.7	4.7	5.4	9.6	32.2	23.1	12.8	2.8	82.8	36.9	48.1	51.9
37406	CHATTANOOGA	18.0	16.2	80.3	82.0	0.2	0.2	0.9	1.0	7.6	8.1	8.6	7.3	6.2	24.7	24.1	11.8	1.6	71.2	35.0	44.4	55.6
37407	CHATTANOOGA	65.4	62.0	29.9	32.7	0.7	0.9	2.6	3.1	7.4	7.0	7.1	6.7	6.5	27.0	24.9	11.6	1.7	74.4	36.5	47.6	52.4
37408	CHATTANOOGA	10.3	9.3	83.4	84.0	1.1	1.1	6.3	6.8	9.6	12.3	10.8	7.2	6.8	23.6	18.9	9.5	1.3	62.7	27.2	52.0	48.0
37409	CHATTANOOGA	53.1	49.7	41.9	44.9	0.6	0.6	4.1	4.8	6.3	6.1	6.6	6.7	7.2	28.7	26.0	10.6	1.9	77.1	36.7	50.2	49.8
37410	CHATTANOOGA	6.1	5.4	91.5	92.1	0.5	0.5	1.9	1.9	9.7	10.4	10.0	7.6	7.2	23.3	19.5	10.7	1.7	65.0	29.1	43.8	56.2
37411	CHATTANOOGA	42.2	39.8	54.9	57.1	0.9	1.0	1.3	1.5	5.9	5.9	6.7	6.9	6.5	28.6	25.8	11.7	2.0	77.2	38.2	46.6	53.4
37412	CHATTANOOGA	93.4	92.1	3.2	3.8	1.7	2.1	1.1	1.4	5.2	5.1	5.5	5.3	5.9	28.8	25.2	16.5	2.6	81.0	40.9	47.0	53.0
37415	CHATTANOOGA	89.5	87.8	6.4	7.5	1.2	1.5	2.2	2.6	5.9	5.6	5.5	5.3	6.4	29.8	24.6	14.9	2.1	80.0	39.2	47.9	52.1
37416	CHATTANOOGA	59.8	56.5	37.3	40.2	1.2	1.4	1.2	1.3	6.0	6.1	6.6	6.4	6.2	28.6	26.5	12.4	1.3	77.5	38.8	46.9	53.1
37419	CHATTANOOGA	98.0	97.7	0.3	0.3	0.7	0.8	0.5	0.6	5.0	5.3	5.8	5.1	4.9	27.1	29.3	15.8	1.7	80.6	43.0	48.9	51.1
37421	CHATTANOOGA	81.8	79.4	13.1	14.6	2.8	3.4	1.7	2.1	5.5	5.6	6.1	5.7	6.4	29.1	26.4	12.9	2.3	79.3	39.5	48.4	51.6
37601	JOHNSON CITY	92.6	92.0	4.6	4.9	0.6	0.7	1.5	1.8	5.9	5.7	5.8	6.3	7.2	28.7	24.9	13.3	2.2	79.2	38.5	47.7	52.3
37604	JOHNSON CITY	90.1	89.1	6.3	6.6	1.4	1.8	1.9	2.3	4.9	4.7	5.2	7.7	10.4	27.4	23.6	13.7	2.4	82.3	36.9	48.8	51.2
37615	JOHNSON CITY	97.4	96.9	0.9	0.9	0.7	0.9	0.9	1.1	6.5	6.3	6.3	5.5	5.7	32.6	26.1	10.0	1.1	77.6	37.5	49.2	50.8
37616	AFTON	97.4	96.9	1.2	1.3	0.3	0.4	1.3	1.7	5.7	5.8	5.9	6.0	6.5	29.5	27.2	12.4	1.1	79.3	39.1	50.3	49.7
37617	BLOUNTVILLE	98.5	98.3	0.5	0.5	0.3	0.3	0.7	0.9	5.7	6.0	6.5	5.4	5.1	29.8	27.9	12.2	1.4	78.5	39.9	50.5	49.5
37618	BLUFF CITY	98.5	98.3	0.5	0.6	0.3	0.4	0.4	0.5	5.6	5.9	6.4	5.7	5.5	29.2	28.5	12.2	1.0	78.5	40.0	50.4	49.6
37620	BRISTOL	96.1	95.7	2.4	2.6	0.5	0.6	0.6	0.7	5.4	5.6	5.9	6.2	6.1	27.1	26.9	15.0	1.8	79.5	40.8	48.8	51.2
37640	BUTLER	98.3	98.1	0.7	0.7	0.1	0.1	0.7	0.8	5.3	5.4	5.6	5.5	5.3	27.9	29.0	14.5	1.5	80.3	41.5	51.7	48.3
37641	CHUCKEY	98.1	97.8	0.5	0.6	0.2	0.2	1.3	1.6	5.6	5.9	6.5	5.8	5.6	29.5	27.4	12.3	1.4	78.5	39.5	49.8	50.3
37642	CHURCH HILL	97.9	97.7	1.2	1.3	0.2	0.2	0.6	0.8	5.9	6.2	6.6	5.7	5.4	29.8	27.2	11.9	1.3	77.8	39.0	49.3	50.7
37643	ELIZABETHTON	97.3	96.9	1.2	1.2	0.3	0.4	0.9	1.1	5.6	5.7	5.9	5.7	5.7	27.9	26.5	14.9	2.2	79.4	40.8	48.1	51.9
37645	MOUNT CARMEL	96.3	95.9	2.2	2.4	0.5	0.7	0.9	1.0	6.9	6.9	6.7	5.3	5.1	28.7	27.3	11.1	2.0	76.1	38.5	47.3	52.7
37650	ERWIN	97.9	97.6	0.1	0.1	0.1	0.1	2.0	2.4	5.6	5.5	5.2	5.3	5.2	25.7	27.3	17.5	2.8	80.6	43.3	48.3	51.7
37656	FALL BRANCH	99.1	98.9	0.2	0.2	0.1	0.1	0.5	0.7	5.7	6.2	6.4	5.3	4.3	28.5	29.6	13.0	1.2	78.5	41.5	49.9	50.1
37657	FLAG POND	99.1	99.0	0.0	0.0	0.0	0.0	0.7	0.8	4.6	4.8	5.2	5.8	5.3	26.5	29.2	16.3	2.2	81.8	43.6	49.6	50.4
37658	HAMPTON	98.9	98.8	0.0	0.0	0.1	0.1	0.6	0.8	5.4	5.6	5.7	5.3	5.1	30.2	28.4	12.8	1.4	80.1	40.1	50.1	49.9
37659	JONESBOROUGH	97.2	96.9	1.5	1.6	0.3	0.4	0.8	1.0	6.3	6.6	6.5	5.3	5.2	30.2	27.9	10.9	1.3	77.3	39.1	49.9	50.1
37660	KINGSPORT	94.4	94.0	3.6	3.7	0.6	0.8	0.9	1.1	5.6	5.6	6.1	5.8	5.1	25.9	27.3	16.1	2.5	79.1	42.1	47.2	52.9
37663	KINGSPORT	97.9	97.5	0.7	0.8	0.6	0.7	0.7	0.8	5.5	6.1	6.7	5.4	4.6	27.3	29.6	13.4	1.4	78.1	41.7	48.8	51.2
37664	KINGSPORT	96.8	96.5	1.5	1.6	0.5	0.6	0.8	1.0	5.6	5.9	6.1	5.7	4.9	25.4	28.3	15.7	2.5	78.9	42.7	47.0	53.0
37665	KINGSPORT	97.9	97.6	0.8	0.9	0.1	0.1	0.7	0.9	5.6	5.6	6.2	5.7	5.2	28.0	26.0	15.7	2.0	79.1	41.0	48.0	52.0
37680	LAUREL BLOOMERY	97.5	97.1	1.2	1.3	0.2	0.3	0.7	0.9	6.4	6.4	6.2	6.3	5.3	27.9	28.5	12.0	1.0	77.2	39.8	49.0	51.0
37681	LIMESTONE	98.0	97.8	0.8	0.8	0.1	0.2	1.4	1.7	5.8	5.9	6.4	5.8	5.6	29.1	27.0	12.6	1.9	78.3	39.7	49.7	50.3
37683	MOUNTAIN CITY	95.7	95.4	3.1	3.3	0.2	0.2	0.8	1.0	4.8	4.9	5.4	5.1	5.4	31.2	27.7	13.6	1.9	81.7	40.9	54.8	45.2
37686	PINEY FLATS	98.9	98.8	0.2	0.2	0.1	0.2	0.4	0.6	6.1	6.5	6.4	5.2	5.1	30.2	28.6	11.1	0.9	77.8	39.4	50.2	49.8
37687	ROAN MOUNTAIN	97.6	97.3	1.4	1.6	0.0	0.0	0.8	1.1	5.7	5.8	5.7	5.7	5.3	29.8	26.7	13.1	2.2	79.3	39.9	52.1	48.0
37688	SHADY VALLEY	98.8	98.7	0.2	0.2	0.1	0.1	0.9	1.1	4.8	5.0	5.2	5.3	4.0	23.2	32.5	17.5	2.5	81.7	46.7	49.3	50.7
37690	TELFORD	98.4	98.2	0.5	0.6	0.1	0.1	1.2	1.4	6.3	6.4	6.6	6.0	6.1	30.5	26.8	10.2	1.0	76.9	38.0	51.1	48.9
37691	TRADE	98.9	98.8	0.0	0.0	0.2	0.3	2.3	2.8	5.7	6.0	6.5	6.0	6.1	26.7	28.7	12.4	2.0	78.3	40.6	51.3	48.7
37692	UNICOI	98.0	97.7	0.1	0.0	0.2	0.2	1.9	2.3	5.7	6.0	6.1	5.2	5.7	28.8	29.2	12.0	1.2	78.9	40.2	51.0	49.0
37694	WATAUGA	98.5	98.4	0.3	0.4	0.2	0.3	1.0	1.2	5.5	5.8	6.0	5.6	5.2	30.1	28.8	12.2	0.9	79.3	40.2	50.6	49.4
37701	ALCOA	78.5	77.6	18.9	19.5	0.3	0.4	1.8	2.1	5.7	6.1	6.5	5.7	5.2	27.3	25.6	15.3	2.7	78.1	40.7	47.1	52.9
37705	ANDERSONVILLE	98.6	98.5	0.1	0.1	0.2	0.2	0.8	1.0	5.7	6.0	6.6	6.2	5.4	26.7	28.7	13.2	1.6	77.8	41.0	48.4	51.6
37708	BEAN STATION	98.7	98.5	0.2	0.2	0.1	0.2	0.8	0.9	6.2	6.3	6.8	5.7	6.1	30.2	26.9	11.0	0.9	77.2	38.1	50.4	49.6
37709	BLAINE	98.1	97.9	0.6	0.6	0.1	0.1	0.8	0.9	6.7	6.8	6.3	5.7	5.9	29.4	26.9	11.5	0.8	76.7	38.0	50.4	49.6
37710	BRICEVILLE	98.7	98.7	0.1	0.1	0.1	0.1	1.5	1.7	5.7	5.7	6.6	6.0	6.9	28.0	27.3	12.6	1.3	78.2	39.0	49.9	50.1
37711	BULLS GAP	98.5	98.3	0.6	0.7	0.1	0.1	0.4	0.5	6.3	6.4	6.8	6.3	5.9	29.1	26.9	11.3	1.1	76.7	38.4	50.2	49.8
37713	BYBEE	97.4	97.2	0.1	0.1	0.1	0.1	1.7	2.1	5.2	5.6	6.8	6.6	6.2	26.5	28.7	13.2	1.3	78.5	41.0	50.5	49.5
37714	CARYVILLE	97.9	97.6	0.1	0.1	0.4	0.4	1.4	1.7	6.4	6.2	6.1	5.3	5.7	29.7	27.4	12.1	1.1	78.2	38.8	50.1	49.9
37715	CLAIRFIELD	99.7	99.7	0.0	0.0	0.2	0.2	0.5	0.7	7.1	7.0	6.9	6.9	5.9	29.9	25.9	9.3	1.1	74.9	35.8	50.6	49.4
37716	CLINTON	96.4	96.1	1.8	1.9	0.3	0.4	0.7	0.9	5.9	5.8	6.6	5.8	6.2	27.9	27.0	13.3	1.7	78.2	40.0	48.4	51.6
37721	CORRYTON	98.2	98.0	0.8	0.9	0.2	0.2	0.4	0.5	6.5	6.6	6.6	5.9	5.7	29.9	27.1	10.7	1.1	76.7	38.7	49.5	50.5
37722	COSBY	98.3	98.0	0.3	0.3	0.1	0.2	1.0	1.2	5.8	6.0	6.0	5.8	5.8	28.3	29.2	11.9	1.2	78.6	39.8	48.7	51.3
37723	CRAB ORCHARD	99.0	98.8	0.0	0.0	0.1	0.1	0.4	0.4	5.9	6.1	6.9	5.8	4.7	28.1	27.8	13.2	1.4	77.5	40.2	50.1	50.0
37724	CUMBERLAND GAP	95.5	95.0	0.8	0.9	0.7	0.8	0.8	1.0	5.1	5.2	6.4	8.6	7.9	27.3	27.3	10.9	1.3	78.3	37.3	48.0	52.0
37725	DANDRIDGE	97.0	96.8	1.8	1.9	0.2	0.2	0.7	0.9	5.7	6.0	6.2	6.0	4.9	28.4	28.3	13.2	1.5	78.3	40.8	50.4	49.6
37726	DEER LODGE	98.5	98.4	0.4	0.3	0.1	0.1	0.7	0.7	5.0	5.9	7.3	7.7	5.9	27.6	27.4	12.0	1.3	76.7	38.8	51.8	48.2
37727	DEL RIO	97.8	97.6	0.6	0.6	0.0	0.0	0.7	0.8	4.8	5.1	6.6	6.3	5.9	26.1	30.3	13.6	1.2	79.8	42.0	50.6	49.4
37729	DUFF	98.4	98.1	0.0	0.0	0.1	0.1	0.9	1.1	6.3	6.3	6.4	6.6	6.7	27.2	27.4	12.0	1.2	77.1	38.7	49.6	50.4
37731	EIDSON	98.1	97.9	0.4	0.4	0.5	0.6	0.2	0.2	6.0	6.2	6.7	5.8	6.2	28.9	27.4	12.0	0.9	77.6	39.7	52.0	48.0
37737	FRIENDSVILLE	97.6	97.3	0.6	0.7	0.5	0.5	0.8	0.9	6.1	6.4	6.6	5.9	5.4	29.3	28.4	10.8	1.1	77.3	39.2	50.1	49.9
37738	GATLINBURG	96.4	95.7	0.2	0.2	1.5	1.9	1.5	1.9	3.3	3.6	4.6	4.7	4.6	25.2	35.3	16.6	2.0	85.5	47.4	49.8	50.2
37742	GREENBACK	97.6	97.2	0.3	0.3	0.4	0.5	0.7	0.9	6.1	6.4	6.4	5.8	5.7	28.3	28.4	11.8	1.2	77.7	39.7	49.8	50.2
37743	GREENEVILLE	95.2	94.9	3.2	3.3	0.3	0.4	0.9	1.0	5.6	5.8	6.3	5.9	5.2	27.5	27.0	14.6	2.2	78.6	40.9	48.8	51.2
37745	GREENEVILLE	95.8	95.3	2.5	2.7	0.4	0.5	1.1	1.3	5.6	5.7	5.8	5.7	6.0	27.8	26.7	14.8	1.9	79.6	40.5	48.2	51.8
37748	HARRIMAN	94.6	94.2	3.5	3.7	0.2	0.3	0.6	0.7	6.0	6.1	6.0	5.7	5.9	27.0	27.2	14.3	1.8	78.4	40.4	48.3	51.7
37752	HARROGATE	98.8	98.6	0.2	0.3	0.4	0.5	0.2	0.2	5.0	5.5	6.5	6.1	5.7	29.0	27.9	12.7	1.8	79.2	40.1	48.2	51.8
37753	HARTFORD	98.0	97.8	0.0	0.0	0.1	0.1	1.4	1.5	5.0	5.1	6.5	6.2	5.6	27.5	29.7	13.6	0.9	79.7	41.4	52.5	47.5
37754	HEISKELL	97.8	97.5	0.2	0.2	0.4	0.5	0.6	0.7	6.0	6.4	7.4	6.5	5.7	29.1	27.0	10.7	1.4	76.2	38.5	49.8	50.3
37755	HELENWOOD	98.2	98.1	0.3	0.2	0.1	0.1	0.4	0.5	6.7	6.7	7.0	6.6	6.9	29.1	24.6	11.1	1.3	75.6	36.6	49.5	50.5
37756	HUNTSVILLE	98.8	98.7	0.1	0.1	0.1	0.2	0.6	0.8	6.5	6.5	6.9	6.5	6.7	29.7	25.3	10.7	1.3	76.2	36.5	50.8	49.2
37757	JACKSBORO	98.1	97.9	0.3	0.3	0.2	0.2	0.7	0.9	6.5	6.4	6.5	6.3	6.1	31.1	24.5	11.5	1.2	76.9	36.9	48.4	51.6
37760	JEFFERSON CITY	92.7	92.0	4.5	4.8	0.6	0.7	2.2	2.7	6.1	5.6	6.0	8.7	11.6	26.4	21.4	12.4	1.9	79.2	34.0	48.5	51.5
37762	JELLICO	96.8	96.6	1.4	1.4	0.5	0.6	0.5	0.6	5.7	5.7	6.0	6.1	6.3	25.1	26.0	16.6	2.6	78.8	41.1	47.1	52.9
37763	KINGSTON	96.3	95.9	1.5	1.6	0.4	0.4	0.8	1.0	5.7	5.9	5.9	5.4	5.5	26.2	28.8	15.1	1.6	79.2	42.0	49.6	50.4
37764	KODAK	97.9	97.6	0.3	0.4	0.3	0.4	0.9	1.1	7.5	7.4	6.7	5.6	5.7	30.8	24.6	10.9	0.7	75.0	36.2	48.4	51.6
	TENNESSEE	80.2	79.4	16.4	16.7	1.0	1.3	2.2	2.6	6.6	6.5	6.8	6.6	7.0	29.0	24.8	11.1	1.5	76.3	36.8	48.9	51.1
	UNITED STATES	75.1	73.6	12.3	12.5	3.8	4.2	12.5	14.1	6.9	6.7	7.2	7.0	7.3	28.6	23.8	10.8	1.7	75.1	36.0	49.1	50.9

#	POST OFFICE NAME	2004 Per Capita Income	2004 HH Income Base	2004 Household Income Distribution (%): Less than $25,000	$25,000 to $49,999	$50,000 to $99,999	$100,000 to $149,999	$150,000 or More	Median Household Income: 2004	2009	2004 National Centile	2004 State Centile	2004 Home Value Base	2004 Home Value Distribution (%): Less than $50,000	$50,000 to $89,999	$90,000 to $174,999	$175,000 to $399,999	$400,000 or More	2004 Median Home Value
37375	SEWANEE	24570	1072	27.7	26.3	26.4	10.7	8.9	46704	52153	66	84	823	17.6	20.7	20.4	32.6	8.8	129018
37376	SHERWOOD	11663	227	47.1	47.1	5.7	0.0	0.0	26164	30183	6	10	207	63.3	29.5	3.4	0.5	3.4	41406
37377	SIGNAL MOUNTAIN	37752	6583	18.3	24.0	30.4	13.7	13.7	59277	67708	84	95	4896	6.5	7.7	29.6	44.0	12.2	196812
37379	SODDY DAISY	22006	9559	23.9	30.5	33.8	9.2	2.6	45904	53255	64	82	8097	17.9	23.9	40.4	15.8	2.0	101989
37380	SOUTH PITTSBURG	17936	2554	41.1	29.0	22.8	4.6	2.6	31720	35027	17	28	1906	24.9	31.7	34.0	8.8	0.7	81711
37381	SPRING CITY	18883	3652	38.5	30.3	22.7	6.3	2.1	32913	36214	21	38	2916	23.5	27.4	31.4	16.3	1.4	88996
37383	SEWANEE	46900	5	0.0	20.0	40.0	40.0	0.0	91155	110555	97	99	3	0.0	0.0	0.0	100.0	0.0	225000
37385	TELLICO PLAINS	16305	3223	42.4	30.4	23.1	3.0	1.2	30972	34157	15	23	2661	34.0	25.4	28.2	11.2	1.2	74216
37387	TRACY CITY	14224	1782	51.2	29.6	16.4	1.6	1.1	24323	26552	4	7	1408	42.6	30.4	21.9	4.6	0.5	59455
37388	TULLAHOMA	22918	10295	32.4	29.7	27.4	6.5	3.9	39027	44199	43	65	7419	15.1	29.6	38.5	14.1	2.7	96913
37391	TURTLETOWN	17937	329	47.4	28.0	17.3	5.8	1.5	26839	29320	7	12	277	24.6	30.0	27.4	15.5	2.5	86795
37396	WHITESIDE	39936	22	27.3	22.7	22.7	13.6	13.6	50000	54564	72	88	19	26.3	5.3	26.3	21.1	21.1	121875
37397	WHITWELL	17198	4419	38.3	35.2	22.2	2.6	1.7	32227	35982	18	31	3646	31.5	31.1	29.3	7.7	0.4	75896
37398	WINCHESTER	21164	5384	33.5	29.5	28.8	6.2	2.0	38899	43835	42	64	4200	17.3	28.1	36.4	15.5	2.6	97252
37402	CHATTANOOGA	17197	2503	72.2	15.0	9.1	2.4	1.3	12706	15293	1	2	33	6.1	0.0	45.5	18.2	30.3	143750
37403	CHATTANOOGA	18135	1485	58.9	22.0	14.9	1.4	2.8	19508	22214	2	3	312	18.3	42.3	18.6	11.9	9.0	74286
37404	CHATTANOOGA	14399	5322	50.1	29.6	16.0	2.2	2.2	24964	28412	5	7	2584	34.5	43.2	16.5	4.3	1.5	60881
37405	CHATTANOOGA	27745	6434	33.1	32.0	23.7	6.1	5.0	36467	41929	33	56	3390	15.0	27.1	33.7	16.9	7.4	105341
37406	CHATTANOOGA	14615	5548	50.0	25.4	20.6	2.6	1.4	25000	28082	5	8	2999	18.7	53.3	25.3	2.6	0.1	73321
37407	CHATTANOOGA	15061	3120	53.6	28.4	13.8	1.8	2.5	22735	26175	3	4	1617	47.9	38.2	10.3	2.9	0.7	51135
37408	CHATTANOOGA	10668	693	71.3	21.2	5.2	0.0	2.3	12352	15000	1	1	129	44.2	40.3	11.6	3.9	0.0	58333
37409	CHATTANOOGA	17700	1195	37.9	34.5	21.4	3.8	2.4	34361	38932	25	45	796	24.6	51.9	20.5	2.4	0.6	64144
37410	CHATTANOOGA	9467	1582	69.1	21.1	7.8	0.6	1.4	14780	17409	1	2	552	41.1	51.3	6.5	1.1	0.0	54153
37411	CHATTANOOGA	23378	7531	31.5	31.3	27.7	5.5	3.9	38161	43870	40	61	4795	6.8	46.8	39.6	6.2	0.7	87343
37412	CHATTANOOGA	23642	9355	25.7	36.6	29.4	6.2	2.2	40615	46838	48	70	6006	4.7	36.0	53.0	6.2	0.2	96423
37415	CHATTANOOGA	26310	10773	27.0	35.2	27.4	6.4	4.1	40501	46104	48	69	6805	6.7	28.4	52.1	10.0	2.7	104092
37416	CHATTANOOGA	25636	6002	21.6	32.0	34.9	7.5	4.0	47426	54585	67	84	4277	3.4	22.8	61.2	9.8	2.9	111009
37419	CHATTANOOGA	25324	2335	27.8	30.6	30.0	7.3	4.3	42599	48838	55	76	1818	15.7	26.4	44.1	9.1	4.7	97579
37421	CHATTANOOGA	30997	18140	19.7	28.3	33.0	11.9	7.1	52264	60575	76	91	11957	3.0	10.1	56.3	25.0	5.6	142792
37601	JOHNSON CITY	21121	15123	38.6	31.9	21.1	5.0	3.4	33290	37133	22	40	9404	15.1	24.4	43.7	14.5	2.3	103894
37604	JOHNSON CITY	22203	13943	38.8	29.4	21.7	5.9	4.1	32809	37045	20	37	8087	11.2	26.1	39.8	21.1	1.9	107177
37615	JOHNSON CITY	25831	6533	25.9	31.0	30.0	8.8	4.4	45829	51807	63	81	4933	9.3	18.4	46.4	22.0	3.9	119421
37616	AFTON	18637	1980	34.6	36.8	22.8	3.0	2.8	35595	39677	30	52	1619	24.4	29.8	34.8	9.0	2.0	85755
37617	BLOUNTVILLE	20906	5354	27.0	34.0	29.3	6.7	3.0	41588	46892	52	74	4432	19.0	20.5	40.6	17.2	2.8	106214
37618	BLUFF CITY	18974	5027	32.6	33.4	27.3	4.7	2.1	37292	42603	36	57	4199	27.3	24.7	34.9	12.0	1.1	87543
37620	BRISTOL	20970	16479	36.4	32.8	23.6	4.6	2.6	34183	38630	25	44	12158	24.8	29.5	35.1	9.8	0.8	84044
37640	BUTLER	14415	1713	51.4	31.6	12.9	2.6	1.5	24135	26756	4	6	1452	40.2	28.6	23.4	6.7	1.2	65032
37641	CHUCKEY	17824	3340	35.2	33.7	25.7	3.8	1.7	35947	39799	31	53	2773	24.5	28.2	34.4	11.1	1.8	86975
37642	CHURCH HILL	19215	5902	32.6	34.2	27.1	4.3	1.8	36520	40636	34	56	4739	22.1	21.2	47.3	8.7	0.7	99313
37643	ELIZABETHTON	16601	14172	41.7	34.1	19.7	3.1	1.4	30012	32905	12	20	10653	22.7	33.0	35.5	8.3	0.6	84363
37645	MOUNT CARMEL	20715	2487	31.3	33.1	27.2	5.8	2.7	38021	41250	39	60	1928	20.7	18.8	50.2	9.0	1.3	102994
37650	ERWIN	17578	5447	38.9	34.3	21.9	4.0	0.9	32374	35948	19	33	4154	21.6	30.7	37.0	10.2	0.5	87139
37656	FALL BRANCH	21927	1499	25.8	33.8	32.8	5.1	2.5	43650	49846	58	78	1273	15.4	23.0	42.5	17.9	1.2	104167
37657	FLAG POND	18658	435	38.6	37.0	15.9	6.4	2.1	31482	35800	16	27	360	31.7	23.6	32.8	11.9	0.0	83448
37658	HAMPTON	14594	2199	45.8	33.3	18.3	1.8	0.8	27282	30139	8	13	1764	39.2	32.9	23.1	4.8	0.0	65063
37659	JONESBOROUGH	21622	9780	28.2	32.8	30.0	6.3	2.7	40673	46141	48	70	8091	11.0	21.3	46.5	17.8	3.4	112862
37660	KINGSPORT	21982	17858	38.0	30.4	22.3	5.9	3.5	33550	37757	23	41	12154	17.1	31.2	37.2	12.1	2.4	92436
37663	KINGSPORT	26585	6054	21.6	28.7	33.8	9.6	6.3	49773	57527	71	88	5104	5.6	12.8	56.2	23.7	1.7	127457
37664	KINGSPORT	23972	11341	31.0	30.3	26.7	8.0	4.0	40313	45381	47	69	8902	12.3	23.2	44.3	18.3	2.0	110065
37665	KINGSPORT	16034	2068	44.6	32.5	18.8	3.7	0.4	28273	31851	9	15	1423	24.5	39.4	33.8	2.0	0.3	75679
37680	LAUREL BLOOMERY	16243	369	42.0	33.6	20.1	2.7	1.6	30086	33375	12	20	311	32.2	37.6	26.1	4.2	0.0	68393
37681	LIMESTONE	17744	2429	33.6	35.0	26.1	3.3	2.1	35365	40065	29	49	2012	17.3	28.5	39.4	12.4	2.5	94804
37683	MOUNTAIN CITY	16540	5023	50.0	28.3	17.4	2.3	2.0	25031	27403	5	8	3884	31.8	29.1	30.1	8.0	1.1	75319
37686	PINEY FLATS	25067	2972	24.4	38.0	26.8	6.0	4.9	41313	47067	51	73	2470	16.7	20.9	35.2	21.9	5.3	109531
37687	ROAN MOUNTAIN	15782	2014	52.0	31.6	12.7	2.0	1.7	23690	25680	4	5	1689	39.1	27.9	28.9	3.0	1.1	65977
37688	SHADY VALLEY	13879	500	51.8	29.8	15.4	2.2	0.8	24220	27491	4	6	431	23.2	35.0	26.0	12.5	3.3	83173
37690	TELFORD	18984	1433	34.5	29.8	27.0	5.9	2.7	35279	40458	29	49	1194	19.0	28.1	39.1	11.3	2.4	94048
37691	TRADE	12768	377	40.9	53.3	5.8	0.0	0.0	30053	33558	12	20	301	28.6	31.2	29.9	7.3	3.0	72692
37692	UNICOI	17719	1903	35.8	31.6	26.8	4.6	1.3	32879	36347	21	37	1526	19.6	21.4	41.4	14.7	2.9	102500
37694	WATAUGA	15430	818	39.2	35.3	22.3	2.7	0.5	31630	34957	17	27	664	27.7	25.2	35.4	11.1	0.6	86667
37701	ALCOA	20709	2781	37.0	29.7	24.2	6.5	2.6	33639	37358	23	42	1922	16.0	31.4	41.2	7.7	3.7	92604
37705	ANDERSONVILLE	23422	2200	27.6	31.4	28.7	8.8	3.5	41924	47286	53	74	1854	11.2	21.6	40.0	22.9	4.3	118795
37708	BEAN STATION	15739	2669	39.9	34.5	21.4	2.6	1.6	32281	35514	19	32	2202	25.8	34.0	29.2	10.1	1.0	79412
37709	BLAINE	18196	1278	37.2	31.4	26.0	3.1	2.4	35088	38478	28	48	1056	25.2	26.4	32.2	14.0	2.2	87763
37710	BRICEVILLE	10835	584	53.4	31.5	14.6	0.5	0.0	22444	25272	3	4	453	60.9	27.4	10.8	0.9	0.0	42500
37711	BULLS GAP	15898	1939	36.8	33.0	27.2	2.4	0.6	34149	38136	25	44	1609	27.0	31.3	34.7	6.5	0.6	79788
37713	BYBEE	19344	692	45.1	32.1	18.8	1.6	2.5	28724	31220	10	16	578	28.2	31.1	31.1	6.9	2.6	77500
37714	CARYVILLE	16635	1821	37.0	37.7	19.9	3.8	1.5	32235	35281	18	32	1435	30.5	31.6	30.0	5.4	2.6	76354
37715	CLAIRFIELD	8796	413	67.3	24.9	7.8	0.0	0.0	17519	20069	1	3	338	80.5	15.1	4.4	0.0	0.0	24643
37716	CLINTON	20140	10744	32.0	30.6	29.1	6.5	1.9	38496	43786	41	62	7923	16.8	26.2	42.1	13.6	1.3	98810
37721	CORRYTON	20655	4151	24.8	32.4	35.0	6.1	1.7	42612	49643	55	77	3504	15.7	23.5	43.6	15.2	2.1	103160
37722	COSBY	16060	2115	41.9	35.9	18.0	2.5	1.8	29458	32808	11	17	1726	25.8	28.9	32.8	10.1	2.4	82768
37723	CRAB ORCHARD	14755	383	40.2	38.6	18.3	2.1	0.8	29493	32795	11	18	325	40.9	29.5	16.9	12.0	0.6	61552
37724	CUMBERLAND GAP	16463	1314	38.7	31.7	24.4	3.7	1.5	31730	35303	17	28	1071	26.2	28.6	33.0	11.9	0.4	83795
37725	DANDRIDGE	21326	5562	29.8	34.5	27.7	5.0	3.1	38683	43013	42	63	4659	23.9	19.6	33.1	20.3	3.1	101363
37726	DEER LODGE	12648	680	50.9	33.1	12.7	2.1	1.3	24552	26650	4	7	560	38.6	39.3	17.7	3.8	0.7	60781
37727	DEL RIO	12748	834	47.4	38.9	12.5	1.2	0.1	26283	29575	6	11	673	44.9	30.6	18.1	5.5	0.9	57500
37729	DUFF	11027	718	55.3	31.8	10.9	1.1	1.0	21292	23245	2	3	573	70.5	21.3	7.9	0.4	0.0	32218
37731	EIDSON	13689	413	46.5	30.3	22.0	1.2	0.0	26598	30271	7	12	363	53.2	14.9	18.2	12.4	1.4	46406
37737	FRIENDSVILLE	23378	2422	21.9	32.5	33.6	8.0	4.0	46295	52237	65	83	2060	13.9	18.9	38.1	22.1	7.1	118131
37738	GATLINBURG	27305	2359	23.3	40.4	26.8	5.4	4.0	40321	45487	47	69	1810	7.7	9.8	37.6	42.0	2.9	163738
37742	GREENBACK	22418	1865	24.3	30.7	34.3	8.3	2.5	45722	51465	63	81	1593	10.7	19.3	41.9	20.9	7.2	120580
37743	GREENEVILLE	18614	10329	39.4	30.3	24.7	3.2	2.4	32540	35974	19	35	7801	19.9	28.5	38.5	10.7	2.5	92135
37745	GREENEVILLE	19163	7329	39.0	33.1	21.1	4.6	2.2	32179	35824	18	31	5404	21.9	26.4	39.0	11.3	1.4	92265
37748	HARRIMAN	18127	7874	38.1	32.5	24.1	3.7	1.6	32987	37255	21	38	5856	26.7	30.1	34.6	7.7	1.1	82762
37752	HARROGATE	16521	2073	35.9	34.4	24.5	4.0	1.2	33485	37044	22	41	1648	25.4	33.2	34.2	6.3	0.9	83472
37753	HARTFORD	10918	332	55.1	36.1	7.2	1.5	0.0	22086	24793	3	4	264	39.8	43.9	13.6	2.7	0.0	63226
37754	HEISKELL	20069	1859	25.8	34.8	30.5	6.4	2.5	41938	48290	53	75	1554	22.8	20.7	36.5	16.2	3.9	96824
37755	HELENWOOD	15330	1469	46.9	30.5	18.6	1.9	2.1	26401	29134	6	11	1156	37.3	31.2	24.7	5.5	1.4	65854
37756	HUNTSVILLE	11902	1018	57.5	28.3	12.4	1.1	0.8	20913	22769	2	3	801	59.3	21.1	16.0	2.9	0.8	42320
37757	JACKSBORO	17771	3639	37.7	33.4	23.0	3.9	2.1	33117	36172	21	39	2790	17.6	33.2	40.0	8.2	0.9	89134
37760	JEFFERSON CITY	19122	4911	37.9	29.7	23.8	6.0	2.7	35008	38118	28	48	3235	13.1	24.3	45.0	15.2	2.5	104923
37762	JELLICO	13101	1514	51.2	34.4	11.3	1.4	1.8	23835	25735	4	6	1026	53.0	34.0	10.3	2.6	0.0	47417
37763	KINGSTON	23344	6004	29.3	31.3	27.9	8.2	3.3	41021	46616	50	71	4820	15.8	25.5	38.9	16.8	3.0	103201
37764	KODAK	19502	3523	27.7	37.8	29.6	3.6	1.4	38614	42537	41	63	2946	25.5	14.6	40.0	18.2	1.7	111966
	TENNESSEE	22498		30.2	30.2	28.1	7.5	4.1	40531	46137				15.0	25.0	39.4	17.3	3.3	104905
	UNITED STATES	25866		24.7	27.1	30.8	10.9	6.5	48124	56710				10.9	15.0	33.7	30.1	10.4	145905

ZIP CODE		FINANCIAL SERVICES				THE HOME						ENTERTAINMENT						PERSONAL			
						Home Improvements		Furnishings													
#	POST OFFICE NAME	Auto Loan	Home Loan	Investments	Retirement Plans	Home Repair	Lawn & Garden	Computers & Hardware	Major Appliances	TV, Radio, Sound Equipment	Furniture	Dine out/ Carry out	Sports Equipment	Fees & Tickets	Toys & Games	Travel	Cable TV	Apparel & Services	Auto Repairs	Health Insurance	Pets & Supplies
37375	SEWANEE	96	102	109	99	102	110	98	100	99	98	122	116	100	125	100	100	119	99	101	114
37376	SHERWOOD	51	34	16	30	39	44	33	41	40	34	47	49	28	44	34	43	42	41	50	58
37377	SIGNAL MOUNTAIN	129	136	141	136	137	143	130	132	127	130	158	154	132	159	131	126	155	131	129	151
37379	SODDY DAISY	90	80	62	76	84	90	75	83	79	76	97	98	73	97	76	81	92	81	89	105
37380	SOUTH PITTSBURG	76	56	35	51	61	70	56	65	64	56	76	76	50	73	56	67	70	64	76	85
37381	SPRING CITY	82	55	25	48	63	72	53	67	64	54	76	80	45	71	54	69	69	66	82	95
37383	SEWANEE	120	137	169	142	135	139	136	131	129	135	163	157	140	167	136	125	161	133	119	143
37385	TELLICO PLAINS	76	51	23	44	58	67	49	62	60	50	70	74	42	66	50	64	64	61	76	88
37387	TRACY CITY	66	44	20	38	50	57	42	53	51	43	60	63	36	57	43	55	55	53	65	75
37388	TULLAHOMA	81	78	73	76	79	86	77	80	80	76	98	93	77	99	78	80	94	79	83	94
37391	TURTLETOWN	74	50	23	43	56	65	48	60	58	49	68	72	41	64	49	62	62	59	74	85
37396	WHITESIDE	128	89	47	84	104	117	88	109	102	87	119	132	75	117	92	107	109	108	130	152
37397	WHITWELL	80	53	24	46	60	70	52	64	62	52	73	77	44	69	52	67	66	64	79	92
37398	WINCHESTER	85	68	47	64	73	83	67	76	74	66	89	88	63	88	68	78	83	74	86	97
37402	CHATTANOOGA	35	30	44	32	30	35	39	35	41	37	51	42	38	49	38	41	49	39	37	39
37403	CHATTANOOGA	51	39	51	41	38	46	57	48	58	52	72	60	51	68	51	56	69	55	50	54
37404	CHATTANOOGA	52	45	49	42	45	52	50	50	55	50	67	56	49	63	49	57	64	52	55	57
37405	CHATTANOOGA	78	74	85	76	74	81	81	79	81	79	101	93	79	97	79	79	97	82	78	88
37406	CHATTANOOGA	52	46	51	42	45	53	50	50	55	51	67	55	50	64	49	58	65	51	56	57
37407	CHATTANOOGA	52	44	48	41	44	52	49	50	55	50	67	56	48	63	48	58	64	52	56	57
37408	CHATTANOOGA	38	31	42	29	30	36	38	36	42	39	52	41	37	50	36	44	51	39	39	41
37409	CHATTANOOGA	59	60	65	58	59	66	61	60	63	60	78	67	63	79	62	64	76	60	63	68
37410	CHATTANOOGA	35	28	34	26	28	33	33	33	37	34	45	36	32	42	32	39	44	34	36	37
37411	CHATTANOOGA	71	73	84	73	72	79	75	74	76	75	95	84	77	95	76	76	93	75	74	82
37412	CHATTANOOGA	67	73	78	71	72	79	72	71	72	70	90	81	74	94	73	73	88	71	72	79
37415	CHATTANOOGA	74	76	85	76	76	82	79	77	78	77	98	90	80	99	79	78	95	78	77	86
37416	CHATTANOOGA	80	88	97	87	87	93	86	85	85	85	107	98	90	110	88	85	105	85	84	94
37419	CHATTANOOGA	81	83	84	82	84	91	81	83	82	80	101	96	83	103	83	82	98	82	85	94
37421	CHATTANOOGA	97	106	120	108	105	110	104	103	100	104	126	119	107	127	105	99	124	103	98	113
37601	JOHNSON CITY	69	63	60	62	64	72	65	67	68	64	83	77	63	82	65	69	79	67	71	78
37604	JOHNSON CITY	70	64	70	65	65	72	71	69	72	69	89	82	69	88	69	72	86	72	71	79
37615	JOHNSON CITY	95	87	72	86	90	97	85	90	88	84	107	105	83	108	85	88	102	88	94	107
37616	AFTON	86	61	33	54	68	78	59	71	69	60	81	85	52	78	60	73	75	70	85	98
37617	BLOUNTVILLE	83	72	56	69	76	83	69	76	74	69	90	89	66	89	70	76	85	75	83	95
37618	BLUFF CITY	83	62	37	56	68	76	59	70	67	60	80	83	53	78	60	71	74	69	82	95
37620	BRISTOL	75	65	52	61	68	76	64	70	69	63	84	81	61	83	65	72	79	69	78	86
37640	BUTLER	58	39	18	34	44	51	38	47	46	38	53	56	32	51	38	49	49	47	58	67
37641	CHUCKEY	80	55	28	48	62	71	53	66	63	54	75	78	46	71	54	68	68	65	80	92
37642	CHURCH HILL	78	61	40	57	67	75	59	68	66	59	79	81	55	78	60	70	74	67	79	90
37643	ELIZABETHTON	67	48	29	44	53	61	49	57	57	49	67	67	43	64	49	60	62	57	68	75
37645	MOUNT CARMEL	74	70	64	69	72	77	67	71	69	67	85	85	66	85	68	69	81	71	74	87
37650	ERWIN	66	51	33	46	55	64	51	58	58	50	69	68	46	67	51	61	64	58	69	76
37656	FALL BRANCH	87	72	50	67	77	84	67	77	74	68	89	92	64	89	69	76	84	75	86	101
37657	FLAG POND	79	53	24	45	60	69	51	63	61	52	72	76	43	68	52	66	65	63	78	90
37658	HAMPTON	63	42	19	37	48	55	41	51	49	42	58	61	35	55	42	53	53	51	63	73
37659	JONESBOROUGH	87	73	53	69	77	85	71	79	76	71	92	92	67	91	71	79	87	77	87	99
37660	KINGSPORT	76	65	58	63	68	77	67	72	72	66	87	83	64	85	67	74	83	72	79	86
37663	KINGSPORT	91	97	98	96	98	103	92	94	90	91	112	109	94	115	94	90	109	92	93	108
37664	KINGSPORT	84	76	64	73	79	88	76	81	80	74	96	93	73	95	76	82	91	80	88	97
37665	KINGSPORT	55	45	35	42	48	56	48	52	53	46	64	58	45	62	48	56	59	52	61	62
37680	LAUREL BLOOMERY	72	49	22	42	55	63	47	59	57	48	66	70	40	63	48	61	60	58	72	83
37681	LIMESTONE	76	58	39	53	63	70	57	66	64	57	76	78	51	72	57	66	71	66	76	87
37683	MOUNTAIN CITY	65	44	21	39	50	58	44	54	52	44	61	63	37	58	44	56	56	53	66	74
37686	PINEY FLATS	105	85	57	79	92	101	80	92	88	80	106	109	75	106	82	92	99	90	104	122
37687	ROAN MOUNTAIN	68	47	25	42	53	62	48	57	56	48	66	67	41	62	48	60	60	57	70	77
37688	SHADY VALLEY	60	40	18	34	45	52	39	48	47	39	55	58	33	52	39	50	50	48	59	69
37690	TELFORD	82	67	45	62	70	76	64	72	69	65	83	85	58	79	64	70	79	72	78	92
37691	TRADE	57	38	17	33	43	50	37	46	44	37	52	55	31	49	37	48	47	45	56	65
37692	UNICOI	71	57	38	53	62	68	54	62	60	55	72	74	51	72	55	63	68	61	70	82
37694	WATAUGA	71	48	22	42	54	62	46	58	56	47	66	69	40	62	47	60	60	57	71	82
37701	ALCOA	63	60	63	57	61	69	63	63	66	62	81	71	63	81	63	68	78	63	68	72
37705	ANDERSONVILLE	95	82	62	75	86	95	77	87	84	77	101	102	74	101	79	87	96	85	97	111
37708	BEAN STATION	71	49	24	42	55	63	47	58	56	47	66	69	40	62	48	60	60	57	71	82
37709	BLAINE	85	57	26	49	64	74	55	69	66	56	78	82	47	73	56	71	71	68	85	97
37710	BRICEVILLE	51	36	18	31	40	45	34	42	41	35	48	50	30	45	35	43	44	42	51	59
37711	BULLS GAP	74	50	23	43	56	65	48	60	58	49	68	72	41	64	49	62	62	59	74	85
37713	BYBEE	87	59	27	51	66	76	57	71	68	58	80	84	48	76	57	74	73	70	87	100
37714	CARYVILLE	75	51	25	45	58	66	50	61	59	50	70	73	43	66	50	63	64	61	75	86
37715	CLAIRFIELD	43	28	13	25	32	37	27	34	33	28	39	41	23	37	28	36	35	34	42	49
37716	CLINTON	74	65	54	61	67	74	64	69	68	63	83	81	61	82	64	70	79	69	75	85
37721	CORRYTON	86	75	55	71	79	85	70	78	74	70	90	92	67	91	71	76	86	76	85	101
37722	COSBY	69	49	28	44	55	63	49	58	57	49	67	68	43	64	50	60	62	58	70	78
37723	CRAB ORCHARD	67	45	20	39	51	59	44	54	53	44	62	65	37	58	44	57	56	54	67	77
37724	CUMBERLAND GAP	71	56	37	51	61	68	53	62	60	54	72	73	49	71	55	63	67	61	72	83
37725	DANDRIDGE	90	71	46	65	76	84	67	78	75	68	90	92	61	87	68	78	84	77	88	103
37726	DEER LODGE	60	40	18	35	46	53	39	49	47	40	55	58	33	52	40	51	50	48	60	69
37727	DEL RIO	57	38	17	33	44	50	37	46	45	38	53	55	32	50	38	48	48	46	57	66
37729	DUFF	52	35	16	30	40	46	34	42	41	34	48	50	29	45	34	44	43	42	52	60
37731	EIDSON	59	40	18	34	45	52	38	48	46	39	54	57	32	51	39	50	49	47	59	68
37737	FRIENDSVILLE	93	87	71	83	89	95	81	88	83	81	102	103	79	103	82	84	98	86	91	108
37738	GATLINBURG	101	79	54	72	89	100	75	90	85	74	100	105	67	99	80	90	93	89	106	123
37742	GREENBACK	93	82	61	77	85	92	76	85	81	77	99	100	73	98	78	82	94	83	91	108
37743	GREENEVILLE	75	56	36	51	61	70	55	65	64	56	76	76	50	73	56	67	70	64	76	86
37745	GREENEVILLE	70	55	40	50	59	68	55	62	62	55	74	72	50	71	56	65	69	62	73	80
37748	HARRIMAN	73	56	37	51	61	69	56	64	63	55	75	75	51	73	56	67	70	64	75	83
37752	HARROGATE	72	53	31	47	58	66	51	61	59	52	70	72	46	68	52	63	65	60	73	83
37753	HARTFORD	49	33	15	28	37	43	31	39	38	32	45	47	27	42	32	41	41	39	49	56
37754	HEISKELL	88	73	50	68	78	84	69	78	75	70	90	93	65	89	70	77	85	77	86	102
37755	HELENWOOD	72	48	22	42	55	63	47	58	56	47	66	70	40	62	47	60	60	58	72	83
37756	HUNTSVILLE	56	38	17	33	43	49	36	46	44	37	52	54	31	49	37	47	47	45	56	65
37757	JACKSBORO	78	56	32	51	62	71	55	66	64	56	76	77	49	73	56	68	70	65	78	88
37760	JEFFERSON CITY	73	61	51	61	63	71	65	68	68	64	83	79	61	81	63	68	79	69	72	80
37762	JELLICO	52	37	26	34	41	48	39	45	45	39	54	52	35	51	39	48	50	45	53	59
37763	KINGSTON	91	72	48	68	78	89	72	82	80	71	95	95	66	93	73	84	88	80	94	105
37764	KODAK	82	73	56	70	74	78	70	76	71	72	88	87	66	83	69	71	84	75	76	91
	TENNESSEE	85	76	68	73	78	85	76	80	79	76	97	94	73	96	75	81	93	80	85	97
	UNITED STATES	100	100	100	100	100	100	100	100	100	100	100	100	100	100	100	100	100	100	100	100

#	POST OFFICE NAME	COUNTY FIPS CODE	POPULATION 2000	2004	2009	% Rate	State Centile	HOUSEHOLDS 2000	2004	2009	% Annual Rate 2000-2004	2004 Average HH Size	FAMILIES 2000	2004	% Annual Rate 2000-2004
37765	KYLES FORD	067	874	807	771	-1.9	0	358	337	330	-1.4	2.39	251	232	-1.8
37766	LA FOLLETTE	013	18513	18532	18668	0.0	22	7644	7862	8098	0.7	2.33	5384	5431	0.2
37769	LAKE CITY	001	6026	6046	6083	0.1	25	2479	2546	2615	0.6	2.33	1749	1756	0.1
37770	LANCING	129	2570	2741	2891	1.5	75	975	1059	1139	2.0	2.56	736	786	1.6
37771	LENOIR CITY	105	13313	14171	14977	1.5	73	5359	5802	6230	1.9	2.41	3732	3955	1.4
37772	LENOIR CITY	105	8757	9236	9748	1.3	67	3535	3801	4078	1.7	2.43	2699	2851	1.3
37774	LOUDON	105	14471	15691	16763	1.9	83	6038	6689	7277	2.4	2.31	4590	5007	2.1
37777	LOUISVILLE	009	10793	11329	11869	1.2	63	4754	5131	5477	1.8	2.18	3014	3164	1.2
37778	LOWLAND	063	136	141	144	0.9	54	52	55	57	1.3	2.56	41	42	0.6
37779	LUTTRELL	173	3805	4140	4612	2.0	85	1410	1569	1785	2.6	2.60	1117	1224	2.2
37801	MARYVILLE	009	18813	19813	20694	1.2	66	7751	8297	8786	1.6	2.37	5503	5775	1.1
37803	MARYVILLE	009	27576	29014	30241	1.2	65	10703	11444	12091	1.6	2.46	8042	8455	1.2
37804	MARYVILLE	009	20959	21422	22092	0.5	42	8134	8450	8837	0.9	2.43	5849	5944	0.4
37806	MASCOT	093	2828	2808	2896	-0.2	12	1155	1161	1210	0.1	2.42	827	811	-0.5
37807	MAYNARDVILLE	173	9166	10094	11331	2.3	90	3461	3881	4438	2.7	2.58	2663	2941	2.4
37809	MIDWAY	059	2002	2067	2133	0.8	49	757	796	835	1.2	2.60	573	592	0.8
37810	MOHAWK	059	1728	1737	1781	0.1	26	694	710	742	0.5	2.45	521	523	0.1
37811	MOORESBURG	073	3471	3797	3988	2.1	87	1403	1568	1675	2.7	2.42	1042	1143	2.2
37813	MORRISTOWN	063	16674	16675	16852	0.0	20	6696	6802	6965	0.4	2.43	4696	4661	-0.2
37814	MORRISTOWN	063	30643	31363	32015	0.6	43	12257	12754	13200	0.9	2.41	8614	8793	0.5
37818	MOSHEIM	059	4813	4908	5045	0.5	39	1949	2035	2135	1.0	2.41	1439	1474	0.6
37819	NEWCOMB	013	545	558	565	0.6	43	219	230	238	1.2	2.43	163	168	0.7
37820	NEW MARKET	089	7031	7534	8134	1.6	77	2638	2883	3162	2.1	2.58	2045	2195	1.7
37821	NEWPORT	029	21440	21892	22375	0.5	41	8864	9255	9643	1.0	2.33	6114	6245	0.5
37825	NEW TAZEWELL	025	7627	8144	8713	1.6	76	3076	3361	3681	2.1	2.40	2242	2403	1.7
37826	NIOTA	107	3759	4117	4322	2.2	88	1515	1689	1795	2.6	2.44	1182	1291	2.1
37829	OAKDALE	129	2066	2094	2148	0.3	34	762	791	830	0.9	2.63	605	618	0.5
37830	OAK RIDGE	001	28148	27920	27937	-0.2	11	12355	12457	12668	0.2	2.21	7941	7814	-0.4
37840	OLIVER SPRINGS	129	10014	10053	10233	0.1	25	4004	4110	4267	0.6	2.45	2958	2982	0.2
37841	ONEIDA	151	8458	8673	8879	0.6	44	3426	3602	3769	1.2	2.39	2410	2485	0.7
37843	PARROTTSVILLE	029	3612	3671	3730	0.4	37	1430	1492	1548	1.0	2.46	1089	1116	0.6
37846	PHILADELPHIA	105	3736	3852	3991	0.7	48	1375	1438	1511	1.1	2.68	1082	1114	0.7
37847	PIONEER	013	2566	2838	3011	2.4	91	937	1066	1157	3.1	2.66	722	807	2.7
37848	POWDER SPRINGS	057	535	538	552	0.1	27	206	211	221	0.6	2.45	155	156	0.2
37849	POWELL	093	21084	22272	23392	1.3	68	8177	8770	9330	1.7	2.49	6135	6434	1.1
37852	ROBBINS	151	2903	2905	2956	0.0	22	1107	1141	1192	0.7	2.54	838	849	0.3
37853	ROCKFORD	009	3815	3691	3742	-0.8	4	1571	1553	1599	-0.3	2.37	1097	1055	-0.9
37854	ROCKWOOD	145	11409	11552	11839	0.3	32	4727	4871	5086	0.7	2.32	3297	3328	0.2
37857	ROGERSVILLE	073	17219	18166	18855	1.3	67	7191	7764	8209	1.8	2.32	5050	5356	1.4
37860	RUSSELLVILLE	063	3251	3580	3782	2.3	90	1280	1442	1549	2.8	2.45	971	1071	2.3
37861	RUTLEDGE	057	7352	7659	7960	1.0	58	2982	3175	3368	1.5	2.36	2177	2275	1.0
37862	SEVIERVILLE	155	17670	19034	20467	1.8	80	7366	8101	8863	2.3	2.31	5003	5374	1.7
37863	PIGEON FORGE	155	5342	5515	5812	0.8	49	2119	2219	2374	1.1	2.43	1505	1545	0.6
37865	SEYMOUR	155	16401	17796	19332	2.1	86	6293	6999	7682	2.5	2.55	4925	5398	2.2
37866	SHARPS CHAPEL	173	1531	1699	1915	2.5	91	630	715	824	3.0	2.38	446	497	2.6
37869	SNEEDVILLE	067	5315	5370	5367	0.2	31	2183	2276	2343	1.0	2.29	1515	1546	0.5
37870	SPEEDWELL	025	4414	4583	4808	0.9	56	1782	1891	2027	1.4	2.42	1356	1416	1.0
37871	STRAWBERRY PLAINS	093	8213	8580	9057	1.0	60	3162	3355	3587	1.4	2.56	2390	2483	0.9
37872	SUNBRIGHT	129	1986	2228	2406	2.7	93	766	881	974	3.4	2.51	568	642	2.9
37873	SURGOINSVILLE	073	3929	4490	4829	3.2	96	1609	1884	2066	3.8	2.38	1210	1391	3.3
37874	SWEETWATER	123	13978	14323	14733	0.6	43	5449	5674	5924	1.0	2.47	3970	4062	0.5
37876	SEVIERVILLE	155	20918	22662	24485	1.9	83	8237	9106	10004	2.4	2.48	6199	6734	2.0
37877	TALBOTT	089	7804	8434	8947	1.8	81	3065	3386	3654	2.4	2.49	2391	2592	1.9
37878	TALLASSEE	009	631	645	664	0.5	42	287	299	312	1.0	2.16	210	214	0.4
37879	TAZEWELL	025	9333	9980	10690	1.6	76	3792	4149	4548	2.1	2.36	2687	2884	1.7
37880	TEN MILE	121	4469	4806	5063	1.7	79	1809	1981	2120	2.2	2.43	1353	1455	1.7
37881	THORN HILL	057	1968	1957	1970	-0.1	14	769	782	805	0.4	2.50	576	575	0.0
37882	TOWNSEND	009	2447	2528	2641	0.8	50	1091	1157	1231	1.4	2.18	774	801	0.8
37885	VONORE	123	3623	3934	4175	2.0	84	1463	1630	1764	2.6	2.41	1105	1208	2.1
37886	WALLAND	009	3931	4188	4419	1.5	74	1580	1710	1828	1.9	2.45	1193	1268	1.4
37887	WARTBURG	129	6673	6683	6765	0.0	23	1952	2000	2075	0.6	2.53	1452	1462	0.2
37888	WASHBURN	057	2258	2307	2393	0.5	41	892	929	984	1.0	2.48	685	703	0.6
37890	WHITE PINE	089	5928	6379	6989	1.7	79	2392	2616	2908	2.1	2.44	1761	1886	1.6
37891	WHITESBURG	063	3225	3420	3552	1.4	70	1284	1393	1471	1.9	2.45	971	1034	1.5
37892	WINFIELD	151	2011	2226	2365	2.4	91	780	881	954	2.9	2.53	586	650	2.5
37902	KNOXVILLE	093	1236	1254	1283	0.3	36	745	763	793	0.6	1.22	63	60	-1.1
37909	KNOXVILLE	093	14453	15391	16329	1.5	73	6772	7349	7912	1.9	1.99	3206	3349	1.0
37912	KNOXVILLE	093	18483	19164	20041	0.9	54	8739	9143	9648	1.1	2.08	5025	5085	0.3
37914	KNOXVILLE	093	20126	20120	20763	0.0	19	8336	8428	8789	0.3	2.36	5497	5412	-0.4
37915	KNOXVILLE	093	5507	5472	5655	-0.2	13	2708	2728	2849	0.2	1.99	1326	1282	-0.8
37916	KNOXVILLE	093	11672	12101	12458	0.9	54	2765	3059	3309	2.4	1.66	324	337	0.9
37917	KNOXVILLE	093	25595	25427	26310	-0.2	13	11881	11921	12470	0.1	2.06	6055	5843	-0.8
37918	KNOXVILLE	093	35987	38359	40809	1.5	74	14711	15809	16982	1.7	2.36	9935	10426	1.1
37919	KNOXVILLE	093	27302	28144	29442	0.7	48	12962	13533	14326	1.0	2.04	6691	6682	0.0
37920	KNOXVILLE	093	38047	38163	39521	0.1	24	16191	16411	17178	0.3	2.28	10031	9861	-0.4
37921	KNOXVILLE	093	26254	26278	27203	0.0	22	10540	10673	11160	0.3	2.44	7106	7010	-0.3
37922	KNOXVILLE	093	43123	47646	51541	2.4	90	15634	17418	19005	2.6	2.72	12558	13730	2.1
37923	KNOXVILLE	093	26741	28181	29842	1.2	66	11658	12468	13363	1.6	2.25	7008	7219	0.7
37924	KNOXVILLE	093	8896	9230	9755	0.9	54	3754	3938	4203	1.1	2.34	2697	2757	0.5
37931	KNOXVILLE	093	19338	21080	22644	2.1	85	7686	8467	9193	2.3	2.48	5731	6190	1.8
37932	KNOXVILLE	093	11129	11850	12613	1.5	73	4238	4562	4902	1.8	2.60	3184	3361	1.3
37938	KNOXVILLE	093	13974	15123	16131	1.9	82	5234	5731	6177	2.2	2.63	4233	4557	1.8
38001	ALAMO	033	4603	4740	4884	0.7	47	1787	1864	1941	1.0	2.45	1245	1269	0.5
38002	ARLINGTON	157	17542	20617	22336	3.9	98	6356	7594	8457	4.3	2.67	5026	5915	3.9
38004	ATOKA	167	12001	13853	15676	3.4	97	4150	4864	5579	3.8	2.85	3397	3924	3.5
38006	BELLS	033	4747	4814	4946	0.3	35	1788	1829	1898	0.5	2.56	1301	1308	0.1
38008	BOLIVAR	069	10290	10545	10868	0.6	43	3844	4031	4251	1.1	2.41	2695	2769	0.6
38011	BRIGHTON	167	8931	10172	11440	3.1	95	3146	3640	4149	3.5	2.78	2577	2936	3.1
38012	BROWNSVILLE	075	15674	15753	16059	0.1	34	5903	6109	6358	0.8	2.54	4208	4267	0.3
38015	BURLISON	167	2740	2941	3213	1.7	78	1049	1145	1268	2.1	2.57	789	843	1.6
38016	CORDOVA	157	29044	34988	38637	4.5	99	11727	14308	15984	4.8	2.44	8080	9658	4.3
38017	COLLIERVILLE	157	35629	40043	42827	2.8	94	11729	13436	14601	3.3	2.97	10076	11402	3.0
38018	CORDOVA	157	24353	28950	31753	4.2	98	9567	11527	12792	4.5	2.47	6708	7856	3.8
38019	COVINGTON	167	15674	16501	17980	1.2	65	5847	6275	6955	1.7	2.58	4241	4461	1.2
38023	DRUMMONDS	167	2410	2639	2917	2.2	88	814	910	1021	2.7	2.90	656	723	2.3
	TENNESSEE					1.0					1.3	2.45			0.9
	UNITED STATES					1.2					1.3	2.58			1.1

# ZIP CODE	POST OFFICE NAME	RACE (%) White 2000	White 2004	Black 2000	Black 2004	Asian/Pacific 2000	Asian/Pacific 2004	% Hispanic Origin 2000	% Hispanic Origin 2004	2004 AGE DISTRIBUTION (%) 0-4	5-9	10-14	15-19	20-24	25-44	45-64	65-84	85+	18+	MEDIAN AGE 2004	% 2004 Males	% 2004 Females
37765	KYLES FORD	98.6	98.6	0.1	0.1	0.1	0.1	0.6	0.6	6.2	6.1	5.6	6.4	5.5	24.3	29.1	15.1	1.7	78.3	42.1	51.2	48.8
37766	LA FOLLETTE	98.4	98.2	0.2	0.2	0.1	0.2	0.5	0.6	5.5	5.6	6.5	6.0	5.8	26.5	26.2	15.9	2.1	78.8	41.0	47.9	52.1
37769	LAKE CITY	98.7	98.5	0.2	0.2	0.1	0.2	0.5	0.6	5.6	5.6	6.6	5.8	5.6	25.9	27.6	15.0	2.5	78.6	41.6	48.4	51.6
37770	LANCING	98.2	98.1	0.5	0.4	0.2	0.2	0.5	0.6	6.0	6.4	7.4	6.3	6.1	29.0	26.7	10.7	1.4	76.3	37.7	50.4	49.7
37771	LENOIR CITY	94.6	93.8	0.9	1.0	0.2	0.3	3.9	4.7	6.6	6.5	6.8	6.3	6.0	28.8	25.1	12.0	2.0	76.3	37.8	48.5	51.5
37772	LENOIR CITY	97.2	96.8	0.8	0.8	0.2	0.3	1.2	1.5	5.6	6.1	6.3	5.3	4.2	26.6	31.4	13.3	1.3	78.8	42.6	49.8	50.2
37774	LOUDON	96.1	95.7	1.5	1.6	0.3	0.3	1.8	2.2	5.0	5.2	5.4	4.7	4.3	22.6	29.7	21.2	1.9	81.5	47.2	48.8	51.2
37777	LOUISVILLE	92.9	92.0	4.7	5.3	0.4	0.5	1.3	1.6	5.1	5.3	5.9	6.1	7.1	32.1	27.6	9.9	1.0	80.0	37.7	50.2	49.8
37778	LOWLAND	94.9	93.6	1.5	1.4	0.0	0.0	5.9	7.8	5.7	5.7	7.1	7.1	5.7	28.4	27.0	12.1	1.4	77.3	39.3	50.4	49.7
37779	LUTTRELL	97.9	97.6	0.2	0.2	0.2	0.2	1.0	1.2	7.5	7.2	6.9	7.0	6.9	29.0	24.7	9.4	1.4	73.8	35.5	49.7	50.3
37801	MARYVILLE	94.9	94.3	2.4	2.6	0.6	0.8	1.3	1.6	6.5	6.5	6.6	6.2	6.2	29.3	25.8	11.7	1.4	76.8	37.8	48.3	51.7
37803	MARYVILLE	96.5	95.9	1.1	1.2	1.3	1.6	0.8	1.0	5.5	5.9	6.7	6.6	5.8	26.2	27.9	13.4	2.1	78.1	40.9	48.1	51.9
37804	MARYVILLE	95.7	95.1	2.0	2.2	0.8	1.0	1.0	1.2	5.9	6.1	6.6	6.1	6.1	27.7	25.2	13.9	2.6	78.1	39.7	47.5	52.5
37806	MASCOT	96.6	96.2	1.9	2.2	0.1	0.1	0.6	0.7	6.0	6.2	6.3	5.6	5.7	28.4	28.3	12.5	1.2	77.9	40.0	48.8	51.2
37807	MAYNARDVILLE	98.7	98.6	0.1	0.1	0.2	0.2	0.7	0.8	6.7	6.7	7.0	6.6	6.4	31.0	24.7	10.0	1.0	75.6	36.7	50.0	50.0
37809	MIDWAY	98.2	97.9	0.4	0.4	0.1	0.2	1.1	1.4	6.6	6.6	6.7	6.3	6.6	28.4	25.6	12.2	1.0	76.4	37.7	49.9	50.1
37810	MOHAWK	98.2	98.0	0.9	0.9	0.0	0.1	0.9	1.0	6.4	6.4	6.9	6.5	6.7	29.0	25.2	11.8	1.3	76.5	37.3	50.0	50.0
37811	MOORESBURG	98.8	98.6	0.2	0.2	0.2	0.2	0.7	0.8	6.3	6.4	6.6	5.9	5.7	28.9	27.8	11.6	0.9	77.3	38.9	50.7	49.4
37813	MORRISTOWN	89.8	88.6	4.6	4.9	0.4	0.5	6.4	7.8	6.9	6.6	6.4	5.8	6.7	29.2	24.7	12.2	1.6	76.6	36.9	48.7	51.3
37814	MORRISTOWN	89.0	87.7	4.9	5.0	0.9	1.1	6.8	8.2	6.5	6.5	6.3	5.5	6.1	29.3	25.6	12.7	1.5	77.5	38.1	49.8	50.2
37818	MOSHEIM	98.6	98.5	0.5	0.5	0.2	0.2	0.6	0.8	6.1	6.3	6.4	5.2	5.8	28.4	28.3	12.5	1.0	78.0	39.8	49.6	50.5
37819	NEWCOMB	98.0	98.0	0.6	0.5	0.0	0.0	0.9	0.9	6.6	6.6	7.0	7.4	5.9	28.1	26.2	11.3	0.9	75.5	36.8	50.5	49.5
37820	NEW MARKET	96.2	95.7	1.4	1.5	0.3	0.4	1.4	1.7	6.3	6.5	7.5	6.1	5.5	29.6	25.7	11.5	1.2	75.7	38.1	50.2	49.8
37821	NEWPORT	95.3	95.0	2.7	2.9	0.2	0.2	1.1	1.4	6.1	6.1	6.2	5.6	5.9	28.4	27.2	13.1	1.6	78.2	39.6	48.4	51.6
37825	NEW TAZEWELL	97.8	97.6	0.7	0.7	0.3	0.3	0.7	0.8	6.2	6.3	6.8	6.4	6.0	29.1	25.7	12.2	1.3	76.8	38.3	49.2	50.8
37826	NIOTA	94.5	93.9	3.6	3.9	0.7	0.9	0.9	1.1	6.4	6.8	7.3	5.9	5.4	29.3	26.6	11.2	1.1	75.8	38.1	49.9	50.1
37829	OAKDALE	98.8	98.7	0.0	0.0	0.2	0.3	0.2	0.2	7.4	7.4	6.8	6.3	6.4	28.8	25.1	10.9	0.8	74.6	36.0	50.5	49.5
37830	OAK RIDGE	87.3	86.0	7.9	8.4	2.1	2.6	1.9	2.3	4.8	5.2	6.7	6.7	5.6	22.0	28.7	17.4	3.0	78.9	44.3	47.0	53.0
37840	OLIVER SPRINGS	96.8	96.6	1.9	2.0	0.2	0.3	0.4	0.5	6.3	6.4	6.7	5.9	6.1	27.8	26.6	12.8	1.4	77.1	39.0	48.9	51.1
37841	ONEIDA	98.5	98.4	0.1	0.1	0.2	0.2	0.6	0.7	7.3	7.3	7.0	6.2	6.6	28.6	24.7	10.9	1.5	74.6	36.1	48.7	51.3
37843	PARROTTSVILLE	96.8	96.4	1.7	1.8	0.3	0.4	0.5	0.7	5.8	5.9	6.2	6.1	6.2	26.7	28.6	13.0	1.4	78.4	40.7	50.4	49.6
37846	PHILADELPHIA	96.2	95.7	1.3	1.4	0.2	0.2	1.6	2.0	7.2	7.2	7.4	6.8	5.7	29.4	25.1	10.4	1.0	74.1	36.5	51.0	49.0
37847	PIONEER	98.3	98.1	0.2	0.2	0.1	0.2	0.7	0.8	7.5	7.3	7.2	6.4	6.3	29.3	25.7	9.6	1.0	74.1	35.5	51.7	48.3
37848	POWDER SPRINGS	98.9	98.9	0.0	0.0	0.2	0.2	0.6	0.6	6.7	6.7	6.7	6.0	6.0	29.6	25.5	11.9	1.1	76.2	37.7	49.6	50.4
37849	POWELL	96.9	96.5	1.3	1.5	0.5	0.6	0.7	0.8	6.1	6.4	6.7	6.3	6.1	28.5	26.7	12.0	1.2	77.2	38.8	48.5	51.5
37852	ROBBINS	98.6	98.4	0.0	0.0	0.0	0.0	0.6	0.7	6.2	6.9	6.8	7.0	7.0	28.6	25.9	10.4	1.1	75.7	36.0	51.4	48.6
37853	ROCKFORD	93.9	93.3	4.3	4.7	0.3	0.4	0.9	1.1	5.4	5.9	6.2	6.0	6.1	28.9	27.8	12.5	1.1	78.8	39.6	48.6	51.4
37854	ROCKWOOD	95.3	95.0	3.2	3.3	0.2	0.3	0.5	0.6	6.0	6.1	6.1	5.6	5.0	25.2	27.7	16.1	2.3	78.4	42.2	47.6	52.4
37857	ROGERSVILLE	96.7	96.4	2.0	2.1	0.2	0.2	0.8	0.9	6.1	6.1	6.0	5.8	5.8	28.4	26.3	13.6	1.9	78.2	39.7	48.7	51.3
37860	RUSSELLVILLE	96.6	96.2	2.2	2.4	0.1	0.2	0.9	1.1	6.2	6.2	6.4	5.9	5.5	30.5	26.5	11.4	1.6	77.7	38.8	50.7	49.3
37861	RUTLEDGE	98.1	97.8	0.4	0.4	0.1	0.1	1.8	2.2	5.7	6.0	6.0	5.4	5.5	29.3	27.2	13.0	1.9	79.0	39.9	50.6	49.4
37862	SEVIERVILLE	96.5	96.0	0.9	0.9	0.8	0.9	1.7	2.1	5.8	5.8	6.1	5.8	5.8	28.1	27.0	13.8	2.0	78.9	40.2	48.3	51.7
37863	PIGEON FORGE	95.5	94.7	0.6	0.7	1.1	1.4	3.3	4.0	6.1	6.1	6.6	5.8	6.5	28.9	24.8	13.5	1.8	77.6	38.4	48.6	51.4
37865	SEYMOUR	97.9	97.6	0.5	0.5	0.4	0.5	0.7	0.9	6.0	6.4	6.9	6.3	5.4	29.2	27.7	11.1	1.0	76.7	38.9	49.2	50.8
37866	SHARPS CHAPEL	98.8	98.8	0.0	0.0	0.1	0.1	0.5	0.7	5.1	5.2	5.6	4.9	5.3	25.5	30.4	16.8	1.1	81.1	44.0	51.1	48.9
37869	SNEEDVILLE	97.8	97.8	0.5	0.5	0.1	0.1	0.4	0.4	5.4	5.5	6.5	6.1	6.6	27.1	26.7	14.2	1.8	79.1	40.1	48.7	51.3
37870	SPEEDWELL	98.9	98.7	0.1	0.1	0.1	0.1	1.0	1.2	4.9	5.4	6.8	5.6	5.2	26.9	28.9	15.0	1.3	79.4	41.9	49.7	50.3
37871	STRAWBERRY PLAINS	96.7	96.3	1.7	1.8	0.2	0.2	0.7	0.9	6.3	6.3	6.5	5.9	5.7	29.7	26.3	12.3	1.1	77.4	38.9	49.4	50.6
37872	SUNBRIGHT	98.1	97.9	0.1	0.1	0.2	0.2	0.9	1.0	7.1	6.9	6.2	6.7	6.6	28.0	27.3	10.1	1.2	75.7	37.0	50.2	49.8
37873	SURGOINSVILLE	98.8	98.6	0.2	0.2	0.0	0.0	1.9	2.2	5.6	5.8	6.6	6.1	5.5	29.9	27.0	12.5	1.1	78.4	39.1	49.9	50.1
37874	SWEETWATER	91.8	91.1	5.1	5.3	0.7	0.9	1.7	2.1	6.2	6.3	7.0	6.6	6.4	27.7	25.3	12.7	1.9	76.6	38.4	48.4	51.6
37876	SEVIERVILLE	98.1	97.9	0.4	0.4	0.3	0.3	0.8	1.0	5.9	6.1	6.4	5.8	5.6	29.3	28.7	11.1	1.0	78.0	39.6	49.8	50.2
37877	TALBOTT	97.3	96.8	0.8	0.8	0.3	0.4	1.3	1.6	6.4	6.6	6.3	5.3	5.2	28.8	27.9	12.5	1.0	77.4	39.8	49.8	50.2
37878	TALLASSEE	98.4	98.3	0.2	0.2	0.5	0.6	0.8	0.8	5.1	5.4	5.3	5.3	4.8	25.3	34.6	13.3	0.9	81.2	44.3	51.2	48.8
37879	TAZEWELL	97.5	97.2	1.4	1.4	0.3	0.3	0.6	0.8	6.0	6.2	6.9	5.8	5.7	28.6	26.1	13.0	1.7	77.4	38.7	47.9	52.1
37880	TEN MILE	97.5	97.3	1.0	1.0	0.2	0.3	0.7	0.8	6.5	6.6	6.1	5.2	5.9	27.1	29.1	12.6	0.9	77.8	39.8	50.8	49.2
37881	THORN HILL	98.6	98.4	0.7	0.8	0.1	0.1	0.4	0.4	5.8	6.1	6.4	6.0	6.3	27.5	28.0	12.8	1.1	78.0	39.3	50.6	49.4
37882	TOWNSEND	97.8	97.5	0.1	0.1	0.3	0.4	1.0	1.2	4.2	4.9	4.0	4.5	3.8	24.1	34.7	17.7	2.1	84.1	47.9	50.1	49.9
37885	VONORE	95.8	95.1	0.2	0.2	0.2	0.3	2.5	3.1	6.8	6.8	6.8	5.8	5.6	28.4	26.8	11.9	1.0	76.1	38.3	50.6	49.4
37886	WALLAND	97.6	97.3	0.1	0.1	0.3	0.4	0.9	1.1	5.2	6.2	6.8	5.7	5.2	28.3	29.9	11.4	1.3	78.4	40.4	50.3	49.7
37887	WARTBURG	93.1	92.6	6.2	6.7	0.1	0.1	0.8	1.0	4.8	5.0	5.6	5.6	7.5	37.0	23.8	9.1	1.6	81.3	36.9	60.4	39.6
37888	WASHBURN	98.6	98.5	0.0	0.0	0.2	0.2	0.7	0.9	6.2	6.2	6.9	6.4	6.3	29.6	25.4	11.7	1.3	76.8	37.8	49.1	50.9
37890	WHITE PINE	97.0	96.4	0.8	1.0	0.2	0.2	1.5	1.9	7.1	6.9	6.3	5.6	5.8	28.1	26.4	12.5	1.1	76.3	38.6	49.7	50.3
37891	WHITESBURG	98.0	97.8	1.0	1.1	0.1	0.1	0.8	1.1	6.4	6.6	6.6	5.9	5.6	30.0	26.5	11.1	1.3	76.8	38.5	50.2	49.8
37892	WINFIELD	98.9	98.7	0.0	0.0	0.1	0.0	0.3	0.4	7.8	7.7	7.1	6.2	6.5	31.9	23.2	8.8	0.9	73.5	34.0	49.7	50.3
37902	KNOXVILLE	80.7	78.3	15.9	17.9	0.9	1.0	1.3	1.4	0.5	0.4	0.2	3.2	22.3	34.9	24.5	12.8	1.4	98.5	38.0	58.1	41.9
37909	KNOXVILLE	88.9	87.1	6.1	7.1	2.1	2.5	2.3	2.8	5.2	4.4	4.3	5.7	13.5	32.9	18.3	12.0	3.7	83.1	33.1	47.1	52.9
37912	KNOXVILLE	89.3	87.7	6.8	7.7	1.6	1.9	1.2	1.5	6.7	6.1	5.3	4.8	7.0	32.0	22.8	13.7	1.7	79.5	36.9	47.4	52.6
37914	KNOXVILLE	56.4	54.9	41.4	42.8	0.3	0.3	0.8	0.9	5.5	5.6	6.6	6.4	5.5	25.0	27.9	15.2	2.4	78.4	42.0	47.2	52.8
37915	KNOXVILLE	13.2	12.1	84.4	85.5	0.1	0.1	1.0	0.9	10.7	8.0	6.5	8.6	8.5	25.5	22.5	8.6	1.2	71.1	30.8	42.6	57.4
37916	KNOXVILLE	84.7	82.0	7.4	8.3	5.6	7.2	1.4	1.7	0.6	0.4	0.3	39.7	41.7	12.6	2.8	1.3	0.6	98.4	21.1	51.9	48.2
37917	KNOXVILLE	82.2	80.6	14.2	15.3	0.6	0.7	1.7	2.0	5.7	5.5	5.8	5.6	6.4	30.2	24.0	14.1	2.8	79.7	39.2	47.6	52.4
37918	KNOXVILLE	94.8	94.1	3.2	3.6	0.5	0.7	1.1	1.3	6.4	6.3	6.0	5.5	5.9	30.2	25.0	12.7	2.1	77.9	38.6	48.1	51.9
37919	KNOXVILLE	90.9	89.4	4.3	4.9	2.7	3.2	1.9	2.3	5.3	5.0	5.2	5.8	8.7	28.9	25.2	13.3	2.7	81.0	38.3	47.9	52.1
37920	KNOXVILLE	93.4	92.6	4.0	4.4	0.5	0.6	1.1	1.4	5.7	5.7	5.7	5.8	8.5	28.9	24.5	13.3	1.8	79.7	38.1	48.9	51.1
37921	KNOXVILLE	76.5	75.2	20.1	21.0	0.7	0.8	1.4	1.6	8.1	7.9	7.2	6.2	7.0	31.5	21.6	9.4	1.1	73.2	33.7	47.4	52.6
37922	KNOXVILLE	93.8	92.6	2.3	2.6	2.5	3.1	1.3	1.5	6.2	7.0	8.0	7.1	5.0	26.0	30.6	9.2	1.0	74.1	40.1	49.2	50.8
37923	KNOXVILLE	90.6	89.2	4.8	5.4	2.5	3.0	1.8	2.2	5.9	5.7	6.4	6.5	7.6	32.8	24.8	9.3	1.0	78.1	36.0	48.8	51.2
37924	KNOXVILLE	92.0	91.0	6.0	6.7	0.5	0.6	1.1	1.4	5.6	5.8	5.9	5.0	5.2	28.4	28.0	14.5	1.5	79.6	41.2	49.0	51.0
37931	KNOXVILLE	95.1	94.5	2.5	2.8	0.9	1.1	1.0	1.2	7.0	7.1	7.0	5.5	5.3	30.8	26.7	9.8	0.8	75.3	38.0	49.1	50.9
37932	KNOXVILLE	93.9	92.9	3.2	3.7	1.4	1.8	1.0	1.2	6.6	6.8	6.8	6.1	5.3	30.4	28.9	8.3	0.7	76.0	38.7	49.0	51.0
37938	KNOXVILLE	98.4	98.0	0.3	0.3	0.3	0.4	0.5	0.6	6.0	6.5	7.0	6.4	5.3	27.9	28.4	11.3	1.2	76.6	40.1	49.2	50.8
38001	ALAMO	83.5	82.6	14.3	14.8	0.1	0.1	2.5	3.2	6.4	6.4	6.9	6.2	6.1	26.5	23.2	15.2	3.2	76.7	39.4	47.0	53.0
38002	ARLINGTON	82.4	78.7	15.4	18.8	0.9	1.1	1.1	1.4	7.3	7.4	6.9	6.1	5.0	31.0	26.7	8.6	0.9	74.4	37.1	49.1	50.9
38004	ATOKA	85.5	84.0	11.9	13.1	0.6	0.7	1.5	1.8	7.5	7.5	8.4	7.7	6.7	30.3	23.9	7.4	0.7	71.9	34.5	49.8	50.2
38006	BELLS	77.1	75.8	15.8	15.8	0.1	0.1	12.4	14.8	7.4	7.2	7.3	6.1	6.3	28.3	22.5	12.2	2.8	74.4	36.1	49.2	50.9
38008	BOLIVAR	50.8	49.1	48.0	49.5	0.4	0.4	0.7	0.8	6.4	6.7	7.2	7.4	6.6	27.2	24.5	11.8	2.2	75.0	37.3	48.6	51.4
38011	BRIGHTON	86.9	85.7	10.9	11.8	0.4	0.5	1.3	1.5	7.1	7.3	8.4	7.5	6.5	28.9	24.5	8.7	1.1	72.6	35.6	49.5	50.5
38012	BROWNSVILLE	44.7	43.3	52.8	53.8	0.2	0.2	3.0	3.6	7.3	7.4	7.9	6.7	7.1	27.0	23.4	11.1	2.1	73.3	35.2	46.5	53.5
38015	BURLISON	93.9	93.4	5.1	5.5	0.1	0.1	0.7	0.7	6.6	6.8	7.2	6.5	6.4	28.1	26.3	11.2	1.0	75.5	37.9	50.1	50.0
38016	CORDOVA	86.4	82.8	8.3	10.7	3.6	4.4	1.9	2.4	7.9	7.7	6.8	5.4	6.0	34.5	23.8	7.0	0.9	74.1	34.7	48.2	51.8
38017	COLLIERVILLE	88.0	86.1	9.3	10.6	1.4	1.8	1.5	1.8	7.3	8.4	9.5	7.8	4.9	28.5	26.6	6.5	0.7	69.6	36.6	49.5	50.6
38018	CORDOVA	86.8	83.5	7.5	9.6	3.9	4.7	1.8	2.3	8.3	7.2	6.5	5.6	6.6	35.0	22.7	6.8	1.3	74.3	33.9	48.6	51.5
38019	COVINGTON	66.1	64.6	32.2	33.5	0.4	0.5	0.8	0.9	7.4	7.2	7.7	7.2	7.1	26.4	23.5	11.7	2.0	73.3	35.8	47.2	52.9
38023	DRUMMONDS	76.1	75.3	22.1	22.7	0.3	0.3	0.7	0.8	6.8	6.9	8.0	8.3	7.2	27.1	26.2	8.6	0.9	73.2	35.6	48.4	51.6
	TENNESSEE	80.2	79.4	16.4	16.7	1.0	1.3	2.2	2.6	6.6	6.5	6.8	6.6	7.0	29.0	24.8	11.1	1.5	76.3	36.8	48.9	51.1
	UNITED STATES	75.1	73.6	12.3	12.5	3.8	4.2	12.5	14.1	6.9	6.7	7.2	7.0	7.3	28.6	23.8	10.8	1.7	75.1	36.0	49.1	50.9

#	POST OFFICE NAME	2004 Per Capita Income	2004 HH Income Base	2004 Household Income Distribution (%): Less than $25,000	$25,000 to $49,999	$50,000 to $99,999	$100,000 to $149,999	$150,000 or More	Median Household Income: 2004	2009	2004 National Centile	2004 State Centile	2004 Home Value Base	2004 Home Value Distribution (%): Less than $50,000	$50,000 to $89,999	$90,000 to $174,999	$175,000 to $399,999	$400,000 or More	2004 Median Home Value
37765	KYLES FORD	11150	337	70.0	22.3	5.6	0.0	2.1	15959	17606	1	2	272	53.3	30.2	16.5	0.0	0.0	48657
37766	LA FOLLETTE	14576	7862	50.2	30.5	15.8	2.3	1.1	24814	27155	4	7	5655	32.5	35.0	24.9	7.1	0.5	68310
37769	LAKE CITY	14667	2546	45.7	33.6	17.4	2.4	0.9	27898	31496	8	14	1798	31.9	31.2	29.3	6.8	0.8	75130
37770	LANCING	13039	1059	45.7	33.4	18.0	2.8	0.0	27000	29801	7	13	894	36.7	35.1	23.5	4.3	0.5	63441
37771	LENOIR CITY	19631	5802	29.8	33.9	29.5	5.2	1.6	38203	43479	40	61	4157	19.9	32.7	34.6	10.3	2.5	86880
37772	LENOIR CITY	28484	3801	20.3	27.2	35.5	10.1	7.0	52343	59251	76	91	3240	7.5	17.9	43.2	22.4	9.0	125260
37774	LOUDON	25106	6689	25.3	29.6	31.0	9.3	4.8	46040	52565	64	82	5478	11.8	23.6	31.0	21.2	12.5	119240
37777	LOUISVILLE	24690	5131	28.0	33.9	26.1	8.5	3.5	39617	44709	45	67	3282	18.3	13.1	38.8	24.7	5.1	126484
37778	LOWLAND	17716	55	29.1	34.6	30.9	3.6	1.8	41344	46732	51	73	45	26.7	20.0	33.3	17.8	2.2	95000
37779	LUTTRELL	15754	1569	40.4	34.9	19.4	2.9	2.4	30521	34456	14	21	1261	33.3	29.3	31.4	5.6	0.4	75583
37801	MARYVILLE	20225	8297	31.4	32.6	28.1	6.1	1.8	37348	42188	37	58	6234	19.3	18.1	45.4	15.5	1.7	106843
37803	MARYVILLE	26137	11444	22.5	29.0	33.5	9.4	5.7	48881	55110	70	86	9305	8.0	12.1	51.7	24.5	3.9	133330
37804	MARYVILLE	19372	8450	30.6	32.6	30.3	5.3	1.3	39771	44792	45	68	6413	12.4	24.0	49.5	13.0	1.1	108154
37806	MASCOT	15807	1161	33.4	39.5	25.0	2.1	0.0	33986	39663	24	43	947	32.4	28.8	27.8	10.1	0.8	71288
37807	MAYNARDVILLE	15222	3881	42.1	33.7	19.4	3.8	1.1	30510	34139	14	21	3078	29.2	28.5	33.1	8.6	0.6	81222
37809	MIDWAY	14271	796	36.4	42.7	18.7	1.3	0.9	31995	36166	18	30	647	23.0	40.7	25.5	8.7	2.2	76096
37810	MOHAWK	15118	710	37.0	41.8	17.2	3.5	0.4	31007	35191	15	24	573	23.0	35.1	31.9	8.4	1.6	81389
37811	MOORESBURG	14684	1568	44.1	33.6	19.1	2.6	0.6	27856	31658	8	14	1317	31.9	30.0	28.6	8.5	1.1	74402
37813	MORRISTOWN	16362	6802	37.9	34.5	23.9	2.7	1.1	32413	36507	19	33	4665	17.5	39.6	36.4	5.9	0.6	84646
37814	MORRISTOWN	23132	12754	32.8	31.1	25.3	6.7	4.1	35919	40392	31	53	9250	12.0	26.9	43.1	15.9	2.1	103698
37818	MOSHEIM	17418	2035	32.3	35.4	28.6	2.8	0.9	35386	39178	29	50	1679	20.9	36.0	35.0	7.0	1.2	82799
37819	NEWCOMB	10646	230	51.3	40.9	7.0	0.4	0.4	23779	25626	4	5	185	60.0	27.6	9.2	3.2	0.0	42600
37820	NEW MARKET	19476	2883	30.0	36.4	27.5	3.9	2.2	36958	41295	35	57	2359	21.2	27.1	38.5	11.3	2.0	92128
37821	NEWPORT	15946	9255	46.7	30.8	17.9	3.2	1.6	26983	29818	7	13	6771	30.4	31.2	30.4	7.4	0.6	76663
37825	NEW TAZEWELL	15507	3361	44.5	31.0	20.3	2.9	1.3	28401	31321	9	16	2659	30.5	30.1	31.3	7.4	0.9	77301
37826	NIOTA	18772	1689	32.4	32.7	29.5	3.6	1.8	37825	42550	39	60	1397	19.4	25.8	40.8	11.4	2.6	96101
37829	OAKDALE	16355	791	31.7	38.9	25.2	1.9	2.3	35508	40168	30	50	673	25.9	39.8	25.0	8.3	1.0	72900
37830	OAK RIDGE	28315	12457	25.1	28.1	28.7	12.0	6.1	46441	52900	65	83	8802	4.7	27.8	44.5	19.8	3.3	114165
37840	OLIVER SPRINGS	18223	4110	35.2	31.7	27.3	5.0	0.8	35340	39800	29	49	3277	29.7	30.2	32.9	6.1	1.1	79121
37841	ONEIDA	16458	3602	45.5	32.6	18.0	2.1	1.8	27475	30061	8	13	2731	34.0	30.4	26.4	7.6	1.7	70457
37843	PARROTTSVILLE	16421	1492	39.7	34.8	20.0	4.4	1.2	31802	35220	17	29	1224	28.8	26.5	31.0	11.7	2.0	83158
37846	PHILADELPHIA	17282	1438	31.4	35.3	27.1	3.7	2.4	37990	43031	39	60	1184	17.2	29.7	38.9	10.0	4.3	93663
37847	PIONEER	12212	1066	54.4	31.2	11.4	1.8	1.1	22394	24918	3	4	868	60.1	22.5	13.1	3.1	1.2	40737
37848	POWDER SPRINGS	14640	211	49.8	28.4	15.6	2.8	3.3	25276	28389	5	9	179	38.6	28.5	21.2	8.4	3.4	66389
37849	POWELL	23603	8770	23.8	28.7	34.2	9.7	3.6	47106	54656	66	84	7224	13.7	19.8	50.5	15.0	0.9	112063
37852	ROBBINS	13283	1141	48.0	33.0	16.5	1.1	1.4	26019	28108	6	10	925	47.2	28.0	19.5	4.5	0.8	52550
37853	ROCKFORD	20253	1553	33.2	33.0	26.7	5.2	2.0	36379	40863	33	55	1165	29.4	21.7	35.3	10.8	2.8	87857
37854	ROCKWOOD	17764	4871	42.1	29.8	23.5	3.2	1.4	31117	34834	15	24	3651	29.9	30.6	28.4	9.9	1.3	75530
37857	ROGERSVILLE	17923	7764	39.9	31.4	23.9	2.8	2.0	32457	36081	19	34	6029	23.1	32.2	32.9	11.1	0.7	83114
37860	RUSSELLVILLE	19914	1442	27.9	36.2	28.4	5.3	2.2	41104	46647	50	71	1184	11.4	23.1	53.3	12.1	0.2	107625
37861	RUTLEDGE	18106	3175	42.1	30.3	21.9	3.5	2.2	29874	33682	12	19	2610	29.8	28.6	28.4	10.9	2.3	80833
37862	SEVIERVILLE	21442	8101	35.8	32.8	22.0	6.1	3.4	35513	38935	30	51	5339	11.7	15.1	40.1	28.9	4.2	131436
37863	PIGEON FORGE	18095	2219	36.8	37.1	19.3	4.2	2.6	32503	36598	19	35	1442	19.1	12.9	38.4	27.5	2.1	124615
37865	SEYMOUR	20889	6999	23.6	34.0	33.4	7.0	2.0	44287	48770	59	79	5696	8.8	16.1	55.6	17.1	2.5	119260
37866	SHARPS CHAPEL	15145	715	50.9	25.6	16.2	6.3	1.0	24166	26523	4	6	607	28.3	33.4	15.2	18.0	5.1	74273
37869	SNEEDVILLE	14400	2276	55.1	28.1	14.0	1.9	1.0	21759	23600	3	4	1786	46.4	26.5	20.4	5.9	0.8	57558
37870	SPEEDWELL	14108	1891	46.2	34.6	16.5	2.0	0.8	27383	30283	8	13	1582	28.8	27.2	31.4	9.5	3.2	82083
37871	STRAWBERRY PLAINS	19578	3355	29.6	34.9	28.6	5.2	1.7	38992	43646	43	64	2771	21.1	25.6	39.7	12.5	1.1	94263
37872	SUNBRIGHT	13454	881	47.3	32.4	16.9	2.6	0.8	26284	28347	6	11	720	42.2	35.4	15.7	3.9	2.8	56667
37873	SURGOINSVILLE	18115	1884	32.9	37.5	24.7	3.8	1.1	38202	42268	40	61	1552	22.8	31.7	36.5	6.8	2.3	85205
37874	SWEETWATER	17653	5674	36.7	32.6	23.3	5.4	2.0	33882	37469	24	42	4484	24.7	30.2	34.3	8.5	2.3	85045
37876	SEVIERVILLE	19838	9106	31.4	34.3	26.9	4.8	2.6	37504	41295	37	59	7446	17.3	18.5	40.0	21.2	2.9	112159
37877	TALBOTT	20277	3386	25.8	34.7	31.4	5.5	2.6	41204	45146	50	72	2868	12.2	26.7	47.7	11.2	2.3	102641
37878	TALLASSEE	22665	299	31.8	38.8	19.4	5.4	4.7	38556	43203	41	62	249	22.9	23.7	29.3	18.1	6.0	96538
37879	TAZEWELL	14880	4149	49.7	29.9	16.9	2.2	1.4	25175	27823	5	8	3186	31.8	37.1	24.5	5.6	1.0	69749
37880	TEN MILE	16878	1981	35.7	36.9	21.9	4.3	1.2	32709	37133	20	36	1644	27.9	24.9	24.8	17.0	5.4	86134
37881	THORN HILL	13239	782	48.2	34.3	15.0	2.3	0.3	25903	29385	6	10	660	34.9	30.5	25.0	9.4	0.3	69508
37882	TOWNSEND	23078	1157	30.6	34.9	25.3	6.2	2.9	39743	45642	45	67	956	15.7	17.8	30.5	26.7	9.3	122269
37885	VONORE	18776	1630	30.9	35.7	27.2	5.0	1.3	37306	41379	37	58	1333	19.5	23.6	32.9	19.1	4.9	101987
37886	WALLAND	19948	1710	28.5	32.5	31.4	6.0	1.7	41568	47118	52	74	1438	23.4	24.8	33.3	15.6	2.9	92476
37887	WARTBURG	14407	2000	40.8	33.9	20.8	3.6	1.1	30546	33354	14	22	1601	26.0	43.2	25.6	5.1	0.1	72135
37888	WASHBURN	14994	929	46.6	33.5	13.1	3.7	3.1	27625	31368	8	14	786	37.8	30.5	23.4	5.2	3.1	66593
37890	WHITE PINE	17543	2616	34.3	36.6	23.6	3.9	1.7	35260	39101	28	49	2094	24.4	25.1	35.8	11.9	2.8	90645
37891	WHITESBURG	17353	1393	37.2	34.2	24.1	3.7	0.9	34392	38486	25	45	1145	21.4	32.9	35.9	8.2	1.6	86040
37892	WINFIELD	16567	881	47.5	32.7	14.9	1.9	3.1	26244	28691	6	10	701	37.1	34.7	19.7	7.0	1.6	62870
37902	KNOXVILLE	16595	763	79.8	8.3	8.7	1.3	2.0	11540	13725	1	1	70	0.0	0.0	62.9	37.1	0.0	163750
37909	KNOXVILLE	26534	7349	31.2	32.6	23.7	8.8	3.8	39245	44277	44	65	2754	2.0	15.0	61.1	19.4	2.6	125285
37912	KNOXVILLE	20839	9143	34.3	35.6	24.5	4.3	1.3	34835	39948	27	47	5100	8.0	36.0	50.9	4.5	0.5	94951
37914	KNOXVILLE	18227	8428	39.3	30.8	23.3	4.8	1.8	33695	38716	23	42	5785	20.0	34.9	35.4	9.2	0.5	84094
37915	KNOXVILLE	11049	2728	74.5	14.6	8.3	1.7	0.8	11585	14460	1	1	577	25.8	55.8	13.0	5.4	0.0	65875
37916	KNOXVILLE	11814	3059	77.5	16.9	5.0	0.2	0.5	12233	14129	1	1	184	12.0	28.3	47.8	12.0	0.0	123214
37917	KNOXVILLE	16748	11921	48.4	31.5	16.1	2.6	1.4	25871	30080	6	10	6227	17.5	54.9	24.6	3.1	0.0	73595
37918	KNOXVILLE	23257	15809	26.8	32.1	30.3	7.7	3.2	42244	49448	54	75	11384	9.3	25.3	51.4	12.9	1.2	104998
37919	KNOXVILLE	40102	13533	31.1	22.6	24.9	10.0	11.4	45085	52469	61	80	7257	5.4	11.6	36.7	30.2	16.1	161810
37920	KNOXVILLE	20945	16411	37.2	29.8	24.1	6.5	2.4	34001	39133	24	43	10774	14.0	33.6	37.9	12.4	2.1	92875
37921	KNOXVILLE	18122	10673	36.5	29.3	27.4	5.2	1.6	35416	41385	29	50	6723	16.5	31.1	47.1	5.1	0.2	91916
37922	KNOXVILLE	39629	17418	9.7	16.6	34.4	21.2	18.0	81795	94517	96	99	15333	1.5	4.2	38.9	44.4	11.1	193349
37923	KNOXVILLE	30660	12468	17.9	28.5	35.3	12.1	6.2	53459	63109	78	92	7473	1.7	10.5	60.9	24.5	2.5	147247
37924	KNOXVILLE	22228	3938	28.1	31.0	32.5	6.0	2.3	43103	50079	56	78	3108	14.6	27.3	44.8	11.7	1.6	98819
37931	KNOXVILLE	25171	8467	17.9	30.4	35.6	12.4	3.7	51359	60568	74	90	6749	13.2	15.4	48.7	21.3	1.3	119464
37932	KNOXVILLE	30939	4562	13.2	24.4	39.4	16.0	7.1	62142	72623	86	96	3792	9.8	10.1	49.3	26.0	4.7	138687
37938	KNOXVILLE	26297	5731	18.2	26.9	39.1	11.9	3.9	54410	63704	79	92	5052	8.4	13.3	55.7	21.4	1.2	125868
38001	ALAMO	17640	1864	40.5	29.2	23.6	3.9	2.8	31994	35563	18	30	1394	21.5	35.1	32.6	10.4	0.4	83741
38002	ARLINGTON	28634	7594	12.7	23.5	42.1	15.1	6.6	63564	73155	87	96	6480	6.3	10.7	39.1	38.8	5.1	164447
38004	ATOKA	22789	4864	19.9	26.6	39.7	10.4	3.4	52797	58718	77	91	4045	9.6	17.7	54.9	17.4	0.4	117671
38006	BELLS	16145	1829	37.9	32.0	25.4	3.1	1.5	32427	36673	19	34	1367	25.1	37.4	29.3	7.7	0.6	77782
38008	BOLIVAR	17290	4031	42.2	29.6	23.7	3.1	1.5	31855	35272	17	29	2812	22.2	43.7	26.8	6.8	0.5	72113
38011	BRIGHTON	20537	3640	21.2	28.1	40.6	8.1	2.0	50539	55841	73	89	3011	9.6	24.2	52.0	13.4	0.8	108050
38012	BROWNSVILLE	16847	6109	41.7	28.6	23.1	4.3	2.3	30690	34347	14	22	4081	16.0	41.0	32.5	9.4	1.1	82591
38015	BURLISON	19891	1145	27.9	29.8	33.3	6.6	2.5	44510	50155	60	79	945	18.4	31.1	40.6	8.7	1.2	90495
38016	CORDOVA	35776	14308	10.8	20.3	40.5	19.0	9.4	69991	81050	91	97	10572	0.5	3.5	44.9	45.8	5.3	176829
38017	COLLIERVILLE	35398	13436	9.3	14.8	34.1	23.2	18.6	85727	99662	96	99	11839	2.4	5.8	23.8	57.2	10.9	214558
38018	CORDOVA	35852	11527	9.3	20.1	40.4	20.6	9.7	72986	83812	92	98	8434	0.7	1.5	54.6	37.6	5.7	165648
38019	COVINGTON	19051	6275	35.8	26.3	29.2	5.9	2.7	38737	44302	42	63	4222	17.5	35.3	36.8	9.4	1.0	86937
38023	DRUMMONDS	18835	910	25.1	35.8	31.4	4.5	3.2	42645	48500	55	77	740	22.7	36.1	33.1	7.7	0.4	81558
	TENNESSEE	22498		30.2	30.2	28.1	7.5	4.1	40531	46137				15.0	25.0	39.4	17.3	3.3	104905
	UNITED STATES	25866		24.7	27.1	30.8	10.9	6.5	48124	56710				10.9	15.0	33.7	30.1	10.4	145905

ZIP CODE #	POST OFFICE NAME	FINANCIAL SERVICES: Auto Loan	Home Loan	Invest-ments	Retire-ment Plans	THE HOME: Home Improvements: Home Repair	Lawn & Garden	Furnishings: Comput-ers & Hard-ware	Major Appli-ances	TV, Radio, Sound Equip-ment	Furni-ture	ENTERTAINMENT: Dine out/Carry out	Sports Equip-ment	Fees & Tickets	Toys & Games	Travel	Cable TV	PERSONAL: Apparel & Services	Auto Repairs	Health Insur-ance	Pets & Supplies
37765	KYLES FORD	50	34	15	29	38	44	32	41	39	33	46	49	28	44	33	42	42	40	50	58
37766	LA FOLLETTE	58	42	27	38	46	54	44	50	51	43	60	58	39	56	44	54	55	50	61	66
37769	LAKE CITY	60	43	27	38	47	55	43	51	50	44	60	59	38	56	43	54	55	51	61	68
37770	LANCING	63	42	19	36	48	55	41	51	49	41	58	61	35	54	41	53	52	50	63	72
37771	LENOIR CITY	77	64	48	61	69	76	63	70	68	62	82	82	60	82	64	71	77	69	78	89
37772	LENOIR CITY	108	97	78	95	103	111	93	102	97	92	118	120	90	120	95	99	112	100	108	126
37774	LOUDON	94	79	60	74	84	96	77	86	84	77	101	96	73	96	79	88	94	85	99	107
37777	LOUISVILLE	80	73	69	73	74	80	76	77	77	75	96	91	74	94	75	76	92	78	78	90
37778	LOWLAND	86	57	26	49	65	75	55	69	67	56	78	83	47	74	56	72	71	68	85	98
37779	LUTTRELL	75	54	29	48	59	67	52	62	60	53	71	74	45	67	52	63	65	62	73	85
37801	MARYVILLE	77	64	51	60	68	75	64	70	69	63	84	82	60	83	64	71	79	69	77	88
37803	MARYVILLE	97	94	86	90	97	104	89	95	91	89	112	110	89	113	91	93	108	93	99	114
37804	MARYVILLE	71	66	58	63	68	75	65	68	69	64	84	79	65	85	66	70	80	68	74	81
37806	MASCOT	72	48	22	42	55	63	46	58	56	47	66	69	40	62	47	60	60	58	72	83
37807	MAYNARDVILLE	71	52	29	46	57	64	50	59	57	51	68	70	44	64	50	60	63	59	70	81
37809	MIDWAY	70	47	21	40	53	61	45	56	54	46	64	67	38	60	46	59	58	56	70	80
37810	MOHAWK	70	47	21	40	53	61	45	56	54	46	64	67	38	60	46	58	58	56	69	80
37811	MOORESBURG	67	45	20	39	51	58	43	54	52	44	61	65	37	58	44	56	56	54	67	77
37813	MORRISTOWN	64	52	39	49	55	62	53	58	58	52	70	68	49	69	53	60	66	58	65	73
37814	MORRISTOWN	91	76	56	72	81	90	75	83	81	74	98	97	70	97	75	84	92	82	92	105
37818	MOSHEIM	77	54	29	48	61	69	52	63	61	53	72	76	46	69	53	65	66	63	76	88
37819	NEWCOMB	49	33	15	28	37	42	31	39	38	32	45	47	27	42	32	41	40	39	48	56
37820	NEW MARKET	81	71	53	68	73	79	68	75	72	69	88	87	65	85	68	73	83	74	79	91
37821	NEWPORT	64	47	30	43	51	59	48	55	55	48	65	65	43	62	48	58	60	55	65	73
37825	NEW TAZEWELL	70	47	22	41	53	61	46	57	55	46	64	68	39	61	46	59	59	56	70	80
37826	NIOTA	83	59	32	53	66	75	57	69	66	58	79	82	50	76	58	71	72	68	83	96
37829	OAKDALE	81	54	25	47	62	71	52	66	63	53	74	78	45	70	53	68	68	65	81	93
37830	OAK RIDGE	85	88	94	86	89	98	88	89	89	87	110	101	90	110	90	90	107	89	92	99
37840	OLIVER SPRINGS	74	60	43	56	64	71	59	66	64	59	77	77	54	75	59	66	72	65	74	84
37841	ONEIDA	73	49	24	43	56	65	49	60	58	49	68	71	42	65	49	62	62	59	73	83
37843	PARROTTSVILLE	76	51	23	44	58	66	49	61	59	50	70	73	42	66	50	64	63	61	76	87
37846	PHILADELPHIA	85	60	31	53	66	75	58	70	67	59	80	83	50	75	58	71	73	69	83	97
37847	PIONEER	61	41	19	35	46	53	40	49	48	40	56	59	34	53	40	51	51	49	61	70
37848	POWDER SPRINGS	70	47	21	41	53	61	45	57	55	46	64	68	39	61	46	59	58	56	70	81
37849	POWELL	88	86	76	84	88	93	82	86	83	81	102	100	81	104	83	83	98	84	88	103
37852	ROBBINS	64	43	19	37	48	56	41	51	50	42	58	61	35	55	42	53	53	51	63	73
37853	ROCKFORD	78	66	49	62	69	76	64	71	68	64	83	84	60	82	64	70	78	70	77	90
37854	ROCKWOOD	68	53	39	48	57	65	54	60	61	53	73	70	50	71	54	64	68	60	71	78
37857	ROGERSVILLE	76	52	26	46	59	68	52	63	61	52	72	75	44	68	52	66	66	63	77	87
37860	RUSSELLVILLE	88	65	36	58	71	80	61	74	71	62	84	88	55	82	63	75	78	73	87	102
37861	RUTLEDGE	79	55	28	49	62	71	53	65	63	54	74	78	46	71	54	67	68	64	79	92
37862	SEVIERVILLE	76	66	58	64	69	77	68	72	72	66	87	83	64	86	68	74	83	72	79	87
37863	PIGEON FORGE	71	60	45	58	63	69	61	66	64	60	77	75	56	73	60	65	73	65	70	79
37865	SEYMOUR	82	75	62	73	78	85	72	77	75	72	92	90	71	93	73	76	88	76	82	95
37866	SHARPS CHAPEL	68	45	21	39	51	59	44	55	53	45	62	65	37	59	45	57	56	54	67	78
37869	SNEEDVILLE	62	42	19	36	47	55	40	50	49	41	57	60	34	54	41	52	52	50	62	72
37870	SPEEDWELL	64	43	20	37	49	56	42	52	50	42	59	62	35	56	42	54	54	51	64	74
37871	STRAWBERRY PLAINS	87	66	41	61	72	80	65	75	72	65	87	88	58	83	65	75	80	74	86	99
37872	SUNBRIGHT	64	43	19	37	48	56	41	51	50	42	58	62	35	55	42	54	53	51	63	73
37873	SURGOINSVILLE	81	54	25	47	62	71	53	66	63	54	74	79	45	70	53	68	68	65	81	93
37874	SWEETWATER	79	56	31	50	63	71	55	66	64	55	76	78	48	72	56	68	70	66	80	91
37876	SEVIERVILLE	80	68	50	65	72	78	66	73	70	66	85	85	62	84	66	72	80	72	79	91
37877	TALBOTT	85	69	47	64	74	82	65	75	72	66	87	89	62	86	67	75	81	73	84	98
37878	TALLASSEE	89	63	34	55	71	81	60	74	71	61	84	88	52	80	62	76	77	73	90	104
37879	TAZEWELL	66	44	21	39	50	58	43	54	52	44	61	64	37	58	44	56	55	53	66	75
37880	TEN MILE	77	52	23	45	58	67	50	62	60	51	71	74	42	67	51	65	64	62	77	88
37881	THORN HILL	62	42	19	36	47	54	40	50	49	41	57	60	34	54	41	52	52	50	62	72
37882	TOWNSEND	84	69	49	63	76	84	64	75	71	64	85	89	59	85	68	75	80	74	87	101
37885	VONORE	85	57	26	49	65	75	55	69	67	56	78	82	47	74	56	72	71	68	85	98
37886	WALLAND	82	68	47	63	72	79	64	72	69	64	84	86	60	82	65	72	79	71	80	95
37887	WARTBURG	61	41	18	35	46	53	39	49	47	40	55	58	33	52	40	51	50	48	60	69
37888	WASHBURN	70	47	21	41	53	61	45	57	55	46	64	68	39	61	46	59	58	56	70	80
37890	WHITE PINE	76	57	32	51	62	69	54	64	62	55	74	76	48	71	55	65	68	64	75	88
37891	WHITESBURG	80	54	25	46	61	70	52	65	63	53	73	77	44	69	53	67	67	64	80	92
37892	WINFIELD	79	53	24	46	60	69	51	64	61	52	72	76	43	68	52	66	66	63	79	90
37902	KNOXVILLE	28	25	37	26	25	30	31	29	33	30	41	34	31	41	31	34	40	31	31	32
37909	KNOXVILLE	73	66	83	71	66	71	80	74	79	77	99	91	77	96	75	74	96	80	69	81
37912	KNOXVILLE	59	58	65	58	58	63	62	60	62	60	78	70	61	77	61	62	75	62	60	67
37914	KNOXVILLE	62	57	56	53	58	66	58	61	63	58	77	68	58	75	59	66	73	61	67	71
37915	KNOXVILLE	31	25	31	23	25	30	29	29	33	30	41	32	29	38	29	35	39	31	33	34
37916	KNOXVILLE	29	18	22	20	17	21	34	25	33	29	41	35	28	37	27	29	39	30	23	28
37917	KNOXVILLE	46	42	49	42	42	48	48	46	50	46	62	53	47	62	47	50	59	48	49	51
37918	KNOXVILLE	78	78	78	77	79	85	77	78	77	76	95	91	77	96	77	77	92	78	79	90
37919	KNOXVILLE	109	112	137	117	111	118	121	114	117	118	147	137	120	145	118	113	144	119	108	126
37920	KNOXVILLE	67	64	66	63	65	72	68	67	69	66	86	78	67	86	67	70	83	68	69	76
37921	KNOXVILLE	63	60	61	59	59	64	62	62	64	62	79	72	61	77	61	63	76	63	62	70
37922	KNOXVILLE	144	172	186	176	167	169	156	154	145	158	183	179	166	188	158	140	182	150	139	170
37923	KNOXVILLE	92	99	116	104	97	100	101	97	96	100	121	115	102	121	99	92	119	98	88	106
37924	KNOXVILLE	81	66	47	62	71	79	63	72	70	63	84	85	59	83	65	73	78	71	82	94
37931	KNOXVILLE	92	95	87	95	95	96	88	91	86	89	107	107	88	107	88	84	104	89	87	106
37932	KNOXVILLE	108	128	132	129	124	122	116	116	108	117	136	136	121	142	117	103	135	113	102	127
37938	KNOXVILLE	97	105	102	103	106	109	96	100	95	96	118	117	100	123	99	94	115	97	97	117
38001	ALAMO	77	54	29	49	61	71	56	66	65	55	76	77	48	72	56	69	69	65	80	88
38002	ARLINGTON	111	120	114	120	118	119	109	112	105	111	131	131	112	134	110	102	129	109	104	128
38004	ATOKA	95	99	91	99	98	98	92	94	89	94	111	111	92	112	91	86	108	93	88	108
38006	BELLS	73	54	32	49	59	68	53	62	61	53	72	74	47	70	53	64	67	62	73	84
38008	BOLIVAR	69	51	37	46	55	65	53	60	61	53	73	69	49	68	53	65	68	60	72	77
38011	BRIGHTON	88	83	69	81	85	89	78	83	80	79	98	99	77	98	79	79	94	82	85	102
38012	BROWNSVILLE	68	54	44	51	57	65	57	62	63	57	76	71	54	74	57	66	72	62	69	76
38015	BURLISON	86	71	48	66	76	83	66	75	72	66	87	90	63	87	68	75	82	74	85	100
38016	CORDOVA	121	135	142	141	130	129	127	125	118	130	150	147	131	151	125	112	149	123	109	137
38017	COLLIERVILLE	148	167	166	172	161	161	152	151	142	156	179	176	158	181	151	136	178	147	135	168
38018	CORDOVA	124	140	146	146	135	135	130	128	121	133	153	150	135	153	128	114	152	126	113	141
38019	COVINGTON	79	65	52	61	68	77	66	72	72	66	87	83	62	85	66	75	82	71	80	89
38023	DRUMMONDS	88	78	60	75	79	85	75	81	77	77	94	94	70	90	74	76	90	81	82	98
	TENNESSEE	85	76	68	73	78	85	76	80	79	76	97	94	73	96	75	81	93	80	85	97
	UNITED STATES	100	100	100	100	100	100	100	100	100	100	100	100	100	100	100	100	100	100	100	100

POPULATION CHANGE

# ZIP CODE / POST OFFICE NAME	COUNTY FIPS CODE	POPULATION 2000	2004	2009	2000-2004 ANNUAL RATE % Rate	State Centile	HOUSEHOLDS 2000	2004	2009	% Annual Rate 2000-2004	2004 Average HH Size	FAMILIES 2000	2004	% Annual Rate 2000-2004
38024 DYERSBURG	045	29301	29826	30532	0.4	38	11590	11944	12371	0.7	2.45	8095	8172	0.2
38028 EADS	047	4638	5511	6212	4.1	98	1683	2044	2354	4.7	2.69	1391	1668	4.4
38030 FINLEY	045	141	155	164	2.3	89	54	60	65	2.5	2.58	40	44	2.3
38034 FRIENDSHIP	033	3470	3486	3553	0.1	26	1441	1467	1510	0.4	2.38	1038	1037	0.0
38037 GATES	075	2101	2164	2221	0.7	48	722	761	798	1.3	2.65	550	570	0.8
38039 GRAND JUNCTION	069	1797	1809	1842	0.2	27	632	649	674	0.6	2.79	485	490	0.2
38040 HALLS	097	5169	5166	5251	0.0	19	2067	2098	2168	0.4	2.45	1482	1474	-0.1
38041 HENNING	097	5460	5658	5799	0.8	53	1191	1300	1386	2.1	2.55	850	910	1.6
38042 HICKORY VALLEY	069	848	911	960	1.7	79	306	337	363	2.3	2.70	234	253	1.9
38044 HORNSBY	069	1230	1234	1254	0.1	25	494	506	524	0.6	2.41	367	369	0.1
38049 MASON	047	4699	4952	5352	1.2	66	1475	1611	1801	2.1	2.73	1121	1202	1.7
38052 MIDDLETON	069	3509	3644	3780	0.9	56	1410	1497	1586	1.4	2.42	1016	1058	1.0
38053 MILLINGTON	157	28726	29849	30948	0.9	56	10048	10637	11182	1.4	2.75	7912	8229	0.9
38057 MOSCOW	047	3831	4028	4400	1.2	65	1329	1425	1594	1.7	2.83	1027	1083	1.3
38058 MUNFORD	167	3211	3515	3876	2.2	87	1136	1265	1416	2.6	2.78	916	1002	2.1
38059 NEWBERN	045	6493	6620	6743	0.5	39	2543	2633	2716	0.8	2.51	1924	1956	0.4
38060 OAKLAND	047	3891	4455	5045	3.2	96	1411	1662	1937	3.9	2.68	1133	1315	3.6
38061 POCAHONTAS	109	1057	1099	1143	0.9	57	436	462	490	1.4	2.38	320	334	1.0
38063 RIPLEY	097	15679	15980	16398	0.5	39	6079	6318	6608	0.9	2.50	4304	4386	0.5
38066 ROSSVILLE	047	2295	2505	2766	2.1	86	851	960	1093	2.9	2.61	645	716	2.5
38067 SAULSBURY	069	1460	1508	1555	0.8	50	594	630	664	1.4	2.39	435	453	1.0
38068 SOMERVILLE	047	10268	11082	12180	1.8	81	3713	4120	4659	2.5	2.61	2765	3012	2.0
38069 STANTON	075	2896	3001	3125	0.8	53	1117	1189	1265	1.5	2.51	812	848	1.0
38075 WHITEVILLE	069	6587	6501	6565	-0.3	9	1191	1187	1235	-0.1	2.88	872	854	-0.5
38076 WILLISTON	047	406	405	428	-0.1	16	150	154	167	0.6	2.63	121	122	0.2
38079 TIPTONVILLE	095	5625	5597	5504	-0.1	15	1480	1505	1499	0.4	2.26	960	953	-0.2
38080 RIDGELY	095	2617	2505	2418	-1.0	2	1051	1020	1001	-0.7	2.37	745	710	-1.1
38103 MEMPHIS	157	7919	9747	10985	5.0	99	3572	4578	5268	6.0	1.67	980	1243	5.8
38104 MEMPHIS	157	24637	24194	24276	-0.4	7	13061	12985	13182	-0.1	1.79	4725	4478	-1.3
38105 MEMPHIS	157	8317	7809	7755	-1.5	1	3445	3298	3324	-1.0	2.12	1541	1384	-2.5
38106 MEMPHIS	157	33644	31743	31531	-1.4	1	12331	11862	11961	-0.9	2.62	8080	7555	-1.6
38107 MEMPHIS	157	21904	20270	20016	-1.8	0	8138	7666	7673	-1.4	2.57	5119	4679	-2.1
38108 MEMPHIS	157	22502	20993	20762	-1.6	1	8499	8066	8089	-1.2	2.58	5578	5138	-1.9
38109 MEMPHIS	157	52307	50886	50980	-0.7	5	17580	17485	17805	-0.1	2.90	13303	12968	-0.6
38111 MEMPHIS	157	43305	43284	43827	0.0	19	18040	18091	18457	0.1	2.27	9774	9530	-0.6
38112 MEMPHIS	157	19887	19143	19087	-0.9	3	7858	7659	7726	-0.6	2.42	4311	4028	-1.6
38114 MEMPHIS	157	34545	32389	32157	-1.5	1	12997	12442	12548	-1.0	2.59	8631	8033	-1.7
38115 MEMPHIS	157	40245	42116	43683	1.1	61	17133	17905	18670	1.0	2.34	9767	9813	0.1
38116 MEMPHIS	157	51019	50987	51387	0.0	19	18087	18232	18543	0.2	2.78	12920	12707	-0.4
38117 MEMPHIS	157	25815	25367	25426	-0.4	7	11763	11741	11920	0.0	2.15	7284	7033	-0.8
38118 MEMPHIS	157	47373	46377	46582	-0.5	6	16162	15777	15907	-0.6	2.89	11668	11131	-1.1
38119 MEMPHIS	157	21989	21962	22092	0.0	18	9740	9893	10087	0.4	2.17	6062	5955	-0.4
38120 MEMPHIS	157	13726	14961	15760	2.1	85	5997	6655	7116	2.5	2.23	3880	4154	1.6
38122 MEMPHIS	157	24641	24225	24337	-0.4	7	10602	10497	10640	-0.2	2.31	6273	5995	-1.1
38125 MEMPHIS	157	23388	26474	28406	3.0	94	8460	9736	10586	3.4	2.72	6716	7578	2.9
38126 MEMPHIS	157	8513	8311	8466	-0.6	5	2972	3164	3419	1.5	2.45	1679	1628	-0.7
38127 MEMPHIS	157	50874	50194	50345	-0.3	8	17252	17172	17389	-0.1	2.91	13090	12771	-0.6
38128 MEMPHIS	157	43834	45107	46222	0.7	47	15992	16556	17111	0.8	2.70	11321	11442	0.3
38131 MEMPHIS	157	1	1	1	0.0	20	0	1	1	0.0	1.00	0	0	0.0
38132 MEMPHIS	157	80	80	80	0.0	20	2	2	2	0.0	2.50	1	1	0.0
38133 MEMPHIS	157	18873	20527	21546	2.0	84	6567	7263	7729	2.4	2.82	5336	5835	2.1
38134 MEMPHIS	157	41692	42459	42977	0.4	39	14509	14942	15354	0.7	2.47	9900	9925	0.1
38135 MEMPHIS	157	24957	26636	27692	1.5	75	8635	9356	9854	1.9	2.83	7160	7645	1.6
38138 GERMANTOWN	157	23796	24348	24779	0.5	42	8864	9273	9592	1.1	2.62	6904	7080	0.6
38139 GERMANTOWN	157	14482	14883	15146	0.6	46	4647	4872	5031	1.1	3.05	4235	4410	1.0
38141 MEMPHIS	157	21922	22278	22588	0.4	37	7672	7892	8090	0.7	2.82	5881	5926	0.2
38152 MEMPHIS	157	597	598	598	0.0	23	11	11	11	0.0	2.55	3	3	0.0
38201 MC KENZIE	017	9836	9922	9972	0.2	30	3890	3992	4059	0.6	2.37	2720	2731	0.1
38220 ATWOOD	017	1988	2056	2091	0.8	52	817	859	882	1.2	2.39	586	604	0.7
38221 BIG SANDY	005	3194	3356	3461	1.2	64	1368	1462	1528	1.6	2.30	1004	1051	1.1
38222 BUCHANAN	079	2322	2432	2498	1.1	62	984	1050	1093	1.5	2.31	738	773	1.1
38224 COTTAGE GROVE	079	1085	1086	1093	0.0	22	407	416	425	0.5	2.61	306	306	0.0
38225 DRESDEN	183	6386	6631	6790	0.9	56	2533	2673	2776	1.3	2.38	1789	1849	0.8
38226 DUKEDOM	183	539	555	560	0.7	47	219	229	234	1.1	2.42	162	166	0.6
38229 GLEASON	183	3055	3036	3031	-0.2	13	1236	1253	1269	0.3	2.42	902	896	-0.2
38230 GREENFIELD	183	3998	3867	3821	-0.8	3	1620	1588	1590	-0.5	2.43	1153	1108	-0.9
38231 HENRY	079	1834	1871	1899	0.5	40	686	715	737	1.0	2.62	527	539	0.5
38232 HORNBEAK	131	2234	2280	2288	0.5	40	911	950	973	1.0	2.40	673	687	0.5
38233 KENTON	053	2826	2738	2693	-0.7	4	1180	1163	1162	-0.3	2.35	839	810	-0.8
38236 MANSFIELD	079	865	929	967	1.7	79	360	395	417	2.2	2.35	260	278	1.6
38237 MARTIN	183	15149	15197	15213	0.1	24	5617	5742	5831	0.5	2.26	3395	3375	-0.1
38240 OBION	131	2275	2304	2306	0.3	33	926	954	970	0.7	2.42	675	681	0.2
38241 PALMERSVILLE	183	1253	1352	1407	1.8	81	500	550	581	2.3	2.46	385	417	1.9
38242 PARIS	079	18870	19248	19636	0.5	40	7963	8230	8495	0.8	2.28	5322	5391	0.3
38251 PURYEAR	079	2900	2809	2806	-0.8	4	1164	1148	1164	-0.3	2.43	854	823	-0.9
38253 RIVES	131	1105	1143	1152	0.8	52	424	448	461	1.3	2.52	331	344	0.9
38255 SHARON	183	2418	2357	2330	-0.6	5	1036	1031	1035	-0.1	2.29	727	707	-0.7
38256 SPRINGVILLE	079	3048	3220	3325	1.3	68	1390	1499	1571	1.8	2.15	951	998	1.1
38257 SOUTH FULTON	131	5066	4867	4767	-0.9	2	2072	2028	2021	-0.5	2.38	1519	1457	-1.0
38258 TREZEVANT	017	1968	1953	1942	-0.2	12	822	830	835	0.2	2.35	578	572	-0.3
38259 TRIMBLE	131	890	876	882	-0.4	8	374	374	382	0.0	2.34	261	255	-0.6
38260 TROY	131	4051	4196	4235	0.8	52	1555	1640	1685	1.3	2.56	1198	1240	0.8
38261 UNION CITY	131	16622	16479	16323	-0.2	11	6805	6878	6938	0.3	2.33	4657	4610	-0.2
38301 JACKSON	113	40114	40039	41498	0.0	17	15793	15999	16839	0.3	2.38	10172	10029	-0.3
38305 JACKSON	113	40300	44099	47404	2.1	87	15459	17230	18812	2.6	2.48	11128	12110	2.0
38310 ADAMSVILLE	109	5377	5406	5477	0.1	27	2192	2241	2305	0.5	2.35	1551	1555	0.1
38311 BATH SPRINGS	039	912	998	1065	2.1	87	375	419	456	2.6	2.38	283	309	2.1
38313 BEECH BLUFF	113	2960	3142	3311	1.4	71	1128	1220	1304	1.9	2.57	890	946	1.5
38315 BETHEL SPRINGS	109	3944	4137	4292	1.1	63	1572	1676	1767	1.5	2.43	1156	1210	1.1
38316 BRADFORD	053	2995	2998	2991	0.0	22	1206	1227	1240	0.4	2.44	875	872	-0.1
38317 BRUCETON	017	2562	2568	2579	0.1	24	1061	1085	1105	0.5	2.26	743	744	0.0
38318 BUENA VISTA	017	419	435	445	0.9	56	166	175	181	1.3	2.47	121	126	1.0
38320 CAMDEN	005	10833	10749	10827	-0.2	12	4473	4520	4625	0.3	2.32	3115	3078	-0.3
38321 CEDAR GROVE	017	1596	1590	1580	-0.1	15	677	687	690	0.4	2.29	492	490	-0.1
38326 COUNCE	071	2423	2505	2550	0.8	52	1064	1124	1162	1.3	2.23	764	790	0.8
TENNESSEE					1.0					1.3	2.45			0.9
UNITED STATES					1.2					1.3	2.58			1.1

POPULATION COMPOSITION

ZIP CODE #	POST OFFICE NAME	RACE (%) White 2000	White 2004	Black 2000	Black 2004	Asian/Pacific 2000	Asian/Pacific 2004	% Hispanic Origin 2000	% Hispanic Origin 2004	2004 AGE DISTRIBUTION (%) 0-4	5-9	10-14	15-19	20-24	25-44	45-64	65-84	85+	18+	MEDIAN AGE 2004	% 2004 Males	% 2004 Females
38024	DYERSBURG	83.5	82.7	14.7	15.2	0.4	0.5	1.2	1.4	6.9	6.8	7.2	6.4	6.5	27.8	24.8	11.6	2.1	75.3	37.3	48.0	52.0
38028	EADS	79.3	76.9	18.4	20.3	0.8	1.0	1.6	1.9	6.3	6.9	7.0	6.3	5.3	26.8	30.5	10.0	0.9	75.7	40.2	50.0	50.1
38030	FINLEY	93.6	93.6	5.7	5.8	0.0	0.0	0.7	0.7	5.2	5.2	5.8	5.8	7.1	28.4	29.0	12.9	0.7	80.0	40.6	51.6	48.4
38034	FRIENDSHIP	85.6	84.9	12.4	12.7	0.0	0.0	2.5	3.0	6.3	6.3	6.9	6.0	6.3	27.7	25.7	12.7	2.0	76.9	39.2	50.1	49.9
38037	GATES	67.7	66.3	30.6	31.8	0.1	0.1	1.8	2.0	7.4	7.4	7.5	6.1	5.8	25.9	23.4	12.5	4.2	73.9	37.8	46.1	53.9
38039	GRAND JUNCTION	37.0	34.7	62.2	64.5	0.0	0.0	0.5	0.6	7.5	7.7	8.5	7.4	6.7	25.7	23.4	11.7	1.4	71.8	34.5	46.4	53.6
38040	HALLS	82.0	81.3	16.6	17.1	0.0	0.0	1.0	1.2	6.8	6.8	7.2	6.5	6.4	27.4	25.5	11.8	1.8	75.4	37.8	48.6	51.4
38041	HENNING	43.4	41.3	53.6	55.4	0.2	0.2	1.1	1.2	4.6	4.7	4.6	4.4	10.6	44.1	19.7	6.5	1.0	83.8	33.8	70.3	29.7
38042	HICKORY VALLEY	47.5	46.0	51.4	52.8	0.0	0.0	0.9	1.1	7.9	8.1	7.7	7.4	6.4	26.1	25.3	10.2	1.0	71.7	35.1	47.4	52.6
38044	HORNSBY	94.6	94.0	4.1	4.5	0.0	0.0	0.4	0.6	5.7	5.9	6.9	5.8	5.7	27.0	28.9	13.0	1.1	78.0	40.9	49.3	50.7
38049	MASON	44.2	42.5	53.2	54.7	0.3	0.3	1.8	1.9	6.1	6.2	7.1	7.0	7.9	32.4	21.9	9.9	1.4	76.2	35.4	54.5	45.5
38052	MIDDLETON	91.4	90.5	7.4	8.1	0.5	0.7	0.4	0.6	6.4	6.4	6.8	6.9	6.5	25.9	26.1	13.6	1.4	76.3	39.0	48.2	51.8
38053	MILLINGTON	77.1	73.3	18.5	21.7	1.4	1.5	3.0	3.5	7.5	7.2	7.7	6.8	6.6	29.3	24.5	9.6	0.9	73.6	35.6	49.8	50.2
38057	MOSCOW	59.2	57.2	38.8	40.5	0.3	0.3	1.6	1.9	6.9	7.1	8.6	7.4	5.7	24.9	26.6	11.3	1.5	72.5	37.8	48.1	51.9
38058	MUNFORD	90.4	89.2	6.7	7.4	0.7	0.9	1.4	1.7	7.0	7.5	8.6	7.7	6.0	28.4	25.5	8.8	0.5	72.2	35.6	49.1	50.9
38059	NEWBERN	91.6	90.7	6.9	7.5	0.3	0.3	1.0	1.2	6.4	6.5	7.4	6.6	6.6	29.1	24.8	11.1	1.5	75.7	37.0	48.4	51.6
38060	OAKLAND	71.2	69.4	26.8	28.3	0.5	0.6	1.2	1.4	6.6	6.9	6.6	5.8	5.5	28.3	28.4	10.8	1.0	76.3	39.0	49.8	50.2
38061	POCAHONTAS	94.6	93.8	4.0	4.4	0.8	1.0	0.8	0.9	7.2	6.9	6.3	6.3	6.1	26.8	26.8	12.4	1.3	75.7	38.3	50.1	50.0
38063	RIPLEY	65.7	64.8	32.4	33.0	0.2	0.3	1.2	1.4	7.6	7.3	7.5	6.8	7.3	27.5	23.9	10.7	1.6	73.7	35.4	47.8	52.2
38066	ROSSVILLE	61.5	59.9	36.8	38.2	0.2	0.2	1.0	1.2	6.4	6.7	6.0	5.5	5.1	26.2	29.1	13.2	1.9	77.6	41.3	50.1	49.9
38067	SAULSBURY	55.6	53.0	43.2	45.6	0.1	0.1	0.4	0.7	7.0	7.5	8.8	6.6	5.9	26.0	24.0	12.9	1.3	72.5	36.1	47.4	52.6
38068	SOMERVILLE	61.0	59.7	37.8	39.1	0.1	0.1	0.7	0.8	7.0	7.0	6.9	7.6	6.2	25.7	25.7	12.0	2.0	74.2	37.9	49.3	50.7
38069	STANTON	43.3	42.4	55.8	56.7	0.0	0.0	0.8	0.9	6.8	7.2	7.7	6.3	6.0	26.8	25.4	12.2	1.5	74.3	37.6	49.4	50.6
38075	WHITEVILLE	39.8	37.4	57.0	58.9	0.3	0.3	1.8	2.1	3.5	3.7	4.2	4.7	11.7	44.1	20.9	6.4	0.9	85.8	34.8	72.6	27.4
38076	WILLISTON	68.5	66.9	30.3	31.6	0.3	0.3	0.5	0.5	7.9	8.2	7.7	6.4	5.2	26.4	26.7	10.4	1.2	72.1	36.8	47.2	52.8
38079	TIPTONVILLE	59.1	58.1	38.6	39.3	0.2	0.2	1.4	1.6	4.2	3.9	3.8	6.2	12.7	36.0	21.9	9.9	1.5	85.1	35.0	66.1	34.0
38080	RIDGELY	86.2	85.8	12.1	12.5	0.0	0.0	1.2	1.4	6.6	6.6	6.9	5.8	5.2	25.9	24.6	15.7	2.6	76.3	39.6	47.6	52.4
38103	MEMPHIS	53.8	51.9	41.3	42.0	3.2	4.2	1.8	2.0	2.8	1.2	1.6	3.9	13.7	44.4	23.4	7.8	1.1	93.2	34.3	59.0	41.1
38104	MEMPHIS	61.7	58.7	29.7	31.8	4.8	5.3	3.3	3.9	5.6	4.7	4.4	5.0	8.6	36.2	24.0	9.6	2.0	82.8	35.9	49.5	50.5
38105	MEMPHIS	11.5	10.0	84.9	86.2	2.2	2.4	1.6	1.6	8.9	7.7	8.6	8.3	9.7	27.4	20.8	7.4	1.4	69.3	29.7	48.7	51.3
38106	MEMPHIS	2.3	1.9	96.5	96.9	0.2	0.2	1.0	1.0	7.5	7.2	8.3	8.0	6.9	23.4	22.5	14.1	2.0	72.3	36.1	45.7	54.3
38107	MEMPHIS	12.2	11.3	85.7	86.4	0.8	0.9	1.1	1.1	7.5	7.9	8.8	8.7	8.5	25.7	21.4	10.0	1.5	70.7	31.4	46.2	53.8
38108	MEMPHIS	25.8	24.7	70.2	70.5	0.6	0.7	4.4	5.4	7.5	7.5	8.0	7.2	6.5	26.5	22.3	12.9	1.6	72.5	35.0	47.9	52.1
38109	MEMPHIS	3.1	2.5	96.1	96.6	0.1	0.1	0.6	0.6	7.2	7.6	8.9	8.2	6.9	23.6	26.0	10.6	1.1	71.2	35.0	45.5	54.5
38111	MEMPHIS	50.2	45.8	44.9	48.6	1.7	1.9	3.9	4.6	6.9	6.5	6.5	7.8	10.2	29.5	20.0	9.8	2.8	76.5	32.7	46.9	53.1
38112	MEMPHIS	39.9	37.7	54.3	55.9	2.8	3.0	3.0	3.5	6.9	6.6	7.2	8.1	8.5	28.2	23.5	9.1	1.9	75.0	33.8	46.8	53.2
38114	MEMPHIS	4.0	3.3	94.7	95.3	0.1	0.1	1.2	1.2	8.5	8.2	8.5	7.5	7.2	25.8	21.7	11.1	1.4	70.2	32.8	45.2	54.8
38115	MEMPHIS	31.1	25.9	60.0	64.0	3.2	3.7	6.2	7.1	8.1	7.2	7.3	6.9	10.3	36.2	16.5	5.8	1.8	73.6	29.8	48.0	52.1
38116	MEMPHIS	7.2	5.8	90.8	92.1	0.2	0.3	1.5	1.6	9.5	8.9	9.0	8.1	9.1	28.3	20.9	5.5	0.8	67.7	28.4	46.0	54.0
38117	MEMPHIS	92.6	91.0	5.0	6.1	1.1	1.3	1.7	2.1	5.7	6.0	5.7	5.1	4.1	26.0	25.3	18.8	3.3	79.3	43.3	46.4	53.6
38118	MEMPHIS	17.5	14.6	76.4	78.8	1.5	1.6	5.6	6.0	9.2	8.8	9.9	9.1	9.0	31.0	17.2	5.3	0.7	66.5	27.5	47.9	52.1
38119	MEMPHIS	83.9	80.2	11.2	13.9	2.9	3.5	2.0	2.5	5.0	4.8	5.1	5.5	7.4	27.7	26.9	15.1	2.6	81.9	41.0	46.8	53.2
38120	MEMPHIS	93.4	91.9	2.9	3.6	2.4	3.0	1.4	1.8	4.9	5.4	5.8	6.0	5.3	22.7	29.0	18.4	2.6	80.0	44.9	47.9	52.1
38122	MEMPHIS	74.4	70.9	18.3	20.5	2.4	2.9	8.0	9.7	7.1	6.5	6.5	5.7	6.8	31.2	21.8	12.6	1.9	76.6	36.0	49.2	50.8
38125	MEMPHIS	53.7	47.9	41.5	46.8	2.8	3.2	1.4	1.7	7.4	7.6	8.0	7.2	5.9	32.5	26.0	5.2	0.3	72.4	35.3	48.6	51.4
38126	MEMPHIS	2.7	2.3	96.4	96.8	0.1	0.1	1.2	1.1	10.4	10.5	10.1	9.1	8.2	24.3	18.1	7.8	1.3	63.8	26.5	49.2	50.8
38127	MEMPHIS	25.7	21.8	72.3	76.1	0.3	0.4	1.3	1.4	9.4	9.0	10.1	9.1	8.1	26.3	20.5	6.7	0.8	65.9	28.4	45.7	54.3
38128	MEMPHIS	35.8	31.4	59.1	62.9	1.0	1.2	4.3	4.8	9.0	8.5	8.9	7.6	8.2	30.2	19.0	7.5	1.1	69.1	30.1	46.9	53.1
38131	MEMPHIS	100.0	100.0	0.0	0.0	0.0	0.0	0.0	0.0	0.0	0.0	0.0	0.0	100.0	0.0	0.0	0.0	0.0	100.0	22.5	100.0	0.0
38132	MEMPHIS	31.3	25.0	68.8	73.8	0.0	0.0	0.0	0.0	0.0	0.0	8.8	3.8	3.8	62.5	21.3	0.0	0.0	88.8	38.9	66.3	33.8
38133	MEMPHIS	86.9	83.7	9.2	11.5	1.9	2.4	2.1	2.8	8.4	8.4	8.7	7.3	5.9	32.0	23.2	5.7	0.4	69.9	33.6	48.7	51.3
38134	MEMPHIS	72.1	67.6	22.5	26.0	2.3	2.7	3.4	4.2	5.8	5.4	5.9	6.5	10.1	34.1	22.8	8.2	1.0	79.3	33.8	52.0	48.0
38135	MEMPHIS	88.7	86.1	8.5	10.5	1.2	1.5	1.4	1.8	7.6	8.0	8.5	7.1	5.4	29.4	25.7	7.6	0.7	71.5	36.1	48.8	51.2
38138	GERMANTOWN	91.7	89.7	3.4	4.3	3.6	4.5	1.1	1.5	4.9	5.9	7.3	7.1	5.1	22.5	34.8	11.5	0.9	77.4	43.3	48.5	51.5
38139	GERMANTOWN	93.0	91.2	2.1	2.7	3.8	4.8	1.1	1.5	5.4	7.8	10.0	9.0	4.0	21.2	35.6	6.5	0.5	70.5	41.4	49.2	50.8
38141	MEMPHIS	35.0	29.5	60.3	65.5	1.7	1.9	3.2	3.6	8.8	8.8	8.9	7.2	6.3	35.9	20.6	3.3	0.3	69.1	31.7	47.8	52.2
38152	MEMPHIS	67.2	61.2	22.1	26.3	8.7	10.2	1.5	1.8	1.7	2.0	2.0	21.4	41.5	17.1	11.0	2.8	0.5	93.0	22.8	42.6	57.4
38201	MC KENZIE	88.9	88.5	8.8	8.9	0.3	0.3	1.8	2.2	6.5	6.1	6.1	6.1	7.3	26.9	24.5	14.1	2.5	77.9	38.7	48.2	51.8
38220	ATWOOD	83.9	82.7	14.4	15.3	0.1	0.1	1.5	1.9	5.3	5.5	6.3	6.4	5.5	27.3	26.2	15.3	2.3	79.2	41.0	49.0	51.0
38221	BIG SANDY	98.8	98.7	0.1	0.1	0.1	0.1	0.8	0.9	5.5	5.7	5.9	5.2	5.0	23.8	30.6	16.8	1.7	79.8	44.3	49.9	50.1
38222	BUCHANAN	98.4	98.2	0.4	0.4	0.3	0.3	0.2	0.2	4.6	5.4	5.6	4.9	5.4	22.1	34.5	16.4	1.1	81.3	46.2	50.5	49.6
38224	COTTAGE GROVE	95.4	94.8	2.9	3.2	0.0	0.0	1.1	1.4	5.8	6.1	7.6	6.5	6.0	26.3	26.5	14.2	1.0	76.4	39.7	50.2	49.8
38225	DRESDEN	95.3	94.9	3.6	3.9	0.2	0.2	0.4	0.5	6.3	6.2	6.1	6.1	6.0	28.1	24.5	13.7	3.0	77.8	39.1	48.8	51.2
38226	DUKEDOM	98.3	98.2	0.0	0.0	0.2	0.2	0.2	0.4	6.0	6.3	7.4	6.1	5.6	27.4	27.4	12.3	1.6	76.4	39.5	50.5	49.6
38229	GLEASON	97.5	97.1	1.3	1.4	0.0	0.0	1.1	1.4	6.9	6.7	7.0	6.9	6.5	28.5	24.2	12.0	1.4	75.3	36.8	49.4	50.6
38230	GREENFIELD	93.6	93.1	5.1	5.5	0.0	0.0	1.2	1.5	7.0	6.8	6.8	5.8	6.6	26.4	25.5	13.5	1.8	76.1	38.6	48.3	51.7
38231	HENRY	90.4	89.3	6.9	7.6	0.1	0.1	3.5	4.3	6.5	6.6	7.0	6.6	6.8	27.7	25.7	11.5	1.4	76.0	37.7	49.9	50.1
38232	HORNBEAK	99.4	99.3	0.1	0.1	0.0	0.0	0.5	0.5	5.5	5.9	6.8	6.5	5.4	27.6	26.5	14.1	1.7	77.6	40.2	50.9	49.1
38233	KENTON	91.4	90.8	7.4	7.9	0.1	0.1	1.3	1.4	6.5	6.8	6.9	5.7	5.3	26.7	24.9	15.3	2.0	76.2	39.5	48.0	52.0
38236	MANSFIELD	88.3	87.1	10.1	11.1	0.1	0.2	1.5	1.7	5.9	5.8	5.5	6.7	6.7	27.1	28.6	12.0	1.7	78.8	40.3	51.6	48.4
38237	MARTIN	83.3	81.9	11.8	12.2	2.9	3.7	1.7	2.0	5.3	4.9	5.2	10.2	15.7	25.4	20.6	10.6	2.1	81.8	30.4	48.6	51.5
38240	OBION	95.7	95.4	3.2	3.4	0.1	0.1	0.4	0.5	6.7	6.6	6.1	5.8	6.5	27.0	26.0	13.6	1.7	77.0	38.9	49.4	50.7
38241	PALMERSVILLE	98.2	98.1	0.0	0.0	0.1	0.2	0.6	0.7	5.8	5.9	6.2	5.8	5.8	27.7	26.6	14.1	2.1	78.7	40.5	50.9	49.1
38242	PARIS	85.6	84.9	12.4	12.8	0.4	0.5	0.9	1.1	5.9	6.0	6.2	5.7	5.7	25.9	25.8	16.1	2.7	78.5	41.3	47.8	52.2
38251	PURYEAR	94.2	93.5	3.9	4.2	0.2	0.2	0.9	1.1	6.2	6.2	6.3	6.0	5.7	26.5	26.3	15.0	1.9	77.6	40.7	50.8	49.2
38253	RIVES	95.0	94.3	2.2	2.5	0.2	0.2	2.4	2.7	6.9	7.1	6.1	5.6	5.5	28.8	27.4	11.2	1.4	76.4	38.6	50.4	49.6
38255	SHARON	94.1	93.7	5.3	5.6	0.1	0.1	0.7	0.9	6.6	6.4	6.0	4.7	6.0	26.3	25.5	16.3	2.3	78.5	40.7	50.2	49.8
38256	SPRINGVILLE	96.9	96.6	2.2	2.4	0.0	0.0	0.5	0.6	3.8	4.1	4.7	4.8	4.8	19.9	33.8	22.3	1.8	84.5	50.2	49.8	50.2
38257	SOUTH FULTON	88.1	86.9	10.8	11.8	0.1	0.2	0.4	0.5	6.4	6.7	6.7	5.1	5.4	24.4	29.1	14.2	2.1	76.9	41.6	48.4	51.6
38258	TREZEVANT	83.9	82.9	14.7	15.6	0.0	0.0	1.3	1.6	5.6	5.7	7.5	6.9	6.0	27.6	24.7	14.6	1.5	77.0	39.7	48.8	51.3
38259	TRIMBLE	98.1	97.7	0.9	1.0	0.0	0.0	0.8	1.0	6.4	6.3	5.7	6.6	6.3	25.5	28.2	12.7	2.4	77.5	39.9	48.6	51.4
38260	TROY	98.8	98.6	0.8	0.8	0.1	0.1	0.8	1.0	6.3	6.5	6.9	5.8	5.8	28.6	27.1	11.5	1.4	76.8	38.4	49.8	50.2
38261	UNION CITY	82.2	81.1	14.9	15.5	0.4	0.5	3.0	3.6	6.5	6.3	6.2	5.7	6.5	27.0	26.2	13.2	2.5	77.5	39.0	48.0	52.0
38301	JACKSON	49.4	47.8	48.7	50.3	0.2	0.3	1.4	1.6	7.2	6.9	7.4	7.1	8.4	26.9	22.3	11.8	2.1	74.6	34.7	47.4	52.6
38305	JACKSON	76.8	74.4	20.1	21.9	1.2	1.4	2.2	2.6	7.1	6.8	7.1	6.7	8.0	30.2	23.5	9.1	1.5	75.2	34.6	48.3	51.7
38310	ADAMSVILLE	97.3	97.1	1.3	1.4	0.1	0.2	0.8	1.0	5.7	5.9	6.7	5.5	5.4	25.3	26.3	16.2	3.1	78.3	41.9	47.6	52.4
38311	BATH SPRINGS	94.3	93.5	3.3	3.6	0.6	0.6	1.9	2.3	5.7	5.7	5.0	5.1	6.2	26.9	28.8	14.7	1.9	80.6	41.8	49.5	50.5
38313	BEECH BLUFF	92.9	92.0	5.6	6.3	0.1	0.1	1.0	1.2	6.5	6.7	6.7	6.3	6.3	30.0	26.5	9.9	1.1	76.4	37.6	51.8	48.2
38315	BETHEL SPRINGS	94.2	93.8	4.3	4.7	0.1	0.2	0.8	1.0	7.0	7.1	7.3	6.1	6.4	26.9	25.7	12.3	1.3	75.0	37.7	49.1	51.0
38316	BRADFORD	94.8	94.5	4.1	4.4	0.0	0.0	0.6	0.6	5.3	5.6	7.2	6.6	6.0	27.5	26.5	13.7	1.8	77.9	39.9	48.7	51.3
38317	BRUCETON	91.5	91.2	7.1	7.4	0.1	0.1	0.6	0.7	5.5	5.6	6.3	5.8	6.0	24.1	25.7	17.1	3.9	78.9	42.3	46.8	53.2
38318	BUENA VISTA	88.3	87.4	9.8	10.3	0.2	0.2	0.5	0.9	5.8	6.2	7.4	6.0	6.0	26.7	26.7	14.0	1.4	76.6	39.1	49.4	50.6
38320	CAMDEN	95.6	95.1	2.9	3.1	0.3	0.4	1.0	1.2	5.0	5.6	6.6	5.5	5.2	25.8	27.3	16.4	2.7	79.5	42.6	48.1	51.9
38321	CEDAR GROVE	92.4	91.8	6.5	7.0	0.0	0.1	0.8	0.9	5.4	5.6	6.0	5.9	5.4	27.4	27.0	15.2	2.4	79.4	41.5	49.3	50.7
38326	COUNCE	98.1	98.1	1.2	1.3	0.1	0.1	0.6	0.7	4.8	5.2	5.1	4.9	3.9	24.5	34.2	16.3	1.2	82.0	46.1	51.5	48.5
	TENNESSEE	80.2	79.4	16.4	16.7	1.0	1.3	2.2	2.6	6.6	6.5	6.8	6.6	7.0	29.0	24.8	11.1	1.5	76.3	36.8	48.9	51.1
	UNITED STATES	75.1	73.6	12.3	12.5	3.8	4.2	12.5	14.1	6.9	6.7	7.2	7.0	7.3	28.6	23.8	10.8	1.7	75.1	36.0	49.1	50.9

ZIP CODE #	POST OFFICE NAME	2004 Per Capita Income	2004 HH Income Base	2004 Household Income Distribution (%): Less than $25,000	$25,000 to $49,999	$50,000 to $99,999	$100,000 to $149,999	$150,000 or More	Median Household Income: 2004	2009	2004 National Centile	2004 State Centile	2004 Home Value Base	2004 Home Value Distribution (%): Less than $50,000	$50,000 to $89,999	$90,000 to $174,999	$175,000 to $399,999	$400,000 or More	2004 Median Home Value
38024	DYERSBURG	18793	11944	36.1	30.2	25.7	5.6	2.4	35783	40236	31	52	8047	18.2	34.4	34.6	11.9	1.0	87230
38028	EADS	31474	2044	15.9	20.8	35.7	15.9	11.8	64991	74337	89	97	1815	8.8	11.9	23.6	40.1	15.7	194352
38030	FINLEY	15156	60	35.0	36.7	28.3	0.0	0.0	40000	45362	46	69	45	48.9	20.0	28.9	2.2	0.0	51667
38034	FRIENDSHIP	16086	1467	42.9	31.8	20.6	3.3	1.4	30459	34029	13	21	1161	33.7	36.8	25.5	4.1	0.0	68771
38037	GATES	16622	761	38.5	31.0	25.6	3.8	1.1	32788	36876	20	37	583	26.8	46.7	22.3	4.3	0.0	70072
38039	GRAND JUNCTION	13851	649	41.3	33.0	22.0	3.1	0.6	29948	33791	12	20	522	42.3	31.0	19.4	7.1	0.2	58511
38040	HALLS	16813	2098	38.6	34.0	23.1	2.9	1.4	31478	35639	16	26	1560	30.6	38.9	23.5	5.6	1.4	69150
38041	HENNING	14507	1300	42.3	28.4	24.1	3.0	2.2	30709	34591	14	22	987	37.9	40.6	14.4	5.5	1.6	62670
38042	HICKORY VALLEY	13432	337	47.5	30.0	18.7	2.4	1.5	27182	30782	7	13	264	40.5	31.4	19.3	8.7	0.0	60333
38044	HORNSBY	19414	506	35.6	36.0	24.1	2.0	2.4	33909	37932	24	43	417	41.0	32.1	17.5	9.4	0.0	62685
38049	MASON	18402	1611	33.7	32.6	24.6	5.5	3.6	38544	44414	41	62	1258	26.5	33.2	29.6	8.1	2.7	80547
38052	MIDDLETON	17781	1497	37.5	35.7	21.6	3.4	1.8	33432	37153	22	40	1182	24.5	33.0	33.3	8.5	0.8	81020
38053	MILLINGTON	22128	10637	20.2	28.6	37.4	10.8	3.0	51025	59535	74	90	7622	10.9	28.2	42.3	17.2	1.4	98129
38057	MOSCOW	20086	1425	28.9	25.7	30.8	11.8	2.8	45680	52414	63	81	1171	13.8	27.7	28.4	24.1	6.2	102995
38058	MUNFORD	21394	1265	22.8	29.3	36.8	8.7	2.5	48217	53404	69	85	1013	8.7	19.6	58.0	13.0	0.8	111014
38059	NEWBERN	18578	2633	30.2	33.8	30.4	4.0	1.8	39488	43683	44	66	1952	13.1	42.8	34.9	8.8	0.4	84307
38060	OAKLAND	24275	1662	19.5	29.3	34.8	10.2	6.2	50932	58596	74	89	1448	12.8	21.3	34.9	25.5	5.5	123302
38061	POCAHONTAS	17709	462	37.2	40.3	18.8	2.0	1.7	33247	37526	22	39	382	43.2	28.8	22.0	5.8	0.3	60606
38063	RIPLEY	16090	6318	39.8	30.4	24.9	3.0	2.0	33726	37782	23	42	4207	24.8	42.5	26.3	6.2	0.3	73410
38066	ROSSVILLE	21419	960	29.7	21.8	33.9	11.3	3.4	48337	55236	69	85	824	10.6	16.6	36.3	30.5	6.1	135246
38067	SAULSBURY	16789	630	43.5	30.5	23.0	1.4	1.6	29862	32733	12	19	504	41.3	34.1	18.9	5.6	0.2	58980
38068	SOMERVILLE	18628	4120	33.0	29.4	28.7	6.3	2.6	38373	43912	41	62	3172	18.4	29.8	30.6	17.5	3.8	92995
38069	STANTON	17571	1189	45.5	31.0	18.3	2.7	2.6	27916	31965	9	14	891	32.8	40.2	20.3	6.7	0.0	64905
38075	WHITEVILLE	12654	1187	39.2	37.4	19.7	1.8	1.9	31678	35680	17	28	918	33.4	38.8	20.0	7.1	0.7	65897
38076	WILLISTON	21697	154	25.3	31.2	31.2	11.0	1.3	42890	50277	56	78	130	11.5	31.5	30.8	20.8	5.4	99000
38079	TIPTONVILLE	13371	1505	52.8	26.5	17.5	2.4	0.9	23410	25562	3	5	906	37.8	42.3	16.2	2.5	1.2	60833
38080	RIDGELY	14431	1020	48.7	28.4	20.9	1.3	0.7	25865	29029	6	9	658	36.2	42.1	15.2	4.7	1.8	61494
38103	MEMPHIS	37657	4578	29.7	23.9	25.5	10.4	10.6	45858	56269	63	82	1019	9.4	5.7	19.6	48.5	16.8	216818
38104	MEMPHIS	28522	12985	38.9	28.2	21.1	6.6	5.2	33342	40184	22	40	4331	8.0	21.8	43.3	23.2	3.8	118572
38105	MEMPHIS	11660	3298	71.7	18.6	6.9	1.9	0.9	12228	15206	1	1	569	44.3	40.3	10.7	4.0	0.7	53652
38106	MEMPHIS	12732	11862	55.7	27.9	12.6	2.3	1.6	21436	25018	2	3	6392	48.3	47.8	3.5	0.2	0.1	50886
38107	MEMPHIS	14614	7666	52.1	27.2	15.2	3.4	2.1	23340	27349	3	5	3772	33.7	45.9	18.7	1.5	0.2	61056
38108	MEMPHIS	12923	8066	52.4	26.7	17.6	2.2	1.1	23362	27278	3	5	4536	45.8	50.4	3.5	0.3	0.0	52092
38109	MEMPHIS	13868	17485	40.9	31.3	23.0	3.7	1.2	31161	36152	15	25	12604	29.5	61.7	8.0	0.7	0.2	60518
38111	MEMPHIS	22640	18091	36.8	31.3	21.5	5.9	4.5	34621	39739	26	46	9848	13.8	50.1	23.0	8.0	5.1	75020
38112	MEMPHIS	20446	7659	41.7	27.3	20.5	5.7	4.9	31521	37030	16	27	3724	27.5	32.4	22.5	14.6	3.0	73746
38114	MEMPHIS	13295	12442	50.8	29.9	15.2	2.7	1.3	24450	28621	4	7	6179	37.0	54.5	7.7	0.7	0.1	56733
38115	MEMPHIS	21535	17905	24.1	36.9	31.1	6.0	1.9	41844	47901	52	74	6432	4.7	32.3	62.2	0.9	0.0	96105
38116	MEMPHIS	16933	18232	34.2	30.8	26.4	6.4	2.1	36166	41581	32	54	8919	7.3	51.5	38.1	2.8	0.4	84221
38117	MEMPHIS	38747	11741	19.1	30.3	28.4	11.5	10.7	50620	59316	73	89	9442	1.1	29.6	41.9	19.2	8.2	116471
38118	MEMPHIS	15375	15777	30.1	36.7	28.7	3.6	0.9	37145	42360	36	57	8274	9.2	73.1	16.7	0.8	0.2	74649
38119	MEMPHIS	39934	9893	11.7	27.0	37.1	13.8	10.4	61756	71518	86	95	6126	0.5	11.0	46.1	36.9	5.5	162378
38120	MEMPHIS	51320	6655	12.4	23.9	29.1	13.7	21.0	70478	82020	91	98	4920	1.0	7.0	25.5	45.8	20.7	231414
38122	MEMPHIS	18792	10497	35.1	35.0	24.6	3.9	1.4	33806	39750	23	42	6590	15.1	68.5	14.7	1.4	0.2	68182
38125	MEMPHIS	33356	9736	6.9	18.5	45.8	19.7	9.1	74669	84441	93	98	8770	0.5	2.5	69.6	22.4	5.0	149197
38126	MEMPHIS	8498	3164	74.4	17.1	6.6	1.6	0.3	11226	13771	1	1	539	55.5	36.7	7.2	0.6	0.0	47862
38127	MEMPHIS	12819	17172	42.3	34.4	19.6	2.9	0.8	29703	33247	12	18	10490	27.2	64.5	6.7	1.6	0.1	60629
38128	MEMPHIS	17927	16556	29.4	33.6	29.1	6.3	1.7	39843	45865	45	68	9727	8.8	52.0	36.9	2.1	0.1	82454
38131	MEMPHIS	0	0	0.0	0.0	0.0	0.0	0.0	0	0	0	0	0	0.0	0.0	0.0	0.0	0.0	0
38132	MEMPHIS	8273	0	0.0	0.0	0.0	0.0	0.0	0	0	0	0	2	0.0	100.0	0.0	0.0	0.0	85000
38133	MEMPHIS	26667	7263	10.7	24.3	42.9	16.0	6.1	64410	75201	88	97	6488	6.5	10.4	59.0	20.2	4.0	123347
38134	MEMPHIS	22904	14942	16.4	32.3	37.7	11.0	2.6	51121	59775	74	90	8450	1.3	20.6	72.4	5.6	0.1	111455
38135	MEMPHIS	27571	9356	10.0	21.1	46.6	16.5	5.9	67708	77608	90	97	8398	1.0	8.0	66.9	23.4	0.7	137272
38138	GERMANTOWN	49268	9273	6.5	13.8	34.9	20.7	24.1	90125	105471	97	99	7733	0.9	3.6	25.9	56.4	13.2	215009
38139	GERMANTOWN	55352	4872	3.9	7.0	23.8	25.0	40.3	129352	150021	100	100	4767	0.4	1.2	7.9	63.4	27.2	291646
38141	MEMPHIS	22745	7892	11.7	28.5	45.2	12.1	2.5	57571	65657	82	94	6644	0.3	28.6	69.0	1.8	0.3	100072
38152	MEMPHIS	6836	11	63.6	27.3	0.0	0.0	9.1	17207	17207	1	2	4	0.0	0.0	50.0	25.0	25.0	187500
38201	MC KENZIE	20183	3992	35.6	34.0	23.0	4.3	3.1	34504	38414	26	46	3022	25.8	35.2	29.7	7.2	2.1	75747
38220	ATWOOD	15858	859	40.2	33.3	22.8	3.0	0.7	31075	34723	15	24	710	30.1	41.8	22.3	5.8	0.0	67037
38221	BIG SANDY	15804	1462	40.4	36.9	19.8	2.0	1.0	29230	32251	11	17	1230	33.6	29.2	23.3	12.8	1.2	74382
38222	BUCHANAN	18210	1050	36.4	36.2	22.0	4.7	0.8	35000	37914	28	48	877	21.7	28.6	26.1	20.3	3.3	89648
38224	COTTAGE GROVE	15106	416	37.7	36.3	22.1	3.1	0.7	31774	35689	17	29	345	27.8	31.9	26.4	11.6	2.3	77639
38225	DRESDEN	18029	2673	36.0	31.9	26.9	3.7	1.6	34676	38684	26	46	2007	24.6	41.6	27.2	5.6	1.1	74216
38226	DUKEDOM	18064	229	29.7	41.1	22.3	3.1	3.9	35113	40000	28	49	192	37.0	24.5	30.7	7.8	0.0	68333
38229	GLEASON	16166	1253	33.3	39.9	22.8	3.3	0.7	32988	37613	21	38	960	31.6	34.7	26.8	5.5	1.5	69905
38230	GREENFIELD	16219	1588	38.6	34.3	22.3	2.6	2.2	31353	35323	16	26	1246	40.3	30.6	24.0	4.9	0.2	61071
38231	HENRY	16345	715	35.5	32.0	26.6	3.6	2.2	34231	37286	25	44	581	28.9	36.0	25.0	7.8	2.4	75438
38232	HORNBEAK	17219	950	34.4	39.2	21.6	3.3	1.6	32779	37711	20	36	780	34.4	41.7	15.8	7.1	1.2	62157
38233	KENTON	18126	1163	36.5	32.0	27.3	3.2	1.0	35541	39436	30	51	904	25.3	46.2	21.1	5.0	2.3	70769
38236	MANSFIELD	17696	395	31.7	39.0	24.8	3.3	1.3	35644	39747	30	52	331	31.7	29.9	30.2	7.6	0.6	74744
38237	MARTIN	18273	5742	40.1	27.8	25.6	4.5	2.0	33536	36972	23	41	3555	13.5	32.8	41.5	11.0	1.2	93573
38240	OBION	16924	954	37.2	34.6	23.2	3.6	1.5	33339	37832	22	40	746	33.0	39.5	22.9	3.8	0.8	63151
38241	PALMERSVILLE	20289	550	37.5	33.6	22.6	2.9	3.5	32250	36545	18	32	461	30.4	40.6	25.0	4.1	0.0	67386
38242	PARIS	18247	8230	38.0	33.2	22.8	4.5	1.5	32417	35809	19	33	5955	22.6	33.1	30.9	12.1	1.4	83748
38251	PURYEAR	17371	1148	31.2	41.4	22.5	3.6	1.4	35414	39396	29	50	947	29.6	35.7	26.1	7.4	1.3	73125
38253	RIVES	18094	448	32.6	35.0	27.0	2.5	2.9	36416	41709	33	55	375	21.3	35.2	32.3	7.5	3.7	81833
38255	SHARON	17814	1031	36.3	32.3	28.5	1.7	1.3	34231	38151	25	44	781	33.6	32.7	28.7	5.1	0.0	67593
38256	SPRINGVILLE	18299	1499	38.4	37.0	20.8	3.1	0.8	32344	35507	19	33	1278	24.6	34.7	30.4	9.2	1.1	80703
38257	SOUTH FULTON	20239	2028	35.3	33.5	22.7	6.2	2.2	35538	39817	30	51	1581	28.0	36.1	26.3	7.9	1.7	72920
38258	TREZEVANT	15978	830	41.0	32.3	23.4	2.9	0.5	30838	34354	14	23	670	40.9	37.0	17.8	4.3	0.0	59531
38259	TRIMBLE	19924	374	30.5	36.4	28.1	3.7	1.3	39036	43473	43	65	270	27.0	40.4	24.4	6.7	1.5	73226
38260	TROY	18452	1640	28.8	36.2	29.8	3.2	2.1	39356	44350	44	66	1352	31.5	35.8	25.7	6.3	0.7	71455
38261	UNION CITY	21623	6878	34.7	28.7	27.7	5.9	3.0	37634	41939	38	59	4594	16.0	38.9	34.9	8.8	1.4	85183
38301	JACKSON	17193	15999	42.8	31.0	20.5	3.6	2.1	29874	34284	12	19	9234	30.1	40.8	24.9	3.8	0.4	70195
38305	JACKSON	28142	17230	18.9	28.7	34.2	11.1	7.1	52166	60362	76	91	12152	5.9	20.4	51.8	18.9	3.1	115107
38310	ADAMSVILLE	18362	2241	38.7	35.3	20.2	3.4	2.4	32442	35981	19	34	1789	31.6	30.1	28.6	9.5	0.2	72820
38311	BATH SPRINGS	18177	419	34.4	32.2	29.4	2.4	1.7	35067	39725	28	48	350	36.9	33.1	20.0	6.9	3.1	66739
38313	BEECH BLUFF	18641	1220	25.6	36.3	32.4	4.8	1.0	41343	46698	51	73	1025	22.2	35.4	33.6	6.7	2.1	80872
38315	BETHEL SPRINGS	18518	1676	39.2	32.3	23.5	2.3	2.7	32320	35920	19	32	1383	42.7	29.8	21.0	6.0	0.5	59853
38316	BRADFORD	18208	1227	36.8	29.5	29.3	3.1	1.3	35511	40244	30	51	1005	30.4	37.7	26.9	5.0	0.1	69598
38317	BRUCETON	18351	1085	37.6	36.5	21.7	3.0	1.3	32502	36194	19	34	837	39.2	38.4	18.5	3.0	1.0	60491
38318	BUENA VISTA	17719	175	34.9	37.1	22.9	2.9	2.3	34387	37863	25	45	147	36.7	37.4	21.8	2.0	2.0	63421
38320	CAMDEN	16666	4520	39.2	35.5	20.7	3.9	0.8	31448	34402	16	26	3541	25.5	36.4	29.9	7.0	1.2	77563
38321	CEDAR GROVE	19720	687	36.4	32.6	26.2	3.1	1.8	35487	39874	29	50	576	39.1	30.4	21.7	8.3	0.5	63571
38326	COUNCE	25051	1124	29.1	33.2	24.2	9.0	4.5	38744	43504	42	64	941	22.5	26.6	32.5	14.2	4.1	91491
	TENNESSEE	22498		30.2	30.2	28.1	7.5	4.1	40531	46137				15.0	25.0	39.4	17.3	3.3	104905
	UNITED STATES	25866		24.7	27.1	30.8	10.9	6.5	48124	56710				10.9	15.0	33.7	30.1	10.4	145905

ZIP CODE #	POST OFFICE NAME	FINANCIAL SERVICES: Auto Loan	Home Loan	Invest-ments	Retire-ment Plans	THE HOME: Home Improvements: Home Repair	Lawn & Garden	Furnishings: Comput-ers & Hard-ware	Major Appli-ances	TV, Radio, Sound Equip-ment	Furni-ture	ENTERTAINMENT: Dine out/ Carry out	Sports Equip-ment	Fees & Tickets	Toys & Games	Travel	Cable TV	PERSONAL: Apparel & Services	Auto Repairs	Health Insur-ance	Pets & Supplies
38024	DYERSBURG	72	61	50	58	64	72	62	67	67	61	81	78	59	80	62	69	77	67	74	82
38028	EADS	127	128	114	127	130	135	117	123	116	118	144	145	119	147	118	115	140	119	122	148
38030	FINLEY	74	49	22	43	56	64	48	60	58	49	68	71	41	64	48	62	61	59	73	85
38034	FRIENDSHIP	72	48	22	42	55	63	47	58	56	47	66	70	40	62	47	60	60	58	72	83
38037	GATES	85	57	26	49	64	74	55	69	66	56	78	82	47	73	56	71	71	68	85	97
38039	GRAND JUNCTION	73	49	22	42	55	63	47	59	57	48	67	70	40	63	48	61	61	58	72	83
38040	HALLS	76	52	25	45	58	68	51	63	61	51	71	74	44	68	52	65	65	62	77	87
38041	HENNING	59	41	21	36	46	53	40	49	47	40	55	58	35	53	40	50	51	48	59	68
38042	HICKORY VALLEY	68	46	21	40	52	60	44	55	53	45	63	66	38	59	45	57	57	55	68	78
38044	HORNSBY	89	59	27	51	67	77	57	72	69	58	81	86	49	77	58	74	74	71	88	102
38049	MASON	95	67	38	59	74	86	65	79	77	67	91	92	58	86	66	82	84	78	95	108
38052	MIDDLETON	77	55	31	50	61	70	54	65	63	55	75	77	48	72	55	67	69	64	77	88
38053	MILLINGTON	88	88	84	86	88	93	86	88	86	86	107	103	86	107	86	86	104	88	87	101
38057	MOSCOW	99	76	47	69	83	93	72	85	81	73	97	101	66	96	74	86	90	83	98	115
38058	MUNFORD	93	86	69	83	89	95	80	87	83	80	101	103	79	103	81	84	97	85	91	109
38059	NEWBERN	75	64	47	61	68	75	62	68	67	61	80	80	59	80	63	69	76	67	76	86
38060	OAKLAND	106	92	68	87	98	105	85	95	91	85	111	114	83	112	88	94	105	93	105	124
38061	POCAHONTAS	79	53	24	46	60	69	51	64	62	52	73	77	44	69	52	67	66	63	79	91
38063	RIPLEY	71	51	30	46	56	65	51	60	59	51	70	71	45	67	51	63	65	60	71	81
38066	ROSSVILLE	93	78	54	72	83	91	72	82	79	73	95	98	69	96	74	82	90	81	92	109
38067	SAULSBURY	76	51	23	44	57	66	49	61	59	50	69	73	42	65	50	64	63	61	75	87
38068	SOMERVILLE	84	63	41	57	69	79	63	73	72	63	86	85	57	82	64	76	79	72	86	96
38069	STANTON	83	56	25	48	63	73	54	67	65	55	76	80	46	72	55	70	69	67	83	95
38075	WHITEVILLE	57	38	17	33	43	49	37	46	44	37	52	55	31	49	37	47	47	45	56	65
38076	WILLISTON	98	77	50	71	84	93	73	85	82	73	98	101	68	97	75	85	91	83	97	114
38079	TIPTONVILLE	49	36	22	34	40	47	39	44	44	37	52	50	34	49	38	46	47	43	52	55
38080	RIDGELY	62	43	22	38	48	56	43	52	51	43	60	61	38	57	44	55	55	52	63	70
38103	MEMPHIS	95	90	165	102	85	96	106	95	110	108	139	116	110	145	105	109	138	102	90	106
38104	MEMPHIS	68	65	88	68	64	70	75	70	76	74	95	84	74	94	73	74	93	74	68	77
38105	MEMPHIS	34	28	36	27	27	32	34	33	37	34	46	38	33	43	33	38	45	35	35	37
38106	MEMPHIS	48	41	44	37	40	49	44	46	50	46	61	49	44	56	44	53	59	47	52	53
38107	MEMPHIS	53	46	53	43	45	53	52	51	56	52	70	57	51	65	50	58	67	53	56	58
38108	MEMPHIS	47	42	45	39	41	48	45	46	50	45	61	50	45	58	45	52	58	47	51	52
38109	MEMPHIS	56	52	58	48	51	60	54	55	59	56	73	58	55	69	55	62	70	55	60	63
38111	MEMPHIS	70	68	83	68	67	74	75	71	76	74	95	83	75	94	73	76	93	74	71	79
38112	MEMPHIS	69	64	75	63	63	71	70	68	73	70	91	78	70	88	69	74	88	71	71	77
38114	MEMPHIS	49	42	48	38	41	49	46	46	51	47	63	51	46	59	45	54	61	48	52	53
38115	MEMPHIS	72	67	77	72	66	69	73	70	71	74	91	84	72	87	70	68	88	73	64	78
38116	MEMPHIS	64	60	73	58	58	67	65	63	69	66	86	71	66	84	64	70	84	65	66	72
38117	MEMPHIS	109	122	138	119	122	133	117	117	116	117	145	132	123	147	121	118	142	116	119	129
38118	MEMPHIS	61	59	67	58	57	62	62	60	64	63	80	70	62	78	60	63	78	62	59	68
38119	MEMPHIS	118	126	144	130	123	130	127	123	122	127	154	145	129	153	125	118	152	125	115	135
38120	MEMPHIS	147	177	219	177	173	184	164	162	156	166	197	185	177	201	170	154	196	160	152	177
38122	MEMPHIS	57	59	65	57	58	64	61	59	62	59	77	68	62	79	61	63	75	60	61	66
38125	MEMPHIS	128	146	145	152	139	136	132	131	121	137	154	153	137	156	130	114	153	127	112	143
38126	MEMPHIS	24	20	24	18	19	23	23	23	26	24	32	25	22	30	22	28	31	24	26	26
38127	MEMPHIS	51	47	56	44	45	52	51	49	55	52	68	56	52	68	50	56	67	51	52	57
38128	MEMPHIS	67	66	74	67	65	69	69	67	69	69	87	78	69	86	68	68	85	69	65	75
38131	MEMPHIS	0	0	0	0	0	0	0	0	0	0	0	0	0	0	0	0	0	0	0	0
38132	MEMPHIS	0	0	0	0	0	0	0	0	0	0	0	0	0	0	0	0	0	0	0	0
38133	MEMPHIS	107	120	117	123	116	115	109	109	101	112	128	127	112	129	108	96	127	106	96	121
38134	MEMPHIS	83	87	97	90	84	87	88	85	84	88	107	101	89	106	86	81	105	87	78	94
38135	MEMPHIS	110	124	123	127	121	119	113	113	106	115	133	132	117	136	112	101	131	110	101	125
38138	GERMANTOWN	167	206	233	208	202	207	186	183	173	187	218	211	200	226	191	169	218	178	168	201
38139	GERMANTOWN	219	277	318	283	269	275	244	238	223	248	283	274	270	295	250	218	286	229	214	263
38141	MEMPHIS	91	99	99	103	95	94	94	92	87	96	111	109	95	110	91	82	109	92	80	101
38152	MEMPHIS	89	54	68	61	53	64	105	77	102	89	127	107	86	114	84	90	119	94	72	88
38201	MC KENZIE	82	63	42	58	68	78	63	72	71	63	85	84	58	82	64	75	79	71	84	94
38220	ATWOOD	71	48	22	42	54	62	46	58	56	47	65	69	40	62	47	60	60	57	71	82
38221	BIG SANDY	68	46	21	39	52	60	44	55	53	45	63	66	38	59	45	57	57	55	68	78
38222	BUCHANAN	74	55	34	49	62	71	52	64	61	53	72	74	46	69	55	65	66	63	77	87
38224	COTTAGE GROVE	74	50	23	43	56	65	48	60	58	49	68	72	41	64	49	62	62	59	74	85
38225	DRESDEN	75	55	33	51	60	70	56	65	64	56	76	75	50	73	56	68	70	64	77	84
38226	DUKEDOM	82	55	25	48	63	72	53	67	64	54	76	80	45	71	54	69	69	66	82	95
38229	GLEASON	73	49	23	43	56	64	48	60	58	49	68	71	41	64	49	62	61	59	73	84
38230	GREENFIELD	72	49	25	44	56	64	49	60	58	49	68	70	42	65	50	63	62	59	73	82
38231	HENRY	81	54	24	47	61	70	52	65	63	53	74	78	44	70	53	68	67	64	80	92
38232	HORNBEAK	78	52	24	45	59	68	50	63	61	51	71	75	43	67	51	65	65	62	77	89
38233	KENTON	79	54	26	47	61	70	52	65	62	53	74	77	45	70	53	67	67	64	79	91
38236	MANSFIELD	78	52	24	45	59	68	51	63	61	52	72	76	43	68	52	66	65	63	78	90
38237	MARTIN	68	54	48	53	56	63	62	61	65	59	79	75	57	76	59	64	75	64	65	75
38240	OBION	77	52	23	44	58	67	50	62	60	51	70	74	42	67	51	65	64	62	77	88
38241	PALMERSVILLE	94	63	28	54	71	82	61	76	73	62	86	91	52	81	62	79	78	75	94	108
38242	PARIS	69	55	40	51	59	67	55	61	61	54	73	71	51	72	55	64	68	61	71	79
38251	PURYEAR	80	53	24	46	60	70	51	64	62	52	73	77	44	69	52	67	66	64	79	91
38253	RIVES	86	58	26	50	65	75	56	70	67	57	79	83	47	75	57	72	72	69	86	99
38255	SHARON	71	51	29	46	56	66	52	61	60	51	71	71	46	67	52	64	65	61	74	80
38256	SPRINGVILLE	66	52	37	47	59	67	49	59	56	50	67	68	45	64	53	60	62	58	71	79
38257	SOUTH FULTON	84	64	40	57	70	79	61	72	70	61	84	85	56	82	62	74	77	71	85	97
38258	TREZEVANT	71	47	21	41	54	62	46	57	55	47	65	68	39	61	47	59	59	57	71	81
38259	TRIMBLE	76	66	49	62	70	76	61	68	66	61	80	82	59	81	63	68	75	67	75	89
38260	TROY	83	63	37	57	69	77	59	71	68	60	81	84	54	79	61	72	75	69	82	96
38261	UNION CITY	74	69	64	66	71	78	70	72	73	68	90	83	69	91	70	75	86	72	77	85
38301	JACKSON	60	53	54	51	54	61	57	58	61	56	75	66	55	73	56	63	71	59	63	68
38305	JACKSON	98	105	111	107	103	107	102	101	98	102	123	118	104	123	101	95	121	101	95	113
38310	ADAMSVILLE	80	54	27	48	61	71	54	66	64	54	76	78	47	71	55	69	69	65	81	91
38311	BATH SPRINGS	82	55	25	47	62	71	53	66	64	54	75	79	45	71	54	68	68	65	81	94
38313	BEECH BLUFF	82	65	43	60	71	78	61	71	68	62	82	85	57	81	63	71	77	70	81	95
38315	BETHEL SPRINGS	85	57	26	49	65	74	55	69	66	56	78	82	47	74	56	72	71	68	85	98
38316	BRADFORD	84	56	25	48	64	73	54	68	65	55	77	81	46	73	55	70	70	67	83	96
38317	BRUCETON	75	53	28	47	59	69	53	64	63	53	74	74	46	69	54	67	67	63	78	85
38318	BUENA VISTA	83	55	25	48	63	72	53	67	64	54	76	80	45	71	54	69	69	66	82	95
38320	CAMDEN	69	49	26	44	54	63	49	59	58	49	68	68	43	64	50	62	62	58	71	79
38321	CEDAR GROVE	86	57	26	49	65	75	55	69	67	56	78	83	47	74	56	72	71	68	85	98
38326	COUNCE	100	72	42	64	82	93	69	85	81	69	95	100	60	92	72	86	87	84	102	118
	TENNESSEE	85	76	68	73	78	85	76	80	79	76	97	94	73	96	75	81	93	80	85	97
	UNITED STATES	100	100	100	100	100	100	100	100	100	100	100	100	100	100	100	100	100	100	100	100

POPULATION CHANGE

# POST OFFICE NAME	COUNTY FIPS CODE	POPULATION 2000	2004	2009	2000-2004 ANNUAL RATE % Rate	State Centile	HOUSEHOLDS 2000	2004	2009	% Annual Rate 2000-2004	2004 Average HH Size	FAMILIES 2000	2004	% Annual Rate 2000-2004
38327 CRUMP	071	513	520	522	0.3	34	223	231	236	0.8	2.25	164	166	0.3
38328 DARDEN	077	812	812	819	0.0	20	336	343	352	0.5	2.37	242	243	0.1
38329 DECATURVILLE	039	3076	3369	3609	2.2	88	1279	1434	1569	2.7	2.29	910	999	2.2
38330 DYER	053	4493	4336	4286	-0.8	3	1810	1774	1778	-0.5	2.38	1301	1251	-0.9
38332 ENVILLE	023	943	967	994	0.6	44	384	399	415	0.9	2.42	280	286	0.5
38333 EVA	005	568	628	664	2.4	91	246	279	300	3.0	2.25	181	200	2.4
38334 FINGER	109	1840	1850	1875	0.1	27	698	714	734	0.5	2.59	540	543	0.1
38337 GADSDEN	033	1475	1559	1629	1.3	68	565	609	646	1.8	2.56	432	457	1.3
38339 GUYS	109	508	525	540	0.8	51	204	215	225	1.2	2.44	151	157	0.9
38340 HENDERSON	023	11287	11746	12166	0.9	57	4006	4245	4460	1.4	2.51	2925	3041	0.9
38341 HOLLADAY	005	2275	2497	2638	2.2	89	912	1017	1089	2.6	2.46	679	743	2.1
38342 HOLLOW ROCK	017	1742	1721	1721	-0.3	9	681	686	694	0.2	2.51	494	489	-0.2
38343 HUMBOLDT	053	16475	16609	16803	0.2	29	6544	6700	6861	0.6	2.43	4616	4648	0.2
38344 HUNTINGDON	017	8928	8881	8868	-0.1	15	3522	3548	3570	0.2	2.42	2538	2509	-0.3
38345 HURON	077	1739	1737	1753	0.0	18	666	678	695	0.4	2.56	503	504	0.1
38347 JACKS CREEK	023	421	452	477	1.7	79	162	176	187	2.0	2.57	121	129	1.5
38348 LAVINIA	017	1102	1104	1099	0.0	23	421	430	432	0.5	2.53	311	312	0.1
38351 LEXINGTON	077	16447	16846	17195	0.6	43	6719	7003	7255	1.0	2.36	4781	4884	0.5
38352 LURAY	023	617	650	678	1.2	66	219	234	246	1.6	2.76	171	180	1.2
38355 MEDINA	113	2597	2847	3007	2.2	88	1048	1160	1238	2.4	2.45	798	868	2.0
38356 MEDON	113	2107	2161	2238	0.6	44	813	854	900	1.2	2.53	619	637	0.7
38357 MICHIE	109	2677	2713	2757	0.3	33	1082	1120	1158	0.8	2.42	798	811	0.4
38358 MILAN	053	11696	11961	12084	0.5	42	4742	4915	5025	0.9	2.37	3278	3329	0.4
38359 MILLEDGEVILLE	109	357	356	358	-0.1	16	167	169	173	0.3	2.11	119	118	-0.2
38361 MORRIS CHAPEL	071	954	950	954	-0.1	15	363	365	369	0.1	2.60	275	272	-0.3
38362 OAKFIELD	113	1190	1448	1642	4.7	99	449	558	644	5.3	2.59	353	430	4.8
38363 PARSONS	039	5886	5841	5957	-0.2	12	2456	2481	2575	0.2	2.30	1658	1633	-0.4
38366 PINSON	113	2328	2514	2675	1.8	81	857	948	1026	2.4	2.63	670	727	1.9
38367 RAMER	109	2986	3029	3091	0.3	36	1218	1260	1309	0.8	2.40	889	902	0.3
38368 REAGAN	077	1547	1606	1653	0.9	55	620	655	683	1.3	2.45	460	477	0.9
38369 RUTHERFORD	053	2179	2147	2124	-0.4	8	896	899	902	0.1	2.39	631	619	-0.5
38370 SALTILLO	071	706	706	703	0.0	20	324	331	334	0.5	2.13	213	212	-0.1
38371 SARDIS	077	1284	1302	1316	0.3	35	532	549	563	0.7	2.37	374	379	0.3
38372 SAVANNAH	071	17180	17209	17252	0.0	23	6953	7127	7263	0.6	2.35	4928	4952	0.1
38374 SCOTTS HILL	077	1959	1956	1984	0.0	17	813	828	853	0.4	2.36	597	596	0.0
38375 SELMER	109	8173	8441	8709	0.8	50	3303	3476	3651	1.2	2.34	2267	2335	0.7
38376 SHILOH	071	422	425	427	0.2	28	175	180	185	0.7	2.36	132	133	0.2
38379 STANTONVILLE	109	1394	1395	1407	0.0	22	568	577	591	0.4	2.41	426	426	0.0
38380 SUGAR TREE	039	528	535	546	0.3	33	247	256	266	0.9	2.09	169	171	0.3
38381 TOONE	069	2365	2678	2899	3.0	94	902	1042	1152	3.5	2.53	635	720	3.0
38382 TRENTON	053	9699	9793	9830	0.2	31	3965	4068	4139	0.6	2.34	2704	2710	0.1
38387 WESTPORT	017	420	467	491	2.5	92	157	179	190	3.1	2.57	120	135	2.8
38388 WILDERSVILLE	077	2663	2733	2786	0.6	45	1031	1079	1118	1.1	2.52	779	802	0.7
38390 YUMA	017	793	827	840	1.0	59	313	333	343	1.5	2.45	235	246	1.1
38391 DENMARK	113	1139	1126	1160	-0.3	10	417	421	440	0.2	2.67	301	296	-0.4
38392 MERCER	113	640	643	664	0.1	26	258	265	279	0.6	2.43	187	188	0.1
38401 COLUMBIA	119	50876	54394	59364	1.6	76	19456	21072	23295	1.9	2.53	14001	14896	1.5
38425 CLIFTON	181	3957	4028	4076	0.4	38	863	915	956	1.4	2.31	608	632	0.9
38449 ARDMORE	055	3641	3903	4060	1.7	77	1439	1580	1673	2.2	2.43	1067	1147	1.7
38450 COLLINWOOD	181	2336	2463	2546	1.3	67	943	1018	1078	1.8	2.42	683	723	1.4
38451 CULLEOKA	119	3864	4141	4498	1.6	77	1376	1500	1651	2.1	2.76	1109	1188	1.6
38452 CYPRESS INN	181	1183	1181	1191	0.0	17	448	457	471	0.5	2.58	361	362	0.1
38453 DELLROSE	103	258	256	256	-0.2	12	106	107	108	0.2	2.39	82	81	-0.3
38454 DUCK RIVER	081	885	909	932	0.6	46	337	351	364	1.0	2.59	261	267	0.5
38456 ETHRIDGE	099	4208	4273	4328	0.4	36	1368	1408	1445	0.7	3.03	1053	1066	0.3
38457 FIVE POINTS	099	859	929	975	1.9	82	337	372	397	2.4	2.50	262	283	1.8
38459 FRANKEWING	103	391	386	385	-0.3	9	156	157	159	0.2	2.46	120	119	-0.2
38460 GOODSPRING	055	1082	1091	1101	0.2	29	420	433	444	0.7	2.52	319	323	0.3
38461 HAMPSHIRE	101	1257	1290	1362	0.6	45	463	485	520	1.1	2.66	363	374	0.7
38462 HOHENWALD	101	9836	10107	10449	0.6	46	3794	3948	4130	0.9	2.50	2759	2817	0.5
38463 IRON CITY	181	2447	2448	2472	0.0	21	942	965	996	0.6	2.54	717	722	0.2
38464 LAWRENCEBURG	099	21742	21682	21915	-0.1	16	8790	8904	9131	0.3	2.39	6198	6145	-0.2
38468 LEOMA	099	4425	4548	4648	0.7	47	1647	1718	1779	1.0	2.65	1307	1342	0.6
38469 LORETTO	099	3940	4070	4175	0.8	50	1541	1619	1685	1.2	2.51	1161	1198	0.7
38471 LUTTS	181	891	872	875	-0.5	6	343	345	355	0.1	2.53	267	264	-0.3
38472 LYNNVILLE	055	2803	2975	3089	1.4	71	1061	1148	1210	1.9	2.59	805	857	1.5
38473 MINOR HILL	055	1111	1177	1220	1.4	70	443	477	501	1.8	2.47	337	357	1.4
38474 MOUNT PLEASANT	119	6963	7184	7727	0.7	49	2740	2875	3136	1.1	2.47	1999	2045	0.5
38475 OLIVEHILL	071	583	590	595	0.3	32	203	211	216	0.9	2.75	155	158	0.5
38476 PRIMM SPRINGS	081	1377	1548	1727	2.8	94	491	561	634	3.2	2.76	384	430	2.7
38477 PROSPECT	055	2383	2401	2435	0.2	29	899	928	959	0.8	2.58	693	704	0.4
38478 PULASKI	055	18385	18549	18833	0.2	30	7454	7662	7902	0.7	2.36	5143	5166	0.1
38481 SAINT JOSEPH	099	848	840	847	-0.2	11	349	353	362	0.3	2.38	257	256	-0.1
38482 SANTA FE	119	1574	1762	1961	2.7	92	611	698	788	3.2	2.52	461	516	2.7
38483 SUMMERTOWN	099	4279	4592	4813	1.7	78	1559	1702	1811	2.1	2.70	1230	1322	1.7
38485 WAYNESBORO	181	6936	6943	7013	0.0	22	2757	2822	2915	0.6	2.37	1957	1964	0.1
38486 WESTPOINT	099	959	959	969	0.0	20	373	382	392	0.6	2.51	282	283	0.1
38487 WILLIAMSPORT	119	671	689	733	0.6	45	255	267	287	1.1	2.58	202	208	0.6
38488 TAFT	103	1988	2079	2118	1.1	61	750	800	827	1.5	2.59	580	607	1.1
38501 COOKEVILLE	141	31902	33432	35130	1.1	62	13219	14064	14991	1.5	2.26	7924	8229	0.8
38504 ALLARDT	049	814	814	824	0.0	20	306	312	323	0.5	2.61	239	240	0.1
38505 COOKEVILLE	141	776	811	837	1.0	61	13	15	17	3.4	2.53	5	6	4.4
38506 COOKEVILLE	141	22248	23174	24198	1.0	58	8720	9245	9806	1.4	2.48	6447	6697	0.9
38541 ALLONS	133	1448	1462	1476	0.2	31	608	628	648	0.8	2.33	462	469	0.4
38542 ALLRED	133	18	19	20	1.3	67	7	8	8	3.2	2.38	5	6	4.4
38543 ALPINE	133	618	607	605	-0.4	7	247	249	253	0.2	2.44	179	177	-0.3
38544 BAXTER	141	6535	6864	7214	1.2	64	2642	2822	3008	1.6	2.43	1900	1987	1.1
38545 BLOOMINGTON SPRINGS	087	1081	1201	1295	2.5	92	404	455	498	2.8	2.62	301	333	2.4
38547 BRUSH CREEK	159	1253	1287	1312	0.6	46	468	491	507	1.1	2.62	362	373	0.7
38548 BUFFALO VALLEY	141	622	678	723	2.1	85	239	265	287	2.5	2.54	178	194	2.1
38549 BYRDSTOWN	137	3419	3442	3423	0.2	27	1461	1509	1539	0.8	2.24	1007	1019	0.3
38551 CELINA	027	4458	4630	4789	0.9	56	1930	2058	2183	1.5	2.21	1296	1352	1.0
38552 CHESTNUT MOUND	159	746	753	761	0.2	30	281	288	294	0.6	2.61	215	216	0.1
38553 CLARKRANGE	049	2187	2496	2716	3.2	95	821	958	1064	3.7	2.60	628	720	3.3
38554 CRAWFORD	133	1394	1456	1493	1.0	60	542	580	606	1.6	2.51	431	453	1.0
TENNESSEE					1.0					1.3	2.45			0.9
UNITED STATES					1.2					1.3	2.58			1.1

ZIP CODE #	POST OFFICE NAME	RACE (%) White 2000	White 2004	Black 2000	Black 2004	Asian/Pacific 2000	Asian/Pacific 2004	% Hispanic Origin 2000	% Hispanic Origin 2004	2004 AGE DISTRIBUTION (%) 0-4	5-9	10-14	15-19	20-24	25-44	45-64	65-84	85+	18+	MEDIAN AGE 2004	% 2004 Males	% 2004 Females
38327	CRUMP	98.1	97.9	0.2	0.2	0.0	0.0	1.0	1.2	6.2	6.5	7.5	5.6	5.6	26.7	26.5	14.0	1.4	76.5	40.0	49.6	50.4
38328	DARDEN	97.9	97.7	0.5	0.5	0.1	0.1	1.4	1.6	6.0	6.2	6.2	5.8	6.0	26.7	28.1	13.4	1.6	78.3	40.5	48.8	51.2
38329	DECATURVILLE	94.0	93.7	4.2	4.3	0.2	0.2	0.9	1.1	5.8	5.9	5.9	5.3	5.6	25.7	27.6	15.4	2.9	79.3	42.0	48.5	51.5
38330	DYER	87.5	86.6	11.4	12.2	0.1	0.1	0.6	0.6	5.8	5.9	6.3	5.8	6.2	25.6	25.4	15.6	3.5	78.5	40.9	46.6	53.4
38332	ENVILLE	97.6	97.5	1.6	1.7	0.0	0.0	0.6	0.7	5.5	5.8	6.7	6.4	5.8	26.9	25.7	16.1	1.1	78.0	40.4	50.4	49.6
38333	EVA	98.6	98.4	0.0	0.0	0.4	0.5	0.7	0.5	4.5	5.7	6.4	6.5	5.3	25.2	30.7	14.5	1.3	79.5	43.0	51.0	49.0
38334	FINGER	95.9	95.7	2.0	2.0	0.1	0.1	0.5	0.5	6.6	6.8	7.4	6.3	6.1	28.4	25.3	11.7	1.4	75.4	36.6	50.0	50.1
38337	GADSDEN	85.6	84.0	12.6	13.9	0.0	0.0	0.8	1.0	5.4	6.3	7.6	6.1	5.6	28.2	28.4	11.0	1.4	76.6	39.3	50.6	49.4
38339	GUYS	88.8	88.6	9.7	9.9	0.0	0.0	1.0	1.1	6.7	6.9	6.7	5.9	5.3	26.1	27.8	13.3	1.3	76.2	39.3	49.3	50.7
38340	HENDERSON	86.3	85.6	11.7	12.2	0.3	0.4	1.1	1.4	7.2	6.7	6.6	8.2	10.4	27.2	20.9	10.9	2.0	76.1	32.3	48.6	51.5
38341	HOLLADAY	96.7	96.4	1.7	1.8	0.2	0.2	1.2	1.4	5.9	6.2	6.9	6.3	5.3	25.7	27.8	15.1	1.0	77.2	40.9	49.8	50.2
38342	HOLLOW ROCK	92.7	92.3	5.6	5.8	0.1	0.1	0.8	1.1	6.3	6.4	7.2	6.2	5.9	27.0	25.3	14.4	1.4	76.4	38.6	49.6	50.4
38343	HUMBOLDT	69.6	69.7	28.7	28.5	0.2	0.2	1.2	1.2	6.5	6.6	6.8	6.0	5.9	26.7	25.1	14.0	2.4	76.5	39.6	48.1	51.9
38344	HUNTINGDON	86.4	85.5	11.6	12.2	0.2	0.2	1.2	1.4	6.1	6.1	6.6	6.4	6.1	26.1	25.6	14.5	2.5	77.1	40.0	47.8	52.2
38345	HURON	95.2	94.9	2.7	2.8	0.1	0.1	0.7	0.9	6.8	6.9	7.1	6.2	6.3	30.6	25.0	10.0	1.0	75.5	36.2	49.7	50.3
38347	JACKS CREEK	88.6	87.8	9.0	9.5	0.2	0.2	0.7	0.9	7.1	7.1	7.7	7.3	6.4	27.4	24.1	11.7	1.1	73.5	35.9	48.7	51.3
38348	LAVINIA	93.9	93.4	5.1	5.4	0.2	0.2	0.7	0.8	6.2	6.3	6.3	5.9	5.4	28.7	26.1	12.6	2.5	77.4	39.1	49.7	50.3
38351	LEXINGTON	88.4	87.8	9.9	10.3	0.2	0.2	1.1	1.3	6.5	6.5	6.8	6.1	6.2	28.5	25.0	12.5	1.8	76.3	38.1	48.2	51.8
38352	LURAY	90.9	90.3	7.3	7.7	0.2	0.2	0.8	0.8	7.1	7.2	7.1	6.6	6.5	28.8	25.1	10.6	1.1	74.8	36.3	50.3	49.7
38355	MEDINA	94.6	93.8	4.1	4.9	0.2	0.2	0.7	0.8	7.5	7.6	7.6	6.0	4.8	32.2	23.9	9.1	1.2	73.5	36.2	48.3	51.7
38356	MEDON	67.7	64.2	30.6	33.9	0.1	0.2	1.0	1.2	6.5	6.6	7.4	6.7	6.2	26.8	26.5	11.9	1.4	75.3	39.1	49.9	50.1
38357	MICHIE	94.6	94.3	4.6	4.8	0.0	0.0	1.0	1.2	5.9	6.0	6.3	6.0	5.8	26.7	27.9	13.7	1.7	78.1	40.7	49.9	50.1
38358	MILAN	81.1	80.8	17.0	17.4	0.3	0.2	1.4	1.4	6.7	6.3	6.6	6.3	6.2	25.8	23.9	15.4	2.7	76.5	39.6	46.7	53.3
38359	MILLEDGEVILLE	95.5	95.5	3.1	3.4	0.0	0.0	0.6	0.6	5.6	5.6	6.7	6.2	5.9	25.0	27.8	15.5	1.7	78.7	41.4	49.4	50.6
38361	MORRIS CHAPEL	88.6	88.0	9.6	10.1	0.2	0.2	0.7	1.0	6.0	5.9	6.3	5.9	6.4	25.1	28.8	13.2	2.4	78.3	41.3	49.9	50.1
38362	OAKFIELD	88.2	86.1	10.3	12.2	0.3	0.3	0.6	0.8	7.1	7.2	7.2	6.8	5.7	33.3	24.4	7.7	0.7	74.4	35.2	49.5	50.5
38363	PARSONS	93.2	92.4	3.9	4.2	0.2	0.3	2.4	2.9	5.7	5.7	6.4	5.5	5.7	25.6	25.8	16.8	2.9	78.8	41.7	48.5	51.5
38366	PINSON	92.2	91.3	6.4	7.2	0.0	0.0	1.1	1.4	6.3	6.5	6.7	6.2	5.5	29.8	27.3	10.6	1.2	76.7	38.2	51.0	49.0
38367	RAMER	92.5	92.2	6.3	6.4	0.1	0.2	0.8	1.0	6.7	6.9	6.8	5.7	5.4	27.5	26.6	13.0	1.4	76.1	38.8	49.7	50.3
38368	REAGAN	97.2	96.9	1.6	1.7	0.1	0.1	0.9	1.1	6.9	6.7	6.9	6.3	6.2	26.6	26.0	13.1	1.4	75.8	38.4	49.9	50.1
38369	RUTHERFORD	85.5	84.5	13.5	14.4	0.1	0.1	0.5	0.6	6.2	6.4	7.3	6.0	5.2	26.2	25.1	15.5	2.2	76.4	40.5	47.5	52.5
38370	SALTILLO	90.2	89.5	8.6	9.4	0.1	0.1	1.1	1.4	3.5	4.3	5.8	4.1	5.2	22.5	33.1	19.1	2.3	84.0	48.3	49.9	50.1
38371	SARDIS	97.1	97.0	2.3	2.4	0.1	0.1	0.7	0.8	6.0	6.1	6.4	5.5	5.4	26.2	27.0	14.9	2.5	78.0	41.1	48.9	51.1
38372	SAVANNAH	94.5	94.1	4.0	4.2	0.2	0.3	1.0	1.3	6.1	6.2	6.6	5.9	6.0	26.5	26.1	14.6	2.1	77.5	39.9	49.0	51.0
38374	SCOTTS HILL	98.7	98.6	0.5	0.5	0.1	0.1	1.5	1.8	6.1	6.2	5.6	5.6	5.8	27.2	26.5	14.7	2.1	78.5	40.5	48.2	51.8
38375	SELMER	87.0	86.3	11.0	11.4	0.2	0.3	1.2	1.4	6.1	6.3	6.9	5.7	5.5	26.8	26.1	14.5	2.2	77.0	40.0	48.4	51.6
38376	SHILOH	95.0	94.8	3.8	4.0	0.2	0.2	1.4	1.7	6.1	6.6	6.6	6.4	5.7	26.8	28.0	12.9	0.9	77.2	39.0	50.4	49.7
38379	STANTONVILLE	95.4	95.0	3.2	3.3	0.1	0.1	0.7	0.9	5.7	6.0	6.4	5.6	5.8	27.6	26.8	14.8	1.4	78.6	40.7	51.1	48.9
38380	SUGAR TREE	97.4	97.0	0.8	0.9	0.2	0.2	1.1	1.3	5.2	5.6	5.6	5.6	4.5	23.2	29.2	20.0	1.1	80.2	45.2	51.6	48.4
38381	TOONE	79.1	77.2	19.7	21.4	0.3	0.3	1.4	1.7	7.5	7.4	7.7	6.2	5.6	26.9	25.3	12.3	1.4	73.8	37.5	50.7	49.3
38382	TRENTON	78.5	77.7	19.8	20.7	0.2	0.2	1.4	1.4	6.1	6.3	6.7	5.9	5.6	26.7	25.6	14.5	2.6	77.4	40.2	48.4	51.6
38387	WESTPORT	81.2	79.9	16.2	17.1	0.7	0.9	0.2	0.2	6.0	6.4	7.5	6.0	6.2	27.0	26.1	12.6	2.1	76.0	38.5	49.9	50.1
38388	WILDERSVILLE	86.1	85.5	12.8	13.4	0.1	0.1	1.0	1.2	6.4	6.6	7.2	6.3	6.3	29.1	26.0	11.0	1.0	76.0	37.3	50.0	50.1
38390	YUMA	88.0	86.7	9.2	10.0	0.6	0.7	1.3	1.5	5.8	6.2	7.1	5.6	6.1	28.7	25.6	13.3	1.7	77.4	38.7	49.7	50.3
38391	DENMARK	38.6	35.2	59.5	62.8	0.1	0.1	0.6	0.8	6.2	6.3	7.5	6.8	7.3	25.9	26.0	12.0	2.0	75.7	38.6	51.5	48.5
38392	MERCER	45.2	41.5	53.1	56.8	0.0	0.0	0.5	0.5	6.2	6.4	7.9	7.2	7.2	26.0	25.8	11.5	1.9	74.7	38.1	51.3	48.7
38401	COLUMBIA	80.2	79.1	16.1	16.6	0.4	0.5	3.8	4.5	7.0	6.8	6.8	7.0	6.7	27.6	25.8	10.8	1.6	75.1	37.1	48.7	51.4
38425	CLIFTON	71.8	70.6	27.1	28.2	0.1	0.1	0.9	1.0	3.0	3.0	3.5	4.0	9.4	46.0	21.9	8.4	1.0	88.5	36.2	73.8	26.2
38449	ARDMORE	91.0	90.0	7.4	8.2	0.2	0.2	0.7	0.9	6.0	6.1	5.9	5.9	5.6	26.7	28.5	13.4	1.9	78.5	41.4	49.3	50.7
38450	COLLINWOOD	98.4	98.3	0.1	0.1	0.2	0.2	0.9	1.1	6.2	6.3	7.1	6.5	6.9	27.1	26.4	12.1	1.3	76.4	37.7	48.8	51.2
38451	CULLEOKA	94.3	93.8	3.8	4.1	0.2	0.3	1.2	1.4	7.0	7.2	7.9	7.3	6.2	29.6	26.5	7.6	0.7	73.3	36.3	49.8	50.2
38452	CYPRESS INN	99.3	99.3	0.1	0.1	0.0	0.0	0.6	0.6	6.6	6.8	7.5	6.5	5.8	27.8	26.3	11.7	1.0	75.1	38.0	50.0	50.0
38453	DELLROSE	96.1	95.3	1.2	1.6	0.4	0.4	0.8	0.4	3.9	4.3	4.7	6.6	7.4	28.1	30.5	12.9	1.6	82.8	42.2	51.6	48.4
38454	DUCK RIVER	96.4	96.0	2.5	2.6	0.1	0.1	1.1	1.3	7.4	7.7	6.7	6.3	5.0	25.5	29.3	11.1	1.1	74.3	38.6	51.1	49.0
38456	ETHRIDGE	98.5	98.3	0.8	0.9	0.1	0.2	0.4	0.5	9.4	9.1	9.7	7.8	6.9	26.1	20.9	9.1	0.9	66.8	30.5	50.2	49.9
38457	FIVE POINTS	97.8	97.5	0.0	0.0	0.7	0.9	0.4	0.4	6.4	6.4	6.9	7.0	6.4	29.4	22.9	13.4	1.4	76.1	37.1	49.5	50.5
38459	FRANKEWING	95.9	95.6	1.3	1.6	0.3	0.3	0.5	0.5	3.9	4.2	4.9	6.7	7.5	27.7	29.8	13.5	1.8	82.6	42.2	51.6	48.5
38460	GOODSPRING	93.8	93.1	4.5	5.0	0.0	0.0	0.5	0.6	7.6	7.7	7.5	6.3	6.4	27.2	25.0	11.0	1.2	73.3	36.0	50.0	50.1
38461	HAMPSHIRE	92.6	91.9	5.2	5.5	0.2	0.2	1.6	1.9	6.1	6.5	7.4	6.8	6.1	27.8	29.4	9.1	0.8	75.9	37.7	50.2	49.8
38462	HOHENWALD	97.3	97.0	1.3	1.3	0.2	0.2	1.2	1.4	6.6	6.7	7.0	7.0	6.5	26.7	25.5	12.4	1.8	75.2	37.9	49.6	50.4
38463	IRON CITY	98.7	98.5	0.5	0.6	0.0	0.0	1.1	1.3	6.1	6.2	7.0	7.3	6.3	29.0	25.5	11.3	1.3	76.3	37.6	50.3	49.8
38464	LAWRENCEBURG	95.6	95.1	2.4	2.5	0.4	0.4	1.2	1.5	6.5	6.4	6.9	6.3	6.1	27.1	24.4	14.1	2.3	76.5	38.8	47.9	52.1
38468	LEOMA	98.0	97.8	0.4	0.4	0.1	0.2	0.5	0.6	6.7	6.8	7.4	6.8	6.2	29.0	24.3	11.6	1.2	74.9	36.6	50.6	49.4
38469	LORETTO	98.2	97.9	0.4	0.4	0.2	0.2	1.1	1.4	6.3	6.4	7.1	6.6	6.0	28.0	24.5	13.6	1.5	76.1	38.2	49.6	50.4
38471	LUTTS	99.4	99.3	0.0	0.0	0.1	0.1	0.1	0.1	5.6	5.7	6.8	7.1	6.2	25.2	28.3	13.2	1.8	77.5	40.4	48.9	51.2
38472	LYNNVILLE	93.3	92.6	4.8	5.2	0.3	0.4	0.8	1.0	5.6	5.8	6.9	7.0	6.8	26.6	28.8	11.4	1.3	77.6	39.6	50.6	49.4
38473	MINOR HILL	97.7	97.6	0.7	0.8	0.0	0.0	1.0	1.0	6.0	6.2	7.7	7.3	6.1	25.1	26.5	13.7	1.4	75.5	39.4	49.1	50.9
38474	MOUNT PLEASANT	83.6	82.4	14.7	15.7	0.2	0.2	1.0	1.2	6.2	6.3	7.3	6.9	6.4	26.9	25.9	12.4	1.8	76.0	38.5	47.5	52.5
38475	OLIVEHILL	97.6	97.3	1.0	1.2	0.0	0.0	1.4	1.9	6.6	6.6	6.8	6.4	6.1	27.5	25.8	12.7	1.5	76.1	38.1	51.0	49.0
38476	PRIMM SPRINGS	96.9	96.5	1.5	1.6	0.1	0.1	0.9	1.2	6.1	6.4	6.6	6.5	6.3	27.3	29.2	10.9	0.8	77.1	39.3	51.0	49.0
38477	PROSPECT	89.1	88.3	9.4	10.0	0.0	0.0	0.7	0.9	6.2	6.4	6.8	6.8	6.5	27.0	27.3	11.6	1.5	76.5	39.2	50.2	49.8
38478	PULASKI	83.1	82.2	15.0	15.7	0.5	0.6	1.0	1.2	6.4	6.4	6.7	6.3	6.2	27.3	25.6	13.0	2.2	76.9	39.0	48.7	51.3
38481	SAINT JOSEPH	98.4	98.1	0.9	1.1	0.0	0.0	1.5	1.8	6.1	6.1	6.7	7.3	6.4	30.6	24.2	11.2	1.6	76.6	37.0	49.3	50.7
38482	SANTA FE	97.1	96.8	1.7	1.8	0.0	0.0	0.8	0.9	7.0	7.2	7.0	5.7	6.1	29.1	26.1	10.7	1.1	75.4	37.3	50.6	49.4
38483	SUMMERTOWN	97.9	97.6	0.8	0.8	0.1	0.2	1.1	1.4	7.0	7.3	7.9	6.7	6.3	29.6	24.6	9.8	0.8	73.8	35.8	50.5	49.5
38485	WAYNESBORO	97.4	97.1	1.0	1.0	0.5	0.6	0.9	1.2	5.4	5.7	6.6	6.2	6.1	26.7	25.5	15.4	2.4	78.4	40.4	49.2	50.8
38486	WESTPOINT	96.5	96.3	2.2	2.4	0.1	0.1	0.2	0.2	5.7	5.6	5.8	7.1	7.4	27.2	27.8	11.8	1.5	78.6	39.3	51.2	48.8
38487	WILLIAMSPORT	91.7	90.9	7.2	7.7	0.0	0.2	1.3	1.5	5.5	6.7	7.6	7.0	5.7	28.2	27.9	10.5	1.2	75.6	38.3	49.6	50.4
38488	TAFT	96.0	95.4	1.1	1.2	0.5	0.6	1.4	1.7	6.0	6.3	6.7	6.7	6.3	27.3	28.1	11.6	1.0	76.9	39.4	50.5	49.5
38501	COOKEVILLE	93.4	92.6	2.1	2.1	1.4	1.7	3.1	3.7	5.9	5.4	5.7	8.3	13.5	27.2	21.0	11.4	1.6	79.7	32.5	50.2	49.9
38504	ALLARDT	98.8	98.7	0.0	0.0	0.0	0.0	0.0	0.0	6.6	7.1	7.4	5.2	5.4	27.9	26.5	12.2	1.7	75.6	38.6	50.7	49.3
38505	COOKEVILLE	86.0	84.3	7.2	7.6	3.6	4.3	3.0	3.7	3.6	1.2	0.7	39.2	40.3	11.1	2.5	1.1	0.3	94.1	20.7	56.6	43.4
38506	COOKEVILLE	96.6	96.2	1.3	1.4	0.6	0.8	1.3	1.6	6.6	6.8	6.8	5.8	5.5	28.5	26.6	11.8	1.6	76.3	38.5	49.0	51.0
38541	ALLONS	99.6	99.6	0.1	0.1	0.0	0.0	0.4	0.5	5.6	5.6	5.9	5.6	4.5	28.0	27.7	15.8	1.3	79.4	41.6	51.1	48.9
38542	ALLRED	100.0	100.0	0.0	0.0	0.0	0.0	0.0	0.0	10.5	10.5	10.5	10.5	5.3	31.6	21.1	0.0	0.0	68.4	31.3	47.4	52.6
38543	ALPINE	98.1	97.9	0.2	0.2	0.2	0.2	1.0	1.2	6.3	6.4	7.1	5.6	5.3	26.4	27.0	14.3	1.7	76.8	40.1	51.4	48.6
38544	BAXTER	98.1	97.9	0.1	0.1	0.2	0.2	1.3	1.5	5.9	6.0	6.6	6.4	6.1	27.9	26.4	13.3	1.4	77.5	39.4	50.2	49.8
38545	BLOOMINGTON SPRINGS	98.6	98.5	0.3	0.3	0.1	0.1	1.0	1.2	6.7	6.7	7.1	6.6	5.8	28.6	25.3	11.8	1.4	75.3	37.6	50.2	49.8
38547	BRUSH CREEK	96.3	95.9	1.8	1.8	0.2	0.2	0.4	0.4	5.8	6.1	6.8	6.5	5.4	31.6	27.5	9.3	1.2	77.4	38.4	51.9	48.1
38548	BUFFALO VALLEY	98.2	97.9	1.0	0.9	0.3	0.4	1.3	1.5	5.0	5.3	6.2	5.8	5.8	26.8	29.2	14.2	1.8	80.1	42.1	50.3	49.7
38549	BYRDSTOWN	99.0	99.0	0.1	0.1	0.0	0.0	1.0	1.0	5.7	5.6	5.4	5.6	5.4	23.5	28.7	17.8	2.3	80.2	44.1	49.0	51.0
38551	CELINA	95.8	95.5	2.3	2.4	0.3	0.4	0.7	0.8	4.9	5.1	6.0	6.0	5.4	26.8	27.7	15.9	2.3	80.6	42.3	47.7	52.3
38552	CHESTNUT MOUND	95.4	95.1	3.0	3.2	0.0	0.0	0.3	0.1	6.4	6.8	7.7	6.2	6.2	29.2	25.1	11.2	1.2	75.2	37.8	51.4	48.6
38553	CLARKRANGE	99.5	99.5	0.1	0.0	0.1	0.1	0.3	0.4	6.9	6.7	7.2	7.0	6.5	29.1	24.6	11.1	1.0	75.0	36.6	50.4	49.6
38554	CRAWFORD	97.9	97.6	0.5	0.6	0.0	0.0	1.2	1.4	6.5	6.6	7.1	6.2	6.5	27.0	28.3	10.7	1.2	76.0	38.0	50.1	49.9
	TENNESSEE	80.2	79.4	16.4	16.7	1.0	1.3	2.2	2.6	6.6	6.5	6.8	6.6	7.0	29.0	24.8	11.1	1.5	76.3	36.8	48.9	51.1
	UNITED STATES	75.1	73.6	12.3	12.5	3.8	4.2	12.5	14.1	6.9	6.7	7.2	7.0	7.3	28.6	23.8	10.8	1.7	75.1	36.0	49.1	50.9

#	POST OFFICE NAME	2004 Per Capita Income	2004 HH Income Base	2004 HOUSEHOLD INCOME DISTRIBUTION (%) Less than $25,000	$25,000 to $49,999	$50,000 to $99,999	$100,000 to $149,999	$150,000 or More	MEDIAN HOUSEHOLD INCOME 2004	2009	2004 National Centile	2004 State Centile	2004 Home Value Base	2004 HOME VALUE DISTRIBUTION (%) Less than $50,000	$50,000 to $89,999	$90,000 to $174,999	$175,000 to $399,999	$400,000 or More	2004 Median Home Value
38327	CRUMP	17033	231	37.7	37.2	21.7	3.0	0.4	32323	36642	19	32	192	30.2	32.8	23.4	13.5	0.0	71875
38328	DARDEN	18182	343	37.6	30.6	25.4	5.3	1.2	33924	36920	24	43	284	27.8	32.8	25.7	12.3	1.4	75000
38329	DECATURVILLE	21118	1434	38.2	34.6	20.9	3.2	3.2	32568	36353	20	35	1183	29.7	36.7	27.1	5.8	0.8	69888
38330	DYER	17682	1774	35.8	35.1	23.2	4.6	1.2	33426	37738	22	40	1362	25.2	41.5	25.6	6.8	1.0	68786
38332	ENVILLE	15909	399	44.1	28.1	22.1	5.5	0.3	28056	31923	9	15	336	39.3	28.9	28.0	3.9	0.0	71515
38333	EVA	18011	279	33.7	38.4	22.6	4.3	1.1	33837	36706	24	42	234	25.6	28.2	33.8	12.0	0.4	86087
38334	FINGER	16052	714	38.5	33.1	24.0	3.1	1.4	33098	36734	21	39	594	34.9	37.4	23.4	4.0	0.3	65811
38337	GADSDEN	18202	609	29.4	33.8	31.4	3.6	1.8	39565	43947	45	67	512	23.1	36.7	27.7	12.3	0.2	78776
38339	GUYS	16987	215	37.2	32.1	24.2	5.1	1.4	32720	35978	20	36	178	32.0	37.1	24.2	6.2	0.6	71429
38340	HENDERSON	18190	4245	32.5	31.6	29.7	4.8	1.4	38428	42705	41	62	3131	24.2	31.8	35.5	7.4	1.1	82966
38341	HOLLADAY	15639	1017	40.7	31.7	24.5	2.5	0.7	30552	33403	14	22	854	45.2	25.8	23.4	5.5	0.1	56406
38342	HOLLOW ROCK	17577	686	36.2	38.9	19.7	2.3	2.9	32284	36515	19	32	564	38.8	39.5	16.1	3.0	2.5	62283
38343	HUMBOLDT	19545	6700	33.5	31.7	26.9	5.9	2.0	36036	40817	32	54	5011	25.2	30.6	34.0	9.6	0.7	82776
38344	HUNTINGDON	18444	3548	39.2	30.6	23.2	4.4	2.7	33011	36610	21	38	2750	27.4	37.6	27.7	6.8	0.6	74034
38345	HURON	17850	678	28.9	39.2	28.2	2.1	1.6	39402	43516	44	66	564	27.0	35.8	28.0	8.9	0.4	77333
38347	JACKS CREEK	18065	176	27.3	35.2	31.8	5.1	0.6	40957	45562	50	71	145	27.6	25.5	38.6	7.6	0.7	87353
38348	LAVINIA	17475	430	37.4	29.5	28.1	2.8	2.1	36654	40695	34	56	353	44.2	25.8	20.4	9.4	0.3	56406
38351	LEXINGTON	19321	7003	35.6	34.1	24.4	3.8	2.1	34833	38351	27	46	5386	23.7	34.5	29.8	11.3	0.8	81111
38352	LURAY	15998	234	30.8	35.5	29.1	4.3	0.4	39402	43551	44	66	196	27.6	29.6	37.2	4.6	1.0	83000
38355	MEDINA	23586	1160	21.6	29.9	36.6	9.8	2.2	48965	56126	70	87	928	14.1	27.2	39.7	17.5	1.6	100926
38356	MEDON	19215	854	33.4	29.6	30.4	5.5	1.1	37733	42458	38	59	713	22.4	34.8	29.9	11.8	1.1	82945
38357	MICHIE	16905	1120	38.8	32.1	23.1	4.5	1.4	31757	35669	17	29	927	33.6	35.6	23.4	7.0	0.4	68333
38358	MILAN	19239	4915	32.9	35.3	24.7	5.0	2.1	35792	40503	31	53	3503	20.8	37.3	32.5	8.8	0.5	81814
38359	MILLEDGEVILLE	22860	169	40.8	35.5	17.8	3.0	3.0	29814	33088	12	19	140	41.4	30.0	23.6	4.3	0.7	62000
38361	MORRIS CHAPEL	12986	365	40.0	42.7	14.8	2.5	0.0	31152	34521	15	25	307	45.9	25.4	19.2	9.5	0.0	53289
38362	OAKFIELD	22851	558	16.9	32.4	39.1	9.3	2.3	50569	58668	73	89	488	12.3	33.8	40.4	13.1	0.4	93115
38363	PARSONS	20257	2481	42.9	30.3	20.7	3.6	2.6	29675	32816	12	18	1881	35.1	34.7	23.1	5.7	1.4	66860
38366	PINSON	19569	948	24.4	32.1	37.2	4.3	2.0	42454	48046	54	76	793	20.8	39.7	30.5	6.7	2.3	80176
38367	RAMER	17083	1260	36.1	35.7	23.7	3.2	1.3	32181	35785	18	31	1032	39.2	31.9	22.7	5.3	1.0	66000
38368	REAGAN	18772	655	40.5	31.0	22.4	4.1	2.0	31491	35464	16	27	551	36.8	30.1	25.8	6.7	0.5	69000
38369	RUTHERFORD	16602	899	35.8	36.8	23.1	3.5	0.8	33602	37925	23	41	711	32.6	38.5	21.2	5.1	2.5	65526
38370	SALTILLO	21175	331	45.3	29.6	18.1	4.8	2.1	28190	30922	9	15	273	42.1	33.7	22.3	1.8	0.0	61042
38371	SARDIS	19103	549	41.0	29.0	24.2	4.9	0.9	32867	36410	21	37	451	41.0	33.5	21.5	3.8	0.2	59878
38372	SAVANNAH	17782	7127	43.5	31.1	19.3	4.3	1.8	29502	33065	11	18	5359	28.6	33.1	26.8	10.7	0.9	75536
38374	SCOTTS HILL	19268	828	33.9	31.5	30.3	2.7	1.6	36027	40372	32	54	686	35.3	32.5	24.2	6.7	1.3	71774
38375	SELMER	19749	3476	39.2	30.8	24.8	3.5	1.6	33158	36080	21	39	2649	31.7	36.2	23.3	7.9	1.0	70900
38376	SHILOH	16136	180	43.3	33.3	16.7	5.6	1.1	30364	33625	13	21	151	29.8	33.8	28.5	7.3	0.7	69643
38379	STANTONVILLE	17367	577	35.9	34.8	23.9	4.3	1.0	34127	38004	24	43	487	38.2	27.5	24.0	8.8	1.4	64881
38380	SUGAR TREE	18547	256	35.2	41.4	18.4	3.9	1.2	31078	35769	15	24	219	51.6	25.6	20.6	2.3	0.0	48871
38381	TOONE	18645	1042	39.4	30.6	23.1	4.1	2.7	32374	35742	19	33	834	31.1	33.9	29.1	5.5	0.4	72836
38382	TRENTON	18548	4068	36.7	29.8	28.0	4.5	1.1	33507	37339	22	41	2941	21.8	33.5	33.8	9.9	1.1	83210
38387	WESTPORT	16465	179	38.0	32.4	25.7	2.8	1.1	32585	37119	20	35	152	38.2	33.6	25.7	2.0	0.7	62667
38388	WILDERSVILLE	19264	1079	33.7	31.3	27.9	4.4	2.7	36443	40492	33	55	897	31.3	27.1	30.4	9.1	2.0	76311
38390	YUMA	16345	333	37.2	33.9	25.2	2.4	1.2	33553	37579	23	41	279	41.6	30.5	23.7	3.9	0.4	61286
38391	DENMARK	15111	421	38.0	36.8	19.2	4.8	1.2	31773	36225	17	29	335	37.0	39.7	17.6	5.7	0.0	61447
38392	MERCER	15721	265	38.1	35.5	23.4	2.6	0.4	33470	37071	22	40	210	36.2	40.0	16.2	6.7	1.0	64500
38401	COLUMBIA	22621	21072	26.1	28.4	31.7	10.2	3.5	45912	52268	64	82	15188	9.7	21.1	46.4	19.7	3.1	117060
38425	CLIFTON	15298	915	41.1	36.1	18.9	1.4	2.5	29329	32023	11	17	698	37.8	32.2	20.9	7.7	1.3	68060
38449	ARDMORE	20654	1580	29.4	34.2	28.2	6.0	2.2	39887	44620	46	68	1296	20.0	32.3	36.0	10.8	0.9	87479
38450	COLLINWOOD	17658	1018	47.4	32.2	16.4	2.3	1.8	26349	28532	6	11	821	41.7	35.1	20.8	2.2	0.2	60848
38451	CULLEOKA	21989	1500	21.0	29.5	36.5	9.2	3.8	49551	56489	71	87	1256	10.0	17.8	50.2	19.6	2.5	122908
38452	CYPRESS INN	13128	457	40.9	39.6	18.2	0.9	0.4	29793	32102	12	19	393	32.8	27.0	32.3	6.1	1.8	79400
38453	DELLROSE	18939	107	29.9	32.7	30.8	4.7	1.9	35832	40554	31	53	94	37.2	31.9	20.2	8.5	2.1	66364
38454	DUCK RIVER	14458	351	41.3	26.5	28.2	4.0	0.0	28517	32419	10	16	295	41.4	15.3	39.0	4.4	0.0	81136
38456	ETHRIDGE	13974	1408	38.3	29.2	26.7	4.6	1.3	32114	35454	18	31	1148	20.5	30.1	34.6	13.2	1.7	89286
38457	FIVE POINTS	18096	372	38.2	34.1	22.3	2.4	3.0	31443	34355	16	26	304	28.3	33.6	30.3	7.6	0.3	72632
38459	FRANKEWING	18417	157	30.6	33.1	30.6	4.5	1.3	35549	40182	30	51	138	37.0	31.2	20.3	10.1	1.5	66471
38460	GOODSPRING	17493	433	29.1	40.4	25.9	2.5	2.1	36562	41183	34	56	359	23.7	36.5	34.5	4.2	1.1	78088
38461	HAMPSHIRE	18437	485	25.4	33.2	33.8	6.0	1.7	42835	47759	56	77	403	21.6	23.1	35.2	18.4	1.7	98600
38462	HOHENWALD	16466	3948	39.4	32.5	23.9	3.3	1.0	32569	35727	20	35	3144	29.0	33.9	30.1	6.6	0.4	74310
38463	IRON CITY	15868	965	39.1	34.9	22.2	2.2	1.7	30968	34214	15	23	818	34.8	35.2	24.3	5.3	0.4	66809
38464	LAWRENCEBURG	19876	8904	37.6	35.0	22.0	2.8	2.7	32862	36087	20	37	6595	15.9	35.0	39.4	8.5	1.3	89192
38468	LEOMA	16956	1718	32.0	37.0	26.0	3.0	2.1	35761	39291	31	52	1413	23.8	27.4	38.7	9.9	0.2	88500
38469	LORETTO	19479	1619	33.7	36.8	23.2	3.6	2.7	34979	38708	27	47	1328	22.2	35.5	32.2	8.8	1.2	82256
38471	LUTTS	12399	345	43.2	45.8	9.6	0.3	1.2	29652	32458	12	18	294	52.7	25.5	19.1	1.4	1.4	46522
38472	LYNNVILLE	20751	1148	27.6	33.9	29.2	7.0	2.4	42571	47809	55	76	951	20.4	32.7	28.3	17.3	1.4	87050
38473	MINOR HILL	17466	477	31.0	32.5	31.7	4.2	0.6	39678	44311	45	67	388	21.1	37.4	33.3	7.0	1.3	82326
38474	MOUNT PLEASANT	18305	2875	31.6	33.2	29.4	4.4	1.5	38623	44174	42	63	2181	18.8	30.4	43.7	6.4	0.7	90893
38475	OLIVEHILL	13729	211	39.3	37.4	18.5	3.8	1.0	31173	35239	15	25	176	36.9	28.4	23.9	10.2	0.6	68889
38476	PRIMM SPRINGS	19585	561	26.9	34.4	29.8	5.2	3.7	42359	49140	54	75	477	14.1	25.6	31.0	21.4	8.0	111706
38477	PROSPECT	18246	928	28.5	36.8	27.8	4.5	2.5	36707	41660	34	57	780	22.3	31.0	32.8	12.1	1.8	86533
38478	PULASKI	20702	7662	33.0	30.5	28.4	5.6	2.6	38037	42470	39	60	5699	14.5	35.2	37.0	11.3	2.0	90344
38481	SAINT JOSEPH	17540	353	39.1	38.5	20.1	0.9	1.4	30883	34367	15	23	287	39.7	38.0	19.5	2.4	0.4	59833
38482	SANTA FE	22915	698	19.8	37.0	34.0	5.2	4.2	44815	51400	61	80	584	15.2	26.2	38.7	15.6	4.3	98621
38483	SUMMERTOWN	16483	1702	29.9	38.5	25.9	3.7	2.1	36065	39935	32	54	1416	23.5	30.3	31.6	13.9	0.6	85610
38485	WAYNESBORO	17275	2822	43.3	37.2	15.3	2.2	2.0	28335	30953	9	15	2249	45.4	32.1	18.7	3.6	0.3	56006
38486	WESTPOINT	14703	382	40.3	35.9	21.5	1.8	0.5	29296	32289	11	17	318	45.0	26.7	26.7	1.6	0.0	60000
38487	WILLIAMSPORT	23694	267	21.4	32.6	34.1	6.7	5.2	46593	52644	65	83	227	13.7	22.0	39.7	21.2	3.5	107372
38488	TAFT	19282	800	30.3	32.5	26.3	8.3	2.8	37851	43264	39	60	664	26.1	25.9	29.5	17.0	1.5	86829
38501	COOKEVILLE	20598	14064	40.7	30.5	20.7	5.0	3.0	31750	35453	17	28	8157	8.6	21.2	47.9	18.8	3.6	114108
38504	ALLARDT	15622	312	35.9	36.9	19.9	6.4	1.0	31062	34304	15	24	270	59.6	14.1	15.9	10.4	0.0	45439
38505	COOKEVILLE	7868	15	73.3	26.7	0.0	0.0	0.0	13868	13886	1	2	1	0.0	0.0	100.0	0.0	0.0	95000
38506	COOKEVILLE	19985	9245	29.2	35.5	26.4	6.2	2.7	38627	43037	42	63	7341	13.0	23.0	44.6	17.1	2.4	109256
38541	ALLONS	14131	628	47.5	30.6	20.7	1.3	0.0	29383	28707	11	17	545	41.7	21.7	25.7	10.5	0.6	66600
38542	ALLRED	12500	8	50.0	25.0	25.0	0.0	0.0	25000	25000	5	8	7	14.3	57.1	28.6	0.0	0.0	82500
38543	ALPINE	14368	249	49.0	26.1	22.5	0.8	1.6	25565	28105	5	9	205	47.3	28.3	20.0	4.4	0.0	53929
38544	BAXTER	17242	2822	36.3	36.9	21.3	4.0	1.5	32488	36625	19	34	2267	19.2	31.8	35.4	11.4	2.2	89017
38545	BLOOMINGTON SPRINGS	18287	455	34.5	35.6	22.4	4.4	3.1	34915	39068	27	47	381	24.9	27.0	37.3	9.2	1.6	87000
38547	BRUSH CREEK	19856	491	20.8	33.4	39.1	5.7	1.0	46922	52354	66	84	427	14.5	20.4	43.3	18.5	3.3	109375
38548	BUFFALO VALLEY	15076	265	36.2	39.6	21.9	1.9	0.4	32458	36131	19	34	223	15.3	30.0	35.9	17.5	1.4	95526
38549	BYRDSTOWN	17041	1509	45.4	32.4	17.3	3.2	1.7	27820	30898	8	14	1230	25.0	31.2	30.9	9.5	3.4	80617
38551	CELINA	15747	2058	49.7	31.9	12.7	3.7	2.0	25180	27530	5	9	1575	35.5	33.9	23.9	6.2	0.6	67139
38552	CHESTNUT MOUND	21103	288	25.4	35.8	31.9	5.9	1.0	41196	45857	50	72	237	15.6	28.7	34.6	19.4	1.7	99643
38553	CLARKRANGE	14049	958	43.7	33.7	18.8	2.5	1.3	28635	31711	10	16	792	34.3	33.6	25.0	6.7	0.4	67000
38554	CRAWFORD	15501	580	46.0	37.2	14.5	1.6	0.7	26829	29907	7	12	488	41.4	25.2	25.8	5.1	2.5	58936
	TENNESSEE	22498		30.2	30.2	28.1	7.5	4.1	40531	46137				15.0	25.0	39.4	17.3	3.3	104905
	UNITED STATES	25866		24.7	27.1	30.8	10.9	6.5	48124	56710				10.9	15.0	33.7	30.1	10.4	145905

ZIP CODE		FINANCIAL SERVICES				THE HOME						ENTERTAINMENT						PERSONAL			
						Home Improvements		Furnishings													
#	POST OFFICE NAME	Auto Loan	Home Loan	Investments	Retirement Plans	Home Repair	Lawn & Garden	Computers & Hardware	Major Appliances	TV, Radio, Sound Equipment	Furniture	Dine out/ Carry out	Sports Equipment	Fees & Tickets	Toys & Games	Travel	Cable TV	Apparel & Services	Auto Repairs	Health Insurance	Pets & Supplies
38327	CRUMP	72	48	22	42	55	63	47	58	56	48	66	70	40	62	47	61	60	58	72	83
38328	DARDEN	81	54	25	47	61	71	52	66	63	53	74	78	45	70	53	68	67	65	81	93
38329	DECATURVILLE	86	63	37	56	70	81	61	74	71	61	84	86	54	81	63	76	77	73	89	100
38330	DYER	80	54	24	46	61	70	52	65	62	53	73	77	44	69	53	67	67	64	80	92
38332	ENVILLE	72	49	23	43	55	63	47	59	56	48	67	70	41	63	48	61	61	58	71	82
38333	EVA	72	53	30	46	59	67	50	61	59	50	69	73	44	67	52	63	63	61	74	86
38334	FINGER	78	53	24	45	59	68	51	63	61	52	72	76	43	68	52	66	65	63	78	90
38337	GADSDEN	75	66	51	63	70	75	61	68	65	61	79	81	60	81	63	67	75	66	74	88
38339	GUYS	78	52	24	45	59	68	50	63	61	51	72	75	43	68	51	66	65	62	78	90
38340	HENDERSON	77	62	43	59	66	75	63	70	69	62	83	81	58	80	63	71	77	69	79	87
38341	HOLLADAY	69	50	29	44	56	64	47	58	55	48	65	69	41	63	49	59	60	57	70	81
38342	HOLLOW ROCK	83	56	25	48	63	72	54	67	65	55	76	80	46	72	55	70	69	66	83	95
38343	HUMBOLDT	78	63	48	59	67	75	63	70	69	63	83	82	59	81	63	72	78	69	79	89
38344	HUNTINGDON	79	58	35	52	64	74	57	68	66	57	79	79	51	75	58	71	72	67	81	90
38345	HURON	86	58	26	50	65	75	56	70	67	57	79	83	47	74	57	72	72	69	86	99
38347	JACKS CREEK	74	67	53	65	67	71	64	69	65	66	80	80	61	76	63	64	77	69	68	82
38348	LAVINIA	84	56	25	48	63	73	54	68	65	55	77	81	46	72	55	70	70	67	83	96
38351	LEXINGTON	81	60	36	54	66	74	58	69	67	59	79	81	52	77	59	70	73	68	81	92
38352	LURAY	80	58	33	52	64	71	56	67	64	57	76	79	49	72	56	67	71	66	78	91
38355	MEDINA	90	82	66	80	85	92	78	84	82	78	100	99	77	101	79	83	95	82	90	104
38356	MEDON	82	67	46	62	72	79	63	72	69	63	83	86	59	83	64	72	78	70	81	95
38357	MICHIE	77	52	23	45	58	67	50	62	60	51	71	74	42	67	51	65	64	62	77	88
38358	MILAN	75	60	43	56	64	73	61	67	67	60	81	79	56	79	61	70	75	67	77	85
38359	MILLEDGEVILLE	91	61	28	52	69	79	59	73	71	60	83	88	50	78	60	76	75	73	90	104
38361	MORRIS CHAPEL	64	43	19	37	48	56	41	51	50	42	58	61	35	55	42	53	53	51	63	73
38362	OAKFIELD	89	88	78	86	89	91	82	86	82	83	102	102	82	103	83	81	98	85	84	103
38363	PARSONS	86	59	29	52	66	77	58	71	69	59	81	84	50	77	59	74	74	71	87	98
38366	PINSON	83	73	55	69	78	84	68	76	72	68	88	90	66	90	70	74	83	74	82	98
38367	RAMER	77	52	23	45	59	67	50	62	60	51	71	75	42	67	51	65	64	62	77	89
38368	REAGAN	85	59	29	52	66	75	57	70	67	58	79	83	49	75	58	72	73	69	84	97
38369	RUTHERFORD	72	52	28	46	57	65	49	60	58	50	68	71	44	66	50	61	63	59	72	83
38370	SALTILLO	85	57	26	49	65	74	55	69	66	56	78	82	47	74	56	71	71	68	85	98
38371	SARDIS	85	57	26	49	65	74	55	69	67	56	78	82	47	74	56	72	71	68	85	98
38372	SAVANNAH	72	53	34	49	58	67	54	62	62	54	74	73	49	71	55	66	68	62	74	82
38374	SCOTTS HILL	86	57	26	49	65	75	55	69	67	56	78	83	47	74	56	72	71	68	85	98
38375	SELMER	85	59	30	52	66	77	59	71	69	59	82	84	51	77	59	74	74	70	87	97
38376	SHILOH	72	48	22	41	54	63	46	58	56	47	66	69	39	62	47	60	60	57	71	82
38379	STANTONVILLE	79	53	24	46	60	69	51	64	62	52	72	76	43	68	52	66	66	63	79	90
38380	SUGAR TREE	66	52	35	47	58	65	49	59	55	48	65	69	43	64	52	59	61	58	69	80
38381	TOONE	89	60	27	52	68	78	58	72	70	59	82	86	49	77	59	75	74	71	89	103
38382	TRENTON	71	57	42	53	61	70	58	64	64	57	77	74	54	76	58	67	72	63	73	81
38387	WESTPORT	80	54	24	46	61	70	52	65	62	53	73	77	44	69	53	67	67	64	80	92
38388	WILDERSVILLE	90	62	31	54	69	80	60	74	71	61	84	88	52	80	61	76	77	73	89	102
38390	YUMA	76	51	23	44	57	66	49	61	59	50	69	73	42	65	50	64	63	61	75	87
38391	DENMARK	76	51	23	44	58	66	49	61	59	50	70	73	42	66	50	64	63	61	76	87
38392	MERCER	72	48	22	41	54	63	46	58	56	47	66	69	39	62	47	60	60	57	72	82
38401	COLUMBIA	85	81	75	79	83	89	79	83	82	79	100	96	79	101	80	82	96	82	86	98
38425	CLIFTON	32	22	10	19	25	28	21	26	25	21	30	31	18	28	21	27	27	26	32	37
38449	ARDMORE	91	66	36	59	73	83	63	76	73	64	87	91	56	84	64	78	80	75	90	105
38450	COLLINWOOD	80	54	24	46	61	70	52	65	63	53	74	78	44	70	53	68	67	64	80	92
38451	CULLEOKA	99	86	63	81	91	98	79	89	85	80	103	106	77	105	82	88	98	87	97	116
38452	CYPRESS INN	64	43	19	37	48	56	41	52	50	42	59	62	35	55	42	54	53	51	64	73
38453	DELLROSE	85	57	26	49	65	75	55	69	67	56	78	82	47	74	56	72	71	68	85	98
38454	DUCK RIVER	70	47	21	41	53	62	46	57	55	46	65	68	39	61	46	59	59	56	70	81
38456	ETHRIDGE	78	55	28	48	61	70	52	64	62	53	73	77	46	70	53	66	67	63	77	89
38457	FIVE POINTS	85	57	26	49	65	74	55	69	66	56	78	82	47	74	56	71	71	68	85	98
38459	FRANKEWING	85	57	26	49	65	74	55	69	67	56	78	82	47	74	56	72	71	68	85	98
38460	GOODSPRING	83	56	25	48	63	72	54	67	65	55	76	80	46	72	55	70	69	66	83	95
38461	HAMPSHIRE	86	66	40	60	72	80	62	73	70	63	84	87	57	82	64	74	78	72	85	99
38462	HOHENWALD	77	52	25	46	59	68	51	63	61	52	72	74	44	68	52	66	65	62	77	87
38463	IRON CITY	76	51	23	44	57	66	49	61	59	50	69	73	42	66	50	64	63	61	75	87
38464	LAWRENCEBURG	81	62	42	57	67	76	62	71	70	62	83	83	57	81	63	73	78	70	82	92
38468	LEOMA	84	57	27	50	64	74	55	68	66	56	77	81	47	73	56	71	71	67	83	96
38469	LORETTO	88	63	33	56	70	80	61	74	72	62	85	87	54	81	62	76	78	73	88	101
38471	LUTTS	59	40	18	34	45	52	38	48	46	39	54	57	32	51	39	50	49	47	59	68
38472	LYNNVILLE	94	72	44	66	79	88	68	80	77	69	92	96	62	90	70	81	86	79	93	109
38473	MINOR HILL	81	54	25	47	62	71	52	66	63	53	74	78	45	70	53	68	68	65	81	93
38474	MOUNT PLEASANT	71	61	48	57	64	72	61	66	65	60	79	76	58	79	61	68	75	65	73	81
38475	OLIVEHILL	71	48	22	41	54	62	46	58	56	47	65	69	39	62	47	60	59	57	71	82
38476	PRIMM SPRINGS	92	74	49	68	80	88	69	80	77	70	92	96	65	92	71	80	86	78	91	107
38477	PROSPECT	88	60	28	52	67	77	57	72	69	59	81	85	49	77	58	74	74	71	88	101
38478	PULASKI	82	65	46	61	70	78	65	72	72	64	86	85	60	84	65	75	80	72	83	94
38481	SAINT JOSEPH	79	53	24	45	60	69	51	64	61	52	72	76	43	68	52	66	65	63	78	90
38482	SANTA FE	93	82	63	78	87	93	76	85	81	76	98	101	75	101	79	83	94	82	92	109
38483	SUMMERTOWN	83	56	26	49	64	73	54	68	65	55	77	81	46	72	55	70	70	67	83	96
38485	WAYNESBORO	78	52	24	45	59	68	50	63	61	51	71	75	43	68	51	66	65	62	78	90
38486	WESTPOINT	70	47	21	40	53	61	45	56	54	46	64	67	38	60	46	58	58	56	69	80
38487	WILLIAMSPORT	98	87	66	83	92	99	81	89	86	81	104	106	79	106	83	88	99	87	97	115
38488	TAFT	83	68	47	64	73	81	65	74	72	65	86	87	62	86	66	74	81	72	83	95
38501	COOKEVILLE	71	59	57	60	61	69	67	67	70	65	86	80	63	83	65	69	81	69	70	80
38504	ALLARDT	77	51	23	44	58	67	50	62	60	51	70	74	42	66	50	64	64	61	76	88
38505	COOKEVILLE	26	16	20	18	15	19	30	22	30	26	37	31	25	33	24	26	35	27	21	25
38506	COOKEVILLE	81	68	50	64	72	80	65	73	71	65	86	87	62	85	66	73	81	72	81	94
38541	ALLONS	62	41	19	36	47	54	40	50	48	41	57	60	34	54	41	52	52	50	62	71
38542	ALLRED	56	37	17	32	42	49	36	45	44	37	51	54	31	48	37	47	47	45	56	64
38543	ALPINE	66	44	20	38	50	58	43	53	51	43	60	64	36	57	43	55	55	53	66	76
38544	BAXTER	78	53	25	46	60	69	51	64	61	52	72	76	44	68	52	66	66	63	78	90
38545	BLOOMINGTON SPRINGS	89	62	31	54	69	79	59	73	70	60	83	87	52	79	60	75	76	72	88	102
38547	BRUSH CREEK	83	74	57	70	78	84	69	76	73	69	89	91	67	90	71	75	84	74	82	98
38548	BUFFALO VALLEY	72	48	22	42	55	63	47	58	56	48	66	70	40	63	48	61	60	58	72	83
38549	BYRDSTOWN	67	49	29	44	54	63	49	58	56	48	66	67	43	63	50	60	61	57	70	77
38551	CELINA	62	43	23	39	49	57	44	53	52	44	61	61	38	57	44	55	55	52	64	70
38552	CHESTNUT MOUND	104	70	32	60	79	91	67	84	81	68	95	100	57	90	68	87	86	83	103	119
38553	CLARKRANGE	69	46	21	40	52	60	45	56	54	45	63	67	38	60	45	58	57	55	69	79
38554	CRAWFORD	73	49	22	42	56	64	47	59	57	48	67	71	40	63	48	62	61	59	73	84
	TENNESSEE	85	76	68	73	78	85	76	80	79	76	97	94	73	96	75	81	93	80	85	97
	UNITED STATES	100	100	100	100	100	100	100	100	100	100	100	100	100	100	100	100	100	100	100	100

TENNESSEE

A 38555-42223

POPULATION CHANGE

ZIP CODE		COUNTY FIPS CODE	POPULATION			2000-2004 ANNUAL RATE		HOUSEHOLDS					FAMILIES		
#	POST OFFICE NAME		2000	2004	2009	% Rate	State Centile	2000	2004	2009	% Annual Rate 2000-2004	2004 Average HH Size	2000	2004	% Annual Rate 2000-2004
38555	CROSSVILLE	035	17879	18152	18935	0.4	36	7325	7619	8135	0.9	2.32	5170	5257	0.4
38556	JAMESTOWN	049	12053	12190	12523	0.3	32	4943	5135	5402	0.9	2.34	3480	3536	0.4
38558	CROSSVILLE	035	5525	5911	6382	1.6	76	2764	3033	3351	2.2	1.95	2200	2378	1.9
38559	DOYLE	185	837	865	887	0.8	51	359	378	393	1.2	2.29	261	270	0.8
38560	ELMWOOD	159	1280	1292	1306	0.2	30	486	498	509	0.6	2.59	371	373	0.1
38562	GAINESBORO	087	6776	6898	7140	0.4	38	2807	2910	3064	0.9	2.32	1944	1973	0.4
38563	GORDONSVILLE	159	2200	2348	2447	1.5	75	869	944	996	2.0	2.49	649	690	1.5
38564	GRANVILLE	087	413	474	519	3.3	96	181	210	233	3.6	2.26	128	146	3.1
38565	GRIMSLEY	049	452	551	620	4.8	99	170	211	242	5.2	2.61	132	161	4.8
38567	HICKMAN	159	804	846	875	1.2	65	317	340	357	1.7	2.49	237	249	1.2
38568	HILHAM	133	1674	1671	1689	0.0	17	692	710	733	0.6	2.33	469	469	0.0
38569	LANCASTER	041	351	366	377	1.0	59	138	146	152	1.3	2.51	104	108	0.9
38570	LIVINGSTON	133	8947	8869	8924	-0.2	11	3705	3750	3848	0.3	2.32	2564	2536	-0.3
38571	CROSSVILLE	035	11153	11874	12645	1.5	73	4357	4749	5170	2.1	2.49	3348	3585	1.6
38572	CROSSVILLE	035	9052	10147	11072	2.7	93	3721	4277	4775	3.3	2.35	2807	3173	2.9
38573	MONROE	133	2190	2116	2099	-0.8	3	894	884	896	-0.3	2.39	664	644	-0.7
38574	MONTEREY	141	6842	7025	7284	0.6	45	2586	2687	2823	0.9	2.57	1929	1966	0.5
38575	MOSS	027	1167	1148	1162	-0.4	8	478	480	497	0.1	2.39	335	330	-0.4
38577	PALL MALL	137	1428	1476	1499	0.8	51	589	623	649	1.3	2.37	431	447	0.9
38578	PLEASANT HILL	035	323	329	341	0.4	39	134	140	149	1.0	2.29	90	92	0.5
38579	QUEBECK	185	1301	1394	1457	1.6	77	512	557	591	2.0	2.50	386	413	1.6
38580	RICKMAN	133	1248	1296	1325	0.9	56	494	524	546	1.4	2.47	382	398	1.0
38581	ROCK ISLAND	175	4299	4257	4260	-0.2	10	1665	1691	1726	0.4	2.49	1255	1249	-0.1
38582	SILVER POINT	141	1015	1063	1110	1.1	61	407	433	459	1.5	2.41	301	314	1.0
38583	SPARTA	185	20676	21333	22051	0.7	49	8243	8667	9103	1.2	2.43	6027	6220	0.7
38585	SPENCER	175	4641	4717	4827	0.4	37	1827	1904	1998	1.0	2.44	1358	1391	0.6
38587	WALLING	185	1084	1108	1138	0.5	42	445	462	481	0.9	2.37	330	337	0.5
38588	WHITLEYVILLE	087	951	962	990	0.3	32	391	404	424	0.8	2.38	258	260	0.2
38589	WILDER	049	55	69	79	5.5	99	23	30	35	6.5	2.30	18	23	5.9
42223	FORT CAMPBELL	125	21235	21545	21902	0.3	36	3798	3952	4093	0.9	3.74	3709	3848	0.9
TENNESSEE						1.0					1.3	2.45			0.9
UNITED STATES						1.2					1.3	2.58			1.1

#	POST OFFICE NAME	RACE (%) White 2000	White 2004	Black 2000	Black 2004	Asian/Pacific 2000	Asian/Pacific 2004	% Hispanic Origin 2000	% Hispanic Origin 2004	0-4	5-9	10-14	15-19	20-24	25-44	45-64	65-84	85+	18+	MEDIAN AGE 2004	% 2004 Males	% 2004 Females
38555	CROSSVILLE	97.6	97.1	0.1	0.1	0.4	0.5	1.8	2.2	6.1	6.1	6.7	6.0	5.9	25.9	24.9	16.5	2.0	77.6	40.4	47.4	52.6
38556	JAMESTOWN	99.2	99.1	0.1	0.2	0.1	0.1	0.6	0.8	6.1	6.2	6.5	6.0	6.0	26.6	27.8	13.1	1.8	77.7	39.9	49.2	50.8
38558	CROSSVILLE	98.6	98.5	0.4	0.4	0.2	0.3	0.5	0.6	2.3	2.2	2.5	2.5	2.4	10.9	27.6	47.3	2.3	91.6	64.9	48.3	51.7
38559	DOYLE	98.7	98.5	0.4	0.5	0.1	0.2	1.1	1.3	5.2	5.4	6.1	6.4	6.7	27.2	27.5	14.1	1.4	79.4	40.7	49.6	50.4
38560	ELMWOOD	95.4	95.1	2.9	3.2	0.0	0.0	0.2	0.3	6.4	6.9	7.8	6.3	6.3	28.6	25.2	11.3	1.3	75.1	37.7	51.4	48.6
38562	GAINESBORO	98.6	98.4	0.2	0.2	0.1	0.1	0.7	0.9	5.6	5.7	6.0	5.4	5.8	27.1	28.1	14.1	2.2	79.5	41.2	49.3	50.7
38563	GORDONSVILLE	95.8	95.4	2.6	2.7	0.1	0.1	1.0	1.2	6.9	6.6	6.5	6.8	6.4	30.2	25.4	9.8	1.3	75.9	37.2	50.2	49.8
38564	GRANVILLE	98.1	97.9	0.0	0.0	0.0	0.0	1.5	1.7	6.1	6.5	6.8	5.9	4.6	24.7	27.9	15.8	1.7	76.8	41.9	51.9	48.1
38565	GRIMSLEY	99.8	99.8	0.0	0.0	0.0	0.0	0.0	0.0	7.4	7.3	6.9	7.1	6.5	29.8	23.2	10.7	1.1	74.1	35.8	50.3	49.7
38567	HICKMAN	95.9	95.5	0.9	1.0	0.5	0.7	1.9	2.1	5.7	5.9	7.0	7.0	6.4	27.4	27.2	12.2	1.3	77.1	39.6	49.5	50.5
38568	HILHAM	98.7	98.6	0.2	0.2	0.2	0.2	0.2	0.2	5.3	5.5	5.9	6.3	6.0	27.5	27.1	14.7	1.6	79.4	40.7	50.5	49.6
38569	LANCASTER	96.3	95.6	0.0	0.0	0.6	0.8	2.0	2.5	4.9	5.5	7.4	6.8	6.3	26.5	28.1	13.4	1.1	77.9	40.5	51.4	48.6
38570	LIVINGSTON	98.6	98.5	0.3	0.3	0.2	0.2	0.6	0.6	5.8	5.8	5.8	5.6	6.2	26.6	26.2	15.7	2.4	79.3	41.1	48.1	51.9
38571	CROSSVILLE	98.3	98.0	0.1	0.1	0.1	0.1	1.3	1.6	5.9	6.2	6.5	5.7	5.2	26.0	26.6	16.5	1.4	77.8	41.3	49.9	50.1
38572	CROSSVILLE	98.0	97.8	0.3	0.3	0.3	0.4	0.9	1.1	5.6	5.6	6.4	5.7	4.9	24.7	28.1	17.4	1.7	78.8	43.1	49.7	50.4
38573	MONROE	99.2	99.2	0.1	0.1	0.1	0.1	0.7	0.9	6.0	6.3	6.5	5.8	4.9	26.8	27.0	15.2	1.6	77.7	40.5	50.5	49.5
38574	MONTEREY	94.4	93.3	0.5	0.6	0.2	0.2	7.9	9.6	6.6	6.7	6.9	6.2	6.6	27.6	25.3	12.4	1.6	75.9	37.8	49.9	50.1
38575	MOSS	98.1	97.9	0.5	0.5	0.3	0.4	1.8	2.0	5.1	5.6	6.6	5.1	5.9	27.7	27.9	14.2	1.9	79.6	41.6	49.0	51.0
38577	PALL MALL	99.5	99.4	0.1	0.1	0.1	0.1	0.3	0.3	6.4	6.1	5.4	5.4	5.7	25.9	28.8	14.8	1.7	79.1	41.7	50.3	49.7
38578	PLEASANT HILL	98.1	97.6	0.3	0.3	0.0	0.3	0.6	0.9	5.5	5.8	6.7	6.1	6.4	24.3	22.5	18.5	4.3	78.4	41.8	47.7	52.3
38579	QUEBECK	99.1	99.0	0.1	0.1	0.1	0.1	0.8	0.9	4.9	5.3	6.7	6.2	5.7	27.3	28.1	14.6	1.4	79.4	41.6	50.4	49.6
38580	RICKMAN	98.6	98.2	0.3	0.3	0.2	0.2	1.2	1.5	7.3	7.1	6.4	5.9	6.0	28.5	26.9	10.7	1.3	75.8	37.4	49.7	50.3
38581	ROCK ISLAND	94.6	93.8	1.8	1.9	0.1	0.1	3.3	4.1	6.3	6.5	6.5	6.3	6.0	28.9	27.2	11.1	1.2	76.9	37.9	51.6	48.4
38582	SILVER POINT	96.9	96.4	2.0	2.2	0.7	0.9	1.4	1.7	5.4	5.5	5.7	5.3	5.3	26.8	28.9	15.1	2.2	79.9	42.7	52.9	47.1
38583	SPARTA	96.3	96.0	1.8	1.9	0.3	0.4	1.2	1.4	6.1	6.1	6.4	6.2	6.0	27.0	26.2	14.1	1.4	77.5	39.8	49.2	50.8
38585	SPENCER	99.1	99.0	0.1	0.1	0.1	0.1	0.3	0.4	6.0	6.2	6.6	5.9	6.3	27.5	27.1	13.1	1.4	77.8	39.6	50.0	50.0
38587	WALLING	97.8	97.7	0.2	0.2	0.1	0.1	0.9	1.1	6.3	6.5	6.4	5.8	5.9	26.9	27.6	13.5	1.1	77.4	39.8	50.8	49.2
38588	WHITLEYVILLE	98.2	98.1	0.2	0.2	0.1	0.1	1.5	1.8	5.4	5.6	5.8	5.4	5.6	24.8	29.7	15.5	2.1	79.9	43.1	49.6	50.4
38589	WILDER	100.0	100.0	0.0	0.0	0.0	0.0	0.0	0.0	7.3	7.3	7.3	7.3	5.8	30.4	21.7	11.6	1.5	75.4	36.3	49.3	50.7
42223	FORT CAMPBELL	61.6	59.2	24.2	24.4	2.7	3.2	12.6	15.1	14.0	10.8	7.1	9.8	22.9	34.2	1.3	0.1	0.0	66.0	21.8	62.1	37.9
	TENNESSEE	80.2	79.4	16.4	16.7	1.0	1.3	2.2	2.6	6.6	6.5	6.8	6.6	7.0	29.0	24.8	11.1	1.5	76.3	36.8	48.9	51.1
	UNITED STATES	75.1	73.6	12.3	12.5	3.8	4.2	12.5	14.1	6.9	6.7	7.2	7.0	7.3	28.6	23.8	10.8	1.7	75.1	36.0	49.1	50.9

TENNESSEE — INCOME

#	POST OFFICE NAME	2004 Per Capita Income	2004 HH Income Base	2004 HOUSEHOLD INCOME DISTRIBUTION (%) Less than $25,000	$25,000 to $49,999	$50,000 to $99,999	$100,000 to $149,999	$150,000 or More	MEDIAN HOUSEHOLD INCOME 2004	2009	2004 National Centile	2004 State Centile	2004 Home Value Base	2004 HOME VALUE DISTRIBUTION (%) Less than $50,000	$50,000 to $89,999	$90,000 to $174,999	$175,000 to $399,999	$400,000 or More	2004 Median Home Value
38555	CROSSVILLE	19908	7619	41.6	30.0	20.7	5.1	2.5	30998	33588	15	23	5340	14.8	28.3	39.5	14.8	2.7	99712
38556	JAMESTOWN	14535	5135	52.4	28.9	14.4	3.1	1.2	23277	25811	3	5	3926	40.4	30.1	20.8	8.0	0.8	61000
38558	CROSSVILLE	28731	3033	20.6	37.1	31.8	6.9	3.6	44681	52060	60	80	2668	7.8	13.1	42.9	33.2	3.0	150979
38559	DOYLE	16950	378	41.5	33.6	19.1	5.0	0.8	29654	32795	12	18	308	22.4	37.0	31.2	9.4	0.0	80000
38560	ELMWOOD	21271	498	25.3	35.7	31.9	6.0	1.0	41136	46108	50	71	410	15.4	28.8	34.9	19.3	1.7	100000
38562	GAINESBORO	16834	2910	44.9	34.2	15.6	3.1	2.3	27991	31084	9	14	2318	28.8	32.5	30.9	6.4	1.3	76578
38563	GORDONSVILLE	19554	944	28.3	30.8	33.6	6.1	1.2	42611	47629	55	77	782	13.9	20.2	46.3	17.3	2.3	108766
38564	GRANVILLE	17085	210	41.4	33.3	20.5	4.8	0.0	30498	32792	13	21	179	21.8	26.8	32.4	14.5	4.5	91923
38565	GRIMSLEY	13793	211	41.7	32.7	23.7	1.9	0.0	30336	33065	13	21	178	38.2	31.5	24.2	5.6	0.6	65000
38567	HICKMAN	18496	340	27.1	35.3	32.9	3.8	0.9	39547	43635	44	67	279	7.9	31.9	38.4	20.4	1.4	102679
38568	HILHAM	13761	710	46.6	37.9	13.4	1.7	0.4	26554	29432	7	12	581	30.5	32.9	26.9	8.4	1.4	74322
38569	LANCASTER	18228	146	24.7	35.6	36.3	2.7	0.7	40400	45000	48	69	121	12.4	27.3	33.1	25.6	1.7	103676
38570	LIVINGSTON	15576	3750	44.4	32.3	20.1	2.2	1.0	28063	30484	9	15	2865	29.1	27.5	34.3	8.7	0.5	83120
38571	CROSSVILLE	16345	4749	34.8	37.3	23.1	3.5	1.4	32691	36346	20	36	3988	22.8	27.4	32.7	14.9	2.2	89739
38572	CROSSVILLE	18619	4277	36.9	35.8	20.9	4.2	2.2	31939	35371	18	30	3554	22.0	30.1	32.9	14.0	1.0	87082
38573	MONROE	19332	884	43.7	33.6	19.3	1.1	2.3	28509	31336	10	16	740	27.8	30.4	29.7	10.8	1.2	79733
38574	MONTEREY	15375	2687	39.5	34.7	22.0	3.0	0.9	31103	35056	15	24	2095	25.2	32.7	29.7	9.7	2.6	82156
38575	MOSS	13723	480	42.5	41.9	14.2	1.3	0.2	28173	31452	9	15	399	49.9	25.8	17.0	7.3	0.0	50278
38577	PALL MALL	13701	623	49.9	30.2	16.7	2.6	0.6	25041	27346	5	8	529	34.8	22.7	29.1	12.1	1.3	78611
38578	PLEASANT HILL	17267	140	39.3	39.3	17.1	2.1	2.1	31212	33728	16	25	104	27.9	34.6	33.7	3.9	0.0	78333
38579	QUEBECK	16832	557	34.7	39.5	20.3	4.9	0.7	34438	37627	26	45	466	19.7	34.8	28.1	16.5	0.9	85116
38580	RICKMAN	16467	524	34.9	37.2	23.9	2.1	1.9	34868	38832	27	47	435	23.5	34.3	30.1	12.2	0.0	83021
38581	ROCK ISLAND	18880	1691	30.2	38.9	27.1	2.9	1.0	37449	41814	37	58	1425	23.9	37.5	30.5	7.0	1.1	79781
38582	SILVER POINT	17234	433	35.8	37.4	22.6	2.1	2.1	34910	38665	27	47	372	29.6	22.3	32.0	12.1	4.0	87308
38583	SPARTA	17082	8667	38.8	33.8	22.3	3.5	1.6	31983	35574	18	30	6814	20.2	31.5	36.6	10.3	1.5	88243
38585	SPENCER	19308	1904	41.0	32.8	22.2	2.1	2.0	30334	34067	13	20	1585	37.4	35.1	21.4	5.6	0.5	63853
38587	WALLING	19333	462	38.3	35.7	20.8	2.4	2.8	31237	35440	16	25	387	19.6	37.0	30.0	12.4	1.0	83929
38588	WHITLEYVILLE	16762	404	39.9	40.4	14.1	2.5	3.2	30730	34163	14	22	314	32.2	33.4	25.2	8.6	0.6	71429
38589	WILDER	15660	30	43.3	30.0	26.7	0.0	0.0	30000	37310	12	20	26	30.8	34.6	34.6	0.0	0.0	70000
42223	FORT CAMPBELL	10677	3952	26.5	51.0	19.5	2.9	0.2	32782	37218	20	37	69	30.4	7.3	58.0	2.9	1.5	95667
	TENNESSEE	22498		30.2	30.2	28.1	7.5	4.1	40531	46137				15.0	25.0	39.4	17.3	3.3	104905
	UNITED STATES	25866		24.7	27.1	30.8	10.9	6.5	48124	56710				10.9	15.0	33.7	30.1	10.4	145905

ZIP CODE		FINANCIAL SERVICES				THE HOME						ENTERTAINMENT						PERSONAL			
						Home Improvements		Furnishings													
#	POST OFFICE NAME	Auto Loan	Home Loan	Invest-ments	Retire-ment Plans	Home Repair	Lawn & Garden	Comput-ers & Hard-ware	Major Appli-ances	TV, Radio, Sound Equip-ment	Furni-ture	Dine out/ Carry out	Sports Equip-ment	Fees & Tickets	Toys & Games	Travel	Cable TV	Apparel & Services	Auto Repairs	Health Insur-ance	Pets & Supplies
38555	CROSSVILLE	78	60	39	56	65	74	61	69	68	60	81	81	55	79	61	72	75	69	81	89
38556	JAMESTOWN	62	43	23	38	48	55	42	51	50	43	59	61	37	56	43	54	54	51	62	71
38558	CROSSVILLE	85	79	75	75	84	99	73	84	78	78	96	82	74	80	80	83	90	81	98	96
38559	DOYLE	73	49	22	42	55	64	47	59	57	48	67	71	40	63	48	61	61	58	73	84
38560	ELMWOOD	104	70	32	60	79	91	67	84	81	68	95	100	57	90	68	87	86	83	104	119
38562	GAINESBORO	74	50	22	43	56	65	48	60	58	49	68	72	41	64	49	62	62	59	74	85
38563	GORDONSVILLE	83	66	43	61	71	78	63	73	69	64	84	86	58	81	64	72	78	71	81	96
38564	GRANVILLE	73	49	22	42	55	63	47	59	57	48	67	70	40	63	48	61	60	58	72	83
38565	GRIMSLEY	68	45	21	39	51	59	44	55	53	45	62	65	37	59	45	57	56	54	68	78
38567	HICKMAN	79	63	41	57	68	75	59	68	66	59	79	82	55	78	60	69	74	67	78	92
38568	HILHAM	60	40	18	35	46	53	39	49	47	40	55	58	33	52	40	51	50	48	60	69
38569	LANCASTER	78	62	41	57	68	74	59	68	65	59	78	81	55	78	60	68	73	66	77	91
38570	LIVINGSTON	67	46	22	40	51	60	45	55	54	45	63	65	38	59	45	58	57	55	68	77
38571	CROSSVILLE	75	52	26	45	59	68	50	62	60	51	70	73	43	66	51	64	64	61	76	86
38572	CROSSVILLE	80	56	29	49	64	73	54	67	64	55	75	79	47	72	56	69	69	66	81	94
38573	MONROE	87	58	26	50	66	76	56	70	68	57	80	84	48	75	57	73	73	70	87	100
38574	MONTEREY	73	51	25	45	57	65	49	60	58	50	69	72	43	65	50	62	63	59	73	84
38575	MOSS	62	41	19	36	47	54	40	50	48	41	57	60	34	53	41	52	51	49	62	71
38577	PALL MALL	61	41	19	35	46	53	40	49	48	40	56	59	34	53	40	51	51	49	61	70
38578	PLEASANT HILL	75	50	23	43	57	66	48	61	59	49	69	72	41	65	49	63	62	60	75	86
38579	QUEBECK	79	53	24	46	60	69	51	64	62	52	73	77	44	69	52	67	66	63	79	91
38580	RICKMAN	77	51	23	44	58	67	50	62	60	50	70	74	42	66	50	64	64	61	76	88
38581	ROCK ISLAND	89	59	27	51	67	78	57	72	69	58	81	86	49	77	58	75	74	71	88	102
38582	SILVER POINT	78	53	24	46	60	69	51	64	61	52	72	76	43	68	52	66	65	63	78	90
38583	SPARTA	77	53	27	47	60	68	51	63	61	52	72	75	45	68	52	65	66	62	76	88
38585	SPENCER	89	60	27	52	68	78	58	72	70	59	82	86	49	77	59	75	74	71	89	102
38587	WALLING	86	58	27	51	66	76	56	70	67	57	79	83	48	75	57	72	72	69	86	99
38588	WHITLEYVILLE	75	50	23	43	57	66	49	61	59	49	69	73	41	65	49	63	63	60	75	86
38589	WILDER	68	45	21	39	51	59	44	55	53	45	62	65	37	59	45	57	56	54	68	78
42223	FORT CAMPBELL	64	41	39	46	37	44	60	52	61	56	76	69	52	68	50	56	73	61	48	59
	TENNESSEE	85	76	68	73	78	85	76	80	79	76	97	94	73	96	75	81	93	80	85	97
	UNITED STATES	100	100	100	100	100	100	100	100	100	100	100	100	100	100	100	100	100	100	100	100

#	POST OFFICE NAME	COUNTY FIPS CODE	POPULATION			2000-2004 ANNUAL RATE		HOUSEHOLDS					FAMILIES		
			2000	2004	2009	% Rate	State Centile	2000	2004	2009	% Annual Rate 2000-2004	2004 Average HH Size	2000	2004	% Annual Rate 2000-2004
75001	ADDISON	113	13718	14976	16398	2.1	69	7407	7975	8584	1.8	1.88	2883	3115	1.8
75002	ALLEN	085	37216	48747	64716	6.6	97	12260	15915	20949	6.3	3.06	10357	13454	6.4
75006	CARROLLTON	113	46784	48799	52444	1.0	42	16973	17254	18134	0.4	2.81	11787	12062	0.5
75007	CARROLLTON	121	50693	58804	73014	3.6	87	17753	20357	24941	3.3	2.88	13741	15718	3.2
75009	CELINA	085	5129	6658	8714	6.3	97	1764	2272	2950	6.1	2.92	1444	1853	6.0
75010	CARROLLTON	121	12884	16998	22533	6.7	98	4858	6381	8380	6.6	2.64	3509	4598	6.6
75013	ALLEN	085	11624	18547	26675	11.6	100	3735	5887	8384	11.3	3.15	3264	5119	11.2
75019	COPPELL	113	35959	40820	45511	3.0	81	12212	13453	14628	2.3	3.03	9753	10778	2.4
75020	DENISON	181	21597	22274	23602	0.7	34	8705	8903	9368	0.5	2.45	5878	6032	0.6
75021	DENISON	181	8034	8540	9211	1.5	56	3115	3289	3525	1.3	2.58	2315	2448	1.3
75022	FLOWER MOUND	121	14287	19095	25377	7.1	98	4573	6004	7855	6.6	3.16	4066	5339	6.6
75023	PLANO	085	45510	50184	60880	2.3	73	16803	18430	22217	2.2	2.71	12736	13875	2.0
75024	PLANO	085	19721	29661	41724	10.1	99	7853	11909	16724	10.3	2.49	5147	7641	9.7
75025	PLANO	085	40821	52481	69128	6.1	97	13874	17473	22596	5.6	3.00	11341	14152	5.4
75028	FLOWER MOUND	121	36715	46593	60591	5.8	96	11737	14716	18887	5.5	3.16	10201	12756	5.4
75032	ROCKWALL	397	14100	19994	29613	8.6	99	4773	6646	9707	8.1	3.01	3940	5488	8.1
75034	FRISCO	121	16681	25675	36766	10.7	99	5905	9041	12826	10.5	2.84	4726	7252	10.6
75035	FRISCO	085	19064	29543	41838	10.9	99	6812	10452	14670	10.6	2.82	5582	8581	10.7
75038	IRVING	113	25977	28183	30917	1.9	66	12877	13688	14726	1.5	2.06	5926	6367	1.7
75039	IRVING	113	2816	3607	4255	6.0	97	1881	2354	2718	5.4	1.53	632	789	5.4
75040	GARLAND	113	55120	57023	60708	0.8	35	16820	17117	17901	0.4	3.32	13736	14008	0.5
75041	GARLAND	113	31076	32095	34197	0.8	34	10587	10661	11108	0.2	2.99	7737	7830	0.3
75042	GARLAND	113	38237	39281	41891	0.6	30	12111	12176	12723	0.1	3.22	9320	9400	0.2
75043	GARLAND	113	53791	58394	63874	2.0	67	19896	21228	22805	1.5	2.72	14217	15127	1.5
75044	GARLAND	113	37147	40259	44129	1.9	66	13661	14443	15489	1.3	2.79	10138	10820	1.5
75048	SACHSE	113	9809	13619	17020	8.0	99	3240	4416	5424	7.6	3.08	2737	3739	7.6
75050	GRAND PRAIRIE	113	38341	39864	42833	0.9	39	14304	14709	15606	0.7	2.69	9315	9559	0.6
75051	GRAND PRAIRIE	113	29090	30631	33020	1.2	49	9435	9733	10291	0.7	3.14	7195	7433	0.8
75052	GRAND PRAIRIE	113	58612	64918	72084	2.4	75	19399	21140	23100	2.0	3.07	15535	16940	2.1
75056	THE COLONY	121	28827	36991	48432	6.0	97	9150	11637	15058	5.8	3.17	7498	9427	5.5
75057	LEWISVILLE	121	11583	14011	17801	4.6	93	4394	5344	6757	4.7	2.61	2722	3275	4.5
75058	GUNTER	181	2118	2388	2631	2.9	80	604	684	755	3.0	3.12	479	543	3.0
75060	IRVING	113	45258	48834	53384	1.8	64	14870	15735	16865	1.3	3.10	11301	11998	1.4
75061	IRVING	113	53362	56598	61030	1.4	54	18778	19407	20470	0.8	2.89	12711	13192	0.9
75062	IRVING	113	40728	42238	45356	0.9	37	15597	15983	16903	0.6	2.61	10088	10327	0.6
75063	IRVING	113	24454	30063	35195	5.0	94	12662	14671	16441	3.5	2.05	5784	7107	5.0
75065	LAKE DALLAS	121	8677	9978	12360	3.3	85	3178	3600	4396	3.0	2.77	2368	2669	2.9
75067	LEWISVILLE	121	49277	58949	74715	4.3	91	19840	23586	29565	4.2	2.49	12422	14605	3.9
75068	LITTLE ELM	121	7087	12884	19858	15.1	100	2428	4329	6568	14.6	2.98	1925	3411	14.4
75069	MC KINNEY	085	25573	30670	38924	4.4	92	8826	10517	13315	4.2	2.82	6019	7202	4.3
75070	MC KINNEY	085	26794	40201	56435	10.0	99	8806	13029	18093	9.7	3.08	7676	11373	9.7
75071	MC KINNEY	085	10553	15052	20698	8.7	99	3499	5082	7038	9.2	2.82	2784	4031	9.1
75074	PLANO	085	37400	44612	56426	4.2	91	12909	15332	19286	4.1	2.88	9377	11151	4.2
75075	PLANO	085	35969	38939	46911	1.9	65	13667	14730	17635	1.8	2.63	10144	10875	1.7
75076	POTTSBORO	181	6743	7419	8109	2.3	73	2828	3097	3367	2.2	2.40	2044	2240	2.2
75077	LEWISVILLE	121	30683	35336	43815	3.4	85	10228	11614	14196	3.0	3.04	8931	10132	3.0
75078	PROSPER	085	2957	3908	5154	6.8	98	937	1226	1602	6.5	3.19	808	1052	6.4
75080	RICHARDSON	113	41105	44164	48907	1.7	61	15895	16833	18398	1.4	2.59	10961	11606	1.4
75081	RICHARDSON	113	32737	34945	37923	1.6	58	12426	13099	13989	1.3	2.65	8800	9233	1.1
75082	RICHARDSON	085	15530	19411	24807	5.4	96	5506	6782	8566	5.0	2.86	4422	5402	4.8
75087	ROCKWALL	397	17428	22272	31411	5.9	97	6120	7767	10883	5.8	2.82	4919	6274	5.9
75088	ROWLETT	113	24500	27989	32322	3.2	83	7794	8759	9951	2.8	3.17	6767	7626	2.9
75089	ROWLETT	113	18356	22888	27168	5.3	95	5957	7289	8479	4.9	3.14	5104	6264	4.9
75090	SHERMAN	181	22354	23571	25358	1.3	50	7974	8321	8898	1.0	2.68	5550	5835	1.2
75092	SHERMAN	181	20427	22425	24603	2.2	72	8499	9300	10171	2.1	2.34	5476	6004	2.2
75093	PLANO	085	44683	55063	70696	5.0	95	16958	20768	26474	4.9	2.64	12268	14982	4.8
75094	PLANO	085	3278	5588	8416	13.4	100	1087	1846	2764	13.3	3.03	957	1614	13.1
75098	WYLIE	085	20729	28324	37784	7.6	98	6997	9520	12610	7.5	2.97	5779	7842	7.5
75102	BARRY	349	629	707	788	2.8	79	232	258	286	2.5	2.74	184	205	2.6
75103	CANTON	467	14623	15683	17164	1.7	61	5624	6002	6542	1.5	2.55	4238	4529	1.6
75104	CEDAR HILL	113	32138	37506	42301	3.7	88	10768	12324	13634	3.2	3.02	8752	10036	3.3
75105	CHATFIELD	349	153	164	179	1.7	60	53	56	61	1.3	2.93	42	44	1.1
75109	CORSICANA	349	2617	3350	3991	6.0	97	915	1162	1371	5.8	2.86	745	941	5.7
75110	CORSICANA	349	28198	29845	32314	1.3	52	10107	10590	11375	1.1	2.69	7088	7437	1.1
75114	CRANDALL	257	3946	4755	5663	4.5	93	1265	1519	1800	4.4	3.12	1043	1250	4.4
75115	DESOTO	113	38014	42796	47630	2.8	80	13834	15275	16678	2.4	2.78	10755	11924	2.5
75116	DUNCANVILLE	113	18259	18398	19442	0.2	17	6583	6505	6746	-0.3	2.82	5123	5076	-0.2
75117	EDGEWOOD	467	4005	4258	4628	1.5	56	1547	1635	1767	1.3	2.60	1201	1271	1.3
75119	ENNIS	139	23930	27133	31979	3.0	81	8011	9004	10532	2.8	2.98	6143	6912	2.8
75124	EUSTACE	213	3410	3854	4313	2.9	81	1280	1433	1591	2.7	2.69	934	1048	2.8
75125	FERRIS	139	6240	7315	8748	3.8	89	1961	2275	2694	3.6	3.19	1538	1785	3.6
75126	FORNEY	257	11055	14547	18166	6.7	98	3664	4776	5917	6.4	3.05	3084	4016	6.4
75127	FRUITVALE	467	1985	2174	2399	2.2	70	720	784	861	2.0	2.77	566	618	2.1
75134	LANCASTER	113	12656	13952	15353	2.3	73	4376	4723	5097	1.8	2.88	3299	3576	1.9
75135	CADDO MILLS	231	4290	4530	4865	1.3	51	1515	1591	1700	1.2	2.85	1216	1279	1.2
75137	DUNCANVILLE	113	17638	18059	19217	0.6	27	6242	6265	6538	0.1	2.86	4920	4958	0.2
75140	GRAND SALINE	467	5927	6101	6530	0.7	32	2172	2218	2360	0.5	2.66	1575	1614	0.6
75141	HUTCHINS	113	2862	2989	3155	1.0	43	961	987	1032	0.6	2.38	691	712	0.6
75142	KAUFMAN	257	17099	19147	22025	2.7	78	5747	6417	7353	2.6	2.93	4554	5085	2.6
75143	KEMP	257	11889	12659	14025	1.5	57	4580	4835	5316	1.3	2.61	3426	3626	1.3
75144	KERENS	349	3151	3429	3763	2.0	68	1227	1327	1442	1.9	2.58	872	946	1.9
75146	LANCASTER	113	15209	16962	18868	2.6	77	5363	5833	6350	2.0	2.83	4022	4402	2.2
75147	MABANK	257	3450	3888	4462	2.9	80	1284	1441	1647	2.8	2.65	899	1007	2.7
75148	MALAKOFF	213	5610	6272	6998	2.7	78	2246	2499	2775	2.5	2.47	1605	1799	2.7
75149	MESQUITE	113	54841	58328	63112	1.5	56	18655	19455	20636	1.0	2.98	14603	15298	1.1
75150	MESQUITE	113	55260	60193	66305	2.0	68	20971	22456	24291	1.6	2.67	14556	15642	1.7
75152	PALMER	139	3032	3631	4401	4.3	92	964	1147	1380	4.2	3.17	807	961	4.2
75153	POWELL	349	118	124	133	1.2	47	43	45	48	1.1	2.76	36	37	0.7
75154	RED OAK	139	25922	29676	34862	3.2	83	8515	9636	11197	3.0	3.08	7155	8105	3.0
75155	RICE	349	2586	2777	3025	1.7	61	910	969	1045	1.5	2.87	716	764	1.5
75156	MABANK	213	15764	17932	20130	3.1	82	6624	7469	8325	2.9	2.40	4704	5320	2.9
75158	SCURRY	257	3869	4642	5515	4.4	92	1336	1598	1890	4.3	2.90	1109	1324	4.3
75159	SEAGOVILLE	113	14353	16368	17858	3.1	82	4516	4895	5303	1.9	2.92	3482	3791	2.0
75160	TERRELL	257	19666	21556	24532	2.2	71	6690	7292	8278	2.1	2.83	4992	5454	2.1
75161	TERRELL	257	5738	6170	6939	1.7	62	2025	2168	2425	1.6	2.83	1646	1759	1.5
	TEXAS					2.2					2.0	2.77			2.1
	UNITED STATES					1.2					1.3	2.58			1.1

ZIP CODE #	POST OFFICE NAME	RACE (%) White 2000	White 2004	Black 2000	Black 2004	Asian/Pacific 2000	Asian/Pacific 2004	% Hispanic Origin 2000	% Hispanic Origin 2004	2004 AGE DISTRIBUTION (%) 0-4	5-9	10-14	15-19	20-24	25-44	45-64	65-84	85+	18+	MEDIAN AGE 2004	% 2004 Males	% 2004 Females
75001	ADDISON	68.4	66.7	9.3	9.0	8.0	8.5	23.0	25.9	6.3	4.6	3.4	3.7	10.3	46.3	20.4	4.9	0.3	84.0	32.8	51.8	48.2
75002	ALLEN	87.1	85.5	4.5	4.7	3.2	3.8	7.5	9.0	9.4	9.6	8.8	7.1	5.4	34.2	21.5	3.7	0.3	67.7	33.1	49.9	50.1
75006	CARROLLTON	68.9	65.8	5.7	5.8	8.8	9.5	31.7	36.0	8.0	7.4	7.1	6.4	7.5	33.3	23.0	6.7	0.6	73.8	33.3	50.1	49.9
75007	CARROLLTON	73.8	71.3	6.8	7.1	12.4	13.8	11.3	12.9	7.4	7.9	8.3	7.1	6.0	32.9	25.8	4.2	0.3	71.9	34.8	49.2	50.8
75009	CELINA	87.3	85.5	3.8	3.7	0.5	0.5	12.6	15.1	7.2	7.6	8.7	7.6	6.4	28.0	24.9	8.3	1.3	71.8	35.8	50.6	49.4
75010	CARROLLTON	74.4	70.8	7.3	7.6	10.6	12.3	11.2	13.8	9.7	8.8	7.5	5.8	5.8	40.7	17.9	3.2	0.5	70.3	32.0	49.4	50.6
75013	ALLEN	88.0	86.5	3.2	3.4	5.6	6.3	4.8	6.1	11.8	11.8	9.5	5.7	3.7	35.8	18.9	2.6	0.3	63.2	32.4	49.8	50.2
75019	COPPELL	83.4	81.1	3.3	3.5	9.2	10.4	6.9	8.8	9.3	10.6	10.0	6.8	3.7	34.7	22.3	2.5	0.2	65.5	34.2	49.4	50.6
75020	DENISON	85.6	84.2	7.6	8.2	0.5	0.6	4.6	5.6	6.2	6.1	6.7	6.4	6.7	24.7	25.6	15.0	2.8	77.3	40.5	47.7	52.3
75021	DENISON	88.5	87.4	4.9	5.2	0.4	0.4	4.3	5.1	6.6	5.9	6.8	6.8	6.9	24.8	27.6	13.2	1.6	76.7	40.3	48.4	51.7
75022	FLOWER MOUND	91.8	90.4	2.2	2.5	3.1	3.8	5.0	6.0	10.5	10.8	8.9	6.6	4.1	31.4	24.1	3.2	0.5	65.0	35.2	49.4	50.6
75023	PLANO	82.2	79.8	4.9	5.1	7.9	9.3	7.2	8.8	6.8	7.4	7.8	6.7	5.7	30.0	29.4	5.5	0.6	73.7	37.0	49.3	50.7
75024	PLANO	72.5	70.1	4.9	5.2	18.6	20.0	5.6	7.0	8.9	8.0	6.9	5.5	6.9	40.3	20.8	2.6	0.1	72.8	32.6	49.7	50.4
75025	PLANO	76.5	73.7	4.9	5.2	14.8	16.7	5.0	6.2	11.1	10.9	8.7	5.6	4.1	37.9	19.3	2.4	0.1	65.7	32.8	49.6	50.4
75028	FLOWER MOUND	89.2	87.6	3.5	3.8	3.2	3.7	6.2	7.5	10.4	10.4	9.1	6.7	4.9	34.6	21.4	2.4	0.2	65.7	33.0	49.5	50.5
75032	ROCKWALL	89.1	87.7	1.5	1.7	1.3	1.4	14.4	16.7	7.7	8.2	8.3	6.7	4.9	29.1	26.8	7.7	0.5	71.6	36.7	51.1	48.9
75034	FRISCO	84.0	82.5	3.3	3.4	1.4	1.8	18.6	20.5	10.6	9.8	7.5	5.7	5.2	35.3	20.6	5.0	0.3	68.6	32.5	49.6	50.4
75035	FRISCO	88.8	87.1	4.1	4.5	3.0	3.4	6.2	7.8	14.0	11.7	6.8	3.8	2.9	45.8	12.6	2.2	0.2	64.9	31.7	49.2	50.8
75038	IRVING	50.7	48.2	23.1	23.1	14.4	15.2	19.1	22.6	7.9	5.8	4.8	5.4	12.6	46.0	15.5	2.1	0.1	78.9	29.3	51.3	48.7
75039	IRVING	78.5	75.2	3.7	4.0	14.1	16.4	7.6	9.7	3.9	2.5	1.8	2.6	11.9	56.6	16.1	4.5	0.1	90.7	32.0	56.1	43.9
75040	GARLAND	62.5	60.0	14.2	13.9	6.2	6.9	30.8	34.6	8.9	8.6	9.1	7.8	7.0	31.3	21.1	5.6	0.6	68.5	31.3	49.6	50.4
75041	GARLAND	67.2	64.3	10.6	10.4	1.4	1.4	38.6	44.4	9.5	8.4	8.1	7.1	8.2	30.9	17.5	9.4	1.1	69.8	30.3	50.2	49.8
75042	GARLAND	54.0	51.3	7.8	7.7	13.9	14.1	37.1	41.4	8.8	8.1	8.1	7.3	8.3	31.6	19.8	7.3	0.7	70.7	30.8	51.5	48.5
75043	GARLAND	71.6	68.3	14.8	15.6	3.5	3.9	14.9	18.3	7.5	6.9	7.4	7.8	8.2	29.8	24.1	7.0	1.3	73.4	33.4	48.0	52.0
75044	GARLAND	70.3	67.3	9.1	9.5	13.1	14.6	10.5	12.8	6.7	7.0	7.5	6.9	6.4	31.0	27.9	6.1	0.5	74.5	35.9	48.7	51.3
75048	SACHSE	86.7	84.7	4.7	4.9	2.4	2.7	8.5	11.0	8.8	8.6	8.5	7.2	5.8	33.7	22.0	5.1	0.3	69.6	33.1	49.5	50.5
75050	GRAND PRAIRIE	65.7	62.6	8.5	8.6	2.2	2.4	38.9	43.4	8.6	7.5	7.3	6.7	9.1	32.9	19.7	7.4	0.9	72.7	30.8	50.4	49.6
75051	GRAND PRAIRIE	58.1	53.7	11.7	12.8	2.5	2.5	45.3	50.8	9.5	9.0	9.2	7.8	7.8	28.7	19.0	8.2	0.9	67.6	29.7	48.7	51.3
75052	GRAND PRAIRIE	61.0	57.6	18.0	18.8	7.1	7.7	23.5	27.1	9.0	8.5	8.3	7.3	7.5	33.3	21.8	4.0	0.3	69.8	31.2	49.1	50.9
75056	THE COLONY	83.3	80.8	5.2	5.6	2.7	3.3	13.4	16.2	8.7	8.5	8.7	7.8	7.1	35.3	20.5	3.2	0.3	69.4	31.1	49.8	50.3
75057	LEWISVILLE	70.1	67.7	5.6	6.3	1.6	2.0	31.2	33.6	7.6	6.4	6.5	6.9	11.7	36.7	17.2	6.1	0.9	75.8	29.9	52.5	47.5
75058	GUNTER	87.6	85.4	0.4	0.5	0.4	0.4	17.0	20.2	6.9	7.0	8.3	8.0	6.9	26.3	22.3	10.4	3.9	72.7	35.8	48.4	51.6
75060	IRVING	68.3	65.1	5.3	5.1	5.3	5.6	38.4	44.2	8.8	8.2	8.3	7.4	8.0	30.7	21.2	6.7	0.7	70.2	31.1	50.5	49.5
75061	IRVING	62.7	59.7	9.0	8.8	4.1	4.3	45.7	51.4	9.0	7.8	7.3	7.0	9.3	34.4	17.5	6.7	1.0	71.9	30.0	51.9	48.1
75062	IRVING	67.5	64.7	9.6	9.8	7.5	7.9	27.1	31.6	7.0	6.1	6.5	7.4	9.6	33.2	20.9	8.8	0.5	76.5	32.7	50.5	49.5
75063	IRVING	67.5	64.6	9.9	10.0	17.3	19.3	8.5	10.7	7.6	6.1	4.7	3.3	8.3	49.0	18.6	2.3	0.1	79.8	32.0	49.9	50.1
75065	LAKE DALLAS	90.7	89.4	2.4	2.7	0.9	1.0	9.1	10.8	7.8	7.5	7.7	7.1	6.5	31.9	24.4	6.7	0.5	72.7	35.0	50.4	49.6
75067	LEWISVILLE	78.1	75.7	7.7	8.2	4.6	5.5	16.1	18.1	9.4	7.9	6.3	5.5	9.8	40.7	16.8	3.3	0.3	73.2	29.8	49.6	50.4
75068	LITTLE ELM	84.8	80.2	1.8	2.3	0.5	0.6	16.7	22.4	10.2	9.2	7.7	6.1	5.8	34.7	20.8	5.1	0.3	69.1	31.3	51.1	48.9
75069	MC KINNEY	65.8	63.7	10.3	9.9	1.1	1.3	30.8	33.8	8.9	8.1	7.6	8.2	9.4	31.6	18.2	6.6	1.3	70.9	29.6	51.1	48.9
75070	MC KINNEY	92.2	91.2	2.7	2.8	2.1	2.4	5.4	6.6	11.0	10.9	9.3	5.8	3.5	34.5	20.4	4.3	0.4	64.7	32.8	49.6	50.4
75071	MC KINNEY	85.3	83.3	6.2	6.6	1.2	1.3	11.0	13.5	9.2	8.6	7.1	5.8	6.4	34.9	20.5	6.4	1.0	71.6	32.3	51.5	48.5
75074	PLANO	72.5	70.3	7.7	7.7	3.9	4.5	26.8	29.4	7.9	7.5	7.4	6.9	8.3	33.0	22.4	6.0	0.6	73.1	32.3	51.2	48.8
75075	PLANO	81.3	78.9	3.6	3.9	8.7	10.0	10.4	11.9	6.4	6.6	6.7	6.3	6.1	30.2	28.5	8.4	0.8	76.5	37.9	49.9	50.1
75076	POTTSBORO	96.5	96.0	0.1	0.1	0.3	0.3	1.8	2.3	4.2	4.6	6.2	6.0	5.3	22.9	33.0	16.7	1.2	81.4	45.5	49.6	50.4
75077	LEWISVILLE	88.6	87.3	4.4	4.6	2.9	3.3	5.7	6.7	7.8	8.7	8.7	7.2	4.3	30.9	27.3	4.7	0.4	70.0	36.4	49.4	50.6
75078	PROSPER	92.5	90.7	0.3	0.4	0.5	0.5	16.2	19.8	9.1	9.2	9.6	7.6	4.6	31.8	21.1	6.1	1.0	67.3	34.1	50.7	49.3
75080	RICHARDSON	80.3	78.1	5.0	4.9	7.2	8.2	13.3	15.9	6.2	6.2	6.7	7.0	8.7	27.6	23.3	12.6	1.7	77.2	36.9	49.3	50.7
75081	RICHARDSON	70.8	67.8	7.9	8.2	14.3	16.0	9.4	11.2	6.3	6.2	6.8	6.7	6.8	30.0	28.1	8.4	0.8	76.5	37.1	49.0	51.0
75082	RICHARDSON	71.7	67.9	6.3	6.7	17.3	19.8	6.3	7.7	8.6	8.7	7.8	5.7	4.9	32.9	25.9	5.1	0.4	71.5	35.7	49.9	50.1
75087	ROCKWALL	90.8	89.7	3.4	3.5	1.5	1.7	7.4	8.7	7.0	7.4	8.0	7.1	6.1	28.1	26.2	8.8	1.3	73.2	37.0	49.8	50.2
75088	ROWLETT	82.2	79.9	8.6	9.2	3.7	4.4	8.3	10.3	7.9	8.3	9.4	8.0	6.0	30.2	24.1	5.2	0.8	69.2	34.3	49.0	51.0
75089	ROWLETT	81.2	79.0	9.6	10.1	2.8	3.1	9.7	12.3	9.5	9.3	9.2	7.0	5.7	34.5	20.2	4.3	0.3	67.5	32.3	49.4	50.6
75090	SHERMAN	75.5	73.9	12.7	13.0	1.0	1.1	15.2	17.3	7.6	6.8	7.3	8.6	9.3	27.4	21.4	9.7	1.9	74.1	32.4	49.2	50.8
75092	SHERMAN	87.8	86.4	5.8	6.3	0.9	1.1	5.3	6.3	6.6	5.9	6.1	6.7	7.9	26.7	23.6	13.7	2.8	77.5	37.8	47.6	52.4
75093	PLANO	81.3	78.8	3.9	4.1	11.3	13.1	4.7	5.7	7.8	8.5	8.3	6.6	5.3	32.0	26.6	4.3	0.8	71.2	35.9	48.9	51.1
75094	PLANO	77.8	76.0	8.3	7.8	8.5	9.8	6.0	8.0	10.1	9.6	7.9	5.1	4.1	37.2	21.1	4.9	0.1	69.2	33.7	50.1	49.9
75098	WYLIE	90.7	88.9	2.2	2.3	0.8	0.9	9.5	12.0	8.7	8.5	8.8	7.2	6.0	33.0	21.4	5.8	0.6	69.6	33.0	49.5	50.5
75102	BARRY	86.2	84.0	5.3	5.8	1.0	1.1	10.3	12.5	7.4	7.2	8.1	8.1	5.7	28.4	24.3	9.9	1.0	72.4	35.8	50.9	49.1
75103	CANTON	93.4	92.6	2.0	2.1	0.3	0.4	4.5	5.4	6.0	6.1	6.4	6.3	5.9	23.3	27.0	16.7	2.4	77.6	42.2	49.2	50.8
75104	CEDAR HILL	56.6	53.4	33.5	34.9	2.0	2.3	12.0	14.9	8.5	8.6	8.8	7.8	6.9	32.3	22.2	4.4	0.6	69.3	32.2	47.5	52.5
75105	CHATFIELD	81.1	78.1	5.9	6.7	0.0	0.0	16.3	19.5	7.9	7.9	8.5	7.9	6.1	29.3	23.8	7.9	0.6	70.7	34.6	50.6	49.4
75109	CORSICANA	88.5	86.7	5.9	6.7	1.2	1.3	5.1	6.5	6.6	7.1	8.7	7.6	5.6	27.3	24.4	11.2	1.5	72.6	37.0	51.5	48.5
75110	CORSICANA	63.4	61.0	20.9	21.3	1.1	1.2	20.3	23.2	7.8	7.2	7.2	8.1	8.3	26.4	21.3	11.2	2.5	73.6	33.6	49.1	51.0
75114	CRANDALL	87.8	85.6	5.3	6.1	0.3	0.3	7.8	9.7	7.4	7.6	9.0	8.1	7.2	29.4	23.2	7.2	0.9	70.9	33.1	49.6	50.4
75115	DESOTO	48.7	46.4	45.2	46.4	1.3	1.4	8.2	10.2	7.3	7.5	8.0	7.3	6.3	27.9	26.7	7.9	1.2	72.7	36.2	47.5	52.5
75116	DUNCANVILLE	66.8	64.0	20.2	20.4	1.9	2.1	18.7	22.9	6.9	6.8	7.7	7.6	7.3	26.5	25.2	10.8	1.2	73.9	35.4	47.5	52.5
75117	EDGEWOOD	93.0	92.2	3.7	4.0	0.1	0.1	4.0	4.7	6.7	6.5	6.9	6.3	6.3	23.3	26.4	15.7	2.0	76.2	41.0	49.3	50.7
75119	ENNIS	72.3	70.0	11.0	11.3	0.3	0.3	28.6	32.1	8.5	7.9	7.8	7.6	8.2	26.9	21.6	9.9	1.8	71.3	32.6	49.6	50.4
75124	EUSTACE	95.9	95.2	0.5	0.6	0.3	0.4	4.1	5.1	6.0	6.3	7.1	6.8	5.8	25.2	25.6	15.7	1.5	76.4	40.4	49.4	50.6
75125	FERRIS	77.8	76.2	11.1	11.0	0.2	0.2	26.8	30.8	8.2	7.9	8.5	8.7	7.6	27.4	23.2	7.8	0.8	70.2	32.4	50.0	50.0
75126	FORNEY	87.9	86.7	5.9	6.3	0.3	0.4	7.4	8.9	7.4	7.9	8.9	7.5	6.0	29.3	24.8	7.6	0.7	71.1	35.2	49.7	50.4
75127	FRUITVALE	95.3	94.6	0.3	0.4	0.1	0.1	4.3	5.1	7.2	7.4	7.8	7.0	5.7	23.8	25.9	13.9	1.3	73.1	38.3	49.9	50.1
75134	LANCASTER	30.9	28.1	57.3	58.6	0.4	0.4	15.0	17.0	8.1	7.8	8.4	8.2	7.5	29.8	21.5	7.5	1.2	70.7	32.0	46.8	53.3
75135	CADDO MILLS	91.8	90.4	3.4	3.7	0.2	0.2	6.7	8.3	7.3	7.4	8.2	7.2	6.1	29.6	24.1	9.2	1.0	72.6	35.5	48.9	51.1
75137	DUNCANVILLE	62.3	59.5	28.3	29.5	2.3	2.6	11.4	14.1	6.0	6.4	7.3	7.5	6.9	26.5	29.5	9.1	0.9	75.4	38.0	47.1	53.0
75140	GRAND SALINE	93.8	93.0	0.4	0.4	0.2	0.3	10.2	11.7	7.0	6.9	7.3	7.2	6.3	24.9	23.0	14.3	3.1	74.3	37.7	50.4	49.6
75141	HUTCHINS	40.1	37.3	42.6	42.2	0.2	0.2	21.5	25.8	7.0	6.6	6.3	8.0	9.4	36.0	20.5	5.6	0.7	75.2	31.7	59.0	41.1
75142	KAUFMAN	81.5	79.2	6.8	7.4	0.4	0.4	17.0	19.6	7.9	7.6	7.8	7.3	7.1	28.1	23.5	9.4	1.4	72.3	34.6	49.5	50.5
75143	KEMP	93.8	92.7	2.1	2.5	0.2	0.2	4.4	5.6	5.9	6.1	7.0	6.8	5.9	24.2	27.5	15.3	1.4	76.9	41.2	49.9	50.1
75144	KERENS	67.0	64.3	26.6	27.9	0.1	0.1	7.1	8.7	7.1	6.9	7.3	7.4	6.6	24.4	24.2	13.5	2.7	74.3	37.9	48.2	51.9
75146	LANCASTER	46.0	41.7	45.5	48.7	0.5	0.5	10.4	12.3	7.9	7.9	8.4	7.2	6.9	30.8	22.5	7.3	1.2	71.3	33.8	47.0	53.0
75147	MABANK	90.6	89.8	4.2	4.8	0.2	0.3	5.6	7.1	7.2	6.7	7.4	7.6	6.9	24.4	22.9	14.5	2.3	74.1	37.5	46.9	53.1
75148	MALAKOFF	84.6	83.7	11.3	11.7	0.3	0.3	6.2	7.2	6.2	6.1	6.2	6.3	5.1	22.7	26.1	18.4	2.9	77.4	43.1	48.4	51.6
75149	MESQUITE	70.5	67.5	15.8	16.5	3.1	3.3	16.9	20.7	8.5	8.2	9.0	7.8	7.4	31.0	20.5	7.0	0.7	69.4	31.6	48.2	51.8
75150	MESQUITE	76.5	73.2	10.5	11.5	4.2	4.8	16.2	19.8	6.9	6.6	7.5	7.9	8.9	30.6	23.4	7.5	0.7	74.4	33.2	48.2	51.8
75152	PALMER	86.8	84.8	2.1	2.3	0.2	0.2	23.5	27.5	7.8	7.7	8.0	8.4	7.4	28.2	24.2	7.7	0.7	71.4	33.3	51.0	49.0
75153	POWELL	77.1	75.8	17.0	17.7	0.0	0.0	6.8	8.9	6.5	6.5	6.5	7.3	6.5	23.4	28.2	14.5	0.8	75.8	40.6	50.0	50.0
75154	RED OAK	81.2	79.3	11.0	11.7	0.6	0.7	13.0	15.4	8.1	8.1	8.9	7.9	6.5	30.1	24.1	5.9	0.4	69.8	33.3	49.3	50.7
75155	RICE	81.3	78.2	6.0	6.4	0.3	0.4	16.4	19.8	7.8	7.7	8.6	7.9	6.2	29.4	23.6	7.9	1.0	71.0	34.4	50.6	49.4
75156	MABANK	94.5	93.6	1.6	1.9	0.4	0.5	3.5	4.4	6.0	5.7	5.8	5.3	4.9	21.8	29.1	19.8	1.7	79.3	45.4	49.8	50.2
75158	SCURRY	93.6	92.3	2.4	2.8	0.1	0.1	4.2	5.4	6.6	6.9	8.6	7.7	6.8	27.4	26.6	8.5	0.8	73.1	36.7	50.0	50.0
75159	SEAGOVILLE	81.2	78.3	8.2	8.6	0.5	0.6	16.4	20.8	7.2	6.8	7.0	6.7	7.3	33.2	23.1	7.9	0.8	75.0	34.1	54.3	45.7
75160	TERRELL	65.8	63.7	23.3	23.8	1.0	1.2	14.5	16.7	7.7	7.6	7.6	7.4	7.8	26.9	23.1	10.1	1.9	72.7	34.4	48.9	51.1
75161	TERRELL	86.8	84.6	7.7	8.9	0.5	0.5	6.8	8.4	6.6	6.7	7.3	7.2	6.8	26.5	27.7	10.5	0.7	75.0	38.2	51.2	48.8
	TEXAS	71.0	69.5	11.5	11.4	2.8	3.1	32.0	34.6	7.9	7.5	7.7	7.5	8.1	29.6	21.9	8.7	1.2	72.6	32.9	49.7	50.3
	UNITED STATES	75.1	73.6	12.3	12.5	3.8	4.2	12.5	14.1	6.9	6.7	7.2	7.0	7.3	28.6	23.8	10.8	1.7	75.1	36.0	49.1	50.9

ZIP CODE				2004 HOUSEHOLD INCOME DISTRIBUTION (%)					MEDIAN HOUSEHOLD INCOME					2004 HOME VALUE DISTRIBUTION (%)					
#	POST OFFICE NAME	2004 Per Capita Income	2004 HH Income Base	Less than $25,000	$25,000 to $49,999	$50,000 to $99,999	$100,000 to $149,999	$150,000 or More	2004	2009	2004 National Centile	2004 State Centile	2004 Home Value Base	Less than $50,000	$50,000 to $89,999	$90,000 to $174,999	$175,000 to $399,999	$400,000 or More	2004 Median Home Value
75001	ADDISON	47220	7975	12.5	27.2	34.6	12.9	12.8	60539	75310	85	87	1551	0.0	1.4	16.9	77.3	4.5	239593
75002	ALLEN	33460	15915	5.8	13.4	41.0	25.9	13.9	85568	104397	96	97	13948	1.7	4.4	48.9	40.5	4.5	166611
75006	CARROLLTON	27133	17254	13.0	25.8	38.2	14.3	8.7	61230	71007	86	88	10176	5.9	14.3	58.4	20.9	0.5	121628
75007	CARROLLTON	33418	20357	6.9	17.6	39.4	22.7	13.5	78783	94954	95	96	14824	0.5	1.6	58.4	37.9	1.7	160744
75009	CELINA	31481	2272	15.1	23.9	31.7	16.9	12.4	63493	74512	87	89	1895	11.2	16.0	28.8	31.6	12.4	145833
75010	CARROLLTON	35538	6381	7.7	18.2	39.0	21.6	13.5	77275	93647	94	95	4042	7.7	2.3	42.5	44.4	3.1	171898
75013	ALLEN	41433	5887	4.6	9.8	25.9	32.9	26.8	110785	129907	99	99	5208	2.0	2.8	12.8	65.3	17.1	239877
75019	COPPELL	47871	13453	4.3	10.4	29.2	22.9	33.2	110922	137499	99	99	10311	2.7	2.8	25.0	55.2	14.2	230356
75020	DENISON	22217	8903	31.6	28.2	28.0	8.8	3.4	40161	45775	47	55	6127	29.4	35.9	26.0	7.8	0.9	69805
75021	DENISON	18653	3289	36.6	27.4	26.8	6.0	3.1	36219	41398	32	39	2470	34.3	29.6	26.4	8.9	0.9	69628
75022	FLOWER MOUND	47535	6004	4.0	6.9	24.0	28.2	37.1	123826	143143	99	100	5712	3.0	1.9	9.7	68.4	17.1	283944
75023	PLANO	37105	18430	6.9	15.8	37.8	24.3	15.2	83214	100248	96	97	13642	1.0	2.2	51.3	44.2	1.4	167415
75024	PLANO	49925	11909	6.0	12.4	32.4	25.5	23.8	98429	116472	98	98	6555	2.6	0.2	7.4	79.4	10.4	252832
75025	PLANO	41973	17473	4.7	9.1	29.3	31.1	25.8	108378	128050	99	99	13770	1.5	0.3	14.1	74.7	9.4	242772
75028	FLOWER MOUND	36713	14716	3.9	9.2	35.7	31.7	19.5	101198	117903	98	98	13694	3.2	1.4	36.9	53.5	5.0	189028
75032	ROCKWALL	38967	6646	8.8	21.9	32.0	18.7	18.7	76902	89359	94	95	5783	8.1	8.4	27.8	39.0	16.7	192269
75034	FRISCO	40153	9041	9.7	19.0	32.7	19.9	18.7	78928	97569	95	96	7019	5.2	10.5	29.8	31.9	22.6	193247
75035	FRISCO	37660	10452	3.1	8.5	42.6	31.8	14.0	94253	111490	98	98	9509	0.6	0.5	37.0	60.9	1.0	186512
75038	IRVING	33398	13688	16.9	34.1	34.6	9.0	5.5	49058	59920	70	76	1548	5.9	8.7	42.1	21.3	22.0	161243
75039	IRVING	77257	2354	5.6	22.3	35.9	18.1	18.0	76809	102236	94	95	338	2.4	2.7	1.5	59.2	34.3	359542
75040	GARLAND	20978	17117	14.6	26.8	39.8	13.5	5.2	58231	66543	83	86	13380	8.3	34.8	52.5	4.3	0.2	97240
75041	GARLAND	17840	10661	21.9	36.4	31.1	8.1	2.6	43556	50075	57	65	6132	7.6	45.3	42.9	4.0	0.3	87588
75042	GARLAND	17259	12176	23.1	32.7	32.7	8.6	2.8	45198	51959	62	68	6797	2.5	45.1	49.1	3.0	0.3	91348
75043	GARLAND	25085	21228	14.7	29.0	38.2	13.0	5.1	56284	65361	81	84	12580	1.9	25.2	62.9	9.5	0.5	108684
75044	GARLAND	32117	14443	9.0	20.5	39.2	19.8	11.4	72287	87625	92	93	10885	0.4	11.9	62.8	23.0	1.9	119429
75048	SACHSE	27591	4416	8.4	17.8	44.4	20.2	9.2	75200	88708	93	94	3875	6.7	9.0	61.9	21.9	0.5	132482
75050	GRAND PRAIRIE	22122	14709	21.7	32.2	32.6	8.9	4.7	46319	54744	65	70	7203	23.7	30.5	35.3	9.4	1.0	81206
75051	GRAND PRAIRIE	15511	9733	32.7	29.5	28.4	7.5	1.9	38994	44691	43	51	5409	20.6	54.7	22.1	2.3	0.4	71037
75052	GRAND PRAIRIE	24859	21140	11.8	21.6	43.3	17.0	6.4	65760	77216	89	90	15816	2.7	22.3	64.0	10.7	0.3	111680
75056	THE COLONY	26018	11637	6.4	20.8	44.5	21.4	7.0	71621	83871	92	93	8868	2.0	13.8	64.5	18.6	1.1	120299
75057	LEWISVILLE	23442	5344	18.6	30.1	38.9	9.1	3.4	51203	61167	74	79	2310	34.5	20.5	36.7	6.8	1.5	81655
75058	GUNTER	19518	684	22.5	26.2	37.4	10.2	3.7	51190	58438	74	79	534	17.6	27.9	32.0	18.0	4.5	96316
75060	IRVING	19392	15735	21.4	29.3	35.7	11.0	2.6	49315	57023	71	76	9797	9.9	33.0	54.0	2.7	0.4	95307
75061	IRVING	18677	19407	23.8	35.1	29.8	8.4	3.1	42416	49770	54	63	7447	11.5	26.8	47.0	14.3	0.5	103196
75062	IRVING	26398	15983	16.0	32.1	35.8	10.6	5.5	51696	61123	75	80	7540	1.7	23.1	62.4	11.6	1.2	108993
75063	IRVING	51901	14671	6.4	20.7	36.5	17.9	18.6	76483	101021	94	95	5598	0.9	0.8	19.2	65.9	13.2	238705
75065	LAKE DALLAS	27770	3600	14.3	25.8	36.3	16.5	7.1	61349	71020	86	88	2760	13.2	12.1	50.3	21.7	2.7	126362
75067	LEWISVILLE	30042	23586	10.9	26.5	39.3	16.9	6.5	62309	73842	87	88	11541	2.1	6.1	57.8	33.1	0.9	144213
75068	LITTLE ELM	27062	4329	15.8	23.7	36.9	14.9	8.8	60781	70315	85	87	3685	18.2	18.4	36.1	20.7	6.6	114719
75069	MC KINNEY	23626	10517	21.5	29.5	31.8	10.4	6.9	48710	60136	70	75	5990	15.8	21.5	35.8	19.8	7.1	113532
75070	MC KINNEY	46696	13029	2.6	8.9	34.2	28.3	26.0	105060	124217	99	99	11929	0.1	0.7	24.7	60.7	13.9	221223
75071	MC KINNEY	28881	5082	14.5	20.1	38.0	18.7	8.7	67069	79007	90	91	3859	6.1	7.7	50.8	30.0	5.3	146953
75074	PLANO	27547	15332	13.4	24.9	38.0	15.9	7.9	63243	74105	87	89	10035	4.9	13.8	58.2	20.9	2.2	124051
75075	PLANO	37817	14730	8.9	18.4	36.0	22.4	14.2	79375	94503	95	96	9873	1.0	2.1	50.9	44.8	1.2	171193
75076	POTTSBORO	25912	3097	21.3	29.2	36.2	8.2	5.0	49347	56488	71	76	2569	21.4	36.6	24.2	16.4	1.4	77689
75077	LEWISVILLE	39387	11614	4.1	10.4	37.6	27.5	20.5	96607	110334	98	98	10689	0.9	0.6	40.5	49.6	8.5	187287
75078	PROSPER	29228	1226	12.8	19.8	34.3	19.4	13.7	72415	84579	92	93	1058	6.1	13.4	39.2	32.2	9.0	154054
75080	RICHARDSON	30572	16833	14.7	24.3	36.0	16.0	9.0	62372	72952	87	88	10931	1.9	7.9	57.8	30.5	1.9	141303
75081	RICHARDSON	32068	13099	11.7	22.0	37.2	19.3	9.8	68526	83171	91	92	8419	2.3	7.2	73.6	16.1	0.8	137448
75082	RICHARDSON	45958	6782	4.8	10.9	29.2	28.7	26.5	106684	124758	99	99	5469	2.4	1.5	18.0	71.4	6.7	223380
75087	ROCKWALL	32563	7767	12.0	16.4	38.2	21.0	12.5	75716	89945	93	94	6318	4.3	6.3	31.4	53.5	4.5	186239
75088	ROWLETT	31624	8759	6.6	15.5	43.1	21.5	13.3	80086	98160	95	96	7949	1.6	7.1	61.4	28.6	1.4	132086
75089	ROWLETT	28434	7289	5.5	15.4	47.5	23.5	8.0	77503	92946	94	95	6772	2.4	6.2	70.9	19.8	0.7	133344
75090	SHERMAN	17938	8321	34.4	30.0	27.4	6.3	1.9	37168	42893	36	43	5412	38.1	33.3	22.0	5.8	0.9	63206
75092	SHERMAN	26603	9300	24.6	31.2	29.9	9.3	5.1	44429	51421	60	67	5559	12.1	25.7	46.0	14.2	1.9	104590
75093	PLANO	65097	20768	5.8	13.0	25.6	18.2	37.4	113064	130925	99	99	14071	0.6	0.6	13.4	44.2	41.3	354415
75094	PLANO	39109	1846	4.1	10.2	37.6	31.5	16.6	96708	114596	98	98	1762	0.8	2.0	23.7	69.0	4.5	205784
75098	WYLIE	28716	9520	10.6	18.8	44.2	18.1	8.3	70049	81304	91	92	8276	16.6	10.9	47.8	22.6	2.1	126198
75102	BARRY	18730	258	25.6	32.2	35.3	5.4	1.6	45882	53031	64	70	217	43.8	24.4	27.2	4.6	0.0	59643
75103	CANTON	20459	6002	31.3	29.4	29.7	6.2	3.4	39614	45121	45	53	4856	23.4	27.7	33.0	13.2	2.7	88349
75104	CEDAR HILL	26425	12324	10.0	22.4	43.0	18.1	6.4	66384	77953	89	91	9917	2.5	21.0	64.2	10.7	1.7	112798
75105	CHATFIELD	16125	56	28.6	37.5	26.8	5.4	1.8	38873	46737	42	51	46	45.7	23.9	26.1	4.4	0.0	60000
75109	CORSICANA	21328	1162	25.0	25.9	34.3	8.9	5.9	47638	53871	67	72	986	31.6	26.4	21.1	18.7	2.2	77571
75110	CORSICANA	17644	10590	39.6	27.1	24.3	5.9	3.0	33232	38442	22	26	6717	36.9	31.4	24.6	5.9	1.1	69466
75114	CRANDALL	22073	1519	15.5	26.0	41.9	12.2	4.5	57344	64920	82	85	1262	13.8	28.8	41.5	15.1	0.8	100124
75115	DESOTO	28521	15275	13.9	23.4	37.1	17.2	8.4	65122	76370	89	90	11645	5.0	11.6	64.0	17.8	1.6	122050
75116	DUNCANVILLE	23149	6505	18.0	30.8	35.2	11.7	4.4	51115	60067	74	79	4454	3.6	38.1	53.8	4.1	0.5	97566
75117	EDGEWOOD	20027	1635	31.5	26.2	30.2	8.0	4.2	43195	49854	56	65	1284	23.3	29.7	32.7	12.5	1.8	84795
75119	ENNIS	19398	9004	24.2	29.3	34.5	8.3	3.8	46793	53426	66	71	6246	19.7	32.7	34.0	11.5	2.1	87170
75124	EUSTACE	17865	1433	32.2	30.6	29.2	5.3	2.7	39831	45854	45	54	1162	36.1	29.5	26.2	6.8	1.5	63194
75125	FERRIS	21055	2275	18.4	31.0	33.3	9.9	7.4	50436	58065	73	78	1759	26.3	41.7	23.2	6.4	2.4	70445
75126	FORNEY	25191	4776	12.6	22.2	42.0	16.3	6.9	66677	75295	90	91	4159	6.1	16.0	45.4	31.2	1.4	133501
75127	FRUITVALE	16281	784	35.2	34.7	23.5	5.1	1.5	35597	41051	30	36	646	31.1	29.7	26.0	10.8	2.3	75536
75134	LANCASTER	18616	4723	22.2	34.8	32.5	7.9	2.6	44666	52006	60	68	3001	11.3	55.5	31.8	0.8	0.6	78993
75135	CADDO MILLS	20907	1591	20.5	29.3	38.9	8.1	3.2	50172	57108	72	77	1261	24.1	31.7	38.0	5.8	0.4	81353
75137	DUNCANVILLE	29322	6265	10.1	24.5	37.5	19.0	8.9	66572	78023	89	91	4728	3.3	23.0	54.6	18.0	1.1	116333
75140	GRAND SALINE	16734	2218	37.6	31.1	25.6	4.0	1.7	35000	40140	28	33	1650	31.2	33.0	26.7	7.0	2.2	70078
75141	HUTCHINS	19308	987	27.4	32.0	31.5	7.3	1.8	41672	49809	52	61	766	53.5	35.4	10.6	0.5	0.0	48058
75142	KAUFMAN	21122	6417	20.6	31.0	34.6	9.5	4.3	48387	55318	69	74	4986	19.5	31.8	36.0	11.1	1.5	88365
75143	KEMP	20318	4835	30.2	30.2	29.3	7.4	3.0	41382	48402	51	59	4004	33.5	29.1	25.5	10.6	1.3	72697
75144	KERENS	16654	1327	38.0	31.4	25.6	3.2	1.9	33302	39045	22	27	969	39.8	35.8	18.6	5.8	0.0	60060
75146	LANCASTER	22795	5833	15.8	29.6	38.3	12.5	3.8	53936	63402	78	82	4000	13.2	27.1	53.4	6.0	0.4	98667
75147	MABANK	18196	1441	30.1	32.8	29.5	6.0	1.6	40424	47158	48	56	1060	35.1	28.1	30.6	5.6	0.7	71719
75148	MALAKOFF	19568	2499	37.5	29.3	22.7	7.2	3.4	33622	38693	23	28	1907	38.0	25.2	25.4	9.7	1.7	64917
75149	MESQUITE	21991	19455	16.7	28.3	39.6	11.5	4.0	54469	63055	79	82	13545	8.6	41.3	44.1	5.2	0.9	90163
75150	MESQUITE	24912	22456	16.0	30.4	36.7	12.4	4.5	53356	62369	77	81	13068	3.0	32.9	60.1	3.8	0.3	101383
75152	PALMER	22686	1147	16.0	28.4	37.9	12.0	5.7	54372	62206	79	82	960	24.2	30.5	27.5	15.8	2.0	81346
75153	POWELL	19365	45	28.9	33.3	26.7	6.7	4.4	39288	48204	44	52	38	23.7	34.2	34.2	7.9	0.0	82500
75154	RED OAK	25309	9636	13.7	23.1	42.7	14.3	6.2	63246	71222	87	89	7995	9.9	18.7	53.5	15.7	2.2	112606
75155	RICE	16351	969	28.7	36.0	28.6	4.4	2.3	39326	45326	44	52	796	42.1	25.6	24.5	5.0	2.8	63684
75156	MABANK	23293	7469	33.0	31.3	25.2	5.9	4.7	37266	43370	36	43	6195	35.2	29.2	24.5	9.3	1.8	71043
75158	SCURRY	24308	1598	15.0	27.5	40.4	12.0	5.1	57134	64519	82	84	1401	19.4	25.2	37.5	15.7	2.1	99321
75159	SEAGOVILLE	20432	4895	20.9	29.4	35.1	10.9	3.7	49641	59258	71	76	3854	35.2	32.5	21.3	9.5	1.6	69430
75160	TERRELL	20310	7292	28.0	28.2	30.0	9.4	4.3	43145	49921	56	65	5006	21.3	30.0	34.6	13.1	1.0	88184
75161	TERRELL	19471	2168	22.4	32.1	34.1	9.7	1.8	47032	54207	66	72	1848	32.9	25.8	33.4	7.2	0.7	76628
	TEXAS	23284		26.2	27.7	29.5	10.3	6.3	45778	54246				21.6	26.1	33.4	15.6	3.4	93683
	UNITED STATES	25866		24.7	27.1	30.8	10.9	6.5	48124	56710				10.9	15.0	33.7	30.1	10.4	145905

#	POST OFFICE NAME	FINANCIAL SERVICES: Auto Loan	FINANCIAL SERVICES: Home Loan	FINANCIAL SERVICES: Invest-ments	FINANCIAL SERVICES: Retire-ment Plans	THE HOME: Home Improvements: Home Repair	THE HOME: Home Improvements: Lawn & Garden	THE HOME: Furnishings: Comput-ers & Hard-ware	THE HOME: Furnishings: Major Appli-ances	THE HOME: Furnishings: TV, Radio, Sound Equip-ment	THE HOME: Furnishings: Furni-ture	ENTERTAINMENT: Dine out/Carry out	ENTERTAINMENT: Sports Equip-ment	ENTERTAINMENT: Fees & Tickets	ENTERTAINMENT: Toys & Games	ENTERTAINMENT: Travel	ENTERTAINMENT: Cable TV	PERSONAL: Apparel & Services	PERSONAL: Auto Repairs	PERSONAL: Health Insur-ance	PERSONAL: Pets & Supplies
75001	ADDISON	120	113	165	127	108	117	128	118	127	130	162	143	129	161	123	122	159	125	107	132
75002	ALLEN	143	164	166	169	157	155	149	147	137	153	174	172	155	177	147	130	173	144	128	162
75006	CARROLLTON	102	105	116	108	101	105	106	103	103	108	130	121	107	129	103	98	129	105	93	113
75007	CARROLLTON	134	151	156	158	145	144	140	138	130	144	165	162	146	166	138	123	164	136	120	152
75009	CELINA	128	140	141	142	139	144	131	132	126	131	157	153	136	161	132	123	155	129	125	148
75010	CARROLLTON	135	151	148	158	145	141	138	137	127	143	161	160	142	161	134	118	159	133	117	149
75013	ALLEN	177	211	223	219	203	202	190	186	173	194	221	216	202	226	190	166	221	180	163	204
75019	COPPELL	197	224	255	236	215	217	211	203	197	215	250	239	222	255	208	188	249	201	179	225
75020	DENISON	74	75	77	73	76	83	75	76	77	73	95	87	76	97	76	78	91	75	79	85
75021	DENISON	71	65	59	63	68	75	66	69	69	64	84	80	65	85	66	71	81	68	74	82
75022	FLOWER MOUND	200	248	266	256	239	240	219	213	199	222	253	247	239	262	221	192	255	206	189	236
75023	PLANO	139	158	166	164	152	152	147	143	136	149	173	168	153	174	145	129	171	141	126	158
75024	PLANO	174	178	210	192	171	175	181	172	172	185	219	206	184	217	174	163	216	176	152	191
75025	PLANO	177	201	203	210	192	189	184	180	169	190	215	211	191	216	180	159	213	177	156	198
75028	FLOWER MOUND	164	189	186	197	180	175	170	167	155	176	197	196	177	199	166	145	196	163	143	184
75032	ROCKWALL	163	186	188	189	182	186	168	168	157	171	198	194	177	201	169	153	197	163	154	189
75034	FRISCO	160	184	190	189	176	175	165	164	153	171	194	191	173	195	164	145	192	160	143	181
75035	FRISCO	152	172	166	180	164	158	155	154	142	162	181	180	160	181	151	132	179	150	131	168
75038	IRVING	97	85	118	96	81	89	100	92	99	102	126	113	97	121	94	94	123	99	83	103
75039	IRVING	149	143	269	164	135	151	169	149	173	172	220	184	176	231	166	171	218	160	140	167
75040	GARLAND	98	103	103	104	100	101	100	100	96	102	121	115	100	121	98	92	120	100	90	109
75041	GARLAND	73	74	78	74	73	76	76	75	75	77	95	87	76	94	74	73	93	77	71	81
75042	GARLAND	75	78	85	76	75	79	78	77	78	80	99	88	79	100	77	76	99	79	73	84
75043	GARLAND	95	101	108	105	98	99	100	97	94	101	120	115	100	119	97	90	118	98	87	107
75044	GARLAND	122	136	147	141	132	133	130	127	121	131	154	149	134	156	128	116	153	126	112	140
75048	SACHSE	118	138	137	142	133	129	124	123	114	127	144	144	129	148	123	107	143	119	106	135
75050	GRAND PRAIRIE	86	80	83	81	78	83	85	84	85	87	107	98	82	102	81	82	105	87	79	93
75051	GRAND PRAIRIE	69	65	67	62	63	68	68	68	70	70	87	77	66	85	66	69	86	70	67	75
75052	GRAND PRAIRIE	108	118	120	122	113	112	111	109	104	114	132	128	113	132	108	98	130	108	95	120
75056	THE COLONY	117	131	129	135	126	123	120	119	111	124	141	140	123	142	118	104	139	117	103	131
75057	LEWISVILLE	90	81	88	86	79	83	88	86	87	90	110	102	85	104	83	82	107	90	78	96
75058	GUNTER	100	86	67	85	91	101	86	93	91	85	110	107	83	110	86	93	104	91	100	113
75060	IRVING	83	85	88	85	83	85	85	85	84	87	106	98	85	107	83	81	105	86	78	92
75061	IRVING	77	71	76	72	69	72	77	75	77	79	98	88	75	95	73	73	97	79	69	82
75062	IRVING	94	95	115	99	92	97	100	96	97	101	124	114	100	123	97	93	122	99	87	105
75063	IRVING	148	143	184	156	137	146	154	145	150	158	191	175	154	186	148	143	188	152	131	162
75065	LAKE DALLAS	110	120	114	121	116	116	111	112	105	113	132	131	112	132	109	100	129	110	101	125
75067	LEWISVILLE	108	107	114	114	103	105	109	106	104	112	132	126	108	128	104	98	130	108	93	117
75068	LITTLE ELM	122	121	104	117	120	124	113	118	111	115	138	137	110	135	112	109	134	117	114	138
75069	MC KINNEY	95	92	98	95	90	95	97	95	95	98	120	112	95	117	94	92	118	98	89	105
75070	MC KINNEY	203	234	234	243	223	218	210	208	192	218	244	242	219	247	206	181	243	202	178	227
75071	MC KINNEY	121	132	125	135	129	128	120	121	113	123	142	142	123	144	119	108	140	118	110	138
75074	PLANO	111	118	124	121	114	116	115	113	110	117	139	132	117	139	112	105	138	113	101	124
75075	PLANO	133	149	171	155	145	149	144	140	136	145	173	164	150	175	143	131	172	140	126	154
75076	POTTSBORO	103	85	61	79	93	103	80	93	88	79	105	109	74	105	84	92	98	91	106	124
75077	LEWISVILLE	163	195	202	202	188	186	174	171	159	178	202	199	185	208	174	152	202	166	149	188
75078	PROSPER	133	150	145	156	144	140	136	135	125	141	158	157	140	159	133	117	157	131	116	148
75080	RICHARDSON	104	112	134	114	110	117	116	110	112	114	141	130	117	141	114	109	139	113	104	121
75081	RICHARDSON	113	127	145	129	124	127	123	120	117	124	148	141	127	151	123	113	147	121	108	132
75082	RICHARDSON	183	212	213	220	203	200	191	188	175	197	223	220	201	226	189	166	222	183	163	207
75087	ROCKWALL	130	142	145	146	139	142	133	133	126	135	159	154	137	159	132	122	156	131	122	148
75088	ROWLETT	140	163	164	170	156	153	147	145	134	151	171	169	154	173	145	127	170	140	125	159
75089	ROWLETT	128	144	139	150	137	133	130	129	120	135	152	151	134	152	127	111	150	126	110	141
75090	SHERMAN	70	64	63	64	65	71	68	68	69	66	86	80	66	85	67	69	83	69	69	79
75092	SHERMAN	89	88	92	89	88	95	89	89	89	88	111	104	89	111	89	89	108	90	89	101
75093	PLANO	232	262	309	274	253	262	249	241	234	254	297	282	263	299	248	225	296	240	216	266
75094	PLANO	169	192	185	200	183	176	173	171	158	180	201	201	178	202	169	148	199	167	145	187
75098	WYLIE	121	136	131	139	131	129	123	124	115	127	145	144	127	146	122	109	143	121	109	137
75102	BARRY	82	74	58	72	74	79	71	76	72	73	89	88	67	84	70	71	85	76	76	90
75103	CANTON	92	67	38	62	75	86	67	80	77	66	91	94	59	87	68	81	83	79	95	107
75104	CEDAR HILL	112	128	127	132	122	120	117	115	108	120	137	136	120	138	115	101	135	113	100	127
75105	CHATFIELD	75	69	54	66	69	72	65	70	66	67	82	81	62	77	64	65	78	70	70	83
75109	CORSICANA	98	88	68	84	90	96	83	90	86	84	105	105	80	103	83	86	100	89	93	111
75110	CORSICANA	70	63	59	61	64	72	66	68	70	66	85	78	64	83	65	71	82	69	72	78
75114	CRANDALL	102	103	93	103	102	104	98	101	95	99	119	118	96	117	96	92	115	100	94	116
75115	DESOTO	110	120	128	124	116	118	115	113	109	117	138	132	118	138	113	104	136	112	102	125
75116	DUNCANVILLE	88	95	103	96	94	98	93	92	90	93	114	108	96	116	93	88	112	92	87	102
75117	EDGEWOOD	88	67	42	64	74	84	68	78	76	66	90	92	61	88	69	79	83	77	91	102
75119	ENNIS	89	80	68	77	81	87	80	84	82	81	102	97	76	99	79	82	98	84	86	98
75124	EUSTACE	89	61	30	54	69	79	59	73	70	59	82	88	50	79	61	75	75	72	89	103
75125	FERRIS	107	95	75	93	97	104	93	99	95	94	117	114	88	112	92	95	112	99	101	118
75126	FORNEY	109	122	118	124	118	117	111	111	103	113	130	130	114	132	110	99	129	108	99	124
75127	FRUITVALE	85	57	26	49	64	74	55	69	66	56	78	82	47	73	56	71	71	68	84	97
75134	LANCASTER	77	75	75	76	74	78	77	77	76	78	96	90	75	93	75	74	93	78	73	85
75135	CADDO MILLS	94	84	65	81	85	93	82	88	84	82	103	101	78	100	81	84	98	87	91	105
75137	DUNCANVILLE	113	128	137	131	125	127	122	120	115	122	145	141	126	147	121	110	143	119	108	132
75140	GRAND SALINE	75	57	37	53	63	73	58	67	66	57	78	78	52	75	59	70	72	67	79	86
75141	HUTCHINS	58	54	46	52	54	58	52	55	53	54	66	63	51	63	52	53	64	55	56	65
75142	KAUFMAN	98	88	70	85	89	96	85	91	88	86	108	106	81	105	85	88	103	91	94	109
75143	KEMP	90	71	49	66	76	86	69	80	76	70	92	91	63	86	70	79	85	79	90	101
75144	KERENS	72	55	35	51	59	68	57	64	64	56	75	73	51	71	57	67	69	64	75	80
75146	LANCASTER	91	94	98	96	92	95	94	93	91	94	114	109	94	114	92	87	112	93	85	103
75147	MABANK	77	65	48	63	68	76	66	71	70	65	85	82	62	82	65	71	80	71	77	86
75148	MALAKOFF	79	63	48	59	67	78	64	71	71	64	85	80	59	79	65	74	79	71	83	89
75149	MESQUITE	91	97	100	100	95	96	95	94	91	95	114	110	96	115	93	87	112	93	85	103
75150	MESQUITE	92	95	104	99	93	95	96	94	92	97	117	111	97	116	94	88	115	95	85	103
75152	PALMER	111	105	86	101	108	114	97	105	100	98	122	124	96	124	99	100	118	103	108	130
75153	POWELL	88	75	55	71	77	83	72	80	75	74	92	93	67	87	71	76	88	79	83	98
75154	RED OAK	111	123	118	125	119	118	112	113	105	115	133	132	114	133	111	100	131	111	101	126
75155	RICE	75	68	53	65	68	72	65	70	66	67	81	80	61	76	64	65	78	69	69	82
75156	MABANK	91	74	54	68	81	93	72	84	80	72	96	94	66	91	75	85	89	83	98	107
75158	SCURRY	113	101	78	96	105	112	94	104	99	95	121	122	91	120	96	100	115	102	109	130
75159	SEAGOVILLE	89	85	72	82	85	89	80	85	80	82	99	99	78	97	80	79	96	84	84	101
75160	TERRELL	85	80	77	78	81	88	80	83	83	81	103	95	80	102	80	84	99	83	85	96
75161	TERRELL	88	80	62	77	80	85	76	82	77	78	95	95	72	91	75	77	92	81	82	98
	TEXAS	94	90	91	90	89	95	92	93	92	93	115	107	90	112	90	90	112	94	89	104
	UNITED STATES	100	100	100	100	100	100	100	100	100	100	100	100	100	100	100	100	100	100	100	100

TEXAS

POPULATION CHANGE

A 75163-75451

# POST OFFICE NAME	COUNTY FIPS CODE	POP 2000	POP 2004	POP 2009	% Rate	State Centile	HH 2000	HH 2004	HH 2009	% Annual Rate 2000-2004	2004 Avg HH Size	FAM 2000	FAM 2004	% Annual Rate 2000-2004
75163 TRINIDAD	213	2585	2753	2984	1.5	57	1128	1189	1279	1.3	2.32	785	829	1.3
75165 WAXAHACHIE	139	28923	33021	39076	3.2	83	9791	11127	13125	3.1	2.85	7564	8617	3.1
75166 LAVON	085	498	552	670	2.5	75	170	187	225	2.3	2.95	136	149	2.2
75167 WAXAHACHIE	139	4764	5557	6649	3.7	88	1532	1779	2118	3.6	3.07	1284	1494	3.6
75169 WILLS POINT	467	12159	13873	15677	3.2	82	4586	5194	5830	3.0	2.65	3404	3868	3.1
75172 WILMER	113	2792	2947	3148	1.3	50	861	893	936	0.9	3.30	646	673	1.0
75173 NEVADA	085	4039	4670	5791	3.5	86	1374	1579	1946	3.3	2.96	1114	1274	3.2
75180 MESQUITE	113	19546	21002	22824	1.7	61	6222	6542	6960	1.2	3.20	4885	5140	1.2
75181 MESQUITE	113	16360	20301	23556	5.2	95	5061	6151	6992	4.7	3.30	4407	5362	4.7
75182 SUNNYVALE	113	3007	3733	4331	5.2	95	1045	1271	1444	4.7	2.94	859	1048	4.8
75189 ROYSE CITY	231	10553	13109	17402	5.2	95	3504	4340	5717	5.2	3.01	2871	3551	5.1
75201 DALLAS	113	2683	3318	3867	5.1	95	1559	1962	2296	5.6	1.47	322	416	6.2
75202 DALLAS	113	1868	2130	2358	3.1	82	807	941	1048	3.7	1.65	167	199	4.2
75203 DALLAS	113	19660	20690	22392	1.2	48	5926	6163	6566	0.9	3.31	4056	4228	1.0
75204 DALLAS	113	21387	24452	27452	3.2	83	10047	11666	13082	3.6	2.05	3554	4012	2.9
75205 DALLAS	113	24287	24385	25593	0.1	15	9972	9869	10235	-0.2	2.20	4984	4925	-0.3
75206 DALLAS	113	39805	42083	45692	1.3	52	20464	21304	22800	1.0	1.97	6803	7091	1.0
75207 DALLAS	113	8150	8153	8156	0.0	13	15	16	18	1.5	2.75	8	9	2.8
75208 DALLAS	113	36138	36516	38545	0.3	19	11157	11067	11463	-0.2	3.28	7297	7259	-0.1
75209 DALLAS	113	14864	15913	17285	1.6	60	6594	6837	7244	0.9	2.32	3481	3661	1.2
75210 DALLAS	113	9360	9226	9624	-0.3	7	3352	3229	3302	-0.9	2.86	2182	2118	-0.7
75211 DALLAS	113	68702	72050	77212	1.1	46	18809	19261	20201	0.6	3.72	14506	14909	0.7
75212 DALLAS	113	22006	22909	24627	1.0	40	5838	5970	6315	0.5	3.79	4691	4804	0.6
75214 DALLAS	113	35500	37486	40466	1.3	51	16091	16634	17601	0.8	2.21	8048	8358	0.9
75215 DALLAS	113	18728	19751	21531	1.3	50	6925	7122	7588	0.7	2.69	4093	4192	0.6
75216 DALLAS	113	49080	50416	53999	0.6	30	16199	16323	17170	0.2	3.06	11868	12022	0.3
75217 DALLAS	113	68324	71162	75923	1.0	43	19323	19651	20515	0.4	3.62	15756	16072	0.5
75218 DALLAS	113	21732	22711	24409	1.0	43	9747	10001	10549	0.6	2.25	5710	5880	0.7
75219 DALLAS	113	22558	25154	27983	2.6	77	11008	12162	13345	2.4	2.06	3855	4253	2.3
75220 DALLAS	113	50432	56367	62560	2.7	78	14907	15897	17094	1.5	3.54	10785	11556	1.6
75223 DALLAS	113	15633	16135	17191	0.8	34	4546	4645	4874	0.5	3.45	3218	3290	0.5
75224 DALLAS	113	32415	32912	34710	0.4	22	9702	9594	9901	-0.3	3.40	7240	7185	-0.2
75225 DALLAS	113	20021	21106	22778	1.3	50	8333	8761	9349	1.2	2.39	5420	5668	1.1
75226 DALLAS	113	2808	3020	3248	1.7	62	1107	1206	1304	2.0	2.05	461	492	1.5
75227 DALLAS	113	50817	53306	56987	1.1	46	15938	16248	16970	0.5	3.24	11912	12196	0.6
75228 DALLAS	113	65647	69112	74628	1.2	49	24098	24712	26081	0.6	2.77	15715	16258	0.8
75229 DALLAS	113	32007	33862	36626	1.3	52	11639	12007	12711	0.7	2.79	8276	8579	0.9
75230 DALLAS	113	27311	29917	33003	2.2	71	13386	14529	15811	2.0	2.05	6720	7202	1.6
75231 DALLAS	113	53237	57841	63445	2.0	67	22533	23409	24862	0.9	2.44	11400	11868	1.0
75232 DALLAS	113	28453	29063	30936	0.5	25	9732	9722	10135	0.0	2.99	7494	7506	0.0
75233 DALLAS	113	13685	14850	16309	1.9	66	4166	4377	4679	1.2	3.35	3101	3275	1.3
75234 DALLAS	113	27899	28007	29443	0.1	15	9774	9620	9922	-0.4	2.90	7009	6928	-0.3
75235 DALLAS	113	17412	19618	21737	2.9	80	5587	6117	6621	2.2	3.06	3165	3517	2.5
75236 DALLAS	113	7198	8519	9649	4.0	90	2602	3026	3369	3.6	2.64	1874	2189	3.7
75237 DALLAS	113	15463	16790	18397	2.0	67	6755	7225	7780	1.6	2.32	3943	4252	1.8
75238 DALLAS	113	31770	33319	35782	1.1	46	12997	13304	13983	0.6	2.48	8412	8657	0.7
75240 DALLAS	113	30520	33517	36963	2.2	72	10966	11654	12543	1.4	2.88	6370	6890	1.9
75241 DALLAS	113	26801	27726	29605	0.8	35	8252	8410	8858	0.5	3.05	6392	6530	0.5
75243 DALLAS	113	58748	61300	65852	1.0	42	26853	27384	28792	0.5	2.21	13723	14097	0.6
75244 DALLAS	113	12006	11961	12583	-0.1	11	4955	4843	4998	-0.5	2.46	3322	3248	-0.5
75246 DALLAS	113	4037	4375	4729	1.9	66	1161	1235	1313	1.5	3.28	620	662	1.6
75247 DALLAS	113	407	429	450	1.3	50	97	107	115	2.3	1.77	61	68	2.6
75248 DALLAS	113	33770	35472	38380	1.2	47	15791	16123	17007	0.5	2.20	9289	9599	0.8
75249 DALLAS	113	9181	9937	10852	1.9	65	2865	3053	3276	1.5	3.24	2406	2567	1.5
75251 DALLAS	113	1542	1845	2099	4.3	91	919	1085	1215	4.0	1.65	332	403	4.7
75252 DALLAS	085	22491	25428	31300	2.9	81	11646	13062	15958	2.7	1.95	5458	6075	2.6
75253 DALLAS	113	15552	16228	17501	1.0	42	5077	5187	5481	0.5	3.12	3850	3948	0.6
75254 DALLAS	113	18567	23277	27917	5.5	96	9819	11505	13132	3.8	2.01	3804	4986	6.6
75261 DALLAS	439	3	3	4	0.0	13	1	1	1	0.0	3.00	1	1	0.0
75287 DALLAS	085	44507	51706	64631	3.6	87	24246	27955	34602	3.4	1.85	9525	10743	2.9
75401 GREENVILLE	231	17332	18021	19301	0.9	39	6224	6434	6853	0.8	2.76	4324	4474	0.8
75402 GREENVILLE	231	14389	15166	16341	1.3	50	5825	6096	6532	1.1	2.43	4162	4370	1.2
75407 PRINCETON	085	9862	11559	14427	3.8	89	3475	4052	5028	3.7	2.84	2716	3154	3.6
75409 ANNA	085	4761	5973	7695	5.5	96	1648	2048	2614	5.3	2.92	1357	1681	5.2
75410 ALBA	499	4808	5432	6176	2.9	80	1911	2151	2438	2.8	2.53	1430	1615	2.9
75411 ARTHUR CITY	277	1888	1966	2077	1.0	40	727	757	799	1.0	2.60	586	612	1.0
75412 BAGWELL	387	998	1011	1032	0.3	20	409	412	420	0.2	2.45	312	315	0.2
75414 BELLS	181	2665	2786	2959	1.1	44	1031	1072	1131	0.9	2.58	787	820	1.0
75415 BEN FRANKLIN	119	151	159	168	1.2	49	53	55	58	0.9	2.89	37	39	1.3
75416 BLOSSOM	277	3810	4075	4370	1.6	59	1453	1551	1660	1.6	2.63	1137	1217	1.6
75417 BOGATA	387	2948	2992	3058	0.4	22	1237	1252	1274	0.3	2.33	835	848	0.4
75418 BONHAM	147	12934	13535	14370	1.1	44	4060	4275	4580	1.2	2.43	2758	2912	1.3
75420 BRASHEAR	223	267	271	283	0.4	22	120	121	126	0.2	2.24	90	91	0.3
75421 BROOKSTON	277	348	366	389	1.2	47	123	129	137	1.1	2.84	97	102	1.2
75422 CAMPBELL	231	2561	3049	3482	4.2	91	962	1138	1292	4.0	2.68	743	879	4.0
75423 CELESTE	231	2349	2492	2683	1.4	55	845	890	952	1.2	2.80	668	704	1.2
75424 BLUE RIDGE	085	2708	2985	3616	2.3	73	938	1027	1235	2.2	2.91	762	832	2.1
75426 CLARKSVILLE	387	6217	6368	6567	0.6	28	2476	2527	2603	0.5	2.44	1707	1749	0.6
75428 COMMERCE	231	9413	9871	10546	1.1	45	3542	3705	3963	1.1	2.36	2047	2143	1.1
75431 COMO	223	2072	2109	2204	0.4	23	736	744	773	0.3	2.78	567	576	0.4
75432 COOPER	119	3804	3971	4199	1.0	43	1475	1528	1604	0.8	2.52	1028	1068	0.9
75433 CUMBY	223	3348	3505	3722	1.1	45	1340	1396	1475	1.0	2.51	981	1027	1.1
75435 DEPORT	277	1946	1975	2065	0.4	22	757	768	805	0.3	2.49	586	597	0.4
75436 DETROIT	387	1744	1794	1848	0.7	31	686	702	721	0.5	2.56	505	518	0.6
75437 DIKE	223	254	262	276	0.7	34	96	98	103	0.5	2.67	77	79	0.6
75438 DODD CITY	147	1345	1433	1547	1.5	57	524	553	590	1.3	2.59	396	419	1.3
75439 ECTOR	147	897	933	994	0.9	39	359	369	390	0.7	2.53	256	263	0.6
75440 EMORY	379	4072	5006	6216	5.0	94	1630	1998	2475	4.9	2.47	1195	1469	5.0
75442 FARMERSVILLE	085	7493	8495	10298	3.0	81	2651	2985	3598	2.8	2.82	2073	2325	2.7
75446 HONEY GROVE	147	2774	2985	3236	1.7	63	1098	1173	1263	1.6	2.47	758	813	1.7
75447 IVANHOE	147	893	937	1003	1.1	46	356	368	390	0.8	2.54	282	293	0.9
75448 KLONDIKE	119	709	745	790	1.2	47	293	305	321	1.0	2.44	205	214	1.0
75449 LADONIA	147	1101	1314	1504	4.3	91	437	516	586	4.0	2.55	315	374	4.1
75450 LAKE CREEK	119	51	55	59	1.8	64	19	20	22	1.2	2.70	14	16	3.2
75451 LEESBURG	063	1477	1524	1599	0.7	34	592	605	628	0.5	2.52	443	454	0.6
TEXAS					2.2					2.0	2.77			2.1
UNITED STATES					1.2					1.3	2.58			1.1

ZIP CODE #	POST OFFICE NAME	RACE (%) White 2000	White 2004	Black 2000	Black 2004	Asian/Pacific 2000	Asian/Pacific 2004	% Hispanic Origin 2000	% Hispanic Origin 2004	2004 AGE DISTRIBUTION (%) 0-4	5-9	10-14	15-19	20-24	25-44	45-64	65-84	85+	18+	MEDIAN AGE 2004	% 2004 Males	% 2004 Females
75163	TRINIDAD	91.1	89.6	5.1	6.0	0.1	0.1	4.4	5.5	4.8	5.1	5.7	5.6	4.0	20.1	29.8	22.8	2.2	80.9	48.7	48.8	51.2
75165	WAXAHACHIE	75.5	73.8	13.3	13.3	0.4	0.4	18.2	21.2	7.6	7.0	7.1	7.8	9.0	28.2	22.8	8.9	1.6	73.8	33.0	49.1	50.9
75166	LAVON	91.8	90.4	1.8	2.0	0.4	0.5	9.2	11.2	7.1	7.6	8.7	7.4	5.8	29.5	26.1	7.3	0.5	71.7	36.5	51.3	48.7
75167	WAXAHACHIE	87.4	85.7	2.4	2.7	0.2	0.2	16.3	18.7	8.7	8.7	8.5	7.4	6.7	29.4	22.9	6.7	1.0	69.4	32.5	50.0	50.0
75169	WILLS POINT	89.5	88.6	4.9	5.0	0.2	0.2	7.4	8.8	6.4	6.7	6.8	6.7	6.2	25.1	25.9	14.1	2.0	76.1	39.9	49.3	50.7
75172	WILMER	47.8	44.9	22.0	22.0	0.0	0.0	47.1	51.7	9.5	8.6	9.4	8.5	8.4	29.9	19.1	6.4	0.3	67.4	28.5	51.5	48.5
75173	NEVADA	92.0	90.5	1.4	1.5	0.2	0.3	9.6	12.0	7.3	7.5	8.5	7.5	6.4	29.2	25.5	7.6	0.6	72.2	35.7	50.8	49.2
75180	MESQUITE	61.6	58.2	19.5	19.5	0.7	0.8	26.1	31.4	9.3	8.7	9.4	9.0	8.8	30.2	18.6	5.6	0.4	67.2	28.3	48.8	51.2
75181	MESQUITE	70.3	67.1	17.0	18.1	5.3	5.9	10.9	13.7	9.5	9.5	10.3	7.9	5.1	35.5	18.7	3.4	0.2	65.5	31.7	48.5	51.5
75182	SUNNYVALE	86.3	84.5	6.6	6.9	2.3	2.7	7.0	8.8	5.1	6.5	10.2	8.5	4.8	26.9	29.8	7.5	0.7	72.3	39.1	49.1	51.0
75189	ROYSE CITY	88.1	86.5	3.4	3.7	0.6	0.8	14.2	16.6	7.8	7.9	8.6	7.7	6.5	29.3	24.1	7.4	0.8	71.0	34.3	50.9	49.2
75201	DALLAS	71.8	68.6	17.5	18.8	3.2	3.7	11.6	14.4	4.7	2.7	3.0	4.5	14.5	51.1	15.8	3.3	0.4	87.4	30.7	51.5	48.5
75202	DALLAS	71.5	68.6	18.5	19.6	2.0	2.4	12.9	15.9	2.3	1.6	2.0	3.8	9.8	57.6	19.3	3.5	0.2	92.5	33.6	56.1	43.9
75203	DALLAS	27.2	26.7	36.0	36.0	0.3	0.3	60.2	61.1	9.8	8.6	8.4	8.0	10.5	31.3	15.3	6.9	1.1	68.7	27.5	54.3	45.7
75204	DALLAS	55.5	55.1	11.6	12.1	5.2	4.8	44.4	45.0	6.2	5.2	4.8	4.9	10.9	46.1	16.2	5.0	0.7	81.1	30.9	55.6	44.5
75205	DALLAS	92.2	90.9	1.7	1.8	2.3	2.7	6.3	8.0	4.8	5.5	6.7	11.5	10.9	27.1	23.4	8.2	2.0	79.4	33.4	46.9	53.1
75206	DALLAS	70.5	67.8	4.9	5.3	3.5	4.0	36.5	39.6	5.9	4.0	3.5	4.2	14.4	47.2	14.7	5.0	1.1	84.6	30.0	55.1	44.9
75207	DALLAS	54.2	52.3	37.4	38.0	0.3	0.3	18.4	22.0	1.0	0.3	0.2	5.3	16.1	64.4	11.6	0.6	0.5	97.3	34.1	71.8	28.2
75208	DALLAS	53.4	51.3	4.6	4.2	0.5	0.5	71.6	75.2	9.4	8.3	8.1	7.7	8.8	31.8	18.7	6.2	1.0	69.6	29.5	52.5	47.6
75209	DALLAS	65.2	62.8	23.0	23.7	1.3	1.4	24.3	28.1	7.3	6.5	5.3	4.4	5.4	34.8	23.0	11.3	2.1	78.2	37.2	49.1	50.9
75210	DALLAS	7.1	7.4	83.4	82.0	0.3	0.3	15.4	17.3	9.6	9.2	8.9	8.1	7.7	27.0	18.9	9.1	1.6	67.4	29.7	46.2	53.8
75211	DALLAS	46.1	44.4	7.9	7.3	1.1	1.1	76.9	80.5	10.7	9.4	9.4	8.4	9.7	30.8	15.6	5.4	0.8	65.6	26.4	51.6	48.4
75212	DALLAS	26.6	27.2	34.3	32.0	1.1	1.0	62.0	64.9	10.8	9.8	10.3	10.5	8.6	25.6	16.4	7.3	0.7	62.1	25.0	49.6	50.4
75214	DALLAS	76.8	73.9	4.4	4.5	1.3	1.4	26.7	30.9	7.1	6.1	5.0	4.7	6.5	37.1	20.8	9.3	3.3	79.0	35.8	49.7	50.3
75215	DALLAS	7.3	8.3	85.6	82.3	0.3	0.3	10.6	14.0	7.2	7.3	8.1	7.5	7.1	26.1	23.0	11.7	2.0	72.8	35.5	47.9	52.1
75216	DALLAS	9.3	9.7	77.6	75.9	0.1	0.1	19.7	21.8	7.3	7.5	8.5	7.9	7.0	25.4	22.7	12.3	1.5	71.9	34.7	46.9	53.1
75217	DALLAS	35.2	33.7	33.4	31.6	0.3	0.4	47.4	52.3	10.1	9.5	9.8	8.8	8.6	28.4	18.3	6.0	0.6	65.2	27.2	49.3	50.7
75218	DALLAS	84.7	82.9	5.3	5.4	1.0	1.2	16.9	20.2	6.3	6.1	5.6	4.7	4.3	30.6	26.0	13.4	3.1	79.2	41.1	47.5	52.5
75219	DALLAS	60.4	58.7	8.5	8.8	7.1	7.2	41.1	43.5	6.7	5.3	4.8	4.8	9.2	43.2	19.7	5.7	0.8	80.6	33.0	57.9	42.1
75220	DALLAS	59.3	58.2	5.2	4.7	0.6	0.6	77.3	80.5	11.5	9.1	7.4	7.0	11.3	36.7	12.8	3.6	0.5	68.1	26.6	55.9	44.1
75223	DALLAS	38.5	38.3	20.1	18.3	0.8	0.8	64.3	67.3	10.1	9.1	8.9	8.1	8.8	31.9	17.4	5.1	0.7	67.2	28.1	52.0	48.0
75224	DALLAS	34.8	33.6	35.0	33.7	0.8	0.8	48.5	52.4	9.8	9.0	9.1	8.9	9.6	28.7	18.1	6.0	1.0	67.1	27.3	49.2	50.8
75225	DALLAS	97.6	97.1	0.4	0.5	0.9	1.1	2.0	2.8	6.5	8.1	8.3	6.2	2.8	22.5	27.4	14.2	4.0	73.0	42.6	46.2	53.8
75226	DALLAS	40.1	37.5	13.3	12.6	0.9	1.0	57.0	61.0	6.9	5.6	5.0	5.2	10.8	38.8	17.6	8.0	2.2	79.6	31.8	59.8	40.2
75227	DALLAS	36.1	34.7	36.7	35.3	1.5	1.5	42.9	47.4	9.8	9.0	9.2	8.2	8.7	30.2	17.5	6.3	1.1	67.1	28.2	48.5	51.6
75228	DALLAS	51.5	49.0	25.2	24.9	4.4	4.6	32.1	36.8	9.0	8.2	7.9	7.0	8.2	30.6	18.2	9.5	1.5	70.9	31.1	48.5	51.5
75229	DALLAS	81.8	80.0	4.3	4.3	3.1	3.3	32.1	36.4	7.3	7.2	7.2	6.2	5.5	27.0	23.6	13.8	2.2	74.5	38.5	50.5	49.5
75230	DALLAS	83.9	82.4	6.1	6.2	2.9	3.2	11.3	13.4	6.1	6.0	4.8	4.4	5.3	28.8	26.0	15.2	3.5	80.5	41.6	47.3	52.7
75231	DALLAS	48.3	47.0	27.0	26.1	1.7	1.8	40.1	44.3	9.9	7.7	6.4	6.5	11.7	39.0	14.4	3.5	1.0	72.6	28.2	52.8	47.2
75232	DALLAS	14.3	14.0	77.9	77.0	0.2	0.2	12.8	14.8	7.0	7.1	8.3	7.8	7.2	25.5	26.9	9.4	0.9	72.9	35.0	46.0	54.0
75233	DALLAS	27.3	25.9	39.7	37.5	0.2	0.2	45.4	50.2	10.1	8.3	7.8	7.6	9.9	29.6	17.5	7.9	1.4	69.5	28.4	49.7	50.3
75234	DALLAS	76.7	74.2	2.5	2.5	3.1	3.2	38.9	43.9	7.3	7.1	7.5	6.7	6.7	28.2	22.6	12.6	1.3	74.1	36.0	49.8	50.2
75235	DALLAS	58.1	57.2	9.5	8.8	3.0	2.8	69.9	74.1	8.7	7.7	7.4	6.7	9.4	37.1	16.7	5.3	1.0	72.4	30.2	57.2	42.8
75236	DALLAS	39.8	37.3	40.2	39.7	5.7	6.0	20.7	25.1	8.5	8.0	9.5	9.4	12.7	30.3	17.0	4.2	0.5	69.6	26.1	47.8	52.2
75237	DALLAS	8.2	8.3	84.3	82.9	0.3	0.3	10.5	12.5	10.7	9.1	9.4	8.4	10.6	34.5	14.7	2.4	0.2	65.9	25.9	43.9	56.1
75238	DALLAS	66.4	64.2	21.7	21.9	1.5	1.6	16.3	19.7	8.4	7.6	7.0	6.2	7.4	30.2	21.2	10.6	1.3	73.2	34.2	47.9	52.1
75240	DALLAS	65.2	64.2	9.0	8.7	3.3	3.4	55.3	59.0	9.2	7.7	6.9	6.7	10.9	38.2	14.2	5.8	0.6	72.6	28.7	54.3	45.7
75241	DALLAS	6.9	6.6	88.1	87.7	0.2	0.2	6.2	7.4	7.0	7.3	7.8	8.0	7.7	26.4	22.8	12.1	0.9	73.0	34.4	48.8	51.2
75243	DALLAS	45.5	43.3	33.6	33.6	9.9	10.5	14.6	17.3	7.8	6.6	6.3	6.0	9.9	37.4	19.1	5.8	1.2	76.1	31.3	48.7	51.3
75244	DALLAS	76.3	74.1	7.5	7.5	4.8	5.3	20.2	23.9	7.2	6.8	6.0	5.9	6.3	27.6	24.8	14.3	1.1	76.4	38.7	49.2	50.8
75246	DALLAS	38.8	36.3	12.8	12.3	3.0	2.9	58.3	62.1	7.8	6.4	6.3	6.3	11.3	36.1	16.6	7.5	1.7	76.1	30.1	57.1	43.0
75247	DALLAS	25.6	23.8	63.4	63.4	1.7	1.9	15.0	17.5	2.6	3.7	3.7	4.9	3.7	35.4	24.2	15.4	6.3	86.3	43.3	58.7	41.3
75248	DALLAS	85.7	84.0	3.6	3.7	6.0	6.8	6.9	8.4	4.5	4.7	5.1	5.4	5.9	28.6	32.8	12.3	0.8	82.3	42.5	49.0	51.0
75249	DALLAS	35.8	34.2	51.3	50.7	2.6	2.9	16.5	19.7	8.4	8.3	8.8	8.0	7.5	31.2	23.8	3.8	0.2	69.4	31.4	47.4	52.6
75251	DALLAS	87.7	86.0	4.1	4.4	4.7	5.4	5.9	7.6	2.9	2.3	1.8	2.8	5.2	50.8	22.3	10.8	1.0	91.1	34.6	50.4	49.6
75252	DALLAS	76.7	74.2	5.9	6.0	12.7	14.3	6.6	8.0	5.6	5.0	4.9	4.8	8.8	40.3	24.6	5.7	0.3	81.8	34.4	49.5	50.5
75253	DALLAS	76.0	72.7	9.8	10.1	0.4	0.4	23.4	28.9	10.1	9.1	8.6	7.4	7.7	31.9	19.1	5.7	0.5	67.8	29.4	50.0	50.0
75254	DALLAS	72.3	72.5	11.3	10.5	7.3	7.4	17.1	18.3	5.6	4.8	4.5	4.4	10.0	42.2	20.0	7.5	1.1	82.6	32.8	49.7	50.3
75261	DALLAS	100.0	100.0	0.0	0.0	0.0	0.0	0.0	0.0	0.0	0.0	0.0	0.0	66.7	33.3	0.0	0.0	0.0	100.0	23.8	66.7	33.3
75287	DALLAS	76.0	73.6	9.8	10.2	7.1	8.0	10.8	12.8	6.1	5.1	4.3	4.6	13.0	46.3	17.9	2.7	0.1	82.2	30.2	49.4	50.6
75401	GREENVILLE	62.7	60.1	23.5	24.4	0.3	0.4	18.4	20.9	8.3	7.8	7.9	7.6	8.0	28.9	19.9	9.8	1.9	71.5	32.0	49.3	50.8
75402	GREENVILLE	90.6	89.3	5.0	5.5	0.8	0.9	4.7	5.8	6.1	6.1	6.6	6.4	5.8	25.3	26.8	14.6	2.4	77.2	41.1	49.2	50.8
75407	PRINCETON	91.8	90.1	0.8	0.9	0.4	0.4	10.2	12.7	7.2	7.4	8.2	7.3	6.2	29.9	24.8	8.4	0.8	72.6	35.7	50.0	50.0
75409	ANNA	89.9	87.7	0.7	0.7	0.5	0.6	13.1	16.4	6.9	7.0	7.6	7.3	6.5	29.2	26.2	8.6	0.9	74.1	36.4	51.6	48.4
75410	ALBA	95.1	94.2	0.6	0.6	0.0	0.0	5.3	6.3	5.7	5.9	6.5	5.7	5.7	22.0	30.6	16.6	1.4	78.5	44.0	50.6	49.5
75411	ARTHUR CITY	94.5	94.0	2.9	3.2	0.0	0.0	1.3	1.5	6.7	7.0	7.1	6.5	5.0	26.0	28.6	11.9	1.2	75.2	39.8	50.0	50.0
75412	BAGWELL	89.3	88.4	8.9	9.7	0.0	0.0	2.3	2.8	5.8	6.2	6.8	5.3	5.3	23.6	28.2	16.7	1.9	78.0	42.6	50.1	50.0
75414	BELLS	94.5	93.8	1.4	1.5	0.4	0.4	1.8	2.2	6.2	6.4	7.7	7.3	5.7	27.6	25.9	11.4	1.9	75.2	38.5	48.9	51.1
75415	BEN FRANKLIN	92.1	91.2	4.0	4.4	0.0	0.0	4.0	5.0	4.4	5.0	6.9	6.9	6.3	25.8	28.9	13.8	1.9	79.3	41.7	52.2	47.8
75416	BLOSSOM	93.6	92.9	3.4	3.7	0.1	0.1	3.8	4.6	6.6	6.9	7.6	6.3	5.5	27.0	27.5	11.3	1.5	75.1	38.6	50.9	49.2
75417	BOGATA	93.1	92.3	3.5	3.8	0.1	0.1	2.8	3.2	5.2	5.1	5.9	6.1	5.9	24.3	26.6	17.5	3.6	80.1	43.4	48.8	51.2
75418	BONHAM	80.7	79.5	13.2	13.5	0.5	0.5	7.5	8.8	5.1	5.1	5.1	5.9	9.7	30.5	22.5	13.0	3.0	81.7	37.7	59.0	41.0
75420	BRASHEAR	92.5	91.5	0.8	0.7	0.0	0.0	7.9	10.0	5.9	6.3	6.3	4.8	5.9	26.2	28.8	14.8	1.1	78.2	41.9	50.9	49.1
75421	BROOKSTON	89.7	88.8	6.9	7.4	0.0	0.0	2.6	3.0	5.7	6.3	8.2	7.7	5.5	25.7	26.2	13.1	1.6	74.9	39.1	48.6	51.4
75422	CAMPBELL	93.3	92.2	2.1	2.4	0.3	0.4	3.9	4.9	5.7	6.2	7.3	7.3	5.7	24.1	29.4	12.9	1.5	75.8	41.0	50.5	49.5
75423	CELESTE	94.1	93.1	1.7	1.9	0.1	0.2	4.1	5.1	6.9	7.0	8.2	7.6	6.9	25.7	26.0	10.0	1.6	73.2	36.5	49.4	50.6
75424	BLUE RIDGE	94.6	93.4	0.2	0.2	0.2	0.3	6.2	7.9	7.0	7.3	8.4	7.4	5.8	28.3	25.6	9.2	0.9	72.6	37.2	49.8	50.2
75426	CLARKSVILLE	64.3	62.8	31.5	32.4	0.2	0.2	6.6	7.6	6.4	6.1	6.7	6.9	6.6	24.3	23.2	16.0	3.8	76.6	40.0	47.6	52.4
75428	COMMERCE	75.1	72.8	17.5	18.7	2.3	2.7	7.3	8.7	6.1	5.4	5.4	10.9	18.4	26.0	17.9	8.2	1.8	79.3	27.2	49.7	50.3
75431	COMO	91.7	90.5	0.7	0.7	0.1	0.1	12.7	14.8	7.0	7.0	7.3	7.8	6.0	25.9	25.3	12.4	1.4	73.6	37.1	50.4	49.6
75432	COOPER	86.3	85.4	10.0	10.5	0.1	0.1	2.7	3.2	6.5	6.8	7.8	7.4	6.0	24.5	23.5	14.0	3.6	74.3	38.4	47.5	52.5
75433	CUMBY	93.6	92.8	0.4	0.3	0.5	0.5	6.2	7.1	6.3	6.3	6.5	5.7	5.3	26.2	27.3	14.6	1.7	77.4	41.1	50.4	49.6
75435	DEPORT	95.1	94.7	1.8	1.9	0.1	0.1	1.2	1.5	6.6	6.5	6.8	6.0	5.8	24.7	25.0	15.4	3.2	76.2	40.6	48.0	52.0
75436	DETROIT	87.3	86.0	8.9	9.7	0.2	0.3	2.2	2.7	6.5	6.7	7.6	6.6	5.6	25.5	26.2	13.6	1.7	75.0	38.5	47.7	52.3
75437	DIKE	89.4	88.2	3.9	3.8	0.0	0.0	8.3	9.5	6.5	6.5	6.9	6.5	6.1	26.7	27.5	11.8	1.5	75.6	39.1	50.8	49.2
75438	DODD CITY	93.2	92.5	3.0	3.3	0.1	0.1	1.0	1.2	5.1	5.6	7.3	6.4	5.7	23.9	27.7	16.4	2.0	78.1	42.7	50.9	49.1
75439	ECTOR	96.0	95.4	0.1	0.1	0.3	0.5	1.7	2.1	5.6	7.3	9.2	6.2	3.8	25.7	24.8	15.5	1.9	73.6	39.0	48.7	51.3
75440	EMORY	90.8	89.8	4.0	4.1	0.2	0.2	6.7	7.8	5.7	5.7	6.3	6.5	6.1	23.8	28.0	15.9	2.2	78.3	42.2	49.8	50.2
75442	FARMERSVILLE	88.8	87.2	4.9	5.1	0.1	0.1	10.9	13.4	7.3	7.2	8.4	7.6	6.9	28.0	23.7	9.2	1.8	72.5	34.9	49.0	51.0
75446	HONEY GROVE	85.0	84.0	10.6	11.2	0.3	0.3	5.2	6.0	5.7	5.6	7.1	6.9	7.0	23.4	23.4	17.5	3.6	77.4	41.3	46.8	53.2
75447	IVANHOE	95.9	95.3	1.1	1.3	0.0	0.1	2.6	3.0	5.2	6.2	6.6	5.6	4.7	22.8	30.2	17.4	1.3	78.1	44.2	50.4	49.6
75448	KLONDIKE	91.8	90.9	4.1	4.4	0.1	0.3	4.2	5.0	4.4	5.0	6.7	6.6	6.3	25.5	28.9	14.6	2.0	80.3	42.3	52.5	47.5
75449	LADONIA	76.9	74.7	18.4	20.1	0.5	0.6	3.4	3.9	7.8	7.5	6.9	5.9	5.5	24.1	26.9	12.9	2.5	74.3	39.2	48.0	52.1
75450	LAKE CREEK	96.1	94.6	2.0	1.8	0.0	0.0	0.0	0.0	5.5	7.3	9.1	9.1	3.6	23.6	27.3	12.7	1.8	72.7	39.4	50.9	49.1
75451	LEESBURG	81.6	79.6	12.5	13.5	0.2	0.2	6.2	7.4	6.4	6.3	5.9	5.8	5.3	24.5	27.8	16.7	1.4	77.9	42.1	50.2	49.8
	TEXAS	71.0	69.5	11.5	11.4	2.8	3.1	32.0	34.6	7.9	7.5	7.7	7.5	8.1	29.6	21.9	8.7	1.2	72.6	32.9	49.7	50.3
	UNITED STATES	75.1	73.6	12.3	12.5	3.8	4.2	12.5	14.1	6.9	6.7	7.2	7.0	7.3	28.6	23.8	10.8	1.7	75.1	36.0	49.1	50.9

INCOME

ZIP CODE				2004 HOUSEHOLD INCOME DISTRIBUTION (%)					MEDIAN HOUSEHOLD INCOME					2004 HOME VALUE DISTRIBUTION (%)					
#	POST OFFICE NAME	2004 Per Capita Income	2004 HH Income Base	Less than $25,000	$25,000 to $49,999	$50,000 to $99,999	$100,000 to $149,999	$150,000 or More	2004	2009	2004 National Centile	2004 State Centile	2004 Home Value Base	Less than $50,000	$50,000 to $89,999	$90,000 to $174,999	$175,000 to $399,999	$400,000 or More	2004 Median Home Value
75163	TRINIDAD	20751	1189	34.6	30.0	29.1	4.0	2.4	35841	41395	31	37	1003	28.0	24.6	26.9	18.2	2.3	85656
75165	WAXAHACHIE	23663	11127	19.8	26.2	37.3	11.2	5.5	53764	61347	78	82	7702	12.7	24.5	45.1	16.2	1.6	106334
75166	LAVON	25228	187	16.6	23.0	43.9	11.2	5.4	58194	67284	83	85	165	10.9	26.7	43.6	16.4	2.4	107917
75167	WAXAHACHIE	23421	1779	16.2	24.5	39.5	12.5	7.4	59824	67296	84	86	1502	23.0	20.4	31.4	19.9	5.2	104293
75169	WILLS POINT	20414	5194	30.6	28.2	31.5	6.6	3.2	41583	47753	52	60	4142	34.0	29.5	27.1	8.3	1.1	72430
75172	WILMER	14225	893	29.9	34.3	29.2	4.9	1.7	37513	43474	37	45	553	68.0	23.7	7.2	1.1	0.0	37389
75173	NEVADA	23002	1579	16.4	26.2	41.8	11.2	4.4	56695	65938	81	84	1368	16.7	25.8	39.6	15.6	2.3	100711
75180	MESQUITE	16305	6542	23.7	36.0	33.5	5.3	1.5	41039	46686	50	58	3852	25.2	56.3	17.1	1.3	0.2	67025
75181	MESQUITE	26836	6151	6.6	14.1	49.4	22.9	7.2	76538	92838	94	95	5878	8.2	4.6	69.8	17.1	0.3	130948
75182	SUNNYVALE	39338	1271	8.1	21.6	32.7	16.8	20.9	75636	92339	93	94	1089	1.2	12.0	33.2	40.3	13.2	183750
75189	ROYSE CITY	25357	4340	16.3	25.2	38.3	13.5	6.7	58409	67673	83	86	3619	16.8	26.5	33.9	18.2	4.6	100256
75201	DALLAS	87053	1962	14.0	17.9	34.1	13.0	21.2	72444	102307	92	93	153	0.0	3.9	17.7	27.5	51.0	402308
75202	DALLAS	58078	941	15.2	19.9	33.8	11.8	19.3	67257	90871	90	91	27	0.0	11.1	0.0	51.9	37.0	275000
75203	DALLAS	9733	6163	51.8	29.4	14.7	3.2	0.9	23872	27628	4	5	1957	50.7	31.2	13.1	4.1	1.0	49550
75204	DALLAS	36674	11666	26.6	25.5	28.6	10.6	8.8	47278	60126	67	72	1998	9.1	21.1	27.3	33.5	9.1	144667
75205	DALLAS	78972	9869	12.8	17.7	24.3	13.0	32.2	86338	116211	97	97	5042	1.3	4.7	5.7	17.5	70.8	662176
75206	DALLAS	33669	21304	21.5	29.7	32.3	10.4	6.0	48803	59885	70	75	4797	5.2	17.3	37.6	34.9	5.0	141712
75207	DALLAS	12823	16	37.5	12.5	50.0	0.0	0.0	47500	54495	67	72	8	37.5	12.5	50.0	0.0	0.0	75000
75208	DALLAS	18951	11067	32.0	29.5	24.2	8.1	6.2	39366	45878	44	52	5465	19.3	33.3	25.2	18.0	4.1	86019
75209	DALLAS	51900	6837	21.3	23.7	24.3	11.0	19.7	57529	69706	82	85	4212	6.1	17.3	19.8	25.9	30.8	230389
75210	DALLAS	9590	3229	64.5	23.3	9.6	1.8	0.7	17337	20854	1	2	1017	64.0	31.3	4.0	0.7	0.0	40686
75211	DALLAS	12845	19261	31.5	34.4	26.8	5.2	2.1	36972	42719	35	42	10062	22.8	55.5	20.6	1.1	0.1	67949
75212	DALLAS	9759	5970	50.0	29.5	16.5	2.7	1.4	24972	28462	5	6	2932	66.0	26.1	7.5	0.3	0.0	40329
75214	DALLAS	41552	16634	17.8	25.4	28.1	14.0	14.8	58549	72024	83	86	8504	2.8	6.1	30.6	47.5	13.0	197186
75215	DALLAS	11073	7122	60.1	24.8	11.1	3.1	1.0	18449	22232	1	2	2503	62.5	26.8	7.8	2.3	0.6	42297
75216	DALLAS	13219	16323	44.5	30.5	20.3	3.1	1.6	28451	32917	9	12	10065	50.1	41.3	7.9	0.6	0.1	49930
75217	DALLAS	12249	19651	34.4	33.5	25.9	4.1	2.1	35419	40197	29	35	12785	31.8	57.0	10.5	0.6	0.1	60020
75218	DALLAS	37845	10001	15.9	26.4	31.6	15.4	10.8	58890	70458	83	86	6679	2.7	17.2	49.5	28.3	2.4	136861
75219	DALLAS	42550	12162	23.9	29.2	26.4	9.4	11.1	46687	58948	65	71	3015	9.4	10.6	28.5	28.6	22.9	180955
75220	DALLAS	19739	15897	31.5	34.4	21.3	6.5	6.4	36804	42001	35	41	4702	8.2	19.4	40.3	17.5	14.7	120107
75223	DALLAS	15526	4645	38.4	27.9	20.3	8.6	4.8	33284	39629	22	27	2452	35.0	32.0	11.9	20.7	0.5	65762
75224	DALLAS	13907	9594	32.4	33.7	25.6	6.0	2.4	37149	42603	36	43	5624	15.8	53.8	27.4	3.0	0.0	74240
75225	DALLAS	92248	8761	9.9	11.1	22.8	14.1	42.2	117889	154477	99	99	6463	1.4	0.5	10.6	24.1	63.5	505664
75226	DALLAS	24619	1206	35.2	21.0	28.4	11.0	4.5	42081	53517	53	62	67	49.3	1.5	20.9	17.9	10.5	75000
75227	DALLAS	14456	16248	32.7	32.4	27.3	5.5	2.1	36542	42088	34	40	9068	16.1	46.9	35.7	1.3	0.0	77634
75228	DALLAS	18188	24712	30.1	33.9	27.3	6.2	2.5	38091	44010	40	47	12139	5.4	46.8	43.7	3.8	0.3	88297
75229	DALLAS	40443	12007	16.4	21.2	26.5	15.5	20.5	69657	82636	91	92	8568	1.7	4.5	36.2	40.9	16.8	194861
75230	DALLAS	59347	14529	19.0	24.4	23.1	11.5	21.9	59563	72752	84	86	7847	4.4	10.2	11.9	41.1	32.4	291872
75231	DALLAS	21400	23409	32.7	37.4	19.6	5.7	4.5	34473	40472	26	31	3351	12.0	14.8	15.8	46.7	10.8	193863
75232	DALLAS	19602	9722	25.8	29.0	31.8	9.8	3.7	44708	51973	60	68	6730	13.1	37.3	46.6	2.9	0.1	89652
75233	DALLAS	16290	4377	29.9	28.6	30.3	7.1	4.0	41700	48443	52	61	2399	5.3	33.3	58.2	3.0	0.2	99175
75234	DALLAS	27153	9620	15.3	27.5	34.5	12.9	9.9	57656	66573	82	85	6702	1.8	23.3	57.8	14.8	2.3	112614
75235	DALLAS	16299	6117	32.2	35.3	24.1	6.4	2.0	36497	42396	34	40	2082	21.3	39.9	30.2	7.0	1.7	79228
75236	DALLAS	18922	3026	23.2	38.9	27.9	8.5	1.5	40927	47230	49	58	1311	23.4	24.2	44.5	6.9	1.0	93424
75237	DALLAS	15797	7225	38.4	40.5	18.5	1.7	0.9	30480	35025	13	17	835	11.1	33.8	48.0	7.1	0.0	96071
75238	DALLAS	29170	13304	19.5	31.4	28.0	12.1	9.1	49164	58936	70	76	6568	0.8	3.8	52.9	40.3	2.2	164065
75240	DALLAS	24524	11654	25.3	32.0	26.4	7.4	8.9	43101	51688	56	65	2879	2.7	19.6	28.7	31.0	17.9	171244
75241	DALLAS	14957	8410	36.6	32.2	23.8	5.5	1.9	34009	39386	24	30	5623	23.1	57.7	18.3	0.7	0.1	68204
75243	DALLAS	28817	27384	22.1	35.3	27.1	8.7	6.9	43587	52101	58	66	7737	10.1	17.2	31.7	36.7	4.3	143866
75244	DALLAS	41347	4843	11.6	23.3	30.1	15.9	19.1	71141	88787	92	92	2849	5.6	3.0	27.2	58.1	6.0	200410
75246	DALLAS	12586	1235	47.0	24.3	19.1	7.7	1.9	26810	31315	7	9	203	11.8	34.0	20.2	30.1	3.9	94250
75247	DALLAS	15559	107	49.5	33.6	14.0	2.8	0.0	25557	30447	5	7	61	62.3	23.0	6.6	8.2	0.0	40625
75248	DALLAS	57976	16123	9.5	19.7	29.7	18.6	22.6	80105	104131	95	96	9303	1.3	5.1	19.4	63.1	11.2	217166
75249	DALLAS	21625	3053	11.5	24.3	43.4	16.9	3.9	62793	72053	87	89	2513	1.4	38.0	55.9	4.7	0.0	96807
75251	DALLAS	71329	1085	8.8	13.9	39.5	18.6	19.3	80971	106673	95	96	318	0.0	0.0	1.6	50.9	47.5	372414
75252	DALLAS	52555	13062	10.8	25.6	29.3	16.7	17.7	69306	85382	91	92	5496	2.3	2.8	14.9	64.9	15.1	234914
75253	DALLAS	16751	5187	25.3	35.9	31.0	5.6	2.2	40534	48347	48	56	3958	57.0	29.8	11.3	1.7	0.3	43117
75254	DALLAS	50576	11505	12.7	28.7	33.3	12.1	13.1	58502	76438	83	86	3178	1.5	12.2	17.9	28.8	39.7	326563
75261	DALLAS	0	0	0.0	0.0	0.0	0.0	0.0	0	0	0	0	0	0.0	0.0	0.0	0.0	0.0	0
75287	DALLAS	44929	27955	12.9	30.8	35.0	11.2	10.2	55604	67477	80	83	6777	0.7	2.0	35.4	44.3	17.6	200699
75401	GREENVILLE	16937	6434	35.9	30.2	27.2	4.3	2.5	35539	41262	30	35	3835	54.1	26.0	16.3	3.3	0.4	46469
75402	GREENVILLE	25458	6096	20.9	27.8	35.8	11.0	4.5	51190	58152	74	79	4232	14.4	30.5	44.2	9.9	1.0	96011
75407	PRINCETON	22365	4052	18.5	27.7	39.0	11.7	3.2	53168	62639	77	81	3255	21.3	32.6	35.8	9.3	1.1	85079
75409	ANNA	24460	2048	15.0	27.5	37.7	13.5	6.4	57106	66683	82	84	1693	15.2	26.6	33.6	20.1	4.4	102162
75410	ALBA	18936	2151	32.6	32.3	27.3	5.3	2.6	36687	42109	34	41	1807	26.6	28.4	30.4	12.3	2.2	83222
75411	ARTHUR CITY	22346	757	26.8	24.4	37.4	7.8	3.6	48461	54895	69	74	654	29.1	24.9	33.3	11.6	1.1	83659
75412	BAGWELL	17392	412	38.4	33.3	21.6	4.1	2.7	31669	35212	17	21	340	54.7	27.7	11.2	5.3	1.2	46000
75414	BELLS	21125	1072	26.8	28.0	34.1	8.8	2.3	44496	51689	60	67	875	21.3	31.8	35.0	10.9	1.1	86513
75415	BEN FRANKLIN	15123	55	36.4	30.9	25.5	5.5	1.8	36087	41645	32	38	46	56.5	21.7	19.6	2.2	0.0	46667
75416	BLOSSOM	18049	1551	35.1	30.1	28.5	5.4	1.0	36336	42147	33	39	1280	38.3	23.9	29.0	8.1	0.8	68750
75417	BOGATA	19792	1252	37.9	29.0	24.0	5.0	4.1	33242	37360	22	26	957	51.6	24.8	17.5	4.6	1.6	48402
75418	BONHAM	17461	4275	36.9	29.6	26.4	4.5	2.7	34241	39330	25	30	2902	34.4	30.4	27.7	6.9	0.7	68190
75420	BRASHEAR	25153	121	29.8	30.6	26.5	9.1	4.1	40844	46556	49	57	103	35.9	30.1	23.3	9.7	1.0	70556
75421	BROOKSTON	18047	129	27.9	31.8	34.1	4.7	1.6	41657	48840	52	60	110	41.8	31.8	18.2	8.2	0.0	61111
75422	CAMPBELL	20984	1138	27.0	29.5	32.0	7.2	4.3	45059	51866	61	68	949	23.8	36.1	29.9	9.1	1.1	79663
75423	CELESTE	19777	890	24.2	28.5	35.7	9.0	2.6	47315	53241	67	72	726	32.8	31.0	26.3	9.1	0.8	70851
75424	BLUE RIDGE	22686	1027	16.9	29.1	36.7	12.9	4.5	54390	64166	79	82	869	18.0	27.6	32.5	19.0	3.0	96525
75426	CLARKSVILLE	15991	2527	43.1	33.8	18.3	3.2	1.5	29212	33117	11	13	1770	58.9	25.4	12.3	2.5	0.9	43203
75428	COMMERCE	18409	3705	44.9	24.9	21.8	5.8	2.7	29025	33178	10	13	1828	36.0	31.2	27.6	4.9	0.3	69839
75431	COMO	25598	744	31.2	33.7	25.3	7.0	2.8	35608	41204	30	36	606	35.6	26.4	26.6	10.2	1.2	72609
75432	COOPER	17922	1528	40.3	27.5	25.7	3.9	2.6	32332	37350	19	23	1103	46.5	29.6	19.6	4.4	0.0	54185
75433	CUMBY	21450	1396	31.6	30.0	27.7	7.9	2.9	39350	45357	44	52	1129	37.0	24.8	27.4	9.6	1.2	70987
75435	DEPORT	14683	768	40.8	38.8	16.4	3.7	0.4	31310	36742	16	20	603	40.0	28.2	23.9	7.3	0.7	63981
75436	DETROIT	17667	702	36.8	28.1	28.8	4.7	1.7	36451	40634	33	40	538	46.7	31.2	14.3	4.8	3.0	53214
75437	DIKE	20871	98	28.6	33.7	26.5	8.2	3.1	40983	47781	50	58	83	30.1	31.3	24.1	13.3	1.2	75625
75438	DODD CITY	22989	553	29.5	28.0	31.1	6.3	5.1	42196	48803	53	62	472	29.9	34.1	26.7	9.1	0.2	74694
75439	ECTOR	20498	369	25.2	31.4	37.9	4.6	0.8	45088	50400	61	68	270	35.2	31.5	24.1	8.5	0.7	70769
75440	EMORY	18746	1998	33.9	32.4	25.2	6.7	1.8	35809	41085	31	37	1582	34.1	26.6	26.0	10.4	3.0	75280
75442	FARMERSVILLE	21355	2985	22.9	27.7	37.0	8.7	3.7	49276	58350	71	76	2304	20.0	31.1	35.4	11.6	2.0	88674
75446	HONEY GROVE	18047	1173	37.0	29.0	26.3	6.0	1.7	35343	40899	29	34	840	38.8	32.4	24.3	3.8	0.7	63867
75447	IVANHOE	24094	368	26.4	29.4	33.4	6.3	4.6	46004	52808	64	70	320	23.4	25.6	39.4	10.3	1.3	91364
75448	KLONDIKE	17844	305	34.8	33.1	25.9	4.9	1.3	36426	41721	33	40	256	60.2	20.3	17.6	2.0	0.0	45593
75449	LADONIA	16387	516	39.3	34.1	20.7	3.9	1.9	34798	40260	27	32	383	49.9	29.2	14.4	6.5	0.0	50152
75450	LAKE CREEK	16744	20	30.0	30.0	35.0	5.0	0.0	42301	54545	54	63	17	23.5	29.4	41.2	5.9	0.0	85000
75451	LEESBURG	18672	605	30.9	39.2	22.3	5.0	2.6	37648	42858	38	45	510	39.6	22.9	27.3	10.2	0.0	64483
	TEXAS	23284		26.2	27.7	29.5	10.3	6.3	45778	54246				21.6	26.1	33.4	15.6	3.4	93683
	UNITED STATES	25866		24.7	27.1	30.8	10.9	6.5	48124	56710				10.9	15.0	33.7	30.1	10.4	145905

ZIP CODE #	POST OFFICE NAME	FINANCIAL SERVICES: Auto Loan	Home Loan	Investments	Retirement Plans	THE HOME: Home Improvements: Home Repair	Lawn & Garden	Furnishings: Computers & Hardware	Major Appliances	TV, Radio, Sound Equipment	Furniture	ENTERTAINMENT: Dine out/Carry out	Sports Equipment	Fees & Tickets	Toys & Games	Travel	Cable TV	PERSONAL: Apparel & Services	Auto Repairs	Health Insurance	Pets & Supplies
75163	TRINIDAD	75	64	53	61	68	81	64	71	69	65	84	74	61	74	66	74	78	70	84	84
75165	WAXAHACHIE	99	98	97	98	97	102	97	98	96	97	120	114	96	119	96	95	116	98	95	112
75166	LAVON	119	106	81	101	112	120	98	109	104	98	127	130	96	129	101	107	121	106	118	140
75167	WAXAHACHIE	107	113	102	114	109	109	104	106	99	107	124	124	104	123	102	94	121	104	96	120
75169	WILLS POINT	90	73	52	69	78	87	71	80	78	71	94	94	67	92	72	80	88	79	89	102
75172	WILMER	72	63	54	61	62	66	65	68	67	68	84	76	61	78	62	64	82	70	65	75
75173	NEVADA	107	100	81	97	102	107	93	100	94	94	116	117	91	116	93	94	112	97	101	122
75180	MESQUITE	74	73	74	74	71	74	75	74	73	76	92	86	73	90	72	71	90	75	69	81
75181	MESQUITE	128	142	134	147	136	132	129	129	119	134	151	150	132	150	126	112	149	125	111	142
75182	SUNNYVALE	158	187	194	194	180	179	168	165	154	172	195	192	178	199	167	146	195	160	144	181
75189	ROYSE CITY	115	114	101	112	113	117	107	112	105	109	131	130	106	128	107	103	128	111	107	130
75201	DALLAS	181	178	327	202	169	189	206	183	209	210	266	224	216	279	203	208	265	195	171	205
75202	DALLAS	156	149	279	171	141	158	176	156	181	179	229	192	183	240	173	179	228	167	146	175
75203	DALLAS	46	38	41	37	38	42	44	44	47	46	59	49	42	56	42	47	58	46	45	48
75204	DALLAS	101	92	144	102	88	97	108	99	111	111	141	120	109	143	104	108	140	107	92	110
75205	DALLAS	239	267	412	280	257	283	276	255	269	278	341	303	295	353	278	266	340	262	238	282
75206	DALLAS	89	81	118	89	78	85	96	88	97	96	122	107	95	122	91	93	121	94	81	97
75207	DALLAS	43	35	35	32	34	40	39	40	44	41	54	44	37	49	38	45	52	42	44	45
75208	DALLAS	88	81	85	80	79	83	87	87	89	91	112	99	84	110	83	85	112	91	81	93
75209	DALLAS	158	168	219	169	163	176	169	165	169	174	214	189	177	216	170	168	213	168	157	181
75210	DALLAS	39	31	37	29	31	37	37	37	42	38	51	41	35	47	35	43	49	39	41	42
75211	DALLAS	69	61	59	59	59	62	66	67	69	70	87	75	63	83	63	66	87	70	63	71
75212	DALLAS	53	45	45	41	43	48	49	50	53	52	65	55	46	59	47	53	64	52	51	55
75214	DALLAS	122	126	169	132	123	131	133	127	131	135	166	150	136	169	131	128	165	131	118	139
75215	DALLAS	43	35	38	32	34	42	40	40	45	41	55	44	38	49	38	47	52	42	46	47
75216	DALLAS	58	51	55	48	50	59	54	55	59	57	73	60	54	68	54	62	71	57	60	63
75217	DALLAS	66	59	54	55	57	60	61	64	64	65	80	69	57	73	58	62	79	65	61	68
75218	DALLAS	109	123	151	123	121	128	122	119	119	121	150	138	126	154	124	118	148	120	114	130
75219	DALLAS	117	107	167	118	102	113	125	115	128	128	163	139	126	164	121	125	161	123	107	127
75220	DALLAS	99	90	94	90	88	92	98	97	100	102	127	111	95	124	93	95	127	102	89	104
75223	DALLAS	75	69	74	68	67	71	75	74	77	78	97	85	73	95	72	74	97	78	70	80
75224	DALLAS	69	62	61	60	60	64	66	67	68	69	85	75	63	79	63	65	84	70	64	72
75225	DALLAS	279	340	459	339	334	363	314	311	301	321	379	351	344	388	329	302	379	305	297	339
75226	DALLAS	77	67	91	72	65	70	79	74	81	81	103	88	78	103	75	77	103	80	68	81
75227	DALLAS	67	63	63	61	61	65	66	66	67	68	84	75	64	82	64	65	83	68	63	72
75228	DALLAS	70	67	75	67	65	70	71	70	72	73	91	81	70	89	69	70	89	72	66	76
75229	DALLAS	145	170	208	166	166	176	161	160	156	164	197	181	170	203	164	154	198	159	148	172
75230	DALLAS	157	171	223	176	168	182	176	168	170	175	214	198	182	215	176	166	213	172	158	184
75231	DALLAS	75	67	78	72	65	69	76	72	75	77	95	87	73	90	71	70	93	77	66	80
75232	DALLAS	80	79	89	75	77	87	80	80	83	82	105	88	83	102	81	85	103	81	83	90
75233	DALLAS	75	74	78	71	72	77	76	76	78	78	98	86	76	97	75	77	97	77	74	83
75234	DALLAS	102	113	131	111	111	116	111	109	109	112	138	125	114	141	112	108	137	110	103	119
75235	DALLAS	72	63	70	65	62	65	71	70	73	74	92	80	68	89	67	69	91	73	64	75
75236	DALLAS	75	66	69	68	65	71	72	71	73	73	92	84	69	87	69	71	89	74	69	81
75237	DALLAS	52	44	55	46	43	48	52	49	54	53	68	59	50	63	49	52	66	53	48	56
75238	DALLAS	99	102	119	106	100	104	105	102	101	106	128	120	106	126	103	97	126	104	93	112
75240	DALLAS	97	92	115	96	89	95	100	96	100	103	128	113	99	126	96	96	127	101	88	106
75241	DALLAS	64	59	66	55	57	67	62	62	67	64	84	67	63	79	62	70	81	64	68	71
75243	DALLAS	90	85	105	92	82	87	93	88	91	94	115	107	92	110	89	86	113	93	80	98
75244	DALLAS	135	147	180	150	144	154	146	142	141	147	178	165	151	177	147	138	176	144	134	156
75246	DALLAS	59	50	52	50	49	52	57	57	60	60	76	65	55	74	54	56	76	60	53	60
75247	DALLAS	47	44	48	41	43	51	45	46	48	47	60	48	46	57	46	51	58	46	50	52
75248	DALLAS	162	188	253	192	182	194	183	176	175	185	222	205	194	229	186	173	221	177	162	192
75249	DALLAS	100	111	109	115	106	104	102	101	95	105	120	119	104	120	100	88	118	100	87	111
75251	DALLAS	152	146	274	167	138	154	172	152	176	175	224	188	180	235	169	175	223	163	142	170
75252	DALLAS	141	136	181	150	131	139	148	138	145	151	184	167	149	181	142	138	181	145	125	154
75253	DALLAS	80	75	64	73	75	80	73	77	73	74	91	89	70	87	72	73	87	76	77	90
75254	DALLAS	140	133	184	146	128	139	148	138	145	150	185	167	148	181	142	139	182	146	126	154
75261	DALLAS	0	0	0	0	0	0	0	0	0	0	0	0	0	0	0	0	0	0	0	0
75287	DALLAS	114	105	152	118	101	109	120	111	119	122	152	135	120	149	115	114	149	118	101	124
75401	GREENVILLE	70	61	55	60	62	70	65	67	68	64	84	77	62	82	64	69	80	67	71	77
75402	GREENVILLE	92	88	82	86	91	98	86	90	88	85	108	104	86	110	87	90	104	88	94	107
75407	PRINCETON	101	90	70	87	92	100	87	94	90	88	110	109	83	107	87	90	105	92	97	113
75409	ANNA	111	103	83	99	108	115	95	104	99	95	121	124	94	124	98	101	116	101	110	132
75410	ALBA	85	62	35	57	70	79	60	73	69	60	81	87	53	79	62	73	75	71	86	100
75411	ARTHUR CITY	102	77	46	70	84	94	73	87	84	74	100	103	67	97	75	88	92	85	101	118
75412	BAGWELL	80	54	24	46	61	70	52	65	63	53	74	78	44	70	53	68	67	64	80	92
75414	BELLS	86	75	58	73	79	87	73	80	78	73	95	93	71	95	74	80	89	78	86	99
75415	BEN FRANKLIN	82	55	25	48	62	72	53	67	64	54	75	79	45	71	54	69	69	66	82	94
75416	BLOSSOM	78	62	44	60	66	75	63	70	69	62	83	81	59	81	63	71	77	69	79	87
75417	BOGATA	75	61	44	59	66	75	62	68	68	60	81	79	58	79	63	71	75	68	78	85
75418	BONHAM	70	59	49	57	62	71	62	66	67	60	81	76	59	79	62	69	76	66	74	79
75420	BRASHEAR	102	71	37	67	83	93	70	87	81	69	95	105	60	93	73	85	87	86	104	121
75421	BROOKSTON	82	73	56	69	77	83	67	75	72	67	87	89	66	89	70	73	83	73	81	97
75422	CAMPBELL	94	78	54	73	84	91	73	83	80	73	96	99	69	96	75	83	90	81	93	110
75423	CELESTE	88	77	59	74	81	89	74	81	79	74	96	95	72	96	75	80	90	79	88	101
75424	BLUE RIDGE	106	94	72	89	99	107	87	96	92	87	112	115	85	115	90	95	107	94	104	124
75426	CLARKSVILLE	66	48	31	45	53	62	51	58	58	50	69	67	45	66	51	62	64	58	69	75
75428	COMMERCE	63	55	64	58	55	61	66	62	66	63	82	76	62	79	62	63	79	66	61	70
75431	COMO	131	91	46	84	105	118	89	111	104	89	122	133	76	118	92	110	111	109	133	155
75432	COOPER	69	59	50	58	62	71	63	67	67	61	80	76	59	77	62	68	75	67	74	78
75433	CUMBY	96	67	36	62	77	88	68	82	79	67	93	97	59	89	69	84	84	81	99	111
75435	DEPORT	58	47	34	46	50	58	50	54	54	48	65	61	46	63	49	56	60	53	61	64
75436	DETROIT	85	57	26	49	64	74	55	69	66	56	78	82	47	74	56	71	71	68	85	98
75437	DIKE	99	74	43	66	81	91	70	84	81	71	96	100	63	93	72	85	89	82	98	115
75438	DODD CITY	103	79	49	75	89	97	76	90	85	75	101	108	69	100	79	88	93	88	103	122
75439	ECTOR	83	68	51	68	73	82	70	76	75	69	91	88	66	90	70	77	85	75	84	92
75440	EMORY	77	61	42	57	67	76	61	69	67	59	80	80	55	78	62	71	74	68	81	89
75442	FARMERSVILLE	94	86	70	85	88	95	83	88	85	83	104	103	81	105	83	85	99	86	91	106
75446	HONEY GROVE	77	55	32	51	61	72	58	67	67	57	79	77	51	74	58	71	72	67	81	86
75447	IVANHOE	110	80	45	72	89	100	76	92	89	77	105	110	68	102	78	94	97	91	110	127
75448	KLONDIKE	82	55	25	47	62	72	53	66	64	54	75	79	45	71	54	69	68	66	82	94
75449	LADONIA	77	52	25	46	59	68	51	63	61	52	72	75	44	68	52	66	66	63	78	88
75450	LAKE CREEK	62	64	74	67	65	68	66	65	63	65	79	77	66	78	65	61	77	66	63	71
75451	LEESBURG	89	59	27	51	67	77	57	72	69	58	81	86	49	77	58	74	74	71	88	102
	TEXAS	94	90	91	90	89	95	92	93	92	93	115	107	90	112	90	90	112	94	89	104
	UNITED STATES	100	100	100	100	100	100	100	100	100	100	100	100	100	100	100	100	100	100	100	100

# POST OFFICE NAME	COUNTY FIPS CODE	POPULATION 2000	2004	2009	2000-2004 ANNUAL RATE % Rate	State Centile	HOUSEHOLDS 2000	2004	2009	% Annual Rate 2000-2004	2004 Average HH Size	FAMILIES 2000	2004	% Annual Rate 2000-2004
75452 LEONARD	147	4067	4312	4658	1.4	54	1524	1596	1706	1.1	2.68	1137	1193	1.1
75453 LONE OAK	231	3248	3448	3798	1.4	55	1267	1335	1464	1.2	2.58	955	1009	1.3
75454 MELISSA	085	2305	2973	3876	6.2	97	821	1049	1357	5.9	2.83	647	823	5.8
75455 MOUNT PLEASANT	449	19213	20335	21713	1.3	52	6352	6622	6967	1.0	2.98	4670	4883	1.1
75457 MOUNT VERNON	159	6552	6760	6958	0.7	34	2520	2592	2664	0.7	2.55	1828	1886	0.7
75459 HOWE	181	3862	4010	4268	0.9	38	1419	1460	1543	0.7	2.75	1121	1152	0.6
75460 PARIS	277	23922	24819	26342	0.9	38	9792	10153	10795	0.9	2.35	6187	6429	0.9
75462 PARIS	277	8166	8926	9683	2.1	70	3095	3380	3658	2.1	2.60	2393	2609	2.1
75468 PATTONVILLE	277	264	270	283	0.5	26	90	92	96	0.5	2.89	73	74	0.3
75469 PECAN GAP	119	504	529	562	1.2	46	215	224	236	1.0	2.36	150	157	1.1
75470 PETTY	277	269	283	301	1.2	48	101	106	113	1.1	2.67	80	84	1.2
75471 PICKTON	223	1837	1896	1998	0.8	34	653	667	698	0.5	2.84	501	513	0.6
75472 POINT	379	2932	3335	3991	3.1	82	1144	1290	1535	2.9	2.58	850	961	2.9
75473 POWDERLY	277	2417	2545	2706	1.2	49	880	926	985	1.2	2.75	713	752	1.3
75474 QUINLAN	231	13999	15336	16821	2.2	71	5270	5732	6247	2.0	2.66	3879	4226	2.0
75476 RAVENNA	147	2039	2146	2301	1.2	48	800	830	879	0.9	2.58	607	631	0.9
75477 ROXTON	277	1151	1191	1254	0.8	36	456	471	495	0.8	2.53	328	340	0.9
75478 SALTILLO	223	359	360	373	0.1	14	138	138	142	0.0	2.61	107	107	0.0
75479 SAVOY	147	1965	2046	2178	1.0	40	736	760	803	0.8	2.56	561	581	0.8
75480 SCROGGINS	159	2368	2446	2526	0.8	35	991	1021	1052	0.7	2.40	755	779	0.7
75481 SULPHUR BLUFF	223	232	239	252	0.7	32	86	88	92	0.5	2.72	68	70	0.7
75482 SULPHUR SPRINGS	223	23590	24996	26803	1.4	54	9116	9606	10257	1.2	2.56	6494	6863	1.3
75486 SUMNER	277	4318	4517	4783	1.1	44	1603	1676	1773	1.1	2.70	1293	1354	1.1
75487 TALCO	449	2034	2058	2149	0.3	19	769	765	785	-0.1	2.69	578	577	0.0
75488 TELEPHONE	147	883	937	1009	1.4	55	346	363	387	1.1	2.58	264	278	1.2
75490 TRENTON	147	2100	2254	2442	1.7	61	775	820	877	1.3	2.75	590	626	1.4
75491 WHITEWRIGHT	181	4870	5015	5310	0.7	32	1802	1840	1935	0.5	2.67	1385	1418	0.6
75492 WINDOM	147	327	351	380	1.7	61	134	142	153	1.4	2.47	99	106	1.6
75493 WINFIELD	449	2467	2565	2708	0.9	39	867	885	917	0.5	2.90	672	688	0.6
75494 WINNSBORO	499	8477	9134	9941	1.8	63	3271	3534	3863	1.8	2.40	2337	2543	2.0
75495 VAN ALSTYNE	181	5555	6131	6742	2.4	74	1978	2163	2361	2.1	2.81	1560	1709	2.2
75496 WOLFE CITY	231	2652	2687	2837	0.3	20	1020	1026	1078	0.1	2.56	729	735	0.2
75497 YANTIS	499	2210	2320	2496	1.2	46	940	984	1056	1.1	2.36	700	735	1.2
75501 TEXARKANA	037	37916	39907	42666	1.2	48	13758	14550	15679	1.4	2.54	9603	10192	1.4
75503 TEXARKANA	037	20293	21868	23621	1.8	63	8073	8664	9363	1.7	2.44	5692	6155	1.9
75550 ANNONA	387	943	959	982	0.4	22	394	399	408	0.3	2.40	270	275	0.4
75551 ATLANTA	067	8836	9148	9547	0.8	36	3473	3606	3783	0.9	2.48	2513	2615	0.5
75554 AVERY	387	1464	1499	1540	0.6	27	625	637	653	0.5	2.35	436	446	0.5
75555 BIVINS	067	2112	2234	2359	1.3	52	812	861	914	1.4	2.59	613	652	1.5
75556 BLOOMBURG	067	846	878	917	0.9	38	341	356	374	1.0	2.47	252	263	1.0
75558 COOKVILLE	449	2579	2659	2794	0.7	33	944	957	988	0.3	2.78	729	741	0.4
75559 DE KALB	037	5769	5870	6140	0.4	23	2356	2396	2506	0.4	2.41	1679	1710	0.4
75560 DOUGLASSVILLE	067	1733	1765	1825	0.4	23	709	725	754	0.5	2.43	503	516	0.6
75561 HOOKS	037	5935	5947	6173	0.1	14	2335	2340	2430	0.1	2.54	1707	1712	0.1
75563 LINDEN	067	5735	5809	5988	0.3	20	2379	2418	2507	0.4	2.33	1584	1615	0.5
75566 MARIETTA	067	1347	1367	1410	0.4	22	565	576	598	0.5	2.37	386	395	0.5
75567 MAUD	037	4862	5037	5300	0.8	37	1846	1912	2012	0.8	2.62	1368	1420	0.9
75568 NAPLES	343	2734	2830	2944	0.8	36	1120	1160	1211	0.8	2.41	761	791	0.9
75569 NASH	037	2266	2485	2698	2.2	71	934	1024	1115	2.2	2.43	666	730	2.2
75570 NEW BOSTON	037	10752	10900	11266	0.3	21	3173	3234	3384	0.5	2.46	2269	2313	0.5
75571 OMAHA	343	1817	1860	1923	0.6	27	715	731	758	0.5	2.50	515	529	0.6
75572 QUEEN CITY	067	4670	4835	5043	0.8	36	1835	1911	2005	1.0	2.53	1323	1381	1.0
75574 SIMMS	037	1489	1535	1611	0.7	33	583	601	631	0.7	2.55	443	457	0.7
75599 TEXARKANA	037	24	25	26	1.0	41	0	0	0	0.0	0.00	0	0	0.0
75601 LONGVIEW	183	14076	14196	14692	0.2	17	5616	5640	5826	0.1	2.36	3547	3570	0.2
75602 LONGVIEW	203	21969	22744	23805	0.8	36	7577	7774	8103	0.6	2.80	5424	5571	0.6
75603 LONGVIEW	183	4354	4416	4574	0.3	21	1757	1775	1831	0.2	2.49	1327	1344	0.3
75604 LONGVIEW	183	27136	28536	30258	1.2	47	10315	10823	11437	1.1	2.63	7552	7928	1.2
75605 LONGVIEW	183	24909	26373	28053	1.4	53	10326	10872	11523	1.2	2.38	6948	7364	1.4
75630 AVINGER	315	3084	3190	3337	0.8	35	1397	1445	1514	0.8	2.19	946	982	0.9
75631 BECKVILLE	365	2606	2664	2766	0.5	26	1013	1039	1085	0.6	2.56	758	779	0.7
75633 CARTHAGE	365	13956	14281	14804	0.5	27	5377	5498	5704	0.5	2.52	3881	3981	0.6
75638 DAINGERFIELD	343	5431	5576	5773	0.6	29	2114	2177	2262	0.7	2.52	1564	1615	0.8
75639 DE BERRY	365	3415	3527	3676	0.8	34	1305	1346	1402	0.7	2.62	949	981	0.8
75640 DIANA	203	2374	2758	3087	3.6	87	887	1030	1152	3.6	2.68	694	807	3.6
75643 GARY	365	1334	1462	1575	2.2	71	530	581	626	2.2	2.52	377	413	2.2
75644 GILMER	459	10728	11334	12189	1.3	51	4051	4277	4600	1.3	2.61	2988	3162	1.3
75645 GILMER	459	7671	8229	8926	1.7	61	2968	3173	3437	1.6	2.57	2230	2389	1.6
75647 GLADEWATER	459	12764	13369	14195	1.1	45	4703	4899	5179	1.0	2.67	3498	3655	1.0
75650 HALLSVILLE	203	7189	7983	8579	2.5	76	2578	2868	3090	2.5	2.78	2010	2233	2.5
75651 HARLETON	203	1729	1778	1828	0.7	31	651	670	690	0.7	2.65	508	523	0.7
75652 HENDERSON	401	14972	15314	15838	0.5	26	5088	5215	5414	0.6	2.57	3691	3789	0.6
75654 HENDERSON	401	9514	10457	11385	2.3	72	3725	4064	4401	2.1	2.54	2689	2960	2.3
75656 HUGHES SPRINGS	067	4687	4808	4987	0.6	29	1839	1894	1976	0.7	2.50	1325	1368	0.8
75657 JEFFERSON	315	9472	9862	10361	1.0	40	3911	4073	4287	1.0	2.40	2673	2792	1.0
75661 KARNACK	203	2641	2583	2619	-0.5	4	1096	1073	1089	-0.5	2.41	771	754	-0.5
75662 KILGORE	183	23905	25424	26928	1.5	56	9100	9621	10142	1.3	2.60	6549	6944	1.4
75667 LANEVILLE	401	3005	2899	2926	-0.8	2	1203	1159	1169	-0.9	2.48	848	817	-0.9
75668 LONE STAR	343	2517	2573	2661	0.5	26	1053	1079	1120	0.6	2.38	745	766	0.7
75669 LONG BRANCH	365	1127	1172	1225	0.9	39	473	493	515	1.0	2.38	340	355	1.0
75670 MARSHALL	203	17824	17768	18193	-0.1	11	6173	6145	6301	-0.1	2.65	4258	4247	-0.1
75672 MARSHALL	203	16563	16485	16831	-0.1	10	6597	6578	6725	-0.1	2.49	4746	4731	-0.1
75681 MOUNT ENTERPRISE	401	2033	1995	2020	-0.4	5	804	789	799	-0.4	2.53	587	576	-0.4
75683 ORE CITY	459	5212	5432	5801	1.0	41	1887	1958	2087	0.9	2.77	1484	1546	1.0
75684 OVERTON	401	6439	6564	6796	0.5	24	2251	2292	2377	0.4	2.60	1659	1690	0.4
75686 PITTSBURG	063	12503	13138	13964	1.2	47	4612	4797	5052	0.9	2.69	3404	3549	1.0
75687 PRICE	401	997	980	990	-0.4	6	354	348	351	-0.4	2.81	263	258	-0.5
75689 SELMAN CITY	401	642	642	648	0.0	13	229	228	230	-0.1	2.79	173	173	0.0
75691 TATUM	401	2909	3113	3280	1.6	60	1054	1124	1182	1.5	2.77	803	859	1.6
75692 WASKOM	203	5044	5272	5474	1.1	44	1859	1944	2020	1.1	2.71	1435	1501	1.1
75693 WHITE OAK	183	6006	6288	6599	1.1	45	2114	2203	2301	1.0	2.83	1679	1751	1.0
75701 TYLER	423	30756	31661	33661	0.7	32	12471	12773	13540	0.6	2.39	8069	8284	0.6
75702 TYLER	423	26095	26795	28377	0.6	29	8175	8299	8735	0.4	3.11	5870	5985	0.5
75703 TYLER	423	30612	33283	36347	2.0	67	13045	14140	15391	1.9	2.32	8406	9104	1.9
75704 TYLER	423	6699	6945	7369	0.9	37	2553	2636	2788	0.8	2.52	1903	1967	0.8
TEXAS					2.2					2.0	2.77			2.1
UNITED STATES					1.2					1.3	2.58			1.1

ZIP CODE #	POST OFFICE NAME	RACE (%) White 2000	White 2004	Black 2000	Black 2004	Asian/Pacific 2000	Asian/Pacific 2004	% Hispanic Origin 2000	% Hispanic Origin 2004	2004 AGE DISTRIBUTION (%) 0-4	5-9	10-14	15-19	20-24	25-44	45-64	65-84	85+	18+	MEDIAN AGE 2004	% 2004 Males	% 2004 Females
75452	LEONARD	90.4	89.1	3.0	3.2	0.1	0.2	5.7	6.9	7.5	7.6	7.9	7.1	6.3	26.0	24.3	11.3	2.1	72.5	36.6	48.9	51.1
75453	LONE OAK	93.9	92.9	2.4	2.7	0.6	0.6	4.0	4.9	5.6	6.1	7.3	6.8	5.2	24.7	27.7	15.3	1.4	76.7	41.4	50.6	49.4
75454	MELISSA	91.1	89.0	0.5	0.5	0.3	0.3	11.0	14.0	7.3	7.5	8.4	7.2	6.1	26.3	27.8	8.5	0.8	72.2	36.9	51.3	48.7
75455	MOUNT PLEASANT	64.2	62.1	12.7	12.5	0.6	0.7	35.0	38.7	9.5	8.6	8.0	7.6	7.5	28.2	18.4	9.9	2.3	69.3	30.9	49.5	50.5
75457	MOUNT VERNON	87.5	86.2	5.3	5.5	0.2	0.2	9.7	11.2	6.1	6.2	7.0	6.4	6.3	24.3	25.8	15.6	2.4	76.9	40.7	48.5	51.5
75459	HOWE	95.2	94.5	0.4	0.4	0.2	0.3	4.4	5.3	8.1	7.9	8.1	7.6	6.7	28.7	23.8	8.3	0.8	71.2	33.9	48.7	51.4
75460	PARIS	73.0	71.3	22.2	23.4	0.6	0.7	4.3	5.0	7.5	6.7	6.6	6.7	7.5	25.9	21.8	14.0	3.3	75.4	36.6	46.7	53.3
75462	PARIS	88.3	87.6	7.6	7.7	0.6	0.7	2.5	3.1	7.8	7.4	7.4	6.8	6.5	26.5	24.5	11.2	2.0	73.4	36.6	47.7	52.3
75468	PATTONVILLE	96.2	95.6	1.5	1.9	0.0	0.0	1.1	1.5	7.4	6.7	7.0	5.9	5.6	26.3	25.6	13.3	2.2	74.8	39.5	48.9	51.1
75469	PECAN GAP	91.9	90.9	4.2	4.4	0.2	0.2	4.2	5.1	4.4	4.9	6.6	6.6	6.4	25.7	28.9	14.4	2.1	80.2	42.3	52.6	47.5
75470	PETTY	90.3	89.4	6.3	6.7	0.0	0.0	2.6	3.5	6.0	6.4	8.1	7.4	5.7	26.5	25.8	12.7	1.4	75.3	39.0	49.1	50.9
75471	PICKTON	84.5	82.7	4.5	4.6	0.0	0.0	18.2	21.0	7.1	7.1	8.0	7.5	6.9	26.1	25.0	11.0	1.3	73.2	35.0	51.3	48.7
75472	POINT	91.8	91.0	2.7	2.8	0.7	0.8	4.3	5.0	6.2	6.3	6.7	6.4	6.1	24.7	27.5	14.6	1.5	76.9	40.7	49.7	50.3
75473	POWDERLY	94.6	94.1	2.7	2.9	0.0	0.0	0.9	1.1	6.9	7.2	7.5	6.3	5.1	27.0	28.1	11.0	0.9	74.5	39.2	49.4	50.6
75474	QUINLAN	94.3	93.3	1.0	1.1	0.2	0.3	5.0	6.2	6.6	6.5	7.3	7.5	6.4	25.6	27.6	11.6	0.9	74.8	38.5	50.2	49.8
75476	RAVENNA	94.5	93.8	1.4	1.5	0.1	0.1	3.4	4.3	5.9	6.2	6.7	6.1	5.2	26.1	27.6	15.2	1.2	77.0	41.4	51.5	48.5
75477	ROXTON	80.9	79.5	15.6	16.6	0.0	0.0	2.8	3.2	7.3	7.3	7.6	7.7	6.1	23.3	22.5	16.0	2.4	73.1	38.3	46.0	54.0
75478	SALTILLO	94.2	93.1	0.6	0.6	0.0	0.0	13.1	15.6	7.5	6.9	7.2	7.2	6.9	26.4	23.9	12.8	1.1	73.6	36.6	51.9	48.1
75479	SAVOY	96.0	95.5	0.3	0.3	0.3	0.4	2.2	2.7	5.6	5.9	7.9	6.5	4.8	24.0	26.6	15.9	2.9	76.4	41.9	48.6	51.4
75480	SCROGGINS	94.2	93.3	0.6	0.7	0.1	0.1	6.8	8.1	5.0	5.0	5.4	5.9	5.0	23.3	29.2	19.5	1.7	81.0	45.4	49.4	50.6
75481	SULPHUR BLUFF	94.8	93.7	0.9	1.3	0.0	0.0	5.2	5.9	6.3	6.3	6.7	6.7	6.7	28.5	25.5	12.6	0.8	76.6	37.5	49.4	50.6
75482	SULPHUR SPRINGS	83.0	81.6	10.3	10.7	0.3	0.4	8.7	10.3	6.8	6.7	7.2	6.6	6.7	26.8	24.2	12.6	2.6	75.3	37.3	48.6	51.4
75486	SUMNER	94.4	93.9	2.5	2.6	0.1	0.1	2.6	3.1	6.5	6.7	7.8	7.0	5.4	25.4	26.8	13.5	0.9	74.6	39.3	51.4	48.6
75487	TALCO	77.4	74.9	15.0	16.2	0.1	0.1	8.4	10.1	6.2	6.5	8.3	6.9	5.9	26.0	25.6	12.7	2.0	74.8	38.5	50.8	49.2
75488	TELEPHONE	95.0	94.2	1.3	1.4	0.0	0.0	3.6	4.3	5.7	5.3	5.6	6.3	6.5	24.9	29.5	15.1	1.3	79.5	42.1	50.8	49.2
75490	TRENTON	89.1	87.8	2.8	2.9	0.1	0.1	8.4	10.0	8.3	8.1	8.3	7.1	6.5	26.6	23.7	10.3	1.2	71.0	35.7	48.8	51.2
75491	WHITEWRIGHT	91.7	90.7	3.8	4.1	0.5	0.6	3.8	4.7	6.8	6.8	7.7	7.5	6.0	26.7	25.2	11.3	2.0	73.8	37.9	48.6	51.5
75492	WINDOM	95.1	94.9	2.8	2.9	0.0	0.0	0.3	0.3	6.6	6.8	7.7	5.7	5.7	23.9	27.4	14.0	2.3	75.5	40.5	49.3	50.7
75493	WINFIELD	82.8	80.0	2.1	2.2	0.1	0.1	20.4	24.3	8.3	8.3	8.5	6.2	5.5	28.5	23.3	10.5	1.0	71.0	34.4	50.2	49.8
75494	WINNSBORO	90.5	89.6	4.3	4.5	0.5	0.6	5.3	6.1	5.1	5.2	6.0	6.1	6.6	25.2	25.3	17.4	3.1	80.2	42.1	51.5	48.5
75495	VAN ALSTYNE	92.8	91.9	2.2	2.3	0.3	0.4	6.1	7.3	7.1	7.3	8.0	7.0	5.5	27.0	25.4	11.1	1.6	73.0	37.7	49.9	50.1
75496	WOLFE CITY	85.7	84.0	10.0	11.1	0.3	0.4	3.9	4.8	7.3	7.0	7.4	7.0	6.7	26.0	22.0	13.8	2.9	74.1	37.1	48.7	51.3
75497	YANTIS	93.4	92.4	2.4	2.7	0.1	0.1	6.9	8.2	4.7	4.8	5.0	4.6	4.4	19.9	33.5	21.8	1.4	82.7	49.6	50.8	49.2
75501	TEXARKANA	62.8	61.9	34.0	34.6	0.4	0.4	5.2	6.0	6.9	6.6	7.0	6.7	7.7	29.7	23.5	10.5	1.5	75.6	35.4	50.7	49.3
75503	TEXARKANA	81.9	80.8	14.6	15.4	1.0	1.1	2.3	2.8	6.0	6.1	7.1	6.5	6.1	25.1	26.3	13.7	3.0	76.6	40.3	46.5	53.5
75550	ANNONA	76.8	74.8	15.1	15.9	0.0	0.0	7.0	8.2	5.6	5.9	6.5	5.7	5.5	23.4	27.8	16.7	2.8	78.7	43.0	49.5	50.5
75551	ATLANTA	76.5	75.5	21.1	21.7	0.3	0.3	1.6	1.9	6.3	6.3	7.0	6.4	7.1	23.0	25.6	15.1	3.3	76.4	40.5	47.1	53.0
75554	AVERY	88.3	87.2	6.8	7.3	0.0	0.0	3.6	4.1	5.7	6.1	6.7	5.5	5.7	23.0	27.0	17.6	2.7	78.1	42.8	48.9	51.1
75555	BIVINS	85.5	84.6	11.6	12.0	0.1	0.2	2.0	2.3	6.8	7.0	7.4	6.2	6.4	24.8	27.3	12.7	1.6	75.0	38.8	50.9	49.1
75556	BLOOMBURG	92.0	91.1	6.3	6.7	0.2	0.5	1.7	1.8	5.9	5.9	6.4	6.7	6.3	24.6	29.0	13.0	2.2	77.9	41.5	48.5	51.5
75558	COOKVILLE	87.9	85.8	1.8	1.9	0.0	0.0	13.0	15.6	7.5	7.0	7.0	8.0	7.0	26.6	25.1	10.8	1.1	73.8	36.3	50.1	49.9
75559	DE KALB	78.4	76.6	18.0	19.2	0.1	0.1	3.0	3.7	6.2	6.4	7.3	6.4	5.6	22.7	26.4	15.8	3.1	76.1	41.5	48.5	51.5
75560	DOUGLASSVILLE	63.7	61.9	34.0	35.6	0.1	0.1	0.9	1.0	5.7	5.9	6.3	6.6	6.1	24.3	30.1	13.1	2.0	78.1	41.8	50.0	50.0
75561	HOOKS	80.7	78.5	14.5	15.9	0.4	0.5	3.0	3.6	7.1	7.2	7.5	6.1	6.5	25.6	26.5	11.8	1.7	74.5	37.6	47.7	52.3
75563	LINDEN	75.9	74.3	22.0	23.3	0.1	0.2	1.6	1.9	5.4	5.4	5.9	6.3	6.3	22.2	27.8	17.6	3.2	79.6	44.0	49.5	50.5
75566	MARIETTA	73.7	72.0	25.4	26.9	0.2	0.2	0.6	0.7	4.5	5.1	6.0	5.5	4.8	21.1	30.3	20.0	2.9	81.2	47.2	49.4	50.6
75567	MAUD	89.7	88.4	8.0	9.0	0.1	0.1	1.5	2.0	6.9	7.0	7.5	6.7	6.4	27.2	26.0	10.9	1.4	74.5	37.7	50.3	49.7
75568	NAPLES	70.0	68.4	27.2	28.4	0.1	0.1	1.8	2.2	6.2	6.2	6.8	6.5	6.9	21.4	25.3	17.7	3.2	76.8	42.0	47.9	52.1
75569	NASH	79.4	76.6	16.2	18.3	0.4	0.5	3.9	4.8	7.4	7.2	7.2	6.1	6.4	29.3	25.4	9.8	1.2	74.6	35.5	48.1	51.9
75570	NEW BOSTON	75.5	73.7	21.8	23.3	0.3	0.4	9.3	10.9	5.5	4.8	5.1	5.5	10.3	36.4	20.6	10.3	1.6	81.5	34.4	60.4	39.6
75571	OMAHA	75.1	73.4	21.2	22.2	0.3	0.3	4.0	4.9	6.8	6.9	7.3	6.1	5.9	23.6	25.8	14.8	2.9	75.2	40.3	48.0	52.0
75572	QUEEN CITY	81.3	80.0	16.4	17.4	0.2	0.2	1.7	2.0	6.8	6.7	7.0	6.4	6.6	26.7	26.6	11.6	1.6	75.6	38.2	48.0	52.0
75574	SIMMS	92.4	91.7	4.6	5.0	0.1	0.1	2.3	2.8	5.5	5.9	7.7	6.3	5.9	27.0	26.6	13.3	1.8	77.0	40.5	48.6	51.4
75599	TEXARKANA	62.5	60.0	33.3	36.0	0.0	0.0	8.3	4.0	8.0	8.0	8.0	8.0	8.0	32.0	24.0	4.0	0.0	76.0	31.3	44.0	56.0
75601	LONGVIEW	71.0	69.0	20.3	20.9	0.8	1.0	11.2	13.0	6.8	6.6	6.4	5.8	6.6	26.8	22.6	15.2	3.2	76.9	38.3	48.3	51.7
75602	LONGVIEW	45.1	44.2	45.3	45.0	0.4	0.5	15.1	17.0	8.4	8.0	8.4	8.6	9.4	27.1	20.2	8.6	1.2	70.6	30.2	49.4	50.6
75603	LONGVIEW	53.0	50.2	41.5	43.7	0.3	0.3	6.4	7.3	5.9	6.2	6.4	5.5	6.3	24.3	30.4	13.7	1.3	78.1	42.0	49.1	50.9
75604	LONGVIEW	83.4	81.5	9.1	9.9	1.0	1.1	9.3	11.0	7.7	7.2	8.1	7.4	7.6	28.0	23.0	9.9	1.0	72.3	33.9	48.4	51.6
75605	LONGVIEW	88.3	86.8	8.2	9.0	0.8	1.0	3.3	4.0	5.8	5.8	6.3	6.7	7.5	26.1	26.3	13.2	2.3	78.1	39.6	47.7	52.3
75630	AVINGER	79.2	78.2	17.3	17.9	0.0	0.0	2.5	2.9	5.1	4.6	5.3	5.1	4.7	20.5	32.6	19.9	2.1	81.8	48.0	50.1	49.9
75631	BECKVILLE	76.8	75.1	16.7	17.4	0.1	0.1	5.7	6.6	7.1	7.0	6.3	5.6	6.9	25.8	28.3	11.5	1.5	76.3	37.7	49.9	50.1
75633	CARTHAGE	79.5	78.4	17.0	17.7	0.3	0.4	3.5	4.1	6.4	6.3	6.8	6.8	7.5	24.0	25.6	14.0	2.7	76.6	39.3	47.5	52.6
75638	DAINGERFIELD	67.5	65.9	27.9	28.9	0.3	0.3	4.0	4.7	5.8	6.0	7.3	7.8	6.5	23.2	25.8	15.4	2.3	76.1	40.6	48.5	51.5
75639	DE BERRY	71.2	69.3	26.4	28.0	0.1	0.1	2.6	3.0	5.7	6.0	7.9	7.0	7.1	24.9	28.8	11.6	1.1	76.1	39.3	50.0	50.0
75640	DIANA	88.1	86.6	9.7	10.7	0.0	0.1	2.2	2.8	6.2	6.4	7.4	7.1	7.4	27.9	25.7	10.8	1.0	75.7	37.6	49.6	50.4
75643	GARY	87.9	86.7	9.2	10.1	0.2	0.1	2.9	3.4	7.1	7.2	7.1	6.2	5.5	24.3	25.0	15.9	1.9	75.0	40.4	50.1	49.9
75644	GILMER	83.5	82.4	12.2	12.7	0.2	0.2	4.2	4.9	6.9	6.8	7.0	6.7	6.4	24.2	25.1	14.4	2.5	75.1	39.0	48.3	51.7
75645	GILMER	86.3	85.1	10.1	10.7	0.1	0.2	3.8	4.5	6.7	6.9	7.4	6.4	6.0	25.4	27.1	12.6	1.7	75.1	39.2	49.7	50.3
75647	GLADEWATER	84.6	83.2	11.7	12.6	0.3	0.4	3.3	4.0	6.7	6.8	7.2	7.1	6.8	25.3	26.2	12.1	1.8	74.8	38.0	48.7	51.3
75650	HALLSVILLE	90.5	89.4	7.1	7.7	0.3	0.3	2.2	2.9	7.1	7.3	8.5	8.1	7.0	28.1	25.1	8.0	0.8	72.0	35.4	48.9	51.1
75651	HARLETON	88.0	86.5	9.6	10.7	0.1	0.1	1.6	2.0	6.2	6.3	7.8	7.5	7.3	26.4	26.6	10.7	1.2	75.3	37.4	50.2	49.8
75652	HENDERSON	67.9	66.3	26.3	27.4	0.3	0.3	8.6	9.6	6.0	5.6	6.2	6.3	7.0	30.6	25.6	10.9	2.0	78.4	38.2	54.6	45.4
75654	HENDERSON	82.0	80.6	10.5	10.5	0.4	0.4	10.6	12.7	6.9	6.4	6.8	6.9	6.2	24.0	24.2	15.7	3.1	75.6	40.1	47.7	52.3
75656	HUGHES SPRINGS	82.4	81.2	15.1	15.9	0.1	0.1	2.7	3.2	6.5	6.0	6.8	6.6	6.6	23.1	25.9	16.0	2.6	76.7	41.2	47.4	52.6
75657	JEFFERSON	71.7	70.2	25.0	26.3	0.3	0.3	2.3	2.7	5.7	5.8	6.2	6.1	5.6	21.9	28.4	17.8	2.4	78.5	44.1	48.6	51.4
75661	KARNACK	63.9	61.1	33.9	36.6	0.2	0.2	1.9	2.2	4.5	5.4	5.9	6.9	5.6	23.2	30.7	15.9	1.9	79.5	44.1	49.4	50.6
75662	KILGORE	78.9	76.6	14.2	15.5	0.5	0.5	7.9	9.3	6.7	6.5	7.0	7.2	7.6	26.2	24.8	12.3	1.8	75.7	37.1	49.1	50.9
75667	LANEVILLE	64.8	62.5	27.3	28.4	0.1	0.1	10.0	11.5	5.9	5.9	6.8	7.2	6.2	22.8	25.7	17.0	2.6	76.9	41.5	51.0	49.0
75668	LONE STAR	77.9	76.5	16.8	17.5	0.2	0.2	5.0	5.9	6.2	6.3	6.9	6.0	5.6	23.2	26.9	17.6	1.3	76.8	41.8	48.2	51.9
75669	LONG BRANCH	86.1	84.9	12.1	12.9	0.1	0.1	1.6	1.9	5.5	5.7	7.3	6.0	5.5	21.8	28.5	17.8	2.0	77.7	43.8	48.2	51.8
75670	MARSHALL	45.9	43.4	46.7	48.3	0.3	0.4	10.2	11.7	7.7	7.0	7.3	8.7	10.4	25.9	20.5	10.2	2.3	73.7	31.3	47.5	52.5
75672	MARSHALL	75.5	72.9	20.4	22.4	0.6	0.7	3.9	4.8	5.9	6.0	6.4	6.6	6.7	24.6	27.4	14.4	2.0	77.6	40.8	48.5	51.5
75681	MOUNT ENTERPRISE	66.1	64.3	31.9	33.6	0.1	0.1	3.3	3.8	5.8	6.3	8.2	6.5	6.2	24.7	25.2	14.9	2.4	75.7	39.2	49.9	50.1
75683	ORE CITY	86.2	85.2	8.4	8.8	0.3	0.3	5.1	6.0	6.9	7.0	7.8	7.4	6.8	26.7	25.0	11.5	1.0	73.8	36.8	49.5	50.5
75684	OVERTON	80.2	78.3	16.3	17.8	0.1	0.1	5.6	6.6	6.4	6.5	6.9	6.4	6.4	27.5	25.2	12.5	2.3	76.3	38.6	52.0	48.0
75686	PITTSBURG	70.4	68.3	18.6	19.0	0.2	0.2	14.9	17.2	7.6	7.4	7.6	6.7	6.3	25.7	23.4	13.4	1.9	73.4	36.6	49.3	50.8
75687	PRICE	68.2	66.2	20.9	21.5	0.4	0.4	15.6	17.4	7.2	6.9	7.6	7.4	7.2	26.5	24.4	11.0	1.7	73.6	36.0	50.6	49.4
75689	SELMAN CITY	83.3	81.6	5.6	6.1	0.2	0.2	11.1	12.9	8.3	7.9	7.5	7.5	7.2	27.4	23.2	9.8	1.3	71.3	33.8	50.8	49.2
75691	TATUM	73.5	71.0	15.6	16.6	0.0	0.0	18.1	20.3	7.1	6.9	7.2	7.5	7.8	27.5	25.0	9.5	1.5	73.9	34.8	50.2	49.8
75692	WASKOM	76.3	73.6	18.6	20.1	0.1	0.1	5.2	6.6	7.3	7.0	6.5	7.3	6.8	25.0	28.1	10.9	1.1	74.9	38.0	50.4	49.6
75693	WHITE OAK	93.3	92.3	2.7	3.1	0.1	0.1	3.8	4.7	7.0	7.0	8.1	8.0	7.2	28.1	24.5	9.3	0.9	72.9	35.4	49.6	50.4
75701	TYLER	72.4	70.0	20.5	21.6	0.6	0.7	11.1	13.3	6.9	6.4	6.8	7.1	7.6	24.3	21.7	15.5	3.9	76.3	37.9	45.2	54.8
75702	TYLER	29.2	27.9	47.4	46.4	0.3	0.3	34.4	37.8	9.7	8.8	8.5	8.3	8.9	27.0	18.7	8.5	1.5	68.0	28.8	48.9	51.1
75703	TYLER	85.6	83.4	10.0	11.4	1.7	1.9	3.4	4.3	6.6	6.3	6.4	6.5	8.3	27.4	24.1	12.4	2.0	77.0	36.5	47.6	52.4
75704	TYLER	68.3	65.0	24.6	26.6	0.5	0.5	9.8	11.9	6.6	6.7	6.5	6.2	7.0	28.7	25.0	12.1	1.3	76.4	37.0	49.6	50.4
	TEXAS	71.0	69.5	11.5	11.4	2.8	3.1	32.0	34.6	7.9	7.5	7.7	7.5	8.1	29.6	21.9	8.7	1.2	72.6	32.9	49.7	50.3
	UNITED STATES	75.1	73.6	12.3	12.5	3.8	4.2	12.5	14.1	6.9	6.7	7.2	7.0	7.3	28.6	23.8	10.8	1.7	75.1	36.0	49.1	50.9

#	POST OFFICE NAME	2004 Per Capita Income	2004 HH Income Base	2004 Household Income Distribution (%): Less than $25,000	$25,000 to $49,999	$50,000 to $99,999	$100,000 to $149,999	$150,000 or More	Median Household Income: 2004	2009	2004 National Centile	2004 State Centile	2004 Home Value Base	2004 Home Value Distribution (%): Less than $50,000	$50,000 to $89,999	$90,000 to $174,999	$175,000 to $399,999	$400,000 or More	2004 Median Home Value
75452	LEONARD	19814	1596	28.0	31.3	32.6	6.2	1.8	43093	49154	56	64	1209	27.4	31.7	31.2	9.0	0.7	78784
75453	LONE OAK	18345	1335	30.4	34.1	28.3	5.2	2.0	38052	44341	39	47	1106	37.3	32.8	21.4	8.4	0.1	64396
75454	MELISSA	31844	1049	16.0	21.5	36.2	13.2	13.2	63895	74493	88	90	876	22.4	18.7	20.9	27.6	10.4	116456
75455	MOUNT PLEASANT	17307	6622	35.8	30.2	24.8	5.2	4.1	35155	40118	28	33	4379	27.0	37.5	25.4	8.7	1.4	74293
75457	MOUNT VERNON	21617	2592	35.4	29.1	23.7	7.0	4.8	36820	41942	35	42	2015	34.3	27.1	26.2	9.9	2.5	74572
75459	HOWE	22016	1460	24.5	27.6	34.0	10.1	3.9	47639	54480	67	72	1151	21.8	30.4	34.0	12.0	1.8	86890
75460	PARIS	19283	10153	43.3	29.8	20.7	3.4	2.9	30063	34761	12	16	5803	44.8	33.6	18.0	3.2	0.4	55689
75462	PARIS	25503	3380	23.5	27.7	33.5	9.5	5.8	48432	55362	69	74	2658	11.1	30.1	43.0	14.5	1.4	98020
75468	PATTONVILLE	12688	92	40.2	40.2	16.3	3.3	0.0	31099	37313	15	19	75	36.0	25.3	26.7	10.7	1.3	71000
75469	PECAN GAP	18440	224	35.7	31.7	25.9	5.4	1.3	36288	41753	33	39	188	58.5	20.7	18.1	2.7	0.0	46098
75470	PETTY	19155	106	28.3	32.1	33.0	4.7	1.9	40755	46955	49	57	91	38.5	33.0	18.7	9.9	0.0	64375
75471	PICKTON	18074	667	33.7	35.2	21.3	5.0	4.8	35359	40473	29	34	502	40.6	34.3	16.9	4.4	3.8	63191
75472	POINT	18079	1290	33.3	29.6	30.2	4.9	1.9	39007	44891	43	51	1064	35.0	37.4	19.9	6.0	1.7	64255
75473	POWDERLY	21280	926	19.3	30.2	40.7	6.8	2.9	50281	56259	72	78	807	17.0	37.9	32.8	11.2	1.1	84733
75474	QUINLAN	20077	5732	28.2	31.0	30.8	7.4	2.6	41096	47769	50	58	4590	40.4	28.4	22.4	8.0	0.9	63163
75476	RAVENNA	20456	830	31.1	28.1	33.1	4.7	3.0	42157	48121	53	62	705	33.9	29.8	27.8	6.7	1.8	69182
75477	ROXTON	16673	471	38.6	27.4	29.5	3.6	0.9	33830	39666	24	29	358	47.8	34.9	13.4	3.9	0.0	53333
75478	SALTILLO	17188	138	31.2	33.3	29.7	4.4	1.5	35000	40399	28	33	115	44.4	27.0	19.1	7.8	1.7	56500
75479	SAVOY	23471	760	26.2	33.6	33.4	4.2	2.6	42036	48031	53	62	591	36.6	32.2	20.1	9.0	2.2	65615
75480	SCROGGINS	20816	1021	28.6	40.5	19.1	8.6	3.2	37437	43395	37	44	853	23.8	26.3	28.6	17.7	3.6	89915
75481	SULPHUR BLUFF	18823	88	30.7	29.6	30.7	6.8	2.3	40747	46872	49	57	74	46.0	24.3	20.3	8.1	1.4	56000
75482	SULPHUR SPRINGS	19735	9606	33.9	32.3	24.5	5.5	3.8	36453	41615	33	40	6769	28.1	32.2	30.0	8.0	1.8	76730
75486	SUMNER	18122	1676	29.9	27.9	36.0	4.7	1.6	40757	46025	49	57	1404	28.4	34.2	27.7	7.9	1.8	73445
75487	TALCO	15063	765	39.5	28.4	27.3	4.8	0.0	35395	40107	29	35	634	51.3	25.2	17.5	5.7	0.3	47895
75488	TELEPHONE	19485	363	35.3	25.1	32.8	5.0	1.9	38152	41721	40	48	293	33.5	26.3	31.4	8.2	0.7	73250
75490	TRENTON	21495	820	25.5	25.6	35.5	10.4	3.1	48976	54936	70	75	635	25.7	26.6	29.5	16.9	1.4	86081
75491	WHITEWRIGHT	20175	1840	24.3	29.5	35.7	8.3	2.2	46322	52791	65	71	1453	22.5	29.3	33.8	12.0	2.4	87056
75492	WINDOM	23077	142	28.9	27.5	31.7	6.3	5.6	43667	50352	58	66	112	42.0	30.4	22.3	4.5	0.9	58182
75493	WINFIELD	20052	885	26.4	32.2	28.1	10.3	2.9	42711	50471	55	63	722	31.9	21.6	30.2	13.2	3.2	84792
75494	WINNSBORO	19044	3534	38.5	32.4	21.8	4.3	3.0	32813	37392	20	25	2766	27.6	37.9	24.4	7.8	2.4	74321
75495	VAN ALSTYNE	22924	2163	20.5	27.7	35.2	11.7	4.9	51585	57860	75	79	1725	13.3	23.0	34.3	27.1	2.3	119703
75496	WOLFE CITY	18241	1026	33.7	31.2	26.7	6.0	2.4	36649	42114	34	41	735	44.1	24.5	26.1	4.6	0.7	58529
75497	YANTIS	24254	984	28.7	33.3	27.9	5.6	4.6	39358	45519	44	52	828	23.0	27.2	29.0	17.9	3.0	89844
75501	TEXARKANA	17298	14570	39.8	28.2	24.9	5.5	1.6	32935	38559	21	25	9530	39.3	34.7	22.9	2.9	0.1	61119
75503	TEXARKANA	30643	8664	23.8	24.9	30.9	12.0	8.3	51442	59692	75	79	6180	14.5	24.8	42.6	14.8	3.3	102714
75550	ANNONA	19025	399	42.9	32.1	19.8	3.5	1.8	30632	35000	14	17	333	49.9	28.8	13.8	6.9	0.6	50200
75551	ATLANTA	19474	3606	37.4	29.7	25.7	4.7	2.6	33033	37787	21	26	2661	32.9	35.0	26.2	5.2	0.7	71264
75554	AVERY	17418	637	45.1	31.2	19.3	2.7	1.7	28599	32266	10	12	499	53.1	28.7	13.4	4.2	0.6	46310
75555	BIVINS	14345	861	39.1	36.2	21.8	2.1	0.7	35392	40570	29	34	746	46.3	29.8	21.3	2.3	0.4	54746
75556	BLOOMBURG	21736	356	35.7	28.9	27.3	5.3	2.8	36353	41716	33	39	285	34.7	27.7	31.2	5.6	0.7	73095
75558	COOKVILLE	19741	957	36.1	27.6	26.9	6.5	3.0	38116	45173	40	47	805	22.4	32.2	28.7	12.9	3.9	79939
75559	DE KALB	16945	2396	42.7	27.3	25.3	3.1	1.7	31108	36077	15	19	1823	48.6	25.1	21.2	3.6	1.6	52008
75560	DOUGLASSVILLE	22945	725	39.2	37.8	15.0	3.7	4.3	30473	35363	13	17	612	40.5	29.7	23.4	5.1	1.3	60698
75561	HOOKS	18696	2340	33.9	32.3	27.2	4.9	1.8	38431	45181	41	49	1821	46.7	31.4	18.7	2.6	0.6	53380
75563	LINDEN	17737	2418	40.9	29.7	23.4	3.7	2.3	31412	36007	16	21	1826	41.8	30.1	21.1	5.8	1.3	58765
75566	MARIETTA	17386	576	46.2	33.9	16.5	1.4	2.1	26641	31188	7	9	491	55.4	29.3	11.8	2.7	0.8	44111
75567	MAUD	18740	1912	32.7	31.1	27.5	6.5	2.1	38287	44785	40	48	1591	43.8	30.6	19.1	5.7	0.8	57190
75568	NAPLES	19430	1160	43.1	28.8	21.0	4.4	2.8	29143	33370	11	13	893	44.6	30.2	21.6	3.3	0.3	56554
75569	NASH	17898	1024	35.5	31.6	27.8	3.4	1.7	35100	40963	28	33	708	46.8	34.6	17.7	1.0	0.0	52738
75570	NEW BOSTON	17447	3234	36.7	28.5	29.7	3.0	2.2	35679	41442	30	36	2314	41.7	36.1	18.9	2.9	0.5	58348
75571	OMAHA	18696	731	41.5	29.8	22.4	4.2	2.1	29861	34390	12	15	566	42.6	35.9	17.5	3.5	0.5	57925
75572	QUEEN CITY	17616	1911	40.1	27.6	26.3	4.4	1.6	32222	36870	18	23	1514	39.6	35.3	21.7	3.3	0.2	60656
75574	SIMMS	21469	601	27.3	36.9	26.8	4.0	5.0	39355	46679	44	52	500	40.4	30.8	24.0	4.4	0.4	59796
75599	TEXARKANA	538	0	0.0	0.0	0.0	0.0	0.0	0	0	0	0	0	0.0	0.0	0.0	0.0	0.0	0
75601	LONGVIEW	21854	5640	32.5	31.1	25.1	7.0	4.4	38082	44218	40	47	3569	23.3	30.4	37.0	8.6	0.7	85846
75602	LONGVIEW	15299	7774	42.1	30.4	21.3	4.5	1.8	30160	34471	13	16	4749	49.2	31.9	15.0	3.1	0.9	50792
75603	LONGVIEW	23084	1775	26.8	29.8	29.0	11.3	3.2	43491	51112	57	65	1509	30.6	31.9	23.6	13.1	0.8	74581
75604	LONGVIEW	22467	10823	27.0	30.6	30.2	7.8	4.5	42839	50318	56	64	7139	20.5	31.9	36.6	9.7	1.4	86973
75605	LONGVIEW	28307	10872	23.2	27.6	32.8	10.0	6.4	49095	56980	70	76	7094	10.9	19.7	52.6	14.6	2.3	110719
75630	AVINGER	19365	1445	43.0	29.5	21.6	4.3	1.7	29701	34638	12	15	1201	48.8	28.8	18.2	3.8	0.4	51686
75631	BECKVILLE	18102	1039	32.7	30.2	28.2	7.4	1.4	37220	42275	36	43	838	41.9	28.4	20.3	8.7	0.7	60408
75633	CARTHAGE	18072	5498	34.3	31.6	24.8	7.5	1.8	36508	41469	34	40	4207	39.2	26.3	27.6	6.4	0.6	67177
75638	DAINGERFIELD	17352	2177	37.2	29.6	26.5	5.0	1.8	35621	40944	30	36	1703	49.4	26.2	22.6	1.8	0.0	50583
75639	DE BERRY	18277	1346	34.7	28.5	28.5	5.9	2.4	35866	40827	31	37	1112	47.3	29.3	19.2	3.7	0.5	53488
75640	DIANA	17652	1030	32.6	33.1	28.5	3.6	2.2	36307	41639	33	39	865	37.7	35.7	21.6	4.6	0.4	64551
75643	GARY	16488	581	44.2	29.6	20.3	4.0	1.9	28853	33088	10	13	488	47.1	26.6	17.0	7.0	2.3	53784
75644	GILMER	18750	4277	35.4	32.7	24.2	4.9	2.8	35387	40285	29	34	3374	36.4	34.1	22.5	5.6	1.4	67609
75645	GILMER	18684	3173	33.0	31.0	28.2	5.5	2.3	38223	43256	40	48	2604	38.3	31.3	22.7	7.2	0.5	66757
75647	GLADEWATER	17977	4899	31.8	32.8	28.0	5.0	2.5	37264	42933	36	43	3747	37.3	31.0	24.2	6.9	0.6	66165
75650	HALLSVILLE	22606	2868	23.1	28.5	37.2	8.7	2.6	48729	54980	70	75	2254	25.6	31.0	30.4	11.7	1.2	81525
75651	HARLETON	18310	670	35.4	31.9	26.0	3.7	3.0	35775	41301	31	37	564	41.8	24.8	25.7	6.6	1.1	60667
75652	HENDERSON	20805	5215	30.8	32.7	26.4	6.5	3.6	37206	42969	36	43	3960	31.5	28.0	28.9	10.1	1.5	76635
75654	HENDERSON	21873	4064	31.6	30.9	28.2	5.4	4.0	38899	44711	42	51	3176	27.3	31.6	30.5	8.7	1.9	78937
75656	HUGHES SPRINGS	17835	1894	39.7	32.3	21.9	4.0	2.2	33585	38475	23	28	1368	43.2	33.0	20.1	3.6	0.2	57500
75657	JEFFERSON	17418	4073	44.3	27.2	21.6	4.6	2.3	29963	34798	12	15	3237	50.4	24.9	19.2	4.4	1.1	49603
75661	KARNACK	22421	1073	38.9	28.9	23.7	3.4	5.2	33829	39955	24	29	886	35.7	28.7	25.1	9.1	1.5	67424
75662	KILGORE	20329	9621	29.9	29.9	29.3	7.5	3.3	40961	47424	50	58	7205	35.9	29.5	28.1	6.2	0.3	68965
75667	LANEVILLE	16034	1159	47.5	26.1	19.8	5.0	1.6	26837	30732	7	9	947	52.1	22.5	19.5	5.7	0.2	47563
75668	LONE STAR	19743	1079	37.2	32.5	22.8	2.6	4.9	33614	39816	23	28	732	49.6	24.2	23.1	2.9	0.3	51071
75669	LONG BRANCH	17260	493	36.3	32.3	26.0	4.7	0.8	35805	41030	31	37	444	46.6	19.8	26.6	6.5	0.5	57143
75670	MARSHALL	14535	6145	45.4	28.8	21.2	3.1	1.6	27913	32112	9	11	3882	53.8	28.2	14.0	3.9	0.2	46909
75672	MARSHALL	22430	6578	31.3	27.4	30.4	7.0	3.9	41974	48179	53	61	5123	29.2	32.6	28.1	9.1	1.0	76193
75681	MOUNT ENTERPRISE	15603	789	42.0	31.9	21.0	3.9	1.1	30556	35035	14	17	649	58.9	21.9	16.6	2.2	0.5	44471
75683	ORE CITY	19485	1958	29.9	32.0	29.8	5.3	3.0	39797	44213	45	53	1608	44.7	27.9	24.3	2.6	0.6	57544
75684	OVERTON	19836	2292	35.7	30.3	26.2	4.4	3.5	36484	41951	33	40	1797	41.6	33.8	18.6	5.3	0.7	59410
75686	PITTSBURG	19535	4797	36.8	30.1	23.0	7.2	2.8	35425	40509	29	35	3608	29.9	32.6	26.3	9.3	1.9	72616
75687	PRICE	14704	348	41.7	33.9	19.5	1.7	3.2	30703	35352	14	18	285	61.4	23.5	12.6	2.5	0.0	35833
75689	SELMAN CITY	15943	228	33.8	32.9	29.0	3.5	0.9	36773	40841	35	41	186	52.2	35.0	11.3	1.6	0.0	46923
75691	TATUM	19019	1124	36.3	33.0	24.1	4.5	2.1	33342	38138	22	27	859	46.5	25.0	21.5	7.0	0.0	53961
75692	WASKOM	17435	1944	32.1	32.2	27.2	6.7	1.9	37552	43369	38	45	1578	38.2	31.8	22.5	7.2	0.3	64745
75693	WHITE OAK	20598	2203	24.9	26.0	36.5	9.0	3.6	48170	55748	69	74	1723	19.4	25.3	48.2	7.1	0.0	93560
75701	TYLER	25216	12773	30.7	29.4	24.8	9.2	6.0	40145	46588	47	55	8094	13.9	39.2	32.6	12.7	1.6	88826
75702	TYLER	12116	8299	44.7	32.1	18.3	3.3	1.6	28236	32192	9	12	4493	48.4	37.5	13.6	0.4	0.2	51319
75703	TYLER	32042	14140	23.3	26.7	30.2	11.2	8.6	49990	57807	72	77	7909	5.6	12.7	52.0	25.1	4.6	131316
75704	TYLER	19287	2636	29.0	34.7	28.0	5.2	3.0	37949	43864	39	46	2112	26.4	40.5	28.0	3.8	1.3	74366
	TEXAS	23284		26.2	27.7	29.5	10.3	6.3	45778	54246				21.6	26.1	33.4	15.6	3.4	93683
	UNITED STATES	25866		24.7	27.1	30.8	10.9	6.5	48124	56710				10.9	15.0	33.7	30.1	10.4	145905

#	POST OFFICE NAME	FINANCIAL SERVICES: Auto Loan	FINANCIAL SERVICES: Home Loan	FINANCIAL SERVICES: Investments	FINANCIAL SERVICES: Retirement Plans	THE HOME: Home Improvements: Home Repair	THE HOME: Home Improvements: Lawn & Garden	THE HOME: Furnishings: Computers & Hardware	THE HOME: Furnishings: Major Appliances	THE HOME: Furnishings: TV, Radio, Sound Equipment	THE HOME: Furnishings: Furniture	ENTERTAINMENT: Dine out/ Carry out	ENTERTAINMENT: Sports Equipment	ENTERTAINMENT: Fees & Tickets	ENTERTAINMENT: Toys & Games	ENTERTAINMENT: Travel	ENTERTAINMENT: Cable TV	PERSONAL: Apparel & Services	PERSONAL: Auto Repairs	PERSONAL: Health Insurance	PERSONAL: Pets & Supplies
75452	LEONARD	84	73	56	71	77	85	72	78	76	71	92	91	69	93	72	77	87	76	84	96
75453	LONE OAK	83	61	35	57	68	77	60	71	69	60	82	84	54	79	61	72	75	71	84	96
75454	MELISSA	127	140	135	138	141	143	126	130	122	126	152	154	131	160	129	121	149	126	125	153
75455	MOUNT PLEASANT	77	69	62	67	69	75	72	74	75	74	93	84	69	90	70	73	90	76	74	83
75457	MOUNT VERNON	94	71	45	66	79	91	71	84	81	70	95	97	63	92	73	86	88	83	100	110
75459	HOWE	94	86	70	84	89	95	82	89	85	83	104	103	80	104	83	86	99	87	92	108
75460	PARIS	69	58	50	56	61	70	63	66	68	61	82	75	59	79	62	70	77	66	74	77
75462	PARIS	96	97	92	95	99	105	92	96	93	92	115	112	93	117	94	94	111	94	97	113
75468	PATTONVILLE	58	48	36	47	51	58	50	54	54	49	65	61	47	63	50	55	60	53	60	64
75469	PECAN GAP	82	55	25	47	62	72	53	66	64	54	75	79	45	71	54	69	68	66	82	94
75470	PETTY	82	73	56	69	77	83	67	75	72	67	87	89	66	89	69	73	83	73	81	96
75471	PICKTON	97	65	29	56	73	84	63	78	75	64	89	93	53	84	64	81	81	77	96	111
75472	POINT	87	59	28	52	67	77	57	71	68	58	80	86	49	77	59	73	73	71	87	101
75473	POWDERLY	93	80	62	78	85	93	79	85	83	78	101	100	76	102	79	85	96	84	93	106
75474	QUINLAN	90	74	52	69	78	84	71	80	76	72	92	94	65	88	71	78	87	79	87	102
75476	RAVENNA	99	67	30	58	76	87	64	80	78	66	91	96	55	86	65	84	83	80	99	114
75477	ROXTON	68	54	37	51	58	67	56	62	62	54	74	71	52	71	56	65	68	62	72	76
75478	SALTILLO	83	57	27	50	65	74	55	69	65	55	77	82	47	73	56	70	70	68	84	97
75479	SAVOY	106	76	45	73	86	100	80	93	90	77	106	108	69	102	81	95	97	92	111	121
75480	SCROGGINS	85	66	44	59	74	83	63	75	71	62	84	88	56	83	66	76	78	74	89	102
75481	SULPHUR BLUFF	80	68	52	67	71	80	70	75	74	68	90	85	66	89	69	76	84	74	81	89
75482	SULPHUR SPRINGS	79	67	56	65	70	79	69	74	73	68	89	85	65	87	69	75	84	73	81	89
75486	SUMNER	83	67	45	62	72	79	63	72	69	63	84	86	59	83	64	72	78	71	82	96
75487	TALCO	76	51	23	44	58	67	49	62	60	50	70	74	42	66	50	64	64	61	76	88
75488	TELEPHONE	92	64	33	59	74	83	63	77	73	62	85	93	53	83	65	76	78	76	93	108
75490	TRENTON	93	81	63	79	86	94	79	86	84	79	102	101	77	103	80	86	97	84	93	107
75491	WHITEWRIGHT	84	76	62	74	79	85	74	79	77	73	94	93	72	94	74	78	89	78	83	96
75492	WINDOM	91	81	62	77	86	92	75	83	80	75	97	99	74	99	77	82	92	81	90	108
75493	WINFIELD	92	81	63	79	83	90	80	86	83	80	101	98	76	98	79	83	96	85	89	101
75494	WINNSBORO	79	57	34	54	64	75	61	70	70	59	82	80	54	78	61	74	75	70	84	89
75495	VAN ALSTYNE	97	92	79	91	95	102	89	94	91	88	112	109	88	113	90	92	107	92	97	112
75496	WOLFE CITY	75	61	44	59	66	75	63	69	69	61	82	79	58	80	63	71	76	68	79	85
75497	YANTIS	90	79	70	75	86	100	74	86	80	78	98	88	73	85	80	85	91	84	101	103
75501	TEXARKANA	65	56	50	53	57	63	58	60	62	58	75	70	55	72	57	63	72	61	65	72
75503	TEXARKANA	104	111	119	112	110	115	109	108	106	108	132	125	111	134	109	104	130	107	103	120
75550	ANNONA	86	58	26	50	65	75	56	70	67	57	79	83	47	75	57	72	72	69	86	99
75551	ATLANTA	79	63	44	60	67	78	65	72	71	63	85	82	60	82	65	75	79	71	83	89
75554	AVERY	77	52	23	45	59	67	50	62	60	51	71	75	42	67	51	65	64	62	77	89
75555	BIVINS	70	47	21	40	53	61	45	57	55	46	64	68	39	61	46	59	58	56	70	80
75556	BLOOMBURG	99	69	34	60	77	88	66	81	78	67	92	97	57	88	67	84	84	80	98	114
75558	COOKVILLE	86	73	57	73	76	86	75	80	80	74	97	91	72	96	74	81	90	79	87	95
75559	DE KALB	71	52	32	47	57	66	52	61	61	52	72	71	47	68	53	64	66	61	73	81
75560	DOUGLASSVILLE	104	70	33	62	80	92	69	85	82	69	96	101	59	91	70	88	88	84	104	119
75561	HOOKS	75	65	49	61	67	75	64	70	68	64	83	80	61	81	64	70	78	69	76	84
75563	LINDEN	72	51	29	47	57	67	54	62	62	52	73	72	47	69	54	66	66	62	76	81
75566	MARIETTA	67	50	33	48	55	66	55	61	62	53	73	68	49	69	55	66	67	61	73	74
75567	MAUD	80	65	46	62	69	78	66	73	72	65	86	84	61	83	65	74	80	72	81	89
75568	NAPLES	80	58	34	54	64	76	61	70	70	59	82	81	54	78	61	74	75	70	85	90
75569	NASH	67	58	46	57	60	68	60	64	63	59	76	73	56	74	59	64	71	63	69	75
75570	NEW BOSTON	56	49	47	47	51	58	52	54	56	51	68	61	50	65	52	57	64	54	59	62
75571	OMAHA	81	58	33	54	65	76	61	71	69	59	82	82	53	78	61	74	74	70	85	93
75572	QUEEN CITY	79	57	32	52	63	72	57	67	65	57	78	78	50	74	57	69	71	66	80	89
75574	SIMMS	98	70	38	66	80	90	69	84	79	68	93	100	60	91	71	83	85	83	99	115
75599	TEXARKANA	0	0	0	0	0	0	0	0	0	0	0	0	0	0	0	0	0	0	0	0
75601	LONGVIEW	71	72	80	71	72	80	74	74	75	73	94	84	75	93	75	77	91	74	76	82
75602	LONGVIEW	62	55	56	53	55	62	60	60	63	59	78	68	58	75	58	64	75	61	63	68
75603	LONGVIEW	104	75	40	66	83	94	72	86	83	72	99	103	63	95	73	89	91	85	103	119
75604	LONGVIEW	83	84	85	84	84	88	84	84	83	83	103	98	84	103	83	81	100	84	81	95
75605	LONGVIEW	96	96	100	98	96	101	97	97	95	96	119	115	96	118	96	92	116	98	93	110
75630	AVINGER	73	55	36	50	61	71	54	64	61	54	73	73	48	69	56	66	67	63	77	85
75631	BECKVILLE	87	59	27	52	67	76	57	71	68	57	80	85	48	76	58	73	72	70	87	100
75633	CARTHAGE	75	60	44	56	65	74	60	68	66	60	80	78	56	77	61	70	74	67	77	85
75638	DAINGERFIELD	75	55	35	51	61	70	57	65	64	56	77	76	51	74	57	68	71	65	76	85
75639	DE BERRY	90	60	27	52	68	79	58	73	70	59	83	87	50	78	59	76	75	72	90	104
75640	DIANA	87	61	31	53	68	78	58	72	69	59	81	85	51	78	59	74	74	71	87	100
75643	GARY	78	52	24	45	59	68	50	63	61	51	72	75	43	68	51	66	65	63	78	90
75644	GILMER	85	63	39	57	69	80	63	73	72	62	85	86	56	82	64	76	78	73	87	97
75645	GILMER	81	64	43	60	69	77	63	72	70	63	83	84	58	80	63	72	78	71	81	92
75647	GLADEWATER	74	66	56	65	68	74	66	70	69	66	84	81	64	83	66	69	80	69	73	83
75650	HALLSVILLE	94	93	82	92	93	96	88	92	87	89	108	108	87	107	87	85	105	91	88	107
75651	HARLETON	83	66	43	61	71	78	63	72	69	64	83	86	58	81	64	72	78	71	81	96
75652	HENDERSON	83	69	53	65	73	81	69	76	75	68	91	90	65	90	70	77	85	76	85	96
75654	HENDERSON	86	76	66	75	81	88	76	82	79	75	96	96	73	95	77	80	91	81	88	100
75656	HUGHES SPRINGS	73	56	42	53	60	70	59	65	66	58	79	75	54	75	59	69	74	66	76	82
75657	JEFFERSON	75	53	28	47	59	69	53	63	62	52	72	74	46	69	53	66	66	63	77	86
75661	KARNACK	100	69	34	60	78	89	66	82	79	67	93	98	57	88	68	85	85	81	100	116
75662	KILGORE	81	72	61	69	74	82	72	77	76	72	93	88	70	91	72	78	89	77	82	91
75667	LANEVILLE	69	49	28	45	54	64	51	60	59	50	70	69	45	66	51	63	63	59	72	77
75668	LONE STAR	80	59	37	56	65	76	62	70	70	60	82	81	55	79	61	73	76	70	83	89
75669	LONG BRANCH	74	53	29	47	60	68	51	62	59	51	70	74	44	67	52	64	64	62	75	87
75670	MARSHALL	57	48	47	46	49	57	53	54	57	52	70	62	51	67	52	59	67	56	59	64
75672	MARSHALL	91	74	57	70	79	89	74	82	80	73	97	96	69	95	75	83	91	82	92	105
75681	MOUNT ENTERPRISE	67	52	36	48	56	63	51	59	57	51	68	70	46	65	51	59	63	59	67	77
75683	ORE CITY	89	73	51	69	78	87	71	80	78	71	94	93	67	93	72	80	88	78	89	102
75684	OVERTON	87	69	48	66	74	84	72	79	78	70	94	90	65	88	71	81	87	79	90	97
75686	PITTSBURG	86	67	49	63	73	83	69	78	77	68	92	90	63	90	70	81	86	77	89	99
75687	PRICE	74	55	31	49	59	66	52	62	60	54	71	74	46	67	53	63	66	62	72	84
75689	SELMAN CITY	71	65	51	62	65	68	62	66	62	63	77	76	58	73	61	61	74	66	66	78
75691	TATUM	89	73	50	68	76	83	70	79	75	72	91	92	64	86	70	76	86	78	85	100
75692	WASKOM	80	65	44	60	69	75	62	71	67	63	81	83	57	78	62	69	77	70	77	91
75693	WHITE OAK	89	81	69	82	83	90	82	85	83	81	102	98	79	101	80	83	97	84	87	99
75701	TYLER	82	83	92	82	84	92	86	86	87	85	108	98	87	108	87	88	105	87	87	95
75702	TYLER	54	48	48	46	47	53	51	52	55	53	68	58	50	64	50	55	66	54	54	58
75703	TYLER	103	106	119	110	104	109	109	105	104	108	132	125	109	130	106	100	129	107	98	117
75704	TYLER	81	68	49	65	71	78	66	73	70	67	86	85	62	82	66	71	81	72	78	91
	TEXAS	94	90	91	90	89	95	92	93	92	93	115	107	90	112	90	90	112	94	89	104
	UNITED STATES	100	100	100	100	100	100	100	100	100	100	100	100	100	100	100	100	100	100	100	100

ZIP CODE		POPULATION			2000-2004 ANNUAL RATE		HOUSEHOLDS					FAMILIES		
# POST OFFICE NAME	COUNTY FIPS CODE	2000	2004	2009	% Rate	State Centile	2000	2004	2009	% Annual Rate 2000-2004	2004 Average HH Size	2000	2004	% Annual Rate 2000-2004
75705 TYLER	423	2042	2146	2302	1.2	47	702	733	782	1.0	2.88	526	550	1.1
75706 TYLER	423	6670	7034	7524	1.3	50	2314	2415	2566	1.0	2.84	1758	1839	1.1
75707 TYLER	423	11169	11889	12862	1.5	57	4328	4582	4934	1.4	2.58	3102	3278	1.3
75708 TYLER	423	5318	6246	7064	3.9	89	1828	2119	2376	3.5	2.93	1391	1618	3.6
75709 TYLER	423	3353	3529	3767	1.2	48	1277	1337	1421	1.1	2.61	970	1017	1.1
75750 ARP	423	3292	3484	3769	1.3	52	1235	1296	1395	1.1	2.66	961	1011	1.2
75751 ATHENS	213	15149	15499	16523	0.5	27	5468	5553	5894	0.4	2.64	3960	4031	0.4
75752 ATHENS	213	6334	6646	7262	1.1	46	2448	2543	2761	0.9	2.58	1842	1917	0.9
75754 BEN WHEELER	467	5364	5793	6343	1.8	64	1998	2149	2345	1.7	2.62	1514	1631	1.8
75755 BIG SANDY	459	3630	3942	4304	2.0	67	1413	1531	1670	1.9	2.57	1026	1115	2.0
75756 BROWNSBORO	213	2199	2405	2644	2.1	70	822	891	972	1.9	2.70	640	695	2.0
75757 BULLARD	073	6579	7328	8073	2.6	77	2594	2887	3171	2.6	2.54	2044	2279	2.6
75758 CHANDLER	213	8369	8873	9591	1.4	54	3307	3476	3732	1.2	2.53	2444	2576	1.3
75760 CUSHING	347	2316	2375	2526	0.6	28	935	955	1010	0.5	2.44	667	681	0.5
75762 FLINT	423	7931	8649	9471	2.1	68	3016	3266	3553	1.9	2.65	2437	2646	2.0
75763 FRANKSTON	001	5786	6275	6851	1.9	66	2293	2474	2692	1.8	2.51	1680	1818	1.9
75765 HAWKINS	499	7160	7682	8346	1.7	61	2838	3056	3335	1.8	2.37	2121	2289	1.8
75766 JACKSONVILLE	073	21403	23215	25318	1.9	66	7788	8375	9067	1.7	2.69	5564	5993	1.8
75770 LARUE	213	2532	2489	2638	-0.4	6	969	944	994	-0.6	2.63	749	733	-0.5
75771 LINDALE	423	14606	16382	18076	2.7	79	5226	5862	6468	2.7	2.61	4044	4550	2.8
75773 MINEOLA	499	9623	10076	10810	1.1	45	3777	3948	4237	1.1	2.51	2748	2876	1.1
75778 MURCHISON	213	3302	3725	4168	2.9	80	1350	1506	1670	2.6	2.47	1025	1146	2.7
75783 QUITMAN	499	7088	7639	8343	1.8	63	2891	3103	3384	1.7	2.39	2084	2239	1.7
75784 REKLAW	073	503	538	580	1.6	59	184	195	209	1.4	2.76	132	141	1.6
75785 RUSK	073	12064	12365	12954	0.6	28	3936	4023	4218	0.5	2.57	2848	2923	0.6
75789 TROUP	073	9414	9874	10562	1.1	46	3466	3608	3832	1.0	2.72	2612	2726	1.0
75790 VAN	467	5157	5434	5875	1.2	49	1920	2007	2158	1.1	2.66	1420	1486	1.1
75791 WHITEHOUSE	423	11842	12830	14019	1.9	65	4099	4399	4774	1.7	2.89	3309	3566	1.8
75792 WINONA	423	2993	3172	3404	1.4	54	1095	1153	1230	1.2	2.75	850	897	1.3
75798 TYLER	423	138	136	139	-0.3	7	22	21	22	-1.1	3.05	14	14	0.0
75799 TYLER	423	266	327	378	5.0	94	140	170	195	4.7	1.91	73	91	5.3
75801 PALESTINE	001	15541	16138	17180	0.9	38	6030	6256	6673	0.9	2.53	4095	4261	0.9
75803 PALESTINE	001	14817	15625	16728	1.3	50	5041	5326	5729	1.3	2.67	3825	4048	1.3
75831 BUFFALO	289	4321	4766	5281	2.3	73	1646	1814	2008	2.3	2.60	1234	1362	2.4
75833 CENTERVILLE	289	3039	3236	3511	1.5	57	1290	1367	1479	1.4	2.33	907	964	1.4
75835 CROCKETT	225	12190	12857	13593	1.3	50	4747	5005	5294	1.3	2.46	3244	3433	1.3
75838 DONIE	161	362	394	444	2.0	68	150	162	183	1.8	2.43	111	121	2.1
75839 ELKHART	001	5647	6242	6857	2.4	75	2174	2411	2654	2.5	2.55	1629	1810	2.5
75840 FAIRFIELD	161	6748	7524	8582	2.6	77	2637	2939	3351	2.6	2.52	1878	2097	2.6
75844 GRAPELAND	225	4866	4931	5117	0.3	20	2004	2024	2097	0.2	2.41	1415	1436	0.4
75845 GROVETON	455	2249	2329	2451	0.8	36	907	937	987	0.8	2.41	621	643	0.8
75846 JEWETT	289	2347	2452	2624	1.0	43	934	971	1035	0.9	2.53	690	719	1.0
75847 KENNARD	225	1928	1946	2015	0.2	18	771	776	801	0.2	2.51	550	555	0.2
75850 LEONA	289	600	645	703	1.7	62	239	255	278	1.5	2.53	170	183	1.8
75851 LOVELADY	225	4772	4823	4910	0.3	19	963	980	1013	0.4	2.49	721	736	0.5
75852 MIDWAY	313	4136	4412	4690	1.5	58	582	686	789	3.9	2.51	422	499	4.0
75853 MONTALBA	001	1193	1270	1366	1.5	57	467	495	532	1.4	2.56	350	373	1.5
75855 OAKWOOD	161	2506	2666	2927	1.5	56	1042	1104	1209	1.4	2.41	744	790	1.4
75856 PENNINGTON	455	637	648	676	0.4	22	265	268	279	0.3	2.41	188	191	0.4
75859 STREETMAN	161	833	937	1067	2.8	79	379	425	482	2.7	2.19	272	306	2.8
75860 TEAGUE	161	6784	7343	8150	1.9	65	2178	2391	2708	2.2	2.49	1529	1684	2.3
75861 TENNESSEE COLONY	001	14696	14675	14775	0.0	12	726	718	755	-0.3	2.62	532	527	-0.2
75862 TRINITY	455	9578	10151	10847	1.4	54	4045	4279	4574	1.3	2.30	2824	2996	1.4
75901 LUFKIN	005	25311	25727	26792	0.4	22	9156	9241	9575	0.2	2.72	6674	6752	0.3
75904 LUFKIN	005	30515	33016	35505	1.9	65	11345	12190	13049	1.7	2.66	8190	8844	1.8
75925 ALTO	073	3313	3372	3537	0.4	23	1259	1273	1327	0.3	2.58	892	906	0.4
75926 APPLE SPRINGS	455	1243	1277	1338	0.6	30	488	499	523	0.5	2.49	352	362	0.7
75928 BON WIER	351	2410	2438	2477	0.3	19	868	881	899	0.4	2.77	667	679	0.4
75929 BROADDUS	405	1993	2034	2109	0.5	25	879	898	932	0.5	2.26	620	635	0.6
75930 BRONSON	403	2201	2254	2330	0.6	27	914	934	964	0.5	2.41	641	657	0.6
75931 BROOKELAND	241	2389	2549	2726	1.5	58	1001	1066	1140	1.5	2.38	754	805	1.6
75932 BURKEVILLE	351	2545	2565	2604	0.2	17	1055	1070	1095	0.3	2.40	735	747	0.4
75933 CALL	351	1881	1900	1940	0.2	18	724	733	751	0.3	2.59	554	563	0.4
75935 CENTER	419	13461	14700	16393	2.1	69	4931	5331	5893	1.9	2.69	3547	3845	1.9
75936 CHESTER	457	1775	1873	1981	1.3	50	702	737	778	1.2	2.54	537	565	1.2
75937 CHIRENO	347	2955	3114	3362	1.2	49	1141	1195	1282	1.1	2.61	868	909	1.1
75938 COLMESNEIL	457	1127	1211	1294	1.7	62	425	455	484	1.6	2.66	318	341	1.7
75939 CORRIGAN	373	4122	4253	4659	0.7	34	1458	1502	1644	0.7	2.79	1087	1122	0.8
75941 DIBOLL	005	8498	8594	8900	0.3	19	2440	2461	2549	0.2	3.05	1966	1985	0.2
75943 DOUGLASS	347	1047	1096	1178	1.1	45	395	411	439	0.9	2.65	291	302	0.9
75946 GARRISON	347	3498	3665	3929	1.1	45	1308	1360	1451	0.9	2.64	950	990	1.0
75948 HEMPHILL	403	4739	4906	5098	0.8	36	2071	2139	2222	0.8	2.26	1477	1530	0.8
75949 HUNTINGTON	005	7940	8162	8507	0.7	30	2950	3018	3132	0.5	2.70	2298	2355	0.6
75951 JASPER	241	16162	16849	17790	1.0	41	6031	6302	6682	1.0	2.55	4335	4544	1.1
75954 JOAQUIN	419	3210	3463	3841	1.8	64	1220	1304	1433	1.6	2.65	901	965	1.6
75956 KIRBYVILLE	241	6546	6880	7302	1.2	47	2540	2673	2846	1.2	2.54	1857	1958	1.3
75959 MILAM	403	2406	2452	2528	0.5	24	1085	1101	1132	0.4	2.23	738	751	0.4
75960 MOSCOW	373	1229	1282	1400	1.0	42	449	467	509	0.9	2.75	337	352	1.0
75961 NACOGDOCHES	347	12802	13510	14645	1.3	50	5100	5338	5749	1.1	2.51	3208	3369	1.2
75962 NACOGDOCHES	347	2863	2868	2875	0.0	14	2	2	2	0.0	2.50	1	1	0.0
75964 NACOGDOCHES	347	18669	19921	21646	1.5	58	6543	6923	7474	1.3	2.80	4661	4940	1.4
75965 NACOGDOCHES	347	15738	17138	18819	2.0	68	6837	7418	8124	1.9	2.18	3582	3942	2.3
75966 NEWTON	351	4754	4869	4988	0.6	27	1623	1671	1723	0.7	2.55	1164	1202	0.8
75968 PINELAND	403	1283	1289	1316	0.1	15	490	491	500	0.1	2.53	351	353	0.1
75969 POLLOK	005	5201	5340	5546	0.6	29	1684	1725	1789	0.6	2.85	1333	1367	0.6
75972 SAN AUGUSTINE	405	6525	6784	7112	0.9	39	2492	2592	2723	0.9	2.51	1758	1834	1.0
75973 SHELBYVILLE	419	3266	3480	3835	1.5	57	1338	1412	1540	1.3	2.46	973	1030	1.4
75974 TENAHA	419	1798	1889	2067	1.2	47	702	730	789	0.9	2.59	509	532	1.1
75975 TIMPSON	419	3442	3763	4205	2.1	70	1381	1495	1653	1.9	2.52	961	1044	2.0
75976 WELLS	073	1697	1743	1837	0.6	30	637	649	679	0.4	2.58	468	479	0.6
75977 WIERGATE	351	269	267	272	-0.1	11	109	109	111	0.0	2.46	76	76	0.0
75979 WOODVILLE	457	10906	11136	11535	0.5	25	3891	3977	4134	0.5	2.40	2726	2795	0.6
75980 ZAVALLA	005	2665	2882	3084	1.9	65	1110	1198	1278	1.8	2.40	803	869	1.9
76001 ARLINGTON	439	21527	27122	32474	5.6	96	6896	8609	10210	5.4	3.14	5909	7367	5.3
76002 ARLINGTON	439	7350	12217	16827	12.7	100	2316	3804	5185	12.4	3.21	2009	3306	12.4
TEXAS					2.2					2.0	2.77			2.1
UNITED STATES					1.2					1.3	2.58			1.1

ZIP CODE #	POST OFFICE NAME	RACE (%) White 2000	White 2004	Black 2000	Black 2004	Asian/Pacific 2000	Asian/Pacific 2004	% Hispanic Origin 2000	% Hispanic Origin 2004	2004 AGE DISTRIBUTION (%) 0-4	5-9	10-14	15-19	20-24	25-44	45-64	65-84	85+	18+	MEDIAN AGE 2004	% 2004 Males	% 2004 Females
75705	TYLER	45.3	43.0	50.3	51.8	0.2	0.2	6.7	8.1	6.8	6.6	7.5	7.3	7.0	25.0	26.6	11.8	1.4	74.3	37.8	48.7	51.3
75706	TYLER	64.7	60.6	20.5	21.5	0.3	0.4	19.9	24.3	7.1	7.2	7.8	7.1	6.8	28.0	24.4	10.6	1.1	73.6	35.3	51.2	48.9
75707	TYLER	85.7	83.6	10.1	11.4	1.1	1.2	4.9	6.1	7.0	6.2	6.3	7.4	9.1	26.5	25.1	11.2	1.1	76.5	35.7	49.2	50.8
75708	TYLER	64.5	60.9	17.7	17.9	0.3	0.3	27.5	32.8	8.7	8.1	8.3	7.6	8.3	27.5	22.3	8.3	0.9	70.1	31.6	49.6	50.4
75709	TYLER	66.3	63.1	29.6	32.0	0.5	0.6	5.0	6.4	6.7	6.9	7.1	6.3	6.2	27.9	26.9	11.0	1.1	75.5	37.9	49.1	50.9
75750	ARP	85.6	83.4	12.2	14.1	0.2	0.1	2.4	3.0	6.5	6.8	7.1	7.2	6.0	25.9	26.9	12.2	1.3	74.8	38.3	50.5	49.5
75751	ATHENS	78.2	77.1	14.3	14.6	0.5	0.6	14.8	16.7	7.5	7.2	7.2	7.6	7.4	25.0	21.8	13.5	2.8	74.0	36.0	48.6	51.4
75752	ATHENS	90.5	88.9	3.7	4.1	0.1	0.2	7.6	9.4	6.8	6.7	6.0	5.8	6.0	23.7	27.9	15.2	1.8	77.0	41.2	49.0	51.0
75754	BEN WHEELER	87.7	86.6	5.7	6.1	0.1	0.1	8.7	10.1	6.5	6.7	6.5	6.0	5.3	23.7	28.4	15.4	1.6	76.5	41.9	50.6	49.4
75755	BIG SANDY	86.0	84.9	9.3	9.8	0.6	0.7	3.4	4.1	7.3	7.1	7.0	7.1	6.5	25.4	25.1	12.8	1.7	74.4	37.9	49.0	51.0
75756	BROWNSBORO	90.3	88.6	4.6	5.4	0.1	0.1	8.2	10.2	7.3	7.2	7.3	6.4	6.4	26.3	25.2	12.7	1.1	74.3	37.5	49.5	50.5
75757	BULLARD	91.2	90.1	5.3	5.7	0.5	0.6	3.0	3.8	6.2	6.4	6.9	6.0	5.1	24.6	27.9	15.8	1.2	76.9	41.5	48.3	51.7
75758	CHANDLER	90.0	88.5	6.4	7.2	0.4	0.5	4.4	5.6	6.6	6.5	6.6	6.1	5.2	24.2	25.6	17.3	1.9	76.5	41.4	48.9	51.1
75760	CUSHING	92.8	91.9	4.3	4.7	0.3	0.3	3.7	4.6	6.3	6.5	7.1	6.2	5.8	23.6	26.9	15.4	2.2	76.3	41.1	48.9	51.1
75762	FLINT	91.2	89.6	5.9	6.9	0.8	0.9	2.6	3.4	6.7	7.0	7.1	5.8	4.3	26.1	27.8	14.1	1.1	75.5	40.9	49.8	50.3
75763	FRANKSTON	87.9	86.1	9.1	10.5	0.2	0.2	3.4	4.2	5.8	5.9	6.5	6.3	5.2	22.9	28.1	17.0	2.2	77.8	43.1	49.1	50.9
75765	HAWKINS	84.4	83.5	12.8	13.2	0.1	0.1	3.0	3.7	4.5	4.5	4.4	6.5	7.8	18.9	29.9	21.9	1.7	83.6	47.6	48.5	51.5
75766	JACKSONVILLE	69.4	67.8	17.7	17.7	0.6	0.7	18.2	20.7	8.2	7.4	7.4	7.5	7.9	25.0	21.6	12.6	2.5	72.9	34.5	48.5	51.5
75770	LARUE	78.0	75.5	18.5	20.5	0.2	0.2	4.5	5.5	6.2	6.3	6.8	6.3	6.3	24.6	27.4	14.6	1.6	77.0	40.3	50.6	49.4
75771	LINDALE	89.8	88.3	6.3	7.0	0.4	0.5	3.8	5.0	5.8	6.0	6.5	8.2	7.3	22.1	25.3	16.5	2.1	77.8	40.6	47.9	52.1
75773	MINEOLA	86.0	84.8	7.1	7.4	0.3	0.3	8.7	10.2	6.6	6.5	7.0	6.2	6.3	21.9	25.2	17.8	2.6	76.2	41.4	48.3	51.7
75778	MURCHISON	92.0	90.6	1.8	2.2	0.2	0.2	6.2	7.7	6.4	6.5	6.4	5.9	5.6	25.2	27.6	15.3	1.1	76.9	41.1	49.7	50.3
75783	QUITMAN	91.7	90.5	4.1	4.6	0.2	0.2	5.0	6.0	5.3	5.4	6.1	5.3	5.0	22.1	27.1	20.2	3.5	79.8	45.6	48.9	51.1
75784	REKLAW	72.8	70.1	16.1	17.3	0.2	0.2	12.1	13.9	6.9	6.9	6.5	6.1	6.1	25.8	25.8	14.3	1.5	76.0	38.6	49.4	50.6
75785	RUSK	76.7	74.9	17.6	18.5	0.5	0.6	7.0	8.1	5.5	5.6	6.5	6.2	6.7	31.2	23.7	12.6	2.1	78.6	38.3	55.2	44.8
75789	TROUP	80.3	78.2	11.3	12.2	0.3	0.3	12.1	14.0	7.3	7.2	7.8	6.9	6.6	26.5	24.0	12.0	1.6	73.4	36.2	49.4	50.7
75790	VAN	94.4	93.7	1.1	1.1	0.2	0.2	7.5	8.8	6.9	6.7	7.2	7.8	6.4	23.9	24.3	14.4	2.6	74.2	38.3	48.6	51.4
75791	WHITEHOUSE	91.7	90.1	5.0	5.9	0.6	0.7	3.1	4.0	7.3	7.4	8.5	8.2	6.8	28.8	23.8	8.4	1.0	71.6	34.8	48.3	51.7
75792	WINONA	77.2	74.8	19.9	21.5	0.1	0.2	5.4	6.9	6.4	6.5	7.1	7.3	7.0	26.8	26.3	11.5	1.1	75.6	37.8	49.8	50.2
75798	TYLER	60.1	55.9	34.8	37.5	0.7	0.7	8.7	10.3	3.7	4.4	3.7	33.1	23.5	14.0	9.6	8.1	0.0	86.8	21.1	48.5	51.5
75799	TYLER	81.2	78.9	13.2	14.7	3.0	3.4	3.0	4.0	6.4	4.0	4.3	10.1	16.2	27.2	21.1	9.8	0.9	82.3	30.9	48.3	51.7
75801	PALESTINE	70.0	67.6	21.4	22.3	0.8	1.0	12.0	13.9	8.0	7.6	7.2	6.7	7.1	25.2	22.8	12.9	2.6	73.1	35.8	47.7	52.3
75803	PALESTINE	73.0	70.8	18.6	19.5	0.4	0.4	11.0	13.0	7.3	7.0	6.8	6.8	7.4	28.4	23.4	11.0	1.8	74.6	35.8	51.4	48.6
75831	BUFFALO	81.6	79.7	9.5	10.0	0.4	0.5	11.7	13.6	7.0	6.9	7.0	6.8	6.5	25.0	25.4	13.5	2.0	74.9	38.5	48.9	51.1
75833	CENTERVILLE	82.6	81.5	14.2	15.0	0.2	0.2	3.7	4.3	4.2	4.6	6.2	6.2	5.3	20.2	30.4	20.2	2.6	80.7	47.0	49.1	50.9
75835	CROCKETT	61.4	59.8	33.3	34.3	0.5	0.5	8.2	9.4	6.3	6.3	7.1	8.1	6.6	22.0	23.9	16.4	3.3	75.1	40.1	47.4	52.6
75838	DONIE	83.2	81.7	11.3	11.7	0.3	0.3	7.2	8.1	4.1	4.3	6.9	6.6	6.1	23.1	28.9	17.8	2.3	80.2	44.4	49.5	50.5
75839	ELKHART	92.6	91.3	5.4	6.3	0.2	0.2	2.4	3.1	6.5	6.4	7.4	6.6	5.9	23.5	25.9	15.0	2.6	75.5	40.5	47.7	52.3
75840	FAIRFIELD	78.1	76.7	15.8	16.3	0.4	0.5	8.4	9.8	6.4	6.2	7.1	6.9	6.2	24.6	26.7	13.7	2.5	76.1	40.4	49.4	50.6
75844	GRAPELAND	84.1	83.5	13.9	14.2	0.1	0.2	2.4	3.0	5.5	5.7	6.6	6.4	6.2	21.4	26.6	18.7	3.0	78.3	43.7	48.9	51.1
75845	GROVETON	83.4	81.8	11.4	12.2	0.0	0.1	7.3	8.5	6.7	6.2	6.7	6.4	6.5	23.7	22.6	18.3	2.9	76.5	40.6	48.1	51.9
75846	JEWETT	85.4	83.9	5.2	5.3	0.0	0.0	12.5	14.4	6.7	6.8	6.8	6.9	6.1	24.1	26.1	15.0	1.6	75.6	40.0	51.1	48.9
75847	KENNARD	78.9	77.9	19.4	20.1	0.2	0.2	1.7	2.0	6.6	6.8	7.2	6.1	5.7	24.2	26.0	15.5	1.9	75.7	40.1	49.2	50.8
75850	LEONA	85.7	84.7	12.0	12.4	0.2	0.2	3.8	4.5	4.8	5.1	6.7	7.4	5.1	20.5	28.2	20.0	2.2	78.8	45.3	51.3	48.7
75851	LOVELADY	70.2	69.7	28.7	29.1	0.0	0.1	12.7	14.7	2.9	3.1	3.4	3.1	3.7	45.1	28.6	8.7	1.4	88.7	41.1	74.3	25.7
75852	MIDWAY	47.3	46.0	38.9	38.9	0.7	0.7	21.6	23.6	2.3	2.5	3.1	4.0	20.1	47.2	13.5	6.4	1.1	90.4	29.4	79.1	20.9
75853	MONTALBA	88.4	86.5	8.2	9.4	0.5	0.6	3.8	4.8	6.7	6.6	6.5	6.4	5.9	25.4	27.2	13.7	1.7	76.0	39.9	50.9	49.1
75855	OAKWOOD	64.2	62.6	32.6	33.8	0.1	0.1	4.2	4.9	5.0	5.2	5.9	6.0	5.5	20.6	29.8	19.5	2.5	80.3	46.3	49.4	50.6
75856	PENNINGTON	90.1	88.9	6.1	6.6	0.5	0.6	4.6	5.4	7.3	6.5	6.2	5.3	4.9	20.7	27.9	18.2	3.1	76.9	44.3	49.9	50.2
75859	STREETMAN	86.2	85.1	9.8	10.4	0.5	0.4	4.7	5.9	5.8	6.1	6.6	6.0	5.2	24.1	28.8	14.9	2.5	78.0	42.7	49.8	50.2
75860	TEAGUE	72.8	71.1	21.0	21.8	0.3	0.3	10.5	12.2	5.0	4.9	5.9	6.4	10.1	31.7	21.2	12.2	2.6	80.6	35.4	57.9	42.1
75861	TENNESSEE COLONY	39.7	35.8	41.9	42.7	0.4	0.4	20.1	23.2	1.0	1.1	1.1	1.8	11.8	65.5	15.7	1.8	0.2	96.1	34.5	93.4	6.6
75862	TRINITY	82.5	81.4	13.2	13.6	0.3	0.4	5.2	6.1	5.6	5.4	5.6	6.1	6.1	21.1	27.3	20.9	2.2	79.9	45.3	49.2	50.8
75901	LUFKIN	70.9	68.7	16.7	17.0	1.0	1.2	16.8	19.3	8.3	7.4	7.1	7.2	8.0	27.6	22.1	10.8	1.6	73.1	33.5	48.7	51.3
75904	LUFKIN	71.7	69.7	18.8	19.3	0.8	0.9	13.0	15.3	7.8	7.3	7.4	7.1	7.6	27.1	22.5	11.1	2.1	73.1	34.5	47.9	52.2
75925	ALTO	68.9	66.4	23.8	25.3	0.2	0.3	8.5	9.9	7.4	6.3	7.5	6.7	5.7	23.6	24.9	15.0	3.0	74.7	39.2	47.9	52.1
75926	APPLE SPRINGS	81.6	80.6	14.9	15.5	0.0	0.0	2.8	3.3	6.7	6.8	6.3	8.5	5.2	25.1	24.4	15.3	1.7	74.2	39.1	51.8	48.2
75928	BON WIER	75.3	74.0	22.2	23.3	0.1	0.1	2.1	2.6	6.8	7.0	7.1	7.1	7.2	25.3	26.2	12.3	1.1	74.7	37.9	50.5	49.6
75929	BROADDUS	96.2	95.9	2.4	2.4	0.0	0.0	2.0	2.4	4.4	4.7	5.8	5.2	4.7	19.6	30.1	23.3	2.2	81.7	49.7	50.0	50.1
75930	BRONSON	97.2	96.9	1.4	1.5	0.0	0.0	1.4	1.6	7.6	7.1	6.7	5.8	5.1	24.2	25.6	15.8	2.1	75.0	40.5	48.8	51.2
75931	BROOKELAND	89.0	88.2	8.0	8.3	0.2	0.2	2.6	3.2	4.9	5.1	6.0	5.7	4.8	21.1	29.8	21.3	1.5	80.5	46.7	49.4	50.7
75932	BURKEVILLE	74.2	73.1	23.1	23.9	0.2	0.3	1.9	2.2	5.5	5.5	6.0	6.2	5.4	20.7	28.4	20.4	1.9	79.2	45.5	49.4	50.6
75933	CALL	72.2	70.8	26.6	27.8	0.1	0.1	2.0	2.4	6.6	6.8	7.4	7.5	7.3	25.6	25.5	12.1	1.3	74.5	37.6	49.2	50.8
75935	CENTER	69.0	66.8	19.9	20.4	0.4	0.4	13.7	15.8	7.5	7.2	7.3	6.6	6.5	26.9	22.3	13.0	2.7	74.0	36.1	48.6	51.4
75936	CHESTER	96.5	96.1	2.3	2.6	0.1	0.1	1.6	1.9	6.5	6.4	6.4	5.7	5.6	23.8	27.0	17.0	1.7	77.3	41.3	49.0	51.0
75937	CHIRENO	92.6	91.7	4.9	5.3	0.0	0.1	3.3	4.0	6.5	6.7	7.5	6.8	5.2	25.8	25.9	14.4	1.1	75.0	39.1	50.1	49.9
75938	COLMESNEIL	90.9	89.4	6.0	6.8	0.1	0.1	3.4	4.2	6.6	6.8	7.3	7.0	5.8	24.0	25.4	15.3	1.9	75.1	40.2	47.2	52.9
75939	CORRIGAN	64.2	61.6	22.4	23.5	0.3	0.3	20.8	23.3	9.0	8.3	8.5	7.6	7.4	24.6	20.9	11.7	2.1	69.7	33.0	49.0	51.0
75941	DIBOLL	65.5	63.4	16.1	15.9	0.2	0.2	31.8	35.7	8.3	7.7	7.7	6.8	7.6	31.7	21.1	7.8	1.4	72.4	32.5	54.6	45.4
75943	DOUGLASS	85.9	84.6	10.5	11.2	0.0	0.0	4.0	4.8	5.8	6.4	7.9	7.2	5.4	23.6	28.7	13.5	1.6	75.1	40.8	49.9	50.1
75946	GARRISON	75.6	74.7	21.7	22.2	0.3	0.3	2.8	3.3	6.7	6.7	7.2	7.0	6.0	25.1	25.2	13.6	2.5	75.1	38.7	49.1	50.9
75948	HEMPHILL	88.6	87.9	8.8	9.2	0.0	0.0	2.2	2.5	4.8	4.7	5.1	5.0	4.6	17.4	28.8	27.1	2.7	82.3	52.4	47.7	52.3
75949	HUNTINGTON	94.1	93.3	3.1	3.4	0.1	0.1	2.7	3.3	7.7	7.6	7.5	7.3	6.3	26.5	24.3	11.8	1.1	72.7	36.0	49.4	50.6
75951	JASPER	63.0	61.0	31.2	32.3	0.6	0.6	6.1	7.1	7.3	6.8	6.8	6.5	7.0	25.4	23.8	14.2	2.1	75.1	37.9	48.8	51.2
75954	JOAQUIN	86.9	85.9	8.6	8.9	0.2	0.2	6.0	7.0	7.4	7.2	7.6	7.2	5.9	26.6	23.7	13.2	1.4	73.6	37.0	49.3	50.7
75956	KIRBYVILLE	85.1	83.8	12.4	13.4	0.2	0.2	2.2	2.6	6.6	6.6	7.3	6.8	5.7	24.7	25.9	14.0	2.3	75.4	39.8	48.2	51.9
75959	MILAM	84.5	83.4	13.9	14.9	0.3	0.4	1.3	1.5	4.3	4.1	4.7	5.5	4.6	16.2	30.8	27.0	2.7	83.6	53.2	49.8	50.2
75960	MOSCOW	68.2	66.2	25.7	27.0	0.2	0.2	8.7	10.1	7.6	7.7	7.5	6.4	6.1	24.0	25.1	14.1	1.4	73.2	37.6	49.6	50.4
75961	NACOGDOCHES	64.5	62.3	29.1	30.2	0.4	0.4	8.8	10.5	6.8	6.9	7.2	7.3	13.6	24.5	21.9	10.2	1.6	74.8	31.5	48.1	51.9
75962	NACOGDOCHES	72.3	69.9	21.5	22.8	1.4	1.6	6.5	7.7	0.1	0.1	0.0	57.7	37.8	3.9	0.4	0.0	0.0	99.6	19.3	43.8	56.2
75964	NACOGDOCHES	66.5	64.4	18.0	18.0	0.5	0.6	23.1	26.5	8.9	8.2	7.9	7.2	7.6	29.0	19.8	9.6	1.7	70.8	31.5	49.8	50.2
75965	NACOGDOCHES	86.2	84.9	9.1	9.8	1.6	1.8	4.5	5.3	5.1	4.6	4.9	7.9	22.1	22.3	20.9	10.5	1.7	82.3	28.9	47.0	53.0
75966	NEWTON	65.0	62.7	28.9	30.3	0.7	0.8	7.8	8.9	6.9	6.8	6.8	7.0	8.8	28.0	22.7	11.4	1.8	75.6	35.2	53.5	46.5
75968	PINELAND	80.3	78.8	16.8	17.8	0.2	0.2	2.3	2.6	5.8	5.9	7.8	6.3	5.4	25.0	23.0	17.8	3.0	76.3	40.8	47.7	52.3
75969	POLLOK	90.6	89.1	4.1	4.4	0.3	0.3	6.2	7.6	6.6	6.7	7.5	7.1	6.7	30.1	25.4	9.0	0.9	74.9	36.0	51.3	48.7
75972	SAN AUGUSTINE	59.2	57.4	37.5	38.8	0.3	0.3	4.2	4.9	6.5	6.5	7.2	6.9	5.9	23.2	23.9	16.2	3.6	75.6	40.3	47.7	52.3
75973	SHELBYVILLE	71.3	69.9	25.1	26.0	0.2	0.2	4.1	4.8	6.3	6.4	6.5	6.2	5.2	24.4	25.5	17.6	1.9	77.1	41.6	47.9	52.1
75974	TENAHA	67.7	66.5	26.0	26.5	0.0	0.0	8.2	9.5	7.3	7.4	8.4	7.3	6.5	25.1	24.0	12.4	1.7	72.6	35.8	48.0	52.0
75975	TIMPSON	77.4	75.8	19.0	20.1	0.1	0.1	5.0	5.9	6.6	5.9	7.4	6.8	6.3	22.6	25.4	16.3	2.7	75.8	40.6	47.7	52.3
75976	WELLS	81.4	79.4	13.0	14.1	0.0	0.0	5.4	6.4	7.3	7.2	6.9	5.5	5.5	25.0	26.0	14.3	2.4	75.9	39.2	49.9	50.1
75977	WIERGATE	40.5	38.8	55.4	56.7	0.0	0.0	4.5	4.5	8.2	8.2	7.5	6.3	5.6	22.4	22.4	17.2	2.2	71.6	37.7	48.5	51.5
75979	WOODVILLE	74.1	72.3	19.9	20.8	0.4	0.4	5.1	6.0	5.4	5.6	6.0	5.5	7.0	28.9	23.3	15.9	2.6	79.6	39.0	53.8	46.2
75980	ZAVALLA	97.9	97.6	0.3	0.3	0.0	0.0	2.2	2.7	6.5	6.6	6.7	5.2	4.8	22.1	27.6	18.7	1.8	76.9	43.4	48.8	51.2
76001	ARLINGTON	78.2	75.0	10.5	11.5	4.3	4.9	10.1	12.9	10.1	9.8	9.0	6.8	5.3	34.4	20.3	3.9	0.3	66.5	32.0	49.2	50.8
76002	ARLINGTON	63.5	58.7	19.2	21.3	8.0	8.8	13.5	16.3	10.7	10.1	9.4	6.9	5.2	39.0	16.5	2.1	0.2	65.5	30.8	49.3	50.7
	TEXAS	71.0	69.5	11.5	11.4	2.8	3.1	32.0	34.6	7.9	7.5	7.7	7.5	8.1	29.6	21.9	8.7	1.2	72.6	32.9	49.7	50.3
	UNITED STATES	75.1	73.6	12.3	12.5	3.8	4.2	12.5	14.1	6.9	6.7	7.2	7.0	7.3	28.6	23.8	10.8	1.7	75.1	36.0	49.1	50.9

#	POST OFFICE NAME	2004 Per Capita Income	2004 HH Income Base	2004 Household Income Distribution (%): Less than $25,000	$25,000 to $49,999	$50,000 to $99,999	$100,000 to $149,999	$150,000 or More	Median Household Income: 2004	2009	2004 National Centile	2004 State Centile	2004 Home Value Base	2004 Home Value Distribution (%): Less than $50,000	$50,000 to $89,999	$90,000 to $174,999	$175,000 to $399,999	$400,000 or More	2004 Median Home Value
75705	TYLER	15711	733	34.0	31.9	26.3	6.1	1.6	35577	41704	30	36	581	31.8	38.6	26.9	2.8	0.0	67899
75706	TYLER	16156	2415	30.1	36.4	27.5	4.4	1.7	38230	44020	40	48	1939	37.1	37.8	20.6	3.5	0.9	63275
75707	TYLER	25758	4582	25.1	25.9	33.6	10.2	5.2	48847	56735	70	75	3235	20.8	27.1	35.9	14.3	2.0	92518
75708	TYLER	14181	2119	34.0	35.7	25.4	3.9	1.0	35392	41790	29	34	1597	43.5	41.6	12.2	2.3	0.4	56946
75709	TYLER	20720	1337	28.7	30.1	28.4	9.3	3.5	40623	47300	48	56	1071	23.0	33.1	34.4	8.7	0.9	83676
75750	ARP	21214	1296	25.5	31.9	31.9	7.2	3.6	43883	51707	58	66	1090	34.3	32.4	24.2	5.6	3.5	69643
75751	ATHENS	20123	5553	34.7	29.6	24.6	6.6	4.6	35988	40709	31	37	3830	31.9	28.9	26.0	12.3	1.0	76773
75752	ATHENS	21604	2543	28.8	29.1	29.5	9.7	3.0	42390	50112	54	63	2036	23.0	28.8	28.3	16.0	3.8	87394
75754	BEN WHEELER	18931	2149	32.2	29.2	30.8	5.6	2.2	39187	44735	43	52	1810	32.8	24.4	27.5	12.5	2.8	79313
75755	BIG SANDY	18835	1531	37.7	31.7	22.7	6.4	1.5	33638	38153	23	28	1184	40.7	32.5	21.6	3.1	2.0	61210
75756	BROWNSBORO	19398	891	30.3	31.5	27.6	7.0	3.6	38671	44813	42	50	750	34.5	27.3	26.8	9.5	1.9	68485
75757	BULLARD	23448	2887	21.9	29.4	34.6	9.4	4.7	48607	57270	69	74	2507	25.7	22.7	29.6	19.0	3.2	94521
75758	CHANDLER	20695	3476	29.3	33.1	27.5	7.2	2.9	38563	44151	41	49	2785	33.2	23.2	34.6	8.8	0.3	77358
75760	CUSHING	16656	955	39.1	35.4	18.5	5.9	1.2	31383	36779	16	20	775	42.1	30.1	23.5	3.7	0.7	59919
75762	FLINT	28976	3266	17.6	26.7	35.7	13.6	6.4	56295	65176	81	84	2807	15.5	15.6	41.2	24.3	3.4	119488
75763	FRANKSTON	19753	2474	33.6	31.5	27.2	5.1	2.6	36401	41672	33	40	2010	38.1	25.9	24.4	10.7	1.0	65621
75765	HAWKINS	21599	3056	25.0	34.7	31.2	6.1	3.0	42342	48617	54	63	2566	28.9	29.6	32.4	8.1	1.1	78406
75766	JACKSONVILLE	16422	8375	40.1	31.3	21.3	4.2	3.2	31671	35863	17	21	5615	38.3	29.1	23.7	7.3	1.6	65025
75770	LARUE	19424	944	32.5	31.5	27.3	5.8	2.9	37214	43108	36	43	801	38.3	30.8	20.0	9.1	1.8	61596
75771	LINDALE	20929	5862	23.9	32.0	32.1	8.4	3.6	44150	52283	59	67	4889	23.6	23.0	36.8	15.3	1.4	95785
75773	MINEOLA	19165	3948	33.5	31.8	26.0	5.4	3.3	36614	41223	34	41	2973	29.0	26.0	33.8	9.4	1.8	83219
75778	MURCHISON	19987	1506	29.0	32.4	29.6	7.4	1.7	39556	45992	45	53	1276	35.0	28.3	26.7	7.8	2.2	69192
75783	QUITMAN	23097	3103	31.1	32.7	26.8	5.0	4.5	37611	42771	38	45	2482	25.5	27.8	32.8	12.2	1.7	85829
75784	REKLAW	15085	195	33.9	38.5	23.1	4.1	0.5	36292	41308	33	39	165	60.0	24.9	7.3	6.1	1.8	44310
75785	RUSK	15253	4023	36.3	36.2	23.3	3.1	1.1	32538	37182	19	24	3084	38.1	34.2	21.5	5.8	0.4	62857
75789	TROUP	17660	3608	33.3	30.4	28.2	5.5	2.6	38679	43908	42	50	2875	41.9	28.8	20.5	7.4	1.4	61411
75790	VAN	20078	2007	29.0	35.5	24.6	7.1	3.8	37936	43427	39	46	1527	27.9	32.2	31.1	7.9	1.0	77553
75791	WHITEHOUSE	23404	4399	18.1	25.4	39.9	11.4	5.1	54685	63839	79	83	3651	18.2	26.9	43.2	8.9	2.8	95407
75792	WINONA	18246	1153	28.3	31.5	31.9	6.4	1.9	39889	47617	46	54	957	33.8	33.0	26.1	6.6	0.5	69085
75798	TYLER	12596	21	42.9	28.6	28.6	0.0	0.0	28571	35000	10	12	13	23.1	61.5	15.4	0.0	0.0	75000
75799	TYLER	43387	170	30.0	22.9	22.9	11.8	12.4	45000	57968	61	68	76	0.0	1.3	36.8	59.2	2.6	202941
75801	PALESTINE	17524	6256	37.0	32.2	24.5	4.2	2.1	33802	38305	23	29	4077	32.6	35.2	23.7	7.6	0.9	68245
75803	PALESTINE	18268	5326	33.8	32.2	26.1	4.5	3.4	37105	42119	36	43	4055	31.6	32.3	26.2	8.7	1.3	71734
75831	BUFFALO	17914	1814	36.7	30.3	25.0	6.0	2.0	34167	39401	25	30	1467	37.2	29.5	24.3	8.7	0.4	67525
75833	CENTERVILLE	21722	1367	41.6	24.8	22.1	6.2	5.3	31597	37477	17	21	1133	38.9	22.2	27.0	8.7	3.2	66458
75835	CROCKETT	17517	5005	42.5	29.5	21.2	4.5	2.3	30634	35266	14	18	3440	40.0	34.3	17.9	7.1	0.7	59556
75838	DONIE	22453	162	40.7	16.1	29.6	10.5	3.1	33447	40782	22	27	138	34.1	23.9	33.3	6.5	2.2	79091
75839	ELKHART	17601	2411	33.8	31.2	27.8	5.5	1.6	35660	40442	30	36	1957	44.1	27.5	21.3	7.1	0.1	58694
75840	FAIRFIELD	20712	2939	34.3	28.1	28.7	6.0	3.0	37112	43652	36	43	2268	30.3	34.5	25.6	8.3	1.4	71250
75844	GRAPELAND	18186	2024	41.5	26.2	25.4	5.4	1.5	31332	35789	16	20	1612	35.7	35.1	21.6	6.6	1.0	63926
75845	GROVETON	16061	937	50.4	27.4	18.1	2.9	1.2	24722	27692	4	6	684	50.4	29.8	18.3	1.2	0.3	49615
75846	JEWETT	22578	971	31.9	27.0	30.1	7.0	4.0	40046	47006	46	54	770	36.5	31.8	22.6	8.1	1.0	67544
75847	KENNARD	17695	776	41.4	27.6	23.1	5.7	2.3	32690	37288	20	24	646	50.5	27.7	14.4	5.7	1.7	49455
75850	LEONA	20267	255	32.9	31.4	24.3	8.6	2.8	36168	42123	32	38	227	34.8	22.9	27.3	9.7	5.3	70714
75851	LOVELADY	15585	980	29.6	35.1	29.9	3.9	1.5	38390	44535	41	49	814	39.9	31.8	21.1	7.1	0.0	57736
75852	MIDWAY	14704	686	37.2	31.1	25.1	3.2	3.5	32872	37419	21	25	547	42.8	22.7	28.2	4.6	1.8	60441
75853	MONTALBA	19455	495	32.9	28.9	29.5	5.7	3.0	38422	44389	41	49	410	36.6	21.7	31.2	8.1	2.4	73889
75855	OAKWOOD	17815	1104	42.1	29.6	20.5	6.2	1.6	31421	37230	16	21	925	30.0	35.4	20.5	11.9	2.3	73214
75856	PENNINGTON	17985	268	47.0	35.8	13.4	1.9	1.9	25985	30193	6	7	221	35.8	30.8	27.6	1.4	4.5	64565
75859	STREETMAN	24680	425	32.7	28.5	28.2	7.3	3.3	40237	46907	47	55	350	37.7	27.7	22.6	10.3	1.7	66563
75860	TEAGUE	18393	2391	36.1	24.8	30.5	6.4	2.1	35682	41943	30	36	1839	41.9	26.6	25.1	6.2	0.2	59901
75861	TENNESSEE COLONY	13764	718	29.9	27.9	35.1	4.5	2.7	39647	45444	45	53	523	36.5	22.4	29.1	11.3	0.8	77444
75862	TRINITY	19229	4279	39.1	32.2	22.3	4.0	2.4	32152	36679	18	23	3373	41.5	34.6	17.8	5.2	0.9	60411
75901	LUFKIN	18741	9241	33.1	29.7	27.4	6.3	3.5	38367	43815	41	49	6213	31.4	35.0	25.0	7.3	1.3	71505
75904	LUFKIN	19459	12190	31.6	30.9	27.2	7.0	3.2	38739	44404	42	50	8449	29.6	30.4	31.7	7.4	0.9	76859
75925	ALTO	16817	1273	39.9	32.7	21.5	4.0	2.0	32292	36660	19	23	1000	46.7	22.9	24.1	5.5	0.8	56600
75926	APPLE SPRINGS	15611	499	42.3	31.9	20.6	4.0	1.2	31331	34570	16	20	425	44.7	30.4	18.4	6.6	0.0	57759
75928	BON WIER	14813	881	44.8	31.9	19.2	2.5	1.6	29023	33234	10	13	746	50.0	32.8	13.9	3.2	0.0	50000
75929	BROADDUS	19497	898	40.3	35.0	17.9	3.0	3.8	30560	35526	14	17	765	47.8	26.5	20.0	5.6	0.0	54342
75930	BRONSON	16569	934	39.6	33.4	22.7	2.7	1.6	32239	36053	18	23	788	49.4	27.2	20.4	3.1	0.0	50833
75931	BROOKELAND	24787	1066	29.1	33.9	27.8	4.2	5.1	38548	45000	41	49	918	31.7	30.5	25.9	10.7	1.2	74085
75932	BURKEVILLE	17659	1070	39.2	30.8	24.3	4.4	1.3	31809	35997	17	22	899	44.4	25.9	20.9	6.3	2.5	59182
75933	CALL	17141	733	43.1	31.4	20.6	3.3	1.6	29832	34028	12	15	611	50.1	32.2	14.4	3.1	0.2	49941
75935	CENTER	17956	5331	36.8	32.2	23.4	4.9	2.7	33320	37900	22	27	4000	44.2	26.7	21.8	6.0	1.4	60520
75936	CHESTER	24299	737	32.6	26.3	30.0	4.6	6.5	38133	43832	40	47	624	48.1	26.6	17.6	6.7	1.0	52727
75937	CHIRENO	20816	1195	36.4	31.5	24.2	5.0	2.9	35273	41432	29	34	997	47.6	28.6	16.7	4.3	2.8	53730
75938	COLMESNEIL	15197	455	40.9	29.9	23.3	4.2	1.8	30875	35373	15	18	383	46.7	26.1	19.6	6.3	1.3	53571
75939	CORRIGAN	14048	1502	42.3	33.2	18.2	4.9	1.4	30289	33936	13	17	1127	53.5	29.1	10.9	5.3	1.2	46938
75941	DIBOLL	13472	2461	34.0	34.2	27.6	3.3	1.0	36146	40554	32	38	1749	46.4	29.6	20.7	2.9	0.3	55165
75943	DOUGLASS	21722	411	24.8	36.3	27.0	8.3	3.7	44315	51271	59	67	343	24.8	23.6	31.8	17.2	2.6	94583
75946	GARRISON	19266	1360	35.7	27.2	27.2	5.7	4.2	37402	44360	37	44	1088	40.4	24.2	24.8	9.0	1.7	67910
75948	HEMPHILL	18215	2139	41.5	33.2	19.5	3.4	2.3	29484	32949	11	14	1801	41.3	25.4	25.3	7.0	1.0	61250
75949	HUNTINGTON	17526	3018	29.9	33.3	30.3	5.6	1.0	37807	43060	39	46	2465	37.2	31.8	23.3	7.2	0.6	66710
75951	JASPER	18553	6302	41.1	27.0	24.8	4.4	2.8	32880	37443	21	25	4668	36.9	31.0	24.7	7.3	0.1	67558
75954	JOAQUIN	16225	1304	39.7	30.2	23.2	5.1	1.8	32066	36328	18	23	1059	44.5	27.7	21.5	3.2	3.1	56724
75956	KIRBYVILLE	17479	2673	38.5	34.5	22.0	3.5	1.7	31779	36254	17	22	2136	42.2	32.4	21.1	4.0	0.3	59540
75959	MILAM	20642	1101	38.9	33.7	19.6	3.1	4.7	31164	35509	15	19	947	42.7	25.6	25.6	5.8	0.4	60211
75960	MOSCOW	14730	467	40.9	32.1	21.2	4.7	1.1	31291	35783	16	20	379	51.2	28.5	12.9	7.1	0.3	48929
75961	NACOGDOCHES	16225	5338	46.7	26.0	19.8	4.7	2.9	27656	32549	8	11	3047	37.6	29.8	23.6	7.3	1.7	70849
75962	NACOGDOCHES	12448	2	100.0	0.0	0.0	0.0	0.0	5000	5000	0	1	0	0.0	0.0	0.0	0.0	0.0	0
75964	NACOGDOCHES	15251	6923	41.2	32.3	19.9	4.2	2.5	31217	36386	16	20	4514	41.5	29.1	22.3	5.7	1.3	64109
75965	NACOGDOCHES	25607	7418	38.8	21.2	24.0	10.0	6.0	37230	45163	36	43	3762	13.4	15.8	45.4	23.0	2.4	121133
75966	NEWTON	14986	1671	42.7	31.4	20.8	3.4	1.7	30189	34017	13	16	1276	46.5	33.8	16.9	2.7	0.2	54737
75968	PINELAND	19605	491	47.7	28.1	17.9	3.1	3.3	26805	29780	7	9	382	53.9	28.5	15.2	2.4	0.0	46591
75969	POLLOK	18389	1725	27.2	33.5	31.1	5.6	2.6	41548	47237	51	60	1452	47.9	27.3	19.3	4.1	1.5	52109
75972	SAN AUGUSTINE	18205	2592	42.7	29.1	21.0	4.7	2.6	30630	34726	14	17	1934	47.1	31.0	15.8	5.8	0.4	54101
75973	SHELBYVILLE	18755	1412	37.7	31.0	22.6	6.7	2.1	33278	37142	22	27	1187	42.5	28.5	22.2	5.9	0.9	61250
75974	TENAHA	14958	730	43.7	30.8	20.6	3.3	1.6	29243	33053	11	14	571	40.6	28.2	23.6	3.0	4.6	58231
75975	TIMPSON	17302	1495	41.4	28.8	21.9	4.4	3.5	31777	35947	17	22	1183	41.1	22.2	28.8	6.9	1.0	64036
75976	WELLS	15015	649	40.7	32.5	22.0	3.2	1.5	31298	35530	16	20	516	48.8	24.8	21.1	4.8	0.4	51714
75977	WIERGATE	12235	109	53.2	30.3	14.7	1.8	0.0	23015	26220	3	4	87	70.1	13.8	14.9	1.2	0.0	27500
75979	WOODVILLE	17087	3977	40.0	30.1	24.1	4.0	1.8	32478	37409	19	23	3110	44.4	27.7	20.6	5.9	1.5	57733
75980	ZAVALLA	17421	1198	39.2	34.1	20.5	4.7	1.4	31550	36206	16	21	1012	48.4	30.0	18.6	3.0	0.0	51882
76001	ARLINGTON	28256	8609	5.6	17.3	45.8	22.1	9.2	75618	87499	93	94	7715	2.2	10.6	57.9	27.7	1.6	125457
76002	ARLINGTON	26126	3804	4.2	14.2	53.2	23.5	4.9	78196	91315	94	95	3632	1.7	9.1	68.5	20.5	0.2	132890
	TEXAS	23284		26.2	27.7	29.5	10.3	6.3	45778	54246				21.6	26.1	33.4	15.6	3.4	93683
	UNITED STATES	25866		24.7	27.1	30.8	10.9	6.5	48124	56710				10.9	15.0	33.7	30.1	10.4	145905

ZIP CODE		FINANCIAL SERVICES				THE HOME						ENTERTAINMENT						PERSONAL			
						Home Improvements		Furnishings													
#	POST OFFICE NAME	Auto Loan	Home Loan	Invest-ments	Retire-ment Plans	Home Repair	Lawn & Garden	Comput-ers & Hard-ware	Major Appli-ances	TV, Radio, Sound Equip-ment	Furni-ture	Dine out/ Carry out	Sports Equip-ment	Fees & Tickets	Toys & Games	Travel	Cable TV	Apparel & Services	Auto Repairs	Health Insur-ance	Pets & Supplies
75705	TYLER	80	61	37	55	65	73	58	68	65	60	78	81	52	74	59	68	73	68	78	91
75706	TYLER	75	64	47	61	66	71	62	69	65	64	80	79	58	76	62	66	76	68	72	84
75707	TYLER	100	92	85	92	93	99	93	95	94	92	117	114	90	115	92	93	112	96	95	113
75708	TYLER	66	59	46	57	60	63	57	62	58	59	72	71	54	68	56	58	69	61	62	73
75709	TYLER	90	75	53	70	80	88	71	80	77	71	93	95	67	93	72	80	88	78	89	104
75750	ARP	89	79	62	77	82	90	77	83	81	77	98	96	74	98	77	82	93	81	88	101
75751	ATHENS	78	75	74	72	75	81	75	77	77	76	95	89	74	94	75	77	92	78	78	88
75752	ATHENS	98	72	43	67	80	90	72	84	81	72	96	100	63	93	73	85	89	84	98	112
75754	BEN WHEELER	83	66	46	63	72	80	66	75	72	66	86	87	60	83	67	74	80	74	84	95
75755	BIG SANDY	81	63	42	60	68	77	64	72	70	63	84	83	59	82	64	73	78	71	81	91
75756	BROWNSBORO	88	73	49	68	76	82	70	78	75	71	90	92	64	85	69	76	85	78	84	99
75757	BULLARD	92	84	71	81	87	97	80	88	84	83	103	96	78	95	82	86	98	86	95	103
75758	CHANDLER	86	71	53	67	75	85	70	78	75	71	91	88	65	86	70	78	85	77	87	96
75760	CUSHING	75	53	27	47	58	66	51	62	59	52	70	73	44	67	51	63	65	61	74	85
75762	FLINT	114	112	102	111	116	122	105	113	106	106	131	130	105	130	108	106	126	110	115	134
75763	FRANKSTON	84	66	44	63	71	79	66	75	72	66	86	87	59	82	66	73	80	74	83	95
75765	HAWKINS	85	71	57	67	77	89	68	78	74	71	91	84	65	82	71	79	84	77	91	96
75766	JACKSONVILLE	68	59	51	56	60	67	60	64	64	60	78	74	57	75	60	65	75	65	69	77
75770	LARUE	93	65	35	60	74	84	64	78	74	64	87	94	55	84	66	78	80	77	93	108
75771	LINDALE	89	77	61	74	81	92	75	83	80	76	97	92	72	90	77	83	91	82	93	100
75773	MINEOLA	82	60	37	57	68	78	63	73	71	61	84	84	55	81	63	75	77	72	87	94
75778	MURCHISON	83	66	45	62	72	80	64	74	71	65	85	86	59	82	66	74	79	73	83	96
75783	QUITMAN	93	72	51	69	80	92	72	84	81	72	96	95	66	91	75	85	89	83	99	107
75784	REKLAW	78	52	24	45	59	68	51	63	61	52	72	76	43	68	52	66	65	63	78	90
75785	RUSK	66	48	27	44	53	61	48	57	55	48	65	66	42	63	48	59	60	56	68	75
75789	TROUP	79	65	46	62	69	77	64	71	69	64	83	83	59	81	64	71	78	70	79	90
75790	VAN	88	70	49	68	76	86	71	80	78	70	93	93	66	92	72	81	86	79	90	100
75791	WHITEHOUSE	99	106	98	107	103	102	98	99	92	100	116	116	98	115	96	88	114	97	89	111
75792	WINONA	81	71	53	68	74	79	67	74	71	68	86	87	64	84	68	71	82	73	78	93
75798	TYLER	51	40	53	46	40	45	56	49	55	53	70	63	51	65	50	51	68	56	46	55
75799	TYLER	115	91	118	102	90	100	126	110	124	118	156	141	115	146	113	114	151	125	102	123
75801	PALESTINE	68	58	52	57	60	67	61	64	64	60	79	74	58	76	60	65	75	65	69	76
75803	PALESTINE	78	68	56	66	71	78	69	73	72	68	88	85	65	85	69	73	83	73	78	87
75831	BUFFALO	75	62	45	59	65	73	63	69	68	63	81	79	58	77	63	69	76	69	76	84
75833	CENTERVILLE	87	65	41	59	72	84	65	76	74	64	88	88	58	84	67	79	81	76	91	101
75835	CROCKETT	69	53	41	50	57	67	58	63	65	56	78	72	52	74	57	68	72	64	74	78
75838	DONIE	88	66	44	64	72	87	73	81	82	70	97	90	65	91	73	87	88	81	97	97
75839	ELKHART	79	56	31	52	63	73	57	68	66	56	78	80	50	74	58	70	71	68	82	91
75840	FAIRFIELD	90	66	42	62	73	85	67	78	77	67	91	91	60	88	68	81	84	78	93	103
75844	GRAPELAND	76	54	31	51	61	71	57	66	65	55	76	77	50	73	57	69	70	66	80	86
75845	GROVETON	68	48	28	44	54	63	50	58	58	49	68	68	44	64	50	62	62	58	71	77
75846	JEWETT	94	79	57	74	84	91	75	85	81	76	97	99	69	94	77	83	92	85	93	109
75847	KENNARD	73	56	38	54	61	71	59	66	65	57	78	75	54	75	59	68	72	65	76	82
75850	LEONA	97	65	29	56	73	84	62	78	75	64	88	93	53	84	63	81	80	77	96	111
75851	LOVELADY	44	38	34	36	41	50	38	44	42	39	51	44	37	45	40	45	47	43	52	49
75852	MIDWAY	48	36	23	34	39	47	39	43	44	37	51	49	34	49	39	46	47	43	52	54
75853	MONTALBA	80	69	52	67	71	77	69	74	71	69	87	85	64	82	68	71	82	74	77	88
75855	OAKWOOD	69	55	41	51	60	71	56	64	63	55	75	71	51	70	58	67	69	64	76	79
75856	PENNINGTON	81	55	25	47	62	71	53	66	64	54	75	79	45	71	54	69	68	65	81	93
75859	STREETMAN	93	70	42	66	78	88	70	82	79	69	93	96	62	91	71	83	86	81	96	108
75860	TEAGUE	65	55	46	52	58	66	58	62	64	57	76	70	55	74	58	66	72	62	70	73
75861	TENNESSEE COLONY	76	60	39	56	63	71	59	67	64	60	77	78	53	73	59	66	72	66	74	85
75862	TRINITY	69	56	43	52	61	70	57	64	62	56	75	71	52	71	58	66	70	63	74	79
75901	LUFKIN	77	70	65	69	71	76	71	74	73	72	90	85	69	88	70	72	87	74	74	85
75904	LUFKIN	78	72	66	70	73	79	72	75	74	72	91	86	70	89	72	74	88	75	77	87
75925	ALTO	72	53	34	51	59	70	58	65	65	55	76	74	51	73	58	69	70	65	78	81
75926	APPLE SPRINGS	74	49	22	43	56	64	48	60	57	49	67	71	41	64	48	62	61	59	73	85
75928	BON WIER	77	52	23	45	59	67	50	62	60	51	71	75	42	67	51	65	64	62	77	89
75929	BROADDUS	80	57	31	50	64	73	54	67	64	55	75	79	47	72	56	69	69	66	81	94
75930	BRONSON	74	51	25	44	58	66	49	61	58	50	69	72	42	65	50	63	63	60	74	86
75931	BROOKELAND	104	77	47	69	87	99	73	90	85	73	100	106	65	98	77	91	93	88	107	124
75932	BURKEVILLE	72	55	37	49	61	69	53	63	61	53	73	73	48	70	55	66	67	63	75	85
75933	CALL	84	56	25	48	63	73	54	68	65	55	77	81	46	72	55	70	70	67	83	96
75935	CENTER	84	61	37	56	68	78	62	73	71	62	85	85	55	81	63	75	78	72	86	96
75936	CHESTER	109	80	48	74	92	103	77	94	88	76	104	112	67	102	81	94	96	93	112	130
75937	CHIRENO	102	68	31	59	77	89	66	83	80	67	94	99	56	88	67	86	85	82	102	117
75938	COLMESNEIL	76	51	24	44	58	67	49	62	59	50	70	73	42	66	50	64	63	61	76	87
75939	CORRIGAN	69	49	29	44	54	62	50	58	58	50	69	69	44	66	50	61	63	58	69	79
75941	DIBOLL	67	54	41	50	56	63	55	61	60	56	73	69	51	68	54	62	69	61	67	74
75943	DOUGLASS	103	74	41	70	85	94	73	89	83	72	98	106	63	95	75	86	90	88	104	122
75946	GARRISON	86	66	43	62	72	82	67	76	75	66	89	88	61	86	67	79	83	75	89	97
75948	HEMPHILL	67	54	41	50	60	69	53	62	60	53	71	69	49	67	56	64	66	61	74	78
75949	HUNTINGTON	80	63	42	59	68	76	62	71	68	62	82	83	57	79	62	71	77	70	79	91
75951	JASPER	78	61	44	57	65	76	63	70	71	62	84	80	58	80	63	74	78	70	82	88
75954	JOAQUIN	81	54	25	47	62	71	52	66	63	53	74	78	45	70	53	68	67	65	81	93
75956	KIRBYVILLE	78	55	33	50	61	71	57	66	66	56	78	78	50	74	57	70	72	66	79	88
75959	MILAM	71	63	58	57	68	80	59	69	65	62	79	71	57	71	64	69	73	67	82	83
75960	MOSCOW	76	51	23	44	58	67	49	62	59	50	70	74	42	66	50	64	63	61	76	87
75961	NACOGDOCHES	62	50	48	49	51	58	57	57	60	56	74	68	52	69	54	60	70	60	60	69
75962	NACOGDOCHES	7	4	5	5	4	5	8	6	8	7	10	9	7	9	7	7	9	8	6	7
75964	NACOGDOCHES	67	57	48	54	58	64	59	62	62	59	76	72	55	73	57	63	72	62	65	74
75965	NACOGDOCHES	82	69	77	73	70	76	85	78	84	80	105	98	79	101	79	80	101	85	76	90
75966	NEWTON	66	48	31	44	53	61	51	57	58	50	69	67	45	66	50	61	64	58	68	75
75968	PINELAND	95	63	29	55	72	83	61	77	74	62	87	91	52	82	62	80	79	76	94	109
75969	POLLOK	90	75	52	70	78	85	71	80	76	72	93	94	66	89	71	78	87	79	87	102
75972	SAN AUGUSTINE	79	57	37	51	62	73	60	68	69	59	82	78	53	76	59	74	75	68	83	88
75973	SHELBYVILLE	84	60	32	52	67	77	57	70	67	57	79	83	49	76	59	72	72	69	85	98
75974	TENAHA	73	49	22	42	55	64	47	59	57	48	67	70	40	63	48	61	61	58	73	84
75975	TIMPSON	78	54	28	48	61	71	55	66	64	54	76	77	47	72	55	69	69	65	80	89
75976	WELLS	73	49	22	42	56	64	47	59	57	48	67	71	40	64	48	62	61	59	73	84
75977	WIERGATE	44	35	37	31	35	43	40	41	46	41	55	44	38	49	39	49	52	43	49	48
75979	WOODVILLE	65	48	32	44	53	62	50	57	57	49	68	66	45	64	51	61	62	57	69	74
75980	ZAVALLA	75	54	32	48	61	70	52	64	60	52	71	75	45	69	54	65	66	63	77	88
76001	ARLINGTON	126	144	140	150	138	133	130	129	119	135	151	151	134	152	127	111	150	125	110	141
76002	ARLINGTON	120	136	131	142	129	125	123	121	112	128	143	142	126	143	119	104	141	118	103	133
	TEXAS	94	90	91	90	89	95	92	93	92	93	115	107	90	112	90	90	112	94	89	104
	UNITED STATES	100	100	100	100	100	100	100	100	100	100	100	100	100	100	100	100	100	100	100	100

TEXAS

A   76006-76207

POPULATION CHANGE

ZIP CODE		POPULATION			2000-2004 ANNUAL RATE		HOUSEHOLDS					FAMILIES		
# POST OFFICE NAME	COUNTY FIPS CODE	2000	2004	2009	% Rate	State Centile	2000	2004	2009	% Annual Rate 2000-2004	2004 Average HH Size	2000	2004	% Annual Rate 2000-2004
76006 ARLINGTON	439	24336	26037	28915	1.6	59	12849	13586	14926	1.3	1.91	5338	5643	1.3
76008 ALEDO	367	8432	9839	11519	3.7	88	2904	3376	3929	3.6	2.91	2449	2842	3.6
76009 ALVARADO	251	18036	19849	22423	2.3	73	6017	6601	7431	2.2	2.97	4814	5287	2.2
76010 ARLINGTON	439	53493	58544	65917	2.2	70	18311	19767	22004	1.8	2.93	12213	13118	1.7
76011 ARLINGTON	439	29704	32584	36486	2.2	71	12262	13263	14699	1.9	2.43	6488	7013	1.9
76012 ARLINGTON	439	25557	27022	29631	1.3	52	9982	10477	11407	1.2	2.51	7126	7467	1.1
76013 ARLINGTON	439	32071	35137	39416	2.2	71	13716	14950	16645	2.1	2.33	8338	9067	2.0
76014 ARLINGTON	439	31332	33687	37335	1.7	62	10400	11106	12208	1.6	3.03	7828	8350	1.5
76015 ARLINGTON	439	15999	16669	18221	1.0	41	6243	6499	7061	1.0	2.54	4307	4469	0.9
76016 ARLINGTON	439	30630	32359	35508	1.3	51	10691	11232	12230	1.2	2.88	8948	9393	1.2
76017 ARLINGTON	439	41752	45838	51412	2.2	72	15425	16866	18784	2.1	2.71	11671	12695	2.0
76018 ARLINGTON	439	23876	27974	32344	3.8	89	7467	8674	9938	3.6	3.22	6280	7293	3.6
76019 ARLINGTON	439	4	4	4	0.0	13	3	3	3	0.0	1.33	2	1	-15.1
76020 AZLE	367	23287	25249	28301	1.9	66	8672	9348	10410	1.8	2.68	6575	7089	1.8
76021 BEDFORD	439	33485	36495	40612	2.1	68	14289	15498	17120	1.9	2.33	8943	9632	1.8
76022 BEDFORD	439	13768	14578	15994	1.4	53	6007	6346	6921	1.3	2.26	3635	3826	1.2
76023 BOYD	497	5481	6020	6775	2.2	72	1973	2149	2401	2.0	2.80	1583	1728	2.1
76028 BURLESON	251	39498	45104	51763	3.2	83	14138	16034	18283	3.0	2.79	11374	12911	3.0
76031 CLEBURNE	251	17057	18708	21074	2.2	71	5676	6180	6923	2.0	2.98	4410	4813	2.1
76033 CLEBURNE	251	21703	23930	27030	2.3	73	8164	8949	10058	2.2	2.63	6022	6615	2.2
76034 COLLEYVILLE	439	19385	22235	25388	3.3	84	6326	7201	8151	3.1	3.08	5719	6506	3.1
76035 CRESSON	221	645	788	928	4.8	94	232	280	328	4.5	2.81	184	222	4.5
76036 CROWLEY	439	12031	15546	19004	6.2	97	4335	5473	6591	5.6	2.83	3405	4358	6.0
76039 EULESS	439	28066	29726	32937	1.4	53	12202	12916	14215	1.4	2.30	7115	7458	1.1
76040 EULESS	439	23221	25719	29003	2.4	75	9937	10974	12293	2.4	2.34	5568	6075	2.1
76041 FORRESTON	139	185	199	228	1.7	62	59	63	71	1.6	3.16	48	51	1.4
76043 GLEN ROSE	425	5395	6090	7060	2.9	80	1923	2162	2498	2.8	2.75	1439	1623	2.9
76044 GODLEY	251	3308	3633	4090	2.2	72	1110	1208	1350	2.0	2.99	901	982	2.1
76048 GRANBURY	221	19390	20520	22477	1.3	52	7583	8032	8814	1.4	2.48	5377	5679	1.3
76049 GRANBURY	221	17838	20456	23295	3.3	84	7116	8123	9228	3.2	2.52	5625	6447	3.3
76050 GRANDVIEW	251	5568	6004	6684	1.8	64	1933	2072	2296	1.7	2.85	1575	1690	1.7
76051 GRAPEVINE	439	41863	47115	53675	2.8	79	15618	17511	19834	2.7	2.68	11285	12571	2.6
76052 HASLET	439	2837	4816	6679	13.3	100	951	1594	2187	12.9	3.02	810	1359	13.0
76053 HURST	439	24376	26408	29643	1.9	65	9620	10325	11477	1.7	2.55	6664	7146	1.7
76054 HURST	439	11930	12616	13924	1.3	52	4419	4634	5069	1.1	2.70	3596	3771	1.1
76055 ITASCA	217	2677	2843	3095	1.4	55	964	1015	1096	1.2	2.73	711	751	1.3
76058 JOSHUA	251	14964	16993	19557	3.0	82	4982	5613	6415	2.9	3.02	4056	4574	2.9
76059 KEENE	251	4637	5124	5759	2.4	74	1526	1690	1904	2.4	2.80	1075	1188	2.4
76060 KENNEDALE	439	5961	6859	7828	3.4	85	2124	2423	2741	3.2	2.81	1503	1712	3.1
76063 MANSFIELD	439	32076	39730	47200	5.2	95	10220	12592	14858	5.0	3.10	8692	10733	5.1
76064 MAYPEARL	139	1185	1317	1537	2.5	76	397	437	506	2.3	3.01	316	348	2.3
76065 MIDLOTHIAN	139	17919	21740	26540	4.7	93	5986	7197	8709	4.4	3.02	4979	5999	4.5
76066 MILLSAP	367	2566	2835	3236	2.4	74	971	1067	1211	2.2	2.66	764	841	2.3
76067 MINERAL WELLS	363	21707	21968	22436	0.3	19	7523	7520	7605	0.0	2.71	5261	5283	0.1
76070 NEMO	425	456	518	603	3.1	82	162	182	211	2.8	2.84	131	148	2.9
76071 NEWARK	497	2836	3102	3482	2.1	70	1008	1094	1218	2.0	2.83	776	844	2.0
76073 PARADISE	497	4416	4858	5472	2.3	73	1552	1696	1898	2.1	2.86	1271	1392	2.2
76077 RAINBOW	425	578	653	757	2.9	80	216	242	280	2.7	2.64	166	186	2.7
76078 RHOME	497	5304	6434	7622	4.7	93	1828	2197	2583	4.4	2.93	1480	1783	4.5
76082 SPRINGTOWN	367	14622	16829	19633	3.4	85	4927	5618	6506	3.1	2.99	3993	4562	3.2
76084 VENUS	251	6799	8051	9408	4.1	90	1874	2246	2647	4.4	3.22	1562	1870	4.3
76085 WEATHERFORD	367	6851	7772	9015	3.0	81	2428	2739	3160	2.9	2.83	1943	2195	2.9
76086 WEATHERFORD	367	17053	18336	20691	1.7	62	6652	7137	8048	1.7	2.46	4459	4782	1.7
76087 WEATHERFORD	367	18060	20921	24517	3.5	87	6526	7520	8763	3.4	2.78	5337	6145	3.4
76088 WEATHERFORD	367	8795	9614	10891	2.1	70	3142	3441	3909	2.2	2.62	2520	2761	2.2
76092 SOUTHLAKE	439	20964	25448	29889	4.7	93	6215	7400	8565	4.2	3.44	5770	6870	4.2
76093 RIO VISTA	251	1716	2025	2364	4.0	90	609	715	830	3.9	2.83	483	566	3.8
76102 FORT WORTH	439	8442	8708	9302	0.7	34	2279	2438	2725	1.6	2.13	1046	1075	0.7
76103 FORT WORTH	439	14368	15141	16576	1.2	49	5226	5417	5862	0.9	2.72	3327	3442	0.8
76104 FORT WORTH	439	17475	17756	19170	0.4	22	5925	5996	6468	0.3	2.70	3620	3657	0.2
76105 FORT WORTH	439	22084	22901	25003	0.9	37	6519	6701	7250	0.7	3.36	4885	5010	0.6
76106 FORT WORTH	439	51833	53833	58675	0.9	38	13224	13568	14652	0.6	3.87	10695	10961	0.6
76107 FORT WORTH	439	26629	27201	29631	0.5	25	12093	12228	13193	0.3	2.21	6383	6428	0.2
76108 FORT WORTH	439	26740	28554	31715	1.6	58	9854	10423	11483	1.3	2.69	7166	7613	1.4
76109 FORT WORTH	439	22219	23237	25363	1.1	44	10381	10829	11778	1.0	2.06	5300	5491	0.8
76110 FORT WORTH	439	32919	34331	37638	1.0	42	10335	10552	11404	0.5	3.23	7178	7326	0.5
76111 FORT WORTH	439	20403	21168	23012	0.9	38	6949	7116	7652	0.6	2.94	4746	4849	0.5
76112 FORT WORTH	439	39239	41823	46255	1.5	57	16570	17597	19332	1.4	2.36	10063	10598	1.2
76114 FORT WORTH	439	24497	24875	26747	0.4	22	8832	8924	9561	0.2	2.60	5956	5999	0.2
76115 FORT WORTH	439	19666	20224	21901	0.7	31	5733	5782	6180	0.2	3.45	4527	4560	0.2
76116 FORT WORTH	439	45031	49079	55343	2.1	68	20089	21753	24487	1.9	2.25	11419	12275	1.7
76117 HALTOM CITY	439	29411	30844	33825	1.1	46	11354	11839	12878	1.0	2.59	7662	7980	1.0
76118 FORT WORTH	439	12674	14116	15957	2.6	77	4712	5171	5778	2.2	2.68	3442	3806	2.4
76119 FORT WORTH	439	40556	42396	46246	1.1	44	12607	13075	14190	0.9	3.08	9551	9871	0.8
76120 FORT WORTH	439	9928	11057	12498	2.6	77	4858	5409	6087	2.6	2.04	2376	2610	2.2
76122 FORT WORTH	439	269	265	282	-0.4	7	2	2	2	0.0	2.50	1	1	0.0
76123 FORT WORTH	439	11137	13916	16592	5.4	95	3426	4245	5015	5.2	3.27	3010	3727	5.2
76126 FORT WORTH	439	15254	15993	17635	1.1	45	5865	6094	6661	0.9	2.61	4535	4708	0.9
76127 NAVAL AIR STATION	439	436	446	469	0.5	26	51	53	57	0.9	5.21	36	37	0.7
76129 FORT WORTH	439	1834	1834	1834	0.0	13	1	1	1	0.0	2.00	0	0	0.0
76131 FORT WORTH	439	7010	8928	10843	5.9	96	2255	2857	3441	5.7	3.12	1872	2383	5.8
76132 FORT WORTH	439	21542	24770	28410	3.3	85	10678	11955	13470	2.7	2.03	4929	5605	3.1
76133 FORT WORTH	439	46158	47850	52136	0.9	37	17818	18338	19814	0.7	2.59	12817	13161	0.6
76134 FORT WORTH	439	18105	19189	21170	1.4	54	6467	6797	7430	1.2	2.81	4955	5209	1.2
76135 FORT WORTH	439	14383	16491	18906	3.3	84	5736	6551	7460	3.2	2.48	3933	4464	3.0
76137 FORT WORTH	439	39511	50327	60876	5.9	96	13812	17426	20873	5.6	2.88	10599	13469	5.8
76140 FORT WORTH	439	18699	20027	22166	1.6	60	6176	6571	7220	1.5	3.03	4881	5186	1.4
76148 FORT WORTH	439	24702	25412	27523	0.7	31	8093	8264	8878	0.5	3.06	6665	6804	0.5
76155 FORT WORTH	439	2626	3014	3434	3.3	84	1699	1927	2171	3.0	1.56	463	520	2.8
76177 FORT WORTH	439	156	288	412	15.5	100	56	101	142	14.9	2.84	47	84	14.6
76179 FORT WORTH	439	20959	25761	30473	5.0	94	7425	9005	10529	4.6	2.86	5967	7235	4.6
76180 NORTH RICHLAND HILLS	439	54305	60030	67448	2.4	75	20289	22136	24590	2.1	2.70	14930	16400	2.2
76201 DENTON	121	24682	27003	32115	2.1	70	10122	11084	13410	2.2	1.98	3668	3901	1.5
76205 DENTON	121	16692	18580	22619	2.6	76	6567	7287	8858	2.5	2.41	3358	3649	2.0
76207 DENTON	121	6781	8278	10576	4.8	94	2639	3170	3991	4.4	2.59	1660	1989	4.4
TEXAS					2.2					2.0	2.77			2.1
UNITED STATES					1.2					1.3	2.58			1.1

ZIP CODE #	POST OFFICE NAME	RACE (%) White 2000	White 2004	Black 2000	Black 2004	Asian/Pacific 2000	Asian/Pacific 2004	% Hispanic Origin 2000	% Hispanic Origin 2004	2004 AGE DISTRIBUTION (%) 0-4	5-9	10-14	15-19	20-24	25-44	45-64	65-84	85+	18+	MEDIAN AGE 2004	% 2004 Males	% 2004 Females
76006	ARLINGTON	70.5	67.0	15.1	16.3	6.7	7.5	11.2	13.9	6.2	4.9	4.7	5.4	12.6	44.8	18.4	2.9	0.2	81.4	30.5	50.9	49.1
76008	ALEDO	95.2	94.2	0.8	1.0	0.7	0.9	4.8	6.1	6.8	8.0	8.9	7.6	5.0	27.6	27.8	8.0	0.6	71.3	37.9	49.3	50.7
76009	ALVARADO	86.9	85.5	3.0	3.0	0.4	0.4	15.2	17.6	7.5	7.2	8.3	8.1	7.2	28.8	24.4	7.8	0.6	71.9	34.2	50.9	49.1
76010	ARLINGTON	50.3	46.8	16.0	15.9	6.3	6.6	39.6	44.7	10.5	8.8	8.5	8.2	11.0	33.0	14.2	5.6	0.4	68.0	26.6	51.8	48.3
76011	ARLINGTON	55.3	52.5	18.3	18.3	4.1	4.3	34.8	39.5	9.2	7.1	6.4	6.9	13.1	37.6	15.0	4.2	0.6	73.7	28.0	51.8	48.2
76012	ARLINGTON	79.8	77.1	8.1	8.6	3.4	3.9	13.4	16.3	6.8	6.5	6.6	6.4	6.4	27.7	26.1	11.8	1.6	76.3	38.2	48.6	51.5
76013	ARLINGTON	78.1	74.9	8.9	9.9	5.5	6.2	10.2	13.0	6.6	5.9	6.0	7.2	10.2	29.3	21.0	12.3	1.6	78.0	34.1	48.8	51.2
76014	ARLINGTON	52.2	48.5	22.5	23.4	12.3	13.0	19.7	23.4	9.1	8.3	8.5	7.5	8.4	33.6	19.7	4.6	0.3	69.6	29.7	49.2	50.8
76015	ARLINGTON	76.7	73.7	10.6	11.7	4.8	5.2	12.0	14.7	7.2	6.7	7.0	6.8	7.9	31.7	23.5	8.2	1.0	75.0	33.8	48.7	51.3
76016	ARLINGTON	85.2	83.1	6.6	7.4	4.0	4.5	5.8	7.4	5.4	6.5	8.3	8.0	5.7	26.1	32.2	7.0	0.8	74.7	39.4	49.3	50.8
76017	ARLINGTON	80.2	77.2	9.7	10.8	4.4	5.0	8.1	10.4	7.6	7.7	8.0	7.1	6.6	32.2	25.3	5.2	0.3	72.3	34.1	49.3	50.7
76018	ARLINGTON	59.7	56.3	20.2	21.2	10.3	11.0	14.6	17.8	9.8	9.4	9.3	7.4	6.2	36.8	18.7	2.3	0.1	66.5	30.7	49.2	50.8
76019	ARLINGTON	75.0	100.0	0.0	0.0	0.0	0.0	0.0	0.0	0.0	0.0	0.0	0.0	50.0	50.0	0.0	0.0	0.0	100.0	25.0	50.0	50.0
76020	AZLE	95.2	94.3	0.4	0.5	0.5	0.5	5.4	6.8	6.7	6.9	7.6	7.0	6.2	27.5	27.0	10.0	1.2	74.4	37.8	49.7	50.3
76021	BEDFORD	88.1	86.0	3.5	4.0	4.2	4.8	6.7	8.8	5.6	5.8	6.5	6.5	7.5	30.9	28.6	7.4	1.2	78.3	37.3	48.2	51.8
76022	BEDFORD	86.6	84.1	4.0	4.6	3.1	3.5	8.5	11.0	6.5	5.9	5.6	5.5	7.5	31.6	24.7	11.0	1.7	78.9	37.0	47.6	52.4
76023	BOYD	93.9	93.2	0.4	0.4	0.3	0.4	7.0	8.2	6.3	6.4	7.5	7.5	6.5	27.6	27.8	9.5	0.8	75.3	37.4	50.2	49.8
76028	BURLESON	94.9	93.9	1.0	1.2	0.5	0.6	5.6	7.0	7.0	7.2	7.7	7.0	5.9	27.6	26.2	10.2	1.3	73.9	37.7	49.0	51.0
76031	CLEBURNE	84.7	83.6	5.0	5.1	0.8	0.8	21.5	24.1	8.3	7.7	7.5	7.5	7.8	28.9	22.4	9.0	0.9	72.2	32.8	50.4	49.7
76033	CLEBURNE	90.8	89.6	2.4	2.6	0.6	0.7	12.8	15.0	7.5	7.0	7.0	7.1	7.2	26.2	23.7	12.0	2.4	74.2	36.2	47.9	52.1
76034	COLLEYVILLE	93.2	92.1	1.3	1.5	3.2	3.7	3.4	4.5	5.5	7.9	10.1	8.3	3.8	22.6	35.2	6.2	0.4	70.8	41.3	49.5	50.5
76035	CRESSON	94.7	93.9	0.5	0.4	0.8	0.9	7.0	8.4	7.6	7.7	7.6	7.1	6.6	28.3	25.4	8.8	0.9	72.8	35.4	49.6	50.4
76036	CROWLEY	92.5	90.5	1.8	2.3	1.1	1.6	7.5	9.6	6.5	7.0	8.6	8.3	6.9	25.9	26.3	9.3	1.3	72.8	37.1	48.1	51.9
76039	EULESS	77.3	74.4	5.1	5.7	9.6	10.5	11.0	13.6	6.8	6.1	6.3	5.8	8.5	39.7	21.7	4.8	0.3	77.3	32.7	49.1	50.9
76040	EULESS	71.2	67.8	10.1	11.1	8.5	9.2	16.1	19.6	8.1	6.6	6.1	6.6	9.5	37.0	19.5	6.0	0.5	75.4	31.8	51.1	48.9
76041	FORRESTON	80.0	76.9	4.3	5.0	0.0	0.0	29.7	34.7	7.0	7.0	8.0	9.1	7.5	27.1	25.1	8.0	1.0	71.9	34.8	52.3	47.7
76043	GLEN ROSE	92.3	91.2	0.3	0.3	0.3	0.3	13.0	15.1	6.4	6.7	7.5	7.6	6.9	25.7	25.8	11.3	2.2	74.8	37.8	50.2	49.8
76044	GODLEY	92.9	91.6	0.6	0.7	0.1	0.1	9.5	11.5	7.8	7.6	7.5	7.5	7.2	28.0	24.8	8.9	0.6	72.2	34.7	50.0	50.0
76048	GRANBURY	93.9	92.9	0.4	0.4	0.3	0.4	9.1	10.9	6.1	6.2	6.6	6.8	6.1	25.0	26.3	14.8	2.1	76.9	40.5	48.9	51.1
76049	GRANBURY	95.6	95.0	0.2	0.3	0.4	0.4	5.8	6.9	5.2	5.6	6.2	5.6	4.8	20.7	29.9	20.6	1.5	79.6	46.3	49.2	50.9
76050	GRANDVIEW	92.9	91.9	3.1	3.3	0.1	0.1	7.4	9.0	7.2	7.2	7.6	7.3	6.4	26.4	25.6	10.5	1.8	73.4	37.1	49.3	50.7
76051	GRAPEVINE	88.3	86.1	2.3	2.7	2.6	3.0	11.4	14.2	7.2	7.5	8.3	7.2	6.6	32.8	25.5	4.5	0.6	72.5	34.8	50.0	50.0
76052	HASLET	91.5	90.6	1.8	2.0	1.2	1.3	8.0	10.0	8.3	8.3	8.3	6.6	5.5	35.6	22.6	4.4	0.3	70.9	34.0	49.5	50.5
76053	HURST	84.0	81.4	5.1	5.4	1.9	2.1	12.6	16.1	7.4	6.7	7.0	6.7	7.4	29.3	22.1	12.3	1.2	75.0	35.7	48.8	51.2
76054	HURST	90.5	88.6	2.0	2.3	2.9	3.3	6.6	8.6	6.1	6.6	6.7	6.2	5.1	24.3	32.1	11.7	1.3	76.7	42.2	48.5	51.6
76055	ITASCA	75.1	72.9	10.6	10.9	0.1	0.1	20.0	23.1	7.4	7.5	7.3	7.0	6.5	25.8	24.0	12.5	2.2	73.5	36.7	49.7	50.3
76058	JOSHUA	92.3	90.9	0.9	1.0	0.4	0.4	9.2	11.1	8.2	7.8	8.4	8.0	7.4	29.0	23.2	7.3	0.6	70.6	33.0	50.4	49.6
76059	KEENE	77.5	75.4	5.9	6.2	4.5	4.8	22.4	26.1	7.6	6.7	6.2	9.3	13.0	26.3	17.9	9.8	3.3	75.7	29.5	47.5	52.5
76060	KENNEDALE	85.9	83.2	5.7	6.6	1.4	1.7	10.4	13.3	7.7	7.5	7.2	7.0	7.4	32.2	23.0	7.3	0.9	73.4	33.7	49.6	50.4
76063	MANSFIELD	86.4	84.3	4.4	4.7	1.2	1.5	12.7	15.3	8.3	8.4	8.6	7.4	6.4	31.2	23.2	5.9	0.6	69.9	33.6	50.6	49.4
76064	MAYPEARL	84.2	81.9	5.9	6.5	0.5	0.5	17.0	20.0	7.4	7.7	8.5	8.4	7.4	29.1	24.0	6.8	0.6	71.2	33.1	49.6	50.4
76065	MIDLOTHIAN	91.6	90.4	2.4	2.8	0.5	0.5	10.1	11.9	7.4	7.5	8.3	8.1	7.0	28.8	25.4	6.8	0.7	71.8	34.5	50.1	49.9
76066	MILLSAP	94.2	93.3	0.4	0.4	0.3	0.4	6.1	7.2	6.4	6.7	7.4	7.3	5.8	26.5	27.8	11.3	0.9	75.1	39.1	50.9	49.1
76067	MINERAL WELLS	83.4	81.2	5.6	6.0	0.6	0.7	15.8	18.4	6.7	6.4	6.9	6.7	7.0	28.5	23.1	12.7	2.1	76.0	37.1	52.1	47.9
76070	NEMO	95.4	94.6	0.4	0.6	0.0	0.2	8.3	10.0	6.8	6.8	7.9	7.7	7.1	25.7	27.4	9.7	1.0	73.6	37.9	50.0	50.0
76071	NEWARK	93.7	92.8	0.3	0.3	0.1	0.2	6.1	7.4	6.9	7.0	8.3	8.0	6.5	29.3	24.0	9.3	0.8	72.8	35.7	48.9	51.1
76073	PARADISE	95.6	94.9	0.2	0.3	0.2	0.2	5.3	6.3	6.7	6.8	8.0	8.3	6.5	27.5	26.9	8.9	0.6	73.5	36.7	50.5	49.5
76077	RAINBOW	90.5	89.0	0.4	0.3	0.4	0.3	17.7	20.5	7.0	7.2	7.7	7.5	7.4	26.0	25.4	10.0	1.8	73.4	35.7	49.6	50.4
76078	RHOME	92.0	90.7	1.0	1.2	0.3	0.3	7.2	8.7	7.9	8.1	8.5	7.3	5.7	31.9	23.7	6.5	0.5	70.9	34.7	50.5	49.5
76082	SPRINGTOWN	94.8	93.9	0.5	0.6	0.3	0.3	5.8	7.1	7.1	7.2	8.5	8.3	6.6	28.6	24.9	8.1	0.7	72.1	35.2	50.2	49.8
76084	VENUS	80.9	78.5	7.2	7.6	2.0	2.2	16.4	19.5	7.4	7.3	7.6	7.1	7.4	33.9	23.6	5.5	0.3	73.1	33.3	55.8	44.2
76085	WEATHERFORD	94.1	93.2	0.6	0.7	0.3	0.3	6.2	7.5	7.1	7.3	7.9	7.4	6.2	28.1	27.1	8.2	0.7	73.1	36.6	49.6	50.4
76086	WEATHERFORD	90.3	88.8	2.2	2.4	0.7	0.9	11.1	13.0	7.1	6.6	6.8	7.2	8.3	26.3	21.5	13.3	3.0	75.6	35.6	47.7	52.3
76087	WEATHERFORD	95.0	94.2	0.4	0.4	0.3	0.4	5.2	6.3	5.6	6.4	7.9	7.1	5.4	24.8	31.0	11.0	0.7	75.6	40.9	50.3	49.7
76088	WEATHERFORD	90.6	89.5	3.3	3.4	0.1	0.2	8.0	9.4	6.2	6.6	7.6	6.7	7.0	29.7	25.7	9.6	1.0	75.5	36.8	53.5	46.5
76092	SOUTHLAKE	94.2	93.1	1.5	1.8	1.9	2.2	3.9	5.1	7.7	10.9	12.0	8.4	3.0	26.7	28.2	2.9	0.2	63.4	36.7	50.0	50.0
76093	RIO VISTA	96.3	95.6	0.2	0.2	0.1	0.1	5.0	6.1	7.8	7.6	7.9	8.4	6.6	28.0	23.8	9.6	0.5	71.7	35.1	51.6	48.4
76102	FORT WORTH	54.2	53.7	34.7	33.9	1.1	1.2	26.3	29.4	6.5	5.2	4.2	6.5	10.6	38.5	16.2	7.6	4.7	81.4	33.1	58.4	41.6
76103	FORT WORTH	54.9	52.0	24.5	24.7	3.0	3.2	29.8	34.3	8.8	8.0	7.7	6.6	6.6	29.5	20.5	9.9	2.6	71.4	33.7	49.0	51.0
76104	FORT WORTH	24.8	23.8	57.1	56.8	2.5	2.4	26.0	28.6	7.6	7.3	7.5	7.2	6.7	26.4	20.9	13.7	2.9	73.0	35.9	48.9	51.1
76105	FORT WORTH	26.8	26.3	50.0	48.7	0.6	0.6	41.1	44.2	10.7	9.5	9.2	8.5	8.9	27.8	17.6	7.1	0.8	65.7	27.2	49.8	50.2
76106	FORT WORTH	52.0	50.2	4.7	4.4	0.4	0.4	82.5	85.5	10.3	9.3	9.0	8.8	9.3	30.9	15.5	6.1	0.7	66.2	26.9	53.1	46.9
76107	FORT WORTH	68.3	66.2	17.2	17.0	0.8	0.8	23.2	27.0	7.1	6.5	6.2	5.7	6.5	30.8	24.2	10.9	2.2	76.8	36.8	48.4	51.6
76108	FORT WORTH	85.9	83.5	4.3	4.7	1.8	2.1	12.8	16.0	7.9	7.3	7.5	7.0	7.4	29.0	23.8	8.9	1.3	73.2	34.7	48.8	51.2
76109	FORT WORTH	91.1	89.7	2.9	3.2	1.7	1.9	6.9	8.8	5.4	4.6	4.9	6.6	11.8	28.0	22.5	13.4	2.9	82.4	35.8	47.1	52.9
76110	FORT WORTH	53.2	50.1	5.0	4.7	3.0	2.9	62.0	67.2	10.0	8.8	8.4	7.9	9.3	31.6	17.6	5.6	0.8	68.2	28.2	52.5	47.5
76111	FORT WORTH	61.5	58.3	6.0	5.6	5.3	5.3	46.5	52.5	9.0	8.5	7.6	6.9	7.6	30.7	19.6	8.6	1.7	70.8	31.7	51.7	48.3
76112	FORT WORTH	43.5	40.6	46.4	47.8	2.8	3.0	10.6	12.7	8.1	7.0	7.1	6.8	8.0	30.4	21.3	9.8	1.6	73.8	33.2	46.6	53.4
76114	FORT WORTH	80.4	77.2	3.3	3.4	0.8	0.9	28.1	33.8	7.2	6.8	7.0	6.5	7.3	29.9	22.1	11.4	1.8	75.2	35.4	46.5	53.5
76115	FORT WORTH	50.3	47.3	9.3	8.9	4.0	3.9	61.0	66.4	11.1	9.8	8.9	8.0	9.0	32.2	14.6	5.8	0.6	65.3	26.7	50.7	49.4
76116	FORT WORTH	76.9	74.0	10.6	11.1	1.9	2.1	18.1	22.6	8.0	6.6	6.0	5.9	8.3	30.7	21.5	11.4	1.7	76.2	34.0	49.0	51.0
76117	HALTOM CITY	77.2	73.7	2.2	2.4	7.7	8.4	21.0	25.7	7.9	7.0	7.0	6.8	8.0	29.1	21.3	11.5	1.5	74.1	33.8	50.0	50.0
76118	FORT WORTH	82.4	78.6	5.0	6.1	4.5	5.5	12.2	15.5	8.8	7.8	7.2	6.3	6.4	31.0	20.4	10.2	2.0	72.4	34.7	47.5	52.5
76119	FORT WORTH	30.2	29.3	55.6	54.7	1.0	1.0	23.2	26.6	9.0	8.5	8.6	7.8	7.4	28.0	21.2	8.7	0.8	69.2	31.3	49.8	50.2
76120	FORT WORTH	62.9	59.5	26.6	28.3	3.9	4.4	9.5	11.7	7.8	6.5	5.6	5.6	10.3	41.9	18.0	4.0	0.3	77.1	30.3	47.4	52.6
76122	FORT WORTH	62.1	57.4	3.4	3.4	6.0	6.0	44.2	50.6	7.9	6.8	6.8	7.9	12.5	40.4	14.0	3.4	0.4	73.2	28.1	52.5	47.6
76123	FORT WORTH	64.4	61.6	23.4	24.7	5.1	5.5	11.0	13.2	9.0	8.7	9.6	9.0	6.5	34.0	20.5	2.6	0.1	66.6	30.7	48.6	51.4
76126	FORT WORTH	90.8	89.2	2.8	3.2	1.8	2.1	6.4	8.3	5.9	6.5	7.2	6.3	4.7	26.3	30.0	12.0	1.1	76.4	41.1	48.3	51.7
76127	NAVAL AIR STATION	73.2	70.2	16.3	17.7	1.8	2.0	9.9	12.6	3.6	4.9	3.6	7.0	24.9	28.5	19.5	7.9	0.2	85.7	28.3	65.0	35.0
76129	FORT WORTH	85.9	83.4	5.3	6.1	3.5	4.1	6.3	8.2	0.0	0.0	0.0	62.1	37.7	0.2	0.1	0.0	0.0	100.0	19.0	35.3	64.7
76131	FORT WORTH	82.0	79.5	2.6	2.8	1.7	1.8	20.6	24.0	9.4	8.9	8.7	7.1	6.6	35.1	19.8	4.2	0.3	68.5	31.2	50.4	49.6
76132	FORT WORTH	80.4	77.9	9.2	10.0	3.8	4.3	9.6	11.7	5.9	5.1	5.3	5.9	11.9	35.0	20.1	8.9	1.9	80.7	32.0	47.4	52.6
76133	FORT WORTH	70.4	67.3	16.2	17.2	3.2	3.5	17.0	20.5	7.2	6.9	7.0	6.7	7.0	27.6	24.1	12.2	1.4	74.8	36.5	47.3	52.7
76134	FORT WORTH	56.7	53.9	31.1	31.8	2.0	2.2	17.0	20.5	7.5	7.4	8.1	7.6	7.0	27.8	23.1	10.6	0.9	72.2	34.5	47.9	52.2
76135	FORT WORTH	87.5	84.8	2.0	2.4	1.1	1.3	12.8	16.4	7.2	6.7	6.5	6.5	7.7	28.9	24.3	10.9	1.3	75.7	36.4	49.3	50.7
76137	FORT WORTH	80.2	77.7	4.9	5.3	6.5	7.3	12.1	14.7	9.9	9.3	8.4	6.8	6.3	37.7	18.7	2.7	0.2	68.2	31.0	49.9	50.1
76140	FORT WORTH	49.1	47.2	39.2	39.3	1.1	1.2	15.4	18.2	8.0	8.0	8.3	7.7	7.1	27.5	23.6	8.9	0.9	70.9	33.4	48.3	51.7
76148	FORT WORTH	86.6	84.3	2.2	2.5	4.2	4.8	10.9	13.9	8.4	8.3	8.7	7.4	6.6	32.9	22.1	5.0	0.6	69.9	32.5	49.4	50.6
76155	FORT WORTH	59.6	56.1	15.7	16.6	15.6	16.7	14.8	18.0	6.2	2.3	0.9	2.3	17.6	55.7	14.5	0.6	0.0	90.1	29.2	56.7	43.3
76177	FORT WORTH	88.5	86.5	1.9	2.1	3.9	4.5	9.0	11.8	8.3	8.3	8.7	6.9	5.9	35.4	21.5	4.5	0.4	70.5	32.6	49.7	50.4
76179	FORT WORTH	86.2	83.1	1.4	1.5	5.0	6.1	10.8	14.3	7.3	7.3	7.6	7.5	6.7	29.7	25.9	7.6	0.5	73.4	35.3	49.3	50.7
76180	NORTH RICHLAND HILLS	88.6	86.8	2.7	3.1	2.7	3.1	9.4	11.7	7.1	6.9	7.6	7.2	7.4	30.0	25.0	7.9	0.9	74.1	35.3	49.3	50.7
76201	DENTON	73.2	70.2	8.6	8.9	6.6	7.5	16.9	19.8	4.5	3.1	3.0	14.7	27.8	26.6	11.9	6.2	2.1	86.6	24.4	50.8	49.2
76205	DENTON	70.4	69.1	13.6	13.2	2.8	3.2	17.0	18.9	5.6	4.9	5.3	7.9	18.8	31.6	18.3	6.9	0.7	80.6	28.2	50.9	49.1
76207	DENTON	81.2	79.4	6.6	6.8	2.0	2.4	12.4	14.6	8.1	7.9	7.3	6.6	9.7	34.4	19.6	5.9	0.6	73.1	30.5	47.9	52.1
	TEXAS	71.0	69.5	11.5	11.4	2.8	3.1	32.0	34.6	7.9	7.5	7.7	7.5	8.1	29.6	21.9	8.7	1.2	72.6	32.9	49.7	50.3
	UNITED STATES	75.1	73.6	12.3	12.5	3.8	4.2	12.5	14.1	6.9	6.7	7.2	7.0	7.3	28.6	23.8	10.8	1.7	75.1	36.0	49.1	50.9

ZIP CODE #	POST OFFICE NAME	2004 Per Capita Income	2004 HH Income Base	2004 Household Income Distribution (%) Less than $25,000	$25,000 to $49,999	$50,000 to $99,999	$100,000 to $149,999	$150,000 or More	Median Household Income 2004	2009	2004 National Centile	2004 State Centile	2004 Home Value Base	2004 Home Value Distribution (%) Less than $50,000	$50,000 to $89,999	$90,000 to $174,999	$175,000 to $399,999	$400,000 or More	2004 Median Home Value
76006	ARLINGTON	39117	13586	13.7	34.8	32.7	11.5	7.3	51189	61717	74	79	2937	12.0	9.5	30.9	40.6	7.0	170678
76008	ALEDO	32657	3376	11.3	20.7	36.9	17.4	13.8	70994	80959	92	92	3021	13.4	11.5	33.0	31.6	10.4	151235
76009	ALVARADO	20016	6601	19.6	29.5	37.7	9.9	3.2	50560	57061	73	78	5351	25.5	34.5	29.0	10.1	0.9	78748
76010	ARLINGTON	14439	19767	34.9	34.9	25.5	3.7	1.1	34629	39269	26	31	6415	17.3	66.2	15.4	0.8	0.4	67946
76011	ARLINGTON	20208	13263	29.7	36.2	25.3	6.1	2.8	37495	44362	37	45	2589	19.5	39.4	16.8	23.1	1.2	75327
76012	ARLINGTON	32296	10477	17.9	25.2	32.7	13.7	10.4	57986	66611	83	85	6871	7.7	12.8	49.1	28.2	2.2	140307
76013	ARLINGTON	26847	14950	26.2	28.9	28.1	11.1	5.7	44906	51904	61	68	7727	1.7	19.7	58.7	17.9	1.9	117220
76014	ARLINGTON	20213	11106	16.3	31.1	39.8	11.1	1.8	51829	60430	75	80	6038	3.6	53.1	42.6	0.7	0.0	86958
76015	ARLINGTON	25022	6499	14.0	32.1	38.0	12.6	3.3	53191	61683	77	81	3649	4.6	30.0	58.8	6.2	0.5	101034
76016	ARLINGTON	35143	11232	6.5	16.3	40.8	22.8	13.6	80248	93460	95	96	9612	2.0	9.3	59.6	24.5	4.6	129900
76017	ARLINGTON	30579	16866	9.1	21.4	42.4	18.7	8.5	69556	79755	91	92	12584	4.1	13.6	65.1	15.2	2.0	119716
76018	ARLINGTON	24489	8674	5.2	20.7	51.0	18.8	4.2	70077	81292	91	92	7642	1.2	17.8	74.6	6.2	0.3	110876
76019	ARLINGTON	0	0	0.0	0.0	0.0	0.0	0.0	0	0	0	0	2	0.0	0.0	100.0	0.0	0.0	112500
76020	AZLE	23053	9348	22.1	28.6	34.4	10.9	4.1	49373	57221	71	76	7528	18.7	30.9	35.4	12.6	2.4	90547
76021	BEDFORD	35296	15498	13.0	24.0	34.1	19.2	9.7	65398	76183	89	90	9072	0.6	3.1	64.9	31.1	0.4	144638
76022	BEDFORD	29082	6346	13.7	34.1	35.2	12.3	4.7	51889	60464	75	80	3506	1.4	24.9	62.9	10.8	0.0	107703
76023	BOYD	20329	2149	24.1	26.7	38.7	8.2	2.3	49303	55647	71	76	1789	22.0	25.5	32.3	16.4	3.9	94450
76028	BURLESON	25198	16034	15.5	25.0	39.5	14.5	5.5	59938	66074	84	87	13285	8.0	27.3	49.1	13.7	2.0	106509
76031	CLEBURNE	17473	6180	28.0	31.2	31.8	6.8	2.4	41489	47682	51	60	4575	29.7	30.1	31.3	8.0	0.8	75846
76033	CLEBURNE	21885	8949	25.1	30.3	32.7	8.1	3.9	44703	50680	60	68	6127	14.1	37.7	36.5	9.9	1.9	87925
76034	COLLEYVILLE	58796	7201	4.5	8.1	21.4	26.2	39.9	129083	149726	100	100	6961	0.4	2.3	14.1	53.2	30.0	296677
76035	CRESSON	21141	280	17.5	31.8	37.9	8.9	3.9	50643	57700	73	78	225	24.0	25.8	34.2	12.0	4.0	90357
76036	CROWLEY	25353	5473	17.9	22.4	36.5	17.1	6.1	58597	68835	83	86	4290	11.2	32.0	31.1	23.7	2.0	98027
76039	EULESS	30998	12916	10.1	27.3	43.8	14.6	4.2	61711	72600	86	88	5893	2.2	25.3	61.6	10.9	0.0	112868
76040	EULESS	25036	10974	18.7	34.2	32.7	12.0	2.5	46980	55481	66	71	4083	6.4	22.4	57.3	13.7	0.2	111641
76041	FORRESTON	18009	63	15.9	34.9	41.3	4.8	3.2	48670	54526	70	75	50	32.0	24.0	32.0	8.0	4.0	76667
76043	GLEN ROSE	20894	2162	25.6	30.2	31.6	9.7	2.9	44493	51219	60	67	1670	23.3	18.6	34.0	17.9	6.2	105469
76044	GODLEY	19860	1208	22.6	27.1	37.4	9.6	3.3	50269	56678	72	78	980	15.7	29.3	36.6	15.8	2.6	96901
76048	GRANBURY	22451	8032	26.3	31.6	30.5	7.7	4.0	42928	49190	56	64	5964	30.0	27.7	29.4	10.9	2.1	78956
76049	GRANBURY	30548	8123	14.0	27.5	35.9	13.8	8.8	58358	67379	83	86	6977	9.9	15.9	38.8	32.0	3.5	138155
76050	GRANDVIEW	22267	2072	22.5	24.0	37.7	11.4	4.3	53156	59387	77	81	1709	17.8	27.2	35.9	15.8	3.3	97566
76051	GRAPEVINE	37325	17511	9.9	19.0	32.4	23.3	15.5	79661	95867	95	96	11472	5.2	4.6	38.1	47.6	4.5	178839
76052	HASLET	32011	1594	8.7	14.3	42.2	24.7	10.0	79402	95462	95	96	1457	4.8	8.8	36.0	42.6	7.9	176035
76053	HURST	22296	10325	19.6	32.3	35.8	10.4	1.9	48270	56079	69	74	6150	4.5	37.7	54.0	3.4	0.5	96426
76054	HURST	36647	4634	7.2	15.3	39.0	26.1	12.3	81984	95224	96	96	3887	2.1	2.0	61.3	33.3	1.4	151769
76055	ITASCA	17845	1015	29.0	32.9	31.0	5.3	1.8	38662	44187	42	50	780	42.4	30.4	18.1	8.0	1.2	59833
76058	JOSHUA	20130	5613	17.6	30.7	40.6	7.8	3.2	50973	58008	74	78	4737	17.8	33.6	37.8	10.3	0.5	88370
76059	KEENE	16771	1690	28.8	33.5	30.1	5.3	2.4	39515	45678	44	53	941	24.0	35.5	35.7	4.0	0.7	76913
76060	KENNEDALE	25052	2423	19.4	28.6	31.7	13.7	6.7	51819	60932	75	80	1462	21.7	17.9	30.5	27.5	2.5	111667
76063	MANSFIELD	30022	12592	10.6	18.6	39.6	19.8	11.5	72962	84095	92	93	10759	9.1	17.5	40.1	29.7	3.7	131604
76064	MAYPEARL	22133	437	18.5	24.9	39.4	11.7	5.5	57876	64621	83	85	337	17.5	20.8	41.8	18.1	1.8	110337
76065	MIDLOTHIAN	25429	7197	12.5	19.6	44.8	16.8	6.4	66449	75445	89	91	6035	7.3	18.5	45.3	25.0	3.9	122674
76066	MILLSAP	21410	1067	22.0	33.3	33.7	8.3	2.7	45765	53540	63	70	895	29.1	27.2	24.8	14.8	4.3	81591
76067	MINERAL WELLS	15569	7520	37.1	32.7	24.8	3.8	1.6	33567	37996	23	28	5114	47.5	29.5	19.0	3.6	0.4	52629
76070	NEMO	22610	182	19.2	24.7	36.3	17.0	2.8	54471	63360	79	83	154	16.2	16.2	36.4	22.7	8.4	120833
76071	NEWARK	18686	1094	28.3	26.1	35.0	8.0	2.6	45267	51432	62	69	888	29.4	25.0	24.9	19.1	1.6	81522
76073	PARADISE	20385	1696	20.5	26.8	40.9	10.0	1.9	51950	59059	75	80	1455	12.7	25.4	38.8	21.4	1.7	110209
76077	RAINBOW	21033	242	24.4	31.8	32.6	8.7	2.5	43745	50306	58	66	185	17.8	18.9	40.0	16.8	6.5	109766
76078	RHOME	20203	2197	18.8	29.6	39.0	9.6	3.1	51270	57866	74	79	1861	13.3	22.7	42.3	18.5	3.2	109510
76082	SPRINGTOWN	19807	5618	20.4	29.4	37.8	9.5	2.9	50101	57664	72	77	4702	14.6	33.1	36.7	13.3	2.2	92793
76084	VENUS	19151	2246	15.5	29.5	41.9	10.2	3.0	53467	60378	78	82	1888	18.4	39.6	34.1	7.2	0.8	82011
76085	WEATHERFORD	21543	2739	18.3	30.9	36.0	10.9	3.9	50587	57968	73	78	2277	14.5	33.6	33.2	15.0	3.7	92514
76086	WEATHERFORD	21407	7137	28.4	31.6	30.3	6.6	3.1	40548	46699	48	56	4613	15.0	31.9	40.2	11.4	1.6	93182
76087	WEATHERFORD	28429	7520	15.9	24.0	35.2	16.0	9.0	61874	70935	86	88	6630	14.0	16.1	35.9	30.4	3.7	136243
76088	WEATHERFORD	23123	3441	18.9	31.9	36.9	8.8	3.5	49246	56808	71	76	2824	20.2	25.3	35.0	16.0	3.5	96702
76092	SOUTHLAKE	57937	7400	3.7	6.7	15.6	22.4	51.7	153314	181774	100	100	7016	3.3	2.2	7.4	32.9	54.2	413506
76093	RIO VISTA	17943	715	26.7	32.3	33.7	5.0	2.2	41982	46950	53	61	586	28.2	36.0	25.8	6.1	3.9	74412
76102	FORT WORTH	20302	2438	49.6	23.1	15.1	6.8	5.5	25366	32395	5	7	389	56.0	20.3	11.3	8.2	4.1	42419
76103	FORT WORTH	17496	5417	32.1	33.8	25.7	6.3	2.1	36234	42114	32	39	3104	28.2	41.3	27.5	2.8	0.2	71572
76104	FORT WORTH	12293	5996	57.0	27.6	12.1	2.0	1.3	20798	24421	2	3	2796	72.8	20.6	5.7	0.3	0.6	38778
76105	FORT WORTH	10025	6701	49.4	32.6	14.4	2.3	1.3	25306	29093	5	6	4013	78.1	19.5	2.0	0.3	0.1	36547
76106	FORT WORTH	11127	13568	35.1	35.2	24.5	3.7	1.5	33889	38685	24	29	7862	62.6	33.4	3.5	0.4	0.1	44730
76107	FORT WORTH	31844	12228	29.7	30.0	24.9	8.1	7.3	40022	47722	46	54	6657	20.1	30.2	23.7	15.7	10.2	89446
76108	FORT WORTH	21169	10423	22.1	32.3	34.0	9.1	2.5	46137	53871	64	70	6977	22.8	37.6	31.7	6.8	1.2	79193
76109	FORT WORTH	45918	10829	21.5	23.6	28.7	10.5	15.7	56231	67153	81	84	5342	4.0	12.4	28.2	41.0	14.5	187248
76110	FORT WORTH	15821	10552	34.3	31.6	23.8	6.7	3.7	36469	42128	33	40	5977	43.5	33.1	12.6	8.3	2.6	54156
76111	FORT WORTH	16040	7116	31.0	35.8	26.3	4.9	1.9	36799	42328	35	41	4568	36.7	46.1	15.1	1.7	0.3	57500
76112	FORT WORTH	21224	17597	31.4	32.8	26.3	6.8	2.8	38057	44143	39	47	8309	17.7	42.0	34.1	5.9	0.4	80613
76114	FORT WORTH	17123	8924	31.9	36.1	26.1	4.4	1.6	35503	41201	30	35	5810	38.8	46.9	13.3	0.7	0.3	58346
76115	FORT WORTH	11597	5782	36.0	39.2	20.7	2.9	1.3	32323	37060	19	23	3131	51.8	42.9	5.1	0.2	0.0	49235
76116	FORT WORTH	26526	21753	28.5	30.9	26.4	8.6	5.6	41308	48661	51	59	8952	10.1	28.4	41.1	17.3	3.1	103709
76117	HALTOM CITY	19339	11839	26.0	35.9	29.7	6.3	2.0	40648	47433	48	57	7164	20.8	55.0	21.0	2.8	0.4	70361
76118	FORT WORTH	23665	5171	17.2	23.6	43.5	13.6	2.1	57490	66652	82	85	3830	4.9	28.8	63.7	2.5	0.2	106544
76119	FORT WORTH	13093	13075	41.3	32.5	21.0	3.4	1.8	30714	35573	14	18	8280	57.4	35.4	6.2	0.8	0.2	46857
76120	FORT WORTH	27002	5409	17.4	40.7	32.0	7.6	2.3	43981	52474	59	66	1471	22.9	30.3	35.4	11.0	0.4	85940
76122	FORT WORTH	2608	0	0.0	0.0	0.0	0.0	0.0	0	0	0	0	0	0.0	0.0	0.0	0.0	0.0	0
76123	FORT WORTH	25328	4245	5.6	17.5	49.9	22.5	4.6	74071	86243	93	94	3689	0.2	13.9	75.5	10.0	0.4	115286
76126	FORT WORTH	29448	6094	10.8	24.3	41.5	17.9	5.4	63176	72261	87	89	4984	5.4	24.1	55.9	12.9	1.6	106639
76127	NAVAL AIR STATION	12568	53	18.9	22.6	41.5	13.2	3.8	63858	73490	88	89	34	11.8	11.8	29.4	47.1	0.0	162500
76129	FORT WORTH	12803	0	0.0	0.0	0.0	0.0	0.0	0	0	0	0	0	0.0	0.0	0.0	0.0	0.0	0
76131	FORT WORTH	24624	2857	11.0	21.1	47.5	15.6	4.8	65056	77281	89	90	2505	10.6	30.9	42.6	13.8	2.2	107093
76132	FORT WORTH	41126	11955	22.6	29.5	27.7	10.5	9.7	47931	57791	68	73	3836	0.9	8.4	25.7	47.0	18.0	215869
76133	FORT WORTH	24671	18338	18.8	29.6	34.7	12.7	4.2	51391	59687	75	79	12371	5.3	38.0	51.4	5.2	0.1	95282
76134	FORT WORTH	20744	6797	18.6	31.5	37.6	10.2	2.1	49858	56907	72	77	5231	10.5	49.6	39.0	0.8	0.1	83981
76135	FORT WORTH	23647	6551	23.9	31.1	33.1	8.4	3.5	45178	52752	62	68	4219	20.1	38.8	32.1	7.6	1.4	80273
76137	FORT WORTH	28538	17426	7.9	20.0	44.4	20.7	7.0	72860	87099	92	93	13359	5.1	15.2	59.3	20.1	0.4	124699
76140	FORT WORTH	18895	6571	20.3	34.5	33.4	9.1	2.8	46397	53466	65	71	5020	24.4	51.8	18.3	4.4	1.1	67855
76148	FORT WORTH	22681	8264	9.8	22.7	49.7	14.8	3.0	63411	73085	87	89	6784	2.7	44.6	51.7	1.0	0.0	91598
76155	FORT WORTH	33480	1927	17.0	37.2	38.5	6.9	0.5	46597	55375	65	71	21	19.1	81.0	0.0	0.0	0.0	59286
76177	FORT WORTH	30414	101	9.9	18.8	43.6	19.8	7.9	72104	83608	92	93	89	18.0	9.0	34.8	32.6	5.6	143056
76179	FORT WORTH	26160	9005	13.7	22.3	41.5	16.6	5.9	62636	71725	87	89	7434	5.8	27.8	47.2	15.2	4.1	106895
76180	NORTH RICHLAND HILLS	29849	22136	12.2	23.3	40.4	16.3	7.8	63968	74610	88	90	15108	4.7	17.3	59.3	17.4	1.3	117836
76201	DENTON	18103	11084	48.4	27.8	17.5	4.1	2.2	25998	31093	6	8	2831	4.5	21.3	65.4	8.3	0.6	109844
76205	DENTON	25165	7287	31.2	29.0	23.2	9.4	7.2	39437	47116	44	52	2810	15.8	14.2	29.3	37.6	3.1	152178
76207	DENTON	26180	3170	17.3	28.5	37.1	11.9	5.3	53688	64138	78	82	1655	11.7	9.7	61.9	13.8	2.8	121265
	TEXAS	23284		26.2	27.7	29.5	10.3	6.3	45778	54246				21.6	26.1	33.4	15.6	3.4	93683
	UNITED STATES	25866		24.7	27.1	30.8	10.9	6.5	48124	56710				10.9	15.0	33.7	30.1	10.4	145905

ZIP CODE #	POST OFFICE NAME	FINANCIAL SERVICES: Auto Loan	FINANCIAL SERVICES: Home Loan	FINANCIAL SERVICES: Invest-ments	FINANCIAL SERVICES: Retire-ment Plans	THE HOME: Home Improvements: Home Repair	THE HOME: Home Improvements: Lawn & Garden	THE HOME: Furnishings: Comput-ers & Hard-ware	THE HOME: Furnishings: Major Appli-ances	THE HOME: Furnishings: TV, Radio, Sound Equip-ment	THE HOME: Furnishings: Furni-ture	ENTERTAINMENT: Dine out/ Carry out	ENTERTAINMENT: Sports Equip-ment	ENTERTAINMENT: Fees & Tickets	ENTERTAINMENT: Toys & Games	ENTERTAINMENT: Travel	ENTERTAINMENT: Cable TV	PERSONAL: Apparel & Services	PERSONAL: Auto Repairs	PERSONAL: Health Insur-ance	PERSONAL: Pets & Supplies
76006	ARLINGTON	108	95	118	106	91	98	109	102	107	111	137	124	105	129	102	100	133	109	92	114
76008	ALEDO	127	155	163	159	150	149	138	136	126	140	160	158	148	166	139	121	160	131	120	150
76009	ALVARADO	94	86	69	83	87	93	82	88	84	84	103	102	78	99	82	83	99	87	89	106
76010	ARLINGTON	60	54	58	55	53	55	61	59	61	62	77	69	58	74	57	57	76	62	54	64
76011	ARLINGTON	72	62	70	67	61	64	71	68	71	73	90	81	68	85	66	66	88	72	61	75
76012	ARLINGTON	108	120	138	121	117	123	118	115	114	118	144	134	122	147	118	111	143	116	107	126
76013	ARLINGTON	84	85	101	89	84	90	92	87	89	90	112	104	91	110	89	85	109	90	81	96
76014	ARLINGTON	86	86	94	90	83	85	89	86	86	90	109	102	87	106	85	81	107	88	77	95
76015	ARLINGTON	87	94	103	97	92	94	92	90	88	93	111	107	94	111	91	84	109	91	82	100
76016	ARLINGTON	135	159	171	163	155	156	146	145	136	147	172	169	154	177	147	131	171	141	130	159
76017	ARLINGTON	117	129	133	136	124	123	121	119	112	124	143	140	125	143	118	106	141	117	103	131
76018	ARLINGTON	113	128	123	133	122	117	115	114	106	120	134	134	119	135	112	98	133	111	97	125
76019	ARLINGTON	0	0	0	0	0	0	0	0	0	0	0	0	0	0	0	0	0	0	0	0
76020	AZLE	91	92	83	90	92	96	87	90	86	88	107	105	86	106	87	85	103	89	88	104
76021	BEDFORD	115	122	134	128	118	121	120	117	114	122	144	138	122	143	117	108	142	118	104	129
76022	BEDFORD	91	92	106	97	91	95	96	93	92	96	117	110	96	115	93	89	114	95	86	102
76023	BOYD	90	81	63	79	82	88	79	84	80	80	99	97	75	95	78	80	94	84	85	100
76028	BURLESON	98	108	109	109	106	108	101	102	96	101	121	119	103	123	101	93	119	100	94	114
76031	CLEBURNE	80	72	62	70	73	78	72	76	74	73	92	87	69	89	71	74	89	76	76	89
76033	CLEBURNE	84	82	77	81	83	89	81	83	82	80	100	97	80	101	81	82	97	83	85	96
76034	COLLEYVILLE	236	297	334	304	288	293	262	256	239	265	304	295	288	317	268	233	307	247	229	283
76035	CRESSON	95	86	68	83	86	91	82	88	83	85	103	102	78	97	81	82	99	88	88	105
76036	CROWLEY	99	111	113	111	109	111	103	103	98	104	123	119	106	124	103	95	121	101	96	115
76039	EULESS	102	101	110	108	97	100	104	100	99	106	126	120	103	122	99	93	123	103	89	111
76040	EULESS	84	79	88	84	76	79	85	82	83	86	105	98	83	101	80	78	103	85	73	90
76041	FORRESTON	88	83	69	81	83	86	80	84	79	81	98	97	76	94	78	78	95	84	82	98
76043	GLEN ROSE	93	81	62	78	85	92	78	85	82	78	100	100	75	99	79	84	95	84	91	105
76044	GODLEY	94	84	65	81	87	93	81	88	84	82	103	102	77	100	81	84	98	86	91	106
76048	GRANBURY	87	78	68	76	81	88	77	83	80	78	98	95	74	94	78	80	93	82	87	99
76049	GRANBURY	118	109	98	105	113	127	104	114	107	108	133	123	102	120	108	110	126	112	123	133
76050	GRANDVIEW	99	90	75	87	93	100	87	93	90	86	110	110	84	110	88	91	105	92	98	115
76051	GRAPEVINE	141	150	159	158	145	147	146	142	137	149	174	168	149	172	142	129	172	142	125	157
76052	HASLET	141	155	145	160	148	144	140	141	130	146	165	164	143	164	137	122	162	137	122	155
76053	HURST	76	81	91	83	80	83	82	80	79	81	100	93	83	101	81	77	98	80	74	87
76054	HURST	131	155	173	158	151	154	143	141	134	144	169	163	152	174	145	130	169	138	127	155
76055	ITASCA	76	65	52	64	68	75	67	72	71	67	86	81	64	84	66	71	82	71	76	83
76058	JOSHUA	92	91	79	89	90	93	85	89	84	87	105	104	83	102	85	82	101	89	86	104
76059	KEENE	66	64	69	65	64	67	69	67	68	68	85	81	68	84	67	65	83	69	63	75
76060	KENNEDALE	103	102	102	105	100	103	101	101	98	103	123	119	100	120	98	94	120	102	94	115
76063	MANSFIELD	134	147	141	149	143	143	135	136	128	138	161	159	138	161	134	122	158	133	123	152
76064	MAYPEARL	101	95	81	97	96	103	93	97	94	94	116	112	92	115	92	93	111	95	97	112
76065	MIDLOTHIAN	110	118	115	120	115	116	110	111	105	112	132	129	112	132	109	100	129	109	101	124
76066	MILLSAP	92	82	62	78	83	89	77	84	80	79	98	98	73	94	77	80	94	83	87	103
76067	MINERAL WELLS	66	56	46	54	59	66	57	61	61	56	74	72	54	73	57	63	70	61	68	75
76070	NEMO	104	91	68	86	97	104	85	94	90	85	109	113	82	111	87	93	104	92	103	122
76071	NEWARK	84	77	60	74	77	81	73	79	74	75	92	91	69	86	72	73	88	78	78	93
76073	PARADISE	93	84	66	81	86	91	80	86	82	81	101	100	76	97	80	81	96	85	88	105
76077	RAINBOW	89	81	63	78	82	87	77	83	78	79	97	96	73	93	76	78	93	82	84	100
76078	RHOME	93	87	70	84	86	90	82	88	82	85	102	101	79	97	81	81	98	87	86	103
76082	SPRINGTOWN	96	85	65	81	86	92	81	88	83	83	102	102	76	98	80	83	98	87	90	107
76084	VENUS	101	94	75	91	93	98	89	95	89	92	110	110	85	105	88	87	106	94	93	111
76085	WEATHERFORD	97	88	68	84	89	95	83	90	86	85	105	105	79	102	83	86	100	89	93	110
76086	WEATHERFORD	80	70	62	70	73	83	74	77	78	72	95	88	71	93	74	80	89	77	85	90
76087	WEATHERFORD	113	122	115	120	121	124	111	115	108	112	134	134	113	137	113	106	132	112	109	133
76088	WEATHERFORD	88	79	61	75	82	88	74	81	78	74	95	95	72	95	75	79	90	79	86	101
76092	SOUTHLAKE	262	326	359	334	316	320	288	281	263	292	334	325	315	347	293	255	337	271	251	311
76093	RIO VISTA	81	74	58	71	74	78	70	75	71	72	88	87	67	83	69	70	84	75	75	89
76102	FORT WORTH	66	62	81	64	61	66	68	66	70	69	88	77	68	86	67	69	86	69	64	73
76103	FORT WORTH	65	65	70	64	64	68	68	67	68	68	85	77	67	85	67	67	84	68	65	72
76104	FORT WORTH	43	35	37	32	35	41	40	40	44	41	54	44	38	50	38	46	52	42	45	46
76105	FORT WORTH	49	42	42	40	41	46	46	47	49	48	61	51	44	56	44	49	60	49	47	51
76106	FORT WORTH	63	54	50	52	52	54	59	60	62	63	78	68	56	74	55	58	78	63	55	64
76107	FORT WORTH	94	96	113	97	95	102	101	98	100	100	125	114	101	124	99	99	123	101	95	108
76108	FORT WORTH	77	83	87	83	82	85	82	81	80	81	100	94	83	103	82	79	98	80	77	89
76109	FORT WORTH	129	137	165	142	135	143	141	136	136	140	171	161	143	169	139	131	168	139	127	149
76110	FORT WORTH	73	65	68	65	64	67	72	72	74	75	93	82	69	90	68	70	92	75	66	77
76111	FORT WORTH	69	63	58	60	62	66	65	67	67	67	84	75	62	80	63	66	82	69	66	74
76112	FORT WORTH	69	67	76	69	66	71	72	69	72	71	90	82	71	88	70	69	88	72	66	77
76114	FORT WORTH	61	60	61	58	61	67	61	62	63	60	78	70	62	80	62	64	76	62	64	70
76115	FORT WORTH	58	50	49	50	49	51	56	56	57	59	73	64	53	69	52	54	72	59	52	60
76116	FORT WORTH	81	81	95	85	80	85	86	83	84	86	106	98	86	104	84	81	104	86	78	91
76117	HALTOM CITY	70	68	71	68	68	73	71	70	72	70	89	82	70	89	70	71	86	71	70	79
76118	FORT WORTH	87	95	101	97	93	95	92	91	88	93	111	106	94	112	91	85	109	90	84	99
76119	FORT WORTH	57	50	50	47	50	56	53	54	56	54	70	61	51	66	52	58	68	55	57	63
76120	FORT WORTH	80	73	82	80	70	74	81	77	78	82	100	93	78	93	75	73	97	81	68	85
76122	FORT WORTH	0	0	0	0	0	0	0	0	0	0	0	0	0	0	0	0	0	0	0	0
76123	FORT WORTH	118	135	131	140	128	124	121	120	111	126	141	140	125	142	118	103	140	116	102	131
76126	FORT WORTH	103	120	126	120	118	119	110	110	104	111	131	128	116	136	112	102	130	107	101	122
76127	NAVAL AIR STATION	104	66	63	76	60	71	98	85	100	92	125	113	84	112	81	91	119	100	78	96
76129	FORT WORTH	0	0	0	0	0	0	0	0	0	0	0	0	0	0	0	0	0	0	0	0
76131	FORT WORTH	110	124	120	129	118	114	112	111	103	117	131	131	115	132	110	96	130	109	95	122
76132	FORT WORTH	116	113	134	121	110	117	124	116	119	123	152	140	123	146	118	113	149	122	106	129
76133	FORT WORTH	86	93	102	95	91	95	92	90	89	92	112	106	94	113	92	86	110	91	84	99
76134	FORT WORTH	81	86	89	86	84	88	83	83	81	84	102	95	85	101	82	79	100	82	78	91
76135	FORT WORTH	84	84	84	85	83	87	84	84	83	84	103	99	83	102	83	80	100	85	80	95
76137	FORT WORTH	118	128	125	134	122	120	119	118	111	124	141	139	121	139	115	103	138	116	102	130
76140	FORT WORTH	83	83	80	82	83	86	81	82	80	81	100	96	80	100	80	78	97	82	79	94
76148	FORT WORTH	97	108	109	112	104	103	101	100	94	103	119	118	103	120	99	89	118	99	87	110
76155	FORT WORTH	77	65	77	73	63	68	76	72	75	78	96	88	73	88	70	70	93	77	64	81
76177	FORT WORTH	128	136	125	139	131	130	125	126	117	129	148	147	126	146	122	111	145	124	113	141
76179	FORT WORTH	103	117	120	119	113	113	108	108	101	110	128	126	111	130	108	97	126	106	96	118
76180	NORTH RICHLAND HILLS	112	120	128	125	117	118	117	115	111	119	140	136	119	140	115	105	138	115	103	126
76201	DENTON	53	42	51	45	41	47	59	50	58	54	73	64	53	68	52	53	70	57	48	56
76205	DENTON	86	74	87	79	73	79	95	83	93	89	116	105	88	111	86	86	112	91	78	93
76207	DENTON	100	94	99	100	91	94	99	96	95	101	121	115	96	115	93	90	118	99	86	108
	TEXAS	94	90	91	90	89	95	92	93	92	93	115	107	90	112	90	90	112	94	89	104
	UNITED STATES	100	100	100	100	100	100	100	100	100	100	100	100	100	100	100	100	100	100	100	100

#	POST OFFICE NAME	COUNTY FIPS CODE	POPULATION 2000	2004	2009	2000-2004 ANNUAL RATE % Rate	State Centile	HOUSEHOLDS 2000	2004	2009	% Annual Rate 2000-2004	2004 Average HH Size	FAMILIES 2000	2004	% Annual Rate 2000-2004
76208	DENTON	121	10739	12969	16486	4.5	93	3741	4468	5604	4.3	2.90	2723	3231	4.1
76209	DENTON	121	22770	26232	32520	3.4	86	8291	9492	11688	3.2	2.68	5426	6155	3.0
76210	DENTON	121	18879	27560	38071	9.3	99	6480	9544	13162	9.5	2.79	5215	7572	9.2
76225	ALVORD	497	2433	2783	3196	3.2	83	939	1067	1219	3.1	2.61	711	810	3.1
76226	ARGYLE	121	7106	8851	11395	5.3	95	2451	3020	3838	5.0	2.93	2073	2544	4.9
76227	AUBREY	121	6840	8943	11882	6.5	97	2455	3168	4152	6.2	2.82	1951	2494	6.0
76228	BELLEVUE	077	1579	1635	1769	0.8	36	614	635	687	0.8	2.57	477	495	0.9
76230	BOWIE	337	9498	9905	10373	1.0	42	3819	3972	4158	0.9	2.44	2709	2824	1.0
76233	COLLINSVILLE	181	2163	2363	2571	2.1	69	824	895	968	2.0	2.60	640	697	2.0
76234	DECATUR	497	12723	14100	15958	2.5	75	4468	4921	5540	2.3	2.81	3483	3840	2.3
76238	ERA	097	320	352	391	2.3	73	106	116	128	2.1	3.03	85	93	2.1
76239	FORESTBURG	337	1241	1296	1364	1.0	43	508	530	557	1.0	2.44	390	407	1.0
76240	GAINESVILLE	097	25451	27379	29984	1.7	62	9688	10353	11276	1.6	2.57	6945	7445	1.7
76245	GORDONVILLE	181	1664	1749	1862	1.2	47	755	787	832	1.0	2.22	528	552	1.1
76247	JUSTIN	121	5585	6679	8440	4.3	91	1868	2235	2808	4.3	2.94	1510	1795	4.2
76248	KELLER	439	27579	37206	46328	7.3	98	8828	11806	14568	7.1	3.15	7717	10262	6.9
76249	KRUM	121	4475	5410	6859	4.6	93	1525	1826	2288	4.3	2.95	1265	1508	4.2
76250	LINDSAY	097	856	913	997	1.5	58	287	304	329	1.4	3.00	227	240	1.3
76251	MONTAGUE	337	699	716	742	0.6	28	281	288	299	0.6	2.37	205	212	0.8
76252	MUENSTER	097	2996	3141	3396	1.1	45	1099	1142	1227	0.9	2.71	805	839	1.0
76255	NOCONA	337	4850	4886	5027	0.2	17	2003	2006	2056	0.0	2.37	1343	1349	0.1
76258	PILOT POINT	121	5674	7221	9367	5.8	96	1972	2491	3200	5.7	2.85	1490	1872	5.5
76259	PONDER	121	2846	3340	4178	3.8	89	957	1115	1380	3.7	2.99	774	898	3.6
76261	RINGGOLD	337	198	193	198	-0.6	4	81	79	81	-0.6	2.44	56	55	-0.4
76262	ROANOKE	121	15977	18367	22376	3.3	85	5752	6579	7948	3.2	2.78	4705	5325	3.0
76263	ROSSTON	097	4	4	5	0.0	13	2	2	2	0.0	2.00	2	2	0.0
76264	SADLER	181	1479	1611	1748	2.0	68	577	624	673	1.9	2.58	447	485	1.9
76265	SAINT JO	337	2155	2264	2381	1.2	47	888	928	969	1.0	2.43	645	676	1.1
76266	SANGER	121	10207	11460	14013	2.8	79	3633	4039	4880	2.5	2.82	2851	3150	2.4
76270	SUNSET	497	1237	1363	1498	2.3	73	493	542	594	2.3	2.47	375	413	2.3
76271	TIOGA	181	1109	1171	1251	1.3	51	431	452	480	1.1	2.59	311	329	1.3
76272	VALLEY VIEW	097	4519	4930	5452	2.1	69	1639	1776	1951	1.9	2.77	1289	1398	1.9
76273	WHITESBORO	181	8376	8966	9677	1.6	60	3189	3387	3630	1.4	2.61	2375	2529	1.5
76301	WICHITA FALLS	485	17640	17899	18416	0.3	21	7298	7371	7567	0.2	2.36	4161	4217	0.3
76302	WICHITA FALLS	485	10960	11888	12731	1.9	66	4192	4581	4919	2.1	2.45	2941	3209	2.1
76305	WICHITA FALLS	485	7097	7235	7374	0.5	24	1305	1350	1398	0.8	2.93	966	999	0.8
76306	WICHITA FALLS	485	16725	16792	17147	0.1	15	6242	6252	6374	0.0	2.66	4483	4501	0.1
76308	WICHITA FALLS	485	18892	19013	19358	0.2	16	7945	7965	8084	0.1	2.29	4906	4952	0.2
76309	WICHITA FALLS	485	13670	14061	14508	0.7	31	5676	5834	6016	0.7	2.37	3600	3713	0.7
76310	WICHITA FALLS	009	15984	16335	16818	0.5	25	6250	6363	6533	0.4	2.53	4510	4601	0.5
76311	SHEPPARD AFB	485	9393	9902	10302	1.3	50	1342	1474	1578	2.2	3.53	1292	1423	2.3
76351	ARCHER CITY	009	1837	1829	1861	-0.1	10	750	745	757	-0.2	2.40	507	503	-0.2
76354	BURKBURNETT	485	11316	11320	11491	0.0	13	4281	4274	4333	0.0	2.63	3224	3223	0.0
76357	BYERS	077	647	669	722	0.8	35	257	266	287	0.8	2.52	196	203	0.8
76360	ELECTRA	487	3796	3731	3770	-0.4	6	1534	1500	1511	-0.5	2.46	1055	1032	-0.5
76363	GOREE	275	386	378	381	-0.5	4	148	145	146	-0.5	2.60	108	106	-0.4
76364	HARROLD	487	261	267	272	0.5	27	107	109	110	0.4	2.45	79	81	0.6
76365	HENRIETTA	077	6117	6675	7427	2.1	69	2422	2637	2933	2.0	2.50	1743	1904	2.1
76366	HOLLIDAY	009	3017	3054	3124	0.3	20	1185	1196	1221	0.2	2.55	881	889	0.2
76367	IOWA PARK	485	9552	9608	9779	0.1	16	3604	3621	3684	0.1	2.51	2756	2769	0.1
76371	MUNDAY	275	1872	1866	1884	-0.1	11	742	739	747	-0.1	2.45	512	512	0.0
76372	NEWCASTLE	503	982	1002	1012	0.5	25	394	400	403	0.4	2.50	287	292	0.4
76373	OKLAUNION	487	185	189	193	0.5	25	63	64	65	0.4	2.95	46	48	1.0
76374	OLNEY	503	4453	4504	4544	0.3	19	1828	1843	1856	0.2	2.38	1219	1231	0.2
76377	PETROLIA	077	1588	1675	1830	1.3	50	613	646	705	1.2	2.59	452	476	1.2
76379	SCOTLAND	009	587	595	608	0.3	21	214	216	221	0.2	2.75	162	164	0.3
76380	SEYMOUR	023	4544	4464	4368	-0.4	6	1969	1916	1861	-0.6	2.30	1283	1255	-0.5
76384	VERNON	487	14092	14183	14338	0.2	16	5317	5316	5341	0.0	2.50	3582	3590	0.1
76388	WEINERT	275	231	223	216	-0.8	2	102	98	96	-0.9	2.27	71	69	-0.7
76389	WINDTHORST	009	1122	1140	1172	0.4	22	380	385	394	0.3	2.96	285	289	0.3
76401	STEPHENVILLE	143	22852	23580	24582	0.7	34	8875	9084	9400	0.6	2.41	5366	5513	0.6
76424	BRECKENRIDGE	429	9163	9267	9406	0.3	19	3442	3465	3505	0.2	2.50	2423	2446	0.2
76426	BRIDGEPORT	497	9517	10404	11625	2.1	70	3196	3490	3904	2.1	2.75	2424	2651	2.1
76427	BRYSON	237	1010	1042	1104	0.7	34	419	430	452	0.6	2.42	306	314	0.6
76429	CADDO	429	160	160	161	0.0	13	68	68	68	0.0	1.85	52	52	0.0
76430	ALBANY	417	2523	2541	2578	0.2	17	986	980	982	-0.1	2.54	710	707	-0.1
76431	CHICO	497	3045	3315	3709	2.0	68	1166	1262	1406	1.9	2.57	890	967	2.0
76432	BLANKET	049	1383	1559	1696	2.9	80	533	599	649	2.8	2.60	407	458	2.8
76433	BLUFF DALE	143	2067	2112	2200	0.5	25	846	855	882	0.3	2.47	640	648	0.3
76435	CARBON	133	504	467	469	-1.8	0	220	202	202	-2.0	2.31	159	147	-1.8
76436	CARLTON	093	554	578	610	1.0	42	224	231	241	0.7	2.43	161	167	0.9
76437	CISCO	133	5421	5612	5807	0.8	36	2149	2213	2275	0.7	2.42	1466	1516	0.8
76442	COMANCHE	093	7554	7879	8331	1.0	42	2908	3006	3152	0.8	2.54	2109	2186	0.9
76443	CROSS PLAINS	059	1831	1873	1928	0.5	27	761	775	796	0.4	2.38	534	545	0.5
76444	DE LEON	093	4108	4240	4459	0.8	34	1685	1720	1791	0.5	2.42	1136	1162	0.5
76445	DESDEMONA	133	469	474	487	0.3	19	191	191	195	0.0	2.48	137	138	0.2
76446	DUBLIN	143	6774	7261	7766	1.7	60	2374	2519	2667	1.4	2.83	1725	1835	1.5
76448	EASTLAND	133	5822	5902	6051	0.3	21	2345	2359	2401	0.1	2.43	1671	1688	0.2
76449	GRAFORD	363	2261	2624	2869	3.6	87	980	1140	1244	3.6	2.30	669	780	3.7
76450	GRAHAM	503	12650	12817	12970	0.3	20	5030	5093	5153	0.3	2.46	3627	3682	0.4
76453	GORDON	363	830	894	935	1.8	63	360	385	401	1.6	2.32	256	273	1.5
76454	GORMAN	133	1704	1718	1756	0.2	17	676	674	683	-0.1	2.49	462	462	0.0
76455	GUSTINE	093	1137	1212	1298	1.5	57	464	491	521	1.3	2.47	334	355	1.5
76457	HICO	143	4021	4103	4258	0.5	25	1557	1564	1601	0.1	2.59	1120	1130	0.2
76458	JACKSBORO	237	6160	6429	6809	1.0	42	2042	2132	2266	1.0	2.51	1451	1519	1.1
76459	JERMYN	237	140	144	153	0.7	31	54	55	58	0.4	2.62	39	40	0.6
76460	LOVING	503	228	230	231	0.2	18	96	96	97	0.0	2.40	75	76	0.3
76462	LIPAN	221	2062	2259	2499	2.2	71	790	861	949	2.1	2.62	590	644	2.1
76463	MINGUS	363	253	276	291	2.1	69	116	126	132	2.0	2.19	80	87	2.0
76464	MORAN	417	466	482	496	0.8	35	203	208	211	0.6	2.32	145	149	0.6
76470	RANGER	133	3450	3528	3635	0.5	26	1351	1373	1405	0.4	2.36	893	909	0.4
76471	RISING STAR	133	1750	1798	1854	0.6	30	741	754	770	0.4	2.33	508	518	0.5
76472	SANTO	363	1447	1495	1529	0.8	35	536	551	562	0.7	2.69	411	424	0.7
76474	SIDNEY	093	96	99	104	0.7	34	36	37	38	0.7	2.68	29	30	0.7
76475	STRAWN	363	1028	1047	1063	0.4	23	417	421	426	0.2	2.49	274	277	0.3
	TEXAS					2.2					2.0	2.77			2.1
	UNITED STATES					1.2					1.3	2.58			1.1

POPULATION COMPOSITION

TEXAS

76208-76475 B

ZIP CODE #	POST OFFICE NAME	RACE (%) White 2000	White 2004	Black 2000	Black 2004	Asian/Pacific 2000	Asian/Pacific 2004	% Hispanic Origin 2000	% Hispanic Origin 2004	2004 AGE DISTRIBUTION (%) 0-4	5-9	10-14	15-19	20-24	25-44	45-64	65-84	85+	18+	MEDIAN AGE 2004	% 2004 Males	% 2004 Females
76208	DENTON	81.7	79.0	5.3	6.0	1.0	1.2	17.8	20.8	9.9	8.8	7.7	7.4	10.3	31.2	19.4	5.0	0.3	69.4	28.6	50.3	49.7
76209	DENTON	78.0	75.6	7.9	8.5	1.5	1.7	18.4	21.1	7.7	7.0	7.1	7.8	11.5	30.8	19.7	7.4	1.1	74.2	29.8	47.0	53.0
76210	DENTON	88.7	87.0	4.3	4.8	2.1	2.5	6.5	7.8	9.7	8.9	6.9	5.4	5.2	36.4	21.7	5.2	0.7	71.0	33.7	49.4	50.6
76225	ALVORD	94.4	93.7	0.4	0.4	0.2	0.2	7.0	8.2	6.8	7.2	7.7	7.0	5.3	27.0	26.8	10.8	1.3	73.7	38.1	50.3	49.7
76226	ARGYLE	91.4	90.4	0.9	1.0	0.5	0.6	8.7	10.1	6.2	7.6	9.0	6.8	4.3	25.8	32.3	7.4	0.6	72.8	40.2	51.1	49.0
76227	AUBREY	91.0	88.6	1.2	1.3	0.3	0.4	9.0	12.2	7.2	7.5	7.5	6.8	5.8	30.7	26.1	7.6	0.6	73.6	36.1	50.7	49.3
76228	BELLEVUE	96.6	96.2	0.1	0.1	0.1	0.1	2.7	3.1	6.1	6.4	7.0	5.9	5.1	24.0	29.7	14.3	1.5	76.8	42.1	50.5	49.5
76230	BOWIE	96.6	96.2	0.1	0.1	0.4	0.4	4.0	4.7	6.4	6.0	6.3	6.7	5.6	23.1	25.3	17.8	2.9	77.2	42.1	47.9	52.1
76233	COLLINSVILLE	94.6	93.5	0.2	0.2	0.1	0.1	5.4	6.6	6.3	6.7	7.7	6.5	6.0	27.5	24.3	13.1	2.0	74.9	38.4	49.6	50.4
76234	DECATUR	88.0	86.1	1.2	1.4	0.4	0.5	14.8	17.4	7.5	7.1	7.7	7.6	6.9	28.0	23.7	9.9	1.8	73.1	35.7	49.9	50.2
76238	ERA	95.3	94.0	0.0	0.3	0.3	0.6	5.6	6.8	6.3	6.5	7.7	8.0	6.0	24.4	27.6	12.2	1.4	74.4	40.0	50.9	49.2
76239	FORESTBURG	95.1	94.1	0.1	0.1	0.1	0.1	5.0	6.3	5.5	5.7	6.6	6.6	5.0	23.0	31.6	14.8	1.2	78.2	43.5	47.6	52.4
76240	GAINESVILLE	86.0	84.4	4.2	4.4	0.4	0.5	12.4	14.4	7.0	6.6	7.1	7.8	6.8	24.3	24.1	14.0	2.3	74.6	37.5	49.0	51.0
76245	GORDONVILLE	96.2	95.5	0.1	0.1	0.4	0.4	2.2	2.8	4.0	4.2	5.3	4.7	4.1	19.3	33.5	22.9	2.1	83.7	50.7	51.5	48.5
76247	JUSTIN	92.0	90.9	0.9	1.0	0.9	1.0	7.3	8.7	7.6	7.6	7.9	7.4	6.5	30.4	24.3	6.9	1.5	72.2	35.3	50.1	49.9
76248	KELLER	92.2	90.1	1.7	2.0	2.6	3.3	5.7	7.9	8.9	9.4	9.5	7.4	5.1	31.5	23.7	4.1	0.3	67.3	33.8	49.5	50.5
76249	KRUM	91.6	90.4	1.1	1.2	0.5	0.5	8.0	9.5	7.5	8.1	8.7	7.6	6.3	31.0	23.8	6.6	0.6	70.7	33.9	49.2	50.8
76250	LINDSAY	98.6	98.3	0.2	0.3	0.1	0.1	1.5	1.9	6.5	6.9	8.7	8.9	7.3	25.4	25.7	9.4	1.2	72.4	35.5	50.4	49.6
76251	MONTAGUE	95.4	94.8	0.7	0.7	0.3	0.3	4.6	5.6	4.5	4.6	5.6	5.9	5.5	25.6	31.7	15.5	1.3	81.6	44.0	52.2	47.8
76252	MUENSTER	97.8	97.4	0.1	0.1	0.3	0.4	2.3	3.0	6.7	6.9	8.0	7.7	5.5	24.6	25.5	12.2	2.9	73.5	39.0	48.7	51.3
76255	NOCONA	94.5	93.6	0.4	0.5	0.3	0.4	9.4	11.2	7.0	6.7	6.2	6.7	5.4	23.1	23.9	17.2	3.8	75.7	41.1	47.5	52.5
76258	PILOT POINT	86.8	85.1	2.9	2.9	0.2	0.2	12.7	14.9	7.1	7.8	8.4	7.5	5.6	29.7	24.1	8.5	1.3	72.0	35.5	50.4	49.6
76259	PONDER	92.5	91.5	0.8	0.9	0.6	0.7	7.0	8.3	7.7	7.8	8.1	7.2	6.1	30.4	26.1	5.9	0.7	71.7	35.4	50.4	49.6
76261	RINGGOLD	97.0	96.9	0.0	0.0	0.0	0.0	3.5	3.6	7.8	6.7	4.2	5.2	5.2	23.8	30.1	14.5	2.6	78.2	42.9	47.7	52.3
76262	ROANOKE	93.7	92.3	1.2	1.4	1.1	1.4	5.5	7.1	7.6	8.0	8.0	6.7	5.3	29.4	28.3	6.3	0.4	72.0	37.1	50.4	49.6
76263	ROSSTON	100.0	100.0	0.0	0.0	0.0	0.0	0.0	0.0	0.0	0.0	0.0	0.0	50.0	50.0	0.0	0.0	0.0	100.0	25.0	50.0	50.0
76264	SADLER	95.7	95.0	0.3	0.3	0.1	0.1	3.1	3.8	6.3	6.3	6.8	6.6	5.7	25.0	27.8	14.7	1.1	76.5	40.8	49.8	50.2
76265	SAINT JO	96.6	96.2	0.1	0.2	0.1	0.1	4.5	5.3	4.8	5.0	6.9	6.3	5.3	19.8	30.3	19.4	2.3	79.6	46.4	48.8	51.2
76266	SANGER	91.8	90.5	1.6	1.8	0.3	0.4	8.6	10.4	7.2	7.3	8.0	7.2	6.7	29.4	25.4	8.0	0.9	72.9	35.7	49.7	50.4
76270	SUNSET	96.2	95.6	0.1	0.1	0.4	0.4	3.3	4.1	5.8	6.2	6.9	6.9	5.3	24.8	29.7	13.3	1.1	76.7	41.4	51.9	48.1
76271	TIOGA	93.6	92.6	0.4	0.4	0.9	1.1	11.2	13.3	8.0	7.7	7.1	5.9	6.4	29.9	24.4	9.4	1.2	73.5	36.1	51.2	48.8
76272	VALLEY VIEW	94.1	93.1	0.4	0.4	0.3	0.3	5.9	7.3	7.0	6.7	7.8	7.3	6.2	27.1	26.6	10.6	0.7	74.0	37.5	50.9	49.2
76273	WHITESBORO	95.7	95.0	0.4	0.4	0.3	0.3	3.3	4.1	6.4	6.6	7.3	7.2	5.9	26.1	25.3	13.1	2.0	75.1	38.8	49.5	50.5
76301	WICHITA FALLS	60.0	58.1	22.9	22.7	1.3	1.4	22.5	25.5	8.0	6.9	7.0	7.1	8.2	26.6	22.3	11.9	2.0	74.1	34.9	48.6	51.4
76302	WICHITA FALLS	85.6	83.5	6.0	6.9	1.1	1.3	11.7	13.5	8.3	6.5	6.6	6.6	9.1	25.6	22.7	12.6	2.0	74.9	34.9	48.3	51.7
76305	WICHITA FALLS	74.9	73.7	21.5	22.1	0.5	0.5	17.8	20.3	3.5	3.5	3.9	8.0	14.6	39.9	18.1	7.6	1.0	85.1	32.7	71.8	28.2
76306	WICHITA FALLS	63.1	60.8	20.0	20.5	3.4	3.8	16.4	18.4	8.2	7.7	8.0	7.5	7.5	28.0	21.5	10.8	0.9	71.7	33.5	49.3	50.7
76308	WICHITA FALLS	87.5	86.0	3.8	4.0	2.7	3.1	6.7	8.0	5.8	5.4	5.9	7.9	11.9	25.9	22.6	12.7	2.0	79.4	35.0	48.1	51.9
76309	WICHITA FALLS	80.3	78.0	4.3	4.5	2.2	2.5	15.6	17.9	7.0	6.8	6.9	6.1	6.7	26.7	23.7	13.1	3.1	75.7	37.7	48.1	51.9
76310	WICHITA FALLS	89.9	88.6	2.6	2.8	2.1	2.4	6.8	8.1	7.0	6.6	7.1	7.0	6.8	28.5	24.9	10.9	1.2	74.9	37.0	48.0	52.0
76311	SHEPPARD AFB	70.2	68.3	16.3	16.8	3.6	4.0	10.2	11.8	8.6	7.3	5.6	25.8	24.2	27.1	1.4	0.1	0.0	76.6	20.6	65.0	35.0
76351	ARCHER CITY	97.1	96.7	0.0	0.0	0.0	0.0	2.9	3.5	6.7	6.7	7.0	6.5	6.2	24.6	24.2	15.5	2.7	75.3	40.1	47.5	52.5
76354	BURKBURNETT	90.9	89.7	2.9	3.1	0.7	0.8	6.2	7.5	7.0	7.0	7.7	7.4	6.3	25.9	24.5	12.9	1.4	73.8	37.8	48.4	51.6
76357	BYERS	92.6	91.5	0.0	0.0	0.0	0.0	6.5	7.3	5.4	6.0	6.7	6.4	5.5	24.5	30.8	13.2	1.5	78.2	42.4	49.3	50.7
76360	ELECTRA	88.8	87.5	4.1	4.3	0.1	0.1	8.1	9.7	6.9	6.8	7.8	7.6	6.3	23.9	23.8	14.3	2.6	73.9	38.8	48.6	51.4
76363	GOREE	75.9	74.9	3.6	3.7	0.0	0.0	27.5	28.3	6.4	6.9	7.7	5.8	3.7	23.3	23.8	19.3	3.2	75.1	42.6	48.7	51.3
76364	HARROLD	88.5	86.5	0.8	0.8	0.0	0.0	8.4	10.5	5.2	6.4	7.9	6.4	4.9	22.1	32.6	13.1	1.5	76.8	42.9	52.1	47.9
76365	HENRIETTA	95.7	95.2	0.6	0.6	0.1	0.1	3.2	3.9	5.9	6.1	6.6	6.6	5.7	23.9	27.6	15.3	2.2	77.3	42.1	48.5	51.5
76366	HOLLIDAY	96.4	95.8	0.1	0.1	0.2	0.2	3.3	4.0	6.6	7.0	7.7	7.5	5.8	26.5	25.2	12.0	1.8	73.9	38.7	49.5	50.5
76367	IOWA PARK	93.9	93.1	2.1	2.1	0.5	0.5	5.5	6.6	6.0	6.2	6.9	7.7	7.4	27.8	23.9	12.6	1.6	76.3	37.8	50.9	49.1
76371	MUNDAY	70.6	70.0	7.6	7.7	0.2	0.2	29.9	30.8	7.5	7.4	8.5	7.5	5.6	22.4	19.8	17.2	4.2	71.2	38.3	46.7	53.3
76372	NEWCASTLE	94.6	93.9	0.8	0.9	0.1	0.1	4.3	5.0	6.1	6.4	7.1	6.6	5.2	25.8	26.0	15.5	1.5	76.5	40.7	50.8	49.2
76373	OKLAUNION	88.7	87.3	0.5	0.5	0.0	0.0	8.7	10.1	5.3	5.8	7.4	6.4	4.8	21.2	33.9	13.8	1.6	77.8	44.4	52.9	47.1
76374	OLNEY	90.9	89.8	2.2	2.3	0.3	0.3	12.3	14.5	6.4	6.2	6.3	7.5	6.5	21.9	23.7	17.6	3.8	76.4	41.8	47.2	52.8
76377	PETROLIA	94.0	93.2	0.4	0.4	0.0	0.0	4.7	5.5	6.6	6.7	7.2	6.3	5.7	25.4	26.4	13.7	2.0	75.7	40.0	46.8	53.3
76379	SCOTLAND	89.4	87.6	0.0	0.0	0.2	0.3	14.8	17.5	8.9	8.9	8.9	6.6	5.6	27.1	20.7	11.8	1.7	69.1	34.4	51.9	48.1
76380	SEYMOUR	91.0	90.8	3.2	3.3	0.7	0.7	9.8	10.2	5.1	5.1	6.5	7.1	5.4	19.7	27.5	20.1	3.7	78.9	45.9	47.9	52.1
76384	VERNON	77.8	75.8	9.2	9.4	0.7	0.8	21.0	24.0	6.9	6.6	6.8	9.5	7.5	23.7	23.0	13.1	3.1	73.9	36.2	49.5	50.5
76388	WEINERT	76.2	73.1	2.6	2.7	0.4	0.5	26.8	31.4	4.9	4.9	6.7	5.4	6.3	22.9	26.9	19.3	2.7	79.8	44.2	48.9	51.1
76389	WINDTHORST	91.4	89.7	0.0	0.0	0.3	0.4	12.0	14.2	8.4	8.5	8.6	6.6	5.7	26.5	22.3	11.8	1.7	70.4	35.4	51.3	48.7
76401	STEPHENVILLE	91.2	90.0	1.1	1.1	0.5	0.6	11.7	13.6	6.3	5.9	6.1	9.6	11.0	28.9	19.5	10.5	2.2	78.1	30.6	49.1	50.9
76424	BRECKENRIDGE	86.5	84.8	2.9	3.0	0.3	0.4	15.3	17.8	6.0	5.5	6.9	7.0	8.3	24.4	24.5	15.2	2.3	77.4	39.1	50.8	49.2
76426	BRIDGEPORT	86.4	84.9	3.2	3.2	0.2	0.2	17.6	20.3	7.0	6.8	7.0	7.3	7.4	28.8	23.5	10.8	1.5	74.8	36.0	50.8	49.2
76427	BRYSON	95.7	95.3	0.4	0.4	0.2	0.2	3.1	3.7	5.2	5.3	6.4	7.5	5.6	24.2	26.9	17.2	1.8	78.6	42.5	50.4	49.6
76429	CADDO	89.4	88.8	6.3	6.3	0.0	0.0	5.0	5.6	3.1	3.1	3.8	6.3	10.0	27.5	30.0	14.4	1.9	86.3	42.5	61.3	38.8
76430	ALBANY	93.5	93.3	0.6	0.6	0.0	0.0	8.3	8.7	6.0	6.4	8.0	7.3	5.9	23.5	26.0	14.1	2.9	75.1	40.8	47.0	53.1
76431	CHICO	94.0	93.3	1.2	1.2	0.1	0.1	6.2	7.2	5.6	6.2	8.3	8.0	5.7	26.3	27.2	11.5	1.3	75.1	38.9	51.4	48.6
76432	BLANKET	93.8	92.7	0.5	0.5	0.1	0.2	7.8	9.4	6.2	6.2	6.9	7.3	6.4	22.3	28.0	15.3	1.5	76.2	41.5	50.7	49.3
76433	BLUFF DALE	95.9	95.2	0.2	0.2	0.2	0.2	6.5	7.9	4.9	5.7	6.7	5.8	4.0	26.2	31.4	14.1	1.3	79.3	42.7	53.1	46.9
76435	CARBON	93.9	92.7	0.0	0.0	0.0	0.0	8.3	9.9	7.3	7.1	6.6	4.1	3.6	20.6	29.8	18.6	2.4	76.5	45.6	52.0	48.0
76436	CARLTON	87.2	84.6	0.2	0.2	0.2	0.4	15.9	19.0	6.1	6.6	6.4	6.1	5.4	21.6	27.5	17.1	3.3	77.3	43.4	51.7	48.3
76437	CISCO	92.0	91.3	2.8	2.8	0.2	0.3	8.3	9.5	5.7	5.5	6.1	8.2	7.9	19.9	26.0	17.7	3.0	79.0	42.4	48.4	51.6
76442	COMANCHE	85.5	83.6	0.8	0.8	0.2	0.2	21.6	24.6	7.0	6.9	7.0	6.5	5.5	23.9	23.2	16.6	3.4	75.1	39.6	48.8	51.2
76443	CROSS PLAINS	96.8	96.4	0.1	0.1	0.0	0.0	3.8	4.6	4.7	4.9	6.0	6.9	6.0	19.6	27.1	20.9	4.0	79.7	46.4	48.2	51.8
76444	DE LEON	90.0	88.5	0.1	0.1	0.1	0.1	19.7	22.6	5.9	6.1	7.3	6.6	5.1	23.1	24.2	17.8	4.0	76.7	42.2	48.7	51.3
76445	DESDEMONA	90.6	89.2	0.0	0.0	0.2	0.2	14.3	16.5	6.3	6.5	6.3	5.7	6.3	22.6	26.0	17.3	3.0	77.6	42.3	49.4	50.6
76446	DUBLIN	81.7	79.5	0.2	0.2	0.1	0.1	28.7	32.2	8.3	7.5	8.5	7.7	5.9	25.9	21.6	12.2	2.4	70.8	34.8	49.2	50.8
76448	EASTLAND	93.2	92.1	1.2	1.3	0.1	0.2	10.6	12.5	6.3	6.0	6.2	6.4	6.6	22.2	26.0	17.6	2.8	77.8	42.4	48.2	51.8
76449	GRAFORD	95.0	94.3	0.0	0.0	0.4	0.5	5.0	6.0	4.3	4.6	6.0	5.3	4.7	20.5	32.9	20.1	1.6	81.8	48.0	50.8	49.2
76450	GRAHAM	90.7	89.5	0.9	0.9	0.3	0.4	10.5	12.2	5.8	5.9	6.8	6.8	5.8	23.1	26.8	16.3	2.7	77.1	42.1	48.4	51.6
76453	GORDON	94.5	93.4	0.1	0.1	0.4	0.6	5.9	7.4	5.3	5.4	5.9	5.6	5.3	20.9	32.2	17.0	2.5	80.1	46.2	47.7	52.4
76454	GORMAN	85.3	83.1	0.1	0.1	0.1	0.1	21.4	24.7	7.0	6.9	7.3	6.5	6.2	21.8	23.6	16.4	4.3	74.5	40.9	48.1	51.9
76455	GUSTINE	88.0	86.1	0.0	0.0	0.0	0.0	21.6	25.3	6.6	6.4	5.7	5.8	5.5	22.9	25.9	18.9	2.4	77.9	42.6	51.8	48.2
76457	HICO	90.9	89.3	0.2	0.2	0.1	0.2	15.0	17.6	6.5	7.1	7.3	6.5	4.9	26.0	24.1	14.8	2.9	75.0	39.2	50.5	49.5
76458	JACKSBORO	85.5	84.0	7.8	8.2	0.3	0.3	9.4	11.1	5.9	5.8	5.8	6.8	8.2	30.8	22.4	12.2	2.2	79.0	37.1	55.7	44.3
76459	JERMYN	95.7	95.8	0.0	0.0	0.0	0.0	2.9	3.5	5.6	5.6	6.3	7.6	5.6	25.0	25.0	17.4	2.1	77.8	41.7	47.9	52.1
76460	LOVING	94.3	93.5	1.3	1.3	0.9	0.9	5.3	6.1	4.8	5.2	6.1	6.1	4.8	20.4	29.1	21.3	2.2	80.4	46.6	51.7	48.3
76462	LIPAN	95.3	94.5	0.2	0.2	0.3	0.4	5.0	6.1	6.8	7.1	6.8	6.4	5.4	25.0	28.5	12.8	1.2	75.4	40.0	49.7	50.3
76463	MINGUS	94.5	93.1	0.0	0.0	0.4	0.7	5.9	7.3	4.7	5.1	6.2	5.8	5.1	20.7	31.9	17.8	2.9	80.1	46.8	46.7	53.3
76464	MORAN	96.4	96.3	0.0	0.0	0.0	0.0	4.7	5.2	3.9	4.4	5.8	5.2	5.0	19.9	29.9	22.6	3.3	82.8	49.7	47.5	52.5
76470	RANGER	87.3	85.8	5.1	5.3	0.5	0.6	11.5	13.4	5.9	5.8	5.4	8.6	10.7	20.0	23.8	17.1	2.7	79.4	39.8	49.5	50.5
76471	RISING STAR	95.3	94.6	0.1	0.1	0.2	0.2	5.3	6.5	5.2	5.1	5.5	6.0	5.3	19.5	27.5	22.0	4.1	80.8	47.6	50.4	49.6
76472	SANTO	94.8	93.8	0.3	0.3	0.4	0.5	5.7	7.0	6.6	6.4	6.0	5.9	4.9	23.1	31.7	13.7	1.8	77.5	43.0	52.4	47.6
76474	SIDNEY	93.8	92.9	0.0	0.0	0.0	0.0	7.3	9.1	4.0	5.1	5.1	7.1	5.1	22.2	29.3	20.2	2.0	82.8	46.3	50.5	49.5
76475	STRAWN	84.6	82.0	0.2	0.2	0.6	0.8	19.4	22.7	7.1	6.5	7.6	7.2	7.6	22.8	24.8	13.7	2.8	74.6	38.2	49.4	50.6
	TEXAS	71.0	69.5	11.5	11.4	2.8	3.1	32.0	34.6	7.9	7.5	7.7	7.5	8.1	29.6	21.9	8.7	1.2	72.6	32.9	49.7	50.3
	UNITED STATES	75.1	73.6	12.3	12.5	3.8	4.2	12.5	14.1	6.9	6.7	7.2	7.0	7.3	28.6	23.8	10.8	1.7	75.1	36.0	49.1	50.9

ZIP CODE #	POST OFFICE NAME	2004 Per Capita Income	2004 HH Income Base	2004 Household Income Distribution (%): Less than $25,000	$25,000 to $49,999	$50,000 to $99,999	$100,000 to $149,999	$150,000 or More	Median Household Income: 2004	2009	2004 National Centile	2004 State Centile	2004 Home Value Base	2004 Home Value Distribution (%): Less than $50,000	$50,000 to $89,999	$90,000 to $174,999	$175,000 to $399,999	$400,000 or More	2004 Median Home Value
76208	DENTON	21486	4468	22.0	32.6	29.4	11.8	4.1	45266	54733	62	69	3039	43.4	9.9	25.3	19.6	1.7	72660
76209	DENTON	21693	9492	23.4	27.0	36.5	9.6	3.5	49521	58159	71	76	5170	8.2	19.5	61.6	10.1	0.6	111537
76210	DENTON	33036	9544	7.9	17.5	41.7	21.2	11.7	77347	92223	94	95	8559	15.1	3.2	37.8	40.2	3.7	164551
76225	ALVORD	22317	1067	27.0	28.3	33.4	8.4	2.9	45332	52131	62	69	880	26.1	27.7	27.5	13.9	4.8	83061
76226	ARGYLE	44949	3020	10.9	16.3	27.0	21.6	24.2	89674	103928	97	97	2663	10.3	5.6	12.0	45.7	26.5	269637
76227	AUBREY	27500	3168	15.2	26.9	35.9	13.8	8.2	58367	67589	83	86	2691	10.8	16.7	40.4	22.6	9.6	124169
76228	BELLEVUE	20711	635	29.1	31.7	30.6	5.0	3.6	40380	44275	47	55	512	38.5	25.2	19.3	14.5	2.5	66596
76230	BOWIE	20580	3972	35.4	32.0	24.4	5.0	3.3	36151	40827	32	38	3044	32.0	35.2	23.2	8.3	1.4	69559
76233	COLLINSVILLE	22276	895	24.7	31.1	33.6	7.2	3.5	44528	50736	60	67	721	18.5	35.5	31.5	11.7	2.9	85870
76234	DECATUR	22865	4921	23.7	27.3	33.4	11.2	4.5	48898	55211	70	75	3824	16.0	18.7	40.9	19.6	4.8	111754
76238	ERA	20905	116	22.4	28.5	36.2	7.8	5.2	48667	54048	70	75	97	15.5	22.7	40.2	19.6	2.1	106618
76239	FORESTBURG	26135	530	28.7	34.2	23.8	7.7	5.7	38836	44236	42	50	435	23.0	28.1	26.9	13.8	8.3	88548
76240	GAINESVILLE	20095	10353	30.9	29.9	29.0	7.2	2.9	40282	46226	47	55	7184	25.8	27.9	30.2	13.1	3.0	83424
76245	GORDONVILLE	25101	787	41.0	29.4	19.8	6.5	3.3	32112	36631	18	23	674	44.2	28.8	17.7	8.9	0.5	58667
76247	JUSTIN	24300	2235	15.7	24.1	41.5	14.1	4.6	58600	68015	83	86	1879	6.4	24.2	46.5	20.7	2.3	114672
76248	KELLER	34272	11806	5.9	12.8	38.1	27.0	16.2	89644	106224	97	97	10805	7.7	7.7	33.9	45.9	4.8	176790
76249	KRUM	24889	1826	13.8	26.6	40.5	14.5	4.6	59799	68230	84	86	1507	13.5	16.9	47.9	19.3	2.4	112567
76250	LINDSAY	20571	304	14.8	26.0	45.1	12.8	1.3	57167	63399	82	84	255	20.0	20.8	43.1	16.1	0.0	104261
76251	MONTAGUE	29999	288	32.3	30.2	26.7	5.6	5.2	38015	42448	39	46	246	37.4	20.7	19.1	17.5	5.3	72500
76252	MUENSTER	23002	1142	22.9	27.9	36.1	8.9	4.2	49182	55428	70	76	944	12.5	29.3	42.0	15.3	1.0	97700
76255	NOCONA	18262	2006	40.9	30.5	21.1	5.2	2.3	33102	38045	21	26	1482	44.0	28.0	21.4	5.5	1.2	57008
76258	PILOT POINT	24603	2491	18.6	26.1	37.6	12.1	5.6	54336	63881	79	82	1905	8.9	23.2	37.0	20.9	10.0	118618
76259	PONDER	24614	1115	16.1	23.5	40.0	14.5	5.9	59949	69176	84	87	935	11.9	21.6	38.7	23.0	4.8	115707
76261	RINGGOLD	15743	79	49.4	29.1	17.7	3.8	0.0	25746	32357	5	7	66	43.9	16.7	28.8	9.1	1.5	60000
76262	ROANOKE	40043	6579	9.4	15.7	32.6	23.6	18.7	85864	101432	96	97	5510	8.8	7.3	24.5	49.5	10.0	193949
76263	ROSSTON	0	0	0.0	0.0	0.0	0.0	0.0	0	0	0	0	0	0.0	0.0	0.0	0.0	0.0	0
76264	SADLER	21376	624	21.6	31.4	37.8	5.6	3.5	46502	52973	65	71	535	27.3	27.3	36.5	8.0	0.9	84024
76265	SAINT JO	19716	928	33.5	26.7	31.1	6.6	2.1	38267	43027	40	48	744	32.4	30.7	26.3	9.4	1.2	72381
76266	SANGER	24796	4039	16.5	27.9	37.9	12.4	5.4	54538	63799	79	83	3129	14.0	24.5	35.8	21.7	4.0	107820
76270	SUNSET	20864	542	30.8	31.0	28.8	7.0	2.4	41183	46811	50	58	458	31.2	24.2	26.6	14.2	3.7	81935
76271	TIOGA	22758	452	16.6	37.4	34.1	8.2	3.8	46655	54043	65	71	356	18.5	31.7	36.0	10.7	3.1	89643
76272	VALLEY VIEW	21967	1776	22.8	29.1	34.2	10.1	3.9	47882	54899	68	73	1418	25.3	22.6	31.8	13.7	6.6	92970
76273	WHITESBORO	20664	3387	30.1	27.8	31.7	7.1	3.3	41664	48094	52	60	2695	28.7	26.4	30.4	12.2	2.3	79913
76301	WICHITA FALLS	16761	7371	46.3	34.0	15.4	2.0	2.4	26798	30428	7	9	3821	67.5	20.4	7.0	3.6	1.5	39010
76302	WICHITA FALLS	19456	4581	34.0	31.5	26.3	5.1	3.1	35566	39713	30	36	2774	18.7	43.2	34.3	3.4	0.5	80030
76305	WICHITA FALLS	14931	1350	31.3	33.9	26.9	6.1	1.8	36973	41340	35	42	1049	40.3	27.1	28.5	3.4	0.7	65225
76306	WICHITA FALLS	16228	6252	32.7	35.2	27.0	4.2	0.9	35630	40403	30	36	3854	43.0	39.6	15.6	1.5	0.4	57765
76308	WICHITA FALLS	26522	7965	25.3	33.3	27.1	7.2	7.1	41913	48657	53	61	4880	14.3	31.3	37.3	14.7	2.4	95658
76309	WICHITA FALLS	22810	5834	28.4	33.7	27.0	7.1	3.8	39350	44615	44	52	3644	35.3	24.7	30.5	9.1	0.4	71550
76310	WICHITA FALLS	23603	6363	20.2	31.9	36.2	8.3	3.4	47985	54612	68	73	4457	7.7	45.3	41.9	4.5	0.6	87816
76311	SHEPPARD AFB	12607	1474	16.2	53.7	28.5	1.6	0.0	40546	45583	48	56	14	0.0	78.6	21.4	0.0	0.0	86364
76351	ARCHER CITY	23245	745	33.2	37.2	22.4	3.5	3.8	35509	41192	30	35	559	53.9	30.2	10.6	4.1	1.3	47095
76354	BURKBURNETT	20418	4274	27.2	30.7	32.0	8.1	2.1	42294	47703	54	62	3225	33.7	34.2	28.6	2.6	0.8	67432
76357	BYERS	19284	266	26.7	36.1	30.1	6.0	1.1	40632	44433	48	56	214	36.5	25.7	29.0	7.0	1.9	71250
76360	ELECTRA	17047	1500	42.7	31.0	19.9	4.0	2.3	29512	33588	11	14	1076	65.8	23.5	8.6	1.9	0.2	35495
76363	GOREE	16854	145	40.7	29.7	22.1	4.8	2.8	31296	35000	16	20	116	57.8	27.6	12.1	1.7	0.9	36667
76364	HARROLD	24228	109	32.1	34.9	22.9	0.0	10.1	36844	41994	35	42	85	38.8	37.7	21.2	0.0	2.4	58636
76365	HENRIETTA	18774	2637	28.4	34.2	29.7	6.5	1.2	40434	44879	48	56	2120	39.6	28.9	25.9	4.9	0.7	63630
76366	HOLLIDAY	20116	1196	31.4	31.2	28.7	5.7	3.1	38492	44102	41	49	936	47.3	28.1	18.1	5.7	0.9	53012
76367	IOWA PARK	21151	3621	21.8	32.7	36.8	6.9	1.8	46439	52154	65	71	2918	30.7	43.6	22.2	3.3	0.2	66228
76371	MUNDAY	14147	739	48.0	30.2	17.9	3.3	0.7	26262	29332	6	8	534	65.0	25.5	8.1	1.1	0.4	35000
76372	NEWCASTLE	21060	400	34.8	37.8	20.3	3.5	3.8	33639	39579	23	28	318	56.9	24.2	12.9	4.4	1.6	44054
76373	OKLAUNION	20152	64	32.8	34.4	23.4	0.0	9.4	36490	41735	34	40	50	36.0	38.0	24.0	0.0	2.0	60000
76374	OLNEY	16784	1843	45.9	29.7	17.3	4.5	2.7	28033	32141	9	12	1194	57.3	23.4	14.6	4.5	0.3	45297
76377	PETROLIA	16410	646	34.7	35.8	24.2	4.0	1.4	35083	39093	28	33	527	52.9	26.4	16.3	3.4	1.0	47905
76379	SCOTLAND	18357	216	28.2	32.4	31.5	6.9	0.9	39146	44323	43	51	173	32.4	33.5	27.2	6.4	0.6	74688
76380	SEYMOUR	18290	1916	45.2	31.2	18.7	3.4	1.6	28085	31688	9	12	1381	56.5	26.2	13.5	3.0	0.9	44576
76384	VERNON	19819	5316	36.6	32.2	22.0	5.7	3.5	33336	39021	22	27	3489	44.9	29.7	20.8	3.9	0.7	55332
76388	WEINERT	18750	98	50.0	26.5	17.4	4.1	2.0	25000	25889	5	6	78	69.2	21.8	6.4	2.6	0.0	31250
76389	WINDTHORST	16637	385	28.8	33.0	30.9	6.0	1.3	38976	43816	43	51	306	35.6	31.4	24.8	7.2	1.0	71538
76401	STEPHENVILLE	20613	9084	37.0	29.9	22.7	7.3	3.1	34701	39690	26	32	5460	25.0	28.2	33.2	11.2	2.4	85797
76424	BRECKENRIDGE	17789	3465	36.1	33.8	22.1	5.3	2.8	33719	38572	23	29	2401	48.9	26.8	16.8	5.3	2.3	51335
76426	BRIDGEPORT	18658	3490	25.5	30.8	33.3	8.1	2.3	43432	49357	57	65	2663	25.0	26.0	31.2	15.9	2.0	88301
76427	BRYSON	21021	430	37.9	32.3	23.5	2.8	3.5	33407	37768	22	27	340	50.0	30.3	15.3	2.4	2.1	50000
76429	CADDO	23418	68	36.8	26.5	26.5	8.8	1.5	33620	37343	23	28	56	35.7	25.0	25.0	12.5	1.8	73333
76430	ALBANY	19643	980	35.2	31.8	26.2	3.8	3.0	34384	40072	25	31	770	49.4	29.4	16.8	4.0	0.5	50735
76431	CHICO	19587	1262	25.8	34.1	30.7	6.9	2.5	42981	49939	56	64	1039	32.3	26.7	27.4	10.6	3.0	75909
76432	BLANKET	19221	599	27.7	32.2	32.7	5.3	2.0	43015	49038	56	64	502	36.9	25.7	27.5	8.8	1.2	72308
76433	BLUFF DALE	25051	855	23.5	30.3	30.9	11.0	4.3	45665	53921	63	69	704	26.6	23.3	25.0	18.9	6.3	90345
76435	CARBON	19560	202	30.2	40.1	23.8	2.0	4.0	37406	41625	37	44	165	41.8	26.1	17.0	13.3	1.8	67222
76436	CARLTON	24893	231	32.9	30.3	23.4	9.5	3.9	38284	44726	40	48	187	28.9	26.7	26.2	12.8	5.4	80455
76437	CISCO	17046	2213	43.4	31.4	18.8	3.9	2.6	29121	32469	11	13	1671	61.9	20.4	13.8	3.4	0.6	40767
76442	COMANCHE	16389	3006	37.9	34.5	21.5	4.6	1.5	33879	38108	24	29	2242	43.4	28.0	21.3	5.6	1.6	58698
76443	CROSS PLAINS	16444	775	42.1	29.0	24.3	4.1	0.5	30133	33168	13	16	608	44.6	27.6	17.1	8.4	2.3	59429
76444	DE LEON	15689	1720	46.1	25.4	23.8	3.8	0.9	28147	31615	9	12	1311	45.4	24.8	20.5	5.9	3.4	54690
76445	DESDEMONA	15921	191	41.9	31.9	20.4	5.2	0.5	29816	33924	12	15	157	38.9	30.6	20.4	7.6	2.6	62692
76446	DUBLIN	16128	2519	38.7	33.5	19.9	5.0	2.9	31853	36325	17	22	1792	44.3	24.9	23.5	5.9	1.5	58240
76448	EASTLAND	19977	2359	36.0	35.0	20.4	4.6	4.1	34043	38565	24	30	1722	44.5	29.0	19.5	4.6	2.4	56250
76449	GRAFORD	21261	1140	33.5	30.9	26.7	6.3	2.6	38398	43296	41	49	953	38.4	20.4	21.7	15.1	4.4	68017
76450	GRAHAM	20476	5093	32.8	31.5	26.0	6.2	3.5	37529	43148	38	45	3837	39.7	28.7	22.5	7.7	1.4	61804
76453	GORDON	27138	385	30.9	26.8	29.4	8.1	4.9	42736	47749	53	62	322	38.8	21.4	22.7	12.7	4.4	70500
76454	GORMAN	14809	674	42.1	34.6	18.4	3.7	1.2	29589	32884	11	14	516	52.9	29.8	12.8	3.9	0.6	46939
76455	GUSTINE	19852	491	42.2	29.5	22.0	4.1	2.2	30787	35230	14	18	388	41.0	22.9	22.2	9.5	4.4	63200
76457	HICO	18535	1564	34.6	30.7	26.2	5.8	2.8	36474	41814	33	40	1184	32.7	25.7	24.1	13.7	3.9	74935
76458	JACKSBORO	18008	2132	32.7	33.7	26.9	4.5	2.3	36368	40721	33	39	1607	44.0	28.8	17.8	6.2	3.2	57659
76459	JERMYN	15990	55	36.4	34.6	23.6	3.6	1.8	33321	38621	22	27	43	51.2	32.6	14.0	0.0	2.3	49000
76460	LOVING	21572	96	35.4	35.4	19.8	5.2	4.2	35381	35980	29	34	79	27.9	20.3	35.4	15.2	1.3	93000
76462	LIPAN	22122	861	25.1	31.8	32.1	7.1	4.0	43142	50437	56	65	727	34.1	25.3	23.0	13.8	3.9	73980
76463	MINGUS	25797	126	31.8	26.2	27.8	8.7	5.6	41313	49220	51	59	105	43.8	20.0	21.9	9.5	4.8	61250
76464	MORAN	18906	208	37.0	34.1	20.2	7.2	1.4	34071	40171	24	30	172	63.4	17.4	7.0	11.1	1.2	38000
76470	RANGER	15173	1373	45.5	33.9	16.0	3.4	1.2	27154	30358	7	10	1006	63.8	16.8	13.4	5.2	0.8	34921
76471	RISING STAR	17386	754	44.2	26.1	22.7	4.4	2.7	29314	32215	11	14	588	54.3	25.0	14.1	6.0	0.7	44681
76472	SANTO	18113	551	30.9	28.7	33.0	5.4	2.0	41833	47098	52	61	468	28.9	25.4	24.8	19.0	1.9	79355
76474	SIDNEY	15808	37	29.7	32.4	35.1	2.7	0.0	40738	50000	49	57	30	13.3	36.7	36.7	10.0	3.3	90000
76475	STRAWN	18502	421	39.2	31.1	22.3	4.3	3.1	33353	38484	22	27	317	65.0	14.8	14.5	4.4	1.3	38173
	TEXAS	23284		26.2	27.7	29.5	10.3	6.3	45778	54246				21.6	26.1	33.4	15.6	3.4	93683
	UNITED STATES	25866		24.7	27.1	30.8	10.9	6.5	48124	56710				10.9	15.0	33.7	30.1	10.4	145905

ZIP CODE #	POST OFFICE NAME	FINANCIAL SERVICES Auto Loan	Home Loan	Invest-ments	Retire-ment Plans	THE HOME Home Improvements Home Repair	Lawn & Garden	Furnishings Comput-ers & Hard-ware	Major Appli-ances	TV, Radio, Sound Equip-ment	Furni-ture	ENTERTAINMENT Dine out/ Carry out	Sports Equip-ment	Fees & Tickets	Toys & Games	Travel	Cable TV	PERSONAL Apparel & Services	Auto Repairs	Health Insur-ance	Pets & Supplies
76208	DENTON	93	91	83	91	90	92	89	90	87	90	108	106	86	105	86	84	105	91	85	104
76209	DENTON	81	82	90	86	81	83	86	82	83	85	104	99	85	103	83	78	102	85	75	91
76210	DENTON	135	147	143	152	142	141	136	136	127	140	161	159	139	160	133	121	159	133	120	151
76225	ALVORD	92	80	62	78	84	92	79	85	83	79	101	99	76	100	79	84	96	84	91	103
76226	ARGYLE	176	214	228	220	208	210	190	186	174	193	221	216	207	229	193	169	222	180	167	208
76227	AUBREY	109	121	117	119	119	120	110	113	105	111	132	131	113	134	111	103	130	110	105	128
76228	BELLEVUE	97	67	35	64	79	88	67	82	77	66	90	99	57	88	69	80	82	81	98	115
76230	BOWIE	83	65	47	62	71	81	67	75	74	65	88	87	61	85	68	77	81	75	87	95
76233	COLLINSVILLE	92	79	61	78	83	93	79	85	84	78	102	99	76	102	79	85	96	84	92	104
76234	DECATUR	98	94	81	93	95	101	90	95	91	91	112	110	89	111	90	90	107	93	95	110
76238	ERA	102	90	69	86	96	103	84	93	89	84	108	110	82	110	86	91	103	90	100	120
76239	FORESTBURG	114	82	46	77	94	105	80	98	91	80	108	117	70	106	83	96	99	96	115	135
76240	GAINESVILLE	79	70	62	68	73	81	71	75	75	71	92	86	69	89	71	76	87	75	81	89
76245	GORDONVILLE	95	74	51	67	84	94	70	84	79	69	94	99	63	93	75	85	87	83	100	115
76247	JUSTIN	113	105	84	101	107	112	99	106	100	100	124	124	95	121	99	100	119	105	107	128
76248	KELLER	152	174	172	180	167	165	157	155	144	162	183	181	164	185	155	137	182	151	135	172
76249	KRUM	108	110	101	110	108	110	105	107	101	107	127	126	103	125	103	97	124	107	99	121
76250	LINDSAY	99	88	67	84	93	100	81	90	86	81	105	108	80	107	84	89	100	88	98	116
76251	MONTAGUE	138	92	42	79	104	120	89	111	107	91	126	133	76	119	90	116	114	110	137	158
76252	MUENSTER	111	81	46	77	93	103	79	96	90	78	106	115	69	105	82	94	97	94	112	132
76255	NOCONA	74	54	33	51	60	71	57	65	65	55	76	75	50	73	57	68	69	65	78	84
76258	PILOT POINT	105	103	91	102	104	110	99	103	99	98	122	119	98	123	99	99	117	101	103	119
76259	PONDER	108	112	103	110	111	114	104	108	101	105	126	125	104	125	104	99	123	106	102	124
76261	RINGGOLD	72	49	22	42	55	63	47	59	56	48	66	70	40	63	48	61	60	58	72	83
76262	ROANOKE	155	174	180	181	169	171	161	159	151	164	191	185	169	193	160	144	189	156	142	177
76263	ROSSTON	0	0	0	0	0	0	0	0	0	0	0	0	0	0	0	0	0	0	0	0
76264	SADLER	92	75	53	69	83	92	70	83	78	70	93	97	64	93	74	82	87	81	95	111
76265	SAINT JO	80	62	41	57	69	79	62	72	70	60	82	83	55	80	64	74	76	71	86	94
76266	SANGER	107	101	85	98	103	109	96	102	98	97	121	119	94	120	97	98	116	101	104	122
76270	SUNSET	91	70	42	63	75	83	66	78	75	68	89	92	60	85	67	78	83	77	89	104
76271	TIOGA	93	80	62	79	84	93	80	86	85	79	103	99	77	103	80	86	97	85	93	104
76272	VALLEY VIEW	97	88	67	84	91	96	82	90	85	83	104	105	79	103	83	86	100	88	94	112
76273	WHITESBORO	88	71	50	67	76	87	72	80	79	70	94	92	67	92	73	82	88	79	92	100
76301	WICHITA FALLS	55	50	53	48	50	57	55	55	59	54	72	63	54	70	54	59	69	56	58	62
76302	WICHITA FALLS	65	67	73	65	66	72	69	68	69	68	86	78	70	86	69	69	84	68	68	74
76305	WICHITA FALLS	62	46	30	42	51	57	46	54	53	46	63	64	41	61	47	55	58	54	63	72
76306	WICHITA FALLS	62	59	59	59	59	63	61	61	61	61	76	71	59	75	60	60	74	62	60	69
76308	WICHITA FALLS	82	86	100	88	85	90	90	86	87	88	109	102	90	110	89	85	107	88	82	95
76309	WICHITA FALLS	72	74	84	75	74	79	78	76	77	76	96	89	78	97	77	76	94	77	74	83
76310	WICHITA FALLS	85	86	88	88	86	89	86	86	84	86	105	101	85	104	84	81	102	86	82	97
76311	SHEPPARD AFB	71	45	43	51	41	49	67	58	68	62	85	77	57	76	55	62	81	68	53	65
76351	ARCHER CITY	94	71	46	68	78	91	74	84	83	72	98	97	66	95	75	87	90	84	99	107
76354	BURKBURNETT	78	77	72	74	78	84	74	77	76	73	93	89	75	95	75	77	90	76	79	90
76357	BYERS	88	61	32	58	71	80	60	75	70	60	82	90	52	80	63	73	75	74	89	104
76360	ELECTRA	65	52	40	50	56	65	57	61	62	55	75	70	52	72	56	65	69	61	70	73
76363	GOREE	71	53	35	51	58	70	59	65	66	56	78	73	52	73	58	70	71	65	78	78
76364	HARROLD	107	75	39	71	87	98	74	92	85	73	100	110	63	98	77	90	91	90	109	128
76365	HENRIETTA	76	62	46	60	67	75	62	69	68	61	82	81	59	81	63	70	76	68	78	87
76366	HOLLIDAY	82	70	54	67	75	83	68	76	73	67	88	88	65	88	70	75	83	74	84	96
76367	IOWA PARK	76	74	65	72	76	80	70	74	71	70	88	87	70	90	71	72	84	73	76	88
76371	MUNDAY	56	42	28	41	46	55	47	51	52	44	62	58	42	58	46	55	56	51	62	62
76372	NEWCASTLE	99	66	30	58	75	87	64	80	77	65	91	96	55	86	65	83	83	79	99	114
76373	OKLAUNION	108	75	39	71	88	98	74	92	86	73	100	111	63	98	77	90	91	91	109	128
76374	OLNEY	66	50	33	48	55	64	53	60	59	51	70	68	48	68	53	62	65	59	70	74
76377	PETROLIA	79	54	26	48	62	70	52	65	62	53	73	78	45	70	54	66	66	64	79	92
76379	SCOTLAND	90	64	35	61	74	83	64	78	73	63	86	93	55	84	66	76	78	77	92	107
76380	SEYMOUR	69	52	35	49	57	68	56	63	63	54	74	71	50	70	56	67	68	62	75	77
76384	VERNON	74	66	62	65	69	77	70	72	73	68	89	83	67	88	70	75	85	73	78	85
76388	WEINERT	69	52	34	50	56	68	57	63	64	54	75	70	51	71	57	68	69	63	75	76
76389	WINDTHORST	86	63	37	60	72	80	63	75	71	62	84	89	55	82	64	74	77	74	88	101
76401	STEPHENVILLE	73	67	68	68	67	72	74	71	74	72	92	85	71	89	71	72	88	74	70	81
76424	BRECKENRIDGE	69	57	44	55	61	69	58	64	63	57	76	73	55	74	59	65	71	63	72	78
76426	BRIDGEPORT	83	72	58	69	75	84	71	78	75	72	92	87	68	87	72	77	87	77	84	93
76427	BRYSON	92	64	34	61	75	84	64	79	73	63	86	95	54	84	66	77	78	77	94	109
76429	CADDO	53	37	19	35	43	48	37	45	42	36	49	55	31	49	38	44	45	45	54	63
76430	ALBANY	88	63	35	60	72	82	64	77	73	62	86	91	55	83	65	77	78	76	91	103
76431	CHICO	88	69	44	63	74	82	65	76	73	67	87	90	59	83	66	76	81	76	86	101
76432	BLANKET	90	63	34	60	74	83	62	77	72	62	84	93	53	83	65	76	77	76	92	107
76433	BLUFF DALE	112	79	42	74	91	102	77	95	89	76	104	115	66	102	80	93	95	94	113	132
76435	CARBON	81	57	32	54	67	75	57	70	65	56	76	83	49	74	59	68	70	69	83	96
76436	CARLTON	113	78	39	71	89	101	76	94	89	76	104	113	65	101	78	94	95	93	114	132
76437	CISCO	68	52	36	49	57	67	55	62	62	53	73	70	49	69	56	65	67	62	73	77
76442	COMANCHE	70	53	33	50	58	67	55	63	61	53	73	72	48	69	55	64	67	63	74	80
76443	CROSS PLAINS	64	48	31	46	52	63	53	58	59	50	69	65	47	65	52	62	63	58	70	71
76444	DE LEON	62	48	33	45	52	60	50	56	56	48	66	65	45	64	51	58	61	56	66	72
76445	DESDEMONA	65	49	32	47	54	63	52	59	58	50	69	67	46	66	52	61	63	59	69	73
76446	DUBLIN	75	60	42	57	63	70	61	68	66	62	80	77	56	75	60	68	76	68	74	82
76448	EASTLAND	81	63	43	61	69	79	65	73	72	63	85	84	59	83	65	75	79	72	84	92
76449	GRAFORD	85	64	40	59	73	82	61	75	70	61	82	88	54	81	65	74	76	73	88	103
76450	GRAHAM	84	64	42	60	71	81	66	75	74	64	88	88	59	85	67	78	81	75	88	97
76453	GORDON	109	83	53	76	94	105	79	96	90	78	106	113	70	105	84	95	98	94	113	132
76454	GORMAN	60	45	29	43	50	59	49	55	55	47	65	62	44	62	49	59	60	55	66	67
76455	GUSTINE	87	64	38	57	72	82	61	74	70	61	83	88	53	81	64	75	77	73	89	103
76457	HICO	84	60	34	57	68	78	62	73	70	60	83	86	54	80	63	74	75	73	87	97
76458	JACKSBORO	82	59	35	56	67	78	62	72	70	60	82	84	54	79	63	74	75	72	86	95
76459	JERMYN	76	53	28	50	62	69	52	65	60	52	71	78	45	69	54	63	64	64	77	90
76460	LOVING	94	65	34	62	76	85	64	80	74	64	87	96	55	85	67	78	79	79	95	111
76462	LIPAN	95	82	60	78	85	91	78	87	82	79	100	101	73	96	78	82	95	86	91	108
76463	MINGUS	96	75	51	68	85	95	71	85	80	70	95	100	63	94	76	86	88	84	101	117
76464	MORAN	71	54	36	52	59	70	59	65	65	56	77	72	53	73	58	69	71	65	78	78
76470	RANGER	59	44	28	42	49	58	48	54	54	46	64	61	43	61	48	57	58	54	65	66
76471	RISING STAR	65	53	42	51	58	68	54	61	59	54	71	65	51	64	56	62	65	60	72	73
76472	SANTO	88	62	32	58	72	81	61	75	70	60	82	91	52	81	63	74	75	74	90	105
76474	SIDNEY	77	53	28	50	62	70	53	65	61	52	71	79	45	70	55	64	65	64	78	91
76475	STRAWN	75	57	38	54	63	74	61	68	68	58	81	77	54	77	61	72	74	68	82	85
	TEXAS	94	90	91	90	89	95	92	93	92	93	115	107	90	112	90	90	112	94	89	104
	UNITED STATES	100	100	100	100	100	100	100	100	100	100	100	100	100	100	100	100	100	100	100	100

TEXAS

A

76476-76687

POPULATION CHANGE

#	POST OFFICE NAME	COUNTY FIPS CODE	POPULATION			2000-2004 ANNUAL RATE		HOUSEHOLDS					FAMILIES		
			2000	2004	2009	% Rate	State Centile	2000	2004	2009	% Annual Rate 2000-2004	2004 Average HH Size	2000	2004	% Annual Rate 2000-2004
76476	TOLAR	221	2156	2496	2854	3.5	86	805	928	1060	3.4	2.65	604	696	3.4
76483	THROCKMORTON	447	1302	1237	1167	-1.2	1	545	511	476	-1.5	2.41	379	357	-1.4
76484	PALO PINTO	363	1099	1133	1157	0.7	33	425	437	444	0.7	2.41	330	339	0.6
76486	PERRIN	237	1671	1796	1937	1.7	62	625	672	726	1.7	2.52	501	539	1.7
76487	POOLVILLE	367	1923	2237	2609	3.6	87	673	778	901	3.5	2.85	549	635	3.5
76490	WHITT	367	86	90	96	1.1	45	35	39	45	2.6	1.00	28	4	-36.7
76491	WOODSON	447	496	488	467	-0.4	6	197	192	181	-0.6	2.48	140	137	-0.5
76501	TEMPLE	027	16069	16703	18406	0.9	39	6187	6417	7047	0.9	2.57	4228	4387	0.9
76502	TEMPLE	027	22114	24645	27790	2.6	77	8781	9779	11012	2.6	2.46	6222	6934	2.6
76504	TEMPLE	027	22485	24196	26896	1.7	63	8857	9514	10584	1.7	2.41	5471	5890	1.8
76511	BARTLETT	027	3129	3210	3519	0.6	29	747	772	878	0.8	2.77	532	549	0.7
76513	BELTON	027	28178	31017	34700	2.3	73	9759	10792	12114	2.4	2.70	7252	8031	2.4
76518	BUCKHOLTS	331	1214	1252	1312	0.7	34	446	457	476	0.6	2.74	330	339	0.6
76519	BURLINGTON	331	1256	1310	1381	1.0	42	513	532	558	0.9	2.46	359	373	0.9
76520	CAMERON	331	7202	7579	8053	1.2	48	2723	2859	3032	1.2	2.57	1871	1970	1.2
76522	COPPERAS COVE	281	34183	36195	38976	1.4	53	11980	12619	13530	1.2	2.85	9370	9907	1.3
76523	DAVILLA	331	1357	1442	1535	1.4	56	517	546	578	1.3	2.64	397	420	1.3
76524	EDDY	309	1730	1814	1923	1.1	45	615	640	674	0.9	2.83	499	520	1.0
76525	EVANT	099	1061	1057	1106	-0.1	11	435	431	449	-0.2	2.45	317	314	-0.2
76526	FLAT	099	356	331	342	-1.7	0	147	136	139	-1.8	2.43	114	105	-1.9
76527	FLORENCE	491	3296	3841	4855	3.7	88	1130	1313	1651	3.6	2.92	903	1044	3.5
76528	GATESVILLE	099	20496	21248	22199	0.9	37	4459	4704	5031	1.3	2.60	3207	3393	1.3
76530	GRANGER	491	2491	2671	3237	1.7	61	941	1006	1216	1.6	2.60	649	690	1.5
76531	HAMILTON	193	5463	5706	6014	1.0	43	2256	2325	2416	0.7	2.38	1558	1609	0.8
76534	HOLLAND	027	2297	2404	2625	1.1	45	838	876	955	1.1	2.74	643	672	1.0
76537	JARRELL	491	2123	2538	3249	4.3	91	729	870	1107	4.3	2.92	562	667	4.1
76538	JONESBORO	099	666	723	772	2.0	67	244	286	320	3.8	1.45	196	144	-7.0
76539	KEMPNER	281	5041	5567	6242	2.4	74	1758	1927	2145	2.2	2.89	1431	1571	2.2
76541	KILLEEN	027	21246	21377	23264	0.1	16	9040	9113	9901	0.2	2.34	5363	5382	0.1
76542	KILLEEN	027	24924	29287	33960	3.9	90	8784	10263	11841	3.7	2.84	6749	7873	3.7
76543	KILLEEN	027	29155	31809	35739	2.1	69	10610	11510	12876	1.9	2.75	7860	8542	2.0
76544	KILLEEN	099	33948	34371	35817	0.3	20	5880	5949	6284	0.3	3.93	5729	5797	0.3
76548	HARKER HEIGHTS	027	17593	19200	21522	2.1	69	6300	6844	7641	2.0	2.79	4788	5196	1.9
76549	KILLEEN	027	19112	24184	29321	5.7	96	6630	8204	9813	5.1	2.95	5154	6414	5.3
76550	LAMPASAS	281	8988	9882	11077	2.3	72	3361	3665	4082	2.1	2.61	2368	2590	2.1
76554	LITTLE RIVER ACADEMY	027	1786	1934	2152	1.9	65	631	681	754	1.8	2.84	496	536	1.8
76556	MILANO	331	2111	2164	2260	0.6	28	818	833	865	0.4	2.60	608	620	0.5
76557	MOODY	027	4861	5080	5423	1.0	43	1762	1832	1945	0.9	2.75	1348	1404	1.0
76559	NOLANVILLE	027	2115	2281	2547	1.8	64	767	825	917	1.7	2.76	578	622	1.7
76561	OGLESBY	099	1244	1280	1343	0.7	31	457	471	495	0.7	2.47	347	357	0.7
76565	POTTSVILLE	193	273	274	284	0.1	15	108	107	109	-0.2	2.56	81	81	0.0
76566	PURMELA	099	560	612	665	2.1	69	223	241	259	1.8	2.54	179	193	1.8
76567	ROCKDALE	331	8504	8992	9566	1.3	52	3181	3337	3530	1.1	2.64	2296	2418	1.2
76569	ROGERS	027	2501	2557	2757	0.5	26	914	932	1001	0.5	2.74	698	712	0.5
76570	ROSEBUD	145	2842	2940	3093	0.8	35	1097	1125	1175	0.6	2.57	771	792	0.6
76571	SALADO	027	5412	6400	7443	4.0	90	2101	2472	2860	3.9	2.59	1678	1969	3.8
76574	TAYLOR	491	16253	17681	21624	2.0	67	5744	6254	7657	2.0	2.73	4216	4559	1.9
76577	THORNDALE	331	2598	2678	2807	0.7	33	1004	1028	1072	0.6	2.61	737	756	0.6
76578	THRALL	491	1399	1610	2026	3.4	85	516	592	741	3.3	2.72	402	458	3.1
76579	TROY	027	3073	3578	4124	3.6	88	1081	1255	1441	3.6	2.85	891	1035	3.6
76621	ABBOTT	217	966	992	1059	0.6	30	373	379	400	0.4	2.62	280	286	0.5
76622	AQUILLA	217	1477	1593	1747	1.8	64	579	620	674	1.6	2.57	451	484	1.7
76624	AXTELL	309	2297	2395	2531	1.0	42	852	883	927	0.8	2.68	657	681	0.9
76626	BLOOMING GROVE	349	1960	2104	2291	1.7	61	770	819	883	1.5	2.56	568	606	1.5
76627	BLUM	217	2488	2623	2842	1.3	50	940	982	1055	1.0	2.67	729	764	1.1
76629	BREMOND	395	1836	2119	2358	3.4	86	748	868	969	3.6	2.38	508	592	3.7
76630	BRUCEVILLE	309	1372	1498	1623	2.1	69	458	496	533	1.9	3.02	378	410	1.9
76631	BYNUM	217	518	549	596	1.4	54	182	191	206	1.1	2.87	143	151	1.3
76632	CHILTON	145	2602	2774	2963	1.5	58	926	982	1041	1.4	2.78	701	744	1.4
76633	CHINA SPRING	309	3390	3892	4333	3.3	84	1152	1312	1448	3.1	2.96	968	1103	3.1
76634	CLIFTON	035	7267	7565	7895	1.0	40	2860	2956	3065	0.8	2.44	2002	2075	0.9
76635	COOLIDGE	293	1248	1344	1442	1.8	63	467	500	533	1.6	2.68	330	354	1.7
76636	COVINGTON	217	843	906	990	1.7	62	308	328	355	1.5	2.73	235	251	1.6
76637	CRANFILLS GAP	035	884	930	977	1.2	48	360	377	394	1.1	2.46	279	293	1.2
76638	CRAWFORD	309	2409	2630	2853	2.1	69	859	929	999	1.9	2.83	701	759	1.9
76639	DAWSON	349	1826	1877	1996	0.7	30	733	746	786	0.4	2.52	516	526	0.5
76640	ELM MOTT	309	3102	3535	3917	3.1	82	1153	1305	1436	3.0	2.70	881	1001	3.1
76641	FROST	349	2185	2287	2457	1.1	45	834	865	920	0.9	2.63	636	660	0.9
76642	GROESBECK	293	6680	7012	7392	1.2	46	2196	2309	2437	1.2	2.58	1567	1652	1.3
76643	HEWITT	309	11176	12524	13797	2.7	79	4042	4486	4899	2.5	2.79	3258	3629	2.6
76645	HILLSBORO	217	10875	11730	12851	1.8	64	3888	4148	4509	1.5	2.71	2697	2886	1.6
76648	HUBBARD	217	2181	2417	2687	2.5	75	849	932	1027	2.2	2.52	578	636	2.3
76649	IREDELL	035	892	913	945	0.6	27	380	385	395	0.3	2.36	276	280	0.3
76651	ITALY	139	2854	3039	3466	1.5	57	966	1021	1158	1.3	2.93	755	798	1.3
76652	KOPPERL	035	1009	1057	1109	1.1	45	389	404	420	0.9	2.62	300	312	0.9
76653	KOSSE	293	929	1001	1072	1.8	63	359	385	409	1.7	2.55	259	279	1.8
76655	LORENA	309	6294	6995	7651	2.5	76	2219	2449	2658	2.4	2.86	1847	2039	2.4
76656	LOTT	145	2145	2226	2345	0.9	38	822	846	883	0.7	2.63	575	593	0.7
76657	MC GREGOR	309	7498	8354	9214	2.6	77	2698	2967	3243	2.3	2.75	2039	2243	2.3
76660	MALONE	217	434	443	472	0.5	25	169	171	181	0.3	2.59	120	122	0.4
76661	MARLIN	145	9238	9476	9873	0.6	29	2929	2997	3126	0.5	2.51	1866	1915	0.6
76664	MART	309	3058	3168	3361	0.8	36	1122	1152	1215	0.6	2.60	774	795	0.6
76665	MERIDIAN	035	2636	2770	2906	1.2	47	980	1019	1060	0.9	2.60	712	742	1.0
76666	MERTENS	217	421	446	484	1.4	54	167	175	189	1.1	2.55	131	138	1.2
76667	MEXIA	293	10105	10350	10810	0.6	28	3620	3665	3800	0.3	2.61	2537	2573	0.3
76670	MILFORD	139	1163	1228	1395	1.3	51	442	462	521	1.1	2.66	313	327	1.0
76671	MORGAN	035	1604	1685	1769	1.2	47	664	691	719	0.9	2.44	476	497	1.0
76673	MOUNT CALM	217	564	669	770	4.1	91	220	259	296	3.9	2.56	160	188	3.9
76676	PENELOPE	217	741	758	807	0.5	27	281	285	301	0.3	2.66	200	204	0.5
76678	PRAIRIE HILL	293	782	831	885	1.4	56	307	325	344	1.4	2.56	225	239	1.4
76679	PURDON	349	835	875	941	1.1	45	314	326	347	0.9	2.68	236	245	0.9
76680	REAGAN	145	734	754	789	0.6	30	311	317	329	0.5	2.38	206	211	0.6
76681	RICHLAND	349	659	692	744	1.2	47	264	274	292	0.9	2.53	198	206	0.9
76682	RIESEL	145	2953	3264	3565	2.4	74	1120	1225	1327	2.1	2.63	843	924	2.2
76687	THORNTON	293	1813	1928	2054	1.5	56	743	787	833	1.4	2.45	565	599	1.4
	TEXAS					2.2					2.0	2.77			2.1
	UNITED STATES					1.2					1.3	2.58			1.1

ZIP CODE #	POST OFFICE NAME	RACE (%) White 2000	White 2004	Black 2000	Black 2004	Asian/Pacific 2000	Asian/Pacific 2004	% Hispanic Origin 2000	% Hispanic Origin 2004	2004 AGE DISTRIBUTION (%) 0-4	5-9	10-14	15-19	20-24	25-44	45-64	65-84	85+	18+	MEDIAN AGE 2004	% 2004 Males	% 2004 Females
76476	TOLAR	94.7	93.7	0.5	0.6	0.2	0.2	5.1	6.2	6.9	6.9	7.1	6.7	6.7	24.4	26.6	12.9	1.8	75.1	38.9	49.0	51.0
76483	THROCKMORTON	91.6	91.1	0.1	0.1	0.1	0.1	10.4	10.8	5.8	6.0	7.4	6.9	5.7	21.7	25.6	17.9	3.2	76.4	42.8	50.0	50.0
76484	PALO PINTO	93.5	92.5	0.6	0.6	0.3	0.3	7.1	8.7	6.8	6.6	6.1	5.7	5.5	26.0	29.0	12.7	1.7	77.1	40.4	53.4	46.6
76486	PERRIN	92.6	91.8	2.9	3.1	0.4	0.4	6.1	7.1	6.3	6.4	7.7	6.9	6.2	28.2	24.9	12.3	1.2	75.5	37.8	54.2	45.8
76487	POOLVILLE	94.9	94.2	1.1	1.3	0.3	0.4	5.6	6.8	7.1	7.2	8.4	8.0	6.6	28.0	24.5	9.5	0.7	72.4	36.0	51.1	49.0
76490	WHITT	60.5	56.7	25.6	27.8	0.0	0.0	15.1	15.6	2.2	2.2	2.2	3.3	8.9	54.4	21.1	5.6	0.0	93.3	36.8	80.0	20.0
76491	WOODSON	93.6	93.2	0.0	0.0	0.0	0.0	6.9	7.6	5.5	5.7	6.6	6.8	5.1	21.1	25.0	20.3	3.9	77.7	44.5	48.6	51.4
76501	TEMPLE	62.0	60.5	23.4	22.8	0.5	0.5	20.5	23.4	7.8	7.6	7.7	6.9	6.3	25.3	23.6	12.6	2.2	72.5	36.7	48.2	51.9
76502	TEMPLE	82.8	80.8	8.1	8.6	1.8	2.1	10.8	12.8	7.2	6.7	6.7	6.5	6.2	26.7	23.6	13.4	3.0	75.6	37.9	47.3	52.7
76504	TEMPLE	67.9	65.4	16.1	16.6	1.8	2.1	21.2	24.1	8.0	6.9	6.8	7.0	8.1	28.7	20.4	11.7	2.5	74.4	33.8	49.2	50.8
76511	BARTLETT	59.1	56.5	22.4	22.5	0.2	0.2	27.1	30.8	4.9	4.8	5.6	7.5	11.3	34.1	19.4	8.9	3.6	81.5	33.8	64.4	35.6
76513	BELTON	80.5	78.8	5.5	5.5	1.1	1.2	18.0	20.2	7.3	7.0	7.5	9.1	9.0	27.3	22.2	9.3	1.3	73.8	32.8	49.3	50.7
76518	BUCKHOLTS	87.5	85.8	0.7	0.8	0.1	0.1	25.1	28.8	6.2	6.5	8.2	7.3	6.3	24.5	25.3	13.6	2.2	74.8	38.3	49.7	50.3
76519	BURLINGTON	81.1	79.3	8.9	9.2	0.1	0.1	17.8	20.6	3.7	4.5	6.5	6.3	5.9	20.7	30.1	19.7	2.7	81.6	46.7	51.6	48.4
76520	CAMERON	72.3	71.0	16.9	17.0	0.2	0.2	23.2	26.1	7.5	7.0	7.4	7.0	6.5	23.3	22.6	14.7	4.1	73.8	38.1	48.0	52.0
76522	COPPERAS COVE	68.3	66.1	18.3	19.0	3.1	3.4	11.2	13.0	10.0	8.1	7.8	7.5	9.7	32.8	17.9	5.9	0.4	69.7	28.5	49.5	50.5
76523	DAVILLA	86.1	84.3	4.7	5.0	0.0	0.0	16.8	19.6	6.6	6.7	7.1	6.7	6.5	26.4	27.1	11.2	1.6	75.5	38.4	51.4	48.6
76524	EDDY	87.9	85.1	0.7	0.8	0.1	0.2	15.4	19.2	7.4	7.6	8.8	8.2	5.4	28.1	24.7	8.9	0.8	71.0	35.8	50.3	49.7
76525	EVANT	92.1	90.7	0.2	0.2	0.6	0.7	8.2	9.7	4.4	4.6	7.2	6.9	4.2	22.8	27.2	20.8	2.0	79.4	45.0	49.7	50.3
76526	FLAT	94.9	94.3	0.3	0.3	0.0	0.0	5.9	7.3	8.2	7.9	4.8	5.4	4.8	25.7	29.3	12.4	1.5	76.4	39.4	51.7	48.3
76527	FLORENCE	92.1	90.7	0.6	0.7	0.2	0.2	13.3	16.2	7.9	7.8	8.2	7.5	6.7	27.4	24.8	8.5	1.1	71.5	34.8	50.2	49.8
76528	GATESVILLE	70.6	69.3	20.6	20.7	0.4	0.5	12.7	14.5	3.9	3.9	4.3	4.9	8.0	45.9	20.3	7.3	1.5	85.1	36.1	42.0	58.0
76530	GRANGER	86.6	85.0	4.9	5.0	0.6	0.6	20.6	24.3	6.4	6.4	6.8	6.7	6.3	26.0	23.8	14.8	2.8	76.0	39.3	49.5	50.5
76531	HAMILTON	95.9	95.3	0.2	0.2	0.2	0.2	5.6	6.6	5.6	5.5	6.7	6.2	5.1	21.2	25.6	19.5	4.7	78.2	44.9	48.0	52.0
76534	HOLLAND	89.9	88.8	3.1	3.1	0.8	0.9	14.4	16.8	7.9	7.5	8.1	9.2	4.7	26.0	25.1	10.5	1.1	70.0	35.7	50.0	50.0
76537	JARRELL	85.0	82.4	1.3	1.4	0.2	0.2	23.5	27.9	6.9	6.9	8.4	7.5	6.5	28.8	24.2	9.6	1.3	73.2	35.1	52.6	47.4
76538	JONESBORO	74.5	72.3	16.1	16.9	1.5	1.8	8.3	9.7	3.0	3.2	4.6	10.5	20.8	33.1	16.0	7.8	1.1	87.0	28.1	65.0	35.0
76539	KEMPNER	85.2	83.8	5.1	5.3	1.3	1.4	10.6	12.4	7.0	6.9	7.7	7.6	7.0	28.7	26.2	8.4	0.6	73.9	35.8	50.3	49.7
76541	KILLEEN	48.2	45.5	29.2	29.6	4.4	4.8	21.3	24.1	10.7	7.5	6.2	6.8	13.3	33.5	14.5	7.0	0.5	72.2	27.1	50.7	49.3
76542	KILLEEN	55.4	52.9	25.7	26.3	5.5	6.0	14.8	17.0	8.8	7.7	7.6	7.0	9.7	35.9	18.9	4.1	0.3	71.8	29.5	49.9	50.1
76543	KILLEEN	44.3	42.2	36.5	36.7	4.8	5.2	16.4	18.6	10.6	8.3	7.5	7.2	12.0	35.0	14.6	4.4	0.4	69.7	26.9	49.5	50.5
76544	KILLEEN	50.8	48.2	31.6	32.3	3.0	3.3	16.7	19.1	12.1	10.5	7.9	11.5	23.3	33.2	1.4	0.1	0.0	66.8	21.7	61.9	38.1
76548	HARKER HEIGHTS	71.2	68.9	14.7	15.3	4.0	4.5	12.3	14.3	9.4	8.4	7.8	7.2	7.5	33.3	19.7	6.1	0.5	70.1	30.6	50.0	50.0
76549	KILLEEN	47.1	44.6	33.0	33.6	5.4	5.6	17.4	20.1	10.2	8.7	8.4	7.4	9.5	37.0	15.0	3.8	0.1	68.3	27.7	49.7	50.3
76550	LAMPASAS	86.9	85.0	1.9	2.0	0.6	0.6	19.3	22.4	7.7	7.0	7.2	7.0	7.1	24.5	22.8	13.7	3.2	73.8	37.1	47.9	52.1
76554	LITTLE RIVER ACADEMY	87.4	85.1	0.5	0.5	0.7	0.8	13.8	16.4	7.1	7.0	7.7	9.2	7.4	28.8	22.4	9.6	0.9	72.7	34.7	49.2	50.8
76556	MILANO	89.2	88.5	8.3	8.8	0.1	0.1	6.0	7.1	5.5	5.6	6.5	6.4	6.6	23.2	29.3	15.4	1.6	78.6	42.6	49.4	50.6
76557	MOODY	87.2	84.8	3.9	4.4	0.1	0.2	12.7	15.7	6.7	6.8	7.5	7.3	6.2	26.2	25.7	11.8	1.8	74.4	38.1	49.7	50.3
76559	NOLANVILLE	81.5	79.5	6.1	6.4	0.9	1.0	16.3	19.3	9.1	8.2	7.9	7.7	7.6	30.3	22.3	6.4	0.6	70.2	31.3	50.7	49.3
76561	OGLESBY	87.1	85.2	3.8	4.0	0.2	0.2	9.9	11.8	6.5	6.2	6.5	7.0	8.4	30.5	23.8	10.0	1.3	76.6	34.5	53.1	46.9
76565	POTTSVILLE	96.7	96.7	0.0	0.0	0.0	0.0	5.9	6.6	4.0	4.0	6.2	6.2	5.1	16.8	31.0	24.1	2.6	82.1	49.6	54.4	45.6
76566	PURMELA	93.4	92.5	1.6	1.8	0.5	0.7	4.1	4.9	6.5	6.9	8.2	6.2	5.2	25.8	26.3	13.2	1.6	74.5	39.8	50.7	49.4
76567	ROCKDALE	75.9	73.9	11.7	12.0	0.4	0.5	19.4	22.3	7.8	7.3	7.6	7.1	6.7	23.5	23.7	13.9	2.4	72.7	36.7	49.0	51.0
76569	ROGERS	84.8	82.9	2.8	2.9	0.2	0.2	17.8	20.5	7.2	7.4	8.3	7.8	6.2	25.5	24.7	11.2	1.8	72.4	37.0	49.4	50.6
76570	ROSEBUD	71.1	68.9	14.3	14.4	0.2	0.2	20.0	22.9	6.5	6.6	7.3	6.9	6.7	21.3	24.6	16.4	3.7	75.2	41.2	49.6	50.4
76571	SALADO	92.5	91.0	0.4	0.5	0.7	0.9	8.4	10.2	5.7	6.2	7.0	6.4	4.5	24.5	30.0	14.4	1.3	76.8	42.1	50.5	49.5
76574	TAYLOR	72.2	70.6	12.0	11.7	0.3	0.4	30.1	33.8	7.7	7.5	7.7	7.1	6.8	27.9	21.9	11.2	2.2	72.8	34.7	49.6	50.4
76577	THORNDALE	89.8	88.7	4.2	4.4	0.1	0.1	12.2	14.2	6.6	6.8	7.8	7.5	6.0	25.3	25.3	13.0	1.8	74.1	38.4	51.5	48.5
76578	THRALL	82.3	79.5	4.5	4.8	0.1	0.1	23.9	28.5	6.8	7.0	8.5	6.8	5.8	27.0	23.7	12.6	1.9	73.5	37.4	49.2	50.8
76579	TROY	89.1	87.3	1.3	1.4	0.4	0.5	13.7	16.4	7.1	7.2	8.1	7.8	6.8	26.8	25.8	9.5	1.0	72.8	36.0	49.3	50.7
76621	ABBOTT	93.6	92.2	1.1	1.3	0.1	0.1	8.2	10.2	6.6	6.7	6.4	6.0	6.2	24.1	26.6	15.3	2.3	76.8	41.0	51.7	48.3
76622	AQUILLA	94.0	93.0	1.3	1.4	0.2	0.3	5.4	6.5	6.7	6.9	6.7	6.0	5.7	23.0	28.3	15.3	1.3	75.9	41.3	50.0	50.0
76624	AXTELL	92.9	91.5	3.2	3.7	0.1	0.1	5.4	6.8	6.7	6.9	6.7	7.1	6.4	25.5	27.7	12.0	1.0	75.0	38.9	50.1	49.9
76626	BLOOMING GROVE	92.4	91.3	3.9	4.4	0.2	0.2	4.1	5.1	5.5	5.6	6.7	7.8	5.8	26.3	26.2	14.2	2.0	77.1	40.7	49.0	51.1
76627	BLUM	94.4	93.4	0.7	0.8	0.0	0.0	6.3	7.7	6.8	6.5	6.1	6.8	6.4	24.6	28.4	13.3	1.1	76.4	40.3	50.3	49.7
76629	BREMOND	81.0	79.1	15.5	16.9	0.1	0.1	3.2	4.0	6.6	6.8	7.2	7.0	5.6	21.9	23.7	17.2	4.2	74.6	41.4	48.8	51.2
76630	BRUCEVILLE	92.1	90.3	0.8	0.9	0.7	0.8	8.5	10.8	6.9	7.0	7.9	8.5	7.0	26.5	26.4	8.7	1.1	73.0	36.2	48.7	51.3
76631	BYNUM	91.1	89.3	1.9	2.0	0.2	0.2	8.9	10.9	6.0	6.4	6.6	5.8	5.8	25.1	25.7	16.4	2.2	77.6	41.3	52.5	47.5
76632	CHILTON	74.3	72.4	12.9	13.3	0.1	0.1	20.2	22.8	7.7	7.8	7.6	7.1	6.1	25.2	24.8	12.2	1.5	72.0	36.7	50.5	49.5
76633	CHINA SPRING	94.6	93.4	1.2	1.3	0.1	0.1	6.5	8.3	6.0	6.9	8.7	7.8	5.8	27.7	27.5	9.1	0.6	73.5	37.1	50.2	49.9
76634	CLIFTON	91.0	89.9	1.8	1.9	0.2	0.2	11.6	13.5	5.8	5.4	6.0	6.3	5.6	20.8	26.6	18.7	4.8	78.8	45.1	48.3	51.8
76635	COOLIDGE	68.8	66.3	16.7	17.1	0.1	0.1	22.9	26.1	8.0	7.5	7.4	7.7	7.7	25.2	22.1	12.4	1.9	72.3	33.8	48.7	51.3
76636	COVINGTON	88.0	85.9	3.4	3.8	0.1	0.2	14.0	16.8	7.8	8.1	7.8	7.6	6.4	25.2	24.5	11.4	1.2	71.3	36.0	50.0	50.0
76637	CRANFILLS GAP	94.1	93.1	1.7	1.8	0.1	0.1	5.9	7.2	5.3	5.5	6.7	7.4	5.2	21.2	30.4	16.0	2.4	77.5	44.3	49.6	50.4
76638	CRAWFORD	92.0	90.2	2.2	2.6	0.2	0.2	6.5	8.2	6.6	7.4	8.0	7.0	5.5	24.9	27.8	11.4	1.4	73.6	39.8	50.0	50.0
76639	DAWSON	85.5	83.7	10.1	11.2	0.1	0.1	5.8	7.1	6.0	6.3	7.0	6.5	5.4	24.0	26.2	16.1	2.6	76.6	41.5	50.1	49.9
76640	ELM MOTT	90.7	88.9	3.7	4.2	0.5	0.6	6.7	8.5	7.2	7.2	7.6	7.4	7.1	26.8	25.8	10.0	0.9	73.3	35.6	51.0	49.0
76641	FROST	85.6	83.9	7.3	7.9	0.5	0.5	8.5	10.2	6.7	6.4	6.1	7.4	6.7	23.4	27.2	14.7	1.4	76.1	40.8	51.4	48.6
76642	GROESBECK	69.8	67.7	17.1	17.4	0.0	0.0	13.9	16.0	6.1	6.0	6.3	6.8	8.9	28.9	21.9	12.7	2.5	77.5	35.8	55.6	44.4
76643	HEWITT	85.3	83.1	6.9	7.6	2.3	2.7	9.0	11.1	7.6	7.8	8.0	6.9	6.2	30.8	24.8	7.4	0.6	72.4	34.8	48.8	51.2
76645	HILLSBORO	74.7	73.0	12.6	12.6	0.5	0.5	23.6	26.7	7.9	6.9	6.9	8.4	7.5	24.3	21.4	13.3	3.4	73.7	34.8	49.5	50.5
76648	HUBBARD	79.5	77.8	15.5	16.5	0.5	0.5	4.2	5.1	7.0	7.2	7.3	6.8	5.7	22.9	24.1	15.8	3.3	73.9	40.5	46.0	54.0
76649	IREDELL	95.5	94.7	0.0	0.0	0.0	0.0	6.3	7.5	6.8	6.2	5.4	5.6	4.7	23.3	26.7	18.5	2.7	78.1	43.8	51.8	48.2
76651	ITALY	76.5	73.8	16.2	17.7	0.1	0.2	12.9	15.3	7.3	7.2	7.7	8.0	7.6	26.7	23.4	10.0	2.0	72.7	34.9	48.4	51.6
76652	KOPPERL	97.5	97.3	0.1	0.1	0.1	0.1	7.1	8.4	5.7	6.3	8.0	6.6	4.7	23.4	28.8	15.0	1.4	75.8	42.0	51.1	48.9
76653	KOSSE	83.3	81.8	10.1	10.7	0.2	0.2	8.3	9.6	5.8	5.9	6.5	6.0	4.8	23.7	27.9	17.2	2.3	77.3	43.0	51.9	48.2
76655	LORENA	90.4	88.6	3.7	4.2	0.5	0.6	7.8	9.8	5.9	6.9	8.5	8.2	5.7	27.5	27.7	8.8	0.9	73.4	37.6	49.9	50.1
76656	LOTT	79.9	78.1	13.3	14.0	0.1	0.1	8.7	10.4	5.4	5.9	8.9	8.5	6.1	23.0	25.9	14.3	2.2	74.7	40.0	50.8	49.2
76657	MC GREGOR	79.2	75.6	8.1	9.2	0.5	0.6	19.6	23.6	7.4	7.3	7.6	7.3	7.2	24.9	23.6	12.0	2.7	73.0	36.9	47.7	52.3
76660	MALONE	85.0	83.1	6.9	7.5	0.0	0.0	12.9	15.6	6.8	6.8	7.0	7.2	6.6	25.5	25.7	12.4	2.0	75.4	38.3	50.1	49.9
76661	MARLIN	45.9	43.8	42.6	43.3	0.2	0.2	16.6	18.9	6.2	6.2	7.2	10.5	6.7	27.9	19.5	13.0	2.7	73.0	34.3	42.4	57.6
76664	MART	74.3	71.8	21.8	23.6	0.0	0.0	5.4	6.5	7.4	7.3	7.4	9.2	6.0	22.5	22.1	14.6	3.6	71.5	37.2	47.1	52.9
76665	MERIDIAN	88.5	87.0	3.2	3.4	0.1	0.1	16.4	19.2	5.7	5.6	7.2	7.0	6.0	22.5	26.8	15.6	3.7	77.0	42.1	48.4	51.6
76666	MERTENS	91.0	89.5	1.9	2.0	0.0	0.0	8.8	11.0	6.3	6.5	6.5	5.8	5.8	24.7	26.2	16.1	2.0	77.4	41.2	52.2	47.8
76667	MEXIA	64.6	62.2	25.7	26.6	0.2	0.2	13.4	15.5	7.2	7.0	7.3	7.4	6.4	25.1	24.0	12.8	2.8	73.7	36.7	48.2	51.8
76670	MILFORD	69.0	65.8	21.2	23.1	0.6	0.7	13.2	15.3	7.1	7.0	7.7	6.8	7.0	25.3	25.7	11.8	1.6	74.1	36.5	49.8	50.2
76671	MORGAN	89.0	87.7	1.3	1.3	0.1	0.1	14.8	17.1	5.5	5.5	6.4	6.4	5.0	21.7	29.9	17.8	1.9	78.8	44.7	52.0	48.0
76673	MOUNT CALM	85.1	83.3	11.4	12.6	0.5	0.6	3.2	4.0	6.9	6.9	6.9	6.6	6.0	23.8	26.3	14.7	2.1	74.9	40.9	46.6	53.4
76676	PENELOPE	85.2	83.1	7.0	7.5	0.0	0.0	12.7	15.3	6.9	6.9	7.0	7.3	6.6	26.1	25.1	12.4	1.9	74.7	37.8	50.0	50.0
76678	PRAIRIE HILL	82.1	80.6	12.2	12.8	0.0	0.0	11.1	12.9	5.9	6.3	6.6	6.9	5.4	23.1	29.0	14.7	2.2	76.3	41.8	49.9	50.1
76679	PURDON	91.5	89.9	2.6	2.9	0.2	0.2	8.0	10.1	7.0	7.1	7.4	6.1	5.4	24.1	26.5	14.9	1.6	74.6	40.0	50.7	49.3
76680	REAGAN	85.2	83.4	9.5	10.2	0.0	0.0	7.0	8.5	4.0	4.5	7.2	6.8	4.8	24.9	28.0	16.8	3.1	80.4	43.7	51.1	48.9
76681	RICHLAND	91.5	90.0	2.6	2.9	0.3	0.3	8.0	9.8	7.1	7.1	7.4	6.1	5.4	24.1	26.5	14.9	1.6	74.6	39.9	50.9	49.1
76682	RIESEL	88.3	86.0	6.1	7.2	0.4	0.5	6.4	7.9	6.1	6.3	7.6	7.1	5.7	25.8	26.3	13.7	1.5	75.4	39.5	50.4	49.6
76687	THORNTON	91.9	90.8	3.5	3.7	0.3	0.4	6.0	7.1	4.8	4.8	6.3	6.4	4.7	22.0	31.1	18.4	1.6	79.9	45.6	51.0	49.0
	TEXAS	71.0	69.5	11.5	11.4	2.8	3.1	32.0	34.6	7.9	7.5	7.7	7.5	8.1	29.6	21.9	8.7	1.2	72.6	32.9	49.7	50.3
	UNITED STATES	75.1	73.6	12.3	12.5	3.8	4.2	12.5	14.1	6.9	6.7	7.2	7.0	7.3	28.6	23.8	10.8	1.7	75.1	36.0	49.1	50.9

INCOME

ZIP CODE #	POST OFFICE NAME	2004 Per Capita Income	2004 HH Income Base	2004 HOUSEHOLD INCOME DISTRIBUTION (%) Less than $25,000	$25,000 to $49,999	$50,000 to $99,999	$100,000 to $149,999	$150,000 or More	MEDIAN HOUSEHOLD INCOME 2004	2009	2004 National Centile	2004 State Centile	2004 Home Value Base	2004 HOME VALUE DISTRIBUTION (%) Less than $50,000	$50,000 to $89,999	$90,000 to $174,999	$175,000 to $399,999	$400,000 or More	2004 Median Home Value
76476	TOLAR	26555	928	23.8	27.9	32.5	9.7	6.0	48429	55093	69	74	755	25.8	25.8	26.8	17.1	4.5	87500
76483	THROCKMORTON	20125	511	37.4	32.7	22.9	3.3	3.7	32601	38491	20	24	384	60.2	26.0	11.7	1.6	0.5	41875
76484	PALO PINTO	20086	437	28.6	32.0	31.6	4.6	3.2	41884	47600	53	61	364	26.4	23.1	27.2	19.8	3.6	91250
76486	PERRIN	18373	672	33.2	31.6	28.4	4.6	2.2	37132	42131	36	43	547	40.6	24.9	20.3	9.9	4.4	65417
76487	POOLVILLE	20731	778	23.4	28.8	36.1	8.6	3.1	48021	55022	68	73	663	19.3	29.7	29.7	18.3	3.0	91711
76490	WHITT	30663	39	25.6	30.8	35.9	7.7	0.0	44071	52583	59	66	32	34.4	18.8	28.1	12.5	6.3	80000
76491	WOODSON	22911	192	38.0	35.9	18.8	3.1	4.2	31103	31971	15	19	149	50.3	24.8	15.4	5.4	4.0	49750
76501	TEMPLE	18999	6417	37.0	30.4	24.8	5.3	2.5	34807	39024	27	32	4071	33.4	33.9	26.7	5.3	0.7	68994
76502	TEMPLE	28585	9779	20.6	27.7	33.8	9.1	8.9	51498	58558	75	79	6777	6.9	23.9	50.6	15.6	3.1	107720
76504	TEMPLE	19141	9514	34.6	37.0	22.0	4.4	2.0	34211	38762	25	30	4515	27.6	42.6	26.1	3.3	0.4	71007
76511	BARTLETT	14838	772	40.5	26.8	25.5	5.3	1.8	32908	38528	21	25	533	33.6	39.2	21.2	4.7	1.3	67727
76513	BELTON	21156	10792	26.1	30.3	30.7	8.5	4.5	43854	50062	58	66	7536	24.7	25.3	33.5	14.2	2.3	90023
76518	BUCKHOLTS	21670	457	25.4	26.9	35.2	6.8	5.7	45583	57842	63	69	370	37.3	21.9	33.0	5.4	2.4	69231
76519	BURLINGTON	15072	532	43.8	31.8	19.2	4.0	1.3	28583	30488	10	12	430	35.4	22.6	21.2	20.9	0.0	74211
76520	CAMERON	19174	2859	41.9	27.1	24.3	4.1	2.5	31030	35905	15	19	1952	42.9	34.5	18.6	2.5	1.5	57943
76522	COPPERAS COVE	19006	12619	21.4	37.3	32.2	6.6	2.6	43275	48152	57	65	7382	12.2	44.7	38.1	4.7	0.3	84797
76523	DAVILLA	19118	546	30.6	28.6	34.6	4.8	1.5	40818	46743	49	57	437	26.5	24.9	29.3	17.4	1.8	87679
76524	EDDY	18814	640	24.2	35.6	30.5	7.5	2.2	41346	48259	51	59	539	38.8	36.7	20.8	3.7	0.0	63516
76525	EVANT	23793	431	35.7	29.0	27.4	4.4	3.5	39239	42854	44	52	348	36.2	24.4	14.1	20.4	4.9	71905
76526	FLAT	20932	136	33.1	23.5	33.8	7.4	2.2	45444	48659	62	69	110	37.3	14.6	30.0	16.4	1.8	83333
76527	FLORENCE	22034	1313	17.4	28.3	37.4	12.4	4.4	54095	60645	78	82	1066	15.2	26.1	25.5	27.5	5.7	109069
76528	GATESVILLE	15861	4704	33.8	31.1	28.0	4.5	2.6	36867	41039	35	42	3413	27.7	35.3	28.5	7.2	1.2	72615
76530	GRANGER	18933	1006	30.6	30.2	30.7	6.3	2.2	39451	45681	44	53	747	31.3	31.6	24.6	10.3	2.1	69833
76531	HAMILTON	19399	2325	34.5	31.7	25.3	5.9	2.5	35603	41060	30	36	1790	38.0	30.3	16.8	9.9	5.0	64860
76534	HOLLAND	18318	876	33.1	28.1	29.1	6.4	3.3	38528	42713	41	49	671	31.6	32.9	23.7	10.7	1.0	72111
76537	JARRELL	19843	870	16.9	35.9	34.4	10.3	2.5	47145	53914	66	72	705	17.6	26.0	41.0	13.9	1.6	96594
76538	JONESBORO	32082	286	21.3	39.5	31.1	3.2	4.9	43957	48180	59	66	232	23.3	28.9	28.9	13.4	5.6	83750
76539	KEMPNER	22229	1927	17.3	35.8	34.0	7.7	5.2	46653	53625	65	71	1578	18.3	20.9	51.1	8.1	1.7	102833
76541	KILLEEN	15610	9113	38.9	41.4	16.1	2.8	0.9	29892	33374	12	15	2637	20.9	59.8	16.2	2.8	0.2	65822
76542	KILLEEN	21376	10263	16.9	31.8	40.0	8.7	2.6	50883	57375	74	78	6513	8.8	25.8	59.3	5.4	0.6	98594
76543	KILLEEN	16891	11510	23.6	43.0	27.2	4.8	1.4	39009	44113	43	51	5724	11.7	56.0	27.5	4.1	0.6	80611
76544	KILLEEN	11095	5949	22.5	55.2	20.4	1.6	0.3	36205	40324	32	39	102	3.9	59.8	36.3	0.0	0.0	86316
76548	HARKER HEIGHTS	23746	6844	20.2	31.4	31.9	11.0	5.5	48236	54828	69	74	3992	20.3	15.2	49.5	14.3	0.6	113896
76549	KILLEEN	16832	8204	21.3	37.1	35.6	5.0	1.0	42835	48339	56	64	5041	8.2	50.1	39.8	1.6	0.3	86474
76550	LAMPASAS	18197	3665	33.8	31.1	27.2	6.6	1.2	36020	40595	32	38	2554	24.0	35.2	29.6	8.7	2.6	77792
76554	LITTLE RIVER ACADEMY	19904	681	24.2	28.6	37.9	6.3	2.9	47937	53641	68	73	551	29.0	31.9	26.1	10.0	2.9	77254
76556	MILANO	19577	833	32.4	30.1	29.4	5.5	2.5	38992	45497	43	51	697	39.2	28.0	21.1	8.9	2.9	63511
76557	MOODY	19191	1832	28.0	32.6	30.4	6.7	2.4	40525	46883	48	56	1492	31.6	30.4	28.4	8.5	1.2	72576
76559	NOLANVILLE	19031	825	23.3	37.9	32.1	4.7	1.9	41506	48161	51	60	600	44.7	27.8	18.8	7.5	1.2	56667
76561	OGLESBY	20576	471	24.2	33.8	33.1	5.7	3.2	42255	46377	54	62	374	36.9	25.1	32.1	4.0	1.9	67059
76565	POTTSVILLE	23230	107	25.2	28.0	31.8	7.5	7.5	42776	50726	55	64	89	12.4	6.7	43.8	32.6	4.5	128125
76566	PURMELA	19976	241	31.5	32.4	28.6	4.2	3.3	39310	42831	44	52	201	25.4	18.4	38.3	12.4	5.5	100481
76567	ROCKDALE	19928	3337	28.0	32.7	30.3	6.7	2.3	41044	47122	50	58	2444	35.8	32.9	24.1	6.6	0.7	64670
76569	ROGERS	18171	932	35.8	24.5	31.6	5.9	2.3	41004	45690	50	58	713	37.5	25.1	28.3	7.3	1.8	67353
76570	ROSEBUD	16264	1125	39.2	32.1	23.1	4.3	1.3	33424	38291	22	27	806	50.7	31.1	13.7	4.5	0.0	49155
76571	SALADO	31696	2472	15.1	22.3	37.3	15.7	9.6	63705	72966	88	89	2152	11.8	12.4	37.7	34.2	4.0	147005
76574	TAYLOR	20596	6254	27.2	27.0	32.7	9.3	3.8	45231	51423	62	68	4326	15.4	28.1	43.3	11.8	1.5	99402
76577	THORNDALE	24763	1028	27.0	32.9	28.8	7.0	4.4	39705	46088	45	53	812	29.1	28.6	32.5	8.1	1.7	79306
76578	THRALL	21901	592	24.7	31.8	32.8	8.1	2.7	43976	50976	59	66	488	21.7	25.6	34.4	15.2	3.1	93250
76579	TROY	21806	1255	19.0	31.2	35.8	9.7	4.4	49830	55875	72	77	1020	19.0	30.1	41.8	6.6	2.6	90909
76621	ABBOTT	18891	379	33.8	24.3	33.0	7.4	1.6	41337	46657	51	59	316	28.5	31.3	25.6	11.1	3.5	76563
76622	AQUILLA	19844	620	29.7	30.8	31.6	5.5	2.4	40992	46648	50	58	505	26.9	35.3	27.5	8.7	1.6	75000
76624	AXTELL	20983	883	19.0	35.6	36.8	6.8	1.8	46867	54026	66	71	748	29.0	31.0	32.4	6.7	0.9	74286
76626	BLOOMING GROVE	20669	819	30.4	26.6	33.3	7.2	2.4	43263	50370	57	65	645	28.7	40.2	27.0	3.6	0.6	71269
76627	BLUM	19018	982	29.9	28.8	32.7	6.6	1.9	42092	48169	53	62	802	32.2	27.1	24.1	13.3	3.4	75238
76629	BREMOND	20426	868	38.6	25.7	25.4	6.3	4.0	35211	40688	28	34	655	35.9	30.5	24.7	8.9	0.0	68056
76630	BRUCEVILLE	21371	496	17.5	28.2	37.3	12.3	4.6	53146	62670	77	81	411	20.4	30.9	37.5	9.7	1.5	88429
76631	BYNUM	19089	191	29.8	25.1	31.9	10.0	3.1	45226	52427	62	68	163	29.5	30.1	25.8	11.0	3.7	77188
76632	CHILTON	18279	982	33.7	32.1	26.6	4.5	3.2	35996	41095	32	38	800	43.9	29.4	18.8	6.8	1.3	58305
76633	CHINA SPRING	23256	1312	18.0	28.1	36.1	12.7	5.2	53580	62654	78	82	1135	13.7	25.2	38.9	19.1	3.1	102799
76634	CLIFTON	21385	2956	32.1	29.9	27.6	6.8	3.6	38052	43474	39	47	2250	30.8	33.1	26.2	7.7	2.2	74381
76635	COOLIDGE	14803	500	43.4	33.0	19.4	1.8	2.4	29377	34366	11	14	348	62.4	17.0	13.2	7.2	0.3	37917
76636	COVINGTON	19814	328	25.9	28.7	36.0	7.6	1.8	44417	50117	60	67	268	31.3	32.1	22.4	13.1	1.1	72400
76637	CRANFILLS GAP	26248	377	23.3	25.5	37.1	9.0	5.0	51053	58807	74	78	311	16.4	30.6	35.1	10.6	7.4	92375
76638	CRAWFORD	25312	929	18.8	27.8	34.1	13.2	6.0	54861	63710	79	83	798	14.3	23.1	38.6	20.3	3.8	110659
76639	DAWSON	16061	746	40.1	29.4	26.4	3.2	0.9	32789	38203	20	25	609	50.3	27.3	16.1	5.6	0.8	49754
76640	ELM MOTT	25688	1305	22.0	29.7	34.6	7.9	5.8	48422	56368	69	74	1085	31.2	28.8	34.1	5.7	0.2	76525
76641	FROST	20407	865	35.0	28.1	28.8	5.9	2.2	38689	44882	42	50	718	41.5	32.0	22.7	3.8	0.0	57349
76642	GROESBECK	16564	2309	37.5	29.8	26.4	4.2	2.2	33702	39200	23	29	1677	42.4	31.5	20.3	5.7	0.1	58070
76643	HEWITT	25878	4486	10.7	23.5	45.2	16.5	4.1	63636	73617	88	89	3329	3.1	23.6	70.2	2.9	0.2	106415
76645	HILLSBORO	15871	4148	37.7	33.8	22.4	4.0	2.2	32591	37009	20	24	2741	36.3	31.8	22.7	8.2	1.0	68326
76648	HUBBARD	18448	932	39.3	28.2	24.4	5.5	2.7	33925	38399	24	30	714	47.6	27.5	19.6	4.5	0.8	53469
76649	IREDELL	17904	385	40.5	27.5	26.2	3.4	2.3	31734	36569	17	22	314	33.1	21.7	23.9	15.3	6.1	76000
76651	ITALY	19455	1021	20.3	30.7	37.8	8.8	2.5	49229	56170	71	76	772	20.9	38.7	29.9	8.6	1.9	79189
76652	KOPPERL	17840	404	30.7	35.2	26.2	6.4	1.5	39067	44279	43	51	331	38.1	28.4	21.2	11.2	1.2	66607
76653	KOSSE	17802	385	38.2	28.1	27.0	4.9	1.8	35442	41760	29	35	300	45.3	28.3	19.7	6.0	0.7	56667
76655	LORENA	26500	2449	13.3	25.1	42.1	13.5	6.0	59337	68091	84	86	2082	14.7	25.4	45.9	12.7	1.4	102644
76656	LOTT	20423	846	38.1	28.8	27.3	4.0	1.8	34300	38868	25	31	663	44.2	24.0	21.0	8.6	2.3	58556
76657	MC GREGOR	26774	2967	26.5	25.0	29.4	9.3	9.8	48229	56346	69	74	2270	33.3	23.1	21.9	16.6	5.1	74771
76660	MALONE	16267	171	38.0	31.0	24.6	5.3	1.2	34161	38493	25	30	140	45.7	28.6	18.6	7.1	0.0	56000
76661	MARLIN	16405	2997	48.5	27.3	17.6	3.9	2.6	26140	30237	6	8	1896	56.0	28.8	9.6	4.4	1.3	46082
76664	MART	17950	1152	37.5	29.0	24.1	6.3	3.0	33755	39257	23	29	845	49.2	29.5	16.2	5.0	0.1	50833
76665	MERIDIAN	22043	1019	30.7	32.8	27.2	5.4	3.9	40284	45707	47	55	769	31.6	27.6	25.6	12.4	2.9	78125
76666	MERTENS	21561	175	29.7	25.1	31.4	10.3	3.4	45251	52302	62	68	149	30.9	29.5	24.8	10.7	4.0	76071
76667	MEXIA	16033	3665	41.1	29.3	23.1	5.2	1.3	30849	35390	14	18	2547	50.6	31.9	13.4	3.8	0.4	49552
76670	MILFORD	18549	462	37.0	24.7	27.3	8.9	2.2	40307	47163	47	55	352	38.6	25.6	24.2	7.7	4.0	66111
76671	MORGAN	18203	691	36.8	32.9	24.6	4.1	1.7	33922	39563	24	29	568	45.4	26.9	20.1	7.0	0.5	56190
76673	MOUNT CALM	18476	259	36.3	27.8	27.0	6.2	2.7	37184	41546	36	43	210	40.5	28.1	24.8	5.7	1.0	64444
76676	PENELOPE	15825	285	38.3	30.5	24.2	5.6	1.4	34473	38471	26	31	233	46.4	27.9	18.9	6.4	0.4	55313
76678	PRAIRIE HILL	16662	325	41.2	32.0	22.8	1.9	2.2	32474	37359	19	23	265	39.3	22.3	23.0	15.1	0.4	66563
76679	PURDON	18186	326	30.1	32.5	30.7	4.6	2.2	39787	46433	45	53	273	29.7	29.7	25.3	13.2	2.2	78750
76680	REAGAN	13256	317	54.6	25.2	15.8	3.5	1.0	21505	24338	2	3	261	54.0	18.8	18.4	5.8	3.1	47083
76681	RICHLAND	19432	274	30.3	32.5	30.7	4.4	2.2	39740	46613	45	53	230	30.0	29.6	25.2	13.0	2.2	78235
76682	RIESEL	18865	1225	28.5	31.8	31.4	6.5	1.9	40805	47367	49	57	1007	34.6	28.6	28.5	6.7	1.7	71790
76687	THORNTON	21855	787	30.6	30.6	28.8	5.8	4.1	41579	47997	52	60	662	30.7	32.0	29.0	7.4	0.9	72333
	TEXAS	23284		26.2	27.7	29.5	10.3	6.3	45778	54246				21.6	26.1	33.4	15.6	3.4	93683
	UNITED STATES	25866		24.7	27.1	30.8	10.9	6.5	48124	56710				10.9	15.0	33.7	30.1	10.4	145905

ZIP CODE #	POST OFFICE NAME	FINANCIAL SERVICES: Auto Loan	Home Loan	Invest-ments	Retire-ment Plans	THE HOME: Home Improvements: Home Repair	Lawn & Garden	Furnishings: Comput-ers & Hard-ware	Major Appli-ances	TV, Radio, Sound Equip-ment	Furni-ture	ENTERTAINMENT: Dine out/ Carry out	Sports Equip-ment	Fees & Tickets	Toys & Games	Travel	Cable TV	PERSONAL: Apparel & Services	Auto Repairs	Health Insur-ance	Pets & Supplies
76476	TOLAR	120	97	65	92	104	113	93	107	100	94	121	126	85	118	94	102	113	106	117	138
76483	THROCKMORTON	81	59	37	57	66	78	64	72	72	61	85	83	56	81	64	76	77	72	87	91
76484	PALO PINTO	90	63	33	59	73	82	62	77	72	61	84	93	53	82	64	75	76	76	91	107
76486	PERRIN	75	52	27	50	61	68	52	64	60	51	70	77	44	69	54	63	64	63	76	89
76487	POOLVILLE	93	84	64	80	84	89	80	86	81	82	100	100	75	95	79	81	96	86	87	103
76490	WHITT	0	0	0	0	0	0	0	0	0	0	0	0	0	0	0	0	0	0	0	0
76491	WOODSON	104	73	38	69	85	95	72	89	83	71	97	107	61	95	74	87	88	87	106	123
76501	TEMPLE	69	64	66	63	65	72	68	68	71	66	87	78	67	87	67	72	84	69	72	78
76502	TEMPLE	95	103	113	103	103	109	100	100	98	100	122	116	103	124	102	97	120	100	98	111
76504	TEMPLE	66	61	64	62	61	66	66	65	67	65	83	76	64	81	64	66	80	67	65	73
76511	BARTLETT	42	33	22	31	36	42	34	38	38	33	45	44	31	44	34	40	42	38	45	48
76513	BELTON	86	83	77	82	83	88	82	84	82	82	102	98	81	101	81	82	99	84	84	97
76518	BUCKHOLTS	107	75	39	71	87	98	74	92	85	73	100	110	63	98	77	90	91	90	109	128
76519	BURLINGTON	60	45	30	43	49	59	50	55	56	47	66	61	44	62	49	59	60	55	66	66
76520	CAMERON	77	63	52	59	66	76	67	71	73	65	88	82	63	86	67	76	83	72	81	86
76522	COPPERAS COVE	82	70	67	74	67	71	80	75	79	78	99	94	74	93	73	74	96	81	69	85
76523	DAVILLA	91	64	33	60	74	83	63	78	73	62	85	94	54	83	65	76	78	77	93	108
76524	EDDY	85	77	61	74	77	82	74	79	75	76	92	91	70	87	73	74	89	79	78	94
76525	EVANT	94	71	47	68	77	93	78	86	88	74	103	97	70	97	77	93	94	86	103	104
76526	FLAT	80	68	53	67	71	80	70	74	74	68	90	85	67	89	69	75	84	73	81	88
76527	FLORENCE	101	95	78	93	96	100	89	95	89	91	111	111	87	108	89	88	107	93	93	113
76528	GATESVILLE	61	46	30	45	51	59	48	55	54	47	64	64	43	62	49	56	59	54	64	70
76530	GRANGER	81	65	46	63	69	77	66	74	71	67	86	85	60	83	66	72	81	74	80	91
76531	HAMILTON	76	59	40	56	65	76	62	70	69	60	81	78	56	76	62	73	75	69	83	86
76534	HOLLAND	80	69	53	67	73	80	67	73	72	67	87	86	65	87	68	73	82	72	80	91
76537	JARRELL	93	83	63	79	87	93	77	85	81	77	99	101	75	100	79	83	94	83	91	108
76538	JONESBORO	111	72	62	79	69	81	99	91	103	93	127	119	85	115	85	96	121	104	89	108
76539	KEMPNER	96	96	85	95	94	96	91	94	89	93	111	110	89	108	89	86	108	94	88	108
76541	KILLEEN	55	41	43	45	39	45	55	49	55	52	69	62	49	64	48	51	66	55	46	55
76542	KILLEEN	90	85	83	90	81	83	90	85	86	89	108	104	87	105	83	80	106	89	76	95
76543	KILLEEN	70	57	56	61	54	59	69	63	69	66	86	79	63	80	62	64	83	70	59	71
76544	KILLEEN	65	41	39	47	38	45	61	53	62	57	78	71	53	70	51	57	75	63	49	60
76548	HARKER HEIGHTS	98	100	93	102	97	99	95	96	91	97	115	112	94	112	93	88	112	96	88	109
76549	KILLEEN	76	57	57	62	53	60	74	66	74	70	93	86	67	87	65	69	90	75	61	75
76550	LAMPASAS	75	62	50	59	66	74	65	70	70	64	84	80	60	81	64	71	80	70	77	84
76554	LITTLE RIVER ACADEMY	85	83	72	80	83	87	79	83	79	80	97	96	77	95	79	77	95	82	81	96
76556	MILANO	85	64	41	62	71	82	67	76	74	65	88	89	60	86	67	78	81	75	89	97
76557	MOODY	84	72	54	69	75	84	72	78	76	71	92	90	68	90	72	78	86	77	85	95
76559	NOLANVILLE	84	76	60	73	76	81	73	78	74	75	91	90	69	86	72	73	87	78	77	92
76561	OGLESBY	79	70	54	67	74	79	65	72	69	65	84	86	64	86	67	71	80	70	78	92
76565	POTTSVILLE	90	84	81	80	89	105	78	89	82	84	103	87	79	85	85	88	96	86	104	101
76566	PURMELA	91	64	34	60	74	83	64	78	73	63	86	93	55	84	66	77	78	77	93	107
76567	ROCKDALE	81	70	59	67	73	81	72	76	77	70	93	88	69	93	72	78	88	76	82	92
76569	ROGERS	79	68	53	67	72	79	67	73	71	66	86	85	65	87	68	73	81	71	79	90
76570	ROSEBUD	72	52	31	47	57	67	54	62	63	53	74	72	48	69	54	67	67	62	76	81
76571	SALADO	123	121	110	117	125	135	111	120	113	113	140	135	112	136	116	116	134	116	127	143
76574	TAYLOR	83	80	73	77	80	86	79	82	80	79	99	94	77	99	79	80	96	82	83	94
76577	THORNDALE	111	83	52	80	93	104	84	97	93	82	111	115	75	109	85	96	102	96	112	128
76578	THRALL	94	82	63	80	86	95	80	87	85	79	103	101	77	104	81	87	97	85	94	107
76579	TROY	92	92	84	92	93	95	87	90	86	87	107	107	87	108	87	84	103	89	87	106
76621	ABBOTT	90	62	32	58	73	81	61	76	71	61	84	92	52	82	64	75	76	75	91	106
76622	AQUILLA	92	64	34	61	75	84	64	79	73	63	86	95	54	84	66	77	78	78	94	110
76624	AXTELL	90	81	62	77	85	90	75	83	79	76	97	98	73	97	77	81	92	81	88	105
76626	BLOOMING GROVE	85	69	49	66	74	85	71	78	77	69	92	89	65	90	71	81	86	77	89	96
76627	BLUM	88	68	44	62	74	83	65	76	73	65	87	89	60	84	66	77	81	74	88	101
76629	BREMOND	79	59	39	57	65	78	66	72	74	62	87	81	59	82	65	78	79	72	87	87
76630	BRUCEVILLE	103	92	71	88	97	103	86	95	90	86	110	112	84	111	88	92	105	93	101	120
76631	BYNUM	99	69	36	65	81	90	68	85	79	68	93	102	58	91	71	83	84	83	101	118
76632	CHILTON	87	66	42	62	72	79	66	78	73	68	88	89	58	83	66	74	83	77	85	98
76633	CHINA SPRING	99	105	98	103	107	109	95	100	94	95	116	118	98	122	98	94	114	97	98	119
76634	CLIFTON	90	67	43	63	75	86	69	80	77	67	92	93	61	89	70	82	84	79	94	105
76635	COOLIDGE	59	48	43	47	50	58	55	56	59	52	71	64	51	69	53	61	67	57	62	65
76636	COVINGTON	85	72	56	72	76	85	74	79	79	73	96	90	71	95	74	80	89	78	86	94
76637	CRANFILLS GAP	117	82	43	77	95	107	81	100	93	80	109	120	69	107	84	98	99	98	119	139
76638	CRAWFORD	104	108	101	107	111	114	99	105	98	98	120	124	100	125	102	97	117	102	104	125
76639	DAWSON	66	49	31	47	54	65	54	60	60	51	71	68	48	67	53	64	65	60	72	74
76640	ELM MOTT	111	99	76	94	105	112	92	101	97	92	118	121	90	121	94	100	113	99	110	131
76641	FROST	97	70	39	63	78	88	67	81	78	68	92	97	60	89	68	83	85	80	96	112
76642	GROESBECK	65	50	35	48	55	62	52	58	58	51	69	69	47	67	52	60	64	59	67	75
76643	HEWITT	100	112	115	115	108	107	105	103	98	107	124	122	107	125	103	93	123	102	91	114
76645	HILLSBORO	65	56	49	54	58	64	59	62	63	59	77	71	56	75	58	64	73	63	66	73
76648	HUBBARD	81	58	34	55	66	76	61	71	69	59	81	83	53	78	61	73	74	71	85	93
76649	IREDELL	68	51	34	49	56	67	57	63	64	54	75	70	51	71	56	67	68	63	75	76
76651	ITALY	90	78	60	76	81	91	78	84	82	77	100	97	75	100	78	84	94	82	91	101
76652	KOPPERL	87	59	28	52	67	77	57	71	68	58	80	85	49	76	58	73	73	70	87	101
76653	KOSSE	75	58	39	54	64	74	60	68	67	58	79	78	53	76	61	71	73	68	81	87
76655	LORENA	111	114	103	111	116	120	104	110	104	103	128	130	105	133	107	104	124	107	110	133
76656	LOTT	94	67	38	63	77	88	69	82	78	67	92	97	59	89	70	83	84	81	98	110
76657	MC GREGOR	117	101	79	97	108	119	99	109	107	97	129	127	95	130	101	110	121	107	121	136
76660	MALONE	66	56	44	56	59	66	58	61	61	57	74	70	55	73	57	62	69	61	67	73
76661	MARLIN	68	52	41	49	56	67	58	63	66	57	78	70	53	73	57	69	72	63	75	75
76664	MART	76	60	42	58	65	76	64	70	70	61	83	80	58	80	63	73	77	69	82	86
76665	MERIDIAN	96	77	55	74	84	94	77	87	84	76	101	101	71	99	78	87	94	86	98	110
76666	MERTENS	99	69	36	66	81	91	69	85	79	68	93	102	59	91	71	83	84	84	101	118
76667	MEXIA	61	53	49	51	54	63	57	59	62	56	75	67	55	73	57	64	71	60	65	68
76670	MILFORD	80	63	44	60	68	79	66	73	72	64	86	83	60	83	66	76	80	72	84	90
76671	MORGAN	78	58	34	52	65	74	55	67	64	55	75	80	48	73	58	68	69	66	81	93
76673	MOUNT CALM	86	60	31	57	70	78	59	73	68	58	80	88	50	78	61	71	73	72	87	102
76676	PENELOPE	66	56	43	56	59	66	58	61	61	56	74	70	55	73	57	62	69	60	67	73
76678	PRAIRIE HILL	69	52	34	50	57	68	57	63	64	54	75	71	51	71	57	68	69	63	75	76
76679	PURDON	88	62	32	58	72	80	61	75	70	60	82	91	52	81	63	74	75	74	90	105
76680	REAGAN	59	40	18	34	45	52	38	48	46	39	54	57	33	51	39	50	49	48	59	68
76681	RICHLAND	89	62	33	59	72	81	61	76	71	61	83	91	52	81	64	74	75	75	90	105
76682	RIESEL	79	67	50	65	70	78	68	74	72	68	87	84	64	84	67	73	82	73	79	88
76687	THORNTON	90	69	47	64	78	89	68	80	77	67	91	93	61	89	71	82	84	79	95	106
	TEXAS	94	90	91	90	89	95	92	93	92	93	115	107	90	112	90	90	112	94	89	104
	UNITED STATES	100	100	100	100	100	100	100	100	100	100	100	100	100	100	100	100	100	100	100	100

ZIP CODE		COUNTY FIPS CODE	POPULATION			2000-2004 ANNUAL RATE		HOUSEHOLDS					FAMILIES		
#	POST OFFICE NAME		2000	2004	2009	% Rate	State Centile	2000	2004	2009	% Annual Rate 2000-2004	2004 Average HH Size	2000	2004	% Annual Rate 2000-2004
76689	VALLEY MILLS	099	5103	5474	5831	1.7	61	1429	1534	1635	1.7	2.87	1103	1191	1.8
76690	WALNUT SPRINGS	035	944	984	1029	1.0	41	336	347	360	0.8	2.84	250	259	0.8
76691	WEST	309	6243	6610	7072	1.4	53	2350	2460	2609	1.1	2.62	1721	1815	1.3
76692	WHITNEY	217	7896	8600	9469	2.0	68	3206	3465	3788	1.8	2.44	2234	2425	2.0
76693	WORTHAM	161	1849	2046	2325	2.4	75	711	785	892	2.4	2.57	495	548	2.4
76701	WACO	309	2209	2226	2272	0.2	17	463	467	483	0.2	2.41	204	205	0.1
76704	WACO	309	7917	8052	8466	0.4	22	3080	3115	3256	0.3	2.50	1922	1948	0.3
76705	WACO	309	27626	29083	31010	1.2	49	9999	10423	11032	1.0	2.69	6836	7149	1.1
76706	WACO	309	32341	33789	35712	1.0	43	11237	11691	12329	0.9	2.57	5828	6108	1.1
76707	WACO	309	17404	17566	18459	0.2	18	5637	5598	5817	-0.2	3.07	3971	3941	-0.2
76708	WACO	309	21057	21483	22618	0.5	24	7851	7975	8362	0.4	2.58	5231	5306	0.3
76710	WACO	309	22556	23826	25543	1.3	51	10591	11162	11919	1.2	2.09	5826	6126	1.2
76711	WACO	309	8619	8734	9144	0.3	20	2852	2864	2979	0.1	2.91	2101	2113	0.1
76712	WOODWAY	309	18874	19981	21336	1.4	53	7325	7693	8155	1.2	2.55	5457	5727	1.1
76801	BROWNWOOD	049	25584	26115	26966	0.5	25	9641	9793	10084	0.4	2.47	6504	6624	0.4
76802	EARLY	049	4821	4889	5062	0.2	21	1754	1766	1822	0.2	2.70	1346	1358	0.2
76820	ART	319	32	32	31	0.0	13	16	16	15	0.0	2.00	12	12	0.0
76821	BALLINGER	399	5283	5339	5412	0.3	19	2010	2020	2041	0.1	2.53	1408	1419	0.2
76823	BANGS	049	2796	2878	2977	0.7	32	1093	1123	1157	0.6	2.49	771	792	0.6
76825	BRADY	307	6891	7060	7293	0.6	28	2728	2785	2868	0.5	2.49	1861	1906	0.6
76827	BROOKESMITH	049	389	420	444	1.8	64	157	172	184	2.2	1.94	129	141	2.1
76828	BURKETT	083	204	201	199	-0.4	7	99	97	95	-0.5	1.81	72	70	-0.7
76831	CASTELL	299	100	107	119	1.6	59	44	47	52	1.6	2.28	34	36	1.4
76832	CHEROKEE	411	622	633	650	0.4	23	222	226	232	0.4	2.11	165	168	0.4
76834	COLEMAN	083	6470	6377	6285	-0.3	7	2708	2654	2604	-0.5	2.36	1798	1768	-0.4
76836	DOOLE	307	54	53	54	-0.4	5	23	23	23	0.0	2.30	17	17	0.0
76837	EDEN	095	2856	2825	2818	-0.3	8	613	600	597	-0.5	2.52	421	414	-0.4
76841	FORT MC KAVETT	327	32	33	33	0.7	34	15	15	16	0.0	2.20	11	11	0.0
76842	FREDONIA	319	83	82	81	-0.3	8	32	31	31	-0.7	2.65	25	25	0.0
76844	GOLDTHWAITE	333	2810	2832	2883	0.2	17	1165	1163	1173	0.0	2.31	768	768	0.0
76845	GOULDBUSK	083	197	193	189	-0.5	4	84	82	80	-0.6	2.35	60	58	-0.8
76848	HEXT	327	78	80	81	0.6	29	34	35	35	0.7	2.29	24	25	1.0
76849	JUNCTION	267	4015	4185	4392	1.0	41	1658	1732	1826	1.0	2.39	1149	1204	1.1
76852	LOHN	307	291	288	293	-0.2	8	113	111	113	-0.4	2.59	83	83	0.0
76853	LOMETA	281	1450	1535	1680	1.4	53	578	609	664	1.2	2.44	406	428	1.3
76854	LONDON	267	416	433	454	1.0	40	186	194	205	1.0	2.17	123	129	1.1
76856	MASON	319	3446	3418	3350	-0.2	9	1488	1469	1439	-0.3	2.30	1019	1009	-0.2
76857	MAY	049	1689	1810	1913	1.6	60	720	769	810	1.6	2.35	538	576	1.6
76858	MELVIN	307	305	302	307	-0.2	8	133	130	132	-0.5	2.09	98	97	-0.2
76859	MENARD	327	2226	2248	2276	0.2	18	932	935	943	0.1	2.36	624	628	0.2
76861	MILES	399	1870	1886	1905	0.2	17	664	666	670	0.1	2.83	524	526	0.1
76862	MILLERSVIEW	095	152	156	157	0.6	29	71	72	73	0.3	2.08	54	55	0.4
76864	MULLIN	333	1558	1626	1686	1.0	42	542	561	577	0.8	2.66	405	421	0.9
76865	NORTON	399	271	273	278	0.2	17	117	118	119	0.2	2.29	86	86	0.0
76866	PAINT ROCK	095	628	644	651	0.6	28	240	245	246	0.5	2.60	182	185	0.4
76869	PONTOTOC	319	145	144	141	-0.2	10	56	55	54	-0.4	2.62	43	43	0.0
76870	PRIDDY	333	130	131	133	0.2	17	41	41	41	0.0	3.17	30	30	0.0
76871	RICHLAND SPRINGS	411	1191	1239	1295	0.9	39	505	522	542	0.8	2.37	357	370	0.9
76872	ROCHELLE	307	831	839	860	0.2	18	357	359	366	0.1	2.34	260	263	0.3
76873	ROCKWOOD	083	54	53	52	-0.4	5	31	30	30	-0.8	1.77	21	21	0.0
76874	ROOSEVELT	267	22	23	23	1.1	44	12	12	13	0.0	1.83	8	8	0.0
76875	ROWENA	399	655	644	643	-0.4	6	274	268	266	-0.5	2.40	192	188	-0.5
76877	SAN SABA	411	4170	4293	4449	0.7	32	1473	1509	1559	0.6	2.57	1032	1060	0.6
76878	SANTA ANNA	083	1590	1549	1519	-0.6	4	663	641	627	-0.8	2.37	436	423	-0.7
76880	STAR	333	648	652	663	0.1	16	252	251	253	-0.1	2.57	194	194	0.0
76882	TALPA	083	273	275	275	0.2	17	127	128	128	0.2	2.13	92	93	0.3
76883	TELEGRAPH	267	19	20	21	1.2	48	9	9	10	0.0	2.11	6	6	0.0
76884	VALERA	083	134	131	128	-0.5	4	57	55	54	-0.8	2.38	41	40	-0.6
76885	VALLEY SPRING	299	289	312	351	1.8	64	127	136	153	1.6	2.29	99	107	1.9
76887	VOCA	307	123	124	126	0.2	17	55	55	56	0.2	2.25	42	42	0.0
76888	VOSS	083	107	105	102	-0.4	5	47	46	45	-0.5	2.28	34	33	-0.7
76890	ZEPHYR	049	889	1034	1141	3.6	87	343	398	438	3.6	2.60	270	314	3.6
76901	SAN ANGELO	451	25675	26300	26957	0.6	28	10046	10250	10502	0.5	2.53	7009	7185	0.6
76903	SAN ANGELO	451	31764	31345	31572	-0.3	8	11768	11616	11721	-0.3	2.62	7815	7745	-0.2
76904	SAN ANGELO	451	30221	31457	32412	1.0	40	12702	13220	13645	0.9	2.31	8096	8453	1.0
76905	SAN ANGELO	451	10664	10752	10941	0.2	17	3710	3737	3804	0.2	2.88	2890	2917	0.2
76908	GOODFELLOW AFB	451	1752	1737	1735	-0.2	9	104	99	98	-1.2	3.24	97	92	-1.2
76909	SAN ANGELO	451	441	440	440	-0.1	11	2	2	2	0.0	7.00	2	1	-15.1
76930	BARNHART	235	165	169	175	0.7	28	65	67	70	0.7	2.52	50	51	0.5
76932	BIG LAKE	383	3326	3266	3249	-0.4	5	1107	1099	1109	-0.2	2.93	872	868	-0.1
76933	BRONTE	081	1657	1783	1960	1.7	63	580	630	703	2.0	2.45	405	441	2.0
76934	CARLSBAD	451	1724	1711	1715	-0.2	9	543	538	540	-0.2	2.75	414	412	-0.1
76935	CHRISTOVAL	451	676	714	737	1.3	51	266	279	288	1.1	2.48	182	192	1.3
76936	ELDORADO	413	2935	2930	2920	0.0	12	1115	1121	1127	0.1	2.57	817	824	0.2
76937	EOLA	095	445	485	509	2.1	68	158	170	176	1.7	2.76	124	134	1.8
76940	MERETA	451	173	179	183	0.8	36	65	67	68	0.7	2.67	52	54	0.9
76941	MERTZON	235	1542	1581	1637	0.6	28	602	619	644	0.7	2.55	454	468	0.7
76943	OZONA	105	4095	4112	4186	0.1	15	1522	1527	1554	0.1	2.66	1113	1120	0.2
76945	ROBERT LEE	081	1882	1996	2195	1.4	54	799	849	937	1.4	2.29	546	581	1.5
76949	SILVER	081	20	22	24	2.3	73	11	12	13	2.1	1.83	8	9	2.8
76950	SONORA	435	4072	4003	3919	-0.4	6	1513	1487	1458	-0.4	2.67	1144	1127	-0.4
76951	STERLING CITY	431	1399	1347	1282	-0.9	1	515	498	477	-0.8	2.65	387	376	-0.7
76955	VANCOURT	451	171	206	227	4.5	92	51	61	67	4.3	3.38	43	52	4.6
77002	HOUSTON	201	13154	13814	14537	1.2	47	1721	2215	2662	6.1	1.50	304	410	7.3
77003	HOUSTON	201	9675	11219	12994	3.6	87	2603	3054	3555	3.8	3.44	1840	2167	3.9
77004	HOUSTON	201	30357	31698	34500	1.0	43	11584	12138	13283	1.1	2.28	5892	6171	1.1
77005	HOUSTON	201	22304	23222	25309	1.0	40	9396	9729	10522	0.8	2.38	5809	5984	0.7
77006	HOUSTON	201	19032	20412	22617	1.7	61	11042	11822	13064	1.6	1.63	2758	2958	1.7
77007	HOUSTON	201	22360	24700	27837	2.4	74	9220	10181	11437	2.4	2.37	4504	4899	2.0
77008	HOUSTON	201	28847	30274	33216	1.1	46	12632	13121	14254	0.9	2.28	6465	6770	1.1
77009	HOUSTON	201	42406	43207	46762	0.4	23	14244	14380	15431	0.2	2.97	9086	9209	0.3
77010	HOUSTON	201	80	84	98	1.2	46	54	63	72	3.7	1.33	5	3	-11.3
77011	HOUSTON	201	22761	23324	25188	0.6	28	6267	6393	6858	0.5	3.58	4916	5018	0.5
77012	HOUSTON	201	25094	26832	29730	1.8	59	6669	7024	7688	1.2	3.80	5398	5701	1.3
77013	HOUSTON	201	18307	20888	24007	3.2	82	5315	6037	6895	3.0	3.27	4164	4734	3.1
	TEXAS					2.2					2.0	2.77			2.1
	UNITED STATES					1.2					1.3	2.58			1.1

ZIP CODE #	POST OFFICE NAME	RACE (%) White 2000	White 2004	Black 2000	Black 2004	Asian/Pacific 2000	Asian/Pacific 2004	% Hispanic Origin 2000	% Hispanic Origin 2004	2004 AGE DISTRIBUTION (%) 0-4	5-9	10-14	15-19	20-24	25-44	45-64	65-84	85+	18+	MEDIAN AGE 2004	% 2004 Males	% 2004 Females
76689	VALLEY MILLS	82.6	80.8	8.8	9.3	0.7	0.8	8.7	10.4	5.2	5.5	6.3	8.1	11.8	28.8	22.6	9.7	2.0	79.6	33.6	56.3	43.7
76690	WALNUT SPRINGS	88.7	87.2	0.1	0.1	0.0	0.0	24.7	28.3	7.2	7.4	8.1	7.4	7.3	22.9	24.7	13.4	1.5	71.9	36.1	51.1	48.9
76691	WEST	94.2	93.1	2.4	2.6	0.2	0.2	6.1	7.7	6.7	6.7	7.1	6.9	6.4	25.3	23.5	14.3	3.0	75.2	39.2	49.1	50.9
76692	WHITNEY	93.6	92.6	2.1	2.3	0.2	0.2	5.8	7.1	5.8	5.8	6.3	5.9	5.3	21.6	28.4	18.6	2.4	78.5	44.6	48.5	51.6
76693	WORTHAM	81.3	79.8	15.4	16.3	0.0	0.0	3.6	4.4	7.9	7.5	7.4	6.6	6.4	24.0	25.3	12.4	2.7	73.5	37.1	47.5	52.5
76701	WACO	55.3	51.3	25.1	25.9	0.7	0.7	26.0	30.3	4.0	3.1	2.2	6.7	14.2	38.4	16.3	9.2	6.0	87.8	34.5	61.7	38.3
76704	WACO	14.6	13.4	78.1	78.6	0.4	0.4	8.5	9.6	10.3	8.5	8.0	8.3	9.4	21.1	19.0	13.1	2.3	68.6	29.3	44.4	55.6
76705	WACO	73.1	70.2	15.8	17.0	0.7	0.7	15.3	18.1	7.9	6.9	6.9	10.3	10.7	26.7	20.2	9.4	1.2	73.8	29.9	52.0	48.0
76706	WACO	68.0	65.4	12.4	12.8	2.8	3.1	25.8	28.9	5.9	5.4	5.7	17.3	23.7	19.9	14.3	7.1	0.9	79.6	23.3	47.6	52.4
76707	WACO	43.5	41.4	33.9	33.4	0.4	0.4	35.7	40.0	10.2	8.8	9.1	8.5	9.1	28.3	17.4	7.2	1.7	66.8	27.8	48.5	51.5
76708	WACO	68.0	66.1	19.6	19.9	0.6	0.6	21.6	24.4	7.6	7.3	8.1	7.5	7.2	26.6	20.4	12.3	3.0	72.3	34.3	47.4	52.6
76710	WACO	78.8	76.0	10.8	11.7	1.2	1.3	13.0	15.7	6.3	5.4	4.8	5.3	8.3	26.1	21.7	18.4	3.8	80.7	39.8	46.2	53.8
76711	WACO	57.0	53.4	11.3	11.4	0.4	0.4	49.1	54.5	9.0	8.2	8.2	7.6	7.8	27.8	19.1	11.0	1.3	70.1	30.8	51.0	49.0
76712	WOODWAY	89.6	87.8	4.5	5.0	2.0	2.3	6.7	8.5	6.3	6.4	7.3	6.8	6.0	26.0	27.1	12.3	1.9	75.8	39.3	48.3	51.7
76801	BROWNWOOD	84.7	83.0	5.2	5.4	0.5	0.5	18.5	21.4	6.5	6.1	6.6	9.0	8.5	24.4	23.2	13.2	2.5	75.7	36.3	49.5	50.5
76802	EARLY	93.8	92.8	0.7	0.8	0.4	0.4	9.7	11.5	6.7	6.7	7.4	7.1	6.4	24.5	25.4	13.4	2.4	74.6	38.9	48.9	51.1
76820	ART	93.8	96.9	0.0	0.0	0.0	0.0	12.5	12.5	6.3	6.3	6.3	6.3	6.3	21.9	25.0	21.9	0.0	81.3	42.5	50.0	50.0
76821	BALLINGER	81.3	81.1	1.7	1.7	0.4	0.4	29.0	29.6	6.4	6.4	7.0	6.8	6.1	22.7	24.8	15.7	4.1	75.7	41.0	48.3	51.7
76823	BANGS	88.3	86.7	4.3	4.6	0.0	0.0	11.3	13.4	6.3	6.4	6.7	7.3	5.1	23.7	26.4	15.1	3.0	76.0	41.0	47.7	52.3
76825	BRADY	83.4	81.4	1.9	1.9	0.2	0.2	29.2	32.9	7.4	7.0	6.9	7.3	6.1	22.0	24.3	15.9	3.2	74.0	39.9	47.1	52.9
76827	BROOKESMITH	90.8	90.0	6.9	7.4	0.0	0.0	10.0	11.9	3.8	4.3	5.0	6.7	7.9	30.0	30.0	10.7	1.7	82.9	40.4	59.5	40.5
76828	BURKETT	95.6	95.5	0.0	0.0	0.0	0.0	5.4	6.0	3.5	3.5	4.5	4.0	4.5	20.9	29.9	21.4	8.0	85.6	50.5	49.8	50.3
76831	CASTELL	97.0	97.2	0.0	0.0	0.0	0.0	5.0	5.6	3.7	3.7	4.7	4.7	3.7	15.9	34.6	27.1	1.9	83.2	53.6	51.4	48.6
76832	CHEROKEE	84.1	82.6	8.4	8.7	0.2	0.2	17.5	20.2	4.3	4.7	7.4	21.6	5.7	15.6	24.3	14.1	2.2	70.1	34.4	59.9	40.1
76834	COLEMAN	86.9	85.2	2.3	2.4	0.3	0.3	14.9	17.3	6.3	6.2	6.2	6.7	6.1	21.2	24.6	18.8	3.9	77.2	42.8	47.7	52.3
76836	DOOLE	87.0	84.9	0.0	0.0	0.0	0.0	22.2	26.4	3.8	3.8	5.7	7.6	5.7	20.8	30.2	20.8	1.9	83.0	46.9	50.9	49.1
76837	EDEN	90.1	90.1	1.3	1.3	0.2	0.2	47.1	48.6	3.6	3.4	3.7	4.3	10.4	43.1	19.7	9.7	2.2	86.9	34.9	69.6	30.4
76841	FORT MC KAVETT	93.8	97.0	0.0	0.0	0.0	0.0	12.5	12.1	3.0	6.1	6.1	6.1	3.0	15.2	39.4	18.2	3.0	84.9	50.8	48.5	51.5
76842	FREDONIA	94.0	95.1	0.0	0.0	0.0	0.0	12.1	12.2	4.9	4.9	6.1	6.1	4.9	18.3	26.8	25.6	2.4	80.5	49.0	47.6	52.4
76844	GOLDTHWAITE	88.2	87.8	0.3	0.3	0.2	0.2	16.4	17.0	6.4	6.1	5.8	6.3	4.9	20.2	25.3	19.2	5.9	77.3	45.3	47.5	52.5
76845	GOULDBUSK	94.9	94.3	0.5	0.5	0.0	0.0	8.1	9.8	4.7	5.2	6.2	5.2	4.7	23.3	27.5	20.7	2.6	80.8	45.5	51.8	48.2
76848	HEXT	93.6	93.8	0.0	0.0	0.0	0.0	14.1	15.0	2.5	3.8	2.5	5.0	3.8	15.0	42.5	22.5	2.5	90.0	55.6	55.0	45.0
76849	JUNCTION	89.6	88.2	0.1	0.1	0.5	0.6	22.0	25.1	6.2	6.2	6.3	6.4	5.4	21.7	27.5	17.9	2.6	77.4	43.5	48.2	51.9
76852	LOHN	87.3	85.1	0.0	0.0	0.0	0.0	22.3	26.4	4.2	4.9	6.9	7.6	5.2	18.8	32.3	17.7	2.4	78.8	46.4	50.7	49.3
76853	LOMETA	89.0	87.8	1.3	1.3	0.2	0.2	18.1	20.7	5.0	6.6	7.8	7.3	5.7	19.8	26.1	18.8	3.1	75.9	43.3	50.2	49.8
76854	LONDON	95.9	95.4	0.0	0.0	0.0	0.0	10.1	11.8	4.6	5.1	4.2	4.4	3.9	18.0	32.3	24.3	3.2	83.1	52.1	49.7	50.4
76856	MASON	91.4	91.1	0.2	0.2	0.1	0.1	21.7	22.5	5.3	5.4	5.8	5.8	4.9	19.5	29.7	19.9	3.8	79.7	47.6	47.8	52.2
76857	MAY	96.7	96.2	0.1	0.1	0.1	0.1	4.5	5.4	4.6	4.7	5.3	5.4	5.3	17.9	30.6	24.5	1.8	82.1	50.0	50.8	49.2
76858	MELVIN	88.5	86.1	0.3	0.3	0.0	0.0	26.2	30.1	3.6	4.3	6.0	7.3	6.3	24.5	30.1	15.9	2.0	81.5	43.6	56.3	43.7
76859	MENARD	87.2	87.0	0.5	0.5	0.4	0.4	32.5	33.5	5.0	5.1	6.3	7.5	6.4	20.1	28.0	18.2	3.6	78.4	44.8	50.1	49.9
76861	MILES	82.6	81.2	0.1	0.1	0.3	0.3	27.5	29.9	5.8	7.0	8.3	7.9	6.1	26.3	25.8	11.2	1.7	73.9	38.2	50.1	50.0
76862	MILLERSVIEW	82.9	82.7	0.0	0.0	0.0	0.0	25.7	26.9	4.5	5.1	5.8	5.1	5.8	23.7	32.1	15.4	2.6	80.8	45.0	52.6	47.4
76864	MULLIN	89.5	89.2	3.2	3.2	0.2	0.2	7.7	8.1	4.3	6.2	8.4	8.7	4.9	18.0	31.3	16.6	1.8	74.7	44.8	55.0	45.0
76865	NORTON	91.5	91.2	0.7	0.7	0.0	0.0	13.3	14.3	5.1	5.1	5.1	6.2	5.5	19.4	31.9	18.7	2.9	80.6	46.8	51.3	48.7
76866	PAINT ROCK	82.6	82.3	0.0	0.0	0.2	0.2	24.8	25.8	5.0	5.3	6.2	5.3	5.9	23.1	29.8	16.8	2.6	80.1	44.4	50.0	50.0
76869	PONTOTOC	94.5	94.4	0.0	0.0	0.0	0.0	12.4	13.2	4.9	5.6	5.6	6.3	4.2	18.8	29.9	22.9	2.1	79.2	48.5	50.0	50.0
76870	PRIDDY	93.9	93.9	0.8	0.8	0.0	0.0	5.4	4.6	4.6	5.3	6.9	7.6	5.3	22.1	26.7	19.1	2.3	77.9	43.4	49.6	50.4
76871	RICHLAND SPRINGS	92.9	91.6	0.1	0.1	0.1	0.1	12.1	14.2	5.0	5.2	6.0	6.5	5.6	18.7	31.1	19.3	2.7	79.7	46.9	52.5	47.5
76872	ROCHELLE	94.1	93.0	0.0	0.0	0.1	0.1	11.3	13.4	4.5	5.5	6.1	5.5	3.6	18.5	35.5	19.1	1.8	80.0	48.4	49.6	50.4
76873	ROCKWOOD	92.6	92.5	1.9	1.9	0.0	0.0	7.4	9.4	3.8	3.8	5.7	5.7	3.8	18.9	28.3	26.4	3.8	86.8	50.6	47.2	52.8
76874	ROOSEVELT	95.5	95.7	0.0	0.0	0.0	0.0	13.6	13.0	8.7	8.7	4.4	4.4	4.4	21.7	34.8	13.0	0.0	78.3	43.8	52.2	47.8
76875	ROWENA	88.4	87.9	0.0	0.0	0.0	0.0	20.0	21.0	5.8	6.1	7.8	5.3	4.7	23.1	24.8	19.1	3.4	77.0	43.4	50.9	49.1
76877	SAN SABA	81.8	79.6	2.8	2.9	0.1	0.1	25.3	28.8	6.0	6.0	7.5	10.9	6.1	20.6	22.8	16.1	4.1	73.6	39.0	49.8	50.2
76878	SANTA ANNA	90.4	89.4	3.1	3.2	0.1	0.1	15.2	17.5	5.9	6.1	6.1	6.3	6.1	20.3	26.2	18.9	4.2	77.7	44.3	48.6	51.4
76880	STAR	92.6	92.3	0.8	0.8	0.0	0.0	12.8	13.5	6.1	6.1	6.3	6.3	5.5	17.8	27.2	20.9	3.8	77.6	46.2	51.4	48.6
76882	TALPA	94.9	94.2	0.4	0.4	0.0	0.0	9.2	10.9	4.7	5.5	6.6	5.1	4.7	24.4	28.0	19.3	1.8	80.0	44.6	53.1	46.9
76883	TELEGRAPH	94.7	95.0	0.0	0.0	0.0	0.0	10.5	15.0	0.0	5.0	0.0	5.0	0.0	10.0	45.0	35.0	0.0	95.0	60.0	45.0	55.0
76884	VALERA	95.5	94.7	0.0	0.0	0.0	0.0	8.2	9.9	5.3	5.3	6.9	5.3	4.6	24.4	26.7	19.1	2.3	77.9	44.2	52.7	47.3
76885	VALLEY SPRING	96.9	96.5	0.4	0.6	0.4	0.3	4.5	5.5	2.9	3.5	4.5	4.8	4.2	18.0	37.5	23.4	1.3	85.9	52.4	50.0	50.0
76887	VOCA	95.9	96.0	0.0	0.0	0.0	0.0	11.4	12.9	4.0	4.8	7.3	5.7	5.7	21.0	31.5	18.6	1.6	79.0	45.9	50.0	50.0
76888	VOSS	95.3	94.3	0.0	0.0	0.0	0.0	8.4	9.5	4.8	5.7	6.7	5.7	4.8	23.8	26.7	20.0	1.9	77.1	44.3	53.3	46.7
76890	ZEPHYR	94.8	93.9	0.0	0.0	0.1	0.1	7.2	8.6	6.5	6.5	5.8	6.5	5.9	22.8	31.0	13.3	1.8	77.3	42.3	51.0	49.0
76901	SAN ANGELO	83.1	80.8	3.3	3.4	0.6	0.7	27.0	31.6	7.2	6.7	7.3	7.4	7.7	28.3	23.3	10.5	1.7	74.3	34.8	48.3	51.8
76903	SAN ANGELO	67.8	65.6	5.5	5.3	0.7	0.7	50.4	54.8	7.8	7.2	7.6	8.0	8.0	25.8	20.4	12.5	2.9	72.7	33.9	48.0	52.0
76904	SAN ANGELO	88.0	86.2	3.3	3.5	1.3	1.5	13.9	17.2	5.9	5.6	6.0	8.0	11.1	24.8	23.9	13.0	1.8	78.9	36.3	47.2	52.8
76905	SAN ANGELO	74.6	72.1	3.8	3.8	1.2	1.3	37.6	42.2	8.1	8.1	8.9	8.3	7.0	28.3	22.3	8.4	0.7	69.6	32.4	49.4	50.6
76908	GOODFELLOW AFB	74.7	71.5	11.6	12.7	2.5	2.8	12.6	15.6	4.7	2.0	1.4	26.4	43.8	21.0	0.5	0.1	0.1	91.0	21.8	71.1	28.9
76909	SAN ANGELO	76.4	72.7	10.4	11.4	1.4	1.6	17.7	22.1	0.7	0.7	0.7	52.7	42.3	2.7	0.2	0.0	0.0	97.3	19.6	44.6	55.5
76930	BARNHART	95.2	95.3	0.0	0.0	0.0	0.0	16.4	16.6	5.9	6.5	5.9	5.9	4.1	23.7	32.0	14.2	1.8	78.1	44.0	49.7	50.3
76932	BIG LAKE	64.6	64.1	3.0	3.1	0.3	0.3	49.5	50.5	8.5	8.2	8.5	9.0	8.0	25.9	21.7	9.2	1.0	68.7	32.2	50.0	50.0
76933	BRONTE	87.0	85.9	4.4	4.4	0.2	0.2	19.6	22.4	4.8	5.1	5.7	13.2	7.7	18.0	23.3	17.7	4.6	76.3	40.9	52.1	48.0
76934	CARLSBAD	89.9	88.0	2.7	3.0	0.2	0.2	13.8	17.3	4.7	5.1	6.6	6.6	6.0	26.5	29.8	13.3	1.3	79.5	41.8	53.4	46.6
76935	CHRISTOVAL	95.0	93.8	0.4	0.6	0.2	0.1	10.8	13.6	4.5	4.8	4.9	6.6	4.5	19.9	30.4	19.1	5.5	81.2	47.6	49.2	50.8
76936	ELDORADO	76.6	76.2	1.5	1.5	0.2	0.2	43.5	44.6	6.5	6.4	7.0	8.4	7.1	22.0	26.3	13.9	2.5	74.7	39.9	49.8	50.2
76937	EOLA	87.0	86.4	0.2	0.2	0.2	0.2	21.6	22.9	5.2	6.6	7.6	6.4	5.2	25.8	27.6	13.8	1.9	76.1	40.5	52.2	47.8
76940	MERETA	85.0	82.1	0.0	0.0	0.0	0.0	25.4	30.7	7.3	7.8	10.6	8.4	5.0	25.7	25.1	9.5	0.6	68.2	35.9	52.0	48.0
76941	MERTZON	90.0	89.8	0.5	0.4	0.0	0.0	25.9	26.7	5.6	6.6	8.0	7.3	4.2	24.5	28.0	14.0	1.7	74.6	41.0	50.1	49.9
76943	OZONA	76.3	76.1	0.7	0.7	0.3	0.3	54.7	55.8	6.8	6.8	8.1	8.2	6.9	23.2	27.2	11.1	1.8	73.0	37.6	49.7	50.3
76945	ROBERT LEE	89.0	87.3	0.2	0.2	0.1	0.1	17.2	20.1	4.8	5.1	6.5	6.4	5.6	19.6	25.6	23.1	3.4	79.3	46.4	47.0	53.0
76949	SILVER	90.0	90.9	0.0	0.0	0.0	0.0	10.0	13.6	0.0	4.6	9.1	4.6	4.6	13.6	36.4	27.3	0.0	86.4	52.5	54.6	45.5
76950	SONORA	75.3	74.9	0.3	0.3	0.2	0.2	51.7	52.8	7.0	7.2	7.8	7.5	6.6	25.1	26.6	11.2	1.1	73.3	37.1	50.2	49.8
76951	STERLING CITY	85.7	85.5	0.1	0.1	0.1	0.1	30.9	31.9	5.1	7.2	10.1	8.8	3.5	28.1	22.5	12.5	2.2	71.5	38.0	48.9	51.1
76955	VANCOURT	93.0	91.3	0.0	0.5	0.6	0.5	13.5	16.0	5.8	8.7	11.2	7.8	3.9	26.2	25.7	9.7	1.0	68.9	37.1	52.9	47.1
77002	HOUSTON	56.3	55.4	39.0	38.6	1.7	2.0	23.5	27.0	1.3	0.8	0.9	8.5	16.4	53.2	15.7	2.9	0.3	94.7	32.4	79.8	20.2
77003	HOUSTON	37.3	36.2	20.2	20.0	1.4	1.5	72.6	73.6	9.6	9.5	8.5	7.7	8.3	28.6	19.6	7.3	1.0	67.7	29.1	53.2	46.8
77004	HOUSTON	16.0	15.9	73.2	71.8	2.8	3.2	11.6	13.7	6.6	6.0	6.3	9.4	12.0	27.0	20.2	10.7	1.9	77.9	31.8	49.2	50.8
77005	HOUSTON	91.7	90.1	1.0	1.2	4.6	5.4	5.5	7.3	6.7	7.9	7.7	5.8	3.6	28.5	30.8	7.3	1.9	74.0	39.7	48.9	51.1
77006	HOUSTON	80.0	76.6	4.5	5.1	4.3	5.0	20.2	24.7	3.1	2.5	2.7	3.6	9.8	47.2	25.4	5.3	0.5	90.0	35.3	57.1	42.9
77007	HOUSTON	59.9	58.3	7.6	7.2	1.9	1.9	53.8	58.3	6.6	5.9	5.8	6.5	7.7	37.5	22.1	6.9	1.0	77.9	33.8	54.3	45.7
77008	HOUSTON	68.5	65.0	4.5	4.4	1.1	1.2	43.4	49.6	6.4	5.8	5.6	5.4	6.6	33.9	23.7	10.4	2.2	79.0	37.1	50.7	49.3
77009	HOUSTON	58.8	57.4	6.2	5.6	0.7	0.7	72.6	76.4	8.0	7.5	7.6	7.3	7.8	32.3	20.3	8.0	1.2	72.6	32.0	52.1	47.9
77010	HOUSTON	55.0	52.4	40.0	39.3	1.3	1.2	23.8	31.0	2.4	1.2	1.2	7.1	13.1	58.3	16.7	0.0	0.0	94.1	34.6	75.0	25.0
77011	HOUSTON	49.1	48.3	1.5	1.5	0.3	0.3	94.5	95.5	9.8	8.9	8.5	7.9	8.7	30.7	17.9	6.9	0.7	68.0	28.6	52.6	47.4
77012	HOUSTON	50.9	50.9	3.4	3.0	1.2	1.1	91.9	93.3	10.8	9.6	9.4	8.7	9.9	30.4	15.8	5.0	0.5	65.1	25.9	53.1	46.9
77013	HOUSTON	42.1	40.1	25.2	25.5	1.1	1.1	59.5	61.5	10.5	9.3	8.8	7.8	9.1	30.8	17.3	5.7	0.6	66.7	27.4	52.1	47.9
	TEXAS	71.0	69.5	11.5	11.4	2.8	3.1	32.0	34.6	7.9	7.5	7.7	7.5	8.1	29.6	21.9	8.7	1.2	72.6	32.9	49.7	50.3
	UNITED STATES	75.1	73.6	12.3	12.5	3.8	4.2	12.5	14.1	6.9	6.7	7.2	7.0	7.3	28.6	23.8	10.8	1.7	75.1	36.0	49.1	50.9

ZIP CODE #	POST OFFICE NAME	2004 Per Capita Income	2004 HH Income Base	2004 Household Income Distribution (%): Less than $25,000	$25,000 to $49,999	$50,000 to $99,999	$100,000 to $149,999	$150,000 or More	Median Household Income: 2004	2009	2004 National Centile	2004 State Centile	2004 Home Value Base	2004 Home Value Distribution (%): Less than $50,000	$50,000 to $89,999	$90,000 to $174,999	$175,000 to $399,999	$400,000 or More	2004 Median Home Value
76689	VALLEY MILLS	19314	1534	23.1	31.8	32.9	8.2	4.0	45176	51555	62	68	1242	21.3	31.2	29.2	15.6	2.7	86026
76690	WALNUT SPRINGS	14675	347	40.1	33.7	19.0	4.9	2.3	30481	34426	13	17	283	59.4	20.9	12.0	6.4	1.4	40185
76691	WEST	21067	2460	27.1	29.9	32.6	7.5	3.0	43649	51039	58	66	1918	30.5	32.2	30.3	6.9	0.2	70000
76692	WHITNEY	20056	3465	36.7	30.0	24.9	5.7	2.8	35330	40576	29	34	2769	39.1	27.2	23.5	9.6	0.7	65360
76693	WORTHAM	16700	785	36.9	30.8	27.4	3.3	1.5	36591	44040	34	41	591	46.4	28.3	22.2	2.7	0.5	54886
76701	WACO	15438	467	54.4	27.8	9.6	3.2	4.9	22557	26063	3	4	163	63.2	12.9	17.8	4.3	1.8	36750
76704	WACO	10266	3115	62.8	24.7	10.1	2.3	0.1	16870	19851	1	2	1219	77.2	18.0	4.8	0.0	0.0	31731
76705	WACO	16277	10423	36.4	33.5	23.4	4.8	1.9	34182	39812	25	30	6246	41.5	34.8	18.9	4.5	0.4	59468
76706	WACO	14215	11691	52.3	25.2	17.2	3.3	2.0	22968	26284	3	4	4912	36.9	32.4	27.4	3.1	0.2	66051
76707	WACO	12077	5598	46.3	33.7	16.4	2.5	1.1	27066	31267	7	10	2792	69.1	23.8	5.8	1.1	0.2	41027
76708	WACO	18514	7975	35.7	30.5	24.4	6.5	3.0	35094	40503	28	33	4857	38.1	28.8	23.7	8.3	1.1	62477
76710	WACO	28915	11162	29.5	31.5	25.5	7.7	5.8	40652	47093	48	57	5778	9.1	40.4	33.4	13.0	4.1	90564
76711	WACO	12338	2864	39.0	41.1	17.5	2.1	0.3	30962	35558	15	19	1762	68.9	29.3	1.3	0.3	0.1	43286
76712	WOODWAY	34229	7693	13.3	24.6	36.3	14.8	11.0	63069	74579	87	89	5306	4.4	18.7	49.9	24.6	2.5	122020
76801	BROWNWOOD	17629	9793	38.6	30.2	24.1	5.1	2.0	33035	37912	21	26	6600	45.2	29.5	19.4	5.1	0.8	55417
76802	EARLY	19817	1766	28.5	31.3	29.1	6.6	4.5	40675	46733	48	57	1420	32.9	33.6	26.3	6.5	0.7	68600
76820	ART	20000	16	31.3	43.8	18.8	6.3	0.0	30000	32320	12	15	13	23.1	23.1	15.4	23.1	15.4	112500
76821	BALLINGER	15587	2020	41.2	32.2	21.6	2.7	2.3	30920	33717	15	19	1504	48.9	26.7	19.4	4.1	1.0	50914
76823	BANGS	16767	1123	38.7	29.7	27.3	2.8	1.6	32293	37046	19	23	860	46.5	29.8	19.3	4.2	0.2	53409
76825	BRADY	15823	2785	45.7	32.3	18.1	2.2	1.8	27784	31149	8	11	1925	56.9	20.0	17.1	4.7	1.3	41551
76827	BROOKESMITH	35132	172	16.9	25.0	37.2	12.2	8.7	57431	65965	82	85	151	17.2	25.2	37.1	17.2	3.3	98846
76828	BURKETT	25001	97	38.1	33.0	18.6	9.3	1.0	33041	37351	21	26	79	31.7	21.5	27.9	16.5	2.5	83750
76831	CASTELL	38063	47	23.4	29.8	31.9	8.5	6.4	46162	56331	64	70	40	17.5	17.5	30.0	22.5	12.5	114286
76832	CHEROKEE	24406	226	35.8	27.0	25.7	4.4	7.1	36046	43015	32	38	174	27.6	28.2	24.7	12.6	6.9	78000
76834	COLEMAN	17146	2654	44.9	31.6	16.9	4.5	2.2	28016	31722	9	11	1838	59.5	23.1	11.5	4.4	1.5	42521
76836	DOOLE	12358	23	60.9	21.7	13.0	4.4	0.0	18526	23559	1	2	19	31.6	21.1	31.6	15.8	0.0	78333
76837	EDEN	17766	600	36.8	30.2	25.3	3.3	4.3	34380	40080	25	31	431	43.9	34.1	16.0	4.2	1.9	55096
76841	FORT MC KAVETT	24545	15	26.7	33.3	26.7	13.3	0.0	37333	45000	37	44	12	25.0	16.7	8.3	25.0	25.0	162500
76842	FREDONIA	17043	31	32.3	35.5	22.6	9.7	0.0	34043	36129	24	30	25	32.0	20.0	20.0	20.0	8.0	87500
76844	GOLDTHWAITE	19025	1163	39.3	28.6	24.0	5.0	3.1	32909	37844	21	25	887	35.0	27.7	24.6	11.1	1.7	70231
76845	GOULDBUSK	22174	82	35.4	30.5	20.7	9.8	3.7	35000	41149	28	33	67	41.8	22.4	19.4	9.0	7.5	66250
76848	HEXT	25219	35	20.0	37.1	28.6	11.4	2.9	41143	47398	50	58	28	28.6	17.9	14.3	17.9	21.4	100000
76849	JUNCTION	19677	1732	37.9	30.4	24.1	4.6	3.1	33054	37772	21	26	1289	37.9	23.6	15.1	15.4	8.1	68882
76852	LOHN	20429	111	48.7	25.2	18.0	4.5	3.6	26117	26910	6	8	91	38.5	18.7	24.2	14.3	4.4	73125
76853	LOMETA	18191	609	37.8	31.0	23.5	5.8	2.0	33787	37948	23	29	456	38.4	24.3	18.6	15.4	3.3	70357
76854	LONDON	22256	194	30.9	28.9	32.5	7.2	0.5	38317	43763	40	48	154	30.5	12.3	21.4	19.5	16.2	108333
76856	MASON	26094	1469	35.1	32.3	22.7	5.6	4.3	35559	41820	30	36	1159	30.9	25.1	24.6	13.9	5.5	77961
76857	MAY	19092	769	35.1	32.8	25.5	4.4	2.2	34748	40109	26	32	657	45.1	27.9	17.8	7.5	1.8	55804
76858	MELVIN	26278	130	46.2	25.4	20.0	5.4	3.1	28421	30486	9	12	105	36.2	20.0	26.7	13.3	3.8	75000
76859	MENARD	17647	935	47.1	28.8	18.0	4.3	1.9	27062	30458	7	10	701	62.2	17.8	9.6	5.4	5.0	41186
76861	MILES	19821	666	27.8	32.4	28.4	6.8	4.7	40621	47298	48	56	539	34.5	35.3	22.6	5.8	1.9	68056
76862	MILLERSVIEW	30326	72	31.9	34.7	23.6	4.2	5.6	35731	41743	30	37	58	41.4	25.9	20.7	8.6	3.5	58333
76864	MULLIN	17630	561	36.5	32.3	24.1	4.1	3.0	34073	38794	24	30	463	36.5	21.2	28.5	10.2	3.7	74167
76865	NORTON	19211	118	34.8	34.8	25.4	2.5	2.5	35323	37084	29	34	96	44.8	16.7	31.3	5.2	2.1	60000
76866	PAINT ROCK	24306	245	30.6	35.1	23.7	4.9	5.7	36056	41857	32	38	197	42.6	24.9	20.3	8.6	3.6	58529
76869	PONTOTOC	22350	55	30.9	36.4	21.8	7.3	3.6	35551	38616	30	36	45	24.4	26.7	20.0	17.8	11.1	88750
76870	PRIDDY	12896	41	41.5	34.2	19.5	4.9	0.0	31294	39067	16	20	34	41.2	23.5	20.6	14.7	0.0	66667
76871	RICHLAND SPRINGS	17957	522	35.6	33.1	24.5	6.3	0.4	35142	38370	28	33	418	36.1	18.7	29.0	12.0	4.3	78571
76872	ROCHELLE	19757	359	32.9	30.6	29.8	5.0	1.7	36483	42044	33	40	295	37.6	20.7	26.1	12.5	3.1	77292
76873	ROCKWOOD	23538	30	43.3	26.7	20.0	10.0	0.0	30000	35000	12	15	24	41.7	16.7	20.8	12.5	8.3	70000
76874	ROOSEVELT	23116	12	33.3	33.3	25.0	8.3	0.0	35000	37321	28	33	9	22.2	0.0	33.3	22.2	22.2	120833
76875	ROWENA	13392	268	47.8	25.8	25.8	0.8	0.0	26494	27543	6	8	209	29.7	36.4	22.5	8.6	2.9	72143
76877	SAN SABA	17498	1509	35.9	35.7	21.2	4.0	3.3	32754	36936	20	24	1108	44.0	31.0	14.9	7.4	2.7	58684
76878	SANTA ANNA	15161	641	46.8	29.8	18.6	3.9	0.9	27371	30700	8	10	459	60.1	20.3	12.4	5.0	2.2	42500
76880	STAR	21724	251	23.9	42.6	19.5	6.0	8.0	40138	45109	47	55	204	31.4	15.7	25.5	24.0	3.4	93750
76882	TALPA	25627	128	30.5	32.0	23.4	7.8	6.3	37054	39375	36	42	104	38.5	24.0	23.1	7.7	6.7	67143
76883	TELEGRAPH	14208	9	44.4	33.3	22.2	0.0	0.0	27247	35000	7	10	7	42.9	0.0	57.1	0.0	0.0	103125
76884	VALERA	22996	55	34.6	32.7	20.0	9.1	3.6	34291	40000	25	30	45	44.4	24.4	17.8	4.4	8.9	61667
76885	VALLEY SPRING	26958	136	19.9	34.6	31.6	7.4	6.6	44309	52353	59	67	116	26.7	12.9	36.2	16.4	7.8	106452
76887	VOCA	20772	55	25.5	32.7	40.0	1.8	0.0	42358	46550	54	63	45	24.4	17.8	35.6	20.0	2.2	104688
76888	VOSS	23657	46	34.8	30.4	19.6	10.9	4.4	35000	42343	28	33	38	44.7	21.1	21.1	5.3	7.9	60000
76890	ZEPHYR	21594	398	28.9	32.4	27.9	8.3	2.5	41204	47177	50	58	335	30.5	32.2	28.4	6.9	2.1	74355
76901	SAN ANGELO	20951	10250	29.2	35.0	28.7	4.1	3.0	39426	44842	44	52	6977	25.7	47.2	22.0	4.2	1.0	67235
76903	SAN ANGELO	14604	11616	44.8	32.7	18.2	2.8	1.6	28111	31704	9	12	6936	48.6	36.0	13.7	0.9	0.8	51011
76904	SAN ANGELO	26846	13220	27.4	27.9	30.3	8.5	5.9	44047	50672	59	66	8079	5.7	25.7	53.2	13.2	2.1	108092
76905	SAN ANGELO	17213	3737	27.0	36.5	29.2	5.4	2.0	39340	44165	44	52	2646	31.5	42.5	20.0	5.0	1.0	67871
76908	GOODFELLOW AFB	12689	99	24.2	49.5	26.3	0.0	0.0	38207	43458	40	48	6	0.0	16.7	83.3	0.0	0.0	100000
76909	SAN ANGELO	12440	2	100.0	0.0	0.0	0.0	0.0	5000	5000	0	1	0	0.0	0.0	0.0	0.0	0.0	0
76930	BARNHART	26834	67	26.9	26.9	28.4	9.0	9.0	46744	53821	66	71	53	30.2	20.8	30.2	17.0	1.9	88333
76932	BIG LAKE	15209	1099	28.4	37.8	28.6	4.5	0.8	36514	40781	34	40	856	47.9	29.4	18.0	3.5	1.2	52727
76933	BRONTE	20313	630	40.0	30.2	20.2	5.7	4.0	31944	36718	18	22	475	45.5	33.3	18.1	1.9	1.3	55658
76934	CARLSBAD	16652	538	29.4	34.6	30.5	3.7	1.9	37663	43096	38	45	455	33.9	34.1	24.2	7.0	0.9	68659
76935	CHRISTOVAL	24600	279	22.2	30.8	35.8	7.9	3.2	47036	54512	66	72	225	17.3	29.3	37.8	12.0	3.6	93571
76936	ELDORADO	19148	1121	35.7	28.8	26.8	6.5	2.2	34583	41827	26	31	840	47.3	25.8	16.0	6.0	5.0	53833
76937	EOLA	23369	170	27.7	32.9	30.0	5.3	4.1	39529	44447	44	53	135	30.4	23.7	28.9	14.1	3.0	83125
76940	MERETA	21225	67	23.9	31.3	35.8	6.0	3.0	44439	46560	60	67	54	27.8	29.6	25.9	11.1	5.6	80000
76941	MERTZON	24005	619	28.9	27.6	30.9	6.5	6.1	42558	51374	55	63	492	32.1	34.4	22.6	8.7	2.2	71702
76943	OZONA	16493	1527	38.4	28.1	27.2	4.7	1.6	32810	39092	20	25	1080	44.9	24.5	23.6	5.3	1.7	57534
76945	ROBERT LEE	20137	849	39.7	28.4	23.0	6.1	2.8	32764	38146	20	25	652	44.3	30.8	18.7	3.7	2.5	56607
76949	SILVER	20682	12	33.3	41.7	25.0	0.0	0.0	35000	37321	28	33	10	30.0	30.0	40.0	0.0	0.0	80000
76950	SONORA	19949	1487	32.6	30.5	25.4	7.6	3.9	38879	44450	42	51	1076	46.1	27.2	17.7	5.4	3.6	54158
76951	STERLING CITY	20148	498	30.9	32.5	27.1	5.6	3.8	38684	44912	42	50	392	35.7	37.8	17.6	7.4	1.5	61579
76955	VANCOURT	16566	61	24.6	31.2	34.4	6.6	3.3	44090	49312	59	66	48	8.3	20.8	47.9	22.9	0.0	112500
77002	HOUSTON	22401	2215	32.1	18.5	25.0	9.8	14.7	48989	63908	70	75	238	22.3	11.3	34.0	25.2	7.1	120833
77003	HOUSTON	10224	3054	53.0	27.6	14.6	3.5	1.2	23009	26940	3	4	943	46.3	36.3	17.1	0.3	0.0	52500
77004	HOUSTON	18177	12138	50.7	22.8	16.4	6.4	3.6	24397	30214	4	5	3749	16.4	23.0	35.6	19.5	5.5	107297
77005	HOUSTON	82163	9729	9.7	13.1	19.1	17.7	40.4	122391	154892	99	100	6892	1.3	1.8	9.6	34.1	53.2	422256
77006	HOUSTON	51393	11822	21.1	26.0	28.2	11.7	13.1	53143	70205	77	81	3356	3.4	7.4	22.6	47.5	19.2	229303
77007	HOUSTON	32645	10181	29.3	23.0	25.9	12.0	9.8	46769	60214	66	71	4330	14.0	19.3	25.7	31.3	9.8	138390
77008	HOUSTON	28002	13121	23.9	29.1	30.3	10.7	6.0	46558	57507	65	71	6779	6.3	16.9	45.5	28.4	2.9	136322
77009	HOUSTON	17688	14380	32.9	29.5	26.0	8.4	3.2	37847	45098	39	46	7684	23.5	33.4	27.9	13.5	1.7	79441
77010	HOUSTON	44111	63	87.3	3.2	0.0	0.0	9.5	10153	12463	0	1	3	0.0	0.0	0.0	33.3	66.7	425000
77011	HOUSTON	9599	6393	46.6	34.5	15.5	2.6	0.9	26901	31353	7	9	2783	56.6	37.9	4.5	1.0	0.0	47680
77012	HOUSTON	10771	7024	45.8	34.3	15.6	2.2	2.0	27071	31538	7	10	2798	44.3	49.9	5.6	0.2	0.0	52809
77013	HOUSTON	13087	6037	33.2	33.8	26.4	5.2	1.4	35482	40951	29	35	2777	22.6	58.3	17.9	1.3	0.0	68793
	TEXAS	23284		26.2	27.7	29.5	10.3	6.3	45778	54246				21.6	26.1	33.4	15.6	3.4	93683
	UNITED STATES	25866		24.7	27.1	30.8	10.9	6.5	48124	56710				10.9	15.0	33.7	30.1	10.4	145905

Copyright © 2004 ESRI BIS. All rights reserved. Reproduction by any method is prohibited.

#	POST OFFICE NAME	FINANCIAL SERVICES: Auto Loan	Home Loan	Investments	Retirement Plans	THE HOME: Home Improvements: Home Repair	Lawn & Garden	Furnishings: Computers & Hardware	Major Appliances	TV, Radio, Sound Equipment	Furniture	ENTERTAINMENT: Dine out/ Carry out	Sports Equipment	Fees & Tickets	Toys & Games	Travel	Cable TV	PERSONAL: Apparel & Services	Auto Repairs	Health Insurance	Pets & Supplies
76689	VALLEY MILLS	91	79	64	78	83	90	79	85	83	78	100	100	75	100	79	83	95	84	90	104
76690	WALNUT SPRINGS	78	52	25	46	60	68	51	64	61	52	71	76	43	68	52	65	65	63	78	90
76691	WEST	86	76	61	73	80	89	75	81	80	73	97	93	73	98	76	83	92	79	89	98
76692	WHITNEY	84	64	42	59	72	82	63	74	71	63	84	85	56	79	65	75	77	73	89	98
76693	WORTHAM	75	53	30	49	59	70	55	64	64	54	75	75	48	71	55	68	68	64	78	84
76701	WACO	34	26	34	29	26	29	38	32	37	35	46	42	34	43	33	34	45	37	30	36
76704	WACO	36	30	35	27	29	35	34	34	39	35	47	38	33	44	33	41	45	36	38	39
76705	WACO	64	58	58	58	58	63	63	62	63	62	79	73	60	76	61	62	76	64	61	71
76706	WACO	52	43	47	43	42	47	55	49	56	52	69	61	51	66	50	53	66	53	48	55
76707	WACO	52	46	50	45	45	51	52	51	55	52	68	58	50	65	50	55	66	53	52	56
76708	WACO	67	63	67	62	64	70	67	67	70	66	86	78	66	85	67	70	83	69	70	76
76710	WACO	82	81	93	82	81	89	87	85	87	85	109	99	86	107	86	86	106	88	85	94
76711	WACO	51	47	46	45	47	51	50	50	52	51	65	56	49	63	49	51	63	51	50	54
76712	WOODWAY	121	131	143	136	128	131	128	125	121	129	153	147	130	153	126	116	151	125	114	138
76801	BROWNWOOD	66	58	54	57	60	66	61	63	64	60	79	74	59	78	61	65	75	64	67	75
76802	EARLY	87	71	53	70	76	86	73	80	78	72	94	92	68	93	73	80	88	78	88	97
76820	ART	68	53	36	48	60	67	50	60	57	50	67	71	45	66	54	61	63	60	71	83
76821	BALLINGER	65	50	33	47	54	62	53	59	59	52	70	67	47	65	52	61	65	59	68	72
76823	BANGS	71	55	36	51	60	68	55	62	61	54	73	73	50	71	55	64	67	62	72	81
76825	BRADY	61	50	42	49	53	60	54	57	58	53	70	66	50	67	53	59	66	58	63	68
76827	BROOKESMITH	127	113	86	107	120	128	105	116	111	105	135	138	102	138	108	114	128	113	125	150
76828	BURKETT	88	61	32	58	71	80	60	75	70	60	82	90	52	80	63	73	74	74	89	104
76831	CASTELL	133	122	114	115	130	152	113	129	120	120	149	129	114	126	123	129	139	126	152	150
76832	CHEROKEE	96	72	48	69	79	95	80	88	89	76	105	98	71	99	79	95	96	88	105	106
76834	COLEMAN	66	50	33	48	55	65	54	60	61	52	71	68	48	68	54	64	65	60	72	75
76836	DOOLE	52	36	19	34	42	47	36	44	41	35	48	53	30	47	37	43	44	43	52	61
76837	EDEN	73	55	36	53	60	72	61	67	68	58	80	75	54	76	60	72	73	67	80	81
76841	FORT MC KAVETT	92	72	49	65	81	91	68	82	77	67	91	96	61	90	72	82	84	80	96	112
76842	FREDONIA	76	60	41	54	68	76	57	68	64	56	76	80	51	75	60	68	70	67	81	93
76844	GOLDTHWAITE	75	55	33	53	62	72	58	67	66	56	78	77	51	74	59	70	71	67	80	86
76845	GOULDBUSK	86	71	53	65	78	89	66	79	74	67	88	88	61	84	71	79	82	77	93	103
76848	HEXT	98	77	52	69	86	97	72	87	82	72	97	102	65	96	77	87	90	86	103	119
76849	JUNCTION	76	61	46	58	67	78	62	70	69	62	82	77	58	76	64	73	76	70	83	86
76852	LOHN	96	67	35	63	78	87	66	82	76	65	89	99	56	88	69	80	81	81	97	114
76853	LOMETA	70	58	47	56	63	75	60	66	65	60	78	70	56	70	61	69	72	66	79	78
76854	LONDON	83	65	44	59	73	82	61	74	69	61	82	86	55	81	65	74	76	73	87	101
76856	MASON	95	78	62	75	83	94	82	89	88	81	106	101	75	100	81	90	99	89	99	106
76857	MAY	78	59	37	54	67	75	56	68	64	56	76	81	50	75	59	68	70	67	81	94
76858	MELVIN	90	63	33	59	73	82	62	77	71	61	84	92	53	82	64	75	76	76	91	107
76859	MENARD	67	54	38	50	57	65	56	62	61	56	73	69	50	69	55	63	69	62	70	75
76861	MILES	98	74	45	70	83	92	71	85	80	71	95	102	64	94	74	83	88	84	98	116
76862	MILLERSVIEW	104	81	55	73	92	103	77	92	87	76	103	108	69	102	82	93	96	91	109	126
76864	MULLIN	87	61	32	57	71	79	60	74	69	59	81	89	51	79	62	73	74	73	88	103
76865	NORTON	80	56	29	53	65	73	55	68	63	54	74	82	47	73	57	67	68	67	81	95
76866	PAINT ROCK	106	83	57	75	94	105	78	94	89	78	105	111	70	104	84	95	98	93	112	129
76869	PONTOTOC	99	78	53	70	88	98	73	88	83	73	98	104	66	97	78	89	91	87	105	121
76870	PRIDDY	74	52	27	49	60	67	51	63	59	50	69	76	43	67	53	62	63	62	75	88
76871	RICHLAND SPRINGS	77	54	28	51	63	70	53	66	61	53	72	79	45	70	55	64	66	65	78	91
76872	ROCHELLE	77	57	35	54	63	74	61	69	69	58	81	79	53	77	61	72	74	69	83	87
76873	ROCKWOOD	63	59	56	56	62	73	54	62	58	58	72	61	55	60	59	62	67	60	73	71
76874	ROOSEVELT	72	59	45	54	65	72	56	66	62	56	74	77	51	73	59	65	69	65	75	87
76875	ROWENA	52	39	26	37	43	51	43	48	48	41	57	53	38	54	43	51	52	47	57	57
76877	SAN SABA	75	56	37	54	62	74	62	68	69	59	82	77	55	77	61	73	75	68	82	83
76878	SANTA ANNA	57	46	34	44	50	59	48	53	53	47	63	58	44	58	49	56	58	53	63	64
76880	STAR	101	71	37	67	83	92	70	87	81	69	95	104	60	93	73	85	86	85	103	120
76882	TALPA	95	72	45	66	82	92	69	83	78	68	92	99	60	91	72	83	85	82	99	115
76883	TELEGRAPH	52	41	30	38	46	52	39	47	44	39	52	53	35	50	42	47	48	46	55	62
76884	VALERA	93	73	50	66	82	92	69	83	78	68	92	97	61	91	73	83	86	82	98	113
76885	VALLEY SPRING	94	88	84	83	93	109	81	92	86	87	107	90	82	89	88	92	100	90	108	105
76887	VOCA	85	59	31	56	69	77	58	72	67	58	79	87	50	77	61	71	72	71	86	101
76888	VOSS	92	72	49	65	81	91	68	82	77	67	91	96	61	90	72	82	84	80	96	112
76890	ZEPHYR	102	71	37	67	83	92	70	87	81	69	95	104	60	93	73	85	86	85	103	121
76901	SAN ANGELO	75	74	73	73	74	79	75	76	76	74	94	88	74	93	75	74	91	77	75	85
76903	SAN ANGELO	53	49	50	47	48	52	52	53	53	53	67	59	50	63	50	53	65	54	52	57
76904	SAN ANGELO	88	84	92	86	85	92	90	88	90	88	112	104	88	108	88	87	108	91	87	99
76905	SAN ANGELO	75	71	61	69	71	74	69	73	69	70	86	84	66	83	68	68	83	72	71	84
76908	GOODFELLOW AFB	63	40	39	46	37	44	60	52	61	56	76	69	51	68	49	55	73	61	48	59
76909	SAN ANGELO	8	5	6	5	5	6	9	7	9	8	11	10	8	10	8	8	11	8	6	8
76930	BARNHART	123	85	45	81	100	112	84	104	97	83	114	126	72	112	88	102	104	103	124	145
76932	BIG LAKE	74	58	41	55	61	67	59	67	64	61	78	76	52	72	58	64	74	68	71	81
76933	BRONTE	86	66	43	62	72	85	69	78	78	66	92	89	62	88	70	82	84	78	93	98
76934	CARLSBAD	76	69	54	66	69	73	66	70	66	68	82	81	62	77	65	66	79	70	70	84
76935	CHRISTOVAL	84	87	101	91	88	92	89	88	86	89	108	104	89	105	89	83	105	89	85	97
76936	ELDORADO	84	64	42	60	69	76	64	75	71	66	86	86	57	80	64	72	81	75	82	94
76937	EOLA	108	81	51	75	93	104	78	95	89	77	105	113	69	103	82	94	97	94	113	131
76940	MERETA	92	80	59	75	85	92	74	84	80	74	96	99	71	98	77	82	91	81	92	109
76941	MERTZON	111	77	41	73	90	101	77	95	88	76	103	114	65	101	79	93	94	93	113	132
76943	OZONA	72	58	42	54	60	64	58	66	63	62	77	74	52	71	57	62	74	67	68	77
76945	ROBERT LEE	77	59	39	55	65	76	61	69	68	59	81	79	54	78	62	73	74	69	83	88
76949	SILVER	64	50	34	46	57	64	48	57	54	47	64	67	43	63	51	58	59	56	68	78
76950	SONORA	84	72	58	68	72	77	72	80	76	77	94	88	66	86	71	75	92	80	79	89
76951	STERLING CITY	97	68	36	64	79	89	67	83	77	66	91	100	57	89	70	81	83	82	99	116
76955	VANCOURT	101	71	37	67	82	92	70	86	80	69	94	104	60	92	72	84	86	85	103	120
77002	HOUSTON	85	77	129	87	74	82	95	84	96	94	122	105	95	123	91	93	120	92	79	94
77003	HOUSTON	51	43	43	40	42	46	47	48	51	50	63	53	45	59	45	50	63	51	48	52
77004	HOUSTON	61	51	61	49	50	59	59	58	65	60	80	66	58	74	57	66	77	61	63	66
77005	HOUSTON	243	298	418	302	291	314	279	271	266	284	336	312	306	349	290	266	338	268	253	297
77006	HOUSTON	111	105	191	120	100	112	126	111	128	127	163	137	129	169	122	126	161	120	104	124
77007	HOUSTON	105	102	138	107	99	105	111	106	113	114	142	125	112	143	109	109	141	111	99	116
77008	HOUSTON	85	89	103	88	87	93	91	89	91	92	114	102	91	113	90	89	112	91	86	97
77009	HOUSTON	76	71	73	69	69	72	74	75	75	78	94	84	71	89	71	72	94	77	70	80
77010	HOUSTON	0	0	0	0	0	0	0	0	0	0	0	0	0	0	0	0	0	0	0	0
77011	HOUSTON	51	43	40	42	42	44	47	49	49	51	62	54	44	59	44	46	62	51	45	51
77012	HOUSTON	60	52	48	50	51	52	57	58	59	61	74	65	53	71	53	56	75	61	53	61
77013	HOUSTON	64	57	55	55	56	59	61	62	64	64	80	70	58	76	58	61	80	65	59	66
	TEXAS	94	90	91	90	89	95	92	93	92	93	115	107	90	112	90	90	112	94	89	104
	UNITED STATES	100	100	100	100	100	100	100	100	100	100	100	100	100	100	100	100	100	100	100	100

POPULATION CHANGE

#	POST OFFICE NAME	COUNTY FIPS CODE	POPULATION			2000-2004 ANNUAL RATE		HOUSEHOLDS					FAMILIES		
			2000	2004	2009	% Rate	State Centile	2000	2004	2009	% Annual Rate 2000-2004	2004 Average HH Size	2000	2004	% Annual Rate 2000-2004
77014	HOUSTON	201	20375	23499	26804	3.4	86	7716	8610	9602	2.6	2.73	4891	5470	2.7
77015	HOUSTON	201	50647	55075	61180	2.0	67	16418	17573	19251	1.6	3.13	12454	13367	1.7
77016	HOUSTON	201	29749	30460	33003	0.6	27	9688	9849	10590	0.4	3.07	7353	7505	0.5
77017	HOUSTON	201	32843	34693	37961	1.3	51	9661	10036	10829	0.9	3.44	7446	7744	0.9
77018	HOUSTON	201	26542	27706	30365	1.0	43	10590	10938	11873	0.8	2.51	6742	6989	0.9
77019	HOUSTON	201	16117	17453	19416	1.9	65	8112	8687	9553	1.6	1.95	3249	3482	1.6
77020	HOUSTON	201	28682	29517	31938	0.7	32	8270	8443	9073	0.5	3.39	6177	6327	0.6
77021	HOUSTON	201	24335	25718	28099	1.3	51	8699	9175	9981	1.3	2.70	5795	6126	1.3
77022	HOUSTON	201	31113	32623	35521	1.1	45	9773	10143	10939	0.9	3.19	6856	7130	0.9
77023	HOUSTON	201	32970	34008	36876	0.7	34	9634	9858	10597	0.5	3.41	7183	7367	0.6
77024	HOUSTON	201	32530	35689	39972	2.2	71	13944	15223	16927	2.1	2.33	8987	9674	1.8
77025	HOUSTON	201	24417	27274	30990	2.6	78	11645	12889	14489	2.4	2.10	6006	6714	2.7
77026	HOUSTON	201	27496	28051	30306	0.5	24	9508	9642	10330	0.3	2.90	6425	6532	0.4
77027	HOUSTON	201	13751	14695	16297	1.6	58	8222	8665	9463	1.2	1.69	2864	3025	1.3
77028	HOUSTON	201	16477	16576	17801	0.1	16	5506	5505	5867	0.0	2.99	4013	4027	0.1
77029	HOUSTON	201	18234	19001	20631	1.0	41	5733	5975	6459	1.0	3.16	4354	4528	0.9
77030	HOUSTON	201	11133	12032	13312	1.8	65	5054	5493	6104	2.0	1.92	2375	2564	1.8
77031	HOUSTON	201	16929	17157	18552	0.3	21	6100	6066	6461	-0.1	2.83	4152	4136	-0.1
77032	HOUSTON	201	10835	12126	13747	2.7	78	3434	3794	4259	2.4	3.09	2604	2870	2.3
77033	HOUSTON	201	27678	28513	30902	0.7	32	8877	9093	9780	0.6	3.12	6759	6932	0.6
77034	HOUSTON	201	26990	29115	32190	1.8	64	9613	10272	11242	1.6	2.83	6642	7122	1.7
77035	HOUSTON	201	37417	39440	43308	1.3	50	13637	14135	15325	0.9	2.78	9135	9499	0.9
77036	HOUSTON	201	75961	83374	92641	2.2	72	28243	30159	32879	1.6	2.74	17961	19251	1.7
77037	HOUSTON	201	17456	18578	20393	1.5	57	5025	5248	5679	1.0	3.52	4121	4308	1.1
77038	HOUSTON	201	21710	23861	26608	2.3	72	6406	6887	7562	1.7	3.45	5117	5512	1.8
77039	HOUSTON	201	27785	30162	33522	2.0	67	7695	8263	9080	1.7	3.64	6340	6814	1.7
77040	HOUSTON	201	38327	41195	45388	1.7	62	14033	15071	16516	1.7	2.72	9949	10650	1.6
77041	HOUSTON	201	25238	29817	34409	4.0	90	7656	8959	10233	3.8	3.32	6305	7399	3.8
77042	HOUSTON	201	35630	38089	42242	1.6	59	17708	18552	20277	1.1	2.05	8373	8848	1.3
77043	HOUSTON	201	24104	25905	28742	1.7	62	8049	8579	9435	1.5	2.99	5969	6389	1.6
77044	HOUSTON	201	13342	15712	18307	3.9	90	4178	4879	5636	3.7	3.22	3397	3979	3.8
77045	HOUSTON	201	24721	26229	28779	1.4	55	7246	7663	8352	1.3	3.41	5940	6295	1.4
77046	HOUSTON	201	471	528	591	2.7	79	307	342	381	2.6	1.54	122	136	2.6
77047	HOUSTON	201	11105	12095	13435	2.0	68	3675	3955	4346	1.7	3.05	2857	3085	1.8
77048	HOUSTON	201	14274	16388	18766	3.3	84	4729	5402	6138	3.2	3.03	3633	4154	3.2
77049	HOUSTON	201	16595	18234	20529	2.2	72	5119	5557	6183	2.0	3.28	4111	4470	2.0
77050	HOUSTON	201	4355	4540	4958	1.0	41	1285	1325	1433	0.7	3.43	1046	1080	0.8
77051	HOUSTON	201	13233	14005	15413	1.3	52	4876	5126	5593	1.2	2.72	3226	3404	1.3
77053	HOUSTON	157	26112	28549	33120	2.1	70	7302	7881	9036	1.8	3.59	6199	6693	1.8
77054	HOUSTON	201	16347	18130	20265	2.5	76	9277	10245	11377	2.4	1.74	3478	3880	2.6
77055	HOUSTON	201	41608	44500	49170	1.6	59	13560	14322	15658	1.3	3.07	9632	10190	1.3
77056	HOUSTON	201	14017	15849	18176	2.9	81	7423	8274	9361	2.6	1.86	3248	3690	3.1
77057	HOUSTON	201	33979	35786	39015	1.2	49	19178	20116	21750	1.1	1.77	6910	7182	0.9
77058	HOUSTON	201	14203	15847	17901	2.6	77	7451	8220	9183	2.3	1.92	3428	3768	2.3
77059	HOUSTON	201	15774	19079	22282	4.6	93	5148	6179	7139	4.4	3.09	4536	5433	4.3
77060	HOUSTON	201	37171	41511	46825	2.6	77	11988	13054	14447	2.0	3.17	8516	9308	2.1
77061	HOUSTON	201	25391	27076	29840	1.5	58	8880	9211	9958	0.9	2.92	6260	6500	0.9
77062	HOUSTON	201	28360	30368	33390	1.6	60	10284	10883	11835	1.3	2.78	7986	8490	1.5
77063	HOUSTON	201	28740	31764	36114	2.4	74	15447	16710	18707	1.9	1.89	6198	6843	2.4
77064	HOUSTON	201	35833	40027	45188	2.6	78	11676	12931	14455	2.4	3.08	9197	10196	2.5
77065	HOUSTON	201	27155	31114	35541	3.3	83	10368	11872	13483	3.2	2.60	7159	8086	2.9
77066	HOUSTON	201	27991	29895	32765	1.6	58	8945	9462	10263	1.3	3.16	7210	7633	1.4
77067	HOUSTON	201	23489	25601	28375	2.1	68	7472	8000	8740	1.6	3.18	5552	5940	1.6
77068	HOUSTON	201	9140	9619	10444	1.2	48	3266	3412	3671	1.0	2.82	2629	2750	1.1
77069	HOUSTON	201	14734	15970	17664	1.9	66	6799	7290	7980	1.7	2.19	4211	4549	1.8
77070	HOUSTON	201	33155	38299	44051	3.5	86	12253	14161	16201	3.5	2.69	9060	10304	3.1
77071	HOUSTON	201	24924	27012	29943	1.9	66	9178	9911	10906	1.8	2.72	6433	6948	1.8
77072	HOUSTON	201	51318	55150	60729	1.7	62	15761	16698	18156	1.4	3.29	12169	12891	1.4
77073	HOUSTON	201	12822	14868	17188	3.5	87	5287	5962	6751	2.9	2.49	3264	3737	3.2
77074	HOUSTON	201	41244	45460	50803	2.3	73	14806	16033	17681	1.9	2.78	9543	10356	1.9
77075	HOUSTON	201	22675	26014	29587	3.3	84	7609	8650	9740	3.1	3.01	5496	6243	3.0
77076	HOUSTON	201	29342	32304	36191	2.3	73	8304	9076	10098	2.1	3.55	6610	7225	2.1
77077	HOUSTON	201	43015	46726	51851	2.0	67	20490	22034	24193	1.7	2.11	11055	11955	1.9
77078	HOUSTON	201	14496	15105	16388	1.0	41	4145	4304	4637	0.9	3.48	3452	3588	0.9
77079	HOUSTON	201	32112	34357	37992	1.6	59	12646	13528	14876	1.6	2.54	9249	9824	1.4
77080	HOUSTON	201	47869	52097	58003	2.0	68	15501	16820	18651	1.9	3.07	11086	11975	1.8
77081	HOUSTON	201	48932	56574	65097	3.5	86	17102	19457	22132	3.1	2.90	10466	11787	2.8
77082	HOUSTON	201	35870	41203	47013	3.3	85	15382	17508	19783	3.1	2.34	8646	9817	3.0
77083	HOUSTON	201	52311	59653	69563	3.1	82	15698	17614	20230	2.8	3.38	13050	14652	2.8
77084	HOUSTON	201	63141	70228	79058	2.5	76	21680	23839	26550	2.3	2.94	16429	18153	2.4
77085	HOUSTON	201	7786	9564	11291	5.0	94	2296	2812	3298	4.9	3.40	1869	2293	4.9
77086	HOUSTON	201	19863	22832	26003	3.3	85	5866	6725	7611	3.3	3.39	4809	5519	3.3
77087	HOUSTON	201	36339	38621	42329	1.4	56	10401	10898	11797	1.1	3.51	8057	8455	1.1
77088	HOUSTON	201	50273	52877	58073	1.2	48	16471	17152	18660	1.0	3.08	12768	13320	1.0
77089	HOUSTON	201	36688	39624	44154	1.8	64	12224	13207	14641	1.8	3.00	9635	10402	1.8
77090	HOUSTON	201	26115	28320	31440	1.9	66	11636	12553	13833	1.8	2.22	6237	6735	1.8
77091	HOUSTON	201	23147	24732	27157	1.6	58	8299	8706	9424	1.1	2.82	5620	5931	1.3
77092	HOUSTON	201	38706	41551	46141	1.7	61	14569	15363	16815	1.3	2.70	9439	9989	1.3
77093	HOUSTON	201	45893	47248	50951	0.7	32	12366	12600	13449	0.4	3.72	9893	10097	0.5
77094	HOUSTON	201	7830	9644	11404	5.0	95	2346	2893	3412	5.1	3.33	2185	2680	4.9
77095	HOUSTON	201	39275	43552	48808	2.5	75	13302	14645	16267	2.3	2.97	10745	11822	2.3
77096	HOUSTON	201	35385	37520	41288	1.4	54	14570	15279	16642	1.1	2.45	9677	10175	1.2
77098	HOUSTON	201	12325	12671	13822	0.7	30	7309	7500	8126	0.6	1.68	2235	2308	0.8
77099	HOUSTON	201	43723	48638	54866	2.5	76	14337	15528	17182	1.9	3.11	10606	11544	2.0
77301	CONROE	339	25012	27794	33361	2.5	76	8115	8936	10653	2.3	3.03	5723	6263	2.1
77302	CONROE	339	12055	14637	18436	4.7	93	4183	5015	6248	4.4	2.91	3403	4068	4.3
77303	CONROE	339	11342	13010	15920	3.3	84	3995	4532	5489	3.0	2.86	3101	3520	3.0
77304	CONROE	339	15288	17735	21855	3.6	87	6383	7307	8917	3.2	2.41	4139	4750	3.3
77306	CONROE	339	8529	9815	12011	3.4	85	2795	3178	3849	3.1	3.08	2165	2457	3.0
77316	MONTGOMERY	339	9812	11516	14224	3.8	89	3551	4114	5027	3.5	2.79	2705	3128	3.5
77318	WILLIS	339	9900	12545	16077	5.7	96	3796	4756	6034	5.5	2.63	3007	3757	5.4
77320	HUNTSVILLE	471	32859	35536	39587	1.9	65	8333	9365	10922	2.8	2.56	5658	6356	2.8
77327	CLEVELAND	291	20977	23060	25931	2.3	72	7342	8005	8949	2.1	2.80	5456	5957	2.1
77328	CLEVELAND	407	11338	12831	15114	3.0	81	3939	4417	5154	2.7	2.90	3130	3516	2.8
77331	COLDSPRING	407	6235	6681	7450	1.6	60	2584	2766	3082	1.6	2.40	1846	1982	1.7
	TEXAS					2.2					2.0	2.77			2.1
	UNITED STATES					1.2					1.3	2.58			1.1

POPULATION COMPOSITION TEXAS
77014-77331 B

ZIP CODE #	POST OFFICE NAME	RACE (%) White 2000	White 2004	Black 2000	Black 2004	Asian/Pacific 2000	Asian/Pacific 2004	% Hispanic Origin 2000	% Hispanic Origin 2004	2004 AGE DISTRIBUTION (%) 0-4	5-9	10-14	15-19	20-24	25-44	45-64	65-84	85+	18+	MEDIAN AGE 2004	% 2004 Males	% 2004 Females
77014	HOUSTON	38.8	35.3	36.2	37.9	10.5	10.9	26.0	28.7	9.7	8.2	7.6	7.2	10.4	38.1	16.4	2.4	0.2	70.7	28.5	49.7	50.3
77015	HOUSTON	56.4	53.6	18.5	18.2	2.2	2.3	43.9	49.4	9.7	8.7	8.5	7.8	8.7	30.4	19.9	5.8	0.4	68.4	28.9	50.0	50.0
77016	HOUSTON	10.3	10.6	79.0	77.7	0.3	0.3	17.4	19.3	7.2	7.8	8.4	7.8	7.2	24.4	25.1	11.3	0.9	71.9	34.8	47.2	52.8
77017	HOUSTON	48.4	46.1	3.0	2.8	4.1	3.9	74.3	78.4	10.1	9.0	9.0	8.5	9.1	30.1	16.4	6.7	1.0	66.8	27.6	51.1	49.0
77018	HOUSTON	70.1	67.0	11.4	11.2	0.9	1.0	31.5	37.7	6.8	6.6	6.4	5.7	5.8	29.4	25.0	12.3	2.1	76.8	38.6	49.5	50.5
77019	HOUSTON	81.6	78.4	6.0	6.8	3.3	3.7	18.9	23.7	4.4	4.4	4.5	5.1	7.0	37.4	27.5	8.5	1.2	83.4	37.2	52.1	47.9
77020	HOUSTON	42.0	42.1	30.7	29.3	0.3	0.2	65.2	67.6	9.2	9.1	9.0	8.3	8.2	28.1	18.9	8.2	1.1	67.7	29.1	51.0	49.0
77021	HOUSTON	9.0	9.1	82.3	81.4	1.2	1.2	12.2	13.7	7.8	7.6	7.8	6.8	6.8	25.5	22.5	13.7	1.5	72.8	35.5	46.4	53.6
77022	HOUSTON	43.2	42.5	24.4	23.0	0.5	0.5	64.1	67.8	9.1	8.5	8.5	7.8	8.0	29.2	18.9	8.8	1.1	69.3	30.3	50.8	49.2
77023	HOUSTON	53.8	52.3	1.9	1.8	1.5	1.4	86.0	88.6	9.9	8.8	8.3	8.0	9.7	31.8	17.3	5.4	0.8	68.5	27.8	52.2	47.8
77024	HOUSTON	88.3	86.3	0.8	0.9	8.1	9.4	5.4	6.9	4.3	5.6	7.3	6.8	4.5	19.9	32.1	16.6	2.9	78.5	45.9	47.1	53.0
77025	HOUSTON	68.2	66.0	12.0	11.8	10.8	12.0	18.0	21.2	6.6	6.1	5.9	5.3	6.5	33.6	23.5	10.0	2.5	78.2	36.3	48.8	51.2
77026	HOUSTON	16.5	17.3	67.5	65.7	0.4	0.3	31.1	33.2	8.3	8.3	8.7	7.5	6.9	25.9	21.0	11.8	1.6	70.2	33.2	48.7	51.3
77027	HOUSTON	89.3	87.7	2.7	3.0	3.7	4.2	9.0	11.3	3.5	3.1	2.6	3.1	8.4	43.1	24.3	9.9	2.0	89.1	36.0	48.7	51.3
77028	HOUSTON	7.1	7.0	84.8	83.9	0.2	0.2	11.7	13.2	7.1	7.3	8.5	7.7	7.1	24.5	24.1	12.5	1.1	72.5	35.5	47.4	52.6
77029	HOUSTON	44.3	41.7	30.2	32.0	0.2	0.2	55.6	57.1	8.5	7.9	8.1	7.9	7.6	26.3	19.7	12.4	1.7	70.7	32.2	48.6	51.4
77030	HOUSTON	72.2	69.3	5.4	5.9	17.0	18.7	8.7	10.6	5.3	4.6	4.1	7.4	11.8	37.7	20.1	7.4	1.7	83.7	33.0	48.4	51.6
77031	HOUSTON	38.1	36.1	37.0	36.5	6.4	6.8	32.2	36.0	9.8	8.3	7.2	6.1	9.1	33.0	20.4	5.4	0.7	71.1	29.9	49.9	50.1
77032	HOUSTON	46.4	43.7	34.1	33.8	1.3	1.5	34.0	39.1	11.1	9.9	8.9	8.0	8.4	31.1	17.1	5.2	0.3	65.2	27.2	48.7	51.3
77033	HOUSTON	6.1	6.4	84.3	83.1	0.8	0.8	13.7	15.3	7.4	7.6	9.2	7.9	6.7	24.6	23.2	12.5	1.0	71.0	34.5	46.1	53.9
77034	HOUSTON	60.8	58.2	9.8	9.6	4.7	5.1	47.0	51.6	9.3	8.3	8.1	7.2	8.8	32.7	18.2	6.9	0.5	70.0	29.6	49.9	50.1
77035	HOUSTON	39.7	38.5	39.7	39.1	5.1	5.3	28.2	31.8	9.4	8.7	8.0	6.8	7.8	31.4	19.6	7.4	0.9	69.8	30.8	47.6	52.5
77036	HOUSTON	37.1	36.2	25.0	23.9	15.0	15.1	44.7	48.7	10.5	8.7	7.4	6.4	9.0	36.9	15.0	5.2	0.8	69.8	28.8	50.7	49.3
77037	HOUSTON	66.3	63.5	3.6	3.5	2.8	2.9	62.4	68.6	9.8	9.2	9.1	7.5	8.3	30.3	18.2	7.2	0.6	67.4	28.8	51.4	48.6
77038	HOUSTON	38.4	37.6	24.7	23.1	6.9	7.1	52.3	56.5	10.8	9.5	9.3	8.7	9.4	31.6	16.6	3.9	0.3	65.3	26.4	50.0	50.0
77039	HOUSTON	48.8	48.0	16.9	15.7	1.8	1.8	60.7	65.8	9.7	8.9	9.6	8.7	9.6	30.0	17.7	5.5	0.4	66.7	27.0	50.6	49.5
77040	HOUSTON	68.7	66.3	10.5	10.7	6.9	7.4	28.8	32.7	7.5	7.4	7.6	7.1	7.5	32.0	24.8	5.6	0.5	73.1	33.5	50.1	49.9
77041	HOUSTON	56.4	53.6	9.8	9.7	13.5	14.0	36.2	41.0	9.2	8.9	8.3	7.1	6.6	32.5	22.4	4.7	0.4	69.1	31.9	50.1	49.9
77042	HOUSTON	62.0	59.4	16.5	16.9	9.7	10.3	21.4	25.5	7.3	5.9	5.0	4.3	9.3	42.3	18.9	6.4	0.6	79.6	31.9	49.3	50.7
77043	HOUSTON	63.1	59.7	6.0	6.1	7.8	8.4	39.6	44.5	8.0	7.6	7.5	7.2	7.9	29.3	21.8	9.9	0.9	72.6	33.2	50.3	49.7
77044	HOUSTON	53.4	51.3	28.1	28.3	0.9	1.2	26.9	29.8	8.9	8.7	9.2	8.0	7.9	30.2	22.0	4.8	0.3	68.1	29.7	49.0	51.0
77045	HOUSTON	17.8	17.8	61.0	59.3	0.8	0.9	33.3	35.9	8.0	8.1	9.2	8.6	8.1	27.2	23.1	7.1	0.5	69.3	30.4	47.1	52.9
77046	HOUSTON	93.2	91.9	1.7	2.1	2.3	2.8	9.3	11.9	2.3	2.3	2.1	1.1	1.0	27.8	34.9	25.8	2.8	93.4	53.3	45.5	54.6
77047	HOUSTON	17.4	17.5	71.5	69.5	0.7	0.7	17.5	20.8	7.7	7.8	8.4	7.1	6.2	26.9	22.1	12.8	1.0	71.8	35.0	47.2	52.8
77048	HOUSTON	5.8	5.6	88.2	87.8	0.4	0.5	7.7	8.8	8.5	9.3	10.5	8.5	7.0	25.2	22.4	8.3	0.5	66.5	30.2	44.3	55.7
77049	HOUSTON	46.8	45.0	27.7	26.5	3.4	3.3	38.1	43.4	8.8	8.5	9.1	9.0	9.1	29.5	21.3	4.5	0.3	68.2	28.4	49.0	51.0
77050	HOUSTON	23.4	23.2	52.5	49.7	0.3	0.3	35.8	40.4	9.9	9.0	8.3	8.2	7.0	26.3	23.9	6.9	0.5	67.9	30.6	49.5	50.6
77051	HOUSTON	2.1	2.3	93.8	93.4	1.1	1.1	3.9	4.6	7.3	7.4	9.1	7.9	6.6	22.4	21.7	15.7	2.1	71.5	36.0	45.7	54.3
77053	HOUSTON	22.0	21.8	53.1	51.7	1.3	1.3	40.2	42.9	8.6	9.0	10.1	9.7	9.0	28.5	20.9	4.0	0.2	66.3	27.5	48.3	51.8
77054	HOUSTON	35.6	32.7	37.1	37.2	19.4	21.3	9.5	11.2	6.4	3.5	2.5	2.9	16.2	51.0	13.8	2.9	1.0	86.4	29.3	47.3	52.8
77055	HOUSTON	68.6	66.3	4.0	3.8	3.6	3.6	55.0	60.1	9.6	8.5	7.8	6.8	8.4	31.3	19.2	7.4	1.0	70.2	30.5	52.0	48.0
77056	HOUSTON	88.3	85.6	2.1	2.4	3.8	4.5	11.2	15.6	4.1	3.9	3.8	4.0	5.4	32.7	28.1	14.0	4.0	85.9	42.3	48.9	51.1
77057	HOUSTON	75.4	73.3	4.6	4.8	5.2	5.7	22.9	25.6	4.9	3.8	3.4	4.0	10.0	43.0	21.9	8.1	1.0	86.0	33.9	50.5	49.5
77058	HOUSTON	78.1	74.3	5.1	5.7	7.5	9.0	12.9	16.0	5.0	4.3	4.5	5.3	9.6	36.3	24.5	9.9	0.7	83.4	35.3	50.3	49.7
77059	HOUSTON	80.6	77.0	2.5	2.8	13.7	16.4	6.0	7.5	7.7	9.2	9.8	7.1	4.2	25.9	30.2	5.6	0.3	68.6	38.3	50.3	49.7
77060	HOUSTON	38.2	37.2	26.5	24.8	1.5	1.5	56.8	61.4	11.5	9.6	9.1	8.1	10.3	33.4	14.3	3.5	0.2	65.1	25.7	51.3	48.7
77061	HOUSTON	34.5	33.1	29.0	27.5	6.6	6.2	47.9	53.0	10.4	9.0	8.3	7.1	8.8	31.1	17.8	6.6	0.9	68.0	28.5	49.8	50.2
77062	HOUSTON	77.5	74.2	4.0	4.4	12.1	13.9	10.0	12.5	7.3	7.8	8.2	7.2	5.7	28.9	27.2	7.3	0.5	72.0	37.0	49.5	50.5
77063	HOUSTON	69.6	66.7	12.1	12.8	6.4	6.8	22.4	26.9	5.9	4.6	3.9	3.9	8.9	41.4	20.8	8.9	1.6	83.6	34.0	50.0	50.0
77064	HOUSTON	64.0	60.7	9.5	9.5	12.4	13.8	25.8	29.8	9.3	8.7	8.2	7.2	6.8	35.3	20.4	3.6	0.4	69.3	31.5	49.7	50.3
77065	HOUSTON	76.4	72.6	8.0	8.9	7.8	9.0	14.3	17.8	8.1	7.7	7.4	6.6	7.7	35.7	22.1	4.1	0.5	72.7	32.3	49.7	50.3
77066	HOUSTON	50.3	48.0	21.2	21.1	12.5	13.1	27.7	31.6	7.3	7.2	8.1	7.9	8.0	30.7	24.9	5.6	0.4	72.5	32.6	49.6	50.5
77067	HOUSTON	27.9	27.9	44.9	43.4	9.2	9.1	35.7	39.3	10.2	9.0	9.2	8.5	9.5	33.9	17.3	2.4	0.2	66.6	27.0	48.7	51.3
77068	HOUSTON	71.7	68.3	12.8	13.7	7.0	7.9	13.2	16.2	5.8	6.0	7.5	7.1	6.6	24.8	32.9	8.6	0.7	76.1	39.9	48.0	52.0
77069	HOUSTON	88.7	86.8	3.6	4.1	4.4	5.2	6.0	7.6	5.2	5.1	5.5	5.5	6.6	25.5	31.9	13.7	1.0	81.0	42.6	48.1	51.9
77070	HOUSTON	82.9	80.0	5.8	6.5	4.7	5.4	12.6	15.8	7.4	7.4	8.0	7.3	6.3	30.8	25.0	6.9	1.0	72.5	34.5	48.8	51.2
77071	HOUSTON	28.7	26.8	54.4	54.7	8.7	9.2	13.6	15.9	8.0	7.6	7.9	7.1	7.3	28.8	24.7	7.7	0.8	72.1	33.9	46.2	53.8
77072	HOUSTON	33.2	32.0	28.6	28.1	18.3	18.2	35.9	39.6	9.1	8.4	8.9	8.6	9.1	31.5	19.2	5.0	0.4	68.5	28.6	48.8	51.3
77073	HOUSTON	66.1	61.8	16.4	17.5	4.6	5.5	25.0	30.2	8.7	7.3	6.4	6.2	11.0	35.5	19.8	4.7	0.3	74.2	29.9	50.4	49.6
77074	HOUSTON	46.1	43.4	21.3	21.5	7.1	7.0	43.1	47.9	9.6	8.3	7.2	6.9	8.9	32.6	17.7	7.3	1.5	70.9	30.2	49.3	50.8
77075	HOUSTON	46.8	44.6	18.2	17.7	5.4	5.5	50.4	55.1	9.8	8.7	7.9	7.3	9.1	33.5	18.2	5.2	0.4	69.3	28.7	50.1	50.0
77076	HOUSTON	61.1	59.1	5.9	5.7	0.7	0.8	74.1	78.5	10.5	9.4	9.0	8.1	8.9	30.2	16.5	6.7	0.7	66.3	27.4	51.3	48.7
77077	HOUSTON	74.8	71.8	9.2	9.9	7.7	8.7	14.5	17.8	6.8	6.4	5.7	4.6	6.3	35.1	26.3	7.7	1.1	78.4	36.3	48.4	51.6
77078	HOUSTON	15.1	14.7	69.5	68.3	0.3	0.3	23.9	26.4	9.3	9.2	10.5	9.5	8.5	26.4	21.0	5.4	0.3	65.2	27.2	47.2	52.8
77079	HOUSTON	82.1	79.2	3.1	3.4	9.1	10.4	10.2	13.2	5.6	6.2	7.5	7.7	6.3	23.2	29.5	13.5	0.7	76.0	41.1	47.9	52.2
77080	HOUSTON	59.7	57.0	5.2	5.1	4.7	4.7	57.9	62.9	9.6	8.4	7.7	6.8	8.8	32.4	17.3	7.9	1.3	70.4	29.8	51.7	48.3
77081	HOUSTON	48.4	47.6	9.1	8.6	4.7	4.6	71.5	74.1	10.7	8.6	7.7	7.0	10.7	40.5	12.5	2.3	0.2	69.0	27.1	54.1	45.9
77082	HOUSTON	53.0	49.8	19.7	20.2	14.3	15.5	22.2	25.9	7.6	6.4	5.7	5.7	9.6	39.4	20.8	4.3	0.6	77.0	31.7	48.6	51.4
77083	HOUSTON	39.5	36.9	24.2	24.7	21.2	21.7	26.3	29.6	8.1	8.3	9.2	8.2	7.6	30.8	23.3	4.2	0.3	69.3	31.1	48.7	51.3
77084	HOUSTON	70.6	66.9	9.1	9.7	6.0	6.7	24.3	29.0	8.7	8.3	8.5	7.9	7.8	32.6	22.4	3.6	0.2	69.4	31.0	49.2	50.8
77085	HOUSTON	25.5	24.0	52.7	54.1	0.9	0.9	38.8	39.5	8.8	8.3	9.0	8.9	8.3	27.5	22.2	6.6	0.5	68.4	29.7	49.4	50.6
77086	HOUSTON	41.8	39.8	26.2	25.7	10.5	10.7	39.2	43.3	9.0	8.2	9.3	8.8	9.0	31.6	20.0	3.9	0.3	68.2	28.4	50.0	50.0
77087	HOUSTON	42.9	42.2	16.2	14.8	1.0	1.0	72.2	75.9	9.5	8.9	9.1	8.3	8.6	29.3	18.6	6.8	1.0	67.6	28.5	50.9	49.1
77088	HOUSTON	25.5	23.5	55.5	56.0	5.9	6.0	21.7	24.1	8.3	8.1	9.0	8.1	7.9	28.5	22.5	7.0	0.6	69.6	31.2	47.2	52.8
77089	HOUSTON	61.3	57.9	12.6	12.9	10.9	11.6	28.1	32.8	7.2	7.2	7.5	7.2	7.5	30.0	24.9	7.8	0.6	73.7	33.7	49.4	50.7
77090	HOUSTON	68.3	64.8	17.5	18.6	4.7	5.2	18.5	22.6	7.2	6.2	6.1	6.6	10.3	36.1	20.1	6.8	0.8	76.9	31.3	49.5	50.5
77091	HOUSTON	21.0	20.3	65.5	64.9	0.7	0.7	21.7	24.4	8.8	8.1	8.6	7.8	8.3	27.5	21.1	8.8	1.2	69.8	30.7	46.8	53.2
77092	HOUSTON	52.2	49.4	19.5	18.6	1.5	1.6	46.3	52.7	9.7	8.2	7.5	6.8	9.1	32.5	19.2	6.6	0.5	70.8	29.7	49.8	50.2
77093	HOUSTON	53.9	52.8	13.0	12.3	0.5	0.5	72.6	76.5	10.2	9.4	9.4	8.4	8.5	29.1	17.5	7.0	0.5	65.8	27.6	51.6	48.4
77094	HOUSTON	84.5	81.4	2.4	3.0	10.8	12.7	5.5	7.2	7.6	9.0	10.6	9.5	5.7	22.5	31.3	3.4	0.3	66.6	36.5	49.4	50.6
77095	HOUSTON	78.9	75.7	6.6	7.3	7.5	8.7	12.3	15.1	8.5	8.7	9.1	7.7	6.1	32.5	24.1	3.1	0.2	68.6	32.8	49.2	50.8
77096	HOUSTON	65.8	64.1	17.2	16.9	5.9	6.6	18.7	21.4	7.2	6.9	7.1	6.5	6.5	26.8	23.7	13.7	1.6	74.8	37.3	47.7	52.3
77098	HOUSTON	85.9	83.7	2.0	2.2	3.5	4.2	16.3	19.2	3.8	2.7	2.5	3.5	8.7	45.1	24.9	7.5	1.3	89.1	35.7	51.6	48.4
77099	HOUSTON	31.9	30.1	29.7	29.4	22.7	23.1	25.9	29.5	8.6	8.3	8.4	7.9	8.2	32.8	20.9	4.7	0.3	69.9	30.2	48.9	51.1
77301	CONROE	63.6	61.3	13.4	13.2	0.8	0.8	41.6	45.8	9.7	8.3	7.4	7.6	10.8	30.7	16.9	7.5	1.2	70.4	28.4	51.3	48.7
77302	CONROE	92.6	91.2	0.9	1.1	0.5	0.5	9.3	11.4	7.6	7.4	7.9	7.4	6.5	26.0	25.8	10.7	0.7	72.5	36.4	49.9	50.1
77303	CONROE	89.8	88.1	1.9	2.1	0.4	0.4	12.7	15.1	8.0	7.6	7.8	7.4	7.5	29.3	23.4	8.3	0.8	71.9	33.3	49.5	50.5
77304	CONROE	89.6	88.3	5.1	5.4	1.1	1.3	10.0	12.0	6.0	5.6	6.1	6.3	8.9	27.3	25.2	12.4	2.2	78.7	37.3	48.4	51.6
77306	CONROE	86.4	83.8	0.5	0.6	0.4	0.4	18.4	22.1	8.6	8.1	8.3	7.4	8.1	28.1	22.6	8.0	0.7	70.4	31.9	51.0	49.0
77316	MONTGOMERY	90.2	88.5	4.2	4.7	0.3	0.4	7.2	9.0	7.3	7.1	7.6	7.1	6.6	27.7	26.9	9.0	0.8	73.6	36.9	49.5	50.5
77318	WILLIS	94.0	92.9	1.5	1.8	0.5	0.6	5.8	7.1	6.0	6.3	6.4	6.6	5.0	23.9	31.2	14.0	0.8	77.1	42.4	49.4	50.6
77320	HUNTSVILLE	66.1	64.7	27.6	28.2	0.6	0.6	15.6	17.4	4.8	4.5	4.7	9.3	12.6	34.6	21.3	7.5	0.8	82.7	33.0	64.7	35.3
77327	CLEVELAND	80.2	78.6	11.3	11.7	0.3	0.4	11.6	13.5	7.7	7.3	7.8	7.2	7.3	27.5	23.6	10.4	1.4	72.9	34.7	50.4	49.6
77328	CLEVELAND	87.8	86.4	3.2	3.2	0.4	0.4	12.8	14.9	8.3	8.1	7.9	7.3	7.5	27.6	23.4	9.0	0.8	71.1	33.4	50.1	49.9
77331	COLDSPRING	81.0	79.8	17.2	18.2	0.2	0.2	3.2	3.6	5.1	5.6	6.5	5.8	4.8	21.9	30.7	18.1	1.5	79.2	45.3	50.7	49.3
	TEXAS	71.0	69.5	11.5	11.4	2.8	3.1	32.0	34.6	7.9	7.5	7.7	7.5	8.1	29.6	21.9	8.7	1.2	72.6	32.9	49.7	50.3
	UNITED STATES	75.1	73.6	12.3	12.5	3.8	4.2	12.5	14.1	6.9	6.7	7.2	7.0	7.3	28.6	23.8	10.8	1.7	75.1	36.0	49.1	50.9

ZIP CODE # POST OFFICE NAME	2004 Per Capita Income	2004 HH Income Base	2004 Household Income Distribution (%): Less than $25,000	$25,000 to $49,999	$50,000 to $99,999	$100,000 to $149,999	$150,000 or More	Median Household Income: 2004	2009	2004 National Centile	2004 State Centile	2004 Home Value Base	2004 Home Value Distribution (%): Less than $50,000	$50,000 to $89,999	$90,000 to $174,999	$175,000 to $399,999	$400,000 or More	2004 Median Home Value
77014 HOUSTON	20909	8610	19.1	33.9	34.4	9.3	3.2	46028	55724	64	70	3723	8.2	14.6	64.7	12.3	0.2	116352
77015 HOUSTON	18869	17573	24.5	31.0	32.1	9.4	3.1	44992	53014	61	68	10501	22.2	35.8	38.3	3.1	0.5	82215
77016 HOUSTON	13682	9849	46.1	29.1	18.8	4.4	1.6	27309	32188	8	10	6518	52.7	39.2	6.8	1.0	0.4	48433
77017 HOUSTON	14062	10036	32.1	34.0	27.0	4.4	2.5	36207	42307	32	39	5306	25.5	57.6	15.7	1.2	0.1	63803
77018 HOUSTON	26383	10938	22.9	27.4	31.9	11.0	6.9	49658	59137	71	77	7684	6.7	20.8	52.4	19.2	1.0	115276
77019 HOUSTON	78715	8687	16.4	18.7	25.7	13.0	26.1	73560	98172	93	93	3564	0.9	6.6	11.3	29.0	52.2	423460
77020 HOUSTON	10779	8443	50.6	27.9	16.9	3.5	1.1	24599	29081	4	5	4293	58.8	36.9	3.9	0.4	0.0	45904
77021 HOUSTON	15634	9175	49.7	25.0	18.3	4.1	2.9	25249	30339	5	6	5102	46.9	32.4	12.4	5.9	2.4	52842
77022 HOUSTON	11563	10143	47.5	30.6	17.0	4.0	0.9	26414	31003	6	8	4719	43.1	45.4	10.1	0.6	0.8	54658
77023 HOUSTON	13575	9858	37.5	31.6	22.6	6.1	2.2	33500	39437	22	28	4732	22.4	49.6	23.0	4.6	0.3	66871
77024 HOUSTON	79709	15223	11.5	15.8	23.7	13.7	35.4	97053	120793	98	98	11055	2.7	7.9	12.3	25.6	51.6	413477
77025 HOUSTON	43179	12889	21.3	22.4	27.8	14.5	14.0	59702	75812	84	86	5618	3.9	10.2	32.9	44.9	8.2	181342
77026 HOUSTON	11223	9642	58.8	25.7	12.4	1.7	1.6	19849	23224	2	3	4264	66.7	25.8	6.7	0.9	0.0	37963
77027 HOUSTON	76589	8665	10.9	20.1	31.5	16.4	21.2	75750	102033	94	94	3135	6.5	5.3	12.0	38.7	37.5	321743
77028 HOUSTON	11760	5505	51.6	28.5	15.9	2.0	2.0	23774	28287	4	5	3758	66.0	27.9	4.6	1.0	0.5	42318
77029 HOUSTON	13708	5975	36.1	34.6	24.0	3.9	1.4	34013	39559	24	30	3929	46.4	49.0	4.5	0.2	0.0	51625
77030 HOUSTON	53293	5493	17.8	18.6	28.5	14.5	20.6	68498	92029	91	92	2065	7.3	6.4	11.5	44.1	30.8	306028
77031 HOUSTON	20930	6066	27.1	31.1	28.3	10.0	3.4	41317	49397	51	59	2632	1.4	22.2	72.6	3.6	0.2	105689
77032 HOUSTON	13127	3794	42.8	28.3	22.4	4.0	2.5	29293	34529	11	14	1737	39.1	46.3	12.7	1.0	0.9	56916
77033 HOUSTON	12895	9093	43.9	32.3	18.8	3.1	1.9	30058	35171	12	16	6012	64.3	29.9	5.2	0.4	0.2	43770
77034 HOUSTON	20468	10272	22.0	35.4	30.3	8.6	3.7	43946	52112	58	66	4992	8.9	55.3	24.9	10.1	0.8	79957
77035 HOUSTON	19624	14135	29.3	31.4	26.1	9.5	3.8	40699	47941	49	57	6436	8.8	31.5	50.5	8.8	0.4	99368
77036 HOUSTON	15303	30159	39.7	35.3	18.4	4.5	2.1	30796	35757	14	18	5573	22.3	18.4	55.6	3.3	0.4	97082
77037 HOUSTON	13517	5248	29.7	33.2	29.4	6.5	1.1	38572	44242	41	49	3757	29.4	52.8	16.5	1.3	0.1	66800
77038 HOUSTON	14317	6887	26.5	36.7	28.7	5.8	2.3	39477	46409	44	53	3375	30.6	55.7	13.0	0.8	0.0	65998
77039 HOUSTON	12809	8263	33.0	31.8	28.1	5.5	1.6	36794	42806	35	41	4740	24.3	59.0	14.2	2.5	0.2	66841
77040 HOUSTON	28288	15071	15.8	27.0	33.1	15.8	8.4	58132	68925	83	85	9197	6.6	30.9	44.1	17.6	0.7	100977
77041 HOUSTON	28174	8959	13.5	22.6	34.4	15.9	13.7	65594	79435	89	90	7727	13.4	29.0	34.7	17.2	5.7	99071
77042 HOUSTON	33682	18552	18.4	32.4	31.0	10.7	7.5	49196	60182	71	76	4473	10.9	8.8	23.3	47.7	9.3	193068
77043 HOUSTON	22483	8579	20.6	27.5	34.1	12.1	5.6	51692	61501	75	80	5157	10.7	27.2	55.4	6.6	0.1	102456
77044 HOUSTON	17983	4879	23.8	27.3	35.4	9.5	4.0	49047	58824	70	75	3885	38.5	34.2	14.7	12.1	0.6	60276
77045 HOUSTON	15331	7663	27.6	31.5	30.6	7.9	2.4	41655	48739	52	60	5301	21.5	66.9	11.2	0.2	0.3	66890
77046 HOUSTON	107536	342	13.2	5.3	21.1	25.4	35.1	118997	152910	99	99	237	0.0	3.4	39.7	40.5	16.5	189224
77047 HOUSTON	16563	3955	30.0	30.3	28.0	10.7	1.0	40760	48734	49	57	3135	40.9	40.0	18.2	0.9	0.0	55600
77048 HOUSTON	14830	5402	42.2	29.2	22.2	4.6	1.8	31406	37018	16	20	3039	40.8	46.4	12.0	0.6	0.2	56901
77049 HOUSTON	16563	5557	21.7	36.9	30.0	9.4	2.1	42137	48530	53	62	3736	18.0	59.7	21.4	1.0	0.0	72843
77050 HOUSTON	14414	1325	29.8	37.5	22.3	6.0	4.4	37297	43107	36	43	989	41.6	42.7	14.4	0.5	0.9	59824
77051 HOUSTON	12492	5126	56.4	24.4	14.4	3.6	1.3	20857	24891	2	3	2821	70.3	23.4	5.3	0.7	0.4	39296
77053 HOUSTON	14298	7881	22.4	35.0	34.4	6.9	1.3	44605	51901	60	68	5631	20.4	59.5	19.3	0.9	0.0	68675
77054 HOUSTON	28182	10245	29.9	32.6	28.1	6.7	2.6	39799	48560	45	54	1738	31.8	44.2	22.0	1.6	0.4	63529
77055 HOUSTON	21741	14322	28.4	29.4	25.4	8.9	7.9	41948	49179	53	61	6829	9.4	27.7	26.9	29.2	6.8	115679
77056 HOUSTON	86545	8274	11.0	16.1	28.1	14.5	30.2	87817	114252	97	97	3871	1.1	4.9	9.2	34.2	50.7	405335
77057 HOUSTON	52819	20116	17.4	25.0	31.6	12.3	13.7	57963	73837	83	85	6449	6.1	14.2	29.0	27.1	23.5	178461
77058 HOUSTON	39010	8220	14.8	26.6	37.2	14.4	7.1	57706	70038	82	85	3104	7.5	13.2	51.2	24.0	4.1	133829
77059 HOUSTON	45487	6179	3.2	6.1	28.6	31.3	30.9	115214	137613	99	99	5698	1.1	0.9	27.3	64.6	6.1	216996
77060 HOUSTON	13090	13054	38.1	35.6	21.7	3.3	1.3	31276	36101	16	20	3517	18.5	60.6	19.7	0.5	0.8	72880
77061 HOUSTON	17640	9211	33.9	34.1	22.6	6.9	2.5	34515	40649	26	31	3629	12.4	36.8	46.3	3.6	0.9	90576
77062 HOUSTON	37879	10883	9.0	16.9	34.3	23.0	16.9	82131	102396	96	96	8140	1.4	4.4	64.2	25.1	4.8	146619
77063 HOUSTON	42796	16710	20.9	27.9	29.9	11.1	10.3	51207	63477	74	79	5090	10.5	12.8	28.3	38.2	10.2	169723
77064 HOUSTON	28350	12931	9.1	20.0	42.4	19.6	8.9	71074	86261	92	92	10094	5.9	24.1	51.4	18.0	0.6	112162
77065 HOUSTON	29930	11872	12.1	21.9	40.0	19.7	6.4	66097	79972	89	91	6668	0.5	18.2	60.8	20.4	0.1	118260
77066 HOUSTON	24112	9462	15.3	23.4	35.6	19.3	6.5	63430	75279	87	89	6997	3.9	30.9	55.5	9.3	0.4	109856
77067 HOUSTON	15924	8000	24.6	35.5	32.2	5.5	2.3	42212	49635	54	62	3617	7.4	57.4	34.8	0.4	0.0	80572
77068 HOUSTON	44425	3412	14.3	13.7	27.0	21.5	23.6	88279	109420	97	97	2653	0.6	1.7	51.1	40.9	5.7	169414
77069 HOUSTON	59398	7290	11.3	19.4	27.3	18.6	23.5	81772	104554	96	96	4495	2.1	7.3	27.7	51.2	11.8	202424
77070 HOUSTON	32819	14161	11.6	20.5	36.3	19.9	11.7	69801	85021	91	92	8988	1.4	11.6	61.3	24.2	1.4	141790
77071 HOUSTON	23984	9911	22.5	27.1	30.8	14.2	5.4	50414	60916	73	78	6278	5.1	26.1	58.1	9.9	0.8	107647
77072 HOUSTON	15034	16698	29.6	35.2	26.4	6.9	1.9	37731	44286	38	45	7611	16.5	55.7	27.4	0.3	0.1	77343
77073 HOUSTON	23802	5962	19.9	32.9	32.2	11.9	3.2	47320	57966	67	72	2584	0.7	13.9	79.3	6.0	0.0	115381
77074 HOUSTON	18259	16033	32.2	34.3	24.6	6.3	2.5	35435	41569	29	35	5733	14.0	47.1	35.6	3.0	0.3	82877
77075 HOUSTON	18966	8650	23.0	33.6	34.5	7.4	1.5	44322	52270	59	67	4601	15.8	48.8	34.0	1.4	0.0	79816
77076 HOUSTON	11582	9076	36.0	36.7	23.2	3.2	0.9	32568	37413	20	24	5246	31.9	57.8	9.7	0.4	0.2	59674
77077 HOUSTON	41703	22034	12.4	26.3	32.7	15.7	13.0	62863	77647	87	89	9912	1.5	5.3	53.1	34.9	5.1	160560
77078 HOUSTON	11343	4304	42.0	27.3	26.7	2.5	1.4	31347	36435	16	20	2543	40.4	50.2	8.3	0.8	0.2	54333
77079 HOUSTON	44423	13528	12.4	18.8	29.4	18.5	21.0	76565	96415	94	95	8926	2.1	9.7	22.7	53.5	12.0	229694
77080 HOUSTON	17112	16820	29.1	33.7	26.0	8.6	2.6	38925	45280	42	51	6507	9.3	29.8	55.6	4.3	1.0	98380
77081 HOUSTON	14153	19457	40.9	35.3	17.5	3.9	2.4	30039	35175	12	16	1371	23.4	13.6	42.7	18.9	1.4	109881
77082 HOUSTON	28841	17508	15.1	31.3	34.6	13.2	5.9	53268	64532	77	81	6833	3.5	26.4	51.0	18.5	0.7	109488
77083 HOUSTON	21137	17614	15.0	24.6	40.6	13.7	6.1	60677	70072	85	87	12790	2.7	33.1	58.0	6.2	0.1	100542
77084 HOUSTON	25859	23839	12.1	24.5	39.3	16.8	7.4	62583	75335	87	88	15852	2.0	29.8	60.0	7.8	0.5	103435
77085 HOUSTON	17023	2812	19.5	32.0	38.2	8.1	2.2	48705	57263	70	75	1971	21.4	50.7	27.1	0.6	0.3	72677
77086 HOUSTON	16278	6725	23.8	32.7	32.8	7.2	3.4	43075	50388	56	64	3849	8.8	68.7	21.2	1.0	0.3	76345
77087 HOUSTON	12638	10898	36.7	33.0	24.1	4.6	1.7	33658	39084	23	28	6197	26.3	60.9	11.7	0.8	0.3	62539
77088 HOUSTON	17514	17152	30.6	26.6	29.3	9.9	3.5	42168	50284	53	62	11089	17.6	39.2	40.3	3.0	0.1	84061
77089 HOUSTON	24588	13207	13.6	25.7	38.8	15.5	6.5	61329	70700	86	88	9525	1.2	34.5	59.8	4.2	0.4	97605
77090 HOUSTON	32154	12553	16.8	31.0	34.3	11.3	6.7	51753	62557	75	80	3823	2.9	16.4	62.8	16.7	1.3	125838
77091 HOUSTON	14921	8706	41.6	29.3	20.4	6.4	2.3	30232	35356	13	16	4122	31.2	29.4	34.4	4.9	0.2	73797
77092 HOUSTON	17510	15363	30.5	36.1	25.6	6.1	1.8	36158	42308	32	38	5790	14.3	41.6	41.5	2.6	0.0	84896
77093 HOUSTON	10598	12600	42.6	32.0	20.4	3.4	1.6	29670	34291	12	15	7831	55.9	38.2	4.9	0.8	0.2	46534
77094 HOUSTON	56453	2893	4.5	6.8	16.5	25.2	47.0	142142	167492	100	100	2793	5.0	0.2	4.8	75.6	14.4	241343
77095 HOUSTON	34753	14645	6.9	15.2	35.1	27.1	15.7	87578	108244	97	97	11461	0.5	8.0	57.8	32.9	0.8	153977
77096 HOUSTON	33217	15279	22.1	26.1	24.5	15.0	12.3	52622	64866	76	80	8043	2.6	4.5	44.4	44.3	4.3	172534
77098 HOUSTON	61512	7500	17.9	23.6	28.7	14.0	15.9	62115	82058	86	88	2215	0.7	3.4	22.7	46.6	26.6	265156
77099 HOUSTON	17010	15528	23.9	34.9	31.2	7.8	2.2	43668	51237	58	66	7928	9.5	48.8	40.3	1.3	0.1	85581
77301 CONROE	15117	8936	35.4	35.0	23.1	4.4	2.1	33565	39372	23	28	4414	34.9	32.9	28.8	2.8	0.6	71170
77302 CONROE	22991	5015	16.8	29.8	36.2	11.6	5.6	53850	64049	78	82	4214	24.8	20.6	40.0	12.6	2.0	97729
77303 CONROE	19622	4532	20.7	34.1	34.5	7.9	2.8	45807	54431	63	70	3419	20.7	38.9	33.1	6.8	0.6	79931
77304 CONROE	31447	7307	19.1	26.1	31.8	14.4	8.6	55566	66293	80	83	4368	9.2	11.3	49.2	24.0	6.3	134656
77306 CONROE	17640	3178	29.2	30.7	30.2	6.4	3.5	41513	50127	51	60	2506	45.3	26.9	23.7	3.8	0.2	55392
77316 MONTGOMERY	21303	4114	22.8	28.9	34.2	10.9	3.2	48364	57514	69	74	3477	18.9	29.2	36.7	12.7	2.5	92314
77318 WILLIS	32433	4756	16.3	20.5	37.7	14.1	11.5	64293	76852	88	90	4096	12.8	13.8	39.8	26.5	7.0	135882
77320 HUNTSVILLE	16583	9365	33.5	29.9	27.8	6.9	1.8	38076	44635	40	47	5899	33.7	25.6	30.8	9.0	0.9	73319
77327 CLEVELAND	17222	8005	35.3	27.1	29.9	5.7	2.1	38597	44333	41	49	5902	42.7	28.3	24.6	4.1	0.3	58821
77328 CLEVELAND	18491	4417	27.6	29.5	32.2	8.1	2.6	42831	50000	56	64	3737	37.3	31.2	24.2	6.5	0.8	65326
77331 COLDSPRING	23794	2766	34.0	29.0	28.0	4.1	5.0	37060	42353	36	42	2282	33.0	28.4	25.5	10.6	2.7	72910
TEXAS	23284		26.2	27.7	29.5	10.3	6.3	45778	54246				21.6	26.1	33.4	15.6	3.4	93683
UNITED STATES	25866		24.7	27.1	30.8	10.9	6.5	48124	56710				10.9	15.0	33.7	30.1	10.4	145905

ZIP CODE #	POST OFFICE NAME	FINANCIAL SERVICES: Auto Loan	FINANCIAL SERVICES: Home Loan	FINANCIAL SERVICES: Invest-ments	FINANCIAL SERVICES: Retire-ment Plans	THE HOME: Home Improvements: Home Repair	THE HOME: Home Improvements: Lawn & Garden	THE HOME: Furnishings: Comput-ers & Hard-ware	THE HOME: Furnishings: Major Appli-ances	THE HOME: Furnishings: TV, Radio, Sound Equip-ment	THE HOME: Furnishings: Furni-ture	ENTERTAINMENT: Dine out/ Carry out	ENTERTAINMENT: Sports Equip-ment	ENTERTAINMENT: Fees & Tickets	ENTERTAINMENT: Toys & Games	ENTERTAINMENT: Travel	ENTERTAINMENT: Cable TV	PERSONAL: Apparel & Services	PERSONAL: Auto Repairs	PERSONAL: Health Insur-ance	PERSONAL: Pets & Supplies
77014	HOUSTON	83	80	86	87	77	78	83	80	79	86	101	96	82	97	79	74	99	83	70	89
77015	HOUSTON	84	79	82	80	77	80	84	83	84	86	106	96	82	103	80	80	105	86	76	90
77016	HOUSTON	60	54	57	50	53	62	56	58	61	59	76	62	57	71	56	64	74	59	63	66
77017	HOUSTON	70	63	62	62	62	64	68	69	69	71	87	78	64	83	64	65	87	72	63	73
77018	HOUSTON	88	95	108	93	93	99	94	93	93	95	117	106	96	118	94	92	116	94	89	101
77019	HOUSTON	200	203	342	222	193	214	224	205	226	229	287	246	235	298	223	224	286	215	191	227
77020	HOUSTON	53	45	45	42	44	49	49	51	53	52	66	56	47	61	47	53	65	53	51	55
77021	HOUSTON	59	54	61	51	53	62	57	57	62	59	77	63	58	73	57	65	75	59	62	66
77022	HOUSTON	55	47	43	44	46	50	50	52	54	53	67	57	47	61	48	53	66	54	52	57
77023	HOUSTON	68	59	55	57	58	60	64	66	67	68	84	73	61	80	60	63	84	69	61	69
77024	HOUSTON	232	284	389	286	277	299	266	259	254	270	320	298	290	332	276	253	321	256	243	283
77025	HOUSTON	116	124	180	130	120	129	130	122	129	131	163	145	136	169	130	127	162	126	114	134
77026	HOUSTON	48	39	39	35	39	46	43	45	49	45	59	49	41	53	42	51	57	47	51	51
77027	HOUSTON	162	169	290	186	161	178	185	168	186	188	236	203	196	247	185	184	235	176	157	187
77028	HOUSTON	50	43	47	39	43	51	47	48	52	48	64	51	46	59	46	55	61	49	54	55
77029	HOUSTON	64	56	53	52	54	60	59	61	63	62	78	66	56	71	57	63	77	63	62	67
77030	HOUSTON	144	149	229	161	145	158	164	151	161	163	203	184	169	206	162	156	202	159	140	167
77031	HOUSTON	79	81	95	80	79	84	83	82	84	85	105	95	84	106	82	83	104	83	78	90
77032	HOUSTON	59	52	52	50	51	56	56	57	59	58	74	65	53	69	54	59	72	59	57	64
77033	HOUSTON	57	52	57	49	51	60	54	55	58	56	73	59	55	68	54	61	70	56	60	63
77034	HOUSTON	82	79	87	81	77	81	83	81	82	85	104	94	82	101	80	78	102	84	74	89
77035	HOUSTON	73	75	90	74	72	77	77	75	77	78	98	87	78	98	76	76	97	77	71	82
77036	HOUSTON	55	52	74	54	50	55	59	56	61	60	77	66	58	79	57	60	77	60	52	61
77037	HOUSTON	72	63	54	59	61	63	65	69	68	71	86	75	61	78	62	65	85	71	65	73
77038	HOUSTON	72	66	67	66	64	68	69	70	70	72	89	80	67	86	67	67	88	72	65	77
77039	HOUSTON	70	61	55	58	59	63	64	67	67	69	84	73	60	77	61	64	83	69	64	71
77040	HOUSTON	108	115	122	120	111	113	112	109	106	114	134	128	114	133	109	101	133	110	97	121
77041	HOUSTON	126	141	155	139	134	139	133	131	129	138	164	149	137	167	132	126	164	131	120	143
77042	HOUSTON	97	90	111	98	87	93	101	95	98	102	125	115	98	119	95	93	122	101	86	105
77043	HOUSTON	89	97	110	94	94	99	95	94	94	98	119	106	97	122	95	93	119	95	88	102
77044	HOUSTON	88	85	73	83	85	88	81	85	80	82	100	99	79	98	80	79	96	84	83	100
77045	HOUSTON	73	70	74	66	68	76	71	72	75	75	94	78	72	90	71	76	92	73	73	80
77046	HOUSTON	209	200	377	230	189	212	237	209	243	241	308	258	247	324	233	240	306	225	196	234
77047	HOUSTON	73	71	71	68	70	78	69	71	71	71	89	78	71	86	70	73	87	71	73	81
77048	HOUSTON	63	57	66	54	55	64	61	60	66	63	82	67	62	79	61	68	80	62	64	69
77049	HOUSTON	80	79	72	78	77	78	77	79	76	79	95	91	75	92	75	72	93	79	73	88
77050	HOUSTON	70	64	66	62	63	69	68	68	71	71	89	75	67	85	66	70	88	70	68	75
77051	HOUSTON	48	42	46	38	41	49	45	46	51	47	62	50	45	57	45	54	60	47	52	53
77053	HOUSTON	73	74	73	73	71	73	73	74	72	76	90	84	72	88	71	69	89	74	68	80
77054	HOUSTON	67	57	83	64	55	61	73	65	73	71	92	81	70	89	68	69	90	72	60	72
77055	HOUSTON	92	91	99	90	89	92	94	93	95	98	120	107	94	120	91	91	120	96	86	100
77056	HOUSTON	209	236	343	248	230	248	236	225	229	239	289	264	252	299	240	227	288	227	210	247
77057	HOUSTON	120	115	192	128	110	122	135	121	136	135	173	149	138	177	131	134	171	130	113	135
77058	HOUSTON	105	101	119	109	98	104	109	104	106	110	134	125	107	129	104	100	131	109	95	116
77059	HOUSTON	184	231	257	237	223	227	203	198	185	206	235	228	224	245	207	180	237	191	177	219
77060	HOUSTON	61	52	53	52	51	54	58	58	60	61	76	67	55	71	55	57	75	61	54	63
77061	HOUSTON	74	66	71	68	65	69	73	72	74	75	93	84	70	90	69	70	92	76	67	79
77062	HOUSTON	145	161	177	166	155	159	153	149	144	156	182	174	158	182	151	138	181	149	134	164
77063	HOUSTON	111	105	142	114	102	111	117	110	116	118	147	132	117	143	113	111	144	116	102	122
77064	HOUSTON	125	136	134	140	129	128	127	126	119	132	151	146	129	150	123	112	150	124	109	137
77065	HOUSTON	111	118	122	124	113	113	114	111	107	117	136	132	115	134	110	100	134	112	97	123
77066	HOUSTON	102	117	127	117	112	114	109	108	104	112	132	124	113	135	109	101	131	106	97	117
77067	HOUSTON	72	70	76	73	67	69	73	71	71	75	91	84	72	88	70	67	89	74	63	78
77068	HOUSTON	163	200	220	204	195	196	181	178	167	181	211	208	194	221	184	162	211	173	159	196
77069	HOUSTON	176	198	223	203	193	202	186	184	177	190	224	211	196	223	188	173	221	182	171	203
77070	HOUSTON	121	136	145	141	133	133	128	126	120	130	152	148	133	153	127	114	150	125	113	139
77071	HOUSTON	87	93	106	94	90	95	93	91	91	94	115	106	95	116	92	89	113	92	85	100
77072	HOUSTON	67	68	78	67	65	69	70	68	70	72	89	78	70	89	68	68	89	70	63	74
77073	HOUSTON	85	79	91	86	77	80	86	82	84	88	107	100	84	101	82	78	104	87	74	92
77074	HOUSTON	69	66	81	67	64	68	72	69	73	74	93	81	71	92	70	71	92	73	65	76
77075	HOUSTON	82	77	81	79	74	77	81	80	81	85	103	93	79	98	77	76	101	83	72	87
77076	HOUSTON	61	53	48	51	51	53	57	59	59	61	74	65	53	69	53	56	74	61	54	62
77077	HOUSTON	121	122	151	130	119	125	128	122	123	129	157	146	129	154	124	118	154	126	111	135
77078	HOUSTON	56	49	55	46	48	54	54	54	58	56	72	59	53	68	52	59	71	56	55	60
77079	HOUSTON	143	171	217	170	166	177	161	158	154	164	194	181	172	200	165	152	195	157	145	172
77080	HOUSTON	73	70	76	70	68	72	74	73	75	77	95	84	73	94	71	72	94	76	68	79
77081	HOUSTON	57	50	60	51	48	51	58	55	60	59	76	65	56	75	54	57	75	59	51	60
77082	HOUSTON	98	94	103	101	90	93	98	94	95	101	121	113	97	115	93	89	118	98	84	105
77083	HOUSTON	100	109	113	113	104	104	104	102	98	107	124	119	105	124	101	92	123	101	89	112
77084	HOUSTON	108	115	118	121	110	110	111	109	104	114	132	129	112	130	107	97	130	109	95	120
77085	HOUSTON	81	84	83	83	82	82	83	83	80	85	101	96	82	100	80	76	100	84	75	90
77086	HOUSTON	76	78	83	77	75	78	79	77	78	80	98	90	78	98	77	75	96	79	72	85
77087	HOUSTON	66	58	53	55	56	59	61	64	64	65	80	69	58	74	58	61	80	66	60	67
77088	HOUSTON	75	75	82	73	73	77	76	75	76	77	96	86	76	94	74	76	94	76	72	83
77089	HOUSTON	100	110	120	111	107	109	106	104	101	107	128	122	109	130	105	97	127	104	94	115
77090	HOUSTON	102	95	114	103	92	98	105	100	102	106	130	120	102	123	99	96	127	105	90	111
77091	HOUSTON	60	54	60	53	52	59	58	58	61	60	77	65	58	72	57	61	74	60	59	65
77092	HOUSTON	67	62	67	63	61	64	67	66	67	69	85	76	65	83	64	64	85	69	61	71
77093	HOUSTON	60	52	45	49	50	53	54	57	57	58	71	62	50	64	51	54	70	59	54	60
77094	HOUSTON	235	293	319	303	284	286	258	252	235	262	299	291	284	311	263	228	302	243	224	279
77095	HOUSTON	146	168	165	175	160	156	151	149	138	156	175	174	157	177	148	129	174	145	127	163
77096	HOUSTON	103	114	150	113	111	120	115	111	115	116	144	129	120	149	117	115	144	113	106	121
77098	HOUSTON	132	126	218	142	120	134	149	133	151	150	192	164	153	197	145	149	190	143	125	148
77099	HOUSTON	72	72	85	75	70	73	76	74	74	78	95	87	75	93	73	71	94	77	67	80
77301	CONROE	65	60	62	59	59	64	64	64	66	65	83	73	62	81	62	65	81	66	63	71
77302	CONROE	100	99	88	97	100	105	93	98	93	95	115	113	92	113	94	92	111	97	97	114
77303	CONROE	85	81	70	79	81	85	79	82	79	79	97	96	76	95	78	77	94	82	81	96
77304	CONROE	104	106	121	109	105	111	109	106	106	109	134	125	109	132	107	104	131	109	101	118
77306	CONROE	86	79	62	76	79	83	75	81	76	77	94	93	71	89	74	75	90	80	80	96
77316	MONTGOMERY	90	85	75	84	86	91	83	87	83	84	103	101	80	100	82	82	99	87	87	102
77318	WILLIS	131	125	105	121	129	136	116	125	118	117	145	148	114	147	118	119	140	123	128	154
77320	HUNTSVILLE	67	59	54	58	60	65	61	63	63	61	78	73	58	74	60	63	74	64	65	74
77327	CLEVELAND	76	65	53	61	67	74	66	71	70	66	85	81	62	82	65	72	81	71	76	86
77328	CLEVELAND	87	76	58	73	78	83	73	80	76	75	93	92	69	88	73	75	89	80	81	96
77331	COLDSPRING	97	74	48	67	83	95	73	86	83	72	98	100	65	95	76	88	90	85	103	115
	TEXAS	94	90	91	90	89	95	92	93	92	93	115	107	90	112	90	90	112	94	89	104
	UNITED STATES	100	100	100	100	100	100	100	100	100	100	100	100	100	100	100	100	100	100	100	100

POPULATION CHANGE

ZIP CODE			POPULATION			2000-2004 ANNUAL RATE		HOUSEHOLDS					FAMILIES		
#	POST OFFICE NAME	COUNTY FIPS CODE	2000	2004	2009	% Rate	State Centile	2000	2004	2009	% Annual Rate 2000-2004	2004 Average HH Size	2000	2004	% Annual Rate 2000-2004
77335	GOODRICH	373	2089	2207	2454	1.3	51	822	866	961	1.2	2.55	599	632	1.3
77336	HUFFMAN	201	8958	9920	11066	2.4	75	3110	3422	3784	2.3	2.90	2506	2760	2.3
77338	HUMBLE	201	20261	21588	23933	1.5	57	7404	7874	8680	1.5	2.72	5227	5496	1.2
77339	HUMBLE	201	31116	32682	36402	1.2	47	11509	12154	13528	1.3	2.69	9063	9478	1.1
77340	HUNTSVILLE	471	25514	28225	32455	2.4	75	8711	9796	11530	2.8	2.35	4826	5479	3.0
77345	HUMBLE	201	22652	27539	32259	4.7	94	7292	8748	10126	4.4	3.15	6410	7703	4.4
77346	HUMBLE	201	27950	32800	37753	3.8	89	9267	10827	12367	3.7	3.03	7950	9290	3.7
77351	LIVINGSTON	373	30445	34022	38376	2.7	78	10923	12292	13982	2.8	2.50	7897	8909	2.9
77354	MAGNOLIA	339	16861	21454	27626	5.8	96	5582	6999	8904	5.5	3.06	4686	5889	5.5
77355	MAGNOLIA	339	12887	15464	19320	4.4	92	4248	5041	6232	4.1	3.07	3475	4120	4.1
77356	MONTGOMERY	339	14246	19418	25772	7.6	98	5899	8003	10542	7.4	2.43	4545	6156	7.4
77357	NEW CANEY	339	17056	19972	24673	3.8	89	5690	6593	8065	3.5	3.02	4544	5248	3.5
77358	NEW WAVERLY	471	4144	4697	5497	3.0	81	1555	1769	2077	3.1	2.58	1120	1273	3.1
77359	OAKHURST	407	258	269	295	1.0	42	105	109	120	0.9	2.47	77	81	1.2
77360	ONALASKA	373	3248	3461	3820	1.5	57	1467	1556	1713	1.4	2.22	1001	1065	1.5
77362	PINEHURST	339	3576	3875	4606	1.9	66	1234	1326	1562	1.7	2.92	1002	1073	1.6
77363	PLANTERSVILLE	185	2150	2401	2751	2.6	77	793	884	1010	2.6	2.71	591	660	2.6
77364	POINTBLANK	407	2719	2913	3249	1.6	60	1204	1289	1437	1.6	2.26	866	930	1.7
77365	PORTER	339	15712	19512	24873	5.2	95	5395	6605	8327	4.9	2.94	4190	5146	5.0
77371	SHEPHERD	407	7638	8923	10441	3.7	88	2736	3194	3737	3.7	2.76	2043	2389	3.8
77372	SPLENDORA	339	9600	11521	14300	4.4	92	3305	3923	4817	4.1	2.94	2611	3100	4.1
77373	SPRING	201	36399	40429	45460	2.5	76	12306	13641	15245	2.5	2.96	9835	10893	2.4
77375	TOMBALL	201	18005	22051	26120	4.9	94	6435	7796	9143	4.6	2.77	4678	5733	4.9
77377	TOMBALL	201	16407	20352	24044	5.2	95	5440	6718	7878	5.1	3.03	4424	5471	5.1
77378	WILLIS	339	10384	12608	15763	4.7	93	3407	4106	5094	4.5	3.04	2639	3173	4.4
77379	SPRING	201	45973	53645	61765	3.7	88	15093	17451	19905	3.5	3.07	12841	14868	3.5
77380	SPRING	339	19320	20711	24812	1.7	60	7745	8237	9776	1.5	2.51	5346	5676	1.4
77381	SPRING	339	34169	39929	49293	3.7	88	11771	13534	16508	3.3	2.92	9535	11024	3.5
77382	SPRING	339	14763	21096	28508	8.8	99	4710	6637	8864	8.4	3.18	4092	5746	8.3
77384	CONROE	339	4600	6429	8649	8.2	99	1618	2256	3018	8.1	2.85	1382	1920	8.0
77385	CONROE	339	9999	12956	16826	6.3	97	3279	4189	5377	5.9	3.09	2770	3535	5.9
77386	SPRING	339	13404	16080	20082	4.4	92	4639	5519	6829	4.2	2.91	3690	4373	4.1
77388	SPRING	201	26632	30096	34069	2.9	81	8934	10066	11322	2.9	2.99	7585	8556	2.9
77389	SPRING	201	13219	15022	16981	3.1	82	4306	4854	5437	2.9	3.09	3666	4141	2.9
77396	HUMBLE	201	23208	26091	29492	2.8	79	6691	7581	8606	3.0	3.09	5346	6055	3.0
77401	BELLAIRE	201	15675	16474	17881	1.2	47	6030	6263	6725	0.9	2.61	4332	4511	1.0
77414	BAY CITY	321	23472	24476	25763	1.0	42	8780	9154	9646	1.0	2.63	6111	6390	1.1
77417	BEASLEY	157	2352	2614	3105	2.5	76	836	918	1076	2.2	2.85	623	684	2.2
77418	BELLVILLE	015	8493	9458	10660	2.6	77	3193	3515	3922	2.3	2.63	2311	2552	2.4
77419	BLESSING	321	1423	1467	1529	0.7	33	497	511	531	0.7	2.87	378	390	0.7
77420	BOLING	481	2151	2285	2418	1.4	55	739	778	818	1.2	2.92	568	600	1.3
77422	BRAZORIA	039	13908	14467	15977	0.9	39	4635	4827	5357	1.0	2.76	3556	3703	1.0
77423	BROOKSHIRE	473	7670	8480	10070	2.4	75	2525	2771	3273	2.2	2.96	1859	2049	2.3
77426	CHAPPELL HILL	477	2363	2412	2491	0.5	25	941	956	983	0.4	2.52	666	678	0.4
77429	CYPRESS	201	35228	42796	50185	4.7	93	12007	14410	16709	4.4	2.97	10047	12162	4.6
77430	DAMON	039	2294	2554	2983	2.6	77	847	934	1082	2.3	2.73	653	723	2.4
77432	DANEVANG	481	347	354	367	0.5	24	88	89	92	0.3	3.98	73	74	0.3
77433	CYPRESS	201	10421	14630	18299	8.3	99	3253	4541	5634	8.2	3.19	2829	3967	8.3
77434	EAGLE LAKE	089	4445	4651	4919	1.1	44	1602	1666	1751	0.9	2.76	1154	1204	1.0
77435	EAST BERNARD	481	6183	6373	6671	0.7	32	2146	2200	2293	0.6	2.85	1620	1665	0.7
77437	EL CAMPO	481	16084	16578	17270	0.7	32	5703	5842	6055	0.6	2.80	4217	4331	0.6
77440	ELMATON	321	505	513	530	0.4	22	206	209	216	0.3	2.45	148	150	0.3
77441	FULSHEAR	157	2704	3125	3787	3.5	86	1003	1143	1366	3.1	2.73	818	936	3.2
77442	GARWOOD	089	2302	2336	2426	0.4	22	892	900	930	0.2	2.60	642	649	0.3
77444	GUY	157	665	718	834	1.8	64	242	259	297	1.6	2.77	185	199	1.7
77445	HEMPSTEAD	473	8734	10747	13492	5.0	94	3182	3872	4816	4.7	2.74	2236	2738	4.9
77447	HOCKLEY	201	9156	10862	12928	4.1	91	3050	3591	4248	3.9	3.01	2474	2916	3.9
77449	KATY	201	38087	48467	58236	5.8	96	11952	15038	17868	5.6	3.21	10005	12607	5.6
77450	KATY	201	48762	59623	71555	4.9	94	15756	19029	22554	4.5	3.13	13549	16481	4.7
77455	LOUISE	481	2409	2423	2500	0.1	16	839	839	861	0.0	2.89	644	645	0.0
77456	MARKHAM	321	2004	2016	2082	0.1	16	703	707	730	0.1	2.85	534	539	0.2
77457	MATAGORDA	321	892	904	933	0.3	20	425	430	444	0.3	2.08	273	278	0.4
77458	MIDFIELD	321	306	317	330	0.8	36	112	115	120	0.6	2.76	86	89	0.8
77459	MISSOURI CITY	157	32842	39236	48551	4.3	91	10742	12534	15237	3.7	3.13	9353	10953	3.8
77461	NEEDVILLE	157	8146	9260	11118	3.1	82	2785	3122	3702	2.7	2.95	2203	2468	2.7
77465	PALACIOS	321	6146	6468	6809	1.2	48	2014	2113	2221	1.1	3.04	1510	1589	1.2
77468	PLEDGER	321	279	260	264	-1.7	0	104	97	98	-1.6	2.68	80	75	-1.5
77469	RICHMOND	157	47110	54693	66040	3.6	87	13814	15991	19288	3.5	3.18	11544	13339	3.5
77471	ROSENBERG	157	28824	32243	38562	2.7	78	9389	10328	12180	2.3	3.10	7243	7983	2.3
77474	SEALY	015	10588	11608	13015	2.2	71	3797	4118	4571	1.9	2.80	2850	3100	2.0
77477	STAFFORD	157	27552	32487	39584	4.0	90	9642	11265	13584	3.7	2.87	7007	8186	3.7
77478	SUGAR LAND	157	49901	58295	71332	3.7	88	16372	18897	22853	3.4	3.06	13644	15731	3.4
77479	SUGAR LAND	157	54986	67517	84377	5.0	94	16385	19845	24511	4.6	3.34	14790	17914	4.6
77480	SWEENY	039	7567	7833	8695	0.8	36	2694	2786	3089	0.8	2.78	2092	2164	0.8
77482	VAN VLECK	321	2531	2593	2721	0.6	28	908	929	974	0.5	2.79	697	715	0.6
77483	WADSWORTH	321	215	216	222	0.1	15	76	76	78	0.0	2.70	53	54	0.4
77484	WALLER	473	13823	15550	18205	2.8	79	3966	4547	5442	3.3	2.81	2929	3354	3.2
77485	WALLIS	015	3405	3515	3907	0.8	34	1243	1269	1395	0.5	2.77	951	972	0.5
77486	WEST COLUMBIA	039	7073	7272	8096	0.7	30	2675	2748	3055	0.6	2.62	1972	2025	0.6
77488	WHARTON	481	14348	15016	15815	1.1	45	5407	5637	5921	1.0	2.58	3713	3888	1.1
77489	MISSOURI CITY	157	32778	34927	40551	1.5	57	10116	10642	12207	1.2	3.27	8523	8953	1.2
77493	KATY	201	15210	16453	18221	1.9	65	4767	5122	5626	1.7	3.20	4018	4319	1.7
77494	KATY	157	10928	14780	19236	7.4	98	3495	4649	5967	6.9	3.17	3004	3985	6.9
77502	PASADENA	201	35355	37041	40400	1.1	45	11534	11930	12865	0.8	3.08	8852	9170	0.8
77503	PASADENA	201	24893	26034	28404	1.1	44	8381	8683	9383	0.8	2.98	6175	6413	0.9
77504	PASADENA	201	19474	21378	23957	2.2	72	7611	8340	9293	2.2	2.52	4974	5479	2.3
77505	PASADENA	201	16759	19764	22864	4.0	90	5522	6471	7425	3.8	3.05	4648	5447	3.8
77506	PASADENA	201	40232	42632	46875	1.4	54	12041	12529	13580	0.9	3.39	9159	9535	1.0
77507	PASADENA	201	190	234	275	5.0	95	66	82	96	5.2	2.72	60	74	5.1
77510	SANTA FE	167	12848	13869	15366	1.8	64	4604	4962	5484	1.8	2.79	3632	3912	1.8
77511	ALVIN	039	42479	47287	54577	2.6	77	14743	16316	18746	2.4	2.89	11220	12434	2.5
77514	ANAHUAC	071	3868	4312	5047	2.6	77	1421	1580	1847	2.5	2.70	1032	1148	2.5
77515	ANGLETON	039	28732	31427	35721	2.1	70	9460	10385	11873	2.2	2.81	7237	7941	2.2
77517	SANTA FE	167	4787	5228	5826	2.1	69	1666	1815	2018	2.0	2.88	1342	1462	2.0
77518	BACLIFF	167	6856	7480	8335	2.1	69	2491	2710	3011	2.0	2.76	1724	1875	2.0
	TEXAS					2.2					2.0	2.77			2.1
	UNITED STATES					1.2					1.3	2.58			1.1

#	POST OFFICE NAME	White 2000	White 2004	Black 2000	Black 2004	Asian/Pacific 2000	Asian/Pacific 2004	% Hispanic Origin 2000	% Hispanic Origin 2004	0-4	5-9	10-14	15-19	20-24	25-44	45-64	65-84	85+	18+	MEDIAN AGE 2004	% 2004 Males	% 2004 Females
77335	GOODRICH	77.2	75.7	15.6	15.8	0.6	0.6	8.9	10.3	6.9	6.7	6.8	6.4	5.9	22.5	26.2	17.0	1.6	75.7	41.0	49.6	50.4
77336	HUFFMAN	94.0	92.7	1.0	1.1	0.7	0.9	6.0	7.8	6.7	6.9	7.9	7.9	6.7	27.4	27.2	8.8	0.6	73.7	36.6	50.6	49.4
77338	HUMBLE	68.6	65.4	16.7	17.4	3.5	3.7	21.8	26.6	8.2	7.6	7.6	6.9	8.8	30.7	22.4	7.1	0.8	72.4	31.8	49.2	50.8
77339	HUMBLE	92.5	91.0	1.9	2.2	2.2	2.6	7.7	10.0	6.7	6.9	7.6	7.0	6.2	27.6	28.9	8.5	0.6	74.6	37.4	49.1	50.9
77340	HUNTSVILLE	72.6	71.1	19.3	19.6	1.2	1.3	13.0	15.6	5.2	4.7	4.5	10.6	21.7	25.4	17.6	9.0	1.4	82.9	27.2	53.8	46.2
77345	HUMBLE	93.5	92.1	1.4	1.6	2.9	3.5	5.2	6.8	6.5	8.2	10.9	9.0	4.5	23.6	31.9	4.7	0.6	68.1	38.5	49.7	50.3
77346	HUMBLE	83.8	81.5	8.0	8.8	2.9	3.3	10.1	12.6	7.8	8.0	8.6	7.5	6.1	31.0	26.2	4.4	0.3	70.9	34.1	49.2	50.8
77351	LIVINGSTON	80.7	79.3	12.4	12.9	0.4	0.5	8.6	10.2	5.7	5.6	5.9	5.8	6.7	26.5	25.3	16.6	2.0	79.2	40.5	52.9	47.1
77354	MAGNOLIA	91.8	90.4	2.5	2.7	0.4	0.4	9.3	11.5	8.3	8.2	8.3	7.1	6.5	30.5	24.6	6.1	0.4	70.8	33.7	49.9	50.1
77355	MAGNOLIA	92.8	91.4	0.7	0.9	0.2	0.3	11.5	14.0	7.4	7.6	8.8	8.0	7.0	28.4	25.8	6.7	0.5	71.3	34.9	49.4	50.6
77356	MONTGOMERY	93.2	92.9	4.0	4.0	0.7	0.8	3.9	4.9	4.6	5.0	5.8	5.3	4.1	21.7	35.0	17.4	1.1	81.2	47.2	49.8	50.2
77357	NEW CANEY	90.9	89.2	1.7	1.9	0.3	0.4	10.7	13.3	8.8	8.1	8.2	7.6	8.1	27.6	23.6	7.6	0.5	70.2	32.1	49.9	50.1
77358	NEW WAVERLY	76.1	74.7	18.9	19.8	0.4	0.5	6.4	7.2	6.5	6.7	7.3	8.6	6.0	23.8	26.5	13.2	1.5	73.7	38.5	50.3	49.7
77359	OAKHURST	78.7	77.3	19.4	20.8	0.0	0.0	1.9	1.9	5.6	6.0	6.3	6.0	4.8	22.3	32.0	15.2	1.9	78.8	44.2	50.9	49.1
77360	ONALASKA	95.4	94.7	2.2	2.4	0.3	0.3	3.0	3.7	4.4	4.3	4.9	5.2	5.3	17.9	30.5	26.0	1.8	83.4	51.3	48.3	51.7
77362	PINEHURST	94.6	93.5	0.8	0.9	0.2	0.2	7.8	9.6	6.0	7.1	8.8	8.1	7.2	26.9	27.8	7.6	0.7	72.9	36.6	49.7	50.3
77363	PLANTERSVILLE	89.9	88.4	4.8	5.3	0.4	0.3	6.8	8.5	6.3	6.4	6.8	6.2	7.1	27.3	29.2	9.8	1.1	76.8	39.0	49.8	50.2
77364	POINTBLANK	83.4	82.3	14.6	15.6	0.2	0.1	2.4	2.7	4.1	4.5	4.9	4.9	4.6	18.1	32.8	24.3	1.8	83.5	51.6	50.0	50.1
77365	PORTER	89.1	86.7	1.3	1.5	0.6	0.7	15.9	19.5	8.8	8.1	8.2	7.2	7.5	28.7	22.8	8.0	0.7	70.6	32.5	49.4	50.6
77371	SHEPHERD	84.0	83.0	10.3	10.6	0.5	0.6	7.6	8.7	7.3	7.0	8.0	7.9	6.9	25.4	24.7	11.4	1.4	72.7	36.6	50.0	50.0
77372	SPLENDORA	93.6	92.5	0.3	0.3	0.4	0.4	8.4	10.3	8.3	8.1	8.6	8.1	7.8	27.3	23.2	8.0	0.6	70.0	32.1	49.5	50.5
77373	SPRING	83.0	80.6	7.0	7.6	1.6	1.8	16.1	19.9	7.5	7.4	8.3	7.8	7.3	31.5	24.7	5.2	0.4	72.0	33.0	48.5	51.5
77375	TOMBALL	86.4	83.3	5.3	6.2	1.0	1.2	11.9	15.4	8.1	7.4	7.2	7.4	7.6	30.3	21.9	8.1	2.1	72.9	33.3	48.6	51.4
77377	TOMBALL	88.3	85.9	2.2	2.6	2.2	2.8	11.9	14.8	8.3	8.4	8.6	7.0	6.1	31.3	24.7	5.2	0.5	70.4	33.6	50.0	50.1
77378	WILLIS	78.0	76.1	11.0	11.0	0.3	0.3	17.7	20.9	8.4	7.9	8.3	7.9	8.1	28.7	22.0	7.8	0.8	70.5	31.8	50.4	49.6
77379	SPRING	85.8	83.5	4.0	4.4	5.2	5.9	8.9	11.3	6.6	7.9	9.8	8.8	5.3	27.3	28.8	5.0	0.4	69.8	36.4	49.6	50.4
77380	SPRING	89.6	87.9	2.9	3.3	2.8	3.1	9.3	11.4	6.4	6.3	7.3	7.3	7.3	27.9	28.3	8.3	0.9	75.6	36.2	48.0	52.0
77381	SPRING	92.9	91.9	1.6	1.9	2.6	3.0	6.0	7.3	6.5	8.2	10.2	8.6	4.8	23.6	30.2	6.5	1.4	69.2	38.9	48.1	51.9
77382	SPRING	92.7	91.5	1.2	1.4	3.4	3.9	6.4	7.9	11.1	11.5	10.3	6.1	2.7	33.9	21.0	3.3	0.2	62.9	33.7	50.1	49.9
77384	CONROE	94.5	93.5	1.2	1.3	1.1	1.3	6.4	7.7	6.7	7.1	7.9	6.4	4.9	27.2	29.0	9.9	0.8	74.3	39.7	49.9	50.1
77385	CONROE	85.9	83.8	6.5	7.3	1.6	1.7	12.4	15.0	8.5	8.4	8.4	7.3	6.1	30.5	23.6	6.8	0.5	70.0	33.8	49.6	50.4
77386	SPRING	87.4	85.1	3.2	3.6	1.5	1.8	13.6	16.7	9.2	8.2	7.1	6.5	8.5	32.9	21.4	5.8	0.4	71.7	32.1	50.2	49.8
77388	SPRING	87.5	85.4	4.0	4.4	3.6	4.1	10.7	13.7	7.2	7.7	8.6	7.6	5.9	28.4	28.2	5.9	0.5	71.6	36.1	49.3	50.7
77389	SPRING	91.7	89.9	1.9	2.3	0.7	0.9	10.3	13.1	7.7	8.1	9.3	8.0	6.0	28.7	25.5	6.2	0.4	69.7	34.6	49.1	50.9
77396	HUMBLE	57.8	54.6	24.2	25.1	2.0	2.1	25.2	29.3	7.8	7.5	7.9	8.4	9.3	34.3	19.8	4.6	0.5	72.1	30.4	54.4	45.7
77401	BELLAIRE	89.1	87.1	0.8	1.0	6.4	7.5	7.8	10.0	6.9	8.0	8.3	6.3	3.9	24.5	30.7	9.2	2.3	72.7	40.8	48.4	51.6
77414	BAY CITY	65.1	63.2	16.4	16.3	0.9	1.0	30.2	33.6	7.6	7.1	7.8	7.7	8.5	25.0	23.9	10.8	1.6	72.8	34.5	49.3	50.7
77417	BEASLEY	49.8	47.5	30.2	29.8	0.5	0.5	32.2	36.9	7.7	7.8	8.2	7.2	6.8	26.4	24.2	10.4	1.3	71.9	34.9	50.2	49.9
77418	BELLVILLE	83.2	81.5	10.4	11.0	0.3	0.4	10.3	12.2	5.9	6.1	7.3	7.4	6.5	23.5	26.8	13.6	2.9	76.0	40.4	48.9	51.1
77419	BLESSING	81.6	79.4	3.0	3.0	0.0	0.0	33.5	38.2	7.2	7.5	9.1	7.4	6.2	26.8	23.0	11.2	1.6	71.6	36.0	52.8	47.2
77420	BOLING	73.4	71.2	6.7	6.9	0.1	0.0	42.0	46.0	6.5	6.9	7.8	7.7	8.4	26.3	24.7	10.6	1.2	73.9	35.6	51.6	48.4
77422	BRAZORIA	74.5	72.8	15.6	16.0	0.4	0.4	12.7	14.8	6.7	6.8	7.4	8.9	8.7	26.5	24.5	9.6	0.9	74.5	34.6	53.2	46.8
77423	BROOKSHIRE	51.1	48.4	27.1	27.9	0.4	0.4	31.5	34.6	8.5	7.6	7.3	7.6	7.5	28.5	23.0	9.0	1.0	72.1	33.2	50.0	50.0
77426	CHAPPELL HILL	68.6	67.4	28.1	28.8	0.4	0.5	4.7	5.5	4.9	5.5	7.5	6.8	5.5	22.3	28.4	17.2	1.9	77.9	43.4	49.2	50.8
77429	CYPRESS	88.9	86.9	3.2	3.5	2.6	3.0	9.6	12.0	8.6	8.9	8.2	7.0	5.5	30.8	26.1	4.6	0.3	69.8	35.0	49.7	50.3
77430	DAMON	88.5	86.8	1.3	1.3	0.5	0.6	15.5	18.4	6.1	6.6	7.4	6.9	6.2	25.8	28.7	11.7	0.7	75.7	39.8	51.5	48.5
77432	DANEVANG	75.2	72.9	3.5	3.4	0.6	0.6	43.2	48.0	8.8	7.9	8.2	8.2	8.2	27.1	21.2	9.0	1.4	70.6	32.5	52.0	48.0
77433	CYPRESS	81.6	79.6	5.4	5.5	3.6	4.1	16.0	18.8	11.5	11.3	9.3	7.1	4.4	35.0	18.2	2.9	0.2	62.8	30.9	50.3	49.8
77434	EAGLE LAKE	55.6	53.9	23.5	23.3	0.0	0.0	39.7	43.6	8.2	7.6	7.6	7.5	7.5	23.7	23.6	12.2	2.2	72.0	35.0	48.6	51.4
77435	EAST BERNARD	69.7	67.8	18.3	18.4	0.3	0.4	19.8	22.7	6.8	7.1	7.6	7.3	6.9	25.5	25.8	11.6	1.5	74.2	37.4	50.6	49.4
77437	EL CAMPO	73.4	71.8	9.0	8.8	0.3	0.3	36.5	40.3	8.0	7.5	7.9	7.4	7.6	25.7	22.5	11.5	1.9	71.9	34.9	49.2	50.8
77440	ELMATON	90.1	88.7	1.0	1.0	0.0	0.0	14.7	17.5	5.1	5.5	6.8	7.2	6.2	25.5	27.1	15.2	1.4	78.4	41.9	52.4	47.6
77441	FULSHEAR	76.0	73.2	14.5	15.8	0.9	1.0	12.4	14.6	5.3	6.2	7.5	6.7	4.9	20.9	33.7	13.8	1.0	76.9	44.0	49.3	50.8
77442	GARWOOD	76.7	74.5	13.3	13.9	0.1	0.1	16.8	19.7	6.0	6.9	7.7	7.4	5.4	22.7	24.1	17.5	2.4	75.0	40.8	51.2	48.8
77444	GUY	83.8	81.3	6.2	6.7	0.2	0.3	15.8	18.9	6.8	7.0	7.9	7.1	6.6	25.8	27.2	10.7	1.0	74.1	38.0	50.0	50.0
77445	HEMPSTEAD	52.4	48.9	33.8	35.4	0.4	0.4	20.4	23.2	7.4	7.1	7.6	7.1	8.8	28.4	22.2	10.0	1.5	73.8	32.7	50.4	49.6
77447	HOCKLEY	81.6	79.5	8.5	8.9	0.5	0.5	16.0	19.3	8.0	8.2	8.6	7.3	6.4	29.9	24.8	6.2	0.7	70.7	33.5	50.1	49.9
77449	KATY	73.0	69.0	8.7	9.5	3.8	4.3	25.3	30.5	9.7	9.3	9.5	8.0	6.5	34.0	19.2	3.4	0.4	66.5	30.6	49.0	51.0
77450	KATY	85.5	83.0	3.3	3.8	6.2	7.4	10.6	13.0	7.6	8.4	9.8	8.4	5.6	28.3	27.5	4.1	0.3	68.7	34.9	48.9	51.1
77455	LOUISE	84.1	82.1	3.5	3.6	0.0	0.0	28.4	32.4	7.1	7.1	9.0	7.4	7.5	27.5	21.8	11.3	1.3	72.3	34.8	51.8	48.2
77456	MARKHAM	85.1	83.9	5.8	5.7	0.1	0.1	27.4	31.1	6.6	7.0	8.7	7.8	7.0	26.6	24.6	10.6	1.1	72.9	36.1	51.0	49.0
77457	MATAGORDA	88.5	87.2	2.6	2.7	0.1	0.1	8.5	10.2	4.4	4.9	5.5	5.3	5.3	20.7	35.6	16.9	1.3	82.1	47.0	51.6	48.5
77458	MIDFIELD	79.7	77.3	3.6	3.5	0.0	0.0	37.6	42.6	7.9	8.2	9.2	7.6	6.3	27.1	21.8	10.4	1.6	70.4	34.4	52.7	47.3
77459	MISSOURI CITY	60.3	56.2	18.8	20.3	13.9	15.4	12.1	14.1	7.9	8.3	8.1	7.1	5.8	27.8	28.3	6.3	0.5	71.2	36.3	49.2	50.9
77461	NEEDVILLE	79.4	76.2	6.5	6.8	0.5	0.5	23.4	28.2	6.9	7.0	8.2	7.8	7.4	27.1	25.5	8.8	1.2	73.0	35.1	49.6	50.4
77465	PALACIOS	60.4	57.9	4.2	4.0	11.6	12.3	47.1	51.0	9.9	8.1	9.3	8.8	7.4	24.1	20.9	10.3	1.3	67.0	30.7	50.3	49.7
77468	PLEDGER	77.4	76.5	16.9	17.3	0.0	0.0	14.0	16.2	4.6	5.0	7.3	9.6	8.9	25.4	27.7	10.4	1.2	77.7	38.1	51.5	48.5
77469	RICHMOND	68.5	66.0	12.2	12.7	2.9	3.3	28.6	32.0	7.7	8.0	8.3	7.5	6.8	30.9	24.4	5.8	0.6	71.4	33.9	52.4	47.6
77471	ROSENBERG	67.6	65.0	7.7	7.8	0.4	0.4	51.9	57.1	8.6	8.1	8.0	7.7	7.9	29.2	21.0	8.5	1.1	70.6	31.5	49.5	50.5
77474	SEALY	77.0	75.3	11.6	11.7	0.3	0.4	21.7	24.9	7.6	7.4	7.6	6.9	7.0	26.3	25.1	10.5	1.7	73.1	36.1	49.3	50.8
77477	STAFFORD	49.8	46.4	16.8	17.7	18.5	19.4	25.4	28.4	7.5	7.2	7.6	7.2	7.9	33.0	23.3	5.8	0.5	73.2	32.2	49.0	51.0
77478	SUGAR LAND	62.2	58.8	8.9	9.8	20.2	21.4	14.8	17.5	7.2	7.6	8.1	7.4	6.2	28.4	27.1	7.0	0.9	72.3	36.0	48.8	51.2
77479	SUGAR LAND	65.0	61.3	6.4	7.2	23.6	25.7	7.6	9.2	8.0	9.3	10.0	8.2	5.2	28.8	26.4	3.7	0.3	66.9	34.7	50.5	49.5
77480	SWEENY	79.0	77.1	13.1	13.6	0.3	0.3	11.6	13.9	6.6	6.9	8.0	7.6	7.2	24.5	25.9	11.8	1.5	73.8	37.1	49.1	50.9
77482	VAN VLECK	74.8	73.3	16.4	16.4	0.1	0.2	20.9	24.6	5.8	5.9	7.4	8.4	7.6	24.8	26.4	12.5	1.4	76.0	38.9	49.9	50.1
77483	WADSWORTH	82.8	80.1	3.7	4.2	0.0	0.0	15.8	18.5	5.1	6.0	7.9	7.9	7.4	25.5	28.7	10.2	1.4	75.9	40.0	56.0	44.0
77484	WALLER	57.3	56.3	33.8	33.2	0.5	0.6	14.5	17.4	6.0	5.8	6.2	13.7	16.5	24.2	19.7	7.1	0.8	78.0	26.3	49.4	50.6
77485	WALLIS	78.1	75.6	9.9	10.4	0.3	0.3	19.3	22.6	7.0	7.3	7.5	7.3	6.1	25.0	27.6	10.9	1.4	73.7	38.4	49.9	50.1
77486	WEST COLUMBIA	78.4	76.5	13.5	14.0	0.4	0.3	13.8	16.2	6.7	6.7	7.6	7.2	7.0	23.8	26.9	12.4	1.8	74.6	38.7	48.0	52.0
77488	WHARTON	60.6	58.9	23.5	23.4	0.6	0.7	28.9	32.4	6.8	6.7	7.6	7.3	7.8	25.2	23.9	12.3	2.4	74.5	36.2	48.6	51.4
77489	MISSOURI CITY	12.9	12.2	76.4	76.4	2.9	3.0	11.4	12.7	6.9	7.4	8.9	9.1	8.1	27.5	27.9	3.9	0.3	71.1	32.6	47.2	52.8
77493	KATY	83.0	80.1	3.7	4.0	0.8	0.9	25.2	30.4	8.3	8.2	8.8	7.8	7.5	29.4	23.3	6.1	0.8	70.0	32.2	50.2	49.9
77494	KATY	86.5	84.9	4.6	4.9	4.1	4.7	9.1	10.9	7.6	8.4	9.8	8.7	5.9	27.0	27.4	4.6	0.6	68.6	35.3	49.0	51.0
77502	PASADENA	71.4	67.6	1.4	1.5	0.9	0.9	50.6	57.7	9.2	8.4	8.3	7.4	8.1	28.4	19.2	9.9	1.0	69.7	30.4	49.4	50.6
77503	PASADENA	73.0	69.2	2.0	2.1	1.1	1.1	46.5	53.6	9.8	8.5	8.3	7.7	9.2	30.8	18.6	6.6	0.6	69.0	28.6	49.9	50.1
77504	PASADENA	78.3	75.0	2.0	2.1	2.4	2.6	32.9	38.6	8.0	7.1	6.9	6.7	8.5	31.3	21.6	8.3	1.6	74.1	32.0	48.7	51.3
77505	PASADENA	85.6	82.7	0.8	0.9	4.8	5.3	19.5	25.3	7.7	7.6	8.4	8.0	7.3	30.9	24.3	5.5	0.3	71.4	33.1	49.2	50.8
77506	PASADENA	58.9	56.1	1.6	1.5	0.9	0.9	73.8	78.8	11.6	10.0	9.3	8.1	9.2	31.0	15.0	5.2	0.6	64.4	26.1	51.3	48.7
77507	PASADENA	87.4	85.0	5.3	6.0	4.2	5.1	8.4	11.1	6.4	7.7	6.8	9.8	3.9	24.4	29.9	10.7	0.4	71.4	40.2	50.0	50.0
77510	SANTA FE	94.2	93.1	0.5	0.6	0.3	0.4	10.6	13.1	6.9	7.0	7.9	7.4	6.6	27.9	25.9	9.6	0.8	73.6	36.5	49.5	50.5
77511	ALVIN	82.2	79.8	1.8	1.9	0.9	0.9	27.5	31.7	8.4	7.9	8.0	7.5	7.9	28.9	22.9	7.8	0.8	71.2	32.3	50.1	49.9
77514	ANAHUAC	63.9	61.0	17.7	18.0	2.6	3.0	20.4	23.1	6.1	6.3	7.0	6.5	6.8	25.7	27.8	12.5	1.4	76.6	39.0	50.9	49.1
77515	ANGLETON	75.0	73.2	11.9	12.0	1.0	0.9	23.4	26.8	7.2	6.9	7.6	7.5	7.3	30.0	24.1	8.3	1.1	73.7	35.0	52.5	47.5
77517	SANTA FE	93.7	92.4	0.4	0.5	0.3	0.3	11.3	14.0	6.9	7.1	7.7	7.1	6.4	27.7	27.6	8.9	0.6	73.9	37.4	50.2	49.8
77518	BACLIFF	83.5	80.9	1.6	1.7	2.8	3.2	22.6	26.6	8.3	7.8	7.8	6.6	6.9	29.9	24.1	7.9	0.6	72.2	34.0	52.4	47.6
	TEXAS	71.0	69.5	11.5	11.4	2.8	3.1	32.0	34.6	7.9	7.5	7.7	7.5	8.1	29.6	21.9	8.7	1.2	72.6	32.9	49.7	50.3
	UNITED STATES	75.1	73.6	12.3	12.5	3.8	4.2	12.5	14.1	6.9	6.7	7.2	7.0	7.3	28.6	23.8	10.8	1.7	75.1	36.0	49.1	50.9

INCOME

#	POST OFFICE NAME	2004 Per Capita Income	2004 HH Income Base	2004 Household Income Distribution (%): Less than $25,000	$25,000 to $49,999	$50,000 to $99,999	$100,000 to $149,999	$150,000 or More	Median Household Income: 2004	2009	2004 National Centile	2004 State Centile	2004 Home Value Base	2004 Home Value Distribution (%): Less than $50,000	$50,000 to $89,999	$90,000 to $174,999	$175,000 to $399,999	$400,000 or More	2004 Median Home Value
77335	GOODRICH	16117	866	41.3	33.0	21.3	2.7	1.7	30596	35472	14	17	720	56.5	22.2	17.5	3.1	0.7	45155
77336	HUFFMAN	25238	3422	17.9	21.1	39.5	16.0	5.5	61325	72721	86	88	2897	21.9	33.1	34.4	10.0	0.7	84355
77338	HUMBLE	20453	7874	23.2	28.3	35.9	10.5	2.2	48524	57034	69	74	4402	7.6	41.4	44.9	5.2	0.9	90617
77339	HUMBLE	37198	12154	8.7	16.9	38.9	21.2	14.3	78432	95376	95	95	9220	0.8	8.1	67.3	20.4	3.4	137646
77340	HUNTSVILLE	20018	9796	37.4	27.9	23.4	7.6	3.8	34424	40106	25	31	5013	27.0	21.9	33.0	16.4	1.6	91786
77345	HUMBLE	48396	8748	5.3	8.6	26.8	28.2	31.1	114429	137120	99	99	7980	1.2	2.4	28.0	59.2	9.2	211738
77346	HUMBLE	32974	10827	6.0	13.3	43.5	25.6	11.6	83836	102682	96	97	9526	0.5	11.1	61.1	26.2	1.2	138000
77351	LIVINGSTON	19613	12292	34.2	31.3	25.8	5.7	3.1	36046	41454	32	38	9805	39.1	28.0	24.5	7.1	1.3	65614
77354	MAGNOLIA	27292	6999	14.6	21.7	37.1	16.5	10.2	64724	78033	88	90	6330	16.4	21.3	29.9	25.2	7.1	117840
77355	MAGNOLIA	24643	5041	16.1	22.9	37.5	14.8	8.8	60927	71342	85	87	4246	15.9	23.5	35.4	21.7	3.5	110018
77356	MONTGOMERY	47967	8003	11.5	18.2	36.2	16.6	17.5	74053	91484	93	94	6913	8.6	10.7	31.4	33.5	15.9	172917
77357	NEW CANEY	18351	6593	25.4	30.8	31.5	9.0	3.5	44452	53805	60	67	5080	37.6	30.0	27.2	4.9	0.3	64321
77358	NEW WAVERLY	21225	1769	34.1	28.6	26.1	6.6	4.6	38118	44932	40	47	1429	32.1	26.9	26.2	12.9	1.9	74714
77359	OAKHURST	20968	109	33.9	34.9	22.0	4.6	4.6	37336	43211	37	44	85	37.7	29.4	24.7	8.2	0.0	65625
77360	ONALASKA	18807	1556	39.8	27.8	26.1	5.8	0.6	31810	36134	17	22	1338	42.9	30.4	19.6	6.7	0.4	58879
77362	PINEHURST	26020	1326	17.6	20.0	37.5	15.8	9.1	62530	73499	87	88	1172	21.9	15.9	34.6	22.9	4.8	116975
77363	PLANTERSVILLE	22356	884	28.1	32.4	26.5	6.9	6.2	38743	44482	42	50	761	34.8	25.2	35.0	4.2	0.8	72647
77364	POINTBLANK	20131	1289	34.9	34.8	23.4	4.4	2.5	35405	40199	29	35	1084	34.2	30.2	27.6	8.0	0.0	71638
77365	PORTER	19767	6605	21.5	33.3	33.6	8.5	3.0	45655	55113	63	69	5109	30.9	32.8	31.8	4.3	0.3	76492
77371	SHEPHERD	14613	3194	40.8	30.3	24.1	3.8	1.1	32699	37189	20	24	2590	49.8	27.0	19.2	2.8	1.2	50298
77372	SPLENDORA	17565	3923	25.9	33.2	31.6	7.4	1.9	43247	51660	57	65	3168	42.6	30.9	23.1	3.3	0.1	60149
77373	SPRING	24876	13641	9.9	22.6	46.4	16.4	4.7	64774	76621	88	90	10571	3.4	50.0	41.4	4.6	0.5	88017
77375	TOMBALL	26299	7796	17.5	26.0	35.2	14.6	6.7	56386	67728	81	84	5491	15.8	21.1	42.2	17.5	3.5	108583
77377	TOMBALL	32246	6718	9.8	19.5	36.3	22.1	12.2	76011	92951	94	94	5809	8.4	12.5	36.4	36.8	6.0	157949
77378	WILLIS	17338	4106	26.6	34.8	28.5	7.0	3.0	41090	49117	50	58	3130	32.1	39.2	21.3	6.5	1.0	68474
77379	SPRING	37883	17451	7.0	12.7	33.3	24.5	22.5	94132	112194	98	98	14859	2.1	5.8	47.8	38.5	5.9	163495
77380	SPRING	40491	8237	16.9	21.7	31.2	14.2	16.0	64506	78055	88	90	4932	0.9	13.4	53.4	21.8	10.6	131620
77381	SPRING	47704	13534	11.6	10.8	24.7	24.1	28.8	104263	125731	98	98	11161	0.7	3.1	35.9	44.1	16.2	201644
77382	SPRING	47956	6637	3.9	6.4	24.6	31.0	34.2	121261	148373	99	100	6190	1.0	1.5	16.6	67.2	13.8	236149
77384	CONROE	31511	2256	13.5	16.3	37.0	21.7	11.5	75764	90092	94	94	2096	6.3	11.7	42.6	34.5	4.9	156058
77385	CONROE	24529	4189	14.0	22.6	38.4	18.0	7.0	64660	76647	88	90	3653	13.6	23.1	50.3	12.8	0.3	109562
77386	SPRING	27414	5519	10.9	22.1	42.2	16.9	8.0	65863	78361	89	90	3972	5.0	15.7	64.9	14.2	0.3	120702
77388	SPRING	31552	10066	6.6	16.4	41.1	24.1	11.9	80171	100328	95	96	8885	2.1	11.5	64.2	21.3	0.9	128725
77389	SPRING	30499	4854	8.6	20.4	37.2	21.7	12.2	76427	91879	94	94	4422	15.8	20.4	39.0	21.4	3.5	115290
77396	HUMBLE	19326	7581	17.8	28.9	38.5	12.2	2.7	52782	61712	77	81	5869	24.0	36.8	36.5	2.0	0.8	79185
77401	BELLAIRE	57616	6263	6.9	13.0	26.0	20.7	33.5	106736	132701	99	99	5155	1.2	1.6	19.8	42.6	34.8	267887
77414	BAY CITY	18402	9154	35.2	28.9	25.1	8.4	2.5	37039	43099	36	42	5532	29.9	38.1	26.1	5.2	0.7	73693
77417	BEASLEY	18084	918	30.4	27.2	30.7	9.2	2.5	41309	51536	51	59	730	36.6	31.5	24.8	5.9	1.2	65357
77418	BELLVILLE	21603	3515	24.3	31.3	30.0	11.3	3.1	44473	51964	60	67	2760	18.2	17.1	33.6	24.8	6.3	115946
77419	BLESSING	17656	511	36.6	29.9	24.1	6.3	3.1	35176	41493	28	34	416	35.3	33.9	24.0	6.5	0.2	61957
77420	BOLING	17695	778	31.8	31.9	27.5	4.9	4.0	36995	43603	35	42	617	43.1	31.9	19.5	3.4	2.1	56159
77422	BRAZORIA	20912	4827	24.4	26.7	34.2	11.6	3.0	48444	56810	69	74	3930	29.8	34.2	25.5	9.9	0.7	73024
77423	BROOKSHIRE	18636	2771	30.2	27.0	27.5	11.2	4.0	41278	49591	51	59	2022	37.4	21.9	21.9	14.4	4.5	69752
77426	CHAPPELL HILL	21153	956	35.4	22.7	27.7	10.8	3.5	38277	43838	40	48	790	28.6	9.4	28.6	29.0	4.4	119663
77429	CYPRESS	37875	14410	7.4	15.0	33.8	24.6	19.3	89258	110602	97	97	12741	2.3	10.0	46.2	35.2	6.3	151046
77430	DAMON	23481	934	20.1	26.2	37.6	13.3	2.8	53104	62958	77	81	801	27.6	22.7	29.6	18.4	1.8	89342
77432	DANEVANG	12236	89	29.2	38.2	21.4	7.9	3.4	40569	46573	48	56	71	42.3	23.9	23.9	8.5	1.4	70833
77433	CYPRESS	30065	4541	6.0	15.1	41.0	27.0	10.9	82308	104274	96	97	4175	3.6	17.3	48.0	30.0	1.1	139432
77434	EAGLE LAKE	15924	1666	37.1	32.1	23.8	3.2	3.8	32365	37935	19	23	1181	48.5	31.3	13.0	5.9	1.2	52011
77435	EAST BERNARD	18972	2200	28.8	30.2	29.0	9.2	2.9	42238	49711	54	62	1751	32.4	26.7	30.6	7.7	2.6	74960
77437	EL CAMPO	16977	5842	34.5	30.1	25.1	7.5	2.7	36773	42407	33	39	4099	34.4	33.5	23.0	8.4	0.8	69815
77440	ELMATON	23416	209	24.4	33.5	27.3	11.0	3.8	42540	50000	55	63	177	35.0	23.2	23.2	17.0	1.7	69286
77441	FULSHEAR	39976	1143	13.8	15.2	28.4	19.0	23.5	83556	101587	96	97	1006	12.6	7.7	17.0	44.3	18.4	228571
77442	GARWOOD	17517	900	43.1	30.4	19.4	4.4	2.6	30000	33933	12	15	733	44.1	29.2	22.0	4.5	0.3	60730
77444	GUY	22600	259	22.4	23.2	38.6	10.8	5.0	52891	62668	77	81	218	23.4	30.3	28.0	16.1	2.3	84667
77445	HEMPSTEAD	18126	3872	37.5	23.5	27.5	7.9	3.6	38839	46607	42	51	2702	27.1	27.5	26.4	15.4	3.5	81975
77447	HOCKLEY	23418	3591	17.2	25.4	36.0	15.6	5.8	57695	67638	82	85	3012	16.1	29.8	35.4	15.3	3.4	99118
77449	KATY	23735	15038	9.5	22.3	45.0	17.9	5.3	66867	79529	90	91	12769	4.9	31.4	59.3	4.3	0.2	102545
77450	KATY	38718	19029	5.7	11.6	32.3	28.5	22.0	100426	119904	98	98	16517	0.4	8.5	44.0	41.7	5.4	169298
77455	LOUISE	17654	839	29.9	29.3	29.6	8.9	2.3	42833	49738	56	64	647	27.7	32.0	26.6	13.3	0.5	76532
77456	MARKHAM	19892	707	20.4	31.4	37.1	9.3	1.8	47867	56718	68	73	573	42.9	34.7	18.5	3.7	0.2	57232
77457	MATAGORDA	23371	430	37.7	25.4	23.3	10.5	3.3	37341	43445	37	44	352	33.8	29.6	26.4	10.2	0.0	71111
77458	MIDFIELD	17876	115	39.1	29.6	23.5	5.2	2.6	32349	38912	19	23	93	35.5	36.6	23.7	4.3	0.0	61250
77459	MISSOURI CITY	36245	12534	6.2	12.3	35.0	27.2	19.3	93483	109608	97	98	11575	4.3	7.1	44.1	40.9	3.8	166204
77461	NEEDVILLE	21670	3122	19.3	25.0	39.2	12.9	3.7	54664	63945	79	83	2519	19.7	29.5	36.6	13.1	1.2	91090
77465	PALACIOS	15978	2113	37.5	27.6	22.8	10.6	1.5	35925	41647	31	37	1521	42.3	28.3	18.3	11.2	0.0	61813
77468	PLEDGER	18213	97	20.6	32.0	40.2	7.2	0.0	45776	53000	63	70	83	26.5	55.4	13.3	4.8	0.0	71471
77469	RICHMOND	26940	15991	13.8	20.2	35.2	17.8	13.1	68767	80242	91	92	12359	11.5	14.8	43.3	25.3	5.1	132984
77471	ROSENBERG	18052	10328	25.8	30.2	32.2	8.7	3.1	43253	52286	57	65	6510	25.0	36.2	31.5	5.9	1.5	78792
77474	SEALY	21033	4118	26.4	28.4	32.3	8.4	4.5	44421	52274	60	67	3178	18.3	28.5	33.1	16.9	3.3	95543
77477	STAFFORD	25035	11265	14.4	26.0	38.1	15.9	5.7	60642	72079	85	87	6490	8.2	16.9	60.7	13.9	0.3	112395
77478	SUGAR LAND	31259	18897	9.6	17.1	38.0	21.3	14.1	77499	91104	94	95	15636	2.4	14.0	45.4	33.9	4.4	142463
77479	SUGAR LAND	40808	19845	5.0	10.4	29.9	27.0	27.7	106202	123331	99	99	18133	1.7	4.0	30.6	52.1	11.7	208713
77480	SWEENY	19880	2786	26.9	25.1	35.3	10.7	2.1	47685	55885	68	73	2173	27.5	32.2	32.8	7.1	0.5	77943
77482	VAN VLECK	19934	929	30.4	26.5	30.4	9.7	3.1	39736	46425	45	53	779	34.3	41.6	20.0	4.1	0.0	66570
77483	WADSWORTH	15338	76	50.0	22.4	14.5	10.5	2.6	25000	27322	5	6	62	33.9	37.1	22.6	6.5	0.0	65000
77484	WALLER	20299	4547	25.2	26.9	31.1	12.3	4.5	47758	56249	68	73	3382	20.4	24.2	32.6	19.0	3.8	99289
77485	WALLIS	23982	1269	25.9	26.3	28.4	11.4	8.1	47906	56938	68	73	1064	21.6	21.7	34.2	19.0	3.5	100305
77486	WEST COLUMBIA	21052	2748	28.8	26.0	31.7	10.0	3.5	43801	51558	58	66	1912	19.5	36.8	33.7	9.8	0.2	81946
77488	WHARTON	18359	5637	37.8	27.2	26.5	5.6	2.9	34221	40023	25	30	3723	36.4	30.8	25.9	5.6	1.3	67991
77489	MISSOURI CITY	21474	10642	11.4	26.6	41.2	17.0	3.8	61262	70565	86	88	8872	4.5	43.5	49.8	2.2	0.1	91297
77493	KATY	24110	5122	15.1	23.0	35.7	18.7	7.6	63462	75224	87	89	4210	8.1	31.1	47.5	12.6	0.8	100480
77494	KATY	34894	4649	8.2	12.4	30.8	26.0	22.6	97115	113943	98	98	4109	2.2	2.9	29.1	61.4	4.5	201784
77502	PASADENA	16897	11930	26.3	32.1	31.7	7.5	2.3	42653	50404	55	63	7639	19.2	53.2	26.7	1.0	0.0	75012
77503	PASADENA	16082	8683	29.5	31.6	31.7	5.5	1.8	40330	46884	47	55	4762	17.1	59.9	21.3	1.4	0.3	73194
77504	PASADENA	23606	8340	24.2	32.3	29.8	10.0	3.7	43312	52099	57	65	3837	21.2	22.2	46.4	9.6	0.6	97137
77505	PASADENA	28234	6471	9.8	14.7	42.9	25.0	7.7	77072	95509	94	95	5497	5.7	15.0	58.6	19.7	0.9	120310
77506	PASADENA	11988	12529	36.5	38.0	20.9	3.2	1.4	32737	37689	20	24	5027	46.7	47.2	5.0	1.0	0.2	51499
77507	PASADENA	44859	82	4.9	9.8	31.7	26.8	26.8	105073	125000	99	99	80	0.0	0.0	32.5	67.5	0.0	187963
77510	SANTA FE	24490	4962	19.2	24.3	36.9	14.5	5.1	56964	66777	82	84	4111	18.5	22.9	42.9	14.2	1.5	101342
77511	ALVIN	21125	16316	22.6	27.1	36.1	10.7	3.5	50282	59067	72	78	11309	26.4	27.2	35.5	10.2	0.6	84753
77514	ANAHUAC	20715	1580	34.6	23.6	28.4	10.4	3.0	42240	49791	54	62	1258	52.2	24.0	17.6	5.6	0.6	47383
77515	ANGLETON	20397	10385	23.0	26.9	35.7	11.8	2.7	50146	58639	72	77	7667	28.1	36.2	28.5	6.4	0.8	74738
77517	SANTA FE	24665	1815	16.1	22.5	40.9	16.5	3.9	61330	72071	86	88	1561	20.5	23.1	40.3	15.2	0.9	98805
77518	BACLIFF	18127	2710	29.6	33.9	26.5	7.2	2.9	37929	46080	39	46	1952	43.6	26.1	18.8	7.2	4.4	58235
	TEXAS	23284		26.2	27.7	29.5	10.3	6.3	45778	54246				21.6	26.1	33.4	15.6	3.4	93683
	UNITED STATES	25866		24.7	27.1	30.8	10.9	6.5	48124	56710				10.9	15.0	33.7	30.1	10.4	145905

#	POST OFFICE NAME	FINANCIAL SERVICES: Auto Loan	Home Loan	Invest-ments	Retire-ment Plans	THE HOME: Home Improvements: Home Repair	Lawn & Garden	Furnishings: Comput-ers & Hard-ware	Major Appli-ances	TV, Radio, Sound Equip-ment	Furni-ture	ENTERTAINMENT: Dine out/ Carry out	Sports Equip-ment	Fees & Tickets	Toys & Games	Travel	Cable TV	PERSONAL: Apparel & Services	Auto Repairs	Health Insur-ance	Pets & Supplies
77335	GOODRICH	72	52	29	47	58	67	52	62	60	51	71	72	45	68	53	64	65	61	75	83
77336	HUFFMAN	105	110	104	108	110	113	102	105	101	102	125	124	104	129	103	99	122	103	102	123
77338	HUMBLE	78	79	85	81	77	79	81	79	78	81	98	93	80	97	78	75	97	80	72	87
77339	HUMBLE	134	152	174	158	148	150	144	141	136	146	172	166	151	176	144	131	171	140	126	155
77340	HUNTSVILLE	72	59	60	60	60	67	71	67	72	68	89	81	65	83	66	69	85	72	68	78
77345	HUMBLE	207	249	260	258	240	238	221	217	202	226	257	252	238	263	222	193	257	210	189	239
77346	HUMBLE	140	162	161	168	155	151	146	144	133	150	170	168	152	171	143	125	168	140	124	158
77351	LIVINGSTON	78	59	39	55	65	76	60	69	68	59	81	79	54	76	61	72	74	69	82	89
77354	MAGNOLIA	124	130	118	131	126	126	120	122	114	123	143	142	120	141	117	109	140	120	111	138
77355	MAGNOLIA	111	116	105	116	114	115	107	110	104	110	129	128	108	129	106	100	126	108	103	125
77356	MONTGOMERY	178	165	151	157	174	201	153	173	162	162	201	176	154	174	164	171	188	168	198	201
77357	NEW CANEY	86	82	68	79	82	85	77	82	77	79	96	95	75	92	77	76	92	81	80	96
77358	NEW WAVERLY	94	72	47	67	78	89	73	83	81	73	97	95	65	90	73	85	89	82	96	105
77359	OAKHURST	85	64	43	61	71	84	68	77	77	65	90	87	61	86	69	81	83	77	92	96
77360	ONALASKA	70	56	41	51	63	71	53	63	59	53	71	72	48	68	57	63	66	62	74	84
77362	PINEHURST	102	122	126	123	119	118	110	109	102	110	128	128	115	134	111	98	127	106	98	121
77363	PLANTERSVILLE	99	87	65	83	88	94	83	90	85	85	105	105	78	99	82	85	100	90	92	110
77364	POINTBLANK	71	61	52	58	66	78	60	68	65	61	79	70	58	69	63	69	73	66	80	80
77365	PORTER	92	85	68	82	85	89	81	86	81	83	100	100	77	96	80	80	97	86	85	102
77371	SHEPHERD	70	55	35	50	58	64	53	61	58	54	70	71	47	66	53	60	65	60	68	79
77372	SPLENDORA	82	75	58	72	75	79	71	77	72	73	89	89	67	84	70	72	85	76	77	91
77373	SPRING	101	114	117	115	110	110	107	106	100	108	127	125	109	129	106	95	125	105	94	117
77375	TOMBALL	105	111	112	115	109	110	106	106	101	108	127	124	107	127	104	96	124	105	96	118
77377	TOMBALL	136	157	156	160	151	149	141	141	131	144	165	164	147	169	140	125	164	137	124	156
77378	WILLIS	84	77	60	74	77	81	73	78	74	75	91	91	69	86	72	73	88	78	78	93
77379	SPRING	158	186	199	193	180	180	169	165	155	172	197	192	180	202	169	149	197	161	145	182
77380	SPRING	139	153	168	159	149	152	147	144	139	150	176	169	152	176	146	133	174	144	129	159
77381	SPRING	186	218	248	225	213	218	202	198	189	205	239	230	215	244	204	183	239	195	180	218
77382	SPRING	217	247	241	258	236	228	223	220	204	231	259	258	230	260	217	190	257	214	187	241
77384	CONROE	119	142	149	142	139	140	129	128	121	129	152	149	136	159	131	118	151	124	117	141
77385	CONROE	108	119	116	120	115	116	109	110	103	111	129	128	111	130	108	98	127	108	99	122
77386	SPRING	112	121	125	126	117	116	116	114	109	119	138	135	118	137	113	103	136	114	100	126
77388	SPRING	128	152	157	155	147	145	137	135	126	139	159	158	144	165	137	120	159	131	119	149
77389	SPRING	134	149	145	151	144	144	136	136	127	139	161	159	140	162	135	122	159	133	122	152
77396	HUMBLE	84	87	80	87	84	85	82	83	79	84	99	97	81	97	80	75	97	83	76	93
77401	BELLAIRE	187	243	303	240	236	246	217	213	202	219	255	245	238	271	226	201	258	207	194	231
77414	BAY CITY	74	65	59	63	66	72	66	70	70	67	86	81	63	82	66	70	82	71	72	83
77417	BEASLEY	87	72	49	67	74	81	69	77	73	70	89	90	63	84	68	74	84	77	82	97
77418	BELLVILLE	96	74	50	71	82	93	75	86	83	73	98	102	67	96	76	86	91	85	99	112
77419	BLESSING	82	67	49	66	71	80	68	75	73	67	88	86	64	87	68	75	82	74	83	92
77420	BOLING	82	70	54	66	72	76	69	77	73	73	91	86	64	85	68	73	88	77	78	89
77422	BRAZORIA	95	84	65	80	89	95	79	88	84	80	102	103	77	102	81	86	97	86	94	111
77423	BROOKSHIRE	83	76	68	73	75	80	78	80	80	79	99	91	74	93	76	79	96	81	79	90
77426	CHAPPELL HILL	91	69	43	64	76	86	69	79	78	68	93	93	62	89	70	82	85	78	93	104
77429	CYPRESS	153	178	187	184	172	171	163	160	151	166	191	188	171	195	162	144	190	157	141	177
77430	DAMON	102	93	74	88	97	103	85	95	90	86	109	112	83	110	87	92	104	92	101	120
77432	DANEVANG	92	61	28	53	70	80	59	74	71	60	84	89	50	79	60	77	76	73	91	105
77433	CYPRESS	138	156	151	163	149	144	141	140	129	147	164	164	145	165	137	120	162	136	119	153
77434	EAGLE LAKE	71	56	39	52	58	67	59	65	65	60	78	72	53	72	58	66	74	66	72	77
77435	EAST BERNARD	87	74	55	70	79	87	72	80	78	71	94	93	68	95	73	80	88	78	89	101
77437	EL CAMPO	77	63	47	60	66	73	64	71	69	65	83	81	58	79	63	70	79	71	76	85
77440	ELMATON	104	73	38	69	85	95	72	89	83	71	97	107	61	95	74	87	88	87	106	123
77441	FULSHEAR	141	175	210	172	171	180	155	156	146	158	184	178	169	191	162	146	184	151	145	173
77442	GARWOOD	84	57	28	52	66	75	56	70	66	56	78	83	48	75	58	70	71	69	84	98
77444	GUY	101	89	68	84	94	101	83	92	88	83	107	110	80	108	85	91	101	90	100	119
77445	HEMPSTEAD	77	69	58	66	70	76	68	72	71	69	87	83	66	84	68	71	83	72	74	86
77447	HOCKLEY	106	105	94	104	104	107	100	103	98	102	122	121	98	119	98	95	118	103	98	119
77449	KATY	109	123	120	128	117	114	112	110	102	116	130	129	115	131	109	96	129	108	94	121
77450	KATY	165	196	203	202	189	187	176	173	161	180	205	202	187	210	176	154	205	168	152	191
77455	LOUISE	94	64	32	59	74	84	63	78	74	63	87	94	54	84	65	78	79	77	94	110
77456	MARKHAM	92	80	59	76	84	90	75	84	80	76	97	99	72	96	77	81	92	83	90	107
77457	MATAGORDA	83	65	44	59	73	82	61	74	69	61	82	86	55	81	65	74	76	73	87	101
77458	MIDFIELD	77	65	51	65	69	77	67	72	71	66	87	82	64	86	67	73	81	71	78	85
77459	MISSOURI CITY	151	183	194	187	177	178	164	162	151	166	191	187	175	197	166	146	191	157	144	178
77461	NEEDVILLE	97	92	79	90	94	101	88	93	90	88	110	109	87	111	89	90	106	91	96	112
77465	PALACIOS	73	66	58	62	64	69	67	71	70	70	87	77	63	81	65	69	85	72	70	77
77468	PLEDGER	78	70	53	66	74	79	64	71	68	64	83	85	63	85	66	70	79	69	77	92
77469	RICHMOND	125	137	137	139	133	134	127	128	121	131	153	146	131	152	126	116	152	126	115	140
77471	ROSENBERG	82	79	73	78	77	81	79	81	79	81	99	92	77	95	77	76	97	81	77	89
77474	SEALY	97	81	58	77	86	94	78	88	84	79	102	103	73	100	79	86	96	86	95	111
77477	STAFFORD	102	101	111	105	98	101	104	101	101	106	128	120	103	124	100	96	125	104	91	112
77478	SUGAR LAND	130	153	165	156	147	147	139	137	129	143	164	160	147	167	139	124	163	134	120	150
77479	SUGAR LAND	186	225	238	233	217	217	200	196	183	204	232	227	216	239	201	175	233	190	172	216
77480	SWEENY	90	75	55	72	80	89	73	82	80	73	96	95	70	95	75	82	90	80	91	103
77482	VAN VLECK	90	74	53	71	80	90	74	82	80	72	96	96	69	95	75	83	90	81	93	104
77483	WADSWORTH	71	55	38	50	62	70	52	63	59	52	70	74	47	69	56	63	65	62	74	86
77484	WALLER	93	87	76	85	88	94	85	89	87	86	107	104	83	105	85	86	103	89	90	105
77485	WALLIS	108	92	73	87	96	105	89	99	94	90	114	116	83	110	89	96	108	98	106	124
77486	WEST COLUMBIA	83	75	65	73	78	86	76	80	79	74	97	92	74	97	76	81	92	79	85	95
77488	WHARTON	70	62	61	61	63	71	66	68	69	65	85	78	63	83	65	70	81	69	72	79
77489	MISSOURI CITY	98	109	109	112	105	104	102	101	95	104	121	120	104	122	100	90	119	100	89	111
77493	KATY	108	123	123	126	118	116	112	111	104	115	132	131	116	133	111	98	130	109	97	122
77494	KATY	149	178	188	184	172	172	160	157	147	163	186	183	171	191	160	140	186	152	139	173
77502	PASADENA	73	73	73	70	71	75	73	74	74	75	92	83	72	91	72	72	92	75	71	80
77503	PASADENA	71	65	61	64	64	67	67	69	68	70	85	79	64	81	65	65	84	70	65	76
77504	PASADENA	86	81	85	84	79	82	86	84	85	87	107	100	84	103	82	80	105	87	77	93
77505	PASADENA	124	136	129	139	131	129	125	125	117	128	147	147	126	147	122	110	145	123	111	139
77506	PASADENA	60	52	48	50	50	52	56	58	59	60	74	64	53	70	53	55	74	60	53	61
77507	PASADENA	166	207	225	214	200	202	183	178	166	185	211	206	201	220	186	161	213	171	158	197
77510	SANTA FE	102	100	89	99	101	106	95	99	95	95	118	117	94	119	95	94	114	98	98	118
77511	ALVIN	90	89	82	88	88	91	86	89	85	87	106	103	84	104	85	83	103	88	85	101
77514	ANAHUAC	97	73	45	67	79	87	72	85	81	75	98	98	64	91	72	84	92	85	95	109
77515	ANGLETON	87	85	76	83	86	90	82	85	82	82	101	99	81	102	82	81	98	84	85	99
77517	SANTA FE	101	108	103	106	108	110	100	103	97	100	121	121	102	125	101	96	118	100	98	120
77518	BACLIFF	76	70	61	70	71	76	70	73	71	70	87	85	68	86	69	70	84	73	73	84
	TEXAS	94	90	91	90	89	95	92	93	92	93	115	107	90	112	90	90	112	94	89	104
	UNITED STATES	100	100	100	100	100	100	100	100	100	100	100	100	100	100	100	100	100	100	100	100

# ZIP CODE POST OFFICE NAME	COUNTY FIPS CODE	POPULATION 2000	2004	2009	2000-2004 ANNUAL RATE % Rate	State Centile	HOUSEHOLDS 2000	2004	2009	% Annual Rate 2000-2004	2004 Average HH Size	FAMILIES 2000	2004	% Annual Rate 2000-2004
77519 BATSON	199	1200	1231	1293	0.6	29	456	469	493	0.7	2.62	349	359	0.7
77520 BAYTOWN	071	48499	51912	58166	1.6	60	16593	17675	19689	1.5	2.91	12378	13260	1.6
77521 BAYTOWN	201	37487	41947	47462	2.7	78	13521	15077	16951	2.6	2.77	10037	11200	2.6
77530 CHANNELVIEW	201	27574	29977	33294	2.0	67	8543	9226	10163	1.8	3.24	6795	7356	1.9
77531 CLUTE	039	14279	15685	17967	2.2	72	5121	5596	6385	2.1	2.77	3637	3974	2.1
77532 CROSBY	201	20262	22210	24713	2.2	71	7150	7788	8592	2.0	2.85	5645	6158	2.1
77534 DANBURY	039	2675	2883	3262	1.8	63	903	973	1101	1.8	2.88	719	775	1.8
77535 DAYTON	291	27221	30491	34457	2.7	79	7953	9015	10290	3.0	2.94	6367	7225	3.0
77536 DEER PARK	201	28559	29687	32385	0.9	39	9631	9935	10743	0.7	2.96	7951	8225	0.8
77538 DEVERS	291	834	908	1015	2.0	68	297	322	357	1.9	2.82	237	257	1.9
77539 DICKINSON	167	27797	31776	36394	3.2	83	10168	11616	13289	3.2	2.72	7325	8385	3.2
77541 FREEPORT	039	18764	19752	22174	1.2	48	6547	6850	7656	1.1	2.87	4776	4997	1.1
77545 FRESNO	157	6148	7679	9671	5.4	95	1757	2162	2686	5.0	3.55	1508	1853	5.0
77546 FRIENDSWOOD	167	38808	43440	49066	2.7	78	13239	14744	16575	2.6	2.93	10676	11911	2.6
77547 GALENA PARK	201	9603	9596	10248	0.0	12	2745	2718	2876	-0.2	3.53	2214	2196	-0.2
77550 GALVESTON	167	30090	31085	33904	0.8	35	12306	12734	13926	0.8	2.32	6799	7009	0.7
77551 GALVESTON	167	20809	21622	23699	0.9	39	8942	9268	10140	0.9	2.33	5428	5614	0.8
77554 GALVESTON	167	8906	10242	11684	3.3	85	3774	4393	5053	3.6	2.16	2326	2696	3.5
77560 HANKAMER	071	326	350	402	1.7	61	115	123	141	1.6	2.85	87	93	1.6
77562 HIGHLANDS	201	9803	10321	11296	1.2	49	3485	3650	3964	1.1	2.82	2732	2864	1.2
77563 HITCHCOCK	167	8658	9144	10061	1.3	51	3469	3662	4028	1.3	2.49	2422	2552	1.2
77564 HULL	291	3777	3993	4392	1.3	52	1382	1452	1587	1.2	2.75	1073	1129	1.2
77565 KEMAH	167	6181	7426	8687	4.4	92	2686	3215	3750	4.3	2.30	1760	2112	4.4
77566 LAKE JACKSON	039	28093	31029	35845	2.4	74	10169	11178	12873	2.3	2.77	7871	8666	2.3
77568 LA MARQUE	167	13728	13803	14901	0.1	15	5248	5271	5680	0.1	2.60	3710	3723	0.1
77571 LA PORTE	201	33752	36101	39706	1.6	59	11609	12334	13458	1.4	2.90	9095	9692	1.5
77573 LEAGUE CITY	167	41407	49681	58297	4.4	92	14543	17353	20272	4.2	2.84	11220	13419	4.3
77575 LIBERTY	291	15424	16430	18131	1.5	57	5559	5887	6466	1.4	2.71	4122	4378	1.4
77577 LIVERPOOL	039	996	1032	1158	0.8	37	401	414	464	0.8	2.47	289	298	0.7
77578 MANVEL	039	5358	6510	7865	4.7	93	1866	2259	2720	4.6	2.88	1537	1861	4.6
77581 PEARLAND	039	29461	33802	39514	3.3	84	10487	11983	13954	3.2	2.81	8356	9539	3.2
77583 ROSHARON	039	18079	21667	25566	4.4	92	3574	4639	5815	6.3	3.24	2913	3796	6.4
77584 PEARLAND	039	30342	40208	50522	6.9	98	10550	13994	17571	6.9	2.87	8587	11374	6.8
77585 SARATOGA	199	1620	1630	1707	0.1	16	610	614	645	0.2	2.65	469	473	0.2
77586 SEABROOK	201	18658	21196	24182	3.1	82	7725	8803	10018	3.1	2.40	5059	5684	2.8
77587 SOUTH HOUSTON	201	15833	16498	17879	1.0	41	4593	4737	5079	0.7	3.48	3696	3820	0.8
77590 TEXAS CITY	167	30310	31618	34531	1.0	42	11142	11601	12653	1.0	2.70	8096	8417	0.9
77591 TEXAS CITY	167	10270	11394	12796	2.5	76	3971	4408	4956	2.5	2.47	2636	2922	2.5
77597 WALLISVILLE	071	1336	1458	1689	2.1	69	483	527	610	2.1	2.77	377	411	2.1
77598 WEBSTER	201	19208	20668	22871	1.7	63	8899	9444	10322	1.4	2.16	4434	4756	1.7
77611 BRIDGE CITY	361	9116	8956	8992	-0.4	6	3364	3311	3326	-0.4	2.70	2611	2571	-0.4
77612 BUNA	241	9886	10296	10881	1.0	40	3673	3821	4039	0.9	2.68	2853	2975	1.0
77614 DEWEYVILLE	351	2775	2818	2874	0.4	22	1044	1063	1088	0.4	2.65	783	800	0.5
77616 FRED	457	2706	2860	3027	1.3	51	1016	1070	1130	1.2	2.67	787	831	1.3
77619 GROVES	245	16570	17029	17559	0.6	30	6541	6686	6865	0.5	2.52	4754	4875	0.5
77622 HAMSHIRE	245	898	919	941	0.6	27	361	368	375	0.5	2.50	279	285	0.5
77624 HILLISTER	457	190	195	204	0.6	29	75	77	80	0.6	2.49	55	56	0.4
77625 KOUNTZE	199	8973	9442	10055	1.2	48	3377	3553	3789	1.2	2.62	2638	2783	1.3
77627 NEDERLAND	245	21513	22108	22755	0.6	30	8415	8612	8833	0.6	2.51	6197	6364	0.6
77630 ORANGE	361	29305	29178	29706	-0.1	10	11266	11203	11411	-0.1	2.55	7986	7977	0.0
77632 ORANGE	361	20484	21686	22648	1.4	53	7531	7951	8305	1.3	2.72	5922	6256	1.3
77640 PORT ARTHUR	245	20642	20249	20541	-0.5	5	8063	7858	7940	-0.6	2.56	5486	5378	-0.6
77642 PORT ARTHUR	245	36887	37987	39249	0.7	32	13662	13984	14386	0.6	2.68	9123	9342	0.6
77650 PORT BOLIVAR	167	3853	4158	4606	1.8	64	1801	1946	2154	1.8	2.14	1139	1230	1.8
77651 PORT NECHES	245	13594	13956	14380	0.6	29	5280	5396	5537	0.5	2.59	3975	4074	0.6
77656 SILSBEE	199	16826	17626	18816	1.1	45	6282	6592	7057	1.1	2.63	4660	4902	1.2
77657 LUMBERTON	199	14699	15327	16230	1.0	42	5360	5593	5934	1.0	2.74	4205	4397	1.1
77659 SOUR LAKE	199	4637	5408	6073	3.7	88	1677	1949	2188	3.6	2.77	1290	1501	3.6
77660 SPURGER	457	1297	1336	1394	0.7	32	516	530	551	0.6	2.52	359	369	0.7
77662 VIDOR	361	27401	28160	28790	0.6	30	9976	10257	10490	0.7	2.72	7654	7869	0.7
77664 WARREN	457	2902	2987	3116	0.7	32	1161	1191	1239	0.6	2.51	901	926	0.7
77665 WINNIE	071	6782	7439	8501	2.2	71	2449	2686	3071	2.2	2.70	1828	2005	2.2
77701 BEAUMONT	245	16501	16471	16777	0.0	12	5785	5745	5838	-0.2	2.72	3751	3733	-0.1
77702 BEAUMONT	245	3051	2973	3004	-0.6	4	1310	1266	1272	-0.8	2.34	722	701	-0.7
77703 BEAUMONT	245	14930	15272	15767	0.5	26	5535	5629	5789	0.4	2.70	3727	3809	0.5
77705 BEAUMONT	245	40530	41385	42140	0.5	25	10599	10714	10936	0.3	2.71	7328	7447	0.4
77706 BEAUMONT	245	25953	26848	27839	0.8	35	11692	12091	12507	0.8	2.21	7163	7424	0.9
77707 BEAUMONT	245	16430	17166	17844	1.0	43	6345	6609	6851	1.0	2.53	4500	4703	1.0
77708 BEAUMONT	245	11784	11925	12261	0.3	19	4467	4502	4614	0.2	2.64	3219	3250	0.2
77710 BEAUMONT	245	12	12	12	0.0	13	5	5	5	0.0	2.40	3	3	0.0
77713 BEAUMONT	245	11441	12101	12703	1.3	52	4349	4616	4849	1.4	2.59	3213	3401	1.4
77801 BRYAN	041	12561	13427	15110	1.6	59	5197	5510	6158	1.4	2.41	2435	2553	1.1
77802 BRYAN	041	19625	21985	25428	2.7	79	8063	8903	10215	2.4	2.41	5031	5603	2.6
77803 BRYAN	041	28040	29525	33022	1.2	49	8572	9000	10073	1.2	3.11	6210	6496	1.1
77807 BRYAN	041	7031	7863	8991	2.7	78	2404	2707	3111	2.8	2.70	1577	1755	2.6
77808 BRYAN	041	7579	8878	10460	3.8	89	2701	3148	3688	3.7	2.82	2084	2415	3.5
77830 ANDERSON	185	2760	3021	3423	2.2	70	1086	1185	1339	2.1	2.51	780	853	2.1
77831 BEDIAS	185	2354	2716	3166	3.4	86	842	962	1115	3.2	2.82	639	731	3.2
77833 BRENHAM	477	25563	26311	27392	0.7	32	9359	9597	9970	0.6	2.56	6560	6745	0.7
77835 BURTON	477	2098	2118	2179	0.2	18	892	896	917	0.1	2.36	615	617	0.1
77836 CALDWELL	051	10391	11900	13819	3.2	83	3936	4480	5174	3.1	2.63	2885	3289	3.1
77837 CALVERT	395	1693	1674	1733	-0.3	8	682	672	695	-0.4	2.46	453	448	-0.3
77840 COLLEGE STATION	041	47641	51543	57575	1.9	65	17330	19054	21717	2.3	2.15	5634	6134	2.0
77845 COLLEGE STATION	041	29081	35547	43082	4.8	94	10636	12835	15400	4.5	2.75	7178	8776	4.8
77850 CONCORD	289	134	138	148	0.7	32	49	50	54	0.5	2.76	35	36	0.7
77853 DIME BOX	287	842	893	974	1.4	54	337	353	381	1.1	2.53	241	253	1.2
77856 FRANKLIN	395	4903	5035	5261	0.6	30	1936	1986	2076	0.6	2.47	1395	1435	0.6
77859 HEARNE	395	7544	7883	8357	1.0	43	2805	2921	3093	1.0	2.67	1993	2081	1.0
77861 IOLA	185	2005	2145	2404	1.6	59	766	819	915	1.6	2.62	572	612	1.6
77864 MADISONVILLE	313	6313	6697	7321	1.4	55	2319	2436	2643	1.2	2.68	1669	1760	1.3
77865 MARQUEZ	289	1356	1413	1515	1.0	41	533	553	591	0.9	2.56	393	409	0.9
77868 NAVASOTA	185	14702	16154	18147	2.2	72	4390	4891	5587	2.6	2.75	3169	3542	2.7
77871 NORMANGEE	289	3019	3212	3485	1.5	56	1288	1366	1478	1.4	2.35	951	1011	1.5
77872 NORTH ZULCH	313	2493	2651	2905	1.5	56	1013	1067	1158	1.2	2.48	747	789	1.3
77873 RICHARDS	339	691	818	993	4.1	90	289	339	408	3.8	2.41	208	245	3.9
TEXAS					2.2					2.0	2.77			2.1
UNITED STATES					1.2					1.3	2.58			1.1

ZIP CODE #	POST OFFICE NAME	RACE (%) White 2000	White 2004	Black 2000	Black 2004	Asian/Pacific 2000	Asian/Pacific 2004	% Hispanic Origin 2000	% Hispanic Origin 2004	2004 AGE DISTRIBUTION (%) 0-4	5-9	10-14	15-19	20-24	25-44	45-64	65-84	85+	18+	MEDIAN AGE 2004	% 2004 Males	% 2004 Females
77519	BATSON	98.0	97.6	0.1	0.1	0.1	0.2	2.3	2.8	7.4	6.7	7.5	7.4	9.1	27.5	23.0	10.2	1.3	74.1	34.2	49.4	50.6
77520	BAYTOWN	71.1	69.6	10.1	10.1	0.7	0.7	35.6	38.5	8.6	8.0	8.3	7.6	7.6	27.8	21.6	9.1	1.5	70.6	32.2	48.8	51.2
77521	BAYTOWN	67.6	64.9	17.2	17.5	1.5	1.7	23.4	27.2	8.4	7.7	7.9	7.4	8.2	29.5	23.0	7.1	0.9	71.6	31.7	48.6	51.4
77530	CHANNELVIEW	63.9	60.5	12.4	12.4	2.0	2.0	37.3	43.3	9.4	8.9	9.3	8.0	7.8	30.7	20.2	5.3	0.4	67.6	29.1	50.0	50.0
77531	CLUTE	68.4	66.1	7.6	7.5	0.9	0.8	41.2	45.5	9.7	8.4	8.0	7.5	9.8	29.9	19.3	6.5	0.9	69.6	28.6	50.2	49.8
77532	CROSBY	76.3	74.4	16.8	17.2	0.4	0.5	9.7	12.3	6.9	7.2	8.0	7.1	6.7	27.0	27.9	8.5	0.7	73.5	36.3	49.8	50.2
77534	DANBURY	88.8	86.9	2.2	2.3	0.3	0.4	15.0	18.1	7.6	7.5	7.7	8.1	7.5	28.4	23.7	8.7	0.7	71.7	33.9	50.7	49.3
77535	DAYTON	79.5	78.0	13.1	13.5	0.3	0.4	10.2	11.9	6.8	6.7	7.6	7.1	7.9	34.4	22.6	6.3	0.6	74.6	33.8	47.6	52.4
77536	DEER PARK	90.0	88.1	1.3	1.4	1.3	1.5	15.3	19.0	6.5	6.9	8.3	8.0	7.3	28.6	26.6	7.3	0.6	73.5	35.2	49.6	50.4
77538	DEVERS	80.0	78.1	8.0	8.3	0.1	0.1	13.0	14.9	7.7	7.8	7.2	6.8	6.5	25.9	26.9	10.4	0.9	73.0	37.0	50.8	49.2
77539	DICKINSON	72.7	69.6	10.8	11.7	2.4	2.6	22.3	25.6	7.7	7.3	7.4	6.9	7.3	29.0	24.9	8.8	0.8	73.4	34.9	50.0	50.0
77541	FREEPORT	70.4	68.5	9.8	9.5	0.4	0.4	39.8	43.9	9.2	8.5	9.0	7.8	7.6	26.9	22.0	8.2	0.8	68.4	30.8	50.9	49.1
77545	FRESNO	40.8	38.2	34.4	34.4	2.4	2.3	38.6	43.0	10.5	9.7	9.2	7.6	7.4	31.8	19.6	3.9	0.3	65.9	29.0	49.7	50.3
77546	FRIENDSWOOD	85.7	83.6	4.3	4.8	4.7	5.3	9.9	12.2	7.4	7.7	8.6	7.6	6.0	28.4	26.6	6.7	1.0	71.3	36.0	48.6	51.4
77547	GALENA PARK	62.2	60.4	8.4	8.1	0.4	0.4	70.8	75.2	9.8	9.0	8.7	8.8	8.9	27.2	18.5	8.1	1.0	67.2	28.2	49.8	50.2
77550	GALVESTON	46.8	44.8	36.1	36.4	3.6	3.8	25.0	28.0	6.8	6.2	6.5	6.6	8.2	30.1	22.2	11.7	1.7	76.8	35.0	48.8	51.2
77551	GALVESTON	68.6	66.2	15.5	16.1	3.1	3.3	30.6	34.4	6.7	6.0	6.8	6.5	8.4	26.3	24.5	13.0	1.8	76.7	37.1	47.3	52.7
77554	GALVESTON	86.1	84.3	6.0	6.6	2.0	2.3	11.2	13.3	5.1	5.3	4.9	7.2	9.2	24.7	30.5	11.8	1.4	82.2	41.1	49.7	50.3
77560	HANKAMER	61.0	58.3	36.2	38.6	0.0	0.0	3.4	4.0	8.0	8.3	7.7	6.0	6.6	24.6	26.3	11.4	1.1	72.6	36.4	48.6	51.4
77562	HIGHLANDS	83.4	81.2	7.9	8.2	0.5	0.5	13.7	17.2	7.3	7.3	8.2	7.2	6.9	28.4	25.2	8.5	1.1	72.7	34.7	49.6	50.4
77563	HITCHCOCK	66.8	64.4	24.6	25.8	0.4	0.4	14.0	16.1	5.8	6.4	6.6	6.2	5.6	26.0	28.5	13.4	1.6	77.4	40.8	49.1	50.9
77564	HULL	90.9	90.1	5.4	5.6	0.0	0.0	4.6	5.4	7.9	7.5	7.8	7.4	6.8	26.0	24.2	10.8	1.5	72.3	35.0	48.6	51.4
77565	KEMAH	86.2	84.4	2.4	2.8	2.1	2.4	14.6	17.0	6.2	6.3	6.3	6.0	5.7	29.5	31.1	7.9	1.0	77.6	39.5	51.3	48.7
77566	LAKE JACKSON	86.5	85.4	3.8	3.8	2.4	2.4	14.5	16.8	7.3	7.6	8.9	8.0	6.3	27.1	25.1	8.8	1.1	71.2	35.7	48.8	51.2
77568	LA MARQUE	56.0	52.9	34.5	36.4	0.5	0.5	15.6	18.0	7.0	6.8	7.1	6.7	7.0	24.8	25.1	13.6	1.9	75.1	37.9	47.4	52.6
77571	LA PORTE	82.0	79.1	6.0	6.3	1.2	1.4	19.8	24.5	7.7	7.5	7.8	7.2	6.9	30.6	24.6	6.7	0.9	72.5	33.7	49.6	50.4
77573	LEAGUE CITY	83.6	81.3	5.2	5.9	3.3	3.8	13.7	16.2	8.3	8.2	8.0	6.9	6.2	32.2	24.1	5.4	0.7	71.2	34.3	49.5	50.5
77575	LIBERTY	73.4	71.6	17.9	18.6	0.4	0.5	10.2	11.8	7.1	7.1	7.7	7.4	7.0	26.3	24.3	11.6	1.5	73.6	36.0	49.5	50.5
77577	LIVERPOOL	91.6	90.0	1.0	1.1	0.1	0.1	7.0	8.6	5.6	5.8	5.8	6.5	5.6	27.9	31.0	10.8	1.0	78.5	40.5	51.9	48.1
77578	MANVEL	83.8	81.7	5.2	5.8	2.1	2.4	18.0	20.4	7.7	7.8	7.6	6.3	5.6	30.0	27.5	7.0	0.5	73.0	36.5	50.7	49.3
77581	PEARLAND	84.1	82.3	4.0	4.3	3.2	3.4	17.0	19.9	7.6	7.5	7.5	6.7	6.6	30.5	24.1	8.5	0.9	73.2	35.3	49.1	50.9
77583	ROSHARON	55.5	54.5	25.2	23.7	2.6	2.9	27.6	31.9	6.1	6.0	6.3	5.5	4.9	40.4	26.0	4.6	0.4	78.2	37.5	65.7	34.3
77584	PEARLAND	73.0	70.6	10.7	11.6	6.6	7.1	18.6	20.7	9.6	9.0	7.2	5.8	5.1	35.1	20.5	7.2	0.5	70.6	34.0	49.1	50.9
77585	SARATOGA	97.5	97.2	0.1	0.1	0.0	0.0	1.7	2.1	5.7	5.8	6.3	6.5	7.4	25.7	27.8	13.4	1.4	78.2	40.6	50.1	49.9
77586	SEABROOK	90.4	88.6	2.2	2.5	2.8	3.3	8.5	11.0	6.0	6.2	6.8	6.5	6.0	31.0	28.1	8.9	0.6	76.8	38.1	51.3	48.7
77587	SOUTH HOUSTON	65.3	63.3	1.0	1.0	0.8	0.7	77.9	82.4	10.6	9.5	8.9	7.9	8.6	30.2	17.5	6.4	0.5	66.3	27.8	51.1	48.9
77590	TEXAS CITY	68.7	65.9	17.7	18.7	0.8	0.9	24.5	28.1	7.4	7.3	7.7	7.3	7.9	26.6	23.7	10.8	1.3	73.2	34.5	48.0	52.1
77591	TEXAS CITY	36.1	33.5	57.3	59.2	1.2	1.3	9.4	10.8	5.6	5.6	6.4	6.6	7.4	25.8	26.1	14.4	2.0	78.4	39.5	45.3	54.7
77597	WALLISVILLE	72.7	70.6	24.8	26.5	0.2	0.1	3.4	4.0	6.8	7.1	7.5	6.3	6.7	26.1	28.5	10.1	1.0	74.6	37.5	48.9	51.1
77598	WEBSTER	71.2	66.9	10.4	11.1	5.2	5.7	19.8	24.7	8.2	6.4	5.8	6.6	11.9	40.1	16.5	3.9	0.6	76.0	29.5	50.5	49.5
77611	BRIDGE CITY	95.3	94.5	0.2	0.3	1.4	1.7	3.7	4.4	6.8	6.8	7.5	7.0	7.2	27.6	25.3	11.0	0.9	74.7	36.3	49.3	50.7
77612	BUNA	94.6	94.0	3.1	3.4	0.2	0.2	1.9	2.3	7.1	7.1	7.4	7.0	6.9	27.7	24.3	11.4	1.0	74.0	36.1	49.1	50.9
77614	DEWEYVILLE	97.2	96.8	0.3	0.3	0.1	0.1	1.7	2.1	7.0	6.9	7.2	6.7	6.9	27.9	26.6	10.1	0.6	74.8	36.0	50.3	49.7
77616	FRED	96.5	95.9	0.9	1.0	0.0	0.0	1.6	2.0	7.8	7.6	6.8	6.3	7.1	27.2	23.9	12.4	1.1	74.1	36.4	50.6	49.4
77619	GROVES	89.8	88.6	4.2	4.4	2.2	2.5	8.1	9.8	6.6	6.2	6.3	6.5	7.0	25.9	23.9	15.0	2.4	77.0	38.9	47.5	52.5
77622	HAMSHIRE	90.4	88.6	5.2	6.1	0.2	0.4	4.7	5.9	6.2	6.1	7.1	7.0	8.2	26.3	26.8	11.3	1.1	76.7	37.1	50.4	49.6
77624	HILLISTER	77.9	75.4	18.4	20.0	0.0	0.5	3.2	3.6	5.6	5.6	6.2	6.2	6.2	22.1	28.2	17.4	2.6	78.5	43.5	48.2	51.8
77625	KOUNTZE	89.2	88.1	8.4	9.1	0.3	0.3	2.3	2.7	6.4	6.5	7.3	7.2	6.3	26.4	26.4	12.1	1.3	75.3	38.2	50.3	49.7
77627	NEDERLAND	92.6	91.2	2.3	2.5	1.8	2.1	5.9	7.4	6.4	6.3	6.7	6.8	7.2	28.0	24.9	12.4	1.3	76.6	37.7	49.9	50.1
77630	ORANGE	73.8	72.1	21.7	22.8	1.3	1.5	4.2	4.8	6.8	6.7	7.3	6.8	7.0	25.8	24.1	13.6	1.9	75.1	37.4	48.7	51.3
77632	ORANGE	93.4	92.2	3.5	4.3	0.5	0.6	3.2	3.8	6.4	6.7	7.7	7.2	6.4	26.5	27.7	10.5	0.9	74.6	38.2	49.7	50.3
77640	PORT ARTHUR	28.4	27.8	64.9	64.6	1.4	1.6	7.0	8.1	6.2	6.2	7.2	7.2	6.8	23.8	25.1	15.7	1.9	76.1	39.8	47.8	52.2
77642	PORT ARTHUR	44.9	42.3	31.9	32.3	8.4	9.0	23.4	25.9	8.9	8.2	8.3	7.4	7.5	26.0	19.9	11.4	2.4	70.2	32.3	47.4	52.6
77650	PORT BOLIVAR	93.7	92.7	0.5	0.5	0.6	0.7	7.0	8.3	3.1	3.5	4.9	4.8	4.5	17.3	37.8	23.0	1.4	85.8	51.4	50.9	49.1
77651	PORT NECHES	94.8	93.7	0.9	1.1	1.6	1.9	5.0	6.4	6.1	6.1	7.0	6.9	7.1	25.6	26.7	13.4	1.3	76.8	39.2	49.1	50.9
77656	SILSBEE	83.5	82.7	14.4	15.0	0.3	0.3	2.5	2.8	7.5	7.3	7.3	6.5	6.8	26.6	24.2	12.0	1.7	73.9	36.4	48.9	51.1
77657	LUMBERTON	97.7	97.3	0.1	0.1	0.2	0.3	2.8	3.4	7.5	7.4	7.8	7.1	7.2	28.6	24.8	8.8	0.8	73.0	34.9	49.4	50.6
77659	SOUR LAKE	94.7	94.0	2.8	3.3	0.3	0.4	2.9	3.5	6.1	6.5	7.4	7.7	6.6	24.3	28.9	11.0	1.4	75.0	39.7	49.5	50.5
77660	SPURGER	92.4	91.5	4.6	5.1	0.1	0.2	1.5	1.8	6.9	7.0	6.5	5.9	5.3	23.4	25.1	18.6	1.4	76.0	41.3	50.5	49.6
77662	VIDOR	97.2	96.8	0.1	0.1	0.3	0.3	3.3	3.9	7.3	7.1	7.3	6.9	7.2	28.1	24.1	11.0	1.2	74.2	35.6	49.2	50.8
77664	WARREN	94.4	93.7	3.6	4.1	0.1	0.1	1.6	1.9	5.2	5.5	7.2	6.8	5.5	22.1	27.9	18.4	1.5	77.8	43.4	49.4	50.7
77665	WINNIE	82.4	79.9	10.4	11.6	0.3	0.4	9.0	10.7	7.0	6.9	7.1	6.8	7.1	27.5	25.3	10.9	1.3	74.8	36.8	51.0	49.0
77701	BEAUMONT	20.9	19.3	64.4	64.8	2.7	2.8	18.2	19.7	7.2	7.2	7.8	9.5	7.4	25.4	22.2	10.9	2.4	71.9	33.8	49.4	50.6
77702	BEAUMONT	55.8	52.3	30.1	31.6	1.8	2.0	18.6	21.4	7.6	6.7	6.7	7.1	9.0	30.7	21.8	9.1	1.4	75.3	33.1	48.9	51.1
77703	BEAUMONT	19.5	17.8	75.9	77.2	0.8	0.8	6.3	7.1	7.8	7.9	9.4	8.1	7.8	25.0	21.9	10.2	1.9	70.0	32.4	46.4	53.6
77705	BEAUMONT	42.7	41.1	51.6	52.6	1.4	1.6	12.3	13.9	5.4	5.1	5.7	6.6	11.3	37.3	20.1	7.7	0.9	80.5	33.0	62.4	37.6
77706	BEAUMONT	82.1	79.8	10.7	11.8	3.9	4.6	5.0	6.0	5.5	5.7	6.1	6.0	6.7	26.1	26.8	14.4	2.6	79.0	40.8	47.1	52.9
77707	BEAUMONT	69.0	66.0	24.0	25.9	3.1	3.6	7.1	8.4	7.2	7.2	7.1	6.1	6.4	27.6	23.7	12.6	2.1	74.8	37.4	46.4	53.6
77708	BEAUMONT	44.7	41.7	50.6	53.0	1.3	1.5	5.0	6.0	9.1	7.9	7.9	7.0	8.6	28.0	22.4	8.0	1.0	70.7	31.6	46.4	53.6
77710	BEAUMONT	25.0	25.0	66.7	75.0	0.0	0.0	0.0	8.3	16.7	16.7	0.0	0.0	33.3	33.3	0.0	0.0	0.0	66.7	22.5	33.3	66.7
77713	BEAUMONT	77.8	74.4	17.5	19.7	1.2	1.5	4.7	6.0	6.5	6.6	7.3	6.6	6.5	28.0	26.2	11.2	1.2	75.6	37.8	49.0	51.0
77801	BRYAN	62.7	59.3	12.5	13.0	5.9	6.3	29.9	33.9	8.8	5.2	4.7	7.9	27.9	30.9	10.5	3.6	0.6	78.6	24.2	53.3	46.7
77802	BRYAN	87.1	85.1	5.8	6.3	1.0	1.1	10.8	13.5	6.6	5.8	5.9	7.0	11.0	27.0	20.9	12.5	3.3	78.2	34.7	47.5	52.5
77803	BRYAN	48.8	46.6	28.5	28.4	0.4	0.4	40.3	44.2	9.0	8.2	8.7	9.0	10.0	30.7	17.4	6.3	0.9	69.0	27.8	49.5	50.5
77807	BRYAN	73.6	70.5	12.3	13.0	1.3	1.5	23.6	27.4	7.5	6.3	5.9	13.9	14.0	29.0	17.6	5.1	0.6	71.2	26.3	54.6	45.4
77808	BRYAN	85.0	81.7	8.4	10.1	0.3	0.4	10.0	12.7	6.8	6.7	7.3	7.1	8.3	29.6	24.8	8.5	0.9	74.9	34.6	50.2	49.8
77830	ANDERSON	83.9	82.3	11.2	12.0	0.2	0.2	6.3	7.9	5.4	5.8	7.0	6.7	5.4	25.8	27.9	14.2	2.0	77.7	40.9	50.4	49.6
77831	BEDIAS	87.0	85.2	8.4	9.2	0.0	0.0	6.4	8.0	6.2	6.6	8.0	7.8	5.5	26.0	26.8	11.7	1.4	74.2	38.9	51.1	48.9
77833	BRENHAM	75.4	74.0	17.5	17.8	1.4	1.6	9.4	11.0	6.6	6.1	6.3	8.1	8.6	24.9	23.6	12.8	3.0	77.0	37.0	48.8	51.3
77835	BURTON	78.3	76.9	16.2	16.6	0.4	0.5	5.9	7.1	5.9	6.0	6.9	5.9	4.4	23.0	26.8	18.4	2.9	77.5	43.6	50.2	49.8
77836	CALDWELL	76.0	73.8	12.2	12.7	0.2	0.2	15.5	17.8	7.1	6.9	7.4	7.0	6.5	25.3	24.4	13.3	2.1	74.3	37.8	49.2	50.8
77837	CALVERT	41.0	39.6	47.8	47.6	0.1	0.1	15.7	18.2	6.2	8.1	9.3	6.6	5.2	21.7	23.8	16.1	3.2	72.0	39.2	47.0	53.0
77840	COLLEGE STATION	78.0	75.1	6.4	6.9	7.9	8.7	11.2	13.9	3.4	2.4	2.1	20.5	45.4	17.2	6.3	2.5	0.3	90.7	22.4	52.0	48.0
77845	COLLEGE STATION	87.3	84.9	3.6	4.0	4.4	5.4	7.7	9.6	7.0	6.7	7.3	8.1	16.3	27.8	20.2	5.8	0.8	74.9	28.1	49.6	50.5
77850	CONCORD	89.6	87.7	4.5	4.4	0.0	0.0	6.7	8.0	5.1	5.1	5.8	6.5	6.5	20.3	31.2	17.4	2.2	79.7	45.4	52.9	47.1
77853	DIME BOX	57.7	54.9	35.8	37.3	0.1	0.1	10.2	12.4	5.6	5.7	7.8	8.4	5.7	23.5	26.5	14.7	2.0	75.8	40.7	48.7	51.3
77856	FRANKLIN	88.6	87.4	7.4	8.0	0.4	0.4	6.3	7.6	6.3	6.8	7.1	6.1	5.3	22.1	27.3	16.5	2.4	76.0	42.4	48.7	51.3
77859	HEARNE	53.6	51.0	31.9	32.6	0.2	0.2	22.9	26.1	8.4	8.1	8.7	7.2	6.9	24.9	22.5	11.5	1.9	70.3	33.8	47.1	52.9
77861	IOLA	94.1	93.1	1.8	1.9	0.1	0.1	7.6	9.4	6.4	6.6	7.0	7.0	5.8	24.2	27.0	14.6	1.5	75.9	40.3	49.1	50.9
77864	MADISONVILLE	68.1	65.5	20.9	21.8	0.4	0.5	16.7	19.6	7.8	6.9	7.1	7.0	6.8	24.4	23.2	13.6	3.2	73.8	36.9	48.7	51.4
77865	MARQUEZ	91.7	90.7	3.5	3.6	0.1	0.1	5.8	6.7	5.4	6.0	6.5	6.4	6.1	22.3	28.2	17.3	1.8	78.2	43.1	50.9	49.1
77868	NAVASOTA	61.9	60.3	27.3	27.6	0.5	0.5	22.2	25.1	6.6	6.3	6.5	6.7	6.9	29.2	24.8	11.0	2.0	76.6	38.0	55.9	44.1
77871	NORMANGEE	89.7	89.0	6.0	6.1	0.1	0.1	5.5	6.5	5.1	5.2	5.4	5.7	4.7	18.5	26.6	26.6	2.3	80.9	48.9	48.1	51.9
77872	NORTH ZULCH	95.8	95.1	1.2	1.3	0.1	0.1	3.9	5.0	5.8	6.0	6.5	6.6	5.1	23.5	28.5	15.9	2.0	77.5	42.7	48.9	51.1
77873	RICHARDS	77.9	76.0	18.4	19.8	0.1	0.2	4.1	4.5	6.2	6.6	7.2	5.9	5.4	24.5	28.6	13.7	2.0	76.2	40.9	50.0	50.0
	TEXAS	71.0	69.5	11.5	11.4	2.8	3.1	32.0	34.6	7.9	7.5	7.7	7.5	8.1	29.6	21.9	8.7	1.2	72.6	32.9	49.7	50.3
	UNITED STATES	75.1	73.6	12.3	12.5	3.8	4.2	12.5	14.1	6.9	6.7	7.2	7.0	7.3	28.6	23.8	10.8	1.7	75.1	36.0	49.1	50.9

INCOME

ZIP CODE #	POST OFFICE NAME	2004 Per Capita Income	2004 HH Income Base	2004 HOUSEHOLD INCOME DISTRIBUTION (%) Less than $25,000	$25,000 to $49,999	$50,000 to $99,999	$100,000 to $149,999	$150,000 or More	MEDIAN HOUSEHOLD INCOME 2004	2009	2004 National Centile	2004 State Centile	2004 Home Value Base	2004 HOME VALUE DISTRIBUTION (%) Less than $50,000	$50,000 to $89,999	$90,000 to $174,999	$175,000 to $399,999	$400,000 or More	2004 Median Home Value
77519	BATSON	19275	469	27.5	36.9	23.5	8.5	3.6	38100	44609	40	47	418	51.9	29.4	11.0	7.7	0.0	48140
77520	BAYTOWN	20329	17675	26.5	27.5	31.7	10.5	3.9	45914	54544	64	70	11837	32.0	33.1	25.6	8.7	0.7	71720
77521	BAYTOWN	23174	15077	21.3	25.0	35.5	13.8	4.4	53566	63743	78	82	9613	19.7	33.7	37.1	8.1	1.4	86470
77530	CHANNELVIEW	17648	9226	20.5	30.7	36.9	9.5	2.5	48976	58095	70	75	6754	22.7	48.3	27.5	1.4	0.2	72141
77531	CLUTE	17578	5596	27.5	35.4	28.6	6.9	1.7	40379	46933	47	55	2769	34.4	42.4	18.8	4.0	0.4	63191
77532	CROSBY	23419	7788	20.0	23.6	36.9	14.4	5.1	58720	68552	83	86	6403	17.6	28.1	44.5	8.8	1.0	94310
77534	DANBURY	21740	973	22.3	23.7	35.9	14.7	3.4	53983	62578	78	82	788	18.2	40.2	33.6	7.7	0.3	81646
77535	DAYTON	18768	9015	22.0	25.8	39.8	9.9	2.5	51726	58777	75	80	7228	28.6	28.8	32.7	9.2	0.8	78914
77536	DEER PARK	28800	9935	11.2	20.1	40.1	21.9	6.7	69264	81797	91	92	8034	4.3	21.6	63.6	10.1	0.4	108953
77538	DEVERS	25016	322	25.5	20.8	37.6	9.0	7.1	52555	58016	76	80	272	37.5	24.6	19.1	18.0	0.7	70714
77539	DICKINSON	22858	11616	24.4	27.0	32.3	12.1	4.2	48100	57591	69	73	8129	20.2	26.1	40.6	11.8	1.3	94624
77541	FREEPORT	16750	6850	33.5	32.1	25.9	6.0	2.5	38111	44269	40	47	4385	50.7	31.4	14.9	2.7	0.3	49442
77545	FRESNO	19399	2162	16.0	24.2	40.0	14.9	5.0	59944	69629	84	87	1864	23.9	16.4	44.9	14.4	0.4	107642
77546	FRIENDSWOOD	32704	14744	8.0	16.5	40.8	23.1	11.5	78488	93931	95	95	12314	1.1	11.0	55.7	28.3	3.9	137694
77547	GALENA PARK	13583	2718	36.8	32.6	25.3	3.1	2.2	34689	40178	26	32	1815	43.0	51.7	4.9	0.4	0.0	53428
77550	GALVESTON	17451	12734	45.8	28.9	18.3	4.7	2.3	28052	33553	9	12	4984	21.8	40.4	28.7	7.4	1.8	78308
77551	GALVESTON	23824	9268	33.4	29.7	24.9	7.8	4.3	39153	46463	43	51	4459	15.1	34.6	34.9	12.7	2.7	90363
77554	GALVESTON	38003	4393	23.7	23.6	26.8	14.4	11.5	55376	66589	80	83	2746	7.7	14.4	31.6	35.4	11.0	156061
77560	HANKAMER	16028	123	34.2	26.0	32.5	4.9	2.4	41769	49546	52	61	110	42.7	29.1	19.1	9.1	0.0	62500
77562	HIGHLANDS	21179	3650	20.1	31.0	34.7	11.7	2.4	48650	58646	70	75	2918	31.3	37.7	26.8	4.0	0.1	71345
77563	HITCHCOCK	22404	3662	29.8	27.9	30.0	9.2	3.1	41263	49137	51	59	2704	27.6	30.4	33.5	8.0	0.6	77186
77564	HULL	17119	1452	30.7	33.3	28.1	6.5	1.3	38094	43484	40	47	1180	51.5	25.7	19.5	2.3	1.0	48636
77565	KEMAH	42969	3215	13.0	19.4	33.6	19.6	14.3	73492	87747	93	93	2272	5.6	17.7	35.2	31.8	9.7	145658
77566	LAKE JACKSON	29699	11178	14.5	20.6	36.0	19.4	9.5	67235	76347	90	91	8167	5.6	23.7	48.3	19.5	2.9	114834
77568	LA MARQUE	19904	5271	30.7	31.3	27.7	7.9	2.4	38432	45453	41	49	3672	26.4	48.8	22.5	2.1	0.2	70633
77571	LA PORTE	25124	12334	14.2	21.8	42.3	16.5	5.3	64238	75742	88	90	9666	10.9	29.3	53.4	5.5	0.9	97034
77573	LEAGUE CITY	30845	17353	9.5	17.0	42.8	21.1	9.6	75543	88306	93	94	13503	4.5	14.5	49.6	29.6	1.8	128945
77575	LIBERTY	18569	5887	32.9	29.7	26.8	7.5	3.2	39928	45188	46	54	4439	37.5	29.6	27.3	5.5	0.2	66052
77577	LIVERPOOL	22398	414	23.2	28.3	36.7	9.7	2.2	47398	57103	67	72	342	28.7	29.2	35.7	5.9	0.6	78571
77578	MANVEL	27758	2259	12.3	20.6	38.8	20.9	7.4	68632	79795	91	92	1999	18.1	19.0	37.6	23.3	2.0	113064
77581	PEARLAND	29511	11983	13.2	21.6	37.8	19.5	7.9	66754	76871	90	91	9228	7.7	11.5	56.7	22.7	1.4	126684
77583	ROSHARON	19476	4639	17.3	25.3	37.3	13.9	6.3	57695	67567	82	85	3899	29.9	21.1	26.0	20.1	3.0	88277
77584	PEARLAND	31188	13994	10.4	17.6	38.4	23.0	10.6	76479	87281	94	94	12515	9.5	11.1	46.5	31.6	1.4	140893
77585	SARATOGA	14066	614	38.8	37.1	20.2	2.9	1.0	31466	35630	16	21	565	58.9	19.8	16.8	2.1	2.3	41293
77586	SEABROOK	38892	8803	9.7	19.6	37.1	21.1	12.5	73154	90141	93	93	5526	1.9	12.4	49.7	32.3	3.7	148397
77587	SOUTH HOUSTON	14020	4737	34.6	32.3	25.9	5.7	1.6	36167	41742	32	38	2810	40.0	49.2	9.5	0.8	0.5	55953
77590	TEXAS CITY	19051	11601	30.5	28.0	30.1	9.5	1.9	41367	49422	51	59	7201	24.6	43.1	27.1	5.1	0.2	74852
77591	TEXAS CITY	20376	4408	33.4	28.2	28.1	7.6	2.7	37867	46076	39	46	2647	19.1	42.9	32.5	5.0	0.5	79321
77597	WALLISVILLE	22345	527	31.3	30.0	23.5	11.2	4.0	42348	49111	54	63	451	41.2	24.4	23.3	10.4	0.7	64500
77598	WEBSTER	24937	9444	20.6	34.2	34.0	9.9	1.3	45839	55309	63	70	2411	11.8	21.7	64.7	1.9	0.0	98995
77611	BRIDGE CITY	20978	3311	22.7	28.4	35.4	11.3	2.2	48735	56268	70	75	2622	24.3	40.1	30.8	4.4	0.5	76398
77612	BUNA	16894	3821	31.1	34.0	28.5	5.3	1.1	36623	41331	34	41	3210	38.7	30.0	24.6	6.5	0.2	64192
77614	DEWEYVILLE	16341	1063	31.8	37.5	27.1	2.4	1.2	37894	41559	39	46	905	49.8	34.1	13.7	1.8	0.6	50238
77616	FRED	16409	1070	34.9	34.6	23.0	5.7	1.9	33441	38569	22	27	919	53.3	24.9	15.7	5.2	0.9	47010
77619	GROVES	24161	6686	23.6	28.6	33.4	10.4	3.9	47877	56076	68	73	4990	26.2	48.0	24.0	1.8	0.0	69120
77622	HAMSHIRE	27682	368	19.6	29.9	35.6	9.8	5.2	50507	59433	73	78	312	28.9	41.4	22.4	7.4	0.0	66905
77624	HILLISTER	17027	77	36.4	31.2	26.0	6.5	0.0	35442	40000	29	35	64	35.9	29.7	21.9	10.9	1.6	70000
77625	KOUNTZE	20348	3553	29.3	28.2	32.2	7.9	2.5	42622	49116	55	63	3000	34.1	29.3	25.2	11.3	0.2	69727
77627	NEDERLAND	25245	8612	19.8	27.8	37.5	10.4	4.5	51833	60927	75	80	6607	18.7	45.0	30.7	5.3	0.3	78514
77630	ORANGE	19304	11203	35.4	27.5	26.7	7.3	3.1	37668	44107	38	45	7646	43.3	29.2	23.0	4.0	0.4	56877
77632	ORANGE	23946	7951	21.0	24.0	37.4	12.9	4.7	55321	62914	80	83	6638	26.6	26.0	35.6	11.5	0.3	86086
77640	PORT ARTHUR	14810	7858	48.8	25.0	20.3	4.2	1.6	25813	30659	6	7	5220	68.1	20.6	9.4	1.3	0.7	35641
77642	PORT ARTHUR	17052	13984	40.3	28.5	23.4	5.7	2.2	33036	38931	21	26	7620	58.0	26.7	13.7	1.3	0.3	44668
77650	PORT BOLIVAR	29454	1946	32.0	26.9	28.9	7.5	4.7	39798	48843	45	53	1617	39.2	28.3	24.3	7.7	0.5	62316
77651	PORT NECHES	25734	5396	19.1	25.8	35.3	15.3	4.5	54678	63864	79	83	4233	21.6	30.8	40.3	7.0	0.3	86967
77656	SILSBEE	20263	6592	29.8	31.0	29.2	7.8	2.3	39481	45068	44	53	5088	41.1	29.1	24.7	4.5	0.6	61850
77657	LUMBERTON	21017	5593	20.4	34.3	32.8	10.5	2.0	45927	52676	64	70	4550	26.9	26.3	35.3	10.9	0.7	85556
77659	SOUR LAKE	22774	1949	28.5	25.5	28.4	12.2	5.4	45250	51507	62	68	1615	29.0	27.2	29.3	13.6	0.8	80688
77660	SPURGER	13560	530	50.0	26.8	20.2	2.1	0.9	25000	28335	5	6	428	72.7	17.3	7.7	2.1	0.2	32969
77662	VIDOR	17965	10257	30.8	32.5	27.9	6.4	2.4	38089	44852	40	47	8119	45.1	33.7	18.6	2.4	0.2	54865
77664	WARREN	20480	1191	29.6	32.0	26.1	9.5	2.8	39966	46582	46	54	1016	33.8	24.7	30.8	10.1	0.6	73710
77665	WINNIE	18673	2686	27.6	31.9	31.0	7.6	2.0	40746	48253	49	57	2081	41.7	27.5	22.2	8.5	0.2	61194
77701	BEAUMONT	14794	5745	48.4	27.9	17.8	3.6	2.3	25897	30491	6	7	3114	64.1	26.3	7.1	1.8	0.7	39277
77702	BEAUMONT	24480	1266	40.3	27.0	21.5	6.0	5.2	31525	38683	16	21	570	24.7	29.1	31.6	13.0	1.6	84884
77703	BEAUMONT	12456	5629	50.5	29.3	17.6	1.7	0.9	24624	28696	4	5	2942	72.2	23.4	4.1	0.3	0.0	38235
77705	BEAUMONT	15363	10714	41.5	27.7	23.1	5.2	2.5	31959	37514	18	22	6474	50.3	28.0	16.9	4.3	0.5	49749
77706	BEAUMONT	35664	12091	20.0	25.3	31.6	14.0	9.2	56547	65807	81	84	7613	5.3	24.0	52.1	14.7	4.1	113225
77707	BEAUMONT	26127	6609	21.7	24.8	35.5	11.4	6.5	53378	62054	77	81	4697	13.6	50.5	25.2	9.3	1.4	78128
77708	BEAUMONT	19495	4502	34.2	30.7	24.5	7.1	3.5	36672	42963	34	41	2629	30.7	41.0	25.1	3.1	0.2	67650
77710	BEAUMONT	3333	5	100.0	0.0	0.0	0.0	0.0	8333	5000	0	1	2	100.0	0.0	0.0	0.0	0.0	45000
77713	BEAUMONT	22968	4616	22.6	27.2	36.7	10.3	3.3	50142	58819	72	77	3548	26.7	28.8	36.1	7.6	0.9	84265
77801	BRYAN	14843	5510	47.6	31.2	17.0	3.1	1.1	26351	31825	6	8	1188	31.4	31.7	32.9	4.0	0.0	73898
77802	BRYAN	26848	8903	25.3	24.8	31.7	11.9	6.3	49900	60674	72	77	5462	5.1	18.8	59.2	16.0	1.0	116295
77803	BRYAN	13276	9000	39.4	32.4	24.0	2.8	1.4	31643	38006	17	21	5100	49.5	38.1	11.5	0.7	0.1	50445
77807	BRYAN	21229	2707	26.0	27.2	34.5	7.9	4.3	47193	58714	67	72	1785	28.4	23.0	39.9	7.0	1.7	87992
77808	BRYAN	22962	3148	20.9	26.2	38.4	11.3	3.1	52636	62735	76	81	2425	27.2	18.9	30.3	19.2	4.5	99847
77830	ANDERSON	20584	1185	34.4	29.5	26.8	6.2	3.2	38771	45291	42	50	982	30.8	30.1	24.5	12.6	1.9	73049
77831	BEDIAS	17163	962	31.4	29.9	30.5	6.0	2.2	37334	43081	37	44	821	30.2	38.1	22.1	9.0	0.6	67067
77833	BRENHAM	20700	9597	30.6	28.1	30.4	7.2	3.7	41590	48378	52	60	6863	19.0	24.8	35.1	17.0	4.1	100058
77835	BURTON	19701	896	33.4	30.7	27.9	6.3	1.8	37502	42151	37	45	738	24.4	8.8	37.8	20.9	8.1	119958
77836	CALDWELL	18881	4480	31.1	33.4	26.8	6.8	2.0	38186	43322	40	48	3451	36.5	25.6	25.9	10.3	1.7	70662
77837	CALVERT	15269	672	54.5	24.7	15.9	2.5	2.4	21938	25557	3	4	415	51.1	26.3	19.8	2.9	0.0	49118
77840	COLLEGE STATION	14585	19054	62.8	19.2	11.6	3.7	2.7	16972	19622	1	2	2969	10.2	23.0	47.6	17.2	2.0	110404
77845	COLLEGE STATION	29758	12835	22.1	18.7	33.3	14.6	11.3	62096	76529	86	88	8316	9.9	5.6	43.7	36.0	4.7	154854
77850	CONCORD	15199	50	44.0	26.0	22.0	6.0	2.0	32354	41541	19	23	41	34.2	31.7	24.4	7.3	2.4	71250
77853	DIME BOX	15617	353	44.8	27.8	22.7	4.0	0.9	28710	32765	10	13	279	41.6	26.2	24.0	6.5	1.8	64219
77856	FRANKLIN	20918	1986	31.6	27.8	28.5	9.5	2.7	42267	48875	54	62	1608	31.3	31.1	24.6	10.3	2.7	72263
77859	HEARNE	14751	2921	42.8	28.3	24.2	3.8	1.0	31010	36068	15	19	1922	41.0	28.1	25.7	4.5	0.8	61761
77861	IOLA	19331	819	28.7	32.7	29.1	6.5	3.1	38647	45354	42	50	689	32.5	29.5	25.1	11.9	1.0	73507
77864	MADISONVILLE	17878	2436	38.2	33.8	19.1	5.1	3.7	31537	36080	16	21	1753	40.3	24.4	26.7	6.7	1.9	63512
77865	MARQUEZ	19807	553	35.3	27.5	28.0	6.2	3.1	38318	45299	40	48	459	35.7	27.7	23.8	9.6	3.3	71375
77868	NAVASOTA	17086	4891	34.9	28.7	27.9	5.2	3.4	37534	43622	38	45	3330	37.0	25.6	24.0	12.0	1.4	69046
77871	NORMANGEE	23659	1366	28.8	31.3	29.1	8.1	2.6	40174	47373	47	55	1158	23.3	19.6	36.0	19.1	2.0	97387
77872	NORTH ZULCH	20966	1067	31.6	34.0	24.8	6.0	3.6	38361	43560	41	48	895	32.6	31.1	20.9	14.5	0.9	73788
77873	RICHARDS	21746	339	33.9	28.6	26.8	7.7	3.0	37219	43961	36	43	282	38.7	22.3	24.1	12.1	2.8	69048
	TEXAS	23284		26.2	27.7	29.5	10.3	6.3	45778	54246				21.6	26.1	33.4	15.6	3.4	93683
	UNITED STATES	25866		24.7	27.1	30.8	10.9	6.5	48124	56710				10.9	15.0	33.7	30.1	10.4	145905

ZIP CODE		FINANCIAL SERVICES				THE HOME						ENTERTAINMENT						PERSONAL			
						Home Improvements		Furnishings													
#	POST OFFICE NAME	Auto Loan	Home Loan	Invest-ments	Retire-ment Plans	Home Repair	Lawn & Garden	Comput-ers & Hard-ware	Major Appli-ances	TV, Radio, Sound Equip-ment	Furni-ture	Dine out/ Carry out	Sports Equip-ment	Fees & Tickets	Toys & Games	Travel	Cable TV	Apparel & Services	Auto Repairs	Health Insur-ance	Pets & Supplies
77519	BATSON	80	73	57	71	73	78	70	75	71	72	87	87	66	83	69	70	84	75	74	89
77520	BAYTOWN	84	82	82	81	81	86	83	84	84	85	105	96	82	102	82	82	103	85	81	93
77521	BAYTOWN	90	92	97	94	90	93	92	91	90	93	113	107	92	111	90	86	110	92	84	101
77530	CHANNELVIEW	85	84	77	82	82	85	80	83	80	83	100	95	78	97	79	77	98	83	78	93
77531	CLUTE	71	66	67	67	64	67	69	69	69	72	87	80	67	83	66	66	86	71	64	76
77532	CROSBY	98	98	90	96	99	104	92	96	93	93	115	112	93	115	93	92	111	95	96	114
77534	DANBURY	101	91	71	87	95	102	84	93	89	84	108	110	83	110	86	90	103	90	99	118
77535	DAYTON	87	79	64	77	80	86	76	82	78	77	96	95	73	93	76	78	92	81	84	98
77536	DEER PARK	113	135	142	135	131	131	124	123	116	124	146	144	129	152	125	111	145	120	110	135
77538	DEVERS	115	101	75	96	102	109	96	105	99	99	122	122	90	115	95	99	116	105	108	128
77539	DICKINSON	90	90	85	89	89	94	88	89	87	89	109	104	87	107	87	86	105	89	87	101
77541	FREEPORT	74	64	56	60	64	69	66	70	69	68	86	78	61	80	64	69	83	71	71	79
77545	FRESNO	100	108	102	110	103	101	100	100	93	104	118	116	101	116	97	88	117	98	87	109
77546	FRIENDSWOOD	131	151	159	156	146	146	139	137	129	141	164	161	145	167	139	124	162	135	122	151
77547	GALENA PARK	70	64	58	60	62	66	66	69	69	70	86	75	63	82	64	67	85	70	66	73
77550	GALVESTON	53	48	57	47	47	53	55	52	57	54	71	61	53	68	53	57	69	55	54	59
77551	GALVESTON	77	74	83	74	72	78	79	78	79	80	99	89	77	95	76	77	98	80	74	85
77554	GALVESTON	131	111	106	109	117	131	118	124	124	116	152	146	110	144	118	125	144	127	133	152
77560	HANKAMER	86	58	26	50	65	75	55	69	67	57	79	83	47	74	56	72	71	69	86	99
77562	HIGHLANDS	95	85	68	82	87	93	81	88	84	83	103	102	78	101	81	84	99	87	91	107
77563	HITCHCOCK	81	78	75	75	79	86	76	79	79	77	98	90	77	97	77	81	94	78	83	93
77564	HULL	85	60	32	54	67	77	59	71	69	60	82	84	52	78	60	73	75	70	85	97
77565	KEMAH	132	148	166	151	144	147	143	140	136	144	172	164	147	175	142	131	170	140	127	154
77566	LAKE JACKSON	111	124	132	127	122	124	119	117	112	119	142	137	123	144	118	109	140	116	107	129
77568	LA MARQUE	70	72	75	69	72	79	72	72	74	71	92	81	74	93	73	75	89	72	75	81
77571	LA PORTE	103	109	109	111	107	110	105	105	101	106	126	123	106	127	104	97	123	104	98	117
77573	LEAGUE CITY	122	137	142	142	132	131	128	126	119	131	151	147	132	152	126	113	150	124	110	138
77575	LIBERTY	87	66	41	61	72	82	66	76	74	66	88	88	59	85	66	78	82	75	88	98
77577	LIVERPOOL	89	79	60	75	84	90	73	81	78	73	95	97	72	96	75	80	90	79	88	105
77578	MANVEL	116	123	114	123	122	124	113	116	109	114	136	136	114	138	113	106	133	113	110	134
77581	PEARLAND	115	129	132	131	125	125	120	119	113	122	142	139	123	144	119	108	141	117	107	132
77583	ROSHARON	105	106	92	104	104	106	98	102	96	101	120	118	97	116	97	93	117	101	96	117
77584	PEARLAND	130	143	136	148	137	134	130	130	121	135	153	152	133	152	127	113	151	127	113	144
77585	SARATOGA	70	47	21	41	53	61	45	57	55	46	64	68	39	61	46	59	59	56	70	81
77586	SEABROOK	129	136	153	144	132	135	136	131	129	138	163	156	138	162	132	122	161	133	117	145
77587	SOUTH HOUSTON	72	63	58	61	61	64	68	70	70	72	88	77	63	83	64	66	88	73	65	74
77590	TEXAS CITY	71	71	75	70	71	76	73	72	73	72	91	83	73	92	72	73	89	73	72	80
77591	TEXAS CITY	73	68	72	68	68	77	71	71	73	72	91	80	71	88	71	74	88	72	74	81
77597	WALLISVILLE	107	84	54	77	89	98	81	93	89	83	107	109	73	101	81	91	100	92	103	121
77598	WEBSTER	79	69	79	76	66	70	79	75	78	81	99	91	75	92	73	72	96	80	67	83
77611	BRIDGE CITY	82	83	77	83	83	87	80	82	79	80	98	96	80	98	80	77	95	81	80	94
77612	BUNA	80	60	36	54	66	74	57	68	65	58	78	81	52	76	58	69	72	67	80	93
77614	DEWEYVILLE	76	58	36	53	62	69	56	65	62	57	75	77	50	71	56	65	70	65	73	86
77616	FRED	83	55	25	48	63	72	53	67	64	54	76	80	45	71	54	69	69	66	82	95
77619	GROVES	82	88	91	85	88	95	86	86	86	84	106	99	88	110	87	87	104	85	87	96
77622	HAMSHIRE	111	98	74	93	104	112	91	101	97	91	118	120	89	120	94	99	112	98	110	131
77624	HILLISTER	70	54	36	50	60	70	55	64	62	54	74	73	49	71	57	66	68	63	76	82
77625	KOUNTZE	95	71	42	64	77	86	68	81	77	69	92	96	61	88	69	81	86	80	93	109
77627	NEDERLAND	90	92	89	90	93	100	89	92	90	88	111	105	90	114	91	91	107	90	93	104
77630	ORANGE	75	65	57	62	67	76	67	71	72	66	87	81	64	85	67	74	83	71	78	85
77632	ORANGE	103	93	74	90	96	103	88	96	92	88	112	112	86	112	89	93	107	94	100	118
77640	PORT ARTHUR	55	47	48	43	48	56	51	52	56	51	69	57	50	64	50	59	65	53	60	61
77642	PORT ARTHUR	63	59	65	58	58	64	64	63	66	64	83	72	63	81	63	66	81	65	64	69
77650	PORT BOLIVAR	107	84	57	76	94	106	79	95	89	78	106	111	71	104	84	95	98	94	112	130
77651	PORT NECHES	90	97	101	97	97	103	94	95	92	93	115	109	97	118	95	92	112	93	92	105
77656	SILSBEE	88	70	50	65	75	85	70	79	78	70	94	91	65	90	70	82	87	78	91	100
77657	LUMBERTON	89	85	71	83	85	88	80	84	80	81	99	99	78	97	79	79	96	84	83	100
77659	SOUR LAKE	98	88	71	84	93	101	85	93	90	84	109	108	82	108	86	92	103	91	101	114
77660	SPURGER	64	43	20	37	49	56	42	52	50	42	59	62	35	56	42	54	54	51	64	74
77662	VIDOR	79	67	49	63	71	78	65	72	70	65	85	84	62	83	66	72	80	71	79	91
77664	WARREN	94	65	32	59	75	85	64	79	74	63	87	95	54	84	65	79	80	78	95	111
77665	WINNIE	85	70	48	66	73	80	67	76	73	68	88	88	63	85	67	74	83	75	82	96
77701	BEAUMONT	57	51	56	48	50	58	55	55	59	57	74	61	55	70	54	61	71	57	59	63
77702	BEAUMONT	76	76	87	76	75	81	82	79	82	80	103	93	82	103	80	81	100	81	77	86
77703	BEAUMONT	47	42	49	40	41	48	46	46	49	47	61	51	46	58	45	51	59	47	49	52
77705	BEAUMONT	62	54	57	52	54	62	58	58	62	58	77	67	57	74	57	63	74	60	62	69
77706	BEAUMONT	104	111	132	115	110	116	115	110	110	113	139	131	116	139	113	107	137	113	103	121
77707	BEAUMONT	90	98	106	97	97	103	95	95	93	95	117	108	98	117	96	92	114	94	92	104
77708	BEAUMONT	69	69	80	68	68	73	73	71	74	73	92	82	73	92	72	73	90	72	69	78
77710	BEAUMONT	11	10	12	10	10	11	11	11	12	11	15	12	11	14	11	12	14	11	11	12
77713	BEAUMONT	90	87	76	85	89	93	82	87	83	82	102	103	81	104	83	83	99	85	88	106
77801	BRYAN	50	37	46	41	37	42	56	46	55	51	69	60	49	64	48	50	66	53	43	52
77802	BRYAN	88	91	103	94	89	94	95	91	92	94	116	108	95	115	93	89	114	93	85	100
77803	BRYAN	60	54	54	54	54	57	59	59	59	59	74	68	56	71	56	57	73	61	56	64
77807	BRYAN	90	80	76	82	78	83	84	84	84	86	105	100	79	98	80	80	102	87	80	97
77808	BRYAN	104	92	73	90	94	99	89	96	91	91	112	112	84	107	88	90	107	96	96	116
77830	ANDERSON	92	66	37	60	74	85	66	79	76	65	89	93	57	86	67	80	82	78	94	107
77831	BEDIAS	89	62	31	54	70	80	59	74	71	60	83	88	51	79	61	76	76	73	90	104
77833	BRENHAM	85	73	60	70	77	85	73	79	78	72	95	93	70	94	74	80	90	79	86	98
77835	BURTON	85	59	30	54	68	77	58	72	67	58	79	86	49	77	60	71	72	71	86	100
77836	CALDWELL	83	64	44	61	69	78	66	74	72	65	87	86	59	83	66	75	81	74	84	94
77837	CALVERT	58	45	37	41	47	57	50	54	57	49	68	59	46	62	49	61	63	54	64	64
77840	COLLEGE STATION	45	30	38	34	30	35	53	40	52	46	64	55	44	59	44	46	61	48	38	46
77845	COLLEGE STATION	117	114	119	119	111	115	123	114	116	120	147	138	119	142	115	109	143	118	103	128
77850	CONCORD	79	53	24	46	60	69	51	64	62	52	72	76	43	68	52	66	66	63	79	91
77853	DIME BOX	74	50	23	43	56	65	48	60	58	49	68	72	41	64	49	62	62	60	74	85
77856	FRANKLIN	88	67	43	62	75	86	67	79	76	65	90	91	59	87	69	81	82	78	94	104
77859	HEARNE	61	51	44	48	52	59	54	57	58	54	70	64	50	65	53	60	67	57	62	67
77861	IOLA	87	68	44	65	74	81	66	77	72	67	86	91	60	83	67	73	81	76	85	100
77864	MADISONVILLE	79	59	42	56	65	75	64	71	71	62	85	82	57	82	64	74	79	71	82	89
77865	MARQUEZ	93	65	33	57	73	84	62	77	74	63	86	92	54	83	64	79	79	76	94	108
77868	NAVASOTA	76	65	53	62	67	74	67	71	71	66	86	82	63	83	66	72	82	71	76	84
77871	NORMANGEE	89	74	59	70	80	94	73	83	80	74	97	88	69	86	76	85	89	82	98	100
77872	NORTH ZULCH	94	66	34	62	77	86	65	80	75	64	88	97	55	86	67	79	80	79	96	112
77873	RICHARDS	88	69	46	65	75	85	68	78	76	68	91	91	63	89	69	79	84	77	90	101
	TEXAS	94	90	91	90	89	95	92	93	92	93	115	107	90	112	90	90	112	94	89	104
	UNITED STATES	100	100	100	100	100	100	100	100	100	100	100	100	100	100	100	100	100	100	100	100

ZIP CODE # / POST OFFICE NAME	COUNTY FIPS CODE	POPULATION 2000	2004	2009	2000-2004 ANNUAL RATE % Rate	State Centile	HOUSEHOLDS 2000	2004	2009	% Annual Rate 2000-2004	2004 Average HH Size	FAMILIES 2000	2004	% Annual Rate 2000-2004
77879 SOMERVILLE	051	6073	6378	7138	1.2	47	2426	2533	2817	1.0	2.52	1687	1765	1.1
77880 WASHINGTON	477	514	940	1280	15.3	100	188	342	463	15.1	2.75	137	248	15.0
77901 VICTORIA	469	41028	41754	42941	0.4	23	14670	14886	15281	0.3	2.74	10163	10325	0.4
77904 VICTORIA	469	23704	24550	25417	0.8	36	8895	9176	9476	0.7	2.65	6785	7016	0.8
77905 VICTORIA	469	14478	15479	16312	1.6	59	4959	5293	5574	1.6	2.88	4012	4287	1.6
77951 BLOOMINGTON	469	3736	3850	3953	0.7	32	1158	1189	1219	0.6	3.24	925	951	0.7
77954 CUERO	123	11294	11698	12174	0.8	36	3822	3956	4117	0.8	2.56	2697	2799	0.9
77957 EDNA	239	9157	9445	9820	0.7	34	3426	3514	3635	0.6	2.63	2440	2511	0.7
77962 GANADO	239	3127	3203	3305	0.6	28	1124	1142	1171	0.4	2.76	846	863	0.5
77963 GOLIAD	175	6460	6908	7506	1.6	59	2468	2641	2877	1.6	2.57	1834	1969	1.7
77964 HALLETTSVILLE	285	6956	7079	7388	0.4	23	2781	2819	2936	0.3	2.43	1939	1970	0.4
77968 INEZ	469	1606	1741	1837	1.9	66	563	610	643	1.9	2.80	455	493	1.9
77971 LOLITA	239	2956	2992	3070	0.3	20	1093	1099	1121	0.1	2.72	837	845	0.2
77974 MEYERSVILLE	123	188	190	195	0.3	19	74	74	76	0.0	2.57	58	58	0.0
77975 MOULTON	285	2522	2561	2665	0.4	22	1024	1034	1072	0.2	2.42	713	721	0.3
77979 PORT LAVACA	057	17678	18111	18701	0.6	28	6353	6474	6657	0.4	2.77	4776	4879	0.5
77983 SEADRIFT	057	2073	2170	2258	1.1	45	757	787	815	0.9	2.75	545	568	1.0
77984 SHINER	285	3650	3823	4038	1.1	45	1507	1578	1665	1.1	2.37	1052	1104	1.1
77990 TIVOLI	391	985	983	978	-0.1	11	395	394	392	-0.1	2.49	295	295	0.0
77994 WESTHOFF	123	373	377	387	0.3	19	148	148	151	0.0	2.55	106	106	0.0
77995 YOAKUM	285	9834	10491	11199	1.5	58	3776	4013	4272	1.4	2.56	2711	2890	1.5
78002 ATASCOSA	029	6446	7142	7910	2.4	75	1986	2183	2405	2.3	3.26	1576	1736	2.3
78003 BANDERA	019	7237	8035	9269	2.5	76	2919	3209	3667	2.3	2.49	2084	2298	2.3
78004 BERGHEIM	259	435	491	582	2.9	80	150	168	198	2.7	2.90	125	140	2.7
78005 BIGFOOT	163	308	317	331	0.7	32	112	116	122	0.8	2.72	84	87	0.8
78006 BOERNE	259	20768	24340	29124	3.8	89	7613	8870	10551	3.7	2.71	5982	6982	3.7
78007 CALLIHAM	311	314	331	331	1.3	50	134	142	142	1.4	2.33	90	95	1.3
78008 CAMPBELLTON	013	501	518	564	0.8	35	203	209	227	0.7	2.48	151	156	0.8
78009 CASTROVILLE	325	6607	7224	8068	2.1	70	2204	2397	2667	2.0	2.98	1784	1943	2.0
78010 CENTER POINT	265	3450	3641	3900	1.3	50	1345	1412	1506	1.2	2.56	972	1023	1.2
78011 CHARLOTTE	013	2128	2224	2431	1.0	43	712	741	806	0.9	3.00	542	565	1.0
78013 COMFORT	259	4124	4757	5703	3.4	86	1513	1720	2039	3.1	2.71	1138	1297	3.1
78014 COTULLA	283	4965	5205	5508	1.1	45	1506	1592	1702	1.3	2.91	1119	1186	1.4
78015 BOERNE	259	6404	7535	8781	3.9	90	2241	2620	3031	3.7	2.86	1982	2317	3.7
78016 DEVINE	325	9045	9999	11242	2.4	75	3068	3379	3787	2.3	2.90	2366	2610	2.3
78017 DILLEY	163	5229	5340	5518	0.5	25	1228	1273	1344	0.9	2.97	943	980	0.9
78019 ENCINAL	283	818	822	851	0.1	15	276	277	288	0.1	2.97	206	207	0.1
78021 FOWLERTON	283	91	93	95	0.5	25	39	40	42	0.6	1.45	28	22	-5.5
78022 GEORGE WEST	297	4509	4589	4766	0.4	23	1644	1678	1750	0.5	2.66	1214	1243	0.6
78023 HELOTES	029	8016	10813	13324	7.3	98	2802	3740	4577	7.0	2.88	2367	3173	7.1
78024 HUNT	265	614	650	694	1.4	53	228	241	258	1.3	2.45	166	176	1.4
78025 INGRAM	265	5725	6171	6682	1.8	63	2257	2416	2603	1.6	2.49	1647	1766	1.7
78026 JOURDANTON	013	5356	6016	6823	2.8	79	1764	1981	2244	2.8	2.94	1379	1551	2.8
78027 KENDALIA	259	343	403	488	3.9	90	141	164	197	3.6	2.46	105	123	3.8
78028 KERRVILLE	265	33641	35574	38116	1.3	52	13893	14650	15675	1.3	2.32	9453	10000	1.3
78039 LA COSTE	325	1680	1741	1889	0.8	37	581	599	647	0.7	2.87	467	482	0.8
78040 LAREDO	479	43292	46709	53468	1.8	64	11901	12814	14665	1.8	3.54	9506	10222	1.7
78041 LAREDO	479	40507	44720	52237	2.4	74	11503	12675	14801	2.3	3.43	9441	10380	2.3
78043 LAREDO	479	34923	38728	45138	2.5	75	9503	10468	12140	2.3	3.70	8047	8858	2.3
78045 LAREDO	479	29150	39772	51355	7.6	98	7765	10697	13860	7.8	3.68	6966	9543	7.7
78046 LAREDO	479	43339	51297	61714	4.1	90	9530	11271	13534	4.0	4.54	9035	10683	4.0
78052 LYTLE	013	5071	5616	6320	2.4	75	1631	1797	2013	2.3	3.12	1304	1439	2.4
78055 MEDINA	019	2139	2286	2576	1.6	59	858	911	1023	1.4	2.37	605	644	1.5
78056 MICO	325	729	792	882	2.0	67	301	325	360	1.8	2.44	243	263	1.9
78057 MOORE	163	866	893	929	0.7	34	335	347	363	0.8	2.55	250	260	0.9
78058 MOUNTAIN HOME	265	310	330	354	1.5	57	130	138	149	1.4	2.17	95	102	1.7
78059 NATALIA	325	5121	6023	7003	3.9	90	1626	1912	2219	3.9	3.14	1305	1536	3.9
78061 PEARSALL	163	9849	10269	10770	1.0	42	3068	3225	3418	1.2	3.01	2366	2494	1.3
78063 PIPE CREEK	019	7733	9078	10779	3.9	89	3012	3506	4126	3.6	2.59	2208	2574	3.7
78064 PLEASANTON	013	13390	14413	16060	1.8	63	4669	5012	5575	1.7	2.85	3566	3834	1.7
78065 POTEET	013	10091	11377	12937	2.9	80	3219	3613	4092	2.8	3.14	2562	2882	2.8
78066 RIO MEDINA	325	682	734	813	1.7	63	240	257	283	1.6	2.86	196	210	1.6
78067 SAN YGNACIO	505	1037	1101	1187	1.4	55	322	343	370	1.5	3.21	247	264	1.6
78069 SOMERSET	013	3726	4179	4708	2.7	79	1188	1323	1482	2.6	3.16	941	1050	2.6
78070 SPRING BRANCH	091	7373	9366	11792	5.8	96	2600	3280	4101	5.6	2.85	2088	2639	5.7
78071 THREE RIVERS	297	5079	5344	5565	1.2	48	1399	1462	1552	1.0	2.65	1032	1082	1.1
78072 TILDEN	311	529	559	559	1.3	51	219	232	232	1.4	2.41	148	157	1.4
78073 VON ORMY	029	7277	8658	9951	4.2	91	2233	2646	3031	4.1	3.27	1804	2139	4.1
78074 WARING	259	31	35	41	2.9	80	13	14	17	1.8	2.50	10	11	2.3
78075 WHITSETT	297	179	190	196	1.4	55	73	77	81	1.3	1.34	54	33	-10.9
78076 ZAPATA	505	11111	11992	13045	1.8	64	3591	3874	4220	1.8	3.09	2911	3147	1.9
78101 ADKINS	029	5787	6220	6828	1.7	62	1994	2140	2347	1.7	2.91	1611	1727	1.7
78102 BEEVILLE	025	30044	31136	32616	0.8	37	8275	8676	9235	1.1	2.72	5963	6268	1.2
78108 CIBOLO	187	7778	9374	11232	4.5	93	2835	3365	3987	4.1	2.79	2230	2644	4.1
78109 CONVERSE	029	22410	25268	28298	2.9	80	7233	8083	9002	2.7	3.10	6008	6721	2.7
78111 ECLETO	255	3	3	3	0.0	13	3	3	3	0.0	1.00	2	0	-100.0
78112 ELMENDORF	029	6940	8067	9157	3.6	87	2070	2375	2673	3.3	3.40	1707	1964	3.4
78113 FALLS CITY	255	1192	1266	1369	1.4	55	456	485	527	1.5	2.60	342	365	1.5
78114 FLORESVILLE	493	15897	18315	21079	3.4	86	5318	6125	7062	3.4	2.93	4289	4956	3.5
78116 GILLETT	255	619	640	681	0.8	35	255	265	283	0.9	2.41	182	190	1.0
78117 HOBSON	255	338	361	390	1.6	58	126	135	146	1.6	2.67	95	101	1.5
78118 KARNES CITY	255	4353	4569	4875	1.2	46	1346	1421	1535	1.3	2.77	978	1035	1.3
78119 KENEDY	255	7492	7763	8140	0.8	37	1720	1836	1995	1.6	2.61	1247	1334	1.6
78121 LA VERNIA	493	7140	7933	8954	2.5	76	2428	2710	3069	2.6	2.89	1977	2205	2.6
78122 LEESVILLE	177	290	307	329	1.4	53	103	108	116	1.1	2.84	79	84	1.5
78123 MC QUEENEY	187	2024	2105	2383	0.9	39	808	835	940	0.8	2.49	594	614	0.8
78124 MARION	187	5431	5598	6245	0.7	33	1832	1873	2073	0.5	2.99	1485	1516	0.5
78130 NEW BRAUNFELS	187	43661	50172	59903	3.3	85	15948	18215	21661	3.2	2.70	11488	13143	3.2
78132 NEW BRAUNFELS	091	11804	13796	16715	3.7	88	4170	4858	5861	3.7	2.81	3454	4021	3.6
78133 CANYON LAKE	091	13493	15835	19244	3.8	89	5640	6579	7947	3.7	2.40	4098	4786	3.7
78140 NIXON	177	3357	3487	3694	0.9	38	1141	1180	1247	0.8	2.86	857	888	0.8
78141 NORDHEIM	123	621	614	632	-0.3	8	253	248	254	-0.5	2.47	182	180	-0.3
78147 POTH	493	3074	3062	3286	-0.1	11	1073	1069	1150	-0.1	2.86	849	844	-0.1
78148 UNIVERSAL CITY	029	14558	15125	16302	0.9	38	5894	6093	6542	0.8	2.48	4156	4302	0.8
78150 UNIVERSAL CITY	029	3816	3705	3890	-0.7	3	1028	990	1045	-0.9	3.22	831	801	-0.9
TEXAS					2.2					2.0	2.77			2.1
UNITED STATES					1.2					1.3	2.58			1.1

#	POST OFFICE NAME	RACE (%) White 2000	White 2004	Black 2000	Black 2004	Asian/Pacific 2000	Asian/Pacific 2004	% Hispanic Origin 2000	% Hispanic Origin 2004	2004 AGE DISTRIBUTION (%) 0-4	5-9	10-14	15-19	20-24	25-44	45-64	65-84	85+	18+	MEDIAN AGE 2004	% 2004 Males	% 2004 Females
77879	SOMERVILLE	70.9	69.0	20.0	20.7	0.2	0.3	13.1	15.1	6.6	6.7	6.7	6.9	6.4	23.5	26.6	14.9	1.8	75.8	40.3	48.9	51.1
77880	WASHINGTON	57.8	56.8	40.5	41.3	0.2	0.1	3.3	3.8	6.6	7.3	8.9	8.2	6.0	22.1	28.3	10.5	2.0	72.1	37.9	50.9	49.2
77901	VICTORIA	64.0	61.9	9.5	9.3	0.6	0.6	53.5	58.0	8.6	7.7	7.9	7.6	8.2	27.5	20.6	10.4	1.6	71.3	32.3	48.6	51.4
77904	VICTORIA	87.4	85.3	3.2	3.5	1.7	1.9	18.8	22.8	6.6	6.7	7.7	7.5	6.2	24.9	27.1	11.5	1.7	74.3	38.6	47.8	52.2
77905	VICTORIA	84.0	82.0	3.1	3.3	0.1	0.2	28.6	32.9	7.2	7.4	8.1	7.1	6.2	27.0	25.6	10.6	0.9	73.0	36.4	50.0	50.0
77951	BLOOMINGTON	59.2	56.7	5.3	5.0	0.2	0.2	60.4	65.0	9.6	9.0	9.7	9.1	7.6	26.5	19.3	8.6	0.7	66.2	29.0	49.4	50.6
77954	CUERO	70.0	68.6	15.7	15.7	0.4	0.4	27.8	31.0	5.6	5.6	6.2	6.3	5.9	28.6	25.6	13.7	2.6	78.6	40.3	53.7	46.3
77957	EDNA	72.6	70.2	10.7	10.9	0.6	0.7	24.5	27.8	7.5	7.2	6.9	7.0	7.5	24.6	23.5	13.5	2.5	74.1	37.4	48.7	51.3
77962	GANADO	79.9	77.9	3.4	3.2	0.2	0.2	29.7	33.6	7.0	7.0	7.2	6.7	6.8	26.4	23.7	13.0	2.3	73.9	37.5	51.1	48.9
77963	GOLIAD	82.4	80.9	4.6	4.6	0.2	0.3	36.1	40.1	5.8	6.2	7.1	6.6	6.0	23.4	27.4	15.4	2.2	76.6	41.7	50.1	49.9
77964	HALLETTSVILLE	87.4	86.2	8.3	8.6	0.1	0.2	7.0	8.5	5.4	5.6	6.1	6.5	5.9	21.9	26.3	18.0	4.4	78.9	44.1	48.9	51.1
77968	INEZ	90.1	88.3	2.0	2.2	0.4	0.4	15.9	19.5	6.6	6.9	8.3	9.3	6.2	25.5	27.4	9.2	0.9	72.0	37.1	49.9	50.1
77971	LOLITA	89.0	87.4	0.7	0.7	0.7	0.7	17.9	21.0	7.1	7.1	7.6	6.7	6.0	26.0	25.0	13.1	1.5	74.3	38.1	49.7	50.3
77974	MEYERSVILLE	95.2	95.3	1.1	1.1	0.0	0.0	6.9	9.0	4.2	5.3	7.4	6.3	5.8	23.7	30.5	15.3	1.6	79.5	43.6	50.5	49.5
77975	MOULTON	95.6	95.0	0.5	0.5	0.0	0.0	10.6	12.5	5.6	5.6	6.2	6.4	5.5	20.8	25.9	19.0	4.8	78.5	44.8	50.3	49.8
77979	PORT LAVACA	77.0	75.2	2.9	2.9	3.0	3.2	44.3	48.4	8.1	7.7	7.8	6.8	6.4	26.5	23.7	11.9	1.1	72.2	35.6	50.7	49.3
77983	SEADRIFT	82.0	79.9	0.6	0.7	7.1	7.6	22.2	26.0	7.8	7.8	8.0	6.4	5.9	22.5	26.7	13.5	1.4	72.4	38.7	50.6	49.5
77984	SHINER	88.6	87.5	8.1	8.6	0.3	0.3	5.3	6.3	5.3	5.6	6.2	5.7	5.3	21.8	26.5	19.3	4.6	79.4	45.2	47.6	52.5
77990	TIVOLI	83.7	83.5	2.2	2.2	0.4	0.4	62.9	64.1	6.3	6.4	6.6	7.2	5.5	24.3	27.2	14.8	1.7	76.1	41.0	51.8	48.2
77994	WESTHOFF	85.5	83.6	5.1	5.6	0.3	0.3	21.2	24.9	5.0	5.6	6.1	6.1	4.5	22.3	27.9	19.9	2.7	79.3	45.3	50.1	49.9
77995	YOAKUM	82.3	80.9	7.7	7.9	0.2	0.2	22.7	25.5	7.2	6.9	7.2	6.7	6.5	24.0	23.5	15.1	2.9	74.5	39.1	48.6	51.4
78002	ATASCOSA	70.5	67.3	0.5	0.5	0.4	0.4	68.5	75.1	8.1	7.7	8.1	8.7	7.7	27.0	22.7	9.1	0.9	70.7	32.6	51.0	49.0
78003	BANDERA	93.9	93.1	0.2	0.3	0.3	0.4	15.3	17.7	5.7	5.9	6.5	6.5	5.6	23.1	29.1	16.1	1.6	77.9	42.9	49.4	50.6
78004	BERGHEIM	97.2	96.7	0.0	0.0	0.0	0.2	9.7	11.2	5.7	6.9	7.5	7.3	5.1	23.0	32.0	11.2	1.2	74.8	41.9	50.3	49.7
78005	BIGFOOT	84.7	83.0	0.3	0.3	0.7	0.6	44.8	50.5	5.7	6.3	8.2	5.7	4.4	24.6	28.7	14.5	1.9	76.0	41.3	51.4	48.6
78006	BOERNE	94.4	93.4	0.3	0.3	0.4	0.4	15.4	18.3	6.0	6.8	7.7	7.1	4.6	23.6	30.5	11.8	1.9	74.8	41.7	48.6	51.4
78007	CALLIHAM	88.5	88.2	1.3	1.2	0.0	0.0	32.2	33.2	3.9	4.5	6.0	7.3	5.4	21.5	32.9	16.0	2.4	81.0	45.6	50.8	49.2
78008	CAMPBELLTON	82.4	80.5	0.2	0.2	0.8	1.0	42.1	47.1	8.1	7.7	6.6	6.0	5.0	25.7	24.7	13.9	2.3	73.9	38.8	51.5	48.5
78009	CASTROVILLE	82.4	80.4	0.5	0.5	0.6	0.6	35.2	39.6	7.6	7.7	8.1	7.4	6.4	27.1	24.6	9.6	1.6	72.1	36.3	50.6	49.4
78010	CENTER POINT	88.7	87.1	0.1	0.1	0.3	0.3	24.0	27.8	6.7	6.6	6.6	6.5	6.1	23.1	27.7	14.8	1.8	76.1	41.3	50.2	49.8
78011	CHARLOTTE	70.5	69.1	0.1	0.1	0.0	0.0	73.5	77.1	9.6	8.4	8.2	8.1	7.6	24.8	22.3	9.7	1.3	69.2	32.1	50.3	49.7
78013	COMFORT	84.1	82.3	0.4	0.4	0.4	0.4	31.7	35.6	7.1	7.1	7.3	6.5	6.4	24.2	26.2	12.7	2.5	74.8	38.3	49.7	50.3
78014	COTULLA	82.4	82.0	3.9	3.7	0.4	0.4	75.8	78.7	7.5	7.3	7.6	8.8	8.3	27.8	21.9	9.7	1.2	72.1	33.0	53.1	46.9
78015	BOERNE	95.9	95.1	0.5	0.5	0.5	0.6	10.4	13.1	4.5	6.1	7.8	7.4	4.1	17.9	35.9	15.5	0.9	76.8	46.3	50.3	49.7
78016	DEVINE	80.6	78.7	0.8	0.9	0.3	0.3	44.5	49.4	7.7	7.4	7.9	7.4	7.0	25.6	24.1	11.3	1.7	72.3	35.3	49.8	50.2
78017	DILLEY	66.3	66.1	14.3	13.5	0.8	0.8	65.5	68.8	6.6	6.6	6.4	6.2	13.4	38.2	15.1	6.7	0.8	76.6	29.4	64.1	35.9
78019	ENCINAL	76.0	75.3	0.4	0.4	0.0	0.0	88.0	90.2	8.5	7.1	8.4	10.6	7.3	24.6	20.2	11.6	1.8	70.0	31.1	50.0	50.0
78021	FOWLERTON	81.3	81.7	13.2	11.8	0.0	0.0	48.4	52.7	4.3	4.3	4.3	6.5	10.8	36.6	23.7	8.6	1.1	83.9	36.4	68.8	31.2
78022	GEORGE WEST	87.1	85.8	0.2	0.2	0.2	0.2	43.9	48.1	6.8	6.6	7.7	6.8	6.5	23.3	26.3	13.7	2.4	74.7	40.1	48.3	51.8
78023	HELOTES	88.1	84.5	1.7	2.0	1.6	1.8	26.6	34.0	6.9	7.0	6.9	6.5	5.5	28.0	28.8	9.5	0.9	75.0	38.7	49.2	50.8
78024	HUNT	94.3	93.5	2.8	2.9	0.3	0.3	14.8	17.7	3.5	4.6	6.6	7.4	6.8	19.1	33.9	16.9	1.2	80.6	46.1	52.6	47.4
78025	INGRAM	94.8	93.9	0.4	0.5	0.5	0.5	10.8	13.0	4.7	4.9	5.8	6.4	5.1	18.9	28.6	23.0	2.6	80.4	47.7	48.9	51.1
78026	JOURDANTON	78.2	76.3	1.0	0.9	0.3	0.3	49.9	54.8	8.3	7.7	8.2	8.3	7.5	27.0	22.0	9.3	1.6	70.5	33.0	49.5	50.5
78027	KENDALIA	93.6	92.8	0.3	0.5	0.3	0.5	12.0	13.9	5.5	6.0	6.2	5.7	3.7	22.8	35.2	13.4	1.5	78.9	45.1	50.6	49.4
78028	KERRVILLE	87.8	86.4	2.2	2.3	0.6	0.7	20.2	23.1	5.5	5.4	6.0	6.4	5.9	20.6	24.6	21.6	4.0	79.1	45.2	47.6	52.4
78039	LA COSTE	81.4	79.9	1.5	1.5	0.3	0.3	46.7	51.3	7.4	7.5	8.9	8.1	6.3	30.0	21.1	9.7	1.2	71.2	33.7	49.9	50.1
78040	LAREDO	82.6	82.4	0.4	0.4	0.2	0.2	96.7	97.2	10.3	9.6	8.9	7.7	7.9	26.4	16.9	10.7	1.7	66.8	28.8	47.4	52.6
78041	LAREDO	84.0	83.8	0.5	0.4	0.9	0.8	91.3	92.6	9.2	8.5	8.3	8.0	8.8	30.0	19.4	7.0	0.9	69.2	29.3	48.5	51.5
78043	LAREDO	81.2	81.0	0.3	0.4	0.3	0.3	95.0	96.0	10.9	10.1	9.5	8.1	8.2	28.8	16.3	7.4	0.8	64.6	27.0	48.3	51.7
78045	LAREDO	81.9	81.6	0.3	0.3	1.0	1.0	90.0	91.5	11.1	10.2	9.9	7.8	7.3	33.5	16.4	3.6	0.3	64.0	27.5	49.0	51.0
78046	LAREDO	80.9	80.8	0.3	0.4	0.1	0.1	97.0	97.5	13.0	12.3	12.1	9.5	8.2	28.6	12.9	3.3	0.2	56.7	22.0	48.9	51.1
78052	LYTLE	71.6	69.7	0.6	0.6	0.4	0.4	60.1	64.5	8.2	8.1	8.2	8.7	7.5	27.0	22.2	9.2	0.9	69.9	32.8	48.8	51.2
78055	MEDINA	95.0	94.6	0.9	1.0	0.2	0.2	8.0	9.3	4.8	5.6	6.6	8.7	4.5	18.2	31.1	17.6	2.9	76.6	46.1	48.6	51.4
78056	MICO	90.1	88.9	0.6	0.5	0.6	0.6	20.6	23.7	6.9	7.3	7.8	6.6	5.6	27.2	27.2	10.5	1.0	73.7	38.7	51.3	48.7
78057	MOORE	84.8	83.1	0.4	0.3	0.2	0.3	45.0	50.1	5.6	6.5	8.4	5.7	4.5	24.9	28.9	13.9	1.7	75.9	40.9	51.2	48.8
78058	MOUNTAIN HOME	91.3	89.7	1.0	1.2	0.3	0.3	12.9	15.2	5.2	5.8	6.7	8.5	4.6	19.7	29.1	18.8	1.8	76.1	44.8	50.9	49.1
78059	NATALIA	70.3	68.9	0.7	0.8	0.4	0.4	62.3	65.9	8.6	8.3	8.8	8.1	6.9	26.0	22.6	9.9	0.9	68.9	32.8	49.6	50.4
78061	PEARSALL	73.3	72.4	0.4	0.4	0.3	0.3	81.6	84.0	8.9	8.5	8.7	8.0	7.5	26.1	21.1	9.8	1.4	69.2	31.4	50.8	49.2
78063	PIPE CREEK	93.8	93.0	0.3	0.3	0.4	0.4	13.5	15.7	5.8	6.3	6.8	6.6	4.7	24.5	30.7	13.6	0.9	76.9	42.3	50.3	49.7
78064	PLEASANTON	78.8	77.1	0.8	0.9	0.6	0.6	48.7	53.0	8.4	8.2	8.1	7.6	6.9	26.2	23.1	10.1	1.4	70.4	33.8	49.1	50.9
78065	POTEET	66.7	65.1	0.4	0.4	0.3	0.3	71.4	74.7	8.8	8.5	9.0	8.4	7.3	26.5	21.4	9.1	0.9	68.3	31.1	49.4	50.6
78066	RIO MEDINA	89.9	88.6	0.6	0.7	0.9	1.0	20.8	24.1	7.0	7.5	7.9	7.0	5.6	27.4	27.3	9.7	0.8	73.3	38.2	51.4	48.6
78067	SAN YGNACIO	80.0	79.7	1.5	1.5	0.1	0.1	90.2	91.7	8.0	7.8	7.8	9.4	8.8	23.7	21.8	11.9	0.8	70.8	31.0	53.1	46.9
78069	SOMERSET	72.0	69.8	0.3	0.3	0.2	0.2	66.8	71.9	8.5	8.3	9.2	7.9	6.9	27.8	21.3	9.2	1.0	68.9	31.6	49.7	50.3
78070	SPRING BRANCH	93.0	91.8	0.7	0.8	0.3	0.4	13.4	16.4	6.1	6.4	8.1	7.5	4.9	26.2	30.6	9.4	0.9	74.3	40.1	49.4	50.6
78071	THREE RIVERS	84.7	83.7	5.4	5.4	0.3	0.3	42.3	47.1	4.2	4.6	5.6	6.1	11.5	33.2	23.6	9.7	1.6	81.9	35.7	62.5	37.5
78072	TILDEN	88.3	88.0	1.3	1.3	0.0	0.0	33.8	34.7	4.1	4.7	5.9	7.7	5.9	21.5	31.7	16.1	2.5	80.7	45.1	50.5	49.6
78073	VON ORMY	67.6	65.3	0.6	0.6	0.6	0.6	73.1	78.4	8.6	8.3	9.9	8.4	7.7	27.5	21.1	7.9	0.6	68.2	30.5	50.2	49.8
78074	WARING	93.6	94.3	0.0	0.0	0.0	0.0	16.1	17.1	5.7	5.7	5.7	5.7	5.7	22.9	31.4	17.1	0.0	82.9	43.8	45.7	54.3
78075	WHITSETT	83.2	82.6	8.9	9.0	0.0	0.0	44.7	50.0	3.2	3.2	4.2	5.3	13.7	39.0	23.2	7.4	1.1	86.3	34.3	72.1	27.9
78076	ZAPATA	84.4	83.9	0.3	0.3	0.2	0.3	84.3	86.4	9.7	9.0	9.2	8.0	7.3	24.2	19.0	12.2	1.5	67.2	30.4	49.0	51.0
78101	ADKINS	86.3	84.3	3.9	4.0	0.5	0.5	20.1	24.7	6.4	6.8	7.8	7.1	6.3	27.5	27.6	9.8	0.8	74.7	37.7	50.2	49.8
78102	BEEVILLE	66.6	65.3	10.6	10.1	0.6	0.6	53.9	57.9	6.1	5.9	6.2	7.2	10.5	35.4	18.8	8.6	1.3	78.0	31.6	60.1	39.9
78108	CIBOLO	82.9	80.4	5.0	5.8	1.5	1.7	19.1	22.9	6.6	6.9	7.8	7.2	6.5	27.6	26.2	10.3	0.9	74.2	37.8	49.1	51.0
78109	CONVERSE	64.3	61.1	18.3	18.9	2.8	2.9	28.7	34.4	8.1	8.1	8.7	8.0	7.3	31.3	22.9	5.4	0.5	70.1	32.3	48.4	51.6
78111	ECLETO	100.0	100.0	0.0	0.0	0.0	0.0	0.0	0.0	0.0	0.0	0.0	0.0	66.7	33.3	0.0	0.0	0.0	100.0	23.8	66.7	33.3
78112	ELMENDORF	66.9	63.9	2.0	2.0	0.4	0.4	65.0	71.6	9.7	9.0	9.5	8.6	7.6	30.0	19.7	5.6	0.3	66.3	29.4	49.3	50.7
78113	FALLS CITY	93.5	92.5	0.2	0.2	0.0	0.0	15.1	17.8	6.6	7.1	7.8	5.9	5.9	26.5	23.4	14.5	2.3	74.9	39.6	50.4	49.6
78114	FLORESVILLE	76.5	74.5	1.5	1.5	0.5	0.5	47.6	51.7	7.2	7.3	8.0	7.5	6.8	27.0	25.1	9.8	1.4	72.8	36.2	49.7	50.3
78116	GILLETT	94.5	93.4	0.0	0.0	0.0	0.0	8.2	10.0	3.8	4.1	5.9	6.7	5.5	20.9	29.5	20.8	2.8	82.0	46.7	49.5	50.5
78117	HOBSON	93.8	92.8	0.0	0.0	0.0	0.0	15.1	18.0	6.9	6.9	8.0	5.8	6.1	26.6	23.3	13.9	2.5	74.5	39.3	50.1	49.9
78118	KARNES CITY	74.8	72.9	4.8	4.9	0.5	0.5	56.7	61.6	6.9	6.5	6.7	7.8	8.7	28.9	19.5	13.0	2.1	75.5	34.1	54.3	45.7
78119	KENEDY	57.0	55.6	19.1	18.6	0.7	0.8	48.6	52.7	4.6	4.3	4.7	5.4	11.8	40.5	17.6	9.0	2.1	83.6	32.7	66.8	33.3
78121	LA VERNIA	89.2	87.7	1.5	1.5	0.3	0.3	16.9	19.9	6.8	7.4	9.0	7.9	6.6	26.1	26.1	8.9	1.3	71.7	36.4	50.2	49.8
78122	LEESVILLE	83.1	81.1	5.2	5.2	0.3	0.3	25.9	29.6	5.9	6.2	7.2	5.5	4.6	23.1	28.3	16.9	2.3	77.5	43.1	51.8	48.2
78123	MC QUEENEY	85.6	83.0	1.4	1.5	0.5	0.5	24.0	29.5	7.4	7.3	6.7	5.7	5.6	28.3	27.2	11.1	0.8	75.2	37.9	51.3	48.7
78124	MARION	83.9	81.5	3.1	3.3	1.0	1.0	23.0	27.6	6.7	6.8	7.8	7.8	6.9	26.9	26.1	10.1	1.0	73.9	36.8	49.8	50.2
78130	NEW BRAUNFELS	84.6	82.8	1.4	1.4	0.6	0.6	33.9	38.4	7.3	7.0	7.0	6.8	6.6	27.7	22.5	12.6	2.5	74.5	36.4	48.3	51.7
78132	NEW BRAUNFELS	90.6	89.1	0.7	0.7	0.4	0.5	16.3	19.3	6.2	6.7	7.7	7.2	5.4	23.8	30.4	11.6	1.1	74.9	40.8	50.3	49.8
78133	CANYON LAKE	94.9	93.9	0.3	0.3	0.2	0.3	9.8	12.2	5.0	5.3	6.1	6.0	4.5	23.4	30.5	17.7	1.4	79.7	44.8	50.0	50.0
78140	NIXON	75.2	73.3	3.1	3.1	0.1	0.1	52.0	56.5	7.9	7.5	8.5	8.4	7.5	25.0	20.5	12.6	2.2	71.2	33.8	50.1	49.9
78141	NORDHEIM	86.6	84.4	0.0	0.0	0.0	0.0	25.3	29.5	4.6	5.1	6.4	5.5	5.4	22.6	27.9	18.7	3.9	80.8	45.3	48.7	51.3
78147	POTH	78.2	75.5	0.6	0.7	0.1	0.2	39.9	44.8	7.2	7.2	7.7	6.9	7.1	26.8	24.3	11.5	1.3	73.3	36.8	50.2	49.8
78148	UNIVERSAL CITY	80.6	78.2	6.4	6.7	3.1	3.4	21.7	26.8	6.4	6.5	6.7	6.4	6.7	27.9	26.3	12.0	1.0	76.5	38.0	49.1	50.9
78150	UNIVERSAL CITY	69.8	66.6	17.2	18.3	3.1	3.3	14.9	19.0	10.2	11.9	11.0	6.9	16.8	37.7	5.4	0.2	0.1	62.8	23.0	55.5	44.5
	TEXAS	71.0	69.5	11.5	11.4	2.8	3.1	32.0	34.6	7.9	7.5	7.7	7.5	8.1	29.6	21.9	8.7	1.2	72.6	32.9	49.7	50.3
	UNITED STATES	75.1	73.6	12.3	12.5	3.8	4.2	12.5	14.1	6.9	6.7	7.2	7.0	7.3	28.6	23.8	10.8	1.7	75.1	36.0	49.1	50.9

ZIP CODE				2004 HOUSEHOLD INCOME DISTRIBUTION (%)					MEDIAN HOUSEHOLD INCOME					2004 HOME VALUE DISTRIBUTION (%)					
#	POST OFFICE NAME	2004 Per Capita Income	2004 HH Income Base	Less than $25,000	$25,000 to $49,999	$50,000 to $99,999	$100,000 to $149,999	$150,000 or More	2004	2009	2004 National Centile	2004 State Centile	2004 Home Value Base	Less than $50,000	$50,000 to $89,999	$90,000 to $174,999	$175,000 to $399,999	$400,000 or More	2004 Median Home Value
77879	SOMERVILLE	19702	2533	37.9	28.8	25.2	4.7	3.4	35158	40014	28	34	2068	44.0	32.9	17.3	5.1	0.7	56851
77880	WASHINGTON	24682	342	27.5	23.4	34.2	8.5	6.4	49215	56898	71	76	287	20.9	23.7	27.2	18.1	10.1	95962
77901	VICTORIA	16675	14886	34.6	34.1	24.1	5.2	2.1	35634	41280	30	36	8462	38.0	40.6	18.2	2.8	0.5	59931
77904	VICTORIA	31051	9176	17.2	22.4	36.7	14.8	8.9	61941	70944	86	88	7011	7.2	20.1	52.1	18.6	2.0	114618
77905	VICTORIA	19551	5293	22.5	27.9	38.2	8.8	2.6	49526	57030	71	76	4469	27.5	30.8	32.9	7.7	1.1	78627
77951	BLOOMINGTON	12717	1189	36.9	33.5	24.2	4.5	0.9	35905	40998	31	37	891	59.9	25.5	11.9	2.7	0.0	43086
77954	CUERO	17150	3956	40.2	29.9	22.8	4.7	2.5	31222	35391	16	20	2959	43.3	25.2	22.4	7.7	1.5	58750
77957	EDNA	18904	3514	32.7	27.8	31.3	6.0	2.2	39250	44843	44	52	2450	36.6	32.1	22.9	8.0	0.4	64825
77962	GANADO	18418	1142	28.3	32.0	29.6	6.3	3.9	40684	48174	49	57	892	35.5	34.5	23.5	5.2	1.2	65795
77963	GOLIAD	20048	2641	34.2	29.3	27.5	6.1	2.9	38048	43406	39	46	2100	36.7	25.0	24.9	10.5	3.0	71857
77964	HALLETTSVILLE	19614	2819	39.8	27.6	23.5	6.4	2.7	33728	38972	23	29	2239	31.1	25.2	27.1	12.9	3.8	78628
77968	INEZ	24149	610	13.0	27.4	41.8	13.6	4.3	59609	67809	84	86	516	21.1	23.8	39.0	15.1	1.0	96047
77971	LOLITA	22314	1099	26.1	28.0	36.7	6.2	3.0	45721	52231	63	69	859	40.1	32.0	23.4	3.8	0.7	58814
77974	MEYERSVILLE	19659	74	28.4	32.4	31.1	6.8	1.4	38635	46565	42	50	61	19.7	26.2	39.3	11.5	3.3	98333
77975	MOULTON	19035	1034	36.5	34.4	23.0	4.1	2.0	33882	39281	24	29	831	29.5	25.9	32.3	10.0	2.4	77841
77979	PORT LAVACA	19864	6474	31.2	28.7	30.3	6.9	3.0	40613	46409	48	56	4793	35.8	32.0	25.6	6.5	0.0	65745
77983	SEADRIFT	16296	787	34.9	33.9	24.3	4.7	2.2	35407	41153	29	35	651	58.2	20.0	17.5	4.3	0.0	42357
77984	SHINER	18007	1578	38.0	31.9	25.4	3.4	1.3	32869	38011	21	25	1237	32.2	33.4	23.9	9.2	1.4	71903
77990	TIVOLI	22683	394	36.6	29.7	24.4	4.6	4.8	35000	40810	28	33	304	62.2	24.0	12.8	0.3	0.7	40513
77994	WESTHOFF	19989	148	33.1	30.4	27.0	4.7	4.7	35733	41887	31	37	122	39.3	25.4	14.8	15.6	4.9	63333
77995	YOAKUM	18976	4013	36.8	32.1	22.2	5.5	3.4	33591	38953	23	28	3036	33.7	30.2	27.8	7.1	1.3	70672
78002	ATASCOSA	13546	2183	34.4	34.8	24.5	5.0	1.3	34595	39384	26	31	1700	38.8	33.4	22.5	4.9	0.4	62458
78003	BANDERA	22375	3209	29.5	30.3	28.8	7.7	3.6	39277	46257	44	52	2600	19.2	22.0	37.0	19.0	2.9	105631
78004	BERGHEIM	37941	168	10.1	16.7	38.7	17.9	16.7	74243	90258	93	94	149	2.0	1.3	31.5	47.7	17.5	202419
78005	BIGFOOT	18044	116	32.8	28.5	25.9	11.2	1.7	38474	44056	41	49	100	48.0	24.0	13.0	15.0	0.0	52857
78006	BOERNE	32139	8870	16.9	20.8	33.3	16.6	12.5	64684	76296	88	90	7380	9.8	6.0	33.3	40.6	10.3	177636
78007	CALLIHAM	28361	142	35.2	30.3	22.5	6.3	5.6	36653	42072	34	41	115	40.9	33.9	11.3	5.2	8.7	57500
78008	CAMPBELLTON	23884	209	41.2	23.4	23.4	7.2	4.8	35941	42366	31	37	172	50.6	13.4	20.4	15.7	0.0	49714
78009	CASTROVILLE	20142	2397	21.2	30.8	34.4	10.4	3.2	47666	53867	68	73	2006	15.5	32.7	33.6	16.4	1.8	93524
78010	CENTER POINT	22257	1412	30.2	30.8	26.8	6.5	5.7	41342	48262	51	59	1130	29.7	22.0	26.1	17.5	4.7	86780
78011	CHARLOTTE	12659	741	45.9	33.1	16.5	2.8	1.8	27568	32030	8	11	568	66.4	19.2	11.1	2.1	1.2	35556
78013	COMFORT	19965	1720	28.8	32.6	27.6	6.9	4.2	40228	49296	47	55	1366	29.0	20.3	23.9	16.7	10.1	91724
78014	COTULLA	12462	1592	50.0	30.2	15.9	3.1	0.8	25000	27032	5	6	1104	66.9	17.8	10.4	3.1	1.7	32115
78015	BOERNE	45448	2620	7.4	11.0	30.0	21.9	29.7	102368	122022	98	98	2465	4.4	5.2	5.6	59.4	25.4	286971
78016	DEVINE	17284	3379	31.5	29.7	29.6	5.5	3.8	37726	42583	38	45	2614	37.0	31.4	22.1	7.3	2.2	66000
78017	DILLEY	11294	1273	53.0	29.4	14.6	1.5	1.5	23167	25775	3	5	812	75.7	15.5	5.8	2.6	0.4	31196
78019	ENCINAL	8267	277	65.3	22.7	10.5	1.4	0.0	18159	20774	1	2	222	73.4	11.7	14.0	0.0	0.9	27333
78021	FOWLERTON	21904	40	45.0	27.5	20.0	7.5	0.0	27261	31091	8	10	32	43.8	15.6	15.6	15.6	9.4	60000
78022	GEORGE WEST	22270	1678	34.9	33.1	23.5	4.8	3.8	35829	41198	31	37	1335	35.6	34.5	20.7	8.5	0.8	66184
78023	HELOTES	34079	3740	6.5	17.6	40.4	22.9	12.6	78656	91988	95	95	3456	4.7	7.8	47.8	35.3	4.5	156472
78024	HUNT	26819	241	22.4	35.7	29.5	4.6	7.9	43338	50346	57	65	161	7.5	14.9	26.7	32.3	18.6	177679
78025	INGRAM	20930	2416	29.2	32.9	28.1	6.3	3.6	40595	46961	48	56	2009	20.4	24.2	35.2	14.2	6.0	99602
78026	JOURDANTON	19280	1981	31.8	34.1	26.4	3.0	4.8	40611	46871	48	56	1562	46.6	28.8	17.5	4.5	2.6	52819
78027	KENDALIA	27945	164	29.3	19.5	34.2	10.4	6.7	51050	61686	74	78	136	17.7	13.2	29.4	17.7	22.1	137500
78028	KERRVILLE	24360	14650	31.5	31.2	25.6	6.7	5.1	38203	43823	40	48	10618	18.7	23.2	35.6	18.7	3.8	104051
78039	LA COSTE	17388	599	24.9	35.1	30.9	7.7	1.5	43004	50045	56	64	505	31.3	35.5	26.7	6.1	0.4	69167
78040	LAREDO	8991	12814	57.5	26.1	13.2	2.0	1.1	20791	23258	2	3	6410	31.3	46.0	20.6	1.9	0.2	63012
78041	LAREDO	17162	12675	35.1	25.6	25.7	8.1	5.6	38675	45460	42	50	7264	13.3	29.7	42.0	11.6	3.4	99155
78043	LAREDO	11779	10468	43.1	32.6	17.1	4.9	2.3	29407	33468	11	14	6772	27.7	36.7	29.8	5.7	0.2	73598
78045	LAREDO	19520	10697	16.2	26.9	38.4	12.5	6.1	56056	65183	81	84	8717	6.6	19.6	58.7	13.7	1.3	114676
78046	LAREDO	7667	11271	47.1	34.0	15.2	3.0	0.7	26388	30332	6	8	9263	37.4	42.9	18.1	1.6	0.1	59302
78052	LYTLE	15565	1797	29.1	33.5	28.2	7.3	1.9	38999	44130	43	51	1394	34.1	32.9	25.1	6.5	1.4	70000
78055	MEDINA	23570	911	31.5	27.3	28.5	8.5	4.2	40541	47490	48	56	735	23.7	15.0	36.1	19.9	5.4	108518
78056	MICO	24677	325	18.8	29.5	37.9	10.5	3.4	51360	57976	74	79	277	12.3	17.0	40.4	26.4	4.0	123724
78057	MOORE	19152	347	33.7	28.2	25.9	10.4	1.7	37914	43675	39	46	298	50.3	23.5	12.1	14.1	0.0	49706
78058	MOUNTAIN HOME	20496	138	31.9	33.3	31.2	2.9	0.7	41171	47057	50	58	113	10.6	29.2	36.3	15.9	8.0	105469
78059	NATALIA	14235	1912	33.7	32.5	27.5	4.8	1.5	36599	42810	34	41	1538	37.3	29.8	22.1	10.4	0.4	68684
78061	PEARSALL	12769	3225	46.0	32.1	17.2	2.8	1.9	27492	31052	8	10	2194	60.0	25.1	12.9	1.2	0.8	43210
78063	PIPE CREEK	23874	3506	23.6	25.8	37.0	9.4	4.3	50520	57533	73	78	2966	18.4	23.0	37.3	19.4	2.0	104176
78064	PLEASANTON	17706	5012	34.3	27.2	28.9	7.4	2.3	38188	42856	40	48	3792	32.2	29.6	29.0	8.3	1.0	73191
78065	POTEET	14675	3613	35.7	32.8	24.4	4.8	2.3	36261	41508	33	39	2744	48.7	29.1	18.3	3.4	0.5	51563
78066	RIO MEDINA	21564	257	16.0	30.4	39.3	10.5	3.9	53696	59826	78	82	216	10.7	18.1	38.9	30.1	2.3	128409
78067	SAN YGNACIO	10143	343	56.6	26.0	11.1	4.4	2.0	20835	24083	2	3	242	65.3	10.7	21.1	2.9	0.0	38333
78069	SOMERSET	14137	1323	32.9	32.5	26.6	6.6	1.4	36413	41205	33	40	993	46.4	32.5	17.3	3.2	0.5	54176
78070	SPRING BRANCH	26686	3280	16.3	21.1	41.5	13.4	7.7	60024	69397	84	87	2958	11.0	24.2	31.7	26.4	6.7	116041
78071	THREE RIVERS	18091	1462	34.9	27.6	28.1	6.6	2.9	38093	42876	40	47	1108	36.0	33.2	26.4	3.9	0.5	70893
78072	TILDEN	26568	232	34.1	31.0	23.3	6.9	4.7	37309	43299	37	44	188	42.0	30.3	12.8	5.3	9.6	59375
78073	VON ORMY	13357	2646	30.5	38.8	25.2	4.1	1.4	37411	44068	37	44	2031	52.1	24.9	18.8	4.0	0.2	47927
78074	WARING	25593	14	14.3	35.7	42.9	0.0	7.1	50000	57100	72	77	11	0.0	27.3	27.3	18.2	27.3	137500
78075	WHITSETT	25046	77	40.3	19.5	31.2	5.2	3.9	35762	40567	31	37	63	46.0	30.2	20.6	3.2	0.0	58333
78076	ZAPATA	12303	3874	45.5	30.6	19.1	2.4	2.4	27788	31309	8	11	2972	55.1	26.7	15.7	2.4	0.2	45546
78101	ADKINS	22729	2140	21.2	25.6	38.3	11.7	3.2	53092	60710	77	81	1841	24.7	24.7	39.2	11.1	0.4	91524
78102	BEEVILLE	14929	8676	38.9	32.5	23.5	3.5	1.6	32483	36753	19	24	5746	38.7	33.8	21.6	5.2	0.8	61600
78108	CIBOLO	25914	3365	17.4	25.0	38.9	12.9	5.8	56316	63233	81	84	2824	17.7	22.8	38.1	20.8	0.6	105601
78109	CONVERSE	21103	8083	12.5	28.7	42.7	12.7	3.4	56438	65052	81	84	6328	11.1	30.7	54.8	3.1	0.3	95683
78111	ECLETO	0	0	0.0	0.0	0.0	0.0	0.0	0	0	0	0	0	0.0	0.0	0.0	0.0	0.0	0
78112	ELMENDORF	14523	2375	23.9	39.1	29.1	6.4	1.5	40670	48577	48	57	2043	36.7	42.9	18.3	1.6	0.5	61602
78113	FALLS CITY	20612	485	30.7	26.4	32.2	7.6	3.1	42362	50254	54	63	401	37.7	24.2	29.7	8.0	0.5	72037
78114	FLORESVILLE	18828	6125	25.5	31.4	31.4	8.0	3.7	43351	50773	57	65	4972	25.3	27.3	34.7	12.3	0.4	85131
78116	GILLETT	23962	265	37.7	21.1	26.4	3.4	11.3	35390	41384	29	34	223	41.7	29.2	19.3	9.9	0.0	65625
78117	HOBSON	19983	135	31.9	26.7	31.9	7.4	2.2	40980	50595	50	58	112	38.4	24.1	29.5	8.0	0.0	71250
78118	KARNES CITY	14524	1421	40.6	28.6	25.3	4.6	0.8	31045	35135	15	19	1011	55.4	29.4	10.9	3.7	0.7	44202
78119	KENEDY	14912	1836	44.9	28.6	21.0	3.7	1.8	27851	31743	8	11	1299	52.4	31.1	12.6	2.9	1.1	47750
78121	LA VERNIA	22402	2710	19.5	27.9	37.3	10.7	4.7	51737	59046	75	80	2368	21.0	26.9	37.6	13.3	1.1	93101
78122	LEESVILLE	20298	108	35.2	34.3	24.1	4.6	1.9	32795	38762	20	25	90	37.8	34.4	15.6	11.1	1.1	65455
78123	MC QUEENEY	25753	835	20.6	31.7	35.3	7.7	4.7	47654	54211	68	72	670	17.9	31.6	25.8	16.4	8.2	91200
78124	MARION	21801	1873	18.5	33.6	33.5	9.1	5.2	48224	54604	69	74	1568	17.7	31.1	33.0	17.0	1.3	91919
78130	NEW BRAUNFELS	20872	18215	23.3	31.9	33.2	8.1	3.7	45544	52235	63	69	12575	16.8	23.4	44.3	14.1	1.4	104942
78132	NEW BRAUNFELS	29411	4858	15.3	24.0	35.8	15.2	9.7	61837	71030	86	88	4272	11.6	9.9	31.4	40.2	6.9	168686
78133	CANYON LAKE	26143	6579	20.1	31.0	36.2	8.8	3.8	48975	57221	70	75	5494	16.1	24.7	38.5	17.5	3.2	104830
78140	NIXON	13840	1180	46.4	31.4	17.6	3.4	1.1	26694	30024	7	9	819	65.2	17.6	9.9	7.0	0.4	36591
78141	NORDHEIM	18212	248	33.9	29.4	31.1	5.7	0.0	39498	45650	44	53	208	37.5	33.2	22.1	5.8	1.4	62273
78147	POTH	17769	1069	31.8	25.6	32.3	7.6	2.7	42769	49170	55	64	846	28.4	33.7	26.4	10.4	1.2	74146
78148	UNIVERSAL CITY	26584	6093	17.7	26.9	36.9	13.5	4.9	55368	63045	80	83	3959	6.2	27.8	54.6	11.0	0.4	106274
78150	UNIVERSAL CITY	15845	990	17.1	45.3	26.6	9.9	1.2	42345	48155	54	63	19	31.6	52.6	15.8	0.0	0.0	55833
	TEXAS	23284		26.2	27.7	29.5	10.3	6.3	45778	54246				21.6	26.1	33.4	15.6	3.4	93683
	UNITED STATES	25866		24.7	27.1	30.8	10.9	6.5	48124	56710				10.9	15.0	33.7	30.1	10.4	145905

ZIP CODE #	POST OFFICE NAME	FINANCIAL SERVICES: Auto Loan	Home Loan	Invest-ments	Retire-ment Plans	THE HOME: Home Improvements: Home Repair	Lawn & Garden	Furnishings: Comput-ers & Hard-ware	Major Appli-ances	TV, Radio, Sound Equip-ment	Furni-ture	ENTERTAINMENT: Dine out/ Carry out	Sports Equip-ment	Fees & Tickets	Toys & Games	Travel	Cable TV	PERSONAL: Apparel & Services	Auto Repairs	Health Insur-ance	Pets & Supplies
77879	SOMERVILLE	83	64	43	60	70	80	65	74	72	64	86	85	59	83	66	76	80	73	85	94
77880	WASHINGTON	109	97	74	92	102	110	89	99	95	89	116	118	88	118	92	97	110	96	107	128
77901	VICTORIA	66	62	59	61	61	65	64	66	66	66	82	74	62	78	62	64	80	67	64	71
77904	VICTORIA	114	123	128	124	121	125	118	118	114	118	143	138	121	144	118	111	140	117	111	131
77905	VICTORIA	93	79	58	75	84	90	75	84	80	75	97	99	71	96	76	82	92	82	91	107
77951	BLOOMINGTON	66	55	42	51	55	58	55	61	59	60	73	67	50	66	53	58	71	62	61	68
77954	CUERO	74	53	31	49	59	69	55	64	63	54	74	75	48	71	55	67	68	64	77	85
77957	EDNA	78	65	52	63	69	78	68	72	73	66	88	84	64	87	68	75	83	72	80	87
77962	GANADO	87	66	43	64	73	82	67	77	74	66	88	91	60	87	68	76	81	76	88	100
77963	GOLIAD	91	66	38	61	74	83	66	79	75	66	89	93	57	85	67	78	82	78	92	105
77964	HALLETTSVILLE	80	59	36	55	65	77	63	72	72	61	85	81	56	80	63	76	77	71	86	90
77968	INEZ	102	101	89	99	105	109	93	101	94	93	115	119	92	118	96	94	111	98	102	123
77971	LOLITA	99	83	61	78	89	99	79	90	86	79	104	105	75	104	82	90	97	88	101	116
77974	MEYERSVILLE	91	64	33	60	74	83	63	78	73	62	85	94	54	83	65	76	78	77	93	108
77975	MOULTON	84	58	29	51	65	76	58	70	69	58	81	82	50	76	59	74	73	70	86	96
77979	PORT LAVACA	87	74	58	70	77	84	74	81	79	75	96	92	69	93	74	80	92	81	86	97
77983	SEADRIFT	82	57	30	50	65	74	55	68	65	56	77	81	47	74	57	70	70	67	83	96
77984	SHINER	74	53	31	49	59	69	55	64	64	54	75	75	48	71	56	67	68	64	78	84
77990	TIVOLI	87	76	63	71	73	77	78	84	81	85	101	89	71	90	74	78	101	86	79	88
77994	WESTHOFF	82	62	41	59	68	81	68	75	77	65	90	84	61	85	68	81	82	75	90	91
77995	YOAKUM	81	62	42	58	68	78	64	72	72	63	85	84	58	82	64	75	79	72	85	93
78002	ATASCOSA	68	60	49	55	57	60	61	66	63	66	79	69	56	70	58	61	78	67	62	68
78003	BANDERA	91	77	55	73	80	87	75	83	80	76	96	97	69	92	75	81	91	83	89	103
78004	BERGHEIM	144	179	190	179	175	173	159	159	148	159	186	186	170	198	163	143	185	153	142	175
78005	BIGFOOT	92	62	28	53	70	81	60	75	72	61	85	89	51	80	61	78	77	74	92	106
78006	BOERNE	118	136	140	137	135	138	125	126	119	124	148	146	131	155	127	117	147	122	119	142
78007	CALLIHAM	117	85	49	79	98	110	83	101	95	82	111	121	72	109	87	100	102	100	120	140
78008	CAMPBELLTON	107	75	39	71	87	98	74	91	85	73	100	110	63	98	77	89	91	90	109	127
78009	CASTROVILLE	92	87	74	84	90	95	82	89	84	83	103	104	80	102	83	84	99	87	91	107
78010	CENTER POINT	95	79	56	76	83	90	77	86	81	78	98	101	70	94	77	81	93	85	91	108
78011	CHARLOTTE	58	51	42	47	49	52	52	56	54	57	68	60	48	60	50	52	67	57	53	59
78013	COMFORT	91	70	47	66	76	84	71	82	79	73	95	94	63	89	71	80	89	82	90	102
78014	COTULLA	56	48	39	45	47	51	49	54	52	53	65	57	45	58	47	51	63	54	53	57
78015	BOERNE	162	213	273	212	207	219	186	184	172	190	218	209	209	229	196	172	221	177	168	201
78016	DEVINE	77	72	60	69	72	75	70	74	71	72	88	84	66	83	69	70	85	74	73	85
78017	DILLEY	46	41	39	39	40	43	44	45	46	45	57	50	42	54	42	45	56	46	44	48
78019	ENCINAL	38	33	27	31	32	33	34	36	35	37	44	39	31	39	32	34	44	37	34	38
78021	FOWLERTON	65	48	31	46	53	64	53	59	60	51	70	67	47	67	53	63	64	59	71	72
78022	GEORGE WEST	99	79	56	75	85	94	79	90	86	80	104	103	72	99	79	88	98	89	99	112
78023	HELOTES	131	158	165	159	154	153	142	141	132	143	166	165	150	173	144	127	165	137	126	155
78024	HUNT	117	92	64	84	104	117	87	104	98	87	117	121	78	114	93	105	108	103	123	142
78025	INGRAM	84	71	56	67	76	88	69	79	75	71	91	85	66	82	72	79	85	78	91	95
78026	JOURDANTON	90	81	65	77	80	84	79	85	81	83	100	95	74	92	77	79	98	85	83	96
78027	KENDALIA	124	87	45	82	101	113	86	106	99	85	116	128	73	113	89	104	106	104	126	148
78028	KERRVILLE	87	78	71	75	81	94	78	85	83	79	101	91	76	93	80	86	95	84	95	97
78039	LA COSTE	78	71	56	68	71	75	68	73	69	70	85	84	64	80	67	68	82	73	72	86
78040	LAREDO	48	42	35	39	40	42	43	46	44	47	56	49	39	49	41	43	55	47	43	48
78041	LAREDO	87	81	75	77	78	81	82	86	84	88	106	93	78	98	79	81	106	88	80	91
78043	LAREDO	66	57	50	54	55	58	60	63	62	65	79	69	56	72	57	59	78	65	59	66
78045	LAREDO	104	104	100	106	100	100	103	103	100	108	127	118	102	124	98	94	127	104	91	111
78046	LAREDO	51	43	41	43	42	44	48	49	50	51	64	55	46	61	45	47	64	51	44	51
78052	LYTLE	73	69	60	66	68	71	67	71	68	71	85	80	65	80	66	67	83	72	69	79
78055	MEDINA	99	75	49	70	85	96	72	87	82	72	97	101	65	93	76	87	89	86	104	118
78056	MICO	90	89	79	87	93	96	82	89	83	82	101	105	81	104	84	83	98	86	90	108
78057	MOORE	92	62	28	53	70	81	60	75	72	61	85	89	51	80	61	78	77	74	92	106
78058	MOUNTAIN HOME	84	58	31	55	68	76	58	71	66	57	78	86	49	76	60	70	71	70	85	99
78059	NATALIA	71	65	51	62	65	69	62	66	63	64	77	77	59	73	61	62	74	66	66	79
78061	PEARSALL	60	51	40	48	51	54	52	57	55	56	68	62	47	61	50	54	67	58	56	63
78063	PIPE CREEK	96	89	74	84	93	101	83	92	86	83	105	106	80	103	86	88	100	90	98	114
78064	PLEASANTON	83	68	50	65	72	77	67	76	72	69	88	88	61	82	67	72	83	76	80	93
78065	POTEET	71	65	53	61	64	67	64	68	65	67	81	76	60	74	62	63	79	69	66	76
78066	RIO MEDINA	80	99	105	99	98	96	88	89	82	88	103	104	94	110	91	80	103	85	80	98
78067	SAN YGNACIO	50	44	36	41	42	44	45	48	46	49	58	51	41	52	43	45	58	49	45	50
78069	SOMERSET	69	62	50	58	60	63	61	66	63	66	79	72	57	71	59	61	78	67	63	72
78070	SPRING BRANCH	110	116	110	114	116	120	107	111	104	108	129	128	108	130	108	103	126	109	107	128
78071	THREE RIVERS	88	67	45	64	73	82	70	80	78	70	93	90	62	87	70	80	87	80	90	98
78072	TILDEN	114	82	46	76	95	106	80	98	92	79	108	117	69	106	83	97	99	97	117	136
78073	VON ORMY	68	60	49	57	59	62	60	65	62	64	77	71	56	70	58	60	76	65	62	71
78074	WARING	116	81	42	76	94	105	80	99	92	79	108	119	68	106	83	97	98	97	118	137
78075	WHITSETT	76	57	38	55	63	75	63	70	71	60	84	78	56	79	63	75	76	70	84	84
78076	ZAPATA	57	51	46	47	50	54	52	56	54	56	68	59	49	61	50	53	67	57	55	59
78101	ADKINS	103	98	80	96	98	102	92	97	92	94	113	113	89	110	91	90	109	96	95	115
78102	BEEVILLE	61	54	48	52	54	58	56	59	59	58	73	66	53	68	55	58	71	60	59	65
78108	CIBOLO	106	109	100	107	107	111	102	105	99	104	124	121	102	123	101	98	121	103	101	120
78109	CONVERSE	93	103	100	106	99	97	96	95	89	98	113	111	97	113	93	84	111	93	83	104
78111	ECLETO	0	0	0	0	0	0	0	0	0	0	0	0	0	0	0	0	0	0	0	0
78112	ELMENDORF	78	71	56	69	71	75	68	73	69	70	85	84	64	80	67	68	82	73	73	87
78113	FALLS CITY	97	68	36	64	79	89	67	83	77	66	91	100	57	89	70	81	83	82	99	115
78114	FLORESVILLE	88	78	60	74	78	84	76	83	79	79	97	94	71	90	75	78	93	83	83	97
78116	GILLETT	105	73	38	69	85	95	72	89	83	71	97	108	62	96	75	87	89	88	106	124
78117	HOBSON	97	67	35	64	79	88	67	82	77	66	90	99	57	88	69	81	82	81	98	115
78118	KARNES CITY	56	45	34	43	46	52	48	52	52	49	63	57	43	57	47	52	60	53	56	59
78119	KENEDY	49	45	43	43	44	47	47	48	49	48	61	54	45	57	46	48	59	49	47	52
78121	LA VERNIA	103	96	77	93	95	100	90	96	91	93	112	112	86	107	89	89	108	96	95	114
78122	LEESVILLE	109	73	33	63	82	95	70	88	85	72	100	105	60	94	71	91	90	87	108	125
78123	MC QUEENEY	103	94	73	90	94	99	89	96	90	92	112	111	84	105	88	89	107	95	95	113
78124	MARION	103	94	74	89	97	103	88	95	91	89	112	112	85	111	89	92	107	94	100	118
78130	NEW BRAUNFELS	83	82	76	80	82	87	79	82	79	80	99	93	78	96	79	79	95	81	82	93
78132	NEW BRAUNFELS	117	126	126	126	126	129	118	121	114	118	141	141	119	143	119	111	138	118	115	137
78133	CANYON LAKE	92	89	88	86	93	104	85	92	87	88	109	98	85	99	89	90	103	90	100	105
78140	NIXON	64	53	40	48	53	57	53	59	57	57	70	65	48	63	51	56	69	60	60	67
78141	NORDHEIM	73	55	36	52	60	72	61	66	68	57	80	75	54	75	60	72	73	66	80	80
78147	POTH	84	66	46	65	72	81	68	76	74	66	88	88	63	87	68	76	82	75	85	95
78148	UNIVERSAL CITY	89	96	105	98	94	98	95	93	91	95	115	108	97	116	94	89	113	93	86	101
78150	UNIVERSAL CITY	85	54	51	62	49	58	80	69	81	75	101	92	68	91	66	74	97	81	64	79
	TEXAS	94	90	91	90	89	95	92	93	92	93	115	107	90	112	90	90	112	94	89	104
	UNITED STATES	100	100	100	100	100	100	100	100	100	100	100	100	100	100	100	100	100	100	100	100

TEXAS

POPULATION CHANGE

A 78151-78382

#	POST OFFICE NAME	COUNTY FIPS CODE	POPULATION			2000-2004 ANNUAL RATE		HOUSEHOLDS					FAMILIES		
			2000	2004	2009	% Rate	State Centile	2000	2004	2009	% Annual Rate 2000-2004	2004 Average HH Size	2000	2004	% Annual Rate 2000-2004
78151	RUNGE	255	1511	1547	1637	0.6	27	574	591	629	0.7	2.62	419	433	0.8
78152	SAINT HEDWIG	029	1830	1869	1981	0.5	25	640	652	690	0.4	2.85	524	534	0.5
78154	SCHERTZ	187	18884	22988	27575	4.7	94	6672	8014	9516	4.4	2.86	5333	6437	4.5
78155	SEGUIN	187	40162	43750	49870	2.0	68	14013	15235	17313	2.0	2.78	10368	11275	2.0
78159	SMILEY	177	926	931	969	0.1	15	364	363	375	-0.1	2.53	262	262	0.0
78160	STOCKDALE	493	3598	3666	3968	0.4	23	1314	1344	1461	0.5	2.67	976	997	0.5
78161	SUTHERLAND SPRINGS	493	997	1065	1176	1.6	58	343	367	406	1.6	2.90	272	290	1.5
78163	BULVERDE	091	7332	8690	10601	4.1	90	2531	2983	3618	3.9	2.91	2124	2503	3.9
78164	YORKTOWN	123	3775	3823	3971	0.3	20	1489	1498	1547	0.1	2.50	1063	1074	0.2
78201	SAN ANTONIO	029	46036	47474	51186	0.7	34	16315	16851	18193	0.8	2.78	10909	11242	0.7
78202	SAN ANTONIO	029	11925	11981	12580	-0.1	11	4066	4014	4237	-0.3	2.88	2620	2591	-0.3
78203	SAN ANTONIO	029	5352	5304	5624	-0.2	9	1737	1702	1798	-0.5	3.09	1218	1198	-0.4
78204	SAN ANTONIO	029	12517	12824	13738	0.6	28	3821	3886	4158	0.4	3.14	2694	2745	0.4
78205	SAN ANTONIO	029	1562	1583	1668	0.3	20	995	1016	1085	0.5	1.19	168	170	0.3
78207	SAN ANTONIO	029	56193	56367	59784	0.1	14	15568	15560	16533	0.0	3.34	11834	11826	0.0
78208	SAN ANTONIO	029	5079	4931	5216	-0.7	3	1628	1574	1662	-0.8	3.03	1118	1079	-0.8
78209	SAN ANTONIO	029	39738	40696	43588	0.6	27	17651	17947	19185	0.4	2.17	9748	9914	0.4
78210	SAN ANTONIO	029	38577	38688	41115	0.1	14	13028	12981	13766	-0.1	2.93	9015	9002	0.0
78211	SAN ANTONIO	029	30627	31302	33514	0.5	25	8476	8638	9226	0.5	3.62	7073	7208	0.5
78212	SAN ANTONIO	029	30936	31059	32927	0.1	15	12039	12021	12770	0.0	2.33	6234	6248	0.1
78213	SAN ANTONIO	029	39025	41433	45274	1.4	55	15961	16859	18343	1.3	2.46	9771	10319	1.3
78214	SAN ANTONIO	029	23808	24686	26574	0.9	37	7560	7816	8398	0.8	3.13	5703	5898	0.8
78215	SAN ANTONIO	029	1376	1482	1611	1.8	63	645	705	775	2.1	1.87	245	267	2.0
78216	SAN ANTONIO	029	34126	36431	39866	1.6	58	15415	16502	18065	1.6	2.20	8451	8986	1.5
78217	SAN ANTONIO	029	30321	31153	33444	0.6	30	12847	13161	14091	0.6	2.35	7866	8065	0.6
78218	SAN ANTONIO	029	30627	31813	34260	0.9	38	12392	12822	13772	0.8	2.46	7789	8074	0.9
78219	SAN ANTONIO	029	14143	14470	15502	0.5	27	5021	5106	5452	0.4	2.83	3755	3826	0.4
78220	SAN ANTONIO	029	17246	17769	19092	0.7	32	6197	6379	6851	0.7	2.73	4414	4547	0.7
78221	SAN ANTONIO	029	34583	36411	39408	1.2	49	10506	11034	11918	1.2	3.26	8510	8935	1.2
78222	SAN ANTONIO	029	14627	16446	18410	2.8	79	4937	5510	6144	2.6	2.93	3785	4243	2.7
78223	SAN ANTONIO	029	42103	44872	49058	1.5	57	14569	15482	16896	1.4	2.84	10543	11201	1.4
78224	SAN ANTONIO	029	15303	15994	17292	1.0	43	4231	4385	4726	0.8	3.57	3605	3738	0.9
78225	SAN ANTONIO	029	13541	13995	15014	0.7	32	4334	4446	4780	0.6	3.13	3392	3480	0.6
78226	SAN ANTONIO	029	8132	8382	8979	0.7	33	2517	2580	2760	0.6	3.07	2069	2116	0.5
78227	SAN ANTONIO	029	39464	42258	46153	1.6	60	12524	13320	14470	1.5	3.17	9792	10434	1.5
78228	SAN ANTONIO	029	59800	61636	66113	0.7	32	18859	19406	20819	0.7	3.06	14333	14768	0.7
78229	SAN ANTONIO	029	29124	31688	35011	2.0	68	14052	15304	16932	2.0	2.01	6195	6705	1.9
78230	SAN ANTONIO	029	36551	38829	42295	1.4	55	15919	16803	18225	1.3	2.30	9822	10371	1.3
78231	SAN ANTONIO	029	8849	9480	10415	1.6	60	3586	3782	4123	1.3	2.51	2479	2622	1.3
78232	SAN ANTONIO	029	34708	39156	43953	2.9	80	14504	16249	18159	2.7	2.39	9589	10695	2.6
78233	SAN ANTONIO	029	36108	39483	43767	2.1	70	12997	14155	15636	2.0	2.78	9753	10641	2.1
78234	SAN ANTONIO	029	5525	5309	5482	-0.9	1	929	869	911	-1.6	3.81	904	845	-1.6
78235	SAN ANTONIO	029	787	780	823	-0.2	9	207	205	218	-0.2	3.38	190	188	-0.3
78236	SAN ANTONIO	029	8017	7948	8039	-0.2	9	337	322	344	-1.1	4.15	305	290	-1.2
78237	SAN ANTONIO	029	36810	37855	40468	0.7	31	10322	10573	11287	0.6	3.51	8403	8612	0.6
78238	SAN ANTONIO	029	21087	22731	24916	1.8	63	8066	8656	9469	1.7	2.62	5402	5785	1.6
78239	SAN ANTONIO	029	26279	26942	28948	0.6	28	9681	9924	10647	0.6	2.69	7184	7351	0.5
78240	SAN ANTONIO	029	42210	50466	58412	4.3	91	18145	21659	25032	4.3	2.30	10369	12377	4.3
78242	SAN ANTONIO	029	27932	29369	31964	1.2	47	7802	8153	8826	1.0	3.60	6461	6756	1.1
78244	SAN ANTONIO	029	19234	22469	25590	3.7	88	5946	6921	7858	3.6	3.25	5040	5867	3.6
78245	SAN ANTONIO	029	31061	34478	38491	2.5	76	10344	11334	12547	2.2	3.03	7975	8787	2.3
78247	SAN ANTONIO	029	38854	42714	47327	2.3	72	13579	14698	16127	1.9	2.89	10743	11630	1.9
78248	SAN ANTONIO	029	13357	16169	18700	4.6	93	5072	6095	7015	4.4	2.65	3755	4506	4.4
78249	SAN ANTONIO	029	33128	38000	42848	3.3	84	11904	13601	15292	3.2	2.75	8521	9742	3.2
78250	SAN ANTONIO	029	50470	55249	61274	2.2	70	16047	17465	19298	2.0	3.16	13355	14541	2.0
78251	SAN ANTONIO	029	24889	33119	40307	7.0	98	8636	11296	13603	6.5	2.93	6449	8517	6.8
78252	SAN ANTONIO	029	6276	6766	7291	1.8	63	1181	1332	1491	2.9	3.26	986	1113	2.9
78253	SAN ANTONIO	029	9646	11590	13364	4.4	92	3162	3785	4350	4.3	3.06	2685	3217	4.4
78254	SAN ANTONIO	029	17086	20482	23696	4.4	92	5748	6850	7893	4.2	2.99	4788	5721	4.3
78255	SAN ANTONIO	029	3974	4596	5200	3.5	86	1504	1736	1960	3.4	2.64	1075	1244	3.5
78256	SAN ANTONIO	029	2747	3281	3768	4.3	91	1166	1381	1577	4.1	2.38	627	756	4.5
78257	SAN ANTONIO	029	2310	2803	3250	4.7	93	898	1076	1238	4.4	2.61	696	785	2.9
78258	SAN ANTONIO	029	18576	29980	39923	11.9	100	6281	9964	13077	11.5	3.01	5267	8337	11.4
78259	SAN ANTONIO	029	9311	12030	14408	6.2	97	2953	3795	4529	6.1	3.14	2644	3399	6.1
78260	SAN ANTONIO	029	1481	2036	2503	7.8	98	531	726	888	7.6	2.80	434	595	7.7
78261	SAN ANTONIO	029	1167	2102	2904	14.9	100	383	688	949	14.8	3.06	343	610	14.5
78263	SAN ANTONIO	029	4669	4995	5423	1.6	59	1609	1713	1854	1.5	2.92	1287	1373	1.5
78264	SAN ANTONIO	029	9239	10282	11557	2.6	76	2849	3154	3533	2.4	3.26	2314	2563	2.4
78266	SAN ANTONIO	091	2675	3134	3800	3.8	89	983	1145	1381	3.7	2.74	848	989	3.7
78332	ALICE	249	27624	28745	30198	0.9	39	9047	9409	9897	0.9	3.01	7083	7383	1.0
78336	ARANSAS PASS	409	12495	13130	14037	1.2	47	4514	4742	5081	1.2	2.73	3290	3462	1.2
78338	ARMSTRONG	261	136	136	136	0.0	13	44	44	44	0.0	3.07	35	35	0.0
78340	BAYSIDE	391	420	409	403	-0.6	3	172	168	165	-0.6	2.43	118	116	-0.4
78343	BISHOP	355	4828	4780	4870	-0.2	8	1625	1594	1613	-0.5	3.00	1272	1251	-0.4
78344	BRUNI	479	469	488	550	0.9	39	148	154	173	0.9	3.15	119	123	0.8
78349	CONCEPCION	131	3246	3236	3253	-0.1	11	1186	1188	1204	0.0	2.72	864	867	0.1
78353	ENCINO	047	650	634	621	-0.6	4	238	232	227	-0.6	2.73	178	174	-0.5
78355	FALFURRIAS	047	7326	7218	7099	-0.4	7	2473	2436	2399	-0.4	2.93	1902	1879	-0.3
78357	FREER	131	3973	3989	4017	0.1	15	1371	1385	1406	0.2	2.88	1034	1047	0.3
78360	GUERRA	247	67	71	77	1.4	54	27	29	31	1.7	2.41	19	20	1.2
78361	HEBBRONVILLE	247	5248	5577	6040	1.4	56	1796	1913	2082	1.5	2.89	1347	1439	1.6
78362	INGLESIDE	409	9598	9994	10612	1.0	40	3075	3208	3426	1.0	2.87	2328	2434	1.1
78363	KINGSVILLE	273	29672	29984	30531	0.3	19	10225	10334	10541	0.3	2.78	7149	7247	0.3
78368	MATHIS	409	11316	11643	12257	0.7	31	3821	3934	4149	0.7	2.95	2972	3065	0.7
78369	MIRANDO CITY	479	1437	1710	2062	4.2	91	390	459	550	3.9	3.72	323	376	3.6
78370	ODEM	409	3468	3488	3640	0.1	16	1092	1098	1149	0.1	3.17	888	895	0.2
78372	ORANGE GROVE	249	5630	5980	6323	1.4	55	1866	1981	2097	1.4	3.02	1454	1547	1.5
78373	PORT ARANSAS	355	3442	3627	3772	1.2	49	1579	1647	1700	1.0	2.20	1025	1075	1.1
78374	PORTLAND	409	18508	20066	21747	1.9	66	6121	6643	7214	1.9	3.01	4955	5391	2.0
78375	PREMONT	249	3872	3924	4046	0.3	20	1316	1333	1374	0.3	2.91	999	1014	0.4
78376	REALITOS	131	479	475	477	-0.2	9	185	185	187	0.0	2.54	140	140	0.0
78377	REFUGIO	391	3903	3880	3852	-0.1	10	1466	1456	1448	-0.2	2.59	1057	1053	-0.1
78379	RIVIERA	273	1869	1905	1934	0.5	24	668	679	690	0.4	2.74	533	543	0.4
78380	ROBSTOWN	355	26540	26127	26541	-0.4	7	7967	7762	7824	-0.6	3.33	6625	6467	-0.6
78382	ROCKPORT	007	19510	21215	23451	2.0	67	8019	8726	9674	2.0	2.40	5605	6116	2.1
	TEXAS					2.2					2.0	2.77			2.1
	UNITED STATES					1.2					1.3	2.58			1.1

295-A

#	POST OFFICE NAME	RACE (%) White 2000	White 2004	Black 2000	Black 2004	Asian/Pacific 2000	Asian/Pacific 2004	% Hispanic Origin 2000	% Hispanic Origin 2004	2004 AGE DISTRIBUTION (%) 0-4	5-9	10-14	15-19	20-24	25-44	45-64	65-84	85+	18+	MEDIAN AGE 2004	% 2004 Males	% 2004 Females
78151	RUNGE	72.6	70.6	1.6	1.6	0.0	0.0	62.5	67.1	8.0	7.5	8.7	7.4	6.1	22.8	22.2	14.5	2.8	70.8	36.9	48.0	52.0
78152	SAINT HEDWIG	89.8	87.9	3.2	3.4	0.2	0.2	13.6	17.6	6.3	6.7	7.4	6.9	5.4	27.9	28.1	10.4	0.9	75.0	39.0	51.7	48.3
78154	SCHERTZ	82.6	80.6	6.3	6.8	2.0	2.1	19.8	23.6	7.5	7.3	7.5	7.6	6.7	28.9	25.2	8.5	0.8	72.7	36.2	48.3	51.7
78155	SEGUIN	73.4	72.0	6.4	5.9	0.7	0.7	40.5	44.1	7.3	7.2	7.5	7.7	7.7	25.7	23.5	11.7	1.8	73.9	35.4	49.1	50.9
78159	SMILEY	83.7	81.7	0.2	0.2	0.0	0.0	40.8	45.9	6.8	6.8	7.3	6.2	6.2	23.6	22.2	17.9	2.9	74.5	40.0	50.0	50.1
78160	STOCKDALE	86.0	84.0	1.2	1.2	0.1	0.1	29.2	33.5	6.5	6.6	6.8	6.6	5.9	24.4	25.9	14.8	2.6	76.3	40.6	50.2	49.8
78161	SUTHERLAND SPRINGS	83.6	81.3	1.0	0.9	0.2	0.2	26.5	30.8	7.0	7.2	7.4	8.0	6.6	25.3	27.2	10.5	0.8	73.5	37.5	49.7	50.3
78163	BULVERDE	93.6	92.5	0.3	0.3	0.5	0.6	13.0	15.9	5.9	7.0	8.0	7.7	3.7	26.0	32.2	8.9	0.6	73.8	40.9	50.8	49.2
78164	YORKTOWN	85.0	82.8	1.9	2.0	0.1	0.1	28.3	32.4	5.1	5.3	6.8	7.0	6.2	22.3	26.0	17.5	3.9	78.3	43.2	48.7	51.3
78201	SAN ANTONIO	69.7	68.7	1.9	1.7	0.6	0.6	83.1	86.4	8.3	7.5	7.4	7.1	7.6	28.8	21.0	10.6	1.8	72.6	33.4	48.8	51.2
78202	SAN ANTONIO	33.3	34.7	43.0	39.6	0.3	0.3	52.0	56.4	8.8	8.2	9.0	7.5	6.9	24.6	19.8	12.8	2.4	69.3	33.4	48.7	51.3
78203	SAN ANTONIO	32.9	33.7	33.8	30.5	0.2	0.1	61.5	65.8	9.4	8.7	8.9	8.5	7.6	26.2	19.0	9.8	1.9	67.7	30.3	48.5	51.6
78204	SAN ANTONIO	59.8	58.8	1.5	1.5	0.2	0.2	90.1	92.1	7.5	7.2	7.4	7.5	7.4	28.9	20.9	11.5	1.7	73.2	33.9	50.5	49.5
78205	SAN ANTONIO	75.7	74.0	7.5	7.3	1.0	1.0	51.3	57.9	2.4	1.7	1.1	1.8	6.3	31.8	28.3	23.3	3.3	94.1	48.1	61.3	38.7
78207	SAN ANTONIO	62.1	61.8	3.0	2.7	0.2	0.2	93.1	94.4	9.4	8.5	8.3	8.4	8.6	28.0	17.6	9.8	1.5	68.9	29.5	51.3	48.7
78208	SAN ANTONIO	55.8	56.3	15.0	13.2	1.0	1.0	74.4	78.4	10.3	8.8	8.8	8.5	8.7	26.8	18.7	8.1	1.3	67.0	28.4	52.2	47.8
78209	SAN ANTONIO	87.6	86.0	3.4	3.5	1.2	1.2	24.4	29.5	6.1	6.1	6.2	5.8	6.2	25.6	24.5	14.9	4.5	78.2	41.0	45.7	54.3
78210	SAN ANTONIO	56.0	55.0	8.1	7.4	0.4	0.4	79.1	82.8	7.9	7.7	8.1	7.8	7.6	27.0	21.5	10.9	1.7	71.4	33.0	48.8	51.2
78211	SAN ANTONIO	60.2	59.5	0.4	0.5	0.2	0.2	95.7	96.6	9.2	8.6	8.8	8.5	8.4	26.9	19.5	9.3	0.9	68.2	29.6	49.8	50.2
78212	SAN ANTONIO	74.1	72.8	2.5	2.4	1.3	1.3	61.0	65.6	5.8	5.4	5.6	8.8	9.7	29.1	21.7	11.2	2.8	79.9	34.9	49.0	51.0
78213	SAN ANTONIO	76.2	74.3	2.7	2.7	1.3	1.3	57.5	63.1	7.4	6.7	6.8	6.8	9.1	29.5	19.9	12.2	1.7	75.2	33.4	47.1	52.9
78214	SAN ANTONIO	57.3	55.9	0.7	0.6	0.3	0.3	88.9	91.4	8.9	8.2	8.3	8.0	7.9	26.7	20.2	10.7	1.3	69.8	31.5	49.1	50.9
78215	SAN ANTONIO	66.3	64.8	9.2	8.4	1.6	1.6	56.3	62.8	5.8	4.5	4.1	4.4	10.3	39.5	20.4	9.4	1.6	83.7	33.9	52.4	47.6
78216	SAN ANTONIO	78.9	76.8	3.7	3.8	1.8	1.9	42.0	47.9	6.6	5.7	5.6	5.8	8.7	32.1	22.3	11.6	1.7	79.0	35.1	48.6	51.5
78217	SAN ANTONIO	75.2	72.5	8.4	8.6	2.7	2.8	31.0	37.4	7.1	6.4	6.6	6.3	8.4	31.2	21.9	10.5	1.5	76.1	34.3	48.5	51.5
78218	SAN ANTONIO	62.1	60.0	16.6	16.4	4.2	4.2	38.7	44.7	8.4	7.4	7.1	6.7	8.5	29.8	20.5	10.5	1.2	73.3	32.5	47.7	52.3
78219	SAN ANTONIO	51.2	49.8	28.7	27.5	2.3	2.3	37.3	43.1	7.7	7.6	8.3	7.9	7.0	26.6	22.9	11.1	1.0	71.6	34.5	47.6	52.4
78220	SAN ANTONIO	27.8	28.0	54.9	52.5	0.2	0.2	31.6	35.7	7.9	7.5	8.1	7.6	6.5	22.8	21.6	15.5	2.5	71.9	36.5	44.4	55.6
78221	SAN ANTONIO	62.9	61.3	0.7	0.7	0.4	0.3	83.6	87.1	8.8	8.3	8.5	8.2	7.6	27.5	20.1	10.0	1.0	69.4	31.2	48.8	51.3
78222	SAN ANTONIO	56.6	54.4	22.8	22.2	0.4	0.4	44.8	51.2	7.7	7.4	8.0	7.8	8.1	25.8	23.7	10.2	1.3	72.2	33.7	47.1	52.9
78223	SAN ANTONIO	64.0	61.7	4.3	4.0	0.5	0.5	67.1	72.8	8.6	8.1	8.4	7.8	7.9	27.8	20.8	9.6	1.0	70.2	31.6	48.5	51.5
78224	SAN ANTONIO	62.4	61.4	1.0	0.9	0.2	0.2	91.5	93.5	9.5	8.6	8.6	8.1	8.8	28.2	19.8	7.6	0.8	68.5	28.9	49.2	50.8
78225	SAN ANTONIO	67.2	66.8	0.4	0.4	0.3	0.2	94.6	95.8	7.9	7.5	7.7	8.1	7.7	26.7	20.5	12.1	1.7	72.0	33.4	48.8	51.2
78226	SAN ANTONIO	62.5	61.2	4.9	4.6	1.1	1.1	77.8	81.3	10.2	8.9	8.6	8.0	12.2	27.4	15.3	9.0	0.5	67.9	26.4	49.5	50.5
78227	SAN ANTONIO	57.5	56.0	6.1	5.5	1.2	1.1	72.8	77.7	9.3	8.6	8.9	8.3	8.1	27.3	18.7	10.0	0.8	68.0	29.7	48.1	51.9
78228	SAN ANTONIO	70.8	69.8	2.4	2.2	0.6	0.5	83.6	86.8	8.2	7.5	7.9	8.0	8.8	26.7	19.8	11.0	2.1	71.9	31.8	47.9	52.1
78229	SAN ANTONIO	67.0	64.6	7.3	7.0	4.1	4.3	49.2	55.5	7.4	5.7	5.1	5.4	13.8	37.7	14.4	8.5	2.1	79.2	29.2	48.1	51.9
78230	SAN ANTONIO	81.2	78.9	3.5	3.6	3.0	3.1	34.1	40.6	6.0	5.8	6.2	6.2	7.6	29.9	24.9	12.1	1.3	78.4	36.7	47.6	52.4
78231	SAN ANTONIO	89.0	87.7	2.3	2.4	2.2	2.4	23.1	28.5	6.3	6.7	7.2	6.5	5.3	28.4	28.6	10.2	0.9	75.7	38.7	47.8	52.2
78232	SAN ANTONIO	88.0	85.9	2.5	2.7	2.3	2.5	19.8	25.2	5.4	5.6	6.2	6.4	6.7	28.2	29.6	10.7	1.3	78.8	39.8	48.6	51.4
78233	SAN ANTONIO	75.5	73.0	8.4	8.5	2.2	2.3	32.7	39.0	7.5	7.4	7.6	6.9	7.3	29.9	24.5	8.4	0.7	73.4	34.4	48.1	52.0
78234	SAN ANTONIO	56.4	53.0	27.3	28.4	4.0	4.2	17.1	21.3	8.2	9.3	8.3	14.1	19.7	35.4	4.8	0.2	0.0	70.8	22.6	54.4	45.6
78235	SAN ANTONIO	62.0	59.0	14.4	14.7	5.7	6.0	25.9	30.6	15.4	10.6	7.6	7.3	13.6	38.7	5.8	1.0	0.0	63.0	23.4	51.4	48.6
78236	SAN ANTONIO	65.2	61.9	18.8	19.8	4.0	4.3	15.4	19.4	2.3	2.5	1.9	36.1	39.8	15.8	1.3	0.3	0.0	91.3	20.9	70.2	29.8
78237	SAN ANTONIO	63.0	62.9	2.8	2.5	0.2	0.2	94.3	95.4	8.8	8.4	8.8	8.7	8.5	26.2	18.6	10.9	1.2	69.0	30.1	48.8	51.2
78238	SAN ANTONIO	67.5	65.4	4.9	4.7	2.1	2.1	61.2	67.4	8.3	7.4	6.7	6.5	9.3	31.0	21.2	8.8	0.9	74.0	31.6	48.2	51.9
78239	SAN ANTONIO	63.9	62.1	19.6	19.2	2.8	2.8	28.4	33.6	7.2	7.2	7.8	6.6	6.0	25.1	23.2	14.8	2.2	73.8	37.4	46.5	53.5
78240	SAN ANTONIO	71.9	69.3	5.2	5.1	4.0	4.0	42.0	48.5	7.4	6.5	6.1	5.9	9.6	36.1	19.2	7.6	1.6	76.8	31.8	47.4	52.6
78242	SAN ANTONIO	59.0	57.4	4.8	4.4	0.9	0.8	80.6	84.3	10.7	10.0	10.6	9.5	9.0	27.4	16.9	5.6	0.3	62.9	25.1	49.2	50.8
78244	SAN ANTONIO	47.9	46.3	28.3	27.7	3.5	3.5	37.2	41.9	8.7	8.7	10.1	8.8	7.7	30.1	21.9	3.8	0.2	66.8	29.9	48.9	51.1
78245	SAN ANTONIO	58.8	56.5	11.3	10.8	3.0	2.9	52.0	58.6	8.9	8.7	9.0	7.3	7.1	32.4	19.5	6.6	0.5	68.8	30.4	48.6	51.4
78247	SAN ANTONIO	81.9	79.5	5.2	5.4	2.2	2.3	27.1	33.4	8.4	8.4	7.8	6.6	5.7	33.8	23.7	5.1	0.5	71.1	34.3	47.8	52.3
78248	SAN ANTONIO	90.7	89.2	1.6	1.7	2.9	3.2	17.4	22.3	7.2	8.2	7.9	6.7	4.8	30.1	29.2	5.8	0.3	72.5	37.1	48.6	51.4
78249	SAN ANTONIO	77.5	75.2	4.0	4.1	4.0	4.1	35.6	42.0	7.5	7.1	7.2	8.9	9.0	31.7	22.4	5.9	0.5	73.9	32.1	48.3	51.8
78250	SAN ANTONIO	70.2	67.7	7.3	7.2	2.3	2.3	47.4	54.2	9.2	8.9	9.2	7.8	6.7	33.3	20.8	3.9	0.3	67.9	31.0	48.2	51.8
78251	SAN ANTONIO	61.0	59.0	11.1	10.7	2.9	2.9	51.7	57.9	9.0	8.1	7.8	7.3	8.2	35.6	19.9	4.0	0.2	70.7	30.3	48.5	51.6
78252	SAN ANTONIO	65.5	63.8	14.6	13.6	1.2	1.3	54.0	60.2	7.0	6.4	6.5	8.9	12.7	42.1	11.8	4.1	0.5	75.6	28.4	66.6	33.4
78253	SAN ANTONIO	77.3	74.4	5.9	6.0	2.9	3.0	32.1	38.8	8.0	7.9	8.5	7.3	7.0	30.8	23.9	6.2	0.5	70.8	33.8	48.7	51.3
78254	SAN ANTONIO	78.9	76.3	5.0	5.1	2.5	2.6	34.0	40.9	8.4	8.3	8.0	7.4	6.6	32.5	23.6	4.7	0.3	70.3	33.0	49.0	51.0
78255	SAN ANTONIO	85.3	83.1	2.1	2.3	2.9	3.1	24.1	30.0	5.1	5.6	6.1	7.2	11.2	24.8	29.0	10.1	1.0	79.4	37.9	50.7	49.4
78256	SAN ANTONIO	75.7	73.0	3.5	3.6	5.3	5.4	29.7	35.8	6.3	6.3	5.5	8.7	20.1	28.0	21.0	4.0	0.2	78.9	26.9	51.1	48.9
78257	SAN ANTONIO	89.7	88.2	1.2	1.3	1.2	1.3	26.0	32.3	5.9	6.6	6.7	5.9	3.9	21.7	34.4	13.5	1.5	77.0	44.5	48.2	51.8
78258	SAN ANTONIO	89.4	87.6	2.3	2.7	2.6	3.0	17.1	21.2	8.9	9.2	8.9	6.9	3.9	29.8	26.1	5.2	1.0	68.4	36.2	48.8	51.2
78259	SAN ANTONIO	88.1	86.1	2.7	2.9	2.6	2.8	18.8	23.9	8.2	8.8	8.8	8.3	5.5	28.7	26.8	4.8	0.3	68.6	35.6	48.7	51.3
78260	SAN ANTONIO	91.6	90.0	0.8	0.9	0.8	0.9	18.8	24.0	6.9	7.9	8.0	6.5	4.6	25.3	31.6	8.7	0.5	73.0	40.4	49.8	50.2
78261	SAN ANTONIO	91.8	90.4	0.7	0.7	2.3	2.5	16.4	21.1	6.5	8.4	10.2	8.4	3.2	26.6	32.4	4.1	0.2	68.7	39.1	51.1	49.0
78263	SAN ANTONIO	84.8	82.5	6.3	6.8	0.3	0.3	21.2	26.5	6.4	6.7	7.3	7.2	6.5	25.5	28.3	11.0	1.1	75.2	39.4	48.9	51.2
78264	SAN ANTONIO	66.5	63.6	0.9	0.9	0.7	0.7	69.1	74.8	8.3	8.6	10.1	8.8	6.4	27.9	22.2	7.2	0.6	67.5	31.3	50.3	49.7
78266	SAN ANTONIO	93.0	91.8	2.0	2.2	1.1	1.2	9.4	11.6	3.9	5.9	7.8	6.9	3.4	18.8	39.3	13.3	0.7	77.8	46.7	49.7	50.3
78332	ALICE	76.7	75.8	0.7	0.7	0.6	0.6	79.3	82.0	8.5	8.3	8.3	8.0	7.4	25.7	21.4	10.7	1.6	69.9	32.4	48.8	51.2
78336	ARANSAS PASS	83.0	80.9	2.8	2.8	0.5	0.6	32.6	38.2	7.9	7.2	7.7	7.4	8.0	25.2	23.5	11.9	1.2	72.6	34.8	50.5	49.5
78338	ARMSTRONG	64.7	64.7	0.7	0.7	0.7	0.7	78.7	79.4	9.6	8.1	8.1	5.9	7.4	25.7	22.8	11.8	0.7	69.9	35.0	52.2	47.8
78340	BAYSIDE	89.1	88.8	1.9	2.0	0.0	0.0	27.4	28.4	6.6	6.6	5.6	4.9	5.9	23.0	32.3	13.5	1.7	79.0	43.6	51.1	48.9
78343	BISHOP	79.5	78.2	1.3	1.2	0.1	0.2	63.7	68.2	7.4	6.9	8.7	8.8	8.0	25.9	22.2	11.0	1.2	71.6	33.5	49.6	50.4
78344	BRUNI	77.8	77.7	0.6	0.6	0.0	0.0	90.8	92.2	9.0	9.0	11.1	8.0	5.9	25.4	19.9	10.7	1.0	65.6	31.2	48.6	51.4
78349	CONCEPCION	82.0	82.1	0.1	0.1	0.1	0.1	93.8	94.0	6.7	6.7	7.3	6.4	6.3	23.2	24.2	16.7	2.5	75.4	40.1	49.5	50.5
78353	ENCINO	86.9	86.8	0.2	0.2	0.0	0.0	93.1	94.2	6.5	6.0	6.5	8.5	7.4	19.7	25.2	18.8	1.4	76.0	41.9	51.7	48.3
78355	FALFURRIAS	74.9	74.4	0.2	0.2	0.2	0.2	91.4	92.6	8.6	8.1	8.8	8.2	6.5	22.7	23.0	12.4	1.8	69.4	34.6	48.3	51.8
78357	FREER	81.8	81.8	0.4	0.4	0.2	0.2	74.0	74.8	8.7	8.3	9.0	9.0	7.3	25.0	21.5	10.2	1.1	68.2	31.7	49.2	50.8
78360	GUERRA	82.1	81.7	1.5	1.4	0.0	0.0	89.6	88.7	7.0	7.0	8.5	8.5	5.6	22.5	22.5	15.5	2.8	71.8	36.9	53.5	46.5
78361	HEBBRONVILLE	80.5	80.1	0.4	0.4	0.2	0.2	90.0	91.4	8.3	8.0	8.5	8.4	7.2	23.9	21.3	12.6	1.9	69.7	33.9	49.6	50.4
78362	INGLESIDE	78.8	76.3	5.0	5.0	2.0	2.1	27.1	32.8	8.6	7.6	7.9	8.1	11.8	31.5	18.0	6.2	0.5	71.4	28.6	53.6	46.4
78363	KINGSVILLE	71.6	70.5	3.9	3.7	1.6	1.7	65.8	69.3	8.0	7.1	6.9	8.6	11.2	28.8	19.1	9.1	1.3	73.8	29.5	50.6	49.5
78368	MATHIS	67.8	66.3	0.9	0.8	0.3	0.3	66.7	70.4	7.7	7.3	8.2	7.7	7.4	23.6	23.3	13.4	1.4	72.1	35.6	49.3	50.7
78369	MIRANDO CITY	84.3	84.4	0.4	0.4	0.1	0.1	93.1	94.4	9.6	9.4	10.9	9.4	7.1	27.2	18.2	7.7	0.6	64.2	28.1	50.3	49.7
78370	ODEM	75.3	73.5	0.2	0.2	0.1	0.1	70.3	75.1	9.0	7.8	8.0	8.3	8.1	25.5	23.5	8.7	1.1	70.1	31.8	48.1	51.9
78372	ORANGE GROVE	85.3	84.0	0.3	0.4	0.6	0.6	56.0	60.9	8.2	8.0	8.2	7.7	7.0	25.9	23.4	10.4	1.2	70.4	34.5	49.0	51.1
78373	PORT ARANSAS	94.0	92.8	0.4	0.5	0.9	1.0	6.0	7.9	3.9	4.2	5.4	5.9	4.0	23.1	37.4	15.5	0.7	82.4	46.8	52.0	48.0
78374	PORTLAND	82.0	80.4	3.4	3.5	1.1	1.2	36.1	39.7	8.6	8.3	8.9	8.1	7.1	29.2	21.5	7.6	0.8	68.9	31.8	49.7	50.3
78375	PREMONT	78.2	77.4	0.4	0.4	0.1	0.1	80.9	83.8	7.5	7.3	8.6	8.5	6.6	23.5	22.3	14.0	1.8	71.3	35.9	50.3	49.7
78376	REALITOS	81.6	81.9	0.0	0.0	0.0	0.0	87.9	88.2	5.5	6.3	6.3	7.2	5.9	18.7	26.5	19.6	4.0	77.9	45.1	50.1	49.9
78377	REFUGIO	77.8	77.8	11.1	11.0	0.5	0.5	41.4	42.4	6.5	6.3	7.4	7.1	6.5	23.9	23.8	15.9	2.6	75.4	39.8	48.4	51.7
78379	RIVIERA	75.8	73.9	0.9	0.9	0.6	0.6	58.5	63.7	6.2	6.3	8.0	8.3	7.2	26.7	25.3	11.1	0.9	74.0	36.7	51.8	48.2
78380	ROBSTOWN	71.8	70.7	0.9	0.9	0.2	0.2	76.2	79.3	8.4	8.1	8.7	8.6	7.8	25.1	22.0	9.8	1.3	69.3	31.7	49.4	50.6
78382	ROCKPORT	87.7	86.2	1.4	1.4	3.2	3.6	19.4	22.2	5.3	5.5	6.3	6.1	5.4	20.7	29.1	19.6	2.0	79.0	45.5	49.3	50.7
	TEXAS	71.0	69.5	11.5	11.4	2.8	3.1	32.0	34.6	7.9	7.5	7.7	7.5	8.1	29.6	21.9	8.7	1.2	72.6	32.9	49.7	50.3
	UNITED STATES	75.1	73.6	12.3	12.5	3.8	4.2	12.5	14.1	6.9	6.7	7.2	7.0	7.3	28.6	23.8	10.8	1.7	75.1	36.0	49.1	50.9

ZIP CODE #	POST OFFICE NAME	2004 Per Capita Income	2004 HH Income Base	2004 HOUSEHOLD INCOME DISTRIBUTION (%) Less than $25,000	$25,000 to $49,999	$50,000 to $99,999	$100,000 to $149,999	$150,000 or More	MEDIAN HOUSEHOLD INCOME 2004	2009	2004 National Centile	2004 State Centile	2004 Home Value Base	2004 HOME VALUE DISTRIBUTION (%) Less than $50,000	$50,000 to $89,999	$90,000 to $174,999	$175,000 to $399,999	$400,000 or More	2004 Median Home Value
78151	RUNGE	13403	591	49.2	29.4	16.9	3.1	1.4	25357	28564	5	6	428	63.6	20.8	11.2	2.8	1.6	33333
78152	SAINT HEDWIG	23208	652	19.3	24.2	39.0	13.5	4.0	56875	65014	82	84	581	21.5	24.3	35.5	15.8	2.9	96447
78154	SCHERTZ	25750	8014	13.7	22.7	43.0	15.0	5.6	62272	70344	86	88	6452	9.3	18.0	55.1	16.9	0.7	125466
78155	SEGUIN	18776	15235	27.7	31.1	31.7	7.0	2.6	41772	47389	52	61	11065	22.9	32.5	32.4	11.2	1.1	82714
78159	SMILEY	13920	363	51.2	31.4	11.0	3.3	3.0	24094	27749	4	5	280	56.4	20.7	21.1	1.8	0.0	43793
78160	STOCKDALE	20518	1344	29.5	28.0	31.9	6.6	4.1	40344	47384	47	55	1054	38.4	27.3	23.1	9.8	1.4	64598
78161	SUTHERLAND SPRINGS	17825	367	24.0	41.1	26.2	5.7	3.0	38344	45000	41	48	303	30.4	23.1	28.1	14.9	3.6	74167
78163	BULVERDE	32837	2983	10.3	18.3	39.6	19.4	12.4	75841	86926	94	94	2748	6.0	9.9	25.3	48.3	10.5	191782
78164	YORKTOWN	18368	1498	38.1	32.6	21.5	5.8	2.0	31684	36018	17	22	1204	46.4	31.7	15.5	5.2	1.1	53583
78201	SAN ANTONIO	14902	16851	41.3	31.9	20.6	4.8	1.4	30545	34772	14	17	9098	34.5	49.8	13.8	1.7	0.2	59559
78202	SAN ANTONIO	9431	4014	59.1	28.0	11.5	1.0	0.5	20538	23373	2	3	2043	64.9	32.8	1.6	0.8	0.0	44340
78203	SAN ANTONIO	9639	1702	53.9	29.9	13.7	1.7	0.9	22859	26014	3	4	940	67.7	30.4	1.8	0.1	0.0	42019
78204	SAN ANTONIO	11611	3886	47.0	31.7	17.7	2.8	0.8	26925	30838	7	9	2324	68.0	24.8	3.8	1.8	1.6	40457
78205	SAN ANTONIO	24028	1016	59.5	24.0	11.8	1.8	3.0	18695	21835	1	2	50	12.0	16.0	2.0	62.0	8.0	200000
78207	SAN ANTONIO	9114	15560	55.2	29.1	13.4	1.8	0.6	22122	25242	3	4	8340	73.6	24.8	1.6	0.2	0.0	38798
78208	SAN ANTONIO	9822	1574	59.5	24.5	13.3	1.8	0.9	20628	24254	2	3	634	71.0	24.0	4.9	0.2	0.0	40000
78209	SAN ANTONIO	38860	17947	22.8	24.6	28.3	13.3	11.1	53050	62301	77	81	10427	4.0	15.3	38.6	30.6	11.5	155247
78210	SAN ANTONIO	13112	12981	42.9	31.5	20.6	3.7	1.3	29582	33632	11	14	7846	48.6	41.6	8.5	1.1	0.2	50736
78211	SAN ANTONIO	9836	8638	45.2	32.8	18.9	2.5	0.6	27719	31515	8	11	5946	68.8	27.4	3.5	0.3	0.1	42365
78212	SAN ANTONIO	26407	12021	36.7	29.6	20.4	6.6	6.8	34674	40900	26	32	5438	21.8	35.7	17.8	13.1	11.6	77666
78213	SAN ANTONIO	21189	16859	28.2	36.5	26.4	5.6	3.3	39173	45269	43	51	8450	10.2	52.5	28.1	8.0	1.2	76871
78214	SAN ANTONIO	11661	7816	46.2	31.9	17.1	3.3	1.4	27010	30934	7	10	4794	59.2	36.4	3.5	0.8	0.0	46119
78215	SAN ANTONIO	24392	705	48.1	29.4	16.3	3.7	2.6	25957	30342	6	7	113	20.4	47.8	30.1	1.8	0.0	83788
78216	SAN ANTONIO	28393	16502	26.5	32.8	25.7	8.8	6.2	41326	48864	51	59	7153	2.3	28.7	41.1	24.0	3.9	111738
78217	SAN ANTONIO	25059	13161	19.9	33.6	34.6	8.3	3.6	47098	54393	66	72	6158	4.1	38.9	52.5	3.2	1.2	95404
78218	SAN ANTONIO	19483	12822	31.9	34.7	25.4	5.6	2.3	36940	43049	35	42	6093	20.2	57.8	12.7	7.8	1.5	68445
78219	SAN ANTONIO	16531	5106	30.1	33.7	29.3	5.6	1.3	37504	43325	37	45	3549	31.9	57.9	9.6	0.3	0.3	60937
78220	SAN ANTONIO	16476	6379	41.9	34.2	19.1	3.1	1.7	30563	34933	14	17	4124	44.1	47.3	7.9	0.6	0.2	53262
78221	SAN ANTONIO	12151	11034	38.0	36.2	21.3	3.4	1.1	31996	36237	18	22	7355	43.7	49.8	6.1	0.4	0.0	53020
78222	SAN ANTONIO	18095	5510	27.6	33.0	29.3	7.9	2.1	40028	46681	46	54	3862	27.5	52.7	18.7	0.9	0.3	67153
78223	SAN ANTONIO	14937	15482	36.1	35.3	23.3	4.2	1.1	33904	39036	24	29	9534	42.5	47.1	9.3	1.0	0.1	54367
78224	SAN ANTONIO	11872	4385	34.8	35.6	25.3	3.7	0.6	35219	40462	28	34	2833	46.6	48.2	4.8	0.3	0.1	51687
78225	SAN ANTONIO	11873	4446	42.7	34.4	19.5	2.8	0.7	29100	32949	11	13	2977	56.4	40.8	2.8	0.0	0.0	47628
78226	SAN ANTONIO	12384	2580	41.8	34.2	18.8	3.3	2.0	30527	34722	14	17	1223	49.6	47.8	2.5	0.1	0.2	50200
78227	SAN ANTONIO	13306	13320	37.5	34.2	23.7	3.3	1.3	32992	37490	21	26	8330	37.7	56.7	5.1	0.3	0.2	56174
78228	SAN ANTONIO	14265	19406	37.0	31.8	24.6	5.1	1.5	34814	39657	27	32	12040	30.3	49.2	19.4	1.0	0.1	63726
78229	SAN ANTONIO	23949	15304	33.9	37.5	21.3	4.4	2.9	34434	40484	26	31	2573	7.2	31.7	44.0	15.2	1.9	100698
78230	SAN ANTONIO	37872	16803	18.5	26.4	29.7	13.3	12.2	55550	66440	80	83	9298	1.3	12.2	51.8	28.6	6.1	144683
78231	SAN ANTONIO	41267	3782	10.4	18.8	35.7	19.1	16.1	76814	91405	94	95	2605	4.4	2.5	56.2	32.9	4.0	156560
78232	SAN ANTONIO	38399	16249	11.5	21.5	35.4	19.3	12.3	70751	84279	92	92	10652	2.1	5.5	62.1	27.3	2.9	146847
78233	SAN ANTONIO	21950	14155	17.1	31.4	37.8	11.3	2.4	51156	59442	74	79	9792	7.6	53.6	38.1	0.7	0.1	84410
78234	SAN ANTONIO	14591	869	8.5	42.9	37.1	8.8	2.8	49045	55855	70	75	21	28.6	9.5	14.3	14.3	33.3	143750
78235	SAN ANTONIO	15585	205	15.6	36.1	41.0	6.3	1.0	48134	54293	69	74	15	53.3	46.7	0.0	0.0	0.0	45000
78236	SAN ANTONIO	12451	322	21.1	49.1	26.1	2.5	1.2	37987	42660	39	46	52	40.4	57.7	1.9	0.0	0.0	54545
78237	SAN ANTONIO	9800	10573	48.4	32.6	15.4	2.9	0.7	25880	29592	6	7	6888	67.7	29.7	2.6	0.0	0.0	42391
78238	SAN ANTONIO	19297	8656	29.3	32.2	30.1	6.2	2.3	40529	46504	48	56	4437	9.4	52.8	36.2	1.3	0.3	82330
78239	SAN ANTONIO	22386	9924	20.5	29.3	34.9	11.8	3.5	50189	57720	72	77	6800	15.4	34.8	44.7	5.0	0.2	89855
78240	SAN ANTONIO	25015	21659	23.3	31.0	31.9	9.8	4.1	45793	53974	63	70	9723	3.0	18.1	71.5	6.6	0.7	108974
78242	SAN ANTONIO	10652	8153	39.7	34.0	22.3	3.2	0.8	31077	35152	15	19	4816	48.9	46.5	4.7	0.0	0.0	50571
78244	SAN ANTONIO	18405	6921	15.6	32.5	39.4	10.2	2.3	51370	59955	75	79	5151	5.4	43.3	49.3	2.0	0.1	91097
78245	SAN ANTONIO	18529	11334	15.4	34.7	40.2	8.4	1.4	49940	57530	72	77	7391	8.9	63.3	27.4	0.3	0.1	78170
78247	SAN ANTONIO	27284	14698	7.4	22.4	47.8	17.6	4.9	66834	78092	90	91	12567	1.0	21.8	72.1	4.9	0.2	110652
78248	SAN ANTONIO	48138	6095	7.9	13.1	28.3	24.6	26.2	101144	120304	98	98	4599	0.6	2.8	20.9	63.0	12.7	228093
78249	SAN ANTONIO	27435	13601	15.9	21.3	38.3	18.0	6.5	63482	74429	87	89	9831	2.3	18.5	65.4	13.3	0.5	116343
78250	SAN ANTONIO	21712	17465	10.5	26.3	46.2	13.8	3.3	60229	68561	85	87	13867	2.0	36.3	60.0	1.6	0.0	97828
78251	SAN ANTONIO	21571	11296	11.8	32.8	41.0	12.0	2.4	54327	63305	79	82	7458	1.7	29.9	63.1	5.3	0.1	102140
78252	SAN ANTONIO	13342	1332	30.7	37.1	27.5	3.0	1.7	37180	43294	36	43	971	56.8	30.5	9.3	3.5	0.0	44843
78253	SAN ANTONIO	25837	3785	10.1	22.1	44.7	17.6	5.6	65875	77195	89	91	3386	18.1	13.8	52.6	15.1	0.5	121191
78254	SAN ANTONIO	29468	6850	5.6	17.5	46.4	21.9	8.7	73726	87095	93	94	5775	0.7	8.6	72.0	17.2	1.5	124600
78255	SAN ANTONIO	38253	1736	15.3	17.1	29.5	22.3	15.8	77658	91559	94	95	1213	3.5	7.5	32.2	48.6	8.2	187277
78256	SAN ANTONIO	33055	1381	28.0	16.9	25.0	17.8	12.3	62715	74521	87	89	595	0.0	6.1	18.2	61.7	14.1	216728
78257	SAN ANTONIO	60039	1076	16.2	25.5	18.4	6.6	33.4	64309	64499	88	90	891	21.4	12.6	4.2	18.0	43.9	340761
78258	SAN ANTONIO	45569	9964	5.7	9.4	31.7	25.8	27.4	104292	126644	98	98	8993	1.6	1.7	22.5	59.5	14.7	220841
78259	SAN ANTONIO	35650	3795	3.4	10.2	35.4	30.5	20.5	101003	120143	98	98	3602	0.8	0.1	51.1	44.6	3.4	173159
78260	SAN ANTONIO	39518	726	13.6	18.5	25.8	22.7	19.4	83655	96155	96	97	661	11.4	8.9	33.6	33.0	13.2	164549
78261	SAN ANTONIO	52619	688	5.1	9.6	30.4	24.9	30.1	106755	124107	99	99	661	0.0	1.1	18.3	55.1	25.6	287030
78263	SAN ANTONIO	21915	1713	16.2	29.0	38.9	12.9	3.0	54898	63669	80	83	1485	17.1	24.8	42.1	15.2	0.9	102277
78264	SAN ANTONIO	14571	3154	33.7	30.1	28.3	5.3	2.8	36899	44109	35	42	2434	49.5	32.5	15.4	2.5	0.2	50607
78266	SAN ANTONIO	43354	1145	9.8	14.2	30.6	23.4	22.0	91192	107158	97	97	1080	5.7	3.0	12.3	64.5	14.4	242217
78332	ALICE	14368	9409	38.8	30.9	23.5	4.8	2.1	32944	37219	21	26	6622	49.7	28.6	18.1	3.3	0.3	50343
78336	ARANSAS PASS	15731	4742	37.2	30.9	26.1	4.5	1.4	34660	40461	26	32	3353	46.6	26.1	21.7	5.2	0.4	54395
78338	ARMSTRONG	14389	44	43.2	38.6	13.6	0.0	4.6	30000	36104	12	15	15	40.0	13.3	40.0	0.0	6.7	75000
78340	BAYSIDE	17531	168	41.1	26.2	23.2	8.9	0.6	32550	38488	19	24	132	49.2	30.3	17.4	0.8	2.3	50833
78343	BISHOP	16876	1594	32.6	29.2	29.4	6.2	2.6	37750	43061	38	46	1195	48.0	33.2	14.9	3.6	0.3	51526
78344	BRUNI	12041	154	43.5	32.5	18.8	4.6	0.7	28687	32783	10	13	119	63.9	25.2	8.4	0.8	1.7	37500
78349	CONCEPCION	14466	1188	53.4	23.5	18.4	2.6	2.1	22959	25744	3	4	1056	70.7	18.2	7.1	3.9	0.1	33909
78353	ENCINO	20597	232	37.9	34.5	21.6	3.0	3.0	31483	37619	16	21	184	62.5	19.6	17.9	0.0	0.0	41481
78355	FALFURRIAS	10834	2436	57.6	22.6	15.7	2.4	1.6	19385	22216	2	3	1714	57.5	28.9	10.9	2.7	0.0	39226
78357	FREER	14354	1385	43.0	28.2	21.7	4.6	2.6	28629	33061	10	13	1076	65.0	21.0	11.7	2.3	0.0	37525
78360	GUERRA	11398	29	65.5	20.7	13.8	0.0	0.0	15670	17200	1	1	18	61.1	38.9	0.0	0.0	0.0	40000
78361	HEBBRONVILLE	14100	1913	44.4	32.8	16.8	3.9	2.0	28621	32361	10	12	1395	62.1	24.2	11.8	1.9	0.0	40534
78362	INGLESIDE	18425	3208	21.8	37.5	30.6	6.8	3.4	43395	49871	57	65	2189	20.0	30.1	44.5	5.4	0.1	89929
78363	KINGSVILLE	15621	10334	40.2	27.9	23.9	5.6	2.5	32580	37464	20	24	5972	41.6	30.4	23.3	4.2	0.5	59882
78368	MATHIS	17592	3934	41.9	29.3	20.8	4.1	3.8	30886	35549	15	19	3027	55.8	23.5	18.2	2.2	0.3	45307
78369	MIRANDO CITY	11059	459	44.9	29.6	16.3	7.4	1.7	29453	33000	11	14	374	57.8	29.1	12.0	1.1	0.0	40938
78370	ODEM	13407	1098	36.4	31.9	26.3	4.1	1.3	35433	40258	29	35	799	46.1	31.3	19.4	3.0	0.3	54565
78372	ORANGE GROVE	14708	1981	36.1	33.3	23.2	5.1	2.3	33718	39070	23	29	1590	44.9	30.2	17.9	5.5	1.5	55548
78373	PORT ARANSAS	29167	1647	27.8	26.8	30.7	8.3	6.4	45691	54200	63	69	1266	17.9	19.4	36.1	19.9	6.7	108553
78374	PORTLAND	21614	6643	18.4	29.1	36.9	11.1	4.6	52142	60000	76	80	4448	13.4	23.1	52.3	10.2	1.0	103231
78375	PREMONT	12646	1333	50.7	25.7	20.0	2.2	1.4	24500	27814	4	5	1004	65.0	22.6	10.3	2.1	0.0	35821
78376	REALITOS	12213	185	57.8	21.6	16.2	3.8	0.5	20613	22846	2	3	165	70.9	20.0	6.1	3.0	0.0	33214
78377	REFUGIO	18213	1456	39.2	25.3	29.2	4.0	2.3	34284	40107	25	30	1043	47.7	26.8	19.0	5.1	1.5	52042
78379	RIVIERA	20442	679	32.1	24.7	27.8	11.8	3.5	41469	49069	51	60	564	41.0	17.2	28.6	11.9	1.4	72571
78380	ROBSTOWN	14263	7762	38.8	28.8	23.3	6.4	2.7	33989	39454	24	30	5861	54.5	23.3	14.5	6.4	1.4	46135
78382	ROCKPORT	23651	8726	35.3	28.7	23.9	7.4	4.7	35931	42259	31	37	6620	31.4	22.8	29.1	13.0	3.9	83284
	TEXAS	23284		26.2	27.7	29.5	10.3	6.3	45778	54246				21.6	26.1	33.4	15.6	3.4	93683
	UNITED STATES	25866		24.7	27.1	30.8	10.9	6.5	48124	56710				10.9	15.0	33.7	30.1	10.4	145905

ZIP CODE #	POST OFFICE NAME	FINANCIAL SERVICES: Auto Loan	FINANCIAL SERVICES: Home Loan	FINANCIAL SERVICES: Invest-ments	FINANCIAL SERVICES: Retire-ment Plans	THE HOME: Home Improvements: Home Repair	THE HOME: Home Improvements: Lawn & Garden	THE HOME: Furnishings: Comput-ers & Hard-ware	THE HOME: Furnishings: Major Appli-ances	THE HOME: Furnishings: TV, Radio, Sound Equip-ment	THE HOME: Furnishings: Furni-ture	ENTERTAINMENT: Dine out/ Carry out	ENTERTAINMENT: Sports Equip-ment	ENTERTAINMENT: Fees & Tickets	ENTERTAINMENT: Toys & Games	ENTERTAINMENT: Travel	ENTERTAINMENT: Cable TV	PERSONAL: Apparel & Services	PERSONAL: Auto Repairs	PERSONAL: Health Insur-ance	PERSONAL: Pets & Supplies
78151	RUNGE	54	47	39	44	45	48	48	52	50	52	63	55	44	55	46	48	62	53	49	54
78152	SAINT HEDWIG	106	94	72	90	99	106	88	97	93	88	113	115	86	115	90	95	108	95	104	123
78154	SCHERTZ	106	114	107	115	111	112	105	107	101	108	127	124	107	127	104	97	124	104	98	119
78155	SEGUIN	79	73	65	71	74	79	73	77	74	74	92	87	70	89	72	74	89	77	77	88
78159	SMILEY	57	43	28	41	47	56	47	52	53	45	62	58	42	59	47	56	57	52	62	63
78160	STOCKDALE	92	70	46	67	77	89	73	82	81	71	96	95	66	93	73	85	88	82	96	104
78161	SUTHERLAND SPRINGS	82	75	59	72	75	79	72	77	72	74	89	89	68	84	71	71	86	76	76	91
78163	BULVERDE	124	154	164	154	152	149	138	137	128	137	160	161	146	171	141	124	160	132	123	152
78164	YORKTOWN	75	56	37	54	61	74	62	68	69	59	82	77	55	77	61	73	75	68	82	83
78201	SAN ANTONIO	61	56	52	53	54	57	58	60	59	61	74	66	54	68	55	57	73	62	57	64
78202	SAN ANTONIO	39	33	34	30	32	37	36	37	40	37	49	41	35	45	35	41	47	39	40	42
78203	SAN ANTONIO	45	38	35	35	37	41	40	43	43	43	54	46	38	48	39	43	53	44	43	46
78204	SAN ANTONIO	53	47	42	44	45	48	48	51	50	52	63	55	45	56	46	48	62	52	49	54
78205	SAN ANTONIO	35	31	43	32	31	35	39	35	40	37	50	42	37	49	37	40	49	39	37	39
78207	SAN ANTONIO	43	37	33	35	36	38	39	41	41	42	51	44	36	45	37	39	50	42	39	43
78208	SAN ANTONIO	44	39	35	36	37	40	40	43	43	44	53	46	37	48	39	42	53	44	41	45
78209	SAN ANTONIO	113	121	150	124	120	130	124	121	122	123	153	140	127	153	125	120	150	123	116	132
78210	SAN ANTONIO	57	51	47	48	49	53	53	56	55	56	69	60	50	62	51	54	68	57	54	59
78211	SAN ANTONIO	55	48	40	44	46	48	49	53	51	53	64	56	45	56	47	49	63	54	50	55
78212	SAN ANTONIO	90	87	95	86	85	91	92	92	93	94	116	104	89	110	89	90	115	95	87	98
78213	SAN ANTONIO	74	70	75	70	68	74	73	74	74	76	93	83	72	88	71	72	91	76	70	80
78214	SAN ANTONIO	56	49	42	45	47	49	50	54	52	54	66	57	46	58	48	51	65	55	51	56
78215	SAN ANTONIO	64	55	77	58	53	59	71	64	72	68	90	79	66	87	66	68	88	71	60	70
78216	SAN ANTONIO	85	83	98	86	81	88	90	86	89	90	112	101	89	109	87	86	110	90	81	95
78217	SAN ANTONIO	81	83	94	86	81	84	85	83	83	85	104	98	86	103	83	79	102	85	76	91
78218	SAN ANTONIO	66	64	73	64	62	67	68	66	69	69	87	77	67	84	66	67	85	69	64	73
78219	SAN ANTONIO	66	66	67	63	65	71	65	66	66	66	82	75	65	80	65	67	80	66	67	75
78220	SAN ANTONIO	63	59	65	56	58	67	61	61	65	63	81	67	62	78	61	68	79	62	67	70
78221	SAN ANTONIO	61	53	44	50	51	54	54	59	57	59	71	62	50	63	52	55	70	60	55	61
78222	SAN ANTONIO	76	77	72	73	76	80	74	77	75	76	93	86	74	92	74	74	91	76	75	85
78223	SAN ANTONIO	63	58	53	55	57	60	59	62	61	62	76	68	56	71	57	59	74	63	60	67
78224	SAN ANTONIO	64	56	48	53	54	57	58	62	61	63	76	67	54	69	55	58	76	64	58	65
78225	SAN ANTONIO	57	50	42	46	48	51	51	55	53	56	67	59	47	59	49	51	66	56	52	58
78226	SAN ANTONIO	57	48	45	48	47	50	53	54	55	56	69	61	49	63	50	52	68	57	50	58
78227	SAN ANTONIO	62	58	53	55	57	60	58	62	60	62	75	67	56	69	57	58	74	62	59	65
78228	SAN ANTONIO	63	59	58	57	58	61	61	63	62	64	78	69	58	74	59	60	77	64	60	67
78229	SAN ANTONIO	68	60	72	66	59	63	72	67	70	70	89	82	68	84	67	66	86	72	61	74
78230	SAN ANTONIO	118	122	147	127	119	127	126	121	122	126	154	142	128	152	124	118	152	124	113	134
78231	SAN ANTONIO	143	148	168	157	144	151	150	144	143	152	182	171	152	177	146	136	179	147	131	160
78232	SAN ANTONIO	126	135	152	141	131	136	133	130	127	135	161	153	136	158	131	121	158	131	118	143
78233	SAN ANTONIO	84	90	95	91	87	89	88	87	84	89	106	102	89	106	86	81	105	87	79	95
78234	SAN ANTONIO	96	61	58	70	56	66	91	78	92	85	115	104	78	103	75	84	110	92	72	89
78235	SAN ANTONIO	86	59	54	64	54	62	80	73	82	77	103	92	70	92	68	76	99	83	67	81
78236	SAN ANTONIO	70	48	44	52	44	51	66	59	67	63	84	76	57	75	56	62	81	68	55	66
78237	SAN ANTONIO	52	46	38	43	44	47	47	51	49	51	61	54	43	54	45	47	61	52	48	53
78238	SAN ANTONIO	71	68	74	68	66	70	72	71	72	73	91	82	70	88	69	69	89	73	66	77
78239	SAN ANTONIO	83	86	94	85	86	92	85	86	84	86	106	96	86	103	86	84	103	86	85	95
78240	SAN ANTONIO	82	79	90	85	77	80	84	81	81	85	103	97	83	99	80	77	101	84	73	90
78242	SAN ANTONIO	57	51	46	48	49	52	53	55	55	56	69	61	50	64	51	53	68	57	52	59
78244	SAN ANTONIO	85	94	92	97	90	88	87	86	81	90	102	102	89	103	85	76	101	85	74	95
78245	SAN ANTONIO	79	86	88	89	83	82	82	80	77	84	97	95	83	97	80	72	96	80	71	88
78247	SAN ANTONIO	111	125	125	129	120	118	115	114	107	118	135	134	118	136	113	101	133	112	99	125
78248	SAN ANTONIO	174	209	216	216	200	199	186	182	169	190	215	212	199	221	185	161	215	176	159	201
78249	SAN ANTONIO	107	115	118	120	111	111	112	108	104	113	132	128	113	131	108	98	130	108	95	119
78250	SAN ANTONIO	98	110	107	114	105	102	100	99	92	104	117	116	103	117	98	86	116	97	85	109
78251	SAN ANTONIO	90	100	99	104	95	93	92	91	85	95	108	107	94	108	90	80	107	90	78	100
78252	SAN ANTONIO	46	44	39	45	43	44	44	44	42	45	53	52	42	51	42	40	52	45	41	50
78253	SAN ANTONIO	113	128	124	133	122	118	116	114	106	120	134	134	119	135	113	99	133	111	97	125
78254	SAN ANTONIO	122	143	144	148	137	134	128	127	117	132	149	148	134	152	127	111	148	123	110	139
78255	SAN ANTONIO	135	142	163	148	141	146	148	141	141	144	177	169	148	176	144	135	174	145	131	156
78256	SAN ANTONIO	106	101	122	109	99	105	117	106	112	113	142	131	114	137	110	105	139	114	97	118
78257	SAN ANTONIO	190	254	347	250	248	268	222	220	207	227	262	248	252	275	237	209	266	212	205	239
78258	SAN ANTONIO	188	215	227	223	209	209	199	196	184	202	234	229	208	235	198	176	231	192	175	215
78259	SAN ANTONIO	160	182	178	190	174	169	164	163	151	171	192	190	170	192	161	141	190	158	139	178
78260	SAN ANTONIO	145	179	197	183	175	178	160	157	147	161	186	180	174	192	163	143	187	152	142	173
78261	SAN ANTONIO	212	264	287	273	255	258	233	226	211	236	269	262	256	280	236	205	272	218	201	251
78263	SAN ANTONIO	96	95	83	92	97	101	88	93	88	88	109	109	88	111	89	88	105	91	93	112
78264	SAN ANTONIO	75	68	56	66	68	72	66	70	67	68	82	81	62	78	65	65	79	70	69	82
78266	SAN ANTONIO	153	185	207	184	184	192	169	170	160	169	201	193	180	205	176	159	199	165	161	185
78332	ALICE	65	60	52	56	58	60	60	64	61	64	77	69	56	70	58	59	76	65	60	67
78336	ARANSAS PASS	67	57	47	55	59	65	59	63	62	59	76	72	55	72	58	63	72	63	66	74
78338	ARMSTRONG	68	59	49	55	57	60	61	65	63	66	79	69	56	70	58	61	78	67	61	68
78340	BAYSIDE	73	56	37	51	64	72	53	65	61	53	72	76	48	71	57	65	67	64	77	89
78343	BISHOP	74	70	64	66	68	72	70	74	72	74	90	79	67	83	68	70	89	74	71	78
78344	BRUNI	58	51	42	47	49	52	52	56	54	57	68	60	48	60	50	52	67	57	53	59
78349	CONCEPCION	60	53	44	49	51	54	54	58	56	59	70	62	50	62	51	54	70	59	55	61
78353	ENCINO	86	76	63	70	73	77	77	84	80	84	101	89	71	89	74	77	100	85	78	87
78355	FALFURRIAS	49	43	35	40	41	43	44	47	45	47	57	50	40	50	41	44	56	48	44	49
78357	FREER	63	56	46	52	54	56	57	61	59	62	74	65	52	65	54	57	73	62	58	64
78360	GUERRA	42	37	31	34	36	38	38	41	39	41	49	43	35	44	36	38	49	42	38	43
78361	HEBBRONVILLE	63	55	46	51	53	56	56	61	58	61	73	64	51	65	53	56	72	62	57	63
78362	INGLESIDE	77	75	75	77	73	76	79	77	77	78	96	92	76	95	75	73	94	79	71	85
78363	KINGSVILLE	63	56	58	56	55	58	63	62	63	63	79	71	59	74	59	60	78	65	58	66
78368	MATHIS	80	70	60	67	70	76	71	77	74	75	92	83	67	83	70	73	89	77	77	85
78369	MIRANDO CITY	63	55	46	51	53	56	56	61	59	62	74	65	52	65	54	57	73	62	57	64
78370	ODEM	66	57	47	54	56	60	58	63	61	62	76	68	54	69	56	60	74	63	61	68
78372	ORANGE GROVE	70	61	47	59	62	68	61	66	63	62	77	75	57	73	60	63	74	66	68	77
78373	PORT ARANSAS	108	86	60	78	96	108	81	97	91	80	108	112	73	106	86	97	101	95	114	131
78374	PORTLAND	91	96	96	97	94	97	93	94	90	94	113	109	93	113	92	87	111	93	87	103
78375	PREMONT	56	50	41	46	48	50	51	55	53	55	66	58	46	58	48	51	65	56	51	57
78376	REALITOS	48	42	35	39	40	42	43	46	44	46	56	49	39	49	41	43	55	47	43	48
78377	REFUGIO	71	61	53	59	65	74	64	68	69	62	84	78	62	85	65	72	79	68	76	81
78379	RIVIERA	87	76	63	71	73	77	78	84	81	84	101	89	71	89	74	78	100	85	79	87
78380	ROBSTOWN	74	65	53	61	64	68	65	70	67	69	84	77	60	77	63	66	82	71	68	78
78382	ROCKPORT	92	76	60	71	82	94	74	85	81	76	99	94	70	91	78	86	92	84	98	106
	TEXAS	94	90	91	90	89	95	92	93	92	93	115	107	90	112	90	90	112	94	89	104
	UNITED STATES	100	100	100	100	100	100	100	100	100	100	100	100	100	100	100	100	100	100	100	100

POPULATION CHANGE

ZIP CODE #	POST OFFICE NAME	COUNTY FIPS CODE	POPULATION 2000	2004	2009	2000-2004 ANNUAL RATE % Rate	State Centile	HOUSEHOLDS 2000	2004	2009	% Annual Rate 2000-2004	2004 Average HH Size	FAMILIES 2000	2004	% Annual Rate 2000-2004
78383	SANDIA	297	2827	3033	3233	1.7	61	1104	1187	1271	1.7	2.53	818	880	1.7
78384	SAN DIEGO	131	6347	6469	6582	0.5	24	1899	1949	1998	0.6	3.03	1445	1486	0.7
78385	SARITA	261	278	279	279	0.1	14	94	94	94	0.0	2.94	76	76	0.0
78387	SINTON	409	9606	10120	10792	1.2	49	3116	3289	3521	1.3	2.97	2403	2540	1.3
78389	SKIDMORE	025	2250	2327	2445	0.8	35	790	818	862	0.8	2.84	611	634	0.9
78390	TAFT	409	6140	6375	6782	0.9	38	1913	1991	2126	0.9	3.14	1510	1573	1.0
78391	TYNAN	025	312	320	334	0.6	29	96	99	103	0.7	3.22	76	79	0.9
78393	WOODSBORO	391	2514	2476	2449	-0.4	7	950	934	924	-0.4	2.64	704	694	-0.3
78401	CORPUS CHRISTI	355	4633	4743	4880	0.6	27	1828	1869	1920	0.5	2.28	859	870	0.3
78402	CORPUS CHRISTI	355	455	453	460	-0.1	10	254	250	252	-0.4	1.81	112	111	-0.2
78404	CORPUS CHRISTI	355	17181	17159	17533	0.0	12	6388	6325	6420	-0.2	2.64	4064	4034	-0.2
78405	CORPUS CHRISTI	355	17340	17079	17393	-0.4	7	5139	4987	5034	-0.7	3.29	3839	3739	-0.6
78406	CORPUS CHRISTI	355	1906	2016	2095	1.3	52	334	362	382	1.9	3.37	261	283	1.9
78407	CORPUS CHRISTI	355	3702	3503	3524	-1.3	1	1153	1076	1074	-1.6	3.11	858	805	-1.5
78408	CORPUS CHRISTI	355	11173	10989	11177	-0.4	6	3660	3565	3598	-0.6	3.04	2692	2630	-0.6
78409	CORPUS CHRISTI	355	3257	3304	3384	0.3	21	1056	1063	1083	0.2	2.98	829	837	0.2
78410	CORPUS CHRISTI	355	22963	24842	26442	1.9	65	7840	8410	8893	1.7	2.92	6252	6713	1.7
78411	CORPUS CHRISTI	355	27741	27826	28433	0.1	14	10548	10459	10602	-0.2	2.64	7400	7357	-0.1
78412	CORPUS CHRISTI	355	34046	34571	35748	0.4	22	13400	13424	13766	0.0	2.52	8793	8869	0.2
78413	CORPUS CHRISTI	355	33397	35529	37298	1.5	56	12644	13283	13827	1.2	2.67	8892	9398	1.3
78414	CORPUS CHRISTI	355	15623	18227	20053	3.7	88	5987	6948	7619	3.6	2.60	4153	4862	3.8
78415	CORPUS CHRISTI	355	38663	39228	40528	0.3	21	12768	12812	13136	0.1	3.01	9656	9724	0.2
78416	CORPUS CHRISTI	355	16344	15939	16172	-0.6	4	4995	4813	4842	-0.9	3.30	4033	3894	-0.8
78417	CORPUS CHRISTI	355	3597	4114	4469	3.2	83	1060	1199	1292	2.9	3.42	868	984	3.0
78418	CORPUS CHRISTI	355	24454	27023	29059	2.4	74	9553	10512	11262	2.3	2.57	6676	7358	2.3
78419	CORPUS CHRISTI	355	2085	2100	2127	0.2	17	487	486	490	-0.1	3.65	452	451	-0.1
78501	MCALLEN	215	57848	64637	76739	2.7	78	18523	20640	24474	2.6	3.10	14169	15817	2.6
78503	MCALLEN	215	17350	19608	23381	2.9	81	4534	5126	6107	2.9	3.80	3861	4353	2.9
78504	MCALLEN	215	32020	39530	49177	5.1	95	10280	12601	15602	4.9	3.12	8249	10172	5.1
78516	ALAMO	215	27390	31492	37759	3.3	85	7604	8680	10358	3.2	3.63	6548	7494	3.2
78520	BROWNSVILLE	061	49175	56078	65932	3.1	82	14079	16024	18849	3.1	3.41	11251	12887	3.3
78521	BROWNSVILLE	061	84729	96518	112996	3.1	82	22209	25249	29517	3.1	3.82	19260	21885	3.1
78526	BROWNSVILLE	061	26356	34862	43752	6.8	98	6766	8946	11208	6.8	3.90	6136	8093	6.7
78536	DELMITA	427	56	54	57	-0.9	2	20	19	21	-1.2	2.84	15	15	0.0
78537	DONNA	215	30072	34514	41462	3.3	84	8151	9276	11080	3.1	3.72	7060	8047	3.1
78538	EDCOUCH	215	20484	22754	26800	2.5	76	5247	5805	6814	2.4	3.92	4641	5139	2.4
78539	EDINBURG	215	45086	51013	60639	3.0	81	12572	14153	16801	2.8	3.52	10648	12040	2.9
78541	EDINBURG	215	39752	45069	53786	3.0	81	9871	11240	13508	3.1	3.77	8339	9510	3.1
78547	GARCIASVILLE	427	64	76	87	4.1	91	18	22	25	4.8	3.45	17	20	3.9
78548	GRULLA	427	352	422	485	4.4	92	82	99	114	4.5	4.26	77	93	4.5
78549	HARGILL	215	1387	1434	1628	0.8	35	410	422	477	0.7	3.40	333	343	0.7
78550	HARLINGEN	061	50440	53339	59635	1.3	52	16263	17246	19352	1.4	3.01	12259	12976	1.4
78552	HARLINGEN	061	29743	32748	37564	2.3	73	9659	10701	12315	2.4	3.04	7909	8751	2.4
78557	HIDALGO	215	7295	8946	11055	4.9	94	1741	2121	2608	4.8	4.21	1576	1922	4.8
78559	LA FERIA	061	11274	12930	15097	3.3	84	3582	4116	4811	3.3	3.14	2907	3334	3.3
78560	LA JOYA	215	9302	10786	12986	3.5	87	2431	2803	3361	3.4	3.85	2179	2513	3.4
78563	LINN	215	1765	1936	2263	2.2	71	589	642	747	2.1	2.96	469	512	2.1
78566	LOS FRESNOS	061	12115	13847	16116	3.2	83	3424	3907	4549	3.2	3.48	2938	3351	3.1
78569	LYFORD	489	3231	3368	3536	1.0	41	947	989	1033	1.0	3.40	804	841	1.1
78570	MERCEDES	215	28688	32772	39168	3.2	83	7575	8643	10307	3.2	3.79	6466	7392	3.2
78572	MISSION	215	60052	76813	97729	6.0	97	17405	22323	28449	6.0	3.44	14793	18926	6.0
78574	MISSION	215	56462	69071	85346	4.9	94	13795	16748	20586	4.7	4.12	12498	15188	4.7
78575	OLMITO	061	3212	3754	4421	3.7	88	1096	1278	1504	3.7	2.94	859	1001	3.7
78577	PHARR	215	48405	56670	68819	3.8	89	13292	15500	18757	3.7	3.65	11290	13204	3.8
78578	PORT ISABEL	061	10839	12250	14169	2.9	81	3458	3931	4567	3.1	3.03	2641	2989	3.0
78580	RAYMONDVILLE	489	12976	13429	14035	0.8	36	3457	3569	3735	0.8	3.46	2819	2916	0.8
78582	RIO GRANDE CITY	427	34329	37934	41978	2.4	74	9108	10096	11227	2.5	3.72	8011	8885	2.5
78583	RIO HONDO	061	5599	6304	7297	2.8	80	1745	1964	2273	2.8	3.21	1433	1611	2.8
78584	ROMA	427	18213	18698	20011	0.6	29	4965	5122	5508	0.7	3.65	4376	4520	0.8
78586	SAN BENITO	061	44152	48457	55439	2.2	71	12279	13427	15335	2.1	3.60	10370	11336	2.1
78588	SAN ISIDRO	427	334	324	341	-0.7	3	130	126	134	-0.7	2.57	99	96	-0.7
78589	SAN JUAN	215	28960	33156	39647	3.2	83	7241	8225	9781	3.0	4.01	6543	7440	3.1
78590	SAN PERLITA	489	1149	1219	1304	1.4	55	342	365	394	1.5	3.34	269	287	1.5
78591	SANTA ELENA	427	236	227	239	-0.9	1	80	77	82	-0.9	2.95	63	60	-1.1
78593	SANTA ROSA	061	4605	4889	5484	1.4	55	1213	1287	1443	1.4	3.80	1048	1111	1.4
78594	SEBASTIAN	489	2462	2512	2607	0.5	24	726	737	763	0.4	3.41	595	606	0.4
78595	SULLIVAN CITY	215	4511	4925	5771	2.1	69	1152	1249	1457	1.9	3.94	1040	1128	1.9
78596	WESLACO	215	52634	60798	73494	3.5	86	14411	16774	20394	3.6	3.60	12156	14108	3.6
78597	SOUTH PADRE ISLAND	061	2836	3265	3817	3.4	85	1418	1635	1899	3.4	2.00	878	1009	3.3
78598	PORT MANSFIELD	489	415	434	457	1.1	44	187	195	205	1.0	2.23	151	158	1.1
78602	BASTROP	021	18499	21419	25163	3.5	86	6390	7413	8746	3.6	2.66	4613	5365	3.6
78605	BERTRAM	053	3389	3874	4629	3.2	83	1224	1385	1639	3.0	2.74	951	1078	3.0
78606	BLANCO	031	4094	4527	5099	2.4	75	1595	1752	1961	2.2	2.53	1133	1250	2.3
78607	BLUFFTON	299	36	40	45	2.5	76	19	21	24	2.4	1.90	13	14	1.8
78608	BRIGGS	053	1344	1595	1944	4.1	91	513	602	726	3.8	2.65	400	471	3.9
78609	BUCHANAN DAM	299	2154	2378	2710	2.4	74	1053	1155	1307	2.2	2.06	690	760	2.3
78610	BUDA	209	13826	16033	20045	3.6	87	4487	5188	6452	3.5	3.09	3767	4362	3.5
78611	BURNET	053	11478	13441	16271	3.8	89	4388	5121	6181	3.7	2.49	3198	3731	3.7
78612	CEDAR CREEK	021	7677	8828	10385	3.3	85	2630	3005	3513	3.2	2.93	2012	2303	3.2
78613	CEDAR PARK	491	34507	47597	65337	7.9	99	11406	15693	21447	7.8	3.02	9479	13007	7.7
78614	COST	177	405	428	458	1.3	51	143	150	160	1.1	2.83	109	114	1.1
78615	COUPLAND	491	1567	1771	2137	2.9	81	566	638	768	2.9	2.77	442	495	2.7
78616	DALE	055	6200	7280	8610	3.9	89	2091	2439	2865	3.7	2.97	1629	1903	3.7
78617	DEL VALLE	453	14136	16269	18615	3.4	85	3662	4290	4960	3.8	3.33	2805	3278	3.7
78618	DOSS	171	64	67	73	1.1	45	31	32	35	0.8	2.09	22	24	2.1
78619	DRIFTWOOD	209	1591	1806	2246	3.0	81	605	687	854	3.0	2.55	472	539	3.2
78620	DRIPPING SPRINGS	209	9734	12320	16131	5.7	96	3362	4251	5544	5.7	2.88	2748	3483	5.7
78621	ELGIN	021	14277	16991	20309	4.2	91	4825	5721	6808	4.1	2.95	3621	4297	4.1
78623	FISCHER	091	437	605	795	8.0	99	166	228	298	7.8	2.65	120	166	7.8
78624	FREDERICKSBURG	171	18675	20272	22428	2.0	67	7653	8314	9222	2.0	2.37	5437	5926	2.1
78626	GEORGETOWN	491	19472	22822	28626	3.8	89	6109	7251	9222	4.1	2.86	4517	5326	4.0
78628	GEORGETOWN	491	26241	32798	42902	5.4	96	10162	12743	16629	5.5	2.57	8319	10391	5.4
78629	GONZALES	177	11974	12678	13577	1.4	53	4395	4626	4929	1.2	2.69	3124	3297	1.3
78631	HARPER	171	1324	1439	1595	2.0	67	549	595	658	1.9	2.42	402	436	1.9
78632	HARWOOD	177	345	364	389	1.3	50	140	147	156	1.2	2.46	104	109	1.1
	TEXAS					2.2					2.0	2.77			2.1
	UNITED STATES					1.2					1.3	2.58			1.1

#	POST OFFICE NAME	RACE (%) White 2000	White 2004	Black 2000	Black 2004	Asian/Pacific 2000	Asian/Pacific 2004	% Hispanic Origin 2000	% Hispanic Origin 2004	2004 AGE DISTRIBUTION (%) 0-4	5-9	10-14	15-19	20-24	25-44	45-64	65-84	85+	18+	MEDIAN AGE 2004	% 2004 Males	% 2004 Females
78383	SANDIA	88.3	87.1	0.3	0.3	0.4	0.4	36.2	40.2	5.7	5.8	6.6	6.4	5.4	20.6	30.5	17.6	1.5	77.6	44.7	50.5	49.5
78384	SAN DIEGO	75.3	75.4	0.9	0.9	0.1	0.1	94.9	95.2	7.9	7.6	8.3	9.3	7.9	26.9	20.7	9.7	1.7	70.3	31.4	51.0	49.0
78385	SARITA	64.4	64.9	0.7	0.7	0.4	0.4	79.1	79.2	9.0	8.2	7.9	6.5	9.3	24.4	22.9	11.1	0.7	71.3	34.1	52.0	48.0
78387	SINTON	74.8	73.3	2.5	2.3	0.1	0.2	66.9	71.8	7.9	7.7	8.0	8.0	7.6	25.7	22.7	11.1	1.3	71.4	33.5	50.4	49.6
78389	SKIDMORE	84.3	82.9	1.4	1.4	0.4	0.3	51.7	56.6	7.0	7.3	8.5	7.4	7.6	23.4	24.4	13.2	1.3	72.2	36.7	52.2	47.8
78390	TAFT	72.8	71.7	2.0	1.9	0.2	0.2	71.9	74.9	8.9	9.4	8.7	8.2	7.5	24.6	21.2	10.3	1.2	67.9	30.7	49.8	50.2
78391	TYNAN	87.2	86.3	1.0	1.3	0.0	0.0	45.2	49.4	5.6	6.9	10.0	7.8	5.3	22.5	25.3	15.3	1.3	71.9	39.5	50.9	49.1
78393	WOODSBORO	81.2	80.9	2.6	2.6	0.1	0.1	45.2	46.2	6.0	5.9	7.9	7.2	6.7	25.1	26.1	13.4	1.7	75.8	38.9	49.0	51.0
78401	CORPUS CHRISTI	55.8	54.8	18.5	17.7	0.5	0.5	57.0	60.8	7.7	6.5	6.2	6.2	7.6	27.5	21.6	12.7	4.0	76.0	36.4	49.4	50.6
78402	CORPUS CHRISTI	83.1	80.6	1.5	1.8	5.5	6.0	21.8	26.7	1.3	2.2	3.8	4.6	3.1	28.3	38.6	17.4	0.7	90.3	48.6	55.2	44.8
78404	CORPUS CHRISTI	69.8	68.0	2.1	2.1	0.5	0.5	65.1	69.3	8.3	7.6	7.0	6.6	7.5	27.8	22.3	10.8	2.2	73.2	34.5	48.7	51.3
78405	CORPUS CHRISTI	58.4	57.8	4.8	4.4	0.2	0.2	88.8	90.5	8.9	8.2	8.5	8.1	7.6	25.7	19.2	11.9	2.0	69.4	31.7	47.9	52.1
78406	CORPUS CHRISTI	50.9	49.3	5.2	4.7	0.2	0.2	73.5	78.5	3.7	3.7	4.8	9.1	14.6	37.1	19.8	6.3	0.9	84.3	31.4	70.7	29.3
78407	CORPUS CHRISTI	52.2	51.8	23.4	21.7	0.2	0.2	58.1	63.0	9.5	9.0	8.7	7.6	8.0	26.0	20.9	9.2	1.1	68.4	30.0	49.8	50.2
78408	CORPUS CHRISTI	58.4	57.0	7.3	6.7	0.6	0.6	74.5	78.4	8.7	8.4	7.7	7.7	7.7	25.6	22.5	10.3	1.5	70.6	32.2	48.7	51.3
78409	CORPUS CHRISTI	68.6	65.8	2.4	2.3	0.8	0.8	60.3	66.5	7.3	7.1	8.2	8.5	7.7	27.5	24.6	7.7	1.4	72.0	33.2	49.6	50.4
78410	CORPUS CHRISTI	81.6	79.1	1.5	1.5	0.5	0.5	37.9	44.4	7.2	7.4	8.8	8.3	7.5	28.2	24.3	7.6	0.7	71.3	33.6	48.9	51.1
78411	CORPUS CHRISTI	75.7	73.6	2.3	2.3	0.9	0.9	53.0	58.6	7.5	7.0	6.8	6.4	7.8	26.5	23.7	12.4	2.0	74.9	36.1	47.4	52.6
78412	CORPUS CHRISTI	77.1	74.9	3.9	4.0	1.6	1.6	42.6	48.7	7.3	6.7	6.7	7.3	9.3	28.2	22.0	11.4	1.3	75.6	33.1	48.1	51.9
78413	CORPUS CHRISTI	77.6	75.1	4.1	4.2	2.8	2.9	40.1	46.6	7.1	6.8	7.3	7.3	8.5	30.0	24.5	7.8	0.8	74.4	33.6	48.6	51.4
78414	CORPUS CHRISTI	76.7	74.1	4.7	4.9	3.2	3.3	37.2	43.6	8.8	8.0	7.0	6.0	7.1	33.2	21.1	7.0	1.9	72.8	33.2	48.3	51.7
78415	CORPUS CHRISTI	67.5	66.1	3.7	3.5	0.7	0.7	74.6	79.0	8.9	8.2	8.0	7.6	8.6	27.8	21.1	8.7	1.0	70.4	30.7	48.9	51.1
78416	CORPUS CHRISTI	56.4	56.4	11.3	10.3	0.2	0.2	85.3	87.1	8.0	7.8	8.5	8.1	7.7	24.5	20.1	14.1	1.1	70.8	33.1	48.4	51.6
78417	CORPUS CHRISTI	57.5	56.4	5.5	5.2	0.3	0.2	83.9	86.7	9.0	8.7	9.6	8.4	8.5	29.8	20.1	5.5	0.4	67.7	28.9	49.6	50.4
78418	CORPUS CHRISTI	82.6	80.6	3.2	3.4	3.2	3.3	19.9	24.0	6.2	6.3	6.7	6.8	6.9	28.1	27.9	10.6	0.5	76.6	38.2	50.8	49.2
78419	CORPUS CHRISTI	64.0	60.5	18.6	19.9	3.8	4.1	20.9	25.2	15.0	12.1	8.4	5.0	15.7	40.9	2.8	0.1	0.0	62.3	23.0	55.1	44.9
78501	MCALLEN	79.7	79.3	0.5	0.5	1.3	1.3	84.1	86.4	9.1	8.3	7.8	7.1	7.9	28.6	19.4	10.3	1.5	70.6	31.1	47.2	52.8
78503	MCALLEN	73.1	73.1	0.5	0.5	1.2	1.2	91.3	92.4	8.7	8.4	8.8	8.4	8.7	27.9	19.5	8.4	1.3	69.0	29.4	47.9	52.1
78504	MCALLEN	79.0	77.6	0.8	0.9	3.3	3.3	68.0	72.4	8.7	8.4	8.8	7.8	7.4	31.0	21.1	6.2	0.7	69.3	31.1	48.2	51.8
78516	ALAMO	86.0	85.7	0.2	0.2	0.1	0.1	86.3	88.4	10.6	9.8	10.0	8.6	7.6	25.4	16.0	11.1	1.0	64.3	27.6	49.3	50.7
78520	BROWNSVILLE	84.0	83.6	0.4	0.4	0.5	0.5	89.7	90.8	9.4	8.8	8.7	8.1	7.6	26.8	18.8	10.4	1.6	68.3	30.4	47.4	52.6
78521	BROWNSVILLE	80.2	79.8	0.3	0.4	0.3	0.3	93.5	94.6	10.7	9.7	9.7	8.9	8.8	27.2	17.3	7.0	0.7	64.5	26.4	47.7	52.3
78526	BROWNSVILLE	83.2	82.6	0.5	0.5	1.2	1.2	89.2	90.6	11.2	10.4	10.3	8.8	7.9	28.4	17.1	5.6	0.3	62.7	26.1	48.2	51.8
78536	DELMITA	85.7	87.0	0.0	0.0	0.0	0.0	94.6	94.4	5.6	5.6	7.4	7.4	7.4	24.1	25.9	14.8	1.9	81.5	40.0	53.7	46.3
78537	DONNA	80.4	80.2	0.3	0.3	0.2	0.1	87.8	89.8	10.4	9.6	9.8	8.8	7.8	24.9	16.5	11.3	0.8	64.8	27.6	48.8	51.2
78538	EDCOUCH	76.8	76.8	0.3	0.3	0.0	0.1	96.7	97.4	11.1	10.1	10.4	9.5	8.4	26.2	16.8	6.9	0.7	62.7	25.4	49.0	51.0
78539	EDINBURG	78.5	78.1	0.5	0.5	0.6	0.6	89.8	91.5	10.6	9.8	9.3	8.4	8.3	29.7	16.9	6.3	0.7	65.3	27.3	49.1	50.9
78541	EDINBURG	65.2	64.5	2.6	2.4	0.3	0.3	90.2	91.9	10.6	9.6	9.4	9.5	10.2	29.8	15.1	5.4	0.5	64.9	25.4	52.0	48.0
78547	GARCIASVILLE	92.2	92.1	0.0	0.0	0.0	0.0	96.9	98.7	10.5	11.8	13.2	9.2	7.9	30.3	13.2	4.0	0.0	56.6	23.3	48.7	51.3
78548	GRULLA	93.2	93.4	0.0	0.0	0.0	0.0	97.4	97.9	12.6	12.8	13.3	9.0	6.9	29.4	11.9	4.0	0.2	55.7	21.7	49.8	50.2
78549	HARGILL	79.9	79.2	0.4	0.5	0.1	0.1	87.7	90.1	9.1	8.9	10.0	8.7	6.8	26.0	19.6	10.0	0.8	66.5	30.3	49.6	50.4
78550	HARLINGEN	78.2	77.3	0.9	0.9	1.0	1.0	75.1	78.0	9.4	8.5	8.5	8.1	7.3	27.0	18.8	10.3	2.1	68.7	30.8	47.9	52.1
78552	HARLINGEN	81.5	80.7	0.6	0.6	0.4	0.4	70.3	73.3	8.2	8.0	8.2	7.4	6.5	23.6	20.5	16.1	1.6	71.1	35.3	48.6	51.5
78557	HIDALGO	83.4	83.3	0.1	0.1	0.1	0.1	97.7	98.2	10.7	10.3	11.0	9.5	8.1	27.5	16.3	6.2	0.4	62.4	25.3	47.6	52.4
78559	LA FERIA	76.0	74.6	0.3	0.3	0.3	0.3	76.7	80.1	8.4	8.1	9.0	7.7	7.4	23.1	20.2	14.6	1.5	69.7	33.5	47.5	52.5
78560	LA JOYA	64.2	63.5	0.2	0.2	0.2	0.3	94.1	95.3	10.9	9.9	9.6	8.5	8.1	27.7	16.1	8.6	0.7	64.4	27.1	48.1	51.9
78563	LINN	77.1	75.8	0.2	0.3	0.1	0.1	78.3	82.4	8.5	8.4	8.8	6.4	5.9	25.2	19.9	15.2	1.7	70.2	34.6	48.9	51.1
78566	LOS FRESNOS	83.2	82.6	0.5	0.5	0.3	0.2	83.5	86.3	9.2	9.3	10.3	9.7	7.8	27.3	18.1	7.7	0.7	65.3	27.9	50.0	50.0
78569	LYFORD	67.3	66.5	0.3	0.2	0.0	0.0	89.3	90.9	8.6	8.1	8.6	9.0	8.4	25.3	20.6	10.3	1.1	69.3	30.5	48.0	52.0
78570	MERCEDES	79.4	79.3	0.3	0.3	0.1	0.1	93.1	93.9	11.2	10.3	10.1	9.2	8.2	24.5	16.9	8.4	1.0	62.8	25.7	48.5	51.5
78572	MISSION	72.9	72.6	0.3	0.3	0.4	0.4	84.9	86.7	10.3	9.3	9.2	7.9	7.5	26.1	16.5	12.1	1.1	66.4	29.2	48.6	51.4
78574	MISSION	79.5	78.8	0.3	0.3	0.4	0.4	91.9	93.3	12.0	11.1	10.9	9.1	8.0	28.6	15.1	4.9	0.4	60.4	24.3	49.2	50.8
78575	OLMITO	91.8	91.5	0.3	0.2	2.3	2.3	70.6	74.6	8.2	8.5	8.7	6.7	5.8	26.4	22.9	11.6	1.3	70.5	34.5	48.8	51.2
78577	PHARR	79.6	79.5	0.2	0.3	0.3	0.3	90.5	91.7	10.9	9.8	9.3	8.0	7.7	26.6	16.2	10.4	1.1	65.2	27.9	47.9	52.1
78578	PORT ISABEL	78.0	76.8	1.0	1.0	0.4	0.3	69.9	73.3	8.5	8.2	8.2	7.6	7.2	27.4	21.5	10.8	0.7	70.5	32.3	49.8	50.2
78580	RAYMONDVILLE	69.8	69.4	3.1	2.9	0.2	0.2	86.1	87.9	8.4	8.2	9.1	8.5	9.2	27.7	18.1	9.8	1.2	69.4	29.3	53.1	46.9
78582	RIO GRANDE CITY	86.4	86.4	0.2	0.2	0.5	0.5	97.6	97.9	11.0	10.2	10.3	9.0	8.1	27.1	16.7	7.1	0.7	63.1	26.1	49.5	50.5
78583	RIO HONDO	80.2	79.7	0.1	0.1	0.5	0.5	81.8	84.7	8.2	8.0	8.8	8.1	6.8	24.7	21.7	12.6	1.0	69.9	33.1	48.8	51.2
78584	ROMA	90.7	90.7	0.1	0.2	0.1	0.1	97.6	98.0	10.3	9.5	10.2	9.2	8.4	25.7	17.8	8.1	0.9	64.4	26.7	47.7	52.3
78586	SAN BENITO	76.4	75.6	0.3	0.3	0.2	0.2	88.7	90.5	10.0	9.4	9.7	8.8	7.8	25.8	18.2	9.4	1.0	65.4	28.3	48.7	51.3
78588	SAN ISIDRO	85.3	85.2	0.0	0.0	0.3	0.3	94.9	95.4	5.3	5.9	7.1	7.1	7.4	23.8	27.2	14.5	1.9	77.2	40.8	51.9	48.2
78589	SAN JUAN	81.8	81.6	0.3	0.3	0.1	0.1	95.8	96.5	11.0	10.3	10.3	9.1	8.6	27.4	16.4	6.2	0.8	62.9	25.5	48.8	51.2
78590	SAN PERLITA	81.6	80.5	1.0	1.0	0.4	0.4	60.4	64.6	7.1	7.1	7.1	6.0	6.7	22.6	24.9	17.3	1.2	75.1	39.1	48.7	51.3
78591	SANTA ELENA	84.8	85.0	0.0	0.0	0.0	0.0	95.8	96.5	4.9	5.7	7.9	6.6	7.5	21.6	28.6	15.9	1.3	77.5	41.8	50.7	49.3
78593	SANTA ROSA	68.8	67.9	0.6	0.6	0.1	0.1	91.8	93.2	10.3	9.5	10.0	9.0	8.3	26.2	17.7	8.2	0.8	64.6	27.0	49.1	50.9
78594	SEBASTIAN	71.7	71.2	0.5	0.5	0.0	0.0	91.6	93.0	9.1	8.8	9.1	8.7	8.6	24.3	21.4	8.9	1.1	67.8	29.4	49.8	50.2
78595	SULLIVAN CITY	65.9	65.5	0.1	0.1	0.0	0.0	98.5	98.8	10.3	9.4	10.2	9.1	9.2	26.8	17.6	6.8	0.7	64.7	26.2	48.2	51.8
78596	WESLACO	80.7	80.1	0.2	0.2	0.7	0.7	88.6	89.9	10.4	9.8	9.6	8.5	7.7	26.2	16.3	9.7	1.8	64.9	27.9	48.2	51.8
78597	SOUTH PADRE ISLAND	95.5	94.8	0.5	0.5	0.3	0.3	18.6	22.1	2.9	2.9	2.4	2.1	2.3	19.6	35.0	31.9	1.1	90.4	57.3	51.7	48.3
78598	PORT MANSFIELD	80.2	79.3	1.0	1.2	0.0	0.0	63.9	68.2	7.6	7.4	7.6	6.2	7.1	23.7	23.7	15.4	1.2	73.3	36.7	48.2	51.8
78602	BASTROP	79.1	77.2	10.7	11.2	0.7	0.8	19.1	22.2	7.1	7.0	6.8	6.3	6.0	30.5	26.0	9.1	1.2	75.1	37.0	53.0	47.1
78605	BERTRAM	91.8	90.3	0.7	0.8	0.2	0.3	12.6	15.0	6.5	6.6	6.2	6.1	5.5	26.6	27.7	12.8	2.1	77.1	40.6	49.4	50.6
78606	BLANCO	89.6	88.3	1.2	1.3	0.2	0.2	17.8	20.5	5.8	6.1	6.7	6.4	5.7	23.3	29.4	14.1	2.7	77.7	42.3	49.6	50.4
78607	BLUFFTON	97.2	95.0	0.0	0.0	0.0	0.0	5.6	5.0	5.0	5.0	5.0	5.0	5.0	15.0	35.0	25.0	0.0	85.0	52.5	50.0	50.0
78608	BRIGGS	90.2	88.5	0.7	0.8	0.2	0.4	13.2	15.8	7.2	7.4	7.2	6.8	5.7	28.3	26.1	10.2	1.2	74.0	37.6	50.2	49.8
78609	BUCHANAN DAM	96.7	96.2	0.2	0.3	0.1	0.0	5.5	6.4	3.0	3.3	3.5	3.7	2.9	13.8	37.3	29.7	2.8	87.7	56.5	49.6	50.4
78610	BUDA	81.9	79.6	2.2	2.3	0.7	0.8	29.4	33.6	7.4	7.9	8.8	8.8	5.7	29.6	26.1	5.4	0.5	70.3	34.6	50.0	50.0
78611	BURNET	90.4	89.4	2.5	2.6	0.4	0.5	11.7	13.4	5.9	5.9	5.9	6.1	5.7	24.0	26.7	17.2	2.6	78.6	42.8	47.0	53.0
78612	CEDAR CREEK	80.3	78.6	7.7	7.9	0.6	0.7	24.5	28.0	7.5	7.4	7.8	7.2	6.7	28.4	26.3	7.8	0.8	72.8	35.5	50.9	49.1
78613	CEDAR PARK	86.5	84.7	3.3	3.6	2.8	3.1	13.1	15.5	10.5	10.2	8.5	6.4	5.3	35.7	19.1	3.8	0.5	66.5	32.2	49.6	50.5
78614	COST	85.2	83.4	1.2	1.4	0.5	0.5	25.4	29.4	7.0	7.0	7.0	6.8	5.1	27.3	23.8	13.8	2.1	74.8	38.5	51.4	48.6
78615	COUPLAND	89.5	88.0	2.6	2.7	0.3	0.3	14.0	16.9	8.0	8.0	7.4	6.6	6.0	27.9	25.1	9.8	1.3	72.7	36.4	49.5	50.5
78616	DALE	76.3	73.9	6.0	6.1	0.2	0.3	32.7	36.8	7.7	7.9	8.3	8.0	6.6	27.1	25.8	8.0	0.6	70.8	35.0	51.4	48.6
78617	DEL VALLE	60.2	57.9	12.1	11.6	1.6	1.6	46.1	51.2	8.5	7.7	7.8	7.9	8.9	35.0	19.3	4.6	0.4	71.6	30.1	55.9	44.1
78618	DOSS	96.9	97.0	0.0	0.0	0.0	0.0	3.1	4.5	1.5	3.0	6.0	4.5	4.5	20.9	32.8	23.9	3.0	89.6	51.8	50.8	49.3
78619	DRIFTWOOD	94.5	93.7	0.5	0.6	0.6	0.7	7.1	8.6	5.4	6.4	7.2	6.6	3.1	24.6	32.6	11.7	2.4	76.7	43.1	50.2	49.8
78620	DRIPPING SPRINGS	94.0	93.0	0.4	0.4	0.6	0.7	8.0	9.6	6.1	7.1	8.6	8.2	4.4	27.2	30.1	7.3	0.9	72.5	39.3	50.4	49.6
78621	ELGIN	76.6	75.6	10.0	9.7	0.5	0.5	31.1	34.2	8.4	7.9	8.0	7.5	6.9	27.0	23.9	9.2	1.3	71.2	34.4	50.2	49.8
78623	FISCHER	93.8	92.6	0.7	0.8	0.2	0.3	11.4	14.1	6.5	6.6	6.8	6.1	4.6	26.5	27.3	14.6	1.2	76.4	41.1	49.8	50.3
78624	FREDERICKSBURG	92.7	91.6	0.2	0.2	0.2	0.2	16.6	19.2	5.2	5.5	6.0	5.6	4.9	19.9	27.5	21.3	4.1	79.9	47.1	47.1	52.9
78626	GEORGETOWN	80.0	77.2	3.9	4.1	0.7	0.8	26.0	30.2	8.2	7.5	7.1	8.7	10.4	29.2	18.6	8.0	2.4	73.2	31.0	49.4	50.6
78628	GEORGETOWN	93.2	92.3	1.6	1.7	0.7	0.8	8.4	10.0	5.6	6.1	6.9	6.1	4.9	22.0	29.2	18.1	1.1	77.4	44.0	48.9	51.1
78629	GONZALES	71.5	69.6	9.7	9.6	0.5	0.5	35.8	39.9	7.3	7.0	7.4	7.3	6.9	25.4	22.9	13.2	2.7	73.7	36.4	49.8	50.2
78631	HARPER	95.2	94.4	0.1	0.1	0.2	0.1	7.3	8.7	4.5	4.5	5.4	5.8	4.2	19.8	32.8	20.9	2.2	82.1	49.2	48.9	51.1
78632	HARWOOD	80.9	78.3	4.1	4.1	0.3	0.3	25.2	29.1	6.0	5.8	6.0	7.7	6.6	24.2	25.6	15.9	2.2	77.5	40.9	50.8	49.2
	TEXAS	71.0	69.5	11.5	11.4	2.8	3.1	32.0	34.6	7.9	7.5	7.7	7.5	8.1	29.6	21.9	8.7	1.2	72.6	32.9	49.7	50.3
	UNITED STATES	75.1	73.6	12.3	12.5	3.8	4.2	12.5	14.1	6.9	6.7	7.2	7.0	7.3	28.6	23.8	10.8	1.7	75.1	36.0	49.1	50.9

INCOME

#	POST OFFICE NAME	2004 Per Capita Income	2004 HH Income Base	2004 Household Income Distribution (%): Less than $25,000	$25,000 to $49,999	$50,000 to $99,999	$100,000 to $149,999	$150,000 or More	Median Household Income: 2004	2009	2004 National Centile	2004 State Centile	2004 Home Value Base	2004 Home Value Distribution (%): Less than $50,000	$50,000 to $89,999	$90,000 to $174,999	$175,000 to $399,999	$400,000 or More	2004 Median Home Value
78383	SANDIA	18995	1187	32.3	34.3	26.4	4.6	2.4	36171	41911	32	38	1005	41.4	33.2	18.1	6.7	0.6	57269
78384	SAN DIEGO	11158	1949	54.0	26.7	15.5	2.9	0.9	22320	25000	3	4	1482	66.3	20.6	9.9	2.9	0.3	31959
78385	SARITA	20314	94	41.5	37.2	14.9	1.1	5.3	31101	31958	15	19	32	43.8	25.0	21.9	0.0	9.4	63333
78387	SINTON	16927	3289	40.6	26.2	24.5	5.4	3.3	32729	37191	20	24	2329	51.0	27.5	18.7	2.8	0.0	49469
78389	SKIDMORE	12691	818	46.1	25.9	24.3	3.7	0.0	27831	31489	8	11	675	56.6	28.0	11.4	2.8	1.2	43154
78390	TAFT	13322	1991	43.4	27.9	21.3	4.8	2.6	29613	33699	11	15	1414	53.0	25.7	16.9	4.4	0.1	48000
78391	TYNAN	12147	99	45.5	25.3	21.2	8.1	0.0	28605	30445	10	12	82	43.9	26.8	23.2	3.7	2.4	57143
78393	WOODSBORO	18049	934	35.3	30.1	25.6	5.9	3.1	34921	41930	27	32	703	56.5	28.5	12.4	2.7	0.0	44770
78401	CORPUS CHRISTI	11617	1869	65.3	22.6	8.6	2.2	1.3	16294	19125	1	1	358	65.6	20.7	11.5	1.7	0.6	39643
78402	CORPUS CHRISTI	31756	250	33.6	27.6	21.2	15.2	2.4	35000	39259	28	33	98	12.2	29.6	49.0	9.2	0.0	93810
78404	CORPUS CHRISTI	19757	6325	38.8	28.3	23.3	5.3	4.4	33402	39619	22	27	3562	26.8	41.4	22.4	7.2	2.2	70057
78405	CORPUS CHRISTI	8918	4987	55.5	30.1	11.9	1.9	0.7	21931	25127	3	3	2948	78.8	18.3	2.5	0.3	0.0	35447
78406	CORPUS CHRISTI	12262	362	34.5	33.4	28.7	3.3	0.0	37463	42583	37	45	248	61.3	31.5	7.3	0.0	0.0	45172
78407	CORPUS CHRISTI	11092	1076	58.5	19.0	16.6	4.6	1.4	19392	22488	2	3	547	60.0	36.6	3.5	0.0	0.0	43876
78408	CORPUS CHRISTI	11541	3565	46.4	33.8	15.8	2.4	1.6	26746	30934	7	9	2221	53.5	42.0	1.6	2.9	0.0	48305
78409	CORPUS CHRISTI	15207	1063	30.8	32.8	30.3	4.8	1.3	38570	44172	41	49	748	41.6	29.1	29.3	0.0	0.0	64167
78410	CORPUS CHRISTI	21658	8410	23.6	23.4	37.0	12.6	3.4	52639	60605	76	81	5898	11.0	35.1	45.3	7.7	1.0	93004
78411	CORPUS CHRISTI	22772	10459	29.2	28.7	30.2	7.5	4.5	42315	49209	54	63	6788	7.8	48.2	36.2	6.6	1.3	85401
78412	CORPUS CHRISTI	24841	13424	26.4	31.4	28.8	7.8	5.7	42894	49894	56	64	7554	10.1	49.7	28.8	8.6	2.8	82230
78413	CORPUS CHRISTI	28321	13283	15.6	24.6	38.2	14.7	7.0	60429	68799	85	87	8268	1.3	12.3	67.1	18.2	1.1	120297
78414	CORPUS CHRISTI	27867	6948	17.9	22.9	38.7	13.8	6.8	59521	68042	84	86	4541	2.3	12.8	64.9	17.4	2.6	119944
78415	CORPUS CHRISTI	14354	12812	35.7	32.8	25.6	4.5	1.5	35285	40706	29	34	7635	26.7	54.0	18.0	1.2	0.1	64120
78416	CORPUS CHRISTI	12960	4813	43.8	34.0	18.1	3.0	1.1	28198	32226	9	12	3230	59.8	38.9	1.4	0.0	0.0	46497
78417	CORPUS CHRISTI	10646	1199	39.5	36.0	20.9	3.6	0.0	30743	34569	14	18	885	49.9	41.5	8.6	0.0	0.0	50040
78418	CORPUS CHRISTI	25376	10512	22.6	27.6	34.7	9.7	5.4	49774	58197	71	77	7167	16.8	30.3	34.0	17.5	1.4	94490
78419	CORPUS CHRISTI	13720	486	18.1	48.4	25.9	4.3	3.3	37129	42319	36	43	30	66.7	0.0	33.3	0.0	0.0	38636
78501	MCALLEN	14141	20640	43.4	27.5	20.9	5.6	2.7	30447	35400	13	17	11897	28.8	40.7	25.3	4.6	0.7	71266
78503	MCALLEN	15549	5126	38.9	30.5	19.3	5.3	6.1	33184	38837	21	26	3505	34.4	43.9	11.7	6.2	3.9	60056
78504	MCALLEN	24185	12601	18.4	23.0	36.2	14.8	7.6	60151	71599	84	87	9134	10.6	22.9	51.2	13.4	1.9	106788
78516	ALAMO	9154	8680	53.5	29.9	13.4	2.0	1.2	23148	26332	3	5	6388	62.5	22.2	13.3	1.8	0.2	41800
78520	BROWNSVILLE	12092	16024	50.0	25.4	17.7	5.1	1.8	25026	28906	5	6	9324	41.0	34.9	19.4	4.2	0.6	57356
78521	BROWNSVILLE	9864	25249	47.9	29.6	16.9	3.9	1.6	26220	29951	6	8	15167	45.7	34.8	15.4	3.7	0.4	53440
78526	BROWNSVILLE	12524	8946	35.5	30.1	25.7	6.1	2.5	35630	40760	30	36	6744	28.8	37.1	28.5	4.8	0.9	74703
78536	DELMITA	12751	19	52.6	26.3	15.8	5.3	0.0	23541	23551	4	5	15	80.0	13.3	6.7	0.0	0.0	27500
78537	DONNA	9117	9276	51.6	31.1	14.1	2.3	1.0	24057	27208	4	5	6530	58.9	27.1	10.5	2.9	0.5	43734
78538	EDCOUCH	7412	5805	57.4	27.2	13.1	1.6	0.7	21165	23845	2	3	4199	65.7	27.5	5.6	0.9	0.3	40187
78539	EDINBURG	13433	14153	40.8	25.8	25.0	5.7	2.7	31826	36827	17	22	9533	36.6	32.5	24.3	5.7	0.9	66067
78541	EDINBURG	9416	11240	49.5	30.4	16.1	3.0	1.1	25282	28599	5	6	7850	51.1	32.3	12.6	3.6	0.3	49240
78547	GARCIASVILLE	4342	22	81.8	13.6	4.6	0.0	0.0	10000	15659	0	1	20	65.0	25.0	10.0	0.0	0.0	42500
78548	GRULLA	4947	99	74.8	16.2	8.1	1.0	0.0	15374	16624	1	1	92	65.2	23.9	8.7	2.2	0.0	42222
78549	HARGILL	9161	422	54.7	28.0	14.7	1.7	1.0	22118	25060	3	4	352	66.5	21.9	9.1	2.0	0.6	37841
78550	HARLINGEN	15820	17246	40.1	27.3	23.2	5.9	3.5	32811	37723	20	25	10374	34.5	33.9	25.3	5.7	0.7	65955
78552	HARLINGEN	16471	10701	33.4	31.6	25.6	5.9	3.4	36630	42855	34	41	8507	41.4	27.7	21.2	8.8	0.9	61613
78557	HIDALGO	6630	2121	56.6	30.5	11.1	1.6	0.3	21589	24525	2	3	1391	29.1	56.4	13.2	1.3	0.0	64921
78559	LA FERIA	13238	4116	43.7	30.5	20.2	4.4	1.3	29334	33752	11	14	3064	52.7	28.8	16.4	2.0	0.2	48080
78560	LA JOYA	8016	2803	53.5	28.9	15.0	1.9	0.7	22870	25880	3	4	1943	55.7	31.4	12.5	0.4	0.0	45508
78563	LINN	11758	642	49.2	31.2	14.3	5.3	0.0	25479	29949	5	7	519	66.5	21.4	12.0	0.2	0.0	38309
78566	LOS FRESNOS	10638	3907	44.7	30.2	20.1	4.1	0.8	27901	31751	8	11	3017	42.4	32.1	18.8	6.0	0.7	56455
78569	LYFORD	11642	989	43.0	32.0	19.7	3.0	2.3	29574	33475	11	14	789	62.7	24.8	11.7	0.8	0.0	41184
78570	MERCEDES	8106	8643	53.5	30.5	13.0	2.1	0.9	22822	25836	3	4	6167	62.2	25.1	10.6	2.0	0.2	40560
78572	MISSION	12139	22323	45.3	28.2	19.4	4.8	2.3	28234	32178	9	12	16556	47.1	30.3	17.7	4.3	0.7	52924
78574	MISSION	9207	16748	50.5	26.7	16.4	4.5	1.9	24639	27804	4	6	12921	51.5	27.1	15.7	4.5	1.2	48730
78575	OLMITO	23669	1278	34.1	21.2	24.8	10.5	9.4	43914	51274	58	66	975	24.7	16.3	36.0	18.9	4.1	109312
78577	PHARR	10863	15500	46.3	28.8	19.5	3.4	2.1	27402	31612	8	10	10698	54.1	31.1	12.2	2.2	0.5	47428
78578	PORT ISABEL	14549	3931	41.5	30.7	19.7	4.6	3.4	30038	34590	12	16	2673	31.8	28.5	26.9	11.0	1.9	73965
78580	RAYMONDVILLE	9679	3569	53.9	28.9	14.0	2.7	0.6	22404	24549	3	4	2393	62.8	25.3	9.9	2.1	0.0	40853
78582	RIO GRANDE CITY	8016	10096	61.8	23.0	11.8	2.7	0.7	18740	20500	1	2	8067	59.3	27.2	11.3	2.0	0.2	43800
78583	RIO HONDO	11130	1964	48.8	28.0	18.9	3.5	0.9	25761	29005	5	7	1451	52.9	30.1	11.2	4.5	1.4	47775
78584	ROMA	7750	5122	66.8	20.3	9.7	1.8	1.5	16353	17545	1	1	3934	54.0	29.1	14.8	1.8	0.4	47006
78586	SAN BENITO	10908	13427	47.3	29.0	18.0	4.0	1.6	26673	30511	7	9	10027	56.6	26.6	12.7	3.6	0.6	44761
78588	SAN ISIDRO	13813	126	56.4	22.2	17.5	4.0	0.0	21442	25978	2	3	102	66.7	14.7	11.8	5.9	1.0	34000
78589	SAN JUAN	8880	8225	50.0	29.5	15.4	3.2	1.9	24988	28123	5	6	5642	51.8	36.3	10.8	0.6	0.5	48669
78590	SAN PERLITA	11517	365	42.7	32.9	19.7	3.0	1.6	30260	35511	13	17	273	53.5	30.4	11.4	4.8	0.0	46607
78591	SANTA ELENA	10750	77	63.6	18.2	14.3	3.9	0.0	16523	20000	1	1	58	63.8	17.2	10.3	8.6	0.0	37500
78593	SANTA ROSA	10462	1287	47.9	31.2	17.0	2.5	1.3	26553	29897	6	8	941	59.6	26.5	11.8	1.9	0.2	43759
78594	SEBASTIAN	12033	737	52.7	31.1	10.3	3.4	2.6	23588	26166	4	5	607	68.0	16.3	10.9	3.6	1.2	41641
78595	SULLIVAN CITY	6107	1249	62.8	26.2	10.1	0.6	0.4	18562	20597	1	2	945	64.8	30.2	3.6	0.9	0.6	42074
78596	WESLACO	10319	16774	46.6	32.9	15.3	3.4	1.8	26989	30936	7	9	11540	54.6	27.6	14.7	2.9	0.2	46190
78597	SOUTH PADRE ISLAND	36644	1635	24.8	24.0	33.4	8.8	9.0	51461	63316	75	79	1304	9.7	20.8	28.9	34.1	6.5	144712
78598	PORT MANSFIELD	16716	195	43.6	33.9	18.5	2.6	1.5	29383	35156	11	14	146	62.3	28.1	8.9	0.7	0.0	41000
78602	BASTROP	21819	7413	22.4	26.6	37.1	9.6	4.3	50949	57429	74	78	5746	16.6	16.3	45.5	18.8	2.7	117749
78605	BERTRAM	23320	1385	21.4	31.6	30.9	11.3	4.9	46982	54468	66	71	1167	13.3	23.7	35.1	18.3	9.7	108726
78606	BLANCO	21287	1752	30.5	29.9	27.7	7.4	4.5	41740	48157	52	61	1371	11.5	21.2	38.9	20.6	7.9	116033
78607	BLUFFTON	23892	21	23.8	28.6	42.9	4.8	0.0	47375	54564	67	72	18	27.8	33.3	33.3	5.6	0.0	75000
78608	BRIGGS	24635	602	25.1	33.7	28.7	7.1	5.3	42867	49622	56	64	506	13.6	22.9	36.6	16.4	10.5	108036
78609	BUCHANAN DAM	28912	1155	27.4	33.2	30.3	4.6	4.6	40104	47060	46	55	950	16.8	21.6	41.6	14.0	6.0	107362
78610	BUDA	25853	5188	9.6	19.8	44.7	19.1	6.8	69520	80794	91	92	4551	10.2	8.9	42.3	35.8	2.9	154601
78611	BURNET	20847	5121	30.5	27.5	31.0	7.7	3.3	42160	48755	53	62	3972	20.1	25.8	30.7	19.3	4.1	97342
78612	CEDAR CREEK	22081	3005	15.9	27.9	40.4	12.0	3.9	55866	62805	81	83	2465	15.2	17.2	47.7	17.1	2.9	114565
78613	CEDAR PARK	30090	15693	6.3	17.8	46.1	21.3	8.6	76869	85594	94	95	13475	1.3	4.1	53.2	39.6	1.8	162696
78614	COST	16647	150	32.7	36.0	23.3	6.0	2.0	35671	40742	30	36	118	27.1	19.5	34.8	11.0	7.6	93636
78615	COUPLAND	23622	638	16.3	29.2	39.7	10.8	4.1	54457	61147	79	82	536	7.8	27.2	34.5	24.8	5.6	122348
78616	DALE	20600	2439	19.2	33.9	34.6	7.3	5.0	47702	54614	68	73	2071	16.7	30.5	39.7	10.4	2.7	93594
78617	DEL VALLE	16728	4290	21.5	31.7	38.9	4.4	3.5	46887	54532	66	71	3025	33.5	25.2	35.0	5.4	1.0	78594
78618	DOSS	23172	32	25.0	34.4	34.4	3.1	3.1	45000	48646	61	68	26	7.7	30.8	30.8	19.2	11.5	125000
78619	DRIFTWOOD	38891	687	11.2	20.8	30.7	18.9	18.3	75723	87981	93	94	607	4.1	12.4	25.4	46.0	12.2	203385
78620	DRIPPING SPRINGS	33312	4251	11.0	15.7	37.6	22.8	12.9	79114	93377	95	96	3786	4.9	7.1	22.3	47.8	17.9	227218
78621	ELGIN	21238	5721	23.6	26.3	37.9	8.5	3.7	50057	56158	72	77	4506	18.9	23.2	40.4	15.5	2.1	103414
78623	FISCHER	27102	228	7.9	34.2	39.9	11.8	6.1	55932	64141	81	84	194	13.4	28.9	46.4	9.3	2.1	101190
78624	FREDERICKSBURG	23843	8314	26.1	33.0	29.6	6.6	4.7	42689	48160	55	63	6523	11.9	17.8	36.9	24.0	9.5	125189
78626	GEORGETOWN	21614	7251	19.6	27.4	37.7	10.9	4.5	52623	59434	76	80	4991	10.7	16.2	45.7	24.1	3.3	127333
78628	GEORGETOWN	34402	12743	10.7	18.9	38.4	21.1	11.0	73524	81958	93	93	10842	1.2	2.4	32.7	56.5	7.3	202891
78629	GONZALES	17023	4626	35.8	29.7	27.0	5.4	2.1	35014	40023	28	33	3274	36.3	25.3	25.3	11.2	2.1	71197
78631	HARPER	27141	595	29.1	30.3	28.6	4.5	7.6	41973	48328	53	61	488	13.9	25.8	27.9	20.5	11.9	112500
78632	HARWOOD	19434	147	41.5	28.6	19.1	3.4	7.5	30660	34434	14	18	122	29.5	20.5	34.4	12.3	3.3	90000
	TEXAS	23284		26.2	27.7	29.5	10.3	6.3	45778	54246				21.6	26.1	33.4	15.6	3.4	93683
	UNITED STATES	25866		24.7	27.1	30.8	10.9	6.5	48124	56710				10.9	15.0	33.7	30.1	10.4	145905

ZIP CODE #	POST OFFICE NAME	FINANCIAL SERVICES: Auto Loan	FINANCIAL SERVICES: Home Loan	FINANCIAL SERVICES: Investments	FINANCIAL SERVICES: Retirement Plans	THE HOME: Home Improvements: Home Repair	THE HOME: Home Improvements: Lawn & Garden	THE HOME: Furnishings: Computers & Hardware	THE HOME: Furnishings: Major Appliances	THE HOME: Furnishings: TV, Radio, Sound Equipment	THE HOME: Furnishings: Furniture	ENTERTAINMENT: Dine out/Carry out	ENTERTAINMENT: Sports Equipment	ENTERTAINMENT: Fees & Tickets	ENTERTAINMENT: Toys & Games	ENTERTAINMENT: Travel	ENTERTAINMENT: Cable TV	PERSONAL: Apparel & Services	PERSONAL: Auto Repairs	PERSONAL: Health Insurance	PERSONAL: Pets & Supplies
78383	SANDIA	79	67	49	62	71	78	63	72	68	64	82	84	58	79	65	70	78	72	80	93
78384	SAN DIEGO	51	45	37	42	43	45	46	49	47	50	60	52	42	53	43	46	59	50	46	51
78385	SARITA	92	81	67	75	78	82	82	89	85	90	107	94	75	95	78	82	106	91	83	93
78387	SINTON	81	67	50	62	68	74	68	76	73	72	90	83	62	82	66	73	87	76	78	86
78389	SKIDMORE	56	48	38	45	47	50	49	53	52	53	64	57	45	58	47	51	63	54	52	57
78390	TAFT	65	57	46	54	56	60	57	62	60	60	74	68	54	69	56	59	72	62	61	68
78391	TYNAN	62	49	36	47	52	59	53	58	58	53	70	64	48	64	52	59	66	58	64	67
78393	WOODSBORO	78	63	45	59	65	70	63	72	68	67	84	81	57	77	62	68	80	72	75	85
78401	CORPUS CHRISTI	35	30	36	30	29	33	36	34	38	36	47	40	34	44	34	37	46	37	35	38
78402	CORPUS CHRISTI	73	77	100	78	76	84	81	78	82	80	103	90	83	103	82	82	101	80	78	85
78404	CORPUS CHRISTI	73	72	76	71	71	74	74	75	74	76	93	85	73	90	73	72	92	77	71	80
78405	CORPUS CHRISTI	44	39	33	36	37	39	40	43	41	43	52	45	36	46	38	40	51	43	40	45
78406	CORPUS CHRISTI	47	41	34	38	40	42	42	45	44	46	55	48	39	48	40	42	54	46	43	47
78407	CORPUS CHRISTI	51	42	41	39	41	47	46	48	50	48	62	52	43	55	44	51	60	50	50	53
78408	CORPUS CHRISTI	53	46	41	43	45	48	48	51	50	51	63	55	45	57	46	49	62	52	49	55
78409	CORPUS CHRISTI	68	64	57	62	62	64	64	67	64	68	81	74	61	74	61	61	80	68	62	71
78410	CORPUS CHRISTI	91	96	93	97	93	94	91	92	87	93	110	107	91	109	90	83	108	91	83	102
78411	CORPUS CHRISTI	81	86	94	84	84	88	85	85	84	86	106	97	86	105	85	83	105	86	81	92
78412	CORPUS CHRISTI	85	86	101	89	85	90	91	88	89	91	113	103	91	111	89	86	110	90	82	96
78413	CORPUS CHRISTI	106	111	119	116	107	110	110	107	104	112	132	126	111	130	107	99	130	108	96	118
78414	CORPUS CHRISTI	101	110	117	115	107	108	105	104	99	107	126	121	108	125	104	95	123	103	94	114
78415	CORPUS CHRISTI	64	59	56	58	57	60	61	63	61	64	77	70	58	71	58	59	76	64	58	67
78416	CORPUS CHRISTI	65	57	49	53	55	58	59	63	61	64	77	67	54	68	56	59	76	64	60	66
78417	CORPUS CHRISTI	56	49	41	45	47	50	50	54	52	54	65	57	46	58	48	50	65	55	51	56
78418	CORPUS CHRISTI	90	94	98	95	93	98	93	93	91	93	114	108	94	113	92	89	111	93	89	103
78419	CORPUS CHRISTI	81	52	49	59	47	56	77	66	78	72	98	88	66	87	63	71	94	78	61	76
78501	MCALLEN	65	60	55	56	58	61	60	64	62	65	78	69	57	72	58	61	78	65	60	67
78503	MCALLEN	86	80	76	77	78	82	82	86	84	87	105	94	78	97	79	81	104	88	81	91
78504	MCALLEN	107	113	116	116	109	110	109	108	104	113	132	125	110	130	106	99	131	108	96	118
78516	ALAMO	49	43	40	41	43	46	45	48	48	49	60	52	43	55	44	46	59	49	47	51
78520	BROWNSVILLE	61	56	51	53	54	56	57	60	58	61	73	65	54	67	55	56	73	61	56	63
78521	BROWNSVILLE	56	49	45	47	48	50	52	54	54	56	68	59	49	63	49	51	68	56	50	57
78526	BROWNSVILLE	70	67	66	66	65	66	68	69	69	72	87	78	67	85	66	65	87	71	63	74
78536	DELMITA	56	49	41	45	47	49	50	54	52	54	65	57	46	57	47	50	64	55	50	56
78537	DONNA	51	45	39	42	44	47	46	50	48	50	61	53	43	55	45	47	60	51	48	52
78538	EDCOUCH	44	39	32	36	38	40	40	43	41	43	52	46	37	46	38	40	52	44	40	45
78539	EDINBURG	71	63	58	61	61	64	66	68	67	70	85	75	62	78	62	64	84	70	63	72
78541	EDINBURG	50	43	39	41	42	44	46	48	48	49	60	53	43	55	44	46	60	50	45	51
78547	GARCIASVILLE	22	18	18	18	18	19	21	21	22	22	27	24	20	27	19	20	28	22	19	22
78548	GRULLA	31	26	25	26	25	26	29	29	31	31	39	34	28	38	27	28	39	31	27	31
78549	HARGILL	48	42	35	39	40	42	43	46	44	47	56	49	39	49	41	43	55	47	43	48
78550	HARLINGEN	71	66	61	64	64	67	67	70	68	70	85	77	63	78	64	65	84	71	65	75
78552	HARLINGEN	77	69	60	64	69	76	68	75	71	72	88	79	64	79	68	71	86	75	76	82
78557	HIDALGO	42	36	32	35	35	36	39	40	40	41	51	44	36	47	36	38	51	42	37	42
78559	LA FERIA	64	56	46	52	54	57	57	62	59	62	74	66	52	66	54	57	73	63	59	65
78560	LA JOYA	47	42	35	39	40	43	42	46	44	46	55	48	39	49	41	43	54	46	44	48
78563	LINN	53	46	39	43	45	47	48	51	50	52	62	55	44	56	45	48	62	52	48	54
78566	LOS FRESNOS	54	48	41	44	46	49	48	52	50	53	63	55	45	56	47	49	63	53	50	55
78569	LYFORD	61	53	44	49	51	54	54	59	56	59	71	62	50	63	52	54	70	60	55	61
78570	MERCEDES	46	40	36	38	39	41	42	45	44	45	55	48	40	51	40	42	55	46	42	47
78572	MISSION	62	57	53	54	56	60	57	61	59	61	74	65	55	67	56	58	73	62	60	65
78574	MISSION	56	49	46	48	48	49	53	54	54	56	69	60	50	65	50	51	69	56	49	57
78575	OLMITO	100	99	95	95	97	102	97	102	97	102	122	111	94	114	96	95	121	102	96	108
78577	PHARR	59	53	48	50	51	55	55	58	57	59	71	62	52	65	53	55	70	59	55	61
78578	PORT ISABEL	65	60	54	58	59	62	61	64	62	64	77	70	58	71	59	60	76	65	61	68
78580	RAYMONDVILLE	50	44	36	41	42	44	45	48	46	49	58	51	41	52	43	45	58	49	45	50
78582	RIO GRANDE CITY	45	39	34	37	38	39	41	43	42	44	53	47	38	49	39	41	53	44	40	45
78583	RIO HONDO	55	48	39	44	47	50	49	53	51	52	64	57	44	57	47	50	63	54	51	57
78584	ROMA	43	38	32	35	36	38	39	41	40	42	51	45	36	46	37	39	50	43	39	43
78586	SAN BENITO	59	53	46	49	52	55	54	58	56	58	70	61	50	62	52	54	69	59	56	61
78588	SAN ISIDRO	54	48	40	44	46	48	49	53	51	53	64	56	45	56	46	49	63	54	49	55
78589	SAN JUAN	53	46	41	44	45	47	49	51	51	53	64	56	46	59	46	49	64	53	48	54
78590	SAN PERLITA	60	52	41	48	52	55	52	57	55	55	68	62	47	62	51	54	66	58	57	64
78591	SANTA ELENA	49	43	35	40	41	43	43	47	45	47	57	50	40	50	41	44	56	48	44	49
78593	SANTA ROSA	61	54	44	50	51	54	55	59	57	59	71	63	50	63	52	55	71	60	55	61
78594	SEBASTIAN	63	55	46	51	53	56	56	61	58	61	73	65	52	65	54	56	73	62	57	63
78595	SULLIVAN CITY	37	32	27	30	31	33	33	36	34	36	43	38	30	38	31	33	43	36	34	37
78596	WESLACO	55	48	45	46	47	50	51	54	53	55	67	58	48	61	49	51	66	55	51	56
78597	SOUTH PADRE ISLAND	111	104	99	98	110	129	96	109	101	103	126	107	97	105	104	108	118	106	128	125
78598	PORT MANSFIELD	57	50	42	46	48	51	51	55	53	56	67	59	47	59	49	51	66	56	52	58
78602	BASTROP	91	88	77	87	88	92	84	88	84	85	104	102	82	102	83	82	100	87	86	102
78605	BERTRAM	103	92	71	88	95	102	87	95	90	88	111	112	83	109	88	91	106	94	99	118
78606	BLANCO	93	69	41	66	77	88	70	82	79	69	93	96	62	91	71	83	86	81	96	108
78607	BLUFFTON	77	60	44	56	67	77	58	70	65	59	78	77	53	72	61	68	71	68	82	89
78608	BRIGGS	104	95	74	91	95	100	90	97	91	93	113	112	85	106	89	90	108	96	96	115
78609	BUCHANAN DAM	93	83	75	79	89	104	77	89	83	82	102	90	77	87	84	88	95	87	105	105
78610	BUDA	116	126	118	128	121	121	115	116	108	118	136	135	117	135	113	103	134	113	104	130
78611	BURNET	86	67	47	64	74	86	70	79	78	68	92	89	64	87	71	82	85	78	93	98
78612	CEDAR CREEK	101	95	78	92	96	100	89	95	90	91	111	111	86	108	89	89	107	94	95	114
78613	CEDAR PARK	129	146	144	152	140	136	133	132	122	137	155	154	137	156	130	115	153	128	113	144
78614	COST	85	60	32	56	69	77	59	73	68	59	80	87	51	78	61	71	73	72	86	100
78615	COUPLAND	103	95	76	91	98	104	88	96	91	89	112	113	86	113	90	92	107	94	100	120
78616	DALE	99	88	67	84	89	95	84	91	86	86	106	106	79	100	83	85	101	91	92	110
78617	DEL VALLE	89	81	67	78	81	86	80	84	81	81	100	97	76	95	78	80	96	84	84	98
78618	DOSS	82	65	44	58	73	82	61	73	69	60	82	86	54	81	65	74	76	72	87	100
78619	DRIFTWOOD	133	164	175	167	160	159	146	144	134	147	170	168	157	179	149	130	170	139	129	160
78620	DRIPPING SPRINGS	134	156	156	162	150	147	140	139	128	144	163	162	146	166	138	121	162	134	120	153
78621	ELGIN	96	90	76	86	90	95	86	92	88	88	109	106	84	106	86	87	106	91	91	107
78623	FISCHER	113	105	84	101	105	110	100	107	100	102	124	123	95	118	99	99	119	106	105	126
78624	FREDERICKSBURG	92	75	58	71	82	95	75	85	83	75	99	94	70	93	78	87	92	84	100	105
78626	GEORGETOWN	93	91	87	92	88	91	90	91	88	93	111	105	88	107	87	84	108	92	84	101
78628	GEORGETOWN	125	134	137	135	134	142	124	128	120	128	151	142	128	145	127	120	147	125	127	143
78629	GONZALES	75	60	42	56	63	70	61	69	67	62	81	77	55	75	61	68	76	69	75	83
78631	HARPER	114	86	54	80	97	110	83	100	94	83	111	117	73	107	87	99	102	99	119	136
78632	HARWOOD	90	60	27	52	68	79	58	73	70	59	83	87	50	78	59	76	75	72	90	103
	TEXAS	94	90	91	90	89	95	92	93	92	93	115	107	90	112	90	90	112	94	89	104
	UNITED STATES	100	100	100	100	100	100	100	100	100	100	100	100	100	100	100	100	100	100	100	100

POPULATION CHANGE

#	POST OFFICE NAME	COUNTY FIPS CODE	POPULATION 2000	2004	2009	2000-2004 ANNUAL RATE % Rate	State Centile	HOUSEHOLDS 2000	2004	2009	% Annual Rate 2000-2004	2004 Average HH Size	FAMILIES 2000	2004	% Annual Rate 2000-2004
78634	HUTTO	491	3774	5931	8626	11.2	99	1235	1925	2778	11.0	3.08	1037	1611	10.9
78635	HYE	031	224	247	279	2.3	73	95	104	116	2.2	2.38	68	74	2.0
78636	JOHNSON CITY	031	3370	3684	4127	2.1	70	1333	1443	1604	1.9	2.52	977	1060	1.9
78638	KINGSBURY	187	1834	1942	2169	1.4	53	681	714	790	1.1	2.71	529	553	1.1
78639	KINGSLAND	299	4666	5284	6092	3.0	81	2135	2406	2764	2.9	2.15	1364	1541	2.9
78640	KYLE	209	15427	21035	28579	7.6	98	4449	6108	8313	7.7	3.36	3706	5096	7.8
78641	LEANDER	453	20233	27390	36448	7.4	98	6857	9230	12184	7.2	2.96	5533	7451	7.3
78642	LIBERTY HILL	491	5560	6739	8666	4.6	93	1816	2203	2826	4.7	3.03	1522	1837	4.5
78643	LLANO	299	5714	6286	7147	2.3	73	2424	2655	3010	2.2	2.31	1677	1843	2.3
78644	LOCKHART	055	15136	17117	19720	2.9	81	4849	5504	6374	3.0	2.84	3658	4163	3.1
78645	LEANDER	453	7554	8677	9880	3.3	84	3202	3669	4148	3.3	2.36	2231	2540	3.1
78648	LULING	055	7317	8018	9126	2.2	71	2617	2854	3236	2.1	2.75	1837	2005	2.1
78650	MC DADE	021	1186	1328	1545	2.7	78	465	516	594	2.5	2.57	325	361	2.5
78652	MANCHACA	453	3388	3602	4158	1.5	56	1117	1172	1340	1.1	3.06	934	987	1.3
78653	MANOR	453	6140	6903	7802	2.8	79	2072	2330	2620	2.8	2.96	1603	1791	2.6
78654	MARBLE FALLS	053	17329	19949	23884	3.4	85	6978	7931	9377	3.1	2.50	5058	5773	3.2
78655	MARTINDALE	055	2049	2302	2657	2.8	79	703	788	906	2.7	2.92	555	623	2.8
78656	MAXWELL	055	3006	3250	3680	1.9	65	1017	1092	1230	1.7	2.98	767	825	1.7
78657	MARBLE FALLS	299	2494	2963	3554	4.1	91	1099	1284	1517	3.7	2.31	812	950	3.8
78659	PAIGE	021	2887	3309	3866	3.3	83	1097	1249	1449	3.1	2.64	826	941	3.1
78660	PFLUGERVILLE	453	35359	45908	55650	6.3	97	11326	14707	17730	6.3	3.11	9359	12095	6.2
78662	RED ROCK	021	1818	2083	2451	3.3	83	648	738	863	3.1	2.82	492	562	3.2
78663	ROUND MOUNTAIN	031	138	153	173	2.5	75	60	66	74	2.3	2.32	45	49	2.0
78664	ROUND ROCK	491	46417	60888	81505	6.6	98	15970	20729	27538	6.3	2.92	11910	15563	6.5
78666	SAN MARCOS	209	51372	61499	77998	4.3	92	17589	21406	27692	4.7	2.55	9340	11278	4.5
78669	SPICEWOOD	453	5376	6203	7193	3.4	86	2188	2513	2888	3.3	2.47	1618	1854	3.3
78671	STONEWALL	171	576	623	688	1.9	65	220	238	263	1.9	2.62	163	177	2.0
78672	TOW	299	1267	1423	1635	2.8	79	632	706	807	2.6	2.02	433	486	2.8
78675	WILLOW CITY	171	109	118	131	1.9	65	38	41	46	1.8	2.88	31	34	2.2
78676	WIMBERLEY	209	9073	11112	14378	4.9	94	3739	4566	5886	4.8	2.42	2692	3304	4.9
78677	WRIGHTSBORO	177	20	21	23	1.2	46	9	9	10	0.0	2.33	7	7	0.0
78681	ROUND ROCK	491	31447	40756	54349	6.3	97	10223	13174	17464	6.2	3.08	8617	11064	6.1
78701	AUSTIN	453	3855	4152	4563	1.8	63	1811	2018	2287	2.6	1.48	385	422	2.2
78702	AUSTIN	453	22489	23570	25851	1.1	45	7222	7530	8206	1.0	3.06	4777	4951	0.9
78703	AUSTIN	453	17449	18183	20020	1.0	41	8679	9057	9940	1.0	1.96	3814	3957	0.9
78704	AUSTIN	453	43117	45473	50186	1.3	50	20562	21616	23745	1.2	2.05	8277	8581	0.9
78705	AUSTIN	453	25376	25550	26962	0.2	16	9409	9472	10194	0.2	1.77	1203	1184	-0.4
78712	AUSTIN	453	400	400	400	0.0	13	0	0	0	0.0	0.00	0	0	0.0
78717	AUSTIN	491	8644	13406	19272	10.9	99	2836	4403	6314	10.9	3.03	2345	3623	10.8
78719	AUSTIN	453	2019	2217	2466	2.2	72	601	660	729	2.2	3.35	487	534	2.2
78721	AUSTIN	453	10111	11118	12443	2.3	72	3093	3393	3774	2.2	3.25	2270	2478	2.1
78722	AUSTIN	453	6213	6297	6816	0.3	21	2830	2862	3084	0.3	2.13	1134	1137	0.1
78723	AUSTIN	453	30320	32396	35672	1.6	58	10512	11105	12098	1.3	2.90	6522	6824	1.1
78724	AUSTIN	453	13141	15389	17757	3.8	89	3601	4191	4796	3.6	3.65	2967	3443	3.6
78725	AUSTIN	453	4155	4584	5059	2.3	73	960	1089	1225	3.0	3.30	763	863	2.9
78726	AUSTIN	453	5710	8338	10699	9.3	99	1977	2839	3596	8.9	2.94	1556	2278	9.4
78727	AUSTIN	453	23131	25986	29454	2.8	79	9878	11136	12569	2.9	2.32	5751	6397	2.5
78728	AUSTIN	453	17294	19981	22984	3.3	85	7940	8969	10200	2.9	2.22	4057	4595	3.0
78729	AUSTIN	491	23646	26918	33485	3.1	82	9446	10694	13222	3.0	2.50	5955	6705	2.8
78730	AUSTIN	453	4686	6070	7329	6.3	97	1909	2455	2935	6.1	2.47	1320	1689	6.0
78731	AUSTIN	453	25926	27042	29566	1.0	42	12649	13162	14299	0.9	2.02	6368	6617	0.9
78732	AUSTIN	453	3824	5374	6751	8.3	99	1434	1938	2373	7.3	2.77	1120	1520	7.5
78733	AUSTIN	453	7774	9748	11676	5.5	96	2503	3115	3696	5.3	3.13	2056	2528	5.0
78734	AUSTIN	453	13172	14697	16503	2.6	77	5191	5804	6488	2.7	2.52	3801	4196	2.4
78735	AUSTIN	453	9599	11174	12903	3.6	88	4195	4909	5659	3.8	2.26	2529	2930	3.5
78736	AUSTIN	453	6134	7123	8157	3.6	87	2266	2637	3007	3.6	2.66	1665	1924	3.5
78737	AUSTIN	209	7237	8525	10530	3.9	90	2486	2928	3597	3.9	2.91	2101	2479	4.0
78738	AUSTIN	453	4180	5420	6583	6.3	97	1519	1978	2393	6.4	2.72	1239	1612	6.4
78739	AUSTIN	453	8602	10368	12085	4.5	93	2635	3185	3699	4.6	3.19	2398	2902	4.6
78741	AUSTIN	453	40661	48969	57673	4.5	92	17080	20363	23736	4.2	2.40	6679	7845	3.9
78742	AUSTIN	453	1473	1609	1787	2.1	69	569	622	687	2.1	2.59	387	420	1.9
78744	AUSTIN	453	34020	36183	39905	1.5	56	10153	10686	11654	1.2	3.38	7326	7685	1.1
78745	AUSTIN	453	53186	57095	63311	1.7	61	20660	22144	24408	1.7	2.55	12621	13426	1.5
78746	AUSTIN	453	28079	30251	33635	1.8	63	10827	11686	12927	1.8	2.58	7582	8081	1.5
78747	AUSTIN	453	4691	6452	8296	7.8	99	1783	2464	3173	7.9	2.61	1350	1864	7.9
78748	AUSTIN	453	25302	28973	33272	3.2	83	9201	10474	11924	3.1	2.76	6779	7755	3.2
78749	AUSTIN	453	28610	34273	40719	4.3	92	10832	13030	15418	4.4	2.62	7585	9149	4.5
78750	AUSTIN	453	24171	27075	32010	2.7	79	9236	10316	12131	2.6	2.61	6781	7531	2.5
78751	AUSTIN	453	14167	14726	16231	0.9	39	7394	7657	8399	0.8	1.87	2036	2078	0.5
78752	AUSTIN	453	17733	19713	22230	2.5	76	6678	7341	8201	2.3	2.65	3366	3666	2.0
78753	AUSTIN	453	38847	45775	53858	3.9	90	14754	17006	19644	3.4	2.68	9007	10360	3.4
78754	AUSTIN	453	4943	5677	6521	3.3	84	2145	2523	2912	3.9	2.25	1252	1421	3.0
78756	AUSTIN	453	7983	8136	8875	0.5	24	4410	4471	4845	0.3	1.81	1510	1509	0.0
78757	AUSTIN	453	23129	23605	25621	0.5	25	10600	10818	11693	0.5	2.16	5405	5442	0.2
78758	AUSTIN	453	45916	50319	56738	2.2	71	19203	20754	23122	1.8	2.40	9863	10596	1.7
78759	AUSTIN	453	37633	39198	42938	1.0	40	18204	18959	20661	1.0	2.06	8946	9183	0.6
78801	UVALDE	463	22057	22976	24127	1.0	41	7118	7402	7769	0.9	3.02	5580	5816	1.0
78827	ASHERTON	127	1692	1717	1743	0.4	22	544	556	571	0.5	3.09	438	448	0.5
78828	BARKSDALE	137	350	344	339	-0.4	6	151	149	148	-0.3	2.30	108	107	-0.2
78829	BATESVILLE	507	1422	1423	1432	0.0	13	413	416	422	0.2	3.42	353	356	0.2
78830	BIG WELLS	127	833	818	814	-0.4	5	290	288	290	-0.2	2.83	216	215	-0.1
78832	BRACKETTVILLE	271	3379	3510	3675	0.9	38	1314	1358	1416	0.8	2.57	941	975	0.8
78833	CAMP WOOD	385	1297	1206	1114	-1.7	0	484	451	418	-1.7	2.59	347	324	-1.6
78834	CARRIZO SPRINGS	127	7706	7748	7792	0.1	15	2466	2508	2555	0.4	3.04	1984	2021	0.4
78837	COMSTOCK	465	569	590	622	0.9	37	242	250	263	0.8	2.36	173	179	0.8
78838	CONCAN	463	132	137	143	0.9	38	50	52	54	0.9	2.58	36	38	1.3
78839	CRYSTAL CITY	507	8474	8558	8674	0.2	18	2487	2529	2587	0.4	3.24	2032	2070	0.4
78840	DEL RIO	465	44246	46916	50306	1.4	54	13895	14716	15785	1.4	3.13	11139	11816	1.4
78843	LAUGHLIN A F B	465	44	44	46	0.0	13	15	15	15	0.0	2.93	12	12	0.0
78850	D HANIS	325	1020	1066	1164	1.0	43	349	363	395	0.9	2.94	274	286	1.0
78851	DRYDEN	443	1084	982	982	-2.3	0	444	406	406	-2.1	2.42	296	271	-2.1
78852	EAGLE PASS	323	46096	50721	56802	2.3	73	12698	13933	15580	2.2	3.63	10925	12001	2.2
78861	HONDO	325	11841	12564	13749	1.4	55	3693	3922	4315	1.4	2.83	2844	3028	1.5
78870	KNIPPA	463	782	815	853	1.0	41	266	276	289	0.9	2.95	197	206	1.1
78872	LA PRYOR	507	1721	1745	1769	0.3	21	536	547	558	0.5	3.19	428	438	0.5
	TEXAS					2.2					2.0	2.77			2.1
	UNITED STATES					1.2					1.3	2.58			1.1

#	POST OFFICE NAME	RACE (%) White 2000	White 2004	Black 2000	Black 2004	Asian/Pacific 2000	Asian/Pacific 2004	% Hispanic Origin 2000	% Hispanic Origin 2004	2004 AGE DISTRIBUTION (%) 0-4	5-9	10-14	15-19	20-24	25-44	45-64	65-84	85+	18+	MEDIAN AGE 2004	% 2004 Males	% 2004 Females
78634	HUTTO	85.7	82.7	3.0	3.4	1.0	1.1	16.0	19.8	8.3	8.6	9.5	7.7	5.6	31.3	23.4	5.1	0.6	68.7	33.3	50.4	49.6
78635	HYE	96.9	96.4	0.5	0.8	0.0	0.0	5.4	6.5	5.7	6.1	5.3	4.5	3.6	23.1	36.8	13.4	1.6	80.2	46.0	51.8	48.2
78636	JOHNSON CITY	92.5	91.4	0.2	0.2	0.2	0.2	13.0	15.1	6.6	6.7	6.3	5.8	4.7	23.3	30.6	13.6	2.3	76.6	42.7	49.2	50.8
78638	KINGSBURY	82.6	79.6	2.0	2.1	0.3	0.4	27.6	33.2	6.4	6.6	7.3	6.8	6.6	26.9	28.5	9.6	1.3	75.3	38.4	51.7	48.3
78639	KINGSLAND	95.7	95.0	0.1	0.2	0.5	0.6	5.9	7.0	4.3	4.1	4.7	4.6	4.5	18.0	27.2	26.9	5.7	83.8	52.5	48.0	52.0
78640	KYLE	65.8	63.6	4.7	4.6	0.3	0.4	52.5	57.3	10.3	9.2	8.7	8.3	7.9	33.0	17.9	4.4	0.4	67.0	28.4	51.3	48.7
78641	LEANDER	88.1	86.2	2.3	2.7	1.1	1.2	13.7	16.5	9.0	8.7	8.5	7.3	6.4	33.2	21.9	4.7	0.4	69.2	32.3	50.3	49.7
78642	LIBERTY HILL	93.2	92.0	0.7	0.8	0.3	0.3	9.7	11.8	7.1	7.8	8.9	7.8	6.0	28.1	26.0	7.7	0.7	71.0	35.9	49.6	50.4
78643	LLANO	95.6	94.9	0.4	0.4	0.2	0.3	6.6	7.9	4.8	5.0	5.7	5.9	4.7	19.5	29.4	21.8	3.3	80.7	48.0	49.1	50.9
78644	LOCKHART	68.6	66.8	10.6	10.4	0.4	0.5	43.2	47.4	7.1	6.8	7.1	7.8	7.5	29.7	22.1	9.8	2.1	73.9	34.6	49.3	50.7
78645	LEANDER	93.6	92.4	0.8	0.8	0.7	0.8	8.0	10.0	5.2	5.7	6.2	5.6	4.0	25.6	30.1	16.2	1.5	79.6	43.8	49.9	50.1
78648	LULING	70.7	68.6	8.7	8.6	0.4	0.5	36.9	40.9	7.9	7.4	7.5	7.6	6.8	24.6	21.4	14.0	3.0	72.5	36.2	48.1	51.9
78650	MC DADE	89.9	88.4	2.5	2.6	0.1	0.1	14.4	17.5	6.6	7.2	7.2	5.4	5.5	26.3	30.4	10.5	0.9	75.5	39.7	51.5	48.5
78652	MANCHACA	86.6	84.8	1.6	1.7	1.6	1.8	18.5	21.5	5.8	6.6	7.5	6.8	5.6	26.7	31.9	8.5	0.6	75.6	40.0	50.3	49.7
78653	MANOR	69.8	66.0	11.6	12.2	0.8	0.8	28.3	33.2	8.0	7.9	7.9	7.2	6.5	28.8	24.9	8.2	0.7	71.8	34.8	50.1	49.9
78654	MARBLE FALLS	88.9	87.3	1.1	1.2	0.4	0.5	16.8	19.5	6.6	6.5	6.3	6.0	5.6	22.0	26.7	18.3	2.1	76.8	42.8	49.3	50.7
78655	MARTINDALE	69.0	66.4	3.5	3.3	0.2	0.2	51.9	57.3	9.3	7.8	8.1	7.7	7.3	29.9	20.9	8.0	0.9	69.9	31.8	51.2	48.8
78656	MAXWELL	66.1	63.7	4.5	4.3	0.3	0.3	52.0	57.0	8.4	7.8	7.8	7.6	7.9	31.5	21.8	6.6	0.7	71.5	31.3	51.7	48.3
78657	MARBLE FALLS	94.4	93.3	0.5	0.5	0.6	0.7	7.9	9.8	4.6	4.4	3.9	3.8	3.9	17.7	31.6	28.3	2.0	85.1	54.9	49.4	50.6
78659	PAIGE	89.1	87.7	3.9	4.0	0.2	0.2	14.8	18.0	7.3	7.6	7.6	6.3	5.5	27.6	27.4	10.0	0.8	73.6	37.9	49.7	50.3
78660	PFLUGERVILLE	71.8	68.8	11.8	12.6	4.6	5.0	21.8	25.4	9.8	9.3	8.7	7.1	6.3	36.5	19.0	3.0	0.4	67.6	31.1	49.3	50.7
78662	RED ROCK	90.4	89.3	3.3	3.5	0.1	0.1	16.3	19.0	8.0	7.7	7.5	8.0	7.0	27.2	26.7	7.3	0.6	71.3	35.1	51.2	48.8
78663	ROUND MOUNTAIN	91.3	89.5	0.0	0.0	0.0	0.0	10.1	11.8	5.9	6.5	5.2	4.6	3.3	22.2	36.0	14.4	2.0	78.4	46.4	48.4	51.6
78664	ROUND ROCK	74.7	72.7	8.9	9.2	2.9	3.2	23.8	26.5	10.2	9.3	8.3	6.9	7.1	37.0	17.2	3.4	0.7	67.8	30.3	49.4	50.6
78666	SAN MARCOS	72.5	70.1	5.2	5.2	1.1	1.2	37.4	41.5	5.9	5.2	5.2	12.1	19.3	28.2	16.3	6.6	1.1	79.9	26.0	50.7	49.3
78669	SPICEWOOD	95.5	94.7	0.3	0.3	0.4	0.5	6.1	7.6	5.3	5.9	6.6	5.6	3.2	26.1	35.5	11.0	0.7	78.6	43.7	51.2	48.8
78671	STONEWALL	91.7	90.4	0.4	0.5	0.2	0.2	17.9	21.0	5.3	5.9	6.4	4.2	4.3	21.2	31.0	19.7	1.9	79.6	47.0	50.6	49.4
78672	TOW	97.8	97.6	0.2	0.1	0.2	0.2	1.8	2.0	2.5	2.5	2.8	3.4	3.4	12.8	35.8	33.8	3.1	90.3	59.3	49.4	50.6
78675	WILLOW CITY	92.7	91.5	0.0	0.0	0.0	0.0	10.1	12.7	5.1	5.1	5.9	5.9	5.1	18.6	30.5	22.0	1.7	78.8	47.5	50.9	49.2
78676	WIMBERLEY	93.8	92.6	0.3	0.4	0.3	0.4	7.8	9.5	4.7	5.3	6.1	6.3	4.7	21.6	32.3	17.3	1.8	79.8	45.7	49.4	50.6
78677	WRIGHTSBORO	85.0	85.7	0.0	0.0	0.0	0.0	20.0	28.6	9.5	9.5	9.5	9.5	4.8	38.1	19.1	0.0	0.0	71.4	28.8	52.4	47.6
78681	ROUND ROCK	82.5	80.0	4.7	5.1	3.9	4.4	15.0	18.1	9.1	9.0	8.7	7.3	6.2	32.3	22.8	4.3	0.4	68.5	32.9	49.8	50.2
78701	AUSTIN	72.0	68.8	12.0	12.8	3.7	4.0	18.4	21.8	1.1	0.7	0.8	3.9	13.8	43.0	22.5	12.4	1.8	96.6	37.1	64.5	35.5
78702	AUSTIN	30.1	29.0	23.8	22.6	0.4	0.4	67.6	70.4	9.1	8.5	8.4	8.2	7.6	28.2	18.2	10.2	1.7	69.2	30.4	50.3	49.7
78703	AUSTIN	91.2	90.0	1.5	1.6	3.0	3.3	7.1	8.7	5.0	4.7	4.6	4.8	6.1	39.9	25.4	7.7	1.8	82.9	36.7	49.5	50.5
78704	AUSTIN	71.9	68.8	4.9	5.0	1.5	1.6	33.9	38.6	6.3	5.0	4.7	6.0	10.7	41.2	19.4	5.7	1.0	81.2	31.8	51.7	48.3
78705	AUSTIN	74.7	71.9	2.7	2.9	15.1	16.5	10.0	12.1	0.8	0.5	0.5	32.3	40.6	19.2	5.0	1.0	0.2	97.7	22.0	52.2	47.8
78712	AUSTIN	61.5	58.5	6.3	6.5	20.8	22.3	15.0	18.0	0.0	0.0	0.0	79.0	20.0	0.8	0.3	0.0	0.0	99.5	18.2	59.3	40.8
78717	AUSTIN	82.7	80.7	4.3	4.6	8.1	9.2	9.6	11.3	10.8	10.7	9.1	6.2	4.8	35.6	19.7	2.8	0.4	65.3	32.5	49.2	50.8
78719	AUSTIN	65.3	62.3	6.1	6.1	0.8	0.8	54.1	59.7	9.5	9.1	9.5	8.3	7.9	29.0	19.9	6.4	0.6	66.9	29.2	51.3	48.7
78721	AUSTIN	23.4	23.5	44.8	42.4	0.2	0.2	50.8	54.2	9.5	8.9	9.2	7.9	7.5	27.1	18.7	10.2	1.1	67.9	29.7	49.7	50.3
78722	AUSTIN	62.1	59.2	22.7	23.6	2.2	2.3	20.2	23.7	4.5	3.8	4.1	5.5	10.2	42.5	17.1	9.6	2.7	84.7	33.1	51.6	48.4
78723	AUSTIN	41.0	39.1	31.6	30.6	1.3	1.4	42.3	46.8	8.9	7.5	6.8	7.0	11.2	33.4	17.6	6.9	0.8	72.9	29.0	52.0	48.0
78724	AUSTIN	28.9	27.5	40.3	39.1	0.3	0.3	45.3	49.2	10.6	9.9	10.3	9.1	9.2	30.5	16.7	3.5	0.2	63.6	25.5	49.6	50.4
78725	AUSTIN	38.4	36.0	38.9	38.3	1.2	1.3	33.7	38.1	7.4	7.1	6.7	7.5	9.3	39.5	18.0	4.2	0.4	74.7	31.2	59.5	40.5
78726	AUSTIN	86.4	84.1	1.8	2.0	8.4	10.1	5.8	7.1	7.9	8.8	9.9	6.6	5.1	31.2	26.1	4.0	0.3	69.1	35.7	50.0	50.0
78727	AUSTIN	75.7	72.9	6.3	6.7	9.1	10.0	14.6	17.4	6.9	6.1	5.7	5.7	8.2	42.1	21.0	3.9	0.4	77.9	32.5	50.9	49.1
78728	AUSTIN	69.2	65.7	9.6	10.2	11.2	12.3	17.1	20.6	8.0	6.5	5.5	5.2	10.3	46.3	15.0	3.1	0.2	77.3	30.3	50.6	49.4
78729	AUSTIN	80.4	78.0	5.0	5.3	7.4	8.2	11.7	14.1	7.4	6.9	7.0	6.6	8.3	38.6	20.9	3.6	0.8	74.7	32.1	49.9	50.1
78730	AUSTIN	91.3	90.0	1.2	1.3	4.8	5.5	6.2	7.7	8.8	9.0	6.9	4.3	2.9	35.0	28.1	4.9	0.2	72.6	37.6	52.3	47.7
78731	AUSTIN	89.6	88.4	1.0	1.1	5.6	6.1	6.6	7.9	4.2	4.3	4.6	4.6	9.6	31.0	25.8	12.9	3.0	84.3	39.2	48.8	51.2
78732	AUSTIN	90.3	88.8	1.5	1.7	4.6	5.3	7.5	9.4	11.9	11.7	7.7	3.9	2.1	39.6	19.9	3.1	0.2	66.1	34.7	51.8	48.2
78733	AUSTIN	90.8	88.8	0.6	0.7	4.3	5.2	7.4	9.2	8.1	10.1	10.6	7.8	3.9	28.7	27.8	2.9	0.2	65.8	35.9	49.9	50.1
78734	AUSTIN	93.3	92.0	0.5	0.6	0.8	0.9	9.5	11.7	5.4	6.5	7.2	6.5	4.3	25.2	32.1	11.5	1.3	76.8	42.4	51.1	48.9
78735	AUSTIN	89.2	87.5	1.3	1.4	3.9	4.3	10.8	13.2	7.1	6.8	5.0	4.2	4.7	40.5	24.1	6.5	1.1	78.6	35.6	50.6	49.5
78736	AUSTIN	88.8	86.6	1.5	1.6	1.4	1.6	14.2	17.6	5.4	6.2	7.4	6.3	5.6	30.4	29.9	7.7	1.2	76.9	39.2	48.8	51.2
78737	AUSTIN	94.1	93.1	0.7	0.8	1.2	1.4	9.4	11.5	5.5	7.2	8.9	8.2	2.6	25.9	33.9	7.2	0.7	72.9	41.2	50.1	49.9
78738	AUSTIN	94.2	92.9	0.7	0.9	2.3	2.9	4.2	5.3	6.4	7.7	7.8	6.1	3.2	25.0	30.1	12.3	1.5	73.9	42.1	49.7	50.4
78739	AUSTIN	87.1	85.2	2.2	2.4	6.0	6.7	10.1	12.4	8.8	9.6	9.7	7.5	4.9	27.2	27.3	4.6	0.3	66.4	35.8	50.3	49.7
78741	AUSTIN	49.5	47.0	8.8	8.6	6.0	5.9	51.6	55.8	7.0	5.0	4.2	9.1	25.6	35.9	10.5	2.5	0.2	81.2	24.8	55.5	44.5
78742	AUSTIN	48.9	45.4	13.3	13.2	0.4	0.4	54.5	59.5	9.6	8.7	8.6	7.2	7.5	34.4	17.9	5.8	0.4	68.9	29.6	52.3	47.7
78744	AUSTIN	46.6	44.3	11.6	11.0	1.4	1.4	64.9	69.1	10.6	9.6	9.4	8.1	10.1	33.6	15.4	3.0	0.2	65.7	26.1	51.2	48.9
78745	AUSTIN	66.4	62.5	5.8	5.9	1.7	1.8	40.3	46.0	7.4	6.6	6.3	6.4	8.9	35.4	21.4	6.9	0.9	76.0	32.2	50.1	49.9
78746	AUSTIN	88.1	86.8	0.6	0.7	7.6	8.2	5.7	7.1	5.7	6.7	8.4	7.9	5.9	27.1	31.0	6.4	1.0	74.0	37.4	50.4	49.7
78747	AUSTIN	79.5	77.2	5.0	5.1	1.0	1.1	31.6	34.7	6.4	6.6	5.6	4.5	4.5	25.8	30.1	15.4	1.0	78.6	42.5	48.6	51.4
78748	AUSTIN	72.9	69.9	5.4	5.6	3.2	3.5	30.3	34.8	8.4	7.7	6.8	6.6	7.3	37.2	21.3	4.4	0.3	73.1	32.2	49.1	50.9
78749	AUSTIN	80.3	77.9	4.1	4.1	5.1	5.8	18.1	21.1	8.4	7.8	7.2	5.7	6.0	38.9	21.4	4.0	0.6	72.9	33.1	49.4	50.6
78750	AUSTIN	84.9	83.0	2.8	3.1	7.1	7.8	9.6	11.9	6.2	6.7	7.1	7.0	6.7	29.3	28.6	7.4	0.9	75.6	37.6	49.4	50.6
78751	AUSTIN	78.5	76.0	2.9	3.1	6.6	7.0	19.3	22.9	3.6	2.8	2.9	4.5	20.1	47.0	14.3	4.2	0.8	89.4	29.2	54.9	45.1
78752	AUSTIN	49.7	47.6	13.4	12.7	2.5	2.6	55.2	59.2	8.6	6.7	5.9	7.7	14.3	36.7	13.1	5.3	1.6	75.2	27.6	54.7	45.3
78753	AUSTIN	49.7	46.2	19.4	19.0	6.0	7.4	36.7	40.2	9.5	8.1	7.3	6.5	9.8	36.6	17.0	4.7	0.6	71.6	29.3	51.0	49.0
78754	AUSTIN	67.4	63.1	15.7	17.2	3.5	3.8	20.5	24.3	7.3	6.6	6.0	5.1	7.5	37.5	21.4	7.9	0.7	77.3	34.3	50.0	50.0
78756	AUSTIN	83.5	81.2	3.2	3.4	2.6	2.9	16.5	19.8	4.8	4.0	4.0	4.1	9.4	41.2	21.8	8.3	2.4	85.1	35.6	49.9	50.1
78757	AUSTIN	81.3	78.9	2.7	2.8	2.1	2.2	22.2	25.7	5.6	5.0	4.8	5.1	7.4	36.6	22.0	11.6	2.0	81.7	36.4	50.0	50.0
78758	AUSTIN	57.0	54.0	11.8	11.8	8.2	8.6	33.4	37.5	7.7	6.1	5.5	6.1	12.2	40.3	16.7	4.8	0.6	77.7	29.4	52.9	47.1
78759	AUSTIN	85.0	82.8	2.6	2.9	7.4	8.5	8.8	10.8	5.3	4.9	4.9	4.8	7.7	40.1	24.0	7.4	1.0	82.0	34.7	50.0	50.0
78801	UVALDE	74.3	73.0	0.4	0.4	0.5	0.6	69.8	73.4	9.2	8.5	8.7	8.2	7.6	25.1	20.2	10.7	1.9	68.6	31.0	48.8	51.2
78827	ASHERTON	76.9	77.1	0.1	0.1	0.1	0.1	90.7	90.8	8.4	7.8	9.6	8.7	6.9	23.0	22.5	11.5	1.6	68.4	32.8	47.5	52.5
78828	BARKSDALE	94.3	93.9	0.0	0.0	0.0	0.0	8.3	9.3	3.5	4.1	6.4	5.2	4.4	15.4	34.0	25.0	2.0	83.1	52.0	50.3	49.7
78829	BATESVILLE	53.7	52.5	0.4	0.5	0.0	0.0	87.6	89.5	9.1	8.6	8.6	9.7	8.6	26.7	19.8	7.9	1.1	68.0	29.0	50.1	49.9
78830	BIG WELLS	79.4	79.3	0.2	0.2	0.4	0.4	88.0	88.5	7.1	8.0	8.9	8.1	3.9	20.1	28.1	13.9	2.0	70.9	40.8	47.8	52.2
78832	BRACKETTVILLE	75.8	73.8	1.7	1.7	0.1	0.1	50.5	54.9	6.2	6.1	7.3	6.7	5.2	19.3	24.5	22.8	2.0	76.0	44.4	50.1	49.9
78833	CAMP WOOD	90.0	88.7	0.4	0.4	0.2	0.3	31.5	35.3	6.0	6.1	7.3	6.9	5.1	21.5	26.9	18.6	1.8	76.5	42.9	50.4	49.6
78834	CARRIZO SPRINGS	76.7	76.8	1.1	1.1	0.9	0.9	83.4	84.0	8.8	8.3	9.3	9.0	7.4	24.1	21.3	10.5	1.4	67.9	31.2	48.7	51.3
78837	COMSTOCK	84.5	81.9	0.0	0.0	0.2	0.2	35.9	42.5	5.3	5.4	5.6	5.4	4.8	20.7	30.2	21.2	1.5	80.2	47.2	51.5	48.5
78838	CONCAN	90.9	89.8	0.0	0.0	0.0	0.0	18.9	23.4	4.4	5.1	7.3	5.1	4.4	20.4	29.9	21.2	2.2	79.6	47.5	51.8	48.2
78839	CRYSTAL CITY	69.1	68.6	0.6	0.6	0.2	0.2	93.3	94.2	9.1	8.7	9.4	9.1	7.9	25.2	19.3	10.0	1.3	67.4	29.3	49.7	50.3
78840	DEL RIO	76.2	75.4	1.6	1.5	0.6	0.6	76.0	78.9	9.1	8.5	8.7	7.9	7.9	26.8	19.9	10.1	1.1	68.7	31.1	49.5	50.6
78843	LAUGHLIN A F B	93.2	90.9	2.3	2.3	0.0	2.3	4.6	6.8	20.5	9.1	4.6	0.0	13.6	52.3	0.0	0.0	0.0	65.9	25.7	59.1	40.9
78850	D HANIS	86.8	85.4	0.3	0.4	0.4	0.4	37.3	41.7	6.3	6.6	7.0	6.3	5.4	21.9	27.7	17.3	1.7	76.5	42.5	51.1	48.9
78851	DRYDEN	88.4	87.2	0.0	0.0	0.7	0.7	48.4	52.8	5.9	5.9	7.2	7.7	5.7	20.4	28.1	17.2	1.8	76.3	43.1	50.8	49.2
78852	EAGLE PASS	70.9	70.7	0.3	0.3	0.4	0.4	95.5	96.1	10.2	9.7	10.5	9.1	7.5	25.2	18.6	8.4	0.9	64.0	27.7	48.1	51.9
78861	HONDO	78.4	77.2	5.7	5.6	0.3	0.3	49.1	52.8	6.8	6.8	7.1	6.5	8.3	30.5	21.1	11.2	1.8	75.2	33.8	54.4	45.6
78870	KNIPPA	76.6	74.0	0.3	0.3	0.3	0.3	46.9	52.4	7.1	7.2	9.2	7.2	6.8	24.7	26.5	9.9	1.4	72.0	34.1	51.2	48.8
78872	LA PRYOR	55.0	53.6	0.1	0.1	0.1	0.1	84.0	86.3	9.5	9.5	10.7	7.9	7.3	24.9	20.6	8.9	0.8	65.1	28.9	48.4	51.6
	TEXAS	71.0	69.5	11.5	11.4	2.8	3.1	32.0	34.6	7.9	7.5	7.7	7.5	8.1	29.6	21.9	8.7	1.2	72.6	32.9	49.7	50.3
	UNITED STATES	75.1	73.6	12.3	12.5	3.8	4.2	12.5	14.1	6.9	6.7	7.2	7.0	7.3	28.6	23.8	10.8	1.7	75.1	36.0	49.1	50.9

#	POST OFFICE NAME	2004 Per Capita Income	2004 HH Income Base	2004 HOUSEHOLD INCOME DISTRIBUTION (%) Less than $25,000	$25,000 to $49,999	$50,000 to $99,999	$100,000 to $149,999	$150,000 or More	MEDIAN HOUSEHOLD INCOME 2004	2009	2004 National Centile	2004 State Centile	2004 Home Value Base	2004 HOME VALUE DISTRIBUTION (%) Less than $50,000	$50,000 to $89,999	$90,000 to $174,999	$175,000 to $399,999	$400,000 or More	2004 Median Home Value
78634	HUTTO	33738	1925	6.6	20.8	40.2	17.4	15.1	74815	83490	93	94	1701	2.5	11.3	41.3	34.9	10.1	161313
78635	HYE	28421	104	21.2	25.0	39.4	9.6	4.8	53555	63312	78	82	85	5.9	27.1	37.7	21.2	8.2	123864
78636	JOHNSON CITY	24380	1443	24.6	28.3	32.6	10.5	4.0	46246	53676	64	70	1169	11.7	24.3	35.0	19.5	9.5	119732
78638	KINGSBURY	23669	714	17.5	30.4	37.5	9.8	4.8	51833	58389	75	80	578	20.1	32.4	32.4	10.0	5.2	87143
78639	KINGSLAND	22122	2406	37.1	35.0	20.2	5.2	2.5	33460	38108	22	28	1922	29.6	23.9	30.0	14.4	2.0	83333
78640	KYLE	19408	6108	14.4	29.3	42.0	11.2	3.1	54675	64270	79	83	4941	22.4	24.1	39.8	11.4	2.4	95491
78641	LEANDER	28410	9230	10.8	22.0	44.9	14.5	7.8	63798	72244	88	89	7931	7.3	10.7	60.6	17.5	3.9	129774
78642	LIBERTY HILL	24378	2203	12.7	26.2	40.0	15.4	5.7	59926	67009	84	87	1871	11.4	19.7	31.0	30.1	7.8	133370
78643	LLANO	25648	2655	27.6	31.9	31.5	5.3	3.8	40635	47165	48	56	2064	23.0	24.8	29.8	16.5	5.9	95769
78644	LOCKHART	17224	5504	28.2	31.1	32.4	6.9	1.4	42647	47315	55	63	3766	19.7	32.6	34.6	10.4	2.8	87402
78645	LEANDER	33772	3669	13.2	27.0	35.1	15.3	9.4	61415	71652	86	88	2838	6.5	11.7	38.7	34.8	8.4	161490
78648	LULING	15755	2854	35.4	34.2	23.6	5.0	1.8	33850	38038	24	29	1917	36.5	31.8	23.8	6.2	1.7	65250
78650	MC DADE	21803	516	27.5	26.6	31.6	11.6	2.7	46491	53350	65	71	414	26.1	29.5	29.0	15.2	0.2	82069
78652	MANCHACA	35713	1172	5.6	14.9	44.9	22.3	12.5	80390	96089	95	96	1080	2.2	3.6	47.8	43.3	3.1	170313
78653	MANOR	26125	2330	17.7	23.9	38.7	12.2	7.6	58108	67217	83	85	1953	20.2	21.3	34.8	20.3	3.3	108873
78654	MARBLE FALLS	24784	7931	25.8	30.4	28.3	9.7	5.9	43714	51174	58	66	6109	17.7	20.0	30.6	25.3	6.6	117096
78655	MARTINDALE	17817	788	24.5	36.8	28.6	7.9	2.3	41168	47186	50	58	619	33.8	23.4	30.2	10.5	2.1	76806
78656	MAXWELL	17296	1092	25.6	34.4	30.0	7.3	2.7	41442	46828	51	60	787	38.5	25.7	27.7	5.8	2.3	68125
78657	MARBLE FALLS	35937	1284	17.7	25.6	30.1	15.6	11.1	55739	66033	80	83	1090	9.8	17.9	25.3	32.8	14.2	164557
78659	PAIGE	23386	1249	20.9	28.5	36.5	8.3	5.8	50471	56927	73	78	1041	19.7	23.5	36.8	17.1	2.9	101620
78660	PFLUGERVILLE	27314	14707	5.9	19.1	48.7	19.4	6.8	72809	85140	92	93	13286	9.3	7.9	58.9	23.6	0.4	139090
78662	RED ROCK	21884	738	19.8	22.9	40.5	14.9	1.9	55710	63605	80	83	600	20.2	27.0	35.8	13.0	4.0	95313
78663	ROUND MOUNTAIN	31306	66	22.7	22.7	31.8	18.2	4.6	57209	65679	82	85	55	7.3	12.7	30.9	30.9	18.2	171875
78664	ROUND ROCK	28439	20729	8.3	22.1	46.6	15.3	7.7	67132	77258	90	91	14374	0.9	3.5	62.6	30.2	2.9	150173
78666	SAN MARCOS	18869	21406	34.9	30.7	25.1	6.6	2.8	36185	42984	32	39	9261	20.9	21.8	35.9	19.3	2.2	103907
78669	SPICEWOOD	41035	2513	13.9	20.5	31.8	16.2	17.7	72032	84129	92	93	2210	8.4	9.2	27.7	32.8	22.0	189324
78671	STONEWALL	20611	238	26.5	41.6	20.6	7.1	4.2	41828	48454	52	61	195	14.9	14.9	26.7	16.9	26.7	133654
78672	TOW	16604	706	47.2	35.3	14.5	2.7	0.4	26659	29881	7	9	603	30.4	27.7	31.3	9.6	1.0	71087
78675	WILLOW CITY	21726	41	19.5	39.0	31.7	7.3	2.4	45544	51367	63	69	34	14.7	14.7	20.6	26.5	23.5	175000
78676	WIMBERLEY	31874	4566	14.5	24.7	37.5	15.2	8.0	59506	70570	84	86	3807	4.9	9.5	37.0	40.4	8.2	171685
78677	WRIGHTSBORO	12262	9	44.4	44.4	11.1	0.0	0.0	27247	40000	7	10	7	0.0	0.0	100.0	0.0	0.0	118750
78681	ROUND ROCK	29966	13174	8.1	15.7	40.7	24.4	11.1	80026	91083	95	96	10761	2.7	1.6	41.0	52.3	2.3	182265
78701	AUSTIN	50498	2018	32.0	26.3	14.4	9.9	17.4	42078	52301	53	62	624	0.3	13.0	20.0	53.2	13.5	218421
78702	AUSTIN	11836	7530	48.1	31.3	16.0	3.0	1.6	26153	30654	6	8	3572	28.1	48.2	20.4	2.5	0.8	69176
78703	AUSTIN	64056	9057	16.2	19.4	26.2	15.2	23.0	72903	96397	92	93	4665	0.3	2.0	8.7	42.3	46.7	382947
78704	AUSTIN	27716	21616	24.4	33.8	28.5	8.6	4.7	41909	51557	53	61	6494	4.4	9.9	37.9	42.8	5.1	169581
78705	AUSTIN	16241	9472	64.0	19.5	10.1	3.8	2.7	16672	20211	1	2	988	2.2	12.4	31.6	38.3	15.6	188014
78712	AUSTIN	12817	0	0.0	0.0	0.0	0.0	0.0	0	0	0	0	0	0.0	0.0	0.0	0.0	0.0	0
78717	AUSTIN	34751	4403	3.8	13.2	37.0	30.5	15.5	93624	108567	98	98	3754	0.4	1.7	27.8	68.3	1.7	220474
78719	AUSTIN	15464	660	21.2	34.1	37.7	5.5	1.5	45564	52157	63	69	473	14.2	40.0	36.8	9.1	0.0	85244
78721	AUSTIN	12101	3393	42.1	30.3	22.8	3.1	1.7	30664	35185	14	18	2013	27.3	48.6	22.2	1.9	0.0	68417
78722	AUSTIN	25172	2862	28.4	29.9	31.3	6.9	3.6	41061	50439	50	58	1201	6.0	13.3	52.3	28.1	0.3	138771
78723	AUSTIN	17323	11105	29.8	33.6	29.3	5.6	1.7	38645	44674	42	50	4704	2.7	24.8	68.5	3.8	0.2	104818
78724	AUSTIN	14167	4191	24.9	35.5	32.4	5.0	2.2	41070	47589	50	58	2833	35.4	33.4	28.1	1.9	1.2	70019
78725	AUSTIN	20349	1089	10.1	34.7	36.8	13.2	5.1	53287	62681	77	81	896	8.5	18.3	66.6	4.5	2.1	108213
78726	AUSTIN	48163	2839	5.7	8.7	26.7	30.9	27.9	111567	136776	99	99	2339	2.1	1.2	7.4	74.2	15.1	286212
78727	AUSTIN	36223	11136	8.3	20.1	44.9	17.5	9.2	69039	82282	91	92	5974	0.7	2.3	63.5	32.6	1.0	148988
78728	AUSTIN	32437	8969	11.7	26.8	40.8	14.7	6.0	60693	73107	85	87	3232	2.7	2.3	64.2	30.9	0.0	156681
78729	AUSTIN	31648	10694	9.4	23.0	43.5	17.0	7.2	67752	78090	90	91	6016	1.3	1.5	52.6	44.4	0.2	169041
78730	AUSTIN	94767	2455	3.7	10.6	19.3	17.4	49.0	145798	182055	100	100	1738	0.0	0.3	0.7	31.1	67.9	480570
78731	AUSTIN	54453	13162	14.7	20.0	27.8	16.6	20.9	74563	94586	93	94	7482	0.5	2.0	13.7	54.1	29.6	309811
78732	AUSTIN	54527	1938	1.5	6.4	25.5	35.1	31.6	122530	148722	99	100	1707	0.6	2.3	5.4	72.2	19.6	280873
78733	AUSTIN	57169	3115	5.6	10.6	27.6	22.9	33.3	110825	131351	99	99	2824	2.4	3.5	15.9	46.5	31.8	293804
78734	AUSTIN	45797	5804	8.4	20.9	31.9	19.4	19.5	79804	97914	95	96	4777	4.4	3.2	24.3	49.1	19.0	238481
78735	AUSTIN	60123	4909	11.3	14.3	31.0	21.0	22.4	87915	111660	97	97	2900	3.9	1.5	20.6	53.8	20.2	232380
78736	AUSTIN	34518	2637	9.7	18.7	44.9	14.2	12.5	67987	79047	90	91	2178	3.7	5.5	60.9	25.8	4.2	141724
78737	AUSTIN	40414	2928	7.7	11.9	31.7	26.6	22.1	97302	114134	98	98	2729	3.4	4.7	16.0	59.9	16.1	240373
78738	AUSTIN	62356	1978	6.1	11.2	24.3	22.1	36.4	116387	140236	99	99	1836	1.0	2.7	8.5	47.7	40.0	356738
78739	AUSTIN	46626	3185	1.4	6.7	27.4	28.4	36.1	119755	145060	99	100	3065	1.1	0.1	5.8	84.8	8.3	249254
78741	AUSTIN	15831	20363	43.8	32.9	19.0	3.2	1.2	29072	34177	10	13	2870	27.6	30.0	34.3	7.8	0.3	77331
78742	AUSTIN	17825	622	28.9	44.9	19.3	3.9	3.1	34091	41201	24	30	286	58.4	18.5	16.8	2.5	3.9	38333
78744	AUSTIN	15643	10686	21.5	37.3	33.6	5.4	2.2	43101	50212	56	65	5717	16.2	42.6	37.9	2.7	0.6	83366
78745	AUSTIN	23494	22144	19.0	31.7	36.2	10.1	3.1	49314	57801	71	76	11789	3.1	18.4	72.3	5.9	0.4	110901
78746	AUSTIN	69224	11686	12.2	14.0	21.5	16.2	36.1	105828	131245	99	99	7888	1.0	0.2	3.9	42.5	52.4	417910
78747	AUSTIN	40593	2464	9.5	19.2	37.1	17.9	16.3	72541	86104	92	93	2179	5.8	11.6	31.1	44.4	7.1	179724
78748	AUSTIN	28210	10474	8.0	22.8	45.7	16.8	6.8	66878	79764	90	91	8072	2.4	4.5	65.8	26.8	0.5	144555
78749	AUSTIN	34775	13030	7.3	14.8	43.9	24.2	9.7	79198	100230	95	96	9534	0.8	0.7	42.6	54.8	1.1	181733
78750	AUSTIN	41673	10316	8.0	18.1	32.1	21.9	19.8	83828	96393	96	97	7124	0.6	1.3	33.8	54.5	9.8	217924
78751	AUSTIN	27698	7657	36.4	28.4	23.0	8.1	4.2	35444	44113	29	35	2039	0.7	10.8	40.1	43.4	5.1	171600
78752	AUSTIN	15528	7341	36.3	33.2	25.5	4.0	0.9	33728	38719	23	29	1881	5.2	24.2	65.4	5.2	0.0	106981
78753	AUSTIN	20684	17006	22.9	31.2	34.8	8.7	2.4	46156	54430	64	70	7359	6.3	13.9	69.7	9.6	0.5	116910
78754	AUSTIN	30260	2523	11.0	31.4	42.3	10.3	5.1	57726	66901	82	85	1346	14.2	16.3	50.5	17.5	1.4	120661
78756	AUSTIN	32892	4471	29.4	28.1	27.0	9.2	6.3	41260	51718	51	59	1437	0.1	4.6	33.0	53.9	8.4	200098
78757	AUSTIN	29199	10818	17.3	30.8	36.8	10.8	4.4	51605	61840	75	79	5767	0.4	7.6	57.1	34.4	0.5	153733
78758	AUSTIN	24624	20754	19.7	32.3	35.2	9.6	3.2	47950	57695	68	73	6166	2.6	12.8	74.9	9.4	0.4	117079
78759	AUSTIN	45639	18959	10.5	21.7	35.5	17.7	14.6	71192	88989	92	93	8670	0.7	1.7	26.0	62.5	9.1	224819
78801	UVALDE	14068	7402	42.3	28.1	22.6	4.7	2.3	30009	34310	12	16	5196	46.9	27.4	17.6	7.2	0.9	53432
78827	ASHERTON	10361	556	50.2	34.2	13.0	1.1	1.6	24883	27175	4	6	393	77.6	15.3	5.1	2.0	0.0	24938
78828	BARKSDALE	21594	149	35.6	27.5	27.5	6.0	3.4	36263	42013	33	39	125	44.8	18.4	17.6	10.4	8.8	55909
78829	BATESVILLE	8832	416	59.1	25.2	12.3	3.4	0.0	20559	23533	2	3	294	79.3	10.9	9.9	0.0	0.0	21500
78830	BIG WELLS	7777	288	69.4	25.7	3.8	0.0	1.0	16551	18517	1	1	237	89.5	5.1	3.8	0.8	0.8	23707
78832	BRACKETTVILLE	17765	1358	40.3	31.7	20.7	4.5	2.9	31591	36246	17	21	1026	48.5	25.8	18.7	5.7	1.3	51667
78833	CAMP WOOD	15398	451	48.6	29.7	18.0	2.4	1.3	25859	28551	6	7	353	50.4	23.0	15.3	7.4	4.0	49483
78834	CARRIZO SPRINGS	11268	2508	49.2	29.4	20.0	1.1	0.3	25435	27119	5	7	1733	61.9	24.0	12.0	1.6	0.5	40528
78837	COMSTOCK	15770	250	44.0	31.6	20.8	2.4	1.2	27769	33105	8	11	206	52.4	31.6	11.2	2.4	2.4	47222
78838	CONCAN	18265	52	34.6	30.8	26.9	5.8	1.9	35000	43205	28	33	42	33.3	23.8	23.8	14.3	4.8	76667
78839	CRYSTAL CITY	8363	2529	61.6	25.3	10.4	1.5	1.2	17252	18376	1	2	1651	74.3	17.5	6.7	1.2	0.3	32796
78840	DEL RIO	13989	14716	40.7	29.9	22.1	5.3	2.0	32053	36799	18	22	9712	38.5	32.2	23.1	5.8	0.5	65481
78843	LAUGHLIN A F B	22601	15	0.0	13.3	66.7	20.0	0.0	64300	69085	88	90	0	0.0	0.0	0.0	0.0	0.0	0
78850	D HANIS	18573	363	28.7	34.4	26.7	7.2	3.0	38141	44008	40	47	297	30.6	28.3	21.2	14.1	5.7	75750
78851	DRYDEN	15781	406	47.5	28.1	17.5	5.7	1.2	26994	31334	7	9	300	70.7	18.7	7.7	0.7	2.3	32885
78852	EAGLE PASS	9903	13933	51.9	28.2	14.8	3.6	1.5	23697	26512	4	5	9341	43.7	36.1	17.7	2.3	0.2	56147
78861	HONDO	16394	3922	34.2	31.0	26.5	6.4	1.8	38285	43520	40	48	2975	28.6	27.8	29.5	12.0	2.1	80619
78870	KNIPPA	15519	276	30.1	36.2	26.8	6.2	0.7	35439	42465	29	35	206	51.5	24.3	16.0	2.9	5.3	48750
78872	LA PRYOR	12033	547	54.7	24.9	17.9	1.1	1.5	22197	25412	3	4	459	81.1	12.0	7.0	0.0	0.0	21136
	TEXAS	23284		26.2	27.7	29.5	10.3	6.3	45778	54246				21.6	26.1	33.4	15.6	3.4	93683
	UNITED STATES	25866		24.7	27.1	30.8	10.9	6.5	48124	56710				10.9	15.0	33.7	30.1	10.4	145905

ZIP CODE #	POST OFFICE NAME	FINANCIAL SERVICES: Auto Loan	FINANCIAL SERVICES: Home Loan	FINANCIAL SERVICES: Investments	FINANCIAL SERVICES: Retirement Plans	THE HOME: Home Improvements: Home Repair	THE HOME: Home Improvements: Lawn & Garden	THE HOME: Furnishings: Computers & Hardware	THE HOME: Furnishings: Major Appliances	THE HOME: Furnishings: TV, Radio, Sound Equipment	THE HOME: Furnishings: Furniture	ENTERTAINMENT: Dine out/ Carry out	ENTERTAINMENT: Sports Equipment	ENTERTAINMENT: Fees & Tickets	ENTERTAINMENT: Toys & Games	ENTERTAINMENT: Travel	ENTERTAINMENT: Cable TV	PERSONAL: Apparel & Services	PERSONAL: Auto Repairs	PERSONAL: Health Insurance	PERSONAL: Pets & Supplies
78634	HUTTO	148	160	155	161	158	161	147	149	141	149	177	176	151	181	148	137	174	146	140	172
78635	HYE	122	85	45	81	99	111	84	104	97	83	114	126	72	112	87	102	104	103	124	145
78636	JOHNSON CITY	106	80	50	77	89	100	80	93	89	79	106	110	72	104	81	92	98	92	107	122
78638	KINGSBURY	103	92	70	88	96	103	85	94	90	86	110	112	83	111	87	92	105	92	101	120
78639	KINGSLAND	72	66	62	61	70	84	63	72	68	66	84	71	62	72	67	73	78	70	85	81
78640	KYLE	99	99	88	99	97	98	93	96	90	97	113	111	92	109	91	87	111	95	89	109
78641	LEANDER	122	133	125	136	128	127	122	122	114	126	144	143	124	143	119	108	141	120	108	136
78642	LIBERTY HILL	115	109	90	106	111	116	102	109	103	103	127	127	100	126	102	102	122	107	109	132
78643	LLANO	94	79	63	75	84	100	80	89	87	80	105	95	76	95	82	92	97	88	104	105
78644	LOCKHART	75	70	61	68	70	75	69	73	71	71	88	82	67	85	69	70	85	73	73	82
78645	LEANDER	116	116	113	115	118	125	111	117	110	112	137	134	110	134	113	110	132	115	117	136
78648	LULING	68	58	46	54	59	65	59	64	63	60	77	71	54	73	58	63	74	64	67	74
78650	MC DADE	101	74	40	66	80	91	71	85	81	72	97	100	62	91	71	86	89	84	99	115
78652	MANCHACA	143	178	191	180	174	173	158	156	146	158	184	182	170	194	161	141	184	151	140	173
78653	MANOR	118	116	98	113	115	119	108	114	107	111	133	132	105	129	107	105	129	113	110	133
78654	MARBLE FALLS	103	81	59	76	89	102	81	93	89	81	107	105	74	100	83	94	100	92	108	118
78655	MARTINDALE	83	76	59	73	76	80	72	77	73	74	90	89	68	85	71	72	86	77	77	92
78656	MAXWELL	82	75	58	72	75	79	71	76	72	73	89	88	67	84	70	71	85	76	76	91
78657	MARBLE FALLS	128	119	106	113	123	140	111	123	115	117	143	129	110	125	116	120	135	121	137	143
78659	PAIGE	102	87	63	83	91	98	82	92	87	83	106	109	77	104	83	88	100	91	98	117
78660	PFLUGERVILLE	123	137	130	142	131	127	124	123	114	129	145	144	127	145	121	107	143	120	106	136
78662	RED ROCK	99	88	67	84	92	99	82	91	86	83	105	107	80	106	84	88	100	89	97	115
78663	ROUND MOUNTAIN	131	92	48	87	107	120	91	112	104	89	122	135	77	120	94	109	112	110	133	156
78664	ROUND ROCK	118	127	130	133	122	122	121	119	113	124	144	140	123	142	118	107	142	119	105	131
78666	SAN MARCOS	71	60	66	62	59	64	76	68	74	71	93	84	69	87	69	69	90	74	63	76
78669	SPICEWOOD	147	154	145	154	157	162	140	148	138	140	170	174	143	176	144	137	166	143	145	176
78671	STONEWALL	98	68	36	64	79	89	67	83	78	67	91	100	57	89	70	81	83	82	99	116
78672	TOW	49	47	49	43	49	60	43	51	47	47	58	47	45	49	48	50	54	49	60	55
78675	WILLOW CITY	95	89	85	84	94	110	82	93	87	88	108	91	83	90	89	93	101	91	109	106
78676	WIMBERLEY	116	113	103	110	118	127	105	114	107	106	131	129	104	128	109	109	125	111	121	137
78677	WRIGHTSBORO	52	36	19	34	42	47	36	44	41	35	48	53	30	47	37	43	44	44	53	61
78681	ROUND ROCK	129	147	148	152	141	139	135	133	124	138	158	156	140	160	132	118	157	130	115	146
78701	AUSTIN	106	96	138	102	93	105	121	105	121	115	152	130	117	150	113	116	148	115	101	117
78702	AUSTIN	53	47	45	44	45	49	50	52	52	52	65	56	47	60	48	52	64	53	51	55
78703	AUSTIN	159	175	283	187	168	183	182	169	180	185	229	201	195	240	185	179	228	174	157	187
78704	AUSTIN	78	71	96	77	69	75	84	77	83	83	106	94	82	103	79	79	103	83	71	85
78705	AUSTIN	45	28	35	31	27	33	53	39	52	45	65	55	44	58	43	46	61	48	36	45
78712	AUSTIN	0	0	0	0	0	0	0	0	0	0	0	0	0	0	0	0	0	0	0	0
78717	AUSTIN	151	171	165	179	163	157	154	153	141	161	180	179	159	180	150	132	178	149	130	167
78719	AUSTIN	82	75	59	72	75	79	72	77	73	74	90	89	68	85	71	72	86	77	76	91
78721	AUSTIN	57	52	52	48	50	55	54	55	57	57	71	59	52	65	52	57	70	57	56	60
78722	AUSTIN	72	63	99	71	61	68	80	71	80	78	101	88	78	100	75	77	99	78	66	79
78723	AUSTIN	69	67	74	67	65	69	71	69	72	72	90	80	71	90	69	69	90	72	65	76
78724	AUSTIN	76	71	70	69	70	76	72	73	74	73	92	83	71	89	71	73	89	74	73	84
78725	AUSTIN	102	110	111	110	106	108	105	104	101	107	127	122	106	126	104	97	125	104	96	116
78726	AUSTIN	188	232	250	240	224	225	205	200	186	208	237	231	224	246	208	180	239	193	177	221
78727	AUSTIN	121	124	130	132	119	120	123	120	116	126	148	142	123	144	118	109	145	121	105	132
78728	AUSTIN	104	105	109	112	100	101	105	102	99	108	127	121	104	122	100	92	124	104	88	112
78729	AUSTIN	113	116	123	124	112	113	116	113	109	119	139	134	116	135	111	103	136	114	100	124
78730	AUSTIN	289	382	506	377	371	396	334	331	310	342	393	374	375	411	352	310	398	318	304	360
78731	AUSTIN	144	153	201	159	150	161	164	152	157	160	198	182	167	199	160	152	196	157	140	167
78732	AUSTIN	214	246	241	256	234	228	221	218	202	229	257	255	229	259	216	189	255	212	186	239
78733	AUSTIN	231	293	338	299	284	291	258	252	236	262	300	290	285	312	265	230	303	243	226	278
78734	AUSTIN	152	180	202	183	176	180	167	164	156	168	197	191	176	202	169	152	196	162	150	180
78735	AUSTIN	178	204	258	211	200	211	196	191	186	198	235	222	208	240	199	182	234	190	177	210
78736	AUSTIN	129	148	147	152	142	139	135	134	125	138	158	157	139	161	133	118	156	131	116	147
78737	AUSTIN	154	192	209	196	186	189	170	166	155	172	197	192	186	204	173	151	199	160	149	184
78738	AUSTIN	215	279	346	280	271	284	244	240	225	249	286	274	273	299	255	223	289	231	219	263
78739	AUSTIN	198	247	269	253	239	242	218	213	199	221	253	246	239	263	222	193	255	206	191	236
78741	AUSTIN	53	41	50	45	40	45	58	50	57	54	72	64	52	66	51	52	70	57	46	56
78742	AUSTIN	65	58	58	56	57	63	65	64	68	65	84	73	61	80	62	67	82	67	65	70
78744	AUSTIN	77	70	69	71	68	71	75	74	75	77	95	88	72	92	71	71	94	78	69	82
78745	AUSTIN	84	85	94	88	82	85	87	85	84	88	107	100	86	105	84	80	105	87	77	93
78746	AUSTIN	229	269	354	277	261	278	257	248	244	260	309	288	277	317	262	240	309	247	228	272
78747	AUSTIN	161	154	143	149	159	179	143	158	147	151	183	163	144	160	150	152	173	154	172	180
78748	AUSTIN	111	122	121	127	116	114	114	112	105	117	134	132	116	133	110	99	132	111	96	123
78749	AUSTIN	128	140	149	148	134	133	133	130	124	137	158	153	136	158	129	117	156	129	113	143
78750	AUSTIN	149	168	179	175	163	165	158	155	147	161	187	182	165	188	157	141	186	153	138	171
78751	AUSTIN	72	55	76	62	54	61	81	67	80	75	101	88	73	95	71	74	97	78	63	76
78752	AUSTIN	59	49	52	51	48	51	60	56	61	60	77	67	56	73	54	56	76	61	51	61
78753	AUSTIN	79	76	86	81	73	76	81	77	78	82	99	93	79	95	77	73	97	80	69	86
78754	AUSTIN	98	97	101	102	95	97	98	96	94	100	119	115	97	116	95	90	117	98	87	109
78756	AUSTIN	79	71	101	78	70	77	88	79	87	85	110	98	85	108	83	83	107	86	74	88
78757	AUSTIN	83	89	108	92	87	92	91	88	89	91	112	104	93	112	91	86	110	90	82	96
78758	AUSTIN	85	78	89	84	75	79	86	82	84	88	107	99	83	102	81	79	105	87	74	91
78759	AUSTIN	127	131	166	141	127	133	136	129	132	138	167	155	139	167	133	126	165	133	118	143
78801	UVALDE	66	58	47	54	57	61	58	63	61	62	76	69	54	69	56	60	74	64	62	69
78827	ASHERTON	49	43	36	40	41	44	44	47	46	48	57	50	40	51	42	44	57	48	45	49
78828	BARKSDALE	76	70	66	67	75	88	65	74	69	69	86	73	66	72	71	74	80	72	87	86
78829	BATESVILLE	46	41	34	38	39	41	41	45	43	45	54	48	38	48	39	42	54	46	42	47
78830	BIG WELLS	34	30	25	27	28	30	30	33	31	33	39	35	28	35	29	30	39	33	31	34
78832	BRACKETTVILLE	70	63	57	59	64	72	61	68	64	66	80	69	59	69	63	65	77	68	72	74
78833	CAMP WOOD	64	54	41	49	56	61	53	60	57	55	70	67	48	65	53	58	67	60	63	72
78834	CARRIZO SPRINGS	52	46	38	43	44	47	47	51	49	51	61	54	43	54	45	47	61	52	48	53
78837	COMSTOCK	63	50	34	45	56	63	47	56	53	46	63	66	42	62	50	56	58	55	66	77
78838	CONCAN	80	64	44	58	71	79	60	72	67	60	80	84	54	79	64	71	75	71	84	97
78839	CRYSTAL CITY	41	36	30	33	34	36	36	39	38	40	47	42	33	42	35	36	47	40	37	41
78840	DEL RIO	67	59	51	57	58	60	61	64	62	65	78	71	57	72	58	60	77	66	61	69
78843	LAUGHLIN A F B	107	68	65	78	62	73	101	87	102	94	128	116	86	115	83	93	123	103	80	99
78850	D HANIS	99	69	36	65	80	90	68	84	78	67	92	101	58	90	71	82	84	83	100	117
78851	DRYDEN	61	49	36	46	52	59	51	57	56	51	67	63	46	63	51	57	63	57	63	68
78852	EAGLE PASS	54	47	41	45	45	47	50	52	52	53	65	57	46	60	47	49	65	54	48	55
78861	HONDO	78	63	45	60	66	72	64	71	68	65	83	81	58	78	63	69	79	71	76	85
78870	KNIPPA	73	67	52	64	67	70	63	68	64	65	79	79	60	75	63	63	76	68	67	81
78872	LA PRYOR	59	52	43	48	50	52	53	57	55	57	69	60	48	61	50	53	68	58	53	59
	TEXAS	94	90	91	90	89	95	92	93	92	93	115	107	90	112	90	90	112	94	89	104
	UNITED STATES	100	100	100	100	100	100	100	100	100	100	100	100	100	100	100	100	100	100	100	100

ZIP CODE		POPULATION			2000-2004 ANNUAL RATE		HOUSEHOLDS					FAMILIES		
#	POST OFFICE NAME	COUNTY FIPS CODE	2000	2004	2009	% Rate	State Centile	2000	2004	2009	% Annual Rate 2000-2004	2004 Average HH Size	2000	2004	% Annual Rate 2000-2004
78873	LEAKEY	385	1267	1177	1085	-1.7	0	551	514	476	-1.6	2.24	374	350	-1.6
78877	QUEMADO	323	1192	1214	1315	0.4	23	388	395	427	0.4	3.07	303	309	0.5
78879	RIO FRIO	385	475	441	407	-1.7	0	209	195	180	-1.6	2.21	148	138	-1.6
78880	ROCKSPRINGS	137	1811	1783	1765	-0.4	7	648	640	638	-0.3	2.74	476	472	-0.2
78881	SABINAL	463	2210	2242	2322	0.3	21	810	820	849	0.3	2.72	604	613	0.4
78883	TARPLEY	019	46	49	56	1.5	57	21	22	25	1.1	2.23	16	17	1.4
78884	UTOPIA	463	745	772	805	0.8	37	315	326	341	0.8	2.32	227	236	0.9
78885	VANDERPOOL	019	308	326	367	1.4	53	141	148	165	1.2	2.20	100	105	1.2
78886	YANCEY	325	518	545	597	1.2	48	177	185	202	1.1	2.90	138	145	1.2
78931	BLEIBLERVILLE	015	183	211	242	3.4	86	78	89	101	3.2	2.37	57	65	3.1
78932	CARMINE	149	509	517	529	0.4	22	208	210	213	0.2	2.43	140	141	0.2
78933	CAT SPRING	089	1300	1376	1484	1.4	53	524	551	590	1.2	2.50	396	417	1.2
78934	COLUMBUS	089	6369	6828	7303	1.7	60	2261	2422	2592	1.6	2.52	1532	1645	1.7
78935	ALLEYTON	089	325	337	354	0.9	37	125	129	135	0.7	2.61	93	97	1.0
78938	ELLINGER	149	261	315	353	4.5	93	118	142	158	4.5	2.22	80	97	4.6
78940	FAYETTEVILLE	149	2496	2677	2858	1.7	61	1022	1090	1156	1.5	2.45	728	778	1.6
78941	FLATONIA	149	2385	2539	2667	1.5	57	908	963	1006	1.4	2.58	637	677	1.4
78942	GIDDINGS	287	7766	8089	8727	1.0	40	2600	2687	2885	0.8	2.78	1871	1936	0.8
78944	INDUSTRY	015	321	363	412	2.9	81	131	146	164	2.6	2.49	96	107	2.6
78945	LA GRANGE	149	10138	10275	10561	0.3	21	4006	4021	4102	0.1	2.50	2829	2848	0.2
78946	LEDBETTER	287	856	894	961	1.0	43	370	381	405	0.7	2.35	259	268	0.8
78947	LEXINGTON	287	3932	4875	5873	5.2	95	1513	1850	2204	4.9	2.64	1139	1395	4.9
78948	LINCOLN	287	1589	1656	1790	1.0	41	621	640	685	0.7	2.59	450	465	0.8
78949	MULDOON	149	372	414	445	2.6	76	152	168	179	2.4	2.46	110	121	2.3
78950	NEW ULM	015	2445	2635	2886	1.8	63	989	1057	1148	1.6	2.49	738	792	1.7
78953	ROSANKY	021	773	893	1051	3.5	86	334	383	448	3.3	2.33	248	285	3.3
78954	ROUND TOP	149	958	981	1011	0.6	27	436	443	454	0.4	2.20	289	295	0.5
78956	SCHULENBURG	149	4716	4845	4993	0.6	30	1882	1918	1964	0.5	2.39	1261	1291	0.6
78957	SMITHVILLE	021	8460	9461	10975	2.7	78	3235	3596	4152	2.5	2.59	2250	2509	2.6
78959	WAELDER	177	1490	1596	1716	1.6	60	562	596	636	1.4	2.68	388	413	1.5
78962	WEIMAR	089	4463	4579	4802	0.6	29	1783	1818	1896	0.5	2.48	1245	1273	0.5
78963	WEST POINT	149	480	550	600	3.3	83	177	202	219	3.2	2.72	130	148	3.1
79001	ADRIAN	359	257	267	283	0.9	38	106	111	118	1.1	2.32	82	86	1.1
79005	BOOKER	295	1507	1558	1610	0.8	35	522	540	556	0.8	2.80	389	403	0.8
79007	BORGER	233	15857	15659	15408	-0.3	8	6123	6038	5942	-0.3	2.56	4445	4397	-0.3
79009	BOVINA	369	2996	3090	3248	0.7	34	951	975	1017	0.6	3.17	790	811	0.6
79011	BRISCOE	483	425	410	401	-0.8	2	165	158	154	-1.0	2.59	123	118	-1.0
79014	CANADIAN	211	3351	3489	3719	1.0	40	1280	1345	1451	1.2	2.49	948	999	1.2
79015	CANYON	381	16906	17301	17905	0.5	27	6429	6565	6796	0.5	2.45	4220	4335	0.6
79016	CANYON	381	443	446	453	0.2	16	0	0	0	0.0	0.00	0	0	0.0
79018	CHANNING	205	651	688	721	1.3	51	237	250	262	1.3	2.75	189	199	1.2
79019	CLAUDE	011	2032	2067	2117	0.4	22	754	760	771	0.2	2.63	577	583	0.2
79022	DALHART	111	8054	8197	8431	0.4	23	3071	3090	3133	0.2	2.62	2178	2198	0.2
79027	DIMMITT	069	6363	6142	5917	-0.8	2	2147	2075	2005	-0.8	2.93	1661	1608	-0.8
79029	DUMAS	341	17839	18218	18622	0.5	25	5962	6021	6093	0.2	2.99	4696	4755	0.3
79031	EARTH	279	1453	1425	1434	-0.5	5	521	508	509	-0.6	2.81	395	387	-0.5
79034	FOLLETT	295	880	872	887	-0.2	9	382	377	383	-0.3	2.31	262	259	-0.3
79035	FRIONA	369	4755	4922	5182	0.8	36	1574	1621	1700	0.7	2.99	1232	1272	0.8
79036	FRITCH	233	5147	5052	4943	-0.4	5	2041	2000	1956	-0.5	2.51	1576	1547	-0.4
79039	GROOM	065	800	799	810	0.0	12	316	315	319	-0.1	2.54	241	241	0.0
79040	GRUVER	195	1861	1887	1932	0.3	21	677	685	701	0.3	2.75	529	536	0.3
79041	HALE CENTER	189	3244	3193	3178	-0.4	7	1143	1118	1109	-0.5	2.81	856	840	-0.4
79042	HAPPY	437	846	855	850	0.3	19	347	349	346	0.1	2.45	241	244	0.3
79043	HART	069	1354	1311	1264	-0.8	3	420	407	393	-0.7	3.22	345	335	-0.7
79044	HARTLEY	205	2291	2324	2358	0.3	21	334	345	357	0.8	2.88	273	282	0.8
79045	HEREFORD	117	18515	18498	18550	0.0	12	6163	6145	6158	-0.1	2.97	4821	4818	-0.1
79046	HIGGINS	295	626	629	639	0.1	15	276	276	280	0.0	2.28	178	179	0.1
79052	KRESS	437	1545	1538	1518	-0.1	10	543	538	530	-0.2	2.86	431	428	-0.2
79056	LIPSCOMB	295	44	44	45	0.0	13	25	25	25	0.0	1.76	16	16	0.0
79057	MCLEAN	179	1122	1091	1062	-0.7	3	456	445	436	-0.6	2.22	280	274	-0.5
79058	MASTERSON	375	185	194	202	1.1	45	76	79	81	0.9	2.44	61	63	0.8
79059	MIAMI	393	887	854	854	-0.9	1	362	350	350	-0.8	2.44	275	267	-0.7
79061	MOBEETIE	483	322	305	295	-1.3	1	139	131	127	-1.4	2.33	101	95	-1.4
79062	MORSE	195	177	178	182	0.1	15	64	64	66	0.0	2.78	48	48	0.0
79063	NAZARETH	069	460	445	429	-0.8	2	159	154	149	-0.8	2.89	125	121	-0.8
79064	OLTON	279	2903	2918	2949	0.1	15	973	973	979	0.0	2.93	760	762	0.1
79065	PAMPA	179	21631	21162	20689	-0.5	4	8342	8132	7935	-0.6	2.40	5776	5649	-0.5
79068	PANHANDLE	065	3786	3874	3971	0.5	27	1395	1429	1468	0.6	2.64	1069	1097	0.6
79070	PERRYTON	357	9006	9171	9367	0.4	23	3261	3291	3335	0.2	2.76	2487	2515	0.3
79072	PLAINVIEW	189	28968	29180	29363	0.2	17	9302	9328	9351	0.1	2.88	7041	7078	0.1
79079	SHAMROCK	483	2579	2585	2572	0.1	14	1098	1096	1087	0.0	2.32	727	729	0.1
79080	SKELLYTOWN	065	682	698	714	0.6	27	264	270	276	0.5	2.59	208	213	0.6
79081	SPEARMAN	195	3331	3381	3463	0.4	22	1264	1282	1313	0.3	2.57	912	928	0.4
79082	SPRINGLAKE	279	338	325	326	-0.9	1	137	131	130	-1.1	2.48	112	107	-1.1
79083	STINNETT	233	2853	2745	2664	-0.9	1	1119	1074	1041	-1.0	2.53	848	817	-0.9
79084	STRATFORD	421	2815	2806	2774	-0.1	11	986	968	944	-0.4	2.82	751	739	-0.4
79085	SUMMERFIELD	069	108	105	102	-0.7	3	35	34	33	-0.7	3.09	28	28	0.0
79086	SUNRAY	341	2136	2151	2179	0.2	16	752	751	755	0.0	2.86	584	584	0.0
79087	TEXLINE	111	763	785	806	0.7	31	279	282	284	0.3	2.78	210	212	0.2
79088	TULIA	437	5987	5901	5809	-0.3	7	2035	1992	1949	-0.5	2.64	1482	1455	-0.4
79092	VEGA	359	1636	1692	1787	0.8	35	526	549	588	1.0	2.63	404	422	0.9
79094	WAYSIDE	011	116	117	120	0.2	17	48	48	49	0.0	2.23	36	36	0.0
79095	WELLINGTON	087	2996	3045	3118	0.4	22	1204	1212	1227	0.2	2.47	846	856	0.3
79096	WHEELER	483	1958	1891	1850	-0.8	2	750	719	702	-1.0	2.51	535	515	-0.9
79097	WHITE DEER	065	1220	1215	1232	-0.1	10	483	480	487	-0.2	2.53	358	356	-0.1
79098	WILDORADO	359	338	347	366	0.6	29	120	124	131	0.8	2.72	93	97	0.8
79101	AMARILLO	375	2852	2901	3055	0.4	22	1176	1193	1258	0.3	2.07	537	543	0.3
79102	AMARILLO	375	9670	10263	11045	1.4	55	4104	4292	4563	1.1	2.36	2376	2496	1.2
79103	AMARILLO	381	10022	10526	11195	1.2	47	3475	3631	3841	1.0	2.90	2731	2847	1.0
79104	AMARILLO	375	7560	8240	9017	2.1	68	2442	2636	2858	1.8	3.11	1822	1968	1.8
79106	AMARILLO	375	28642	29220	30678	0.5	24	12151	12316	12850	0.3	2.29	7269	7361	0.3
79107	AMARILLO	375	31908	34164	37285	1.6	60	10488	11157	12081	1.5	3.05	7810	8282	1.4
79108	AMARILLO	375	16097	17069	18185	1.4	54	4063	4314	4624	1.4	2.85	3138	3334	1.4
79109	AMARILLO	381	43887	45646	48127	0.9	39	19109	19830	20873	0.9	2.29	12161	12629	0.9
79110	AMARILLO	381	17946	18515	19650	0.7	34	6791	6979	7391	0.6	2.64	5014	5171	0.7
	TEXAS					2.2					2.0	2.77			2.1
	UNITED STATES					1.2					1.3	2.58			1.1

ZIP CODE #	POST OFFICE NAME	RACE (%) White 2000	White 2004	Black 2000	Black 2004	Asian/Pacific 2000	Asian/Pacific 2004	% Hispanic Origin 2000	% Hispanic Origin 2004	2004 AGE DISTRIBUTION (%) 0-4	5-9	10-14	15-19	20-24	25-44	45-64	65-84	85+	18+	MEDIAN AGE 2004	% 2004 Males	% 2004 Females
78873	LEAKEY	93.0	91.8	0.1	0.1	0.2	0.3	16.3	19.1	4.5	4.8	6.4	6.1	5.4	19.5	29.6	20.8	2.9	80.5	47.4	48.3	51.7
78877	QUEMADO	70.0	68.5	0.5	0.5	0.0	0.1	75.9	79.1	7.4	8.1	8.6	8.2	6.3	22.4	25.3	12.7	1.1	70.8	36.8	51.7	48.4
78879	RIO FRIO	91.4	90.3	0.0	0.0	0.2	0.2	14.7	17.5	3.4	3.9	5.2	5.4	4.1	18.4	34.0	23.1	2.5	83.9	51.4	49.9	50.1
78880	ROCKSPRINGS	81.1	80.9	0.9	1.0	0.2	0.2	52.2	53.5	6.3	7.4	9.3	7.8	6.4	23.1	24.8	13.6	1.4	71.8	37.9	50.8	49.2
78881	SABINAL	82.4	80.8	0.1	0.0	0.1	0.1	53.0	57.7	6.8	6.9	8.7	7.4	6.0	24.8	23.6	14.2	1.7	72.9	37.7	50.0	50.0
78883	TARPLEY	95.7	95.9	0.0	0.0	0.0	0.0	8.7	12.2	8.2	8.2	8.2	8.2	4.1	22.5	26.5	14.3	0.0	75.5	39.2	51.0	49.0
78884	UTOPIA	91.7	90.2	0.0	0.0	0.1	0.1	17.9	21.5	4.5	5.3	7.1	5.4	3.8	20.1	30.4	20.7	2.6	79.9	48.0	51.9	48.1
78885	VANDERPOOL	95.8	94.8	0.3	0.3	0.3	0.3	8.1	9.2	4.3	4.9	5.2	6.1	3.1	18.1	35.3	20.6	2.5	81.6	50.4	50.0	50.0
78886	YANCEY	85.3	83.7	0.8	0.9	0.8	0.9	32.2	36.3	5.7	5.9	7.3	6.6	4.8	24.4	27.5	15.2	2.6	76.0	41.7	46.6	53.4
78931	BLEIBLERVILLE	93.4	92.9	2.7	2.8	0.0	0.0	5.5	6.2	5.7	5.7	5.7	5.7	5.2	23.2	29.9	15.6	3.3	79.2	44.2	49.8	50.2
78932	CARMINE	93.1	92.1	4.1	4.5	0.0	0.0	4.3	5.2	4.5	4.6	5.6	5.8	5.4	18.0	31.5	20.9	3.7	81.8	48.9	48.6	51.5
78933	CAT SPRING	86.5	85.0	7.4	7.8	0.2	0.2	10.0	11.8	6.2	6.3	7.1	6.9	4.7	23.8	29.3	14.0	1.7	75.9	41.7	50.1	49.9
78934	COLUMBUS	70.5	68.3	16.0	16.3	0.3	0.4	17.7	20.5	6.5	6.2	6.5	7.1	9.0	23.8	22.1	14.8	4.0	77.2	37.5	48.1	51.9
78935	ALLEYTON	91.7	90.2	2.2	2.7	0.0	0.3	6.8	8.3	5.0	5.6	7.1	7.1	2.7	23.4	32.3	15.4	1.2	77.2	44.3	51.0	49.0
78938	ELLINGER	93.5	93.0	1.2	1.3	0.0	0.3	6.1	7.6	4.4	5.1	5.7	5.7	5.4	21.9	31.4	16.8	3.5	81.9	46.1	49.8	50.2
78940	FAYETTEVILLE	92.6	91.6	2.8	3.0	0.3	0.3	5.4	6.6	4.6	5.5	6.9	5.8	5.4	22.7	28.4	17.5	3.2	79.6	44.4	50.6	49.4
78941	FLATONIA	80.0	78.1	5.6	5.6	0.2	0.2	27.1	30.3	6.5	6.5	7.1	6.0	6.3	22.9	25.7	15.4	3.5	76.0	41.4	50.3	49.7
78942	GIDDINGS	71.3	68.5	11.2	11.2	0.5	0.6	27.7	32.1	8.0	7.2	7.2	10.6	8.2	24.6	20.2	11.2	2.7	71.3	32.3	51.7	48.3
78944	INDUSTRY	91.6	90.4	4.4	4.7	0.0	0.3	6.2	7.2	5.8	6.3	6.1	5.5	5.2	24.0	28.9	14.9	3.3	78.5	43.1	50.1	49.9
78945	LA GRANGE	82.9	81.1	7.7	8.1	0.4	0.4	13.0	15.2	5.9	6.0	6.6	6.3	6.3	23.4	25.5	16.3	3.7	77.7	42.1	48.5	51.5
78946	LEDBETTER	72.7	70.1	20.2	21.4	0.1	0.2	10.2	12.4	5.5	5.7	7.3	7.2	6.0	22.7	27.2	16.1	2.4	77.1	42.0	49.2	50.8
78947	LEXINGTON	90.2	88.4	4.3	5.1	0.1	0.1	8.7	10.4	7.0	6.9	7.1	7.6	6.4	25.8	26.1	11.8	1.4	74.4	38.4	49.4	50.6
78948	LINCOLN	77.3	74.9	19.8	21.6	0.0	0.0	6.4	8.0	6.0	6.2	7.1	7.3	5.4	24.1	27.2	14.9	1.8	76.2	40.9	48.8	51.2
78949	MULDOON	88.2	86.5	3.0	3.1	0.3	0.5	13.2	15.5	5.1	5.6	7.3	5.8	4.6	20.5	31.2	17.2	2.9	78.5	45.7	50.5	49.5
78950	NEW ULM	90.4	89.2	4.7	5.0	0.2	0.2	6.7	8.2	5.1	5.7	6.7	5.9	4.7	23.2	30.2	16.1	2.4	78.8	44.1	51.2	48.8
78953	ROSANKY	86.9	85.7	6.3	6.6	0.3	0.5	10.1	12.1	6.3	6.6	6.9	6.4	5.3	26.1	28.8	12.4	1.2	76.0	40.4	50.3	49.7
78954	ROUND TOP	92.7	91.9	3.7	3.9	0.2	0.2	4.8	5.9	4.2	4.5	5.7	5.7	5.1	18.4	31.5	21.3	3.7	82.2	49.1	48.3	51.7
78956	SCHULENBURG	83.4	81.8	9.9	10.3	0.2	0.3	11.0	12.9	5.4	5.8	6.5	5.7	4.9	21.2	26.2	18.2	6.2	78.7	45.4	47.6	52.4
78957	SMITHVILLE	84.0	82.6	9.2	9.5	0.3	0.4	12.9	15.2	6.8	7.0	7.5	6.8	5.7	25.8	25.0	13.3	2.1	74.3	38.9	49.0	51.0
78959	WAELDER	58.1	57.0	18.1	17.3	0.2	0.2	48.8	52.6	6.9	6.8	7.1	6.8	6.9	24.1	24.7	14.7	2.1	75.2	39.1	50.8	49.2
78962	WEIMAR	79.4	77.6	12.3	12.7	0.4	0.5	12.8	15.2	5.6	5.9	6.7	7.0	5.3	20.8	27.6	17.8	3.3	77.5	44.1	48.3	51.7
78963	WEST POINT	87.5	86.6	6.3	6.6	0.0	0.0	12.3	14.4	5.8	6.2	7.1	6.9	5.6	26.6	26.0	13.5	2.4	76.9	40.8	49.6	50.4
79001	ADRIAN	87.2	86.9	1.6	1.5	0.8	0.8	14.8	15.0	7.1	7.9	7.5	6.0	5.2	28.1	26.6	10.9	0.8	73.0	37.5	49.1	50.9
79005	BOOKER	73.9	73.4	0.5	0.5	0.1	0.1	35.4	36.1	7.7	8.2	8.3	7.1	8.3	26.4	19.0	12.5	2.6	71.0	33.9	49.0	51.0
79007	BORGER	83.3	81.5	3.4	3.5	0.5	0.5	19.2	22.1	7.6	7.2	7.2	7.0	8.2	23.7	23.9	13.2	2.1	73.9	36.0	48.9	51.1
79009	BOVINA	61.5	58.6	1.0	0.9	0.2	0.2	55.1	59.3	9.4	9.2	10.1	8.3	6.8	25.7	20.5	8.7	1.2	66.3	30.3	50.7	49.4
79011	BRISCOE	96.7	96.6	0.0	0.0	0.2	0.2	3.8	3.9	7.3	7.6	7.6	5.9	6.6	23.4	28.1	11.5	2.2	74.4	39.1	50.2	49.8
79014	CANADIAN	87.7	86.0	1.6	1.6	0.3	0.3	15.6	18.0	5.8	5.9	7.0	9.1	6.2	22.8	28.6	12.5	2.2	74.7	40.1	50.6	49.4
79015	CANYON	90.0	88.6	1.4	1.5	1.6	1.8	9.5	11.2	6.7	6.4	6.2	10.3	13.9	25.7	20.3	9.0	1.6	76.7	29.1	49.2	50.8
79016	CANYON	81.0	78.5	4.7	4.9	4.5	5.2	14.0	16.6	4.7	3.4	3.1	22.2	30.5	19.7	10.1	5.4	0.9	85.9	22.7	47.8	52.2
79018	CHANNING	94.2	93.2	0.8	0.9	0.2	0.2	7.4	8.7	8.0	7.9	8.1	7.7	5.7	26.6	24.6	10.3	1.2	70.5	35.6	50.6	49.4
79019	CLAUDE	95.5	95.4	0.3	0.3	0.0	0.0	5.3	5.5	5.5	6.5	6.4	6.9	5.4	23.2	27.3	15.4	3.4	76.9	42.2	48.7	51.3
79022	DALHART	85.8	84.1	1.4	1.4	0.3	0.4	22.2	25.2	8.3	7.9	8.2	7.1	6.3	27.3	22.3	10.6	1.9	70.9	34.1	49.6	50.4
79027	DIMMITT	77.4	75.6	2.3	2.2	0.0	0.0	50.1	54.5	8.7	8.1	8.9	8.1	7.4	23.0	22.8	11.5	1.5	69.0	33.0	49.8	50.2
79029	DUMAS	62.7	59.6	0.7	0.7	1.0	1.0	49.2	53.5	9.8	8.8	9.0	8.1	8.0	27.2	19.0	9.0	1.3	67.4	30.0	50.4	49.6
79031	EARTH	76.6	74.5	2.3	2.2	0.0	0.0	46.3	51.1	7.9	7.8	7.8	8.1	7.1	23.6	23.4	13.0	1.4	71.4	35.0	48.4	51.7
79034	FOLLETT	91.0	90.9	0.6	0.6	0.0	0.0	8.9	8.9	5.7	6.1	7.0	6.3	5.2	20.3	30.1	16.2	3.2	77.2	44.7	49.3	50.7
79035	FRIONA	63.7	60.7	1.2	1.2	0.4	0.4	53.7	58.3	9.1	8.5	8.6	8.5	7.3	25.1	20.8	9.9	2.2	68.5	31.6	49.7	50.3
79036	FRITCH	95.6	95.0	0.5	0.5	0.2	0.2	4.7	5.7	5.9	6.4	7.3	6.7	6.3	23.0	29.3	13.7	1.4	76.2	41.3	49.6	50.4
79039	GROOM	95.5	95.4	0.0	0.0	0.1	0.1	5.8	6.0	5.4	5.8	8.0	6.0	6.0	24.0	26.2	16.8	1.9	77.2	41.2	51.3	48.7
79040	GRUVER	77.4	77.0	0.0	0.0	0.1	0.1	32.5	33.4	7.1	7.3	8.9	6.9	6.0	26.4	24.2	11.9	1.4	72.4	36.7	50.6	49.4
79041	HALE CENTER	80.3	80.0	4.0	4.0	0.0	0.0	50.1	51.6	8.6	7.7	8.6	7.9	6.5	25.0	20.4	12.5	2.8	70.2	34.4	49.6	50.4
79042	HAPPY	89.4	89.2	0.4	0.4	0.0	0.0	16.3	17.0	6.4	6.4	6.2	6.4	6.0	25.6	26.4	14.4	2.1	77.1	39.5	48.4	51.6
79043	HART	60.2	58.0	3.2	3.0	0.1	0.1	70.2	74.5	10.1	9.9	9.2	8.2	7.9	24.0	20.6	9.5	0.7	65.8	28.8	51.3	48.7
79044	HARTLEY	61.2	57.5	19.1	19.8	0.1	0.2	22.9	26.3	3.5	3.6	3.2	3.1	3.2	47.6	31.3	4.1	0.3	87.7	40.3	79.6	20.4
79045	HEREFORD	72.2	72.0	1.5	1.5	0.4	0.4	57.5	58.5	9.2	8.9	9.3	7.9	7.3	25.2	20.3	10.4	1.6	67.7	30.9	49.0	51.0
79046	HIGGINS	92.3	92.4	0.6	0.6	0.0	0.0	3.2	3.3	4.5	4.8	4.9	5.3	5.6	18.1	32.1	21.0	3.8	81.4	48.8	48.7	51.4
79052	KRESS	69.4	68.8	3.2	3.2	0.5	0.5	43.5	44.7	7.7	7.7	7.9	7.0	6.6	25.9	22.6	13.1	1.4	72.4	35.7	51.0	49.0
79056	LIPSCOMB	93.2	93.2	0.0	0.0	0.0	0.0	4.6	2.3	4.6	4.6	4.6	4.6	4.6	18.2	34.1	20.5	4.6	86.4	50.0	50.0	50.0
79057	MCLEAN	96.1	95.3	0.3	0.3	0.2	0.2	3.7	4.8	6.1	6.1	6.1	4.3	5.1	18.5	23.6	22.3	7.8	78.9	48.0	46.8	53.3
79058	MASTERSON	86.0	84.0	0.5	0.5	0.5	0.5	17.3	20.6	6.2	6.7	7.2	7.2	6.7	27.8	26.3	11.3	0.5	74.7	38.1	50.5	49.5
79059	MIAMI	96.5	96.4	0.3	0.4	0.1	0.1	3.2	3.3	4.9	5.0	9.5	7.1	2.7	23.2	33.4	12.5	1.6	75.5	43.4	50.0	50.0
79061	MOBEETIE	95.0	94.8	0.0	0.0	0.3	0.3	8.7	9.2	3.9	4.9	7.2	5.9	4.6	20.0	33.1	18.4	2.0	81.0	47.2	49.8	50.2
79062	MORSE	89.8	89.9	0.0	0.0	1.1	1.1	23.7	24.2	5.6	5.6	7.3	6.7	5.1	24.2	29.8	14.6	1.1	77.5	42.5	50.6	49.4
79063	NAZARETH	91.3	89.4	0.4	0.5	0.0	0.0	17.6	21.4	6.5	7.6	8.8	9.7	4.3	27.2	23.4	11.9	0.7	70.1	36.0	52.4	47.6
79064	OLTON	70.8	68.8	1.9	1.9	0.1	0.1	55.9	60.2	8.6	8.3	8.2	8.0	7.0	22.4	20.7	13.9	3.0	69.3	34.3	50.0	50.0
79065	PAMPA	81.4	79.5	6.1	6.4	0.4	0.5	13.5	15.6	6.0	5.9	6.6	6.7	7.2	26.1	24.0	14.9	2.7	77.7	39.3	51.4	48.6
79068	PANHANDLE	92.7	92.6	0.9	0.9	0.2	0.2	8.2	8.5	6.8	6.6	8.1	7.9	5.8	23.4	25.7	13.3	2.5	73.2	40.0	48.5	51.6
79070	PERRYTON	86.2	84.6	0.1	0.1	0.4	0.5	31.8	35.7	8.4	8.0	8.0	7.4	6.8	27.5	22.6	9.9	1.4	70.8	33.7	50.3	49.7
79072	PLAINVIEW	64.1	63.8	6.6	6.5	0.4	0.4	48.1	49.0	8.8	7.9	7.8	8.4	9.1	27.0	19.0	10.2	1.7	70.9	30.8	51.0	49.0
79079	SHAMROCK	86.2	86.0	4.7	4.7	1.1	1.1	12.0	12.4	5.9	5.8	6.4	6.8	5.7	19.8	26.5	19.7	3.6	78.0	44.8	47.2	52.8
79080	SKELLYTOWN	93.8	93.8	0.4	0.4	0.2	0.1	5.6	5.9	5.3	5.6	6.0	6.7	7.6	20.1	31.1	15.6	2.0	78.8	44.0	48.4	51.6
79081	SPEARMAN	80.7	80.3	0.1	0.1	0.3	0.3	31.3	32.2	7.1	7.3	7.9	6.5	6.1	24.6	23.9	13.9	2.6	73.3	38.1	48.5	51.5
79082	SPRINGLAKE	83.7	81.5	0.9	0.9	0.0	0.0	28.7	33.5	7.1	7.4	6.5	4.3	6.2	25.2	26.2	16.0	1.2	76.3	39.9	50.8	49.2
79083	STINNETT	91.9	90.7	0.2	0.3	0.1	0.2	7.5	9.1	5.9	5.9	7.2	7.4	6.8	24.4	27.3	13.6	1.4	76.2	40.1	50.5	49.5
79084	STRATFORD	82.6	82.2	0.5	0.5	0.0	0.0	28.0	28.8	7.1	7.4	9.0	7.3	5.6	26.3	23.8	11.5	2.0	71.6	36.1	51.0	49.0
79085	SUMMERFIELD	78.7	77.1	0.0	0.0	0.0	0.0	52.8	59.1	7.6	7.6	9.5	8.6	7.6	26.7	21.9	9.5	1.0	68.6	33.8	51.4	48.6
79086	SUNRAY	72.5	68.8	0.9	1.0	0.2	0.2	34.9	40.0	8.0	8.5	9.3	8.1	6.7	27.5	21.9	9.0	1.0	68.8	32.6	51.0	49.1
79087	TEXLINE	92.3	91.2	0.0	0.0	0.0	0.0	21.8	24.7	8.9	9.3	8.7	5.6	5.9	26.8	23.8	9.9	1.2	69.6	35.5	49.3	50.7
79088	TULIA	69.9	69.3	7.3	7.4	0.1	0.1	35.8	36.7	7.8	7.4	7.0	7.9	8.5	25.6	20.1	13.6	2.2	73.2	33.7	53.1	46.9
79092	VEGA	91.9	91.7	2.0	2.0	0.2	0.2	9.9	10.3	6.0	7.5	12.8	13.1	4.1	20.9	24.2	10.2	1.2	63.7	32.1	53.3	46.8
79094	WAYSIDE	94.8	94.9	0.0	0.0	0.0	0.0	6.9	6.8	6.0	6.0	6.0	6.8	5.1	23.9	24.8	16.2	5.1	76.9	42.5	50.4	49.6
79095	WELLINGTON	79.0	78.7	5.7	5.7	0.2	0.2	21.2	21.8	6.3	6.5	7.4	7.6	5.8	21.6	23.8	17.4	3.6	75.1	41.3	48.7	51.3
79096	WHEELER	86.9	86.6	1.3	1.3	0.2	0.2	15.9	16.5	6.8	6.7	6.6	6.2	5.9	22.2	26.7	14.4	4.5	75.9	41.8	48.4	51.6
79097	WHITE DEER	96.1	95.9	0.1	0.1	0.0	0.0	5.0	5.3	6.2	6.5	7.6	7.0	5.6	25.8	25.8	13.7	1.7	75.5	40.0	48.6	51.4
79098	WILDORADO	87.9	87.3	1.5	1.4	0.6	0.6	15.1	15.6	8.1	7.8	7.2	6.3	5.5	28.0	25.7	10.7	0.9	72.3	36.5	49.9	50.1
79101	AMARILLO	74.6	72.0	7.3	7.6	0.7	0.9	23.4	26.7	7.9	6.1	5.0	6.3	9.2	28.6	20.5	9.2	7.2	78.2	35.7	49.2	50.8
79102	AMARILLO	77.4	74.8	3.6	3.8	0.4	0.5	31.4	35.6	8.6	7.4	6.8	6.5	8.0	28.1	20.6	10.8	3.1	73.4	33.5	48.0	52.1
79103	AMARILLO	76.2	73.6	1.9	1.9	0.2	0.2	41.7	46.1	9.0	8.6	8.3	7.8	7.2	27.4	21.2	10.0	0.6	69.3	31.8	47.9	52.1
79104	AMARILLO	57.6	54.6	2.1	2.1	1.3	1.6	61.4	66.2	10.9	9.5	8.9	8.3	8.2	28.2	18.0	6.9	1.1	65.5	27.7	50.0	50.0
79106	AMARILLO	84.0	82.0	4.7	5.0	0.9	1.1	15.2	17.6	7.2	6.4	6.4	6.1	8.0	26.8	21.1	14.6	3.3	76.6	36.6	47.0	53.1
79107	AMARILLO	45.3	42.9	20.4	19.9	7.1	7.5	38.8	43.0	10.3	9.6	9.8	8.2	7.6	27.3	18.2	8.1	0.8	65.3	28.1	48.6	51.4
79108	AMARILLO	74.1	71.8	13.4	13.7	0.5	0.6	14.4	16.7	5.0	5.0	5.5	7.9	8.2	36.4	23.7	7.6	0.7	81.3	35.9	62.5	37.5
79109	AMARILLO	90.8	89.5	1.9	2.0	1.0	1.1	9.2	10.8	6.5	6.2	6.4	6.8	8.0	26.7	25.2	12.5	1.7	76.9	37.4	47.9	52.1
79110	AMARILLO	87.9	86.5	1.8	1.9	0.6	0.6	14.2	16.3	8.5	8.1	8.1	6.9	6.4	31.0	21.5	8.7	0.8	71.1	32.7	48.9	51.2
	TEXAS	71.0	69.5	11.5	11.4	2.8	3.1	32.0	34.6	7.9	7.5	7.7	7.5	8.1	29.6	21.9	8.7	1.2	72.6	32.9	49.7	50.3
	UNITED STATES	75.1	73.6	12.3	12.5	3.8	4.2	12.5	14.1	6.9	6.7	7.2	7.0	7.3	28.6	23.8	10.8	1.7	75.1	36.0	49.1	50.9

ZIP CODE #	POST OFFICE NAME	2004 Per Capita Income	2004 HH Income Base	2004 HOUSEHOLD INCOME DISTRIBUTION (%) Less than $25,000	$25,000 to $49,999	$50,000 to $99,999	$100,000 to $149,999	$150,000 or More	MEDIAN HOUSEHOLD INCOME 2004	2009	2004 National Centile	2004 State Centile	2004 Home Value Base	2004 HOME VALUE DISTRIBUTION (%) Less than $50,000	$50,000 to $89,999	$90,000 to $174,999	$175,000 to $399,999	$400,000 or More	2004 Median Home Value
78873	LEAKEY	17397	514	43.6	30.9	20.8	3.5	1.2	29378	32383	11	14	400	26.3	28.0	26.3	13.0	6.5	81053
78877	QUEMADO	9652	395	60.3	19.0	18.0	2.8	0.0	18177	20763	1	2	297	47.8	36.4	9.1	6.7	0.0	58125
78879	RIO FRIO	19905	195	36.4	32.3	25.6	4.1	1.5	33892	37819	24	29	157	19.8	25.5	31.9	14.0	8.9	97500
78880	ROCKSPRINGS	13500	640	47.2	28.0	20.2	3.3	1.4	26902	30803	7	9	475	51.6	23.2	13.5	6.5	5.3	48256
78881	SABINAL	15423	820	43.2	31.6	18.4	4.9	2.0	30934	35969	15	19	656	57.2	24.4	13.6	3.7	1.2	43380
78883	TARPLEY	26327	22	18.2	27.3	40.9	13.6	0.0	52835	57172	77	81	18	0.0	22.2	33.3	44.4	0.0	162500
78884	UTOPIA	20470	326	35.3	30.4	27.9	3.7	2.8	35563	42840	30	36	265	29.1	24.5	26.8	15.9	3.8	83214
78885	VANDERPOOL	29065	148	27.0	29.1	31.1	9.5	3.4	44219	52440	59	67	121	19.0	16.5	33.9	23.1	7.4	115972
78886	YANCEY	21302	185	24.9	29.7	31.4	8.7	5.4	46812	54072	66	71	155	21.9	20.7	40.0	15.5	1.9	102365
78931	BLEIBLERVILLE	23077	89	34.8	28.1	29.2	5.6	2.3	40313	48392	47	55	74	17.6	32.4	25.7	13.5	10.8	90000
78932	CARMINE	29613	210	27.1	29.5	30.5	7.1	5.7	45296	52570	62	69	179	15.1	20.7	32.4	22.9	8.9	116477
78933	CAT SPRING	23823	551	23.4	29.0	35.0	7.6	4.9	47818	54996	68	73	450	17.6	23.1	28.7	25.3	5.3	110294
78934	COLUMBUS	19563	2422	36.5	24.1	29.2	6.6	3.7	38570	45537	41	49	1669	30.9	24.7	29.7	13.1	1.7	81190
78935	ALLEYTON	25346	129	17.1	27.9	41.1	8.5	5.4	54958	62888	80	83	107	16.8	15.9	29.9	31.8	5.6	141071
78938	ELLINGER	19268	142	40.9	29.6	21.8	4.9	2.8	31513	36006	16	21	118	18.6	31.4	29.7	15.3	5.1	90000
78940	FAYETTEVILLE	22062	1090	33.7	28.4	28.3	6.0	3.8	39819	46526	45	54	909	23.2	25.3	30.5	16.8	4.2	93000
78941	FLATONIA	17346	963	37.7	30.7	23.2	6.8	1.7	35085	40818	28	33	770	32.6	25.1	27.0	11.7	3.6	76140
78942	GIDDINGS	18659	2687	30.6	33.0	26.8	6.5	3.1	38819	43349	42	50	1942	32.1	25.4	30.3	11.0	1.2	78182
78944	INDUSTRY	21994	146	32.2	28.1	30.8	6.2	2.7	41232	47373	51	58	120	15.0	30.8	28.3	15.0	10.8	101471
78945	LA GRANGE	21372	4021	30.4	27.3	30.6	8.1	3.6	41911	48509	53	61	3017	19.9	27.9	32.7	15.7	3.9	93994
78946	LEDBETTER	20220	381	40.4	28.6	24.4	4.5	2.1	33050	38569	21	26	310	35.8	22.3	24.8	13.2	3.9	74500
78947	LEXINGTON	23191	1850	23.4	31.8	33.1	7.3	4.4	45968	51976	64	70	1549	25.5	22.2	35.6	14.5	2.2	93480
78948	LINCOLN	20159	640	32.0	34.2	26.4	5.6	1.7	36506	41702	34	40	555	29.6	19.8	38.0	11.2	1.4	91129
78949	MULDOON	19256	168	35.1	28.0	27.4	9.5	0.0	39218	45865	43	52	143	20.3	21.7	35.7	15.4	7.0	106618
78950	NEW ULM	25880	1057	25.6	26.7	34.0	8.8	4.9	47472	54694	67	72	883	18.4	19.9	29.9	23.7	8.2	117876
78953	ROSANKY	23823	383	26.4	30.3	30.6	9.4	3.4	44443	50928	60	67	321	19.3	21.2	36.5	17.8	5.3	106920
78954	ROUND TOP	30491	443	31.4	29.4	27.5	6.6	5.2	41446	49055	51	60	377	18.3	22.8	30.8	20.4	7.7	106389
78956	SCHULENBURG	24031	1918	34.9	30.6	25.7	4.9	4.0	36037	41776	32	38	1433	22.7	32.8	31.1	11.8	1.7	81649
78957	SMITHVILLE	19576	3596	32.5	28.1	28.1	8.2	3.2	41483	47942	51	60	2715	24.0	24.2	37.3	13.0	1.6	93299
78959	WAELDER	16167	596	46.1	29.5	18.3	3.0	3.0	27290	31853	8	10	451	58.1	14.4	18.9	6.2	2.4	40395
78962	WEIMAR	20944	1818	34.8	27.3	27.3	6.6	4.1	37645	44340	38	45	1473	27.4	33.3	24.4	12.5	2.5	76893
78963	WEST POINT	20460	202	12.9	33.2	46.0	7.4	0.5	51495	58217	75	79	170	20.6	28.2	38.2	11.2	1.8	91111
79001	ADRIAN	20659	111	32.4	31.5	24.3	7.2	4.5	36139	38441	32	38	72	41.7	27.8	22.2	4.2	4.2	66667
79005	BOOKER	15831	540	34.6	31.1	27.8	5.2	1.3	36362	42266	33	39	395	50.1	31.4	17.0	1.5	0.0	49878
79007	BORGER	19634	6038	28.4	32.1	30.2	6.9	2.4	40242	45575	47	55	4420	50.3	25.1	18.2	5.8	0.7	49794
79009	BOVINA	14341	975	35.7	38.1	18.9	5.0	2.4	32178	36945	18	23	669	52.3	24.7	15.0	7.5	0.6	47847
79011	BRISCOE	17439	158	33.5	35.4	24.1	1.9	5.1	34611	34652	26	31	114	49.1	19.3	20.2	7.0	4.4	51667
79014	CANADIAN	19856	1345	29.4	31.8	30.3	6.2	2.3	39834	45742	45	54	1055	34.7	31.8	23.8	7.7	2.1	68407
79015	CANYON	21578	6565	28.9	29.0	30.0	8.0	4.0	41495	48397	51	60	3810	15.8	27.5	40.9	13.8	2.1	99663
79016	CANYON	4131	0	0.0	0.0	0.0	0.0	0.0	0	0	0	0	0	0.0	0.0	0.0	0.0	0.0	0
79018	CHANNING	18584	250	22.4	35.6	33.2	6.8	2.0	44502	50568	60	67	168	43.5	23.2	25.6	6.0	1.8	57857
79019	CLAUDE	19903	760	27.1	31.1	31.5	8.4	2.0	43019	49027	56	64	608	30.8	25.8	31.6	10.4	1.5	78462
79022	DALHART	19350	3090	31.8	31.3	27.4	5.2	4.3	37015	42432	35	42	2216	29.9	34.3	26.9	8.4	0.5	70222
79027	DIMMITT	16797	2075	36.8	33.1	20.3	6.9	2.9	34652	39876	26	31	1470	39.1	32.3	20.7	7.1	0.8	62000
79029	DUMAS	16904	6021	30.6	33.4	28.7	5.0	2.4	38673	43421	42	50	4121	36.4	29.9	28.7	4.8	0.2	65159
79031	EARTH	17181	508	41.7	31.9	18.9	3.5	3.9	30220	33716	13	16	385	62.1	21.8	14.6	1.6	0.0	33906
79034	FOLLETT	20781	377	30.8	32.6	26.8	6.9	2.9	37059	43524	36	42	294	50.0	27.2	17.4	5.1	0.3	50000
79035	FRIONA	17045	1621	33.5	31.1	26.3	4.6	4.6	36558	41555	34	40	1158	38.3	31.2	25.1	4.2	1.3	62184
79036	FRITCH	20934	2000	25.5	32.9	32.1	8.1	1.5	44537	51018	60	67	1699	43.1	32.9	20.5	3.2	0.4	56912
79039	GROOM	19759	315	28.3	31.4	34.6	4.4	1.3	40647	45399	48	57	259	37.5	33.6	25.1	3.1	0.8	69792
79040	GRUVER	21855	685	28.5	35.3	26.7	5.4	4.1	39236	44348	44	52	520	37.1	23.5	31.2	6.7	1.5	75000
79041	HALE CENTER	16806	1118	39.4	30.8	22.5	4.0	3.3	32615	37020	20	24	765	52.3	24.1	18.6	5.1	0.0	47892
79042	HAPPY	17046	349	30.1	42.4	22.1	4.9	0.6	33119	38844	21	26	273	57.5	20.5	18.0	4.0	0.0	42115
79043	HART	12369	407	35.4	38.8	22.1	2.7	1.0	32502	36864	19	24	294	57.8	23.5	17.0	1.7	0.0	39677
79044	HARTLEY	16906	345	17.4	33.0	33.6	10.7	5.2	49517	54578	71	76	242	30.6	26.9	19.8	21.9	0.8	77143
79045	HEREFORD	15108	6145	37.0	34.3	22.0	4.3	2.3	32814	36743	20	25	4227	44.1	29.9	21.7	3.4	1.0	56698
79046	HIGGINS	21613	276	38.0	28.3	23.6	5.1	5.1	33370	38088	22	27	218	56.4	20.2	18.8	3.2	1.4	40000
79052	KRESS	17552	538	28.1	39.2	25.1	5.0	2.6	37514	42941	38	45	406	51.5	25.1	16.5	5.4	1.5	48636
79056	LIPSCOMB	27961	25	44.0	24.0	20.0	8.0	4.0	31106	41122	15	19	20	60.0	20.0	20.0	0.0	0.0	35000
79057	MCLEAN	17287	445	42.5	28.8	23.8	4.3	0.7	30424	34565	13	17	341	67.2	19.1	9.7	3.5	0.6	35100
79058	MASTERSON	25853	79	22.8	29.1	35.4	7.6	5.1	48003	56016	68	73	61	19.7	19.7	50.8	9.8	0.0	102679
79059	MIAMI	23992	350	24.3	25.1	37.7	8.6	4.3	50374	55853	73	78	278	32.4	40.3	20.5	5.8	1.1	64583
79061	MOBEETIE	18972	131	28.2	38.9	25.2	5.3	2.3	35835	36182	31	37	107	38.3	20.6	28.0	9.4	3.7	73125
79062	MORSE	17756	64	26.6	37.5	25.0	9.4	1.6	38101	42920	40	47	46	39.1	26.1	34.8	0.0	0.0	63333
79063	NAZARETH	20577	154	25.3	33.1	26.6	9.1	5.8	45310	51522	62	69	122	27.9	31.2	23.0	12.3	5.7	78182
79064	OLTON	13639	973	38.9	37.1	18.7	3.6	1.8	31363	35770	16	20	726	59.0	22.3	12.0	6.5	0.3	43229
79065	PAMPA	20059	8132	34.4	32.4	24.1	6.6	2.6	35822	41212	31	37	5977	56.8	21.6	17.4	3.4	0.8	44906
79068	PANHANDLE	24259	1429	20.2	30.9	36.5	8.9	3.5	48907	55549	70	75	1187	33.7	29.7	27.7	7.9	0.9	71804
79070	PERRYTON	19442	3291	28.3	28.2	33.4	7.1	3.0	43488	50144	57	65	2431	43.9	28.1	21.5	5.8	0.7	56077
79072	PLAINVIEW	15903	9328	35.0	32.7	24.9	5.0	2.4	35321	39841	29	34	6162	34.7	32.3	25.8	6.6	0.6	68147
79079	SHAMROCK	16484	1096	41.8	31.0	22.6	3.7	0.9	31831	35313	17	22	819	59.3	24.5	13.7	2.0	0.5	40893
79080	SKELLYTOWN	18025	270	32.2	32.6	27.8	4.1	3.3	37924	43839	39	46	229	65.5	23.6	7.0	3.1	0.9	34028
79081	SPEARMAN	19956	1282	32.5	27.9	30.9	5.2	3.6	40465	46138	48	56	984	52.9	25.1	19.7	1.5	0.8	48095
79082	SPRINGLAKE	30782	131	35.9	29.8	19.1	8.4	6.9	36785	42005	35	41	93	40.9	24.7	30.1	4.3	0.0	62083
79083	STINNETT	19178	1074	30.8	31.3	29.8	5.8	2.3	38599	43665	41	49	858	52.9	30.8	13.1	2.6	0.7	46795
79084	STRATFORD	20001	968	28.4	37.3	25.7	4.6	4.0	37324	42303	37	44	754	42.4	32.8	19.4	4.9	0.5	59048
79085	SUMMERFIELD	13429	34	38.2	32.4	23.5	5.9	0.0	35000	40731	28	33	25	40.0	40.0	16.0	4.0	0.0	62500
79086	SUNRAY	19700	751	28.8	31.7	31.3	5.2	3.1	37470	41928	37	45	544	47.1	28.1	20.2	4.2	0.4	52667
79087	TEXLINE	16620	282	32.6	39.7	18.8	6.0	2.8	35773	40332	31	37	179	43.0	34.6	15.6	6.7	0.0	58929
79088	TULIA	16467	1992	37.2	32.9	23.2	4.8	1.9	32934	36700	21	25	1367	51.4	23.3	19.4	5.6	0.4	49049
79092	VEGA	17473	549	28.8	37.0	27.5	3.3	3.5	38519	44221	41	49	363	44.4	34.7	15.4	4.7	0.8	56613
79094	WAYSIDE	20256	48	35.4	25.0	35.4	4.2	0.0	40000	43655	46	54	37	46.0	21.6	24.3	5.4	2.7	55000
79095	WELLINGTON	17108	1212	44.2	29.6	17.9	5.6	2.6	28891	32668	10	13	903	55.2	27.8	14.1	2.4	0.6	44946
79096	WHEELER	21191	719	29.1	36.3	26.3	4.6	3.8	36864	42545	35	42	584	49.1	27.9	19.2	2.9	0.9	50962
79097	WHITE DEER	20632	480	24.6	38.1	31.0	3.1	3.1	41296	46392	51	59	401	38.4	36.7	21.7	3.2	0.0	61618
79098	WILDORADO	17443	124	33.1	32.3	24.2	6.5	4.0	36514	38963	34	40	79	38.0	25.3	25.3	6.3	5.1	74167
79101	AMARILLO	17223	1193	47.2	33.5	14.8	2.1	2.5	26279	30216	6	8	384	43.0	40.6	14.6	1.8	0.0	54576
79102	AMARILLO	20676	4292	38.4	31.7	22.9	3.5	3.5	31629	35859	17	21	2252	28.3	37.7	26.6	6.2	1.2	70277
79103	AMARILLO	14695	3631	30.7	34.8	30.7	2.9	0.9	37307	42403	37	44	2748	28.4	63.3	7.3	1.0	0.0	62697
79104	AMARILLO	12515	2636	39.0	40.2	16.5	2.5	1.8	31249	34842	16	20	1679	63.9	32.8	3.2	0.2	0.0	42250
79106	AMARILLO	21044	12316	35.8	33.7	22.2	5.2	3.1	34472	39504	26	31	6895	22.2	34.3	35.2	7.1	1.2	82840
79107	AMARILLO	12295	11157	46.2	32.2	17.6	2.7	1.3	27060	30303	7	10	6692	66.3	30.8	2.0	0.9	0.0	43204
79108	AMARILLO	16264	4314	28.0	33.1	31.0	5.5	2.5	41282	47238	51	59	3439	28.1	34.1	32.3	5.4	0.2	79409
79109	AMARILLO	28715	19830	25.4	26.5	32.4	11.1	4.7	47767	54356	68	73	12277	2.9	24.0	58.3	13.1	1.7	112455
79110	AMARILLO	20654	6979	21.3	33.9	37.3	5.7	1.8	45401	52065	62	69	5149	19.1	45.0	33.1	2.6	0.2	77071
	TEXAS	23284		26.2	27.7	29.5	10.3	6.3	45778	54246				21.6	26.1	33.4	15.6	3.4	93683
	UNITED STATES	25866		24.7	27.1	30.8	10.9	6.5	48124	56710				10.9	15.0	33.7	30.1	10.4	145905

SPENDING POTENTIAL INDICES TEXAS
78873-79110 D

ZIP CODE #	POST OFFICE NAME	FINANCIAL SERVICES Auto Loan	Home Loan	Investments	Retirement Plans	THE HOME Home Improvements Home Repair	Lawn & Garden	Furnishings Computers & Hardware	Major Appliances	TV, Radio, Sound Equipment	Furniture	ENTERTAINMENT Dine out/Carry out	Sports Equipment	Fees & Tickets	Toys & Games	Travel	Cable TV	PERSONAL Apparel & Services	Auto Repairs	Health Insurance	Pets & Supplies
78873	LEAKEY	65	51	34	47	57	65	50	59	57	49	67	68	45	65	52	60	62	58	70	77
78877	QUEMADO	45	40	33	37	38	40	41	44	42	44	53	47	38	47	39	41	53	45	41	46
78879	RIO FRIO	75	59	40	53	66	75	56	67	63	55	74	78	50	74	59	67	69	66	79	92
78880	ROCKSPRINGS	58	50	40	46	51	55	50	55	53	53	65	60	46	59	49	53	63	56	56	63
78881	SABINAL	66	57	45	52	56	60	57	62	60	61	74	68	52	67	55	59	73	63	62	69
78883	TARPLEY	106	74	40	70	86	97	73	90	84	72	99	109	63	97	76	89	90	89	107	126
78884	UTOPIA	81	64	43	57	72	81	60	72	68	59	80	85	54	79	64	73	75	71	85	99
78885	VANDERPOOL	103	87	71	81	96	110	82	96	90	84	109	104	77	100	88	96	101	94	113	122
78886	YANCEY	112	78	41	74	91	102	78	96	89	77	105	116	66	103	80	94	96	94	114	133
78931	BLEIBLERVILLE	99	69	36	65	81	90	68	84	79	67	92	102	58	90	71	83	84	83	101	118
78932	CARMINE	95	105	112	100	105	116	101	102	102	99	126	114	105	130	105	105	123	100	106	112
78933	CAT SPRING	106	77	43	72	88	98	75	91	85	74	101	109	66	99	77	90	93	89	107	125
78934	COLUMBUS	78	65	58	65	69	78	70	74	75	68	91	85	66	89	70	77	85	74	81	87
78935	ALLEYTON	120	84	44	79	97	109	83	102	95	82	112	123	71	109	86	100	102	101	122	142
78938	ELLINGER	77	54	28	51	63	70	53	66	61	53	72	79	46	71	55	64	66	65	79	92
78940	FAYETTEVILLE	94	68	40	64	78	89	69	82	79	68	93	97	60	90	71	83	85	81	98	110
78941	FLATONIA	83	57	28	51	65	74	55	69	65	56	77	82	47	74	57	70	70	68	83	97
78942	GIDDINGS	86	70	51	67	74	82	71	79	77	72	93	90	65	89	70	78	88	79	85	96
78944	INDUSTRY	98	70	39	65	81	91	68	84	78	68	92	101	59	90	71	83	84	83	100	117
78945	LA GRANGE	90	68	44	65	76	86	70	81	78	69	93	94	63	89	71	82	86	81	94	103
78946	LEDBETTER	85	59	31	54	67	77	60	72	70	59	82	85	52	78	61	74	75	71	87	98
78947	LEXINGTON	101	82	58	80	88	97	82	91	88	81	106	106	75	103	82	89	99	90	100	114
78948	LINCOLN	97	66	32	59	75	86	64	80	76	65	89	96	55	86	66	81	81	79	97	112
78949	MULDOON	86	60	31	57	70	78	59	73	68	58	80	88	51	78	61	72	73	72	87	102
78950	NEW ULM	115	83	47	77	95	107	81	99	92	80	109	118	70	107	84	98	100	98	118	137
78953	ROSANKY	96	74	46	70	82	91	71	84	79	71	94	101	64	93	73	82	87	83	96	113
78954	ROUND TOP	96	92	86	88	96	108	92	97	96	90	117	109	91	118	94	100	112	95	106	112
78956	SCHULENBURG	97	75	54	73	83	94	78	88	86	76	102	103	70	98	79	89	94	88	101	111
78957	SMITHVILLE	80	69	54	66	72	80	69	75	73	68	89	87	65	87	69	75	84	74	81	91
78959	WAELDER	81	55	25	48	62	71	53	66	63	54	75	79	45	71	54	68	68	65	81	94
78962	WEIMAR	90	66	40	62	75	86	67	79	76	65	89	93	59	87	69	80	82	78	94	106
78963	WEST POINT	101	70	37	66	82	92	69	86	80	69	94	104	59	92	72	84	86	85	102	120
79001	ADRIAN	88	61	32	58	72	80	61	75	70	60	82	90	52	80	63	73	75	74	89	104
79005	BOOKER	70	60	47	55	59	62	61	67	64	65	79	72	55	71	58	62	78	67	65	72
79007	BORGER	77	68	57	66	70	77	69	73	72	69	88	84	65	86	68	73	84	73	77	86
79009	BOVINA	75	60	42	56	62	67	60	69	65	63	79	77	54	73	59	65	76	69	72	81
79011	BRISCOE	82	57	30	54	67	75	56	70	65	56	76	84	48	75	59	68	70	69	83	97
79014	CANADIAN	88	63	35	59	72	82	64	76	73	62	86	90	55	83	65	77	78	76	91	102
79015	CANYON	75	71	79	74	71	75	80	75	78	77	98	92	77	96	76	74	95	79	70	85
79016	CANYON	0	0	0	0	0	0	0	0	0	0	0	0	0	0	0	0	0	0	0	0
79018	CHANNING	93	65	34	61	75	84	64	79	74	63	86	95	54	85	66	77	79	78	94	110
79019	CLAUDE	96	67	35	63	78	87	66	82	76	65	89	99	56	88	69	80	81	81	97	114
79022	DALHART	73	68	66	67	69	75	70	72	72	70	89	84	69	89	70	72	86	73	74	83
79027	DIMMITT	76	67	57	64	68	72	67	73	70	70	86	81	63	81	66	69	84	73	73	82
79029	DUMAS	76	69	61	67	70	74	70	73	72	72	89	83	67	87	68	71	87	74	73	83
79031	EARTH	77	64	49	60	64	68	65	72	69	69	85	79	59	77	63	68	83	73	71	80
79034	FOLLETT	87	61	32	57	71	79	60	74	69	59	81	89	51	79	62	73	74	73	88	103
79035	FRIONA	85	67	47	63	70	76	67	77	73	70	89	87	60	83	67	73	85	78	81	93
79036	FRITCH	91	70	44	66	78	87	67	80	75	66	89	95	61	89	70	78	83	78	92	108
79039	GROOM	91	63	33	60	74	83	63	77	72	62	85	93	53	83	65	76	77	76	92	108
79040	GRUVER	109	76	40	72	89	99	75	93	87	74	102	112	64	100	78	91	93	92	111	129
79041	HALE CENTER	76	63	47	59	64	68	64	71	68	68	84	78	57	76	62	67	81	72	72	81
79042	HAPPY	76	53	28	50	61	69	52	64	60	51	70	78	44	69	54	63	64	63	77	90
79043	HART	62	53	43	50	52	55	54	59	57	59	71	64	50	63	52	55	70	60	57	64
79044	HARTLEY	50	35	18	33	41	46	35	43	40	34	47	51	29	46	36	42	43	42	51	59
79045	HEREFORD	70	60	48	57	61	65	61	67	64	64	79	74	56	73	59	63	77	67	67	75
79046	HIGGINS	79	60	39	57	65	78	66	73	74	63	87	81	59	82	65	78	79	73	87	88
79052	KRESS	83	66	46	61	69	75	66	76	72	69	87	86	59	81	65	72	84	76	80	92
79056	LIPSCOMB	79	60	39	57	65	78	66	73	74	63	87	81	59	82	65	78	79	73	87	88
79057	MCLEAN	64	48	31	46	52	63	53	58	59	50	70	65	47	66	52	63	64	58	70	70
79058	MASTERSON	102	90	69	86	96	103	84	93	89	84	108	110	82	110	86	91	103	90	100	120
79059	MIAMI	97	80	58	78	88	95	77	88	82	76	99	106	71	99	79	84	93	87	97	116
79061	MOBEETIE	80	56	29	53	65	73	55	68	63	54	74	82	47	73	57	67	68	67	81	95
79062	MORSE	89	62	33	59	73	81	62	76	71	61	83	92	53	82	64	75	76	75	91	106
79063	NAZARETH	108	75	39	71	88	98	74	92	85	73	100	111	63	98	77	90	91	90	109	128
79064	OLTON	63	53	41	50	53	57	54	60	57	58	71	65	49	64	52	56	69	61	59	66
79065	PAMPA	67	65	64	63	66	74	66	68	69	65	84	77	66	84	67	70	81	68	72	78
79068	PANHANDLE	110	86	56	82	95	105	84	97	93	83	111	116	77	110	86	96	103	96	111	129
79070	PERRYTON	84	74	59	72	76	82	73	79	77	74	94	91	70	91	73	77	90	79	82	93
79072	PLAINVIEW	65	61	57	59	60	64	62	65	64	64	79	73	60	75	61	62	78	66	63	71
79079	SHAMROCK	63	47	30	45	52	61	51	57	57	49	67	65	45	64	51	60	61	57	68	71
79080	SKELLYTOWN	84	59	31	56	69	77	58	72	67	57	79	87	50	77	60	70	72	71	86	100
79081	SPEARMAN	88	66	41	62	72	81	67	78	75	67	90	90	59	85	68	78	83	78	89	100
79082	SPRINGLAKE	138	97	52	91	112	125	96	118	110	95	129	141	82	126	99	115	118	116	139	163
79083	STINNETT	84	63	38	59	69	79	63	73	71	62	84	86	56	82	63	74	78	72	85	96
79084	STRATFORD	94	74	51	73	81	91	75	85	82	74	99	99	69	97	76	85	92	84	96	107
79085	SUMMERFIELD	64	56	46	52	54	56	57	62	59	62	74	65	52	66	54	57	74	63	58	64
79086	SUNRAY	88	75	60	73	77	84	77	83	81	79	100	92	73	95	75	81	96	83	85	94
79087	TEXLINE	84	58	31	55	68	76	58	71	67	57	78	86	49	76	60	70	71	70	85	99
79088	TULIA	74	57	38	54	61	68	59	67	65	60	78	76	52	73	58	66	73	67	74	83
79092	VEGA	84	62	37	60	71	78	61	73	69	61	81	88	54	80	63	71	75	72	84	99
79094	WAYSIDE	84	59	31	56	69	77	58	72	67	57	79	87	50	77	60	70	72	71	86	100
79095	WELLINGTON	67	54	40	52	59	68	57	63	62	55	74	71	52	72	57	65	69	62	73	76
79096	WHEELER	90	66	41	63	74	87	71	81	81	68	95	92	63	90	71	85	86	81	97	102
79097	WHITE DEER	95	66	35	62	77	86	65	81	75	64	88	97	56	86	68	79	80	79	96	112
79098	WILDORADO	86	60	32	57	70	79	60	74	69	59	80	89	51	79	62	72	73	73	88	103
79101	AMARILLO	43	44	50	45	44	47	46	45	45	45	57	54	46	56	46	44	55	46	44	49
79102	AMARILLO	67	66	71	65	65	70	70	69	70	69	87	79	68	85	68	68	85	71	67	74
79103	AMARILLO	59	59	59	58	58	62	60	60	61	60	75	69	60	75	59	60	73	61	59	67
79104	AMARILLO	59	52	44	48	50	53	53	57	55	58	70	61	49	62	51	53	69	59	54	60
79106	AMARILLO	66	64	73	65	64	70	70	67	70	68	88	79	69	87	69	69	85	70	67	74
79107	AMARILLO	54	49	48	46	47	52	52	53	54	54	68	58	50	64	50	54	67	54	52	57
79108	AMARILLO	77	68	53	65	70	76	66	71	69	66	84	83	63	82	66	70	80	71	76	87
79109	AMARILLO	88	93	105	95	91	96	95	92	92	94	116	109	96	116	94	89	114	94	86	101
79110	AMARILLO	73	80	85	81	78	80	79	77	76	78	95	92	80	97	78	72	94	78	71	85
	TEXAS	94	90	91	90	89	95	92	93	92	93	115	107	90	112	90	90	112	94	89	104
	UNITED STATES	100	100	100	100	100	100	100	100	100	100	100	100	100	100	100	100	100	100	100	100

ZIP CODE			POPULATION			2000-2004 ANNUAL RATE		HOUSEHOLDS					FAMILIES		
# POST OFFICE NAME	COUNTY FIPS CODE		2000	2004	2009	% Rate	State Centile	2000	2004	2009	% Annual Rate 2000-2004	2004 Average HH Size	2000	2004	% Annual Rate 2000-2004
79111 AMARILLO	375		1931	1975	2070	0.5	26	604	645	696	1.6	2.76	506	543	1.7
79118 AMARILLO	381		12128	13560	14703	2.7	78	4269	4789	5204	2.7	2.80	3378	3791	2.8
79119 AMARILLO	381		4345	5097	5659	3.8	89	1492	1730	1904	3.5	2.92	1211	1402	3.5
79121 AMARILLO	381		7564	7872	8216	0.9	39	3137	3281	3432	1.1	2.38	2246	2347	1.0
79124 AMARILLO	375		5946	6914	7774	3.6	87	2266	2621	2925	3.5	2.59	1829	2114	3.5
79201 CHILDRESS	075		7604	7618	7631	0.0	14	2444	2429	2419	-0.1	2.44	1628	1622	-0.1
79220 AFTON	125		123	121	120	-0.4	6	52	51	50	-0.5	1.59	36	34	-1.3
79225 CHILLICOTHE	197		1117	1097	1068	-0.4	6	446	435	422	-0.6	2.52	310	304	-0.5
79226 CLARENDON	129		3033	3144	3299	0.9	37	1241	1282	1341	0.8	2.29	838	869	0.9
79227 CROWELL	155		1709	1661	1612	-0.7	3	702	677	652	-0.9	2.39	465	449	-0.8
79229 DICKENS	125		588	580	573	-0.3	7	244	239	234	-0.5	1.63	168	165	-0.4
79230 DODSON	075		171	166	165	-0.7	3	73	70	69	-1.0	2.09	57	55	-0.8
79234 FLOMOT	345		77	76	75	-0.3	8	30	29	29	-0.8	2.62	21	21	0.0
79235 FLOYDADA	153		4720	4720	4705	0.0	13	1688	1675	1661	-0.2	2.76	1284	1279	-0.1
79237 HEDLEY	129		786	794	823	0.2	18	332	333	343	0.1	2.38	215	216	0.1
79239 LAKEVIEW	191		286	281	282	-0.4	6	109	105	103	-0.9	2.68	76	73	-0.9
79241 LOCKNEY	153		3051	2973	2929	-0.6	4	1042	1007	988	-0.8	2.91	827	801	-0.8
79243 MCADOO	125		103	102	100	-0.2	8	50	49	48	-0.5	1.39	34	24	-7.9
79244 MATADOR	345		1011	992	973	-0.5	5	431	420	409	-0.6	2.36	310	303	-0.5
79245 MEMPHIS	191		2804	2828	2858	0.2	17	1146	1136	1129	-0.2	2.45	748	745	-0.1
79247 ODELL	487		71	82	89	3.5	86	28	32	35	3.2	2.56	21	24	3.2
79248 PADUCAH	269		2260	2204	2162	-0.6	4	928	905	890	-0.6	2.33	639	625	-0.5
79250 PETERSBURG	189		1572	1546	1538	-0.4	6	548	536	532	-0.5	2.88	432	424	-0.4
79251 QUAIL	087		68	66	65	-0.7	3	26	25	24	-0.9	2.64	20	19	-1.2
79252 QUANAH	197		3607	3501	3401	-0.7	3	1497	1448	1403	-0.8	2.37	1009	979	-0.7
79255 QUITAQUE	045		568	564	570	-0.2	9	236	233	234	-0.3	2.42	157	156	-0.2
79256 ROARING SPRINGS	345		338	335	329	-0.2	9	145	143	140	-0.3	2.34	103	102	-0.2
79257 SILVERTON	045		1222	1245	1271	0.4	23	488	494	501	0.3	2.52	354	359	0.3
79259 TELL	075		61	61	61	0.0	13	22	22	22	0.0	2.55	17	4	-28.9
79261 TURKEY	191		692	710	723	0.6	29	293	295	296	0.2	2.41	189	192	0.4
79311 ABERNATHY	189		3558	3546	3576	-0.1	11	1249	1239	1247	-0.2	2.86	1020	1015	-0.1
79312 AMHERST	279		1132	1100	1105	-0.7	3	406	392	391	-0.8	2.73	311	301	-0.8
79313 ANTON	219		1550	1560	1577	0.2	16	544	550	559	0.3	2.84	417	423	0.3
79316 BROWNFIELD	445		11562	11501	11547	-0.1	10	3887	3877	3902	-0.1	2.72	2918	2920	0.0
79320 BULA	017		63	61	60	-0.8	3	19	18	18	-1.3	3.39	15	14	-1.6
79322 CROSBYTON	107		2439	2401	2354	-0.4	7	909	894	876	-0.4	2.62	659	650	-0.3
79323 DENVER CITY	501		5286	5389	5543	0.5	24	1792	1830	1886	0.5	2.92	1468	1502	0.5
79324 ENOCHS	017		66	64	64	-0.7	3	24	23	23	-1.0	2.78	18	18	0.0
79325 FARWELL	369		2265	2317	2422	0.5	27	797	812	846	0.4	2.76	594	608	0.6
79326 FIELDTON	279		18	18	18	0.0	13	9	9	9	0.0	2.00	7	7	0.0
79329 IDALOU	303		4875	4977	5219	0.5	25	1742	1773	1857	0.4	2.80	1344	1371	0.5
79331 LAMESA	115		13801	13494	13164	-0.5	4	4295	4179	4062	-0.6	2.69	3157	3080	-0.6
79336 LEVELLAND	219		19658	19797	20132	0.2	17	6926	7010	7180	0.3	2.74	5258	5334	0.3
79339 LITTLEFIELD	279		7627	7779	7940	0.5	24	2831	2866	2909	0.3	2.65	2055	2086	0.4
79342 LOOP	165		386	388	397	0.1	15	123	123	126	0.0	3.15	104	104	0.0
79343 LORENZO	107		1834	1801	1764	-0.4	5	633	620	606	-0.5	2.90	470	462	-0.4
79344 MAPLE	017		162	157	155	-0.7	3	58	56	55	-0.8	2.80	45	43	-1.1
79345 MEADOW	445		1179	1172	1173	-0.1	10	383	380	381	-0.2	3.08	321	320	-0.1
79346 MORTON	079		2930	2798	2614	-1.1	1	1046	1002	941	-1.0	2.73	816	784	-0.9
79347 MULESHOE	017		6303	6263	6238	-0.2	10	2247	2225	2215	-0.2	2.79	1700	1687	-0.2
79351 ODONNELL	305		1266	1249	1249	-0.3	7	458	450	450	-0.4	2.78	344	339	-0.3
79353 PEP	219		32	32	32	0.0	13	14	14	14	0.0	2.29	10	10	0.0
79355 PLAINS	501		2036	2036	2065	0.0	13	677	675	686	-0.1	3.01	540	539	-0.1
79356 POST	169		4872	5059	5325	0.9	38	1663	1736	1843	1.0	2.65	1218	1275	1.1
79357 RALLS	107		2799	2740	2680	-0.5	4	970	944	921	-0.6	2.87	737	720	-0.6
79358 ROPESVILLE	219		1476	1536	1581	0.9	39	510	533	552	1.0	2.88	403	422	1.1
79359 SEAGRAVES	165		3181	3189	3266	0.1	14	1082	1083	1108	0.0	2.94	841	842	0.0
79360 SEMINOLE	165		10900	11265	11724	0.8	35	3476	3575	3705	0.7	3.12	2811	2897	0.7
79363 SHALLOWATER	303		5585	5957	6377	1.5	58	1929	2054	2197	1.5	2.90	1530	1632	1.5
79364 SLATON	303		7311	7401	7741	0.3	20	2703	2728	2852	0.2	2.67	1960	1983	0.3
79366 RANSOM CANYON	303		1016	1038	1085	0.5	25	407	415	434	0.5	2.50	307	314	0.5
79370 SPUR	125		1948	1916	1884	-0.4	6	634	620	608	-0.5	2.68	400	393	-0.4
79371 SUDAN	279		1238	1369	1458	2.4	75	483	532	563	2.3	2.57	352	389	2.4
79373 TAHOKA	305		4236	4229	4239	0.0	12	1539	1529	1526	-0.2	2.74	1154	1150	-0.1
79376 TOKIO	445		20	20	20	0.0	13	8	8	8	0.0	2.50	7	7	0.0
79377 WELCH	115		518	510	497	-0.4	7	180	177	172	-0.4	2.88	143	141	-0.3
79379 WHITEFACE	079		800	771	724	-0.9	2	263	254	240	-0.8	2.98	201	195	-0.7
79381 WILSON	305		1048	1046	1050	0.0	12	357	354	354	-0.2	2.95	280	278	-0.2
79382 WOLFFORTH	303		3861	4200	4549	2.0	67	1338	1451	1571	1.9	2.86	1091	1186	2.0
79401 LUBBOCK	303		9268	9225	9610	-0.1	10	3851	3799	3960	-0.3	2.18	1578	1562	-0.2
79403 LUBBOCK	303		17140	17673	18690	0.7	33	5522	5684	6012	0.7	3.04	4290	4428	0.8
79404 LUBBOCK	303		11164	11424	12030	0.6	27	3434	3520	3720	0.6	2.99	2555	2623	0.6
79407 LUBBOCK	303		15731	17267	18907	2.2	72	6432	7112	7840	2.4	2.34	3759	4184	2.6
79409 LUBBOCK	303		4470	4489	4504	0.1	15	41	56	68	7.6	1.30	8	11	7.8
79410 LUBBOCK	303		9760	9531	9915	-0.6	4	4266	4164	4338	-0.6	2.21	2229	2181	-0.5
79411 LUBBOCK	303		8234	8417	8866	0.5	26	3103	3159	3319	0.4	2.65	1838	1876	0.5
79412 LUBBOCK	303		15142	15787	16766	1.0	42	5748	5978	6340	0.9	2.61	3904	4069	1.0
79413 LUBBOCK	303		20564	21147	22304	0.7	31	8717	8937	9416	0.6	2.35	5653	5820	0.7
79414 LUBBOCK	303		16968	17502	18601	0.7	34	7514	7731	8210	0.7	2.25	4114	4253	0.8
79415 LUBBOCK	303		15045	16130	17448	1.7	60	5592	6150	6761	2.3	2.53	3282	3564	2.0
79416 LUBBOCK	303		23905	26122	28465	2.1	69	9560	10422	11356	2.1	2.47	5911	6440	2.0
79423 LUBBOCK	303		23825	25830	27965	1.9	66	9196	9970	10797	1.9	2.58	6787	7366	1.9
79424 LUBBOCK	303		28024	31316	34547	2.7	78	11154	12383	13637	2.5	2.50	7741	8634	2.6
79501 ANSON	253		3598	3730	3909	0.9	37	1335	1379	1439	0.8	2.62	986	1020	0.8
79502 ASPERMONT	433		1423	1349	1245	-1.3	1	582	552	511	-1.2	2.37	404	385	-1.1
79503 AVOCA	253		242	275	303	3.1	82	93	105	115	2.9	2.62	65	74	3.1
79504 BAIRD	059		2484	2528	2606	0.4	23	1018	1031	1059	0.3	2.40	681	691	0.3
79506 BLACKWELL	353		844	873	911	0.8	35	386	401	420	0.9	2.18	269	280	0.8
79508 BUFFALO GAP	441		1126	1174	1211	1.0	42	434	448	456	0.8	2.61	343	355	0.8
79510 CLYDE	059		7520	7786	8079	0.8	36	2866	2953	3054	0.7	2.62	2212	2285	0.8
79511 COAHOMA	227		1482	1486	1513	0.1	14	572	575	586	0.1	2.58	431	434	0.2
79512 COLORADO CITY	335		8161	8149	8167	0.0	12	2234	2226	2231	-0.1	2.47	1574	1572	0.0
79517 FLUVANNA	033		246	263	274	1.6	59	106	114	119	1.7	2.31	83	90	1.9
79518 GIRARD	263		128	130	131	0.4	22	54	55	55	0.4	2.36	40	41	0.6
79519 GOLDSBORO	083		47	49	49	1.0	42	19	20	20	1.2	2.45	14	15	1.6
TEXAS						2.2					2.0	2.77			2.1
UNITED STATES						1.2					1.3	2.58			1.1

ZIP CODE		RACE (%)								2004 AGE DISTRIBUTION (%)										MEDIAN AGE		
#	POST OFFICE NAME	White		Black		Asian/Pacific		% Hispanic Origin														
		2000	2004	2000	2004	2000	2004	2000	2004	0-4	5-9	10-14	15-19	20-24	25-44	45-64	65-84	85+	18+	2004	% 2004 Males	% 2004 Females
79111	AMARILLO	80.4	77.8	7.1	7.7	1.4	1.8	15.6	18.4	11.3	9.1	9.2	10.3	10.9	33.2	13.8	2.0	0.1	65.0	24.6	52.5	47.5
79118	AMARILLO	89.7	88.1	1.1	1.2	0.3	0.4	11.2	13.4	7.7	7.4	8.0	8.4	7.4	28.0	24.8	7.8	0.5	71.6	33.6	50.6	49.4
79119	AMARILLO	92.8	91.6	1.2	1.3	1.2	1.4	7.6	9.1	7.7	8.0	8.4	7.3	5.4	28.5	24.8	9.1	0.8	71.2	36.0	48.8	51.2
79121	AMARILLO	92.4	91.3	1.3	1.4	3.0	3.4	6.3	7.6	4.8	5.8	7.5	7.1	5.7	24.6	30.6	12.7	1.2	77.4	41.7	48.2	51.8
79124	AMARILLO	93.4	92.2	1.6	1.8	1.1	1.4	5.4	6.5	6.6	6.9	6.5	5.8	5.0	25.5	30.1	12.3	1.4	76.5	41.4	48.6	51.4
79201	CHILDRESS	68.0	67.4	13.9	14.0	0.4	0.4	20.4	21.0	5.9	5.8	5.7	7.3	9.4	30.0	20.9	12.6	2.5	78.5	36.3	58.7	41.3
79220	AFTON	80.5	80.2	12.2	12.4	0.0	0.0	20.3	20.7	3.3	3.3	4.1	4.1	11.6	37.2	23.1	10.7	2.5	85.1	36.6	65.3	34.7
79225	CHILLICOTHE	87.6	86.3	4.5	4.7	0.2	0.2	11.2	12.9	5.8	5.9	7.8	8.2	6.8	23.6	24.2	15.0	2.8	75.5	39.3	47.4	52.6
79226	CLARENDON	91.0	90.1	4.8	5.0	0.1	0.2	5.8	6.8	5.0	5.0	6.3	6.6	7.7	20.6	26.0	19.5	3.3	80.4	44.1	48.9	51.1
79227	CROWELL	84.6	84.1	3.2	3.3	0.2	0.2	16.2	16.8	6.1	6.1	7.3	6.2	6.2	21.0	24.7	17.2	5.1	76.2	42.6	47.0	53.0
79229	DICKENS	80.3	79.8	12.2	12.4	0.2	0.2	20.2	20.9	3.1	3.3	4.0	4.3	11.2	39.5	21.4	11.2	2.1	86.4	35.9	66.9	33.1
79230	DODSON	83.6	83.1	5.9	6.0	0.0	0.0	11.1	11.5	3.6	3.6	5.4	6.6	6.6	24.7	28.9	18.1	2.4	83.1	44.6	56.6	43.4
79234	FLOMOT	90.9	90.8	1.3	1.3	0.0	0.0	10.4	11.8	6.6	6.6	4.0	5.3	5.3	19.7	26.3	23.7	2.6	82.9	46.7	52.6	47.4
79235	FLOYDADA	73.4	73.1	3.9	4.0	0.2	0.2	46.3	47.2	8.3	8.1	8.8	7.2	6.3	23.5	21.6	13.5	2.6	70.0	35.3	48.8	51.2
79237	HEDLEY	93.0	92.1	0.9	0.9	0.0	0.0	8.7	10.2	5.8	6.1	7.3	6.9	5.0	21.2	25.7	19.7	2.4	76.5	43.0	48.4	51.6
79239	LAKEVIEW	61.5	60.9	4.9	5.0	0.0	0.0	42.0	43.1	7.8	7.5	6.4	8.5	5.0	22.4	22.4	16.4	3.6	73.0	39.6	53.7	46.3
79241	LOCKNEY	75.3	74.9	2.5	2.5	0.2	0.2	45.4	46.6	8.8	8.4	8.5	8.4	6.0	23.9	21.1	12.3	2.7	68.9	34.2	48.3	51.7
79243	MCADOO	80.6	79.4	12.6	12.8	0.0	0.0	19.4	20.6	2.9	3.9	3.9	4.9	11.8	40.2	20.6	9.8	2.0	87.3	35.0	66.7	33.3
79244	MATADOR	86.1	85.8	4.5	4.5	0.4	0.4	12.5	12.8	5.9	6.2	6.7	6.7	6.0	19.6	26.6	19.6	3.0	77.3	44.4	50.4	49.6
79245	MEMPHIS	72.0	71.4	9.2	9.3	0.1	0.1	26.0	26.8	7.6	7.1	7.7	6.3	6.3	21.2	22.6	17.6	3.6	73.5	40.2	47.1	52.9
79247	ODELL	88.7	87.8	1.4	1.2	0.0	0.0	12.7	13.4	4.9	7.3	11.0	7.3	3.7	25.6	24.4	14.6	1.2	70.7	37.9	48.8	51.2
79248	PADUCAH	83.5	83.2	8.3	8.4	0.0	0.0	17.4	18.0	5.4	5.8	7.4	6.9	5.0	21.7	25.3	18.7	3.8	76.4	43.6	47.3	52.7
79250	PETERSBURG	65.9	65.3	2.1	2.1	0.0	0.0	54.8	56.1	8.4	7.4	7.9	7.4	7.8	24.1	22.5	12.5	2.1	71.8	34.3	49.2	50.8
79251	QUAIL	91.2	92.4	0.0	0.0	0.0	0.0	8.8	9.1	3.0	4.6	6.1	6.1	6.1	21.2	31.8	19.7	1.5	86.4	47.0	48.5	51.5
79252	QUANAH	84.8	83.1	4.9	5.1	0.3	0.4	15.5	18.0	7.1	6.2	5.9	6.5	6.9	21.7	25.2	16.8	3.9	76.5	41.7	47.8	52.2
79255	QUITAQUE	80.6	80.3	4.9	5.0	0.0	0.0	25.7	26.2	4.3	7.3	8.5	7.6	3.9	21.5	28.4	16.5	2.1	75.2	42.6	48.9	51.1
79256	ROARING SPRINGS	90.5	90.5	1.2	1.2	0.0	0.0	11.5	11.9	6.3	6.0	4.8	4.5	5.1	20.6	26.9	23.3	2.7	80.9	47.1	51.3	48.7
79257	SILVERTON	84.6	84.2	1.1	1.1	0.1	0.1	21.4	22.3	7.7	7.7	7.0	6.2	5.5	22.7	23.8	17.1	2.4	73.7	40.0	49.1	50.9
79259	TELL	45.9	45.9	31.2	31.2	0.0	0.0	23.0	23.0	3.3	3.3	1.6	9.8	11.5	44.3	21.3	4.9	0.0	90.2	35.3	85.3	14.8
79261	TURKEY	76.2	75.9	5.8	5.8	0.3	0.3	27.6	28.2	7.9	7.8	7.9	5.5	5.1	20.7	24.2	17.3	3.7	73.2	41.0	51.0	49.0
79311	ABERNATHY	78.5	77.2	2.2	2.3	0.1	0.2	39.0	41.2	8.1	7.9	8.0	7.1	6.7	25.2	22.6	12.9	1.6	71.9	35.9	49.3	50.7
79312	AMHERST	74.0	71.6	6.8	6.7	0.0	0.0	33.6	38.2	8.5	8.0	7.2	6.1	5.6	23.2	22.1	16.6	2.7	71.9	38.2	49.3	50.7
79313	ANTON	74.9	72.1	4.5	4.7	0.0	0.0	41.2	46.2	7.9	7.2	8.4	9.0	7.5	24.3	20.9	13.3	1.5	71.0	34.9	49.2	50.8
79316	BROWNFIELD	76.1	75.8	5.5	5.5	0.2	0.2	44.0	44.9	7.7	6.9	7.0	7.6	8.0	26.3	22.2	12.5	2.0	73.9	35.3	52.3	47.7
79320	BULA	71.4	68.9	1.6	1.6	0.0	0.0	36.5	37.7	4.9	6.6	6.6	8.2	6.6	23.0	29.5	14.8	0.0	77.1	41.5	54.1	45.9
79322	CROSBYTON	66.6	63.9	5.0	5.0	0.3	0.3	41.9	46.1	8.3	7.0	7.3	6.8	6.8	22.5	23.5	15.1	2.7	73.0	37.1	46.9	53.1
79323	DENVER CITY	69.3	66.5	1.7	1.8	0.2	0.2	45.4	49.8	8.2	7.7	8.0	8.6	8.0	24.6	23.3	10.5	1.3	70.6	34.4	48.3	51.7
79324	ENOCHS	71.2	70.3	1.5	1.6	0.0	0.0	37.9	37.5	4.7	6.3	6.3	7.8	6.3	21.9	32.8	14.1	0.0	78.1	43.0	53.1	46.9
79325	FARWELL	76.9	74.0	0.6	0.6	0.6	0.7	32.0	36.2	7.8	7.7	8.0	7.3	6.0	24.8	22.0	13.5	2.9	72.0	36.8	48.5	51.5
79326	FIELDTON	88.9	88.9	0.0	0.0	0.0	0.0	22.2	27.8	11.1	11.1	11.1	5.6	0.0	27.8	27.8	5.6	0.0	66.7	35.0	50.0	50.0
79329	IDALOU	77.2	73.5	1.1	1.1	0.3	0.3	32.2	37.7	6.6	6.7	8.3	8.6	5.6	24.8	26.1	11.7	1.6	72.9	38.2	49.6	50.5
79331	LAMESA	71.7	70.4	9.4	9.1	0.2	0.2	49.4	53.5	6.6	6.1	6.7	7.1	8.1	30.7	21.2	11.5	2.1	76.3	35.3	56.1	43.9
79336	LEVELLAND	73.6	71.2	3.9	3.9	0.2	0.2	37.0	41.1	7.7	7.0	7.6	8.2	9.7	25.3	22.0	10.6	1.8	73.3	32.7	49.0	51.0
79339	LITTLEFIELD	78.4	76.8	5.2	5.2	0.2	0.2	42.3	46.5	7.7	7.4	7.5	7.1	7.7	23.7	21.7	14.2	3.0	72.8	36.4	49.1	50.9
79342	LOOP	80.6	78.1	0.5	0.5	0.0	0.0	35.2	40.5	8.8	9.0	7.0	8.8	7.2	26.8	21.7	10.3	0.5	69.6	31.8	49.2	50.8
79343	LORENZO	67.1	64.7	5.3	5.2	0.1	0.1	50.9	55.5	8.2	8.3	9.3	7.9	6.2	25.2	22.8	10.9	1.3	69.5	33.0	49.8	50.2
79344	MAPLE	71.0	70.7	1.2	1.3	0.0	0.0	36.4	38.2	6.4	6.4	7.0	8.3	5.7	24.2	26.1	14.7	1.3	75.2	39.7	51.6	48.4
79345	MEADOW	80.9	80.3	0.4	0.4	0.2	0.2	45.3	47.2	8.4	7.9	7.8	7.3	6.7	27.6	22.9	10.5	0.9	71.3	33.9	51.9	48.1
79346	MORTON	62.1	59.1	5.1	5.0	0.3	0.4	46.4	50.7	7.7	7.0	8.2	8.6	6.8	24.2	21.9	13.4	2.3	71.4	35.8	49.0	51.0
79347	MULESHOE	66.5	66.0	1.3	1.3	0.1	0.1	47.8	48.8	8.5	8.1	8.1	7.5	6.9	23.7	22.4	12.8	2.0	70.7	34.7	49.2	50.9
79351	ODONNELL	68.3	67.7	1.1	1.1	0.5	0.5	55.1	56.5	7.5	7.3	7.8	8.7	7.3	23.2	23.0	13.9	1.5	72.3	36.7	50.4	49.6
79353	PEP	75.0	71.9	0.0	0.0	0.0	0.0	40.6	43.8	6.3	6.3	6.3	6.3	6.3	31.3	25.0	12.5	0.0	81.3	40.0	53.1	46.9
79355	PLAINS	74.0	71.5	0.5	0.5	0.1	0.1	47.4	51.9	7.3	7.8	8.7	8.1	7.0	25.8	23.6	10.4	1.2	70.7	35.3	49.9	50.1
79356	POST	74.8	72.5	4.8	4.8	0.1	0.1	37.2	41.3	6.6	6.7	8.2	8.2	6.2	27.5	22.4	12.0	2.2	73.1	35.3	52.8	47.2
79357	RALLS	59.1	55.9	1.9	1.9	0.0	0.0	53.7	58.2	8.5	7.4	9.2	8.7	7.2	22.9	21.0	12.8	2.5	68.9	33.2	47.6	52.5
79358	ROPESVILLE	84.4	82.4	1.0	1.0	0.2	0.3	36.0	40.7	8.5	8.7	8.6	6.4	5.4	27.5	22.3	11.5	1.2	70.3	35.4	52.0	48.1
79359	SEAGRAVES	69.4	67.5	4.7	4.6	0.0	0.0	51.7	56.4	8.1	8.1	8.7	8.3	6.8	25.4	22.5	10.6	1.6	70.0	33.4	48.9	51.1
79360	SEMINOLE	83.4	81.4	1.6	1.7	0.2	0.2	31.1	35.2	9.1	8.6	9.3	9.7	8.4	25.9	19.4	8.7	1.1	66.8	28.9	49.4	50.7
79363	SHALLOWATER	85.1	82.0	0.6	0.7	0.1	0.1	22.6	27.6	7.3	7.5	8.3	8.8	6.8	27.7	23.3	9.4	1.0	71.1	34.3	49.2	50.8
79364	SLATON	74.8	72.0	7.0	7.2	0.3	0.3	38.4	43.7	8.0	7.6	7.6	7.1	7.0	23.7	23.4	13.2	2.4	72.5	35.7	47.4	52.6
79366	RANSOM CANYON	89.4	87.0	1.4	1.5	0.2	0.4	16.0	19.8	5.1	5.6	6.1	6.1	6.0	23.2	34.0	13.2	0.8	79.6	43.8	49.5	50.5
79370	SPUR	76.5	76.0	6.5	6.6	0.4	0.4	25.4	26.2	4.9	4.9	5.2	5.4	7.6	26.9	24.5	16.6	3.9	81.3	41.5	53.2	46.8
79371	SUDAN	73.6	70.8	5.1	5.1	0.0	0.0	31.7	36.0	7.1	6.8	7.4	8.3	6.8	22.0	23.7	15.3	2.6	73.5	38.9	46.4	53.6
79373	TAHOKA	77.3	76.9	3.9	3.9	0.1	0.1	41.3	42.3	7.5	7.6	8.6	8.0	6.4	24.8	22.6	12.6	1.8	71.2	36.2	49.6	50.4
79376	TOKIO	80.0	80.0	0.0	0.0	0.0	0.0	35.0	35.0	10.0	10.0	10.0	10.0	10.0	35.0	15.0	0.0	0.0	70.0	25.0	55.0	45.0
79377	WELCH	87.8	86.1	0.0	0.0	0.6	0.6	37.1	42.6	7.1	7.7	9.2	6.7	5.1	25.9	23.5	14.1	0.8	72.0	37.5	51.0	49.0
79379	WHITEFACE	73.1	70.3	2.5	2.5	0.1	0.1	35.9	40.2	5.7	5.5	9.2	11.2	7.0	26.2	23.1	11.2	1.0	72.0	36.9	47.2	52.8
79381	WILSON	77.3	77.0	0.7	0.7	0.0	0.0	45.5	46.6	8.3	7.7	7.7	8.0	8.7	22.7	25.1	10.8	1.0	70.9	34.9	51.6	48.4
79382	WOLFFORTH	87.1	84.8	1.0	1.1	0.4	0.5	19.9	23.8	7.5	7.6	8.1	7.3	6.6	29.8	24.2	7.9	0.9	72.1	34.7	48.5	51.5
79401	LUBBOCK	50.4	47.9	15.8	15.8	6.4	6.5	46.8	51.0	7.5	6.0	5.6	8.2	15.7	37.5	14.4	4.4	0.7	77.1	27.4	57.0	43.0
79403	LUBBOCK	42.0	39.9	32.5	31.9	0.1	0.1	37.9	41.8	8.6	8.7	9.3	8.7	7.0	25.8	20.9	10.1	0.9	67.9	30.8	48.6	51.4
79404	LUBBOCK	44.1	42.4	25.4	25.0	0.2	0.2	49.4	52.7	8.6	8.5	8.5	7.8	7.1	29.2	20.8	8.7	0.9	69.6	31.7	52.6	47.4
79407	LUBBOCK	82.3	79.3	4.7	5.0	1.0	1.1	21.9	26.7	7.3	6.7	6.4	8.5	13.5	30.2	18.3	8.0	1.2	76.1	28.5	47.9	52.1
79409	LUBBOCK	88.6	86.6	4.3	4.8	2.6	3.1	7.9	9.8	0.1	0.0	0.0	71.4	25.0	3.4	0.2	0.0	0.0	99.6	18.5	51.0	49.0
79410	LUBBOCK	85.3	82.7	4.0	4.4	1.2	1.3	15.8	19.2	5.8	5.1	5.6	6.6	14.0	30.8	18.4	10.6	3.3	80.2	30.9	48.9	51.1
79411	LUBBOCK	57.7	54.5	8.7	8.7	0.6	0.6	52.5	57.4	9.5	8.1	7.8	8.3	10.1	31.6	17.2	6.0	1.5	69.9	27.8	49.9	50.1
79412	LUBBOCK	61.0	57.6	10.5	10.7	0.6	0.6	43.3	48.2	9.8	8.4	7.5	7.4	8.1	27.9	17.9	11.3	1.7	69.9	30.2	47.3	52.7
79413	LUBBOCK	87.4	85.5	3.6	3.9	0.8	1.0	15.6	18.7	5.7	5.5	6.0	6.9	7.4	25.4	22.7	17.5	2.9	79.0	39.7	46.5	53.6
79414	LUBBOCK	80.1	77.0	4.9	5.4	1.9	2.1	21.5	25.9	7.7	5.9	5.3	6.9	14.3	30.6	17.9	9.8	1.7	78.0	29.1	47.4	52.6
79415	LUBBOCK	52.6	50.6	5.0	5.1	1.2	1.4	64.8	66.9	8.3	7.5	7.3	8.8	14.6	28.0	17.2	7.4	1.0	72.5	26.8	50.5	49.5
79416	LUBBOCK	82.4	79.2	4.1	4.6	2.1	2.3	18.8	22.7	6.9	6.3	6.7	7.9	13.3	29.8	19.0	8.5	1.7	76.3	29.4	48.5	51.6
79423	LUBBOCK	86.6	84.0	3.2	3.6	0.9	1.1	15.7	19.3	7.2	7.0	7.0	6.5	6.7	31.1	24.7	8.9	0.8	74.9	34.8	48.7	51.4
79424	LUBBOCK	91.5	89.8	1.3	1.6	2.3	2.6	8.5	10.8	6.0	6.3	7.0	7.3	7.5	29.4	26.0	9.1	1.4	76.2	35.9	48.5	51.5
79501	ANSON	79.0	76.3	2.6	2.8	0.8	0.8	27.8	31.8	6.9	6.9	7.1	7.4	6.5	23.0	23.2	15.2	3.8	74.4	39.1	48.2	51.8
79502	ASPERMONT	87.1	85.5	3.4	3.6	0.4	0.4	12.3	14.3	5.9	5.8	5.9	6.0	7.0	21.6	25.4	18.2	4.3	78.8	43.4	46.8	53.2
79503	AVOCA	78.9	76.7	5.8	6.2	0.0	0.0	27.7	31.6	7.6	7.3	6.6	7.3	6.9	21.5	23.3	17.5	2.2	74.2	40.1	47.6	52.4
79504	BAIRD	92.4	91.2	0.1	0.2	0.6	0.7	10.6	12.5	4.6	5.0	7.0	6.5	6.0	23.7	27.3	17.0	2.9	79.2	43.2	49.6	50.4
79506	BLACKWELL	90.8	89.2	1.0	0.9	0.0	0.0	10.6	12.6	5.6	5.7	6.0	5.7	5.5	19.5	29.2	20.6	2.2	79.3	46.3	48.7	51.3
79508	BUFFALO GAP	95.3	94.4	0.5	0.6	0.3	0.3	4.7	6.0	5.0	7.5	9.2	6.7	3.0	28.1	30.3	9.0	1.1	73.7	40.5	49.1	50.9
79510	CLYDE	95.4	94.8	0.3	0.4	0.3	0.4	5.0	6.0	6.3	6.3	7.2	7.7	6.4	24.0	26.2	14.4	1.6	75.4	40.1	48.4	51.6
79511	COAHOMA	90.4	88.9	0.3	0.3	0.1	0.1	20.6	24.0	5.3	5.7	8.1	7.8	6.8	24.0	26.1	15.1	1.1	76.1	40.2	48.9	51.1
79512	COLORADO CITY	74.3	74.1	14.6	14.7	0.4	0.4	31.0	31.9	4.6	4.5	4.9	7.7	9.5	31.8	24.2	10.7	2.3	82.4	37.6	64.1	35.9
79517	FLUVANNA	93.1	93.2	0.0	0.0	0.4	0.4	13.8	16.0	4.2	4.9	6.1	6.5	5.3	22.4	32.3	16.7	1.5	80.6	45.3	50.2	49.8
79518	GIRARD	93.8	93.9	0.0	0.0	0.0	0.0	8.6	9.2	4.6	4.6	6.2	7.7	6.2	20.8	26.2	20.8	3.1	80.0	45.0	51.5	48.5
79519	GOLDSBORO	93.6	95.9	0.0	0.0	0.0	0.0	4.3	8.2	4.1	6.1	8.2	4.1	4.1	20.4	30.6	20.4	2.0	81.6	46.9	51.0	49.0
	TEXAS	71.0	69.5	11.5	11.4	2.8	3.1	32.0	34.6	7.9	7.5	7.7	7.5	8.1	29.6	21.9	8.7	1.2	72.6	32.9	49.7	50.3
	UNITED STATES	75.1	73.6	12.3	12.5	3.8	4.2	12.5	14.1	6.9	6.7	7.2	7.0	7.3	28.6	23.8	10.8	1.7	75.1	36.0	49.1	50.9

ZIP CODE #	POST OFFICE NAME	2004 Per Capita Income	2004 HH Income Base	2004 HOUSEHOLD INCOME DISTRIBUTION (%) Less than $25,000	$25,000 to $49,999	$50,000 to $99,999	$100,000 to $149,999	$150,000 or More	MEDIAN HOUSEHOLD INCOME 2004	2009	2004 National Centile	2004 State Centile	2004 Home Value Base	2004 HOME VALUE DISTRIBUTION (%) Less than $50,000	$50,000 to $89,999	$90,000 to $174,999	$175,000 to $399,999	$400,000 or More	2004 Median Home Value
79111	AMARILLO	17778	645	19.2	37.7	37.4	4.3	1.4	47152	54108	66	72	59	47.5	22.0	17.0	13.6	0.0	53000
79118	AMARILLO	20818	4789	19.9	32.5	35.8	8.0	4.0	47672	55675	68	73	3841	36.1	22.0	28.1	11.5	2.2	75488
79119	AMARILLO	26999	1730	15.1	25.1	34.5	16.2	9.0	60739	69415	85	87	1572	22.2	10.2	30.6	32.8	4.2	148007
79121	AMARILLO	41133	3281	15.5	21.6	32.4	16.2	14.4	68211	77920	90	91	2386	4.0	3.2	56.7	30.9	5.1	150939
79124	AMARILLO	36392	2621	12.1	20.9	40.1	16.2	10.8	68270	81937	90	91	2213	9.9	12.7	43.0	30.3	4.1	140749
79201	CHILDRESS	15935	2429	40.1	31.5	24.3	2.4	1.7	31555	35838	17	21	1700	46.4	34.4	15.4	3.8	0.0	53804
79220	AFTON	21752	51	49.0	25.5	19.6	3.9	2.0	26131	30000	6	8	40	60.0	22.5	15.0	2.5	0.0	42000
79225	CHILLICOTHE	18088	435	38.9	33.3	20.7	4.4	2.8	32925	37924	21	25	315	69.8	18.7	9.5	1.6	0.3	35583
79226	CLARENDON	18908	1282	37.4	32.5	22.3	5.8	2.1	33596	38344	23	28	952	42.9	32.4	19.5	3.7	1.6	59855
79227	CROWELL	16863	677	43.4	32.5	18.9	2.5	2.7	30043	33551	12	16	504	68.5	20.6	10.3	0.2	0.4	33378
79229	DICKENS	21371	239	47.3	26.8	18.8	4.2	2.9	28097	30369	9	12	188	56.9	25.0	15.4	2.7	0.0	42353
79230	DODSON	22510	70	31.4	31.4	27.1	7.1	2.9	38887	42336	42	51	57	43.9	31.6	21.1	3.5	0.0	57000
79234	FLOMOT	15417	29	41.4	34.5	17.2	6.9	0.0	29028	31116	10	13	23	56.5	26.1	17.4	0.0	0.0	42500
79235	FLOYDADA	15500	1675	43.0	27.2	21.4	6.2	2.3	29483	34062	11	14	1211	57.8	25.9	14.0	2.2	0.0	41637
79237	HEDLEY	18519	333	42.0	33.3	19.2	3.6	1.8	32564	36490	19	24	263	56.7	22.1	14.5	6.8	0.0	41250
79239	LAKEVIEW	12034	105	47.6	32.4	18.1	1.9	0.0	27327	28351	8	10	83	69.9	15.7	3.6	6.0	4.8	28409
79241	LOCKNEY	18064	1007	36.9	29.7	22.4	7.7	3.3	33643	40679	23	28	730	47.3	29.0	17.8	4.9	1.0	53226
79243	MCADOO	24188	49	49.0	26.5	18.4	4.1	2.0	26129	28160	6	8	39	59.0	23.1	15.4	2.6	0.0	41250
79244	MATADOR	18405	420	38.6	32.9	21.7	4.8	2.1	32680	38788	20	24	315	71.1	17.5	10.5	0.6	0.3	37214
79245	MEMPHIS	13185	1136	50.4	31.3	15.4	2.6	0.4	24792	27075	4	6	805	68.6	21.2	9.3	0.9	0.0	34226
79247	ODELL	16555	32	28.1	40.6	21.9	9.4	0.0	35000	40735	28	33	24	33.3	29.2	29.2	8.3	0.0	65000
79248	PADUCAH	18010	905	43.8	31.6	19.6	3.3	1.8	30114	33827	13	16	612	66.5	19.1	10.6	3.8	0.0	36100
79250	PETERSBURG	16864	536	35.5	34.1	22.0	4.3	4.1	33636	38270	23	28	387	62.3	22.5	12.7	1.8	0.8	41364
79251	QUAIL	15985	25	36.0	36.0	20.0	8.0	0.0	33600	40000	23	28	21	42.9	33.3	23.8	0.0	0.0	57500
79252	QUANAH	20453	1448	39.0	30.3	22.5	4.3	3.9	31705	36024	17	22	1027	65.0	21.8	11.4	1.6	0.2	39006
79255	QUITAQUE	15764	233	42.1	30.0	23.2	4.7	0.0	31994	35373	18	22	180	60.6	28.9	9.4	0.0	1.1	39167
79256	ROARING SPRINGS	16905	143	42.7	31.5	17.5	7.0	1.4	28893	30884	10	13	112	55.4	23.2	19.6	0.9	0.9	41429
79257	SILVERTON	16358	494	36.0	35.0	23.3	4.3	1.4	33262	37057	22	27	391	55.8	28.6	12.8	1.5	1.3	42742
79259	TELL	25138	22	36.4	22.7	36.4	4.6	0.0	40000	45000	46	54	18	33.3	33.3	27.8	5.6	0.0	75000
79261	TURKEY	14954	295	54.9	26.1	16.6	1.0	1.4	22391	24154	3	4	235	88.1	5.1	6.4	0.4	0.0	21023
79311	ABERNATHY	17686	1239	30.8	33.8	26.2	6.0	3.2	38166	43485	40	48	905	41.2	32.8	22.0	4.0	0.0	61933
79312	AMHERST	16777	392	40.3	27.6	23.0	6.4	2.8	33363	37658	22	27	309	62.5	20.4	12.6	3.9	0.7	34274
79313	ANTON	15924	550	39.3	29.1	25.6	2.7	3.3	35133	40639	28	33	396	58.8	27.3	11.1	2.8	0.0	44167
79316	BROWNFIELD	16380	3877	41.6	29.6	21.1	5.3	2.4	31524	36617	16	21	2727	46.4	31.2	18.4	3.7	0.2	53495
79320	BULA	14170	18	33.3	22.2	38.9	5.6	0.0	40000	40000	46	54	11	54.6	27.3	18.2	0.0	0.0	47500
79322	CROSBYTON	19676	894	42.4	31.4	15.1	5.0	6.0	30270	35081	13	17	628	57.2	29.9	11.8	1.1	0.0	42742
79323	DENVER CITY	17577	1830	36.2	29.0	25.0	5.4	4.4	36313	42189	33	39	1397	60.8	23.8	12.2	2.7	0.5	43370
79324	ENOCHS	17060	23	30.4	30.4	26.1	8.7	4.4	36108	33593	32	38	14	42.9	28.6	28.6	0.0	0.0	55000
79325	FARWELL	15424	812	36.5	36.6	21.6	4.2	1.2	32591	35897	20	24	637	35.6	30.9	24.0	8.8	0.6	67456
79326	FIELDTON	23333	9	11.1	55.6	33.3	0.0	0.0	42288	54495	54	62	7	0.0	14.3	57.1	28.6	0.0	131250
79329	IDALOU	19714	1773	27.3	34.2	27.2	7.7	3.5	40083	46153	46	55	1316	34.1	28.5	29.0	7.5	0.8	69923
79331	LAMESA	17706	4179	40.7	32.5	19.3	4.1	3.4	30756	34525	14	18	2990	53.0	26.6	16.3	4.0	0.2	47335
79336	LEVELLAND	17362	7010	34.3	33.3	24.9	5.0	2.5	34758	39277	27	32	5070	43.3	29.6	23.3	3.6	0.2	57338
79339	LITTLEFIELD	18033	2866	41.6	31.3	20.2	4.6	2.3	30890	35232	15	19	2072	55.9	25.2	16.8	1.7	0.2	44225
79342	LOOP	16560	123	32.5	33.3	21.1	4.9	8.1	37325	43187	37	44	93	51.6	30.1	17.2	1.1	0.0	49118
79343	LORENZO	14612	620	45.5	25.5	22.1	4.2	2.7	29804	34281	12	15	454	56.8	22.3	19.2	1.8	0.0	45303
79344	MAPLE	16806	56	35.7	26.8	30.4	5.4	1.8	35000	37348	28	33	35	45.7	25.7	22.9	5.7	0.0	53750
79345	MEADOW	14994	380	35.3	31.1	29.2	3.4	1.1	32019	36996	18	22	299	52.5	25.1	17.1	5.0	0.3	46429
79346	MORTON	15140	1002	42.0	32.5	18.4	4.2	2.9	29927	33857	12	15	763	69.7	17.6	10.2	2.1	0.4	33654
79347	MULESHOE	14686	2225	40.1	32.2	21.9	3.6	2.2	31508	34921	16	21	1620	54.5	25.5	16.7	3.0	0.3	44895
79351	ODONNELL	17126	450	42.9	27.8	18.4	7.8	3.1	30586	36854	14	17	329	66.9	19.5	12.2	1.2	0.3	33241
79353	PEP	20781	14	35.7	28.6	21.4	14.3	0.0	35000	45000	28	33	10	30.0	30.0	40.0	0.0	0.0	80000
79355	PLAINS	17170	675	32.0	33.0	25.8	5.3	3.9	37004	42321	35	42	531	48.6	28.1	18.6	4.5	0.2	51500
79356	POST	15437	1736	40.9	34.2	17.5	6.0	1.5	30880	33949	15	18	1219	50.2	28.4	14.7	5.9	0.8	49862
79357	RALLS	16080	944	44.8	33.9	15.8	3.9	1.6	28025	31742	9	11	663	60.0	28.8	9.1	1.1	1.1	41582
79358	ROPESVILLE	20314	533	29.8	36.0	24.2	6.0	3.9	37330	42580	37	44	412	40.5	34.2	18.9	5.8	0.5	61500
79359	SEAGRAVES	15598	1083	39.4	33.3	20.8	3.3	3.1	32604	37229	20	24	795	59.8	24.8	14.6	0.9	0.0	38922
79360	SEMINOLE	14889	3575	35.9	31.9	24.5	4.9	2.8	34296	39108	25	31	2786	45.7	29.9	20.3	3.6	0.6	54636
79363	SHALLOWATER	19346	2054	23.6	35.5	30.8	7.4	2.7	43268	50704	57	65	1623	33.8	29.6	27.8	8.4	0.4	74477
79364	SLATON	18164	2728	38.7	31.0	21.6	5.7	3.0	32881	37648	21	25	1909	48.7	28.3	14.9	6.9	1.1	51667
79366	RANSOM CANYON	32825	415	21.2	29.2	29.9	12.5	7.2	49679	57978	71	77	349	20.6	24.1	32.7	20.3	2.3	99250
79370	SPUR	14228	620	42.7	33.6	20.2	2.6	1.0	29873	32919	12	15	462	71.7	23.6	4.3	0.4	0.0	27955
79371	SUDAN	20961	532	33.7	29.5	25.2	7.7	4.0	37332	43643	37	44	399	59.2	27.6	11.8	1.0	0.5	42065
79373	TAHOKA	16062	1529	43.4	24.3	23.5	5.8	2.9	30096	35871	12	16	1127	50.8	24.5	20.7	3.8	0.3	49309
79376	TOKIO	14750	8	50.0	12.5	37.5	0.0	0.0	25000	32500	5	6	6	33.3	33.3	33.3	0.0	0.0	65000
79377	WELCH	19889	177	28.3	36.7	29.9	4.0	1.1	40099	45450	46	55	138	48.6	30.4	19.6	1.5	0.0	52857
79379	WHITEFACE	17474	254	33.1	32.7	25.2	5.5	3.5	37328	42713	37	44	185	66.5	24.3	8.1	1.1	0.0	39167
79381	WILSON	18216	354	33.6	29.1	26.6	7.3	3.4	35499	44634	29	35	268	50.4	22.0	23.1	3.7	0.8	49615
79382	WOLFFORTH	20757	1451	23.2	33.2	29.6	9.7	4.4	45676	53379	63	69	1187	32.8	32.8	21.7	11.5	1.3	64703
79401	LUBBOCK	11805	3799	66.9	23.1	8.2	1.6	0.2	17725	20442	1	2	772	58.9	34.5	6.6	0.0	0.0	44851
79403	LUBBOCK	13806	5684	44.3	31.9	18.2	2.6	3.0	29111	33648	11	13	3962	67.3	20.9	8.5	2.4	0.8	38363
79404	LUBBOCK	12966	3520	42.6	36.1	17.0	3.0	1.5	30000	33731	12	15	2223	65.3	22.9	8.0	2.9	0.9	38681
79407	LUBBOCK	20992	7112	38.3	31.6	22.6	4.1	3.5	33015	38349	21	26	3576	30.5	39.3	20.7	6.4	3.1	67821
79409	LUBBOCK	12871	56	60.7	39.3	0.0	0.0	0.0	9032	10645	0	1	0	0.0	0.0	0.0	0.0	0.0	0
79410	LUBBOCK	22088	4164	36.0	29.9	25.9	5.8	2.5	34310	40698	25	31	2086	18.5	41.5	31.4	7.8	0.9	78828
79411	LUBBOCK	12788	3159	48.6	30.8	16.9	2.9	0.8	25808	30067	6	7	1293	66.2	24.6	9.2	0.0	0.0	39034
79412	LUBBOCK	15037	5978	40.1	34.0	21.5	3.1	1.3	30708	35463	14	18	3168	43.6	39.5	16.9	0.0	0.0	54420
79413	LUBBOCK	24615	8937	27.3	32.2	27.6	8.3	4.6	41972	48509	53	61	5749	12.2	38.3	43.4	6.0	0.1	89410
79414	LUBBOCK	18151	7731	40.9	29.3	24.3	4.2	1.4	31306	36547	16	20	3194	19.4	63.5	16.5	0.6	0.0	69638
79415	LUBBOCK	12111	6150	56.2	27.5	13.8	1.9	0.6	21459	23952	2	3	2691	72.9	17.4	7.1	2.4	0.2	37402
79416	LUBBOCK	23604	10422	31.6	28.9	28.5	6.5	4.6	39690	46247	45	53	5877	11.7	46.2	29.2	11.2	1.7	82137
79423	LUBBOCK	27580	9970	17.9	28.9	34.6	11.2	7.5	53205	62422	77	81	7566	12.6	32.8	41.5	12.0	1.1	94929
79424	LUBBOCK	32586	12383	19.8	20.6	35.8	13.7	10.1	60968	70659	85	87	8587	5.2	14.9	55.9	21.2	2.9	121582
79501	ANSON	17447	1379	40.5	33.1	19.3	4.1	3.1	31171	35220	15	19	1004	64.6	18.9	11.6	2.7	2.2	38072
79502	ASPERMONT	17363	552	40.8	31.5	21.2	4.5	2.0	31808	36685	17	22	422	68.7	21.3	7.1	1.2	1.7	37093
79503	AVOCA	14920	105	41.0	35.2	17.1	5.7	1.0	30236	34056	13	16	72	51.4	27.8	18.1	1.4	1.4	48750
79504	BAIRD	16951	1031	40.7	29.5	24.4	3.8	1.7	32242	35633	18	23	794	46.0	29.7	18.3	5.0	1.0	54051
79506	BLACKWELL	20821	401	34.2	33.9	23.9	6.5	1.5	35066	42589	28	33	314	47.5	28.0	19.4	3.5	1.6	52963
79508	BUFFALO GAP	27006	448	17.2	27.5	37.5	13.0	4.9	56939	64456	82	84	388	26.3	19.3	36.3	15.5	2.6	98095
79510	CLYDE	17733	2953	29.3	38.0	26.1	5.0	1.7	37834	42178	39	46	2395	37.6	36.5	21.5	4.1	0.3	63284
79511	COAHOMA	18668	575	29.0	33.4	30.8	4.7	2.1	39836	46299	45	54	472	49.4	31.1	17.6	1.7	0.2	50625
79512	COLORADO CITY	16241	2226	45.2	30.8	19.7	2.1	2.2	27880	30932	8	11	1604	61.9	24.8	11.0	2.2	0.1	39375
79517	FLUVANNA	20680	114	32.5	34.2	25.4	7.0	0.9	36156	43301	32	38	91	37.4	31.9	28.6	1.1	1.1	73500
79518	GIRARD	18442	55	41.8	30.9	18.2	5.5	3.6	29415	34291	11	14	43	48.8	37.2	11.6	2.3	0.0	51000
79519	GOLDSBORO	17857	20	35.0	25.0	35.0	5.0	0.0	40000	45000	46	54	17	47.1	23.5	29.4	0.0	0.0	55000
	TEXAS	23284		26.2	27.7	29.5	10.3	6.3	45778	54246				21.6	26.1	33.4	15.6	3.4	93683
	UNITED STATES	25866		24.7	27.1	30.8	10.9	6.5	48124	56710				10.9	15.0	33.7	30.1	10.4	145905

SPENDING POTENTIAL INDICES TEXAS

79111-79519 D

ZIP CODE #	POST OFFICE NAME	FINANCIAL SERVICES: Auto Loan	FINANCIAL SERVICES: Home Loan	FINANCIAL SERVICES: Invest-ments	FINANCIAL SERVICES: Retire-ment Plans	THE HOME: Home Improvements: Home Repair	THE HOME: Home Improvements: Lawn & Garden	THE HOME: Furnishings: Comput-ers & Hard-ware	THE HOME: Furnishings: Major Appli-ances	THE HOME: Furnishings: TV, Radio, Sound Equip-ment	THE HOME: Furnishings: Furni-ture	ENTERTAINMENT: Dine out/ Carry out	ENTERTAINMENT: Sports Equip-ment	ENTERTAINMENT: Fees & Tickets	ENTERTAINMENT: Toys & Games	ENTERTAINMENT: Travel	ENTERTAINMENT: Cable TV	PERSONAL: Apparel & Services	PERSONAL: Auto Repairs	PERSONAL: Health Insur-ance	PERSONAL: Pets & Supplies
79111	AMARILLO	60	66	66	67	63	63	62	62	58	63	74	73	63	74	61	55	73	62	54	68
79118	AMARILLO	90	85	69	83	85	89	80	86	81	82	100	99	77	96	80	79	96	85	84	101
79119	AMARILLO	113	123	117	121	121	123	112	115	108	114	135	134	114	136	113	105	132	113	108	131
79121	AMARILLO	134	148	161	153	145	149	142	140	134	143	169	164	147	170	141	129	167	139	128	155
79124	AMARILLO	130	148	152	147	147	149	135	137	129	135	161	161	141	169	138	127	159	133	128	156
79201	CHILDRESS	58	45	31	43	49	57	49	53	54	47	64	61	44	61	48	56	59	53	62	65
79220	AFTON	67	50	33	48	55	66	56	61	63	53	74	69	50	69	55	66	67	61	74	74
79225	CHILLICOTHE	75	56	36	53	61	73	61	68	68	58	80	77	54	76	60	72	73	68	81	84
79226	CLARENDON	73	56	37	52	62	72	58	66	65	56	77	75	52	74	59	69	71	66	79	84
79227	CROWELL	68	50	31	48	56	65	53	61	60	51	71	70	47	67	53	63	65	60	73	77
79229	DICKENS	67	50	33	48	55	66	56	61	63	53	74	69	50	70	55	66	67	61	74	74
79230	DODSON	79	55	29	52	64	72	54	67	62	53	73	81	46	72	56	65	67	66	80	93
79234	FLOMOT	65	49	32	47	54	64	54	60	61	51	72	67	48	67	54	64	65	60	71	72
79235	FLOYDADA	67	58	46	54	59	64	57	64	61	60	75	71	53	71	57	61	72	64	66	74
79237	HEDLEY	71	54	35	51	59	70	59	65	66	56	78	73	53	74	59	70	71	65	78	79
79239	LAKEVIEW	52	39	26	37	43	51	43	48	48	41	57	53	39	54	43	51	52	48	57	57
79241	LOCKNEY	85	70	52	65	71	76	70	79	75	75	93	88	63	85	69	75	90	80	81	91
79243	MCADOO	67	50	33	48	55	66	56	61	63	53	74	69	50	69	55	66	67	61	74	74
79244	MATADOR	70	53	35	51	58	69	58	64	65	55	77	72	52	73	58	69	70	64	77	77
79245	MEMPHIS	52	39	26	38	43	51	43	48	49	41	57	54	39	54	43	51	52	48	57	58
79247	ODELL	77	54	28	51	62	70	53	65	61	52	72	79	45	70	55	64	65	65	78	91
79248	PADUCAH	72	52	32	50	59	69	56	64	63	53	74	74	49	71	56	66	67	64	76	82
79250	PETERSBURG	74	66	54	61	63	66	67	72	69	73	87	77	61	77	64	67	86	73	68	75
79251	QUAIL	76	53	28	50	62	70	53	65	61	52	71	78	45	70	55	64	65	64	78	91
79252	QUANAH	81	60	38	57	66	78	65	73	73	62	86	83	57	81	65	77	78	73	87	91
79255	QUITAQUE	69	48	25	46	56	63	48	59	55	47	64	71	41	63	49	58	59	58	70	82
79256	ROARING SPRINGS	64	48	32	46	53	63	53	58	60	50	70	66	47	66	53	63	64	58	70	71
79257	SILVERTON	75	52	27	49	61	68	51	64	59	51	70	77	44	68	53	62	63	63	76	89
79259	TELL	0	0	0	0	0	0	0	0	0	0	0	0	0	0	0	0	0	0	0	0
79261	TURKEY	58	44	29	42	48	57	48	53	54	46	64	60	43	60	48	57	58	53	64	64
79311	ABERNATHY	85	66	45	63	71	78	66	76	73	68	88	88	60	84	66	74	83	76	83	95
79312	AMHERST	84	58	31	55	68	76	58	71	66	57	78	86	49	76	60	70	71	70	85	99
79313	ANTON	82	57	30	54	66	74	56	70	65	56	76	84	48	75	58	68	69	69	83	97
79316	BROWNFIELD	69	58	44	54	59	64	58	65	62	61	76	72	53	71	57	62	73	65	67	75
79320	BULA	87	61	32	57	71	79	60	74	69	59	81	89	51	79	62	72	74	73	88	103
79322	CROSBYTON	84	66	47	62	71	81	69	77	76	68	91	87	62	86	69	79	85	77	88	94
79323	DENVER CITY	84	68	48	63	70	76	68	78	74	72	90	87	61	83	67	73	87	78	81	92
79324	ENOCHS	86	60	31	57	70	78	59	73	68	59	80	88	51	78	61	72	73	72	87	102
79325	FARWELL	74	55	34	52	61	67	55	65	61	56	74	76	48	70	56	63	69	65	73	84
79326	FIELDTON	84	59	31	56	69	77	58	72	67	58	79	87	50	77	60	70	72	71	86	100
79329	IDALOU	96	72	44	68	79	87	71	84	79	72	94	99	63	90	72	81	88	84	94	110
79331	LAMESA	68	61	52	58	62	67	62	67	65	64	80	73	59	75	61	65	78	67	68	74
79336	LEVELLAND	73	65	56	62	65	71	66	70	68	67	84	79	62	80	65	68	81	70	71	80
79339	LITTLEFIELD	78	61	42	57	65	74	64	72	71	64	85	80	57	79	63	73	79	72	80	86
79342	LOOP	95	66	35	62	77	86	65	81	75	64	88	97	56	86	68	79	80	79	96	112
79343	LORENZO	68	56	42	52	57	61	57	64	61	61	75	70	51	68	55	60	73	64	64	72
79344	MAPLE	85	60	31	56	69	78	59	73	68	58	79	88	50	78	61	71	72	72	87	101
79345	MEADOW	74	61	47	57	62	66	62	69	66	66	82	76	56	74	60	65	80	70	69	78
79346	MORTON	66	55	42	51	55	59	56	62	59	60	73	68	51	66	54	58	72	63	62	69
79347	MULESHOE	66	52	37	49	55	61	55	61	60	55	72	69	49	68	54	61	68	61	66	72
79351	ODONNELL	76	63	48	59	64	68	64	71	68	68	84	78	58	76	62	67	82	72	71	80
79353	PEP	86	60	31	57	70	78	59	73	68	59	80	88	51	79	61	72	73	72	87	102
79355	PLAINS	83	68	51	64	69	74	69	78	74	74	91	85	62	83	67	73	88	78	78	89
79356	POST	70	54	36	50	58	64	54	63	60	56	72	72	48	68	54	61	68	63	69	78
79357	RALLS	73	62	48	57	61	65	62	69	66	67	82	75	57	74	60	65	80	70	68	77
79358	ROPESVILLE	106	74	39	70	86	96	73	90	84	72	99	109	62	97	76	88	90	89	108	126
79359	SEAGRAVES	74	62	46	58	63	68	62	69	65	65	80	77	56	74	60	65	77	69	70	81
79360	SEMINOLE	75	64	48	60	65	69	63	70	66	66	81	78	57	75	62	65	78	70	71	82
79363	SHALLOWATER	85	79	70	77	79	84	78	82	79	79	98	95	75	94	77	78	94	82	81	94
79364	SLATON	78	62	44	59	65	75	65	72	71	65	86	81	59	80	64	73	81	72	80	85
79366	RANSOM CANYON	149	104	54	98	121	135	102	127	118	101	138	153	87	136	106	124	126	125	151	176
79370	SPUR	62	47	31	45	51	62	52	57	58	49	69	64	46	65	51	62	62	57	68	69
79371	SUDAN	88	66	43	63	72	86	72	80	81	68	95	90	64	90	71	85	87	80	96	97
79373	TAHOKA	76	57	35	53	62	69	57	67	63	58	76	78	50	72	57	65	71	67	75	87
79376	TOKIO	67	47	24	44	54	61	46	57	53	45	62	69	39	61	48	56	57	56	68	79
79377	WELCH	104	72	38	68	84	94	72	88	82	71	97	107	61	95	74	86	88	87	105	123
79379	WHITEFACE	84	69	50	68	74	83	70	77	76	69	91	89	66	90	70	77	85	76	86	95
79381	WILSON	89	70	49	66	74	80	71	81	77	74	94	91	63	87	70	77	90	82	85	98
79382	WOLFFORTH	85	89	85	90	88	90	85	86	82	86	103	100	86	104	84	80	100	85	81	97
79401	LUBBOCK	34	25	32	28	25	28	37	32	37	34	46	40	33	43	32	34	44	36	30	35
79403	LUBBOCK	64	54	50	50	55	62	56	60	61	58	75	67	54	70	56	63	72	61	64	70
79404	LUBBOCK	59	52	46	48	51	56	53	56	56	56	69	62	50	63	51	56	67	57	57	63
79407	LUBBOCK	70	64	70	66	63	68	73	69	72	71	90	83	69	87	69	69	87	73	66	78
79409	LUBBOCK	30	18	23	21	18	22	35	26	34	30	43	36	29	38	28	30	40	32	24	29
79410	LUBBOCK	67	59	74	64	58	63	74	67	72	70	91	84	70	87	68	67	89	73	62	74
79411	LUBBOCK	47	44	45	43	43	46	48	48	49	48	61	55	46	58	46	47	60	49	46	51
79412	LUBBOCK	55	51	53	50	51	56	55	55	57	55	71	63	54	69	54	57	69	56	56	60
79413	LUBBOCK	76	82	92	81	82	88	82	81	81	81	102	93	85	103	83	81	99	81	80	89
79414	LUBBOCK	55	50	60	53	50	54	61	55	60	58	75	69	58	73	57	56	73	59	52	61
79415	LUBBOCK	45	36	35	36	36	39	45	42	45	44	57	50	40	52	41	42	55	46	40	47
79416	LUBBOCK	80	77	88	81	76	80	87	81	84	84	106	98	84	103	82	79	103	85	75	89
79423	LUBBOCK	100	109	110	110	106	108	103	103	97	104	122	120	104	123	102	94	120	102	94	114
79424	LUBBOCK	113	119	128	124	116	119	120	116	114	120	143	138	120	142	116	108	141	117	105	128
79501	ANSON	74	56	40	54	61	72	62	68	69	59	81	78	55	78	61	72	75	68	79	83
79502	ASPERMONT	71	51	31	49	58	67	54	62	61	52	72	72	47	69	54	64	66	62	75	81
79503	AVOCA	64	48	31	46	52	62	52	58	58	50	69	66	46	65	52	62	63	58	69	71
79504	BAIRD	66	50	34	48	55	65	55	60	61	53	72	68	49	68	54	64	66	60	71	73
79506	BLACKWELL	75	57	38	54	64	74	59	68	66	57	78	77	53	76	60	71	72	67	81	87
79508	BUFFALO GAP	92	114	121	114	112	110	102	101	94	101	118	119	108	126	104	91	118	98	91	112
79510	CLYDE	79	62	41	60	68	75	61	70	67	61	80	83	55	77	62	68	74	70	78	91
79511	COAHOMA	83	60	35	57	68	78	62	73	71	60	83	85	54	80	63	75	76	72	87	96
79512	COLORADO CITY	55	44	34	42	47	53	48	52	52	47	62	58	43	59	47	53	59	52	58	61
79517	FLUVANNA	86	60	32	57	70	79	60	74	69	59	80	89	51	79	62	72	73	73	88	103
79518	GIRARD	79	55	29	52	64	72	54	67	63	54	73	81	46	72	56	66	67	66	80	94
79519	GOLDSBORO	75	58	38	52	65	73	55	66	62	54	74	78	49	73	58	66	68	65	79	91
	TEXAS	94	90	91	90	89	95	92	93	92	93	115	107	90	112	90	90	112	94	89	104
	UNITED STATES	100	100	100	100	100	100	100	100	100	100	100	100	100	100	100	100	100	100	100	100

 Copyright © 2004 ESRI BIS. All rights reserved. Reproduction by any method is prohibited.

ZIP CODE		COUNTY FIPS CODE	POPULATION			2000-2004 ANNUAL RATE		HOUSEHOLDS					FAMILIES		
#	POST OFFICE NAME		2000	2004	2009	% Rate	State Centile	2000	2004	2009	% Annual Rate 2000-2004	2004 Average HH Size	2000	2004	% Annual Rate 2000-2004
79520	HAMLIN	253	2570	2546	2627	-0.2	9	1048	1034	1063	-0.3	2.42	718	709	-0.3
79521	HASKELL	207	3570	3516	3449	-0.4	7	1487	1463	1436	-0.4	2.34	1010	998	-0.3
79525	HAWLEY	253	2630	2817	3009	1.6	60	928	987	1049	1.5	2.85	750	797	1.4
79526	HERMLEIGH	415	907	901	903	-0.2	10	361	360	360	-0.1	2.39	261	261	0.0
79527	IRA	415	282	280	280	-0.2	9	113	113	113	0.0	2.46	89	88	-0.3
79528	JAYTON	263	591	589	588	-0.1	11	240	240	239	0.0	2.30	164	164	0.0
79529	KNOX CITY	275	1456	1465	1484	0.2	16	583	585	592	0.1	2.39	392	394	0.1
79530	LAWN	441	648	677	699	1.0	43	256	267	275	1.0	2.54	197	206	1.1
79532	LORAINE	335	1144	1191	1219	1.0	40	449	466	478	0.9	2.49	315	328	1.0
79533	LUEDERS	253	466	461	476	-0.3	8	199	196	202	-0.4	2.33	138	136	-0.3
79534	MC CAULLEY	151	226	228	233	0.2	18	92	93	96	0.3	2.45	65	66	0.4
79535	MARYNEAL	353	170	164	160	-0.8	2	66	64	62	-0.7	2.56	52	51	-0.5
79536	MERKEL	441	5066	4984	5091	-0.4	6	1906	1866	1900	-0.5	2.64	1427	1405	-0.4
79537	NOLAN	353	152	151	149	-0.2	10	56	56	55	0.0	2.70	38	38	0.0
79538	NOVICE	083	229	236	238	0.7	32	91	93	94	0.5	2.54	68	70	0.7
79539	O BRIEN	207	280	270	262	-0.9	2	109	105	102	-0.9	2.56	76	74	-0.6
79540	OLD GLORY	433	270	242	218	-2.5	0	131	118	106	-2.4	2.05	89	80	-2.5
79541	OVALO	441	705	750	782	1.5	56	260	275	285	1.3	2.72	204	216	1.4
79543	ROBY	151	1299	1313	1341	0.3	19	522	528	540	0.3	2.44	372	378	0.4
79544	ROCHESTER	207	583	562	546	-0.9	2	247	238	231	-0.9	2.35	173	167	-0.8
79545	ROSCOE	353	1826	1756	1716	-0.9	1	684	657	641	-0.9	2.61	527	507	-0.9
79546	ROTAN	151	2130	2152	2198	0.2	18	885	896	920	0.3	2.34	597	607	0.4
79547	RULE	207	862	843	824	-0.5	4	364	355	348	-0.6	2.37	253	248	-0.5
79548	RULE	207	296	286	279	-0.8	2	131	127	123	-0.7	2.25	92	89	-0.8
79549	SNYDER	263	15171	15059	15104	-0.2	9	5283	5262	5293	-0.1	2.55	3810	3806	0.0
79553	STAMFORD	207	4199	4301	4507	0.6	28	1634	1667	1739	0.5	2.48	1163	1188	0.5
79556	SWEETWATER	353	13569	13472	13377	-0.2	9	5314	5274	5246	-0.2	2.47	3649	3636	-0.1
79560	SYLVESTER	151	220	223	229	0.3	21	101	103	105	0.5	2.17	73	74	0.3
79561	TRENT	441	511	539	560	1.3	50	199	210	217	1.3	2.57	143	151	1.3
79562	TUSCOLA	441	2270	2512	2677	2.4	75	869	953	1008	2.2	2.63	694	762	2.2
79563	TYE	441	1127	1089	1097	-0.8	2	412	397	399	-0.9	2.73	311	301	-0.8
79565	WESTBROOK	335	400	404	407	0.2	18	157	158	159	0.2	2.56	110	111	0.2
79566	WINGATE	399	357	356	360	-0.1	11	157	156	156	-0.2	2.28	119	118	-0.2
79567	WINTERS	399	3756	3743	3765	-0.1	11	1448	1434	1435	-0.2	2.58	1027	1019	-0.2
79601	ABILENE	253	21562	22016	22674	0.5	25	6993	7247	7558	0.8	2.22	4024	4163	0.8
79602	ABILENE	441	19536	20066	20692	0.6	30	6965	7132	7350	0.6	2.63	4963	5111	0.7
79603	ABILENE	441	24208	24374	24968	0.2	16	8780	8814	9018	0.1	2.72	6397	6446	0.2
79605	ABILENE	441	29605	29549	30059	0.0	12	11849	11790	11984	-0.1	2.44	8094	8070	-0.1
79606	ABILENE	441	20659	22285	23598	1.8	64	8485	9050	9525	1.5	2.44	5721	6193	1.9
79607	DYESS AFB	441	4969	4839	4867	-0.6	3	1123	1083	1081	-0.9	3.64	1096	1057	-0.9
79697	ABILENE	441	451	448	452	-0.2	10	1	1	1	0.0	3.00	1	1	0.0
79698	ABILENE	441	710	712	715	0.1	14	16	16	16	0.0	2.56	10	10	0.0
79699	ABILENE	441	1956	2202	2367	2.8	80	198	251	286	5.7	4.61	62	82	6.8
79701	MIDLAND	329	24444	24374	24950	-0.1	11	8329	8268	8431	-0.2	2.87	5945	5903	-0.2
79703	MIDLAND	329	18442	18269	18650	-0.2	9	6749	6674	6790	-0.3	2.74	4985	4926	-0.3
79705	MIDLAND	329	29136	30111	31356	0.8	35	11207	11550	11996	0.7	2.58	8036	8280	0.7
79706	MIDLAND	329	15292	16645	17726	2.0	68	5149	5592	5948	2.0	2.98	4177	4537	2.0
79707	MIDLAND	329	26692	28844	31160	1.8	65	10612	11318	12131	1.5	2.51	7234	7795	1.8
79713	ACKERLY	115	675	642	617	-1.2	1	253	240	230	-1.2	2.67	205	194	-1.3
79714	ANDREWS	003	13004	13574	14439	1.0	42	4601	4821	5158	1.1	2.80	3519	3697	1.2
79718	BALMORHEA	389	1257	1213	1186	-0.8	2	462	449	442	-0.7	2.70	332	323	-0.6
79719	BARSTOW	475	880	871	877	-0.2	8	239	237	242	-0.2	2.83	169	169	0.0
79720	BIG SPRING	227	32077	33274	34193	0.9	38	10808	11037	11404	0.5	2.53	7505	7688	0.6
79730	COYANOSA	371	312	313	316	0.1	14	100	101	103	0.2	3.10	82	83	0.3
79731	CRANE	103	3996	3920	3903	-0.5	5	1360	1331	1326	-0.5	2.91	1083	1063	-0.4
79734	FORT DAVIS	243	1932	1947	1950	0.2	18	787	790	787	0.1	2.38	551	555	0.2
79735	FORT STOCKTON	371	13962	14091	14291	0.2	18	4191	4259	4359	0.4	2.84	3261	3323	0.4
79738	GAIL	033	516	497	497	-0.9	2	193	187	187	-0.7	2.66	143	139	-0.7
79739	GARDEN CITY	173	1299	1261	1202	-0.7	3	448	439	424	-0.5	2.87	330	324	-0.4
79741	GOLDSMITH	135	337	335	348	-0.1	10	135	134	138	-0.2	2.50	103	100	-0.7
79742	GRANDFALLS	475	566	540	542	-1.1	1	211	203	206	-0.9	2.66	152	147	-0.8
79743	IMPERIAL	371	678	681	686	0.1	15	239	241	245	0.2	2.83	196	198	0.2
79744	IRAAN	371	1526	1507	1516	-0.3	8	530	525	531	-0.2	2.78	417	413	-0.2
79745	KERMIT	495	6196	6135	6122	-0.2	8	2223	2210	2220	-0.1	2.73	1692	1687	-0.1
79748	KNOTT	227	276	272	277	-0.3	7	92	91	92	-0.3	2.99	71	70	-0.3
79749	LENORAH	317	452	442	438	-0.5	4	157	154	153	-0.5	2.87	119	118	-0.2
79752	MC CAMEY	461	2169	2106	2087	-0.7	3	808	794	798	-0.4	2.62	587	577	-0.4
79754	MENTONE	301	67	64	64	-1.1	1	31	30	30	-0.8	2.13	20	19	-1.2
79755	MIDKIFF	461	1235	1225	1225	-0.2	9	448	450	458	0.1	2.71	347	349	0.1
79756	MONAHANS	475	9321	9334	9460	0.0	13	3451	3479	3558	0.2	2.64	2565	2593	0.3
79758	GARDENDALE	135	1635	1736	1846	1.4	55	631	666	707	1.3	2.61	501	537	1.7
79761	ODESSA	135	29224	30142	31811	0.7	34	10849	11188	11801	0.7	2.63	7526	7776	0.8
79762	ODESSA	135	34268	36302	38890	1.4	54	13681	14486	15504	1.4	2.49	9408	9951	1.3
79763	ODESSA	135	30422	31615	33239	0.9	39	10011	10331	10816	0.7	3.03	7716	8003	0.9
79764	ODESSA	135	18050	18558	19560	0.7	31	6388	6543	6881	0.6	2.83	4752	4887	0.7
79765	ODESSA	135	4862	5161	5461	1.4	55	1720	1821	1922	1.4	2.73	1302	1379	1.4
79766	ODESSA	135	4179	4867	5434	3.7	88	1078	1264	1419	3.8	3.47	923	1089	4.0
79772	PECOS	389	11880	11619	11446	-0.5	4	3629	3558	3520	-0.5	2.94	2798	2749	-0.4
79777	PYOTE	475	142	140	142	-0.3	7	63	63	64	0.0	1.71	45	44	-0.5
79781	SHEFFIELD	371	332	329	331	-0.2	9	94	93	94	-0.3	3.34	74	73	-0.3
79782	STANTON	317	3919	3928	3938	0.1	14	1351	1355	1362	0.1	2.84	1047	1054	0.2
79783	TARZAN	317	515	513	513	-0.1	11	166	165	166	-0.1	3.11	132	132	0.0
79789	WINK	495	977	946	934	-0.8	3	361	351	348	-0.7	2.61	278	270	-0.7
79821	ANTHONY	141	6250	6969	7574	2.6	77	1331	1544	1726	3.6	3.56	1145	1329	3.6
79830	ALPINE	043	7960	8373	8936	1.2	48	3280	3464	3720	1.3	2.30	1972	2092	1.4
79832	ALPINE	043	52	55	59	1.3	52	4	4	5	0.0	2.50	2	2	0.0
79834	BIG BEND NATIONAL PARK	043	224	237	253	1.3	52	109	115	124	1.3	2.02	66	71	1.7
79835	CANUTILLO	141	10704	11831	12856	2.4	74	2838	3184	3499	2.7	3.71	2469	2765	2.7
79836	CLINT	141	17102	18300	19613	1.6	60	4542	4930	5341	2.0	3.71	4028	4368	1.9
79837	DELL CITY	229	625	613	642	-0.5	5	241	235	243	-0.6	2.61	182	178	-0.5
79839	FORT HANCOCK	229	1817	1984	2161	2.1	69	525	569	613	1.9	3.49	430	466	1.9
79842	MARATHON	043	555	560	585	0.2	18	238	241	253	0.3	2.32	153	156	0.5
79843	MARFA	377	2655	2660	2875	0.0	14	1073	1083	1177	0.2	2.37	701	704	0.1
79845	PRESIDIO	377	4633	5375	6202	3.6	87	1451	1692	1953	3.7	3.18	1159	1347	3.6
79847	SALT FLAT	109	165	162	157	-0.4	5	79	78	77	-0.3	2.06	49	49	0.0
	TEXAS					2.2					2.0	2.77			2.1
	UNITED STATES					1.2					1.3	2.58			1.1

ZIP CODE #	POST OFFICE NAME	RACE (%) White 2000	White 2004	Black 2000	Black 2004	Asian/Pacific 2000	Asian/Pacific 2004	% Hispanic Origin 2000	% Hispanic Origin 2004	2004 AGE DISTRIBUTION (%) 0-4	5-9	10-14	15-19	20-24	25-44	45-64	65-84	85+	18+	MEDIAN AGE 2004	% 2004 Males	% 2004 Females
79520	HAMLIN	81.8	79.3	5.5	6.0	0.7	0.8	19.5	22.7	6.0	6.2	7.5	6.4	6.1	21.0	25.7	17.1	4.0	76.0	42.3	47.3	52.7
79521	HASKELL	82.1	80.0	3.4	3.5	0.1	0.1	20.7	23.7	5.8	5.6	6.4	7.0	6.1	19.7	24.5	20.1	4.8	77.7	44.6	45.9	54.1
79525	HAWLEY	94.5	93.6	0.5	0.6	0.5	0.5	6.2	7.6	6.8	7.0	8.2	7.6	6.6	26.7	25.1	11.2	0.8	73.3	36.8	50.3	49.7
79526	HERMLEIGH	92.0	90.3	1.5	1.7	0.3	0.3	17.3	21.1	6.2	5.9	5.1	8.8	9.3	22.0	27.6	13.1	2.0	79.3	40.4	50.5	49.5
79527	IRA	95.7	95.4	0.0	0.0	0.0	0.0	12.4	15.0	4.3	5.4	7.9	6.8	5.7	23.9	29.6	14.6	1.8	78.2	42.4	51.4	48.6
79528	JAYTON	96.3	96.4	0.2	0.2	0.0	0.0	9.1	9.5	3.4	4.4	6.5	5.9	2.6	19.9	29.7	21.6	6.1	82.3	51.3	46.2	53.8
79529	KNOX CITY	72.4	71.9	8.9	8.9	0.4	0.4	22.5	23.2	6.9	6.1	6.1	8.1	6.6	19.3	23.5	19.3	4.2	75.4	42.8	45.9	54.1
79530	LAWN	96.5	96.0	0.0	0.0	0.5	0.6	5.4	6.8	3.7	6.2	9.6	7.7	3.3	24.5	27.5	14.2	3.4	75.3	41.8	49.8	50.2
79532	LORAINE	69.2	68.9	4.2	4.2	0.1	0.1	38.6	39.6	5.9	5.8	7.6	7.0	6.4	20.5	24.1	19.2	3.6	76.7	42.7	47.7	52.3
79533	LUEDERS	93.1	92.0	1.1	1.1	0.0	0.0	6.7	8.2	6.5	6.7	7.4	6.9	6.5	25.6	25.4	13.9	1.1	74.8	39.6	51.0	49.0
79534	MC CAULLEY	89.8	89.0	1.3	1.3	0.4	0.4	13.3	13.6	4.8	5.3	7.0	6.1	5.7	21.1	27.2	20.2	2.6	78.5	45.0	50.9	49.1
79535	MARYNEAL	92.9	92.1	0.0	0.0	0.0	0.0	11.2	13.4	4.3	6.1	9.2	7.3	2.4	24.4	28.7	16.5	1.2	74.4	42.7	51.2	48.8
79536	MERKEL	91.8	90.6	0.9	0.9	0.3	0.4	11.1	13.3	6.1	6.4	7.6	7.3	6.7	25.8	25.7	12.5	1.9	75.4	38.9	48.6	51.4
79537	NOLAN	86.8	84.8	1.3	1.3	0.0	0.0	15.1	19.2	8.0	8.6	6.0	6.0	6.6	19.9	25.2	17.9	2.0	73.5	40.8	48.3	51.7
79538	NOVICE	93.9	92.8	0.0	0.0	0.9	0.9	6.1	7.6	5.5	5.5	5.9	5.1	4.7	17.8	29.2	24.2	2.1	80.1	48.4	51.3	48.7
79539	O BRIEN	76.1	72.6	2.5	3.0	0.7	0.7	27.1	31.5	5.2	4.8	6.3	5.6	6.3	23.0	27.4	18.9	2.6	79.6	44.2	50.4	49.6
79540	OLD GLORY	94.1	93.4	0.7	0.8	0.0	0.0	8.9	10.3	3.3	3.3	4.6	5.0	3.3	18.6	28.5	28.1	5.4	85.5	53.3	51.2	48.8
79541	OVALO	96.2	95.3	0.3	0.3	0.4	0.4	5.1	6.3	4.4	6.9	9.3	7.5	3.2	26.0	28.5	12.0	2.1	74.3	40.9	49.9	50.1
79543	ROBY	89.8	89.6	1.8	1.8	0.0	0.0	16.5	17.1	6.6	6.8	7.4	5.5	5.0	20.9	25.4	19.4	3.1	75.9	43.4	47.8	52.2
79544	ROCHESTER	76.2	72.6	2.6	2.9	0.5	0.7	27.1	31.3	5.0	4.8	6.4	5.5	6.2	23.3	26.7	19.4	2.7	80.3	44.1	49.3	50.7
79545	ROSCOE	79.7	76.4	0.9	0.9	0.1	0.1	30.4	35.5	5.8	6.5	9.4	7.4	5.5	22.6	24.3	15.6	3.1	73.5	39.4	48.0	52.1
79546	ROTAN	76.6	76.2	4.3	4.4	0.2	0.2	28.4	29.2	6.4	6.1	6.7	6.6	6.1	20.9	24.4	19.0	3.9	77.0	42.9	47.8	52.2
79547	RULE	87.8	86.2	1.9	1.9	0.0	0.0	18.0	20.8	4.9	4.9	6.2	8.3	5.6	19.3	26.1	21.7	3.1	78.9	45.6	49.8	50.2
79548	RULE	89.2	87.8	1.4	1.4	0.0	0.0	13.9	16.4	3.9	4.6	5.9	7.0	4.9	17.5	29.0	23.8	3.5	81.5	48.6	47.2	52.8
79549	SNYDER	80.3	78.6	6.4	6.5	0.2	0.2	28.6	32.2	6.4	6.3	6.5	8.1	8.0	25.6	23.8	13.1	2.2	76.5	37.0	52.4	47.6
79553	STAMFORD	76.9	74.6	7.0	7.4	0.1	0.1	23.7	27.4	6.5	6.3	7.3	7.1	6.2	21.3	24.2	17.4	3.6	75.3	41.2	47.9	52.1
79556	SWEETWATER	78.1	76.1	5.3	5.3	0.3	0.4	28.1	31.4	7.0	6.6	7.1	7.4	7.4	24.1	24.6	13.7	2.3	75.1	37.6	48.8	51.2
79560	SYLVESTER	90.5	90.6	1.8	1.8	0.0	0.0	11.4	11.7	4.5	5.4	5.8	5.8	4.0	22.4	29.2	19.3	3.6	80.7	46.5	50.7	49.3
79561	TRENT	91.8	90.2	1.4	1.5	0.2	0.2	11.9	14.7	4.5	6.5	8.9	9.3	4.1	26.0	25.2	13.4	2.2	73.8	39.8	47.5	52.5
79562	TUSCOLA	96.2	95.4	0.4	0.4	0.1	0.2	4.9	6.3	5.0	7.1	8.7	7.8	3.6	26.6	29.2	11.0	1.1	73.8	40.3	49.9	50.1
79563	TYE	92.4	90.9	1.2	1.2	0.6	0.6	10.3	12.9	7.1	7.4	8.4	6.9	6.4	27.0	27.4	8.8	0.6	72.5	36.9	48.7	51.3
79565	WESTBROOK	94.8	95.1	0.0	0.0	0.0	0.0	10.0	10.4	5.0	4.7	5.5	5.9	5.2	20.3	31.4	20.3	1.7	81.4	47.1	49.5	50.5
79566	WINGATE	93.0	92.7	0.6	0.6	0.0	0.0	9.8	10.7	5.3	6.2	7.0	6.5	4.8	21.6	30.6	15.5	2.5	77.3	44.1	49.7	50.3
79567	WINTERS	79.5	79.0	1.8	1.8	0.4	0.4	32.6	33.8	7.4	6.9	7.5	7.1	7.3	21.6	23.8	15.6	2.9	73.7	38.7	47.7	52.3
79601	ABILENE	76.0	74.7	14.7	15.0	1.1	1.2	19.6	21.7	4.3	3.9	4.3	10.2	17.1	29.7	19.0	10.0	1.6	83.3	30.8	59.1	41.0
79602	ABILENE	83.6	82.1	5.3	5.4	1.2	1.3	17.0	19.4	7.1	7.1	7.9	7.6	7.2	29.9	23.0	9.1	1.0	73.2	34.1	49.9	50.2
79603	ABILENE	68.5	65.6	9.8	10.0	0.7	0.8	35.2	40.0	8.6	7.6	8.0	7.7	7.8	25.1	21.0	12.4	1.7	71.1	33.0	47.4	52.6
79605	ABILENE	81.5	79.1	6.5	6.8	1.3	1.5	14.6	17.6	7.7	6.7	7.0	7.1	8.4	26.7	21.1	13.0	2.3	74.3	34.7	47.5	52.5
79606	ABILENE	87.3	85.8	4.8	5.0	2.1	2.4	8.2	9.9	6.6	6.5	7.5	6.9	8.9	30.2	23.0	8.9	1.4	75.1	34.5	49.0	51.0
79607	DYESS AFB	72.0	68.9	12.8	13.6	3.3	3.6	13.4	16.1	15.7	10.4	7.2	7.5	20.5	37.2	1.4	0.1	0.0	63.7	22.3	55.6	44.4
79697	ABILENE	83.4	80.8	4.4	4.9	1.3	1.6	16.2	19.9	8.3	5.1	4.9	11.8	22.5	28.4	12.5	5.4	1.1	79.9	24.4	51.6	48.4
79698	ABILENE	84.2	81.6	4.9	5.5	0.1	0.1	19.2	23.2	3.2	2.7	3.8	31.7	32.7	11.5	9.3	4.8	0.3	88.3	21.3	44.5	55.5
79699	ABILENE	89.2	87.7	4.8	5.2	2.3	2.7	5.3	6.5	1.3	1.3	2.1	34.6	35.2	10.8	5.6	5.0	4.1	93.2	21.5	44.1	56.0
79701	MIDLAND	59.3	57.2	12.3	12.1	0.4	0.4	50.0	53.9	9.0	8.4	8.7	8.5	8.0	25.0	19.8	10.7	2.0	68.6	31.3	48.3	51.7
79703	MIDLAND	78.5	75.0	4.7	5.1	0.9	1.0	32.1	38.0	8.7	8.3	8.5	7.8	8.3	28.5	20.3	8.9	0.8	69.7	30.9	48.1	51.9
79705	MIDLAND	77.4	75.8	10.9	10.8	0.8	0.8	23.2	26.4	7.0	7.0	7.7	8.0	7.3	22.7	25.2	13.6	1.5	73.4	37.7	47.6	52.4
79706	MIDLAND	85.2	82.6	0.7	0.8	0.3	0.3	31.7	37.1	7.5	7.5	8.6	8.8	7.9	26.4	24.9	7.8	0.6	70.9	33.3	49.8	50.2
79707	MIDLAND	87.5	85.6	3.6	4.1	1.9	2.1	13.6	16.3	6.6	6.2	7.6	8.7	8.9	25.8	26.3	8.6	1.3	74.3	35.5	48.4	51.6
79713	ACKERLY	76.0	72.4	0.4	0.5	0.4	0.5	31.6	36.5	5.5	6.9	7.8	8.3	4.4	24.5	31.2	11.5	0.2	74.6	41.5	51.4	48.6
79714	ANDREWS	77.1	74.9	1.7	1.7	0.7	0.8	40.0	44.2	7.7	7.3	8.2	8.9	7.7	25.1	22.8	11.1	1.2	71.1	34.5	49.3	50.8
79718	BALMORHEA	78.4	77.7	0.0	0.0	0.0	0.0	81.9	84.8	6.8	6.3	8.7	9.6	6.1	21.2	22.6	17.2	1.7	71.8	37.0	50.6	49.4
79719	BARSTOW	75.7	75.7	8.9	8.8	0.2	0.2	55.2	56.4	4.8	6.1	6.8	23.9	6.2	17.2	20.2	13.3	1.5	63.2	28.4	63.5	36.5
79720	BIG SPRING	79.7	78.0	4.3	4.3	0.6	0.7	38.2	42.3	6.1	5.6	6.4	6.7	8.1	30.5	22.3	12.3	1.9	77.9	36.3	55.0	45.0
79730	COYANOSA	87.2	85.6	0.3	0.3	0.6	0.6	52.2	57.2	7.7	7.7	8.0	8.3	7.4	22.0	26.5	11.2	1.3	71.3	36.9	50.2	49.8
79731	CRANE	73.7	73.2	2.9	3.0	0.4	0.4	43.9	45.0	7.9	7.9	8.7	8.3	7.4	24.1	24.4	10.0	1.5	70.3	35.3	48.8	51.2
79734	FORT DAVIS	90.6	90.5	1.0	1.0	0.1	0.1	33.4	34.5	4.5	5.0	7.1	8.5	4.0	22.8	32.0	14.4	1.8	77.3	43.7	51.2	48.8
79735	FORT STOCKTON	73.1	72.0	5.0	4.8	0.6	0.6	64.7	68.3	6.8	6.5	7.3	8.8	10.7	27.9	21.2	9.6	1.2	74.5	31.5	55.7	44.3
79738	GAIL	90.5	90.1	0.2	0.2	0.0	0.0	11.8	12.5	4.0	4.4	6.4	7.0	6.4	25.0	28.2	17.1	1.4	80.5	43.2	50.9	49.1
79739	GARDEN CITY	77.1	76.5	0.5	0.5	0.2	0.2	30.3	31.2	8.8	8.5	8.8	7.3	6.6	25.9	24.5	8.9	0.8	69.6	35.2	52.9	47.1
79741	GOLDSMITH	82.2	79.4	0.3	0.3	0.0	0.0	37.7	44.2	7.8	8.4	7.8	6.6	6.9	24.8	24.5	12.5	0.9	71.6	35.4	51.6	48.4
79742	GRANDFALLS	73.3	72.8	0.2	0.2	0.0	0.0	45.9	47.0	8.0	7.6	8.2	7.6	7.6	23.2	23.0	13.3	1.7	71.5	36.2	47.8	52.2
79743	IMPERIAL	87.3	86.2	0.2	0.2	0.6	0.6	52.2	57.3	7.8	7.5	8.7	8.4	7.3	22.2	26.1	10.9	1.2	70.6	36.1	49.8	50.2
79744	IRAAN	90.6	89.6	1.5	1.5	0.0	0.0	37.9	42.5	6.8	7.1	7.6	9.5	7.9	27.5	23.6	8.8	1.3	72.4	33.9	53.6	46.4
79745	KERMIT	73.3	72.9	2.0	2.0	0.2	0.2	46.7	47.6	7.6	7.3	7.9	8.3	7.2	24.5	22.5	12.9	1.8	72.0	35.4	49.0	51.0
79748	KNOTT	82.6	80.2	0.7	0.7	0.0	0.0	27.9	32.7	5.2	5.5	6.6	5.9	5.5	23.5	28.7	17.3	1.8	78.3	43.1	50.4	49.6
79749	LENORAH	77.9	77.2	0.0	0.0	0.0	0.0	34.1	35.3	9.1	9.1	7.0	7.0	7.5	24.0	22.2	12.2	2.0	70.8	34.6	51.1	48.9
79752	MC CAMEY	74.3	73.8	1.5	1.5	0.1	0.1	48.8	49.9	6.3	6.9	8.2	8.2	7.5	22.6	24.7	13.8	1.9	73.5	38.0	48.9	51.1
79754	MENTONE	89.6	89.1	0.0	0.0	0.0	0.0	10.5	10.9	3.1	3.1	9.4	4.7	1.6	25.0	35.9	17.2	0.0	79.7	46.4	53.1	46.9
79755	MIDKIFF	84.0	83.5	1.9	1.9	0.2	0.2	31.6	32.8	5.5	5.7	7.2	8.2	7.8	20.5	30.9	13.1	1.1	76.4	41.4	49.6	50.5
79756	MONAHANS	80.6	80.4	4.4	4.4	0.3	0.3	40.3	41.4	6.8	7.2	8.5	8.3	6.2	24.6	24.4	12.5	1.6	72.3	37.0	48.8	51.2
79758	GARDENDALE	90.7	88.7	0.6	0.6	0.2	0.3	12.2	15.2	5.8	6.3	6.2	6.5	5.9	23.4	32.3	12.5	0.9	77.7	42.6	50.9	49.1
79761	ODESSA	68.4	67.3	8.7	8.5	0.7	0.8	46.6	49.3	8.3	7.4	7.6	7.5	8.9	25.0	21.9	11.7	1.7	72.3	33.0	48.7	51.3
79762	ODESSA	83.2	81.1	3.9	4.1	1.2	1.4	24.5	28.3	7.6	6.9	7.3	7.6	8.8	26.7	23.1	10.9	1.2	73.8	33.9	47.7	52.3
79763	ODESSA	67.0	64.7	4.1	4.0	0.3	0.3	57.6	62.6	8.6	8.4	9.5	8.9	8.5	26.0	20.7	8.2	1.2	68.1	29.7	48.4	51.6
79764	ODESSA	75.0	71.9	1.6	1.6	0.4	0.4	42.3	48.1	8.6	8.1	8.4	8.0	8.6	27.0	22.1	8.6	0.5	70.1	30.9	49.7	50.3
79765	ODESSA	80.5	77.3	1.5	1.7	2.0	2.1	24.9	29.8	7.5	6.8	8.0	7.9	7.7	27.6	23.8	9.2	1.4	72.7	35.4	49.8	50.2
79766	ODESSA	67.5	65.1	2.2	2.2	0.2	0.2	68.0	73.5	7.9	7.5	8.6	10.0	9.9	29.7	19.8	6.4	0.3	70.1	28.8	53.2	46.9
79772	PECOS	79.4	78.6	2.3	2.2	0.4	0.4	72.5	75.6	7.1	7.5	8.1	9.6	8.5	25.0	22.2	10.7	1.3	71.3	32.4	53.1	46.9
79777	PYOTE	76.1	75.7	9.2	8.6	0.0	0.0	55.6	56.4	5.0	5.7	6.4	23.6	5.7	18.6	20.7	12.9	1.4	63.6	30.0	63.6	36.4
79781	SHEFFIELD	89.5	88.8	2.7	2.7	0.0	0.0	40.1	45.0	6.7	6.7	7.3	9.4	8.2	27.1	25.2	8.2	1.2	73.9	33.4	53.8	46.2
79782	STANTON	78.7	78.3	1.9	1.9	0.2	0.2	42.8	43.9	8.7	8.8	8.9	7.6	6.4	25.4	20.8	11.7	1.7	68.4	33.5	48.7	51.3
79783	TARZAN	85.6	85.2	0.0	0.0	0.0	0.0	22.9	23.8	9.4	9.2	9.4	7.6	5.3	25.0	25.0	8.4	1.0	67.1	34.4	51.9	48.2
79789	WINK	84.3	83.8	0.8	0.9	0.0	0.0	26.9	28.0	5.8	5.9	8.1	8.3	7.9	25.7	26.9	10.3	1.2	75.3	37.7	48.5	51.5
79821	ANTHONY	80.9	81.1	2.6	2.2	0.2	0.3	86.4	89.1	7.6	7.3	8.1	8.4	9.6	35.3	18.2	4.9	0.5	71.9	30.0	60.2	39.8
79830	ALPINE	80.6	78.9	1.3	1.3	0.5	0.5	43.5	47.8	5.8	5.8	6.2	7.7	9.5	25.7	24.7	13.0	1.6	78.6	35.5	49.5	50.5
79832	ALPINE	84.6	83.6	1.9	1.8	0.0	1.8	28.9	30.9	3.6	5.5	5.5	7.3	12.7	23.6	25.5	14.6	1.8	85.5	37.5	47.3	52.7
79834	BIG BEND NATIONAL PARK	85.7	84.0	0.9	0.8	0.5	0.4	38.4	43.5	5.1	5.5	5.1	6.3	5.9	24.1	30.0	16.9	1.3	81.9	43.3	51.9	48.1
79835	CANUTILLO	92.4	91.9	0.5	0.5	0.1	0.1	91.6	92.7	9.9	10.0	10.5	9.3	8.1	27.5	17.7	6.5	0.4	63.7	26.6	49.4	50.6
79836	CLINT	79.8	79.5	0.4	0.4	0.0	0.1	93.5	94.8	10.7	10.1	10.9	9.7	8.5	25.9	17.4	6.3	0.5	62.2	25.0	48.9	51.1
79837	DELL CITY	67.4	64.6	1.1	1.3	0.3	0.3	58.9	63.1	5.7	6.2	9.3	7.8	6.2	21.4	26.8	16.0	0.7	73.7	39.7	50.2	49.8
79839	FORT HANCOCK	93.5	93.3	0.2	0.2	0.2	0.2	85.4	87.2	10.2	9.3	10.2	9.2	8.9	25.8	18.3	7.7	0.5	64.6	27.0	52.2	47.8
79842	MARATHON	85.2	83.9	0.7	0.7	0.0	0.0	48.8	53.8	2.9	3.4	5.4	7.5	7.1	19.1	35.5	17.5	1.6	83.8	48.1	52.0	48.0
79843	MARFA	90.3	89.9	0.6	0.7	0.1	0.1	69.1	71.6	5.7	6.1	7.9	6.9	6.4	24.6	25.1	15.2	2.1	76.1	39.0	50.6	49.4
79845	PRESIDIO	81.9	81.9	0.1	0.1	0.1	0.1	93.1	93.9	9.2	8.8	11.1	9.8	6.3	24.4	18.9	10.3	1.2	64.4	29.6	47.7	52.3
79847	SALT FLAT	89.7	88.3	0.6	1.2	0.6	0.6	34.6	38.9	3.7	4.3	5.6	5.6	5.6	27.8	32.1	14.8	0.6	82.7	43.6	56.2	43.8
	TEXAS	71.0	69.5	11.5	11.4	2.8	3.1	32.0	34.6	7.9	7.5	7.7	7.5	8.1	29.6	21.9	8.7	1.2	72.6	32.9	49.7	50.3
	UNITED STATES	75.1	73.6	12.3	12.5	3.8	4.2	12.5	14.1	6.9	6.7	7.2	7.0	7.3	28.6	23.8	10.8	1.7	75.1	36.0	49.1	50.9

#	POST OFFICE NAME	2004 Per Capita Income	2004 HH Income Base	2004 Household Income Distribution (%) Less than $25,000	$25,000 to $49,999	$50,000 to $99,999	$100,000 to $149,999	$150,000 or More	Median Household Income 2004	2009	2004 National Centile	2004 State Centile	2004 Home Value Base	2004 Home Value Distribution (%) Less than $50,000	$50,000 to $89,999	$90,000 to $174,999	$175,000 to $399,999	$400,000 or More	2004 Median Home Value
79520	HAMLIN	17961	1034	42.6	31.2	20.2	3.5	2.5	30682	34699	14	18	774	60.6	25.6	13.2	0.7	0.0	38194
79521	HASKELL	16287	1463	48.5	28.2	16.7	5.3	1.3	25909	30185	6	7	1061	62.1	24.4	12.5	0.9	0.0	42351
79525	HAWLEY	17029	987	28.1	35.9	28.1	5.5	2.5	39709	44175	45	53	828	48.1	28.7	16.9	5.2	1.1	52462
79526	HERMLEIGH	19314	360	35.3	26.7	31.1	5.6	1.4	35640	41281	30	36	285	44.6	27.4	22.5	5.6	0.0	55741
79527	IRA	21630	113	31.9	31.9	25.7	6.2	4.4	37019	46399	36	42	90	38.9	27.8	30.0	3.3	0.0	63333
79528	JAYTON	20896	240	31.7	33.3	26.7	7.5	0.8	36777	41978	35	41	183	71.0	21.9	5.5	1.6	0.0	29375
79529	KNOX CITY	16648	585	43.8	32.3	18.0	3.8	2.2	28472	32198	9	12	429	59.4	25.6	14.0	0.5	0.5	37717
79530	LAWN	21252	267	27.7	39.7	25.5	3.8	3.4	39505	45558	44	53	226	47.8	26.6	19.0	5.3	1.3	53333
79532	LORAINE	25118	466	46.6	29.8	15.7	3.2	4.7	26740	31102	7	9	354	62.7	18.9	15.8	2.3	0.3	32500
79533	LUEDERS	18290	196	32.1	41.3	19.4	5.6	1.5	34730	40637	26	32	162	64.2	19.8	13.6	2.5	0.0	39643
79534	MC CAULLEY	18282	93	34.4	33.3	25.8	3.2	3.2	36400	42589	33	40	74	50.0	20.3	21.6	6.8	1.4	50000
79535	MARYNEAL	19341	64	32.8	29.7	31.3	3.1	3.1	40000	42346	46	54	51	37.3	39.2	19.6	3.9	0.0	60833
79536	MERKEL	17773	1866	30.2	38.7	23.3	5.1	2.8	37463	43109	37	45	1437	56.4	24.6	15.4	3.3	0.3	42795
79537	NOLAN	15525	56	41.1	33.9	19.6	3.6	1.8	30870	36713	14	18	41	63.4	17.1	14.6	2.4	2.4	37500
79538	NOVICE	22004	93	31.2	35.5	23.7	6.5	3.2	38050	45000	39	47	78	46.2	23.1	21.8	5.1	3.9	55000
79539	O BRIEN	16555	105	51.4	26.7	16.2	3.8	1.9	23914	27313	4	5	83	67.5	24.1	6.0	2.4	0.0	33500
79540	OLD GLORY	28773	118	40.7	22.0	28.0	5.9	3.4	37868	41991	39	46	96	36.5	32.3	18.8	10.4	2.1	68182
79541	OVALO	22345	275	22.9	33.1	32.4	8.0	3.6	45131	51842	62	68	235	37.5	24.3	25.5	10.2	2.6	71786
79543	ROBY	18843	528	37.1	32.4	24.8	3.4	2.3	35416	40000	29	35	411	54.0	29.4	10.7	4.9	1.0	45286
79544	ROCHESTER	18019	238	50.0	26.5	16.4	3.8	3.4	25000	28100	5	6	188	62.8	23.9	8.0	4.3	1.1	37500
79545	ROSCOE	15369	657	42.6	28.2	23.9	3.8	1.5	30056	33918	12	16	504	57.5	28.0	12.5	1.8	0.2	40952
79546	ROTAN	15746	896	46.2	27.8	22.3	2.2	1.5	27638	31539	8	11	643	66.1	21.3	9.3	2.5	0.8	36394
79547	RULE	16795	355	44.2	30.4	20.3	3.1	2.0	28977	33255	10	13	286	69.6	18.5	10.5	1.4	0.0	29792
79548	RULE	20819	127	44.9	23.6	22.8	4.7	3.9	28942	32763	10	13	102	46.1	31.4	19.6	2.9	0.0	60000
79549	SNYDER	18897	5262	35.1	29.9	26.8	4.8	3.4	36324	42222	33	39	3846	49.7	23.3	22.3	4.3	0.4	50493
79553	STAMFORD	16812	1667	43.6	29.5	18.7	5.6	2.7	29528	33339	11	14	1214	57.0	26.2	14.1	2.1	0.7	40341
79556	SWEETWATER	16561	5274	43.5	28.9	21.2	3.8	2.6	30109	34100	13	16	3403	56.9	25.5	14.0	3.1	0.5	42726
79560	SYLVESTER	22090	103	34.0	35.9	19.4	7.8	2.9	33699	37873	23	29	83	53.0	20.5	19.3	7.2	0.0	46429
79561	TRENT	19269	210	27.1	35.7	30.5	5.2	1.4	41390	47574	51	59	173	60.1	28.3	11.6	0.0	0.0	38281
79562	TUSCOLA	24156	953	19.7	29.5	36.8	10.1	3.9	50706	57199	73	78	818	30.4	23.7	30.6	13.3	2.0	84516
79563	TYE	23573	397	32.5	29.5	28.0	6.1	4.0	38087	43877	40	47	302	58.9	21.5	15.2	4.0	0.3	38889
79565	WESTBROOK	17029	158	34.2	33.5	26.6	4.4	1.3	35443	39689	29	35	131	47.3	28.2	19.9	4.6	0.0	52188
79566	WINGATE	22612	156	30.1	32.1	29.5	5.8	2.6	38795	45000	42	50	130	41.5	16.9	31.5	8.5	1.5	70000
79567	WINTERS	14504	1434	41.5	31.5	23.6	2.4	1.1	30725	33652	14	18	1045	62.0	19.1	15.9	2.3	0.7	40704
79601	ABILENE	17737	7247	42.7	27.8	22.6	4.9	2.2	29866	34058	12	15	3873	41.3	27.4	25.7	4.8	0.8	63548
79602	ABILENE	19687	7132	32.0	29.7	27.9	6.5	3.9	38781	43714	42	50	4907	37.6	27.9	23.7	9.6	1.2	66723
79603	ABILENE	16846	8814	36.9	35.9	21.3	3.8	2.1	33444	37704	22	27	5732	56.7	35.2	7.8	0.3	0.0	45266
79605	ABILENE	21072	11790	29.0	36.3	25.9	5.1	3.8	37969	43080	39	46	7332	31.8	41.2	21.3	4.7	1.0	67014
79606	ABILENE	27146	9050	21.9	28.3	34.8	9.7	5.3	49756	57091	71	77	5500	8.2	25.0	53.2	11.8	1.8	106378
79607	DYESS AFB	11749	1083	17.1	56.2	25.6	1.1	0.0	37187	41403	36	43	15	100.0	0.0	0.0	0.0	0.0	45000
79697	ABILENE	3339	0	0.0	0.0	0.0	0.0	0.0	0	0	0	0	0	0.0	0.0	0.0	0.0	0.0	0
79698	ABILENE	7446	16	56.3	31.3	12.5	0.0	0.0	22205	25000	3	4	6	50.0	16.7	33.3	0.0	0.0	60000
79699	ABILENE	11175	251	48.2	18.3	22.7	6.8	4.0	26571	30968	7	9	68	17.7	19.1	39.7	23.5	0.0	122500
79701	MIDLAND	16780	8268	40.6	30.6	19.7	5.3	3.8	31107	35922	15	19	5538	57.2	24.1	15.1	3.2	0.4	43372
79703	MIDLAND	17844	6674	24.1	36.9	31.7	6.0	1.4	41473	48794	51	60	4495	37.8	55.5	5.6	1.0	0.1	55681
79705	MIDLAND	29198	11550	24.2	24.4	29.7	12.9	8.8	51658	61891	75	80	8029	20.0	22.4	43.0	12.0	2.5	98601
79706	MIDLAND	19336	5592	26.5	30.1	32.4	7.3	3.7	42863	51878	56	64	4591	43.3	29.2	22.5	4.8	0.2	57398
79707	MIDLAND	30619	11318	20.8	23.1	30.8	14.5	10.9	57610	69453	82	85	6739	4.0	28.1	46.9	19.2	1.9	106830
79713	ACKERLY	25606	240	24.2	32.9	22.1	10.0	10.8	46302	53933	65	70	185	24.9	43.8	27.0	4.3	0.0	73889
79714	ANDREWS	17925	4821	32.8	33.8	26.6	4.0	2.8	37338	41547	37	44	3667	53.6	24.1	18.2	3.7	0.4	47481
79718	BALMORHEA	8712	449	67.3	22.5	9.1	0.7	0.5	17433	19471	1	2	317	82.7	12.6	4.7	0.0	0.0	26810
79719	BARSTOW	10556	237	51.9	33.8	13.5	0.8	0.0	23755	27744	4	5	181	87.9	9.4	2.8	0.0	0.0	14766
79720	BIG SPRING	17546	11037	37.4	31.0	23.4	5.6	2.6	34665	39433	26	32	7437	53.9	24.5	17.8	3.4	0.4	46888
79730	COYANOSA	13445	101	46.5	22.8	22.8	5.0	3.0	26537	30311	6	8	88	75.0	6.8	11.4	3.4	3.4	25000
79731	CRANE	17656	1331	34.1	30.5	25.5	8.1	1.7	36673	41847	34	41	1066	58.2	29.5	9.9	1.7	0.8	45029
79734	FORT DAVIS	22548	790	33.4	30.5	26.3	5.3	4.4	36875	42864	35	42	564	26.1	18.8	30.1	17.0	8.0	96304
79735	FORT STOCKTON	13956	4259	38.3	32.3	24.6	3.9	0.9	31385	35788	16	20	3104	53.7	29.2	12.6	4.2	0.3	47150
79738	GAIL	20310	187	35.3	25.7	25.7	9.1	4.3	35249	43846	28	34	144	41.0	26.4	25.0	3.5	4.2	60000
79739	GARDEN CITY	24116	439	28.7	29.8	26.9	6.6	8.0	41583	50973	52	60	290	31.7	24.1	34.1	7.9	2.1	75625
79741	GOLDSMITH	20491	134	27.6	32.1	32.8	4.5	3.0	41667	48898	52	61	103	65.1	30.1	4.9	0.0	0.0	36042
79742	GRANDFALLS	12144	203	48.8	30.1	18.7	2.5	0.0	26643	30648	7	9	147	76.9	13.6	8.2	1.4	0.0	24205
79743	IMPERIAL	14769	241	45.2	23.7	23.2	4.6	3.3	27159	30384	7	10	209	72.7	8.6	12.0	3.8	2.9	27813
79744	IRAAN	18567	525	25.3	28.4	36.0	9.1	1.1	45327	50847	62	69	383	49.1	35.3	13.1	2.6	0.0	50946
79745	KERMIT	15574	2210	35.8	37.3	22.6	3.2	1.1	33179	36481	21	26	1824	72.8	22.2	4.7	0.2	0.3	33346
79748	KNOTT	18108	91	36.3	34.1	18.7	4.4	6.6	31986	36696	18	22	67	41.8	19.4	35.8	3.0	0.0	71250
79749	LENORAH	18140	154	34.4	25.3	24.0	13.6	2.6	39187	45462	43	52	126	25.4	38.9	26.2	9.5	0.0	78235
79752	MC CAMEY	15757	794	40.8	30.5	23.2	4.5	1.0	30922	35841	15	19	619	69.1	23.8	6.5	0.2	0.5	35573
79754	MENTONE	26484	30	26.7	23.3	36.7	10.0	3.3	50000	50000	72	77	25	80.0	8.0	0.0	12.0	0.0	12500
79755	MIDKIFF	18853	450	34.4	25.8	32.2	3.8	3.8	40667	45976	48	57	343	65.0	24.5	8.2	2.0	0.3	38750
79756	MONAHANS	17967	3479	37.1	30.3	24.7	5.4	2.6	34606	40000	26	31	2653	60.2	23.7	14.3	1.6	0.3	41979
79758	GARDENDALE	30048	666	17.9	24.2	39.6	13.2	5.1	60216	66905	85	87	591	23.0	25.7	37.2	11.3	2.7	92885
79761	ODESSA	17759	11188	38.6	31.7	21.2	5.1	3.4	33126	37603	21	26	7098	49.7	30.0	17.3	2.8	0.3	50372
79762	ODESSA	22171	14486	30.2	31.1	27.6	7.3	3.8	39965	44850	46	54	8907	32.3	38.3	25.0	3.9	0.5	65012
79763	ODESSA	12582	10331	40.1	35.5	20.7	2.6	1.2	30789	34671	14	18	7116	68.8	24.4	6.4	0.4	0.0	38316
79764	ODESSA	14824	6543	37.1	35.1	22.7	3.5	1.5	33593	38223	23	28	4715	66.6	22.1	10.3	0.9	0.1	36871
79765	ODESSA	30746	1821	24.9	26.0	28.8	11.0	9.3	48439	56205	69	74	1242	25.4	26.8	25.0	19.3	3.5	84000
79766	ODESSA	12589	1264	34.6	31.3	29.2	4.0	1.0	34872	39768	27	32	1050	60.1	22.7	15.4	1.8	0.0	40783
79772	PECOS	12977	3558	46.9	31.8	17.1	2.9	1.3	26753	29750	7	9	2561	76.7	17.1	5.2	0.8	0.2	28895
79777	PYOTE	15442	63	52.4	33.3	12.7	1.6	0.0	23295	27308	3	5	48	89.6	8.3	2.1	0.0	0.0	14444
79781	SHEFFIELD	14437	93	29.0	31.2	32.3	7.5	0.0	41408	46714	51	59	67	47.8	38.8	11.9	1.5	0.0	51500
79782	STANTON	18382	1355	33.6	34.1	23.2	5.5	3.7	35914	40580	31	37	1032	47.6	25.1	24.2	2.6	0.5	53623
79783	TARZAN	20121	165	29.7	33.9	26.1	3.0	7.3	36652	41394	34	41	113	26.6	31.0	36.3	6.2	0.0	81500
79789	WINK	19976	351	32.8	22.5	36.2	6.0	2.6	43558	48678	57	65	295	69.2	21.4	7.8	0.7	1.0	37375
79821	ANTHONY	11906	1544	43.9	34.1	17.0	3.1	1.8	28180	32079	9	12	1114	37.9	46.7	13.9	1.4	0.1	59926
79830	ALPINE	17250	3464	41.1	30.5	22.1	4.7	1.6	30261	33789	13	17	2159	33.0	26.8	26.4	11.0	2.8	76775
79832	ALPINE	777	4	100.0	0.0	0.0	0.0	0.0	5000	5000	0	1	2	0.0	0.0	100.0	0.0	0.0	112500
79834	BIG BEND NATIONAL PARK	23096	115	29.6	35.7	25.2	8.7	0.9	37757	43887	38	46	71	29.6	12.7	33.8	15.5	8.5	107292
79835	CANUTILLO	9046	3184	50.4	32.0	14.2	2.8	0.5	24813	28417	4	6	2300	52.0	36.2	10.0	1.4	0.4	48607
79836	CLINT	8834	4930	50.6	33.4	12.2	2.6	1.2	24630	27952	4	5	3485	55.2	30.8	11.9	2.2	0.0	45883
79837	DELL CITY	12643	235	54.9	26.4	14.5	2.1	2.1	22733	25564	3	4	164	72.6	16.5	9.2	1.8	0.0	33750
79839	FORT HANCOCK	8087	569	62.6	23.0	10.5	3.0	0.9	19238	20758	2	2	454	77.8	16.7	5.5	0.0	0.0	31250
79842	MARATHON	22242	241	46.1	19.5	24.5	5.8	4.2	27987	31128	9	11	190	45.3	27.9	14.7	10.0	2.1	62353
79843	MARFA	16018	1083	46.8	26.7	21.0	3.8	1.8	27270	30733	8	10	780	47.2	29.5	17.6	4.0	1.8	54231
79845	PRESIDIO	8044	1692	62.2	26.7	8.9	2.0	0.1	19155	21075	2	2	1131	72.9	21.9	4.0	1.0	0.2	33294
79847	SALT FLAT	19609	78	30.8	37.2	32.1	0.0	0.0	36998	42313	35	42	40	47.5	22.5	7.5	20.0	2.5	52000
	TEXAS	23284		26.2	27.7	29.5	10.3	6.3	45778	54246				21.6	26.1	33.4	15.6	3.4	93683
	UNITED STATES	25866		24.7	27.1	30.8	10.9	6.5	48124	56710				10.9	15.0	33.7	30.1	10.4	145905

ZIP CODE		FINANCIAL SERVICES				THE HOME						ENTERTAINMENT						PERSONAL			
						Home Improvements		Furnishings													
#	POST OFFICE NAME	Auto Loan	Home Loan	Invest-ments	Retire-ment Plans	Home Repair	Lawn & Garden	Comput-ers & Hard-ware	Major Appli-ances	TV, Radio, Sound Equip-ment	Furni-ture	Dine out/ Carry out	Sports Equip-ment	Fees & Tickets	Toys & Games	Travel	Cable TV	Apparel & Services	Auto Repairs	Health Insur-ance	Pets & Supplies
79520	HAMLIN	71	53	35	51	58	70	59	65	66	56	77	73	52	73	58	69	71	65	77	78
79521	HASKELL	60	47	35	45	51	60	51	56	57	49	68	63	47	65	51	60	63	56	65	68
79525	HAWLEY	80	68	49	65	71	76	65	73	69	67	83	85	60	80	65	69	79	72	76	91
79526	HERMLEIGH	77	57	36	55	63	75	62	70	70	59	82	79	55	78	62	74	75	69	83	86
79527	IRA	97	68	35	64	79	88	67	82	77	66	90	99	57	88	69	81	82	81	98	115
79528	JAYTON	82	60	38	58	67	79	65	73	73	62	86	84	58	82	65	77	79	73	88	92
79529	KNOX CITY	65	49	32	47	53	64	54	59	61	51	71	67	48	67	53	64	65	59	71	72
79530	LAWN	97	68	36	64	79	89	67	83	77	66	91	100	57	89	70	81	83	82	99	116
79532	LORAINE	102	77	51	74	84	101	85	93	95	80	112	105	76	106	84	100	102	93	112	113
79533	LUEDERS	76	53	28	50	62	70	53	65	61	52	72	78	45	70	55	64	65	64	78	90
79534	MC CAULLEY	81	57	30	53	66	74	56	69	64	55	76	83	48	74	58	68	69	68	82	96
79535	MARYNEAL	88	62	34	59	72	81	63	76	72	61	84	91	54	82	64	75	77	75	91	104
79536	MERKEL	76	62	45	61	66	74	63	70	68	63	82	80	59	80	63	70	77	69	77	85
79537	NOLAN	68	51	33	49	56	67	56	62	63	53	74	69	50	70	56	67	68	62	74	75
79538	NOVICE	95	74	51	67	84	94	70	84	79	69	94	99	63	93	75	85	87	83	100	115
79539	O BRIEN	68	51	34	49	56	68	57	63	64	54	75	70	51	71	56	67	69	63	75	76
79540	OLD GLORY	95	72	47	69	78	94	79	87	89	75	104	98	70	99	78	94	95	87	104	106
79541	OVALO	99	84	63	82	92	99	80	92	85	79	102	109	75	104	83	87	97	90	100	119
79543	ROBY	79	57	34	54	65	75	60	70	68	58	80	81	52	77	61	72	73	69	83	90
79544	ROCHESTER	68	51	34	49	56	68	57	63	64	54	75	70	51	71	56	67	69	63	75	76
79545	ROSCOE	67	51	34	49	56	65	53	60	59	52	70	69	48	68	54	62	65	60	70	75
79546	ROTAN	62	45	28	43	51	60	49	55	55	47	65	63	43	62	49	58	59	55	66	70
79547	RULE	64	48	32	46	53	63	54	59	60	51	71	66	48	67	53	63	64	59	71	71
79548	RULE	76	57	37	55	62	75	63	69	71	60	83	78	56	78	62	75	76	69	83	84
79549	SNYDER	70	63	54	60	64	70	64	68	67	64	82	77	60	79	63	67	79	68	71	78
79553	STAMFORD	67	52	37	49	56	66	57	62	63	54	75	70	51	71	56	66	69	62	72	74
79556	SWEETWATER	63	52	44	50	54	61	56	59	60	56	73	68	52	70	55	61	70	60	64	69
79560	SYLVESTER	85	60	33	57	69	78	60	73	69	59	81	88	52	79	62	73	74	72	87	100
79561	TRENT	77	66	51	65	69	78	68	72	72	66	87	82	65	86	67	73	81	71	78	85
79562	TUSCOLA	102	89	68	87	96	102	84	95	89	84	107	113	80	108	87	90	102	93	102	122
79563	TYE	103	94	73	90	94	99	89	96	90	92	112	111	84	105	88	89	107	95	95	113
79565	WESTBROOK	74	58	39	52	65	73	55	66	62	54	73	77	49	72	58	66	68	65	78	90
79566	WINGATE	83	72	55	70	78	83	68	78	72	68	87	92	64	88	70	74	82	76	84	100
79567	WINTERS	64	47	28	44	52	59	48	56	55	48	65	65	42	61	48	57	60	56	66	73
79601	ABILENE	58	50	55	51	50	56	61	56	61	57	76	68	57	73	57	59	73	60	56	64
79602	ABILENE	75	74	74	74	73	78	75	75	75	75	93	88	74	92	74	73	91	76	73	85
79603	ABILENE	66	62	59	59	62	67	64	66	66	64	82	74	62	79	63	66	79	67	67	72
79605	ABILENE	70	71	78	71	71	76	74	73	74	73	92	85	74	92	73	72	89	74	71	80
79606	ABILENE	94	93	99	97	92	95	97	94	93	96	117	113	95	115	93	89	114	96	87	106
79607	DYESS AFB	67	43	41	49	39	46	64	55	65	59	81	73	55	72	52	59	77	65	51	62
79697	ABILENE	0	0	0	0	0	0	0	0	0	0	0	0	0	0	0	0	0	0	0	0
79698	ABILENE	36	22	28	25	22	26	43	31	42	36	52	44	35	47	34	37	49	38	29	36
79699	ABILENE	63	39	49	44	38	46	75	55	73	63	91	76	61	81	60	64	85	67	51	63
79701	MIDLAND	68	66	66	63	64	68	67	69	68	70	86	76	65	81	66	67	84	70	67	74
79703	MIDLAND	68	69	72	70	68	70	70	69	68	71	86	81	69	85	68	65	84	70	64	76
79705	MIDLAND	105	109	117	109	108	114	107	108	105	109	132	123	108	128	107	103	129	108	104	119
79706	MIDLAND	90	83	67	80	83	88	80	85	80	82	99	98	75	94	79	79	96	85	84	100
79707	MIDLAND	108	112	123	117	108	112	113	109	107	113	136	129	114	134	109	102	134	111	98	121
79713	ACKERLY	124	87	45	82	101	113	85	106	98	84	115	127	73	113	89	103	105	104	126	147
79714	ANDREWS	78	70	57	66	70	74	69	74	71	72	88	83	65	83	68	70	85	74	74	84
79718	BALMORHEA	36	32	26	29	30	32	32	35	34	35	42	37	30	37	31	32	42	36	33	36
79719	BARSTOW	43	38	31	35	36	38	38	42	40	42	50	44	35	44	37	38	50	42	39	43
79720	BIG SPRING	66	59	54	57	61	67	61	64	64	60	79	74	58	77	61	65	75	65	68	75
79730	COYANOSA	64	56	47	52	54	57	57	62	59	62	75	66	52	66	54	57	74	63	58	64
79731	CRANE	79	70	58	66	70	75	70	76	73	74	91	84	65	84	69	72	89	77	75	85
79734	FORT DAVIS	88	73	56	67	76	82	72	82	78	75	95	91	65	88	72	79	92	82	86	97
79735	FORT STOCKTON	60	55	49	52	53	56	56	59	57	59	71	64	52	65	54	55	71	60	55	62
79738	GAIL	98	68	36	64	79	89	67	83	78	67	91	100	57	89	70	81	83	82	99	116
79739	GARDEN CITY	125	88	46	83	102	114	86	107	100	85	117	129	74	114	90	105	106	105	127	149
79741	GOLDSMITH	82	74	58	71	74	79	71	76	72	73	89	88	67	84	70	71	85	76	75	90
79742	GRANDFALLS	49	44	36	40	42	44	44	48	46	48	58	51	41	51	42	44	57	49	45	50
79743	IMPERIAL	64	56	47	52	54	57	57	62	60	62	75	66	53	66	55	57	74	63	58	65
79744	IRAAN	94	66	34	62	77	86	65	80	75	64	88	97	56	86	67	79	80	79	96	112
79745	KERMIT	65	57	47	54	57	62	58	63	61	61	75	69	54	70	57	61	73	63	63	70
79748	KNOTT	98	68	36	65	80	89	68	84	78	67	91	101	58	89	70	82	83	82	99	116
79749	LENORAH	94	66	34	62	77	86	65	80	75	64	88	97	55	86	67	79	80	79	96	112
79752	MC CAMEY	70	54	35	50	58	63	54	63	59	55	71	72	47	67	54	60	68	63	68	79
79754	MENTONE	91	81	61	77	85	91	74	83	79	74	96	98	73	98	77	81	91	80	89	107
79755	MIDKIFF	86	63	38	60	71	83	67	77	76	64	89	89	59	85	67	80	81	76	92	98
79756	MONAHANS	75	64	50	61	67	73	64	71	68	65	83	80	59	79	64	69	79	71	76	84
79758	GARDENDALE	114	119	109	116	121	125	108	113	107	108	132	134	110	138	111	107	129	110	113	136
79761	ODESSA	67	64	64	62	63	68	66	67	67	67	83	75	64	80	65	67	82	68	67	74
79762	ODESSA	77	78	82	78	77	81	79	79	78	79	97	92	78	96	77	75	95	80	75	87
79763	ODESSA	58	52	44	49	51	54	53	56	54	55	68	62	49	62	51	53	66	57	54	61
79764	ODESSA	65	58	49	57	58	62	58	61	59	60	74	71	55	70	57	59	71	62	61	72
79765	ODESSA	117	132	137	134	129	128	124	123	116	125	147	146	127	150	123	111	145	122	109	136
79766	ODESSA	67	60	50	56	58	61	60	65	62	65	78	70	56	70	58	60	77	66	61	69
79772	PECOS	59	51	43	48	49	52	52	57	54	57	68	60	48	60	50	53	68	58	53	59
79777	PYOTE	43	37	31	35	36	38	38	41	40	41	50	44	35	44	36	38	49	42	39	43
79781	SHEFFIELD	88	61	32	58	71	80	61	75	70	60	82	90	52	80	63	73	75	74	89	104
79782	STANTON	91	68	42	64	75	82	68	80	75	69	90	93	59	86	68	77	84	80	89	104
79783	TARZAN	113	79	41	75	92	103	78	97	90	77	105	116	67	103	81	94	96	95	115	134
79789	WINK	95	67	35	63	78	87	66	81	76	65	89	98	56	87	68	80	81	80	97	113
79821	ANTHONY	62	54	48	51	52	54	57	60	60	62	75	66	53	70	54	57	75	62	55	63
79830	ALPINE	59	52	50	52	53	58	57	58	58	56	72	66	53	69	55	57	69	59	58	64
79832	ALPINE	8	6	5	6	6	7	7	7	8	7	9	8	6	8	7	8	8	7	8	9
79834	BIG BEND NATIONAL PARK	75	58	41	56	63	75	64	69	70	61	83	78	57	79	63	74	76	69	82	83
79835	CANUTILLO	50	42	39	41	41	43	47	48	48	50	61	53	44	58	44	46	61	50	44	50
79836	CLINT	48	42	38	40	41	42	45	47	47	48	60	52	43	56	43	44	60	49	43	49
79837	DELL CITY	51	44	37	41	43	45	45	49	47	49	59	52	42	52	43	45	59	50	46	51
79839	FORT HANCOCK	43	38	32	35	37	38	39	42	40	42	50	44	36	45	37	39	50	43	39	44
79842	MARATHON	83	63	42	60	69	82	69	76	78	66	91	86	62	86	69	82	83	76	91	92
79843	MARFA	59	52	43	48	50	52	52	57	55	57	68	60	48	60	50	53	68	58	53	59
79845	PRESIDIO	39	34	29	32	33	35	35	38	36	38	46	40	32	40	33	35	45	39	36	40
79847	SALT FLAT	72	52	29	49	59	65	51	62	58	52	69	74	44	67	53	61	64	62	72	84
	TEXAS	94	90	91	90	89	95	92	93	92	93	115	107	90	112	90	90	112	94	89	104
	UNITED STATES	100	100	100	100	100	100	100	100	100	100	100	100	100	100	100	100	100	100	100	100

POPULATION CHANGE

#	POST OFFICE NAME	COUNTY FIPS CODE	POPULATION 2000	2004	2009	2000-2004 ANNUAL RATE % Rate	State Centile	HOUSEHOLDS 2000	2004	2009	% Annual Rate 2000-2004	2004 Average HH Size	FAMILIES 2000	2004	% Annual Rate 2000-2004
79849	SAN ELIZARIO	141	11285	12963	14352	3.3	85	2676	3123	3498	3.7	4.15	2483	2899	3.7
79851	SIERRA BLANCA	229	762	797	847	1.1	44	273	284	299	0.9	2.69	187	195	1.0
79852	TERLINGUA	043	75	79	85	1.2	49	38	40	43	1.2	1.98	23	24	1.0
79854	VALENTINE	243	275	261	255	-1.2	1	109	103	100	-1.3	2.53	82	78	-1.2
79855	VAN HORN	109	2827	2714	2597	-1.0	1	984	956	929	-0.7	2.83	756	736	-0.6
79901	EL PASO	141	14012	13765	14460	-0.4	6	4514	4478	4776	-0.2	2.84	2935	2909	-0.2
79902	EL PASO	141	22993	23155	24477	0.2	17	9052	9326	10006	0.7	2.44	5178	5299	0.5
79903	EL PASO	141	18941	19489	20725	0.7	31	6437	6738	7253	1.1	2.87	4609	4798	1.0
79904	EL PASO	141	33248	32666	33856	-0.4	6	10805	10749	11256	-0.1	3.03	8369	8312	-0.2
79905	EL PASO	141	28357	29167	30963	0.7	31	8514	8921	9594	1.1	3.25	6679	6985	1.1
79906	EL PASO	141	6808	7408	8172	2.0	68	1350	1568	1836	3.6	3.08	1251	1459	3.7
79907	EL PASO	141	55173	55746	58365	0.2	18	15287	15721	16674	0.7	3.53	13376	13738	0.6
79908	EL PASO	141	1060	1051	1048	-0.2	9	303	243	245	-5.1	2.64	282	226	-5.1
79912	EL PASO	141	64276	70293	76469	2.1	70	23902	26198	28639	2.2	2.67	16853	18489	2.2
79915	EL PASO	141	42410	42040	43930	-0.2	9	12760	12912	13686	0.3	3.22	10502	10597	0.2
79916	EL PASO	141	726	890	1016	4.9	94	13	17	20	6.5	2.59	10	13	6.4
79918	EL PASO	141	212	210	210	-0.2	9	0	0	0	0.0	0.00	0	0	0.0
79922	EL PASO	141	8783	8882	9291	0.3	19	2770	2852	3026	0.7	3.07	2315	2382	0.7
79924	EL PASO	141	56486	57578	60719	0.5	24	18713	19308	20565	0.7	2.98	14668	15124	0.7
79925	EL PASO	141	41272	41894	44093	0.4	22	15356	15861	16912	0.8	2.60	10831	11125	0.6
79927	EL PASO	141	33328	35222	37444	1.3	51	8289	8919	9605	1.7	3.95	7618	8191	1.7
79928	EL PASO	141	18977	24121	28074	5.8	96	4904	6253	7315	5.9	3.78	4420	5633	5.9
79930	EL PASO	141	28340	28636	30031	0.2	18	9370	9610	10195	0.6	2.95	6950	7111	0.5
79932	EL PASO	141	16832	17851	19025	1.4	54	5234	5644	6091	1.8	3.16	4276	4599	1.7
79934	EL PASO	141	10641	13143	15117	5.1	95	3163	3925	4542	5.2	3.35	2793	3473	5.3
79935	EL PASO	141	19295	19081	19942	-0.3	8	6584	6622	7015	0.1	2.83	4979	4991	0.1
79936	EL PASO	141	92393	106008	118361	3.3	84	27000	31123	34969	3.4	3.39	23389	26968	3.4
79938	EL PASO	141	19288	24580	28671	5.9	96	4287	5664	6777	6.8	3.85	3792	5001	6.7
79968	EL PASO	141	482	456	456	-1.3	1	52	43	43	-4.4	2.70	43	35	-4.7
	TEXAS UNITED STATES					2.2 / 1.2					2.0 / 1.3	2.77 / 2.58			2.1 / 1.1

ZIP CODE		RACE (%)							2004 AGE DISTRIBUTION (%)										MEDIAN AGE		
		White		Black		Asian/Pacific		% Hispanic Origin													% 2004 Males	% 2004 Females
#	POST OFFICE NAME	2000	2004	2000	2004	2000	2004	2000	2004	0-4	5-9	10-14	15-19	20-24	25-44	45-64	65-84	85+	18+	2004		
79849	SAN ELIZARIO	91.8	91.9	0.2	0.2	0.0	0.0	97.4	97.9	10.7	10.2	11.8	10.8	8.6	27.1	15.9	4.6	0.3	60.3	23.8	49.6	50.4
79851	SIERRA BLANCA	87.8	87.0	0.0	0.0	0.1	0.1	62.3	65.8	9.3	6.4	6.8	7.0	7.3	28.4	23.8	9.0	2.0	73.8	34.9	49.3	50.7
79852	TERLINGUA	85.3	83.5	1.3	1.3	0.0	0.0	40.0	44.3	5.1	5.1	5.1	5.1	5.1	24.1	32.9	16.5	1.3	84.8	45.3	49.4	50.6
79854	VALENTINE	90.2	90.0	0.4	0.4	0.0	0.0	50.2	51.7	1.9	8.1	10.0	6.5	0.4	21.5	32.6	17.2	1.9	75.9	45.9	51.3	48.7
79855	VAN HORN	67.8	66.3	0.7	0.8	0.6	0.6	74.4	77.5	7.9	7.9	9.2	8.8	8.1	24.2	24.2	10.9	0.9	69.8	32.4	50.3	49.7
79901	EL PASO	79.0	78.7	0.8	0.8	0.2	0.2	95.8	96.5	8.3	8.6	8.6	8.9	8.7	22.4	18.6	14.1	2.0	69.5	30.6	47.4	52.6
79902	EL PASO	80.1	79.5	1.6	1.6	1.6	1.6	75.7	78.0	7.3	6.5	6.3	6.4	8.2	28.6	22.0	12.6	2.3	76.3	35.0	48.4	51.6
79903	EL PASO	78.3	78.0	1.2	1.1	0.3	0.3	89.8	91.2	7.2	7.2	7.6	7.0	6.3	25.4	21.6	15.3	2.4	73.6	36.7	46.0	54.0
79904	EL PASO	66.2	65.5	6.9	6.7	1.4	1.4	69.3	72.3	10.6	9.2	8.6	7.5	7.8	27.4	17.9	10.0	1.0	67.1	29.0	47.8	52.2
79905	EL PASO	76.3	76.3	1.0	0.9	0.3	0.3	95.8	96.6	8.8	8.5	8.4	7.8	7.0	24.3	19.3	14.4	1.6	69.6	32.5	46.8	53.2
79906	EL PASO	59.8	56.7	23.0	23.4	2.7	2.9	22.1	26.2	13.3	8.0	4.8	9.8	30.7	30.3	2.4	0.6	0.1	72.1	22.3	63.1	36.9
79907	EL PASO	70.2	70.0	0.7	0.7	0.2	0.2	94.5	95.4	8.5	8.2	8.9	8.6	9.1	26.0	21.3	8.7	0.8	69.2	29.4	47.2	52.8
79908	EL PASO	56.0	54.9	30.9	30.8	4.0	4.2	19.1	22.4	6.4	7.1	12.8	8.9	9.0	47.1	8.3	0.5	0.0	67.6	28.8	59.3	40.7
79912	EL PASO	81.0	80.0	2.0	1.9	2.8	2.9	55.0	60.0	8.4	7.9	7.8	6.9	7.4	30.6	21.7	8.1	1.2	71.5	33.0	47.8	52.2
79915	EL PASO	70.2	69.9	1.8	1.6	0.3	0.3	93.5	94.5	8.4	8.0	8.1	7.6	7.4	25.6	19.8	14.0	1.3	70.9	32.9	47.2	52.8
79916	EL PASO	55.0	52.8	25.8	25.4	2.8	2.9	25.1	29.0	14.6	9.2	6.3	7.6	27.3	31.9	2.7	0.3	0.0	67.5	22.2	60.2	39.8
79918	EL PASO	56.1	54.8	31.1	31.0	3.8	4.3	19.3	22.4	6.7	7.1	12.9	8.6	9.1	47.6	8.1	0.0	0.0	67.6	28.5	59.5	40.5
79922	EL PASO	84.9	84.2	0.7	0.6	1.1	1.1	53.4	57.2	6.9	7.8	8.6	7.7	5.7	23.6	28.8	9.9	1.0	71.7	38.2	48.7	51.3
79924	EL PASO	65.8	64.8	8.7	8.2	2.5	2.5	59.2	63.8	7.9	7.8	8.8	8.3	7.6	25.8	22.3	10.9	0.8	70.5	32.7	46.8	53.2
79925	EL PASO	78.0	77.5	3.6	3.3	1.2	1.2	69.2	73.1	7.0	6.4	6.8	7.2	8.8	27.2	21.9	13.4	1.5	75.7	34.7	48.4	51.6
79927	EL PASO	73.6	73.5	0.4	0.4	0.1	0.1	96.3	96.9	9.5	9.0	9.9	9.7	8.8	26.9	19.8	6.1	0.4	65.7	27.2	48.4	51.6
79928	EL PASO	75.9	75.5	1.2	1.2	0.3	0.3	86.2	88.4	11.1	10.5	11.3	9.3	7.9	30.2	15.6	3.9	0.3	61.4	25.0	49.6	50.4
79930	EL PASO	76.9	76.6	2.0	1.9	0.5	0.5	87.3	89.2	8.6	7.9	7.5	7.2	7.4	26.6	20.2	12.8	1.9	71.8	33.3	47.2	52.8
79932	EL PASO	82.9	82.4	1.0	1.0	0.5	0.5	69.2	72.8	8.6	8.7	9.7	8.2	6.8	26.3	23.0	8.0	0.7	67.8	31.7	48.2	51.8
79934	EL PASO	62.8	61.4	14.6	14.3	3.1	3.2	47.6	52.3	9.1	9.9	10.9	8.7	6.2	34.7	17.5	2.9	0.2	64.6	29.2	49.0	51.0
79935	EL PASO	74.5	74.1	3.8	3.5	1.1	1.1	72.9	76.4	8.3	7.6	7.2	8.1	9.1	27.3	22.6	9.1	0.9	72.3	31.2	46.6	53.4
79936	EL PASO	69.3	68.5	2.4	2.2	1.1	1.1	81.4	84.2	9.8	9.4	9.7	8.2	7.6	32.3	18.5	4.0	0.5	66.0	28.4	48.1	51.9
79938	EL PASO	68.2	66.9	2.9	2.5	0.5	0.5	84.4	87.2	9.6	9.4	9.8	10.0	11.3	31.5	14.7	3.5	0.2	65.8	25.0	54.9	45.2
79968	EL PASO	68.3	68.4	9.1	8.3	9.3	9.2	57.9	62.3	4.4	1.8	1.3	18.9	17.5	18.0	4.2	20.0	14.0	91.2	29.5	45.6	54.4
	TEXAS	71.0	69.5	11.5	11.4	2.8	3.1	32.0	34.6	7.9	7.5	7.7	7.5	8.1	29.6	21.9	8.7	1.2	72.6	32.9	49.7	50.3
	UNITED STATES	75.1	73.6	12.3	12.5	3.8	4.2	12.5	14.1	6.9	6.7	7.2	7.0	7.3	28.6	23.8	10.8	1.7	75.1	36.0	49.1	50.9

ZIP CODE		2004 Per Capita Income	2004 HH Income Base	2004 HOUSEHOLD INCOME DISTRIBUTION (%)					MEDIAN HOUSEHOLD INCOME				2004 Home Value Base	2004 HOME VALUE DISTRIBUTION (%)					2004 Median Home Value
#	POST OFFICE NAME			Less than $25,000	$25,000 to $49,999	$50,000 to $99,999	$100,000 to $149,999	$150,000 or More	2004	2009	2004 National Centile	2004 State Centile		Less than $50,000	$50,000 to $89,999	$90,000 to $174,999	$175,000 to $399,999	$400,000 or More	
79849	SAN ELIZARIO	7035	3123	56.4	29.0	12.9	1.4	0.3	22385	25573	3	4	2627	50.7	39.1	8.9	1.0	0.4	49541
79851	SIERRA BLANCA	15972	284	32.4	41.2	20.4	3.2	2.8	33165	38812	21	26	206	53.4	32.0	13.6	1.0	0.0	43000
79852	TERLINGUA	23478	40	32.5	37.5	20.0	10.0	0.0	36096	41698	32	38	24	29.2	16.7	29.2	16.7	8.3	100000
79854	VALENTINE	18973	103	35.0	31.1	22.3	6.8	4.9	38813	43438	42	50	56	82.1	14.3	0.0	0.0	3.6	23750
79855	VAN HORN	12708	956	45.3	33.1	18.4	1.9	1.4	27838	30928	8	11	675	67.1	23.9	6.7	1.8	0.6	38708
79901	EL PASO	6640	4478	81.5	14.5	3.6	0.3	0.3	10830	11900	1	1	541	54.0	34.0	9.8	1.9	0.4	47933
79902	EL PASO	19079	9326	48.5	24.8	15.4	5.5	5.7	25906	30405	6	7	3394	6.5	32.4	46.9	11.6	2.7	100982
79903	EL PASO	13331	6738	48.1	29.0	17.6	3.8	1.5	25989	29575	6	8	4048	12.0	65.8	20.1	1.8	0.3	70553
79904	EL PASO	13849	10749	41.8	33.2	18.1	5.1	1.8	30200	34088	13	16	5351	21.0	51.9	22.6	4.5	0.0	66960
79905	EL PASO	9311	8921	61.3	25.6	10.4	1.7	1.1	19317	21602	2	2	4192	31.8	58.5	9.3	0.2	0.1	60000
79906	EL PASO	13469	1568	32.1	44.3	18.8	3.0	1.8	32790	36603	20	25	96	8.3	79.2	12.5	0.0	0.0	67000
79907	EL PASO	10781	15721	42.8	34.0	19.3	2.9	1.0	29372	33132	11	14	10290	20.9	65.3	12.5	1.2	0.1	66002
79908	EL PASO	17987	243	4.9	52.7	35.0	2.9	4.5	47417	53923	67	72	5	0.0	100.0	0.0	0.0	0.0	76250
79912	EL PASO	28764	26198	20.7	23.1	34.8	12.7	8.7	56547	66732	81	84	16017	1.2	19.1	57.7	19.4	2.7	117218
79915	EL PASO	10837	12912	48.3	30.7	17.6	2.5	1.0	25934	29367	6	7	7632	18.4	69.0	12.1	0.4	0.2	65478
79916	EL PASO	3673	17	47.1	47.1	5.9	0.0	0.0	25651	30000	5	7	16	68.8	25.0	6.3	0.0	0.0	35000
79918	EL PASO	4993	0	0.0	0.0	0.0	0.0	0.0	0	0	0	0	0	0.0	0.0	0.0	0.0	0.0	0
79922	EL PASO	39744	2852	18.5	18.2	27.1	15.3	21.0	71497	86260	92	93	2399	7.2	28.6	23.4	29.9	10.9	133781
79924	EL PASO	15522	19308	31.3	33.6	28.3	5.3	1.5	37588	43370	38	45	13269	13.9	68.4	17.4	0.3	0.1	70542
79925	EL PASO	20294	15861	28.5	31.1	29.7	8.0	2.7	41450	48475	51	60	8928	3.3	41.3	53.0	2.4	0.1	93279
79927	EL PASO	8586	8919	45.1	35.7	16.7	2.0	0.6	27511	31378	8	11	6996	37.3	48.1	12.3	2.0	0.3	59911
79928	EL PASO	11866	6253	38.5	31.6	22.9	5.0	2.0	32097	36899	18	23	5489	35.0	39.1	23.8	2.1	0.0	65827
79930	EL PASO	13025	9610	47.4	30.5	16.8	3.6	1.6	26306	30079	6	8	5354	15.6	64.2	18.8	1.2	0.3	69573
79932	EL PASO	23375	5644	30.4	27.0	24.5	8.2	9.9	42444	49224	54	63	4135	17.7	25.9	33.1	20.4	2.9	98791
79934	EL PASO	18959	3925	14.4	32.1	39.3	11.1	3.1	52423	61075	76	80	3132	7.0	41.3	46.5	5.2	0.0	91145
79935	EL PASO	19676	6622	30.3	27.1	28.0	11.3	3.3	42311	49499	54	63	3626	1.9	36.9	56.5	4.8	0.0	98450
79936	EL PASO	17494	31123	19.6	32.4	36.2	8.8	3.0	48270	55521	69	74	24446	3.5	47.9	41.8	6.2	0.7	89233
79938	EL PASO	10982	5664	33.7	41.6	19.4	4.1	1.2	33285	38222	22	27	4857	39.7	40.6	16.4	3.2	0.1	61829
79968	EL PASO	11679	43	74.4	14.0	4.7	7.0	0.0	10661	12046	1	1	1	0.0	0.0	0.0	100.0	0.0	350000
	TEXAS	23284		26.2	27.7	29.5	10.3	6.3	45778	54246				21.6	26.1	33.4	15.6	3.4	93683
	UNITED STATES	25866		24.7	27.1	30.8	10.9	6.5	48124	56710				10.9	15.0	33.7	30.1	10.4	145905

ZIP CODE		FINANCIAL SERVICES				THE HOME							ENTERTAINMENT						PERSONAL			
						Home Improvements		Furnishings														
#	POST OFFICE NAME	Auto Loan	Home Loan	Invest-ments	Retire-ment Plans	Home Repair	Lawn & Garden	Comput-ers & Hard-ware	Major Appli-ances	TV, Radio, Sound Equip-ment	Furni-ture	Dine out/ Carry out	Sports Equip-ment	Fees & Tickets	Toys & Games	Travel	Cable TV	Apparel & Services	Auto Repairs	Health Insur-ance	Pets & Supplies
79849	SAN ELIZARIO	42	36	35	36	35	36	41	40	42	43	53	46	39	52	38	39	54	43	37	43
79851	SIERRA BLANCA	66	58	49	54	56	59	60	64	62	65	78	68	55	69	57	60	77	66	60	67
79852	TERLINGUA	75	56	37	54	62	74	62	68	70	59	82	77	55	77	62	74	75	68	82	83
79854	VALENTINE	87	61	32	57	71	79	60	74	69	59	81	89	51	79	62	73	74	73	88	103
79855	VAN HORN	56	48	39	45	47	50	49	54	51	53	64	57	45	57	47	50	63	54	51	57
79901	EL PASO	25	22	22	21	21	23	24	25	25	25	31	27	22	29	23	24	31	26	23	26
79902	EL PASO	65	62	68	62	61	64	66	66	67	68	84	75	64	81	64	64	83	68	62	71
79903	EL PASO	57	51	46	48	49	52	53	56	55	57	69	60	49	62	51	53	68	57	53	59
79904	EL PASO	61	55	52	53	54	57	59	60	60	61	76	67	56	71	56	58	75	62	57	64
79905	EL PASO	46	40	34	38	39	40	42	44	43	45	54	48	38	49	39	41	54	45	41	46
79906	EL PASO	68	45	42	50	41	48	64	56	65	61	82	74	55	73	54	60	78	66	52	64
79907	EL PASO	58	50	43	47	49	51	52	56	54	57	68	60	48	61	50	52	68	57	52	58
79908	EL PASO	90	57	55	66	53	62	86	74	87	80	109	98	73	97	70	79	104	87	68	84
79912	EL PASO	108	112	119	116	108	111	111	109	106	114	135	128	111	132	108	101	133	110	98	120
79915	EL PASO	53	46	39	43	45	47	48	51	50	52	63	55	44	56	45	48	62	52	48	54
79916	EL PASO	43	37	31	35	36	38	38	41	40	42	50	44	35	44	36	38	49	42	39	43
79918	EL PASO	0	0	0	0	0	0	0	0	0	0	0	0	0	0	0	0	0	0	0	0
79922	EL PASO	161	192	216	189	185	192	175	174	167	179	211	197	186	216	178	164	212	171	160	189
79924	EL PASO	67	64	61	61	62	66	64	67	65	68	82	74	62	77	63	64	81	68	64	72
79925	EL PASO	74	73	79	73	71	76	75	75	75	77	94	85	74	91	73	73	93	76	71	81
79927	EL PASO	51	45	39	42	43	45	47	49	49	50	61	53	43	55	44	46	61	51	46	52
79928	EL PASO	64	58	57	58	57	58	63	63	64	66	81	73	61	80	59	60	81	66	56	67
79930	EL PASO	58	51	44	48	49	52	53	56	55	57	69	61	49	62	50	53	69	58	53	59
79932	EL PASO	105	108	105	107	105	106	105	106	102	109	129	120	104	125	102	98	128	106	97	114
79934	EL PASO	93	100	93	103	96	95	92	93	86	95	109	108	92	107	89	81	107	91	82	103
79935	EL PASO	79	77	79	76	75	78	79	80	79	82	100	89	77	97	76	76	99	81	74	85
79936	EL PASO	85	86	84	86	83	83	84	85	83	88	105	97	84	103	81	78	104	86	76	91
79938	EL PASO	61	53	48	51	51	53	57	59	60	61	75	66	54	71	54	56	75	62	54	62
79968	EL PASO	31	24	32	28	24	27	34	30	34	32	42	38	31	39	30	31	41	34	28	33
	TEXAS	94	90	91	90	89	95	92	93	92	93	115	107	90	112	90	90	112	94	89	104
	UNITED STATES	100	100	100	100	100	100	100	100	100	100	100	100	100	100	100	100	100	100	100	100

POPULATION CHANGE

# POST OFFICE NAME	COUNTY FIPS CODE	POPULATION 2000	2004	2009	2000-2004 ANNUAL RATE % Rate	State Centile	HOUSEHOLDS 2000	2004	2009	% Annual Rate 2000-2004	2004 Average HH Size	FAMILIES 2000	2004	% Annual Rate 2000-2004
84001 ALTAMONT	013	142	153	165	1.8	54	44	49	55	2.6	3.12	36	40	2.5
84003 AMERICAN FORK	049	30741	35080	40873	3.2	81	7902	9167	10841	3.6	3.79	6984	8018	3.3
84004 ALPINE	049	7521	8802	10366	3.8	88	1761	2106	2521	4.3	4.18	1646	1955	4.1
84006 BINGHAM CANYON	035	726	730	742	0.1	17	273	276	282	0.3	2.64	192	181	-1.4
84007 BLUEBELL	013	1365	1435	1536	1.2	41	439	476	526	1.9	3.01	359	384	1.6
84010 BOUNTIFUL	011	44308	45184	48494	0.5	24	14358	15031	16496	1.1	2.97	11523	11847	0.7
84013 CEDAR VALLEY	049	2352	3008	3818	6.0	97	637	812	1033	5.9	3.66	537	680	5.7
84014 CENTERVILLE	011	14556	14930	15936	0.6	29	4134	4374	4782	1.3	3.41	3529	3677	1.0
84015 CLEARFIELD	011	46413	52216	58660	2.8	75	13972	16018	18364	3.3	3.18	11413	12967	3.1
84017 COALVILLE	043	3300	3637	4223	2.3	70	1084	1218	1438	2.8	2.95	887	984	2.5
84018 CROYDON	029	134	147	161	2.2	67	36	40	44	2.5	3.67	32	35	2.1
84020 DRAPER	035	25324	31425	35717	5.2	95	6330	8303	9736	6.6	3.33	5446	7032	6.2
84021 DUCHESNE	013	2663	2824	3032	1.4	45	829	911	1011	2.2	2.92	645	699	1.9
84022 DUGWAY	045	2105	2461	2940	3.7	87	376	506	679	7.2	2.92	284	375	6.8
84023 DUTCH JOHN	009	210	215	215	0.6	26	86	91	91	1.3	2.16	61	63	0.8
84025 FARMINGTON	011	12288	13693	15204	2.6	74	3142	3627	4141	3.4	3.62	2831	3233	3.2
84026 FORT DUCHESNE	047	1727	1727	1803	0.0	13	494	509	547	0.7	3.34	406	413	0.4
84028 GARDEN CITY	033	503	614	768	4.8	94	190	239	308	5.6	2.56	152	189	5.3
84029 GRANTSVILLE	045	6470	7871	10022	4.7	93	1979	2467	3194	5.3	3.12	1628	1996	4.9
84031 HANNA	013	55	60	66	2.1	61	17	19	22	2.7	3.16	13	14	1.8
84032 HEBER CITY	051	11602	14200	17906	4.9	95	3582	4463	5721	5.3	3.15	2926	3597	5.0
84033 HENEFER	043	785	863	1002	2.3	68	251	282	332	2.8	3.05	205	227	2.4
84035 JENSEN	047	593	628	671	1.4	43	197	216	238	2.2	2.91	163	176	1.8
84036 KAMAS	043	4420	5119	6098	3.5	85	1435	1697	2055	4.0	3.02	1135	1319	3.6
84037 KAYSVILLE	011	25668	27028	29361	1.2	41	6903	7392	8170	1.6	3.64	6073	6446	1.4
84038 LAKETOWN	033	432	524	653	4.7	92	140	175	224	5.4	2.98	113	139	5.0
84039 LAPOINT	047	342	343	356	0.1	15	110	114	122	0.8	3.01	92	94	0.5
84040 LAYTON	011	23053	25006	27555	1.9	56	6412	7122	8010	2.5	3.50	5767	6331	2.2
84041 LAYTON	011	35952	39588	44065	2.3	70	12032	13460	15232	2.7	2.94	9165	10066	2.2
84042 LINDON	049	8373	9530	11060	3.1	79	1939	2240	2635	3.5	4.23	1791	2053	3.3
84043 LEHI	049	23404	34633	46816	9.7	100	6246	9233	12548	9.6	3.74	5631	8292	9.5
84044 MAGNA	035	22103	23185	24265	1.1	39	6405	6854	7273	1.6	3.38	5301	5573	1.2
84046 MANILA	009	711	727	727	0.5	25	254	268	268	1.3	2.49	179	185	0.8
84047 MIDVALE	035	27924	28336	29325	0.4	21	10633	10973	11495	0.7	2.57	6954	6922	-0.1
84049 MIDWAY	051	2720	2815	3268	0.8	34	901	959	1138	1.5	2.94	724	757	1.1
84050 MORGAN	029	6995	7602	8282	2.0	59	2010	2218	2448	2.3	3.43	1750	1914	2.1
84051 MOUNTAIN HOME	013	453	496	543	2.2	64	190	215	242	3.0	2.31	141	157	2.6
84052 MYTON	013	1073	1141	1229	1.5	48	329	359	398	2.1	3.18	276	297	1.7
84053 NEOLA	013	813	879	953	1.9	56	253	282	316	2.6	3.05	213	235	2.3
84054 NORTH SALT LAKE	011	8143	8843	9707	2.0	58	2670	2963	3315	2.5	2.98	2100	2290	2.1
84056 HILL AFB	011	4785	5632	6410	3.9	89	1158	1427	1683	5.0	3.51	1140	1403	5.0
84057 OREM	049	35342	37328	41735	1.3	42	9903	10695	12172	1.8	3.46	8131	8611	1.4
84058 OREM	049	28033	31180	35944	2.5	72	8133	9328	10992	3.3	3.33	6259	6974	2.6
84060 PARK CITY	043	7468	8444	9950	2.9	77	2739	3100	3674	3.0	2.72	1709	1880	2.3
84061 PEOA	043	581	663	784	3.2	81	178	207	249	3.6	3.19	146	167	3.2
84062 PLEASANT GROVE	049	26625	30821	36221	3.5	84	6817	7994	9514	3.8	3.85	6064	7053	3.6
84063 RANDLETT	047	76	75	78	-0.3	5	27	28	30	0.9	2.68	21	22	1.1
84064 RANDOLPH	033	665	753	907	3.0	77	203	234	288	3.4	3.16	163	186	3.2
84065 RIVERTON	035	33237	42145	49185	5.8	96	8406	10943	13007	6.4	3.84	7759	9949	6.0
84066 ROOSEVELT	013	7793	8238	8838	1.3	43	2443	2652	2923	2.0	3.10	1990	2133	1.7
84067 ROY	057	33885	36788	40373	2.0	57	10963	12083	13411	2.3	3.03	8870	9639	2.0
84069 RUSH VALLEY	045	445	508	629	3.2	81	148	172	216	3.6	2.95	113	128	3.0
84070 SANDY	035	22233	22808	23761	0.6	29	7171	7558	8015	1.2	2.96	5415	5545	0.6
84071 STOCKTON	045	712	812	1005	3.1	80	243	283	355	3.7	2.87	186	211	3.0
84072 TABIONA	013	479	525	574	2.2	65	159	180	203	3.0	2.92	118	131	2.5
84073 TALMAGE	013	334	358	387	1.7	53	113	126	140	2.6	2.73	86	95	2.4
84074 TOOELE	045	28975	36233	46966	5.4	96	9333	11730	15290	5.5	3.07	7458	9257	5.2
84075 SYRACUSE	011	9607	12512	15122	6.4	98	2540	3386	4174	7.0	3.70	2294	3027	6.7
84076 TRIDELL	047	350	351	364	0.1	15	95	99	105	1.0	3.55	79	81	0.6
84078 VERNAL	047	20394	21739	23342	1.5	49	6725	7354	8108	2.1	2.93	5346	5764	1.5
84080 VERNON	045	288	328	405	3.1	79	94	109	137	3.5	3.01	74	84	3.0
84082 WALLSBURG	051	866	1218	1637	8.4	100	253	364	498	8.9	3.35	214	305	8.7
84083 WENDOVER	045	2008	2296	2816	3.2	82	586	678	837	3.5	3.39	440	498	3.0
84084 WEST JORDAN	035	45168	52420	58309	3.6	86	12350	14664	16550	4.1	3.56	10743	12604	3.8
84085 WHITEROCKS	047	943	958	1000	0.4	22	282	296	317	1.2	3.24	229	237	0.8
84086 WOODRUFF	033	361	410	494	3.0	78	112	130	160	3.6	3.15	94	108	3.3
84087 WOODS CROSS	011	9819	10715	11907	2.1	62	2759	3104	3531	2.8	3.45	2412	2680	2.5
84088 WEST JORDAN	035	39354	45316	49830	3.4	83	10748	12598	14030	3.8	3.58	9345	10811	3.5
84092 SANDY	035	29990	30764	31965	0.6	29	8068	8483	8963	1.2	3.61	7346	7653	1.0
84093 SANDY	035	26025	25512	26082	-0.5	4	7445	7486	7780	0.1	3.41	6561	6506	-0.2
84094 SANDY	035	28576	28233	28789	-0.3	5	8480	8596	8910	0.3	3.28	7090	7065	-0.1
84095 SOUTH JORDAN	035	30305	35701	39679	3.9	89	7922	9546	10769	4.5	3.74	7023	8372	4.2
84097 OREM	049	21085	22390	25153	1.4	47	5396	5839	6667	1.9	3.79	4741	5069	1.6
84098 PARK CITY	043	13226	16021	19567	4.6	92	4659	5741	7110	5.0	2.79	3433	4147	4.6
84101 SALT LAKE CITY	035	3243	3609	3872	2.6	72	1202	1356	1474	2.9	2.11	416	446	1.7
84102 SALT LAKE CITY	035	16843	17535	18319	1.0	37	8232	8708	9214	1.3	1.96	2927	2872	-0.5
84103 SALT LAKE CITY	035	22598	22524	23201	-0.1	9	10804	10940	11407	0.3	2.03	4997	4810	-0.9
84104 SALT LAKE CITY	035	22549	22598	23116	0.1	14	6572	6520	6662	-0.2	3.42	4818	4652	-0.8
84105 SALT LAKE CITY	035	22628	22092	22508	-0.6	3	9789	9755	10081	-0.1	2.23	5312	5031	-1.3
84106 SALT LAKE CITY	035	33072	32633	33355	-0.3	5	13448	13512	13993	0.1	2.37	8188	7883	-0.9
84107 SALT LAKE CITY	035	30762	30644	31391	-0.1	8	12634	12771	13230	0.3	2.38	7919	7686	-0.7
84108 SALT LAKE CITY	035	20092	19573	19935	-0.6	2	7576	7504	7741	-0.2	2.54	5451	5246	-0.9
84109 SALT LAKE CITY	035	23889	23286	23683	-0.6	3	8604	8543	8801	-0.2	2.70	6089	5867	-0.9
84111 SALT LAKE CITY	035	10573	11307	11961	1.6	51	5165	5526	5879	1.6	1.95	1842	1853	0.1
84112 SALT LAKE CITY	035	1465	1463	1477	0.0	11	68	69	71	0.3	2.57	44	43	-0.5
84113 SALT LAKE CITY	035	566	566	571	0.0	13	226	232	239	0.6	1.32	169	84	-15.2
84115 SALT LAKE CITY	035	24351	24280	24908	-0.1	10	9825	9866	10203	0.1	2.40	5379	5147	-1.0
84116 SALT LAKE CITY	035	31760	32870	34357	0.8	34	9706	9950	10396	0.6	3.28	7033	7013	-0.1
84117 SALT LAKE CITY	035	23274	23743	24692	0.5	24	9399	9760	10291	0.9	2.40	5994	6013	0.1
84118 SALT LAKE CITY	035	64003	64304	66513	0.1	16	17791	18249	19132	0.6	3.52	15342	15525	0.3
84119 SALT LAKE CITY	035	49155	51280	53570	1.0	38	15974	16938	17917	1.4	2.89	11196	11508	0.7
84120 SALT LAKE CITY	035	45173	45007	46026	-0.1	8	12543	12688	13122	0.3	3.54	10819	10788	-0.1
84121 SALT LAKE CITY	035	43178	42358	43373	-0.5	4	15044	15069	15662	0.0	2.80	11425	11181	-0.5
84123 SALT LAKE CITY	035	35157	37644	39992	1.6	52	12737	13945	15037	2.2	2.69	8742	9246	1.3
84124 SALT LAKE CITY	035	21251	21005	21479	-0.3	6	7726	7813	8113	0.3	2.66	5669	5561	-0.5
UTAH					1.8					2.2	3.09			1.8
UNITED STATES					1.2					1.3	2.58			1.1

ZIP CODE #	POST OFFICE NAME	RACE (%) White 2000	White 2004	Black 2000	Black 2004	Asian/Pacific 2000	Asian/Pacific 2004	% Hispanic Origin 2000	% Hispanic Origin 2004	2004 AGE DISTRIBUTION (%) 0-4	5-9	10-14	15-19	20-24	25-44	45-64	65-84	85+	18+	MEDIAN AGE 2004	% 2004 Males	% 2004 Females
84001	ALTAMONT	97.2	96.7	0.0	0.0	0.0	0.0	1.4	1.3	8.5	7.8	9.8	7.8	5.9	23.5	24.2	11.1	1.3	68.6	33.6	52.9	47.1
84003	AMERICAN FORK	95.9	95.5	0.2	0.2	0.8	0.9	3.8	4.3	12.0	11.5	10.8	8.9	6.7	28.5	15.3	5.5	0.9	60.0	25.1	50.3	49.7
84004	ALPINE	97.5	97.3	0.2	0.2	0.5	0.6	1.8	2.0	9.4	12.4	14.4	11.3	4.1	24.5	18.7	4.8	0.5	55.9	23.1	50.2	49.8
84006	BINGHAM CANYON	93.3	92.6	0.0	0.0	0.7	0.7	8.5	10.0	8.9	8.8	8.1	6.6	5.8	29.5	20.1	9.5	2.9	70.3	33.2	48.2	51.8
84007	BLUEBELL	95.4	95.2	0.0	0.0	0.2	0.2	1.5	1.7	9.3	8.8	8.9	8.9	6.8	23.1	23.1	10.2	1.0	67.5	31.3	51.2	48.8
84010	BOUNTIFUL	94.9	94.5	0.3	0.3	1.6	1.7	3.5	3.9	8.8	7.9	7.6	7.2	8.3	26.1	20.2	12.3	1.7	71.4	31.7	48.7	51.3
84013	CEDAR VALLEY	93.7	93.6	0.2	0.2	0.2	0.2	7.3	7.6	15.4	11.9	9.2	7.1	7.0	30.5	13.5	4.8	0.6	58.9	24.6	50.7	49.3
84014	CENTERVILLE	97.1	96.9	0.2	0.2	1.0	1.1	1.9	2.2	8.8	9.3	9.9	9.3	7.6	26.3	21.5	6.7	0.7	66.1	28.8	49.5	50.5
84015	CLEARFIELD	87.9	87.2	1.9	1.9	2.4	2.6	8.8	9.6	11.6	9.7	8.5	8.5	9.6	31.2	15.1	5.2	0.6	65.3	26.0	50.4	49.6
84017	COALVILLE	95.1	94.5	0.1	0.1	0.3	0.3	5.1	5.8	9.3	9.1	9.1	7.6	7.2	28.0	20.7	8.0	1.2	67.7	30.5	51.2	48.8
84018	CROYDON	97.0	97.3	0.0	0.0	0.0	0.0	1.5	2.7	9.5	8.8	11.6	8.8	8.2	23.8	22.5	6.8	0.0	64.6	28.2	51.0	49.0
84020	DRAPER	91.2	90.7	1.5	1.6	1.7	1.9	5.9	6.6	10.9	9.9	8.3	6.4	7.3	38.0	15.5	3.3	0.5	66.9	28.7	55.1	45.0
84021	DUCHESNE	93.3	92.9	0.3	0.3	0.5	0.5	4.1	4.5	9.2	8.6	8.9	8.8	8.3	25.3	21.5	8.7	0.7	67.6	29.7	53.3	46.7
84022	DUGWAY	63.5	61.3	14.4	15.9	3.2	3.5	6.0	7.0	6.3	6.5	5.5	29.7	17.3	22.8	11.1	0.7	0.1	66.5	20.6	34.1	65.9
84023	DUTCH JOHN	94.8	94.9	0.5	0.5	0.0	0.0	5.2	4.7	7.0	6.5	5.6	5.1	6.1	27.0	28.8	13.0	0.9	77.2	40.2	54.9	45.1
84025	FARMINGTON	95.7	95.5	0.4	0.4	1.0	1.1	2.9	3.3	8.4	9.3	10.6	10.4	7.9	26.8	20.9	5.0	0.7	64.8	27.6	52.0	48.0
84026	FORT DUCHESNE	37.2	34.9	0.1	0.1	0.2	0.2	3.5	3.5	8.6	8.9	11.5	10.0	7.8	27.2	19.7	6.1	0.3	64.3	27.6	49.5	50.6
84028	GARDEN CITY	97.0	96.7	0.0	0.0	0.8	0.8	2.0	2.4	7.2	6.8	7.0	6.7	7.3	18.6	30.3	14.0	2.1	74.9	41.9	49.4	50.7
84029	GRANTSVILLE	94.1	93.5	0.7	0.8	0.4	0.4	4.9	5.8	10.3	10.1	9.2	8.7	8.0	27.8	17.9	7.0	0.9	65.0	27.4	49.7	50.3
84031	HANNA	98.2	98.3	0.0	0.0	0.0	0.0	3.6	3.3	6.7	6.7	11.7	6.7	6.7	16.7	28.3	16.7	0.0	71.7	41.3	51.7	48.3
84032	HEBER CITY	95.3	94.9	0.3	0.3	0.4	0.4	5.5	6.1	10.1	9.3	8.8	7.6	7.5	30.1	18.7	6.9	1.0	67.0	29.3	50.6	49.5
84033	HENEFER	95.9	95.4	0.1	0.1	0.4	0.5	4.2	4.9	9.2	8.8	8.7	7.9	6.8	28.9	20.9	8.1	0.8	68.3	30.9	51.3	48.7
84035	JENSEN	97.1	97.0	0.2	0.2	0.0	0.2	1.9	1.9	7.8	8.0	9.2	9.1	8.8	26.0	23.7	7.0	0.5	69.4	30.4	52.1	47.9
84036	KAMAS	97.3	97.0	0.2	0.2	0.2	0.2	3.5	4.1	8.3	8.4	9.6	7.9	6.5	29.0	22.4	7.1	0.9	68.8	32.3	50.5	49.5
84037	KAYSVILLE	96.8	96.6	0.3	0.3	0.8	0.9	2.7	3.1	10.3	10.7	10.6	9.2	7.0	26.6	18.3	6.4	0.8	62.3	26.8	49.9	50.1
84038	LAKETOWN	97.2	97.1	0.0	0.0	0.7	0.8	2.1	2.1	7.3	6.9	7.4	7.1	7.1	18.9	30.2	13.2	2.1	74.2	41.1	49.6	50.4
84039	LAPOINT	80.7	79.3	0.0	0.0	0.0	0.0	3.2	3.5	10.5	9.6	10.2	9.9	5.8	23.9	20.7	8.5	0.9	62.7	28.1	49.9	50.2
84040	LAYTON	93.2	92.6	1.2	1.4	1.8	2.0	4.0	4.5	8.7	9.2	10.3	9.5	7.3	27.1	22.2	5.2	0.5	65.8	29.2	50.0	50.0
84041	LAYTON	87.6	86.7	1.9	2.0	2.7	3.0	9.2	10.2	12.1	9.5	8.1	7.3	9.9	32.3	15.1	5.4	0.5	66.2	26.6	50.1	49.9
84042	LINDON	95.7	95.1	0.2	0.2	0.9	1.0	3.3	3.9	11.7	12.8	12.1	9.8	4.5	30.1	14.5	4.2	0.5	57.2	24.1	50.4	49.6
84043	LEHI	95.7	95.3	0.3	0.3	0.9	1.0	3.0	3.7	16.6	12.8	8.8	6.4	6.1	34.9	10.7	3.2	0.5	57.7	24.4	50.0	50.0
84044	MAGNA	86.2	84.8	0.7	0.8	2.0	2.2	15.0	17.1	11.2	10.2	9.0	8.1	8.3	32.2	15.1	5.2	0.6	64.5	26.6	50.3	49.7
84046	MANILA	94.5	94.5	0.7	0.7	0.1	0.1	5.1	5.4	6.9	6.5	5.6	5.1	6.3	26.7	29.2	12.9	0.8	78.0	40.2	56.0	44.0
84047	MIDVALE	82.9	81.5	1.1	1.3	2.6	2.8	20.0	22.0	9.5	7.8	6.2	6.2	10.4	34.0	17.0	8.0	1.0	73.1	29.2	50.5	49.5
84049	MIDWAY	97.1	96.9	0.1	0.1	0.6	0.6	3.1	3.5	8.5	8.6	8.2	7.9	6.8	25.7	24.2	9.1	1.0	69.9	32.6	51.6	48.5
84050	MORGAN	98.1	98.0	0.0	0.0	0.2	0.2	1.4	1.6	9.0	8.7	9.5	9.2	8.5	24.0	21.7	8.6	0.9	67.0	29.8	50.5	49.5
84051	MOUNTAIN HOME	97.6	97.6	0.0	0.0	0.2	0.2	2.9	3.2	6.9	7.1	7.3	7.5	5.9	19.0	27.8	17.9	0.8	74.6	42.3	51.6	48.4
84052	MYTON	81.9	81.2	0.1	0.1	0.4	0.4	8.6	9.5	8.4	10.3	9.6	9.2	9.0	23.3	21.1	8.2	0.8	65.4	27.9	51.5	48.5
84053	NEOLA	85.2	85.1	0.1	0.1	0.4	0.3	2.2	2.5	8.5	8.7	9.0	10.1	7.1	23.3	22.8	9.7	0.9	66.7	30.9	50.1	49.9
84054	NORTH SALT LAKE	93.2	92.7	0.3	0.4	1.7	1.9	6.0	6.6	10.0	8.6	7.7	7.2	9.1	29.1	19.6	7.8	0.9	69.4	29.0	50.1	49.9
84056	HILL AFB	77.9	76.5	8.6	9.2	3.6	3.9	9.3	10.3	15.2	10.8	8.4	5.8	16.6	41.2	2.0	0.1	0.0	62.9	23.0	55.3	44.7
84057	OREM	89.2	88.1	0.4	0.4	2.5	2.7	10.7	12.1	12.2	10.5	9.7	8.7	8.5	31.2	13.4	4.9	1.0	62.5	25.2	49.5	50.5
84058	OREM	90.7	89.6	0.4	0.4	2.4	2.7	8.2	9.6	11.0	9.0	8.4	9.7	12.4	29.8	13.9	4.9	0.9	66.5	24.8	49.4	50.6
84060	PARK CITY	80.6	78.1	0.4	0.5	1.9	2.0	19.5	22.2	5.3	5.5	6.6	6.2	9.0	36.2	26.2	4.8	0.3	78.9	33.2	54.3	45.7
84061	PEOA	96.0	95.6	0.2	0.2	0.3	0.5	4.7	5.4	8.5	8.6	9.7	8.8	7.2	26.4	23.4	6.6	0.9	67.9	31.7	51.0	49.0
84062	PLEASANT GROVE	95.3	94.8	0.3	0.3	0.9	1.0	4.3	4.9	13.5	12.5	10.5	8.1	6.0	31.1	13.3	4.5	0.5	58.3	24.5	50.1	49.9
84063	RANDLETT	52.6	50.7	0.0	0.0	0.0	0.0	9.2	8.0	8.0	8.0	8.0	10.7	8.0	24.0	24.0	8.0	1.3	72.0	29.6	52.0	48.0
84064	RANDOLPH	99.1	98.9	0.0	0.0	0.2	0.1	2.1	2.4	8.9	8.8	10.1	10.2	7.7	23.0	21.5	8.9	0.9	65.2	30.1	51.1	48.9
84065	RIVERTON	96.4	95.9	0.2	0.2	0.8	0.9	3.2	3.8	12.8	11.3	10.4	8.4	7.3	31.7	14.7	3.1	0.3	60.1	24.9	50.5	49.5
84066	ROOSEVELT	88.5	88.1	0.2	0.2	0.3	0.3	3.1	3.5	10.5	9.8	9.8	9.7	7.9	25.0	19.3	7.3	0.8	63.7	26.8	49.8	50.2
84067	ROY	90.8	89.6	1.2	1.3	1.9	2.1	7.6	9.1	10.5	9.1	8.3	7.4	8.0	31.6	17.3	7.1	0.7	67.6	28.5	49.4	50.6
84069	RUSH VALLEY	90.3	89.4	0.0	0.0	0.5	0.4	7.2	8.5	8.1	8.1	8.3	6.9	6.7	24.4	26.2	10.4	1.0	71.7	34.5	51.2	48.8
84070	SANDY	90.8	89.8	0.7	0.9	2.5	2.8	7.5	8.7	9.7	8.7	7.6	7.0	8.4	31.9	17.9	6.9	1.9	69.8	29.4	49.5	50.5
84071	STOCKTON	94.9	94.3	0.0	0.0	0.3	0.4	5.9	6.9	8.6	6.8	8.5	9.4	7.3	24.5	24.8	9.2	1.0	70.2	33.1	51.9	48.2
84072	TABIONA	97.7	97.5	0.0	0.0	0.2	0.2	2.7	3.2	6.9	7.1	7.6	7.4	5.9	18.7	28.0	17.7	0.8	73.9	42.1	51.8	48.2
84073	TALMAGE	96.4	96.7	0.0	0.0	0.3	0.3	3.0	3.4	8.7	8.4	8.1	7.8	7.0	23.2	22.6	13.4	0.8	70.4	33.6	52.5	47.5
84074	TOOELE	92.2	91.3	0.5	0.6	0.7	0.8	9.0	10.4	12.3	10.5	8.4	6.9	7.0	31.5	16.7	6.0	0.8	64.5	27.9	49.8	50.2
84075	SYRACUSE	93.8	93.5	0.6	0.6	1.8	1.9	4.3	4.7	12.2	10.6	9.8	8.4	8.0	31.3	15.8	3.6	0.3	62.2	25.6	50.8	49.2
84076	TRIDELL	80.6	78.9	0.0	0.0	0.0	0.0	3.1	3.4	10.5	9.1	10.5	9.7	5.7	23.7	20.8	8.8	1.1	63.0	28.5	49.9	50.1
84078	VERNAL	94.3	93.9	0.1	0.1	0.3	0.3	3.7	4.2	9.0	8.5	8.9	8.9	8.3	25.2	21.0	9.3	1.2	68.3	29.8	49.8	50.2
84080	VERNON	94.1	93.3	0.0	0.0	0.4	0.3	5.9	7.3	7.6	7.6	8.2	7.0	6.7	22.9	27.4	11.6	0.9	72.9	36.2	50.6	49.4
84082	WALLSBURG	95.8	95.5	0.1	0.2	0.4	0.4	6.1	6.9	7.9	8.0	8.3	8.0	7.2	27.3	24.3	8.5	0.6	70.9	32.6	51.2	48.8
84083	WENDOVER	53.3	50.5	1.0	1.1	0.9	1.0	53.9	57.5	12.4	10.8	10.2	9.1	9.4	28.8	14.4	4.7	0.4	61.2	24.0	52.1	47.9
84084	WEST JORDAN	88.1	86.9	0.6	0.7	3.1	3.4	11.6	13.2	11.6	10.1	9.5	8.3	8.8	32.7	16.1	2.8	0.3	63.7	25.9	50.3	49.8
84085	WHITEROCKS	38.2	36.1	0.0	0.0	0.0	0.0	1.9	2.0	8.5	9.6	11.6	10.3	7.4	25.5	20.2	6.6	0.4	64.1	27.1	48.3	51.7
84086	WOODRUFF	99.2	99.0	0.0	0.0	0.0	0.0	0.8	1.0	8.8	9.0	11.5	11.0	6.6	23.4	19.3	8.3	2.2	64.2	28.6	53.2	46.8
84087	WOODS CROSS	96.3	96.1	0.2	0.2	1.0	1.1	2.7	3.2	10.6	9.7	9.3	8.7	8.2	30.9	18.3	4.0	0.4	65.1	27.0	49.1	50.9
84088	WEST JORDAN	89.4	88.3	0.7	0.8	2.9	3.2	8.6	9.9	12.8	10.9	9.5	8.1	8.4	33.1	14.3	2.7	0.4	61.8	25.2	49.6	50.4
84092	SANDY	95.5	95.0	0.4	0.5	1.9	2.2	2.5	2.9	7.1	9.4	11.3	10.1	6.1	25.3	26.7	3.9	0.4	65.7	31.9	51.1	48.9
84093	SANDY	95.1	94.6	0.4	0.4	2.3	2.6	2.7	3.2	6.7	7.4	9.0	9.3	7.8	24.4	28.6	6.3	0.5	71.2	33.5	50.8	49.2
84094	SANDY	92.9	92.1	0.5	0.6	2.4	2.7	5.3	6.1	9.2	9.3	9.5	8.1	6.9	31.0	20.2	5.3	0.5	66.9	29.6	49.8	50.2
84095	SOUTH JORDAN	95.3	94.8	0.3	0.4	1.6	1.7	3.4	4.1	9.0	10.2	11.6	10.3	6.7	28.0	19.3	4.5	0.5	62.5	26.9	50.1	49.9
84097	OREM	93.7	93.1	0.2	0.2	1.8	2.0	5.5	6.3	9.0	10.2	11.3	11.1	7.2	25.1	17.9	7.3	0.8	62.1	25.8	49.4	50.6
84098	PARK CITY	95.1	94.6	0.2	0.2	1.0	1.1	4.3	4.9	7.2	7.6	8.6	7.8	6.4	30.3	28.9	3.1	0.1	71.8	35.7	50.9	49.1
84101	SALT LAKE CITY	68.9	66.6	5.4	5.8	3.5	3.7	29.9	33.3	6.2	5.1	4.1	4.7	10.5	41.1	20.9	6.5	1.0	82.4	33.0	61.7	38.3
84102	SALT LAKE CITY	81.0	79.6	2.0	2.2	5.9	6.5	12.2	13.6	5.2	3.5	3.0	5.3	18.7	41.2	14.4	6.5	2.3	86.4	28.9	52.0	48.0
84103	SALT LAKE CITY	90.3	89.5	0.9	1.1	2.9	3.2	7.8	8.7	5.5	4.6	4.3	5.2	10.5	35.1	21.8	10.9	2.2	82.9	34.0	49.2	50.8
84104	SALT LAKE CITY	56.1	54.1	2.8	3.1	11.9	12.2	40.6	43.6	10.9	9.5	8.6	7.9	8.9	30.5	15.8	7.0	0.9	66.4	27.2	52.2	47.8
84105	SALT LAKE CITY	91.1	90.2	0.9	1.0	2.6	2.9	6.0	7.0	6.7	5.7	5.3	5.6	10.2	37.9	20.4	6.5	1.7	79.3	32.5	48.7	51.3
84106	SALT LAKE CITY	89.9	88.9	1.3	1.5	2.6	2.9	7.2	8.3	8.4	7.2	5.8	5.9	7.2	32.6	18.4	11.0	3.6	75.1	33.3	48.1	51.9
84107	SALT LAKE CITY	89.3	88.3	1.1	1.3	2.9	3.2	9.1	10.5	8.1	6.8	6.0	6.1	8.9	31.7	19.2	11.5	1.7	75.8	32.1	48.9	51.1
84108	SALT LAKE CITY	92.3	91.5	0.6	0.7	4.3	4.9	2.8	3.3	7.9	6.2	6.1	6.8	9.6	28.1	20.7	12.0	2.6	76.5	32.7	48.8	51.2
84109	SALT LAKE CITY	95.0	94.5	0.4	0.5	2.3	2.5	2.5	2.9	6.7	6.4	6.8	7.0	7.9	26.3	21.8	14.4	2.6	75.9	36.1	48.8	51.2
84111	SALT LAKE CITY	74.9	73.2	3.2	3.4	3.7	4.0	23.4	26.1	6.8	5.1	4.4	5.5	11.6	37.3	18.0	9.5	2.0	81.2	31.9	52.1	47.9
84112	SALT LAKE CITY	81.9	80.1	1.0	1.2	12.2	13.5	3.2	3.7	11.7	4.2	2.7	20.6	23.2	26.0	7.7	3.3	0.7	79.7	22.3	51.2	48.8
84113	SALT LAKE CITY	79.5	77.6	1.2	1.4	13.8	15.2	3.4	4.1	13.3	3.9	2.1	23.1	24.0	27.6	4.1	1.6	0.4	79.2	21.6	51.4	48.6
84115	SALT LAKE CITY	75.6	73.7	2.5	2.8	4.1	4.4	23.3	26.2	9.7	7.6	6.0	6.0	9.8	34.8	16.9	7.5	1.8	73.5	30.3	50.8	49.2
84116	SALT LAKE CITY	65.1	63.3	3.3	3.5	7.9	8.2	39.2	42.4	10.9	9.1	8.0	7.0	9.2	32.4	15.6	7.1	0.8	68.0	27.9	51.6	48.4
84117	SALT LAKE CITY	93.4	92.8	0.8	0.9	2.5	2.8	3.7	4.3	6.4	5.9	5.7	6.0	7.8	26.8	23.6	14.8	2.9	78.4	37.4	47.0	53.0
84118	SALT LAKE CITY	83.3	81.8	0.7	0.8	4.5	4.9	16.4	18.5	10.5	9.6	9.3	8.4	8.6	31.5	17.1	4.7	0.3	65.5	27.0	50.5	49.6
84119	SALT LAKE CITY	75.4	73.3	1.6	1.8	6.8	7.3	21.0	23.6	9.7	8.2	7.1	7.1	10.3	32.6	17.8	6.7	0.5	71.0	28.5	52.2	47.8
84120	SALT LAKE CITY	78.3	76.5	1.0	1.1	8.8	9.5	17.9	20.1	10.3	9.4	8.8	7.9	8.5	30.3	19.0	5.4	0.4	66.7	27.9	50.2	49.8
84121	SALT LAKE CITY	93.9	93.3	0.6	0.7	2.5	2.9	2.9	3.4	6.4	6.5	7.2	7.1	7.5	28.1	25.6	10.6	1.0	75.6	35.3	49.8	50.2
84123	SALT LAKE CITY	87.3	85.8	1.2	1.4	3.6	4.0	10.4	12.1	8.6	7.7	7.3	7.4	10.2	31.5	19.1	7.4	0.8	72.1	29.1	49.2	50.8
84124	SALT LAKE CITY	93.4	92.8	0.6	0.6	2.6	2.9	3.6	4.1	6.4	5.9	6.8	7.0	7.7	25.6	22.9	15.4	2.3	76.7	37.5	48.7	51.3
	UTAH	89.2	88.6	0.8	0.9	2.3	2.5	9.0	10.0	9.9	8.8	8.3	8.3	9.3	29.3	17.7	7.2	1.0	68.3	27.9	50.0	50.0
	UNITED STATES	75.1	73.6	12.3	12.5	3.8	4.2	12.5	14.1	6.9	6.7	7.2	7.0	7.3	28.6	23.8	10.8	1.7	75.1	36.0	49.1	50.9

ZIP CODE #	POST OFFICE NAME	2004 Per Capita Income	2004 HH Income Base	2004 HOUSEHOLD INCOME DISTRIBUTION (%) Less than $25,000	$25,000 to $49,999	$50,000 to $99,999	$100,000 to $149,999	$150,000 or More	MEDIAN HOUSEHOLD INCOME 2004	2009	2004 National Centile	2004 State Centile	2004 Home Value Base	2004 HOME VALUE DISTRIBUTION (%) Less than $50,000	$50,000 to $89,999	$90,000 to $174,999	$175,000 to $399,999	$400,000 or More	2004 Median Home Value
84001	ALTAMONT	14714	49	28.6	34.7	32.7	4.1	0.0	35746	39427	31	21	42	14.3	23.8	47.6	14.3	0.0	98333
84003	AMERICAN FORK	20928	9167	10.6	23.3	40.8	16.9	8.5	65500	78620	89	89	7625	1.4	1.7	37.9	51.2	7.9	190251
84004	ALPINE	26566	2106	7.2	14.4	37.6	21.7	19.2	83425	106237	96	98	1912	0.3	0.3	10.7	57.0	31.7	331507
84006	BINGHAM CANYON	21277	276	31.9	22.1	31.5	10.5	4.0	47096	53112	66	56	224	0.0	0.9	89.7	4.5	4.9	121842
84007	BLUEBELL	14082	476	29.2	39.7	27.1	2.7	1.3	36054	40405	32	21	421	12.8	28.5	49.4	8.6	0.7	95615
84010	BOUNTIFUL	29802	15031	12.7	24.5	37.2	14.8	10.9	63285	74903	87	87	11371	0.9	1.3	35.5	52.7	9.6	195059
84013	CEDAR VALLEY	16391	812	16.1	32.6	40.2	8.6	2.5	50712	58346	73	64	733	5.7	12.0	45.4	33.2	3.7	156152
84014	CENTERVILLE	25389	4374	8.3	20.6	40.9	21.7	8.6	73703	86266	93	95	3800	1.8	2.1	29.8	62.4	3.8	200637
84015	CLEARFIELD	19277	16018	14.0	30.1	43.4	10.4	2.1	54063	62701	78	74	12306	3.2	6.1	70.2	19.7	0.9	137956
84017	COALVILLE	23724	1218	13.1	33.5	37.8	10.2	5.5	53104	63953	77	72	1023	10.1	7.4	37.7	36.9	7.9	158689
84018	CROYDON	24820	40	10.0	17.5	40.0	20.0	12.5	75000	85755	93	95	36	0.0	0.0	19.4	72.2	8.3	243750
84020	DRAPER	29171	8303	6.3	17.1	36.7	26.1	13.8	83604	104305	96	99	6998	1.8	0.4	12.6	66.3	18.9	263268
84021	DUCHESNE	15087	911	29.3	41.5	24.0	3.7	1.4	36385	41677	33	23	737	21.2	27.4	44.6	5.4	1.4	90972
84022	DUGWAY	18035	506	17.0	28.7	45.7	8.7	0.0	53186	59205	77	73	27	22.2	29.6	18.5	3.7	25.9	59375
84023	DUTCH JOHN	20928	91	31.9	30.8	28.6	7.7	1.1	35566	43004	30	20	65	21.5	36.9	26.2	10.8	4.6	82143
84025	FARMINGTON	29097	3627	5.5	17.9	37.1	23.1	16.4	83395	99714	96	98	3235	0.5	1.3	19.9	65.7	12.6	228009
84026	FORT DUCHESNE	9342	509	49.7	33.0	15.1	1.8	0.4	25146	27990	5	3	387	35.4	26.1	28.9	9.3	0.3	75968
84028	GARDEN CITY	27344	239	20.9	29.7	31.4	11.3	6.7	49410	58921	71	61	203	3.9	17.2	60.1	13.3	5.4	122384
84029	GRANTSVILLE	18498	2467	19.9	29.9	38.3	9.3	2.6	50199	54573	72	63	1985	6.3	7.3	55.4	30.2	0.8	144954
84031	HANNA	9375	19	47.4	36.8	15.8	0.0	0.0	26070	27273	6	3	17	0.0	23.5	58.8	17.7	0.0	107500
84032	HEBER CITY	23107	4463	14.7	28.6	40.6	8.9	7.1	55027	64207	80	75	3596	4.4	5.1	26.5	49.8	14.2	205690
84033	HENEFER	23041	282	12.1	27.7	41.5	13.1	5.7	56029	68884	81	76	245	3.3	4.9	38.0	41.6	12.2	182197
84035	JENSEN	18021	216	18.5	42.6	30.1	6.0	2.8	38897	45000	42	35	183	20.8	26.2	46.5	4.4	2.2	92750
84036	KAMAS	22921	1697	14.4	28.8	38.1	13.7	5.0	57098	69297	82	79	1441	4.4	5.2	26.0	50.7	13.8	213049
84037	KAYSVILLE	23810	7392	10.7	18.6	41.3	21.2	8.2	73764	86954	93	95	6296	1.6	1.9	33.1	56.8	6.6	196982
84038	LAKETOWN	22771	175	21.1	31.4	30.3	10.9	6.3	47814	57222	68	58	148	4.7	18.9	60.8	11.5	4.1	117143
84039	LAPOINT	14302	114	27.2	41.2	27.2	4.4	0.0	41098	46110	50	42	97	16.5	38.1	38.1	7.2	0.0	85000
84040	LAYTON	27364	7122	7.4	16.6	41.2	23.0	11.9	79165	92661	95	96	6463	3.5	2.3	30.3	56.9	7.1	199338
84041	LAYTON	20648	13460	17.2	30.4	40.5	9.9	2.0	51669	60729	75	67	9163	9.2	7.9	63.8	18.3	0.9	134533
84042	LINDON	22187	2240	7.6	24.8	38.3	18.6	10.8	70652	85532	91	94	1983	2.5	0.0	16.5	65.9	15.1	253015
84043	LEHI	18925	9233	11.1	25.8	44.5	13.9	4.7	60434	70103	85	82	7859	1.6	1.6	48.0	43.7	5.1	173868
84044	MAGNA	17110	6854	15.6	35.1	38.4	9.5	1.4	49553	58412	71	61	5640	3.4	8.0	83.0	5.4	0.2	123861
84046	MANILA	18445	268	31.3	31.7	29.1	6.7	1.1	36417	45349	33	24	192	19.3	42.2	24.5	9.9	4.2	79545
84047	MIDVALE	22103	10973	20.1	35.0	33.5	8.8	2.6	46250	54591	64	55	5522	2.6	3.6	61.1	31.1	1.6	153600
84049	MIDWAY	28087	959	12.7	31.0	34.7	12.7	8.9	55713	64850	80	76	810	1.9	0.7	18.6	57.2	21.6	259091
84050	MORGAN	21102	2218	13.3	28.5	38.1	13.1	7.1	58009	68259	83	81	1976	2.1	2.8	30.6	56.2	8.4	200000
84051	MOUNTAIN HOME	15429	215	40.9	38.6	17.7	1.9	0.9	28718	32519	10	8	188	17.6	23.9	39.4	15.4	3.7	96667
84052	MYTON	13670	359	40.7	33.2	20.9	2.8	2.5	30357	33840	13	11	297	31.3	24.6	35.4	7.4	1.4	81250
84053	NEOLA	16639	282	23.4	38.7	30.9	3.6	3.6	40898	45250	49	42	242	9.1	27.7	50.8	9.5	2.9	98889
84054	NORTH SALT LAKE	26540	2963	13.5	30.2	32.7	13.4	10.1	57394	68063	82	79	2262	15.1	7.2	32.1	28.8	16.8	168219
84056	HILL AFB	13318	1427	17.0	54.0	24.5	3.4	1.1	39982	44557	46	39	9	0.0	0.0	33.3	66.7	0.0	181250
84057	OREM	18488	10695	17.2	31.4	35.4	11.6	4.3	51082	60453	74	66	7152	5.0	2.9	55.7	35.2	1.2	159194
84058	OREM	20258	9328	17.4	30.8	34.5	11.0	6.4	51434	61092	75	67	5507	3.8	1.8	46.4	42.3	5.7	172466
84060	PARK CITY	54533	3100	11.8	19.1	29.7	13.2	26.2	79432	108787	95	97	1884	0.7	0.8	8.8	32.0	57.6	463717
84061	PEOA	24991	207	11.1	27.5	39.1	14.5	7.7	60931	74690	85	83	177	2.8	5.7	23.7	52.0	15.8	219167
84062	PLEASANT GROVE	18980	7994	11.0	25.6	41.1	17.1	5.3	62164	75024	86	84	6570	2.0	1.2	37.3	57.4	2.2	191346
84063	RANDLETT	12051	28	53.6	28.6	14.3	3.6	0.0	22272	20000	3	2	21	47.6	19.1	28.6	4.8	0.0	52500
84064	RANDOLPH	14444	234	26.5	34.6	34.6	1.7	2.6	38763	44631	42	35	192	25.5	39.6	34.9	0.0	0.0	73684
84065	RIVERTON	21142	10943	6.2	16.8	51.8	19.8	5.5	72127	84756	92	94	10254	0.7	0.7	30.2	62.9	5.4	198053
84066	ROOSEVELT	14559	2652	33.6	35.4	25.0	4.0	2.0	35513	40176	30	20	2153	14.4	32.0	41.5	10.5	1.6	92429
84067	ROY	21270	12083	12.6	28.5	44.5	11.8	2.6	56885	65854	82	79	10165	4.2	6.7	76.2	12.4	0.5	134072
84069	RUSH VALLEY	16867	172	20.9	36.6	36.1	5.2	1.2	45000	49212	61	52	140	14.3	17.1	35.7	27.1	5.7	131250
84070	SANDY	21220	7558	15.8	31.4	37.4	11.5	3.9	52347	62026	76	71	5261	8.8	5.2	56.4	28.6	1.1	152827
84071	STOCKTON	19548	283	24.7	32.2	33.9	7.1	2.1	46116	49829	64	54	246	9.8	24.0	43.9	20.3	2.0	116250
84072	TABIONA	12199	180	40.6	38.9	18.3	1.1	1.1	28883	33294	10	8	158	17.1	23.4	39.9	15.8	3.8	97500
84073	TALMAGE	15063	126	33.3	38.9	23.0	2.4	2.4	33333	38353	22	14	108	16.7	24.1	44.4	12.0	2.8	96667
84074	TOOELE	19357	11730	15.3	31.3	41.7	9.8	2.0	52242	58539	76	70	9756	4.0	7.2	58.6	29.3	0.9	146187
84075	SYRACUSE	19407	3386	8.3	23.9	49.8	15.1	3.0	63281	74160	87	87	2981	0.2	1.3	53.0	42.9	2.6	168952
84076	TRIDELL	11962	99	29.3	40.4	26.3	4.0	0.0	40583	46583	48	41	84	17.9	39.3	36.9	6.0	0.0	82500
84078	VERNAL	17291	7354	28.2	33.0	30.3	5.9	2.6	40465	47009	48	40	5542	11.7	28.9	48.7	10.0	0.7	97806
84080	VERNON	17153	109	19.3	34.9	40.4	3.7	1.8	47033	51130	66	56	95	11.6	15.8	37.9	31.6	3.2	136458
84082	WALLSBURG	23617	364	13.7	22.3	44.5	11.5	8.0	62405	72506	87	85	314	4.5	3.2	14.3	62.4	15.6	263542
84083	WENDOVER	12533	678	32.6	40.1	21.4	5.8	0.2	33566	38512	23	15	336	47.0	24.4	17.6	5.7	5.4	53333
84084	WEST JORDAN	19624	14664	8.6	25.8	49.1	13.0	3.6	62150	73108	86	84	12814	0.8	1.7	69.8	27.4	0.3	153785
84085	WHITEROCKS	8739	296	56.8	27.7	13.2	2.4	0.0	21333	23632	2	1	242	39.7	24.8	26.9	8.7	0.0	65294
84086	WOODRUFF	14051	130	21.5	43.9	30.8	3.9	0.0	38570	44564	41	34	106	17.9	42.5	37.7	0.0	1.9	84211
84087	WOODS CROSS	20632	3104	9.8	24.1	48.7	13.9	3.5	62566	72332	87	86	2746	1.5	5.4	50.7	41.0	1.5	168179
84088	WEST JORDAN	21230	12598	8.1	25.5	45.1	17.3	4.1	64147	76108	88	88	10190	4.0	2.5	42.7	49.9	1.0	176129
84092	SANDY	36136	8483	4.7	10.4	34.3	28.1	22.5	100691	121477	98	100	8045	0.2	0.1	9.6	69.4	20.8	266801
84093	SANDY	33896	7486	5.4	17.0	36.0	24.7	17.0	85655	103556	96	99	6960	0.8	0.9	18.6	65.8	13.9	231945
84094	SANDY	23693	8596	9.3	20.6	44.8	20.4	5.0	69312	81834	91	92	7247	0.6	0.8	51.0	46.7	0.9	172426
84095	SOUTH JORDAN	25755	9546	6.3	14.2	42.3	28.2	9.0	82948	102608	96	97	8385	0.5	0.6	14.0	77.6	7.3	242301
84097	OREM	22237	5839	11.4	22.5	37.3	18.6	10.2	67426	81452	90	90	4836	0.7	0.8	38.8	52.4	7.3	190962
84098	PARK CITY	48980	5741	7.0	12.5	30.5	23.1	26.8	99897	135579	98	100	4561	0.3	0.0	4.6	49.1	45.9	382570
84101	SALT LAKE CITY	17164	1356	44.6	29.7	21.2	3.4	1.2	28295	36438	9	7	261	0.0	28.7	49.4	15.3	6.5	100658
84102	SALT LAKE CITY	24061	8708	36.1	33.7	21.4	5.5	3.3	34277	42052	25	16	2368	1.4	5.8	48.7	37.5	6.7	164275
84103	SALT LAKE CITY	38878	10940	26.6	28.0	24.5	9.3	11.5	45071	55018	61	52	4636	0.6	2.4	21.1	49.6	26.2	256061
84104	SALT LAKE CITY	12839	6520	32.4	36.0	25.5	4.5	1.6	34829	41340	27	18	3779	5.8	19.6	68.9	5.5	0.2	112895
84105	SALT LAKE CITY	33020	9755	18.9	26.0	35.0	14.0	6.1	55188	68332	80	75	5880	0.7	2.2	38.7	52.5	5.9	187037
84106	SALT LAKE CITY	26115	13512	20.8	31.8	33.5	9.3	4.6	47536	56302	67	57	8449	0.9	3.0	48.1	45.2	2.8	172190
84107	SALT LAKE CITY	25187	12771	22.5	33.0	31.9	7.9	4.6	45449	53853	62	54	6651	4.2	7.5	50.4	34.9	3.2	157661
84108	SALT LAKE CITY	38790	7504	13.8	21.8	30.6	17.0	16.9	69712	86328	91	93	5238	0.0	0.1	12.4	66.4	21.2	260037
84109	SALT LAKE CITY	32014	8543	14.5	24.5	33.4	16.5	11.2	64483	78378	88	88	6715	0.0	0.9	23.2	65.0	10.9	218408
84111	SALT LAKE CITY	19750	5526	47.5	29.2	18.1	3.2	2.0	26417	32516	6	5	1358	2.7	12.4	64.2	18.9	1.7	130517
84112	SALT LAKE CITY	12801	69	30.4	15.9	13.0	10.1	30.4	62189	72168	86	85	43	2.3	0.0	2.3	25.6	69.8	526786
84113	SALT LAKE CITY	25537	232	51.7	31.9	9.9	1.7	4.7	24253	26360	4	2	18	0.0	0.0	0.0	11.1	88.9	750000
84115	SALT LAKE CITY	17826	9866	35.5	35.0	23.4	4.2	1.9	33547	40891	23	14	3594	3.4	8.6	80.1	7.4	0.6	123379
84116	SALT LAKE CITY	14967	9950	29.2	31.8	30.2	7.5	1.4	39963	47094	46	38	5790	5.2	7.2	77.3	10.0	0.3	128357
84117	SALT LAKE CITY	33928	9760	15.5	27.6	32.9	13.9	10.2	57710	68220	82	80	6520	2.5	6.0	25.3	52.5	13.7	212569
84118	SALT LAKE CITY	19058	18249	10.5	30.6	44.1	11.7	3.2	56790	66690	81	78	15404	1.2	2.2	80.9	15.1	0.7	138621
84119	SALT LAKE CITY	17847	16938	23.9	33.7	32.9	7.8	1.7	43902	51810	58	49	9935	10.4	9.4	68.7	11.2	0.3	128275
84120	SALT LAKE CITY	18391	12688	12.0	28.3	45.3	11.8	2.6	57931	68348	83	80	10152	2.8	2.4	81.0	13.2	0.5	139765
84121	SALT LAKE CITY	38426	15069	10.4	21.0	34.1	18.6	16.0	75196	91079	93	96	11695	0.1	1.2	25.9	57.0	15.8	219300
84123	SALT LAKE CITY	22156	13945	19.3	32.4	34.7	10.6	3.0	48663	57113	70	59	8240	10.9	8.6	45.9	34.0	0.6	151503
84124	SALT LAKE CITY	34905	7813	13.0	22.4	33.9	17.4	13.3	65042	79154	89	89	5900	0.3	0.6	18.0	65.8	15.3	239532
	UTAH	21907		18.7	28.9	35.1	11.8	5.5	52040	61244				4.3	6.7	48.5	35.1	5.4	159338
	UNITED STATES	25866		24.7	27.1	30.8	10.9	6.5	48124	56710				10.9	15.0	33.7	30.1	10.4	145905

#	POST OFFICE NAME	FINANCIAL SERVICES: Auto Loan	FINANCIAL SERVICES: Home Loan	FINANCIAL SERVICES: Invest-ments	FINANCIAL SERVICES: Retire-ment Plans	THE HOME: Home Improvements: Home Repair	THE HOME: Home Improvements: Lawn & Garden	THE HOME: Furnishings: Comput-ers & Hard-ware	THE HOME: Furnishings: Major Appli-ances	THE HOME: Furnishings: TV, Radio, Sound Equip-ment	THE HOME: Furnishings: Furni-ture	ENTERTAINMENT: Dine out/ Carry out	ENTERTAINMENT: Sports Equip-ment	ENTERTAINMENT: Fees & Tickets	ENTERTAINMENT: Toys & Games	ENTERTAINMENT: Travel	ENTERTAINMENT: Cable TV	PERSONAL: Apparel & Services	PERSONAL: Auto Repairs	PERSONAL: Health Insur-ance	PERSONAL: Pets & Supplies
84001	ALTAMONT	83	58	30	55	68	76	57	71	66	57	77	85	49	76	59	69	71	70	84	99
84003	AMERICAN FORK	110	124	126	127	120	119	115	114	108	117	136	134	119	138	114	102	135	112	101	125
84004	ALPINE	152	180	184	185	174	171	161	159	148	165	187	186	170	193	161	141	187	154	139	175
84006	BINGHAM CANYON	72	79	83	74	79	88	78	77	80	75	100	86	82	108	80	83	96	75	83	85
84007	BLUEBELL	77	54	28	51	62	70	53	65	61	52	72	79	45	70	55	64	65	65	78	91
84010	BOUNTIFUL	118	132	145	133	130	135	128	126	122	127	154	146	132	156	128	119	152	125	118	138
84013	CEDAR VALLEY	91	88	76	90	89	93	84	88	84	85	103	102	83	103	83	82	99	86	86	102
84014	CENTERVILLE	117	136	140	139	132	130	126	124	117	126	148	146	130	152	125	112	146	122	110	136
84015	CLEARFIELD	87	92	93	95	89	90	89	88	85	90	107	104	90	107	87	80	105	88	79	97
84017	COALVILLE	114	94	70	93	101	111	94	104	101	93	122	123	88	120	95	102	114	103	113	130
84018	CROYDON	118	147	156	147	145	143	131	131	122	131	153	153	140	163	134	118	153	126	117	145
84020	DRAPER	132	152	149	157	145	141	136	135	125	141	159	158	141	161	134	117	157	131	116	148
84021	DUCHESNE	75	59	38	56	64	71	58	67	63	57	75	79	52	73	58	64	70	66	74	86
84022	DUGWAY	80	87	88	89	84	84	84	82	78	84	99	98	84	100	82	74	97	82	73	90
84023	DUTCH JOHN	79	62	42	56	69	78	58	70	66	58	78	82	52	77	62	70	73	69	83	96
84025	FARMINGTON	146	172	178	176	166	165	156	154	144	158	182	179	164	187	156	137	181	149	135	169
84026	FORT DUCHESNE	45	39	37	38	40	45	43	43	46	42	56	50	41	55	42	46	53	44	46	49
84028	GARDEN CITY	119	93	64	84	105	118	88	106	99	87	118	124	79	116	94	106	110	104	125	145
84029	GRANTSVILLE	87	86	76	86	86	89	81	84	80	82	100	99	81	100	81	79	96	83	82	98
84031	HANNA	50	39	27	36	44	50	37	45	42	37	50	52	33	49	40	45	46	44	53	61
84032	HEBER CITY	107	109	100	109	110	112	102	106	100	103	124	125	101	125	102	98	121	104	103	124
84033	HENEFER	100	107	104	108	104	104	102	102	96	103	121	121	101	122	100	91	119	101	92	114
84035	JENSEN	83	76	59	73	76	80	73	78	73	75	91	90	69	85	71	72	87	77	77	92
84036	KAMAS	105	100	87	96	104	110	94	102	96	94	117	120	91	118	96	97	113	100	105	126
84037	KAYSVILLE	116	137	143	138	133	133	125	124	117	127	148	145	131	152	126	113	147	121	112	136
84038	LAKETOWN	116	90	60	82	102	114	85	103	97	84	114	121	76	113	91	103	106	101	122	141
84039	LAPOINT	78	55	29	52	63	71	54	66	62	53	73	80	46	71	56	65	66	65	79	92
84040	LAYTON	132	155	156	158	149	146	139	138	128	142	162	162	145	167	139	122	161	134	120	152
84041	LAYTON	87	88	91	92	85	86	88	86	84	90	107	102	87	104	85	79	104	87	77	95
84042	LINDON	131	152	150	157	146	142	137	136	126	141	159	159	142	162	135	118	158	132	117	149
84043	LEHI	102	111	107	115	107	105	103	102	96	106	122	120	105	121	100	90	119	101	90	113
84044	MAGNA	82	85	83	85	83	86	83	83	80	83	101	96	83	101	81	78	98	82	78	92
84046	MANILA	79	62	42	56	70	78	58	70	66	58	78	82	52	77	62	71	73	69	83	96
84047	MIDVALE	79	78	86	81	76	80	82	79	80	82	101	94	81	99	79	76	99	82	73	87
84049	MIDWAY	116	127	123	124	129	132	115	120	112	114	138	141	117	145	118	112	136	116	117	141
84050	MORGAN	108	107	94	105	111	115	99	106	99	98	122	126	99	126	101	100	118	103	108	130
84051	MOUNTAIN HOME	60	47	32	43	53	60	45	54	51	44	60	63	40	59	48	54	56	53	64	74
84052	MYTON	71	61	44	59	63	68	59	65	61	60	75	76	54	71	59	61	71	65	68	80
84053	NEOLA	92	64	34	61	75	84	63	78	73	63	86	95	54	84	66	77	78	77	93	109
84054	NORTH SALT LAKE	113	121	118	122	118	119	114	115	108	115	136	135	115	136	112	104	134	113	104	128
84056	HILL AFB	74	47	45	54	43	51	70	60	71	65	88	80	60	79	57	65	85	71	56	68
84057	OREM	90	94	98	97	91	93	93	91	88	94	112	107	93	111	90	84	109	92	83	101
84058	OREM	94	94	104	99	91	95	99	94	94	99	120	113	97	116	94	89	117	97	85	105
84060	PARK CITY	210	210	248	212	211	228	207	209	206	209	258	246	210	259	210	206	252	211	206	246
84061	PEOA	110	124	124	124	124	124	114	116	108	113	135	137	117	141	115	105	133	113	107	132
84062	PLEASANT GROVE	104	113	111	117	109	108	106	105	99	109	126	124	108	126	103	93	123	104	92	116
84063	RANDLETT	61	41	18	35	46	53	39	49	47	40	56	59	33	53	40	51	51	49	61	70
84064	RANDOLPH	83	58	30	54	67	75	57	70	66	56	77	85	49	75	59	69	70	69	84	98
84065	RIVERTON	116	130	125	135	125	122	118	117	109	122	138	138	121	139	115	102	136	114	101	130
84066	ROOSEVELT	74	60	42	58	64	72	60	67	65	60	78	78	56	77	60	66	73	66	74	84
84067	ROY	91	98	97	99	95	98	92	93	89	94	111	107	94	111	92	85	109	92	86	103
84069	RUSH VALLEY	77	70	58	68	74	79	67	72	70	66	85	86	66	87	68	71	82	71	76	90
84070	SANDY	90	91	93	93	90	92	91	90	88	91	110	107	90	109	89	84	107	91	84	101
84071	STOCKTON	90	80	61	76	85	91	74	82	79	74	95	98	72	98	76	81	91	80	89	106
84072	TABIONA	60	47	32	43	53	60	45	54	51	44	60	63	40	59	48	54	56	53	64	74
84073	TALMAGE	70	54	36	50	60	68	52	62	59	52	70	73	47	69	55	62	65	61	72	83
84074	TOOELE	85	91	87	92	89	90	85	86	82	87	102	100	86	103	84	79	100	85	79	96
84075	SYRACUSE	102	114	111	118	109	106	105	104	97	108	123	122	107	123	102	90	121	102	89	114
84076	TRIDELL	77	54	28	51	62	70	53	65	61	52	72	79	45	70	55	64	65	65	78	91
84078	VERNAL	79	69	56	68	72	78	69	74	72	69	88	87	66	87	69	72	83	74	78	90
84080	VERNON	83	74	56	70	78	83	68	75	72	68	88	90	67	90	70	74	84	73	82	97
84082	WALLSBURG	105	126	130	125	125	124	112	114	106	112	133	133	118	140	115	104	132	110	105	129
84083	WENDOVER	61	53	52	54	53	56	59	59	61	61	77	69	57	76	56	58	76	62	55	64
84084	WEST JORDAN	98	109	110	113	105	103	102	100	95	104	120	119	104	121	100	89	119	99	87	110
84085	WHITEROCKS	43	33	35	31	34	40	38	39	42	38	52	45	36	50	37	44	49	40	43	47
84086	WOODRUFF	80	56	29	53	65	73	55	68	64	55	75	82	47	73	57	67	68	67	81	95
84087	WOODS CROSS	99	113	113	115	109	107	103	102	96	105	121	120	107	124	102	91	120	100	90	113
84088	WEST JORDAN	108	122	119	126	116	113	111	110	102	115	130	129	114	130	108	96	128	108	94	120
84092	SANDY	173	213	229	217	207	209	188	185	173	190	219	215	204	229	192	168	220	179	167	207
84093	SANDY	150	187	202	190	183	183	166	164	153	167	194	191	180	204	170	149	194	159	147	182
84094	SANDY	107	121	124	124	117	116	113	112	105	115	133	132	116	135	112	100	132	110	98	123
84095	SOUTH JORDAN	134	153	156	159	147	145	140	138	129	144	164	162	146	165	138	122	163	135	120	152
84097	OREM	113	130	139	132	127	130	121	120	115	122	145	140	127	148	122	112	143	118	110	133
84098	PARK CITY	190	223	226	231	213	210	199	196	182	205	231	228	210	235	197	172	230	190	169	215
84101	SALT LAKE CITY	50	42	52	45	42	47	54	49	55	51	69	60	51	66	50	53	67	54	49	55
84102	SALT LAKE CITY	65	53	69	59	53	58	72	63	71	67	89	81	66	83	65	65	86	71	59	71
84103	SALT LAKE CITY	103	101	139	107	99	108	116	107	114	113	144	130	115	144	112	110	142	114	100	118
84104	SALT LAKE CITY	62	58	58	57	57	59	61	62	62	64	78	70	59	75	59	60	78	64	58	66
84105	SALT LAKE CITY	96	103	127	108	102	106	108	103	104	106	131	124	109	132	106	99	129	106	94	112
84106	SALT LAKE CITY	82	88	102	90	87	91	90	87	87	88	109	103	91	110	89	85	107	89	83	95
84107	SALT LAKE CITY	81	81	96	84	79	84	87	83	85	86	107	99	87	106	85	82	105	86	78	91
84108	SALT LAKE CITY	127	148	181	149	145	152	145	140	138	144	174	165	151	178	146	134	172	141	129	152
84109	SALT LAKE CITY	111	129	150	127	127	136	124	122	120	123	150	140	130	154	127	119	148	121	118	133
84111	SALT LAKE CITY	52	46	59	50	46	50	57	52	57	54	71	64	54	69	54	54	69	57	50	57
84112	SALT LAKE CITY	177	195	263	199	190	209	205	190	195	200	246	226	212	245	202	188	244	196	176	208
84113	SALT LAKE CITY	63	39	50	44	39	47	75	55	72	63	90	76	61	82	60	64	85	67	51	63
84115	SALT LAKE CITY	59	55	64	57	54	58	62	59	62	61	78	70	60	76	59	60	75	62	56	65
84116	SALT LAKE CITY	69	68	70	68	67	69	69	69	69	72	87	79	69	86	67	66	86	70	64	75
84117	SALT LAKE CITY	107	117	140	120	116	123	117	115	114	117	143	133	121	143	118	112	141	116	110	126
84118	SALT LAKE CITY	93	102	103	104	99	100	97	96	92	98	116	112	99	118	96	88	114	95	87	106
84119	SALT LAKE CITY	70	69	73	70	67	71	72	70	71	71	89	83	71	88	70	69	87	72	67	78
84120	SALT LAKE CITY	90	98	100	99	96	97	94	93	89	94	113	109	95	114	93	86	111	92	85	103
84121	SALT LAKE CITY	144	163	181	165	160	166	154	152	147	155	185	176	161	188	156	144	183	151	142	169
84123	SALT LAKE CITY	85	84	91	88	82	85	86	84	83	88	105	99	85	102	83	79	103	86	77	94
84124	SALT LAKE CITY	123	137	160	140	135	142	134	131	128	134	162	153	139	163	135	125	160	132	123	144
	UTAH	96	98	100	99	97	100	97	97	94	97	118	114	97	118	95	91	115	97	91	109
	UNITED STATES	100	100	100	100	100	100	100	100	100	100	100	100	100	100	100	100	100	100	100	100

POPULATION CHANGE

#	POST OFFICE NAME	COUNTY FIPS CODE	POPULATION 2000	POPULATION 2004	POPULATION 2009	2000-2004 ANNUAL RATE % Rate	2000-2004 ANNUAL RATE State Centile	HOUSEHOLDS 2000	HOUSEHOLDS 2004	HOUSEHOLDS 2009	% Annual Rate 2000-2004	2004 Average HH Size	FAMILIES 2000	FAMILIES 2004	% Annual Rate 2000-2004
84128	SALT LAKE CITY	035	21150	22012	22965	0.9	37	5597	5963	6319	1.5	3.69	4974	5229	1.2
84302	BRIGHAM CITY	003	21156	21714	22572	0.6	30	6660	6942	7319	1.0	3.08	5380	5536	0.7
84305	CLARKSTON	005	730	731	764	0.0	13	218	223	237	0.5	3.28	184	185	0.1
84306	COLLINSTON	003	443	521	578	3.9	89	128	153	173	4.3	3.41	108	128	4.1
84307	CORINNE	003	1151	1225	1285	1.5	48	347	377	402	2.0	3.25	295	317	1.7
84308	CORNISH	005	240	243	256	0.3	19	64	66	70	0.7	3.68	55	56	0.4
84309	DEWEYVILLE	003	376	482	558	6.0	98	134	175	206	6.5	2.75	113	145	6.0
84310	EDEN	057	2932	3223	3545	2.3	68	880	989	1103	2.8	3.25	724	801	2.4
84311	FIELDING	003	652	657	668	0.2	17	203	209	216	0.7	3.14	174	177	0.4
84312	GARLAND	003	3669	3721	3799	0.3	20	1068	1104	1145	0.8	3.37	896	916	0.5
84313	GROUSE CREEK	003	138	137	140	-0.2	7	50	51	52	0.5	2.69	36	36	0.0
84314	HONEYVILLE	003	1721	1850	1955	1.7	53	517	566	606	2.2	3.27	445	481	1.9
84315	HOOPER	057	4306	4973	5619	3.5	84	1262	1489	1707	4.0	3.34	1119	1306	3.7
84317	HUNTSVILLE	057	2481	2879	3258	3.6	86	770	910	1043	4.0	3.15	651	758	3.7
84318	HYDE PARK	005	3009	3312	3645	2.3	69	779	878	983	2.9	3.77	684	762	2.6
84319	HYRUM	005	6914	7242	7846	1.1	39	1842	1960	2152	1.5	3.69	1641	1727	1.2
84320	LEWISTON	005	2287	2331	2460	0.5	23	641	664	710	0.8	3.51	538	549	0.5
84321	LOGAN	005	34672	36543	39599	1.2	42	11655	12396	13583	1.5	2.91	7877	8175	0.9
84322	LOGAN	005	333	400	459	4.4	91	66	82	96	5.2	4.61	6	7	3.7
84324	MANTUA	003	805	804	820	0.0	11	221	225	233	0.4	3.56	193	195	0.2
84325	MENDON	005	1501	1594	1722	1.4	47	425	460	505	1.9	3.47	379	406	1.6
84328	PARADISE	005	1173	1210	1293	0.7	32	326	342	371	1.1	3.54	279	289	0.8
84329	PARK VALLEY	003	283	282	287	-0.1	9	90	91	94	0.3	3.10	65	65	0.0
84330	PLYMOUTH	003	356	370	383	0.9	36	115	122	128	1.4	3.03	98	102	1.0
84331	PORTAGE	003	322	334	346	0.9	35	86	91	96	1.3	3.67	73	76	1.0
84332	PROVIDENCE	005	6118	7175	8150	3.8	88	1693	2035	2353	4.4	3.52	1478	1757	4.2
84333	RICHMOND	005	2304	2463	2668	1.6	50	692	757	833	2.1	3.25	594	640	1.8
84335	SMITHFIELD	005	9540	10223	11112	1.6	52	2711	2972	3284	2.2	3.44	2341	2532	1.9
84336	SNOWVILLE	003	606	601	612	-0.2	6	182	184	191	0.3	3.27	154	154	0.0
84337	TREMONTON	003	8872	9409	9856	1.4	45	2622	2827	3001	1.8	3.31	2199	2342	1.5
84338	TRENTON	005	514	545	589	1.4	45	155	168	184	1.9	3.27	132	141	1.6
84339	WELLSVILLE	005	3671	3987	4354	2.0	58	1024	1135	1258	2.5	3.51	904	990	2.2
84340	WILLARD	003	2202	2453	2637	2.6	73	722	816	889	2.9	3.01	582	649	2.6
84341	LOGAN	005	18379	20153	22197	2.2	66	5252	5925	6687	2.9	3.12	3925	4347	2.4
84401	OGDEN	057	30928	32449	35053	1.1	40	10257	10751	11669	1.1	2.90	6823	7004	0.6
84403	OGDEN	057	34886	36290	38938	0.9	36	12203	12791	13842	1.1	2.78	8764	8958	0.5
84404	OGDEN	057	44875	49255	54288	2.2	67	15648	17415	19397	2.6	2.81	11563	12613	2.1
84405	OGDEN	057	25608	27608	30208	1.8	55	8727	9515	10519	2.1	2.85	6674	7152	1.6
84408	OGDEN	057	138	150	162	2.0	59	40	47	53	3.9	2.04	29	33	3.1
84414	OGDEN	057	20895	22802	24994	2.1	62	6068	6763	7515	2.6	3.37	5358	5903	2.3
84501	PRICE	007	12547	12197	11937	-0.7	2	4407	4385	4376	-0.1	2.67	3198	3128	-0.5
84510	ANETH	037	4000	3982	4020	-0.1	7	1015	1030	1062	0.4	3.87	846	849	0.1
84511	BLANDING	037	4635	4770	4895	0.7	31	1384	1467	1546	1.4	3.19	1074	1122	1.0
84520	EAST CARBON	007	1804	1827	1817	0.3	20	726	752	763	0.8	2.43	493	498	0.2
84523	FERRON	015	2373	2377	2406	0.0	14	779	810	848	0.9	2.87	627	643	0.6
84525	GREEN RIVER	015	1090	1101	1117	0.2	18	385	395	410	0.6	2.79	276	278	0.2
84526	HELPER	007	4154	4013	3912	-0.8	1	1619	1609	1602	-0.2	2.47	1158	1121	-0.8
84528	HUNTINGTON	015	7499	7584	7716	0.3	19	2349	2450	2571	1.0	3.08	1925	1983	0.7
84531	MEXICAN HAT	037	775	773	780	-0.1	11	178	180	185	0.3	4.29	152	153	0.2
84532	MOAB	019	8321	8715	9112	1.1	38	3353	3605	3859	1.7	2.39	2122	2225	1.1
84533	LAKE POWELL	037	126	128	131	0.4	22	59	62	65	1.2	2.06	36	37	0.7
84535	MONTICELLO	037	3008	3006	3038	0.0	12	964	986	1021	0.5	2.90	723	727	0.1
84536	MONUMENT VALLEY	037	1710	1728	1756	0.3	18	424	437	453	0.7	3.95	356	362	0.4
84540	THOMPSON	019	219	223	227	0.4	23	100	105	110	1.2	2.12	64	66	0.7
84542	WELLINGTON	007	1919	1914	1890	-0.1	11	662	682	690	0.7	2.80	531	538	0.3
84601	PROVO	049	27800	30420	34717	2.1	63	8584	9469	10923	2.3	3.17	6565	7070	1.8
84604	PROVO	049	48194	52302	59041	1.9	57	12077	13525	15759	2.7	3.39	8282	8912	1.7
84606	PROVO	049	29687	32079	36374	1.8	55	8673	9529	10972	2.2	3.30	5217	5542	1.4
84621	AXTELL	039	203	211	222	0.9	36	68	72	76	1.4	2.93	54	56	0.9
84622	CENTERFIELD	039	1250	1320	1400	1.3	42	380	405	433	1.5	3.26	305	322	1.3
84624	DELTA	027	6661	6777	6915	0.4	22	1998	2079	2167	0.9	3.24	1628	1673	0.6
84627	EPHRAIM	039	4680	5404	5996	3.4	84	1178	1392	1571	4.0	3.56	796	924	3.6
84628	EUREKA	023	794	868	965	2.1	63	286	314	350	2.2	2.76	202	217	1.7
84629	FAIRVIEW	039	3151	3391	3635	1.7	53	956	1044	1131	2.1	3.24	786	850	1.9
84630	FAYETTE	039	239	249	261	1.0	37	76	80	85	1.2	3.11	60	63	1.2
84631	FILLMORE	027	4452	4568	4681	0.6	30	1445	1511	1577	1.1	2.95	1138	1172	0.7
84634	GUNNISON	039	2441	2476	2547	0.3	21	520	538	566	0.8	3.13	417	427	0.6
84635	HINCKLEY	027	859	862	876	0.1	16	261	269	280	0.7	3.20	218	222	0.4
84642	MANTI	039	4157	4283	4484	0.7	31	1276	1335	1411	1.1	3.17	1015	1049	0.8
84645	MONA	023	1432	1633	1854	3.1	80	343	392	447	3.2	4.17	304	345	3.0
84647	MOUNT PLEASANT	039	6642	6789	7125	0.5	25	2093	2165	2294	0.8	3.10	1632	1666	0.5
84648	NEPHI	023	5744	6256	6936	2.0	60	1745	1913	2127	2.2	3.22	1419	1535	1.9
84650	OASIS	027	233	241	249	0.8	32	73	78	82	1.6	3.09	60	63	1.2
84651	PAYSON	049	16846	19121	22186	3.0	78	4664	5411	6385	3.6	3.53	3993	4563	3.2
84653	SALEM	049	5845	6743	7882	3.4	83	1487	1755	2088	4.0	3.84	1341	1565	3.7
84654	SALINA	041	4549	4654	4788	0.5	26	1465	1523	1590	0.9	3.06	1207	1238	0.6
84655	SANTAQUIN	049	6258	7245	8481	3.5	85	1644	1942	2312	4.0	3.69	1453	1693	3.5
84660	SPANISH FORK	049	23569	27390	32335	3.6	87	6475	7622	9121	3.9	3.54	5609	6532	3.7
84663	SPRINGVILLE	049	20098	22229	25537	2.4	71	5876	6581	7651	2.7	3.37	4943	5448	2.3
84664	MAPLETON	049	6094	7411	8995	4.7	93	1509	1881	2325	5.3	3.94	1382	1712	5.2
84701	RICHFIELD	041	9797	10105	10427	0.7	32	3111	3279	3444	1.3	2.96	2500	2600	0.9
84710	ALTON	025	264	298	327	2.9	75	87	100	113	3.3	2.96	55	62	2.9
84712	ANTIMONY	017	190	202	218	1.5	47	52	56	61	1.8	3.52	42	45	1.6
84713	BEAVER	001	3132	3325	3561	1.4	47	1099	1193	1302	2.0	2.67	854	913	1.6
84714	BERYL	021	692	771	850	2.6	74	206	235	263	3.2	3.26	166	186	2.7
84716	BOULDER	017	253	279	309	2.3	71	91	103	116	3.0	2.71	64	70	2.1
84717	BRYCE CANYON	017	1049	1114	1205	1.4	47	336	361	396	1.7	3.01	273	289	1.4
84719	BRIAN HEAD	021	118	129	140	2.1	63	55	61	67	2.5	2.11	42	46	2.2
84720	CEDAR CITY	021	29046	31946	35179	2.3	69	9035	10130	11346	2.7	3.09	6842	7545	2.3
84722	CENTRAL	053	2021	2271	2649	2.8	74	639	740	884	3.5	3.07	532	606	3.1
84726	ESCALANTE	017	949	1012	1099	1.5	50	347	377	417	2.0	2.68	241	257	1.5
84728	GARRISON	027	200	193	195	-0.8	0	63	62	64	-0.4	3.11	49	47	-1.0
84729	GLENDALE	025	359	393	424	2.2	64	118	133	147	2.9	2.95	90	100	2.5
84731	GREENVILLE	001	298	319	343	1.6	52	40	43	47	1.7	6.56	33	35	1.4
84734	HANKSVILLE	055	711	766	817	1.8	54	298	332	366	2.6	2.30	203	220	1.9
	UTAH					1.8					2.2	3.09			1.8
	UNITED STATES					1.2					1.3	2.58			1.1

#	ZIP CODE POST OFFICE NAME	RACE (%) White 2000	White 2004	Black 2000	Black 2004	Asian/Pacific 2000	Asian/Pacific 2004	% Hispanic Origin 2000	% Hispanic Origin 2004	2004 AGE DISTRIBUTION (%) 0-4	5-9	10-14	15-19	20-24	25-44	45-64	65-84	85+	18+	MEDIAN AGE 2004	% 2004 Males	% 2004 Females
84128	SALT LAKE CITY	84.1	82.4	0.9	1.0	3.3	3.5	15.3	17.4	12.6	10.8	9.4	7.8	8.2	33.6	15.0	2.5	0.2	62.4	25.6	50.6	49.5
84302	BRIGHAM CITY	91.9	91.2	0.2	0.2	0.8	0.9	7.1	8.0	9.8	8.8	9.1	8.4	7.8	26.0	18.7	10.0	1.4	67.1	29.1	50.3	49.7
84305	CLARKSTON	95.9	95.6	0.0	0.0	0.0	0.0	2.1	2.3	9.4	9.4	10.3	8.9	7.4	25.3	19.3	8.3	1.6	65.4	28.4	52.7	47.3
84306	COLLINSTON	96.4	96.2	0.0	0.0	0.9	1.2	2.9	3.5	8.1	8.1	9.8	9.0	8.3	24.2	21.9	9.4	1.3	68.3	30.3	50.5	49.5
84307	CORINNE	92.4	91.5	0.1	0.1	1.8	2.0	6.3	7.2	9.1	9.2	9.4	8.2	8.2	25.5	22.3	7.3	0.9	67.2	29.2	50.9	49.1
84308	CORNISH	95.4	94.7	0.0	0.0	0.8	0.8	6.3	7.0	11.5	9.1	8.2	11.1	7.8	23.5	19.8	7.8	1.2	64.2	26.5	50.6	49.4
84309	DEWEYVILLE	96.5	96.1	0.0	0.0	0.8	1.0	3.5	3.9	8.3	7.9	9.5	8.7	7.9	24.5	22.0	9.8	1.5	68.9	31.0	50.4	49.6
84310	EDEN	97.2	96.9	0.2	0.3	0.8	0.9	2.1	2.7	6.8	7.5	9.0	8.4	7.2	24.5	28.1	7.7	0.7	71.3	36.0	52.0	48.0
84311	FIELDING	96.8	96.7	0.0	0.0	0.9	1.1	2.6	3.0	8.7	9.0	10.5	9.3	8.1	24.1	20.7	8.7	1.1	65.9	28.6	50.5	49.5
84312	GARLAND	92.7	91.9	0.0	0.0	1.8	2.0	5.7	6.5	11.3	10.6	10.4	8.5	7.1	26.2	17.4	7.4	1.1	62.4	26.6	50.3	49.7
84313	GROUSE CREEK	92.8	92.7	0.0	0.0	0.7	0.7	13.0	14.6	10.2	9.5	11.0	8.8	5.8	25.6	16.8	11.0	1.5	64.2	28.3	54.0	46.0
84314	HONEYVILLE	94.5	94.1	0.0	0.0	1.9	2.1	4.4	4.9	9.2	8.9	10.8	9.1	6.5	25.1	20.1	9.0	1.2	65.3	29.8	51.1	48.9
84315	HOOPER	97.2	96.7	0.2	0.3	0.7	0.7	2.6	3.2	8.2	7.9	8.7	9.1	8.0	26.4	24.4	6.4	0.8	69.6	31.1	50.7	49.3
84317	HUNTSVILLE	97.7	97.4	0.2	0.2	0.5	0.6	2.5	3.1	6.6	8.3	9.3	9.4	7.0	22.8	26.8	8.7	1.2	69.6	35.6	51.3	48.7
84318	HYDE PARK	97.5	97.2	0.2	0.3	0.8	0.9	1.9	2.3	10.5	9.6	11.3	11.1	7.2	25.6	19.0	4.6	1.2	61.5	25.3	50.7	49.3
84319	HYRUM	89.0	88.1	0.2	0.2	0.6	0.6	12.6	14.0	13.5	11.6	9.7	8.2	7.8	28.7	15.5	4.6	0.4	60.3	24.5	50.6	49.4
84320	LEWISTON	95.3	94.7	0.1	0.2	0.2	0.2	4.9	5.7	10.9	10.3	10.3	10.1	7.4	25.9	16.5	6.8	1.8	62.3	25.8	50.5	49.5
84321	LOGAN	90.1	89.2	0.4	0.5	2.6	2.9	8.7	9.7	10.0	7.1	5.8	7.9	20.5	29.0	11.9	6.1	1.7	73.8	24.7	48.4	51.6
84322	LOGAN	96.4	96.0	0.3	0.3	2.1	2.3	2.7	3.0	0.5	0.3	0.3	38.0	51.3	9.0	0.3	0.5	0.0	96.3	21.1	19.3	80.8
84324	MANTUA	96.4	96.4	0.6	0.6	0.3	0.3	0.9	1.0	6.8	9.1	12.1	13.3	5.9	22.6	21.9	7.7	0.6	62.2	30.7	52.5	47.5
84325	MENDON	97.1	97.0	0.0	0.0	0.1	0.1	1.9	2.1	10.4	9.8	11.0	8.4	7.2	25.5	21.1	5.8	0.9	62.7	27.3	50.8	49.2
84328	PARADISE	98.4	98.4	0.3	0.3	0.7	0.7	1.9	2.0	9.9	10.0	10.0	8.9	7.3	26.0	21.3	5.5	1.1	64.6	27.9	51.6	48.4
84329	PARK VALLEY	92.9	92.2	0.0	0.0	0.7	0.7	13.1	14.9	9.6	8.9	12.8	9.2	6.0	25.2	16.3	11.0	1.1	62.8	27.5	52.8	47.2
84330	PLYMOUTH	98.0	98.1	0.0	0.0	0.3	0.3	3.1	3.5	10.3	11.4	12.4	9.5	5.7	25.1	18.7	6.0	1.1	59.2	25.7	48.4	51.6
84331	PORTAGE	98.1	97.9	0.0	0.0	0.3	0.3	3.1	3.3	10.5	11.4	11.1	9.6	5.7	25.5	18.9	6.6	0.9	60.5	26.6	49.4	50.6
84332	PROVIDENCE	96.3	96.0	0.1	0.1	0.7	0.7	2.7	3.1	10.3	10.5	9.9	9.0	7.0	27.6	19.2	5.6	1.0	63.9	27.3	49.9	50.1
84333	RICHMOND	96.4	96.1	0.2	0.2	0.2	0.2	2.7	3.2	10.2	9.7	9.9	9.1	7.8	24.8	19.9	7.7	0.9	64.4	27.8	49.7	50.4
84335	SMITHFIELD	95.4	94.8	0.1	0.1	0.6	0.7	5.1	5.9	10.8	9.6	10.0	9.6	7.9	26.5	17.8	6.8	1.0	63.3	26.6	49.9	50.1
84336	SNOWVILLE	94.6	93.8	0.3	0.3	0.7	0.7	7.3	8.2	10.3	10.5	12.3	10.2	6.3	26.8	17.1	6.0	0.5	60.2	25.3	51.9	48.1
84337	TREMONTON	92.9	92.2	0.2	0.2	1.2	1.4	7.5	8.4	10.8	9.8	10.0	9.0	8.1	26.2	17.4	7.5	1.3	63.8	26.6	50.6	49.4
84338	TRENTON	94.8	94.1	0.0	0.0	0.4	0.4	7.4	8.4	12.3	10.3	9.0	9.0	7.5	26.2	17.4	7.0	1.3	62.8	26.4	49.7	50.3
84339	WELLSVILLE	96.6	96.2	0.0	0.0	0.3	0.3	3.7	4.3	10.6	10.7	10.4	8.3	7.1	28.8	16.8	6.1	1.1	63.0	26.8	50.7	49.3
84340	WILLARD	95.6	95.1	0.1	0.1	0.7	0.8	4.6	5.3	8.6	8.5	8.4	7.2	7.8	25.8	23.4	9.5	0.7	70.2	32.4	50.1	49.9
84341	LOGAN	90.7	89.8	0.8	0.9	4.8	5.2	4.2	4.9	10.2	7.3	6.6	12.8	19.1	27.0	11.4	4.7	0.8	72.2	23.4	48.6	51.4
84401	OGDEN	74.8	73.3	2.8	2.9	1.3	1.4	30.2	32.5	10.2	8.6	7.9	7.4	8.9	31.2	18.0	6.7	1.2	69.3	28.7	52.9	47.2
84403	OGDEN	85.1	83.8	1.5	1.7	2.0	2.2	15.3	17.0	8.8	7.8	7.1	7.4	9.0	27.9	19.7	10.5	1.9	72.4	30.6	49.8	50.2
84404	OGDEN	88.7	87.4	1.2	1.4	1.1	1.2	11.3	13.1	9.6	8.6	7.9	7.4	8.1	29.1	19.0	9.0	1.3	69.5	29.8	49.3	50.7
84405	OGDEN	91.8	90.9	1.4	1.6	1.4	1.5	6.4	7.5	8.7	8.1	7.7	7.9	8.2	27.9	20.0	10.1	1.5	70.8	30.5	49.4	50.6
84408	OGDEN	87.0	86.0	2.9	3.3	6.5	7.3	4.4	6.0	4.0	3.3	3.3	21.3	23.3	16.7	12.7	14.0	1.3	88.7	23.9	46.0	54.0
84414	OGDEN	95.9	95.2	0.4	0.4	0.8	0.9	3.8	4.6	8.9	8.6	9.5	9.2	7.9	25.9	21.4	8.0	0.7	67.4	29.6	50.2	49.8
84501	PRICE	91.7	91.1	0.3	0.3	0.5	0.5	9.4	10.5	8.1	7.5	7.8	9.0	9.1	24.6	22.2	10.0	1.8	71.8	31.5	48.8	51.2
84510	ANETH	1.7	1.6	0.0	0.1	0.0	0.0	0.6	0.6	11.0	10.4	12.2	11.6	7.7	24.7	15.8	6.1	0.6	59.2	23.1	49.8	50.2
84511	BLANDING	65.0	64.0	0.2	0.2	0.2	0.2	3.5	3.9	10.2	10.4	11.2	9.1	6.4	24.4	19.6	7.1	1.6	62.4	27.0	49.2	50.8
84520	EAST CARBON	83.3	81.6	0.2	0.2	0.1	0.1	20.7	23.2	5.9	6.1	7.4	7.3	6.2	21.6	26.9	15.9	2.7	76.2	41.6	47.4	52.7
84523	FERRON	97.6	97.6	0.3	0.3	0.3	0.3	1.3	1.3	7.4	7.1	9.1	8.8	7.7	20.7	25.7	10.8	2.8	70.4	36.2	49.8	50.2
84525	GREEN RIVER	90.2	90.3	0.6	0.6	1.2	1.2	16.7	16.7	9.1	8.9	9.1	8.2	7.0	26.8	19.2	10.6	1.2	67.9	31.2	49.4	50.6
84526	HELPER	91.0	90.2	0.4	0.5	0.3	0.3	10.9	12.3	7.0	6.7	7.0	7.3	7.2	24.7	25.2	12.7	2.2	75.0	37.4	49.5	50.5
84528	HUNTINGTON	95.8	95.7	0.1	0.1	0.3	0.3	4.8	4.9	9.3	8.6	9.2	8.9	9.1	23.7	22.3	8.0	0.9	67.2	28.7	50.6	49.4
84531	MEXICAN HAT	3.7	3.5	0.1	0.1	0.0	0.0	0.4	0.5	11.4	12.8	11.6	9.4	7.5	27.6	14.0	5.1	0.7	58.3	23.2	49.6	50.5
84532	MOAB	92.4	92.1	0.3	0.3	0.3	0.3	5.5	6.2	7.0	6.9	7.1	7.4	6.4	26.5	26.3	11.1	1.4	74.3	37.2	48.8	51.2
84533	LAKE POWELL	43.7	43.0	0.0	0.0	0.0	0.0	3.2	3.1	7.8	7.8	9.4	7.8	7.0	30.5	22.7	7.0	0.0	71.1	32.2	50.8	49.2
84535	MONTICELLO	83.8	82.7	0.2	0.2	0.7	0.8	10.9	12.2	8.8	8.4	9.4	8.6	6.7	25.7	21.9	9.6	1.1	67.9	31.3	51.7	48.3
84536	MONUMENT VALLEY	3.1	3.0	0.1	0.1	0.1	0.1	0.4	0.3	11.1	13.4	11.9	9.4	7.0	26.5	14.8	5.5	0.5	57.6	23.0	49.4	50.6
84540	THOMPSON	94.1	93.3	0.5	0.5	0.5	0.5	6.4	7.2	7.2	7.6	7.6	6.3	5.8	26.5	27.8	10.3	0.9	73.5	37.0	49.8	50.2
84542	WELLINGTON	94.5	93.9	0.3	0.4	0.2	0.2	4.7	5.4	8.6	8.3	8.1	7.5	8.7	26.7	23.1	8.3	0.8	70.5	30.2	49.5	50.5
84601	PROVO	83.4	82.0	0.5	0.6	2.4	2.6	18.5	20.6	13.8	9.5	6.8	6.7	12.6	35.6	10.3	4.1	0.7	66.4	25.2	50.0	50.0
84604	PROVO	91.8	91.0	0.5	0.5	2.8	3.1	5.2	6.1	6.9	4.6	5.1	21.0	21.7	22.8	10.5	6.3	1.1	79.9	22.9	47.3	52.7
84606	PROVO	88.1	86.8	0.4	0.5	2.6	2.9	11.4	13.2	9.0	4.9	3.3	9.3	34.8	29.6	5.8	2.7	0.6	81.0	23.4	45.7	54.3
84621	AXTELL	90.6	89.6	0.0	0.0	0.0	0.0	8.4	9.5	9.0	9.5	10.4	8.1	8.5	22.3	19.4	11.9	1.0	65.4	28.7	50.2	49.8
84622	CENTERFIELD	93.1	92.5	0.1	0.1	0.1	0.1	7.5	8.4	9.7	8.8	11.3	9.0	9.6	23.2	18.9	8.4	1.1	63.6	26.5	51.3	48.7
84624	DELTA	94.9	94.5	0.1	0.1	0.5	0.5	6.7	7.6	9.5	9.2	10.2	9.7	7.7	22.2	20.8	9.2	1.4	64.5	28.4	51.1	48.9
84627	EPHRAIM	89.5	88.5	0.4	0.5	1.8	1.9	9.5	10.6	8.0	5.6	6.4	20.8	25.3	14.8	12.8	5.0	1.1	75.9	21.8	45.6	54.4
84628	EUREKA	91.2	90.8	0.5	0.6	0.6	0.6	5.2	5.8	8.6	10.5	8.9	8.3	5.5	29.3	19.5	9.1	0.4	66.1	30.0	50.0	50.0
84629	FAIRVIEW	94.5	94.0	0.1	0.1	0.6	0.7	4.5	5.0	9.3	9.3	10.1	8.6	6.9	23.7	20.5	10.3	1.3	65.9	29.8	49.9	50.1
84630	FAYETTE	90.4	90.0	0.0	0.0	0.0	0.0	8.4	9.2	8.8	9.2	10.0	9.6	8.4	22.1	19.3	11.7	0.8	65.1	28.2	51.0	49.0
84631	FILLMORE	92.6	92.1	0.1	0.1	1.1	1.2	8.2	9.2	8.2	7.7	9.1	8.8	8.2	21.3	21.9	12.6	2.1	69.3	32.7	51.1	49.0
84634	GUNNISON	88.0	87.1	1.8	2.0	1.4	1.5	7.5	8.2	7.0	6.0	6.7	6.2	13.1	34.3	17.7	7.8	1.2	76.4	30.7	67.2	32.8
84635	HINCKLEY	96.2	95.8	0.2	0.2	0.1	0.1	4.2	4.8	7.8	7.7	10.0	9.7	8.5	21.1	24.0	10.3	0.9	68.2	32.2	52.8	47.2
84642	MANTI	96.6	96.4	0.1	0.1	0.4	0.4	2.8	3.2	12.1	8.6	9.4	7.6	9.8	21.2	18.6	10.7	2.1	64.9	27.0	49.5	50.5
84645	MONA	98.5	98.5	0.0	0.0	0.1	0.1	1.2	1.3	14.2	12.7	11.7	9.8	6.9	24.0	15.2	5.0	0.6	55.0	21.2	48.5	51.5
84647	MOUNT PLEASANT	92.6	92.0	0.1	0.1	0.5	0.5	7.5	8.3	9.1	8.9	9.8	9.3	7.8	23.4	20.0	10.1	1.7	66.0	29.3	49.7	50.3
84648	NEPHI	97.1	96.9	0.1	0.1	0.4	0.5	2.5	2.9	11.9	10.4	9.3	8.0	6.8	25.5	17.9	8.5	1.8	63.1	27.6	50.3	49.7
84650	OASIS	94.0	93.8	0.4	0.4	0.9	0.8	4.3	5.0	10.4	8.7	7.9	10.0	8.3	19.9	23.7	10.0	1.2	66.0	29.1	51.5	48.6
84651	PAYSON	94.4	93.8	0.1	0.1	0.7	0.7	5.9	6.9	12.4	10.9	10.2	8.5	8.0	27.9	15.2	6.1	0.9	61.4	25.1	50.8	49.3
84653	SALEM	97.0	96.8	0.1	0.1	0.4	0.4	2.8	3.2	9.8	12.0	12.1	10.4	4.4	25.7	18.3	6.7	0.6	59.3	26.1	50.3	49.7
84654	SALINA	97.4	97.3	0.1	0.1	0.4	0.4	2.2	2.4	9.9	9.1	9.2	8.2	7.9	25.1	19.5	9.8	1.3	66.8	29.2	49.7	50.3
84655	SANTAQUIN	90.6	89.3	0.1	0.2	0.3	0.3	10.7	12.3	14.9	12.2	9.7	7.8	7.4	29.3	13.6	4.5	0.5	58.3	23.7	51.2	48.8
84660	SPANISH FORK	95.5	95.0	0.2	0.2	0.6	0.7	4.1	4.9	13.4	11.7	9.7	7.8	6.5	31.8	13.3	5.1	0.7	60.4	25.5	50.5	49.5
84663	SPRINGVILLE	94.6	93.9	0.1	0.1	0.7	0.8	4.8	5.6	13.3	11.7	8.8	7.2	6.7	31.2	13.9	6.3	1.0	61.8	26.2	49.5	50.5
84664	MAPLETON	97.4	96.8	0.1	0.2	0.6	0.8	2.0	2.7	10.2	12.2	11.3	9.6	5.3	26.1	18.3	6.4	0.7	60.1	26.3	50.2	49.8
84701	RICHFIELD	95.3	95.2	0.3	0.3	0.4	0.4	2.2	2.5	9.3	8.4	8.5	9.7	8.1	22.8	20.4	10.9	2.0	67.3	29.7	49.8	50.2
84710	ALTON	92.4	93.0	0.0	0.0	0.0	0.0	1.9	1.7	7.4	7.4	7.1	6.4	4.7	27.5	29.2	10.4	0.0	72.8	37.2	52.4	47.7
84712	ANTIMONY	95.8	96.5	0.0	0.0	0.0	0.0	2.6	2.0	10.4	9.4	8.9	6.9	6.4	21.3	21.3	13.4	2.0	65.8	32.7	51.0	49.0
84713	BEAVER	94.1	93.6	0.4	0.4	0.4	0.4	5.2	6.0	8.8	8.5	8.3	6.6	6.4	25.4	22.1	12.0	2.0	70.2	33.1	52.1	47.9
84714	BERYL	89.9	89.1	0.7	0.8	0.0	0.0	8.5	9.5	10.6	10.3	9.3	9.0	7.9	23.5	20.2	8.7	0.5	63.9	27.6	52.1	47.9
84716	BOULDER	95.3	95.3	0.0	0.0	0.8	0.7	3.2	3.6	7.9	7.9	8.2	7.5	7.5	23.7	25.1	10.8	1.4	71.7	34.9	51.3	48.8
84717	BRYCE CANYON	96.1	96.0	0.0	0.0	0.3	0.3	2.2	2.3	10.4	9.4	9.1	7.3	6.3	21.1	21.6	12.8	2.1	65.5	32.2	50.5	49.5
84719	BRIAN HEAD	96.6	96.1	0.0	0.8	0.0	0.0	4.2	5.4	6.2	6.2	8.5	10.1	5.4	21.7	28.7	11.6	1.6	72.9	38.2	54.3	45.7
84720	CEDAR CITY	92.7	92.3	0.4	0.4	1.2	1.2	4.0	4.5	10.2	8.6	7.7	10.0	13.8	26.6	15.8	6.6	0.8	69.1	24.9	49.5	50.5
84722	CENTRAL	95.9	95.6	0.1	0.0	0.3	0.3	2.0	2.4	8.9	8.5	8.9	9.8	7.7	20.2	21.9	13.1	1.0	67.7	31.8	50.5	49.5
84726	ESCALANTE	94.6	94.6	0.0	0.0	0.7	0.8	3.9	4.3	8.1	7.6	8.0	6.8	7.0	23.1	26.6	11.6	1.2	72.1	36.3	51.3	48.7
84728	GARRISON	82.0	80.3	0.0	0.0	1.0	1.0	16.5	18.1	8.3	7.3	11.9	12.4	10.9	19.7	20.2	8.3	1.0	64.8	24.6	48.7	51.3
84729	GLENDALE	98.1	98.2	0.0	0.0	0.0	0.0	2.5	2.5	8.1	8.4	9.9	9.7	6.6	19.9	22.4	13.2	1.8	67.9	32.5	51.9	48.1
84731	GREENVILLE	94.3	94.4	1.3	1.3	1.3	1.3	4.7	5.3	7.8	7.2	6.9	7.5	6.9	27.0	23.8	11.9	0.9	73.4	35.8	58.9	41.1
84734	HANKSVILLE	93.7	93.6	0.0	0.0	0.3	0.3	1.7	1.8	9.3	8.8	8.2	7.1	5.9	23.5	27.4	9.0	0.9	68.9	34.5	50.7	49.4
	UTAH	89.2	88.6	0.8	0.9	2.3	2.5	9.0	10.0	9.9	8.8	8.3	8.3	9.3	29.3	17.7	7.2	1.0	68.3	27.9	50.0	50.0
	UNITED STATES	75.1	73.6	12.3	12.5	3.8	4.2	12.5	14.1	6.9	6.7	7.2	7.0	7.3	28.6	23.8	10.8	1.7	75.1	36.0	49.1	50.9

ZIP CODE #	POST OFFICE NAME	2004 Per Capita Income	2004 HH Income Base	2004 HOUSEHOLD INCOME DISTRIBUTION (%) Less than $25,000	$25,000 to $49,999	$50,000 to $99,999	$100,000 to $149,999	$150,000 or More	MEDIAN HOUSEHOLD INCOME 2004	2009	2004 National Centile	2004 State Centile	2004 Home Value Base	2004 HOME VALUE DISTRIBUTION (%) Less than $50,000	$50,000 to $89,999	$90,000 to $174,999	$175,000 to $399,999	$400,000 or More	2004 Median Home Value
84128	SALT LAKE CITY	17509	5963	9.2	29.0	49.2	11.5	1.1	58771	68001	83	81	5272	2.6	3.8	82.2	11.2	0.2	139421
84302	BRIGHAM CITY	18667	6942	18.3	31.4	39.5	8.7	2.1	50211	56982	72	64	5396	2.8	7.1	69.2	19.8	1.2	135905
84305	CLARKSTON	15121	223	16.1	42.2	36.8	4.0	0.9	45326	51454	62	53	205	6.3	18.1	66.3	9.3	0.0	112910
84306	COLLINSTON	17212	153	17.0	32.7	39.2	9.2	2.0	50210	55912	72	63	133	1.5	9.8	60.9	24.1	3.8	141204
84307	CORINNE	17791	377	17.5	30.8	43.8	6.1	1.9	51054	55555	74	66	325	3.1	15.7	62.5	18.5	0.3	122768
84308	CORNISH	16371	66	15.2	43.9	31.8	4.6	4.6	45000	51634	61	52	53	1.9	18.9	58.5	18.9	1.9	126786
84309	DEWEYVILLE	22405	175	17.1	33.1	37.1	10.9	1.7	49831	56602	72	62	155	0.0	7.7	56.8	31.0	4.5	149597
84310	EDEN	25517	989	9.2	18.8	42.8	19.5	9.7	69935	82420	91	93	889	0.8	1.7	21.7	63.6	12.3	239969
84311	FIELDING	17169	209	18.2	31.6	43.1	6.7	0.5	50129	55159	72	63	179	3.4	16.8	65.9	12.3	1.7	124702
84312	GARLAND	15781	1104	16.6	37.3	38.7	6.7	0.7	46662	51670	65	55	938	4.5	15.9	65.4	13.8	0.5	121653
84313	GROUSE CREEK	14164	51	27.5	60.8	7.8	3.9	0.0	29244	33782	11	9	34	38.2	11.8	20.6	8.8	20.6	80000
84314	HONEYVILLE	17810	566	16.6	33.8	39.2	8.8	1.6	49691	54530	71	62	504	2.8	12.7	58.3	25.0	1.2	136813
84315	HOOPER	23895	1489	8.6	23.6	45.5	16.9	5.4	67032	77728	90	90	1401	0.4	4.4	48.3	44.7	2.4	170850
84317	HUNTSVILLE	25797	910	10.2	18.9	43.1	18.6	9.2	69011	80548	91	92	816	1.0	2.1	24.0	58.6	14.3	238298
84318	HYDE PARK	21797	878	9.9	31.2	38.6	14.1	6.2	56495	67062	81	78	782	2.6	2.4	57.9	33.1	4.0	161202
84319	HYRUM	17410	1960	13.9	37.0	35.9	8.3	5.0	49387	57408	71	60	1681	7.3	4.1	67.9	18.9	1.8	135812
84320	LEWISTON	14718	664	20.8	40.4	30.9	5.7	2.3	42847	48747	56	47	556	2.3	12.8	62.1	20.9	2.0	123592
84321	LOGAN	17715	12396	30.3	34.4	26.2	6.0	3.1	36858	44185	35	26	6052	5.7	8.5	60.3	23.1	2.4	137442
84322	LOGAN	6816	82	47.6	42.7	7.3	2.4	0.0	26252	27282	6	4	1	0.0	0.0	100.0	0.0	0.0	137500
84324	MANTUA	20012	225	9.3	22.7	49.3	15.6	3.1	64527	72672	88	89	210	0.5	1.4	60.0	33.8	4.3	161413
84325	MENDON	21164	460	8.0	29.1	45.4	10.9	6.5	61788	71886	86	84	400	3.0	0.8	42.3	47.5	6.5	185811
84328	PARADISE	18875	342	16.4	29.8	36.3	12.3	5.3	52884	61437	77	72	316	1.3	1.6	45.3	49.4	2.5	177727
84329	PARK VALLEY	12386	91	29.7	57.1	8.8	4.4	0.0	29829	33654	12	10	61	39.3	13.1	18.0	9.8	19.7	66250
84330	PLYMOUTH	18805	122	17.2	27.1	45.9	9.0	0.8	54136	60567	79	74	108	5.6	20.4	54.6	19.4	0.0	127778
84331	PORTAGE	15578	91	16.5	25.3	48.4	8.8	1.1	56352	61552	81	77	81	7.4	21.0	53.1	18.5	0.0	123958
84332	PROVIDENCE	22240	2035	11.9	24.9	45.4	12.8	5.0	61451	71370	86	83	1826	1.5	7.4	46.4	40.4	4.3	166336
84333	RICHMOND	16658	757	18.2	34.7	38.7	6.6	1.7	48057	54209	68	58	647	6.2	8.0	64.3	19.3	2.2	131644
84335	SMITHFIELD	18440	2972	17.4	29.4	41.1	8.4	3.6	51848	60046	75	68	2554	4.6	3.8	62.6	26.8	2.2	146935
84336	SNOWVILLE	15645	184	20.7	35.3	35.9	7.6	0.5	44145	48254	59	50	156	7.1	13.5	63.5	14.7	1.3	119853
84337	TREMONTON	17771	2827	19.2	29.7	38.7	9.9	2.5	50745	56722	73	65	2306	4.9	9.6	66.1	18.1	1.3	130647
84338	TRENTON	15478	168	24.4	38.7	30.4	3.6	3.0	41675	46537	52	44	135	3.7	12.6	54.8	27.4	1.5	139881
84339	WELLSVILLE	19130	1135	13.4	30.8	41.9	10.1	3.9	53948	62571	78	73	995	1.1	4.2	65.1	27.4	2.1	151227
84340	WILLARD	20154	816	17.0	30.4	38.7	11.4	2.5	52204	57948	76	70	707	9.3	7.4	51.3	29.4	2.6	142976
84341	LOGAN	17988	5925	26.0	32.6	28.4	7.9	5.1	41523	49319	51	43	3094	8.2	3.2	51.1	33.7	3.7	156629
84401	OGDEN	17430	10751	32.8	30.8	26.5	7.5	2.5	37675	45294	38	31	6009	5.1	20.0	53.9	19.8	1.3	117077
84403	OGDEN	25876	12791	22.1	29.6	30.3	9.9	8.2	48357	56718	69	58	8847	1.3	11.4	53.4	28.3	5.7	143486
84404	OGDEN	19270	17415	22.9	34.8	32.5	8.0	1.9	44557	51628	60	51	12775	7.8	14.6	63.1	13.4	1.1	116702
84405	OGDEN	22852	9515	17.0	28.4	36.1	14.6	3.8	54004	63066	78	74	7191	6.2	5.6	57.5	29.2	1.5	142330
84408	OGDEN	29841	47	31.9	25.5	14.9	17.0	10.6	44080	51776	59	49	40	0.0	0.0	65.0	35.0	0.0	161364
84414	OGDEN	25035	6763	6.6	24.4	43.2	19.4	6.5	68895	80903	91	91	6190	1.0	2.7	53.9	39.2	3.2	165418
84501	PRICE	18433	4385	30.3	29.1	30.9	8.2	1.4	41377	49270	51	42	3296	7.5	25.6	53.5	12.2	1.2	105274
84510	ANETH	8227	1030	61.2	19.6	15.7	1.8	1.8	15471	17105	1	0	900	75.8	13.3	9.4	0.7	0.8	17500
84511	BLANDING	14352	1467	33.3	31.8	27.7	5.7	1.5	37290	44146	36	27	1058	18.8	30.2	42.3	7.8	0.9	91122
84520	EAST CARBON	15805	752	42.0	33.1	19.7	4.5	0.7	29241	33599	11	9	621	30.0	59.7	9.5	0.8	0.0	59881
84523	FERRON	17197	810	27.7	32.5	30.9	8.2	0.9	41966	47874	53	45	675	15.4	38.8	39.6	5.5	0.7	86647
84525	GREEN RIVER	13984	395	34.2	39.0	24.6	2.0	0.3	34030	39534	24	16	311	25.1	36.3	32.5	4.2	1.9	79853
84526	HELPER	18457	1609	35.2	31.3	25.1	6.7	1.7	34832	39845	27	18	1274	9.8	35.5	44.0	10.0	0.7	93226
84528	HUNTINGTON	16392	2450	24.8	32.4	35.4	6.4	1.1	45348	50743	62	53	2052	16.2	28.6	49.6	5.6	0.2	94737
84531	MEXICAN HAT	8605	180	47.8	27.2	20.6	2.2	2.2	26167	31652	6	4	150	66.7	16.0	17.3	0.0	0.0	21000
84532	MOAB	21001	3605	32.8	34.0	24.2	5.5	3.4	36692	42721	34	25	2577	15.5	13.1	51.5	16.5	3.5	117482
84533	LAKE POWELL	18508	62	48.4	24.2	22.6	4.8	0.0	26514	36160	6	5	35	40.0	25.7	20.0	5.7	8.6	61250
84535	MONTICELLO	16984	986	28.8	35.3	27.7	5.7	2.5	37373	44122	37	29	772	17.1	17.8	54.0	9.5	1.7	107857
84536	MONUMENT VALLEY	8369	437	53.3	21.1	21.5	2.3	1.8	21660	24588	2	1	340	66.8	18.2	12.9	2.1	0.0	25682
84540	THOMPSON	18836	105	40.0	35.2	19.1	4.8	1.0	28535	33094	10	7	86	18.6	16.3	37.2	23.3	4.7	122727
84542	WELLINGTON	18747	682	26.3	29.6	34.5	8.1	1.6	42604	50363	55	47	561	9.6	27.1	46.5	16.0	0.7	103154
84601	PROVO	14952	9469	28.0	36.1	28.6	5.9	1.4	40474	47937	48	40	4846	8.6	6.7	65.8	18.6	0.3	141359
84604	PROVO	19085	13525	26.0	30.6	25.3	11.6	6.5	43417	50311	57	48	6615	0.6	0.8	31.2	57.0	10.5	210544
84606	PROVO	12559	9529	37.6	37.8	19.1	3.9	1.6	31346	36105	16	11	2551	1.3	5.2	65.4	26.0	2.1	153145
84621	AXTELL	15179	72	43.1	34.7	18.1	2.8	1.4	27510	30613	8	6	53	0.0	20.8	60.4	17.0	1.9	122321
84622	CENTERFIELD	14451	405	31.6	38.5	24.2	4.7	1.0	36432	40293	33	25	327	10.7	22.3	50.2	16.2	0.6	108627
84624	DELTA	16225	2079	27.7	28.5	36.6	5.1	2.2	44190	50566	59	50	1686	11.7	34.1	47.5	5.9	0.8	93646
84627	EPHRAIM	12888	1392	32.0	35.9	24.4	6.1	1.6	33654	40551	23	15	793	10.1	9.5	61.4	18.8	0.3	127300
84628	EUREKA	15235	314	34.1	30.6	30.9	4.5	0.0	35279	42021	29	19	229	28.8	38.4	24.9	6.6	1.3	72097
84629	FAIRVIEW	14646	1044	28.5	34.0	31.3	4.7	1.5	39413	44861	44	37	873	6.8	18.9	53.2	19.9	1.3	116497
84630	FAYETTE	14376	80	42.5	35.0	18.8	2.5	1.3	27739	31381	8	6	59	0.0	22.0	59.3	17.0	1.7	122500
84631	FILLMORE	15169	1511	30.4	38.1	25.8	4.2	1.6	36923	43052	35	26	1211	11.6	31.3	48.6	7.6	1.0	96553
84634	GUNNISON	16732	538	28.8	36.8	24.7	7.6	2.0	37382	43149	37	29	437	4.8	19.5	62.2	13.3	0.2	111758
84635	HINCKLEY	15940	269	26.8	30.9	35.7	3.0	3.7	43227	50000	57	48	231	11.7	31.6	49.4	6.1	1.3	97381
84642	MANTI	16063	1335	32.0	33.5	28.3	3.9	2.3	38156	43606	40	33	982	4.4	19.5	57.2	17.0	1.9	119344
84645	MONA	14085	392	20.4	28.3	40.3	5.9	5.1	50723	55893	73	65	314	5.7	5.7	50.6	36.9	1.0	158898
84647	MOUNT PLEASANT	14624	2165	30.8	36.3	26.6	4.8	1.5	37759	42622	38	32	1763	8.3	16.3	56.8	17.5	1.1	117229
84648	NEPHI	14807	1913	28.1	34.9	29.8	5.9	1.4	41383	46269	51	43	1548	5.4	12.2	61.1	18.7	2.6	129093
84650	OASIS	16583	78	32.1	28.2	34.6	2.6	2.6	41962	49200	53	44	67	11.9	22.4	55.2	10.5	0.0	108173
84651	PAYSON	17590	5411	19.3	27.8	40.4	9.1	3.4	51953	60717	75	69	4311	4.4	5.8	54.1	31.9	3.9	155916
84653	SALEM	22883	1755	12.0	23.5	39.8	16.2	8.5	62988	73327	87	86	1554	0.2	3.0	34.6	52.2	10.0	206207
84654	SALINA	16386	1523	25.9	36.5	30.3	4.1	3.2	42118	47657	53	46	1290	6.7	24.7	58.6	7.8	2.2	108384
84655	SANTAQUIN	15787	1942	13.1	38.8	38.4	7.8	1.9	48927	55584	70	60	1666	6.3	6.0	62.9	22.0	2.8	150975
84660	SPANISH FORK	18980	7622	13.6	28.1	44.4	10.4	3.5	56111	66149	81	77	6096	1.9	3.0	54.0	38.1	2.9	164178
84663	SPRINGVILLE	18554	6581	16.2	30.9	37.9	12.3	2.7	52204	61097	76	70	5034	5.1	4.7	49.2	38.5	2.6	164519
84664	MAPLETON	21083	1881	10.1	20.4	42.4	19.1	8.0	68823	82091	91	91	1741	0.5	1.6	18.4	67.8	11.8	236337
84701	RICHFIELD	16960	3279	26.1	35.2	30.8	5.8	2.1	40321	46249	47	39	2652	5.8	19.9	60.0	13.3	0.9	111094
84710	ALTON	14942	100	33.0	31.0	31.0	5.0	0.0	34360	39646	25	17	61	6.6	9.8	37.7	34.4	11.5	164583
84712	ANTIMONY	13335	56	25.0	35.7	33.9	5.4	0.0	43207	45562	57	47	46	13.0	28.3	50.0	4.4	4.4	98000
84713	BEAVER	17731	1193	28.5	39.6	25.8	4.7	1.4	37487	42285	37	30	964	5.3	22.2	59.8	12.7	0.1	111687
84714	BERYL	11622	235	40.9	28.5	27.2	3.4	0.0	31672	34125	17	12	185	20.5	19.5	53.5	6.0	0.5	98043
84716	BOULDER	15688	103	34.0	35.9	25.2	4.9	0.0	35314	38621	29	19	80	15.0	12.5	48.8	18.8	5.0	117647
84717	BRYCE CANYON	15529	361	24.9	36.3	32.4	6.1	0.3	42593	48864	55	46	294	12.6	28.2	50.3	4.8	4.1	97941
84719	BRIAN HEAD	23869	61	32.8	32.8	23.0	4.9	6.6	36721	42985	34	26	52	13.5	23.1	48.1	13.5	1.9	105769
84720	CEDAR CITY	16257	10130	29.9	35.9	25.2	6.9	2.1	37672	43693	38	31	6653	6.3	9.8	61.2	21.7	1.1	124441
84722	CENTRAL	17969	740	23.8	36.5	29.3	5.7	4.7	42001	48593	53	45	634	4.1	13.6	53.2	27.8	1.4	132031
84726	ESCALANTE	15078	377	35.3	34.8	26.8	3.2	0.0	34728	38409	26	17	301	12.6	17.3	53.2	14.3	2.7	112500
84728	GARRISON	8575	62	40.3	59.7	0.0	0.0	0.0	27144	32508	7	5	27	33.3	63.0	3.7	0.0	0.0	56429
84729	GLENDALE	14757	133	33.1	37.6	26.3	2.3	0.8	37351	42795	37	28	116	5.2	31.9	50.0	11.2	1.7	103906
84731	GREENVILLE	12893	43	27.9	34.9	30.2	2.3	4.7	36146	43653	32	22	36	2.8	27.8	52.8	8.3	8.3	103571
84734	HANKSVILLE	17918	332	36.1	31.9	27.7	4.2	0.0	33786	38509	23	16	224	17.4	13.4	44.6	19.6	4.9	114634
	UTAH	21907		18.7	28.9	35.1	11.8	5.5	52040	61244				4.3	6.7	48.5	35.1	5.4	159338
	UNITED STATES	25866		24.7	27.1	30.8	10.9	6.5	48124	56710				10.9	15.0	33.7	30.1	10.4	145905

#	POST OFFICE NAME	FINANCIAL SERVICES: Auto Loan	Home Loan	Invest-ments	Retire-ment Plans	THE HOME: Home Improvements: Home Repair	Lawn & Garden	Furnishings: Comput-ers & Hard-ware	Major Appli-ances	TV, Radio, Sound Equip-ment	Furni-ture	ENTERTAINMENT: Dine out/Carry out	Sports Equip-ment	Fees & Tickets	Toys & Games	Travel	Cable TV	PERSONAL: Apparel & Services	Auto Repairs	Health Insur-ance	Pets & Supplies
84128	SALT LAKE CITY	91	101	100	104	97	95	94	93	88	96	111	110	96	111	92	82	109	92	81	102
84302	BRIGHAM CITY	84	83	76	83	84	89	81	83	81	80	100	97	80	101	80	80	96	82	83	96
84305	CLARKSTON	79	71	54	67	75	80	65	72	69	65	84	86	64	86	67	71	80	71	78	93
84306	COLLINSTON	94	84	64	79	88	95	77	86	82	77	100	102	76	102	80	84	95	83	93	110
84307	CORINNE	93	82	63	78	87	93	76	84	81	76	98	101	75	101	78	83	94	82	91	109
84308	CORNISH	84	92	92	94	89	88	88	87	82	89	104	103	88	104	86	78	102	87	77	96
84309	DEWEYVILLE	99	88	67	84	93	100	81	90	86	81	105	107	80	107	84	89	100	88	98	116
84310	EDEN	108	134	142	134	132	130	119	119	111	119	139	140	127	148	122	107	139	115	107	132
84311	FIELDING	86	77	59	73	81	87	71	79	76	71	92	94	70	94	73	77	87	77	85	102
84312	GARLAND	84	73	56	71	77	85	72	78	76	71	92	90	69	93	72	77	87	76	84	96
84313	GROUSE CREEK	65	51	35	46	57	64	48	58	54	47	64	67	43	63	51	58	59	57	68	79
84314	HONEYVILLE	93	83	63	79	88	94	77	85	81	77	99	101	75	101	79	84	94	83	92	110
84315	HOOPER	104	129	136	129	126	124	115	115	106	115	134	134	122	142	117	103	134	111	102	127
84317	HUNTSVILLE	106	132	140	132	129	127	117	117	109	117	137	137	125	146	120	105	136	113	105	129
84318	HYDE PARK	109	133	139	134	130	127	119	118	110	119	138	138	126	146	120	106	138	114	105	130
84319	HYRUM	89	99	99	100	96	95	94	93	88	94	111	110	94	112	92	83	109	92	82	102
84320	LEWISTON	79	71	59	71	74	80	71	75	74	70	90	87	69	90	71	74	85	74	79	89
84321	LOGAN	71	66	75	70	64	69	77	70	75	74	94	87	74	91	72	70	91	75	65	78
84322	LOGAN	41	25	32	28	25	30	49	36	47	41	59	50	40	53	39	41	55	43	33	41
84324	MANTUA	93	115	122	115	113	112	103	103	95	102	120	120	109	128	105	93	120	99	92	113
84325	MENDON	96	118	125	118	116	114	106	105	98	105	123	123	112	131	108	95	123	102	94	116
84328	PARADISE	90	96	110	100	97	100	96	95	92	95	115	112	97	114	96	89	112	96	90	105
84329	PARK VALLEY	65	51	35	46	57	65	48	58	54	48	65	68	43	64	51	58	60	57	69	79
84330	PLYMOUTH	91	81	62	77	86	92	75	83	80	75	97	99	74	99	77	82	92	81	90	108
84331	PORTAGE	92	82	62	77	86	92	75	84	80	75	97	100	74	99	78	82	93	81	90	108
84332	PROVIDENCE	106	122	126	124	119	118	114	113	106	114	134	133	117	137	113	101	132	111	100	124
84333	RICHMOND	87	77	59	73	82	87	72	79	76	72	92	94	70	94	74	78	88	77	86	102
84335	SMITHFIELD	90	96	93	97	95	96	91	92	87	91	109	108	91	110	90	84	106	91	85	104
84336	SNOWVILLE	82	73	55	69	77	83	67	75	72	67	87	89	66	89	69	73	83	73	81	97
84337	TREMONTON	91	85	71	83	87	92	80	86	82	80	101	102	79	102	81	82	97	84	88	105
84338	TRENTON	84	68	48	66	74	80	66	76	71	66	85	91	60	84	67	72	80	75	82	98
84339	WELLSVILLE	94	103	103	105	99	98	98	97	92	99	116	115	98	116	96	86	114	97	85	107
84340	WILLARD	97	86	66	82	91	98	80	89	85	80	103	105	78	105	82	87	98	86	96	114
84341	LOGAN	79	73	84	78	71	75	85	77	82	82	103	96	81	99	79	76	100	82	70	86
84401	OGDEN	68	67	71	67	67	71	71	69	71	70	88	81	70	89	69	69	87	71	67	76
84403	OGDEN	96	103	113	104	103	108	104	102	101	103	127	119	105	129	104	99	124	103	97	112
84404	OGDEN	75	77	79	77	76	80	77	77	76	76	95	90	77	95	76	74	92	77	74	86
84405	OGDEN	90	95	98	96	94	98	93	93	91	93	114	108	95	116	93	89	111	92	89	103
84408	OGDEN	98	114	126	108	113	123	108	108	107	107	134	121	114	139	113	110	131	106	110	118
84414	OGDEN	116	131	132	132	129	129	121	121	114	122	144	142	125	148	121	111	142	119	111	136
84501	PRICE	74	66	58	64	68	76	68	71	71	67	87	82	65	85	68	73	82	72	77	84
84510	ANETH	49	43	36	40	41	43	44	47	45	48	57	50	40	50	42	44	56	48	44	49
84511	BLANDING	65	68	66	69	66	67	66	66	63	66	79	78	65	79	65	60	77	66	60	73
84520	EAST CARBON	62	47	31	45	51	61	52	57	58	49	68	64	46	64	51	61	62	57	68	68
84523	FERRON	89	62	33	59	73	81	62	76	71	61	83	92	53	82	64	75	76	75	91	106
84525	GREEN RIVER	61	52	41	52	55	61	53	57	56	53	68	65	51	67	53	57	64	56	61	67
84526	HELPER	76	58	38	55	64	73	60	68	67	59	79	79	54	76	61	70	73	68	79	86
84528	HUNTINGTON	83	69	51	67	74	80	67	75	72	67	87	89	63	85	68	73	81	74	81	95
84531	MEXICAN HAT	57	50	41	46	48	50	51	55	53	55	66	58	47	58	48	51	66	56	51	57
84532	MOAB	79	69	56	67	72	77	69	74	71	68	87	87	65	85	68	71	83	74	77	90
84533	LAKE POWELL	61	55	43	53	55	59	53	57	53	54	66	65	50	62	52	53	63	56	56	67
84535	MONTICELLO	82	67	46	64	71	78	66	74	71	66	85	87	60	82	66	72	80	73	81	94
84536	MONUMENT VALLEY	49	43	39	41	42	45	46	48	48	48	60	52	43	55	44	47	59	49	46	51
84540	THOMPSON	64	58	46	56	58	61	55	59	56	57	69	69	52	65	55	55	66	59	59	70
84542	WELLINGTON	81	71	58	71	74	82	72	77	76	71	92	88	70	91	72	76	87	76	81	90
84601	PROVO	66	64	70	68	62	64	70	66	67	69	85	80	68	82	66	63	83	69	59	73
84604	PROVO	90	82	97	86	81	89	101	89	97	94	122	110	95	117	93	91	118	96	84	99
84606	PROVO	58	44	53	49	43	48	65	53	63	59	79	70	57	73	56	57	76	61	49	60
84621	AXTELL	81	56	29	53	65	73	56	69	64	55	75	83	47	74	58	67	68	68	82	96
84622	CENTERFIELD	85	59	31	56	69	78	59	73	68	58	79	88	50	78	61	71	72	72	87	101
84624	DELTA	91	67	41	65	76	86	68	80	76	67	90	95	60	88	69	79	83	79	93	106
84627	EPHRAIM	61	49	59	53	49	54	71	59	68	63	86	76	63	82	62	62	82	66	54	65
84628	EUREKA	66	56	44	56	59	66	58	61	61	57	74	70	55	73	57	62	69	61	67	73
84629	FAIRVIEW	80	62	42	59	69	78	61	71	68	60	81	83	56	80	63	71	75	70	82	93
84630	FAYETTE	81	57	30	53	66	74	56	69	64	55	75	83	48	74	58	68	69	68	82	96
84631	FILLMORE	78	57	33	55	65	73	57	68	64	56	76	81	50	75	58	67	70	67	80	92
84634	GUNNISON	89	66	42	63	73	86	72	80	81	68	95	91	64	90	71	85	87	80	96	99
84635	HINCKLEY	92	65	34	61	75	84	64	79	73	63	86	95	54	84	66	77	79	78	94	110
84642	MANTI	92	64	34	61	75	84	64	78	73	63	86	95	54	84	66	77	78	77	93	109
84645	MONA	82	90	90	91	87	86	86	85	80	86	101	100	86	102	84	75	100	84	74	93
84647	MOUNT PLEASANT	77	59	38	57	65	73	59	68	65	58	78	80	54	77	60	68	72	67	78	88
84648	NEPHI	80	62	41	60	68	76	63	71	69	62	82	83	57	81	63	71	76	70	81	91
84650	OASIS	93	65	34	61	75	84	64	79	74	63	86	95	55	85	66	77	79	78	94	110
84651	PAYSON	91	91	84	92	91	94	88	90	86	88	107	106	87	108	87	84	104	89	86	103
84653	SALEM	126	136	129	136	136	138	123	127	119	124	148	149	127	153	125	117	146	123	121	148
84654	SALINA	87	64	38	62	73	81	64	76	72	63	85	90	57	84	66	75	78	75	89	102
84655	SANTAQUIN	85	87	82	88	86	87	83	85	80	84	100	101	82	100	82	77	98	84	78	97
84660	SPANISH FORK	98	102	95	103	100	103	96	98	93	97	116	114	97	117	95	90	113	96	92	110
84663	SPRINGVILLE	86	95	98	96	93	93	90	89	85	91	108	105	92	110	89	82	106	88	81	98
84664	MAPLETON	113	134	137	137	130	127	120	120	111	122	140	140	126	145	120	106	139	116	105	132
84701	RICHFIELD	81	67	50	65	72	81	67	75	72	66	87	86	62	84	68	74	81	74	83	93
84710	ALTON	75	59	40	53	66	74	55	67	63	55	74	78	50	73	59	67	69	66	79	91
84712	ANTIMONY	84	59	32	56	69	77	58	72	67	58	79	87	50	77	61	71	72	71	86	100
84713	BEAVER	80	62	41	59	69	77	62	71	68	61	82	84	56	80	63	71	76	70	82	93
84714	BERYL	67	49	29	47	56	62	48	58	54	47	64	70	42	63	50	57	59	57	68	79
84716	BOULDER	77	54	28	51	63	70	53	66	61	52	72	79	45	70	55	64	65	65	78	91
84717	BRYCE CANYON	85	59	31	56	69	77	58	72	67	58	79	87	50	77	61	71	72	71	86	100
84719	BRIAN HEAD	86	67	46	61	76	85	63	76	72	63	85	89	57	84	68	77	79	75	90	104
84720	CEDAR CITY	73	69	68	71	69	72	73	71	71	71	89	86	70	87	70	68	86	73	67	82
84722	CENTRAL	98	71	41	66	82	92	69	85	79	68	93	100	60	91	72	83	85	83	100	116
84726	ESCALANTE	69	52	33	50	58	66	52	61	58	52	69	72	47	68	53	61	64	60	70	80
84728	GARRISON	48	34	18	32	39	44	33	41	38	33	45	50	28	44	35	40	41	41	49	57
84729	GLENDALE	79	55	29	52	64	72	54	67	63	54	74	81	46	72	56	66	67	66	80	94
84731	GREENVILLE	147	105	58	98	121	136	103	126	118	101	139	152	88	136	107	124	127	125	150	175
84734	HANKSVILLE	69	56	39	53	61	67	54	62	58	54	70	73	49	68	55	60	66	62	69	81
	UTAH	96	98	100	99	97	100	97	97	94	97	118	114	97	118	95	91	115	97	91	109
	UNITED STATES	100	100	100	100	100	100	100	100	100	100	100	100	100	100	100	100	100	100	100	100

UTAH

A 84737-84790

POPULATION CHANGE

ZIP CODE		COUNTY FIPS CODE	POPULATION			2000-2004 ANNUAL RATE		HOUSEHOLDS					FAMILIES		
#	POST OFFICE NAME		2000	2004	2009	% Rate	State Centile	2000	2004	2009	% Annual Rate 2000-2004	2004 Average HH Size	2000	2004	% Annual Rate 2000-2004
84737	HURRICANE	053	13777	16301	19504	4.0	90	4304	5280	6493	4.9	3.06	3397	4089	4.5
84738	IVINS	053	4220	5734	7317	7.5	99	1354	1896	2479	8.2	3.02	1158	1599	7.9
84739	JOSEPH	041	493	557	602	2.9	76	147	169	185	3.3	3.30	126	143	3.0
84741	KANAB	025	4578	4693	4917	0.6	28	1717	1824	1978	1.4	2.54	1258	1312	1.0
84743	KINGSTON	031	972	977	978	0.1	16	332	338	341	0.4	2.87	252	253	0.1
84745	LA VERKIN	053	3920	4294	4941	2.2	65	1213	1350	1579	2.6	3.16	980	1071	2.1
84747	LOA	055	1158	1187	1217	0.6	27	369	389	409	1.3	3.03	296	308	0.9
84750	MARYSVALE	031	463	450	444	-0.7	1	177	176	176	-0.1	2.50	138	134	-0.7
84751	MILFORD	001	2575	2702	2880	1.1	40	843	889	956	1.3	3.02	644	668	0.9
84753	MODENA	021	32	35	39	2.1	63	16	18	20	2.8	1.94	13	14	1.8
84754	MONROE	041	3949	4087	4235	0.8	34	1338	1407	1479	1.2	2.89	1057	1095	0.8
84755	MOUNT CARMEL	025	17	19	20	2.7	74	8	9	10	2.8	2.11	6	7	3.7
84756	NEWCASTLE	021	365	401	439	2.2	68	102	115	128	2.9	3.48	81	90	2.5
84757	NEW HARMONY	053	229	303	382	6.8	99	81	109	139	7.2	2.78	71	93	6.6
84758	ORDERVILLE	025	631	692	747	2.2	67	207	234	259	2.9	2.96	156	173	2.5
84759	PANGUITCH	017	2167	2309	2500	1.5	49	689	748	826	2.0	2.96	536	574	1.6
84760	PARAGONAH	021	609	663	723	2.0	59	199	220	243	2.4	3.01	153	166	1.9
84761	PAROWAN	021	2621	2718	2884	0.9	35	905	962	1040	1.5	2.80	693	722	1.0
84765	SANTA CLARA	053	4746	5668	6820	4.3	90	1294	1581	1941	4.8	3.59	1193	1446	4.6
84766	SEVIER	041	54	61	66	2.9	76	20	23	25	3.3	2.65	17	19	2.7
84770	SAINT GEORGE	053	29773	32488	37489	2.1	61	10580	11793	13916	2.6	2.69	7589	8264	2.0
84772	SUMMIT	021	296	314	337	1.4	45	109	118	129	1.9	2.64	84	89	1.4
84773	TEASDALE	055	532	545	559	0.6	26	222	234	246	1.3	2.33	160	165	0.7
84775	TORREY	055	432	443	454	0.6	28	162	171	180	1.3	2.59	117	121	0.8
84780	WASHINGTON	053	8112	10370	12843	6.0	97	2585	3433	4381	6.9	2.92	2096	2736	6.5
84781	PINE VALLEY	053	71	85	102	4.3	91	29	35	43	4.5	2.43	24	29	4.6
84782	VEYO	053	839	962	1133	3.3	82	277	323	388	3.7	2.98	235	269	3.2
84783	DAMMERON VALLEY	053	1360	1670	2034	5.0	95	382	480	597	5.5	3.48	340	420	5.1
84790	SAINT GEORGE	053	21286	25985	31663	4.8	94	7201	9013	11222	5.4	2.87	5814	7150	5.0
UTAH						1.8					2.2	3.09			1.8
UNITED STATES						1.2					1.3	2.58			1.1

ZIP CODE # / POST OFFICE NAME	White 2000	White 2004	Black 2000	Black 2004	Asian/Pacific 2000	Asian/Pacific 2004	% Hispanic Origin 2000	% Hispanic Origin 2004	0-4	5-9	10-14	15-19	20-24	25-44	45-64	65-84	85+	18+	MEDIAN AGE 2004	% 2004 Males	% 2004 Females
84737 HURRICANE	95.5	95.2	0.1	0.2	0.7	0.7	3.1	3.5	11.5	9.5	8.5	7.6	6.2	22.0	20.3	13.0	1.4	65.8	30.6	49.7	50.3
84738 IVINS	94.2	93.7	0.1	0.1	0.7	0.8	3.8	4.4	10.7	9.4	8.1	6.3	5.3	25.9	20.5	12.9	1.0	67.7	31.9	49.6	50.4
84739 JOSEPH	89.7	89.1	1.0	1.3	0.6	0.5	6.9	7.7	12.4	9.7	9.2	7.2	7.0	23.2	20.5	10.6	0.4	63.7	28.3	50.3	49.7
84741 KANAB	96.0	95.7	0.0	0.0	0.3	0.4	2.3	2.6	6.4	6.4	7.3	7.7	6.6	19.3	28.5	15.6	2.2	75.1	42.0	48.8	51.3
84743 KINGSTON	95.7	95.7	0.1	0.1	0.3	0.3	5.0	4.8	8.4	7.6	9.1	8.0	4.4	19.7	25.5	14.5	2.9	68.8	39.0	50.6	49.4
84745 LA VERKIN	94.4	94.0	0.1	0.1	0.3	0.4	4.3	5.0	9.7	9.3	9.9	8.7	6.9	23.9	19.6	10.7	1.5	65.8	29.7	49.8	50.2
84747 LOA	98.4	98.4	0.4	0.3	0.4	0.3	2.1	2.1	10.9	10.5	9.4	7.1	7.1	23.2	20.6	9.3	2.0	64.5	28.9	51.5	48.5
84750 MARYSVALE	95.5	95.3	0.2	0.2	0.2	0.2	3.2	3.8	7.1	7.6	6.9	7.3	5.1	21.6	26.9	15.1	2.4	73.6	40.0	52.7	47.3
84751 MILFORD	92.1	91.5	0.0	0.0	1.0	1.1	6.0	6.8	11.5	10.0	9.7	8.4	7.4	23.4	18.8	9.1	1.6	63.1	27.3	51.0	49.0
84753 MODENA	90.6	88.6	0.0	0.0	0.0	0.0	9.4	8.6	11.4	11.4	8.6	8.6	8.6	22.9	22.9	5.7	0.0	65.7	26.3	54.3	45.7
84754 MONROE	95.1	94.8	0.3	0.4	0.3	0.3	3.2	3.7	9.0	8.4	8.4	7.9	7.3	22.3	23.1	12.1	1.5	69.3	33.3	50.0	50.0
84755 MOUNT CARMEL	100.0	100.0	0.0	0.0	0.0	0.0	0.0	0.0	10.5	10.5	10.5	10.5	10.5	26.3	21.1	0.0	0.0	68.4	23.8	47.4	52.6
84756 NEWCASTLE	89.3	88.3	0.8	1.0	0.0	0.0	9.0	10.2	10.7	10.2	9.5	9.0	8.0	23.4	20.2	8.7	0.3	63.6	27.3	52.4	47.6
84757 NEW HARMONY	96.1	96.0	0.0	0.0	0.0	0.0	4.4	5.0	5.6	5.6	6.9	7.6	5.6	19.5	31.0	16.8	1.3	77.2	44.4	51.2	48.8
84758 ORDERVILLE	97.6	97.7	0.0	0.0	0.0	0.0	2.4	2.8	8.1	8.4	9.7	9.4	6.5	20.5	22.8	13.0	1.6	67.8	33.1	51.7	48.3
84759 PANGUITCH	94.4	94.0	0.4	0.4	0.4	0.4	2.8	3.2	8.8	8.5	7.6	7.5	7.3	23.1	23.4	12.5	1.3	70.1	33.6	51.4	48.6
84760 PARAGONAH	96.4	96.1	0.3	0.5	0.3	0.3	4.4	5.3	6.5	6.8	8.6	8.0	5.4	21.7	29.0	12.5	1.5	73.2	39.6	52.5	47.5
84761 PAROWAN	96.4	96.1	0.0	0.0	0.3	0.3	3.1	3.6	8.0	7.8	8.4	7.6	6.9	22.0	23.2	13.8	2.3	70.4	35.7	49.9	50.1
84765 SANTA CLARA	96.7	96.4	0.2	0.2	0.8	0.9	2.2	2.5	9.6	10.6	12.4	10.9	4.5	24.6	18.3	8.4	0.8	60.3	27.0	50.7	49.3
84766 SEVIER	88.9	88.5	1.9	1.6	0.0	0.0	7.4	6.6	14.8	9.8	9.8	6.6	6.6	21.3	18.0	13.1	0.0	59.0	26.9	52.5	47.5
84770 SAINT GEORGE	90.6	89.9	0.3	0.4	1.2	1.2	8.6	9.8	10.0	7.5	6.7	8.4	9.9	24.1	16.1	14.4	2.8	71.9	29.5	48.5	51.5
84772 SUMMIT	96.3	96.2	0.0	0.3	0.0	0.0	4.1	4.1	7.3	7.3	8.6	8.0	6.4	21.3	26.1	13.1	1.9	71.7	37.2	51.0	49.0
84773 TEASDALE	97.4	97.3	0.0	0.0	0.2	0.2	2.3	2.4	6.4	6.4	6.8	6.4	5.1	23.1	27.5	16.5	1.7	76.5	41.2	50.5	49.5
84775 TORREY	97.5	97.5	0.0	0.0	0.0	0.0	2.3	2.5	6.3	6.3	6.8	6.3	5.0	23.0	28.2	16.5	1.6	76.5	41.7	50.1	49.9
84780 WASHINGTON	94.2	93.7	0.4	0.4	0.4	0.4	4.8	5.5	9.4	7.8	7.9	7.7	7.0	24.0	18.7	16.0	1.6	70.2	32.3	50.9	49.1
84781 PINE VALLEY	97.2	97.7	0.0	0.0	0.0	0.0	2.8	1.2	7.1	7.1	7.1	5.9	5.9	21.2	30.6	15.3	0.0	75.3	42.1	52.9	47.1
84782 VEYO	91.9	91.6	0.0	0.0	0.6	0.7	2.6	2.7	7.5	7.5	7.7	7.9	5.5	21.7	27.0	14.5	0.7	72.4	39.9	50.3	49.7
84783 DAMMERON VALLEY	96.2	96.1	0.1	0.1	0.3	0.4	2.8	3.1	10.0	11.2	11.1	7.9	4.4	26.7	20.1	8.1	0.6	62.3	30.3	49.6	50.4
84790 SAINT GEORGE	95.0	94.5	0.1	0.1	1.1	1.2	3.8	4.5	8.3	7.6	8.2	7.6	7.0	22.0	19.7	17.7	1.9	71.3	34.8	48.7	51.3
UTAH	89.2	88.6	0.8	0.9	2.3	2.5	9.0	10.0	9.9	8.8	8.3	8.3	9.3	29.3	17.7	7.2	1.0	68.3	27.9	50.0	50.0
UNITED STATES	75.1	73.6	12.3	12.5	3.8	4.2	12.5	14.1	6.9	6.7	7.2	7.0	7.3	28.6	23.8	10.8	1.7	75.1	36.0	49.1	50.9

ZIP CODE		2004 Per Capita Income	2004 HH Income Base	2004 HOUSEHOLD INCOME DISTRIBUTION (%)					MEDIAN HOUSEHOLD INCOME				2004 Home Value Base	2004 HOME VALUE DISTRIBUTION (%)					2004 Median Home Value
#	POST OFFICE NAME			Less than $25,000	$25,000 to $49,999	$50,000 to $99,999	$100,000 to $149,999	$150,000 or More	2004	2009	2004 National Centile	2004 State Centile		Less than $50,000	$50,000 to $89,999	$90,000 to $174,999	$175,000 to $399,999	$400,000 or More	
84737	HURRICANE	15685	5280	28.0	36.1	28.6	5.3	2.1	37956	43327	39	32	4169	11.5	13.9	45.0	24.5	5.1	133682
84738	IVINS	19992	1896	18.2	39.6	30.6	7.7	4.0	45381	52180	62	53	1640	2.0	5.9	63.8	23.3	5.0	143732
84739	JOSEPH	12599	169	29.6	41.4	24.3	4.1	0.6	39168	44176	43	36	142	10.6	19.0	45.1	25.4	0.0	113000
84741	KANAB	18303	1824	27.1	39.1	27.5	4.9	1.3	37815	43452	39	32	1467	10.3	14.4	51.5	22.8	1.0	120881
84743	KINGSTON	13383	338	38.8	37.0	19.5	4.1	0.6	31820	36729	17	12	283	14.1	32.9	45.9	6.4	0.7	93148
84745	LA VERKIN	14593	1350	26.9	38.7	28.4	4.7	1.3	39248	45153	44	37	1125	7.6	11.0	60.0	19.0	2.4	128962
84747	LOA	18942	389	35.2	32.4	24.2	5.1	3.1	38063	41854	39	33	324	4.0	22.2	59.3	13.6	0.9	109639
84750	MARYSVALE	15690	176	36.9	35.2	23.3	3.4	1.1	32290	36758	19	13	151	17.2	31.1	42.4	4.6	4.6	91389
84751	MILFORD	18308	889	28.7	35.6	29.5	4.3	2.0	39300	44603	44	37	702	11.4	33.1	50.3	4.1	1.1	93645
84753	MODENA	19490	18	44.4	27.8	22.2	5.6	0.0	30000	30000	12	10	14	7.1	28.6	64.3	0.0	0.0	100000
84754	MONROE	15591	1407	30.1	39.1	26.1	3.1	1.7	35840	40750	31	21	1207	9.2	25.9	50.8	13.7	0.5	106849
84755	MOUNT CARMEL	16711	9	33.3	44.4	22.2	0.0	0.0	32265	50000	18	13	8	0.0	37.5	62.5	0.0	0.0	100000
84756	NEWCASTLE	10802	115	41.7	27.8	26.1	4.4	0.0	31629	32695	17	11	90	20.0	21.1	55.6	3.3	0.0	97273
84757	NEW HARMONY	21494	109	28.4	19.3	35.8	11.9	4.6	51760	61054	75	68	98	4.1	6.1	28.6	52.0	9.2	197917
84758	ORDERVILLE	14731	234	37.6	36.7	26.9	2.1	1.7	38637	42831	42	34	201	5.5	30.9	49.3	11.0	3.5	105134
84759	PANGUITCH	15196	748	27.5	36.0	31.6	4.6	0.4	39565	45331	45	38	625	9.0	32.3	48.0	9.0	1.8	98385
84760	PARAGONAH	16804	220	32.7	32.7	24.6	5.0	5.0	36406	43141	33	24	188	14.4	23.4	45.2	14.9	2.1	105233
84761	PAROWAN	17396	962	29.3	38.3	24.5	5.8	2.1	37486	43006	37	30	796	3.3	17.5	63.8	14.8	0.6	118444
84765	SANTA CLARA	20066	1581	11.3	26.1	43.0	16.4	3.2	60246	70381	85	82	1407	0.3	1.6	49.6	44.0	4.5	173310
84766	SEVIER	15652	23	26.1	43.5	26.1	4.4	0.0	40703	45714	49	41	19	5.3	21.1	52.6	21.1	0.0	112500
84770	SAINT GEORGE	18405	11793	30.9	35.1	24.9	6.4	2.8	36927	43412	35	27	7340	7.8	12.9	49.3	27.8	2.3	132696
84772	SUMMIT	18679	118	30.5	35.6	25.4	5.1	3.4	37332	43083	37	28	99	7.1	19.2	56.6	16.2	1.0	114352
84773	TEASDALE	19496	234	28.2	38.9	25.6	6.0	1.3	36206	43273	32	22	194	7.7	15.0	50.0	20.1	7.2	124324
84775	TORREY	17503	171	28.1	38.6	25.7	6.4	1.2	36246	43056	33	23	142	8.5	15.5	47.9	21.1	7.0	125000
84780	WASHINGTON	16530	3433	26.6	39.6	26.4	4.8	2.6	39080	43948	43	36	2763	6.6	14.2	53.9	23.3	2.1	126329
84781	PINE VALLEY	29489	35	22.9	22.9	34.3	11.4	8.6	52516	67828	76	71	32	3.1	0.0	50.0	43.8	3.1	168750
84782	VEYO	20725	323	22.6	28.5	31.3	13.3	4.3	48818	58092	70	59	286	5.9	11.2	32.2	46.2	4.6	177000
84783	DAMMERON VALLEY	17503	480	14.6	32.3	40.2	11.0	1.9	51914	60461	75	68	442	1.8	4.3	29.9	60.2	3.9	200952
84790	SAINT GEORGE	23505	9013	18.8	34.2	32.2	9.6	5.2	47236	55421	67	57	7293	2.8	3.4	46.1	41.1	6.5	171579
	UTAH	21907		18.7	28.9	35.1	11.8	5.5	52040	61244				4.3	6.7	48.5	35.1	5.4	159338
	UNITED STATES	25866		24.7	27.1	30.8	10.9	6.5	48124	56710				10.9	15.0	33.7	30.1	10.4	145905

SPENDING POTENTIAL INDICES

UTAH

84737-84790 **D**

ZIP CODE		FINANCIAL SERVICES				THE HOME						ENTERTAINMENT						PERSONAL			
						Home Improvements		Furnishings													
#	POST OFFICE NAME	Auto Loan	Home Loan	Investments	Retirement Plans	Home Repair	Lawn & Garden	Computers & Hardware	Major Appliances	TV, Radio, Sound Equipment	Furniture	Dine out/ Carry out	Sports Equipment	Fees & Tickets	Toys & Games	Travel	Cable TV	Apparel & Services	Auto Repairs	Health Insurance	Pets & Supplies
84737	HURRICANE	80	65	47	62	70	78	63	72	68	64	82	83	58	78	65	70	77	71	81	92
84738	IVINS	90	87	79	87	88	94	85	88	85	85	105	100	84	103	84	84	101	87	88	100
84739	JOSEPH	75	52	27	50	61	68	52	64	60	51	70	77	44	69	54	63	64	63	76	89
84741	KANAB	79	62	40	59	67	74	61	70	67	61	80	83	55	77	62	69	74	70	79	91
84743	KINGSTON	68	49	28	46	57	64	48	59	55	47	65	71	41	64	50	58	59	58	70	82
84745	LA VERKIN	73	64	53	63	67	71	63	68	65	64	79	80	59	76	63	65	76	68	71	83
84747	LOA	104	73	38	69	85	95	72	89	83	71	97	107	61	95	74	87	88	87	106	124
84750	MARYSVALE	67	52	36	47	59	66	49	59	56	49	66	69	44	65	52	59	61	58	70	81
84751	MILFORD	95	71	44	69	80	90	71	84	80	70	95	99	64	93	73	83	87	82	96	110
84753	MODENA	68	49	27	46	56	62	48	58	54	47	64	70	41	63	49	57	59	57	69	80
84754	MONROE	79	58	33	55	66	74	57	69	65	57	77	82	50	75	59	68	70	68	81	93
84755	MOUNT CARMEL	63	45	24	42	52	58	44	54	51	44	59	65	38	58	46	53	54	54	65	75
84756	NEWCASTLE	67	48	26	45	55	62	47	58	54	47	63	69	41	62	49	56	58	57	68	80
84757	NEW HARMONY	91	85	81	80	90	106	78	89	83	84	103	87	79	86	85	88	96	86	104	102
84758	ORDERVILLE	79	55	30	52	64	72	54	67	63	54	73	81	47	72	57	66	67	66	80	93
84759	PANGUITCH	77	59	38	54	67	75	56	68	64	56	76	80	50	74	60	68	70	67	81	94
84760	PARAGONAH	86	67	46	61	76	85	64	77	72	63	85	90	57	84	68	77	79	75	90	105
84761	PAROWAN	88	62	32	58	72	80	61	75	70	60	82	91	52	80	63	73	75	74	89	105
84765	SANTA CLARA	99	115	115	118	112	110	104	104	97	106	122	121	108	126	104	92	121	101	92	115
84766	SEVIER	75	52	27	50	61	68	52	64	60	51	70	77	44	69	54	63	64	63	76	89
84770	SAINT GEORGE	76	66	59	65	68	77	68	72	71	69	88	82	65	82	68	72	83	73	77	85
84772	SUMMIT	87	64	38	59	73	82	62	76	71	61	83	90	54	82	65	75	77	75	90	105
84773	TEASDALE	77	60	41	55	68	76	57	69	64	56	76	80	51	75	61	69	71	68	81	94
84775	TORREY	77	60	41	54	68	76	57	69	64	56	76	80	51	75	61	69	71	67	81	94
84780	WASHINGTON	75	66	56	64	69	80	65	71	69	66	84	76	63	77	67	72	79	70	80	83
84781	PINE VALLEY	121	95	65	86	107	121	90	108	102	89	120	127	80	119	96	109	112	107	128	148
84782	VEYO	109	80	46	74	91	103	77	94	88	76	104	113	67	102	81	93	95	93	112	131
84783	DAMMERON VALLEY	91	93	84	95	92	92	86	89	83	89	104	105	86	104	85	79	101	87	82	103
84790	SAINT GEORGE	99	98	91	95	100	109	93	99	94	95	117	108	93	110	95	96	111	97	104	113
UTAH		96	98	100	99	97	100	97	97	94	97	118	114	97	118	95	91	115	97	91	109
UNITED STATES		100	100	100	100	100	100	100	100	100	100	100	100	100	100	100	100	100	100	100	100

304-D Copyright © 2004 ESRI BIS. All rights reserved. Reproduction by any method is prohibited.

VERMONT

A 05001-05442

POPULATION CHANGE

#	POST OFFICE NAME	COUNTY FIPS CODE	POPULATION 2000	2004	2009	% Rate	State Centile	HOUSEHOLDS 2000	2004	2009	% Annual Rate 2000-2004	2004 Average HH Size	FAMILIES 2000	2004	% Annual Rate 2000-2004
05001	WHITE RIVER JUNCTION	027	10694	11169	11737	1.0	72	4635	4938	5287	1.5	2.25	2888	3057	1.4
05032	BETHEL	027	2524	2596	2702	0.7	52	1035	1089	1157	1.2	2.38	699	732	1.1
05033	BRADFORD	017	2786	2883	2983	0.8	63	1094	1160	1226	1.4	2.43	741	782	1.3
05034	BRIDGEWATER	027	120	123	128	0.6	41	50	52	55	0.9	2.37	32	33	0.7
05035	BRIDGEWATER CORNERS	027	720	740	770	0.7	50	287	300	319	1.1	2.47	183	191	1.0
05036	BROOKFIELD	017	944	945	961	0.0	8	379	389	404	0.6	2.41	280	286	0.5
05037	BROWNSVILLE	027	495	515	540	0.9	70	206	218	233	1.3	2.36	148	156	1.3
05038	CHELSEA	017	1255	1276	1308	0.4	25	492	514	539	1.0	2.38	325	337	0.9
05039	CORINTH	017	1128	1191	1247	1.3	80	414	448	479	1.9	2.66	318	343	1.8
05040	EAST CORINTH	017	464	491	514	1.3	83	169	183	196	1.9	2.68	128	138	1.8
05041	EAST RANDOLPH	017	217	222	228	0.5	39	85	90	95	1.4	1.74	60	64	1.5
05042	EAST RYEGATE	005	451	465	489	0.7	57	172	181	195	1.2	2.57	129	135	1.1
05043	EAST THETFORD	017	492	520	544	1.3	82	199	213	226	1.6	2.44	139	149	1.7
05045	FAIRLEE	017	1624	1640	1682	0.2	15	655	674	704	0.7	2.42	450	461	0.6
05046	GROTON	005	907	991	1073	2.1	94	352	395	438	2.8	2.51	262	292	2.6
05048	HARTLAND	027	2102	2156	2240	0.6	43	816	852	901	1.0	2.53	587	611	1.0
05051	NEWBURY	017	434	450	466	0.9	65	179	189	200	1.3	2.38	108	113	1.1
05052	NORTH HARTLAND	027	259	266	277	0.6	48	95	99	105	1.0	2.69	68	70	0.7
05053	NORTH POMFRET	027	190	195	203	0.6	45	72	75	80	1.0	2.60	51	53	0.9
05055	NORWICH	027	3322	3543	3761	1.5	87	1287	1389	1496	1.8	2.55	887	953	1.7
05056	PLYMOUTH	027	356	381	405	1.6	88	166	181	196	2.1	2.10	112	121	1.8
05058	POST MILLS	017	333	352	368	1.3	82	128	138	146	1.8	2.55	91	98	1.8
05060	RANDOLPH	017	4618	4763	4928	0.7	58	1875	1977	2084	1.3	2.39	1210	1268	1.1
05061	RANDOLPH CENTER	017	1592	1630	1672	0.6	39	435	459	484	1.3	2.69	307	322	1.1
05062	READING	027	709	749	790	1.3	80	291	311	333	1.6	2.41	208	221	1.4
05065	SHARON	027	1151	1190	1242	0.8	62	455	478	507	1.2	2.49	312	327	1.1
05067	SOUTH POMFRET	027	183	188	196	0.6	49	72	75	80	1.0	2.51	51	53	0.9
05068	SOUTH ROYALTON	027	3103	3214	3357	0.8	64	1362	1442	1537	1.4	2.22	774	813	1.2
05069	SOUTH RYEGATE	017	1179	1252	1327	1.4	85	450	490	531	2.0	2.56	337	365	1.9
05070	SOUTH STRAFFORD	017	401	415	429	0.8	63	162	171	181	1.3	2.43	114	120	1.2
05071	SOUTH WOODSTOCK	027	388	396	411	0.5	35	172	180	191	1.1	2.17	116	120	0.8
05072	STRAFFORD	017	621	642	664	0.8	62	253	268	283	1.4	2.40	179	189	1.3
05073	TAFTSVILLE	027	113	116	121	0.6	46	50	52	55	0.9	2.23	36	37	0.7
05075	THETFORD CENTER	017	1661	1764	1852	1.4	86	647	698	745	1.8	2.53	460	494	1.7
05077	TUNBRIDGE	017	1118	1160	1202	0.9	66	440	467	495	1.4	2.48	310	328	1.3
05079	VERSHIRE	017	584	620	650	1.4	85	242	262	281	1.9	2.36	161	174	1.8
05081	WELLS RIVER	017	997	1039	1082	1.0	71	426	454	482	1.5	2.29	288	305	1.4
05083	WEST FAIRLEE	017	258	266	275	0.7	57	101	106	112	1.1	2.51	71	74	1.0
05084	WEST HARTFORD	017	164	169	176	0.7	54	60	63	67	1.2	2.68	43	45	1.1
05086	WEST TOPSHAM	017	1247	1279	1317	0.6	43	464	486	511	1.1	2.63	357	372	1.0
05089	WINDSOR	027	5260	5376	5572	0.5	36	2177	2270	2400	1.0	2.24	1402	1455	0.9
05091	WOODSTOCK	027	3720	3796	3930	0.5	35	1569	1636	1728	1.0	2.25	1005	1041	0.8
05101	BELLOWS FALLS	025	4943	5150	5375	1.0	70	2027	2163	2309	1.5	2.36	1259	1336	1.4
05141	CAMBRIDGEPORT	025	67	69	72	0.7	53	29	31	33	1.6	2.23	19	20	1.2
05142	CAVENDISH	027	801	816	845	0.4	30	335	349	368	1.0	2.32	233	242	0.9
05143	CHESTER	027	4539	4693	4896	0.8	62	1932	2044	2178	1.3	2.29	1284	1352	1.2
05146	GRAFTON	025	602	624	650	0.9	65	259	275	293	1.4	2.27	168	178	1.4
05148	LONDONDERRY	003	1374	1430	1498	0.9	70	556	587	625	1.3	2.44	373	392	1.2
05149	LUDLOW	027	2639	2836	3022	1.7	90	1144	1256	1367	2.2	2.21	714	779	2.1
05150	NORTH SPRINGFIELD	027	781	829	876	1.4	84	343	372	402	1.9	2.13	223	241	1.8
05151	PERKINSVILLE	027	1463	1556	1649	1.5	87	609	660	714	1.9	2.36	431	465	1.8
05152	PERU	003	158	167	178	1.3	82	57	60	65	1.2	2.78	42	44	1.1
05153	PROCTORSVILLE	027	739	753	779	0.4	30	308	320	337	0.9	2.34	216	223	0.8
05154	SAXTONS RIVER	025	538	540	551	0.1	11	218	223	232	0.5	2.42	158	161	0.4
05155	SOUTH LONDONDERRY	025	918	948	984	0.8	60	422	445	471	1.3	2.13	269	282	1.1
05156	SPRINGFIELD	027	8954	9245	9666	0.8	60	3803	3998	4256	1.2	2.30	2477	2594	1.1
05158	WESTMINSTER	025	849	875	908	0.7	54	326	344	363	1.3	2.54	221	232	1.2
05161	WESTON	027	570	584	607	0.6	40	251	263	279	1.1	2.19	162	169	1.0
05201	BENNINGTON	003	15338	16339	17603	1.5	87	6146	6696	7380	2.0	2.32	3888	4241	2.1
05250	ARLINGTON	003	3480	3602	3794	0.8	63	1446	1532	1648	1.4	2.35	988	1040	1.2
05251	DORSET	003	1455	1481	1545	0.4	28	629	651	693	0.8	2.27	442	454	0.6
05252	EAST ARLINGTON	003	129	133	140	0.7	57	66	70	75	1.4	1.90	45	47	1.0
05253	EAST DORSET	003	588	598	624	0.4	26	230	238	253	0.8	2.51	161	166	0.7
05255	MANCHESTER CENTER	003	4184	4442	4739	1.4	85	1822	1972	2144	1.9	2.22	1159	1244	1.7
05257	NORTH BENNINGTON	003	2316	2463	2628	1.5	87	765	844	932	2.3	2.46	517	563	2.0
05260	NORTH POWNAL	003	380	388	405	0.5	35	124	130	138	1.1	2.98	87	91	1.1
05261	POWNAL	003	2480	2598	2753	1.1	74	971	1037	1120	1.6	2.51	717	762	1.4
05262	SHAFTSBURY	003	2978	3046	3187	0.5	38	1156	1208	1287	1.0	2.52	860	893	0.9
05301	BRATTLEBORO	025	16519	16819	17372	0.4	28	7110	7392	7801	0.9	2.19	4085	4221	0.8
05340	BONDVILLE	003	591	635	681	1.7	89	260	283	308	2.0	2.24	172	185	1.7
05341	EAST DOVER	025	358	376	394	1.2	76	141	152	163	1.8	2.47	86	92	1.6
05342	JACKSONVILLE	025	696	718	746	0.7	58	282	298	316	1.3	2.41	201	211	1.2
05343	JAMAICA	025	867	908	951	1.1	73	380	408	437	1.7	2.23	228	243	1.5
05345	NEWFANE	025	1490	1511	1554	0.3	22	611	633	664	0.8	2.39	409	422	0.7
05346	PUTNEY	025	5418	5537	5710	0.5	36	2089	2181	2297	1.0	2.40	1368	1420	0.9
05350	READSBORO	003	809	818	850	0.3	17	321	330	349	0.7	2.40	225	230	0.5
05351	SOUTH NEWFANE	025	301	304	311	0.2	15	129	134	140	0.9	2.07	86	89	0.8
05352	STAMFORD	003	813	835	875	0.6	48	313	328	350	1.1	2.55	235	245	1.0
05353	TOWNSHEND	025	1083	1098	1128	0.3	20	435	451	473	0.9	2.37	296	305	0.7
05354	VERNON	025	2141	2200	2279	0.6	49	741	775	819	1.1	2.72	574	598	1.0
05355	WARDSBORO	025	740	777	814	1.2	76	310	333	357	1.7	2.33	204	218	1.6
05356	WEST DOVER	025	1051	1106	1161	1.2	77	468	504	541	1.8	2.19	285	305	1.6
05358	WEST HALIFAX	025	261	276	290	1.3	82	102	110	118	1.8	2.51	68	73	1.7
05359	WEST TOWNSHEND	025	406	417	431	0.6	48	179	189	200	1.3	2.19	115	121	1.2
05360	WEST WARDSBORO	025	244	272	294	2.6	98	106	121	133	3.2	2.25	66	75	3.1
05361	WHITINGHAM	025	755	780	810	0.8	61	300	317	337	1.3	2.46	216	227	1.2
05362	WILLIAMSVILLE	025	292	295	303	0.2	16	117	121	127	0.8	2.44	80	82	0.6
05363	WILMINGTON	025	2260	2305	2378	0.5	33	1007	1050	1105	1.0	2.20	609	632	0.9
05401	BURLINGTON	007	38489	39459	41015	0.6	42	15925	16649	17665	1.1	2.15	7080	7288	0.7
05403	SOUTH BURLINGTON	007	15581	17022	18195	2.1	93	6240	6986	7626	2.7	2.27	3723	4151	2.6
05404	WINOOSKI	007	6561	6461	6600	-0.4	2	2944	2952	3067	0.1	2.17	1467	1460	-0.1
05405	BURLINGTON	007	515	521	526	0.3	19	9	9	10	0.0	2.56	3	3	0.0
05440	ALBURG	013	1952	2238	2565	3.3	99	791	927	1083	3.8	2.41	529	618	3.7
05441	BAKERSFIELD	011	381	409	438	1.7	89	144	157	171	2.1	2.61	107	116	1.9
05442	BELVIDERE CENTER	015	265	272	289	0.6	46	97	101	109	1.0	2.65	67	69	0.7
	VERMONT					0.8					1.3	2.40			1.2
	UNITED STATES					1.2					1.3	2.58			1.1

ZIP CODE		RACE (%)						% Hispanic Origin		2004 AGE DISTRIBUTION (%)										MEDIAN AGE		
#	POST OFFICE NAME	White		Black		Asian/Pacific																
		2000	2004	2000	2004	2000	2004	2000	2004	0-4	5-9	10-14	15-19	20-24	25-44	45-64	65-84	85+	18+	2004	% 2004 Males	% 2004 Females
05001	WHITE RIVER JUNCTION	97.0	96.7	0.5	0.7	0.9	1.2	0.8	0.9	5.2	5.4	7.0	6.7	6.1	25.7	29.0	13.3	1.8	78.0	41.4	47.4	52.6
05032	BETHEL	98.1	97.9	0.2	0.2	0.4	0.5	1.2	1.2	5.6	5.7	6.7	7.4	5.1	25.6	30.6	12.0	1.4	77.5	41.4	49.0	51.0
05033	BRADFORD	97.7	97.6	0.5	0.5	0.4	0.4	0.6	0.6	6.0	6.4	6.6	7.2	6.2	23.6	27.9	13.8	2.5	76.3	41.5	47.8	52.2
05034	BRIDGEWATER	98.3	98.4	0.0	0.0	0.8	0.8	0.0	0.0	4.1	4.9	6.5	6.5	5.7	26.0	33.3	11.4	1.6	79.7	43.0	52.9	47.2
05035	BRIDGEWATER CORNERS	98.5	98.5	0.0	0.0	0.4	0.5	0.1	0.1	4.3	5.1	6.4	6.5	5.7	25.5	32.2	12.4	1.9	79.3	43.0	51.4	48.7
05036	BROOKFIELD	97.7	97.4	0.2	0.2	1.0	1.2	0.1	0.1	5.6	6.2	7.0	6.1	5.8	24.7	32.1	11.6	0.9	77.5	41.3	50.4	49.6
05037	BROWNSVILLE	98.4	98.3	0.2	0.4	0.2	0.2	1.6	1.8	4.5	5.1	5.6	5.1	4.9	19.8	39.4	14.2	1.6	81.8	47.7	50.3	49.7
05038	CHELSEA	98.1	98.1	0.2	0.2	0.1	0.1	0.5	0.5	5.3	6.0	7.5	6.5	4.4	24.1	29.0	13.9	3.5	76.6	42.6	50.8	49.2
05039	CORINTH	98.8	98.7	0.2	0.3	0.0	0.0	1.0	1.1	5.5	6.1	7.9	7.9	5.6	25.1	28.3	12.2	1.4	75.7	40.5	49.9	50.1
05040	EAST CORINTH	98.3	98.4	0.2	0.4	0.4	0.4	0.7	0.6	5.5	6.5	7.9	7.3	5.1	26.5	28.3	11.6	1.2	75.2	40.5	49.7	50.3
05041	EAST RANDOLPH	97.2	96.9	0.5	0.5	0.9	0.9	0.9	0.5	4.1	4.1	5.4	13.5	18.5	24.8	21.2	7.2	1.4	83.8	27.5	56.8	43.2
05042	EAST RYEGATE	98.5	98.3	0.0	0.0	0.4	0.4	0.0	0.2	4.1	5.0	8.0	7.1	5.8	23.4	32.3	12.5	1.9	78.5	42.6	52.5	47.5
05043	EAST THETFORD	97.8	97.7	0.4	0.6	0.4	0.6	0.4	0.6	6.0	6.9	7.5	6.7	4.4	27.5	31.4	8.5	1.2	75.4	39.9	49.0	51.0
05045	FAIRLEE	97.7	97.5	0.3	0.2	0.5	0.6	0.5	0.6	5.9	6.3	7.0	6.2	5.1	25.9	31.6	11.0	1.2	77.0	41.7	49.6	50.4
05046	GROTON	96.6	96.5	0.0	0.0	0.0	0.0	0.3	0.4	6.0	6.6	7.9	7.2	5.7	23.6	28.2	13.3	1.7	75.2	40.7	46.3	53.7
05048	HARTLAND	98.6	98.4	0.1	0.1	0.4	0.6	0.7	0.7	4.7	5.6	7.8	7.5	5.2	26.1	31.6	10.5	1.0	77.0	41.4	50.0	50.0
05051	NEWBURY	97.7	97.8	0.0	0.0	0.0	0.0	0.2	0.2	4.4	6.0	7.6	6.9	5.1	22.0	29.1	17.1	1.8	76.9	43.9	48.2	51.8
05052	NORTH HARTLAND	98.5	98.5	0.0	0.0	0.4	0.8	0.8	0.8	5.3	6.0	9.0	7.9	5.6	27.8	28.2	9.0	1.1	75.2	39.8	49.3	50.8
05053	NORTH POMFRET	97.9	98.0	0.0	0.0	1.1	1.0	1.6	2.1	4.6	6.2	7.2	7.2	4.1	23.1	31.3	15.4	1.0	76.9	43.8	49.2	50.8
05055	NORWICH	95.9	95.4	0.5	0.6	1.7	2.1	0.8	0.8	4.5	5.9	8.7	9.7	4.6	20.9	34.3	10.0	1.4	74.0	42.3	49.1	51.0
05056	PLYMOUTH	99.2	99.5	0.3	0.3	0.0	0.0	0.0	0.0	3.7	4.5	5.0	4.2	2.9	23.4	34.4	20.2	1.8	84.3	49.2	52.5	47.5
05058	POST MILLS	97.6	97.2	0.3	0.6	0.6	0.9	0.3	0.3	6.3	7.4	7.4	6.8	5.1	25.9	30.7	9.7	0.9	75.0	40.2	48.3	51.7
05060	RANDOLPH	98.0	97.8	0.1	0.2	0.6	0.7	0.5	0.6	5.7	5.4	6.4	7.2	7.0	23.7	29.1	13.1	2.3	77.9	41.4	48.1	51.9
05061	RANDOLPH CENTER	97.5	97.2	0.3	0.4	0.8	0.9	0.5	0.7	4.6	4.3	5.8	12.2	16.9	24.5	22.3	8.0	1.4	82.3	28.8	55.8	44.2
05062	READING	98.5	98.5	0.4	0.4	0.1	0.1	1.0	1.2	5.2	5.6	7.1	5.9	3.9	23.6	34.5	13.2	1.1	78.5	44.3	48.3	51.7
05065	SHARON	97.1	96.8	0.6	0.7	0.7	0.8	1.0	1.0	6.2	7.1	7.7	7.3	5.1	26.9	30.8	8.1	0.8	74.3	39.3	50.4	49.6
05067	SOUTH POMFRET	98.4	97.9	0.0	0.0	1.1	1.1	1.6	2.1	4.8	5.9	7.5	6.9	4.3	21.3	32.5	16.0	1.1	77.1	44.7	48.4	51.6
05068	SOUTH ROYALTON	97.3	96.9	0.7	0.8	0.8	1.0	0.9	1.0	4.8	4.9	6.6	7.2	7.4	31.6	26.3	10.1	1.2	79.3	36.8	50.2	49.8
05069	SOUTH RYEGATE	97.9	97.5	0.3	0.4	0.4	0.6	0.2	0.2	4.8	5.5	7.3	6.8	5.2	24.7	31.3	13.0	1.4	78.3	42.5	51.4	48.6
05070	SOUTH STRAFFORD	98.3	98.3	0.3	0.2	0.3	0.5	0.8	0.5	5.3	6.5	8.7	7.0	4.3	23.6	32.3	11.6	0.7	75.4	41.9	49.9	50.1
05071	SOUTH WOODSTOCK	97.9	97.5	0.8	0.8	0.5	0.8	1.3	1.3	3.3	4.0	7.1	7.8	3.5	21.2	37.1	13.9	2.0	79.6	46.4	49.2	50.8
05072	STRAFFORD	98.6	98.4	0.2	0.2	0.3	0.3	0.5	0.6	5.5	6.4	8.9	6.7	4.4	23.1	32.1	12.3	0.8	75.2	42.1	50.6	49.4
05073	TAFTSVILLE	98.2	97.4	0.0	0.0	0.9	1.7	0.9	1.7	5.2	6.0	7.8	6.9	3.5	21.6	33.6	14.7	0.9	75.9	44.5	49.1	50.9
05075	THETFORD CENTER	97.6	97.3	0.4	0.5	0.6	0.7	0.5	0.6	6.2	7.1	7.4	6.8	4.9	25.7	31.3	9.6	1.0	75.0	40.5	48.9	51.1
05077	TUNBRIDGE	99.0	98.9	0.3	0.3	0.2	0.3	1.0	1.0	5.8	7.3	7.2	4.4	4.9	28.4	28.2	12.1	1.8	76.7	39.8	49.8	50.2
05079	VERSHIRE	98.3	98.1	0.3	0.3	0.3	0.5	0.3	0.3	5.8	6.0	6.1	7.9	6.0	28.9	28.6	10.7	0.2	77.3	40.0	49.5	50.5
05081	WELLS RIVER	97.7	97.6	0.2	0.3	0.1	0.2	0.2	0.3	4.6	5.3	7.0	6.5	5.2	22.2	30.7	16.4	2.0	78.8	44.4	48.5	51.5
05083	WEST FAIRLEE	98.5	98.9	0.0	0.0	0.4	0.4	0.0	0.0	6.8	6.8	7.1	7.1	5.6	30.1	27.4	8.7	0.4	74.8	37.2	50.4	49.6
05084	WEST HARTFORD	98.2	97.6	0.0	0.0	1.2	1.2	1.2	1.8	4.7	6.5	7.1	7.1	4.1	21.3	34.3	14.2	0.6	77.5	44.5	46.8	53.3
05086	WEST TOPSHAM	98.6	98.4	0.2	0.3	0.5	0.6	0.8	0.9	6.1	6.2	8.1	7.3	5.3	28.4	27.6	10.0	1.0	74.8	38.6	48.9	51.1
05089	WINDSOR	98.0	97.8	0.2	0.2	0.3	0.3	1.0	1.1	4.8	5.1	6.3	6.4	5.6	24.1	28.7	15.5	3.5	79.6	43.6	48.4	51.6
05091	WOODSTOCK	98.2	97.9	0.3	0.4	0.6	0.8	0.7	0.8	3.6	4.4	6.3	6.9	4.3	21.6	34.6	15.4	3.0	80.8	46.5	48.7	51.3
05101	BELLOWS FALLS	97.2	96.9	0.3	0.4	0.6	0.7	1.2	1.3	6.0	5.9	6.8	7.4	7.2	24.6	27.2	12.6	2.3	76.8	39.7	48.7	51.3
05141	CAMBRIDGEPORT	98.5	98.6	0.0	0.0	0.0	0.0	0.0	1.5	5.8	5.8	4.4	4.4	4.4	24.6	29.0	18.8	2.9	84.1	45.4	56.5	43.5
05142	CAVENDISH	97.6	97.6	0.1	0.1	0.9	1.1	1.0	1.1	4.9	5.4	6.6	4.5	3.9	26.4	31.4	14.8	2.1	80.2	44.1	49.8	50.3
05143	CHESTER	98.5	98.4	0.3	0.3	0.3	0.4	0.8	0.9	4.5	5.4	6.7	6.8	5.0	23.3	31.7	14.8	1.8	78.8	44.1	48.9	51.1
05146	GRAFTON	98.2	98.2	0.0	0.0	0.3	0.5	1.0	1.0	5.5	5.5	5.1	5.0	5.0	23.2	33.5	15.7	1.6	80.8	45.5	52.1	47.9
05148	LONDONDERRY	98.5	98.5	0.1	0.1	0.4	0.6	0.5	0.5	5.2	6.2	5.7	6.2	4.0	25.0	31.4	14.8	1.5	78.7	43.7	51.0	49.0
05149	LUDLOW	98.5	98.4	0.2	0.2	0.4	0.5	0.2	0.2	4.4	4.8	5.9	6.1	5.9	23.0	31.5	16.2	2.3	81.1	45.0	49.7	50.4
05150	NORTH SPRINGFIELD	98.6	98.6	0.0	0.0	0.4	0.5	0.6	0.7	4.3	4.3	5.0	5.8	5.8	22.8	28.2	19.3	4.5	82.6	46.3	47.5	52.5
05151	PERKINSVILLE	98.4	98.4	0.1	0.1	0.2	0.3	0.8	1.0	4.6	5.4	6.8	5.3	4.1	24.3	32.8	14.6	2.1	79.8	44.7	49.0	51.0
05152	PERU	98.1	98.2	0.0	0.0	0.6	0.6	0.6	0.6	6.0	7.2	6.0	7.2	1.8	24.0	33.5	13.2	1.2	76.1	43.8	50.3	49.7
05153	PROCTORSVILLE	98.0	97.9	0.1	0.1	0.7	0.8	1.0	0.9	5.3	5.7	6.8	4.8	4.1	26.6	30.8	14.2	1.7	79.2	43.2	49.8	50.2
05154	SAXTONS RIVER	98.3	98.5	0.0	0.0	0.4	0.6	0.9	0.9	5.0	5.7	7.0	6.9	5.2	22.4	33.3	13.0	1.5	78.3	43.5	49.1	50.9
05155	SOUTH LONDONDERRY	98.5	98.4	0.1	0.1	0.4	0.5	0.4	0.5	5.3	5.8	5.5	5.5	4.6	26.3	30.4	15.0	1.7	79.9	43.2	51.4	48.6
05156	SPRINGFIELD	97.6	97.3	0.3	0.3	0.8	1.0	0.7	0.8	5.5	5.6	6.1	6.9	6.1	23.3	28.5	15.1	2.9	78.5	42.8	47.9	52.1
05158	WESTMINSTER	97.5	97.4	0.4	0.5	0.2	0.2	0.7	0.7	5.5	6.2	7.3	7.9	5.8	24.9	31.0	9.9	1.5	76.1	40.5	48.7	51.3
05161	WESTON	97.5	97.4	0.2	0.2	0.5	0.7	1.2	1.2	3.9	4.5	5.1	5.3	3.8	19.9	34.1	22.1	1.4	82.9	50.0	52.1	48.0
05201	BENNINGTON	97.3	97.0	0.6	0.7	0.8	1.0	0.9	1.0	5.9	6.0	6.6	6.9	6.8	26.0	24.9	14.0	3.0	77.4	39.7	47.2	52.8
05250	ARLINGTON	98.4	98.1	0.2	0.3	0.6	0.7	0.5	0.6	5.0	5.3	6.8	6.3	4.3	23.8	30.8	15.5	2.2	78.8	44.1	48.5	51.5
05251	DORSET	99.0	98.9	0.4	0.5	0.1	0.2	0.4	0.4	3.4	5.1	6.6	6.9	3.4	20.9	34.0	17.6	2.1	80.0	47.3	49.8	50.2
05252	EAST ARLINGTON	97.7	98.5	0.0	0.0	0.8	0.8	0.0	0.8	6.0	6.0	6.8	6.0	5.3	25.6	27.1	15.0	2.3	76.7	41.6	48.1	51.9
05253	EAST DORSET	99.0	98.7	0.5	0.5	0.2	0.2	0.3	0.5	3.5	5.0	6.5	6.9	3.3	21.1	33.8	17.7	2.2	79.8	47.3	49.8	50.2
05255	MANCHESTER CENTER	97.9	97.8	0.4	0.4	0.3	0.5	1.7	1.9	4.3	5.3	6.8	6.4	4.0	21.4	32.0	16.9	2.9	78.5	46.1	46.9	53.1
05257	NORTH BENNINGTON	96.2	95.6	0.5	0.7	1.6	2.0	1.1	1.1	5.6	5.3	6.2	8.6	12.2	24.7	22.9	11.9	2.5	79.7	34.4	45.0	55.0
05260	NORTH POWNAL	98.7	98.7	0.0	0.0	0.3	0.3	0.5	0.5	5.2	5.7	7.7	6.2	4.9	26.3	30.9	12.6	0.5	77.3	41.6	50.0	50.0
05261	POWNAL	97.4	97.2	0.3	0.4	0.7	0.9	0.4	0.4	5.8	6.2	7.4	6.7	5.7	27.7	28.7	11.1	0.9	76.0	39.5	51.2	48.8
05262	SHAFTSBURY	98.7	98.6	0.2	0.3	0.3	0.4	0.9	1.0	5.1	5.9	7.2	6.8	4.8	24.7	32.1	12.1	1.4	77.6	42.3	48.9	51.2
05301	BRATTLEBORO	95.0	94.4	0.8	1.0	1.4	1.8	1.4	1.6	4.8	5.2	6.6	7.0	6.8	25.2	29.3	12.5	2.7	79.1	41.6	46.9	53.1
05340	BONDVILLE	98.3	98.3	0.5	0.5	0.2	0.2	2.7	3.0	4.1	4.4	3.8	4.4	4.1	25.0	34.8	18.1	1.3	85.0	47.4	49.3	50.7
05341	EAST DOVER	98.0	97.9	0.0	0.0	0.8	1.1	1.1	1.3	5.1	5.6	5.9	6.9	5.9	25.0	33.2	11.7	0.8	79.0	42.5	52.1	47.9
05342	JACKSONVILLE	98.7	98.8	0.0	0.0	0.0	0.1	0.7	0.8	5.9	5.7	7.4	6.6	5.0	25.4	30.9	12.0	1.3	76.7	41.6	49.3	50.7
05343	JAMAICA	98.5	98.5	0.0	0.0	0.5	0.6	0.6	0.6	6.1	6.6	6.2	4.3	3.1	30.8	29.4	12.1	1.4	78.2	41.1	52.3	47.7
05345	NEWFANE	97.9	97.9	0.1	0.1	0.3	0.4	1.0	1.1	6.0	5.2	7.0	5.8	4.6	24.9	34.9	10.8	0.9	78.0	43.0	48.3	51.7
05346	PUTNEY	96.9	96.5	0.7	0.9	0.6	0.7	1.1	1.1	4.9	5.3	7.2	7.9	8.3	26.2	29.8	9.5	1.1	78.5	39.2	50.2	49.9
05350	READSBORO	98.8	98.8	0.0	0.0	0.3	0.2	1.1	1.1	4.8	4.8	7.2	7.8	6.7	22.3	28.5	15.9	2.1	77.4	42.9	50.5	49.5
05351	SOUTH NEWFANE	97.7	98.0	0.0	0.0	1.0	1.0	1.0	1.0	3.6	4.0	5.9	10.9	10.5	19.7	34.2	9.9	1.3	81.9	42.2	47.7	52.3
05352	STAMFORD	98.5	98.4	0.0	0.0	0.4	0.5	0.3	0.2	5.0	5.9	8.0	6.8	4.3	22.2	33.7	13.3	0.8	76.9	43.9	50.7	49.3
05353	TOWNSHEND	97.8	97.6	0.3	0.4	0.3	0.4	0.7	0.9	6.3	6.4	6.0	5.6	4.0	24.0	32.3	13.2	2.3	77.5	43.8	47.5	52.5
05354	VERNON	98.6	98.5	0.3	0.4	0.2	0.2	0.8	0.9	6.1	6.8	7.9	6.7	5.0	25.4	28.7	10.8	2.8	74.6	40.8	50.3	49.7
05355	WARDSBORO	98.5	98.5	0.4	0.4	0.1	0.1	0.5	0.6	5.5	6.1	6.6	6.1	5.5	26.3	31.8	11.8	0.4	78.1	41.7	52.5	47.5
05356	WEST DOVER	97.5	97.3	0.1	0.1	1.1	1.5	1.2	1.4	4.7	5.0	5.9	7.3	6.2	24.3	34.2	11.6	0.9	79.9	43.1	51.7	48.3
05358	WEST HALIFAX	97.3	97.1	0.0	0.0	0.4	0.4	1.2	1.1	5.4	4.4	7.6	6.5	5.1	23.6	33.3	12.7	1.5	77.5	43.7	49.3	50.7
05359	WEST TOWNSHEND	98.0	98.1	0.3	0.2	0.3	0.2	0.7	0.7	5.5	5.8	5.0	4.8	3.8	24.9	32.6	15.4	2.2	80.6	45.1	51.6	48.4
05360	WEST WARDSBORO	98.4	98.9	0.0	0.0	0.0	0.0	1.6	1.8	5.5	6.3	7.0	5.2	4.0	27.2	32.4	12.1	0.4	77.6	42.2	52.6	47.4
05361	WHITINGHAM	99.2	99.4	0.0	0.0	0.0	0.0	0.8	0.8	5.6	5.5	8.0	6.0	4.7	25.1	32.3	11.4	1.3	77.3	41.9	49.6	50.4
05362	WILLIAMSVILLE	99.0	99.7	0.0	0.0	0.0	0.0	1.0	1.0	4.1	4.4	6.8	6.1	5.4	22.7	38.0	11.2	1.4	80.7	45.2	47.8	52.2
05363	WILMINGTON	97.8	97.7	0.2	0.3	0.6	0.7	0.9	1.0	4.6	4.6	5.9	6.6	5.5	24.6	33.9	12.8	1.5	80.9	43.9	50.5	49.5
05401	BURLINGTON	92.3	91.3	1.8	2.1	2.7	3.3	1.4	1.5	4.6	4.1	4.6	9.0	18.0	30.4	18.6	8.8	2.0	83.9	29.9	48.4	51.6
05403	SOUTH BURLINGTON	93.7	92.6	0.8	1.0	3.4	4.3	1.2	1.3	4.9	5.3	6.2	11.3	6.5	28.2	24.2	11.3	2.3	79.6	37.3	47.1	52.9
05404	WINOOSKI	90.6	89.0	1.3	1.5	5.4	6.8	1.1	1.2	6.3	5.6	6.1	5.9	8.2	34.7	19.6	11.9	1.8	78.8	34.4	48.5	51.5
05405	BURLINGTON	94.8	93.9	1.2	1.3	1.9	2.3	2.5	2.7	0.8	0.6	0.6	48.9	37.8	5.4	4.0	1.5	0.4	97.3	19.9	48.4	51.6
05440	ALBURG	96.7	96.4	0.0	0.0	0.2	0.2	0.2	0.2	6.8	6.6	6.4	6.6	5.1	26.7	28.1	12.7	1.1	76.2	40.2	50.7	49.3
05441	BAKERSFIELD	97.9	97.8	0.3	0.2	0.0	0.0	0.0	0.0	7.6	8.3	9.1	5.9	6.4	26.7	26.9	8.3	1.0	71.4	36.4	49.1	50.9
05442	BELVIDERE CENTER	98.1	97.8	0.0	0.0	0.4	0.4	0.0	0.0	6.3	7.0	10.3	5.9	5.5	29.8	24.6	9.6	1.1	72.4	36.5	53.3	46.7
	VERMONT	96.8	96.4	0.5	0.6	0.9	1.1	0.9	1.0	5.5	5.9	6.9	7.5	7.2	26.5	27.5	11.2	1.8	77.5	39.1	49.1	50.9
	UNITED STATES	75.1	73.6	12.3	12.5	3.8	4.2	12.5	14.1	6.9	6.7	7.2	7.0	7.3	28.6	23.8	10.8	1.7	75.1	36.0	49.1	50.9

INCOME

ZIP CODE #	POST OFFICE NAME	2004 Per Capita Income	2004 HH Income Base	2004 Household Income Distribution (%): Less than $25,000	$25,000 to $49,999	$50,000 to $99,999	$100,000 to $149,999	$150,000 or More	Median Household Income: 2004	2009	2004 National Centile	2004 State Centile	2004 Home Value Base	2004 Home Value Distribution (%): Less than $50,000	$50,000 to $89,999	$90,000 to $174,999	$175,000 to $399,999	$400,000 or More	2004 Median Home Value
05001	WHITE RIVER JUNCTION	26579	4938	24.9	27.6	33.5	8.8	5.3	47439	53492	67	70	3365	7.5	6.7	45.4	34.6	5.9	157178
05032	BETHEL	22101	1089	27.4	33.9	29.2	5.1	4.4	39511	45280	44	29	808	7.6	11.0	44.9	30.7	5.8	143056
05033	BRADFORD	21113	1160	31.1	29.7	30.5	6.0	2.7	40825	45773	49	37	844	4.4	9.1	57.6	26.4	2.5	132974
05034	BRIDGEWATER	24640	52	23.1	34.6	32.7	5.8	3.9	45000	49091	61	57	39	0.0	10.3	51.3	25.6	12.8	147500
05035	BRIDGEWATER CORNERS	23714	300	25.3	33.7	31.0	7.0	3.0	43015	49277	56	46	228	3.5	7.9	49.6	25.9	13.2	150000
05036	BROOKFIELD	25323	389	18.0	31.9	36.5	9.5	4.1	50099	54368	72	76	334	3.3	9.3	45.5	36.5	5.4	155714
05037	BROWNSVILLE	31630	218	16.1	22.0	44.5	11.0	6.4	60748	67069	85	96	184	0.5	2.2	26.1	52.7	18.5	237097
05038	CHELSEA	18393	514	33.1	33.7	27.6	4.9	0.8	35634	39608	30	13	403	5.5	9.9	59.8	23.1	1.7	132774
05039	CORINTH	16436	448	29.9	38.8	26.1	3.4	1.8	35733	39926	31	13	381	8.1	13.4	50.7	23.4	4.5	123191
05040	EAST CORINTH	19311	183	25.1	36.6	31.7	4.4	2.2	41042	46783	50	38	157	7.0	13.4	53.5	22.9	3.2	126705
05041	EAST RANDOLPH	34442	90	15.6	27.8	45.6	6.7	4.4	54924	63388	80	89	73	1.4	5.5	57.5	34.3	1.4	146591
05042	EAST RYEGATE	20666	181	24.3	40.9	28.2	3.9	2.8	40126	45916	47	34	156	4.5	23.1	48.1	23.1	1.3	115625
05043	EAST THETFORD	24680	213	19.3	29.6	38.5	9.9	2.8	50947	56523	74	80	182	5.0	2.8	36.3	49.5	6.6	187500
05045	FAIRLEE	21423	674	21.8	31.6	39.6	5.6	1.3	47239	51902	67	68	519	4.8	7.7	41.2	42.0	4.2	167724
05046	GROTON	17010	395	28.6	39.0	28.4	3.8	0.3	37928	42969	39	25	333	5.4	19.5	53.8	18.0	3.3	118906
05048	HARTLAND	25363	852	16.7	29.3	39.9	9.2	4.9	52394	58508	76	85	721	6.5	6.9	37.0	43.0	6.5	174069
05051	NEWBURY	15081	189	40.2	37.6	20.1	2.1	0.0	28850	31246	10	2	133	8.3	14.3	52.6	23.3	1.5	129375
05052	NORTH HARTLAND	21422	99	14.1	34.3	42.4	6.1	3.0	50855	55764	74	79	80	10.0	15.0	38.8	32.5	3.8	145000
05053	NORTH POMFRET	31902	75	16.0	22.7	41.3	9.3	10.7	60425	69740	85	94	59	0.0	3.4	23.7	45.8	27.1	262500
05055	NORWICH	42550	1389	13.3	20.1	34.0	14.7	17.9	73347	83758	93	100	1096	0.3	1.7	17.0	44.7	36.3	334498
05056	PLYMOUTH	29284	181	27.6	27.6	30.9	11.1	2.8	45616	51337	63	60	155	5.8	5.8	28.4	40.0	20.0	214130
05058	POST MILLS	24233	138	18.8	29.7	37.0	10.9	3.6	51110	55376	74	82	114	6.1	6.1	37.7	41.2	8.8	175000
05060	RANDOLPH	21363	1977	29.0	32.0	30.1	6.8	2.1	39823	44151	45	32	1377	10.4	9.3	59.0	19.4	2.0	127414
05061	RANDOLPH CENTER	22878	459	18.5	25.1	46.0	7.4	3.1	54363	61287	79	89	376	2.7	5.3	58.2	30.9	2.9	147581
05062	READING	25496	311	21.9	28.3	38.6	7.4	3.9	49853	55595	72	75	261	4.2	6.9	38.7	40.2	10.0	175368
05065	SHARON	23816	478	25.1	30.3	31.4	8.0	5.2	45166	50222	62	58	388	7.7	9.8	50.8	23.7	8.0	144257
05067	SOUTH POMFRET	33090	75	16.0	22.7	41.3	9.3	10.7	60425	69740	85	94	59	0.0	3.4	23.7	45.8	27.1	262500
05068	SOUTH ROYALTON	21240	1442	34.8	31.0	26.4	5.0	2.8	35607	39657	30	12	860	8.8	11.4	40.6	31.4	7.8	148364
05069	SOUTH RYEGATE	21451	490	24.1	35.5	32.5	4.7	3.3	42636	47815	55	44	417	5.3	18.0	49.9	24.7	2.2	124826
05070	SOUTH STRAFFORD	26089	171	19.9	29.8	36.3	8.2	5.9	50190	55580	72	77	146	3.4	6.9	31.5	46.6	11.6	196429
05071	SOUTH WOODSTOCK	33714	180	17.8	31.1	33.9	9.4	7.8	50929	58002	74	80	147	6.8	2.7	23.1	42.2	25.2	241071
05072	STRAFFORD	26711	268	19.0	28.7	38.1	8.2	6.0	51456	56759	75	84	231	3.5	5.6	28.1	49.4	13.4	207653
05073	TAFTSVILLE	32737	52	17.3	25.0	38.5	9.6	9.6	56202	66606	81	90	41	0.0	2.4	26.8	43.9	26.8	256250
05075	THETFORD CENTER	25239	698	17.8	29.1	37.4	11.5	4.3	52651	58036	76	85	592	4.1	3.7	34.1	49.2	9.0	191667
05077	TUNBRIDGE	22723	467	26.3	29.6	37.0	3.6	3.4	44654	49875	60	54	386	7.0	9.3	45.6	34.2	3.9	150000
05079	VERSHIRE	19466	262	24.8	38.2	30.9	5.3	0.8	41437	46342	51	39	214	8.4	27.6	44.4	18.2	1.4	102857
05081	WELLS RIVER	19670	454	30.6	40.3	23.6	3.3	2.2	34471	38175	26	9	333	4.5	13.5	54.4	24.6	3.0	134198
05083	WEST FAIRLEE	19701	106	22.6	36.8	33.0	5.7	1.9	42704	48453	55	44	83	8.4	19.3	48.2	19.3	4.8	125962
05084	WEST HARTFORD	30675	63	15.9	22.2	42.9	9.5	9.5	60450	66580	85	95	49	0.0	4.1	24.5	44.9	26.5	255000
05086	WEST TOPSHAM	17993	486	23.5	38.5	32.7	3.9	1.4	41240	46235	51	39	420	9.1	16.7	56.4	16.0	1.9	115432
05089	WINDSOR	22816	2270	27.9	32.8	29.0	7.2	3.0	41440	47089	51	39	1537	8.5	9.1	53.5	24.3	4.6	128190
05091	WOODSTOCK	31857	1636	19.0	26.8	34.6	11.2	8.5	53553	61697	78	87	1249	2.6	2.7	23.9	45.9	24.9	241711
05101	BELLOWS FALLS	20036	2163	35.4	27.8	30.8	4.7	1.3	35795	40450	31	14	1286	4.4	12.7	65.6	14.9	2.4	121835
05141	CAMBRIDGEPORT	24961	31	22.6	35.5	35.5	3.2	3.2	45731	50787	63	61	25	0.0	12.0	44.0	36.0	8.0	156250
05142	CAVENDISH	20723	349	26.7	37.0	29.8	4.0	2.6	39031	44277	43	27	289	6.9	14.5	54.3	19.0	5.2	126944
05143	CHESTER	24234	2044	26.3	30.2	33.6	7.1	2.7	44154	50227	59	51	1581	4.1	9.3	49.1	31.3	6.2	148663
05146	GRAFTON	23854	275	24.4	34.2	33.8	4.7	2.9	45090	50830	61	58	225	4.9	11.6	41.8	33.8	8.0	155729
05148	LONDONDERRY	28446	587	23.9	29.6	32.5	7.7	6.3	47404	53471	67	69	464	3.2	5.0	29.5	42.0	20.3	207937
05149	LUDLOW	26889	1256	29.6	30.2	31.1	4.9	4.1	41028	46185	50	38	922	6.8	5.0	42.6	36.0	9.5	167235
05150	NORTH SPRINGFIELD	24723	372	16.1	40.3	36.8	4.6	2.2	46584	52654	65	65	304	3.3	16.5	67.4	12.5	0.3	112766
05151	PERKINSVILLE	24826	660	26.5	30.6	33.3	4.9	4.7	45903	50837	64	61	562	12.5	13.0	51.4	19.6	3.6	128723
05152	PERU	27754	60	21.7	26.7	31.7	8.3	11.7	51409	56641	75	83	48	8.3	2.1	12.5	45.8	31.3	280000
05153	PROCTORSVILLE	21171	320	26.3	35.6	30.9	5.0	2.2	40222	45565	47	35	264	7.2	12.9	53.8	21.2	4.9	128947
05154	SAXTONS RIVER	30521	223	20.6	37.2	29.6	7.6	4.9	44833	50275	61	55	184	3.8	9.2	61.4	19.6	6.0	137500
05155	SOUTH LONDONDERRY	29982	445	24.3	32.1	32.4	6.5	4.7	46122	52209	64	63	347	2.0	6.6	38.9	38.0	14.4	180313
05156	SPRINGFIELD	21384	3998	30.6	33.3	27.8	6.7	1.6	37614	43079	38	23	2757	4.0	18.5	59.8	15.1	2.6	114667
05158	WESTMINSTER	21812	344	27.3	24.4	39.0	6.1	3.2	48216	53207	69	72	281	7.5	11.0	52.7	25.6	3.2	135061
05161	WESTON	33792	263	22.8	29.3	29.7	9.5	8.8	48253	53861	69	73	217	3.7	3.7	28.6	47.9	16.1	221154
05201	BENNINGTON	20375	6696	33.6	30.4	27.3	5.8	2.9	37832	43283	39	24	4443	10.9	9.3	56.8	21.0	2.1	131393
05250	ARLINGTON	25697	1532	26.0	30.9	30.4	7.1	5.6	44527	50842	60	53	1194	3.7	5.0	39.2	44.1	8.0	179960
05251	DORSET	37556	651	19.8	24.6	31.0	10.1	14.4	57662	63510	82	91	536	1.5	1.9	20.3	41.8	34.5	290196
05252	EAST ARLINGTON	26963	70	30.0	30.0	31.4	7.1	1.4	40000	44312	46	34	53	1.9	9.4	49.1	35.9	3.8	155357
05253	EAST DORSET	34064	238	19.8	24.4	31.1	10.1	14.7	57992	62474	83	92	196	1.0	2.6	20.4	41.3	34.7	286842
05255	MANCHESTER CENTER	35453	1972	20.9	24.1	33.7	12.0	9.3	53287	61301	77	87	1432	5.7	3.4	16.5	51.1	23.4	246283
05257	NORTH BENNINGTON	19262	844	31.6	28.4	29.5	7.6	2.8	42194	47949	53	41	598	1.5	8.4	57.7	27.6	4.9	145800
05260	NORTH POWNAL	17213	130	27.7	26.9	36.2	7.7	1.5	46845	51568	66	65	100	5.0	8.0	58.0	24.0	5.0	134524
05261	POWNAL	19535	1037	23.4	39.5	31.4	3.5	2.1	41684	46601	52	41	859	24.0	8.5	46.9	16.7	4.0	122681
05262	SHAFTSBURY	25548	1208	20.3	28.7	34.4	12.6	4.0	50893	57208	74	80	1049	1.1	3.7	53.1	34.3	7.8	165539
05301	BRATTLEBORO	22759	7392	32.1	29.7	28.0	6.9	3.3	38215	43211	40	25	4657	6.9	8.0	47.1	34.0	4.0	155413
05340	BONDVILLE	36168	283	17.0	23.3	33.2	11.0	15.6	62651	69291	87	96	232	0.9	5.2	23.3	57.3	13.4	241176
05341	EAST DOVER	24502	152	20.4	29.6	38.2	7.2	4.6	50000	54222	72	76	115	5.2	5.2	33.0	46.1	10.4	190625
05342	JACKSONVILLE	23935	298	21.8	36.9	33.6	4.4	3.4	42326	48200	54	43	251	2.8	13.9	46.2	33.5	3.6	147813
05343	JAMAICA	27027	408	28.4	31.6	26.5	5.9	7.6	39568	45120	45	29	328	2.1	6.7	41.2	39.6	10.4	175000
05345	NEWFANE	23697	633	23.5	30.2	34.9	8.2	3.2	47056	53213	66	67	530	7.9	5.7	44.5	37.7	4.2	159191
05346	PUTNEY	23389	2181	24.0	30.1	34.9	7.0	4.0	46475	52556	65	64	1653	9.1	9.3	41.8	34.8	5.0	153617
05350	READSBORO	20300	330	30.9	28.2	32.1	6.4	2.4	39638	46913	45	30	226	1.8	27.0	56.6	12.8	1.8	111628
05351	SOUTH NEWFANE	29149	134	22.4	30.6	32.8	9.0	5.2	48025	54173	68	72	115	1.7	4.4	37.4	48.7	7.8	190625
05352	STAMFORD	22510	328	21.3	22.9	46.7	7.6	1.5	53231	59640	77	86	285	3.2	8.4	46.7	40.4	1.4	157197
05353	TOWNSHEND	22087	451	26.4	34.2	30.6	5.1	3.8	43103	49600	56	47	368	1.9	5.4	47.8	41.0	3.8	167460
05354	VERNON	22704	775	16.5	25.7	43.9	10.3	3.6	54976	61844	80	89	666	2.6	5.3	39.5	48.8	3.9	178879
05355	WARDSBORO	20525	333	26.7	38.1	27.6	4.2	3.3	38659	44039	42	27	278	4.7	16.9	46.8	26.6	5.0	135870
05356	WEST DOVER	27615	504	22.0	29.8	35.5	7.1	5.6	48214	53508	69	72	376	4.3	4.0	31.9	49.7	10.1	199342
05358	WEST HALIFAX	20757	110	27.3	37.3	26.4	4.6	4.6	40434	45493	48	35	94	5.3	16.0	46.8	30.9	1.1	138462
05359	WEST TOWNSHEND	24701	189	24.9	33.9	32.3	4.8	4.2	44831	50543	61	55	152	3.3	9.2	43.4	36.8	7.2	163158
05360	WEST WARDSBORO	27407	121	19.0	41.3	24.8	5.8	9.1	42096	47790	53	41	104	5.8	8.7	43.3	35.6	6.7	162500
05361	WHITINGHAM	25799	317	21.1	35.3	34.7	5.1	3.8	43628	49861	58	50	266	2.6	11.7	44.7	36.5	4.5	156250
05362	WILLIAMSVILLE	26735	121	24.0	24.8	35.5	10.7	5.0	50958	56553	74	81	106	1.9	4.7	40.6	50.0	2.8	180769
05363	WILMINGTON	28160	1050	29.4	30.2	29.1	5.7	5.6	40789	46132	49	37	723	2.8	7.2	46.6	36.0	7.5	164674
05401	BURLINGTON	22120	16649	32.4	32.1	25.9	6.5	3.1	37259	43481	36	21	7019	1.9	2.6	48.4	41.9	5.3	171034
05403	SOUTH BURLINGTON	29493	6986	15.6	27.5	36.9	14.0	6.0	57017	64584	82	91	4519	0.2	2.1	43.7	49.5	4.6	181109
05404	WINOOSKI	19319	2952	36.8	31.5	26.2	4.3	1.3	33750	38284	23	8	1319	0.5	2.7	69.0	27.1	0.7	153618
05405	BURLINGTON	9481	9	55.6	11.1	33.3	0.0	0.0	22222	22500	3	1	3	0.0	0.0	0.0	100.0	0.0	350000
05440	ALBURG	18721	927	31.5	35.1	27.2	4.6	1.6	36980	41492	35	19	756	10.6	21.2	46.6	19.2	2.5	114212
05441	BAKERSFIELD	18853	157	23.6	36.9	34.4	3.8	1.3	43268	49092	57	48	134	4.5	13.4	59.0	22.4	0.8	132000
05442	BELVIDERE CENTER	19951	101	23.8	34.7	31.7	6.9	3.0	43819	48648	58	50	84	11.9	15.5	41.7	23.8	7.1	131250
	VERMONT	23579		25.6	30.1	32.7	7.7	3.9	44976	50578				5.7	9.3	47.1	32.6	5.3	151623
	UNITED STATES	25866		24.7	27.1	30.8	10.9	6.5	48124	56710				10.9	15.0	33.7	30.1	10.4	145905

ZIP CODE #	POST OFFICE NAME	FINANCIAL SERVICES: Auto Loan	FINANCIAL SERVICES: Home Loan	FINANCIAL SERVICES: Investments	FINANCIAL SERVICES: Retirement Plans	THE HOME: Home Improvements: Home Repair	THE HOME: Home Improvements: Lawn & Garden	THE HOME: Furnishings: Computers & Hardware	THE HOME: Furnishings: Major Appliances	THE HOME: Furnishings: TV, Radio, Sound Equipment	THE HOME: Furnishings: Furniture	ENTERTAINMENT: Dine out/Carry out	ENTERTAINMENT: Sports Equipment	ENTERTAINMENT: Fees & Tickets	ENTERTAINMENT: Toys & Games	ENTERTAINMENT: Travel	ENTERTAINMENT: Cable TV	PERSONAL: Apparel & Services	PERSONAL: Auto Repairs	PERSONAL: Health Insurance	PERSONAL: Pets & Supplies
05001	WHITE RIVER JUNCTION	86	84	84	82	86	93	83	86	84	82	104	101	82	104	84	85	100	86	89	101
05032	BETHEL	88	69	46	66	76	85	69	79	76	68	90	93	62	89	70	79	84	78	90	102
05033	BRADFORD	83	67	47	64	72	83	69	76	76	67	91	87	64	88	69	79	84	76	87	94
05034	BRIDGEWATER	99	78	53	70	87	98	73	88	83	72	98	103	65	97	78	88	91	87	104	120
05035	BRIDGEWATER CORNERS	99	78	53	70	88	98	73	88	83	73	98	103	66	97	78	89	91	87	105	121
05036	BROOKFIELD	98	87	68	83	92	99	81	89	86	81	104	107	80	107	83	88	99	87	96	115
05037	BROWNSVILLE	127	99	68	90	112	126	94	113	106	93	126	132	84	124	100	113	117	111	134	154
05038	CHELSEA	80	56	30	53	65	73	56	68	64	55	75	83	48	74	58	67	69	68	81	95
05039	CORINTH	79	55	29	52	64	72	55	67	63	54	74	81	47	72	57	66	67	66	80	94
05040	EAST CORINTH	88	70	45	65	77	85	66	78	74	66	88	93	61	88	69	77	82	76	89	105
05041	EAST RANDOLPH	98	112	138	116	110	113	111	107	105	110	133	128	114	136	111	102	131	108	98	117
05042	EAST RYEGATE	96	67	35	63	78	88	66	82	76	65	90	99	57	88	69	80	82	81	98	114
05043	EAST THETFORD	82	94	96	95	91	90	87	87	82	88	103	103	90	106	87	78	102	85	77	96
05045	FAIRLEE	87	70	50	67	77	84	68	78	74	67	88	93	62	88	69	76	82	77	87	103
05046	GROTON	72	57	39	51	64	72	54	64	61	53	72	75	48	71	57	65	67	64	76	88
05048	HARTLAND	92	98	92	95	99	102	89	93	88	89	109	109	91	113	91	88	106	90	92	110
05051	NEWBURY	60	44	27	42	49	58	47	54	53	45	63	61	42	60	47	56	57	53	64	67
05052	NORTH HARTLAND	92	82	63	78	87	93	76	84	81	76	98	100	74	100	78	83	93	82	91	109
05053	NORTH POMFRET	107	129	145	128	128	135	118	119	112	118	141	134	126	142	123	111	139	115	113	129
05055	NORWICH	139	165	192	166	163	170	155	154	147	155	186	178	163	189	159	145	184	152	144	168
05056	PLYMOUTH	105	82	56	74	92	104	77	93	87	77	104	109	69	102	82	93	96	92	110	127
05058	POST MILLS	84	95	99	95	95	96	88	89	84	87	105	105	91	110	89	82	103	86	83	101
05060	RANDOLPH	77	71	60	67	75	82	68	74	73	67	88	86	67	92	70	75	84	72	81	91
05061	RANDOLPH CENTER	100	101	109	102	103	108	100	102	99	99	123	122	99	125	101	98	119	103	101	120
05062	READING	110	78	42	73	91	101	77	95	88	76	104	114	66	102	80	93	95	93	112	131
05065	SHARON	95	85	65	81	89	96	78	87	83	78	101	103	77	103	81	85	96	84	93	111
05067	SOUTH POMFRET	107	129	145	128	128	135	118	119	112	118	141	134	126	142	123	111	139	115	113	129
05068	SOUTH ROYALTON	69	60	61	61	62	67	67	67	68	64	84	81	63	82	65	66	81	69	67	79
05069	SOUTH RYEGATE	96	72	44	66	81	91	69	83	78	68	92	99	61	91	72	82	85	82	98	115
05070	SOUTH STRAFFORD	113	81	45	77	93	104	80	97	91	79	107	117	69	105	82	95	98	96	114	134
05071	SOUTH WOODSTOCK	94	108	133	112	106	109	107	103	102	106	128	123	110	131	107	98	127	105	94	113
05072	STRAFFORD	116	81	42	76	94	105	80	99	92	79	108	119	68	106	83	97	98	97	118	137
05073	TAFTSVILLE	94	113	128	112	113	118	104	104	98	104	124	118	111	125	108	98	123	102	100	114
05075	THETFORD CENTER	85	100	105	100	98	98	92	92	86	92	108	108	95	113	93	83	107	90	83	102
05077	TUNBRIDGE	102	71	37	67	83	93	70	87	81	70	95	105	60	93	73	85	87	86	104	121
05079	VERSHIRE	83	58	30	55	68	76	57	71	66	57	78	86	49	76	60	69	71	70	85	99
05081	WELLS RIVER	79	57	33	54	66	74	57	69	65	56	76	81	49	75	59	69	70	68	82	93
05083	WEST FAIRLEE	82	69	49	65	74	80	64	73	70	64	84	88	61	85	66	72	79	72	81	96
05084	WEST HARTFORD	106	128	144	127	127	133	117	118	111	117	139	133	125	141	122	110	138	115	112	128
05086	WEST TOPSHAM	76	67	50	64	71	77	62	69	66	62	81	83	61	82	64	68	76	68	75	90
05089	WINDSOR	81	69	56	66	73	83	71	77	76	69	92	88	67	90	71	79	86	77	86	93
05091	WOODSTOCK	97	107	122	107	107	112	103	104	101	103	126	121	106	129	105	100	124	103	100	117
05101	BELLOWS FALLS	72	63	52	60	66	74	64	69	69	62	83	80	61	83	65	71	78	68	76	83
05141	CAMBRIDGEPORT	94	74	50	67	83	93	70	84	79	69	93	98	62	92	74	84	87	83	99	115
05142	CAVENDISH	85	63	37	59	71	79	61	74	69	60	82	88	54	81	63	72	75	72	86	101
05143	CHESTER	91	74	53	69	81	91	72	82	80	71	95	96	67	94	75	84	89	81	95	107
05146	GRAFTON	91	73	51	67	81	90	69	81	77	68	91	95	63	91	73	81	85	80	94	110
05148	LONDONDERRY	118	92	63	83	104	117	87	105	98	86	117	123	78	115	93	105	108	103	124	143
05149	LUDLOW	102	80	55	72	90	101	75	91	85	75	101	106	67	100	80	91	94	90	108	124
05150	NORTH SPRINGFIELD	70	77	81	73	77	85	75	74	76	72	95	83	79	101	77	79	92	73	79	82
05151	PERKINSVILLE	98	81	55	75	87	95	76	86	83	76	100	103	72	100	78	86	94	85	97	115
05152	PERU	131	103	70	93	116	130	97	117	110	96	130	137	87	128	103	117	121	115	138	160
05153	PROCTORSVILLE	86	66	42	63	74	81	63	75	71	63	84	90	58	84	66	73	78	74	86	101
05154	SAXTONS RIVER	134	93	49	88	109	122	92	114	106	91	125	137	79	122	96	112	114	112	136	159
05155	SOUTH LONDONDERRY	108	85	58	77	96	107	80	97	91	79	107	113	72	106	85	97	100	95	114	132
05156	SPRINGFIELD	73	66	57	64	69	78	67	71	71	65	86	80	66	87	68	73	82	70	78	83
05158	WESTMINSTER	89	79	60	75	84	90	73	81	78	73	94	97	72	96	75	80	90	79	88	105
05161	WESTON	127	99	68	90	112	126	94	113	106	93	126	132	84	124	100	113	117	111	133	154
05201	BENNINGTON	68	65	64	64	66	73	67	68	69	66	85	78	67	86	67	70	82	68	71	78
05250	ARLINGTON	104	78	49	75	88	98	78	91	87	77	103	108	70	102	80	90	95	90	106	121
05251	DORSET	145	114	77	103	128	144	107	129	121	106	144	151	96	142	114	130	134	127	153	177
05252	EAST ARLINGTON	87	66	43	64	73	83	67	77	74	66	88	90	61	87	68	76	82	76	88	100
05253	EAST DORSET	145	114	78	103	128	144	107	129	121	106	144	151	96	142	114	130	134	127	153	177
05255	MANCHESTER CENTER	122	111	99	106	119	130	105	117	111	105	135	136	101	134	110	115	128	116	128	148
05257	NORTH BENNINGTON	73	72	71	71	73	79	71	73	72	70	88	86	70	89	71	72	85	73	74	86
05260	NORTH POWNAL	82	73	56	69	77	83	68	75	72	68	87	89	66	89	70	74	83	73	81	97
05261	POWNAL	84	66	42	61	72	80	62	73	70	63	84	87	58	83	64	73	78	71	84	98
05262	SHAFTSBURY	97	94	82	91	98	104	87	94	89	87	110	110	87	112	90	91	105	91	98	115
05301	BRATTLEBORO	70	70	75	70	71	76	71	72	72	70	89	85	71	90	72	71	86	72	71	83
05340	BONDVILLE	138	108	74	97	122	137	102	123	115	101	137	144	91	135	109	123	127	121	145	168
05341	EAST DOVER	103	81	55	73	91	102	76	92	86	75	102	107	68	101	81	92	95	90	108	125
05342	JACKSONVILLE	98	77	52	69	86	97	72	87	82	72	97	102	65	96	77	87	90	86	103	119
05343	JAMAICA	102	80	55	72	90	101	75	91	85	75	101	106	67	100	80	91	94	90	107	124
05345	NEWFANE	82	81	81	80	83	88	78	81	79	77	97	97	77	99	79	79	94	81	83	98
05346	PUTNEY	88	82	71	80	85	91	78	84	81	78	100	99	77	101	80	82	95	82	88	102
05350	READSBORO	89	62	33	59	73	81	62	76	71	61	83	92	53	82	64	75	76	75	91	106
05351	SOUTH NEWFANE	108	85	58	77	96	107	80	96	91	79	107	113	72	106	85	97	100	95	114	132
05352	STAMFORD	92	82	62	78	86	93	76	84	80	76	98	100	74	100	78	82	93	82	91	108
05353	TOWNSHEND	95	68	38	64	78	87	67	82	76	66	90	98	58	88	69	80	82	80	96	113
05354	VERNON	101	90	68	85	95	102	83	92	88	83	107	110	81	110	86	90	102	90	100	119
05355	WARDSBORO	81	64	43	57	72	81	60	72	68	60	81	85	54	80	64	73	75	71	86	99
05356	WEST DOVER	103	81	55	73	91	102	76	92	86	75	102	107	68	101	81	92	95	90	108	125
05358	WEST HALIFAX	88	69	47	63	78	88	65	79	74	65	88	92	58	86	70	79	81	78	93	108
05359	WEST TOWNSHEND	94	71	45	65	81	91	68	83	77	67	91	98	60	90	72	82	85	81	98	114
05360	WEST WARDSBORO	105	82	56	74	92	104	77	93	87	77	104	109	69	102	82	93	96	92	110	127
05361	WHITINGHAM	108	84	58	76	95	107	80	96	90	79	107	112	71	105	85	96	99	94	113	131
05362	WILLIAMSVILLE	111	87	59	78	98	110	82	98	93	81	110	115	73	108	87	99	102	97	116	135
05363	WILMINGTON	105	82	56	74	93	104	78	93	88	77	104	109	69	103	83	94	97	92	110	128
05401	BURLINGTON	67	61	75	64	60	66	75	67	73	70	92	83	71	89	69	69	89	72	63	74
05403	SOUTH BURLINGTON	94	99	116	104	97	102	101	98	97	101	123	116	102	121	99	94	120	100	91	108
05404	WINOOSKI	55	52	63	54	52	56	61	57	61	58	76	69	59	76	59	59	74	60	55	62
05405	BURLINGTON	45	28	35	31	27	33	53	39	52	45	65	55	44	58	43	46	61	48	36	45
05440	ALBURG	77	60	41	54	68	76	57	68	64	56	76	80	51	75	60	69	71	67	81	93
05441	BAKERSFIELD	79	70	53	67	74	79	65	72	69	65	84	86	63	85	67	70	79	70	78	93
05442	BELVIDERE CENTER	83	71	55	71	74	84	73	78	77	71	94	89	70	93	72	78	88	77	84	92
	VERMONT	85	80	74	78	82	89	79	83	81	78	100	98	77	100	80	82	96	83	86	99
	UNITED STATES	100	100	100	100	100	100	100	100	100	100	100	100	100	100	100	100	100	100	100	100

VERMONT

A 05443-05766

POPULATION CHANGE

# ZIP CODE / POST OFFICE NAME	COUNTY FIPS CODE	POPULATION 2000	2004	2009	2000-2004 ANNUAL RATE % Rate	State Centile	HOUSEHOLDS 2000	2004	2009	% Annual Rate 2000-2004	2004 Average HH Size	FAMILIES 2000	2004	% Annual Rate 2000-2004
05443 BRISTOL	001	6258	6361	6592	0.4	24	2381	2463	2601	0.8	2.57	1707	1758	0.7
05444 CAMBRIDGE	011	1679	1734	1832	0.8	60	624	656	704	1.2	2.64	450	469	1.0
05445 CHARLOTTE	007	3565	3605	3694	0.3	17	1286	1323	1379	0.7	2.72	990	1014	0.6
05446 COLCHESTER	007	17404	18026	18772	0.8	64	6293	6658	7076	1.3	2.46	4289	4518	1.2
05447 EAST BERKSHIRE	011	102	112	121	2.2	95	36	40	44	2.5	2.80	27	30	2.5
05448 EAST FAIRFIELD	011	941	988	1048	1.2	76	344	368	397	1.6	2.68	265	283	1.6
05450 ENOSBURG FALLS	011	5378	5615	5935	1.0	72	1974	2087	2236	1.3	2.67	1428	1503	1.2
05452 ESSEX JUNCTION	007	18367	19074	19900	0.9	67	6922	7303	7744	1.3	2.58	4961	5226	1.2
05454 FAIRFAX	011	4219	4547	4886	1.8	91	1381	1515	1657	2.2	2.85	1096	1198	2.1
05455 FAIRFIELD	011	847	886	937	1.1	73	280	299	323	1.6	2.95	221	236	1.6
05456 FERRISBURG	001	1259	1284	1325	0.5	33	466	486	511	1.0	2.64	345	357	0.8
05457 FRANKLIN	011	1430	1571	1706	2.2	95	484	541	596	2.7	2.87	388	432	2.6
05458 GRAND ISLE	013	1955	2184	2470	2.6	98	772	875	1007	3.0	2.50	572	646	2.9
05459 HIGHGATE CENTER	011	1905	2117	2313	2.5	96	668	757	841	3.0	2.80	514	580	2.9
05461 HINESBURG	007	4434	4555	4709	0.6	49	1625	1697	1783	1.0	2.68	1197	1246	1.0
05462 HUNTINGTON	007	1809	1824	1865	0.2	14	670	688	717	0.6	2.65	495	507	0.6
05463 ISLE LA MOTTE	013	488	503	546	0.7	54	202	214	238	1.4	2.35	143	151	1.3
05464 JEFFERSONVILLE	015	2487	2613	2803	1.2	76	991	1065	1164	1.7	2.45	703	751	1.6
05465 JERICHO	007	5415	5372	5502	-0.2	4	1902	1922	2003	0.3	2.80	1512	1524	0.2
05468 MILTON	007	11995	12479	13029	0.9	70	4174	4434	4713	1.4	2.81	3309	3502	1.3
05471 MONTGOMERY CENTER	011	804	830	871	0.8	58	330	345	368	1.1	2.40	232	241	0.9
05472 NEW HAVEN	001	1793	1844	1913	0.7	52	663	692	730	1.0	2.66	501	521	0.9
05473 NORTH FERRISBURG	001	1300	1349	1406	0.9	66	505	534	567	1.3	2.53	383	404	1.3
05474 NORTH HERO	013	810	877	976	1.9	92	333	370	421	2.5	2.37	237	263	2.5
05476 RICHFORD	011	2780	2894	3067	1.0	70	1072	1136	1224	1.4	2.51	741	780	1.2
05477 RICHMOND	007	4589	4513	4614	-0.4	2	1698	1697	1761	0.0	2.65	1240	1234	-0.1
05478 SAINT ALBANS	011	14418	15063	15971	1.0	72	5613	5956	6413	1.4	2.49	3803	4015	1.3
05482 SHELBURNE	007	6965	7066	7274	0.3	22	2644	2725	2849	0.7	2.54	1855	1904	0.6
05483 SHELDON	011	1348	1402	1479	0.9	68	461	488	524	1.4	2.85	370	390	1.3
05486 SOUTH HERO	013	1695	1758	1913	0.9	65	662	699	775	1.3	2.52	472	496	1.2
05487 STARKSBORO	001	1528	1562	1618	0.5	37	532	548	574	0.7	2.85	387	397	0.6
05488 SWANTON	011	7283	7692	8184	1.3	80	2762	2970	3211	1.7	2.58	2015	2156	1.6
05489 UNDERHILL	007	3418	3386	3469	-0.2	3	1213	1223	1275	0.2	2.77	977	982	0.1
05491 VERGENNES	001	6038	6150	6340	0.4	29	2178	2256	2367	0.8	2.58	1566	1616	0.7
05492 WATERVILLE	015	797	823	875	0.8	60	295	310	334	1.2	2.62	205	213	0.9
05494 WESTFORD	007	1563	1582	1623	0.3	20	536	551	574	0.7	2.87	416	427	0.6
05495 WILLISTON	007	8350	9133	9765	2.1	94	3179	3535	3837	2.5	2.56	2336	2587	2.4
05602 MONTPELIER	023	12207	12447	12771	0.5	33	5392	5602	5864	0.9	2.18	3126	3235	0.8
05640 ADAMANT	023	276	292	304	1.3	83	111	121	129	2.1	2.41	74	79	1.6
05641 BARRE	023	16571	16756	17138	0.3	17	6989	7211	7521	0.7	2.27	4344	4469	0.7
05647 CABOT	023	943	967	989	0.6	42	349	366	382	1.1	2.64	246	256	0.9
05648 CALAIS	023	239	253	263	1.4	83	98	107	114	2.1	2.36	65	70	1.8
05649 EAST BARRE	017	605	609	616	0.2	13	240	248	256	0.8	2.44	170	174	0.6
05650 EAST CALAIS	023	880	875	888	-0.1	5	369	378	392	0.6	2.31	248	251	0.3
05651 EAST MONTPELIER	023	1401	1428	1455	0.5	31	538	561	583	1.0	2.54	383	397	0.9
05652 EDEN	015	808	829	878	0.6	45	287	300	324	1.1	2.76	218	227	1.0
05653 EDEN MILLS	015	363	372	395	0.6	41	135	141	152	1.0	2.64	103	107	0.9
05654 GRANITEVILLE	023	1653	1786	1880	1.8	91	645	713	765	2.4	2.50	463	509	2.3
05655 HYDE PARK	015	2942	3241	3568	2.3	96	1174	1324	1487	2.9	2.44	800	897	2.7
05656 JOHNSON	015	3169	3202	3347	0.2	16	1132	1169	1253	0.8	2.37	648	664	0.6
05658 MARSHFIELD	023	1309	1332	1356	0.4	26	503	523	544	0.9	2.55	359	371	0.8
05660 MORETOWN	023	1788	1864	1922	1.0	71	697	741	779	1.5	2.51	457	481	1.2
05661 MORRISVILLE	015	5299	5683	6168	1.7	89	2154	2356	2605	2.1	2.36	1357	1474	2.0
05663 NORTHFIELD	023	6524	6622	6754	0.4	23	2092	2181	2283	1.0	2.43	1417	1467	0.8
05666 NORTH MONTPELIER	023	76	78	80	0.6	45	28	29	31	0.8	2.69	20	20	0.0
05667 PLAINFIELD	023	2423	2433	2463	0.1	11	940	967	1000	0.7	2.41	640	653	0.5
05669 ROXBURY	023	409	401	405	-0.5	1	161	162	167	0.2	2.48	116	116	0.0
05672 STOWE	015	4339	4652	5047	1.7	88	1905	2062	2265	1.9	2.25	1130	1214	1.7
05673 WAITSFIELD	023	2158	2210	2258	0.6	39	967	1012	1056	1.1	2.18	642	667	0.9
05674 WARREN	023	1680	1706	1735	0.4	24	741	765	791	0.8	2.23	436	446	0.5
05675 WASHINGTON	017	1073	1097	1127	0.5	37	418	438	461	1.1	2.50	298	312	1.1
05676 WATERBURY	023	4223	4337	4446	0.6	48	1763	1845	1928	1.1	2.31	1104	1145	0.9
05677 WATERBURY CENTER	023	2168	2240	2299	0.8	61	836	881	922	1.2	2.54	617	646	1.1
05679 WILLIAMSTOWN	017	3040	3109	3197	0.5	38	1180	1233	1293	1.0	2.52	843	877	0.9
05680 WOLCOTT	015	2165	2503	2824	3.5	100	811	957	1099	4.0	2.61	592	695	3.9
05681 WOODBURY	023	399	397	401	-0.1	5	158	162	168	0.6	2.45	101	102	0.2
05682 WORCESTER	023	1252	1278	1311	0.5	35	473	493	516	1.0	2.59	343	355	0.8
05701 RUTLAND	021	21539	21843	22387	0.3	22	9173	9486	9916	0.8	2.22	5415	5565	0.6
05730 BELMONT	021	359	358	364	-0.1	7	144	146	152	0.3	2.45	100	101	0.2
05732 BOMOSEEN	021	1134	1143	1162	0.2	14	461	475	493	0.7	2.21	306	314	0.6
05733 BRANDON	021	5452	5607	5786	0.7	52	2191	2305	2428	1.2	2.43	1515	1586	1.1
05734 BRIDPORT	001	1149	1210	1273	1.2	78	431	464	498	1.8	2.61	325	349	1.7
05735 CASTLETON	021	2688	2712	2756	0.2	14	863	888	922	0.7	2.70	565	578	0.5
05736 CENTER RUTLAND	021	626	631	641	0.2	14	283	293	304	0.8	2.15	196	202	0.7
05737 CHITTENDEN	021	507	638	729	5.6	100	195	250	291	6.0	2.55	149	189	5.8
05738 CUTTINGSVILLE	021	1047	1097	1140	1.1	74	415	446	473	1.7	2.39	315	336	1.5
05739 DANBY	021	1169	1172	1191	0.1	9	473	483	501	0.5	2.43	332	337	0.5
05742 EAST WALLINGFORD	021	605	607	617	0.1	10	238	244	254	0.6	2.48	174	177	0.4
05743 FAIR HAVEN	021	4683	4773	4897	0.5	31	1863	1936	2024	0.9	2.41	1264	1307	0.8
05744 FLORENCE	021	446	447	455	0.1	9	172	176	182	0.5	2.54	111	113	0.4
05746 GAYSVILLE	027	25	26	27	0.9	68	10	10	11	0.0	2.60	7	7	0.0
05747 GRANVILLE	001	303	304	311	0.1	10	127	130	135	0.6	2.34	85	86	0.3
05748 HANCOCK	001	343	344	352	0.1	9	149	153	159	0.6	2.25	99	101	0.5
05751 KILLINGTON	021	1105	1122	1146	0.4	24	505	522	543	0.8	2.15	285	292	0.6
05753 MIDDLEBURY	001	10276	10558	10968	0.6	49	3446	3633	3882	1.3	2.29	2109	2210	1.1
05757 MIDDLETOWN SPRINGS	021	1184	1219	1254	0.7	53	466	492	518	1.3	2.48	338	356	1.2
05758 MOUNT HOLLY	021	741	738	751	-0.1	6	294	299	310	0.4	2.47	204	206	0.2
05759 NORTH CLARENDON	021	2262	2288	2340	0.3	19	950	986	1032	0.9	2.31	652	673	0.8
05760 ORWELL	001	1544	1629	1711	1.3	78	575	622	667	1.9	2.60	432	464	1.7
05761 PAWLET	021	991	1003	1025	0.3	20	395	407	424	0.7	2.46	280	287	0.6
05762 PITTSFIELD	021	525	585	631	2.6	97	214	241	263	2.8	2.43	147	165	2.8
05763 PITTSFORD	021	3186	3310	3435	0.9	67	1297	1369	1444	1.3	2.41	910	958	1.2
05764 POULTNEY	021	4121	4196	4284	0.4	29	1466	1527	1594	1.0	2.32	956	989	0.8
05765 PROCTOR	021	1980	1966	1997	-0.2	4	797	806	834	0.3	2.44	559	562	0.1
05766 RIPTON	001	542	552	569	0.4	29	202	209	218	0.8	2.56	144	148	0.7
VERMONT					0.8					1.3	2.40			1.2
UNITED STATES					1.2					1.3	2.58			1.1

ZIP CODE #	POST OFFICE NAME	RACE (%) White 2000	White 2004	Black 2000	Black 2004	Asian/Pacific 2000	Asian/Pacific 2004	% Hispanic Origin 2000	% Hispanic Origin 2004	2004 AGE DISTRIBUTION (%) 0-4	5-9	10-14	15-19	20-24	25-44	45-64	65-84	85+	18+	MEDIAN AGE 2004	% 2004 Males	% 2004 Females
05443	BRISTOL	98.2	97.9	0.2	0.3	0.5	0.7	0.6	0.7	6.2	7.0	8.2	6.9	5.4	27.4	29.3	8.5	1.2	74.2	38.5	49.4	50.6
05444	CAMBRIDGE	97.0	96.8	0.2	0.2	0.2	0.3	0.7	0.7	7.0	7.5	7.9	5.7	5.0	32.6	26.6	6.9	0.7	73.9	36.5	51.5	48.5
05445	CHARLOTTE	97.9	97.7	0.2	0.3	0.6	0.8	0.7	0.8	5.3	7.2	9.7	7.3	3.3	24.9	33.3	8.4	0.5	72.7	40.6	49.5	50.5
05446	COLCHESTER	96.6	96.1	0.6	0.7	1.6	2.0	1.1	1.2	5.8	5.9	6.2	9.5	10.2	29.3	25.6	6.8	0.6	78.5	34.2	48.8	51.2
05447	EAST BERKSHIRE	98.0	96.4	1.0	0.9	0.0	0.0	0.0	0.9	7.1	7.1	7.1	7.1	5.4	27.7	27.7	9.8	0.9	73.2	38.8	50.9	49.1
05448	EAST FAIRFIELD	97.1	97.2	0.0	0.1	0.2	0.3	0.7	0.8	7.4	8.1	8.4	6.6	5.6	28.4	27.4	7.5	0.6	72.0	36.6	50.8	49.2
05450	ENOSBURG FALLS	96.5	96.3	0.2	0.3	0.2	0.2	0.6	0.6	6.5	7.0	8.4	6.9	6.1	27.0	26.2	10.2	1.7	73.7	37.7	49.6	50.4
05452	ESSEX JUNCTION	95.4	94.6	0.9	1.0	2.3	2.9	0.9	0.9	6.1	6.6	7.9	7.7	6.4	28.2	28.2	8.0	0.9	74.1	37.5	49.1	50.9
05454	FAIRFAX	97.7	97.5	0.5	0.6	0.3	0.5	0.7	0.7	6.9	7.7	8.6	6.9	5.2	34.5	24.9	5.0	0.4	72.5	35.8	53.4	46.6
05455	FAIRFIELD	97.2	97.1	0.0	0.0	0.4	0.3	1.2	1.4	7.0	7.5	8.2	7.3	5.6	28.4	27.8	7.5	0.7	72.6	37.0	49.4	50.6
05456	FERRISBURG	97.7	97.4	0.2	0.2	0.5	0.6	0.6	0.7	6.2	6.9	7.5	5.6	4.4	27.2	29.8	11.1	1.3	75.9	40.8	49.5	50.5
05457	FRANKLIN	96.6	96.4	0.3	0.3	0.2	0.3	0.1	0.1	6.8	7.3	8.9	7.3	5.1	28.2	26.0	9.2	1.2	72.1	37.2	50.2	49.8
05458	GRAND ISLE	97.5	97.5	0.2	0.2	0.4	0.4	0.6	0.6	5.7	5.7	8.1	5.8	4.3	26.8	32.7	10.4	0.7	76.8	41.8	50.2	49.8
05459	HIGHGATE CENTER	93.0	92.7	0.1	0.1	0.2	0.2	0.2	0.1	7.0	8.1	8.2	7.2	6.5	29.5	23.1	10.0	0.4	72.2	35.7	49.5	50.5
05461	HINESBURG	97.9	97.8	0.1	0.1	0.5	0.6	0.8	0.8	6.8	7.4	7.8	7.0	5.3	32.0	27.3	5.9	0.6	73.7	36.8	49.5	50.5
05462	HUNTINGTON	97.5	97.3	0.4	0.4	0.5	0.6	0.4	0.4	6.7	7.1	8.1	6.9	2.9	34.6	27.9	5.1	0.8	72.8	37.2	49.7	50.3
05463	ISLE LA MOTTE	97.8	97.6	0.0	0.0	0.2	0.2	0.0	0.0	5.4	5.2	7.4	7.0	2.6	24.1	30.8	15.7	2.0	77.1	44.0	48.1	51.9
05464	JEFFERSONVILLE	96.5	96.3	0.2	0.3	0.1	0.2	0.7	0.7	6.2	6.7	7.0	5.3	4.7	34.3	26.4	8.5	0.8	76.4	37.5	50.8	49.3
05465	JERICHO	97.5	97.2	0.6	0.8	0.6	0.8	1.1	1.2	6.7	7.6	8.8	7.2	5.0	27.4	30.2	6.4	0.8	72.4	38.6	49.6	50.4
05468	MILTON	98.2	98.0	0.2	0.3	0.3	0.4	0.6	0.7	7.2	7.7	8.3	6.6	5.7	31.9	26.0	5.9	0.5	72.4	36.1	50.2	49.8
05471	MONTGOMERY CENTER	96.9	96.8	0.3	0.2	0.0	0.0	0.6	0.5	6.4	6.6	5.8	5.1	4.2	23.4	34.9	12.2	1.5	78.1	44.0	51.0	49.0
05472	NEW HAVEN	98.3	98.2	0.2	0.3	0.1	0.1	0.8	1.0	6.1	6.9	7.8	6.1	5.8	28.5	29.7	8.2	0.9	75.4	39.3	51.1	48.9
05473	NORTH FERRISBURG	98.1	97.9	0.2	0.2	0.5	0.6	0.5	0.7	6.7	7.5	7.5	6.1	4.4	27.9	30.5	8.6	1.0	74.6	40.0	49.8	50.2
05474	NORTH HERO	97.5	97.4	0.3	0.3	0.4	0.5	0.6	0.7	4.3	4.5	6.3	6.6	3.5	24.2	38.2	11.5	0.9	79.9	45.3	50.4	49.6
05476	RICHFORD	97.6	97.6	0.4	0.4	0.0	0.0	0.7	0.7	7.2	7.2	7.4	6.0	5.4	25.7	25.6	13.4	2.3	74.7	39.1	49.0	51.0
05477	RICHMOND	98.3	98.1	0.1	0.1	0.5	0.7	0.8	0.9	6.7	7.3	8.6	7.2	4.7	29.5	28.9	6.4	0.6	72.4	37.8	49.1	50.9
05478	SAINT ALBANS	96.5	96.3	0.3	0.4	0.4	0.4	0.7	0.8	7.3	7.3	7.2	6.8	6.0	28.7	23.7	11.4	1.7	73.9	36.9	48.8	51.2
05482	SHELBURNE	97.6	97.3	0.2	0.3	1.0	1.3	0.9	0.9	6.0	7.1	8.3	7.0	4.3	21.9	29.7	12.5	3.3	74.1	42.3	47.9	52.2
05483	SHELDON	94.9	94.6	0.0	0.1	0.2	0.3	0.7	0.7	7.1	7.4	8.4	8.2	5.7	29.3	25.1	8.0	0.7	71.2	36.1	49.8	50.2
05486	SOUTH HERO	97.9	97.8	0.2	0.3	0.3	0.3	0.5	0.5	4.6	6.6	7.2	6.7	4.1	26.6	33.0	10.5	0.8	76.7	41.9	49.7	50.3
05487	STARKSBORO	96.7	96.4	0.2	0.2	0.7	0.8	0.3	0.3	7.5	8.7	9.0	6.2	5.8	30.7	25.7	5.7	0.7	70.6	34.3	48.5	51.5
05488	SWANTON	92.9	92.3	0.5	0.5	0.4	0.5	0.5	0.5	7.0	7.2	7.8	6.6	6.0	27.9	25.8	10.5	1.2	73.8	37.4	49.2	50.8
05489	UNDERHILL	98.5	98.3	0.3	0.3	0.2	0.3	0.7	0.9	5.6	6.5	9.0	7.9	4.0	29.3	31.2	6.0	0.6	73.5	39.4	50.2	49.8
05491	VERGENNES	95.9	95.6	1.0	1.2	0.4	0.6	1.6	1.7	6.2	6.5	7.1	10.3	6.9	25.5	25.9	10.1	1.6	74.2	36.9	50.2	49.8
05492	WATERVILLE	97.7	97.7	0.0	0.0	0.3	0.2	0.1	0.1	6.4	7.1	9.0	6.1	5.4	30.6	24.9	9.5	1.1	73.3	36.8	52.3	47.8
05494	WESTFORD	98.1	98.0	0.3	0.4	0.5	0.5	1.0	1.2	7.0	8.0	8.9	7.1	4.2	29.1	29.3	5.9	0.5	71.6	38.2	50.3	49.7
05495	WILLISTON	97.5	97.1	0.5	0.6	1.1	1.4	1.0	1.1	6.5	7.1	8.2	7.1	4.3	26.8	28.1	11.0	1.0	73.4	39.9	48.8	51.2
05602	MONTPELIER	96.7	96.4	0.6	0.7	0.7	0.9	1.1	1.2	4.7	5.0	6.4	7.1	6.9	25.7	30.5	11.5	2.2	79.4	41.4	47.0	53.1
05640	ADAMANT	97.1	96.6	0.0	0.0	0.4	0.7	0.0	0.0	4.5	5.8	6.2	6.5	4.5	22.3	39.4	10.3	0.7	79.5	45.2	50.0	50.0
05641	BARRE	97.8	97.6	0.3	0.4	0.4	0.5	1.5	1.7	5.8	5.7	6.8	6.6	6.1	26.1	26.5	13.5	3.0	77.7	40.6	47.5	52.5
05647	CABOT	96.0	96.0	0.1	0.1	0.3	0.4	0.6	0.7	5.0	5.6	7.9	8.5	6.7	24.6	31.1	9.7	0.9	76.4	39.8	49.4	50.6
05648	CALAIS	97.1	97.2	0.0	0.0	0.4	0.4	0.0	0.0	4.4	5.9	6.3	6.7	4.7	23.3	37.9	9.9	0.8	78.7	44.0	49.8	50.2
05649	EAST BARRE	99.2	99.2	0.2	0.2	0.2	0.3	1.3	1.5	4.6	5.1	8.1	6.7	4.9	27.6	28.7	12.5	1.8	77.3	40.6	49.6	50.4
05650	EAST CALAIS	94.3	93.9	0.5	0.6	0.3	0.6	0.7	0.8	4.5	5.4	7.2	7.2	5.3	25.4	36.0	8.3	0.8	78.4	41.6	50.7	49.3
05651	EAST MONTPELIER	96.7	96.4	0.6	0.8	0.4	0.5	1.2	1.3	5.1	5.8	6.9	6.7	6.2	24.2	32.1	11.5	1.4	77.9	41.5	48.8	51.2
05652	EDEN	95.7	95.4	0.1	0.1	0.5	0.6	1.1	1.3	6.8	7.1	8.4	8.4	5.8	30.3	25.1	7.5	0.6	72.3	35.3	50.9	49.1
05653	EDEN MILLS	95.6	95.4	0.3	0.3	0.6	0.5	1.4	1.3	6.7	7.3	8.3	8.6	5.9	29.8	25.0	7.5	0.8	72.9	35.0	51.3	48.7
05654	GRANITEVILLE	97.9	97.7	0.2	0.3	0.3	0.4	2.1	2.2	6.4	6.4	6.6	6.6	6.1	26.2	26.5	13.6	1.6	76.6	40.0	48.8	51.2
05655	HYDE PARK	97.8	97.5	0.5	0.6	0.4	0.5	0.8	0.9	6.0	6.3	6.8	6.6	6.0	27.2	27.7	11.9	1.5	76.9	38.9	49.5	50.5
05656	JOHNSON	96.6	96.3	0.6	0.7	0.7	0.8	0.8	0.8	6.1	5.1	5.3	12.9	17.1	25.6	19.6	7.2	1.2	79.8	27.0	51.2	48.8
05658	MARSHFIELD	96.3	96.1	0.6	0.7	0.4	0.5	0.7	0.8	6.5	7.1	7.7	7.0	5.6	24.9	31.2	9.4	0.8	74.4	39.4	50.7	49.3
05660	MORETOWN	98.0	97.9	0.2	0.2	0.4	0.5	1.0	1.0	5.6	6.1	6.9	6.5	5.7	27.8	31.0	9.2	1.1	77.4	40.5	50.9	49.1
05661	MORRISVILLE	97.5	97.3	0.3	0.4	0.5	0.6	0.8	0.8	4.9	5.2	7.3	7.4	6.2	26.7	27.1	12.2	2.9	77.7	40.4	48.1	51.9
05663	NORTHFIELD	95.5	94.9	0.9	1.1	1.2	1.6	2.1	2.2	4.7	5.0	5.6	10.8	15.5	24.6	22.0	9.4	2.5	81.3	31.7	54.2	45.8
05666	NORTH MONTPELIER	97.4	98.7	0.0	0.0	0.0	0.0	1.3	1.3	5.1	5.1	7.7	6.4	6.4	25.6	29.5	12.8	1.3	78.2	40.0	48.7	51.3
05667	PLAINFIELD	96.4	96.1	0.7	0.9	0.4	0.5	1.1	1.1	5.8	6.0	6.8	7.5	7.5	26.6	29.6	8.9	1.3	77.1	38.4	48.8	51.2
05669	ROXBURY	94.1	94.0	0.5	0.5	0.0	0.0	1.2	1.3	5.7	6.2	6.5	5.0	4.7	26.9	35.2	9.0	0.8	78.8	42.3	50.4	49.6
05672	STOWE	97.5	97.2	0.3	0.3	0.4	0.5	1.1	1.2	4.0	4.5	6.7	6.2	6.1	26.1	31.7	13.1	1.6	80.9	42.7	50.7	49.3
05673	WAITSFIELD	97.5	97.3	0.9	1.0	0.4	0.5	1.1	1.2	5.3	5.7	6.5	5.4	5.1	28.3	31.2	11.4	1.1	79.4	41.8	49.4	50.6
05674	WARREN	98.0	97.9	0.2	0.2	0.2	0.3	1.0	1.1	4.1	5.2	6.9	7.2	3.5	28.4	33.9	10.2	0.6	78.5	41.8	51.2	48.8
05675	WASHINGTON	97.3	97.2	0.5	0.6	0.2	0.3	0.7	0.7	3.7	6.2	7.8	7.9	4.7	27.3	32.2	9.5	0.7	76.7	40.7	51.1	49.0
05676	WATERBURY	97.8	97.5	0.2	0.3	0.7	0.9	0.6	0.6	6.2	6.4	6.9	6.2	4.7	31.1	27.6	9.5	1.5	76.3	39.0	49.8	50.2
05677	WATERBURY CENTER	98.1	97.8	0.3	0.3	0.5	0.6	0.7	0.9	6.1	7.1	7.6	6.5	4.1	27.8	31.1	8.8	0.9	75.0	40.1	50.0	50.0
05679	WILLIAMSTOWN	98.3	98.1	0.1	0.1	0.1	0.2	0.8	0.8	6.5	6.8	7.1	6.4	5.4	30.1	27.2	9.6	0.9	75.6	38.1	51.2	48.8
05680	WOLCOTT	98.7	98.5	0.1	0.0	0.3	0.3	0.4	0.4	6.6	7.0	8.3	7.4	6.0	30.5	26.3	7.1	0.9	73.2	36.1	50.7	49.3
05681	WOODBURY	91.5	91.4	0.3	0.5	0.8	1.0	1.0	1.0	4.5	5.5	6.1	7.1	5.5	25.4	38.0	7.1	0.8	80.1	41.8	53.2	46.9
05682	WORCESTER	97.6	97.6	0.1	0.1	0.1	0.1	0.8	0.9	4.5	6.6	8.5	6.7	5.1	26.7	35.1	6.2	0.7	76.0	40.5	49.8	50.2
05701	RUTLAND	97.9	97.7	0.4	0.5	0.5	0.6	0.9	0.9	5.3	5.4	6.4	6.9	6.1	25.2	27.1	14.5	3.3	78.8	41.6	47.6	52.4
05730	BELMONT	98.1	97.5	0.3	0.3	0.3	0.3	0.3	0.3	5.3	5.9	7.3	6.7	5.3	26.5	30.7	11.2	1.1	77.1	40.7	50.3	49.7
05732	BOMOSEEN	98.1	97.7	0.1	0.1	0.5	0.8	1.2	1.2	3.6	4.9	6.1	10.4	13.0	21.0	29.5	10.5	1.1	81.3	37.9	49.7	50.3
05733	BRANDON	98.8	98.8	0.2	0.2	0.2	0.2	0.3	0.3	5.1	5.6	7.2	6.6	5.3	26.6	29.9	12.1	1.6	77.9	41.5	48.7	51.4
05734	BRIDPORT	98.4	98.2	0.1	0.1	0.4	0.5	0.1	0.1	6.6	7.2	7.8	6.0	5.3	26.9	28.4	10.5	1.4	74.7	38.6	51.9	48.1
05735	CASTLETON	97.7	97.5	0.3	0.3	0.6	0.7	1.1	1.2	3.8	5.0	5.9	12.1	14.6	21.4	26.6	9.7	1.1	81.3	34.6	49.7	50.3
05736	CENTER RUTLAND	99.4	99.1	0.2	0.2	0.3	0.3	0.5	0.6	3.7	4.6	6.5	7.0	4.3	21.2	34.2	16.0	2.5	80.8	46.6	49.5	50.6
05737	CHITTENDEN	98.4	98.6	0.2	0.2	0.2	0.2	0.2	0.3	6.6	6.9	6.0	6.7	6.3	24.5	33.7	8.0	1.4	76.5	41.7	50.2	49.8
05738	CUTTINGSVILLE	98.3	98.2	0.2	0.2	0.3	0.4	1.3	1.5	4.5	5.3	6.9	6.8	4.7	23.3	34.9	12.7	1.0	78.4	44.1	50.5	49.5
05739	DANBY	98.7	98.5	0.0	0.0	0.2	0.3	0.5	0.7	6.0	6.4	7.1	6.2	4.7	28.7	27.6	11.9	1.5	76.7	39.2	51.6	48.4
05742	EAST WALLINGFORD	98.7	98.5	0.2	0.2	0.2	0.3	0.3	0.3	5.3	5.4	5.6	6.8	5.3	24.9	33.8	11.9	1.2	78.8	43.1	50.1	49.9
05743	FAIR HAVEN	97.6	97.4	0.5	0.5	0.4	0.5	0.9	1.0	6.0	6.2	6.8	7.8	7.3	26.0	27.3	11.1	1.6	76.0	38.3	49.1	50.9
05744	FLORENCE	98.7	98.7	0.2	0.2	0.5	0.5	0.5	0.5	4.9	5.4	6.5	6.7	5.8	26.0	29.5	13.4	1.8	78.8	42.1	49.7	50.3
05746	GAYSVILLE	100.0	100.0	0.0	0.0	0.0	0.0	0.0	0.0	7.7	7.7	7.7	7.7	3.9	30.8	30.8	3.9	0.0	76.9	35.0	50.0	50.0
05747	GRANVILLE	97.0	96.7	0.0	0.0	0.3	0.7	1.0	0.3	4.6	5.3	7.2	6.3	5.3	28.3	30.6	11.2	1.3	79.0	40.8	52.0	48.0
05748	HANCOCK	97.1	96.8	0.3	0.3	0.6	0.6	0.9	0.6	4.7	5.5	7.0	6.4	5.2	28.5	29.7	11.6	1.5	79.1	40.7	51.5	48.6
05751	KILLINGTON	97.7	97.4	0.4	0.5	0.6	0.8	0.9	1.0	3.6	4.5	6.3	5.6	5.0	27.9	34.0	12.7	0.5	82.1	43.4	53.2	46.8
05753	MIDDLEBURY	95.1	94.5	0.9	1.1	1.6	2.0	1.9	2.0	4.2	4.6	5.5	13.0	17.4	19.2	22.7	11.4	2.2	82.4	31.7	48.0	52.0
05757	MIDDLETOWN SPRINGS	98.1	97.9	0.3	0.5	0.3	0.4	0.5	0.4	5.7	6.3	7.3	5.4	4.9	24.5	32.7	11.7	1.5	77.4	42.5	47.3	52.7
05758	MOUNT HOLLY	98.0	97.8	0.1	0.1	0.1	0.3	0.1	0.1	5.2	5.8	7.3	6.9	5.2	26.8	30.1	11.7	1.1	77.6	40.6	50.3	49.7
05759	NORTH CLARENDON	98.0	97.7	0.3	0.4	0.7	0.8	0.5	0.5	4.2	5.0	6.6	6.2	5.5	24.0	35.5	11.7	1.4	80.3	44.1	48.8	51.2
05760	ORWELL	98.6	98.5	0.3	0.3	0.4	0.5	0.8	0.9	6.4	7.1	7.7	6.4	5.3	25.7	29.3	10.9	1.3	74.6	40.0	49.4	50.6
05761	PAWLET	99.0	98.8	0.2	0.2	0.1	0.1	0.4	0.6	5.5	5.8	7.4	6.2	3.9	27.3	30.2	12.7	1.1	77.1	41.1	51.1	49.0
05762	PITTSFIELD	98.5	98.5	0.0	0.2	0.2	0.2	0.4	0.3	5.6	6.2	5.8	5.8	4.4	26.5	33.7	10.9	1.0	79.2	42.8	50.6	49.4
05763	PITTSFORD	99.0	98.9	0.2	0.3	0.2	0.2	0.4	0.5	5.6	6.1	6.3	6.3	5.4	26.4	31.2	11.1	1.7	78.0	41.7	50.3	49.7
05764	POULTNEY	97.2	96.9	0.6	0.7	0.9	1.1	0.7	0.7	4.8	4.7	6.3	9.3	13.2	25.2	22.3	12.4	1.9	80.9	34.8	49.5	50.5
05765	PROCTOR	99.0	99.1	0.2	0.2	0.1	0.1	0.6	0.6	5.8	6.1	7.5	7.0	5.6	25.1	27.5	13.2	2.2	76.4	40.7	46.9	53.1
05766	RIPTON	97.2	97.5	0.2	0.2	0.6	0.5	0.7	0.7	6.0	6.5	6.5	6.5	4.7	27.0	33.7	7.6	1.5	75.5	41.3	52.4	47.6
	VERMONT	96.8	96.4	0.5	0.6	0.9	1.1	0.9	1.0	5.5	5.9	6.9	7.5	7.2	26.5	27.5	11.2	1.8	77.5	39.1	49.1	50.9
	UNITED STATES	75.1	73.6	12.3	12.5	3.8	4.2	12.5	14.1	6.9	6.7	7.2	7.0	7.3	28.6	23.8	10.8	1.7	75.1	36.0	49.1	50.9

ZIP CODE #	POST OFFICE NAME	2004 Per Capita Income	2004 HH Income Base	2004 HOUSEHOLD INCOME DISTRIBUTION (%) Less than $25,000	$25,000 to $49,999	$50,000 to $99,999	$100,000 to $149,999	$150,000 or More	MEDIAN HOUSEHOLD INCOME 2004	2009	2004 National Centile	2004 State Centile	2004 Home Value Base	2004 HOME VALUE DISTRIBUTION (%) Less than $50,000	$50,000 to $89,999	$90,000 to $174,999	$175,000 to $399,999	$400,000 or More	2004 Median Home Value
05443	BRISTOL	23033	2463	20.5	29.3	39.5	6.9	3.8	50124	54938	72	76	1935	7.3	8.0	47.3	35.2	2.3	155995
05444	CAMBRIDGE	22086	656	16.8	31.6	41.3	7.9	2.4	51011	55898	74	81	516	1.6	5.6	52.3	37.8	2.7	161080
05445	CHARLOTTE	42941	1323	14.4	15.9	40.0	14.1	15.6	70790	78834	92	99	1166	0.0	0.8	10.8	45.1	43.3	357838
05446	COLCHESTER	26491	6658	15.4	25.3	42.0	11.7	5.6	58059	67101	83	93	4678	11.1	3.9	35.3	45.7	3.9	174391
05447	EAST BERKSHIRE	17213	40	27.5	35.0	30.0	7.5	0.0	41519	43191	51	40	33	9.1	15.2	51.5	24.2	0.0	118056
05448	EAST FAIRFIELD	20814	368	22.6	29.9	38.9	6.3	2.5	47722	52355	68	70	316	2.9	10.4	59.8	25.6	1.3	139754
05450	ENOSBURG FALLS	18104	2087	28.7	36.1	29.2	4.1	1.9	39097	42889	43	28	1629	9.0	18.2	53.4	18.1	1.4	119092
05452	ESSEX JUNCTION	29793	7303	10.5	24.7	42.7	15.0	7.2	63648	72371	88	97	5580	0.5	2.1	38.8	53.6	5.0	190313
05454	FAIRFAX	22163	1515	12.7	25.7	50.2	8.8	2.6	58580	63400	83	93	1320	1.4	5.3	49.4	41.1	2.8	165868
05455	FAIRFIELD	19162	299	24.1	26.1	40.5	6.4	3.0	49773	52778	71	75	255	2.4	10.2	62.4	23.1	2.0	137750
05456	FERRISBURG	25261	486	15.6	25.3	41.2	13.4	4.5	57835	63765	82	91	410	0.5	8.8	34.6	44.4	11.7	191892
05457	FRANKLIN	18593	541	20.2	36.4	35.3	6.3	1.9	44600	49513	60	54	457	5.3	12.7	58.9	19.5	3.7	130540
05458	GRAND ISLE	26380	875	16.5	28.7	40.7	9.1	5.0	53841	61491	78	88	743	4.6	5.0	37.3	42.3	10.9	180390
05459	HIGHGATE CENTER	18584	757	21.5	33.2	38.8	5.2	1.3	46574	51851	65	64	621	9.7	11.0	63.0	14.8	1.6	118908
05461	HINESBURG	25296	1697	14.9	30.0	38.5	12.0	4.7	54053	60446	78	88	1430	13.4	4.8	32.5	46.9	2.5	173851
05462	HUNTINGTON	22649	688	17.0	28.5	43.6	8.4	2.5	53489	61040	78	87	610	3.0	8.2	52.1	33.3	3.4	156591
05463	ISLE LA MOTTE	22752	214	28.5	30.4	31.3	6.1	3.7	40000	46060	46	34	178	12.4	7.3	43.3	30.3	6.7	138333
05464	JEFFERSONVILLE	23356	1065	18.6	32.3	38.7	8.1	2.4	49161	54106	70	74	794	1.4	6.7	46.9	41.1	4.0	168036
05465	JERICHO	27606	1922	11.1	20.8	44.0	18.1	6.0	67909	75614	90	98	1728	1.7	0.9	37.8	55.4	4.2	193498
05468	MILTON	22665	4434	14.8	28.0	44.8	9.5	2.9	55486	62575	80	90	3815	7.3	4.0	48.1	39.0	1.7	162341
05471	MONTGOMERY CENTER	18480	345	33.6	31.0	29.6	4.1	1.7	36971	41556	35	18	287	7.0	17.4	55.8	18.5	1.4	118654
05472	NEW HAVEN	24117	692	16.3	30.4	40.5	8.4	4.5	52261	57919	76	84	589	1.9	5.6	43.0	41.3	8.3	174313
05473	NORTH FERRISBURG	27228	534	14.8	24.7	43.1	12.7	4.7	58201	64450	83	93	461	1.7	5.9	41.0	43.0	8.5	178869
05474	NORTH HERO	31287	370	18.7	30.0	37.8	6.5	7.0	51336	59094	74	83	312	0.3	6.1	33.3	52.2	8.0	192778
05476	RICHFORD	15901	1136	40.2	32.4	23.9	2.4	1.1	31250	34482	16	5	835	21.3	31.0	39.2	8.1	0.4	86953
05477	RICHMOND	28699	1697	12.9	22.5	43.0	14.9	6.8	64023	72469	88	97	1375	10.8	3.5	38.4	44.2	3.1	170888
05478	SAINT ALBANS	20494	5956	24.9	32.0	35.8	5.8	1.6	44886	49912	61	56	3952	4.5	7.1	61.1	24.9	2.4	140888
05482	SHELBURNE	42430	2725	11.1	19.6	37.0	15.9	16.5	74914	83601	93	100	2220	3.2	3.8	15.3	57.1	20.6	239556
05483	SHELDON	18830	488	22.8	32.4	39.1	4.5	1.2	46103	51222	64	62	413	5.3	11.4	62.5	18.2	2.7	130945
05486	SOUTH HERO	29939	699	18.2	25.8	36.2	12.3	7.6	57919	64159	83	92	573	2.3	1.8	28.1	53.1	14.8	223571
05487	STARKSBORO	19564	548	17.5	35.0	39.2	5.8	2.4	48481	54168	69	73	462	20.8	9.5	40.3	27.1	2.4	138235
05488	SWANTON	20684	2970	24.6	30.6	35.5	6.8	2.5	45271	50314	62	59	2289	5.4	9.8	56.7	26.8	1.3	139497
05489	UNDERHILL	29747	1223	11.4	20.2	42.4	19.0	7.0	69951	78601	91	99	1128	1.9	0.5	27.9	62.5	7.2	209266
05491	VERGENNES	20827	2256	22.6	28.5	39.5	7.2	2.2	48878	53718	70	74	1746	6.0	5.7	51.1	31.6	5.7	154874
05492	WATERVILLE	20344	310	23.6	34.5	31.9	7.1	2.9	43948	49041	58	50	254	11.0	13.4	43.7	26.0	5.9	135526
05494	WESTFORD	26135	551	9.1	26.1	44.7	14.2	6.0	64884	75000	88	98	500	5.4	4.2	40.2	47.4	2.8	175347
05495	WILLISTON	33544	3535	10.7	20.6	41.9	15.6	11.2	68366	79543	90	98	2838	4.0	2.1	27.1	58.8	8.1	213054
05602	MONTPELIER	25439	5602	26.5	29.2	32.0	8.2	4.1	44558	50315	60	54	3647	3.9	8.2	50.3	35.8	1.9	152786
05640	ADAMANT	26037	121	16.5	32.2	43.0	5.0	3.3	50577	56745	73	78	105	1.0	7.6	39.1	45.7	6.7	179464
05641	BARRE	22343	7211	30.6	29.3	30.7	6.8	2.6	39750	45262	45	31	4606	2.6	9.8	67.4	19.3	1.1	131027
05647	CABOT	20881	366	27.1	27.1	36.1	6.0	3.8	46318	52389	65	63	310	4.2	18.7	53.2	18.7	5.2	135648
05648	CALAIS	26531	107	15.9	31.8	43.0	5.6	3.7	51085	56699	74	82	93	1.1	7.5	37.6	46.2	7.5	181731
05649	EAST BARRE	25223	248	18.2	34.3	33.1	9.3	5.2	47723	54310	68	70	200	4.5	14.0	67.5	12.0	2.0	122917
05650	EAST CALAIS	23712	378	20.6	33.3	37.6	5.8	2.7	46858	52474	66	66	323	4.6	13.3	45.8	33.1	3.1	147635
05651	EAST MONTPELIER	24436	561	20.0	28.9	36.2	10.0	5.0	50792	58899	73	78	413	8.7	6.5	41.7	40.4	2.7	159840
05652	EDEN	15559	300	29.0	37.3	30.0	2.7	1.0	37839	41203	39	24	250	14.4	21.6	49.6	14.4	0.0	105556
05653	EDEN MILLS	16070	141	29.1	39.0	27.7	2.8	1.4	37080	40000	36	20	118	15.3	22.0	48.3	14.4	0.0	103125
05654	GRANITEVILLE	21873	713	23.3	35.5	29.9	8.4	3.0	44260	50215	59	52	533	5.6	11.8	62.5	19.5	0.6	123989
05655	HYDE PARK	23422	1324	23.0	35.1	31.3	7.6	3.0	42635	48504	55	43	1021	10.5	13.9	44.3	27.2	4.1	134806
05656	JOHNSON	17699	1169	37.2	30.0	26.5	5.0	1.3	33688	36919	23	8	702	19.7	14.7	46.0	18.8	0.9	113618
05658	MARSHFIELD	21181	523	25.4	32.1	33.8	5.7	2.9	45055	50795	61	57	435	6.4	18.4	46.9	24.4	3.9	127500
05660	MORETOWN	24882	741	18.4	27.3	41.6	8.4	4.5	53009	60333	77	85	583	5.3	8.2	33.8	43.6	9.1	180167
05661	MORRISVILLE	19925	2356	29.5	36.9	25.6	5.8	2.2	36852	41370	35	18	1632	5.3	8.5	51.8	31.5	3.0	149226
05663	NORTHFIELD	19754	2181	23.8	29.8	37.8	7.6	1.1	46954	54020	66	67	1541	9.4	11.4	55.9	22.5	0.8	135215
05666	NORTH MONTPELIER	21804	29	24.1	31.0	31.0	10.3	3.5	46137	58065	64	63	20	10.0	5.0	50.0	35.0	0.0	150000
05667	PLAINFIELD	21756	967	22.2	33.4	35.4	6.4	2.6	45728	52078	63	60	726	6.2	13.9	49.2	27.8	2.9	141441
05669	ROXBURY	20447	162	25.3	28.4	40.1	3.1	3.1	47124	52386	66	68	139	1.4	22.3	60.4	15.1	0.7	118092
05672	STOWE	40135	2062	18.3	22.8	34.5	13.2	11.1	61692	72296	86	96	1412	0.6	2.8	15.8	50.3	30.5	298795
05673	WAITSFIELD	30249	1012	19.5	26.0	38.3	10.4	5.8	53099	60593	77	86	769	5.6	3.0	23.8	52.9	14.7	212838
05674	WARREN	33657	765	23.7	25.0	36.7	6.8	7.8	50889	56540	74	79	563	2.7	4.6	32.5	41.7	18.5	202016
05675	WASHINGTON	21012	438	21.7	34.7	37.2	4.1	2.3	46091	51837	64	62	374	9.4	17.7	47.9	22.2	2.9	121930
05676	WATERBURY	25491	1845	23.4	31.5	32.0	9.5	3.6	45906	51417	64	61	1255	8.5	6.6	44.2	37.0	3.8	157868
05677	WATERBURY CENTER	31812	881	13.6	29.5	32.4	16.4	8.2	60476	63851	85	95	760	6.6	4.2	29.2	51.2	8.8	191814
05679	WILLIAMSTOWN	20664	1233	24.1	33.5	35.5	4.1	2.8	42891	47666	56	45	1028	12.9	13.2	54.2	18.1	1.6	119340
05680	WOLCOTT	19171	957	25.0	35.5	32.5	4.7	2.3	40329	43781	47	35	805	7.2	13.4	51.2	22.9	5.3	131250
05681	WOODBURY	20243	162	27.8	35.8	29.0	4.9	2.5	37355	42734	37	22	137	7.3	19.7	48.2	21.9	2.9	118534
05682	WORCESTER	22054	493	18.9	33.9	36.3	7.9	3.0	46945	52485	66	67	416	5.8	10.8	51.0	30.3	2.2	146831
05701	RUTLAND	20801	9486	34.9	29.2	28.4	5.2	2.3	35997	40063	32	15	5720	2.4	9.6	60.9	25.4	1.7	136139
05730	BELMONT	22433	146	24.0	34.9	32.9	6.2	2.1	43384	50000	60	53	125	6.4	16.8	41.6	31.2	4.0	145536
05732	BOMOSEEN	25072	475	26.3	29.5	33.5	5.5	5.3	45507	50938	63	59	356	6.5	8.2	53.4	27.8	4.2	143333
05733	BRANDON	23218	2305	26.4	35.8	30.1	4.7	3.1	39711	44669	45	31	1812	7.6	11.2	57.1	22.3	1.8	127613
05734	BRIDPORT	22209	464	21.8	31.3	35.8	7.8	3.5	47359	52560	67	69	365	0.3	9.6	50.7	31.2	8.2	158958
05735	CASTLETON	18880	888	28.5	30.5	31.4	5.3	4.3	42304	47567	54	42	658	9.6	9.3	52.7	26.0	2.4	139474
05736	CENTER RUTLAND	32699	293	22.5	27.0	31.4	11.3	7.9	50611	53976	73	78	250	2.8	5.6	39.6	41.6	10.4	179167
05737	CHITTENDEN	23851	250	18.8	33.2	34.0	9.2	4.8	48739	54059	70	74	212	2.4	7.6	40.1	42.9	7.1	175000
05738	CUTTINGSVILLE	25752	446	19.5	28.7	34.8	11.9	5.2	51399	55797	75	83	387	3.4	6.2	41.3	43.4	5.7	173011
05739	DANBY	19081	483	30.6	34.2	29.4	3.7	2.1	39625	43666	45	30	390	14.9	12.1	41.8	25.6	5.6	124658
05742	EAST WALLINGFORD	22964	244	20.9	32.8	35.3	8.2	2.9	47947	53306	68	71	210	2.9	10.5	43.8	37.6	5.2	162903
05743	FAIR HAVEN	20785	1936	30.8	31.3	31.4	4.3	2.3	40503	45625	48	36	1412	9.5	15.9	57.3	15.7	1.7	117057
05744	FLORENCE	19934	176	27.3	36.4	29.0	5.7	1.7	39593	45752	45	30	121	3.3	9.9	62.0	22.3	2.5	136932
05746	GAYSVILLE	18846	10	10.0	50.0	40.0	0.0	0.0	45000	54545	61	57	9	0.0	11.1	66.7	22.2	0.0	120833
05747	GRANVILLE	18175	130	32.3	33.1	30.0	3.9	0.8	36307	40980	33	16	105	10.5	24.8	48.6	13.3	2.9	112500
05748	HANCOCK	18889	153	32.0	34.0	28.8	4.6	0.7	36796	40856	35	17	124	12.1	25.0	46.8	12.9	3.2	110000
05751	KILLINGTON	36868	522	23.8	25.9	27.8	11.7	10.9	50461	56920	73	77	376	0.5	6.9	14.1	62.8	15.7	273810
05753	MIDDLEBURY	23213	3633	28.1	30.5	29.5	7.3	4.7	42948	47763	56	46	2477	3.8	5.8	41.9	40.8	7.7	172507
05757	MIDDLETOWN SPRINGS	20130	492	25.4	35.4	31.5	6.1	1.6	39376	43913	44	28	413	5.1	10.7	46.7	32.2	5.3	152412
05758	MOUNT HOLLY	22249	299	24.1	34.8	32.1	6.4	2.7	44233	49675	59	52	257	5.5	16.7	42.8	31.1	3.9	144397
05759	NORTH CLARENDON	22788	986	25.8	30.8	34.1	7.2	2.1	45257	50302	62	59	808	11.1	9.2	48.0	29.0	2.7	136468
05760	ORWELL	21312	622	24.0	36.5	30.1	6.9	2.6	43566	48543	57	49	503	3.6	8.8	52.1	29.6	6.0	152344
05761	PAWLET	23033	407	26.3	36.9	26.3	6.1	4.4	40667	45480	48	36	318	5.7	10.7	38.7	37.7	7.2	162097
05762	PITTSFIELD	23984	241	21.2	32.0	34.9	7.5	4.6	47761	52619	68	71	197	2.0	9.1	39.6	43.7	5.6	173558
05763	PITTSFORD	22153	1369	21.3	37.0	32.0	7.2	2.5	45057	50289	61	57	1073	4.6	8.6	55.2	28.3	3.4	144786
05764	POULTNEY	17524	1527	34.6	32.7	27.2	4.0	1.5	35430	38820	29	11	1064	8.0	12.4	63.1	14.1	2.4	119040
05765	PROCTOR	21555	806	28.0	28.8	35.1	5.6	2.5	43448	49859	57	49	615	0.5	11.2	73.0	14.0	1.3	123681
05766	RIPTON	19849	209	24.9	31.6	34.0	8.1	1.4	43420	47785	57	48	165	1.8	8.5	52.7	34.6	2.4	156466
	VERMONT	23579		25.6	30.1	32.7	7.7	3.9	44976	50578				5.7	9.3	47.1	32.6	5.3	151623
	UNITED STATES	25866		24.7	27.1	30.8	10.9	6.5	48124	56710				10.9	15.0	33.7	30.1	10.4	145905

ZIP CODE #	POST OFFICE NAME	FINANCIAL SERVICES: Auto Loan	Home Loan	Investments	Retirement Plans	THE HOME: Home Improvements: Home Repair	Lawn & Garden	Furnishings: Computers & Hardware	Major Appliances	TV, Radio, Sound Equipment	Furniture	ENTERTAINMENT: Dine out/ Carry out	Sports Equipment	Fees & Tickets	Toys & Games	Travel	Cable TV	PERSONAL: Apparel & Services	Auto Repairs	Health Insurance	Pets & Supplies
05443	BRISTOL	90	84	72	84	86	93	82	86	84	81	103	100	81	104	82	84	98	85	88	102
05444	CAMBRIDGE	81	89	89	91	86	85	85	84	80	86	101	100	85	101	83	75	99	84	74	93
05445	CHARLOTTE	152	190	203	192	186	184	169	167	156	169	196	195	181	208	172	151	197	161	149	185
05446	COLCHESTER	96	101	105	103	100	101	99	98	95	99	119	117	99	120	98	91	117	99	90	110
05447	EAST BERKSHIRE	77	69	52	65	73	78	64	70	67	64	82	84	62	84	65	69	78	69	76	91
05448	EAST FAIRFIELD	86	81	68	79	84	88	76	81	78	76	95	97	75	97	77	78	92	80	84	101
05450	ENOSBURG FALLS	78	66	48	63	71	78	64	71	69	63	83	83	61	83	65	72	78	70	80	90
05452	ESSEX JUNCTION	105	120	126	123	117	116	112	111	105	113	133	130	116	136	111	101	131	109	99	121
05454	FAIRFAX	91	101	100	104	97	96	94	94	88	96	111	110	96	111	92	82	109	92	81	103
05455	FAIRFIELD	90	81	62	77	85	91	75	83	79	75	96	98	74	98	77	81	92	81	89	106
05456	FERRISBURG	101	98	86	93	103	109	90	98	92	89	112	115	88	115	94	94	108	96	103	123
05457	FRANKLIN	88	75	55	70	81	88	69	79	75	69	91	94	66	92	72	79	86	78	89	105
05458	GRAND ISLE	106	94	72	89	99	106	87	96	92	87	112	115	85	114	89	95	107	94	104	124
05459	HIGHGATE CENTER	83	75	58	72	77	82	70	77	73	71	89	90	68	87	71	73	85	75	79	95
05461	HINESBURG	92	106	109	107	103	102	98	98	92	99	116	115	101	119	98	88	115	96	87	108
05462	HUNTINGTON	84	92	92	93	89	88	87	87	82	88	103	103	88	104	85	77	102	86	76	95
05463	ISLE LA MOTTE	91	71	48	64	80	90	67	81	76	66	90	95	60	89	72	81	84	80	96	111
05464	JEFFERSONVILLE	80	88	88	89	85	84	83	83	78	84	99	98	84	99	82	74	97	82	73	91
05465	JERICHO	101	124	131	124	122	120	111	111	103	111	130	130	118	138	113	100	129	107	99	122
05468	MILTON	92	97	92	98	94	94	92	93	87	93	110	109	91	109	90	83	108	92	83	103
05471	MONTGOMERY CENTER	75	59	40	53	67	75	56	67	63	55	75	79	50	74	59	67	69	66	79	92
05472	NEW HAVEN	100	94	76	90	98	103	86	94	89	86	109	111	85	112	88	91	105	91	99	118
05473	NORTH FERRISBURG	97	105	102	103	107	110	95	100	93	95	115	117	97	120	99	94	113	97	98	119
05474	NORTH HERO	126	99	67	89	111	125	93	112	105	92	125	131	83	123	99	112	116	110	132	153
05476	RICHFORD	66	53	38	48	57	65	51	59	58	51	69	68	48	70	53	61	65	58	68	77
05477	RICHMOND	103	119	123	121	116	115	111	110	103	111	130	130	114	134	110	98	129	108	97	121
05478	SAINT ALBANS	74	71	69	71	73	77	72	73	73	70	90	86	71	91	72	72	87	73	74	85
05482	SHELBURNE	146	165	185	172	163	168	158	155	148	158	187	181	165	188	158	144	185	154	144	171
05483	SHELDON	86	77	59	73	81	87	71	79	75	71	92	94	70	94	73	77	87	77	85	102
05486	SOUTH HERO	128	100	68	90	113	127	94	114	107	94	127	133	84	125	101	114	118	112	135	156
05487	STARKSBORO	84	83	73	82	81	84	79	82	77	80	96	95	77	94	78	75	93	81	77	94
05488	SWANTON	86	73	55	70	78	86	71	79	76	70	92	92	68	92	72	78	87	77	87	99
05489	UNDERHILL	107	133	141	133	131	129	119	118	110	118	138	138	126	147	121	107	138	114	106	131
05491	VERGENNES	87	76	59	74	80	88	74	81	78	73	95	94	71	96	75	80	90	79	87	100
05492	WATERVILLE	83	72	59	72	75	84	74	78	77	73	94	90	71	93	73	78	89	77	83	91
05494	WESTFORD	97	121	129	121	119	117	108	108	100	108	126	126	115	134	111	97	126	104	96	119
05495	WILLISTON	120	139	137	142	134	131	125	125	116	128	146	146	130	150	124	110	145	121	109	138
05602	MONTPELIER	74	81	93	82	80	84	80	79	78	79	97	92	82	100	81	76	96	79	75	87
05640	ADAMANT	80	92	113	95	91	93	91	88	86	90	109	105	94	112	91	84	108	89	80	96
05641	BARRE	71	71	73	70	72	79	72	72	73	70	90	83	72	91	72	74	87	72	75	83
05647	CABOT	89	79	60	75	83	89	73	81	77	73	94	96	71	96	75	79	89	79	87	104
05648	CALAIS	80	92	113	95	90	93	91	88	86	90	109	105	93	111	91	84	108	89	80	96
05649	EAST BARRE	106	81	53	78	92	101	79	94	88	78	104	112	71	103	82	91	97	92	108	126
05650	EAST CALAIS	81	80	75	78	81	85	76	80	76	76	94	95	74	94	77	75	91	80	79	96
05651	EAST MONTPELIER	80	93	111	95	91	93	90	87	85	89	107	104	93	111	91	82	106	88	79	96
05652	EDEN	68	62	49	60	62	66	59	64	60	61	74	74	56	70	59	60	71	63	64	76
05653	EDEN MILLS	67	62	48	59	62	65	59	63	59	60	73	73	55	69	58	59	70	63	62	75
05654	GRANITEVILLE	79	77	70	73	80	87	74	77	78	72	95	89	76	100	76	80	91	76	83	92
05655	HYDE PARK	84	81	72	81	83	90	80	83	81	79	99	96	79	101	80	81	95	81	85	96
05656	JOHNSON	59	55	66	59	55	58	65	60	64	62	80	75	63	79	62	60	78	64	56	66
05658	MARSHFIELD	87	77	58	72	81	87	71	79	76	71	92	94	69	93	73	78	87	77	86	102
05660	MORETOWN	90	92	89	92	93	95	88	91	86	88	107	107	87	108	88	84	104	90	87	106
05661	MORRISVILLE	73	63	50	62	66	73	66	69	69	64	83	79	61	80	65	70	78	69	75	81
05663	NORTHFIELD	76	75	75	75	76	81	74	76	74	73	92	89	74	93	74	74	89	76	76	88
05666	NORTH MONTPELIER	75	86	106	89	85	87	85	82	81	84	102	98	87	104	85	78	101	83	75	90
05667	PLAINFIELD	73	78	86	79	78	81	76	76	74	76	92	91	77	94	76	72	90	76	72	87
05669	ROXBURY	86	67	46	61	76	85	63	76	72	63	85	90	57	84	68	77	79	75	90	105
05672	STOWE	141	123	109	119	132	145	120	134	127	119	154	157	113	152	124	131	146	133	146	168
05673	WAITSFIELD	94	98	97	96	101	105	91	96	91	91	112	113	92	115	94	91	109	94	96	115
05674	WARREN	127	100	68	90	112	126	94	113	107	93	126	133	84	125	100	114	117	112	134	155
05675	WASHINGTON	85	74	55	70	79	85	69	77	74	69	89	92	67	91	71	76	85	75	84	100
05676	WATERBURY	79	88	95	90	87	87	86	84	82	85	103	100	88	106	86	78	101	84	76	92
05677	WATERBURY CENTER	105	131	139	131	128	126	116	116	108	116	136	136	124	145	119	105	136	112	104	128
05679	WILLIAMSTOWN	84	74	57	71	79	84	69	76	73	69	89	91	67	91	71	75	84	74	82	98
05680	WOLCOTT	70	77	77	78	74	73	73	72	68	74	86	86	73	87	71	64	85	72	64	79
05681	WOODBURY	84	66	45	60	74	83	62	75	70	62	83	88	56	82	66	75	78	74	89	103
05682	WORCESTER	78	88	91	90	86	85	83	82	78	83	98	97	85	100	82	74	97	81	73	90
05701	RUTLAND	64	64	68	63	65	71	66	66	67	64	83	76	66	84	66	68	80	66	68	74
05730	BELMONT	93	73	50	66	82	93	69	83	78	68	93	97	62	91	74	83	86	82	98	114
05732	BOMOSEEN	95	77	56	73	84	95	76	86	83	75	100	100	70	99	78	87	93	85	99	111
05733	BRANDON	91	76	57	72	82	91	74	83	81	73	97	97	70	96	76	84	91	82	93	106
05734	BRIDPORT	105	73	38	69	85	95	72	89	83	71	98	108	62	96	75	87	89	88	106	124
05735	CASTLETON	87	71	53	68	77	87	71	79	77	70	92	92	66	91	72	80	86	78	89	100
05736	CENTER RUTLAND	127	89	47	84	104	116	88	109	101	87	119	131	75	116	91	106	108	107	129	151
05737	CHITTENDEN	79	98	104	98	97	95	88	87	81	87	102	102	93	109	90	79	102	84	78	97
05738	CUTTINGSVILLE	81	101	107	101	99	98	90	90	83	90	105	105	96	112	92	81	105	87	80	99
05739	DANBY	79	60	38	56	68	76	59	70	66	58	79	83	53	79	61	70	73	69	82	94
05742	EAST WALLINGFORD	93	80	59	75	86	93	74	84	80	74	97	100	71	98	77	83	91	82	93	110
05743	FAIR HAVEN	80	67	52	66	72	81	68	74	73	67	88	85	65	88	69	75	83	73	82	90
05744	FLORENCE	77	68	55	67	71	80	69	73	73	68	89	83	67	89	69	75	84	72	79	86
05746	GAYSVILLE	83	65	44	59	73	82	61	74	70	61	82	87	55	81	66	74	77	73	88	101
05747	GRANVILLE	72	57	39	51	64	72	53	64	60	53	71	75	48	71	57	64	66	63	76	88
05748	HANCOCK	72	56	39	51	64	71	53	64	60	53	71	75	48	71	57	64	66	63	76	88
05751	KILLINGTON	134	105	72	95	119	133	99	120	112	98	133	140	89	132	106	120	124	118	142	164
05753	MIDDLEBURY	88	80	80	79	82	91	85	86	86	82	106	102	81	105	84	86	102	87	89	102
05757	MIDDLETOWN SPRINGS	87	65	40	62	74	81	64	76	71	63	84	91	56	83	66	74	78	75	88	103
05758	MOUNT HOLLY	93	73	50	66	82	92	69	83	78	68	92	97	62	91	73	83	86	82	98	113
05759	NORTH CLARENDON	83	75	60	72	79	85	70	77	74	70	90	91	69	92	72	76	86	75	83	97
05760	ORWELL	97	71	42	68	81	90	71	84	80	70	95	100	63	93	73	83	87	83	98	113
05761	PAWLET	103	72	38	68	84	94	71	88	82	70	96	106	60	94	73	86	87	86	104	122
05762	PITTSFIELD	88	85	74	81	90	95	78	86	80	77	98	101	76	100	82	82	94	84	91	107
05763	PITTSFORD	82	76	62	74	79	85	72	78	75	72	92	91	71	94	74	76	88	76	82	95
05764	POULTNEY	73	55	35	52	61	70	56	65	63	55	75	75	50	72	57	66	69	64	76	84
05765	PROCTOR	68	75	80	71	76	83	73	73	74	71	92	82	76	97	76	76	89	72	77	81
05766	RIPTON	66	75	93	78	74	76	75	72	71	74	89	86	77	92	75	69	88	73	66	79
	VERMONT	85	80	74	78	82	89	79	83	81	78	100	98	77	100	80	82	96	83	86	99
	UNITED STATES	100	100	100	100	100	100	100	100	100	100	100	100	100	100	100	100	100	100	100	100

VERMONT

POPULATION CHANGE

A 05767-05907

ZIP CODE		POPULATION			2000-2004 ANNUAL RATE		HOUSEHOLDS					FAMILIES		
# POST OFFICE NAME	COUNTY FIPS CODE	2000	2004	2009	% Rate	State Centile	2000	2004	2009	% Annual Rate 2000-2004	2004 Average HH Size	2000	2004	% Annual Rate 2000-2004
05767 ROCHESTER	027	1337	1365	1415	0.5	35	585	612	649	1.1	2.21	377	392	0.9
05769 SALISBURY	001	1157	1298	1411	2.7	98	464	536	595	3.5	2.40	330	379	3.3
05770 SHOREHAM	001	988	1091	1176	2.4	96	362	409	449	2.9	2.67	274	309	2.9
05772 STOCKBRIDGE	027	647	667	696	0.7	57	270	283	302	1.1	2.36	185	194	1.1
05773 WALLINGFORD	021	2328	2358	2409	0.3	20	940	975	1019	0.9	2.40	674	695	0.7
05774 WELLS	021	1007	1038	1069	0.7	57	421	442	463	1.2	2.35	302	315	1.0
05775 WEST PAWLET	021	671	727	768	1.9	93	275	302	324	2.2	2.41	186	203	2.1
05776 WEST RUPERT	003	697	725	765	0.9	68	292	309	332	1.3	2.35	200	210	1.2
05777 WEST RUTLAND	021	3513	3578	3660	0.4	29	1380	1437	1500	1.0	2.49	942	974	0.8
05778 WHITING	001	723	779	829	1.8	90	272	299	324	2.3	2.61	198	217	2.2
05819 SAINT JOHNSBURY	005	9126	9597	10186	1.2	77	3779	4062	4407	1.7	2.27	2366	2532	1.6
05820 ALBANY	019	618	624	636	0.2	15	244	254	266	1.0	2.46	172	178	0.8
05821 BARNET	005	1505	1542	1614	0.6	40	576	603	645	1.1	2.48	400	416	0.9
05822 BARTON	019	1802	1832	1877	0.4	25	736	769	809	1.0	2.37	479	498	0.9
05824 CONCORD	009	1125	1181	1221	1.2	76	443	475	501	1.7	2.46	303	324	1.6
05825 COVENTRY	019	137	141	146	0.7	52	45	47	50	1.0	3.00	34	36	1.4
05826 CRAFTSBURY	019	824	823	838	0.0	7	310	318	333	0.6	2.37	219	223	0.4
05827 CRAFTSBURY COMMON	019	398	398	406	0.0	8	153	157	165	0.6	2.36	108	110	0.4
05828 DANVILLE	005	1743	1827	1935	1.1	74	677	724	781	1.6	2.51	487	518	1.5
05829 DERBY	019	1548	1555	1591	0.1	12	648	668	700	0.7	2.30	460	472	0.6
05830 DERBY LINE	019	1682	1720	1768	0.5	38	671	698	732	0.9	2.46	484	502	0.9
05832 EAST BURKE	005	574	606	645	1.3	78	256	277	302	1.9	2.19	177	190	1.7
05833 EAST CHARLESTON	019	189	190	193	0.1	12	76	78	82	0.6	2.44	55	56	0.4
05836 EAST HARDWICK	005	843	840	875	-0.1	6	319	323	342	0.3	2.60	225	227	0.2
05837 EAST HAVEN	009	301	296	294	-0.4	2	119	120	121	0.2	2.47	87	87	0.0
05839 GLOVER	019	670	680	695	0.4	23	258	269	282	1.0	2.42	181	187	0.8
05841 GREENSBORO	019	475	474	482	-0.1	7	193	198	207	0.6	2.31	133	135	0.4
05842 GREENSBORO BEND	005	453	467	487	0.7	57	184	194	208	1.3	2.36	131	138	1.2
05843 HARDWICK	005	2686	2738	2872	0.5	31	1029	1061	1130	0.7	2.58	725	745	0.6
05845 IRASBURG	019	973	1083	1165	2.6	97	367	420	465	3.2	2.58	287	327	3.1
05846 ISLAND POND	009	1354	1336	1334	-0.3	3	572	575	585	0.1	2.32	387	387	0.0
05847 LOWELL	019	743	764	787	0.7	52	272	286	303	1.2	2.67	206	215	1.0
05850 LYNDON CENTER	005	166	169	177	0.4	28	70	72	77	0.7	2.26	38	39	0.6
05851 LYNDONVILLE	005	6049	6269	6583	0.8	64	2256	2388	2562	1.4	2.41	1504	1585	1.2
05853 MORGAN	019	670	711	745	1.4	84	248	268	286	1.8	2.65	184	198	1.7
05855 NEWPORT	019	7843	8004	8209	0.5	35	3153	3304	3479	1.1	2.30	1983	2066	1.0
05857 NEWPORT CENTER	019	1477	1514	1558	0.6	41	572	605	640	1.3	2.50	426	449	1.2
05858 NORTH CONCORD	009	386	393	397	0.4	28	150	155	160	0.8	2.52	106	109	0.7
05859 NORTH TROY	019	1920	1953	2001	0.4	26	742	779	821	1.2	2.50	521	545	1.1
05860 ORLEANS	019	2229	2292	2360	0.7	52	910	956	1008	1.2	2.31	621	649	1.0
05862 PEACHAM	005	195	200	209	0.6	43	87	91	98	1.1	2.20	61	64	1.1
05866 SHEFFIELD	005	787	851	916	1.9	91	297	329	362	2.4	2.59	222	245	2.4
05867 SUTTON	005	990	1071	1154	1.9	92	362	401	441	2.4	2.67	259	286	2.4
05868 TROY	019	72	73	75	0.3	22	34	36	38	1.4	2.03	25	26	0.9
05871 WEST BURKE	005	1457	1540	1640	1.3	82	571	617	670	1.8	2.50	420	451	1.7
05872 WEST CHARLESTON	019	651	654	666	0.1	12	259	267	279	0.7	2.45	187	191	0.5
05873 WEST DANVILLE	005	1062	1084	1138	0.5	35	417	435	466	1.0	2.49	300	312	0.9
05874 WESTFIELD	019	459	472	486	0.7	52	180	191	202	1.4	2.43	129	136	1.3
05875 WEST GLOVER	019	522	528	540	0.3	19	215	224	235	1.0	2.30	149	155	0.9
05901 AVERILL	009	8	9	9	2.8	99	3	3	4	0.0	3.00	2	2	0.0
05902 BEECHER FALLS	009	508	497	494	-0.5	1	214	214	216	0.0	2.32	149	148	-0.2
05903 CANAAN	009	570	557	555	-0.5	0	227	226	229	-0.1	2.46	158	157	-0.2
05904 GILMAN	009	37	38	38	0.6	48	14	14	15	0.0	2.64	10	10	0.0
05905 GUILDHALL	009	819	865	893	1.3	80	331	358	376	1.9	2.42	232	249	1.7
05906 LUNENBURG	009	1459	1450	1449	-0.2	4	568	575	584	0.3	2.50	403	406	0.2
05907 NORTON	009	218	237	248	2.0	93	93	103	110	2.4	2.30	64	71	2.5
VERMONT					0.8					1.3	2.40			1.2
UNITED STATES					1.2					1.3	2.58			1.1

#	POST OFFICE NAME	White 2000	White 2004	Black 2000	Black 2004	Asian/Pacific 2000	Asian/Pacific 2004	% Hispanic Origin 2000	% Hispanic Origin 2004	0-4	5-9	10-14	15-19	20-24	25-44	45-64	65-84	85+	18+	MEDIAN AGE 2004	% 2004 Males	% 2004 Females
05767	ROCHESTER	98.4	98.4	0.2	0.2	0.2	0.3	1.1	1.2	4.1	5.4	6.2	6.2	5.1	22.9	32.7	15.4	2.1	79.7	45.1	48.6	51.4
05769	SALISBURY	98.2	98.2	0.0	0.0	0.3	0.3	0.4	0.3	5.9	6.2	6.9	6.4	4.9	26.3	30.8	11.6	1.2	76.5	41.0	50.2	49.8
05770	SHOREHAM	98.6	98.4	0.6	0.7	0.3	0.5	0.5	0.6	4.9	6.6	8.2	8.3	4.7	25.9	29.0	11.6	1.0	74.4	40.1	49.9	50.1
05772	STOCKBRIDGE	98.3	98.1	0.6	0.8	0.6	0.8	0.5	0.5	6.5	6.8	6.0	4.5	3.9	25.5	31.8	13.2	2.0	77.8	43.4	51.3	48.7
05773	WALLINGFORD	98.4	98.3	0.1	0.1	0.3	0.4	0.5	0.6	5.0	5.3	6.1	6.6	5.4	25.0	32.7	12.4	1.5	79.2	43.0	48.9	51.1
05774	WELLS	98.7	98.7	0.4	0.4	0.0	0.0	0.9	1.1	4.1	4.3	6.3	6.3	5.1	22.5	32.8	16.9	1.9	81.5	45.9	49.1	50.9
05775	WEST PAWLET	98.5	98.4	0.3	0.4	0.0	0.0	1.2	1.4	5.9	6.5	8.0	6.2	4.8	23.3	29.0	13.9	2.5	75.7	42.0	52.1	47.9
05776	WEST RUPERT	99.0	98.8	0.3	0.4	0.4	0.4	0.7	0.8	3.7	4.1	6.5	6.1	4.4	21.7	32.6	18.2	2.8	81.8	47.2	49.7	50.3
05777	WEST RUTLAND	98.2	97.9	0.3	0.4	0.6	0.8	0.5	0.5	4.9	5.5	6.7	6.5	6.3	26.9	29.6	12.1	1.6	79.0	41.1	49.2	50.8
05778	WHITING	98.3	98.1	0.3	0.4	0.4	0.5	0.6	0.5	5.4	6.3	6.9	6.9	5.7	25.6	30.4	11.7	1.2	76.9	41.0	50.2	49.8
05819	SAINT JOHNSBURY	96.7	96.4	0.5	0.6	0.6	0.7	1.0	1.1	5.3	5.4	6.3	7.2	7.0	24.9	26.9	14.3	2.8	78.9	40.9	49.1	50.9
05820	ALBANY	97.6	97.4	0.2	0.2	0.2	0.2	0.2	0.2	7.7	7.4	6.1	6.1	4.8	26.8	29.7	10.4	1.1	75.0	39.7	51.0	49.0
05821	BARNET	97.3	97.1	0.5	0.7	0.5	0.6	0.5	0.5	4.9	5.6	6.9	7.7	5.6	22.1	32.5	13.0	1.7	77.7	43.3	50.3	49.7
05822	BARTON	97.3	97.2	0.4	0.5	0.1	0.1	0.3	0.3	4.5	5.0	7.3	7.3	6.4	24.6	29.1	13.6	2.2	78.7	41.5	49.3	50.7
05824	CONCORD	97.1	97.0	0.1	0.2	0.2	0.3	1.2	1.0	7.2	7.3	6.8	6.0	4.8	27.4	28.0	11.6	0.9	74.8	39.1	50.2	49.8
05825	COVENTRY	97.8	97.9	0.0	0.7	0.0	0.0	0.7	0.7	6.4	6.4	7.1	7.1	7.1	27.0	30.5	7.8	0.7	75.2	37.8	51.8	48.2
05826	CRAFTSBURY	96.7	96.5	0.4	0.5	0.5	0.5	1.1	1.3	5.0	5.7	6.3	5.2	4.7	26.1	27.2	15.9	3.8	80.3	42.8	47.6	52.4
05827	CRAFTSBURY COMMON	97.0	96.5	0.3	0.5	0.3	0.5	1.0	1.3	5.3	5.8	6.3	5.5	5.0	26.4	27.4	15.1	3.3	79.9	42.2	48.7	51.3
05828	DANVILLE	99.1	99.0	0.2	0.2	0.1	0.2	0.5	0.5	5.4	6.4	7.8	6.7	4.3	22.9	31.0	13.3	2.2	76.2	42.8	47.8	52.2
05829	DERBY	97.6	97.6	0.2	0.2	0.3	0.4	0.8	0.8	6.4	6.7	7.4	6.8	5.7	23.5	28.0	13.3	2.2	75.0	40.9	50.6	49.4
05830	DERBY LINE	97.6	97.4	0.3	0.4	0.4	0.5	0.3	0.4	6.3	6.9	8.0	6.7	5.4	25.2	27.5	12.2	1.7	74.1	39.4	49.0	51.0
05832	EAST BURKE	96.7	96.4	0.4	0.5	0.2	0.2	1.1	1.0	5.9	6.3	6.3	5.1	4.5	26.6	33.3	11.1	1.0	78.6	42.1	51.0	49.0
05833	EAST CHARLESTON	96.3	95.8	0.0	0.0	0.5	0.5	0.5	0.5	4.2	5.3	7.4	5.8	6.3	23.7	35.3	11.1	1.1	79.5	42.9	48.4	51.6
05836	EAST HARDWICK	98.1	97.9	0.1	0.1	0.1	0.2	0.4	0.4	6.4	7.0	8.0	6.8	5.6	26.9	27.9	10.1	1.3	74.3	38.7	49.5	50.5
05837	EAST HAVEN	97.3	97.0	0.3	0.3	0.3	0.3	0.7	0.7	5.4	5.7	6.8	6.4	5.4	26.0	28.7	13.9	1.7	78.0	41.9	48.3	51.7
05839	GLOVER	96.4	96.2	0.2	0.2	0.2	0.3	0.6	0.7	5.3	3.7	7.1	6.6	4.3	21.0	37.7	11.6	2.8	79.7	46.0	50.3	49.7
05841	GREENSBORO	96.4	96.2	0.2	0.2	0.0	0.0	0.6	0.6	4.6	5.1	5.1	6.8	4.0	25.3	29.8	15.0	4.4	80.2	44.4	46.6	53.4
05842	GREENSBORO BEND	96.9	97.0	0.0	0.0	0.0	0.0	0.7	0.6	5.1	5.6	6.2	7.1	4.5	25.5	30.6	12.6	2.8	78.2	42.5	48.6	51.4
05843	HARDWICK	97.8	97.7	0.1	0.1	0.1	0.1	0.4	0.5	6.7	7.0	8.8	7.6	6.2	26.3	25.9	10.4	1.1	72.8	37.2	48.7	51.3
05845	IRASBURG	98.6	98.4	0.1	0.1	0.0	0.2	0.3	0.4	6.4	6.8	7.9	6.4	5.5	28.6	26.2	11.4	0.8	75.0	38.8	48.9	51.2
05846	ISLAND POND	95.3	95.3	0.2	0.2	0.4	0.5	0.3	0.3	4.9	5.5	7.8	6.7	6.7	22.3	28.6	15.5	2.1	77.8	42.0	48.7	51.4
05847	LOWELL	98.0	97.8	1.2	1.3	0.0	0.0	1.2	1.3	6.2	6.0	9.2	7.5	5.6	27.9	26.4	10.5	0.8	72.9	36.9	50.8	49.2
05850	LYNDON CENTER	97.6	98.2	0.0	0.0	0.6	0.6	1.2	1.2	5.3	4.7	5.9	10.1	10.7	30.8	20.7	10.1	1.8	78.7	31.5	50.3	49.7
05851	LYNDONVILLE	97.7	97.5	0.3	0.3	0.6	0.7	0.5	0.5	5.0	5.1	6.4	10.1	10.3	23.9	25.7	11.6	1.9	79.3	36.9	50.4	49.6
05853	MORGAN	97.6	97.3	0.5	0.4	0.2	0.3	0.6	0.7	6.1	7.2	9.4	7.5	3.8	26.6	29.0	10.0	0.6	71.2	38.5	50.1	49.9
05855	NEWPORT	96.7	96.4	0.6	0.8	0.5	0.6	1.1	1.2	5.8	6.0	6.6	6.7	6.5	25.4	26.4	14.2	2.4	77.4	40.3	49.9	50.1
05857	NEWPORT CENTER	97.4	97.2	0.3	0.3	0.3	0.5	0.5	0.6	5.2	5.6	8.0	6.3	5.3	26.4	30.7	12.0	0.6	77.2	41.0	49.1	51.0
05858	NORTH CONCORD	97.2	97.5	0.3	0.3	0.3	0.3	1.0	0.8	6.6	6.9	6.9	6.4	5.3	26.2	27.7	12.7	1.3	75.6	39.6	48.9	51.2
05859	NORTH TROY	98.0	97.9	0.1	0.1	0.3	0.4	0.5	0.5	5.5	5.7	6.4	7.1	6.6	27.0	28.5	11.6	1.3	77.9	39.5	50.6	49.4
05860	ORLEANS	97.4	97.1	0.2	0.3	0.4	0.4	0.3	0.4	5.4	5.8	7.1	6.1	6.0	24.0	29.4	13.6	2.8	77.9	42.2	49.7	50.3
05862	PEACHAM	98.5	98.5	0.5	0.5	0.5	0.5	1.0	1.0	3.5	6.0	10.0	7.0	3.0	18.5	36.0	14.5	1.5	76.0	45.9	50.0	50.0
05866	SHEFFIELD	97.7	97.4	0.1	0.1	0.1	0.1	0.9	0.8	5.5	6.1	7.6	7.3	5.1	26.2	31.7	9.8	0.7	76.3	40.3	51.4	48.7
05867	SUTTON	98.0	97.9	0.1	0.1	0.2	0.3	0.4	0.6	6.3	7.1	7.8	6.8	5.9	26.1	28.5	10.7	0.8	73.6	38.8	50.2	49.8
05868	TROY	97.2	98.6	0.0	0.0	0.0	0.0	0.3	0.0	5.5	5.5	5.5	8.2	8.2	30.1	24.7	11.6	1.4	76.7	37.1	52.1	48.0
05871	WEST BURKE	97.5	97.3	0.1	0.2	0.2	0.4	1.2	1.3	6.5	7.1	7.5	6.7	5.8	27.5	28.2	9.7	1.0	74.6	37.1	52.0	48.1
05872	WEST CHARLESTON	96.5	96.3	0.0	0.0	0.3	0.5	0.5	0.5	4.4	5.4	7.3	5.8	6.4	24.3	34.3	11.0	1.1	79.2	42.1	49.2	50.8
05873	WEST DANVILLE	98.6	98.4	0.4	0.5	0.1	0.2	0.5	0.5	5.4	6.5	8.2	6.8	4.5	24.4	31.2	11.5	1.6	75.6	41.5	49.1	50.9
05874	WESTFIELD	97.0	97.3	0.2	0.2	0.2	0.4	1.1	1.1	5.1	5.7	6.4	5.5	4.9	24.2	34.3	12.7	1.3	78.6	43.8	50.0	50.0
05875	WEST GLOVER	96.7	96.4	0.4	0.4	0.2	0.2	0.4	0.6	5.9	4.9	6.8	6.6	4.7	23.3	33.7	11.7	2.3	78.0	43.5	50.4	49.6
05901	AVERILL	100.0	100.0	0.0	0.0	0.0	0.0	0.0	0.0	0.0	0.0	0.0	0.0	22.2	77.8	0.0	0.0	0.0	100.0	31.3	55.6	44.4
05902	BEECHER FALLS	95.9	96.0	0.2	0.2	0.0	0.0	0.2	0.2	4.8	5.4	8.1	8.3	7.0	24.6	29.4	10.9	1.6	76.9	40.7	50.7	49.3
05903	CANAAN	95.8	95.7	0.2	0.2	0.2	0.2	0.4	0.4	4.9	5.4	7.9	8.1	6.8	25.0	29.4	11.1	1.4	77.0	40.9	49.9	50.1
05904	GILMAN	97.3	97.4	0.0	0.0	0.0	0.0	0.0	0.0	5.3	5.3	5.3	5.3	5.3	31.6	21.1	21.1	0.0	84.2	41.3	52.6	47.4
05905	GUILDHALL	96.7	96.8	0.2	0.2	0.2	0.2	0.1	0.2	4.3	6.1	7.9	6.4	3.7	24.5	30.3	15.4	1.5	77.9	43.4	51.9	48.1
05906	LUNENBURG	97.5	97.5	0.1	0.1	0.2	0.2	0.6	0.6	5.9	5.9	7.0	7.5	5.8	28.1	25.7	12.9	1.5	76.1	39.2	51.5	48.6
05907	NORTON	96.8	96.2	0.5	0.4	0.5	0.4	0.0	0.0	3.8	6.3	8.4	6.3	3.4	23.6	31.2	15.2	1.7	77.2	43.9	53.6	46.4
	VERMONT	96.8	96.4	0.5	0.6	0.9	1.1	0.9	1.0	5.5	5.9	6.9	7.5	7.2	26.5	27.5	11.2	1.8	77.5	39.1	49.1	50.9
	UNITED STATES	75.1	73.6	12.3	12.5	3.8	4.2	12.5	14.1	6.9	6.7	7.2	7.0	7.3	28.6	23.8	10.8	1.7	75.1	36.0	49.1	50.9

VERMONT

INCOME

C 05767-05907

# POST OFFICE NAME	2004 Per Capita Income	2004 HH Income Base	Less than $25,000	$25,000 to $49,999	$50,000 to $99,999	$100,000 to $149,999	$150,000 or More	2004	2009	2004 National Centile	2004 State Centile	2004 Home Value Base	Less than $50,000	$50,000 to $89,999	$90,000 to $174,999	$175,000 to $399,999	$400,000 or More	2004 Median Home Value
05767 ROCHESTER	23382	612	24.0	39.2	27.9	5.7	3.1	40909	46700	49	37	447	5.8	13.0	46.1	31.5	3.6	140720
05769 SALISBURY	23200	536	23.3	33.0	34.7	4.5	4.5	44328	49643	60	52	443	4.5	8.6	43.8	36.6	6.6	161623
05770 SHOREHAM	20048	409	21.8	36.7	32.0	7.3	2.2	42958	47921	56	46	325	4.9	10.2	44.6	33.5	6.8	155793
05772 STOCKBRIDGE	23493	283	23.7	36.4	31.8	5.3	2.8	42209	47753	54	42	247	6.5	12.6	50.6	27.9	2.4	134583
05773 WALLINGFORD	20733	975	26.4	32.7	32.8	6.3	1.9	43446	48400	57	48	805	3.9	12.1	52.8	28.6	2.7	142101
05774 WELLS	18941	442	33.9	32.1	28.5	3.6	1.8	35866	39902	31	15	373	8.6	11.0	52.8	24.7	3.0	130227
05775 WEST PAWLET	22262	302	31.5	30.1	29.5	5.3	3.6	37585	41963	38	22	232	1.7	16.4	45.3	28.5	8.2	150000
05776 WEST RUPERT	23817	309	26.2	33.3	30.1	4.5	5.8	42358	48006	54	43	256	4.7	4.3	46.5	34.4	10.2	166250
05777 WEST RUTLAND	19915	1437	26.6	33.1	33.3	5.5	1.5	42758	48205	55	45	1118	3.7	10.9	67.2	17.2	1.1	126968
05778 WHITING	25112	299	22.1	31.4	31.8	8.7	6.0	46600	51714	65	65	250	3.2	9.6	40.4	36.0	10.8	169595
05819 SAINT JOHNSBURY	19799	4062	37.2	27.7	27.9	4.5	2.7	35847	40356	31	14	2615	4.7	16.1	60.1	17.4	1.7	120313
05820 ALBANY	17494	254	34.7	35.8	24.4	3.9	1.2	33531	36519	22	7	208	17.8	20.7	43.8	17.8	0.0	103788
05821 BARNET	20127	603	30.7	32.8	27.4	7.0	2.2	39766	44036	45	32	504	2.6	13.3	52.0	29.2	3.0	133582
05822 BARTON	15759	769	40.3	38.1	17.6	2.6	1.4	31301	34402	16	5	573	11.0	23.2	48.5	16.1	1.2	108995
05824 CONCORD	18065	475	29.5	34.5	32.2	2.7	1.1	39420	43850	44	28	391	11.0	24.6	49.4	14.1	1.0	104972
05825 COVENTRY	13809	47	36.2	38.3	23.4	2.1	0.0	34284	40000	25	9	38	18.4	21.1	47.4	13.2	0.0	103125
05826 CRAFTSBURY	18822	318	35.5	32.7	24.2	4.4	3.1	37354	41392	37	22	261	10.3	15.7	44.1	26.1	3.8	124219
05827 CRAFTSBURY COMMON	18825	157	35.0	33.1	24.8	4.5	2.6	37043	40282	36	20	129	10.9	17.1	45.7	24.0	2.3	120313
05828 DANVILLE	21360	724	23.1	31.4	36.3	6.2	3.0	46935	52061	66	66	613	2.6	13.9	52.7	28.4	2.5	136883
05829 DERBY	19548	668	34.4	33.4	25.9	4.2	2.1	35483	39058	29	12	548	15.0	16.2	49.1	18.3	1.5	116346
05830 DERBY LINE	16977	698	30.4	43.3	21.4	4.3	0.7	35140	40438	28	10	532	7.0	21.4	59.0	11.5	1.1	107624
05832 EAST BURKE	23187	277	27.4	31.8	33.9	4.3	2.5	41664	46543	52	40	223	4.9	13.0	54.3	23.3	4.5	132292
05833 EAST CHARLESTON	16790	78	39.7	34.6	19.2	3.9	2.6	30729	32312	14	4	63	14.3	22.2	46.0	17.5	0.0	107955
05836 EAST HARDWICK	17219	323	31.9	34.4	27.2	5.0	1.6	38422	41860	41	26	259	8.1	19.3	54.1	18.2	0.4	116189
05837 EAST HAVEN	16936	120	35.8	36.7	20.8	4.2	2.5	32700	35215	20	6	102	9.8	31.4	42.2	14.7	2.0	101136
05839 GLOVER	17433	269	30.1	34.6	30.9	3.0	1.5	37200	41745	36	21	230	7.4	23.9	45.7	21.3	1.7	112000
05841 GREENSBORO	20904	198	28.3	40.9	22.7	5.1	3.0	37828	43254	39	23	162	6.2	13.6	31.5	30.3	18.5	169444
05842 GREENSBORO BEND	19336	194	29.9	37.6	26.3	4.1	2.1	36628	41411	34	17	161	9.3	18.6	39.1	23.0	9.9	122845
05843 HARDWICK	16662	1061	34.8	35.3	23.9	3.9	2.1	35711	39274	30	13	791	11.6	26.8	48.8	12.4	0.4	103770
05845 IRASBURG	18514	420	26.0	40.7	26.4	3.8	3.1	38623	42349	42	26	341	8.5	19.7	53.7	16.7	1.5	112639
05846 ISLAND POND	14778	575	44.5	34.8	17.4	3.1	0.2	27428	29206	8	1	406	8.6	41.4	38.4	10.8	0.7	90000
05847 LOWELL	13599	286	40.6	39.2	17.5	1.1	1.8	29409	31572	11	2	240	14.6	32.9	47.1	4.2	1.3	92500
05850 LYNDON CENTER	14361	72	44.4	31.9	22.2	1.4	0.0	30000	31725	12	3	29	3.5	13.8	75.9	6.9	0.0	118750
05851 LYNDONVILLE	18673	2388	30.4	34.8	28.4	3.6	2.8	37177	41560	36	20	1729	12.2	16.7	54.9	14.8	1.5	115895
05853 MORGAN	15487	268	34.3	36.6	23.1	5.2	0.8	36666	37037	23	7	221	12.7	18.6	42.1	23.5	3.2	116159
05855 NEWPORT	18456	3304	40.3	27.7	26.2	4.2	1.7	31838	35013	17	6	2129	5.7	22.2	50.3	19.2	2.7	114508
05857 NEWPORT CENTER	19560	605	26.8	37.7	26.9	5.3	3.3	37917	42078	39	24	513	6.2	20.7	47.4	21.4	4.3	120916
05858 NORTH CONCORD	16792	155	33.6	36.8	25.8	3.2	0.7	35165	37559	28	10	130	11.5	30.0	46.2	12.3	0.0	99167
05859 NORTH TROY	16261	779	35.0	36.7	23.9	3.5	0.9	35407	39689	29	11	599	7.4	26.2	47.6	17.2	1.7	108912
05860 ORLEANS	16506	956	39.2	35.8	21.2	2.9	0.8	30504	33393	14	4	732	8.3	30.2	48.0	11.2	2.3	102397
05862 PEACHAM	24206	91	28.6	30.8	30.8	8.8	1.1	43057	48444	56	47	76	0.0	9.2	42.1	44.7	4.0	171429
05866 SHEFFIELD	16141	329	31.9	32.8	31.9	3.0	0.3	35300	38846	29	11	280	13.6	25.0	47.9	13.2	0.4	104032
05867 SUTTON	16924	401	28.4	36.2	30.7	4.0	0.8	38574	43587	41	26	343	8.2	12.5	56.3	12.8	0.3	108875
05868 TROY	22256	36	30.6	33.3	30.6	5.6	0.0	40000	42361	46	34	30	3.3	16.7	60.0	20.0	0.0	128571
05871 WEST BURKE	21560	617	32.1	33.2	25.5	4.5	4.7	36984	40757	35	19	506	7.5	20.4	57.7	13.8	0.6	113036
05872 WEST CHARLESTON	16623	267	41.2	34.1	18.4	3.8	2.6	30107	32058	12	4	217	13.8	21.2	47.0	17.1	0.9	109295
05873 WEST DANVILLE	21004	435	24.4	34.9	31.0	7.1	2.5	44071	48835	59	51	368	3.8	16.3	49.7	28.3	1.9	135000
05874 WESTFIELD	18424	191	30.9	35.1	27.2	4.2	2.6	35937	40000	31	15	162	10.5	14.2	49.4	21.6	4.3	121094
05875 WEST GLOVER	17957	224	33.9	35.3	26.8	3.1	0.9	35000	39128	28	9	185	11.4	22.7	44.3	20.0	1.6	109926
05901 AVERILL	0	0	0.0	0.0	0.0	0.0	0.0	0	0	0	0	2	0.0	0.0	100.0	0.0	0.0	112500
05902 BEECHER FALLS	17003	214	34.6	36.9	27.1	0.9	0.5	36485	40694	33	16	168	8.9	25.0	56.0	9.5	0.6	105978
05903 CANAAN	16093	226	35.0	37.2	25.7	1.3	0.9	36630	40730	34	17	178	9.6	25.8	53.9	9.6	1.1	104545
05904 GILMAN	14934	14	28.6	35.7	35.7	0.0	0.0	40000	42343	46	34	11	9.1	36.4	54.6	0.0	0.0	95000
05905 GUILDHALL	16388	358	41.9	32.1	21.0	3.4	1.7	30000	31904	12	3	304	8.6	29.9	48.7	9.9	3.0	101250
05906 LUNENBURG	15571	575	35.3	36.7	25.2	2.1	0.7	33538	37097	23	7	469	16.2	32.8	41.8	8.7	0.4	91023
05907 NORTON	16921	103	41.8	31.1	21.4	3.9	1.9	29673	31492	12	2	87	8.1	28.7	50.6	9.2	3.5	102344
VERMONT	23579		25.6	30.1	32.7	7.7	3.9	44976	50578				5.7	9.3	47.1	32.6	5.3	151623
UNITED STATES	25866		24.7	27.1	30.8	10.9	6.5	48124	56710				10.9	15.0	33.7	30.1	10.4	145905

#	POST OFFICE NAME	FINANCIAL SERVICES				THE HOME						ENTERTAINMENT						PERSONAL			
						Home Improvements		Furnishings													
		Auto Loan	Home Loan	Invest- ments	Retire- ment Plans	Home Repair	Lawn & Garden	Comput- ers & Hard- ware	Major Appli- ances	TV, Radio, Sound Equip- ment	Furni- ture	Dine out/ Carry out	Sports Equip- ment	Fees & Tickets	Toys & Games	Travel	Cable TV	Apparel & Services	Auto Repairs	Health Insur- ance	Pets & Supplies
05767	ROCHESTER	91	67	40	62	77	86	65	79	74	64	87	94	57	86	68	78	80	78	94	109
05769	SALISBURY	94	74	51	68	83	94	71	84	80	70	94	98	64	93	75	85	88	83	99	114
05770	SHOREHAM	97	68	35	64	79	88	67	83	77	66	90	99	57	88	69	81	82	81	98	115
05772	STOCKBRIDGE	94	74	50	66	83	93	69	84	79	69	93	98	62	92	74	84	87	82	99	114
05773	WALLINGFORD	74	71	63	67	74	81	67	72	70	66	85	84	66	87	70	72	82	71	78	89
05774	WELLS	75	59	40	53	67	75	56	67	63	55	75	79	50	74	59	67	70	66	79	92
05775	WEST PAWLET	97	68	35	64	79	88	67	83	77	66	90	100	57	89	69	81	82	82	98	115
05776	WEST RUPERT	95	74	51	67	84	94	70	84	79	69	94	99	63	93	75	85	87	83	100	115
05777	WEST RUTLAND	72	69	62	67	71	78	68	70	71	66	87	81	68	90	69	72	83	69	75	82
05778	WHITING	117	83	46	78	96	108	82	101	94	81	110	121	70	108	85	99	101	99	119	139
05819	SAINT JOHNSBURY	69	60	55	60	63	71	62	66	66	61	80	76	60	79	63	67	76	66	71	79
05820	ALBANY	81	54	25	47	61	71	52	65	63	53	74	78	44	70	53	68	67	65	81	93
05821	BARNET	88	66	41	61	75	84	63	77	72	63	85	91	56	84	67	77	79	76	91	106
05822	BARTON	64	46	28	44	52	61	49	56	55	47	65	65	42	62	49	58	59	56	67	73
05824	CONCORD	76	59	40	54	67	75	56	67	63	55	75	79	50	74	60	68	70	66	80	92
05825	COVENTRY	66	60	47	58	60	63	57	61	58	59	72	71	54	68	57	57	69	61	61	73
05826	CRAFTSBURY	83	58	31	55	68	76	58	71	66	57	78	86	49	76	60	70	71	70	85	99
05827	CRAFTSBURY COMMON	83	58	29	54	67	75	57	70	66	56	77	84	48	75	59	69	70	69	84	98
05828	DANVILLE	97	68	36	64	79	89	67	83	77	66	91	100	57	89	70	81	83	82	99	115
05829	DERBY	78	60	38	55	65	73	58	67	65	58	78	79	53	76	59	68	72	66	78	89
05830	DERBY LINE	61	57	51	53	60	67	55	59	60	54	73	68	55	76	58	63	69	58	67	73
05832	EAST BURKE	86	67	46	61	76	85	64	76	72	63	86	89	58	85	68	77	80	75	90	104
05833	EAST CHARLESTON	69	54	37	49	61	69	51	62	58	51	69	72	46	68	55	62	64	61	73	85
05836	EAST HARDWICK	71	59	45	58	63	71	60	66	65	59	78	76	57	77	61	66	73	65	73	81
05837	EAST HAVEN	71	56	38	50	63	70	52	63	59	52	70	74	47	69	56	63	65	62	75	86
05839	GLOVER	73	57	39	51	64	72	54	65	61	53	72	76	48	71	57	65	67	64	76	88
05841	GREENSBORO	83	65	44	59	74	83	62	74	70	61	83	87	55	81	66	74	77	73	88	101
05842	GREENSBORO BEND	76	63	45	58	69	76	59	69	65	59	79	81	55	78	62	68	73	67	78	91
05843	HARDWICK	68	57	44	57	60	68	58	63	62	57	75	72	56	75	58	63	71	62	69	75
05845	IRASBURG	86	60	32	57	70	79	60	74	69	59	81	89	51	79	62	72	73	73	88	102
05846	ISLAND POND	58	46	31	41	51	58	43	52	49	43	58	61	39	57	46	52	54	51	61	71
05847	LOWELL	62	48	33	44	54	61	46	55	52	45	61	64	41	60	49	55	57	54	65	75
05850	LYNDON CENTER	43	45	51	46	44	46	48	46	46	46	58	55	48	59	47	44	57	47	42	49
05851	LYNDONVILLE	73	62	48	60	66	74	63	68	67	61	81	79	59	80	63	69	76	67	76	84
05853	MORGAN	70	55	37	49	62	69	52	62	58	51	69	73	46	68	55	62	64	61	73	85
05855	NEWPORT	67	55	44	53	58	67	59	63	63	57	76	72	54	74	58	65	72	63	70	75
05857	NEWPORT CENTER	85	65	41	62	73	80	62	74	70	62	83	89	57	83	65	72	77	73	85	100
05858	NORTH CONCORD	72	56	38	51	63	71	53	64	60	53	71	75	48	70	57	64	66	63	76	88
05859	NORTH TROY	65	55	42	53	59	65	54	60	58	53	70	70	51	70	55	60	66	59	66	75
05860	ORLEANS	64	49	33	46	55	63	50	58	56	49	67	66	45	64	51	60	61	57	69	75
05862	PEACHAM	90	71	48	64	80	90	67	80	76	66	89	94	60	88	71	81	83	79	95	110
05866	SHEFFIELD	67	60	45	57	63	67	55	61	58	55	71	73	54	73	57	60	68	59	66	79
05867	SUTTON	77	60	41	54	68	76	57	68	64	56	76	80	51	75	60	69	71	67	81	93
05868	TROY	73	64	48	61	68	73	59	66	63	59	77	79	58	78	61	65	73	64	72	86
05871	WEST BURKE	87	71	53	69	77	87	71	80	77	70	93	92	66	92	73	80	87	78	90	100
05872	WEST CHARLESTON	69	54	37	49	61	69	51	62	58	51	68	72	46	68	54	62	64	61	73	84
05873	WEST DANVILLE	91	68	42	63	78	87	65	80	75	65	88	95	57	87	69	79	81	78	94	110
05874	WESTFIELD	77	60	41	54	68	76	57	68	64	56	76	80	51	75	60	68	71	67	81	93
05875	WEST GLOVER	73	54	33	48	61	69	52	63	60	52	71	74	46	69	54	64	65	62	75	86
05901	AVERILL	0	0	0	0	0	0	0	0	0	0	0	0	0	0	0	0	0	0	0	0
05902	BEECHER FALLS	62	52	41	52	55	62	54	58	57	53	69	66	52	69	54	58	65	57	62	68
05903	CANAAN	62	53	41	53	55	62	54	58	58	53	70	66	52	69	54	58	65	57	63	68
05904	GILMAN	73	52	28	45	58	67	49	61	58	50	69	72	43	66	51	63	63	60	74	85
05905	GUILDHALL	67	53	36	48	59	67	50	60	56	49	67	70	44	66	53	60	62	59	71	82
05906	LUNENBURG	71	50	28	44	57	65	48	59	57	48	67	70	42	64	50	61	61	59	72	83
05907	NORTON	66	52	35	47	58	66	49	59	55	48	65	69	44	65	52	59	61	58	70	80
	VERMONT	85	80	74	78	82	89	79	83	81	78	100	98	77	100	80	82	96	83	86	99
	UNITED STATES	100	100	100	100	100	100	100	100	100	100	100	100	100	100	100	100	100	100	100	100

ZIP CODE			POPULATION			2000-2004 ANNUAL RATE		HOUSEHOLDS					FAMILIES		
#	POST OFFICE NAME	COUNTY FIPS CODE	2000	2004	2009	% Rate	State Centile	2000	2004	2009	% Annual Rate 2000-2004	2004 Average HH Size	2000	2004	% Annual Rate 2000-2004
20105	ALDIE	107	1451	2538	4006	14.1	100	560	990	1572	14.4	2.56	408	712	14.0
20106	AMISSVILLE	157	3511	4039	4617	3.4	92	1238	1448	1676	3.8	2.79	999	1161	3.6
20107	ARCOLA	107	21	40	66	16.4	100	7	14	22	17.7	2.86	5	10	17.7
20109	MANASSAS	153	29650	34916	43332	3.9	95	11079	13100	16352	4.0	2.66	7165	8293	3.5
20110	MANASSAS	683	39152	42466	46435	1.9	78	12924	14061	15405	2.0	2.96	9458	10195	1.8
20111	MANASSAS	153	24227	27622	33374	3.1	90	7782	8918	10837	3.3	3.07	6219	7056	3.0
20112	MANASSAS	153	17782	21993	28023	5.1	97	5616	6947	8892	5.1	3.16	4945	6076	5.0
20115	MARSHALL	061	5473	6091	6999	2.6	85	2051	2333	2734	3.1	2.60	1544	1738	2.8
20117	MIDDLEBURG	107	3186	3526	4797	2.4	84	1399	1561	2140	2.6	2.25	897	972	1.9
20119	CATLETT	061	4051	4552	5262	2.8	88	1433	1639	1926	3.2	2.77	1132	1279	2.9
20120	CENTREVILLE	059	34542	37229	40466	1.8	75	11690	12568	13691	1.7	2.96	8895	9596	1.8
20121	CENTREVILLE	059	26043	25638	26244	-0.4	14	9579	9229	9364	-0.9	2.78	6509	6253	-0.9
20124	CLIFTON	059	14680	14964	15493	0.5	40	4609	4648	4797	0.2	3.22	3909	3926	0.1
20129	PAEONIAN SPRINGS	107	325	332	414	0.5	43	120	123	154	0.6	2.67	98	99	0.2
20130	PARIS	043	128	142	162	2.5	85	55	62	72	2.9	2.27	40	45	2.8
20132	PURCELLVILLE	107	8907	12568	18224	8.4	99	3110	4392	6380	8.5	2.85	2482	3463	8.2
20135	BLUEMONT	043	2731	3053	3675	2.7	87	1082	1224	1487	2.9	2.49	776	865	2.6
20136	BRISTOW	153	7720	13021	18977	13.1	99	2464	4182	6139	13.3	3.09	2103	3526	12.9
20137	BROAD RUN	061	2172	2550	3053	3.9	95	753	895	1087	4.2	2.85	603	711	4.0
20141	ROUND HILL	107	2968	3720	5171	5.5	97	1033	1302	1817	5.6	2.86	833	1040	5.4
20143	CATHARPIN	153	974	1577	2282	12.0	99	319	530	780	12.7	2.97	267	436	12.2
20144	DELAPLANE	061	1060	1154	1308	2.0	79	443	493	570	2.6	2.31	313	343	2.2
20147	ASHBURN	107	27795	54919	91015	17.4	100	9355	18634	31021	17.6	2.95	7233	14093	17.0
20148	ASHBURN	107	4077	8321	13882	18.3	100	1297	2680	4505	18.6	3.10	1096	2247	18.4
20151	CHANTILLY	059	17164	18396	19396	1.6	72	5283	5624	5921	1.5	3.26	4417	4736	1.7
20152	CHANTILLY	107	6430	12137	19678	16.1	100	2386	4561	7448	16.5	2.66	1816	3429	16.1
20155	GAINESVILLE	153	7494	12864	18913	13.6	99	2746	4819	7186	14.2	2.67	2199	3807	13.8
20158	HAMILTON	107	3224	3741	4983	3.6	93	1163	1352	1804	3.6	2.76	908	1046	3.4
20164	STERLING	107	34192	35689	46799	1.0	58	11649	12268	16170	1.2	2.91	8580	8907	0.9
20165	STERLING	107	27742	33031	44607	4.2	96	9827	11851	16124	4.5	2.78	7548	8972	4.2
20166	STERLING	107	4041	4631	6204	3.3	91	1533	1783	2405	3.6	2.60	1125	1290	3.3
20169	HAYMARKET	153	5934	8259	11164	8.1	99	2040	2892	3959	8.6	2.83	1664	2316	8.1
20170	HERNDON	059	37105	35039	35575	-1.3	1	11569	10859	11013	-1.5	3.23	8927	8387	-1.5
20171	HERNDON	059	33968	39160	43655	3.4	92	11028	13017	14712	4.0	3.01	9121	10690	3.8
20175	LEESBURG	107	16943	20348	27701	4.4	96	6352	7577	10330	4.2	2.65	4458	5277	4.1
20176	LEESBURG	107	20755	28419	41883	7.7	99	7461	10587	15974	8.6	2.65	5411	7438	7.8
20180	LOVETTSVILLE	107	4252	5786	8239	7.5	99	1492	2053	2943	7.8	2.81	1204	1641	7.6
20181	NOKESVILLE	153	7516	8681	10618	3.5	92	2515	2939	3630	3.7	2.95	2109	2434	3.4
20184	UPPERVILLE	107	901	904	1084	0.1	27	409	418	508	0.5	2.16	280	279	-0.1
20186	WARRENTON	061	11323	12929	15012	3.2	91	4365	5079	6010	3.6	2.48	3048	3480	3.2
20187	WARRENTON	061	12069	14120	16619	3.8	94	4006	4785	5737	4.3	2.93	3279	3885	4.1
20190	RESTON	059	14253	18639	21874	6.5	98	6337	8474	10086	7.1	2.14	3333	4346	6.4
20191	RESTON	059	28881	30518	32188	1.3	64	11373	12164	12904	1.6	2.51	7580	7978	1.2
20194	RESTON	059	13674	15926	17376	3.7	93	5763	6680	7291	3.5	2.38	3689	4305	3.7
20197	WATERFORD	107	1195	1489	2049	5.3	97	410	512	708	5.4	2.87	344	428	5.3
20198	THE PLAINS	061	2180	2196	2438	0.2	30	913	942	1066	0.7	2.33	609	617	0.3
22003	ANNANDALE	059	53605	52408	53064	-0.5	10	19304	18636	18803	-0.8	2.79	13856	13314	-0.9
22015	BURKE	059	41823	41149	41819	-0.4	13	14050	13844	14115	-0.4	2.96	11272	11037	-0.5
22026	DUMFRIES	153	23231	28003	35086	4.5	96	7804	9480	11971	4.7	2.95	6023	7218	4.4
22027	DUNN LORING	059	1643	1723	1812	1.1	61	533	568	601	1.5	3.01	386	409	1.4
22030	FAIRFAX	059	39509	47831	55392	4.6	96	13169	16900	20274	6.1	2.57	9118	11270	5.1
22031	FAIRFAX	059	26878	29140	31682	1.9	78	9988	10812	11788	1.9	2.66	6567	7044	1.7
22032	FAIRFAX	059	29165	29146	29857	0.0	23	9703	9686	9950	0.0	2.99	8137	8088	-0.1
22033	FAIRFAX	059	33194	36443	39159	2.2	82	13587	15020	16258	2.4	2.42	8370	9131	2.1
22039	FAIRFAX STATION	059	19825	20228	21012	0.5	41	6092	6201	6442	0.4	3.26	5689	5784	0.4
22041	FALLS CHURCH	059	24550	25216	26574	0.6	47	8863	9388	10033	1.4	2.67	5340	5484	0.6
22042	FALLS CHURCH	059	30396	30692	31803	0.2	32	11128	11299	11737	0.4	2.72	7246	7260	0.1
22043	FALLS CHURCH	059	23224	23607	24262	0.4	38	9131	9289	9571	0.4	2.53	5733	5758	0.1
22044	FALLS CHURCH	059	12217	13047	13735	1.6	70	4817	5097	5348	1.3	2.55	2974	3138	1.3
22046	FALLS CHURCH	610	13900	14197	14594	0.5	43	5664	5791	5962	0.5	2.44	3514	3540	0.2
22060	FORT BELVOIR	059	8216	8893	9625	1.9	77	2456	2670	2898	2.0	3.21	2173	2353	1.9
22066	GREAT FALLS	059	16713	18055	19161	1.8	76	5306	5717	6073	1.8	3.16	4787	5140	1.7
22067	GREENWAY	059	225	212	213	-1.4	1	77	73	73	-1.3	2.75	64	60	-1.5
22079	LORTON	059	21793	26781	32841	5.0	97	7022	9932	12154	8.5	2.68	4921	6856	8.1
22101	MC LEAN	059	28176	29057	30138	0.7	50	10478	10885	11356	0.9	2.66	8014	8248	0.7
22102	MC LEAN	059	18751	19319	20168	0.7	49	8539	8852	9297	0.9	2.18	4795	4910	0.6
22124	OAKTON	059	13765	14430	15062	1.1	61	5237	5507	5770	1.2	2.62	3843	4022	1.1
22134	QUANTICO	153	6906	6935	7967	0.1	28	1684	1723	2064	0.5	3.22	1459	1467	0.1
22150	SPRINGFIELD	059	22208	23120	24870	1.0	56	7358	7649	8243	0.9	3.01	5424	5587	0.7
22151	SPRINGFIELD	059	16619	16246	16433	-0.5	10	5767	5594	5651	-0.7	2.90	4396	4245	-0.8
22152	SPRINGFIELD	059	27547	28147	29273	0.5	43	9961	10272	10751	0.7	2.74	7579	7746	0.5
22153	SPRINGFIELD	059	31093	33653	36645	1.9	77	10148	11028	12061	2.0	3.05	8547	9191	1.7
22172	TRIANGLE	153	4975	5722	7001	3.4	92	1974	2269	2788	3.3	2.51	1315	1477	2.8
22180	VIENNA	059	21927	22938	23984	1.1	59	8172	8613	9061	1.2	2.65	5930	6149	0.9
22181	VIENNA	059	14469	14354	14581	-0.2	18	5120	5071	5162	-0.2	2.81	4099	4039	-0.4
22182	VIENNA	059	22662	23142	24085	0.5	42	7812	8104	8526	0.9	2.85	6342	6502	0.6
22191	WOODBRIDGE	153	39690	47327	59011	4.2	96	13283	15916	19979	4.4	2.96	9774	11537	4.0
22192	WOODBRIDGE	153	49162	56717	69578	3.4	92	17878	20814	25758	3.6	2.72	13089	15021	3.3
22193	WOODBRIDGE	153	61929	71472	87866	3.4	92	19514	22681	28088	3.6	3.15	15983	18409	3.4
22201	ARLINGTON	013	26614	29984	32704	2.9	89	14511	16471	18015	3.0	1.78	4648	5139	2.4
22202	ARLINGTON	013	18215	19306	20218	1.4	66	10214	10668	11126	1.0	1.79	3472	3647	1.2
22203	ARLINGTON	013	18046	19061	19907	1.3	64	8404	8986	9458	1.6	2.09	3417	3542	0.9
22204	ARLINGTON	013	50191	49058	49345	-0.5	10	20220	19494	19501	-0.9	2.50	10542	10075	-1.1
22205	ARLINGTON	013	16872	16208	16208	-0.9	3	6990	6754	6777	-0.8	2.39	4274	4092	-1.0
22206	ARLINGTON	013	16489	18232	19550	2.4	84	8123	8935	9562	2.3	2.04	3272	3581	2.2
22207	ARLINGTON	013	28885	28189	28335	-0.6	9	11141	10883	10957	-0.6	2.51	7438	7204	-0.8
22209	ARLINGTON	013	10320	11046	11610	1.6	71	6025	6374	6669	1.3	1.72	1651	1730	1.1
22211	FT MYER	013	2622	2628	2645	0.1	26	464	477	490	0.7	2.05	262	257	-0.5
22213	ARLINGTON	013	2447	2471	2521	0.2	32	1005	1010	1046	0.1	2.43	675	672	-0.1
22301	ALEXANDRIA	510	11434	10682	10750	-1.6	1	5195	4942	5039	-1.2	2.10	2682	2477	-1.9
22302	ALEXANDRIA	510	17233	17545	18264	0.4	40	9001	9279	9747	0.7	1.87	3868	3856	-0.1
22303	ALEXANDRIA	059	12710	14928	16513	3.9	95	6216	7403	8272	4.2	2.02	2744	3130	3.2
22304	ALEXANDRIA	510	41217	45664	50170	2.4	84	19978	22200	24603	2.5	2.04	8836	9667	2.3
22305	ALEXANDRIA	510	15738	17487	19324	2.5	85	6089	6607	7194	1.9	2.64	3392	3604	1.4
22306	ALEXANDRIA	059	26977	26195	26564	-0.7	7	10230	9799	9904	-1.0	2.65	6668	6360	-1.1
	VIRGINIA					1.4					1.7	2.51			1.4
	UNITED STATES					1.2					1.3	2.58			1.1

ZIP CODE #	POST OFFICE NAME	RACE (%) White 2000	White 2004	Black 2000	Black 2004	Asian/Pacific 2000	Asian/Pacific 2004	% Hispanic Origin 2000	% Hispanic Origin 2004	2004 AGE DISTRIBUTION (%) 0-4	5-9	10-14	15-19	20-24	25-44	45-64	65-84	85+	18+	MEDIAN AGE 2004	% 2004 Males	% 2004 Females
20105	ALDIE	86.0	84.0	8.4	8.8	2.5	3.2	3.4	4.9	9.1	8.6	6.5	4.7	3.4	34.5	24.0	8.3	0.9	72.8	36.4	50.0	50.0
20106	AMISSVILLE	93.0	92.1	4.6	4.9	0.3	0.4	1.7	2.0	6.5	7.3	7.8	6.0	4.0	27.5	28.9	11.3	0.9	74.7	40.4	50.7	49.3
20107	ARCOLA	90.5	85.0	4.8	5.0	4.8	5.0	0.0	5.0	10.0	10.0	5.0	5.0	5.0	37.5	22.5	5.0	0.0	75.0	35.0	50.0	50.0
20109	MANASSAS	65.4	61.3	16.3	16.9	4.6	5.2	16.4	20.4	9.3	8.2	7.3	6.4	8.1	37.0	18.2	5.0	0.5	71.4	30.6	50.0	50.0
20110	MANASSAS	73.4	70.9	12.3	12.4	3.5	4.0	14.2	17.0	8.5	8.2	8.4	6.9	7.0	33.1	21.9	5.4	0.6	70.6	32.4	50.8	49.2
20111	MANASSAS	77.7	75.0	8.8	9.0	3.1	3.6	13.5	16.3	9.2	8.7	7.7	6.3	5.9	34.3	21.5	5.9	0.6	70.4	33.1	50.4	49.7
20112	MANASSAS	86.7	83.7	6.8	8.1	2.2	2.7	4.2	5.8	7.3	8.1	8.7	7.4	5.4	29.5	28.6	4.6	0.3	71.0	36.3	50.6	49.4
20115	MARSHALL	89.6	88.6	7.8	8.3	0.4	0.5	2.1	2.6	4.7	5.4	6.4	6.2	4.2	25.6	34.0	12.2	1.3	79.5	43.6	49.9	50.1
20117	MIDDLEBURG	83.9	81.8	13.2	14.5	0.5	0.6	3.6	4.6	5.0	5.3	6.2	6.4	5.1	24.3	32.1	13.8	1.8	79.4	43.7	47.5	52.5
20119	CATLETT	89.2	88.2	8.4	8.9	0.5	0.6	1.3	1.7	6.0	6.6	7.1	6.6	5.0	26.9	29.7	11.1	1.0	76.0	40.4	51.0	49.0
20120	CENTREVILLE	75.8	71.5	7.1	7.4	11.8	14.6	6.6	8.4	8.4	8.8	8.6	6.9	5.8	34.4	22.9	3.9	0.4	69.8	33.5	49.5	50.6
20121	CENTREVILLE	65.9	62.0	10.2	10.5	16.0	17.9	10.1	12.8	9.7	8.6	7.1	5.8	7.0	42.3	16.8	2.6	0.1	71.1	31.1	49.5	50.5
20124	CLIFTON	84.2	81.6	2.9	3.2	9.6	11.2	3.4	4.6	5.9	7.9	9.2	8.4	5.1	26.3	32.0	4.9	0.4	71.3	37.8	49.7	50.3
20129	PAEONIAN SPRINGS	94.5	93.7	3.4	3.9	0.6	0.6	1.2	1.5	5.7	6.9	9.3	7.2	3.0	21.1	33.4	11.8	1.5	72.6	43.2	47.3	52.7
20130	PARIS	92.2	91.6	5.5	6.3	0.0	0.0	1.6	2.1	4.9	6.3	7.0	6.3	3.5	29.6	30.3	11.3	0.7	77.5	41.6	49.3	50.7
20132	PURCELLVILLE	92.9	91.5	4.1	4.7	0.9	1.1	1.7	2.4	7.0	8.1	9.4	7.1	4.0	26.6	27.7	8.9	1.3	70.7	38.7	48.9	51.1
20135	BLUEMONT	95.3	94.8	2.1	2.2	0.3	0.4	1.4	1.8	6.1	6.9	6.6	6.0	4.0	28.0	32.1	9.7	0.6	76.7	41.5	49.7	50.3
20136	BRISTOW	88.1	85.6	6.5	7.6	2.5	3.1	3.9	5.3	12.9	11.7	8.0	5.3	3.7	39.6	15.7	2.9	0.2	63.6	31.6	49.9	50.1
20137	BROAD RUN	93.0	92.3	4.8	5.1	0.9	1.1	1.5	1.9	6.1	7.1	8.1	6.2	3.9	24.6	33.1	9.8	1.0	74.4	41.8	48.6	51.4
20141	ROUND HILL	94.1	93.6	3.3	3.3	0.6	0.7	1.6	2.2	7.2	8.3	8.4	6.4	3.7	26.3	30.1	8.9	0.7	72.0	40.2	49.7	50.3
20143	CATHARPIN	92.7	92.1	2.9	3.0	1.4	1.7	1.8	2.2	4.6	5.2	5.7	5.1	3.5	18.5	36.5	19.9	1.0	81.1	50.5	49.7	50.4
20144	DELAPLANE	85.5	84.1	11.7	12.7	0.4	0.4	3.4	4.3	5.5	5.9	6.0	5.8	4.7	27.5	31.2	11.8	1.7	78.9	42.0	49.2	50.8
20147	ASHBURN	83.7	81.1	6.5	7.1	5.7	6.9	4.4	5.9	12.1	11.7	8.9	5.1	3.4	39.1	16.6	2.9	0.2	64.0	32.1	49.1	50.9
20148	ASHBURN	85.4	83.0	5.7	6.3	5.6	6.7	3.5	4.8	12.7	12.4	9.2	5.0	3.2	38.5	17.0	1.8	0.1	62.4	31.7	49.4	50.6
20151	CHANTILLY	72.4	68.9	5.3	5.4	15.0	17.0	10.4	12.9	7.9	8.7	9.2	7.1	5.3	30.0	27.0	4.6	0.2	69.7	35.1	50.8	49.2
20152	CHANTILLY	86.6	84.2	4.9	5.4	4.7	5.6	5.2	7.0	12.6	10.9	5.7	3.1	2.6	45.4	15.7	3.6	0.3	68.7	32.7	49.2	50.8
20155	GAINESVILLE	90.2	88.8	5.4	5.7	1.6	2.0	3.1	4.1	9.0	8.7	6.6	4.8	3.9	32.1	25.8	8.7	0.4	72.6	36.7	49.7	50.3
20158	HAMILTON	95.5	94.7	2.3	2.5	0.7	0.9	1.7	2.4	6.3	7.4	8.0	6.6	4.0	24.1	32.4	9.9	1.4	74.0	41.7	49.4	50.6
20164	STERLING	71.8	67.7	9.3	9.7	9.8	11.3	11.8	15.4	8.2	8.0	7.7	6.4	6.6	35.4	22.7	4.7	0.4	72.3	33.4	50.3	49.7
20165	STERLING	83.6	80.7	5.4	5.8	6.9	8.3	4.8	6.4	10.1	10.1	8.1	5.0	3.7	36.1	21.9	4.2	0.8	68.4	34.9	48.7	51.3
20166	STERLING	72.5	69.4	10.0	10.4	9.7	10.8	10.7	13.7	8.9	8.1	6.6	6.0	7.5	37.5	21.1	4.0	0.3	72.8	32.3	49.9	50.1
20169	HAYMARKET	92.7	91.1	4.0	4.8	1.3	1.7	1.6	2.2	7.2	7.6	7.5	5.8	4.5	30.6	29.2	7.1	0.5	74.0	38.2	50.4	49.6
20170	HERNDON	64.4	60.8	8.5	8.6	12.8	13.8	19.1	22.9	7.9	8.3	8.1	7.0	7.0	33.5	24.6	3.5	0.3	71.5	32.8	51.7	48.3
20171	HERNDON	74.9	69.1	5.3	6.1	14.9	18.2	5.6	8.1	8.4	8.6	8.6	7.1	6.0	32.4	25.5	3.2	0.2	69.9	33.7	49.9	50.1
20175	LEESBURG	88.4	87.1	6.5	6.7	2.0	2.4	4.0	5.2	8.7	8.7	7.6	5.8	4.8	32.8	24.3	6.8	0.8	71.3	35.9	49.7	50.3
20176	LEESBURG	81.7	78.4	9.1	9.5	3.7	5.1	6.5	8.5	10.2	9.7	7.6	5.2	4.4	37.7	19.2	5.2	0.8	69.0	33.1	49.3	50.8
20180	LOVETTSVILLE	97.0	96.3	0.8	0.9	0.8	0.9	1.3	1.8	5.5	7.8	9.3	7.0	3.2	25.6	31.7	8.9	1.1	72.8	40.9	49.6	50.4
20181	NOKESVILLE	93.6	92.5	3.1	3.5	0.9	1.1	2.3	3.1	6.1	6.7	7.0	6.8	5.2	27.2	31.3	9.0	0.7	75.8	40.2	50.4	49.7
20184	UPPERVILLE	87.8	86.3	8.4	9.2	0.6	0.7	3.4	4.4	5.6	6.1	6.3	5.8	4.7	25.4	33.0	12.1	1.1	78.4	42.9	49.2	50.8
20186	WARRENTON	84.3	83.0	12.6	13.3	0.9	1.1	2.3	2.9	6.2	6.4	7.1	6.4	5.4	26.9	27.3	12.3	2.0	76.2	40.4	48.4	51.6
20187	WARRENTON	91.0	90.3	6.1	6.3	0.8	0.9	1.7	2.1	6.6	7.4	8.3	6.9	4.8	26.1	29.5	9.0	1.3	73.1	39.7	49.9	50.1
20190	RESTON	71.2	68.7	10.0	10.1	9.7	11.0	12.1	14.4	5.7	5.1	5.1	4.8	6.0	35.2	23.7	11.2	3.4	81.2	37.5	48.0	52.0
20191	RESTON	70.0	68.5	10.4	10.4	10.7	11.0	12.0	14.0	6.5	6.5	6.0	5.6	6.0	31.5	29.4	7.8	0.7	77.6	37.9	49.3	50.8
20194	RESTON	83.2	80.7	5.4	5.9	7.8	9.1	4.3	5.7	7.6	7.6	6.9	5.4	4.5	34.9	28.6	4.3	0.3	74.5	37.0	48.6	51.4
20197	WATERFORD	95.6	95.1	2.3	2.3	0.8	0.9	1.9	2.6	6.3	7.8	9.1	7.6	3.5	22.4	32.6	9.6	1.1	71.3	41.7	49.6	50.4
20198	THE PLAINS	90.8	89.9	6.5	7.0	0.1	0.1	3.4	4.5	5.0	5.3	6.3	5.8	5.2	26.2	31.1	13.3	1.8	79.9	42.8	47.2	52.8
22003	ANNANDALE	65.6	62.2	5.7	5.7	19.0	20.8	13.4	16.3	6.2	6.4	6.4	5.8	5.6	28.7	27.7	11.9	1.3	77.4	39.6	48.5	51.5
22015	BURKE	72.9	69.2	5.0	5.2	15.5	17.7	8.5	10.8	5.8	6.7	7.5	7.1	5.9	27.6	32.4	6.2	0.9	75.6	38.7	48.7	51.3
22026	DUMFRIES	63.6	61.0	26.6	27.4	3.1	3.6	7.6	9.3	9.1	8.8	8.6	7.3	6.8	32.4	22.7	4.0	0.3	69.0	31.8	48.9	51.1
22027	DUNN LORING	68.5	63.5	3.3	3.4	20.3	23.9	7.4	8.5	8.2	8.2	5.8	4.4	3.5	36.9	25.0	7.5	0.6	75.1	37.2	49.2	50.8
22030	FAIRFAX	71.3	67.1	7.5	7.7	13.6	16.6	9.9	11.4	5.9	5.7	5.3	8.3	9.0	33.7	23.1	8.2	1.0	79.9	34.7	50.4	49.6
22031	FAIRFAX	63.3	60.3	5.4	5.4	21.6	23.5	13.5	15.4	6.2	6.1	5.9	5.6	7.0	32.3	24.5	9.7	2.8	78.5	37.1	49.5	50.5
22032	FAIRFAX	77.4	74.2	4.2	4.4	14.0	16.2	5.7	7.3	5.6	6.4	7.3	7.0	5.3	25.5	32.2	10.0	0.7	76.3	40.9	49.5	50.5
22033	FAIRFAX	75.1	70.9	5.1	5.6	15.4	18.2	5.5	7.1	6.7	6.4	5.7	4.7	7.0	40.6	23.0	5.3	0.6	78.3	33.9	49.2	50.8
22039	FAIRFAX STATION	83.3	81.0	3.9	4.1	9.9	11.4	3.3	4.4	5.3	7.7	10.0	7.8	4.2	19.9	37.9	6.8	0.4	71.8	42.3	50.4	49.6
22041	FALLS CHURCH	49.9	48.6	10.0	9.9	12.9	13.0	37.7	39.2	7.2	6.6	5.9	5.3	7.2	35.1	21.7	8.7	2.2	77.1	34.8	50.8	49.3
22042	FALLS CHURCH	61.4	57.8	4.8	4.8	19.3	20.9	22.4	25.7	6.7	6.3	5.8	5.2	6.4	35.8	24.4	8.5	1.0	78.1	36.3	50.0	50.0
22043	FALLS CHURCH	69.9	66.7	5.0	4.9	15.8	17.4	13.8	16.9	5.9	5.7	5.4	5.2	5.7	37.1	24.8	9.1	1.1	79.8	36.5	49.9	50.1
22044	FALLS CHURCH	63.0	61.9	5.0	4.6	15.5	15.5	28.4	32.1	6.5	6.3	6.0	5.1	6.0	33.9	25.5	9.4	1.3	78.2	37.1	50.6	49.4
22046	FALLS CHURCH	81.2	79.1	3.5	3.5	8.4	9.2	10.9	13.3	5.8	6.0	6.6	6.8	6.2	28.0	29.3	9.7	1.9	77.3	39.8	49.5	50.5
22060	FORT BELVOIR	55.5	52.5	31.5	32.3	3.3	3.6	10.3	13.2	13.5	13.9	11.0	6.5	7.8	38.1	7.0	1.6	0.7	57.4	23.3	50.7	49.3
22066	GREAT FALLS	86.1	83.7	1.9	2.1	9.1	10.8	2.5	3.4	6.5	8.4	9.6	7.4	3.9	19.8	35.3	8.5	0.6	70.6	41.8	50.5	49.6
22067	GREENWAY	83.1	80.7	2.2	2.4	10.2	12.3	2.2	3.3	4.7	5.7	7.6	6.6	2.8	20.8	38.2	12.7	0.9	78.3	46.3	48.6	51.4
22079	LORTON	54.5	57.9	30.0	22.5	7.4	9.0	9.0	12.5	7.8	7.6	7.7	6.3	6.2	33.7	24.2	5.5	1.1	73.1	34.6	48.7	51.3
22101	MC LEAN	84.1	81.3	1.7	1.8	10.9	12.9	3.9	5.2	5.6	6.8	7.4	6.4	3.9	19.9	32.6	14.9	2.5	76.0	45.0	47.9	52.1
22102	MC LEAN	75.9	72.2	2.8	3.0	15.8	18.3	5.5	7.0	4.3	4.8	5.7	5.6	7.2	32.5	27.8	11.2	1.0	81.9	38.4	48.1	51.9
22124	OAKTON	86.4	83.8	3.2	3.5	7.2	8.7	4.6	6.1	5.7	6.6	7.2	6.5	5.0	26.5	33.7	8.3	0.5	76.3	40.6	47.9	52.1
22134	QUANTICO	72.1	68.7	16.6	17.6	2.9	3.5	9.0	11.3	14.3	9.3	5.9	6.5	26.7	32.2	4.3	0.8	0.1	68.0	22.6	60.0	40.0
22150	SPRINGFIELD	57.4	54.0	7.4	7.3	21.9	24.2	18.7	20.8	6.8	6.9	6.8	5.8	5.8	31.3	24.4	10.7	1.7	76.0	37.2	49.9	50.1
22151	SPRINGFIELD	71.4	67.3	4.6	4.7	16.6	18.9	9.6	12.1	6.8	7.2	7.2	5.8	4.8	29.0	26.7	11.7	1.0	75.2	39.4	49.8	50.2
22152	SPRINGFIELD	74.0	70.6	5.6	6.0	14.3	16.0	7.9	10.1	5.7	6.4	7.3	6.5	5.3	28.1	30.3	9.9	0.5	76.5	40.2	48.3	51.7
22153	SPRINGFIELD	72.3	67.7	9.2	10.5	12.0	13.8	6.9	9.0	6.9	7.6	8.4	7.1	5.6	28.0	31.3	4.9	0.3	72.7	37.3	48.9	51.1
22172	TRIANGLE	64.0	60.9	25.8	26.9	3.0	3.5	7.4	9.3	9.2	8.0	7.0	6.8	7.9	31.6	22.1	6.9	0.5	71.8	31.6	50.2	49.8
22180	VIENNA	77.1	73.0	3.5	3.8	12.8	15.2	8.9	11.3	6.4	6.5	6.1	5.2	5.4	30.7	26.7	11.9	1.1	77.7	39.2	50.2	49.8
22181	VIENNA	82.9	80.0	2.7	3.0	10.1	11.8	5.9	7.8	5.9	6.7	7.0	6.0	4.7	26.1	32.5	10.2	0.9	76.5	41.3	49.8	50.2
22182	VIENNA	79.4	75.8	2.9	3.1	12.9	15.3	3.5	4.8	7.3	8.3	7.4	5.7	3.7	26.3	31.1	9.5	0.8	73.4	40.5	49.3	50.7
22191	WOODBRIDGE	55.2	51.8	26.0	26.5	5.0	5.5	17.4	20.7	9.4	8.5	8.2	7.1	8.5	33.2	18.5	6.0	0.6	69.5	30.1	49.9	50.1
22192	WOODBRIDGE	72.9	69.9	16.4	17.4	4.5	5.3	7.0	8.9	7.2	7.3	7.9	7.2	6.8	31.7	26.6	4.6	0.7	73.1	34.6	48.2	51.8
22193	WOODBRIDGE	58.8	55.4	27.4	28.5	5.1	5.8	9.4	11.5	8.1	8.1	9.0	7.8	6.9	32.2	23.4	4.3	0.2	69.9	32.2	49.2	50.8
22201	ARLINGTON	77.8	75.1	5.1	5.3	8.6	9.8	11.3	13.8	3.7	2.9	2.7	3.1	7.8	51.9	21.0	5.8	1.0	88.8	34.2	51.6	48.4
22202	ARLINGTON	70.8	67.4	8.1	8.4	12.5	13.9	11.9	14.9	3.3	2.6	2.4	2.2	7.3	42.2	26.8	11.4	1.8	90.5	38.9	50.9	49.1
22203	ARLINGTON	68.6	65.2	4.6	4.6	11.2	12.3	25.5	29.7	4.8	4.2	3.7	3.8	7.9	41.3	21.0	10.0	3.5	85.2	36.0	51.1	48.9
22204	ARLINGTON	49.7	46.7	17.3	16.5	10.2	10.8	33.0	37.9	7.0	6.1	5.8	5.4	7.7	39.7	20.9	6.4	1.0	78.1	33.7	50.7	49.3
22205	ARLINGTON	84.8	82.4	2.9	3.0	6.4	7.5	8.6	10.8	6.3	6.5	5.8	4.9	4.4	34.8	27.4	8.4	1.6	78.3	38.2	49.5	50.5
22206	ARLINGTON	65.0	59.9	14.5	15.9	5.9	6.5	19.8	24.2	5.3	4.3	4.8	4.4	7.0	45.2	23.3	5.1	0.6	83.0	34.7	47.1	52.9
22207	ARLINGTON	85.3	83.3	4.8	4.9	4.6	5.4	7.4	9.3	5.9	6.5	6.3	5.7	4.9	27.7	28.7	11.7	2.6	78.0	40.8	48.7	51.3
22209	ARLINGTON	67.9	63.9	5.7	5.9	13.6	14.8	18.4	23.3	3.2	2.5	2.4	3.0	11.0	52.6	20.1	4.8	0.5	90.3	33.3	54.8	45.2
22211	FT MYER	63.2	59.3	21.9	22.8	3.1	3.5	11.2	14.2	4.3	2.2	2.4	10.7	34.5	34.9	9.9	1.0	0.1	89.9	24.4	75.7	24.4
22213	ARLINGTON	88.9	86.1	1.5	1.6	5.6	6.8	5.9	8.3	6.1	6.4	6.3	4.4	3.7	30.8	27.8	11.9	2.6	78.1	40.6	48.5	51.5
22301	ALEXANDRIA	80.7	78.8	13.2	13.9	2.0	2.3	6.0	7.3	6.1	5.2	4.6	3.8	3.8	39.0	26.0	9.4	2.0	81.5	38.7	47.6	52.4
22302	ALEXANDRIA	74.2	71.0	11.2	11.8	5.5	6.4	8.2	9.8	5.8	5.2	4.0	3.2	5.0	39.0	26.0	9.9	2.0	83.1	38.8	46.4	53.6
22303	ALEXANDRIA	65.6	60.7	14.8	15.9	7.2	8.1	16.5	20.6	5.4	4.9	4.7	4.6	6.4	39.1	24.9	9.1	0.9	82.4	36.9	50.5	49.5
22304	ALEXANDRIA	54.4	52.8	24.4	23.7	8.8	9.6	15.0	17.4	6.1	5.1	4.2	4.1	7.3	42.2	21.9	8.1	1.0	82.2	35.2	48.1	51.9
22305	ALEXANDRIA	42.4	37.9	25.9	26.1	3.2	3.1	36.6	42.2	7.8	7.0	6.6	5.7	8.7	39.2	20.1	4.5	0.5	75.5	31.9	53.4	46.6
22306	ALEXANDRIA	50.9	48.4	26.9	26.3	8.1	8.7	19.1	22.8	7.7	7.2	7.1	6.5	6.8	32.8	23.1	8.0	0.8	74.1	34.5	49.1	51.0
	VIRGINIA	72.3	70.7	19.6	19.9	3.7	4.3	4.7	5.7	6.5	6.6	6.9	6.9	7.0	29.7	24.9	10.1	1.4	76.2	36.6	49.1	50.9
	UNITED STATES	75.1	73.6	12.3	12.5	3.8	4.2	12.5	14.1	6.9	6.7	7.2	7.0	7.3	28.6	23.8	10.8	1.7	75.1	36.0	49.1	50.9

#	POST OFFICE NAME	2004 Per Capita Income	2004 HH Income Base	2004 Household Income Distribution (%): Less than $25,000	$25,000 to $49,999	$50,000 to $99,999	$100,000 to $149,999	$150,000 or More	Median Household Income: 2004	2009	2004 National Centile	2004 State Centile	2004 Home Value Base	2004 Home Value Distribution (%): Less than $50,000	$50,000 to $89,999	$90,000 to $174,999	$175,000 to $399,999	$400,000 or More	2004 Median Home Value
20105	ALDIE	49514	990	6.8	12.1	33.4	23.9	23.7	95560	115348	98	95	803	0.0	0.0	2.6	46.5	50.9	406000
20106	AMISSVILLE	30066	1448	15.6	18.9	35.9	19.1	10.5	70187	86031	91	85	1282	1.6	1.4	20.1	57.8	19.0	266092
20107	ARCOLA	42722	14	0.0	0.0	42.9	28.6	28.6	110913	140387	99	98	12	0.0	0.0	0.0	66.7	33.3	360000
20109	MANASSAS	26805	13100	11.3	26.0	42.7	15.9	4.2	61571	72304	86	80	6754	0.5	1.7	40.1	56.1	1.6	191043
20110	MANASSAS	29949	14061	8.9	19.7	41.4	20.8	9.3	73983	86520	93	87	10029	1.3	2.2	26.2	64.9	5.5	230750
20111	MANASSAS	28518	8918	8.3	18.0	43.2	21.3	9.3	75701	85985	93	89	7146	2.1	1.0	29.2	58.1	9.6	214169
20112	MANASSAS	37985	6947	3.2	8.0	33.7	34.1	21.0	105206	127254	99	97	6608	3.2	0.3	5.6	65.3	25.7	322022
20115	MARSHALL	47361	2333	12.6	19.0	30.9	20.4	17.1	78615	101364	95	90	1911	0.5	0.5	14.4	48.0	36.6	334733
20117	MIDDLEBURG	56443	1561	14.9	17.0	30.2	16.6	21.2	75900	95224	94	89	940	0.0	1.7	4.9	35.4	58.0	491463
20119	CATLETT	32261	1639	11.8	22.1	34.4	19.7	12.0	69494	86453	91	85	1354	0.9	1.2	14.1	64.3	19.6	271018
20120	CENTREVILLE	40723	12568	3.7	11.2	32.0	30.3	22.8	103786	129365	98	97	9717	0.9	0.3	10.7	60.7	27.5	296858
20121	CENTREVILLE	35379	9229	3.8	15.3	42.5	26.9	11.6	84395	105500	96	92	5966	1.2	1.0	16.6	65.4	15.9	235095
20124	CLIFTON	58189	4648	2.9	8.6	17.9	26.5	44.2	137686	167840	100	99	4039	0.9	0.4	2.6	21.7	74.4	518588
20129	PAEONIAN SPRINGS	57985	123	8.1	4.9	16.3	30.1	40.7	135250	161902	100	99	109	0.0	3.7	13.8	23.9	58.7	486364
20130	PARIS	38592	62	14.5	19.4	35.5	21.0	9.7	72428	85739	92	86	51	0.0	0.0	23.5	49.0	27.5	275000
20132	PURCELLVILLE	37904	4392	8.7	14.9	33.5	26.3	16.6	87188	105367	97	93	3687	0.3	0.7	4.8	51.3	42.9	366216
20135	BLUEMONT	36240	1224	9.1	19.4	37.8	21.7	12.0	75265	90865	93	88	1034	1.6	3.5	19.5	47.8	27.6	250971
20136	BRISTOW	38590	4182	3.6	7.5	42.7	30.0	16.2	95170	115516	98	95	3910	0.3	0.2	7.5	76.6	15.4	299919
20137	BROAD RUN	44205	895	6.5	15.0	31.5	23.2	23.8	93994	118768	98	95	788	0.1	0.0	4.6	52.5	42.8	350435
20141	ROUND HILL	38996	1302	6.2	13.1	32.6	31.6	16.5	96398	115471	98	95	1161	0.3	0.6	8.1	48.7	42.4	364024
20143	CATHARPIN	45436	530	2.1	5.5	40.8	28.1	23.6	101970	120263	98	96	498	3.0	0.0	1.6	48.2	47.2	390541
20144	DELAPLANE	43625	493	15.4	25.4	30.0	16.8	12.4	63146	78729	87	81	355	0.6	0.0	22.0	43.4	34.1	296250
20147	ASHBURN	43485	18634	2.6	9.6	34.2	31.3	22.3	104127	123849	98	97	16179	0.1	0.2	5.1	58.3	36.3	328041
20148	ASHBURN	52569	2680	2.0	5.8	27.5	31.6	33.2	121363	143031	99	99	2456	0.0	0.0	0.0	42.6	57.4	437787
20151	CHANTILLY	37707	5624	2.8	9.4	31.9	32.1	23.7	106596	130044	99	97	4955	6.9	1.8	10.9	52.0	28.4	306255
20152	CHANTILLY	41476	4561	3.3	10.5	38.2	29.4	18.6	96808	115396	98	95	4083	0.0	0.0	2.6	61.4	36.0	343904
20155	GAINESVILLE	46301	4819	3.5	11.3	37.4	27.3	20.6	96539	113407	98	95	4385	6.6	1.1	6.9	53.3	32.1	319949
20158	HAMILTON	47496	1352	8.8	13.5	26.4	27.3	24.0	101524	122094	98	96	1195	0.9	0.7	8.7	49.7	40.0	342271
20164	STERLING	32233	12268	5.5	15.9	43.9	24.6	10.2	80816	94582	95	91	9123	0.5	0.4	17.8	76.7	4.6	242880
20165	STERLING	48439	11851	2.6	8.7	31.0	32.6	25.1	109343	129983	99	98	10165	0.4	0.2	5.4	61.2	32.7	340866
20166	STERLING	37319	1783	3.8	16.0	41.8	28.5	9.9	85631	102252	96	92	1461	1.3	0.5	7.2	83.6	7.4	260440
20169	HAYMARKET	38988	2892	4.0	10.7	38.5	28.3	18.6	94948	109836	98	95	2631	1.8	0.4	9.2	65.7	23.0	279989
20170	HERNDON	39071	10859	4.8	12.2	32.2	29.2	21.6	100855	123872	98	96	7752	0.2	0.5	14.6	63.1	21.6	291888
20171	HERNDON	50210	13017	2.2	7.5	25.8	31.7	32.8	120283	147030	99	98	9856	0.9	0.1	2.2	53.1	43.7	379628
20175	LEESBURG	41928	7577	9.0	15.4	32.6	22.3	20.7	87290	106036	97	93	5715	1.7	0.8	13.0	49.2	35.3	302035
20176	LEESBURG	39578	10587	6.5	16.5	40.0	23.2	13.9	81751	98003	95	91	7383	1.6	0.7	14.4	52.9	30.4	294522
20180	LOVETTSVILLE	38314	2053	7.6	12.7	36.2	27.3	16.2	89846	108928	97	94	1827	0.2	0.9	9.2	51.2	38.5	334938
20181	NOKESVILLE	36455	2939	4.7	12.9	37.5	29.2	15.7	92470	112429	97	94	2637	0.1	0.3	6.0	71.6	22.0	304457
20184	UPPERVILLE	50103	418	11.7	21.8	32.3	17.7	16.5	71836	89550	92	86	280	1.8	1.1	11.8	36.4	48.9	392105
20186	WARRENTON	36017	5079	13.0	16.6	38.3	20.9	11.3	73602	89230	93	87	3848	0.4	0.9	18.6	61.0	19.1	261284
20187	WARRENTON	37049	4785	6.1	13.8	36.9	25.7	17.6	89228	109794	97	93	4252	0.0	0.2	9.2	71.5	19.2	275762
20190	RESTON	48992	8474	11.4	15.9	33.7	21.9	17.1	82755	105831	96	91	4037	0.0	0.6	19.1	62.7	17.7	253278
20191	RESTON	52677	12164	6.9	11.8	32.0	25.0	24.3	98541	124251	98	96	8575	0.3	2.0	19.8	47.6	30.4	276625
20194	RESTON	74387	6680	3.0	7.4	27.5	25.9	36.2	121412	151984	99	99	4639	0.0	0.2	5.5	44.7	49.6	398158
20197	WATERFORD	59441	512	5.3	10.6	22.9	24.0	37.3	125300	151153	100	99	458	1.1	0.9	6.3	26.4	65.3	536885
20198	THE PLAINS	72197	942	17.1	18.9	26.3	15.7	22.0	75161	101569	93	88	554	1.3	0.5	10.1	44.4	43.7	365686
22003	ANNANDALE	39893	18636	7.7	13.8	33.5	26.0	19.0	90471	114518	97	94	13094	1.1	2.3	9.2	57.7	29.8	328660
22015	BURKE	41815	13844	3.9	9.1	31.7	31.1	24.2	106020	129752	99	97	11571	0.7	0.2	8.7	68.0	22.5	304861
22026	DUMFRIES	30503	9480	9.1	19.1	39.6	21.7	10.6	76601	87006	94	89	6859	2.0	1.3	26.3	63.5	6.8	219731
22027	DUNN LORING	47327	568	1.6	9.7	27.3	29.1	32.4	116442	146304	99	98	479	3.3	0.0	0.2	36.3	60.1	457059
22030	FAIRFAX	45882	16900	5.3	13.2	33.4	26.0	22.1	96461	121706	98	95	11477	1.6	0.8	4.7	60.7	32.4	325175
22031	FAIRFAX	40669	10812	8.0	14.4	35.3	23.8	18.5	86654	110119	97	92	6154	0.4	1.2	7.1	55.7	35.6	313490
22032	FAIRFAX	40904	9686	2.8	8.0	31.4	34.5	23.4	108933	134002	99	98	8736	0.6	0.1	1.9	72.6	24.9	343219
22033	FAIRFAX	50721	15020	4.2	12.8	33.6	28.1	21.4	98880	120509	98	96	8923	0.4	0.2	8.2	68.2	23.0	302768
22039	FAIRFAX STATION	66783	6201	1.3	2.9	14.4	26.9	54.5	157879	190312	100	100	5964	0.7	0.3	0.7	14.1	84.3	579127
22041	FALLS CHURCH	35699	9388	12.7	21.8	35.9	15.9	13.7	67351	86154	90	84	4163	0.9	2.7	25.3	47.9	23.3	247808
22042	FALLS CHURCH	35881	11299	8.2	17.5	37.1	23.5	13.8	79856	101449	95	91	7369	0.7	1.0	10.4	74.2	13.7	273181
22043	FALLS CHURCH	45881	9289	5.9	14.5	36.6	22.6	20.5	88205	112207	97	93	5713	0.9	0.2	8.2	63.0	27.7	298318
22044	FALLS CHURCH	44192	5097	13.6	17.2	29.2	18.5	21.6	79540	104693	95	91	2734	0.7	4.0	14.5	36.6	44.3	375743
22046	FALLS CHURCH	49039	5791	7.8	13.9	32.1	25.0	21.2	92030	117172	97	94	3936	0.3	0.8	10.6	50.1	38.2	356530
22060	FORT BELVOIR	18920	2670	13.2	34.5	39.5	9.9	2.9	51381	62248	75	68	268	0.0	3.0	24.3	72.0	0.8	211468
22066	GREAT FALLS	97694	5717	1.9	3.7	11.2	19.0	64.2	192006	234334	100	100	5442	0.3	0.4	0.6	8.4	90.4	791465
22067	GREENWAY	124247	73	0.0	2.7	16.4	23.3	57.5	177340	209026	100	100	67	4.5	0.0	6.0	3.0	86.6	1000001
22079	LORTON	35260	9932	6.7	20.7	39.2	21.7	11.7	74626	91679	93	88	6593	0.4	1.4	27.6	48.9	21.7	229860
22101	MC LEAN	89751	10885	4.2	6.4	16.8	22.8	49.9	149670	185354	100	100	9286	0.1	0.2	0.9	18.6	80.2	589272
22102	MC LEAN	83745	8852	6.4	11.0	30.7	21.8	30.2	103107	130912	98	97	4570	0.1	0.8	17.8	25.5	55.8	506401
22124	OAKTON	79426	5507	2.5	7.4	21.0	20.2	48.9	146850	178444	100	100	4485	0.0	0.0	7.2	28.9	63.9	523410
22134	QUANTICO	15954	1723	18.3	39.3	34.2	7.8	0.4	44404	52341	60	52	132	31.8	6.1	53.8	8.3	0.0	105102
22150	SPRINGFIELD	32573	7649	6.5	15.2	39.7	26.1	12.5	83662	105323	96	92	5341	0.6	0.0	2.6	88.0	8.9	270807
22151	SPRINGFIELD	37187	5594	4.4	13.4	36.7	29.9	15.6	92494	114022	97	94	4690	1.0	0.5	1.0	93.3	4.3	281001
22152	SPRINGFIELD	43782	10272	3.6	11.1	36.5	28.3	20.5	98056	120977	98	96	8485	0.6	0.5	9.8	74.0	15.2	289849
22153	SPRINGFIELD	42450	11028	3.0	7.4	33.4	30.7	25.5	107896	130689	99	97	9295	0.3	0.2	6.2	73.3	20.1	311663
22172	TRIANGLE	25651	2269	16.8	33.4	31.1	14.1	4.5	49745	61334	71	65	1166	3.1	1.0	29.1	61.2	5.7	210211
22180	VIENNA	46706	8613	4.3	11.7	32.3	28.4	23.2	101986	127385	98	96	6705	0.4	0.1	3.2	65.8	30.6	347376
22181	VIENNA	66442	5071	2.7	6.5	20.9	26.4	43.5	136953	169622	100	99	4221	0.0	0.0	2.8	31.3	65.9	471209
22182	VIENNA	70400	8104	5.5	5.8	18.5	21.9	48.3	145091	177267	100	99	6977	0.4	0.1	0.4	21.1	78.0	530704
22191	WOODBRIDGE	23705	15916	10.3	29.6	40.1	14.8	5.2	58961	69695	84	79	9080	3.2	0.7	41.5	52.2	2.3	180805
22192	WOODBRIDGE	37195	20814	5.3	16.6	38.9	24.6	14.6	83490	98467	96	92	15029	1.1	1.2	23.0	64.6	10.1	230881
22193	WOODBRIDGE	27600	22681	6.0	17.5	45.3	23.4	7.7	77550	89503	94	90	18110	0.5	0.3	26.0	70.5	2.7	212000
22201	ARLINGTON	60378	16471	9.4	16.7	35.0	20.4	18.4	81393	107445	95	91	5262	0.3	1.3	15.4	45.4	37.6	340673
22202	ARLINGTON	56861	10668	10.8	14.9	38.3	20.6	15.5	79352	103620	95	90	3132	0.0	2.5	12.1	43.2	42.2	360995
22203	ARLINGTON	43995	8986	14.7	17.3	34.5	19.7	13.9	72313	92503	92	86	2893	0.6	3.8	13.3	53.3	29.0	323747
22204	ARLINGTON	30039	19494	14.6	27.4	35.2	14.8	8.0	56960	71384	82	77	7082	1.2	4.2	19.4	61.5	13.8	247540
22205	ARLINGTON	57113	6754	6.4	11.4	26.6	26.6	29.0	108381	137762	99	97	4731	0.1	0.1	1.4	52.9	45.4	387593
22206	ARLINGTON	47090	8935	7.4	19.9	39.9	20.8	12.0	75648	94008	93	89	4238	0.4	0.8	19.7	74.0	5.1	225015
22207	ARLINGTON	68147	10883	5.2	8.7	23.7	25.6	36.8	124095	156119	99	99	8394	0.1	0.5	2.5	25.5	71.4	503663
22209	ARLINGTON	55914	6374	13.9	23.7	33.7	14.4	14.3	65635	86520	89	83	1439	1.5	6.6	18.7	37.5	35.7	254775
22211	FT MYER	25364	477	14.9	24.7	31.9	17.6	10.9	64347	84162	88	82	79	0.0	1.3	36.7	32.9	29.1	253125
22213	ARLINGTON	55689	1010	2.3	6.3	30.5	31.7	29.2	115590	146806	99	98	841	0.2	0.0	0.1	57.9	41.7	375528
22301	ALEXANDRIA	60404	4942	7.4	15.2	30.4	22.3	24.7	93601	128699	98	94	3024	0.3	0.2	6.7	54.3	38.4	341374
22302	ALEXANDRIA	55016	9279	9.1	19.6	36.0	20.0	15.4	75310	97155	93	89	4882	0.0	3.1	36.0	33.7	27.3	210531
22303	ALEXANDRIA	42928	7403	9.6	23.3	41.2	18.0	8.0	66038	82536	89	83	3032	0.1	2.0	31.9	60.0	6.0	212048
22304	ALEXANDRIA	39732	22200	14.0	25.5	35.6	15.5	9.4	61638	78779	86	80	8041	0.6	2.3	34.8	44.8	17.6	219183
22305	ALEXANDRIA	30121	6607	14.0	27.5	33.8	13.5	11.1	58533	75000	83	78	2379	0.3	2.5	26.6	39.7	31.0	262888
22306	ALEXANDRIA	30400	9799	16.0	23.5	33.6	16.5	10.4	62520	79169	87	81	5152	16.3	1.6	8.1	58.6	15.3	247631
	VIRGINIA	30454		19.8	25.2	32.5	13.6	8.9	55216	67801				6.8	10.4	35.8	36.5	10.5	166226
	UNITED STATES	25866		24.7	27.1	30.8	10.9	6.5	48124	56710				10.9	15.0	33.7	30.1	10.4	145905

ZIP CODE #	POST OFFICE NAME	FINANCIAL SERVICES				THE HOME						ENTERTAINMENT						PERSONAL			
						Home Improvements		Furnishings													
		Auto Loan	Home Loan	Invest-ments	Retire-ment Plans	Home Repair	Lawn & Garden	Comput-ers & Hard-ware	Major Appli-ances	TV, Radio, Sound Equip-ment	Furni-ture	Dine out/ Carry out	Sports Equip-ment	Fees & Tickets	Toys & Games	Travel	Cable TV	Apparel & Services	Auto Repairs	Health Insur-ance	Pets & Supplies
20105	ALDIE	173	203	211	207	197	197	183	182	170	188	215	210	193	218	184	163	213	177	163	199
20106	AMISSVILLE	126	124	109	122	129	134	114	124	115	114	141	147	113	145	118	116	136	121	126	151
20107	ARCOLA	171	199	198	207	190	186	178	175	163	184	207	205	187	209	175	153	206	170	151	193
20109	MANASSAS	102	98	110	105	95	99	104	100	100	105	127	120	102	121	99	94	124	104	90	111
20110	MANASSAS	125	133	141	139	129	130	130	127	123	132	156	149	132	154	126	116	154	127	112	140
20111	MANASSAS	122	134	141	139	129	130	128	125	120	130	152	147	131	153	125	114	150	124	110	138
20112	MANASSAS	164	196	201	202	188	186	175	172	159	179	203	200	185	208	174	152	202	166	149	189
20115	MARSHALL	171	184	191	184	188	195	173	179	169	172	210	209	176	214	177	168	205	175	175	206
20117	MIDDLEBURG	163	191	227	195	189	194	183	180	174	183	219	211	191	224	186	170	217	179	166	196
20119	CATLETT	115	141	153	140	139	139	128	127	120	127	151	148	136	161	131	118	151	123	116	140
20120	CENTREVILLE	167	190	201	199	182	181	175	171	162	180	206	201	184	209	173	154	205	168	149	189
20121	CENTREVILLE	142	148	151	157	141	140	144	140	134	148	171	166	144	167	137	125	168	141	121	154
20124	CLIFTON	244	295	356	302	286	299	270	263	250	274	318	303	293	326	275	244	320	257	238	289
20129	PAEONIAN SPRINGS	206	256	278	265	248	250	226	220	205	229	262	255	248	272	230	199	264	212	196	244
20130	PARIS	132	129	116	127	135	140	120	130	121	119	148	154	119	153	124	122	143	127	132	159
20132	PURCELLVILLE	147	175	182	180	169	168	157	155	144	160	183	180	167	188	158	138	182	150	137	170
20135	BLUEMONT	117	144	157	145	141	140	130	129	121	130	152	151	138	161	133	117	152	125	116	142
20136	BRISTOW	171	194	188	202	185	179	175	173	160	182	204	203	180	205	171	149	202	169	147	190
20137	BROAD RUN	165	204	224	209	198	199	182	178	167	184	212	207	198	221	185	162	213	172	159	197
20141	ROUND HILL	145	180	193	181	176	175	161	159	148	161	187	186	172	198	164	144	187	154	142	176
20143	CATHARPIN	192	206	211	205	208	228	186	196	182	194	230	208	197	214	195	186	223	190	203	221
20144	DELAPLANE	165	136	108	133	148	161	134	152	144	133	173	182	124	172	137	147	163	151	166	196
20147	ASHBURN	184	205	199	214	195	189	187	185	172	195	219	217	192	218	182	160	216	181	157	203
20148	ASHBURN	234	265	256	276	252	243	239	236	218	248	278	276	246	278	233	203	275	230	201	258
20151	CHANTILLY	169	190	204	195	184	188	177	174	167	181	212	202	186	214	176	161	211	172	156	193
20152	CHANTILLY	158	179	172	187	170	164	161	160	148	168	188	187	166	188	157	137	186	156	136	175
20155	GAINESVILLE	176	195	192	198	190	194	176	179	166	182	210	203	183	206	177	161	207	174	165	200
20158	HAMILTON	172	213	228	215	208	207	189	188	175	190	220	219	203	233	193	169	221	181	167	207
20164	STERLING	131	143	149	149	138	138	136	133	128	139	162	158	139	161	133	121	160	133	118	147
20165	STERLING	188	210	217	219	204	203	196	194	182	201	230	227	202	230	193	172	227	190	172	212
20166	STERLING	138	157	154	164	150	146	142	140	129	147	165	164	147	166	139	121	163	136	119	153
20169	HAYMARKET	150	180	187	185	174	173	161	158	147	164	187	185	171	193	161	141	187	153	140	175
20170	HERNDON	169	193	220	199	185	189	182	176	171	185	218	205	191	223	181	166	218	175	157	194
20171	HERNDON	207	241	257	251	232	232	219	214	202	225	257	250	233	260	218	192	256	210	188	236
20175	LEESBURG	158	172	177	181	165	164	163	159	152	168	193	188	167	192	159	143	191	159	139	176
20176	LEESBURG	151	161	166	170	154	153	154	150	144	159	183	178	157	181	149	135	181	150	131	166
20180	LOVETTSVILLE	140	174	185	174	171	169	155	155	144	155	181	181	165	193	159	140	181	149	139	171
20181	NOKESVILLE	142	174	184	176	170	168	155	154	143	156	181	180	166	191	158	138	181	149	137	170
20184	UPPERVILLE	139	161	193	166	159	162	157	152	148	156	187	181	162	193	158	144	185	153	138	167
20186	WARRENTON	117	138	160	141	136	138	131	128	123	130	155	151	137	161	133	120	154	127	117	141
20187	WARRENTON	141	175	188	176	172	170	157	156	146	157	183	182	168	194	160	141	183	151	140	172
20190	RESTON	139	145	206	156	141	151	153	145	150	154	190	173	158	194	152	147	188	149	135	160
20191	RESTON	171	198	242	201	192	201	190	185	181	192	229	216	199	233	191	176	227	186	169	202
20194	RESTON	239	262	315	280	253	262	257	244	242	261	309	289	270	312	253	233	308	246	219	272
20197	WATERFORD	227	283	307	292	274	276	249	243	227	253	289	281	274	300	253	220	291	234	216	269
20198	THE PLAINS	215	248	303	256	244	250	244	236	231	242	291	281	251	299	245	224	288	238	214	258
22003	ANNANDALE	134	173	229	168	166	173	160	157	152	161	192	182	171	206	166	151	194	156	139	167
22015	BURKE	164	192	217	196	185	190	178	174	167	181	213	201	190	218	179	163	213	172	157	191
22026	DUMFRIES	129	137	139	144	132	132	131	129	123	135	156	152	133	154	127	115	153	128	113	142
22027	DUNN LORING	184	235	266	239	227	230	207	201	189	209	240	232	228	253	212	184	243	194	179	221
22030	FAIRFAX	158	179	257	187	172	183	181	170	176	183	222	202	191	233	182	173	222	173	155	186
22031	FAIRFAX	135	155	220	159	149	158	156	149	152	157	192	176	163	201	158	150	192	152	135	162
22032	FAIRFAX	154	202	235	199	194	198	177	174	163	179	206	200	193	220	182	161	209	168	155	188
22033	FAIRFAX	163	173	233	186	166	174	177	167	172	180	218	200	184	222	175	166	216	171	151	185
22039	FAIRFAX STATION	275	356	440	358	346	362	312	307	287	318	365	350	349	382	325	285	369	295	279	336
22041	FALLS CHURCH	119	123	195	127	118	130	134	125	138	137	175	147	137	182	134	139	175	132	119	138
22042	FALLS CHURCH	117	142	203	140	136	145	138	132	136	140	172	153	147	185	142	136	173	134	121	143
22043	FALLS CHURCH	142	167	248	170	159	170	166	156	163	168	206	183	177	221	169	163	207	159	143	170
22044	FALLS CHURCH	131	157	248	153	150	165	157	148	160	159	203	171	168	222	163	164	205	152	142	162
22046	FALLS CHURCH	143	187	247	180	180	188	171	167	164	173	206	192	185	224	178	164	209	165	151	179
22060	FORT BELVOIR	95	67	68	75	63	72	92	82	92	87	116	106	81	105	79	85	111	93	76	92
22066	GREAT FALLS	379	503	668	497	489	523	439	435	408	450	517	491	495	542	465	409	524	418	401	473
22067	GREENWAY	434	584	801	572	569	614	509	504	474	520	599	567	578	631	542	478	609	484	468	548
22079	LORTON	134	135	148	143	131	135	138	133	131	140	167	159	137	162	133	124	164	137	120	148
22101	MC LEAN	284	389	528	375	377	404	340	336	319	346	402	379	383	432	362	323	409	324	310	362
22102	MC LEAN	227	248	402	265	239	263	260	241	258	264	327	286	278	343	263	258	327	248	226	266
22124	OAKTON	257	314	445	320	305	328	297	287	283	302	358	332	325	375	307	282	360	284	265	313
22134	QUANTICO	81	53	55	61	50	58	78	68	79	73	99	90	68	89	66	72	95	79	63	77
22150	SPRINGFIELD	123	142	189	143	138	145	140	137	136	142	172	160	145	178	142	134	172	139	125	147
22151	SPRINGFIELD	123	177	233	164	169	177	154	152	145	155	182	172	170	203	163	147	186	147	136	161
22152	SPRINGFIELD	151	194	228	193	187	189	173	170	161	175	203	197	187	215	177	157	204	165	150	184
22153	SPRINGFIELD	177	211	218	218	203	201	188	185	172	193	219	215	201	224	188	164	219	179	161	203
22172	TRIANGLE	89	95	99	98	92	92	94	92	89	94	113	110	94	113	91	84	111	93	82	101
22180	VIENNA	140	200	280	189	191	201	177	173	168	179	211	197	197	237	188	171	216	168	154	183
22181	VIENNA	224	307	409	299	297	314	268	264	250	272	315	299	301	339	284	251	321	254	240	285
22182	VIENNA	250	320	411	321	313	330	288	283	268	292	339	324	317	354	300	266	342	275	260	309
22191	WOODBRIDGE	100	96	105	101	92	97	102	98	99	103	126	117	100	122	97	94	123	102	88	108
22192	WOODBRIDGE	142	155	163	163	149	149	147	144	137	151	175	170	151	174	144	130	172	143	126	159
22193	WOODBRIDGE	121	136	138	141	131	130	127	125	117	129	149	147	130	150	124	111	147	123	109	137
22201	ARLINGTON	137	138	241	155	132	146	156	141	158	158	200	172	163	209	155	156	199	149	131	157
22202	ARLINGTON	127	130	230	144	124	137	146	132	148	148	188	160	153	198	145	147	187	139	123	146
22203	ARLINGTON	111	117	206	124	112	125	130	119	135	131	171	142	136	183	132	137	171	126	115	131
22204	ARLINGTON	92	94	156	98	90	100	106	97	109	106	139	116	108	146	106	111	139	103	93	107
22205	ARLINGTON	159	208	305	204	198	211	195	187	189	197	238	217	213	261	204	190	241	186	169	200
22206	ARLINGTON	122	118	206	132	112	125	137	123	140	139	178	150	141	185	134	139	176	131	116	137
22207	ARLINGTON	210	270	385	268	261	279	249	241	238	253	301	277	275	323	261	240	304	238	222	261
22209	ARLINGTON	120	116	221	132	110	123	137	121	141	139	180	149	143	190	136	141	179	130	114	136
22211	FT MYER	118	97	153	112	91	104	125	109	127	123	161	139	121	159	115	122	157	122	102	123
22213	ARLINGTON	153	225	298	210	215	224	194	192	183	195	229	218	216	257	207	185	234	185	171	202
22301	ALEXANDRIA	161	176	278	189	170	183	185	172	183	188	232	206	196	244	187	181	231	177	158	189
22302	ALEXANDRIA	129	137	222	147	132	146	147	136	148	149	187	162	156	196	148	148	186	142	129	150
22303	ALEXANDRIA	109	112	186	121	107	118	123	113	124	125	158	134	129	165	123	124	157	118	106	125
22304	ALEXANDRIA	107	104	154	113	100	110	116	108	117	118	148	130	118	149	114	114	146	114	101	120
22305	ALEXANDRIA	97	100	165	102	96	107	111	103	115	113	147	121	113	153	111	118	147	109	100	113
22306	ALEXANDRIA	113	115	128	119	112	117	116	114	113	118	143	134	117	139	113	108	140	116	105	127
	VIRGINIA	112	109	113	109	109	117	108	110	109	109	136	129	108	135	108	109	132	110	109	128
	UNITED STATES	100	100	100	100	100	100	100	100	100	100	100	100	100	100	100	100	100	100	100	100

POPULATION CHANGE

ZIP CODE		COUNTY FIPS CODE	POPULATION			2000-2004 ANNUAL RATE		HOUSEHOLDS					FAMILIES		
#	POST OFFICE NAME		2000	2004	2009	% Rate	State Centile	2000	2004	2009	% Annual Rate 2000-2004	2004 Average HH Size	2000	2004	% Annual Rate 2000-2004
22307	ALEXANDRIA	059	10169	12085	13362	4.2	95	4732	5761	6469	4.7	2.10	2656	3088	3.6
22308	ALEXANDRIA	059	12088	13034	13777	1.8	75	4613	4989	5293	1.9	2.59	3625	3896	1.7
22309	ALEXANDRIA	059	28084	28031	29093	0.0	22	10388	10432	10859	0.1	2.69	7354	7325	-0.1
22310	ALEXANDRIA	059	25779	27750	29549	1.8	74	10211	10995	11744	1.8	2.52	6694	7129	1.5
22311	ALEXANDRIA	510	15436	16847	18055	2.1	80	7243	7833	8393	1.9	2.09	3113	3326	1.6
22312	ALEXANDRIA	059	27696	30063	32511	2.0	79	10038	10874	11769	1.9	2.75	6587	7020	1.5
22314	ALEXANDRIA	510	24585	26254	28093	1.6	70	13407	14655	15947	2.1	1.75	5329	5650	1.4
22315	ALEXANDRIA	059	26012	28090	29895	1.8	75	10578	11467	12252	1.9	2.45	6909	7425	1.7
22401	FREDERICKSBURG	630	19283	19569	20063	0.4	37	8104	8407	8822	0.9	2.05	3926	3974	0.3
22405	FREDERICKSBURG	179	23216	27224	34167	3.8	95	8091	9616	12213	4.2	2.80	6312	7416	3.9
22406	FREDERICKSBURG	179	11183	15204	20510	7.5	98	3996	5517	7525	7.9	2.75	3050	4158	7.6
22407	FREDERICKSBURG	177	40237	49280	63386	4.9	96	13811	17142	22396	5.2	2.85	10759	13264	5.1
22408	FREDERICKSBURG	177	18470	24301	32343	6.7	98	6685	8947	12105	7.1	2.71	5052	6677	6.8
22427	BOWLING GREEN	033	2772	2751	2847	-0.2	18	1050	1061	1120	0.3	2.52	733	728	-0.2
22432	BURGESS	133	566	638	709	2.9	89	237	270	304	3.1	2.36	167	188	2.8
22433	BURR HILL	137	403	461	534	3.2	91	147	171	201	3.6	2.70	118	136	3.4
22435	CALLAO	133	2346	2433	2582	0.9	54	999	1053	1135	1.3	2.30	690	716	0.9
22436	CARET	057	403	404	415	0.1	26	160	164	171	0.6	2.46	117	118	0.2
22437	CENTER CROSS	057	470	481	499	0.6	44	199	207	219	0.9	2.32	139	143	0.7
22438	CHAMPLAIN	057	549	551	566	0.1	27	212	217	228	0.6	2.53	155	157	0.3
22443	COLONIAL BEACH	193	7528	7894	8290	1.1	61	3110	3306	3525	1.5	2.36	2076	2171	1.1
22448	DAHLGREN	099	958	1301	1619	7.5	98	198	297	390	10.0	3.64	196	294	10.0
22454	DUNNSVILLE	057	2150	2178	2251	0.3	36	870	894	941	0.6	2.44	619	628	0.3
22460	FARNHAM	159	1455	1497	1555	0.7	48	590	624	667	1.3	2.20	417	435	1.0
22469	HAGUE	193	2253	2308	2392	0.6	45	912	956	1011	1.1	2.41	635	657	0.8
22473	HEATHSVILLE	133	4590	4934	5346	1.7	73	2022	2208	2430	2.1	2.23	1404	1511	1.7
22476	HUSTLE	057	390	391	402	0.1	26	136	139	146	0.5	2.81	99	100	0.2
22480	IRVINGTON	103	770	781	792	0.3	37	247	252	258	0.5	2.33	176	176	0.0
22482	KILMARNOCK	133	2178	2221	2305	0.5	41	1001	1037	1094	0.8	2.08	690	705	0.5
22485	KING GEORGE	099	15847	17371	19665	2.2	81	5894	6577	7564	2.6	2.62	4329	4749	2.2
22488	KINSALE	193	1439	1432	1472	-0.1	20	592	603	633	0.4	2.37	415	418	0.2
22503	LANCASTER	103	4547	4650	4762	0.5	44	1980	2068	2158	1.0	2.23	1353	1391	0.7
22504	LANEVIEW	057	186	190	198	0.5	43	69	72	76	1.0	2.64	48	50	1.0
22508	LOCUST GROVE	137	7520	8782	10317	3.7	94	3090	3680	4404	4.2	2.39	2391	2811	3.9
22509	LORETTO	057	71	71	73	0.0	24	34	35	36	0.7	2.03	25	25	0.0
22511	LOTTSBURG	133	1283	1342	1434	1.1	59	591	627	680	1.4	2.14	410	428	1.0
22514	MILFORD	033	2343	2374	2463	0.3	36	893	923	975	0.8	2.57	667	680	0.5
22520	MONTROSS	193	5279	5435	5656	0.7	48	2129	2227	2356	1.1	2.43	1489	1536	0.7
22534	PARTLOW	177	2061	2581	3352	5.4	97	696	890	1177	6.0	2.90	555	702	5.7
22535	PORT ROYAL	033	780	776	794	-0.1	20	202	205	216	0.4	2.38	146	145	-0.2
22538	RAPPAHANNOCK ACADEMY	033	292	290	301	-0.2	19	114	115	122	0.2	2.49	82	82	0.0
22539	REEDVILLE	133	2342	2561	2800	2.1	81	1090	1212	1346	2.5	2.11	744	814	2.1
22542	RHOADESVILLE	137	1510	1675	1909	2.5	85	552	621	721	2.8	2.70	432	481	2.6
22546	RUTHER GLEN	033	9841	10682	11536	2.0	79	3572	3960	4362	2.5	2.68	2753	3016	2.2
22553	SPOTSYLVANIA	177	26186	31071	39365	4.1	95	8803	10653	13734	4.6	2.92	7245	8683	4.4
22554	STAFFORD	179	37912	45832	58389	4.6	96	12000	14635	18825	4.8	3.09	10025	12142	4.6
22556	STAFFORD	179	20255	25223	32522	5.3	97	6136	7742	10114	5.6	3.17	5135	6443	5.5
22560	TAPPAHANNOCK	057	5674	6033	6398	1.5	67	2279	2475	2679	2.0	2.37	1511	1615	1.6
22567	UNIONVILLE	137	2441	2805	3258	3.3	91	901	1056	1251	3.8	2.65	691	799	3.5
22572	WARSAW	159	7382	7593	7859	0.7	48	2369	2513	2686	1.4	2.38	1597	1668	1.0
22576	WEEMS	103	2358	2297	2309	-0.6	8	1024	1014	1036	-0.2	2.18	684	667	-0.6
22578	WHITE STONE	103	2799	2917	3009	1.0	57	1260	1330	1392	1.3	2.16	863	898	0.9
22579	WICOMICO CHURCH	133	236	249	266	1.3	64	103	110	120	1.6	2.26	72	76	1.3
22580	WOODFORD	033	5323	5603	6081	1.2	62	1942	2085	2307	1.7	2.66	1448	1536	1.4
22601	WINCHESTER	840	24456	25514	26746	1.0	57	10327	10893	11537	1.3	2.26	5863	6062	0.8
22602	WINCHESTER	069	21139	23568	26471	2.6	86	7874	8918	10168	3.0	2.63	6002	6714	2.7
22603	WINCHESTER	069	10814	11815	13128	2.1	80	4177	4653	5267	2.6	2.44	3056	3363	2.3
22610	BENTONVILLE	187	1628	1742	1892	1.6	71	660	715	784	1.9	2.44	482	514	1.5
22611	BERRYVILLE	043	7584	8213	9009	1.9	77	2934	3279	3709	2.7	2.46	2088	2301	2.3
22620	BOYCE	043	2425	2541	2741	1.1	60	987	1062	1177	1.7	2.38	708	752	1.4
22624	CLEAR BROOK	069	2823	3189	3598	2.9	89	1036	1194	1372	3.4	2.67	820	937	3.2
22625	CROSS JUNCTION	069	2739	3102	3506	3.0	90	957	1104	1270	3.4	2.75	757	864	3.2
22627	FLINT HILL	157	484	505	521	1.0	57	219	232	243	1.4	2.18	160	167	1.0
22630	FRONT ROYAL	187	25598	27338	29696	1.6	70	9745	10514	11534	1.8	2.55	6819	7252	1.5
22637	GORE	069	2007	2058	2205	0.6	45	756	790	862	1.0	2.57	594	615	0.8
22639	HUME	061	499	606	726	4.7	96	204	253	309	5.2	2.38	155	191	5.0
22640	HUNTLY	157	639	667	689	1.0	58	252	266	279	1.3	2.51	179	187	1.0
22641	STRASBURG	171	163	190	215	3.7	94	67	79	91	4.0	2.41	51	60	3.9
22642	LINDEN	061	3575	3905	4307	2.1	80	1332	1471	1639	2.4	2.65	952	1036	2.0
22643	MARKHAM	061	356	400	460	2.8	88	138	158	186	3.2	2.47	100	113	2.9
22644	MAURERTOWN	171	1981	2095	2261	1.3	65	747	804	882	1.8	2.58	571	608	1.5
22645	MIDDLETOWN	069	2979	3231	3563	1.9	78	1196	1319	1476	2.3	2.44	873	950	2.0
22649	MIDDLETOWN	187	35	43	50	5.0	97	17	21	25	5.1	2.05	13	16	5.0
22650	RILEYVILLE	139	986	974	973	-0.3	16	392	396	404	0.2	2.45	285	284	-0.1
22652	FORT VALLEY	171	1139	1278	1422	2.8	87	468	533	601	3.1	2.40	343	386	2.8
22654	STAR TANNERY	069	457	485	530	1.4	67	188	202	223	1.7	2.40	138	147	1.5
22655	STEPHENS CITY	069	13713	15067	16801	2.2	82	5045	5623	6361	2.6	2.68	3835	4233	2.4
22656	STEPHENSON	069	1661	1754	1912	1.3	64	616	661	732	1.7	2.65	478	507	1.4
22657	STRASBURG	171	8025	8851	9766	2.3	83	3363	3762	4203	2.7	2.35	2287	2520	2.3
22660	TOMS BROOK	171	1450	1511	1616	1.0	56	570	604	656	1.4	2.48	432	452	1.1
22663	WHITE POST	043	1842	1883	2004	0.5	43	607	635	692	1.1	2.75	454	469	0.8
22664	WOODSTOCK	171	7342	7943	8671	1.9	76	2966	3250	3600	2.2	2.35	2031	2191	1.8
22701	CULPEPER	047	21576	23888	27479	2.4	84	8211	9239	10806	2.8	2.54	5858	6489	2.4
22709	ARODA	113	1467	1570	1700	1.6	71	523	574	637	2.2	2.67	398	431	1.9
22712	BEALETON	061	6445	7182	8243	2.6	86	2174	2456	2862	2.9	2.91	1720	1921	2.6
22713	BOSTON	047	856	976	1121	3.1	90	313	363	423	3.6	2.69	243	278	3.2
22714	BRANDY STATION	047	519	559	639	1.8	74	189	207	240	2.2	2.70	137	147	1.7
22715	BRIGHTWOOD	113	1177	1262	1369	1.7	72	443	485	539	2.2	2.57	352	381	1.9
22716	CASTLETON	157	660	691	714	1.1	60	260	278	291	1.6	2.49	190	200	1.2
22718	ELKWOOD	047	631	671	757	1.5	68	224	243	279	1.9	2.71	174	185	1.5
22720	GOLDVEIN	061	1333	1360	1491	0.5	41	448	464	517	0.8	2.92	364	373	0.6
22722	HAYWOOD	113	253	271	294	1.6	71	86	94	105	2.1	2.85	68	74	2.0
22724	JEFFERSONTON	047	1851	2335	2862	5.6	98	621	799	997	6.1	2.92	520	662	5.9
22725	LEON	113	387	415	450	1.7	72	145	159	176	2.2	2.58	115	125	2.0
22726	LIGNUM	047	527	560	630	1.4	67	173	188	215	2.0	2.90	140	149	1.5
	VIRGINIA					1.4					1.7	2.51			1.4
	UNITED STATES					1.2					1.3	2.58			1.1

ZIP CODE #	POST OFFICE NAME	RACE (%) White 2000	White 2004	Black 2000	Black 2004	Asian/Pacific 2000	Asian/Pacific 2004	% Hispanic Origin 2000	% Hispanic Origin 2004	2004 AGE DISTRIBUTION (%) 0-4	5-9	10-14	15-19	20-24	25-44	45-64	65-84	85+	18+	MEDIAN AGE 2004	% 2004 Males	% 2004 Females
22307	ALEXANDRIA	83.2	81.9	7.8	7.7	2.9	3.3	7.8	9.6	5.0	5.3	5.2	4.4	3.9	29.0	30.0	14.6	2.8	81.8	43.6	46.6	53.4
22308	ALEXANDRIA	90.3	89.1	4.3	4.5	2.9	3.4	2.7	3.6	6.2	7.5	7.8	5.6	3.0	19.0	31.4	17.4	2.2	74.8	45.5	48.1	51.9
22309	ALEXANDRIA	54.8	54.4	27.4	25.9	6.5	7.0	14.2	16.3	7.0	6.8	7.0	6.7	6.8	28.6	26.4	10.1	0.7	75.1	37.1	48.4	51.6
22310	ALEXANDRIA	69.5	65.8	11.7	12.4	9.9	11.2	11.0	13.7	6.5	6.4	6.0	5.1	5.4	33.6	27.4	9.0	0.7	78.0	38.3	48.7	51.3
22311	ALEXANDRIA	50.1	48.1	24.9	23.7	9.4	10.5	16.9	19.9	6.1	5.3	4.7	4.9	8.6	40.0	19.8	7.0	3.7	81.2	34.5	49.2	50.8
22312	ALEXANDRIA	47.7	45.4	22.1	21.4	13.2	14.2	21.8	25.3	7.6	7.1	6.5	5.8	6.8	34.5	23.6	7.4	0.8	75.4	34.7	49.4	50.6
22314	ALEXANDRIA	71.7	70.1	22.6	23.2	2.2	2.6	5.1	6.2	4.1	3.9	3.2	3.1	5.0	42.1	27.5	10.0	1.1	86.9	38.9	47.8	52.2
22315	ALEXANDRIA	69.7	66.3	13.9	14.6	10.1	11.7	7.6	9.5	7.3	7.1	6.0	4.8	4.7	38.5	26.7	4.8	0.2	76.6	36.6	48.2	51.8
22401	FREDERICKSBURG	73.2	71.2	20.4	21.3	1.6	1.8	4.9	6.0	5.8	4.7	4.6	11.4	14.7	26.6	19.5	10.9	1.9	82.2	30.5	45.1	54.9
22405	FREDERICKSBURG	88.5	87.5	7.5	7.8	1.2	1.4	2.3	2.8	6.9	7.1	8.2	6.8	6.0	28.1	25.8	9.7	1.3	73.4	37.0	49.3	50.7
22406	FREDERICKSBURG	85.5	83.5	9.4	10.3	1.5	1.8	2.5	3.3	8.3	8.0	7.8	6.6	6.2	32.5	23.6	6.6	0.6	71.9	33.9	50.0	50.1
22407	FREDERICKSBURG	81.8	80.1	12.9	13.7	1.8	2.1	3.5	4.3	7.7	7.6	8.4	7.6	6.7	30.0	23.7	7.2	1.2	71.5	33.9	48.8	51.2
22408	FREDERICKSBURG	82.7	81.2	12.4	13.1	1.4	1.7	3.1	3.8	8.8	8.3	7.8	6.1	5.9	32.5	21.6	8.4	0.7	71.3	33.4	48.6	51.4
22427	BOWLING GREEN	63.5	61.5	32.0	33.3	0.7	0.8	2.4	2.9	5.7	5.9	6.7	5.8	5.1	25.6	26.7	15.4	3.1	77.8	41.8	47.3	52.7
22432	BURGESS	65.0	62.4	33.8	36.2	0.0	0.0	1.8	2.0	4.1	4.6	5.8	5.3	4.7	19.8	31.0	22.6	2.2	82.6	49.0	47.2	52.8
22433	BURR HILL	89.6	88.9	8.4	9.1	0.3	0.2	1.5	2.0	7.2	7.2	7.4	7.4	4.6	27.8	28.6	8.7	1.3	73.5	38.7	49.5	50.5
22435	CALLAO	75.6	74.0	23.1	24.4	0.0	0.1	1.1	1.3	5.2	5.5	6.0	5.3	4.6	23.8	28.5	18.6	2.5	80.1	44.7	47.7	52.3
22436	CARET	33.8	31.7	62.8	64.9	0.5	0.5	0.5	0.3	4.7	5.5	7.4	5.7	4.7	26.5	29.5	14.4	1.7	78.7	41.5	47.5	52.5
22437	CENTER CROSS	73.8	71.9	25.1	26.6	0.2	0.2	0.9	1.3	4.6	4.6	5.6	5.6	4.6	21.8	34.1	17.3	1.9	82.1	46.9	47.2	52.8
22438	CHAMPLAIN	41.0	38.8	55.4	57.4	0.6	0.5	0.7	0.9	4.9	5.6	7.1	5.8	4.9	25.4	29.8	14.7	1.8	79.0	42.4	48.1	51.9
22443	COLONIAL BEACH	78.2	76.1	17.0	18.2	0.4	0.5	4.6	5.6	5.5	5.9	6.7	6.2	4.5	23.1	28.4	17.5	2.2	77.9	43.8	48.3	51.7
22448	DAHLGREN	76.9	74.9	15.9	16.8	1.7	2.0	6.9	8.4	14.2	12.5	6.8	7.1	19.7	37.1	2.4	0.2	0.0	65.2	22.4	60.0	40.0
22454	DUNNSVILLE	71.9	70.0	25.3	26.7	0.5	0.6	0.7	0.8	5.1	5.4	6.4	6.3	5.3	24.8	29.9	14.9	1.9	79.3	42.9	48.9	51.1
22460	FARNHAM	69.8	68.1	28.5	29.8	0.5	0.5	1.0	1.2	4.0	4.3	6.0	5.5	5.3	25.3	27.9	17.7	4.0	82.0	44.7	50.2	49.8
22469	HAGUE	50.7	48.5	47.6	49.7	0.3	0.3	1.5	1.8	5.2	5.5	6.0	6.3	5.4	22.1	31.5	16.5	1.5	79.6	44.7	47.6	52.4
22473	HEATHSVILLE	64.5	62.6	34.2	36.0	0.2	0.3	1.0	1.1	4.8	5.0	5.4	4.9	4.0	19.3	30.6	23.4	2.6	81.9	49.7	48.5	51.5
22476	HUSTLE	33.6	31.7	62.8	64.7	0.5	0.5	0.5	0.3	4.6	5.6	7.4	5.9	4.9	25.8	29.4	14.6	1.8	78.5	41.8	47.3	52.7
22480	IRVINGTON	88.7	87.5	11.2	12.4	0.1	0.1	0.0	0.0	2.3	2.4	3.6	3.5	3.1	11.1	26.6	33.7	13.7	89.5	63.2	42.9	57.1
22482	KILMARNOCK	75.2	73.4	23.1	24.5	0.4	0.5	0.7	1.0	3.7	4.0	5.0	4.1	3.6	15.5	30.0	29.5	4.6	84.6	56.0	46.0	54.0
22485	KING GEORGE	77.7	76.2	18.9	20.0	1.0	1.2	1.5	1.8	7.2	7.4	7.4	6.6	5.7	29.2	26.0	9.3	1.2	73.9	37.3	49.5	50.5
22488	KINSALE	41.4	39.0	57.0	59.2	0.1	0.1	0.9	1.1	4.3	4.8	6.3	6.7	5.0	20.6	31.8	18.4	2.1	80.5	46.5	47.6	52.4
22503	LANCASTER	60.3	58.4	38.4	40.2	0.4	0.4	0.8	1.0	4.2	4.6	5.8	5.4	4.7	19.7	30.7	22.3	2.6	81.9	48.6	46.7	53.3
22504	LANEVIEW	73.7	72.6	24.7	26.8	0.0	0.0	1.1	1.1	4.2	4.7	5.8	5.8	4.2	22.1	33.7	17.4	2.1	81.6	46.9	47.4	52.6
22508	LOCUST GROVE	92.3	91.5	5.3	5.7	0.7	0.8	1.6	2.0	5.3	5.5	6.1	5.0	4.0	20.9	29.2	22.8	1.3	80.0	47.2	48.3	51.7
22509	LORETTO	33.8	32.4	63.4	64.8	0.0	0.0	0.0	0.0	5.6	5.6	7.0	5.6	5.6	28.2	25.4	15.5	1.4	78.9	39.6	49.3	50.7
22511	LOTTSBURG	80.1	78.8	18.9	20.0	0.5	0.6	0.8	0.9	4.0	4.4	5.3	4.8	3.2	18.9	31.7	25.0	2.7	83.2	52.5	47.1	52.9
22514	MILFORD	59.8	57.9	35.2	36.7	0.4	0.5	1.1	1.2	6.2	6.5	7.2	6.1	5.2	26.1	27.8	13.3	1.6	76.2	40.5	48.7	51.3
22520	MONTROSS	60.6	58.5	35.6	37.2	0.4	0.5	3.5	4.3	4.8	5.1	6.4	6.0	5.0	22.3	29.8	18.4	2.3	79.9	45.4	48.1	51.9
22534	PARTLOW	85.5	84.3	10.7	11.3	0.9	1.0	0.9	1.1	7.0	7.1	7.9	6.9	6.2	29.2	26.7	8.1	0.9	73.7	36.7	50.1	49.9
22535	PORT ROYAL	55.4	54.1	42.2	43.0	0.1	0.1	3.2	3.7	5.2	4.6	4.0	5.2	13.5	39.8	18.9	8.0	0.8	84.7	33.2	66.0	34.0
22538	RAPPAHANNOCK ACADEMY	75.7	74.1	20.9	21.7	0.3	0.3	2.7	3.1	7.9	7.9	6.2	4.5	4.8	29.7	24.5	13.1	1.4	75.2	38.6	49.0	51.0
22539	REEDVILLE	82.7	82.0	16.5	17.1	0.1	0.1	0.8	0.9	3.2	3.4	4.3	3.6	3.8	14.6	34.3	29.7	3.2	87.1	57.1	48.5	51.5
22542	RHOADESVILLE	87.0	86.0	11.2	11.9	0.3	0.4	1.3	1.7	7.0	7.2	7.3	6.9	5.4	27.9	26.7	10.4	1.1	74.2	38.1	50.0	50.0
22546	RUTHER GLEN	63.2	61.4	34.2	35.6	0.4	0.4	1.2	1.4	6.5	6.9	7.4	6.5	5.5	29.1	27.1	10.0	1.0	75.2	38.1	50.2	49.8
22553	SPOTSYLVANIA	84.2	83.1	12.0	12.5	1.0	1.2	2.0	2.5	7.3	7.8	8.7	7.5	6.0	29.1	25.8	7.3	0.6	71.6	35.6	50.1	50.0
22554	STAFFORD	77.5	75.8	15.6	16.2	2.1	2.4	4.7	5.8	8.3	8.4	9.1	7.7	6.8	32.0	22.9	4.2	0.4	69.1	32.3	49.8	50.2
22556	STAFFORD	81.1	79.2	12.6	13.4	1.8	2.1	3.7	4.6	8.1	8.3	9.5	8.3	7.9	31.6	22.5	3.7	0.3	69.0	31.3	51.2	48.8
22560	TAPPAHANNOCK	56.2	54.1	40.7	42.3	1.2	1.3	0.8	0.9	5.4	5.6	7.4	6.1	5.3	26.8	25.5	15.2	2.7	77.8	40.8	46.8	53.2
22567	UNIONVILLE	83.3	81.9	15.1	16.3	0.3	0.3	1.0	1.3	6.2	6.5	6.9	6.4	5.5	27.8	26.8	12.6	1.4	76.5	40.1	50.3	49.7
22572	WARSAW	62.9	61.0	35.1	36.6	0.4	0.4	2.3	2.8	4.3	4.4	4.8	5.3	6.8	31.9	26.0	13.8	2.7	83.1	40.8	57.4	42.6
22576	WEEMS	64.3	62.0	34.4	36.5	0.3	0.4	0.8	1.0	5.4	5.4	5.4	5.3	4.7	18.0	27.9	23.5	4.6	80.6	49.4	46.2	53.9
22578	WHITE STONE	81.5	80.0	17.3	18.5	0.5	0.7	0.2	0.3	4.0	4.2	4.8	4.9	3.8	17.3	32.0	25.9	3.2	84.0	52.7	48.6	51.4
22579	WICOMICO CHURCH	71.6	70.7	26.7	28.1	0.0	0.0	0.9	0.4	4.8	4.4	4.8	4.0	4.8	16.9	30.9	26.9	2.4	83.1	51.9	48.2	51.8
22580	WOODFORD	68.0	66.0	29.2	30.8	0.5	0.6	1.0	1.2	6.7	6.7	7.3	6.2	5.5	26.7	27.0	12.3	1.7	75.4	39.4	49.2	50.9
22601	WINCHESTER	82.2	80.4	10.4	10.9	1.6	1.9	6.3	7.8	6.2	5.7	6.2	6.6	8.7	30.2	22.5	12.2	1.8	78.6	35.6	48.9	51.2
22602	WINCHESTER	94.5	93.7	2.8	3.0	0.8	0.9	1.8	2.3	6.8	7.0	7.6	6.4	5.5	30.0	25.5	10.3	0.9	74.5	37.4	49.7	50.3
22603	WINCHESTER	95.3	94.7	2.7	2.9	0.5	0.6	1.0	1.4	5.8	6.1	7.0	6.6	5.1	28.9	27.4	11.0	2.2	76.9	39.9	50.5	49.5
22610	BENTONVILLE	97.1	96.7	1.8	2.0	0.0	0.0	0.6	0.8	5.2	5.7	6.8	6.2	4.5	25.1	29.1	15.1	2.2	78.3	43.0	49.8	50.2
22611	BERRYVILLE	90.8	89.9	7.0	7.5	0.6	0.7	1.5	1.9	5.4	6.1	7.7	6.0	4.5	25.1	28.1	14.8	2.4	77.0	42.4	48.0	52.0
22620	BOYCE	90.7	89.9	7.0	7.4	0.6	0.6	1.5	2.0	4.1	5.4	7.2	6.0	4.2	25.3	32.7	13.7	1.5	79.5	43.8	51.4	48.6
22624	CLEAR BROOK	96.4	96.0	2.0	2.1	0.3	0.3	1.1	1.4	5.2	6.4	7.3	7.3	4.8	26.9	31.0	10.1	0.9	76.4	40.9	51.3	48.7
22625	CROSS JUNCTION	97.7	97.4	0.7	0.8	0.4	0.4	0.4	0.6	5.9	6.4	7.2	6.6	4.7	28.1	29.0	10.9	1.2	76.1	40.2	50.9	49.1
22627	FLINT HILL	94.6	94.3	3.7	4.0	0.2	0.2	1.2	1.6	5.5	6.3	7.5	6.1	4.4	24.2	31.3	13.5	1.2	77.0	42.6	49.5	50.5
22630	FRONT ROYAL	91.8	90.9	5.6	6.0	0.5	0.6	1.7	2.1	6.7	6.7	7.3	6.9	6.2	27.6	25.6	11.5	1.6	75.2	38.1	48.9	51.1
22637	GORE	97.4	97.0	0.9	0.9	0.7	0.7	0.5	0.6	6.0	6.5	6.7	6.0	4.7	27.3	29.0	12.7	1.2	77.0	40.9	50.2	49.8
22639	HUME	90.0	89.1	7.4	7.8	0.6	0.7	1.8	2.2	4.5	5.3	6.6	6.4	4.3	23.3	35.3	12.9	1.5	79.5	44.8	49.0	51.0
22640	HUNTLY	96.6	96.4	2.5	2.7	0.2	0.2	0.3	0.5	5.9	6.9	7.5	6.6	4.2	22.8	31.5	13.5	1.2	75.7	42.7	49.0	51.0
22641	STRASBURG	98.2	98.4	0.6	0.5	0.6	0.5	1.2	1.1	6.3	6.3	6.3	5.3	4.2	25.8	27.9	16.3	1.6	77.9	42.5	49.5	50.5
22642	LINDEN	94.2	93.3	3.5	3.9	0.4	0.4	1.6	2.2	7.7	7.9	7.7	5.8	4.7	33.4	25.8	6.5	0.5	73.0	36.9	51.1	48.9
22643	MARKHAM	83.7	82.5	13.5	14.3	0.3	0.3	2.8	3.8	5.3	5.8	6.3	6.3	4.8	27.5	31.3	11.3	1.8	78.5	41.5	48.8	51.3
22644	MAURERTOWN	98.2	97.9	0.4	0.4	0.2	0.2	1.1	1.5	5.4	5.8	6.4	5.6	4.6	26.9	28.8	15.1	1.5	79.0	42.3	50.0	50.0
22645	MIDDLETOWN	96.7	96.5	2.0	2.0	0.3	0.4	0.9	1.2	5.1	5.7	7.2	5.9	5.3	27.5	29.5	12.4	1.5	78.4	41.5	50.0	50.1
22649	MIDDLETOWN	100.0	100.0	0.0	0.0	0.0	0.0	0.0	0.0	4.7	4.7	4.7	4.7	4.7	23.3	37.2	16.3	0.0	86.1	46.9	46.5	53.5
22650	RILEYVILLE	97.3	96.8	1.3	1.4	0.6	0.6	0.4	0.6	4.6	5.0	6.1	6.0	5.1	26.5	31.1	14.2	1.4	80.0	43.0	51.8	48.3
22652	FORT VALLEY	97.6	97.2	0.1	0.1	0.3	0.4	1.1	1.5	4.9	5.6	6.7	5.4	3.9	21.8	35.2	15.3	1.2	79.3	45.8	51.3	48.7
22654	STAR TANNERY	98.7	98.6	0.2	0.2	0.2	0.2	0.4	0.6	5.8	6.8	7.8	6.4	4.7	26.6	29.3	11.8	0.8	75.9	41.1	51.3	48.7
22655	STEPHENS CITY	94.7	94.1	2.9	3.1	0.9	1.1	1.8	2.2	7.4	7.4	8.0	7.0	6.5	31.0	24.0	7.9	0.7	72.9	35.0	48.9	51.1
22656	STEPHENSON	97.4	97.0	1.2	1.3	0.2	0.3	0.9	1.1	5.3	6.0	7.8	7.6	4.6	27.5	28.8	11.4	1.0	76.2	40.5	50.7	49.3
22657	STRASBURG	95.6	95.0	2.5	2.7	0.5	0.5	1.1	1.5	5.9	6.1	7.3	6.1	5.3	28.2	26.0	13.6	1.6	76.9	39.8	48.6	51.4
22660	TOMS BROOK	97.4	96.8	0.6	0.5	0.2	0.3	1.1	1.6	5.6	6.1	6.6	5.6	4.6	28.0	28.1	14.0	1.5	78.4	41.5	50.4	49.6
22663	WHITE POST	86.2	84.4	8.4	9.1	0.2	0.3	9.7	12.1	5.7	6.3	7.0	6.7	8.0	28.7	26.2	10.1	1.3	76.9	36.7	56.7	43.3
22664	WOODSTOCK	94.2	93.1	1.7	1.8	0.3	0.3	5.0	6.4	5.6	5.6	6.3	5.9	5.6	24.5	25.1	17.8	3.5	78.6	42.4	47.2	52.8
22701	CULPEPER	76.8	74.8	19.1	20.4	0.9	1.0	3.0	3.7	6.7	6.7	7.4	6.6	6.6	28.1	24.6	11.6	1.7	75.1	37.2	48.6	51.4
22709	ARODA	83.1	81.8	14.6	15.5	0.5	0.6	0.9	1.1	6.1	6.4	7.0	6.6	6.1	25.2	28.0	12.6	2.0	76.3	40.5	48.8	51.2
22712	BEALETON	86.7	85.3	10.1	11.0	0.5	0.6	2.2	2.8	8.3	8.4	8.7	7.0	5.8	32.0	22.7	6.4	0.7	70.0	34.6	49.6	50.5
22713	BOSTON	87.0	85.3	10.6	11.9	0.1	0.2	1.3	1.5	5.5	5.6	6.9	6.5	4.8	28.6	30.7	10.5	0.9	77.8	40.8	49.0	51.0
22714	BRANDY STATION	80.4	78.5	15.0	15.9	0.0	0.0	4.8	6.1	6.3	6.6	8.1	6.3	6.4	28.4	26.7	9.7	1.6	75.1	37.4	50.8	49.2
22715	BRIGHTWOOD	92.2	91.5	6.6	7.1	0.3	0.4	0.7	0.9	6.1	6.2	6.1	5.9	5.1	26.2	29.0	13.5	2.0	77.6	41.4	49.1	50.9
22716	CASTLETON	93.9	93.3	3.9	4.3	0.0	0.0	1.5	1.9	5.1	4.3	7.2	5.6	3.8	25.8	35.3	11.7	1.2	79.2	44.0	49.8	50.2
22718	ELKWOOD	78.5	76.2	16.6	17.9	0.8	0.9	3.3	4.5	5.8	7.0	8.8	6.7	5.8	28.5	25.8	10.1	1.5	74.2	37.4	50.5	49.5
22720	GOLDVEIN	92.1	91.1	5.9	6.4	0.5	0.7	1.0	1.3	6.2	6.8	7.8	7.4	5.8	29.1	28.0	8.0	0.9	74.6	38.3	50.4	49.6
22722	HAYWOOD	92.1	91.5	6.7	7.0	0.4	0.4	0.8	0.7	5.9	6.3	5.9	5.9	5.2	26.2	28.8	13.7	2.2	77.9	41.6	49.8	50.2
22724	JEFFERSONTON	85.6	83.9	12.4	13.8	0.3	0.3	1.2	1.6	7.0	7.7	8.0	6.7	4.5	27.7	28.0	9.7	0.8	73.1	38.9	50.0	50.0
22725	LEON	92.3	91.3	6.7	7.2	0.3	0.2	0.8	0.7	6.0	6.3	6.0	5.8	5.1	26.0	28.9	13.7	2.2	77.8	41.4	49.4	50.6
22726	LIGNUM	78.0	75.2	17.1	18.6	1.1	1.4	2.5	3.4	5.5	7.1	9.1	7.1	5.2	28.4	25.7	10.2	1.6	73.9	37.6	50.2	49.8
	VIRGINIA	72.3	70.7	19.6	19.9	3.7	4.3	4.7	5.7	6.5	6.6	6.9	6.9	7.0	29.7	24.9	10.1	1.4	76.2	36.6	49.1	50.9
	UNITED STATES	75.1	73.6	12.3	12.5	3.8	4.2	12.5	14.1	6.9	6.7	7.2	7.0	7.3	28.6	23.8	10.8	1.7	75.1	36.0	49.1	50.9

#	ZIP CODE POST OFFICE NAME	2004 Per Capita Income	2004 HH Income Base	2004 HOUSEHOLD INCOME DISTRIBUTION (%) Less than $25,000	$25,000 to $49,999	$50,000 to $99,999	$100,000 to $149,999	$150,000 or More	MEDIAN HOUSEHOLD INCOME 2004	2009	2004 National Centile	2004 State Centile	2004 Home Value Base	2004 HOME VALUE DISTRIBUTION (%) Less than $50,000	$50,000 to $89,999	$90,000 to $174,999	$175,000 to $399,999	$400,000 or More	2004 Median Home Value
22307	ALEXANDRIA	61860	5761	8.4	16.3	31.4	21.4	22.6	87668	115117	97	93	4180	1.4	1.6	26.9	30.3	39.8	316339
22308	ALEXANDRIA	56151	4989	5.1	6.9	25.4	29.5	33.2	119848	151269	99	98	4527	0.3	0.0	0.8	51.7	47.2	392591
22309	ALEXANDRIA	38900	10432	9.3	20.4	34.7	20.3	15.2	75682	94401	93	89	6716	3.2	4.4	14.2	53.0	25.2	281913
22310	ALEXANDRIA	43526	10995	4.7	11.9	38.1	26.9	18.6	92603	115039	97	94	8100	1.1	0.3	9.9	70.9	17.8	265811
22311	ALEXANDRIA	35826	7833	13.4	31.0	36.2	11.4	8.1	55300	68667	80	75	1404	0.0	1.4	4.7	71.6	22.3	311791
22312	ALEXANDRIA	34757	10874	11.9	22.3	33.7	19.4	12.7	71015	89454	92	85	5576	1.0	4.5	14.5	60.4	19.7	281350
22314	ALEXANDRIA	79091	14655	11.6	13.1	30.2	18.1	27.1	90040	126774	97	94	7151	0.1	0.1	10.8	39.5	49.5	396796
22315	ALEXANDRIA	45478	11467	2.8	10.1	40.2	29.9	17.0	95350	116625	98	95	8144	0.3	0.8	7.0	78.8	13.1	277700
22401	FREDERICKSBURG	29463	8407	28.5	29.1	26.5	8.5	7.3	41737	53507	52	44	3167	1.8	4.6	35.1	48.1	10.3	200314
22405	FREDERICKSBURG	30331	9616	9.5	21.2	41.7	19.3	8.2	70453	81954	91	85	7926	1.3	1.5	28.6	61.9	6.8	207269
22406	FREDERICKSBURG	32926	5517	9.0	18.1	43.9	20.1	8.9	73936	84059	93	87	4089	1.6	1.3	19.8	64.6	12.8	248934
22407	FREDERICKSBURG	28263	17142	9.7	22.1	42.8	18.9	6.4	68421	79321	91	85	13602	2.3	1.2	29.2	62.9	4.4	202552
22408	FREDERICKSBURG	27855	8947	12.5	24.7	40.9	15.5	6.5	63422	74700	87	82	7379	7.5	1.9	29.5	56.8	4.3	195640
22427	BOWLING GREEN	22225	1061	27.1	29.8	30.4	9.2	3.5	41860	49879	52	44	800	8.4	12.0	42.4	34.1	3.1	147250
22432	BURGESS	29524	270	24.1	25.2	30.7	10.4	9.6	50590	61591	73	67	225	8.9	9.3	36.4	29.3	16.0	157500
22433	BURR HILL	25241	171	16.4	31.6	39.2	8.2	4.7	51880	60258	75	69	146	2.1	8.2	50.0	31.5	8.2	161111
22435	CALLAO	23885	1053	29.8	31.2	30.2	6.4	2.4	38437	46797	41	34	886	16.6	17.3	42.1	19.6	4.4	109219
22436	CARET	21445	164	26.2	28.1	34.2	9.8	1.8	46020	53945	64	56	137	13.1	29.2	29.2	26.3	2.2	103289
22437	CENTER CROSS	24144	207	21.7	32.9	31.4	10.1	3.9	44841	54795	61	53	174	14.4	11.5	33.3	33.9	6.9	121795
22438	CHAMPLAIN	22070	217	25.4	28.6	33.2	9.7	3.2	46825	54098	66	58	182	13.2	21.4	33.0	27.5	5.0	118478
22443	COLONIAL BEACH	26178	3306	30.9	26.9	31.0	6.4	4.8	42209	50389	54	45	2475	6.5	8.1	53.7	27.8	3.9	137999
22448	DAHLGREN	14556	297	12.8	46.5	34.3	4.7	1.7	46025	52545	64	56	7	0.0	0.0	28.6	71.4	0.0	275000
22454	DUNNSVILLE	19702	894	29.3	27.7	34.5	8.5	0.0	42537	49642	55	47	735	3.7	14.8	45.4	33.3	2.7	137833
22460	FARNHAM	23370	624	35.3	26.3	28.9	4.5	5.1	38940	47130	43	36	517	7.9	23.0	41.4	22.8	4.8	117578
22469	HAGUE	21907	956	35.9	26.8	28.9	5.9	2.6	38840	47035	42	36	784	12.0	28.1	36.5	21.7	1.8	111522
22473	HEATHSVILLE	29477	2208	31.6	22.1	29.3	9.3	7.8	44929	55851	61	54	1895	11.0	13.9	26.0	36.4	12.7	170516
22476	HUSTLE	18834	139	25.9	27.3	35.3	9.4	2.2	46668	52909	65	57	116	13.8	30.2	26.7	26.7	2.6	100000
22480	IRVINGTON	48450	252	15.1	25.4	27.8	14.7	17.1	61129	87918	85	80	218	1.4	9.2	30.3	39.5	19.7	210811
22482	KILMARNOCK	31784	1037	25.3	26.4	26.2	13.8	8.3	47243	62683	67	59	880	5.8	9.3	27.1	34.2	23.6	210563
22485	KING GEORGE	27656	6577	15.1	26.0	38.3	14.6	6.0	57453	70203	82	77	5222	7.9	4.5	31.8	48.0	7.8	187645
22488	KINSALE	21651	603	36.3	27.0	23.9	8.5	4.3	32830	41094	20	15	501	14.4	15.6	39.3	26.0	4.8	130208
22503	LANCASTER	22891	2068	37.6	27.7	24.4	7.6	2.7	32667	41991	20	15	1741	16.7	14.2	27.7	28.4	12.9	137675
22504	LANEVIEW	21313	72	22.2	30.6	33.3	9.7	4.2	46563	55263	65	57	61	14.8	11.5	32.8	34.4	6.6	122115
22508	LOCUST GROVE	35607	3680	9.0	28.1	41.5	13.6	7.8	61144	73655	85	80	3234	2.3	3.0	32.5	54.0	8.3	201355
22509	LORETTO	25930	35	25.7	28.6	37.1	8.6	0.0	46148	57113	64	56	29	10.3	27.6	27.6	34.5	0.0	109375
22511	LOTTSBURG	33330	627	20.3	25.4	36.5	9.7	8.1	52951	64116	77	71	543	10.1	15.5	28.7	35.5	10.1	153241
22514	MILFORD	21165	923	23.2	34.0	32.0	8.7	2.2	42462	50416	54	46	766	8.9	14.0	41.5	33.4	2.2	135366
22520	MONTROSS	23186	2227	27.0	31.1	32.3	7.0	2.7	43918	51228	58	51	1818	12.2	10.8	40.3	30.8	6.0	144208
22534	PARTLOW	20773	890	18.7	27.3	41.0	11.4	1.7	54364	63601	79	73	761	3.9	4.3	44.4	44.9	2.4	170764
22535	PORT ROYAL	22798	205	27.3	37.1	22.4	6.8	6.3	38351	45376	41	34	169	26.0	5.9	34.3	22.5	11.2	131250
22538	RAPPAHANNOCK ACADEMY	26107	115	27.0	36.5	23.5	6.1	7.0	38957	45648	43	37	95	25.3	6.3	33.7	22.1	12.6	133750
22539	REEDVILLE	30010	1212	20.2	32.3	29.7	11.1	6.8	48505	57437	69	62	1058	2.1	12.5	29.9	40.6	14.9	193438
22542	RHOADESVILLE	22642	621	22.9	31.6	34.5	7.6	3.5	47137	54285	66	59	531	5.7	7.9	41.6	39.7	5.1	165317
22546	RUTHER GLEN	22645	3960	19.5	30.7	35.7	10.5	3.7	49870	57880	72	65	3329	4.6	10.9	54.0	28.5	2.0	132380
22553	SPOTSYLVANIA	26618	10653	11.6	22.0	43.7	16.4	6.4	65803	76650	89	83	9259	1.9	3.2	36.6	50.8	7.6	189311
22554	STAFFORD	29977	14635	5.3	16.0	44.9	23.4	10.4	80694	92697	95	91	11981	3.4	0.8	11.5	77.0	7.3	258496
22556	STAFFORD	27396	7742	9.2	15.9	44.8	21.3	8.8	76395	85856	94	89	6475	4.9	1.6	16.1	71.6	5.8	231223
22560	TAPPAHANNOCK	22141	2475	27.3	31.6	30.8	7.6	2.8	42902	49940	56	48	1841	12.2	12.8	41.3	27.6	6.1	139006
22567	UNIONVILLE	21382	1056	24.2	32.6	31.1	9.2	3.0	44141	51630	59	51	898	6.9	9.0	42.5	36.3	5.2	152108
22572	WARSAW	20072	2513	31.9	29.5	28.6	7.9	2.2	39500	46762	44	38	1922	12.2	14.8	42.8	25.7	4.5	126981
22576	WEEMS	29560	1014	28.5	32.3	21.5	8.9	8.9	38324	50309	40	33	795	10.4	16.1	29.8	27.8	15.9	141886
22578	WHITE STONE	46070	1330	22.9	22.1	26.9	13.5	14.6	56049	79501	81	76	1122	5.4	12.2	25.0	33.2	24.3	216204
22579	WICOMICO CHURCH	27809	110	30.9	19.1	34.6	8.2	7.3	50000	60000	72	65	92	4.4	10.9	25.0	41.3	18.5	225000
22580	WOODFORD	21365	2085	21.3	32.6	35.7	7.9	2.6	46666	54575	65	57	1698	10.0	10.4	48.8	26.2	4.7	135648
22601	WINCHESTER	26885	10893	28.0	31.7	27.1	7.6	5.7	40610	50050	48	41	5526	3.4	4.7	50.9	35.3	5.7	154772
22602	WINCHESTER	26206	8918	14.7	30.3	37.8	12.0	5.1	54477	63672	79	73	7199	5.6	6.1	43.3	40.4	4.5	165428
22603	WINCHESTER	26812	4653	17.5	29.7	37.1	10.2	5.6	52205	61110	76	70	3783	9.2	5.9	38.8	40.1	6.0	165765
22610	BENTONVILLE	25513	715	19.3	32.3	35.1	10.5	2.8	48865	56862	70	63	605	5.1	5.1	39.8	42.8	7.1	174813
22611	BERRYVILLE	29496	3279	16.5	25.1	38.1	15.5	4.8	57551	67695	82	78	2515	0.6	4.7	25.6	57.2	11.8	230172
22620	BOYCE	34813	1062	16.3	21.4	35.3	15.7	11.3	64370	78049	88	83	867	0.7	3.7	29.0	42.3	24.3	233263
22624	CLEAR BROOK	24612	1194	17.5	32.9	34.8	9.1	5.8	49594	59621	71	64	1047	7.1	4.5	35.7	44.7	8.0	182345
22625	CROSS JUNCTION	24328	1104	11.3	28.9	44.0	11.0	4.8	58080	67372	83	78	959	3.7	5.8	38.9	47.6	4.1	178051
22627	FLINT HILL	33595	232	18.5	24.6	35.8	12.1	9.1	57282	70465	82	77	193	1.6	6.2	33.2	38.9	20.2	213542
22630	FRONT ROYAL	23294	10514	21.6	30.8	34.0	10.1	3.4	47565	55871	67	60	7544	2.4	4.7	48.2	40.9	3.8	164960
22637	GORE	21128	790	22.2	28.7	39.5	8.2	1.4	49257	57189	71	63	665	3.6	7.8	46.5	37.4	4.7	156514
22639	HUME	53863	253	15.4	21.3	26.1	20.2	17.0	72310	97816	92	86	220	0.0	0.0	15.9	43.6	40.5	353333
22640	HUNTLY	27682	266	16.9	25.6	40.6	10.2	6.8	58074	71175	83	78	217	0.0	8.8	40.6	31.3	19.4	182500
22641	STRASBURG	26650	79	10.1	35.4	40.5	10.1	3.8	53905	59555	78	72	67	1.5	6.0	49.3	41.8	1.5	158929
22642	LINDEN	27143	1471	10.3	26.4	46.2	13.4	3.8	62063	71746	86	81	1273	0.9	1.7	47.5	45.2	4.8	174950
22643	MARKHAM	38221	158	17.1	26.0	28.5	17.1	11.4	60000	75000	84	79	120	0.8	0.0	25.0	41.7	32.5	250000
22644	MAURERTOWN	24093	804	21.1	31.0	36.0	8.1	3.9	48476	55498	69	62	681	5.4	7.6	54.3	27.6	5.0	143668
22645	MIDDLETOWN	26579	1319	16.7	35.7	35.9	7.9	3.9	48031	56691	68	61	1076	1.8	6.1	49.4	37.3	5.5	157432
22649	MIDDLETOWN	28140	21	14.3	28.6	52.4	4.8	0.0	54416	61445	79	73	17	0.0	5.9	41.2	47.1	5.9	181250
22650	RILEYVILLE	22387	396	19.7	36.9	34.1	6.1	3.3	44420	50942	60	52	339	0.6	24.2	40.7	26.3	8.3	137868
22652	FORT VALLEY	29604	533	21.0	22.7	32.3	17.6	6.4	54981	66707	80	74	451	3.3	7.1	35.3	44.8	9.5	189338
22654	STAR TANNERY	28827	202	9.4	30.7	41.6	12.4	5.9	56967	67359	82	77	176	8.0	8.0	39.2	38.1	6.8	158929
22655	STEPHENS CITY	24154	5623	16.6	25.6	43.5	11.3	3.0	56948	65661	82	76	4523	2.6	6.4	45.7	43.2	2.1	166620
22656	STEPHENSON	24413	661	15.7	38.3	30.3	12.3	3.5	47334	55377	67	59	572	24.1	4.2	25.4	42.8	3.5	165455
22657	STRASBURG	23960	3762	22.6	34.2	32.9	6.4	3.9	45739	52480	63	55	2683	2.4	8.4	56.1	30.7	2.4	143966
22660	TOMS BROOK	26926	604	16.7	31.5	41.6	5.6	4.6	50844	57731	74	67	509	4.5	7.5	51.7	29.5	6.9	153006
22663	WHITE POST	28106	635	18.4	30.2	33.9	10.1	7.4	51405	61100	75	68	475	11.6	3.6	25.1	46.7	13.1	207941
22664	WOODSTOCK	23594	3250	23.8	35.7	30.9	6.7	3.0	42098	48472	53	45	2214	2.3	7.5	50.2	36.4	3.6	156478
22701	CULPEPER	23948	9239	22.8	28.2	35.1	9.9	4.1	49116	58402	70	63	6186	4.2	2.7	37.9	48.6	6.6	185989
22709	ARODA	22528	574	21.4	29.3	37.5	8.0	3.8	49294	56086	71	64	459	5.2	8.9	38.1	42.5	5.2	167905
22712	BEALETON	24914	2456	11.6	26.7	41.3	15.0	5.4	60631	72272	85	80	1986	6.9	3.3	22.9	58.8	8.1	203219
22713	BOSTON	23981	363	18.2	29.8	33.6	14.1	4.4	52103	62117	76	69	312	1.9	1.0	35.9	50.3	10.9	199306
22714	BRANDY STATION	29426	207	18.8	34.3	32.4	7.3	7.3	47928	56386	68	61	147	2.7	2.0	31.3	49.7	14.3	209821
22715	BRIGHTWOOD	23137	485	25.8	31.3	29.9	7.4	5.6	43042	50947	56	49	418	5.3	6.5	47.6	35.2	5.5	154255
22716	CASTLETON	29524	278	18.0	25.2	33.1	14.4	9.4	55866	70630	81	75	229	2.2	2.6	34.9	41.5	18.8	213889
22718	ELKWOOD	23960	243	16.9	37.9	31.7	9.1	4.5	47090	54911	66	58	200	4.0	5.0	35.0	45.5	10.5	188043
22720	GOLDVEIN	30987	464	11.4	13.2	41.2	24.1	10.1	78480	93954	95	90	416	1.2	1.2	15.9	73.8	7.9	243878
22722	HAYWOOD	20936	94	25.5	30.9	31.9	7.5	4.3	43909	51270	58	51	81	4.9	7.4	48.2	34.6	4.9	151389
22724	JEFFERSONTON	27134	799	12.0	17.0	42.8	22.4	5.8	72793	84881	92	87	712	0.6	1.4	23.5	59.3	15.3	245528
22725	LEON	23030	159	25.8	30.8	30.8	7.6	5.0	43319	50522	57	49	137	5.1	6.6	48.2	35.0	5.1	152500
22726	LIGNUM	19658	188	16.0	38.8	31.9	10.6	2.7	47018	54287	66	58	167	4.2	6.6	37.1	43.1	9.0	179167
	VIRGINIA	30454		19.8	25.2	32.5	13.6	8.9	55216	67801				6.8	10.4	35.8	36.5	10.5	166226
	UNITED STATES	25866		24.7	27.1	30.8	10.9	6.5	48124	56710				10.9	15.0	33.7	30.1	10.4	145905

ZIP CODE #	POST OFFICE NAME	FINANCIAL SERVICES: Auto Loan	FINANCIAL SERVICES: Home Loan	FINANCIAL SERVICES: Invest-ments	FINANCIAL SERVICES: Retire-ment Plans	THE HOME: Home Improvements: Home Repair	THE HOME: Home Improvements: Lawn & Garden	THE HOME: Furnishings: Comput-ers & Hard-ware	THE HOME: Furnishings: Major Appli-ances	THE HOME: Furnishings: TV, Radio, Sound Equip-ment	THE HOME: Furnishings: Furni-ture	ENTERTAINMENT: Dine out/ Carry out	ENTERTAINMENT: Sports Equip-ment	ENTERTAINMENT: Fees & Tickets	ENTERTAINMENT: Toys & Games	ENTERTAINMENT: Travel	ENTERTAINMENT: Cable TV	PERSONAL: Apparel & Services	PERSONAL: Auto Repairs	PERSONAL: Health Insur-ance	PERSONAL: Pets & Supplies
22307	ALEXANDRIA	161	188	271	194	182	195	186	177	180	187	227	208	198	238	189	178	227	179	164	193
22308	ALEXANDRIA	174	238	306	229	230	243	209	206	196	211	246	234	231	265	221	197	250	199	189	222
22309	ALEXANDRIA	136	151	186	153	147	155	149	145	145	151	183	169	154	186	150	142	182	147	134	159
22310	ALEXANDRIA	140	165	212	167	158	165	158	152	151	160	191	178	167	200	159	148	191	153	136	165
22311	ALEXANDRIA	106	101	123	108	97	104	110	105	108	112	137	126	108	131	105	102	134	111	95	116
22312	ALEXANDRIA	113	129	201	128	123	135	134	126	137	135	173	148	140	187	137	139	174	131	120	138
22314	ALEXANDRIA	177	184	303	200	176	194	201	184	202	204	256	221	211	266	201	200	254	192	173	204
22315	ALEXANDRIA	153	172	192	179	164	164	162	157	151	166	192	185	168	195	159	144	191	156	137	172
22401	FREDERICKSBURG	87	82	100	86	80	87	94	87	93	92	117	106	91	113	89	88	114	93	82	97
22405	FREDERICKSBURG	115	133	140	135	129	129	124	122	116	125	146	143	129	150	123	111	145	120	109	134
22406	FREDERICKSBURG	130	135	139	141	131	133	131	129	124	134	157	153	132	156	127	118	155	129	116	145
22407	FREDERICKSBURG	113	124	127	129	120	119	118	116	110	120	139	137	119	139	115	104	137	115	102	128
22408	FREDERICKSBURG	109	119	114	122	115	113	109	109	102	112	129	128	111	129	107	97	127	107	97	122
22427	BOWLING GREEN	90	76	58	70	81	91	74	83	81	73	98	96	70	96	76	85	92	82	94	105
22432	BURGESS	106	99	95	94	105	123	91	104	97	98	120	102	93	100	99	103	113	101	122	119
22433	BURR HILL	109	97	74	92	103	110	90	99	95	90	116	118	88	118	92	98	110	97	108	128
22435	CALLAO	86	71	57	68	76	90	73	81	80	73	96	88	69	88	75	84	89	81	95	96
22436	CARET	99	67	30	57	75	87	64	80	78	66	91	96	55	86	65	84	83	80	99	114
22437	CENTER CROSS	95	75	51	67	84	94	70	85	80	70	94	99	63	93	75	85	88	83	100	116
22438	CHAMPLAIN	99	72	42	66	79	91	71	84	82	71	97	99	64	94	72	86	89	83	99	112
22443	COLONIAL BEACH	102	80	54	75	88	101	81	93	91	79	107	107	73	104	83	96	99	92	109	118
22448	DAHLGREN	84	53	51	61	49	58	79	68	80	74	101	91	68	90	65	73	96	81	63	78
22454	DUNNSVILLE	79	61	41	57	68	78	62	72	70	60	83	82	56	80	64	75	76	71	85	92
22460	FARNHAM	81	69	60	68	73	82	73	77	77	71	93	89	68	89	72	78	87	77	85	91
22469	HAGUE	94	68	39	60	77	88	66	80	77	66	90	94	57	87	68	82	83	79	97	111
22473	HEATHSVILLE	106	91	75	84	98	114	84	99	92	88	113	104	81	100	91	99	105	96	117	122
22476	HUSTLE	100	67	30	58	76	87	64	81	78	66	91	96	55	86	66	84	83	80	99	114
22480	IRVINGTON	209	195	187	185	207	244	181	206	191	194	238	201	183	198	197	204	222	200	241	235
22482	KILMARNOCK	102	94	89	90	100	118	88	100	93	94	116	99	89	97	95	100	108	97	117	115
22485	KING GEORGE	107	108	99	107	109	113	101	105	100	101	124	124	101	127	102	99	121	103	104	125
22488	KINSALE	87	65	41	60	73	84	66	77	75	65	89	89	58	85	68	80	81	76	92	101
22503	LANCASTER	79	67	56	65	71	83	69	75	74	68	90	82	65	82	70	78	83	75	87	88
22504	LANEVIEW	95	75	51	68	84	95	71	85	80	70	95	100	63	93	75	85	88	84	100	116
22508	LOCUST GROVE	130	121	112	116	128	146	112	126	118	118	146	130	113	129	120	124	137	122	143	148
22509	LORETTO	99	66	30	57	75	86	64	80	77	65	91	96	54	86	65	83	82	79	99	114
22511	LOTTSBURG	108	101	97	96	107	126	93	106	99	100	123	104	95	102	102	106	115	103	124	121
22514	MILFORD	94	73	47	66	80	89	69	81	78	70	93	96	64	92	71	82	87	80	94	109
22520	MONTROSS	88	78	65	71	82	93	74	83	80	75	97	93	72	94	77	85	92	81	94	103
22534	PARTLOW	96	87	67	83	88	94	82	89	84	84	104	104	78	100	82	84	99	88	91	108
22535	PORT ROYAL	118	79	36	68	90	103	76	96	92	78	108	114	65	102	78	99	99	95	118	136
22538	RAPPAHANNOCK ACADEMY	122	82	37	70	92	106	79	99	95	80	112	118	67	106	80	102	101	98	121	140
22539	REEDVILLE	96	90	86	85	95	112	83	95	88	89	109	93	84	91	90	94	102	92	111	108
22542	RHOADESVILLE	104	82	54	78	91	100	78	92	87	78	104	110	72	104	81	90	97	90	104	123
22546	RUTHER GLEN	95	88	72	85	90	95	82	89	85	83	104	106	80	105	83	85	100	87	91	110
22553	SPOTSYLVANIA	113	120	111	120	118	119	110	113	106	112	132	132	111	133	110	103	129	110	105	130
22554	STAFFORD	131	149	149	155	143	141	136	134	125	140	159	157	141	160	133	118	157	131	116	148
22556	STAFFORD	126	139	133	143	134	133	127	127	119	131	150	149	130	150	125	112	148	124	113	142
22560	TAPPAHANNOCK	84	71	52	69	74	83	72	78	77	71	93	89	67	90	71	79	87	77	86	94
22567	UNIONVILLE	99	75	45	69	83	93	72	85	81	72	97	102	65	95	74	85	89	84	99	116
22572	WARSAW	87	62	36	58	70	82	65	76	75	64	88	88	57	84	66	80	80	75	92	99
22576	WEEMS	101	83	71	77	87	105	87	95	97	88	117	101	82	104	88	103	108	95	113	112
22578	WHITE STONE	152	141	136	134	149	176	132	150	140	141	174	147	133	145	143	150	163	145	175	171
22579	WICOMICO CHURCH	95	89	85	85	94	111	82	94	87	88	109	92	84	90	90	93	102	91	110	107
22580	WOODFORD	95	78	55	73	84	92	74	84	81	75	98	100	70	97	76	84	92	83	94	110
22601	WINCHESTER	86	82	87	83	82	89	88	86	88	86	110	101	86	109	86	87	106	88	86	96
22602	WINCHESTER	101	104	96	105	103	106	98	100	95	99	119	117	98	119	97	93	115	98	95	115
22603	WINCHESTER	103	96	81	94	99	104	91	97	93	91	114	115	89	114	92	93	109	96	100	119
22610	BENTONVILLE	108	82	50	77	92	102	79	94	89	78	105	113	71	104	82	92	97	93	109	128
22611	BERRYVILLE	100	106	106	104	107	115	102	104	102	101	126	119	105	130	104	103	123	102	105	118
22620	BOYCE	107	125	136	121	124	132	117	117	114	116	143	133	124	149	121	115	141	114	115	128
22624	CLEAR BROOK	100	97	82	94	100	105	89	96	91	89	112	113	89	114	91	92	108	93	98	118
22625	CROSS JUNCTION	96	103	97	101	105	107	94	98	92	93	114	115	96	119	96	91	111	94	95	116
22627	FLINT HILL	124	99	65	94	109	119	94	110	104	93	124	131	87	124	97	107	116	107	124	147
22630	FRONT ROYAL	85	85	82	84	86	91	84	85	84	82	104	99	84	106	84	84	100	85	86	98
22637	GORE	83	80	67	77	83	87	73	79	75	73	92	94	73	95	75	76	89	77	82	99
22639	HUME	183	191	190	187	197	210	178	188	176	178	218	216	180	219	185	178	212	183	191	220
22640	HUNTLY	111	99	75	94	105	112	91	101	97	91	118	121	90	121	94	100	112	99	110	131
22641	STRASBURG	103	91	70	87	97	104	84	94	90	84	109	112	83	111	87	92	104	91	101	121
22642	LINDEN	105	110	104	113	108	108	103	105	98	105	123	124	103	123	101	93	120	103	95	119
22643	MARKHAM	174	121	63	114	141	158	120	148	138	118	162	178	102	159	124	145	147	146	176	206
22644	MAURERTOWN	100	89	67	84	94	101	82	91	87	82	106	109	80	108	85	90	101	89	99	118
22645	MIDDLETOWN	104	93	71	88	98	105	86	95	91	86	111	113	84	113	88	93	105	92	103	123
22649	MIDDLETOWN	92	82	63	78	87	93	76	84	81	76	98	100	74	100	78	83	93	82	91	109
22650	RILEYVILLE	90	76	56	71	83	90	71	81	77	71	93	96	67	94	74	81	88	80	91	107
22652	FORT VALLEY	126	91	52	85	105	118	89	109	102	88	120	130	77	117	93	107	110	107	129	151
22654	STAR TANNERY	111	99	75	94	104	112	91	101	97	91	118	121	89	120	94	99	112	98	109	131
22655	STEPHENS CITY	96	99	90	100	97	99	92	94	89	93	111	110	92	111	91	86	108	92	88	108
22656	STEPHENSON	102	95	76	91	97	102	87	95	90	88	110	112	86	111	89	90	106	92	98	118
22657	STRASBURG	89	78	60	75	82	90	75	82	80	75	97	96	73	98	76	82	92	81	90	103
22660	TOMS BROOK	107	96	73	91	101	108	88	98	94	88	114	117	87	116	91	96	108	95	106	126
22663	WHITE POST	125	112	89	109	115	125	109	117	113	109	139	135	105	136	109	114	132	116	123	141
22664	WOODSTOCK	88	74	56	70	79	90	75	82	82	73	98	94	71	96	76	86	91	81	94	100
22701	CULPEPER	87	83	78	82	85	92	84	86	86	82	106	100	83	107	84	86	102	86	89	99
22709	ARODA	97	86	66	82	91	98	80	89	85	80	103	106	78	105	82	87	98	86	96	114
22712	BEALETON	100	112	113	114	109	107	106	105	99	106	125	124	107	126	104	94	123	104	92	115
22713	BOSTON	95	94	86	91	97	104	87	93	89	87	110	109	89	112	90	91	106	91	97	113
22714	BRANDY STATION	123	107	85	106	111	125	109	116	115	107	139	132	105	138	108	116	131	114	124	136
22715	BRIGHTWOOD	96	85	65	81	90	96	79	87	84	79	102	104	77	104	81	86	97	85	94	113
22716	CASTLETON	102	109	111	108	112	119	102	107	100	102	124	122	104	125	106	101	121	104	108	124
22718	ELKWOOD	102	87	68	87	91	103	89	95	95	88	115	109	86	114	89	96	108	94	103	113
22720	GOLDVEIN	118	146	156	147	144	142	131	130	121	130	152	152	139	162	134	117	152	126	117	144
22722	HAYWOOD	96	85	65	81	90	97	79	87	84	79	102	104	77	104	81	86	97	85	95	113
22724	JEFFERSONTON	103	128	136	128	126	124	114	114	106	114	133	133	122	142	117	103	133	110	102	126
22725	LEON	95	85	65	81	90	96	79	87	83	79	101	104	77	104	81	86	96	85	94	112
22726	LIGNUM	90	76	59	76	80	90	78	84	83	77	101	95	75	100	78	84	94	82	91	99
	VIRGINIA	112	109	113	109	109	117	108	110	109	109	136	129	108	135	108	109	132	110	109	128
	UNITED STATES	100	100	100	100	100	100	100	100	100	100	100	100	100	100	100	100	100	100	100	100

#	POST OFFICE NAME	COUNTY FIPS CODE	POPULATION			2000-2004 ANNUAL RATE		HOUSEHOLDS					FAMILIES		
			2000	2004	2009	% Rate	State Centile	2000	2004	2009	% Annual Rate 2000-2004	2004 Average HH Size	2000	2004	% Annual Rate 2000-2004
22727	MADISON	113	4186	4399	4720	1.2	61	1680	1813	1997	1.8	2.40	1190	1266	1.5
22728	MIDLAND	061	2786	3034	3442	2.0	79	980	1088	1257	2.5	2.77	766	841	2.2
22729	MITCHELLS	047	126	130	136	0.7	51	46	51	58	2.5	2.55	33	4	-39.1
22730	OAKPARK	113	980	1051	1138	1.7	72	331	364	405	2.3	2.79	250	272	2.0
22731	PRATTS	113	99	105	113	1.4	66	43	47	52	2.1	2.19	30	32	1.5
22732	RADIANT	113	1181	1267	1373	1.7	72	398	438	487	2.3	2.80	302	329	2.0
22733	RAPIDAN	047	2469	2620	2844	1.4	67	397	454	534	3.2	3.24	300	337	2.8
22734	REMINGTON	061	2452	2768	3202	2.9	89	854	977	1146	3.2	2.83	677	765	2.9
22735	REVA	047	1290	1495	1733	3.5	92	478	565	668	4.0	2.64	373	435	3.7
22736	RICHARDSVILLE	047	456	485	545	1.5	68	146	158	181	1.9	2.99	118	126	1.6
22737	RIXEYVILLE	047	2531	2966	3514	3.8	95	884	1056	1272	4.3	2.81	734	868	4.0
22738	ROCHELLE	113	462	493	534	1.5	69	189	207	229	2.2	2.36	145	156	1.7
22740	SPERRYVILLE	157	2404	2493	2613	0.9	54	970	1029	1099	1.4	2.42	692	724	1.1
22741	STEVENSBURG	047	145	146	164	0.2	29	53	54	62	0.4	2.69	36	37	0.7
22742	SUMERDUCK	061	1723	1747	1910	0.3	37	580	597	662	0.7	2.93	474	483	0.4
22743	SYRIA	113	216	227	243	1.2	62	105	113	124	1.7	2.01	77	81	1.2
22746	VIEWTOWN	047	617	721	837	3.7	94	223	266	313	4.2	2.71	183	217	4.1
22747	WASHINGTON	157	1248	1261	1284	0.2	33	506	521	539	0.7	2.41	356	361	0.3
22749	WOODVILLE	157	451	470	485	1.0	57	189	201	211	1.5	2.34	134	140	1.0
22801	HARRISONBURG	165	33099	36156	38493	2.1	80	10063	11169	12021	2.5	2.68	5304	5933	2.7
22802	HARRISONBURG	165	21970	22641	23378	0.7	49	8517	8839	9152	0.9	2.45	5280	5334	0.2
22807	HARRISONBURG	660	409	403	403	-0.4	14	43	40	40	-1.7	2.23	21	19	-2.3
22810	BASYE	171	967	1041	1134	1.8	74	449	491	542	2.1	2.12	316	341	1.8
22811	BERGTON	165	363	390	414	1.7	73	155	170	183	2.2	2.29	118	128	1.9
22812	BRIDGEWATER	165	8671	8650	8893	-0.1	21	2987	3011	3145	0.2	2.52	2160	2150	-0.1
22815	BROADWAY	165	7309	7240	7492	-0.2	18	2794	2806	2944	0.1	2.56	2086	2071	-0.2
22820	CRIDERS	165	259	274	289	1.3	65	105	113	121	1.7	2.42	80	85	1.4
22821	DAYTON	165	5417	5377	5565	-0.2	18	1936	1938	2027	0.0	2.77	1473	1449	-0.4
22824	EDINBURG	171	5365	5681	6160	1.4	65	2162	2320	2548	1.7	2.45	1575	1670	1.4
22827	ELKTON	165	10989	11508	12149	1.1	60	4283	4572	4904	1.6	2.51	3122	3276	1.1
22830	FULKS RUN	165	1579	1725	1862	2.1	80	588	652	713	2.5	2.64	451	494	2.2
22831	HINTON	165	885	857	877	-0.8	6	345	339	352	-0.4	2.53	269	261	-0.7
22832	KEEZLETOWN	165	1280	1308	1382	0.5	43	495	513	550	0.8	2.55	359	364	0.3
22834	LINVILLE	165	1598	1574	1616	-0.4	14	585	585	609	0.0	2.69	456	451	-0.3
22835	LURAY	139	11675	12002	12324	0.7	48	4721	4944	5182	1.1	2.38	3300	3408	0.8
22840	MC GAHEYSVILLE	165	2892	3370	3723	3.7	94	1112	1317	1475	4.1	2.56	854	998	3.7
22841	MOUNT CRAWFORD	165	2696	2857	3030	1.4	66	1000	1073	1152	1.7	2.65	770	819	1.5
22842	MOUNT JACKSON	171	4503	4668	5013	0.9	54	1805	1893	2057	1.1	2.46	1281	1325	0.8
22843	MOUNT SOLON	015	2483	2566	2717	0.8	52	903	943	1012	1.0	2.72	717	741	0.8
22844	NEW MARKET	171	3943	4156	4520	1.3	63	1627	1744	1930	1.7	2.29	1114	1177	1.3
22845	ORKNEY SPRINGS	171	59	64	69	1.9	78	30	33	36	2.3	1.94	21	23	2.2
22846	PENN LAIRD	165	619	721	795	3.7	93	228	268	300	3.9	2.69	180	209	3.6
22847	QUICKSBURG	171	676	707	758	1.1	59	254	270	293	1.5	2.62	199	208	1.1
22849	SHENANDOAH	139	4933	5003	5063	0.3	37	1986	2074	2154	1.0	2.41	1440	1484	0.7
22851	STANLEY	139	5295	5302	5354	0.0	25	2085	2136	2205	0.6	2.48	1525	1543	0.3
22853	TIMBERVILLE	165	4532	4465	4594	-0.4	14	1772	1773	1852	0.0	2.47	1294	1279	-0.3
22901	CHARLOTTESVILLE	003	30200	32427	35524	1.7	73	13182	14358	15953	2.0	2.22	7806	8297	1.5
22902	CHARLOTTESVILLE	003	18586	18593	18931	0.0	24	8095	8243	8516	0.4	2.19	4488	4498	0.1
22903	CHARLOTTESVILLE	003	37952	38171	38319	0.1	29	13457	13739	14044	0.5	2.30	5989	6046	0.2
22904	CHARLOTTESVILLE	003	116	116	124	0.0	24	42	43	47	0.6	2.70	10	10	0.0
22911	CHARLOTTESVILLE	003	12228	14232	16252	3.6	93	4375	5180	6009	4.1	2.70	3327	3886	3.7
22920	AFTON	125	4319	4470	4751	0.8	53	1755	1859	2019	1.4	2.39	1258	1314	1.0
22922	ARRINGTON	125	1832	1888	2008	0.7	49	737	775	843	1.2	2.40	540	554	0.8
22923	BARBOURSVILLE	003	3872	4241	4778	2.2	81	1471	1636	1868	2.5	2.59	1124	1234	2.2
22931	COVESVILLE	003	325	349	385	1.7	73	127	140	157	2.3	2.48	94	102	1.9
22932	CROZET	003	5242	5582	6092	1.5	69	1949	2116	2354	2.0	2.50	1414	1511	1.6
22935	DYKE	079	996	1082	1205	2.0	79	380	418	471	2.3	2.58	296	322	2.0
22936	EARLYSVILLE	003	4769	5148	5722	1.8	75	1775	1951	2201	2.3	2.64	1409	1529	1.9
22937	ESMONT	003	1058	1157	1297	2.1	81	410	458	523	2.6	2.52	286	314	2.2
22938	FABER	125	1344	1493	1638	2.5	85	512	583	655	3.1	2.50	358	402	2.8
22939	FISHERSVILLE	015	3388	3800	4206	2.7	87	1293	1509	1721	3.7	2.36	1009	1160	3.3
22940	FREE UNION	003	1087	1179	1300	1.9	78	341	379	426	2.5	2.95	253	276	2.1
22942	GORDONSVILLE	109	6971	7549	8638	1.9	77	2775	3066	3580	2.4	2.44	1989	2168	2.1
22943	GREENWOOD	003	614	604	647	-0.4	13	247	248	270	0.1	2.44	176	174	-0.3
22946	KEENE	003	51	48	51	-1.4	1	23	22	24	-1.0	2.18	16	15	-1.5
22947	KESWICK	003	3670	3970	4441	1.9	76	1484	1652	1900	2.6	2.34	1112	1220	2.2
22948	LOCUST DALE	113	152	163	177	1.7	72	41	45	50	2.2	3.47	31	34	2.2
22949	LOVINGSTON	125	1608	1766	1932	2.2	82	665	750	842	2.9	2.29	444	495	2.6
22952	LYNDHURST	015	2520	2626	2794	1.0	56	990	1049	1134	1.4	2.49	753	789	1.1
22958	NELLYSFORD	125	775	821	876	1.4	66	347	377	413	2.0	2.17	247	264	1.6
22959	NORTH GARDEN	003	2008	2105	2304	1.1	61	762	813	905	1.5	2.55	552	581	1.2
22960	ORANGE	137	9325	10546	12141	2.9	90	3604	4176	4927	3.5	2.42	2507	2866	3.2
22963	PALMYRA	065	10882	13784	18155	5.7	98	4235	5488	7383	6.3	2.48	3334	4273	6.0
22964	PINEY RIVER	125	181	193	206	1.5	69	80	87	96	2.0	2.16	57	62	2.0
22967	ROSELAND	125	2180	2392	2593	2.2	82	893	1004	1114	2.8	2.36	631	699	2.4
22968	RUCKERSVILLE	079	8373	9785	11457	3.7	94	2999	3539	4181	4.0	2.74	2365	2761	3.7
22969	SCHUYLER	125	1171	1257	1360	1.7	73	465	508	560	2.1	2.47	332	357	1.7
22971	SHIPMAN	125	1056	1123	1200	1.5	68	417	455	500	2.1	2.36	285	307	1.8
22972	SOMERSET	137	272	278	308	0.5	43	116	122	138	1.2	2.26	84	87	0.8
22973	STANARDSVILLE	079	4773	5174	5833	1.9	78	1826	2009	2292	2.3	2.55	1352	1466	1.9
22974	TROY	065	3816	4718	5971	5.1	97	1115	1434	1886	6.1	2.89	858	1088	5.8
22976	TYRO	125	435	446	467	0.6	45	171	179	192	1.1	2.49	116	120	0.8
22980	WAYNESBORO	015	29755	31313	32948	1.2	62	12280	13106	13965	1.5	2.36	8491	8956	1.3
23002	AMELIA COURT HOUSE	007	8818	9500	10260	1.8	74	3258	3570	3919	2.2	2.63	2443	2642	1.9
23004	ARVONIA	029	1270	1288	1314	0.3	37	476	495	515	0.9	2.60	348	357	0.6
23005	ASHLAND	085	14193	15082	16414	1.4	67	5179	5603	6206	1.9	2.45	3718	3963	1.5
23009	AYLETT	101	4851	5306	5801	2.1	81	1768	1969	2188	2.6	2.69	1405	1548	2.3
23011	BARHAMSVILLE	127	803	919	1052	3.2	91	300	358	427	4.3	2.13	227	268	4.0
23015	BEAVERDAM	085	3714	4184	4775	2.8	88	1327	1520	1756	3.3	2.74	1069	1209	2.9
23021	BOHANNON	115	192	197	203	0.6	46	78	81	84	0.9	2.40	57	59	0.8
23022	BREMO BLUFF	065	1309	1463	1807	2.7	86	463	530	672	3.2	2.65	335	378	2.9
23023	BRUINGTON	097	223	229	236	0.6	47	97	102	107	1.2	2.25	69	72	1.0
23024	BUMPASS	109	6239	7062	8252	3.0	90	2425	2807	3348	3.5	2.50	1829	2092	3.2
23025	CARDINAL	115	657	675	696	0.6	47	278	288	299	0.8	2.30	204	209	0.6
23027	CARTERSVILLE	049	1239	1226	1218	-0.3	17	471	478	487	0.4	2.56	334	333	-0.1
	VIRGINIA					1.4					1.7	2.51			1.4
	UNITED STATES					1.2					1.3	2.58			1.1

#	ZIP CODE POST OFFICE NAME	RACE (%) White 2000	White 2004	Black 2000	Black 2004	Asian/Pacific 2000	Asian/Pacific 2004	% Hispanic Origin 2000	% Hispanic Origin 2004	2004 AGE DISTRIBUTION (%) 0-4	5-9	10-14	15-19	20-24	25-44	45-64	65-84	85+	18+	MEDIAN AGE 2004	% 2004 Males	% 2004 Females
22727	MADISON	86.9	85.9	11.6	12.4	0.4	0.5	0.4	0.5	5.5	6.0	6.6	5.6	5.0	26.3	28.6	14.3	2.2	78.5	42.1	48.3	51.7
22728	MIDLAND	88.2	87.1	9.6	10.3	0.4	0.5	1.3	1.6	6.3	6.8	7.6	6.9	5.4	28.4	28.4	9.4	0.8	74.8	38.6	50.4	49.6
22729	MITCHELLS	52.4	49.2	46.8	50.0	0.0	0.0	0.8	1.5	1.5	1.5	2.3	9.2	8.5	52.3	20.8	3.9	0.0	89.2	36.0	83.9	16.2
22730	OAKPARK	83.2	81.8	14.3	15.1	0.9	1.1	1.3	1.5	6.3	6.4	6.8	6.4	5.3	26.6	27.4	12.8	2.1	76.5	40.4	48.3	51.7
22731	PRATTS	82.8	81.9	15.2	16.2	1.0	1.0	0.0	0.0	5.7	5.7	7.6	4.8	5.7	28.6	24.8	14.3	2.9	77.1	41.5	45.7	54.3
22732	RADIANT	81.1	79.7	15.9	16.9	0.9	1.1	1.4	1.7	6.2	6.6	7.0	6.7	5.8	25.7	27.9	12.2	2.0	76.0	40.3	48.6	51.4
22733	RAPIDAN	60.0	57.9	38.3	40.0	0.4	0.4	1.2	1.5	3.0	3.3	3.7	8.3	7.6	43.4	22.7	7.0	1.0	84.7	36.5	72.0	28.0
22734	REMINGTON	84.3	82.6	12.1	13.1	0.6	0.7	2.7	3.5	9.0	8.9	9.0	7.3	6.0	33.0	21.1	5.4	0.5	68.5	32.7	48.9	51.1
22735	REVA	87.1	85.6	11.1	12.4	0.2	0.2	1.0	1.3	5.9	6.3	6.2	6.4	5.4	29.0	29.0	10.8	1.3	77.7	39.7	49.1	50.9
22736	RICHARDSVILLE	77.9	75.1	17.1	18.6	1.1	1.4	2.4	3.5	5.6	7.2	8.9	7.0	5.2	28.5	25.8	10.5	1.4	74.0	37.8	50.3	49.7
22737	RIXEYVILLE	89.5	88.2	8.2	9.0	0.2	0.3	1.2	1.6	6.8	7.4	7.9	6.4	4.6	29.1	27.2	9.8	0.8	73.8	38.4	49.6	50.4
22738	ROCHELLE	85.1	84.0	13.2	14.0	0.0	0.0	0.2	0.4	5.9	6.3	7.1	6.3	6.5	24.5	28.2	13.2	2.0	76.9	41.0	48.9	51.1
22740	SPERRYVILLE	91.1	90.3	7.0	7.5	0.3	0.4	0.9	1.1	4.9	5.1	6.5	5.4	4.7	24.2	34.0	13.6	1.7	80.1	44.5	49.2	50.8
22741	STEVENSBURG	66.2	63.7	27.6	29.5	0.0	0.7	4.8	5.5	7.5	7.5	7.5	6.9	7.5	28.1	23.3	10.3	1.4	73.3	35.0	51.4	48.6
22742	SUMERDUCK	93.4	92.7	4.5	4.9	0.6	0.6	0.9	1.3	6.3	6.8	8.0	7.3	6.0	30.1	27.1	7.7	0.9	74.5	37.8	50.4	49.6
22743	SYRIA	91.7	90.8	6.5	7.1	0.5	0.4	0.9	0.9	5.3	5.7	6.2	5.7	4.9	25.1	30.8	14.5	1.8	79.3	43.3	50.2	49.8
22746	VIEWTOWN	93.2	92.1	4.4	4.9	0.3	0.4	1.6	1.8	6.8	7.5	7.9	6.1	3.9	28.0	28.2	10.8	0.8	73.9	39.9	50.8	49.2
22747	WASHINGTON	90.0	89.0	8.0	8.6	0.3	0.4	1.1	1.4	4.4	4.7	5.9	5.1	4.5	22.9	36.6	14.3	1.7	81.8	46.4	49.6	50.4
22749	WOODVILLE	92.5	91.7	5.3	5.7	0.2	0.2	1.1	1.3	4.9	4.5	7.5	5.1	3.8	24.9	36.0	12.1	1.3	79.8	44.6	50.0	50.0
22801	HARRISONBURG	88.0	86.7	4.2	4.1	3.0	3.3	6.6	8.4	4.6	4.3	4.2	16.6	26.8	18.5	15.2	7.8	1.8	84.3	23.8	47.1	52.9
22802	HARRISONBURG	87.4	85.7	5.3	5.6	1.6	1.8	11.3	13.7	6.2	5.9	6.0	7.1	9.6	29.7	21.6	11.8	2.1	78.6	34.5	49.1	50.9
22807	HARRISONBURG	91.0	89.8	5.4	5.7	1.7	2.0	2.2	2.7	0.3	0.3	2.0	40.2	47.2	3.2	5.7	1.0	0.3	96.5	20.8	49.6	50.4
22810	BASYE	97.0	96.5	0.8	0.9	0.5	0.6	1.3	1.5	4.5	4.9	5.3	4.3	4.2	21.1	35.0	19.3	1.3	82.7	48.6	50.9	49.1
22811	BERGTON	98.9	98.5	0.0	0.0	0.3	0.3	0.8	1.0	4.6	4.9	5.6	4.6	4.6	25.9	33.6	14.4	1.8	82.1	44.9	51.8	48.2
22812	BRIDGEWATER	96.5	96.1	1.7	1.8	0.4	0.4	2.2	2.7	5.5	5.7	6.5	9.6	10.5	24.2	22.0	12.7	3.3	78.9	36.3	47.7	52.3
22815	BROADWAY	98.0	97.7	0.4	0.4	0.4	0.4	1.9	2.3	6.3	6.6	6.9	6.0	5.3	28.3	27.0	12.4	1.1	76.5	39.2	49.2	50.8
22820	CRIDERS	98.8	99.3	0.0	0.0	0.0	0.0	0.8	1.1	4.7	5.5	5.8	4.7	4.7	26.3	32.5	13.9	1.8	80.7	44.0	52.6	47.5
22821	DAYTON	96.9	96.3	0.6	0.6	0.2	0.2	3.6	4.6	7.8	7.7	7.8	6.4	5.5	29.2	22.8	11.4	1.4	72.7	35.7	50.6	49.4
22824	EDINBURG	96.5	95.9	0.2	0.2	0.2	0.2	3.9	4.8	5.8	6.1	6.3	5.4	5.1	25.9	28.5	15.2	1.8	78.6	42.1	49.1	50.9
22827	ELKTON	96.4	96.0	2.3	2.5	0.2	0.3	1.1	1.4	6.4	6.4	6.6	6.1	6.1	28.7	25.9	12.6	1.2	76.9	38.9	49.2	50.8
22830	FULKS RUN	98.7	98.6	0.3	0.3	0.1	0.1	0.4	0.5	6.3	6.6	6.9	5.9	6.3	29.1	26.3	11.4	1.2	76.6	38.0	53.0	47.0
22831	HINTON	98.5	98.3	0.3	0.4	0.3	0.5	0.6	0.6	6.5	6.3	6.4	6.1	6.9	27.9	26.1	12.5	1.3	77.0	38.6	51.3	48.7
22832	KEEZLETOWN	97.1	96.9	1.4	1.4	0.1	0.2	4.1	4.4	5.3	5.9	6.3	6.4	5.1	27.8	30.1	12.3	0.9	78.7	41.1	50.9	49.1
22834	LINVILLE	98.3	98.0	0.1	0.1	0.6	0.7	0.9	1.0	5.7	6.4	7.3	6.2	5.3	27.9	28.0	12.1	1.1	76.8	39.7	49.8	50.3
22835	LURAY	94.6	94.1	3.6	3.8	0.4	0.4	1.2	1.5	5.3	5.6	6.4	5.8	5.4	26.7	26.6	15.8	2.4	79.2	41.7	49.0	51.0
22840	MC GAHEYSVILLE	93.7	93.2	4.1	4.2	0.3	0.4	2.2	2.7	6.0	6.6	7.2	6.1	4.8	29.3	27.7	11.4	0.8	76.4	39.7	50.6	49.4
22841	MOUNT CRAWFORD	97.2	96.9	0.7	0.7	0.5	0.5	3.3	3.9	6.0	6.3	6.4	6.7	5.7	26.5	29.5	11.5	1.5	77.2	40.3	49.6	50.4
22842	MOUNT JACKSON	94.1	92.8	0.5	0.5	0.3	0.4	6.6	8.2	5.7	6.0	6.6	5.3	5.1	25.7	28.8	15.4	1.5	78.6	42.2	50.5	49.5
22843	MOUNT SOLON	97.1	96.7	1.1	1.2	0.1	0.1	2.7	3.4	7.7	7.4	6.8	5.8	5.4	29.0	25.2	11.5	1.1	74.4	37.5	50.6	49.4
22844	NEW MARKET	95.9	94.9	0.7	0.8	0.7	0.8	3.6	5.0	5.0	5.1	5.9	5.7	5.4	23.7	29.0	17.4	2.8	80.6	44.4	47.6	52.4
22845	ORKNEY SPRINGS	96.6	96.9	0.0	1.6	0.0	0.0	0.0	1.6	4.7	6.3	6.3	4.7	3.1	20.3	34.4	20.3	0.0	82.8	48.0	54.7	45.3
22846	PENN LAIRD	95.5	94.9	1.9	1.9	0.2	0.3	4.4	5.3	6.0	6.7	7.9	6.5	6.1	28.2	26.5	11.1	1.1	75.5	38.7	50.8	49.2
22847	QUICKSBURG	97.9	97.5	0.3	0.3	0.3	0.3	2.2	2.8	4.4	5.2	7.1	5.9	4.8	27.2	30.4	13.7	1.3	79.6	42.5	50.5	49.5
22849	SHENANDOAH	97.3	96.9	1.3	1.5	0.2	0.2	0.9	1.2	5.7	5.9	6.6	6.1	5.9	28.1	27.2	13.3	1.4	78.1	39.8	48.9	51.1
22851	STANLEY	98.4	97.9	0.1	0.1	0.1	0.2	1.2	1.6	6.5	6.5	6.8	6.1	6.2	29.3	25.8	11.7	1.1	76.6	37.9	49.7	50.3
22853	TIMBERVILLE	97.9	97.5	0.4	0.4	0.2	0.2	3.5	4.4	5.4	5.8	6.9	6.1	5.5	27.5	26.8	14.0	2.1	78.2	40.5	49.5	50.5
22901	CHARLOTTESVILLE	81.6	79.9	11.8	12.2	3.6	4.3	3.2	4.0	5.7	6.0	6.6	6.6	6.2	27.6	25.5	13.5	2.4	77.6	39.0	46.4	53.6
22902	CHARLOTTESVILLE	75.8	74.1	19.8	20.8	1.1	1.4	3.1	3.7	6.7	6.4	6.5	5.7	6.2	33.7	24.0	9.6	1.4	77.0	36.4	48.4	51.7
22903	CHARLOTTESVILLE	70.9	69.1	18.8	19.2	7.3	8.2	2.4	2.9	3.9	3.7	4.2	18.4	20.6	25.3	15.3	7.4	1.3	85.8	24.8	47.6	52.5
22904	CHARLOTTESVILLE	58.6	55.2	19.8	19.8	19.0	21.6	3.5	4.3	4.3	2.6	1.7	6.9	41.4	35.3	7.8	0.0	0.0	90.5	24.2	55.2	44.8
22911	CHARLOTTESVILLE	88.0	86.4	7.7	8.1	2.5	3.3	1.6	2.1	7.3	7.9	8.6	7.2	5.3	27.1	25.0	10.0	1.6	71.2	37.4	47.8	52.2
22920	AFTON	91.5	90.5	6.7	7.3	0.4	0.5	1.9	2.3	4.8	5.4	5.7	5.4	4.7	24.2	34.6	14.0	1.3	80.8	44.9	49.1	50.9
22922	ARRINGTON	72.9	71.1	24.5	25.9	0.2	0.2	2.5	3.1	5.0	5.5	6.5	6.3	5.4	24.1	29.8	15.7	1.9	79.0	43.2	49.3	50.7
22923	BARBOURSVILLE	88.1	87.0	9.5	10.1	0.5	0.6	1.5	1.8	7.3	7.7	7.4	6.2	4.7	30.2	26.8	9.0	0.8	73.7	37.8	49.9	50.1
22931	COVESVILLE	84.9	83.4	12.6	13.5	0.3	0.3	4.0	5.2	6.0	6.3	6.9	6.3	5.7	25.5	29.8	12.3	1.2	77.1	41.2	49.0	51.0
22932	CROZET	91.8	90.8	5.5	6.0	0.8	1.0	2.0	2.6	6.1	6.8	7.3	6.5	5.0	25.3	28.7	13.0	1.4	75.6	41.0	47.2	52.8
22935	DYKE	97.4	97.0	1.0	1.1	0.4	0.5	0.8	0.9	5.6	6.3	7.3	6.8	5.4	26.8	29.8	11.2	0.8	76.3	40.3	50.2	49.8
22936	EARLYSVILLE	95.7	95.0	2.6	3.0	0.7	0.8	1.0	1.4	5.5	6.7	7.9	6.8	4.6	22.8	32.4	12.3	1.0	75.6	42.5	49.1	51.0
22937	ESMONT	66.4	63.7	31.5	33.5	0.1	0.1	1.5	1.9	5.6	6.0	6.7	6.2	5.4	25.7	30.0	13.0	1.5	78.1	41.8	48.1	51.9
22938	FABER	84.8	83.5	12.9	13.7	0.4	0.4	2.2	3.0	5.8	5.9	5.5	5.9	5.5	23.7	31.4	14.2	2.1	79.0	43.6	48.8	51.2
22939	FISHERSVILLE	94.2	93.3	4.0	4.5	0.6	0.7	0.9	1.1	6.4	6.2	6.1	5.2	5.3	26.0	29.0	13.4	2.5	78.0	42.1	48.4	51.6
22940	FREE UNION	95.8	95.2	2.3	2.5	0.6	0.7	1.2	1.6	5.2	5.8	6.8	6.7	5.5	25.5	32.1	11.5	1.0	78.0	41.6	49.0	51.0
22942	GORDONSVILLE	78.1	76.3	19.7	21.1	0.3	0.4	1.0	1.2	6.2	6.5	6.5	5.6	5.1	28.7	27.7	12.1	1.5	77.3	40.2	47.9	52.1
22943	GREENWOOD	89.7	88.7	8.1	8.8	0.7	0.7	2.6	3.3	5.6	7.0	8.3	6.6	4.8	24.2	32.0	10.4	1.2	74.8	40.9	47.5	52.5
22946	KEENE	66.7	64.6	31.4	33.3	0.0	0.0	0.0	0.0	4.2	4.2	6.3	8.3	6.3	22.9	33.3	12.5	2.1	85.4	43.8	45.8	54.2
22947	KESWICK	83.8	81.9	14.4	15.8	0.7	0.8	1.2	1.6	4.8	5.7	6.8	5.5	4.1	24.7	32.7	14.6	1.1	79.2	44.1	48.0	52.0
22948	LOCUST DALE	79.6	77.9	17.1	18.4	1.3	1.8	2.0	2.5	6.8	6.8	6.8	6.8	5.5	27.0	26.4	12.3	1.8	75.5	39.4	48.5	51.5
22949	LOVINGSTON	82.3	81.1	14.5	15.2	0.5	0.5	3.6	4.3	5.6	5.5	5.4	6.3	5.7	21.7	30.7	16.5	2.7	79.6	44.9	48.6	51.4
22952	LYNDHURST	95.0	94.3	2.9	3.2	0.4	0.5	1.7	2.2	6.3	6.7	6.8	5.9	4.8	28.3	29.3	10.6	1.3	76.3	40.0	49.4	50.6
22958	NELLYSFORD	90.7	89.9	7.2	7.7	0.5	0.5	1.2	1.5	4.3	4.6	5.5	4.8	4.3	20.3	35.9	19.2	1.1	82.6	48.6	49.1	50.9
22959	NORTH GARDEN	84.3	83.0	13.0	13.6	0.4	0.4	5.0	6.1	6.0	6.3	6.9	6.5	5.0	25.9	30.5	11.6	1.3	76.6	41.3	48.5	51.5
22960	ORANGE	79.0	77.3	19.3	20.7	0.3	0.3	1.2	1.5	6.3	6.3	6.3	5.9	5.7	27.3	25.1	14.6	2.7	77.6	40.4	48.0	52.0
22963	PALMYRA	85.3	84.4	12.4	12.9	0.4	0.5	1.3	1.6	6.6	7.0	7.0	5.3	3.8	28.0	24.9	16.5	1.0	75.9	40.6	47.6	52.4
22964	PINEY RIVER	66.3	64.3	30.4	31.6	0.0	0.0	5.0	5.7	4.2	4.7	5.7	6.7	5.7	24.4	30.6	16.1	2.1	80.3	44.2	50.3	49.7
22967	ROSELAND	80.8	79.5	17.0	17.9	0.2	0.3	2.7	3.1	4.6	5.0	5.9	6.1	5.0	23.1	32.0	16.6	1.8	80.7	45.3	49.5	50.5
22968	RUCKERSVILLE	90.3	89.4	7.1	7.5	0.5	0.6	1.5	1.9	8.4	8.2	8.0	6.4	5.1	33.3	21.9	7.5	1.1	71.2	34.6	49.4	50.7
22969	SCHUYLER	82.3	80.4	15.1	16.5	0.2	0.2	1.8	2.2	6.7	6.8	6.2	6.0	5.2	26.3	28.8	12.9	1.3	76.8	41.1	49.1	50.9
22971	SHIPMAN	77.1	75.7	18.6	19.3	0.3	0.3	2.7	3.4	6.4	6.3	5.7	5.8	5.5	24.0	27.8	15.5	2.9	77.7	42.4	48.7	51.3
22972	SOMERSET	83.1	82.0	15.1	16.2	0.4	0.4	0.7	1.4	6.1	6.1	6.1	5.8	5.0	27.3	29.1	12.6	1.8	77.3	41.1	47.5	52.5
22973	STANARDSVILLE	92.1	91.2	5.7	6.2	0.5	0.5	0.9	1.2	5.5	5.5	7.1	6.3	5.5	27.5	29.0	12.0	1.6	78.0	40.7	49.4	50.6
22974	TROY	76.1	73.4	21.8	24.2	0.6	0.7	1.0	1.2	6.4	6.5	5.9	4.9	5.2	36.6	25.5	8.5	0.7	78.2	37.8	43.1	56.9
22976	TYRO	91.3	90.4	7.1	7.6	0.5	0.5	3.0	3.8	4.9	4.9	5.4	6.5	6.1	25.8	30.9	14.1	1.4	80.7	42.7	48.7	51.4
22980	WAYNESBORO	89.5	88.6	7.7	8.1	0.5	0.6	2.5	3.1	6.3	6.2	6.9	6.2	5.7	26.0	26.2	14.4	2.0	76.7	40.1	47.8	52.2
23002	AMELIA COURT HOUSE	70.9	69.1	27.8	29.3	0.2	0.2	0.7	0.9	6.4	6.5	6.7	6.3	5.4	27.4	27.1	12.1	2.0	76.3	40.0	49.0	51.0
23004	ARVONIA	58.6	56.4	39.8	41.7	0.1	0.2	0.3	0.4	6.0	6.3	7.8	7.2	5.0	27.6	26.6	12.3	1.4	75.5	39.1	48.0	52.0
23005	ASHLAND	82.0	80.7	15.6	16.5	0.6	0.7	1.4	1.7	5.2	5.6	6.6	9.5	9.8	24.1	25.9	11.7	1.7	78.2	38.1	49.0	51.1
23009	AYLETT	77.8	76.2	19.4	20.6	0.2	0.3	0.8	0.9	8.0	7.8	6.8	5.7	5.5	32.7	25.4	7.4	0.8	73.9	36.0	49.9	50.1
23011	BARHAMSVILLE	67.3	65.6	30.5	31.9	0.4	0.4	1.5	1.7	3.6	4.0	6.6	7.8	6.2	35.0	25.6	9.9	1.2	81.5	38.8	54.4	45.6
23015	BEAVERDAM	86.2	85.0	12.0	12.9	0.4	0.5	0.6	0.7	6.5	7.2	7.4	6.6	4.8	27.3	29.0	10.0	1.3	74.5	39.6	49.3	50.7
23021	BOHANNON	84.9	83.8	14.1	14.7	0.0	0.0	1.0	0.5	4.6	5.1	5.6	5.1	4.1	21.8	32.5	17.8	3.6	81.7	47.7	48.2	51.8
23022	BREMO BLUFF	62.2	59.3	36.3	39.1	0.9	1.0	0.7	0.8	5.3	5.6	6.6	6.4	5.8	24.1	27.6	15.2	3.4	78.6	42.6	48.0	52.0
23023	BRUINGTON	56.5	54.2	40.4	41.9	0.5	0.4	0.9	0.9	5.2	6.1	6.6	6.1	5.2	25.8	29.7	13.5	1.8	77.7	42.0	49.3	50.7
23024	BUMPASS	84.8	83.6	13.4	14.3	0.3	0.3	0.7	0.8	6.0	6.4	7.0	6.0	5.2	28.8	29.1	10.7	0.8	76.8	39.9	49.8	50.2
23025	CARDINAL	85.1	84.0	13.9	14.8	0.0	0.0	0.8	1.2	4.7	5.2	5.5	5.2	4.2	21.9	32.4	17.3	3.6	80.9	47.3	48.4	51.6
23027	CARTERSVILLE	67.2	65.3	30.5	32.0	0.1	0.1	1.5	1.9	7.7	7.8	7.6	5.2	4.7	27.9	24.6	13.3	1.4	73.7	38.2	48.5	51.5
	VIRGINIA	72.3	70.7	19.6	19.9	3.7	4.3	4.7	5.7	6.5	6.6	6.9	6.9	7.0	29.7	24.9	10.1	1.4	76.2	36.6	49.1	50.9
	UNITED STATES	75.1	73.6	12.3	12.5	3.8	4.2	12.5	14.1	6.9	6.7	7.2	7.0	7.3	28.6	23.8	10.8	1.7	75.1	36.0	49.1	50.9

ZIP CODE #	POST OFFICE NAME	2004 Per Capita Income	2004 HH Income Base	2004 HOUSEHOLD INCOME DISTRIBUTION (%) Less than $25,000	$25,000 to $49,999	$50,000 to $99,999	$100,000 to $149,999	$150,000 or More	MEDIAN HOUSEHOLD INCOME 2004	2009	2004 National Centile	2004 State Centile	2004 Home Value Base	2004 HOME VALUE DISTRIBUTION (%) Less than $50,000	$50,000 to $89,999	$90,000 to $174,999	$175,000 to $399,999	$400,000 or More	2004 Median Home Value
22727	MADISON	23535	1813	23.9	32.8	31.3	8.3	3.7	44775	52055	61	53	1456	6.3	8.2	38.7	40.7	6.1	165600
22728	MIDLAND	30825	1088	9.3	22.9	41.1	17.4	9.4	66965	80694	90	84	871	0.6	1.0	13.2	67.7	17.5	262413
22729	MITCHELLS	28635	51	11.8	29.4	37.3	15.7	5.9	58824	69988	83	79	39	15.4	0.0	18.0	59.0	7.7	225000
22730	OAKPARK	23467	364	20.6	30.8	35.7	7.1	5.8	48648	56679	70	62	278	3.2	9.7	40.7	42.5	4.0	165741
22731	PRATTS	28002	47	23.4	27.7	36.2	8.5	4.3	48660	57178	70	62	36	2.8	8.3	38.9	41.7	8.3	175000
22732	RADIANT	23261	438	18.7	30.6	38.8	7.1	4.8	50388	57639	73	66	333	3.6	9.9	37.5	44.4	4.5	171983
22733	RAPIDAN	19213	454	14.5	31.7	34.4	12.6	6.8	54044	63265	78	73	337	7.7	3.0	29.7	47.2	12.5	198897
22734	REMINGTON	23037	977	14.6	29.2	39.7	12.6	3.9	54335	65102	79	73	767	12.4	4.6	28.8	50.2	4.0	181348
22735	REVA	21439	565	21.4	34.5	30.6	11.3	2.1	44458	52497	60	52	490	2.5	2.7	42.5	43.5	9.0	180172
22736	RICHARDSVILLE	19166	158	16.5	39.9	30.4	10.8	2.5	46286	54013	65	56	140	4.3	5.7	37.1	42.9	10.0	180882
22737	RIXEYVILLE	26831	1056	14.4	21.4	39.7	17.4	7.1	66204	79039	89	84	934	4.9	1.1	26.2	58.5	9.3	224713
22738	ROCHELLE	23080	207	24.2	27.5	37.2	8.7	2.4	48134	53896	69	61	176	7.4	7.4	38.6	40.3	6.3	163462
22740	SPERRYVILLE	26269	1029	20.2	33.2	30.9	10.6	5.1	47620	56380	67	60	822	3.7	5.8	33.1	42.5	15.0	192941
22741	STEVENSBURG	20875	54	25.9	31.5	27.8	9.3	5.6	41541	46555	51	43	34	0.0	0.0	29.4	64.7	5.9	213636
22742	SUMERDUCK	31120	597	10.2	12.9	43.1	24.6	9.2	79542	94691	95	91	541	0.4	0.2	16.1	78.7	4.6	239685
22743	SYRIA	26942	113	22.1	38.9	27.4	9.7	1.8	42780	50884	55	47	95	7.4	9.5	40.0	36.8	6.3	156944
22746	VIEWTOWN	30765	266	15.0	18.1	36.5	20.3	10.2	72443	87952	92	86	237	1.3	1.3	19.4	59.9	18.1	268382
22747	WASHINGTON	31741	521	19.0	29.4	32.1	9.6	10.0	51412	64437	75	68	401	0.8	4.7	22.0	43.1	29.4	243852
22749	WOODVILLE	28658	201	17.9	27.9	35.8	12.4	6.0	53581	66355	78	72	156	0.6	2.6	32.1	48.7	16.0	215217
22801	HARRISONBURG	21637	11169	31.1	25.8	27.5	10.1	5.6	42228	52534	54	45	5764	4.4	2.7	28.8	57.1	7.1	202195
22802	HARRISONBURG	22920	8839	31.2	32.7	26.4	5.3	4.5	38687	45910	42	35	4789	8.1	5.3	53.1	29.0	4.5	143245
22807	HARRISONBURG	27285	40	0.0	30.0	30.0	17.5	22.5	85357	115191	96	92	30	0.0	0.0	0.0	100.0	0.0	213158
22810	BASYE	30764	491	19.1	29.7	34.2	10.8	6.1	50961	61630	74	67	416	4.1	10.6	42.8	36.8	5.8	146552
22811	BERGTON	21597	170	24.7	42.4	25.9	2.9	4.1	37314	43121	37	30	141	7.1	14.2	68.1	9.2	1.4	116563
22812	BRIDGEWATER	23166	3011	17.7	34.1	35.8	8.7	3.6	48407	55883	69	61	2263	2.4	3.7	42.5	45.8	5.6	177555
22815	BROADWAY	20558	2806	24.6	36.2	30.6	6.3	2.3	43039	49504	56	48	2274	7.5	9.2	56.7	23.6	3.1	134598
22820	CRIDERS	20735	113	24.8	43.4	23.9	3.5	4.4	36848	42896	35	29	94	7.5	18.1	61.7	11.7	1.1	115909
22821	DAYTON	21121	1938	23.8	36.9	30.8	5.4	3.2	43110	49575	56	49	1478	4.7	10.3	44.8	35.6	4.7	152914
22824	EDINBURG	23336	2320	20.7	36.0	32.5	8.0	2.8	44859	51090	61	53	1813	5.1	8.6	44.4	37.1	4.8	152803
22827	ELKTON	19864	4572	27.7	34.1	30.1	5.8	2.3	40274	46356	47	40	3597	11.0	10.1	46.9	29.4	2.6	135492
22830	FULKS RUN	17660	652	27.3	42.3	23.9	4.8	1.7	36629	41493	34	28	531	8.3	27.7	42.6	18.5	3.0	114833
22831	HINTON	19692	339	31.0	37.8	25.7	1.8	3.8	40208	45739	47	40	268	4.5	22.0	53.4	19.4	0.8	121111
22832	KEEZLETOWN	24763	513	18.1	28.1	38.8	11.1	3.9	53164	61518	77	71	425	6.8	7.1	43.5	36.7	5.9	160682
22834	LINVILLE	21427	585	21.0	30.4	38.5	6.3	3.8	48566	54567	69	62	483	4.6	7.9	55.9	28.0	3.7	144016
22835	LURAY	21010	4944	31.2	32.6	28.5	5.8	2.0	40055	45230	46	39	3702	5.5	14.3	51.4	25.0	3.8	135938
22840	MC GAHEYSVILLE	27358	1317	13.9	29.0	39.0	12.7	5.4	56622	65682	81	76	1126	4.7	6.4	37.9	46.0	5.0	177148
22841	MOUNT CRAWFORD	28778	1073	15.7	29.5	39.0	9.5	6.4	54479	63936	79	73	901	5.6	10.2	34.5	41.2	8.6	174421
22842	MOUNT JACKSON	22853	1893	23.7	33.3	32.3	6.8	3.9	44372	50973	60	52	1499	8.3	9.5	46.4	30.9	4.9	139090
22843	MOUNT SOLON	25497	943	21.0	28.8	37.3	6.7	6.2	50084	56723	72	65	785	8.3	9.9	40.8	38.1	2.9	152690
22844	NEW MARKET	24434	1744	27.4	30.7	31.0	7.1	3.7	43776	50470	58	51	1245	5.6	6.9	45.5	37.6	4.4	155865
22845	ORKNEY SPRINGS	33434	33	18.2	30.3	30.3	12.1	9.1	51421	63142	75	68	28	0.0	10.7	53.6	32.1	3.6	137500
22846	PENN LAIRD	23484	268	17.2	33.2	35.5	10.1	4.1	49753	59046	71	65	219	5.0	3.7	55.7	22.4	13.2	146221
22847	QUICKSBURG	18613	270	24.4	40.4	28.5	4.8	1.9	39522	45531	44	38	227	6.2	11.9	43.6	32.2	6.2	152917
22849	SHENANDOAH	20546	2074	30.8	34.4	24.7	6.9	3.3	38422	44034	41	34	1645	7.9	18.4	52.1	19.8	1.8	118567
22851	STANLEY	16621	2136	35.5	37.2	21.9	4.1	1.3	34260	38782	25	19	1644	15.0	14.9	48.5	18.3	3.2	117093
22853	TIMBERVILLE	21218	1773	24.5	36.6	29.6	7.3	2.0	42487	49210	55	46	1391	5.8	11.6	58.2	22.4	2.2	129729
22901	CHARLOTTESVILLE	39289	14358	18.0	25.0	31.6	13.8	11.7	57716	73809	82	78	8166	1.6	2.2	28.2	51.5	16.5	218333
22902	CHARLOTTESVILLE	27723	8243	25.2	29.8	30.6	9.8	4.6	45502	57500	63	55	4534	7.7	6.6	43.5	38.4	3.7	154118
22903	CHARLOTTESVILLE	27388	13739	34.2	24.6	24.1	9.4	7.7	39406	50838	44	38	5368	1.7	7.6	31.9	40.1	18.6	203668
22904	CHARLOTTESVILLE	9327	43	53.5	34.9	11.6	0.0	0.0	22882	26671	3	3	0	0.0	0.0	0.0	0.0	0.0	0
22911	CHARLOTTESVILLE	36720	5180	10.7	19.9	39.6	17.2	12.6	74674	91041	93	88	4154	6.1	1.1	18.2	64.8	9.9	231131
22920	AFTON	33924	1859	16.4	25.1	36.6	14.2	7.7	57244	73766	82	77	1533	6.5	8.6	33.8	38.3	12.9	179972
22922	ARRINGTON	24967	775	31.9	32.5	26.2	4.4	5.0	37135	46328	36	30	640	13.9	19.5	40.5	23.1	3.0	115263
22923	BARBOURSVILLE	26052	1636	16.3	31.9	36.4	10.2	5.3	51519	60326	75	68	1388	9.3	4.5	43.3	34.7	8.3	158103
22931	COVESVILLE	22570	140	22.1	31.4	32.1	11.4	2.9	47564	56790	67	60	115	0.0	13.9	37.4	40.0	8.7	170833
22932	CROZET	26519	2116	17.3	27.5	38.3	11.3	5.6	53943	66823	78	72	1695	7.0	4.7	40.9	37.6	9.7	168569
22935	DYKE	29939	418	20.8	24.4	32.3	12.7	9.8	55462	68477	80	75	350	3.4	8.0	40.3	33.1	15.1	170000
22936	EARLYSVILLE	39065	1951	9.8	19.0	34.0	21.8	15.3	79506	104122	95	90	1764	2.4	2.4	18.3	51.8	25.1	246449
22937	ESMONT	23944	458	28.6	24.7	34.1	10.0	2.6	47503	58219	67	60	380	9.0	13.4	41.8	27.6	8.2	137083
22938	FABER	23678	583	22.1	31.4	33.6	8.2	4.6	46766	55744	66	58	472	7.2	10.8	38.4	35.8	7.8	156707
22939	FISHERSVILLE	26601	1509	23.1	23.8	35.6	12.9	4.6	52253	59755	76	70	1217	5.9	3.4	30.2	56.1	4.4	194676
22940	FREE UNION	30994	379	15.6	29.6	29.8	11.9	13.2	54828	70078	79	74	304	2.3	7.9	26.3	40.8	22.7	215789
22942	GORDONSVILLE	24463	3066	23.1	31.4	32.0	10.1	3.5	46061	53598	64	56	2483	6.6	9.6	50.8	26.3	6.7	141542
22943	GREENWOOD	25924	248	12.5	27.4	45.2	13.7	1.2	57428	70838	82	77	200	2.0	6.0	38.5	42.0	11.5	189583
22946	KEENE	25729	22	22.7	27.3	36.4	13.6	0.0	50000	60000	72	65	18	0.0	11.1	50.0	27.8	11.1	150000
22947	KESWICK	47487	1652	10.7	22.0	31.9	16.6	18.8	74268	94657	93	88	1436	1.3	2.3	30.3	34.5	31.6	238535
22948	LOCUST DALE	20416	45	13.3	31.1	40.0	6.7	8.9	53625	60000	78	72	32	0.0	12.5	37.5	43.8	6.3	175000
22949	LOVINGSTON	24748	750	24.3	34.0	28.7	6.5	6.5	41426	51532	51	42	560	4.1	14.1	37.5	37.5	6.8	153947
22952	LYNDHURST	23127	1049	20.1	24.4	43.8	9.7	2.0	52822	60558	77	70	907	10.4	4.5	46.5	36.5	2.1	147500
22958	NELLYSFORD	47855	377	20.2	22.8	30.2	13.3	13.5	58651	79132	83	79	316	7.9	8.9	26.3	36.1	20.9	204545
22959	NORTH GARDEN	25194	813	21.2	27.9	32.4	13.8	4.8	50938	65634	74	67	640	1.6	7.7	35.9	44.2	10.6	191489
22960	ORANGE	22618	4176	28.9	28.9	29.3	9.0	4.0	42028	50189	53	44	2919	6.4	10.0	48.4	30.2	5.1	143028
22963	PALMYRA	27505	5488	13.7	27.0	41.0	14.6	3.8	57476	66972	82	78	4740	2.2	3.9	45.1	44.9	3.9	173063
22964	PINEY RIVER	23290	87	35.6	24.1	29.9	4.6	5.8	38368	50000	41	34	72	19.4	11.1	34.7	31.9	2.8	128571
22967	ROSELAND	29910	1004	28.0	27.5	29.9	7.6	7.1	44648	54300	60	53	822	12.9	16.1	30.3	33.2	7.5	142014
22968	RUCKERSVILLE	22846	3539	12.6	31.3	43.4	10.0	2.7	53980	61022	78	72	3024	6.4	3.8	52.9	34.9	2.1	152703
22969	SCHUYLER	22069	508	30.7	32.9	25.6	7.9	3.0	39259	47358	44	37	426	14.1	17.6	35.5	29.1	3.8	123077
22971	SHIPMAN	23744	455	24.0	35.4	29.2	7.0	4.4	42253	51890	54	45	362	13.0	24.6	36.2	23.2	3.0	111364
22972	SOMERSET	26125	122	23.0	28.7	36.9	8.2	3.3	48638	57104	70	62	98	11.2	8.2	48.0	25.5	7.1	137500
22973	STANARDSVILLE	22698	2009	20.7	28.8	37.3	10.5	2.7	50340	56449	73	66	1643	3.1	8.2	53.0	32.1	3.7	148140
22974	TROY	22454	1434	19.5	27.6	37.9	9.8	5.3	52030	60047	76	69	1224	5.4	6.0	45.3	34.4	9.0	160000
22976	TYRO	24561	179	27.9	32.4	30.2	6.7	2.8	35754	41758	31	25	144	28.5	16.7	32.6	19.4	2.8	97778
22980	WAYNESBORO	23268	13106	27.6	31.2	29.8	8.1	3.4	43029	50486	56	48	9198	7.0	10.4	49.1	30.8	2.8	139521
23002	AMELIA COURT HOUSE	23779	3570	19.6	33.9	32.9	9.7	3.9	47184	54784	67	59	2949	9.3	10.7	47.7	30.7	1.7	136971
23004	ARVONIA	17279	495	39.0	33.1	19.4	5.1	3.4	35054	39896	28	23	395	32.7	23.3	33.2	7.9	3.0	80208
23005	ASHLAND	29268	5603	19.9	25.4	32.8	13.5	8.5	55246	66804	80	74	4092	10.6	5.9	32.0	45.7	5.8	178307
23009	AYLETT	26044	1969	14.4	26.2	43.0	12.9	3.6	57384	65638	82	77	1716	3.7	3.2	49.4	40.5	3.2	162442
23011	BARHAMSVILLE	36155	358	22.4	30.7	29.6	9.8	7.5	47242	58144	67	59	317	6.0	6.6	44.2	38.5	4.7	161563
23015	BEAVERDAM	28579	1520	13.4	23.0	39.4	17.1	7.1	63617	76143	88	82	1306	2.2	10.4	35.2	45.0	7.2	180370
23021	BOHANNON	29850	81	21.0	32.1	34.6	6.2	6.2	47762	57843	68	60	68	7.4	11.8	45.6	26.5	8.8	136111
23022	BREMO BLUFF	24458	530	26.6	37.2	26.2	4.3	5.7	40909	46642	49	41	407	13.3	18.9	43.5	20.6	3.7	112500
23023	BRUINGTON	24356	102	28.4	26.5	31.4	7.8	5.9	43912	51630	58	51	85	17.7	14.1	42.4	21.2	4.7	123958
23024	BUMPASS	26192	2807	20.5	28.9	35.8	9.2	5.7	50490	59407	73	66	2397	3.9	10.4	46.1	33.4	6.2	150541
23025	CARDINAL	31037	288	20.5	30.9	37.2	6.9	4.5	48949	57434	70	63	242	6.6	11.6	45.9	26.5	9.5	138636
23027	CARTERSVILLE	20501	478	21.8	26.2	44.1	8.0	0.0	51089	58508	74	67	382	10.0	18.6	43.5	26.2	1.8	133333
	VIRGINIA	30454		19.8	25.2	32.5	13.6	8.9	55216	67801				6.8	10.4	35.8	36.5	10.5	166226
	UNITED STATES	25866		24.7	27.1	30.8	10.9	6.5	48124	56710				10.9	15.0	33.7	30.1	10.4	145905

ZIP CODE		FINANCIAL SERVICES				THE HOME						ENTERTAINMENT						PERSONAL			
						Home Improvements		Furnishings													
#	POST OFFICE NAME	Auto Loan	Home Loan	Invest-ments	Retire-ment Plans	Home Repair	Lawn & Garden	Comput-ers & Hard-ware	Major Appli-ances	TV, Radio, Sound Equip-ment	Furni-ture	Dine out/ Carry out	Sports Equip-ment	Fees & Tickets	Toys & Games	Travel	Cable TV	Apparel & Services	Auto Repairs	Health Insur-ance	Pets & Supplies
22727	MADISON	90	78	60	76	83	91	76	83	81	75	98	97	74	99	77	82	92	81	90	103
22728	MIDLAND	114	134	140	135	131	130	124	123	116	124	146	145	129	152	124	111	145	120	110	135
22729	MITCHELLS	0	0	0	0	0	0	0	0	0	0	0	0	0	0	0	0	0	0	0	0
22730	OAKPARK	106	93	71	89	99	107	88	97	93	88	114	115	86	115	90	96	108	95	105	123
22731	PRATTS	96	82	64	82	86	97	84	90	90	83	109	103	81	108	84	91	102	89	98	106
22732	RADIANT	105	94	71	89	99	106	87	96	92	87	112	115	85	114	89	94	106	94	104	124
22733	RAPIDAN	74	65	50	63	68	75	64	69	68	63	82	80	62	82	64	69	77	68	75	85
22734	REMINGTON	91	100	100	101	97	96	95	94	89	95	112	111	95	113	93	84	110	93	83	104
22735	REVA	90	81	62	77	85	91	75	83	79	75	96	98	73	98	77	81	92	80	89	106
22736	RICHARDSVILLE	90	76	60	76	80	90	79	84	83	77	101	96	75	100	78	85	95	83	91	99
22737	RIXEYVILLE	110	114	105	112	116	120	104	109	103	104	127	129	106	133	107	103	124	106	108	131
22738	ROCHELLE	87	78	59	74	82	88	72	80	76	72	93	95	70	95	74	78	88	78	86	103
22740	SPERRYVILLE	97	90	77	86	95	103	85	93	89	85	108	108	84	110	88	91	104	91	100	115
22741	STEVENSBURG	88	74	58	74	78	88	77	82	81	75	99	93	73	98	76	83	92	81	89	97
22742	SUMERDUCK	118	147	156	147	144	142	131	131	121	131	153	153	140	163	134	118	153	126	117	144
22743	SYRIA	87	77	58	73	81	87	71	79	76	71	92	94	70	94	73	78	88	77	86	102
22746	VIEWTOWN	120	127	119	125	130	132	116	122	114	115	140	144	117	146	119	113	137	119	120	145
22747	WASHINGTON	129	101	69	96	113	125	98	115	109	97	130	137	90	130	102	114	121	114	133	153
22749	WOODVILLE	86	102	114	99	101	108	95	95	92	94	115	107	100	118	99	92	113	93	93	103
22801	HARRISONBURG	89	75	81	79	74	81	92	83	90	87	113	104	85	107	84	85	108	90	79	96
22802	HARRISONBURG	82	75	78	76	75	82	80	80	81	79	101	95	78	99	78	80	98	82	80	92
22807	HARRISONBURG	192	204	265	205	200	222	214	205	215	212	271	236	219	273	216	216	265	212	205	225
22810	BASYE	111	87	59	78	98	110	82	99	93	81	110	115	73	108	87	99	102	97	117	135
22811	BERGTON	93	62	28	54	71	81	60	75	73	61	85	90	51	81	61	78	78	75	93	107
22812	BRIDGEWATER	90	84	80	82	86	94	83	87	86	83	106	101	83	107	84	88	102	86	91	104
22815	BROADWAY	90	71	46	65	77	85	68	78	76	68	91	93	63	89	69	79	85	77	90	104
22820	CRIDERS	95	63	29	55	72	83	61	77	74	62	87	91	52	82	62	80	79	76	94	109
22821	DAYTON	93	78	60	77	83	93	79	86	84	78	102	99	75	102	79	86	96	84	94	104
22824	EDINBURG	91	78	60	74	83	92	75	83	82	75	99	97	73	100	77	85	93	82	93	105
22827	ELKTON	84	66	45	60	71	80	64	74	72	64	87	86	60	86	65	76	81	72	85	96
22830	FULKS RUN	88	59	27	51	67	77	57	71	69	58	80	85	48	76	58	74	73	70	88	101
22831	HINTON	90	64	34	57	72	81	62	75	72	63	86	89	55	82	63	77	79	74	90	104
22832	KEEZLETOWN	105	86	61	79	95	105	81	94	89	80	107	111	75	107	85	94	100	93	108	126
22834	LINVILLE	91	83	66	80	87	93	77	84	80	77	98	100	76	100	79	82	94	82	89	107
22835	LURAY	82	65	44	60	70	81	66	74	73	64	88	85	60	86	66	78	81	73	87	94
22840	MC GAHEYSVILLE	113	99	75	94	105	114	92	103	98	92	119	122	89	121	95	101	113	100	112	133
22841	MOUNT CRAWFORD	119	112	91	107	114	121	104	112	106	105	131	132	102	130	105	107	126	110	115	137
22842	MOUNT JACKSON	90	75	56	73	80	90	75	83	81	74	98	95	71	97	76	84	92	82	92	102
22843	MOUNT SOLON	119	94	60	86	102	113	88	103	99	89	119	123	82	117	91	104	111	101	118	139
22844	NEW MARKET	90	74	55	73	79	90	77	83	83	75	99	95	72	98	77	85	93	82	93	101
22845	ORKNEY SPRINGS	110	86	59	78	97	109	81	98	92	81	109	115	73	108	87	98	101	97	116	134
22846	PENN LAIRD	101	90	68	85	95	102	83	92	88	83	108	110	81	110	86	91	102	90	100	120
22847	QUICKSBURG	76	65	51	65	69	77	66	71	70	65	85	82	64	85	66	72	80	70	77	85
22849	SHENANDOAH	83	66	44	60	71	80	64	73	72	64	86	86	59	85	65	75	80	72	84	96
22851	STANLEY	77	52	24	45	59	68	50	63	61	51	71	75	43	67	51	65	65	62	77	89
22853	TIMBERVILLE	88	71	48	67	76	85	69	78	76	69	91	91	64	90	70	79	85	76	88	101
22901	CHARLOTTESVILLE	119	124	145	129	121	128	127	123	123	127	155	145	129	153	125	118	152	126	114	135
22902	CHARLOTTESVILLE	84	87	96	88	85	90	87	86	86	88	108	100	88	108	86	85	106	87	82	96
22903	CHARLOTTESVILLE	94	81	97	86	80	88	104	91	102	97	128	114	97	122	95	95	123	100	86	102
22904	CHARLOTTESVILLE	36	22	27	25	21	26	42	31	41	35	51	43	34	46	34	36	48	38	29	35
22911	CHARLOTTESVILLE	143	157	151	161	152	152	144	145	136	148	171	169	148	172	142	130	168	141	130	161
22920	AFTON	120	117	107	112	122	130	110	118	113	109	139	139	109	142	114	115	134	116	123	145
22922	ARRINGTON	108	78	44	69	87	98	75	90	88	76	104	107	67	101	77	93	96	89	108	124
22923	BARBOURSVILLE	103	100	84	97	102	106	93	99	93	94	115	116	92	115	94	93	111	97	99	119
22931	COVESVILLE	91	73	52	72	79	89	75	83	81	73	97	96	69	96	75	83	91	82	93	103
22932	CROZET	96	98	96	96	101	108	94	98	94	93	116	113	95	119	96	96	112	96	100	114
22935	DYKE	112	118	109	115	120	123	107	112	106	107	131	132	110	137	110	106	128	109	111	134
22936	EARLYSVILLE	134	163	176	163	161	163	147	148	138	147	174	171	156	181	152	136	173	143	136	163
22937	ESMONT	90	80	67	77	84	95	83	88	88	80	106	100	79	104	83	91	99	87	97	103
22938	FABER	87	86	79	82	88	96	81	86	84	81	103	99	82	105	84	86	99	84	90	102
22939	FISHERSVILLE	98	91	78	87	94	101	87	93	91	87	112	110	86	113	89	92	107	91	98	114
22940	FREE UNION	145	134	114	130	142	152	126	139	130	125	159	163	123	160	130	133	151	136	148	173
22942	GORDONSVILLE	94	81	64	79	85	95	81	87	86	80	104	101	78	104	81	88	98	86	95	106
22943	GREENWOOD	87	95	94	92	95	99	88	90	87	87	108	105	91	113	90	87	106	88	89	105
22946	KEENE	71	86	95	84	85	87	80	79	76	79	96	91	85	102	82	75	96	77	74	86
22947	KESWICK	151	172	182	168	172	181	159	162	154	158	193	185	167	198	164	155	190	157	158	182
22948	LOCUST DALE	115	102	78	97	108	116	94	105	100	94	122	125	92	124	97	103	116	102	113	135
22949	LOVINGSTON	81	80	76	78	82	91	79	82	81	78	100	93	80	102	80	83	96	80	86	94
22952	LYNDHURST	92	82	63	78	87	93	76	84	81	76	98	100	74	100	78	83	93	82	91	109
22958	NELLYSFORD	173	141	100	130	155	173	133	156	148	132	176	183	122	175	140	156	165	153	180	208
22959	NORTH GARDEN	107	86	62	84	95	104	85	97	92	84	110	115	78	110	87	95	103	95	108	125
22960	ORANGE	89	73	54	68	78	89	73	82	81	72	97	94	68	94	74	84	90	81	93	102
22963	PALMYRA	95	99	98	95	101	110	94	97	96	93	118	111	97	122	97	98	115	95	101	112
22964	PINEY RIVER	96	64	29	55	73	84	62	77	75	63	88	92	53	83	63	80	80	77	95	110
22967	ROSELAND	121	94	60	86	103	116	91	106	102	90	122	125	82	119	93	107	113	104	123	141
22968	RUCKERSVILLE	91	94	88	94	93	94	89	91	86	90	108	108	89	108	88	83	105	90	84	104
22969	SCHUYLER	97	69	39	63	77	88	69	82	80	69	95	96	61	91	70	85	87	81	97	110
22971	SHIPMAN	81	79	74	73	81	91	76	80	81	75	99	91	77	103	79	85	95	79	88	95
22972	SOMERSET	94	81	61	78	85	95	79	87	85	78	103	101	76	102	80	87	96	85	95	107
22973	STANARDSVILLE	93	83	63	79	87	94	77	85	81	77	99	101	75	101	79	83	94	83	92	109
22974	TROY	106	97	78	93	102	109	90	99	95	90	115	117	89	118	93	97	110	96	105	125
22976	TYRO	99	74	49	71	81	97	82	90	92	78	108	101	73	102	81	97	99	90	108	109
22980	WAYNESBORO	82	76	68	72	78	86	75	79	79	74	96	91	74	96	76	81	92	79	85	94
23002	AMELIA COURT HOUSE	103	87	62	82	93	101	82	92	89	82	108	110	78	108	84	92	101	90	103	120
23004	ARVONIA	85	57	26	49	64	74	55	68	66	56	78	82	47	73	56	71	70	68	84	97
23005	ASHLAND	103	110	113	109	110	117	106	107	104	106	129	123	108	131	107	103	126	106	105	120
23009	AYLETT	101	106	100	106	106	108	99	102	96	99	120	120	100	123	99	94	117	100	96	118
23011	BARHAMSVILLE	139	104	69	100	114	137	116	127	129	109	152	142	103	144	114	137	139	127	152	153
23015	BEAVERDAM	114	119	109	116	121	125	108	114	107	108	133	134	110	138	111	107	129	110	113	137
23021	BOHANNON	130	91	48	86	106	118	90	111	103	89	121	134	77	119	93	108	111	109	132	154
23022	BREMO BLUFF	100	86	68	82	91	105	89	95	96	85	116	108	84	115	89	101	108	94	109	114
23023	BRUINGTON	97	73	43	66	80	89	69	82	79	70	94	98	63	92	70	83	87	80	96	112
23024	BUMPASS	107	92	68	86	99	107	85	97	92	85	112	115	82	113	89	96	105	95	108	127
23025	CARDINAL	130	91	48	86	106	119	90	111	104	89	121	134	77	119	93	109	111	110	132	155
23027	CARTERSVILLE	83	70	53	69	73	83	72	77	76	70	92	88	68	91	71	78	86	76	84	92
	VIRGINIA	112	109	113	109	109	117	108	110	109	109	136	129	108	135	108	109	132	110	109	128
	UNITED STATES	100	100	100	100	100	100	100	100	100	100	100	100	100	100	100	100	100	100	100	100

#	POST OFFICE NAME	COUNTY FIPS CODE	POPULATION 2000	2004	2009	% Rate	State Centile	HOUSEHOLDS 2000	2004	2009	% Annual Rate 2000-2004	2004 Average HH Size	FAMILIES 2000	2004	% Annual Rate 2000-2004
23030	CHARLES CITY	036	5409	5700	6043	1.2	63	2094	2271	2479	1.9	2.51	1544	1654	1.6
23032	CHURCH VIEW	119	526	522	528	-0.2	18	227	230	237	0.3	2.27	158	158	0.0
23035	COBBS CREEK	115	1449	1507	1565	0.9	56	641	673	705	1.2	2.24	471	488	0.8
23038	COLUMBIA	075	1726	1868	2088	1.9	77	682	754	858	2.4	2.47	490	534	2.0
23039	CROZIER	075	950	1073	1239	2.9	89	402	465	549	3.5	2.30	308	352	3.2
23040	CUMBERLAND	049	4294	4768	5128	2.5	85	1570	1784	1960	3.1	2.64	1161	1304	2.8
23043	DELTAVILLE	119	1470	1516	1555	0.7	50	711	747	779	1.2	2.03	455	470	0.8
23045	DIGGS	115	292	301	311	0.7	50	127	132	138	0.9	2.26	93	96	0.8
23047	DOSWELL	085	1947	2026	2184	0.9	56	701	738	805	1.2	2.73	549	570	0.9
23050	DUTTON	115	315	349	376	2.4	84	125	141	154	2.9	2.47	96	107	2.6
23055	FORK UNION	065	621	699	871	2.8	88	243	279	354	3.3	2.51	181	205	3.0
23056	FOSTER	115	297	305	315	0.6	47	119	123	128	0.8	2.43	87	89	0.5
23059	GLEN ALLEN	085	15259	19298	22589	5.7	98	5825	7446	8805	6.0	2.59	4283	5448	5.8
23060	GLEN ALLEN	087	27269	30563	33455	2.7	87	10670	12141	13453	3.1	2.50	7475	8371	2.7
23061	GLOUCESTER	073	19099	21124	23077	2.4	84	6960	7806	8648	2.7	2.67	5357	5935	2.4
23062	GLOUCESTER POINT	073	2523	2311	2361	-2.0	0	1090	1019	1058	-1.6	2.27	742	680	-2.0
23063	GOOCHLAND	075	3789	4137	4678	2.1	80	1447	1618	1874	2.7	2.49	1053	1163	2.4
23065	GUM SPRING	075	1379	1495	1690	1.9	78	535	592	682	2.4	2.52	405	443	2.1
23066	GWYNN	115	685	692	708	0.2	33	333	340	351	0.5	2.04	211	211	0.0
23069	HANOVER	085	3301	3526	3807	1.6	70	923	1013	1122	2.2	3.01	738	800	1.9
23070	HARDYVILLE	119	848	889	921	1.1	61	395	424	447	1.7	2.10	272	287	1.3
23071	HARTFIELD	119	785	852	899	2.0	79	344	379	406	2.3	2.25	249	271	2.0
23072	HAYES	073	11870	11971	12550	0.2	32	4597	4739	5052	0.7	2.52	3398	3446	0.3
23075	HIGHLAND SPRINGS	087	9990	10007	10389	0.0	25	3881	3943	4144	0.4	2.52	2740	2741	0.0
23079	JAMAICA	119	470	472	479	0.1	28	199	205	211	0.7	2.30	142	144	0.3
23083	JETERSVILLE	007	2117	2165	2291	0.5	44	791	823	885	0.9	2.63	593	609	0.6
23084	KENTS STORE	065	1163	1343	1670	3.4	92	464	545	687	3.9	2.46	353	409	3.5
23085	KING AND QUEEN COURT	097	575	587	601	0.5	42	216	226	237	1.1	2.60	155	160	0.8
23086	KING WILLIAM	101	2666	2871	3114	1.8	74	1018	1117	1232	2.2	2.57	798	866	1.9
23089	LANEXA	127	4560	5162	5988	3.0	90	1699	1962	2324	3.4	2.56	1272	1451	3.2
23091	LITTLE PLYMOUTH	097	100	102	104	0.5	41	37	39	40	1.3	2.62	27	28	0.9
23092	LOCUST HILL	119	41	46	50	2.7	87	20	23	25	3.3	2.00	14	16	3.2
23093	LOUISA	109	9794	11018	12701	2.8	88	3805	4362	5126	3.3	2.49	2693	3046	2.9
23102	MAIDENS	075	2525	2681	2953	1.4	67	823	905	1041	2.3	2.40	622	675	1.9
23103	MANAKIN SABOT	075	3326	3823	4448	3.3	91	1311	1541	1833	3.9	2.44	1048	1218	3.6
23106	MANQUIN	101	1059	1161	1272	2.2	81	367	410	457	2.6	2.83	301	334	2.5
23109	MATHEWS	115	1106	1136	1171	0.6	47	461	478	497	0.9	2.33	339	346	0.5
23110	MATTAPONI	097	367	376	387	0.6	45	146	153	160	1.1	2.46	111	115	0.8
23111	MECHANICSVILLE	085	30888	34564	38938	2.7	87	11707	13254	15075	3.0	2.60	8975	10046	2.7
23112	MIDLOTHIAN	041	40046	45476	51435	3.0	90	14237	16306	18625	3.2	2.79	11236	12709	2.9
23113	MIDLOTHIAN	041	19327	21540	24207	2.6	86	6796	7705	8796	3.0	2.76	5626	6349	2.9
23114	MIDLOTHIAN	041	11809	12613	13914	1.6	70	3894	4268	4798	2.2	2.93	3317	3595	1.9
23116	MECHANICSVILLE	085	23706	26873	30513	3.0	90	8020	9110	10386	3.0	2.93	6816	7688	2.9
23117	MINERAL	109	7364	7929	9010	1.8	74	2884	3164	3664	2.2	2.50	2149	2330	1.9
23119	MOON	115	674	701	728	0.9	56	277	291	305	1.2	2.41	203	211	0.9
23120	MOSELEY	041	3184	3569	4019	2.7	87	1064	1206	1373	3.0	2.96	902	1012	2.7
23123	NEW CANTON	029	1587	1616	1650	0.4	40	637	666	695	1.1	2.43	458	472	0.7
23124	NEW KENT	127	2210	2470	2823	2.7	86	784	889	1031	3.0	2.75	639	717	2.8
23125	NEW POINT	115	112	114	117	0.4	40	53	54	56	0.4	2.11	36	37	0.7
23126	NEWTOWN	097	992	1027	1061	0.8	53	393	416	440	1.4	2.47	278	290	1.0
23128	NORTH	115	2033	2197	2338	1.8	76	811	883	947	2.0	2.48	611	658	1.8
23129	OILVILLE	075	336	390	456	3.6	93	135	160	191	4.1	2.44	105	123	3.8
23130	ONEMO	115	461	472	485	0.6	45	193	199	207	0.7	2.34	138	141	0.5
23138	PORT HAYWOOD	115	631	643	660	0.4	40	273	281	291	0.7	2.28	191	193	0.3
23139	POWHATAN	145	20495	22985	26261	2.7	87	6588	7607	8940	3.4	2.70	5351	6124	3.2
23140	PROVIDENCE FORGE	127	2710	2815	3039	0.9	55	1029	1092	1203	1.4	2.58	793	832	1.1
23141	QUINTON	127	5506	6143	7022	2.6	86	2031	2301	2670	3.0	2.67	1641	1844	2.8
23146	ROCKVILLE	085	3085	3249	3552	1.2	62	1138	1222	1357	1.7	2.65	917	972	1.4
23148	SAINT STEPHENS CHURC	097	829	855	883	0.7	50	308	324	343	1.2	2.64	221	229	0.8
23149	SALUDA	119	3490	3706	3889	1.4	67	1340	1447	1540	1.8	2.43	950	1014	1.6
23150	SANDSTON	087	11374	11820	12493	0.9	55	4585	4841	5180	1.3	2.43	3342	3481	1.0
23153	SANDY HOOK	075	1074	1186	1352	2.4	83	409	460	535	2.8	2.58	313	347	2.5
23156	SHACKLEFORDS	097	2468	2499	2559	0.3	34	1027	1064	1114	0.8	2.35	719	735	0.5
23160	STATE FARM	075	715	721	730	0.2	32	5	5	5	0.0	2.60	4	4	0.0
23161	STEVENSVILLE	097	78	79	81	0.3	36	30	31	33	0.8	2.55	22	22	0.0
23163	SUSAN	115	750	762	782	0.4	38	332	341	352	0.6	2.23	228	231	0.3
23168	TOANO	095	4017	4691	5605	3.7	94	1480	1763	2144	4.2	2.66	1174	1382	3.9
23169	TOPPING	119	1691	1751	1800	0.8	53	712	746	775	1.1	2.34	480	496	0.8
23173	UNIVERSITY OF RICHMO	760	1671	1672	1672	0.0	24	1	1	1	0.0	3.00	1	1	0.0
23175	URBANNA	119	733	735	747	0.1	26	335	344	357	0.6	1.96	232	235	0.3
23176	WAKE	119	484	496	507	0.6	45	189	196	203	0.9	2.53	135	138	0.5
23177	WALKERTON	097	1264	1297	1339	0.6	46	515	541	570	1.2	2.40	368	381	0.8
23180	WATER VIEW	119	235	238	242	0.3	36	92	95	99	0.8	2.51	67	68	0.4
23181	WEST POINT	101	4376	4658	5037	1.5	68	1685	1826	2012	1.9	2.45	1268	1356	1.6
23185	WILLIAMSBURG	095	38733	42598	48661	2.3	82	14784	16654	19549	2.8	2.32	10100	11228	2.5
23186	WILLIAMSBURG	830	1489	1485	1501	-0.1	21	15	15	16	0.0	2.53	6	6	0.0
23188	WILLIAMSBURG	095	23744	27665	32883	3.7	94	9221	11023	13411	4.3	2.45	6755	7944	3.9
23192	MONTPELIER	085	5612	6215	6953	2.4	84	2003	2256	2554	2.8	2.75	1639	1825	2.6
23219	RICHMOND	760	1916	1987	2006	0.9	54	923	989	1019	1.6	1.68	215	213	-0.2
23220	RICHMOND	760	29476	29125	28623	-0.3	16	13208	13205	13096	0.0	1.92	4492	4329	-0.9
23221	RICHMOND	760	14319	14030	13689	-0.5	11	7858	7768	7650	-0.3	1.79	2764	2677	-0.8
23222	RICHMOND	087	28441	27213	26700	-1.0	3	10818	10452	10356	-0.8	2.56	7053	6717	-1.1
23223	RICHMOND	087	43192	43341	43954	0.1	27	16802	17142	17625	0.5	2.39	10429	10408	-0.1
23224	RICHMOND	760	31376	30555	29916	-0.6	8	12213	11929	11762	-0.6	2.54	7937	7646	-0.9
23225	RICHMOND	760	38127	38409	38398	0.2	30	18041	18288	18420	0.3	2.07	9225	9166	-0.2
23226	RICHMOND	760	16399	16140	16214	-0.4	14	7029	6974	7074	-0.2	2.12	3843	3738	-0.7
23227	RICHMOND	087	21639	21692	22085	0.1	26	10072	10161	10414	0.2	2.06	5316	5258	-0.3
23228	RICHMOND	087	31408	32236	33964	0.6	46	14401	15059	16108	1.1	2.06	7674	7788	0.4
23229	RICHMOND	087	31362	31341	32628	0.0	23	13190	13413	14157	0.4	2.32	8675	8670	0.0
23230	RICHMOND	087	6551	6536	6714	-0.1	22	3014	3047	3158	0.3	2.08	1528	1501	-0.4
23231	RICHMOND	087	27211	28920	30537	1.4	67	10452	11264	12036	1.8	2.56	7510	7974	1.4
23233	RICHMOND	087	50321	54054	58257	1.7	73	19560	21078	22870	1.8	2.51	13464	14339	1.5
23234	RICHMOND	041	37201	38500	40883	0.8	53	13984	14608	15675	1.0	2.62	9869	10163	0.7
23235	RICHMOND	041	29619	29657	31226	0.0	25	11940	12139	12950	0.4	2.39	8300	8301	0.0
23236	RICHMOND	041	25045	25501	27456	0.4	40	9124	9471	10365	0.9	2.68	7213	7409	0.6
	VIRGINIA					1.4					1.7	2.51			1.4
	UNITED STATES					1.2					1.3	2.58			1.1

#	POST OFFICE NAME	RACE (%) White 2000	White 2004	Black 2000	Black 2004	Asian/Pacific 2000	Asian/Pacific 2004	% Hispanic Origin 2000	% Hispanic Origin 2004	2004 AGE DISTRIBUTION (%) 0-4	5-9	10-14	15-19	20-24	25-44	45-64	65-84	85+	18+	MEDIAN AGE 2004	% 2004 Males	% 2004 Females
23030	CHARLES CITY	36.6	34.9	55.8	57.1	0.1	0.1	0.6	0.8	5.5	6.0	6.1	5.6	5.6	26.6	31.2	12.4	1.0	79.2	42.0	49.7	50.3
23032	CHURCH VIEW	66.2	64.2	32.3	34.1	0.2	0.2	0.4	0.4	3.8	4.4	6.5	6.3	4.2	22.4	32.0	18.4	1.9	81.2	46.4	47.9	52.1
23035	COBBS CREEK	87.1	86.0	11.2	11.9	0.1	0.2	0.8	1.0	4.6	5.0	5.6	4.6	4.3	22.8	32.1	18.7	2.3	81.6	46.9	48.5	51.5
23038	COLUMBIA	64.3	62.1	32.6	34.3	0.6	0.7	1.5	1.7	5.8	5.9	6.8	6.8	5.1	28.3	27.8	12.3	1.3	77.3	40.3	48.7	51.3
23039	CROZIER	78.5	76.5	20.1	21.8	0.6	0.8	0.8	0.9	4.9	5.9	6.1	4.9	3.5	26.3	35.0	11.9	1.5	80.1	44.2	50.7	49.3
23040	CUMBERLAND	58.4	56.9	39.6	40.8	0.1	0.2	1.9	2.2	6.0	6.7	8.0	7.2	5.1	27.4	26.1	12.1	1.5	74.5	38.5	47.8	52.2
23043	DELTAVILLE	95.4	94.9	3.4	3.7	0.2	0.2	0.3	0.4	2.6	3.0	4.6	3.5	2.4	16.1	36.3	27.5	4.0	87.7	56.5	48.2	51.9
23045	DIGGS	85.6	84.7	13.0	13.6	0.0	0.0	0.7	1.3	4.7	5.3	5.7	5.0	4.3	22.3	32.2	17.6	3.0	80.7	46.9	48.5	51.5
23047	DOSWELL	76.4	74.2	21.4	23.3	0.1	0.1	0.8	1.1	5.2	5.8	6.8	7.4	5.1	24.8	31.9	11.6	1.4	76.9	42.2	49.5	50.5
23050	DUTTON	86.4	85.4	11.1	11.8	0.3	0.6	1.3	1.4	5.4	5.7	6.9	6.0	4.6	25.2	30.1	14.3	1.7	78.5	42.7	49.0	51.0
23055	FORK UNION	58.0	54.7	40.3	43.2	0.3	0.4	0.8	0.7	5.4	5.7	6.3	7.6	5.7	24.6	28.2	14.9	1.6	78.0	41.7	47.8	52.2
23056	FOSTER	84.9	84.3	13.8	14.8	0.0	0.0	0.7	1.3	4.9	5.3	5.6	5.3	3.9	21.6	33.1	17.1	3.3	80.7	47.4	47.5	52.5
23059	GLEN ALLEN	85.2	83.9	9.5	9.7	3.4	4.2	1.7	2.1	9.0	9.2	7.9	5.8	4.1	33.0	23.6	6.9	0.6	70.2	36.0	49.6	50.4
23060	GLEN ALLEN	74.4	71.8	18.1	19.4	5.3	6.1	1.7	2.1	8.2	7.8	7.0	5.8	5.9	34.8	23.1	6.6	0.9	73.4	35.2	47.7	52.3
23061	GLOUCESTER	85.1	83.9	12.0	12.7	0.5	0.6	1.6	2.0	6.0	6.4	7.9	7.1	5.7	27.4	27.1	10.7	1.7	75.2	39.6	49.0	51.0
23062	GLOUCESTER POINT	90.4	89.6	5.7	5.9	1.4	1.6	1.6	2.0	5.2	5.2	5.8	6.7	6.1	27.8	29.7	12.4	1.2	79.8	40.9	49.2	50.8
23063	GOOCHLAND	60.3	57.7	37.7	40.0	0.2	0.2	1.0	1.1	5.7	6.0	6.6	6.8	4.7	25.4	29.1	13.8	1.9	76.9	41.9	48.4	51.6
23065	GUM SPRING	78.4	76.7	19.7	21.2	0.4	0.4	0.8	0.9	6.2	6.8	6.6	5.5	4.0	29.6	29.8	10.3	1.2	76.9	40.7	49.4	50.6
23066	GWYNN	97.4	97.0	0.4	0.4	0.7	0.9	0.3	0.4	3.9	3.9	3.5	3.5	3.3	17.2	34.7	26.3	3.8	86.7	55.5	49.4	50.6
23069	HANOVER	70.3	68.8	28.1	29.5	0.3	0.3	0.9	1.2	3.9	4.8	6.3	11.9	6.2	25.9	29.6	10.7	0.8	76.1	39.9	55.8	44.2
23070	HARDYVILLE	92.7	92.0	5.4	5.9	0.2	0.3	0.2	0.5	3.5	4.2	5.5	3.9	2.7	18.8	33.2	26.1	2.1	84.3	53.4	48.3	51.7
23071	HARTFIELD	76.1	74.2	22.3	23.8	0.1	0.1	0.4	0.6	4.5	5.6	7.2	6.8	3.3	23.6	30.8	16.4	1.9	78.1	44.4	48.8	51.2
23072	HAYES	88.5	87.7	8.4	8.7	1.0	1.2	1.6	2.0	6.0	6.1	6.9	6.6	5.7	27.5	28.5	11.5	1.2	77.0	39.8	49.5	50.5
23075	HIGHLAND SPRINGS	49.8	46.6	46.2	48.9	0.6	0.7	1.6	2.0	7.8	7.7	8.2	7.0	6.9	29.6	22.8	8.8	1.3	71.9	33.9	46.0	54.0
23079	JAMAICA	64.7	62.5	33.4	35.2	0.2	0.2	0.6	0.6	4.0	4.7	6.6	6.8	4.0	23.1	32.6	16.3	1.9	80.3	45.4	48.9	51.1
23083	JETERSVILLE	71.1	69.9	27.3	28.3	0.3	0.4	1.1	1.4	6.2	6.5	7.5	6.7	5.6	27.6	27.3	11.2	1.2	75.6	38.9	51.1	48.9
23084	KENTS STORE	63.9	61.0	33.2	35.7	0.3	0.3	1.2	1.5	6.3	6.6	7.4	6.9	5.1	26.4	27.7	12.4	1.3	75.3	39.9	48.2	51.8
23085	KING AND QUEEN COURT	57.9	56.1	39.5	41.2	0.2	0.2	0.9	1.2	5.5	6.0	6.1	5.8	5.3	23.7	32.4	13.5	1.9	78.9	43.5	48.9	51.1
23086	KING WILLIAM	68.8	67.5	26.7	27.6	0.2	0.2	0.6	0.7	7.1	7.1	6.6	6.0	5.3	29.7	26.9	10.3	1.1	75.6	38.2	50.2	49.8
23089	LANEXA	81.9	80.2	15.2	16.5	0.3	0.4	1.4	1.7	5.3	5.8	6.3	6.2	4.9	28.1	30.6	11.7	1.1	78.8	41.6	51.1	48.9
23091	LITTLE PLYMOUTH	60.0	58.8	38.0	39.2	0.0	0.0	0.0	1.0	5.9	5.9	5.9	5.9	5.9	22.6	32.4	13.7	2.0	77.5	43.8	49.0	51.0
23092	LOCUST HILL	75.6	73.9	22.0	23.9	0.0	0.0	0.0	0.0	4.4	4.4	6.5	8.7	4.4	23.9	28.3	17.4	2.2	84.8	43.8	52.2	47.8
23093	LOUISA	70.5	68.8	27.5	29.0	0.3	0.3	0.8	0.9	6.2	6.3	7.0	6.3	5.5	26.9	27.0	13.0	1.9	76.6	40.5	48.8	51.2
23102	MAIDENS	68.5	67.0	30.5	31.9	0.2	0.3	0.5	0.6	4.5	5.2	5.2	4.4	4.8	37.4	29.1	8.3	1.2	82.4	40.0	53.0	47.0
23103	MANAKIN SABOT	83.3	81.4	15.2	16.8	0.8	0.9	1.1	1.3	4.9	6.1	6.0	5.6	3.0	22.6	35.5	15.3	1.1	78.9	46.0	49.9	50.1
23106	MANQUIN	68.2	66.2	29.5	31.1	0.1	0.2	0.7	0.9	7.0	7.0	7.0	6.4	6.2	28.8	28.2	8.8	0.8	75.2	37.8	50.7	49.4
23109	MATHEWS	85.0	83.9	13.9	14.8	0.1	0.1	0.8	1.1	4.8	5.2	5.6	5.2	4.2	21.9	32.3	17.3	3.5	80.7	47.1	48.4	51.6
23110	MATTAPONI	82.0	80.9	15.0	16.0	0.0	0.0	0.3	0.0	4.5	5.1	7.2	5.1	4.5	28.2	29.5	13.8	2.1	80.1	42.3	50.3	49.7
23111	MECHANICSVILLE	91.1	90.2	6.4	6.9	0.8	1.0	1.1	1.4	6.9	7.3	7.6	6.4	5.4	30.0	25.1	10.0	1.2	74.0	37.4	48.4	51.6
23112	MIDLOTHIAN	87.4	85.7	8.8	9.6	2.0	2.3	1.8	2.4	7.7	8.1	9.0	7.5	5.5	30.3	25.6	5.7	0.6	70.3	35.2	48.6	51.4
23113	MIDLOTHIAN	90.8	89.5	5.0	5.5	2.7	3.3	1.4	1.8	4.9	6.8	9.0	7.9	3.9	21.1	35.3	9.5	1.5	73.6	43.0	48.7	51.3
23114	MIDLOTHIAN	89.7	88.0	5.4	6.0	3.6	4.4	1.3	1.8	6.6	8.2	9.8	8.0	4.5	28.0	28.7	5.2	0.9	69.6	37.4	49.3	50.7
23116	MECHANICSVILLE	91.1	90.0	6.4	7.0	1.2	1.4	0.9	1.2	7.3	8.2	9.1	7.1	4.5	26.8	28.5	8.0	0.7	70.7	38.5	49.7	50.3
23117	MINERAL	78.3	76.9	19.8	21.0	0.3	0.4	0.8	1.0	5.2	6.0	6.5	5.6	4.7	25.7	31.9	13.2	1.2	78.8	42.9	50.4	49.6
23119	MOON	87.1	86.0	11.1	12.0	0.2	0.1	0.7	1.0	4.7	5.0	5.7	4.7	4.3	22.7	32.2	18.5	2.1	81.5	46.8	48.4	51.6
23120	MOSELEY	93.6	92.4	4.8	5.6	0.8	1.0	0.9	1.1	6.4	7.3	8.3	6.8	4.3	26.7	30.7	8.7	0.8	73.3	39.7	49.2	50.8
23123	NEW CANTON	54.5	52.3	43.6	45.5	0.1	0.1	1.7	2.0	5.3	5.6	7.5	6.9	5.3	26.4	26.7	14.7	1.6	77.4	40.7	47.7	52.4
23124	NEW KENT	77.1	75.3	20.2	21.5	0.5	0.5	0.8	1.1	6.3	7.1	7.4	6.4	4.8	29.4	29.0	8.7	0.9	75.0	39.0	49.7	50.3
23125	NEW POINT	88.4	87.7	10.7	11.4	0.0	0.0	0.9	1.8	4.4	5.3	5.3	5.3	5.3	19.3	30.7	21.9	2.6	79.8	48.0	50.0	50.0
23126	NEWTOWN	54.7	52.5	40.9	42.8	0.5	0.6	0.8	0.9	5.5	5.8	6.3	6.0	5.3	26.7	28.5	14.2	1.7	78.9	42.0	49.4	50.6
23128	NORTH	86.2	85.2	11.7	12.4	0.3	0.4	1.1	1.3	5.2	5.6	6.5	5.6	4.5	24.7	30.6	15.3	2.0	79.0	43.8	49.3	50.8
23129	OILVILLE	81.3	79.5	18.2	20.0	0.0	0.0	0.6	0.8	4.9	6.2	7.4	5.4	2.6	23.6	36.4	12.1	1.5	77.7	45.0	49.2	50.8
23130	ONEMO	86.1	85.2	12.6	13.6	0.2	0.2	0.9	1.3	4.7	5.1	5.3	5.3	4.2	21.2	32.4	18.6	3.2	81.4	47.8	48.5	51.5
23138	PORT HAYWOOD	87.5	86.8	11.3	12.0	0.2	0.3	1.0	1.2	4.5	4.8	5.3	5.4	4.7	20.4	31.9	20.1	3.0	81.8	48.0	49.0	51.0
23139	POWHATAN	80.4	79.1	18.1	19.1	0.2	0.2	0.8	1.0	5.9	6.3	6.7	6.9	5.7	32.4	27.1	8.3	0.8	76.9	37.9	55.0	45.0
23140	PROVIDENCE FORGE	53.1	51.7	34.9	35.5	0.2	0.3	1.4	1.7	5.3	6.4	7.1	6.0	4.9	28.7	29.6	11.2	1.0	77.5	40.7	49.2	50.8
23141	QUINTON	86.6	85.6	10.1	10.6	0.8	0.9	1.2	1.5	6.0	6.7	7.2	6.4	4.6	28.4	31.5	8.8	0.5	76.0	40.4	49.4	50.6
23146	ROCKVILLE	87.5	86.1	11.2	12.3	0.6	0.6	0.5	0.6	6.0	7.1	7.5	5.6	3.5	25.7	32.1	11.2	1.3	75.6	42.2	48.5	51.5
23148	SAINT STEPHENS CHURC	55.0	52.9	40.9	42.6	0.4	0.5	0.8	0.9	5.5	5.7	7.1	6.1	4.9	26.9	28.7	13.5	1.6	77.8	41.5	49.1	50.9
23149	SALUDA	78.3	76.9	20.1	21.2	0.1	0.1	0.9	1.2	3.9	4.8	6.4	6.3	4.5	23.5	31.4	16.6	2.7	80.9	45.4	48.5	51.5
23150	SANDSTON	81.9	79.7	14.8	16.4	0.5	0.5	1.7	2.1	6.2	6.3	6.8	6.3	5.8	28.3	27.0	12.1	1.2	76.7	39.1	47.5	52.5
23153	SANDY HOOK	75.8	73.7	21.7	23.4	0.6	0.7	1.0	1.2	7.0	7.4	6.9	5.7	3.7	31.2	27.8	9.1	1.2	75.0	39.5	48.8	51.2
23156	SHACKLEFORDS	66.2	64.5	31.6	32.9	0.2	0.2	1.1	1.3	5.3	5.5	6.4	5.8	5.0	25.9	28.8	14.5	2.7	79.1	42.6	48.1	51.9
23160	STATE FARM	35.0	32.6	64.9	67.0	0.1	0.1	0.4	0.6	0.4	0.4	0.7	0.8	9.7	73.8	13.7	0.4	0.0	98.2	35.2	61.3	38.7
23161	STEVENSVILLE	59.0	55.7	39.7	41.8	0.0	0.0	0.0	1.3	5.1	6.3	6.3	6.3	5.1	24.1	29.1	15.2	2.5	78.5	42.9	51.9	48.1
23163	SUSAN	88.3	87.4	10.5	11.3	0.3	0.3	1.1	1.3	4.5	4.7	5.1	5.6	4.7	20.0	32.0	20.7	2.6	82.6	48.3	49.2	50.8
23168	TOANO	76.2	74.2	21.6	23.1	0.7	0.8	1.0	1.3	6.6	7.0	7.6	7.3	5.9	27.0	28.7	9.2	0.8	74.3	39.0	49.3	50.7
23169	TOPPING	77.0	75.3	21.9	23.4	0.1	0.1	0.8	1.0	4.7	5.0	5.8	5.8	4.4	22.7	32.0	17.7	1.8	80.6	46.0	48.6	51.4
23173	UNIVERSITY OF RICHMO	89.1	86.8	5.6	6.5	1.4	1.7	2.3	3.1	0.1	0.1	0.1	43.1	54.6	1.1	0.8	0.3	0.0	99.5	20.6	48.2	51.8
23175	URBANNA	65.1	62.7	33.7	35.7	0.1	0.3	0.4	0.5	3.5	4.0	5.7	5.6	4.8	22.3	31.7	19.2	3.3	83.4	47.7	48.0	52.0
23176	WAKE	81.2	79.8	18.2	19.6	0.2	0.2	0.4	0.6	5.2	5.4	6.3	6.1	4.0	24.2	30.4	16.3	2.0	79.4	44.2	47.0	53.0
23177	WALKERTON	54.3	52.2	41.8	43.6	0.2	0.3	0.8	0.9	5.6	6.1	6.3	5.9	5.0	25.3	30.2	13.9	1.8	78.3	42.5	49.5	50.5
23180	WATER VIEW	63.4	61.8	34.0	36.1	0.0	0.0	0.9	0.8	3.8	5.0	6.7	7.1	3.8	24.0	33.2	14.3	2.1	79.4	44.7	49.6	50.4
23181	WEST POINT	75.7	73.9	20.7	22.1	0.8	0.9	1.4	1.7	5.3	5.9	7.4	6.9	5.1	25.6	27.0	14.7	2.2	76.6	41.2	48.0	52.0
23185	WILLIAMSBURG	81.1	80.0	14.0	14.3	2.5	2.9	1.9	2.3	4.5	4.7	5.7	8.9	10.7	21.6	25.6	15.9	2.3	81.6	40.5	47.3	52.7
23186	WILLIAMSBURG	84.5	82.7	6.9	7.2	6.5	7.7	3.0	3.7	0.5	0.2	0.3	39.3	49.4	3.1	2.4	3.1	1.8	98.6	21.0	45.2	54.8
23188	WILLIAMSBURG	80.1	78.1	16.0	17.3	1.6	2.0	1.9	2.4	5.8	5.9	6.6	6.2	5.8	26.4	27.4	14.6	1.4	77.9	40.9	47.9	52.1
23192	MONTPELIER	82.4	81.0	16.2	17.4	0.4	0.4	0.5	0.6	6.5	7.3	8.0	6.6	4.4	26.5	29.7	10.0	1.0	74.0	40.3	49.2	50.8
23219	RICHMOND	21.6	21.2	73.5	73.1	1.7	2.1	1.0	1.2	4.1	5.5	5.9	6.4	11.3	32.9	20.2	12.3	1.3	81.5	33.9	52.1	47.9
23220	RICHMOND	48.4	45.8	45.5	47.0	3.2	3.7	1.9	2.3	3.9	3.6	3.6	11.3	17.6	31.5	18.6	8.6	1.4	86.9	29.6	48.5	51.5
23221	RICHMOND	83.3	81.2	12.9	14.3	1.6	1.8	1.6	2.1	4.1	3.6	3.2	3.5	8.8	41.9	22.4	10.5	2.0	87.2	35.8	48.7	51.4
23222	RICHMOND	8.5	7.7	89.5	90.1	0.3	0.4	1.0	1.1	6.5	7.0	8.5	7.5	5.8	25.4	24.3	13.4	1.7	73.4	38.1	45.3	54.7
23223	RICHMOND	13.8	13.0	84.2	84.8	0.3	0.4	1.0	1.1	7.4	7.0	7.6	7.3	7.6	28.4	22.7	10.5	1.6	73.5	34.6	46.5	53.5
23224	RICHMOND	17.5	15.4	75.2	76.3	1.2	1.3	6.0	6.9	8.2	8.1	8.6	7.3	7.5	29.0	21.7	8.8	0.9	70.8	32.1	46.4	53.6
23225	RICHMOND	46.5	42.8	47.0	49.8	2.0	2.2	3.7	4.5	6.4	5.9	5.9	5.8	7.3	32.4	22.7	11.3	2.2	78.4	36.2	45.7	54.3
23226	RICHMOND	88.4	86.5	5.9	6.7	2.5	2.9	3.2	4.1	5.2	5.0	4.9	7.3	8.4	29.6	22.1	14.4	3.2	82.2	37.7	46.8	53.2
23227	RICHMOND	49.4	46.4	47.0	49.6	1.3	1.4	1.5	1.8	6.0	5.2	5.6	5.4	6.9	28.7	24.1	13.3	4.9	80.1	39.9	44.7	55.3
23228	RICHMOND	69.8	66.5	22.0	24.0	4.0	4.5	3.5	4.2	5.7	5.3	5.4	5.4	7.7	33.5	21.3	13.2	2.6	80.5	37.2	46.8	53.3
23229	RICHMOND	89.9	88.1	5.1	6.0	3.2	3.8	1.9	2.5	5.4	5.8	6.7	6.2	5.5	25.2	26.2	16.4	2.5	78.2	41.7	47.1	52.9
23230	RICHMOND	66.5	63.8	17.3	18.4	9.3	10.0	8.3	9.7	5.9	5.3	5.3	5.5	6.9	33.5	21.1	13.7	2.8	80.1	37.3	49.0	51.0
23231	RICHMOND	47.7	44.7	49.4	52.1	0.5	0.5	1.1	1.3	6.9	7.2	7.8	6.9	6.5	28.0	26.4	9.2	1.2	74.0	36.7	46.8	53.2
23233	RICHMOND	89.4	87.7	4.5	5.1	4.4	5.2	1.8	2.3	6.8	7.5	7.9	6.6	4.8	28.3	27.2	8.8	2.3	73.5	38.3	47.3	52.7
23234	RICHMOND	44.4	42.1	46.4	47.3	2.7	3.1	7.2	8.6	7.4	7.4	7.7	6.9	7.2	29.9	23.8	8.9	0.8	73.3	34.3	48.3	51.7
23235	RICHMOND	80.3	77.8	14.9	16.5	2.2	2.6	2.1	2.8	5.2	5.8	6.7	7.6	5.3	24.1	29.5	14.2	1.7	77.2	42.0	47.7	52.3
23236	RICHMOND	78.4	76.3	16.0	17.1	3.1	3.7	1.7	2.1	5.9	6.5	7.3	7.0	5.8	27.1	30.7	9.0	0.7	75.8	39.2	48.5	51.5
	VIRGINIA	72.3	70.7	19.6	19.9	3.7	4.3	4.7	5.7	6.5	6.6	6.9	6.9	7.0	29.7	24.9	10.1	1.4	76.2	36.6	49.1	50.9
	UNITED STATES	75.1	73.6	12.3	12.5	3.8	4.2	12.5	14.1	6.9	6.7	7.2	7.0	7.3	28.6	23.8	10.8	1.7	75.1	36.0	49.1	50.9

INCOME

ZIP CODE #	POST OFFICE NAME	2004 Per Capita Income	2004 HH Income Base	2004 HOUSEHOLD INCOME DISTRIBUTION (%) Less than $25,000	$25,000 to $49,999	$50,000 to $99,999	$100,000 to $149,999	$150,000 or More	MEDIAN HOUSEHOLD INCOME 2004	2009	2004 National Centile	2004 State Centile	2004 Home Value Base	2004 HOME VALUE DISTRIBUTION (%) Less than $50,000	$50,000 to $89,999	$90,000 to $174,999	$175,000 to $399,999	$400,000 or More	2004 Median Home Value
23030	CHARLES CITY	23027	2271	24.0	28.3	35.8	8.7	3.2	47824	56932	68	61	1880	15.4	22.6	41.2	17.2	3.6	107983
23032	CHURCH VIEW	20708	230	30.4	34.4	27.0	7.4	0.9	38761	45449	42	35	191	10.5	14.7	49.7	24.1	1.1	120608
23035	COBBS CREEK	33269	673	18.4	27.0	37.6	10.9	6.1	53422	63080	78	71	561	4.1	12.3	34.8	39.8	9.1	171615
23038	COLUMBIA	25830	754	33.3	24.9	25.3	11.8	4.6	42684	52231	55	47	616	8.3	19.3	42.9	25.0	4.6	121591
23039	CROZIER	41777	465	10.8	20.7	37.9	18.3	12.5	69980	92195	91	85	408	0.0	1.5	40.0	41.9	16.7	200000
23040	CUMBERLAND	17392	1784	30.2	33.7	28.8	6.9	0.4	38934	45399	43	36	1473	16.2	17.8	42.2	20.6	3.3	111131
23043	DELTAVILLE	39060	747	22.6	32.3	30.7	8.0	6.4	46425	54701	65	57	636	7.9	9.4	21.2	49.4	12.1	211504
23045	DIGGS	32287	132	19.7	29.6	37.1	8.3	5.3	50544	59249	73	66	110	7.3	10.9	40.0	31.8	10.0	150000
23047	DOSWELL	31058	738	14.8	16.1	37.8	18.7	12.6	73847	85907	93	87	601	3.0	6.5	27.1	55.1	8.3	204481
23050	DUTTON	29008	141	12.1	27.7	45.4	10.6	4.3	57704	65025	82	78	123	3.3	10.6	43.9	37.4	4.9	159167
23055	FORK UNION	22245	279	25.5	39.1	22.9	7.2	5.4	41721	47817	52	44	221	7.7	18.6	42.5	26.2	5.0	133173
23056	FOSTER	29418	123	20.3	30.9	37.4	6.5	4.9	49078	55954	70	63	103	8.7	11.7	44.7	26.2	8.7	136607
23059	GLEN ALLEN	47554	7446	7.3	15.1	33.3	22.6	21.7	89004	115500	97	93	5642	2.4	2.2	18.1	60.1	17.2	253702
23060	GLEN ALLEN	34234	12141	9.8	20.8	42.1	20.0	7.3	69873	84062	91	85	9707	0.4	3.9	49.9	45.4	0.4	169161
23061	GLOUCESTER	23876	7806	17.0	31.2	38.6	9.1	4.1	51361	59098	74	68	6564	6.6	8.9	51.5	29.4	3.6	140819
23062	GLOUCESTER POINT	30149	1019	16.2	27.6	39.6	11.7	5.0	54149	62284	79	73	707	3.5	0.6	52.9	37.6	5.4	162985
23063	GOOCHLAND	25265	1618	23.1	25.6	34.6	12.9	3.9	51111	63609	74	67	1355	7.8	12.3	42.0	33.1	4.8	147930
23065	GUM SPRING	28067	592	16.6	24.5	39.2	15.0	4.7	59366	71353	84	79	515	5.2	6.8	49.1	34.6	4.3	156331
23066	GWYNN	28016	340	22.9	30.0	35.6	8.5	2.9	46560	55217	65	57	290	1.7	17.9	51.0	27.2	2.1	123235
23069	HANOVER	23070	1013	16.7	23.4	37.1	16.7	6.1	62300	75000	86	81	878	4.6	6.6	41.3	44.2	3.3	169762
23070	HARDYVILLE	28777	424	15.6	32.8	40.1	9.0	2.6	51533	60805	75	69	365	14.5	4.4	28.8	44.9	7.4	181439
23071	HARTFIELD	27407	379	27.2	26.1	28.0	11.6	7.1	45770	57315	63	55	314	7.0	5.4	43.6	31.5	12.4	162162
23072	HAYES	24160	4739	21.2	26.5	37.4	11.2	3.7	51601	59218	75	69	3737	8.9	8.5	49.2	29.5	4.0	141285
23075	HIGHLAND SPRINGS	21644	3943	23.4	32.0	35.8	6.4	2.4	45193	54439	62	54	2483	1.8	33.2	60.8	4.1	0.2	99907
23079	JAMAICA	20294	205	30.2	37.1	24.9	6.3	1.5	38108	45187	40	33	170	5.9	13.5	50.6	28.2	1.8	127419
23083	JETERSVILLE	19240	823	25.8	34.6	31.2	6.0	2.4	42322	48823	54	45	684	13.3	14.8	33.8	36.7	1.5	139683
23084	KENTS STORE	27872	545	23.5	27.0	31.6	12.7	5.3	49510	56404	71	64	461	6.7	13.9	47.9	27.3	4.1	132112
23085	KING AND QUEEN COURT	22547	226	25.7	25.7	34.5	7.1	7.1	48747	59034	70	62	190	20.5	10.0	39.0	23.7	6.8	127941
23086	KING WILLIAM	25049	1117	15.8	26.4	47.5	8.9	1.4	54850	62754	79	74	944	4.9	5.9	55.7	31.0	2.4	146904
23089	LANEXA	25838	1962	16.4	28.1	38.4	11.3	5.9	55857	67379	81	75	1672	6.8	12.1	39.9	34.8	6.5	154237
23091	LITTLE PLYMOUTH	22545	39	23.1	25.6	35.9	7.7	7.7	51440	65159	75	68	33	24.2	6.1	36.4	27.3	6.1	127500
23092	LOCUST HILL	31837	23	30.4	21.7	30.4	8.7	8.7	47380	62035	67	60	19	0.0	5.3	57.9	26.3	10.5	143750
23093	LOUISA	23416	4362	28.0	30.6	30.4	6.9	4.1	42821	50199	55	48	3334	8.3	8.3	50.3	28.9	4.2	138530
23102	MAIDENS	29819	905	14.1	20.8	38.3	18.5	8.3	68377	84950	90	84	787	2.7	2.5	43.0	44.7	7.1	179215
23103	MANAKIN SABOT	58296	1541	7.5	18.5	28.3	18.8	27.0	89217	130873	97	93	1380	0.5	0.7	29.4	41.2	28.3	253211
23106	MANQUIN	26540	410	13.9	29.8	41.5	11.5	3.4	55285	63260	80	74	356	5.6	2.8	54.5	35.4	1.7	151042
23109	MATHEWS	30586	478	20.1	31.4	37.2	6.9	4.4	48926	56863	70	63	402	7.0	11.2	46.5	25.9	9.5	137037
23110	MATTAPONI	20987	153	22.2	39.9	28.8	7.2	2.0	45109	51232	61	54	132	15.2	6.8	52.3	22.7	3.0	125000
23111	MECHANICSVILLE	29202	13254	10.7	25.0	44.2	15.0	5.2	64016	75351	88	82	10957	0.5	1.0	51.7	44.5	2.4	171212
23112	MIDLOTHIAN	32846	16306	7.0	18.0	45.1	19.8	10.2	75219	88041	93	88	13569	0.5	2.2	52.6	42.2	2.5	166902
23113	MIDLOTHIAN	51452	7705	5.4	12.3	27.9	22.1	32.4	107893	134772	99	97	6842	0.4	0.4	20.5	59.1	19.6	286255
23114	MIDLOTHIAN	36656	4268	4.0	11.1	43.2	28.3	13.4	88540	107036	97	93	3970	0.5	0.0	30.8	68.0	0.8	200307
23116	MECHANICSVILLE	34549	9110	7.1	13.0	41.8	24.3	13.9	83505	100945	96	92	8309	0.6	1.7	24.9	66.3	6.6	217598
23117	MINERAL	23831	3164	22.9	29.4	33.3	9.3	5.1	47904	56682	68	61	2662	8.6	10.0	43.5	30.6	7.3	143669
23119	MOON	30909	291	18.6	26.8	38.1	10.7	5.8	53478	63481	78	71	243	4.1	11.9	35.0	39.5	9.5	172024
23120	MOSELEY	34558	1206	10.5	17.1	40.5	23.4	8.5	75913	90991	94	89	1106	1.6	4.3	33.5	51.2	9.4	197852
23123	NEW CANTON	18365	666	35.9	30.5	27.6	4.4	1.7	38105	43658	40	33	526	15.6	28.1	43.9	10.3	2.1	97857
23124	NEW KENT	26972	889	10.4	24.2	42.9	16.3	6.3	64178	75397	88	82	802	3.5	6.7	39.0	49.0	1.8	176181
23125	NEW POINT	26950	54	27.8	27.8	37.0	5.6	1.9	40000	50000	46	39	46	2.2	8.7	58.7	23.9	6.5	142500
23126	NEWTOWN	20501	416	32.2	28.1	29.3	7.7	2.6	38877	46048	42	36	343	14.3	19.2	43.2	19.2	4.1	118510
23128	NORTH	29223	883	15.6	28.2	41.6	9.9	4.8	54513	63716	79	74	757	4.4	10.7	42.0	36.1	6.9	158281
23129	OILVILLE	45688	160	8.8	13.1	43.1	10.6	24.4	78201	106256	94	90	143	0.0	0.7	30.8	52.5	16.1	221296
23130	ONEMO	28060	199	22.1	30.2	37.7	6.5	3.5	47823	54998	68	60	167	6.0	10.2	50.3	25.2	8.4	139732
23138	PORT HAYWOOD	26364	281	25.3	28.1	36.7	6.8	3.2	45230	52614	62	54	237	3.8	9.3	55.3	24.5	7.2	140691
23139	POWHATAN	31517	7607	12.6	25.5	38.7	15.6	7.6	62444	76157	87	81	6714	1.9	4.4	43.0	45.5	5.1	176453
23140	PROVIDENCE FORGE	23703	1092	21.2	25.0	39.1	11.9	2.8	54520	63988	79	74	936	9.3	17.6	43.1	28.0	2.0	123490
23141	QUINTON	28708	2301	9.3	20.8	47.8	16.1	6.0	69487	79824	91	85	2065	2.9	7.7	41.9	46.6	0.9	170900
23146	ROCKVILLE	36515	1222	9.2	16.8	42.7	19.2	12.2	78541	96082	95	90	1104	0.5	3.4	28.1	54.9	13.1	222105
23148	SAINT STEPHENS CHURC	19566	324	30.6	30.9	28.4	6.8	3.4	39346	47080	44	37	269	11.9	17.5	46.5	19.7	4.5	122443
23149	SALUDA	31383	1447	23.2	27.1	33.3	8.7	7.7	49764	59735	71	65	1190	6.0	11.3	40.6	35.0	7.2	150526
23150	SANDSTON	26434	4841	15.7	30.7	39.1	10.7	3.9	52878	63930	77	70	3691	6.1	13.3	59.8	20.3	0.5	127055
23153	SANDY HOOK	27733	460	14.1	23.0	38.5	21.1	3.3	65580	80710	89	83	405	4.4	7.9	46.4	38.5	2.7	158864
23156	SHACKLEFORDS	19596	1064	28.2	40.2	24.6	5.8	1.1	38766	44590	42	35	854	12.7	18.4	47.3	19.3	2.3	116061
23160	STATE FARM	14810	5	20.0	0.0	20.0	40.0	20.0	110555	150000	99	98	3	33.3	0.0	0.0	66.7	0.0	275000
23161	STEVENSVILLE	23873	31	22.6	29.0	35.5	6.5	6.5	48639	61509	70	62	26	15.4	7.7	46.2	26.9	3.9	133333
23163	SUSAN	25256	341	26.4	27.3	37.5	6.5	2.4	43158	50411	56	49	288	2.8	8.0	59.7	24.0	5.6	141045
23168	TOANO	25294	1763	16.3	24.8	42.0	12.0	4.9	58092	70766	83	78	1485	8.0	4.4	49.4	33.9	4.3	156593
23169	TOPPING	23320	746	29.6	39.1	23.2	4.7	3.4	37941	45445	39	32	618	12.6	12.6	32.9	35.6	6.3	144583
23173	UNIVERSITY OF RICHMO	15421	0	0.0	0.0	0.0	0.0	0.0	0	0	0	0	0	0.0	0.0	0.0	0.0	0.0	0
23175	URBANNA	33150	344	27.3	27.6	32.0	7.6	5.5	44133	52915	59	51	288	13.2	16.0	43.8	23.3	3.8	117857
23176	WAKE	25014	196	29.6	32.7	25.0	8.2	4.6	41044	48259	50	42	161	9.9	13.0	28.0	39.1	9.9	172500
23177	WALKERTON	22648	541	28.5	26.4	33.3	7.4	4.4	44452	52973	60	52	452	16.6	14.2	42.0	22.1	5.1	126603
23180	WATER VIEW	18726	95	29.5	37.9	24.2	6.3	2.1	37537	46393	38	31	79	2.5	13.9	51.9	29.1	2.5	128906
23181	WEST POINT	30068	1826	19.8	26.6	34.7	13.1	5.9	53273	62764	77	71	1512	3.2	13.7	43.4	36.0	3.7	147424
23185	WILLIAMSBURG	39951	16654	15.8	22.4	31.1	16.6	14.1	64491	83192	88	83	11964	5.6	5.3	27.4	42.5	19.3	218155
23186	WILLIAMSBURG	14572	15	33.3	26.7	20.0	13.3	6.7	37333	40000	37	31	6	0.0	0.0	0.0	66.7	33.3	350000
23188	WILLIAMSBURG	32807	11023	15.4	21.2	37.8	17.2	8.5	64316	79521	88	82	8071	2.9	3.3	34.6	48.1	11.1	197154
23192	MONTPELIER	29005	2256	11.8	21.1	42.8	17.2	7.1	66021	77621	89	83	1982	1.7	7.4	27.3	51.4	12.3	210108
23219	RICHMOND	13950	989	72.8	19.1	5.8	0.6	1.7	12525	14123	1	1	60	16.7	15.0	56.7	10.0	1.7	108750
23220	RICHMOND	28934	13205	42.1	24.5	19.8	6.8	6.8	31871	41305	17	13	3944	4.4	23.4	35.2	29.4	7.5	124246
23221	RICHMOND	48925	7768	20.9	29.5	26.1	11.5	12.1	49645	69835	71	64	3428	0.5	7.2	32.9	41.3	18.1	202947
23222	RICHMOND	17967	10452	35.4	33.3	23.9	4.9	2.4	33979	41210	24	18	5931	5.7	48.5	40.7	4.7	0.4	87910
23223	RICHMOND	18142	17142	38.5	30.1	24.0	5.4	2.0	32629	39515	20	14	7955	6.3	34.0	48.9	10.5	0.4	98556
23224	RICHMOND	17418	11929	37.9	33.8	22.7	4.2	1.4	31978	38099	18	13	5616	13.4	48.4	35.8	2.2	0.2	82297
23225	RICHMOND	26461	18288	27.4	33.6	27.6	7.5	4.0	40558	49452	48	41	7898	3.7	22.3	50.2	22.2	1.5	118890
23226	RICHMOND	49576	6974	14.6	26.9	28.0	13.5	17.0	61066	81727	85	80	5010	0.9	7.8	41.9	33.4	16.0	173573
23227	RICHMOND	29522	10161	26.8	28.9	30.9	8.9	4.5	45465	55634	62	55	5357	0.6	7.1	63.4	28.1	0.8	141567
23228	RICHMOND	27062	15059	21.2	35.7	32.5	8.1	2.6	44872	53541	61	53	7626	1.1	16.9	69.1	12.7	0.2	117619
23229	RICHMOND	42361	13413	12.6	23.1	35.3	15.3	13.7	64749	80822	88	83	9637	0.3	1.2	45.6	41.7	11.2	182284
23230	RICHMOND	27413	3047	26.1	31.5	30.3	8.0	4.1	42812	52479	55	48	1539	0.6	9.8	67.3	21.3	1.1	123474
23231	RICHMOND	26600	11264	20.4	27.7	36.5	11.3	4.1	51756	63687	75	69	7992	2.1	20.7	53.6	22.5	1.2	123858
23233	RICHMOND	46373	21078	6.9	17.1	35.1	21.6	19.4	84503	109127	96	92	15648	0.3	2.0	28.2	57.5	11.9	218057
23234	RICHMOND	21816	14608	21.8	32.4	35.0	7.9	2.9	46814	55717	66	58	9156	4.4	23.3	59.4	12.8	0.1	111088
23235	RICHMOND	34340	12139	10.1	23.9	40.7	18.0	7.3	66361	79697	89	84	9618	2.0	4.8	55.0	36.8	1.4	159636
23236	RICHMOND	33733	9471	7.0	19.3	42.9	20.5	10.2	74260	87358	93	88	8418	0.2	3.2	58.4	34.8	3.5	158232
	VIRGINIA	30454		19.8	25.2	32.5	13.6	8.9	55216	67801				6.8	10.4	35.8	36.5	10.5	166226
	UNITED STATES	25866		24.7	27.1	30.8	10.9	6.5	48124	56710				10.9	15.0	33.7	30.1	10.4	145905

ZIP CODE #	POST OFFICE NAME	FINANCIAL SERVICES: Auto Loan	FINANCIAL SERVICES: Home Loan	FINANCIAL SERVICES: Invest-ments	FINANCIAL SERVICES: Retire-ment Plans	THE HOME: Home Improvements: Home Repair	THE HOME: Home Improvements: Lawn & Garden	THE HOME: Furnishings: Comput-ers & Hard-ware	THE HOME: Furnishings: Major Appli-ances	THE HOME: Furnishings: TV, Radio, Sound Equip-ment	THE HOME: Furnishings: Furni-ture	ENTERTAINMENT: Dine out/ Carry out	ENTERTAINMENT: Sports Equip-ment	ENTERTAINMENT: Fees & Tickets	ENTERTAINMENT: Toys & Games	ENTERTAINMENT: Travel	ENTERTAINMENT: Cable TV	PERSONAL: Apparel & Services	PERSONAL: Auto Repairs	PERSONAL: Health Insur-ance	PERSONAL: Pets & Supplies
23030	CHARLES CITY	98	77	52	70	83	93	74	85	83	75	100	100	69	97	75	88	93	84	99	114
23032	CHURCH VIEW	85	60	33	53	68	78	58	71	68	58	80	85	50	77	60	73	74	70	87	100
23035	COBBS CREEK	94	110	122	104	109	119	104	104	104	103	129	116	110	134	108	106	127	102	106	113
23038	COLUMBIA	104	88	65	82	94	104	83	94	91	83	110	111	80	110	86	95	103	92	105	122
23039	CROZIER	124	153	166	152	151	152	138	138	129	138	162	159	147	169	142	126	161	133	127	151
23040	CUMBERLAND	79	61	39	57	65	73	60	69	67	60	80	80	54	77	60	69	74	68	78	89
23043	DELTAVILLE	131	107	81	98	119	135	101	119	112	102	134	134	93	127	108	120	125	117	141	156
23045	DIGGS	116	99	78	94	107	119	96	109	104	95	125	127	90	125	100	108	117	107	122	138
23047	DOSWELL	112	132	138	130	131	134	120	121	116	120	144	140	127	152	124	115	143	118	116	136
23050	DUTTON	95	108	114	106	105	110	102	102	99	102	124	117	106	127	104	98	122	101	97	111
23055	FORK UNION	71	79	84	75	79	88	77	76	79	75	98	85	82	105	80	82	95	75	81	84
23056	FOSTER	131	91	48	86	106	119	90	111	104	89	122	134	77	119	93	109	111	110	133	155
23059	GLEN ALLEN	171	193	198	199	187	184	179	177	166	183	211	208	184	213	177	158	208	174	155	195
23060	GLEN ALLEN	121	133	134	138	127	126	125	123	117	128	148	144	127	148	122	110	146	122	108	135
23061	GLOUCESTER	93	95	90	93	94	98	90	93	88	91	110	108	90	109	90	87	107	92	90	106
23062	GLOUCESTER POINT	91	103	108	101	101	104	98	97	94	98	118	112	101	121	98	92	116	96	92	106
23063	GOOCHLAND	100	86	67	84	91	101	86	93	91	84	110	107	82	110	86	94	104	91	102	113
23065	GUM SPRING	106	106	93	103	109	113	96	103	98	96	120	122	98	124	99	98	116	100	105	126
23066	GWYNN	97	76	52	68	85	96	72	86	81	71	96	101	64	95	76	86	89	85	102	118
23069	HANOVER	110	108	95	103	111	117	99	106	101	99	124	125	99	126	102	102	119	104	110	130
23070	HARDYVILLE	91	85	82	81	91	107	79	90	84	85	104	88	80	86	86	89	97	87	105	103
23071	HARTFIELD	109	80	48	71	91	103	76	93	89	76	105	110	67	102	80	95	96	92	112	130
23072	HAYES	85	89	88	87	89	93	86	87	85	86	106	102	86	107	86	84	103	87	85	99
23075	HIGHLAND SPRINGS	72	74	84	74	73	78	78	75	78	77	97	88	79	99	77	76	95	76	73	83
23079	JAMAICA	81	61	39	55	69	78	58	71	67	58	79	83	51	77	61	72	73	70	84	98
23083	JETERSVILLE	86	70	47	64	75	82	65	75	72	65	87	89	61	86	67	75	81	73	85	100
23084	KENTS STORE	102	95	83	92	98	109	93	99	98	92	119	113	92	120	95	100	114	97	106	117
23085	KING AND QUEEN COURT	97	82	58	77	87	95	76	86	83	76	100	103	73	101	78	86	94	84	96	113
23086	KING WILLIAM	104	91	69	86	96	102	85	95	91	86	110	113	82	110	87	92	105	93	101	121
23089	LANEXA	105	96	76	92	100	107	90	98	94	90	114	116	88	116	91	95	109	95	103	123
23091	LITTLE PLYMOUTH	96	83	62	79	88	95	77	86	83	77	100	103	75	102	80	85	95	84	95	112
23092	LOCUST HILL	108	85	58	76	95	107	80	96	90	79	107	113	71	106	85	97	100	95	114	132
23093	LOUISA	96	78	55	74	84	95	77	87	85	76	101	101	72	100	78	88	94	85	99	110
23102	MAIDENS	102	118	119	117	117	118	107	108	101	106	127	127	111	133	109	100	125	105	101	123
23103	MANAKIN SABOT	185	226	252	224	224	232	205	206	193	206	243	235	219	250	213	192	242	200	194	225
23106	MANQUIN	120	107	82	102	113	121	99	110	105	99	128	131	97	131	102	108	122	107	119	142
23109	MATHEWS	130	91	48	86	106	119	90	111	103	89	121	134	77	119	93	109	111	110	132	155
23110	MATTAPONI	97	65	29	56	74	85	63	78	76	64	89	94	53	84	64	82	81	78	97	111
23111	MECHANICSVILLE	106	116	118	119	114	115	109	109	104	110	130	127	112	133	108	100	128	107	99	121
23112	MIDLOTHIAN	127	145	148	150	140	139	133	132	123	136	156	154	138	158	132	117	154	129	116	145
23113	MIDLOTHIAN	187	230	254	234	223	227	207	202	191	208	242	234	224	252	211	186	243	196	183	223
23114	MIDLOTHIAN	146	176	183	182	169	168	157	154	143	160	182	179	167	187	157	137	182	149	134	170
23116	MECHANICSVILLE	137	164	169	167	159	156	147	146	136	149	172	171	155	178	148	130	171	142	129	161
23117	MINERAL	100	81	56	74	89	99	76	89	84	76	101	105	70	100	80	89	94	87	103	120
23119	MOON	94	110	122	104	109	119	104	104	103	103	129	116	110	134	108	106	127	102	106	113
23120	MOSELEY	134	164	173	165	161	159	147	147	137	147	172	172	156	182	150	132	172	142	131	162
23123	NEW CANTON	84	56	25	48	64	73	54	68	65	55	77	81	46	73	55	71	70	67	84	96
23124	NEW KENT	107	114	107	112	115	118	103	108	102	103	126	127	106	131	106	101	123	104	106	128
23125	NEW POINT	97	76	52	68	85	96	71	86	81	71	96	101	64	94	76	86	89	85	102	118
23126	NEWTOWN	95	64	29	55	72	83	62	77	74	63	87	92	52	82	63	80	79	76	95	109
23128	NORTH	102	105	103	102	107	114	100	104	101	100	125	120	101	127	103	102	121	103	106	120
23129	OILVILLE	145	180	191	180	177	174	160	160	149	160	187	187	171	199	164	144	187	154	143	177
23130	ONEMO	117	85	50	79	98	110	83	101	95	82	111	121	72	109	87	100	102	100	120	140
23138	PORT HAYWOOD	104	79	51	72	90	101	75	91	86	75	101	108	67	100	80	91	94	90	108	126
23139	POWHATAN	125	136	132	135	136	139	125	128	121	125	151	151	128	157	127	119	148	125	122	148
23140	PROVIDENCE FORGE	97	85	68	80	90	98	80	89	86	81	105	105	78	105	82	89	100	88	98	114
23141	QUINTON	109	117	112	116	118	120	107	111	104	107	130	131	110	135	109	103	127	108	107	130
23146	ROCKVILLE	128	155	162	155	153	152	139	139	130	138	163	163	147	173	142	126	162	134	127	156
23148	SAINT STEPHENS CHURC	94	67	36	59	75	85	64	78	75	65	89	93	56	85	65	80	82	77	93	108
23149	SALUDA	125	106	84	100	113	129	104	117	112	105	136	127	98	124	107	117	127	115	132	141
23150	SANDSTON	89	92	92	90	93	100	90	91	90	89	112	104	92	116	91	91	109	90	92	103
23153	SANDY HOOK	97	113	114	112	112	112	101	103	96	101	120	121	106	127	104	94	119	99	96	117
23156	SHACKLEFORDS	83	57	29	51	64	75	58	69	68	58	80	82	50	76	58	73	73	69	85	94
23160	STATE FARM	0	0	0	0	0	0	0	0	0	0	0	0	0	0	0	0	0	0	0	0
23161	STEVENSVILLE	97	87	66	82	92	98	80	89	85	80	104	106	79	106	83	87	98	87	96	115
23163	SUSAN	96	75	51	68	85	95	71	85	80	70	95	100	63	94	75	86	88	84	101	117
23168	TOANO	94	103	102	104	100	100	97	97	92	98	116	115	98	117	96	87	114	96	87	108
23169	TOPPING	94	72	48	65	82	92	68	83	78	68	92	97	61	91	73	83	85	81	98	113
23173	UNIVERSITY OF RICHMO	0	0	0	0	0	0	0	0	0	0	0	0	0	0	0	0	0	0	0	0
23175	URBANNA	118	84	47	77	94	110	87	102	101	86	119	118	76	112	88	108	108	101	124	133
23176	WAKE	113	82	46	72	93	105	78	96	91	79	108	114	68	104	81	98	99	95	116	134
23177	WALKERTON	96	72	42	65	79	89	68	81	78	69	93	97	62	91	70	83	86	80	96	111
23180	WATER VIEW	80	62	43	56	70	79	59	71	67	58	79	83	53	78	63	71	73	70	84	97
23181	WEST POINT	120	104	78	100	110	120	100	110	107	99	130	129	97	130	102	110	122	108	120	138
23185	WILLIAMSBURG	135	138	148	139	138	147	139	138	136	139	171	158	139	164	138	134	165	139	136	154
23186	WILLIAMSBURG	82	50	63	57	49	60	98	71	95	82	118	100	79	106	78	83	111	87	66	81
23188	WILLIAMSBURG	114	116	127	120	116	122	116	116	113	117	142	135	117	139	115	110	138	117	110	130
23192	MONTPELIER	114	119	116	118	121	125	111	115	110	111	136	136	113	139	113	109	132	113	114	136
23219	RICHMOND	30	25	35	27	25	29	33	30	34	31	42	36	31	41	31	33	41	33	30	33
23220	RICHMOND	81	65	90	70	64	74	88	77	90	84	112	96	82	107	80	86	109	85	75	87
23221	RICHMOND	115	107	161	118	104	115	128	116	128	126	162	143	127	161	123	123	159	125	109	129
23222	RICHMOND	63	59	68	56	58	67	63	62	67	64	84	68	64	81	63	69	81	64	66	71
23223	RICHMOND	60	56	66	54	55	62	60	59	64	61	79	67	60	77	59	65	77	61	62	67
23224	RICHMOND	61	55	65	54	54	61	62	60	65	62	81	68	61	78	60	65	79	62	61	67
23225	RICHMOND	74	72	87	75	71	77	79	75	79	78	99	89	78	97	77	77	97	79	73	83
23226	RICHMOND	143	161	202	164	159	168	160	155	155	159	195	182	167	199	162	152	193	156	146	170
23227	RICHMOND	81	82	101	84	81	88	89	85	88	87	111	100	89	110	87	86	108	88	82	93
23228	RICHMOND	75	78	91	80	77	82	81	78	80	81	101	92	82	101	80	78	99	80	75	86
23229	RICHMOND	127	145	173	145	143	152	141	138	136	140	171	159	147	174	143	135	169	138	132	151
23230	RICHMOND	76	74	90	76	73	80	84	78	83	81	104	94	82	103	81	81	101	83	77	87
23231	RICHMOND	93	97	102	95	96	101	96	96	96	96	120	112	98	122	96	95	117	96	94	108
23233	RICHMOND	160	179	199	186	175	178	171	167	160	173	203	197	177	204	170	154	201	167	151	184
23234	RICHMOND	78	79	87	80	77	83	81	80	81	82	102	92	82	101	80	80	99	81	77	88
23235	RICHMOND	108	126	140	126	125	129	119	118	113	118	142	136	125	147	121	112	141	116	111	129
23236	RICHMOND	123	143	150	145	139	139	131	130	122	133	154	152	137	158	131	117	153	127	116	143
	VIRGINIA	112	109	113	109	109	117	108	110	109	109	136	129	108	135	108	109	132	110	109	128
	UNITED STATES	100	100	100	100	100	100	100	100	100	100	100	100	100	100	100	100	100	100	100	100

POPULATION CHANGE

#	POST OFFICE NAME	COUNTY FIPS CODE	POPULATION			2000-2004 ANNUAL RATE		HOUSEHOLDS					FAMILIES		
			2000	2004	2009	% Rate	State Centile	2000	2004	2009	% Annual Rate 2000-2004	2004 Average HH Size	2000	2004	% Annual Rate 2000-2004
23237 RICHMOND		041	20528	21743	23751	1.4	65	7572	8138	9012	1.7	2.66	5616	5940	1.3
23294 RICHMOND		087	15505	16953	18435	2.1	80	7452	8419	9352	2.9	2.00	3731	3983	1.6
23298 RICHMOND		760	427	427	427	0.0	24	0	0	0	0.0	0.00	0	0	0.0
23301 ACCOMAC		001	2204	2220	2252	0.2	30	785	795	811	0.3	2.60	534	533	0.0
23302 ASSAWOMAN		001	129	125	126	-0.7	6	41	40	41	-0.6	3.08	29	28	-0.8
23306 BELLE HAVEN		001	1045	1045	1061	0.0	24	448	454	465	0.3	2.28	312	312	0.0
23307 BIRDSNEST		131	940	961	969	0.5	43	369	384	393	0.9	2.46	259	265	0.5
23308 BLOXOM		001	2615	2700	2775	0.8	51	951	988	1021	0.9	2.61	665	680	0.5
23310 CAPE CHARLES		131	6086	6048	6010	-0.2	19	2446	2464	2483	0.2	2.38	1565	1550	-0.2
23314 CARROLLTON		093	4561	5012	5524	2.2	82	1728	1928	2158	2.6	2.60	1412	1560	2.4
23315 CARRSVILLE		093	1531	1617	1749	1.3	64	601	646	711	1.7	2.48	421	446	1.4
23320 CHESAPEAKE		550	44431	47687	50493	1.7	73	17061	18580	19923	2.0	2.52	11978	12846	1.7
23321 CHESAPEAKE		550	30068	30985	32262	0.7	49	10678	11207	11838	1.1	2.76	8639	8971	0.9
23322 CHESAPEAKE		550	54317	59489	63893	2.2	81	16801	18626	20227	2.5	3.05	14564	16021	2.3
23323 CHESAPEAKE		550	31645	33683	35733	1.5	68	10547	11356	12172	1.8	2.93	8551	9143	1.6
23324 CHESAPEAKE		550	21706	21984	22804	0.3	36	8347	8646	9109	0.8	2.53	5637	5693	0.2
23325 CHESAPEAKE		550	16892	16705	17110	-0.3	16	6422	6473	6723	0.2	2.57	4756	4722	-0.2
23336 CHINCOTEAGUE ISLAND		001	4324	4462	4585	0.7	51	2068	2154	2229	1.0	2.06	1244	1271	0.5
23337 WALLOPS ISLAND		001	428	441	457	0.7	49	178	184	192	0.8	2.39	125	128	0.6
23350 EXMORE		131	3868	3849	3829	-0.1	20	1637	1658	1675	0.3	2.31	1125	1121	-0.1
23354 FRANKTOWN		131	347	341	337	-0.4	12	140	140	141	0.0	2.24	97	95	-0.5
23356 GREENBACKVILLE		001	612	678	723	2.4	84	299	333	358	2.6	2.03	214	235	2.2
23357 GREENBUSH		001	669	669	679	0.0	24	239	241	247	0.2	2.63	156	155	-0.2
23359 HALLWOOD		001	888	893	907	0.1	29	317	320	327	0.2	2.69	231	230	-0.1
23395 HORNTOWN		001	406	450	480	2.5	85	134	149	160	2.5	3.01	96	105	2.1
23404 LOCUSTVILLE		001	29	29	29	0.0	24	14	14	14	0.0	2.07	9	9	0.0
23405 MACHIPONGO		131	926	942	947	0.4	39	394	406	414	0.7	2.25	275	279	0.3
23409 MEARS		001	165	170	174	0.7	49	66	68	70	0.7	2.49	47	48	0.5
23410 MELFA		001	2905	2964	3033	0.5	41	1217	1254	1293	0.7	2.35	846	860	0.4
23413 NASSAWADOX		131	929	931	930	0.1	26	336	344	349	0.6	2.49	227	228	0.1
23415 NEW CHURCH		001	5848	6322	6671	1.9	76	2159	2346	2490	2.0	2.69	1525	1632	1.6
23416 OAK HALL		001	860	827	832	-0.9	4	347	337	342	-0.7	2.44	241	230	-1.1
23417 ONANCOCK		001	4177	4198	4264	0.1	28	1778	1806	1850	0.4	2.24	1163	1163	0.0
23418 ONLEY		001	925	928	941	0.1	27	380	386	395	0.4	2.40	253	253	0.0
23420 PAINTER		001	3421	3447	3499	0.2	30	1310	1339	1373	0.5	2.49	906	913	0.2
23421 PARKSLEY		001	4207	4303	4403	0.5	44	1583	1632	1681	0.7	2.54	1083	1100	0.4
23426 SANFORD		001	607	590	595	-0.7	8	270	265	269	-0.4	2.23	188	182	-0.8
23430 SMITHFIELD		093	15108	16350	17879	1.9	77	5693	6274	6981	2.3	2.59	4404	4798	2.0
23432 SUFFOLK		800	1448	1527	1758	1.3	63	542	585	685	1.8	2.61	424	451	1.5
23433 SUFFOLK		800	1230	1297	1493	1.3	63	496	535	627	1.8	2.42	388	413	1.5
23434 SUFFOLK		800	39675	45894	55415	3.5	92	14685	17220	21096	3.8	2.62	10812	12515	3.5
23435 SUFFOLK		800	15117	19008	23916	5.5	97	5200	6687	8566	6.1	2.82	4302	5465	5.8
23436 SUFFOLK		800	782	824	949	1.2	63	296	319	374	1.8	2.58	232	246	1.4
23437 SUFFOLK		800	3991	4420	5222	2.4	84	1509	1708	2052	3.0	2.59	1156	1286	2.5
23438 SUFFOLK		800	1448	1566	1827	1.9	76	556	616	732	2.4	2.54	417	454	2.0
23440 TANGIER		001	691	697	707	0.2	32	280	286	293	0.5	2.44	209	211	0.2
23442 TEMPERANCEVILLE		001	1145	1128	1142	-0.4	14	433	430	438	-0.2	2.59	309	303	-0.5
23451 VIRGINIA BEACH		810	41485	42187	43137	0.4	39	19213	19986	20868	0.9	2.04	9976	10055	0.2
23452 VIRGINIA BEACH		810	61450	60362	60880	-0.4	12	22417	22586	23282	0.2	2.65	16394	16219	-0.3
23453 VIRGINIA BEACH		810	33240	37270	40322	2.7	87	11089	12686	13994	3.2	2.94	8535	9624	2.9
23454 VIRGINIA BEACH		810	60469	61550	63040	0.4	40	22123	23029	24071	1.0	2.64	15892	16320	0.6
23455 VIRGINIA BEACH		810	44609	44028	44462	-0.3	15	18241	18432	18998	0.3	2.38	12183	12066	-0.2
23456 VIRGINIA BEACH		810	43960	50295	54847	3.2	91	13463	15630	17291	3.6	3.15	11662	13409	3.3
23457 VIRGINIA BEACH		810	3785	3730	3755	-0.3	15	1371	1377	1413	0.1	2.70	1082	1072	-0.2
23459 VIRGINIA BEACH		810	1043	1011	1010	-0.7	7	182	176	179	-0.8	3.46	171	165	-0.8
23460 VIRGINIA BEACH		810	1561	1455	1440	-1.6	0	86	58	54	-8.9	3.57	83	56	-8.8
23461 VIRGINIA BEACH		810	843	872	891	0.8	52	21	23	24	2.2	2.57	19	20	1.2
23462 VIRGINIA BEACH		810	58229	57760	58603	-0.2	18	21892	22201	22985	0.3	2.59	15277	15180	-0.2
23463 VIRGINIA BEACH		810	26	24	24	-1.9	0	9	9	9	0.0	2.67	5	5	0.0
23464 VIRGINIA BEACH		810	70610	72236	74461	0.5	44	23825	24895	26166	1.0	2.89	19189	19863	0.8
23487 WINDSOR		093	5708	6044	6536	1.4	65	2188	2355	2588	1.8	2.56	1642	1747	1.5
23502 NORFOLK		710	21234	21320	21471	0.1	28	7718	7854	8019	0.4	2.56	5324	5343	0.1
23503 NORFOLK		710	30586	31997	32913	1.1	59	13328	14127	14722	1.4	2.25	7451	7760	1.0
23504 NORFOLK		710	23430	22882	22933	-0.6	10	8078	7977	8100	-0.3	2.64	5230	5052	-0.8
23505 NORFOLK		710	27083	27007	27085	-0.1	21	11586	11697	11889	0.2	2.17	6630	6576	-0.2
23507 NORFOLK		710	6472	6681	6829	0.8	51	3408	3597	3742	1.3	1.79	1236	1269	0.6
23508 NORFOLK		710	17837	17768	17880	-0.1	21	6481	6517	6646	0.1	2.48	3461	3405	-0.4
23509 NORFOLK		710	12710	12783	12862	0.1	29	4957	5045	5141	0.4	2.51	3151	3149	0.0
23510 NORFOLK		710	5287	5725	5988	1.9	77	1924	2204	2390	3.3	1.89	920	1013	2.3
23511 NORFOLK		710	18873	19082	19197	0.3	33	661	700	726	1.4	6.25	645	682	1.3
23513 NORFOLK		710	29528	29938	30313	0.3	36	11257	11586	11901	0.7	2.58	7425	7521	0.3
23517 NORFOLK		710	4235	4214	4246	-0.1	20	2178	2212	2269	0.4	1.83	786	772	-0.4
23518 NORFOLK		710	29566	29011	29099	-0.4	12	11944	11888	12099	-0.1	2.44	7790	7659	-0.4
23521 NORFOLK		810	4087	4005	4008	-0.5	11	576	571	585	-0.2	3.93	526	519	-0.3
23523 NORFOLK		710	7513	7603	7716	0.3	34	2672	2761	2850	0.8	2.75	1854	1884	0.4
23601 NEWPORT NEWS		700	25009	25730	26263	0.7	48	10297	10681	11013	0.9	2.37	6560	6700	0.5
23602 NEWPORT NEWS		700	41538	43556	44856	1.1	61	16183	17314	18136	1.6	2.46	11048	11624	1.2
23603 NEWPORT NEWS		700	3729	3736	3775	0.0	25	1328	1359	1397	0.5	2.48	887	893	0.2
23604 FORT EUSTIS		700	5738	5067	4932	-2.9	0	965	785	755	-4.7	3.65	946	769	-4.8
23605 NEWPORT NEWS		700	14728	14298	14135	-0.7	7	6271	6184	6204	-0.3	2.30	3842	3717	-0.8
23606 NEWPORT NEWS		700	25714	25373	25310	-0.3	15	11037	11053	11191	0.0	2.23	6690	6562	-0.5
23607 NEWPORT NEWS		700	25785	24491	24120	-1.2	2	9975	9614	9604	-0.9	2.45	6180	5843	-1.3
23608 NEWPORT NEWS		700	41506	43311	44465	1.0	58	15144	15916	16511	1.2	2.71	11132	11548	0.9
23651 FORT MONROE		650	1253	1183	1147	-1.3	1	363	347	341	-1.1	3.18	338	322	-1.1
23661 HAMPTON		650	14347	13857	13567	-0.8	5	5728	5598	5551	-0.5	2.42	3778	3640	-0.9
23662 POQUOSON		735	11566	11810	12086	0.5	42	4166	4328	4503	0.9	2.71	3370	3470	0.7
23663 HAMPTON		650	13390	13800	13986	0.7	49	4959	5134	5247	0.8	2.67	3467	3574	0.7
23664 HAMPTON		650	10152	9834	9628	-0.8	6	4293	4224	4196	-0.4	2.32	2783	2706	-0.7
23665 HAMPTON		650	13432	13093	13292	-0.6	9	1428	1347	1412	-1.4	3.69	1393	1317	-1.3
23666 HAMPTON		650	48699	50750	51628	1.0	57	19731	20951	21655	1.4	2.40	12903	13404	0.9
23668 HAMPTON		650	453	450	448	-0.2	19	4	4	4	0.0	2.50	1	1	0.0
23669 HAMPTON		650	45361	43871	43032	-0.8	6	16927	16517	16377	-0.6	2.48	11377	10966	-0.9
23690 YORKTOWN		199	2725	2917	3178	1.6	71	930	1020	1139	2.2	2.53	664	719	1.9
23692 YORKTOWN		199	16630	18106	20039	2.0	79	6404	7102	7992	2.5	2.53	4932	5389	2.1
23693 YORKTOWN		199	19758	23228	26688	3.9	95	6770	8030	9331	4.1	2.89	5485	6475	4.0
VIRGINIA						1.4					1.7	2.51			1.4
UNITED STATES						1.2					1.3	2.58			1.1

ZIP CODE #	POST OFFICE NAME	RACE (%) White 2000	White 2004	Black 2000	Black 2004	Asian/Pacific 2000	Asian/Pacific 2004	% Hispanic Origin 2000	% Hispanic Origin 2004	2004 AGE DISTRIBUTION (%) 0-4	5-9	10-14	15-19	20-24	25-44	45-64	65-84	85+	18+	MEDIAN AGE 2004	% 2004 Males	% 2004 Females
23237	RICHMOND	75.2	72.6	17.6	18.8	1.9	2.3	5.3	6.6	7.2	7.3	7.7	6.9	7.2	30.2	25.5	7.3	0.7	73.7	35.1	49.0	51.0
23294	RICHMOND	70.5	67.1	14.2	15.4	10.9	12.3	3.6	4.4	5.4	4.5	4.6	4.9	11.2	40.2	19.5	8.8	0.9	82.7	32.4	47.3	52.7
23298	RICHMOND	30.4	26.7	51.8	54.3	12.9	13.6	3.0	3.5	0.0	0.0	0.2	29.3	44.5	23.2	2.6	0.2	0.0	99.3	22.3	32.8	67.2
23301	ACCOMAC	47.1	44.1	40.7	41.3	1.5	1.5	12.3	15.1	6.6	6.3	5.8	6.4	7.3	28.0	24.0	13.7	1.9	77.8	37.6	53.1	46.9
23302	ASSAWOMAN	49.6	46.4	45.0	47.2	0.0	0.0	6.2	6.4	6.4	6.4	7.2	6.4	6.4	27.2	24.8	13.6	1.6	75.2	38.4	49.6	50.4
23306	BELLE HAVEN	53.6	51.2	45.0	47.2	0.3	0.3	1.2	1.6	5.2	5.8	7.0	6.2	4.9	21.7	28.5	18.7	2.0	78.1	44.4	45.1	54.9
23307	BIRDSNEST	39.4	38.7	56.6	57.0	0.1	0.1	3.7	3.9	6.4	6.1	5.9	6.4	6.2	21.2	26.2	19.0	2.5	77.7	43.5	46.1	53.9
23308	BLOXOM	52.9	50.4	35.8	36.2	0.1	0.2	13.5	16.2	7.8	7.5	6.8	6.3	6.5	27.2	23.9	12.0	1.9	74.4	35.9	49.2	50.9
23310	CAPE CHARLES	53.4	52.6	42.3	43.1	0.3	0.3	4.4	4.4	5.6	5.8	6.9	6.8	5.8	22.9	26.6	17.4	2.4	77.6	42.5	47.5	52.5
23314	CARROLLTON	84.6	83.2	13.8	14.8	0.5	0.6	1.1	1.4	5.5	6.4	7.2	6.3	4.2	27.7	29.7	12.3	0.7	76.9	41.5	50.0	50.0
23315	CARRSVILLE	71.5	69.7	27.6	29.4	0.2	0.3	0.3	0.3	5.0	5.7	7.4	6.6	5.2	25.5	28.6	14.6	1.6	77.7	42.0	47.3	52.7
23320	CHESAPEAKE	63.9	61.2	29.2	30.7	3.4	4.0	2.9	3.5	7.6	6.9	6.9	6.4	7.2	32.7	23.2	8.2	1.0	74.8	34.7	47.2	52.8
23321	CHESAPEAKE	68.9	66.4	26.3	28.1	2.5	2.9	1.7	2.0	6.6	6.8	8.0	7.7	6.5	26.9	27.0	9.5	0.9	73.8	37.2	48.1	51.9
23322	CHESAPEAKE	85.1	83.3	11.3	12.5	1.3	1.6	1.9	2.4	6.5	7.6	8.9	8.6	6.6	29.5	25.9	5.9	0.5	71.5	35.8	51.5	48.6
23323	CHESAPEAKE	59.1	56.7	37.0	38.8	1.1	1.3	2.0	2.5	8.0	7.7	8.1	7.3	6.9	30.3	22.6	8.1	1.0	71.6	34.6	48.5	51.5
23324	CHESAPEAKE	42.6	40.3	54.0	55.8	1.0	1.1	1.4	1.6	8.0	7.4	8.3	7.8	7.2	26.1	20.9	13.0	1.3	71.4	34.0	45.2	54.9
23325	CHESAPEAKE	58.5	56.3	37.5	39.2	1.2	1.4	1.9	2.2	7.1	6.8	6.7	6.5	7.1	28.5	23.8	12.2	1.3	75.5	36.4	47.5	52.5
23336	CHINCOTEAGUE ISLAND	96.9	96.5	1.0	1.1	0.3	0.3	0.5	0.7	4.3	4.4	4.7	4.6	4.0	23.1	33.5	19.5	2.0	83.8	48.0	49.1	50.9
23337	WALLOPS ISLAND	58.4	56.2	38.1	39.5	0.0	0.2	3.0	4.1	6.6	7.3	8.4	6.1	5.9	27.7	24.3	12.5	1.4	73.9	37.1	50.3	49.7
23350	EXMORE	59.1	58.6	37.7	38.2	0.3	0.3	2.6	2.7	5.1	5.5	6.3	6.5	5.5	21.5	28.8	18.0	2.8	78.9	44.7	47.3	52.7
23354	FRANKTOWN	46.1	45.5	52.2	53.1	0.0	0.0	1.2	1.2	5.3	5.6	6.2	5.0	4.7	19.1	28.2	21.1	5.0	79.5	47.8	46.0	54.0
23356	GREENBACKVILLE	64.7	62.2	31.4	33.2	0.2	0.2	3.8	4.7	7.5	8.6	9.6	6.1	5.8	29.2	22.0	10.5	0.9	70.5	34.1	51.2	48.8
23357	GREENBUSH	39.2	36.6	50.8	51.4	0.0	0.0	11.7	14.1	5.8	5.7	6.9	6.9	7.9	26.8	25.0	12.9	2.2	77.3	37.5	51.7	48.3
23359	HALLWOOD	55.4	53.0	32.7	32.9	0.1	0.1	12.8	15.3	7.1	6.9	7.3	6.3	6.8	28.1	24.9	11.2	1.5	75.0	35.5	48.8	51.2
23395	HORNTOWN	64.8	62.4	31.5	33.1	0.3	0.2	3.9	4.7	7.3	8.4	10.0	6.2	6.0	28.7	22.0	10.4	0.9	70.4	33.9	51.8	48.2
23404	LOCUSTVILLE	55.2	58.6	41.4	41.4	0.0	0.0	6.9	3.5	6.9	6.9	6.9	6.9	6.9	27.6	27.6	10.3	0.0	79.3	36.3	51.7	48.3
23405	MACHIPONGO	40.8	40.2	55.4	55.8	0.1	0.1	3.5	3.4	6.2	6.1	5.8	6.1	6.1	21.1	26.2	19.5	3.0	78.1	44.2	46.2	53.8
23409	MEARS	75.2	72.4	15.8	15.9	0.0	0.6	11.5	13.5	6.5	6.5	6.5	5.9	6.5	28.2	25.3	12.9	1.8	76.5	38.2	50.6	49.4
23410	MELFA	58.0	55.6	39.2	41.2	0.1	0.2	3.1	3.6	5.9	6.2	6.8	6.1	5.9	25.2	26.8	15.3	1.9	77.3	41.2	47.2	52.8
23413	NASSAWADOX	57.2	56.6	40.6	41.3	0.2	0.2	1.5	1.6	5.6	5.6	5.5	5.5	5.3	19.6	27.1	20.8	5.2	79.8	47.1	46.6	53.4
23415	NEW CHURCH	59.3	57.0	37.0	38.5	0.3	0.3	3.3	4.2	7.4	8.3	9.5	6.2	5.7	29.4	21.9	10.6	1.0	70.8	34.3	50.6	49.4
23416	OAK HALL	54.3	51.6	42.8	44.7	0.0	0.2	2.6	3.3	5.4	5.8	7.1	5.9	5.9	26.7	26.7	14.6	1.7	77.8	40.7	48.4	51.6
23417	ONANCOCK	73.6	71.5	24.3	25.9	0.3	0.3	1.8	2.3	4.8	5.2	6.1	5.8	5.0	20.4	28.8	20.2	3.8	80.4	46.8	46.2	53.8
23418	ONLEY	61.2	58.6	35.1	37.0	0.3	0.3	3.5	4.1	5.4	5.6	6.5	6.3	5.3	23.4	29.0	16.0	2.7	78.7	43.4	47.2	52.8
23420	PAINTER	51.3	48.5	43.3	45.0	0.1	0.1	6.0	7.3	5.7	6.1	6.8	6.6	6.0	24.6	27.2	15.4	1.7	77.7	41.1	48.1	51.9
23421	PARKSLEY	55.9	53.5	36.8	37.7	0.3	0.4	10.6	12.9	6.3	6.4	7.2	6.9	6.5	25.1	24.1	14.6	2.9	75.8	38.5	48.1	51.9
23426	SANFORD	82.9	81.4	14.8	15.9	0.0	0.0	1.2	1.5	3.9	4.4	6.4	4.9	5.3	23.6	31.9	17.1	2.5	82.2	45.7	48.5	51.5
23430	SMITHFIELD	65.2	63.5	32.8	34.2	0.4	0.5	0.8	1.0	6.3	6.9	7.2	6.1	4.8	26.7	28.9	11.5	1.6	75.6	40.7	48.8	51.2
23432	SUFFOLK	73.8	71.1	23.9	26.3	1.2	1.4	0.3	0.3	4.4	5.3	6.6	6.2	4.1	22.7	34.5	14.6	1.6	79.8	45.4	49.5	50.5
23433	SUFFOLK	73.8	71.2	23.9	26.2	1.1	1.3	0.2	0.4	4.4	5.3	6.7	6.2	4.1	22.7	34.4	14.6	1.6	79.7	45.3	49.5	50.5
23434	SUFFOLK	47.9	46.8	50.0	50.8	0.5	0.6	1.1	1.3	7.3	7.4	7.9	7.1	6.1	28.4	23.6	10.8	1.5	73.0	36.4	47.2	52.8
23435	SUFFOLK	59.2	55.6	36.3	39.3	1.7	1.9	2.0	2.2	8.8	8.5	7.9	6.5	5.2	32.6	22.3	7.3	1.0	70.7	34.9	48.8	51.2
23436	SUFFOLK	73.8	71.2	23.9	26.2	1.3	1.3	0.3	0.4	4.4	5.3	6.7	6.2	4.1	22.6	34.3	14.7	1.7	79.7	45.4	49.8	50.2
23437	SUFFOLK	71.0	68.4	27.3	29.8	0.2	0.2	0.9	1.0	5.4	5.8	6.9	6.5	4.9	26.6	29.2	13.1	1.6	77.9	41.8	48.3	51.7
23438	SUFFOLK	63.8	60.7	34.6	37.6	0.2	0.2	0.8	0.9	4.9	5.6	7.0	5.8	5.0	25.0	32.4	13.0	1.3	78.9	43.0	50.1	49.9
23440	TANGIER	99.1	99.0	0.9	1.0	0.0	0.0	0.0	0.0	5.2	5.5	5.5	5.6	4.5	26.4	28.1	18.1	1.3	80.5	43.6	52.2	47.8
23442	TEMPERANCEVILLE	59.8	57.3	34.8	36.1	0.1	0.2	5.4	6.7	5.9	6.0	7.0	6.2	6.6	27.2	26.2	13.4	1.6	77.0	39.2	48.5	51.5
23451	VIRGINIA BEACH	84.7	83.1	10.1	10.7	1.6	1.9	3.1	3.9	5.9	5.4	5.0	5.4	8.4	32.6	23.0	11.3	3.1	81.0	36.6	50.2	49.8
23452	VIRGINIA BEACH	74.0	71.8	17.8	18.6	3.4	4.0	4.3	5.2	7.0	6.9	7.7	7.3	7.3	31.1	22.5	9.4	0.8	73.9	34.3	48.8	51.2
23453	VIRGINIA BEACH	59.0	56.7	26.3	26.7	8.5	9.5	5.5	6.5	8.7	8.5	8.5	7.8	8.4	35.6	18.5	3.8	0.2	69.4	29.6	49.2	50.8
23454	VIRGINIA BEACH	80.1	78.5	13.1	13.6	2.4	2.7	4.7	5.7	7.4	7.2	7.9	7.5	8.3	31.9	21.3	7.4	1.1	73.0	32.8	49.2	50.8
23455	VIRGINIA BEACH	77.7	75.7	14.1	14.8	4.1	4.7	3.6	4.3	6.4	6.4	6.6	5.9	6.4	30.5	23.7	12.7	1.4	76.9	37.3	48.9	51.1
23456	VIRGINIA BEACH	71.9	70.2	16.2	16.4	7.7	8.6	4.0	4.8	8.2	8.4	8.8	7.7	6.1	34.2	22.1	4.2	0.3	69.8	33.6	50.2	49.8
23457	VIRGINIA BEACH	90.0	89.0	7.9	8.5	0.2	0.3	0.8	1.0	4.8	5.6	6.8	7.3	4.7	27.2	30.6	11.6	1.4	78.3	41.9	49.5	50.5
23459	VIRGINIA BEACH	44.1	41.6	42.9	43.4	1.7	1.9	13.1	15.2	11.5	8.7	4.5	7.7	33.3	32.4	1.6	0.3	0.0	73.9	22.7	59.0	41.1
23460	VIRGINIA BEACH	67.6	64.7	20.1	20.9	2.4	2.7	9.9	11.8	2.7	3.5	2.1	22.4	41.2	26.6	1.6	0.0	0.0	90.9	22.4	80.1	19.9
23461	VIRGINIA BEACH	66.6	63.8	21.5	22.4	2.4	2.8	8.2	9.8	13.3	12.8	8.4	11.4	13.1	35.3	4.7	1.0	0.0	62.3	21.6	57.2	42.8
23462	VIRGINIA BEACH	59.9	57.0	31.0	32.4	4.0	4.6	4.5	5.3	8.0	7.2	7.7	7.4	8.7	33.6	19.1	7.6	0.6	72.6	31.4	48.7	51.3
23463	VIRGINIA BEACH	69.2	70.8	19.2	16.7	3.9	4.2	7.7	8.3	16.7	8.3	8.3	0.0	16.7	45.8	4.2	0.0	0.0	66.7	25.0	54.2	45.8
23464	VIRGINIA BEACH	65.1	62.2	21.3	22.1	9.2	10.6	3.6	4.4	6.4	7.0	8.4	8.2	7.0	29.8	25.5	7.1	0.7	73.0	35.0	48.7	51.3
23487	WINDSOR	75.8	73.8	22.4	24.0	0.3	0.3	1.1	1.3	5.4	6.0	7.6	7.0	5.8	28.1	28.2	10.8	1.1	76.7	39.5	49.4	50.6
23502	NORFOLK	45.2	42.8	47.8	49.2	3.2	3.6	3.2	3.8	6.8	6.4	6.5	7.5	8.2	28.5	21.8	12.1	2.1	76.5	35.0	48.2	51.8
23503	NORFOLK	71.8	68.9	19.1	20.4	2.8	3.3	5.2	6.2	7.6	6.4	6.6	6.4	10.1	32.6	20.9	8.4	1.1	75.9	32.5	50.9	49.1
23504	NORFOLK	4.8	4.5	93.2	93.3	0.3	0.3	1.2	1.3	8.8	8.8	9.4	11.8	9.5	22.1	17.9	9.6	2.0	68.0	26.5	42.3	57.7
23505	NORFOLK	58.2	55.4	31.6	33.0	4.0	4.5	5.2	6.2	7.8	6.2	5.3	7.0	15.6	29.5	16.9	9.9	1.9	77.6	29.1	51.0	49.0
23507	NORFOLK	87.3	85.3	7.0	7.8	3.1	3.8	2.2	2.8	3.9	3.1	3.1	4.9	9.1	39.1	25.5	9.2	2.2	87.0	35.9	49.3	50.7
23508	NORFOLK	51.5	49.3	41.6	43.0	3.7	4.2	2.0	2.4	5.3	5.8	5.9	13.3	16.1	26.1	18.1	8.2	1.3	79.6	27.4	49.7	50.3
23509	NORFOLK	43.9	41.5	51.9	53.7	1.2	1.4	2.2	2.6	6.6	6.6	7.5	7.1	6.7	26.7	24.3	12.6	2.0	74.9	37.8	47.6	52.4
23510	NORFOLK	31.6	31.8	65.7	65.0	1.2	1.5	1.4	1.6	7.3	6.2	5.1	5.7	10.1	37.8	18.6	8.2	1.2	79.2	32.8	54.7	45.3
23511	NORFOLK	54.2	50.5	33.8	35.6	2.9	3.2	10.0	11.8	3.8	3.9	2.7	14.6	48.2	25.3	1.5	0.1	0.0	88.8	22.6	80.5	19.6
23513	NORFOLK	34.8	32.2	57.5	59.1	3.8	4.2	2.7	3.1	7.6	7.2	8.1	7.8	8.7	29.0	21.1	9.2	1.2	72.4	32.1	47.8	52.2
23517	NORFOLK	61.2	59.9	33.2	33.5	2.3	2.7	2.8	3.3	3.8	3.7	4.3	5.4	9.5	38.4	23.0	10.3	1.7	85.3	35.0	50.5	49.6
23518	NORFOLK	66.2	63.2	23.9	25.2	4.4	5.2	4.1	5.0	7.8	6.6	6.7	6.3	8.5	29.3	21.8	11.8	1.2	75.3	34.6	49.7	50.3
23521	NORFOLK	63.3	60.6	25.6	26.5	2.7	3.1	8.3	10.0	8.8	9.3	6.6	14.3	23.8	32.9	3.8	0.5	0.1	72.6	22.3	65.7	34.3
23523	NORFOLK	1.7	1.5	96.7	96.8	0.1	0.1	1.0	1.1	7.9	9.5	10.8	9.2	6.9	22.5	20.0	11.6	1.7	65.9	30.7	42.2	57.8
23601	NEWPORT NEWS	69.8	66.5	25.0	27.3	1.5	1.7	2.9	3.6	7.6	7.3	7.2	6.4	6.9	30.1	21.4	11.1	2.1	74.1	35.5	47.7	52.3
23602	NEWPORT NEWS	59.4	56.9	31.2	32.4	3.8	4.3	4.6	5.4	7.6	6.9	7.3	7.0	7.7	31.1	21.9	9.2	1.4	74.0	34.0	47.8	52.2
23603	NEWPORT NEWS	62.5	59.1	28.9	31.0	1.9	2.1	6.8	8.2	9.5	6.8	5.8	10.4	14.7	31.6	16.1	4.8	0.3	73.3	26.4	52.0	48.0
23604	FORT EUSTIS	54.2	50.7	29.9	30.9	2.3	2.6	15.0	17.6	12.2	9.3	5.3	13.0	25.8	32.8	1.5	0.1	0.0	71.5	22.0	62.5	37.5
23605	NEWPORT NEWS	46.0	43.6	49.4	51.2	1.1	1.2	2.3	2.6	7.2	6.5	7.1	7.1	9.1	30.7	21.4	10.0	1.0	75.1	33.4	48.4	51.6
23606	NEWPORT NEWS	75.0	71.9	19.2	21.2	2.0	2.3	3.3	4.1	6.7	6.1	6.1	8.0	9.9	28.5	21.0	12.1	1.8	77.6	34.0	47.7	52.3
23607	NEWPORT NEWS	10.3	10.0	86.8	86.8	0.3	0.3	1.4	1.6	7.7	7.5	8.7	8.3	7.4	25.4	22.3	11.2	1.5	71.0	34.0	47.3	52.7
23608	NEWPORT NEWS	52.3	49.1	37.5	39.3	3.8	4.2	5.9	7.0	8.8	7.9	8.1	8.0	9.5	32.0	19.8	5.6	0.4	70.4	29.8	48.8	51.2
23651	FORT MONROE	63.1	60.4	24.7	25.4	1.8	2.0	10.7	12.8	14.4	12.5	8.3	4.9	11.8	37.7	10.1	0.3	0.0	61.7	24.2	52.2	47.8
23661	HAMPTON	31.9	30.8	65.1	66.0	0.7	0.7	1.3	1.4	5.3	5.8	7.2	7.2	6.0	24.9	27.9	13.5	2.3	77.2	41.0	47.4	52.6
23662	POQUOSON	96.3	95.6	0.7	0.7	1.6	1.9	1.1	1.4	5.0	6.0	8.2	7.8	5.5	23.9	30.6	11.6	1.6	75.9	41.6	50.3	49.7
23663	HAMPTON	45.6	44.0	48.3	49.0	1.5	1.7	2.8	3.3	7.5	7.3	8.8	8.3	7.6	27.6	23.0	9.1	0.8	71.2	33.1	47.9	52.1
23664	HAMPTON	78.5	76.9	17.1	17.9	1.3	1.5	2.2	2.7	5.6	6.0	7.2	6.3	5.1	28.3	28.5	12.0	1.1	77.3	40.4	50.1	49.9
23665	HAMPTON	67.6	65.1	24.9	26.1	2.3	2.6	5.2	6.3	5.8	5.2	4.9	5.2	17.3	55.7	5.7	0.1	0.0	81.7	29.2	66.4	33.6
23666	HAMPTON	49.4	46.9	43.9	45.4	2.7	3.1	3.0	3.6	6.9	6.4	6.6	6.5	8.7	31.3	22.0	10.3	1.5	76.2	34.6	47.9	52.1
23668	HAMPTON	6.2	5.8	90.3	90.2	0.2	0.4	2.7	2.9	0.7	0.4	0.2	48.7	34.4	6.0	6.0	3.1	0.4	98.0	20.0	42.4	57.6
23669	HAMPTON	46.7	44.7	47.8	49.1	1.8	2.0	2.7	3.2	6.4	6.4	7.1	10.4	9.7	25.8	23.1	10.2	0.9	75.9	33.4	47.2	52.8
23690	YORKTOWN	43.2	40.7	50.6	52.3	1.0	1.1	4.2	4.9	8.2	7.7	8.1	9.2	13.3	25.3	18.5	8.8	1.0	71.9	27.6	51.6	48.4
23692	YORKTOWN	89.7	88.3	5.7	6.3	2.5	2.9	1.9	2.4	5.0	5.6	7.0	6.6	5.3	24.7	31.6	12.9	1.3	78.1	42.7	48.7	51.3
23693	YORKTOWN	79.9	77.8	10.9	11.6	5.6	6.4	2.9	3.6	6.3	7.1	9.0	8.7	6.5	28.9	27.8	5.3	0.4	71.9	36.3	49.2	50.8
	VIRGINIA	72.3	70.7	19.6	19.9	3.7	4.3	4.7	5.7	6.5	6.6	6.9	6.9	7.0	29.7	24.9	10.1	1.4	76.2	36.6	49.1	50.9
	UNITED STATES	75.1	73.6	12.3	12.5	3.8	4.2	12.5	14.1	6.9	6.7	7.2	7.0	7.3	28.6	23.8	10.8	1.7	75.1	36.0	49.1	50.9

INCOME

ZIP CODE #	POST OFFICE NAME	2004 Per Capita Income	2004 HH Income Base	2004 HOUSEHOLD INCOME DISTRIBUTION (%) Less than $25,000	$25,000 to $49,999	$50,000 to $99,999	$100,000 to $149,999	$150,000 or More	MEDIAN HOUSEHOLD INCOME 2004	2009	2004 National Centile	2004 State Centile	2004 Home Value Base	2004 HOME VALUE DISTRIBUTION (%) Less than $50,000	$50,000 to $89,999	$90,000 to $174,999	$175,000 to $399,999	$400,000 or More	2004 Median Home Value
23237	RICHMOND	24182	8138	16.6	28.2	41.2	11.3	2.8	54018	63454	78	73	5908	5.4	17.4	62.9	14.2	0.1	115376
23294	RICHMOND	29563	8419	15.7	35.0	36.6	10.5	2.2	49407	58210	71	64	2939	0.5	3.7	81.6	13.6	0.7	137708
23298	RICHMOND	15534	0	0.0	0.0	0.0	0.0	0.0	0	0	0	0	0	0.0	0.0	0.0	0.0	0.0	0
23301	ACCOMAC	20001	795	32.0	35.5	22.6	6.2	3.8	35503	41282	30	24	569	17.8	17.1	41.3	18.8	5.1	111089
23302	ASSAWOMAN	12286	40	32.5	45.0	20.0	2.5	0.0	33835	40541	24	18	31	32.3	19.4	45.2	3.2	0.0	85000
23306	BELLE HAVEN	21237	454	36.8	29.3	24.9	6.8	2.2	38192	45373	40	33	349	17.2	20.9	31.5	21.8	8.6	120833
23307	BIRDSNEST	18146	384	44.0	26.8	20.3	5.0	3.9	28542	34455	10	7	295	17.3	17.3	38.6	17.0	9.8	115625
23308	BLOXOM	15349	988	46.4	31.3	18.0	3.3	1.0	27010	30862	7	5	752	35.2	27.4	23.8	12.1	1.5	66000
23310	CAPE CHARLES	20367	2464	40.2	31.5	19.8	4.1	4.4	31892	38169	18	13	1725	19.9	21.5	33.8	19.7	5.1	105143
23314	CARROLLTON	29793	1928	15.6	17.1	43.8	15.8	7.8	66747	78586	90	84	1670	7.1	3.1	26.3	55.8	7.8	204970
23315	CARRSVILLE	22666	646	24.2	29.6	37.5	7.3	1.6	45794	54237	63	56	520	15.0	15.6	39.6	27.1	2.7	119375
23320	CHESAPEAKE	28035	18580	13.7	28.2	40.3	13.0	4.9	57420	66793	82	77	12747	3.5	7.4	49.8	37.4	1.9	152110
23321	CHESAPEAKE	27902	11207	11.9	25.0	40.6	16.3	6.3	63303	74036	87	82	8496	1.7	5.8	46.0	44.3	2.3	167998
23322	CHESAPEAKE	27503	18626	7.0	18.2	46.2	21.1	7.4	74840	84627	93	88	16253	0.7	2.0	28.2	66.1	3.0	200634
23323	CHESAPEAKE	21884	11356	16.0	26.4	42.8	11.3	3.6	56754	65815	81	76	9249	5.6	7.0	57.5	29.4	0.5	139894
23324	CHESAPEAKE	16617	8646	39.8	32.9	21.3	4.1	1.9	32243	38385	18	14	4345	12.7	27.8	56.9	2.1	0.6	96373
23325	CHESAPEAKE	23776	6473	20.6	29.2	37.9	9.6	2.6	50085	60103	72	66	4277	0.6	13.1	63.7	22.1	0.5	124640
23336	CHINCOTEAGUE ISLAND	25367	2154	34.2	34.7	19.5	9.0	2.6	34029	41233	24	19	1748	7.5	13.8	44.1	30.2	4.4	142606
23337	WALLOPS ISLAND	15854	184	33.2	42.4	21.2	3.3	0.0	33633	37425	23	17	144	27.8	16.7	44.4	9.7	1.4	95333
23350	EXMORE	21678	1658	38.1	29.7	22.5	4.6	5.1	34452	41582	26	20	1199	17.0	22.4	38.0	17.9	4.8	106525
23354	FRANKTOWN	26538	140	33.6	26.4	25.7	7.1	7.1	40000	51171	46	39	108	18.5	19.4	26.9	21.3	13.9	114286
23356	GREENBACKVILLE	17990	333	37.2	38.4	20.7	3.6	0.0	31314	34657	16	12	257	26.1	17.1	42.4	12.5	2.0	94487
23357	GREENBUSH	15544	241	39.8	29.5	24.1	5.0	1.7	30558	35683	14	11	167	22.8	32.9	29.3	14.4	0.6	83214
23359	HALLWOOD	15180	320	43.4	32.2	18.1	5.6	0.6	28303	32486	9	7	243	41.2	29.2	21.0	7.0	1.7	59773
23395	HORNTOWN	12161	149	38.3	38.3	20.1	3.4	0.0	30876	33860	15	11	115	26.1	17.4	41.7	13.0	1.7	94167
23404	LOCUSTVILLE	17069	14	42.9	21.4	35.7	0.0	0.0	32500	37500	19	14	10	10.0	30.0	40.0	20.0	0.0	100000
23405	MACHIPONGO	21632	406	42.1	25.6	21.9	5.7	4.7	30000	37350	12	10	310	16.5	16.5	37.1	18.7	11.3	118229
23409	MEARS	15738	68	39.7	33.8	22.1	4.4	0.0	30000	34051	12	10	53	39.6	28.3	22.6	9.4	0.0	61250
23410	MELFA	20561	1254	35.5	30.9	25.5	5.4	2.6	36639	44261	34	28	949	19.2	23.7	37.4	17.1	2.6	99507
23413	NASSAWADOX	24064	344	34.9	25.0	26.2	7.6	6.4	38717	48167	42	35	257	14.0	14.4	36.6	23.4	11.7	120833
23415	NEW CHURCH	14112	2346	38.5	36.2	20.7	4.3	0.3	31467	35125	16	12	1792	31.4	15.4	41.4	10.3	1.6	92511
23416	OAK HALL	16007	337	28.5	47.2	21.7	2.7	0.0	35387	40392	29	24	267	30.7	15.7	46.1	7.1	0.4	96786
23417	ONANCOCK	28568	1806	30.0	28.2	28.2	7.4	6.3	43054	52289	56	49	1365	8.1	13.7	39.3	31.0	7.9	140543
23418	ONLEY	21449	386	35.2	28.5	26.2	6.2	3.9	37708	45430	38	32	270	7.8	18.5	45.6	26.7	1.5	124390
23420	PAINTER	19064	1339	38.5	28.8	25.0	5.3	2.4	35450	42190	29	24	1070	23.6	21.8	29.8	19.6	5.1	97424
23421	PARKSLEY	16926	1632	34.4	34.7	25.6	3.6	1.7	34903	40141	27	22	1192	30.0	20.5	34.7	13.7	1.2	89020
23426	SANFORD	18844	265	43.4	25.3	22.6	6.8	1.9	29839	35866	12	9	219	40.6	23.3	21.9	13.2	0.9	60750
23430	SMITHFIELD	25017	6274	22.4	24.1	35.6	13.6	4.3	53228	63533	77	71	5065	10.8	10.7	32.9	41.4	4.2	161973
23432	SUFFOLK	41809	585	15.4	19.0	30.8	20.0	14.9	72536	93373	92	87	517	6.4	10.3	25.0	47.6	10.8	205137
23433	SUFFOLK	45045	535	15.3	19.3	30.5	20.0	15.0	72294	92813	92	86	473	6.1	10.2	25.0	47.8	11.0	207090
23434	SUFFOLK	21377	17220	30.6	28.0	29.9	7.8	3.7	41066	49755	50	42	11753	10.4	15.9	49.8	22.0	2.0	126256
23435	SUFFOLK	25389	6687	13.0	25.3	42.2	14.9	4.6	59660	69528	84	79	5735	4.1	5.0	34.4	54.0	2.6	183567
23436	SUFFOLK	42313	319	15.4	19.1	30.4	20.1	15.1	72259	92293	92	86	282	6.7	10.3	25.2	46.8	11.0	203750
23437	SUFFOLK	23397	1708	20.0	27.3	40.8	8.5	3.3	51762	61766	75	69	1431	7.9	18.2	45.7	27.5	0.6	128757
23438	SUFFOLK	23156	616	25.7	31.0	33.0	8.1	2.3	42419	51066	54	46	508	8.1	15.2	46.1	29.5	1.2	129825
23440	TANGIER	34828	286	39.2	25.5	24.5	1.8	9.1	31721	39315	17	13	261	28.4	31.0	33.7	4.6	2.3	81833
23442	TEMPERANCEVILLE	16405	430	32.6	41.2	21.2	4.7	0.5	33800	38706	23	18	337	32.1	22.0	37.4	7.7	0.9	82500
23451	VIRGINIA BEACH	42110	19986	18.1	29.2	28.6	12.5	11.6	53115	64975	77	71	10186	2.7	4.6	23.9	47.3	21.5	237961
23452	VIRGINIA BEACH	26641	22586	14.5	32.4	36.0	10.6	6.6	52408	61935	76	70	14295	0.2	6.4	61.0	25.0	7.5	144699
23453	VIRGINIA BEACH	20269	12686	15.8	33.5	38.6	9.5	2.6	50570	58866	73	67	8127	1.2	16.2	57.9	24.0	0.6	137825
23454	VIRGINIA BEACH	30666	23029	13.6	30.3	35.1	12.2	8.8	55733	65819	80	75	14982	2.4	5.3	42.7	39.2	10.5	174372
23455	VIRGINIA BEACH	32508	18432	15.7	28.3	34.7	13.1	8.2	55816	67220	80	75	11518	1.5	2.7	44.0	45.1	6.7	179311
23456	VIRGINIA BEACH	27312	15630	5.7	17.2	50.6	18.8	7.7	73025	86058	92	87	13857	0.3	2.1	36.8	57.6	3.2	193005
23457	VIRGINIA BEACH	28599	1377	12.1	19.8	44.2	17.3	6.5	63801	75664	88	82	1186	6.8	3.2	25.6	56.7	7.8	213976
23459	VIRGINIA BEACH	13745	176	21.0	48.3	29.0	1.7	0.0	35967	41041	31	26	9	0.0	0.0	0.0	100.0	0.0	310000
23460	VIRGINIA BEACH	15350	58	3.5	58.6	37.9	0.0	0.0	43500	48900	57	50	44	63.6	9.1	20.5	0.0	6.8	36667
23461	VIRGINIA BEACH	4547	23	8.7	56.5	26.1	8.7	0.0	42851	52860	56	48	6	0.0	0.0	33.3	66.7	0.0	216667
23462	VIRGINIA BEACH	21542	22201	17.6	36.5	36.2	7.8	1.9	47126	54212	66	59	12521	5.7	12.0	68.3	13.7	0.3	122703
23463	VIRGINIA BEACH	6042	9	77.8	22.2	0.0	0.0	0.0	17182	17182	1	1	0	0.0	0.0	0.0	0.0	0.0	0
23464	VIRGINIA BEACH	24961	24895	10.3	25.8	44.3	15.0	4.6	61691	72391	86	80	19000	0.3	5.9	59.2	34.3	0.3	156598
23487	WINDSOR	23227	2355	20.0	31.5	36.5	9.6	2.4	48839	57396	70	62	1968	26.3	11.0	34.3	25.8	2.6	119796
23502	NORFOLK	21634	7854	24.1	34.3	31.3	6.6	3.7	44057	52043	59	51	4739	2.6	12.4	70.5	13.3	1.3	120098
23503	NORFOLK	21931	14127	27.6	37.4	27.0	6.0	2.1	38484	45467	41	34	6266	0.7	11.0	71.7	15.4	1.2	121449
23504	NORFOLK	13351	7977	59.5	21.9	14.0	2.3	2.3	18596	22203	1	1	2505	9.8	32.6	49.3	8.1	0.2	97189
23505	NORFOLK	26666	11697	32.6	32.4	23.5	6.3	5.2	35980	42527	31	26	4671	3.8	18.2	46.5	25.1	6.5	125461
23507	NORFOLK	51865	3597	21.1	23.3	27.4	12.0	16.2	56252	79075	81	76	1358	0.0	5.1	19.2	57.8	17.9	237662
23508	NORFOLK	27917	6517	33.9	25.2	21.1	10.7	9.0	39059	48674	43	37	3212	3.7	11.6	36.1	43.4	5.2	171486
23509	NORFOLK	22324	5045	29.8	32.3	25.6	8.3	4.0	40038	47295	46	39	3267	1.1	24.7	58.3	11.0	4.9	108032
23510	NORFOLK	27321	2204	39.7	23.7	21.3	6.5	8.7	34706	43979	26	21	461	1.1	0.9	22.3	55.3	20.4	263679
23511	NORFOLK	13929	700	16.1	54.3	22.7	5.3	1.6	40114	46211	46	39	22	0.0	0.0	100.0	0.0	0.0	125000
23513	NORFOLK	17185	11586	34.1	35.2	25.4	3.9	1.5	35093	40514	28	23	6000	3.8	31.3	62.7	2.3	0.0	99879
23517	NORFOLK	30485	2212	31.4	32.1	22.6	7.7	6.2	38847	48855	42	36	704	2.8	19.7	31.4	43.5	2.6	165411
23518	NORFOLK	22007	11888	25.6	34.1	30.0	7.1	3.2	41523	49365	51	43	6875	5.3	6.0	70.1	17.0	1.6	124323
23521	NORFOLK	14939	571	15.2	45.7	29.1	6.7	3.3	43388	50862	57	50	69	0.0	1.5	71.0	23.2	4.4	147656
23523	NORFOLK	11044	2761	58.7	24.7	13.4	2.4	0.8	20108	23277	2	2	1052	13.8	39.1	43.5	3.1	0.5	87778
23601	NEWPORT NEWS	22661	10681	26.8	33.6	31.3	6.0	2.5	41569	48598	52	43	6022	0.5	5.3	82.4	11.2	0.6	123330
23602	NEWPORT NEWS	24397	17314	19.5	31.0	35.9	10.3	3.3	49557	58011	71	64	9943	3.8	7.0	62.9	25.4	0.9	139250
23603	NEWPORT NEWS	19210	1359	22.3	38.4	33.7	4.1	1.5	41822	47844	52	44	508	1.8	12.0	60.6	24.6	1.0	120253
23604	FORT EUSTIS	13549	785	22.6	51.2	22.8	2.6	0.9	36370	41611	33	28	47	34.0	42.6	23.4	0.0	0.0	73125
23605	NEWPORT NEWS	18662	6184	34.2	34.8	26.5	3.8	0.7	34939	40451	27	22	2980	8.9	30.9	56.9	3.4	0.0	96335
23606	NEWPORT NEWS	28453	11053	21.8	33.3	29.9	9.5	5.6	45828	52850	63	56	5796	7.5	6.2	46.3	35.8	4.2	157542
23607	NEWPORT NEWS	15008	9614	53.9	24.5	16.2	3.3	2.1	22248	26508	3	3	3777	13.0	43.0	38.5	5.2	0.3	86109
23608	NEWPORT NEWS	19882	15916	20.4	33.1	36.8	8.1	1.6	47121	53721	66	59	8765	5.5	11.2	65.8	17.1	0.4	131371
23651	FORT MONROE	19678	347	18.2	36.0	28.2	12.1	5.5	46428	55106	65	57	7	0.0	0.0	100.0	0.0	0.0	103125
23661	HAMPTON	23319	5598	29.0	30.7	30.0	6.8	3.5	41638	49726	52	43	4018	2.7	31.4	55.7	9.5	0.7	104247
23662	POQUOSON	31927	4328	10.6	19.5	41.5	18.5	10.0	71310	83734	92	86	3619	5.1	2.2	31.1	54.5	7.2	197378
23663	HAMPTON	19062	5134	30.4	30.7	32.4	4.2	2.4	39687	47475	45	38	3233	2.4	35.4	58.4	3.1	0.7	97933
23664	HAMPTON	29684	4224	22.0	25.2	33.0	13.5	6.4	53547	65076	78	72	2999	3.7	10.9	57.0	24.1	4.3	129870
23665	HAMPTON	15183	1347	10.0	53.4	26.1	9.4	1.0	42470	49025	55	46	32	0.0	12.5	87.5	0.0	0.0	118750
23666	HAMPTON	24179	20951	19.5	32.5	36.9	8.3	2.8	48381	55785	69	61	11896	3.2	10.0	66.0	20.5	0.4	127843
23668	HAMPTON	12630	4	100.0	0.0	0.0	0.0	0.0	10000	10000	0	1	0	0.0	0.0	0.0	0.0	0.0	0
23669	HAMPTON	22800	16517	27.4	28.2	31.4	9.1	3.9	44311	52079	59	52	9623	1.9	16.2	60.6	19.9	1.5	125254
23690	YORKTOWN	18484	1020	38.7	32.7	21.3	5.3	2.1	31856	37652	17	13	470	11.5	19.8	38.9	27.2	2.6	115625
23692	YORKTOWN	33886	7102	9.0	22.0	38.7	21.8	8.7	73087	85455	92	87	5926	2.6	2.0	34.3	55.6	5.6	192052
23693	YORKTOWN	30817	8030	6.6	19.7	40.1	23.6	10.1	78936	93678	95	90	6490	2.0	0.9	30.9	62.4	3.8	216244
	VIRGINIA	30454		19.8	25.2	32.5	13.6	8.9	55216	67801				6.8	10.4	35.8	36.5	10.5	166226
	UNITED STATES	25866		24.7	27.1	30.8	10.9	6.5	48124	56710				10.9	15.0	33.7	30.1	10.4	145905

ZIP CODE		FINANCIAL SERVICES				THE HOME						ENTERTAINMENT						PERSONAL			
						Home Improvements		Furnishings													
#	POST OFFICE NAME	Auto Loan	Home Loan	Invest-ments	Retire-ment Plans	Home Repair	Lawn & Garden	Comput-ers & Hard-ware	Major Appli-ances	TV, Radio, Sound Equip-ment	Furni-ture	Dine out/ Carry out	Sports Equip-ment	Fees & Tickets	Toys & Games	Travel	Cable TV	Apparel & Services	Auto Repairs	Health Insur-ance	Pets & Supplies
23237	RICHMOND	90	95	95	94	93	96	92	92	90	92	112	107	93	114	91	88	110	91	87	103
23294	RICHMOND	81	78	102	84	75	80	86	80	84	87	107	97	85	105	82	81	105	85	74	89
23298	RICHMOND	0	0	0	0	0	0	0	0	0	0	0	0	0	0	0	0	0	0	0	0
23301	ACCOMAC	99	66	31	58	75	87	65	80	78	66	91	96	55	86	66	84	83	80	99	113
23302	ASSAWOMAN	71	47	21	41	54	62	46	57	55	47	65	68	39	61	46	59	59	57	70	81
23306	BELLE HAVEN	90	61	30	55	70	80	60	74	71	60	83	89	51	80	61	75	75	74	90	105
23307	BIRDSNEST	77	55	32	51	61	72	58	67	67	56	78	77	51	74	58	71	71	67	81	86
23308	BLOXOM	75	51	23	44	57	66	49	61	59	50	69	73	41	65	50	63	63	60	75	87
23310	CAPE CHARLES	82	60	36	56	66	78	64	73	73	62	86	83	56	81	64	77	78	72	88	91
23314	CARROLLTON	109	120	115	118	121	123	108	112	105	108	131	132	112	137	111	104	128	108	108	132
23315	CARRSVILLE	102	73	40	65	82	92	70	85	82	71	97	101	62	93	71	87	89	84	102	118
23320	CHESAPEAKE	102	108	109	112	103	104	103	102	97	106	124	119	104	122	100	92	121	101	90	112
23321	CHESAPEAKE	104	117	125	118	114	117	110	109	105	111	133	127	114	136	111	103	131	108	101	121
23322	CHESAPEAKE	118	136	138	140	131	129	124	123	115	127	146	144	129	149	123	109	144	120	108	135
23323	CHESAPEAKE	91	97	96	97	94	97	92	92	89	93	111	106	93	111	91	86	109	91	86	103
23324	CHESAPEAKE	57	54	62	52	53	60	58	57	61	58	76	65	58	75	58	62	74	59	60	64
23325	CHESAPEAKE	81	87	94	84	86	93	86	85	86	85	107	97	89	111	87	87	105	84	85	94
23336	CHINCOTEAGUE ISLAND	89	70	47	63	78	88	66	79	74	65	88	93	59	87	70	79	82	78	94	108
23337	WALLOPS ISLAND	71	48	22	41	54	62	46	58	56	47	65	69	39	62	47	60	59	57	71	82
23350	EXMORE	82	62	41	59	68	81	66	74	74	63	88	84	59	84	67	79	80	74	89	92
23354	FRANKTOWN	99	75	49	72	82	98	83	91	93	78	109	102	74	103	82	98	99	91	109	110
23356	GREENBACKVILLE	69	46	21	40	52	60	44	56	54	45	63	66	38	60	45	58	57	55	69	79
23357	GREENBUSH	76	51	24	45	58	67	50	62	60	51	71	74	43	67	51	65	64	61	76	87
23359	HALLWOOD	77	51	23	44	58	67	50	62	60	51	70	74	42	66	50	65	64	61	77	88
23395	HORNTOWN	69	46	21	40	52	60	45	56	54	45	63	67	38	60	45	58	57	55	69	79
23404	LOCUSTVILLE	57	43	28	41	47	56	48	52	53	45	63	59	42	59	47	56	57	52	63	63
23405	MACHIPONGO	83	60	36	56	67	79	64	73	73	62	86	84	56	81	64	78	79	73	88	93
23409	MEARS	74	49	22	43	56	64	48	60	58	49	68	71	41	64	48	62	61	59	73	85
23410	MELFA	80	60	39	58	66	77	64	72	72	62	85	82	58	81	64	75	78	71	84	89
23413	NASSAWADOX	102	75	48	71	83	99	82	91	92	78	109	103	72	103	81	98	99	91	110	113
23415	NEW CHURCH	71	48	22	41	54	62	46	58	56	47	65	69	39	62	47	60	59	57	71	82
23416	OAK HALL	74	49	22	42	56	64	48	59	57	48	67	71	40	64	48	62	61	59	73	84
23417	ONANCOCK	98	84	68	80	89	104	88	95	96	85	114	106	83	111	89	100	107	94	108	111
23418	ONLEY	83	63	42	60	69	82	69	76	77	66	91	85	62	86	69	82	83	76	91	92
23420	PAINTER	88	60	29	53	68	78	59	73	70	59	82	87	50	78	60	75	75	72	89	102
23421	PARKSLEY	77	54	28	48	60	70	54	65	64	54	75	76	47	71	55	68	68	64	79	88
23426	SANFORD	79	53	24	46	60	69	51	64	62	52	72	76	43	68	52	66	66	63	79	91
23430	SMITHFIELD	102	91	75	86	95	103	86	95	92	87	111	111	84	111	88	94	106	93	102	119
23432	SUFFOLK	140	169	191	168	169	177	155	156	147	156	185	176	165	187	162	146	183	152	149	170
23433	SUFFOLK	140	170	191	168	169	177	155	156	147	156	185	177	165	188	162	146	183	152	149	170
23434	SUFFOLK	82	77	74	73	77	84	77	80	81	78	99	91	76	97	77	82	95	80	83	93
23435	SUFFOLK	102	110	107	111	109	111	102	104	98	103	123	121	105	124	103	96	120	101	98	117
23436	SUFFOLK	140	170	191	168	169	177	156	156	147	156	185	177	165	188	162	147	183	152	149	170
23437	SUFFOLK	87	90	84	86	91	96	83	87	84	83	103	102	85	108	85	84	101	85	88	104
23438	SUFFOLK	94	84	64	80	89	95	78	86	82	78	100	102	76	102	80	84	95	84	93	111
23440	TANGIER	160	107	48	92	121	140	103	129	125	105	146	154	88	138	105	134	133	128	159	183
23442	TEMPERANCEVILLE	80	54	24	46	61	70	52	65	63	53	73	77	44	69	53	67	67	64	80	92
23451	VIRGINIA BEACH	121	116	137	121	114	123	127	121	125	126	157	145	125	152	123	121	153	127	115	134
23452	VIRGINIA BEACH	96	102	114	105	99	103	102	99	98	103	124	117	104	124	100	94	122	101	91	110
23453	VIRGINIA BEACH	85	86	88	89	82	83	87	84	83	88	105	101	86	103	83	78	103	86	75	93
23454	VIRGINIA BEACH	115	116	123	122	112	116	119	115	114	119	144	137	118	140	114	108	141	117	104	127
23455	VIRGINIA BEACH	105	110	123	112	108	115	111	109	108	111	136	127	113	134	110	105	133	110	103	120
23456	VIRGINIA BEACH	123	136	131	141	131	128	124	123	115	128	145	145	127	146	121	108	143	120	107	137
23457	VIRGINIA BEACH	105	120	122	118	120	121	109	111	105	109	131	130	115	138	112	103	129	107	105	126
23459	VIRGINIA BEACH	69	44	43	51	41	48	65	57	66	61	83	75	56	74	54	61	79	67	52	64
23460	VIRGINIA BEACH	75	48	46	55	44	52	71	61	72	66	90	82	61	81	59	66	86	72	57	70
23461	VIRGINIA BEACH	84	54	51	61	49	58	80	69	81	74	101	92	68	91	66	74	97	81	64	78
23462	VIRGINIA BEACH	80	76	82	79	74	78	81	78	79	81	100	93	79	96	77	76	97	81	73	87
23463	VIRGINIA BEACH	23	14	18	16	14	17	27	20	26	23	33	27	22	29	21	23	31	24	18	23
23464	VIRGINIA BEACH	98	109	116	112	106	108	105	103	99	105	125	121	107	126	103	95	123	102	92	113
23487	WINDSOR	95	86	66	82	88	93	81	88	83	82	102	103	77	100	81	84	98	87	91	108
23502	NORFOLK	77	75	82	74	74	82	79	77	81	78	101	89	80	101	78	81	98	79	78	87
23503	NORFOLK	68	63	72	66	61	67	72	68	72	70	90	82	70	88	68	68	87	72	64	75
23504	NORFOLK	48	41	50	38	40	47	47	46	52	48	64	51	46	61	46	54	62	48	50	53
23505	NORFOLK	83	71	83	76	69	77	87	80	87	84	109	99	82	105	81	83	106	87	76	89
23507	NORFOLK	123	121	190	134	117	127	138	125	137	137	173	154	140	178	134	133	171	133	116	139
23508	NORFOLK	95	92	115	92	89	99	106	97	106	102	132	117	103	129	101	103	129	103	94	108
23509	NORFOLK	74	77	89	75	76	84	78	77	80	78	100	87	81	101	79	81	98	77	78	85
23510	NORFOLK	73	64	103	67	61	70	77	70	82	78	103	84	77	103	74	83	101	76	71	80
23511	NORFOLK	79	50	48	58	46	55	75	65	76	70	95	86	64	85	62	70	91	77	60	74
23513	NORFOLK	60	58	67	58	57	63	62	60	64	62	80	70	63	79	61	63	78	62	60	68
23517	NORFOLK	77	67	92	71	65	74	82	76	84	80	105	91	79	101	78	82	102	82	75	85
23518	NORFOLK	72	71	80	72	70	76	77	74	77	75	96	87	77	96	75	76	94	76	72	81
23521	NORFOLK	89	60	59	68	56	65	85	75	86	80	107	98	74	97	72	79	103	87	69	84
23523	NORFOLK	44	35	40	31	34	42	40	41	46	41	56	45	39	51	39	49	54	43	47	48
23601	NEWPORT NEWS	74	73	81	73	73	78	77	75	77	76	96	88	76	95	75	76	93	77	74	84
23602	NEWPORT NEWS	84	86	94	89	84	87	87	85	84	88	107	100	88	105	85	81	105	86	78	94
23603	NEWPORT NEWS	71	66	65	69	63	65	72	68	69	71	87	84	68	84	66	64	85	72	61	75
23604	FORT EUSTIS	70	44	42	51	40	48	66	57	67	61	84	76	56	75	54	61	80	67	53	65
23605	NEWPORT NEWS	60	56	59	57	55	60	62	59	62	60	77	71	60	77	59	60	75	62	58	66
23606	NEWPORT NEWS	87	88	103	92	86	91	93	89	90	92	114	106	93	113	91	87	112	92	83	98
23607	NEWPORT NEWS	50	44	53	41	43	51	49	49	54	50	67	54	49	63	48	56	64	51	53	55
23608	NEWPORT NEWS	78	76	78	79	73	76	79	76	76	79	96	91	77	93	75	72	93	78	69	85
23651	FORT MONROE	102	65	62	74	59	70	97	83	98	90	123	111	83	110	80	90	117	98	77	95
23661	HAMPTON	77	78	86	74	77	86	78	78	81	79	101	86	81	100	79	83	98	78	82	88
23662	POQUOSON	116	134	142	134	132	135	124	125	118	125	148	144	129	150	126	115	146	122	116	137
23663	HAMPTON	67	69	79	68	68	74	71	69	73	71	91	80	74	93	71	73	89	70	70	77
23664	HAMPTON	91	101	109	100	100	104	98	97	96	97	120	113	101	124	99	95	118	96	93	107
23665	HAMPTON	66	42	40	48	38	46	63	54	64	58	79	72	54	71	52	58	76	64	50	61
23666	HAMPTON	82	82	87	85	80	84	84	82	81	84	103	96	84	101	81	78	100	83	76	90
23668	HAMPTON	12	8	10	9	7	9	15	11	14	12	18	15	12	16	12	12	17	13	10	12
23669	HAMPTON	77	78	89	77	77	84	81	79	82	81	103	91	83	102	81	83	101	81	79	88
23690	YORKTOWN	71	56	57	53	56	67	65	66	72	64	87	75	61	83	63	75	83	68	73	77
23692	YORKTOWN	117	133	137	133	132	136	123	124	117	123	147	142	128	149	125	115	144	121	117	137
23693	YORKTOWN	124	140	143	145	134	133	130	127	120	133	153	150	134	154	127	114	151	125	111	140
	VIRGINIA	112	109	113	109	109	117	108	110	109	109	136	129	108	135	108	109	132	110	109	128
	UNITED STATES	100	100	100	100	100	100	100	100	100	100	100	100	100	100	100	100	100	100	100	100

VIRGINIA

POPULATION CHANGE

A 23696-24011

#	POST OFFICE NAME	COUNTY FIPS CODE	POPULATION			2000-2004 ANNUAL RATE		HOUSEHOLDS					FAMILIES		
			2000	2004	2009	% Rate	State Centile	2000	2004	2009	% Annual Rate 2000-2004	2004 Average HH Size	2000	2004	% Annual Rate 2000-2004
23696	SEAFORD	199	3432	3614	3954	1.2	62	1287	1370	1520	1.5	2.58	1005	1059	1.2
23701	PORTSMOUTH	740	27122	26162	25414	-0.8	5	10335	10148	10014	-0.4	2.48	7184	6947	-0.8
23702	PORTSMOUTH	740	11665	11490	11275	-0.4	14	4500	4475	4443	-0.1	2.57	3050	2985	-0.5
23703	PORTSMOUTH	740	27625	27920	27702	0.3	33	9673	9938	10010	0.6	2.57	7022	7133	0.4
23704	PORTSMOUTH	740	19160	18449	17925	-0.9	4	7423	7254	7147	-0.5	2.41	4441	4231	-1.1
23707	PORTSMOUTH	740	14773	14643	14384	-0.2	18	6224	6250	6221	0.1	2.30	3773	3714	-0.4
23708	PORTSMOUTH	740	200	200	200	0.0	24	9	9	9	0.0	2.33	5	5	0.0
23709	PORTSMOUTH	740	20	20	20	0.0	24	6	6	6	0.0	3.33	6	6	0.0
23801	FORT LEE	149	7269	7008	6963	-0.9	4	1401	1347	1354	-0.9	3.22	1224	1170	-1.1
23803	PETERSBURG	041	39522	39531	40108	0.0	24	15303	15523	15962	0.3	2.44	10104	10130	0.1
23805	PETERSBURG	149	18087	18170	17959	0.1	28	7285	7392	7382	0.3	2.40	4859	4873	0.1
23806	PETERSBURG	041	1695	1688	1703	-0.1	21	11	11	12	0.0	2.55	6	6	0.0
23821	ALBERTA	025	1555	1609	1621	0.8	53	635	673	693	1.4	2.34	433	452	1.0
23824	BLACKSTONE	135	6877	6887	6966	0.0	25	2693	2731	2799	0.3	2.44	1808	1803	-0.1
23827	BOYKINS	175	1459	1465	1464	0.1	28	593	608	618	0.6	2.41	412	416	0.2
23828	BRANCHVILLE	175	534	544	547	0.4	40	210	218	223	0.9	2.50	145	149	0.6
23829	CAPRON	175	2531	2570	2593	0.4	38	471	497	515	1.3	2.41	332	346	1.0
23830	CARSON	053	1069	1193	1287	2.6	86	425	482	529	3.0	2.48	315	354	2.8
23831	CHESTER	041	25895	28895	32485	2.6	86	9595	10882	12416	3.0	2.65	7384	8237	2.6
23832	CHESTERFIELD	041	24265	28561	33073	3.9	95	8182	9878	11670	4.5	2.80	6435	7683	4.3
23833	CHURCH ROAD	053	1929	2072	2225	1.7	73	713	783	859	2.2	2.53	543	589	1.9
23834	COLONIAL HEIGHTS	041	24026	25405	26899	1.3	64	9599	10269	10989	1.6	2.45	6775	7184	1.4
23836	CHESTER	041	8264	9594	10976	3.6	93	3015	3543	4100	3.9	2.70	2348	2706	3.4
23837	COURTLAND	175	3886	3814	3793	-0.4	12	1538	1536	1554	0.0	2.35	1074	1058	-0.4
23838	CHESTERFIELD	041	9751	11428	13087	3.8	95	3372	4011	4657	4.2	2.84	2917	3443	4.0
23839	DENDRON	181	629	649	684	0.7	51	231	241	257	1.0	2.69	173	178	0.7
23840	DEWITT	053	1462	1542	1643	1.3	63	550	595	649	1.9	2.55	408	436	1.6
23841	DINWIDDIE	053	3499	3682	3917	1.2	62	1339	1446	1573	1.8	2.54	1027	1097	1.6
23842	DISPUTANTA	149	5264	5548	5608	1.2	63	1905	1975	2027	0.9	2.52	1501	1542	0.6
23843	DOLPHIN	025	573	562	549	-0.5	12	241	242	242	0.1	2.31	168	167	-0.1
23844	DREWRYVILLE	175	766	862	915	2.8	88	285	326	351	3.2	2.64	204	230	2.9
23845	EBONY	025	488	482	473	-0.3	16	217	220	220	0.3	2.19	146	145	-0.2
23846	ELBERON	181	844	878	928	0.9	56	292	308	330	1.3	2.85	219	228	1.0
23847	EMPORIA	081	16594	17430	18555	1.2	61	5328	5776	6357	1.9	2.52	3616	3863	1.6
23850	FORD	053	1229	1280	1354	1.0	56	473	504	545	1.6	2.54	336	353	1.2
23851	FRANKLIN	175	13306	13062	12936	-0.4	12	5313	5322	5374	0.0	2.40	3637	3589	-0.3
23856	FREEMAN	025	1275	1256	1230	-0.4	14	485	488	488	0.2	2.52	343	340	-0.2
23857	GASBURG	025	577	573	562	-0.2	19	256	261	262	0.5	2.19	180	181	0.1
23860	HOPEWELL	149	26459	26682	27060	0.2	32	10542	10782	11099	0.5	2.44	7286	7339	0.2
23866	IVOR	175	2151	2177	2206	0.3	34	826	852	878	0.7	2.56	617	627	0.4
23867	JARRATT	183	2135	2149	2177	0.2	29	886	928	984	1.1	1.81	604	623	0.7
23868	LAWRENCEVILLE	025	7981	7817	7679	-0.5	11	2044	2013	1996	-0.4	2.48	1388	1346	-0.7
23872	MC KENNEY	053	2167	2294	2456	1.4	65	830	896	979	1.8	2.53	611	650	1.5
23874	NEWSOMS	175	1054	1007	994	-1.1	2	426	416	417	-0.6	2.42	309	297	-0.9
23875	PRINCE GEORGE	149	9750	10538	11047	1.9	76	3666	4008	4250	2.1	2.61	2817	3055	1.9
23876	RAWLINGS	025	538	515	498	-1.0	3	211	207	205	-0.5	2.49	148	143	-0.8
23878	SEDLEY	175	997	1065	1101	1.6	70	378	410	431	1.9	2.56	283	303	1.6
23879	SKIPPERS	081	575	616	674	1.6	71	229	253	284	2.4	2.43	164	179	2.1
23881	SPRING GROVE	181	4620	6295	6430	7.6	99	998	1049	1117	1.2	2.69	715	741	0.8
23882	STONY CREEK	183	2336	2413	2474	0.8	52	963	1020	1069	1.4	2.35	666	695	1.0
23883	SURRY	181	2178	2352	2539	1.8	75	838	917	1002	2.1	2.56	612	662	1.9
23885	SUTHERLAND	053	2613	2660	2787	0.4	40	982	1021	1091	0.9	2.59	775	798	0.7
23887	VALENTINES	025	608	606	595	-0.1	21	270	276	278	0.5	2.20	194	196	0.2
23888	WAKEFIELD	183	2665	2615	2616	-0.4	12	1088	1085	1105	-0.1	2.38	759	746	-0.4
23889	WARFIELD	025	576	560	545	-0.7	8	235	234	234	-0.1	2.39	164	161	-0.4
23890	WAVERLY	183	6891	6984	7054	0.3	36	1748	1833	1902	1.1	2.55	1204	1245	0.8
23893	WHITE PLAINS	025	646	640	628	-0.2	18	270	274	275	0.4	2.33	187	187	0.0
23894	WILSONS	053	390	397	414	0.4	40	167	174	186	1.0	2.28	119	122	0.6
23897	YALE	183	546	532	528	-0.6	8	221	220	223	-0.1	2.42	161	158	-0.4
23898	ZUNI	093	1792	1852	1961	0.8	52	667	704	760	1.3	2.58	514	536	1.0
23901	FARMVILLE	049	13621	13738	14097	0.2	32	5142	5309	5585	0.8	2.19	3261	3296	0.3
23909	FARMVILLE	147	2243	2262	2294	0.2	32	0	0	0	0.0	0.00	0	0	0.0
23915	BASKERVILLE	117	858	925	976	1.8	75	337	368	396	2.1	1.96	238	257	1.8
23917	BOYDTON	117	4323	4482	4625	0.9	54	1255	1349	1434	1.7	2.68	877	929	1.4
23919	BRACEY	117	1868	1994	2088	1.6	69	870	945	1006	2.0	2.11	624	669	1.7
23920	BRODNAX	025	3140	3149	3137	0.1	26	1221	1248	1267	0.5	2.52	838	844	0.2
23921	BUCKINGHAM	029	2120	2135	2178	0.2	30	883	909	947	0.7	2.32	581	589	0.3
23922	BURKEVILLE	135	3628	3742	3831	0.7	49	889	942	988	1.4	2.82	613	640	1.0
23923	CHARLOTTE COURT HOUS	037	2208	2294	2421	0.9	55	877	931	1005	1.4	2.42	609	639	1.1
23924	CHASE CITY	117	6422	6697	6988	1.0	57	2705	2872	3050	1.4	2.29	1797	1876	1.0
23927	CLARKSVILLE	117	4431	4588	4759	0.8	53	1969	2079	2198	1.3	2.20	1348	1404	1.0
23930	CREWE	135	6004	6082	6164	0.3	36	2401	2483	2561	0.8	2.32	1682	1713	0.4
23934	CULLEN	037	661	691	731	1.1	58	262	279	302	1.5	2.47	177	186	1.2
23936	DILLWYN	029	6862	7086	7284	0.8	51	1877	2003	2120	1.5	2.48	1328	1398	1.2
23937	DRAKES BRANCH	037	1382	1467	1566	1.4	67	573	624	684	2.0	2.29	383	410	1.6
23938	DUNDAS	025	575	600	609	1.0	58	236	254	265	1.7	2.35	164	174	1.4
23942	GREEN BAY	147	983	1037	1091	1.3	64	419	452	485	1.8	2.10	288	306	1.4
23944	KENBRIDGE	111	4550	4540	4541	-0.1	22	1851	1888	1922	0.5	2.39	1248	1253	0.1
23947	KEYSVILLE	111	4193	4414	4645	1.2	62	1736	1871	2015	1.9	2.31	1182	1252	1.4
23950	LA CROSSE	117	3276	3291	3364	0.1	28	1317	1345	1399	0.5	2.43	929	935	0.2
23952	LUNENBURG	111	114	114	114	0.0	24	48	49	50	0.5	1.37	32	22	-8.4
23954	MEHERRIN	147	1733	1813	1890	1.1	59	664	710	755	1.6	2.54	471	497	1.3
23958	PAMPLIN	147	2745	2843	2953	0.8	53	1084	1144	1211	1.3	2.40	791	823	0.9
23959	PHENIX	037	919	955	1008	0.9	55	355	375	404	1.3	2.53	261	273	1.1
23960	PROSPECT	147	1989	2125	2260	1.6	70	750	818	889	2.1	2.48	517	553	1.6
23962	RANDOLPH	037	672	686	713	0.5	42	266	278	295	1.0	2.41	185	191	0.8
23963	RED HOUSE	037	699	745	795	1.5	69	260	284	309	2.1	2.61	190	205	1.8
23964	RED OAK	037	1155	1225	1305	1.4	66	458	496	540	1.9	2.46	323	345	1.6
23966	RICE	147	2062	2131	2235	0.8	52	815	863	925	1.4	2.43	556	579	1.1
23967	SAXE	037	1450	1494	1571	0.7	49	546	576	620	1.3	2.58	400	416	0.9
23968	SKIPWITH	117	957	1021	1075	1.5	69	377	408	437	1.9	2.50	273	291	1.5
23970	SOUTH HILL	117	7824	7852	8031	0.1	27	3148	3208	3338	0.5	2.34	2165	2177	0.1
23974	VICTORIA	111	5085	5080	5077	0.0	23	1689	1722	1750	0.5	2.36	1117	1119	0.0
23976	WYLLIESBURG	037	565	584	616	0.8	52	229	243	261	1.4	2.40	161	168	1.0
24011	ROANOKE	770	52	50	49	-0.9	4	17	14	13	-4.5	2.57	3	1	-22.8
	VIRGINIA					1.4					1.7	2.51			1.4
	UNITED STATES					1.2					1.3	2.58			1.1

ZIP CODE #	POST OFFICE NAME	RACE (%) White 2000	White 2004	Black 2000	Black 2004	Asian/Pacific 2000	Asian/Pacific 2004	% Hispanic Origin 2000	% Hispanic Origin 2004	2004 AGE DISTRIBUTION (%) 0-4	5-9	10-14	15-19	20-24	25-44	45-64	65-84	85+	18+	MEDIAN AGE 2004	% 2004 Males	% 2004 Females
23696	SEAFORD	94.2	93.3	3.4	4.0	0.8	1.0	1.6	2.1	5.8	6.7	7.3	5.8	3.8	24.4	31.9	13.3	1.1	76.6	43.0	49.9	50.1
23701	PORTSMOUTH	44.0	42.6	53.5	54.5	0.5	0.6	1.0	1.1	5.9	6.0	6.6	6.2	6.5	27.1	23.8	16.0	1.9	77.8	39.3	47.8	52.2
23702	PORTSMOUTH	54.7	51.2	40.9	43.7	0.7	0.8	2.1	2.5	8.7	8.0	8.3	7.6	7.8	30.1	20.1	8.2	1.2	70.4	31.2	48.0	52.0
23703	PORTSMOUTH	55.7	52.2	39.3	42.2	1.6	1.8	2.9	3.4	6.8	6.5	6.8	9.0	11.5	28.7	20.8	8.7	1.3	75.8	31.6	51.6	48.4
23704	PORTSMOUTH	20.3	19.5	77.3	77.8	0.5	0.6	1.3	1.4	7.5	6.8	7.3	8.2	7.0	25.7	22.2	12.9	2.4	73.2	35.8	46.7	53.3
23707	PORTSMOUTH	56.9	55.3	39.9	41.0	0.6	0.6	1.2	1.4	7.9	7.3	7.1	6.3	6.5	28.4	22.3	11.7	2.4	73.9	35.9	46.2	53.8
23708	PORTSMOUTH	47.0	43.0	36.5	39.0	7.0	7.5	13.0	15.0	1.0	1.0	1.0	10.5	48.0	34.5	4.0	0.0	0.0	97.0	23.8	68.5	31.5
23709	PORTSMOUTH	90.0	90.0	10.0	10.0	0.0	0.0	0.0	0.0	0.0	10.0	15.0	10.0	5.0	15.0	35.0	10.0	0.0	65.0	43.3	45.0	55.0
23801	FORT LEE	39.7	38.1	46.9	46.1	2.8	3.1	11.4	13.3	9.5	7.1	6.0	16.2	24.7	33.9	2.4	0.2	0.1	74.8	22.3	58.3	41.7
23803	PETERSBURG	33.4	33.2	64.3	64.1	0.4	0.5	1.4	1.6	6.4	6.5	7.6	7.6	6.4	27.7	24.8	11.8	1.4	75.2	37.1	47.3	52.7
23805	PETERSBURG	41.8	40.8	55.1	55.6	1.2	1.4	1.3	1.5	5.4	5.6	6.8	6.8	6.3	25.6	27.2	14.0	2.3	77.9	40.5	46.7	53.3
23806	PETERSBURG	4.5	4.0	92.5	92.6	0.1	0.1	2.4	2.6	0.3	0.2	1.7	52.8	37.0	5.2	2.2	0.4	0.2	96.5	19.5	40.6	59.4
23821	ALBERTA	45.5	44.0	53.1	54.4	0.7	0.8	1.5	1.7	4.9	5.2	6.3	7.0	6.3	24.0	29.2	15.2	1.9	79.4	42.6	47.7	52.3
23824	BLACKSTONE	55.5	53.7	41.3	42.5	0.6	0.7	2.5	3.0	6.2	6.2	6.6	6.4	5.6	24.8	25.9	15.5	2.9	76.9	41.3	47.4	52.6
23827	BOYKINS	47.4	46.4	51.4	52.4	0.1	0.1	1.0	0.9	5.5	5.7	6.4	6.4	5.9	23.9	27.7	16.5	2.1	78.6	42.9	48.7	51.3
23828	BRANCHVILLE	45.9	45.0	52.8	53.9	0.2	0.2	0.9	0.7	5.5	5.7	6.4	6.4	5.9	23.4	27.8	16.7	2.2	78.5	43.0	48.4	51.7
23829	CAPRON	38.8	38.0	60.3	61.1	0.4	0.4	0.6	0.5	2.6	2.8	3.2	6.5	20.1	30.5	23.6	9.9	0.8	89.0	33.7	76.0	24.1
23830	CARSON	67.5	66.3	30.8	31.8	0.3	0.3	0.8	0.9	5.4	6.0	7.0	6.4	6.2	26.6	29.8	11.6	1.3	77.8	40.5	49.1	50.9
23831	CHESTER	81.8	78.9	13.2	15.0	2.3	2.7	2.7	3.4	6.9	7.0	7.6	7.0	6.2	28.8	27.6	8.1	0.7	74.1	37.1	48.8	51.3
23832	CHESTERFIELD	73.4	72.0	21.9	22.5	1.6	1.9	2.5	3.0	7.5	7.5	7.8	7.4	6.6	32.1	25.0	5.5	0.6	72.6	34.6	48.6	51.4
23833	CHURCH ROAD	77.4	75.8	21.2	22.5	0.1	0.1	0.6	0.8	6.2	6.4	6.2	5.9	4.4	31.2	28.3	10.1	1.3	77.0	39.7	52.9	47.1
23834	COLONIAL HEIGHTS	82.2	80.0	13.2	14.6	2.4	2.8	1.8	2.3	6.6	6.4	7.1	6.7	6.4	27.2	24.7	13.2	1.8	75.8	38.2	47.3	52.7
23836	CHESTER	82.8	80.0	10.9	11.9	3.8	4.9	2.3	3.0	7.0	7.4	7.9	6.7	5.5	28.2	28.4	8.3	0.5	73.4	38.2	49.5	50.5
23837	COURTLAND	63.4	62.7	35.5	36.2	0.3	0.3	0.4	0.5	5.1	5.4	6.6	6.3	5.8	26.5	28.0	14.1	2.3	78.8	41.8	50.6	49.5
23838	CHESTERFIELD	87.7	86.2	9.9	11.0	1.1	1.3	0.8	1.1	5.7	6.9	8.0	6.9	4.8	25.2	34.6	7.5	0.6	75.1	41.5	50.5	49.5
23839	DENDRON	48.5	46.7	50.2	52.1	0.0	0.0	0.6	0.6	6.5	6.6	7.4	7.1	5.1	25.1	28.5	11.6	2.2	74.9	40.4	47.5	52.5
23840	DEWITT	63.0	61.0	35.8	37.6	0.1	0.1	0.4	0.4	4.6	5.3	7.2	6.2	5.0	24.8	32.1	13.4	1.5	78.5	43.3	51.2	48.8
23841	DINWIDDIE	55.7	53.6	43.1	45.0	0.2	0.3	0.5	0.6	5.2	5.8	6.5	5.8	5.2	25.5	30.7	13.9	1.4	79.0	42.5	49.2	50.8
23842	DISPUTANTA	68.5	66.6	29.0	30.3	0.8	1.0	1.6	2.1	5.0	5.5	7.0	6.6	6.3	32.2	27.0	9.5	0.9	78.2	38.3	54.9	45.1
23843	DOLPHIN	39.3	36.8	59.5	61.7	0.0	0.0	0.7	0.7	4.8	5.5	6.6	6.2	5.9	23.7	29.4	16.0	2.0	79.9	43.0	48.0	52.0
23844	DREWRYVILLE	44.5	43.6	54.6	55.5	0.0	0.0	0.7	0.7	6.4	6.6	7.8	7.1	5.6	24.4	25.6	15.2	1.4	74.7	40.4	47.0	53.0
23845	EBONY	59.0	56.4	40.0	42.1	0.0	0.0	0.6	0.8	4.6	5.0	5.8	4.8	4.4	23.2	31.7	18.5	2.1	81.5	46.4	46.9	53.1
23846	ELBERON	49.8	47.8	48.2	49.7	0.0	0.0	1.0	1.0	5.8	6.2	7.7	7.1	5.2	25.6	28.5	12.1	1.8	76.0	40.9	47.0	53.0
23847	EMPORIA	39.8	38.1	58.8	60.4	0.5	0.6	1.2	1.4	4.9	5.0	5.8	6.3	6.1	31.8	25.1	12.8	2.2	80.3	39.3	55.1	44.9
23850	FORD	66.1	64.2	32.6	34.1	0.1	0.2	0.4	0.5	4.8	5.5	7.3	6.0	4.8	26.9	29.1	14.0	1.6	78.4	42.3	49.4	50.6
23851	FRANKLIN	50.3	49.0	48.1	49.3	0.5	0.6	0.6	0.6	5.5	5.8	7.4	7.2	6.2	24.5	26.6	14.3	2.7	76.9	40.8	45.8	54.2
23856	FREEMAN	31.1	29.2	67.7	69.4	0.1	0.1	1.9	2.2	6.0	6.5	7.8	6.6	5.4	25.2	25.7	14.6	2.2	75.6	40.1	46.1	53.9
23857	GASBURG	66.4	64.4	32.9	34.9	0.0	0.0	0.7	0.9	5.4	5.6	5.1	4.7	3.8	22.3	31.9	19.4	1.8	81.0	47.1	49.9	50.1
23860	HOPEWELL	63.8	61.8	31.9	33.1	1.1	1.2	2.9	3.5	7.1	6.9	7.5	6.6	6.8	27.3	23.9	12.1	1.7	74.3	36.3	47.4	52.6
23866	IVOR	64.2	63.1	34.3	35.4	0.1	0.1	0.7	0.7	5.4	5.9	6.8	7.3	5.2	24.8	29.4	13.5	1.8	77.4	41.9	49.1	50.9
23867	JARRATT	32.9	31.6	66.0	67.2	0.3	0.3	0.6	0.7	4.5	4.7	5.1	5.8	6.1	35.1	25.0	12.3	1.4	82.1	39.4	59.1	40.9
23868	LAWRENCEVILLE	35.8	34.0	62.9	64.6	0.2	0.2	1.3	1.6	4.1	4.1	4.4	6.3	10.1	37.8	21.8	10.0	1.5	84.7	35.5	60.8	39.2
23872	MC KENNEY	62.5	60.5	36.2	38.1	0.3	0.4	1.1	1.2	5.0	5.6	7.2	5.7	4.8	25.2	30.6	13.9	2.1	78.5	42.9	49.7	50.4
23874	NEWSOMS	57.1	56.1	41.8	42.7	0.1	0.1	0.9	0.8	5.6	6.2	6.7	5.7	5.3	26.4	28.5	14.0	1.8	78.2	41.9	47.9	52.1
23875	PRINCE GEORGE	67.1	65.5	27.5	28.0	2.1	2.5	3.1	3.8	6.2	6.3	8.2	7.9	6.3	29.1	27.2	8.5	0.6	74.4	36.9	49.3	50.7
23876	RAWLINGS	42.2	40.4	56.9	58.6	0.6	0.6	2.0	2.3	5.6	6.0	7.0	6.8	5.4	25.1	27.6	14.8	1.8	77.3	41.5	47.8	52.2
23878	SEDLEY	69.9	69.7	28.6	28.9	0.2	0.2	0.8	0.8	5.8	6.1	7.0	6.4	5.2	27.5	27.2	12.9	2.0	77.1	40.7	49.5	50.5
23879	SKIPPERS	44.7	42.4	54.3	56.5	0.0	0.0	1.0	1.1	5.4	5.5	6.2	6.7	5.7	25.3	29.4	14.5	1.5	78.7	42.0	49.4	50.7
23881	SPRING GROVE	44.3	40.9	51.0	52.8	1.0	1.3	5.4	7.5	2.5	2.6	3.0	4.9	10.9	48.0	20.8	6.6	0.7	89.8	35.2	75.3	24.7
23882	STONY CREEK	42.3	41.0	56.3	57.6	0.1	0.1	0.6	0.5	5.1	5.6	6.3	6.1	5.1	25.8	30.5	13.7	1.8	79.4	42.7	48.6	51.4
23883	SURRY	45.0	43.0	53.8	55.5	0.2	0.2	0.6	0.8	5.3	6.2	7.9	6.9	5.7	26.8	28.7	11.4	1.2	76.3	40.2	48.8	51.2
23885	SUTHERLAND	74.9	73.6	24.0	25.2	0.3	0.3	0.5	0.6	5.1	5.7	6.9	6.0	4.9	27.4	30.4	12.6	1.0	78.5	41.7	51.1	48.9
23887	VALENTINES	76.2	74.4	23.5	25.1	0.2	0.2	0.5	0.7	5.6	5.6	4.0	3.6	3.0	20.3	34.2	22.0	1.8	82.8	50.5	51.2	48.8
23888	WAKEFIELD	47.7	46.5	51.0	52.0	0.1	0.1	0.6	0.6	6.1	6.3	7.2	6.5	5.7	25.6	27.1	13.5	2.0	76.4	40.6	47.9	52.1
23889	WARFIELD	40.8	38.6	58.0	59.8	0.2	0.2	1.0	1.4	5.0	5.5	6.6	6.1	5.7	23.9	29.3	15.7	2.1	79.3	42.9	48.0	52.0
23890	WAVERLY	32.5	32.2	66.0	66.3	0.1	0.1	1.1	1.1	3.9	4.1	5.0	4.9	9.1	37.8	23.9	9.6	1.7	83.8	36.9	64.3	35.7
23893	WHITE PLAINS	53.3	50.9	46.3	48.4	0.0	0.0	0.9	1.1	5.8	6.1	6.7	6.3	5.3	25.3	28.3	15.0	1.3	77.5	41.1	48.3	51.7
23894	WILSONS	66.4	64.5	32.1	33.8	0.3	0.3	0.5	0.5	4.8	5.8	7.6	5.8	4.8	26.2	28.7	14.6	1.8	78.3	42.4	48.9	51.1
23897	YALE	51.3	50.0	48.0	49.1	0.2	0.2	0.4	0.4	6.0	7.0	7.7	6.2	4.3	25.8	25.2	16.2	1.7	75.6	40.9	50.0	50.0
23898	ZUNI	77.2	75.9	21.4	22.6	0.3	0.3	0.8	1.0	5.5	5.9	6.8	7.0	5.9	27.4	29.6	10.9	1.1	77.3	40.3	49.8	50.2
23901	FARMVILLE	63.9	62.1	34.0	35.5	0.7	0.8	1.1	1.3	5.2	5.3	5.7	10.8	12.4	22.7	22.0	13.2	2.9	80.6	34.9	49.9	50.1
23909	FARMVILLE	84.4	83.1	11.5	12.1	2.0	2.4	1.2	1.4	1.8	1.9	2.2	35.1	33.2	7.6	9.9	7.0	1.5	92.7	21.4	38.1	61.9
23915	BASKERVILLE	55.7	54.0	42.8	44.2	0.1	0.2	1.9	2.4	4.0	4.3	5.5	6.0	6.6	36.0	25.0	11.4	1.3	82.6	38.9	59.7	40.3
23917	BOYDTON	51.4	48.9	47.4	49.6	0.2	0.2	0.6	0.7	3.6	3.9	4.8	5.0	6.2	33.2	27.4	14.5	1.5	84.7	41.4	57.7	42.3
23919	BRACEY	80.4	78.6	18.2	19.7	0.1	0.2	1.2	1.5	4.8	4.8	4.7	4.4	4.6	20.7	32.6	22.0	1.6	83.1	49.3	48.8	51.3
23920	BRODNAX	48.7	46.8	50.1	51.8	0.3	0.3	0.9	1.1	6.4	6.4	6.5	6.4	6.1	25.3	27.4	14.1	1.5	76.9	40.3	48.5	51.5
23921	BUCKINGHAM	67.0	65.0	30.8	32.5	0.3	0.3	0.6	0.8	5.4	5.6	6.0	6.5	5.5	24.5	29.4	15.2	1.8	78.7	42.6	48.3	51.7
23922	BURKEVILLE	47.4	45.4	50.9	52.6	0.4	0.6	1.0	1.2	3.9	4.1	4.8	5.3	8.9	35.1	22.6	13.4	1.8	84.0	37.9	61.8	38.2
23923	CHARLOTTE COURT HOUS	63.0	61.2	35.0	36.5	0.1	0.1	1.5	1.9	5.8	6.0	6.9	6.5	5.8	24.8	27.3	15.3	1.7	77.2	41.2	49.7	50.4
23924	CHASE CITY	53.9	52.3	44.3	45.7	0.2	0.3	1.2	1.4	5.9	6.2	6.9	6.3	5.4	24.7	26.4	16.1	2.2	77.1	41.4	47.5	52.5
23927	CLARKSVILLE	66.2	64.3	32.3	34.0	0.1	0.2	0.8	1.0	5.1	5.3	5.8	5.4	4.5	23.0	29.6	19.5	1.9	80.5	45.7	47.7	52.4
23930	CREWE	65.0	62.9	33.5	35.4	0.2	0.2	0.9	1.1	6.1	6.2	7.0	6.7	6.4	26.6	24.9	14.1	2.2	76.7	39.1	50.4	49.6
23934	CULLEN	59.3	57.5	39.3	41.1	0.0	0.0	0.6	1.0	5.6	6.1	6.5	7.0	5.6	24.0	28.8	14.6	1.7	77.6	41.7	49.5	50.5
23936	DILLWYN	54.6	52.8	43.8	45.4	0.2	0.2	0.8	0.9	4.2	4.5	5.3	5.9	6.9	37.2	24.6	10.0	1.6	82.1	38.1	62.8	37.2
23937	DRAKES BRANCH	68.0	66.1	30.8	32.5	0.1	0.1	2.0	2.3	4.8	6.1	7.6	6.1	5.1	25.5	26.8	15.1	2.7	77.4	41.3	47.6	52.4
23938	DUNDAS	60.9	59.2	37.4	39.0	0.5	0.5	1.7	1.7	5.7	5.8	6.2	7.0	5.8	24.0	29.2	14.8	1.5	77.8	42.1	49.7	50.3
23942	GREEN BAY	63.2	61.5	34.8	36.2	0.2	0.3	0.7	0.9	4.4	5.1	6.9	6.6	6.1	29.8	25.8	13.6	1.6	79.6	40.0	54.5	45.5
23944	KENBRIDGE	57.4	56.7	40.0	40.8	0.3	0.3	2.5	2.5	5.6	5.8	6.2	6.4	5.8	23.2	28.6	16.5	2.1	78.6	43.0	49.6	50.4
23947	KEYSVILLE	67.0	65.6	31.2	32.4	0.1	0.1	1.8	2.1	5.2	5.6	7.1	6.4	5.3	23.8	28.6	15.6	2.4	77.9	42.7	48.0	52.0
23950	LA CROSSE	59.0	57.2	39.3	40.8	0.2	0.2	1.8	2.2	5.6	5.7	5.7	5.9	5.2	25.5	28.8	16.3	1.5	79.5	42.7	48.6	51.4
23952	LUNENBURG	59.7	59.7	38.6	39.5	0.0	0.0	0.9	0.9	3.5	3.5	3.5	4.4	7.9	42.1	22.8	11.4	0.9	87.7	37.9	68.4	31.6
23954	MEHERRIN	53.8	52.2	44.7	46.2	0.1	0.1	0.5	0.6	5.7	6.1	7.2	7.3	6.3	24.2	28.8	12.9	1.5	76.5	40.6	49.5	50.5
23958	PAMPLIN	65.2	63.2	33.8	35.6	0.1	0.1	1.0	1.1	6.1	6.6	7.4	7.8	7.4	24.1	26.0	13.1	1.6	76.1	38.7	51.5	48.5
23959	PHENIX	74.7	73.2	24.2	25.3	0.0	0.0	1.4	1.7	5.7	5.5	6.1	7.0	7.2	24.2	25.3	17.0	2.1	78.4	41.3	48.4	51.6
23960	PROSPECT	54.7	52.8	44.2	45.9	0.3	0.3	0.6	0.8	6.5	6.7	7.2	8.5	7.9	25.2	23.6	12.7	1.7	75.6	37.7	51.2	48.8
23962	RANDOLPH	59.7	57.9	39.0	40.7	0.0	0.0	1.0	1.2	5.5	5.5	7.1	6.6	5.5	24.2	26.2	17.2	2.0	77.7	41.9	49.6	50.4
23963	RED HOUSE	67.2	65.5	30.5	32.0	0.1	0.1	1.7	2.0	6.3	6.4	7.4	6.3	6.2	25.6	26.3	14.1	1.3	75.8	39.9	49.4	50.6
23964	RED OAK	60.4	58.4	37.5	39.1	1.0	1.1	1.6	2.0	6.1	6.7	7.6	5.7	6.0	24.8	26.5	14.6	2.0	76.2	40.5	48.7	51.3
23966	RICE	59.0	57.0	39.2	40.9	0.5	0.6	1.0	1.2	5.8	6.0	6.7	6.4	6.4	26.1	27.3	13.3	2.0	77.6	39.8	47.3	52.8
23967	SAXE	63.2	61.6	35.5	37.1	0.1	0.1	1.9	2.3	5.9	6.8	7.9	6.5	5.4	26.8	25.4	13.7	1.5	75.4	38.7	47.3	52.7
23968	SKIPWITH	67.8	65.3	30.5	32.6	0.2	0.3	1.0	1.3	5.3	5.8	6.3	5.7	4.7	24.2	29.1	17.6	1.4	79.0	43.8	49.0	51.0
23970	SOUTH HILL	55.5	53.5	42.3	44.1	0.8	0.9	1.5	1.8	6.1	5.9	6.2	6.2	6.1	26.2	25.6	15.1	2.7	77.9	40.9	47.3	52.7
23974	VICTORIA	57.3	56.5	40.5	41.2	0.3	0.3	1.7	1.7	4.1	4.4	5.1	5.8	6.8	32.4	25.8	13.8	1.8	83.0	40.2	58.5	41.5
23976	WYLLIESBURG	63.5	61.8	35.4	37.0	0.2	0.2	0.9	1.0	6.7	7.0	7.4	5.7	5.7	26.5	25.3	14.0	1.7	75.7	38.6	49.3	50.7
24011	ROANOKE	44.2	40.0	51.9	58.0	0.0	0.0	0.0	0.0	0.0	0.0	0.0	4.0	26.0	54.0	16.0	0.0	0.0	100.0	31.4	80.0	20.0
	VIRGINIA	72.3	70.7	19.6	19.9	3.7	4.3	4.7	5.7	6.5	6.6	6.9	6.9	7.0	29.7	24.9	10.1	1.4	76.2	36.6	49.1	50.9
	UNITED STATES	75.1	73.6	12.3	12.5	3.8	4.2	12.5	14.1	6.9	6.7	7.2	7.0	7.3	28.6	23.8	10.8	1.7	75.1	36.0	49.1	50.9

 Copyright © 2004 ESRI BIS. All rights reserved. Reproduction by any method is prohibited.

ZIP CODE #	POST OFFICE NAME	2004 Per Capita Income	2004 HH Income Base	2004 Household Income Distribution (%) Less than $25,000	$25,000 to $49,999	$50,000 to $99,999	$100,000 to $149,999	$150,000 or More	Median Household Income 2004	2009	2004 National Centile	2004 State Centile	2004 Home Value Base	2004 Home Value Distribution (%) Less than $50,000	$50,000 to $89,999	$90,000 to $174,999	$175,000 to $399,999	$400,000 or More	2004 Median Home Value
23696	SEAFORD	36910	1370	8.0	20.6	38.3	22.4	10.7	78594	94298	95	90	1243	0.3	4.3	26.5	64.3	4.7	210457
23701	PORTSMOUTH	20332	10148	26.8	34.3	30.4	6.5	2.0	41614	48815	52	43	6860	1.7	27.4	63.0	7.3	0.7	105507
23702	PORTSMOUTH	15034	4475	37.7	36.7	22.1	2.4	1.1	32634	37185	20	14	2262	5.4	49.4	44.8	0.4	0.0	87762
23703	PORTSMOUTH	22934	9938	17.9	31.6	37.3	9.9	3.3	50421	58242	73	66	6554	0.9	11.8	62.4	23.8	1.0	139036
23704	PORTSMOUTH	17580	7254	44.0	29.2	20.1	4.5	2.2	28534	33324	10	7	3369	8.8	40.8	41.5	8.0	0.9	90339
23707	PORTSMOUTH	19086	6250	37.5	31.0	25.5	4.5	1.5	34167	39628	25	19	3411	2.0	31.4	56.1	10.1	0.4	104758
23708	PORTSMOUTH	15800	9	44.4	22.2	33.3	0.0	0.0	27247	54495	7	6	4	0.0	0.0	100.0	0.0	0.0	125000
23709	PORTSMOUTH	30000	6	0.0	0.0	50.0	50.0	0.0	100000	113247	98	96	0	0.0	0.0	0.0	0.0	0.0	0
23801	FORT LEE	15226	1347	19.2	42.2	33.6	5.0	0.0	42161	49004	53	45	44	11.4	36.4	52.3	0.0	0.0	92000
23803	PETERSBURG	19364	15523	33.9	31.2	26.6	6.0	2.4	36879	44561	35	29	9195	15.0	29.4	46.3	8.5	0.7	95511
23805	PETERSBURG	26080	7392	20.2	30.3	35.5	9.4	4.6	49580	58967	71	64	5083	5.6	23.4	52.7	16.6	1.7	112223
23806	PETERSBURG	13722	11	54.6	45.5	0.0	0.0	0.0	22247	26288	3	2	5	0.0	40.0	60.0	0.0	0.0	112500
23821	ALBERTA	21656	673	37.0	30.3	25.4	4.6	2.7	33897	39287	24	18	537	19.0	29.2	35.6	14.7	1.5	94318
23824	BLACKSTONE	20932	2731	37.5	26.3	27.8	4.8	3.6	35061	42358	28	23	1955	21.2	23.9	36.8	15.8	2.4	102127
23827	BOYKINS	18671	608	37.3	30.4	26.6	3.3	2.3	33803	39426	23	18	438	15.5	27.2	42.2	14.4	0.7	100962
23828	BRANCHVILLE	17437	218	38.5	30.3	25.7	3.2	2.3	32824	38250	20	15	155	16.8	27.1	41.3	14.2	0.7	99500
23829	CAPRON	18265	497	31.0	29.2	32.8	5.8	1.2	38864	45099	42	36	389	15.2	24.7	35.2	24.4	0.5	102500
23830	CARSON	22165	482	22.8	30.3	36.1	7.3	3.5	47703	54159	68	60	379	21.4	15.0	38.8	23.8	1.1	120192
23831	CHESTER	30595	10882	12.4	21.6	40.9	18.5	6.7	66989	79201	90	84	8568	8.8	4.2	45.7	40.0	1.2	158760
23832	CHESTERFIELD	27249	9878	6.0	25.4	46.0	17.3	5.4	67071	78871	90	84	8172	0.2	3.5	65.3	29.8	1.2	143145
23833	CHURCH ROAD	24001	783	19.5	27.8	37.3	13.0	2.3	52370	61820	76	70	672	8.9	10.9	51.5	26.6	2.1	136792
23834	COLONIAL HEIGHTS	27729	10269	17.1	29.1	37.1	12.8	3.9	53536	63956	78	72	7452	1.5	16.7	58.2	23.0	0.6	124443
23836	CHESTER	33651	3543	10.2	21.0	39.3	19.4	10.2	73418	85762	93	87	3103	10.3	4.4	48.2	33.2	3.9	146064
23837	COURTLAND	25390	1536	27.7	28.4	31.5	8.8	3.7	44767	52862	61	53	1151	9.0	16.9	49.4	23.3	1.5	127500
23838	CHESTERFIELD	38849	4011	6.7	15.1	37.0	25.6	15.6	86092	104804	96	92	3782	2.5	3.6	32.4	50.7	10.9	208696
23839	DENDRON	17418	241	27.4	35.3	30.7	5.4	1.2	44314	50484	59	52	197	19.3	24.9	29.4	18.8	7.6	104167
23840	DEWITT	26557	595	20.0	25.7	41.5	8.2	4.5	53577	62093	78	72	497	12.3	23.3	46.1	15.9	2.4	111376
23841	DINWIDDIE	29125	1446	21.3	22.5	38.3	11.8	6.1	55894	65113	81	75	1202	9.3	23.5	45.5	19.7	1.9	117500
23842	DISPUTANTA	28510	1975	17.0	23.1	38.9	16.0	5.0	58632	68894	83	79	1702	9.6	6.8	49.7	32.3	1.7	148646
23843	DOLPHIN	21547	242	31.0	28.9	30.6	6.2	3.3	40463	46660	48	41	198	13.6	25.3	33.3	22.7	5.1	110938
23844	DREWRYVILLE	14390	326	37.7	35.3	24.9	1.8	0.3	31945	36805	18	13	249	26.5	21.7	32.1	19.7	0.0	93750
23845	EBONY	17068	220	40.9	37.3	16.4	5.5	0.0	28832	33809	10	7	180	39.4	8.9	23.9	22.8	5.0	100000
23846	ELBERON	17500	308	25.3	33.8	35.7	2.9	2.3	42831	50000	56	48	254	18.1	17.3	42.9	19.3	2.4	109906
23847	EMPORIA	18277	5776	35.3	32.2	25.5	4.5	2.5	35425	40630	29	24	4018	18.2	27.6	42.9	10.3	1.0	95107
23850	FORD	21975	504	23.0	28.4	39.3	7.1	2.2	47210	54873	67	59	417	12.5	20.9	35.3	28.3	3.1	125765
23851	FRANKLIN	22394	5322	35.1	27.3	25.5	8.2	3.9	37824	46569	39	32	3346	9.8	17.9	45.4	24.6	2.3	125542
23856	FREEMAN	17197	488	34.4	31.4	28.1	4.7	1.4	37389	42418	37	31	385	18.4	32.7	30.9	14.3	3.6	88953
23857	GASBURG	23703	261	24.9	36.8	27.6	7.3	3.5	42761	50687	55	47	218	16.1	11.0	31.7	34.9	6.4	141304
23860	HOPEWELL	21699	10782	28.7	31.8	29.3	8.0	2.3	40385	47222	47	41	6782	5.5	28.9	51.1	13.0	1.6	106092
23866	IVOR	18731	852	32.2	29.9	29.7	5.6	2.6	39420	47103	44	38	697	8.8	15.2	45.5	27.7	2.9	124756
23867	JARRATT	25466	928	33.3	33.4	25.5	5.5	2.3	34087	39739	24	19	698	21.1	24.2	40.4	12.8	1.6	96875
23868	LAWRENCEVILLE	16984	2013	35.7	30.7	27.4	3.8	2.5	35980	41005	31	26	1547	16.5	30.0	39.0	12.9	1.6	94325
23872	MC KENNEY	22321	896	23.4	30.0	36.4	8.2	2.0	45406	52628	62	55	708	14.7	29.9	39.4	14.4	1.6	96786
23874	NEWSOMS	23268	416	25.0	34.9	33.4	3.6	3.1	41739	49862	52	44	345	12.2	23.8	47.5	13.6	2.9	105784
23875	PRINCE GEORGE	25018	4008	17.3	25.5	41.3	12.2	3.8	55555	64097	80	75	3237	16.2	4.4	53.3	24.7	1.5	134444
23876	RAWLINGS	20091	207	40.1	24.2	28.0	4.8	2.9	31889	37350	18	13	159	18.2	30.2	32.7	17.0	1.9	95000
23878	SEDLEY	19410	410	31.7	30.0	31.0	5.9	1.5	42482	50443	55	46	325	10.8	12.9	44.9	30.2	1.2	133073
23879	SKIPPERS	18611	253	34.8	33.6	25.3	4.4	2.0	36277	41544	33	27	201	24.9	31.8	35.8	7.5	0.0	81563
23881	SPRING GROVE	17929	1049	30.0	25.3	34.9	6.2	3.6	43161	50236	56	49	801	6.7	15.6	45.1	29.2	3.4	137950
23882	STONY CREEK	22960	1020	32.6	28.5	28.9	6.3	3.7	37937	45794	39	32	785	21.8	24.0	41.7	12.6	0.0	95076
23883	SURRY	19984	917	23.5	35.4	33.5	6.8	0.9	43095	49330	56	49	763	24.8	10.9	40.0	20.3	4.1	116996
23885	SUTHERLAND	30020	1021	14.2	25.0	38.7	16.3	5.9	59946	69714	84	79	887	3.8	13.6	52.7	25.0	4.9	137588
23887	VALENTINES	28131	276	18.1	33.0	33.7	9.4	5.8	49269	61019	71	64	236	5.9	5.9	31.4	48.7	8.1	188793
23888	WAKEFIELD	18100	1085	36.8	31.6	25.2	5.3	1.2	34342	40041	25	20	809	22.3	20.0	39.8	16.1	1.9	104435
23889	WARFIELD	20068	234	35.5	26.5	28.6	6.0	3.4	36989	43743	35	29	186	14.5	28.0	31.7	22.0	3.8	105147
23890	WAVERLY	17803	1833	31.8	29.2	29.4	7.9	1.8	38445	46017	41	34	1340	17.7	22.3	43.1	15.5	1.4	107622
23893	WHITE PLAINS	17355	274	31.8	44.9	19.0	3.7	0.7	35000	40330	28	23	219	28.8	21.0	35.6	11.0	3.7	90313
23894	WILSONS	24055	174	23.0	28.7	39.7	6.3	2.3	46903	53470	66	58	143	13.3	22.4	32.9	28.0	3.5	122794
23897	YALE	18060	220	28.2	39.1	25.9	6.8	0.0	38534	45871	41	34	168	9.5	29.2	45.8	15.5	0.0	102083
23898	ZUNI	23399	704	21.2	29.0	37.9	9.7	2.3	49888	58196	72	65	599	18.0	11.5	37.9	31.4	1.2	131055
23901	FARMVILLE	21673	5309	37.6	28.9	24.5	5.5	3.5	34517	40433	26	21	3575	10.6	18.8	39.9	27.6	3.1	125318
23909	FARMVILLE	10008	0	0.0	0.0	0.0	0.0	0.0	0	0	0	0	0	0.0	0.0	0.0	0.0	0.0	0
23915	BASKERVILLE	26505	368	29.6	40.8	21.2	3.8	4.6	35563	40742	30	25	278	13.0	21.6	49.6	14.8	1.1	106818
23917	BOYDTON	20157	1349	31.4	35.9	22.5	5.3	4.9	38173	45140	40	33	1088	14.5	22.9	37.6	22.2	2.8	107143
23919	BRACEY	23129	945	29.1	34.3	26.1	7.9	2.5	38828	47011	42	35	796	18.6	11.1	39.6	26.0	4.8	122650
23920	BRODNAX	18134	1248	36.2	34.9	23.2	3.7	2.1	34800	39899	27	22	955	26.6	21.1	39.6	11.9	0.8	92446
23921	BUCKINGHAM	18601	909	33.3	34.0	25.6	5.6	1.4	34878	41198	27	22	712	13.2	17.7	44.7	22.9	1.5	124769
23922	BURKEVILLE	15555	942	36.1	29.7	27.8	4.9	1.5	37514	45000	38	31	747	15.5	20.2	44.6	18.2	1.5	112793
23923	CHARLOTTE COURT HOUS	19365	931	36.5	33.0	24.5	2.8	3.2	34095	39129	24	19	772	14.8	18.4	47.0	16.1	3.8	114286
23924	CHASE CITY	17687	2872	45.3	29.8	18.5	4.2	2.2	28316	32708	9	7	2089	23.9	29.6	34.9	9.9	1.7	86415
23927	CLARKSVILLE	25091	2079	28.0	32.0	29.3	7.8	2.8	40736	48561	49	41	1656	10.3	14.2	48.3	23.5	3.8	131019
23930	CREWE	20214	2483	34.7	32.0	25.8	5.8	1.8	37229	43619	36	30	1795	10.7	24.2	48.8	15.3	1.1	108910
23934	CULLEN	20762	279	34.8	37.6	20.1	3.2	4.3	33111	38447	21	16	229	12.7	23.6	48.9	12.2	2.6	108239
23936	DILLWYN	17226	2003	38.2	29.5	23.7	6.9	1.7	33056	38746	21	16	1561	19.3	21.3	38.6	19.2	1.6	108033
23937	DRAKES BRANCH	19593	624	38.9	36.1	17.8	4.0	3.2	31930	36756	18	13	479	25.3	25.1	35.5	13.2	1.0	89659
23938	DUNDAS	20737	254	36.2	32.3	26.8	2.8	2.0	32442	37632	19	14	207	29.0	21.7	35.8	12.6	1.0	88929
23942	GREEN BAY	21565	452	38.9	28.5	25.0	2.9	4.7	37240	45808	36	30	366	19.7	21.6	35.8	15.3	7.7	111735
23944	KENBRIDGE	19136	1888	39.0	28.1	27.0	3.4	2.5	32594	37875	20	14	1440	22.7	23.6	38.5	14.1	1.1	95464
23947	KEYSVILLE	19759	1871	39.1	31.6	22.7	3.2	3.5	31944	36919	18	13	1459	18.8	20.4	43.1	16.0	1.6	108616
23950	LA CROSSE	19764	1345	34.2	35.1	22.2	5.1	3.4	35496	41350	29	24	1074	22.7	18.2	40.2	16.6	2.3	102660
23952	LUNENBURG	23606	49	36.7	36.7	20.4	6.1	0.0	35546	41536	30	25	39	20.5	28.2	43.6	7.7	0.0	95000
23954	MEHERRIN	17890	710	40.1	28.6	23.2	5.4	2.7	32739	39305	20	15	580	21.7	22.4	31.0	21.2	3.6	103125
23958	PAMPLIN	22351	1144	33.1	34.0	25.3	4.6	3.0	36166	41990	32	27	918	16.0	23.4	41.6	16.3	2.6	110200
23959	PHENIX	17198	375	42.9	20.3	31.7	4.3	0.8	33292	36807	22	16	299	17.4	28.1	44.5	9.7	0.3	97105
23960	PROSPECT	18531	818	32.6	32.0	26.0	8.3	1.0	38267	44318	40	33	642	10.9	19.0	36.9	27.4	5.8	129000
23962	RANDOLPH	16373	278	43.5	32.4	19.1	2.9	2.2	30257	36204	13	10	227	29.1	16.3	45.8	8.8	0.0	95250
23963	RED HOUSE	17875	284	34.5	27.8	32.0	3.5	2.1	36971	42215	35	29	234	15.4	22.2	39.7	17.5	5.1	112500
23964	RED OAK	14191	496	43.4	32.9	19.8	4.0	0.0	29117	33076	11	8	390	39.0	13.3	36.9	9.5	1.3	86250
23966	RICE	21031	863	32.3	33.3	23.3	6.8	4.3	39948	47087	46	39	615	16.3	14.5	30.7	35.5	3.1	141595
23967	SAXE	15482	576	38.7	36.6	20.3	4.0	0.4	33252	38015	22	16	464	29.1	24.1	28.7	14.9	3.2	86053
23968	SKIPWITH	18695	408	35.8	29.9	25.5	7.6	1.2	35291	40469	29	23	329	19.8	21.6	35.6	20.1	3.0	105449
23970	SOUTH HILL	22338	3208	33.4	33.2	24.6	5.1	3.8	36848	42948	35	29	2263	14.5	22.2	37.3	22.9	3.2	116425
23974	VICTORIA	16118	1722	43.2	32.9	19.4	3.1	1.4	29269	33716	11	8	1293	23.4	31.9	34.0	10.1	0.5	81543
23976	WYLLIESBURG	15794	243	37.5	35.8	22.2	4.5	0.0	32679	37316	20	15	183	26.8	27.9	32.8	9.3	3.3	86136
24011	ROANOKE	22168	14	57.1	21.4	14.3	7.1	0.0	20000	18462	2	1	1	0.0	100.0	0.0	0.0	0.0	75000
	VIRGINIA	30454		19.8	25.2	32.5	13.6	8.9	55216	67801				6.8	10.4	35.8	36.5	10.5	166226
	UNITED STATES	25866		24.7	27.1	30.8	10.9	6.5	48124	56710				10.9	15.0	33.7	30.1	10.4	145905

ZIP CODE		FINANCIAL SERVICES				THE HOME						ENTERTAINMENT						PERSONAL			
						Home Improvements		Furnishings													
#	POST OFFICE NAME	Auto Loan	Home Loan	Invest-ments	Retire-ment Plans	Home Repair	Lawn & Garden	Comput-ers & Hard-ware	Major Appli-ances	TV, Radio, Sound Equip-ment	Furni-ture	Dine out/ Carry out	Sports Equip-ment	Fees & Tickets	Toys & Games	Travel	Cable TV	Apparel & Services	Auto Repairs	Health Insur-ance	Pets & Supplies
23696	SEAFORD	125	152	167	152	151	154	138	138	129	138	163	159	147	169	143	127	162	134	128	152
23701	PORTSMOUTH	68	70	76	67	69	78	70	70	72	70	90	77	73	90	71	74	88	70	74	78
23702	PORTSMOUTH	51	50	57	49	50	55	54	52	56	53	70	60	55	71	54	56	68	54	54	58
23703	PORTSMOUTH	83	89	96	90	87	90	87	86	84	88	106	100	89	106	86	81	104	86	79	94
23704	PORTSMOUTH	58	54	64	52	53	61	58	58	62	59	77	64	59	74	58	64	75	60	62	65
23707	PORTSMOUTH	59	58	67	57	58	64	62	60	64	61	79	69	62	80	61	64	77	61	62	67
23708	PORTSMOUTH	51	49	61	47	47	54	52	51	55	53	69	57	54	69	52	56	68	52	52	57
23709	PORTSMOUTH	170	133	91	120	150	168	125	151	142	124	168	177	112	166	134	152	156	149	179	207
23801	FORT LEE	77	49	47	56	45	53	73	63	74	68	93	84	63	83	60	68	89	74	58	72
23803	PETERSBURG	66	62	66	59	61	69	65	65	68	65	84	73	65	82	64	70	82	66	69	74
23805	PETERSBURG	85	89	96	87	89	96	88	88	89	88	111	101	90	112	89	89	108	88	89	99
23806	PETERSBURG	30	18	23	20	18	21	35	26	34	29	42	36	28	38	28	30	40	31	24	29
23821	ALBERTA	95	65	31	56	73	84	62	77	75	64	88	92	53	83	63	80	80	77	95	109
23824	BLACKSTONE	80	66	54	61	69	79	68	74	75	68	91	86	64	88	68	79	86	74	84	91
23827	BOYKINS	83	57	28	50	64	74	55	68	66	56	78	81	48	74	56	71	71	67	83	95
23828	BRANCHVILLE	80	55	28	48	62	71	54	66	64	54	75	78	47	72	55	68	69	65	80	92
23829	CAPRON	77	68	56	62	72	81	66	72	73	65	89	83	65	91	68	77	84	71	83	90
23830	CARSON	97	73	42	65	80	90	69	82	79	70	94	98	62	92	70	84	87	81	97	113
23831	CHESTER	114	124	125	126	121	122	117	116	111	119	140	136	119	140	115	106	137	115	106	129
23832	CHESTERFIELD	109	120	121	125	115	114	113	111	105	115	133	131	115	133	110	98	131	110	96	122
23833	CHURCH ROAD	104	84	58	78	91	100	80	91	88	80	106	109	75	105	81	91	99	89	103	121
23834	COLONIAL HEIGHTS	92	98	103	97	98	104	96	96	96	95	119	110	99	123	97	96	116	95	95	106
23836	CHESTER	132	139	131	139	136	138	130	132	125	132	156	154	130	156	129	121	153	130	122	149
23837	COURTLAND	95	78	57	74	83	96	80	88	88	78	105	100	75	103	81	92	98	87	101	107
23838	CHESTERFIELD	148	179	188	182	173	172	160	157	147	162	187	183	171	194	161	142	187	152	139	173
23839	DENDRON	88	59	27	51	67	77	57	71	69	58	81	85	49	76	58	74	74	71	88	101
23840	DEWITT	115	93	64	87	101	110	88	101	97	88	117	120	83	116	90	101	109	99	114	133
23841	DINWIDDIE	130	99	60	90	108	121	94	111	107	95	127	132	85	124	96	112	118	109	129	151
23842	DISPUTANTA	104	101	88	99	103	107	95	100	95	96	118	119	94	119	96	95	114	99	100	121
23843	DOLPHIN	93	63	29	55	71	82	61	76	73	62	86	90	52	81	62	78	78	75	93	107
23844	DREWRYVILLE	72	48	22	41	54	63	46	58	56	47	66	69	39	62	47	60	60	57	71	82
23845	EBONY	70	47	21	41	53	61	45	57	55	46	64	68	39	61	46	59	59	56	70	81
23846	ELBERON	85	68	46	63	74	81	64	74	71	64	85	88	60	85	66	74	80	72	84	99
23847	EMPORIA	66	53	40	49	56	64	54	59	60	53	72	69	50	70	54	62	67	59	68	75
23850	FORD	82	77	78	77	79	85	77	81	78	77	97	95	75	94	77	78	93	81	83	95
23851	FRANKLIN	84	71	63	67	74	83	72	78	79	73	95	89	69	91	72	82	90	78	86	95
23856	FREEMAN	73	53	39	46	56	67	55	63	65	56	77	71	50	71	55	70	72	63	76	81
23857	GASBURG	87	70	53	64	76	89	66	78	74	69	90	84	63	79	70	79	83	77	94	99
23860	HOPEWELL	74	71	70	69	72	80	74	74	76	72	94	85	73	94	73	78	90	75	79	84
23866	IVOR	90	60	28	52	68	79	58	73	70	59	83	87	50	78	59	76	75	72	90	103
23867	JARRATT	55	37	17	32	41	48	35	44	43	36	50	53	30	47	36	46	45	44	54	63
23868	LAWRENCEVILLE	73	55	40	50	59	69	57	65	65	57	77	74	51	72	57	68	72	65	75	83
23872	MC KENNEY	88	78	65	74	82	90	76	83	81	76	98	96	74	98	77	83	93	81	89	102
23874	NEWSOMS	106	71	32	61	80	93	69	86	83	70	97	102	58	92	70	89	88	85	106	122
23875	PRINCE GEORGE	95	98	92	98	97	99	93	95	90	94	113	112	93	113	92	87	110	94	89	108
23876	RAWLINGS	94	63	29	54	71	82	61	76	73	62	86	91	52	81	62	79	78	75	94	108
23878	SEDLEY	82	64	45	62	69	79	66	73	73	65	87	84	61	85	66	76	81	73	84	91
23879	SKIPPERS	85	57	26	49	65	75	55	69	67	56	78	82	47	74	56	72	71	68	85	98
23881	SPRING GROVE	90	74	53	68	81	90	69	81	76	69	91	95	64	91	73	80	86	79	93	108
23882	STONY CREEK	99	69	35	60	77	89	67	82	79	68	93	97	58	89	68	85	85	81	99	114
23883	SURRY	93	67	36	59	74	84	64	77	74	64	88	92	56	85	65	79	81	76	93	108
23885	SUTHERLAND	115	115	103	110	118	125	106	113	108	106	133	132	107	136	109	110	128	110	117	137
23887	VALENTINES	94	88	84	83	93	109	81	92	86	87	106	90	82	89	88	91	100	89	108	105
23888	WAKEFIELD	75	52	28	47	59	69	54	64	63	53	74	74	47	70	54	67	67	63	77	85
23889	WARFIELD	90	61	27	52	69	79	58	73	71	60	83	87	50	78	59	76	75	72	90	104
23890	WAVERLY	71	52	34	47	57	66	53	61	62	53	73	71	48	69	53	66	67	61	74	80
23893	WHITE PLAINS	76	51	23	44	58	67	49	62	59	50	70	74	42	66	50	64	63	61	76	87
23894	WILSONS	78	76	80	78	78	83	77	79	77	77	95	93	76	93	77	76	92	79	79	90
23897	YALE	80	55	27	50	64	72	54	67	63	54	74	81	46	72	56	67	68	66	81	94
23898	ZUNI	99	85	63	81	89	96	81	90	86	82	105	106	77	102	82	87	99	89	96	113
23901	FARMVILLE	81	64	48	60	69	79	66	73	73	65	87	84	60	83	66	77	81	73	85	92
23909	FARMVILLE	0	0	0	0	0	0	0	0	0	0	0	0	0	0	0	0	0	0	0	0
23915	BASKERVILLE	109	73	33	63	83	95	71	88	85	72	100	105	60	95	72	92	91	87	109	125
23917	BOYDTON	104	73	38	64	82	94	70	86	83	71	97	103	60	93	72	89	89	85	105	121
23919	BRACEY	84	65	43	58	73	82	61	74	69	61	82	87	54	81	65	74	76	73	88	101
23920	BRODNAX	83	57	31	50	64	74	56	68	67	58	79	81	49	75	57	72	73	68	84	95
23921	BUCKINGHAM	72	55	36	52	60	69	57	64	64	56	76	74	52	73	57	66	70	63	74	81
23922	BURKEVILLE	70	51	30	48	57	67	54	62	62	52	73	71	47	69	54	65	66	62	75	79
23923	CHARLOTTE COURT HOUS	82	60	38	55	67	76	60	70	68	60	81	83	53	77	60	72	75	70	83	94
23924	CHASE CITY	72	50	29	44	56	65	51	60	60	51	71	70	45	66	51	65	65	60	74	82
23927	CLARKSVILLE	94	72	46	65	78	90	71	82	81	70	96	96	64	93	72	86	89	82	98	108
23930	CREWE	71	55	38	52	60	70	58	64	64	56	76	73	53	74	58	68	71	64	75	80
23934	CULLEN	97	65	29	56	73	84	62	78	75	64	88	93	53	84	63	81	80	77	96	111
23936	DILLWYN	69	48	25	43	54	62	48	58	57	48	67	68	42	63	49	60	61	58	70	78
23937	DRAKES BRANCH	83	57	29	50	64	74	55	68	66	56	78	82	48	74	56	71	71	68	83	96
23938	DUNDAS	92	62	28	53	70	80	59	74	72	61	84	89	51	80	60	77	76	74	92	105
23942	GREEN BAY	85	58	29	51	65	76	58	70	68	58	80	83	50	76	58	73	73	70	86	97
23944	KENBRIDGE	85	57	27	50	65	75	56	69	67	57	79	83	48	75	57	72	72	69	85	97
23947	KEYSVILLE	81	57	31	51	64	74	58	69	68	57	80	81	50	75	58	72	73	68	84	92
23950	LA CROSSE	88	62	32	54	70	79	59	73	70	60	83	87	51	79	61	75	76	72	89	102
23952	LUNENBURG	64	48	32	46	53	63	53	59	60	51	70	66	47	66	53	63	64	59	70	71
23954	MEHERRIN	86	57	26	49	65	75	55	69	67	56	78	83	47	74	56	72	71	69	85	98
23958	PAMPLIN	98	70	39	62	78	88	68	82	79	68	93	97	60	90	69	84	86	81	97	112
23959	PHENIX	82	55	25	47	62	72	53	66	64	54	75	79	45	71	54	69	68	66	82	94
23960	PROSPECT	78	57	34	53	63	74	61	69	69	59	81	78	53	77	60	73	74	69	83	87
23962	RANDOLPH	65	52	41	50	56	62	52	58	56	52	68	69	48	65	52	58	64	58	65	74
23963	RED HOUSE	88	59	27	51	67	77	57	71	68	58	80	85	48	76	58	74	73	70	87	101
23964	RED OAK	66	44	20	38	50	57	42	53	51	43	60	63	36	57	43	55	55	52	65	75
23966	RICE	92	64	33	57	72	84	64	77	76	64	89	91	56	84	65	81	81	77	95	105
23967	SAXE	75	50	23	43	57	66	49	61	59	50	69	73	41	65	49	63	63	60	75	86
23968	SKIPWITH	88	59	27	51	67	77	57	71	69	58	81	85	48	76	58	74	73	70	88	101
23970	SOUTH HILL	87	69	51	64	74	84	69	78	77	70	93	89	65	89	70	80	87	77	88	98
23974	VICTORIA	67	47	26	43	53	62	49	57	57	48	67	66	43	63	49	61	61	57	70	75
23976	WYLLIESBURG	71	48	22	41	54	62	46	58	56	47	65	69	39	62	47	60	59	57	71	82
24011	ROANOKE	0	0	0	0	0	0	0	0	0	0	0	0	0	0	0	0	0	0	0	0
	VIRGINIA	112	109	113	109	109	117	108	110	109	109	136	129	108	135	108	109	132	110	109	128
	UNITED STATES	100	100	100	100	100	100	100	100	100	100	100	100	100	100	100	100	100	100	100	100

POPULATION CHANGE

# POST OFFICE NAME	COUNTY FIPS CODE	POPULATION 2000	2004	2009	2000-2004 ANNUAL RATE % Rate	State Centile	HOUSEHOLDS 2000	2004	2009	% Annual Rate 2000-2004	2004 Average HH Size	FAMILIES 2000	2004	% Annual Rate 2000-2004
24012 ROANOKE	770	27089	26808	26508	-0.3	17	12128	12153	12179	0.1	2.16	7412	7296	-0.4
24013 ROANOKE	770	8094	7865	7639	-0.7	8	3191	3161	3124	-0.2	2.44	1980	1916	-0.8
24014 ROANOKE	161	20858	21666	22117	0.9	55	9494	9990	10343	1.2	2.15	5864	6078	0.9
24015 ROANOKE	770	15270	14783	14304	-0.8	6	7332	7182	7045	-0.5	2.03	3834	3660	-1.1
24016 ROANOKE	770	9847	9310	8940	-1.3	1	4111	3908	3785	-1.2	2.05	1803	1676	-1.7
24017 ROANOKE	770	23216	22586	21916	-0.7	8	9480	9394	9270	-0.2	2.36	6154	5980	-0.7
24018 ROANOKE	161	30478	31785	32994	1.0	57	12978	13817	14602	1.5	2.29	8804	9250	1.2
24019 ROANOKE	161	25154	26211	27226	1.0	56	9669	10238	10802	1.4	2.46	7103	7430	1.1
24020 ROANOKE	161	216	221	225	0.5	44	59	64	69	1.9	1.25	31	22	-7.8
24053 ARARAT	141	2317	2552	2734	2.3	83	963	1081	1180	2.8	2.36	708	783	2.4
24054 AXTON	089	6227	6706	6919	1.8	74	2394	2635	2776	2.3	2.54	1818	1976	2.0
24055 BASSETT	089	14455	13880	13489	-1.0	3	5898	5786	5744	-0.5	2.38	4227	4087	-0.8
24059 BENT MOUNTAIN	161	895	891	908	-0.1	20	351	356	369	0.3	2.50	257	258	0.1
24060 BLACKSBURG	121	48416	50587	52968	1.0	58	16855	17985	19229	1.5	2.34	7176	7478	1.0
24064 BLUE RIDGE	019	4278	4566	4877	1.5	69	1607	1748	1897	2.0	2.61	1298	1395	1.7
24065 BOONES MILL	067	5829	6110	6460	1.1	60	2361	2520	2712	1.6	2.42	1761	1855	1.2
24066 BUCHANAN	023	4472	4534	4683	0.3	36	1837	1893	1984	0.7	2.38	1345	1364	0.3
24067 CALLAWAY	067	2188	2485	2752	3.0	90	830	964	1088	3.6	2.53	629	723	3.3
24069 CASCADE	143	2060	2090	2106	0.3	37	788	818	841	0.9	2.53	596	610	0.6
24070 CATAWBA	045	1857	1874	1914	0.2	32	716	737	766	0.7	2.43	542	551	0.4
24072 CHECK	063	1356	1499	1651	2.4	84	559	627	701	2.7	2.39	419	463	2.4
24073 CHRISTIANSBURG	121	24719	25504	26649	0.7	51	10065	10530	11152	1.1	2.38	6984	7206	0.7
24076 CLAUDVILLE	141	1319	1347	1383	0.5	43	553	576	602	1.0	2.34	398	409	0.6
24077 CLOVERDALE	023	577	637	686	2.4	83	245	273	297	2.6	2.33	172	187	2.0
24078 COLLINSVILLE	089	6715	6567	6411	-0.5	10	3003	2992	2979	-0.1	2.16	1912	1869	-0.5
24079 COPPER HILL	063	1793	1988	2194	2.5	85	731	824	924	2.9	2.41	534	594	2.5
24082 CRITZ	141	330	346	360	1.1	61	128	137	145	1.6	2.53	96	102	1.4
24083 DALEVILLE	023	2188	2341	2480	1.6	70	856	932	1003	2.0	2.51	711	767	1.8
24084 DUBLIN	155	10999	11227	11319	0.5	41	4300	4508	4655	1.1	2.31	3021	3126	0.8
24085 EAGLE ROCK	023	2415	2380	2436	-0.3	15	983	990	1031	0.2	2.38	709	702	-0.2
24086 EGGLESTON	071	378	373	387	-0.3	15	153	154	163	0.2	2.42	114	113	-0.2
24087 ELLISTON	121	3920	4028	4191	0.6	47	1544	1613	1703	1.0	2.50	1129	1164	0.7
24088 FERRUM	067	4441	4855	5248	2.1	80	1568	1772	1970	2.9	2.42	1127	1254	2.5
24089 FIELDALE	089	2622	2456	2357	-1.5	1	1147	1102	1082	-0.9	2.20	812	767	-1.3
24090 FINCASTLE	023	4374	4649	4944	1.5	67	1685	1820	1966	1.8	2.48	1312	1401	1.6
24091 FLOYD	063	6327	6607	7060	1.0	58	2701	2868	3115	1.4	2.28	1884	1967	1.0
24092 GLADE HILL	067	2608	2791	2996	1.6	71	1065	1160	1266	2.0	2.41	787	846	1.7
24093 GLEN LYN	071	140	148	157	1.3	64	54	58	63	1.7	2.55	40	43	1.7
24094 GOLDBOND	071	114	126	138	2.4	83	47	53	59	2.9	2.38	34	38	2.7
24095 GOODVIEW	019	3347	3506	3751	1.1	60	1295	1377	1494	1.5	2.55	1021	1073	1.2
24101 HARDY	067	4431	4596	4848	0.9	54	1734	1833	1967	1.3	2.51	1378	1441	1.1
24102 HENRY	067	1638	1797	1951	2.2	82	661	741	821	2.7	2.39	483	535	2.4
24104 HUDDLESTON	019	3020	3404	3788	2.9	89	1307	1507	1709	3.4	2.26	986	1125	3.2
24105 INDIAN VALLEY	063	581	627	681	1.8	75	235	257	284	2.1	2.44	179	194	1.9
24112 MARTINSVILLE	089	36468	35403	34269	-0.7	7	15103	14922	14695	-0.3	2.31	10172	9906	-0.6
24120 MEADOWS OF DAN	141	2438	2502	2589	0.6	46	1069	1119	1180	1.1	2.23	753	777	0.7
24121 MONETA	019	8766	9503	10322	1.9	78	3713	4102	4534	2.4	2.30	2857	3118	2.1
24122 MONTVALE	019	2317	2408	2562	0.9	55	926	978	1058	1.3	2.43	688	718	1.0
24124 NARROWS	071	5300	5527	5834	1.0	57	2195	2331	2507	1.4	2.36	1562	1636	1.1
24127 NEW CASTLE	045	4040	4161	4272	0.7	49	1630	1709	1781	1.1	2.41	1193	1235	0.8
24128 NEWPORT	071	1361	1363	1414	0.0	25	591	605	641	0.6	2.25	411	415	0.2
24131 PAINT BANK	045	143	147	150	0.7	48	52	54	57	0.9	2.69	39	40	0.6
24133 PATRICK SPRINGS	141	3027	3131	3238	0.8	52	1234	1301	1370	1.3	2.41	922	959	0.9
24134 PEARISBURG	071	5498	5979	6477	2.0	79	2344	2596	2864	2.4	2.30	1625	1773	2.1
24136 PEMBROKE	071	2997	3146	3344	1.2	61	1249	1335	1446	1.6	2.36	856	903	1.3
24137 PENHOOK	067	2376	2586	2788	2.0	79	1012	1122	1231	2.5	2.30	745	814	2.1
24138 PILOT	121	1432	1477	1541	0.7	50	551	578	613	1.1	2.51	425	441	0.9
24139 PITTSVILLE	143	539	553	562	0.6	46	220	231	240	1.2	2.39	158	163	0.7
24141 RADFORD	155	20298	19818	19260	-0.6	10	8892	8876	8815	0.0	2.07	4824	4731	-0.5
24142 RADFORD	750	2755	2711	2649	-0.4	13	8	8	8	0.0	2.50	1	1	0.0
24147 RICH CREEK	071	865	840	867	-0.7	7	366	360	378	-0.4	2.23	256	248	-0.7
24148 RIDGEWAY	089	8321	8635	8690	0.9	54	3430	3641	3745	1.4	2.37	2492	2607	1.1
24149 RINER	121	2351	2371	2435	0.2	32	932	953	992	0.5	2.49	720	729	0.3
24150 RIPPLEMEAD	071	342	370	398	1.9	76	146	161	177	2.3	2.30	104	113	2.0
24151 ROCKY MOUNT	067	17816	18729	20005	1.2	62	7148	7655	8330	1.6	2.39	5017	5306	1.3
24153 SALEM	161	35522	36043	36792	0.3	37	14069	14468	14969	0.7	2.34	9686	9818	0.3
24161 SANDY LEVEL	143	392	402	408	0.6	45	165	173	180	1.1	2.32	117	121	0.8
24162 SHAWSVILLE	121	2301	2231	2266	-0.7	7	883	870	898	-0.4	2.41	650	631	-0.7
24165 SPENCER	141	1536	1504	1498	-0.5	11	673	676	688	0.1	2.22	480	475	-0.3
24167 STAFFORDSVILLE	071	407	409	422	0.1	28	163	166	175	0.4	2.46	122	123	0.2
24168 STANLEYTOWN	089	235	239	239	0.4	39	96	101	104	1.2	2.22	64	66	0.7
24171 STUART	141	8361	8433	8625	0.2	32	3498	3596	3749	0.7	2.28	2433	2464	0.3
24174 THAXTON	019	2087	2212	2382	1.4	66	853	921	1008	1.8	2.40	612	652	1.5
24175 TROUTVILLE	023	7374	7719	8130	1.1	60	2743	2920	3126	1.5	2.54	2192	2317	1.3
24176 UNION HALL	067	1210	1277	1361	1.3	64	509	548	594	1.8	2.33	388	412	1.4
24179 VINTON	019	19228	19452	20197	0.3	33	7847	8053	8488	0.6	2.39	5751	5827	0.3
24184 WIRTZ	067	2776	3045	3310	2.2	82	1113	1243	1375	2.6	2.45	848	934	2.3
24185 WOOLWINE	141	880	903	929	0.6	46	377	394	412	1.0	2.29	265	272	0.6
24201 BRISTOL	520	16632	16244	15786	-0.6	10	7335	7297	7228	-0.1	2.14	4570	4465	-0.6
24202 BRISTOL	191	11766	12599	13329	1.6	71	4817	5263	5681	2.1	2.39	3628	3916	1.8
24210 ABINGDON	191	14812	14742	15144	-0.1	20	6455	6575	6913	0.4	2.16	4178	4178	0.0
24211 ABINGDON	191	8847	9519	10106	1.7	73	3668	4036	4381	2.3	2.33	2683	2913	2.0
24216 APPALACHIA	195	3399	3536	3591	0.9	56	1421	1520	1570	1.6	2.33	973	1025	1.2
24217 BEE	051	376	367	362	-0.6	9	157	158	159	0.2	2.32	115	114	-0.2
24219 BIG STONE GAP	195	10939	11118	11149	0.4	38	4419	4589	4667	0.9	2.38	3164	3242	0.6
24220 BIRCHLEAF	051	1050	1050	1048	0.0	24	394	405	412	0.7	2.59	311	316	0.4
24221 BLACKWATER	105	1054	1037	1016	-0.4	13	444	443	443	-0.1	2.34	320	315	-0.4
24224 CASTLEWOOD	167	8613	8313	8272	-0.8	5	3484	3433	3490	-0.4	2.40	2602	2536	-0.6
24225 CLEVELAND	167	1951	1851	1836	-1.2	2	808	782	793	-0.8	2.37	585	563	-0.9
24226 CLINCHCO	051	1729	1703	1688	-0.4	14	711	721	731	0.3	2.36	526	526	0.0
24228 CLINTWOOD	051	7748	7696	7656	-0.2	19	3231	3303	3361	0.5	2.29	2300	2319	0.2
24230 COEBURN	195	9370	9437	9444	0.2	30	3660	3774	3838	0.7	2.44	2717	2769	0.5
24236 DAMASCUS	191	3127	3261	3405	1.0	57	1383	1474	1572	1.5	2.21	927	966	1.0
24237 DANTE	051	996	960	950	-0.9	4	418	415	421	-0.2	2.31	306	300	-0.5
24239 DAVENPORT	027	26	25	24	-0.9	4	8	8	8	0.0	3.13	6	6	0.0
VIRGINIA					1.4					1.7	2.51			1.4
UNITED STATES					1.2					1.3	2.58			1.1

ZIP CODE #	POST OFFICE NAME	RACE (%) White 2000	White 2004	Black 2000	Black 2004	Asian/Pacific 2000	Asian/Pacific 2004	% Hispanic Origin 2000	% Hispanic Origin 2004	2004 AGE DISTRIBUTION (%) 0-4	5-9	10-14	15-19	20-24	25-44	45-64	65-84	85+	18+	MEDIAN AGE 2004	% 2004 Males	% 2004 Females
24012	ROANOKE	82.9	81.2	12.6	13.5	1.7	2.0	1.8	2.3	6.3	6.3	6.1	5.1	5.2	28.6	24.8	15.0	2.7	78.3	39.9	47.3	52.8
24013	ROANOKE	90.9	89.4	5.3	6.1	0.9	1.1	1.4	1.7	7.0	6.9	7.6	7.1	6.4	29.3	22.8	11.2	1.7	74.1	36.0	49.6	50.4
24014	ROANOKE	93.0	91.8	3.9	4.4	1.6	1.9	1.1	1.4	5.1	5.3	6.0	5.9	5.4	26.9	29.0	14.3	2.2	80.1	42.1	47.3	52.8
24015	ROANOKE	92.5	91.1	4.7	5.5	1.0	1.2	1.2	1.5	6.5	6.0	5.7	5.5	5.9	32.5	23.9	11.6	2.5	78.6	37.8	46.7	53.3
24016	ROANOKE	46.8	43.1	47.9	50.9	0.8	0.9	2.4	2.8	5.9	5.7	6.4	6.8	8.4	33.4	21.7	9.1	2.7	78.3	35.1	50.6	49.4
24017	ROANOKE	29.9	27.2	66.4	68.7	0.9	1.0	1.2	1.4	7.0	7.1	7.9	6.7	6.2	24.9	25.0	13.2	1.9	73.8	37.4	45.5	54.6
24018	ROANOKE	94.0	93.1	2.2	2.4	2.5	2.9	1.2	1.6	5.1	5.7	6.9	6.2	4.9	24.0	29.4	15.4	2.4	78.5	43.3	47.3	52.7
24019	ROANOKE	90.5	89.4	6.6	7.1	1.4	1.7	0.9	1.1	5.7	6.1	6.6	6.5	5.5	25.7	27.9	14.1	2.0	78.0	41.1	46.9	53.1
24020	ROANOKE	81.5	79.6	13.0	13.6	2.8	3.2	2.8	3.6	1.8	2.3	1.8	29.9	26.2	14.9	15.4	7.2	0.5	92.3	22.7	24.4	75.6
24053	ARARAT	92.4	91.5	4.5	4.9	0.4	0.4	2.5	3.1	6.1	6.3	6.2	5.3	5.8	29.1	25.6	14.3	1.4	78.2	39.4	51.5	48.5
24054	AXTON	64.4	63.8	32.9	33.1	0.2	0.3	3.6	4.6	6.5	6.6	6.8	6.4	6.0	28.9	26.2	11.5	1.0	76.3	38.2	48.8	51.2
24055	BASSETT	83.4	82.1	13.2	13.7	0.2	0.3	5.0	6.4	5.6	5.6	5.9	5.9	5.7	27.9	26.5	15.2	1.7	79.3	40.9	49.7	50.3
24059	BENT MOUNTAIN	94.4	93.8	2.9	3.1	0.7	0.8	1.2	1.5	4.3	7.0	7.0	8.3	4.8	23.3	33.9	10.4	1.0	76.9	42.2	50.2	49.8
24060	BLACKSBURG	86.3	84.4	4.0	4.2	6.7	7.8	2.1	2.5	3.5	3.4	4.0	24.8	18.0	25.2	13.9	6.2	1.0	86.2	24.0	53.2	46.8
24064	BLUE RIDGE	96.1	95.5	2.2	2.4	0.7	0.8	0.5	0.6	5.7	6.3	6.7	6.2	4.5	27.3	31.3	11.2	0.9	77.5	41.5	48.9	51.1
24065	BOONES MILL	94.4	93.8	3.9	4.2	0.4	0.5	1.1	1.3	5.4	5.9	6.6	5.7	4.4	27.4	30.1	13.1	1.4	78.5	41.9	49.3	50.7
24066	BUCHANAN	95.1	94.6	3.8	4.0	0.2	0.3	0.4	0.6	5.2	5.7	6.0	5.6	4.4	28.1	29.3	14.1	1.5	79.4	42.2	48.9	51.1
24067	CALLAWAY	95.1	94.5	3.5	3.8	0.4	0.5	0.7	0.8	6.0	6.4	6.3	6.3	5.5	27.7	29.3	11.1	1.5	77.8	39.9	49.6	50.4
24069	CASCADE	57.2	54.8	41.5	43.7	0.2	0.1	1.2	1.4	5.8	6.1	6.7	6.4	5.7	28.2	27.2	12.5	1.5	77.2	40.3	49.2	50.8
24070	CATAWBA	96.8	96.6	1.7	1.8	0.1	0.1	0.3	0.3	5.4	6.2	6.7	5.8	4.4	27.4	29.0	13.2	1.8	77.9	42.0	50.5	49.5
24072	CHECK	97.4	97.0	1.7	1.9	0.2	0.1	0.7	0.9	6.7	7.1	6.7	5.5	4.5	28.2	28.5	11.4	1.5	76.1	39.7	50.1	49.9
24073	CHRISTIANSBURG	94.4	93.8	3.8	4.1	0.4	0.4	0.9	1.2	6.8	6.7	6.5	6.3	5.6	32.0	24.5	10.5	1.2	76.1	36.4	48.9	51.2
24076	CLAUDVILLE	91.5	90.6	6.1	6.5	0.2	0.2	2.1	2.5	5.9	6.2	6.5	5.1	5.7	26.1	29.3	13.4	1.8	78.3	41.0	50.3	49.7
24077	CLOVERDALE	91.2	90.0	6.4	7.2	0.9	1.1	0.5	0.6	5.2	6.0	6.8	6.0	5.0	24.2	31.7	13.7	1.6	78.3	43.3	49.0	51.0
24078	COLLINSVILLE	84.1	82.7	12.1	12.7	0.8	1.0	3.7	4.7	5.9	5.8	5.9	5.5	5.5	29.2	24.9	15.2	2.1	79.0	40.0	47.7	52.3
24079	COPPER HILL	95.9	95.3	2.8	3.1	0.2	0.2	0.8	1.0	6.0	6.2	6.0	5.4	4.8	26.8	30.4	12.6	1.7	78.4	41.2	49.6	50.4
24082	CRITZ	83.0	82.1	15.8	16.8	0.0	0.0	0.6	0.6	6.4	6.4	7.2	6.7	5.8	30.4	25.7	10.1	1.5	76.0	37.4	48.8	51.2
24083	DALEVILLE	97.0	96.6	2.1	2.2	0.4	0.5	0.8	1.1	5.8	6.7	6.8	5.6	4.1	22.5	33.1	14.3	1.2	77.2	44.1	50.3	49.7
24084	DUBLIN	92.9	92.8	5.6	5.7	0.3	0.3	0.5	0.5	5.2	5.2	5.2	5.1	5.4	30.6	29.8	11.7	1.6	81.2	40.7	51.1	48.9
24085	EAGLE ROCK	94.5	94.1	4.1	4.4	0.0	0.0	0.7	0.8	5.5	5.8	5.8	5.5	4.6	25.0	31.4	14.9	1.6	79.5	43.7	50.6	49.4
24086	EGGLESTON	97.1	97.3	1.9	1.9	0.0	0.0	0.3	0.5	5.4	5.9	6.4	5.1	5.1	27.4	30.3	12.6	1.9	79.1	41.9	54.7	45.3
24087	ELLISTON	95.3	94.8	2.4	2.5	0.3	0.3	1.2	1.4	6.8	6.7	7.2	6.4	6.2	29.5	27.4	8.9	0.9	75.1	37.3	50.9	49.1
24088	FERRUM	93.1	92.4	5.4	5.9	0.2	0.2	1.3	1.6	5.2	5.4	5.8	11.3	11.3	25.6	23.9	10.2	1.4	80.1	34.3	50.4	49.6
24089	FIELDALE	77.1	75.5	20.3	21.5	0.3	0.3	4.5	5.7	5.5	5.5	6.2	6.4	5.7	27.4	25.4	16.0	2.0	79.0	40.8	49.1	50.9
24090	FINCASTLE	95.1	94.6	3.6	3.8	0.3	0.3	0.6	0.7	4.8	5.3	5.7	6.0	5.2	25.8	32.6	13.0	1.6	80.3	43.4	50.5	49.5
24091	FLOYD	95.9	95.5	2.8	2.9	0.1	0.1	1.6	2.1	5.4	5.7	6.2	5.4	4.9	26.4	28.3	15.2	2.7	79.6	42.4	48.5	51.5
24092	GLADE HILL	89.2	87.7	9.1	10.3	0.1	0.1	1.8	2.3	5.6	5.9	6.2	5.4	5.2	27.5	29.7	13.5	1.1	79.0	41.9	49.6	50.4
24093	GLEN LYN	98.6	98.0	0.7	0.7	0.0	0.0	0.7	0.7	4.7	5.4	5.4	6.8	6.1	25.7	29.1	15.5	1.4	80.4	42.5	51.4	48.7
24094	GOLDBOND	94.7	94.4	4.4	4.8	0.0	0.0	0.0	0.8	5.6	5.6	6.4	5.6	4.0	28.6	29.4	13.5	1.6	77.8	41.5	51.6	48.4
24095	GOODVIEW	95.3	94.9	3.5	3.7	0.2	0.2	0.7	0.8	5.8	6.6	7.2	5.7	4.4	28.7	30.6	10.3	0.7	76.8	40.3	50.7	49.3
24101	HARDY	95.2	94.5	3.8	4.2	0.2	0.2	0.8	1.0	5.2	5.9	6.5	5.4	3.9	26.5	33.4	12.2	1.0	79.0	43.0	51.0	49.0
24102	HENRY	93.8	93.8	4.8	4.6	0.7	0.8	1.1	1.4	5.6	6.0	6.3	5.5	5.1	27.4	28.8	13.6	1.8	78.5	41.2	49.0	51.0
24104	HUDDLESTON	92.3	91.9	6.1	6.3	0.3	0.4	0.7	0.9	4.6	4.9	5.1	4.6	4.0	21.6	31.8	21.9	1.6	82.6	48.5	50.2	49.9
24105	INDIAN VALLEY	98.3	97.9	0.9	1.0	0.0	0.0	0.9	1.1	6.4	6.5	6.7	6.5	6.5	26.6	28.1	10.9	1.8	76.6	38.4	51.7	48.3
24112	MARTINSVILLE	61.7	59.7	35.9	37.5	0.5	0.6	2.6	3.2	5.4	5.6	6.3	6.2	5.6	26.4	27.3	15.0	2.3	78.9	41.5	47.6	52.4
24120	MEADOWS OF DAN	96.7	96.2	1.4	1.4	0.2	0.3	2.2	2.7	5.0	5.3	5.9	5.0	4.7	25.3	28.2	18.1	2.4	80.6	44.1	50.0	50.0
24121	MONETA	93.8	93.2	4.9	5.3	0.2	0.2	1.0	1.2	4.4	4.7	5.3	4.6	3.8	23.2	34.5	18.3	1.1	82.7	47.4	50.6	49.4
24122	MONTVALE	96.6	96.2	2.0	2.2	0.3	0.3	0.3	0.3	5.4	5.8	6.0	6.5	4.8	29.4	29.8	10.8	1.5	78.6	41.0	51.5	48.6
24124	NARROWS	97.9	97.7	1.3	1.3	0.1	0.2	0.6	0.9	6.0	5.9	5.9	5.8	5.4	26.1	27.2	15.5	2.2	78.6	41.5	48.7	51.3
24127	NEW CASTLE	98.9	98.8	0.2	0.2	0.2	0.2	0.3	0.4	5.6	6.1	6.6	6.2	5.0	27.4	28.9	12.8	1.4	77.5	41.0	51.1	48.9
24128	NEWPORT	98.2	98.2	0.2	0.2	0.2	0.2	0.5	0.7	4.2	4.8	5.7	5.3	4.6	29.5	32.8	11.9	1.4	82.3	42.6	50.5	49.5
24131	PAINT BANK	98.6	99.3	0.0	0.0	0.0	0.0	0.0	0.7	5.4	5.4	6.8	7.5	6.1	27.2	29.3	11.6	0.7	77.6	39.8	51.0	49.0
24133	PATRICK SPRINGS	91.8	91.0	6.8	7.3	0.1	0.2	0.8	1.1	6.0	6.3	6.8	6.0	5.7	28.7	27.7	11.8	1.1	77.2	39.2	49.4	50.7
24134	PEARISBURG	96.8	96.4	2.0	2.1	0.3	0.3	0.6	0.8	5.7	5.9	6.3	5.6	5.0	26.4	27.3	15.7	2.1	78.4	41.8	49.2	50.8
24136	PEMBROKE	96.3	96.0	2.9	3.1	0.1	0.1	0.6	0.8	5.2	5.6	6.2	5.7	5.0	29.0	28.7	13.1	1.6	79.6	41.0	49.6	50.4
24137	PENHOOK	81.7	79.6	17.1	19.0	0.1	0.2	0.8	1.0	5.4	5.6	5.9	5.3	5.0	25.4	31.4	14.7	1.4	79.9	43.5	50.0	50.0
24138	PILOT	98.7	98.6	0.6	0.6	0.2	0.3	0.8	1.0	5.9	6.3	6.6	5.8	5.1	28.4	29.3	11.1	1.5	77.6	40.4	50.0	50.0
24139	PITTSVILLE	78.7	76.7	19.7	21.2	0.0	0.0	0.6	1.1	5.2	5.2	5.8	5.8	5.2	25.5	30.9	14.8	1.5	80.5	43.3	49.4	50.6
24141	RADFORD	90.4	89.6	6.9	7.2	1.0	1.2	0.9	1.1	4.6	4.6	4.9	9.9	17.6	24.0	21.8	11.0	1.6	83.1	31.8	47.4	52.6
24142	RADFORD	88.2	86.9	7.6	8.0	1.6	1.9	1.9	2.4	0.5	0.4	0.4	40.9	48.7	5.5	2.2	1.1	0.3	98.3	20.8	41.4	58.6
24147	RICH CREEK	99.0	98.8	0.6	0.6	0.2	0.2	1.0	1.3	6.3	6.0	5.6	5.2	5.4	24.8	26.1	17.4	3.3	78.7	42.6	48.5	51.6
24148	RIDGEWAY	79.9	78.5	18.3	19.4	0.5	0.5	1.2	1.4	5.5	5.8	6.6	6.0	4.9	28.1	28.7	13.3	1.2	78.5	41.1	49.4	50.6
24149	RINER	99.1	98.9	0.3	0.3	0.1	0.2	1.0	1.3	5.3	6.6	7.4	8.1	3.6	28.9	29.0	10.2	1.0	75.5	39.1	49.0	51.0
24150	RIPPLEMEAD	95.6	95.4	3.8	4.1	0.0	0.0	0.6	0.8	5.7	6.0	6.0	5.1	4.6	28.7	28.7	13.8	1.6	79.2	41.3	50.0	50.0
24151	ROCKY MOUNT	82.1	80.8	15.6	16.5	0.6	0.7	1.5	1.9	5.9	6.2	6.7	6.1	5.6	27.9	26.4	13.2	1.9	77.3	39.8	48.5	51.5
24153	SALEM	93.5	92.8	4.6	4.9	0.8	1.0	0.8	0.9	4.6	5.1	6.2	7.3	6.5	24.8	27.6	15.2	2.7	80.3	42.1	47.4	52.7
24161	SANDY LEVEL	80.9	78.9	16.3	17.9	0.0	0.0	0.8	0.8	5.0	4.7	4.0	4.5	4.0	23.6	34.3	18.2	1.7	83.3	47.9	49.5	50.5
24162	SHAWSVILLE	96.3	95.8	2.7	2.9	0.2	0.2	0.7	1.0	4.8	5.2	5.7	5.3	5.4	27.4	29.8	14.0	2.5	81.0	42.4	49.5	50.5
24165	SPENCER	80.7	79.1	18.0	19.4	0.1	0.1	0.9	1.1	5.5	5.6	5.9	5.5	4.7	28.9	27.9	14.4	1.5	79.7	41.2	48.5	51.5
24167	STAFFORDSVILLE	97.8	97.8	1.5	1.5	0.3	0.2	0.7	1.0	6.9	6.9	5.9	5.9	5.9	26.9	27.1	13.0	1.7	77.5	39.9	51.3	48.7
24168	STANLEYTOWN	84.3	82.4	11.1	12.1	0.4	0.4	7.2	9.2	3.8	4.2	4.6	6.3	5.4	25.1	26.4	20.1	4.2	83.3	45.4	47.7	52.3
24171	STUART	90.9	90.0	7.1	7.6	0.2	0.2	2.0	2.5	5.8	5.7	5.7	5.3	5.3	26.1	27.6	15.6	3.0	79.6	42.4	48.8	51.2
24174	THAXTON	97.4	97.1	1.5	1.6	0.1	0.2	0.9	1.0	5.1	5.7	6.7	5.8	5.0	29.2	29.0	12.1	1.5	78.8	40.9	50.4	49.6
24175	TROUTVILLE	94.9	94.4	3.5	3.7	0.5	0.6	0.5	0.7	5.5	6.0	6.1	5.8	4.6	25.8	31.8	13.3	1.2	78.7	42.9	51.3	48.7
24176	UNION HALL	89.3	87.7	9.4	10.7	0.2	0.2	0.9	1.2	4.5	4.6	4.9	4.5	4.6	22.7	35.8	17.3	1.0	83.2	47.5	50.2	49.8
24179	VINTON	96.3	95.8	2.0	2.2	0.5	0.6	0.8	1.1	5.9	6.1	6.4	5.9	5.7	26.8	28.4	13.1	1.9	78.1	41.0	48.3	51.7
24184	WIRTZ	94.7	94.1	3.5	3.8	0.2	0.3	0.9	1.3	5.1	6.0	6.9	5.9	4.6	27.4	30.2	12.8	1.1	78.1	41.4	50.2	49.9
24185	WOOLWINE	95.1	94.5	2.6	2.8	0.1	0.1	2.4	3.0	5.1	5.3	5.4	5.5	5.0	25.5	29.2	16.8	2.1	80.6	43.8	51.1	49.0
24201	BRISTOL	92.3	91.5	5.8	6.2	0.4	0.5	1.0	1.2	5.4	5.3	5.7	5.9	6.1	25.7	25.3	17.6	3.0	80.2	42.1	45.4	54.6
24202	BRISTOL	98.6	98.4	0.5	0.5	0.2	0.2	0.6	0.8	5.1	5.6	6.4	5.5	5.2	27.5	29.3	14.2	1.2	79.4	41.8	49.5	50.5
24210	ABINGDON	96.7	96.2	2.0	2.1	0.4	0.4	0.8	1.0	5.1	5.1	5.4	5.3	5.7	26.9	27.9	15.9	2.7	81.3	42.7	47.0	53.0
24211	ABINGDON	98.4	98.1	0.6	0.6	0.3	0.4	0.6	0.7	5.0	5.7	6.0	5.8	4.9	27.3	29.9	14.2	1.3	79.7	42.3	49.2	50.9
24216	APPALACHIA	95.7	95.3	3.2	3.5	0.2	0.2	0.8	1.1	6.0	6.0	6.6	6.0	6.1	25.9	27.1	14.3	2.0	77.9	39.4	47.5	52.5
24217	BEE	99.5	99.2	0.0	0.0	0.0	0.0	1.1	1.4	5.5	5.7	7.1	7.1	6.0	26.2	28.6	12.5	1.4	77.4	40.8	51.8	48.2
24219	BIG STONE GAP	96.2	95.8	2.3	2.5	0.4	0.5	0.5	0.6	6.0	6.3	6.7	5.8	6.4	26.2	27.9	12.8	2.1	77.5	39.6	48.3	51.7
24220	BIRCHLEAF	99.7	99.6	0.0	0.0	0.0	0.0	0.2	0.2	5.5	7.3	7.0	6.5	6.0	29.1	27.2	10.5	0.9	76.0	38.1	50.5	49.5
24221	BLACKWATER	98.9	98.8	0.1	0.1	0.0	0.0	0.4	0.4	5.3	5.4	5.5	5.4	5.4	25.8	28.8	15.8	2.5	80.5	43.1	50.1	49.9
24224	CASTLEWOOD	98.4	98.3	0.8	0.9	0.1	0.1	0.5	0.7	5.3	5.5	6.2	5.7	6.0	27.5	28.7	13.7	1.4	79.6	41.1	49.2	50.8
24225	CLEVELAND	98.9	98.8	0.4	0.4	0.1	0.1	0.6	0.8	5.3	5.6	5.9	5.7	5.4	27.8	29.3	13.6	1.5	79.7	41.2	50.6	49.4
24226	CLINCHCO	98.4	98.2	0.8	0.8	0.1	0.1	0.4	0.4	5.2	5.5	6.1	6.2	5.9	26.6	29.6	13.5	1.4	79.4	41.4	49.3	50.7
24228	CLINTWOOD	98.7	98.5	0.5	0.5	0.1	0.2	0.4	0.5	5.4	5.6	5.3	5.4	6.0	26.3	29.4	14.6	2.1	80.6	42.4	48.8	51.2
24230	COEBURN	96.2	95.7	2.5	2.7	0.1	0.2	1.0	1.2	5.6	5.9	6.4	7.0	6.8	28.0	26.9	12.1	1.3	78.0	38.4	50.4	49.7
24236	DAMASCUS	98.8	98.6	0.5	0.6	0.1	0.2	0.6	0.8	4.9	5.2	6.6	5.5	5.6	26.3	28.6	15.7	1.7	80.0	42.0	48.2	51.8
24237	DANTE	97.9	97.8	1.4	1.5	0.0	0.0	0.4	0.4	5.3	5.2	5.8	6.3	6.2	25.8	29.1	14.4	2.0	79.7	41.6	50.8	49.2
24239	DAVENPORT	100.0	100.0	0.0	0.0	0.0	0.0	0.0	0.0	4.0	8.0	8.0	8.0	8.0	32.0	32.0	0.0	0.0	80.0	33.8	48.0	52.0
	VIRGINIA	72.3	70.7	19.6	19.9	3.7	4.3	4.7	5.7	6.5	6.6	6.9	6.9	7.0	29.7	24.9	10.1	1.4	76.2	36.6	49.1	50.9
	UNITED STATES	75.1	73.6	12.3	12.5	3.8	4.2	12.5	14.1	6.9	6.7	7.2	7.0	7.3	28.6	23.8	10.8	1.7	75.1	36.0	49.1	50.9

#	POST OFFICE NAME	2004 Per Capita Income	2004 HH Income Base	2004 Household Income Distribution (%) Less than $25,000	$25,000 to $49,999	$50,000 to $99,999	$100,000 to $149,999	$150,000 or More	Median Household Income 2004	2009	2004 National Centile	2004 State Centile	2004 Home Value Base	2004 Home Value Distribution (%) Less than $50,000	$50,000 to $89,999	$90,000 to $174,999	$175,000 to $399,999	$400,000 or More	2004 Median Home Value
24012	ROANOKE	21166	12153	31.6	33.8	28.3	5.5	0.9	36951	42817	35	29	7422	4.9	27.1	56.7	11.0	0.3	104759
24013	ROANOKE	13486	3161	47.9	35.2	14.1	2.0	0.8	25993	29443	6	4	1699	32.8	57.0	9.7	0.5	0.0	59653
24014	ROANOKE	40412	9990	20.0	28.7	29.0	10.3	12.0	51217	63024	74	67	6594	5.9	16.9	37.4	31.4	8.4	139100
24015	ROANOKE	27896	7182	23.3	35.6	30.2	7.5	3.4	42450	51201	54	46	4155	1.7	14.4	69.0	14.4	0.5	123766
24016	ROANOKE	16092	3908	56.6	26.2	13.7	2.6	1.0	20765	23636	2	2	1244	36.6	33.8	22.5	6.8	0.2	63366
24017	ROANOKE	17414	9394	41.4	31.7	22.4	3.2	1.4	30158	35476	13	10	5513	10.8	47.4	39.5	2.0	0.4	84337
24018	ROANOKE	37382	13817	13.4	24.9	35.4	16.2	10.1	62611	76614	87	81	10182	0.7	3.5	49.9	42.0	3.9	168454
24019	ROANOKE	27844	10238	14.4	28.0	42.1	11.3	4.3	56184	65777	81	76	8377	3.1	8.2	62.9	24.7	1.1	135576
24020	ROANOKE	18907	64	46.9	31.3	21.9	0.0	0.0	27308	34081	8	6	26	30.8	30.8	26.9	11.5	0.0	66667
24053	ARARAT	21708	1081	39.5	35.9	19.3	2.9	2.4	29325	33655	11	9	874	22.1	17.6	48.5	10.0	1.8	104333
24054	AXTON	18181	2635	31.3	33.8	29.1	3.6	2.2	40170	45846	47	40	2168	24.8	25.6	38.0	9.8	1.9	89484
24055	BASSETT	19754	5786	36.2	33.6	23.4	4.8	2.1	34048	39041	24	19	4574	19.7	23.5	45.5	10.6	0.7	98179
24059	BENT MOUNTAIN	37984	356	16.0	28.1	34.3	9.8	11.8	56625	68098	81	76	307	7.8	2.9	45.3	40.7	3.3	161397
24060	BLACKSBURG	22003	17985	41.9	24.0	20.4	8.0	5.8	31604	39776	17	12	6911	12.9	5.7	26.6	47.3	7.6	186675
24064	BLUE RIDGE	26120	1748	17.7	25.7	38.3	13.4	4.8	57104	66862	82	77	1556	9.3	8.4	49.5	32.5	0.4	148761
24065	BOONES MILL	24010	2520	25.7	28.1	35.1	7.3	3.9	46396	54746	65	57	2099	10.6	15.3	43.8	27.2	3.1	134840
24066	BUCHANAN	21919	1893	24.0	36.1	31.6	6.4	1.9	43273	50914	57	49	1569	12.9	21.7	44.5	19.8	1.2	110510
24067	CALLAWAY	23563	964	19.5	33.8	34.1	7.7	4.9	46680	55178	65	58	817	10.2	13.2	37.5	34.6	4.5	149116
24069	CASCADE	17637	818	33.0	29.1	33.7	2.2	2.0	40294	46092	47	40	665	20.3	35.3	34.9	8.6	0.9	85370
24070	CATAWBA	21738	737	23.7	34.5	30.9	9.4	1.5	43963	50676	59	51	618	7.4	16.2	36.1	35.3	5.0	143878
24072	CHECK	18989	627	27.0	35.7	33.2	3.4	0.8	39094	45061	43	37	532	13.4	21.6	36.7	26.3	2.1	124603
24073	CHRISTIANSBURG	23225	10530	23.8	30.9	35.1	8.0	2.2	46259	55314	64	56	7753	12.6	11.2	45.6	28.4	2.2	137590
24076	CLAUDVILLE	19354	576	36.3	36.5	22.2	3.0	2.1	34613	40000	26	21	469	19.0	35.0	35.6	10.0	0.4	86373
24077	CLOVERDALE	28381	273	21.3	28.2	34.4	9.5	6.6	50549	60509	73	66	228	13.6	14.5	33.8	34.2	4.0	142391
24078	COLLINSVILLE	20821	2992	33.7	33.8	26.5	4.4	1.6	34819	39639	27	22	1974	14.9	20.2	48.8	14.8	1.2	109988
24079	COPPER HILL	19229	824	28.3	35.0	31.1	5.1	0.6	41657	47907	52	43	694	15.7	18.3	40.9	22.1	3.0	120202
24082	CRITZ	14156	137	42.3	34.3	20.4	2.9	0.0	28286	31427	9	7	112	28.6	15.2	33.0	23.2	0.0	104412
24083	DALEVILLE	38034	932	11.9	16.3	40.3	14.2	17.3	70879	88043	92	85	845	3.6	0.8	34.4	51.0	10.2	197288
24084	DUBLIN	22149	4508	26.0	31.2	34.5	6.3	2.0	44560	51588	60	52	3481	11.8	15.5	50.7	20.1	1.9	121274
24085	EAGLE ROCK	22040	990	28.8	32.8	31.1	5.2	2.1	41043	48970	50	41	846	24.4	24.9	36.5	12.5	1.7	90870
24086	EGGLESTON	19985	154	37.0	30.5	24.0	6.5	2.0	33769	41027	23	17	132	25.0	20.5	42.4	8.3	3.8	103000
24087	ELLISTON	21663	1613	27.2	34.6	28.2	5.3	4.8	42768	51164	55	47	1334	35.7	11.8	33.1	15.7	3.7	100578
24088	FERRUM	20904	1772	27.4	37.3	26.9	4.5	3.9	39265	46345	44	37	1447	19.1	15.8	44.6	19.8	0.7	116250
24089	FIELDALE	17733	1102	40.0	37.4	17.9	4.1	0.6	30250	35052	13	10	875	21.3	30.9	41.8	5.4	0.7	87239
24090	FINCASTLE	25988	1820	19.2	25.8	37.7	12.9	4.5	54581	65111	79	74	1564	7.0	10.7	38.8	38.9	4.6	157653
24091	FLOYD	20492	2868	34.1	32.6	27.0	3.5	2.8	33695	38962	23	17	2308	16.9	14.6	47.4	17.6	3.4	117651
24092	GLADE HILL	26077	1160	30.3	29.5	28.6	6.5	5.2	42353	50398	54	46	942	11.8	14.5	42.6	24.0	7.1	131954
24093	GLEN LYN	18908	58	31.0	34.5	29.3	1.7	3.5	38875	45765	42	36	47	27.7	17.0	38.3	17.0	0.0	101389
24094	GOLDBOND	19177	53	26.4	35.9	32.1	5.7	0.0	41719	47371	52	44	45	22.2	26.7	40.0	11.1	0.0	91250
24095	GOODVIEW	23018	1377	14.8	37.8	37.0	7.6	2.8	48900	56947	70	63	1178	6.3	17.7	45.6	27.8	2.6	136326
24101	HARDY	26985	1833	19.1	23.7	39.8	11.7	5.7	55158	67014	80	74	1591	6.6	5.5	38.3	43.8	5.8	174076
24102	HENRY	18494	741	33.1	38.7	22.8	3.2	2.2	36974	42782	35	29	612	23.0	11.9	45.1	18.0	2.0	118947
24104	HUDDLESTON	24629	1507	19.0	34.2	37.6	5.9	3.2	47111	55532	66	59	1284	6.1	11.0	32.1	41.0	9.8	177331
24105	INDIAN VALLEY	17074	257	30.4	35.0	30.4	3.9	0.4	35747	39484	31	25	219	22.4	26.5	33.3	13.2	4.6	92778
24112	MARTINSVILLE	22030	14922	35.4	31.6	24.1	5.5	3.4	35425	41705	29	24	10492	14.5	23.9	43.7	15.9	2.0	104807
24120	MEADOWS OF DAN	19171	1119	39.1	36.3	20.0	2.8	1.9	30575	35158	14	11	923	19.5	19.3	43.7	15.3	2.3	107153
24121	MONETA	35130	4102	19.5	29.9	33.5	8.4	8.7	50500	60740	73	66	3556	8.9	9.4	34.4	32.1	15.2	166392
24122	MONTVALE	20575	978	25.9	34.8	31.2	3.5	4.7	40148	47411	47	40	819	20.5	18.1	44.9	16.5	0.0	106371
24124	NARROWS	21350	2331	33.2	32.3	28.3	3.9	2.3	37132	42785	36	30	1832	18.2	31.4	40.1	10.0	0.3	90702
24127	NEW CASTLE	20397	1709	27.4	36.5	28.0	5.8	2.3	41145	45848	50	42	1410	10.8	15.9	40.1	27.1	6.2	130132
24128	NEWPORT	29871	605	28.1	26.5	31.4	8.1	6.0	44705	53266	60	53	500	21.6	20.0	29.6	21.4	7.4	109091
24131	PAINT BANK	15421	54	25.9	46.3	24.1	3.7	0.0	38870	42716	42	36	44	13.6	20.5	43.2	22.7	0.0	105556
24133	PATRICK SPRINGS	19138	1301	34.0	32.3	27.7	3.9	2.2	35914	41027	31	26	1059	18.4	22.3	40.5	17.1	1.7	105260
24134	PEARISBURG	22597	2596	29.9	33.1	29.1	5.1	2.9	39815	46068	45	38	2013	12.6	25.5	46.1	13.8	1.9	107432
24136	PEMBROKE	23136	1335	30.6	31.5	28.2	6.0	3.7	40373	47302	47	40	1050	21.2	24.4	38.5	13.6	2.3	95750
24137	PENHOOK	27216	1122	26.6	30.4	30.8	7.6	4.7	43707	51669	58	50	937	16.4	17.8	34.7	23.6	7.5	123355
24138	PILOT	25464	578	18.7	41.9	30.6	5.9	2.9	41937	50157	53	44	493	13.2	14.8	47.5	24.1	0.4	124513
24139	PITTSVILLE	17950	231	34.2	33.8	26.4	3.9	1.7	34839	40509	27	22	191	27.2	26.2	33.5	11.0	2.1	86579
24141	RADFORD	23919	8876	37.6	26.9	26.3	5.5	3.8	35814	43849	31	25	4927	9.0	14.2	50.5	23.7	2.7	126851
24142	RADFORD	8758	8	100.0	0.0	0.0	0.0	0.0	8000	8000	0	0	0	0.0	0.0	0.0	0.0	0.0	0
24147	RICH CREEK	23595	360	27.5	37.8	28.1	3.6	3.1	38049	43667	39	32	261	20.7	30.3	42.5	5.8	0.8	88913
24148	RIDGEWAY	21386	3641	29.7	35.3	26.5	5.0	3.5	38942	45010	43	36	2985	24.1	18.5	38.7	17.6	1.2	101723
24149	RINER	25203	953	19.5	34.8	35.5	6.6	3.6	45258	54699	62	55	815	11.8	10.8	42.7	30.6	4.2	139382
24150	RIPPLEMEAD	20701	161	31.7	35.4	26.7	4.4	1.9	37590	43640	38	32	131	20.6	24.4	42.0	13.0	0.0	95417
24151	ROCKY MOUNT	20439	7655	33.4	30.1	27.5	6.4	2.6	38244	45300	40	33	5881	13.4	17.1	41.4	25.9	2.3	124110
24153	SALEM	25495	14468	22.9	30.5	31.7	10.2	4.7	46981	55340	66	58	10624	6.3	15.0	52.7	23.6	2.4	125038
24161	SANDY LEVEL	19982	173	29.5	38.2	24.9	5.2	2.3	35280	43652	29	23	144	34.0	13.2	31.3	17.4	4.2	95000
24162	SHAWSVILLE	28155	870	20.2	38.2	32.1	6.0	3.6	45000	53043	61	54	693	11.1	13.6	52.5	21.7	1.2	122736
24165	SPENCER	25275	676	29.3	34.8	27.5	6.4	2.1	40138	45492	47	40	560	23.6	22.9	35.2	16.4	2.0	94651
24167	STAFFORDSVILLE	21218	166	28.3	34.9	28.3	5.4	3.0	40337	46734	47	40	141	13.5	31.9	45.4	7.8	1.4	95909
24168	STANLEYTOWN	31092	101	34.7	29.7	19.8	8.9	6.9	35370	40000	29	23	73	13.7	24.7	34.3	20.6	6.9	116071
24171	STUART	18601	3596	36.6	34.8	22.9	3.9	1.9	34174	39280	25	19	2825	20.4	20.4	40.7	16.9	1.7	105069
24174	THAXTON	19527	921	23.9	41.2	27.8	6.0	1.2	40028	46655	46	39	770	21.4	17.0	42.7	18.1	0.8	108273
24175	TROUTVILLE	29968	2920	15.2	22.2	40.6	14.1	7.9	62272	74359	86	81	2590	3.3	8.6	38.1	45.5	4.5	175085
24176	UNION HALL	43414	548	23.0	24.1	28.3	11.5	13.1	52875	67118	77	70	454	7.5	13.7	26.7	28.6	23.6	188889
24179	VINTON	22483	8053	22.0	34.1	34.1	7.7	2.1	45463	52866	62	55	6222	8.6	14.1	58.0	19.1	0.2	121668
24184	WIRTZ	32861	1243	23.5	34.0	25.0	8.0	9.5	44887	54053	61	53	1035	11.4	6.9	36.3	34.2	11.2	161506
24185	WOOLWINE	16862	394	39.9	36.8	18.5	3.3	1.5	29584	34088	11	9	325	16.6	14.2	49.5	17.2	2.5	109628
24201	BRISTOL	22414	7297	40.5	32.1	20.2	3.9	3.3	31269	36057	16	12	4777	16.0	35.7	41.1	6.5	0.8	88368
24202	BRISTOL	23472	5263	29.8	34.0	27.5	5.4	3.3	39526	46781	44	38	4342	15.7	25.3	44.4	13.3	1.3	102270
24210	ABINGDON	24918	6575	34.7	31.0	24.3	5.3	4.7	35713	42566	30	25	4403	16.5	18.9	46.0	15.4	3.3	108734
24211	ABINGDON	28686	4036	22.1	26.9	35.3	10.1	5.5	50861	60923	74	67	3327	11.8	14.6	37.8	31.2	4.7	140888
24216	APPALACHIA	14890	1520	51.3	28.6	15.7	2.6	1.8	24177	27971	4	3	1116	52.3	31.3	15.7	0.5	0.2	48700
24217	BEE	13313	158	53.8	24.7	20.9	0.6	0.0	22266	24638	3	3	127	40.2	31.5	23.6	4.7	0.0	64333
24219	BIG STONE GAP	19583	4589	42.8	25.4	24.3	4.3	3.2	31200	36981	15	12	3398	20.8	24.5	42.2	10.9	1.6	95896
24220	BIRCHLEAF	12373	405	51.4	28.2	16.5	4.0	0.0	24218	26884	4	3	341	39.6	34.3	25.5	0.6	0.0	61842
24221	BLACKWATER	16130	443	39.7	33.6	21.4	5.2	0.0	30209	35367	13	10	372	45.4	27.2	18.0	8.6	0.8	54857
24224	CASTLEWOOD	17839	3433	40.6	34.8	18.8	4.0	1.9	30423	35696	13	10	2762	31.8	24.4	35.2	7.5	1.2	81192
24225	CLEVELAND	17178	782	44.8	30.4	19.8	4.1	0.9	27463	30979	8	6	637	36.1	27.8	29.5	5.5	1.1	69681
24226	CLINCHCO	16655	721	46.1	35.4	14.6	2.1	1.9	26699	30037	7	5	584	43.2	31.3	22.4	2.9	0.2	56154
24228	CLINTWOOD	15490	3303	47.2	31.4	17.5	2.3	1.6	26523	29808	6	5	2613	35.6	26.8	29.3	7.3	1.0	72714
24230	COEBURN	16273	3774	43.3	34.4	17.2	3.0	2.2	29007	33525	10	8	2975	32.5	29.8	29.4	7.9	0.5	75884
24236	DAMASCUS	19922	1474	41.1	33.2	21.0	2.4	2.2	30451	35476	13	11	1058	28.7	28.8	32.7	9.7	0.0	81919
24237	DANTE	18166	415	49.4	34.5	11.6	1.7	2.9	25227	28108	5	4	345	55.7	24.9	16.5	2.9	0.0	45568
24239	DAVENPORT	6400	8	62.5	25.0	12.5	0.0	0.0	15000	15000	1	1	7	14.3	14.3	71.4	0.0	0.0	106250
	VIRGINIA	30454		19.8	25.2	32.5	13.6	8.9	55216	67801				6.8	10.4	35.8	36.5	10.5	166226
	UNITED STATES	25866		24.7	27.1	30.8	10.9	6.5	48124	56710				10.9	15.0	33.7	30.1	10.4	145905

ZIP CODE		FINANCIAL SERVICES				THE HOME						ENTERTAINMENT						PERSONAL			
						Home Improvements		Furnishings													
#	POST OFFICE NAME	Auto Loan	Home Loan	Investments	Retirement Plans	Home Repair	Lawn & Garden	Computers & Hardware	Major Appliances	TV, Radio, Sound Equipment	Furniture	Dine out/ Carry out	Sports Equipment	Fees & Tickets	Toys & Games	Travel	Cable TV	Apparel & Services	Auto Repairs	Health Insurance	Pets & Supplies
24012	ROANOKE	64	62	62	61	63	69	64	65	66	62	81	75	64	82	64	67	78	65	67	73
24013	ROANOKE	44	41	45	40	41	47	46	44	48	44	60	51	46	60	45	49	58	46	47	49
24014	ROANOKE	121	121	131	121	122	132	123	123	123	121	153	143	123	154	123	123	148	124	124	140
24015	ROANOKE	74	79	93	81	78	82	82	79	80	81	100	94	83	102	81	77	99	81	74	86
24016	ROANOKE	45	38	46	39	38	43	46	44	48	45	60	52	44	57	44	47	58	47	44	49
24017	ROANOKE	57	53	59	50	52	60	56	56	60	57	74	62	57	73	56	62	72	57	60	64
24018	ROANOKE	116	127	141	130	125	130	123	121	118	124	149	142	127	149	123	114	146	121	113	134
24019	ROANOKE	97	103	101	101	104	109	98	100	97	97	120	116	100	123	99	96	117	98	99	115
24020	ROANOKE	42	33	44	38	33	37	46	41	46	43	58	52	42	54	42	42	56	46	38	45
24053	ARARAT	96	65	29	56	73	84	62	78	75	64	88	93	53	84	63	81	80	77	96	111
24054	AXTON	87	58	26	50	66	76	56	70	68	57	80	84	48	75	57	73	72	70	87	100
24055	BASSETT	87	60	30	53	68	77	58	71	69	59	81	85	50	77	59	74	74	71	87	100
24059	BENT MOUNTAIN	124	153	162	153	151	149	137	137	127	136	159	160	145	170	140	123	159	132	122	151
24060	BLACKSBURG	75	61	73	65	60	67	84	71	82	77	103	91	76	97	75	76	98	80	68	81
24064	BLUE RIDGE	94	105	105	104	104	106	97	98	93	96	116	114	100	121	98	92	114	95	93	111
24065	BOONES MILL	93	83	63	79	88	94	77	85	81	77	99	101	75	101	79	83	94	83	92	110
24066	BUCHANAN	89	70	46	65	76	84	68	78	75	68	90	92	63	89	69	78	84	76	88	102
24067	CALLAWAY	96	85	65	81	90	97	79	88	84	79	102	104	78	104	81	86	97	85	95	112
24069	CASCADE	84	56	26	49	64	74	54	68	66	55	77	81	46	73	55	71	70	67	84	97
24070	CATAWBA	97	68	35	63	79	88	67	83	77	66	91	99	57	88	69	81	82	81	99	115
24072	CHECK	83	59	30	52	65	74	56	69	66	57	78	82	49	75	57	71	72	68	83	96
24073	CHRISTIANSBURG	84	80	69	78	81	86	77	81	78	77	96	94	75	95	77	78	92	80	82	95
24076	CLAUDVILLE	85	57	26	49	65	74	55	69	66	56	78	82	47	74	56	72	71	68	85	98
24077	CLOVERDALE	106	94	74	88	99	106	87	98	93	88	113	116	84	113	89	96	107	96	106	125
24078	COLLINSVILLE	70	59	47	58	62	70	62	65	66	60	80	75	59	79	61	67	75	65	71	78
24079	COPPER HILL	83	61	35	55	68	76	58	70	67	59	80	83	52	77	59	71	74	68	82	96
24082	CRITZ	67	45	20	39	51	59	43	54	53	44	62	65	37	58	44	57	56	54	67	77
24083	DALEVILLE	135	148	142	145	149	151	133	138	130	133	161	163	138	169	137	129	158	134	133	162
24084	DUBLIN	86	71	51	67	76	84	69	77	75	68	90	90	65	90	70	77	84	76	86	99
24085	EAGLE ROCK	92	70	43	63	77	86	66	79	76	67	90	94	60	88	68	80	83	78	92	108
24086	EGGLESTON	91	61	28	53	69	80	59	74	71	60	83	88	50	79	60	77	76	73	91	105
24087	ELLISTON	84	80	66	77	80	84	75	80	75	76	93	93	72	91	75	75	89	78	79	95
24088	FERRUM	91	68	41	62	75	85	66	78	76	67	90	92	60	88	67	80	83	77	91	105
24089	FIELDALE	66	51	33	45	56	63	50	58	57	50	68	68	46	67	51	61	63	57	68	77
24090	FINCASTLE	97	98	87	95	100	104	89	95	90	89	110	112	90	114	92	90	107	92	96	116
24091	FLOYD	86	60	31	53	68	77	58	71	68	59	81	85	50	77	59	73	74	70	86	99
24092	GLADE HILL	114	81	43	71	91	104	77	95	91	78	108	113	68	103	80	98	99	94	115	133
24093	GLEN LYN	91	61	28	52	69	79	59	73	71	60	83	88	50	79	60	76	76	73	90	104
24094	GOLDBOND	86	57	26	50	65	75	55	69	67	57	79	83	47	74	56	72	71	69	86	99
24095	GOODVIEW	94	84	64	80	88	94	78	86	82	78	100	102	76	101	80	84	95	84	92	109
24101	HARDY	108	96	73	92	102	109	89	99	95	89	115	118	87	118	92	97	109	96	107	128
24102	HENRY	83	56	25	48	63	73	54	67	65	55	76	81	46	72	55	70	69	67	83	96
24104	HUDDLESTON	89	77	62	73	83	92	73	82	78	74	95	93	70	91	76	82	90	80	93	103
24105	INDIAN VALLEY	78	53	24	45	59	69	51	63	61	52	72	76	43	68	52	66	65	63	78	90
24112	MARTINSVILLE	83	67	51	62	71	81	67	75	75	67	90	87	63	87	68	78	84	75	86	95
24120	MEADOWS OF DAN	80	54	24	46	61	70	52	65	63	53	74	78	44	70	53	68	67	64	80	92
24121	MONETA	130	113	93	107	120	136	107	121	114	111	139	131	103	125	112	119	131	119	137	148
24122	MONTVALE	80	72	56	69	74	79	68	74	70	69	86	87	65	85	68	71	82	73	77	92
24124	NARROWS	80	67	51	60	71	81	65	73	73	65	88	84	63	89	67	77	82	72	84	92
24127	NEW CASTLE	91	62	31	57	72	81	61	76	72	61	84	91	52	81	63	76	76	75	91	106
24128	NEWPORT	116	89	56	85	100	110	86	102	96	85	114	122	78	114	89	100	106	100	117	137
24131	PAINT BANK	78	52	24	45	59	68	51	63	61	52	72	76	43	68	51	66	65	63	78	90
24133	PATRICK SPRINGS	87	58	26	50	66	76	56	70	68	57	79	84	48	75	57	73	72	69	86	100
24134	PEARISBURG	76	71	63	66	73	83	70	74	75	68	91	84	69	93	72	78	86	73	83	88
24136	PEMBROKE	95	71	42	65	78	88	70	82	79	70	94	97	63	91	70	83	87	81	96	109
24137	PENHOOK	114	81	44	71	91	104	77	95	91	78	107	113	67	103	80	98	98	94	116	133
24138	PILOT	109	88	59	81	95	105	83	95	92	83	110	114	78	110	85	96	103	93	108	127
24139	PITTSVILLE	77	55	31	49	62	71	53	65	62	54	74	77	46	71	55	67	67	64	78	90
24141	RADFORD	75	63	59	63	65	73	73	71	75	69	92	85	68	90	69	74	88	74	73	84
24142	RADFORD	14	8	11	9	8	10	16	12	16	14	20	17	13	18	13	14	18	15	11	14
24147	RICH CREEK	95	66	35	60	74	87	68	80	79	67	93	94	59	88	68	85	85	80	98	107
24148	RIDGEWAY	93	65	33	56	73	83	62	77	74	63	88	91	54	83	63	80	80	76	94	107
24149	RINER	102	88	65	84	94	102	82	92	88	82	107	110	79	108	85	91	101	90	101	120
24150	RIPPLEMEAD	87	59	30	53	67	78	59	72	70	59	83	85	51	78	60	75	75	71	88	99
24151	ROCKY MOUNT	86	65	39	59	71	80	63	73	71	63	85	87	57	83	64	75	78	72	86	99
24153	SALEM	87	87	84	85	89	96	84	88	86	84	106	101	85	107	86	87	102	87	91	102
24161	SANDY LEVEL	80	61	40	55	69	78	58	70	66	58	78	82	51	77	61	71	73	69	84	97
24162	SHAWSVILLE	119	95	62	87	103	113	89	104	100	90	119	123	83	118	91	104	112	102	118	139
24165	SPENCER	106	71	32	61	80	92	68	86	83	70	97	102	58	92	70	89	88	85	105	122
24167	STAFFORDSVILLE	98	66	30	57	75	86	64	80	77	65	90	95	54	85	65	83	82	79	98	113
24168	STANLEYTOWN	134	90	41	77	102	117	87	108	105	88	123	129	74	116	88	113	112	107	133	154
24171	STUART	79	54	25	47	60	70	52	65	63	53	74	77	45	70	53	67	67	64	79	90
24174	THAXTON	82	63	38	58	68	75	60	71	67	61	80	84	54	77	61	69	75	70	80	94
24175	TROUTVILLE	110	119	113	117	121	123	108	112	106	108	131	132	111	137	111	105	128	109	109	133
24176	UNION HALL	175	133	86	119	150	170	126	153	144	126	171	180	112	167	134	155	158	151	182	211
24179	VINTON	80	76	67	74	78	84	74	78	76	74	93	90	73	94	75	77	90	77	81	92
24184	WIRTZ	132	112	82	104	121	133	104	119	113	104	136	141	99	137	109	118	128	117	134	157
24185	WOOLWINE	73	49	22	42	55	64	47	59	57	48	67	70	40	63	48	61	61	58	72	83
24201	BRISTOL	71	62	59	61	65	74	67	69	71	65	86	79	64	84	67	72	81	70	75	81
24202	BRISTOL	100	73	41	66	81	92	70	84	81	71	97	100	63	93	72	86	89	83	100	115
24210	ABINGDON	85	72	59	67	76	87	72	79	79	71	95	91	69	93	74	83	90	79	90	98
24211	ABINGDON	104	95	79	92	100	108	90	98	94	90	115	114	89	116	92	96	110	96	104	121
24216	APPALACHIA	56	42	27	40	46	55	46	51	52	44	61	57	41	58	46	55	56	51	61	62
24217	BEE	58	39	18	34	44	51	38	47	45	38	53	56	32	50	38	49	48	47	58	67
24219	BIG STONE GAP	78	60	39	57	65	75	62	70	68	61	81	80	56	78	62	71	75	69	80	88
24220	BIRCHLEAF	60	40	18	35	46	53	39	49	47	40	55	58	33	52	40	51	50	48	60	69
24221	BLACKWATER	66	47	26	43	52	61	49	57	56	48	66	65	42	62	49	60	60	56	69	74
24224	CASTLEWOOD	76	55	32	49	61	69	54	64	63	54	74	76	48	70	55	66	68	64	77	87
24225	CLEVELAND	77	51	23	44	58	67	49	62	60	50	70	74	42	66	50	64	64	61	76	88
24226	CLINCHCO	72	49	25	44	55	64	49	59	58	49	68	70	42	64	50	62	62	59	73	81
24228	CLINTWOOD	64	44	22	39	50	58	44	54	52	44	62	63	38	58	45	56	56	53	66	73
24230	COEBURN	74	50	23	43	57	65	49	60	58	49	69	72	41	65	49	63	62	60	74	85
24236	DAMASCUS	78	55	30	49	61	71	56	66	65	55	77	77	49	72	56	70	70	66	80	88
24237	DANTE	75	52	28	47	58	68	53	63	62	53	73	74	46	69	53	67	67	63	77	85
24239	DAVENPORT	38	25	11	22	29	33	24	30	29	25	34	36	21	33	25	32	31	30	38	43
	VIRGINIA	112	109	113	109	109	117	108	110	109	109	136	129	108	135	108	109	132	110	109	128
	UNITED STATES	100	100	100	100	100	100	100	100	100	100	100	100	100	100	100	100	100	100	100	100

POPULATION CHANGE

# POST OFFICE NAME	COUNTY FIPS CODE	POPULATION 2000	2004	2009	% Rate	State Centile	HOUSEHOLDS 2000	2004	2009	% Annual Rate 2000-2004	2004 Average HH Size	FAMILIES 2000	2004	% Annual Rate 2000-2004
24243 DRYDEN	105	2322	2286	2236	-0.4	14	855	862	865	0.2	2.56	634	631	-0.1
24244 DUFFIELD	169	5599	5489	5403	-0.5	12	2201	2204	2220	0.0	2.39	1610	1593	-0.3
24245 DUNGANNON	169	1162	1159	1152	-0.1	21	495	503	511	0.4	2.30	364	365	0.1
24248 EWING	105	2414	2346	2281	-0.7	8	1006	1001	997	-0.1	2.34	713	699	-0.5
24250 FORT BLACKMORE	169	1312	1293	1277	-0.3	15	536	540	547	0.2	2.39	405	404	-0.1
24251 GATE CITY	169	7996	8065	8081	0.2	32	3429	3539	3629	0.8	2.26	2403	2441	0.4
24256 HAYSI	051	3206	3135	3085	-0.5	10	1326	1335	1346	0.2	2.35	972	965	-0.2
24258 HILTONS	169	2720	2729	2719	0.1	27	1135	1168	1191	0.7	2.34	822	836	0.4
24260 HONAKER	167	5756	5466	5401	-1.2	2	2302	2242	2270	-0.6	2.43	1755	1692	-0.9
24263 JONESVILLE	105	6236	6326	6292	0.3	37	2642	2748	2799	0.9	2.29	1809	1853	0.6
24265 KEOKEE	105	1554	1472	1417	-1.3	1	608	591	584	-0.7	2.48	437	419	-1.0
24266 LEBANON	167	7180	7514	7703	1.1	60	2882	3093	3254	1.7	2.32	2061	2180	1.3
24269 MC CLURE	051	78	79	79	0.3	36	34	35	36	0.7	2.26	26	26	0.0
24270 MENDOTA	191	690	706	730	0.5	44	278	292	309	1.2	2.42	212	220	0.9
24271 NICKELSVILLE	169	2900	2799	2742	-0.8	5	1186	1172	1176	-0.3	2.38	858	837	-0.6
24272 NORA	051	573	583	586	0.4	39	223	234	240	1.1	2.49	164	169	0.7
24273 NORTON	195	5438	5536	5612	0.4	40	2367	2476	2574	1.1	2.21	1545	1593	0.7
24277 PENNINGTON GAP	105	5478	6908	6753	5.6	98	2334	2303	2288	-0.3	2.26	1604	1560	-0.7
24279 POUND	195	4979	5117	5162	0.7	48	1970	2072	2119	1.2	2.47	1494	1553	0.9
24280 ROSEDALE	167	4054	4083	4117	0.2	30	1209	1245	1286	0.7	2.42	951	971	0.5
24281 ROSE HILL	105	2335	2280	2222	-0.6	10	975	974	971	0.0	2.34	688	678	-0.3
24282 SAINT CHARLES	105	367	350	338	-1.1	2	148	145	144	-0.5	2.37	107	103	-0.9
24283 SAINT PAUL	195	2240	2287	2302	0.5	42	951	1000	1024	1.2	2.29	668	692	0.8
24290 WEBER CITY	169	1978	2111	2170	1.5	69	878	961	1013	2.2	2.13	617	667	1.9
24292 WHITETOP	077	619	592	595	-1.0	3	267	256	264	-1.0	1.69	184	174	-1.3
24293 WISE	195	10979	11453	11660	1.0	57	4261	4577	4739	1.7	2.36	3017	3194	1.4
24301 PULASKI	155	15302	15059	14946	-0.4	13	6559	6571	6653	0.0	2.27	4424	4358	-0.4
24311 ATKINS	173	1458	1412	1386	-0.8	6	613	606	604	-0.3	2.33	432	422	-0.6
24312 AUSTINVILLE	035	2244	2395	2562	1.5	69	935	1017	1110	2.0	2.33	705	757	1.7
24313 BARREN SPRINGS	197	675	686	703	0.4	38	263	275	288	1.1	2.49	200	206	0.7
24314 BASTIAN	021	1525	1553	1596	0.4	40	610	637	671	1.0	2.41	467	483	0.8
24315 BLAND	021	3605	3715	3835	0.7	49	1227	1300	1382	1.4	2.40	897	938	1.1
24316 BROADFORD	173	22	21	21	-1.1	2	9	9	9	0.0	2.33	6	6	0.0
24317 CANA	035	3519	3541	3671	0.2	29	1462	1505	1592	0.7	2.34	1067	1084	0.4
24318 CERES	021	768	775	790	0.2	32	323	334	348	0.8	2.32	233	238	0.5
24319 CHILHOWIE	173	6603	6562	6529	-0.2	19	2584	2621	2647	0.3	2.40	1904	1908	0.1
24322 CRIPPLE CREEK	197	100	99	101	-0.2	17	48	49	51	0.5	2.02	34	34	0.0
24323 CROCKETT	197	521	587	637	2.9	89	204	234	260	3.3	2.51	151	170	2.8
24324 DRAPER	155	1678	1698	1708	0.3	34	689	714	735	0.8	2.38	510	521	0.5
24325 DUGSPUR	035	1325	1357	1422	0.6	45	568	590	628	0.9	2.28	414	423	0.5
24326 ELK CREEK	077	1202	1141	1152	-1.2	2	536	520	536	-0.7	2.19	386	370	-1.0
24328 FANCY GAP	035	2286	2347	2461	0.6	46	960	1007	1077	1.1	2.33	722	749	0.9
24330 FRIES	077	4119	4075	4174	-0.3	17	1765	1782	1865	0.2	2.29	1243	1237	-0.1
24333 GALAX	077	17648	17577	17749	-0.1	21	7539	7625	7823	0.3	2.29	5165	5181	0.1
24340 GLADE SPRING	191	5376	5431	5611	0.2	33	2148	2231	2366	0.9	2.29	1562	1598	0.5
24343 HILLSVILLE	035	9353	9456	9905	0.3	33	3895	4000	4270	0.6	2.28	2731	2764	0.3
24347 HIWASSEE	155	1644	1658	1656	0.2	32	670	693	708	0.8	2.39	507	517	0.5
24348 INDEPENDENCE	077	3922	3949	4063	0.2	29	1676	1720	1806	0.6	2.23	1135	1148	0.3
24350 IVANHOE	197	1229	1224	1259	-0.1	21	504	514	541	0.5	2.38	362	363	0.1
24351 LAMBSBURG	035	637	686	739	1.8	74	247	271	297	2.2	2.53	182	197	1.9
24352 LAUREL FORK	035	666	674	700	0.3	34	276	284	302	0.7	2.31	199	202	0.4
24354 MARION	173	16992	17328	17564	0.5	42	6936	7232	7440	1.0	2.28	4825	4959	0.7
24360 MAX MEADOWS	197	5911	6293	6639	1.5	68	2336	2547	2750	2.1	2.46	1804	1942	1.8
24361 MEADOWVIEW	191	5592	5774	5987	0.8	51	2001	2118	2250	1.4	2.56	1493	1557	1.0
24363 MOUTH OF WILSON	077	1540	1498	1518	-0.7	8	691	685	709	-0.2	2.07	474	462	-0.6
24366 ROCKY GAP	021	570	581	598	0.5	40	237	248	263	1.1	2.23	183	190	0.9
24368 RURAL RETREAT	197	5150	5389	5607	1.1	59	2067	2210	2347	1.6	2.44	1511	1592	1.2
24370 SALTVILLE	173	6860	6689	6608	-0.6	9	2821	2813	2825	-0.1	2.38	2073	2043	-0.3
24374 SPEEDWELL	197	627	633	650	0.2	32	253	262	275	0.8	2.42	183	186	0.4
24375 SUGAR GROVE	173	1332	1326	1316	-0.1	20	567	575	578	0.3	2.31	400	400	0.0
24377 TANNERSVILLE	185	297	304	309	0.6	44	115	121	126	1.2	2.51	94	98	1.0
24378 TROUTDALE	077	2397	2301	2303	-1.0	3	597	577	589	-0.8	2.59	427	408	-1.1
24380 WILLIS	063	2704	2934	3203	1.9	78	1086	1198	1330	2.3	2.45	791	862	2.0
24381 WOODLAWN	035	3010	3449	3841	3.3	91	1233	1456	1663	4.0	2.30	886	1033	3.7
24382 WYTHEVILLE	197	14009	14168	14589	0.3	33	6065	6275	6609	0.8	2.20	4013	4083	0.4
24401 STAUNTON	015	34491	34420	34336	-0.1	22	13836	13967	14088	0.2	2.26	8800	8767	-0.1
24413 BLUE GRASS	091	176	174	170	-0.3	16	74	75	75	0.3	2.32	50	50	0.0
24416 BUENA VISTA	163	8746	8722	8725	-0.1	21	3491	3543	3607	0.4	2.38	2452	2454	0.0
24421 CHURCHVILLE	015	2829	2909	3071	0.7	48	1092	1139	1220	1.0	2.53	857	885	0.8
24422 CLIFTON FORGE	005	7129	6830	6586	-1.0	3	3021	2961	2922	-0.5	2.23	1985	1910	-0.9
24426 COVINGTON	005	15942	15375	14712	-0.9	5	6638	6525	6367	-0.4	2.32	4639	4511	-0.7
24430 CRAIGSVILLE	015	2586	2622	2721	0.3	37	734	757	805	0.7	2.59	517	525	0.4
24431 CRIMORA	015	2432	2507	2653	0.7	50	956	1000	1074	1.1	2.50	713	737	0.8
24432 DEERFIELD	015	354	354	369	0.0	24	156	158	167	0.3	2.24	106	106	0.0
24433 DOE HILL	091	289	285	278	-0.3	15	119	121	121	0.4	2.36	79	79	0.0
24435 FAIRFIELD	163	1673	1690	1762	0.2	33	677	695	735	0.6	2.43	499	506	0.3
24437 FORT DEFIANCE	015	726	769	825	1.4	65	268	287	313	1.6	2.68	219	233	1.5
24439 GOSHEN	163	1305	1312	1358	0.1	29	541	555	585	0.6	2.18	381	386	0.3
24440 GREENVILLE	015	2286	2655	2973	3.6	93	626	770	899	5.0	2.76	482	586	4.7
24441 GROTTOES	015	5688	6021	6380	1.4	65	2229	2399	2579	1.7	2.51	1641	1744	1.4
24442 HEAD WATERS	091	101	100	97	-0.2	17	43	44	44	0.5	2.27	29	28	-0.8
24445 HOT SPRINGS	017	2590	2557	2525	-0.3	16	1071	1079	1089	0.2	2.30	759	755	-0.1
24450 LEXINGTON	163	15431	16140	16788	1.1	59	5713	6088	6445	1.5	2.27	3552	3761	1.4
24458 MC DOWELL	091	336	332	324	-0.3	16	157	159	159	0.3	2.09	105	104	-0.2
24459 MIDDLEBROOK	015	650	658	688	0.3	34	246	254	270	0.8	2.59	186	190	0.5
24460 MILLBORO	017	1849	1862	1859	0.2	29	707	727	741	0.7	2.36	514	521	0.3
24464 MONTEBELLO	125	156	160	167	0.6	46	68	71	76	1.0	2.25	46	48	1.0
24465 MONTEREY	091	1431	1408	1375	-0.4	13	651	654	653	0.1	2.15	442	438	-0.2
24467 MOUNT SIDNEY	015	2039	2290	2534	2.8	88	788	895	1004	3.0	2.56	623	701	2.8
24468 MUSTOE	091	211	208	204	-0.3	15	90	91	91	0.3	2.29	61	61	0.0
24471 PORT REPUBLIC	165	1127	1272	1387	2.9	89	451	515	567	3.2	2.47	352	397	2.9
24472 RAPHINE	015	2939	3127	3355	1.5	68	1208	1309	1427	1.9	2.39	886	947	1.6
24473 ROCKBRIDGE BATHS	163	828	859	910	0.9	54	347	366	394	1.3	2.34	251	261	0.8
24477 STUARTS DRAFT	015	8219	8696	9349	1.3	65	3052	3287	3595	1.8	2.61	2423	2584	1.5
24479 SWOOPE	015	1771	1712	1787	-0.8	5	675	661	701	-0.5	2.59	530	514	-0.7
VIRGINIA					1.4					1.7	2.51			1.4
UNITED STATES					1.2					1.3	2.58			1.1

# ZIP CODE	POST OFFICE NAME	RACE (%) White 2000	White 2004	Black 2000	Black 2004	Asian/Pacific 2000	Asian/Pacific 2004	% Hispanic Origin 2000	% Hispanic Origin 2004	2004 AGE DISTRIBUTION (%) 0-4	5-9	10-14	15-19	20-24	25-44	45-64	65-84	85+	18+	MEDIAN AGE 2004	% 2004 Males	% 2004 Females
24243	DRYDEN	98.8	98.6	0.3	0.4	0.1	0.1	0.1	0.2	6.3	6.4	6.8	6.1	5.3	27.7	27.1	12.4	1.9	76.6	39.2	48.7	51.3
24244	DUFFIELD	98.8	98.7	0.4	0.4	0.1	0.1	0.4	0.4	5.3	5.5	6.1	5.8	5.4	26.2	27.6	15.5	2.7	79.6	42.1	48.8	51.2
24245	DUNGANNON	99.2	99.2	0.3	0.3	0.0	0.0	0.2	0.2	5.7	5.9	6.6	6.2	5.5	26.6	28.2	13.6	1.8	78.0	40.4	48.2	51.8
24248	EWING	99.2	99.0	0.2	0.2	0.0	0.0	0.8	0.9	5.4	5.8	6.3	5.8	5.2	25.3	29.2	15.3	1.8	79.0	42.4	47.4	52.6
24250	FORT BLACKMORE	99.2	99.2	0.1	0.1	0.0	0.0	0.5	0.5	4.8	5.1	5.7	5.5	5.0	27.9	28.2	16.0	1.8	81.0	42.7	50.5	49.5
24251	GATE CITY	97.9	97.9	1.2	1.2	0.1	0.1	0.5	0.5	5.2	5.4	5.7	5.3	5.2	26.4	27.8	16.8	2.2	80.5	42.9	48.3	51.7
24256	HAYSI	99.4	99.3	0.2	0.2	0.0	0.0	0.5	0.8	5.7	5.8	6.0	6.0	6.6	26.5	30.0	12.4	1.1	79.0	41.0	48.5	51.6
24258	HILTONS	99.3	99.3	0.1	0.1	0.0	0.0	0.3	0.2	5.1	5.5	6.3	5.5	4.8	28.6	28.7	13.9	1.6	79.6	41.2	50.3	49.7
24260	HONAKER	99.3	99.2	0.1	0.1	0.0	0.0	0.9	1.1	5.3	5.9	6.3	5.6	5.7	28.5	29.4	11.9	1.5	79.2	40.4	49.4	50.6
24263	JONESVILLE	98.3	98.1	0.5	0.5	0.2	0.2	0.5	0.7	5.9	5.7	5.6	5.9	5.7	25.7	28.1	15.1	2.3	79.3	41.9	49.1	50.9
24265	KEOKEE	98.5	98.3	0.3	0.3	0.1	0.1	0.5	0.5	5.3	6.1	7.2	6.7	6.1	29.4	26.8	11.3	1.2	77.0	38.0	51.8	48.2
24266	LEBANON	97.1	96.8	2.1	2.2	0.0	0.1	0.4	0.5	5.6	5.7	5.8	5.3	6.2	28.4	26.6	14.1	2.3	79.6	40.5	48.2	51.8
24269	MC CLURE	100.0	100.0	0.0	0.0	0.0	0.0	0.0	0.0	5.1	5.1	6.3	5.1	7.6	30.4	27.9	11.4	1.3	83.5	38.8	49.4	50.6
24270	MENDOTA	97.4	97.2	0.0	0.0	0.3	0.3	1.3	1.4	5.1	5.5	6.9	5.7	5.5	27.2	29.2	13.3	1.6	78.9	41.6	49.4	50.6
24271	NICKELSVILLE	98.8	98.7	0.2	0.2	0.1	0.1	0.7	0.8	5.7	5.8	5.9	5.3	5.5	26.8	28.0	15.1	2.0	79.5	41.7	49.0	51.0
24272	NORA	99.5	99.5	0.2	0.2	0.0	0.0	0.5	0.7	5.3	5.5	6.2	6.9	7.6	27.8	27.6	11.8	1.4	79.1	38.8	50.8	49.2
24273	NORTON	93.7	93.6	4.5	4.6	0.9	0.9	0.8	0.8	5.2	5.5	6.4	5.5	6.3	27.6	27.8	13.9	1.9	79.6	40.3	46.7	53.3
24277	PENNINGTON GAP	97.6	97.4	0.9	0.8	0.3	0.5	0.6	0.8	5.5	5.7	5.8	6.4	5.9	27.5	27.9	13.5	2.0	79.4	40.8	49.9	50.1
24279	POUND	99.3	99.2	0.0	0.0	0.1	0.1	0.6	0.7	5.7	6.0	6.6	5.8	5.8	28.3	28.2	12.2	1.4	78.2	40.0	49.9	50.1
24280	ROSEDALE	81.7	80.7	16.9	17.6	0.0	0.1	2.1	2.6	4.5	4.7	4.3	4.7	8.2	39.5	25.1	8.2	0.7	83.5	36.4	63.0	37.0
24281	ROSE HILL	99.1	98.9	0.2	0.2	0.1	0.1	0.6	0.7	5.5	5.7	6.4	5.8	5.6	26.7	27.0	15.3	1.9	78.8	41.3	48.4	51.6
24282	SAINT CHARLES	99.2	99.1	0.5	0.6	0.0	0.0	0.3	0.3	5.7	6.3	7.4	7.1	6.0	28.3	26.9	10.9	1.4	76.3	37.6	50.3	49.7
24283	SAINT PAUL	98.0	97.7	0.7	0.7	0.3	0.4	0.3	0.4	6.0	6.0	6.2	5.8	6.3	26.5	27.5	14.0	1.8	78.4	40.6	47.5	52.5
24290	WEBER CITY	98.0	98.1	0.7	0.7	0.1	0.1	0.3	0.3	4.5	4.6	5.0	4.6	5.0	24.3	29.7	19.0	3.4	83.2	46.5	46.2	53.8
24292	WHITETOP	78.7	77.2	20.7	22.0	0.2	0.2	0.5	0.3	3.7	4.2	4.4	3.6	8.1	37.7	24.3	12.3	1.7	85.6	38.4	63.2	36.8
24293	WISE	97.6	97.2	1.0	1.1	0.5	0.6	0.9	1.1	5.8	5.6	5.9	6.4	8.2	29.2	26.3	11.5	1.3	79.6	37.5	49.3	50.8
24301	PULASKI	91.3	91.0	6.3	6.5	0.5	0.5	1.5	1.6	5.6	5.9	6.2	5.3	5.1	26.4	28.0	15.5	2.1	79.3	41.9	48.5	51.5
24311	ATKINS	99.2	99.2	0.1	0.1	0.1	0.1	0.9	0.9	6.2	6.0	6.4	6.6	5.8	28.9	26.6	12.2	1.4	77.5	38.9	48.8	51.2
24312	AUSTINVILLE	98.9	98.7	0.5	0.5	0.0	0.0	1.0	1.4	5.2	5.6	6.4	5.9	5.2	29.1	26.5	14.2	1.9	78.8	40.4	50.8	49.2
24313	BARREN SPRINGS	99.4	99.1	0.3	0.3	0.0	0.0	0.2	0.2	5.1	5.5	6.4	5.3	4.7	30.6	28.0	13.0	1.5	79.7	39.7	51.2	48.8
24314	BASTIAN	99.0	98.8	0.4	0.5	0.0	0.0	0.2	0.2	4.3	4.7	6.1	5.6	6.1	26.7	30.1	14.7	1.8	81.3	42.8	50.7	49.3
24315	BLAND	92.1	91.5	6.6	7.1	0.3	0.3	0.6	0.8	4.2	4.5	4.9	5.1	5.7	32.9	29.3	12.1	1.4	83.5	40.7	58.8	41.2
24316	BROADFORD	100.0	100.0	0.0	0.0	0.0	0.0	0.0	0.0	9.5	9.5	9.5	4.8	0.0	38.1	28.6	0.0	0.0	71.4	33.8	47.6	52.4
24317	CANA	98.1	97.7	0.2	0.2	0.1	0.1	1.4	1.8	6.0	6.1	6.0	5.5	5.4	28.5	26.8	14.5	1.3	78.7	40.2	50.3	49.7
24318	CERES	99.1	99.1	0.0	0.0	0.0	0.0	0.5	0.4	6.7	6.7	6.1	5.4	4.7	26.7	28.1	13.8	1.8	77.0	40.8	49.9	50.1
24319	CHILHOWIE	96.9	96.8	1.6	1.7	0.2	0.2	1.0	1.1	5.2	5.7	6.8	5.4	5.2	27.8	26.8	14.5	2.7	78.9	41.0	48.7	51.3
24322	CRIPPLE CREEK	98.0	98.0	1.0	1.0	0.0	0.0	1.0	1.0	5.1	5.1	6.1	5.1	5.1	26.3	29.3	16.2	2.0	80.8	43.4	51.5	48.5
24323	CROCKETT	98.1	97.6	0.2	0.3	0.2	0.2	0.6	1.0	6.6	6.6	7.2	5.6	6.8	30.0	24.7	10.9	1.5	76.2	36.8	48.0	52.0
24324	DRAPER	94.9	94.5	3.5	3.9	0.5	0.5	0.5	0.5	5.4	5.8	6.0	5.3	4.8	27.8	29.6	14.3	1.1	79.6	42.0	51.2	48.8
24325	DUGSPUR	98.3	98.1	0.0	0.0	0.3	0.4	1.0	1.3	5.1	5.4	5.7	4.9	4.9	25.6	28.5	17.4	2.6	80.6	44.0	48.3	51.7
24326	ELK CREEK	97.2	96.8	1.5	1.7	0.2	0.3	0.8	1.1	4.6	5.1	6.1	5.6	4.7	24.6	30.5	17.1	1.8	80.9	44.6	50.0	50.0
24328	FANCY GAP	97.8	97.3	0.2	0.2	0.0	0.0	2.1	2.8	5.6	7.2	6.2	5.2	4.7	29.2	27.1	13.4	1.4	77.6	39.5	51.0	49.0
24330	FRIES	97.5	97.2	0.8	0.9	0.0	0.0	1.6	1.9	5.4	6.1	6.7	5.1	5.2	26.4	27.3	15.8	2.2	78.7	41.6	49.3	50.7
24333	GALAX	92.2	91.7	3.9	3.9	0.3	0.4	5.5	6.3	5.9	6.1	6.3	5.6	5.2	26.9	26.9	15.1	2.0	78.2	40.8	48.9	51.2
24340	GLADE SPRING	96.5	96.0	2.6	2.9	0.3	0.3	0.5	0.7	4.8	4.9	5.5	8.1	9.1	25.1	27.3	13.7	1.5	81.4	40.0	49.1	50.9
24343	HILLSVILLE	98.0	97.6	0.4	0.4	0.1	0.2	1.6	2.0	5.3	5.6	5.5	5.0	5.0	27.3	27.6	16.1	2.6	80.5	42.6	49.2	50.9
24347	HIWASSEE	97.4	97.4	2.0	2.1	0.1	0.1	0.4	0.4	5.4	5.8	6.0	6.3	4.2	27.7	30.1	13.2	1.3	78.8	41.7	51.2	48.8
24348	INDEPENDENCE	95.2	94.3	3.0	3.4	0.1	0.1	2.0	2.6	5.0	5.1	5.3	5.1	5.0	25.6	28.9	17.1	3.0	81.6	44.4	49.5	50.5
24350	IVANHOE	97.0	96.6	1.9	2.1	0.2	0.3	0.7	0.9	5.1	6.0	6.1	4.8	4.9	27.0	30.4	13.8	2.0	79.8	42.2	50.7	49.4
24351	LAMBSBURG	98.1	97.7	0.3	0.4	0.0	0.2	1.6	2.2	6.0	6.1	6.1	6.1	5.5	28.0	27.0	13.7	1.5	77.8	39.8	50.2	49.9
24352	LAUREL FORK	98.1	97.6	0.3	0.3	0.0	0.0	2.0	2.5	4.5	4.8	5.6	5.0	4.8	23.2	29.2	20.0	3.0	81.9	46.5	48.5	51.5
24354	MARION	95.8	95.8	2.8	2.8	0.3	0.3	1.0	1.0	5.5	5.4	5.9	5.9	6.0	26.8	27.1	15.4	2.0	79.7	41.3	48.6	51.4
24360	MAX MEADOWS	97.4	97.0	1.4	1.6	0.3	0.3	0.5	0.6	5.5	5.9	6.3	5.6	5.6	30.0	27.9	11.9	1.3	78.9	39.4	49.5	50.5
24361	MEADOWVIEW	96.8	96.3	2.0	2.2	0.5	0.5	0.5	0.7	5.1	5.1	5.4	7.8	8.9	26.7	27.3	12.2	1.5	81.0	39.0	49.9	50.1
24363	MOUTH OF WILSON	94.9	94.5	4.4	4.7	0.1	0.1	0.7	0.9	4.5	4.9	4.7	4.1	5.3	26.8	30.0	17.3	2.3	83.4	44.8	52.6	47.4
24366	ROCKY GAP	97.5	97.1	1.4	1.6	0.0	0.0	0.5	0.7	3.4	3.8	5.7	5.7	6.2	26.9	29.3	16.2	2.9	83.1	43.9	49.2	50.8
24368	RURAL RETREAT	98.2	97.9	0.6	0.7	0.3	0.4	0.6	0.7	6.1	6.2	6.9	6.1	5.9	29.2	25.9	12.2	1.5	77.1	38.5	49.2	50.8
24370	SALTVILLE	99.0	98.9	0.4	0.4	0.0	0.0	0.5	0.5	5.0	5.4	6.5	5.7	5.3	27.0	27.8	15.6	1.6	79.5	41.8	49.3	50.7
24374	SPEEDWELL	98.4	98.3	0.6	0.6	0.2	0.2	1.0	1.1	5.7	5.9	6.8	6.0	5.7	27.7	27.8	13.0	1.6	77.9	40.3	50.4	49.6
24375	SUGAR GROVE	96.1	96.0	2.6	2.6	0.0	0.0	0.7	0.7	5.3	5.7	7.4	6.6	5.5	28.8	26.0	13.2	1.5	77.6	38.5	50.2	49.8
24377	TANNERSVILLE	99.3	99.0	0.0	0.0	0.0	0.0	0.3	0.3	4.3	4.6	5.9	6.6	5.6	27.0	34.2	10.9	1.0	81.3	42.4	51.0	49.0
24378	TROUTDALE	71.4	69.5	27.5	29.2	0.2	0.3	0.5	0.6	3.0	3.3	3.7	3.8	9.8	40.6	23.5	11.2	1.3	88.0	37.1	67.7	32.3
24380	WILLIS	97.9	97.4	0.6	0.7	0.0	0.0	1.4	1.8	5.2	5.6	6.1	5.8	5.6	26.7	28.3	14.6	2.2	79.6	41.9	51.4	48.6
24381	WOODLAWN	97.3	97.0	1.0	1.0	0.1	0.1	2.0	2.5	5.7	6.0	6.0	5.7	5.0	28.5	27.8	14.0	1.4	78.9	40.7	50.4	49.6
24382	WYTHEVILLE	93.8	93.2	4.6	5.0	0.5	0.6	0.6	0.7	5.2	5.3	5.6	5.6	5.6	26.9	27.4	15.9	2.6	80.5	42.2	46.7	53.3
24401	STAUNTON	86.8	86.0	10.8	11.2	0.5	0.5	1.1	1.4	5.2	5.2	5.6	6.4	6.8	26.4	26.8	15.0	2.6	80.4	41.3	47.6	52.4
24413	BLUE GRASS	99.4	99.4	0.0	0.0	0.6	0.6	0.0	0.0	4.0	4.6	6.3	4.6	4.0	21.3	34.5	18.4	2.3	81.6	48.0	51.2	48.9
24416	BUENA VISTA	94.5	93.9	4.0	4.3	0.4	0.5	1.0	1.2	6.1	6.0	6.3	6.2	6.5	26.6	26.2	14.1	2.0	78.2	39.5	47.4	52.7
24421	CHURCHVILLE	98.1	97.9	0.7	0.8	0.2	0.2	1.2	1.5	5.3	5.8	6.8	6.4	5.3	25.8	31.2	11.9	1.5	77.9	41.8	49.8	50.2
24422	CLIFTON FORGE	88.2	87.0	9.9	10.7	0.1	0.1	0.7	0.9	5.4	5.6	6.3	5.3	5.2	24.0	26.5	18.4	3.3	79.4	43.8	46.7	53.3
24426	COVINGTON	91.5	91.0	6.7	6.9	0.4	0.5	0.5	0.6	5.9	6.0	6.3	5.7	5.4	25.7	27.9	15.0	2.3	78.3	41.8	49.4	50.6
24430	CRAIGSVILLE	80.6	79.4	18.1	19.1	0.1	0.1	0.3	0.4	4.5	4.4	4.9	5.1	7.9	36.4	25.4	10.1	1.2	82.8	38.3	60.9	39.1
24431	CRIMORA	97.4	97.0	1.1	1.2	0.2	0.3	1.0	1.4	5.8	5.9	7.7	7.5	6.3	28.4	26.3	11.3	0.7	75.9	38.2	49.4	50.6
24432	DEERFIELD	98.6	98.6	0.3	0.3	0.3	0.3	0.3	0.3	3.4	4.5	7.3	5.7	4.0	23.2	34.5	15.3	2.3	80.8	46.1	52.0	48.0
24433	DOE HILL	99.3	99.3	0.0	0.0	0.0	0.0	0.7	0.7	3.2	3.5	6.7	5.6	3.5	24.6	30.5	20.0	2.5	82.5	46.8	50.9	49.1
24435	FAIRFIELD	96.8	96.5	2.0	2.3	0.3	0.4	0.4	0.4	6.2	6.4	6.4	5.8	5.7	27.8	27.9	12.8	1.1	77.6	40.5	50.9	49.1
24437	FORT DEFIANCE	98.1	97.7	1.2	1.3	0.1	0.4	0.6	0.8	5.1	5.9	7.2	6.9	5.1	25.0	30.4	13.1	1.4	77.8	42.3	50.5	49.5
24439	GOSHEN	92.8	92.2	6.4	6.9	0.2	0.2	0.5	0.6	4.9	5.0	5.6	5.6	6.0	27.9	29.9	13.7	1.5	80.9	42.1	53.7	46.3
24440	GREENVILLE	85.1	83.9	13.2	14.1	0.4	0.5	0.7	0.9	4.2	4.9	5.4	4.7	7.7	36.7	26.0	9.5	0.9	82.2	37.9	61.6	38.4
24441	GROTTOES	95.9	95.5	2.9	3.0	0.1	0.2	1.6	2.0	7.2	7.4	7.1	5.8	5.2	30.6	25.3	10.5	0.9	74.7	37.0	49.5	50.5
24442	HEAD WATERS	99.0	100.0	0.0	0.0	0.0	0.0	0.0	0.0	3.0	4.0	7.0	6.0	4.0	23.0	30.0	20.0	3.0	80.0	46.7	51.0	49.0
24445	HOT SPRINGS	94.9	94.8	3.8	3.9	0.5	0.6	0.4	0.4	4.6	5.8	6.9	5.6	3.7	25.6	29.3	16.4	2.2	78.9	43.7	48.3	51.7
24450	LEXINGTON	91.8	91.3	5.7	5.9	1.2	1.4	1.0	1.3	4.1	4.1	4.6	11.5	14.0	20.9	23.9	14.8	2.1	84.2	36.5	52.4	47.6
24458	MC DOWELL	99.1	99.1	0.3	0.3	0.0	0.0	0.6	0.6	3.0	4.2	6.3	5.7	3.3	24.4	30.7	19.9	2.4	82.8	46.8	50.9	49.1
24459	MIDDLEBROOK	97.9	97.6	1.2	1.4	0.2	0.2	0.3	0.3	5.3	5.6	6.5	6.2	6.1	24.0	31.0	13.5	1.7	78.6	43.1	51.7	48.3
24460	MILLBORO	88.9	88.7	9.5	9.7	0.5	0.5	0.5	0.5	4.2	5.1	5.8	5.8	4.4	29.2	30.8	13.6	1.3	80.9	42.6	52.7	47.3
24464	MONTEBELLO	91.0	90.6	7.1	7.5	0.6	0.6	3.2	3.8	5.0	5.0	5.6	6.3	5.6	25.6	31.9	13.8	1.3	80.6	42.9	49.4	50.6
24465	MONTEREY	99.2	99.1	0.1	0.1	0.1	0.1	0.6	0.6	4.0	4.5	5.4	5.2	4.1	20.5	34.7	19.1	2.6	82.9	48.5	48.7	51.3
24467	MOUNT SIDNEY	99.0	98.9	0.2	0.2	0.2	0.2	0.5	0.8	4.4	5.1	6.6	6.9	5.5	23.7	33.2	12.7	1.9	79.7	43.8	49.5	50.5
24468	MUSTOE	99.5	99.5	0.0	0.0	0.5	0.5	0.0	0.0	3.4	4.3	6.3	4.8	4.3	21.2	35.1	18.3	2.4	83.2	48.0	50.5	49.5
24471	PORT REPUBLIC	97.8	97.6	0.8	0.8	0.4	0.4	1.8	2.1	5.8	6.4	6.6	6.5	5.5	26.7	30.2	10.9	1.3	77.2	40.4	49.8	50.2
24472	RAPHINE	97.9	97.5	1.2	1.3	0.4	0.5	0.3	0.4	5.2	5.5	6.1	5.5	5.5	27.3	29.5	14.1	1.4	79.8	42.2	50.3	49.7
24473	ROCKBRIDGE BATHS	97.7	97.4	1.2	1.3	0.1	0.2	0.7	0.9	4.8	5.1	6.4	5.9	6.4	23.3	30.5	15.7	1.9	79.9	43.8	50.1	49.9
24477	STUARTS DRAFT	96.2	95.8	2.5	2.7	0.2	0.3	1.0	1.3	6.1	6.3	7.0	6.5	5.6	27.6	27.5	12.0	1.3	76.6	39.8	49.1	50.9
24479	SWOOPE	96.7	96.4	2.4	2.5	0.3	0.4	0.8	1.0	4.7	5.4	6.6	6.9	6.0	25.1	30.8	13.4	1.1	79.2	42.4	49.9	50.1
	VIRGINIA	72.3	70.7	19.6	19.9	3.7	4.3	4.7	5.7	6.5	6.6	6.9	6.9	7.0	29.7	24.9	10.1	1.4	76.2	36.6	49.1	50.9
	UNITED STATES	75.1	73.6	12.3	12.5	3.8	4.2	12.5	14.1	6.9	6.7	7.2	7.0	7.3	28.6	23.8	10.8	1.7	75.1	36.0	49.1	50.9

ZIP CODE #	POST OFFICE NAME	2004 Per Capita Income	2004 HH Income Base	2004 Household Income Distribution (%): Less than $25,000	$25,000 to $49,999	$50,000 to $99,999	$100,000 to $149,999	$150,000 or More	Median Household Income: 2004	2009	2004 National Centile	2004 State Centile	2004 Home Value Base	2004 Home Value Distribution (%): Less than $50,000	$50,000 to $89,999	$90,000 to $174,999	$175,000 to $399,999	$400,000 or More	2004 Median Home Value
24243	DRYDEN	15829	862	44.8	28.8	18.6	5.8	2.1	28281	33059	9	6	660	28.2	28.8	32.4	10.3	0.3	80800
24244	DUFFIELD	14374	2204	44.3	32.1	22.0	1.3	0.3	28087	32168	9	6	1743	36.4	27.1	28.9	6.9	0.7	73292
24245	DUNGANNON	14878	503	53.7	26.0	16.9	2.6	0.8	23068	25742	3	3	397	44.8	29.2	21.4	4.3	0.3	57321
24248	EWING	19704	1001	44.3	30.1	18.7	4.2	2.8	30167	35673	13	10	804	32.6	21.6	33.0	10.8	2.0	81500
24250	FORT BLACKMORE	13720	540	49.1	30.6	17.4	3.0	0.0	25569	28882	5	4	444	45.5	25.0	22.5	6.5	0.5	58333
24251	GATE CITY	20691	3539	37.1	31.6	23.2	6.1	2.0	33682	39088	23	17	2721	24.9	29.0	35.8	9.3	1.0	85413
24256	HAYSI	13897	1335	51.4	33.2	13.5	1.5	0.5	24200	26850	4	3	1054	42.6	31.3	22.9	2.6	0.7	57429
24258	HILTONS	18027	1168	39.6	28.0	26.3	4.5	1.7	33372	38902	22	16	953	25.7	30.1	27.0	16.4	0.8	83148
24260	HONAKER	18220	2242	45.8	30.7	18.9	2.7	1.9	27214	30832	7	5	1817	36.7	27.3	30.1	5.2	0.7	67233
24263	JONESVILLE	17376	2748	48.7	27.7	16.1	5.4	2.1	25702	29984	5	4	1947	24.2	26.6	36.6	11.6	0.9	89068
24265	KEOKEE	12369	591	56.4	27.6	12.9	2.0	1.2	22001	25082	3	2	470	61.7	19.4	17.2	1.7	0.0	37353
24266	LEBANON	20859	3093	35.1	32.1	24.3	6.2	2.2	34957	40439	27	22	2363	23.5	19.6	41.9	12.9	2.1	100219
24269	MC CLURE	16010	35	48.6	25.7	22.9	2.9	0.0	26114	30000	6	4	27	48.2	25.9	25.9	0.0	0.0	51667
24270	MENDOTA	19025	292	38.4	36.6	21.9	1.0	2.1	30740	36135	14	11	236	27.1	31.8	27.1	11.4	2.5	81600
24271	NICKELSVILLE	15949	1172	41.8	32.8	21.5	3.3	0.6	30486	35115	13	11	926	28.7	28.9	31.0	10.6	0.8	80897
24272	NORA	15610	234	44.9	32.1	19.2	2.1	1.7	27786	31410	8	6	200	43.5	22.0	28.5	6.0	0.0	66667
24273	NORTON	19842	2476	45.8	27.5	19.1	5.5	2.2	28170	33597	9	6	1652	28.2	29.9	32.5	8.7	0.8	79318
24277	PENNINGTON GAP	16423	2303	49.2	29.2	16.6	3.0	2.0	25457	29490	5	4	1658	33.9	26.8	28.8	9.8	0.7	76100
24279	POUND	15824	2072	40.0	34.3	21.8	2.7	1.3	31042	35890	15	12	1662	34.2	25.6	32.2	7.2	0.8	75392
24280	ROSEDALE	18385	1245	30.2	32.1	29.0	8.0	0.6	39428	45506	44	38	1046	16.6	21.7	43.4	16.1	2.2	108375
24281	ROSE HILL	15128	974	54.2	26.4	14.8	2.7	2.0	22226	25999	3	2	756	33.5	29.0	30.2	6.5	0.9	70455
24282	SAINT CHARLES	10937	145	61.4	29.7	8.3	0.7	0.0	19605	22068	2	1	111	69.4	18.9	10.8	0.9	0.0	27750
24283	SAINT PAUL	17196	1000	44.6	31.8	18.9	3.3	1.4	28971	34216	10	8	731	36.4	25.4	31.5	6.3	0.4	70357
24290	WEBER CITY	21492	961	35.0	37.9	21.6	4.1	1.5	34414	39259	25	20	699	17.9	28.8	44.2	9.2	0.0	93730
24292	WHITETOP	20242	256	41.8	32.4	22.3	2.7	0.8	29069	33258	10	8	217	24.4	20.7	26.3	26.7	1.8	96563
24293	WISE	19141	4577	38.7	31.4	22.8	4.3	2.7	33054	38560	21	15	3581	29.5	21.1	34.9	13.8	0.7	88825
24301	PULASKI	24254	6571	37.5	29.2	25.4	4.2	3.6	34434	40859	26	20	4624	18.5	27.1	35.6	17.0	1.8	96733
24311	ATKINS	22070	606	36.0	34.0	23.9	3.3	2.8	32324	37213	19	14	474	34.0	20.9	30.0	13.7	1.5	78182
24312	AUSTINVILLE	19628	1017	36.4	37.0	21.7	3.0	2.0	35861	40779	31	26	830	21.2	34.5	35.8	7.8	0.7	84891
24313	BARREN SPRINGS	17059	275	32.4	34.6	29.5	3.6	0.0	36310	40852	33	27	231	28.6	35.1	23.8	12.6	0.0	77292
24314	BASTIAN	25766	637	25.6	40.2	23.1	8.5	2.7	37401	45043	37	31	538	25.5	24.9	39.2	8.9	1.5	89524
24315	BLAND	18518	1300	37.0	28.2	28.0	5.7	1.2	33819	40366	23	18	1088	21.2	23.4	43.8	10.9	0.6	99206
24316	BROADFORD	15357	9	44.4	22.2	33.3	0.0	0.0	27247	27247	7	6	7	14.3	42.9	42.9	0.0	0.0	85000
24317	CANA	16788	1505	41.8	35.4	17.6	3.2	2.0	29883	34841	12	9	1263	23.8	34.7	31.8	7.0	2.9	81270
24318	CERES	19786	334	38.9	33.8	17.1	6.9	3.3	32478	38566	19	14	282	29.1	18.8	37.2	12.1	2.8	92222
24319	CHILHOWIE	18687	2621	34.6	35.2	24.7	3.7	1.9	34495	39914	26	21	2020	23.5	22.1	42.4	10.7	1.3	96544
24322	CRIPPLE CREEK	23704	49	32.7	36.7	22.5	4.1	4.1	34417	39294	25	20	40	22.5	27.5	37.5	10.0	2.5	90000
24323	CROCKETT	21455	234	32.5	35.9	23.9	5.1	2.6	36053	42189	32	26	191	17.8	26.2	42.4	12.0	1.6	96765
24324	DRAPER	20165	714	33.2	31.7	25.5	8.4	1.3	35485	41527	29	24	606	21.1	18.2	35.8	23.9	1.0	109884
24325	DUGSPUR	22655	590	35.8	27.1	29.3	2.9	4.9	36373	42900	33	28	499	14.8	25.7	30.3	24.3	5.0	106926
24326	ELK CREEK	30124	520	30.8	34.6	27.3	2.9	4.4	37354	43300	37	31	444	13.5	32.0	40.3	13.7	0.5	100305
24328	FANCY GAP	20062	1007	35.6	36.9	20.7	3.4	3.5	33534	39061	23	17	843	18.2	33.2	36.4	10.8	1.4	88647
24330	FRIES	17793	1782	43.8	35.9	17.4	1.3	1.6	28465	32405	9	7	1426	30.6	36.0	27.0	6.0	0.4	70254
24333	GALAX	21391	7625	35.6	35.2	22.7	3.3	3.2	34027	39630	24	18	5965	24.5	25.6	37.6	10.7	1.5	89780
24340	GLADE SPRING	20178	2231	34.4	33.2	24.8	5.2	2.4	36624	43080	34	28	1766	21.2	31.1	34.5	10.7	2.5	87796
24343	HILLSVILLE	22120	4000	36.2	30.8	25.9	4.0	3.1	35107	40419	28	23	3097	15.7	22.3	42.4	18.1	1.5	108505
24347	HIWASSEE	19741	693	31.9	30.0	32.5	3.6	2.0	38754	45000	42	35	581	19.6	19.1	37.2	23.1	1.0	107813
24348	INDEPENDENCE	19821	1720	39.1	33.7	20.2	4.7	2.2	31306	36129	16	12	1333	18.6	20.6	37.2	21.6	2.0	109304
24350	IVANHOE	14697	514	42.2	35.4	19.8	2.5	0.0	28590	32820	10	7	428	27.6	43.7	19.4	8.2	1.2	73725
24351	LAMBSBURG	16468	271	39.1	38.0	19.2	2.2	1.5	33126	38867	21	16	227	24.7	32.2	33.9	7.5	1.8	80882
24352	LAUREL FORK	22693	284	30.3	32.4	30.6	2.5	4.2	38633	45989	42	35	243	9.1	29.6	38.7	17.7	4.9	107880
24354	MARION	20360	7232	35.3	33.7	22.8	5.3	2.9	33805	39459	23	18	5300	20.8	24.0	41.6	12.6	1.1	97722
24360	MAX MEADOWS	21276	2547	25.4	34.0	31.5	6.2	3.0	43360	50076	57	50	2148	21.3	23.8	36.6	17.9	0.3	97394
24361	MEADOWVIEW	18905	2118	33.6	33.5	25.8	5.0	2.1	36331	42614	33	27	1691	23.0	27.0	36.0	12.2	1.9	90040
24363	MOUTH OF WILSON	19499	685	37.1	32.9	24.1	5.1	0.9	33500	37872	22	16	575	13.7	26.3	33.7	24.9	1.4	107314
24366	ROCKY GAP	31564	248	20.6	38.7	26.2	8.9	5.7	42979	52299	56	48	209	19.6	17.7	43.5	15.8	3.4	106389
24368	RURAL RETREAT	23390	2210	30.5	33.4	27.9	3.8	4.5	37419	44328	37	31	1833	19.2	24.2	43.5	11.6	1.5	97993
24370	SALTVILLE	17476	2813	38.0	34.3	23.6	3.1	1.1	32722	37556	20	15	2225	29.6	31.2	32.2	6.4	0.6	78676
24374	SPEEDWELL	23078	262	34.7	37.0	19.1	3.1	6.1	33232	39575	22	16	217	19.8	29.0	36.9	11.5	2.8	91563
24375	SUGAR GROVE	20052	575	35.5	32.4	25.0	3.1	4.0	35765	41188	31	25	457	34.1	21.4	32.0	12.3	0.2	73542
24377	TANNERSVILLE	18583	121	19.8	44.6	27.3	8.3	0.0	40661	47069	48	41	102	31.4	20.6	39.2	8.8	0.0	85000
24378	TROUTDALE	19018	577	34.0	33.3	26.3	3.3	3.1	34377	40075	25	20	489	18.2	25.6	39.1	16.0	1.2	100694
24380	WILLIS	18142	1198	34.1	34.8	24.1	4.6	2.4	33705	38281	23	17	1011	15.4	24.4	34.0	23.2	2.9	104907
24381	WOODLAWN	18507	1456	33.9	37.2	24.7	2.6	1.7	36182	40942	32	27	1179	19.2	27.5	42.8	9.2	1.4	93990
24382	WYTHEVILLE	22904	6275	37.0	30.3	24.4	4.8	3.5	34787	41199	27	21	4501	17.2	21.6	40.2	19.4	1.5	108526
24401	STAUNTON	24791	13967	27.9	29.5	30.9	7.3	4.4	42795	51614	55	47	9549	3.5	11.8	52.3	28.7	3.8	140259
24413	BLUE GRASS	19196	75	36.0	37.3	20.0	2.7	4.0	32725	38029	20	15	62	6.5	19.4	32.3	32.3	9.7	145000
24416	BUENA VISTA	19899	3543	31.6	34.5	26.6	5.3	2.1	37948	43140	39	32	2660	13.2	20.9	48.3	15.2	2.3	107933
24421	CHURCHVILLE	27144	1139	16.3	31.6	37.3	11.6	3.2	51473	58671	75	68	983	5.5	8.8	44.1	35.5	6.2	157435
24422	CLIFTON FORGE	19354	2961	39.1	31.8	22.8	4.1	2.2	33754	38383	23	17	2118	22.7	31.4	37.2	8.1	0.7	84941
24426	COVINGTON	23019	6525	28.8	31.9	31.5	5.2	2.6	40055	46277	46	39	5032	18.7	30.5	37.9	12.4	0.6	91331
24430	CRAIGSVILLE	15594	757	38.7	37.3	20.7	1.6	1.7	32916	37456	21	15	558	22.4	28.1	40.7	8.8	0.0	89474
24431	CRIMORA	22008	1000	26.1	34.3	28.9	6.5	4.2	42572	48600	55	47	879	40.1	8.1	31.3	18.8	1.8	93837
24432	DEERFIELD	20597	158	22.2	43.7	26.6	7.6	0.0	37899	43405	39	32	134	11.2	17.2	44.8	22.4	4.5	118269
24433	DOE HILL	15348	121	41.3	38.0	16.5	4.1	0.0	28880	34059	10	8	102	3.9	32.4	34.3	21.6	7.8	120455
24435	FAIRFIELD	22363	695	21.4	35.3	34.0	6.5	2.9	46005	51723	64	56	563	11.4	8.2	42.5	28.2	9.8	138690
24437	FORT DEFIANCE	25624	287	18.1	25.1	40.8	11.2	4.9	56049	64034	81	76	245	3.3	2.5	34.7	51.4	8.2	194583
24439	GOSHEN	22247	555	32.6	33.5	25.6	6.7	1.6	36366	41107	33	27	437	18.3	15.3	31.4	26.5	8.5	125781
24440	GREENVILLE	20568	770	15.6	38.7	33.8	7.3	4.7	48026	54752	68	61	659	17.9	12.9	42.5	23.8	2.9	127894
24441	GROTTOES	21067	2399	23.1	33.3	35.4	7.2	1.0	44080	50379	59	51	1915	12.2	9.9	50.4	25.8	1.7	132711
24442	HEAD WATERS	15806	44	38.6	38.6	18.2	4.6	0.0	30000	33170	12	10	37	2.7	32.4	35.1	21.6	8.1	121875
24445	HOT SPRINGS	30324	1079	24.0	30.4	34.4	5.8	5.4	45139	52731	62	54	887	10.5	19.1	47.6	20.6	2.3	116172
24450	LEXINGTON	25037	6088	30.1	29.4	26.2	9.3	5.0	41874	50265	53	44	4164	5.1	8.7	37.8	39.2	9.2	170060
24458	MC DOWELL	17829	159	39.0	39.0	17.6	4.4	0.0	30179	34230	13	10	133	4.5	29.3	36.1	21.8	8.3	124167
24459	MIDDLEBROOK	24466	254	24.8	22.4	40.2	5.5	7.1	51894	60000	75	69	212	2.4	10.9	26.4	46.7	13.7	208929
24460	MILLBORO	30060	727	20.6	39.3	26.7	7.4	5.9	41404	50797	51	42	597	9.7	15.8	32.3	37.7	4.5	153066
24464	MONTEBELLO	27184	71	28.2	31.0	31.0	7.0	2.8	36732	40000	34	28	57	28.1	17.5	31.6	19.3	3.5	98333
24465	MONTEREY	21638	654	32.4	38.1	23.4	2.9	3.2	36601	40982	34	28	535	11.4	16.5	39.8	26.7	5.6	128125
24467	MOUNT SIDNEY	27841	895	20.5	25.1	38.6	10.7	5.1	53683	61143	78	72	763	0.9	5.2	39.1	50.2	4.6	185489
24468	MUSTOE	19530	91	33.0	39.6	19.8	3.3	4.4	33934	37858	24	18	75	5.3	21.3	32.0	29.3	12.0	143750
24471	PORT REPUBLIC	26106	515	15.9	30.7	40.0	10.3	3.1	52943	61730	77	70	433	7.4	7.4	43.2	32.8	9.2	157398
24472	RAPHINE	24637	1309	22.8	31.3	34.1	7.4	4.4	46531	52952	65	57	1088	10.3	9.4	37.0	36.0	7.3	151899
24473	ROCKBRIDGE BATHS	24426	366	27.3	33.9	28.7	7.1	3.0	41394	47139	51	42	301	11.6	7.6	31.9	36.5	12.3	171196
24477	STUARTS DRAFT	22664	3287	15.6	30.2	41.9	11.3	1.1	53231	60811	77	71	2765	3.0	6.9	54.2	35.2	0.8	154723
24479	SWOOPE	21717	661	23.8	26.6	39.0	8.2	2.4	49607	55916	71	64	563	9.1	13.3	43.0	30.6	4.1	127926
	VIRGINIA	30454		19.8	25.2	32.5	13.6	8.9	55216	67801				6.8	10.4	35.8	36.5	10.5	166226
	UNITED STATES	25866		24.7	27.1	30.8	10.9	6.5	48124	56710				10.9	15.0	33.7	30.1	10.4	145905

ZIP CODE	FINANCIAL SERVICES				THE HOME						ENTERTAINMENT						PERSONAL			
					Home Improvements		Furnishings													
# POST OFFICE NAME	Auto Loan	Home Loan	Invest-ments	Retire-ment Plans	Home Repair	Lawn & Garden	Comput-ers & Hard-ware	Major Appli-ances	TV, Radio, Sound Equip-ment	Furni-ture	Dine out/ Carry out	Sports Equip-ment	Fees & Tickets	Toys & Games	Travel	Cable TV	Apparel & Services	Auto Repairs	Health Insur-ance	Pets & Supplies
24243 DRYDEN	74	52	27	46	58	66	51	61	59	51	70	72	44	67	51	63	64	61	74	84
24244 DUFFIELD	63	43	21	38	48	56	43	52	51	43	59	61	37	56	43	54	54	51	64	72
24245 DUNGANNON	64	43	20	37	49	56	42	52	50	42	59	62	35	56	42	54	54	52	64	74
24248 EWING	87	58	26	50	66	76	56	70	68	57	80	84	48	75	57	73	72	70	87	100
24250 FORT BLACKMORE	62	41	19	36	47	54	40	50	48	41	57	60	34	54	41	52	51	49	62	71
24251 GATE CITY	80	58	35	54	64	75	61	70	70	59	82	80	54	78	61	74	75	70	84	89
24256 HAYSI	61	41	19	36	47	54	40	50	48	40	56	59	34	53	40	52	51	49	61	71
24258 HILTONS	79	53	24	46	60	69	51	64	62	52	73	77	44	69	52	67	66	63	79	91
24260 HONAKER	83	56	25	48	63	73	54	67	65	55	76	81	46	72	55	70	69	67	83	96
24263 JONESVILLE	68	49	29	45	54	64	52	59	59	50	70	68	45	66	52	63	64	59	72	76
24265 KEOKEE	54	38	20	34	42	50	39	46	45	38	53	54	34	50	39	48	48	46	56	62
24266 LEBANON	85	60	34	55	67	79	63	73	73	62	86	85	55	81	63	78	78	73	89	96
24269 MC CLURE	68	46	21	39	52	59	44	55	53	45	62	66	37	59	45	57	57	54	68	78
24270 MENDOTA	87	58	26	50	66	76	56	70	68	57	79	84	48	75	57	73	72	69	86	99
24271 NICKELSVILLE	71	48	22	41	54	62	46	58	56	47	65	69	39	62	47	60	59	57	71	82
24272 NORA	73	49	22	42	56	64	47	59	57	48	67	71	40	63	48	62	61	59	73	84
24273 NORTON	73	53	37	50	59	69	58	64	65	56	78	74	51	74	57	69	71	65	77	82
24277 PENNINGTON GAP	66	47	25	42	52	61	48	56	56	47	66	66	41	62	48	60	60	56	69	75
24279 POUND	73	49	23	43	55	64	48	59	57	48	67	71	41	64	49	62	61	59	73	83
24280 ROSEDALE	88	59	27	51	67	77	57	71	69	58	81	85	48	76	58	74	73	71	88	101
24281 ROSE HILL	66	45	21	39	50	58	43	54	52	44	61	64	37	58	44	56	56	53	66	76
24282 SAINT CHARLES	48	32	15	28	37	42	31	39	38	32	44	47	27	42	32	41	40	39	48	55
24283 SAINT PAUL	67	48	28	45	54	63	51	59	59	50	69	67	45	65	51	62	63	58	71	76
24290 WEBER CITY	78	57	34	53	62	74	61	69	69	58	81	78	53	77	60	73	74	69	83	87
24292 WHITETOP	43	28	13	25	32	37	27	34	33	28	39	41	23	37	28	36	35	34	42	49
24293 WISE	76	58	37	55	63	73	60	68	67	59	80	78	54	75	60	70	74	68	79	85
24301 PULASKI	87	73	57	69	77	87	73	80	80	72	96	93	69	95	74	83	91	80	90	100
24311 ATKINS	97	65	29	56	73	85	63	78	76	64	89	94	53	84	64	81	81	77	96	111
24312 AUSTINVILLE	77	61	42	56	66	74	59	67	66	59	79	79	55	79	60	70	74	66	78	89
24313 BARREN SPRINGS	80	54	24	46	61	70	52	65	62	53	73	77	44	69	53	67	67	64	80	92
24314 BASTIAN	117	79	36	68	89	102	76	95	92	77	107	113	64	102	77	99	98	94	117	135
24315 BLAND	81	57	31	51	63	74	58	69	68	57	80	80	51	75	58	73	73	68	84	92
24316 BROADFORD	67	45	20	39	51	59	44	54	53	44	62	65	37	58	44	57	56	54	67	77
24317 CANA	74	50	22	43	56	65	48	60	58	49	68	71	41	64	49	62	62	59	74	85
24318 CERES	86	58	26	50	66	75	56	70	67	57	79	83	48	75	57	73	72	69	86	99
24319 CHILHOWIE	84	58	27	50	65	74	55	69	66	56	78	82	48	74	56	71	71	68	84	97
24322 CRIPPLE CREEK	78	58	38	56	64	76	64	71	72	61	85	80	57	80	63	76	77	71	85	86
24323 CROCKETT	90	70	47	67	76	86	71	80	78	70	94	93	65	92	71	81	87	79	91	101
24324 DRAPER	82	65	43	60	71	78	61	71	68	62	82	85	57	81	63	71	77	70	81	95
24325 DUGSPUR	90	70	43	63	76	85	66	77	74	66	89	92	60	87	67	78	83	76	90	105
24326 ELK CREEK	124	83	38	72	94	109	80	101	97	82	114	120	68	108	82	105	104	100	124	143
24328 FANCY GAP	85	60	32	52	68	77	57	71	68	58	80	84	50	77	59	73	73	70	86	100
24330 FRIES	75	51	25	45	57	67	50	62	60	51	70	73	43	67	51	64	64	61	76	85
24333 GALAX	90	62	32	55	70	80	61	74	72	62	85	88	53	80	62	77	78	73	89	103
24340 GLADE SPRING	85	60	31	53	67	76	58	71	69	59	81	84	51	77	59	73	74	70	85	97
24343 HILLSVILLE	85	66	45	62	72	82	67	75	74	66	89	87	61	86	67	78	82	75	88	96
24347 HIWASSEE	82	63	39	58	69	77	60	70	68	60	81	84	55	80	61	71	75	69	82	96
24348 INDEPENDENCE	80	57	31	51	64	73	55	67	65	56	76	80	48	73	57	69	70	66	81	93
24350 IVANHOE	66	44	20	38	50	58	43	53	51	43	60	64	36	57	43	55	55	53	66	76
24351 LAMBSBURG	78	53	24	45	60	69	51	63	61	52	72	76	43	68	52	66	65	63	78	90
24352 LAUREL FORK	93	71	43	64	77	86	67	79	76	67	91	94	61	89	68	80	84	78	92	108
24354 MARION	79	62	41	56	67	76	60	70	68	60	81	82	55	79	61	72	76	69	81	91
24360 MAX MEADOWS	89	72	48	66	78	85	67	78	75	68	90	93	63	89	69	78	84	76	88	104
24361 MEADOWVIEW	89	63	32	56	70	80	61	74	72	62	85	88	53	81	62	76	77	73	89	102
24363 MOUTH OF WILSON	69	48	23	42	54	62	46	57	55	47	65	68	40	62	47	59	59	56	69	79
24366 ROCKY GAP	136	91	41	79	103	119	88	110	106	90	125	131	75	118	89	114	113	109	135	156
24368 RURAL RETREAT	98	74	46	69	80	92	74	85	83	74	99	99	67	96	74	87	92	84	99	111
24370 SALTVILLE	78	52	24	45	59	68	51	63	61	51	72	76	43	68	51	66	65	63	78	90
24374 SPEEDWELL	98	69	38	63	77	90	71	84	83	70	97	97	62	92	72	88	89	83	102	110
24375 SUGAR GROVE	87	58	26	50	66	76	56	70	68	57	80	84	48	75	57	73	72	70	87	100
24377 TANNERSVILLE	75	67	51	63	70	75	62	68	65	62	79	81	60	81	63	67	76	66	74	88
24378 TROUTDALE	87	58	26	50	66	76	56	70	68	57	80	84	48	75	57	73	72	70	87	100
24380 WILLIS	83	56	26	49	64	73	54	68	65	55	77	81	46	73	55	70	70	67	83	96
24381 WOODLAWN	80	54	25	47	61	70	52	65	63	53	74	77	45	70	53	68	67	64	80	92
24382 WYTHEVILLE	84	65	44	61	71	81	67	75	74	65	89	86	61	86	67	78	82	74	87	95
24401 STAUNTON	83	79	76	77	81	88	80	82	82	78	101	95	79	101	80	83	97	82	86	95
24413 BLUE GRASS	76	59	40	53	67	75	56	67	63	55	75	79	50	74	60	68	70	66	80	92
24416 BUENA VISTA	76	63	48	60	67	75	64	70	69	63	84	80	60	82	64	72	78	69	78	85
24421 CHURCHVILLE	112	97	72	92	104	112	90	101	97	91	118	121	88	119	93	100	111	99	111	132
24422 CLIFTON FORGE	69	56	41	53	60	69	58	63	64	56	76	72	54	75	58	67	71	63	74	78
24426 COVINGTON	84	73	58	68	77	86	71	78	77	70	93	90	69	95	73	80	88	76	87	97
24430 CRAIGSVILLE	52	35	16	30	39	45	33	42	40	34	47	50	28	45	34	43	43	41	51	59
24431 CRIMORA	88	80	62	76	81	86	75	81	77	77	95	95	72	92	75	77	91	81	83	99
24432 DEERFIELD	78	61	42	55	69	78	58	70	66	57	78	82	52	77	62	70	72	69	82	95
24433 DOE HILL	61	48	33	43	54	61	45	55	51	45	61	64	41	60	48	55	57	54	65	75
24435 FAIRFIELD	86	76	58	73	80	87	73	79	77	72	94	93	71	95	74	79	89	78	86	100
24437 FORT DEFIANCE	110	98	75	93	103	111	90	100	96	91	117	120	89	119	93	99	111	98	109	129
24439 GOSHEN	71	55	36	53	61	68	55	63	61	55	73	75	50	72	56	63	68	63	72	82
24440 GREENVILLE	110	78	41	69	87	99	74	91	87	76	103	108	66	99	76	93	95	89	109	126
24441 GROTTOES	89	73	51	68	78	85	69	78	75	70	91	93	65	89	70	77	85	77	86	102
24442 HEAD WATERS	61	48	33	43	54	60	45	54	51	45	60	64	40	60	48	54	56	53	64	74
24445 HOT SPRINGS	116	92	63	89	100	113	94	105	103	92	123	122	86	120	94	107	114	104	120	133
24450 LEXINGTON	91	79	72	77	83	93	83	86	87	81	106	101	79	103	83	87	101	87	93	104
24458 MC DOWELL	63	50	34	45	56	63	47	56	53	46	63	66	42	62	50	56	58	55	67	77
24459 MIDDLEBROOK	102	90	69	86	96	102	84	93	89	84	108	110	82	110	86	91	103	90	100	120
24460 MILLBORO	125	98	67	88	110	124	93	111	105	92	124	130	83	123	99	112	115	110	132	152
24464 MONTEBELLO	99	74	49	71	81	97	82	90	92	78	108	101	73	102	81	97	99	90	108	109
24465 MONTEREY	77	59	39	55	65	76	61	69	68	59	81	79	54	78	62	73	74	69	83	89
24467 MOUNT SIDNEY	106	107	95	104	109	114	97	103	98	97	121	122	99	125	100	98	117	100	105	126
24468 MUSTOE	76	59	40	54	67	75	56	67	63	55	75	79	50	74	60	68	70	66	80	92
24471 PORT REPUBLIC	107	90	64	84	96	105	84	95	91	84	110	113	80	111	86	94	104	93	105	125
24472 RAPHINE	96	81	59	78	87	95	77	87	83	77	101	103	74	102	79	86	95	85	96	112
24473 ROCKBRIDGE BATHS	102	73	41	69	84	94	72	88	82	71	97	105	63	95	75	86	89	86	103	120
24477 STUARTS DRAFT	93	84	68	80	88	96	79	86	84	79	102	102	78	104	81	86	97	84	93	109
24479 SWOOPE	96	77	51	71	83	91	72	83	80	73	96	99	68	96	74	84	90	82	95	111
VIRGINIA	112	109	113	109	109	117	108	110	109	109	136	129	108	135	108	109	132	110	109	128
UNITED STATES	100	100	100	100	100	100	100	100	100	100	100	100	100	100	100	100	100	100	100	100

ZIP CODE		POPULATION			2000-2004 ANNUAL RATE		HOUSEHOLDS					FAMILIES		
# POST OFFICE NAME	COUNTY FIPS CODE	2000	2004	2009	% Rate	State Centile	2000	2004	2009	% Annual Rate 2000-2004	2004 Average HH Size	2000	2004	% Annual Rate 2000-2004
24482 VERONA	015	4765	4987	5338	1.1	60	1967	2099	2285	1.5	2.38	1395	1468	1.2
24483 VESUVIUS	163	612	630	657	0.7	48	270	284	302	1.2	2.22	199	207	0.9
24484 WARM SPRINGS	017	941	943	940	0.1	26	394	403	409	0.5	2.31	277	279	0.2
24485 WEST AUGUSTA	015	870	882	924	0.3	36	349	359	381	0.7	2.46	251	255	0.4
24486 WEYERS CAVE	015	2099	2337	2573	2.6	85	786	882	983	2.8	2.65	626	696	2.5
24487 WILLIAMSVILLE	017	142	145	145	0.5	42	59	61	63	0.8	2.38	44	45	0.5
24501 LYNCHBURG	031	22189	21967	22061	-0.2	17	9141	9183	9370	0.1	2.22	5311	5224	-0.4
24502 LYNCHBURG	680	37287	38783	39979	0.9	56	14436	15322	16094	1.4	2.32	9657	10103	1.1
24503 LYNCHBURG	019	18184	18672	19133	0.6	47	7460	7747	8031	0.9	2.28	4871	4961	0.4
24504 LYNCHBURG	031	10043	9762	9767	-0.7	8	3702	3662	3729	-0.3	2.43	2306	2239	-0.7
24517 ALTAVISTA	031	4871	4851	5019	-0.1	21	2088	2114	2229	0.3	2.26	1378	1379	0.0
24520 ALTON	083	2727	2822	2855	0.8	53	1061	1125	1163	1.4	2.51	793	829	1.1
24521 AMHERST	009	10149	10280	10375	0.3	36	3666	3782	3877	0.7	2.40	2583	2630	0.4
24522 APPOMATTOX	011	10068	10297	10503	0.5	44	3906	4060	4201	0.9	2.50	2945	3027	0.7
24523 BEDFORD	019	18984	19584	20485	0.7	50	7587	7949	8433	1.1	2.36	5325	5514	0.8
24526 BIG ISLAND	019	1379	1557	1734	2.9	89	557	639	722	3.3	2.44	425	482	3.0
24527 BLAIRS	143	2018	2000	2010	-0.2	18	755	766	784	0.3	2.61	598	599	0.0
24528 BROOKNEAL	031	3836	3882	4041	0.3	34	1502	1542	1635	0.6	2.47	1058	1070	0.3
24529 BUFFALO JUNCTION	117	1745	1753	1798	0.1	28	727	747	783	0.6	2.35	520	525	0.2
24530 CALLANDS	143	1486	1517	1538	0.5	42	621	651	673	1.1	2.33	443	457	0.7
24531 CHATHAM	143	8398	8208	8209	-0.5	10	3442	3438	3503	0.0	2.31	2371	2331	-0.4
24534 CLOVER	083	1903	1884	1861	-0.2	17	753	762	769	0.3	2.47	539	538	0.0
24536 COLEMAN FALLS	019	306	313	330	0.5	44	123	127	136	0.8	2.46	92	94	0.5
24538 CONCORD	031	4113	4167	4266	0.3	36	1556	1607	1677	0.8	2.59	1197	1225	0.6
24539 CRYSTAL HILL	083	195	209	215	1.6	72	93	102	107	2.2	2.04	62	67	1.8
24540 DANVILLE	143	35552	36005	35838	0.3	36	14600	15019	15168	0.7	2.33	9951	10109	0.4
24541 DANVILLE	143	31267	29881	28784	-1.1	3	13243	12844	12550	-0.7	2.27	8514	8147	-1.0
24549 DRY FORK	143	3771	3995	4153	1.4	66	1494	1614	1707	1.8	2.48	1155	1236	1.6
24550 EVINGTON	031	5726	5986	6265	1.1	58	2278	2429	2593	1.5	2.46	1680	1766	1.2
24551 FOREST	019	15306	16564	17986	1.9	77	5787	6344	6979	2.2	2.61	4425	4797	1.9
24553 GLADSTONE	125	2139	2115	2151	-0.3	16	812	818	847	0.2	2.59	613	611	-0.1
24554 GLADYS	031	3884	3982	4151	0.6	45	1535	1612	1718	1.2	2.46	1140	1182	0.9
24555 GLASGOW	163	1680	1736	1819	0.8	52	723	758	805	1.1	2.26	499	515	0.8
24556 GOODE	019	2526	2783	3057	2.3	83	949	1055	1173	2.5	2.64	787	867	2.3
24557 GRETNA	143	8483	8342	8348	-0.4	13	3472	3491	3561	0.1	2.37	2447	2423	0.2
24558 HALIFAX	083	6746	6742	6705	0.0	23	2603	2666	2710	0.6	2.42	1866	1879	0.2
24562 HOWARDSVILLE	125	75	81	88	1.8	76	27	30	33	2.5	2.70	19	21	2.4
24563 HURT	143	5221	5058	5040	-0.7	6	2196	2183	2220	-0.1	2.32	1577	1543	-0.5
24565 JAVA	143	1567	1546	1543	-0.3	15	596	602	613	0.2	2.57	450	449	-0.1
24566 KEELING	143	1568	1724	1815	2.3	82	610	686	735	2.8	2.51	453	502	2.5
24569 LONG ISLAND	143	978	941	941	-0.9	4	369	364	371	-0.3	2.59	276	269	-0.6
24570 LOWRY	019	66	67	71	0.4	37	26	27	29	0.9	2.48	19	19	0.0
24571 LYNCH STATION	031	1865	1863	1923	0.0	22	751	765	805	0.4	2.44	551	553	0.1
24572 MADISON HEIGHTS	009	16390	16592	16730	0.3	34	6279	6486	6642	0.8	2.45	4593	4682	0.5
24574 MONROE	009	4415	4433	4485	0.1	28	1615	1665	1717	0.7	2.61	1189	1209	0.4
24577 NATHALIE	083	5472	5341	5246	-0.6	9	2172	2167	2176	-0.1	2.46	1577	1553	-0.4
24578 NATURAL BRIDGE	163	1135	1153	1196	0.4	38	456	470	494	0.7	2.37	331	336	0.4
24579 NATURAL BRIDGE STATI	163	1734	1844	1964	1.5	68	687	739	798	1.7	2.41	479	507	1.4
24580 NELSON	117	661	696	726	1.2	62	272	293	312	1.8	2.38	193	205	1.4
24586 RINGGOLD	143	4395	4745	4979	1.8	75	1731	1914	2048	2.4	2.48	1292	1412	2.1
24588 RUSTBURG	031	8945	9595	10191	1.7	72	3445	3775	4095	2.2	2.49	2515	2721	1.9
24589 SCOTTSBURG	083	2593	2588	2567	-0.1	22	1036	1057	1071	0.5	2.44	757	761	0.1
24590 SCOTTSVILLE	029	7154	7824	8991	2.1	81	2761	3073	3585	2.6	2.54	1974	2169	2.2
24592 SOUTH BOSTON	083	13615	13488	13388	-0.2	18	5631	5674	5740	0.2	2.27	3714	3690	-0.2
24593 SPOUT SPRING	011	827	832	844	0.1	29	321	329	340	0.6	2.51	241	244	0.3
24594 SUTHERLIN	143	1717	1739	1749	0.3	36	669	695	713	0.9	2.50	506	520	0.6
24597 VERNON HILL	083	1235	1240	1237	0.1	28	490	504	514	0.7	2.45	357	363	0.4
24598 VIRGILINA	083	2185	2181	2175	0.0	22	896	913	928	0.4	2.39	642	646	0.2
24599 WINGINA	029	837	851	883	0.4	38	342	354	375	0.8	2.39	246	251	0.5
24602 BANDY	185	2097	2046	2041	-0.6	9	854	855	874	0.0	2.39	631	622	-0.4
24603 BIG ROCK	027	1022	1001	972	-0.5	11	415	420	422	0.3	2.38	322	323	0.1
24605 BLUEFIELD	185	10779	10807	10887	0.1	26	4462	4575	4720	0.6	2.29	3139	3172	0.3
24609 CEDAR BLUFF	185	2461	2482	2507	0.2	32	1035	1071	1108	0.8	2.30	762	778	0.5
24613 FALLS MILLS	185	798	782	781	-0.5	11	328	329	337	0.1	2.38	224	222	-0.2
24614 GRUNDY	027	8629	8321	8031	-0.9	5	3442	3417	3400	-0.2	2.36	2535	2486	-0.5
24620 HURLEY	027	4128	3970	3826	-0.9	4	1634	1625	1621	-0.1	2.43	1256	1236	-0.4
24622 JEWELL RIDGE	027	891	852	824	-1.1	3	359	355	355	-0.3	2.40	269	263	-0.5
24627 MAVISDALE	027	114	111	107	-0.6	8	47	47	47	0.0	2.32	34	34	0.0
24630 NORTH TAZEWELL	185	6748	6864	6969	0.4	39	2801	2920	3037	1.0	2.35	2075	2136	0.7
24631 OAKWOOD	027	3593	3466	3363	-0.8	5	1124	1104	1093	-0.4	2.32	832	806	-0.7
24634 PILGRIMS KNOB	027	576	563	546	-0.5	10	225	227	227	0.2	2.48	173	172	-0.1
24637 POUNDING MILL	185	4622	4675	4722	0.3	33	1811	1876	1939	0.8	2.49	1456	1493	0.6
24639 RAVEN	027	4041	3958	3939	-0.5	11	1641	1657	1696	0.2	2.39	1231	1226	-0.1
24641 RICHLANDS	185	6658	6629	6713	-0.1	21	2878	2935	3047	0.5	2.26	1954	1965	0.1
24646 ROWE	027	1162	1139	1105	-0.5	12	464	468	468	0.2	2.43	369	369	0.0
24649 SWORDS CREEK	167	2702	2572	2553	-1.2	2	1073	1046	1063	-0.6	2.46	842	813	-0.8
24651 TAZEWELL	185	7172	7255	7333	0.3	33	2780	2882	2986	0.9	2.35	1993	2037	0.5
24656 VANSANT	027	3883	3754	3625	-0.8	5	1577	1574	1570	0.0	2.38	1192	1176	-0.3
24657 WHITEWOOD	027	589	571	551	-0.7	7	237	237	237	0.0	2.41	187	185	-0.3
VIRGINIA					1.4					1.7	2.51			1.4
UNITED STATES					1.2					1.3	2.58			1.1

ZIP CODE #	POST OFFICE NAME	RACE (%) White 2000	White 2004	Black 2000	Black 2004	Asian/Pacific 2000	Asian/Pacific 2004	% Hispanic Origin 2000	% Hispanic Origin 2004	2004 AGE DISTRIBUTION (%) 0-4	5-9	10-14	15-19	20-24	25-44	45-64	65-84	85+	18+	MEDIAN AGE 2004	% 2004 Males	% 2004 Females
24482	VERONA	95.7	95.2	2.6	2.8	0.5	0.6	0.6	0.8	5.7	6.0	6.4	6.3	6.1	25.9	29.9	12.6	1.3	78.2	40.8	49.8	50.2
24483	VESUVIUS	93.0	91.9	5.9	6.7	0.2	0.2	0.7	0.8	5.7	5.9	6.5	5.9	4.9	27.6	29.2	13.0	1.3	78.3	41.1	50.6	49.4
24484	WARM SPRINGS	93.4	93.3	4.9	5.0	0.3	0.3	0.2	0.2	4.2	5.5	6.2	5.9	3.4	25.1	31.9	16.0	1.7	80.0	44.8	50.5	49.5
24485	WEST AUGUSTA	98.9	98.9	0.3	0.3	0.2	0.2	0.1	0.2	4.4	5.1	7.4	5.9	4.8	25.2	32.5	13.0	1.7	79.5	43.4	50.7	49.3
24486	WEYERS CAVE	98.0	97.8	0.5	0.6	0.1	0.0	0.7	0.9	6.3	6.9	7.9	6.5	5.1	26.4	29.1	10.6	1.3	74.8	40.2	51.1	48.9
24487	WILLIAMSVILLE	95.1	95.2	3.5	3.5	0.0	0.0	0.0	0.0	4.1	5.5	6.2	6.2	2.8	24.8	33.8	15.2	1.4	80.0	45.2	51.0	49.0
24501	LYNCHBURG	58.3	55.6	37.8	40.0	1.4	1.6	1.1	1.3	6.5	6.3	6.9	8.7	8.7	26.8	21.2	12.6	2.3	76.3	34.0	46.0	54.0
24502	LYNCHBURG	83.8	81.7	12.2	13.5	1.7	2.0	1.6	2.0	5.8	5.7	5.8	8.9	9.9	26.5	22.9	12.6	1.9	79.3	35.2	47.5	52.6
24503	LYNCHBURG	83.8	82.8	13.8	14.5	0.8	1.0	0.8	1.0	5.4	5.9	6.8	7.8	6.4	22.8	26.3	14.8	3.8	77.7	41.6	45.1	54.9
24504	LYNCHBURG	39.7	38.2	58.1	59.3	0.2	0.3	1.0	1.1	5.5	6.0	6.9	6.8	6.3	27.6	26.1	12.6	2.3	77.7	39.2	49.4	50.6
24517	ALTAVISTA	75.7	74.1	23.1	24.5	0.2	0.2	0.8	0.9	5.3	5.5	6.6	6.4	5.9	23.4	27.6	16.2	3.1	78.6	42.8	46.1	53.9
24520	ALTON	59.9	58.6	38.5	39.5	0.2	0.3	1.0	1.3	6.1	6.5	7.4	6.1	5.4	25.7	27.6	13.8	1.6	76.4	40.5	49.1	50.9
24521	AMHERST	75.0	73.6	22.6	23.7	0.4	0.5	1.2	1.4	5.4	5.7	6.3	9.6	9.4	23.7	25.1	12.5	2.4	78.6	37.4	45.3	54.7
24522	APPOMATTOX	75.7	74.2	23.2	24.5	0.2	0.2	0.5	0.6	6.3	6.5	7.0	6.1	5.6	26.3	26.9	13.6	1.8	76.5	40.1	48.4	51.6
24523	BEDFORD	83.5	82.9	14.9	15.5	0.4	0.4	0.7	0.8	5.4	5.7	6.5	5.9	5.1	25.9	27.2	15.7	2.7	78.7	42.3	48.9	51.1
24526	BIG ISLAND	86.0	85.0	12.5	13.3	0.2	0.2	1.0	1.2	4.8	5.5	6.4	5.5	4.8	26.3	31.3	13.7	1.7	80.0	43.1	50.0	50.0
24527	BLAIRS	63.8	61.9	34.1	35.7	0.4	0.4	1.8	2.1	5.4	5.8	6.2	6.6	6.2	26.8	30.5	11.4	1.4	78.9	40.7	49.5	50.5
24528	BROOKNEAL	67.8	66.2	31.2	32.7	0.0	0.0	1.4	1.6	6.0	6.4	7.4	7.2	5.7	24.2	25.0	15.6	2.5	75.4	40.6	47.4	52.6
24529	BUFFALO JUNCTION	66.4	64.6	31.8	33.3	0.2	0.2	1.4	1.8	5.4	5.8	6.8	5.8	4.9	23.3	29.0	17.6	1.6	78.6	43.9	49.1	50.9
24530	CALLANDS	74.1	72.6	24.8	26.1	0.1	0.1	1.2	1.3	5.5	5.7	6.4	6.1	5.5	27.4	29.0	12.9	1.5	78.6	41.3	48.9	51.2
24531	CHATHAM	68.5	66.4	30.1	32.0	0.2	0.2	1.0	1.2	5.0	5.2	5.8	5.8	5.4	26.0	29.1	15.2	2.4	80.2	43.0	49.0	51.1
24534	CLOVER	50.2	48.4	48.6	50.3	0.1	0.1	1.1	1.2	6.4	6.6	7.5	6.4	5.1	23.5	27.4	15.2	1.9	75.6	41.2	48.9	51.1
24536	COLEMAN FALLS	90.9	90.1	8.2	8.6	0.0	0.0	1.0	1.3	6.1	6.7	6.7	5.1	4.2	26.8	31.6	11.8	1.0	76.7	41.6	50.8	49.2
24538	CONCORD	80.4	78.8	17.8	19.1	0.2	0.2	0.7	1.0	6.4	6.6	6.8	6.4	6.1	27.4	27.7	11.4	1.1	76.2	38.8	49.8	50.2
24539	CRYSTAL HILL	66.7	65.1	31.8	33.5	0.0	0.0	0.5	0.5	6.7	6.2	6.7	5.7	6.2	25.4	27.3	13.4	2.4	77.0	41.0	50.7	49.3
24540	DANVILLE	61.3	59.8	36.8	37.9	0.5	0.6	1.3	1.7	6.3	6.3	6.4	6.1	5.8	25.7	25.9	15.1	2.5	77.3	40.6	46.6	53.4
24541	DANVILLE	61.3	60.3	36.9	37.5	0.6	0.6	1.4	1.7	5.8	5.9	6.4	6.7	6.1	24.7	26.8	15.3	2.2	77.9	41.2	47.3	52.7
24549	DRY FORK	83.0	81.6	15.7	16.8	0.2	0.3	1.1	1.2	5.8	6.2	6.5	6.1	5.5	28.2	28.5	11.8	1.3	77.8	40.5	50.2	49.8
24550	EVINGTON	84.7	83.4	13.6	14.6	0.3	0.4	0.8	1.0	6.2	6.5	7.1	6.2	5.4	27.9	28.2	11.6	1.0	76.5	39.6	49.6	50.4
24551	FOREST	91.9	91.1	5.8	6.2	1.1	1.3	0.9	1.1	6.5	6.9	7.8	6.9	5.6	27.4	28.8	9.5	0.8	74.6	38.8	49.2	50.9
24553	GLADSTONE	73.0	71.2	25.2	26.7	0.1	0.2	0.6	0.7	5.4	6.2	7.8	6.3	5.1	25.3	28.5	14.0	1.4	76.6	40.8	48.8	51.3
24554	GLADYS	75.5	74.2	23.4	24.5	0.1	0.1	0.8	0.9	4.9	5.7	7.0	7.0	5.5	26.7	27.4	14.1	1.7	77.9	41.0	49.6	50.4
24555	GLASGOW	87.1	85.9	10.4	11.1	0.4	0.4	0.5	0.6	5.0	5.4	6.6	6.0	5.4	24.7	27.9	17.2	1.8	79.2	43.0	49.4	50.6
24556	GOODE	89.8	88.9	8.4	9.1	0.3	0.3	1.2	1.5	5.9	6.5	7.7	6.4	4.5	25.9	30.4	11.5	1.2	75.9	41.4	49.2	50.8
24557	GRETNA	73.1	71.3	26.0	27.6	0.1	0.2	0.8	0.9	5.1	5.4	6.3	6.1	5.7	24.7	28.9	15.8	2.1	79.5	43.0	48.3	51.7
24558	HALIFAX	61.7	59.5	36.9	38.8	0.2	0.2	1.1	1.3	5.7	6.0	6.8	5.8	5.6	26.5	28.4	13.8	1.5	77.9	41.0	49.3	50.7
24562	HOWARDSVILLE	78.7	76.5	18.7	21.0	0.0	0.0	1.3	2.5	7.4	7.4	6.2	4.9	4.9	27.2	28.4	12.4	1.2	75.3	40.9	48.2	51.9
24563	HURT	77.3	75.3	21.7	23.6	0.2	0.2	0.6	0.8	5.3	5.6	6.5	5.4	5.7	27.7	27.3	14.8	1.6	79.2	40.9	48.2	51.8
24565	JAVA	49.2	46.9	48.5	50.5	0.2	0.2	2.4	2.9	5.9	6.1	7.0	6.5	5.6	25.4	28.9	12.9	1.7	77.0	41.4	47.9	52.1
24566	KEELING	80.0	78.7	18.5	19.7	0.0	0.0	1.7	2.0	6.4	6.6	6.2	5.6	6.6	27.8	28.9	10.7	1.2	77.4	39.4	49.4	50.6
24569	LONG ISLAND	61.5	59.1	37.1	39.2	0.0	0.0	1.8	2.1	5.7	6.0	6.8	6.9	6.0	25.2	28.8	12.5	2.1	77.2	40.5	50.2	49.8
24570	LOWRY	72.7	71.6	27.3	28.4	0.0	0.0	0.0	1.5	4.5	4.5	7.5	6.0	6.0	29.9	28.4	11.9	1.5	77.6	41.6	52.2	47.8
24571	LYNCH STATION	82.5	81.1	16.0	17.0	0.1	0.2	0.4	0.5	5.7	6.0	6.4	6.8	5.7	26.2	27.8	13.8	1.6	77.7	40.9	49.4	50.6
24572	MADISON HEIGHTS	78.5	76.9	18.8	20.1	0.4	0.5	0.9	1.0	5.9	6.1	6.6	5.9	5.5	28.5	27.1	13.2	1.3	77.8	40.0	48.6	51.4
24574	MONROE	80.1	79.0	17.4	18.2	0.2	0.3	0.9	1.2	5.9	6.3	6.9	6.8	5.8	26.3	28.1	12.7	1.3	76.9	39.9	50.0	50.0
24577	NATHALIE	57.5	55.7	41.3	42.8	0.0	0.0	1.0	1.2	6.0	6.4	6.9	5.5	5.6	25.0	28.0	14.5	2.2	77.4	41.4	49.1	50.9
24578	NATURAL BRIDGE	92.6	91.9	5.6	6.1	0.5	0.6	0.2	0.1	4.4	4.9	5.0	5.5	4.8	23.2	31.7	18.7	1.7	82.0	46.3	51.3	48.7
24579	NATURAL BRIDGE STATI	92.2	91.3	4.3	4.6	0.3	0.3	0.9	1.1	7.4	7.3	6.0	7.7	5.5	27.7	23.4	13.9	1.1	73.9	37.6	51.7	48.3
24580	NELSON	72.6	70.8	26.8	28.6	0.0	0.0	0.8	1.0	5.3	5.6	6.8	5.5	5.5	26.6	28.5	14.8	1.6	79.0	42.0	50.9	49.1
24586	RINGGOLD	78.4	76.3	20.5	22.4	0.1	0.1	1.1	1.3	5.5	5.8	5.9	6.1	5.8	27.5	29.7	12.6	1.3	79.3	41.3	49.5	50.5
24588	RUSTBURG	84.8	83.8	13.7	14.5	0.2	0.3	0.5	0.7	6.0	6.5	7.1	6.0	5.3	30.4	27.1	10.6	0.9	76.6	38.1	50.3	49.7
24589	SCOTTSBURG	69.7	68.0	28.7	30.1	0.1	0.1	1.4	1.7	6.4	6.5	6.8	5.9	5.3	25.0	28.0	14.4	1.7	76.7	40.9	49.7	50.3
24590	SCOTTSVILLE	77.5	76.0	20.7	21.9	0.2	0.2	0.9	1.1	6.3	6.5	7.1	6.5	5.4	27.4	28.4	11.1	1.3	76.2	39.4	49.1	50.9
24592	SOUTH BOSTON	58.9	56.8	39.0	40.8	0.5	0.5	1.5	1.8	6.1	6.3	6.6	5.8	5.3	24.2	26.8	15.8	3.0	77.3	41.9	46.3	53.7
24593	SPOUT SPRING	77.2	75.5	21.3	22.6	0.5	0.5	0.5	0.7	5.8	6.0	6.6	5.7	5.8	26.2	28.4	14.2	1.4	78.1	40.8	50.6	49.4
24594	SUTHERLIN	75.5	74.0	23.7	25.1	0.1	0.1	1.3	1.6	6.5	6.6	6.6	6.6	6.2	28.1	27.8	10.6	1.2	76.4	38.6	50.5	49.5
24597	VERNON HILL	47.5	46.1	50.7	51.7	0.0	0.0	1.9	2.3	5.1	5.6	7.2	6.4	6.3	25.2	28.4	14.2	1.7	77.9	41.2	48.6	51.5
24598	VIRGILINA	78.7	76.9	20.2	21.7	0.1	0.2	0.7	0.8	4.8	5.3	6.1	5.7	5.2	24.7	30.2	15.8	2.3	80.2	43.8	49.1	50.9
24599	WINGINA	75.8	74.0	21.9	23.2	0.0	0.0	1.2	1.4	5.9	6.0	6.7	6.5	5.5	24.2	28.8	14.8	1.7	77.3	42.3	49.2	50.8
24602	BANDY	97.9	97.6	1.2	1.3	0.1	0.2	0.3	0.4	4.9	5.5	6.4	5.3	5.6	25.4	30.0	15.2	1.7	80.1	43.0	49.2	50.8
24603	BIG ROCK	99.8	99.8	0.0	0.0	0.0	0.0	0.0	0.1	5.5	5.7	6.2	4.3	5.5	27.5	31.0	12.8	1.6	80.2	42.1	48.8	51.3
24605	BLUEFIELD	94.2	93.5	3.7	3.9	0.9	1.1	0.7	0.8	4.7	5.0	5.8	6.4	6.3	23.7	29.2	16.5	2.4	81.2	43.6	47.8	52.2
24609	CEDAR BLUFF	99.0	99.0	0.1	0.1	0.2	0.2	0.8	0.9	5.7	5.8	5.5	5.3	5.8	27.9	29.3	13.5	1.2	79.7	41.0	47.9	52.1
24613	FALLS MILLS	83.5	82.2	14.5	15.4	0.1	0.1	1.8	1.9	6.5	5.9	6.4	6.3	6.3	25.3	27.2	14.3	1.8	77.9	40.4	47.2	52.8
24614	GRUNDY	96.7	96.3	2.4	2.6	0.3	0.3	0.5	0.7	4.8	5.7	6.8	6.7	5.3	27.0	29.5	12.9	1.4	78.4	41.2	48.5	51.5
24620	HURLEY	99.4	99.4	0.1	0.1	0.1	0.1	0.5	0.6	5.1	5.6	6.4	7.3	5.7	29.6	29.2	10.2	0.9	78.2	39.5	49.4	50.6
24622	JEWELL RIDGE	99.2	99.1	0.0	0.0	0.0	0.0	0.2	0.1	4.8	5.3	6.5	7.2	5.4	26.1	30.8	12.4	1.6	79.1	41.7	50.8	49.2
24627	MAVISDALE	99.1	100.0	0.0	0.0	0.0	0.0	0.0	0.0	4.5	4.5	5.4	9.9	7.2	27.9	29.7	9.9	0.9	79.3	39.8	50.5	49.6
24630	NORTH TAZEWELL	96.7	96.2	2.0	2.2	0.4	0.5	0.4	0.5	5.1	5.8	6.4	5.4	5.4	26.1	30.5	13.8	1.7	79.4	42.3	48.8	51.2
24631	OAKWOOD	85.5	84.3	13.8	14.8	0.2	0.3	0.8	0.9	3.1	3.9	4.8	5.7	8.4	36.9	28.1	8.3	0.8	84.8	38.4	61.4	38.6
24634	PILGRIMS KNOB	99.0	98.6	0.0	0.0	0.2	0.2	0.5	0.7	5.3	5.9	5.9	8.4	6.2	27.4	31.3	8.4	1.4	78.2	39.6	49.4	50.6
24637	POUNDING MILL	99.0	98.8	0.2	0.2	0.2	0.3	0.5	0.6	5.2	5.8	6.6	5.5	5.4	27.3	32.1	11.1	1.1	79.0	41.5	48.7	51.3
24639	RAVEN	98.3	98.0	0.1	0.1	1.1	1.3	0.5	0.7	5.6	5.8	6.4	5.4	6.0	28.3	29.9	11.8	0.9	79.0	40.2	49.5	50.5
24641	RICHLANDS	98.4	98.1	0.1	0.1	0.8	1.0	0.4	0.6	5.6	5.6	5.7	5.4	6.2	26.4	28.9	14.5	1.7	79.8	41.8	46.6	53.4
24646	ROWE	99.7	99.7	0.0	0.0	0.0	0.0	0.2	0.3	4.6	5.2	6.1	7.1	6.4	28.6	29.6	11.2	1.2	79.5	40.6	50.3	49.7
24649	SWORDS CREEK	98.9	98.7	0.0	0.0	0.0	0.0	0.8	1.0	5.4	5.6	6.0	5.4	5.9	30.2	29.9	10.8	1.0	79.9	39.7	48.6	51.4
24651	TAZEWELL	94.0	93.4	4.5	4.9	0.4	0.5	0.3	0.4	5.1	5.4	5.8	5.3	6.0	26.7	28.5	14.6	2.6	80.4	42.1	48.4	51.6
24656	VANSANT	99.6	99.6	0.1	0.1	0.0	0.0	0.4	0.5	5.1	5.4	5.6	6.8	6.1	28.1	30.1	11.8	1.2	79.7	41.0	49.6	50.4
24657	WHITEWOOD	99.0	98.8	0.0	0.0	0.0	0.2	0.3	0.4	5.3	6.1	6.0	7.5	5.6	27.5	31.4	9.3	1.4	78.1	40.1	50.3	49.7
	VIRGINIA	72.3	70.7	19.6	19.9	3.7	4.3	4.7	5.7	6.5	6.6	6.9	6.9	7.0	29.7	24.9	10.1	1.4	76.2	36.6	49.1	50.9
	UNITED STATES	75.1	73.6	12.3	12.5	3.8	4.2	12.5	14.1	6.9	6.7	7.2	7.0	7.3	28.6	23.8	10.8	1.7	75.1	36.0	49.1	50.9

#	POST OFFICE NAME	2004 Per Capita Income	2004 HH Income Base	2004 Household Income Distribution (%): Less than $25,000	$25,000 to $49,999	$50,000 to $99,999	$100,000 to $149,999	$150,000 or More	Median Household Income: 2004	2009	2004 National Centile	2004 State Centile	2004 Home Value Base	2004 Home Value Distribution (%): Less than $50,000	$50,000 to $89,999	$90,000 to $174,999	$175,000 to $399,999	$400,000 or More	2004 Median Home Value
24482	VERONA	22415	2099	18.1	40.7	31.8	8.2	1.2	43450	50694	57	50	1620	9.1	4.1	53.5	31.1	2.4	143599
24483	VESUVIUS	23366	284	26.1	36.3	27.5	6.3	3.9	41632	47335	52	43	232	16.0	22.8	47.0	14.2	0.0	106111
24484	WARM SPRINGS	25404	403	24.8	39.0	27.5	5.5	3.2	39110	47249	43	37	326	9.8	18.7	37.7	30.1	3.7	131081
24485	WEST AUGUSTA	21212	359	21.5	37.1	29.3	11.1	1.1	42117	48407	53	45	304	7.2	11.2	48.4	27.6	5.6	139881
24486	WEYERS CAVE	25542	882	21.8	25.7	38.0	10.7	3.9	51612	58876	75	69	751	1.9	3.9	42.9	45.0	6.4	178547
24487	WILLIAMSVILLE	20278	61	26.2	36.1	29.5	6.6	1.6	38342	47375	41	33	50	4.0	16.0	34.0	42.0	4.0	162500
24501	LYNCHBURG	19966	9183	43.1	30.9	19.8	3.4	2.7	29389	34857	11	9	4467	25.4	43.6	24.8	5.7	0.5	74343
24502	LYNCHBURG	22836	15322	23.8	32.3	33.3	8.5	2.1	44894	53103	61	54	10729	5.9	14.1	65.1	14.4	0.5	122946
24503	LYNCHBURG	36468	7747	20.8	22.0	30.8	13.8	12.6	59472	77407	84	79	5452	5.1	9.0	38.7	40.1	7.2	168781
24504	LYNCHBURG	16123	3662	42.7	30.0	21.6	4.6	1.1	29957	35310	12	9	2213	32.2	28.0	29.6	9.8	0.4	77167
24517	ALTAVISTA	21555	2114	32.8	29.5	27.0	8.0	2.7	37382	43441	37	31	1481	14.9	30.5	40.7	13.2	0.9	97020
24520	ALTON	17072	1125	38.1	30.7	25.2	5.5	0.4	35885	42323	31	26	928	14.2	26.9	46.1	10.7	2.1	100980
24521	AMHERST	22591	3782	27.8	29.6	31.5	7.6	3.5	43183	49638	56	49	2972	14.3	20.0	42.6	21.1	2.1	112354
24522	APPOMATTOX	22346	4060	29.1	30.0	31.5	6.2	3.2	42291	49623	54	45	3270	13.3	19.9	40.9	23.0	2.9	119486
24523	BEDFORD	21414	7949	29.6	31.9	29.0	6.9	2.7	39782	47665	45	38	6128	13.0	18.8	44.5	21.4	2.4	114965
24526	BIG ISLAND	28552	639	26.3	24.9	33.3	9.7	5.8	49116	57446	70	63	546	16.1	24.7	31.5	22.0	5.7	106452
24527	BLAIRS	17944	766	29.0	38.0	25.7	5.1	2.2	37096	42199	36	30	639	21.6	26.8	39.4	10.6	1.6	91981
24528	BROOKNEAL	18218	1542	38.9	28.8	25.6	4.5	2.3	34083	39584	24	19	1152	30.0	29.9	33.0	6.8	0.4	76947
24529	BUFFALO JUNCTION	22132	747	35.6	27.6	25.3	8.7	2.8	35476	41151	29	24	594	20.0	17.2	38.2	21.4	3.2	114925
24530	CALLANDS	21751	651	32.0	38.1	20.4	6.0	3.5	36154	42048	32	26	537	27.0	31.5	37.6	3.0	0.9	81875
24531	CHATHAM	23034	3438	33.0	32.0	25.7	5.9	3.4	37208	42881	36	30	2700	24.0	30.0	34.9	10.2	1.0	86157
24534	CLOVER	16126	762	47.1	32.8	15.5	1.6	3.0	26735	31388	7	5	602	26.3	26.6	35.4	11.6	0.2	86792
24536	COLEMAN FALLS	28962	127	21.3	20.5	39.4	12.6	6.3	61761	76429	86	81	109	8.3	17.4	27.5	31.2	15.6	167045
24538	CONCORD	19905	1607	23.2	35.8	33.1	7.3	0.5	43666	50620	58	50	1357	16.7	17.6	45.0	19.2	1.5	113724
24539	CRYSTAL HILL	18612	102	40.2	35.3	19.6	4.9	0.0	30902	35450	15	11	79	15.2	29.1	39.2	15.2	1.3	99000
24540	DANVILLE	19668	15019	34.5	31.3	27.3	5.1	1.7	36233	42878	32	27	10420	21.5	30.8	40.1	7.3	0.5	87879
24541	DANVILLE	24709	12844	38.5	26.9	23.6	6.1	5.0	33694	41310	23	17	8119	21.2	30.4	33.3	13.5	1.8	88562
24549	DRY FORK	21440	1614	25.8	31.6	33.2	6.8	2.5	43351	50220	57	50	1361	19.3	21.8	39.9	17.1	1.9	103377
24550	EVINGTON	22823	2429	29.2	28.4	31.0	8.0	3.4	42453	49767	54	46	2006	21.8	17.8	41.4	17.3	1.7	107817
24551	FOREST	30675	6344	12.0	24.8	37.9	17.1	8.1	64027	77547	88	82	5233	3.2	3.4	45.0	44.5	3.9	172180
24553	GLADSTONE	21081	818	31.2	33.4	28.2	4.5	2.7	36601	43452	34	28	692	15.2	22.3	48.8	12.0	1.7	106414
24554	GLADYS	19379	1612	34.0	30.5	29.0	4.9	1.7	36580	42406	34	28	1315	27.5	24.2	39.2	8.3	0.8	87656
24555	GLASGOW	19228	758	33.6	34.3	27.0	3.7	1.3	35994	40042	32	26	578	16.3	17.7	39.6	24.4	2.1	113438
24556	GOODE	28641	1055	17.9	21.0	42.9	11.3	6.9	60925	70753	85	80	948	5.5	7.7	31.9	49.3	5.7	185491
24557	GRETNA	18041	3491	35.2	34.3	25.7	3.6	1.2	34836	39942	27	22	2755	24.1	35.6	33.9	6.2	0.2	82379
24558	HALIFAX	21403	2666	31.6	32.0	27.6	6.4	2.4	38323	44862	40	33	2174	17.4	24.1	39.3	16.7	2.5	103357
24562	HOWARDSVILLE	20340	30	30.0	33.3	26.7	6.7	3.3	41492	43636	51	42	25	16.0	16.0	36.0	28.0	4.0	120833
24563	HURT	19311	2183	32.5	31.2	31.7	3.9	0.6	39100	44446	43	37	1769	24.6	38.4	34.5	2.1	0.3	78940
24565	JAVA	17062	602	37.0	31.6	23.3	6.3	1.8	36821	42572	35	29	485	29.5	35.3	26.8	7.2	1.2	74778
24566	KEELING	16704	686	34.1	34.3	26.2	5.0	0.4	34534	39597	26	21	564	23.1	35.8	35.5	5.5	0.2	83151
24569	LONG ISLAND	17281	364	35.7	33.8	24.7	5.0	0.8	34762	40530	27	21	295	25.8	32.2	34.2	7.8	0.0	82419
24570	LOWRY	20149	27	22.2	37.0	37.0	3.7	0.0	42380	54514	54	46	23	4.4	30.4	39.1	21.7	4.4	120833
24571	LYNCH STATION	20915	765	28.6	36.9	22.0	9.9	2.6	38836	45054	42	35	643	19.1	20.8	33.0	26.3	0.8	107902
24572	MADISON HEIGHTS	20368	6486	27.5	33.9	30.7	6.0	1.9	41687	47657	52	43	4999	10.9	21.5	55.3	11.8	0.5	108028
24574	MONROE	21503	1665	23.2	32.9	33.4	6.9	3.7	45229	52089	62	54	1378	12.6	17.6	48.7	19.8	1.2	116022
24577	NATHALIE	17921	2167	42.4	31.2	20.9	3.2	2.4	28866	34168	10	8	1725	20.4	20.8	47.6	10.3	1.0	99472
24578	NATURAL BRIDGE	21330	470	28.9	35.1	28.7	4.3	3.0	38443	43089	41	34	386	6.5	12.4	35.0	42.2	3.9	161111
24579	NATURAL BRIDGE STATI	20256	739	36.0	31.3	26.4	4.2	2.2	35532	39488	30	25	612	31.4	24.7	36.6	6.1	1.3	79429
24580	NELSON	20914	293	37.2	23.6	27.3	8.2	3.8	34474	45946	26	20	243	23.9	15.6	48.6	11.9	0.0	101276
24586	RINGGOLD	19942	1914	29.0	31.6	33.8	4.6	1.1	42684	48884	55	47	1580	25.6	30.1	33.9	10.4	0.0	83077
24588	RUSTBURG	21550	3775	25.4	30.3	34.5	7.6	2.2	45356	52320	62	55	3154	25.5	18.2	38.8	16.7	0.7	102603
24589	SCOTTSBURG	18992	1057	34.9	32.5	26.8	4.0	1.8	37349	43528	37	31	846	24.5	22.0	36.8	15.4	1.4	95455
24590	SCOTTSVILLE	20958	3073	25.8	32.4	31.8	7.6	2.3	43381	51083	57	50	2393	8.9	14.1	49.2	23.1	4.7	131047
24592	SOUTH BOSTON	20827	5674	36.8	30.7	25.0	4.6	3.1	34608	41018	26	21	4079	12.0	27.4	43.6	15.7	1.4	104614
24593	SPOUT SPRING	24061	329	26.8	29.8	32.8	5.5	5.2	45101	52427	61	54	269	12.6	13.0	38.7	33.8	1.9	135417
24594	SUTHERLIN	21205	695	28.4	41.0	23.0	5.0	2.6	40429	45885	48	41	570	28.6	21.4	36.8	12.6	0.5	90000
24597	VERNON HILL	24332	504	35.9	27.8	27.6	4.8	4.0	37257	43832	36	30	408	14.2	30.6	37.8	14.7	2.7	95250
24598	VIRGILINA	23512	913	31.7	27.4	30.2	7.5	3.3	41240	48369	51	42	760	14.6	21.7	50.8	11.7	1.2	104360
24599	WINGINA	20686	354	34.5	38.1	18.6	6.5	2.3	34779	40654	27	21	292	25.0	18.2	38.0	17.8	1.0	101613
24602	BANDY	15014	855	42.3	38.5	15.2	3.4	0.6	28840	32560	10	8	689	53.1	23.8	19.6	3.3	0.2	47737
24603	BIG ROCK	15045	420	44.1	33.1	18.1	4.8	0.0	29050	34206	10	8	339	46.6	20.9	27.4	5.0	0.0	55750
24605	BLUEFIELD	22924	4575	34.9	33.3	21.5	5.8	4.5	34493	40654	26	20	3588	27.6	23.5	33.6	12.9	2.3	88104
24609	CEDAR BLUFF	17985	1071	40.3	35.8	18.7	3.4	1.9	30023	34662	12	10	839	27.9	28.8	31.5	11.1	0.7	81308
24613	FALLS MILLS	13353	329	45.9	36.5	15.5	1.8	0.3	26643	29895	7	5	222	39.6	31.5	22.5	6.3	0.0	64000
24614	GRUNDY	15902	3417	48.1	27.9	19.0	3.6	1.5	26115	30389	6	5	2681	39.1	24.3	30.1	5.9	0.6	71425
24620	HURLEY	12522	1625	56.0	28.1	12.4	3.2	0.3	21636	24446	2	2	1325	53.3	22.3	20.9	3.2	0.3	47315
24622	JEWELL RIDGE	14461	355	51.8	24.5	18.6	3.7	1.4	23572	26752	4	3	283	38.9	30.7	18.4	8.5	3.5	62143
24627	MAVISDALE	15154	47	46.8	31.9	14.9	6.4	0.0	26671	30738	7	5	39	46.2	33.3	20.5	0.0	0.0	57500
24630	NORTH TAZEWELL	17724	2920	39.9	33.7	21.1	3.0	2.3	30685	35954	14	11	2341	31.1	26.9	33.4	8.1	0.6	78988
24631	OAKWOOD	18000	1104	42.5	30.2	20.7	4.4	2.4	31136	36853	15	12	859	42.3	24.7	24.8	7.9	0.4	63816
24634	PILGRIMS KNOB	13877	227	55.1	22.5	18.1	2.2	2.2	22011	25635	3	2	182	35.7	22.0	29.7	11.0	1.7	76667
24637	POUNDING MILL	19655	1876	31.1	35.1	27.2	5.0	1.6	36317	42394	33	27	1571	22.3	22.5	44.0	10.1	1.2	101768
24639	RAVEN	14263	1657	55.5	26.3	14.1	2.8	1.3	22013	24728	3	2	1281	45.3	24.1	22.8	7.4	0.4	55762
24641	RICHLANDS	17429	2935	48.2	27.9	16.7	5.0	2.3	26061	29928	6	4	2142	36.5	25.0	31.0	6.9	0.7	71915
24646	ROWE	12971	468	53.2	26.3	18.4	2.1	0.0	23561	26630	4	3	398	36.9	26.6	28.6	7.0	0.8	66154
24649	SWORDS CREEK	13278	1046	48.3	32.2	16.2	2.8	0.6	25654	28423	5	4	866	50.5	25.1	19.9	4.6	0.0	49529
24651	TAZEWELL	18679	2882	34.3	33.5	24.8	5.5	2.0	35249	41640	28	23	2129	17.7	27.1	37.1	16.2	1.9	99449
24656	VANSANT	15341	1574	45.4	33.9	17.3	2.7	0.6	27135	30917	7	5	1289	40.7	28.1	27.6	3.4	0.2	62944
24657	WHITEWOOD	12054	237	61.6	21.9	14.4	0.4	1.7	18080	20115	1	1	193	39.9	25.9	21.8	10.4	2.1	63750
	VIRGINIA	30454		19.8	25.2	32.5	13.6	8.9	55216	67801				6.8	10.4	35.8	36.5	10.5	166226
	UNITED STATES	25866		24.7	27.1	30.8	10.9	6.5	48124	56710				10.9	15.0	33.7	30.1	10.4	145905

#	POST OFFICE NAME	FINANCIAL SERVICES				THE HOME						ENTERTAINMENT						PERSONAL			
						Home Improvements		Furnishings													
		Auto Loan	Home Loan	Invest-ments	Retire-ment Plans	Home Repair	Lawn & Garden	Comput-ers & Hard-ware	Major Appli-ances	TV, Radio, Sound Equip-ment	Furni-ture	Dine out/ Carry out	Sports Equip-ment	Fees & Tickets	Toys & Games	Travel	Cable TV	Apparel & Services	Auto Repairs	Health Insur-ance	Pets & Supplies
24482	VERONA	84	75	60	73	79	86	71	78	75	71	91	91	70	93	73	76	87	76	83	97
24483	VESUVIUS	95	66	34	59	74	85	64	78	76	65	90	93	56	86	65	81	82	77	94	108
24484	WARM SPRINGS	98	76	53	71	85	97	76	88	85	74	101	102	69	99	79	90	94	87	104	115
24485	WEST AUGUSTA	86	71	51	66	78	86	67	78	74	67	88	92	62	88	70	77	83	76	88	104
24486	WEYERS CAVE	102	100	86	97	104	108	92	98	93	92	115	117	92	119	94	94	111	95	101	122
24487	WILLIAMSVILLE	82	64	44	58	72	81	60	73	68	60	81	85	54	80	64	73	75	72	86	100
24501	LYNCHBURG	63	58	62	56	58	65	63	62	66	62	81	72	61	80	62	66	78	64	65	71
24502	LYNCHBURG	78	76	72	75	77	83	76	78	77	75	95	90	76	96	76	77	92	77	79	89
24503	LYNCHBURG	115	123	137	123	122	130	122	121	120	121	149	140	125	150	122	118	146	121	117	134
24504	LYNCHBURG	60	49	45	44	50	59	52	55	58	52	70	62	49	65	51	62	67	56	64	67
24517	ALTAVISTA	81	63	47	56	67	77	63	71	72	63	86	82	58	81	63	76	80	71	84	92
24520	ALTON	81	54	25	47	61	70	52	65	63	53	74	78	44	70	53	68	67	64	80	92
24521	AMHERST	94	74	49	70	80	91	74	84	82	73	98	98	68	95	74	86	91	83	96	108
24522	APPOMATTOX	97	74	46	67	81	91	71	84	81	72	97	99	65	95	73	86	90	82	98	112
24523	BEDFORD	83	68	50	64	73	82	67	75	74	67	89	87	63	86	68	77	83	74	85	95
24526	BIG ISLAND	111	99	76	94	105	112	92	102	97	92	118	121	90	121	94	100	113	99	110	131
24527	BLAIRS	88	59	27	51	67	77	57	71	69	58	81	85	48	76	58	74	73	71	88	101
24528	BROOKNEAL	85	57	26	49	64	74	55	69	66	56	78	82	47	74	56	71	71	68	85	98
24529	BUFFALO JUNCTION	93	67	39	59	74	85	65	78	76	66	90	92	58	86	66	81	83	77	94	107
24530	CALLANDS	95	64	29	55	72	83	62	77	74	63	87	92	52	83	63	80	79	76	95	110
24531	CHATHAM	98	67	34	59	76	88	67	81	79	67	93	96	58	88	68	85	85	81	100	112
24534	CLOVER	75	50	23	43	57	66	49	61	59	49	69	73	41	65	49	63	62	60	75	86
24536	COLEMAN FALLS	114	102	77	97	107	115	94	104	100	94	121	124	92	124	97	102	115	101	113	134
24538	CONCORD	88	71	47	65	75	83	67	77	73	68	89	91	62	86	68	76	83	76	86	101
24539	CRYSTAL HILL	72	48	22	41	54	63	46	58	56	47	66	69	39	62	47	60	60	57	71	82
24540	DANVILLE	73	60	48	56	63	72	61	67	67	61	81	76	58	78	61	71	76	66	76	83
24541	DANVILLE	84	74	71	70	76	86	76	80	82	76	100	92	74	98	77	85	95	81	88	95
24549	DRY FORK	94	70	41	63	77	87	67	80	77	67	91	95	60	89	68	81	84	78	94	109
24550	EVINGTON	100	74	42	67	82	91	71	85	81	72	97	101	63	93	72	86	89	83	99	116
24551	FOREST	112	125	123	126	122	122	115	116	108	116	136	136	118	140	115	104	134	113	105	130
24553	GLADSTONE	98	70	38	63	77	89	69	82	80	69	95	97	60	90	69	85	87	81	98	111
24554	GLADYS	90	60	28	52	68	79	58	73	70	59	82	87	50	78	59	75	75	72	89	103
24555	GLASGOW	80	56	29	50	63	71	54	66	64	55	75	78	47	72	55	68	69	65	79	91
24556	GOODE	113	114	101	111	116	120	104	110	104	104	128	130	105	132	106	104	124	107	110	133
24557	GRETNA	81	54	24	47	61	70	52	65	63	53	74	78	44	70	53	68	67	64	80	92
24558	HALIFAX	94	67	36	60	74	85	66	79	77	66	91	93	58	87	67	82	83	78	95	107
24562	HOWARDSVILLE	98	68	36	61	77	89	69	83	81	69	96	97	60	90	70	87	87	82	101	112
24563	HURT	84	56	26	49	64	74	54	68	66	55	77	81	46	73	55	71	70	67	84	97
24565	JAVA	83	55	25	48	63	72	53	67	64	54	76	80	45	71	54	69	69	66	82	95
24566	KEELING	79	53	24	46	60	69	51	64	62	52	72	76	43	68	52	66	66	63	79	91
24569	LONG ISLAND	84	56	26	49	64	73	54	68	66	55	77	81	46	73	55	71	70	67	84	97
24570	LOWRY	80	71	54	68	75	81	66	73	70	66	85	87	65	87	68	72	81	71	79	94
24571	LYNCH STATION	93	66	35	58	73	83	63	77	74	64	88	91	56	84	64	79	81	76	92	106
24572	MADISON HEIGHTS	79	67	49	63	71	79	65	72	70	64	85	84	62	84	66	73	80	71	81	91
24574	MONROE	96	75	49	70	81	91	73	84	81	73	97	99	67	96	74	85	91	83	96	110
24577	NATHALIE	83	56	25	48	63	73	54	67	65	55	76	80	46	72	55	70	69	67	83	95
24578	NATURAL BRIDGE	91	66	38	60	73	83	64	77	74	65	88	91	57	85	65	79	81	76	91	104
24579	NATURAL BRIDGE STATI	89	63	34	56	70	80	62	74	72	62	85	88	54	82	62	77	78	73	89	101
24580	NELSON	94	63	28	54	71	82	60	76	73	62	86	90	51	81	61	79	78	75	93	107
24586	RINGGOLD	87	66	40	60	72	81	63	74	71	63	85	88	57	83	64	75	79	73	86	100
24588	RUSTBURG	88	77	57	73	79	85	72	80	76	73	93	94	69	91	73	77	88	79	84	100
24589	SCOTTSBURG	86	59	29	52	67	76	57	70	68	58	80	84	50	76	58	73	73	69	85	99
24590	SCOTTSVILLE	85	73	55	69	78	85	71	78	76	70	92	92	68	92	72	79	87	77	87	99
24592	SOUTH BOSTON	79	62	43	57	66	76	62	70	70	62	84	81	57	80	63	74	78	70	82	89
24593	SPOUT SPRING	111	78	40	69	87	99	75	92	88	76	104	109	65	100	76	94	96	90	111	128
24594	SUTHERLIN	97	69	36	61	77	87	66	80	77	67	91	96	58	88	67	82	84	79	96	111
24597	VERNON HILL	112	75	34	65	85	98	73	91	88	74	103	109	62	97	74	95	94	90	112	129
24598	VIRGILINA	104	72	36	63	81	92	69	85	82	70	97	102	60	92	70	88	88	84	103	119
24599	WINGINA	92	63	30	54	71	81	61	75	73	62	86	89	52	81	62	78	78	74	92	106
24602	BANDY	68	45	21	39	51	59	44	55	53	45	62	65	37	59	44	57	56	54	67	78
24603	BIG ROCK	61	44	26	41	49	58	46	54	53	45	63	62	41	59	46	57	57	53	65	69
24605	BLUEFIELD	85	69	52	64	74	85	70	78	77	69	93	89	65	90	71	81	86	77	90	97
24609	CEDAR BLUFF	75	53	28	47	59	67	52	63	61	53	72	74	45	68	53	64	66	62	75	85
24613	FALLS MILLS	50	39	31	37	41	48	42	45	47	41	57	53	39	55	42	49	53	46	52	56
24614	GRUNDY	67	48	26	42	53	61	47	57	55	47	65	66	41	62	48	59	60	56	69	77
24620	HURLEY	57	38	17	33	43	50	37	46	45	38	52	55	31	49	38	48	47	46	57	66
24622	JEWELL RIDGE	65	44	20	38	50	57	42	53	51	43	60	63	36	57	43	55	54	52	65	75
24627	MAVISDALE	67	45	20	38	50	58	43	54	52	44	61	64	37	58	44	56	55	53	66	76
24630	NORTH TAZEWELL	77	53	26	47	60	68	51	63	61	52	72	76	44	68	52	65	65	62	77	89
24631	OAKWOOD	82	55	25	47	62	72	53	66	64	54	75	79	45	71	54	69	68	66	82	94
24634	PILGRIMS KNOB	65	43	20	37	49	57	42	52	51	43	59	63	36	56	43	54	54	52	65	74
24637	POUNDING MILL	83	67	45	62	72	78	64	73	70	65	84	86	59	82	64	72	79	72	81	95
24639	RAVEN	64	43	19	37	49	56	41	52	50	42	59	62	35	56	42	54	53	51	64	74
24641	RICHLANDS	69	49	27	44	54	64	50	59	58	49	69	69	44	65	50	62	63	59	72	78
24646	ROWE	59	40	18	34	45	52	38	48	46	39	54	57	33	51	39	50	49	48	59	68
24649	SWORDS CREEK	61	41	19	36	47	54	40	50	48	40	56	59	34	53	40	52	51	49	61	71
24651	TAZEWELL	77	56	33	52	62	72	57	67	65	57	77	78	50	73	58	69	71	66	79	87
24656	VANSANT	69	46	21	40	52	60	44	56	54	45	63	66	38	59	45	58	57	55	68	79
24657	WHITEWOOD	55	37	17	32	41	48	35	44	43	36	50	53	30	47	36	46	46	44	54	63
	VIRGINIA	112	109	113	109	109	117	108	110	109	109	136	129	108	135	108	109	132	110	109	128
	UNITED STATES	100	100	100	100	100	100	100	100	100	100	100	100	100	100	100	100	100	100	100	100

POPULATION CHANGE

ZIP CODE			POPULATION			2000-2004 ANNUAL RATE		HOUSEHOLDS					FAMILIES		
#	POST OFFICE NAME	COUNTY FIPS CODE	2000	2004	2009	% Rate	State Centile	2000	2004	2009	% Annual Rate 2000-2004	2004 Average HH Size	2000	2004	% Annual Rate 2000-2004
98001	AUBURN	033	25644	26336	26862	0.6	44	8876	9233	9494	0.9	2.85	6870	7103	0.8
98002	AUBURN	033	30897	31410	32005	0.4	36	12616	12952	13287	0.6	2.38	7577	7670	0.3
98003	FEDERAL WAY	033	41671	44876	47094	1.8	79	16645	17972	18896	1.8	2.47	10470	11185	1.6
98004	BELLEVUE	033	22265	22616	23107	0.4	35	10316	10779	11205	1.0	2.06	5806	5836	0.1
98005	BELLEVUE	033	16824	17257	17639	0.6	43	7460	7769	8010	1.0	2.19	4400	4512	0.6
98006	BELLEVUE	033	34925	37137	38760	1.5	72	12904	13815	14501	1.6	2.69	9954	10671	1.7
98007	BELLEVUE	033	23223	23460	23821	0.2	29	10303	10491	10702	0.4	2.23	5689	5715	0.1
98008	BELLEVUE	033	24179	24391	24912	0.2	27	9337	9521	9796	0.5	2.54	6624	6707	0.3
98010	BLACK DIAMOND	033	4289	4521	4664	1.3	66	1571	1662	1721	1.3	2.72	1221	1287	1.3
98011	BOTHELL	033	26611	27918	28846	1.1	62	10520	11189	11665	1.5	2.48	6983	7385	1.3
98012	BOTHELL	061	39244	42522	45905	1.9	81	14653	16097	17542	2.2	2.64	10644	11605	2.1
98014	CARNATION	033	6858	7220	7455	1.2	64	2364	2505	2598	1.4	2.88	1871	1976	1.3
98019	DUVALL	033	8188	8911	9311	2.0	83	2829	3115	3280	2.3	2.85	2290	2511	2.2
98020	EDMONDS	061	18184	18261	19095	0.1	22	8046	8209	8677	0.5	2.21	5112	5176	0.3
98021	BOTHELL	061	22549	23127	24338	0.6	43	8234	8592	9143	1.0	2.68	6176	6396	0.8
98022	ENUMCLAW	033	21798	22752	23388	1.0	59	8031	8422	8694	1.1	2.67	5792	6050	1.0
98023	FEDERAL WAY	033	48611	51429	53558	1.3	68	17435	18520	19342	1.4	2.77	12740	13431	1.3
98024	FALL CITY	033	4297	4783	5077	2.6	90	1627	1832	1959	2.8	2.61	1215	1359	2.7
98026	EDMONDS	061	35659	36458	38316	0.5	39	13811	14361	15277	0.9	2.52	9696	10003	0.7
98027	ISSAQUAH	033	24518	26258	27379	1.6	76	9546	10432	11008	2.1	2.48	6716	7277	1.9
98028	KENMORE	033	18633	19340	20025	0.9	52	7307	7785	8184	1.5	2.47	4985	5206	1.0
98029	ISSAQUAH	033	14444	18110	20668	5.5	100	5393	6794	7788	5.6	2.65	3997	4935	5.1
98030	KENT	033	31101	32840	34245	1.3	67	11447	12058	12597	1.2	2.70	7736	8144	1.2
98031	KENT	033	34302	35367	36254	0.7	47	12188	12671	13066	0.9	2.78	8943	9223	0.7
98032	KENT	033	28021	29853	30993	1.5	73	12023	12867	13415	1.6	2.29	6598	6995	1.4
98033	KIRKLAND	033	30939	31052	31572	0.1	22	13929	14139	14505	0.4	2.17	7843	7948	0.3
98034	KIRKLAND	033	39885	39880	40429	0.0	20	16147	16388	16768	0.4	2.40	10104	10156	0.1
98036	LYNNWOOD	061	32688	33481	35330	0.6	42	12253	12727	13564	0.9	2.61	8145	8403	0.7
98037	LYNNWOOD	061	41689	46049	50527	2.4	88	16356	18363	20385	2.8	2.49	10648	11761	2.4
98038	MAPLE VALLEY	033	22372	24253	25421	1.9	82	7625	8334	8784	2.1	2.91	6234	6789	2.0
98039	MEDINA	033	3011	2909	2894	-0.8	3	1111	1079	1077	-0.7	2.70	904	873	-0.8
98040	MERCER ISLAND	033	22036	22229	22533	0.2	27	8437	8581	8748	0.4	2.56	6273	6348	0.3
98042	KENT	033	37780	40469	42125	1.6	76	12726	13811	14495	1.9	2.93	10409	11246	1.8
98043	MOUNTLAKE TERRACE	061	20404	21262	22606	1.0	55	7981	8477	9132	1.4	2.49	5053	5310	1.2
98045	NORTH BEND	033	13770	14784	15390	1.7	78	5083	5493	5750	1.8	2.67	3799	4081	1.7
98047	PACIFIC	033	4920	4801	4788	-0.6	6	1740	1705	1707	-0.5	2.81	1265	1232	-0.6
98051	RAVENSDALE	033	2878	3024	3098	1.2	64	1024	1088	1123	1.4	2.78	771	815	1.3
98052	REDMOND	033	50000	53945	56698	1.8	80	20598	22628	24013	2.2	2.35	12654	13702	1.9
98053	REDMOND	033	11417	12910	13853	2.9	95	3708	4220	4552	3.1	3.06	3174	3603	3.0
98055	RENTON	033	27626	27951	28296	0.3	31	12062	12245	12444	0.4	2.26	6604	6653	0.2
98056	RENTON	033	27141	29107	30323	1.7	77	11716	12710	13341	1.9	2.28	6967	7464	1.6
98058	RENTON	033	37300	38933	40207	1.0	59	13446	14250	14854	1.4	2.73	10154	10692	1.2
98059	RENTON	033	22901	23903	24509	1.0	59	8578	9078	9392	1.3	2.63	6268	6563	1.1
98065	SNOQUALMIE	033	4358	5262	5899	4.5	99	1548	1882	2121	4.7	2.70	1155	1399	4.6
98070	VASHON	033	10123	10198	10310	0.2	25	4193	4283	4370	0.5	2.37	2839	2878	0.3
98072	WOODINVILLE	033	20438	20836	21312	0.5	38	7287	7566	7823	0.9	2.75	5516	5669	0.7
98074	SAMMAMISH	033	20306	22789	24474	2.8	93	6738	7631	8242	3.0	2.99	5745	6479	2.9
98075	SAMMAMISH	033	13771	16563	18435	4.4	99	4376	5219	5795	4.2	3.16	3800	4501	4.1
98077	WOODINVILLE	033	14500	16459	17710	3.0	95	4555	5204	5628	3.2	3.16	4050	4605	3.1
98092	AUBURN	033	25766	28163	29950	2.1	84	8812	9722	10404	2.3	2.89	6935	7623	2.3
98101	SEATTLE	033	9145	9778	10187	1.6	75	6022	6527	6859	1.9	1.28	1032	1095	1.4
98102	SEATTLE	033	20626	20764	20996	0.2	24	13320	13558	13811	0.4	1.52	2594	2558	-0.3
98103	SEATTLE	033	41970	41534	41713	-0.3	13	21156	21163	21414	0.0	1.94	7783	7666	-0.4
98104	SEATTLE	033	13119	13661	14028	1.0	55	5414	5799	6072	1.6	1.52	1170	1251	1.6
98105	SEATTLE	033	37271	37173	37391	-0.1	17	14959	15027	15209	0.1	2.12	5464	5451	-0.1
98106	SEATTLE	033	23051	23065	23304	0.0	20	8423	8477	8606	0.2	2.72	5322	5308	-0.1
98107	SEATTLE	033	19162	19013	19140	-0.2	14	10186	10231	10385	0.1	1.83	3724	3686	-0.2
98108	SEATTLE	033	21704	21561	21688	-0.2	14	7258	7175	7219	-0.3	2.96	4809	4727	-0.4
98109	SEATTLE	033	14855	15550	16022	1.1	60	8595	9133	9502	1.4	1.62	2411	2500	0.9
98110	BAINBRIDGE ISLAND	035	20308	21634	22566	1.5	73	7979	8562	8988	1.7	2.51	5785	6163	1.5
98112	SEATTLE	033	19674	19566	19719	-0.1	15	9378	9440	9594	0.2	2.05	4235	4205	-0.2
98115	SEATTLE	033	42929	42376	42482	-0.3	12	19231	19130	19292	-0.1	2.18	10193	10034	-0.4
98116	SEATTLE	033	20404	20331	20447	-0.1	17	10339	10456	10612	0.3	1.93	4861	4850	-0.1
98117	SEATTLE	033	29505	28727	28664	-0.6	5	13059	12830	12887	-0.4	2.21	7245	7045	-0.7
98118	SEATTLE	033	40727	41615	42515	0.5	39	13940	14265	14610	0.5	2.86	9275	9424	0.4
98119	SEATTLE	033	20774	20943	21184	0.2	26	10900	11199	11463	0.6	1.67	3388	3368	-0.1
98121	SEATTLE	033	8557	10037	10931	3.8	98	5908	7097	7824	4.4	1.29	885	1054	4.2
98122	SEATTLE	033	27879	28411	28888	0.5	38	13443	13956	14430	0.9	1.85	4126	4150	0.1
98125	SEATTLE	033	34994	34988	35293	0.0	20	15967	16115	16358	0.2	2.15	7983	7925	-0.2
98126	SEATTLE	033	19779	19303	19315	-0.6	6	8743	8670	8757	-0.2	2.18	4704	4595	-0.6
98133	SEATTLE	033	42769	43235	43707	0.3	30	19068	19470	19816	0.5	2.17	9937	9991	0.1
98134	SEATTLE	033	1350	1331	1331	-0.3	11	432	423	425	-0.5	2.04	157	152	-0.8
98136	SEATTLE	033	13800	13430	13404	-0.6	4	6641	6540	6579	-0.4	2.04	3373	3282	-0.6
98144	SEATTLE	033	24943	24845	24996	-0.1	16	9746	9791	9914	0.1	2.46	5438	5388	-0.2
98146	SEATTLE	033	25724	26017	26386	0.3	31	9782	9896	10050	0.3	2.61	6406	6424	0.1
98148	SEATTLE	033	8644	9477	10045	2.2	86	3803	4199	4470	2.4	2.26	2121	2317	2.1
98155	SEATTLE	033	33372	33187	33311	-0.1	15	12899	12962	13106	0.1	2.49	8552	8520	-0.1
98158	SEATTLE	033	1	1	1	0.0	20	1	1	1	0.0	1.00	1	0	-100.0
98166	SEATTLE	033	21139	20994	21116	-0.2	14	8984	8966	9064	-0.1	2.33	5848	5807	-0.2
98168	SEATTLE	033	30786	30920	31276	0.1	22	11693	11747	11896	0.1	2.62	7183	7128	-0.2
98177	SEATTLE	033	18741	18974	19208	0.3	31	7405	7584	7740	0.6	2.44	5134	5220	0.4
98178	SEATTLE	033	20744	20724	20831	0.0	18	7887	7918	7989	0.1	2.61	5268	5244	-0.1
98188	SEATTLE	033	21856	22152	22488	0.3	32	9288	9428	9591	0.4	2.35	5276	5288	0.1
98195	SEATTLE	033	2182	2182	2182	0.0	20	0	0	0	0.0	0.00	0	0	0.0
98198	SEATTLE	033	33533	34106	34700	0.4	36	12564	12746	13038	0.3	2.49	7996	8029	0.1
98199	SEATTLE	033	19156	19065	19228	-0.1	16	9077	9103	9230	0.1	2.08	4782	4745	-0.2
98201	EVERETT	061	30286	29946	31055	-0.3	12	11812	11826	12458	0.0	2.23	6169	6110	-0.2
98203	EVERETT	061	32093	33061	35003	0.7	46	12388	12911	13802	1.0	2.52	8396	8674	0.8
98204	EVERETT	061	30907	33355	36065	1.8	80	12650	13777	15030	2.0	2.41	7315	7846	1.7
98205	EVERETT	061	16213	17266	18368	1.5	72	5490	5899	6323	1.7	2.92	4283	4570	1.5
98208	EVERETT	061	45469	50783	55755	2.6	92	16763	18928	20952	2.9	2.67	12129	13696	2.9
98220	ACME	073	512	527	556	0.7	45	182	189	201	0.9	2.79	133	136	0.5
98221	ANACORTES	057	18824	19599	20515	1.0	55	7912	8290	8707	1.1	2.34	5473	5712	1.0
98223	ARLINGTON	061	34466	38695	42462	2.8	93	12264	13964	15488	3.1	2.76	9306	10529	3.0
98224	BARING	033	77	76	76	-0.3	12	33	33	33	0.0	2.30	18	18	0.0
	WASHINGTON					1.1					1.3	2.52			1.2
	UNITED STATES					1.2					1.3	2.58			1.1

317-A

ZIP CODE #	POST OFFICE NAME	RACE (%) White 2000	White 2004	Black 2000	Black 2004	Asian/Pacific 2000	Asian/Pacific 2004	% Hispanic Origin 2000	% Hispanic Origin 2004	2004 AGE DISTRIBUTION (%) 0-4	5-9	10-14	15-19	20-24	25-44	45-64	65-84	85+	18+	MEDIAN AGE 2004	% 2004 Males	% 2004 Females
98001	AUBURN	84.1	82.8	2.8	2.9	6.4	6.9	4.2	5.0	6.4	7.2	8.4	7.4	5.8	29.3	27.4	7.6	0.7	73.4	37.2	50.3	49.7
98002	AUBURN	82.6	81.0	2.4	2.6	3.7	4.1	8.2	9.7	7.7	6.9	7.2	6.8	7.9	29.5	21.3	10.9	1.9	74.1	34.4	49.3	50.7
98003	FEDERAL WAY	68.3	65.6	8.5	9.1	12.0	12.9	8.5	10.0	7.9	7.3	7.1	6.5	8.2	30.5	22.3	9.0	1.1	74.0	33.6	48.6	51.4
98004	BELLEVUE	85.2	83.7	1.3	1.3	9.6	10.7	3.2	3.7	4.5	4.7	5.2	4.9	5.1	26.4	27.5	17.6	4.1	82.6	44.5	47.6	52.4
98005	BELLEVUE	74.8	72.6	2.0	2.1	17.0	18.5	5.3	6.3	5.2	4.8	4.9	5.0	7.2	33.2	25.6	12.1	2.1	82.3	38.6	50.1	49.9
98006	BELLEVUE	75.0	72.8	1.6	1.7	19.1	20.8	2.7	3.2	5.9	6.7	7.8	6.5	5.2	26.8	30.1	10.2	0.8	75.6	40.1	49.7	50.3
98007	BELLEVUE	65.1	62.7	2.8	2.9	22.7	24.0	9.6	10.9	6.1	5.2	5.1	5.9	9.1	37.2	20.3	9.9	1.3	80.3	33.8	51.2	48.8
98008	BELLEVUE	77.8	75.8	1.9	2.0	14.1	15.4	5.8	6.6	5.8	6.0	6.3	5.7	5.2	28.5	27.4	13.6	1.6	78.4	40.7	49.7	50.3
98010	BLACK DIAMOND	93.8	93.4	0.1	0.1	0.9	1.0	2.2	2.6	7.0	7.4	8.1	6.6	5.1	29.8	27.5	7.8	0.8	73.2	37.8	51.1	48.9
98011	BOTHELL	86.9	85.5	1.3	1.4	6.0	6.6	4.8	5.6	6.6	6.5	6.9	6.7	7.0	31.8	26.0	7.3	1.1	75.9	35.9	49.0	51.0
98012	BOTHELL	85.0	83.6	1.3	1.3	8.8	9.5	4.0	4.7	7.1	7.2	7.7	6.8	6.8	31.6	25.3	6.7	0.7	73.7	35.1	49.4	50.7
98014	CARNATION	93.4	92.8	0.2	0.2	2.0	2.2	3.0	3.6	7.5	8.7	9.2	7.0	4.6	31.1	26.6	4.9	0.6	70.0	36.9	51.0	49.0
98019	DUVALL	93.8	93.0	0.4	0.5	1.7	1.9	3.9	4.6	8.2	8.8	8.3	6.7	5.0	34.3	24.5	4.0	0.3	70.4	35.5	50.3	49.7
98020	EDMONDS	91.4	90.5	0.9	0.9	4.1	4.6	2.3	2.8	4.3	4.7	5.5	5.2	4.9	22.3	30.2	19.8	3.1	82.4	47.0	46.0	54.0
98021	BOTHELL	88.0	87.0	1.0	1.0	6.4	6.9	3.2	3.8	6.0	6.7	7.8	7.1	5.6	29.0	28.1	8.5	1.1	75.0	38.2	49.3	50.7
98022	ENUMCLAW	93.1	92.4	0.3	0.3	0.8	0.9	3.8	4.5	6.3	7.1	8.5	8.2	5.9	26.8	25.8	9.5	1.9	72.9	37.5	49.3	50.7
98023	FEDERAL WAY	71.0	68.2	7.0	7.4	13.7	15.5	6.1	7.0	7.8	7.8	8.2	7.4	7.5	30.8	23.7	6.1	0.6	71.7	33.2	49.4	50.6
98024	FALL CITY	94.3	93.6	0.2	0.3	1.2	1.4	2.7	3.2	5.2	6.8	8.4	6.8	4.4	28.1	30.8	8.4	1.1	75.2	40.3	50.9	49.1
98026	EDMONDS	84.3	83.1	1.6	1.7	8.2	8.9	3.9	4.6	6.0	6.3	7.0	6.6	6.3	26.9	29.2	10.6	1.2	76.7	39.8	48.7	51.3
98027	ISSAQUAH	89.4	88.1	0.9	1.0	5.4	6.1	3.3	3.9	6.0	6.6	7.4	6.4	5.4	29.2	30.0	8.0	1.2	75.9	39.2	49.5	50.5
98028	KENMORE	86.5	85.2	1.4	1.5	7.6	8.1	3.5	4.4	5.7	5.9	6.7	6.5	6.2	29.7	28.2	9.9	1.2	77.8	38.8	49.5	50.5
98029	ISSAQUAH	81.7	80.7	0.8	0.8	13.5	14.2	2.7	3.1	8.8	9.4	8.9	6.2	3.8	31.3	21.7	7.8	2.1	68.9	36.1	48.1	51.9
98030	KENT	70.4	68.2	8.9	9.2	10.4	11.5	7.1	8.2	9.2	8.4	8.3	6.9	7.7	32.5	20.4	5.7	0.9	69.9	30.9	49.0	51.0
98031	KENT	70.3	68.3	6.0	6.3	15.2	16.3	5.3	6.2	7.7	7.8	8.4	7.4	7.0	31.2	23.5	6.6	0.7	71.6	33.8	49.7	50.3
98032	KENT	69.5	67.4	9.0	9.3	9.1	9.6	10.6	12.3	7.7	6.9	6.1	6.0	8.1	33.9	22.2	8.2	1.0	76.0	33.7	50.2	49.9
98033	KIRKLAND	87.6	86.3	1.2	1.3	6.9	7.5	3.2	3.8	5.2	5.2	5.2	5.4	6.0	34.7	27.7	9.4	1.2	81.5	38.6	49.2	50.8
98034	KIRKLAND	82.4	80.7	1.8	2.0	9.7	10.6	5.1	6.1	6.3	6.3	6.3	6.3	6.5	34.2	25.4	7.5	1.3	77.4	36.2	49.1	50.9
98036	LYNNWOOD	78.2	76.8	2.6	2.7	11.3	12.0	6.4	7.3	7.1	6.9	7.2	6.9	7.7	30.5	24.3	7.8	1.5	74.7	35.2	49.6	50.4
98037	LYNNWOOD	77.4	75.4	2.5	2.6	12.9	14.0	5.1	6.0	7.3	6.5	6.7	6.5	8.6	31.5	23.3	8.5	1.2	75.9	34.0	49.3	50.7
98038	MAPLE VALLEY	92.1	91.2	1.0	1.1	2.2	2.5	2.9	3.6	8.0	8.4	9.2	7.3	4.8	31.5	24.9	5.5	0.4	69.6	35.5	50.2	49.8
98039	MEDINA	92.6	91.8	0.2	0.2	5.0	5.5	1.4	1.7	6.8	8.3	8.8	6.5	3.0	21.0	29.7	14.4	1.6	71.9	42.8	49.1	51.0
98040	MERCER ISLAND	84.1	82.6	1.1	1.2	11.9	13.1	1.9	2.2	4.3	5.8	8.3	7.9	4.8	17.4	32.3	16.2	3.1	76.5	45.9	48.0	52.0
98042	KENT	87.8	86.7	2.2	2.4	4.4	4.7	3.5	4.2	6.7	7.6	9.0	7.9	5.6	29.4	27.0	6.3	0.5	71.7	36.2	50.4	49.6
98043	MOUNTLAKE TERRACE	77.8	76.1	2.5	2.6	11.3	12.0	5.7	6.7	6.5	6.2	7.1	6.8	8.0	33.8	22.4	8.2	1.1	76.2	34.4	49.4	50.6
98045	NORTH BEND	93.5	92.9	0.5	0.6	1.8	2.0	2.7	3.2	8.1	8.4	8.1	6.3	4.3	33.6	24.3	5.8	1.1	71.3	36.1	51.3	48.7
98047	PACIFIC	85.2	83.7	1.5	1.7	5.1	5.6	6.3	7.5	8.6	8.1	8.4	7.5	8.1	32.2	21.4	5.4	0.4	70.6	31.5	49.6	50.4
98051	RAVENSDALE	95.1	94.5	0.6	0.6	0.6	0.7	1.8	2.2	5.0	7.8	9.7	7.9	3.5	31.8	28.7	5.2	0.4	72.6	38.4	52.4	47.6
98052	REDMOND	80.1	78.2	1.4	1.5	12.6	13.6	5.5	6.4	6.3	6.0	6.1	5.8	7.1	35.4	24.0	7.1	2.2	78.0	35.4	50.1	49.9
98053	REDMOND	91.1	90.3	0.7	0.8	4.4	4.8	2.8	3.3	7.6	9.1	9.7	7.5	4.0	28.6	28.8	4.3	0.3	68.6	37.3	51.3	48.7
98055	RENTON	62.6	60.3	11.6	12.0	16.5	17.7	6.5	7.5	6.6	5.9	5.9	5.7	7.8	33.3	23.6	9.3	1.9	78.3	35.6	49.6	50.4
98056	RENTON	74.9	72.5	4.9	5.3	11.6	12.6	7.4	8.7	7.0	6.3	5.9	5.0	6.6	34.4	23.0	10.1	1.7	77.8	36.3	49.4	50.7
98058	RENTON	76.2	74.2	5.0	5.3	12.5	13.6	3.6	4.2	6.7	7.2	7.8	7.0	6.2	29.6	27.6	7.4	0.5	74.0	36.8	49.8	50.2
98059	RENTON	81.2	79.4	2.5	2.7	10.3	11.3	4.6	5.5	6.8	6.9	7.1	6.3	6.2	32.3	27.0	6.9	0.6	75.5	36.6	50.4	49.6
98065	SNOQUALMIE	90.1	88.1	1.2	1.6	2.0	2.2	3.5	4.6	8.0	7.3	10.2	8.7	5.0	29.7	25.0	5.4	0.7	68.5	34.3	52.0	48.0
98070	VASHON	93.6	93.0	0.5	0.5	1.6	1.8	2.6	3.1	4.4	5.5	7.0	6.5	4.4	20.9	37.3	12.4	1.6	78.8	45.6	48.6	51.4
98072	WOODINVILLE	88.3	86.9	0.8	0.9	4.9	5.4	5.1	6.1	6.0	6.8	8.4	7.6	5.7	27.7	30.2	6.6	1.1	73.9	38.0	50.0	50.0
98074	SAMMAMISH	87.7	86.2	0.9	1.0	7.9	8.9	2.6	3.0	8.0	9.0	9.3	7.5	4.4	30.7	27.1	3.7	0.3	68.7	35.9	50.7	49.3
98075	SAMMAMISH	88.5	87.2	0.7	0.8	7.7	8.6	2.3	2.7	8.1	9.8	9.6	6.8	3.3	27.5	27.4	6.7	0.8	68.0	37.7	50.1	49.9
98077	WOODINVILLE	91.6	90.5	0.7	0.7	4.1	4.6	2.7	3.3	6.6	8.8	10.8	8.6	3.6	25.9	31.3	4.1	0.3	67.9	38.2	51.0	49.0
98092	AUBURN	85.7	84.6	1.7	1.9	3.6	4.1	4.3	4.9	7.4	7.9	8.5	7.4	6.3	29.7	26.0	6.4	0.5	71.6	35.3	50.4	49.7
98101	SEATTLE	72.7	70.4	10.4	11.2	8.2	9.0	5.3	6.2	1.4	1.0	0.9	2.1	9.5	39.2	26.1	14.0	5.7	95.9	42.4	53.3	46.7
98102	SEATTLE	84.9	83.4	3.3	3.6	6.3	6.9	3.9	4.7	1.8	1.2	1.1	2.2	12.2	52.9	21.2	6.4	1.0	95.1	33.8	54.1	45.9
98103	SEATTLE	85.3	84.0	2.3	2.4	6.4	7.0	4.0	4.7	4.1	3.2	3.1	3.3	8.6	47.1	22.9	6.2	1.5	87.8	34.8	49.6	50.5
98104	SEATTLE	49.4	46.6	20.1	20.8	20.5	22.2	7.5	8.3	2.3	1.8	1.7	3.4	9.5	42.9	24.9	11.3	2.1	92.9	39.2	65.3	34.7
98105	SEATTLE	79.0	77.3	2.0	2.1	13.0	14.1	3.7	4.3	3.4	3.1	2.8	12.7	25.1	30.5	15.6	5.6	1.2	88.9	26.3	51.1	48.9
98106	SEATTLE	47.7	45.2	11.7	12.0	24.6	25.6	10.8	12.2	7.4	6.7	7.5	7.2	8.2	33.2	22.4	6.6	0.9	74.1	33.0	49.7	50.3
98107	SEATTLE	87.2	85.8	2.0	2.1	4.0	4.4	4.7	5.6	3.7	3.3	3.4	3.1	7.2	42.5	24.3	9.8	2.7	87.8	37.7	48.2	51.8
98108	SEATTLE	26.4	24.9	14.7	14.6	44.1	45.1	12.8	14.1	6.8	6.5	7.2	6.8	7.7	30.4	22.8	10.2	1.6	75.5	34.9	50.8	49.2
98109	SEATTLE	86.5	85.1	3.1	3.5	5.7	6.2	3.3	3.9	3.0	2.2	2.0	2.5	8.2	47.6	23.5	8.4	2.6	91.5	36.4	49.8	50.2
98110	BAINBRIDGE ISLAND	92.9	92.1	0.3	0.3	2.5	2.8	2.2	2.6	4.8	6.3	8.2	7.3	4.0	19.4	36.2	11.7	2.1	75.8	45.0	48.6	51.5
98112	SEATTLE	83.0	81.9	8.9	9.2	3.9	4.2	2.7	3.1	4.6	4.4	4.6	4.4	5.4	36.3	27.8	10.2	2.4	83.6	39.3	48.0	52.1
98115	SEATTLE	84.4	82.8	1.8	2.0	8.6	9.4	3.0	3.5	5.1	4.9	4.8	4.4	5.8	36.0	25.8	10.7	2.4	82.4	38.6	48.3	51.7
98116	SEATTLE	88.8	87.8	1.7	1.8	3.9	4.2	3.4	4.0	4.5	4.4	4.3	3.9	4.3	34.3	29.2	12.4	2.9	84.6	42.1	47.9	52.1
98117	SEATTLE	87.8	86.7	1.5	1.6	4.9	5.3	3.7	4.4	5.1	5.1	5.1	4.7	4.8	35.1	28.2	9.5	2.4	81.9	40.0	48.1	51.9
98118	SEATTLE	27.2	25.6	26.0	26.1	35.6	36.5	7.0	7.7	6.5	6.4	7.1	7.3	7.4	28.5	24.7	10.4	1.7	75.6	36.2	49.1	50.9
98119	SEATTLE	88.3	87.1	2.0	2.2	4.8	5.3	3.2	3.8	2.6	2.2	2.6	7.2	11.5	42.0	21.7	7.9	2.3	91.1	34.6	47.3	52.8
98121	SEATTLE	75.4	73.6	8.5	9.0	8.4	9.2	5.2	5.9	1.1	0.6	0.6	4.6	11.7	44.1	25.8	9.8	1.7	97.3	37.8	57.8	42.2
98122	SEATTLE	57.6	55.7	25.1	25.6	7.7	8.3	7.1	8.2	3.6	3.1	3.3	7.1	12.4	41.4	20.1	7.6	1.5	87.2	33.6	52.2	47.9
98125	SEATTLE	70.7	68.4	5.0	5.3	15.3	16.6	5.8	6.8	4.8	4.5	4.6	5.0	7.6	34.1	24.8	11.5	3.0	83.2	38.2	48.8	51.2
98126	SEATTLE	70.8	69.6	7.9	8.0	11.7	12.1	6.5	7.4	6.3	6.0	5.7	5.2	5.8	34.0	24.9	9.4	2.7	78.8	38.1	48.1	51.9
98133	SEATTLE	73.0	70.8	4.2	4.5	14.8	16.0	5.2	6.0	4.7	4.6	5.2	5.7	7.5	31.7	25.1	12.2	3.3	82.2	39.2	48.3	51.7
98134	SEATTLE	47.8	46.1	17.4	17.7	22.2	22.9	9.0	10.3	2.9	2.2	1.7	2.3	8.1	34.9	34.3	10.9	2.9	92.2	43.5	62.6	37.4
98136	SEATTLE	87.8	86.5	2.4	2.6	4.2	4.5	3.9	4.7	4.9	4.9	4.7	4.1	4.6	33.2	28.5	11.8	3.3	83.1	41.8	47.2	52.8
98144	SEATTLE	35.4	33.2	22.2	22.8	31.2	32.3	8.5	9.3	5.4	5.4	6.1	6.2	6.6	32.4	24.3	11.5	2.2	79.2	37.7	49.3	50.7
98146	SEATTLE	64.7	62.0	5.6	5.9	17.0	18.0	11.2	13.1	6.8	6.7	6.8	6.2	6.6	29.3	25.6	10.3	1.7	75.9	37.4	49.7	50.3
98148	SEATTLE	73.2	71.1	6.0	6.3	9.0	9.6	10.3	11.8	6.5	6.0	6.4	6.4	8.3	30.6	25.0	9.8	1.0	77.3	36.5	49.8	50.2
98155	SEATTLE	78.6	76.8	2.8	2.9	12.0	13.1	3.5	4.1	5.2	5.6	6.3	6.5	6.2	28.2	29.2	11.1	1.8	78.8	40.4	48.6	51.4
98158	SEATTLE	0.0	0.0	0.0	0.0	0.0	0.0	0.0	0.0	0.0	0.0	0.0	0.0	100.0	0.0	0.0	0.0	0.0	100.0	22.5	100.0	0.0
98166	SEATTLE	84.1	82.7	3.4	3.6	4.6	5.0	7.6	8.8	5.1	5.4	6.4	6.5	5.9	23.5	30.0	14.8	2.3	79.1	43.1	48.4	51.6
98168	SEATTLE	62.7	60.3	8.0	8.3	13.7	14.4	13.6	15.5	7.4	6.7	7.0	6.9	7.8	31.5	23.1	8.5	1.2	74.8	34.6	51.3	48.7
98177	SEATTLE	87.3	86.1	1.3	1.4	6.9	7.6	2.6	3.1	4.4	5.2	6.2	6.2	5.1	21.5	32.1	15.6	3.7	80.3	45.8	47.5	52.5
98178	SEATTLE	40.3	38.1	26.7	27.2	24.5	25.6	4.4	5.0	5.8	6.2	7.1	6.5	6.3	28.8	26.1	11.7	1.7	77.0	38.4	49.2	50.8
98188	SEATTLE	61.6	59.3	10.7	11.1	13.9	14.5	11.4	13.0	6.9	6.1	6.3	6.1	8.0	32.6	23.7	9.2	1.1	77.3	35.3	51.8	48.2
98195	SEATTLE	57.2	54.3	2.8	2.8	30.9	32.9	3.2	3.8	0.0	0.0	0.0	49.7	39.1	10.8	0.4	0.0	0.0	99.8	20.0	52.8	47.2
98198	SEATTLE	70.9	69.2	8.4	8.7	10.3	10.9	8.9	10.1	6.6	6.2	6.5	6.3	7.5	30.4	22.8	10.7	3.1	76.9	36.5	49.5	50.6
98199	SEATTLE	87.3	86.1	1.7	1.8	6.1	6.7	3.4	4.0	5.3	5.3	4.8	4.2	4.6	32.2	29.0	12.2	2.6	82.2	41.4	48.3	51.7
98201	EVERETT	83.0	81.7	3.5	3.6	4.0	4.4	6.6	7.7	6.6	5.8	5.9	7.0	11.4	31.1	21.1	8.7	2.5	78.1	33.2	53.2	46.8
98203	EVERETT	85.8	84.6	2.0	2.1	6.0	6.5	5.0	5.8	7.2	7.0	7.3	6.3	6.5	30.1	24.4	9.4	1.7	74.5	36.3	49.3	50.7
98204	EVERETT	74.8	73.2	4.2	4.3	9.2	9.6	10.8	12.1	9.0	7.2	6.9	7.0	11.2	34.5	17.6	6.0	0.7	73.0	29.2	50.8	49.2
98205	EVERETT	91.2	90.2	1.0	1.0	2.2	2.5	4.2	5.1	9.1	8.9	8.9	7.2	5.7	33.8	20.3	5.5	0.6	68.6	32.7	50.4	49.6
98208	EVERETT	82.0	80.5	2.7	2.9	8.4	9.1	4.9	5.8	8.4	7.9	7.6	6.7	7.2	32.1	22.5	6.8	0.9	72.1	33.6	49.4	50.7
98220	ACME	89.1	88.1	0.2	0.2	0.6	0.6	4.9	6.1	4.2	6.1	10.4	8.7	5.9	24.5	30.4	8.9	1.0	73.2	38.5	50.9	49.2
98221	ANACORTES	93.4	92.8	0.3	0.3	1.6	1.7	2.7	3.3	4.9	5.4	6.5	6.4	4.8	21.3	30.4	17.6	2.8	79.1	45.5	48.8	51.2
98223	ARLINGTON	92.5	91.8	0.6	0.6	1.7	1.8	3.6	4.3	7.1	7.3	8.1	7.5	6.3	28.2	26.2	8.2	1.1	72.9	36.1	50.1	49.9
98224	BARING	92.2	92.1	0.0	0.0	1.3	1.3	1.3	2.6	2.6	5.3	5.3	5.3	2.6	31.6	35.5	11.8	0.0	82.9	44.1	55.3	44.7
	WASHINGTON	81.8	80.6	3.2	3.3	5.9	6.3	7.5	8.6	6.7	6.6	7.1	7.0	7.6	28.7	24.9	9.8	1.6	75.4	36.1	49.7	50.3
	UNITED STATES	75.1	73.6	12.3	12.5	3.8	4.2	12.5	14.1	6.9	6.7	7.2	7.0	7.3	28.6	23.8	10.8	1.7	75.1	36.0	49.1	50.9

#	ZIP CODE / POST OFFICE NAME	2004 Per Capita Income	2004 HH Income Base	2004 HOUSEHOLD INCOME DISTRIBUTION (%) Less than $25,000	$25,000 to $49,999	$50,000 to $99,999	$100,000 to $149,999	$150,000 or More	MEDIAN HOUSEHOLD INCOME 2004	2009	2004 National Centile	2004 State Centile	2004 Home Value Base	2004 HOME VALUE DISTRIBUTION (%) Less than $50,000	$50,000 to $89,999	$90,000 to $174,999	$175,000 to $399,999	$400,000 or More	2004 Median Home Value
98001	AUBURN	27524	9233	13.0	20.6	43.1	17.9	5.4	66744	78404	90	91	7751	0.9	1.0	29.3	63.3	5.6	202690
98002	AUBURN	21056	12952	29.5	32.6	29.7	6.8	1.5	40147	45541	47	41	6494	18.3	11.2	39.8	29.8	1.0	141601
98003	FEDERAL WAY	24004	17972	21.8	31.2	33.5	9.1	4.4	47533	54053	67	61	9625	9.1	6.8	29.6	49.1	5.4	183343
98004	BELLEVUE	58706	10779	13.8	21.5	30.6	15.9	18.3	70149	83818	91	93	6432	0.0	0.2	4.9	33.0	61.9	470872
98005	BELLEVUE	41841	7769	13.4	21.6	34.9	16.9	13.3	66586	79104	90	90	4293	0.3	0.1	8.3	40.6	50.7	403228
98006	BELLEVUE	50169	13815	6.5	13.6	32.9	22.9	24.1	93982	114524	98	99	11109	1.3	1.1	4.4	39.5	53.7	417745
98007	BELLEVUE	32986	10491	18.2	25.5	36.1	13.6	6.6	55413	65381	80	77	4427	1.9	1.9	14.9	64.4	16.8	285049
98008	BELLEVUE	42604	9521	10.8	19.4	35.1	20.0	14.7	76150	90766	94	97	7162	1.2	0.4	4.1	65.9	28.4	318655
98010	BLACK DIAMOND	32053	1662	13.8	19.3	39.0	20.7	7.2	71754	82765	92	95	1488	6.9	2.7	18.8	55.0	16.6	231907
98011	BOTHELL	32838	11189	12.3	23.0	37.8	18.4	8.6	67749	79646	90	92	7653	4.4	0.6	11.8	68.5	14.7	271509
98012	BOTHELL	32142	16097	9.8	21.3	41.1	19.2	8.6	70746	80841	92	93	11480	3.5	1.7	7.4	65.9	21.5	282413
98014	CARNATION	37732	2505	8.3	20.4	36.7	21.7	12.9	75116	89178	93	96	2229	1.7	0.5	6.0	58.3	33.6	318556
98019	DUVALL	37712	3115	7.3	19.3	38.1	21.1	14.2	79556	93642	95	98	2834	4.5	2.3	5.3	60.1	28.0	311723
98020	EDMONDS	39781	8209	15.8	23.1	34.2	15.0	11.9	62315	70962	87	86	6007	0.7	0.4	5.9	61.7	31.3	313310
98021	BOTHELL	29737	8592	11.7	20.2	40.4	21.1	6.6	71217	80453	92	94	7176	4.6	3.8	8.2	70.1	13.2	261883
98022	ENUMCLAW	26080	8422	19.2	22.2	38.3	14.6	5.7	59806	68441	84	83	6501	5.8	3.6	18.4	56.7	15.6	223909
98023	FEDERAL WAY	27320	18520	12.8	23.5	41.3	15.7	6.7	64149	75679	88	88	11978	1.0	0.7	19.8	69.3	9.1	220410
98024	FALL CITY	33311	1832	12.7	21.0	35.6	20.7	9.9	71688	81895	92	95	1592	4.2	1.4	6.9	56.0	31.6	301347
98026	EDMONDS	30944	14361	13.8	24.9	36.3	17.2	7.9	62898	72109	87	87	10381	1.2	0.4	9.1	72.0	17.3	272495
98027	ISSAQUAH	42039	10432	10.2	18.4	34.3	20.6	16.6	78761	92883	95	98	8006	1.4	1.1	6.8	45.2	45.5	380176
98028	KENMORE	37000	7785	12.9	21.9	37.3	15.3	12.6	69106	80725	91	93	5622	6.8	0.9	4.5	60.3	27.5	293851
98029	ISSAQUAH	43353	6794	9.5	14.5	34.0	22.5	19.5	86553	103557	97	98	5437	1.6	0.0	4.8	54.6	39.1	366898
98030	KENT	23585	12058	20.9	28.6	36.0	10.4	4.2	50474	57130	73	68	6412	4.6	2.1	20.6	67.3	5.5	216676
98031	KENT	25560	12671	14.1	24.8	38.8	17.4	5.0	61359	70537	86	85	8266	2.9	4.2	17.3	71.3	4.4	219405
98032	KENT	25148	12867	23.3	27.9	35.7	9.8	3.3	48637	55809	70	64	5897	9.2	1.8	30.2	55.4	3.4	188932
98033	KIRKLAND	53070	14139	9.2	16.1	38.3	20.1	16.3	78633	98152	95	97	9162	0.2	0.6	3.7	50.7	44.9	379698
98034	KIRKLAND	34843	16388	11.2	22.3	40.4	17.8	8.3	67735	79432	90	92	10613	0.6	1.5	14.2	66.2	17.6	278028
98036	LYNNWOOD	24728	12727	16.7	28.3	36.8	14.2	4.0	54634	62133	79	76	7948	3.6	1.7	14.6	74.0	6.2	234927
98037	LYNNWOOD	24969	18363	17.6	29.6	37.4	12.1	3.3	52551	59019	76	72	10454	10.5	4.4	10.3	68.9	6.0	232271
98038	MAPLE VALLEY	31669	8334	7.3	17.1	44.5	21.7	9.4	77739	90937	94	97	7484	0.5	0.5	10.7	71.2	17.1	261624
98039	MEDINA	98186	1079	7.1	8.1	18.2	17.0	49.7	148594	173112	100	100	990	0.0	0.0	0.0	3.6	96.4	1000001
98040	MERCER ISLAND	63467	8581	9.0	13.3	25.5	20.3	31.9	104175	127280	98	99	6939	0.4	0.3	1.7	13.3	84.4	697298
98042	KENT	29642	13811	6.8	20.3	45.3	19.4	8.4	74649	86137	93	96	12175	2.8	2.2	19.5	60.5	15.1	232940
98043	MOUNTLAKE TERRACE	24899	8477	14.7	30.5	42.1	9.8	2.9	53096	61404	77	73	5203	2.1	0.9	23.8	71.5	1.8	211392
98045	NORTH BEND	31660	5493	12.5	18.0	39.4	20.0	10.1	73699	84717	93	96	4545	2.8	1.7	10.0	60.9	24.6	278998
98047	PACIFIC	21713	1705	16.5	30.4	38.7	12.1	2.3	52338	61511	76	72	1104	2.3	0.2	49.8	47.6	0.1	172776
98051	RAVENSDALE	28650	1088	8.7	23.3	46.3	17.2	4.5	65681	76464	89	90	968	5.3	1.9	14.4	65.4	13.1	263568
98052	REDMOND	44785	22628	9.7	18.5	36.9	19.6	15.2	77386	91003	94	97	13316	3.2	1.6	8.5	53.9	32.8	334959
98053	REDMOND	50585	4220	5.6	10.1	31.7	22.4	30.3	104432	125257	98	99	3941	1.2	0.7	3.6	28.3	66.3	489972
98055	RENTON	26517	12245	22.2	30.3	32.8	10.4	4.4	47821	54885	68	62	6031	3.5	4.0	26.2	61.8	4.6	206807
98056	RENTON	30638	12710	18.7	24.3	37.0	13.5	6.5	56976	65408	82	79	7474	2.9	5.7	19.9	56.0	15.6	232276
98058	RENTON	31105	14250	10.1	20.8	41.0	20.0	8.1	70826	82147	92	94	11121	2.4	2.7	15.7	69.6	9.6	234518
98059	RENTON	32319	9078	10.6	20.1	41.5	18.1	9.7	71173	82388	92	94	6817	2.5	2.0	12.9	65.3	17.4	249483
98065	SNOQUALMIE	29187	1882	13.7	19.3	40.4	19.3	7.3	68195	81537	90	92	1525	3.3	1.0	11.1	57.3	27.4	278067
98070	VASHON	37210	4283	15.7	21.4	35.8	15.7	11.4	64853	76954	88	89	3488	0.0	1.0	8.6	54.7	35.7	332976
98072	WOODINVILLE	41844	7566	8.4	15.2	36.7	23.0	16.7	83031	98701	96	98	6183	1.0	0.7	7.5	48.4	42.4	365280
98074	SAMMAMISH	47026	7631	4.0	10.2	31.1	27.9	26.8	106926	127439	99	100	6832	0.5	0.2	0.9	41.6	56.9	421069
98075	SAMMAMISH	52440	5219	4.7	9.4	26.9	24.5	34.5	115990	135382	99	100	4812	0.5	0.1	0.9	24.6	74.0	517722
98077	WOODINVILLE	45809	5204	5.8	12.5	30.3	23.7	27.8	102190	120967	98	99	4907	0.5	0.1	3.1	32.2	64.1	468812
98092	AUBURN	28880	9722	11.7	19.6	41.5	18.8	8.4	71347	83293	92	95	8084	5.4	4.2	14.6	64.0	11.8	239124
98101	SEATTLE	49101	6527	37.6	28.8	19.1	6.9	7.6	33586	41869	23	13	1406	1.6	0.9	11.4	47.2	38.9	339535
98102	SEATTLE	49795	13558	19.2	31.6	31.7	9.3	8.3	49329	63100	71	65	3591	0.5	0.9	15.7	37.6	45.4	365240
98103	SEATTLE	39934	21163	15.4	27.1	34.7	13.9	8.9	57356	71362	82	79	8912	0.5	0.4	7.6	58.0	33.6	340139
98104	SEATTLE	20564	5799	60.7	21.2	13.4	2.5	2.3	18009	22056	1	1	341	1.5	1.8	12.0	39.0	45.8	373148
98105	SEATTLE	34228	15027	30.1	23.3	24.4	10.9	11.4	45469	54168	63	55	5657	0.1	0.6	5.8	37.8	55.7	430714
98106	SEATTLE	20467	8477	26.3	27.8	32.7	10.5	2.8	46295	54242	65	57	4499	1.6	1.1	34.0	60.2	3.1	192251
98107	SEATTLE	34424	10231	19.8	30.0	33.5	11.9	4.9	50209	61374	72	67	3819	2.3	1.1	6.6	66.0	24.0	304388
98108	SEATTLE	19831	7175	26.2	30.3	30.2	9.4	3.9	43201	51100	56	49	3961	3.7	2.1	26.9	63.2	4.2	210134
98109	SEATTLE	50428	9133	16.1	28.1	30.1	14.2	11.6	58292	73385	83	82	3018	1.3	0.8	9.9	37.1	50.9	405660
98110	BAINBRIDGE ISLAND	43636	8562	13.9	19.2	30.4	17.9	18.5	76882	89532	94	97	7024	0.5	0.6	6.0	43.2	49.7	398426
98112	SEATTLE	64214	9440	16.9	19.3	25.5	15.3	23.0	72499	90285	92	95	5477	0.3	0.1	2.1	24.7	72.8	579561
98115	SEATTLE	41292	19130	13.8	21.1	34.7	18.4	12.0	68429	84700	91	93	12571	0.8	0.4	5.5	56.6	36.8	352984
98116	SEATTLE	46225	10456	13.8	23.2	33.1	18.5	11.5	67242	83712	90	91	6069	0.2	0.2	3.4	56.1	40.1	361600
98117	SEATTLE	37369	12830	12.3	23.1	38.2	17.3	9.1	65364	80811	89	89	8861	0.5	0.2	4.0	68.6	26.7	321676
98118	SEATTLE	22835	14265	23.1	26.5	33.1	11.8	5.6	50336	59887	73	67	8585	1.6	0.9	21.5	61.8	14.3	232355
98119	SEATTLE	49872	11199	15.7	26.7	31.9	14.3	11.5	57785	73105	82	80	4029	0.7	1.2	7.4	33.6	57.2	435169
98121	SEATTLE	51104	7097	36.0	26.3	21.5	8.0	8.3	36852	46308	35	27	1398	1.5	0.6	14.2	47.2	36.4	292803
98122	SEATTLE	32552	13956	32.4	29.2	23.8	7.8	6.8	38461	47550	41	34	4661	0.6	1.0	11.8	51.7	34.9	324058
98125	SEATTLE	29940	16115	24.2	28.2	30.8	10.7	6.1	47390	55205	67	61	8191	0.9	0.5	10.0	70.8	17.8	269145
98126	SEATTLE	31467	8670	22.6	22.9	34.4	13.2	7.0	54461	66178	79	75	4987	0.6	0.5	16.6	65.2	17.1	251786
98133	SEATTLE	27363	19470	22.9	30.5	32.1	10.7	3.9	47026	54896	66	59	10578	3.4	0.8	13.2	76.3	6.4	243201
98134	SEATTLE	25608	423	23.9	31.0	30.0	11.8	3.3	43162	55694	56	49	105	6.7	5.7	10.5	65.7	11.4	205469
98136	SEATTLE	45415	6540	15.4	22.8	34.4	15.8	11.5	65497	80513	89	90	4002	0.3	0.0	4.7	57.5	37.5	346652
98144	SEATTLE	27840	9791	28.5	25.3	28.4	10.3	7.5	45552	53615	63	55	4989	2.7	1.1	12.8	57.0	26.5	273042
98146	SEATTLE	25007	9896	20.7	26.7	35.8	12.0	4.8	52020	61874	76	72	6167	1.0	1.5	26.4	57.5	13.7	218595
98148	SEATTLE	24979	4199	21.7	36.3	30.1	9.1	2.9	43652	50000	58	50	1943	1.0	7.3	29.9	58.5	3.4	191027
98155	SEATTLE	31710	12962	12.6	25.0	37.4	16.6	8.4	62522	75058	87	87	9478	1.4	0.8	10.7	72.6	14.6	251706
98158	SEATTLE	0	0	0.0	0.0	0.0	0.0	0.0	0	0	0	0	0	0.0	0.0	0.0	0.0	0.0	0
98166	SEATTLE	32456	8966	20.4	26.8	28.9	15.2	8.6	53733	63026	78	74	6067	0.5	0.9	13.7	55.0	29.9	288006
98168	SEATTLE	21687	11747	22.4	32.6	32.9	9.8	2.3	45911	53776	64	56	6622	3.5	3.0	46.4	45.0	2.1	171374
98177	SEATTLE	39647	7584	13.3	20.9	34.3	17.9	13.7	70957	84432	92	94	6001	0.4	0.2	4.2	51.7	43.6	371015
98178	SEATTLE	25786	7918	16.8	28.3	36.8	13.5	4.6	54309	64185	79	75	5686	3.2	1.6	26.7	62.5	6.0	211243
98188	SEATTLE	24868	9428	22.3	32.7	33.1	8.9	3.1	45085	50901	61	53	4731	9.6	4.8	30.5	51.2	3.9	183827
98195	SEATTLE	17520	0	0.0	0.0	0.0	0.0	0.0	0	0	0	0	0	0.0	0.0	0.0	0.0	0.0	0
98198	SEATTLE	25159	12746	17.8	31.8	35.1	11.1	4.2	50436	58298	73	68	7301	6.2	2.3	24.7	59.4	7.4	203066
98199	SEATTLE	45783	9103	11.6	23.1	32.6	18.6	14.1	68987	85817	91	93	5728	0.2	0.3	6.5	38.1	55.1	427858
98201	EVERETT	21668	11826	32.8	31.0	27.9	5.7	2.6	37288	42893	36	28	5177	1.6	0.4	40.3	52.2	5.5	188002
98203	EVERETT	27155	12911	16.4	27.0	38.4	13.3	4.9	56373	64362	81	78	8653	2.0	2.0	21.4	65.1	9.5	218619
98204	EVERETT	19907	13777	25.7	37.9	29.9	5.2	1.2	40426	44778	48	42	4708	11.4	9.5	38.1	39.0	2.1	160391
98205	EVERETT	24927	5899	10.2	22.9	45.6	16.6	4.8	64060	73343	88	88	4948	2.7	2.8	20.5	66.8	7.3	217088
98208	EVERETT	27484	18928	12.9	25.1	40.7	15.6	5.7	61629	70424	86	85	13071	3.1	3.5	10.9	78.2	4.3	239593
98220	ACME	19583	189	25.4	28.6	37.6	4.2	4.2	46968	51345	66	59	152	0.0	9.2	38.8	46.7	5.3	178571
98221	ANACORTES	28599	8290	19.7	33.2	31.5	9.8	5.9	47641	53893	68	62	6279	1.3	0.8	22.9	57.0	17.9	231911
98223	ARLINGTON	24224	13964	15.1	26.2	43.1	12.3	3.4	58098	65143	83	81	11146	4.4	4.0	21.5	60.9	9.3	220248
98224	BARING	22884	33	24.2	30.3	39.4	6.1	0.0	47321	58510	67	61	26	0.0	26.9	50.0	23.1	0.0	116667
	WASHINGTON	26555		21.6	27.8	33.4	11.4	5.9	50585	57953				4.6	5.9	31.3	45.6	12.6	195701
	UNITED STATES	25866		24.7	27.1	30.8	10.9	6.5	48124	56710				10.9	15.0	33.7	30.1	10.4	145905

#	POST OFFICE NAME	FINANCIAL SERVICES: Auto Loan	Home Loan	Investments	Retirement Plans	THE HOME: Home Improvements: Home Repair	Lawn & Garden	Furnishings: Computers & Hardware	Major Appliances	TV, Radio, Sound Equipment	Furniture	ENTERTAINMENT: Dine out/Carry out	Sports Equipment	Fees & Tickets	Toys & Games	Travel	Cable TV	PERSONAL: Apparel & Services	Auto Repairs	Health Insurance	Pets & Supplies
98001	AUBURN	105	120	126	121	117	118	113	112	107	113	135	131	117	139	113	103	133	111	101	123
98002	AUBURN	70	68	73	69	67	73	71	71	72	71	89	82	70	87	70	70	87	72	70	79
98003	FEDERAL WAY	83	83	93	87	81	85	86	83	83	87	105	98	86	103	83	80	103	85	77	92
98004	BELLEVUE	153	179	237	179	175	189	174	169	169	175	213	195	185	221	179	169	212	170	161	184
98005	BELLEVUE	118	132	177	137	129	136	133	127	128	133	162	151	138	166	134	126	161	129	118	139
98006	BELLEVUE	172	214	254	214	207	213	194	190	181	197	229	220	209	240	199	177	230	186	171	207
98007	BELLEVUE	100	99	126	105	96	102	106	101	104	108	132	120	106	130	103	100	130	106	93	112
98008	BELLEVUE	129	173	222	166	168	175	156	154	147	156	184	177	168	199	163	147	186	151	140	164
98010	BLACK DIAMOND	120	136	136	136	133	134	125	126	118	126	148	147	129	152	126	114	146	123	115	140
98011	BOTHELL	112	123	133	127	120	121	118	116	112	120	141	138	121	142	117	107	139	116	104	128
98012	BOTHELL	119	127	134	132	123	125	123	121	116	125	147	142	125	146	120	111	145	121	109	134
98014	CARNATION	151	175	175	180	168	164	158	157	146	162	185	184	164	188	156	137	183	153	136	172
98019	DUVALL	150	174	173	179	167	163	157	155	144	161	183	182	163	186	155	136	181	151	134	170
98020	EDMONDS	118	130	150	129	130	141	124	126	121	126	152	140	129	148	128	122	149	125	125	139
98021	BOTHELL	111	122	127	125	120	122	114	114	109	116	137	132	118	138	114	105	135	113	105	127
98022	ENUMCLAW	99	103	102	104	103	107	99	101	96	99	120	119	99	121	99	94	117	100	97	115
98023	FEDERAL WAY	105	110	120	115	107	109	110	107	105	111	133	127	111	131	107	99	130	109	96	118
98024	FALL CITY	123	134	129	133	135	138	121	125	118	121	147	147	126	153	124	117	144	121	121	148
98026	EDMONDS	105	117	130	120	114	117	113	110	107	113	135	130	116	137	112	103	134	110	100	122
98027	ISSAQUAH	140	163	183	168	158	160	152	148	142	154	180	174	161	184	152	136	179	147	132	163
98028	KENMORE	122	139	157	142	136	140	132	130	125	133	158	152	137	160	133	121	156	129	119	143
98029	ISSAQUAH	160	183	188	188	177	179	166	166	155	171	196	189	174	195	166	149	194	162	150	182
98030	KENT	91	91	98	96	88	89	93	90	89	95	113	107	92	109	89	83	110	92	80	99
98031	KENT	99	104	112	108	101	103	103	101	98	104	124	118	104	123	100	94	122	102	91	111
98032	KENT	80	77	89	81	76	80	83	80	82	83	104	95	82	101	80	79	101	83	75	89
98033	KIRKLAND	149	169	222	176	164	171	167	160	160	168	203	189	175	211	168	157	202	161	145	175
98034	KIRKLAND	116	122	136	128	119	122	122	119	116	123	147	141	123	146	119	111	145	120	107	131
98036	LYNNWOOD	88	93	104	97	91	93	94	91	89	94	113	108	95	113	92	86	111	92	83	100
98037	LYNNWOOD	86	89	98	93	86	89	90	88	86	91	109	104	90	108	88	82	107	89	79	97
98038	MAPLE VALLEY	127	148	150	152	143	140	134	133	123	137	156	155	140	160	133	117	155	129	115	146
98039	MEDINA	320	431	591	423	421	454	376	373	350	384	443	419	427	466	401	353	450	358	346	405
98040	MERCER ISLAND	202	255	333	252	250	267	233	230	221	236	278	263	255	290	244	221	279	226	215	250
98042	KENT	119	137	139	139	133	132	126	125	117	127	148	146	130	151	125	112	146	122	111	138
98043	MOUNTLAKE TERRACE	86	86	97	91	84	87	90	87	87	91	110	104	90	108	87	83	108	90	79	96
98045	NORTH BEND	119	134	134	138	129	128	123	122	115	126	145	143	126	147	121	109	143	119	108	135
98047	PACIFIC	87	88	92	92	86	87	89	87	85	90	107	104	88	105	86	80	105	88	77	96
98051	RAVENSDALE	117	120	108	118	122	125	110	116	109	111	135	136	111	139	112	109	131	113	114	138
98052	REDMOND	143	150	187	158	145	153	153	147	148	155	187	174	157	187	150	142	185	150	134	162
98053	REDMOND	207	253	269	261	244	244	224	219	204	228	260	254	243	269	226	197	261	212	193	242
98055	RENTON	83	82	95	87	80	84	87	84	84	88	107	100	86	104	84	80	104	87	77	93
98056	RENTON	93	100	118	102	97	101	101	98	97	101	123	115	102	124	100	94	121	99	90	107
98058	RENTON	114	129	141	132	125	127	123	120	116	124	147	141	127	149	122	111	145	119	108	132
98059	RENTON	117	130	137	134	126	126	123	121	116	125	147	143	127	148	122	110	145	120	107	134
98065	SNOQUALMIE	106	122	134	126	119	119	116	113	108	116	137	134	120	141	115	104	136	112	101	124
98070	VASHON	117	133	145	132	133	139	126	126	121	125	151	145	130	154	129	120	149	124	122	140
98072	WOODINVILLE	156	181	194	187	176	177	167	164	154	169	196	192	176	200	167	148	195	160	146	181
98074	SAMMAMISH	190	230	243	237	221	220	204	200	186	208	237	232	220	243	205	178	237	193	175	220
98075	SAMMAMISH	223	272	288	281	262	262	241	236	220	246	280	273	261	288	243	211	281	228	208	260
98077	WOODINVILLE	190	237	257	244	230	231	209	205	191	212	243	237	229	253	213	185	245	197	182	227
98092	AUBURN	117	129	129	132	125	126	120	120	114	122	143	141	123	145	119	109	141	118	108	134
98101	SEATTLE	91	80	128	90	78	88	101	90	103	99	130	111	99	129	96	100	127	99	87	100
98102	SEATTLE	97	92	161	104	88	98	110	97	111	110	141	120	112	145	106	109	139	105	91	109
98103	SEATTLE	101	101	151	110	98	105	113	104	112	113	141	126	114	143	110	108	139	109	96	115
98104	SEATTLE	39	34	49	36	33	39	43	39	45	41	56	47	42	55	41	44	54	43	40	43
98105	SEATTLE	105	91	125	99	89	99	120	102	117	112	147	130	113	142	109	109	142	113	95	114
98106	SEATTLE	75	75	88	76	73	78	79	76	79	80	100	89	79	99	77	77	98	79	72	84
98107	SEATTLE	83	84	112	89	82	88	92	86	90	91	114	104	92	114	90	87	112	90	80	95
98108	SEATTLE	74	80	109	88	82	80	87	85	80	85	101	106	84	99	86	74	101	89	72	89
98109	SEATTLE	106	106	181	118	101	111	121	109	122	122	155	134	125	161	119	120	154	116	101	121
98110	BAINBRIDGE ISLAND	143	171	194	174	167	174	158	154	148	159	187	177	169	192	161	145	187	151	143	170
98112	SEATTLE	166	191	272	197	185	198	190	181	184	192	232	213	202	242	193	181	232	183	167	198
98115	SEATTLE	114	134	173	136	131	136	131	126	125	130	158	149	137	164	133	123	157	127	116	137
98116	SEATTLE	113	130	171	134	126	132	129	124	124	129	157	147	134	163	130	121	156	125	113	135
98117	SEATTLE	106	122	150	125	120	124	120	116	114	119	144	137	124	148	121	112	143	117	107	127
98118	SEATTLE	78	93	134	97	93	93	96	92	90	94	114	113	96	118	97	87	114	96	81	98
98119	SEATTLE	114	112	187	125	107	118	129	116	130	130	165	143	133	170	126	127	163	124	108	129
98121	SEATTLE	91	82	138	93	78	88	102	90	103	101	131	112	101	132	97	100	128	98	84	100
98122	SEATTLE	84	76	102	83	75	82	94	84	92	90	116	105	90	112	87	87	113	92	78	93
98125	SEATTLE	84	87	110	90	85	91	94	89	91	92	115	107	94	115	92	88	113	93	83	97
98126	SEATTLE	88	96	119	98	94	99	97	94	95	97	119	111	99	121	97	92	118	96	87	103
98133	SEATTLE	79	81	100	85	80	85	87	82	85	86	107	98	87	106	85	82	105	86	77	91
98134	SEATTLE	80	64	84	73	64	71	89	78	87	83	109	100	81	102	80	80	106	88	72	87
98136	SEATTLE	119	135	168	138	132	139	134	129	128	133	162	152	138	165	135	126	160	131	120	141
98144	SEATTLE	84	95	137	101	95	97	101	97	96	99	121	119	101	122	102	92	120	101	86	104
98146	SEATTLE	85	94	113	93	92	97	93	91	91	94	115	105	96	118	93	90	114	92	86	99
98148	SEATTLE	78	76	87	79	74	79	81	78	80	81	101	92	81	99	78	77	99	81	73	86
98155	SEATTLE	104	119	139	120	116	120	115	112	110	115	139	132	119	142	116	107	137	113	103	123
98158	SEATTLE	0	0	0	0	0	0	0	0	0	0	0	0	0	0	0	0	0	0	0	0
98166	SEATTLE	98	110	126	109	109	116	108	106	105	107	132	122	112	134	110	105	130	106	103	116
98168	SEATTLE	77	77	90	78	75	80	81	78	81	81	102	92	81	102	79	79	100	81	74	86
98177	SEATTLE	125	148	175	147	146	154	140	138	134	140	169	159	148	173	144	133	167	137	131	151
98178	SEATTLE	87	97	115	95	95	100	95	94	94	96	118	107	99	122	96	93	117	94	89	102
98188	SEATTLE	81	80	91	83	78	82	84	81	82	85	104	96	84	102	81	79	102	84	75	90
98195	SEATTLE	0	0	0	0	0	0	0	0	0	0	0	0	0	0	0	0	0	0	0	0
98198	SEATTLE	85	88	97	90	86	89	89	87	86	89	109	102	90	109	87	83	107	88	81	96
98199	SEATTLE	118	140	193	142	136	144	137	131	132	138	167	154	145	175	140	131	167	132	121	143
98201	EVERETT	66	65	77	67	65	69	72	68	71	70	89	82	71	89	70	69	87	71	65	75
98203	EVERETT	95	101	107	104	99	101	99	98	95	100	120	116	100	121	98	91	117	98	90	108
98204	EVERETT	70	63	70	68	61	64	70	67	68	71	86	81	67	81	65	64	84	70	61	75
98205	EVERETT	105	113	109	116	110	109	105	106	99	107	125	125	106	126	103	94	122	104	95	119
98208	EVERETT	102	110	117	115	106	107	107	104	101	109	128	123	109	127	104	96	126	104	93	115
98220	ACME	85	79	65	77	82	86	74	80	76	74	93	95	73	95	75	76	89	78	82	99
98221	ANACORTES	94	97	98	95	100	108	93	97	93	92	115	110	94	116	96	95	112	95	100	111
98223	ARLINGTON	98	99	92	100	99	102	94	97	92	95	115	114	95	116	94	90	112	95	92	112
98224	BARING	89	70	48	63	79	89	66	80	75	66	89	93	59	88	70	80	82	78	94	109
	WASHINGTON	94	96	103	97	95	100	96	95	94	96	118	112	96	118	95	92	115	96	91	107
	UNITED STATES	100	100	100	100	100	100	100	100	100	100	100	100	100	100	100	100	100	100	100	100

#	POST OFFICE NAME	COUNTY FIPS CODE	POPULATION 2000	POPULATION 2004	POPULATION 2009	2000-2004 ANNUAL RATE % Rate	2000-2004 ANNUAL RATE State Centile	HOUSEHOLDS 2000	HOUSEHOLDS 2004	HOUSEHOLDS 2009	% Annual Rate 2000-2004	2004 Average HH Size	FAMILIES 2000	FAMILIES 2004	% Annual Rate 2000-2004
98225	BELLINGHAM	073	42197	43184	45565	0.6	41	17740	18347	19594	0.8	2.11	7807	7932	0.4
98226	BELLINGHAM	073	30936	34513	37921	2.6	91	11600	13131	14562	3.0	2.62	8204	9190	2.7
98229	BELLINGHAM	073	25639	27491	29696	1.7	77	10448	11268	12229	1.8	2.43	6756	7199	1.5
98230	BLAINE	073	10786	11914	13037	2.4	88	4369	4891	5401	2.7	2.42	3068	3396	2.4
98232	BOW	057	3645	4003	4301	2.2	87	1373	1526	1649	2.5	2.61	1033	1141	2.4
98233	BURLINGTON	057	12466	13906	15020	2.6	91	4576	5109	5519	2.6	2.68	3288	3650	2.5
98236	CLINTON	029	5343	6005	6592	2.8	93	2165	2459	2732	3.0	2.44	1584	1787	2.9
98237	CONCRETE	057	4111	4252	4436	0.8	50	1558	1621	1694	0.9	2.62	1107	1145	0.8
98239	COUPEVILLE	029	5959	6340	6754	1.5	72	2572	2768	2983	1.7	2.24	1787	1915	1.6
98240	CUSTER	073	2994	3280	3569	2.2	85	1034	1145	1255	2.4	2.86	807	887	2.3
98241	DARRINGTON	061	1906	1896	1972	-0.1	15	767	775	816	0.2	2.44	507	507	0.0
98244	DEMING	073	2363	2384	2506	0.2	27	862	878	931	0.4	2.71	625	629	0.2
98245	EASTSOUND	055	3605	3915	4352	2.0	82	1686	1862	2098	2.4	2.10	1009	1106	2.2
98247	EVERSON	073	7975	8992	9951	2.9	94	2655	3008	3344	3.0	2.99	2100	2365	2.8
98248	FERNDALE	073	18492	19784	21327	1.6	75	6607	7133	7738	1.8	2.76	4990	5342	1.6
98249	FREELAND	029	3756	4170	4557	2.5	89	1644	1837	2024	2.7	2.27	1123	1249	2.5
98250	FRIDAY HARBOR	055	6889	7820	8883	3.0	95	3056	3503	4024	3.3	2.20	1922	2190	3.1
98251	GOLD BAR	061	4487	4713	4992	1.2	63	1678	1770	1885	1.3	2.65	1160	1214	1.1
98252	GRANITE FALLS	061	6716	7256	7807	1.8	80	2406	2616	2831	2.0	2.77	1773	1913	1.8
98253	GREENBANK	029	1338	1395	1471	1.0	56	618	648	689	1.1	2.15	436	455	1.0
98257	LA CONNER	057	3609	3812	4013	1.3	67	1561	1657	1748	1.4	2.30	1088	1150	1.3
98258	LAKE STEVENS	061	18273	20136	21849	2.3	88	6315	7041	7711	2.6	2.85	4904	5433	2.4
98260	LANGLEY	029	5205	5558	5965	1.6	74	2216	2391	2594	1.8	2.32	1492	1602	1.7
98261	LOPEZ ISLAND	055	2412	2707	3061	2.8	93	1130	1292	1484	3.2	2.09	715	812	3.0
98262	LUMMI ISLAND	073	812	907	997	2.6	92	381	431	478	2.9	2.10	224	250	2.6
98264	LYNDEN	073	16245	17677	19216	2.0	83	5691	6264	6862	2.3	2.80	4355	4756	2.1
98266	MAPLE FALLS	073	2679	3314	3846	5.1	99	865	1067	1238	5.1	3.11	635	775	4.8
98267	MARBLEMOUNT	057	363	366	375	0.2	26	145	147	151	0.3	2.48	96	97	0.2
98270	MARYSVILLE	061	34613	37965	41242	2.2	86	12483	13683	15015	2.2	2.75	9151	10051	2.2
98271	MARYSVILLE	061	23217	25558	27899	2.3	87	7959	8878	9787	2.6	2.87	6227	6909	2.5
98272	MONROE	061	23407	25898	28132	2.4	89	7427	8297	9104	2.6	2.89	5643	6284	2.6
98273	MOUNT VERNON	057	25579	27079	28679	1.4	69	9173	9663	10213	1.2	2.76	6237	6528	1.1
98274	MOUNT VERNON	057	13324	14169	14998	1.5	72	4896	5196	5485	1.4	2.66	3544	3746	1.3
98275	MUKILTEO	061	17999	19209	20572	1.5	74	6748	7275	7856	1.8	2.64	4977	5299	1.5
98277	OAK HARBOR	029	34599	35341	37185	0.5	39	12934	13409	14296	0.9	2.62	9530	9844	0.8
98278	OAK HARBOR	029	2037	2010	2041	-0.3	12	291	287	303	-0.3	2.99	266	263	-0.3
98279	OLGA	055	976	1055	1169	1.9	81	476	523	589	2.2	2.01	298	325	2.1
98281	POINT ROBERTS	073	1308	1524	1725	3.7	98	607	703	795	3.5	2.17	373	426	3.2
98282	CAMANO ISLAND	029	13358	15080	16605	2.9	94	5360	6039	6680	2.9	2.50	4033	4532	2.8
98283	ROCKPORT	057	257	266	276	0.8	51	105	110	115	1.1	2.42	72	75	1.0
98284	SEDRO WOOLLEY	057	22292	23254	24387	1.0	57	8171	8573	9022	1.1	2.63	5836	6091	1.0
98288	SKYKOMISH	033	347	342	341	-0.3	11	163	162	163	-0.1	2.10	91	89	-0.5
98290	SNOHOMISH	061	29945	32259	34768	1.8	79	10568	11522	12546	2.1	2.75	8002	8707	2.0
98292	STANWOOD	061	17350	19048	20648	2.2	86	6221	6870	7496	2.4	2.72	4640	5084	2.2
98294	SULTAN	061	5991	6495	6970	1.9	82	2232	2451	2656	2.2	2.65	1582	1724	2.0
98295	SUMAS	073	2206	2243	2401	0.4	36	764	778	835	0.4	2.87	566	570	0.2
98296	SNOHOMISH	061	19547	22251	24661	3.1	96	6398	7368	8240	3.4	3.02	5382	6184	3.3
98303	ANDERSON ISLAND	053	900	990	1074	2.3	87	421	463	501	2.3	2.14	288	314	2.1
98304	ASHFORD	053	813	833	864	0.6	42	368	378	392	0.6	2.20	238	241	0.3
98305	BEAVER	009	536	514	516	-1.0	2	229	223	226	-0.6	2.30	159	153	-0.9
98310	BREMERTON	035	18740	18366	18587	-0.5	8	8187	8107	8270	-0.2	2.23	4765	4646	-0.6
98311	BREMERTON	035	23733	23685	24044	-0.1	17	8459	8571	8790	0.3	2.75	6486	6529	0.2
98312	BREMERTON	035	30831	30313	30754	-0.4	9	12163	12016	12264	-0.3	2.49	8080	7953	-0.4
98315	SILVERDALE	035	6486	6887	7150	1.4	71	1099	1222	1305	2.5	3.68	1088	1210	2.5
98320	BRINNON	031	1189	1195	1232	0.1	23	570	581	607	0.5	2.06	367	371	0.3
98321	BUCKLEY	053	16347	17762	19143	2.0	83	5504	5983	6440	2.0	2.89	4274	4612	1.8
98323	CARBONADO	053	725	792	856	2.1	84	230	252	271	2.2	3.14	176	192	2.1
98325	CHIMACUM	031	1650	1714	1783	0.9	53	633	665	699	1.2	2.58	452	469	0.9
98326	CLALLAM BAY	009	1529	1546	1569	0.3	30	286	294	306	0.7	2.78	184	188	0.5
98327	DUPONT	053	2270	2983	3536	6.6	100	918	1206	1426	6.6	2.47	635	824	6.3
98328	EATONVILLE	053	8693	9637	10501	2.5	89	3095	3425	3722	2.4	2.80	2381	2614	2.2
98329	GIG HARBOR	053	9550	10498	11375	2.3	87	3369	3695	3992	2.2	2.84	2639	2875	2.0
98330	ELBE	053	387	396	408	0.5	40	164	169	174	0.7	2.34	107	109	0.4
98331	FORKS	009	6650	6619	6736	-0.1	16	2318	2323	2386	0.1	2.69	1637	1631	-0.1
98332	GIG HARBOR	053	13068	14369	15581	2.3	87	4724	5197	5634	2.3	2.62	3680	4033	2.2
98333	FOX ISLAND	053	2803	2952	3130	1.2	65	1048	1101	1164	1.2	2.68	848	886	1.0
98335	GIG HARBOR	053	23015	24972	26903	1.9	82	8826	9587	10324	2.0	2.57	6619	7129	1.8
98336	GLENOMA	041	1139	1113	1108	-0.5	6	444	441	444	-0.2	2.52	325	320	-0.4
98337	BREMERTON	035	8263	7933	7963	-1.0	2	2847	2719	2749	-1.1	2.18	1336	1252	-1.5
98338	GRAHAM	053	21594	24454	26965	3.0	95	7244	8198	9028	3.0	2.97	5895	6642	2.9
98339	PORT HADLOCK	031	3091	3226	3376	1.0	59	1245	1311	1386	1.2	2.44	843	880	1.0
98340	HANSVILLE	035	1980	2134	2236	1.8	79	861	935	987	2.0	2.28	633	681	1.7
98342	INDIANOLA	035	1859	1936	2025	1.0	55	725	758	796	1.1	2.55	543	563	0.9
98345	KEYPORT	035	403	394	398	-0.5	7	151	149	152	-0.3	2.60	110	108	-0.4
98346	KINGSTON	035	8152	8673	9063	1.5	72	3095	3327	3503	1.7	2.61	2284	2435	1.5
98349	LAKEBAY	053	5543	5719	6021	0.7	48	1554	1605	1709	0.8	2.64	1123	1150	0.6
98351	LONGBRANCH	053	908	994	1089	2.2	85	390	425	463	2.0	2.34	284	307	1.9
98354	MILTON	053	5714	6361	6920	2.6	90	2359	2626	2854	2.6	2.39	1555	1709	2.3
98355	MINERAL	041	565	569	569	0.2	25	236	241	244	0.5	2.36	158	161	0.4
98356	MORTON	041	1989	1945	1938	-0.5	7	828	819	822	-0.3	2.34	562	551	-0.5
98358	NORDLAND	031	837	866	898	0.8	50	395	413	434	1.1	2.10	268	278	0.9
98359	OLALLA	035	5179	5529	5786	1.6	74	1794	1938	2047	1.8	2.83	1441	1547	1.7
98360	ORTING	053	7613	8515	9321	2.7	92	2635	2942	3215	2.6	2.84	2033	2251	2.4
98361	PACKWOOD	041	846	833	834	-0.4	11	400	399	403	-0.1	2.09	270	267	-0.3
98362	PORT ANGELES	009	20991	21508	22119	0.6	42	9159	9504	9883	0.9	2.23	5777	5971	0.8
98363	PORT ANGELES	009	12271	12436	12685	0.3	32	4944	5064	5220	0.6	2.44	3412	3481	0.5
98365	PORT LUDLOW	031	3679	4178	4575	3.0	96	1728	1992	2210	3.4	2.08	1283	1469	3.2
98366	PORT ORCHARD	035	31534	32652	33697	0.8	51	11711	12272	12776	1.1	2.58	8233	8553	0.9
98367	PORT ORCHARD	035	23193	24865	26120	1.7	77	8154	8854	9385	2.0	2.80	6526	7035	1.8
98368	PORT TOWNSEND	031	12806	13221	13732	0.8	49	5965	6242	6564	1.1	2.10	3610	3751	0.9
98370	POULSBO	035	24455	26137	27343	1.6	75	9389	10098	10624	1.7	2.56	6849	7318	1.6
98371	PUYALLUP	053	19366	20628	22062	1.5	73	7668	8146	8688	1.4	2.51	5239	5522	1.3
98372	PUYALLUP	053	21730	22833	24201	1.2	64	8572	8987	9504	1.1	2.50	5690	5923	1.0
98373	PUYALLUP	053	16273	19018	21340	3.7	98	6243	7293	8168	3.7	2.61	4529	5253	3.6
98374	PUYALLUP	053	29419	33681	37546	3.2	96	10364	11854	13190	3.2	2.84	7997	9036	2.9
	WASHINGTON					1.1					1.3	2.52			1.2
	UNITED STATES					1.2					1.3	2.58			1.1

ZIP CODE #	POST OFFICE NAME	RACE (%) White 2000	White 2004	Black 2000	Black 2004	Asian/Pacific 2000	Asian/Pacific 2004	% Hispanic Origin 2000	% Hispanic Origin 2004	2004 AGE DISTRIBUTION (%) 0-4	5-9	10-14	15-19	20-24	25-44	45-64	65-84	85+	18+	MEDIAN AGE 2004	% 2004 Males	% 2004 Females
98225	BELLINGHAM	88.4	87.3	0.9	0.9	3.9	4.3	4.4	5.1	4.2	3.9	3.9	10.6	20.3	26.3	19.3	8.9	2.8	85.6	28.9	47.9	52.1
98226	BELLINGHAM	84.0	83.5	0.8	0.8	3.8	4.2	4.7	5.4	6.7	6.7	7.2	7.0	7.9	26.9	25.8	10.3	1.5	75.3	36.3	49.4	50.6
98229	BELLINGHAM	90.2	89.3	0.8	0.8	3.3	3.6	3.8	4.4	5.8	5.6	6.1	6.1	9.0	28.3	26.6	11.2	1.4	79.1	36.8	49.3	50.7
98230	BLAINE	91.1	90.3	1.0	1.1	2.6	2.8	4.3	5.0	6.0	6.5	7.2	6.6	5.3	24.7	28.9	13.7	1.1	76.2	41.0	49.8	50.2
98232	BOW	92.9	92.2	0.1	0.1	1.8	2.0	6.1	6.8	4.8	5.7	6.9	6.5	4.9	23.8	34.8	11.2	1.6	78.6	43.3	50.1	49.9
98233	BURLINGTON	83.0	81.1	0.5	0.5	1.9	2.0	16.7	19.2	7.8	7.3	7.7	6.9	7.7	28.1	21.9	10.8	1.8	73.0	34.1	50.0	50.0
98236	CLINTON	94.4	93.8	0.5	0.6	1.2	1.4	2.2	2.6	4.6	5.5	7.3	6.4	4.9	21.0	34.5	14.3	1.5	78.4	45.2	49.3	50.7
98237	CONCRETE	93.5	92.9	0.2	0.2	0.6	0.6	2.0	2.4	7.0	6.8	8.0	7.4	6.2	25.1	27.4	11.4	0.7	73.5	38.2	50.7	49.3
98239	COUPEVILLE	92.3	91.3	1.1	1.3	1.7	2.0	3.2	3.9	4.7	5.1	5.8	5.3	4.0	21.8	31.5	18.9	2.9	80.8	47.1	48.6	51.4
98240	CUSTER	92.5	91.8	0.5	0.6	1.3	1.4	5.6	6.6	6.2	7.0	8.0	7.9	5.6	25.9	30.5	8.6	0.6	73.8	38.9	51.4	48.6
98241	DARRINGTON	93.5	93.0	0.2	0.2	0.5	0.6	1.3	1.5	5.6	5.9	7.3	7.3	6.7	24.6	27.1	13.8	1.6	76.2	40.3	49.6	50.4
98244	DEMING	89.7	89.1	0.3	0.3	0.6	0.6	3.0	3.4	6.1	8.5	9.3	6.9	5.2	26.9	28.0	8.5	0.6	71.5	36.6	51.4	48.6
98245	EASTSOUND	94.5	94.0	0.3	0.3	1.2	1.3	1.8	2.2	3.9	4.4	5.9	5.0	3.1	20.5	40.5	15.2	1.6	82.4	48.8	49.5	50.5
98247	EVERSON	86.4	84.9	0.3	0.3	1.2	1.4	10.6	12.4	7.8	8.4	9.4	8.2	6.4	27.8	23.6	7.4	0.9	69.1	33.0	50.1	49.9
98248	FERNDALE	86.8	85.9	0.6	0.7	1.8	1.9	7.5	8.6	7.4	7.6	8.3	7.3	6.1	27.3	26.2	8.9	1.0	72.0	36.1	49.8	50.2
98249	FREELAND	95.0	94.4	0.3	0.4	1.3	1.5	1.8	2.2	3.6	4.4	5.8	5.3	3.1	19.0	36.8	19.6	2.3	83.0	50.0	48.1	51.9
98250	FRIDAY HARBOR	95.1	94.7	0.3	0.3	1.0	1.1	2.8	3.3	3.6	4.5	6.1	6.2	3.8	19.9	36.4	16.9	2.6	81.6	48.4	48.7	51.3
98251	GOLD BAR	92.9	92.2	0.4	0.4	1.2	1.3	2.8	3.3	7.5	7.7	8.4	6.7	5.3	32.5	24.6	6.8	0.5	72.2	35.8	52.2	47.8
98252	GRANITE FALLS	93.3	92.8	0.3	0.4	1.1	1.1	3.7	4.4	7.6	8.0	9.3	7.8	5.8	31.8	23.4	5.8	0.6	70.2	34.0	50.5	49.5
98253	GREENBANK	94.0	93.3	0.3	0.4	1.4	1.6	1.7	2.2	3.8	4.4	4.4	3.9	2.7	16.1	39.6	22.9	2.3	85.1	53.7	48.9	51.1
98257	LA CONNER	78.0	77.1	0.3	0.2	0.5	0.5	4.0	4.6	4.5	4.7	5.1	5.3	4.6	18.1	31.2	23.3	3.0	82.5	50.5	48.0	52.1
98258	LAKE STEVENS	93.4	92.8	0.6	0.7	1.2	1.3	2.9	3.6	7.5	8.2	9.1	8.0	5.7	31.6	23.4	6.0	0.6	70.1	34.3	50.5	49.5
98260	LANGLEY	94.9	94.2	0.4	0.4	1.6	1.8	1.8	2.2	4.3	5.3	7.5	7.0	4.1	19.8	35.4	15.0	1.7	78.3	46.0	47.3	52.7
98261	LOPEZ ISLAND	95.2	94.8	0.1	0.1	0.8	0.9	2.3	2.8	3.1	4.0	5.3	4.4	3.7	16.3	41.2	20.1	1.8	84.6	51.7	49.5	50.5
98262	LUMMI ISLAND	95.8	95.4	0.5	0.6	0.5	0.6	0.7	0.9	3.8	3.5	7.0	5.5	1.8	20.8	41.6	14.9	1.2	82.4	48.2	49.0	51.1
98264	LYNDEN	91.9	91.0	0.3	0.3	2.0	2.1	7.0	8.0	7.3	7.4	8.3	8.1	6.6	25.2	22.3	12.4	2.5	71.8	35.7	48.9	51.1
98266	MAPLE FALLS	91.8	91.0	0.3	0.3	0.6	0.6	3.7	4.4	8.9	10.1	11.3	7.5	6.5	29.4	20.1	5.8	0.4	65.1	29.4	51.3	48.7
98267	MARBLEMOUNT	94.2	93.7	0.3	0.3	0.0	0.0	1.4	1.9	5.5	7.1	7.4	8.7	4.1	24.0	31.7	10.4	1.1	74.6	41.0	51.1	48.9
98270	MARYSVILLE	88.6	87.5	1.0	1.1	4.1	4.6	4.6	5.4	8.4	8.0	8.5	7.2	6.9	30.4	20.8	8.2	1.7	70.7	33.5	48.9	51.1
98271	MARYSVILLE	83.2	82.9	0.5	0.5	2.2	2.4	4.2	4.9	6.9	7.2	8.7	7.6	6.2	28.7	26.3	7.9	0.7	72.5	36.3	50.5	49.5
98272	MONROE	89.4	88.5	1.9	1.9	1.9	2.1	7.2	8.5	8.6	8.2	7.8	6.4	6.4	33.9	21.4	6.2	1.2	71.6	33.7	53.1	46.9
98273	MOUNT VERNON	77.9	75.7	0.6	0.6	2.5	2.6	22.5	25.5	7.9	7.2	7.8	7.6	9.0	27.5	22.3	9.3	1.5	72.9	32.5	50.1	49.9
98274	MOUNT VERNON	86.4	84.9	0.5	0.5	1.8	1.9	11.8	13.6	6.8	6.8	7.6	6.7	6.4	26.7	24.3	11.8	2.9	74.7	37.8	48.7	51.3
98275	MUKILTEO	82.3	80.8	1.7	1.8	10.6	11.5	3.0	3.6	5.9	6.7	8.3	7.7	6.4	28.4	29.4	6.6	0.6	74.2	37.3	49.5	50.5
98277	OAK HARBOR	80.8	79.0	3.8	4.1	7.7	8.4	5.4	6.4	8.7	7.5	7.4	6.5	8.6	30.4	20.1	9.7	1.2	72.6	32.4	50.2	49.8
98278	OAK HARBOR	66.9	63.9	10.0	10.6	11.5	12.5	11.0	12.7	8.1	2.8	1.3	11.1	49.0	25.4	1.8	0.4	0.2	86.8	22.7	68.0	32.0
98279	OLGA	95.3	94.9	0.1	0.1	0.8	0.9	2.0	2.4	3.4	4.1	4.8	4.5	2.5	18.9	40.7	19.3	1.9	84.8	50.9	46.8	53.2
98281	POINT ROBERTS	94.9	94.6	0.6	0.7	2.1	2.2	1.3	1.6	5.6	6.3	6.2	4.0	2.5	24.6	36.6	12.9	1.3	79.3	45.4	50.0	50.0
98282	CAMANO ISLAND	95.6	95.1	0.3	0.3	0.9	1.0	2.1	2.5	5.3	6.0	7.2	6.0	4.2	22.6	30.0	17.1	1.7	77.8	44.3	49.8	50.2
98283	ROCKPORT	93.8	92.9	0.4	0.4	0.0	0.0	1.6	1.9	5.6	7.1	7.5	7.9	4.5	24.4	31.2	10.9	0.8	74.8	40.7	51.9	48.1
98284	SEDRO WOOLLEY	92.0	91.4	0.5	0.5	0.9	0.9	5.4	6.3	6.9	6.8	7.4	7.2	6.9	27.8	24.7	10.5	1.8	74.5	36.4	49.7	50.3
98288	SKYKOMISH	91.9	90.9	0.6	0.6	1.2	1.5	2.0	2.6	3.5	5.0	5.3	5.9	3.5	29.8	32.8	13.7	0.6	81.9	43.6	52.1	48.0
98290	SNOHOMISH	94.6	94.2	0.4	0.4	1.2	1.3	3.0	3.5	6.4	7.0	8.2	7.5	5.8	28.0	28.1	7.8	1.2	73.6	37.8	50.3	49.7
98292	STANWOOD	94.3	93.8	0.4	0.4	1.0	1.1	3.1	3.7	6.3	7.3	8.4	7.1	5.2	27.5	25.9	9.8	2.4	73.3	38.4	50.0	50.0
98294	SULTAN	92.0	91.3	0.3	0.3	1.3	1.4	3.8	4.5	7.3	7.4	8.5	7.0	5.8	30.6	24.4	7.9	1.1	72.4	35.8	51.5	48.5
98295	SUMAS	89.1	88.1	0.1	0.1	2.3	2.4	7.8	8.9	7.6	7.7	9.2	8.8	7.5	27.2	22.2	8.8	1.1	69.4	32.8	50.7	49.3
98296	SNOHOMISH	91.2	90.2	0.5	0.6	3.9	4.4	2.9	3.4	7.7	8.7	9.2	6.9	4.7	30.8	26.7	4.9	0.5	69.8	36.4	50.3	49.7
98303	ANDERSON ISLAND	96.0	95.6	0.4	0.5	1.2	1.4	2.1	2.5	4.2	4.4	5.5	4.2	3.1	14.0	33.4	28.9	2.1	83.2	54.6	50.4	49.6
98304	ASHFORD	93.1	92.3	0.4	0.4	0.7	0.7	2.6	3.2	4.1	5.4	7.9	6.8	4.0	26.5	31.6	12.7	1.0	77.8	42.6	50.8	49.2
98305	BEAVER	93.1	92.4	0.4	0.4	0.8	0.8	0.8	1.0	5.3	4.1	7.0	7.8	4.9	21.6	37.0	11.3	1.2	77.8	44.7	51.2	48.8
98310	BREMERTON	78.4	76.8	5.2	5.5	7.1	7.5	4.5	5.2	7.0	6.2	6.3	6.0	7.6	27.5	21.8	14.1	3.6	77.0	37.3	47.5	52.5
98311	BREMERTON	78.6	76.9	3.7	4.0	10.1	10.8	3.7	4.3	6.7	7.0	8.0	7.8	7.3	27.3	26.3	8.6	1.1	73.4	35.6	49.5	50.5
98312	BREMERTON	80.6	79.3	5.0	5.2	5.3	5.7	5.1	5.9	8.0	7.3	7.2	6.6	8.0	28.9	23.4	9.1	1.4	73.5	34.1	50.3	49.7
98315	SILVERDALE	76.9	75.1	8.0	8.4	5.4	5.8	10.2	11.8	12.3	7.3	5.5	5.7	22.1	44.6	2.4	0.2	0.0	72.9	24.4	66.2	33.8
98320	BRINNON	90.8	90.0	0.3	0.3	0.8	0.8	1.9	2.3	2.5	3.1	4.3	4.4	3.8	14.4	36.7	28.3	2.7	87.3	54.3	51.6	48.4
98321	BUCKLEY	94.0	93.2	0.6	0.7	1.0	1.2	2.5	3.0	7.9	7.7	8.1	7.3	6.1	31.2	24.5	6.6	0.7	71.6	34.9	50.6	49.4
98323	CARBONADO	95.5	95.1	0.4	0.5	0.4	0.5	1.9	2.3	9.1	7.8	8.6	7.3	4.4	32.8	24.5	4.9	0.5	69.7	34.1	52.3	47.7
98325	CHIMACUM	91.7	91.0	0.5	0.5	1.1	1.2	2.2	2.5	5.4	6.3	7.8	7.5	5.8	23.2	31.5	11.5	1.0	75.8	41.2	50.4	49.6
98326	CLALLAM BAY	73.8	72.3	13.9	14.8	2.9	2.9	8.8	10.6	3.0	2.9	4.0	14.0	13.5	35.5	20.8	5.8	0.6	83.4	31.7	75.5	24.5
98327	DUPONT	78.4	76.5	5.7	6.1	8.2	8.9	4.9	5.7	9.0	8.5	6.5	5.2	4.6	37.0	21.7	7.1	0.5	72.3	34.6	48.8	51.2
98328	EATONVILLE	92.1	91.3	0.5	0.5	1.4	1.6	3.0	3.6	6.1	6.8	8.4	7.6	5.7	26.7	28.6	9.1	1.0	73.9	38.7	50.9	49.1
98329	GIG HARBOR	92.2	91.4	0.7	0.7	1.5	1.6	2.2	2.7	6.5	7.1	8.4	7.4	6.0	26.8	28.8	8.3	0.7	73.2	37.9	50.9	49.1
98330	ELBE	93.8	92.9	0.3	0.3	1.0	1.0	2.3	3.0	4.0	5.6	7.6	6.6	4.0	26.5	31.1	13.4	1.3	78.0	42.8	51.3	48.7
98331	FORKS	77.0	75.6	1.4	1.4	1.4	1.4	12.3	14.5	7.2	6.9	8.1	8.0	8.4	27.4	25.7	7.5	0.7	73.0	33.4	55.0	45.0
98332	GIG HARBOR	91.8	90.8	1.9	2.0	1.9	2.2	2.8	3.4	5.0	5.7	7.2	6.5	5.0	25.9	31.2	12.2	1.4	78.0	42.0	46.4	53.6
98333	FOX ISLAND	94.1	93.4	0.6	0.7	1.8	2.0	1.9	2.2	5.3	6.8	8.2	7.1	3.5	21.8	34.5	11.7	1.2	75.0	43.7	50.1	49.9
98335	GIG HARBOR	93.0	92.1	0.9	1.1	2.2	2.5	2.7	3.3	5.6	6.3	7.3	6.9	5.5	22.7	31.3	12.4	2.1	76.5	42.4	48.3	51.7
98336	GLENOMA	95.7	95.2	0.3	0.5	0.2	0.2	2.3	2.9	5.5	5.9	7.6	8.1	5.8	22.0	29.6	14.4	1.2	76.1	41.7	50.4	49.6
98337	BREMERTON	71.5	69.4	9.9	10.6	5.7	6.1	10.0	11.7	5.7	4.8	4.8	9.3	23.6	30.1	16.5	4.7	0.7	82.1	26.0	60.9	39.1
98338	GRAHAM	89.4	88.2	1.6	1.8	2.4	2.7	3.2	3.9	7.3	7.8	8.8	8.0	5.9	29.8	25.5	6.4	0.5	70.9	35.4	50.7	49.3
98339	PORT HADLOCK	90.7	89.7	0.3	0.3	1.5	1.7	2.5	3.0	5.2	5.6	7.2	7.0	6.4	24.1	30.6	12.5	1.5	77.7	41.6	49.9	50.1
98340	HANSVILLE	93.9	93.4	0.2	0.2	1.6	1.7	2.0	2.3	5.3	5.6	5.2	4.6	3.1	22.0	34.4	18.0	1.9	80.5	47.6	49.2	50.8
98342	INDIANOLA	88.0	86.8	0.5	0.6	1.7	1.9	2.7	3.2	6.7	7.2	8.4	7.3	5.9	29.2	27.6	7.0	0.5	73.1	37.1	49.7	50.3
98345	KEYPORT	89.6	88.8	1.0	1.0	3.5	3.8	2.7	3.6	5.3	5.8	6.4	5.8	4.8	25.9	32.0	12.4	1.5	78.4	42.7	51.0	49.0
98346	KINGSTON	86.1	85.9	0.4	0.5	1.7	1.8	2.8	3.3	6.4	6.7	7.5	7.2	6.1	25.6	29.8	10.0	0.8	75.0	39.6	50.1	49.9
98349	LAKEBAY	87.8	87.1	6.5	6.7	0.9	0.9	5.3	6.2	4.3	4.6	5.4	5.6	6.7	34.0	29.0	10.0	0.5	82.7	39.7	62.2	37.8
98351	LONGBRANCH	93.7	92.9	0.4	0.6	0.7	0.8	3.3	4.0	5.9	6.5	7.3	6.8	5.0	23.5	30.9	13.0	0.9	75.9	41.9	49.0	51.0
98354	MILTON	88.8	87.8	1.4	1.5	3.9	4.3	3.5	4.2	5.8	6.4	7.6	6.7	6.7	29.4	25.0	10.1	2.4	76.0	37.9	48.7	51.3
98355	MINERAL	96.5	96.3	0.2	0.2	0.7	0.7	1.4	1.8	3.0	5.1	6.9	6.0	3.2	24.6	33.9	15.6	1.8	80.5	45.5	51.7	48.3
98356	MORTON	95.5	95.1	0.3	0.3	0.8	0.8	1.6	1.8	5.3	6.5	6.5	6.4	5.2	22.1	26.8	17.6	3.5	77.3	43.6	48.7	51.3
98358	NORDLAND	96.5	96.1	0.0	0.0	1.1	1.2	1.9	2.1	2.8	3.0	4.3	4.2	3.0	14.2	41.9	24.5	2.2	87.2	54.7	49.8	50.2
98359	OLALLA	90.9	90.0	0.6	0.6	1.7	1.8	3.0	3.5	6.0	6.6	8.3	7.9	6.1	26.3	29.9	8.4	0.6	74.0	38.5	50.8	49.2
98360	ORTING	92.9	92.1	0.5	0.5	1.2	1.3	3.1	3.8	7.8	8.2	8.6	7.2	5.2	31.2	22.1	8.8	1.0	70.7	34.9	51.7	48.3
98361	PACKWOOD	97.8	97.6	0.0	0.0	0.2	0.2	1.2	1.6	3.8	3.8	4.6	5.6	4.6	17.8	36.9	21.3	1.7	84.4	50.3	50.2	49.8
98362	PORT ANGELES	93.2	92.7	0.5	0.5	1.1	1.2	2.0	2.3	4.8	5.1	6.4	6.8	5.8	22.0	29.6	16.7	2.7	79.5	44.3	48.8	51.2
98363	PORT ANGELES	88.7	88.0	0.5	0.6	1.2	1.3	2.2	2.6	6.2	6.5	7.3	7.3	5.7	23.7	29.6	11.8	1.9	75.4	40.9	49.0	51.0
98365	PORT LUDLOW	94.9	94.5	0.4	0.4	1.3	1.4	1.7	2.0	2.4	3.0	3.7	3.2	2.3	13.4	37.3	32.5	2.2	88.7	58.7	49.9	50.1
98366	PORT ORCHARD	86.2	85.1	2.3	2.4	4.3	4.6	4.1	4.9	6.7	6.5	7.4	7.2	7.9	28.0	24.8	9.8	1.6	75.1	36.1	50.3	49.7
98367	PORT ORCHARD	89.5	88.5	1.1	1.2	3.4	3.7	3.1	3.7	6.2	7.1	8.2	7.3	5.4	27.1	29.4	8.7	0.8	73.9	38.7	50.7	49.3
98368	PORT TOWNSEND	93.8	93.2	0.5	0.5	1.5	1.6	1.9	2.3	3.9	4.5	5.4	5.5	4.4	18.3	36.0	19.0	3.1	82.7	49.6	47.2	52.8
98370	POULSBO	90.1	89.2	0.8	0.8	2.8	3.1	3.4	4.0	6.0	6.5	7.4	6.6	5.6	24.8	29.5	11.4	2.1	76.0	40.8	49.3	50.7
98371	PUYALLUP	89.5	88.1	1.3	1.5	2.8	3.1	4.4	5.3	6.0	6.2	7.0	6.7	6.1	26.7	27.1	12.1	2.1	76.6	39.7	49.0	51.0
98372	PUYALLUP	89.6	88.4	1.2	1.3	3.1	3.5	4.2	5.1	6.4	6.4	7.2	7.0	7.6	28.4	25.4	9.9	1.8	75.9	36.9	48.9	51.2
98373	PUYALLUP	87.3	85.7	2.5	2.7	3.6	4.1	3.7	4.5	7.1	6.9	7.5	6.9	7.4	31.3	24.0	8.2	0.8	74.4	34.3	49.4	50.6
98374	PUYALLUP	88.1	86.6	1.9	2.2	3.6	4.0	4.1	5.1	8.0	7.7	8.5	7.7	7.4	30.3	23.1	6.4	1.0	71.1	33.0	48.7	51.3
	WASHINGTON	81.8	80.6	3.2	3.3	5.9	6.3	7.5	8.6	6.7	6.6	7.1	7.0	7.6	28.7	24.9	9.8	1.6	75.4	36.1	49.7	50.3
	UNITED STATES	75.1	73.6	12.3	12.5	3.8	4.2	12.5	14.1	6.9	6.7	7.2	7.0	7.3	28.6	23.8	10.8	1.7	75.1	36.0	49.1	50.9

ZIP CODE #	POST OFFICE NAME	2004 Per Capita Income	2004 HH Income Base	2004 HOUSEHOLD INCOME DISTRIBUTION (%) Less than $25,000	$25,000 to $49,999	$50,000 to $99,999	$100,000 to $149,999	$150,000 or More	MEDIAN HOUSEHOLD INCOME 2004	2009	2004 National Centile	2004 State Centile	2004 Home Value Base	2004 HOME VALUE DISTRIBUTION (%) Less than $50,000	$50,000 to $89,999	$90,000 to $174,999	$175,000 to $399,999	$400,000 or More	2004 Median Home Value
98225	BELLINGHAM	22939	18347	40.4	28.8	21.9	5.3	3.7	31998	36256	18	9	7723	2.5	4.1	39.4	44.2	9.8	181667
98226	BELLINGHAM	23339	13131	21.8	30.8	33.2	10.0	4.1	47850	53703	68	63	9395	3.6	3.7	26.3	57.3	9.2	205941
98229	BELLINGHAM	26425	11268	23.6	27.3	32.1	11.2	5.9	49038	55959	70	65	7476	6.7	3.8	22.7	53.4	13.4	209950
98230	BLAINE	26153	4891	22.9	31.5	32.9	7.9	4.8	46748	52866	66	58	3676	6.9	6.9	36.9	37.7	11.5	173427
98232	BOW	28615	1526	16.7	23.3	39.7	12.8	7.5	57364	66618	82	79	1326	4.1	2.0	16.5	60.5	16.9	234970
98233	BURLINGTON	23910	5109	22.2	30.0	36.6	9.0	2.2	48292	53987	69	64	3468	2.4	4.9	35.8	52.6	4.3	186338
98236	CLINTON	27970	2459	20.8	28.1	33.5	11.0	6.6	50961	56328	74	69	2061	1.4	0.5	20.0	57.0	21.2	250827
98237	CONCRETE	17692	1621	34.6	33.1	25.3	5.4	1.6	36385	39687	33	24	1245	10.1	11.8	41.5	34.8	1.8	146074
98239	COUPEVILLE	26357	2768	18.9	28.7	40.0	8.9	3.5	51557	58120	75	70	2197	5.0	2.2	28.5	54.1	10.2	204579
98240	CUSTER	24607	1145	18.6	28.4	38.7	10.1	4.2	53123	59729	77	73	984	2.5	5.0	28.0	56.4	8.1	198675
98241	DARRINGTON	18659	775	35.0	29.4	29.3	3.7	2.6	34431	37691	25	17	584	5.7	8.6	59.9	24.3	1.5	132558
98244	DEMING	23793	878	26.0	25.6	35.8	7.6	5.0	48137	53364	69	63	733	4.0	6.7	40.3	41.5	7.6	173452
98245	EASTSOUND	39107	1862	28.4	26.4	26.4	6.9	12.0	45241	51349	62	53	1431	0.0	1.8	15.7	38.2	44.4	350613
98247	EVERSON	18692	3008	20.4	34.8	35.4	6.7	2.7	45916	50948	64	56	2411	4.7	4.9	39.8	44.7	6.0	176215
98248	FERNDALE	21325	7133	21.7	31.2	35.1	8.8	3.2	47302	52347	67	60	5614	6.2	4.1	32.5	50.3	7.0	186142
98249	FREELAND	27051	1837	18.0	34.9	32.6	9.3	5.3	47606	52867	67	62	1530	1.4	1.3	18.2	55.9	23.2	247781
98250	FRIDAY HARBOR	39017	3503	20.8	29.4	31.5	9.2	9.1	49796	58417	72	66	2669	3.7	2.1	7.5	40.7	46.0	363021
98251	GOLD BAR	22085	1770	17.9	32.0	38.4	9.2	2.5	50074	56620	72	67	1486	9.6	6.3	43.8	36.1	4.3	161303
98252	GRANITE FALLS	23187	2616	16.1	25.5	44.0	10.9	3.4	56178	63434	81	78	2100	2.6	5.1	28.0	58.1	6.3	197872
98253	GREENBANK	31727	648	17.1	23.9	41.8	12.5	4.6	56519	65011	81	79	552	0.7	1.6	21.9	56.9	18.8	242149
98257	LA CONNER	29912	1657	21.9	27.6	32.2	10.4	7.9	50411	57931	73	68	1299	3.9	1.8	19.8	56.0	18.6	231490
98258	LAKE STEVENS	26286	7041	12.0	19.9	46.0	16.0	6.1	65392	75252	89	89	5769	1.3	2.2	13.6	72.5	10.4	236259
98260	LANGLEY	27156	2391	22.5	30.1	31.0	9.9	6.5	47884	53262	68	63	1912	0.5	2.8	21.2	56.6	18.9	243959
98261	LOPEZ ISLAND	33853	1292	21.8	34.9	29.0	8.8	5.5	43930	51820	58	50	1052	2.1	2.0	13.8	37.9	44.2	359333
98262	LUMMI ISLAND	32147	431	28.8	24.1	29.9	8.8	8.4	46235	52791	64	57	350	0.0	2.0	23.1	52.0	22.9	251923
98264	LYNDEN	22373	6264	20.4	31.9	35.1	7.8	4.8	48163	54561	69	63	4513	2.3	2.3	26.2	62.1	7.3	203168
98266	MAPLE FALLS	15701	1067	30.7	36.3	23.8	5.1	4.1	40017	45091	46	40	834	24.1	26.0	28.2	12.8	8.9	89839
98267	MARBLEMOUNT	29816	147	31.3	26.5	28.6	8.8	4.8	40459	43316	48	42	119	13.5	10.9	35.3	36.1	4.2	137500
98270	MARYSVILLE	23594	13683	15.8	27.3	40.0	13.4	3.5	56780	64718	81	79	9816	3.6	3.3	20.0	70.8	2.3	213115
98271	MARYSVILLE	23250	8878	14.6	24.7	44.3	13.0	3.4	60580	67726	85	84	7578	9.1	4.5	24.6	54.4	7.3	197334
98272	MONROE	24388	8297	14.0	22.3	43.1	15.1	5.6	61801	70510	86	85	6189	0.9	1.1	12.4	72.5	13.1	239632
98273	MOUNT VERNON	23213	9663	25.2	31.8	30.6	7.4	5.1	44082	48960	59	51	6012	5.8	4.1	34.6	48.7	6.8	186763
98274	MOUNT VERNON	26349	5196	18.3	28.6	36.4	11.2	5.5	52672	60993	76	72	3872	3.9	2.9	32.2	50.7	10.4	200945
98275	MUKILTEO	33004	7275	9.5	21.3	38.0	20.5	10.7	72943	83680	92	96	5087	0.5	1.0	4.7	62.5	31.4	330206
98277	OAK HARBOR	22081	13409	21.1	33.6	34.5	7.5	3.3	46210	51680	64	57	8032	7.0	3.0	32.6	53.1	4.2	187895
98278	OAK HARBOR	14636	287	47.4	40.1	10.5	2.1	0.0	25570	28437	5	2	20	0.0	0.0	50.0	50.0	0.0	187500
98279	OLGA	37623	523	19.9	24.7	32.5	13.0	9.9	58752	69839	83	82	438	0.0	0.7	6.9	34.0	58.5	436275
98281	POINT ROBERTS	26822	703	30.0	30.0	28.0	8.5	3.4	39097	43825	43	37	548	4.4	10.2	42.9	30.5	12.0	158197
98282	CAMANO ISLAND	27528	6039	16.5	24.4	40.1	13.8	5.3	59027	65160	84	82	5240	0.5	1.3	25.5	53.7	19.0	230633
98283	ROCKPORT	21090	110	32.7	30.0	27.3	7.3	2.7	37326	40318	37	29	90	12.2	11.1	40.0	34.4	2.2	140625
98284	SEDRO WOOLLEY	22353	8573	23.2	32.0	32.6	8.5	3.6	45730	51073	63	55	6505	7.3	5.0	43.1	39.5	5.1	165704
98288	SKYKOMISH	25174	162	22.2	29.6	39.5	6.8	1.9	48727	53982	70	64	129	8.5	24.8	41.1	22.5	3.1	115341
98290	SNOHOMISH	28365	11522	12.6	22.4	39.9	17.3	7.8	66800	76622	90	91	9310	1.6	1.1	12.6	65.8	19.0	262834
98292	STANWOOD	26478	6870	15.7	25.3	41.4	12.1	5.5	59828	65899	84	83	5521	1.8	3.2	15.9	64.0	15.1	233446
98294	SULTAN	22974	2451	17.8	28.5	40.9	9.8	3.0	52888	60790	77	73	1947	6.2	4.1	24.9	55.3	9.6	203048
98295	SUMAS	18316	778	27.9	34.2	29.2	4.8	4.0	41772	46307	52	46	567	7.4	10.4	37.6	37.4	7.2	164967
98296	SNOHOMISH	33181	7368	7.3	14.0	41.0	25.0	12.6	83355	99625	96	98	6810	2.0	0.6	5.1	62.6	29.7	320415
98303	ANDERSON ISLAND	29176	463	33.1	24.8	31.3	5.2	5.6	42538	49265	55	48	410	2.4	6.1	31.7	40.7	19.0	207746
98304	ASHFORD	22395	378	27.8	33.3	31.0	4.8	3.2	39631	44010	45	38	310	7.7	10.0	43.2	29.7	9.4	148404
98305	BEAVER	18683	223	26.9	41.7	28.7	2.7	0.0	37633	41300	38	30	180	17.8	5.6	45.0	29.4	2.2	147093
98310	BREMERTON	21586	8107	30.1	33.3	28.4	6.3	2.0	38983	43891	43	37	4271	2.5	5.2	65.2	24.8	2.2	140967
98311	BREMERTON	24202	8571	14.0	27.3	42.7	12.4	3.6	57629	65336	82	80	6407	6.8	3.4	51.8	35.0	2.9	162117
98312	BREMERTON	22710	12016	25.3	32.0	30.4	8.1	4.3	44173	50681	59	51	7106	4.6	8.5	49.4	33.9	3.7	147965
98315	SILVERDALE	13168	1222	21.1	57.7	19.4	1.2	0.7	36595	40655	34	26	32	0.0	3.1	34.4	59.4	3.1	210000
98320	BRINNON	20272	561	40.1	34.8	18.6	4.8	1.7	31567	34930	17	8	498	8.4	22.3	33.7	25.5	10.0	129268
98321	BUCKLEY	23209	5983	13.7	26.0	43.9	13.0	3.4	60062	66286	84	84	4987	5.6	4.2	32.6	51.3	6.3	189198
98323	CARBONADO	22652	252	11.9	25.0	46.4	13.1	3.6	62445	68928	87	87	219	3.7	4.1	36.5	48.9	6.9	184766
98325	CHIMACUM	18995	665	32.5	29.2	28.9	7.1	2.4	42290	46296	54	47	518	12.4	9.1	40.5	33.8	4.3	146610
98326	CLALLAM BAY	16657	294	34.4	38.8	22.5	1.7	2.7	33854	36893	24	15	187	15.5	20.9	49.7	12.8	1.1	105592
98327	DUPONT	27996	1206	9.0	21.2	53.4	13.8	2.6	62690	71095	87	87	879	1.6	0.8	24.9	71.8	0.9	207154
98328	EATONVILLE	23366	3425	15.5	32.1	36.6	11.1	4.8	51911	57865	75	71	2906	4.4	4.7	35.0	46.2	9.8	187991
98329	GIG HARBOR	24426	3695	12.9	28.4	41.9	12.9	3.9	57562	64131	82	80	3191	1.2	5.9	45.4	40.6	6.9	170859
98330	ELBE	20187	169	30.2	33.1	29.0	4.7	3.0	38105	41929	40	33	136	8.8	14.0	42.7	27.2	7.4	140000
98331	FORKS	16161	2323	32.1	33.9	29.4	3.6	1.0	37253	40063	36	28	1733	21.5	14.8	49.7	13.0	0.9	106054
98332	GIG HARBOR	33162	5197	12.4	22.3	38.6	16.0	10.7	66971	76790	90	91	4525	3.9	1.4	17.0	54.8	22.9	239441
98333	FOX ISLAND	38199	1101	4.8	15.6	45.1	20.0	14.5	78905	95737	95	98	1012	1.3	0.7	9.3	53.5	35.3	325126
98335	GIG HARBOR	33641	9587	12.5	25.0	35.9	14.8	11.9	65060	73710	89	89	7580	2.1	0.1	13.2	61.8	22.8	252609
98336	GLENOMA	16615	441	35.8	31.5	26.5	4.3	1.8	35066	37617	28	19	348	19.5	14.4	37.9	28.2	0.0	120909
98337	BREMERTON	17479	2719	40.8	36.0	19.0	2.8	1.4	30328	34622	13	5	1012	2.7	23.5	66.7	6.6	0.5	107792
98338	GRAHAM	22788	8198	13.5	26.6	43.9	12.8	3.2	59274	65832	84	83	7183	5.5	8.0	31.1	49.9	5.5	184336
98339	PORT HADLOCK	18066	1311	36.2	31.4	25.4	4.6	2.4	35017	38396	28	19	1027	11.9	6.5	49.0	27.2	5.5	143406
98340	HANSVILLE	34097	935	17.2	21.9	38.8	14.2	7.8	62064	72670	86	86	817	1.6	1.7	21.4	57.9	17.4	223964
98342	INDIANOLA	27210	758	15.8	25.6	43.5	11.9	3.2	58056	65144	83	81	655	0.5	2.9	51.3	35.9	9.5	168801
98345	KEYPORT	27180	149	13.4	28.9	36.2	17.5	4.0	60273	67633	85	84	121	5.8	5.8	24.0	44.6	19.8	226786
98346	KINGSTON	26132	3327	16.1	30.3	36.7	12.2	4.8	53995	61364	78	74	2644	4.4	4.2	30.8	48.7	12.0	198500
98349	LAKEBAY	22491	1605	24.9	26.7	31.2	10.7	6.7	48466	52720	69	64	1358	3.5	3.4	36.2	40.8	16.1	190000
98351	LONGBRANCH	26657	425	29.2	22.8	30.8	11.1	6.1	47059	49863	66	59	361	3.9	2.8	39.3	39.6	14.4	183056
98354	MILTON	25609	2626	17.5	28.6	40.3	11.4	2.2	53089	60322	77	73	1697	0.1	6.3	27.1	64.1	2.5	197191
98355	MINERAL	17349	241	35.3	33.6	25.7	3.7	1.7	33787	35935	23	14	197	8.1	25.9	44.2	19.3	2.5	116250
98356	MORTON	19654	819	32.7	34.3	27.1	3.4	2.4	35713	38339	30	21	606	7.9	18.2	50.0	22.1	1.8	122244
98358	NORDLAND	27048	413	13.8	45.8	30.3	6.8	3.4	42478	50000	55	47	358	4.2	0.0	10.9	50.0	34.9	343750
98359	OLALLA	24684	1938	19.8	29.5	36.1	10.8	3.8	50596	56964	73	69	1684	3.7	5.9	46.0	40.0	4.3	164397
98360	ORTING	24103	2942	13.9	24.2	45.1	13.6	3.2	61685	68234	86	85	2528	1.5	6.0	40.1	49.5	3.0	178412
98361	PACKWOOD	24762	399	32.1	42.6	17.0	4.0	4.3	36621	40563	34	26	322	12.7	10.6	49.7	24.8	2.2	124675
98362	PORT ANGELES	22046	9504	33.0	30.2	27.7	5.8	3.3	38463	42231	41	34	6662	3.5	7.4	50.1	34.1	5.0	152768
98363	PORT ANGELES	20626	5064	26.7	34.3	30.6	5.7	2.7	41053	45615	50	44	3796	5.3	5.9	51.7	32.2	4.9	152808
98365	PORT LUDLOW	35540	1992	12.0	31.5	40.3	10.7	5.5	55379	65367	80	77	1754	1.7	3.8	19.0	53.5	22.1	260238
98366	PORT ORCHARD	22350	12272	22.1	29.1	36.0	10.0	2.8	48868	55604	70	64	8059	2.8	4.7	52.8	35.9	3.8	160130
98367	PORT ORCHARD	24355	8854	15.2	25.1	43.0	12.3	4.3	58423	65456	83	82	7814	3.4	5.2	42.3	44.2	4.9	173452
98368	PORT TOWNSEND	27225	6242	30.9	29.0	27.6	8.4	4.1	40372	44364	47	41	4603	6.3	3.2	31.2	47.0	12.3	201557
98370	POULSBO	26411	10098	16.9	26.5	37.8	14.2	4.6	56688	63702	81	79	7929	3.5	3.7	27.5	55.5	9.9	208454
98371	PUYALLUP	25510	8146	20.1	30.0	33.9	11.1	5.0	49931	55266	72	66	6140	10.2	2.2	27.6	57.1	2.9	191685
98372	PUYALLUP	25094	8987	19.2	29.5	35.8	11.1	4.4	51149	56950	74	69	5674	7.5	3.0	28.4	53.9	7.2	196555
98373	PUYALLUP	25608	7293	12.9	29.1	41.1	13.2	3.8	58067	64042	83	81	4792	2.8	1.4	24.8	69.8	1.3	202795
98374	PUYALLUP	25221	11854	12.7	24.6	44.3	12.7	5.7	61887	67962	86	86	8588	6.0	2.8	23.1	64.4	3.7	202066
	WASHINGTON	26555		21.6	27.8	33.4	11.4	5.9	50585	57953				4.6	5.9	31.3	45.6	12.6	195701
	UNITED STATES	25866		24.7	27.1	30.8	10.9	6.5	48124	56710				10.9	15.0	33.7	30.1	10.4	145905

ZIP CODE # POST OFFICE NAME	FINANCIAL SERVICES				THE HOME						ENTERTAINMENT						PERSONAL			
					Home Improvements		Furnishings													
	Auto Loan	Home Loan	Invest-ments	Retire-ment Plans	Home Repair	Lawn & Garden	Comput-ers & Hard-ware	Major Appli-ances	TV, Radio, Sound Equip-ment	Furni-ture	Dine out/ Carry out	Sports Equip-ment	Fees & Tickets	Toys & Games	Travel	Cable TV	Apparel & Services	Auto Repairs	Health Insur-ance	Pets & Supplies
98225 BELLINGHAM	67	59	72	63	58	64	75	66	74	70	92	83	70	89	69	69	89	73	63	73
98226 BELLINGHAM	86	89	91	89	89	92	86	87	85	86	106	103	87	107	86	83	103	87	84	100
98229 BELLINGHAM	84	93	107	95	91	94	93	90	89	92	112	107	95	114	93	86	111	91	83	99
98230 BLAINE	99	88	73	84	94	105	84	94	90	85	109	105	81	104	87	93	102	92	105	116
98232 BOW	101	116	121	116	116	117	107	108	101	107	127	126	111	131	109	99	125	105	100	121
98233 BURLINGTON	92	92	93	94	92	97	92	92	90	92	112	108	92	112	91	88	109	92	88	103
98236 CLINTON	104	97	85	94	102	110	92	100	95	92	116	116	90	116	95	97	111	98	107	123
98237 CONCRETE	80	61	38	56	66	75	60	69	67	60	80	81	54	77	60	70	74	69	80	91
98239 COUPEVILLE	84	84	82	80	86	98	81	86	84	81	103	92	82	100	85	88	99	84	94	97
98240 CUSTER	109	103	85	99	106	112	95	103	98	95	120	122	94	123	97	99	115	100	107	129
98241 DARRINGTON	75	58	38	55	63	73	60	67	67	58	80	77	55	77	60	71	73	67	79	84
98244 DEMING	95	97	90	96	96	98	91	94	89	92	111	111	91	112	91	86	108	93	89	109
98245 EASTSOUND	139	110	76	99	123	138	103	124	117	103	138	145	93	136	110	125	129	122	147	169
98247 EVERSON	85	80	68	79	82	87	77	81	78	77	97	95	76	97	77	78	92	80	82	97
98248 FERNDALE	92	82	66	79	86	92	80	86	83	79	102	101	77	102	80	84	97	85	91	106
98249 FREELAND	93	86	78	81	92	104	81	91	86	83	105	98	80	98	86	91	99	89	103	109
98250 FRIDAY HARBOR	138	119	98	113	128	146	114	130	122	117	149	140	109	135	119	128	139	127	148	158
98251 GOLD BAR	91	85	71	82	86	91	81	87	82	82	101	101	77	98	81	81	97	86	87	104
98252 GRANITE FALLS	92	97	93	97	95	96	92	93	88	93	110	110	92	111	91	85	108	92	85	105
98253 GREENBANK	100	98	97	93	102	118	91	100	95	96	118	101	93	104	98	100	112	98	114	113
98257 LA CONNER	100	98	100	96	102	115	93	101	95	97	118	107	94	107	98	98	113	99	110	115
98258 LAKE STEVENS	106	116	114	119	113	113	108	108	102	110	128	128	110	129	107	97	126	107	97	121
98260 LANGLEY	93	90	84	87	93	100	86	92	88	86	108	106	85	108	88	89	104	91	96	109
98261 LOPEZ ISLAND	120	94	64	85	106	119	89	107	100	88	119	125	79	118	95	107	111	105	126	146
98262 LUMMI ISLAND	115	90	61	81	101	114	85	102	96	84	114	120	76	112	90	103	106	101	121	140
98264 LYNDEN	97	86	75	85	90	98	86	92	89	85	108	109	81	106	86	89	102	92	97	112
98266 MAPLE FALLS	77	71	56	68	71	75	67	72	68	69	84	84	64	80	67	67	81	72	72	86
98267 MARBLEMOUNT	121	105	77	99	111	120	97	109	104	97	126	130	94	128	100	107	120	106	119	142
98270 MARYSVILLE	92	96	97	98	94	97	93	93	90	94	113	109	94	113	92	87	110	93	86	104
98271 MARYSVILLE	95	101	99	101	99	102	95	97	92	97	115	113	96	114	95	89	112	96	91	109
98272 MONROE	99	108	112	112	105	105	103	102	97	105	123	121	105	124	102	92	121	101	91	112
98273 MOUNT VERNON	94	90	85	89	91	97	89	93	90	90	112	108	87	110	89	89	108	93	93	106
98274 MOUNT VERNON	96	103	111	104	104	108	100	101	97	99	121	119	102	123	101	95	118	100	97	114
98275 MUKILTEO	119	133	145	139	129	130	126	123	118	128	150	145	132	151	125	112	149	122	109	136
98277 OAK HARBOR	84	79	79	81	76	81	84	81	83	83	103	98	81	101	80	79	101	84	76	91
98278 OAK HARBOR	52	33	31	38	30	36	49	42	49	45	62	56	42	55	40	45	59	50	39	48
98279 OLGA	118	106	95	99	114	133	98	113	106	104	130	116	97	113	107	113	121	111	133	135
98281 POINT ROBERTS	99	77	53	70	87	98	73	88	83	72	98	103	65	97	78	88	91	87	104	120
98282 CAMANO ISLAND	102	100	92	96	104	114	92	101	95	94	117	112	93	114	97	98	112	98	108	121
98283 ROCKPORT	89	68	42	62	75	83	65	76	73	65	87	91	59	86	66	77	81	75	88	103
98284 SEDRO WOOLLEY	89	85	74	84	86	91	82	86	83	82	102	101	81	102	82	82	98	85	87	102
98288 SKYKOMISH	90	71	48	64	79	89	67	80	75	66	89	94	59	88	71	80	83	79	95	110
98290 SNOHOMISH	106	121	125	122	119	119	113	112	106	113	134	132	116	138	113	103	132	110	103	125
98292 STANWOOD	102	109	109	110	109	111	103	105	100	103	124	123	105	126	103	97	121	103	99	119
98294 SULTAN	90	89	80	89	90	93	85	89	85	85	105	104	84	105	85	83	101	88	86	104
98295 SUMAS	82	72	57	71	75	82	72	77	75	71	92	88	69	91	71	76	87	76	82	91
98296 SNOHOMISH	136	162	166	166	157	154	145	144	134	148	169	168	153	175	145	127	168	139	126	158
98303 ANDERSON ISLAND	95	88	85	84	94	110	82	93	86	88	108	91	83	89	89	92	101	90	109	106
98304 ASHFORD	79	66	50	64	70	79	66	73	71	65	86	83	63	85	67	73	80	71	80	89
98305 BEAVER	78	54	28	51	63	71	54	66	62	53	73	80	46	71	56	65	66	65	79	93
98310 BREMERTON	64	67	75	67	67	73	69	68	68	67	85	79	69	86	69	68	82	68	67	75
98311 BREMERTON	90	104	108	105	101	101	96	96	90	97	114	113	100	117	96	86	113	94	85	105
98312 BREMERTON	79	78	83	79	77	82	81	80	80	80	100	94	81	100	80	79	98	81	77	89
98315 SILVERDALE	64	41	40	47	38	45	61	53	62	57	77	70	52	69	50	56	74	62	49	60
98320 BRINNON	71	55	38	50	62	70	52	63	59	52	70	74	47	69	56	63	65	62	75	86
98321 BUCKLEY	97	104	98	104	101	102	97	98	92	98	116	115	97	116	96	88	114	97	89	111
98323 CARBONADO	99	109	109	111	105	104	104	103	97	105	123	122	104	123	101	92	121	102	90	113
98325 CHIMACUM	78	71	55	68	72	76	67	72	69	68	84	84	64	81	67	68	81	72	73	88
98326 CLALLAM BAY	19	15	10	14	17	19	14	17	16	14	19	20	13	19	15	17	18	17	20	24
98327 DUPONT	100	111	107	116	106	103	101	100	93	105	118	117	103	118	98	86	116	98	85	110
98328 EATONVILLE	101	93	77	90	96	103	89	96	92	90	113	111	87	113	90	93	108	94	99	115
98329 GIG HARBOR	100	105	99	104	104	106	98	101	95	99	118	119	99	120	98	92	116	99	95	116
98330 ELBE	76	63	46	60	68	76	62	70	68	61	82	81	58	81	64	70	76	69	79	88
98331 FORKS	67	61	50	60	61	66	60	63	61	60	75	73	57	73	59	61	72	63	64	74
98332 GIG HARBOR	118	138	146	136	137	142	126	127	121	126	151	147	133	158	130	120	149	124	121	142
98333 FOX ISLAND	132	162	177	162	160	163	147	147	137	147	173	169	156	180	151	135	172	142	136	161
98335 GIG HARBOR	113	133	149	135	131	133	125	123	118	124	149	144	131	154	127	115	147	121	113	136
98336 GLENOMA	79	53	24	46	60	69	51	64	62	52	72	76	43	68	52	66	66	63	79	91
98337 BREMERTON	51	48	57	51	48	51	56	52	55	54	69	64	54	68	53	52	67	55	48	57
98338 GRAHAM	99	103	94	103	102	103	96	99	93	98	116	116	96	115	95	90	113	97	92	113
98339 PORT HADLOCK	69	61	49	60	63	70	60	65	63	61	77	73	58	73	60	63	73	64	69	76
98340 HANSVILLE	116	112	109	107	117	136	103	116	107	110	134	115	105	114	111	114	126	112	132	132
98342 INDIANOLA	99	110	108	114	105	103	102	101	94	104	119	118	103	119	99	88	117	99	86	110
98345 KEYPORT	90	109	121	107	107	109	101	100	97	100	122	116	108	129	104	95	121	98	93	109
98346 KINGSTON	92	106	110	106	104	106	98	98	92	98	116	114	101	118	99	89	114	96	90	109
98349 LAKEBAY	104	87	63	81	94	103	83	95	89	83	108	110	76	104	85	92	101	94	105	123
98351 LONGBRANCH	101	89	67	84	91	98	84	93	88	86	107	108	79	102	85	88	102	92	97	115
98354 MILTON	85	90	93	92	89	92	88	88	85	88	106	103	89	107	87	82	104	88	83	97
98355 MINERAL	71	54	34	48	61	69	51	62	59	51	69	73	45	68	54	63	64	61	74	85
98356 MORTON	79	57	34	54	64	74	60	69	68	58	80	80	52	76	60	72	73	69	83	89
98358 NORDLAND	86	80	77	76	85	100	74	85	79	80	98	83	75	81	81	84	91	82	99	97
98359 OLALLA	106	103	89	101	103	107	98	103	97	99	121	120	95	118	97	95	117	102	99	120
98360 ORTING	104	104	90	104	102	105	97	101	95	100	118	117	96	116	96	92	114	99	95	115
98361 PACKWOOD	88	69	47	62	77	87	65	78	73	64	87	91	58	86	69	78	81	77	92	107
98362 PORT ANGELES	75	65	57	63	69	78	67	72	71	66	86	81	64	83	68	74	81	72	81	85
98363 PORT ANGELES	77	68	60	67	72	78	68	74	71	67	87	87	65	87	69	72	83	73	79	90
98365 PORT LUDLOW	113	105	100	100	111	131	97	111	103	104	128	109	99	107	106	110	120	107	129	127
98366 PORT ORCHARD	79	85	89	86	85	87	83	83	80	82	100	97	84	102	83	78	98	82	78	92
98367 PORT ORCHARD	99	103	96	102	103	106	96	99	94	96	117	116	97	118	97	92	114	97	95	115
98368 PORT TOWNSEND	82	82	83	80	83	92	79	83	80	80	99	91	79	94	81	81	95	82	87	94
98370 POULSBO	89	105	114	105	104	106	97	97	92	97	115	112	102	119	99	90	114	95	90	107
98371 PUYALLUP	89	94	94	93	95	99	90	92	89	89	111	107	92	113	91	89	108	91	91	105
98372 PUYALLUP	90	90	93	93	89	93	90	90	88	91	110	105	90	108	88	85	107	90	85	101
98373 PUYALLUP	93	97	104	101	94	96	97	94	92	98	117	112	98	116	94	87	115	95	84	104
98374 PUYALLUP	100	108	113	111	105	107	103	102	98	105	124	119	105	123	102	94	121	102	93	113
WASHINGTON	94	96	103	97	95	100	96	95	94	96	118	112	96	118	95	92	115	96	91	107
UNITED STATES	100	100	100	100	100	100	100	100	100	100	100	100	100	100	100	100	100	100	100	100

POPULATION CHANGE

#	POST OFFICE NAME	COUNTY FIPS CODE	POPULATION			2000-2004 ANNUAL RATE		HOUSEHOLDS					FAMILIES		
			2000	2004	2009	% Rate	State Centile	2000	2004	2009	% Annual Rate 2000-2004	2004 Average HH Size	2000	2004	% Annual Rate 2000-2004
98375	PUYALLUP	053	14169	16962	19372	4.3	99	4706	5651	6455	4.4	2.99	3844	4573	4.2
98376	QUILCENE	031	1753	1771	1823	0.2	29	758	776	809	0.6	2.28	498	505	0.3
98377	RANDLE	041	2475	2386	2371	-0.9	3	1034	1012	1015	-0.5	2.36	709	687	-0.7
98380	SEABECK	035	4187	4496	4706	1.7	78	1507	1635	1726	1.9	2.75	1185	1279	1.8
98381	SEKIU	009	1872	1886	1937	0.2	26	691	703	730	0.4	2.48	464	469	0.3
98382	SEQUIM	009	21535	23125	24244	1.7	78	9844	10684	11312	2.0	2.14	6662	7178	1.8
98383	SILVERDALE	035	20010	22179	23868	2.5	89	7243	8195	8928	3.0	2.64	5287	5910	2.7
98387	SPANAWAY	053	34149	39099	43501	3.2	96	11501	13026	14391	3.0	2.99	9065	10255	2.9
98388	STEILACOOM	053	5915	6074	6351	0.6	44	2517	2584	2696	0.6	2.35	1727	1755	0.4
98390	SUMNER	053	43606	49101	54360	2.8	94	15422	17300	19094	2.7	2.83	11844	13246	2.7
98392	SUQUAMISH	035	2443	2664	2811	2.1	84	990	1092	1162	2.3	2.44	662	723	2.1
98394	VAUGHN	053	742	759	803	0.5	40	299	307	324	0.6	2.46	219	223	0.4
98402	TACOMA	053	4361	4621	4884	1.4	69	2006	2186	2355	2.0	1.53	360	388	1.8
98403	TACOMA	053	7560	7503	7809	-0.2	14	4135	4081	4235	-0.3	1.81	1606	1571	-0.5
98404	TACOMA	053	30881	31605	33281	0.6	41	10240	10443	10960	0.5	2.99	7320	7399	0.3
98405	TACOMA	053	23901	24202	25317	0.3	31	9654	9799	10265	0.4	2.35	5126	5125	0.0
98406	TACOMA	053	22602	22947	24153	0.4	34	9538	9670	10177	0.3	2.23	5494	5498	0.0
98407	TACOMA	053	19511	19565	20368	0.1	21	8358	8371	8697	0.0	2.31	5116	5063	-0.2
98408	TACOMA	053	19124	19298	20223	0.2	27	7202	7252	7584	0.2	2.62	4750	4727	-0.1
98409	TACOMA	053	22151	22980	24269	0.9	52	8751	9054	9537	0.8	2.51	5393	5510	0.5
98416	TACOMA	053	953	964	980	0.3	31	13	13	14	0.0	2.54	7	7	0.0
98418	TACOMA	053	10405	10192	10568	-0.5	8	3886	3794	3923	-0.6	2.65	2492	2407	-0.8
98421	TACOMA	053	603	643	676	1.5	74	33	38	43	3.4	2.55	17	19	2.7
98422	TACOMA	053	19086	20382	21864	1.6	74	7140	7622	8178	1.6	2.65	5405	5709	1.3
98424	TACOMA	053	5683	5976	6381	1.2	64	2456	2569	2734	1.1	2.31	1376	1421	0.8
98430	CAMP MURRAY	053	15	18	20	4.4	99	11	13	15	4.0	1.38	6	6	0.0
98433	TACOMA	053	19686	19650	20225	0.0	18	3581	3571	3739	-0.1	3.76	3495	3482	-0.1
98438	MCCHORD AFB	053	513	502	519	-0.5	7	52	51	53	-0.5	2.57	51	49	-0.9
98439	LAKEWOOD	053	6292	6293	6589	0.0	20	2042	2045	2149	0.0	2.81	1581	1566	-0.2
98443	TACOMA	053	5575	5717	6003	0.6	43	2058	2109	2208	0.6	2.70	1565	1591	0.4
98444	TACOMA	053	31122	32226	34003	0.8	51	11575	11967	12627	0.8	2.55	7446	7619	0.5
98445	TACOMA	053	24630	26977	29247	2.2	85	8930	9780	10587	2.2	2.75	6676	7240	1.9
98446	TACOMA	053	8070	8518	9069	1.3	66	3005	3169	3367	1.3	2.67	2266	2367	1.0
98447	TACOMA	053	81	78	82	-0.9	2	36	35	36	-0.7	2.23	20	20	0.0
98465	TACOMA	053	7222	7408	7758	0.6	43	3332	3405	3559	0.5	2.14	1716	1734	0.3
98466	TACOMA	053	24991	25740	27099	0.7	46	10742	11065	11632	0.7	2.32	6816	6947	0.5
98467	UNIVERSITY PLACE	053	14777	15506	16518	1.1	62	5719	5992	6370	1.1	2.55	4076	4228	0.9
98498	LAKEWOOD	053	28442	29561	31334	0.9	54	11176	11619	12316	0.9	2.43	7519	7724	0.6
98499	LAKEWOOD	053	29117	30907	33091	1.4	70	12230	12941	13811	1.3	2.37	7419	7748	1.0
98501	OLYMPIA	067	33584	34779	36585	0.8	52	14078	14666	15529	1.0	2.35	8688	9030	0.9
98502	OLYMPIA	067	25536	26790	28366	1.1	64	10687	11349	12149	1.4	2.26	6379	6679	1.1
98503	LACEY	067	33300	35297	37439	1.4	69	13199	14112	15094	1.6	2.47	8926	9501	1.5
98505	OLYMPIA	067	651	718	770	2.3	88	4	5	5	5.4	2.60	3	3	0.0
98506	OLYMPIA	067	16989	17847	18836	1.2	64	7246	7685	8183	1.4	2.25	4219	4454	1.3
98512	OLYMPIA	067	24008	25334	26794	1.3	66	9594	10254	10952	1.6	2.42	6455	6829	1.3
98513	OLYMPIA	067	23984	25459	27048	1.4	70	8686	9336	10008	1.7	2.73	6773	7252	1.6
98516	OLYMPIA	067	13878	14568	15298	1.2	63	5287	5624	5962	1.5	2.59	3877	4105	1.4
98520	ABERDEEN	027	21485	20931	20499	-0.6	5	8512	8283	8117	-0.6	2.50	5591	5417	-0.7
98524	ALLYN	045	1633	1823	1977	2.6	91	699	789	863	2.9	2.31	515	577	2.7
98526	AMANDA PARK	027	453	446	439	-0.4	10	167	165	163	-0.3	2.70	124	122	-0.4
98528	BELFAIR	045	7763	7889	8169	0.4	35	3004	3075	3204	0.6	2.55	2129	2164	0.4
98531	CENTRALIA	041	21453	21510	21729	0.1	21	8462	8526	8655	0.2	2.45	5502	5505	0.0
98532	CHEHALIS	041	21107	21814	22308	0.8	49	7803	8130	8361	1.0	2.62	5705	5924	0.9
98533	CINEBAR	041	588	604	612	0.6	44	225	235	240	1.0	2.57	164	170	0.9
98535	COPALIS BEACH	027	227	214	206	-1.4	1	97	92	89	-1.2	2.33	60	56	-1.6
98536	COPALIS CROSSING	027	639	645	641	0.2	28	297	301	301	0.3	2.14	188	188	0.0
98537	COSMOPOLIS	027	2052	2046	2024	-0.1	17	814	814	807	0.0	2.51	581	577	-0.2
98538	CURTIS	041	330	338	342	0.6	42	124	128	131	0.8	2.64	97	100	0.7
98541	ELMA	027	9240	9506	9590	0.7	45	3468	3580	3624	0.8	2.64	2458	2525	0.6
98542	ETHEL	041	499	521	532	1.0	59	185	195	201	1.3	2.67	143	149	1.0
98546	GRAPEVIEW	045	1870	1996	2115	1.6	74	808	869	926	1.7	2.30	597	637	1.5
98547	GRAYLAND	027	1778	1792	1785	0.2	26	848	863	867	0.4	2.08	496	500	0.2
98548	HOODSPORT	045	1809	1867	1942	0.8	49	883	919	962	0.9	2.03	581	600	0.8
98550	HOQUIAM	027	11611	11351	11140	-0.5	7	4571	4482	4410	-0.5	2.51	2955	2882	-0.6
98552	HUMPTULIPS	027	252	262	265	0.9	54	96	100	102	1.0	2.62	73	75	0.6
98555	LILLIWAUP	045	440	455	474	0.8	50	227	237	248	1.0	1.92	145	150	0.8
98557	MCCLEARY	027	2628	2725	2748	0.9	52	1023	1068	1082	1.0	2.48	734	762	0.9
98560	MATLOCK	045	152	162	171	1.5	73	56	61	65	2.0	2.66	39	41	1.2
98562	MOCLIPS	027	598	598	591	0.0	20	265	267	265	0.2	2.24	142	141	-0.2
98563	MONTESANO	031	7455	7327	7204	-0.4	9	2936	2913	2884	-0.2	2.46	2090	2061	-0.3
98564	MOSSYROCK	041	2303	2287	2287	-0.2	14	878	880	885	0.1	2.60	645	641	-0.2
98568	OAKVILLE	027	2334	2442	2472	1.1	60	796	834	847	1.1	2.93	591	615	0.9
98569	OCEAN SHORES	027	4083	4505	4682	2.3	88	1919	2130	2225	2.5	2.12	1278	1406	2.3
98570	ONALASKA	041	3708	3750	3773	0.3	31	1363	1398	1419	0.6	2.68	1032	1051	0.4
98571	PACIFIC BEACH	027	125	126	125	0.2	26	46	47	47	0.5	2.68	28	28	0.0
98572	PE ELL	041	871	887	894	0.4	37	329	336	340	0.5	2.64	239	242	0.3
98575	QUINAULT	027	499	462	442	-1.8	0	190	177	170	-1.7	2.61	135	125	-1.8
98576	RAINIER	067	3620	3776	3990	1.0	57	1337	1415	1509	1.3	2.67	997	1048	1.2
98577	RAYMOND	049	6461	6547	6682	0.3	32	2614	2680	2768	0.6	2.42	1771	1804	0.4
98579	ROCHESTER	067	9979	11291	12328	3.0	95	3511	4021	4430	3.2	2.76	2699	3069	3.1
98580	ROY	053	8927	9884	10764	2.4	89	3067	3399	3697	2.5	2.89	2422	2665	2.3
98581	RYDERWOOD	015	422	426	426	0.2	28	242	247	248	0.5	1.72	164	166	0.3
98582	SALKUM	041	329	345	354	1.1	61	139	147	152	1.3	2.35	107	112	1.1
98584	SHELTON	045	31589	33098	34848	1.1	60	11473	12146	12921	1.4	2.54	8154	8601	1.3
98585	SILVER CREEK	041	597	606	610	0.4	34	238	245	249	0.7	2.47	176	180	0.5
98586	SOUTH BEND	049	2450	2405	2393	-0.4	9	959	945	948	-0.4	2.47	651	638	-0.5
98587	TAHOLAH	027	909	935	938	0.7	45	266	276	279	0.9	3.39	206	213	0.7
98588	TAHUYA	045	1651	1692	1757	0.6	42	695	716	747	0.7	2.36	472	482	0.5
98589	TENINO	067	6746	7334	7855	2.0	83	2475	2728	2950	2.3	2.69	1879	2057	2.2
98590	TOKELAND	049	450	449	448	-0.1	17	196	197	198	0.1	2.28	127	127	0.0
98591	TOLEDO	041	2856	2791	2783	-0.5	6	1067	1053	1057	-0.3	2.65	803	788	-0.4
98592	UNION	045	1309	1382	1458	1.3	67	601	638	678	1.4	2.17	432	456	1.3
98593	VADER	041	925	1041	1108	2.8	93	322	362	385	2.8	2.88	244	273	2.7
98595	WESTPORT	027	2793	2845	2840	0.4	37	1312	1347	1352	0.6	2.11	732	745	0.4
98596	WINLOCK	041	6636	7032	7254	1.4	69	2414	2576	2671	1.5	2.73	1838	1951	1.4
	WASHINGTON					1.1					1.3	2.52			1.2
	UNITED STATES					1.2					1.3	2.58			1.1

ZIP CODE #	POST OFFICE NAME	RACE (%) White 2000	White 2004	Black 2000	Black 2004	Asian/Pacific 2000	Asian/Pacific 2004	% Hispanic Origin 2000	% Hispanic Origin 2004	2004 AGE DISTRIBUTION (%) 0-4	5-9	10-14	15-19	20-24	25-44	45-64	65-84	85+	18+	MEDIAN AGE 2004	% 2004 Males	% 2004 Females
98375	PUYALLUP	86.7	85.6	2.4	2.6	4.1	4.5	4.4	5.1	7.8	7.9	9.1	7.9	6.6	30.6	23.3	6.1	0.6	70.2	33.7	49.7	50.3
98376	QUILCENE	89.6	88.8	0.8	0.8	0.9	1.0	1.6	1.9	3.3	6.6	6.9	6.3	3.4	21.3	36.8	13.8	1.5	79.0	46.0	50.4	49.6
98377	RANDLE	96.0	95.7	0.3	0.3	0.3	0.3	2.0	2.3	4.8	5.7	6.9	6.8	4.2	21.4	32.7	15.8	1.6	78.3	45.1	50.8	49.2
98380	SEABECK	92.1	91.4	0.3	0.3	1.9	2.1	3.0	3.6	5.1	5.7	8.9	8.0	5.4	26.5	31.2	8.5	0.7	75.1	40.1	52.0	48.0
98381	SEKIU	31.2	29.5	2.1	2.3	0.6	0.6	6.2	6.7	8.6	7.5	9.1	9.5	8.5	29.0	21.3	6.1	0.4	69.3	30.0	56.3	43.7
98382	SEQUIM	94.3	93.8	0.2	0.2	1.4	1.6	2.3	2.7	4.0	4.2	4.7	4.3	3.8	14.6	30.3	29.5	4.7	84.5	55.5	47.0	53.0
98383	SILVERDALE	79.7	77.9	3.0	3.4	10.2	10.8	4.3	5.2	6.8	6.6	7.3	7.8	11.5	28.6	23.2	7.1	1.1	74.7	31.9	50.5	49.5
98387	SPANAWAY	76.6	74.5	7.0	7.5	6.6	7.2	5.2	6.2	8.4	8.0	8.6	7.8	7.0	31.6	22.1	6.2	0.4	70.2	32.4	49.7	50.4
98388	STEILACOOM	78.2	76.3	6.5	7.0	7.1	7.8	5.3	6.3	5.6	5.5	6.1	6.2	6.2	27.3	27.3	14.7	1.2	79.2	40.4	48.6	51.4
98390	SUMNER	93.1	92.2	0.6	0.7	1.5	1.7	3.6	4.3	7.2	7.4	8.6	7.8	6.5	30.3	24.9	6.6	0.7	71.9	35.3	50.2	49.8
98392	SUQUAMISH	80.5	79.2	0.4	0.5	2.7	3.0	3.1	3.7	6.5	7.0	6.9	6.4	6.0	27.1	30.0	8.9	1.2	75.7	38.9	49.7	50.3
98394	VAUGHN	94.7	94.1	0.1	0.1	1.1	1.2	2.0	2.6	5.1	5.5	7.6	6.6	3.7	23.1	34.7	12.9	0.8	77.7	44.1	51.0	49.0
98402	TACOMA	68.8	66.7	16.3	17.2	5.7	6.2	5.1	5.8	3.3	2.8	2.4	3.2	7.6	42.1	22.9	11.7	4.1	90.7	39.6	59.9	40.1
98403	TACOMA	86.7	85.3	4.0	4.3	2.6	2.8	3.8	4.5	4.8	4.1	4.4	5.1	8.2	35.8	26.1	9.6	1.8	83.7	37.2	47.6	52.4
98404	TACOMA	53.4	51.2	12.8	13.2	14.4	15.1	13.1	14.8	8.4	8.1	9.0	8.5	7.6	28.0	20.9	8.3	1.3	69.3	31.4	49.3	50.7
98405	TACOMA	59.1	57.4	21.5	22.2	8.1	8.3	6.2	7.1	7.3	6.5	7.3	7.6	7.9	29.7	20.6	9.8	3.3	74.4	34.1	48.0	52.0
98406	TACOMA	85.3	84.0	4.6	4.9	3.9	4.3	3.3	4.0	5.0	4.8	5.6	8.1	9.7	25.5	24.4	13.1	3.8	80.5	38.7	46.9	53.1
98407	TACOMA	85.9	84.6	4.5	4.8	3.3	3.6	3.3	4.0	5.2	5.2	6.1	6.6	6.4	26.5	28.2	12.9	2.9	79.5	41.2	47.6	52.4
98408	TACOMA	68.5	66.2	10.3	10.8	9.9	10.6	6.8	7.8	7.0	6.6	7.7	7.3	7.2	28.6	23.3	10.7	1.7	74.2	35.8	49.0	51.0
98409	TACOMA	63.4	61.0	15.4	16.2	7.7	8.1	9.3	10.7	8.9	7.7	7.6	7.5	9.5	31.2	19.0	7.4	1.4	71.5	30.2	49.1	51.0
98416	TACOMA	83.4	81.9	1.1	1.1	8.4	9.2	2.0	2.4	1.6	0.9	1.9	42.4	38.4	6.6	5.5	2.4	0.3	94.1	20.4	39.1	60.9
98418	TACOMA	68.3	65.9	10.3	10.9	8.3	8.8	8.0	9.4	8.1	7.2	7.7	7.9	8.0	30.6	21.5	7.7	1.3	72.3	32.8	50.0	50.0
98421	TACOMA	90.9	90.1	2.0	2.2	1.7	1.9	1.7	2.0	0.6	1.4	3.0	6.1	12.4	43.4	28.8	4.0	0.3	93.5	34.5	70.5	29.6
98422	TACOMA	79.4	77.4	5.2	5.6	8.6	9.5	3.8	4.6	7.6	7.4	7.6	6.6	6.1	31.6	25.7	6.7	0.5	73.1	35.8	49.8	50.2
98424	TACOMA	72.0	69.3	6.0	6.6	7.0	7.8	11.8	13.4	8.7	6.8	6.6	6.3	10.1	33.5	19.9	7.3	0.8	74.3	30.9	51.3	48.7
98430	CAMP MURRAY	66.7	66.7	13.3	11.1	0.0	0.0	13.3	11.1	11.1	5.6	5.6	5.6	11.1	44.4	16.7	0.0	0.0	77.8	30.0	55.6	44.4
98433	TACOMA	60.5	57.9	20.3	21.3	5.2	5.5	13.1	15.1	12.6	9.4	6.4	8.5	25.1	35.3	2.2	0.4	0.1	69.3	22.6	63.4	36.6
98438	MCCHORD AFB	76.4	74.1	8.6	9.2	4.7	5.2	8.2	9.8	13.2	11.0	8.2	6.8	21.7	37.3	2.0	0.0	0.0	65.1	22.5	56.0	44.0
98439	LAKEWOOD	70.8	68.3	12.2	13.1	4.9	5.2	10.0	11.7	13.1	10.2	7.8	7.8	18.3	34.6	6.5	1.5	0.1	65.4	23.0	52.4	47.6
98443	TACOMA	89.5	88.5	2.0	2.2	2.0	2.2	3.1	3.7	5.3	5.8	7.3	7.5	5.7	25.3	29.8	11.6	1.6	76.7	41.0	49.6	50.4
98444	TACOMA	64.4	62.1	12.6	13.2	11.3	12.0	7.2	8.3	8.4	7.0	6.7	8.7	12.7	28.9	18.6	8.1	1.1	74.1	28.7	48.4	51.6
98445	TACOMA	73.2	70.9	8.2	8.9	8.5	9.2	5.0	6.0	7.1	6.6	7.7	7.4	7.4	28.1	24.4	10.3	1.0	74.0	35.9	49.0	51.0
98446	TACOMA	85.5	84.0	3.1	3.4	4.0	4.4	3.5	4.3	6.2	6.5	7.4	6.6	5.8	28.0	26.7	11.5	1.4	75.9	38.9	49.7	50.3
98447	TACOMA	80.3	78.2	0.0	0.0	11.1	11.5	1.2	2.6	2.6	2.6	1.3	1.3	9.0	44.9	24.4	14.1	0.0	93.6	35.0	46.2	53.9
98465	TACOMA	76.0	74.0	9.3	9.9	6.7	7.4	5.0	5.9	5.6	5.1	5.5	5.9	8.3	28.5	24.3	13.5	3.3	80.4	38.7	47.9	52.1
98466	TACOMA	79.6	77.8	8.1	8.7	5.6	6.2	3.6	4.3	5.7	5.5	6.6	7.0	7.6	26.3	26.0	13.9	1.6	78.1	39.1	47.1	52.9
98467	UNIVERSITY PLACE	70.9	68.4	10.3	10.8	10.6	11.8	4.6	5.4	7.4	7.1	7.6	7.2	7.5	27.4	26.0	8.8	1.2	73.5	35.1	47.9	52.2
98498	LAKEWOOD	69.8	67.6	11.0	11.6	9.4	10.2	6.1	7.1	6.0	5.6	6.2	6.4	7.7	26.5	25.9	14.4	1.4	78.5	39.5	49.1	50.9
98499	LAKEWOOD	59.5	56.6	13.5	14.3	12.9	13.7	10.4	11.9	8.2	6.8	6.5	6.6	9.5	29.1	21.0	11.0	1.3	74.8	32.8	48.8	51.2
98501	OLYMPIA	88.8	87.8	1.2	1.3	4.0	4.4	3.8	4.5	5.8	6.0	6.9	6.7	7.6	27.5	27.7	10.1	1.6	77.3	38.2	48.5	51.5
98502	OLYMPIA	86.4	85.2	1.6	1.7	6.1	6.6	3.9	4.7	5.0	5.1	6.0	7.2	10.4	26.9	27.0	10.5	1.8	80.3	36.8	48.3	51.7
98503	LACEY	79.9	78.5	4.4	4.5	7.3	7.9	6.2	7.2	7.3	6.8	7.0	6.6	7.8	27.7	23.1	11.0	2.6	74.9	35.4	47.9	52.1
98505	OLYMPIA	86.9	85.9	1.7	1.8	5.2	5.7	2.3	2.7	4.3	5.2	5.6	15.3	24.9	21.9	19.4	3.3	0.1	82.0	23.9	50.7	49.3
98506	OLYMPIA	88.5	87.9	1.6	1.6	4.0	4.3	3.5	4.0	5.3	5.3	6.0	6.1	7.0	27.8	27.7	11.9	2.8	79.7	40.0	48.1	51.9
98512	OLYMPIA	90.3	89.5	1.4	1.5	3.0	3.3	3.2	3.7	5.4	5.5	6.5	7.3	8.0	27.5	28.2	9.9	1.7	78.2	38.7	49.9	50.1
98513	OLYMPIA	78.0	76.5	4.6	4.9	7.5	8.0	5.3	6.2	6.8	7.1	7.3	6.7	6.6	29.5	27.1	8.1	0.8	74.7	36.5	49.0	51.0
98516	OLYMPIA	80.2	79.0	4.2	4.2	8.4	8.9	4.8	5.5	6.4	6.8	7.2	6.3	6.3	26.6	29.8	9.6	1.0	75.8	38.8	49.6	50.5
98520	ABERDEEN	87.0	86.9	0.4	0.4	1.9	2.0	7.5	7.6	6.9	6.6	6.9	7.1	7.5	24.9	25.5	12.5	2.0	75.3	37.5	49.6	50.4
98524	ALLYN	92.9	92.4	0.4	0.5	1.0	1.0	2.0	2.5	4.1	4.4	5.4	5.2	4.7	15.0	35.4	24.0	1.8	82.9	51.0	51.1	48.9
98526	AMANDA PARK	47.9	46.0	0.0	0.0	0.4	0.5	6.8	7.2	7.2	7.9	9.4	7.9	6.7	24.7	27.6	8.1	0.7	70.4	33.8	53.8	46.2
98528	BELFAIR	90.2	89.2	0.7	0.7	2.4	2.6	3.7	4.5	5.8	6.1	7.5	7.1	5.6	25.4	29.0	12.4	1.1	75.9	40.5	50.3	49.7
98531	CENTRALIA	90.5	89.5	0.5	0.5	1.2	1.3	8.7	10.2	7.3	6.3	6.4	7.2	8.1	24.1	23.3	14.0	3.4	75.8	37.5	48.3	51.7
98532	CHEHALIS	92.9	92.2	0.6	0.7	1.0	1.1	5.0	5.8	6.7	6.8	7.3	7.8	7.3	24.8	25.5	11.8	2.0	74.2	37.0	50.2	49.8
98533	CINEBAR	95.8	95.4	0.2	0.2	0.5	0.7	2.0	2.2	4.1	7.3	7.1	6.8	4.8	22.4	31.0	15.6	1.0	76.8	43.2	50.7	49.3
98535	COPALIS BEACH	90.8	90.7	0.4	0.5	0.9	0.9	1.8	1.4	4.7	5.1	5.1	4.2	4.2	18.7	38.8	17.3	1.9	82.2	49.1	50.0	50.0
98536	COPALIS CROSSING	90.1	90.2	0.2	0.2	2.0	2.0	1.7	1.7	3.9	4.0	5.1	6.4	5.6	17.1	35.5	21.1	1.4	83.1	49.0	49.2	50.9
98537	COSMOPOLIS	91.4	91.3	0.1	0.1	1.8	1.8	3.2	3.3	5.9	6.4	7.7	6.4	6.3	25.8	27.9	12.2	1.6	76.2	40.2	49.5	50.5
98538	CURTIS	92.7	92.3	0.0	0.0	0.3	0.3	4.2	4.7	5.6	6.2	7.7	7.7	6.5	20.4	30.5	13.0	2.4	75.2	42.1	50.0	50.0
98541	ELMA	91.7	91.6	0.5	0.5	1.2	1.2	3.7	3.8	6.6	6.5	7.4	8.0	7.2	25.6	24.9	12.3	1.4	74.5	37.4	50.2	49.8
98542	ETHEL	94.6	94.2	0.0	0.0	0.8	0.8	3.6	4.4	6.3	6.5	7.1	7.1	6.0	22.5	29.0	14.2	1.3	75.6	41.2	51.1	48.9
98546	GRAPEVIEW	93.8	93.5	0.6	0.6	0.9	0.9	1.9	2.2	3.8	4.2	5.5	5.3	4.0	18.8	33.9	22.9	1.7	83.0	49.8	50.2	49.9
98547	GRAYLAND	92.4	92.2	0.3	0.3	1.2	1.2	2.3	2.5	3.3	3.7	4.6	4.5	4.1	20.2	35.3	21.9	2.5	85.7	50.8	51.3	48.7
98548	HOODSPORT	92.4	91.8	0.3	0.4	1.1	1.1	1.7	2.1	2.6	3.0	4.3	4.8	3.8	15.4	35.0	29.2	1.7	87.0	55.4	50.0	50.0
98550	HOQUIAM	90.1	90.0	0.3	0.3	1.1	1.2	5.1	5.2	6.6	6.6	7.3	7.2	7.2	24.7	26.0	11.9	2.5	75.0	38.1	49.3	50.7
98552	HUMPTULIPS	89.7	89.7	0.4	0.4	0.0	0.0	6.4	6.5	5.7	6.9	8.0	6.5	6.1	24.1	31.7	10.3	0.8	74.4	40.3	51.5	48.5
98555	LILLIWAUP	92.1	91.2	0.2	0.4	1.1	1.3	2.1	2.2	2.4	2.6	3.5	5.1	3.5	13.4	37.1	29.7	2.6	88.4	56.9	49.9	50.1
98557	MCCLEARY	94.1	94.1	0.2	0.2	0.4	0.4	2.0	2.1	6.5	6.7	6.8	6.9	5.7	25.8	26.5	12.3	2.8	75.6	39.3	48.5	51.5
98560	MATLOCK	92.8	92.6	0.0	0.0	1.3	1.9	0.0	0.0	1.9	3.1	5.6	7.4	4.9	20.4	40.1	16.7	0.0	85.2	48.4	50.6	49.4
98562	MOCLIPS	64.7	64.6	0.2	0.2	1.3	1.3	7.2	7.5	5.2	5.5	5.9	5.2	4.4	22.7	35.8	13.9	1.5	79.9	45.7	51.7	48.3
98563	MONTESANO	94.3	94.3	0.1	0.1	0.9	0.9	2.0	2.1	5.8	6.0	6.5	6.8	6.5	25.2	28.8	12.7	1.7	77.5	40.9	49.8	50.2
98564	MOSSYROCK	94.1	93.7	0.3	0.3	0.4	0.4	3.7	4.3	5.8	6.0	7.6	7.1	5.3	22.9	29.3	14.7	1.4	76.0	41.7	50.1	49.9
98568	OAKVILLE	74.9	74.9	0.4	0.4	0.6	0.6	5.1	5.4	8.3	8.1	8.0	7.8	7.0	25.1	24.6	10.2	0.9	70.9	34.5	49.7	50.3
98569	OCEAN SHORES	92.4	92.4	0.6	0.6	1.3	1.3	1.7	1.8	4.3	4.7	4.5	3.8	3.7	17.7	32.9	26.2	2.2	84.2	52.8	48.4	51.6
98570	ONALASKA	95.3	94.8	0.1	0.2	0.4	0.4	3.2	3.9	5.7	6.1	6.8	7.0	6.3	24.1	28.9	13.7	1.5	77.2	41.0	51.1	48.9
98571	PACIFIC BEACH	86.4	86.5	0.0	0.0	1.6	1.6	2.4	2.4	4.0	4.8	4.8	5.6	5.6	17.5	37.3	19.1	1.6	81.8	49.2	49.2	50.8
98572	PE ELL	94.3	93.8	0.3	0.3	1.0	1.1	1.8	2.3	7.6	7.8	8.6	7.3	5.5	23.3	26.4	11.7	1.8	71.5	37.2	51.3	48.7
98575	QUINAULT	85.8	85.7	0.0	0.0	0.2	0.2	9.8	10.0	4.1	5.2	7.8	7.8	6.9	22.3	31.4	13.4	1.1	78.4	42.0	52.4	47.6
98576	RAINIER	93.1	92.6	0.7	0.6	0.9	1.0	2.7	3.2	5.7	6.0	7.3	7.9	6.3	27.3	29.3	9.5	0.7	76.0	39.1	49.0	51.0
98577	RAYMOND	88.8	88.0	0.2	0.2	4.0	4.3	6.1	6.8	5.7	5.9	6.5	7.1	6.2	21.3	28.3	16.2	2.7	77.5	42.9	49.6	50.4
98579	ROCHESTER	90.4	89.7	0.7	0.7	0.8	0.8	6.9	7.9	7.4	7.5	7.6	7.5	6.4	28.2	25.4	9.2	0.9	72.7	35.5	51.0	49.0
98580	ROY	90.0	89.1	1.0	1.1	1.8	1.9	3.8	4.5	6.2	6.9	8.5	8.1	6.0	28.4	27.6	7.7	0.7	73.3	37.2	50.6	49.4
98581	RYDERWOOD	95.0	94.4	1.0	0.9	0.5	0.7	1.9	2.4	4.0	3.5	3.1	3.5	4.0	14.6	28.4	35.5	3.5	87.8	59.2	48.8	51.2
98582	SALKUM	95.1	94.5	0.0	0.0	0.6	0.9	3.7	4.4	6.4	6.7	7.0	7.0	5.8	22.6	28.4	14.8	1.5	75.7	41.2	51.0	49.0
98584	SHELTON	86.7	85.9	1.6	1.6	1.4	1.5	5.9	6.8	5.8	5.8	6.5	6.6	7.2	25.8	26.1	14.2	2.0	78.0	39.8	52.3	47.7
98585	SILVER CREEK	95.0	94.6	0.2	0.2	0.3	0.5	3.5	4.0	4.8	5.9	7.1	7.3	5.0	22.4	31.5	14.7	1.3	77.2	43.2	50.3	49.7
98586	SOUTH BEND	84.0	82.7	0.1	0.2	3.5	3.8	7.8	9.1	5.8	5.9	7.0	7.1	6.0	22.0	26.4	17.2	2.7	76.8	42.1	49.9	50.1
98587	TAHOLAH	18.9	18.8	0.0	0.0	0.7	0.6	4.7	4.8	9.2	9.7	10.5	8.1	6.7	26.5	23.7	5.0	0.4	64.6	29.1	54.8	45.2
98588	TAHUYA	91.8	91.1	0.2	0.2	1.8	2.0	3.0	3.6	3.8	4.8	6.8	6.3	4.0	24.3	33.5	15.4	1.2	81.0	45.0	52.0	48.1
98589	TENINO	92.5	91.8	0.5	0.6	1.4	1.5	3.2	3.8	5.6	6.0	7.4	7.4	6.6	26.7	28.8	10.4	1.1	76.5	39.3	50.4	49.7
98590	TOKELAND	85.3	84.2	0.2	0.2	2.4	2.7	6.0	6.9	5.6	5.8	6.5	6.2	4.9	20.7	28.5	19.6	2.2	78.2	45.2	51.0	49.0
98591	TOLEDO	94.9	94.6	0.3	0.3	0.4	0.4	2.9	3.5	6.5	6.5	7.2	7.4	6.4	23.7	27.8	12.9	1.7	75.4	39.9	50.0	50.0
98592	UNION	93.4	93.0	0.2	0.1	0.9	1.0	2.4	2.8	4.2	4.9	5.4	4.6	2.6	19.5	36.4	21.1	1.5	82.6	50.3	49.9	50.1
98593	VADER	93.5	92.9	0.0	0.0	0.1	0.2	4.4	5.3	7.1	7.3	7.9	7.6	5.8	23.7	27.2	12.1	1.3	73.0	38.6	49.1	50.9
98595	WESTPORT	93.2	93.2	0.3	0.3	0.8	0.8	2.5	2.6	4.3	4.6	5.6	5.9	5.0	20.9	32.9	18.9	1.9	81.9	47.0	50.0	50.0
98596	WINLOCK	92.7	92.0	0.2	0.2	0.7	0.7	5.1	6.0	6.9	7.1	7.8	7.5	6.4	24.0	26.8	12.3	1.2	73.5	38.2	49.3	50.7
	WASHINGTON	81.8	80.6	3.2	3.3	5.9	6.3	7.5	8.6	6.7	6.6	7.1	7.0	7.6	28.7	24.9	9.8	1.6	75.4	36.1	49.7	50.3
	UNITED STATES	75.1	73.6	12.3	12.5	3.8	4.2	12.5	14.1	6.9	6.7	7.2	7.0	7.3	28.6	23.8	10.8	1.7	75.1	36.0	49.1	50.9

#	POST OFFICE NAME	2004 Per Capita Income	2004 HH Income Base	2004 Household Income Distribution (%): Less than $25,000	$25,000 to $49,999	$50,000 to $99,999	$100,000 to $149,999	$150,000 or More	Median Household Income: 2004	2009	2004 National Centile	2004 State Centile	2004 Home Value Base	2004 Home Value Distribution (%): Less than $50,000	$50,000 to $89,999	$90,000 to $174,999	$175,000 to $399,999	$400,000 or More	2004 Median Home Value
98375	PUYALLUP	24473	5651	9.6	25.5	44.5	16.0	4.5	64432	72269	88	88	4815	8.0	6.0	29.5	55.4	1.1	186286
98376	QUILCENE	23095	776	29.9	30.7	29.5	6.6	3.4	41326	45157	51	45	636	6.3	12.1	32.4	41.5	7.7	173188
98377	RANDLE	18154	1012	37.1	40.2	17.8	3.3	1.7	32936	36161	21	12	811	19.1	16.3	45.0	19.1	0.5	111336
98380	SEABECK	25624	1635	14.7	20.3	46.5	14.1	4.3	61940	70355	86	86	1442	0.6	3.5	42.7	42.0	11.2	182566
98381	SEKIU	15670	703	42.5	30.6	22.3	3.1	1.4	30556	33886	14	7	482	13.9	18.9	51.0	15.6	0.6	109223
98382	SEQUIM	25327	10684	27.2	33.9	29.4	5.6	4.0	41165	45711	50	45	8520	6.5	5.1	36.4	43.8	8.2	179502
98383	SILVERDALE	25789	8195	15.2	30.4	37.7	12.4	4.3	53947	60239	78	74	4617	2.7	1.5	28.7	60.0	7.1	201626
98387	SPANAWAY	21113	13026	16.1	27.1	43.7	10.5	2.7	56381	63851	81	78	10375	7.3	5.7	45.3	39.9	1.9	164299
98388	STEILACOOM	31698	2584	16.1	30.9	29.6	12.2	11.2	53398	60766	78	74	1698	0.2	1.6	27.6	52.9	17.7	221617
98390	SUMNER	25756	17300	12.7	24.3	42.5	15.5	5.1	63142	71865	87	87	14102	2.8	5.4	30.0	52.9	8.9	195877
98392	SUQUAMISH	24877	1092	19.0	30.4	35.4	12.1	3.1	50506	56638	73	68	842	4.2	8.2	51.5	29.0	7.1	144729
98394	VAUGHN	25996	307	19.2	28.7	35.5	10.8	5.9	51723	57887	75	71	263	2.3	4.9	33.8	43.4	15.6	195259
98402	TACOMA	17841	2186	66.7	21.1	9.7	1.1	1.4	16919	20190	1	1	124	7.3	8.9	43.6	28.2	12.1	157353
98403	TACOMA	34526	4081	26.5	32.2	24.9	9.4	7.1	41512	49163	51	45	1512	1.1	1.4	19.5	51.1	27.0	275641
98404	TACOMA	15400	10443	31.9	33.4	28.4	4.9	1.6	37600	42642	38	30	6265	3.5	11.6	69.7	14.7	0.6	124356
98405	TACOMA	17986	9799	38.5	31.4	24.0	5.0	1.2	33574	38095	23	13	4465	1.7	9.3	68.2	20.2	0.6	133746
98406	TACOMA	27708	9670	23.9	27.3	33.8	9.9	5.1	48895	55325	70	65	6234	0.9	1.7	38.4	54.9	4.1	187281
98407	TACOMA	28336	8371	19.9	28.0	35.1	12.1	5.0	51737	59286	75	71	5703	0.9	2.0	40.2	49.5	7.4	185177
98408	TACOMA	19783	7252	23.3	35.3	32.7	6.5	2.2	43515	50160	57	50	5028	1.1	6.2	75.0	17.3	0.3	134129
98409	TACOMA	17422	9054	29.8	38.5	26.3	4.0	1.4	36050	40960	32	22	3944	1.6	9.0	79.0	10.1	0.4	119168
98416	TACOMA	11886	13	30.8	15.4	53.9	0.0	0.0	54580	33008	79	75	7	0.0	0.0	14.3	85.7	0.0	225000
98418	TACOMA	17898	3794	25.8	36.7	31.8	4.6	1.0	39965	47303	46	39	2256	1.7	7.1	81.1	10.1	0.0	121947
98421	TACOMA	14137	38	18.4	31.6	34.2	5.3	10.5	50000	56612	72	67	30	23.3	13.3	20.0	20.0	23.3	125000
98422	TACOMA	34110	7622	9.1	19.9	41.9	18.5	10.7	71644	82222	92	95	5889	1.7	0.6	17.1	65.1	15.5	240915
98424	TACOMA	20035	2569	28.5	39.1	25.0	5.8	1.6	37441	41029	37	30	913	14.0	3.8	26.4	49.3	6.5	187153
98430	CAMP MURRAY	18518	13	46.2	53.9	0.0	0.0	0.0	26024	28535	6	2	4	0.0	0.0	100.0	0.0	0.0	112500
98433	TACOMA	13342	3571	19.0	54.6	23.4	2.4	0.6	35742	39432	31	21	72	31.9	22.2	16.7	29.2	0.0	76250
98438	MCCHORD AFB	7356	51	15.7	52.9	27.5	2.0	2.0	37294	40553	36	28	0	0.0	0.0	0.0	0.0	0.0	0
98439	LAKEWOOD	13094	2045	37.2	43.8	15.9	2.2	0.9	30497	33102	13	6	188	70.2	11.2	1.1	7.5	10.1	26875
98443	TACOMA	25940	2109	16.5	24.2	40.7	13.4	5.2	59677	65862	84	83	1816	5.6	2.5	32.4	54.2	5.3	189931
98444	TACOMA	17865	11967	32.4	35.0	26.6	4.6	1.3	35759	39781	31	21	5351	6.0	6.8	61.2	25.0	1.0	140965
98445	TACOMA	22118	9780	19.2	29.1	39.0	9.4	3.3	51276	58535	74	70	7111	5.6	4.1	46.6	42.4	1.4	167343
98446	TACOMA	27641	3169	14.6	28.2	38.3	12.4	6.5	58795	64653	83	82	2647	4.5	3.2	32.1	54.1	6.1	189419
98447	TACOMA	34915	35	0.0	45.7	25.7	17.1	11.4	70763	78919	92	94	18	0.0	0.0	44.4	55.6	0.0	256250
98465	TACOMA	22415	3405	35.7	28.6	25.5	8.1	2.2	34874	38149	27	18	1597	1.4	4.1	43.3	42.4	8.8	177372
98466	TACOMA	28405	11065	19.1	29.6	34.4	11.3	5.6	51185	57693	74	69	6311	0.2	1.8	30.4	60.2	7.4	202524
98467	UNIVERSITY PLACE	29399	5992	17.6	28.7	31.7	15.1	7.0	55006	61210	80	76	3743	2.1	2.0	17.1	72.0	6.9	231018
98498	LAKEWOOD	26124	11619	24.0	28.8	31.1	10.6	5.5	47039	52873	66	59	7176	0.7	3.2	39.3	50.8	6.0	184971
98499	LAKEWOOD	20395	12941	33.8	33.6	24.1	6.0	2.6	35491	38795	29	20	5671	16.8	3.9	39.0	34.0	6.3	155163
98501	OLYMPIA	27254	14666	23.1	26.7	34.1	11.0	5.1	50144	56034	72	67	9290	4.8	2.8	34.5	52.9	5.0	188361
98502	OLYMPIA	30424	11349	23.1	26.1	31.2	12.1	7.5	50686	56872	73	69	6967	4.0	3.7	26.9	49.9	15.5	214465
98503	LACEY	23617	14112	20.6	29.6	38.1	9.8	1.9	49749	55646	71	66	8727	5.1	3.5	55.4	34.2	1.8	159256
98505	OLYMPIA	4532	5	0.0	0.0	100.0	0.0	0.0	87500	110555	97	99	4	0.0	0.0	0.0	100.0	0.0	300000
98506	OLYMPIA	26804	7685	20.9	29.6	35.6	10.1	3.8	49505	56049	71	65	4895	3.9	3.9	42.5	42.0	7.6	174324
98512	OLYMPIA	28171	10254	17.1	28.5	36.8	12.6	5.1	54599	61104	79	75	7187	10.1	3.3	34.3	48.8	3.6	180125
98513	OLYMPIA	25267	9336	11.8	26.3	45.3	12.6	4.2	60125	67096	84	84	7717	6.3	6.4	44.9	39.0	3.4	164642
98516	OLYMPIA	28659	5624	16.0	24.9	38.3	14.7	6.2	59535	66648	84	83	4339	5.3	4.0	33.3	46.9	10.5	191868
98520	ABERDEEN	18990	8283	34.5	30.2	27.0	5.6	2.7	36708	40717	34	26	5488	11.8	19.8	47.5	19.4	1.6	112347
98524	ALLYN	26208	789	27.0	21.3	35.2	11.7	4.8	51313	55457	74	70	697	6.3	7.5	25.3	51.9	9.0	204167
98526	AMANDA PARK	15184	165	36.4	35.2	22.4	5.5	0.6	32841	35783	20	12	122	26.2	22.1	38.5	11.5	1.6	92000
98528	BELFAIR	22273	3075	22.9	30.1	34.1	9.3	3.6	46507	50092	65	58	2533	5.6	9.6	39.4	35.7	9.8	166223
98531	CENTRALIA	19876	8526	34.3	31.7	26.0	5.0	3.0	36438	40950	33	25	5335	8.6	13.8	50.6	26.0	1.1	132699
98532	CHEHALIS	20467	8130	26.6	32.2	31.4	6.9	3.0	42793	47056	55	48	6100	3.8	9.8	44.1	37.6	4.7	160127
98533	CINEBAR	17001	235	43.4	26.0	22.6	4.7	3.4	32675	33903	20	11	196	5.6	29.6	36.7	22.5	5.6	135484
98535	COPALIS BEACH	13550	92	46.7	35.9	16.3	1.1	0.0	26294	30232	6	3	77	6.5	19.5	49.4	24.7	0.0	127083
98536	COPALIS CROSSING	18973	301	41.9	28.9	24.3	4.0	1.0	34723	36480	26	18	229	13.5	21.0	37.6	27.1	0.9	108418
98537	COSMOPOLIS	19813	814	27.3	32.1	33.1	6.0	1.6	42879	46986	56	48	666	9.3	16.2	51.5	22.5	0.5	116568
98538	CURTIS	19616	128	31.3	28.9	32.8	3.9	3.1	36307	39227	33	24	106	5.7	13.2	38.7	36.8	5.7	152778
98541	ELMA	17161	3580	30.5	34.1	29.2	5.1	1.1	38878	42875	42	36	2641	12.0	15.5	42.9	26.7	2.9	124870
98542	ETHEL	15257	195	28.2	43.1	26.2	1.5	1.0	36441	39860	33	25	157	4.5	10.8	40.8	39.5	4.5	162500
98546	GRAPEVIEW	24112	869	22.0	36.1	30.2	8.6	3.1	44682	49734	60	52	749	4.9	6.4	26.2	45.3	17.2	215361
98547	GRAYLAND	22175	863	38.5	31.4	21.1	5.5	3.6	33810	37061	23	14	691	16.4	22.9	43.4	16.4	1.0	102562
98548	HOODSPORT	21714	919	28.3	39.8	27.3	3.3	1.3	37782	41526	38	31	781	5.1	13.2	47.3	33.0	1.4	144032
98550	HOQUIAM	17798	4482	35.3	34.7	24.3	4.4	1.4	34813	38078	27	18	2961	10.4	26.4	46.0	16.1	1.2	104434
98552	HUMPTULIPS	17859	100	34.0	34.0	24.0	6.0	2.0	35000	36706	28	19	79	10.1	21.5	48.1	17.7	2.5	115132
98555	LILLIWAUP	21206	237	30.8	41.8	24.9	1.7	0.8	37986	40377	39	32	199	5.5	13.1	45.7	33.2	2.5	150431
98557	MCCLEARY	18020	1068	28.1	40.3	26.1	4.6	0.9	37956	41095	39	32	814	5.0	17.6	54.8	19.7	3.0	123711
98560	MATLOCK	18123	61	23.0	31.2	41.0	4.9	0.0	44305	45564	59	51	52	5.8	13.5	46.2	30.8	3.9	143750
98562	MOCLIPS	17000	267	38.6	34.8	20.2	6.4	0.0	30516	33375	14	6	182	18.7	17.6	29.7	31.3	2.8	112069
98563	MONTESANO	22118	2913	26.8	30.0	31.8	9.7	1.8	45245	49123	62	54	2330	8.6	11.0	45.4	30.9	4.1	146942
98564	MOSSYROCK	15989	880	33.2	36.6	26.8	2.4	1.0	35803	38640	31	21	698	11.6	8.0	42.6	34.1	3.7	147917
98568	OAKVILLE	15861	834	30.2	35.1	28.5	4.8	1.3	37994	41642	39	33	667	11.2	15.3	42.1	25.2	6.2	124375
98569	OCEAN SHORES	21467	2130	35.9	30.0	26.2	5.6	2.3	36834	40302	35	27	1715	2.0	8.8	48.2	37.8	3.2	158944
98570	ONALASKA	16607	1398	30.5	39.6	23.2	5.2	1.5	37962	41227	39	32	1140	10.1	13.9	37.5	32.2	6.3	145833
98571	PACIFIC BEACH	14839	47	40.4	31.9	23.4	4.3	0.0	33636	36149	23	14	35	14.3	17.1	42.9	25.7	0.0	109722
98572	PE ELL	14961	336	36.9	36.3	23.5	2.7	0.6	31706	34185	17	8	279	9.0	21.5	55.2	12.9	1.4	113799
98575	QUINAULT	18322	177	31.1	32.8	26.6	7.3	2.3	37597	39563	38	30	125	19.2	26.4	36.8	16.8	0.8	100833
98576	RAINIER	20632	1415	21.1	34.6	34.8	7.6	1.9	45796	51047	63	56	1180	2.0	8.5	51.5	29.9	8.1	154624
98577	RAYMOND	17405	2680	37.3	32.0	25.2	4.5	1.0	34319	37266	25	17	2054	11.7	22.6	46.8	17.4	1.6	108314
98579	ROCHESTER	20499	4021	19.1	36.7	32.3	9.4	2.6	46420	51945	65	58	3316	7.5	8.0	48.4	35.0	1.1	152879
98580	ROY	20764	3399	17.7	30.6	38.2	10.2	3.3	51331	57239	74	70	2876	4.0	8.5	38.7	42.3	6.6	172995
98581	RYDERWOOD	24969	247	41.3	31.6	19.4	4.5	3.2	30101	33332	12	5	222	11.7	27.5	38.7	20.3	1.8	105714
98582	SALKUM	18233	147	27.9	44.2	24.5	2.0	1.4	36100	38865	32	23	119	6.7	16.0	37.8	32.8	6.7	152679
98584	SHELTON	19473	12146	27.7	33.1	31.2	6.0	2.0	41958	46085	53	47	9420	5.5	11.0	50.0	29.3	4.2	140203
98585	SILVER CREEK	18819	245	33.5	33.1	26.1	4.1	3.3	37350	39823	37	29	203	7.9	18.2	38.4	29.1	6.4	150417
98586	SOUTH BEND	17986	945	36.0	34.9	22.8	3.7	2.7	33959	37698	24	15	695	11.5	24.9	45.9	16.4	1.3	108534
98587	TAHOLAH	10490	276	40.6	36.6	18.8	4.0	0.0	30492	32949	13	6	211	30.8	20.9	37.9	8.1	2.4	87813
98588	TAHUYA	23238	716	20.3	37.3	33.1	5.9	3.5	44880	48676	61	52	614	10.4	16.5	38.8	24.9	9.5	142667
98589	TENINO	21812	2728	19.7	33.0	36.4	8.5	2.5	47777	52177	68	62	2261	10.0	9.6	40.0	38.2	2.2	155649
98590	TOKELAND	19892	197	36.0	33.5	22.3	4.6	3.6	36328	40000	33	24	151	10.6	22.5	50.3	13.9	2.7	108882
98591	TOLEDO	18650	1053	27.0	38.1	28.9	3.7	2.4	39725	42121	45	39	834	3.6	11.0	45.2	36.9	3.2	149292
98592	UNION	27429	638	24.5	28.7	32.8	7.5	6.6	45603	50000	63	55	543	3.5	5.0	36.3	45.3	9.9	185795
98593	VADER	16508	362	29.3	30.9	33.2	4.4	2.2	40000	41845	46	40	305	7.2	16.4	45.9	24.6	5.9	124144
98595	WESTPORT	20732	1347	37.5	32.4	22.9	4.6	2.6	32819	35784	20	11	1025	17.1	17.7	41.1	22.0	2.2	115519
98596	WINLOCK	17685	2576	27.7	33.9	31.5	5.7	1.3	41045	44478	50	44	2123	5.9	13.9	43.0	33.3	4.0	148363
	WASHINGTON	26555		21.6	27.8	33.4	11.4	5.9	50585	57953				4.6	5.9	31.3	45.6	12.6	195701
	UNITED STATES	25866		24.7	27.1	30.8	10.9	6.5	48124	56710				10.9	15.0	33.7	30.1	10.4	145905

ZIP CODE #	POST OFFICE NAME	Financial Services: Auto Loan	Financial Services: Home Loan	Financial Services: Investments	Financial Services: Retirement Plans	The Home: Home Improvements: Home Repair	The Home: Home Improvements: Lawn & Garden	The Home: Furnishings: Computers & Hardware	The Home: Furnishings: Major Appliances	The Home: Furnishings: TV, Radio, Sound Equipment	The Home: Furnishings: Furniture	Entertainment: Dine out/Carry out	Entertainment: Sports Equipment	Entertainment: Fees & Tickets	Entertainment: Toys & Games	Entertainment: Travel	Entertainment: Cable TV	Personal: Apparel & Services	Personal: Auto Repairs	Personal: Health Insurance	Personal: Pets & Supplies
98375	PUYALLUP	109	112	101	113	110	111	104	107	100	107	126	125	104	124	103	96	123	105	98	122
98376	QUILCENE	93	68	40	64	78	87	66	81	75	65	89	96	58	87	69	79	82	79	95	111
98377	RANDLE	78	55	29	48	62	71	53	65	62	53	73	77	45	70	54	67	67	64	79	91
98380	SEABECK	104	105	96	102	106	111	97	102	97	98	120	120	98	122	99	97	117	100	102	122
98381	SEKIU	49	43	37	42	44	48	44	46	46	44	56	54	42	54	44	46	54	47	48	55
98382	SEQUIM	82	76	74	72	81	95	71	81	76	76	94	82	72	81	77	80	88	79	94	93
98383	SILVERDALE	99	94	99	100	90	95	101	95	97	100	123	115	98	119	95	92	120	100	87	106
98387	SPANAWAY	90	96	93	97	93	94	91	91	87	92	109	107	92	109	89	83	107	90	83	101
98388	STEILACOOM	97	112	127	112	111	115	107	105	102	107	128	122	111	131	109	100	127	104	99	115
98390	SUMNER	103	113	111	114	110	111	105	105	99	106	125	123	107	126	104	96	123	103	96	117
98392	SUQUAMISH	81	91	100	94	89	89	88	86	83	88	105	103	90	106	87	79	103	86	77	95
98394	VAUGHN	107	87	61	79	96	107	81	96	90	81	108	113	74	107	86	96	101	94	111	129
98402	TACOMA	36	34	44	36	34	38	39	37	40	38	50	44	38	48	38	39	48	39	37	41
98403	TACOMA	83	78	105	85	77	83	93	85	91	90	115	104	90	112	88	87	112	91	79	94
98404	TACOMA	61	62	70	61	61	65	65	63	66	64	82	74	65	83	64	64	80	65	62	70
98405	TACOMA	55	53	62	53	52	57	59	56	60	57	74	66	58	74	57	59	72	58	56	62
98406	TACOMA	82	89	105	90	88	93	91	88	88	89	111	103	92	112	91	87	109	89	84	96
98407	TACOMA	85	95	109	95	94	98	94	92	91	93	115	107	97	118	95	90	113	92	87	100
98408	TACOMA	68	73	79	73	72	76	74	72	73	72	92	85	75	95	74	72	90	73	70	79
98409	TACOMA	59	59	66	61	58	61	63	61	62	62	78	72	63	78	61	60	76	62	58	66
98416	TACOMA	78	48	60	54	47	57	93	68	90	78	112	95	76	101	74	79	106	83	63	78
98418	TACOMA	61	65	75	67	65	67	69	66	67	67	84	79	69	86	68	64	82	67	62	71
98421	TACOMA	115	102	78	97	108	116	95	105	100	95	122	125	93	125	97	103	116	102	113	135
98422	TACOMA	126	145	146	148	140	137	132	131	122	134	154	154	136	158	131	116	153	128	114	144
98424	TACOMA	68	60	66	65	59	62	67	64	66	68	84	78	64	78	63	62	81	68	59	73
98430	CAMP MURRAY	35	31	34	30	31	35	36	35	38	35	47	40	35	46	35	38	45	36	36	38
98433	TACOMA	69	44	42	50	40	47	65	56	66	61	83	75	56	74	54	60	79	66	52	64
98438	MCCHORD AFB	74	47	45	54	43	51	70	60	71	65	88	80	60	79	57	65	85	71	56	68
98439	LAKEWOOD	53	38	44	41	36	42	53	47	54	50	68	60	47	62	46	51	65	54	45	53
98443	TACOMA	92	109	115	107	108	110	99	100	95	99	119	116	105	126	102	94	118	97	94	112
98444	TACOMA	62	59	66	61	59	63	66	63	66	64	82	75	64	81	63	64	80	65	61	70
98445	TACOMA	82	89	93	89	88	91	87	86	84	86	106	101	89	109	87	82	103	86	82	95
98446	TACOMA	99	113	117	111	112	115	105	106	101	105	127	123	109	132	107	100	125	103	100	118
98447	TACOMA	99	115	127	109	114	124	109	109	108	107	135	121	115	140	113	111	132	107	111	118
98465	TACOMA	63	64	78	66	63	68	70	66	68	68	86	79	69	85	68	66	84	69	63	72
98466	TACOMA	87	93	107	94	91	97	95	92	92	94	116	108	96	117	94	90	114	93	87	101
98467	UNIVERSITY PLACE	103	111	121	115	108	110	109	107	104	110	131	127	111	132	107	99	129	107	96	118
98498	LAKEWOOD	85	91	103	91	90	96	92	90	90	91	113	104	94	114	92	89	111	91	87	99
98499	LAKEWOOD	67	62	71	63	62	69	69	67	70	68	87	78	67	85	67	70	85	69	67	74
98501	OLYMPIA	86	92	102	94	91	94	93	90	89	92	112	107	94	114	92	86	110	91	84	100
98502	OLYMPIA	93	97	115	100	96	100	101	97	98	100	124	116	102	123	100	95	121	100	91	108
98503	LACEY	81	84	90	86	82	86	84	83	81	84	103	97	84	101	83	79	100	84	77	92
98505	OLYMPIA	112	128	158	133	126	129	127	123	120	126	152	146	130	156	127	116	150	124	111	134
98506	OLYMPIA	81	88	97	90	88	91	88	86	85	87	106	101	89	107	88	82	104	87	82	95
98512	OLYMPIA	95	100	107	103	98	100	99	97	95	99	120	115	99	119	97	91	117	98	89	109
98513	OLYMPIA	96	107	106	108	104	104	99	99	94	101	118	116	101	119	98	90	116	98	90	110
98516	OLYMPIA	103	110	114	113	108	111	107	106	102	107	128	124	108	129	105	99	126	105	98	117
98520	ABERDEEN	67	63	63	61	65	72	66	67	68	64	84	77	65	84	66	69	80	68	71	77
98524	ALLYN	95	84	74	79	91	105	78	91	84	82	104	94	77	91	85	90	97	88	106	110
98526	AMANDA PARK	67	57	42	54	60	66	54	61	58	55	70	71	50	68	55	59	66	61	66	78
98528	BELFAIR	92	80	60	75	84	92	75	84	80	76	97	98	71	94	77	82	92	83	92	107
98531	CENTRALIA	71	65	62	65	67	74	68	70	70	67	86	81	66	85	68	71	82	70	73	80
98532	CHEHALIS	81	76	67	73	78	84	74	78	76	73	93	92	72	93	74	76	89	77	81	94
98533	CINEBAR	82	55	25	48	62	72	53	67	64	54	75	79	45	71	54	69	68	66	82	94
98535	COPALIS BEACH	53	42	29	38	47	53	40	48	45	39	53	56	35	52	42	48	49	47	56	65
98536	COPALIS CROSSING	69	54	37	49	61	68	51	61	58	51	68	72	46	68	54	62	64	61	73	84
98537	COSMOPOLIS	72	71	66	70	73	78	69	72	70	68	86	83	69	88	70	70	83	70	73	83
98538	CURTIS	94	65	34	62	76	85	65	80	74	64	87	96	55	86	67	78	80	79	95	111
98541	ELMA	74	61	45	57	64	71	60	67	65	60	79	78	56	77	60	67	74	66	74	85
98542	ETHEL	75	51	26	47	59	67	50	63	59	50	69	75	43	67	52	62	63	62	75	88
98546	GRAPEVIEW	90	76	58	71	83	92	72	83	78	73	94	94	68	91	75	82	88	81	94	107
98547	GRAYLAND	78	61	41	55	69	77	58	70	65	57	78	81	52	77	61	70	72	68	82	95
98548	HOODSPORT	71	60	49	56	66	76	56	66	62	58	75	72	54	69	61	66	70	65	78	84
98550	HOQUIAM	66	57	54	56	60	67	61	63	65	60	79	73	58	78	61	66	75	64	69	75
98552	HUMPTULIPS	86	60	31	52	68	77	57	71	68	58	80	85	49	77	59	73	73	70	87	100
98555	LILLIWAUP	62	58	55	55	61	72	53	61	56	57	70	59	54	58	58	60	66	59	71	69
98557	MCCLEARY	71	59	43	57	62	70	61	66	65	60	79	75	57	75	60	67	73	65	73	79
98560	MATLOCK	82	64	44	58	72	81	60	73	68	60	81	85	54	80	64	73	75	72	86	99
98562	MOCLIPS	65	51	35	46	57	64	48	58	54	47	64	67	43	63	51	58	60	57	68	79
98563	MONTESANO	84	76	62	73	80	87	74	80	78	72	94	93	71	95	75	80	89	78	87	98
98564	MOSSYROCK	69	53	34	50	57	66	55	62	61	54	73	71	50	70	55	64	67	61	72	77
98568	OAKVILLE	73	63	49	62	65	73	64	68	67	63	81	78	61	80	63	68	77	67	73	80
98569	OCEAN SHORES	73	61	50	58	67	74	59	68	64	59	77	79	55	76	62	67	73	67	76	87
98570	ONALASKA	80	58	32	52	64	72	56	67	65	57	77	80	49	73	57	68	71	67	79	92
98571	PACIFIC BEACH	67	53	36	48	60	67	50	60	56	49	67	70	45	66	53	60	62	59	71	82
98572	PE ELL	62	52	40	52	55	62	54	58	57	53	69	66	51	69	53	58	65	57	63	69
98575	QUINAULT	81	64	43	57	72	80	60	72	68	59	80	85	54	79	64	73	75	71	85	99
98576	RAINIER	82	83	73	81	82	85	77	81	76	78	94	94	76	93	77	75	92	80	78	94
98577	RAYMOND	70	52	34	50	58	67	56	63	62	54	74	72	50	71	56	65	67	62	74	78
98579	ROCHESTER	88	82	68	80	82	87	79	84	80	80	98	97	75	94	78	79	94	83	83	99
98580	ROY	93	88	73	87	88	92	84	89	84	86	104	103	81	100	83	82	100	88	86	103
98581	RYDERWOOD	63	60	64	55	64	77	56	65	60	61	75	61	57	63	61	65	70	63	77	70
98582	SALKUM	78	54	27	50	63	70	53	66	62	53	73	79	45	70	55	65	66	65	79	92
98584	SHELTON	75	68	59	66	71	77	67	72	70	67	86	83	65	84	68	71	82	71	76	87
98585	SILVER CREEK	87	59	27	51	67	77	57	71	68	58	80	85	48	76	58	73	73	70	87	101
98586	SOUTH BEND	72	54	36	52	59	71	60	66	67	57	79	74	53	74	59	71	72	66	79	79
98587	TAHOLAH	57	52	40	50	52	54	49	53	50	51	61	61	46	58	48	49	59	53	52	63
98588	TAHUYA	93	73	50	66	82	92	69	83	78	68	92	97	62	91	73	83	86	82	98	113
98589	TENINO	95	83	62	79	87	94	78	86	82	78	100	102	75	100	79	84	95	85	93	110
98590	TOKELAND	75	57	38	53	63	74	59	68	67	57	79	77	53	76	60	71	72	67	81	85
98591	TOLEDO	78	68	52	66	72	79	66	72	70	66	85	84	64	86	67	72	81	71	78	90
98592	UNION	103	78	50	71	89	99	74	90	85	74	100	107	66	99	79	90	93	89	107	124
98593	VADER	78	67	49	64	69	74	64	71	67	66	82	83	59	78	64	67	78	71	74	88
98595	WESTPORT	71	53	35	51	58	70	59	65	66	56	77	72	52	73	58	69	70	64	77	78
98596	WINLOCK	78	66	49	64	70	77	65	71	69	65	83	83	61	82	65	70	78	70	77	89
	WASHINGTON	94	96	103	97	95	100	96	95	94	96	118	112	96	118	95	92	115	96	91	107
	UNITED STATES	100	100	100	100	100	100	100	100	100	100	100	100	100	100	100	100	100	100	100	100

A   98597-98932

#	POST OFFICE NAME	COUNTY FIPS CODE	POPULATION 2000	2004	2009	2000-2004 ANNUAL RATE % Rate	State Centile	HOUSEHOLDS 2000	2004	2009	% Annual Rate 2000-2004	2004 Average HH Size	FAMILIES 2000	2004	% Annual Rate 2000-2004
98597	YELM	067	14017	15231	16332	2.0	83	5134	5639	6097	2.2	2.69	3759	4096	2.0
98601	AMBOY	011	2505	2709	2973	1.9	81	814	891	985	2.2	3.04	660	718	2.0
98602	APPLETON	039	119	133	143	2.7	92	48	55	59	3.3	2.42	37	42	3.0
98603	ARIEL	015	945	988	1006	1.1	59	333	351	359	1.3	2.81	256	267	1.0
98604	BATTLE GROUND	011	23916	27790	31679	3.6	98	7799	9176	10549	3.9	2.98	6392	7476	3.8
98605	BINGEN	059	630	645	659	0.6	41	221	229	236	0.8	2.82	163	168	0.7
98606	BRUSH PRAIRIE	011	9104	10183	11413	2.7	92	2918	3307	3738	3.0	3.08	2450	2765	2.9
98607	CAMAS	011	18367	21835	25275	4.2	98	6470	7711	8951	4.2	2.82	5048	6012	4.2
98610	CARSON	059	2341	2414	2479	0.7	48	882	916	948	0.9	2.63	640	661	0.8
98611	CASTLE ROCK	015	8628	8754	8820	0.3	33	3269	3349	3390	0.6	2.60	2472	2514	0.4
98612	CATHLAMET	069	2569	2632	2656	0.6	42	1054	1091	1106	0.8	2.36	732	755	0.7
98613	CENTERVILLE	039	861	891	908	0.8	51	347	364	375	1.1	2.45	248	259	1.0
98616	COUGAR	015	96	101	104	1.2	64	41	44	45	1.7	2.30	31	33	1.5
98617	DALLESPORT	039	207	214	218	0.8	50	73	76	78	1.0	2.82	52	54	0.9
98619	GLENWOOD	039	534	540	544	0.3	30	208	213	217	0.6	2.54	156	158	0.3
98620	GOLDENDALE	039	6922	7144	7303	0.8	49	2694	2815	2908	1.0	2.48	1875	1949	0.9
98621	GRAYS RIVER	069	206	202	200	-0.5	8	80	79	79	-0.3	2.56	61	60	-0.4
98624	ILWACO	049	1283	1278	1276	-0.1	16	534	539	545	0.2	2.34	335	336	0.1
98625	KALAMA	015	4773	5103	5274	1.6	75	1839	1994	2077	1.9	2.56	1384	1489	1.7
98626	KELSO	015	22552	23033	23428	0.5	39	8478	8684	8853	0.6	2.63	6048	6184	0.5
98628	KLICKITAT	039	308	290	290	-1.4	1	98	94	95	-1.0	2.97	73	69	-1.3
98629	LA CENTER	011	6696	7471	8336	2.6	91	2227	2514	2825	2.9	2.97	1823	2045	2.7
98631	LONG BEACH	049	4089	4046	4035	-0.3	13	1933	1932	1947	0.0	2.07	1134	1128	-0.1
98632	LONGVIEW	015	46791	47479	48111	0.3	33	18536	18904	19224	0.5	2.46	12330	12501	0.3
98635	LYLE	039	2904	3044	3139	1.1	61	1130	1198	1247	1.4	2.52	831	876	1.3
98638	NASELLE	049	2005	1956	1943	-0.6	5	803	793	797	-0.3	2.32	572	563	-0.4
98640	OCEAN PARK	049	3751	4028	4181	1.7	78	1818	1967	2061	1.9	2.05	1159	1247	1.7
98642	RIDGEFIELD	011	11797	13237	14839	2.8	93	4226	4841	5495	3.3	2.72	3362	3817	3.0
98643	ROSBURG	069	401	392	389	-0.5	7	167	165	164	-0.3	2.38	128	126	-0.4
98645	SILVERLAKE	015	1239	1259	1268	0.4	35	466	479	485	0.7	2.62	372	380	0.5
98647	SKAMOKAWA	069	416	419	419	0.2	25	160	162	163	0.3	2.59	116	118	0.4
98648	STEVENSON	059	3845	3894	3969	0.3	32	1507	1545	1591	0.6	2.48	1061	1081	0.4
98649	TOUTLE	015	673	691	697	0.6	44	237	246	250	0.9	2.81	186	192	0.8
98650	TROUT LAKE	039	792	788	792	-0.1	15	316	320	325	0.3	2.46	226	228	0.2
98651	UNDERWOOD	059	905	926	947	0.5	40	362	374	386	0.8	2.48	271	279	0.7
98660	VANCOUVER	011	10483	10604	11334	0.3	31	4309	4404	4767	0.5	2.18	2202	2199	0.0
98661	VANCOUVER	011	36273	38073	41347	1.2	63	14681	15433	16817	1.2	2.45	8860	9218	0.4
98662	VANCOUVER	011	24241	26466	29236	2.1	84	8850	9798	10921	2.4	2.67	6286	6888	2.2
98663	VANCOUVER	011	13960	14002	14923	0.1	21	5615	5678	6093	0.3	2.42	3516	3513	0.0
98664	VANCOUVER	011	20559	21448	23235	1.0	57	8272	8758	9581	1.4	2.42	5460	5705	1.1
98665	VANCOUVER	011	20221	21209	23021	1.1	62	7974	8433	9208	1.3	2.51	5332	5583	1.1
98671	WASHOUGAL	059	14746	16100	17702	2.1	84	5507	6075	6728	2.3	2.65	4094	4486	2.2
98672	WHITE SALMON	039	5700	5805	5879	0.4	37	2273	2349	2402	0.8	2.46	1593	1639	0.7
98674	WOODLAND	015	9094	9669	10182	1.5	71	3224	3448	3653	1.6	2.76	2457	2614	1.5
98675	YACOLT	011	5451	5602	6036	0.7	44	1545	1599	1736	0.8	3.42	1271	1308	0.7
98682	VANCOUVER	011	41846	48218	54852	3.4	97	14041	16326	18683	3.6	2.95	10870	12549	3.4
98683	VANCOUVER	011	28195	32566	37246	3.5	97	11391	13276	15276	3.7	2.44	7704	8903	3.5
98684	VANCOUVER	011	21443	24569	27879	3.3	96	7661	8895	10177	3.6	2.76	5674	6532	3.4
98685	VANCOUVER	011	21282	23006	25333	1.9	81	7807	8518	9442	2.1	2.70	5910	6405	1.9
98686	VANCOUVER	011	14122	15461	17144	2.2	85	5100	5651	6315	2.4	2.73	4044	4446	2.3
98801	WENATCHEE	007	36653	37809	38820	0.7	48	13845	14164	14422	0.5	2.62	9359	9535	0.4
98802	EAST WENATCHEE	017	23564	24957	26526	1.4	69	8608	9117	9678	1.4	2.71	6488	6852	1.3
98812	BREWSTER	047	3873	3936	3997	0.4	35	1203	1212	1225	0.2	3.20	927	932	0.1
98813	BRIDGEPORT	017	3286	3317	3440	0.2	28	1077	1079	1115	0.0	3.07	836	833	-0.1
98814	CARLTON	047	439	488	520	2.5	90	189	212	227	2.7	2.30	134	149	2.5
98815	CASHMERE	007	8346	8706	9002	1.0	57	2946	3057	3141	0.9	2.80	2137	2204	0.7
98816	CHELAN	007	6254	6383	6507	0.5	38	2468	2511	2547	0.4	2.50	1695	1712	0.2
98822	ENTIAT	007	2098	2132	2173	0.4	35	779	791	803	0.4	2.69	563	570	0.3
98823	EPHRATA	025	9562	10126	10573	1.4	69	3439	3624	3754	1.2	2.73	2507	2632	1.2
98826	LEAVENWORTH	007	6141	6638	6977	1.9	81	2534	2741	2872	1.9	2.42	1765	1897	1.7
98827	LOOMIS	047	528	551	567	1.0	59	191	200	206	1.1	2.67	142	148	1.0
98828	MALAGA	007	1991	2025	2054	0.4	36	682	694	701	0.4	2.92	542	549	0.4
98830	MANSFIELD	017	634	621	641	-0.5	8	275	270	278	-0.4	2.29	182	176	-0.8
98831	MANSON	007	3248	3394	3492	1.0	59	1114	1159	1187	0.9	2.89	830	859	0.8
98832	MARLIN	025	715	716	724	0.0	20	241	240	241	-0.1	2.69	177	175	-0.3
98833	MAZAMA	047	228	264	286	3.5	97	108	127	139	3.9	2.08	72	84	3.7
98834	METHOW	047	832	865	887	0.9	54	302	315	324	1.0	2.69	231	241	1.0
98837	MOSES LAKE	025	32005	33628	35138	1.2	64	11251	11796	12245	1.1	2.80	8091	8441	1.0
98840	OKANOGAN	047	5298	5360	5427	0.3	31	1979	2012	2042	0.4	2.56	1410	1426	0.3
98841	OMAK	047	7763	7896	8017	0.4	36	2940	3008	3069	0.5	2.56	2074	2114	0.5
98843	ORONDO	017	1614	1657	1724	0.6	44	513	528	550	0.7	3.08	414	424	0.6
98844	OROVILLE	047	3999	4042	4103	0.3	29	1605	1630	1659	0.4	2.45	1091	1103	0.3
98845	PALISADES	017	61	64	68	1.1	62	22	23	25	1.1	2.78	17	18	1.4
98846	PATEROS	047	755	767	777	0.4	35	273	276	278	0.3	2.65	190	191	0.1
98847	PESHASTIN	007	1779	1830	1868	0.7	45	614	630	639	0.6	2.89	448	457	0.5
98848	QUINCY	025	9969	10534	10987	1.3	68	3086	3217	3313	1.0	3.25	2476	2571	0.9
98849	RIVERSIDE	047	1857	1958	2024	1.3	66	720	766	800	1.5	2.51	518	549	1.2
98850	ROCK ISLAND	017	1438	1602	1742	2.6	91	465	513	555	2.3	3.12	367	404	2.3
98851	SOAP LAKE	025	4059	4217	4357	0.9	53	1641	1688	1726	0.7	2.47	1066	1089	0.5
98852	STEHEKIN	007	106	123	135	3.6	98	39	46	50	4.0	2.59	18	21	3.7
98855	TONASKET	047	5450	5673	5825	1.0	55	2086	2184	2255	1.1	2.51	1447	1508	1.0
98856	TWISP	047	2430	2616	2738	1.8	78	1098	1194	1256	2.0	2.19	712	773	2.0
98857	WARDEN	025	3820	4055	4241	1.4	70	1149	1214	1261	1.3	3.34	936	987	1.3
98858	WATERVILLE	017	1819	1857	1928	0.5	39	687	704	731	0.6	2.62	512	522	0.5
98859	WAUCONDA	047	321	337	348	1.2	63	138	146	152	1.3	2.30	96	102	1.4
98862	WINTHROP	047	1509	1564	1601	0.9	52	693	725	747	1.1	2.14	446	464	0.9
98901	YAKIMA	077	28417	28599	28805	0.2	24	9080	9074	9064	0.0	3.00	6371	6334	-0.1
98902	YAKIMA	077	43506	42971	43034	-0.3	12	16756	16430	16321	-0.5	2.56	10500	10201	-0.7
98903	YAKIMA	077	12517	12735	12888	0.4	36	4519	4584	4608	0.3	2.73	3321	3350	0.2
98908	YAKIMA	077	31703	33203	34185	1.1	60	12201	12732	13024	1.0	2.59	9018	9367	0.9
98922	CLE ELUM	037	7382	7721	8086	1.1	60	3188	3364	3539	1.3	2.29	2088	2192	1.2
98923	COWICHE	077	1338	1391	1418	0.9	54	405	418	423	0.8	3.29	346	356	0.7
98926	ELLENSBURG	037	25326	26915	28557	1.4	71	9956	10671	11413	1.7	2.32	5509	5862	1.5
98930	GRANDVIEW	077	12833	12907	12972	0.1	23	3776	3771	3759	0.0	3.39	3089	3074	-0.1
98932	GRANGER	077	4276	4560	4723	1.5	74	1054	1111	1138	1.3	4.09	902	949	1.2
	WASHINGTON					1.1					1.3	2.52			1.2
	UNITED STATES					1.2					1.3	2.58			1.1

   320-A

ZIP CODE #	POST OFFICE NAME	RACE (%) White 2000	White 2004	Black 2000	Black 2004	Asian/Pacific 2000	Asian/Pacific 2004	% Hispanic Origin 2000	% Hispanic Origin 2004	2004 AGE DISTRIBUTION (%) 0-4	5-9	10-14	15-19	20-24	25-44	45-64	65-84	85+	18+	MEDIAN AGE 2004	% 2004 Males	% 2004 Females
98597	YELM	89.4	88.5	1.2	1.3	1.9	2.0	4.4	5.2	7.3	7.3	8.2	7.4	6.6	28.3	24.1	9.8	0.9	72.5	35.6	48.8	51.2
98601	AMBOY	95.3	94.8	0.4	0.5	0.7	0.8	1.9	2.3	7.9	8.5	9.4	8.3	6.6	25.5	25.8	7.4	0.6	69.1	33.9	51.0	49.0
98602	APPLETON	94.1	93.2	0.0	0.0	1.7	1.5	4.2	3.8	4.5	5.3	6.0	6.0	4.5	24.8	34.6	12.0	2.3	79.7	44.5	53.4	46.6
98603	ARIEL	96.0	95.6	0.1	0.1	0.6	0.6	1.7	1.9	6.2	7.1	8.8	7.1	4.9	25.9	30.5	8.9	0.7	73.5	39.0	51.6	48.4
98604	BATTLE GROUND	94.6	94.1	0.6	0.6	0.9	1.0	3.0	3.7	8.7	8.5	8.8	8.1	6.5	27.8	23.9	6.7	1.0	68.8	32.9	50.2	49.8
98605	BINGEN	90.5	89.5	0.2	0.2	0.3	0.3	9.1	10.7	6.5	7.8	7.8	6.4	4.3	27.3	29.3	9.8	0.9	73.8	39.5	51.8	48.2
98606	BRUSH PRAIRIE	95.2	94.8	0.3	0.3	1.3	1.4	1.8	2.1	6.2	7.5	9.7	8.4	5.6	22.9	32.0	7.1	0.7	71.4	39.0	50.8	49.2
98607	CAMAS	92.6	91.7	0.6	0.6	3.3	3.7	2.6	3.1	8.2	8.5	8.6	7.3	5.3	28.4	25.0	7.8	1.0	70.3	35.8	49.5	50.5
98610	CARSON	89.5	88.9	0.4	0.5	0.9	1.0	5.2	6.0	6.8	7.7	7.3	6.8	7.6	26.2	26.7	9.6	1.4	73.7	37.5	49.0	51.0
98611	CASTLE ROCK	94.4	93.9	0.3	0.3	0.7	0.7	2.3	2.7	5.7	6.0	7.4	6.9	5.7	23.9	29.6	13.4	1.4	76.7	41.5	49.5	50.5
98612	CATHLAMET	94.1	94.1	0.3	0.3	0.4	0.4	2.0	2.0	5.6	5.6	5.8	5.9	5.3	19.3	30.8	19.2	2.6	79.3	46.9	49.6	50.4
98613	CENTERVILLE	84.9	84.3	0.2	0.2	0.6	0.7	3.7	4.4	6.5	6.9	6.4	7.1	5.4	21.7	30.3	14.0	1.8	76.1	42.3	51.7	48.3
98616	COUGAR	96.9	97.0	0.0	0.0	0.0	0.0	0.0	1.0	6.9	6.9	11.9	5.9	4.0	23.8	31.7	8.9	0.0	68.3	38.9	50.5	49.5
98617	DALLESPORT	87.4	86.5	0.0	0.0	1.5	1.9	4.8	5.6	6.1	6.5	7.5	7.0	6.1	21.5	31.3	12.6	1.4	75.2	41.4	48.6	51.4
98619	GLENWOOD	81.1	80.6	0.8	0.7	0.2	0.2	3.0	3.3	6.1	6.3	6.5	8.3	6.5	22.8	30.9	11.7	0.9	75.2	40.7	49.6	50.4
98620	GOLDENDALE	88.3	87.5	0.3	0.4	0.9	0.9	5.0	5.9	6.3	6.3	7.3	7.0	6.1	22.2	29.0	13.6	2.2	75.6	41.1	49.2	50.8
98621	GRAYS RIVER	91.3	91.1	0.0	0.0	1.0	1.0	4.4	4.5	5.0	5.5	5.9	5.9	5.0	22.8	35.2	12.9	2.0	79.7	45.0	50.5	49.5
98624	ILWACO	93.6	92.8	0.2	0.2	0.7	0.8	4.7	5.6	4.1	4.5	5.5	5.9	4.4	20.3	33.1	19.8	2.4	82.3	48.4	48.7	51.3
98625	KALAMA	95.8	95.5	0.4	0.5	0.5	0.5	1.8	2.2	5.4	6.1	7.8	6.8	5.1	24.3	31.5	12.3	0.9	76.6	41.6	50.5	49.5
98626	KELSO	92.0	91.3	0.5	0.5	0.9	1.0	4.7	5.5	7.1	6.9	7.9	7.3	7.1	27.2	24.3	10.6	1.5	73.7	35.6	50.0	50.1
98628	KLICKITAT	93.5	92.8	0.3	0.3	0.7	1.0	2.0	2.8	8.6	8.3	9.0	7.2	6.9	24.5	26.6	7.9	1.0	68.3	33.5	49.7	50.3
98629	LA CENTER	94.0	93.3	0.3	0.3	1.0	1.0	3.4	4.2	7.4	7.6	8.1	7.8	6.5	26.3	28.3	7.3	0.7	72.0	36.7	50.6	49.4
98631	LONG BEACH	93.2	92.4	0.1	0.1	1.1	1.2	4.1	5.0	3.9	4.3	5.0	5.4	4.5	18.7	32.4	23.1	2.8	83.6	50.4	47.8	52.2
98632	LONGVIEW	90.4	89.6	0.6	0.7	2.1	2.3	5.0	5.8	6.8	6.6	7.4	6.9	7.1	25.7	25.3	11.9	2.3	75.1	37.4	48.9	51.1
98635	LYLE	89.9	89.4	0.2	0.2	1.6	1.7	4.1	4.8	6.1	6.6	7.2	6.6	5.9	22.3	31.5	12.0	1.8	75.7	41.9	49.3	50.7
98638	NASELLE	90.6	89.9	0.7	0.7	0.8	0.9	3.1	3.6	4.2	4.6	6.2	10.8	4.3	20.3	31.2	16.8	1.6	76.8	44.7	52.9	47.1
98640	OCEAN PARK	94.8	94.2	0.1	0.2	0.5	0.6	4.0	4.8	3.1	3.4	4.2	4.2	4.0	14.5	33.2	30.5	3.0	86.9	56.5	49.7	50.3
98642	RIDGEFIELD	94.5	94.0	0.4	0.5	1.4	1.5	2.2	2.6	5.5	6.4	8.1	7.3	5.4	23.6	31.9	10.7	1.2	75.3	41.5	49.6	50.4
98643	ROSBURG	91.0	91.1	0.0	0.0	1.0	1.0	4.5	4.6	4.9	5.4	6.1	5.6	4.9	22.7	35.0	13.8	1.8	79.9	45.4	50.8	49.2
98645	SILVERLAKE	94.6	94.0	0.2	0.2	0.7	0.8	2.3	2.7	5.6	6.0	7.9	7.2	6.8	24.5	30.6	10.6	1.0	76.2	40.4	50.6	49.4
98647	SKAMOKAWA	94.5	94.8	0.2	0.2	0.2	0.2	2.4	2.2	5.0	5.5	7.2	8.1	5.5	22.7	34.6	11.0	0.5	76.6	42.6	51.6	48.5
98648	STEVENSON	92.3	91.8	0.2	0.3	0.9	1.0	3.0	3.5	5.4	5.8	6.5	7.7	7.3	23.4	30.1	12.3	1.5	77.6	41.1	48.7	51.3
98649	TOUTLE	92.7	92.0	0.2	0.1	0.6	0.6	3.7	4.3	4.6	5.4	7.2	7.2	6.4	23.6	33.6	11.7	0.3	78.4	42.2	49.6	50.4
98650	TROUT LAKE	93.4	92.6	0.0	0.0	0.9	0.9	4.6	5.5	4.4	5.5	8.3	8.0	6.6	21.8	33.6	10.4	1.4	76.5	42.1	51.0	49.0
98651	UNDERWOOD	92.3	91.3	0.1	0.1	0.2	0.2	7.5	9.0	6.4	7.7	7.8	6.2	3.8	27.3	29.8	10.2	1.0	74.2	40.2	52.1	48.0
98660	VANCOUVER	88.5	87.4	2.4	2.5	1.6	1.7	6.4	7.7	6.3	5.7	6.3	6.8	7.3	32.6	23.4	9.8	1.9	77.7	36.2	52.0	48.0
98661	VANCOUVER	81.8	80.3	3.2	3.3	4.0	4.2	9.8	11.4	8.5	7.3	7.1	6.5	8.2	29.7	21.8	9.5	1.5	73.5	32.9	49.3	50.8
98662	VANCOUVER	88.0	87.1	2.0	2.1	4.5	4.7	4.3	5.1	7.6	7.4	7.8	6.8	6.9	29.4	24.2	8.4	1.6	73.1	34.7	48.9	51.1
98663	VANCOUVER	88.2	87.2	2.0	2.1	2.3	2.4	6.4	7.5	6.9	6.5	6.5	6.7	7.0	28.5	25.0	10.6	2.3	76.1	37.1	49.6	50.4
98664	VANCOUVER	87.5	86.5	2.3	2.5	4.1	4.3	4.9	5.7	7.0	6.6	6.5	6.0	7.0	28.9	24.4	11.7	2.0	76.4	36.7	47.9	52.1
98665	VANCOUVER	87.4	85.8	2.5	2.7	2.4	2.6	7.2	9.0	7.6	7.2	7.0	6.7	6.8	27.3	24.7	10.9	1.8	74.2	36.4	49.3	50.7
98671	WASHOUGAL	94.4	93.9	0.3	0.4	0.9	1.0	2.3	2.7	7.4	7.5	7.5	7.2	6.2	26.8	27.5	8.7	1.2	73.1	37.0	50.1	49.9
98672	WHITE SALMON	86.6	85.0	0.1	0.1	0.7	0.8	12.7	14.8	6.6	6.8	7.4	7.4	5.8	24.5	28.1	11.7	1.7	74.3	39.7	50.0	50.0
98674	WOODLAND	93.1	92.4	0.2	0.2	0.7	0.8	6.5	7.4	7.5	7.7	7.5	6.8	6.4	26.9	25.3	10.1	1.8	73.1	36.7	51.0	49.0
98675	YACOLT	94.4	93.9	0.9	1.0	0.8	0.8	2.2	2.6	8.8	9.1	10.2	8.7	6.1	26.6	23.2	6.6	0.7	66.3	31.8	52.4	47.6
98682	VANCOUVER	87.2	86.2	1.9	1.9	4.9	5.2	4.3	5.0	10.0	9.1	8.9	7.2	7.6	33.0	19.3	4.6	0.4	67.6	29.8	49.7	50.3
98683	VANCOUVER	82.7	81.1	2.3	2.5	9.1	9.9	4.5	5.3	8.0	7.6	7.2	6.0	6.5	31.0	21.7	10.2	1.9	73.6	34.5	48.4	51.6
98684	VANCOUVER	87.2	86.2	2.0	2.1	5.2	5.5	4.3	5.0	8.7	8.2	8.1	7.3	7.3	31.9	22.3	5.7	0.6	70.6	31.8	49.8	50.2
98685	VANCOUVER	91.8	91.2	1.2	1.2	2.8	2.9	3.1	3.7	5.9	6.9	8.4	7.9	6.1	25.2	29.6	9.0	1.0	73.7	39.1	49.2	50.8
98686	VANCOUVER	92.8	92.3	1.0	1.1	2.3	2.5	4.5	5.1	6.5	7.1	8.1	7.4	6.0	26.1	29.5	8.7	0.7	73.7	38.3	49.1	50.9
98801	WENATCHEE	82.3	80.4	0.3	0.4	1.0	1.1	19.9	22.6	7.7	7.3	7.5	7.0	7.3	26.3	23.1	11.4	2.4	73.3	35.4	49.3	50.7
98802	EAST WENATCHEE	88.2	86.7	0.3	0.3	0.7	0.8	14.2	16.8	7.2	7.2	8.0	7.4	6.8	25.5	24.7	11.5	1.8	73.1	36.7	49.1	50.9
98812	BREWSTER	60.8	57.8	0.9	0.9	0.5	0.5	48.6	53.1	9.5	8.7	9.5	8.4	8.2	25.6	19.5	8.6	2.0	67.3	29.3	51.1	48.9
98813	BRIDGEPORT	68.5	66.4	0.4	0.4	0.3	0.3	50.1	54.8	10.5	10.0	9.1	7.6	7.2	26.1	20.0	8.6	0.9	65.8	29.3	51.7	48.3
98814	CARLTON	96.1	95.7	0.2	0.2	0.2	0.2	1.6	1.6	4.5	4.7	6.6	6.4	3.3	20.9	39.6	12.5	1.6	80.1	46.8	51.2	48.8
98815	CASHMERE	87.3	85.6	0.2	0.2	0.5	0.5	19.1	22.2	7.0	7.1	8.1	7.8	7.0	25.5	24.3	11.1	2.2	72.8	36.7	50.0	50.0
98816	CHELAN	80.8	78.1	0.1	0.1	0.5	0.5	22.3	26.0	6.3	6.1	7.8	7.1	6.3	22.5	27.8	13.9	2.2	75.3	40.6	50.5	49.5
98822	ENTIAT	81.5	78.9	0.5	0.5	0.6	0.7	18.5	21.5	7.6	8.0	8.9	7.7	6.1	25.7	25.3	10.0	0.8	70.5	36.1	50.3	49.7
98823	EPHRATA	90.2	88.6	0.3	0.3	0.7	0.8	11.2	13.8	7.2	7.2	8.4	8.5	7.2	24.9	23.5	11.2	2.0	71.5	35.4	50.0	50.0
98826	LEAVENWORTH	94.3	93.6	0.1	0.2	0.4	0.4	5.3	6.2	5.4	5.6	6.3	6.4	5.0	21.8	33.0	14.5	2.0	78.6	44.7	49.6	50.4
98827	LOOMIS	82.6	80.0	0.2	0.4	0.6	0.5	18.9	22.5	7.4	7.4	7.8	6.2	5.8	24.9	25.2	14.2	1.1	73.3	38.2	51.2	48.8
98828	MALAGA	89.8	88.1	0.1	0.2	0.9	0.9	12.6	14.9	6.3	7.1	9.2	8.6	6.5	26.3	27.8	7.6	0.6	72.1	36.5	51.2	48.8
98830	MANSFIELD	91.2	90.3	0.0	0.0	0.3	0.3	6.5	7.7	6.8	6.8	6.0	5.5	4.2	21.1	31.2	15.1	3.4	76.7	44.8	47.5	52.5
98831	MANSON	72.7	69.6	0.1	0.1	0.3	0.3	36.8	41.6	8.0	8.3	8.9	8.5	5.7	24.9	23.9	10.4	1.5	69.0	34.4	50.4	49.6
98832	MARLIN	90.5	89.1	0.8	1.0	1.4	1.5	7.0	8.7	6.3	6.7	8.5	6.2	5.5	24.4	29.5	11.6	1.4	74.4	40.2	51.3	48.7
98833	MAZAMA	97.8	97.7	0.0	0.0	2.2	2.3	0.4	0.4	2.7	5.3	4.2	2.3	3.0	28.8	40.9	12.5	0.4	86.0	46.6	47.7	52.3
98834	METHOW	89.4	88.4	0.2	0.2	1.0	1.0	18.4	21.9	6.8	6.9	7.2	6.9	6.9	23.0	30.1	10.9	1.3	74.9	39.0	50.2	49.8
98837	MOSES LAKE	79.4	77.3	1.9	1.9	1.2	1.3	21.2	24.5	8.8	8.2	8.1	8.0	7.7	26.6	21.8	9.5	1.4	70.2	31.9	50.0	50.1
98840	OKANOGAN	78.9	77.2	0.3	0.3	0.3	0.3	12.5	14.9	6.1	6.0	7.5	7.8	7.1	23.9	26.4	13.2	2.0	75.2	39.0	50.0	50.0
98841	OMAK	72.8	71.0	0.2	0.2	0.9	1.0	11.3	13.4	6.5	6.2	8.0	8.0	7.7	24.9	24.4	12.6	1.7	74.3	36.5	48.8	51.3
98843	ORONDO	67.5	64.4	0.4	0.5	0.5	0.5	45.6	50.8	9.9	9.7	9.0	7.7	6.3	28.9	21.1	6.9	0.5	66.6	30.9	53.2	46.8
98844	OROVILLE	85.1	83.3	0.3	0.3	0.6	0.6	14.0	16.7	6.6	6.7	7.8	6.9	5.3	23.0	27.1	15.0	1.5	74.0	40.6	50.4	49.7
98845	PALISADES	91.8	90.6	0.0	0.0	0.0	1.6	6.6	6.3	4.7	6.3	9.4	7.8	1.6	23.4	32.8	14.1	0.0	73.4	43.3	53.1	46.9
98846	PATEROS	76.8	73.9	0.0	0.0	0.4	0.4	31.7	36.4	8.1	8.2	8.2	6.5	6.1	27.1	21.1	12.5	2.1	72.5	34.0	49.9	50.1
98847	PESHASTIN	82.9	80.5	0.2	0.3	0.6	0.6	21.9	25.5	6.4	6.7	8.6	8.5	7.5	26.7	25.4	9.4	0.9	72.8	36.0	50.7	49.3
98848	QUINCY	72.5	70.4	0.2	0.2	0.8	0.8	48.5	53.2	9.9	9.1	8.9	7.9	7.8	26.0	20.2	9.3	1.0	67.2	29.8	52.7	47.3
98849	RIVERSIDE	88.4	86.9	0.2	0.2	0.3	0.3	8.2	9.9	5.2	5.4	6.6	7.1	5.0	22.8	33.0	13.4	1.5	77.8	43.6	51.1	48.9
98850	ROCK ISLAND	69.6	66.0	0.5	0.5	0.6	0.6	34.0	38.8	10.4	8.9	8.1	8.3	7.2	27.0	21.2	8.4	0.5	67.6	30.6	50.6	49.4
98851	SOAP LAKE	89.6	88.1	0.8	0.9	0.3	0.3	9.6	11.9	7.5	7.4	7.7	6.7	5.2	20.8	24.4	18.0	2.4	73.2	40.9	49.1	50.9
98852	STEHEKIN	96.2	95.9	0.0	0.0	1.9	2.4	2.8	4.1	4.1	8.9	8.1	4.1	8.9	33.3	30.1	2.4	0.0	75.6	37.2	51.2	48.8
98855	TONASKET	85.0	82.9	0.2	0.2	0.5	0.6	13.3	15.8	6.0	6.2	7.5	7.4	5.8	20.7	30.5	13.7	2.2	75.2	42.5	49.5	50.5
98856	TWISP	96.4	96.1	0.0	0.0	0.4	0.4	1.7	2.1	4.4	4.3	6.2	6.7	4.6	21.6	36.7	13.7	1.9	80.2	46.1	49.3	50.7
98857	WARDEN	55.4	52.4	0.2	0.2	0.7	0.8	53.7	57.7	11.1	10.0	8.9	7.9	7.4	26.6	19.3	8.0	0.9	65.2	28.3	51.7	48.3
98858	WATERVILLE	90.8	89.5	0.7	0.7	0.4	0.5	7.8	9.3	5.9	7.0	8.5	7.5	4.5	22.2	29.1	13.1	2.3	73.8	41.8	49.6	50.4
98859	WAUCONDA	92.2	91.7	0.0	0.0	0.3	0.3	3.7	4.8	3.6	3.9	8.0	7.7	5.6	18.4	39.5	13.1	0.3	79.2	46.3	50.7	49.3
98862	WINTHROP	97.2	96.9	0.3	0.3	0.4	0.5	1.7	2.1	4.0	3.8	6.7	4.9	4.0	21.4	39.8	14.3	1.2	82.1	47.3	50.1	49.9
98901	YAKIMA	59.7	57.1	2.6	2.5	0.8	0.8	43.3	47.1	9.4	8.6	9.0	8.1	8.0	28.0	19.6	8.1	1.2	68.1	29.8	51.4	48.6
98902	YAKIMA	74.2	71.1	1.6	1.7	1.3	1.4	28.3	32.7	9.1	8.0	7.2	6.6	8.0	27.9	19.5	10.7	3.1	72.0	32.4	48.1	51.9
98903	YAKIMA	81.0	78.2	0.4	0.4	0.6	0.7	18.8	22.6	6.7	6.9	8.0	6.9	6.3	26.3	25.6	11.5	1.7	74.0	37.3	50.6	49.4
98908	YAKIMA	89.6	88.0	0.8	0.8	1.7	1.8	10.0	12.4	6.1	6.5	7.7	7.0	6.0	24.3	27.4	12.9	2.1	75.3	39.9	48.4	51.6
98922	CLE ELUM	95.9	95.5	0.3	0.3	0.6	0.7	2.3	2.7	5.0	5.6	6.2	6.0	5.0	22.3	33.5	14.5	1.9	79.4	44.9	50.4	49.6
98923	COWICHE	83.6	80.9	0.2	0.1	0.3	0.3	33.0	38.9	9.1	8.6	9.4	7.8	7.5	27.6	21.1	8.5	0.5	68.3	31.0	49.5	50.5
98926	ELLENSBURG	90.5	89.6	0.8	0.9	2.9	3.1	5.8	6.8	5.1	4.7	5.3	10.1	20.3	23.8	19.9	9.0	1.8	81.5	27.8	49.4	50.6
98930	GRANDVIEW	56.2	52.9	0.6	0.6	0.8	0.8	60.7	66.0	10.5	9.7	9.3	8.1	8.3	27.2	18.3	7.5	1.3	65.5	27.8	50.0	50.0
98932	GRANGER	37.0	33.6	0.1	0.0	0.2	0.2	66.5	70.5	12.1	10.7	10.3	8.4	9.2	26.1	16.6	6.1	0.5	61.9	24.6	52.4	47.6
	WASHINGTON	81.8	80.6	3.2	3.3	5.9	6.3	7.5	8.6	6.7	6.6	7.1	7.0	7.6	28.7	24.9	9.8	1.6	75.4	36.1	49.7	50.3
	UNITED STATES	75.1	73.6	12.3	12.5	3.8	4.2	12.5	14.1	6.9	6.7	7.2	7.0	7.3	28.6	23.8	10.8	1.7	75.1	36.0	49.1	50.9

INCOME

ZIP CODE #	POST OFFICE NAME	2004 Per Capita Income	2004 HH Income Base	2004 Household Income Distribution (%): Less than $25,000	$25,000 to $49,999	$50,000 to $99,999	$100,000 to $149,999	$150,000 or More	Median Household Income: 2004	2009	2004 National Centile	2004 State Centile	2004 Home Value Base	2004 Home Value Distribution (%): Less than $50,000	$50,000 to $89,999	$90,000 to $174,999	$175,000 to $399,999	$400,000 or More	2004 Median Home Value
98597	YELM	19678	5639	25.1	30.7	35.5	6.8	2.0	45229	50312	62	53	4418	4.3	13.1	49.5	29.7	3.4	149695
98601	AMBOY	19179	891	19.4	30.0	39.3	8.6	2.7	50443	55844	73	68	770	6.0	2.6	21.7	58.8	10.9	214241
98602	APPLETON	18877	55	30.9	36.4	25.5	7.3	0.0	38652	44089	42	35	47	8.5	14.9	40.4	27.7	8.5	142500
98603	ARIEL	17407	351	29.9	30.2	33.1	5.1	1.7	40587	41717	48	42	294	7.1	7.5	34.0	50.0	1.4	177381
98604	BATTLE GROUND	23208	9176	15.1	22.9	42.3	14.5	5.2	61057	68364	85	85	7880	4.4	1.8	26.4	57.3	10.2	216789
98605	BINGEN	19697	229	30.1	28.0	28.4	9.2	4.4	42529	46154	55	48	183	1.6	5.5	36.1	45.9	10.9	190625
98606	BRUSH PRAIRIE	29588	3307	8.5	20.7	40.9	16.5	13.4	70585	81646	91	93	3029	5.3	1.8	9.7	61.4	21.9	286205
98607	CAMAS	31365	7711	11.7	22.2	38.2	17.2	10.8	68152	79125	90	92	6331	1.9	1.4	22.0	57.5	17.2	237114
98610	CARSON	16348	916	31.4	36.8	27.2	2.8	1.8	37374	41625	37	29	705	14.8	4.0	47.2	32.1	2.0	149437
98611	CASTLE ROCK	21278	3349	22.4	31.3	35.6	8.7	2.1	47437	51783	67	61	2742	4.5	8.5	44.2	39.2	3.6	161166
98612	CATHLAMET	23674	1091	23.7	33.4	34.6	5.0	3.3	44040	47969	59	51	863	6.5	11.7	32.8	42.3	6.7	172739
98613	CENTERVILLE	17420	364	39.3	29.7	26.7	2.5	1.9	34380	36945	25	17	294	16.7	21.4	32.3	21.1	8.5	113021
98616	COUGAR	17445	44	34.1	31.8	31.8	2.3	0.0	32347	34413	19	10	36	11.1	8.3	30.6	50.0	0.0	175000
98617	DALLESPORT	17427	76	34.2	32.9	25.0	5.3	2.6	37840	40000	39	31	59	11.9	22.0	45.8	18.6	1.7	114423
98619	GLENWOOD	18626	213	27.2	34.3	31.9	4.7	1.9	41684	44812	52	46	154	9.1	14.3	46.1	24.7	5.8	133000
98620	GOLDENDALE	17335	2815	37.7	30.8	26.1	4.1	1.4	33234	36591	22	12	2006	7.2	16.3	50.1	23.5	3.0	124934
98621	GRAYS RIVER	18811	79	26.6	34.2	32.9	5.1	1.3	39637	42615	45	39	65	7.7	10.8	41.5	36.9	3.1	147917
98624	ILWACO	20037	539	37.9	31.5	22.5	4.6	3.5	34559	38755	26	17	421	7.4	13.5	43.5	32.3	3.3	143750
98625	KALAMA	21566	1994	26.2	27.0	34.1	8.9	3.8	46092	49351	64	57	1639	4.8	7.0	38.9	43.4	5.9	173412
98626	KELSO	19335	8684	30.0	29.4	31.4	6.7	2.5	41786	46133	52	46	6078	9.4	9.8	46.9	31.5	2.4	143537
98628	KLICKITAT	13451	94	40.4	30.9	23.4	5.3	0.0	35000	35767	28	19	64	6.3	32.8	37.5	20.3	3.1	110000
98629	LA CENTER	22383	2514	13.5	27.2	41.6	14.0	3.7	58037	64258	83	81	2209	3.6	1.6	22.1	63.3	9.3	228432
98631	LONG BEACH	22539	1932	37.9	34.0	21.5	4.2	2.4	33151	36796	21	12	1396	5.9	12.8	46.1	30.2	5.0	144764
98632	LONGVIEW	21465	18904	29.1	29.8	30.1	8.0	3.0	41853	47071	52	47	12218	5.0	7.5	46.8	37.9	2.8	159146
98635	LYLE	18828	1198	32.0	33.2	27.6	5.7	1.5	38651	41483	42	35	931	9.1	17.9	42.6	25.8	4.5	130322
98638	NASELLE	21346	793	30.1	33.8	26.5	5.9	3.7	38861	43555	42	36	649	5.2	10.5	45.6	35.9	2.8	146314
98640	OCEAN PARK	19250	1967	40.8	35.7	18.9	3.2	1.5	30299	32894	13	5	1643	9.4	16.1	45.7	25.6	3.4	124414
98642	RIDGEFIELD	28882	4841	14.8	24.8	35.2	15.3	9.9	63426	71470	87	88	4081	2.4	1.6	15.6	59.5	20.8	266932
98643	ROSBURG	20374	165	26.7	32.7	35.8	3.6	1.2	39828	43268	45	39	136	6.6	9.6	43.4	36.0	4.4	150000
98645	SILVERLAKE	22102	479	18.2	35.7	38.4	6.1	1.7	48503	54225	69	64	408	3.7	4.9	48.8	40.7	2.0	163462
98647	SKAMOKAWA	16309	162	29.0	38.9	30.9	1.2	0.0	38616	41323	41	35	134	9.0	22.4	33.6	35.1	0.0	129545
98648	STEVENSON	19554	1545	30.2	32.0	30.1	5.2	2.5	38975	43067	43	37	1096	6.0	5.2	39.6	41.4	7.8	173602
98649	TOUTLE	17500	246	28.5	30.5	35.4	4.9	0.8	45805	47758	63	56	209	0.5	12.9	45.5	37.8	3.4	154891
98650	TROUT LAKE	20934	320	27.5	32.2	32.2	5.6	2.5	40892	44392	49	43	245	2.5	5.7	33.1	44.9	13.9	200862
98651	UNDERWOOD	23786	374	28.1	26.2	30.5	10.2	5.1	45268	49452	62	54	306	2.9	4.3	34.0	47.4	11.4	193750
98660	VANCOUVER	19671	4404	39.1	28.3	25.5	5.0	2.1	33394	38043	22	13	2089	6.0	4.5	56.7	30.4	2.4	150378
98661	VANCOUVER	19831	15433	32.4	34.0	25.3	6.2	2.1	36109	40474	32	23	6917	3.4	3.5	54.0	34.7	4.5	160856
98662	VANCOUVER	23244	9798	17.1	31.2	38.3	9.4	4.0	51188	57719	74	69	6705	3.3	1.9	51.4	39.6	3.9	167503
98663	VANCOUVER	21814	5678	25.8	31.4	31.2	9.5	2.1	45000	51072	61	53	3465	3.1	3.6	54.4	37.6	1.2	161077
98664	VANCOUVER	26384	8758	17.9	32.7	34.6	10.5	4.4	49517	55584	71	66	5650	0.7	0.8	47.4	44.1	7.0	176778
98665	VANCOUVER	24523	8433	22.3	30.4	32.6	9.6	5.1	47551	52735	67	62	5496	6.3	5.8	32.4	51.6	3.9	182842
98671	WASHOUGAL	23735	6075	17.2	31.2	37.8	9.7	4.1	51305	57027	74	70	4657	5.5	3.2	34.2	48.3	8.8	190255
98672	WHITE SALMON	19706	2349	29.8	34.8	27.0	6.3	2.0	38982	43158	43	37	1750	3.1	8.5	41.8	38.4	8.2	165625
98674	WOODLAND	21648	3448	20.9	29.3	36.7	9.8	3.3	49800	54684	72	66	2707	4.1	5.2	34.2	49.4	7.1	186612
98675	YACOLT	18750	1599	14.6	25.5	43.6	13.1	3.3	56497	63563	81	78	1385	2.5	2.6	29.8	51.8	13.3	223032
98682	VANCOUVER	21083	16326	13.0	30.7	43.8	10.2	2.3	54984	62128	80	76	12129	4.0	3.4	50.3	40.2	2.1	167377
98683	VANCOUVER	28348	13276	15.4	28.1	38.8	11.8	5.8	55813	63014	80	78	8593	2.6	2.0	26.0	63.1	6.4	204043
98684	VANCOUVER	22763	8895	15.0	28.8	41.6	12.5	2.1	55430	62135	80	77	5649	4.1	2.0	48.3	43.6	2.1	170260
98685	VANCOUVER	28845	8518	14.5	20.7	39.1	17.0	8.8	65670	74540	89	90	6840	3.3	1.7	27.9	59.2	7.9	205198
98686	VANCOUVER	28276	5651	14.1	22.8	37.7	16.9	8.5	64631	72455	88	89	4507	2.3	1.2	22.7	65.3	8.5	218603
98801	WENATCHEE	23007	14164	29.0	29.8	27.9	8.1	5.3	41132	47579	50	44	9437	4.0	5.4	42.5	42.1	6.1	171834
98802	EAST WENATCHEE	20303	9117	25.4	29.0	35.5	7.8	2.3	45592	50735	63	55	6787	5.7	4.2	43.8	43.7	2.7	169937
98812	BREWSTER	12859	1212	46.4	31.5	15.9	4.0	2.2	27033	29802	7	3	753	11.7	14.5	51.8	21.1	0.9	121554
98813	BRIDGEPORT	12358	1079	39.6	40.0	17.2	2.6	0.7	30305	34187	13	5	740	26.1	28.9	34.9	7.7	2.4	82885
98814	CARLTON	20817	212	29.3	35.9	26.4	7.1	1.4	40453	43947	48	42	176	1.7	8.0	38.1	41.5	10.8	181250
98815	CASHMERE	19007	3057	27.4	31.9	29.2	8.6	2.9	40799	46753	49	43	2110	5.5	6.9	35.6	44.0	8.0	179884
98816	CHELAN	21801	2511	33.4	30.3	24.2	7.4	4.7	36704	42124	34	26	1690	5.1	3.1	34.9	40.9	16.0	193831
98822	ENTIAT	18829	791	30.1	31.7	29.1	4.9	4.2	38644	43810	42	35	586	5.1	6.3	50.0	33.1	5.5	156180
98823	EPHRATA	19350	3624	26.7	33.3	28.9	8.0	3.2	40085	44411	46	40	2738	9.9	15.5	52.3	20.6	1.9	118893
98826	LEAVENWORTH	26484	2741	24.3	30.0	30.7	9.7	5.4	45596	51630	63	55	2093	1.6	2.5	28.3	54.3	13.3	209686
98827	LOOMIS	13191	200	47.5	30.5	17.5	3.0	1.5	26139	27842	6	3	145	5.5	24.8	39.3	20.0	10.3	131250
98828	MALAGA	22010	694	20.0	24.6	40.8	8.8	5.8	53940	61523	78	74	579	3.5	4.0	41.8	42.1	8.6	176731
98830	MANSFIELD	18440	270	40.0	26.3	27.4	5.6	0.7	35831	36260	31	21	203	15.3	39.9	32.5	9.4	3.0	84474
98831	MANSON	16329	1159	33.5	33.4	25.5	5.1	2.6	36034	40386	32	22	834	10.8	5.4	27.1	42.3	14.4	190556
98832	MARLIN	15983	240	31.3	38.8	22.9	7.1	0.0	33918	36454	24	15	188	15.4	21.3	35.6	22.3	5.3	111458
98833	MAZAMA	78743	127	22.1	12.6	29.1	14.2	22.1	67792	86663	90	92	107	0.0	5.6	29.9	58.9	5.6	238750
98834	METHOW	24688	315	24.8	30.2	33.0	7.0	5.1	47148	52306	66	60	223	1.8	9.0	45.3	39.0	4.9	165878
98837	MOSES LAKE	18551	11796	27.8	34.3	27.1	7.9	2.9	40764	45198	49	43	8205	10.6	14.9	46.8	24.7	2.9	122256
98840	OKANOGAN	15889	2012	40.4	34.3	19.2	4.0	2.0	31224	34564	16	7	1416	7.6	24.6	45.8	20.1	2.1	113401
98841	OMAK	16435	3008	37.4	32.7	24.8	3.9	1.3	33903	36220	24	15	2114	10.4	19.9	53.3	13.5	2.9	109397
98843	ORONDO	18890	528	32.4	35.6	19.7	7.8	4.6	35839	39728	31	22	324	9.6	3.1	25.3	36.4	25.6	225714
98844	OROVILLE	15015	1630	44.2	34.4	16.6	3.7	1.2	28513	30886	10	4	1146	14.3	21.9	42.7	17.8	3.3	108333
98845	PALISADES	17070	23	21.7	34.8	39.1	4.4	0.0	46120	54473	64	57	18	5.6	22.2	38.9	33.3	0.0	137500
98846	PATEROS	15301	276	35.5	39.1	19.9	5.1	0.4	32532	34283	19	10	200	9.5	12.5	51.0	26.0	1.0	132813
98847	PESHASTIN	22074	630	23.2	28.7	33.0	9.2	5.9	48210	54698	69	63	419	6.4	4.5	33.9	46.5	8.6	193534
98848	QUINCY	14558	3217	27.8	40.4	25.3	4.6	2.0	37386	41451	37	30	2233	10.7	12.2	50.7	22.3	4.1	127418
98849	RIVERSIDE	16349	766	38.6	35.0	21.5	2.4	2.5	31475	34297	16	8	618	13.6	23.6	39.0	18.6	5.2	110381
98850	ROCK ISLAND	15149	513	32.8	36.8	23.6	4.9	2.0	34604	38742	26	18	394	10.9	15.2	46.2	23.1	4.6	124662
98851	SOAP LAKE	14822	1688	46.8	29.9	19.6	2.6	1.2	26560	28433	7	3	1138	11.5	30.2	39.1	18.0	1.1	106143
98852	STEHEKIN	12468	46	45.7	43.5	6.5	0.0	4.4	31099	27500	15	7	19	0.0	0.0	73.7	15.8	10.5	144643
98855	TONASKET	15317	2184	42.8	33.5	19.2	2.8	1.8	29105	31268	11	4	1602	18.9	20.5	41.2	15.3	4.1	107538
98856	TWISP	19859	1194	34.4	37.4	22.0	3.9	2.4	34071	38127	24	16	914	8.6	9.9	35.5	37.1	9.0	164286
98857	WARDEN	14220	1214	30.2	35.9	26.4	5.5	2.0	38276	41443	40	33	856	10.1	22.3	45.2	21.9	0.6	108886
98858	WATERVILLE	21830	704	25.7	35.1	30.7	5.5	3.0	40630	44575	48	42	565	6.9	16.3	54.7	20.4	1.8	119981
98859	WAUCONDA	17584	146	46.6	25.3	24.7	2.7	0.7	27588	30000	8	4	126	20.6	15.9	42.9	15.9	4.8	109483
98862	WINTHROP	26084	725	29.2	35.9	24.3	4.4	6.2	38963	43142	43	36	587	5.1	7.7	32.0	42.6	12.6	186213
98901	YAKIMA	14918	9074	40.8	30.0	21.2	5.1	2.8	30718	33932	14	7	5353	17.0	18.2	42.9	20.2	1.7	112771
98902	YAKIMA	17837	16430	36.3	33.4	22.9	5.2	2.2	33640	38236	23	14	9165	8.8	17.1	63.3	9.6	1.3	112811
98903	YAKIMA	19015	4584	28.1	31.7	30.5	7.4	2.3	41814	46571	52	46	3531	16.9	18.9	42.4	19.3	2.5	110757
98908	YAKIMA	27990	12732	19.2	27.5	34.7	11.3	7.3	52825	60976	77	73	9791	6.0	4.7	47.8	35.6	5.9	162008
98922	CLE ELUM	26971	3364	26.3	29.1	30.3	8.9	5.4	45840	52445	63	56	2619	3.1	7.6	43.2	36.5	9.7	166921
98923	COWICHE	17819	418	22.0	33.7	30.6	10.8	2.9	45345	51149	62	54	294	6.5	21.1	50.0	18.7	3.7	125481
98926	ELLENSBURG	21114	10671	40.6	26.8	23.9	5.7	3.1	32715	37046	20	11	5572	6.7	4.5	43.3	39.3	6.2	165103
98930	GRANDVIEW	14632	3771	29.7	32.1	30.2	6.0	2.0	37693	42198	38	31	2729	13.2	26.4	46.7	12.5	1.2	98442
98932	GRANGER	10060	1111	36.7	36.2	21.3	4.9	0.9	32714	36035	20	11	792	12.8	17.8	47.5	19.7	2.3	107470
	WASHINGTON	26555		21.6	27.8	33.4	11.4	5.9	50585	57953				4.6	5.9	31.3	45.6	12.6	195701
	UNITED STATES	25866		24.7	27.1	30.8	10.9	6.5	48124	56710				10.9	15.0	33.7	30.1	10.4	145905

#	POST OFFICE NAME	FINANCIAL SERVICES: Auto Loan	Home Loan	Investments	Retirement Plans	THE HOME: Home Improvements: Home Repair	Lawn & Garden	Furnishings: Computers & Hardware	Major Appliances	TV, Radio, Sound Equipment	Furniture	ENTERTAINMENT: Dine out/Carry out	Sports Equipment	Fees & Tickets	Toys & Games	Travel	Cable TV	PERSONAL: Apparel & Services	Auto Repairs	Health Insurance	Pets & Supplies
98597	YELM	83	77	63	75	78	81	73	78	74	75	91	91	70	88	73	73	88	78	77	93
98601	AMBOY	92	85	67	82	86	90	80	86	81	82	100	100	77	97	80	81	96	85	86	103
98602	APPLETON	72	60	47	60	63	72	62	67	66	61	80	76	59	79	62	67	75	66	73	80
98603	ARIEL	78	71	55	68	72	76	67	72	69	68	84	84	64	81	67	68	81	72	74	88
98604	BATTLE GROUND	94	108	111	109	106	105	100	100	94	100	118	117	103	122	100	91	117	98	90	111
98605	BINGEN	98	71	40	67	81	91	70	85	80	69	94	101	61	93	72	83	86	84	99	115
98606	BRUSH PRAIRIE	120	147	155	148	144	142	131	131	122	132	153	153	139	162	134	117	153	126	117	144
98607	CAMAS	125	136	135	137	133	135	127	127	121	128	152	149	130	155	126	117	149	125	118	143
98610	CARSON	68	62	48	60	63	66	59	64	60	61	74	74	56	70	59	60	71	63	64	76
98611	CASTLE ROCK	84	79	68	76	82	88	74	80	77	74	95	94	74	96	76	78	91	79	85	99
98612	CATHLAMET	78	79	77	75	80	89	78	80	80	76	98	90	78	98	79	82	94	79	85	91
98613	CENTERVILLE	77	54	28	50	63	70	53	66	61	53	72	79	45	70	55	65	66	65	79	92
98616	COUGAR	64	58	45	56	58	61	55	59	56	57	69	69	52	65	55	55	67	59	59	70
98617	DALLESPORT	92	62	28	54	70	81	60	75	72	61	85	89	51	80	61	77	77	74	92	106
98619	GLENWOOD	85	60	31	56	70	78	59	73	68	58	80	88	50	78	61	71	73	72	87	101
98620	GOLDENDALE	72	55	37	52	60	68	57	64	63	56	75	74	51	73	57	66	70	63	73	81
98621	GRAYS RIVER	86	61	33	58	71	79	60	74	69	60	81	89	52	79	62	72	74	73	87	102
98624	ILWACO	81	62	40	56	70	79	59	71	67	58	79	84	52	78	62	71	73	70	84	98
98625	KALAMA	88	78	60	75	81	88	74	81	78	74	95	95	72	95	75	79	90	79	86	100
98626	KELSO	73	70	68	69	71	76	71	72	72	70	89	85	70	90	71	72	86	73	73	83
98628	KLICKITAT	55	48	51	48	48	55	56	54	59	54	72	63	54	71	54	59	69	56	57	60
98629	LA CENTER	94	102	99	102	100	101	95	96	91	95	114	114	96	116	95	87	111	95	88	109
98631	LONG BEACH	79	62	42	56	70	79	59	71	66	58	79	83	52	78	62	71	73	70	83	97
98632	LONGVIEW	72	72	76	71	73	79	73	74	74	72	92	86	74	93	74	74	89	74	75	84
98635	LYLE	80	63	42	59	67	75	62	71	69	63	83	83	57	79	62	71	77	70	79	90
98638	NASELLE	86	62	36	59	70	81	65	76	73	63	86	88	56	83	66	77	79	75	90	99
98640	OCEAN PARK	65	53	40	48	59	67	50	60	56	50	67	67	46	64	53	60	62	58	70	78
98642	RIDGEFIELD	103	126	133	126	123	122	113	113	106	113	133	132	120	141	116	102	132	109	101	125
98643	ROSBURG	88	61	32	58	71	80	60	75	70	60	82	90	52	80	63	73	74	74	89	104
98645	SILVERLAKE	93	84	65	80	86	91	79	86	81	80	100	100	76	97	79	81	95	84	88	105
98647	SKAMOKAWA	67	61	48	59	61	65	58	63	59	60	73	72	55	69	58	58	70	62	62	75
98648	STEVENSON	77	67	53	64	71	78	65	72	69	64	84	83	62	84	66	71	79	70	79	89
98649	TOUTLE	79	70	54	67	74	79	65	72	69	65	84	85	64	85	67	70	80	70	77	92
98650	TROUT LAKE	93	65	34	62	76	85	64	80	74	64	87	96	55	85	67	78	79	78	95	111
98651	UNDERWOOD	107	74	39	70	87	97	73	91	85	73	99	110	63	97	76	89	91	90	108	127
98660	VANCOUVER	57	56	66	57	56	60	61	59	61	60	76	70	61	76	60	60	74	61	57	65
98661	VANCOUVER	67	64	68	65	64	69	69	68	70	68	87	80	68	86	67	68	84	70	66	75
98662	VANCOUVER	86	91	97	94	89	91	90	89	86	90	108	105	90	108	88	82	106	89	81	98
98663	VANCOUVER	71	74	81	75	74	78	76	74	75	74	93	88	76	95	75	73	91	75	72	82
98664	VANCOUVER	87	91	100	93	90	94	92	91	89	92	112	107	93	112	91	87	110	92	85	100
98665	VANCOUVER	84	88	97	92	87	90	89	87	85	89	108	102	90	107	87	82	106	88	80	96
98671	WASHOUGAL	91	91	85	90	93	97	88	91	88	87	108	107	88	111	88	87	105	89	90	106
98672	WHITE SALMON	82	62	39	60	69	78	63	73	70	62	84	86	57	82	64	73	77	72	84	95
98674	WOODLAND	94	84	66	80	88	95	80	87	85	80	103	103	78	104	81	86	98	85	93	109
98675	YACOLT	92	98	93	98	96	97	92	93	88	93	110	109	92	110	91	85	108	92	86	106
98682	VANCOUVER	89	93	95	97	90	90	91	89	85	92	108	106	91	107	88	80	106	89	79	99
98683	VANCOUVER	98	100	107	105	98	100	100	98	96	102	121	117	100	118	97	91	118	99	89	110
98684	VANCOUVER	89	92	95	95	89	91	91	90	87	92	110	106	91	108	88	82	107	91	81	99
98685	VANCOUVER	104	123	131	125	120	119	112	111	105	113	132	130	118	137	113	101	132	108	99	123
98686	VANCOUVER	105	119	123	121	117	117	111	111	105	111	132	131	114	136	111	101	130	109	101	124
98801	WENATCHEE	84	85	87	84	85	90	85	86	85	85	106	100	85	106	85	84	103	86	84	96
98802	EAST WENATCHEE	78	80	78	80	80	84	78	79	77	77	95	93	78	96	78	76	93	79	77	90
98812	BREWSTER	60	55	52	54	54	57	57	59	58	60	73	67	55	69	55	56	72	60	55	64
98813	BRIDGEPORT	58	51	43	49	50	53	52	55	54	55	67	62	49	63	50	52	66	56	53	61
98814	CARLTON	84	62	38	57	71	80	60	73	68	59	81	87	52	79	63	72	74	72	87	101
98815	CASHMERE	87	71	53	69	76	83	71	79	76	71	92	93	65	89	71	77	86	79	85	100
98816	CHELAN	89	70	52	67	76	86	72	81	79	71	95	94	65	92	73	82	89	81	91	102
98822	ENTIAT	85	69	47	66	74	80	67	76	72	68	86	90	61	83	68	73	81	76	83	98
98823	EPHRATA	84	72	55	70	74	82	72	78	76	72	92	89	68	89	72	77	87	77	83	93
98826	LEAVENWORTH	102	87	70	82	94	107	84	95	91	85	110	105	80	104	88	95	103	93	109	118
98827	LOOMIS	58	46	32	43	51	58	45	52	50	44	59	61	41	59	47	53	55	51	61	69
98828	MALAGA	97	96	83	93	96	99	90	94	89	92	110	109	88	108	90	87	107	93	91	110
98830	MANSFIELD	70	52	32	49	58	68	56	63	63	53	74	72	49	70	56	66	67	63	75	79
98831	MANSON	79	61	42	58	65	71	62	71	67	64	82	81	55	76	61	68	78	71	76	87
98832	MARLIN	77	54	28	51	63	70	53	66	61	53	72	79	45	70	55	64	65	65	78	92
98833	MAZAMA	278	218	148	196	245	275	205	247	232	203	275	290	184	272	219	248	256	244	292	338
98834	METHOW	112	89	61	81	99	112	85	101	95	84	113	118	76	111	89	101	105	99	118	136
98837	MOSES LAKE	77	72	66	71	73	79	72	75	74	72	91	87	70	89	72	73	87	75	76	87
98840	OKANOGAN	66	50	35	48	55	63	54	60	60	52	71	68	48	68	53	62	66	60	69	74
98841	OMAK	65	55	44	53	56	64	58	61	61	57	74	70	54	71	57	63	70	62	66	72
98843	ORONDO	96	76	54	71	80	87	77	88	83	81	102	99	69	94	76	84	98	88	92	105
98844	OROVILLE	59	46	34	43	50	58	48	54	54	47	64	62	44	62	49	56	60	54	62	68
98845	PALISADES	86	60	31	57	70	78	59	73	68	59	80	88	51	79	61	72	73	72	87	102
98846	PATEROS	63	53	42	53	56	63	55	59	58	54	71	67	53	70	55	59	66	58	64	69
98847	PESHASTIN	96	94	83	93	95	98	89	93	88	89	110	110	88	110	89	87	106	91	91	110
98848	QUINCY	73	63	52	61	64	69	64	68	67	66	83	79	61	81	63	66	81	69	69	81
98849	RIVERSIDE	67	58	43	55	60	65	55	61	58	56	71	71	52	67	56	58	67	61	64	76
98850	ROCK ISLAND	67	66	71	68	67	71	67	68	66	67	82	80	66	80	67	64	79	69	67	77
98851	SOAP LAKE	59	49	36	47	51	57	50	54	53	49	64	62	46	60	49	54	60	54	59	65
98852	STEHEKIN	54	42	29	38	47	53	40	48	45	39	53	56	36	53	42	48	50	47	57	65
98855	TONASKET	63	49	33	46	53	62	50	57	56	49	66	65	45	64	51	59	61	57	67	72
98856	TWISP	74	55	35	51	62	71	56	65	63	54	75	76	49	72	57	67	68	65	78	86
98857	WARDEN	75	59	48	58	62	66	64	68	69	66	84	80	58	83	61	67	82	71	70	81
98858	WATERVILLE	103	72	38	68	84	94	71	88	82	71	96	106	61	95	74	86	88	87	105	123
98859	WAUCONDA	69	54	37	49	61	68	51	61	57	50	68	72	45	67	54	61	63	60	72	84
98862	WINTHROP	96	74	49	67	84	94	70	85	80	70	94	100	62	93	75	85	87	84	100	116
98901	YAKIMA	67	60	54	58	60	63	61	64	63	63	79	73	58	76	60	62	77	65	63	72
98902	YAKIMA	62	60	66	60	60	65	65	63	66	64	82	74	64	81	64	64	79	65	63	70
98903	YAKIMA	79	73	62	70	74	80	71	76	73	72	90	87	69	88	71	74	87	75	78	89
98908	YAKIMA	103	108	107	107	108	112	102	105	100	103	125	122	103	126	103	99	122	104	101	120
98922	CLE ELUM	102	79	55	74	88	101	81	92	90	79	107	106	73	104	83	95	99	91	108	118
98923	COWICHE	86	87	80	87	87	88	83	86	81	84	101	102	81	101	82	78	98	85	80	99
98926	ELLENSBURG	71	62	65	64	62	68	73	68	73	69	90	85	68	88	69	69	87	72	67	79
98930	GRANDVIEW	77	67	55	64	67	71	68	73	70	71	87	82	63	81	66	69	85	74	72	83
98932	GRANGER	62	54	47	52	53	55	57	60	59	61	74	66	53	68	54	56	73	61	56	64
	WASHINGTON	94	96	103	97	95	100	96	95	94	96	118	112	96	118	95	92	115	96	91	107
	UNITED STATES	100	100	100	100	100	100	100	100	100	100	100	100	100	100	100	100	100	100	100	100

A 98933-99181

# POST OFFICE NAME	COUNTY FIPS CODE	POPULATION 2000	2004	2009	2000-2004 ANNUAL RATE % Rate	State Centile	HOUSEHOLDS 2000	2004	2009	% Annual Rate 2000-2004	2004 Average HH Size	FAMILIES 2000	2004	% Annual Rate 2000-2004
98933 HARRAH	077	1200	1251	1282	1.0	55	346	360	367	0.9	3.47	283	293	0.8
98935 MABTON	077	3835	4022	4127	1.1	62	967	1009	1028	1.0	3.95	828	862	1.0
98936 MOXEE	077	3720	3792	3832	0.5	38	1261	1284	1291	0.4	2.94	990	1002	0.3
98937 NACHES	077	4309	4445	4568	0.7	48	1628	1676	1713	0.7	2.64	1233	1264	0.6
98938 OUTLOOK	077	1793	1871	1914	1.0	59	518	537	545	0.9	3.48	432	446	0.8
98942 SELAH	077	15503	16098	16419	0.9	53	5429	5634	5717	0.9	2.83	4283	4419	0.7
98944 SUNNYSIDE	077	19743	20350	20691	0.7	47	5494	5603	5641	0.5	3.59	4402	4465	0.3
98946 THORP	037	611	658	698	1.8	79	227	247	263	2.0	2.66	182	197	1.9
98947 TIETON	077	2506	2710	2826	1.9	81	780	833	859	1.6	3.25	614	652	1.4
98948 TOPPENISH	077	12677	12679	12766	0.0	20	3362	3320	3306	-0.3	3.76	2735	2689	-0.4
98951 WAPATO	077	13970	14068	14113	0.2	24	3812	3811	3807	0.0	3.66	3122	3107	-0.1
98952 WHITE SWAN	077	2696	2776	2823	0.7	45	634	648	654	0.5	4.12	538	548	0.4
98953 ZILLAH	077	6141	6485	6687	1.3	67	1998	2100	2151	1.2	3.07	1602	1675	1.1
99003 CHATTAROY	063	4265	4513	4695	1.3	68	1520	1623	1697	1.6	2.77	1243	1317	1.4
99004 CHENEY	063	14600	15813	16575	1.9	81	5252	5770	6103	2.2	2.45	3190	3503	2.2
99005 COLBERT	063	6642	7142	7461	1.7	78	2161	2346	2464	2.0	3.03	1876	2028	1.9
99006 DEER PARK	063	8284	8571	8762	0.8	50	2987	3110	3192	1.0	2.74	2258	2334	0.8
99008 EDWALL	043	530	542	545	0.5	40	194	199	200	0.6	2.72	141	144	0.5
99009 ELK	063	2942	3068	3153	1.0	56	1045	1103	1143	1.3	2.78	818	857	1.1
99011 FAIRCHILD AIR FORCE	063	4361	4223	4216	-0.8	4	1072	1043	1048	-0.6	3.33	1050	1021	-0.7
99012 FAIRFIELD	063	1037	1012	1014	-0.6	6	377	371	373	-0.4	2.62	282	276	-0.5
99013 FORD	065	1010	1052	1079	1.0	55	370	391	405	1.3	2.69	278	292	1.2
99016 GREENACRES	063	8685	9522	10050	2.2	86	3289	3655	3888	2.5	2.57	2334	2555	2.2
99017 LAMONT	075	261	251	250	-0.9	2	99	96	96	-0.7	2.61	75	73	-0.6
99018 LATAH	063	221	215	215	-0.7	4	87	85	86	-0.6	2.40	65	63	-0.7
99019 LIBERTY LAKE	063	5069	5865	6397	3.5	97	1928	2229	2443	3.5	2.63	1485	1703	3.3
99021 MEAD	063	8557	9155	9550	1.6	75	3048	3273	3424	1.7	2.79	2368	2539	1.7
99022 MEDICAL LAKE	063	7567	7985	8274	1.3	66	2462	2627	2742	1.5	2.65	1846	1957	1.4
99023 MICA	063	129	134	137	0.9	53	48	50	52	1.0	2.66	40	42	1.2
99025 NEWMAN LAKE	063	4756	4791	4841	0.2	25	1575	1603	1630	0.4	2.97	1304	1319	0.3
99026 NINE MILE FALLS	063	7852	8361	8704	1.5	72	2680	2896	3043	1.8	2.86	2244	2414	1.7
99027 OTIS ORCHARDS	063	5185	5222	5271	0.2	25	1959	1993	2023	0.4	2.62	1482	1498	0.3
99029 REARDAN	043	1447	1469	1474	0.4	34	535	546	552	0.5	2.68	419	426	0.4
99030 ROCKFORD	063	834	825	828	-0.3	13	301	301	304	0.0	2.71	233	231	-0.2
99031 SPANGLE	063	989	1019	1043	0.7	46	368	381	392	0.8	2.67	280	289	0.7
99032 SPRAGUE	043	765	777	777	0.4	35	318	324	323	0.4	2.39	221	223	0.2
99033 TEKOA	075	996	960	959	-0.9	3	390	378	380	-0.7	2.40	273	264	-0.8
99034 TUMTUM	065	609	633	649	0.9	54	237	251	260	1.4	2.52	175	183	1.1
99036 VALLEYFORD	063	1302	1295	1303	-0.1	15	451	453	458	0.1	2.85	366	366	0.0
99037 VERADALE	063	9533	10544	11240	2.4	88	3380	3773	4040	2.6	2.77	2601	2884	2.5
99040 WELLPINIT	065	1001	1045	1073	1.0	59	302	319	331	1.3	3.28	231	243	1.2
99101 ADDY	065	1460	1524	1566	1.0	59	534	565	587	1.3	2.70	410	431	1.2
99103 ALMIRA	043	725	732	729	0.2	28	299	305	307	0.5	2.40	213	216	0.3
99105 BENGE	001	23	23	23	0.0	20	10	10	10	0.0	2.30	7	7	0.0
99107 BOYDS	019	197	203	206	0.7	46	83	87	89	1.1	2.33	62	65	1.1
99109 CHEWELAH	065	4727	4874	4977	0.7	47	1833	1909	1965	1.0	2.52	1288	1337	0.9
99110 CLAYTON	065	2164	2237	2287	0.8	49	760	794	819	1.0	2.81	583	605	0.9
99111 COLFAX	075	4132	4180	4264	0.3	31	1681	1718	1772	0.5	2.32	1108	1134	0.6
99113 COLTON	075	843	826	829	-0.5	8	316	311	314	-0.4	2.66	231	227	-0.4
99114 COLVILLE	065	12306	12296	12422	0.0	18	4792	4849	4944	0.3	2.48	3323	3340	0.1
99115 COULEE CITY	025	1002	993	1010	-0.2	13	459	453	457	-0.3	2.19	297	290	-0.6
99116 COULEE DAM	047	4346	4372	4425	0.1	23	1531	1546	1569	0.2	2.81	1114	1122	0.2
99117 CRESTON	043	649	664	667	0.5	40	282	291	295	0.7	2.28	200	206	0.7
99118 CURLEW	019	1071	1078	1078	0.2	24	372	383	389	0.7	2.56	257	263	0.5
99119 CUSICK	051	628	672	713	1.6	76	256	276	294	1.8	2.43	188	202	1.7
99121 DANVILLE	019	60	60	61	0.0	20	20	21	21	1.2	2.86	14	14	0.0
99122 DAVENPORT	043	3095	3124	3119	0.2	28	1263	1281	1284	0.3	2.38	868	878	0.3
99123 ELECTRIC CITY	025	1088	1092	1108	0.1	22	452	452	455	0.0	2.42	340	338	-0.1
99125 ENDICOTT	075	953	915	912	-1.0	2	269	259	260	-0.9	3.05	192	185	-0.9
99126 EVANS	065	459	468	474	0.5	38	158	164	168	0.9	2.85	121	124	0.6
99128 FARMINGTON	075	358	345	344	-0.9	3	151	146	146	-0.8	2.34	103	100	-0.7
99129 FRUITLAND	065	676	712	735	1.2	65	243	259	270	1.5	2.75	184	195	1.4
99130 GARFIELD	075	888	846	843	-1.1	1	349	335	337	-1.0	2.53	246	237	-0.9
99131 GIFFORD	065	218	235	245	1.8	79	95	103	108	1.9	2.27	71	77	1.9
99133 GRAND COULEE	017	1266	1209	1222	-1.1	2	565	537	540	-1.2	2.20	357	337	-1.4
99134 HARRINGTON	043	721	708	697	-0.4	9	302	298	295	-0.3	2.36	213	209	-0.5
99135 HARTLINE	025	348	347	353	-0.1	17	137	136	137	-0.2	2.55	99	97	-0.5
99136 HAY	075	12	11	11	-2.0	0	6	6	6	0.0	1.83	5	4	-5.1
99137 HUNTERS	065	422	455	475	1.8	79	143	155	163	1.9	2.93	107	115	1.7
99138 INCHELIUM	019	1173	1185	1189	0.2	29	438	452	460	0.7	2.62	303	311	0.6
99139 IONE	051	1451	1472	1525	0.3	33	600	618	647	0.7	2.37	419	429	0.6
99140 KELLER	019	472	473	472	0.1	21	176	180	183	0.5	2.63	119	121	0.4
99141 KETTLE FALLS	065	5347	5526	5638	0.8	49	2111	2217	2287	1.2	2.49	1524	1591	1.0
99143 LACROSSE	075	864	807	801	-1.6	1	359	337	338	-1.5	2.39	251	236	-1.4
99147 LINCOLN	043	35	36	36	0.7	45	17	18	18	1.4	2.00	12	12	0.0
99148 LOON LAKE	065	2274	2319	2352	0.5	38	907	930	949	0.6	2.49	672	685	0.5
99150 MALO	019	361	372	378	0.7	46	140	148	152	1.3	2.19	101	106	1.1
99153 METALINE FALLS	051	663	652	669	-0.4	10	301	300	312	-0.1	2.17	173	171	-0.3
99156 NEWPORT	051	8274	8631	9015	1.0	57	3211	3394	3589	1.3	2.52	2277	2392	1.2
99157 NORTHPORT	065	193	199	202	0.7	47	73	76	78	1.0	2.62	54	56	0.9
99158 OAKESDALE	075	593	579	580	-0.6	6	234	229	231	-0.5	2.53	171	167	-0.6
99159 ODESSA	043	1405	1382	1366	-0.4	10	573	564	558	-0.4	2.37	395	386	-0.5
99161 PALOUSE	075	1332	1255	1248	-1.4	1	566	539	542	-1.1	2.33	397	378	-1.2
99163 PULLMAN	075	25954	26861	27700	0.8	51	9657	10176	10673	1.2	2.22	4155	4379	1.2
99164 PULLMAN	075	855	829	825	-0.7	4	74	65	64	-3.0	2.60	61	54	-2.8
99166 REPUBLIC	019	2978	3137	3220	1.2	65	1215	1305	1357	1.7	2.35	847	905	1.6
99167 RICE	065	637	667	687	1.1	60	243	257	267	1.3	2.57	186	196	1.2
99169 RITZVILLE	001	2722	2648	2639	-0.7	4	1095	1066	1059	-0.6	2.32	720	695	-0.8
99170 ROSALIA	075	1356	1375	1390	0.3	33	526	534	543	0.4	2.57	381	386	0.3
99171 SAINT JOHN	075	1058	1020	1018	-0.9	3	458	441	444	-0.9	1.98	321	309	-0.9
99173 SPRINGDALE	065	945	986	1013	1.0	57	346	365	377	1.3	2.69	265	277	1.1
99176 THORNTON	075	165	162	163	-0.4	9	66	65	65	-0.4	2.46	49	48	-0.5
99179 UNIONTOWN	075	390	382	383	-0.5	8	156	153	155	-0.5	2.50	114	112	-0.4
99180 USK	051	547	587	623	1.7	77	210	228	244	2.0	2.56	157	169	1.8
99181 VALLEY	065	2007	2016	2036	0.1	22	739	748	762	0.3	2.69	545	549	0.2
WASHINGTON					1.1					1.3	2.52			1.2
UNITED STATES					1.2					1.3	2.58			1.1

#	POST OFFICE NAME	RACE (%) White 2000	White 2004	Black 2000	Black 2004	Asian/Pacific 2000	Asian/Pacific 2004	% Hispanic Origin 2000	% Hispanic Origin 2004	2004 AGE DISTRIBUTION (%) 0-4	5-9	10-14	15-19	20-24	25-44	45-64	65-84	85+	18+	MEDIAN AGE 2004	% 2004 Males	% 2004 Females
98933	HARRAH	40.9	38.1	0.3	0.2	1.8	1.8	35.8	41.2	9.3	10.2	9.3	8.3	7.1	26.3	22.1	7.0	0.5	65.8	29.5	51.7	48.3
98935	MABTON	36.6	33.7	0.2	0.2	0.6	0.6	68.8	72.3	9.9	9.2	10.7	10.0	9.4	25.5	17.3	7.3	0.7	64.0	25.6	51.9	48.1
98936	MOXEE	76.6	72.8	0.7	0.7	0.4	0.4	25.5	30.6	7.4	8.1	8.2	7.3	6.3	27.6	25.1	9.3	0.8	71.5	34.9	51.1	48.9
98937	NACHES	90.4	88.7	0.2	0.2	0.4	0.5	10.4	12.8	6.1	6.5	7.9	6.9	5.7	25.0	28.7	12.0	1.3	75.3	40.1	51.6	48.4
98938	OUTLOOK	59.0	54.1	0.2	0.2	0.5	0.5	48.0	54.0	9.1	8.7	10.1	8.8	7.9	24.8	22.2	7.5	1.0	66.8	30.4	51.2	48.8
98942	SELAH	89.8	87.9	0.5	0.6	0.7	0.8	9.9	12.3	7.4	7.6	8.3	7.6	6.7	27.5	25.0	8.9	1.1	71.8	35.3	49.5	50.5
98944	SUNNYSIDE	46.9	43.6	0.4	0.4	0.6	0.6	67.4	72.1	11.6	10.4	9.7	8.0	8.7	26.5	16.2	7.3	1.6	63.3	26.0	50.6	49.4
98946	THORP	94.9	94.5	0.2	0.2	0.7	0.6	3.4	3.8	4.9	5.9	8.2	7.1	4.9	22.0	33.6	12.5	0.9	76.6	43.2	50.0	50.0
98947	TIETON	70.1	66.1	0.4	0.4	0.4	0.5	40.6	46.9	9.6	9.3	9.5	7.8	8.0	27.4	19.6	7.8	1.0	66.9	29.2	50.6	49.4
98948	TOPPENISH	32.1	30.2	0.5	0.5	0.7	0.7	63.8	68.1	10.8	10.0	10.3	9.4	8.5	26.9	16.5	6.7	1.1	63.2	25.8	51.5	48.5
98951	WAPATO	33.9	32.0	0.3	0.3	2.3	2.3	50.9	55.4	10.2	9.6	9.7	8.9	8.3	26.6	18.3	7.5	1.0	65.1	27.4	51.4	48.7
98952	WHITE SWAN	25.4	24.4	0.4	0.4	0.4	0.4	13.7	15.7	10.4	9.8	10.2	12.5	9.8	23.9	17.7	5.4	0.4	62.3	23.6	52.2	47.8
98953	ZILLAH	70.1	66.8	0.6	0.6	0.8	0.8	33.0	37.8	9.0	8.7	8.7	8.2	6.9	26.0	22.1	9.3	1.1	68.6	32.2	50.1	49.9
99003	CHATTAROY	96.5	96.3	0.1	0.1	0.4	0.4	1.3	1.6	5.2	6.5	8.7	8.9	5.2	23.8	31.8	9.0	0.9	73.6	40.5	50.5	49.6
99004	CHENEY	89.0	88.3	1.5	1.5	4.4	4.6	3.5	4.0	5.0	5.1	5.9	12.3	19.4	21.7	22.0	7.4	1.1	80.4	26.8	48.4	51.6
99005	COLBERT	96.6	96.3	0.2	0.2	0.7	0.7	1.6	1.9	5.8	7.4	10.0	8.3	4.1	24.3	30.6	8.5	0.9	71.0	39.9	48.9	51.1
99006	DEER PARK	95.1	94.7	0.2	0.2	0.4	0.4	2.0	2.5	6.7	6.9	8.4	8.2	6.7	24.5	25.8	11.2	1.6	72.6	37.6	49.6	50.4
99008	EDWALL	95.3	95.0	0.2	0.2	0.4	0.4	2.1	2.2	5.9	6.5	7.6	6.6	5.9	22.1	31.6	12.6	1.3	75.8	42.0	50.6	49.5
99009	ELK	95.8	95.3	0.1	0.1	0.5	0.6	1.1	1.3	5.8	6.3	8.0	8.4	7.5	24.1	30.3	8.9	0.7	74.6	38.9	50.3	49.7
99011	FAIRCHILD AIR FORCE	78.2	76.4	7.9	8.4	3.9	4.2	8.5	9.9	14.0	9.6	7.3	7.5	22.4	36.3	2.2	0.5	0.2	66.8	22.6	56.2	43.8
99012	FAIRFIELD	96.6	96.5	0.4	0.4	0.2	0.2	2.0	2.3	4.8	5.3	6.6	8.0	6.3	22.9	29.0	14.0	3.0	77.3	42.4	50.8	49.2
99013	FORD	58.8	58.5	0.4	0.5	0.9	1.0	2.8	3.0	7.9	8.1	9.0	8.8	6.3	24.9	26.1	8.4	0.6	69.6	34.4	50.6	49.4
99016	GREENACRES	95.3	94.8	0.5	0.5	1.0	1.1	2.1	2.5	6.2	6.7	8.0	7.3	5.6	26.4	26.8	10.6	2.3	74.3	38.8	49.3	50.7
99017	LAMONT	97.3	96.8	0.0	0.0	0.4	0.4	2.3	2.4	6.8	7.2	7.6	6.0	5.6	21.5	28.3	14.7	2.4	74.1	42.1	50.6	49.4
99018	LATAH	95.9	95.8	0.5	0.5	0.5	0.5	2.3	2.8	4.7	5.1	6.5	7.9	6.1	22.3	29.8	14.4	3.3	77.7	43.4	50.7	49.3
99019	LIBERTY LAKE	94.0	93.0	0.7	0.8	2.6	3.0	2.1	2.6	8.8	8.6	7.7	6.0	4.8	29.2	26.0	8.2	0.7	71.0	36.1	49.8	50.2
99021	MEAD	95.7	95.4	0.4	0.4	0.8	0.9	1.7	2.1	6.5	7.1	9.0	8.6	6.1	25.5	27.6	8.7	1.0	71.9	37.7	50.1	50.0
99022	MEDICAL LAKE	91.5	90.9	2.6	2.7	1.5	1.6	3.3	3.9	4.7	5.2	7.1	8.4	7.3	28.6	28.9	9.1	0.8	77.8	39.0	51.3	48.7
99023	MICA	97.7	97.8	0.0	0.0	0.0	0.8	0.0	0.8	4.5	6.7	9.7	9.0	5.2	20.9	37.3	6.0	0.8	73.1	41.7	49.3	50.8
99025	NEWMAN LAKE	95.1	94.6	0.3	0.4	1.0	1.1	1.7	2.1	6.5	7.4	9.7	9.1	5.5	29.0	27.0	5.4	0.4	70.1	36.3	50.9	49.1
99026	NINE MILE FALLS	95.1	94.7	0.5	0.5	1.0	1.2	1.4	1.7	6.1	7.2	9.0	8.2	5.8	26.7	29.1	7.2	0.7	72.3	38.1	50.4	49.6
99027	OTIS ORCHARDS	95.2	94.8	0.2	0.2	1.1	1.2	1.7	2.1	5.4	6.4	8.1	8.4	5.2	26.4	28.8	10.3	0.9	74.6	39.6	49.7	50.3
99029	REARDAN	94.0	93.9	0.3	0.3	0.7	0.8	1.9	2.1	6.0	6.7	7.8	6.5	5.4	24.0	30.9	11.8	0.9	75.4	40.8	52.4	47.6
99030	ROCKFORD	98.0	97.7	0.1	0.1	0.1	0.1	0.6	0.7	4.9	5.8	7.6	7.9	7.2	21.6	31.2	12.1	1.8	76.0	42.1	49.3	50.7
99031	SPANGLE	96.9	96.7	0.2	0.2	0.4	0.5	1.4	1.8	5.9	6.5	7.4	7.1	5.5	24.2	31.2	11.1	1.2	75.9	41.2	51.6	48.4
99032	SPRAGUE	95.7	95.8	0.0	0.0	0.1	0.1	2.6	2.6	6.1	6.7	7.3	6.7	5.5	21.6	30.6	13.8	1.7	75.7	42.4	50.6	49.4
99033	TEKOA	94.1	93.8	0.3	0.3	1.2	1.3	1.3	1.7	6.4	6.6	7.1	7.5	5.1	19.5	25.7	18.0	4.2	74.6	43.3	46.7	53.3
99034	TUMTUM	93.6	93.2	0.5	0.5	1.0	1.1	1.3	1.4	5.7	6.8	8.1	6.8	5.1	24.2	32.4	10.3	0.8	75.2	40.9	50.4	49.6
99036	VALLEYFORD	97.6	97.5	0.0	0.1	0.3	0.4	0.7	0.9	4.6	7.6	9.1	9.2	3.6	24.5	32.9	7.9	0.7	72.4	41.0	51.1	48.9
99037	VERADALE	93.4	92.8	0.9	1.0	2.6	2.8	2.1	2.5	6.5	7.0	8.8	8.0	6.9	25.9	25.8	9.5	1.6	72.6	36.9	49.1	50.9
99040	WELLPINIT	18.2	18.2	0.3	0.3	0.7	0.8	4.4	4.6	10.0	9.4	10.2	10.4	7.7	25.7	19.9	6.4	0.4	63.7	26.9	48.9	51.1
99101	ADDY	94.3	93.9	0.2	0.2	0.9	0.9	1.3	1.5	5.6	6.4	8.0	7.9	5.5	22.1	32.0	11.4	1.1	74.7	41.6	50.7	49.3
99103	ALMIRA	95.5	95.5	0.3	0.3	0.7	0.7	1.0	1.0	6.0	6.2	6.6	6.3	5.1	23.8	30.6	14.2	1.4	77.5	42.7	50.4	49.6
99105	BENGE	95.7	100.0	0.0	0.0	0.0	0.0	4.4	0.0	4.4	8.7	8.7	8.7	8.7	17.4	34.8	8.7	0.0	78.3	41.3	52.2	47.8
99107	BOYDS	91.9	90.2	0.0	0.5	0.5	0.5	2.5	3.0	4.9	5.4	6.4	5.9	4.4	19.2	35.0	17.7	1.0	79.3	47.3	51.7	48.3
99109	CHEWELAH	93.9	93.5	0.1	0.1	0.6	0.7	1.7	2.0	5.5	6.1	7.9	8.3	5.9	19.6	29.4	14.9	2.5	75.0	42.6	49.9	50.1
99110	CLAYTON	94.1	93.7	0.3	0.3	0.6	0.6	1.4	1.6	5.8	6.6	8.1	7.5	6.1	22.9	31.1	11.0	1.0	74.8	40.8	50.4	49.6
99111	COLFAX	95.2	95.0	0.2	0.2	1.6	1.6	1.6	1.9	5.8	6.0	7.2	6.8	5.4	23.5	26.1	15.1	4.2	76.3	42.0	49.6	50.5
99113	COLTON	96.9	96.5	0.0	0.0	1.0	1.1	2.3	2.5	7.4	7.9	8.6	5.5	4.8	24.5	27.6	12.5	1.3	72.6	40.0	50.0	50.0
99114	COLVILLE	93.9	93.5	0.2	0.2	0.6	0.6	1.9	2.2	6.1	6.1	7.0	7.6	6.7	21.1	29.4	13.2	2.7	75.9	41.5	48.4	51.6
99115	COULEE CITY	95.7	95.5	0.6	0.6	0.7	0.7	2.5	3.0	4.3	4.2	5.1	6.7	6.6	19.7	32.7	18.7	1.9	82.2	47.2	51.7	48.3
99116	COULEE DAM	34.5	33.4	0.2	0.2	0.2	0.2	6.0	6.8	7.2	7.3	9.1	8.4	7.4	23.5	25.4	10.6	1.1	71.0	34.1	50.4	49.6
99117	CRESTON	91.4	91.4	0.6	0.6	0.5	0.5	1.2	1.4	4.4	5.1	6.8	6.5	3.6	17.8	34.0	19.9	2.0	79.7	48.4	50.9	49.1
99118	CURLEW	84.6	83.3	0.3	0.3	0.6	0.7	3.4	4.0	4.1	5.6	8.0	14.0	5.6	18.9	32.9	9.7	1.2	73.2	40.7	54.7	45.3
99119	CUSICK	83.0	83.2	0.2	0.2	0.3	0.3	1.1	1.0	5.7	6.7	7.1	6.9	4.6	21.9	31.3	15.0	0.9	76.2	43.1	50.7	49.3
99121	DANVILLE	85.0	85.0	0.0	0.0	0.0	0.0	1.7	1.7	5.0	5.0	8.3	8.3	3.3	21.7	35.0	11.7	1.7	75.0	44.0	50.0	50.0
99122	DAVENPORT	95.9	95.8	0.3	0.3	0.3	0.3	2.1	2.1	6.2	6.4	7.0	6.3	5.2	19.4	28.4	17.4	3.8	76.3	44.7	48.5	51.5
99123	ELECTRIC CITY	90.7	90.2	0.2	0.2	0.8	0.9	2.0	2.6	4.3	5.1	6.7	6.3	4.5	17.8	37.4	16.5	1.5	80.0	48.2	48.7	51.3
99125	ENDICOTT	93.6	93.1	0.5	0.6	2.7	2.8	2.5	2.8	5.5	5.5	6.3	6.8	10.2	25.5	23.5	14.3	2.5	78.7	37.5	51.5	48.5
99126	EVANS	91.1	90.6	0.4	0.4	0.7	0.6	2.0	2.1	5.3	6.6	7.7	8.8	7.3	19.7	33.3	10.5	0.9	74.2	41.2	50.6	49.4
99128	FARMINGTON	96.7	96.2	0.0	0.0	0.6	0.6	2.0	2.6	5.2	6.4	7.8	7.0	4.6	20.6	30.7	14.2	3.5	75.9	43.9	50.7	49.3
99129	FRUITLAND	41.6	42.0	0.3	0.3	0.4	0.6	3.3	3.5	8.3	8.2	9.3	8.6	6.9	22.9	25.6	9.6	0.8	68.0	33.0	46.9	53.1
99130	GARFIELD	97.0	96.7	0.0	0.0	0.1	0.1	1.1	1.3	5.4	6.7	7.9	9.3	3.6	24.4	28.1	12.7	1.9	72.9	41.4	49.2	50.8
99131	GIFFORD	92.7	91.9	0.5	0.4	0.0	0.0	1.4	1.3	6.8	7.2	9.4	6.0	4.7	17.9	33.6	13.2	1.3	71.9	43.4	47.7	52.3
99133	GRAND COULEE	84.1	83.2	0.9	0.9	1.1	1.2	5.0	5.9	5.5	5.4	5.3	6.6	5.9	18.2	30.9	19.4	2.9	79.7	47.2	48.1	51.9
99134	HARRINGTON	96.4	96.3	0.1	0.1	0.1	0.1	2.8	2.8	5.7	6.1	6.9	7.5	5.4	20.9	30.1	15.1	2.4	76.0	43.4	51.6	48.5
99135	HARTLINE	95.7	95.4	0.0	0.0	0.6	0.6	3.2	4.0	3.8	4.6	6.3	6.3	4.3	21.3	35.7	16.4	1.2	81.3	47.2	52.7	47.3
99136	HAY	100.0	100.0	0.0	0.0	0.0	0.0	0.0	0.0	0.0	18.2	0.0	0.0	18.2	18.2	45.5	0.0	0.0	81.8	28.8	81.8	18.2
99137	HUNTERS	92.4	92.1	0.5	0.4	0.2	0.2	1.0	1.1	6.6	7.3	7.9	6.2	4.8	18.7	33.6	13.6	1.3	73.4	43.9	48.1	51.9
99138	INCHELIUM	26.6	25.2	0.0	0.0	0.1	0.1	2.1	2.4	6.6	6.7	7.7	8.4	6.9	25.5	25.2	12.4	0.8	74.1	35.7	49.5	50.6
99139	IONE	91.7	91.4	0.1	0.1	0.6	0.5	1.9	2.2	5.2	7.1	7.9	6.7	3.3	21.5	32.3	14.7	1.3	75.5	44.0	50.4	49.6
99140	KELLER	25.0	23.7	0.2	0.2	0.0	0.0	3.2	3.2	8.9	8.7	9.1	5.7	6.8	24.5	24.1	11.8	0.4	69.8	35.1	53.7	46.3
99141	KETTLE FALLS	92.2	91.7	0.3	0.3	0.5	0.5	2.2	2.6	6.0	6.5	7.3	7.2	6.3	20.8	30.8	13.7	1.4	75.3	41.7	50.2	49.8
99143	LACROSSE	95.8	95.7	0.0	0.0	0.7	0.7	0.8	0.9	6.3	7.1	7.3	6.8	3.6	21.9	29.0	15.5	2.5	74.7	43.3	52.5	47.5
99147	LINCOLN	91.4	91.7	0.0	0.0	0.0	0.0	0.0	0.0	5.6	5.6	5.6	5.6	5.6	13.9	36.1	22.2	0.0	83.3	48.8	50.0	50.0
99148	LOON LAKE	93.8	93.5	0.4	0.4	0.6	0.7	1.5	1.8	4.6	6.4	7.6	7.9	5.5	20.7	32.5	13.9	1.0	76.0	43.3	50.2	49.9
99150	MALO	86.7	85.8	0.3	0.3	0.8	0.8	4.4	4.8	4.8	6.5	7.0	15.3	7.5	19.9	29.3	8.3	1.3	71.8	36.1	55.7	44.4
99153	METALINE FALLS	95.0	94.9	0.0	0.0	0.8	0.8	1.4	1.7	5.1	5.8	6.4	7.2	4.5	18.3	34.4	16.6	1.8	78.4	46.5	50.2	49.9
99156	NEWPORT	94.5	94.1	0.2	0.2	0.9	1.0	2.3	2.7	5.6	6.0	8.0	7.7	4.0	22.3	32.2	13.1	1.3	75.1	42.9	50.2	49.8
99157	NORTHPORT	91.7	91.5	1.0	1.0	0.5	0.5	2.6	3.0	5.0	6.0	6.5	7.0	6.0	19.1	36.2	13.1	1.0	76.9	45.1	50.3	49.8
99158	OAKESDALE	98.2	98.1	0.0	0.0	0.2	0.2	1.9	2.1	5.0	5.7	7.4	7.4	5.4	22.6	30.9	13.5	2.1	77.2	43.0	50.6	49.4
99159	ODESSA	97.2	97.1	0.1	0.1	0.1	0.1	1.8	1.8	5.1	5.4	6.9	7.5	5.1	19.5	26.7	19.3	4.7	77.4	45.5	49.0	51.0
99161	PALOUSE	96.8	96.7	0.0	0.0	0.2	0.2	1.0	1.1	4.4	5.5	7.5	8.0	5.8	24.8	30.3	12.1	1.7	77.4	42.0	48.5	51.5
99163	PULLMAN	84.4	83.3	2.2	2.3	8.0	8.5	3.7	4.3	4.4	3.5	3.5	13.8	34.3	22.5	12.9	4.4	0.8	86.4	23.6	50.7	49.3
99164	PULLMAN	75.1	73.7	2.7	2.8	17.0	17.9	4.7	5.3	3.4	1.6	1.9	38.4	31.5	21.7	1.3	0.2	0.0	92.3	20.8	61.5	38.5
99166	REPUBLIC	91.6	91.0	0.3	0.3	0.4	0.4	2.7	3.1	5.2	5.9	7.7	7.3	4.7	21.8	34.2	12.1	1.2	76.6	43.3	50.8	49.2
99167	RICE	92.9	92.7	0.3	0.3	0.6	0.6	1.1	1.4	5.7	6.5	7.5	6.8	5.6	18.7	33.9	14.1	1.4	75.4	44.5	49.9	50.1
99169	RITZVILLE	95.6	95.1	0.2	0.2	0.5	0.5	3.5	4.3	5.2	5.5	6.8	6.8	5.6	20.9	28.8	16.7	3.7	78.0	44.4	50.1	49.9
99170	ROSALIA	97.1	97.0	0.3	0.3	0.2	0.2	1.0	1.2	7.4	7.5	7.4	7.1	5.1	23.6	26.9	13.3	1.8	73.3	40.1	50.4	49.6
99171	SAINT JOHN	93.4	92.8	0.7	0.7	2.8	3.0	2.6	2.9	5.4	5.4	6.2	7.0	10.3	25.8	23.2	14.2	2.6	79.3	37.2	51.4	48.6
99173	SPRINGDALE	89.5	89.2	0.4	0.4	0.5	0.6	2.4	2.7	6.1	6.8	8.9	7.7	6.4	21.6	29.9	11.7	0.9	73.0	40.0	52.4	47.6
99176	THORNTON	98.2	97.5	0.0	0.0	0.6	0.6	1.8	2.5	4.9	5.6	6.8	7.4	5.6	22.8	31.5	13.6	1.9	77.8	43.2	51.2	48.8
99179	UNIONTOWN	97.2	96.9	0.0	0.0	0.8	0.8	2.3	2.6	7.6	7.9	8.6	5.5	4.7	24.6	27.2	12.6	1.3	72.8	39.8	50.0	50.0
99180	USK	93.1	93.0	0.2	0.2	0.7	0.9	1.3	1.7	5.1	6.6	8.5	7.5	3.4	21.3	32.9	14.0	0.7	75.1	43.5	50.9	49.1
99181	VALLEY	94.8	94.5	0.2	0.2	0.6	0.6	2.1	2.4	6.0	7.0	8.1	7.6	6.3	21.1	31.6	11.5	0.8	73.4	41.0	51.1	48.9
	WASHINGTON	81.8	80.6	3.2	3.3	5.9	6.3	7.5	8.6	6.7	6.6	7.1	7.0	7.6	28.7	24.9	9.8	1.6	75.4	36.1	49.7	50.3
	UNITED STATES	75.1	73.6	12.3	12.5	3.8	4.2	12.5	14.1	6.9	6.7	7.2	7.0	7.3	28.6	23.8	10.8	1.7	75.1	36.0	49.1	50.9

#	POST OFFICE NAME	2004 Per Capita Income	2004 HH Income Base	2004 Household Income Distribution (%): Less than $25,000	$25,000 to $49,999	$50,000 to $99,999	$100,000 to $149,999	$150,000 or More	Median Household Income: 2004	2009	2004 National Centile	2004 State Centile	2004 Home Value Base	2004 Home Value Distribution (%): Less than $50,000	$50,000 to $89,999	$90,000 to $174,999	$175,000 to $399,999	$400,000 or More	2004 Median Home Value
98933	HARRAH	15055	360	27.2	29.7	31.1	10.0	1.9	45000	48888	61	53	258	9.3	13.2	57.8	15.5	4.3	119907
98935	MABTON	10552	1009	35.0	37.8	22.0	3.8	1.5	33586	36451	23	13	684	17.8	31.1	41.1	9.4	0.6	90897
98936	MOXEE	18061	1284	22.0	34.0	32.6	9.7	1.6	44572	49908	60	52	989	11.0	19.1	44.8	21.7	3.3	121797
98937	NACHES	20628	1676	24.8	32.3	34.6	6.2	2.2	43496	48200	57	50	1340	9.3	15.9	49.3	23.4	2.2	124654
98938	OUTLOOK	13740	537	30.5	32.6	28.3	6.3	2.2	39505	44003	44	38	392	13.0	5.9	56.1	22.2	2.8	126613
98942	SELAH	20513	5634	21.0	30.0	36.5	9.7	2.8	49133	54827	70	65	4265	4.9	8.6	53.7	31.4	1.4	150549
98944	SUNNYSIDE	12248	5603	37.0	33.0	23.2	5.0	1.8	32841	36251	20	12	3460	18.1	20.6	50.4	9.3	1.6	101936
98946	THORP	27479	247	13.8	30.8	37.3	12.6	5.7	55420	64280	80	77	208	4.3	4.3	29.3	50.5	11.5	211250
98947	TIETON	16076	833	31.5	33.4	27.6	5.5	2.0	38505	42923	41	34	628	5.7	21.0	55.4	14.7	3.2	117885
98948	TOPPENISH	10515	3320	39.3	36.7	19.3	3.4	1.3	30351	33199	13	6	2179	13.2	25.3	54.3	6.7	0.5	100161
98951	WAPATO	11874	3811	37.0	35.3	20.9	4.4	2.4	32777	36369	20	11	2490	13.9	27.1	43.2	13.9	1.9	101338
98952	WHITE SWAN	10869	648	38.3	26.1	27.3	7.6	0.8	34159	37117	25	16	425	15.3	20.9	48.5	13.7	1.7	97405
98953	ZILLAH	16677	2100	29.4	34.1	26.9	7.1	2.6	40360	45062	47	41	1482	8.0	11.8	49.6	27.6	3.0	134845
99003	CHATTAROY	21245	1623	25.9	29.9	32.3	9.3	2.5	45326	48826	62	54	1457	5.9	9.7	44.5	33.5	6.4	160652
99004	CHENEY	18887	5770	36.6	27.7	27.2	6.8	1.8	34549	37518	26	17	3279	6.9	12.1	52.3	26.6	2.3	140086
99005	COLBERT	26586	2346	14.3	21.0	38.8	18.3	7.5	64488	73957	88	88	2201	2.3	4.5	38.9	44.7	9.5	184388
99006	DEER PARK	19312	3110	28.0	31.9	30.6	6.8	2.8	42368	46393	54	47	2518	6.4	13.6	57.7	20.7	1.6	126261
99008	EDWALL	18664	199	26.1	37.7	27.1	7.0	2.0	38214	41519	40	33	157	14.0	17.2	47.1	19.8	1.9	114732
99009	ELK	18657	1103	28.9	34.3	27.7	6.6	2.5	41281	45491	51	45	972	9.1	13.2	44.8	27.4	5.7	145800
99011	FAIRCHILD AIR FORCE	13404	1043	19.0	59.3	18.7	2.3	0.8	36225	40382	32	23	19	0.0	100.0	0.0	0.0	0.0	64063
99012	FAIRFIELD	17649	371	29.7	34.2	29.1	5.4	1.6	40101	42015	46	41	297	12.5	22.9	47.1	14.5	3.0	108532
99013	FORD	15939	391	36.6	32.5	25.8	3.8	1.3	35942	40465	31	22	296	13.2	18.9	44.3	21.6	2.0	112500
99016	GREENACRES	20675	3655	24.1	34.1	32.2	6.8	2.9	44470	50017	60	52	2939	6.4	18.5	51.2	21.2	2.7	121913
99017	LAMONT	16929	96	31.3	40.6	20.8	4.2	3.1	33852	37685	24	15	70	25.7	25.7	30.0	14.3	4.3	88000
99018	LATAH	19230	85	31.8	34.1	27.1	5.9	1.2	37343	40000	37	29	67	14.9	26.9	41.8	14.9	1.5	100962
99019	LIBERTY LAKE	35193	2229	10.6	19.8	45.8	15.7	8.2	67479	77597	90	91	1893	2.2	3.0	38.6	49.3	7.0	188405
99021	MEAD	23132	3273	19.2	25.5	38.3	12.5	4.5	55131	62281	80	76	2970	13.7	14.5	38.1	31.5	2.2	141497
99022	MEDICAL LAKE	21240	2627	20.8	27.1	40.2	9.7	2.2	51687	58223	75	71	1996	7.6	9.3	54.2	26.6	2.3	137346
99023	MICA	29801	50	12.0	26.0	38.0	14.0	10.0	62035	72010	86	86	47	2.1	8.5	25.5	48.9	14.9	210714
99025	NEWMAN LAKE	21574	1603	16.2	26.6	43.7	9.8	3.7	55034	62221	80	76	1487	3.8	7.1	61.9	24.7	2.4	134375
99026	NINE MILE FALLS	23151	2896	13.6	26.8	43.6	12.4	3.6	57780	64221	82	80	2666	2.9	4.2	41.9	48.4	2.6	176527
99027	OTIS ORCHARDS	19597	1993	21.9	36.9	33.0	6.9	1.3	43271	46659	57	49	1820	16.5	10.6	58.0	13.9	1.0	116774
99029	REARDAN	22520	546	20.5	32.8	35.5	7.9	3.3	47283	52309	67	60	446	9.6	8.1	44.4	37.7	0.2	151724
99030	ROCKFORD	19291	301	24.9	31.6	33.2	8.3	2.0	44390	48981	60	52	260	4.6	14.2	53.5	21.2	6.5	132143
99031	SPANGLE	21409	381	19.2	34.9	35.4	8.7	1.8	47478	52260	67	61	316	8.5	11.1	48.1	26.0	6.3	141667
99032	SPRAGUE	19362	324	29.9	36.4	25.0	6.8	1.9	36137	39472	32	23	253	18.2	22.1	38.3	19.0	2.4	99800
99033	TEKOA	17172	378	35.7	38.4	20.6	4.0	1.3	33994	38752	24	16	279	22.2	25.8	43.4	7.5	1.1	92895
99034	TUMTUM	18573	251	32.7	32.3	29.5	4.0	1.6	39639	43321	45	39	213	8.9	13.2	47.4	27.7	2.8	128646
99036	VALLEYFORD	25288	453	16.8	22.7	38.6	13.9	8.0	59632	69484	84	83	416	1.4	7.2	34.6	42.6	14.2	190556
99037	VERADALE	25914	3773	17.6	28.4	38.1	11.1	4.8	53319	60534	77	74	2833	2.4	4.8	53.2	36.2	3.3	158380
99040	WELLPINIT	11143	319	42.0	33.9	20.1	3.8	0.3	30583	35273	14	7	213	20.2	30.1	39.0	10.3	0.5	89783
99101	ADDY	17143	565	33.6	36.6	23.0	4.8	2.0	35446	39065	29	20	468	15.6	11.3	38.3	30.1	4.7	131452
99103	ALMIRA	20088	305	30.5	38.0	22.3	6.9	2.3	35342	38737	29	20	240	27.5	21.7	28.3	20.4	2.1	92857
99105	BENGE	17826	10	30.0	40.0	30.0	0.0	0.0	40000	37500	46	40	7	14.3	42.9	42.9	0.0	0.0	85000
99107	BOYDS	19564	87	28.7	36.8	29.9	4.6	0.0	38438	43276	41	34	74	9.5	18.9	43.2	25.7	2.7	130556
99109	CHEWELAH	18196	1909	36.8	29.6	27.6	3.8	2.3	34122	37400	24	16	1370	5.8	14.6	43.7	32.9	3.0	137893
99110	CLAYTON	18305	794	30.5	31.1	32.0	4.5	1.9	43007	45409	56	48	675	5.3	9.2	52.4	30.2	2.8	143924
99111	COLFAX	22178	1718	25.6	34.9	31.7	6.1	1.6	41429	48423	51	45	1226	7.3	13.3	52.6	24.8	2.0	122656
99113	COLTON	21198	311	16.7	36.7	36.0	8.7	1.9	47229	52883	67	60	254	13.4	5.5	51.6	28.0	1.6	129808
99114	COLVILLE	19473	4849	35.4	31.4	26.2	4.5	2.6	35262	38645	28	20	3514	8.7	13.0	49.4	27.1	1.8	128141
99115	COULEE CITY	18226	453	40.2	30.5	24.9	3.1	1.3	33296	35085	22	12	360	15.6	29.2	36.9	16.9	1.4	99048
99116	COULEE DAM	14885	1546	34.7	35.8	24.1	4.3	1.0	33995	37738	24	16	1124	21.1	24.9	41.9	9.8	2.3	95114
99117	CRESTON	18038	291	35.7	35.4	23.4	3.1	2.4	35237	38335	28	19	234	15.4	28.2	29.5	22.7	4.3	101515
99118	CURLEW	15912	383	38.6	30.8	25.6	3.7	1.3	31873	35084	17	9	309	17.2	23.3	41.4	14.2	3.9	111218
99119	CUSICK	16516	276	43.1	26.8	24.6	4.0	1.5	30460	34374	13	6	228	20.6	16.2	32.9	25.0	5.3	121154
99121	DANVILLE	14717	21	33.3	28.6	33.3	4.8	0.0	37357	33586	37	29	18	5.6	33.3	44.4	11.1	5.6	125000
99122	DAVENPORT	21934	1281	28.7	32.9	29.0	6.5	2.9	41343	46117	51	45	969	10.3	17.5	46.7	24.2	1.3	120217
99123	ELECTRIC CITY	19731	452	36.3	20.8	35.0	7.1	0.9	40000	41437	46	40	365	15.1	19.7	46.6	18.6	0.0	106568
99125	ENDICOTT	15604	259	28.6	38.6	25.9	5.4	1.5	37698	43481	38	31	202	18.3	28.7	33.7	15.8	3.5	94615
99126	EVANS	14213	164	37.8	38.4	19.5	2.4	1.8	33606	36123	23	13	137	8.0	11.7	56.9	21.2	2.2	123790
99128	FARMINGTON	20015	146	24.7	41.1	27.4	5.5	1.4	38983	44384	43	37	112	12.5	30.4	41.1	10.7	5.4	96667
99129	FRUITLAND	13801	259	39.8	35.1	20.5	4.3	0.4	32312	35790	19	10	205	15.1	24.9	36.1	20.5	3.4	107917
99130	GARFIELD	17807	335	30.2	37.3	26.6	4.5	1.5	38321	43516	40	33	258	10.9	28.3	46.9	10.9	3.1	101103
99131	GIFFORD	17286	103	40.8	33.0	20.4	4.9	1.0	31126	35000	15	7	85	12.9	15.3	37.7	27.1	7.1	135577
99133	GRAND COULEE	16578	537	47.1	26.6	22.9	3.2	0.2	27314	27968	8	3	377	26.0	24.7	35.5	13.0	0.8	88810
99134	HARRINGTON	19961	298	30.5	35.9	24.8	6.0	2.7	36320	39643	33	24	232	19.8	28.5	31.9	16.4	3.5	95000
99135	HARTLINE	20284	136	25.7	33.1	32.4	6.6	2.2	43985	47914	59	51	111	9.9	19.8	35.1	29.7	5.4	141346
99136	HAY	35682	6	0.0	16.7	83.3	0.0	0.0	65822	65822	89	90	4	0.0	0.0	50.0	50.0	0.0	200000
99137	HUNTERS	13446	155	39.4	34.2	20.7	4.5	1.3	32331	35247	19	10	128	13.3	18.0	35.2	26.6	7.0	131250
99138	INCHELIUM	13890	452	48.5	29.2	17.5	4.2	0.7	25771	28045	6	2	333	16.5	27.3	34.5	12.6	9.0	104303
99139	IONE	18112	618	42.2	31.2	21.7	3.9	1.0	31474	35179	16	8	496	18.8	23.4	35.3	18.6	4.0	106452
99140	KELLER	10882	180	53.3	30.0	16.1	0.6	0.0	22060	25196	3	1	133	25.6	28.6	33.1	9.8	3.0	84500
99141	KETTLE FALLS	16806	2217	34.6	34.8	26.3	3.3	0.9	35720	39837	30	21	1726	7.3	16.5	52.6	20.7	2.8	121168
99143	LACROSSE	18125	337	29.1	38.6	28.2	3.6	0.6	35300	40000	29	20	252	25.0	22.2	39.3	13.5	0.0	93500
99147	LINCOLN	20045	18	33.3	38.9	27.8	0.0	0.0	36408	40000	33	25	15	6.7	26.7	40.0	26.7	0.0	112500
99148	LOON LAKE	19017	930	31.0	35.0	26.1	5.9	2.0	38741	42029	42	36	781	9.9	13.6	42.6	30.7	3.2	136925
99150	MALO	17600	148	39.9	32.4	23.7	3.4	0.7	32086	35808	18	9	116	21.6	18.1	38.8	20.7	0.9	107353
99153	METALINE FALLS	16576	300	50.7	28.0	18.0	2.3	1.0	24609	27092	4	2	219	11.4	29.7	41.1	15.1	2.7	105903
99156	NEWPORT	18469	3394	34.6	31.9	25.0	6.1	2.4	36518	40733	34	26	2705	8.4	15.4	41.7	30.9	3.6	134697
99157	NORTHPORT	15251	76	35.5	34.2	25.0	4.0	1.3	35000	34057	28	19	63	3.2	19.1	49.2	25.4	3.2	121094
99158	OAKESDALE	19781	229	28.4	36.2	29.7	5.2	0.4	37846	43135	39	31	181	13.8	27.1	43.1	13.8	2.2	99706
99159	ODESSA	19258	564	29.6	36.2	27.3	5.5	1.4	37888	42210	39	31	454	13.7	35.2	38.6	11.5	1.1	91563
99161	PALOUSE	20771	539	24.5	36.4	31.7	5.4	2.0	41067	47839	50	44	411	8.5	14.1	56.2	19.2	2.0	117841
99163	PULLMAN	19245	10176	48.7	21.5	19.6	6.9	3.4	26031	30078	6	2	3600	8.7	5.6	36.8	44.4	4.5	173246
99164	PULLMAN	15771	65	60.0	35.4	4.6	0.0	0.0	20288	23341	2	1	0	0.0	0.0	0.0	0.0	0.0	0
99166	REPUBLIC	19464	1305	38.9	32.2	23.4	3.5	2.0	32262	35542	18	9	985	16.6	20.8	40.8	19.6	2.2	108015
99167	RICE	16777	257	30.0	37.0	29.6	3.1	0.4	36485	40821	33	25	214	7.5	15.0	42.5	28.0	7.0	135714
99169	RITZVILLE	19961	1066	34.2	33.4	25.1	4.4	2.8	37982	39945	39	32	800	10.1	29.5	49.0	11.1	0.3	102210
99170	ROSALIA	16356	534	30.3	38.2	27.7	2.6	1.1	37098	41389	36	27	424	21.0	22.2	43.9	9.4	3.5	96444
99171	SAINT JOHN	23114	441	27.2	38.3	27.2	5.9	1.4	39138	45308	43	38	354	15.3	29.9	37.0	15.0	2.8	96800
99173	SPRINGDALE	14735	365	41.6	29.0	25.2	2.7	1.4	31246	32906	16	8	302	13.3	18.2	39.4	26.2	3.0	128289
99176	THORNTON	17648	65	29.2	36.9	29.2	4.6	0.0	36891	42330	35	27	52	17.3	26.9	40.4	13.5	1.9	96000
99179	UNIONTOWN	22518	153	17.0	36.6	36.0	8.5	2.0	47104	53667	66	60	126	14.3	5.6	50.8	27.0	2.4	128846
99180	USK	16543	228	37.7	29.8	26.3	4.8	1.3	33811	37314	23	14	186	17.2	19.4	30.1	28.0	5.4	131250
99181	VALLEY	15422	748	37.7	35.2	21.5	4.6	1.1	34211	36898	25	17	617	14.1	18.6	39.7	23.0	4.5	119971
	WASHINGTON	26555		21.6	27.8	33.4	11.4	5.9	50585	57953				4.6	5.9	31.3	45.6	12.6	195701
	UNITED STATES	25866		24.7	27.1	30.8	10.9	6.5	48124	56710				10.9	15.0	33.7	30.1	10.4	145905

ZIP CODE		FINANCIAL SERVICES				THE HOME						ENTERTAINMENT						PERSONAL			
						Home Improvements		Furnishings													
#	POST OFFICE NAME	Auto Loan	Home Loan	Invest-ments	Retire-ment Plans	Home Repair	Lawn & Garden	Comput-ers & Hard-ware	Major Appli-ances	TV, Radio, Sound Equip-ment	Furni-ture	Dine out/ Carry out	Sports Equip-ment	Fees & Tickets	Toys & Games	Travel	Cable TV	Apparel & Services	Auto Repairs	Health Insur-ance	Pets & Supplies
98933	HARRAH	78	73	64	70	71	74	73	77	74	77	92	85	69	85	70	71	91	77	72	82
98935	MABTON	64	56	45	52	54	57	57	62	59	61	74	66	52	66	54	57	73	63	59	65
98936	MOXEE	84	76	59	73	76	82	73	78	75	75	92	90	69	88	72	74	88	78	79	93
98937	NACHES	90	73	52	69	79	88	71	81	78	71	94	94	66	93	73	81	88	79	91	104
98938	OUTLOOK	75	67	54	63	66	69	66	71	67	69	84	79	61	77	64	66	82	71	69	79
98942	SELAH	83	84	83	85	84	87	83	84	81	83	101	99	82	100	82	78	98	84	80	95
98944	SUNNYSIDE	65	57	52	55	56	58	61	63	63	64	79	70	57	75	57	60	79	65	58	67
98946	THORP	120	101	74	97	110	119	96	110	103	95	123	131	89	124	99	106	116	108	121	144
98947	TIETON	82	70	56	66	70	75	71	78	75	75	93	85	66	85	69	74	90	78	77	86
98948	TOPPENISH	58	51	47	49	49	51	54	56	56	58	71	62	51	67	51	53	71	58	51	59
98951	WAPATO	66	58	48	55	57	61	59	64	62	63	77	69	55	71	57	60	76	64	62	69
98952	WHITE SWAN	68	64	52	62	63	66	61	65	61	62	75	75	58	72	60	60	73	64	63	76
98953	ZILLAH	80	69	54	67	72	79	69	75	73	69	90	86	66	88	69	74	85	74	79	90
99003	CHATTAROY	89	88	76	85	89	92	81	86	81	82	100	101	81	101	82	81	97	84	85	103
99004	CHENEY	69	57	57	59	59	64	68	65	68	64	84	81	62	81	64	65	81	69	64	77
99005	COLBERT	105	130	138	130	128	126	116	116	108	116	135	136	123	144	119	105	135	112	104	128
99006	DEER PARK	82	74	59	72	76	83	73	78	75	72	92	90	70	90	72	76	87	77	81	92
99008	EDWALL	90	66	37	62	75	83	64	78	73	64	86	93	56	84	66	76	79	77	91	106
99009	ELK	83	75	58	72	76	80	71	77	73	73	89	89	68	86	71	72	86	76	77	93
99011	FAIRCHILD AIR FORCE	67	42	41	49	39	46	63	55	64	59	80	73	54	72	52	59	77	64	50	62
99012	FAIRFIELD	84	58	31	55	68	76	58	71	66	57	78	86	49	76	60	70	71	70	85	99
99013	FORD	64	58	52	56	58	63	60	61	62	59	76	71	57	73	59	62	73	62	63	72
99016	GREENACRES	80	78	69	77	78	82	75	78	74	76	92	91	73	90	74	73	89	77	76	90
99017	LAMONT	80	56	29	53	65	73	55	68	64	55	75	82	47	73	57	67	68	67	81	95
99018	LATAH	84	58	31	55	68	76	58	71	67	57	78	86	49	76	60	70	71	70	85	99
99019	LIBERTY LAKE	128	148	148	151	142	140	134	133	124	137	158	155	139	161	133	119	156	129	117	146
99021	MEAD	96	98	88	97	97	99	91	95	89	93	110	110	90	109	90	86	108	93	89	109
99022	MEDICAL LAKE	76	84	87	83	83	85	80	80	77	80	96	94	82	99	80	75	95	79	75	89
99023	MICA	103	129	137	129	126	125	115	114	106	114	134	134	122	142	117	103	134	110	102	126
99025	NEWMAN LAKE	87	100	103	101	98	97	93	92	87	93	109	109	95	113	93	83	108	90	83	102
99026	NINE MILE FALLS	93	102	102	104	100	100	96	96	90	97	114	113	97	114	95	87	112	95	87	107
99027	OTIS ORCHARDS	74	78	75	77	77	79	73	75	70	74	88	86	73	87	73	69	86	74	71	85
99029	REARDAN	102	81	56	77	90	99	78	91	85	77	102	108	70	101	81	89	95	90	104	122
99030	ROCKFORD	88	71	48	68	78	85	68	79	74	67	88	95	62	88	70	76	82	78	89	105
99031	SPANGLE	92	80	61	78	87	92	76	86	80	75	96	103	71	98	78	82	91	84	93	111
99032	SPRAGUE	84	58	31	55	68	76	58	71	66	57	78	86	49	76	60	70	71	70	85	99
99033	TEKOA	67	50	33	48	55	66	55	61	62	52	73	69	49	69	55	65	66	61	73	75
99034	TUMTUM	75	67	51	64	68	73	64	70	66	65	81	81	60	77	64	66	77	69	72	85
99036	VALLEYFORD	95	115	120	115	114	113	103	104	97	103	121	122	109	129	106	94	120	100	95	116
99037	VERADALE	98	108	116	112	105	107	104	102	98	105	124	120	107	125	103	94	123	102	92	113
99040	WELLPINIT	52	47	46	46	47	52	51	51	53	50	66	59	49	64	50	53	63	52	52	57
99101	ADDY	79	62	40	59	69	75	59	69	66	59	78	83	54	78	61	68	73	68	79	93
99103	ALMIRA	87	61	32	58	71	79	60	74	69	59	81	90	51	80	62	73	74	73	89	104
99105	BENGE	74	52	27	49	60	68	51	63	59	51	69	76	44	68	53	62	63	62	75	88
99107	BOYDS	83	58	30	54	67	75	57	70	66	56	77	85	49	75	59	69	70	69	84	98
99109	CHEWELAH	74	57	44	55	63	72	60	67	67	59	80	78	55	78	61	70	74	67	78	85
99110	CLAYTON	83	74	57	70	75	81	70	77	72	71	89	89	66	85	70	72	85	76	79	94
99111	COLFAX	78	71	64	69	74	82	71	76	74	69	90	88	68	89	72	75	85	75	82	91
99113	COLTON	101	71	38	67	83	93	70	87	81	70	95	105	60	93	73	85	87	86	103	120
99114	COLVILLE	77	65	50	63	69	77	65	71	70	64	84	83	61	82	66	71	79	71	79	88
99115	COULEE CITY	65	50	33	47	55	65	53	59	59	51	70	67	47	67	53	63	64	59	71	74
99116	COULEE DAM	62	56	50	54	57	64	57	60	60	57	73	68	55	72	57	62	70	60	64	70
99117	CRESTON	70	55	37	49	62	69	52	62	58	51	69	73	46	68	55	62	64	61	74	85
99118	CURLEW	70	53	33	51	59	65	52	62	58	52	69	73	46	67	53	59	64	61	70	82
99119	CUSICK	66	51	34	47	57	66	52	60	58	50	69	69	46	67	53	62	64	59	71	77
99121	DANVILLE	76	53	28	50	62	69	52	65	60	52	71	78	45	69	54	63	65	64	77	90
99122	DAVENPORT	89	67	42	62	75	86	67	79	76	66	90	92	59	87	69	81	82	78	94	105
99123	ELECTRIC CITY	77	58	38	55	63	76	64	70	72	61	84	79	57	80	63	76	77	70	84	85
99125	ENDICOTT	80	58	34	55	65	76	61	70	69	59	81	82	53	78	61	73	74	70	84	91
99126	EVANS	66	57	42	55	59	63	55	61	57	56	70	71	51	66	55	57	66	60	63	75
99128	FARMINGTON	84	59	32	56	68	77	59	72	68	58	80	86	51	78	61	71	73	71	86	98
99129	FRUITLAND	63	53	37	50	55	59	51	57	53	52	65	67	46	62	51	54	61	57	60	72
99130	GARFIELD	81	57	30	54	66	74	56	69	65	55	76	84	48	74	58	68	69	68	83	97
99131	GIFFORD	71	50	26	47	58	65	49	61	57	49	66	73	42	65	51	59	61	60	72	85
99133	GRAND COULEE	59	44	29	43	49	58	49	54	55	46	64	61	43	61	48	58	59	54	65	66
99134	HARRINGTON	85	60	31	56	70	78	59	73	68	58	80	88	50	78	61	71	73	72	87	101
99135	HARTLINE	88	69	47	62	78	87	65	78	73	64	87	92	58	86	69	78	81	77	92	107
99136	HAY	118	83	43	78	96	108	82	101	94	81	110	122	70	108	85	99	101	100	120	141
99137	HUNTERS	71	50	26	47	58	65	49	61	57	49	66	73	42	65	51	59	61	60	72	85
99138	INCHELIUM	59	44	29	42	48	58	49	54	55	46	65	60	44	61	48	58	59	54	64	65
99139	IONE	76	56	34	50	63	72	53	65	62	53	73	77	47	71	56	66	67	64	78	90
99140	KELLER	40	35	37	34	35	40	40	39	43	39	52	45	39	51	39	43	50	41	41	43
99141	KETTLE FALLS	71	55	36	53	60	67	55	63	60	54	72	74	50	70	55	62	67	62	71	81
99143	LACROSSE	78	55	29	52	64	71	54	67	62	53	73	80	46	72	56	65	67	66	79	93
99147	LINCOLN	68	53	36	48	60	67	50	61	57	50	67	71	45	67	54	61	63	60	72	83
99148	LOON LAKE	79	64	45	59	71	78	61	71	67	61	80	83	55	78	64	71	75	70	82	95
99150	MALO	64	53	37	51	56	61	51	58	54	52	66	68	47	63	52	55	62	57	62	73
99153	METALINE FALLS	60	45	29	42	49	58	47	53	53	45	63	61	42	60	47	57	58	53	64	67
99156	NEWPORT	76	61	45	58	67	76	61	69	67	60	80	81	55	78	63	70	74	69	80	90
99157	NORTHPORT	72	50	26	48	59	66	50	62	57	49	67	74	43	66	52	60	61	61	73	86
99158	OAKESDALE	91	63	33	60	74	82	62	77	72	62	84	93	53	83	65	75	77	76	92	107
99159	ODESSA	76	56	35	54	62	73	60	68	68	58	80	78	53	76	60	72	73	68	82	86
99161	PALOUSE	88	61	32	58	71	80	60	75	70	60	82	90	52	80	63	73	74	74	89	104
99163	PULLMAN	60	50	60	53	49	54	67	57	65	62	82	74	61	77	60	60	78	64	53	64
99164	PULLMAN	33	20	25	23	20	24	39	28	38	33	47	39	31	42	31	33	44	35	26	32
99166	REPUBLIC	79	59	36	55	66	75	58	69	66	58	78	82	51	76	60	69	72	69	82	93
99167	RICE	74	58	37	54	64	70	55	65	61	55	73	77	50	73	57	64	68	63	74	87
99169	RITZVILLE	78	57	36	55	64	75	62	70	69	59	82	80	54	78	62	73	75	70	84	88
99170	ROSALIA	76	53	28	50	62	69	53	65	61	52	71	78	45	70	55	64	65	64	77	90
99171	SAINT JOHN	79	58	36	56	65	76	63	71	71	60	83	81	55	79	63	75	76	71	85	89
99173	SPRINGDALE	72	51	26	44	57	65	49	60	58	50	68	71	42	65	50	62	63	59	72	83
99176	THORNTON	78	55	29	52	63	71	55	67	63	54	74	80	47	72	56	66	67	66	80	92
99179	UNIONTOWN	102	71	37	67	83	93	70	87	81	69	95	105	60	93	73	85	86	86	103	121
99180	USK	70	53	36	50	59	69	55	63	62	53	74	72	49	71	56	66	68	63	75	80
99181	VALLEY	71	56	38	51	61	68	53	62	59	54	71	73	48	68	55	62	66	62	71	83
	WASHINGTON	94	96	103	97	95	100	96	95	94	96	118	112	96	118	95	92	115	96	91	107
	UNITED STATES	100	100	100	100	100	100	100	100	100	100	100	100	100	100	100	100	100	100	100	100

WASHINGTON

A 99185-99403

POPULATION CHANGE

ZIP CODE		COUNTY FIPS CODE	POPULATION			2000-2004 ANNUAL RATE		HOUSEHOLDS					FAMILIES		
#	POST OFFICE NAME		2000	2004	2009	% Rate	State Centile	2000	2004	2009	% Annual Rate 2000-2004	2004 Average HH Size	2000	2004	% Annual Rate 2000-2004
99185	WILBUR	043	1309	1303	1291	-0.1	16	541	542	540	0.0	2.39	374	372	-0.1
99201	SPOKANE	063	11368	11197	11260	-0.4	11	5262	5154	5183	-0.5	1.92	1898	1839	-0.7
99202	SPOKANE	063	19043	18888	19031	-0.2	13	7101	7062	7140	-0.1	2.37	3798	3722	-0.5
99203	SPOKANE	063	20502	20042	20107	-0.5	7	8920	8788	8859	-0.4	2.27	5722	5575	-0.6
99204	SPOKANE	063	9707	9547	9608	-0.4	10	5427	5328	5368	-0.4	1.70	1646	1589	-0.8
99205	SPOKANE	063	43020	43124	43596	0.1	21	17689	17848	18113	0.2	2.38	11056	11025	-0.1
99206	SPOKANE	063	32144	32938	33664	0.6	42	12552	12964	13319	0.8	2.51	8534	8737	0.6
99207	SPOKANE	063	29925	29818	30049	-0.1	17	12085	12071	12183	0.0	2.44	6978	6889	-0.3
99208	SPOKANE	063	40551	43021	45026	1.4	70	15784	16878	17750	1.6	2.51	10952	11632	1.4
99212	SPOKANE	063	17811	18048	18437	0.3	32	7811	7958	8168	0.4	2.25	4783	4831	0.2
99216	SPOKANE	063	21929	23181	24078	1.3	68	8858	9480	9937	1.6	2.41	5739	6067	1.3
99217	SPOKANE	063	15911	16777	17457	1.3	66	6025	6443	6767	1.6	2.58	4066	4291	1.3
99218	SPOKANE	063	12090	12262	12551	0.3	33	4723	4864	5024	0.7	2.39	3256	3279	0.2
99223	SPOKANE	063	26849	28022	28873	1.0	59	10538	11083	11478	1.2	2.51	7206	7532	1.1
99224	SPOKANE	063	17501	18413	19051	1.2	64	6171	6595	6886	1.6	2.39	4154	4429	1.5
99251	SPOKANE	063	845	852	857	0.2	26	14	14	15	0.0	2.57	10	11	2.3
99301	PASCO	021	44079	51224	60386	3.5	97	13606	15608	18273	3.3	3.25	10582	12111	3.2
99320	BENTON CITY	005	8218	9021	9931	2.2	86	2771	3059	3376	2.4	2.95	2196	2410	2.2
99321	BEVERLY	025	620	679	723	2.2	85	154	165	173	1.6	4.08	124	133	1.7
99322	BICKLETON	039	275	306	324	2.6	90	102	114	121	2.7	2.66	77	86	2.6
99323	BURBANK	071	685	1461	2077	19.5	100	228	489	696	19.7	2.99	191	406	19.4
99324	COLLEGE PLACE	071	7914	8159	8304	0.7	47	2982	3115	3196	1.0	2.28	1954	2012	0.7
99326	CONNELL	021	3669	3853	4272	1.2	63	991	1037	1151	1.1	3.21	789	818	0.9
99328	DAYTON	013	3687	3702	3646	0.1	22	1532	1555	1547	0.4	2.33	1025	1036	0.3
99330	ELTOPIA	021	896	959	1086	1.6	76	279	295	329	1.3	3.25	229	240	1.1
99336	KENNEWICK	005	39146	41366	44896	1.3	68	15360	16289	17735	1.4	2.51	9754	10227	1.1
99337	KENNEWICK	005	25812	28056	30913	2.0	83	9054	9911	10962	2.2	2.82	7187	7821	2.0
99338	KENNEWICK	005	7789	8379	9138	1.7	78	2546	2753	3012	1.9	3.04	2182	2361	1.9
99341	LIND	001	873	889	899	0.4	37	335	341	343	0.4	2.61	251	253	0.2
99343	MESA	021	2904	3070	3454	1.3	68	737	769	854	1.0	3.97	634	658	0.9
99344	OTHELLO	001	13972	14454	14815	0.8	50	4092	4212	4283	0.7	3.42	3382	3466	0.6
99347	POMEROY	023	2458	2472	2480	0.1	23	1013	1023	1030	0.2	2.38	690	692	0.1
99348	PRESCOTT	071	1591	1794	1915	2.9	94	457	510	541	2.6	3.47	373	412	2.4
99349	MATTAWA	025	5612	5919	6168	1.3	66	1332	1374	1406	0.7	4.31	1132	1164	0.7
99350	PROSSER	005	12093	12830	13860	1.4	70	3838	4078	4409	1.4	3.13	3054	3234	1.2
99352	RICHLAND	005	39884	43480	47919	2.1	83	15921	17374	19167	2.1	2.49	11016	11993	2.0
99353	WEST RICHLAND	005	9515	10721	11955	2.9	94	3363	3770	4191	2.7	2.84	2665	2969	2.6
99356	ROOSEVELT	039	239	266	282	2.6	90	99	110	117	2.5	2.39	75	83	2.4
99357	ROYAL CITY	025	3736	3967	4148	1.4	71	994	1038	1070	1.0	3.82	823	856	0.9
99360	TOUCHET	071	1470	1505	1528	0.6	41	495	509	518	0.7	2.96	411	419	0.5
99361	WAITSBURG	071	2304	2306	2306	0.0	20	895	903	907	0.2	2.55	631	630	0.0
99362	WALLA WALLA	071	38531	38921	39711	0.2	29	13729	13948	14302	0.4	2.49	8957	9017	0.2
99371	WASHTUCNA	001	485	478	478	-0.3	11	199	197	196	-0.2	2.43	147	144	-0.5
99401	ANATONE	003	213	215	211	0.2	28	77	78	78	0.3	2.76	60	60	0.0
99402	ASOTIN	003	1404	1412	1388	0.1	23	540	547	544	0.3	2.58	416	419	0.2
99403	CLARKSTON	003	18986	18709	18255	-0.4	11	7767	7722	7620	-0.1	2.38	5189	5135	-0.3
	WASHINGTON					1.1					1.3	2.52			1.2
	UNITED STATES					1.2					1.3	2.58			1.1

#	POST OFFICE NAME	White 2000	White 2004	Black 2000	Black 2004	Asian/Pacific 2000	Asian/Pacific 2004	% Hispanic Origin 2000	% Hispanic Origin 2004	0-4	5-9	10-14	15-19	20-24	25-44	45-64	65-84	85+	18+	MEDIAN AGE 2004	% 2004 Males	% 2004 Females
99185	WILBUR	95.7	95.6	0.1	0.1	0.5	0.5	1.5	1.5	5.6	5.5	5.8	6.5	5.7	18.7	30.7	18.4	3.2	78.5	46.6	48.3	51.7
99201	SPOKANE	84.8	83.7	3.4	3.6	1.8	1.9	4.1	4.8	5.4	4.9	5.4	7.2	9.4	31.8	23.7	10.4	1.9	80.2	36.1	54.4	45.6
99202	SPOKANE	82.3	80.9	4.6	4.9	3.7	4.0	4.4	5.2	7.1	6.3	6.6	9.8	12.0	26.5	19.4	8.9	3.4	76.5	30.4	48.5	51.5
99203	SPOKANE	93.7	93.1	1.0	1.1	1.8	1.9	2.2	2.7	6.1	6.4	7.1	6.3	5.4	25.3	28.0	12.6	2.9	76.4	40.4	46.7	53.3
99204	SPOKANE	88.0	87.0	2.6	2.8	2.5	2.6	3.4	4.0	5.5	3.7	3.5	5.2	13.8	33.0	22.2	10.0	3.1	85.1	33.9	47.3	52.8
99205	SPOKANE	91.7	91.0	1.4	1.5	1.9	2.0	2.8	3.3	7.3	6.9	6.9	6.8	7.1	29.7	21.7	11.6	2.0	75.0	35.2	48.0	52.0
99206	SPOKANE	93.7	93.1	0.9	1.0	1.3	1.5	2.6	3.1	6.7	6.7	7.6	7.3	7.0	26.5	25.4	10.9	1.9	74.3	36.7	48.7	51.3
99207	SPOKANE	86.8	85.7	2.6	2.8	2.6	2.8	3.7	4.4	8.4	7.2	7.3	7.2	10.0	30.5	18.5	8.7	2.3	72.9	30.8	48.0	52.0
99208	SPOKANE	92.4	91.8	1.4	1.4	2.2	2.4	2.3	2.7	6.3	6.3	7.3	7.7	8.1	23.6	26.5	12.1	2.2	75.5	38.6	48.2	51.8
99212	SPOKANE	92.6	91.9	1.0	1.1	1.6	1.8	2.3	2.8	6.2	6.1	6.6	6.2	6.7	27.3	27.4	11.8	1.8	77.4	39.2	50.2	49.8
99216	SPOKANE	93.4	92.8	0.9	1.0	1.8	2.0	2.5	3.0	7.1	6.7	7.0	7.2	7.7	27.5	23.0	11.3	2.4	74.7	35.5	48.1	51.9
99217	SPOKANE	90.9	90.2	0.9	1.0	2.5	2.7	2.6	3.1	7.1	6.8	7.5	7.1	7.8	27.9	24.4	10.1	1.4	74.4	35.4	49.7	50.4
99218	SPOKANE	92.9	92.2	1.0	1.1	2.1	2.3	2.4	2.8	6.0	5.8	6.7	9.1	10.8	22.7	25.1	11.2	2.6	77.1	35.8	46.9	53.1
99223	SPOKANE	92.6	91.9	1.5	1.6	2.4	2.7	2.0	2.4	6.2	6.6	7.6	7.2	6.2	24.5	27.2	11.9	2.6	75.0	39.6	47.7	52.3
99224	SPOKANE	88.5	88.0	3.7	3.7	2.1	2.3	4.6	5.3	5.5	5.5	5.7	6.3	7.5	32.7	26.1	9.4	1.3	79.9	37.4	55.7	44.3
99251	SPOKANE	92.0	91.3	1.0	1.1	2.6	2.8	2.3	2.7	3.2	3.6	4.9	23.6	19.7	13.0	20.1	10.6	1.3	85.1	23.7	44.3	55.8
99301	PASCO	62.1	60.2	2.5	2.4	1.6	1.6	45.4	48.7	10.0	9.1	9.0	8.0	8.2	27.1	20.1	7.6	1.0	67.1	29.1	51.5	48.5
99320	BENTON CITY	88.5	86.7	0.3	0.3	0.9	1.0	13.7	16.3	7.9	8.2	9.1	8.4	6.8	26.7	25.4	6.9	0.5	69.4	33.5	50.9	49.1
99321	BEVERLY	59.4	56.1	0.0	0.0	0.5	0.4	60.7	66.1	12.1	10.8	10.3	8.8	9.9	29.9	14.4	3.7	0.2	61.3	24.1	54.2	45.8
99322	BICKLETON	77.8	75.8	1.5	1.3	1.8	1.6	24.7	28.1	7.5	8.2	7.5	6.5	4.6	27.5	26.1	10.8	1.3	72.9	36.0	53.3	46.7
99323	BURBANK	94.7	94.3	0.0	0.0	1.0	1.1	3.5	4.3	5.3	6.0	7.9	8.0	5.9	23.8	32.7	9.5	1.0	75.8	41.1	49.4	50.6
99324	COLLEGE PLACE	86.1	84.1	1.5	1.6	2.1	2.3	14.1	17.0	6.6	5.7	5.9	9.4	14.9	22.7	18.4	13.2	3.3	78.5	30.7	48.3	51.7
99326	CONNELL	66.8	62.2	3.2	3.4	3.8	3.6	39.4	47.0	9.3	8.4	8.0	9.2	9.5	31.0	18.7	5.3	0.6	68.4	28.4	57.2	42.9
99328	DAYTON	93.6	93.5	0.2	0.2	0.5	0.5	6.7	6.8	5.6	5.9	6.9	6.5	5.9	22.0	28.8	15.9	2.4	77.5	42.9	48.2	51.8
99330	ELTOPIA	79.2	74.4	0.2	0.3	0.9	0.8	31.3	39.3	9.4	9.1	8.8	7.7	8.1	28.8	20.4	7.1	0.6	68.1	29.3	53.5	46.5
99336	KENNEWICK	79.9	77.6	1.2	1.2	2.1	2.2	19.0	22.0	9.2	7.4	7.4	7.2	9.9	28.5	20.1	8.7	1.5	71.7	30.5	49.5	50.5
99337	KENNEWICK	90.4	89.2	0.6	0.7	1.5	1.6	8.5	10.1	6.7	7.1	8.3	7.8	7.0	24.7	27.6	9.5	1.3	72.9	37.2	49.7	50.3
99338	KENNEWICK	92.5	91.6	0.5	0.6	1.5	1.6	6.3	7.5	6.0	7.5	9.6	9.5	5.7	24.0	30.8	6.4	0.5	70.7	37.9	50.5	49.6
99341	LIND	89.6	88.1	0.1	0.1	0.3	0.3	11.5	13.7	7.0	7.7	10.1	6.8	5.4	22.8	26.6	12.3	1.5	70.6	38.9	51.9	48.1
99343	MESA	71.1	66.6	0.2	0.2	0.7	0.7	47.1	55.3	12.1	10.1	10.0	10.1	9.8	26.6	15.9	5.1	0.5	61.3	24.0	53.0	47.0
99344	OTHELLO	57.7	54.9	0.3	0.3	0.7	0.7	58.9	63.6	11.1	9.9	9.6	8.3	8.7	26.8	18.0	6.8	0.7	64.3	26.6	51.5	48.5
99347	POMEROY	96.4	96.4	0.0	0.0	0.7	0.7	2.0	2.0	4.5	5.2	7.1	7.4	6.4	19.5	28.8	18.0	3.1	78.5	44.9	49.7	50.3
99348	PRESCOTT	52.0	47.7	0.5	0.5	0.4	0.5	53.4	58.8	12.4	10.8	9.1	8.6	8.0	30.9	14.8	5.1	0.3	62.0	25.7	53.8	46.2
99349	MATTAWA	44.8	41.9	0.1	0.1	0.9	0.8	71.6	76.1	11.9	10.5	10.2	8.0	9.6	32.1	12.4	4.9	0.3	62.5	24.8	55.7	44.3
99350	PROSSER	75.5	72.7	0.3	0.3	0.9	0.9	34.5	39.0	8.3	8.5	8.9	8.6	7.6	25.5	22.3	9.1	1.2	68.8	31.8	50.3	49.7
99352	RICHLAND	89.7	88.7	1.4	1.4	4.1	4.4	4.7	5.7	6.6	6.5	7.7	7.3	6.5	24.8	27.6	11.3	1.7	74.6	38.7	48.9	51.1
99353	WEST RICHLAND	93.5	92.8	0.4	0.5	1.8	1.9	4.7	5.7	8.4	8.4	8.4	7.4	6.3	28.1	25.8	6.8	0.5	70.0	34.7	50.0	50.0
99356	ROOSEVELT	77.8	75.9	1.3	1.5	1.7	1.5	24.7	28.2	7.1	7.9	9.8	6.4	4.5	26.3	26.3	10.5	1.1	71.8	35.3	51.9	48.1
99357	ROYAL CITY	69.2	67.3	0.2	0.2	0.5	0.5	63.1	68.1	11.5	10.5	10.3	8.9	8.9	29.4	14.6	5.3	0.6	62.0	25.0	54.4	45.7
99360	TOUCHET	90.7	89.1	0.1	0.1	0.3	0.3	15.1	18.3	7.9	8.2	8.5	7.8	5.3	26.5	24.3	10.3	1.3	70.5	36.4	52.0	48.0
99361	WAITSBURG	93.8	93.0	0.4	0.4	0.6	0.6	4.7	5.8	5.9	6.4	8.1	7.6	5.4	22.1	28.8	14.2	1.6	74.9	41.5	50.0	50.0
99362	WALLA WALLA	85.5	84.1	2.1	2.1	1.4	1.4	15.5	17.9	6.0	5.7	6.5	8.3	10.3	24.8	23.2	12.4	3.0	77.9	36.2	51.5	48.5
99371	WASHTUCNA	96.5	96.2	0.0	0.0	0.0	0.0	3.5	4.2	4.6	5.2	6.7	6.3	5.4	21.3	32.4	16.5	1.5	79.3	45.2	51.1	49.0
99401	ANATONE	97.2	97.2	0.0	0.0	0.5	0.5	0.9	1.4	5.1	6.5	8.8	7.9	4.2	23.7	29.3	13.0	1.1	74.0	41.5	49.3	50.7
99402	ASOTIN	97.5	97.3	0.1	0.2	0.3	0.3	1.1	1.2	5.0	6.4	8.7	8.2	4.1	23.4	29.7	13.2	1.3	74.0	41.7	49.7	50.4
99403	CLARKSTON	95.5	95.1	0.2	0.2	0.6	0.6	2.0	2.4	7.0	6.6	6.9	6.4	6.9	24.3	25.3	13.8	2.9	75.6	39.2	47.8	52.2
	WASHINGTON	81.8	80.6	3.2	3.3	5.9	6.3	7.5	8.6	6.7	6.6	7.1	7.0	7.6	28.7	24.9	9.8	1.6	75.4	36.1	49.7	50.3
	UNITED STATES	75.1	73.6	12.3	12.5	3.8	4.2	12.5	14.1	6.9	6.7	7.2	7.0	7.3	28.6	23.8	10.8	1.7	75.1	36.0	49.1	50.9

# ZIP CODE POST OFFICE NAME	2004 Per Capita Income	2004 HH Income Base	2004 HOUSEHOLD INCOME DISTRIBUTION (%)					MEDIAN HOUSEHOLD INCOME				2004 Home Value Base	2004 HOME VALUE DISTRIBUTION (%)					2004 Median Home Value
			Less than $25,000	$25,000 to $49,999	$50,000 to $99,999	$100,000 to $149,999	$150,000 or More	2004	2009	2004 National Centile	2004 State Centile		Less than $50,000	$50,000 to $89,999	$90,000 to $174,999	$175,000 to $399,999	$400,000 or More	
99185 WILBUR	17763	542	34.5	33.6	27.1	3.5	1.3	35861	38475	31	22	415	16.1	29.2	44.8	8.7	1.2	95909
99201 SPOKANE	15063	5154	61.2	24.8	11.8	1.2	1.0	18785	21424	1	1	1507	20.6	43.6	29.5	5.4	0.9	81555
99202 SPOKANE	17050	7062	43.5	32.5	19.6	2.9	1.4	28934	32431	10	4	3516	4.4	36.6	53.2	4.9	1.0	96900
99203 SPOKANE	32607	8788	21.3	26.9	31.1	12.2	8.5	51991	58382	75	72	6552	0.3	4.2	60.1	30.5	5.0	153314
99204 SPOKANE	19655	5328	52.6	30.4	11.8	3.3	1.9	23399	25885	3	2	1105	2.7	14.2	57.3	24.3	1.5	137798
99205 SPOKANE	19387	17848	27.8	37.6	28.8	4.8	1.1	38801	44498	42	36	12541	0.8	23.7	70.7	4.4	0.4	106351
99206 SPOKANE	22210	12964	25.1	32.0	31.8	8.2	3.0	43962	49173	59	50	8509	4.0	7.1	67.0	19.6	2.2	135379
99207 SPOKANE	15208	12071	40.9	36.9	19.0	2.5	0.7	30078	34157	12	5	6345	2.6	49.4	46.7	1.3	0.0	88974
99208 SPOKANE	25531	16878	23.3	29.7	31.9	10.5	4.6	47229	53404	67	60	11825	2.4	8.9	57.9	28.5	2.3	147735
99212 SPOKANE	22421	7958	30.1	31.9	28.5	6.3	3.3	38652	43543	42	35	5417	8.3	19.4	56.1	14.9	1.3	113201
99216 SPOKANE	20059	9480	25.8	35.5	31.9	5.4	1.4	40304	44739	47	41	5794	2.8	9.9	79.0	7.7	0.6	124064
99217 SPOKANE	20548	6443	27.8	33.7	28.3	6.4	3.9	38922	44044	42	36	4344	6.9	19.5	49.6	21.1	2.9	115408
99218 SPOKANE	26109	4864	25.0	29.2	29.3	11.8	4.8	46326	50684	65	58	3087	0.8	5.1	59.6	32.7	1.9	160035
99223 SPOKANE	30132	11083	19.6	25.6	32.9	13.9	8.1	55740	62444	80	77	8189	1.0	5.2	48.8	40.2	4.8	168039
99224 SPOKANE	23683	6595	25.1	32.2	29.1	9.0	4.7	43093	48790	56	49	4636	15.7	11.3	38.2	30.3	4.6	138592
99251 SPOKANE	6736	14	14.3	28.6	42.9	7.1	7.1	54416	63080	79	75	12	0.0	0.0	66.7	33.3	0.0	158333
99301 PASCO	18445	15608	28.4	28.8	30.0	9.2	3.7	43896	49367	58	50	10462	8.1	16.6	54.0	18.7	2.5	121673
99320 BENTON CITY	20859	3059	19.0	29.1	38.9	9.9	3.0	51561	58490	75	71	2597	10.4	16.9	51.6	20.0	1.2	117478
99321 BEVERLY	7594	165	42.4	42.4	13.9	1.2	0.0	27711	30672	8	4	79	15.2	27.9	30.4	17.7	8.9	97857
99322 BICKLETON	20578	114	27.2	27.2	36.8	5.3	3.5	47060	51491	66	59	84	7.1	22.6	45.2	16.7	8.3	116667
99323 BURBANK	21783	489	15.5	26.0	42.7	10.0	5.7	57483	62031	82	80	442	1.1	12.2	42.5	44.1	0.0	165580
99324 COLLEGE PLACE	18339	3115	39.1	28.4	26.5	4.7	1.4	32582	36222	20	10	1685	9.2	16.2	43.7	29.6	1.3	136954
99326 CONNELL	15703	1037	30.1	35.1	27.9	4.4	2.5	37951	42258	39	32	688	25.2	27.8	43.2	3.1	0.9	85918
99328 DAYTON	20300	1555	32.4	34.2	26.2	5.5	1.7	37261	41348	36	28	1173	8.7	25.2	45.5	19.0	1.6	110883
99330 ELTOPIA	17142	295	30.2	31.5	27.1	7.8	3.4	41053	43504	50	44	213	10.8	22.1	34.7	23.0	9.4	125543
99336 KENNEWICK	20070	16289	28.9	33.4	28.9	7.0	1.8	39106	44052	43	38	8580	9.3	19.1	58.1	13.1	0.4	114277
99337 KENNEWICK	24959	9911	14.7	27.7	39.7	13.6	4.3	57800	65728	82	81	8174	7.8	9.2	55.7	25.3	2.1	140851
99338 KENNEWICK	27801	2753	7.9	18.4	45.2	20.6	8.0	75014	85123	93	96	2477	6.9	2.9	34.2	52.4	3.6	184784
99341 LIND	18056	341	27.9	39.6	27.0	3.8	1.8	40873	42653	49	43	270	23.7	31.5	38.5	5.9	0.4	84815
99343 MESA	14010	769	30.2	38.8	20.9	6.5	3.6	36828	40707	35	26	506	19.4	19.0	31.2	18.8	11.7	112654
99344 OTHELLO	13766	4212	29.4	40.1	25.1	3.9	1.5	36099	39490	32	23	2894	18.4	17.2	47.0	14.0	3.4	108417
99347 POMEROY	18913	1023	34.2	29.4	29.3	5.8	1.3	36293	41305	33	24	768	19.9	28.1	35.2	16.5	0.3	92830
99348 PRESCOTT	12211	510	31.0	37.8	27.1	2.8	1.4	37196	41259	36	28	200	24.0	22.0	40.0	4.5	9.5	96154
99349 MATTAWA	11695	1374	27.4	43.5	21.6	5.9	1.5	37034	40969	36	27	846	14.4	14.7	55.2	15.7	0.0	113782
99350 PROSSER	16590	4078	26.1	31.5	33.2	6.7	2.4	43049	48999	56	49	3061	10.5	12.2	52.6	22.4	2.3	123457
99352 RICHLAND	29275	17374	17.7	23.6	36.8	14.8	7.0	60140	68655	84	84	12296	4.0	9.6	47.4	36.6	2.5	153664
99353 WEST RICHLAND	25749	3770	15.0	22.4	43.2	15.6	3.8	63182	71406	87	88	3256	11.7	9.4	44.6	32.9	1.4	141166
99356 ROOSEVELT	22962	110	27.3	28.2	35.5	5.5	3.6	46518	50287	65	58	81	7.4	22.2	44.4	17.3	8.6	116912
99357 ROYAL CITY	11315	1038	36.7	35.7	21.7	4.6	1.3	32279	35709	19	9	632	24.2	18.7	39.2	13.1	4.8	99184
99360 TOUCHET	17887	509	23.6	33.4	33.0	8.5	1.6	45291	49593	62	54	384	7.0	11.2	43.2	31.8	6.8	147656
99361 WAITSBURG	19210	903	32.1	32.3	28.2	5.4	1.9	38472	41620	41	34	739	10.7	13.8	49.8	20.0	5.7	117697
99362 WALLA WALLA	20226	13948	32.8	28.3	28.6	7.6	2.8	39426	44402	44	38	9114	5.3	12.6	48.4	30.2	3.7	139119
99371 WASHTUCNA	19503	197	27.4	36.0	28.9	5.6	2.0	41562	43048	52	46	141	22.0	29.8	34.8	9.9	3.6	87500
99401 ANATONE	19100	78	29.5	29.5	32.1	5.1	3.9	40000	45908	46	40	61	9.8	11.5	42.6	29.5	6.6	137500
99402 ASOTIN	20657	547	28.3	30.2	32.2	6.2	3.1	40788	45000	49	43	434	10.4	10.6	42.2	30.0	6.9	137019
99403 CLARKSTON	20376	7722	33.1	33.3	24.4	6.6	2.6	36406	40490	33	25	5189	8.4	16.8	51.3	20.3	3.1	120418
WASHINGTON	26555		21.6	27.8	33.4	11.4	5.9	50585	57953				4.6	5.9	31.3	45.6	12.6	195701
UNITED STATES	25866		24.7	27.1	30.8	10.9	6.5	48124	56710				10.9	15.0	33.7	30.1	10.4	145905

| ZIP CODE | | FINANCIAL SERVICES | | | | THE HOME | | | | | | ENTERTAINMENT | | | | | | PERSONAL | | | |
| | | | | | | Home Improvements | | Furnishings | | | | | | | | | | | | | |
#	POST OFFICE NAME	Auto Loan	Home Loan	Invest-ments	Retire-ment Plans	Home Repair	Lawn & Garden	Comput-ers & Hard-ware	Major Appli-ances	TV, Radio, Sound Equip-ment	Furni-ture	Dine out/ Carry out	Sports Equip-ment	Fees & Tickets	Toys & Games	Travel	Cable TV	Apparel & Services	Auto Repairs	Health Insur-ance	Pets & Supplies
99185	WILBUR	70	52	34	50	58	68	56	63	63	54	74	72	50	71	56	67	68	63	76	79
99201	SPOKANE	38	34	41	35	34	38	41	38	42	39	52	45	39	50	39	41	50	41	39	42
99202	SPOKANE	53	50	59	51	50	54	58	54	59	56	73	65	57	72	56	57	71	57	53	60
99203	SPOKANE	95	109	130	111	108	113	107	104	102	106	128	122	110	131	108	100	127	105	98	114
99204	SPOKANE	46	38	49	43	38	42	51	45	50	48	62	57	47	59	46	46	61	50	42	50
99205	SPOKANE	60	64	71	64	64	68	66	64	65	64	81	75	67	84	66	64	79	65	62	70
99206	SPOKANE	74	80	88	81	79	82	80	78	78	79	98	92	82	100	80	76	96	79	74	86
99207	SPOKANE	49	48	55	49	48	51	54	51	53	52	66	61	52	66	52	51	65	53	49	56
99208	SPOKANE	85	93	104	94	92	95	93	90	89	91	112	106	95	114	92	87	110	91	85	99
99212	SPOKANE	67	71	78	71	71	75	72	71	71	70	89	83	74	91	72	70	87	71	69	78
99216	SPOKANE	65	68	78	70	67	70	70	68	68	69	85	80	70	85	69	65	83	69	63	74
99217	SPOKANE	73	73	78	74	73	77	76	74	75	74	94	88	76	94	75	73	91	76	72	84
99218	SPOKANE	84	92	104	94	91	95	92	90	88	90	110	105	93	111	91	85	108	90	84	98
99223	SPOKANE	100	112	126	115	111	114	109	107	104	108	131	125	112	134	109	101	129	107	99	118
99224	SPOKANE	77	72	70	72	73	79	73	75	74	73	91	88	71	89	73	73	88	76	75	87
99251	SPOKANE	81	98	108	96	96	98	91	90	87	90	109	104	97	116	93	86	109	88	84	98
99301	PASCO	86	85	82	84	83	86	84	86	84	87	105	98	83	104	82	80	104	86	80	94
99320	BENTON CITY	92	93	83	93	91	93	87	90	85	89	106	105	86	103	86	82	103	89	84	103
99321	BEVERLY	44	37	37	37	37	38	43	42	44	45	56	49	41	55	40	41	57	45	39	45
99322	BICKLETON	87	79	62	76	79	84	76	81	77	78	95	94	72	89	75	76	91	81	81	96
99323	BURBANK	84	105	112	105	103	102	94	93	87	93	109	109	100	116	96	84	109	90	84	103
99324	COLLEGE PLACE	59	54	57	54	55	62	60	59	61	57	75	69	58	73	59	61	72	61	61	66
99326	CONNELL	71	68	64	66	66	68	70	72	70	72	88	80	67	83	67	67	87	73	66	76
99328	DAYTON	80	60	39	58	67	77	62	71	69	60	82	83	56	80	63	73	76	70	83	91
99330	ELTOPIA	89	81	63	78	81	85	77	83	78	79	96	95	73	91	76	77	93	82	82	98
99336	KENNEWICK	68	68	76	70	67	71	73	70	72	72	90	83	72	89	71	69	88	72	66	77
99337	KENNEWICK	101	105	101	104	104	107	100	102	97	101	122	119	100	121	99	95	119	101	96	115
99338	KENNEWICK	116	134	136	135	132	132	121	122	114	122	143	142	127	148	123	110	142	118	111	136
99341	LIND	85	59	31	56	69	78	59	73	68	58	79	88	50	78	61	71	72	72	86	101
99343	MESA	83	72	67	72	72	74	77	79	79	81	100	91	74	97	73	75	99	82	73	86
99344	OTHELLO	71	63	56	60	62	65	65	68	67	68	84	76	61	80	62	65	83	69	65	75
99347	POMEROY	75	56	36	53	62	73	59	67	67	57	78	77	52	75	60	70	72	67	80	85
99348	PRESCOTT	61	52	51	52	51	52	59	58	61	62	77	67	56	75	55	57	78	62	53	62
99349	MATTAWA	73	62	61	62	61	63	70	70	73	74	92	80	67	90	65	68	93	74	63	74
99350	PROSSER	81	74	61	71	75	80	72	77	73	73	90	88	68	86	71	73	86	76	77	91
99352	RICHLAND	97	105	117	107	104	109	105	103	101	104	127	120	107	128	105	98	124	103	97	113
99353	WEST RICHLAND	108	114	105	116	110	110	105	107	100	109	125	125	105	123	103	95	123	105	96	120
99356	ROOSEVELT	88	80	62	77	80	84	76	82	77	78	95	94	72	90	75	76	91	81	81	97
99357	ROYAL CITY	65	57	51	56	56	58	60	61	62	63	77	71	57	75	57	59	77	64	58	68
99360	TOUCHET	94	68	39	65	78	87	67	81	76	66	89	97	59	88	69	79	82	80	95	111
99361	WAITSBURG	83	61	37	58	68	79	64	74	72	62	85	85	56	82	64	76	78	73	88	95
99362	WALLA WALLA	71	70	74	70	71	77	72	73	72	71	90	84	71	88	72	72	87	73	73	82
99371	WASHTUCNA	86	60	31	56	70	78	59	73	68	58	80	88	50	78	61	71	73	72	87	102
99401	ANATONE	88	72	50	69	79	86	68	78	74	68	89	94	64	90	70	77	84	77	88	104
99402	ASOTIN	88	74	52	70	80	87	69	79	75	69	91	94	66	92	72	78	85	77	88	104
99403	CLARKSTON	75	64	52	62	68	76	66	71	70	64	85	82	62	83	66	72	80	71	78	85
	WASHINGTON	94	96	103	97	95	100	96	95	94	96	118	112	96	118	95	92	115	96	91	107
	UNITED STATES	100	100	100	100	100	100	100	100	100	100	100	100	100	100	100	100	100	100	100	100

POPULATION CHANGE

ZIP CODE			POPULATION			2000-2004 ANNUAL RATE		HOUSEHOLDS					FAMILIES		
#	POST OFFICE NAME	COUNTY FIPS CODE	2000	2004	2009	% Rate	State Centile	2000	2004	2009	% Annual Rate 2000-2004	2004 Average HH Size	2000	2004	% Annual Rate 2000-2004
24701	BLUEFIELD	055	20762	20370	20043	-0.5	27	8985	9015	9071	0.1	2.24	5835	5605	-0.9
24712	ATHENS	055	2021	2024	2016	0.0	59	615	629	639	0.5	2.18	421	414	-0.4
24714	BEESON	055	239	238	235	-0.1	48	99	101	102	0.5	2.36	73	73	0.0
24715	BRAMWELL	055	500	461	441	-1.9	1	221	210	206	-1.2	2.20	142	128	-2.4
24726	HERNDON	109	1926	1836	1763	-1.1	8	783	771	764	-0.4	2.38	568	540	-1.2
24731	KEGLEY	055	101	99	97	-0.5	26	31	31	31	0.0	3.19	23	22	-1.0
24733	LASHMEET	055	732	704	686	-0.9	12	282	278	277	-0.3	2.52	213	203	-1.1
24736	MATOAKA	055	1122	1066	1031	-1.2	6	446	435	431	-0.6	2.45	337	317	-1.4
24740	PRINCETON	055	30331	30510	30377	0.1	65	13001	13359	13588	0.6	2.26	8761	8650	-0.3
24747	ROCK	055	5007	4848	4736	-0.8	16	2001	1989	1991	-0.1	2.44	1512	1456	-0.9
24801	WELCH	047	8399	7940	7452	-1.3	5	3483	3378	3261	-0.7	2.27	2307	2145	-1.7
24815	BERWIND	047	3394	3226	3031	-1.2	6	1361	1334	1294	-0.5	2.41	960	907	-1.3
24818	BRENTON	109	2357	2292	2218	-0.7	19	923	925	925	0.1	2.48	676	656	-0.7
24822	CLEAR FORK	109	694	677	655	-0.6	22	273	275	275	0.2	2.46	214	209	-0.6
24823	COAL MOUNTAIN	109	115	112	109	-0.6	20	44	44	44	0.0	2.55	35	34	-0.7
24827	CYCLONE	109	2012	1959	1897	-0.6	20	787	791	792	0.1	2.48	616	603	-0.5
24828	DAVY	047	2333	2199	2059	-1.4	4	909	885	856	-0.6	2.48	673	634	-1.4
24834	FANROCK	109	114	111	107	-0.6	20	47	47	48	0.0	2.36	35	34	-0.7
24839	HANOVER	109	1409	1383	1344	-0.4	28	580	588	590	0.3	2.35	417	408	-0.5
24844	IAEGER	047	4491	4283	4042	-1.1	9	1839	1816	1772	-0.3	2.35	1354	1293	-1.1
24849	JESSE	109	357	346	335	-0.7	17	145	145	145	0.0	2.39	106	103	-0.7
24850	JOLO	047	2561	2463	2326	-0.9	12	1068	1066	1042	0.0	2.31	786	759	-0.8
24859	MARIANNA	109	831	799	770	-0.9	12	327	325	324	-0.1	2.46	230	221	-0.9
24860	MATHENY	109	675	659	639	-0.6	23	293	295	294	0.2	2.23	223	218	-0.5
24862	MOHAWK	047	1353	1288	1210	-1.2	7	540	532	518	-0.4	2.42	414	395	-1.1
24868	NORTHFORK	047	3209	3059	2877	-1.1	8	1321	1296	1257	-0.5	2.35	892	840	-1.4
24869	NORTH SPRING	109	134	130	126	-0.7	18	56	57	57	0.4	2.28	41	40	-0.6
24870	OCEANA	109	3573	3463	3347	-0.7	17	1453	1450	1445	-0.1	2.39	1126	1093	-0.7
24873	PAYNESVILLE	047	1601	1555	1474	-0.7	18	634	633	618	0.0	2.46	457	440	-0.9
24874	PINEVILLE	109	3773	3642	3516	-0.8	14	1606	1605	1601	0.0	2.23	1133	1092	-0.9
24882	SIMON	109	647	631	612	-0.6	22	246	248	248	0.2	2.54	191	187	-0.5
24884	SQUIRE	047	747	705	663	-1.4	4	310	302	293	-0.6	2.33	224	210	-1.5
24901	LEWISBURG	025	7954	8369	8620	1.2	90	3547	3816	4014	1.7	2.15	2271	2334	0.7
24910	ALDERSON	089	4934	4921	4906	-0.1	52	1489	1511	1532	0.4	2.44	1012	987	-0.6
24915	ARBOVALE	075	540	535	526	-0.2	42	222	225	226	0.3	2.37	139	135	-0.7
24916	ASBURY	025	732	737	739	0.2	67	297	304	311	0.6	2.42	224	222	-0.2
24917	AUTO	025	371	569	569	10.6	100	108	110	112	0.4	3.11	77	76	-0.3
24918	BALLARD	063	1275	1287	1291	0.2	69	506	523	533	0.8	2.46	379	379	0.0
24920	BARTOW	075	516	504	492	-0.6	23	214	213	212	-0.1	2.37	153	147	-0.9
24925	CALDWELL	025	211	210	210	-0.1	47	99	101	103	0.5	2.08	74	73	-0.3
24927	CASS	075	900	888	871	-0.3	35	388	391	391	0.2	2.25	249	240	-0.9
24931	CRAWLEY	025	1122	1125	1126	0.1	61	455	465	475	0.5	2.42	348	346	-0.1
24934	DUNMORE	075	225	222	217	-0.3	35	104	105	105	0.2	2.10	73	70	-1.0
24935	FOREST HILL	089	290	289	284	-0.1	49	126	129	130	0.6	2.19	91	89	-0.5
24936	FORT SPRING	025	285	291	294	0.5	80	116	121	124	1.0	2.40	86	86	0.0
24938	FRANKFORD	025	1195	1199	1202	0.1	62	472	484	494	0.6	2.47	365	364	-0.1
24941	GAP MILLS	063	672	670	670	-0.1	50	280	285	289	0.4	2.35	199	196	-0.4
24943	GRASSY MEADOWS	025	200	205	208	0.6	82	79	83	85	1.2	2.47	60	61	0.4
24944	GREEN BANK	075	461	455	446	-0.3	35	181	183	183	0.3	2.49	130	126	-0.7
24945	GREENVILLE	063	1361	1383	1393	0.4	77	542	564	577	0.9	2.39	387	389	0.1
24946	HILLSBORO	075	1540	1525	1501	-0.2	41	564	571	573	0.3	2.36	389	379	-0.6
24950	KIEFFER	025	7	7	7	0.0	57	3	3	3	0.0	2.33	2	2	0.0
24951	LINDSIDE	063	808	809	809	0.0	59	343	352	358	0.6	2.17	239	236	-0.3
24954	MARLINTON	075	4166	4116	4041	-0.3	37	1825	1837	1837	0.2	2.18	1167	1124	-0.9
24957	MAXWELTON	025	108	109	110	0.2	69	47	48	50	0.5	2.27	36	36	0.0
24962	PENCE SPRINGS	089	294	291	285	-0.2	40	121	122	122	0.2	2.38	87	85	-0.6
24963	PETERSTOWN	063	4121	4134	4140	0.1	61	1740	1788	1819	0.6	2.31	1244	1235	-0.2
24966	RENICK	025	1648	1779	1781	1.8	94	657	670	685	0.5	2.42	481	475	-0.3
24970	RONCEVERTE	025	5207	5156	5158	-0.2	41	2128	2150	2196	0.2	2.33	1445	1405	-0.7
24974	SECONDCREEK	063	458	460	460	0.1	63	187	191	194	0.5	2.40	141	140	-0.2
24976	SINKS GROVE	063	1231	1237	1239	0.1	63	470	481	488	0.6	2.52	347	344	-0.2
24977	SMOOT	025	887	895	899	0.2	69	349	359	368	0.7	2.49	257	256	-0.1
24981	TALCOTT	089	748	748	736	0.0	57	321	329	332	0.6	2.26	223	219	-0.4
24983	UNION	063	2152	2149	2151	0.0	54	910	934	948	0.5	2.29	627	615	-0.5
24984	WAITEVILLE	063	201	199	198	-0.2	40	83	84	84	0.3	2.37	59	57	-0.8
24985	WAYSIDE	063	534	534	529	0.0	57	222	226	228	0.4	2.11	158	155	-0.5
24986	WHITE SULPHUR SPRING	025	4697	5195	5193	2.4	97	2110	2140	2187	0.3	2.11	1363	1325	-0.7
24991	WILLIAMSBURG	025	777	785	789	0.2	71	304	313	321	0.7	2.50	230	230	0.0
24993	WOLFCREEK	063	215	214	214	-0.1	47	86	87	88	0.3	1.54	60	52	-3.3
25003	ALUM CREEK	039	2561	2503	2494	-0.5	23	1032	1034	1057	0.1	2.42	774	751	-0.7
25005	AMMA	087	407	400	407	-0.4	30	156	156	162	0.0	2.56	120	117	-0.6
25007	ARNETT	081	370	357	353	-0.8	14	133	132	133	-0.2	2.70	99	94	-1.2
25008	ARTIE	081	571	562	562	-0.4	32	220	224	230	0.4	2.51	168	166	-0.3
25009	ASHFORD	005	579	583	585	0.2	67	222	229	236	0.7	2.55	168	168	0.0
25010	BALD KNOB	005	547	526	521	-0.9	12	235	233	238	-0.2	2.26	170	163	-1.0
25015	BELLE	039	7068	6612	6255	-1.6	2	2996	2861	2762	-1.1	2.31	2053	1879	-2.1
25019	BICKMORE	015	629	627	632	-0.1	50	243	249	257	0.6	2.52	185	185	0.0
25021	BIM	005	803	768	761	-1.0	10	334	330	336	-0.3	2.33	240	228	-1.2
25024	BLOOMINGROSE	005	684	687	688	0.1	63	272	279	286	0.6	2.46	194	192	-0.2
25025	BLOUNT	039	687	688	670	0.0	59	266	273	272	0.6	2.52	211	211	0.0
25028	BOB WHITE	005	511	505	503	-0.3	37	207	210	216	0.3	2.42	149	146	-0.5
25030	BOMONT	015	138	139	140	0.2	67	56	58	60	0.8	2.40	43	43	0.0
25033	BUFFALO	079	2273	2393	2514	1.2	90	916	992	1067	1.9	2.40	668	697	1.0
25035	CABIN CREEK	039	1171	1084	1021	-1.8	1	481	457	441	-1.2	2.37	327	297	-2.2
25039	CEDAR GROVE	039	2670	2502	2368	-1.5	3	1135	1086	1049	-1.0	2.29	791	724	-2.1
25043	CLAY	015	2570	2595	2622	0.2	70	1027	1060	1096	0.8	2.42	711	707	-0.1
25044	CLEAR CREEK	081	20	20	21	0.0	57	7	7	8	0.0	2.86	5	5	0.0
25045	CLENDENIN	039	5672	5640	5520	-0.1	46	2270	2307	2306	0.4	2.44	1664	1630	-0.5
25046	CLIO	087	521	512	521	-0.4	30	199	199	207	0.0	2.57	154	150	-0.6
25047	CLOTHIER	045	1282	1239	1198	-0.8	15	529	525	522	-0.2	2.32	387	372	-0.9
25048	COLCORD	081	300	291	289	-0.7	18	117	117	119	0.0	2.49	90	87	-0.8
25049	COMFORT	005	389	392	393	0.2	68	152	156	161	0.6	2.51	109	108	-0.2
25051	COSTA	005	453	452	451	-0.1	52	179	183	188	0.5	2.47	137	136	-0.2
25053	DANVILLE	005	3852	3916	3971	0.4	77	1502	1565	1625	1.0	2.47	1093	1103	0.2
25059	DIXIE	067	657	617	606	-1.5	3	254	246	248	-0.8	2.40	194	183	-1.4
	WEST VIRGINIA					0.2					0.6	2.35			-0.3
	UNITED STATES					1.2					1.3	2.58			1.1

ZIP CODE #	POST OFFICE NAME	RACE (%) White 2000	White 2004	Black 2000	Black 2004	Asian/Pacific 2000	Asian/Pacific 2004	% Hispanic Origin 2000	% Hispanic Origin 2004	2004 AGE DISTRIBUTION (%) 0-4	5-9	10-14	15-19	20-24	25-44	45-64	65-84	85+	18+	MEDIAN AGE 2004	% 2004 Males	% 2004 Females
24701	BLUEFIELD	85.5	85.0	12.9	13.2	0.4	0.5	0.5	0.5	5.8	5.8	5.8	5.4	5.9	25.2	27.3	16.4	2.6	79.4	42.1	47.3	52.7
24712	ATHENS	93.5	93.0	4.0	4.0	1.4	1.8	0.7	0.8	3.1	3.3	4.4	16.7	21.5	19.8	19.5	10.6	1.2	87.0	25.9	55.8	44.2
24714	BEESON	99.2	99.6	0.0	0.0	0.0	0.0	0.0	0.0	5.5	5.5	5.9	5.9	8.4	27.7	28.6	10.9	1.7	79.4	38.8	47.5	52.5
24715	BRAMWELL	90.4	90.0	7.4	7.8	0.0	0.0	0.4	0.2	5.0	5.0	6.3	6.1	5.4	22.8	29.3	17.1	3.0	79.8	44.5	48.4	51.6
24726	HERNDON	97.0	96.8	1.5	1.5	0.1	0.1	0.7	0.8	4.8	5.2	6.0	5.3	5.9	25.9	29.7	15.6	1.5	80.7	42.5	50.8	49.2
24731	KEGLEY	99.0	99.0	0.0	0.0	0.0	0.0	0.0	0.0	6.1	6.1	7.1	5.1	6.1	25.3	30.3	13.1	1.0	77.8	41.1	50.5	49.5
24733	LASHMEET	98.8	98.6	0.1	0.1	0.1	0.1	0.3	0.3	6.1	6.1	6.7	6.0	6.1	28.3	26.0	12.9	1.9	77.4	38.1	48.0	52.0
24736	MATOAKA	98.5	98.3	0.4	0.4	0.3	0.4	0.3	0.3	5.2	5.4	6.9	6.1	6.2	28.0	27.2	13.7	1.3	78.8	39.5	49.9	50.1
24740	PRINCETON	95.5	95.2	2.7	2.7	0.6	0.8	0.4	0.4	5.8	5.7	5.6	5.4	5.9	26.5	27.1	15.6	2.4	79.7	41.4	47.2	52.8
24747	ROCK	98.1	98.0	0.9	1.0	0.1	0.1	0.6	0.6	5.7	5.9	6.1	5.4	5.7	26.7	30.1	12.9	1.6	79.0	41.3	50.8	49.2
24801	WELCH	78.1	77.5	20.3	20.8	0.1	0.2	0.7	0.7	4.8	4.9	5.7	6.3	6.3	22.2	28.7	18.2	3.1	80.8	44.9	46.4	53.6
24815	BERWIND	95.5	95.4	3.7	3.8	0.0	0.0	0.2	0.3	5.7	6.0	6.6	7.1	6.4	25.3	28.5	12.5	1.9	77.3	40.5	48.4	51.6
24818	BRENTON	99.1	99.0	0.1	0.1	0.1	0.1	0.7	0.7	6.2	6.2	5.9	5.9	7.1	25.5	31.3	10.9	1.1	78.3	40.4	49.7	50.4
24822	CLEAR FORK	99.3	99.3	0.1	0.2	0.0	0.0	0.7	0.7	5.8	5.6	5.9	5.8	6.1	29.3	28.7	12.1	0.9	79.5	39.3	51.0	49.0
24823	COAL MOUNTAIN	99.1	99.1	0.0	0.0	0.0	0.0	0.9	0.9	5.4	5.4	5.4	5.4	5.4	29.5	32.1	10.7	0.9	78.6	40.6	52.7	47.3
24827	CYCLONE	99.6	99.4	0.0	0.1	0.1	0.1	0.6	0.6	5.6	5.7	5.9	5.8	6.1	28.8	29.1	12.1	1.0	79.4	39.7	50.0	50.0
24828	DAVY	97.4	97.2	2.0	2.1	0.1	0.2	0.4	0.4	5.3	5.5	6.6	6.1	6.8	27.0	30.1	11.1	1.5	79.2	40.3	49.4	50.6
24834	FANROCK	99.1	99.1	0.0	0.0	0.0	0.0	0.0	0.0	5.4	5.4	5.4	5.4	5.4	25.2	36.0	10.8	0.9	79.3	43.4	47.8	52.3
24839	HANOVER	99.6	99.6	0.1	0.1	0.0	0.0	0.9	1.0	6.2	6.4	6.2	6.1	6.1	29.4	29.1	10.0	0.7	77.6	38.8	49.3	50.7
24844	IAEGER	98.3	98.2	0.9	1.0	0.0	0.1	0.6	0.7	5.1	5.9	6.4	6.4	5.9	27.9	30.2	11.2	1.1	78.7	40.3	48.7	51.3
24849	JESSE	99.2	99.1	0.0	0.0	0.0	0.3	0.6	0.6	4.6	5.2	5.8	5.8	5.8	22.8	33.5	15.0	1.5	80.6	45.0	49.7	50.3
24850	JOLO	99.5	99.4	0.1	0.2	0.0	0.0	0.2	0.2	5.6	6.5	7.2	7.2	5.1	27.0	29.6	10.7	1.1	76.3	39.5	48.0	52.1
24859	MARIANNA	99.2	99.3	0.1	0.1	0.1	0.1	0.8	0.8	5.3	5.3	5.6	5.8	6.4	24.2	31.8	14.1	1.6	80.6	43.2	49.3	50.7
24860	MATHENY	99.3	99.4	0.0	0.0	0.0	0.0	0.4	0.5	4.7	5.2	5.8	5.8	6.4	23.1	34.1	13.8	1.2	81.2	44.4	51.1	48.9
24862	MOHAWK	99.7	99.7	0.0	0.0	0.0	0.0	0.2	0.2	4.7	5.5	6.8	6.6	5.5	29.0	31.0	10.3	0.7	78.7	39.4	51.3	48.7
24868	NORTHFORK	61.4	60.7	37.2	37.8	0.0	0.0	0.6	0.7	5.4	5.5	6.6	6.6	6.3	23.1	28.1	15.5	2.9	78.3	42.3	46.8	53.3
24869	NORTH SPRING	98.5	99.2	0.0	0.0	0.0	0.0	0.0	0.0	6.2	6.2	6.2	5.4	5.4	26.9	30.8	11.5	1.5	77.7	41.0	49.2	50.8
24870	OCEANA	99.4	99.3	0.0	0.0	0.0	0.1	0.4	0.4	5.4	6.0	6.2	5.8	5.8	26.9	30.5	12.4	1.0	78.8	41.0	49.5	50.5
24873	PAYNESVILLE	93.5	93.4	5.6	5.6	0.1	0.1	0.4	0.4	5.2	5.5	6.7	7.0	6.1	25.7	30.2	12.3	1.4	78.3	41.1	48.0	52.0
24874	PINEVILLE	98.9	98.7	0.3	0.3	0.1	0.2	0.4	0.4	5.7	5.9	5.3	5.4	5.7	24.5	30.9	14.7	2.0	79.9	43.4	48.2	51.8
24882	SIMON	99.2	99.2	0.2	0.2	0.0	0.0	0.8	0.8	5.7	5.7	5.9	5.9	6.2	29.2	28.5	12.0	1.0	79.4	39.2	51.2	48.8
24884	SQUIRE	93.2	93.1	5.8	5.8	0.0	0.0	0.1	0.1	4.5	5.0	6.7	6.1	5.7	24.0	31.6	14.6	1.8	80.1	43.7	51.4	48.7
24901	LEWISBURG	94.3	94.0	3.8	3.8	0.3	0.5	0.7	0.7	5.1	5.4	5.8	5.5	5.2	24.1	29.7	15.9	3.4	80.4	44.3	46.6	53.4
24910	ALDERSON	82.7	82.4	15.8	16.0	0.3	0.3	1.1	1.1	4.2	4.4	4.9	4.7	6.7	36.1	25.7	11.7	1.8	83.7	39.4	37.2	62.8
24915	ARBOVALE	98.7	98.7	0.2	0.2	0.2	0.2	0.6	0.8	4.9	4.9	5.4	5.1	3.7	29.2	31.2	14.6	1.1	81.7	43.2	53.5	46.5
24916	ASBURY	97.8	97.6	0.3	0.3	0.3	0.3	0.3	0.3	5.3	5.6	6.2	5.6	5.3	24.7	33.4	12.6	1.4	79.5	43.4	48.3	51.7
24917	AUTO	97.0	96.8	1.9	1.9	0.3	0.4	0.8	0.7	5.6	4.6	5.3	6.7	10.4	23.4	27.6	14.8	1.8	81.4	40.6	53.8	46.2
24918	BALLARD	98.5	98.5	0.4	0.4	0.1	0.1	0.2	0.2	6.0	6.1	6.4	6.1	5.8	27.3	26.8	14.1	1.6	78.2	39.4	50.0	50.0
24920	BARTOW	99.0	99.0	0.8	0.8	0.2	0.2	0.4	0.4	5.0	5.2	7.5	6.2	6.0	24.8	29.4	13.9	2.2	78.6	42.0	51.8	48.2
24925	CALDWELL	98.6	99.1	0.0	0.0	0.0	0.0	0.0	0.0	6.7	6.7	6.2	5.7	4.8	27.6	28.6	12.4	1.4	77.1	40.0	50.0	50.0
24927	CASS	98.7	98.8	0.4	0.5	0.1	0.1	0.6	0.6	5.0	5.2	5.7	5.3	4.4	27.1	30.2	15.0	2.1	80.9	43.3	52.3	47.8
24931	CRAWLEY	99.3	99.2	0.1	0.1	0.1	0.1	0.5	0.4	5.3	5.8	6.0	5.8	5.2	25.8	30.1	14.3	1.6	79.3	42.7	50.3	49.7
24934	DUNMORE	98.7	98.7	0.4	0.5	0.4	0.5	0.4	0.5	5.0	4.5	7.2	6.3	4.1	24.3	28.4	18.9	1.4	79.3	44.3	50.5	49.6
24935	FOREST HILL	97.9	97.9	0.7	0.7	0.0	0.4	0.0	0.0	4.5	5.2	6.6	5.2	4.5	23.2	27.7	20.1	3.1	79.9	45.7	50.5	49.5
24936	FORT SPRING	99.0	99.0	0.0	0.0	0.0	0.0	0.0	0.0	7.6	7.6	6.9	5.5	4.8	27.5	27.5	11.7	1.0	74.2	38.8	48.5	51.6
24938	FRANKFORD	98.0	97.8	0.8	0.8	0.1	0.2	0.6	0.6	5.4	6.0	5.8	5.6	5.0	25.7	30.9	13.9	1.6	79.2	42.7	49.7	50.3
24941	GAP MILLS	97.3	97.3	1.5	1.5	0.0	0.0	0.2	0.2	5.8	6.1	6.3	5.4	5.8	24.8	31.3	13.3	1.2	78.7	41.8	49.9	50.2
24943	GRASSY MEADOWS	98.5	99.0	0.0	0.0	0.0	0.0	1.0	1.0	6.8	6.8	7.8	4.9	5.9	27.3	26.8	12.2	1.5	75.1	38.8	49.8	50.2
24944	GREEN BANK	98.9	98.9	0.2	0.2	0.2	0.2	0.4	0.4	4.6	4.6	7.5	6.8	4.0	24.4	28.6	18.7	0.9	78.2	44.1	51.7	48.4
24945	GREENVILLE	97.0	97.1	1.3	1.3	0.2	0.1	0.2	0.2	4.6	4.9	6.3	6.0	5.6	25.2	29.6	15.7	2.1	80.4	43.1	49.4	50.6
24946	HILLSBORO	97.3	97.3	1.7	1.7	0.0	0.0	0.5	0.5	3.7	4.1	5.2	4.7	5.2	30.6	30.6	14.2	1.8	83.6	43.0	55.9	44.1
24950	KIEFFER	100.0	100.0	0.0	0.0	0.0	0.0	0.0	0.0	0.0	0.0	0.0	0.0	28.6	71.4	0.0	0.0	0.0	100.0	28.8	57.1	42.9
24951	LINDSIDE	97.4	97.5	1.1	1.1	0.0	0.0	0.4	0.4	5.4	5.7	5.3	4.7	4.8	24.0	29.4	16.9	3.7	80.8	45.1	48.7	51.3
24954	MARLINTON	98.3	98.3	0.8	0.8	0.2	0.2	0.3	0.3	5.2	5.5	6.0	5.4	4.8	25.0	28.6	16.4	3.1	79.9	43.7	49.8	50.2
24957	MAXWELTON	97.2	96.3	0.9	0.9	0.0	0.9	0.0	0.9	5.5	5.5	7.3	6.4	5.5	22.9	31.2	13.8	1.8	76.2	42.8	50.5	49.5
24962	PENCE SPRINGS	98.0	97.9	1.4	1.4	0.0	0.0	0.0	0.0	5.5	5.8	6.9	5.5	4.5	26.8	27.5	15.8	1.7	77.7	41.9	48.1	51.9
24963	PETERSTOWN	98.5	98.5	0.4	0.4	0.1	0.1	0.3	0.3	5.8	5.9	6.1	5.8	5.4	27.0	26.7	15.5	1.9	78.8	40.6	49.3	50.8
24966	RENICK	97.8	97.4	0.8	0.9	0.2	0.3	0.4	0.5	5.6	5.7	6.4	6.3	6.4	22.8	30.2	14.8	1.9	78.5	42.9	50.5	49.5
24970	RONCEVERTE	94.2	94.0	4.0	4.1	0.3	0.4	0.9	1.0	6.1	6.2	6.2	6.0	5.4	26.6	26.4	15.1	2.2	77.8	40.6	48.5	51.5
24974	SECONDCREEK	98.5	98.7	0.0	0.0	0.2	0.2	0.2	0.2	6.1	6.1	7.0	6.1	5.9	27.4	29.4	11.3	0.9	77.2	40.8	49.8	50.2
24976	SINKS GROVE	97.3	97.3	1.3	1.3	0.3	0.3	0.2	0.2	5.9	6.1	6.5	5.9	5.6	28.1	28.6	12.3	1.1	77.9	40.9	48.9	51.1
24977	SMOOT	99.0	98.9	0.1	0.1	0.0	0.0	0.6	0.6	6.0	6.4	6.6	5.0	5.6	25.5	28.9	14.2	1.8	78.0	41.7	51.0	49.1
24981	TALCOTT	93.2	92.8	5.6	5.9	0.1	0.1	0.4	0.3	4.8	5.2	6.6	5.9	5.5	25.4	28.5	16.3	1.9	79.6	42.7	49.6	50.4
24983	UNION	96.9	96.8	1.7	1.7	0.1	0.1	0.1	0.1	5.3	5.3	6.0	6.0	5.4	24.0	29.0	16.8	2.3	79.8	43.5	49.0	51.0
24984	WAITEVILLE	97.5	98.0	1.0	1.0	0.0	0.0	0.0	0.0	5.5	6.0	6.0	5.0	5.5	23.1	32.7	14.6	1.5	79.4	44.0	49.8	50.3
24985	WAYSIDE	92.0	91.6	6.9	7.1	0.2	0.2	0.6	0.6	4.5	4.7	6.2	5.6	5.4	30.3	27.3	14.2	1.7	80.5	41.2	43.6	56.4
24986	WHITE SULPHUR SPRING	90.6	90.8	7.7	7.3	0.2	0.3	0.7	0.7	5.0	4.7	5.5	5.6	6.9	24.6	28.4	17.2	2.2	81.7	43.6	48.2	51.8
24991	WILLIAMSBURG	97.2	96.7	0.8	0.8	0.3	0.4	0.4	0.5	5.6	6.2	6.8	6.5	5.5	24.0	30.5	13.3	1.8	77.1	42.1	50.3	49.7
24993	WOLFCREEK	76.3	75.7	21.9	22.4	0.5	0.5	1.4	0.9	2.8	3.3	3.7	4.2	7.0	40.7	25.7	10.8	1.9	87.4	39.5	32.2	67.8
25003	ALUM CREEK	98.4	98.3	0.2	0.2	0.2	0.3	0.3	0.4	5.9	6.2	6.3	5.1	5.6	28.7	29.7	11.4	1.2	78.6	40.2	49.7	50.3
25005	AMMA	98.5	98.0	0.0	0.0	0.3	0.5	0.3	0.3	4.8	5.5	6.5	6.5	5.8	26.3	32.8	11.0	1.0	79.5	41.7	49.8	50.3
25007	ARNETT	99.7	99.4	0.3	0.3	0.0	0.0	0.3	0.3	5.3	5.9	7.0	5.9	6.7	25.8	30.0	12.3	1.1	78.4	40.5	51.0	49.0
25008	ARTIE	99.8	99.8	0.0	0.0	0.0	0.0	0.0	0.0	4.6	5.2	7.8	7.7	5.5	27.2	27.6	12.6	1.8	77.8	40.0	49.8	50.2
25009	ASHFORD	98.5	98.6	0.0	0.0	0.0	0.0	0.4	0.3	6.7	6.9	6.9	5.8	5.7	27.1	28.5	11.3	1.2	76.2	38.6	49.9	50.1
25010	BALD KNOB	99.3	99.2	0.0	0.0	0.0	0.0	0.2	0.2	4.8	5.3	6.1	4.9	4.4	26.1	32.5	14.6	1.3	80.8	43.8	48.1	51.9
25015	BELLE	97.5	97.3	0.6	0.6	0.0	0.1	0.6	0.6	5.7	5.9	6.1	5.5	5.9	26.8	27.1	14.7	2.3	79.0	40.9	48.0	52.0
25019	BICKMORE	97.5	97.5	0.2	0.2	0.0	0.0	0.0	0.0	5.6	6.1	7.0	6.7	6.2	27.4	27.9	12.0	1.1	77.5	39.1	51.2	48.8
25021	BIM	99.8	99.7	0.0	0.0	0.0	0.0	0.5	0.5	4.8	5.3	6.1	5.5	4.6	25.1	33.5	13.8	1.3	80.1	43.8	49.6	50.4
25024	BLOOMINGROSE	98.4	98.5	0.3	0.3	0.2	0.2	0.4	0.4	7.4	7.9	7.7	5.2	3.9	31.2	23.6	11.4	1.8	73.8	35.4	49.2	50.8
25025	BLOUNT	98.8	98.7	0.3	0.3	0.2	0.2	0.0	0.0	6.3	6.3	6.4	5.4	6.4	28.1	28.3	12.1	0.9	77.8	38.9	51.0	49.0
25028	BOB WHITE	98.8	98.6	1.0	1.0	0.0	0.0	0.6	0.6	4.0	4.4	5.9	5.7	6.5	24.4	33.7	14.1	1.4	82.2	44.3	49.7	50.3
25030	BOMONT	99.3	98.6	0.0	0.0	0.0	0.0	0.0	0.0	5.0	5.8	7.9	7.9	6.5	25.9	27.3	13.0	0.7	76.3	39.2	51.8	48.2
25033	BUFFALO	98.2	98.2	0.1	0.1	0.1	0.1	0.7	0.8	5.4	5.6	6.2	6.2	5.9	28.4	29.0	11.9	1.3	79.0	40.2	49.9	50.1
25035	CABIN CREEK	98.8	98.6	0.4	0.5	0.0	0.0	0.3	0.4	4.9	5.3	5.8	5.3	4.9	26.9	28.8	16.8	1.5	80.8	43.0	50.1	49.9
25039	CEDAR GROVE	94.3	94.1	4.2	4.4	0.2	0.2	0.5	0.5	5.4	5.7	5.7	5.4	5.3	25.6	28.2	16.5	2.2	79.9	42.7	48.2	51.8
25043	CLAY	98.4	98.4	0.0	0.0	0.0	0.0	0.4	0.4	6.6	6.4	7.2	6.7	7.1	26.3	24.8	13.3	1.6	75.6	37.2	48.9	51.1
25044	CLEAR CREEK	100.0	100.0	0.0	0.0	0.0	0.0	0.0	0.0	10.0	10.0	10.0	10.0	10.0	35.0	15.0	0.0	0.0	70.0	25.0	50.0	50.0
25045	CLENDENIN	98.6	98.4	0.1	0.1	0.1	0.1	0.3	0.3	5.9	5.9	5.7	5.7	6.1	25.7	29.1	14.2	1.7	79.0	41.6	49.5	50.5
25046	CLIO	98.5	98.2	0.0	0.0	0.2	0.4	0.2	0.2	4.7	5.3	6.5	6.6	5.9	26.2	33.2	10.6	1.2	79.7	41.8	49.8	50.2
25047	CLOTHIER	96.3	96.1	2.9	2.9	0.2	0.2	0.9	1.0	6.4	6.3	6.7	5.4	6.5	27.2	27.2	12.8	1.6	77.2	38.9	46.3	53.7
25048	COLCORD	99.7	100.0	0.0	0.0	0.0	0.0	0.0	0.0	4.5	5.2	7.9	7.9	5.5	26.5	28.5	12.4	1.7	78.4	40.3	50.2	49.8
25049	COMFORT	98.5	98.7	0.3	0.3	0.0	0.0	0.5	0.5	7.1	7.4	7.1	5.1	4.3	31.1	24.2	12.0	1.5	75.3	36.3	48.7	51.3
25051	COSTA	98.9	98.7	0.2	0.2	0.0	0.0	0.9	0.7	4.9	5.5	6.0	5.8	6.6	26.1	30.8	12.2	2.2	80.1	41.6	51.3	48.7
25053	DANVILLE	98.7	98.8	0.4	0.4	0.2	0.2	0.3	0.3	6.3	6.4	6.5	6.1	6.3	27.6	27.9	11.3	1.6	77.0	38.7	49.2	50.8
25059	DIXIE	98.0	97.9	0.8	0.8	0.0	0.0	0.2	0.2	5.2	5.4	6.2	6.0	7.0	28.5	26.7	14.1	1.0	79.9	39.7	52.4	47.7
	WEST VIRGINIA	95.1	94.8	3.2	3.2	0.5	0.7	0.7	0.7	5.6	5.8	6.2	6.3	6.7	26.7	27.1	13.7	1.9	78.9	40.1	48.8	51.2
	UNITED STATES	75.1	73.6	12.3	12.5	3.8	4.2	12.5	14.1	6.9	6.7	7.2	7.0	7.3	28.6	23.8	10.8	1.7	75.1	36.0	49.1	50.9

#	ZIP CODE / POST OFFICE NAME	2004 Per Capita Income	2004 HH Income Base	2004 Household Income Distribution (%): Less than $25,000	$25,000 to $49,999	$50,000 to $99,999	$100,000 to $149,999	$150,000 or More	Median Household Income: 2004	2009	2004 National Centile	2004 State Centile	2004 Home Value Base	2004 Home Value Distribution (%): Less than $50,000	$50,000 to $89,999	$90,000 to $174,999	$175,000 to $399,999	$400,000 or More	2004 Median Home Value
24701	BLUEFIELD	18720	9015	42.8	32.0	18.9	3.8	2.6	29822	33960	12	52	6725	36.3	32.9	25.0	5.0	0.7	68025
24712	ATHENS	14934	629	40.2	29.7	24.2	4.1	1.8	32262	36711	18	68	476	29.8	32.4	27.5	10.3	0.0	78182
24714	BEESON	25325	101	56.4	16.8	20.8	4.0	2.0	21782	25000	3	9	87	41.4	26.4	18.4	10.3	3.5	64583
24715	BRAMWELL	12638	210	56.2	29.5	12.4	1.0	1.0	21196	24307	2	8	176	54.6	30.7	11.9	1.7	1.1	44667
24726	HERNDON	19727	771	48.8	25.0	17.3	4.9	4.0	25982	31380	6	28	643	65.5	27.7	5.1	1.7	0.0	36371
24731	KEGLEY	9899	31	41.9	35.5	22.6	0.0	0.0	30716	37296	14	58	27	37.0	33.3	18.5	7.4	3.7	62500
24733	LASHMEET	11581	278	54.7	27.3	16.6	1.4	0.0	22414	26375	3	12	227	73.1	13.7	10.6	2.2	0.4	32885
24736	MATOAKA	15138	435	51.7	32.6	11.5	1.8	2.3	24049	27713	4	18	367	77.7	15.0	6.8	0.3	0.3	25671
24740	PRINCETON	18713	13359	42.6	29.8	21.6	3.7	2.2	30372	34807	13	55	10224	31.7	32.3	27.2	8.1	0.7	73803
24747	ROCK	14365	1989	44.5	35.7	17.7	1.7	0.5	28305	32192	9	42	1667	48.8	29.0	17.9	3.4	1.0	51404
24801	WELCH	14065	3378	57.0	25.5	14.4	1.5	1.7	20787	23183	2	6	2465	77.5	15.4	6.3	0.8	0.0	26007
24815	BERWIND	10912	1334	65.8	25.0	7.1	1.2	0.9	17570	19787	1	2	1056	82.7	13.8	3.4	0.1	0.0	24097
24818	BRENTON	16032	925	50.6	23.1	22.6	2.7	1.0	24481	28533	4	20	736	48.6	34.2	15.0	2.2	0.0	51852
24822	CLEAR FORK	13537	275	49.1	26.9	20.7	3.3	0.0	25510	30128	5	25	229	53.7	27.1	17.9	1.3	0.0	45750
24823	COAL MOUNTAIN	13138	44	47.7	27.3	20.5	4.6	0.0	26493	30000	6	30	37	54.1	24.3	21.6	0.0	0.0	45000
24827	CYCLONE	15200	791	45.6	30.5	20.6	2.7	0.6	27830	32383	8	39	661	56.7	25.6	16.6	1.1	0.0	44295
24828	DAVY	10448	885	63.1	26.4	8.7	1.2	0.6	17748	20054	1	3	712	83.2	11.8	4.5	0.6	0.0	22095
24834	FANROCK	15588	47	46.8	27.7	19.2	6.4	0.0	28622	30000	10	44	38	50.0	29.0	15.8	5.3	0.0	50000
24839	HANOVER	14317	588	53.7	21.8	20.6	2.9	1.0	22267	25498	3	11	490	66.9	15.1	16.5	1.4	0.0	40778
24844	IAEGER	11735	1816	61.5	26.4	9.6	1.4	1.1	18877	20928	1	3	1496	67.8	21.9	9.4	0.9	0.0	33309
24849	JESSE	15000	145	50.3	29.7	14.5	3.5	2.1	24843	29028	4	21	118	48.3	33.1	17.0	1.7	0.0	51176
24850	JOLO	10750	1066	67.1	23.7	6.9	0.3	2.1	15577	17102	1	1	864	73.6	14.4	10.8	1.3	0.0	31825
24859	MARIANNA	16201	325	50.8	25.9	17.9	4.3	1.2	24516	29010	4	20	263	51.0	31.9	14.5	1.5	1.1	49219
24860	MATHENY	20725	295	51.5	22.4	18.0	3.7	4.4	24109	28659	4	18	246	45.5	37.8	14.6	2.0	0.0	54231
24862	MOHAWK	8986	532	68.2	27.6	2.8	0.6	0.8	17391	19239	1	2	440	73.0	18.4	8.2	0.5	0.0	33125
24868	NORTHFORK	9888	1296	67.0	23.4	8.6	0.8	0.2	16831	18260	1	2	1018	87.7	8.8	3.4	0.0	0.0	20680
24869	NORTH SPRING	15798	57	50.9	26.3	17.5	5.3	0.0	24271	31147	4	19	47	55.3	23.4	17.0	4.3	0.0	47500
24870	OCEANA	17609	1450	45.2	28.9	20.8	3.2	1.9	28391	33345	9	43	1217	46.9	33.3	18.4	1.4	0.0	53409
24873	PAYNESVILLE	10525	633	61.9	27.5	9.6	0.6	0.3	19654	21642	2	4	523	83.8	14.0	1.9	0.4	0.0	20694
24874	PINEVILLE	17044	1605	45.8	30.2	17.9	4.7	1.4	27281	31934	8	34	1269	48.2	31.1	16.9	3.0	0.8	51836
24882	SIMON	13127	248	50.0	25.8	21.4	2.8	0.0	25000	29287	5	22	206	50.0	29.6	17.5	2.9	0.0	50000
24884	SQUIRE	11382	302	59.3	31.8	8.3	0.7	0.0	20725	23098	2	6	252	87.3	7.5	5.2	0.0	0.0	23621
24901	LEWISBURG	24240	3816	40.8	27.3	21.1	5.8	5.0	32057	36857	18	66	2908	18.7	15.9	38.3	22.5	4.6	117528
24910	ALDERSON	13482	1511	48.8	30.2	16.4	2.6	2.0	25541	28890	5	25	1214	31.8	33.0	28.3	5.8	1.1	72088
24915	ARBOVALE	18694	225	32.0	33.3	28.0	5.8	0.9	35945	42163	31	80	186	29.0	27.4	22.0	19.4	2.2	79412
24916	ASBURY	17563	304	41.1	29.0	22.7	3.6	3.6	35000	40105	28	77	259	30.9	30.1	27.4	7.3	4.3	73462
24917	AUTO	9496	110	36.4	43.6	16.4	1.8	1.8	30348	33253	13	54	93	29.0	34.4	30.1	5.4	1.1	76111
24918	BALLARD	22926	523	40.3	31.4	21.6	3.8	2.9	31494	36449	16	62	442	28.1	33.7	35.3	2.7	0.2	76842
24920	BARTOW	13301	213	54.5	31.5	9.9	2.8	1.4	23189	25877	3	14	172	39.0	38.4	21.5	1.2	0.0	61429
24925	CALDWELL	24416	101	27.7	43.6	20.8	3.0	5.0	36156	41105	32	81	87	19.5	24.1	43.7	10.3	2.3	94583
24927	CASS	17358	391	39.9	32.5	22.3	4.6	0.8	30472	34407	13	55	316	30.4	32.3	21.8	13.6	1.9	75484
24931	CRAWLEY	21049	465	34.6	33.3	22.2	5.4	4.5	37512	42072	37	85	398	19.6	28.4	49.3	2.8	0.0	92963
24934	DUNMORE	18260	105	39.1	34.3	21.0	3.8	1.9	33805	37765	23	72	89	25.8	19.1	46.1	6.7	2.3	99000
24935	FOREST HILL	15176	129	48.8	31.0	16.3	3.9	0.0	25824	29470	6	27	106	23.6	35.9	34.9	5.7	0.0	78000
24936	FORT SPRING	16828	121	35.5	38.0	23.1	0.8	2.5	31766	35555	17	65	101	20.8	23.8	42.6	9.9	3.0	95500
24938	FRANKFORD	21447	484	35.3	30.4	28.9	2.3	3.1	33815	38257	23	72	415	21.9	21.5	40.7	12.5	3.4	97237
24941	GAP MILLS	22198	285	37.5	35.4	21.1	2.8	3.2	35072	40520	28	77	240	32.5	38.3	19.2	6.7	3.3	66857
24943	GRASSY MEADOWS	19224	83	48.2	26.5	20.5	2.4	2.4	25928	30306	6	28	72	27.8	20.8	36.1	13.9	1.4	91429
24944	GREEN BANK	15929	183	38.8	35.0	20.8	4.4	1.1	35110	41042	28	77	158	27.2	16.5	46.8	7.6	1.9	102000
24945	GREENVILLE	24064	564	44.5	31.4	19.3	2.0	2.8	28258	32637	9	41	484	35.5	30.8	30.8	1.0	1.9	70000
24946	HILLSBORO	16184	571	40.8	35.0	20.0	3.3	0.9	32631	35785	20	68	484	31.8	35.3	21.5	8.1	3.3	70222
24950	KIEFFER	2143	3	100.0	0.0	0.0	0.0	0.0	5000	0	0	1	0	0.0	0.0	0.0	0.0	0.0	0
24951	LINDSIDE	27414	352	45.2	28.7	21.3	1.4	3.4	29153	33305	11	48	306	29.4	41.8	28.4	0.3	0.0	66053
24954	MARLINTON	16981	1837	44.2	33.4	17.9	3.8	0.8	27868	31394	8	39	1461	29.5	33.7	26.6	8.3	2.0	75731
24957	MAXWELTON	23601	48	35.4	31.3	22.9	4.2	6.3	36112	40000	32	81	40	22.5	17.5	40.0	20.0	0.0	100000
24962	PENCE SPRINGS	12862	122	59.0	19.7	20.5	0.0	0.8	18777	21302	1	3	105	40.0	18.1	33.3	4.8	3.8	67000
24963	PETERSTOWN	20686	1788	39.3	32.3	22.4	4.1	1.9	32028	36891	18	66	1480	26.4	30.3	36.6	6.4	0.4	82143
24966	RENICK	17101	670	44.8	32.2	18.1	1.9	3.0	28323	32003	9	42	566	32.5	26.9	29.5	10.4	0.7	78571
24970	RONCEVERTE	18125	2150	40.1	33.9	19.5	3.8	2.7	30032	34170	12	53	1673	28.5	30.0	32.8	6.5	2.3	80929
24974	SECONDCREEK	19391	191	31.4	35.6	24.1	6.8	2.1	40615	45734	48	91	172	33.7	27.3	26.2	9.9	2.9	78750
24976	SINKS GROVE	17527	481	33.5	36.0	23.1	5.6	1.9	37063	41674	36	84	422	30.1	28.7	28.2	10.4	2.6	80976
24977	SMOOT	17322	359	40.4	34.0	20.9	3.1	1.7	31685	35222	17	64	308	32.8	21.4	37.7	7.1	1.0	84800
24981	TALCOTT	13901	329	56.2	25.8	15.8	0.9	1.2	20287	22738	2	5	272	44.5	23.9	25.0	4.4	2.2	55769
24983	UNION	17705	934	40.6	33.0	21.3	4.3	0.9	29563	34180	11	51	761	24.4	35.0	27.9	11.6	1.2	80714
24984	WAITEVILLE	20188	84	35.7	39.3	19.1	2.4	3.6	36169	42018	32	81	71	31.0	42.3	15.5	7.0	4.2	65000
24985	WAYSIDE	17105	226	52.2	26.6	18.6	0.9	1.8	23557	27147	4	16	194	39.2	22.2	30.4	4.6	3.6	69000
24986	WHITE SULPHUR SPRING	15727	2140	41.1	36.3	19.0	2.9	0.8	30140	33873	13	53	1607	27.3	36.9	29.9	5.7	0.3	77514
24991	WILLIAMSBURG	22691	313	36.1	36.1	18.9	3.8	5.1	32914	37335	21	70	263	28.5	22.1	34.6	13.7	1.1	89250
24993	WOLFCREEK	18194	87	39.1	41.4	14.9	3.5	1.2	27858	32556	8	39	73	31.5	35.6	26.0	6.9	0.0	73571
25003	ALUM CREEK	22603	1034	36.3	27.5	26.5	5.4	4.4	37344	44264	37	85	876	32.0	25.2	30.7	10.4	1.7	79107
25005	AMMA	14414	156	46.2	30.1	18.6	4.5	0.6	26539	29268	6	30	135	25.2	34.1	29.6	11.1	0.0	76500
25007	ARNETT	16511	132	43.9	32.6	16.7	3.0	3.8	28128	31110	9	40	106	49.1	26.4	17.9	3.8	2.8	51429
25008	ARTIE	12535	224	55.8	23.7	16.5	4.0	0.0	21526	24713	2	8	183	47.5	37.2	14.8	0.6	0.0	52045
25009	ASHFORD	14485	229	47.6	26.2	21.4	4.4	0.4	26540	30633	6	30	185	35.1	33.5	29.7	1.6	0.0	69722
25010	BALD KNOB	16122	233	46.4	20.6	31.8	1.3	0.0	31615	37094	17	63	191	59.7	29.8	8.9	1.6	0.0	44032
25015	BELLE	18107	2861	36.3	33.4	25.1	4.3	0.9	33949	40055	24	73	2173	34.7	35.6	28.1	1.6	0.1	68291
25019	BICKMORE	11381	249	54.6	28.1	14.5	2.4	0.4	21233	24100	2	8	207	54.1	27.1	18.4	0.5	0.0	33500
25021	BIM	15818	330	45.2	25.2	27.6	2.1	0.0	30598	35702	14	57	268	54.1	31.7	12.7	0.4	1.1	46944
25024	BLOOMINGROSE	29282	279	43.0	25.8	24.4	2.9	3.9	33096	40349	21	71	220	56.4	24.6	15.0	4.1	0.0	40000
25025	BLOUNT	16318	273	35.5	30.4	29.3	4.0	0.7	36977	43066	35	84	228	50.9	33.8	13.6	1.8	0.0	49048
25028	BOB WHITE	15196	210	46.2	27.6	22.9	3.3	0.0	27464	31970	8	36	170	49.4	30.0	18.2	0.0	2.4	50500
25030	BOMONT	13024	58	46.6	37.9	15.5	0.0	0.0	26454	26793	6	30	47	53.2	27.7	17.0	2.1	0.0	47857
25033	BUFFALO	17262	992	41.1	30.9	23.1	3.9	1.0	30341	35259	13	54	834	41.3	28.2	24.3	5.3	1.0	62885
25035	CABIN CREEK	18666	457	43.3	37.9	17.1	0.7	1.1	27566	31740	8	37	353	52.7	32.6	14.5	0.0	0.3	47625
25039	CEDAR GROVE	17717	1086	41.2	27.7	26.4	3.4	1.3	32851	39425	20	69	833	46.6	34.9	17.8	0.7	0.0	53608
25043	CLAY	13476	1060	55.2	26.2	14.6	2.7	1.2	21405	25100	2	8	771	41.9	34.9	19.8	2.9	0.5	61533
25044	CLEAR CREEK	5500	7	100.0	0.0	0.0	0.0	0.0	15855	25000	1	1	6	33.3	66.7	0.0	0.0	0.0	60000
25045	CLENDENIN	16504	2307	42.6	28.7	23.5	4.6	0.7	30023	35543	12	53	1904	39.9	33.1	21.6	4.7	0.7	61176
25046	CLIO	14365	199	47.2	29.7	18.1	4.0	1.0	26124	29557	6	28	172	26.7	34.9	27.3	11.1	0.0	73846
25047	CLOTHIER	19210	525	43.2	29.0	21.5	4.0	2.3	29481	35000	11	50	394	40.6	34.8	22.1	2.5	0.0	60769
25048	COLCORD	12627	117	58.1	20.5	17.1	4.3	0.0	20206	22706	2	5	94	46.8	36.2	16.0	1.1	0.0	52500
25049	COMFORT	25843	156	45.5	25.0	23.1	3.2	3.2	29294	34602	11	49	124	50.8	27.4	18.6	3.2	0.0	48889
25051	COSTA	11799	183	54.6	30.1	14.2	1.1	0.0	22603	26377	3	12	165	53.9	27.9	11.5	6.7	0.0	47045
25053	DANVILLE	16523	1565	42.6	28.2	24.2	3.8	1.2	30629	35707	14	57	1223	33.8	29.1	29.4	7.4	0.3	69086
25059	DIXIE	20530	246	46.3	31.3	17.9	2.0	2.4	27038	30000	7	33	205	42.0	33.7	24.4	0.0	0.0	62955
	WEST VIRGINIA	19262		38.4	30.0	24.1	5.2	2.4	33458	38993				29.0	29.1	31.1	9.6	1.3	80023
	UNITED STATES	25866		24.7	27.1	30.8	10.9	6.5	48124	56710				10.9	15.0	33.7	30.1	10.4	145905

ZIP CODE #	POST OFFICE NAME	FINANCIAL SERVICES: Auto Loan	Home Loan	Investments	Retirement Plans	THE HOME: Home Improvements: Home Repair	Lawn & Garden	Furnishings: Computers & Hardware	Major Appliances	TV, Radio, Sound Equipment	Furniture	ENTERTAINMENT: Dine out/Carry out	Sports Equipment	Fees & Tickets	Toys & Games	Travel	Cable TV	PERSONAL: Apparel & Services	Auto Repairs	Health Insurance	Pets & Supplies
24701	BLUEFIELD	66	56	46	52	59	67	56	61	61	55	74	70	53	71	57	64	69	61	69	75
24712	ATHENS	70	47	31	44	52	61	56	59	62	53	74	72	48	69	53	63	68	61	68	77
24714	BEESON	96	72	48	69	79	95	80	88	90	76	106	99	71	100	79	95	96	88	106	107
24715	BRAMWELL	45	34	22	32	37	44	37	41	42	35	49	46	33	46	37	44	45	41	49	49
24726	HERNDON	85	59	30	52	66	76	59	71	70	59	82	83	51	77	59	74	74	70	87	96
24731	KEGLEY	60	40	18	34	45	52	38	48	46	39	55	57	33	52	39	50	50	48	59	68
24733	LASHMEET	54	37	18	32	41	48	36	44	43	36	51	52	31	48	37	46	46	44	54	61
24736	MATOAKA	69	47	22	40	53	61	45	56	55	46	64	67	39	60	46	59	58	56	69	79
24740	PRINCETON	71	54	36	50	58	68	56	63	63	55	75	72	50	71	56	66	69	63	74	80
24747	ROCK	64	44	23	38	49	57	43	53	52	44	61	62	37	57	44	55	56	52	65	74
24801	WELCH	48	39	38	36	40	48	44	46	49	43	59	50	41	54	43	52	55	47	53	53
24815	BERWIND	46	33	19	29	36	42	33	39	39	33	46	45	29	43	34	42	42	39	48	52
24818	BRENTON	75	50	23	43	57	65	48	60	58	49	69	72	41	65	49	63	62	60	74	86
24822	CLEAR FORK	63	42	19	36	48	55	41	51	49	41	57	61	34	54	41	53	52	50	63	72
24823	COAL MOUNTAIN	63	42	19	36	48	55	41	51	49	41	58	61	35	55	41	53	52	50	63	72
24827	CYCLONE	71	47	22	41	54	62	46	57	55	47	65	68	39	61	47	60	59	57	71	81
24828	DAVY	47	32	16	29	37	42	32	39	38	32	45	46	28	42	33	41	41	39	48	54
24834	FANROCK	69	46	21	40	53	61	45	56	54	46	63	67	38	60	46	58	58	55	69	80
24839	HANOVER	63	42	19	37	48	55	41	51	49	42	58	61	35	55	42	53	53	51	63	73
24844	IAEGER	51	35	17	30	39	45	34	42	41	34	48	50	29	45	35	44	44	42	51	58
24849	JESSE	58	43	29	42	47	57	48	53	54	46	63	59	43	60	48	57	58	53	63	64
24850	JOLO	47	31	14	27	35	41	30	38	36	31	43	45	26	40	31	39	39	37	47	54
24859	MARIANNA	66	49	30	46	54	64	53	59	60	50	70	67	46	66	52	63	64	59	71	74
24860	MATHENY	83	58	30	51	65	75	58	70	68	58	80	82	50	76	59	73	73	69	85	95
24862	MOHAWK	41	27	12	24	31	36	26	33	32	27	38	40	23	35	27	34	34	33	41	47
24868	NORTHFORK	35	27	27	24	28	34	30	32	35	31	43	35	29	38	30	38	40	33	38	38
24869	NORTH SPRING	68	45	21	39	51	59	44	55	53	45	62	66	37	59	45	57	56	54	68	78
24870	OCEANA	77	53	26	46	59	69	52	64	62	52	73	75	45	69	53	67	66	63	78	87
24873	PAYNESVILLE	45	32	19	28	35	41	33	38	38	33	45	45	29	42	33	41	42	38	47	51
24874	PINEVILLE	65	47	28	44	52	62	50	57	57	49	67	65	44	64	50	61	61	57	69	73
24882	SIMON	63	42	19	36	48	55	41	51	49	41	58	61	35	54	41	53	52	50	63	72
24884	SQUIRE	40	31	32	28	31	39	35	37	40	36	49	40	33	43	34	43	46	38	44	43
24901	LEWISBURG	85	70	54	67	76	87	70	79	76	70	91	88	65	86	72	79	85	78	91	97
24910	ALDERSON	52	38	23	35	42	50	40	46	46	39	54	53	35	51	40	49	49	46	55	59
24915	ARBOVALE	75	59	40	53	66	75	56	67	63	55	75	78	50	74	59	67	69	66	79	92
24916	ASBURY	80	54	24	46	61	70	52	65	63	53	73	77	44	69	53	67	67	64	80	92
24917	AUTO	60	47	32	42	53	59	44	53	50	44	59	62	39	58	47	53	55	52	63	73
24918	BALLARD	104	72	37	63	80	92	70	85	82	71	97	102	60	92	71	88	89	85	103	119
24920	BARTOW	59	40	18	34	45	52	38	48	46	39	54	57	33	51	39	50	49	47	59	68
24925	CALDWELL	92	64	34	61	75	84	63	78	73	63	86	94	54	84	66	77	78	77	93	109
24927	CASS	68	52	33	46	58	66	49	59	56	49	66	70	43	65	52	60	61	59	71	82
24931	CRAWLEY	96	64	29	56	73	84	62	78	75	63	88	93	53	83	63	80	80	77	95	110
24934	DUNMORE	65	51	35	46	58	65	48	58	55	48	65	68	43	64	51	58	60	57	69	80
24935	FOREST HILL	57	45	31	40	50	57	42	51	48	42	57	60	38	56	45	51	53	50	60	70
24936	FORT SPRING	66	49	32	47	54	65	54	60	61	51	72	67	48	67	54	64	65	60	72	73
24938	FRANKFORD	99	67	32	59	76	87	65	81	78	66	91	97	55	87	67	83	83	80	99	115
24941	GAP MILLS	89	69	47	63	78	88	65	79	74	65	88	92	59	87	70	79	82	78	93	108
24943	GRASSY MEADOWS	89	60	27	52	68	78	58	72	70	59	82	86	49	77	59	75	74	72	89	103
24944	GREEN BANK	67	53	36	48	59	67	50	60	56	49	67	70	44	66	53	60	62	59	71	82
24945	GREENVILLE	94	76	61	73	82	90	76	85	82	76	100	101	70	95	76	85	93	85	94	108
24946	HILLSBORO	69	54	37	49	61	69	52	62	59	51	70	72	46	68	55	63	64	61	73	84
24950	KIEFFER	9	6	3	5	7	8	6	8	7	6	9	9	5	8	6	8	8	8	9	11
24951	LINDSIDE	116	78	36	68	89	102	76	94	91	77	107	113	65	101	77	98	98	94	116	133
24954	MARLINTON	64	48	30	44	54	62	48	57	55	47	65	66	42	62	50	58	59	56	68	75
24957	MAXWELTON	97	68	35	64	79	88	67	83	77	66	90	100	57	89	69	81	82	82	98	115
24962	PENCE SPRINGS	52	41	28	37	46	52	38	46	43	38	52	54	34	51	41	46	48	46	55	63
24963	PETERSTOWN	85	60	32	54	67	78	60	72	71	60	83	84	52	79	61	76	76	71	88	96
24966	RENICK	75	55	33	52	62	71	57	66	64	55	75	77	49	73	58	68	69	66	79	87
24970	RONCEVERTE	74	53	31	50	60	69	56	65	64	54	75	75	49	71	56	67	68	64	78	84
24974	SECONDCREEK	88	59	27	51	67	77	57	71	69	58	80	85	48	76	58	74	73	70	87	101
24976	SINKS GROVE	79	54	27	47	60	70	53	65	63	54	74	77	46	70	54	68	68	64	80	90
24977	SMOOT	76	54	29	48	60	70	55	65	64	54	75	76	48	71	55	68	69	64	79	86
24981	TALCOTT	52	41	28	38	45	52	41	47	46	40	54	54	37	53	42	49	50	47	56	61
24983	UNION	69	51	32	47	57	66	52	61	59	51	70	70	46	67	53	63	64	60	73	80
24984	WAITEVILLE	81	64	43	57	72	80	60	72	68	59	80	85	54	79	64	73	75	71	85	99
24985	WAYSIDE	50	41	33	39	45	50	40	46	43	39	52	54	37	51	42	45	49	45	52	60
24986	WHITE SULPHUR SPRING	59	45	29	42	49	58	48	54	54	46	63	61	42	60	48	57	58	53	64	67
24991	WILLIAMSBURG	104	72	36	66	83	94	70	87	82	70	97	105	60	94	73	87	88	86	105	122
24993	WOLFCREEK	25	17	8	14	19	22	16	20	19	16	23	24	14	22	16	21	21	20	25	29
25003	ALUM CREEK	97	72	42	65	78	88	70	82	79	71	95	97	62	90	70	83	88	81	95	110
25005	AMMA	69	47	21	40	53	61	45	56	54	46	64	67	38	60	46	58	58	56	69	80
25007	ARNETT	84	56	26	49	64	73	54	68	66	55	77	81	46	73	55	71	70	67	84	97
25008	ARTIE	59	40	18	34	45	52	38	48	46	39	54	57	33	51	39	50	49	47	59	68
25009	ASHFORD	69	47	21	40	53	61	45	56	54	46	64	67	38	60	46	58	58	56	69	80
25010	BALD KNOB	69	46	21	40	52	60	44	55	53	45	63	66	38	59	45	58	57	55	68	79
25015	BELLE	64	55	44	51	58	67	56	60	61	54	73	68	53	73	57	64	69	60	69	73
25019	BICKMORE	54	36	16	31	41	47	35	44	42	36	49	52	30	47	35	45	45	43	54	62
25021	BIM	66	46	24	41	51	60	46	56	54	46	64	65	40	60	47	58	58	55	68	75
25024	BLOOMINGROSE	136	91	41	78	103	119	88	110	106	89	124	131	75	118	89	114	113	109	135	156
25025	BLOUNT	72	55	33	50	59	66	53	62	59	54	71	73	47	67	53	62	66	61	70	82
25028	BOB WHITE	59	44	29	43	48	58	49	54	55	47	65	60	44	61	49	58	59	54	65	65
25030	BOMONT	59	39	18	34	45	51	38	48	46	39	54	57	32	51	39	49	49	47	59	67
25033	BUFFALO	75	55	31	49	60	67	52	63	60	53	72	74	46	68	53	63	66	62	73	85
25035	CABIN CREEK	77	55	30	50	61	72	57	66	66	56	77	77	49	73	57	70	70	66	81	87
25039	CEDAR GROVE	65	52	38	48	56	65	54	59	60	52	72	68	50	71	54	63	66	59	70	73
25043	CLAY	57	40	23	37	45	53	42	49	49	41	57	56	37	54	42	52	52	49	59	63
25044	CLEAR CREEK	30	20	9	17	22	26	19	24	23	19	27	29	16	26	19	25	25	24	29	34
25045	CLENDENIN	64	51	37	48	55	64	54	59	59	52	71	67	50	68	54	63	65	59	69	72
25046	CLIO	69	47	21	40	53	61	45	56	54	46	64	67	38	60	46	58	58	56	69	80
25047	CLOTHIER	74	55	35	52	60	72	60	67	68	57	79	75	53	75	59	72	72	67	80	82
25048	COLCORD	59	40	18	34	45	52	38	48	46	39	54	57	33	51	39	50	49	47	59	68
25049	COMFORT	122	82	37	71	93	107	79	99	95	81	112	118	67	106	80	103	102	98	122	140
25051	COSTA	55	37	17	32	42	48	35	44	43	36	50	53	30	47	36	46	46	44	55	63
25053	DANVILLE	77	52	24	46	59	68	50	63	60	51	71	75	43	67	52	64	64	62	77	89
25059	DIXIE	87	58	26	50	66	76	56	70	68	57	80	84	48	75	57	73	72	70	87	100
	WEST VIRGINIA	73	60	47	57	64	72	61	67	67	60	80	78	57	78	61	69	75	67	76	84
	UNITED STATES	100	100	100	100	100	100	100	100	100	100	100	100	100	100	100	100	100	100	100	100

#	POST OFFICE NAME	COUNTY FIPS CODE	POPULATION			2000-2004 ANNUAL RATE		HOUSEHOLDS					FAMILIES		
			2000	2004	2009	% Rate	State Centile	2000	2004	2009	% Annual Rate 2000-2004	2004 Average HH Size	2000	2004	% Annual Rate 2000-2004
25060	DOROTHY	081	464	446	441	-0.9	11	187	185	187	-0.3	2.41	143	138	-0.8
25062	DRY CREEK	081	1200	1174	1165	-0.5	24	473	475	484	0.1	2.47	349	339	-0.7
25063	DUCK	015	1059	1074	1088	0.3	75	415	431	446	0.9	2.44	292	293	0.1
25064	DUNBAR	039	10557	9942	9443	-1.4	3	4732	4535	4383	-1.0	2.08	2780	2519	-2.3
25071	ELKVIEW	039	11064	11421	11341	0.8	85	4508	4769	4841	1.3	2.39	3313	3375	0.4
25075	ESKDALE	039	2238	2059	1934	-1.9	1	901	852	820	-1.3	2.42	637	578	-2.3
25079	FALLING ROCK	039	27	25	23	-1.8	1	11	10	10	-2.2	2.40	8	7	-3.1
25081	FOSTER	005	2309	2359	2385	0.5	81	906	949	983	1.1	2.48	690	700	0.3
25082	FRAZIERS BOTTOM	079	1458	1505	1560	0.8	85	562	594	627	1.3	2.53	440	452	0.6
25083	GALLAGHER	039	2232	2077	1960	-1.7	2	932	888	857	-1.1	2.34	631	575	-2.2
25085	GAULEY BRIDGE	019	934	918	913	-0.4	30	405	407	412	0.1	2.23	282	272	-0.9
25088	GLEN	015	156	157	158	0.2	66	62	64	66	0.8	2.45	48	48	0.0
25093	GORDON	005	198	194	194	-0.5	25	82	83	85	0.3	2.34	52	50	-0.9
25103	HANSFORD	039	128	117	110	-2.1	0	58	55	52	-1.2	2.13	41	37	-2.4
25106	HENDERSON	053	498	471	465	-1.3	5	204	197	195	-0.8	2.39	151	141	-1.6
25107	HERNSHAW	039	629	589	558	-1.5	3	262	252	243	-0.9	2.34	196	182	-1.7
25108	HEWETT	005	1849	1855	1848	0.1	62	708	727	741	0.6	2.55	537	535	-0.1
25111	INDORE	015	1182	1179	1187	-0.1	52	438	448	463	0.5	2.63	341	340	-0.1
25113	IVYDALE	015	173	174	176	0.1	65	69	71	73	0.7	2.45	48	48	0.0
25114	JEFFREY	005	486	484	483	-0.1	48	184	188	192	0.5	2.57	136	134	-0.4
25115	KANAWHA FALLS	019	89	89	88	0.0	57	36	37	37	0.7	2.38	28	27	-0.9
25118	KIMBERLY	019	163	160	159	-0.4	28	65	65	65	0.0	1.57	46	40	-3.2
25119	KINCAID	019	434	419	415	-0.8	14	172	170	172	-0.3	2.46	121	116	-1.0
25121	LAKE	045	964	919	884	-1.1	8	376	370	366	-0.4	2.48	295	283	-1.0
25123	LEON	053	2993	2989	2991	0.0	54	1190	1218	1236	0.6	2.45	881	871	-0.3
25124	LIBERTY	079	1100	1086	1109	-0.3	36	432	438	457	0.2	2.48	335	330	-0.4
25125	LIZEMORES	015	624	623	628	0.0	53	234	240	248	0.6	2.60	184	183	-0.1
25130	MADISON	005	4259	4188	4179	-0.4	31	1840	1854	1897	0.2	2.26	1280	1242	-0.7
25132	MAMMOTH	039	341	339	330	-0.1	45	131	133	132	0.4	2.53	102	100	-0.5
25133	MAYSEL	015	551	558	566	0.3	73	221	229	237	0.8	2.44	164	164	0.0
25136	MONTGOMERY	019	9349	9209	9157	-0.4	33	3430	3447	3494	0.1	2.27	2224	2136	-1.0
25140	NAOMA	081	1143	1113	1102	-0.6	20	456	457	465	0.1	2.44	339	329	-0.7
25141	NEBO	015	299	303	307	0.3	74	123	128	132	0.9	2.30	85	85	0.0
25142	NELLIS	005	830	849	859	0.5	81	312	326	338	1.0	2.60	242	246	0.4
25143	NITRO	039	9866	9558	9320	-0.7	17	4268	4205	4174	-0.4	2.27	2787	2625	-1.4
25148	ORGAS	005	900	906	907	0.2	67	366	377	387	0.7	2.40	261	260	-0.1
25150	OVAPA	015	710	724	736	0.5	79	252	263	273	1.0	2.75	186	188	0.3
25154	PEYTONA	005	618	619	619	0.0	60	239	246	252	0.7	2.52	182	181	-0.1
25159	POCA	079	6686	6648	6837	-0.1	46	2629	2670	2801	0.4	2.49	1985	1954	-0.4
25160	POND GAP	039	636	625	605	-0.4	30	238	239	236	0.1	2.59	184	179	-0.7
25161	POWELLTON	019	836	825	822	-0.3	35	315	318	323	0.2	2.59	245	241	-0.4
25164	PROCIOUS	015	1036	1044	1054	0.2	68	402	413	427	0.6	2.53	299	298	-0.1
25165	RACINE	005	630	635	637	0.2	68	258	267	274	0.8	2.38	194	195	0.1
25168	RED HOUSE	079	3956	4002	4108	0.3	73	1612	1670	1750	0.8	2.40	1211	1218	0.1
25169	RIDGEVIEW	005	21	22	22	1.1	88	6	6	7	0.0	3.67	5	5	0.0
25173	ROBSON	019	308	298	295	-0.8	16	125	124	125	-0.2	2.40	90	86	-1.1
25174	ROCK CREEK	081	228	220	217	-0.8	14	80	79	80	-0.3	2.78	59	57	-0.8
25177	SAINT ALBANS	039	25196	23825	22664	-1.3	5	10505	10121	9812	-0.9	2.33	7275	6729	-1.8
25180	SAXON	081	161	156	155	-0.7	17	54	54	55	0.0	2.89	41	39	-1.2
25181	SETH	005	1858	1859	1863	0.0	58	726	745	766	0.6	2.49	509	503	-0.3
25187	SOUTHSIDE	053	667	718	745	1.8	94	271	299	313	2.3	2.40	200	213	1.5
25193	SYLVESTER	005	1519	1498	1495	-0.3	34	673	682	697	0.3	2.20	469	456	-0.7
25202	TORNADO	039	1336	1276	1223	-1.1	9	510	498	487	-0.6	2.56	396	375	-1.3
25204	TWILIGHT	005	476	460	457	-0.8	15	205	205	210	0.0	2.24	148	143	-0.8
25209	WHITESVILLE	081	418	473	503	3.0	98	168	195	213	3.6	2.43	125	141	2.9
25213	WINFIELD	079	4992	5294	5581	1.4	91	2001	2174	2344	2.0	2.41	1516	1605	1.4
25214	WINIFREDE	039	14	13	12	-1.7	2	6	6	5	0.0	2.17	5	4	-5.1
25231	ADVENT	035	140	150	159	1.6	94	49	53	57	1.9	2.83	38	40	1.2
25234	ARNOLDSBURG	013	1764	1745	1719	-0.3	39	724	731	736	0.2	2.38	528	516	-0.5
25235	CHLOE	013	931	927	918	-0.1	48	377	385	390	0.5	2.39	273	269	-0.4
25239	COTTAGEVILLE	035	1414	1488	1550	1.2	90	556	599	637	1.8	2.48	436	456	1.1
25241	EVANS	035	1476	1492	1521	0.3	72	563	583	608	0.8	2.56	435	438	0.2
25243	GANDEEVILLE	087	884	968	1044	2.2	96	345	385	422	2.6	2.51	265	288	2.0
25244	GAY	035	1151	1154	1171	0.1	61	431	443	459	0.7	2.60	341	340	-0.1
25245	GIVEN	035	1569	1683	1774	1.7	94	588	646	696	2.2	2.61	475	509	1.6
25248	KENNA	035	2981	3105	3234	1.0	88	1141	1215	1292	1.5	2.56	892	924	0.8
25251	LEFT HAND	087	407	400	407	-0.4	30	154	154	160	0.0	2.59	116	112	-0.8
25252	LE ROY	035	691	691	701	0.0	57	262	268	278	0.5	2.58	209	208	-0.1
25253	LETART	053	4559	4508	4474	-0.3	39	1867	1890	1897	0.3	2.37	1383	1354	-0.5
25259	LOONEYVILLE	087	498	497	504	-0.1	52	182	185	191	0.4	2.69	139	137	-0.3
25260	MASON	053	2672	2650	2632	-0.2	44	1089	1103	1106	0.3	2.33	753	732	-0.7
25261	MILLSTONE	013	760	752	741	-0.3	39	298	301	303	0.2	2.49	215	210	-0.6
25262	MILLWOOD	035	1404	1440	1484	0.6	82	543	569	597	1.1	2.53	428	436	0.4
25264	MOUNT ALTO	035	368	391	410	1.4	92	141	154	165	2.1	2.54	111	118	1.5
25266	NEWTON	087	895	881	891	-0.4	32	347	348	358	0.1	2.53	246	237	-0.9
25267	NORMANTOWN	021	733	734	720	0.0	59	298	298	299	0.0	2.40	220	213	-0.8
25268	ORMA	013	645	640	631	-0.2	44	259	263	266	0.4	2.43	189	186	-0.4
25270	REEDY	087	1968	1930	1962	-0.5	26	788	789	818	0.0	2.44	582	564	-0.7
25271	RIPLEY	035	6995	7354	7715	1.2	89	2844	3044	3256	1.6	2.36	1991	2060	0.8
25275	SANDYVILLE	035	1751	1775	1813	0.3	74	692	717	748	0.8	2.48	526	527	0.0
25276	SPENCER	087	7769	8274	8784	1.5	92	3149	3415	3693	1.9	2.39	2206	2313	1.1
25279	STATTS MILLS	035	369	408	438	2.4	97	135	152	167	2.8	2.68	106	117	2.4
25281	TARIFF	087	179	177	180	-0.3	39	82	83	85	0.3	2.13	59	58	-0.4
25285	WALLBACK	015	569	578	586	0.4	77	214	222	231	0.9	2.59	156	157	0.2
25286	WALTON	087	1711	1695	1726	-0.2	42	674	679	702	0.2	2.49	522	510	-0.6
25287	WEST COLUMBIA	053	1026	1063	1082	0.8	86	333	356	366	1.6	2.93	260	270	0.9
25301	CHARLESTON	039	3272	3112	2981	-1.2	6	1867	1792	1733	-1.0	1.45	476	412	-3.3
25302	CHARLESTON	039	16510	15932	15312	-0.8	14	7730	7596	7443	-0.4	2.10	4445	4149	-1.6
25303	CHARLESTON	039	7261	6916	6591	-1.1	7	3320	3231	3140	-0.6	2.14	2060	1906	-1.8
25304	CHARLESTON	039	8859	8731	8479	-0.3	33	3973	3974	3922	0.0	2.05	2266	2157	-1.2
25306	CHARLESTON	039	7490	7452	7269	-0.1	46	3186	3249	3241	0.5	2.28	2213	2171	-0.5
25309	CHARLESTON	039	12442	11868	11359	-1.1	9	5381	5223	5090	-0.7	2.19	3429	3165	-1.9
25311	CHARLESTON	039	10693	10571	10295	-0.3	38	4956	4988	4947	0.2	2.05	2585	2466	-1.1
25312	CHARLESTON	039	16265	15713	15100	-0.8	15	6807	6725	6603	-0.3	2.34	4677	4447	-1.1
25313	CHARLESTON	039	11838	12422	12408	1.1	89	4785	5131	5238	1.7	2.42	3458	3566	0.7
	WEST VIRGINIA					0.2					0.6	2.35			-0.3
	UNITED STATES					1.2					1.3	2.58			1.1

ZIP CODE #	POST OFFICE NAME	RACE (%) White 2000	White 2004	Black 2000	Black 2004	Asian/Pacific 2000	Asian/Pacific 2004	% Hispanic Origin 2000	% Hispanic Origin 2004	2004 AGE DISTRIBUTION (%) 0-4	5-9	10-14	15-19	20-24	25-44	45-64	65-84	85+	18+	MEDIAN AGE 2004	% 2004 Males	% 2004 Females
25060	DOROTHY	99.8	100.0	0.0	0.0	0.0	0.0	0.0	0.0	4.3	4.9	7.6	7.9	5.6	26.2	28.9	12.8	1.8	78.3	40.9	50.5	49.6
25062	DRY CREEK	99.2	99.1	0.0	0.0	0.1	0.1	0.3	0.3	5.8	6.1	6.3	5.5	5.1	24.6	33.0	12.4	1.2	78.5	41.6	49.4	50.6
25063	DUCK	98.4	98.2	0.1	0.1	0.1	0.2	0.3	0.4	5.8	5.8	6.6	6.0	5.9	26.4	27.1	14.3	2.3	78.2	40.8	50.4	49.6
25064	DUNBAR	78.8	78.2	17.8	17.8	1.4	1.9	0.6	0.6	5.4	5.3	5.1	6.3	6.9	26.0	25.8	15.9	3.3	81.0	41.3	46.8	53.2
25071	ELKVIEW	98.7	98.5	0.3	0.3	0.2	0.3	0.4	0.5	5.8	6.1	6.2	5.2	5.3	27.5	29.4	13.1	1.4	78.7	41.1	49.4	50.6
25075	ESKDALE	98.1	98.0	1.1	1.1	0.1	0.2	0.5	0.5	5.3	5.5	6.2	5.9	6.1	26.5	28.0	14.9	1.5	79.5	41.2	50.2	49.8
25079	FALLING ROCK	96.3	96.0	0.0	0.0	0.0	0.0	0.0	0.0	8.0	8.0	8.0	8.0	8.0	32.0	28.0	0.0	0.0	76.0	31.3	48.0	52.0
25081	FOSTER	98.6	98.6	0.6	0.6	0.1	0.1	0.4	0.4	6.5	6.6	5.9	5.3	5.5	27.2	29.8	11.9	1.3	77.6	40.0	49.2	50.8
25082	FRAZIERS BOTTOM	98.6	98.6	0.4	0.4	0.1	0.1	0.4	0.4	5.5	5.5	5.8	6.0	6.1	28.0	31.0	11.1	1.0	79.6	40.9	50.4	49.6
25083	GALLAGHER	89.4	88.9	8.7	8.9	0.5	0.7	0.5	0.5	5.0	5.1	5.9	5.3	6.8	25.4	28.3	16.3	1.9	81.0	41.9	48.0	52.0
25085	GAULEY BRIDGE	95.3	95.3	3.0	3.1	0.3	0.3	1.0	1.0	6.2	6.0	5.3	4.3	6.9	25.9	27.6	15.1	2.7	80.0	40.8	48.9	51.1
25088	GLEN	98.7	98.7	0.0	0.0	0.0	0.0	0.0	0.0	4.5	5.1	7.6	7.6	6.4	27.4	26.8	14.0	0.6	77.7	40.8	50.3	49.7
25093	GORDON	99.0	99.0	0.5	0.5	0.0	0.0	0.5	0.5	5.2	6.2	6.7	5.7	6.2	25.8	29.4	12.9	2.1	78.4	41.1	49.5	50.5
25103	HANSFORD	96.9	95.7	2.3	2.6	0.0	0.0	0.8	0.0	5.1	5.1	6.0	6.0	6.0	26.5	29.1	15.4	0.9	78.6	41.6	50.4	49.6
25106	HENDERSON	98.4	98.5	0.0	0.0	0.0	0.0	0.4	0.2	5.9	6.4	6.6	6.4	6.2	26.8	27.6	13.0	1.3	77.3	39.5	48.4	51.6
25107	HERNSHAW	98.1	98.0	0.0	0.0	0.0	0.0	0.5	0.7	5.9	6.5	7.3	4.8	5.1	29.4	27.5	12.6	1.0	77.4	38.9	50.9	49.1
25108	HEWETT	99.2	99.2	0.2	0.2	0.0	0.0	0.2	0.2	5.7	5.9	7.3	6.3	6.5	27.9	27.4	11.7	1.4	77.2	39.0	49.7	50.4
25111	INDORE	96.7	96.6	0.1	0.1	0.0	0.0	0.2	0.2	5.7	5.9	7.1	7.2	6.5	27.1	27.4	11.9	1.2	76.8	38.6	51.1	48.9
25113	IVYDALE	98.3	98.9	0.0	0.0	0.0	0.0	1.2	0.6	6.9	6.3	7.5	6.9	6.9	26.4	24.1	13.8	1.2	74.7	36.5	51.2	48.9
25114	JEFFREY	97.1	97.1	2.3	2.3	0.0	0.0	1.0	1.0	7.6	7.2	6.2	6.2	6.4	26.2	28.3	10.3	1.5	75.2	37.4	49.8	50.2
25115	KANAWHA FALLS	97.8	96.6	1.1	1.1	0.0	0.0	0.0	1.1	5.6	5.6	5.6	6.7	5.6	28.1	28.1	13.5	1.1	77.5	40.4	51.7	48.3
25118	KIMBERLY	84.1	84.4	12.9	13.1	1.2	1.3	0.0	0.0	5.0	3.8	3.8	10.6	21.9	24.4	19.4	10.0	1.3	86.9	27.0	56.9	43.1
25119	KINCAID	86.4	86.4	11.8	11.7	0.2	0.2	0.5	0.5	6.2	6.0	6.0	6.2	6.4	26.7	27.7	13.4	1.4	78.3	39.9	49.4	50.6
25121	LAKE	98.1	98.2	1.5	1.4	0.1	0.1	0.4	0.4	6.8	6.8	5.4	4.8	6.2	27.4	30.8	10.2	1.6	78.4	39.7	49.1	50.9
25123	LEON	99.6	99.6	0.1	0.1	0.0	0.0	0.4	0.4	5.3	5.5	6.4	6.3	6.2	26.9	29.1	13.0	1.3	79.0	41.0	51.5	48.5
25124	LIBERTY	99.1	99.0	0.4	0.4	0.2	0.2	0.4	0.4	7.2	7.0	5.6	4.7	5.7	28.9	27.7	12.1	1.1	77.4	39.0	51.0	49.0
25125	LIZEMORES	97.0	97.0	0.0	0.0	0.0	0.0	0.2	0.2	5.6	5.6	7.4	7.7	6.7	26.8	27.0	12.2	1.0	76.6	38.5	50.7	49.3
25130	MADISON	97.4	97.3	2.0	2.0	0.2	0.2	0.6	0.6	6.1	6.3	6.0	5.6	6.0	25.8	29.8	12.8	1.6	78.1	40.8	48.0	52.0
25132	MAMMOTH	98.0	97.6	0.9	0.9	0.0	0.0	0.0	0.3	5.3	5.6	6.2	5.9	6.2	27.1	29.2	13.6	0.9	79.1	40.3	51.3	48.7
25133	MAYSEL	98.6	98.8	0.0	0.0	0.0	0.0	0.7	0.7	6.5	6.6	7.5	6.8	6.3	27.6	26.3	11.1	1.3	75.3	37.4	48.9	51.1
25136	MONTGOMERY	87.8	87.6	9.6	9.7	0.9	0.9	0.4	0.4	4.9	4.8	4.6	5.0	8.4	29.3	26.2	14.3	2.6	83.5	40.2	54.8	45.2
25140	NAOMA	99.2	99.1	0.1	0.1	0.0	0.0	0.2	0.2	4.9	5.3	6.4	5.2	7.0	23.6	32.6	13.4	1.6	80.7	43.2	51.0	49.0
25141	NEBO	98.7	98.7	0.0	0.0	0.0	0.0	0.0	0.0	5.6	5.6	6.6	5.9	5.9	25.7	26.7	15.2	2.6	78.6	41.3	50.8	49.2
25142	NELLIS	99.2	99.2	0.0	0.0	0.0	0.1	0.5	0.5	7.1	7.0	6.6	6.0	5.9	30.9	25.8	9.5	1.3	75.5	35.9	50.4	49.6
25143	NITRO	96.0	95.7	2.1	2.2	0.5	0.6	0.6	0.6	5.8	5.8	5.8	5.0	5.9	28.0	27.2	14.7	1.9	79.6	40.5	47.7	52.3
25148	ORGAS	99.2	99.2	0.2	0.2	0.0	0.0	0.3	0.4	7.1	6.4	5.2	5.6	6.1	24.4	28.2	15.3	1.8	77.9	41.5	47.4	52.7
25150	OVAPA	97.8	97.7	0.0	0.0	0.0	0.0	0.4	0.4	6.4	6.5	7.2	6.9	6.2	28.2	25.8	11.5	1.4	75.8	37.6	48.9	51.1
25154	PEYTONA	98.7	98.7	0.2	0.2	0.0	0.0	0.7	0.7	5.7	6.1	6.1	5.7	6.1	26.2	30.5	11.8	1.8	78.5	40.9	50.2	49.8
25159	POCA	98.4	98.3	0.7	0.7	0.1	0.1	0.3	0.4	6.7	6.7	6.4	6.3	5.8	29.1	28.1	10.1	1.0	76.4	38.2	50.1	49.9
25160	POND GAP	98.4	98.4	0.3	0.3	0.0	0.0	0.3	0.2	5.3	5.8	6.2	5.8	6.1	27.0	29.9	13.0	1.0	78.9	40.4	51.0	49.0
25161	POWELLTON	90.0	89.9	7.5	7.6	0.4	0.4	0.4	0.4	6.2	6.4	5.9	5.9	6.1	26.7	30.9	10.4	1.5	77.8	40.0	49.0	51.0
25164	PROCIOUS	99.4	99.4	0.2	0.2	0.0	0.0	1.1	1.1	6.5	6.8	7.7	6.9	6.2	27.1	27.1	10.5	1.2	74.8	37.2	49.2	50.8
25165	RACINE	98.4	98.6	0.2	0.2	0.0	0.0	0.3	0.3	6.6	6.8	6.6	5.5	5.7	27.2	28.8	11.5	1.3	76.5	39.0	49.5	50.6
25168	RED HOUSE	99.1	99.0	0.1	0.1	0.2	0.3	0.7	0.7	5.6	5.6	6.4	6.1	5.9	28.4	27.3	13.3	1.4	78.8	40.3	49.5	50.5
25169	RIDGEVIEW	100.0	100.0	0.0	0.0	0.0	0.0	0.0	0.0	9.1	9.1	9.1	9.1	9.1	36.4	18.2	0.0	0.0	72.7	27.5	50.0	50.0
25173	ROBSON	85.7	85.6	12.0	12.1	0.3	0.3	0.3	0.3	6.0	6.0	6.0	6.4	6.4	26.9	27.9	13.1	1.3	77.9	39.7	48.7	51.3
25174	ROCK CREEK	99.6	100.0	0.0	0.0	0.0	0.0	0.0	0.0	5.5	5.9	7.3	5.9	6.8	25.9	29.1	12.3	1.4	77.7	40.0	51.4	48.6
25177	SAINT ALBANS	94.7	94.2	3.3	3.5	0.4	0.5	0.6	0.6	6.1	5.8	6.0	5.8	5.7	26.3	26.8	15.6	2.2	78.6	41.2	47.6	52.4
25180	SAXON	99.4	100.0	0.0	0.0	0.0	0.0	0.0	0.0	5.8	5.8	7.1	6.4	7.1	26.3	29.5	11.5	0.6	77.6	39.0	51.3	48.7
25181	SETH	98.8	98.7	0.7	0.7	0.1	0.1	0.6	0.7	5.8	6.0	6.1	5.3	6.0	26.4	29.6	13.2	1.6	78.8	41.0	49.3	50.7
25187	SOUTHSIDE	99.4	99.3	0.2	0.1	0.0	0.0	0.5	0.6	5.3	5.6	6.0	6.1	6.1	26.9	29.0	13.7	1.4	79.4	42.0	50.7	49.3
25193	SYLVESTER	98.4	98.4	0.8	0.8	0.0	0.0	0.6	0.5	5.3	5.5	5.7	5.3	6.3	26.5	30.4	13.2	1.6	80.2	41.7	50.9	49.1
25202	TORNADO	97.2	96.9	0.8	0.8	0.5	0.7	0.5	0.5	6.7	7.0	6.7	6.1	5.9	30.1	27.4	9.3	0.9	75.6	37.5	49.7	50.3
25204	TWILIGHT	99.2	98.9	0.2	0.2	0.0	0.0	0.2	0.2	4.6	5.0	6.1	4.8	4.8	26.5	32.4	14.6	1.3	81.1	43.7	47.8	52.2
25209	WHITESVILLE	99.3	99.4	0.0	0.0	0.0	0.0	0.2	0.2	6.1	6.3	8.3	6.1	5.3	29.8	25.8	11.0	1.3	75.5	37.5	48.6	51.4
25213	WINFIELD	98.8	98.7	0.2	0.2	0.3	0.5	0.3	0.3	6.2	6.5	6.5	6.0	4.8	28.8	29.4	10.6	1.2	77.1	39.9	48.7	51.3
25214	WINIFREDE	100.0	100.0	0.0	0.0	0.0	0.0	0.0	0.0	0.0	0.0	0.0	0.0	0.0	30.8	69.2	0.0	0.0	100.0	49.2	76.9	23.1
25231	ADVENT	99.3	100.0	0.0	0.0	0.0	0.0	0.0	0.0	6.7	6.7	6.0	6.0	5.3	27.3	30.0	10.7	1.3	76.7	40.0	50.7	49.3
25234	ARNOLDSBURG	98.8	98.7	0.2	0.2	0.0	0.0	0.9	0.9	5.2	5.4	6.3	6.4	6.3	24.8	28.3	15.0	2.4	79.3	42.3	50.0	50.0
25235	CHLOE	99.1	99.0	0.1	0.1	0.1	0.1	0.2	0.2	6.0	5.9	5.6	5.4	6.3	25.4	29.6	13.8	2.1	78.8	41.9	51.5	48.5
25239	COTTAGEVILLE	99.0	98.8	0.1	0.1	0.1	0.3	0.1	0.1	5.5	5.8	6.2	5.7	5.7	29.4	26.8	13.8	1.1	79.0	40.0	50.3	49.7
25241	EVANS	98.8	98.5	0.1	0.1	0.6	0.8	0.4	0.4	6.4	6.8	7.4	6.4	5.8	28.4	25.7	12.5	0.7	75.7	37.6	48.5	51.5
25243	GANDEEVILLE	98.5	98.4	0.2	0.3	0.1	0.2	0.3	0.3	5.0	5.0	5.6	7.2	5.6	26.6	30.9	12.8	1.5	79.9	41.5	51.2	48.8
25244	GAY	99.4	99.5	0.0	0.0	0.0	0.0	0.0	0.0	6.0	6.5	7.1	6.0	5.2	27.3	28.8	11.8	1.4	76.6	40.1	52.1	47.9
25245	GIVEN	98.3	98.0	0.1	0.1	0.3	0.4	0.1	0.1	6.5	6.8	6.8	6.3	6.3	28.1	28.1	10.2	0.9	76.0	38.4	50.0	50.0
25248	KENNA	99.4	99.3	0.0	0.0	0.1	0.2	0.2	0.2	6.4	6.5	6.1	5.8	5.5	28.0	29.8	10.6	1.3	77.5	39.8	50.0	50.0
25251	LEFT HAND	98.8	98.8	0.0	0.0	0.3	0.3	0.5	0.3	5.3	6.0	6.5	6.3	5.8	26.5	32.0	10.3	1.5	78.3	41.1	49.8	50.3
25252	LE ROY	99.1	99.1	0.1	0.1	0.0	0.0	0.0	0.0	4.8	5.1	7.2	8.0	6.5	26.8	28.5	11.6	1.6	78.3	39.8	51.5	48.5
25253	LETART	99.0	98.9	0.2	0.2	0.1	0.1	0.3	0.3	5.8	6.1	6.2	5.8	5.7	26.6	27.7	14.7	1.4	78.4	41.0	49.8	50.2
25259	LOONEYVILLE	99.0	98.8	0.4	0.4	0.0	0.0	1.4	1.2	5.2	5.8	6.4	6.4	6.2	25.6	31.4	12.1	0.8	78.5	40.4	50.9	49.1
25260	MASON	97.9	97.9	0.3	0.3	0.2	0.2	0.3	0.3	6.0	6.2	6.2	5.3	5.7	25.3	26.5	17.1	1.8	78.6	41.8	50.2	49.8
25261	MILLSTONE	99.0	98.9	0.1	0.1	0.1	0.1	1.1	1.2	4.9	5.1	5.7	6.7	6.0	24.9	30.9	13.3	2.7	80.5	43.0	49.2	50.8
25262	MILLWOOD	99.2	99.0	0.1	0.1	0.1	0.2	0.1	0.1	7.2	7.4	7.2	5.6	5.7	29.6	23.9	12.6	0.9	74.8	36.7	49.2	50.8
25264	MOUNT ALTO	98.9	98.7	0.0	0.0	0.3	0.3	0.0	0.0	4.1	4.4	5.1	5.9	5.6	29.4	28.9	15.4	1.3	82.6	42.7	51.2	48.9
25266	NEWTON	99.2	99.2	0.0	0.0	0.1	0.1	0.5	0.5	6.9	6.8	6.6	5.5	5.2	26.9	28.8	11.5	1.8	76.2	40.0	50.7	49.3
25267	NORMANTOWN	98.1	98.0	0.4	0.5	0.0	0.1	0.8	0.7	4.6	4.9	5.7	6.5	6.3	25.8	30.4	13.9	1.9	81.1	42.6	51.1	48.9
25268	ORMA	99.1	99.1	0.2	0.2	0.2	0.2	0.3	0.2	5.9	5.9	5.6	5.5	6.3	25.5	29.4	13.9	2.0	78.9	41.9	51.4	48.6
25270	REEDY	99.4	99.3	0.1	0.1	0.0	0.0	0.4	0.4	6.3	6.2	5.3	5.4	5.7	25.1	30.0	14.5	1.5	78.6	42.1	49.4	50.6
25271	RIPLEY	98.5	98.4	0.0	0.0	0.2	0.2	0.5	0.5	6.3	6.3	6.4	6.1	5.9	26.1	25.1	15.5	2.3	77.5	39.9	47.1	52.9
25275	SANDYVILLE	98.9	98.8	0.1	0.1	0.1	0.1	0.1	0.1	6.1	6.4	7.2	6.3	5.2	29.1	25.3	13.3	1.1	76.4	38.7	49.5	50.5
25276	SPENCER	98.3	98.1	0.3	0.3	0.3	0.5	0.8	0.8	5.9	5.9	6.1	6.4	6.5	25.1	27.1	14.7	2.3	78.1	40.7	48.9	51.1
25279	STATTS MILLS	99.2	99.3	0.0	0.0	0.0	0.0	0.0	0.0	7.1	7.4	7.6	6.1	5.6	29.4	26.0	9.8	1.0	74.3	37.0	49.8	50.3
25281	TARIFF	98.9	99.4	0.0	0.0	0.0	0.0	1.1	1.1	6.2	6.8	6.2	5.7	5.7	26.6	29.4	11.9	1.7	77.4	40.2	50.3	49.7
25285	WALLBACK	98.2	98.3	0.0	0.0	0.0	0.0	0.7	0.5	6.2	6.4	7.1	6.6	6.2	27.3	26.5	11.9	1.7	76.1	38.5	49.3	50.7
25286	WALTON	98.5	98.4	0.1	0.1	0.1	0.2	0.8	0.9	5.0	5.1	5.7	6.5	6.9	28.7	28.3	12.3	1.5	80.6	40.4	50.7	49.3
25287	WEST COLUMBIA	97.9	97.8	0.5	0.6	0.4	0.4	0.8	0.7	5.3	5.8	7.2	5.9	5.6	25.6	30.4	13.2	1.0	78.0	41.4	49.0	51.0
25301	CHARLESTON	63.5	62.3	31.0	31.6	1.5	2.0	1.0	0.9	4.5	3.8	3.3	3.4	5.6	26.4	26.1	20.7	6.4	86.6	47.1	43.4	56.6
25302	CHARLESTON	84.3	83.7	13.1	13.4	0.5	0.7	0.5	0.5	5.4	5.5	5.8	5.5	5.3	26.5	27.5	15.7	2.9	79.8	42.4	46.4	53.6
25303	CHARLESTON	91.2	90.6	6.1	6.3	1.0	1.4	0.4	0.5	5.2	5.5	5.4	5.3	5.4	26.7	28.5	15.6	2.5	80.6	42.8	46.4	53.6
25304	CHARLESTON	89.3	87.9	6.3	6.6	2.7	3.6	0.9	0.9	3.8	4.2	5.1	6.1	6.8	25.0	27.0	17.7	4.2	83.6	44.3	45.7	54.3
25306	CHARLESTON	87.0	87.1	10.4	10.2	0.2	0.3	0.6	0.6	5.6	5.7	5.5	5.7	6.0	26.6	28.2	14.7	1.9	79.8	41.4	47.2	52.8
25309	CHARLESTON	92.0	91.2	5.8	6.1	0.7	1.0	0.6	0.6	5.7	5.7	5.6	5.2	5.7	27.1	27.3	15.4	2.5	80.0	41.8	47.3	52.7
25311	CHARLESTON	75.1	74.4	20.3	20.6	1.3	1.6	1.1	1.1	5.9	5.5	5.5	6.4	7.0	28.7	27.1	12.0	1.9	79.3	39.0	47.9	52.1
25312	CHARLESTON	89.0	88.9	9.3	9.2	0.3	0.4	0.5	0.5	5.8	6.1	6.2	5.9	6.0	28.3	27.6	12.7	1.4	78.4	40.0	48.6	51.4
25313	CHARLESTON	94.1	93.2	3.4	3.6	1.3	1.8	0.6	0.6	5.9	6.0	6.8	6.4	6.3	29.0	27.7	10.9	1.0	77.3	38.5	48.6	51.4
	WEST VIRGINIA	95.1	94.8	3.2	3.2	0.5	0.7	0.7	0.7	5.6	5.8	6.2	6.3	6.7	26.7	27.1	13.7	1.9	78.9	40.1	48.8	51.2
	UNITED STATES	75.1	73.6	12.3	12.5	3.8	4.2	12.5	14.1	6.9	6.7	7.2	7.0	7.3	28.6	23.8	10.8	1.7	75.1	36.0	49.1	50.9

#	POST OFFICE NAME	2004 Per Capita Income	2004 HH Income Base	2004 Household Income Distribution (%): Less than $25,000	$25,000 to $49,999	$50,000 to $99,999	$100,000 to $149,999	$150,000 or More	Median Household Income: 2004	2009	2004 National Centile	2004 State Centile	2004 Home Value Base	2004 Home Value Distribution (%): Less than $50,000	$50,000 to $89,999	$90,000 to $174,999	$175,000 to $399,999	$400,000 or More	2004 Median Home Value
25060	DOROTHY	13011	185	57.3	20.5	17.8	4.3	0.0	20869	23157	2	7	148	46.6	35.8	16.9	0.7	0.0	52778
25062	DRY CREEK	17783	475	43.4	24.4	26.1	4.6	1.5	30575	35194	14	56	392	50.5	27.8	18.9	2.6	0.3	49756
25063	DUCK	11782	431	54.3	29.0	14.2	2.1	0.5	22588	25464	3	12	352	46.3	32.7	15.9	4.8	0.3	55417
25064	DUNBAR	21559	4535	34.2	29.6	27.9	6.6	1.8	38909	46304	42	88	2929	16.7	42.6	37.8	2.6	0.3	84007
25071	ELKVIEW	19820	4769	32.5	29.5	29.5	6.9	1.5	38569	46204	41	87	3912	28.4	26.6	34.8	9.6	0.7	84438
25075	ESKDALE	16166	852	52.9	24.2	20.2	1.8	0.9	23232	27489	3	14	698	50.4	39.8	8.2	1.6	0.0	49286
25079	FALLING ROCK	15950	10	40.0	30.0	30.0	0.0	0.0	35000	40000	28	77	8	37.5	62.5	0.0	0.0	0.0	55000
25081	FOSTER	17006	949	39.5	32.0	23.2	4.1	1.2	30678	35473	14	57	784	37.4	25.8	28.4	7.7	0.8	69718
25082	FRAZIERS BOTTOM	24541	594	25.1	30.3	30.8	8.8	5.1	45264	52457	62	96	509	25.5	22.6	26.9	24.8	0.2	92111
25083	GALLAGHER	17094	888	40.1	32.0	22.5	4.8	0.6	32164	38304	18	67	650	43.5	37.5	17.1	1.9	0.0	58077
25085	GAULEY BRIDGE	18843	407	39.3	28.8	26.8	3.2	2.0	32053	37044	18	66	292	39.0	32.5	23.0	5.5	0.0	64643
25088	GLEN	11814	64	50.0	32.8	17.2	0.0	0.0	25000	27614	5	22	52	63.5	23.1	11.5	1.9	0.0	42222
25093	GORDON	15686	83	49.4	20.5	26.5	3.6	0.0	25551	28340	5	25	66	57.6	25.8	16.7	0.0	0.0	44444
25103	HANSFORD	13440	55	52.7	30.9	16.4	0.0	0.0	22906	23568	3	13	45	73.3	20.0	6.7	0.0	0.0	30833
25106	HENDERSON	14506	197	49.2	34.5	11.2	1.5	3.6	25294	29484	5	23	159	53.5	25.2	20.1	0.6	0.6	42143
25107	HERNSHAW	16646	252	44.4	29.4	21.8	2.4	2.0	29287	34354	11	49	211	52.1	29.4	15.6	1.0	1.9	47857
25108	HEWETT	12123	727	51.6	30.4	16.4	0.6	1.1	24055	27835	4	18	601	24.6	36.1	34.9	3.5	0.8	80652
25111	INDORE	11483	448	50.2	29.5	18.5	1.3	0.5	24834	27155	4	21	370	56.8	28.1	13.0	2.2	0.0	44048
25113	IVYDALE	11935	71	59.2	21.1	16.9	2.8	0.0	20291	23195	2	5	54	42.6	37.0	16.7	3.7	0.0	60000
25114	JEFFREY	13977	188	43.6	33.5	19.2	2.1	1.6	29181	33040	11	48	148	33.8	33.1	29.1	4.1	0.0	71333
25115	KANAWHA FALLS	17659	37	37.8	24.3	32.4	2.7	2.7	34054	41146	24	73	32	43.8	21.9	21.9	12.5	0.0	60000
25118	KIMBERLY	14953	65	56.9	27.7	12.3	3.1	0.0	21065	25427	2	7	54	48.2	38.9	13.0	0.0	0.0	53333
25119	KINCAID	13679	170	46.5	36.5	15.9	0.6	0.6	26285	30000	6	29	139	56.1	25.2	15.1	2.9	0.7	44688
25121	LAKE	14848	370	44.6	29.5	23.0	3.0	0.0	27629	32508	8	37	313	33.2	33.9	29.7	3.2	0.0	68600
25123	LEON	14553	1218	45.2	31.0	21.1	2.3	0.4	27976	32131	9	40	1043	39.3	29.6	25.0	5.0	1.1	64133
25124	LIBERTY	18288	438	35.8	25.1	30.4	8.2	0.5	35237	43276	28	77	399	25.1	27.6	37.6	9.3	0.5	84750
25125	LIZEMORES	11728	240	48.3	30.8	19.6	0.8	0.4	25591	27563	5	25	198	58.6	27.3	12.1	2.0	0.0	44333
25130	MADISON	19797	1854	38.8	29.0	25.6	4.1	2.6	32038	37656	18	66	1372	31.9	26.5	32.8	7.7	1.2	76437
25132	MAMMOTH	15232	133	44.4	25.6	25.6	3.8	0.8	28218	34297	9	41	109	59.6	26.6	13.8	0.0	0.0	40455
25133	MAYSEL	17761	229	41.9	32.8	20.1	3.9	1.3	30737	34810	14	58	187	32.6	34.2	27.3	5.4	0.5	71667
25136	MONTGOMERY	15604	3447	45.8	29.0	20.0	3.6	1.7	27567	31813	8	37	2473	41.0	35.1	19.7	4.0	0.2	60241
25140	NAOMA	17112	457	45.1	30.9	19.0	2.8	2.2	28019	32574	9	40	356	50.0	28.1	18.3	2.3	1.4	50000
25141	NEBO	11932	128	56.3	28.1	13.3	2.3	0.0	21675	25000	2	9	104	45.2	36.5	15.4	2.9	0.0	58333
25142	NELLIS	12764	326	41.7	41.4	16.0	0.6	0.3	29415	33707	11	50	268	55.6	14.2	20.2	10.1	0.0	42500
25143	NITRO	22110	4205	30.4	30.7	30.0	6.2	2.8	38751	46889	42	88	3078	18.1	43.0	33.6	4.7	0.7	81500
25148	ORGAS	21746	377	44.8	21.8	27.1	4.5	1.9	29354	33982	11	50	312	38.8	31.7	28.5	1.0	0.0	71923
25150	OVAPA	17130	263	43.7	28.1	21.7	3.8	2.7	28582	32188	10	44	212	33.5	36.3	28.3	1.9	0.0	70000
25154	PEYTONA	13037	246	51.6	28.5	17.5	2.4	0.0	24084	28318	4	18	214	46.3	29.9	19.2	4.7	0.0	56667
25159	POCA	20596	2670	28.7	29.6	32.1	7.7	1.9	41465	48689	51	93	2288	31.5	25.4	35.5	6.6	1.0	81980
25160	POND GAP	14694	239	45.2	25.1	25.1	3.4	1.3	27821	33319	8	38	195	61.5	24.1	13.3	1.0	0.0	38676
25161	POWELLTON	17496	318	39.3	32.4	22.6	3.5	2.2	35000	40334	28	77	268	41.0	32.1	22.4	4.1	0.4	60909
25164	PROCIOUS	15399	413	38.7	38.3	18.4	3.9	0.7	34672	39311	26	75	342	31.9	32.8	25.4	8.8	1.2	73929
25165	RACINE	17042	267	46.1	26.6	22.1	4.5	0.8	27562	32331	8	36	217	36.9	32.3	28.6	2.3	0.0	68333
25168	RED HOUSE	20429	1670	31.4	31.6	30.0	5.8	1.2	38739	45632	42	87	1399	24.5	26.8	41.9	6.1	0.7	88391
25169	RIDGEVIEW	5341	6	66.7	33.3	0.0	0.0	0.0	20000	27208	2	4	0	0.0	0.0	0.0	0.0	0.0	0
25173	ROBSON	14919	124	46.0	37.1	15.3	0.8	0.8	26555	31528	7	31	102	52.9	27.5	14.7	3.9	1.0	47273
25174	ROCK CREEK	12648	79	46.8	31.7	16.5	3.8	1.3	26582	30730	7	31	63	49.2	27.0	17.5	3.2	3.2	51250
25177	SAINT ALBANS	21232	10121	29.6	31.1	30.2	7.4	1.7	40890	48426	49	92	7873	20.0	40.8	34.1	4.9	0.2	81383
25180	SAXON	13141	54	42.6	33.3	18.5	3.7	1.9	28849	34291	10	46	44	47.7	27.3	18.2	4.6	2.3	53333
25181	SETH	16159	745	46.2	24.2	24.3	4.3	1.1	27780	32844	8	38	603	43.1	29.7	24.1	3.0	0.2	62674
25187	SOUTHSIDE	14195	299	50.5	20.7	27.1	1.0	0.7	24488	29067	4	20	256	36.7	24.6	32.8	5.9	0.0	66786
25193	SYLVESTER	15942	682	54.7	21.1	20.4	3.4	0.4	21648	25678	2	9	550	48.6	31.5	18.6	1.5	0.0	51509
25202	TORNADO	23839	498	16.1	29.7	41.6	10.0	2.6	52704	62999	76	98	437	14.9	35.2	42.1	7.3	0.5	89907
25204	TWILIGHT	15946	205	48.3	19.5	31.2	1.0	0.0	29313	35569	11	49	169	61.5	27.8	8.9	1.8	0.0	43710
25209	WHITESVILLE	13112	195	45.1	38.5	14.4	2.1	0.0	27573	31174	8	37	173	49.7	43.9	5.8	0.6	0.0	50217
25213	WINFIELD	26615	2174	17.6	29.8	35.1	13.1	4.6	52665	62490	76	98	1928	15.3	13.7	46.9	21.1	3.0	120833
25214	WINIFREDE	9423	6	66.7	33.3	0.0	0.0	0.0	21941	23678	3	10	5	60.0	40.0	0.0	0.0	0.0	47500
25231	ADVENT	14215	53	37.7	32.1	26.4	3.8	0.0	32945	39298	21	70	46	26.1	23.9	28.3	21.7	0.0	90000
25234	ARNOLDSBURG	13369	731	51.9	28.5	16.8	2.5	0.4	23949	27123	4	17	592	39.9	31.6	23.3	2.7	2.5	61373
25235	CHLOE	11489	385	57.4	28.1	12.5	2.1	0.0	21059	24111	2	7	311	43.4	35.4	20.6	0.6	0.0	56833
25239	COTTAGEVILLE	18204	599	32.9	31.6	33.1	2.2	0.3	38472	43191	41	87	513	25.5	22.6	41.9	8.6	1.4	92209
25241	EVANS	20455	583	33.5	32.3	23.2	7.2	4.0	39265	43753	44	89	496	16.9	32.3	34.9	13.3	2.6	91026
25243	GANDEEVILLE	14486	385	44.7	33.8	16.4	3.9	1.3	27620	31848	8	37	329	30.4	32.5	28.9	6.4	1.8	76406
25244	GAY	15475	443	38.4	33.2	23.9	4.1	0.5	35922	40657	31	80	388	39.4	30.2	20.1	8.3	2.1	67586
25245	GIVEN	21224	646	23.4	29.9	36.7	9.3	0.8	47781	52877	68	97	583	19.9	24.5	31.6	23.7	0.3	103373
25248	KENNA	16630	1215	34.3	31.0	29.3	5.4	0.0	36643	41335	34	83	1066	22.8	22.5	34.2	19.8	0.8	99091
25251	LEFT HAND	13889	154	48.7	27.3	18.8	4.6	0.7	25522	28567	5	25	132	30.3	33.3	26.5	9.9	0.0	69286
25252	LE ROY	14744	268	30.6	45.9	22.4	1.1	0.0	35791	41251	31	80	243	26.8	43.2	26.8	3.3	0.0	75645
25253	LETART	17059	1890	41.3	28.7	25.0	4.2	0.9	31174	36413	15	61	1603	32.3	34.6	29.0	3.1	1.0	71326
25259	LOONEYVILLE	11341	185	56.2	27.0	14.1	2.7	0.0	22100	25293	3	11	156	43.0	29.5	20.5	7.1	0.0	60833
25260	MASON	15640	1103	41.5	32.9	22.0	3.4	0.2	29618	34307	11	51	863	47.3	26.8	20.9	5.0	0.1	53615
25261	MILLSTONE	14464	301	46.5	29.2	20.3	3.0	1.0	26890	30966	7	32	243	42.0	29.6	22.6	2.5	3.3	61471
25262	MILLWOOD	21490	569	23.0	35.0	36.2	3.9	1.9	44396	49296	60	95	485	25.4	25.4	40.2	8.7	0.4	89186
25264	MOUNT ALTO	15338	154	39.6	29.9	27.9	2.6	0.0	36381	41250	33	82	133	24.1	20.3	45.1	8.3	2.3	96818
25266	NEWTON	13024	348	52.6	24.1	19.5	3.7	0.0	23427	26555	3	15	288	41.7	31.3	21.5	5.6	0.0	58000
25267	NORMANTOWN	14212	298	52.0	25.5	17.8	2.0	2.7	23789	26959	4	17	251	31.1	40.2	23.5	5.2	0.0	67727
25268	ORMA	11379	263	56.3	28.5	12.9	2.3	0.0	21587	23739	2	8	212	42.0	35.4	22.6	0.0	0.0	57727
25270	REEDY	17106	789	38.7	32.2	23.1	3.7	2.4	31073	35090	15	61	704	27.1	29.6	32.2	10.9	0.1	80408
25271	RIPLEY	18310	3044	40.3	30.9	22.5	4.4	1.9	31337	36231	16	62	2324	20.0	29.2	39.9	10.5	0.5	90963
25275	SANDYVILLE	20179	717	34.2	33.2	26.4	4.7	1.5	39572	44420	45	90	593	29.0	30.5	33.4	6.1	1.0	79886
25276	SPENCER	15154	3415	48.2	30.4	15.8	4.2	1.4	25977	29595	6	28	2600	35.5	32.0	24.3	7.6	0.6	70649
25279	STATTS MILLS	15104	152	36.8	31.6	27.6	4.0	0.0	37334	41457	37	85	125	32.8	27.2	28.0	10.4	1.6	80385
25281	TARIFF	15102	83	53.0	24.1	19.3	3.6	0.0	23385	25700	3	15	69	43.5	30.4	20.3	5.8	0.0	57500
25285	WALLBACK	16134	222	45.1	30.2	19.8	3.6	1.4	27849	31180	8	39	180	35.0	36.1	25.0	3.9	0.0	67692
25286	WALTON	16608	679	41.2	33.7	19.0	5.3	0.7	30382	35000	13	55	578	38.8	35.0	20.6	5.5	0.2	62031
25287	WEST COLUMBIA	17773	356	28.9	31.7	28.9	6.7	3.7	41084	47051	50	93	323	22.6	31.9	31.0	14.2	0.3	85735
25301	CHARLESTON	20357	1792	62.4	19.5	11.9	3.1	3.0	15904	18524	1	1	303	11.9	34.0	39.3	13.2	1.7	95435
25302	CHARLESTON	23733	7596	35.9	29.1	25.2	7.1	2.8	35604	42469	30	79	4918	18.5	35.9	36.8	8.0	0.8	85562
25303	CHARLESTON	30843	3231	25.8	26.7	30.0	11.1	6.3	47371	57167	67	97	2317	7.4	24.2	56.0	11.9	0.6	106848
25304	CHARLESTON	37116	3974	25.0	28.1	28.3	8.5	10.2	46700	56001	65	96	2670	7.8	15.4	45.7	23.0	8.2	125702
25306	CHARLESTON	16828	3249	41.1	31.1	23.9	3.2	0.8	30474	35751	13	55	2459	37.1	40.5	21.1	1.0	0.3	64614
25309	CHARLESTON	25418	5223	32.8	28.7	27.3	7.5	3.6	37799	45234	39	86	3777	20.3	35.2	36.2	7.1	1.2	84734
25311	CHARLESTON	26313	4988	42.7	27.0	18.3	5.9	6.1	29290	34507	11	49	2769	22.8	27.6	30.2	14.9	4.5	89344
25312	CHARLESTON	19769	6725	39.2	28.7	24.8	5.2	2.1	33235	39009	22	71	5010	32.5	33.0	29.2	5.2	0.2	71515
25313	CHARLESTON	26631	5131	21.4	27.9	34.1	12.6	4.0	50588	60492	73	98	3987	14.3	26.7	48.4	10.1	0.6	99688
	WEST VIRGINIA	19262		38.4	30.0	24.1	5.2	2.4	33458	38993				29.0	29.1	31.1	9.6	1.3	80023
	UNITED STATES	25866		24.7	27.1	30.8	10.9	6.5	48124	56710				10.9	15.0	33.7	30.1	10.4	145905

#	POST OFFICE NAME	FINANCIAL SERVICES: Auto Loan	Home Loan	Invest-ments	Retire-ment Plans	THE HOME: Home Improvements: Home Repair	Lawn & Garden	Furnishings: Comput-ers & Hard-ware	Major Appli-ances	TV, Radio, Sound Equip-ment	Furni-ture	ENTERTAINMENT: Dine out/ Carry out	Sports Equip-ment	Fees & Tickets	Toys & Games	Travel	Cable TV	PERSONAL: Apparel & Services	Auto Repairs	Health Insur-ance	Pets & Supplies
25060	DOROTHY	59	40	18	34	45	52	38	48	46	39	54	57	32	51	39	50	49	47	59	68
25062	DRY CREEK	83	55	25	48	63	72	53	67	65	54	76	80	45	72	54	70	69	66	82	95
25063	DUCK	55	37	17	32	41	48	35	44	43	36	50	53	30	47	36	46	45	44	54	63
25064	DUNBAR	63	63	67	62	63	70	65	65	67	63	82	74	65	83	66	67	79	66	68	72
25071	ELKVIEW	81	63	40	58	68	77	61	71	69	61	82	83	56	80	62	72	76	70	82	93
25075	ESKDALE	66	50	32	45	55	63	50	58	57	50	68	67	45	65	51	61	63	58	69	76
25079	FALLING ROCK	64	48	32	46	53	63	53	59	60	51	70	66	47	66	53	63	64	59	70	71
25081	FOSTER	79	53	24	46	60	69	51	64	62	52	73	77	44	69	52	67	66	64	79	91
25082	FRAZIERS BOTTOM	102	87	64	82	93	101	81	91	88	81	106	109	78	107	84	90	100	89	100	119
25083	GALLAGHER	60	53	44	50	56	64	54	58	58	52	70	65	52	69	55	61	66	57	66	69
25085	GAULEY BRIDGE	66	50	33	48	55	65	55	61	62	52	73	68	49	69	55	65	66	61	73	73
25088	GLEN	55	37	17	32	41	48	35	44	43	36	50	53	30	47	36	46	45	44	54	63
25093	GORDON	69	46	21	40	52	60	45	56	54	45	63	67	38	60	45	58	57	55	69	79
25103	HANSFORD	46	35	23	33	38	45	38	42	43	36	51	47	34	48	38	45	46	42	51	51
25106	HENDERSON	65	44	20	38	50	57	42	53	51	43	60	63	36	57	43	55	54	52	65	75
25107	HERNSHAW	73	49	22	42	56	64	47	59	57	48	67	71	40	63	48	62	61	59	73	84
25108	HEWETT	55	38	20	35	43	50	39	47	46	39	54	54	34	51	39	49	49	46	57	63
25111	INDORE	57	38	17	33	43	50	37	46	44	37	52	55	31	49	37	48	47	46	57	65
25113	IVYDALE	47	35	23	34	39	47	39	43	44	37	52	48	35	49	39	46	47	43	52	52
25114	JEFFREY	67	45	22	39	51	59	44	55	53	45	62	65	38	59	45	57	57	54	67	76
25115	KANAWHA FALLS	66	56	44	56	59	66	58	62	61	57	74	70	55	74	57	62	70	61	67	73
25118	KIMBERLY	50	37	25	36	41	49	41	45	46	39	54	51	37	51	41	49	50	45	54	55
25119	KINCAID	56	41	26	39	45	54	45	50	51	43	59	57	40	56	44	54	54	50	60	62
25121	LAKE	69	47	21	40	53	61	45	56	54	46	64	67	38	60	46	58	58	56	69	80
25123	LEON	67	45	21	39	51	59	44	54	52	44	62	65	37	58	44	56	56	54	67	77
25124	LIBERTY	82	59	32	53	66	74	56	68	66	57	78	82	50	75	58	70	72	67	81	95
25125	LIZEMORES	57	38	17	33	43	50	37	46	45	38	53	55	32	50	38	48	48	46	57	66
25130	MADISON	79	56	30	51	63	73	57	68	66	56	77	79	49	74	58	70	70	67	82	90
25132	MAMMOTH	73	49	22	42	55	64	47	59	57	48	67	70	40	63	48	61	61	58	72	83
25133	MAYSEL	81	55	25	47	62	71	53	66	64	54	75	79	45	71	54	68	68	65	81	94
25136	MONTGOMERY	57	44	34	42	48	56	48	52	53	46	63	59	43	61	48	56	58	52	61	64
25140	NAOMA	73	52	28	47	57	67	53	63	62	52	73	73	46	69	53	66	66	62	76	82
25141	NEBO	52	35	16	30	40	46	34	42	41	34	48	51	29	45	34	44	44	42	52	60
25142	NELLIS	62	42	19	36	47	55	40	51	49	41	57	60	34	54	41	53	52	50	62	72
25143	NITRO	71	69	65	66	72	79	69	71	72	67	88	81	69	91	70	74	84	70	77	83
25148	ORGAS	98	66	30	57	75	86	64	80	77	65	90	95	54	85	65	83	82	79	98	113
25150	OVAPA	89	59	27	51	67	78	57	72	69	58	81	86	49	77	58	75	74	71	88	102
25154	PEYTONA	62	41	19	36	47	54	40	50	48	41	57	60	34	53	41	52	51	49	62	71
25159	POCA	85	70	50	65	75	82	67	76	73	67	88	89	63	86	68	76	83	75	85	98
25160	POND GAP	72	48	22	42	55	63	47	58	56	47	66	70	40	62	47	61	60	58	72	83
25161	POWELLTON	85	57	26	49	65	75	55	69	67	56	78	83	47	74	56	72	71	68	85	98
25164	PROCIOUS	73	49	22	42	56	64	47	59	57	48	67	71	40	63	48	62	61	59	73	84
25165	RACINE	76	51	23	44	58	67	49	62	60	50	70	74	42	66	50	64	64	61	76	88
25168	RED HOUSE	81	66	46	63	70	78	65	73	70	65	85	84	61	82	65	72	80	72	80	91
25169	RIDGEVIEW	37	25	11	21	28	32	24	30	29	24	34	36	20	32	24	31	31	30	37	42
25173	ROBSON	60	44	27	41	48	57	47	53	54	45	63	60	42	60	47	57	58	53	64	67
25174	ROCK CREEK	66	44	20	38	50	58	43	54	52	44	61	64	36	57	44	56	55	53	66	76
25177	SAINT ALBANS	71	69	67	66	70	78	69	71	71	67	87	81	68	88	70	73	84	70	75	82
25180	SAXON	71	48	22	41	54	62	46	58	56	47	65	69	39	62	47	60	59	57	71	82
25181	SETH	76	51	23	44	58	66	49	61	59	50	70	73	42	66	50	64	63	61	76	87
25187	SOUTHSIDE	64	43	19	37	49	56	41	52	50	42	59	62	35	56	42	54	53	51	64	74
25193	SYLVESTER	66	44	20	38	50	58	43	53	51	43	60	64	36	57	43	55	55	53	66	76
25202	TORNADO	85	92	92	91	91	93	87	88	84	87	105	103	88	107	87	82	103	87	82	99
25204	TWILIGHT	67	45	20	39	51	59	44	54	53	44	62	65	37	58	44	57	56	54	67	77
25209	WHITESVILLE	60	40	18	35	45	52	39	48	47	39	55	58	33	52	39	50	50	48	60	69
25213	WINFIELD	99	95	81	92	99	104	87	94	89	87	110	112	87	113	90	90	106	91	97	117
25214	WINIFREDE	38	26	12	22	29	34	25	31	30	25	35	37	21	33	25	32	32	31	38	44
25231	ADVENT	76	51	23	44	57	66	49	61	59	50	69	73	42	66	50	64	63	61	75	87
25234	ARNOLDSBURG	59	40	19	35	45	52	39	48	47	40	55	57	34	52	40	50	50	48	59	67
25235	CHLOE	52	35	16	30	39	45	33	42	40	34	47	50	29	45	34	44	43	41	52	60
25239	COTTAGEVILLE	80	60	35	54	66	74	57	68	65	57	78	81	51	76	58	69	72	67	80	93
25241	EVANS	84	74	56	70	79	84	69	77	73	69	89	91	67	91	71	75	85	75	83	99
25243	GANDEEVILLE	67	47	23	41	52	60	45	55	53	45	63	66	39	60	46	57	57	55	67	78
25244	GAY	76	51	23	44	57	66	49	61	59	50	70	73	42	66	50	64	63	61	75	87
25245	GIVEN	90	78	58	74	82	89	73	81	78	73	94	97	70	95	74	80	90	80	88	105
25248	KENNA	77	56	31	49	62	70	53	64	62	54	73	76	47	71	54	65	67	63	76	89
25251	LEFT HAND	68	45	21	39	51	59	44	55	53	45	62	66	37	59	45	57	56	54	68	78
25252	LE ROY	72	48	22	41	54	63	46	58	56	47	66	69	39	62	47	60	60	57	71	82
25253	LETART	72	52	29	47	57	66	52	61	60	51	70	71	45	67	52	63	65	60	73	82
25259	LOONEYVILLE	57	38	17	33	44	50	37	46	45	38	53	55	32	50	38	48	48	46	57	66
25260	MASON	65	46	26	42	51	60	48	56	55	47	65	64	41	61	48	59	59	55	67	73
25261	MILLSTONE	66	45	22	40	51	59	45	55	53	45	63	65	38	59	45	57	57	54	67	75
25262	MILLWOOD	88	77	57	73	82	88	71	80	76	71	93	95	69	94	73	79	88	78	87	104
25264	MOUNT ALTO	73	49	22	42	56	64	47	59	57	48	67	71	40	63	48	62	61	59	73	84
25266	NEWTON	62	42	19	36	47	54	40	50	48	41	57	60	34	54	41	52	52	50	62	71
25267	NORMANTOWN	65	44	20	38	49	57	42	53	51	43	60	63	36	56	43	55	54	52	65	74
25268	ORMA	52	35	16	30	39	45	34	42	41	34	48	50	29	45	34	44	43	42	52	60
25270	REEDY	68	54	37	51	58	67	56	62	61	54	73	71	51	71	56	64	68	61	72	76
25271	RIPLEY	67	59	48	57	61	69	60	64	63	59	77	73	57	74	60	65	72	64	70	75
25275	SANDYVILLE	94	63	29	54	71	82	61	76	73	62	86	91	52	81	62	79	78	75	94	108
25276	SPENCER	63	45	25	41	50	59	47	55	54	46	64	63	41	60	47	58	58	54	66	72
25279	STATTS MILLS	71	55	33	50	58	65	52	61	58	54	70	72	47	66	52	60	65	61	69	80
25281	TARIFF	61	41	18	35	46	53	39	49	47	40	56	59	33	52	40	51	50	49	60	70
25285	WALLBACK	79	53	24	46	60	69	51	64	62	52	72	76	43	68	52	66	66	63	79	91
25286	WALTON	77	52	25	47	60	68	51	63	60	51	71	76	43	68	52	65	65	63	77	89
25287	WEST COLUMBIA	88	73	52	68	78	85	68	78	75	69	90	93	65	90	70	77	85	76	87	102
25301	CHARLESTON	42	37	55	39	38	44	47	43	50	45	62	51	46	61	46	50	60	47	47	48
25302	CHARLESTON	66	68	79	67	68	75	70	69	71	68	88	79	71	89	71	71	85	70	70	77
25303	CHARLESTON	86	95	106	93	95	103	93	93	92	92	115	106	96	117	95	93	112	92	93	102
25304	CHARLESTON	105	112	131	112	112	121	114	112	113	112	142	129	116	143	115	114	138	113	111	124
25306	CHARLESTON	64	48	31	44	52	61	51	57	57	49	68	65	45	64	50	61	62	57	68	71
25309	CHARLESTON	81	79	79	77	80	89	79	82	81	79	100	92	79	98	80	83	96	81	86	93
25311	CHARLESTON	79	70	76	69	71	80	77	76	81	75	99	89	74	97	75	82	95	79	81	89
25312	CHARLESTON	70	62	53	58	64	72	62	66	67	61	81	76	60	81	62	69	77	65	73	81
25313	CHARLESTON	89	96	95	94	96	100	90	92	89	89	111	107	93	115	92	89	108	90	91	106
	WEST VIRGINIA	73	60	47	57	64	72	61	67	67	60	80	78	57	78	61	69	75	67	76	84
	UNITED STATES	100	100	100	100	100	100	100	100	100	100	100	100	100	100	100	100	100	100	100	100

# POST OFFICE NAME	COUNTY FIPS CODE	POPULATION 2000	2004	2009	2000-2004 ANNUAL RATE % Rate	State Centile	HOUSEHOLDS 2000	2004	2009	% Annual Rate 2000-2004	2004 Average HH Size	FAMILIES 2000	2004	% Annual Rate 2000-2004
25314 CHARLESTON	039	15001	14488	13928	-0.8	14	6323	6251	6139	-0.3	2.29	4301	4065	-1.3
25315 CHARLESTON	039	3946	3684	3486	-1.6	2	1752	1682	1630	-1.0	2.15	1125	1027	-2.1
25320 CHARLESTON	039	5915	6085	6033	0.7	84	2282	2401	2431	1.2	2.49	1751	1783	0.4
25401 MARTINSBURG	003	43594	49695	58445	3.1	98	17482	20264	24227	3.5	2.40	11570	12864	2.5
25411 BERKELEY SPRINGS	065	10954	12063	13613	2.3	96	4537	5087	5849	2.7	2.34	3187	3450	1.9
25413 BUNKER HILL	003	6418	7587	9084	4.0	99	2365	2836	3442	4.4	2.68	1816	2113	3.6
25414 CHARLES TOWN	037	17617	20045	23246	3.1	98	6943	8050	9517	3.5	2.48	4801	5367	2.7
25419 FALLING WATERS	003	7145	8478	10167	4.1	99	2747	3306	4018	4.5	2.56	2054	2393	3.7
25420 GERRARDSTOWN	003	3350	3577	4068	1.6	92	1216	1318	1520	1.9	2.71	938	987	1.2
25422 GREAT CACAPON	065	1408	1552	1751	2.3	96	603	682	785	2.9	2.28	406	440	1.9
25425 HARPERS FERRY	037	8087	9186	10604	3.0	98	3163	3668	4317	3.6	2.50	2258	2525	2.7
25427 HEDGESVILLE	003	10935	12150	14045	2.5	97	4077	4612	5416	2.9	2.63	3073	3368	2.2
25428 INWOOD	003	5435	6300	7473	3.5	98	2047	2408	2896	3.9	2.62	1556	1775	3.2
25430 KEARNEYSVILLE	037	5642	6022	6728	1.6	92	2049	2237	2556	2.1	2.63	1554	1646	1.4
25431 LEVELS	027	147	153	158	1.0	87	58	62	65	1.6	2.47	40	41	0.6
25434 PAW PAW	027	1875	2085	2300	2.5	97	753	858	966	3.1	2.42	537	588	2.2
25437 POINTS	027	121	125	128	0.8	85	49	52	54	1.4	2.37	36	36	0.0
25438 RANSON	037	3396	3752	4271	2.4	97	1377	1548	1795	2.8	2.42	917	985	1.7
25442 SHENANDOAH JUNCTION	037	1487	1613	1816	1.9	95	547	605	694	2.4	2.65	400	427	1.6
25443 SHEPHERDSTOWN	037	5765	6282	7019	2.0	95	2009	2265	2624	2.9	2.34	1307	1415	1.9
25444 SLANESVILLE	027	771	825	869	1.6	93	281	308	330	2.2	2.67	206	218	1.3
25446 SUMMIT POINT	037	958	1048	1185	2.1	96	362	404	467	2.6	2.59	285	310	2.0
25501 ALKOL	043	1486	1509	1568	0.4	76	598	625	668	1.0	2.41	437	442	0.3
25502 APPLE GROVE	053	1614	1695	1732	1.2	89	646	694	717	1.7	2.44	479	498	0.9
25503 ASHTON	053	779	808	820	0.9	87	310	329	337	1.4	2.46	233	240	0.7
25504 BARBOURSVILLE	011	10879	11232	11304	0.8	85	4367	4599	4715	1.2	2.41	3167	3218	0.4
25505 BIG CREEK	045	699	732	734	1.1	88	257	276	284	1.7	2.65	212	222	1.1
25506 BRANCHLAND	043	2727	2919	3077	1.6	93	1090	1198	1294	2.3	2.44	811	862	1.5
25508 CHAPMANVILLE	045	11326	11359	11193	0.1	61	4407	4544	4603	0.7	2.47	3268	3259	-0.1
25510 CULLODEN	011	4861	4891	4893	0.1	65	1881	1942	1985	0.8	2.46	1447	1440	-0.1
25511 DUNLOW	099	694	705	714	0.4	77	262	274	284	1.1	2.57	200	203	0.4
25512 EAST LYNN	099	1629	1611	1619	-0.3	39	657	667	688	0.4	2.41	476	467	-0.5
25514 FORT GAY	099	4441	4595	4697	0.8	85	1684	1781	1861	1.3	2.58	1290	1323	0.6
25515 GALLIPOLIS FERRY	053	2271	2275	2276	0.0	60	909	932	943	0.6	2.44	677	673	-0.1
25517 GENOA	099	2622	2696	2748	0.7	84	975	1027	1070	1.2	2.63	740	755	0.5
25520 GLENWOOD	011	2307	2326	2316	0.2	68	895	923	932	0.7	2.51	680	676	-0.1
25521 GRIFFITHSVILLE	043	686	725	768	1.3	91	257	277	301	1.8	2.62	194	203	1.1
25523 HAMLIN	043	3276	3377	3530	0.7	84	1333	1406	1506	1.3	2.36	971	991	0.5
25524 HARTS	043	2124	2176	2271	0.6	82	778	821	882	1.3	2.65	630	650	0.7
25526 HURRICANE	079	19045	20425	21650	1.7	94	7250	7891	8503	2.0	2.57	5599	5924	1.3
25529 JULIAN	005	1395	1424	1439	0.5	80	550	576	595	1.1	2.39	399	404	0.3
25530 KENOVA	099	7878	7777	7851	-0.3	36	3413	3440	3550	0.2	2.25	2304	2237	-0.7
25534 KIAHSVILLE	099	337	337	340	0.0	57	124	127	132	0.6	2.65	90	89	-0.3
25535 LAVALETTE	099	3818	3800	3826	-0.1	47	1538	1568	1615	0.5	2.40	1187	1175	-0.2
25537 LESAGE	011	1698	1668	1632	-0.4	28	663	666	665	0.1	2.48	494	474	-1.0
25540 MIDKIFF	043	128	136	145	1.4	92	43	47	51	2.1	2.89	32	34	1.4
25541 MILTON	011	7740	7968	8017	0.7	84	3149	3318	3409	1.2	2.38	2294	2321	0.3
25544 MYRA	043	247	260	275	1.2	90	91	98	106	1.8	2.64	65	67	0.7
25545 ONA	011	5412	5798	5942	1.6	93	2027	2220	2322	2.2	2.59	1589	1679	1.3
25547 PECKS MILL	045	907	858	822	-1.3	5	370	362	357	-0.5	2.37	285	271	-1.2
25550 POINT PLEASANT	053	7948	7848	7817	-0.3	36	3406	3432	3451	0.2	2.24	2281	2211	-0.7
25555 PRICHARD	099	979	996	1009	0.4	78	377	392	406	0.9	2.54	291	294	0.2
25557 RANGER	043	4576	4745	4978	0.9	87	1737	1856	2003	1.6	2.56	1318	1366	0.9
25559 SALT ROCK	011	1591	1773	1849	2.6	98	607	697	743	3.3	2.54	484	538	2.5
25560 SCOTT DEPOT	079	7799	8016	8382	0.7	84	2979	3136	3350	1.2	2.54	2321	2370	0.5
25564 SOD	043	2419	2589	2762	1.6	93	969	1066	1167	2.3	2.43	742	792	1.6
25565 SPURLOCKVILLE	043	666	676	704	0.4	75	252	264	283	1.1	2.56	195	198	0.4
25567 SUMERCO	043	703	741	786	1.3	91	280	302	328	1.8	2.45	218	229	1.2
25570 WAYNE	099	5433	5532	5602	0.4	78	2169	2262	2344	1.0	2.43	1598	1609	0.2
25571 WEST HAMLIN	043	1887	1971	2076	1.0	88	718	766	826	1.5	2.57	547	566	0.8
25572 WOODVILLE	043	48	48	50	0.0	57	21	22	23	1.1	2.18	15	15	0.0
25573 YAWKEY	043	643	652	680	0.3	75	273	284	305	0.9	2.30	197	198	0.1
25601 LOGAN	045	10857	10437	10079	-0.9	12	4412	4353	4319	-0.3	2.32	3055	2904	-1.2
25607 AMHERSTDALE	045	2545	2429	2338	-1.1	9	962	947	939	-0.4	2.56	743	711	-1.0
25608 BAISDEN	059	1985	1996	2024	0.1	64	790	825	868	1.0	2.42	600	607	0.3
25617 DAVIN	045	1529	1477	1428	-0.8	15	585	582	580	-0.1	2.54	466	452	-0.7
25621 GILBERT	059	1997	1986	2011	-0.1	46	841	867	909	0.7	2.29	615	614	-0.1
25632 LYBURN	045	460	423	401	-2.0	1	172	163	159	-1.3	2.55	123	112	-2.2
25635 MAN	045	3989	3810	3667	-1.1	9	1586	1563	1549	-0.3	2.43	1177	1123	-1.1
25638 OMAR	045	2335	2205	2113	-1.3	4	900	875	863	-0.7	2.50	682	643	-1.4
25650 VERNER	059	1161	1151	1165	-0.2	43	463	476	500	0.7	2.41	342	341	-0.1
25651 WHARNCLIFFE	059	369	369	374	0.0	57	140	145	152	0.8	2.54	107	107	0.0
25654 YOLYN	045	1072	954	892	-2.7	0	418	383	369	-2.0	2.49	313	278	-2.8
25661 WILLIAMSON	059	7377	7359	7456	-0.1	52	3164	3257	3412	0.7	2.23	2105	2081	-0.3
25666 BREEDEN	059	622	636	647	0.5	81	241	255	269	1.3	2.49	186	191	0.6
25669 CRUM	099	794	787	790	-0.2	42	297	303	312	0.5	2.59	220	218	-0.2
25670 DELBARTON	059	3790	3840	3910	0.3	74	1439	1508	1587	1.1	2.54	1085	1101	0.4
25671 DINGESS	059	1936	1963	1992	0.3	75	711	748	786	1.2	2.62	548	559	0.5
25674 KERMIT	059	3067	3011	3031	-0.4	28	1172	1189	1235	0.3	2.53	883	868	-0.4
25676 LENORE	059	2229	2202	2221	-0.3	37	862	883	923	0.6	2.49	654	650	-0.1
25678 MATEWAN	059	2324	2319	2349	-0.1	52	947	975	1022	0.7	2.38	679	674	-0.2
25682 MEADOR	059	1878	1889	1918	0.1	65	715	743	780	0.9	2.54	548	552	0.2
25694 THACKER	059	907	920	933	0.3	75	346	363	380	1.1	2.53	265	270	0.4
25699 WILSONDALE	099	933	916	918	-0.4	28	364	368	378	0.3	2.48	277	271	-0.5
25701 HUNTINGTON	011	23444	22972	22570	-0.5	25	11067	11026	11015	-0.1	2.00	5474	5168	-1.3
25702 HUNTINGTON	011	7650	7140	6846	-1.6	2	3406	3243	3168	-1.2	2.18	2071	1848	-2.7
25703 HUNTINGTON	011	5569	5368	5231	-0.9	13	2447	2396	2372	-0.5	2.15	1003	883	-3.0
25704 HUNTINGTON	099	17184	17141	17199	-0.1	52	7226	7350	7518	0.4	2.32	4900	4798	-0.5
25705 HUNTINGTON	011	21689	21057	20555	-0.7	18	9330	9278	9247	-0.1	2.25	6239	5877	-1.4
25755 HUNTINGTON	011	1491	1488	1486	-0.1	52	0	0	0	0.0	0.00	0	0	
25801 BECKLEY	081	37312	37530	37797	0.1	65	15987	16424	16914	0.6	2.24	10495	10337	-0.4
25811 AMIGO	109	437	413	396	-1.3	5	195	190	188	-0.6	2.17	136	127	-1.6
25812 ANSTED	019	162	159	159	-0.4	28	65	65	66	0.0	2.45	45	44	-0.5
25813 BEAVER	081	5848	5965	5995	0.5	80	1371	1428	1474	1.0	3.42	1026	1039	0.3
25817 BOLT	081	358	358	357	0.0	57	134	138	140	0.7	2.59	106	106	0.0
WEST VIRGINIA					0.2					0.6	2.35			-0.3
UNITED STATES					1.2					1.3	2.58			1.1

#	POST OFFICE NAME	RACE (%) White 2000	White 2004	Black 2000	Black 2004	Asian/Pacific 2000	Asian/Pacific 2004	% Hispanic Origin 2000	% Hispanic Origin 2004	2004 AGE DISTRIBUTION (%) 0-4	5-9	10-14	15-19	20-24	25-44	45-64	65-84	85+	18+	MEDIAN AGE 2004	% 2004 Males	% 2004 Females
25314	CHARLESTON	91.8	90.5	3.6	3.7	3.3	4.4	0.7	0.7	5.1	6.0	7.0	6.2	4.8	24.2	31.1	14.0	1.7	78.0	42.9	47.9	52.2
25315	CHARLESTON	94.3	94.1	4.5	4.6	0.1	0.2	0.4	0.4	5.1	5.5	5.5	4.7	4.6	26.2	27.3	18.1	3.0	81.0	44.0	46.6	53.4
25320	CHARLESTON	98.8	98.6	0.3	0.4	0.1	0.2	0.4	0.4	5.8	6.0	6.2	5.5	5.9	27.9	28.9	12.3	1.5	78.6	40.6	49.5	50.5
25401	MARTINSBURG	89.8	89.4	7.1	7.2	0.6	0.8	1.9	1.9	7.0	6.9	6.8	6.3	6.3	29.5	24.6	11.2	1.4	75.4	36.6	49.2	50.8
25411	BERKELEY SPRINGS	98.7	98.6	0.3	0.3	0.1	0.2	0.7	0.7	5.8	6.2	6.3	5.3	4.9	25.9	27.6	16.2	1.8	78.5	42.2	48.9	51.1
25413	BUNKER HILL	96.7	96.5	1.3	1.3	0.3	0.4	1.1	1.2	6.3	6.6	7.7	7.0	6.1	30.1	26.4	9.1	0.7	75.1	37.2	49.5	50.5
25414	CHARLES TOWN	90.4	90.0	6.8	6.9	0.6	0.8	1.7	1.7	7.1	7.2	6.7	6.0	5.7	29.1	25.6	11.1	1.6	75.4	38.1	49.0	51.0
25419	FALLING WATERS	97.3	97.1	0.9	1.0	0.4	0.5	1.1	1.1	5.7	5.9	7.4	7.0	6.6	29.6	27.9	9.5	0.5	76.6	38.2	50.3	49.7
25420	GERRARDSTOWN	97.0	96.7	1.0	1.0	0.2	0.3	1.4	1.4	6.8	7.1	8.1	7.1	6.4	33.1	24.6	6.6	0.4	73.7	35.2	50.2	49.9
25422	GREAT CACAPON	98.7	98.5	0.4	0.3	0.0	0.0	0.6	0.6	4.7	5.2	5.9	5.4	5.0	21.7	33.2	17.7	1.2	80.9	46.2	50.1	49.9
25425	HARPERS FERRY	95.3	94.8	2.2	2.3	0.6	0.9	1.5	1.5	6.0	6.3	6.3	5.9	5.3	29.2	29.6	10.5	0.9	77.7	40.1	50.3	49.7
25427	HEDGESVILLE	97.6	97.3	0.9	0.9	0.2	0.3	0.9	0.9	5.9	6.5	7.9	6.7	5.4	29.1	28.4	9.6	0.6	75.4	38.4	50.6	49.4
25428	INWOOD	95.9	95.6	2.0	2.1	0.4	0.6	1.1	1.1	6.5	6.9	7.7	6.5	5.8	31.6	25.3	9.1	0.7	74.9	36.3	49.5	50.5
25430	KEARNEYSVILLE	92.9	92.5	4.0	4.1	0.4	0.5	2.2	2.3	5.8	6.5	7.0	7.3	5.9	28.5	28.7	9.4	0.8	76.0	38.5	50.6	49.4
25431	LEVELS	98.6	99.4	0.7	0.7	0.0	0.0	0.0	0.7	8.5	7.8	7.2	5.9	5.2	24.2	28.8	11.8	0.7	72.6	36.9	49.7	50.3
25434	PAW PAW	95.5	95.4	3.0	3.1	0.1	0.1	1.6	1.5	6.1	6.4	6.7	6.4	5.1	25.7	27.8	14.4	1.5	76.9	39.9	50.5	49.5
25437	POINTS	99.2	99.2	0.0	0.0	0.0	0.0	1.7	0.8	4.0	5.6	8.0	6.4	4.8	24.8	28.0	16.8	1.6	77.6	42.5	52.8	47.2
25438	RANSON	83.8	83.4	12.7	12.7	0.3	0.5	2.7	2.8	6.7	6.5	7.0	6.5	7.3	29.8	24.8	10.6	0.8	75.8	36.1	48.4	51.6
25442	SHENANDOAH JUNCTION	87.4	87.2	10.2	10.2	0.5	0.7	0.9	0.8	6.1	6.1	5.9	6.6	6.3	27.3	29.5	10.9	1.3	77.9	40.1	50.0	50.0
25443	SHEPHERDSTOWN	89.3	88.6	7.2	7.2	1.4	1.9	1.5	1.4	3.6	4.3	5.2	12.3	14.9	22.0	26.2	10.1	1.5	83.3	34.3	49.7	50.3
25444	SLANESVILLE	98.3	98.3	0.7	0.6	0.0	0.0	0.9	0.9	6.2	6.6	7.0	6.8	5.3	25.2	29.6	12.1	1.2	76.1	40.0	51.6	48.4
25446	SUMMIT POINT	92.9	92.5	5.7	5.8	0.4	0.7	1.2	1.2	7.0	7.7	7.4	5.8	3.9	31.8	28.4	7.4	0.7	74.1	38.3	50.1	49.9
25501	ALKOL	98.5	98.4	0.0	0.0	0.1	0.1	0.5	0.5	5.9	6.7	5.7	5.6	7.4	29.6	26.2	11.9	1.2	78.5	38.5	51.4	48.6
25502	APPLE GROVE	99.2	99.2	0.1	0.1	0.2	0.2	0.6	0.6	5.7	5.9	6.5	5.8	6.5	28.7	28.1	11.7	1.0	78.5	39.3	51.5	48.5
25503	ASHTON	99.1	99.1	0.1	0.1	0.1	0.1	0.8	0.7	6.4	6.6	6.4	5.2	6.1	29.3	28.2	10.6	1.1	77.2	38.7	50.9	49.1
25504	BARBOURSVILLE	98.6	98.3	0.3	0.3	0.4	0.5	0.5	0.5	5.8	6.0	6.2	5.9	6.1	27.4	28.1	13.2	1.5	78.4	40.2	48.4	51.6
25505	BIG CREEK	98.9	98.8	0.1	0.1	0.6	0.7	0.6	0.6	7.0	7.2	7.5	4.5	5.9	33.9	24.6	8.9	0.6	75.4	35.0	50.4	49.6
25506	BRANCHLAND	99.2	99.0	0.0	0.0	0.2	0.2	0.8	0.8	6.1	6.2	6.7	6.2	6.3	29.2	25.6	12.4	1.4	77.3	38.4	49.8	50.2
25508	CHAPMANVILLE	98.3	98.1	0.6	0.6	0.4	0.6	0.5	0.5	5.6	6.0	6.2	5.6	6.2	27.7	28.8	12.5	1.4	78.8	39.7	49.2	50.8
25510	CULLODEN	98.8	98.6	0.3	0.3	0.3	0.4	0.3	0.3	5.8	6.0	6.1	5.7	5.3	28.5	27.6	13.1	1.8	78.6	39.9	49.3	50.7
25511	DUNLOW	98.9	98.9	0.0	0.0	0.0	0.0	0.3	0.3	5.8	7.5	8.2	6.5	5.3	28.5	26.5	10.8	0.9	74.5	37.3	53.8	46.2
25512	EAST LYNN	99.1	99.0	0.1	0.1	0.1	0.1	0.4	0.4	6.0	6.3	6.7	6.0	6.2	26.4	27.6	13.0	1.7	77.3	39.6	51.3	48.7
25514	FORT GAY	98.8	98.6	0.1	0.1	0.1	0.2	0.5	0.6	6.7	6.9	7.1	6.4	6.5	28.5	25.4	11.1	1.4	75.6	36.5	49.9	50.1
25515	GALLIPOLIS FERRY	98.8	98.8	0.0	0.0	0.1	0.1	0.5	0.5	5.7	5.9	6.2	5.8	6.6	28.7	28.7	11.2	1.2	78.6	39.7	49.9	50.1
25517	GENOA	99.0	98.9	0.1	0.1	0.1	0.1	0.3	0.3	6.8	7.4	8.5	6.9	6.7	27.5	24.4	10.7	1.0	73.1	35.5	51.4	48.6
25520	GLENWOOD	99.1	99.1	0.2	0.2	0.1	0.1	0.6	0.6	6.5	6.7	6.6	5.3	5.6	29.5	27.5	11.2	1.1	77.0	38.7	50.0	50.0
25521	GRIFFITHSVILLE	99.0	98.9	0.2	0.1	0.2	0.1	0.3	0.1	7.7	7.2	6.2	5.2	6.3	29.0	25.2	11.5	1.7	75.6	36.7	48.4	51.6
25523	HAMLIN	99.2	99.1	0.1	0.1	0.0	0.0	0.7	0.7	5.7	5.6	6.0	5.9	6.3	27.0	27.0	14.3	2.3	79.2	40.8	47.4	52.6
25524	HARTS	99.1	99.1	0.0	0.0	0.1	0.2	0.2	0.2	5.7	6.2	6.6	6.7	7.1	29.6	26.7	10.5	0.9	77.2	37.5	51.6	48.4
25526	HURRICANE	97.2	96.8	0.8	0.8	1.1	1.5	0.6	0.6	7.1	7.2	7.3	6.2	5.6	28.5	26.4	10.3	1.2	74.4	37.7	48.8	51.2
25529	JULIAN	98.9	98.8	0.1	0.1	0.2	0.2	0.4	0.4	6.1	6.3	6.0	5.3	5.4	28.6	28.0	12.3	2.2	78.2	39.8	49.6	50.4
25530	KENOVA	98.7	98.6	0.1	0.1	0.3	0.4	0.5	0.5	5.1	5.4	5.9	5.9	5.7	26.0	27.1	16.8	2.1	79.8	42.1	46.7	53.3
25534	KIAHSVILLE	98.5	98.5	0.0	0.0	0.0	0.0	0.0	0.3	5.0	7.1	8.6	6.5	3.6	28.8	26.4	12.8	1.2	75.4	39.0	52.5	47.5
25535	LAVALETTE	99.0	98.8	0.1	0.1	0.2	0.3	0.4	0.3	5.1	6.5	6.2	5.4	5.1	28.2	27.5	13.5	1.5	78.0	39.7	50.0	50.0
25537	LESAGE	99.4	99.3	0.1	0.1	0.1	0.1	0.7	0.7	6.4	6.4	6.1	5.6	5.0	29.4	27.1	12.9	1.1	77.5	39.2	49.5	50.5
25540	MIDKIFF	99.2	99.3	0.0	0.0	0.0	0.0	1.6	2.2	7.4	7.4	7.4	5.2	5.9	27.2	25.0	13.2	1.5	73.5	38.1	52.2	47.8
25541	MILTON	99.0	98.8	0.2	0.3	0.2	0.3	0.5	0.5	5.8	6.0	6.3	5.4	5.5	28.2	27.2	13.9	1.8	78.6	39.9	48.5	51.5
25544	MYRA	99.6	99.6	0.0	0.0	0.0	0.0	0.4	0.4	5.4	5.0	5.8	7.3	6.9	27.3	29.2	11.5	1.5	79.2	40.8	50.8	49.2
25545	ONA	98.7	98.5	0.2	0.2	0.4	0.5	0.5	0.5	6.1	6.5	6.7	6.0	5.4	28.4	27.9	12.0	1.2	77.0	39.4	48.8	51.2
25547	PECKS MILL	99.0	98.7	0.0	0.0	0.2	0.4	0.1	0.1	4.9	4.6	3.7	5.7	7.0	22.7	31.9	17.7	1.8	83.2	45.7	48.4	51.6
25550	POINT PLEASANT	97.2	97.1	1.3	1.3	0.6	0.7	0.5	0.5	5.8	5.8	6.1	5.6	5.9	24.0	27.6	17.0	2.3	79.1	42.5	46.7	53.3
25555	PRICHARD	99.2	99.1	0.1	0.1	0.1	0.1	0.3	0.3	6.3	6.7	7.2	5.7	6.0	29.3	26.4	10.9	1.3	76.1	36.8	51.1	48.9
25557	RANGER	99.2	99.1	0.0	0.0	0.0	0.0	0.5	0.6	6.0	6.4	7.0	6.5	6.4	29.0	26.0	11.6	1.0	76.8	37.5	50.6	49.4
25559	SALT ROCK	98.9	98.6	0.2	0.3	0.3	0.5	0.6	0.6	6.2	6.4	6.8	6.2	6.3	29.8	27.6	9.6	1.1	76.9	37.8	49.7	50.3
25560	SCOTT DEPOT	97.8	97.5	0.5	0.5	0.7	1.0	0.6	0.6	6.0	6.7	7.6	6.3	5.0	26.9	28.1	11.8	1.6	75.7	40.0	49.1	50.9
25564	SOD	98.9	98.8	0.2	0.2	0.1	0.2	0.5	0.4	5.5	5.6	5.2	5.3	6.1	28.6	29.9	12.5	1.4	80.6	40.9	49.7	50.3
25565	SPURLOCKVILLE	99.3	99.4	0.0	0.0	0.0	0.0	0.0	0.2	5.6	6.1	7.0	6.2	6.4	29.0	26.6	11.8	1.3	77.2	38.5	51.5	48.5
25567	SUMERCO	97.9	97.8	0.1	0.1	0.4	0.4	0.6	0.4	7.4	7.4	5.7	4.6	5.3	28.7	27.7	12.0	1.2	76.7	38.3	50.5	49.5
25570	WAYNE	98.7	98.5	0.1	0.1	0.2	0.3	0.5	0.5	6.2	6.4	6.4	5.9	5.9	28.1	26.2	13.3	1.6	77.5	38.9	48.9	51.1
25571	WEST HAMLIN	99.3	99.1	0.0	0.0	0.1	0.2	0.7	0.8	6.2	6.4	8.1	6.8	5.9	28.8	24.5	11.7	1.6	75.5	37.2	47.8	52.2
25572	WOODVILLE	97.9	100.0	0.0	0.0	0.0	0.0	0.0	0.0	4.2	4.2	6.3	6.3	4.2	31.3	27.1	16.7	0.0	85.4	42.0	47.9	52.1
25573	YAWKEY	98.6	98.5	0.0	0.0	0.3	0.3	0.9	1.1	6.4	6.3	6.0	5.8	5.4	29.0	25.9	14.0	1.2	77.8	39.2	48.8	51.2
25601	LOGAN	93.5	93.2	5.1	5.3	0.3	0.4	0.5	0.5	5.2	5.4	5.8	5.6	6.2	26.7	28.0	15.3	1.8	80.3	41.4	48.4	51.6
25607	AMHERSTDALE	97.1	97.0	2.3	2.4	0.0	0.0	0.8	0.8	6.1	6.1	5.7	5.6	7.2	26.0	31.1	11.2	1.0	78.7	40.5	49.9	50.1
25608	BAISDEN	98.8	98.8	0.3	0.3	0.1	0.1	0.3	0.3	6.0	6.0	6.0	5.8	6.3	30.7	28.2	10.3	0.7	78.6	38.2	50.2	49.8
25617	DAVIN	96.8	96.5	2.4	2.4	0.3	0.5	0.6	0.6	5.8	6.0	6.0	6.0	6.5	27.7	28.6	12.7	0.8	78.7	39.7	50.2	49.8
25621	GILBERT	99.2	99.1	0.1	0.1	0.2	0.2	0.5	0.5	6.1	6.0	6.5	5.3	5.9	30.8	27.1	11.5	0.8	78.4	38.9	49.2	50.8
25632	LYBURN	95.2	95.0	3.9	4.0	0.2	0.2	0.4	0.5	6.2	5.9	5.7	5.0	6.2	26.5	29.3	13.7	1.7	79.4	41.5	48.9	51.1
25635	MAN	95.4	95.0	3.1	3.1	0.8	1.0	0.4	0.4	5.8	5.9	5.8	5.8	6.1	27.7	28.6	13.2	1.2	79.0	40.2	49.1	50.9
25638	OMAR	97.6	97.5	1.9	2.0	0.0	0.0	1.3	1.4	5.9	6.3	6.7	5.3	6.4	26.6	28.8	12.7	1.3	77.6	39.8	47.7	52.3
25650	VERNER	99.7	99.5	0.1	0.1	0.1	0.1	0.7	0.7	6.0	5.9	7.0	5.7	6.0	29.8	27.3	11.7	0.7	78.0	39.0	50.2	49.8
25651	WHARNCLIFFE	99.2	99.5	0.3	0.3	0.0	0.0	0.0	0.3	6.2	6.0	5.7	6.2	6.8	29.0	29.3	10.0	0.8	78.3	38.4	51.2	48.8
25654	YOLYN	97.7	97.5	2.0	2.0	0.0	0.0	0.5	0.6	5.1	5.4	5.7	4.8	6.3	24.6	31.9	14.7	1.6	80.8	43.7	49.6	50.4
25661	WILLIAMSON	91.3	91.2	6.8	6.9	0.5	0.5	0.6	0.6	5.5	5.5	5.6	6.1	6.6	24.9	28.5	15.3	1.9	79.8	42.0	46.9	53.1
25666	BREEDEN	98.2	98.3	0.0	0.0	0.2	0.2	0.2	0.3	6.3	7.9	7.1	6.1	8.0	28.9	26.3	8.3	1.1	74.7	34.8	51.4	48.6
25669	CRUM	99.4	99.4	0.3	0.3	0.1	0.1	0.3	0.4	4.3	7.6	9.5	6.2	5.5	31.1	23.9	10.9	0.9	75.0	36.2	50.3	49.7
25670	DELBARTON	98.2	98.2	0.4	0.4	0.1	0.1	0.4	0.4	5.8	6.3	7.0	6.6	7.1	28.2	27.1	10.9	1.0	76.7	38.0	49.2	50.8
25671	DINGESS	98.7	98.7	0.1	0.1	0.2	0.2	0.4	0.4	5.9	7.3	7.2	6.4	7.2	28.9	27.7	8.5	0.9	75.6	35.9	50.4	49.6
25674	KERMIT	98.9	98.9	0.3	0.3	0.2	0.2	0.4	0.5	5.7	6.2	7.4	6.7	7.1	28.9	25.8	11.0	1.1	76.5	37.0	49.4	50.6
25676	LENORE	99.4	99.4	0.1	0.1	0.0	0.1	0.4	0.4	5.0	6.0	7.4	6.7	7.3	28.7	28.7	9.6	0.8	77.7	37.8	49.3	50.7
25678	MATEWAN	95.7	95.6	2.7	2.7	0.1	0.1	0.6	0.6	6.1	6.3	6.9	6.8	6.4	27.5	27.3	11.4	1.3	76.5	38.0	48.0	52.0
25682	MEADOR	97.1	97.0	1.7	1.6	0.2	0.2	0.5	0.5	6.3	6.2	7.0	6.5	6.0	28.9	27.3	10.9	1.0	76.4	37.9	48.8	51.2
25694	THACKER	96.0	95.8	3.4	3.5	0.1	0.2	0.1	0.1	6.1	6.4	7.3	6.6	7.5	27.9	27.6	9.4	1.2	76.2	37.0	48.6	51.4
25699	WILSONDALE	98.9	98.8	0.5	0.6	0.1	0.1	0.2	0.3	5.2	6.2	7.6	6.8	6.3	28.2	26.8	12.0	0.9	76.9	38.1	50.1	49.9
25701	HUNTINGTON	87.5	86.8	9.2	9.3	1.2	1.6	1.0	1.0	4.5	4.5	4.8	5.7	10.8	26.7	23.9	16.0	3.2	83.3	39.6	48.5	51.5
25702	HUNTINGTON	96.9	96.5	1.3	1.3	0.3	0.5	0.5	0.6	5.3	5.3	5.7	5.3	6.5	27.0	25.8	16.6	2.6	80.6	41.1	46.7	53.3
25703	HUNTINGTON	79.4	78.9	17.3	17.4	0.9	1.3	1.2	1.2	4.2	4.2	4.2	11.5	27.9	21.5	16.5	8.6	1.5	85.3	24.7	47.4	52.6
25704	HUNTINGTON	97.7	97.5	0.6	0.6	0.4	0.5	0.7	0.7	5.8	5.7	5.9	5.7	6.4	27.1	25.6	15.7	2.1	79.2	40.2	47.6	52.4
25705	HUNTINGTON	94.3	93.4	2.7	3.0	1.3	1.8	0.5	0.5	6.0	5.9	5.9	5.7	6.2	26.9	26.3	15.5	1.7	78.8	40.1	47.4	52.6
25755	HUNTINGTON	85.0	83.7	12.5	13.6	0.8	1.0	0.9	1.0	0.0	0.0	0.0	57.3	40.5	1.8	0.3	0.1	0.0	99.7	19.4	45.3	54.7
25801	BECKLEY	84.7	84.1	12.8	12.9	1.2	1.6	0.7	0.7	5.5	5.5	5.9	5.9	6.2	24.9	27.9	15.7	2.5	79.5	42.1	46.8	53.3
25811	AMIGO	95.7	95.6	2.8	2.7	0.5	0.5	0.7	0.7	5.1	5.3	6.1	4.8	5.6	23.5	29.8	18.2	1.7	80.6	44.7	48.4	51.6
25812	ANSTED	97.5	97.5	1.9	1.9	0.0	0.0	1.2	1.3	6.3	6.3	6.3	5.0	6.9	23.3	27.7	16.4	1.9	77.4	41.4	48.4	51.6
25813	BEAVER	87.6	87.2	10.9	11.1	0.8	1.0	2.5	2.4	4.7	5.0	5.1	4.7	6.4	35.0	28.0	10.1	1.2	82.4	38.5	57.8	42.2
25817	BOLT	99.4	99.4	0.0	0.0	0.0	0.0	0.8	0.6	5.6	6.2	6.2	5.9	6.2	27.1	30.5	11.2	1.4	78.8	40.0	49.4	50.6
	WEST VIRGINIA	95.1	94.8	3.2	3.2	0.5	0.7	0.7	0.7	5.6	5.8	6.2	6.3	6.7	26.7	27.1	13.7	1.9	78.9	40.1	48.8	51.2
	UNITED STATES	75.1	73.6	12.3	12.5	3.8	4.2	12.5	14.1	6.9	6.7	7.2	7.0	7.3	28.6	23.8	10.8	1.7	75.1	36.0	49.1	50.9

#	POST OFFICE NAME	2004 Per Capita Income	2004 HH Income Base	2004 HH Income Dist. (%) Less than $25,000	$25,000 to $49,999	$50,000 to $99,999	$100,000 to $149,999	$150,000 or More	Median HH Income 2004	Median HH Income 2009	2004 National Centile	2004 State Centile	2004 Home Value Base	2004 Home Value Dist. (%) Less than $50,000	$50,000 to $89,999	$90,000 to $174,999	$175,000 to $399,999	$400,000 or More	2004 Median Home Value
25314	CHARLESTON	45210	6251	15.0	21.6	29.9	17.4	16.2	68790	83464	91	100	5073	7.0	11.8	39.9	32.7	8.6	155220
25315	CHARLESTON	19195	1682	38.8	35.7	21.3	3.5	0.8	32952	38706	21	70	1163	39.4	37.4	20.7	1.7	0.8	61822
25320	CHARLESTON	21395	2401	30.5	28.0	32.7	6.7	2.0	41121	48792	50	93	2023	32.7	29.5	28.9	8.6	0.4	76351
25401	MARTINSBURG	20405	20264	28.2	32.7	31.0	6.0	2.1	40984	46976	50	92	14113	15.5	11.8	44.9	25.2	2.5	131239
25411	BERKELEY SPRINGS	21310	5087	28.9	33.9	29.2	5.5	2.5	39272	44628	44	89	4169	16.0	18.4	48.0	16.3	1.4	111234
25413	BUNKER HILL	21576	2836	19.4	30.9	36.7	10.5	2.4	49691	55860	71	98	2416	11.7	9.8	49.5	27.0	2.0	141067
25414	CHARLES TOWN	24459	8050	24.9	24.8	36.4	10.1	3.7	50211	59820	72	98	6101	6.1	6.7	40.5	41.5	5.2	166239
25419	FALLING WATERS	20650	3306	23.4	28.5	39.5	7.4	1.2	48355	54229	69	97	2818	22.4	9.2	32.8	33.6	2.0	143430
25420	GERRARDSTOWN	19230	1318	20.0	35.9	36.2	6.1	1.8	44958	51261	61	96	1120	16.5	12.6	44.9	20.9	5.1	122577
25422	GREAT CACAPON	21275	682	36.5	38.0	22.6	1.3	1.6	34055	38407	24	74	588	26.9	27.7	32.3	11.7	1.4	85909
25425	HARPERS FERRY	26694	3668	20.3	24.9	35.1	14.3	5.5	54845	64593	79	99	3052	6.6	9.1	34.2	42.1	8.0	175186
25427	HEDGESVILLE	21558	4612	21.6	31.9	35.9	8.1	2.5	47309	53788	67	97	3984	16.9	9.5	39.4	29.6	4.5	135941
25428	INWOOD	21451	2408	22.5	31.5	34.1	9.3	2.6	46143	51813	64	96	2083	17.6	6.3	44.6	27.9	3.7	141280
25430	KEARNEYSVILLE	21508	2237	20.0	30.8	37.2	10.2	1.7	49311	58153	71	98	1912	16.5	14.5	38.9	26.9	3.2	131769
25431	LEVELS	15699	62	33.9	35.5	29.0	1.6	0.0	33871	37321	24	73	53	22.6	35.9	34.0	5.7	1.9	78750
25434	PAW PAW	18662	858	33.0	35.6	27.2	2.7	1.6	37961	42357	39	86	679	31.4	32.3	30.8	4.6	1.0	68700
25437	POINTS	20504	52	34.6	30.8	25.0	3.9	5.8	37321	42334	37	84	45	17.8	42.2	31.1	4.4	4.4	84375
25438	RANSON	17062	1548	38.4	30.1	26.0	4.3	1.2	35990	42731	32	81	1049	16.2	17.4	53.1	11.8	1.5	114592
25442	SHENANDOAH JUNCTION	26921	605	14.7	24.6	38.5	17.4	4.8	62872	72440	87	100	481	11.6	7.1	28.3	43.7	9.4	184797
25443	SHEPHERDSTOWN	26701	2265	21.2	22.4	36.1	12.8	7.5	56409	66423	81	99	1659	2.8	5.1	30.9	48.5	12.8	217905
25444	SLANESVILLE	16827	308	29.9	38.3	25.7	3.3	2.9	40153	44733	47	91	265	24.5	32.5	34.7	6.8	1.5	81957
25446	SUMMIT POINT	25311	404	14.9	27.5	39.6	15.8	2.2	58671	69155	83	100	353	3.7	11.3	28.3	51.0	5.7	190461
25501	ALKOL	10608	625	65.1	22.2	11.7	0.8	0.2	18896	21492	1	4	506	44.5	30.6	18.8	6.1	0.0	55490
25502	APPLE GROVE	18824	694	43.7	24.6	27.1	2.5	2.2	30746	35670	14	58	583	37.4	32.1	23.5	5.5	1.5	68143
25503	ASHTON	17346	329	45.3	25.8	23.7	4.3	0.9	28355	33976	9	43	280	41.1	22.5	26.1	9.6	0.7	70526
25504	BARBOURSVILLE	22499	4599	29.5	29.3	30.5	8.5	2.3	41801	49961	52	94	3744	15.5	28.4	44.2	11.2	0.8	95596
25505	BIG CREEK	17491	276	37.7	26.5	29.0	3.6	3.3	40571	47112	48	91	219	44.8	14.6	28.8	7.8	4.1	74500
25506	BRANCHLAND	13909	1198	48.6	28.9	19.4	2.8	0.4	25897	30394	6	27	954	41.7	27.5	24.3	5.9	0.6	61692
25508	CHAPMANVILLE	17800	4544	45.8	25.4	22.0	4.4	2.5	27918	32923	9	40	3566	30.8	28.8	30.7	9.1	0.6	79776
25510	CULLODEN	21559	1942	24.8	34.4	30.2	8.5	2.1	42385	50021	54	94	1669	21.0	29.4	38.2	10.1	1.3	89561
25511	DUNLOW	11933	274	58.8	23.4	15.3	0.7	1.8	21232	24359	2	8	227	56.0	24.2	18.5	1.3	0.0	41000
25512	EAST LYNN	12803	668	54.8	25.9	16.2	3.0	0.2	22241	25846	3	11	538	44.6	31.8	22.9	0.7	0.0	60000
25514	FORT GAY	13689	1781	43.7	33.5	20.2	2.2	0.4	29223	33949	11	48	1430	41.3	29.9	24.2	4.5	0.2	61250
25515	GALLIPOLIS FERRY	16668	932	43.0	30.6	21.1	2.8	2.5	30486	35480	13	56	787	37.7	31.3	27.5	1.8	1.8	68661
25517	GENOA	14576	1027	53.5	26.6	16.0	1.4	2.6	22624	26134	3	12	853	43.7	26.3	26.5	3.5	0.0	60192
25520	GLENWOOD	16621	923	40.5	29.0	24.2	5.1	1.2	31504	37105	16	63	790	38.2	21.5	29.9	8.4	2.0	73400
25521	GRIFFITHSVILLE	17428	277	51.6	20.2	24.9	1.4	1.8	24130	28228	4	19	219	41.6	29.2	25.6	3.7	0.0	64200
25523	HAMLIN	19442	1406	44.7	30.6	18.9	2.8	3.0	28581	33853	10	44	1083	25.4	33.1	31.8	9.1	0.7	79253
25524	HARTS	11926	821	53.5	26.2	16.3	4.0	0.0	22858	26366	3	13	670	47.5	37.2	12.4	2.8	0.2	54857
25526	HURRICANE	25813	7891	21.9	25.0	34.0	13.4	5.8	52857	62532	77	99	6541	10.7	20.4	39.4	26.7	2.8	118590
25529	JULIAN	14614	576	45.8	31.6	20.0	2.3	0.4	26838	30899	7	32	453	42.4	26.9	22.3	8.4	0.0	60735
25530	KENOVA	19502	3440	41.0	29.1	23.6	4.5	1.9	30708	36122	14	58	2508	23.7	34.8	35.9	5.2	0.4	82140
25534	KIAHSVILLE	10983	127	57.5	22.8	18.9	0.8	0.0	22047	25272	3	10	103	49.5	29.1	21.4	0.0	0.0	50714
25535	LAVALETTE	18567	1568	34.9	27.9	30.6	5.6	1.1	38053	44743	39	86	1335	25.2	27.7	39.2	7.0	0.8	85928
25537	LESAGE	16152	666	39.0	34.4	19.8	6.3	0.5	31758	37222	17	64	567	32.5	34.7	25.2	5.6	1.9	68581
25540	MIDKIFF	9171	47	59.6	29.8	10.6	0.0	0.0	20406	24492	2	5	39	46.2	18.0	28.2	7.7	0.0	55000
25541	MILTON	18639	3318	32.0	35.0	26.6	5.0	1.3	36554	42615	34	82	2698	27.5	27.5	35.2	8.8	1.1	83709
25544	MYRA	13275	98	43.9	33.7	21.4	1.0	0.0	27766	32310	8	38	79	36.7	29.1	25.3	8.9	0.0	67727
25545	ONA	19761	2220	30.1	29.1	31.1	7.6	2.3	41544	49639	51	93	1918	23.9	21.0	38.8	13.3	3.0	95904
25547	PECKS MILL	13974	362	48.9	28.7	21.8	0.6	0.0	25615	30272	5	25	297	36.4	33.3	30.3	0.0	0.0	66719
25550	POINT PLEASANT	18973	3432	41.1	31.5	19.3	5.8	2.3	31033	36051	15	60	2504	22.4	35.9	33.0	7.8	1.0	81557
25555	PRICHARD	16408	392	33.2	38.3	24.0	3.3	1.3	34824	41401	27	76	329	30.7	32.5	26.1	10.6	0.0	70652
25557	RANGER	11381	1856	55.7	26.5	15.7	1.8	0.3	21080	24357	2	7	1502	53.0	29.8	15.4	1.5	0.4	47594
25559	SALT ROCK	19092	697	29.1	30.9	31.3	7.9	0.9	40680	47443	48	92	605	28.4	28.8	30.3	12.6	0.0	81635
25560	SCOTT DEPOT	27797	3136	17.4	28.7	36.6	12.3	5.1	53523	63475	78	99	2759	10.2	13.9	52.8	21.0	2.2	125361
25564	SOD	18835	1066	44.5	22.8	25.8	5.3	1.7	30838	37149	14	59	914	28.9	24.6	37.4	8.9	0.2	84839
25565	SPURLOCKVILLE	11619	264	58.0	24.2	14.4	3.4	0.0	19177	22841	2	4	213	54.9	22.5	17.4	5.2	0.0	45625
25567	SUMERCO	15203	302	45.0	26.8	24.5	3.3	0.3	28599	33477	10	44	245	38.0	32.2	26.5	3.3	0.0	63250
25570	WAYNE	15499	2262	44.6	26.7	24.5	3.3	0.9	28884	33315	10	46	1812	35.1	28.6	30.5	5.5	0.3	71975
25571	WEST HAMLIN	14852	766	46.3	28.6	20.9	3.1	1.0	27342	31934	8	35	593	27.0	41.7	27.0	4.2	0.2	70929
25572	WOODVILLE	13270	22	50.0	31.8	18.2	0.0	0.0	25000	26087	5	22	18	33.3	33.3	33.3	0.0	0.0	73333
25573	YAWKEY	14924	284	50.4	28.5	19.7	1.1	0.4	24827	28260	4	20	227	37.0	33.0	26.9	3.1	0.0	68448
25601	LOGAN	17494	4353	46.6	28.5	18.7	4.0	2.3	26978	31729	7	32	3191	36.2	36.6	23.1	3.9	0.2	66417
25607	AMHERSTDALE	16534	947	45.0	22.2	27.6	3.0	2.3	29227	34933	11	48	807	43.3	28.8	24.4	3.6	0.0	60362
25608	BAISDEN	14176	825	51.2	28.6	17.2	2.3	0.7	24121	27551	4	19	715	44.3	27.8	22.2	5.3	0.0	59872
25617	DAVIN	13595	582	47.3	29.0	21.3	2.4	0.0	26267	30317	6	29	473	52.4	29.2	15.6	2.8	0.0	47195
25621	GILBERT	15208	867	49.3	29.6	16.3	3.1	1.7	25428	29568	5	24	715	50.9	26.0	17.2	5.7	0.1	48879
25632	LYBURN	15567	163	49.7	26.4	19.0	2.5	2.5	25138	28900	5	22	125	38.4	32.0	26.4	3.2	0.0	66875
25635	MAN	15856	1563	48.6	26.2	20.2	2.9	2.2	25813	30024	6	26	1227	44.3	29.0	23.3	3.3	0.1	58198
25638	OMAR	13075	875	53.0	28.2	15.3	2.7	0.7	23489	27354	4	15	694	40.5	37.6	18.3	3.6	0.0	56226
25650	VERNER	13339	476	54.8	25.6	15.3	2.5	1.7	22016	25724	3	10	386	56.2	22.3	15.8	5.2	0.5	44667
25651	WHARNCLIFFE	11812	145	60.7	26.2	11.0	1.4	0.7	17426	20424	1	2	121	40.5	28.9	26.5	4.1	0.0	70455
25654	YOLYN	18489	383	37.1	29.0	26.9	5.2	1.8	37780	44085	38	86	319	34.2	32.3	28.2	5.3	0.0	71296
25661	WILLIAMSON	16897	3257	49.5	25.8	19.2	3.5	2.0	25358	30265	5	24	2241	34.2	32.4	29.4	3.8	0.3	71766
25666	BREEDEN	12714	255	52.6	26.3	17.7	1.2	2.4	22757	26257	3	13	210	51.9	30.5	15.7	1.9	0.0	48095
25669	CRUM	24357	303	57.1	26.4	9.9	3.3	3.3	20272	22686	2	5	253	45.1	19.4	33.2	2.4	0.0	62917
25670	DELBARTON	14783	1508	46.9	32.3	16.1	3.1	1.7	26634	31000	7	31	1236	41.2	32.2	22.9	3.6	0.1	61504
25671	DINGESS	12690	748	51.7	27.8	16.7	2.3	1.5	23497	27430	4	16	614	46.4	29.2	19.1	5.4	0.0	55238
25674	KERMIT	12393	1189	56.4	25.0	16.5	1.3	0.9	20684	23907	2	6	955	45.9	33.0	19.2	1.7	0.3	56475
25676	LENORE	13698	883	52.7	28.0	14.5	3.6	1.3	23129	26789	3	14	723	36.9	29.1	27.1	6.9	0.0	72895
25678	MATEWAN	14765	975	57.6	21.3	18.0	1.2	1.9	20682	24197	2	5	725	38.6	37.9	21.4	1.9	0.1	62803
25682	MEADOR	12315	743	54.6	26.9	15.5	2.3	0.7	22061	25671	3	10	589	39.2	38.4	20.0	2.4	0.0	63727
25694	THACKER	11621	363	55.1	28.9	13.5	2.5	0.0	21691	25478	2	9	290	51.0	29.7	16.6	2.4	0.3	49032
25699	WILSONDALE	11879	368	57.1	24.2	16.9	1.4	0.5	20898	24444	2	7	299	51.8	29.4	17.1	1.7	0.0	47800
25701	HUNTINGTON	23067	11026	45.6	25.0	20.8	5.2	3.4	28590	33967	10	44	6058	15.9	31.2	37.9	13.0	2.0	93308
25702	HUNTINGTON	15741	3243	50.0	30.8	16.5	1.6	1.1	25023	29473	5	22	2091	36.4	37.1	21.6	4.7	0.2	63553
25703	HUNTINGTON	13231	2396	64.2	20.6	11.6	2.6	1.1	15971	18476	1	2	855	42.8	37.4	17.9	1.3	0.6	55491
25704	HUNTINGTON	17743	7350	41.5	29.9	22.4	4.1	2.1	30240	36035	13	53	5281	25.1	37.3	31.6	4.9	1.0	78163
25705	HUNTINGTON	24977	9278	34.0	27.6	25.5	7.7	5.2	38086	44805	40	87	6685	13.8	33.5	39.7	11.3	1.8	93035
25755	HUNTINGTON	6555	0	0.0	0.0	0.0	0.0	0.0	0	0	0	0	0	0.0	0.0	0.0	0.0	0.0	0
25801	BECKLEY	20267	16424	40.1	29.0	22.6	5.4	2.9	32197	37615	18	67	11915	24.5	32.5	33.3	8.8	0.9	82628
25811	AMIGO	20035	190	46.3	28.4	16.3	5.8	3.2	26973	31121	7	32	154	58.4	26.6	14.3	0.7	0.0	44091
25812	ANSTED	16281	65	44.6	35.4	15.4	1.5	3.1	27692	31818	8	37	50	52.0	32.0	16.0	0.0	0.0	48333
25813	BEAVER	13446	1428	29.2	29.8	32.9	5.9	2.2	40440	48669	48	91	1214	18.0	20.0	41.0	18.7	2.2	107598
25817	BOLT	23808	138	29.7	30.4	30.4	6.5	2.9	39523	46325	44	89	118	23.7	31.4	35.6	8.5	0.9	83333
	WEST VIRGINIA	19262		38.4	30.0	24.1	5.2	2.4	33458	38993				29.0	29.1	31.1	9.6	1.3	80023
	UNITED STATES	25866		24.7	27.1	30.8	10.9	6.5	48124	56710				10.9	15.0	33.7	30.1	10.4	145905

ZIP CODE #	POST OFFICE NAME	FINANCIAL SERVICES: Auto Loan	Home Loan	Investments	Retirement Plans	THE HOME: Home Improvements: Home Repair	Lawn & Garden	Furnishings: Computers & Hardware	Major Appliances	TV, Radio, Sound Equipment	Furniture	ENTERTAINMENT: Dine out/ Carry out	Sports Equipment	Fees & Tickets	Toys & Games	Travel	Cable TV	PERSONAL: Apparel & Services	Auto Repairs	Health Insurance	Pets & Supplies
25314	CHARLESTON	136	158	176	157	157	166	149	149	143	148	179	170	156	181	153	142	176	147	144	164
25315	CHARLESTON	68	51	35	48	55	66	55	61	63	53	74	69	50	69	55	67	68	61	74	75
25320	CHARLESTON	90	72	49	68	76	86	71	80	78	71	94	93	66	91	71	81	87	79	90	101
25401	MARTINSBURG	74	68	60	65	69	76	68	71	71	67	87	82	66	82	68	72	83	71	75	84
25411	BERKELEY SPRINGS	87	66	40	61	72	82	64	75	73	64	87	88	58	84	65	77	80	74	88	100
25413	BUNKER HILL	88	84	71	81	87	92	78	84	80	78	98	99	78	101	80	81	94	82	87	104
25414	CHARLES TOWN	86	87	86	87	88	93	86	87	85	85	105	102	86	107	86	84	102	86	86	99
25419	FALLING WATERS	85	76	57	72	78	84	71	78	74	72	91	92	68	90	72	75	86	77	82	98
25420	GERRARDSTOWN	83	75	58	72	77	82	70	77	73	71	89	90	68	88	71	74	85	76	80	95
25422	GREAT CACAPON	82	64	44	58	73	81	61	73	69	60	81	86	54	80	65	73	76	72	87	100
25425	HARPERS FERRY	94	101	100	100	101	103	94	96	92	94	114	113	96	117	95	90	112	95	92	111
25427	HEDGESVILLE	92	80	60	75	85	93	74	84	80	74	96	99	71	98	77	82	91	82	92	109
25428	INWOOD	88	79	62	77	82	89	76	82	79	76	97	96	74	97	77	80	92	81	87	101
25430	KEARNEYSVILLE	92	82	63	78	86	92	76	84	80	77	98	100	74	99	78	82	93	82	90	107
25431	LEVELS	66	52	35	47	58	65	49	59	55	48	65	69	43	64	52	59	61	58	69	80
25434	PAW PAW	84	58	29	50	65	75	55	69	66	56	78	82	48	74	57	71	71	68	84	97
25437	POINTS	83	65	45	59	74	83	62	74	70	61	83	87	55	82	66	74	77	73	88	101
25438	RANSON	65	55	43	53	57	64	56	60	60	55	72	71	52	70	56	61	68	61	66	73
25442	SHENANDOAH JUNCTION	104	106	102	104	108	112	99	103	99	99	122	122	100	126	101	99	119	101	103	123
25443	SHEPHERDSTOWN	91	104	126	107	103	106	102	100	98	102	123	118	106	127	103	95	122	100	92	109
25444	SLANESVILLE	82	58	31	51	65	75	55	68	65	56	77	81	48	74	57	70	71	67	83	95
25446	SUMMIT POINT	105	94	71	89	99	106	87	96	92	87	112	114	85	114	89	94	106	93	104	124
25501	ALKOL	48	32	15	28	37	42	31	39	38	32	44	47	27	42	32	41	40	39	48	55
25502	APPLE GROVE	87	58	26	50	66	76	56	70	68	57	79	84	48	75	57	73	72	69	86	99
25503	ASHTON	80	54	24	46	61	70	52	65	63	53	73	77	44	69	53	67	67	64	80	92
25504	BARBOURSVILLE	82	76	66	73	80	87	74	79	78	73	94	91	73	95	76	80	90	78	86	95
25505	BIG CREEK	74	67	52	64	67	71	64	69	65	66	80	79	60	76	63	65	77	69	69	82
25506	BRANCHLAND	64	43	20	37	48	56	41	52	50	42	58	62	35	55	42	53	53	51	63	73
25508	CHAPMANVILLE	76	57	36	51	62	72	57	66	65	56	77	77	51	74	57	69	71	65	78	86
25510	CULLODEN	89	72	50	68	77	86	71	80	78	71	94	93	66	92	71	80	87	78	90	102
25511	DUNLOW	58	39	18	33	44	50	37	47	45	38	53	56	32	50	38	49	48	46	58	66
25512	EAST LYNN	58	39	18	34	44	51	38	47	45	38	53	56	32	50	38	49	48	47	58	67
25514	FORT GAY	66	45	20	38	50	58	43	54	52	44	61	64	37	58	44	56	55	53	66	76
25515	GALLIPOLIS FERRY	77	51	23	44	58	67	49	62	60	50	70	74	42	66	50	64	64	61	76	88
25517	GENOA	72	48	22	42	55	63	47	58	56	47	66	70	40	62	47	61	60	58	72	83
25520	GLENWOOD	77	54	26	47	60	69	51	63	61	52	72	76	45	69	52	65	66	63	77	89
25521	GRIFFITHSVILLE	86	58	26	50	65	75	55	69	67	57	79	83	47	74	56	72	71	69	86	99
25523	HAMLIN	83	58	30	52	65	76	58	70	69	58	81	82	50	76	59	74	73	69	85	95
25524	HARTS	60	40	18	34	45	52	38	48	46	39	55	57	33	52	39	50	50	48	59	68
25526	HURRICANE	99	101	91	99	101	104	93	97	92	94	114	113	94	116	93	91	110	94	95	114
25529	JULIAN	67	45	20	39	51	59	43	54	52	44	61	65	37	58	44	56	56	54	67	77
25530	KENOVA	71	56	38	53	61	70	59	65	65	57	77	74	54	74	59	68	71	64	76	80
25534	KIAHSVILLE	55	37	17	32	42	48	35	44	43	36	50	53	30	47	36	46	46	44	55	63
25535	LAVALETTE	77	57	35	53	63	72	58	67	66	57	78	78	52	75	58	70	72	66	79	87
25537	LESAGE	76	51	23	44	57	66	49	61	59	50	69	73	42	66	50	64	63	61	75	87
25540	MIDKIFF	50	33	15	29	38	44	32	40	39	33	46	48	27	43	33	42	42	40	50	57
25541	MILTON	73	59	42	56	63	71	59	66	65	58	78	76	55	75	59	67	72	65	75	83
25544	MYRA	66	44	20	38	50	58	43	53	52	44	61	64	36	57	43	56	55	53	66	76
25545	ONA	79	74	63	70	77	81	69	75	72	70	88	88	68	89	71	73	85	74	79	93
25547	PECKS MILL	62	42	19	36	47	54	40	50	49	41	57	60	34	54	41	52	52	50	62	72
25550	POINT PLEASANT	62	57	54	55	59	67	59	61	62	57	76	70	57	75	59	64	72	61	67	72
25555	PRICHARD	79	53	24	45	60	69	51	63	61	52	72	76	43	68	52	66	65	63	78	90
25557	RANGER	55	37	17	32	42	48	35	44	43	36	50	53	30	47	36	46	46	44	55	63
25559	SALT ROCK	84	66	42	60	72	79	62	72	69	62	83	86	57	82	63	73	78	71	83	97
25560	SCOTT DEPOT	100	106	106	106	107	110	99	102	97	99	121	121	101	124	101	96	118	100	99	119
25564	SOD	83	58	31	52	65	74	57	69	67	58	79	82	50	76	58	71	73	68	83	94
25565	SPURLOCKVILLE	56	38	17	32	42	49	36	45	44	37	51	54	31	48	37	47	47	45	56	64
25567	SUMERCO	67	48	25	43	53	61	47	56	55	47	65	66	41	62	47	58	59	56	67	77
25570	WAYNE	71	48	22	41	54	62	46	57	55	47	65	69	39	62	47	60	59	57	71	82
25571	WEST HAMLIN	72	48	22	42	55	63	46	58	56	47	66	69	40	62	47	60	60	57	72	82
25572	WOODVILLE	55	37	17	31	41	48	35	44	43	36	50	53	30	47	36	46	45	44	54	63
25573	YAWKEY	65	43	20	37	49	56	42	52	50	42	59	62	35	56	42	54	54	52	64	74
25601	LOGAN	63	51	43	49	54	64	56	60	62	54	74	67	52	70	56	65	69	60	69	71
25607	AMHERSTDALE	79	53	25	46	60	70	52	64	62	53	73	77	44	69	53	67	66	64	79	91
25608	BAISDEN	65	43	20	37	49	56	42	52	50	43	59	62	36	56	42	54	54	52	64	74
25617	DAVIN	61	45	28	41	49	55	44	52	50	44	60	62	39	57	44	53	55	51	61	70
25621	GILBERT	66	44	20	38	50	57	42	53	51	43	60	63	36	57	43	55	55	52	65	75
25632	LYBURN	70	50	27	45	55	65	51	60	60	50	70	70	45	66	51	64	64	60	73	79
25635	MAN	61	49	37	47	52	61	52	57	57	50	68	65	48	65	52	59	63	57	65	69
25638	OMAR	58	42	24	38	46	53	42	49	48	42	57	57	37	54	42	51	52	49	58	65
25650	VERNER	61	41	18	35	46	53	39	49	47	40	56	59	33	53	40	51	50	49	60	70
25651	WHARNCLIFFE	57	38	17	33	43	49	37	46	44	37	52	55	31	49	37	48	47	45	56	65
25654	YOLYN	83	57	30	51	64	75	58	69	68	58	80	81	50	76	58	73	73	69	85	94
25661	WILLIAMSON	64	48	33	44	53	61	49	56	56	49	66	65	44	63	49	59	61	56	67	73
25666	BREEDEN	60	40	18	34	45	52	39	48	47	39	55	58	33	52	39	50	50	48	59	69
25669	CRUM	119	80	36	69	90	104	77	96	93	78	109	115	65	103	78	100	99	95	119	137
25670	DELBARTON	71	47	21	41	54	62	46	57	55	47	65	68	39	61	47	59	59	57	70	81
25671	DINGESS	63	42	19	36	48	55	41	51	49	41	57	61	34	54	41	53	52	50	62	72
25674	KERMIT	59	40	18	34	45	52	38	48	46	39	54	57	32	51	39	50	49	47	59	68
25676	LENORE	64	43	20	37	49	56	42	52	50	42	59	62	35	56	42	54	54	51	64	74
25678	MATEWAN	66	44	20	38	50	58	43	53	52	44	61	64	36	57	43	56	55	53	66	76
25682	MEADOR	59	39	18	34	45	51	38	48	46	39	54	57	32	51	39	50	49	47	59	68
25694	THACKER	55	37	17	32	42	48	36	45	43	37	51	54	30	48	36	47	46	44	55	64
25699	WILSONDALE	56	37	17	32	42	49	36	45	43	37	51	54	31	48	37	47	46	44	55	64
25701	HUNTINGTON	66	60	66	61	61	68	68	66	69	65	85	77	65	83	66	68	82	68	67	74
25702	HUNTINGTON	55	42	32	40	45	54	46	50	51	44	61	57	42	58	46	54	56	51	59	61
25703	HUNTINGTON	41	32	36	32	32	37	44	38	45	40	55	47	39	51	39	43	52	42	39	43
25704	HUNTINGTON	63	52	44	51	55	64	56	59	61	54	73	68	52	71	56	63	68	60	67	71
25705	HUNTINGTON	79	78	81	76	79	87	79	80	81	78	99	92	79	99	79	82	96	80	83	91
25755	HUNTINGTON	0	0	0	0	0	0	0	0	0	0	0	0	0	0	0	0	0	0	0	0
25801	BECKLEY	70	59	49	56	62	72	62	66	67	60	81	75	59	78	62	70	76	66	75	79
25811	AMIGO	70	53	35	51	58	69	59	64	66	55	77	72	52	73	58	69	70	64	77	78
25812	ANSTED	64	48	32	46	53	63	54	59	60	51	70	66	48	67	53	63	64	59	70	71
25813	BEAVER	76	71	61	69	74	81	70	75	73	69	88	86	68	88	71	74	84	73	80	88
25817	BOLT	116	78	35	67	88	102	75	94	91	77	107	112	64	101	76	98	97	93	116	133
	WEST VIRGINIA	73	60	47	57	64	72	61	67	67	60	80	78	57	78	61	69	75	67	76	84
	UNITED STATES	100	100	100	100	100	100	100	100	100	100	100	100	100	100	100	100	100	100	100	100

ZIP CODE			POPULATION			2000-2004 ANNUAL RATE		HOUSEHOLDS					FAMILIES		
#	POST OFFICE NAME	COUNTY FIPS CODE	2000	2004	2009	% Rate	State Centile	2000	2004	2009	% Annual Rate 2000-2004	2004 Average HH Size	2000	2004	% Annual Rate 2000-2004
25820	CAMP CREEK	055	37	38	38	0.6	83	14	15	15	1.6	2.47	11	11	0.0
25823	COAL CITY	081	1024	1025	1024	0.0	58	410	421	430	0.6	2.43	317	316	-0.1
25825	COOL RIDGE	081	1860	1876	1881	0.2	68	706	730	750	0.8	2.57	557	560	0.1
25827	CRAB ORCHARD	081	5037	4951	4917	-0.4	30	2134	2155	2194	0.2	2.30	1502	1460	-0.7
25831	DANESE	019	1420	1422	1421	0.0	59	566	580	592	0.6	2.45	400	395	-0.3
25832	DANIELS	081	3428	3466	3463	0.3	72	1472	1522	1561	0.8	1.87	1007	1001	-0.1
25837	EDMOND	019	146	147	147	0.2	67	62	64	65	0.8	2.30	46	46	0.0
25839	FAIRDALE	081	326	326	325	0.0	57	126	129	132	0.6	2.53	100	100	0.0
25840	FAYETTEVILLE	019	7695	7720	7739	0.1	62	3088	3166	3239	0.6	2.41	2198	2173	-0.3
25841	FLAT TOP	055	722	738	739	0.5	81	290	304	311	1.1	2.41	223	227	0.4
25843	GHENT	081	970	980	982	0.2	71	408	422	433	0.8	2.32	321	323	0.2
25844	GLEN DANIEL	081	2312	2291	2280	-0.2	42	885	900	918	0.4	2.55	681	672	-0.3
25845	GLEN FORK	109	304	295	285	-0.7	18	129	129	129	0.0	2.28	91	88	-0.8
25847	GLEN MORGAN	081	2640	2597	2581	-0.4	31	1071	1081	1101	0.2	2.39	732	710	-0.7
25848	GLEN ROGERS	109	278	265	255	-1.1	8	108	106	105	-0.4	2.50	84	80	-1.1
25854	HICO	019	699	680	677	-0.7	19	284	283	287	-0.1	2.40	213	206	-0.8
25856	JONBEN	081	84	84	84	0.0	57	31	32	33	0.8	2.63	24	24	0.0
25857	JOSEPHINE	081	352	341	338	-0.7	17	135	134	136	-0.2	2.54	102	98	-0.9
25862	LANSING	019	91	90	89	-0.3	39	38	38	39	0.0	2.37	26	25	-0.9
25864	LAYLAND	081	83	87	89	1.1	88	31	33	35	1.5	2.64	23	23	0.0
25865	LESTER	081	963	940	932	-0.6	23	399	400	407	0.1	2.35	295	286	-0.7
25868	LOOKOUT	019	290	284	283	-0.5	25	116	116	118	0.0	2.45	86	83	-0.8
25870	MABEN	109	362	345	332	-1.1	7	142	139	138	-0.5	2.47	102	96	-1.4
25876	SAULSVILLE	109	623	594	570	-1.1	8	250	246	244	-0.4	2.41	193	184	-1.1
25880	MOUNT HOPE	019	8206	8168	8151	-0.1	47	3182	3239	3303	0.4	2.43	2242	2201	-0.4
25882	MULLENS	109	2438	2371	2297	-0.7	19	1054	1052	1048	0.0	2.20	713	684	-1.0
25901	OAK HILL	019	14913	15015	15093	0.2	67	6180	6331	6481	0.6	2.33	4203	4143	-0.3
25902	ODD	081	553	541	536	-0.5	24	207	208	211	0.1	2.60	156	152	-0.6
25908	PRINCEWICK	081	355	346	343	-0.6	22	150	150	153	0.0	2.31	108	105	-0.7
25913	RAVENCLIFF	109	1400	1364	1321	-0.6	21	517	519	518	0.1	2.63	405	395	-0.6
25915	RHODELL	081	1128	1087	1075	-0.9	12	426	420	426	-0.3	2.59	315	301	-1.1
25917	SCARBRO	019	1518	1501	1496	-0.3	39	601	606	615	0.2	2.48	429	417	-0.7
25918	SHADY SPRING	081	4424	4476	4467	0.3	73	1809	1866	1910	0.7	1.87	1316	1311	-0.1
25920	SLAB FORK	081	818	804	799	-0.4	30	324	327	333	0.2	2.46	254	250	-0.4
25922	SPANISHBURG	055	1119	1122	1112	0.1	61	424	435	440	0.6	2.58	318	316	-0.2
25928	STEPHENSON	109	264	249	238	-1.4	4	106	103	102	-0.7	2.42	77	72	-1.6
25932	SURVEYOR	081	330	326	324	-0.3	37	141	143	145	0.3	2.28	102	99	-0.7
25936	THURMOND	019	14	14	14	0.0	57	9	9	9	0.0	1.56	6	5	-4.2
25938	VICTOR	019	2372	2384	2387	0.1	63	925	948	968	0.6	2.46	680	674	-0.2
25951	HINTON	089	5886	5740	5599	-0.6	22	2570	2564	2558	-0.1	2.20	1634	1559	-1.1
25958	CHARMCO	025	638	625	624	-0.5	25	263	264	269	0.1	2.30	182	176	-0.8
25962	RAINELLE	025	3831	3753	3742	-0.5	25	1632	1629	1656	0.0	2.27	1103	1060	-0.9
25965	ELTON	089	207	205	201	-0.2	41	81	82	83	0.3	2.50	57	56	-0.4
25966	GREEN SULPHUR SPRING	089	669	660	646	-0.3	35	288	292	294	0.3	2.26	202	197	-0.6
25969	JUMPING BRANCH	089	1139	1125	1102	-0.3	37	465	472	473	0.4	2.36	353	348	-0.3
25971	LERONA	055	484	483	478	-0.1	52	184	188	191	0.5	2.53	138	136	-0.3
25976	MEADOW BRIDGE	019	1647	1700	1722	0.8	85	676	714	739	1.3	2.38	497	507	0.5
25977	MEADOW CREEK	089	192	190	186	-0.3	39	84	85	86	0.3	2.24	59	58	-0.4
25978	NIMITZ	089	608	599	586	-0.4	33	242	245	246	0.3	2.42	185	182	-0.4
25979	PIPESTEM	089	592	584	572	-0.3	35	244	247	248	0.3	2.36	183	180	-0.4
25981	QUINWOOD	025	1708	1637	1626	-1.0	11	699	684	693	-0.5	2.39	528	502	-1.2
25984	RUPERT	025	1440	1428	1428	-0.2	43	587	594	608	0.3	2.39	394	384	-0.6
25985	SANDSTONE	089	408	399	390	-0.5	24	182	183	184	0.1	2.18	124	120	-0.8
25986	SPRING DALE	019	92	97	99	1.3	91	40	43	45	1.7	2.23	29	30	0.8
25989	WHITE OAK	081	462	473	476	0.6	81	184	192	198	1.0	2.26	143	145	0.3
26003	WHEELING	069	46968	45494	43852	-0.8	16	19514	19169	18715	-0.4	2.24	12071	11329	-1.5
26031	BENWOOD	051	2406	2399	2372	-0.1	50	1013	1026	1031	0.3	2.34	668	654	-0.5
26032	BETHANY	009	1092	1093	1088	0.0	58	225	231	235	0.6	2.88	150	147	-0.5
26033	CAMERON	051	2641	2552	2486	-0.8	15	1048	1031	1022	-0.4	2.42	733	694	-1.3
26034	CHESTER	029	6050	5785	5486	-1.1	10	2469	2414	2341	-0.5	2.36	1740	1642	-1.4
26035	COLLIERS	009	2229	2237	2239	0.1	62	864	892	917	0.8	2.51	667	667	0.0
26036	DALLAS	051	876	861	845	-0.4	30	333	334	334	0.1	2.58	258	251	-0.7
26037	FOLLANSBEE	009	7428	7337	7319	-0.3	37	3047	3090	3162	0.3	2.32	2139	2088	-0.6
26038	GLEN DALE	051	3283	3191	3116	-0.7	19	1370	1360	1353	-0.2	2.35	1002	961	-1.0
26039	GLEN EASTON	051	2228	2185	2142	-0.5	26	800	803	802	0.1	2.71	631	616	-0.6
26040	MCMECHEN	051	1937	1843	1784	-1.2	6	865	841	830	-0.7	2.18	560	521	-1.7
26041	MOUNDSVILLE	051	17425	17284	17059	-0.2	44	6976	7051	7086	0.3	2.35	4851	4719	-0.7
26047	NEW CUMBERLAND	029	6721	6418	6080	-1.1	9	2742	2691	2615	-0.4	2.38	2009	1908	-1.2
26050	NEWELL	029	2502	2382	2254	-1.2	7	1029	1000	967	-0.7	2.38	698	651	-1.6
26055	PROCTOR	103	1716	1654	1604	-0.9	13	644	636	632	-0.3	2.60	499	478	-1.0
26059	TRIADELPHIA	069	2563	2474	2371	-0.8	14	1034	1018	992	-0.4	2.42	758	720	-1.2
26060	VALLEY GROVE	069	1764	1707	1641	-0.8	16	676	667	651	-0.3	2.35	476	452	-1.2
26062	WEIRTON	029	21380	20732	19922	-0.7	17	9338	9257	9101	-0.2	2.21	6183	5866	-1.2
26070	WELLSBURG	009	10712	10816	10924	0.2	70	4360	4498	4646	0.7	2.34	3077	3068	-0.1
26101	PARKERSBURG	107	31116	30993	30926	-0.1	49	13129	13313	13462	0.3	2.29	8404	8150	-0.7
26104	PARKERSBURG	107	18097	17590	17339	-0.7	19	7699	7654	7666	-0.1	2.24	5033	4772	-1.3
26105	VIENNA	107	12317	12040	11877	-0.5	24	5316	5315	5325	0.0	2.23	3575	3417	-1.1
26133	BELLEVILLE	107	1216	1197	1183	-0.4	32	446	450	452	0.2	2.66	360	353	-0.5
26134	BELMONT	073	1560	1570	1589	0.2	66	599	613	632	0.6	2.47	449	446	-0.2
26136	BIG BEND	013	837	825	811	-0.3	33	337	340	343	0.2	2.42	243	237	-0.6
26137	BIG SPRINGS	021	669	658	647	-0.4	31	265	267	268	0.2	2.46	192	186	-0.7
26138	BROHARD	105	6	6	6	0.0	57	3	3	3	0.0	2.00	2	2	0.0
26141	CRESTON	105	365	364	361	-0.1	52	145	148	150	0.5	2.44	103	102	-0.2
26142	DAVISVILLE	107	2267	2798	3116	5.1	99	829	1023	1146	5.1	2.74	651	786	4.5
26143	ELIZABETH	105	3394	3396	3429	0.0	58	1331	1353	1385	0.4	2.49	983	968	-0.4
26146	FRIENDLY	095	937	986	1016	1.2	90	367	395	416	1.8	2.50	280	293	1.1
26147	GRANTSVILLE	013	1732	1702	1672	-0.4	30	720	723	726	0.1	2.33	500	484	-0.8
26148	MACFARLAN	085	461	462	463	0.1	60	189	193	195	0.5	2.39	139	137	-0.3
26149	MIDDLEBOURNE	095	2711	2715	2723	0.0	59	1074	1099	1125	0.5	2.46	793	785	-0.2
26150	MINERAL WELLS	107	5794	6107	6252	1.3	91	2213	2383	2479	1.8	2.56	1730	1809	1.1
26151	MOUNT ZION	013	234	230	226	-0.4	30	105	105	106	0.0	2.17	73	70	-1.0
26152	MUNDAY	105	161	165	167	0.6	82	63	66	67	1.1	2.50	47	47	0.0
26155	NEW MARTINSVILLE	103	6963	6935	6816	-0.1	49	2872	2918	2926	0.4	2.32	1975	1931	-0.5
26159	PADEN CITY	103	3368	3349	3300	-0.1	46	1380	1396	1402	0.3	2.38	1012	989	-0.5
26160	PALESTINE	105	922	940	950	0.5	79	354	368	377	0.9	2.55	264	266	0.2
	WEST VIRGINIA					0.2					0.6	2.35			-0.3
	UNITED STATES					1.2					1.3	2.58			1.1

POPULATION COMPOSITION WEST VIRGINIA

25820-26160 B

ZIP CODE #	POST OFFICE NAME	RACE (%) White 2000	White 2004	Black 2000	Black 2004	Asian/Pacific 2000	Asian/Pacific 2004	% Hispanic Origin 2000	% Hispanic Origin 2004	2004 AGE DISTRIBUTION (%) 0-4	5-9	10-14	15-19	20-24	25-44	45-64	65-84	85+	18+	MEDIAN AGE 2004	% 2004 Males	% 2004 Females
25820	CAMP CREEK	100.0	100.0	0.0	0.0	0.0	0.0	0.0	0.0	5.3	5.3	5.3	5.3	5.3	21.1	31.6	21.1	0.0	84.2	46.3	42.1	57.9
25823	COAL CITY	98.0	97.9	1.1	1.1	0.0	0.1	0.5	0.4	4.9	5.5	7.3	6.1	5.9	27.6	27.3	13.9	1.7	78.5	40.1	48.6	51.4
25825	COOL RIDGE	98.9	98.8	0.4	0.4	0.2	0.2	0.4	0.4	5.5	5.8	6.9	6.1	5.3	28.2	29.9	11.1	1.2	77.8	40.1	49.6	50.4
25827	CRAB ORCHARD	97.8	97.6	1.1	1.1	0.1	0.2	0.3	0.3	5.5	5.8	6.3	5.3	5.4	27.8	28.4	14.0	1.7	79.2	40.5	47.4	52.6
25831	DANESE	98.7	98.7	0.2	0.2	0.3	0.3	0.5	0.5	6.0	6.0	6.3	6.5	6.1	26.4	27.6	13.6	1.6	77.9	39.8	49.8	50.2
25832	DANIELS	89.6	89.0	9.1	9.3	0.7	0.9	2.2	2.2	4.7	4.8	4.5	4.5	6.1	33.6	24.8	14.0	3.1	83.0	39.4	55.2	44.8
25837	EDMOND	99.3	100.0	0.0	0.0	0.0	0.0	0.0	0.0	5.4	6.1	6.1	6.8	5.4	25.9	29.3	12.9	2.0	78.2	41.1	49.7	50.3
25839	FAIRDALE	99.4	99.4	0.0	0.0	0.0	0.0	0.6	0.6	5.5	6.1	6.1	5.8	6.1	26.7	30.7	11.4	1.5	78.5	40.4	49.1	50.9
25840	FAYETTEVILLE	96.4	96.3	2.6	2.7	0.1	0.1	0.6	0.6	5.5	5.8	6.3	6.2	6.1	25.5	28.6	14.2	1.9	78.6	41.4	49.1	50.9
25841	FLAT TOP	99.5	99.6	0.0	0.0	0.1	0.1	0.3	0.3	6.4	6.5	5.2	4.6	5.8	27.1	29.8	12.9	1.8	78.9	40.9	48.8	51.2
25843	GHENT	99.2	99.2	0.1	0.1	0.3	0.4	0.4	0.4	5.4	5.4	6.0	5.5	5.1	26.9	32.7	11.6	1.3	79.6	42.0	49.9	50.1
25844	GLEN DANIEL	96.7	96.6	2.6	2.6	0.0	0.0	0.5	0.5	5.9	6.1	6.2	6.0	6.4	26.8	30.0	11.0	1.5	78.2	39.6	49.8	50.2
25845	GLEN FORK	99.0	99.0	0.0	0.0	0.3	0.3	0.3	0.3	5.4	5.4	5.1	5.4	5.8	23.1	31.5	16.6	1.7	80.7	44.9	48.8	51.2
25847	GLEN MORGAN	95.1	95.0	3.4	3.3	0.5	0.6	0.8	0.9	5.9	5.8	5.4	5.0	5.6	26.6	29.3	14.7	1.7	79.9	41.9	48.4	51.6
25848	GLEN ROGERS	98.6	98.5	1.4	1.5	0.0	0.0	0.0	0.0	5.3	5.3	6.4	6.4	6.8	26.4	30.9	11.3	1.1	78.9	40.8	51.3	48.7
25854	HICO	99.3	99.3	0.1	0.2	0.0	0.0	0.9	0.9	5.4	5.7	5.9	5.0	5.9	25.2	30.3	14.9	1.8	80.2	42.5	49.7	50.3
25856	JONBEN	97.6	97.6	1.2	1.2	0.0	0.0	0.0	0.0	4.8	4.8	7.1	6.0	6.0	29.8	25.0	15.5	1.2	77.4	40.0	48.8	51.2
25857	JOSEPHINE	95.7	95.3	2.8	2.9	0.0	0.0	0.9	0.9	6.2	6.5	7.6	6.2	5.9	28.7	26.7	10.9	1.5	76.0	37.7	49.3	50.7
25862	LANSING	98.9	98.9	0.0	0.0	0.0	0.0	0.0	0.0	5.6	5.6	6.7	6.7	6.7	26.7	26.7	14.4	1.1	75.6	40.0	53.3	46.7
25864	LAYLAND	94.0	94.3	4.8	4.6	0.0	0.0	0.0	1.2	5.8	5.8	4.6	6.9	6.9	25.3	31.0	12.6	1.2	77.0	41.3	50.6	49.4
25865	LESTER	93.2	93.0	5.8	6.0	0.0	0.0	0.0	0.0	5.9	6.0	6.1	6.0	6.6	26.9	30.3	10.9	1.5	78.6	39.8	50.1	49.9
25868	LOOKOUT	99.3	99.7	0.0	0.0	0.0	0.0	0.7	0.4	5.3	5.6	6.0	6.0	6.0	25.0	30.3	14.1	1.8	79.6	42.1	50.0	50.0
25870	MABEN	96.7	96.8	2.2	2.3	0.3	0.3	0.3	0.3	5.2	5.5	6.4	5.5	5.8	24.4	29.3	16.2	1.7	79.4	42.9	49.3	50.7
25876	SAULSVILLE	98.4	98.5	1.4	1.5	0.0	0.0	0.0	0.2	5.1	5.6	6.6	6.4	6.7	26.1	31.5	11.1	1.0	79.3	40.9	51.0	49.0
25880	MOUNT HOPE	90.6	90.5	7.2	7.1	0.4	0.5	0.8	0.8	6.4	6.7	6.9	6.1	6.9	28.0	25.8	11.5	1.8	76.6	37.1	48.0	52.0
25882	MULLENS	96.3	96.1	2.6	2.7	0.2	0.3	0.4	0.4	5.4	5.4	5.4	5.4	5.8	24.3	28.3	17.7	2.4	80.4	43.6	49.1	50.9
25901	OAK HILL	92.3	92.2	5.8	5.9	0.3	0.3	0.9	0.9	5.7	5.8	6.2	5.9	6.2	26.4	26.9	14.8	2.3	78.7	40.9	48.3	51.7
25902	ODD	96.6	96.7	2.0	2.0	0.0	0.0	0.7	0.6	6.1	6.3	6.8	5.9	5.4	29.2	26.6	12.4	1.3	77.1	38.8	49.5	50.5
25908	PRINCEWICK	96.1	96.2	2.3	2.3	0.0	0.0	1.1	1.2	6.7	6.7	6.4	4.6	5.8	25.4	29.2	14.2	1.2	77.5	41.0	50.6	49.4
25913	RAVENCLIFF	98.5	98.4	0.5	0.5	0.1	0.1	0.3	0.3	6.6	6.6	6.5	6.3	6.2	27.0	29.3	10.6	1.0	76.5	38.7	49.6	50.4
25915	RHODELL	94.4	94.3	3.9	4.0	0.0	0.0	0.9	0.9	7.4	7.5	7.1	5.9	5.2	28.1	25.8	12.0	1.2	74.5	37.3	50.0	50.1
25917	SCARBRO	94.9	94.9	3.8	3.8	0.1	0.1	0.7	0.6	6.4	6.4	6.3	5.5	6.1	27.3	27.6	12.9	1.6	77.7	40.3	49.2	50.8
25918	SHADY SPRING	86.4	85.9	12.1	12.4	0.6	0.7	2.9	3.0	4.3	4.5	4.4	4.5	7.1	36.5	26.6	10.9	1.2	84.1	38.4	60.3	39.7
25920	SLAB FORK	97.7	97.6	1.5	1.4	0.1	0.1	0.2	0.1	5.6	5.7	6.0	6.3	5.9	28.9	29.0	11.4	1.2	78.9	39.6	49.6	50.4
25922	SPANISHBURG	99.0	98.9	0.2	0.2	0.1	0.1	0.3	0.3	6.5	6.4	6.3	5.8	7.1	29.5	25.8	11.1	1.4	77.3	37.1	50.5	49.6
25928	STEPHENSON	95.8	96.0	3.0	2.8	0.0	0.0	1.5	1.6	4.4	4.8	5.2	5.2	6.4	24.5	32.5	15.7	1.2	81.9	44.5	51.8	48.2
25932	SURVEYOR	92.7	92.3	6.4	6.4	0.0	0.0	0.3	0.3	5.8	5.8	6.1	5.5	6.4	26.7	30.7	11.4	1.5	79.1	40.2	50.3	49.7
25936	THURMOND	100.0	100.0	0.0	0.0	0.0	0.0	0.0	0.0	14.3	14.3	0.0	14.3	21.4	0.0	35.7	0.0	0.0	71.4	21.7	78.6	21.4
25938	VICTOR	98.0	98.0	1.4	1.4	0.0	0.0	0.5	0.5	5.5	5.7	6.4	5.7	6.5	26.4	26.9	14.2	2.6	78.9	40.7	49.0	51.0
25951	HINTON	95.8	95.6	2.7	2.7	0.2	0.3	0.5	0.6	4.6	4.9	5.9	5.4	5.9	23.1	27.7	19.0	3.6	81.4	45.2	47.9	52.1
25958	CHARMCO	96.6	96.5	1.6	1.6	0.2	0.2	0.5	0.5	5.6	5.6	6.2	5.6	6.4	24.2	27.2	16.2	3.0	79.7	42.3	50.1	49.9
25962	RAINELLE	97.6	97.3	0.8	0.8	0.1	0.1	0.7	0.7	5.1	5.3	5.8	5.3	5.5	22.6	29.2	18.4	2.7	80.7	45.2	48.2	51.9
25965	ELTON	99.0	99.0	0.0	0.0	0.0	0.0	0.5	1.0	3.4	4.4	5.4	4.9	5.9	23.4	31.2	19.5	2.0	83.9	46.7	52.2	47.8
25966	GREEN SULPHUR SPRING	98.5	98.3	0.2	0.2	0.2	0.2	0.9	0.9	3.8	4.2	5.3	5.2	6.1	23.2	31.8	18.6	1.8	83.3	46.4	51.5	48.5
25969	JUMPING BRANCH	99.2	99.1	0.1	0.1	0.0	0.0	0.2	0.2	4.9	5.3	5.6	4.6	5.6	25.7	31.3	14.6	2.4	80.9	43.8	49.9	50.1
25971	LERONA	99.0	99.2	0.4	0.4	0.0	0.0	0.8	0.6	4.8	5.4	6.4	5.0	5.6	26.5	28.6	15.9	1.9	79.7	42.8	48.7	51.4
25976	MEADOW BRIDGE	99.0	99.1	0.2	0.2	0.2	0.2	0.3	0.3	4.9	5.1	6.1	6.4	5.9	26.3	28.7	15.3	1.5	79.9	41.9	48.4	51.7
25977	MEADOW CREEK	99.0	99.0	0.0	0.0	0.0	0.0	0.5	0.5	3.7	3.7	5.8	4.7	6.3	22.6	31.6	20.0	1.6	83.7	46.9	51.6	48.4
25978	NIMITZ	99.3	99.3	0.0	0.0	0.0	0.0	0.2	0.2	5.0	5.5	5.3	4.2	5.5	25.7	31.4	15.0	2.3	81.1	44.1	49.6	50.4
25979	PIPESTEM	99.0	98.8	0.2	0.2	0.2	0.2	1.2	1.2	5.5	5.8	6.3	5.3	6.9	24.1	29.8	14.7	1.5	79.1	42.4	49.7	50.3
25981	QUINWOOD	95.3	95.1	2.5	2.6	0.1	0.1	0.6	0.6	5.9	5.9	5.6	5.9	5.3	24.3	28.9	16.6	1.7	78.9	43.1	49.9	50.2
25984	RUPERT	96.9	96.8	1.0	1.1	0.0	0.0	0.7	0.7	6.0	6.3	6.7	5.7	6.2	24.4	28.3	13.7	2.6	77.6	41.3	48.8	51.2
25985	SANDSTONE	97.6	97.5	0.5	0.5	0.0	0.0	1.0	1.0	4.0	4.5	4.5	5.8	5.8	22.8	33.8	17.3	1.5	83.5	46.5	51.4	48.6
25986	SPRING DALE	100.0	100.0	0.0	0.0	0.0	0.0	0.0	0.0	5.2	5.2	6.2	6.2	6.2	25.8	28.9	15.5	1.0	77.3	41.8	47.4	52.6
25989	WHITE OAK	94.6	94.5	4.8	4.7	0.2	0.2	1.1	1.1	5.7	5.9	6.1	5.7	5.5	31.3	27.9	10.8	1.1	78.7	38.7	53.7	46.3
26003	WHEELING	94.5	94.1	3.6	3.6	0.8	1.1	0.5	0.5	5.1	5.2	6.1	6.9	7.2	23.8	26.8	16.2	2.8	79.9	42.0	46.7	53.3
26031	BENWOOD	98.5	98.5	0.8	0.8	0.1	0.1	0.3	0.3	6.2	6.3	5.9	6.1	5.6	26.3	25.9	15.1	2.5	77.9	39.8	46.4	53.7
26032	BETHANY	95.9	96.0	2.1	2.1	1.2	1.2	0.5	0.6	3.8	3.1	3.9	18.0	27.7	16.1	19.1	7.2	1.0	87.0	23.8	51.3	48.7
26033	CAMERON	98.0	98.0	0.3	0.4	0.0	0.0	0.3	0.3	5.6	5.6	6.7	6.3	6.4	23.1	27.6	15.5	3.0	78.1	42.4	48.8	51.2
26034	CHESTER	98.9	98.8	0.1	0.1	0.4	0.5	0.9	0.9	5.7	5.8	6.2	5.5	5.4	26.2	27.7	15.2	2.3	79.0	41.8	48.1	51.9
26035	COLLIERS	98.5	98.5	0.4	0.4	0.3	0.3	0.6	0.6	4.7	5.1	6.4	5.7	5.3	26.8	31.3	13.8	1.1	80.4	42.6	50.2	49.8
26036	DALLAS	98.4	98.3	0.7	0.7	0.1	0.1	0.2	0.2	6.2	6.4	6.4	6.2	5.9	25.4	29.2	13.4	1.1	77.2	40.3	50.2	49.8
26037	FOLLANSBEE	98.8	98.7	0.3	0.3	0.2	0.2	0.4	0.4	5.2	5.5	6.0	5.5	5.6	25.0	28.0	16.6	2.7	79.9	43.1	47.2	52.8
26038	GLEN DALE	98.7	98.4	0.0	0.0	0.6	0.9	0.6	0.6	4.0	4.7	6.5	5.8	5.1	22.0	31.6	18.1	2.2	81.1	46.1	47.6	52.4
26039	GLEN EASTON	98.7	98.7	0.1	0.1	0.3	0.3	0.5	0.5	6.0	6.4	8.3	6.6	6.2	28.6	28.2	9.1	0.8	75.2	37.4	50.4	49.6
26040	MCMECHEN	98.6	98.4	0.4	0.4	0.1	0.2	0.4	0.4	4.1	4.6	6.1	6.0	5.7	22.9	28.2	20.0	2.4	81.3	45.4	47.3	52.7
26041	MOUNDSVILLE	98.3	98.2	0.5	0.5	0.3	0.4	0.9	0.9	5.3	5.6	6.3	5.9	5.5	26.4	28.0	14.9	2.1	79.1	41.7	48.8	51.2
26047	NEW CUMBERLAND	98.6	98.5	0.3	0.3	0.3	0.4	0.7	0.7	5.1	5.6	6.3	5.4	5.1	26.6	30.7	13.9	1.3	79.7	42.3	49.8	50.2
26050	NEWELL	98.8	98.7	0.2	0.2	0.0	0.1	0.7	0.7	6.6	6.6	6.5	5.5	6.5	26.1	27.1	13.9	1.3	77.0	38.6	49.2	50.8
26055	PROCTOR	98.8	98.7	0.2	0.2	0.1	0.1	0.4	0.4	5.1	6.4	7.2	6.5	4.9	28.1	28.9	11.7	1.3	77.1	40.4	51.9	48.1
26059	TRIADELPHIA	98.5	98.4	0.7	0.7	0.2	0.2	0.3	0.2	6.1	6.4	6.8	6.1	5.2	27.5	29.1	11.8	1.1	76.8	39.7	50.4	49.6
26060	VALLEY GROVE	98.4	98.2	0.9	0.9	0.2	0.2	0.4	0.4	5.7	5.8	5.9	7.7	9.6	27.1	26.5	10.8	1.0	79.1	36.5	50.7	49.3
26062	WEIRTON	94.7	94.5	3.7	3.8	0.6	0.7	0.7	0.7	4.9	5.1	5.5	5.2	5.0	25.0	27.4	19.0	3.0	81.4	44.6	47.3	52.7
26070	WELLSBURG	98.0	98.1	0.9	0.8	0.2	0.2	0.3	0.3	5.0	5.4	6.1	5.9	6.3	25.0	28.3	15.9	2.2	80.2	42.4	48.5	51.5
26101	PARKERSBURG	96.6	96.6	1.5	1.6	0.4	0.4	0.7	0.7	6.2	5.9	6.1	6.2	6.5	27.1	25.5	14.2	2.3	78.1	39.6	47.6	52.4
26104	PARKERSBURG	97.3	97.3	1.1	1.1	0.7	0.7	0.6	0.6	5.4	5.5	6.0	5.6	5.5	26.1	27.2	15.8	3.0	79.8	42.1	47.3	52.8
26105	VIENNA	96.7	96.6	1.0	1.0	1.4	1.5	0.5	0.5	5.1	5.5	6.5	5.6	5.6	24.5	28.0	16.7	2.5	79.5	43.1	47.0	53.0
26133	BELLEVILLE	98.8	98.7	0.0	0.0	0.1	0.1	0.8	0.8	5.1	5.4	6.9	7.1	6.3	27.2	29.8	11.3	0.9	78.5	40.5	50.5	49.5
26134	BELMONT	98.7	98.5	0.3	0.3	0.2	0.2	0.5	0.5	6.3	6.5	6.8	5.5	6.2	25.5	26.9	13.9	2.4	77.1	39.8	46.9	53.1
26136	BIG BEND	98.7	98.7	0.0	0.0	0.1	0.1	0.4	0.4	4.9	4.7	4.9	6.4	7.4	25.1	30.9	14.2	1.6	82.2	43.0	49.0	51.0
26137	BIG SPRINGS	99.1	98.9	0.0	0.0	0.3	0.3	0.3	0.2	5.9	5.6	5.3	4.9	6.4	26.1	28.7	15.4	1.7	80.4	42.2	49.4	50.6
26138	BROHARD	100.0	100.0	0.0	0.0	0.0	0.0	0.0	0.0	0.0	0.0	0.0	0.0	33.3	66.7	0.0	0.0	0.0	100.0	27.5	50.0	50.0
26141	CRESTON	98.6	98.9	0.0	0.0	0.3	0.3	0.3	0.3	5.0	4.4	5.8	6.9	6.9	23.9	29.1	15.7	2.5	80.5	43.3	49.2	50.8
26142	DAVISVILLE	98.7	98.5	0.5	0.6	0.1	0.1	0.8	0.8	6.8	7.2	8.5	6.7	6.0	31.5	24.4	8.4	0.6	73.3	34.8	49.7	50.3
26143	ELIZABETH	98.7	98.7	0.2	0.2	0.0	0.0	0.2	0.2	6.1	6.4	7.2	6.5	5.9	27.7	26.2	12.5	1.5	76.1	39.2	50.4	49.6
26146	FRIENDLY	99.2	99.1	0.0	0.0	0.1	0.1	0.4	0.4	6.2	6.4	6.1	5.9	4.6	27.1	28.9	13.4	1.5	77.7	40.7	47.9	52.1
26147	GRANTSVILLE	98.9	98.9	0.1	0.1	0.2	0.2	0.5	0.5	4.8	4.7	5.6	6.4	7.1	23.4	29.4	15.9	2.6	81.0	43.6	49.8	50.2
26148	MACFARLAN	98.9	98.9	0.2	0.2	0.0	0.0	0.4	0.2	4.3	4.8	6.5	6.9	5.6	24.5	30.1	15.4	2.0	79.9	43.5	51.3	48.7
26149	MIDDLEBOURNE	99.4	99.4	0.0	0.0	0.0	0.0	0.4	0.4	4.6	5.1	6.5	6.7	5.8	25.3	31.1	13.2	1.8	79.3	42.2	49.3	50.7
26150	MINERAL WELLS	98.7	98.7	0.3	0.3	0.2	0.2	0.4	0.3	6.5	6.8	7.4	6.2	6.0	28.6	28.2	9.6	0.7	75.5	38.2	49.5	50.5
26151	MOUNT ZION	98.7	99.1	0.0	0.0	0.0	0.0	0.9	0.4	4.8	4.8	5.7	6.5	6.5	23.0	30.4	15.2	3.0	80.4	44.1	48.7	51.3
26152	MUNDAY	98.1	98.8	0.6	0.6	0.0	0.0	0.0	0.6	5.5	6.1	6.7	6.1	5.5	27.3	28.5	12.7	1.8	77.6	40.2	52.1	47.9
26155	NEW MARTINSVILLE	98.6	98.3	0.1	0.1	0.7	1.0	0.5	0.5	5.6	5.8	6.3	6.3	5.5	23.9	28.3	15.7	2.6	78.4	42.8	47.8	52.2
26159	PADEN CITY	99.2	99.1	0.2	0.2	0.2	0.2	0.5	0.5	5.8	6.5	5.9	6.0	5.8	23.9	27.2	17.1	2.0	77.8	42.3	48.3	51.8
26160	PALESTINE	98.7	98.7	0.1	0.1	0.3	0.3	0.2	0.3	4.9	4.6	6.2	6.9	6.4	25.0	29.3	14.9	1.9	79.5	42.7	50.0	50.0
	WEST VIRGINIA	95.1	94.8	3.2	3.2	0.5	0.7	0.7	0.7	5.6	5.8	6.2	6.3	6.7	26.7	27.1	13.7	1.9	78.9	40.1	48.8	51.2
	UNITED STATES	75.1	73.6	12.3	12.5	3.8	4.2	12.5	14.1	6.9	6.7	7.2	7.0	7.3	28.6	23.8	10.8	1.7	75.1	36.0	49.1	50.9

WEST VIRGINIA

INCOME

C 25820-26160

#	POST OFFICE NAME	2004 Per Capita Income	2004 HH Income Base	2004 Household Income Distribution (%): Less than $25,000	$25,000 to $49,999	$50,000 to $99,999	$100,000 to $149,999	$150,000 or More	Median Household Income: 2004	2009	2004 National Centile	2004 State Centile	2004 Home Value Base	2004 Home Value Distribution (%): Less than $50,000	$50,000 to $89,999	$90,000 to $174,999	$175,000 to $399,999	$400,000 or More	2004 Median Home Value
25820	CAMP CREEK	14503	15	40.0	26.7	33.3	0.0	0.0	37333	47351	37	84	13	23.1	30.8	30.8	15.4	0.0	85000
25823	COAL CITY	13381	421	44.9	39.9	13.5	1.7	0.0	28290	32865	9	42	355	42.5	36.6	18.9	1.4	0.6	58281
25825	COOL RIDGE	14777	730	41.8	33.3	19.5	4.4	1.1	29633	34265	11	51	621	34.5	29.2	23.4	11.3	1.8	69762
25827	CRAB ORCHARD	19558	2155	43.8	27.9	24.4	2.1	1.9	29054	33855	10	47	1703	39.0	35.9	23.0	1.8	0.3	61054
25831	DANESE	11972	580	51.4	31.9	15.7	1.0	0.0	24110	26941	4	18	488	51.8	25.0	19.1	4.1	0.0	48364
25832	DANIELS	25427	1522	35.7	31.3	24.0	3.8	5.1	33881	39448	24	73	1215	26.3	25.3	34.9	11.2	2.3	88088
25837	EDMOND	14423	64	53.1	28.1	17.2	1.6	0.0	23341	26862	3	15	54	42.6	29.6	25.9	1.9	0.0	60000
25839	FAIRDALE	24752	129	28.7	31.8	29.5	7.0	3.1	39759	46559	45	90	111	25.2	31.5	34.2	8.1	0.9	81667
25840	FAYETTEVILLE	18537	3166	41.7	28.2	23.6	4.6	1.9	30336	34509	13	54	2578	32.1	32.2	26.1	9.4	0.2	70427
25841	FLAT TOP	19806	304	43.4	18.8	32.6	4.3	1.0	33225	34785	22	71	263	28.9	20.5	32.7	17.5	0.4	90682
25843	GHENT	21654	422	31.0	31.5	27.7	5.7	4.0	41208	50196	50	93	377	21.0	20.2	38.7	18.6	1.6	103084
25844	GLEN DANIEL	21098	900	35.3	29.1	27.7	5.2	2.7	36513	42045	34	82	757	32.4	32.6	27.6	6.6	0.8	71583
25845	GLEN FORK	16076	129	41.1	35.7	17.8	4.7	0.8	28372	33363	9	43	104	43.3	32.7	20.2	3.9	0.0	55385
25847	GLEN MORGAN	16691	1081	41.5	29.5	24.3	4.2	0.5	29109	34023	11	47	850	41.1	37.1	18.7	2.9	0.2	60370
25848	GLEN ROGERS	14677	106	49.1	24.5	24.5	0.9	0.9	25621	30446	5	26	89	51.7	30.3	14.6	1.1	2.3	48125
25854	HICO	16642	283	40.3	27.2	27.6	5.0	0.0	30309	34874	13	54	243	44.0	28.4	22.2	5.4	0.0	63000
25856	JONBEN	12432	32	43.8	37.5	15.6	3.1	0.0	30000	33618	12	52	27	44.4	33.3	22.2	0.0	0.0	55000
25857	JOSEPHINE	10248	134	57.5	31.3	10.5	0.8	0.0	20699	24023	2	6	108	66.7	25.0	5.6	1.9	0.9	25000
25862	LANSING	16833	38	50.0	31.6	15.8	0.0	2.6	25000	32308	5	22	31	35.5	35.5	22.6	6.5	0.0	62500
25864	LAYLAND	12361	33	45.5	36.4	18.2	0.0	0.0	27273	33622	8	34	27	48.2	33.3	18.5	0.0	0.0	52500
25865	LESTER	17381	400	43.8	25.8	26.3	3.3	1.0	29384	34335	11	50	327	39.8	33.9	24.2	1.8	0.3	64861
25868	LOOKOUT	14861	116	48.3	26.7	22.4	2.6	0.0	25862	30482	6	27	98	48.0	26.5	20.4	5.1	0.0	54000
25870	MABEN	16350	139	45.3	29.5	19.4	2.9	2.9	27747	34299	8	38	115	53.0	29.6	14.8	1.7	0.9	47308
25876	SAULSVILLE	15133	246	49.6	24.0	24.4	1.2	0.8	25288	30000	5	23	207	52.7	30.0	13.5	1.9	1.9	47105
25880	MOUNT HOPE	16600	3239	44.8	29.7	20.6	3.3	1.5	28132	32274	9	41	2378	44.0	31.0	21.5	2.7	0.9	57010
25882	MULLENS	18860	1052	44.5	28.3	20.6	3.8	2.8	28962	34791	10	46	815	52.6	36.0	10.2	1.0	0.3	48162
25901	OAK HILL	15456	6331	47.5	30.1	18.2	2.8	1.4	26559	30537	7	31	4665	38.6	35.8	22.0	3.1	0.5	61188
25902	ODD	10474	208	56.7	29.3	12.0	1.9	0.0	20945	23741	2	7	169	69.8	20.1	4.1	5.9	0.0	29500
25908	PRINCEWICK	15177	150	51.3	23.3	20.7	4.7	0.0	24290	27668	4	19	124	59.7	30.7	9.7	0.0	0.0	40000
25913	RAVENCLIFF	14767	519	46.8	30.1	19.5	2.3	1.4	26480	30930	6	30	431	49.2	29.5	18.6	2.3	0.5	51061
25915	RHODELL	8812	420	64.3	27.4	7.4	1.0	0.0	18182	20712	1	3	338	84.3	11.8	1.5	2.4	0.0	19333
25917	SCARBRO	13284	606	49.3	29.2	19.1	2.0	0.3	25324	28449	5	24	483	52.0	29.6	15.9	1.9	0.6	48956
25918	SHADY SPRING	21166	1866	39.7	27.8	24.3	5.2	3.1	31928	36833	18	65	1584	25.1	26.6	34.3	10.9	3.2	87672
25920	SLAB FORK	15618	327	44.0	27.8	24.5	3.7	0.0	29132	33976	11	48	267	37.1	31.5	29.6	1.1	0.8	67031
25922	SPANISHBURG	15424	435	44.8	32.6	19.1	3.0	0.5	28225	32236	9	41	374	40.9	27.5	24.6	6.4	0.5	65385
25928	STEPHENSON	19502	103	52.4	17.5	17.5	9.7	2.9	23666	26679	4	16	82	67.1	23.2	7.3	2.4	0.0	39000
25932	SURVEYOR	17149	143	45.5	28.0	23.1	2.8	0.7	28453	33821	9	43	118	42.4	33.1	22.9	1.7	0.0	63000
25936	THURMOND	13036	9	66.7	22.2	11.1	0.0	0.0	17182	22222	1	2	7	57.1	42.9	0.0	0.0	0.0	45000
25938	VICTOR	16900	948	40.6	33.4	20.2	4.3	1.5	30604	34664	14	57	787	44.0	33.0	20.3	2.4	0.3	58190
25951	HINTON	15027	2564	52.5	28.4	15.1	2.7	1.3	23538	27054	4	16	1899	35.6	33.1	24.5	6.4	0.5	68107
25958	CHARMCO	15637	264	46.2	29.9	20.5	1.1	2.3	28422	32343	9	43	202	38.6	36.6	22.3	2.5	0.0	67368
25962	RAINELLE	16898	1629	48.5	32.0	15.2	2.5	1.9	25883	29419	6	27	1266	45.7	29.2	21.5	3.3	0.3	55000
25965	ELTON	11757	82	48.8	37.8	9.8	3.7	0.0	25407	27581	5	24	68	47.1	32.4	17.7	2.9	0.0	55000
25966	GREEN SULPHUR SPRING	12421	292	52.1	35.3	10.3	2.4	0.0	23748	26351	4	17	243	46.1	33.3	17.3	3.3	0.0	55938
25969	JUMPING BRANCH	16588	472	43.2	25.4	25.0	4.9	1.5	28855	32238	10	46	402	33.3	24.1	34.6	6.5	1.5	80625
25971	LERONA	16468	188	39.9	28.7	25.5	4.3	1.6	35368	39086	29	78	158	32.9	27.2	27.2	12.7	0.0	79333
25976	MEADOW BRIDGE	13844	714	45.2	36.3	16.4	2.1	0.0	27775	31456	8	38	611	46.5	20.6	25.4	7.5	0.0	54778
25977	MEADOW CREEK	13216	85	49.4	36.5	10.6	3.5	0.0	25202	27907	5	23	70	47.1	34.3	15.7	2.9	0.0	55000
25978	NIMITZ	16200	245	44.1	24.1	25.7	4.9	1.2	28449	31665	9	43	208	35.6	20.7	35.6	6.7	1.4	80714
25979	PIPESTEM	14088	247	47.4	33.6	17.8	1.2	0.0	26363	30226	6	29	206	31.6	30.6	28.6	9.2	0.0	70714
25981	QUINWOOD	11771	684	54.2	33.9	10.2	1.2	0.4	22546	25754	3	12	565	59.5	26.6	12.2	1.8	0.0	42357
25984	RUPERT	12820	594	50.3	34.0	13.6	1.7	0.3	24806	27802	4	20	458	45.4	36.5	14.4	3.5	0.2	54667
25985	SANDSTONE	11338	183	60.1	29.0	9.8	1.1	0.0	18432	20298	1	3	154	42.2	33.8	19.5	4.6	0.0	59231
25986	SPRING DALE	14958	43	48.8	32.6	16.3	2.3	0.0	25725	29054	5	26	37	48.7	21.6	24.3	5.4	0.0	51667
25989	WHITE OAK	17119	192	41.7	30.7	20.8	5.2	1.6	28840	33599	10	45	163	31.3	28.2	26.4	11.7	2.5	73750
26003	WHEELING	20941	19169	37.4	28.1	25.4	5.9	3.2	35384	41834	29	78	13672	25.4	36.0	29.2	8.2	1.2	77978
26031	BENWOOD	17956	1026	43.5	26.6	26.0	3.2	0.7	28899	33463	10	46	735	45.7	32.8	20.4	0.8	0.3	53000
26032	BETHANY	13666	231	28.1	33.3	28.1	7.4	3.0	37621	43262	38	86	173	13.3	30.6	54.9	1.2	0.0	94565
26033	CAMERON	15515	1031	41.3	30.2	24.7	3.6	0.2	31601	36823	17	63	789	53.0	30.8	14.3	1.1	0.8	46867
26034	CHESTER	18714	2414	34.3	34.4	26.4	3.1	1.8	34934	39782	27	76	1913	32.2	37.1	26.0	4.3	0.4	70304
26035	COLLIERS	18958	892	29.2	34.2	29.2	6.2	1.4	39104	44283	43	89	770	29.4	26.8	38.7	4.8	0.4	80962
26036	DALLAS	17455	334	28.7	37.1	28.4	4.5	1.2	37068	43167	36	84	277	26.4	32.5	36.8	4.0	0.4	80926
26037	FOLLANSBEE	18994	3090	31.9	35.1	26.7	5.0	1.4	37566	42910	38	85	2408	28.1	34.3	31.8	5.4	0.5	78255
26038	GLEN DALE	26800	1360	22.4	29.9	31.3	12.1	4.4	47788	55464	68	97	1183	13.6	33.4	41.4	10.4	1.2	93060
26039	GLEN EASTON	19444	803	28.6	25.5	38.4	5.5	2.0	44458	51043	60	96	686	31.9	36.7	26.1	5.0	0.3	70820
26040	MCMECHEN	17770	841	42.2	31.8	22.6	2.5	1.0	30385	35444	13	55	616	54.4	38.2	6.8	0.7	0.0	48043
26041	MOUNDSVILLE	18233	7051	40.2	29.2	24.2	4.6	1.9	31864	37407	17	65	5341	35.7	40.9	20.3	2.8	0.2	63287
26047	NEW CUMBERLAND	20841	2691	27.9	36.8	28.2	5.2	1.9	39407	44882	44	89	2289	27.4	31.0	34.3	5.9	1.4	81244
26050	NEWELL	15917	1000	38.4	34.7	24.0	2.3	0.6	32107	35566	18	67	727	54.2	28.8	16.0	1.1	0.0	47123
26055	PROCTOR	20037	636	32.2	27.0	30.7	7.4	2.7	41819	47922	52	94	555	28.3	35.1	29.6	6.1	0.9	75278
26059	TRIADELPHIA	20967	1018	30.2	30.6	31.4	4.7	3.1	40638	47110	48	92	856	34.8	32.1	25.0	7.2	0.8	68955
26060	VALLEY GROVE	19438	667	31.5	32.5	29.1	4.5	2.4	38939	45363	43	88	544	34.2	34.7	23.5	6.4	1.1	68889
26062	WEIRTON	22187	9257	30.8	32.5	28.7	6.0	2.1	39468	44995	44	89	7037	16.5	40.8	35.6	6.5	0.5	83783
26070	WELLSBURG	20438	4498	33.0	33.6	26.1	4.4	2.9	35455	40080	29	79	3577	31.4	34.7	30.3	3.4	0.3	68971
26101	PARKERSBURG	18291	13313	41.4	30.5	21.9	5.0	1.3	30716	35675	14	58	8830	25.6	40.1	30.0	4.2	0.3	73451
26104	PARKERSBURG	21510	7654	32.4	31.6	26.7	6.9	2.5	37541	43698	38	85	5692	18.1	33.8	36.5	11.0	0.7	88076
26105	VIENNA	28420	5315	27.2	30.0	26.3	10.4	6.3	43621	51243	58	95	4209	10.7	32.9	39.4	13.5	3.5	96771
26133	BELLEVILLE	16411	450	31.8	37.1	25.3	5.1	0.7	36187	41630	32	82	403	24.1	32.0	30.8	13.2	0.0	83875
26134	BELMONT	19410	613	35.4	31.3	25.0	6.2	2.1	37026	40735	36	84	475	25.5	24.2	44.6	5.5	0.2	90357
26136	BIG BEND	12811	340	54.1	24.7	20.0	1.2	0.0	22170	25309	3	11	269	50.2	41.3	6.7	1.9	0.0	49886
26137	BIG SPRINGS	14218	267	44.9	30.7	21.4	3.0	0.0	27470	32076	8	36	215	38.1	21.9	36.7	3.3	0.0	67083
26138	BROHARD	0	0	0.0	0.0	0.0	0.0	0.0	0	0	0	0	3	0.0	0.0	100.0	0.0	0.0	112500
26141	CRESTON	14578	148	46.6	31.1	19.6	2.7	0.0	27302	31217	8	35	121	40.5	36.4	17.4	3.3	2.5	61364
26142	DAVISVILLE	16594	1023	23.9	42.7	28.5	4.3	0.7	37908	45347	39	86	862	30.3	39.2	21.8	8.2	0.5	61620
26143	ELIZABETH	16194	1353	36.5	37.5	21.4	3.2	1.4	32708	35931	20	69	1110	35.8	30.9	28.6	4.8	0.0	70482
26146	FRIENDLY	17751	395	35.2	31.4	27.9	4.6	1.0	35408	40000	29	78	341	36.4	31.7	25.8	5.9	0.3	70893
26147	GRANTSVILLE	14385	723	51.9	23.4	22.3	1.9	0.6	23521	26826	4	16	554	50.7	28.7	18.2	1.3	1.1	49467
26148	MACFARLAN	15792	193	43.5	33.7	18.1	2.1	2.6	30551	34237	14	56	163	46.0	22.7	23.3	6.1	1.8	56500
26149	MIDDLEBOURNE	17009	1099	36.5	34.1	23.7	5.0	0.7	31913	36732	18	65	926	27.5	34.2	31.1	6.5	0.7	79176
26150	MINERAL WELLS	20790	2383	21.1	38.3	29.6	9.0	2.0	42649	49125	55	94	2049	20.9	26.7	33.4	16.7	2.4	92360
26151	MOUNT ZION	16766	105	48.6	26.7	20.0	3.8	1.0	25814	29061	6	27	82	48.8	28.1	17.1	2.4	3.7	52000
26152	MUNDAY	13848	66	39.4	39.4	18.2	3.0	0.0	31245	34518	16	62	57	40.4	24.6	33.3	1.8	0.0	66250
26155	NEW MARTINSVILLE	21681	2918	35.6	26.1	28.4	6.4	3.4	38625	44924	42	87	2209	23.6	28.3	39.6	8.5	0.0	87798
26159	PADEN CITY	20114	1396	35.6	32.5	26.4	4.7	0.9	35673	40832	30	79	1140	27.6	40.6	29.3	2.5	0.0	74222
26160	PALESTINE	14957	368	36.7	39.4	20.1	3.8	0.0	34132	36540	24	74	322	27.0	39.8	24.5	4.7	4.0	75405
	WEST VIRGINIA	19262		38.4	30.0	24.1	5.2	2.4	33458	38993				29.0	29.1	31.1	9.6	1.3	80023
	UNITED STATES	25866		24.7	27.1	30.8	10.9	6.5	48124	56710				10.9	15.0	33.7	30.1	10.4	145905

ZIP CODE #	POST OFFICE NAME	FINANCIAL SERVICES: Auto Loan	FINANCIAL SERVICES: Home Loan	FINANCIAL SERVICES: Investments	FINANCIAL SERVICES: Retirement Plans	THE HOME: Home Improvements: Home Repair	THE HOME: Home Improvements: Lawn & Garden	THE HOME: Furnishings: Computers & Hardware	THE HOME: Furnishings: Major Appliances	THE HOME: Furnishings: TV, Radio, Sound Equipment	THE HOME: Furnishings: Furniture	ENTERTAINMENT: Dine out/Carry out	ENTERTAINMENT: Sports Equipment	ENTERTAINMENT: Fees & Tickets	ENTERTAINMENT: Toys & Games	ENTERTAINMENT: Travel	ENTERTAINMENT: Cable TV	PERSONAL: Apparel & Services	PERSONAL: Auto Repairs	PERSONAL: Health Insurance	PERSONAL: Pets & Supplies
25820	CAMP CREEK	63	48	31	43	53	61	46	55	53	46	63	64	41	61	48	56	58	55	66	74
25823	COAL CITY	56	40	24	37	44	52	42	49	49	41	57	56	37	54	42	52	52	48	59	62
25825	COOL RIDGE	70	49	25	42	55	63	47	58	55	47	65	69	40	62	48	59	59	57	70	81
25827	CRAB ORCHARD	78	56	33	52	62	73	58	67	66	57	78	78	51	75	58	71	72	67	81	88
25831	DANESE	55	37	17	32	42	48	36	45	43	36	51	53	30	48	36	46	46	44	55	63
25832	DANIELS	82	72	68	73	76	85	77	80	80	75	97	92	73	93	76	81	91	80	86	92
25837	EDMOND	62	42	19	36	47	54	40	50	49	41	57	60	34	54	41	52	52	50	62	72
25839	FAIRDALE	118	79	36	68	89	103	76	95	92	78	108	114	65	102	77	99	98	94	117	135
25840	FAYETTEVILLE	72	57	41	54	62	72	60	66	66	58	79	75	55	76	60	70	73	66	77	81
25841	FLAT TOP	81	63	43	57	71	80	61	72	69	60	81	84	54	80	64	73	75	71	86	97
25843	GHENT	86	67	44	60	75	84	63	76	72	62	85	89	56	83	67	77	79	75	90	104
25844	GLEN DANIEL	101	68	31	58	77	88	65	82	79	67	93	98	56	88	66	85	84	81	101	116
25845	GLEN FORK	59	45	29	43	49	58	49	54	55	47	65	61	44	61	49	58	59	54	65	65
25847	GLEN MORGAN	70	50	27	45	55	65	51	60	59	50	70	70	45	66	51	63	64	60	73	79
25848	GLEN ROGERS	69	46	21	40	52	60	45	56	54	45	63	67	38	60	45	58	58	55	69	79
25854	HICO	64	50	35	49	54	63	54	59	59	52	71	66	49	68	53	62	65	58	68	71
25856	JONBEN	55	40	24	37	44	52	43	49	49	41	57	56	38	54	43	52	52	48	59	62
25857	JOSEPHINE	49	33	15	28	37	43	32	40	38	32	45	47	27	43	32	41	41	39	49	56
25862	LANSING	64	48	32	46	53	63	54	59	60	51	71	66	48	67	53	63	64	59	71	71
25864	LAYLAND	61	41	19	35	47	54	40	50	48	40	56	59	34	53	40	52	51	49	61	70
25865	LESTER	77	52	23	44	58	67	50	62	60	51	70	74	42	67	51	65	64	62	77	88
25868	LOOKOUT	64	45	24	41	50	59	46	55	54	46	63	64	40	60	46	58	58	54	67	73
25870	MABEN	69	50	29	46	55	65	53	60	60	51	71	69	46	67	53	64	65	60	73	77
25876	SAULSVILLE	69	46	21	40	52	60	45	56	54	45	63	66	38	60	45	58	57	55	68	79
25880	MOUNT HOPE	66	53	39	51	56	64	56	60	61	54	73	69	52	70	55	63	68	60	68	73
25882	MULLENS	68	51	34	49	56	67	57	62	63	54	75	70	50	70	56	67	68	62	75	75
25901	OAK HILL	59	44	29	42	48	58	49	54	55	46	64	60	43	61	48	58	59	54	64	65
25902	ODD	51	34	16	30	39	45	33	41	40	34	47	49	28	44	34	43	43	41	51	58
25908	PRINCEWICK	66	44	20	38	50	58	43	53	51	43	60	64	36	57	43	55	55	53	66	76
25913	RAVENCLIFF	71	49	24	43	55	63	48	59	57	48	67	69	42	64	49	61	61	58	72	80
25915	RHODELL	43	29	13	25	33	38	28	35	34	28	39	41	24	37	28	36	36	34	43	49
25917	SCARBRO	56	40	24	38	45	53	43	49	49	42	58	56	38	55	43	52	53	49	59	62
25918	SHADY SPRING	80	58	35	54	64	76	62	70	70	60	83	80	54	78	61	75	76	70	85	90
25920	SLAB FORK	72	48	22	42	55	63	47	58	56	48	66	70	40	63	48	61	60	58	72	83
25922	SPANISHBURG	72	50	26	44	56	65	49	60	59	50	69	71	43	65	50	63	63	60	73	83
25928	STEPHENSON	76	57	38	55	63	75	63	70	71	60	83	78	56	79	63	75	76	70	83	84
25932	SURVEYOR	71	49	25	43	55	64	49	59	58	49	68	69	42	64	49	62	62	59	72	80
25936	THURMOND	38	26	12	22	29	33	25	31	30	25	35	37	21	33	25	32	32	31	38	44
25938	VICTOR	72	53	33	50	58	68	55	63	62	54	74	73	49	71	55	65	68	62	74	81
25951	HINTON	52	41	35	38	44	51	44	48	49	43	59	55	40	56	44	52	55	49	56	59
25958	CHARMCO	59	44	29	43	48	58	49	54	55	47	65	60	44	61	49	58	59	54	65	65
25962	RAINELLE	65	47	29	44	52	62	51	57	58	49	68	65	45	64	51	61	62	57	69	72
25965	ELTON	48	36	23	34	39	47	39	43	44	37	52	49	35	49	39	47	47	43	52	53
25966	GREEN SULPHUR SPRING	47	34	21	32	38	45	37	42	42	36	49	48	32	47	37	45	45	42	50	53
25969	JUMPING BRANCH	74	50	23	43	56	65	48	60	58	49	68	72	41	64	49	62	62	59	74	85
25971	LERONA	78	54	26	47	61	69	51	64	61	52	72	76	44	69	53	66	66	63	78	90
25976	MEADOW BRIDGE	62	42	19	36	47	54	40	50	48	41	57	60	34	54	41	52	52	50	62	71
25977	MEADOW CREEK	48	36	24	34	39	47	40	44	44	38	52	49	35	49	39	47	48	44	52	53
25978	NIMITZ	74	50	23	43	56	65	48	60	58	49	68	72	41	64	49	62	62	59	74	85
25979	PIPESTEM	54	40	27	39	44	53	45	49	50	42	59	55	40	56	44	53	54	49	59	59
25981	QUINWOOD	49	35	20	32	39	45	36	42	42	35	49	49	32	47	36	45	45	42	51	55
25984	RUPERT	52	38	23	35	42	49	40	46	46	39	54	52	36	51	40	49	49	46	55	58
25985	SANDSTONE	46	31	15	27	35	41	30	38	36	31	43	45	26	40	31	39	39	37	46	53
25986	SPRING DALE	63	43	19	37	48	55	41	51	50	42	58	61	35	55	42	53	53	51	63	73
25989	WHITE OAK	73	51	26	45	57	66	51	62	60	51	71	72	44	67	52	65	65	61	75	83
26003	WHEELING	68	65	68	64	66	74	68	68	70	66	86	78	67	86	68	72	83	69	73	78
26031	BENWOOD	64	54	45	52	56	64	57	60	62	55	74	69	54	73	57	63	70	60	67	72
26032	BETHANY	67	76	94	79	75	77	76	73	72	75	91	87	78	93	76	69	90	74	66	80
26033	CAMERON	66	47	26	43	52	62	49	57	56	48	66	66	43	63	49	60	60	57	69	75
26034	CHESTER	69	61	49	56	64	71	59	64	64	58	78	74	57	80	60	67	73	63	73	80
26035	COLLIERS	87	61	32	54	69	78	59	72	69	60	82	86	52	78	60	74	75	71	87	100
26036	DALLAS	77	55	32	51	62	73	58	67	67	57	79	77	51	74	58	71	72	67	82	87
26037	FOLLANSBEE	67	60	51	56	63	71	60	64	65	58	79	73	59	80	61	68	74	63	72	77
26038	GLEN DALE	87	92	91	87	93	101	86	89	88	85	108	102	89	112	89	90	105	87	93	103
26039	GLEN EASTON	89	72	50	67	78	86	68	78	75	68	90	93	63	90	70	79	84	77	89	104
26040	MCMECHEN	56	52	48	50	54	62	53	56	56	52	68	62	52	68	54	58	64	55	62	64
26041	MOUNDSVILLE	66	58	50	55	61	69	59	63	64	58	77	72	58	78	60	66	73	63	71	75
26047	NEW CUMBERLAND	79	68	52	64	72	80	66	72	71	65	86	85	63	87	67	73	81	71	80	91
26050	NEWELL	61	51	39	47	54	60	50	55	55	50	66	64	47	66	51	57	62	54	62	69
26055	PROCTOR	90	70	44	64	77	85	66	78	75	67	89	93	61	88	68	78	83	76	90	105
26059	TRIADELPHIA	75	70	61	67	73	81	69	72	73	67	89	83	69	92	70	75	85	71	79	86
26060	VALLEY GROVE	69	64	62	63	66	73	67	68	70	65	86	79	66	87	67	70	82	68	71	79
26062	WEIRTON	66	69	71	66	70	78	68	69	70	67	87	78	70	90	70	73	84	68	74	77
26070	WELLSBURG	77	65	49	61	69	78	65	71	71	63	85	82	62	84	66	74	80	70	80	88
26101	PARKERSBURG	61	55	51	52	57	65	58	59	62	56	75	68	56	75	58	64	71	60	66	69
26104	PARKERSBURG	75	65	53	62	69	78	66	71	71	64	86	81	63	85	67	74	81	70	80	85
26105	VIENNA	89	91	90	88	93	102	89	92	90	87	111	104	90	112	91	93	107	90	97	104
26133	BELLEVILLE	82	55	25	47	62	72	53	66	64	54	75	79	45	71	54	69	68	66	82	94
26134	BELMONT	79	62	43	59	67	78	66	72	73	63	86	82	60	83	66	76	79	72	85	89
26136	BIG BEND	58	39	18	34	44	51	38	47	46	39	54	56	32	51	39	49	49	47	58	67
26137	BIG SPRINGS	58	45	30	41	50	57	45	52	51	44	60	60	41	58	47	54	56	52	62	68
26138	BROHARD	0	0	0	0	0	0	0	0	0	0	0	0	0	0	0	0	0	0	0	0
26141	CRESTON	61	45	28	42	51	59	46	54	52	45	62	62	41	59	47	56	57	53	64	70
26142	DAVISVILLE	67	65	59	63	66	69	63	65	64	63	79	77	62	80	63	64	76	65	66	77
26143	ELIZABETH	73	52	29	47	57	66	51	61	59	51	70	72	45	67	52	63	64	60	73	83
26146	FRIENDLY	82	56	27	49	64	73	54	67	65	55	76	80	46	72	55	70	69	67	83	95
26147	GRANTSVILLE	55	41	26	39	45	54	45	50	51	43	60	56	40	56	45	54	54	50	60	61
26148	MACFARLAN	71	48	22	41	54	62	46	58	56	47	65	69	39	62	47	60	59	57	71	82
26149	MIDDLEBOURNE	78	53	25	46	60	69	51	64	61	52	72	76	44	68	52	66	66	63	78	90
26150	MINERAL WELLS	88	74	53	70	79	86	70	79	75	70	91	93	66	91	71	78	86	77	87	103
26151	MOUNT ZION	62	45	27	42	50	59	48	55	55	46	64	62	42	61	47	58	58	54	66	70
26152	MUNDAY	65	44	20	38	49	57	42	53	51	43	60	63	36	56	43	55	54	52	65	75
26155	NEW MARTINSVILLE	83	68	49	63	73	83	67	75	74	66	89	87	62	86	68	78	83	75	87	96
26159	PADEN CITY	78	58	38	56	64	77	65	71	72	61	85	80	58	80	64	77	78	71	85	86
26160	PALESTINE	66	50	32	45	57	64	48	58	55	47	65	68	42	63	50	58	60	57	69	80
	WEST VIRGINIA	73	60	47	57	64	72	61	67	67	60	80	78	57	78	61	69	75	67	76	84
	UNITED STATES	100	100	100	100	100	100	100	100	100	100	100	100	100	100	100	100	100	100	100	100

ZIP CODE		POPULATION			2000-2004 ANNUAL RATE		HOUSEHOLDS					FAMILIES		
# POST OFFICE NAME	COUNTY FIPS CODE	2000	2004	2009	% Rate	State Centile	2000	2004	2009	% Annual Rate 2000-2004	2004 Average HH Size	2000	2004	% Annual Rate 2000-2004
26161 PETROLEUM	085	479	481	482	0.1	63	186	190	193	0.5	2.53	136	134	-0.4
26164 RAVENSWOOD	035	7419	7386	7512	-0.1	48	3005	3058	3175	0.4	2.36	2135	2092	-0.5
26167 READER	103	2155	2101	2040	-0.6	22	839	836	829	-0.1	2.51	627	605	-0.8
26169 ROCKPORT	107	1097	1076	1062	-0.5	27	399	398	398	-0.1	2.70	322	313	-0.7
26170 SAINT MARYS	073	5427	5462	5533	0.2	66	2092	2142	2205	0.6	2.46	1533	1519	-0.2
26173 SHERMAN	035	385	383	390	-0.1	46	155	158	165	0.5	2.42	118	117	-0.2
26175 SISTERSVILLE	095	3601	3669	3746	0.4	79	1456	1514	1577	0.9	2.38	1045	1050	0.1
26178 SMITHVILLE	085	565	564	565	0.0	53	226	230	233	0.4	2.45	167	165	-0.3
26180 WALKER	107	3556	3534	3523	-0.2	45	1333	1354	1372	0.4	2.57	1021	999	-0.5
26181 WASHINGTON	107	6013	6159	6244	0.6	82	2287	2411	2491	1.3	2.55	1861	1913	0.7
26184 WAVERLY	107	2357	2370	2372	0.1	64	877	904	921	0.7	2.58	683	682	0.0
26186 WILEYVILLE	103	253	244	236	-0.9	13	98	97	95	-0.2	2.52	75	71	-1.3
26187 WILLIAMSTOWN	107	5669	5617	5575	-0.2	42	2310	2335	2353	0.3	2.40	1689	1648	-0.6
26201 BUCKHANNON	097	17295	17320	17339	0.0	59	6622	6765	6879	0.5	2.36	4588	4514	-0.4
26202 FENWICK	067	349	340	336	-0.6	21	132	132	134	0.0	2.58	103	100	-0.7
26203 ERBACON	101	234	227	223	-0.7	18	98	98	99	0.0	2.27	72	70	-0.7
26205 CRAIGSVILLE	067	3789	3784	3768	0.0	54	1540	1573	1603	0.5	2.41	1126	1113	-0.3
26206 COWEN	101	3073	3044	3013	-0.2	42	1235	1257	1273	0.4	2.38	905	891	-0.4
26208 CAMDEN ON GAULEY	101	1112	1089	1073	-0.5	25	430	433	437	0.2	2.51	313	304	-0.7
26210 ADRIAN	097	912	920	921	0.2	69	357	369	376	0.8	2.49	267	266	-0.1
26215 CLEVELAND	097	423	416	413	-0.4	31	166	167	169	0.1	2.49	124	121	-0.6
26217 DIANA	101	830	809	795	-0.6	22	347	348	351	0.1	2.32	244	236	-0.8
26218 FRENCH CREEK	097	2360	2341	2332	-0.2	44	907	922	934	0.4	2.54	677	666	-0.4
26222 HACKER VALLEY	101	629	614	605	-0.6	23	252	253	256	0.1	2.43	188	183	-0.6
26224 HELVETIA	083	203	194	189	-1.1	10	84	82	81	-0.6	2.37	59	56	-1.2
26228 KANAWHA HEAD	097	173	171	170	-0.3	38	63	64	65	0.4	2.67	45	44	-0.5
26230 PICKENS	083	225	215	208	-1.1	10	95	92	91	-0.8	2.15	67	63	-1.4
26234 ROCK CAVE	097	639	633	630	-0.2	42	261	265	269	0.4	2.39	185	181	-0.5
26236 SELBYVILLE	097	28	28	28	0.0	57	13	13	13	0.0	2.15	9	9	0.0
26237 TALLMANSVILLE	097	476	473	471	-0.2	45	180	183	184	0.4	2.58	145	144	-0.2
26238 VOLGA	001	1284	1307	1318	0.4	78	488	507	518	0.9	2.58	369	372	0.2
26241 ELKINS	083	13613	13429	13227	-0.3	35	5656	5683	5700	0.1	2.25	3619	3481	-0.9
26250 BELINGTON	001	5319	5379	5409	0.3	72	2100	2167	2202	0.7	2.46	1531	1527	-0.1
26253 BEVERLY	083	3816	3771	3713	-0.3	37	1470	1480	1485	0.2	2.50	1103	1074	-0.6
26254 BOWDEN	083	150	150	148	0.0	57	65	67	67	0.7	2.24	48	47	-0.5
26257 COALTON	083	1440	1428	1407	-0.2	43	556	561	563	0.2	2.55	425	415	-0.6
26260 DAVIS	093	1240	1157	1099	-1.6	2	551	525	510	-1.1	2.13	360	328	-2.2
26261 RICHWOOD	067	3629	3435	3377	-1.3	6	1501	1448	1456	-0.8	2.29	1018	944	-1.8
26263 DRYFORK	083	260	260	256	0.0	57	111	114	114	0.6	2.28	81	80	-0.3
26264 DURBIN	075	88	86	84	-0.5	23	34	34	34	0.0	2.53	24	23	-1.0
26266 UPPERGLADE	101	402	402	399	0.0	57	150	155	158	0.8	2.59	106	105	-0.2
26267 ELLAMORE	097	448	444	440	-0.2	42	163	165	166	0.3	2.68	130	128	-0.4
26268 GLADY	083	608	604	595	-0.2	45	249	253	255	0.4	2.34	185	181	-0.5
26269 HAMBLETON	093	809	769	735	-1.2	6	308	299	292	-0.7	2.57	231	218	-1.4
26270 HARMAN	083	579	579	572	0.0	57	242	248	250	0.6	2.33	178	176	-0.3
26271 HENDRICKS	093	328	309	295	-1.4	4	129	124	121	-0.9	2.49	98	91	-1.7
26273 HUTTONSVILLE	083	1429	1401	1379	-0.5	26	234	234	234	0.0	4.17	174	168	-0.8
26276 KERENS	083	587	625	635	1.5	92	215	234	242	2.0	2.67	158	165	1.0
26278 MABIE	083	418	417	412	-0.1	52	146	148	149	0.3	2.82	112	110	-0.4
26280 MILL CREEK	083	1966	1940	1912	-0.3	35	757	758	758	0.0	2.05	575	557	-0.8
26282 MONTERVILLE	083	68	65	64	-1.1	10	26	26	25	0.0	2.50	17	16	-1.4
26283 MONTROSE	083	1120	1161	1166	0.9	86	438	464	476	1.4	2.50	327	334	0.5
26287 PARSONS	093	3395	3401	3341	0.0	60	1418	1455	1461	0.6	2.34	1021	1008	-0.3
26288 WEBSTER SPRINGS	101	3430	3381	3339	-0.3	33	1495	1517	1534	0.3	2.23	986	959	-0.7
26289 RED CREEK	093	278	262	249	-1.4	4	118	114	111	-0.8	2.30	83	77	-1.8
26291 SLATYFORK	075	581	591	587	0.4	77	262	271	274	0.8	2.18	173	172	-0.1
26292 THOMAS	093	823	762	723	-1.8	1	347	326	314	-1.5	2.05	203	180	-2.8
26293 VALLEY BEND	083	973	994	994	0.5	80	379	394	401	0.9	2.52	290	292	0.2
26294 VALLEY HEAD	083	948	932	915	-0.4	30	400	400	399	0.0	2.33	274	263	-1.0
26296 WHITMER	083	378	374	368	-0.3	39	156	158	159	0.3	2.37	114	111	-0.6
26301 CLARKSBURG	033	32088	32489	33082	0.3	73	13668	14060	14549	0.7	2.27	8737	8604	-0.4
26320 ALMA	095	1268	1214	1204	-1.0	11	517	506	511	-0.5	2.40	395	376	-1.2
26321 ALUM BRIDGE	041	758	739	726	-0.6	22	302	301	301	-0.1	2.46	219	210	-1.0
26325 AUBURN	085	275	277	278	0.2	67	104	107	109	0.7	2.59	76	75	-0.3
26327 BEREA	085	123	124	125	0.2	68	48	50	51	1.0	2.48	35	35	0.0
26330 BRIDGEPORT	033	13095	13460	13751	0.7	84	5223	5467	5680	1.1	2.44	3729	3758	0.2
26332 BRISTOL	033	2251	2247	2271	0.0	53	885	904	931	0.5	2.48	676	669	-0.2
26335 BURNSVILLE	007	1446	1461	1471	0.2	71	583	602	618	0.8	2.41	408	405	-0.2
26337 CAIRO	085	1396	1407	1413	0.2	68	566	580	591	0.6	2.42	407	403	-0.2
26338 CAMDEN	041	624	609	600	-0.6	23	238	238	240	0.0	2.56	166	160	-0.9
26339 CENTER POINT	017	176	177	174	0.1	64	72	74	73	0.3	2.42	50	49	-0.5
26342 COXS MILLS	021	731	805	792	2.3	96	302	303	304	0.1	2.34	211	204	-0.8
26343 CRAWFORD	041	637	660	672	0.8	86	245	261	272	1.5	2.53	182	187	0.6
26346 ELLENBORO	085	837	846	852	0.3	72	329	338	345	0.6	2.50	253	253	0.0
26347 FLEMINGTON	091	2574	2559	2545	-0.1	45	974	985	994	0.3	2.60	740	726	-0.5
26348 FOLSOM	103	351	336	323	-1.0	11	130	127	125	-0.6	2.65	95	89	-1.5
26351 GLENVILLE	021	2541	3796	3797	9.9	100	941	977	998	0.9	2.21	521	514	-0.3
26354 GRAFTON	091	10236	10134	10064	-0.2	40	4062	4091	4130	0.2	2.37	2799	2714	-0.7
26362 HARRISVILLE	085	3308	3286	3288	-0.2	45	1367	1383	1405	0.3	2.32	959	935	-0.6
26372 HORNER	041	271	325	355	4.4	99	112	139	155	5.2	2.34	87	104	4.3
26374 INDEPENDENCE	077	1267	1263	1260	-0.1	50	488	498	507	0.5	2.42	370	365	-0.3
26376 IRELAND	007	401	396	392	-0.3	37	154	156	158	0.3	2.54	113	110	-0.6
26377 JACKSONBURG	103	596	568	552	-1.1	7	232	226	224	-0.6	2.51	178	168	-1.4
26378 JANE LEW	041	5000	4963	4932	-0.2	44	2033	2058	2084	0.3	2.37	1450	1416	-0.6
26384 LINN	021	735	719	706	-0.5	24	284	284	285	0.0	2.53	216	210	-0.7
26385 LOST CREEK	033	3511	3580	3637	0.5	79	1318	1372	1419	1.0	2.61	1038	1050	0.3
26386 LUMBERPORT	033	2278	2285	2307	0.1	61	864	884	909	0.5	2.56	652	646	-0.2
26404 MEADOWBROOK	033	1065	1076	1088	0.2	71	427	439	453	0.7	2.45	307	304	-0.2
26405 MOATSVILLE	001	1304	1272	1258	-0.6	22	517	516	517	-0.1	2.47	392	379	-0.8
26408 MOUNT CLARE	033	1655	1671	1690	0.2	70	644	666	687	0.8	2.51	490	492	0.1
26410 NEWBURG	077	1374	1361	1351	-0.1	42	478	485	492	0.3	2.68	358	352	-0.4
26411 NEW MILTON	017	858	855	838	-0.1	49	328	332	330	0.3	2.57	244	239	-0.5
26412 ORLANDO	041	395	509	572	6.2	100	145	192	220	6.8	2.65	110	140	5.8
26415 PENNSBORO	085	3062	3145	3195	0.6	83	1231	1288	1329	1.1	2.44	872	879	0.2
26416 PHILIPPI	001	7772	7742	7728	-0.1	49	3054	3093	3115	0.3	2.38	2110	2057	-0.6
WEST VIRGINIA					0.2					0.6	2.35			-0.3
UNITED STATES					1.2					1.3	2.58			1.1

ZIP CODE #	POST OFFICE NAME	RACE (%) White 2000	White 2004	Black 2000	Black 2004	Asian/Pacific 2000	Asian/Pacific 2004	% Hispanic Origin 2000	% Hispanic Origin 2004	2004 AGE DISTRIBUTION (%) 0-4	5-9	10-14	15-19	20-24	25-44	45-64	65-84	85+	18+	MEDIAN AGE 2004	% 2004 Males	% 2004 Females
26161	PETROLEUM	99.2	99.0	0.2	0.2	0.0	0.0	0.4	0.4	4.8	5.0	6.2	6.4	5.8	25.4	30.2	14.6	1.7	79.8	42.9	50.5	49.5
26164	RAVENSWOOD	98.4	98.2	0.2	0.2	0.4	0.6	0.4	0.4	5.9	5.9	6.5	6.4	6.0	24.1	25.1	17.9	2.3	77.7	41.7	47.7	52.3
26167	READER	99.3	99.2	0.1	0.1	0.1	0.2	0.4	0.4	6.2	6.7	7.6	6.2	5.6	26.0	27.8	12.7	1.3	75.6	39.3	50.6	49.4
26169	ROCKPORT	98.6	98.6	0.0	0.0	0.1	0.1	0.3	0.3	4.8	6.8	10.1	7.1	4.7	27.2	28.1	9.4	1.8	73.7	38.0	51.5	48.5
26170	SAINT MARYS	98.2	98.2	0.6	0.6	0.2	0.2	0.3	0.3	5.7	6.1	6.8	5.6	5.9	27.3	27.5	13.3	1.7	77.8	40.1	51.4	48.6
26173	SHERMAN	99.0	99.0	0.0	0.0	0.0	0.0	0.0	0.0	4.4	5.0	6.3	6.0	5.5	26.4	30.8	14.1	1.6	81.2	42.8	51.4	48.6
26175	SISTERSVILLE	99.4	99.4	0.0	0.0	0.1	0.1	0.5	0.5	5.4	5.8	5.8	6.4	5.2	24.3	28.7	16.0	2.4	78.9	43.1	48.4	51.6
26178	SMITHVILLE	98.9	98.8	0.4	0.4	0.0	0.0	0.4	0.4	4.3	4.6	6.7	6.9	5.5	25.2	29.8	15.1	2.0	80.1	43.2	50.7	49.3
26180	WALKER	98.3	98.2	0.3	0.3	0.2	0.2	0.6	0.6	5.6	6.2	7.4	7.4	6.0	28.8	27.2	10.4	1.1	75.8	38.6	51.6	48.4
26181	WASHINGTON	98.5	98.4	0.4	0.4	0.3	0.3	0.5	0.5	5.6	6.1	6.8	6.0	4.9	26.1	31.3	12.2	1.0	77.7	41.7	50.6	49.4
26184	WAVERLY	97.8	97.7	0.8	0.8	0.5	0.5	0.4	0.4	6.2	6.6	7.6	6.5	6.0	28.9	27.8	9.4	0.9	76.0	37.7	50.0	50.0
26186	WILEYVILLE	98.8	98.8	0.0	0.0	0.0	0.0	0.0	0.0	6.2	6.2	7.0	5.3	5.7	27.9	27.5	12.3	2.1	77.1	39.2	49.6	50.4
26187	WILLIAMSTOWN	98.4	98.3	0.4	0.4	0.4	0.4	0.4	0.4	5.5	5.9	6.6	6.3	5.4	26.2	28.4	14.1	1.6	78.1	41.3	47.8	52.2
26201	BUCKHANNON	97.9	97.9	0.8	0.8	0.4	0.4	0.6	0.6	5.3	5.5	6.1	8.6	9.0	24.1	26.0	13.1	2.4	79.7	38.4	48.0	52.0
26202	FENWICK	99.1	99.1	0.0	0.0	0.6	0.6	0.9	0.6	5.6	6.2	6.5	6.2	5.6	26.2	29.4	13.2	1.2	77.7	41.0	49.1	50.9
26203	ERBACON	99.6	99.6	0.0	0.0	0.0	0.0	0.9	0.9	4.9	6.2	7.1	6.2	5.7	26.4	28.2	12.8	2.6	77.5	40.2	51.5	48.5
26205	CRAIGSVILLE	98.8	98.8	0.1	0.1	0.1	0.1	0.2	0.2	6.1	6.4	6.6	5.9	5.9	26.9	27.9	13.2	1.2	77.3	39.7	49.4	50.6
26206	COWEN	99.1	99.1	0.0	0.0	0.1	0.1	0.3	0.3	5.8	6.1	7.1	6.2	5.7	26.5	28.0	12.7	2.0	77.1	39.7	50.2	49.8
26208	CAMDEN ON GAULEY	99.2	99.3	0.0	0.0	0.1	0.1	0.2	0.3	4.9	5.2	6.8	6.1	6.3	25.5	30.9	12.7	1.7	79.3	41.7	49.2	50.8
26210	ADRIAN	99.6	99.5	0.0	0.0	0.1	0.1	0.4	0.5	5.8	6.1	7.5	5.7	6.1	27.2	28.8	11.3	1.6	77.2	39.8	49.4	50.7
26215	CLEVELAND	98.8	99.0	0.5	0.5	0.0	0.0	0.7	0.5	5.8	6.3	6.7	5.8	4.8	25.5	27.9	15.1	2.2	77.6	42.0	50.5	49.5
26217	DIANA	99.6	99.8	0.0	0.0	0.0	0.0	0.2	0.3	5.1	5.2	6.1	6.7	6.3	22.9	30.9	15.2	1.7	79.6	43.5	49.0	51.1
26218	FRENCH CREEK	98.9	98.9	0.1	0.1	0.4	0.4	0.3	0.3	5.7	5.9	6.6	6.5	6.1	26.9	28.3	12.2	1.8	77.9	40.2	51.1	48.9
26222	HACKER VALLEY	99.4	99.4	0.0	0.0	0.0	0.0	0.6	0.7	4.1	4.6	6.4	6.8	6.0	25.7	26.4	17.8	2.3	80.8	42.6	50.5	49.5
26224	HELVETIA	99.5	100.0	0.0	0.0	0.0	0.0	0.0	0.0	4.6	5.2	6.2	6.7	6.2	24.2	28.9	16.5	1.6	80.9	43.1	54.1	45.9
26228	KANAWHA HEAD	100.0	100.0	0.0	0.0	0.0	0.0	0.0	0.6	4.7	5.3	8.2	5.9	5.3	26.3	28.7	14.6	1.2	77.8	41.0	52.6	47.4
26230	PICKENS	98.2	98.1	1.8	1.9	0.0	0.0	0.4	0.5	3.7	4.7	6.1	6.1	7.0	27.0	29.8	14.4	1.4	82.8	42.5	58.1	41.9
26234	ROCK CAVE	99.8	99.7	0.0	0.0	0.2	0.2	0.3	0.5	4.4	5.2	7.6	5.7	5.2	28.1	28.3	14.2	1.3	79.3	41.4	53.2	46.8
26236	SELBYVILLE	100.0	100.0	0.0	0.0	0.0	0.0	0.0	0.0	3.6	7.1	7.1	7.1	7.1	28.6	28.6	10.7	0.0	82.1	37.5	53.6	46.4
26237	TALLMANSVILLE	98.1	98.3	0.0	0.0	0.4	0.4	0.2	0.2	5.7	6.1	6.1	6.3	6.1	27.3	27.1	13.1	2.1	78.2	39.3	52.2	47.8
26238	VOLGA	99.3	99.3	0.2	0.2	0.0	0.0	0.4	0.4	5.2	5.7	6.9	6.3	5.7	26.7	30.0	11.9	1.6	78.4	40.6	50.3	49.7
26241	ELKINS	97.7	97.4	0.7	0.7	0.7	0.9	0.8	0.8	5.1	5.4	6.0	6.9	6.8	25.1	27.0	15.0	2.9	79.6	41.4	48.2	51.8
26250	BELINGTON	98.8	98.8	0.1	0.1	0.1	0.1	0.4	0.4	5.8	6.1	6.9	6.2	5.4	26.0	26.6	14.9	2.2	77.3	40.8	50.2	49.8
26253	BEVERLY	99.0	98.8	0.2	0.2	0.2	0.3	0.6	0.6	6.3	6.7	7.5	6.1	5.3	28.3	26.4	11.5	2.0	75.5	38.4	48.6	51.4
26254	BOWDEN	98.7	98.7	0.7	0.7	0.0	0.0	0.7	0.0	4.7	6.0	6.0	5.3	4.0	28.0	30.0	14.0	2.0	79.3	42.5	51.3	48.7
26257	COALTON	98.5	98.4	1.0	1.0	0.1	0.1	0.4	0.4	6.1	6.7	8.1	6.1	5.0	28.1	26.0	12.3	1.6	75.3	38.5	50.4	49.6
26260	DAVIS	98.2	98.1	0.2	0.2	0.0	0.0	0.3	0.4	3.6	4.4	6.7	7.7	4.5	23.7	29.3	18.2	1.9	79.6	44.7	49.9	50.1
26261	RICHWOOD	98.8	98.8	0.1	0.1	0.3	0.3	0.5	0.5	4.7	4.8	5.5	6.3	5.9	22.5	28.4	18.3	3.6	81.2	45.2	47.3	52.8
26263	DRYFORK	98.9	98.9	0.4	0.4	0.0	0.0	0.4	0.4	5.0	5.4	5.4	5.4	4.6	27.7	31.2	13.9	1.5	80.4	42.9	52.3	47.7
26264	DURBIN	98.9	98.8	1.1	1.2	0.0	0.0	0.0	0.0	4.7	4.7	7.0	7.0	5.8	24.4	27.9	16.3	2.3	76.7	42.5	52.3	47.7
26266	UPPERGLADE	99.8	99.8	0.0	0.0	0.0	0.0	0.5	0.5	6.7	7.0	7.0	6.0	5.0	28.6	26.6	11.9	1.2	75.9	37.3	51.7	48.3
26267	ELLAMORE	98.9	99.1	0.5	0.5	0.0	0.0	0.7	0.7	6.1	6.5	7.4	6.3	5.6	27.3	27.3	11.9	1.6	75.7	38.8	49.8	50.2
26268	GLADY	98.7	98.5	0.2	0.2	0.0	0.0	0.3	0.2	5.8	6.0	6.3	5.5	4.5	26.8	29.6	13.4	2.2	78.6	42.2	48.8	51.2
26269	HAMBLETON	99.6	99.7	0.0	0.0	0.0	0.0	0.0	0.0	5.7	6.0	7.4	4.9	4.8	29.9	27.6	12.5	1.6	77.8	40.0	49.9	50.1
26270	HARMAN	98.6	98.6	0.5	0.5	0.0	0.0	0.5	0.5	5.0	5.4	5.7	5.4	4.5	27.8	31.1	13.5	1.7	80.5	42.7	51.6	48.4
26271	HENDRICKS	99.1	99.7	0.0	0.0	0.0	0.0	0.0	0.0	5.5	5.5	6.5	6.2	6.5	24.3	28.5	14.9	2.3	78.6	42.1	47.3	52.8
26273	HUTTONSVILLE	92.8	92.5	6.7	6.9	0.1	0.1	0.6	0.8	3.4	3.6	4.7	5.1	9.1	38.3	24.8	9.6	1.4	85.5	37.6	65.0	35.1
26276	KERENS	98.0	97.9	0.0	0.0	0.5	0.6	0.7	0.6	5.6	6.4	6.1	5.6	5.3	27.4	28.6	13.6	1.4	78.1	41.0	50.4	49.6
26278	MABIE	99.0	99.0	0.0	0.0	0.0	0.0	0.7	0.7	4.8	6.7	7.9	6.7	4.8	26.4	27.6	13.7	1.4	76.0	40.2	50.1	49.9
26280	MILL CREEK	94.7	94.4	4.3	4.4	0.2	0.2	0.5	0.4	5.1	5.2	5.7	5.4	8.1	36.7	23.8	8.9	1.2	80.7	36.2	59.3	40.7
26282	MONTERVILLE	100.0	100.0	0.0	0.0	0.0	0.0	0.0	0.0	3.1	6.2	6.2	6.2	6.2	26.2	26.2	16.9	3.1	84.6	42.5	50.8	49.2
26283	MONTROSE	98.0	97.9	0.0	0.0	0.5	0.5	0.8	0.9	5.4	6.8	6.4	5.9	5.6	27.7	28.3	12.7	1.2	77.4	39.9	51.2	48.8
26287	PARSONS	99.0	98.9	0.1	0.1	0.2	0.2	0.3	0.3	5.1	5.7	6.6	5.1	5.7	26.0	28.0	15.8	2.2	79.5	42.6	49.2	50.8
26288	WEBSTER SPRINGS	99.0	98.9	0.0	0.0	0.1	0.2	0.4	0.4	4.6	5.0	6.2	5.8	6.1	24.5	31.3	14.5	2.2	80.7	43.6	48.5	51.5
26289	RED CREEK	98.9	98.9	0.0	0.0	0.0	0.0	0.4	0.4	3.8	3.4	5.7	5.7	3.4	22.9	38.2	16.4	0.4	83.6	47.6	51.9	48.1
26291	SLATYFORK	99.1	99.2	0.0	0.0	0.0	0.0	0.7	0.5	6.3	6.4	6.1	5.6	4.6	28.6	30.6	10.3	1.5	77.7	40.7	53.5	46.5
26292	THOMAS	99.2	99.1	0.0	0.0	0.0	0.0	0.0	0.0	4.3	4.7	4.5	3.9	3.7	21.7	26.9	23.0	7.4	84.0	51.1	45.1	54.9
26293	VALLEY BEND	99.3	99.3	0.1	0.1	0.1	0.1	1.5	1.4	4.9	8.1	9.2	5.5	4.1	29.0	25.8	12.2	1.3	74.3	38.0	47.5	52.5
26294	VALLEY HEAD	99.4	99.3	0.0	0.0	0.0	0.0	0.5	0.6	4.5	4.8	6.0	6.1	5.9	24.3	32.2	14.3	1.9	80.8	44.0	50.9	49.1
26296	WHITMER	98.4	98.7	0.0	0.0	0.0	0.0	0.0	0.3	5.6	5.9	6.2	5.1	4.6	28.1	29.7	13.4	1.6	79.1	42.1	48.9	51.1
26301	CLARKSBURG	95.6	95.4	2.6	2.6	0.3	0.5	1.0	1.0	5.9	5.7	6.3	5.7	6.0	26.5	25.9	15.2	2.9	78.6	40.9	47.4	52.6
26320	ALMA	99.1	99.2	0.0	0.0	0.2	0.2	0.3	0.3	5.7	6.1	6.8	5.5	4.9	24.5	29.9	14.8	1.7	77.9	42.4	49.8	50.3
26321	ALUM BRIDGE	98.9	98.8	0.1	0.1	0.0	0.0	0.3	0.3	5.4	6.2	6.9	6.9	6.1	26.1	28.3	12.5	1.6	77.1	40.0	50.6	49.4
26325	AUBURN	98.2	98.2	0.0	0.0	0.4	0.4	0.4	0.4	5.4	6.1	7.9	6.5	5.4	23.8	28.2	14.8	1.8	76.5	41.6	52.0	48.0
26327	BEREA	98.4	97.6	0.0	0.0	0.0	0.8	0.0	0.0	5.7	6.5	7.3	6.5	5.7	24.2	27.4	15.3	1.6	75.8	41.1	50.8	49.2
26330	BRIDGEPORT	97.3	96.9	1.2	1.2	0.8	1.1	1.2	1.2	5.5	5.9	7.0	6.4	5.4	25.4	28.3	14.1	2.1	77.5	41.5	47.9	52.2
26332	BRISTOL	97.8	97.6	0.4	0.5	0.4	0.6	0.8	0.8	5.7	5.6	6.2	6.3	6.4	25.0	30.0	13.3	1.7	78.8	41.7	49.1	50.9
26335	BURNSVILLE	98.8	98.7	0.4	0.3	0.1	0.1	0.5	0.6	6.3	6.6	7.1	5.7	5.1	27.1	26.6	13.1	2.3	76.5	39.5	50.8	49.2
26337	CAIRO	99.4	99.4	0.1	0.1	0.1	0.1	0.5	0.5	6.2	6.2	6.0	5.5	6.1	26.2	28.9	13.4	1.5	78.3	40.8	49.2	50.8
26338	CAMDEN	98.7	98.5	0.2	0.2	0.0	0.0	0.6	0.7	5.4	6.6	7.2	6.4	5.3	26.3	28.9	13.0	1.0	76.7	40.5	51.7	48.3
26339	CENTER POINT	98.9	98.9	0.0	0.0	0.0	0.0	1.1	0.6	6.2	6.8	7.3	6.8	5.1	25.4	27.7	13.6	1.1	75.1	39.8	52.0	48.0
26342	COXS MILLS	98.5	98.3	0.3	0.4	0.1	0.3	0.1	0.3	6.0	5.5	5.1	5.8	8.1	24.7	27.8	14.9	2.1	80.6	41.4	48.6	51.4
26343	CRAWFORD	98.9	98.9	0.2	0.2	0.2	0.2	0.5	0.5	6.1	6.8	7.3	5.6	5.3	26.8	28.0	12.6	1.5	76.5	39.6	51.8	48.2
26346	ELLENBORO	98.6	98.1	0.1	0.1	0.2	0.5	0.4	0.4	6.6	6.4	5.8	5.6	6.7	28.5	28.8	10.5	1.1	78.0	38.6	50.1	49.9
26347	FLEMINGTON	98.9	98.9	0.3	0.3	0.1	0.1	0.8	0.8	5.4	5.7	6.5	6.5	6.9	27.8	27.5	12.3	1.5	78.5	39.2	50.9	49.1
26348	FOLSOM	99.4	99.4	0.0	0.0	0.0	0.0	0.3	0.3	6.6	6.9	6.9	5.1	6.0	26.2	26.2	15.2	1.2	76.2	39.3	49.4	50.6
26351	GLENVILLE	94.9	95.2	2.1	1.7	1.5	1.6	1.0	1.0	4.3	3.7	4.8	11.8	17.2	20.3	22.8	12.1	3.0	83.8	32.9	50.5	49.6
26354	GRAFTON	98.1	98.1	0.9	0.9	0.1	0.1	0.5	0.5	5.0	5.2	6.0	6.5	6.1	26.9	26.6	15.3	2.4	79.7	41.2	48.7	51.3
26362	HARRISVILLE	98.6	98.5	0.1	0.1	0.2	0.2	0.5	0.6	5.5	5.6	6.2	5.3	5.5	26.8	27.5	14.8	2.9	79.7	41.9	48.5	51.6
26372	HORNER	98.5	98.2	0.0	0.3	0.0	0.0	0.7	0.6	6.2	6.5	6.8	5.9	5.2	28.0	29.5	10.8	1.2	76.9	39.3	50.2	49.9
26374	INDEPENDENCE	98.6	98.6	0.2	0.2	0.1	0.1	0.6	0.6	5.5	5.8	5.9	5.5	5.3	26.7	29.0	14.7	1.7	79.3	42.1	49.6	50.4
26376	IRELAND	98.8	99.0	0.0	0.0	0.3	0.3	0.5	0.3	6.1	7.1	7.3	5.3	5.8	26.3	28.8	11.9	1.5	76.0	39.4	53.8	46.2
26377	JACKSONBURG	99.3	99.3	0.0	0.0	0.0	0.0	0.7	0.5	5.8	6.2	6.3	5.5	5.8	24.8	28.5	15.1	1.9	78.5	41.8	49.1	50.9
26378	JANE LEW	99.0	99.1	0.0	0.0	0.1	0.1	0.4	0.3	5.6	5.9	6.9	5.6	5.3	27.0	27.2	14.0	2.6	78.0	41.0	48.2	51.8
26384	LINN	99.2	99.2	0.0	0.0	0.0	0.0	0.5	0.6	6.7	6.3	6.4	6.8	6.3	27.4	24.1	14.1	2.1	76.9	38.1	51.7	48.3
26385	LOST CREEK	98.7	98.6	0.1	0.1	0.1	0.1	0.7	0.7	6.2	6.5	7.6	6.2	5.4	29.5	27.1	10.4	1.2	75.8	38.3	49.8	50.3
26386	LUMBERPORT	99.1	99.0	0.1	0.1	0.1	0.1	0.8	0.8	5.7	6.4	7.1	6.5	4.7	27.6	27.6	12.3	2.1	76.6	40.0	49.8	50.2
26404	MEADOWBROOK	98.1	97.9	0.8	0.8	0.1	0.2	1.5	1.5	7.0	7.0	7.7	6.5	5.7	27.2	23.5	13.4	2.0	74.3	37.5	47.8	52.2
26405	MOATSVILLE	96.9	96.9	0.3	0.3	0.2	0.2	0.5	0.6	4.0	5.2	6.3	6.7	4.8	26.7	31.1	13.6	1.7	80.0	42.8	51.8	48.2
26408	MOUNT CLARE	98.2	98.0	0.5	0.5	0.4	0.6	1.0	1.0	5.6	6.0	7.1	6.1	5.0	26.5	30.6	11.7	1.6	77.6	41.5	47.8	52.2
26410	NEWBURG	98.7	98.7	0.2	0.2	0.0	0.0	0.6	0.6	5.0	5.3	6.4	6.3	5.8	26.4	28.3	14.9	1.6	79.5	41.9	50.9	49.1
26411	NEW MILTON	98.3	98.4	0.0	0.0	0.2	0.2	0.7	0.8	5.6	6.2	7.0	5.7	5.4	25.2	30.1	13.0	1.9	77.7	41.7	52.2	47.8
26412	ORLANDO	98.2	98.0	0.3	0.2	0.0	0.2	0.5	0.6	6.5	6.5	6.5	5.9	5.3	28.5	29.5	10.2	1.2	77.0	38.7	49.9	50.1
26415	PENNSBORO	98.5	98.4	0.2	0.2	0.1	0.1	0.5	0.5	5.8	5.9	6.7	6.0	6.4	25.8	28.3	13.4	1.8	77.9	40.6	48.6	51.4
26416	PHILIPPI	96.2	96.2	0.8	0.8	0.4	0.5	0.5	0.5	5.6	5.7	6.4	7.1	7.5	26.7	25.7	13.1	2.4	78.6	38.3	48.4	51.7
	WEST VIRGINIA	95.1	94.8	3.2	3.2	0.5	0.7	0.7	0.7	5.6	5.8	6.2	6.3	6.7	26.7	27.1	13.7	1.9	78.9	40.1	48.8	51.2
	UNITED STATES	75.1	73.6	12.3	12.5	3.8	4.2	12.5	14.1	6.9	6.7	7.2	7.0	7.3	28.6	23.8	10.8	1.7	75.1	36.0	49.1	50.9

ZIP CODE #	POST OFFICE NAME	2004 Per Capita Income	2004 HH Income Base	2004 Household Income Distribution (%): Less than $25,000	$25,000 to $49,999	$50,000 to $99,999	$100,000 to $149,999	$150,000 or More	Median Household Income: 2004	2009	2004 National Centile	2004 State Centile	2004 Home Value Base	2004 Home Value Distribution (%): Less than $50,000	$50,000 to $89,999	$90,000 to $174,999	$175,000 to $399,999	$400,000 or More	2004 Median Home Value
26161	PETROLEUM	15331	190	43.2	32.6	20.5	2.1	1.6	30365	34743	13	54	161	44.1	24.8	23.6	5.6	1.9	58636
26164	RAVENSWOOD	19246	3058	34.0	34.3	23.8	6.3	1.6	36619	41539	34	83	2336	19.8	36.8	33.0	8.7	1.7	84762
26167	READER	16745	836	38.0	30.6	26.9	3.7	0.7	34046	39719	24	73	703	32.7	37.6	27.5	2.3	0.0	71250
26169	ROCKPORT	15220	398	36.2	34.7	24.1	4.3	0.8	34136	40372	24	74	338	23.4	35.8	32.8	7.1	0.9	83404
26170	SAINT MARYS	18931	2142	33.9	34.1	24.9	5.7	1.4	36058	40380	32	81	1734	31.6	25.8	34.1	6.6	1.9	80922
26173	SHERMAN	21622	158	24.7	37.3	28.5	5.7	3.8	40815	45224	49	92	139	17.3	28.8	32.4	18.7	2.9	102885
26175	SISTERSVILLE	18643	1514	36.8	31.9	23.7	5.3	2.3	33728	38767	23	72	1230	34.2	31.4	28.7	5.4	0.4	71915
26178	SMITHVILLE	14323	230	45.2	35.2	17.0	1.3	1.3	27852	31556	8	39	193	45.1	25.9	22.8	5.2	1.0	57917
26180	WALKER	16881	1354	35.1	35.7	22.6	5.0	1.6	35916	40402	31	80	1182	34.8	30.9	26.9	6.8	0.7	69000
26181	WASHINGTON	25095	2411	18.0	26.0	39.2	12.3	4.4	55428	66140	80	99	2201	12.6	22.4	53.0	11.8	0.2	104510
26184	WAVERLY	20977	904	28.7	27.8	33.0	7.5	3.1	41554	48559	52	93	789	30.5	22.3	37.0	9.4	0.8	85588
26186	WILEYVILLE	14741	97	42.3	28.9	26.8	2.1	0.0	30562	34440	14	56	83	39.8	25.3	33.7	1.2	0.0	73571
26187	WILLIAMSTOWN	23030	2335	25.8	29.9	32.1	9.5	2.7	43626	51254	58	95	1955	13.6	28.2	49.1	8.4	0.7	97595
26201	BUCKHANNON	16565	6765	39.5	31.8	23.5	3.8	1.5	31684	35710	17	64	5091	20.2	34.6	34.9	8.9	1.4	85745
26202	FENWICK	13730	132	47.0	34.1	13.6	5.3	0.0	26619	30000	7	31	112	51.8	25.0	21.4	1.8	0.0	46667
26203	ERBACON	12526	98	57.1	22.5	17.4	2.0	1.0	20000	22706	2	4	78	53.9	37.2	9.0	0.0	0.0	47500
26205	CRAIGSVILLE	15846	1573	44.3	32.3	19.4	2.2	1.8	28265	32131	9	42	1280	40.8	31.4	26.2	1.3	0.4	61068
26206	COWEN	13694	1257	54.3	28.1	15.8	1.0	1.0	22162	25026	3	11	1012	51.4	31.8	14.4	2.2	0.2	49152
26208	CAMDEN ON GAULEY	13553	433	52.7	28.6	15.9	2.1	0.7	23272	26467	3	14	349	51.6	35.8	7.7	4.9	0.0	48962
26210	ADRIAN	15634	369	37.1	39.6	20.1	2.4	0.8	32064	36081	18	67	312	25.6	31.4	38.5	2.9	1.6	81538
26215	CLEVELAND	12306	167	49.7	34.1	13.2	3.0	0.0	25241	27320	5	23	144	34.7	31.3	27.1	6.9	0.0	71667
26217	DIANA	10552	348	65.2	23.6	10.3	0.9	0.0	18620	21185	1	3	285	54.4	34.4	10.5	0.0	0.7	47727
26218	FRENCH CREEK	13918	922	47.0	32.8	16.5	2.8	1.0	26802	30548	7	32	785	35.5	30.8	25.7	6.5	1.4	69527
26222	HACKER VALLEY	15288	253	36.8	45.1	14.6	2.4	1.2	31099	35229	15	61	217	42.9	36.4	19.8	0.9	0.0	56458
26224	HELVETIA	13302	82	51.2	32.9	13.4	2.4	0.0	24330	26362	4	19	68	42.7	27.9	23.5	1.5	4.4	60000
26228	KANAWHA HEAD	11456	64	54.7	32.8	10.9	0.0	1.6	23049	27252	3	14	55	41.8	34.6	21.8	0.0	1.8	63571
26230	PICKENS	13896	92	50.0	34.8	13.0	2.2	0.0	25000	27263	5	22	76	43.4	26.3	25.0	1.3	4.0	58333
26234	ROCK CAVE	12648	265	55.1	31.7	11.7	0.0	1.5	22780	26368	3	13	227	39.2	35.7	22.9	0.9	1.3	65536
26236	SELBYVILLE	11696	13	61.5	30.8	7.7	0.0	0.0	22072	27290	3	10	11	45.5	27.3	27.3	0.0	0.0	65000
26237	TALLMANSVILLE	13414	183	49.2	26.8	21.3	0.6	2.2	25262	28120	5	23	153	51.0	34.0	15.0	0.0	0.0	48929
26238	VOLGA	14086	507	41.2	35.3	20.1	3.4	0.0	30895	34108	15	60	435	30.6	39.8	22.5	7.1	0.0	71444
26241	ELKINS	19527	5683	39.5	32.6	21.5	4.3	2.2	31960	35623	18	66	4035	19.9	31.4	39.0	8.6	1.1	88585
26250	BELINGTON	13677	2167	48.7	30.1	18.6	1.4	1.1	25761	29203	5	26	1752	40.2	33.5	23.2	2.5	0.6	60000
26253	BEVERLY	16613	1480	37.4	34.4	23.7	3.1	1.4	32698	36711	20	69	1210	29.3	28.1	31.2	9.8	1.6	81262
26254	BOWDEN	18750	67	38.8	34.3	22.4	3.0	1.5	30922	34518	15	60	57	35.1	15.8	40.4	8.8	0.0	88333
26257	COALTON	12125	561	51.9	26.4	21.4	0.4	0.0	24005	26782	4	18	503	42.0	31.8	18.3	6.0	2.0	60714
26260	DAVIS	24409	525	41.9	26.3	22.5	4.8	4.6	30693	35000	14	57	402	27.6	26.4	31.1	14.9	0.0	82727
26261	RICHWOOD	13804	1448	51.1	31.1	14.0	3.0	0.9	24340	27644	4	19	1113	62.2	24.9	11.3	1.6	0.0	38838
26263	DRYFORK	18673	114	38.6	32.5	23.7	3.5	1.8	31194	35485	15	61	96	36.5	16.7	37.5	9.4	0.0	84000
26264	DURBIN	12192	34	55.9	29.4	8.8	2.9	2.9	22687	25000	3	13	28	42.9	39.3	17.9	0.0	0.0	56667
26266	UPPERGLADE	14171	155	54.8	30.3	13.6	0.0	1.3	21657	23121	2	9	127	52.8	27.6	18.9	0.8	0.0	48478
26267	ELLAMORE	13568	165	45.5	30.3	22.4	1.2	0.6	27459	31019	8	35	144	34.7	34.0	22.9	6.3	2.1	73077
26268	GLADY	17241	253	40.7	30.4	24.1	2.8	2.0	31465	34848	16	62	218	26.2	20.6	44.0	8.3	0.9	92593
26269	HAMBLETON	17100	299	35.1	41.8	15.4	5.0	2.7	34294	39307	25	75	256	32.0	30.1	28.5	8.2	1.2	75238
26270	HARMAN	21190	248	38.7	32.7	23.0	3.6	2.0	31224	35000	16	61	209	36.8	15.3	38.3	9.6	0.0	85500
26271	HENDRICKS	20324	124	45.2	33.1	16.9	2.4	2.4	27065	30899	7	33	109	40.4	41.3	17.4	0.9	0.0	58077
26273	HUTTONSVILLE	7647	234	49.6	32.1	15.8	2.6	0.0	25171	28509	5	22	200	42.5	30.5	22.0	2.5	2.5	60000
26276	KERENS	14341	234	39.3	36.3	21.4	2.1	0.9	31667	35000	17	64	190	28.4	27.4	34.7	9.0	0.5	82143
26278	MABIE	12196	148	43.9	35.1	19.6	1.4	0.0	27566	31423	8	37	129	27.9	38.0	24.0	9.3	0.8	72500
26280	MILL CREEK	16115	758	42.7	35.5	19.8	0.9	1.1	28648	32112	10	44	605	45.8	29.9	18.4	5.8	0.2	54636
26282	MONTERVILLE	9538	26	65.4	26.9	7.7	0.0	0.0	18896	30699	1	4	22	40.9	27.3	27.3	4.6	0.0	70000
26283	MONTROSE	14922	464	38.6	36.9	22.6	1.5	0.4	31628	35674	17	63	389	29.8	29.8	31.1	9.3	0.0	77361
26287	PARSONS	17489	1455	43.7	36.2	16.2	2.2	1.7	29262	32416	11	48	1201	36.7	31.6	27.1	4.4	0.2	66862
26288	WEBSTER SPRINGS	15549	1517	54.1	27.4	14.6	2.3	1.6	22385	25423	3	11	1175	50.6	33.9	13.7	1.3	0.5	49540
26289	RED CREEK	23924	114	38.6	18.4	28.1	7.0	7.9	34292	43677	25	74	94	17.0	16.0	39.4	27.7	0.0	127500
26291	SLATYFORK	18266	271	43.5	25.8	24.7	5.5	0.4	29544	33383	11	50	226	31.9	23.0	25.2	18.1	1.8	81538
26292	THOMAS	14244	326	54.6	26.7	16.0	1.8	0.9	23014	26403	3	13	245	38.8	33.1	24.1	4.1	0.0	64107
26293	VALLEY BEND	14894	394	36.6	39.1	21.8	2.5	0.0	31598	35254	17	63	318	30.2	30.8	32.4	6.6	0.0	81860
26294	VALLEY HEAD	16423	400	50.5	29.3	14.5	2.3	3.5	24761	28246	4	20	339	39.8	28.6	22.7	7.1	1.8	67292
26296	WHITMER	16275	158	44.3	29.1	23.4	1.9	1.3	28968	33733	10	46	136	27.9	21.3	44.1	6.6	0.0	90526
26301	CLARKSBURG	18602	14060	42.5	30.8	21.2	3.9	1.6	30078	34799	12	53	9974	32.8	35.2	26.3	4.9	0.8	68902
26320	ALMA	14823	506	42.5	36.6	18.4	1.8	0.8	29573	34010	11	51	438	35.2	31.1	23.5	8.7	1.6	69655
26321	ALUM BRIDGE	15000	301	44.9	32.2	18.9	2.7	1.3	27539	31397	8	36	238	35.3	26.5	34.0	3.4	0.8	73684
26325	AUBURN	20302	107	56.1	26.2	13.1	0.9	3.7	21789	25572	3	9	91	45.1	24.2	19.8	8.8	2.2	57500
26327	BEREA	13911	50	58.0	24.0	14.0	2.0	2.0	20837	25418	2	6	43	41.9	20.9	20.9	11.6	4.7	61667
26330	BRIDGEPORT	24929	5467	24.0	28.4	33.8	9.8	4.0	47493	55131	67	97	4497	13.9	17.0	43.6	23.4	2.1	116690
26332	BRISTOL	19640	904	30.3	34.9	27.5	4.8	2.5	39890	45627	46	90	772	22.9	29.0	35.4	11.1	1.6	87761
26335	BURNSVILLE	13984	602	46.7	35.9	13.6	3.0	0.8	26923	31009	7	32	489	41.3	34.6	20.5	3.3	0.4	62451
26337	CAIRO	17277	580	36.6	33.3	26.2	2.9	1.0	33715	38718	23	72	495	39.0	32.1	21.8	4.9	2.2	62209
26338	CAMDEN	12574	238	47.9	36.1	14.3	1.3	0.4	26032	29508	6	28	189	45.0	31.2	18.5	5.3	0.0	57917
26339	CENTER POINT	13743	73	45.2	35.6	17.8	0.0	1.4	28329	30437	9	42	61	41.0	31.2	26.2	1.6	0.0	59167
26342	COXS MILLS	14806	303	41.3	36.6	16.8	4.3	1.0	29315	33437	11	49	235	28.9	20.9	43.4	6.0	0.9	90200
26343	CRAWFORD	12921	261	48.7	33.3	15.3	2.3	0.4	25850	29722	6	27	215	35.4	34.4	25.1	4.7	0.5	66429
26346	ELLENBORO	17178	338	31.4	38.8	26.0	2.7	1.2	35650	39599	30	79	288	42.0	30.6	20.1	6.3	1.0	61923
26347	FLEMINGTON	15174	985	42.2	31.6	21.8	2.5	1.8	29024	32385	10	47	821	42.6	27.2	21.8	6.7	1.7	60789
26348	FOLSOM	23294	127	47.2	29.1	18.1	3.2	2.4	26560	30733	7	31	103	65.1	27.2	2.9	4.9	0.0	38438
26351	GLENVILLE	12258	977	51.6	26.9	17.3	3.1	1.1	23957	27686	4	17	588	27.7	32.0	29.6	9.2	1.5	77292
26354	GRAFTON	14615	4091	44.0	32.9	19.8	2.7	0.6	28131	31575	9	41	3177	37.4	31.7	25.2	4.9	0.8	66779
26362	HARRISVILLE	18016	1383	41.4	30.8	23.8	3.3	0.7	31147	35460	15	61	1092	34.5	33.3	25.6	5.4	1.1	69352
26372	HORNER	16581	139	40.3	37.4	17.3	4.3	0.7	31778	35749	17	65	116	31.0	27.6	30.2	9.5	1.7	78000
26374	INDEPENDENCE	18220	498	33.7	30.9	28.5	5.2	1.6	36573	41399	34	82	434	33.6	24.2	34.3	6.9	0.9	81707
26376	IRELAND	13785	156	48.1	31.4	18.0	2.6	0.0	26003	30396	6	28	124	29.0	44.4	21.8	4.8	0.0	65000
26377	JACKSONBURG	15096	226	43.8	31.4	21.2	2.2	1.3	28738	33608	10	45	186	48.9	32.3	17.2	1.6	0.0	51111
26378	JANE LEW	16574	2058	39.2	34.4	22.0	3.4	1.0	32036	36132	18	66	1622	27.7	31.2	31.8	8.4	0.9	81000
26384	LINN	14472	284	53.5	24.3	14.8	6.0	1.4	23441	27175	3	15	227	36.1	37.4	26.4	0.0	0.0	68077
26385	LOST CREEK	19948	1372	29.8	32.2	28.4	5.9	3.6	39608	45720	45	90	1170	21.7	27.0	40.0	10.0	1.3	91456
26386	LUMBERPORT	19237	884	35.9	27.4	29.8	5.0	2.0	34909	40778	27	76	743	39.3	31.8	24.2	4.2	0.5	65000
26404	MEADOWBROOK	13689	439	42.8	36.0	20.1	0.7	0.5	27841	32220	8	39	337	49.6	32.3	15.7	2.4	0.0	50417
26405	MOATSVILLE	14701	516	39.9	40.5	14.9	4.1	0.6	28684	32414	10	45	451	34.8	28.2	30.6	6.4	0.0	65889
26408	MOUNT CLARE	25640	666	20.4	26.3	37.7	11.3	4.4	54493	65597	79	99	586	10.2	19.6	42.2	24.2	3.8	123626
26410	NEWBURG	13494	485	44.7	30.5	20.4	3.1	1.2	28996	32243	10	47	416	44.7	30.5	20.9	3.9	0.0	57097
26411	NEW MILTON	18999	332	36.8	34.0	23.8	3.6	1.8	33354	36699	22	71	278	24.1	34.5	30.2	9.7	1.4	72500
26412	ORLANDO	13829	192	41.7	38.5	14.6	4.2	1.0	30365	34247	13	54	159	36.5	27.0	27.7	6.3	2.5	70417
26415	PENNSBORO	17198	1288	40.5	33.9	20.8	3.3	1.6	31348	35479	16	62	1023	44.1	26.9	23.1	5.5	0.5	56954
26416	PHILIPPI	14344	3093	46.1	31.7	18.1	3.5	0.7	27521	30936	8	36	2338	35.1	30.8	28.2	5.6	0.4	70169
	WEST VIRGINIA	19262		38.4	30.0	24.1	5.2	2.4	33458	38993				29.0	29.1	31.1	9.6	1.3	80023
	UNITED STATES	25866		24.7	27.1	30.8	10.9	6.5	48124	56710				10.9	15.0	33.7	30.1	10.4	145905

ZIP CODE #	POST OFFICE NAME	FINANCIAL SERVICES: Auto Loan	FINANCIAL SERVICES: Home Loan	FINANCIAL SERVICES: Invest-ments	FINANCIAL SERVICES: Retire-ment Plans	THE HOME: Home Improvements: Home Repair	THE HOME: Home Improvements: Lawn & Garden	THE HOME: Furnishings: Comput-ers & Hard-ware	THE HOME: Furnishings: Major Appli-ances	THE HOME: Furnishings: TV, Radio, Sound Equip-ment	THE HOME: Furnishings: Furni-ture	ENTERTAINMENT: Dine out/ Carry out	ENTERTAINMENT: Sports Equip-ment	ENTERTAINMENT: Fees & Tickets	ENTERTAINMENT: Toys & Games	ENTERTAINMENT: Travel	ENTERTAINMENT: Cable TV	PERSONAL: Apparel & Services	PERSONAL: Auto Repairs	PERSONAL: Health Insur-ance	PERSONAL: Pets & Supplies
26161	PETROLEUM	73	49	22	42	55	64	47	59	57	48	67	71	40	63	48	61	61	58	73	84
26164	RAVENSWOOD	73	60	48	56	64	73	61	67	67	60	81	78	57	79	62	70	76	67	76	84
26167	READER	76	54	28	47	60	69	52	64	62	53	73	75	46	69	53	66	66	63	77	87
26169	ROCKPORT	76	53	27	46	59	67	51	62	60	52	71	74	44	67	52	64	65	62	75	87
26170	SAINT MARYS	78	63	44	60	67	76	63	70	69	63	83	82	59	80	63	71	77	70	79	88
26173	SHERMAN	86	73	53	69	78	85	68	77	74	68	89	92	66	90	70	76	84	75	85	100
26175	SISTERSVILLE	73	59	44	54	64	73	58	66	65	58	78	76	54	76	60	69	73	65	77	84
26178	SMITHVILLE	66	44	20	38	50	58	43	53	52	44	61	64	36	57	43	56	55	53	66	76
26180	WALKER	80	56	29	49	63	72	54	66	64	55	75	79	47	72	55	68	69	65	80	93
26181	WASHINGTON	100	93	77	89	97	103	86	94	89	86	109	111	84	111	88	91	104	92	99	118
26184	WAVERLY	93	75	49	69	81	89	70	81	78	70	94	97	65	93	72	82	87	80	93	109
26186	WILEYVILLE	70	47	21	40	53	61	45	56	54	46	64	67	38	60	46	59	58	56	70	80
26187	WILLIAMSTOWN	80	79	72	74	81	89	75	79	78	74	96	91	76	99	77	80	92	77	85	95
26201	BUCKHANNON	67	51	38	48	56	64	54	60	60	53	72	70	49	70	54	63	67	60	69	76
26202	FENWICK	67	45	20	38	51	58	43	54	52	44	61	64	37	58	44	56	55	53	66	76
26203	ERBACON	54	36	16	31	41	47	35	44	42	36	49	52	30	47	35	45	45	43	54	62
26205	CRAIGSVILLE	72	48	22	41	54	63	46	58	56	47	66	69	40	62	47	60	60	57	71	82
26206	COWEN	62	41	19	36	47	54	40	50	48	41	57	60	34	54	41	52	52	50	62	70
26208	CAMDEN ON GAULEY	64	43	19	37	49	56	41	52	50	42	59	62	35	56	42	54	53	51	64	74
26210	ADRIAN	73	49	22	42	56	64	47	59	57	48	67	71	40	64	48	62	61	59	73	84
26215	CLEVELAND	58	39	18	33	44	50	37	47	45	38	53	56	32	50	38	48	48	46	57	66
26217	DIANA	44	31	16	27	34	40	31	37	36	31	43	43	27	40	31	39	39	37	45	50
26218	FRENCH CREEK	67	45	20	38	50	58	43	54	52	44	61	64	37	58	44	56	55	53	66	76
26222	HACKER VALLEY	70	47	21	40	53	61	45	56	55	46	64	67	38	60	46	59	58	56	70	80
26224	HELVETIA	54	42	27	37	47	53	39	48	45	39	53	56	35	52	42	48	49	47	57	65
26228	KANAWHA HEAD	58	39	17	33	44	50	37	47	45	38	53	56	32	50	38	48	48	46	57	66
26230	PICKENS	54	41	26	37	46	52	39	47	45	39	53	56	35	52	41	48	49	47	56	65
26234	ROCK CAVE	57	38	17	33	43	50	37	46	44	37	52	55	31	49	37	48	47	46	57	65
26236	SELBYVILLE	47	32	14	27	36	41	31	38	37	31	43	46	26	41	31	40	39	38	47	54
26237	TALLMANSVILLE	65	44	20	38	50	57	42	53	51	43	60	63	36	57	43	55	54	52	65	75
26238	VOLGA	63	45	26	41	50	59	47	54	54	46	64	63	41	60	47	58	58	54	66	71
26241	ELKINS	71	59	47	56	63	72	61	66	66	59	79	75	57	78	61	69	74	66	75	81
26250	BELINGTON	60	42	22	38	47	55	43	51	50	42	59	59	37	56	43	53	54	51	62	68
26253	BEVERLY	76	55	29	48	61	69	52	63	61	53	72	76	46	69	53	65	66	62	76	88
26254	BOWDEN	71	56	38	50	63	71	53	63	60	52	71	74	47	70	56	64	66	62	75	87
26257	COALTON	58	39	18	34	44	51	38	47	45	38	53	56	32	50	38	49	48	46	58	67
26260	DAVIS	88	68	45	63	75	87	69	80	78	67	92	91	62	89	71	83	85	79	95	102
26261	RICHWOOD	54	39	24	37	44	52	42	48	48	41	57	55	37	53	42	51	52	48	58	61
26263	DRYFORK	72	57	39	51	64	72	53	64	60	53	72	75	48	71	57	65	67	63	76	88
26264	DURBIN	58	39	18	34	44	51	38	47	45	38	53	56	32	50	38	49	48	46	58	67
26266	UPPERGLADE	69	46	21	40	52	60	45	56	54	46	63	67	38	60	45	58	58	55	69	79
26267	ELLAMORE	69	46	21	40	52	60	44	56	54	45	63	66	38	59	45	58	57	55	68	79
26268	GLADY	69	55	38	50	61	68	52	61	58	51	69	72	47	68	55	61	64	60	71	83
26269	HAMBLETON	81	55	27	48	62	72	54	67	65	55	76	79	47	72	55	70	69	66	82	92
26270	HARMAN	84	66	45	59	74	83	62	75	70	61	83	88	55	82	66	75	77	74	88	102
26271	HENDRICKS	82	61	40	59	67	81	68	75	76	64	90	84	61	85	67	81	82	75	90	90
26273	HUTTONSVILLE	59	44	26	39	49	56	42	51	48	42	57	60	36	55	44	52	52	50	61	70
26276	KERENS	66	48	28	44	53	62	49	57	57	48	67	67	44	64	49	60	61	57	69	75
26278	MABIE	64	44	21	38	49	57	42	52	50	43	59	62	36	56	43	54	54	52	64	74
26280	MILL CREEK	71	48	22	41	54	62	46	58	55	47	65	69	39	62	47	60	59	57	71	82
26282	MONTERVILLE	40	32	22	29	36	40	30	36	34	30	40	42	27	40	32	36	37	35	43	49
26283	MONTROSE	68	47	23	41	52	61	47	56	55	47	65	66	40	61	47	59	59	56	69	77
26287	PARSONS	69	51	32	47	56	66	53	61	61	52	71	70	47	68	54	64	65	61	73	78
26288	WEBSTER SPRINGS	60	43	24	39	48	56	44	52	52	44	61	60	39	57	45	55	55	52	63	68
26289	RED CREEK	93	73	50	66	82	93	69	83	78	68	92	97	62	91	74	83	86	82	98	114
26291	SLATYFORK	68	53	36	48	60	67	50	60	56	49	67	70	45	66	53	60	62	59	71	82
26292	THOMAS	51	38	25	37	42	50	42	46	47	40	56	52	38	52	42	50	51	46	56	56
26293	VALLEY BEND	71	47	21	41	54	62	46	57	55	47	65	68	39	61	47	59	59	57	70	81
26294	VALLEY HEAD	65	51	35	46	57	64	48	58	54	48	64	68	43	64	51	58	60	57	68	79
26296	WHITMER	65	51	35	46	58	65	48	58	55	48	65	68	43	64	52	58	60	57	69	80
26301	CLARKSBURG	64	54	46	52	57	67	58	61	63	56	76	69	55	74	58	66	71	61	70	73
26320	ALMA	64	46	26	41	52	59	44	54	51	44	61	64	38	58	46	55	56	53	65	75
26321	ALUM BRIDGE	66	46	24	41	51	60	46	55	55	46	64	65	40	61	47	58	58	55	68	75
26325	AUBURN	99	66	30	57	75	86	64	80	77	65	91	96	54	86	65	83	82	79	99	114
26327	BEREA	65	44	20	38	49	57	42	53	51	43	60	63	36	56	43	55	54	52	65	75
26330	BRIDGEPORT	94	86	73	82	91	99	82	90	86	82	105	105	80	104	84	88	100	89	97	111
26332	BRISTOL	88	61	32	57	70	80	61	75	71	60	83	89	53	81	63	75	76	74	90	102
26335	BURNSVILLE	57	42	25	39	46	54	44	50	51	43	59	58	39	56	44	54	54	50	61	64
26337	CAIRO	79	53	24	46	60	69	51	64	62	52	72	76	43	68	52	66	66	63	79	90
26338	CAMDEN	61	41	18	35	46	53	39	49	47	40	55	59	33	52	40	51	50	48	60	70
26339	CENTER POINT	54	40	27	39	44	53	45	49	50	42	59	55	40	56	44	53	54	49	59	59
26342	COXS MILLS	61	47	32	44	52	60	49	55	54	47	64	64	43	62	50	57	59	55	65	72
26343	CRAWFORD	62	41	19	36	47	54	40	50	48	41	56	59	34	53	40	52	51	49	61	71
26346	ELLENBORO	81	54	25	47	61	71	52	65	63	53	74	78	45	70	53	68	67	65	81	93
26347	FLEMINGTON	74	50	23	43	56	65	48	60	58	49	68	72	41	64	49	62	62	59	74	85
26348	FOLSOM	116	78	35	67	88	101	75	94	91	76	106	112	64	100	76	98	97	93	116	133
26351	GLENVILLE	57	40	31	40	43	52	52	51	56	48	67	61	45	62	48	56	62	54	57	62
26354	GRAFTON	58	45	30	42	49	57	47	52	52	45	62	60	43	60	47	55	57	52	62	65
26362	HARRISVILLE	77	53	27	47	59	69	53	64	63	53	74	75	46	70	54	67	67	64	78	87
26372	HORNER	71	50	26	44	56	64	48	59	56	49	67	70	42	64	49	60	61	58	70	82
26374	INDEPENDENCE	81	59	33	53	64	73	58	68	66	58	79	80	51	75	58	70	72	67	80	92
26376	IRELAND	64	45	24	39	51	58	43	53	51	43	60	63	37	57	44	55	55	53	65	75
26377	JACKSONBURG	69	49	27	43	55	63	47	58	55	47	65	68	41	62	48	59	59	57	70	81
26378	JANE LEW	65	50	34	48	55	64	53	59	59	51	69	67	48	67	53	62	64	58	69	73
26384	LINN	68	46	22	40	52	60	45	56	54	46	63	66	38	60	46	58	58	55	68	78
26385	LOST CREEK	86	71	50	68	76	84	68	77	74	68	89	91	65	89	70	76	84	75	86	99
26386	LUMBERPORT	93	62	28	54	71	81	60	75	73	61	85	90	51	81	61	78	78	75	93	107
26404	MEADOWBROOK	55	41	26	39	45	54	45	50	50	43	59	56	40	56	44	53	54	50	60	61
26405	MOATSVILLE	68	46	21	39	52	60	44	55	53	45	62	66	38	59	45	57	57	55	68	78
26408	MOUNT CLARE	90	98	94	96	99	101	90	93	88	89	109	109	92	113	92	88	107	90	91	108
26410	NEWBURG	70	47	21	40	53	61	45	56	54	46	64	67	38	60	46	59	58	56	69	80
26411	NEW MILTON	92	62	28	53	70	80	60	74	72	61	84	89	51	80	61	77	77	74	92	105
26412	ORLANDO	69	46	21	40	52	60	45	56	54	45	63	67	38	60	45	58	57	55	69	79
26415	PENNSBORO	79	53	24	46	60	69	51	64	62	52	72	76	43	68	52	66	66	63	79	91
26416	PHILIPPI	60	43	28	40	48	56	45	52	52	44	61	61	40	59	45	55	56	52	62	69
	WEST VIRGINIA	73	60	47	57	64	72	61	67	67	60	80	78	57	78	61	69	75	67	76	84
	UNITED STATES	100	100	100	100	100	100	100	100	100	100	100	100	100	100	100	100	100	100	100	100

#	POST OFFICE NAME	COUNTY FIPS CODE	POPULATION			2000-2004 ANNUAL RATE		HOUSEHOLDS					FAMILIES		
			2000	2004	2009	% Rate	State Centile	2000	2004	2009	% Annual Rate 2000-2004	2004 Average HH Size	2000	2004	% Annual Rate 2000-2004
26419	PINE GROVE	103	724	692	666	-1.1	10	294	288	283	-0.5	2.40	220	208	-1.3
26421	PULLMAN	085	269	269	270	0.0	57	104	106	108	0.5	2.54	79	78	-0.3
26425	ROWLESBURG	077	670	652	642	-0.6	20	262	261	263	-0.1	2.50	176	168	-1.1
26426	SALEM	017	6020	5929	5878	-0.4	32	2199	2201	2218	0.0	2.42	1505	1452	-0.8
26430	SAND FORK	021	659	642	629	-0.6	21	255	255	256	0.0	2.52	192	186	-0.7
26431	SHINNSTON	033	6081	6089	6163	0.0	59	2445	2490	2562	0.4	2.44	1765	1736	-0.4
26437	SMITHFIELD	103	706	673	648	-1.1	8	289	281	276	-0.7	2.40	214	202	-1.4
26440	THORNTON	091	1145	1144	1139	0.0	54	461	470	477	0.5	2.42	330	325	-0.4
26443	TROY	021	105	103	101	-0.5	27	45	45	45	0.0	2.29	32	31	-0.7
26444	TUNNELTON	077	3120	3074	3043	-0.4	33	1245	1255	1271	0.2	2.45	910	887	-0.6
26447	WALKERSVILLE	041	1364	1507	1584	2.4	97	547	618	663	2.9	2.44	400	437	2.1
26448	WALLACE	033	1427	1430	1444	0.1	60	538	552	568	0.6	2.59	401	397	-0.2
26451	WEST MILFORD	033	1799	1819	1842	0.3	72	642	663	684	0.8	2.73	507	509	0.1
26452	WESTON	041	9423	9183	9047	-0.6	21	3933	3906	3919	-0.2	2.31	2649	2525	-1.1
26456	WEST UNION	017	3242	3210	3142	-0.2	41	1284	1291	1283	0.1	2.49	928	901	-0.7
26501	MORGANTOWN	061	22769	22547	22867	-0.2	41	9369	9412	9741	0.1	2.28	5731	5451	-1.2
26505	MORGANTOWN	061	31297	32414	33512	0.8	86	13129	13952	14778	1.4	2.00	5021	4924	-0.5
26506	MORGANTOWN	061	496	515	530	0.9	87	283	303	319	1.6	1.66	41	39	-1.2
26508	MORGANTOWN	061	22884	23988	25011	1.1	88	8968	9536	10108	1.5	2.51	6409	6579	0.6
26519	ALBRIGHT	077	1256	1264	1263	0.2	66	493	508	520	0.7	2.49	361	360	-0.1
26521	BLACKSVILLE	061	344	418	466	4.7	99	144	178	203	5.1	2.31	112	134	4.3
26525	BRUCETON MILLS	077	4109	4169	4185	0.3	75	1643	1707	1754	0.9	2.44	1196	1201	0.1
26529	CORE	061	402	491	550	4.8	99	153	192	219	5.5	2.56	119	144	4.6
26537	KINGWOOD	077	6458	6362	6305	-0.4	33	2543	2558	2590	0.1	2.41	1798	1744	-0.7
26541	MAIDSVILLE	061	756	753	759	-0.1	49	272	278	287	0.5	2.71	201	198	-0.4
26542	MASONTOWN	077	759	764	766	0.2	66	285	294	301	0.7	2.60	213	212	-0.1
26546	PURSGLOVE	061	230	229	232	-0.1	48	92	94	97	0.5	2.44	70	69	-0.3
26547	REEDSVILLE	077	3650	3663	3658	0.1	62	1507	1550	1585	0.7	2.36	1076	1069	-0.2
26554	FAIRMONT	049	41687	41214	40718	-0.3	38	17673	17802	17893	0.2	2.25	11154	10748	-0.9
26560	BAXTER	049	427	419	412	-0.4	28	173	174	174	0.1	2.41	123	119	-0.8
26561	BIG RUN	103	570	543	523	-1.1	7	216	210	206	-0.7	2.59	164	155	-1.3
26562	BURTON	061	806	780	767	-0.8	16	339	335	336	-0.3	2.33	229	218	-1.2
26568	ENTERPRISE	033	1476	1481	1491	0.1	62	558	570	584	0.5	2.60	427	422	-0.3
26570	FAIRVIEW	061	2256	2288	2308	0.3	75	901	932	958	0.8	2.45	679	681	0.1
26571	FARMINGTON	049	3431	3310	3236	-0.8	14	1404	1386	1381	-0.3	2.39	1018	969	-1.2
26575	HUNDRED	103	1033	993	957	-0.9	12	433	425	419	-0.4	2.34	271	253	-1.6
26581	LITTLETON	103	520	501	483	-0.9	12	190	187	185	-0.4	2.68	144	138	-1.0
26582	MANNINGTON	049	5337	5366	5342	0.1	64	2151	2203	2233	0.6	2.44	1578	1559	-0.3
26585	METZ	049	864	874	870	0.3	73	332	342	347	0.7	2.56	241	240	-0.1
26587	RACHEL	049	307	301	296	-0.5	26	115	115	115	0.0	2.62	85	82	-0.8
26588	RIVESVILLE	049	3255	3223	3188	-0.2	41	1303	1311	1322	0.1	2.40	941	914	-0.7
26590	WANA	061	680	713	747	1.1	89	244	260	278	1.5	2.74	192	199	0.9
26591	WORTHINGTON	049	1376	1365	1349	-0.2	44	512	520	523	0.4	2.60	379	372	-0.4
26601	SUTTON	007	5087	5134	5191	0.2	69	1847	1901	1955	0.7	2.55	1308	1298	-0.2
26610	BIRCH RIVER	067	1496	1485	1474	-0.2	44	579	589	599	0.4	2.52	428	421	-0.4
26611	CEDARVILLE	021	385	381	378	-0.3	39	145	147	149	0.3	2.59	111	109	-0.4
26615	COPEN	007	253	257	260	0.4	77	95	99	102	1.0	2.60	69	69	0.0
26617	DILLE	015	399	403	408	0.2	70	162	167	173	0.7	2.40	124	125	0.2
26619	EXCHANGE	007	269	274	277	0.4	78	104	109	113	1.1	2.51	78	80	0.6
26621	FLATWOODS	007	855	868	877	0.4	76	350	366	378	1.1	1.92	246	248	0.2
26623	FRAMETOWN	007	1723	1745	1759	0.3	73	682	706	725	0.8	2.47	502	503	0.1
26624	GASSAWAY	007	3006	2992	3001	-0.1	47	1263	1279	1303	0.3	2.34	875	854	-0.6
26627	HEATERS	007	247	250	253	0.3	73	101	106	109	1.1	1.66	71	72	0.3
26629	LITTLE BIRCH	007	539	566	582	1.2	89	216	232	243	1.7	2.44	163	170	1.0
26631	NAPIER	007	187	190	192	0.4	77	78	81	84	0.9	2.32	55	55	0.0
26636	ROSEDALE	021	498	487	478	-0.5	24	201	201	202	0.0	2.42	147	142	-0.8
26638	SHOCK	021	182	177	173	-0.7	19	68	68	68	0.0	2.60	49	47	-1.0
26639	STRANGE CREEK	007	236	237	238	0.1	63	97	100	102	0.7	2.37	70	69	-0.3
26641	WILSIE	007	143	145	147	0.3	75	59	61	63	0.8	2.38	44	44	0.0
26651	SUMMERSVILLE	067	6758	7101	7308	1.2	89	2846	3058	3221	1.7	2.30	1921	1987	0.8
26656	BELVA	067	349	327	321	-1.5	3	140	135	136	-0.9	2.42	107	100	-1.6
26660	CALVIN	067	771	779	779	0.2	71	290	300	307	0.8	2.60	228	229	0.1
26662	CANVAS	067	1372	1350	1337	-0.4	31	521	528	537	0.3	2.55	398	391	-0.4
26667	DRENNEN	067	203	196	194	-0.8	14	87	86	87	-0.3	2.28	64	61	-1.1
26674	JODIE	019	426	425	424	-0.1	52	170	173	176	0.4	2.38	123	120	-0.6
26675	KESLERS CROSS LANES	067	1048	1030	1020	-0.4	30	413	418	424	0.3	2.46	302	294	-0.6
26676	LEIVASY	067	971	964	957	-0.2	44	411	420	428	0.5	2.30	315	312	-0.2
26678	MOUNT LOOKOUT	067	1189	1208	1210	0.4	77	450	469	483	1.0	2.58	357	363	0.4
26679	MOUNT NEBO	067	1883	1900	1898	0.2	69	751	779	799	0.9	2.44	582	588	0.2
26680	NALLEN	019	65	61	60	-1.5	3	29	28	28	-0.8	2.18	21	20	-1.1
26681	NETTIE	067	1226	1205	1193	-0.4	30	481	486	494	0.2	2.48	369	362	-0.5
26684	POOL	067	153	156	156	0.5	79	60	63	64	1.2	2.48	47	48	0.5
26690	SWISS	067	556	526	517	-1.3	5	218	212	214	-0.7	2.48	164	154	-1.5
26691	TIOGA	067	318	325	327	0.5	81	119	123	123	1.0	2.73	86	87	0.3
26704	AUGUSTA	027	3497	3742	3941	1.6	93	1359	1488	1595	2.2	2.47	1013	1072	1.3
26705	AURORA	077	909	891	881	-0.5	26	357	358	362	0.1	2.49	273	266	-0.6
26710	BURLINGTON	057	4090	4202	4383	0.6	83	1533	1606	1708	1.1	2.60	1213	1239	0.5
26711	CAPON BRIDGE	027	1314	1392	1459	1.4	91	551	597	637	1.9	2.31	397	414	1.0
26714	DELRAY	027	843	919	977	2.1	95	313	349	378	2.6	2.63	230	248	1.8
26716	EGLON	077	647	638	633	-0.3	34	244	246	250	0.2	2.59	182	178	-0.5
26717	ELK GARDEN	057	1059	1041	1074	-0.4	30	410	410	431	0.0	2.54	313	304	-0.7
26719	FORT ASHBY	057	2199	2240	2324	0.4	79	865	901	955	1.0	2.45	615	619	0.2
26720	GORMANIA	023	694	674	672	-0.7	18	293	292	297	-0.1	2.31	210	202	-0.9
26722	GREEN SPRING	027	761	777	801	0.5	80	313	328	344	1.1	2.37	216	217	0.1
26726	KEYSER	057	9327	10229	11070	2.2	96	3792	4256	4711	2.8	2.30	2513	2712	1.8
26731	LAHMANSVILLE	023	545	544	546	0.0	53	228	233	239	0.5	2.33	165	163	-0.3
26739	MOUNT STORM	023	834	828	829	-0.2	44	344	349	357	0.3	2.37	252	248	-0.4
26743	NEW CREEK	057	1550	1591	1658	0.6	82	598	628	669	1.2	2.53	442	449	0.4
26750	PIEDMONT	057	1050	1035	1066	-0.3	33	435	433	454	-0.1	2.39	281	269	-1.0
26753	RIDGELEY	057	6426	6547	6826	0.4	79	2580	2685	2856	0.9	2.43	1939	1961	0.3
26755	RIO	027	427	457	481	1.6	93	161	176	189	2.1	2.59	124	132	1.5
26757	ROMNEY	027	5570	5655	5811	0.4	76	2269	2348	2455	0.8	2.28	1482	1471	-0.2
26761	SHANKS	027	1131	1191	1243	1.2	90	383	411	436	1.7	2.87	291	303	1.0
26763	SPRINGFIELD	027	1483	1506	1550	0.4	76	605	629	660	0.9	2.36	430	431	0.1
26764	TERRA ALTA	077	5066	5146	5172	0.4	77	1985	2066	2129	1.0	2.44	1428	1435	0.1
	WEST VIRGINIA					0.2					0.6	2.35			-0.3
	UNITED STATES					1.2					1.3	2.58			1.1

ZIP CODE #	POST OFFICE NAME	RACE (%) White 2000	White 2004	Black 2000	Black 2004	Asian/Pacific 2000	Asian/Pacific 2004	% Hispanic Origin 2000	% Hispanic Origin 2004	2004 AGE DISTRIBUTION (%) 0-4	5-9	10-14	15-19	20-24	25-44	45-64	65-84	85+	18+	MEDIAN AGE 2004	% 2004 Males	% 2004 Females
26419	PINE GROVE	99.5	99.4	0.0	0.0	0.0	0.0	0.6	0.6	5.8	6.5	7.2	5.8	6.4	25.7	27.8	12.9	2.0	76.7	39.6	48.7	51.3
26421	PULLMAN	97.8	97.4	0.0	0.0	0.4	0.4	0.4	0.4	4.8	4.8	6.7	7.8	6.7	25.3	30.5	11.9	1.5	79.2	41.1	48.7	51.3
26425	ROWLESBURG	98.8	98.9	0.0	0.0	0.2	0.2	0.0	0.2	5.4	5.5	6.4	6.8	5.5	25.0	27.2	16.1	2.2	78.7	41.7	48.6	51.4
26426	SALEM	93.6	92.4	1.5	1.5	3.3	4.4	0.8	0.9	5.5	5.5	6.2	8.4	10.1	25.6	24.2	12.6	2.0	78.2	36.0	49.9	50.1
26430	SAND FORK	99.1	99.1	0.0	0.0	0.2	0.2	0.6	0.6	5.3	5.0	5.5	7.3	7.3	28.0	26.2	13.6	1.9	79.6	40.7	49.8	50.2
26431	SHINNSTON	98.5	98.3	0.5	0.5	0.2	0.2	0.8	0.8	5.7	6.1	6.4	5.5	6.1	26.7	27.6	14.1	1.9	78.5	40.6	48.5	51.5
26437	SMITHFIELD	99.4	99.4	0.0	0.0	0.0	0.0	0.7	0.6	6.4	6.5	6.7	5.2	5.8	26.8	26.8	14.6	1.3	77.1	39.8	49.3	50.7
26440	THORNTON	98.5	98.5	0.2	0.2	0.4	0.4	0.6	0.6	4.6	4.9	6.5	6.5	5.4	26.8	28.6	14.7	2.1	79.8	42.0	50.5	49.5
26443	TROY	99.1	99.0	0.0	0.0	0.0	0.0	0.0	0.0	4.9	5.8	6.8	5.8	6.8	24.3	30.1	12.6	2.9	76.7	42.2	49.5	50.5
26444	TUNNELTON	99.1	99.1	0.1	0.1	0.1	0.1	0.6	0.6	5.3	5.6	6.7	6.5	5.9	26.9	26.8	13.2	1.4	78.4	40.8	50.3	49.7
26447	WALKERSVILLE	98.5	98.5	0.2	0.1	0.1	0.1	0.5	0.5	5.8	6.4	6.7	5.7	5.2	27.4	29.6	11.6	1.5	77.6	40.0	51.2	48.8
26448	WALLACE	98.5	98.5	0.1	0.1	0.2	0.2	0.7	0.7	4.6	6.2	7.5	6.6	6.1	29.2	28.0	10.6	1.3	77.3	38.8	51.4	48.6
26451	WEST MILFORD	98.6	98.6	0.2	0.2	0.1	0.1	0.7	0.7	6.5	6.7	7.5	6.9	6.1	27.8	26.9	10.5	1.1	74.7	37.9	49.9	50.1
26452	WESTON	98.4	98.4	0.2	0.2	0.5	0.5	0.6	0.6	5.0	5.3	6.1	5.7	5.5	26.5	28.1	15.5	2.4	80.3	42.3	48.2	51.8
26456	WEST UNION	98.4	98.4	0.0	0.0	0.1	0.1	0.4	0.4	6.5	6.3	6.2	5.8	6.5	25.1	26.3	15.3	2.0	77.3	41.0	48.3	51.7
26501	MORGANTOWN	91.7	91.0	5.4	5.6	1.0	1.3	0.8	0.9	5.3	5.2	5.7	5.7	9.1	30.9	25.1	11.6	1.5	80.8	37.0	51.2	48.8
26505	MORGANTOWN	89.0	87.3	3.8	3.8	4.8	6.4	1.4	1.4	3.2	2.7	3.0	15.3	28.5	22.8	14.6	8.1	1.8	89.0	24.5	51.2	48.8
26506	MORGANTOWN	72.2	67.4	5.4	5.2	17.9	23.1	3.0	3.1	2.5	1.8	1.8	9.3	46.0	27.8	3.1	3.7	4.1	91.8	23.8	56.5	43.5
26508	MORGANTOWN	96.6	96.1	1.1	1.1	1.0	1.4	0.7	0.7	6.6	6.8	6.9	5.8	6.1	30.2	27.4	9.2	1.0	76.2	37.6	49.3	50.8
26519	ALBRIGHT	98.8	98.8	0.2	0.2	0.1	0.1	0.3	0.3	5.2	5.7	6.6	5.4	5.7	28.8	29.7	11.6	1.4	79.2	40.6	51.1	48.9
26521	BLACKSVILLE	98.3	98.1	0.9	1.0	0.0	0.2	0.0	0.0	5.3	5.7	6.7	4.8	6.2	25.8	30.1	13.9	1.4	79.2	41.8	50.7	49.3
26525	BRUCETON MILLS	98.9	99.0	0.0	0.0	0.2	0.2	0.5	0.5	5.6	5.8	6.3	5.9	5.8	29.3	27.8	11.9	1.7	78.7	40.0	50.0	50.0
26529	CORE	99.3	99.2	0.0	0.0	0.0	0.2	0.0	0.0	5.3	5.7	6.5	5.1	6.3	25.5	29.7	14.5	1.4	79.4	42.0	49.9	50.1
26537	KINGWOOD	98.0	98.0	0.9	0.9	0.3	0.4	0.5	0.5	5.4	5.7	6.4	6.6	6.1	26.1	27.1	13.9	2.8	78.1	40.7	48.3	51.7
26541	MAIDSVILLE	97.2	97.0	1.3	1.3	0.1	0.3	0.4	0.4	6.0	6.5	8.6	5.8	6.0	28.4	28.8	9.2	0.7	75.3	38.5	49.4	50.6
26542	MASONTOWN	99.1	99.0	0.0	0.0	0.3	0.4	0.4	0.3	6.5	6.7	6.8	6.8	6.3	27.2	26.6	11.8	1.3	76.1	38.6	51.8	48.2
26546	PURSGLOVE	98.3	98.3	0.4	0.4	0.4	0.4	0.4	0.4	6.6	6.6	7.0	6.6	7.9	30.1	25.3	8.7	1.3	75.6	36.3	48.5	51.5
26547	REEDSVILLE	99.4	99.4	0.0	0.0	0.1	0.1	1.0	1.0	6.5	6.5	5.7	5.9	6.0	27.7	27.1	13.1	1.5	77.8	39.0	48.5	51.5
26554	FAIRMONT	94.1	93.8	4.0	4.1	0.5	0.7	0.7	0.7	5.2	5.2	5.6	5.8	7.9	26.1	26.1	15.3	2.9	81.0	40.6	47.5	52.5
26560	BAXTER	95.1	94.8	3.5	3.6	0.2	0.2	0.7	0.7	4.5	5.0	6.4	5.7	5.7	26.0	29.1	15.0	2.4	80.7	42.5	46.8	53.2
26561	BIG RUN	99.8	99.8	0.0	0.0	0.0	0.0	0.5	0.6	5.0	6.3	8.1	5.9	5.9	25.8	28.0	13.3	1.8	76.6	40.3	52.7	47.3
26562	BURTON	98.5	98.5	0.5	0.5	0.0	0.0	0.3	0.3	4.7	5.1	6.3	6.2	6.7	23.7	29.5	15.4	2.4	80.0	43.0	49.5	50.5
26568	ENTERPRISE	98.9	98.9	0.4	0.4	0.0	0.0	0.8	0.7	6.7	6.8	7.2	6.2	5.7	28.9	25.0	12.6	1.0	75.4	37.6	49.4	50.6
26570	FAIRVIEW	98.8	98.7	0.2	0.2	0.0	0.0	0.6	0.6	5.8	6.1	6.5	5.3	5.3	26.6	28.5	14.3	1.5	78.3	41.1	49.4	50.6
26571	FARMINGTON	96.5	96.3	2.3	2.4	0.1	0.1	0.5	0.5	5.3	5.3	6.2	6.1	5.8	26.0	28.5	14.7	2.1	79.5	41.7	49.0	51.0
26575	HUNDRED	98.4	98.3	0.1	0.1	0.0	0.0	0.1	0.1	4.3	4.7	7.2	7.7	6.5	22.8	28.7	15.9	2.3	79.2	42.8	49.5	50.6
26581	LITTLETON	98.7	98.6	0.2	0.2	0.0	0.0	0.0	0.0	5.8	6.0	6.8	5.2	6.0	27.2	28.1	13.0	2.0	78.0	39.9	49.5	50.5
26582	MANNINGTON	98.4	98.2	0.4	0.4	0.1	0.2	0.7	0.7	5.8	5.9	6.5	5.7	5.6	26.0	27.8	14.5	2.2	78.4	41.0	47.9	52.1
26585	METZ	98.7	98.6	0.0	0.0	0.1	0.1	0.8	0.8	5.0	5.6	7.6	6.4	5.6	24.6	29.2	14.0	2.1	77.7	41.5	48.5	51.5
26587	RACHEL	98.4	98.3	1.0	1.0	0.0	0.0	0.3	0.3	5.7	5.7	6.3	5.0	5.7	24.6	29.6	15.3	2.3	78.7	42.5	47.8	52.2
26588	RIVESVILLE	97.0	96.8	2.2	2.4	0.2	0.2	0.5	0.5	4.9	5.1	6.0	5.8	6.0	27.3	28.4	14.2	2.4	80.6	41.7	49.6	50.4
26590	WANA	98.4	98.5	0.6	0.6	0.0	0.0	0.3	0.3	5.9	6.0	6.7	5.2	6.3	26.5	28.5	13.0	1.8	78.4	40.3	50.2	49.8
26591	WORTHINGTON	98.5	98.3	0.9	0.9	0.2	0.2	0.5	0.5	4.2	4.6	6.7	6.3	6.3	27.2	29.7	13.2	1.8	80.7	41.7	49.3	50.7
26601	SUTTON	97.1	96.9	1.1	1.1	0.1	0.2	0.5	0.5	5.0	5.3	5.9	6.3	6.4	27.7	28.2	13.1	2.1	79.9	40.6	51.7	48.3
26610	BIRCH RIVER	98.5	98.5	0.0	0.0	0.3	0.3	0.4	0.4	5.0	5.3	7.2	7.3	6.7	28.8	26.0	12.0	1.8	78.1	39.4	51.5	48.5
26611	CEDARVILLE	97.9	98.2	0.8	0.8	0.0	0.0	0.8	0.5	5.5	5.8	6.6	6.3	6.6	26.8	27.6	13.4	1.6	78.2	40.4	51.2	48.8
26615	COPEN	98.4	98.1	0.4	0.4	0.0	0.4	0.4	0.4	7.0	7.0	6.6	5.8	6.2	26.9	26.9	11.7	2.0	75.5	38.3	49.8	50.2
26617	DILLE	99.3	99.3	0.0	0.0	0.0	0.0	0.0	0.0	5.7	6.2	7.2	6.0	6.7	27.8	26.8	12.2	1.5	77.2	38.6	50.9	49.1
26619	EXCHANGE	98.1	98.2	0.4	0.4	0.4	0.4	0.4	0.4	7.3	6.9	6.2	5.8	6.6	26.6	27.7	11.0	1.8	76.3	38.2	50.0	50.0
26621	FLATWOODS	97.3	96.9	1.8	1.8	0.4	0.5	0.1	0.1	3.7	4.0	4.7	5.0	7.3	33.1	28.9	11.2	2.2	84.3	40.6	57.4	42.6
26623	FRAMETOWN	98.5	98.3	0.2	0.2	0.3	0.3	0.4	0.4	6.2	6.5	7.1	6.1	5.3	25.9	27.2	13.9	1.8	76.5	40.0	49.5	50.5
26624	GASSAWAY	99.1	99.0	0.2	0.2	0.1	0.1	0.5	0.5	4.8	5.4	6.7	6.1	4.9	25.3	28.1	15.9	2.9	79.4	43.1	48.5	51.5
26627	HEATERS	96.4	95.6	2.8	2.8	0.4	0.4	0.0	0.0	3.2	3.6	4.4	4.4	8.4	36.4	26.8	10.4	2.4	86.0	39.3	60.4	39.6
26629	LITTLE BIRCH	97.4	97.4	0.6	0.5	0.2	0.2	0.9	1.1	6.0	6.0	7.8	7.4	6.2	26.9	25.8	12.4	1.6	75.4	38.7	51.1	48.9
26631	NAPIER	98.9	98.4	0.5	0.5	0.0	0.0	0.0	0.5	4.2	4.7	5.8	5.8	5.3	26.8	32.6	12.6	2.1	81.6	43.3	51.6	48.4
26636	ROSEDALE	98.4	98.6	0.2	0.2	0.0	0.0	0.6	0.8	4.9	5.1	5.5	6.2	6.2	25.7	31.4	13.1	1.9	80.7	42.7	51.3	48.7
26638	SHOCK	98.4	98.3	0.0	0.0	0.0	0.0	1.1	1.1	4.5	4.5	5.7	6.2	5.7	24.9	33.9	12.4	2.3	81.4	44.0	50.3	49.7
26639	STRANGE CREEK	99.6	99.6	0.4	0.4	0.0	0.0	0.0	0.0	6.3	7.2	8.4	6.3	5.1	23.2	26.2	15.2	2.1	73.8	39.8	48.5	51.5
26641	WILSIE	97.9	97.2	0.0	0.0	0.7	0.7	0.0	0.7	6.2	6.2	6.9	6.2	5.5	26.9	26.9	13.1	2.1	76.6	39.8	49.0	51.0
26651	SUMMERSVILLE	98.5	98.5	0.0	0.0	0.4	0.4	0.9	0.8	5.3	5.5	6.3	6.7	6.3	25.3	28.0	14.6	2.1	78.9	41.5	48.0	52.1
26656	BELVA	98.9	98.5	0.0	0.0	0.0	0.0	0.3	0.3	5.5	5.5	6.1	6.1	7.0	26.9	26.3	15.3	1.2	79.2	40.3	50.5	49.5
26660	CALVIN	98.7	98.8	0.0	0.0	0.4	0.4	0.1	0.0	5.8	5.9	6.3	6.3	5.8	27.5	28.6	12.6	1.3	78.1	40.1	49.4	50.6
26662	CANVAS	99.1	99.1	0.1	0.1	0.2	0.2	0.3	0.3	5.2	5.6	6.6	6.4	5.6	27.1	29.6	12.7	1.2	78.7	41.0	49.7	50.3
26667	DRENNEN	99.0	99.0	0.0	0.0	0.0	0.0	1.0	1.0	5.6	5.6	5.1	5.1	6.1	29.6	28.1	13.8	1.0	80.6	40.3	49.0	51.0
26674	JODIE	97.4	97.4	2.1	2.1	0.0	0.0	0.5	0.5	5.4	5.4	6.4	5.7	6.6	25.9	26.1	15.1	3.5	79.3	41.4	48.7	51.3
26675	KESLERS CROSS LANES	99.5	99.5	0.0	0.0	0.0	0.0	0.9	0.9	7.4	7.3	6.8	5.3	5.3	32.0	25.0	9.8	1.1	75.2	36.1	49.9	50.1
26676	LEIVASY	99.3	99.5	0.0	0.0	0.1	0.1	0.2	0.2	5.6	6.0	6.3	5.8	5.3	27.2	28.8	13.7	1.2	78.5	41.1	51.1	48.9
26678	MOUNT LOOKOUT	99.5	99.5	0.1	0.1	0.0	0.0	0.4	0.4	5.1	5.6	6.7	6.5	5.2	27.1	31.5	10.9	1.5	78.6	41.1	49.4	50.6
26679	MOUNT NEBO	99.3	99.4	0.0	0.0	0.1	0.1	0.2	0.2	5.4	6.3	6.1	6.3	5.6	28.5	29.0	11.5	1.4	78.2	39.6	50.6	49.4
26680	NALLEN	100.0	100.0	0.0	0.0	0.0	0.0	0.0	1.6	4.9	4.9	4.9	4.9	6.6	23.0	31.2	18.0	1.6	85.3	45.4	50.8	49.2
26681	NETTIE	99.1	99.2	0.1	0.1	0.2	0.2	0.4	0.3	5.2	5.6	6.6	6.3	5.6	27.0	29.5	12.8	1.2	78.7	41.1	49.8	50.2
26684	POOL	99.4	99.4	0.0	0.0	0.0	0.0	0.0	0.0	5.1	5.8	6.4	6.4	5.1	26.9	32.1	10.9	1.3	78.9	40.9	48.7	51.3
26690	SWISS	98.7	98.7	0.0	0.0	0.0	0.0	0.5	0.6	4.9	5.1	5.5	5.5	6.8	27.4	27.6	16.0	1.1	81.0	41.5	50.2	49.8
26691	TIOGA	98.4	98.8	0.0	0.0	0.0	0.0	0.3	0.3	5.9	6.2	6.8	6.8	6.5	27.4	27.1	12.0	1.5	76.9	39.4	50.2	49.9
26704	AUGUSTA	98.3	98.1	0.5	0.5	0.1	0.2	0.6	0.6	6.7	6.7	6.9	6.4	6.3	27.7	25.5	12.6	1.3	75.6	38.5	51.4	48.6
26705	AURORA	99.2	99.3	0.1	0.1	0.1	0.1	0.8	0.6	4.8	5.2	7.1	7.2	5.8	23.6	30.1	14.4	1.9	78.6	42.5	51.1	48.9
26710	BURLINGTON	98.8	98.7	0.4	0.4	0.1	0.2	0.4	0.5	5.4	6.0	7.7	6.7	5.7	27.8	27.9	11.8	1.1	76.7	39.1	51.1	48.9
26711	CAPON BRIDGE	97.7	97.7	1.5	1.5	0.2	0.1	0.4	0.3	5.1	5.8	7.6	6.6	5.0	26.7	30.2	11.9	1.3	77.2	41.5	51.5	48.5
26714	DELRAY	97.9	97.8	0.6	0.5	0.1	0.1	0.2	0.3	7.5	7.3	7.5	6.3	6.4	26.9	24.7	12.7	0.7	73.5	37.2	52.2	47.8
26716	EGLON	99.5	99.5	0.3	0.3	0.0	0.0	0.3	0.3	5.0	5.3	6.7	6.6	5.0	24.5	30.1	15.2	1.6	78.8	43.0	52.0	48.0
26717	ELK GARDEN	96.5	96.4	2.7	2.8	0.0	0.0	0.9	0.9	4.7	5.0	6.9	6.5	7.0	26.9	28.2	13.2	1.5	79.3	40.8	52.2	47.8
26719	FORT ASHBY	98.8	98.7	0.2	0.2	0.2	0.3	0.5	0.5	5.6	5.9	6.7	6.1	5.1	27.2	26.9	14.5	1.9	77.9	40.6	49.1	50.9
26720	GORMANIA	97.6	97.2	0.7	0.7	0.1	0.2	0.4	0.5	4.9	5.3	4.9	5.2	6.1	24.6	32.8	14.1	2.1	81.9	44.1	49.0	51.0
26722	GREEN SPRING	99.0	99.0	0.5	0.5	0.1	0.1	0.5	0.4	7.0	7.3	7.0	6.3	5.0	24.5	29.0	12.9	1.2	74.9	39.0	49.7	50.3
26726	KEYSER	93.3	93.1	4.8	4.9	0.4	0.5	0.6	0.6	6.0	5.7	6.0	6.3	7.9	24.9	25.6	15.0	2.7	79.3	39.7	48.3	51.8
26731	LAHMANSVILLE	99.1	99.1	0.4	0.4	0.0	0.0	0.6	0.4	6.3	6.4	5.3	5.2	5.2	26.1	30.3	13.8	1.5	79.2	41.8	51.7	48.4
26739	MOUNT STORM	98.8	98.7	0.2	0.2	0.1	0.1	0.2	0.2	5.6	5.8	5.4	5.3	5.4	26.0	30.9	14.1	1.5	80.2	42.5	51.5	48.6
26743	NEW CREEK	97.6	97.4	0.7	0.7	0.3	0.4	0.5	0.5	5.6	5.8	6.7	6.5	6.1	25.1	30.0	13.1	1.2	77.7	41.2	50.2	49.8
26750	PIEDMONT	81.2	81.3	15.4	15.4	0.0	0.0	1.6	1.6	6.8	6.3	7.3	7.4	7.5	26.4	24.8	12.0	1.5	75.2	36.6	48.4	51.6
26753	RIDGELEY	99.2	99.2	0.2	0.2	0.1	0.1	0.7	0.7	5.8	6.2	6.8	6.0	4.9	26.9	29.1	12.8	1.5	77.4	40.4	48.8	51.2
26755	RIO	98.1	98.0	0.7	0.7	0.0	0.2	0.2	0.2	7.0	7.0	7.9	7.0	6.4	26.9	25.2	11.8	0.9	73.7	37.4	49.7	50.3
26757	ROMNEY	97.4	97.2	1.4	1.4	0.3	0.5	0.7	0.7	5.7	6.1	7.0	7.1	5.9	25.0	25.8	15.1	2.4	76.6	40.2	47.8	52.2
26761	SHANKS	98.1	97.9	0.7	0.7	0.2	0.3	0.4	0.5	6.5	6.5	7.4	7.1	6.5	26.8	26.4	11.8	1.3	75.3	38.2	49.2	50.8
26763	SPRINGFIELD	99.1	99.1	0.3	0.3	0.1	0.2	0.4	0.4	5.6	6.0	6.8	6.4	5.1	25.0	29.6	14.0	1.5	77.4	41.4	50.1	49.9
26764	TERRA ALTA	99.0	99.0	0.2	0.2	0.1	0.1	0.6	0.6	5.9	6.0	6.4	7.3	6.1	24.9	28.2	13.8	1.5	77.1	40.3	50.3	49.7
	WEST VIRGINIA	95.1	94.8	3.2	3.2	0.5	0.7	0.7	0.7	5.6	5.8	6.2	6.3	6.7	26.7	27.1	13.7	1.9	78.9	40.1	48.8	51.2
	UNITED STATES	75.1	73.6	12.3	12.5	3.8	4.2	12.5	14.1	6.9	6.7	7.2	7.0	7.3	28.6	23.8	10.8	1.7	75.1	36.0	49.1	50.9

#	POST OFFICE NAME	2004 Per Capita Income	2004 HH Income Base	2004 Household Income Distribution (%): Less than $25,000	$25,000 to $49,999	$50,000 to $99,999	$100,000 to $149,999	$150,000 or More	Median Household Income: 2004	2009	2004 National Centile	2004 State Centile	2004 Home Value Base	2004 Home Value Distribution (%): Less than $50,000	$50,000 to $89,999	$90,000 to $174,999	$175,000 to $399,999	$400,000 or More	2004 Median Home Value
26419	PINE GROVE	17747	288	41.0	32.6	21.5	3.5	1.4	31057	36476	15	60	224	46.0	31.7	21.0	1.3	0.0	53750
26421	PULLMAN	16562	106	42.5	25.5	26.4	5.7	0.0	30000	35000	12	52	91	39.6	23.1	23.1	11.0	3.3	69375
26425	ROWLESBURG	15221	261	42.2	36.0	18.8	1.2	1.9	29601	33205	11	51	195	57.4	28.2	12.8	1.5	0.0	45972
26426	SALEM	15565	2201	45.3	32.8	16.9	2.6	2.5	27756	31455	8	38	1625	38.3	29.1	26.5	5.7	0.5	66106
26430	SAND FORK	13182	255	52.6	27.8	16.5	0.8	2.4	23752	26537	4	17	206	39.8	21.4	35.0	3.9	0.0	65000
26431	SHINNSTON	17269	2490	39.5	30.4	24.3	3.8	2.0	32330	37426	19	68	2031	33.0	34.4	25.3	6.9	0.5	69703
26437	SMITHFIELD	23523	281	43.8	29.9	21.4	3.2	1.8	28836	33078	10	45	230	59.6	28.7	7.4	4.4	0.0	42414
26440	THORNTON	14132	470	47.5	33.6	15.3	2.3	1.3	26318	29921	6	29	380	44.0	29.5	21.8	4.7	0.0	56216
26443	TROY	16930	45	44.4	33.3	17.8	2.2	2.2	27912	32320	8	40	35	25.7	22.9	42.9	5.7	2.9	91250
26444	TUNNELTON	13291	1255	47.0	36.0	14.3	1.9	0.7	26292	29636	6	29	1077	54.6	28.4	13.7	2.6	0.7	45875
26447	WALKERSVILLE	14887	618	43.5	37.2	15.7	2.8	0.8	28247	32120	9	41	506	32.8	34.2	25.7	5.9	1.4	70238
26448	WALLACE	15571	552	44.2	31.2	19.4	2.9	2.4	28290	31908	9	42	460	50.0	22.2	22.8	4.1	0.9	50000
26451	WEST MILFORD	16019	663	34.2	37.6	23.8	3.3	1.1	35541	41243	30	79	555	33.9	34.6	26.1	5.4	0.0	68690
26452	WESTON	16419	3906	41.5	34.5	19.6	3.2	1.2	30450	34418	13	55	2881	30.5	33.2	29.2	7.0	0.2	75114
26456	WEST UNION	14030	1291	45.8	33.5	18.1	2.2	0.4	27104	30498	7	34	1019	39.0	27.2	28.3	5.4	0.2	66954
26501	MORGANTOWN	18162	9412	39.4	29.9	23.7	5.8	1.3	32620	39432	20	68	6501	26.5	29.1	33.5	10.2	0.8	83403
26505	MORGANTOWN	18755	13952	51.8	21.4	17.6	5.8	3.4	23412	28552	3	15	5549	18.4	14.2	42.8	22.7	2.1	116931
26506	MORGANTOWN	14648	303	74.6	13.2	7.9	2.3	2.0	13244	15477	1	1	18	50.0	16.7	16.7	0.0	16.7	55000
26508	MORGANTOWN	24680	9536	25.8	29.8	28.6	10.8	5.1	45469	54009	63	96	7859	23.4	17.7	34.2	20.5	4.2	107355
26519	ALBRIGHT	15948	508	37.8	38.2	20.5	2.2	1.4	32240	36344	18	67	428	25.9	36.9	29.7	6.3	1.2	76000
26521	BLACKSVILLE	23004	178	30.3	36.0	27.5	2.3	3.9	40000	47354	46	90	153	34.0	30.7	32.7	2.6	0.0	71250
26525	BRUCETON MILLS	17977	1707	35.1	34.7	24.3	3.2	2.8	35941	40355	31	80	1449	24.8	28.6	34.6	10.9	1.1	86221
26529	CORE	21055	192	30.2	35.4	28.7	2.1	3.7	40341	47177	47	91	165	32.7	29.7	35.2	2.4	0.0	73462
26537	KINGWOOD	16231	2558	41.0	31.7	21.1	4.8	1.4	30761	34409	14	59	2031	29.1	33.3	30.1	7.3	0.2	76906
26541	MAIDSVILLE	15101	278	34.2	35.6	25.5	3.6	1.1	32503	38428	19	68	236	36.4	22.9	34.8	5.9	0.0	72500
26542	MASONTOWN	15249	294	40.5	35.4	21.1	2.7	0.3	30840	34879	14	59	254	26.8	38.2	26.4	8.3	0.4	69048
26546	PURSGLOVE	16237	94	39.4	26.6	30.9	3.2	0.0	31687	37326	17	64	78	47.4	24.4	25.6	0.0	2.6	54000
26547	REEDSVILLE	16894	1550	38.7	30.5	27.3	2.9	0.7	32874	36508	21	70	1273	30.5	31.7	32.8	4.3	0.8	77571
26554	FAIRMONT	19493	17802	38.8	29.2	24.3	5.5	2.2	33246	38851	22	71	13004	24.8	32.6	33.7	8.2	0.8	82139
26560	BAXTER	14851	174	50.0	23.6	23.0	3.5	0.0	25000	30000	5	22	144	31.3	40.3	27.1	0.7	0.7	68125
26561	BIG RUN	16227	210	31.4	36.2	28.6	3.8	0.0	36709	41988	34	83	179	41.3	30.2	27.4	1.1	0.0	61364
26562	BURTON	17826	335	43.0	23.3	26.9	4.8	2.1	30703	35952	14	58	266	35.0	32.0	27.1	3.8	2.3	66429
26568	ENTERPRISE	15602	570	40.9	30.4	24.6	2.5	1.8	31056	35671	15	60	472	44.1	30.5	20.1	5.3	0.0	55714
26570	FAIRVIEW	17647	932	33.2	35.5	27.4	2.3	1.7	34766	40291	27	75	779	41.6	32.5	23.2	2.6	0.1	58973
26571	FARMINGTON	17353	1386	38.7	33.5	23.8	3.6	0.4	30838	35784	14	59	1119	39.2	38.1	20.1	2.2	0.4	57259
26575	HUNDRED	14969	425	49.4	26.8	19.8	2.8	1.2	25400	28890	5	24	333	61.6	20.1	16.2	0.9	1.2	41250
26581	LITTLETON	14096	187	40.1	31.0	26.2	2.7	0.0	32906	37677	21	70	160	43.1	20.6	34.4	1.9	0.0	72000
26582	MANNINGTON	17283	2203	41.8	31.7	22.8	3.1	0.7	30544	35297	14	56	1788	48.2	31.4	17.8	2.6	0.0	51988
26585	METZ	17231	342	36.3	36.0	24.0	2.9	0.9	32801	38007	20	69	278	47.1	24.1	25.9	2.5	0.4	54706
26587	RACHEL	15865	115	31.3	41.7	24.4	2.6	0.0	36641	42781	34	83	91	29.7	53.9	16.5	0.0	0.0	60833
26588	RIVESVILLE	16975	1311	38.8	28.5	28.2	3.8	0.6	32915	38328	21	70	1060	30.6	35.6	29.0	4.6	0.3	70357
26590	WANA	17814	260	33.5	28.1	32.3	3.1	3.1	38914	47613	42	88	226	33.2	29.7	32.3	4.0	0.9	71667
26591	WORTHINGTON	14956	520	45.2	28.5	21.2	4.0	1.2	27926	32170	9	40	425	44.9	28.0	17.4	9.2	0.5	54778
26601	SUTTON	14255	1901	48.8	27.6	18.4	3.6	1.6	25640	29177	5	26	1485	40.3	28.6	24.2	5.5	1.4	63571
26610	BIRCH RIVER	15519	589	46.0	34.5	14.4	2.0	3.1	26995	30788	7	33	488	49.6	32.4	16.6	1.4	0.0	50645
26611	CEDARVILLE	10174	147	57.1	29.9	12.9	0.0	0.0	20812	23165	2	6	122	38.5	45.1	11.5	4.1	0.8	59333
26615	COPEN	12658	99	44.4	38.4	15.2	2.0	0.0	28789	30628	10	45	81	45.7	34.6	14.8	3.7	1.2	58750
26617	DILLE	12994	167	53.3	34.7	9.6	0.6	1.8	22039	24754	3	10	137	52.6	35.8	11.7	0.0	0.0	47083
26619	EXCHANGE	13197	109	47.7	34.9	16.5	0.9	0.0	26389	31406	6	30	90	43.3	37.8	11.1	5.6	2.2	61333
26621	FLATWOODS	20622	366	38.0	35.5	18.6	3.6	4.4	31783	35936	17	65	300	28.3	30.0	30.7	10.0	1.0	79583
26623	FRAMETOWN	13330	706	49.3	29.6	18.6	1.7	0.9	25352	28491	5	24	595	40.3	27.9	21.3	9.2	1.2	60833
26624	GASSAWAY	17981	1279	46.1	26.0	23.1	3.1	1.7	27399	31410	8	35	1020	37.9	31.9	22.9	3.8	3.4	64455
26627	HEATERS	22786	106	34.9	34.9	20.8	4.7	4.7	35482	42346	29	79	86	31.4	22.1	33.7	11.6	1.2	84000
26629	LITTLE BIRCH	13951	232	52.6	24.6	18.1	3.5	1.3	23727	26707	4	16	195	54.9	21.5	19.0	3.1	1.5	46724
26631	NAPIER	17431	81	44.4	38.3	13.6	1.2	2.5	26986	30955	7	33	68	23.5	45.6	25.0	4.4	1.5	75000
26636	ROSEDALE	15136	201	49.8	25.4	18.9	2.5	3.5	25165	28502	5	22	169	32.5	36.1	26.6	4.7	0.0	69250
26638	SHOCK	17116	68	42.7	25.0	25.0	2.9	4.4	31534	37380	16	63	58	27.6	32.8	32.8	6.9	0.0	78333
26639	STRANGE CREEK	13159	100	52.0	26.0	21.0	1.0	0.0	23139	26949	3	14	84	27.4	36.9	25.0	10.7	0.0	69167
26641	WILSIE	14022	61	47.5	32.8	16.4	1.6	1.6	26322	29420	6	29	51	43.1	25.5	19.6	9.8	2.0	57000
26651	SUMMERSVILLE	22416	3058	37.2	31.3	23.5	3.9	4.2	34190	39876	25	74	2336	26.6	28.3	33.7	9.2	2.3	82467
26656	BELVA	22638	135	45.9	31.1	18.5	1.5	3.0	27284	30434	8	34	112	42.9	31.3	25.0	0.9	0.0	62727
26660	CALVIN	15069	300	43.3	34.7	18.3	1.3	2.3	29044	32591	10	47	268	38.8	31.3	27.2	2.6	0.0	61111
26662	CANVAS	15171	528	42.2	33.7	19.1	3.6	1.3	30221	34294	13	53	469	39.0	27.5	29.0	3.6	0.9	67000
26667	DRENNEN	24477	86	46.5	26.7	19.8	3.5	3.5	27299	31907	8	34	73	42.5	31.5	23.3	2.7	0.0	59167
26674	JODIE	17233	173	41.0	36.4	16.8	4.1	1.7	30889	35000	15	59	141	53.2	29.8	15.6	1.4	0.0	47632
26675	KESLERS CROSS LANES	13613	418	47.4	28.7	22.5	1.4	0.0	27015	29778	7	33	353	41.1	42.2	13.6	0.6	2.6	56848
26676	LEIVASY	18787	420	43.1	31.2	21.0	2.6	2.1	30934	35202	15	60	369	41.5	25.5	27.4	3.8	1.9	65370
26678	MOUNT LOOKOUT	16007	469	37.5	38.0	17.5	5.5	1.5	31657	36108	17	64	410	30.0	32.7	26.3	11.0	0.0	76136
26679	MOUNT NEBO	18867	779	37.2	34.0	22.7	3.6	2.4	35037	39930	28	77	679	34.0	33.1	27.0	5.0	0.9	69058
26680	NALLEN	18532	28	39.3	28.6	28.6	3.6	0.0	30000	35000	12	52	24	58.3	20.8	16.7	4.2	0.0	46000
26681	NETTIE	15469	486	42.6	33.7	18.5	3.9	1.2	29842	33849	12	52	429	40.8	27.3	27.7	3.5	0.7	65167
26684	POOL	15064	63	39.7	36.5	19.1	4.8	0.0	31338	37825	16	62	55	29.1	36.4	25.5	9.1	0.0	75000
26690	SWISS	24088	212	45.8	29.7	17.9	2.8	3.8	27280	30289	8	34	178	43.3	29.2	25.8	1.7	0.0	61875
26691	TIOGA	15631	119	41.2	36.1	17.7	2.5	2.5	30830	34597	14	59	100	38.0	31.0	26.0	5.0	0.0	66667
26704	AUGUSTA	15191	1488	37.6	32.1	28.7	1.1	0.5	33369	36919	22	72	1262	24.1	28.7	36.9	8.2	2.1	86930
26705	AURORA	13075	358	48.3	34.9	13.7	2.0	1.1	25727	29054	5	26	312	35.3	38.5	23.7	1.9	0.6	64483
26710	BURLINGTON	18312	1606	29.5	36.2	27.6	4.6	2.1	38742	43971	42	87	1401	21.7	32.3	34.3	10.3	1.4	85174
26711	CAPON BRIDGE	23062	597	21.8	37.0	35.0	3.2	3.0	44193	49560	59	95	508	17.9	26.0	45.3	9.3	1.6	101000
26714	DELRAY	14655	349	38.4	26.4	34.7	0.6	0.0	36074	39457	32	81	291	32.0	29.9	27.5	7.2	3.4	73409
26716	EGLON	11949	246	49.2	35.4	12.6	1.6	1.2	25292	28307	5	23	213	34.7	40.4	24.4	0.5	0.0	69000
26717	ELK GARDEN	13503	410	43.7	37.1	17.3	1.5	0.5	29077	32735	10	47	352	49.4	31.5	15.9	3.1	0.0	50556
26719	FORT ASHBY	16913	901	34.6	33.4	27.4	4.2	0.3	33979	39042	24	73	754	22.6	19.8	48.7	8.5	0.5	97250
26720	GORMANIA	17272	292	45.9	30.8	17.1	3.4	2.7	29565	32886	11	51	245	39.6	24.9	29.0	6.1	0.4	67250
26722	GREEN SPRING	16390	328	35.4	34.2	27.7	2.7	0.0	34317	37661	25	75	280	26.1	36.1	30.7	5.0	2.1	78462
26726	KEYSER	16764	4256	43.2	30.4	22.5	3.0	1.0	29882	34225	12	52	2983	22.9	40.6	32.6	3.6	0.3	77705
26731	LAHMANSVILLE	17752	233	37.8	32.2	24.9	3.9	1.3	32835	36191	20	69	196	26.5	28.1	29.6	14.8	1.0	83571
26739	MOUNT STORM	19884	349	34.4	34.7	22.6	5.4	2.9	36576	39882	34	83	298	29.2	26.9	28.2	14.1	1.7	79565
26743	NEW CREEK	20064	628	30.1	28.2	32.0	6.9	2.9	42286	47236	54	94	548	28.8	18.8	33.2	19.2	0.0	94643
26750	PIEDMONT	12710	433	53.4	27.9	16.2	2.1	0.5	22571	26110	3	12	257	55.3	29.6	15.2	0.0	0.0	44375
26753	RIDGELEY	20107	2685	29.1	33.9	29.6	5.7	1.8	40369	45483	47	91	2284	18.4	24.7	44.9	10.9	1.1	98154
26755	RIO	15055	176	33.5	37.5	26.7	2.3	0.0	34281	38238	25	74	148	29.7	29.1	31.8	8.1	1.4	77500
26757	ROMNEY	16851	2348	40.6	32.1	22.4	3.1	1.9	30580	34240	14	56	1704	21.0	33.3	34.7	9.4	1.6	85706
26761	SHANKS	14057	411	33.1	38.0	25.8	2.7	0.5	34466	38493	26	75	336	25.6	29.2	33.0	10.4	1.8	84286
26763	SPRINGFIELD	16289	629	36.3	34.7	25.9	2.9	0.3	32598	36347	20	68	539	23.4	32.3	36.6	5.2	2.6	84245
26764	TERRA ALTA	15296	2066	43.0	34.9	18.5	2.8	0.9	28762	32564	10	45	1660	38.3	34.8	21.2	5.5	0.3	61854
	WEST VIRGINIA	19262		38.4	30.0	24.1	5.2	2.4	33458	38993				29.0	29.1	31.1	9.6	1.3	80023
	UNITED STATES	25866		24.7	27.1	30.8	10.9	6.5	48124	56710				10.9	15.0	33.7	30.1	10.4	145905

ZIP CODE #	POST OFFICE NAME	FINANCIAL SERVICES: Auto Loan	Home Loan	Invest-ments	Retire-ment Plans	THE HOME: Home Improvements: Home Repair	Lawn & Garden	Furnishings: Comput-ers & Hard-ware	Major Appli-ances	TV, Radio, Sound Equip-ment	Furni-ture	ENTERTAINMENT: Dine out/ Carry out	Sports Equip-ment	Fees & Tickets	Toys & Games	Travel	Cable TV	PERSONAL: Apparel & Services	Auto Repairs	Health Insur-ance	Pets & Supplies
26419	PINE GROVE	80	54	24	46	61	70	52	65	63	53	74	78	44	69	53	67	67	64	80	92
26421	PULLMAN	79	53	24	46	60	69	51	64	62	52	72	76	44	69	52	66	66	63	79	91
26425	ROWLESBURG	72	48	22	41	54	63	46	58	56	47	66	69	39	62	47	60	60	57	71	82
26426	SALEM	66	49	35	46	53	63	52	58	59	51	71	68	47	67	52	63	65	59	70	75
26430	SAND FORK	62	42	19	36	47	55	40	51	49	41	57	60	34	54	41	53	52	50	62	72
26431	SHINNSTON	73	54	33	49	59	68	54	63	62	54	73	73	48	70	55	66	68	63	75	83
26437	SMITHFIELD	106	71	32	61	80	93	69	86	83	70	97	102	58	92	70	89	88	85	106	122
26440	THORNTON	63	43	21	38	48	56	42	52	51	43	59	62	36	56	43	54	54	52	64	72
26443	TROY	64	47	29	45	52	62	51	58	58	49	68	65	45	64	51	62	62	57	69	72
26444	TUNNELTON	61	41	19	35	46	54	40	50	48	40	56	59	34	53	40	51	51	49	61	70
26447	WALKERSVILLE	66	46	24	41	52	60	45	55	53	45	62	65	39	59	46	57	57	54	67	77
26448	WALLACE	76	51	23	44	58	66	49	61	59	50	70	73	42	66	50	64	63	61	76	87
26451	WEST MILFORD	80	56	28	51	64	72	54	67	64	54	75	80	47	72	56	67	68	66	81	94
26452	WESTON	64	48	31	45	52	62	50	57	57	49	67	65	45	64	50	60	62	57	68	72
26456	WEST UNION	61	44	25	40	49	57	44	52	51	44	60	61	39	58	45	55	55	52	63	70
26501	MORGANTOWN	64	55	53	54	57	63	59	60	62	58	76	72	56	74	58	62	72	62	64	73
26505	MORGANTOWN	57	44	54	48	44	50	65	54	63	58	79	70	57	74	56	58	76	61	51	60
26506	MORGANTOWN	35	21	27	24	21	25	41	30	40	35	50	42	34	45	33	35	47	37	28	34
26508	MORGANTOWN	93	90	81	88	91	96	86	90	86	87	107	105	84	105	86	86	103	90	90	107
26519	ALBRIGHT	75	50	23	43	57	65	48	60	58	49	68	72	41	65	49	63	62	60	74	86
26521	BLACKSVILLE	70	79	85	75	79	86	75	76	75	74	93	85	79	96	78	77	91	74	78	83
26525	BRUCETON MILLS	83	55	25	48	63	72	53	67	64	54	76	80	45	72	54	69	69	66	82	95
26529	CORE	68	80	88	76	79	86	75	75	75	74	93	84	80	97	78	77	92	74	77	82
26537	KINGWOOD	65	51	36	48	55	64	53	59	58	52	70	67	48	67	53	61	65	58	68	73
26541	MAIDSVILLE	77	52	23	44	58	67	50	62	60	51	71	74	42	67	51	65	64	62	77	88
26542	MASONTOWN	73	51	25	45	57	65	49	60	58	50	68	72	42	65	50	62	63	60	72	84
26546	PURSGLOVE	63	57	45	55	57	61	55	59	55	56	68	68	52	65	54	55	66	58	58	70
26547	REEDSVILLE	67	52	34	49	56	64	52	59	58	52	70	68	48	67	53	61	64	58	68	75
26554	FAIRMONT	64	60	57	58	61	69	62	63	64	60	79	73	60	78	62	66	75	64	68	74
26560	BAXTER	57	44	29	42	48	57	48	53	54	46	63	59	43	60	48	57	58	53	63	63
26561	BIG RUN	79	53	24	46	60	69	51	64	62	52	72	76	43	68	52	66	66	63	79	91
26562	BURTON	71	51	30	47	57	67	54	62	62	52	73	71	47	69	54	66	66	62	75	80
26568	ENTERPRISE	76	51	23	44	58	67	49	62	60	50	70	74	42	66	50	64	64	61	76	88
26570	FAIRVIEW	68	55	40	52	59	69	58	64	64	56	76	72	53	73	58	68	70	63	75	77
26571	FARMINGTON	67	52	35	48	56	66	55	61	62	53	73	69	50	70	55	65	67	61	72	76
26575	HUNDRED	62	43	23	39	49	57	44	53	52	44	61	61	38	58	44	55	55	52	64	71
26581	LITTLETON	71	48	22	41	54	62	46	57	55	47	65	69	39	62	47	60	59	57	71	82
26582	MANNINGTON	68	55	40	50	59	68	55	62	62	54	74	71	51	72	56	65	68	61	72	77
26585	METZ	78	55	29	49	61	71	56	66	65	55	77	77	48	72	56	70	70	66	81	89
26587	RACHEL	53	58	61	55	59	65	57	57	59	55	74	63	61	80	59	62	71	56	61	63
26588	RIVESVILLE	60	55	49	53	58	66	56	59	60	54	73	67	55	73	57	62	69	58	66	69
26590	WANA	82	65	45	58	70	80	62	72	71	63	84	85	58	82	64	75	79	71	84	95
26591	WORTHINGTON	68	48	27	44	54	63	50	59	58	49	68	68	44	64	50	62	62	58	71	77
26601	SUTTON	65	47	27	43	52	61	48	56	55	47	65	65	42	62	48	59	60	56	68	74
26610	BIRCH RIVER	74	49	22	43	56	64	48	60	57	49	67	71	41	64	48	62	61	59	73	85
26611	CEDARVILLE	50	33	15	29	38	43	32	40	39	33	45	48	27	43	33	42	41	40	49	57
26615	COPEN	58	41	22	37	46	53	42	49	49	41	57	58	36	54	42	52	52	49	60	66
26617	DILLE	59	39	18	34	45	51	38	48	46	39	54	57	32	51	39	49	49	47	59	68
26619	EXCHANGE	62	42	19	36	47	55	40	50	49	41	57	60	34	54	41	52	52	50	62	71
26621	FLATWOODS	75	58	38	54	64	74	60	68	68	58	80	78	54	76	61	72	73	68	81	86
26623	FRAMETOWN	62	42	19	36	47	54	40	50	48	41	57	60	34	54	41	52	52	50	62	71
26624	GASSAWAY	71	52	31	48	57	68	55	63	63	53	74	71	48	70	55	67	67	62	76	79
26627	HEATERS	79	59	39	57	65	78	66	72	74	62	87	81	59	82	65	78	79	72	87	87
26629	LITTLE BIRCH	64	43	19	37	49	56	41	52	50	42	59	62	35	55	42	54	53	51	64	74
26631	NAPIER	69	54	37	49	61	68	51	61	58	51	69	72	46	68	54	62	64	60	73	84
26636	ROSEDALE	69	46	21	40	52	60	45	56	54	45	63	67	38	60	45	58	57	55	69	79
26638	SHOCK	84	56	25	48	64	73	54	68	65	55	77	81	46	73	55	70	70	67	84	96
26639	STRANGE CREEK	59	39	18	34	45	51	38	47	46	39	54	57	32	51	39	49	49	47	58	67
26641	WILSIE	63	42	19	36	48	55	41	51	49	41	57	61	35	54	41	53	52	50	63	72
26651	SUMMERSVILLE	91	66	38	61	73	84	66	78	76	66	90	91	59	86	67	80	83	77	93	103
26656	BELVA	101	69	33	60	77	90	68	83	81	68	95	98	58	90	69	87	86	82	102	115
26660	CALVIN	74	49	22	43	56	64	48	60	57	49	67	71	41	64	48	62	61	59	73	85
26662	CANVAS	73	49	22	42	55	64	47	59	57	48	67	71	40	63	48	61	61	58	73	84
26667	DRENNEN	95	69	40	63	76	90	72	83	83	70	98	96	64	92	72	89	89	83	101	107
26674	JODIE	75	52	27	47	58	68	53	63	62	52	73	74	45	69	53	66	66	63	77	85
26675	KESLERS CROSS LANES	63	42	19	36	48	55	41	51	49	42	58	61	35	55	42	53	53	51	63	72
26676	LEIVASY	81	54	25	47	62	71	52	66	63	54	74	78	45	70	53	68	68	65	81	93
26678	MOUNT LOOKOUT	66	60	47	58	60	63	57	61	58	59	71	71	54	67	56	57	68	61	61	73
26679	MOUNT NEBO	86	58	27	50	66	76	56	70	68	57	79	84	48	75	57	73	72	69	86	99
26680	NALLEN	65	49	32	47	54	64	54	60	61	51	71	67	48	67	54	64	65	60	71	72
26681	NETTIE	72	48	22	42	55	63	47	58	56	48	66	70	40	62	47	61	60	58	72	83
26684	POOL	63	52	36	49	54	58	50	56	53	51	64	65	46	61	49	54	61	55	59	70
26690	SWISS	105	74	41	67	82	97	76	90	89	75	104	104	67	99	77	95	95	89	109	118
26691	TIOGA	80	54	24	46	61	70	52	65	63	53	74	78	44	70	53	68	67	64	80	92
26704	AUGUSTA	71	48	22	41	54	62	46	58	56	47	65	69	39	62	47	60	59	57	71	82
26705	AURORA	61	41	19	35	46	54	40	50	48	40	56	59	34	53	40	51	51	49	61	70
26710	BURLINGTON	89	61	29	53	69	78	59	73	70	60	82	87	50	78	60	75	75	72	89	102
26711	CAPON BRIDGE	86	76	58	73	81	87	71	78	75	71	91	93	69	93	73	77	87	76	85	101
26714	DELRAY	73	49	22	42	55	63	47	59	57	48	67	70	40	63	48	61	60	58	72	83
26716	EGLON	58	39	18	34	44	51	38	47	46	38	53	56	32	51	38	49	49	47	58	67
26717	ELK GARDEN	64	43	20	38	49	56	42	52	50	43	59	62	36	56	43	54	54	52	64	74
26719	FORT ASHBY	78	53	25	46	60	69	51	64	61	52	72	76	44	68	52	66	66	63	78	90
26720	GORMANIA	75	50	23	43	57	66	49	61	59	49	69	72	41	65	49	63	62	60	75	86
26722	GREEN SPRING	65	50	34	46	56	64	50	58	56	49	66	67	45	65	52	60	61	58	69	77
26726	KEYSER	64	50	34	47	54	63	52	58	59	51	70	66	48	67	52	62	64	58	69	72
26731	LAHMANSVILLE	78	52	24	45	59	68	50	63	61	51	71	75	43	68	51	66	65	62	78	90
26739	MOUNT STORM	89	59	27	51	67	78	57	72	69	58	81	86	49	77	58	75	74	71	88	102
26743	NEW CREEK	82	72	54	68	76	82	67	74	71	67	87	89	65	88	69	73	82	72	81	96
26750	PIEDMONT	47	37	32	35	39	45	41	43	45	40	54	51	38	53	40	46	51	44	48	53
26753	RIDGELEY	76	67	53	64	70	78	66	71	70	65	85	82	64	86	67	72	80	70	78	87
26755	RIO	74	49	22	43	56	64	48	59	57	48	67	71	40	64	48	62	61	59	73	84
26757	ROMNEY	68	49	34	45	54	63	51	59	58	50	69	69	45	67	51	62	64	59	70	78
26761	SHANKS	76	51	24	45	58	67	50	62	59	50	70	74	42	66	51	63	63	61	76	88
26763	SPRINGFIELD	68	49	28	44	55	64	49	58	57	49	67	68	43	64	50	61	61	58	71	79
26764	TERRA ALTA	63	46	31	43	51	59	50	56	56	48	67	64	44	63	49	59	61	56	66	70
	WEST VIRGINIA	73	60	47	57	64	72	61	67	67	60	80	78	57	78	61	69	75	67	76	84
	UNITED STATES	100	100	100	100	100	100	100	100	100	100	100	100	100	100	100	100	100	100	100	100

A 26767-26884

#	POST OFFICE NAME	COUNTY FIPS CODE	POPULATION			2000-2004 ANNUAL RATE		HOUSEHOLDS					FAMILIES		
			2000	2004	2009	% Rate	State Centile	2000	2004	2009	% Annual Rate 2000-2004	2004 Average HH Size	2000	2004	% Annual Rate 2000-2004
26767	WILEY FORD	057	1095	1092	1132	-0.1	52	463	470	497	0.4	2.32	309	302	-0.5
26801	BAKER	031	1410	1452	1490	0.7	84	574	606	634	1.3	2.35	386	391	0.3
26802	BRANDYWINE	071	975	976	977	0.0	58	413	424	435	0.6	2.28	277	272	-0.4
26804	CIRCLEVILLE	071	615	608	607	-0.3	38	254	258	264	0.4	2.33	182	178	-0.5
26807	FRANKLIN	071	2842	2869	2888	0.2	69	1160	1196	1232	0.7	2.32	807	803	-0.1
26808	HIGH VIEW	027	1280	1372	1446	1.7	94	503	549	588	2.1	2.47	365	384	1.2
26810	LOST CITY	031	424	441	455	0.9	87	192	204	214	1.4	2.16	134	136	0.4
26812	MATHIAS	031	1395	1433	1469	0.6	83	572	600	626	1.1	2.39	409	411	0.1
26814	RIVERTON	071	298	294	294	-0.3	35	116	118	121	0.4	2.47	83	81	-0.6
26815	SUGAR GROVE	071	1318	1324	1326	0.1	63	499	513	525	0.7	2.48	354	351	-0.2
26817	BLOOMERY	027	1039	1129	1198	2.0	95	396	439	474	2.5	2.57	296	317	1.6
26818	FISHER	031	2	2	2	0.0	57	1	1	1	0.0	2.00	1	1	0.0
26824	JUNCTION	027	201	203	208	0.2	70	86	89	93	0.8	2.28	62	62	0.0
26833	MAYSVILLE	023	3102	3134	3156	0.2	71	1185	1223	1254	0.8	2.56	933	938	0.1
26836	MOOREFIELD	031	7235	7498	7744	0.8	86	2955	3116	3266	1.3	2.41	2012	2045	0.4
26838	MILAM	031	32	35	36	2.1	95	14	15	16	1.6	2.33	11	11	0.0
26845	OLD FIELDS	031	132	137	141	0.9	87	52	55	58	1.3	2.49	38	39	0.6
26847	PETERSBURG	023	6000	6148	6249	0.6	82	2491	2615	2710	1.2	2.30	1676	1690	0.2
26851	WARDENSVILLE	031	2036	2111	2173	0.9	86	844	892	933	1.3	2.32	574	583	0.4
26852	PURGITSVILLE	027	750	763	782	0.4	78	296	309	323	1.0	2.46	214	215	0.1
26855	CABINS	023	87	88	89	0.3	73	37	38	39	0.6	2.32	29	29	0.0
26865	YELLOW SPRING	027	187	202	213	1.8	95	74	81	87	2.2	2.46	54	57	1.3
26866	UPPER TRACT	071	1098	1094	1096	-0.1	49	463	474	486	0.6	2.31	338	334	-0.3
26884	SENECA ROCKS	071	1066	1062	1063	-0.1	49	450	458	469	0.4	2.32	318	312	-0.5
	WEST VIRGINIA					0.2					0.6	2.35			-0.3
	UNITED STATES					1.2					1.3	2.58			1.1

#	POST OFFICE NAME	White 2000	White 2004	Black 2000	Black 2004	Asian/Pacific 2000	Asian/Pacific 2004	% Hispanic Origin 2000	% Hispanic Origin 2004	0-4	5-9	10-14	15-19	20-24	25-44	45-64	65-84	85+	18+	MEDIAN AGE 2004	% 2004 Males	% 2004 Females
26767	WILEY FORD	99.1	99.1	0.3	0.3	0.1	0.1	0.2	0.2	3.8	4.5	7.2	7.1	4.4	25.6	28.6	17.2	1.6	80.0	43.3	48.4	51.7
26801	BAKER	98.6	98.5	0.6	0.6	0.1	0.1	0.4	0.3	5.7	5.7	5.5	5.5	5.2	26.3	29.8	14.1	2.3	80.0	42.5	50.2	49.8
26802	BRANDYWINE	96.8	96.7	1.5	1.5	0.5	0.5	0.5	0.6	7.2	7.2	6.6	5.7	4.7	29.9	26.3	11.3	1.1	75.4	37.4	50.8	49.2
26804	CIRCLEVILLE	99.4	99.5	0.0	0.0	0.0	0.0	0.0	0.0	4.9	4.8	6.6	6.9	4.4	27.0	26.8	16.6	2.0	79.4	41.1	53.0	47.0
26807	FRANKLIN	94.9	94.9	3.2	3.2	0.1	0.1	0.7	0.7	4.9	5.4	6.0	5.9	4.8	23.5	28.6	17.2	3.8	80.1	44.7	48.7	51.3
26808	HIGH VIEW	98.5	98.5	0.9	0.8	0.2	0.2	0.7	0.7	6.3	6.8	7.5	5.9	4.2	28.4	27.0	12.9	1.0	75.3	39.8	50.2	49.9
26810	LOST CITY	98.8	99.1	0.2	0.2	0.0	0.0	0.7	0.5	5.2	5.9	6.8	4.8	4.3	24.7	32.4	13.8	2.0	79.1	43.9	49.4	50.6
26812	MATHIAS	98.6	98.5	0.4	0.4	0.1	0.1	0.3	0.4	5.2	5.8	6.7	5.1	5.0	25.0	31.1	14.7	1.5	79.1	43.4	48.4	51.6
26814	RIVERTON	99.7	99.3	0.0	0.0	0.0	0.0	0.0	0.0	4.8	4.8	6.5	6.8	4.8	27.2	26.9	16.3	2.0	79.6	41.1	52.7	47.3
26815	SUGAR GROVE	92.6	92.6	5.0	5.0	0.4	0.4	2.6	2.6	7.1	7.2	7.0	5.7	6.2	30.5	23.6	11.4	1.4	75.2	35.9	51.4	48.6
26817	BLOOMERY	98.1	98.0	0.7	0.7	0.1	0.1	0.5	0.4	6.8	7.2	6.7	5.8	4.6	27.9	27.8	12.1	1.2	75.7	39.7	50.4	49.6
26818	FISHER	100.0	100.0	0.0	0.0	0.0	0.0	0.0	0.0	0.0	0.0	0.0	0.0	100.0	0.0	0.0	0.0	0.0	100.0	22.5	50.0	50.0
26824	JUNCTION	97.5	98.0	0.0	0.0	0.5	0.5	0.0	0.0	5.4	5.9	6.9	5.4	5.4	26.1	29.1	14.3	1.5	78.8	41.5	49.8	50.3
26833	MAYSVILLE	98.8	98.7	0.3	0.3	0.1	0.2	0.5	0.5	6.8	7.1	6.8	6.0	5.2	28.8	27.1	11.0	1.2	75.7	37.9	50.5	49.5
26836	MOOREFIELD	95.7	95.6	2.9	2.9	0.2	0.3	0.8	0.8	6.3	6.5	7.1	6.1	5.6	28.5	25.7	13.0	1.3	76.4	38.7	49.6	50.5
26838	MILAM	100.0	100.0	0.0	0.0	0.0	0.0	0.0	0.0	5.7	5.7	5.7	5.7	5.7	28.6	22.9	20.0	0.0	82.9	41.9	51.4	48.6
26845	OLD FIELDS	98.5	98.5	0.8	0.7	0.0	0.0	0.0	0.0	5.8	5.8	7.3	7.3	6.6	27.0	28.5	10.2	1.5	76.6	39.3	51.1	48.9
26847	PETERSBURG	98.1	97.9	1.0	1.0	0.2	0.3	0.7	0.7	6.0	6.2	6.1	5.4	5.3	27.0	26.2	15.3	2.5	78.4	40.9	48.8	51.2
26851	WARDENSVILLE	98.2	98.0	1.0	1.0	0.1	0.1	0.5	0.5	5.8	6.0	6.6	6.0	4.3	28.0	26.7	14.8	1.9	77.9	41.3	50.3	49.7
26852	PURGITSVILLE	97.6	97.4	0.1	0.1	0.3	0.4	0.1	0.1	5.1	5.5	7.2	5.4	5.4	26.5	28.4	15.2	1.3	79.7	41.7	50.3	49.7
26855	CABINS	98.9	100.0	0.0	0.0	0.0	0.0	0.0	1.1	6.8	6.8	6.8	5.7	5.7	29.6	26.1	11.4	1.1	73.9	37.5	48.9	51.1
26865	YELLOW SPRING	98.9	99.0	0.5	0.5	0.0	0.5	1.1	0.5	6.9	6.9	6.9	5.5	4.0	29.7	25.7	13.4	1.0	74.8	39.3	50.0	50.0
26866	UPPER TRACT	99.4	99.4	0.1	0.1	0.1	0.1	0.8	0.8	3.8	4.4	6.2	4.9	4.6	25.8	30.5	18.0	1.8	82.5	45.2	51.8	48.2
26884	SENECA ROCKS	98.7	98.7	0.0	0.0	0.3	0.3	0.4	0.4	4.5	4.9	5.3	5.0	5.6	25.5	29.2	17.1	2.9	82.4	44.5	50.5	49.5
	WEST VIRGINIA	95.1	94.8	3.2	3.2	0.5	0.7	0.7	0.7	5.6	5.8	6.2	6.3	6.7	26.7	27.1	13.7	1.9	78.9	40.1	48.8	51.2
	UNITED STATES	75.1	73.6	12.3	12.5	3.8	4.2	12.5	14.1	6.9	6.7	7.2	7.0	7.3	28.6	23.8	10.8	1.7	75.1	36.0	49.1	50.9

#	POST OFFICE NAME	2004 Per Capita Income	2004 HH Income Base	2004 HOUSEHOLD INCOME DISTRIBUTION (%)					MEDIAN HOUSEHOLD INCOME				2004 Home Value Base	2004 HOME VALUE DISTRIBUTION (%)					2004 Median Home Value
				Less than $25,000	$25,000 to $49,999	$50,000 to $99,999	$100,000 to $149,999	$150,000 or More	2004	2009	2004 National Centile	2004 State Centile		Less than $50,000	$50,000 to $89,999	$90,000 to $174,999	$175,000 to $399,999	$400,000 or More	
26767	WILEY FORD	17651	470	33.2	42.3	20.2	2.8	1.5	36216	41526	32	82	383	26.4	34.5	32.1	7.1	0.0	79875
26801	BAKER	18561	606	31.4	33.7	30.4	4.3	0.3	37577	43182	38	85	521	23.4	23.0	33.4	12.9	7.3	96167
26802	BRANDYWINE	17685	424	36.1	38.9	19.3	4.0	1.7	35367	38629	29	78	352	32.7	22.4	33.8	8.8	2.3	83333
26804	CIRCLEVILLE	13753	258	44.2	41.9	10.9	3.1	0.0	27332	30999	8	35	221	33.9	29.9	33.0	3.2	0.0	74167
26807	FRANKLIN	19200	1196	33.0	40.6	20.8	2.4	3.1	34682	38115	26	75	953	16.0	32.2	41.1	10.4	0.3	92273
26808	HIGH VIEW	21317	549	20.6	42.8	28.6	3.8	4.2	44095	49402	59	95	470	14.9	28.3	43.4	13.4	0.0	101168
26810	LOST CITY	21857	204	35.3	29.4	27.5	3.9	3.9	40733	45643	49	92	188	27.7	20.2	44.2	8.0	0.0	94444
26812	MATHIAS	17854	600	35.7	32.8	25.2	4.5	1.8	38766	41993	42	88	528	23.7	26.3	37.5	12.5	0.0	90000
26814	RIVERTON	13059	118	44.1	41.5	11.0	3.4	0.0	27442	31072	8	35	101	35.6	28.7	32.7	3.0	0.0	73125
26815	SUGAR GROVE	15726	513	30.0	38.0	30.8	1.2	0.0	35392	38192	29	78	386	25.7	25.1	43.8	3.1	2.3	89189
26817	BLOOMERY	18536	439	31.0	32.8	29.2	3.4	3.6	39039	42549	43	88	381	14.2	18.4	50.1	12.6	4.7	115512
26818	FISHER	0	0	0.0	0.0	0.0	0.0	0.0	0	0	0	0	0	0.0	0.0	0.0	0.0	0.0	0
26824	JUNCTION	16420	89	37.1	39.3	22.5	1.1	0.0	35268	38050	29	77	77	42.9	15.6	32.5	9.1	0.0	68333
26833	MAYSVILLE	16424	1223	37.2	35.3	22.9	2.8	1.8	32798	37080	20	69	1065	22.1	28.5	38.1	10.0	1.3	89356
26836	MOOREFIELD	17449	3116	36.0	35.9	22.5	4.1	1.6	33372	37342	22	72	2426	32.6	26.7	31.0	8.2	1.5	79740
26838	MILAM	22071	15	26.7	33.3	26.7	13.3	0.0	42343	40000	54	94	13	23.1	30.8	46.2	0.0	0.0	85000
26845	OLD FIELDS	17051	55	34.6	38.2	20.0	5.5	1.8	33321	36818	22	71	49	26.5	18.4	28.6	18.4	8.2	102083
26847	PETERSBURG	19133	2615	41.0	32.4	23.1	2.0	1.5	30627	34425	14	57	2044	24.3	25.6	41.2	7.5	1.3	90049
26851	WARDENSVILLE	20231	892	27.1	35.0	30.9	5.7	1.2	40152	44374	47	90	739	11.8	31.9	43.0	11.4	1.9	96458
26852	PURGITSVILLE	14636	309	36.6	41.1	21.7	0.7	0.0	35400	39876	29	78	270	43.7	13.0	33.7	9.6	0.0	66667
26855	CABINS	18282	38	34.2	36.8	26.3	2.6	0.0	35000	35736	28	77	33	24.2	21.2	48.5	6.1	0.0	95000
26865	YELLOW SPRING	21195	81	21.0	44.4	27.2	3.7	3.7	43439	49644	57	95	70	14.3	27.1	44.3	14.3	0.0	103125
26866	UPPER TRACT	26137	474	31.4	36.3	22.4	3.4	6.5	35990	39849	32	81	419	23.9	34.1	27.7	10.0	4.3	79605
26884	SENECA ROCKS	16535	458	42.4	36.2	17.3	2.0	2.2	29274	32289	11	49	392	25.5	19.4	38.0	14.5	2.6	97143
	WEST VIRGINIA	19262		38.4	30.0	24.1	5.2	2.4	33458	38993				29.0	29.1	31.1	9.6	1.3	80023
	UNITED STATES	25866		24.7	27.1	30.8	10.9	6.5	48124	56710				10.9	15.0	33.7	30.1	10.4	145905

# POST OFFICE NAME	FINANCIAL SERVICES				THE HOME						ENTERTAINMENT						PERSONAL			
					Home Improvements		Furnishings													
	Auto Loan	Home Loan	Invest-ments	Retire-ment Plans	Home Repair	Lawn & Garden	Comput-ers & Hard-ware	Major Appli-ances	TV, Radio, Sound Equip-ment	Furni-ture	Dine out/ Carry out	Sports Equip-ment	Fees & Tickets	Toys & Games	Travel	Cable TV	Apparel & Services	Auto Repairs	Health Insur-ance	Pets & Supplies
26767 WILEY FORD	53	57	60	54	58	64	57	56	59	54	73	62	60	79	58	61	70	55	60	62
26801 BAKER	77	58	37	52	65	74	55	67	63	55	75	79	49	73	58	68	69	66	80	92
26802 BRANDYWINE	68	54	38	50	60	67	52	61	58	51	69	71	47	68	54	61	64	60	71	81
26804 CIRCLEVILLE	61	41	19	35	46	53	39	49	47	40	56	59	33	53	40	51	51	49	60	70
26807 FRANKLIN	80	58	33	52	65	75	57	69	67	57	78	80	50	75	59	71	72	68	83	92
26808 HIGH VIEW	85	76	58	72	80	86	70	78	74	70	90	92	69	92	72	76	86	76	84	100
26810 LOST CITY	80	63	43	57	71	80	59	71	67	59	79	84	53	78	63	72	74	70	84	98
26812 MATHIAS	77	55	30	48	62	71	53	65	62	53	73	77	46	70	55	66	67	64	78	90
26814 RIVERTON	61	41	18	35	46	53	39	49	48	40	56	59	33	53	40	51	51	49	61	70
26815 SUGAR GROVE	62	53	41	53	56	63	55	58	58	54	70	66	52	70	54	59	66	57	63	69
26817 BLOOMERY	78	67	49	63	71	77	62	70	67	62	81	83	60	82	64	69	77	68	77	91
26818 FISHER	0	0	0	0	0	0	0	0	0	0	0	0	0	0	0	0	0	0	0	0
26824 JUNCTION	71	47	21	41	53	62	46	57	55	46	65	68	39	61	46	59	59	56	70	81
26833 MAYSVILLE	79	53	24	46	60	69	51	64	62	52	73	77	44	69	52	67	66	63	79	91
26836 MOOREFIELD	77	53	27	47	60	69	52	63	62	53	73	75	45	69	53	66	66	63	77	88
26838 MILAM	97	65	29	56	74	85	63	78	76	64	89	94	53	84	64	81	81	78	97	111
26845 OLD FIELDS	80	54	24	46	61	70	52	65	62	53	73	77	44	69	53	67	67	64	80	92
26847 PETERSBURG	79	55	30	50	62	72	57	67	66	56	78	78	49	73	57	71	71	67	82	89
26851 WARDENSVILLE	81	63	43	57	71	80	60	72	67	59	80	84	53	79	64	72	74	71	85	98
26852 PURGITSVILLE	68	45	21	39	51	59	44	55	53	45	62	66	37	59	45	57	56	54	68	78
26855 CABINS	80	53	24	46	60	70	52	64	62	52	73	77	44	69	52	67	66	64	79	91
26865 YELLOW SPRING	84	75	57	71	79	85	69	77	74	69	90	92	68	92	72	76	85	75	83	99
26866 UPPER TRACT	103	80	54	72	90	101	76	91	86	75	102	107	68	100	81	92	94	90	108	125
26884 SENECA ROCKS	72	48	22	42	55	63	47	58	56	48	66	70	40	62	47	61	60	58	72	83
WEST VIRGINIA	73	60	47	57	64	72	61	67	67	60	80	78	57	78	61	69	75	67	76	84
UNITED STATES	100	100	100	100	100	100	100	100	100	100	100	100	100	100	100	100	100	100	100	100

329-D

#	POST OFFICE NAME	COUNTY FIPS CODE	POPULATION			2000-2004 ANNUAL RATE		HOUSEHOLDS					FAMILIES		
			2000	2004	2009	% Rate	State Centile	2000	2004	2009	% Annual Rate 2000-2004	2004 Average HH Size	2000	2004	% Annual Rate 2000-2004
53001	ADELL	117	1888	2060	2169	2.1	87	687	776	838	2.9	2.65	537	597	2.5
53002	ALLENTON	131	2236	2397	2539	1.7	79	796	883	961	2.5	2.70	628	690	2.2
53004	BELGIUM	089	3046	3395	3656	2.6	93	1083	1234	1361	3.1	2.69	835	944	2.9
53005	BROOKFIELD	133	20049	20750	21693	0.8	47	7352	7827	8403	1.5	2.62	5943	6264	1.3
53006	BROWNSVILLE	027	2227	2324	2407	1.0	57	817	878	933	1.7	2.65	640	681	1.5
53007	BUTLER	133	1850	1892	1962	0.5	36	903	948	1009	1.2	1.99	453	462	0.5
53010	CAMPBELLSPORT	039	7098	7332	7541	0.8	46	2613	2797	2962	1.6	2.58	1962	2072	1.3
53011	CASCADE	117	1961	2010	2069	0.6	38	767	810	854	1.3	2.48	593	620	1.1
53012	CEDARBURG	089	17718	18451	19262	1.0	55	6695	7149	7650	1.6	2.55	5020	5293	1.3
53013	CEDAR GROVE	117	3116	3232	3321	0.9	49	1125	1203	1266	1.6	2.68	898	950	1.3
53014	CHILTON	015	8163	8702	9478	1.5	75	3109	3431	3859	2.4	2.49	2197	2383	1.9
53015	CLEVELAND	071	2683	2691	2702	0.1	18	979	1012	1042	0.8	2.65	748	764	0.5
53017	COLGATE	131	4863	5196	5495	1.6	77	1655	1826	1986	2.3	2.84	1409	1545	2.2
53018	DELAFIELD	133	7381	7974	8471	1.8	83	2476	2761	3018	2.6	2.75	2017	2226	2.4
53019	EDEN	039	1939	1950	1983	0.1	20	688	715	748	0.9	2.73	521	536	0.7
53020	ELKHART LAKE	117	3551	3630	3703	0.5	35	1330	1399	1462	1.2	2.56	1009	1048	0.9
53021	FREDONIA	089	4178	4360	4559	1.3	68	1467	1604	1731	2.1	2.48	1154	1248	1.9
53022	GERMANTOWN	131	17222	19138	20694	2.5	92	6539	7438	8229	3.1	2.56	4865	5484	2.9
53023	GLENBEULAH	117	2595	2604	2613	0.1	18	499	516	531	0.8	3.16	403	412	0.5
53024	GRAFTON	089	14631	15459	16271	1.3	69	5685	6196	6703	2.1	2.49	4184	4519	1.8
53027	HARTFORD	131	19118	20148	21212	1.2	66	7175	7803	8446	2.0	2.56	5289	5679	1.7
53029	HARTLAND	133	18269	19343	20380	1.4	71	6560	7149	7737	2.0	2.71	5148	5544	1.8
53032	HORICON	027	4777	4782	4895	0.0	16	1854	1908	2003	0.7	2.50	1342	1364	0.4
53033	HUBERTUS	131	5228	5276	5456	0.2	24	1868	1953	2079	1.1	2.70	1576	1633	0.8
53034	HUSTISFORD	027	939	953	971	0.4	29	390	409	428	1.1	2.33	255	262	0.6
53035	IRON RIDGE	027	2833	2928	3024	0.8	46	1015	1078	1141	1.4	2.72	772	810	1.1
53036	IXONIA	055	2203	2458	2672	2.6	93	796	915	1022	3.3	2.68	648	739	3.1
53037	JACKSON	131	6931	7161	7434	0.8	46	2628	2807	2997	1.6	2.55	1990	2099	1.3
53038	JOHNSON CREEK	055	2853	2983	3152	1.1	59	1086	1169	1266	1.8	2.55	787	836	1.4
53039	JUNEAU	027	5431	5416	5504	-0.1	12	1929	1978	2066	0.6	2.50	1393	1409	0.3
53040	KEWASKUM	131	7104	7431	7774	1.1	59	2556	2755	2960	1.8	2.67	2021	2155	1.5
53042	KIEL	071	6742	6930	7117	0.7	41	2615	2749	2889	1.2	2.52	1885	1954	0.9
53044	KOHLER	117	2010	2057	2104	0.6	37	773	813	851	1.2	2.53	610	635	1.0
53045	BROOKFIELD	133	21499	22978	24433	1.6	77	7815	8667	9508	2.5	2.60	6056	6621	2.1
53046	LANNON	133	1041	1044	1075	0.1	18	438	454	482	0.9	2.30	328	337	0.6
53048	LOMIRA	027	2609	2658	2715	0.4	32	950	995	1043	1.1	2.62	685	708	0.8
53049	MALONE	039	2462	2499	2549	0.4	29	887	930	975	1.1	2.55	711	738	0.9
53050	MAYVILLE	027	7010	7190	7401	0.6	39	2715	2884	3057	1.4	2.46	1915	2002	1.1
53051	MENOMONEE FALLS	133	32634	34243	36190	1.1	63	12839	13847	15020	1.8	2.46	9255	9900	1.6
53057	MOUNT CALVARY	039	2014	2012	2033	0.0	14	551	569	594	0.8	2.74	424	433	0.5
53058	NASHOTAH	133	2815	2959	3101	1.2	64	1089	1170	1254	1.7	2.52	805	855	1.4
53059	NEOSHO	027	1845	2036	2175	2.3	90	649	740	812	3.1	2.75	517	583	2.9
53061	NEW HOLSTEIN	015	4958	4940	5272	-0.1	11	1948	2017	2227	0.8	2.37	1380	1404	0.4
53063	NEWTON	071	1744	1751	1760	0.1	18	603	623	643	0.8	2.71	484	496	0.6
53065	OAKFIELD	039	2088	2051	2072	-0.4	5	725	734	761	0.3	2.79	575	576	0.0
53066	OCONOMOWOC	133	28800	29714	30942	0.7	45	10828	11494	12297	1.4	2.53	8032	8412	1.1
53069	OKAUCHEE	133	833	821	839	-0.3	7	369	373	390	0.3	2.20	232	230	-0.2
53070	OOSTBURG	117	4522	4774	4933	1.3	67	1625	1765	1865	2.0	2.70	1282	1374	1.6
53072	PEWAUKEE	133	21049	22561	23962	1.7	79	8569	9527	10434	2.5	2.34	5845	6375	2.1
53073	PLYMOUTH	117	13966	14338	14626	0.6	40	5328	5620	5866	1.3	2.39	3725	3861	0.9
53074	PORT WASHINGTON	089	12123	12246	12572	0.2	25	4719	4909	5180	0.9	2.42	3211	3293	0.6
53075	RANDOM LAKE	117	3945	4033	4099	0.5	35	1161	1227	1279	1.3	2.96	862	898	1.0
53076	RICHFIELD	131	3301	3345	3455	0.3	27	1132	1183	1257	1.0	2.82	964	998	0.8
53078	RUBICON	027	1656	1708	1757	0.7	45	547	582	616	1.5	2.93	447	472	1.3
53079	SAINT CLOUD	039	1753	1749	1775	-0.1	12	635	656	685	0.8	2.61	478	486	0.4
53080	SAUKVILLE	089	5977	6143	6373	0.7	41	2248	2389	2551	1.4	2.57	1657	1740	1.2
53081	SHEBOYGAN	117	44023	43884	44206	-0.1	12	17839	18213	18736	0.5	2.35	11066	11081	0.0
53083	SHEBOYGAN	117	19157	20024	20747	1.1	59	7520	8034	8492	1.6	2.48	5370	5685	1.4
53085	SHEBOYGAN FALLS	117	10406	10590	10790	0.4	31	4062	4257	4443	1.1	2.42	2909	3003	0.8
53086	SLINGER	131	7131	7432	7762	1.0	56	2604	2791	2990	1.7	2.64	1926	2041	1.4
53089	SUSSEX	133	16069	16872	17713	1.2	63	5872	6358	6860	1.9	2.65	4645	4985	1.7
53090	WEST BEND	131	20134	21244	22384	1.3	67	7339	8005	8674	2.1	2.63	5538	5971	1.8
53091	THERESA	027	2128	2205	2282	0.8	48	787	843	898	1.6	2.62	614	650	1.4
53092	THIENSVILLE	089	20314	20780	21519	0.5	36	7685	8094	8613	1.2	2.54	5947	6201	1.0
53093	WALDO	117	1830	1821	1837	-0.1	10	655	672	695	0.6	2.63	523	531	0.4
53094	WATERTOWN	055	16868	17597	18552	1.0	57	6183	6594	7114	1.5	2.55	4407	4644	1.2
53095	WEST BEND	131	24800	25353	26874	0.5	35	9756	10293	11016	1.3	2.39	6727	7004	1.0
53097	MEQUON	089	4866	5043	5222	0.8	48	1716	1823	1934	1.4	2.76	1386	1455	1.2
53098	WATERTOWN	027	11468	12043	12533	1.2	63	4262	4613	4932	1.9	2.53	3097	3319	1.6
53103	BIG BEND	133	3922	4020	4191	0.6	38	1336	1419	1524	1.4	2.83	1138	1199	1.2
53104	BRISTOL	059	5363	5747	6130	1.6	79	2012	2215	2414	2.3	2.59	1478	1605	2.0
53105	BURLINGTON	101	28700	29897	30978	1.0	55	10570	11256	11899	1.5	2.62	7786	8193	1.2
53108	CALEDONIA	101	3100	3162	3211	0.5	33	1190	1252	1306	1.2	2.52	925	962	0.9
53110	CUDAHY	079	18429	17927	17596	-0.7	2	7888	7892	7929	0.0	2.26	4894	4810	-0.4
53114	DARIEN	127	2802	2803	2928	0.0	15	957	977	1039	0.5	2.81	739	746	0.2
53115	DELAVAN	127	14811	15497	16567	1.1	60	5570	5893	6379	1.3	2.60	3857	4020	1.0
53118	DOUSMAN	133	6949	7306	7697	1.2	64	2526	2772	3024	2.2	2.58	1983	2154	2.0
53119	EAGLE	133	4648	5031	5353	1.9	85	1564	1736	1894	2.5	2.90	1312	1444	2.3
53120	EAST TROY	127	8873	9501	10170	1.6	78	3291	3613	3944	2.2	2.60	2513	2728	2.0
53121	ELKHORN	127	15587	16868	18181	1.9	85	5750	6372	7005	2.5	2.54	4125	4511	2.1
53122	ELM GROVE	133	6369	6323	6476	-0.2	9	2494	2537	2665	0.4	2.43	1815	1820	0.1
53125	FONTANA	127	1854	1975	2116	1.5	74	805	874	954	2.0	2.14	556	595	1.6
53126	FRANKSVILLE	101	6045	6293	6455	1.0	54	2136	2285	2401	1.6	2.74	1758	1862	1.4
53128	GENOA CITY	127	6771	7241	7763	1.6	78	2448	2652	2882	1.9	2.70	1768	1890	1.6
53129	GREENDALE	079	14221	13987	13780	-0.4	6	5938	6062	6139	0.5	2.29	4156	4172	0.1
53130	HALES CORNERS	079	7695	7571	7456	-0.4	6	3239	3272	3294	0.2	2.28	2111	2096	-0.2
53132	FRANKLIN	079	29465	30676	31102	1.0	54	10592	11247	11608	1.4	2.54	7690	8069	1.1
53137	HELENVILLE	055	1439	1570	1697	2.1	87	510	574	637	2.8	2.71	395	439	2.5
53139	KANSASVILLE	101	2599	2677	2736	0.7	43	956	1012	1059	1.4	2.62	718	751	1.1
53140	KENOSHA	059	28837	29726	31313	0.7	44	11133	11718	12596	1.2	2.40	6722	6917	0.7
53142	KENOSHA	059	27847	30143	32527	1.9	85	10641	11765	12937	2.4	2.54	7609	8311	2.1
53143	KENOSHA	059	25488	25779	27001	0.3	26	9735	10071	10766	0.8	2.49	6299	6395	0.4
53144	KENOSHA	059	21506	23074	24709	1.7	80	7841	8644	9482	2.3	2.51	5225	5667	1.9
53146	NEW BERLIN	133	7547	7748	8080	0.6	40	2803	2982	3207	1.5	2.59	2219	2328	1.1
53147	LAKE GENEVA	127	14919	15879	17099	1.5	74	6171	6693	7329	1.9	2.35	3969	4233	1.5
	WISCONSIN					0.8					1.4	2.44			1.1
	UNITED STATES					1.2					1.3	2.58			1.1

ZIP CODE		RACE (%)						% Hispanic Origin		2004 AGE DISTRIBUTION (%)										MEDIAN AGE		
#	POST OFFICE NAME	White 2000	White 2004	Black 2000	Black 2004	Asian/Pacific 2000	Asian/Pacific 2004	2000	2004	0-4	5-9	10-14	15-19	20-24	25-44	45-64	65-84	85+	18+	2004	% 2004 Males	% 2004 Females
53001	ADELL	98.1	97.7	0.1	0.2	0.4	0.5	1.4	1.7	5.5	7.1	7.3	7.3	6.2	26.8	28.6	10.2	1.0	75.4	38.6	51.5	48.5
53002	ALLENTON	99.2	99.2	0.0	0.0	0.1	0.1	0.8	0.8	6.3	6.4	7.6	6.8	6.5	30.3	27.0	8.4	0.8	75.4	37.7	51.6	48.4
53004	BELGIUM	97.1	96.8	0.3	0.3	0.4	0.4	2.6	3.0	7.9	8.2	8.3	6.7	5.7	30.4	22.5	9.3	1.2	71.5	35.7	50.9	49.1
53005	BROOKFIELD	94.4	93.4	0.9	1.0	3.6	4.5	1.3	1.6	5.1	6.1	7.5	7.0	4.8	20.1	30.1	17.2	2.3	76.5	44.7	48.6	51.4
53006	BROWNSVILLE	98.3	98.0	0.1	0.2	0.6	0.7	1.1	1.3	6.9	7.0	7.1	7.1	5.9	30.3	24.0	10.6	1.1	74.6	36.9	51.5	48.5
53007	BUTLER	97.4	97.2	0.3	0.3	0.7	0.7	0.9	1.0	4.6	4.6	6.1	5.4	5.9	28.7	22.8	18.5	3.5	81.6	41.7	47.7	52.3
53010	CAMPBELLSPORT	98.2	98.0	0.1	0.1	0.2	0.3	0.9	1.0	5.5	5.6	6.8	7.1	6.0	28.7	25.9	12.0	2.4	77.5	39.7	50.1	49.9
53011	CASCADE	98.5	98.3	0.1	0.1	0.3	0.4	1.0	1.2	5.9	6.2	6.5	6.3	5.8	26.1	30.6	11.8	0.8	77.6	41.4	51.5	48.5
53012	CEDARBURG	98.3	98.1	0.2	0.3	0.6	0.8	0.8	1.0	6.4	6.9	8.0	7.2	4.9	24.2	28.3	11.7	2.4	73.9	40.9	48.5	51.5
53013	CEDAR GROVE	98.3	98.1	0.2	0.2	0.2	0.2	2.1	2.5	8.0	8.2	7.2	7.1	5.6	25.5	26.0	11.3	1.1	71.9	37.5	50.1	49.9
53014	CHILTON	98.5	98.3	0.3	0.3	0.2	0.3	0.8	0.9	6.0	6.4	7.4	7.0	6.4	27.9	24.9	11.9	2.1	75.5	38.1	51.2	48.8
53015	CLEVELAND	98.3	98.2	0.2	0.2	0.2	0.2	1.3	1.5	6.4	6.6	6.6	6.9	5.8	27.5	28.3	10.5	1.5	76.2	39.4	52.1	47.9
53017	COLGATE	98.4	98.2	0.3	0.3	0.4	0.5	0.9	1.0	5.9	7.1	8.0	6.8	4.6	26.5	31.7	8.8	0.6	74.5	40.9	50.6	49.4
53018	DELAFIELD	94.1	93.5	3.1	3.3	0.7	0.8	1.7	1.9	6.0	7.0	8.7	11.1	5.1	22.9	31.2	7.0	1.1	69.8	38.7	51.8	48.2
53019	EDEN	98.4	98.2	0.1	0.1	0.2	0.2	2.5	2.9	5.7	6.6	8.4	7.7	6.0	28.7	25.8	10.2	0.9	74.5	37.4	52.7	47.3
53020	ELKHART LAKE	98.9	98.7	0.1	0.1	0.2	0.2	0.8	0.9	5.5	5.9	5.7	6.1	5.7	27.1	31.7	10.8	1.5	78.8	41.9	50.7	49.3
53021	FREDONIA	97.5	97.2	0.6	0.7	0.4	0.5	1.2	1.4	6.5	6.2	6.5	10.1	10.8	27.3	24.8	7.2	0.7	76.3	33.7	49.8	50.2
53022	GERMANTOWN	95.7	95.1	1.4	1.6	1.7	2.1	1.1	1.2	7.3	7.7	7.9	6.4	5.4	30.7	25.5	8.4	0.8	73.0	37.0	49.2	50.8
53023	GLENBEULAH	78.3	75.8	19.4	21.9	0.2	0.3	3.5	4.0	4.2	4.4	4.8	6.2	11.7	42.3	20.8	5.2	0.5	83.5	34.2	70.0	30.0
53024	GRAFTON	97.9	97.6	0.3	0.3	0.7	0.9	1.4	1.6	6.0	6.4	7.5	6.7	5.8	26.8	28.8	10.7	1.2	75.8	39.7	49.7	50.3
53027	HARTFORD	97.6	97.4	0.2	0.2	0.4	0.5	1.9	2.2	7.1	7.0	7.4	7.2	6.2	29.9	23.7	10.0	1.5	74.0	36.8	50.0	50.0
53029	HARTLAND	98.2	97.9	0.2	0.3	0.5	0.6	1.2	1.4	6.6	7.2	8.4	8.2	6.2	27.4	27.4	7.8	0.8	72.7	37.0	49.4	50.6
53032	HORICON	98.1	97.9	0.3	0.4	0.2	0.3	1.6	1.8	5.8	6.2	6.8	7.2	6.9	28.0	26.8	10.8	1.6	76.8	38.4	49.9	50.1
53033	HUBERTUS	98.7	98.5	0.2	0.3	0.5	0.6	0.5	0.6	5.1	6.7	7.2	6.5	4.9	26.0	34.2	9.0	0.5	76.8	41.9	51.7	48.3
53034	HUSTISFORD	99.3	99.2	0.1	0.1	0.1	0.1	1.2	1.5	7.2	6.6	6.1	6.4	6.6	26.7	25.1	13.0	2.3	76.2	38.9	49.6	50.4
53035	IRON RIDGE	99.1	98.8	0.1	0.1	0.1	0.1	0.7	0.8	6.7	7.0	8.2	8.0	6.5	28.4	24.3	9.9	1.1	73.1	36.5	51.2	48.8
53036	IXONIA	98.5	98.2	0.1	0.1	0.4	0.5	0.9	1.1	5.9	6.6	7.2	6.6	5.4	27.3	29.6	10.4	1.0	76.2	40.1	51.2	48.8
53037	JACKSON	98.9	98.7	0.1	0.1	0.2	0.2	0.9	1.1	8.0	7.6	7.2	6.0	5.7	32.6	23.0	9.0	1.0	73.3	35.8	49.9	50.1
53038	JOHNSON CREEK	96.5	95.9	0.3	0.3	0.2	0.2	3.1	3.6	6.9	7.2	7.1	6.1	6.0	32.5	24.0	9.4	0.9	75.0	35.6	50.7	49.3
53039	JUNEAU	97.9	97.6	0.2	0.3	0.2	0.3	2.4	2.8	6.2	6.3	6.3	6.0	6.4	28.2	24.6	13.2	2.8	77.6	39.3	51.3	48.7
53040	KEWASKUM	98.6	98.4	0.2	0.2	0.3	0.3	0.8	0.9	6.4	6.7	7.5	7.1	6.9	29.0	25.1	9.9	1.4	74.9	37.0	50.2	49.8
53042	KIEL	98.4	98.1	0.1	0.1	0.3	0.4	0.9	1.1	6.7	6.8	7.8	7.1	5.6	27.8	24.9	11.6	1.6	74.1	37.9	49.3	50.7
53044	KOHLER	97.3	96.7	0.1	0.1	1.7	2.3	1.0	1.2	6.9	7.8	8.3	6.9	3.8	24.6	29.9	10.2	1.7	72.5	40.4	48.3	51.7
53045	BROOKFIELD	94.0	92.8	0.8	0.9	4.0	5.0	1.0	1.2	5.4	6.8	8.3	7.4	4.0	20.2	30.2	15.1	2.7	74.3	43.8	47.6	52.4
53046	LANNON	98.1	97.9	0.7	0.8	0.4	0.5	1.0	1.1	5.5	6.0	6.2	6.4	5.4	26.6	29.7	13.3	0.9	78.5	41.7	51.8	48.2
53048	LOMIRA	98.5	98.2	0.2	0.2	0.2	0.2	2.0	2.2	7.6	7.4	7.6	7.4	6.4	30.7	20.9	9.9	2.2	72.6	34.8	50.4	49.6
53049	MALONE	97.5	97.2	0.8	0.9	0.4	0.5	1.1	1.3	4.5	5.0	6.9	7.3	6.4	25.4	29.6	13.3	1.6	78.7	41.6	50.8	49.2
53050	MAYVILLE	98.4	98.1	0.1	0.1	0.4	0.5	1.3	1.5	5.9	6.1	7.3	7.6	6.2	27.7	24.0	12.7	2.6	75.9	38.9	50.6	49.4
53051	MENOMONEE FALLS	96.5	96.0	1.5	1.7	0.9	1.1	1.2	1.4	6.5	6.9	7.0	6.2	4.9	26.9	25.5	14.2	2.0	75.6	40.5	48.5	51.5
53057	MOUNT CALVARY	92.7	91.6	0.4	0.5	2.8	3.4	3.7	4.3	4.3	5.0	6.1	14.0	5.5	21.5	24.0	15.0	4.7	73.8	40.6	54.6	45.4
53058	NASHOTAH	98.7	98.4	0.1	0.1	0.4	0.5	1.3	1.6	6.4	6.9	7.2	6.3	4.7	24.7	30.0	12.0	1.7	75.4	41.2	49.6	50.4
53059	NEOSHO	98.8	98.6	0.0	0.1	0.3	0.3	0.5	0.6	6.9	7.2	7.3	6.6	5.9	28.4	27.8	9.0	0.9	74.6	38.4	51.3	48.7
53061	NEW HOLSTEIN	98.7	98.4	0.0	0.0	0.2	0.3	0.6	0.8	5.1	5.4	6.6	6.4	5.7	26.1	27.1	14.3	3.3	78.9	41.5	49.1	50.9
53063	NEWTON	98.3	98.2	0.1	0.1	0.3	0.3	1.3	1.4	5.8	6.3	7.4	6.7	6.1	25.9	27.1	12.7	2.1	76.2	40.4	50.4	49.6
53065	OAKFIELD	98.7	98.5	0.1	0.1	0.3	0.3	1.7	2.0	6.2	6.6	8.1	8.2	6.0	27.7	26.8	9.2	1.2	74.0	37.5	51.2	48.8
53066	OCONOMOWOC	97.9	97.6	0.4	0.4	0.5	0.6	1.3	1.5	6.0	6.5	7.2	7.1	5.3	26.3	28.1	11.3	2.3	75.8	40.4	49.2	50.8
53069	OKAUCHEE	98.2	98.2	0.1	0.1	0.2	0.2	0.5	0.5	4.5	4.6	5.6	6.2	6.3	30.9	29.8	10.4	1.6	81.6	40.3	52.0	48.0
53070	OOSTBURG	98.7	98.5	0.1	0.2	0.4	0.4	1.1	1.3	7.0	7.3	7.7	6.9	5.8	26.1	25.7	12.0	1.5	73.5	38.2	50.6	49.4
53072	PEWAUKEE	97.0	96.5	0.4	0.4	1.3	1.7	1.1	1.3	6.4	6.6	6.5	5.6	5.6	29.8	27.5	10.4	1.5	76.8	39.1	49.1	51.0
53073	PLYMOUTH	96.9	96.4	1.6	1.7	0.6	0.7	1.0	1.2	5.7	5.9	6.8	7.6	8.3	26.2	26.0	11.1	2.4	77.3	38.4	50.5	49.5
53074	PORT WASHINGTON	97.0	96.6	0.8	0.9	0.5	0.6	1.5	1.7	6.7	6.5	6.9	7.2	6.8	28.7	24.2	11.0	2.0	75.2	37.3	49.4	50.6
53075	RANDOM LAKE	97.6	97.3	0.4	0.5	0.3	0.4	1.3	1.6	5.2	5.5	6.9	10.7	12.7	24.6	24.1	9.6	0.9	78.0	34.7	49.4	50.6
53076	RICHFIELD	97.6	97.2	0.4	0.4	1.2	1.5	1.0	1.2	7.1	7.7	7.5	6.8	5.4	26.8	29.3	8.6	0.8	73.5	38.9	51.1	48.9
53078	RUBICON	98.4	98.2	0.1	0.2	0.2	0.2	0.9	1.1	6.1	6.7	7.7	7.7	6.6	27.4	27.5	9.5	0.8	74.9	38.1	51.3	48.7
53079	SAINT CLOUD	98.8	98.7	0.1	0.1	0.2	0.3	0.8	1.0	5.2	5.6	7.9	7.7	5.8	27.3	26.4	12.6	1.6	76.3	39.6	51.2	48.8
53080	SAUKVILLE	97.7	97.4	0.5	0.5	0.5	0.6	1.9	2.2	7.0	7.2	7.6	6.9	6.1	30.9	25.6	8.0	0.8	74.0	36.3	51.3	48.7
53081	SHEBOYGAN	87.1	84.7	0.9	1.1	6.7	8.3	6.4	7.4	7.1	6.5	7.0	6.9	7.7	28.5	21.7	12.1	2.6	75.3	35.8	49.5	50.5
53083	SHEBOYGAN	95.0	94.0	0.2	0.3	2.9	3.7	2.0	2.3	6.5	6.8	7.3	6.7	5.8	27.0	26.7	11.1	2.0	75.2	38.8	49.3	50.7
53085	SHEBOYGAN FALLS	98.2	97.9	0.3	0.3	0.4	0.6	0.8	1.0	5.8	5.9	6.9	6.8	6.1	27.2	26.8	12.0	2.6	77.2	40.0	49.0	51.0
53086	SLINGER	98.3	98.1	0.2	0.3	0.3	0.4	1.1	1.4	6.4	6.9	7.8	7.5	5.9	29.0	25.7	9.5	1.3	73.9	37.9	50.1	49.9
53089	SUSSEX	97.7	97.3	0.5	0.6	0.6	0.8	1.2	1.5	7.6	7.6	7.7	6.5	5.8	28.6	25.8	9.5	1.0	73.0	37.6	49.2	50.8
53090	WEST BEND	97.8	97.5	0.2	0.3	0.4	0.5	1.6	1.9	7.3	7.2	7.1	7.0	6.8	30.6	24.6	8.4	1.1	74.0	35.8	50.4	49.6
53091	THERESA	98.4	98.1	0.1	0.1	0.2	0.3	0.9	1.1	6.6	6.9	7.8	6.8	5.8	29.4	24.7	11.1	1.0	74.5	37.7	51.0	49.0
53092	THIENSVILLE	94.3	93.3	2.1	2.4	2.3	2.9	1.2	1.3	5.1	6.3	7.8	7.4	4.7	19.1	33.4	14.2	1.9	75.8	44.7	48.7	51.3
53093	WALDO	98.2	97.9	0.2	0.2	0.4	0.5	0.9	1.1	6.4	6.8	6.9	6.7	5.4	26.3	28.8	11.3	1.4	75.7	40.1	51.3	48.7
53094	WATERTOWN	95.7	95.2	0.3	0.3	0.6	0.7	4.9	5.6	7.3	6.8	6.8	7.2	8.2	29.2	22.7	10.4	1.5	75.0	34.9	49.0	51.0
53095	WEST BEND	97.9	97.6	0.3	0.3	0.5	0.6	1.4	1.7	6.4	6.4	6.6	6.3	6.3	26.6	24.7	13.3	3.5	76.7	39.5	48.5	51.5
53097	MEQUON	95.4	94.5	1.8	2.0	2.1	2.6	1.2	1.4	5.3	7.4	8.9	6.9	3.5	23.3	32.0	11.6	1.1	73.8	42.4	49.6	50.4
53098	WATERTOWN	97.6	97.2	0.2	0.2	0.6	0.7	2.9	3.4	6.1	6.1	7.1	7.1	6.4	27.4	23.1	13.0	3.7	76.3	38.5	49.3	50.8
53103	BIG BEND	98.3	98.1	0.2	0.2	0.3	0.3	1.2	1.5	5.0	6.2	8.1	6.9	5.5	25.8	33.4	8.2	0.9	76.4	41.0	52.0	48.0
53104	BRISTOL	97.4	96.9	0.3	0.4	0.9	1.1	2.4	2.9	5.7	6.3	7.7	6.8	4.9	28.3	27.9	11.1	1.3	75.8	39.7	49.9	50.1
53105	BURLINGTON	97.1	96.4	0.4	0.5	0.4	0.5	2.9	3.7	6.4	6.7	7.6	7.2	6.3	27.6	26.3	10.3	1.6	74.6	38.0	49.8	50.3
53108	CALEDONIA	97.7	97.3	0.6	0.8	0.1	0.1	1.6	2.1	5.1	5.5	6.0	5.5	4.8	26.3	31.0	14.9	0.9	80.0	43.2	52.1	47.9
53110	CUDAHY	93.9	92.5	1.0	1.3	0.9	1.2	4.7	5.8	6.3	6.1	6.3	6.0	6.3	28.8	24.1	14.2	1.9	77.7	39.0	48.7	51.3
53114	DARIEN	94.3	93.3	0.4	0.4	0.1	0.2	10.6	12.2	7.7	7.9	7.6	7.2	6.4	28.0	26.0	8.0	1.2	72.1	35.4	52.1	47.9
53115	DELAVAN	89.1	87.5	0.9	1.0	0.7	0.9	14.5	16.7	7.1	6.7	7.6	7.5	7.1	27.9	23.8	10.7	1.7	73.7	35.8	49.7	50.3
53118	DOUSMAN	97.4	97.0	0.6	0.7	0.4	0.6	1.4	1.7	5.8	6.6	7.7	8.4	5.6	24.5	30.0	9.3	2.3	74.3	40.5	50.1	49.9
53119	EAGLE	97.3	96.9	0.4	0.5	0.3	0.4	1.5	1.9	7.9	8.6	8.8	6.4	4.7	30.4	26.2	6.5	0.6	70.7	36.5	48.9	51.1
53120	EAST TROY	97.8	97.4	0.2	0.2	0.4	0.5	1.9	2.3	6.5	6.8	7.3	6.8	5.5	27.9	27.3	10.5	1.6	75.2	38.9	50.1	50.0
53121	ELKHORN	96.1	95.5	0.5	0.5	0.6	0.7	4.3	5.0	6.6	6.6	7.4	7.0	6.3	28.3	24.5	11.1	2.2	74.9	37.8	49.8	50.2
53122	ELM GROVE	97.2	96.7	0.4	0.5	1.6	1.9	1.2	1.4	4.9	6.0	7.6	7.0	4.3	15.9	30.9	20.1	3.3	76.6	47.3	47.1	52.9
53125	FONTANA	98.2	97.7	0.2	0.3	0.8	1.0	2.3	2.9	5.2	5.5	6.1	5.4	4.2	20.8	29.2	19.1	4.6	79.8	46.9	48.4	51.7
53126	FRANKSVILLE	96.8	96.1	0.8	1.0	0.9	1.2	1.8	2.3	6.3	6.8	8.0	6.8	4.7	26.6	29.7	10.3	1.0	74.5	40.4	51.0	49.0
53128	GENOA CITY	96.9	96.4	0.7	0.8	0.4	0.5	2.9	3.5	8.2	8.0	8.5	7.2	6.2	30.8	21.6	8.2	1.3	70.5	34.2	50.2	49.8
53129	GREENDALE	96.2	95.1	0.3	0.5	2.1	2.8	2.4	2.9	5.0	5.3	6.1	6.5	5.4	21.3	28.6	19.0	2.8	79.3	45.3	46.9	53.1
53130	HALES CORNERS	97.1	96.3	0.2	0.4	1.0	1.4	2.1	2.6	4.6	4.8	6.4	6.8	6.6	25.0	27.5	15.2	3.1	79.8	42.3	47.8	52.2
53132	FRANKLIN	90.8	89.1	5.2	5.8	2.1	2.9	2.7	3.3	5.6	6.0	6.4	6.9	6.5	29.6	28.4	9.7	0.9	77.8	39.1	52.1	47.9
53137	HELENVILLE	98.3	98.2	0.1	0.1	0.1	0.1	2.0	2.2	6.0	6.9	6.8	6.6	5.3	29.0	29.0	9.6	0.9	75.9	39.4	51.2	48.9
53139	KANSASVILLE	96.3	95.5	0.5	0.6	0.7	0.9	4.0	5.0	5.6	6.4	8.6	7.3	5.3	30.5	26.8	8.6	0.9	74.7	38.1	50.0	50.0
53140	KENOSHA	81.2	78.8	9.0	10.2	0.8	0.9	12.1	14.0	7.7	6.7	6.9	8.4	10.0	28.9	19.3	10.2	2.0	74.6	32.1	49.5	50.5
53142	KENOSHA	92.4	90.9	2.4	2.9	1.4	1.8	4.9	5.9	7.0	7.0	7.5	6.6	5.5	29.7	24.1	10.8	1.8	74.2	37.3	48.5	51.5
53143	KENOSHA	82.8	81.0	8.3	9.2	0.7	0.8	11.0	12.4	7.5	7.2	8.0	7.2	7.0	28.8	21.5	10.6	2.3	72.9	34.8	48.8	51.2
53144	KENOSHA	82.4	80.4	8.8	9.7	1.4	1.6	8.6	9.8	7.1	6.9	6.9	8.1	9.0	30.1	22.2	8.4	1.3	74.9	33.4	50.3	49.7
53146	NEW BERLIN	96.3	95.5	0.2	0.2	2.0	2.6	1.7	2.1	6.1	6.6	6.7	6.0	4.8	27.5	29.3	12.1	0.9	76.7	40.7	49.8	50.2
53147	LAKE GENEVA	93.1	92.3	1.0	1.1	0.8	1.0	9.6	10.9	5.5	5.7	6.6	6.1	5.8	26.9	27.8	13.6	1.9	78.4	40.7	49.8	50.2
	WISCONSIN	88.9	88.0	5.7	6.0	1.7	2.1	3.6	4.0	6.4	6.5	7.1	7.3	7.7	27.6	24.5	11.1	1.9	75.8	36.9	49.5	50.5
	UNITED STATES	75.1	73.6	12.3	12.5	3.8	4.2	12.5	14.1	6.9	6.7	7.2	7.0	7.3	28.6	23.8	10.8	1.7	75.1	36.0	49.1	50.9

WISCONSIN

INCOME

C   53001-53147

ZIP CODE		2004 Per Capita Income	2004 HH Income Base	2004 HOUSEHOLD INCOME DISTRIBUTION (%)					MEDIAN HOUSEHOLD INCOME				2004 Home Value Base	2004 HOME VALUE DISTRIBUTION (%)					2004 Median Home Value
#	POST OFFICE NAME			Less than $25,000	$25,000 to $49,999	$50,000 to $99,999	$100,000 to $149,999	$150,000 or More	2004	2009	2004 National Centile	2004 State Centile		Less than $50,000	$50,000 to $89,999	$90,000 to $174,999	$175,000 to $399,999	$400,000 or More	
53001	ADELL	24817	776	14.1	28.1	43.7	10.3	3.9	56000	62783	81	79	648	1.5	5.9	54.2	35.8	2.6	156061
53002	ALLENTON	25289	883	12.0	18.9	51.9	14.6	2.6	64300	75374	88	92	701	0.7	3.9	37.2	53.9	4.3	190293
53004	BELGIUM	27674	1234	10.6	24.7	45.2	14.5	4.9	62126	76183	86	90	1002	0.7	2.1	42.8	46.2	8.2	181962
53005	BROOKFIELD	40107	7827	8.1	17.4	38.4	20.9	15.2	79089	94856	95	99	7215	0.3	0.6	18.8	71.6	8.8	223551
53006	BROWNSVILLE	24648	878	13.9	27.1	45.0	10.7	3.3	57831	63841	82	82	722	2.8	8.3	48.1	37.7	3.2	158163
53007	BUTLER	26613	948	24.4	33.2	33.8	6.7	2.0	44592	54511	60	47	490	0.0	2.0	78.2	19.8	0.0	143440
53010	CAMPBELLSPORT	23878	2797	16.0	28.4	43.1	9.9	2.5	54316	60459	79	75	2313	4.0	5.0	49.6	39.0	2.4	161771
53011	CASCADE	26432	810	12.6	29.4	43.3	11.1	3.6	56633	63183	81	80	717	3.1	7.8	51.6	33.5	4.0	148929
53012	CEDARBURG	34747	7149	11.8	20.3	37.5	18.5	12.0	71471	86152	92	96	5511	0.2	0.1	19.0	68.8	11.9	233140
53013	CEDAR GROVE	25291	1203	10.7	29.8	44.6	9.6	5.2	57780	64611	82	82	1026	0.3	3.3	65.9	27.8	2.7	145392
53014	CHILTON	23342	3431	18.1	31.4	40.7	7.1	2.7	50396	56049	73	65	2744	4.4	21.2	53.8	19.3	1.4	119703
53015	CLEVELAND	23880	1012	15.6	25.5	46.2	10.0	2.8	58719	63741	83	83	872	8.8	7.9	56.5	24.7	2.1	132601
53017	COLGATE	35447	1826	7.6	16.8	40.2	23.9	11.6	78538	91384	95	99	1733	1.7	2.4	12.7	68.3	14.9	243007
53018	DELAFIELD	39410	2761	10.1	13.0	30.9	26.5	19.5	91467	106408	97	100	2355	0.6	0.2	16.0	57.1	26.2	290799
53019	EDEN	22727	715	15.1	31.1	42.5	8.0	3.4	52442	58832	76	70	616	17.5	6.2	46.8	26.5	3.1	135606
53020	ELKHART LAKE	29509	1399	9.2	27.2	45.2	12.3	6.2	61857	69029	86	90	1210	1.7	7.2	47.9	35.5	7.6	159160
53021	FREDONIA	26764	1604	9.9	23.2	49.9	13.7	3.3	63176	76856	87	91	1274	0.0	1.3	39.3	53.9	5.6	190513
53022	GERMANTOWN	29663	7438	9.9	22.0	44.1	18.4	5.6	66281	76733	89	94	5798	1.5	4.9	26.6	64.8	2.3	206357
53023	GLENBEULAH	18212	516	11.2	29.1	44.6	10.5	4.7	57436	64595	82	81	449	2.9	12.3	47.2	33.0	4.7	148284
53024	GRAFTON	33713	6196	12.4	23.0	38.2	16.8	9.6	65143	79854	89	93	4600	1.4	0.9	32.3	57.0	8.4	196833
53027	HARTFORD	27595	7803	15.3	23.9	41.9	13.5	5.5	60859	69797	85	88	5855	0.7	0.9	38.7	54.2	5.5	190099
53029	HARTLAND	39133	7149	9.3	16.7	39.7	20.0	14.3	77841	92269	94	98	5482	0.2	0.8	17.2	56.9	25.0	257132
53032	HORICON	25799	1908	14.7	30.2	40.3	12.0	2.9	54492	60953	79	75	1502	3.3	14.4	58.1	23.1	1.2	125342
53033	HUBERTUS	35084	1953	5.6	15.1	45.5	24.9	8.9	79800	94195	95	99	1851	0.0	1.0	19.1	71.0	8.9	226143
53034	HUSTISFORD	25986	409	20.8	27.4	40.6	7.3	3.9	51595	57430	75	68	261	0.8	5.4	60.9	32.2	0.8	149702
53035	IRON RIDGE	22816	1078	16.1	29.6	40.9	10.3	3.1	52691	59271	76	71	886	11.1	3.7	48.7	34.9	1.7	151575
53036	IXONIA	26799	915	9.8	27.9	44.5	13.3	4.5	59335	67075	84	84	781	1.8	4.4	36.0	50.3	7.6	188851
53037	JACKSON	27889	2807	11.3	22.8	48.1	12.8	5.1	61206	70285	86	88	2272	11.5	4.9	26.5	53.9	3.3	186313
53038	JOHNSON CREEK	24204	1169	16.5	31.6	38.8	9.3	3.9	51364	57909	74	68	917	20.3	5.6	37.1	33.3	3.8	149679
53039	JUNEAU	22320	1978	19.0	31.0	38.9	8.1	2.9	49958	55439	72	64	1529	2.7	9.7	58.9	27.1	1.7	135964
53040	KEWASKUM	25905	2755	11.4	25.6	45.1	14.2	3.7	61813	71004	86	89	2108	0.5	2.6	43.3	49.3	4.4	181150
53042	KIEL	25947	2749	18.7	27.7	42.6	7.3	3.7	53164	59633	77	72	2239	4.6	11.1	57.2	24.7	2.4	128727
53044	KOHLER	42174	813	12.2	15.6	40.0	21.9	10.3	75060	86794	93	98	752	0.0	2.5	54.0	40.2	3.3	161685
53045	BROOKFIELD	47337	8667	8.6	16.1	32.6	20.4	22.4	87165	103307	97	99	7344	0.3	0.3	12.2	65.6	21.5	258879
53046	LANNON	32753	454	12.1	24.2	41.2	16.3	6.2	63438	75993	87	92	404	6.7	10.9	34.7	42.1	3.0	167647
53048	LOMIRA	23020	995	19.1	28.2	42.8	7.5	2.3	51853	57820	75	69	738	12.3	8.1	52.6	26.0	1.0	137179
53049	MALONE	24519	930	14.7	28.9	43.4	8.5	4.4	54948	61182	80	77	830	2.5	5.5	50.8	37.6	3.5	160200
53050	MAYVILLE	22742	2884	19.8	31.4	38.3	8.3	2.2	49031	54302	70	62	2104	2.7	8.5	65.7	22.2	1.0	132733
53051	MENOMONEE FALLS	32229	13847	12.5	22.4	40.5	18.1	6.6	64967	78280	88	93	10893	1.2	1.4	34.1	58.1	5.1	193852
53057	MOUNT CALVARY	19977	569	17.1	27.2	43.6	9.5	2.6	54742	60132	79	76	493	2.0	9.1	57.0	29.0	2.8	144500
53058	NASHOTAH	39065	1170	11.3	21.2	36.1	19.3	12.1	71571	85767	92	96	866	0.2	0.6	14.3	57.3	27.6	281679
53059	NEOSHO	25956	740	11.8	27.3	44.5	11.5	5.0	59569	65662	84	85	628	0.8	3.8	48.1	43.3	4.0	170991
53061	NEW HOLSTEIN	24022	2017	17.5	31.4	42.6	6.5	2.0	50707	56919	73	66	1626	6.6	21.8	56.9	14.3	0.4	109360
53063	NEWTON	24515	623	14.0	26.0	44.6	11.6	3.9	59905	65087	84	85	559	4.7	10.6	50.3	31.0	3.6	145658
53065	OAKFIELD	24279	734	12.5	27.7	44.8	11.0	4.0	57353	63337	82	80	636	4.3	4.7	55.5	34.6	0.9	152670
53066	OCONOMOWOC	35645	11494	12.1	21.0	39.0	17.9	10.0	67935	81238	90	95	9055	1.0	1.5	28.0	52.3	17.2	220653
53069	OKAUCHEE	35551	373	15.3	25.5	38.9	12.3	8.0	60621	70310	85	87	246	0.0	0.0	19.9	50.0	30.1	287097
53070	OOSTBURG	24821	1765	12.5	30.1	42.5	9.9	5.0	57371	63222	82	81	1485	0.1	4.6	59.9	32.5	3.0	143724
53072	PEWAUKEE	40113	9527	8.1	21.2	38.5	20.3	12.0	73979	87986	93	97	6936	0.5	1.3	28.1	52.2	18.0	228812
53073	PLYMOUTH	26891	5620	18.3	28.5	40.1	8.4	4.7	52663	59230	76	71	4183	3.5	7.4	60.9	25.4	2.8	139475
53074	PORT WASHINGTON	29436	4909	14.4	21.9	44.7	14.3	4.8	62521	76410	87	91	3265	0.9	0.5	50.1	45.1	3.5	173311
53075	RANDOM LAKE	21207	1227	16.2	29.4	41.4	9.0	4.0	53399	60254	78	72	941	0.3	5.0	54.0	38.3	2.4	160513
53076	RICHFIELD	31602	1183	9.8	14.5	43.9	22.2	9.6	76738	86335	94	98	1066	2.7	1.1	17.1	66.9	12.2	239030
53078	RUBICON	23073	582	10.7	29.0	43.1	13.6	3.6	57639	64435	82	81	508	1.2	1.4	40.4	51.4	5.7	187162
53079	SAINT CLOUD	23558	656	16.5	28.2	42.5	10.2	2.6	54825	60431	79	76	566	3.7	10.8	54.4	27.7	3.4	136337
53080	SAUKVILLE	27966	2389	14.1	21.3	43.1	17.4	4.1	64091	77525	88	92	1692	0.0	2.0	42.7	51.2	4.1	183624
53081	SHEBOYGAN	22157	18213	23.9	33.0	35.4	5.8	1.9	44539	50469	60	47	11111	5.3	26.7	58.5	8.8	0.8	105451
53083	SHEBOYGAN	27314	8034	17.3	26.6	40.8	10.1	5.2	55095	62420	80	77	6193	1.1	12.9	60.4	23.0	2.6	130164
53085	SHEBOYGAN FALLS	26042	4257	15.0	29.2	43.3	9.5	3.0	53644	61555	78	73	3183	8.6	10.2	55.4	24.7	1.2	125875
53086	SLINGER	27119	2791	14.3	22.0	44.3	13.7	5.8	61206	71277	86	88	2162	8.7	1.7	28.7	52.3	8.7	198606
53089	SUSSEX	30294	6358	10.6	17.5	44.9	21.5	5.6	71440	84700	92	96	5119	6.9	1.4	19.3	68.8	3.7	214753
53090	WEST BEND	25637	8005	11.9	23.6	47.5	14.1	2.9	61363	70666	86	89	6127	1.1	1.7	47.7	47.3	2.2	174299
53091	THERESA	22598	843	15.5	27.2	47.9	7.0	2.4	55331	61680	80	78	735	7.5	13.6	52.5	24.0	2.5	134248
53092	THIENSVILLE	59818	8094	7.4	15.0	29.5	19.7	28.4	95566	115594	98	100	7000	0.4	1.4	12.6	53.5	32.2	292072
53093	WALDO	25579	672	11.0	30.1	46.0	9.8	3.1	56507	63373	81	79	571	2.8	9.5	57.1	28.7	1.9	141709
53094	WATERTOWN	22523	6594	20.0	31.7	37.8	7.6	2.9	48478	54744	69	60	4630	2.3	5.6	59.6	30.1	2.5	146083
53095	WEST BEND	30289	10293	14.4	28.1	37.9	12.7	7.0	58678	65979	83	83	7052	0.4	1.7	39.8	49.1	9.0	189070
53097	MEQUON	45310	1823	6.3	17.6	31.9	24.7	19.6	89992	109360	97	100	1651	0.0	0.1	9.6	63.7	26.7	282167
53098	WATERTOWN	22401	4613	19.0	29.8	40.6	8.3	2.2	50685	56312	73	66	3472	0.9	8.8	60.8	26.8	2.7	143759
53103	BIG BEND	28831	1419	5.5	16.4	52.0	21.9	4.2	73411	86862	93	97	1307	0.3	1.3	25.4	68.3	4.7	212440
53104	BRISTOL	28114	2215	13.1	25.6	40.7	15.4	5.3	60357	70403	85	87	1895	10.6	4.5	31.7	46.4	6.8	182221
53105	BURLINGTON	26547	11256	15.5	25.9	41.4	12.4	4.8	58007	67210	83	82	8736	3.9	6.1	48.2	37.6	4.2	159735
53108	CALEDONIA	28996	1252	11.3	25.9	39.4	18.5	5.0	65241	76411	89	93	1142	0.1	10.2	46.1	39.7	4.0	159874
53110	CUDAHY	23096	7892	23.8	32.3	34.3	8.5	1.0	45292	52835	62	50	4850	2.3	7.1	78.5	11.7	0.4	126279
53114	DARIEN	22176	977	16.8	27.1	42.2	11.2	2.8	54749	63696	79	76	779	5.1	6.4	57.0	27.7	3.7	142691
53115	DELAVAN	23302	5893	20.2	30.8	36.6	9.3	3.1	49107	57023	70	62	3908	2.7	11.0	54.9	28.6	2.8	140362
53118	DOUSMAN	33329	2772	9.4	19.5	39.7	23.7	7.7	71642	86029	92	96	2247	3.8	2.2	20.9	64.0	9.1	229019
53119	EAGLE	28976	1736	7.7	17.5	49.1	18.7	7.0	71365	84938	92	95	1596	0.8	1.3	29.2	61.7	7.1	208938
53120	EAST TROY	27695	3613	12.8	24.0	45.5	13.2	4.5	61302	71605	86	89	2980	5.7	5.1	37.6	44.7	6.9	178175
53121	ELKHORN	25990	6372	18.7	28.6	36.9	11.3	4.6	52662	61247	76	71	4512	3.9	4.1	45.9	39.6	6.5	167874
53122	ELM GROVE	54108	2537	12.6	12.4	29.6	18.0	27.4	89200	104798	97	100	2199	0.5	0.7	9.9	60.2	28.7	313401
53125	FONTANA	38971	874	15.2	22.2	37.5	14.9	10.2	62276	74226	86	90	719	0.6	1.1	27.7	57.2	13.5	224132
53126	FRANKSVILLE	30154	2285	10.2	20.2	46.1	18.0	5.5	68606	79552	91	95	2021	0.8	3.9	38.9	49.6	6.7	188670
53128	GENOA CITY	21676	2652	17.6	29.8	41.3	9.4	2.0	51701	60500	75	68	2183	3.5	10.1	61.8	22.6	2.0	138086
53129	GREENDALE	33139	6062	16.1	23.3	38.6	16.0	5.9	61191	71020	86	88	4508	0.2	0.5	46.7	49.8	2.8	178520
53130	HALES CORNERS	29744	3272	15.7	23.0	41.2	17.0	3.1	61860	74578	86	90	2060	1.3	0.9	45.1	51.0	1.8	178377
53132	FRANKLIN	32872	11247	11.1	18.6	40.8	20.3	9.1	72707	85269	92	97	8990	1.9	1.3	38.3	56.2	2.4	185806
53137	HELENVILLE	24456	574	13.4	28.1	45.1	9.8	3.7	57284	63796	82	80	502	7.8	5.0	33.9	48.4	5.0	182727
53139	KANSASVILLE	27509	1012	13.0	29.0	39.0	12.7	6.3	56679	65641	81	80	883	5.3	6.8	40.9	39.5	7.5	167952
53140	KENOSHA	19948	11718	31.4	29.6	30.2	7.5	1.4	39359	46571	44	26	5943	2.3	12.2	72.2	12.5	0.7	121952
53142	KENOSHA	26787	11765	15.9	24.4	40.0	15.8	3.8	60235	70619	85	86	9306	2.7	3.5	59.7	33.2	0.9	151643
53143	KENOSHA	23286	10071	24.8	29.1	35.1	7.9	3.1	46060	54832	64	53	6465	5.9	11.6	70.0	11.7	0.7	122103
53144	KENOSHA	24980	8644	20.4	28.7	33.9	12.9	4.1	50656	60752	73	66	5309	4.0	5.4	53.1	34.9	2.7	150501
53146	NEW BERLIN	32649	2982	8.2	20.0	41.2	22.8	7.8	71895	85563	92	96	2568	1.1	0.5	34.9	59.1	4.4	194538
53147	LAKE GENEVA	27808	6693	20.7	28.5	34.4	10.8	5.7	50717	60140	73	66	4693	4.5	7.2	44.3	34.8	9.3	160805
	WISCONSIN	25041		22.2	28.8	35.0	9.6	4.2	48930	56561				7.0	14.9	46.8	27.8	3.6	134326
	UNITED STATES	25866		24.7	27.1	30.8	10.9	6.5	48124	56710				10.9	15.0	33.7	30.1	10.4	145905

330-C

ZIP CODE #	POST OFFICE NAME	FINANCIAL SERVICES: Auto Loan	Home Loan	Invest-ments	Retire-ment Plans	THE HOME: Home Improvements: Home Repair	Lawn & Garden	Furnishings: Comput-ers & Hard-ware	Major Appli-ances	TV, Radio, Sound Equip-ment	Furni-ture	ENTERTAINMENT: Dine out/ Carry out	Sports Equip-ment	Fees & Tickets	Toys & Games	Travel	Cable TV	PERSONAL: Apparel & Services	Auto Repairs	Health Insur-ance	Pets & Supplies
53001	ADELL	106	94	72	89	99	106	87	96	92	87	112	115	85	115	89	95	107	94	104	124
53002	ALLENTON	92	108	112	109	105	104	99	99	92	99	116	116	103	121	100	88	115	96	88	109
53004	BELGIUM	120	108	84	103	114	122	100	110	105	100	128	131	98	131	103	108	122	107	118	141
53005	BROOKFIELD	135	166	190	165	164	170	151	151	143	152	179	172	162	186	157	141	179	147	141	164
53006	BROWNSVILLE	105	93	71	88	98	105	86	95	91	86	111	114	84	113	89	94	106	93	103	123
53007	BUTLER	72	73	80	71	74	81	73	73	75	72	93	85	75	96	75	77	91	74	76	84
53010	CAMPBELLSPORT	99	89	67	84	94	100	82	91	87	82	106	108	80	108	84	89	100	88	98	117
53011	CASCADE	105	94	71	89	99	106	86	96	92	86	112	114	85	114	89	94	106	93	104	124
53012	CEDARBURG	117	136	154	139	134	136	129	127	121	128	153	149	134	157	130	118	151	125	115	139
53013	CEDAR GROVE	109	97	74	92	102	110	89	99	95	89	116	118	88	118	92	97	110	97	107	128
53014	CHILTON	93	81	62	79	85	94	79	86	83	78	101	100	76	102	80	85	96	84	93	106
53015	CLEVELAND	102	90	69	86	95	102	83	93	89	84	108	110	82	110	86	91	103	90	100	119
53017	COLGATE	135	161	165	160	159	158	144	145	135	143	169	170	152	180	147	132	168	140	133	164
53018	DELAFIELD	147	182	196	185	178	177	162	160	149	163	188	186	175	198	165	144	189	154	143	177
53019	EDEN	97	90	71	86	94	100	82	90	86	82	105	108	82	108	85	88	101	88	96	115
53020	ELKHART LAKE	124	107	80	100	115	124	99	112	107	99	129	133	95	131	103	111	122	110	124	147
53021	FREDONIA	105	104	90	101	107	112	95	102	96	95	118	120	96	123	98	97	114	99	104	125
53022	GERMANTOWN	108	115	118	119	111	112	110	108	104	112	132	128	111	132	108	99	129	108	98	121
53023	GLENBEULAH	111	98	75	93	104	111	91	101	97	91	117	120	89	120	94	99	112	98	109	130
53024	GRAFTON	109	131	143	131	128	129	121	119	114	120	143	139	127	151	123	111	142	117	109	131
53027	HARTFORD	101	103	98	102	104	110	99	102	99	98	123	118	101	126	100	99	119	100	102	117
53029	HARTLAND	143	168	177	171	163	162	153	151	142	155	180	177	161	185	153	136	179	148	134	167
53032	HORICON	103	91	69	87	96	104	86	94	91	86	111	111	84	112	88	93	105	92	102	119
53033	HUBERTUS	123	153	162	153	150	148	136	136	126	136	159	159	145	169	140	123	159	131	122	150
53034	HUSTISFORD	97	86	66	82	91	98	80	88	85	80	103	105	78	105	82	87	98	86	96	114
53035	IRON RIDGE	99	88	67	84	93	100	82	91	87	82	106	108	80	108	84	89	100	88	98	117
53036	IXONIA	99	112	111	111	113	113	101	104	97	101	121	122	106	128	104	96	119	100	98	120
53037	JACKSON	103	107	100	107	106	108	101	103	98	101	122	122	101	123	100	95	119	102	97	119
53038	JOHNSON CREEK	95	85	69	84	89	98	84	90	88	83	107	104	82	108	85	89	101	88	96	108
53039	JUNEAU	92	80	62	78	85	93	78	85	83	77	101	99	76	101	79	85	95	83	92	105
53040	KEWASKUM	104	104	91	101	106	110	95	101	96	95	118	120	96	122	97	96	114	98	102	123
53042	KIEL	105	93	71	89	99	106	86	96	92	86	111	114	84	114	89	94	106	93	103	123
53044	KOHLER	139	172	183	172	169	167	154	153	142	153	179	179	164	191	157	138	179	148	137	169
53045	BROOKFIELD	158	198	234	197	193	201	179	177	167	180	211	202	194	221	185	166	212	172	163	192
53046	LANNON	117	110	90	105	115	121	101	110	105	101	128	130	101	132	104	106	123	107	115	138
53048	LOMIRA	98	87	66	82	92	98	80	89	85	80	104	106	79	106	83	87	99	87	96	115
53049	MALONE	97	95	82	92	98	103	87	93	89	87	109	111	88	113	90	89	105	91	96	115
53050	MAYVILLE	90	76	57	74	81	90	75	82	81	74	98	96	72	97	76	83	92	81	91	103
53051	MENOMONEE FALLS	107	119	125	119	118	122	113	113	109	113	137	131	117	141	114	108	134	111	108	126
53057	MOUNT CALVARY	98	87	66	83	92	98	80	89	85	80	104	106	79	106	83	87	99	87	96	115
53058	NASHOTAH	127	152	177	154	149	151	142	140	134	142	168	165	150	176	145	130	168	138	126	153
53059	NEOSHO	114	102	78	97	108	115	94	104	100	94	122	124	92	124	97	103	116	102	113	135
53061	NEW HOLSTEIN	93	82	63	78	87	93	76	84	81	76	98	101	75	101	78	83	94	82	91	109
53063	NEWTON	109	97	74	92	102	109	89	99	95	89	115	118	88	118	92	97	110	96	107	128
53065	OAKFIELD	109	97	74	92	102	110	89	99	95	89	116	118	88	118	92	97	110	96	107	128
53066	OCONOMOWOC	122	139	149	139	138	142	130	130	125	130	157	151	136	162	132	123	154	128	123	145
53069	OKAUCHEE	100	114	141	119	113	116	113	110	108	113	136	131	117	139	114	104	134	111	100	120
53070	OOSTBURG	107	96	73	91	101	108	88	98	94	88	114	117	87	117	91	96	108	95	106	126
53072	PEWAUKEE	124	146	163	149	143	144	137	134	128	137	162	157	143	167	138	124	161	132	121	147
53073	PLYMOUTH	99	94	83	92	97	105	91	96	94	90	115	112	91	118	92	95	110	94	100	115
53074	PORT WASHINGTON	101	109	108	109	108	111	103	104	99	102	124	123	105	127	103	97	122	103	98	119
53075	RANDOM LAKE	105	94	72	89	99	106	87	96	92	87	112	114	85	114	89	94	106	93	103	123
53076	RICHFIELD	119	143	148	143	140	139	128	128	120	128	150	151	135	159	130	116	149	124	116	143
53078	RUBICON	109	97	74	92	102	109	89	99	95	89	115	118	87	118	92	97	110	96	107	128
53079	SAINT CLOUD	100	89	67	84	94	100	82	91	87	82	106	108	80	108	84	89	101	88	98	117
53080	SAUKVILLE	96	113	118	113	111	110	103	103	97	103	122	121	108	128	105	94	121	100	93	114
53081	SHEBOYGAN	74	70	69	70	72	79	74	74	76	71	93	86	73	94	73	76	89	74	77	84
53083	SHEBOYGAN	99	97	88	96	100	106	94	98	95	92	117	115	93	119	95	96	112	96	100	116
53085	SHEBOYGAN FALLS	105	90	65	84	96	104	83	94	90	84	109	112	80	110	86	93	103	92	104	123
53086	SLINGER	111	102	84	101	105	113	98	105	102	98	124	122	97	125	99	102	118	102	109	126
53089	SUSSEX	110	124	125	125	123	123	115	115	109	115	137	136	119	142	115	105	135	113	106	130
53090	WEST BEND	97	102	98	103	101	103	96	98	93	97	116	115	97	118	96	91	113	96	92	112
53091	THERESA	94	85	66	81	89	95	78	86	83	78	101	103	77	103	81	84	96	84	93	111
53092	THIENSVILLE	198	239	285	241	236	248	218	217	206	221	260	247	235	264	226	204	259	212	204	239
53093	WALDO	109	97	74	93	103	110	90	100	96	90	116	119	88	119	93	98	111	97	108	129
53094	WATERTOWN	86	82	76	81	83	90	81	84	83	80	102	99	80	103	81	83	98	83	86	99
53095	WEST BEND	100	108	114	107	108	114	104	105	102	103	128	121	107	131	105	102	125	104	103	118
53097	MEQUON	163	200	221	202	196	202	180	178	167	181	211	203	194	217	185	164	211	172	165	195
53098	WATERTOWN	86	82	73	80	84	91	79	84	81	79	99	95	78	99	80	82	95	82	87	99
53103	BIG BEND	112	128	127	126	128	129	115	118	110	115	138	139	120	145	118	109	136	114	111	136
53104	BRISTOL	111	106	92	105	110	114	100	107	101	100	124	127	98	126	101	100	119	105	108	131
53105	BURLINGTON	101	103	97	102	105	109	98	101	97	97	120	119	99	123	99	96	117	99	100	118
53108	CALEDONIA	103	112	108	109	112	115	102	105	100	101	124	124	105	130	105	99	122	102	103	123
53110	CUDAHY	70	72	76	71	73	79	73	73	74	71	92	84	75	95	74	75	89	73	75	81
53114	DARIEN	101	89	68	85	94	102	83	92	88	83	107	109	81	109	85	90	102	90	100	118
53115	DELAVAN	93	85	73	83	88	95	83	89	86	82	106	103	81	106	84	87	101	87	93	107
53118	DOUSMAN	119	136	137	136	134	133	125	126	118	125	148	148	129	153	126	114	146	123	114	141
53119	EAGLE	116	135	136	138	130	128	122	121	112	124	142	142	127	146	121	107	141	117	106	133
53120	EAST TROY	108	107	93	104	110	115	99	105	100	98	123	124	99	127	101	101	119	102	108	128
53121	ELKHORN	98	95	89	94	98	104	94	97	95	92	117	115	92	119	94	95	112	96	99	115
53122	ELM GROVE	172	209	239	207	208	218	191	192	180	192	227	217	204	231	199	180	225	186	182	209
53125	FONTANA	144	115	81	106	128	144	111	130	124	110	147	151	101	145	116	131	137	128	151	173
53126	FRANKSVILLE	121	125	116	123	127	131	114	120	114	115	141	141	117	146	117	113	137	116	118	143
53128	GENOA CITY	90	84	71	83	86	91	81	86	83	81	102	100	79	102	81	82	97	85	87	102
53129	GREENDALE	102	114	124	112	114	122	107	109	104	108	131	122	112	130	111	105	128	107	109	120
53130	HALES CORNERS	88	103	119	103	102	106	98	97	94	97	118	112	102	122	100	92	116	96	91	105
53132	FRANKLIN	114	133	144	135	131	131	124	122	116	124	147	144	129	152	125	113	146	120	111	136
53137	HELENVILLE	107	95	72	90	100	108	88	97	93	88	113	116	86	116	90	96	108	95	105	126
53139	KANSASVILLE	107	108	99	107	109	111	101	105	100	102	124	125	101	126	102	98	120	103	101	124
53140	KENOSHA	66	65	73	66	64	70	70	67	70	68	88	79	69	88	69	69	85	69	67	74
53142	KENOSHA	91	101	109	101	100	104	98	97	94	97	118	113	101	121	99	92	116	96	92	107
53143	KENOSHA	79	83	89	82	82	87	84	83	83	82	103	96	85	105	84	82	101	83	81	91
53144	KENOSHA	91	90	93	92	90	94	92	91	91	91	114	108	92	114	90	89	111	92	88	103
53146	NEW BERLIN	109	133	147	133	130	130	122	121	114	121	144	141	129	152	124	111	143	118	109	132
53147	LAKE GENEVA	102	89	78	87	94	103	88	96	93	88	113	112	84	112	90	95	108	96	103	119
	WISCONSIN	89	86	85	86	88	94	86	88	87	85	108	103	86	109	86	87	104	88	89	103
	UNITED STATES	100	100	100	100	100	100	100	100	100	100	100	100	100	100	100	100	100	100	100	100

WISCONSIN

POPULATION CHANGE

# POST OFFICE NAME	COUNTY FIPS CODE	POPULATION 2000	2004	2009	2000-2004 ANNUAL RATE % Rate	State Centile	HOUSEHOLDS 2000	2004	2009	% Annual Rate 2000-2004	2004 Average HH Size	FAMILIES 2000	2004	% Annual Rate 2000-2004
53149 MUKWONAGO	133	16712	17775	18779	1.5	73	5857	6440	7005	2.3	2.74	4732	5160	2.1
53150 MUSKEGO	133	21999	22937	23964	1.0	56	7749	8343	8971	1.8	2.71	6284	6689	1.5
53151 NEW BERLIN	133	30615	31926	33387	1.0	56	11671	12537	13472	1.7	2.53	8780	9343	1.5
53153 NORTH PRAIRIE	133	1985	2260	2469	3.1	96	680	800	900	3.9	2.83	579	675	3.7
53154 OAK CREEK	079	28456	31417	32761	2.4	90	11239	12668	13468	2.9	2.47	7525	8383	2.6
53156 PALMYRA	055	3051	3167	3330	0.9	50	1173	1249	1345	1.5	2.53	841	885	1.2
53158 PLEASANT PRAIRIE	059	12239	13520	14661	2.4	91	4334	4902	5422	2.9	2.74	3397	3800	2.7
53168 SALEM	059	8239	8702	9252	1.3	68	2946	3176	3439	1.8	2.74	2225	2367	1.5
53170 SILVER LAKE	059	2000	2229	2425	2.6	93	715	811	898	3.0	2.74	508	568	2.7
53172 SOUTH MILWAUKEE	079	21256	20726	20340	-0.6	3	8694	8685	8706	0.0	2.34	5620	5525	-0.4
53177 STURTEVANT	101	7121	7129	7182	0.0	16	2212	2284	2367	0.8	2.50	1577	1603	0.4
53178 SULLIVAN	055	2871	2980	3158	0.9	50	1138	1222	1331	1.7	2.44	846	897	1.4
53179 TREVOR	059	4692	5157	5573	2.3	90	1676	1871	2055	2.6	2.75	1259	1390	2.4
53181 TWIN LAKES	059	6565	6818	7150	0.9	51	2472	2631	2815	1.5	2.58	1821	1913	1.2
53182 UNION GROVE	101	8740	9209	9510	1.2	66	2983	3247	3444	2.0	2.56	2220	2384	1.7
53183 WALES	133	2444	2443	2502	0.0	14	831	860	907	0.8	2.84	730	752	0.7
53184 WALWORTH	127	3884	4408	4861	3.0	95	1327	1542	1732	3.6	2.78	953	1092	3.3
53185 WATERFORD	101	16487	17932	18797	2.0	86	5901	6569	7036	2.6	2.73	4656	5121	2.3
53186 WAUKESHA	133	33575	33991	35166	0.3	27	13560	14140	15042	1.0	2.32	8456	8676	0.6
53188 WAUKESHA	133	33734	34931	36367	0.8	48	12910	13803	14801	1.6	2.43	8683	9158	1.3
53189 WAUKESHA	133	21926	23675	25340	1.8	83	7691	8546	9396	2.5	2.77	6222	6841	2.3
53190 WHITEWATER	127	18069	18823	19792	1.0	55	5835	6252	6768	1.6	2.43	3029	3189	1.2
53191 WILLIAMS BAY	127	2180	2362	2556	1.9	85	925	1016	1116	2.2	2.24	609	658	1.8
53202 MILWAUKEE	079	20967	21002	20896	0.0	17	13637	14021	14257	0.7	1.37	2234	2193	-0.4
53203 MILWAUKEE	079	331	355	364	1.7	80	219	240	251	2.2	1.36	45	47	1.0
53204 MILWAUKEE	079	42716	43111	43089	0.2	24	12549	12665	12770	0.2	3.35	8488	8439	-0.1
53205 MILWAUKEE	079	10441	9743	9406	-1.6	0	3545	3384	3333	-1.1	2.80	2244	2123	-1.3
53206 MILWAUKEE	079	33259	31621	30875	-1.2	0	10764	10524	10514	-0.5	2.99	7629	7358	-0.9
53207 MILWAUKEE	079	36569	35588	34927	-0.6	2	16197	16190	16254	0.0	2.19	9179	9000	-0.5
53208 MILWAUKEE	079	35005	33389	32511	-1.1	1	12837	12544	12462	-0.5	2.61	7126	6776	-1.2
53209 MILWAUKEE	079	48529	47472	46728	-0.5	3	19031	19048	19135	0.0	2.46	12428	12185	-0.5
53210 MILWAUKEE	079	30181	28785	27998	-1.1	1	10280	9977	9873	-0.7	2.85	7048	6723	-1.1
53211 MILWAUKEE	079	35013	34082	33443	-0.6	2	15791	15715	15729	-0.1	2.02	6596	6392	-0.7
53212 MILWAUKEE	079	31144	30781	30693	-0.3	8	12220	12378	12600	0.3	2.45	6469	6462	0.0
53213 MILWAUKEE	079	26194	25417	24894	-0.7	2	11325	11269	11275	-0.1	2.23	6663	6496	-0.6
53214 MILWAUKEE	079	35630	34863	34287	-0.5	3	15903	15967	16048	0.1	2.14	8582	8437	-0.4
53215 MILWAUKEE	079	54428	55661	55845	0.5	36	19196	19688	19956	0.6	2.81	12389	12494	0.2
53216 MILWAUKEE	079	34104	34040	33870	0.0	13	13164	13332	13480	0.3	2.55	8723	8715	0.0
53217 MILWAUKEE	079	29637	29651	29500	0.0	15	11816	12101	12290	0.6	2.40	8311	8393	0.2
53218 MILWAUKEE	079	41287	41584	41475	0.2	22	14601	14887	15072	0.5	2.78	10421	10480	0.1
53219 MILWAUKEE	079	33947	33351	32872	-0.4	5	15690	15797	15903	0.2	2.09	8943	8821	-0.3
53220 MILWAUKEE	079	25179	25162	25021	0.0	14	11163	11422	11592	0.5	2.14	6613	6662	0.2
53221 MILWAUKEE	079	35081	34528	34036	-0.4	7	15156	15312	15427	0.2	2.22	9378	9301	-0.2
53222 MILWAUKEE	079	24500	24379	24176	-0.1	10	11067	11232	11349	0.4	2.13	6266	6229	-0.1
53223 MILWAUKEE	079	30080	29965	29732	-0.1	11	12593	12836	13000	0.5	2.26	7678	7677	0.0
53224 MILWAUKEE	079	19855	20217	20291	0.4	31	7194	7401	7532	0.7	2.70	4859	4915	0.3
53225 MILWAUKEE	079	25499	26041	26166	0.5	34	9959	10335	10559	0.9	2.46	6630	6748	0.4
53226 MILWAUKEE	079	19021	18724	18475	-0.4	7	8336	8437	8514	0.3	2.11	4967	4919	-0.2
53227 MILWAUKEE	079	23822	23748	23559	-0.1	12	10923	11205	11374	0.6	2.07	6069	6095	0.1
53228 MILWAUKEE	079	13839	13921	13870	0.1	21	5740	5952	6077	0.9	2.30	3613	3678	0.4
53233 MILWAUKEE	079	15541	15137	14903	-0.6	2	5076	4989	4971	-0.4	1.87	1228	1146	-1.6
53235 MILWAUKEE	079	8921	8840	8728	-0.2	8	4158	4244	4291	0.5	2.05	2224	2222	0.0
53402 RACINE	101	33246	33274	33652	0.0	16	12818	13126	13568	0.6	2.51	9163	9276	0.3
53403 RACINE	101	27353	26905	27045	-0.4	6	10441	10471	10747	0.1	2.49	6603	6513	-0.3
53404 RACINE	101	16850	16538	16596	-0.4	4	5730	5753	5895	0.1	2.75	3976	3921	-0.3
53405 RACINE	101	25764	25338	25402	-0.4	6	10178	10231	10480	0.1	2.47	6992	6905	-0.3
53406 RACINE	101	22818	23680	24423	0.9	50	9384	10035	10610	1.6	2.29	6273	6599	1.2
53502 ALBANY	045	2175	2292	2407	1.2	66	826	891	956	1.8	2.57	601	639	1.5
53503 ARENA	049	1780	1902	2027	1.6	77	668	733	801	2.2	2.59	502	546	2.0
53504 ARGYLE	065	2129	2218	2293	1.0	55	823	875	924	1.5	2.53	589	618	1.1
53505 AVALON	105	311	306	308	-0.4	6	116	117	121	0.2	2.62	86	86	0.0
53506 AVOCA	049	1023	1031	1063	0.2	23	398	411	434	0.8	2.51	274	279	0.4
53507 BARNEVELD	049	1897	1978	2079	1.0	56	697	744	800	1.6	2.64	534	564	1.3
53508 BELLEVILLE	025	4288	4571	4894	1.5	75	1624	1778	1948	2.2	2.56	1226	1319	1.7
53510 BELMONT	065	1370	1409	1438	0.7	42	547	582	611	1.5	2.42	377	397	1.2
53511 BELOIT	105	47129	47619	48465	0.2	25	17819	18352	19020	0.7	2.52	12249	12434	0.4
53515 BLACK EARTH	025	2137	2259	2422	1.3	69	813	880	964	1.9	2.53	592	630	1.5
53516 BLANCHARDVILLE	065	1917	2003	2082	1.0	58	752	803	854	1.6	2.46	526	555	1.3
53517 BLUE MOUNDS	025	1649	1776	1919	1.8	82	623	687	757	2.3	2.58	482	524	2.0
53518 BLUE RIVER	103	1520	1541	1556	0.3	28	598	625	644	1.0	2.46	437	450	0.7
53520 BRODHEAD	105	6606	7039	7448	1.5	75	2478	2702	2918	2.1	2.59	1839	1976	1.7
53521 BROOKLYN	045	3030	3326	3595	2.2	89	1107	1245	1376	2.8	2.66	885	982	2.5
53522 BROWNTOWN	045	1274	1229	1251	-0.8	1	479	475	496	-0.2	2.58	370	361	-0.6
53523 CAMBRIDGE	025	4716	4997	5339	1.4	72	1851	2006	2190	1.9	2.47	1325	1413	1.5
53525 CLINTON	105	3911	4052	4185	0.8	48	1399	1477	1553	1.3	2.69	1041	1083	0.9
53526 COBB	049	531	552	579	0.9	53	223	238	256	1.5	2.32	160	168	1.2
53527 COTTAGE GROVE	025	7670	8223	8879	1.7	79	2690	2968	3281	2.3	2.76	2146	2337	2.0
53528 CROSS PLAINS	025	4964	5147	5505	0.9	49	1875	1998	2188	1.5	2.57	1391	1460	1.2
53529 DANE	025	1707	1797	1922	1.2	65	587	635	696	1.9	2.83	458	488	1.5
53530 DARLINGTON	065	4321	4303	4337	-0.1	10	1662	1692	1745	0.4	2.47	1162	1167	0.1
53531 DEERFIELD	025	3619	3780	4022	1.0	58	1268	1361	1483	1.7	2.70	973	1028	1.3
53532 DE FOREST	025	11936	13112	14388	2.2	89	4252	4785	5368	2.8	2.73	3341	3707	2.5
53533 DODGEVILLE	049	6466	6884	7322	1.5	74	2548	2783	3033	2.1	2.42	1730	1863	1.8
53534 EDGERTON	105	10532	10918	11319	0.9	49	4191	4435	4683	1.3	2.45	2879	2999	1.0
53536 EVANSVILLE	105	7222	7712	8048	1.6	76	2736	2976	3159	2.0	2.55	1952	2091	1.6
53538 FORT ATKINSON	055	17548	18355	19437	1.1	59	6981	7498	8134	1.7	2.41	4735	5014	1.4
53541 GRATIOT	065	1023	1040	1054	0.4	30	379	398	414	1.2	2.60	286	296	0.8
53543 HIGHLAND	049	1725	1742	1798	0.2	24	644	669	707	0.9	2.59	466	478	0.6
53544 HOLLANDALE	049	768	762	790	-0.2	9	300	306	325	0.5	2.47	220	222	0.2
53545 JANESVILLE	105	23506	23528	23889	0.0	16	9478	9716	10069	0.6	2.35	6047	6100	0.2
53546 JANESVILLE	105	28080	29352	30383	1.1	59	10816	11615	12282	1.7	2.49	7659	8087	1.3
53548 JANESVILLE	105	19092	19174	19514	0.1	19	7523	7726	8023	0.6	2.41	5010	5088	0.4
53549 JEFFERSON	055	10044	10317	10783	0.6	41	3739	3939	4223	1.2	2.42	2526	2622	0.9
53550 JUDA	045	1328	1347	1385	0.3	28	463	483	509	1.0	2.79	382	395	0.8
53551 LAKE MILLS	055	7205	7645	8152	1.4	72	2808	3050	3326	2.0	2.48	1991	2135	1.7
WISCONSIN					0.8					1.4	2.44			1.1
UNITED STATES					1.2					1.3	2.58			1.1

ZIP CODE #	POST OFFICE NAME	RACE (%) White 2000	White 2004	Black 2000	Black 2004	Asian/Pacific 2000	Asian/Pacific 2004	% Hispanic Origin 2000	% Hispanic Origin 2004	2004 AGE DISTRIBUTION (%) 0-4	5-9	10-14	15-19	20-24	25-44	45-64	65-84	85+	18+	MEDIAN AGE 2004	% 2004 Males	% 2004 Females
53149	MUKWONAGO	98.1	97.8	0.3	0.3	0.4	0.5	1.6	1.9	6.4	7.1	8.1	7.7	6.6	27.9	28.1	6.9	1.2	73.5	37.2	50.0	50.0
53150	MUSKEGO	98.1	97.8	0.2	0.2	0.5	0.6	1.3	1.6	6.7	7.1	7.8	6.7	5.3	28.1	27.9	8.9	1.7	74.2	38.9	49.4	50.6
53151	NEW BERLIN	95.7	94.8	0.5	0.6	2.5	3.1	1.5	1.8	5.9	6.4	6.9	6.7	5.6	25.6	29.2	12.2	1.5	76.4	41.0	48.7	51.3
53153	NORTH PRAIRIE	98.4	98.2	0.1	0.0	0.2	0.3	1.3	1.6	5.6	6.5	8.3	7.4	5.4	27.5	31.2	7.5	0.7	74.9	39.6	50.0	50.0
53154	OAK CREEK	92.0	89.7	1.8	2.7	2.4	3.1	4.5	5.4	6.9	6.5	6.6	6.6	8.1	32.4	23.8	8.4	0.9	76.1	35.2	49.8	50.2
53156	PALMYRA	95.8	95.2	0.2	0.2	0.1	0.2	5.2	6.2	6.7	6.8	6.6	6.2	5.8	29.3	26.3	10.9	1.5	76.3	38.3	49.0	51.0
53158	PLEASANT PRAIRIE	93.6	92.5	1.5	1.9	1.6	1.9	3.6	4.3	6.6	7.0	8.3	7.3	5.7	29.8	26.6	8.0	0.7	73.2	37.0	50.6	49.4
53168	SALEM	97.1	96.6	0.4	0.5	0.5	0.6	3.0	3.6	6.5	6.7	8.7	7.7	6.5	30.5	25.0	7.6	0.9	73.2	36.5	50.9	49.1
53170	SILVER LAKE	97.0	96.5	0.3	0.4	0.3	0.3	3.3	4.0	6.5	6.9	9.3	7.8	6.4	28.2	25.3	8.5	1.3	72.2	36.7	50.5	49.5
53172	SOUTH MILWAUKEE	94.8	93.5	1.0	1.5	0.7	1.0	4.0	4.9	6.2	6.0	6.8	6.8	6.6	27.9	23.7	13.5	2.6	77.0	38.9	48.5	51.5
53177	STURTEVANT	84.6	81.6	11.8	14.3	0.5	0.6	4.8	5.7	5.5	5.3	5.6	5.9	8.8	36.0	23.3	8.7	1.0	80.3	36.1	60.4	39.6
53178	SULLIVAN	98.3	98.1	0.1	0.1	0.2	0.2	0.9	1.1	6.0	6.4	6.7	5.4	4.8	30.5	28.0	11.1	1.1	77.6	39.8	50.4	49.6
53179	TREVOR	97.4	96.9	0.5	0.6	0.3	0.4	2.7	3.3	7.4	7.6	8.5	7.1	5.4	32.6	23.3	7.3	0.9	72.0	35.9	51.1	48.9
53181	TWIN LAKES	97.5	97.1	0.3	0.4	0.5	0.6	2.4	3.0	6.3	6.5	7.7	7.3	6.1	27.8	26.2	10.7	1.4	74.8	38.1	49.7	50.3
53182	UNION GROVE	95.2	94.3	2.2	2.5	0.5	0.6	2.3	2.9	5.9	6.0	7.2	7.7	6.4	30.6	25.4	9.4	1.4	75.6	37.6	47.9	52.1
53183	WALES	98.5	98.2	0.1	0.2	0.3	0.3	1.2	1.4	5.9	7.0	8.7	8.2	6.0	24.7	32.7	6.4	0.4	73.3	39.8	50.2	49.8
53184	WALWORTH	97.7	97.2	0.5	0.5	0.5	0.6	5.0	5.9	5.7	5.9	8.0	7.1	6.3	26.0	26.0	12.4	2.6	75.8	39.8	49.7	50.3
53185	WATERFORD	98.3	97.9	0.3	0.4	0.3	0.3	1.7	2.1	7.2	7.6	7.9	6.9	5.3	29.5	26.0	8.8	0.8	72.8	37.8	50.6	49.4
53186	WAUKESHA	90.6	89.3	1.0	1.1	2.4	2.8	9.7	11.0	6.7	6.3	6.2	7.3	8.8	29.2	23.2	10.5	1.8	77.1	35.0	48.4	51.6
53188	WAUKESHA	93.5	92.5	1.3	1.4	1.8	2.2	5.5	6.5	6.7	6.6	6.5	6.4	7.2	30.2	24.6	9.5	2.4	76.3	36.6	49.2	50.8
53189	WAUKESHA	95.3	94.6	0.8	0.8	1.3	1.7	4.1	4.7	7.2	7.6	8.3	7.5	6.4	28.2	28.0	6.5	0.5	72.2	36.3	49.8	50.2
53190	WHITEWATER	93.3	92.2	1.8	2.0	1.2	1.5	6.1	7.2	3.7	3.6	4.3	15.1	28.7	18.3	16.1	8.1	2.1	85.4	24.0	49.8	50.2
53191	WILLIAMS BAY	98.5	98.2	0.4	0.4	0.5	0.6	2.7	3.3	5.1	5.4	6.7	6.5	4.8	23.0	28.9	16.9	2.7	78.4	44.0	49.0	51.0
53202	MILWAUKEE	83.7	79.2	8.8	11.8	3.6	4.7	3.4	4.1	1.6	1.1	0.8	3.1	12.5	46.2	20.1	11.1	3.4	96.1	34.6	54.8	45.2
53203	MILWAUKEE	77.6	71.8	12.7	16.3	6.3	7.9	2.7	3.1	1.4	0.6	0.3	0.9	10.7	58.9	21.4	5.1	0.9	97.5	34.4	59.4	40.6
53204	MILWAUKEE	44.3	40.7	8.2	9.5	3.4	3.8	64.4	67.0	10.7	9.0	9.4	9.1	10.9	30.3	14.8	5.1	0.8	65.6	25.6	53.1	46.9
53205	MILWAUKEE	4.5	3.4	86.6	88.2	5.5	5.3	4.0	3.6	10.7	11.1	12.4	10.8	7.7	23.9	15.9	6.9	0.7	59.1	23.3	45.5	54.5
53206	MILWAUKEE	1.5	1.1	96.0	96.7	0.4	0.4	1.3	1.2	9.8	10.0	11.7	9.9	7.0	24.2	18.2	8.3	0.8	62.1	26.3	45.2	54.9
53207	MILWAUKEE	90.1	88.2	1.4	1.9	1.1	1.4	10.4	12.2	6.3	6.0	6.1	5.8	6.2	31.5	25.1	11.5	1.7	78.2	38.1	49.4	50.6
53208	MILWAUKEE	33.9	30.1	51.0	55.0	8.5	8.7	5.8	5.9	9.4	9.4	10.1	9.3	7.9	28.3	19.3	5.4	1.0	65.6	28.0	48.3	51.8
53209	MILWAUKEE	32.4	29.0	63.3	66.5	1.4	1.6	2.3	2.4	7.7	7.9	8.9	7.9	6.9	25.6	22.5	10.7	2.0	70.5	33.7	45.1	54.9
53210	MILWAUKEE	25.2	21.7	68.9	72.4	2.2	2.3	2.9	3.0	9.6	10.1	10.9	9.4	7.6	28.0	18.3	5.1	1.1	63.4	26.9	45.4	54.6
53211	MILWAUKEE	91.0	88.5	2.5	3.5	3.6	4.7	2.6	3.1	3.8	3.4	4.1	9.2	18.1	30.3	20.5	8.3	2.2	86.1	30.4	48.1	52.0
53212	MILWAUKEE	27.7	23.6	63.3	67.3	0.7	0.8	10.3	10.4	9.0	8.3	9.3	8.3	8.9	29.3	18.8	7.3	0.8	68.4	28.8	47.1	53.0
53213	MILWAUKEE	93.6	91.9	2.2	3.0	1.7	2.2	2.3	2.8	6.8	6.6	6.6	6.9	6.0	31.0	24.2	9.3	2.6	75.8	37.0	46.6	53.4
53214	MILWAUKEE	91.8	89.7	2.1	2.9	1.6	2.1	5.2	6.3	6.1	5.7	6.0	6.3	7.4	31.7	23.4	11.2	2.1	78.4	37.1	49.8	50.2
53215	MILWAUKEE	63.5	59.2	3.9	4.8	4.1	4.8	38.4	42.4	9.4	8.2	8.2	7.7	8.9	29.9	18.0	8.2	1.6	69.6	29.8	49.8	50.2
53216	MILWAUKEE	19.8	15.4	75.3	79.9	1.4	1.5	2.2	2.2	8.1	8.4	9.5	8.6	7.5	26.7	22.8	7.6	1.1	68.7	31.5	44.8	55.2
53217	MILWAUKEE	93.0	91.0	2.7	3.7	2.9	3.8	1.7	2.0	5.8	6.7	7.3	6.9	4.8	21.8	29.8	14.6	2.4	75.9	42.9	47.9	52.2
53218	MILWAUKEE	30.6	24.4	59.4	65.5	5.9	6.2	3.0	3.0	9.1	9.3	10.4	8.7	7.2	26.5	20.1	7.9	0.9	65.7	29.4	45.9	54.1
53219	MILWAUKEE	94.6	93.3	0.9	1.3	0.8	1.0	4.5	5.5	5.8	5.6	5.3	5.1	5.7	29.5	24.3	15.9	3.0	80.3	40.8	47.5	52.5
53220	MILWAUKEE	93.2	91.5	1.0	1.4	2.1	2.8	4.9	6.0	5.1	5.1	5.4	5.2	5.6	27.4	24.4	18.8	3.1	81.2	42.5	47.1	53.0
53221	MILWAUKEE	88.8	86.2	2.1	2.8	2.6	3.4	7.9	9.6	6.0	5.7	5.6	5.4	6.4	27.7	24.8	16.0	2.6	79.6	40.5	47.6	52.4
53222	MILWAUKEE	87.4	83.9	7.5	10.0	2.0	2.5	2.8	3.3	6.5	6.2	5.6	4.6	4.8	28.9	22.7	16.6	4.1	78.9	40.8	45.2	54.8
53223	MILWAUKEE	61.3	53.9	32.0	38.8	2.9	3.4	2.8	3.0	6.2	6.3	6.9	6.3	5.7	26.4	24.8	13.9	3.4	76.6	39.4	46.3	53.7
53224	MILWAUKEE	48.8	40.8	44.1	51.9	2.6	2.9	3.9	4.0	9.2	8.8	9.0	7.7	7.4	28.2	19.2	8.3	2.2	68.2	30.2	46.7	53.3
53225	MILWAUKEE	55.9	49.0	37.3	43.9	2.4	2.8	3.2	3.5	9.4	8.3	7.8	6.6	7.4	28.9	19.3	10.0	2.2	70.3	32.1	46.6	53.4
53226	MILWAUKEE	93.9	92.2	1.9	2.5	2.5	3.3	1.6	2.0	5.7	5.7	5.7	6.1	5.5	25.8	25.0	16.3	4.2	79.1	42.0	46.6	53.4
53227	MILWAUKEE	92.9	91.0	2.1	2.9	2.1	2.8	3.2	3.9	5.4	5.2	5.4	5.2	6.1	29.2	22.9	16.7	3.8	80.9	40.7	47.5	52.5
53228	MILWAUKEE	95.6	94.3	0.6	1.0	1.9	2.6	2.9	3.6	5.1	5.2	6.2	5.7	6.0	27.0	26.9	14.4	3.6	79.8	41.5	47.1	52.9
53233	MILWAUKEE	53.5	48.0	35.0	39.7	6.2	7.0	4.9	5.1	4.2	2.8	2.5	19.9	33.1	22.1	11.4	3.6	0.4	88.7	23.1	53.7	46.3
53235	MILWAUKEE	93.7	92.2	1.0	1.4	1.1	1.5	4.7	5.7	4.6	4.6	5.8	5.8	6.8	28.9	26.3	14.8	2.6	81.6	41.3	49.1	51.0
53402	RACINE	87.5	85.2	6.0	7.2	1.1	1.4	6.9	8.3	7.6	7.4	7.3	6.6	6.4	27.2	25.2	10.7	1.7	73.5	37.1	48.4	51.6
53403	RACINE	61.0	57.4	28.7	31.2	0.9	1.1	15.5	16.9	7.4	7.1	7.9	7.8	8.3	27.4	23.0	9.7	1.3	72.9	33.8	49.9	50.1
53404	RACINE	54.9	51.7	27.7	29.7	0.5	0.6	21.3	23.0	8.9	8.0	8.3	8.9	9.9	25.9	19.3	9.2	1.7	70.2	29.6	50.2	49.8
53405	RACINE	85.0	81.6	8.1	9.9	0.6	0.8	8.2	10.2	7.3	6.8	7.2	6.9	6.8	27.8	24.6	11.0	1.6	74.5	36.8	48.6	51.4
53406	RACINE	86.9	84.4	8.7	10.5	1.3	1.5	4.5	5.4	5.5	5.5	6.2	6.1	6.5	23.0	27.8	16.0	3.3	79.0	43.0	46.9	53.1
53502	ALBANY	98.3	98.0	0.1	0.1	0.3	0.4	1.0	1.3	5.9	6.4	7.3	6.9	5.9	27.6	28.0	10.9	1.1	75.7	38.6	51.1	49.0
53503	ARENA	98.7	98.4	0.0	0.0	0.9	1.2	0.8	0.9	6.2	6.6	7.2	6.4	5.5	29.3	28.7	9.5	0.6	76.1	38.5	51.6	48.4
53504	ARGYLE	98.9	98.8	0.2	0.2	0.1	0.1	0.8	1.0	6.6	7.1	7.8	6.3	5.3	26.7	24.6	13.8	1.9	74.0	39.8	52.2	47.8
53505	AVALON	99.7	100.0	0.0	0.0	0.0	0.0	1.9	2.3	6.2	6.5	7.5	6.2	5.2	26.1	29.7	11.4	1.0	75.8	40.6	50.7	49.4
53506	AVOCA	98.3	98.2	0.2	0.2	0.6	0.8	0.3	0.4	5.4	6.4	8.2	7.9	5.8	27.0	26.5	11.5	1.4	75.1	39.1	50.5	49.5
53507	BARNEVELD	98.8	98.7	0.3	0.3	0.1	0.1	0.3	0.2	6.7	7.1	8.0	7.3	5.2	32.2	25.1	7.3	1.1	73.4	37.1	52.0	48.0
53508	BELLEVILLE	98.6	98.3	0.2	0.2	0.3	0.4	0.5	0.6	7.0	7.3	7.9	6.7	5.3	29.5	25.9	9.1	1.3	73.3	37.8	50.4	49.6
53510	BELMONT	98.9	98.8	0.1	0.1	0.4	0.5	0.5	0.5	6.4	6.2	6.7	7.0	7.2	26.3	24.3	14.0	2.0	76.2	38.3	50.5	49.5
53511	BELOIT	79.8	77.4	12.7	14.2	1.0	1.2	7.4	8.3	7.0	6.8	7.5	7.6	7.7	26.2	23.7	11.6	1.9	74.5	35.8	48.5	51.5
53515	BLACK EARTH	97.3	96.8	0.1	0.2	0.5	0.6	1.5	1.9	6.0	6.4	7.8	7.4	6.2	26.7	27.0	10.1	2.4	74.9	39.0	50.6	49.4
53516	BLANCHARDVILLE	99.1	99.0	0.1	0.1	0.2	0.2	0.4	0.5	6.3	6.7	7.6	6.5	4.9	27.4	25.6	12.5	2.4	74.9	40.1	49.8	50.2
53517	BLUE MOUNDS	98.4	98.1	0.1	0.1	0.5	0.6	0.5	0.6	6.9	7.7	7.7	6.7	4.3	28.3	29.7	7.9	0.7	73.4	39.3	50.8	49.2
53518	BLUE RIVER	99.0	98.8	0.1	0.1	0.2	0.2	0.7	0.8	5.7	6.0	7.3	6.8	5.8	24.2	29.3	13.4	1.4	76.6	41.4	52.4	47.6
53520	BRODHEAD	97.9	97.6	0.4	0.4	0.2	0.2	1.0	1.2	6.7	7.1	7.9	7.2	5.8	26.8	25.4	11.2	2.0	73.8	37.7	49.5	50.5
53521	BROOKLYN	98.0	97.6	0.3	0.3	0.5	0.6	0.9	1.1	6.6	7.8	8.7	6.3	4.5	29.2	28.9	7.0	1.0	72.6	38.7	51.1	48.9
53522	BROWNTOWN	99.1	99.0	0.2	0.2	0.1	0.1	0.7	0.7	5.8	6.7	7.9	7.0	5.5	26.4	28.9	10.7	1.1	74.8	40.0	51.6	48.4
53523	CAMBRIDGE	97.6	97.2	0.3	0.4	0.6	0.8	1.5	1.8	6.1	6.7	7.0	6.8	5.2	26.5	28.5	11.3	1.8	75.6	40.4	50.6	49.5
53525	CLINTON	95.9	95.2	0.4	0.5	0.6	0.8	3.5	4.1	6.4	7.2	7.9	7.4	6.6	26.1	26.3	9.9	2.3	73.9	37.2	49.8	50.3
53526	COBB	98.7	98.6	0.0	0.0	0.2	0.4	0.4	0.2	6.7	7.1	7.8	6.2	5.8	25.5	26.6	12.7	1.6	74.8	39.0	53.6	46.4
53527	COTTAGE GROVE	96.7	96.0	1.2	1.5	0.7	0.9	1.5	1.7	8.3	8.7	8.2	6.6	5.2	32.4	24.2	5.6	0.8	70.3	35.1	50.6	49.4
53528	CROSS PLAINS	98.5	98.2	0.3	0.4	0.3	0.4	0.4	0.6	6.7	7.1	8.6	6.6	5.6	29.3	26.5	8.7	1.0	73.5	37.2	50.0	50.0
53529	DANE	97.4	96.7	0.2	0.3	1.1	1.5	1.0	1.3	8.0	8.4	7.8	6.9	4.9	31.2	24.3	8.0	0.7	71.6	35.8	51.1	48.9
53530	DARLINGTON	99.0	98.8	0.1	0.1	0.2	0.2	1.0	1.2	6.2	6.3	7.1	6.9	6.4	24.7	24.2	15.0	3.1	75.9	40.1	49.1	50.9
53531	DEERFIELD	94.8	93.9	2.0	2.4	0.9	1.1	2.1	2.5	6.9	7.4	7.8	7.0	5.2	31.1	25.3	8.3	1.0	73.1	37.2	52.2	47.8
53532	DE FOREST	96.1	95.3	1.1	1.2	0.8	1.1	1.8	2.2	7.6	7.7	8.3	7.2	6.1	30.6	24.9	6.7	0.9	71.5	35.3	48.6	51.4
53533	DODGEVILLE	98.3	98.1	0.3	0.3	0.5	0.6	0.3	0.4	7.0	6.8	7.3	6.8	6.0	27.4	24.1	12.4	2.3	74.3	38.6	48.5	51.5
53534	EDGERTON	97.6	97.2	0.2	0.2	0.3	0.4	2.4	2.9	5.9	6.3	7.4	6.7	5.6	28.1	26.6	11.5	1.9	76.1	39.1	50.5	49.6
53536	EVANSVILLE	97.7	97.3	0.2	0.2	0.4	0.5	1.4	1.7	7.7	7.7	8.1	6.7	5.6	29.0	23.5	9.7	2.0	72.3	36.8	49.2	50.8
53538	FORT ATKINSON	96.8	96.3	0.3	0.3	0.5	0.6	3.4	4.0	6.1	6.0	6.6	6.5	6.8	28.1	26.3	11.5	2.2	77.2	38.9	49.3	50.7
53541	GRATIOT	98.8	98.8	0.7	0.8	0.0	0.0	0.1	0.0	6.0	4.9	7.7	8.5	6.1	26.4	26.4	12.7	1.4	76.2	40.0	51.7	48.3
53543	HIGHLAND	99.5	99.5	0.1	0.1	0.1	0.2	0.2	0.3	6.1	6.4	7.1	6.7	5.9	29.0	24.3	13.1	1.4	75.8	38.8	50.8	49.3
53544	HOLLANDALE	99.2	99.1	0.1	0.1	0.0	0.0	0.3	0.4	5.0	6.2	8.1	7.6	3.8	28.6	27.4	11.4	1.8	75.6	40.2	51.8	48.2
53545	JANESVILLE	96.0	95.2	1.3	1.6	0.7	0.9	2.3	2.8	6.4	6.3	6.9	6.6	6.4	28.2	24.1	13.0	2.3	76.3	37.9	49.0	51.0
53546	JANESVILLE	95.9	94.9	1.3	1.6	0.8	1.1	2.4	2.9	7.3	7.2	7.3	6.6	6.2	30.3	23.9	9.9	1.4	74.1	35.8	49.5	50.5
53548	JANESVILLE	94.0	93.0	1.6	2.0	1.3	1.5	2.7	3.1	6.7	6.6	7.3	7.4	6.8	28.9	24.4	10.4	1.6	74.8	36.6	50.0	50.0
53549	JEFFERSON	95.4	94.7	0.4	0.5	0.4	0.5	5.3	6.3	5.8	5.7	6.1	6.5	6.5	30.0	24.2	12.6	2.8	78.7	38.7	49.8	50.2
53550	JUDA	98.1	97.6	0.1	0.1	0.9	1.1	0.5	0.6	6.6	6.9	7.4	7.0	6.2	27.5	26.4	11.1	1.0	74.8	38.8	49.5	50.5
53551	LAKE MILLS	97.5	97.1	0.2	0.2	0.8	1.0	2.3	2.8	6.6	6.8	7.2	7.2	6.0	27.0	25.7	11.3	2.2	74.6	38.2	49.3	50.7
	WISCONSIN	88.9	88.0	5.7	6.0	1.7	2.1	3.6	4.0	6.4	6.5	7.1	7.3	7.7	27.6	24.5	11.1	1.9	75.8	36.9	49.5	50.5
	UNITED STATES	75.1	73.6	12.3	12.5	3.8	4.2	12.5	14.1	6.9	6.7	7.2	7.0	7.3	28.6	23.8	10.8	1.7	75.1	36.0	49.1	50.9

ZIP CODE #	POST OFFICE NAME	2004 Per Capita Income	2004 HH Income Base	2004 HOUSEHOLD INCOME DISTRIBUTION (%) Less than $25,000	$25,000 to $49,999	$50,000 to $99,999	$100,000 to $149,999	$150,000 or More	MEDIAN HOUSEHOLD INCOME 2004	2009	2004 National Centile	2004 State Centile	2004 Home Value Base	2004 HOME VALUE DISTRIBUTION (%) Less than $50,000	$50,000 to $89,999	$90,000 to $174,999	$175,000 to $399,999	$400,000 or More	2004 Median Home Value
53149	MUKWONAGO	31574	6440	9.5	16.7	44.9	21.4	7.6	74062	87629	93	97	5407	0.8	1.0	26.2	65.6	6.4	212840
53150	MUSKEGO	31151	8343	8.9	17.5	46.4	19.2	8.0	73029	86102	92	97	7133	0.4	0.4	27.2	67.9	4.2	212716
53151	NEW BERLIN	36491	12537	8.5	18.8	39.3	21.0	12.4	76446	89922	94	98	10057	0.3	1.0	25.0	68.1	5.5	210496
53153	NORTH PRAIRIE	31025	800	5.6	19.4	45.9	23.3	5.9	75295	88253	93	98	716	0.0	2.0	33.8	58.8	5.5	201818
53154	OAK CREEK	27614	12668	14.3	23.4	43.3	14.9	4.1	60886	72622	85	88	7988	3.0	2.0	52.1	42.5	0.5	167696
53156	PALMYRA	24794	1249	16.3	29.9	40.8	9.3	3.8	52760	59136	77	71	1015	6.2	5.4	47.1	37.3	3.9	159309
53158	PLEASANT PRAIRIE	31235	4902	10.0	21.3	40.4	18.8	9.5	71785	82848	92	96	4243	7.3	3.9	31.8	51.9	5.1	189567
53168	SALEM	27316	3176	12.9	23.5	41.8	16.8	5.1	64492	76717	88	93	2673	5.4	6.0	48.9	35.1	4.6	154830
53170	SILVER LAKE	24496	811	18.6	22.4	41.9	13.6	3.5	58765	68814	83	83	623	8.0	9.8	50.7	29.1	2.4	142316
53172	SOUTH MILWAUKEE	24761	8685	19.9	30.0	38.1	9.7	2.4	50092	59572	72	64	5591	0.9	6.4	73.1	19.4	0.2	133290
53177	STURTEVANT	23434	2284	15.2	24.2	46.5	11.9	2.2	58958	69190	84	84	1708	8.6	9.1	62.8	17.8	1.8	123258
53178	SULLIVAN	26541	1222	16.4	28.7	41.0	10.2	3.8	54359	60928	79	75	1018	12.4	10.7	26.1	43.6	7.2	176835
53179	TREVOR	22661	1871	18.4	27.7	38.4	12.4	3.0	53644	62913	78	73	1607	2.9	8.5	51.7	34.4	2.6	153268
53181	TWIN LAKES	26460	2631	16.2	25.0	39.0	15.2	4.6	60132	71395	84	86	2061	0.1	2.6	45.1	44.8	7.4	179745
53182	UNION GROVE	25218	3247	14.4	21.5	47.6	12.8	3.8	59302	70556	84	84	2447	8.2	4.5	47.7	35.5	4.2	159505
53183	WALES	37853	860	4.4	12.1	43.1	28.3	12.1	86098	102552	96	99	790	0.0	0.6	10.8	78.5	10.1	244301
53184	WALWORTH	23667	1542	17.3	28.4	38.7	12.0	3.7	54035	62946	78	74	1112	1.3	4.6	54.3	34.6	5.2	159218
53185	WATERFORD	28366	6569	10.5	20.1	45.6	18.2	5.6	69429	80098	91	95	5564	1.2	3.7	36.5	55.0	3.7	188494
53186	WAUKESHA	28390	14140	18.1	26.7	37.5	12.9	4.9	54846	65507	79	76	8363	0.6	2.9	46.5	47.8	2.3	175198
53188	WAUKESHA	30352	13803	14.8	22.3	40.7	15.8	6.4	62624	75670	87	91	8948	1.4	0.9	40.1	54.3	3.3	190225
53189	WAUKESHA	30982	8546	8.4	20.4	43.0	19.7	8.6	73171	86265	93	97	6736	0.4	0.6	22.9	69.0	7.1	221661
53190	WHITEWATER	20147	6252	28.9	30.7	29.3	7.7	3.4	41703	47857	52	37	3253	8.7	5.6	44.4	37.2	4.1	158479
53191	WILLIAMS BAY	36309	1016	20.4	23.2	32.8	15.3	8.4	57530	67035	82	81	778	1.7	3.0	32.7	53.5	9.3	206000
53202	MILWAUKEE	38172	14021	36.5	29.4	22.8	6.7	4.7	35145	41992	28	8	2349	3.7	10.9	43.7	31.8	9.9	161714
53203	MILWAUKEE	50595	240	29.6	18.8	27.5	10.4	13.8	51287	62436	74	68	46	0.0	0.0	0.0	87.0	13.0	244118
53204	MILWAUKEE	10724	12665	45.3	33.6	17.2	2.9	0.9	27645	32934	8	1	3689	45.4	43.6	9.6	1.3	0.1	52856
53205	MILWAUKEE	9351	3384	64.5	23.2	10.4	1.4	0.5	17120	20572	1	1	852	50.7	33.5	12.9	1.2	1.8	49608
53206	MILWAUKEE	11027	10524	53.3	29.4	13.9	1.9	1.5	22802	26610	3	1	4047	68.2	25.9	4.5	1.2	0.3	41962
53207	MILWAUKEE	24354	16190	23.4	32.5	35.0	7.6	1.6	45198	53700	62	49	10153	2.4	18.3	70.4	8.5	0.4	113605
53208	MILWAUKEE	15366	12544	42.1	30.0	21.6	4.8	1.6	30179	35889	13	2	4267	18.9	29.3	44.5	7.2	0.2	92492
53209	MILWAUKEE	19973	19048	33.9	31.9	25.0	6.2	3.0	36004	40193	32	11	10446	18.6	40.7	26.8	13.6	0.3	76357
53210	MILWAUKEE	15978	9977	35.0	30.9	26.2	6.0	1.9	35567	40868	30	10	4532	16.3	40.6	37.2	5.6	0.3	83261
53211	MILWAUKEE	35143	15715	22.8	28.4	28.5	10.5	9.9	48716	58122	70	61	6750	0.6	3.4	26.7	57.6	11.6	214182
53212	MILWAUKEE	14902	12378	47.3	30.8	17.6	3.1	1.2	26554	31198	7	1	3916	39.0	38.8	18.4	2.8	0.9	58000
53213	MILWAUKEE	32806	11269	15.0	26.4	38.3	13.4	6.9	58488	70280	83	82	7456	0.6	5.4	56.7	35.7	1.7	158274
53214	MILWAUKEE	23950	15967	24.9	33.5	33.4	6.7	1.5	43333	51026	57	42	8898	3.3	16.7	75.7	4.1	0.2	111768
53215	MILWAUKEE	16246	19688	32.8	33.3	27.4	5.1	1.5	36784	43395	35	15	9292	9.8	42.0	44.5	3.5	0.3	88588
53216	MILWAUKEE	17268	13332	35.3	31.8	26.4	4.9	1.6	35161	39123	28	8	7352	13.3	53.7	30.9	2.1	0.0	78692
53217	MILWAUKEE	51087	12101	12.2	17.1	31.2	17.6	21.9	80793	95604	95	99	9725	0.3	1.3	22.8	57.3	18.3	233271
53218	MILWAUKEE	15723	14887	34.1	33.9	26.7	4.0	1.4	35109	39377	28	8	8607	12.8	64.4	21.9	0.8	0.1	72113
53219	MILWAUKEE	24773	15797	23.4	32.7	35.3	7.5	1.1	45272	52855	62	50	10355	0.5	9.0	80.9	9.3	0.3	120178
53220	MILWAUKEE	26017	11422	19.9	33.5	36.9	7.9	1.9	47416	55184	67	57	7070	0.5	4.3	75.6	19.4	0.2	137295
53221	MILWAUKEE	24924	15312	21.8	32.0	35.2	8.8	2.2	46740	54883	66	55	9771	4.3	9.7	68.0	17.6	0.4	129264
53222	MILWAUKEE	26174	11232	22.2	31.8	35.1	8.2	2.7	46224	54277	64	53	7929	0.4	16.2	70.2	12.5	0.7	116245
53223	MILWAUKEE	25386	12836	21.4	29.9	35.8	9.4	3.4	48702	56534	70	61	7915	3.2	24.9	60.3	11.1	0.5	111778
53224	MILWAUKEE	20762	7401	25.3	28.6	34.2	9.2	2.7	46174	54543	64	53	3791	7.5	16.1	61.9	13.8	0.7	117054
53225	MILWAUKEE	21053	10335	24.1	33.4	33.4	7.0	2.1	43251	50496	57	42	5162	1.9	21.4	67.7	8.6	0.5	113118
53226	MILWAUKEE	35833	8437	16.1	25.2	36.7	15.0	7.0	60532	70097	85	87	5888	0.3	1.6	51.3	46.0	0.8	171036
53227	MILWAUKEE	25421	11205	23.6	33.3	34.4	6.8	1.8	44257	51254	59	46	6228	4.8	4.0	72.1	18.9	0.2	134527
53228	MILWAUKEE	28603	5952	17.9	26.9	35.9	15.5	3.8	56316	65871	81	79	3750	0.2	6.2	46.7	46.0	0.9	170880
53233	MILWAUKEE	12526	4989	69.3	22.5	6.5	0.9	0.9	15093	17118	1	0	231	44.2	41.1	5.6	8.2	0.9	53462
53235	MILWAUKEE	25496	4244	25.9	34.4	31.1	6.1	2.5	41678	48826	52	36	2490	0.9	7.1	85.8	6.1	0.0	116604
53402	RACINE	28550	13126	16.8	25.9	39.3	12.9	5.2	57475	66483	82	81	9744	2.0	13.3	56.6	25.5	2.6	126116
53403	RACINE	21847	10471	29.5	29.6	30.7	7.3	2.9	41885	50177	53	37	6030	11.0	26.2	45.4	16.1	1.3	100896
53404	RACINE	18096	5753	33.7	27.6	28.9	7.0	2.8	38073	45598	40	21	3118	8.8	31.3	52.7	7.1	0.2	97769
53405	RACINE	24370	10231	20.2	28.4	38.9	9.2	3.4	51015	59691	74	67	7542	2.2	23.0	63.5	10.9	0.5	108636
53406	RACINE	28028	10035	22.3	25.0	35.1	12.6	5.1	52588	60467	76	71	6917	0.4	7.6	65.5	25.7	0.9	139321
53502	ALBANY	23652	891	17.0	32.1	39.3	8.0	3.7	50731	57092	73	66	699	3.7	17.9	52.5	23.2	2.7	124919
53503	ARENA	24040	733	18.0	26.3	45.2	8.5	2.1	54082	62176	78	74	605	7.4	7.9	50.6	27.8	6.3	145421
53504	ARGYLE	20211	875	22.6	35.7	35.5	4.5	1.7	43541	49880	57	43	712	9.3	20.7	45.5	19.8	4.8	115345
53505	AVALON	28009	117	12.0	23.9	46.2	12.8	5.1	62164	70500	86	90	91	5.5	16.5	38.5	27.5	12.1	143056
53506	AVOCA	20894	411	31.4	31.1	28.7	6.1	2.7	38301	43461	40	22	330	29.4	21.8	26.1	18.5	4.2	87500
53507	BARNEVELD	25303	744	16.9	23.7	44.8	11.7	3.0	58924	65965	83	84	628	2.4	4.9	49.7	36.5	6.5	162912
53508	BELLEVILLE	26871	1778	11.9	27.1	44.4	12.4	4.3	60499	70666	85	87	1384	2.0	4.9	49.3	39.0	4.8	166732
53510	BELMONT	19066	582	29.0	34.2	31.1	4.1	1.6	38806	43486	42	24	435	14.5	23.7	50.6	8.1	3.2	102904
53511	BELOIT	21055	18352	26.1	30.6	33.2	7.6	2.4	43659	50645	58	44	12827	14.3	38.8	37.4	9.0	0.6	86919
53515	BLACK EARTH	26269	880	14.6	25.0	46.6	10.5	3.4	58429	70181	83	82	674	4.5	4.3	49.6	36.9	4.8	162931
53516	BLANCHARDVILLE	23065	803	21.2	28.9	38.7	8.5	2.7	49929	55244	72	64	666	7.7	17.0	41.6	28.4	5.4	126596
53517	BLUE MOUNDS	30909	687	13.3	26.2	39.7	14.3	6.6	59599	69404	84	85	604	16.2	5.6	23.3	42.7	12.1	185821
53518	BLUE RIVER	19354	625	30.2	33.0	29.9	5.0	1.9	39469	43939	44	27	512	17.4	25.8	38.3	17.2	1.4	99722
53520	BRODHEAD	20930	2702	22.8	29.6	38.1	7.8	1.7	47686	53589	68	58	2178	8.8	19.2	52.3	18.5	1.2	116384
53521	BROOKLYN	27730	1245	10.1	23.8	46.5	15.0	4.6	63497	73535	87	92	1110	2.3	4.1	37.4	48.8	7.3	187593
53522	BROWNTOWN	21559	475	20.2	35.6	35.2	5.9	3.2	46336	51493	65	53	384	10.7	16.2	40.6	28.1	4.4	127439
53523	CAMBRIDGE	27571	2006	15.6	24.0	42.3	13.8	4.3	60258	68369	85	86	1689	6.3	5.2	38.0	42.7	7.9	176250
53525	CLINTON	23448	1477	18.8	24.7	42.5	11.1	2.8	55737	63911	80	78	1128	7.7	10.2	60.9	19.6	1.6	127093
53526	COBB	20986	238	25.6	41.2	26.9	5.0	1.3	40205	45246	47	30	191	4.7	25.7	57.1	11.0	1.6	108726
53527	COTTAGE GROVE	30718	2968	8.6	14.1	50.5	20.5	6.3	76735	89971	94	98	2510	0.6	1.4	35.4	59.2	3.5	191579
53528	CROSS PLAINS	30347	1998	8.6	22.0	47.9	14.7	6.9	65861	78655	89	93	1502	0.7	2.6	36.2	51.1	9.4	192401
53529	DANE	25991	635	12.3	20.9	49.8	12.8	4.3	63123	74332	87	91	516	1.9	2.1	42.6	48.1	5.2	180743
53530	DARLINGTON	19296	1692	29.1	32.3	31.8	5.7	1.1	40488	45837	48	32	1301	9.9	33.6	42.2	12.2	2.1	97613
53531	DEERFIELD	26223	1361	12.7	23.4	46.5	12.6	4.9	61749	72790	86	89	1158	1.0	2.2	48.7	44.0	4.2	172250
53532	DE FOREST	27978	4785	9.2	21.2	47.8	17.6	4.2	67894	81032	90	94	3886	0.2	1.1	47.1	48.0	3.5	177145
53533	DODGEVILLE	24302	2783	20.2	31.9	36.0	9.0	2.9	47919	55451	68	58	2024	5.6	13.4	58.9	19.7	2.4	118357
53534	EDGERTON	26060	4435	17.8	26.1	42.6	9.9	3.6	55127	63719	80	77	3440	2.9	13.3	58.2	23.7	2.0	128416
53536	EVANSVILLE	24573	2976	17.8	27.6	41.6	9.9	3.1	54106	62160	79	74	2312	7.3	7.1	59.0	24.8	1.8	134674
53538	FORT ATKINSON	25659	7498	19.0	28.6	39.4	9.0	4.0	51787	59248	75	69	5341	3.0	5.7	56.8	32.0	2.5	150135
53541	GRATIOT	19819	398	21.9	33.9	34.9	7.8	1.5	45666	50620	63	51	317	15.8	27.8	37.5	12.6	6.3	96212
53543	HIGHLAND	19027	669	25.4	35.3	32.6	5.2	1.5	41680	46948	52	37	544	10.9	20.8	47.4	18.8	2.2	111916
53544	HOLLANDALE	21637	306	25.5	28.4	35.3	8.5	2.3	45000	50915	61	49	249	5.6	20.1	42.6	26.5	5.2	129688
53545	JANESVILLE	26309	9716	19.1	29.9	36.8	10.2	4.0	50713	57869	73	66	6533	0.7	12.3	72.5	13.2	1.3	118733
53546	JANESVILLE	26973	11615	13.9	27.6	41.2	12.8	4.5	57638	66356	82	81	8794	10.0	10.0	62.3	17.1	0.7	121823
53548	JANESVILLE	24623	7726	21.3	30.7	34.1	10.1	3.8	48031	55556	68	59	5448	4.3	23.3	54.4	16.5	1.5	114856
53549	JEFFERSON	23591	3939	19.4	32.4	36.8	8.7	2.7	48581	55491	69	60	2756	6.4	6.6	53.2	31.4	2.4	148073
53550	JUDA	22397	483	17.0	37.3	38.5	4.4	2.9	48064	54003	68	59	392	7.9	12.5	46.9	24.5	8.2	128788
53551	LAKE MILLS	25490	3050	18.7	28.6	38.5	11.1	3.2	51771	58644	75	69	2316	6.9	3.3	49.3	35.5	5.0	163223
	WISCONSIN	25041		22.2	28.8	35.0	9.6	4.2	48930	56561				7.0	14.9	46.8	27.8	3.6	134326
	UNITED STATES	25866		24.7	27.1	30.8	10.9	6.5	48124	56710				10.9	15.0	33.7	30.1	10.4	145905

#	POST OFFICE NAME	FINANCIAL SERVICES: Auto Loan	Home Loan	Invest-ments	Retire-ment Plans	THE HOME: Home Improvements: Home Repair	Lawn & Garden	Furnishings: Comput-ers & Hard-ware	Major Appli-ances	TV, Radio, Sound Equip-ment	Furni-ture	ENTERTAINMENT: Dine out/ Carry out	Sports Equip-ment	Fees & Tickets	Toys & Games	Travel	Cable TV	PERSONAL: Apparel & Services	Auto Repairs	Health Insur-ance	Pets & Supplies
53149	MUKWONAGO	115	135	145	137	133	133	125	124	117	125	148	146	131	153	126	113	146	122	112	137
53150	MUSKEGO	116	137	140	140	133	130	124	123	114	126	144	144	129	149	123	109	143	119	107	135
53151	NEW BERLIN	121	145	159	146	142	144	133	132	125	133	157	153	141	164	136	122	157	129	121	145
53153	NORTH PRAIRIE	114	142	150	142	139	137	126	126	117	126	147	147	134	157	129	114	147	121	113	139
53154	OAK CREEK	97	99	104	102	97	100	98	97	95	99	119	115	98	119	96	91	117	98	90	110
53156	PALMYRA	97	89	72	87	92	100	85	91	89	84	108	107	84	110	86	90	103	89	97	112
53158	PLEASANT PRAIRIE	114	138	144	139	135	133	124	124	115	124	145	145	131	152	126	111	144	120	111	136
53168	SALEM	110	113	103	113	113	115	105	109	103	106	128	128	105	129	105	100	124	107	103	127
53170	SILVER LAKE	99	96	87	97	97	102	95	98	95	95	117	114	93	117	94	93	113	97	96	111
53172	SOUTH MILWAUKEE	77	83	89	82	83	89	83	82	82	81	102	94	85	106	84	82	100	82	82	91
53177	STURTEVANT	98	93	81	91	95	103	90	95	93	90	114	110	89	115	91	93	109	94	98	113
53178	SULLIVAN	101	94	75	90	98	104	86	94	90	86	110	112	86	113	89	92	105	92	100	120
53179	TREVOR	95	89	75	88	91	97	86	91	88	86	108	107	84	108	86	87	103	89	93	109
53181	TWIN LAKES	105	98	82	94	103	110	92	100	96	91	116	118	90	118	95	98	111	98	106	125
53182	UNION GROVE	99	99	92	98	101	104	95	98	95	94	117	117	95	120	95	93	114	97	97	116
53183	WALES	140	174	184	174	170	168	155	154	143	154	180	181	165	192	158	139	180	149	138	171
53184	WALWORTH	105	91	70	89	96	106	90	98	96	89	116	113	86	116	90	98	109	96	106	119
53185	WATERFORD	107	123	122	124	120	118	111	112	104	113	131	131	115	135	111	100	130	109	100	125
53186	WAUKESHA	90	96	109	98	94	99	97	94	93	96	118	111	98	118	96	90	115	96	88	104
53188	WAUKESHA	103	110	120	113	108	112	109	107	104	109	131	126	111	132	108	101	129	107	99	118
53189	WAUKESHA	116	133	139	136	130	129	124	123	116	125	147	144	128	150	124	111	145	121	110	135
53190	WHITEWATER	75	67	72	69	67	73	80	73	78	75	98	90	74	95	74	75	94	78	71	84
53191	WILLIAMS BAY	126	116	108	111	123	133	112	122	117	111	142	144	107	143	116	120	136	121	131	153
53202	MILWAUKEE	73	64	104	73	62	69	81	72	82	80	104	90	80	103	77	79	102	79	67	80
53203	MILWAUKEE	90	86	162	99	82	91	102	90	105	104	133	111	106	140	100	104	132	97	84	101
53204	MILWAUKEE	51	44	44	44	43	45	50	49	52	52	66	57	48	64	47	49	66	52	46	53
53205	MILWAUKEE	36	30	39	28	29	34	35	34	39	36	49	38	34	46	34	41	47	36	37	39
53206	MILWAUKEE	46	39	47	36	38	45	44	44	50	46	61	49	44	58	43	52	59	46	48	50
53207	MILWAUKEE	69	75	84	74	75	80	76	74	75	74	94	86	78	98	76	75	92	74	73	81
53208	MILWAUKEE	54	50	63	49	49	55	56	54	59	56	74	63	56	73	55	59	72	57	55	60
53209	MILWAUKEE	67	65	76	63	63	71	68	67	71	69	89	76	69	88	68	73	87	68	69	75
53210	MILWAUKEE	61	58	70	57	56	63	63	61	67	64	83	71	64	82	62	67	81	63	62	69
53211	MILWAUKEE	98	94	123	100	92	100	111	100	108	106	136	123	108	133	105	102	133	107	93	111
53212	MILWAUKEE	51	42	53	42	42	48	51	49	55	51	68	57	49	64	49	55	66	52	50	55
53213	MILWAUKEE	95	108	129	111	106	109	106	103	101	105	128	122	110	131	107	98	126	104	95	112
53214	MILWAUKEE	67	72	82	73	71	75	74	72	73	72	91	85	75	94	74	71	89	73	69	78
53215	MILWAUKEE	62	59	64	59	59	63	65	63	66	64	82	73	64	82	63	64	81	65	62	68
53216	MILWAUKEE	59	56	66	55	55	62	61	59	64	61	80	67	62	80	60	65	78	61	61	67
53217	MILWAUKEE	156	192	237	192	188	197	178	175	169	179	213	201	191	221	184	167	213	172	162	190
53218	MILWAUKEE	58	57	67	55	55	62	61	59	63	61	79	67	62	80	60	64	77	60	60	66
53219	MILWAUKEE	67	73	82	72	72	78	74	72	74	72	92	83	76	96	75	74	90	72	72	79
53220	MILWAUKEE	72	79	93	78	78	86	80	78	80	78	100	89	83	103	81	81	98	78	78	85
53221	MILWAUKEE	73	79	88	77	78	84	78	77	78	77	98	89	81	101	80	79	95	78	78	86
53222	MILWAUKEE	72	79	92	79	79	85	80	78	79	78	99	90	82	102	81	79	97	78	77	85
53223	MILWAUKEE	77	82	94	83	81	85	84	81	82	83	102	96	85	103	83	80	101	82	77	89
53224	MILWAUKEE	77	77	88	78	76	81	80	78	80	80	100	91	81	99	79	78	98	80	75	87
53225	MILWAUKEE	70	71	82	70	69	75	74	72	75	74	94	83	75	94	73	74	92	73	70	80
53226	MILWAUKEE	100	114	136	114	112	119	111	109	108	111	136	126	116	140	113	108	134	109	105	119
53227	MILWAUKEE	69	73	86	73	72	78	76	73	76	74	95	85	77	97	76	75	93	75	73	80
53228	MILWAUKEE	86	99	112	99	98	101	95	94	91	94	114	109	99	118	96	90	113	93	89	103
53233	MILWAUKEE	33	23	30	25	22	26	38	30	38	34	47	40	33	43	32	34	45	35	29	34
53235	MILWAUKEE	68	73	86	72	72	78	75	72	75	73	93	84	77	96	75	74	91	73	72	79
53402	RACINE	97	105	110	104	104	109	103	102	100	101	125	118	105	128	103	99	123	101	98	112
53403	RACINE	72	73	80	71	72	79	76	74	77	74	96	86	77	97	75	77	93	75	75	82
53404	RACINE	69	66	72	64	65	72	71	69	73	70	91	80	71	91	70	74	88	71	71	77
53405	RACINE	80	86	91	86	86	90	86	85	84	84	105	99	87	108	86	83	103	85	82	93
53406	RACINE	85	96	107	94	95	100	92	91	91	91	113	105	96	117	94	91	112	91	89	101
53502	ALBANY	95	83	65	82	87	96	82	89	87	81	106	103	80	106	83	88	100	87	95	108
53503	ARENA	98	90	72	86	95	100	83	91	87	83	106	108	82	109	85	89	101	89	97	116
53504	ARGYLE	90	67	39	63	76	84	65	78	73	64	87	94	57	86	67	76	80	77	91	107
53505	AVALON	117	104	80	99	110	118	97	107	103	97	125	128	95	127	99	105	119	104	116	138
53506	AVOCA	98	66	31	59	76	86	64	80	76	65	90	96	55	86	66	82	82	79	98	113
53507	BARNEVELD	93	104	104	105	100	99	97	97	91	98	115	114	99	117	96	86	113	96	85	107
53508	BELLEVILLE	96	108	108	111	104	102	100	100	93	102	118	117	102	120	99	88	117	98	87	109
53510	BELMONT	73	63	48	61	67	73	62	67	66	61	80	79	60	80	62	67	75	66	73	83
53511	BELOIT	74	73	75	72	74	81	75	75	77	73	95	87	76	97	75	77	92	75	77	85
53515	BLACK EARTH	86	104	114	103	102	103	96	95	91	95	114	110	102	121	98	89	114	92	87	104
53516	BLANCHARDVILLE	96	77	54	75	86	93	74	87	81	73	96	104	68	97	77	83	90	85	97	114
53517	BLUE MOUNDS	105	128	135	129	126	124	115	115	107	115	134	135	122	142	117	103	134	111	102	127
53518	BLUE RIVER	81	64	42	61	71	78	61	71	68	61	81	86	56	81	63	70	75	70	81	96
53520	BRODHEAD	83	76	63	73	79	87	73	78	77	72	94	91	73	97	75	79	90	77	84	96
53521	BROOKLYN	100	117	121	119	113	112	107	106	100	108	126	125	112	129	107	95	125	104	94	117
53522	BROWNTOWN	90	79	58	75	84	90	73	82	78	73	95	97	71	96	75	80	90	80	89	106
53523	CAMBRIDGE	92	106	109	104	105	107	97	98	93	96	116	114	101	123	99	92	115	95	92	111
53525	CLINTON	99	90	73	88	94	102	86	93	90	85	109	109	85	111	87	91	104	91	98	114
53526	COBB	88	61	32	58	72	80	61	75	70	60	82	91	52	80	63	73	75	74	89	105
53527	COTTAGE GROVE	119	138	136	142	132	128	124	123	114	127	144	144	128	147	122	107	143	119	106	135
53528	CROSS PLAINS	107	121	124	123	118	116	113	112	106	114	134	133	116	137	112	101	132	111	99	124
53529	DANE	101	114	116	116	111	109	107	106	100	108	126	125	109	128	106	95	124	105	94	117
53530	DARLINGTON	80	62	41	58	69	78	62	72	70	61	83	84	56	82	64	73	77	71	84	94
53531	DEERFIELD	99	111	112	112	107	106	105	104	98	105	124	123	106	125	103	93	122	103	91	114
53532	DE FOREST	105	122	123	124	118	116	111	110	103	112	130	130	115	134	110	98	129	108	97	121
53533	DODGEVILLE	89	82	72	80	85	92	81	86	84	80	103	102	79	104	82	84	98	86	90	104
53534	EDGERTON	98	91	76	88	95	102	86	93	90	86	110	109	85	112	88	91	105	91	98	115
53536	EVANSVILLE	86	92	97	93	91	93	91	90	87	90	110	107	92	112	90	84	108	90	83	100
53538	FORT ATKINSON	93	88	78	87	90	97	86	90	88	85	108	105	85	109	87	88	103	89	93	106
53541	GRATIOT	84	73	54	69	78	84	68	76	73	68	88	91	65	89	70	75	83	74	83	99
53543	HIGHLAND	89	62	33	59	73	81	62	76	71	61	83	92	53	82	64	74	76	75	91	106
53544	HOLLANDALE	95	69	41	66	79	87	68	82	77	68	91	99	60	89	70	80	83	81	95	112
53545	JANESVILLE	84	89	96	89	89	94	89	88	88	87	109	103	91	113	90	87	107	88	86	98
53546	JANESVILLE	98	100	96	100	99	102	96	97	94	96	117	114	96	118	95	91	114	96	93	112
53548	JANESVILLE	84	85	86	84	86	91	84	85	85	83	105	99	85	108	85	85	102	85	85	97
53549	JEFFERSON	90	81	68	80	85	94	81	86	85	80	104	99	79	105	81	87	98	84	92	103
53550	JUDA	98	90	71	86	95	101	83	91	87	83	106	108	82	109	85	89	101	89	97	116
53551	LAKE MILLS	99	89	73	87	94	101	85	93	89	85	109	111	82	110	87	91	103	92	100	117
	WISCONSIN	89	86	85	86	88	94	86	88	87	85	108	103	86	109	86	87	104	88	89	103
	UNITED STATES	100	100	100	100	100	100	100	100	100	100	100	100	100	100	100	100	100	100	100	100

WISCONSIN

POPULATION CHANGE

A 53553-53950

# POST OFFICE NAME	COUNTY FIPS CODE	POPULATION 2000	2004	2009	2000-2004 ANNUAL RATE % Rate	State Centile	HOUSEHOLDS 2000	2004	2009	% Annual Rate 2000-2004	2004 Average HH Size	FAMILIES 2000	2004	% Annual Rate 2000-2004
53553 LINDEN	049	712	820	908	3.4	96	252	297	337	3.9	2.63	187	218	3.7
53554 LIVINGSTON	043	1011	1009	1010	-0.1	12	391	399	406	0.5	2.53	265	266	0.1
53555 LODI	021	7716	7920	8224	0.6	40	2970	3123	3315	1.2	2.50	2160	2239	0.9
53556 LONE ROCK	103	2756	2715	2712	-0.4	7	1104	1120	1142	0.3	2.40	765	762	-0.1
53557 LOWELL	027	230	235	240	0.5	34	84	88	92	1.1	2.67	62	65	1.1
53558 MC FARLAND	025	9239	9835	10623	1.5	74	3465	3785	4179	2.1	2.59	2542	2728	1.7
53559 MARSHALL	025	5730	6085	6534	1.4	73	2102	2277	2492	1.9	2.66	1597	1703	1.5
53560 MAZOMANIE	025	3454	3582	3833	0.9	49	1319	1401	1530	1.4	2.55	1010	1058	1.1
53561 MERRIMAC	111	1613	1730	1866	1.7	80	697	770	851	2.4	2.25	486	529	2.0
53562 MIDDLETON	025	19458	21119	23133	2.0	86	8341	9309	10439	2.6	2.26	5071	5546	2.1
53563 MILTON	105	9334	9706	10011	0.9	53	3509	3731	3923	1.5	2.59	2618	2759	1.2
53565 MINERAL POINT	049	4593	4809	5062	1.1	61	1787	1918	2068	1.7	2.46	1231	1303	1.4
53566 MONROE	045	14610	14887	15504	0.4	32	6014	6251	6638	0.9	2.33	3877	3967	0.5
53569 MONTFORT	043	1180	1194	1209	0.3	26	423	436	448	0.7	2.73	304	310	0.5
53570 MONTICELLO	045	2335	2469	2599	1.3	70	919	997	1074	1.9	2.45	647	694	1.7
53572 MOUNT HOREB	025	8435	9014	9718	1.6	77	3165	3446	3789	2.0	2.57	2281	2443	1.6
53573 MUSCODA	043	3456	3573	3650	0.8	46	1377	1462	1522	1.4	2.39	946	990	1.1
53574 NEW GLARUS	045	3131	3381	3597	1.8	83	1217	1349	1469	2.5	2.46	868	949	2.1
53575 OREGON	025	13623	14390	15401	1.3	69	4746	5144	5640	1.9	2.64	3643	3889	1.6
53576 ORFORDVILLE	105	2184	2330	2448	1.5	75	778	853	916	2.2	2.71	608	658	1.9
53577 PLAIN	111	1355	1397	1485	0.7	44	533	566	615	1.4	2.47	395	414	1.1
53578 PRAIRIE DU SAC	111	4955	5191	5550	1.1	61	1937	2080	2273	1.7	2.46	1331	1409	1.4
53579 REESEVILLE	027	2106	2172	2233	0.7	45	809	859	907	1.4	2.53	584	611	1.1
53580 REWEY	049	616	634	661	0.7	43	215	226	240	1.2	2.81	160	166	0.9
53581 RICHLAND CENTER	103	9992	10082	10148	0.2	23	4066	4205	4307	0.8	2.34	2626	2679	0.5
53582 RIDGEWAY	049	1103	1126	1171	0.5	33	431	452	481	1.1	2.47	315	327	0.9
53583 SAUK CITY	111	5310	5521	5894	0.9	53	2094	2228	2431	1.5	2.46	1463	1542	1.3
53585 SHARON	127	2313	2565	2794	2.5	91	852	970	1077	3.1	2.64	645	725	2.8
53586 SHULLSBURG	065	2097	2102	2120	0.1	17	832	856	884	0.7	2.43	572	580	0.3
53587 SOUTH WAYNE	065	1295	1301	1309	0.1	19	506	524	542	0.8	2.48	363	371	0.5
53588 SPRING GREEN	111	3943	4098	4361	0.9	52	1514	1618	1764	1.6	2.49	1057	1113	1.2
53589 STOUGHTON	025	19286	20351	21929	1.3	67	7332	7906	8701	1.8	2.52	5224	5539	1.4
53590 SUN PRAIRIE	025	25600	29085	32485	3.1	95	9685	11288	12898	3.7	2.56	6909	7938	3.3
53593 VERONA	025	12848	15673	18205	4.8	99	4589	5734	6813	5.4	2.71	3479	4286	5.0
53594 WATERLOO	055	4949	5145	5403	0.9	53	1846	1964	2109	1.5	2.58	1319	1381	1.1
53597 WAUNAKEE	025	13269	14341	15581	1.8	84	4876	5396	5991	2.4	2.63	3587	3903	2.0
53598 WINDSOR	025	1901	2025	2180	1.5	74	727	792	870	2.0	2.55	551	593	1.7
53703 MADISON	025	26697	27717	29581	0.9	51	12693	13479	14776	1.4	1.81	1587	1558	-0.4
53704 MADISON	025	44280	47247	51606	1.5	75	20114	21962	24523	2.1	2.11	10247	10876	1.4
53705 MADISON	025	23385	23955	25715	0.6	37	10952	11624	12807	1.4	2.04	6064	6172	0.4
53706 MADISON	025	6692	6692	6696	0.0	15	20	19	21	-1.2	3.37	2	2	0.0
53711 MADISON	025	44447	46551	50137	1.1	61	18209	19490	21428	1.6	2.36	11164	11668	1.0
53713 MADISON	025	20828	21446	23028	0.7	43	8985	9387	10252	1.0	2.25	4411	4462	0.3
53714 MADISON	025	15597	15711	16661	0.2	22	6607	6846	7439	0.8	2.26	3989	4040	0.3
53715 MADISON	025	10430	10509	11099	0.2	23	4487	4630	5013	0.7	2.16	962	947	-0.4
53716 MADISON	025	19209	19176	20258	0.0	13	8109	8334	9021	0.7	2.29	5179	5204	0.1
53717 MADISON	025	10612	11914	13293	2.8	94	4853	5626	6439	3.5	2.11	2721	3068	2.9
53718 MADISON	025	3555	5484	7090	10.7	100	1554	2511	3352	12.0	2.17	1029	1610	11.1
53719 MADISON	025	18560	22611	26238	4.8	99	8199	10237	12150	5.4	2.18	4426	5420	4.9
53726 MADISON	025	5095	5342	5715	1.1	62	2207	2388	2622	1.9	2.13	756	788	1.0
53801 BAGLEY	043	837	831	825	-0.2	9	358	367	373	0.6	2.26	263	266	0.3
53803 BENTON	065	106	109	111	0.7	42	37	39	41	1.3	2.79	26	28	1.8
53804 BLOOMINGTON	043	1601	1583	1576	-0.3	8	616	629	640	0.5	2.52	438	441	0.2
53805 BOSCOBEL	043	5223	5250	5271	0.1	20	1977	2043	2095	0.8	2.45	1344	1368	0.4
53806 CASSVILLE	043	1986	1975	1971	-0.1	10	831	850	865	0.5	2.32	566	571	0.2
53807 CUBA CITY	043	6587	6600	6619	0.1	17	2462	2550	2618	0.8	2.52	1783	1823	0.5
53809 FENNIMORE	043	3871	3827	3803	-0.3	8	1531	1557	1579	0.4	2.41	1037	1038	0.0
53810 GLEN HAVEN	043	500	491	487	-0.4	4	186	189	192	0.4	2.60	142	143	0.2
53811 HAZEL GREEN	043	3629	3622	3623	-0.1	12	1321	1367	1400	0.8	2.58	981	1003	0.5
53813 LANCASTER	043	6304	6176	6138	-0.5	4	2396	2406	2436	0.1	2.46	1634	1620	-0.2
53816 MOUNT HOPE	043	573	567	567	-0.3	8	234	239	244	0.5	2.37	168	169	0.1
53818 PLATTEVILLE	043	13428	13502	13540	0.1	20	4527	4683	4793	0.8	2.37	2651	2701	0.4
53820 POTOSI	043	2752	2801	2821	0.4	31	1049	1104	1137	1.2	2.54	777	808	0.9
53821 PRAIRIE DU CHIEN	023	8528	8494	8625	-0.1	11	3338	3407	3550	0.5	2.32	2186	2195	0.1
53825 STITZER	043	453	459	459	0.3	27	152	157	161	0.8	2.92	116	119	0.6
53826 WAUZEKA	023	1638	1718	1783	1.1	63	596	646	689	1.9	2.65	432	462	1.6
53827 WOODMAN	043	407	394	390	-0.8	1	159	159	161	0.0	2.48	112	111	-0.2
53901 PORTAGE	021	13463	13819	14349	0.6	40	5264	5550	5902	1.3	2.30	3355	3490	0.9
53910 ADAMS	001	3549	3871	4135	2.1	87	1457	1628	1771	2.7	2.34	927	1020	2.3
53911 ARLINGTON	021	1398	1487	1571	1.5	73	522	571	617	2.1	2.60	400	433	1.9
53913 BARABOO	111	18797	20309	22177	1.8	84	7613	8411	9387	2.4	2.37	4998	5446	2.0
53916 BEAVER DAM	027	20981	21555	22266	0.6	41	8578	9002	9505	1.1	2.37	5706	5910	0.8
53919 BRANDON	039	2790	2875	2952	0.7	44	983	1036	1087	1.2	2.78	792	825	1.0
53920 BRIGGSVILLE	077	521	534	557	0.6	38	226	238	254	1.2	2.23	170	177	1.0
53922 BURNETT	027	981	949	958	-0.8	1	357	354	366	-0.2	2.68	286	281	-0.4
53923 CAMBRIA	021	2608	2661	2767	0.5	33	906	941	998	0.9	2.83	679	697	0.6
53924 CAZENOVIA	103	1622	1629	1638	0.1	19	592	612	627	0.8	2.66	437	444	0.4
53925 COLUMBUS	021	7296	7488	7743	0.6	39	2850	2998	3171	1.2	2.46	1976	2047	0.8
53926 DALTON	047	1433	1543	1610	1.8	82	475	524	560	2.3	2.94	357	390	2.1
53929 ELROY	057	2978	3050	3209	0.6	37	1160	1216	1309	1.1	2.41	796	821	0.7
53930 ENDEAVOR	077	1293	1332	1400	0.7	43	464	489	526	1.2	2.70	341	356	1.0
53932 FALL RIVER	021	2155	2303	2432	1.6	77	799	874	943	2.1	2.63	594	641	1.8
53933 FOX LAKE	027	3901	4111	4267	1.2	66	1103	1210	1301	2.2	2.53	748	807	1.8
53934 FRIENDSHIP	001	4555	4805	5035	1.3	67	1952	2120	2270	2.0	2.19	1311	1401	1.6
53936 GRAND MARSH	001	1062	1189	1288	2.7	94	439	502	553	3.2	2.37	295	333	2.9
53937 HILLPOINT	111	995	1016	1068	0.5	33	329	345	370	1.1	2.94	266	277	1.0
53939 KINGSTON	047	169	183	189	1.9	85	77	86	91	2.6	2.13	58	63	2.0
53941 LA VALLE	111	2639	2830	3072	1.7	80	965	1056	1170	2.1	2.68	761	826	2.0
53943 LOGANVILLE	111	1033	1061	1125	0.6	41	377	398	431	1.3	2.67	290	303	1.1
53944 LYNDON STATION	057	1697	1886	2077	2.5	92	680	779	879	3.3	2.41	495	559	2.9
53946 MARKESAN	047	4286	4148	4070	-0.8	1	1735	1727	1737	-0.1	2.39	1251	1230	-0.4
53947 MARQUETTE	047	169	165	162	-0.6	3	69	69	70	0.0	2.39	49	48	-0.5
53948 MAUSTON	057	7739	8069	8581	1.0	56	3123	3343	3646	1.6	2.37	2096	2209	1.2
53949 MONTELLO	077	7116	7075	7393	-0.1	9	2458	2506	2709	0.5	2.28	1668	1676	0.1
53950 NEW LISBON	057	4143	4436	4808	1.6	78	1708	1876	2082	2.2	2.35	1180	1282	2.0
WISCONSIN					0.8					1.4	2.44			1.1
UNITED STATES					1.2					1.3	2.58			1.1

ZIP CODE #	POST OFFICE NAME	RACE (%) White 2000	White 2004	Black 2000	Black 2004	Asian/Pacific 2000	Asian/Pacific 2004	% Hispanic Origin 2000	% Hispanic Origin 2004	2004 AGE DISTRIBUTION (%) 0-4	5-9	10-14	15-19	20-24	25-44	45-64	65-84	85+	18+	MEDIAN AGE 2004	% 2004 Males	% 2004 Females
53553	LINDEN	99.0	98.9	0.3	0.2	0.0	0.0	0.1	0.1	7.2	7.4	8.4	6.5	5.0	27.6	23.5	11.5	2.9	72.8	37.6	49.9	50.1
53554	LIVINGSTON	99.6	99.6	0.0	0.0	0.0	0.0	0.2	0.3	6.1	6.4	7.9	5.9	6.1	28.4	24.5	12.5	2.1	75.9	38.2	50.4	49.7
53555	LODI	98.4	98.2	0.2	0.3	0.3	0.4	0.7	0.8	6.8	6.8	7.4	6.1	5.1	28.0	27.0	10.9	2.0	75.1	39.6	50.3	49.7
53556	LONE ROCK	98.4	98.3	0.2	0.2	0.2	0.3	1.0	1.1	6.2	6.5	7.0	7.2	6.3	27.5	26.2	11.5	1.7	76.0	38.2	50.0	50.0
53557	LOWELL	97.4	97.0	0.0	0.4	0.4	0.4	2.2	2.6	7.7	7.7	6.4	6.0	5.5	31.1	23.8	10.6	1.3	74.9	37.9	52.3	47.7
53558	MC FARLAND	97.1	96.5	0.4	0.4	0.8	1.0	1.4	1.8	5.8	6.6	7.7	7.2	5.9	26.5	31.2	8.3	0.9	75.1	40.1	50.3	49.7
53559	MARSHALL	95.4	94.5	0.8	0.9	0.3	0.4	4.0	4.9	8.0	8.1	8.2	6.5	5.4	29.3	24.3	8.9	1.3	71.7	35.8	50.5	49.5
53560	MAZOMANIE	97.4	97.1	0.5	0.5	0.2	0.3	1.4	1.8	6.3	6.9	7.4	6.6	4.8	28.7	28.8	9.4	1.1	75.2	39.2	50.3	49.7
53561	MERRIMAC	98.7	98.6	0.3	0.3	0.2	0.2	0.7	0.8	4.5	5.1	6.1	5.7	4.5	23.9	34.7	14.2	1.2	80.8	45.1	50.8	49.3
53562	MIDDLETON	93.1	91.9	1.7	1.9	2.4	3.2	2.3	2.8	5.5	5.6	6.8	6.8	7.3	29.1	29.4	8.4	1.4	77.6	38.2	48.6	51.4
53563	MILTON	98.0	97.6	0.2	0.3	0.5	0.6	1.2	1.4	6.1	6.5	7.8	7.4	6.5	28.0	27.1	9.3	1.3	74.9	37.7	50.1	49.9
53565	MINERAL POINT	98.7	98.6	0.2	0.2	0.3	0.4	0.5	0.6	6.7	7.0	7.2	6.4	5.6	27.3	25.4	12.0	2.4	74.9	38.7	49.3	50.7
53566	MONROE	98.0	97.8	0.3	0.3	0.3	0.4	1.2	1.3	6.1	6.3	7.1	6.9	6.3	25.8	25.2	13.6	2.8	76.0	39.8	48.3	51.7
53569	MONTFORT	99.0	98.9	0.2	0.2	0.2	0.2	0.2	0.2	5.6	7.4	10.3	8.5	5.4	25.9	23.3	12.6	1.2	71.3	37.0	50.5	49.5
53570	MONTICELLO	98.5	98.4	0.2	0.2	0.1	0.1	0.6	0.8	6.7	7.1	6.6	6.3	5.2	27.3	27.8	11.0	2.1	75.6	39.5	50.5	49.5
53572	MOUNT HOREB	98.1	97.8	0.3	0.3	0.4	0.5	0.7	0.8	7.5	7.6	7.8	7.0	5.7	29.1	23.8	9.4	2.2	72.7	36.6	48.9	51.1
53573	MUSCODA	98.5	98.5	0.2	0.2	0.2	0.2	1.0	1.0	5.9	6.1	7.1	6.8	5.9	25.4	26.7	13.4	2.9	76.8	40.3	51.1	48.9
53574	NEW GLARUS	98.5	98.3	0.1	0.2	0.3	0.4	1.0	1.2	6.6	7.1	7.8	6.5	4.9	27.1	25.4	11.8	3.0	74.2	39.7	48.9	51.1
53575	OREGON	95.0	94.3	3.3	3.7	0.6	0.8	1.0	1.2	6.8	7.5	7.8	6.5	5.8	31.1	26.8	6.8	1.0	73.7	36.8	52.1	47.9
53576	ORFORDVILLE	97.9	97.6	0.2	0.3	0.1	0.1	1.5	1.7	6.4	7.1	8.5	7.1	5.5	28.1	26.3	9.6	1.4	73.2	37.6	49.7	50.3
53577	PLAIN	98.8	98.6	0.2	0.1	0.0	0.0	0.9	1.1	7.0	7.4	7.9	6.4	5.2	25.1	26.9	12.4	1.7	73.7	40.0	52.5	47.5
53578	PRAIRIE DU SAC	97.7	97.4	0.2	0.2	0.4	0.5	2.5	2.9	6.4	6.5	7.4	7.1	5.4	27.6	25.1	11.9	2.5	75.1	38.5	49.7	50.3
53579	REESEVILLE	97.4	97.1	0.6	0.7	0.2	0.2	2.1	2.5	6.9	7.1	7.4	6.5	6.5	29.4	25.0	10.2	1.0	74.6	37.3	52.4	47.6
53580	REWEY	98.7	98.6	0.2	0.2	0.0	0.0	0.3	0.5	7.9	9.2	10.4	7.1	4.4	27.1	24.8	8.7	0.5	67.8	35.3	49.5	50.5
53581	RICHLAND CENTER	98.3	98.1	0.2	0.2	0.3	0.4	1.0	1.1	5.6	5.8	6.4	7.1	7.7	23.5	25.3	15.3	3.4	78.1	40.7	48.7	51.3
53582	RIDGEWAY	98.9	98.7	0.1	0.1	0.5	0.7	0.1	0.1	6.4	6.9	7.8	6.1	4.5	28.5	28.7	10.1	0.9	75.0	39.8	50.7	49.3
53583	SAUK CITY	98.0	97.8	0.2	0.2	0.2	0.2	2.2	2.5	6.5	6.6	7.0	7.4	6.0	27.8	25.9	11.0	1.9	75.4	38.7	50.1	49.9
53585	SHARON	95.3	94.4	0.4	0.4	0.4	0.5	5.4	6.6	6.6	7.3	8.8	7.4	5.1	28.2	26.2	9.6	0.9	72.5	37.5	51.1	48.9
53586	SHULLSBURG	99.2	99.1	0.1	0.1	0.4	0.5	0.0	0.0	6.2	6.4	7.3	6.7	6.1	24.9	26.0	14.2	2.2	76.1	40.2	49.7	50.3
53587	SOUTH WAYNE	99.6	99.6	0.1	0.2	0.0	0.0	0.6	0.7	5.8	6.2	7.8	7.2	5.9	26.4	26.8	12.7	1.3	75.6	40.0	51.7	48.4
53588	SPRING GREEN	98.8	98.7	0.1	0.2	0.1	0.2	0.7	0.8	6.0	6.2	6.9	7.4	5.7	25.5	27.4	12.5	2.5	76.0	40.6	49.5	50.5
53589	STOUGHTON	97.2	96.7	0.7	0.8	0.7	0.9	1.1	1.4	7.1	7.1	7.6	6.9	5.7	28.1	25.2	10.1	2.3	73.7	37.9	48.6	51.5
53590	SUN PRAIRIE	93.7	92.6	2.6	2.9	1.2	1.6	2.4	2.8	7.8	7.5	7.3	6.9	7.0	31.1	23.5	7.6	1.3	72.9	34.6	49.0	51.0
53593	VERONA	97.0	96.3	0.7	0.9	1.0	1.3	0.9	1.1	6.3	7.3	8.8	7.6	5.1	27.7	28.8	7.2	1.3	71.9	38.3	49.2	50.8
53594	WATERLOO	94.9	94.2	0.8	0.9	0.3	0.4	5.7	6.6	6.7	6.5	7.5	7.7	6.6	29.3	24.8	9.6	1.4	74.4	36.7	50.6	49.4
53597	WAUNAKEE	97.9	97.5	0.4	0.5	0.6	0.8	0.9	1.2	7.0	7.4	8.5	7.5	5.5	28.7	24.4	9.3	1.7	72.3	37.0	49.3	50.7
53598	WINDSOR	95.6	94.7	0.6	0.8	1.3	1.8	1.4	1.7	7.9	7.5	6.7	6.2	5.9	32.4	25.2	7.6	0.6	73.9	35.9	49.8	50.2
53703	MADISON	86.6	84.0	4.7	5.4	5.0	6.6	3.6	4.3	1.1	0.8	1.1	9.2	48.7	27.7	8.3	2.1	0.9	96.2	23.9	53.2	46.8
53704	MADISON	84.5	82.2	7.0	8.1	3.3	4.1	4.7	5.4	6.0	5.3	5.2	5.9	8.3	34.8	24.6	8.6	1.3	80.1	35.8	48.7	51.3
53705	MADISON	81.0	78.1	2.3	2.6	13.1	15.4	3.3	3.6	5.1	4.8	5.4	5.8	7.7	28.7	26.1	13.6	2.9	81.0	39.6	46.9	53.1
53706	MADISON	90.0	87.8	1.5	1.8	5.3	6.9	2.1	2.5	0.0	0.0	0.0	73.1	26.2	0.4	0.2	0.0	0.0	99.7	18.4	45.2	54.8
53711	MADISON	85.0	82.5	6.6	7.5	4.2	5.2	3.9	4.7	6.2	6.3	6.7	6.8	8.9	29.0	25.8	8.8	1.7	76.9	35.9	48.5	51.5
53713	MADISON	61.9	58.3	17.8	19.3	7.3	8.5	15.4	16.8	7.8	6.3	6.2	6.8	12.5	36.6	18.1	5.1	0.6	76.1	29.2	51.1	48.9
53714	MADISON	88.3	86.5	5.8	6.6	2.1	2.6	3.4	4.0	5.7	5.7	6.3	6.1	7.0	31.3	25.6	10.7	1.6	78.8	38.0	48.7	51.3
53715	MADISON	82.7	79.6	3.9	4.5	9.6	11.8	3.6	4.1	1.7	1.4	1.8	6.8	45.8	22.5	12.2	5.7	2.1	93.6	24.2	52.9	47.1
53716	MADISON	93.3	92.0	2.6	3.1	1.2	1.6	2.4	2.9	4.9	5.3	6.3	6.7	5.9	26.9	29.0	13.4	1.5	79.4	41.4	48.5	51.5
53717	MADISON	86.3	84.3	4.0	4.3	6.0	7.5	3.6	4.0	5.7	5.5	6.6	6.9	7.2	29.9	27.8	9.5	1.1	77.7	36.8	47.6	52.4
53718	MADISON	95.3	94.3	1.8	2.1	1.0	1.3	1.6	1.9	5.2	5.3	5.6	5.4	5.9	32.5	29.9	9.3	0.9	80.3	39.4	49.9	50.1
53719	MADISON	86.3	84.0	4.7	5.2	5.0	6.2	4.6	5.3	7.8	6.6	5.5	5.2	7.8	43.1	18.0	4.8	1.2	76.9	31.7	49.3	50.7
53726	MADISON	85.5	82.0	1.5	1.7	10.1	13.1	2.5	2.9	2.5	2.2	2.8	7.9	37.0	25.4	16.9	4.6	0.6	90.7	24.7	52.0	48.0
53801	BAGLEY	98.0	98.1	0.0	0.0	0.2	0.2	0.8	0.8	4.7	5.1	6.7	7.2	5.1	22.9	28.4	18.4	1.6	79.1	44.0	51.3	48.7
53803	BENTON	98.1	98.2	0.0	0.0	0.9	1.8	0.0	0.0	5.5	6.4	6.4	7.3	6.4	24.8	31.2	11.0	0.9	76.2	41.3	51.4	48.6
53804	BLOOMINGTON	99.4	99.5	0.0	0.0	0.1	0.1	0.3	0.3	5.2	5.7	8.4	7.8	5.4	25.1	25.6	14.9	2.0	75.5	40.3	50.7	49.3
53805	BOSCOBEL	96.6	96.5	2.2	2.3	0.2	0.2	0.9	0.9	6.3	6.4	7.2	6.6	7.4	27.0	23.6	12.9	2.6	76.0	37.7	50.9	49.1
53806	CASSVILLE	99.2	99.3	0.1	0.1	0.1	0.1	0.3	0.3	4.7	5.2	7.5	7.7	5.2	23.3	26.5	17.7	2.1	77.5	42.7	50.3	49.7
53807	CUBA CITY	99.2	99.2	0.1	0.1	0.3	0.3	0.2	0.2	6.2	6.6	7.2	6.5	6.0	25.5	25.6	14.1	2.4	75.7	39.9	49.6	50.4
53809	FENNIMORE	99.1	99.0	0.1	0.1	0.3	0.3	0.8	0.8	6.1	6.0	7.1	7.6	7.1	25.2	23.9	14.0	3.1	76.4	39.1	50.0	50.0
53810	GLEN HAVEN	99.4	99.6	0.0	0.0	0.0	0.0	0.2	0.2	4.9	5.5	7.3	6.9	5.3	25.5	25.5	17.7	1.4	77.8	41.9	51.5	48.5
53811	HAZEL GREEN	99.2	99.1	0.1	0.1	0.2	0.3	0.3	0.3	6.1	6.6	7.0	7.3	6.2	24.7	26.7	13.3	2.2	75.7	40.0	48.2	51.8
53813	LANCASTER	99.3	99.3	0.1	0.1	0.2	0.2	0.4	0.4	5.7	5.8	7.1	7.5	6.6	24.9	25.2	14.2	3.0	76.6	40.0	49.2	50.8
53816	MOUNT HOPE	99.8	99.8	0.0	0.0	0.0	0.0	0.4	0.4	5.1	5.3	6.5	6.7	6.9	25.2	29.1	13.9	1.2	78.7	41.5	52.4	47.6
53818	PLATTEVILLE	96.6	96.6	0.9	1.0	1.3	1.3	0.7	0.8	4.0	4.2	5.0	13.5	22.9	19.5	19.0	10.0	2.0	83.3	25.4	53.8	46.2
53820	POTOSI	99.3	99.3	0.0	0.0	0.1	0.1	0.6	0.5	5.9	6.4	7.9	6.9	5.6	26.1	27.4	12.4	1.4	75.4	39.4	51.9	48.1
53821	PRAIRIE DU CHIEN	96.1	95.6	2.6	2.9	0.3	0.3	0.7	0.8	6.0	6.3	6.7	8.1	7.3	24.4	25.2	13.5	2.5	75.8	38.7	50.9	49.1
53825	STITZER	99.3	99.4	0.2	0.2	0.2	0.2	0.4	0.4	7.4	8.1	8.3	8.3	5.9	26.4	24.8	9.8	1.1	70.4	35.7	52.7	47.3
53826	WAUZEKA	99.2	99.1	0.0	0.0	0.3	0.4	0.6	0.5	8.0	8.0	7.9	6.8	7.0	26.3	24.2	11.0	0.8	71.5	35.3	51.2	48.8
53827	WOODMAN	99.8	99.8	0.0	0.0	0.0	0.0	0.5	0.5	5.3	5.3	5.6	5.8	7.9	24.9	28.9	14.7	1.5	80.7	42.0	52.3	47.7
53901	PORTAGE	94.4	93.7	2.9	3.2	0.6	0.7	2.7	3.0	5.6	5.5	6.3	6.9	7.9	28.3	24.5	12.6	2.5	78.5	38.4	51.3	48.8
53910	ADAMS	97.2	96.9	0.3	0.4	0.3	0.4	1.8	2.1	6.2	6.4	6.9	6.3	5.2	24.3	25.0	17.0	2.8	76.6	41.6	49.2	50.8
53911	ARLINGTON	98.9	98.8	0.1	0.1	0.1	0.1	1.1	1.2	6.7	7.1	6.7	6.1	5.4	26.8	29.1	10.7	1.4	75.7	40.2	52.3	47.8
53913	BARABOO	96.6	96.3	0.4	0.5	0.4	0.5	1.9	2.2	6.6	6.5	7.0	6.6	6.6	28.3	25.0	11.2	2.3	75.9	37.6	49.2	50.8
53916	BEAVER DAM	96.2	95.7	0.4	0.4	0.6	0.7	3.9	4.6	6.8	6.6	6.6	6.6	6.5	27.1	25.0	12.5	2.3	75.9	38.6	49.2	50.8
53919	BRANDON	99.2	99.1	0.1	0.1	0.1	0.1	0.7	0.8	7.8	7.8	8.1	7.0	6.0	27.4	23.5	11.3	1.2	72.1	36.6	50.2	49.8
53920	BRIGGSVILLE	97.3	97.2	0.6	0.8	0.2	0.2	1.2	1.3	5.2	5.8	6.6	6.2	3.8	24.9	28.8	17.4	1.3	78.5	43.6	50.2	49.8
53922	BURNETT	98.6	98.3	0.2	0.2	0.1	0.2	1.1	1.3	6.9	7.0	6.7	7.2	6.0	25.1	29.0	10.8	1.5	75.0	39.6	52.2	47.8
53923	CAMBRIA	97.0	96.7	0.1	0.1	0.1	0.1	2.8	3.1	7.9	7.6	8.0	7.4	6.6	25.5	24.3	11.1	1.6	72.0	36.2	50.5	49.5
53924	CAZENOVIA	98.7	98.6	0.1	0.1	0.3	0.3	0.5	0.6	6.3	6.7	8.0	6.7	6.1	25.0	26.4	13.5	1.2	74.8	39.5	52.0	48.0
53925	COLUMBUS	98.2	97.9	0.4	0.5	0.3	0.3	1.2	1.5	6.4	6.3	7.0	7.2	6.8	26.8	24.6	12.3	2.6	75.5	38.6	49.2	50.9
53926	DALTON	97.7	97.7	0.1	0.1	0.1	0.1	1.4	1.4	7.6	7.7	8.0	7.8	6.9	25.2	24.2	11.0	1.8	71.8	36.2	49.4	50.6
53929	ELROY	98.8	98.7	0.2	0.3	0.2	0.2	0.7	0.8	5.7	6.0	7.3	6.8	6.2	24.2	26.1	14.2	3.4	76.1	41.2	50.0	50.0
53930	ENDEAVOR	96.8	96.8	0.3	0.5	0.4	0.4	2.4	2.5	6.8	6.9	8.0	8.1	5.9	27.3	23.6	12.3	1.1	73.3	37.0	49.9	50.2
53932	FALL RIVER	98.3	98.0	0.4	0.4	0.2	0.3	1.1	1.4	7.3	7.3	7.1	6.8	5.8	30.8	24.3	9.3	1.4	74.1	36.8	50.2	49.8
53933	FOX LAKE	85.5	83.4	12.5	14.5	0.2	0.2	3.3	3.8	3.3	3.7	5.0	5.8	8.2	36.9	24.3	11.2	1.7	84.6	37.9	63.1	36.9
53934	FRIENDSHIP	97.7	97.4	0.2	0.3	0.4	0.5	1.5	1.8	4.4	4.5	5.5	5.6	4.9	21.3	29.2	21.8	2.8	82.2	47.6	50.7	49.3
53936	GRAND MARSH	97.5	97.1	0.4	0.4	0.2	0.3	2.2	2.5	5.2	5.6	6.5	5.6	4.6	24.3	28.6	18.1	1.5	79.2	44.0	51.7	48.3
53937	HILLPOINT	99.2	99.3	0.1	0.1	0.0	0.0	1.1	1.4	7.0	7.4	8.3	8.0	6.5	26.2	25.6	9.8	1.3	72.5	37.1	52.0	48.0
53939	KINGSTON	97.6	97.8	0.0	0.0	0.0	0.0	1.2	1.1	8.2	7.7	8.2	8.2	7.1	25.7	22.4	10.9	1.6	70.5	34.3	48.6	51.4
53941	LA VALLE	98.7	98.6	0.2	0.2	0.0	0.0	1.0	1.2	6.8	7.2	7.4	7.4	5.4	24.1	26.0	14.5	1.4	73.8	39.6	50.3	49.8
53943	LOGANVILLE	99.2	99.2	0.0	0.0	0.0	0.0	1.7	2.2	7.3	7.4	7.5	6.6	5.9	26.5	26.6	11.3	1.0	73.9	38.3	51.6	48.4
53944	LYNDON STATION	91.2	90.7	0.7	0.7	0.2	0.3	1.7	2.0	6.2	6.4	7.3	7.0	5.7	25.8	27.9	12.6	1.1	75.6	40.0	51.4	48.6
53946	MARKESAN	98.8	98.7	0.2	0.3	0.1	0.1	1.5	1.6	6.0	5.8	5.9	6.4	6.1	24.0	27.8	16.1	2.0	78.4	42.3	50.4	49.6
53947	MARQUETTE	98.2	98.8	0.0	0.0	0.0	0.0	1.2	1.2	5.5	5.5	5.5	4.9	4.2	20.6	32.7	19.4	1.8	80.0	47.5	52.1	47.9
53948	MAUSTON	97.0	96.6	0.5	0.6	0.8	1.0	1.5	1.7	6.0	6.0	6.7	7.0	6.4	25.3	25.5	14.6	2.7	77.0	40.5	49.2	50.8
53949	MONTELLO	88.6	88.2	7.2	7.7	0.4	0.4	4.1	4.2	4.2	4.2	4.5	5.1	6.4	31.2	26.2	16.4	1.8	83.8	41.9	59.3	40.7
53950	NEW LISBON	97.8	97.5	0.1	0.2	0.5	0.6	1.0	1.2	5.9	5.9	6.7	6.6	5.7	23.9	27.8	15.6	1.9	77.4	42.0	50.3	49.8
	WISCONSIN	88.9	88.0	5.7	6.0	1.7	2.1	3.6	4.0	6.4	6.5	7.1	7.3	7.7	27.6	24.5	11.1	1.9	75.8	36.9	49.5	50.5
	UNITED STATES	75.1	73.6	12.3	12.5	3.8	4.2	12.5	14.1	6.9	6.7	7.2	7.0	7.3	28.6	23.8	10.8	1.7	75.1	36.0	49.1	50.9

ZIP CODE #	POST OFFICE NAME	2004 Per Capita Income	2004 HH Income Base	2004 HOUSEHOLD INCOME DISTRIBUTION (%) Less than $25,000	$25,000 to $49,999	$50,000 to $99,999	$100,000 to $149,999	$150,000 or More	MEDIAN HOUSEHOLD INCOME 2004	2009	2004 National Centile	2004 State Centile	2004 Home Value Base	2004 HOME VALUE DISTRIBUTION (%) Less than $50,000	$50,000 to $89,999	$90,000 to $174,999	$175,000 to $399,999	$400,000 or More	2004 Median Home Value
53553	LINDEN	19734	297	24.6	32.7	33.7	6.4	2.7	41839	47205	52	37	237	17.3	19.8	36.7	21.5	4.6	112500
53554	LIVINGSTON	18249	399	32.3	32.3	29.1	4.8	1.5	38908	42519	42	25	318	18.6	27.7	39.9	10.7	3.1	94615
53555	LODI	28187	3123	15.4	25.5	42.1	12.4	4.7	59429	66082	84	85	2477	3.9	3.9	38.3	46.8	7.1	183234
53556	LONE ROCK	22154	1120	21.6	35.2	35.5	5.4	2.3	43838	50000	58	44	897	19.3	20.1	43.6	14.3	2.8	104514
53557	LOWELL	20392	88	20.5	28.4	44.3	5.7	1.1	50665	54931	73	66	72	4.2	9.7	52.8	33.3	0.0	140000
53558	MC FARLAND	31630	3785	9.9	20.7	44.9	17.8	6.7	69570	80605	91	95	3055	1.0	1.6	34.7	56.4	6.4	191338
53559	MARSHALL	25362	2277	13.1	27.8	45.7	9.8	3.7	57478	66859	82	81	1897	16.8	5.2	36.0	38.1	4.0	162115
53560	MAZOMANIE	28026	1401	11.4	25.8	45.5	13.2	4.1	61845	73580	86	90	1171	5.4	6.0	45.6	38.2	4.9	162345
53561	MERRIMAC	28808	770	18.3	28.1	38.8	9.7	5.1	52479	60476	76	70	649	6.5	7.6	36.1	42.1	7.9	174798
53562	MIDDLETON	38292	9309	13.9	23.7	35.1	15.6	11.7	63405	76142	87	92	5834	0.5	1.7	25.4	56.9	15.5	222782
53563	MILTON	26448	3731	13.6	27.6	40.2	15.3	3.3	58850	67423	83	84	2910	2.4	9.1	55.9	30.7	1.9	142550
53565	MINERAL POINT	22310	1918	22.0	31.7	36.6	7.1	2.7	46921	53132	66	55	1454	7.0	18.7	49.2	21.6	3.4	118750
53566	MONROE	24534	6251	25.7	32.0	32.4	6.1	3.8	43838	50000	58	44	4392	4.2	17.4	57.4	19.5	1.6	120045
53569	MONTFORT	16939	436	27.8	39.5	26.8	4.6	1.4	38817	43080	42	25	357	17.1	28.9	40.9	11.5	1.7	96304
53570	MONTICELLO	25096	997	19.2	27.9	41.1	7.3	4.5	52271	58932	76	70	790	3.7	11.0	55.1	26.0	4.3	131566
53572	MOUNT HOREB	28077	3446	12.6	24.6	45.4	12.6	4.8	61975	73251	86	90	2547	1.6	1.8	37.0	51.9	7.7	189248
53573	MUSCODA	19897	1462	32.4	32.7	28.5	4.5	1.9	37306	41755	37	18	1166	23.6	32.8	30.7	11.0	2.0	82211
53574	NEW GLARUS	25720	1349	16.7	29.1	40.1	9.3	4.8	54035	60998	78	74	1080	4.5	4.7	49.0	36.5	5.3	159864
53575	OREGON	29290	5144	9.2	21.8	45.7	17.2	6.1	67081	80307	90	94	4251	3.0	1.8	35.3	55.3	4.6	189361
53576	ORFORDVILLE	24315	853	16.1	27.4	41.5	11.6	3.4	55155	63219	80	77	722	4.9	16.9	52.5	23.4	2.4	121141
53577	PLAIN	23403	566	23.3	30.6	34.3	8.1	3.7	46342	50222	65	53	455	3.3	10.1	48.4	31.9	6.4	143910
53578	PRAIRIE DU SAC	26933	2080	19.5	31.2	32.7	11.2	5.5	49452	56819	71	63	1488	3.7	4.6	46.3	41.4	4.0	168883
53579	REESEVILLE	21504	859	19.4	30.2	42.8	5.5	2.1	50218	56086	72	65	691	9.0	10.9	51.2	26.5	2.5	132738
53580	REWEY	17722	226	27.4	35.8	31.0	3.1	2.7	40216	45000	47	30	176	18.8	19.9	34.1	19.9	7.4	105263
53581	RICHLAND CENTER	19388	4205	34.4	33.6	25.7	4.6	1.8	35218	39766	28	9	2930	12.5	29.3	44.4	12.0	1.8	99339
53582	RIDGEWAY	22567	452	22.1	29.4	38.1	8.2	2.2	48685	54497	70	61	371	4.6	14.6	44.7	28.6	7.6	140885
53583	SAUK CITY	24860	2228	20.9	28.9	38.1	9.3	3.0	50184	57737	72	65	1629	1.4	4.1	54.3	35.7	4.5	157772
53585	SHARON	21182	970	17.7	33.3	39.3	7.7	2.0	49056	57323	70	62	770	0.8	11.6	59.0	23.3	5.5	136964
53586	SHULLSBURG	19005	856	30.8	33.8	28.6	5.1	1.6	38565	43562	41	23	665	16.4	33.8	39.7	8.0	2.1	89667
53587	SOUTH WAYNE	20688	524	27.1	32.6	30.7	7.4	2.1	42355	47183	54	39	414	13.5	26.8	43.0	13.0	3.6	103533
53588	SPRING GREEN	24422	1618	19.8	29.1	38.4	8.1	4.6	50738	57225	73	67	1265	6.5	11.8	47.2	30.5	4.0	143219
53589	STOUGHTON	27668	7906	14.8	25.0	41.5	13.6	5.1	60081	71494	84	86	6038	2.6	3.0	48.1	42.3	4.0	169841
53590	SUN PRAIRIE	28657	11288	11.9	24.7	43.3	14.8	5.3	62753	75870	87	91	7790	0.6	1.4	43.3	52.4	2.3	182047
53593	VERONA	36163	5734	10.2	16.3	42.3	19.9	11.3	75796	89168	94	98	4575	0.9	0.6	27.0	58.3	13.2	217768
53594	WATERLOO	25693	1964	15.4	28.6	41.6	9.8	4.6	55010	62154	80	77	1463	7.3	6.3	51.7	32.3	2.5	152203
53597	WAUNAKEE	32049	5396	9.0	23.2	43.3	16.9	7.6	65313	77645	89	93	3924	1.8	0.1	24.9	67.2	6.1	212147
53598	WINDSOR	35501	792	6.9	25.3	43.1	16.4	8.3	64939	77153	88	93	589	0.0	1.9	46.5	48.9	2.7	177399
53703	MADISON	18091	13479	55.2	27.2	13.1	3.0	1.6	21806	25369	3	1	1513	0.7	5.3	39.3	46.3	8.4	183938
53704	MADISON	28590	21962	19.7	32.1	35.9	8.5	3.8	48196	56949	69	59	11871	2.7	6.0	62.2	26.3	2.8	145136
53705	MADISON	38058	11624	21.6	25.9	29.6	11.8	11.1	52665	62557	76	71	6320	0.7	1.3	32.8	56.4	8.8	199691
53706	MADISON	12064	19	89.5	10.5	0.0	0.0	0.0	14566	17391	1	0	0	0.0	0.0	0.0	0.0	0.0	0
53711	MADISON	32740	19490	14.5	24.5	37.9	14.6	8.5	61481	72551	86	89	12075	0.7	1.2	38.5	53.4	6.2	187979
53713	MADISON	22932	9387	28.3	37.0	25.9	5.8	3.0	37451	43958	37	19	2976	17.5	10.5	44.2	21.5	6.3	128263
53714	MADISON	26406	6846	14.5	30.8	42.4	10.6	1.7	53326	63758	77	72	4444	1.5	2.7	75.3	20.0	0.5	140043
53715	MADISON	16310	4630	47.9	30.4	16.7	3.9	1.1	26360	31633	6	1	1061	1.9	3.2	58.7	33.5	2.7	157560
53716	MADISON	28836	8334	13.7	25.4	45.0	12.5	3.3	58517	68142	83	83	6243	1.0	0.6	63.6	31.4	3.4	157600
53717	MADISON	43956	5626	12.6	23.3	32.9	17.0	14.3	68095	82925	90	95	3324	1.3	0.8	21.1	64.2	12.6	235020
53718	MADISON	38007	2511	8.4	22.3	43.6	18.1	7.7	72615	84155	92	97	1788	0.5	0.3	37.6	55.7	6.0	192772
53719	MADISON	32686	10237	11.2	27.6	41.9	13.3	5.9	60907	74935	85	88	4659	1.4	2.5	31.1	59.3	5.6	193007
53726	MADISON	28342	2388	46.0	15.6	19.4	10.8	8.2	29108	34239	11	2	805	0.0	0.0	7.2	71.4	21.4	279369
53801	BAGLEY	18410	367	37.1	37.1	21.3	2.5	2.2	31910	35753	18	2	297	22.6	28.6	25.9	18.5	4.4	87308
53803	BENTON	17225	39	28.2	28.2	35.9	7.7	0.0	43645	48654	58	43	31	6.5	12.9	58.1	19.4	3.2	117188
53804	BLOOMINGTON	18924	629	29.9	37.0	26.7	4.9	1.4	38439	42341	41	22	511	26.0	30.9	29.0	11.4	2.7	79405
53805	BOSCOBEL	17619	2043	33.6	36.8	25.4	2.7	1.5	36739	41011	34	15	1493	19.2	32.2	36.5	10.5	1.7	88534
53806	CASSVILLE	18338	850	37.4	35.7	21.7	3.8	1.5	33343	37247	22	5	649	26.7	34.4	29.4	8.5	1.1	78559
53807	CUBA CITY	20842	2550	24.2	33.9	33.2	6.5	2.2	43434	48919	57	43	2023	7.0	26.4	51.2	12.8	2.6	108606
53809	FENNIMORE	19991	1557	30.1	34.4	29.0	5.2	1.4	39019	43176	43	25	1149	15.7	30.3	38.1	13.1	2.9	96643
53810	GLEN HAVEN	16032	189	35.5	36.5	23.3	4.2	0.5	33691	37154	23	5	150	20.7	26.7	30.0	18.7	4.0	95000
53811	HAZEL GREEN	20692	1367	22.1	34.5	34.4	6.7	2.3	44068	49586	59	45	1085	11.2	25.0	46.2	15.5	2.2	106804
53813	LANCASTER	19339	2406	30.4	32.5	29.3	5.7	2.1	38439	42464	41	22	1788	10.5	28.2	45.6	14.3	1.5	102305
53816	MOUNT HOPE	19730	239	28.9	37.2	27.2	5.0	1.7	39176	42334	43	26	191	28.8	24.6	28.3	14.7	3.7	82778
53818	PLATTEVILLE	19965	4683	29.6	31.8	29.3	7.0	2.4	40794	45605	49	33	2709	7.3	19.4	54.3	16.6	2.4	115273
53820	POTOSI	19785	1104	23.9	35.7	33.5	5.8	1.1	42436	47454	54	40	913	15.2	25.0	43.6	14.9	1.3	103542
53821	PRAIRIE DU CHIEN	21782	3407	30.7	31.8	28.7	5.7	3.1	39613	45159	45	27	2611	17.9	25.1	44.2	11.6	1.2	100227
53825	STITZER	17426	157	26.8	33.8	30.6	6.4	2.6	42099	45759	53	38	127	15.0	16.5	44.1	21.3	3.2	115761
53826	WAUZEKA	18655	646	28.5	31.4	33.4	5.4	1.2	40762	45245	49	33	528	23.7	26.1	37.1	10.8	2.3	90278
53827	WOODMAN	18366	159	27.0	38.4	29.6	4.4	0.6	39762	43515	45	28	127	32.3	24.4	26.8	13.4	3.2	76111
53901	PORTAGE	22749	5550	24.6	31.8	35.1	6.0	2.5	44699	50685	60	48	3704	6.7	13.3	56.0	21.7	2.3	123502
53910	ADAMS	17816	1628	37.7	34.3	22.7	3.9	1.4	32787	36416	20	3	1213	22.8	34.7	35.5	6.6	0.3	81757
53911	ARLINGTON	25463	571	13.5	28.9	43.1	10.2	4.4	56232	63382	81	79	435	0.9	4.1	47.6	43.5	3.9	171062
53913	BARABOO	23150	8411	23.7	32.4	34.9	6.4	2.7	45277	51198	62	50	6060	11.4	14.9	48.3	22.8	2.6	122141
53916	BEAVER DAM	23255	9002	21.8	33.4	35.6	6.6	2.6	45980	51556	64	52	6330	7.0	13.0	55.7	22.8	1.4	122604
53919	BRANDON	20484	1036	19.0	29.1	42.5	7.2	2.2	51220	56884	74	67	885	4.2	20.9	51.4	22.3	1.2	120304
53920	BRIGGSVILLE	23607	238	18.5	35.7	39.1	5.9	0.8	46735	52266	66	55	200	6.0	20.5	48.5	21.5	3.5	118085
53922	BURNETT	25024	354	15.0	24.9	45.5	12.4	2.3	59676	64922	84	85	305	3.6	12.1	46.6	33.1	4.6	152679
53923	CAMBRIA	18665	941	22.4	34.2	36.0	5.4	1.9	45035	50886	61	49	751	8.4	19.2	49.0	20.4	3.1	119196
53924	CAZENOVIA	19270	612	28.9	32.7	30.7	4.1	3.6	40000	44604	46	29	497	17.5	20.3	42.3	17.7	2.2	108644
53925	COLUMBUS	25762	2998	19.0	28.1	42.2	8.3	2.5	52067	59691	76	70	2110	4.1	5.6	52.8	33.6	4.0	152328
53926	DALTON	16907	524	21.0	39.1	33.8	4.2	1.9	42691	47692	55	40	441	7.7	24.5	44.9	20.6	2.3	115309
53929	ELROY	20349	1216	28.7	32.5	32.0	4.6	2.2	40267	44432	47	31	924	17.5	35.0	33.6	11.9	2.1	87195
53930	ENDEAVOR	18478	489	26.6	28.8	38.9	3.9	1.8	45388	47521	62	50	407	15.7	17.7	49.9	14.5	2.2	110842
53932	FALL RIVER	23189	874	18.2	27.2	41.4	10.6	2.5	53431	60284	78	73	712	7.7	8.6	47.1	35.1	1.5	150000
53933	FOX LAKE	19419	1210	20.3	34.6	36.3	6.0	2.9	45972	51675	64	52	996	4.9	16.5	45.8	28.8	4.0	131111
53934	FRIENDSHIP	19665	2120	36.0	35.0	23.3	4.0	1.8	32330	36408	19	3	1737	21.8	32.6	33.9	10.7	1.0	84650
53936	GRAND MARSH	18407	502	30.3	38.7	26.1	3.8	1.2	36387	41132	33	13	418	23.4	25.6	38.5	11.7	0.7	91739
53937	HILLPOINT	17293	345	26.1	31.3	34.5	7.0	1.2	44219	48584	59	46	286	5.9	12.9	43.0	28.0	10.1	144853
53939	KINGSTON	22926	86	19.8	39.5	33.7	3.5	3.5	43150	47772	56	41	72	8.3	29.2	43.1	18.1	1.4	108929
53941	LA VALLE	21362	1056	20.8	33.6	34.5	7.6	3.5	47217	52918	67	56	905	8.1	15.8	45.6	27.3	3.2	135335
53943	LOGANVILLE	19407	398	21.9	34.7	35.4	5.8	2.3	43674	48161	58	44	312	5.5	15.1	48.4	23.1	8.0	123571
53944	LYNDON STATION	21408	779	24.4	36.3	30.7	5.9	2.7	40876	45508	49	34	638	16.5	20.4	42.2	18.2	2.8	111634
53946	MARKESAN	23964	1727	22.2	32.7	34.8	7.2	3.1	45914	51071	64	52	1356	4.6	19.1	49.8	19.7	6.9	122475
53947	MARQUETTE	21984	69	26.1	31.9	37.7	4.4	0.0	42739	48646	55	41	59	3.4	15.3	42.4	32.2	6.8	151786
53948	MAUSTON	21207	3343	30.2	34.9	27.8	4.8	2.5	38528	43254	41	23	2449	20.9	33.5	32.6	11.6	1.4	84401
53949	MONTELLO	18085	2506	30.5	36.7	27.7	3.6	1.6	37676	40980	38	19	2046	12.6	22.0	47.0	16.6	1.8	109606
53950	NEW LISBON	22418	1876	29.9	34.4	29.2	4.3	2.3	38728	43054	42	24	1488	18.2	32.1	37.0	11.6	1.1	89704
	WISCONSIN	25041		22.2	28.8	35.0	9.6	4.2	48930	56561				7.0	14.9	46.8	27.8	3.6	134326
	UNITED STATES	25866		24.7	27.1	30.8	10.9	6.5	48124	56710				10.9	15.0	33.7	30.1	10.4	145905

ZIP CODE #	POST OFFICE NAME	FINANCIAL SERVICES: Auto Loan	FINANCIAL SERVICES: Home Loan	FINANCIAL SERVICES: Invest-ments	FINANCIAL SERVICES: Retire-ment Plans	THE HOME: Home Improvements: Home Repair	THE HOME: Home Improvements: Lawn & Garden	THE HOME: Furnishings: Comput-ers & Hard-ware	THE HOME: Furnishings: Major Appli-ances	THE HOME: Furnishings: TV, Radio, Sound Equip-ment	THE HOME: Furnishings: Furni-ture	ENTERTAINMENT: Dine out/ Carry out	ENTERTAINMENT: Sports Equip-ment	ENTERTAINMENT: Fees & Tickets	ENTERTAINMENT: Toys & Games	ENTERTAINMENT: Travel	ENTERTAINMENT: Cable TV	PERSONAL: Apparel & Services	PERSONAL: Auto Repairs	PERSONAL: Health Insur-ance	PERSONAL: Pets & Supplies
53553	LINDEN	83	70	54	70	74	83	72	77	77	71	93	88	69	92	72	78	87	76	84	92
53554	LIVINGSTON	84	58	30	55	68	76	58	71	66	57	78	86	49	76	60	70	71	70	85	99
53555	LODI	103	107	100	106	108	111	99	103	97	99	121	122	100	124	101	96	118	101	100	122
53556	LONE ROCK	84	74	60	72	78	85	72	78	76	71	92	91	70	93	73	77	87	76	83	96
53557	LOWELL	87	77	59	74	82	88	72	80	76	72	93	95	70	95	74	78	88	77	86	102
53558	MC FARLAND	108	129	140	130	126	127	118	117	111	118	139	136	124	146	120	108	139	114	106	129
53559	MARSHALL	100	101	91	99	103	106	93	98	93	93	115	116	94	118	95	92	112	96	97	118
53560	MAZOMANIE	96	112	116	112	109	108	103	103	97	104	122	121	107	126	104	93	121	101	92	114
53561	MERRIMAC	107	89	65	83	97	107	83	96	91	83	110	114	78	110	87	95	103	94	109	128
53562	MIDDLETON	114	127	152	132	124	127	126	121	119	126	151	145	129	152	125	115	149	123	110	133
53563	MILTON	99	102	95	101	102	106	96	99	95	96	118	117	97	120	97	94	114	97	97	115
53565	MINERAL POINT	92	73	51	71	80	89	73	82	80	72	95	97	68	95	74	82	89	81	93	105
53566	MONROE	86	79	70	76	82	90	79	83	83	77	101	96	77	102	80	84	96	82	89	99
53569	MONTFORT	83	59	31	56	68	76	58	71	67	57	78	86	50	77	60	70	71	70	85	99
53570	MONTICELLO	97	85	66	83	89	98	83	90	88	82	107	105	81	108	84	90	101	88	97	111
53572	MOUNT HOREB	99	115	118	117	112	110	106	105	98	107	124	123	110	128	105	94	123	102	93	115
53573	MUSCODA	82	62	40	59	69	77	62	72	69	62	83	85	56	81	63	72	77	71	83	94
53574	NEW GLARUS	90	96	92	96	95	98	91	92	88	91	110	108	92	112	91	86	107	91	88	104
53575	OREGON	109	126	133	130	122	121	116	114	108	118	136	134	121	139	115	103	135	112	101	126
53576	ORFORDVILLE	106	94	72	90	100	107	87	97	92	87	113	115	86	115	90	95	107	94	104	124
53577	PLAIN	103	74	42	70	85	95	73	88	83	72	98	106	64	96	75	86	90	87	104	122
53578	PRAIRIE DU SAC	98	93	83	91	97	106	91	97	94	90	115	111	90	117	93	96	110	95	103	114
53579	REESEVILLE	85	75	59	73	79	87	73	79	77	73	94	92	71	95	74	79	89	78	85	97
53580	REWEY	90	63	33	59	73	82	62	77	71	61	84	92	53	82	64	75	76	76	91	107
53581	RICHLAND CENTER	71	59	47	57	63	72	62	66	67	60	80	77	58	79	62	69	75	66	74	81
53582	RIDGEWAY	88	81	65	78	85	90	75	82	78	75	95	97	74	98	77	79	91	79	86	103
53583	SAUK CITY	92	87	75	86	89	97	85	89	87	83	106	103	83	107	85	87	101	87	93	105
53585	SHARON	88	77	59	75	81	89	75	82	80	75	97	95	73	97	76	82	92	80	89	100
53586	SHULLSBURG	76	61	44	60	66	74	62	69	67	61	80	80	57	80	62	69	75	68	77	87
53587	SOUTH WAYNE	85	71	51	68	77	83	67	76	72	67	87	91	64	88	69	74	82	74	84	100
53588	SPRING GREEN	106	81	50	77	91	100	78	93	87	77	104	111	70	103	81	91	96	91	107	126
53589	STOUGHTON	96	106	110	107	104	105	102	101	97	101	121	119	103	124	101	93	119	100	92	112
53590	SUN PRAIRIE	102	110	115	114	108	109	106	105	101	107	127	124	108	129	105	96	125	105	95	116
53593	VERONA	134	157	163	162	152	150	143	141	132	146	167	164	150	172	142	126	166	137	124	155
53594	WATERLOO	100	96	83	95	97	103	93	97	94	92	115	114	91	116	92	93	111	96	98	114
53597	WAUNAKEE	116	133	138	136	129	128	123	121	115	124	145	142	128	149	122	110	143	119	108	134
53598	WINDSOR	121	135	152	139	132	133	132	129	124	132	157	153	134	159	131	119	155	129	115	141
53703	MADISON	47	32	44	37	32	37	55	43	54	48	67	58	47	62	46	48	64	51	40	48
53704	MADISON	82	82	98	87	81	86	89	85	86	88	109	101	88	107	86	82	106	88	78	93
53705	MADISON	103	106	133	111	104	112	114	107	110	112	139	129	114	137	111	106	137	112	100	118
53706	MADISON	25	15	19	17	15	18	29	21	28	25	35	30	24	32	23	25	33	26	20	24
53711	MADISON	104	112	129	116	109	113	113	109	108	113	136	129	115	136	111	103	134	110	99	120
53713	MADISON	74	64	77	71	62	67	77	71	75	76	95	87	73	89	71	70	93	77	64	79
53714	MADISON	80	85	95	86	83	88	86	84	84	85	106	98	88	108	86	82	104	85	80	92
53715	MADISON	49	36	47	40	36	41	56	46	55	50	69	60	49	64	49	50	66	53	43	51
53716	MADISON	86	99	112	99	97	101	95	93	91	95	114	108	99	118	96	90	113	92	88	102
53717	MADISON	129	128	150	137	125	131	135	129	130	136	165	155	134	160	130	123	162	134	117	143
53718	MADISON	107	124	147	128	122	124	120	117	113	120	143	139	124	147	120	109	141	117	105	128
53719	MADISON	104	100	109	109	96	99	105	101	100	107	128	121	103	122	99	94	125	104	89	112
53726	MADISON	83	65	92	71	63	73	99	78	96	88	121	103	88	115	86	88	116	90	72	88
53801	BAGLEY	75	53	28	50	61	69	52	64	60	51	70	78	44	69	54	63	64	63	77	90
53803	BENTON	87	61	32	57	71	79	60	74	69	59	81	90	51	80	62	73	74	73	88	103
53804	BLOOMINGTON	72	64	53	60	69	76	63	69	68	61	83	80	61	86	65	71	78	68	78	86
53805	BOSCOBEL	69	58	45	56	62	70	59	64	63	57	76	74	56	75	59	66	71	63	72	79
53806	CASSVILLE	70	54	36	51	59	68	56	63	63	54	74	72	51	72	57	66	68	63	74	79
53807	CUBA CITY	85	71	52	69	76	85	71	78	77	70	92	90	67	91	72	79	86	77	87	96
53809	FENNIMORE	81	61	39	59	68	78	64	73	71	62	84	84	57	81	64	75	77	72	85	93
53810	GLEN HAVEN	75	53	28	50	61	69	52	64	60	51	70	77	44	69	54	63	64	63	77	89
53811	HAZEL GREEN	87	73	54	71	78	86	72	79	77	71	93	93	68	93	73	79	87	78	87	100
53813	LANCASTER	76	63	48	61	68	77	65	71	70	63	85	81	61	84	65	73	79	70	80	86
53816	MOUNT HOPE	85	59	31	56	69	77	58	72	67	58	79	87	50	77	61	71	72	71	86	101
53818	PLATTEVILLE	74	64	67	65	65	73	73	71	75	70	92	87	69	90	70	73	89	75	73	84
53820	POTOSI	80	71	54	68	75	81	66	73	70	66	86	87	65	87	68	72	81	71	79	94
53821	PRAIRIE DU CHIEN	81	69	55	66	74	84	70	76	75	68	91	87	66	91	71	79	85	75	86	93
53825	STITZER	92	64	34	61	75	84	64	79	73	63	86	95	54	84	66	77	78	77	94	109
53826	WAUZEKA	80	65	47	64	70	79	66	73	72	65	86	85	62	85	66	73	80	72	81	90
53827	WOODMAN	81	58	32	55	67	75	57	70	65	57	77	84	50	76	59	68	70	69	82	96
53901	PORTAGE	83	74	62	72	77	85	74	79	78	73	95	91	71	94	74	79	90	78	85	94
53910	ADAMS	70	54	36	50	60	69	54	63	61	53	72	72	48	70	56	65	66	62	75	81
53911	ARLINGTON	106	95	73	90	100	107	88	97	93	88	113	115	86	115	90	95	107	94	105	125
53913	BARABOO	83	77	67	76	80	86	76	80	78	75	96	94	74	96	77	79	92	80	84	96
53916	BEAVER DAM	84	77	66	75	80	87	75	80	79	74	96	93	74	97	76	80	92	79	85	96
53919	BRANDON	90	79	61	76	83	91	76	83	81	75	98	97	74	99	77	82	93	81	90	104
53920	BRIGGSVILLE	94	68	39	63	78	88	66	81	76	65	89	97	57	87	69	80	82	80	96	112
53922	BURNETT	107	96	73	91	101	108	88	98	94	88	114	117	87	117	91	96	109	95	106	126
53923	CAMBRIA	87	71	51	69	77	85	70	78	75	69	91	92	65	91	71	77	85	77	87	100
53924	CAZENOVIA	86	70	48	67	77	83	66	76	72	66	87	91	62	88	69	75	82	75	85	101
53925	COLUMBUS	96	89	77	88	92	99	88	92	91	87	111	107	87	112	88	91	106	91	96	109
53926	DALTON	79	70	54	67	74	80	66	73	70	66	85	86	64	86	67	72	81	71	79	92
53929	ELROY	76	67	55	65	71	80	67	72	72	65	87	83	65	89	68	74	82	71	80	88
53930	ENDEAVOR	82	70	51	66	75	81	65	74	70	65	85	88	63	86	67	73	80	72	82	97
53932	FALL RIVER	98	87	66	83	92	99	80	89	85	80	104	106	79	106	83	88	99	87	96	115
53933	FOX LAKE	74	59	42	54	66	73	56	66	62	55	74	77	51	74	59	66	69	65	76	89
53934	FRIENDSHIP	73	57	39	52	64	73	56	66	63	55	74	76	50	73	58	67	69	65	78	87
53936	GRAND MARSH	74	58	40	52	65	73	55	66	62	54	73	77	49	72	58	66	68	65	78	90
53937	HILLPOINT	82	72	55	69	77	82	67	75	71	67	87	89	65	88	69	73	82	73	81	97
53939	KINGSTON	78	70	53	66	74	79	64	71	68	64	83	85	63	85	66	70	79	69	77	92
53941	LA VALLE	97	77	53	71	86	95	73	86	81	72	97	102	67	96	76	85	90	84	99	116
53943	LOGANVILLE	92	67	38	63	76	85	65	79	74	64	87	95	57	86	68	77	80	78	93	109
53944	LYNDON STATION	89	70	44	64	76	84	66	77	74	66	89	92	61	87	67	78	83	75	88	104
53946	MARKESAN	92	77	57	74	83	93	75	84	81	74	98	98	71	98	77	84	92	83	94	108
53947	MARQUETTE	89	70	48	63	79	88	66	79	75	65	88	93	59	87	70	80	82	78	94	109
53948	MAUSTON	81	68	51	65	72	81	67	74	73	66	88	86	64	87	68	76	82	73	83	92
53949	MONTELLO	65	50	33	47	55	63	51	58	57	50	68	67	46	66	52	60	63	58	68	74
53950	NEW LISBON	86	71	51	67	76	85	70	78	76	69	91	91	65	89	71	79	85	77	88	100
	WISCONSIN	89	86	85	86	88	94	86	88	87	85	108	103	86	109	86	87	104	88	89	103
	UNITED STATES	100	100	100	100	100	100	100	100	100	100	100	100	100	100	100	100	100	100	100	100

#	POST OFFICE NAME	COUNTY FIPS CODE	POPULATION			2000-2004 ANNUAL RATE		HOUSEHOLDS					FAMILIES		
			2000	2004	2009	% Rate	State Centile	2000	2004	2009	% Annual Rate 2000-2004	2004 Average HH Size	2000	2004	% Annual Rate 2000-2004
53951	NORTH FREEDOM	111	1540	1605	1717	1.0	56	571	608	664	1.5	2.63	425	447	1.2
53952	OXFORD	077	2658	2685	2849	0.2	25	1105	1142	1235	0.8	2.35	768	783	0.5
53954	PARDEEVILLE	021	6660	6959	7275	1.0	58	2543	2734	2925	1.7	2.50	1839	1951	1.4
53955	POYNETTE	021	5505	5815	6124	1.3	69	2193	2374	2555	1.9	2.45	1544	1649	1.6
53956	RANDOLPH	021	3236	3278	3364	0.3	27	1190	1247	1319	1.1	2.38	860	886	0.7
53959	REEDSBURG	111	11560	12652	13891	2.2	88	4469	5004	5620	2.7	2.47	3066	3388	2.4
53960	RIO	021	3200	3633	3965	3.0	95	1227	1420	1581	3.5	2.53	912	1043	3.2
53961	ROCK SPRINGS	111	715	768	835	1.7	81	262	289	321	2.3	2.65	206	224	2.0
53963	WAUPUN	039	13722	13796	14025	0.1	20	4300	4439	4644	0.8	2.44	3021	3078	0.4
53964	WESTFIELD	077	3156	3195	3413	0.3	27	1308	1359	1485	0.9	2.34	888	911	0.6
53965	WISCONSIN DELLS	001	9691	10691	11545	2.1	88	3937	4399	4845	2.7	2.40	2673	2950	2.4
53968	WONEWOC	057	2541	2613	2759	0.7	42	1000	1048	1129	1.1	2.48	716	741	0.8
54001	AMERY	095	7846	8550	9405	2.0	86	3122	3493	3941	2.7	2.40	2183	2417	2.4
54002	BALDWIN	109	4751	5690	7032	4.3	98	1812	2228	2825	5.0	2.52	1293	1569	4.7
54003	BELDENVILLE	093	1036	1246	1435	4.4	99	367	454	535	5.1	2.74	286	348	4.7
54004	CLAYTON	005	2505	2564	2685	0.6	37	938	986	1058	1.2	2.60	690	716	0.9
54005	CLEAR LAKE	095	2809	3044	3343	1.9	85	1043	1160	1304	2.5	2.62	709	776	2.2
54006	CUSHING	095	1831	1940	2098	1.4	72	707	771	855	2.1	2.52	519	557	1.7
54007	DEER PARK	109	1282	1404	1627	2.2	89	453	510	607	2.8	2.75	354	395	2.6
54009	DRESSER	095	1968	2230	2501	3.0	95	766	886	1014	3.5	2.51	553	632	3.2
54011	ELLSWORTH	093	6128	6702	7356	2.1	88	2304	2587	2911	2.8	2.54	1641	1816	2.4
54013	GLENWOOD CITY	109	3318	3768	4535	3.0	95	1183	1378	1702	3.7	2.70	881	1016	3.4
54014	HAGER CITY	093	2043	2267	2520	2.5	91	767	874	996	3.1	2.59	587	662	2.9
54015	HAMMOND	109	1910	2504	3230	6.6	100	682	926	1188	7.5	2.65	523	703	7.2
54016	HUDSON	109	22756	26831	32937	4.0	98	8358	10127	12761	4.6	2.63	6150	7374	4.4
54017	NEW RICHMOND	109	11941	14033	17164	3.9	98	4503	5455	6867	4.6	2.51	3050	3638	4.2
54020	OSCEOLA	095	6198	7292	8325	3.9	98	2297	2764	3224	4.5	2.63	1665	1975	4.1
54021	PRESCOTT	093	5563	5854	6294	1.2	65	2016	2173	2392	1.8	2.67	1508	1602	1.4
54022	RIVER FALLS	093	19014	20570	22885	1.9	84	6503	7291	8414	2.7	2.52	4140	4580	2.4
54023	ROBERTS	109	2489	3112	3933	5.4	99	894	1155	1502	6.2	2.69	673	857	5.9
54024	SAINT CROIX FALLS	095	3610	3682	3936	0.5	33	1482	1556	1707	1.2	2.29	951	981	0.7
54025	SOMERSET	109	4868	5974	7487	4.9	99	1795	2260	2901	5.6	2.64	1341	1667	5.3
54026	STAR PRAIRIE	095	1635	1787	2028	2.1	88	583	654	760	2.7	2.73	448	497	2.5
54027	WILSON	109	801	930	1134	3.6	97	298	356	445	4.3	2.61	234	277	4.1
54028	WOODVILLE	109	2085	2417	2940	3.5	97	791	944	1179	4.3	2.51	575	678	4.0
54082	HOULTON	109	1337	1490	1781	2.6	93	499	568	696	3.1	2.62	387	437	2.9
54101	ABRAMS	083	2445	2858	3298	3.7	97	875	1056	1252	4.5	2.70	666	794	4.2
54102	AMBERG	075	934	910	923	-0.6	3	421	422	440	0.1	2.16	275	271	-0.3
54103	ARMSTRONG CREEK	041	517	521	535	0.2	23	231	237	249	0.6	2.20	148	150	0.3
54104	ATHELSTANE	075	1035	1062	1090	0.6	39	455	482	509	1.4	2.20	314	326	0.9
54106	BLACK CREEK	087	4915	5190	5541	1.3	68	1790	1960	2154	2.2	2.65	1369	1474	1.8
54107	BONDUEL	115	3290	3473	3635	1.3	67	1252	1357	1452	1.9	2.55	926	989	1.6
54110	BRILLION	015	5222	5358	5759	0.6	39	1952	2069	2290	1.4	2.58	1438	1502	1.0
54111	CECIL	115	2079	2143	2230	0.7	44	817	866	924	1.4	2.47	616	645	1.1
54112	COLEMAN	075	2401	2574	2749	1.7	79	944	1047	1152	2.5	2.46	677	740	2.1
54113	COMBINED LOCKS	087	2412	2872	3263	4.2	98	880	1080	1259	4.9	2.65	728	882	4.6
54114	CRIVITZ	075	4968	5393	5731	2.0	86	2179	2444	2677	2.7	2.17	1486	1640	2.4
54115	DE PERE	009	30959	33774	36479	2.1	87	11206	12639	14048	2.9	2.54	7879	8742	2.5
54119	DUNBAR	075	1242	1262	1282	0.4	30	246	260	273	1.3	3.13	173	179	0.8
54120	FENCE	037	445	447	450	0.1	19	207	216	225	1.0	2.07	134	138	0.7
54121	FLORENCE	037	2893	2896	2900	0.0	16	1205	1244	1285	0.8	2.28	812	827	0.4
54124	GILLETT	083	3625	3829	4186	1.3	69	1417	1523	1698	1.7	2.49	999	1059	1.4
54125	GOODMAN	075	736	762	785	0.8	48	317	338	358	1.5	2.25	214	224	1.1
54126	GREENLEAF	009	3534	3852	4153	2.1	87	1175	1321	1460	2.8	2.91	953	1059	2.5
54128	GRESHAM	115	1957	2012	2068	0.7	41	697	732	769	1.2	2.72	515	533	0.8
54129	HILBERT	015	4039	4399	4921	2.0	86	1461	1640	1888	2.8	2.68	1087	1204	2.4
54130	KAUKAUNA	087	21383	22821	24596	1.5	75	7841	8622	9542	2.3	2.62	5690	6177	2.0
54135	KESHENA	078	4173	4319	4491	0.8	47	1248	1328	1418	1.5	3.22	984	1039	1.3
54136	KIMBERLY	087	5829	6066	6460	0.9	54	2322	2486	2716	1.6	2.44	1587	1667	1.2
54137	KRAKOW	115	1035	1157	1260	2.7	93	390	449	500	3.4	2.58	309	352	3.1
54138	LAKEWOOD	083	911	1066	1229	3.8	97	413	494	582	4.3	2.16	290	342	4.0
54139	LENA	083	3124	3406	3788	2.1	87	1217	1362	1552	2.7	2.49	870	960	2.3
54140	LITTLE CHUTE	087	8945	9315	9888	1.0	55	3300	3539	3856	1.7	2.61	2359	2486	1.2
54141	LITTLE SUAMICO	083	1905	2078	2311	2.1	87	722	807	919	2.7	2.57	562	622	2.4
54143	MARINETTE	075	15961	15561	15744	-0.6	3	6690	6704	6968	0.1	2.27	4237	4179	-0.3
54149	MOUNTAIN	083	1262	1507	1755	4.3	98	581	711	847	4.9	2.12	396	478	4.5
54150	NEOPIT	078	16	16	16	0.0	15	6	6	6	0.0	2.67	5	5	0.0
54151	NIAGARA	075	4247	4886	5382	3.4	96	1697	2022	2297	4.2	2.39	1170	1369	3.8
54153	OCONTO	083	7319	7812	8622	1.6	76	2875	3153	3570	2.2	2.43	1992	2154	1.9
54154	OCONTO FALLS	083	5073	5308	5756	1.1	60	1991	2133	2369	1.6	2.44	1352	1429	1.3
54155	ONEIDA	087	4174	4467	4780	1.6	78	1372	1512	1658	2.3	2.95	1149	1252	2.0
54156	PEMBINE	075	1813	1825	1858	0.2	21	762	792	831	0.9	2.10	524	537	0.6
54157	PESHTIGO	075	5555	5552	5651	0.0	14	2098	2147	2243	0.5	2.43	1499	1511	0.2
54159	PORTERFIELD	075	1558	1649	1724	1.3	71	625	685	738	2.2	2.41	480	520	1.9
54161	POUND	075	2783	3208	3568	3.4	97	1124	1334	1525	4.1	2.40	794	929	3.8
54162	PULASKI	115	8003	8994	9847	2.8	94	2845	3288	3687	3.5	2.72	2170	2475	3.1
54165	SEYMOUR	087	7189	7427	7829	0.8	46	2558	2723	2945	1.5	2.69	1930	2023	1.1
54166	SHAWANO	115	16171	16252	16605	0.1	20	6656	6866	7179	0.7	2.28	4387	4456	0.4
54169	SHERWOOD	015	1521	1937	2311	5.9	100	559	734	901	6.6	2.64	454	590	6.4
54170	SHIOCTON	087	3780	4149	4519	2.2	89	1382	1568	1754	3.0	2.62	1056	1178	2.6
54171	SOBIESKI	083	2722	2971	3305	2.1	87	1017	1158	2.7	2.92	757	841	2.5	
54173	SUAMICO	009	3398	3917	4346	3.4	97	1207	1426	1619	4.0	2.74	996	1164	3.7
54174	SURING	083	3067	3253	3564	1.4	72	1265	1373	1539	2.0	2.33	881	942	1.6
54175	TOWNSEND	083	984	1127	1286	3.2	96	451	529	618	3.8	2.13	318	368	3.5
54177	WAUSAUKEE	075	3310	3361	3443	0.4	29	1364	1423	1496	1.0	2.36	948	975	0.7
54180	WRIGHTSTOWN	009	1759	2074	2329	4.0	98	645	783	901	4.7	2.65	489	587	4.4
54201	ALGOMA	061	5673	5629	5765	-0.2	9	2351	2402	2526	0.5	2.31	1564	1574	0.2
54202	BAILEYS HARBOR	029	1228	1308	1396	1.5	74	591	651	717	2.3	2.01	381	412	1.9
54204	BRUSSELS	029	1678	1787	1908	1.5	74	628	689	757	2.2	2.59	483	524	1.9
54205	CASCO	061	2116	2185	2269	0.8	45	750	800	853	1.5	2.73	596	628	1.2
54208	DENMARK	009	5792	6197	6603	1.6	78	2107	2321	2536	2.3	2.66	1587	1722	1.9
54209	EGG HARBOR	029	1183	1237	1305	1.1	59	502	546	596	2.0	2.27	357	383	1.7
54210	ELLISON BAY	029	943	981	1033	0.9	53	420	448	485	1.5	2.19	298	313	1.2
54212	FISH CREEK	029	1055	1102	1164	1.0	58	466	502	547	1.8	2.20	319	339	1.4
54213	FORESTVILLE	029	1328	1464	1590	2.3	90	510	578	646	3.0	2.53	386	433	2.7
	WISCONSIN					0.8					1.4	2.44			1.1
	UNITED STATES					1.2					1.3	2.58			1.1

ZIP CODE #	POST OFFICE NAME	RACE (%) White 2000	White 2004	Black 2000	Black 2004	Asian/Pacific 2000	Asian/Pacific 2004	% Hispanic Origin 2000	% Hispanic Origin 2004	2004 AGE DISTRIBUTION (%) 0-4	5-9	10-14	15-19	20-24	25-44	45-64	65-84	85+	18+	MEDIAN AGE 2004	% 2004 Males	% 2004 Females
53951	NORTH FREEDOM	97.0	96.6	0.1	0.1	0.2	0.3	3.3	3.8	7.2	7.7	7.8	7.0	5.3	28.9	25.2	9.7	1.3	73.0	36.7	51.5	48.5
53952	OXFORD	97.7	97.5	0.5	0.6	0.6	0.6	1.5	1.6	5.3	5.4	6.4	6.0	5.1	24.1	28.7	17.2	1.9	79.1	43.7	50.7	49.4
53954	PARDEEVILLE	98.2	97.9	0.2	0.2	0.4	0.5	1.6	1.9	6.6	6.8	7.1	6.4	5.3	26.4	26.3	13.1	2.0	75.4	39.7	50.9	49.1
53955	POYNETTE	97.7	97.4	0.1	0.1	0.2	0.3	1.0	1.2	6.2	6.6	7.4	6.5	5.3	28.8	27.8	10.1	1.3	75.6	39.1	52.1	47.9
53956	RANDOLPH	95.3	94.5	3.2	3.8	0.2	0.2	1.8	2.1	6.0	6.1	6.7	6.5	7.1	27.7	23.2	13.6	3.1	77.3	38.3	53.5	46.5
53959	REEDSBURG	97.6	97.4	0.1	0.2	0.2	0.3	1.3	1.5	6.9	6.8	7.3	7.1	6.3	27.5	23.4	12.3	2.6	74.6	37.3	49.2	50.8
53960	RIO	98.1	97.9	0.1	0.1	0.4	0.5	1.4	1.7	6.2	6.5	7.3	6.6	5.7	27.6	27.0	11.4	1.9	75.9	40.0	50.4	49.6
53961	ROCK SPRINGS	98.7	98.6	0.1	0.1	0.1	0.1	1.3	1.4	5.5	5.6	6.4	6.5	6.3	28.3	29.0	11.2	1.3	78.7	40.3	51.0	49.0
53963	WAUPUN	88.0	86.7	9.9	11.1	0.3	0.4	2.6	2.9	5.2	5.2	6.0	6.6	8.6	34.2	21.9	10.5	1.9	80.0	35.9	59.2	40.8
53964	WESTFIELD	97.8	97.7	0.3	0.3	0.2	0.2	2.0	2.0	5.9	6.0	6.3	6.0	5.9	24.7	27.5	15.8	2.2	78.0	42.1	51.0	49.0
53965	WISCONSIN DELLS	95.7	95.4	0.4	0.5	0.3	0.4	1.5	1.7	5.1	5.4	6.3	6.3	5.6	25.0	29.2	15.2	2.2	79.5	42.8	49.4	50.6
53968	WONEWOC	98.8	98.7	0.1	0.1	0.1	0.2	0.9	1.0	6.1	6.8	7.9	6.6	5.4	24.9	25.4	14.7	2.3	74.7	40.3	49.2	50.8
54001	AMERY	98.5	98.3	0.1	0.1	0.3	0.4	0.7	0.8	5.4	6.1	7.3	6.7	5.5	23.9	27.5	14.7	3.0	76.8	41.9	48.9	51.1
54002	BALDWIN	98.1	97.8	0.1	0.1	0.6	0.8	0.6	0.7	6.5	6.5	6.6	7.2	7.8	26.7	24.2	12.3	2.3	75.7	37.3	49.0	51.0
54003	BELDENVILLE	98.8	98.6	0.2	0.2	0.3	0.3	0.7	0.7	5.7	7.5	7.5	7.5	5.2	29.6	28.8	7.5	0.8	74.6	38.4	51.0	49.0
54004	CLAYTON	98.2	98.1	0.2	0.2	0.3	0.4	0.4	0.5	6.6	6.9	8.2	7.1	6.7	27.4	25.8	10.3	1.1	73.9	37.0	51.6	48.4
54005	CLEAR LAKE	98.4	98.2	0.1	0.1	0.1	0.1	1.6	1.8	6.4	6.7	8.3	7.5	6.8	27.2	24.1	11.1	2.1	74.0	37.1	51.0	49.1
54006	CUSHING	98.5	98.3	0.2	0.3	0.6	0.7	0.6	0.6	5.5	6.0	7.4	7.1	5.7	25.3	30.4	11.3	1.2	76.7	41.1	51.1	48.9
54007	DEER PARK	98.7	98.7	0.0	0.0	0.4	0.4	0.4	0.4	7.1	6.5	7.6	7.5	5.6	28.2	27.2	9.8	0.6	73.6	37.6	52.2	47.8
54009	DRESSER	98.5	98.4	0.2	0.2	0.1	0.1	0.8	0.9	7.2	7.5	7.5	6.1	5.2	30.0	25.4	9.8	1.4	73.9	37.3	50.5	49.5
54011	ELLSWORTH	98.4	98.2	0.1	0.1	0.2	0.2	0.9	1.0	6.7	6.9	7.1	6.8	6.6	29.0	25.0	10.0	2.1	75.3	37.1	50.4	49.6
54013	GLENWOOD CITY	98.3	98.0	0.1	0.1	0.8	1.0	0.5	0.6	6.1	6.8	8.4	7.9	5.7	27.5	24.9	11.0	1.7	73.1	37.4	51.0	49.0
54014	HAGER CITY	98.6	98.4	0.2	0.2	0.2	0.2	0.6	0.8	6.4	6.7	6.8	6.5	5.8	28.8	28.3	9.9	0.9	76.2	38.8	52.9	47.1
54015	HAMMOND	98.5	98.4	0.1	0.1	0.3	0.3	0.4	0.4	6.6	6.5	7.6	8.0	8.0	28.5	24.2	8.5	2.2	74.1	35.5	48.9	51.1
54016	HUDSON	97.8	97.4	0.3	0.3	0.7	0.9	0.9	1.0	7.4	7.5	7.7	6.7	6.3	31.1	25.8	6.5	1.0	73.1	35.6	50.3	49.7
54017	NEW RICHMOND	97.8	97.5	0.6	0.6	0.4	0.5	0.8	1.0	7.1	6.9	7.5	7.0	7.5	29.9	22.8	9.6	1.7	74.2	34.9	49.8	50.2
54020	OSCEOLA	98.1	97.8	0.3	0.3	0.3	0.3	0.8	1.0	7.1	7.5	8.2	7.5	6.8	29.9	23.5	8.4	1.2	72.3	35.5	50.2	49.8
54021	PRESCOTT	98.5	98.2	0.2	0.2	0.2	0.3	1.0	1.2	6.8	6.9	7.5	7.3	7.1	29.4	25.0	8.7	1.3	74.3	36.4	50.4	49.6
54022	RIVER FALLS	97.2	96.8	0.4	0.5	0.8	1.0	0.9	1.0	5.3	5.5	5.9	11.5	17.6	25.4	20.5	6.5	1.6	79.5	27.9	47.3	52.7
54023	ROBERTS	98.5	98.3	0.2	0.3	0.4	0.5	0.6	0.8	6.6	6.9	7.6	6.7	7.0	31.5	26.5	6.6	0.6	74.9	36.2	50.6	49.4
54024	SAINT CROIX FALLS	98.3	98.0	0.2	0.2	0.4	0.5	1.0	1.1	5.9	6.1	6.9	6.7	5.8	25.2	26.3	13.4	3.6	76.5	40.9	49.7	50.4
54025	SOMERSET	97.7	97.3	0.3	0.3	0.6	0.8	0.6	0.7	7.6	7.8	8.1	7.0	5.9	32.5	24.0	6.4	0.6	72.2	34.7	51.0	49.0
54026	STAR PRAIRIE	98.0	97.8	0.1	0.1	0.7	0.9	0.6	0.6	7.1	7.4	7.5	6.7	5.7	29.7	27.1	8.0	0.8	73.9	37.2	51.0	49.0
54027	WILSON	97.1	96.7	0.0	0.0	1.6	2.2	0.5	0.5	5.9	6.7	8.5	7.0	6.0	27.6	27.1	10.5	0.7	74.2	38.4	51.9	48.1
54028	WOODVILLE	97.7	97.3	0.0	0.0	1.0	1.2	0.8	1.0	7.0	7.6	7.9	6.4	5.7	29.7	23.3	10.2	2.2	73.4	36.4	50.1	49.9
54082	HOULTON	97.5	97.3	0.2	0.2	1.1	1.2	0.8	0.8	6.7	7.5	8.1	6.7	5.0	29.7	28.3	7.6	0.5	73.5	37.8	51.8	48.2
54101	ABRAMS	98.2	98.1	0.1	0.1	0.1	0.1	0.6	0.7	6.3	7.0	7.0	6.3	4.8	30.2	29.0	8.6	0.8	75.8	39.2	51.4	48.6
54102	AMBERG	96.6	96.4	1.1	1.2	0.2	0.2	1.1	1.2	4.7	4.8	6.3	7.0	3.6	20.7	32.8	18.8	1.3	79.9	46.6	51.5	48.5
54103	ARMSTRONG CREEK	95.7	95.4	0.6	0.8	0.4	0.4	1.2	1.3	6.0	6.1	6.7	6.5	5.6	22.1	26.3	18.0	2.7	77.2	42.8	49.9	50.1
54104	ATHELSTANE	98.1	97.9	0.2	0.3	0.1	0.2	0.6	0.8	4.0	4.3	5.7	5.1	4.1	18.3	34.8	22.4	1.5	82.9	51.0	52.7	47.3
54106	BLACK CREEK	97.7	97.4	0.0	0.0	0.3	0.4	1.1	1.3	7.1	7.2	7.5	6.4	6.2	30.5	25.3	8.5	1.3	74.3	36.5	51.7	48.3
54107	BONDUEL	97.4	97.0	0.1	0.1	0.2	0.3	1.0	1.1	7.5	7.5	7.4	6.3	5.4	28.7	22.8	12.7	1.8	73.6	37.0	51.1	48.9
54110	BRILLION	98.4	98.2	0.1	0.1	0.2	0.2	0.6	0.7	6.5	6.8	8.0	7.1	6.0	28.9	24.4	10.7	1.6	74.2	36.9	50.0	50.0
54111	CECIL	96.1	95.6	0.1	0.1	0.1	0.2	1.1	1.3	5.6	5.8	6.4	6.3	5.4	23.7	28.3	16.6	2.0	78.3	43.2	51.4	48.6
54112	COLEMAN	98.8	98.7	0.0	0.0	0.1	0.1	0.6	0.8	6.0	6.1	6.8	7.4	6.1	24.4	26.7	14.2	2.3	76.2	40.9	51.4	48.6
54113	COMBINED LOCKS	98.2	97.8	0.2	0.2	0.6	0.8	1.2	1.4	9.6	9.5	8.6	5.8	4.7	31.8	20.6	9.1	0.4	68.0	34.8	50.1	49.9
54114	CRIVITZ	98.0	97.6	0.2	0.2	0.2	0.2	0.8	1.0	4.6	4.9	6.0	5.7	4.5	21.1	30.7	19.8	2.8	80.9	47.1	51.1	49.0
54115	DE PERE	94.5	94.0	0.4	0.5	0.7	0.9	1.1	1.3	7.1	7.1	7.5	8.0	8.8	29.2	22.1	8.7	1.5	74.3	34.1	49.2	50.8
54119	DUNBAR	97.6	97.2	0.1	0.2	0.6	0.8	1.1	1.2	4.2	3.7	4.7	14.9	21.9	22.1	18.8	9.1	0.7	84.6	25.4	48.3	51.7
54120	FENCE	97.8	97.8	0.2	0.2	0.7	0.7	0.2	0.2	3.4	3.6	5.2	5.6	4.3	20.6	35.8	20.1	1.6	84.6	48.7	52.4	47.7
54121	FLORENCE	98.0	97.9	0.1	0.2	0.3	0.3	0.4	0.4	4.7	5.9	6.9	6.3	3.7	25.0	29.2	15.3	3.1	78.3	43.7	51.1	48.9
54124	GILLETT	96.9	96.6	0.1	0.2	0.1	0.2	0.5	0.6	6.1	6.4	7.4	7.1	5.9	26.1	25.4	13.1	2.5	75.6	39.9	50.4	49.6
54125	GOODMAN	97.4	97.1	0.4	0.4	0.4	0.5	0.8	1.1	4.3	4.9	6.4	6.0	4.6	20.3	30.7	20.9	1.8	80.7	47.3	51.3	48.7
54126	GREENLEAF	98.4	98.1	0.2	0.2	0.2	0.2	0.8	1.0	7.8	8.3	8.3	6.7	5.7	30.0	24.4	7.9	0.8	71.4	35.5	51.3	48.7
54128	GRESHAM	68.3	66.8	0.1	0.2	0.2	0.2	2.3	2.5	7.3	7.4	8.6	6.9	6.1	25.6	24.6	12.4	1.3	71.8	37.3	49.4	50.6
54129	HILBERT	98.1	97.8	0.0	0.0	0.6	0.8	0.7	0.8	6.6	7.1	8.0	6.8	6.3	27.8	25.9	10.6	1.1	73.9	37.8	50.8	49.2
54130	KAUKAUNA	96.6	96.1	0.2	0.3	1.5	1.8	0.7	0.9	6.9	7.0	7.8	7.5	6.9	29.3	23.4	9.3	1.9	73.5	36.1	50.0	50.0
54135	KESHENA	12.4	11.8	0.1	0.1	0.0	0.0	2.8	2.9	9.8	9.6	10.6	9.7	7.3	22.8	20.8	9.3	0.3	63.4	28.2	49.2	50.9
54136	KIMBERLY	97.7	97.4	0.2	0.3	0.8	1.0	0.7	0.9	6.8	6.6	7.6	6.5	6.1	31.2	21.1	12.5	1.6	74.8	36.6	49.4	50.6
54137	KRAKOW	98.3	98.0	0.1	0.2	0.4	0.5	0.4	0.4	7.6	7.8	8.0	6.4	5.7	28.7	23.9	10.7	1.1	72.6	36.7	50.7	49.3
54138	LAKEWOOD	97.6	97.5	0.0	0.0	0.1	0.1	0.7	0.8	2.8	3.2	4.7	4.2	3.6	16.6	34.4	28.8	1.7	86.6	54.6	51.6	48.4
54139	LENA	98.4	98.3	0.1	0.1	0.2	0.2	0.6	0.7	5.9	6.3	7.8	6.9	5.2	29.4	24.8	11.8	1.8	75.2	39.1	52.1	47.9
54140	LITTLE CHUTE	96.6	96.0	0.1	0.1	0.9	1.2	2.0	2.3	8.0	7.5	7.8	7.7	7.7	31.0	20.6	8.3	1.4	71.8	32.7	49.2	50.8
54141	LITTLE SUAMICO	97.6	97.4	0.7	0.8	0.3	0.4	0.8	0.9	6.5	7.0	8.1	7.5	6.0	30.6	26.9	6.6	0.8	73.8	37.1	51.7	48.3
54143	MARINETTE	97.8	97.6	0.3	0.3	0.3	0.4	0.8	0.9	5.6	5.6	6.5	6.8	7.0	25.4	26.5	13.4	3.3	78.3	40.7	48.2	51.8
54149	MOUNTAIN	97.7	97.5	0.0	0.0	0.2	0.3	0.6	0.8	3.1	3.4	4.8	4.8	4.8	17.6	33.6	26.1	1.9	85.8	52.1	51.5	48.5
54150	NEOPIT	0.0	0.0	0.0	0.0	0.0	0.0	0.0	0.0	12.5	12.5	12.5	12.5	6.3	37.5	6.3	0.0	0.0	62.5	20.0	43.8	56.3
54151	NIAGARA	98.9	98.9	0.1	0.1	0.2	0.2	0.9	1.1	5.2	6.3	8.3	8.0	4.6	26.9	25.2	13.1	2.5	75.0	39.8	49.5	50.5
54153	OCONTO	97.6	97.3	0.1	0.1	0.3	0.4	0.9	1.1	6.1	6.5	7.1	7.6	6.1	27.0	25.1	12.2	2.4	75.4	38.5	49.7	50.3
54154	OCONTO FALLS	98.4	98.2	0.1	0.2	0.2	0.3	0.4	0.5	6.4	6.4	7.4	7.2	6.3	26.8	24.1	12.5	3.0	75.3	39.0	48.8	51.2
54155	ONEIDA	71.3	69.7	0.2	0.2	0.4	0.5	1.7	1.9	6.8	7.6	8.9	8.0	6.0	23.5	30.7	7.8	0.7	71.6	38.4	48.6	51.4
54156	PEMBINE	97.3	97.0	0.5	0.5	0.4	0.6	1.2	1.4	4.0	4.7	6.3	9.5	8.2	22.8	27.3	15.8	1.3	80.5	41.7	50.5	49.5
54157	PESHTIGO	98.4	98.2	0.1	0.1	0.4	0.5	0.6	0.7	6.1	6.3	6.8	6.5	5.8	24.9	24.8	14.6	4.2	76.7	41.2	48.3	51.7
54159	PORTERFIELD	98.4	98.2	0.1	0.2	0.1	0.1	0.3	0.4	5.0	5.5	6.4	6.2	5.9	25.4	31.4	13.0	1.3	79.3	42.8	51.6	48.4
54161	POUND	98.7	98.6	0.1	0.1	0.1	0.2	0.8	0.8	5.2	5.4	6.6	6.8	4.6	23.6	28.6	17.2	1.9	78.6	43.6	51.5	48.5
54162	PULASKI	98.2	97.9	0.2	0.2	0.4	0.5	0.7	0.9	7.2	7.2	8.1	7.5	6.8	29.7	22.9	9.2	1.3	72.7	35.6	50.8	49.2
54165	SEYMOUR	92.5	92.0	0.1	0.1	0.2	0.2	1.1	1.3	7.4	7.4	8.0	7.7	6.6	29.4	22.6	8.9	2.1	72.3	35.4	50.0	50.0
54166	SHAWANO	91.2	90.5	0.2	0.3	0.5	0.6	1.4	1.6	6.0	5.9	6.1	6.4	5.6	25.3	25.5	16.1	3.1	77.9	41.5	49.3	50.7
54169	SHERWOOD	98.5	98.1	0.2	0.3	0.8	1.0	0.6	0.7	8.0	8.4	7.7	6.5	4.8	29.5	25.9	8.5	0.7	71.6	37.5	50.5	49.5
54170	SHIOCTON	97.1	96.7	0.1	0.1	0.1	0.1	3.1	3.6	7.1	7.3	7.6	6.7	5.2	31.1	24.9	9.2	0.9	73.9	37.0	53.0	47.1
54171	SOBIESKI	98.3	98.1	0.2	0.3	0.2	0.2	0.7	0.8	7.4	7.8	8.7	7.6	6.3	29.9	25.6	6.1	0.6	71.4	36.2	50.9	49.1
54173	SUAMICO	97.5	97.1	0.2	0.2	0.6	0.7	0.8	1.1	6.8	7.9	8.1	6.6	3.9	31.7	28.7	5.5	0.7	72.9	37.9	51.5	48.5
54174	SURING	96.6	96.3	0.1	0.1	0.2	0.3	0.5	0.6	5.1	5.2	6.8	6.5	5.4	23.7	26.5	18.0	2.7	78.4	43.3	50.2	49.8
54175	TOWNSEND	97.7	97.4	0.1	0.1	0.1	0.1	0.5	0.6	2.7	3.1	4.9	4.2	3.3	16.0	34.4	29.9	1.6	86.8	55.4	51.4	48.6
54177	WAUSAUKEE	98.0	97.7	0.3	0.4	0.2	0.3	0.4	0.5	4.6	5.1	6.7	6.6	5.0	21.2	31.6	17.5	1.7	79.6	45.5	50.5	49.5
54180	WRIGHTSTOWN	97.5	96.9	0.2	0.3	0.8	1.1	1.6	1.9	9.5	8.8	8.3	6.6	6.5	34.5	18.3	6.8	0.9	68.9	32.1	50.7	49.3
54201	ALGOMA	98.3	98.1	0.1	0.1	0.1	0.1	1.2	1.4	5.2	5.7	6.5	6.4	6.0	25.5	27.0	14.4	3.3	78.7	41.6	49.2	50.8
54202	BAILEYS HARBOR	98.4	98.2	0.1	0.1	0.2	0.3	1.5	1.7	3.4	4.3	5.1	5.1	4.1	22.1	34.8	19.3	1.8	84.1	48.1	49.5	50.5
54204	BRUSSELS	98.4	98.1	0.3	0.4	0.4	0.5	0.4	0.5	6.0	7.1	7.2	5.9	5.3	27.6	29.4	10.5	1.0	75.9	39.8	50.3	49.8
54205	CASCO	98.0	97.9	0.1	0.1	0.1	0.1	1.2	1.3	6.3	6.6	7.3	7.3	6.7	28.3	24.8	11.1	1.7	75.2	37.5	50.4	49.6
54208	DENMARK	98.4	98.2	0.2	0.2	0.3	0.4	0.5	0.6	6.9	7.3	8.1	7.0	6.5	28.2	25.4	9.3	1.5	73.3	36.9	51.1	48.9
54209	EGG HARBOR	97.9	97.6	0.2	0.2	0.4	0.6	0.9	0.9	3.2	4.5	5.3	5.9	3.8	21.5	36.1	18.0	1.6	83.2	48.1	50.1	49.9
54210	ELLISON BAY	99.3	99.1	0.0	0.0	0.1	0.2	0.6	0.8	3.8	4.4	5.4	4.8	3.4	17.6	34.9	23.2	2.6	83.5	52.0	48.4	51.6
54212	FISH CREEK	98.3	97.9	0.2	0.2	0.2	0.2	1.2	1.5	4.2	4.5	4.7	3.9	3.6	19.2	37.6	21.0	1.4	84.1	51.1	49.9	50.1
54213	FORESTVILLE	98.0	97.9	0.3	0.3	0.3	0.4	0.3	0.3	5.7	6.3	7.9	6.4	5.9	27.4	27.5	11.1	1.8	76.2	39.8	51.0	49.0
	WISCONSIN	88.9	88.0	5.7	6.0	1.7	2.1	3.6	4.0	6.4	6.5	7.1	7.3	7.7	27.6	24.5	11.1	1.9	75.8	36.9	49.5	50.5
	UNITED STATES	75.1	73.6	12.3	12.5	3.8	4.2	12.5	14.1	6.9	6.7	7.2	7.0	7.3	28.6	23.8	10.8	1.7	75.1	36.0	49.1	50.9

#	POST OFFICE NAME	2004 Per Capita Income	2004 HH Income Base	2004 Household Income Distribution (%): Less than $25,000	$25,000 to $49,999	$50,000 to $99,999	$100,000 to $149,999	$150,000 or More	Median Household Income: 2004	2009	2004 National Centile	2004 State Centile	2004 Home Value Base	2004 Home Value Distribution (%): Less than $50,000	$50,000 to $89,999	$90,000 to $174,999	$175,000 to $399,999	$400,000 or More	2004 Median Home Value
53951	NORTH FREEDOM	21917	608	24.8	27.6	37.3	6.4	3.8	47836	53947	68	58	517	14.5	18.4	35.6	27.5	4.1	113705
53952	OXFORD	20012	1142	26.4	36.7	31.6	4.1	1.2	40350	45389	47	31	933	14.2	25.2	43.1	15.7	1.9	106445
53954	PARDEEVILLE	24308	2734	20.9	31.0	37.7	6.9	3.6	48550	54787	69	60	2186	4.4	7.6	50.7	34.9	2.3	150862
53955	POYNETTE	26230	2374	17.4	26.5	42.5	9.8	3.8	55164	61949	80	78	1897	6.0	4.6	45.3	39.8	4.3	165283
53956	RANDOLPH	22802	1247	20.3	33.0	36.9	7.4	2.4	47163	53265	66	56	975	4.0	13.7	58.4	20.7	3.2	125083
53959	REEDSBURG	22352	5004	22.9	32.1	34.6	7.5	3.0	46076	51587	64	53	3577	11.8	12.4	51.6	21.5	2.7	121037
53960	RIO	23157	1420	15.8	32.1	41.3	8.7	2.2	51893	57942	75	69	1180	4.8	9.2	51.2	31.5	3.4	145652
53961	ROCK SPRINGS	23639	289	18.3	26.6	40.5	10.7	3.8	54185	61444	79	75	246	4.1	18.7	38.6	33.7	4.9	141667
53963	WAUPUN	20510	4439	20.1	32.5	38.7	7.0	1.6	47727	53857	68	58	3385	3.7	18.1	59.6	17.9	0.7	117651
53964	WESTFIELD	20628	1359	32.5	34.4	26.3	4.0	2.9	36595	40523	34	14	1063	12.8	25.1	43.7	16.1	2.4	105699
53965	WISCONSIN DELLS	22530	4399	24.2	34.6	32.0	6.2	2.9	42494	48331	55	40	3391	16.7	18.5	42.4	19.2	3.2	113153
53968	WONEWOC	20193	1048	27.6	38.7	26.4	4.4	3.0	38426	43067	41	22	831	16.4	28.8	37.6	15.6	1.7	95260
54001	AMERY	23059	3493	24.2	31.4	33.3	8.7	2.5	45732	52698	63	51	2839	8.6	15.5	47.9	25.2	2.8	129589
54002	BALDWIN	24655	2228	18.3	30.2	37.4	11.3	2.8	51285	58974	74	67	1540	5.8	5.7	36.5	45.8	6.2	178934
54003	BELDENVILLE	24577	454	14.3	24.9	45.6	11.2	4.0	60000	66159	84	86	401	2.5	6.7	30.9	48.4	11.5	199688
54004	CLAYTON	19657	986	25.3	33.0	34.3	5.6	1.9	42575	46778	55	40	814	15.2	21.9	44.5	17.2	1.2	108491
54005	CLEAR LAKE	19531	1160	26.4	32.1	33.9	5.8	1.9	43270	49041	57	42	939	18.6	18.0	45.6	16.6	1.2	108854
54006	CUSHING	20375	771	21.8	35.3	35.5	6.2	1.2	44949	51141	61	48	666	12.9	18.2	46.4	21.5	1.1	117986
54007	DEER PARK	22972	510	15.7	27.8	44.7	9.4	2.4	55519	64403	80	78	439	5.2	10.0	47.2	33.7	3.9	155254
54009	DRESSER	24915	886	16.6	34.2	37.3	8.4	3.6	49373	56320	71	63	702	8.6	10.5	51.3	27.5	2.1	132632
54011	ELLSWORTH	23075	2587	18.6	28.2	42.0	8.8	2.4	52288	60064	76	70	2029	7.3	9.8	41.3	36.3	5.3	155174
54013	GLENWOOD CITY	22646	1378	20.8	30.2	35.8	10.2	3.1	49131	57201	70	62	1137	9.8	14.3	37.3	32.9	5.8	143339
54014	HAGER CITY	26199	874	14.2	25.4	44.5	12.8	3.1	58613	65373	83	83	756	6.5	8.6	39.4	38.1	7.4	163961
54015	HAMMOND	24348	926	14.9	26.1	44.3	11.9	2.8	58307	69799	83	82	692	6.7	4.9	40.2	41.9	6.4	171429
54016	HUDSON	33449	10127	9.8	18.2	40.8	21.0	10.2	74896	87311	93	98	7798	0.7	1.8	17.9	64.6	15.1	245582
54017	NEW RICHMOND	24647	5455	17.4	27.6	40.0	12.6	2.5	54025	64010	78	74	3960	5.8	3.1	41.8	44.1	5.2	173763
54020	OSCEOLA	23616	2764	16.5	28.4	40.7	11.6	2.8	54499	61825	79	76	2138	7.1	7.9	47.5	34.2	3.3	150000
54021	PRESCOTT	27850	2173	10.8	24.3	46.9	13.9	4.2	63717	73588	88	92	1648	3.8	1.5	27.0	56.0	11.7	206846
54022	RIVER FALLS	24633	7291	18.9	25.3	38.5	12.8	4.6	55689	64569	80	78	4498	2.8	2.3	27.1	57.3	10.5	210115
54023	ROBERTS	26362	1155	12.6	24.9	43.8	14.6	4.2	60495	71386	85	87	972	17.0	5.6	21.3	47.3	8.9	190152
54024	SAINT CROIX FALLS	23437	1556	27.3	29.0	33.2	7.7	2.9	44044	50027	59	45	1189	10.4	14.2	49.1	23.6	2.6	126683
54025	SOMERSET	28539	2260	11.6	25.2	42.7	15.4	5.1	60992	71817	85	88	1812	3.7	2.4	27.4	56.3	10.2	212174
54026	STAR PRAIRIE	24809	654	11.3	25.1	46.2	14.2	3.2	60847	70343	85	87	580	2.6	6.7	38.8	45.9	6.0	178571
54027	WILSON	25513	356	13.5	27.5	41.9	13.2	3.9	58692	67460	83	83	325	5.9	7.7	34.8	44.3	7.4	180288
54028	WOODVILLE	24994	944	16.5	31.6	36.7	12.2	3.1	51710	60047	75	68	728	14.3	6.7	35.7	37.6	5.6	157500
54082	HOULTON	35553	568	9.0	12.7	44.2	25.4	8.8	78751	93035	95	99	504	10.1	0.6	11.5	60.3	17.5	246610
54101	ABRAMS	23701	1056	13.6	28.3	45.3	10.0	2.8	55534	62387	80	78	966	6.5	14.3	45.0	31.6	2.6	140559
54102	AMBERG	20628	422	38.2	34.4	21.8	3.6	2.1	32315	36297	19	3	355	26.8	27.6	36.3	9.3	0.0	84038
54103	ARMSTRONG CREEK	19121	237	35.4	33.3	26.2	3.8	1.3	33529	37810	22	5	183	18.0	38.8	36.1	7.1	0.0	82188
54104	ATHELSTANE	20250	482	31.5	37.8	25.3	4.6	0.8	35896	40835	31	11	422	24.9	31.8	28.4	12.6	2.4	81515
54106	BLACK CREEK	23319	1960	16.5	28.7	44.0	8.5	2.2	53331	60677	77	72	1645	7.4	15.2	50.2	24.4	2.8	123604
54107	BONDUEL	21700	1357	20.6	35.3	34.7	6.7	2.7	45433	51116	62	50	1111	5.5	17.3	56.4	18.5	2.3	117746
54110	BRILLION	24633	2069	18.0	29.1	42.3	7.2	3.5	52095	58510	76	70	1680	10.3	21.0	55.5	12.0	1.3	109005
54111	CECIL	21911	866	23.6	32.3	34.5	7.3	2.3	43604	48519	58	43	728	10.6	21.7	42.3	22.4	3.0	115000
54112	COLEMAN	19973	1047	29.2	32.2	31.3	5.8	1.4	41130	46014	50	35	829	15.1	27.9	44.5	11.5	1.1	102177
54113	COMBINED LOCKS	29861	1080	10.2	25.3	44.4	14.5	5.7	62632	71075	87	91	967	0.4	8.4	58.3	30.4	2.5	136547
54114	CRIVITZ	20425	2444	31.5	35.7	26.3	5.6	1.0	36965	41668	35	16	1995	15.4	28.9	38.1	15.3	2.3	98731
54115	DE PERE	28964	12639	15.1	25.4	40.4	13.0	6.0	58731	67324	83	83	9255	1.8	6.4	53.0	34.3	4.5	154496
54119	DUNBAR	13465	260	32.7	35.4	26.2	4.2	1.5	36430	40661	33	13	211	23.2	33.7	33.7	9.5	0.0	80938
54120	FENCE	23702	216	34.3	36.6	23.2	3.7	2.3	33996	39868	24	6	194	25.3	30.9	29.4	12.4	2.1	81429
54121	FLORENCE	21227	1244	31.4	31.5	30.1	5.2	1.8	39718	44273	45	28	1027	19.4	22.1	38.7	17.7	2.1	106953
54124	GILLETT	20064	1523	27.6	34.1	32.2	4.1	1.9	40801	45951	49	33	1220	18.3	34.4	35.0	11.1	1.2	87381
54125	GOODMAN	19488	338	33.4	37.6	23.7	3.6	1.8	35167	39034	28	8	285	29.8	30.9	30.5	8.4	0.4	75682
54126	GREENLEAF	23767	1321	10.5	27.3	46.3	11.1	4.8	59328	68575	84	84	1177	6.2	10.1	46.9	33.0	3.8	146185
54128	GRESHAM	17052	732	29.5	31.4	32.9	5.2	1.0	39679	44227	45	28	598	17.2	24.6	46.7	9.7	1.8	100000
54129	HILBERT	23806	1640	15.3	29.8	41.7	9.3	4.0	53687	60480	78	73	1384	9.9	17.7	50.6	18.6	3.2	118959
54130	KAUKAUNA	23626	8622	16.2	27.4	43.2	10.3	2.8	54569	63064	79	76	6688	1.2	14.8	63.7	18.8	1.5	120736
54135	KESHENA	11942	1328	37.1	34.3	24.6	3.9	0.2	32848	36892	20	4	962	33.5	27.1	26.4	12.2	0.8	73385
54136	KIMBERLY	24472	2486	18.2	29.0	42.0	8.2	2.5	51629	59494	75	68	1974	1.1	16.6	72.0	10.1	0.2	111497
54137	KRAKOW	22843	449	16.7	33.6	38.8	8.2	2.7	49765	56348	71	64	408	5.9	16.9	49.3	25.0	2.9	123077
54138	LAKEWOOD	21301	494	32.8	33.6	27.3	4.5	1.8	34867	41015	27	7	444	12.8	20.1	40.1	24.3	2.7	116875
54139	LENA	20796	1362	27.0	30.8	33.8	6.2	2.1	43206	48417	56	41	1121	14.5	26.6	41.0	16.5	1.4	103895
54140	LITTLE CHUTE	24908	3539	16.9	31.3	39.2	8.8	3.8	51612	58925	75	68	2431	7.5	15.0	64.8	12.6	0.2	117678
54141	LITTLE SUAMICO	25888	807	9.4	27.5	49.0	11.4	2.7	60250	66765	85	86	734	9.8	11.7	48.0	29.0	1.5	138433
54143	MARINETTE	21811	6704	29.2	32.9	29.3	6.2	2.4	38936	43490	43	25	4923	21.0	36.7	32.1	9.8	0.5	79676
54149	MOUNTAIN	21375	711	28.8	39.0	28.0	3.1	1.1	37421	43815	37	19	610	16.6	24.1	40.0	16.9	2.5	104924
54150	NEOPIT	12977	6	33.3	50.0	16.7	0.0	0.0	35000	31982	28	8	4	0.0	100.0	0.0	0.0	0.0	55000
54151	NIAGARA	20202	2022	29.9	33.5	29.1	6.3	1.1	38679	43867	42	24	1633	23.6	32.3	35.9	7.8	0.4	81075
54153	OCONTO	22654	3153	26.6	31.8	33.5	5.4	2.7	43160	49087	56	41	2406	10.4	32.3	40.4	15.7	1.2	101430
54154	OCONTO FALLS	20745	2133	24.8	32.4	34.4	7.0	1.5	44848	50698	61	48	1553	9.7	25.3	45.1	18.6	1.3	109466
54155	ONEIDA	28816	1512	13.4	21.5	37.8	16.2	11.0	67587	77722	90	94	1326	2.0	8.0	38.8	42.6	8.5	177930
54156	PEMBINE	20757	792	33.2	34.9	25.3	4.9	1.8	36493	41153	34	13	661	24.2	29.7	37.1	8.6	0.5	85278
54157	PESHTIGO	19642	2147	26.4	34.6	31.0	6.8	1.2	41129	45881	50	35	1685	12.8	30.1	40.7	15.8	0.7	99640
54159	PORTERFIELD	21328	685	22.8	31.8	38.5	6.0	0.9	46581	52144	65	54	629	12.1	25.1	47.2	14.2	1.4	108972
54161	POUND	18834	1334	30.9	35.0	28.0	5.0	1.2	38139	43326	40	21	1091	14.9	28.7	37.6	17.4	1.5	99400
54162	PULASKI	22393	3288	20.4	24.6	41.3	11.3	2.4	55062	62965	80	77	2627	5.2	11.1	51.9	29.9	1.9	137325
54165	SEYMOUR	22440	2723	15.5	29.4	42.6	10.2	2.3	53748	61124	78	74	2157	3.6	13.2	56.1	25.5	1.7	127604
54166	SHAWANO	21796	6866	28.8	34.9	27.8	5.6	3.0	39632	44428	45	28	5040	8.4	26.1	47.9	16.3	1.4	108106
54169	SHERWOOD	30436	734	10.9	19.8	47.4	13.2	8.7	66585	75049	90	94	656	1.7	4.9	45.0	43.3	5.2	172500
54170	SHIOCTON	22821	1568	15.0	29.0	45.3	8.6	2.1	54708	62011	79	76	1350	8.3	18.7	47.7	22.8	2.4	120848
54171	SOBIESKI	25288	1017	12.8	19.7	47.6	14.6	5.4	64244	72974	88	92	958	5.9	7.9	42.2	42.3	1.8	164205
54173	SUAMICO	30936	1426	6.5	16.6	53.7	14.7	8.5	70226	81867	91	95	1270	0.3	5.0	38.3	47.9	8.5	186188
54174	SURING	20341	1373	29.8	34.9	29.5	4.2	1.7	38000	43274	39	20	1119	17.0	33.4	34.3	13.3	2.0	89458
54175	TOWNSEND	20851	529	34.8	33.3	25.5	4.7	1.7	32911	38410	21	4	482	13.7	19.3	39.2	25.1	2.7	119079
54177	WAUSAUKEE	18963	1423	33.0	35.2	27.0	4.2	0.6	36804	41100	35	15	1207	22.9	24.1	39.4	12.8	0.9	96293
54180	WRIGHTSTOWN	26763	783	13.7	26.7	41.6	12.4	5.6	59472	68384	84	85	630	1.6	8.4	56.2	31.6	2.2	141919
54201	ALGOMA	21295	2402	27.0	32.8	33.3	5.7	1.3	42517	48344	55	40	1871	10.3	29.1	44.3	14.3	2.0	102751
54202	BAILEYS HARBOR	29097	651	20.7	35.2	32.1	8.6	3.4	46626	54943	65	54	547	4.6	4.0	33.6	43.3	14.4	204261
54204	BRUSSELS	22945	689	21.3	29.3	35.6	11.3	2.5	49904	57410	71	63	596	7.4	15.3	43.6	26.5	7.2	133904
54205	CASCO	20327	800	21.6	29.8	39.5	6.6	2.5	48970	54325	70	61	668	4.9	15.3	52.7	24.4	2.7	131378
54208	DENMARK	23360	2321	17.5	29.5	40.4	9.2	3.4	52489	60195	76	70	1853	5.0	14.1	52.5	25.5	3.0	128350
54209	EGG HARBOR	31806	546	21.6	29.7	31.9	9.9	7.0	48986	57955	70	62	465	4.1	7.1	31.6	37.4	19.8	198929
54210	ELLISON BAY	29628	448	21.4	29.2	35.9	7.1	6.3	49445	57832	71	63	384	0.5	4.7	31.0	43.5	20.3	221569
54212	FISH CREEK	34828	502	18.7	28.3	32.5	11.4	9.2	53093	64260	77	72	443	1.4	2.7	25.3	49.4	21.2	250532
54213	FORESTVILLE	22844	578	22.3	30.3	37.2	8.3	1.9	48069	55016	68	59	495	7.3	21.0	46.3	23.6	1.8	116984
	WISCONSIN	25041		22.2	28.8	35.0	9.6	4.2	48930	56561				7.0	14.9	46.8	27.8	3.6	134326
	UNITED STATES	25866		24.7	27.1	30.8	10.9	6.5	48124	56710				10.9	15.0	33.7	30.1	10.4	145905

SPENDING POTENTIAL INDICES WISCONSIN
53951-54213 D

ZIP CODE #	POST OFFICE NAME	FINANCIAL SERVICES: Auto Loan	Home Loan	Invest-ments	Retire-ment Plans	THE HOME: Home Improvements: Home Repair	Lawn & Garden	Furnishings: Comput-ers & Hard-ware	Major Appli-ances	TV, Radio, Sound Equip-ment	Furni-ture	ENTERTAINMENT: Dine out/Carry out	Sports Equip-ment	Fees & Tickets	Toys & Games	Travel	Cable TV	PERSONAL: Apparel & Services	Auto Repairs	Health Insur-ance	Pets & Supplies
53951	NORTH FREEDOM	86	85	74	83	87	92	79	84	80	79	99	99	79	101	81	81	95	82	86	101
53952	OXFORD	78	62	44	58	69	78	60	70	67	60	80	82	55	79	63	71	75	69	81	93
53954	PARDEEVILLE	100	84	60	80	90	99	81	91	87	80	105	107	76	106	82	90	99	89	101	117
53955	POYNETTE	101	89	70	87	94	102	86	94	91	86	111	110	84	112	87	93	105	92	101	116
53956	RANDOLPH	80	68	51	66	73	80	67	73	71	66	86	86	64	87	68	73	81	72	80	92
53959	REEDSBURG	86	76	62	75	79	87	76	81	80	75	98	94	74	98	76	81	92	80	86	97
53960	RIO	94	84	64	80	89	95	78	86	83	78	100	103	76	102	80	85	95	84	93	111
53961	ROCK SPRINGS	97	92	76	88	95	101	84	91	87	84	106	109	84	110	87	88	102	89	96	115
53963	WAUPUN	73	64	51	62	68	75	63	68	67	62	81	79	61	82	64	69	77	66	74	83
53964	WESTFIELD	80	64	44	60	70	79	63	72	69	62	83	84	57	82	64	73	77	71	83	94
53965	WISCONSIN DELLS	89	73	53	69	79	88	71	81	78	70	93	94	66	92	73	81	87	80	92	104
53968	WONEWOC	77	69	57	66	73	80	67	72	71	65	86	84	66	90	69	74	82	71	80	90
54001	AMERY	87	76	62	74	81	89	75	82	79	74	96	96	71	95	76	81	91	81	89	102
54002	BALDWIN	93	87	75	86	90	99	87	91	89	84	108	105	84	108	87	91	103	90	97	106
54003	BELDENVILLE	98	102	94	100	104	107	93	98	92	93	114	115	95	119	95	92	111	95	97	117
54004	CLAYTON	80	71	58	70	75	81	69	74	72	68	88	87	67	89	70	73	84	73	79	92
54005	CLEAR LAKE	81	69	54	68	73	81	69	75	73	68	89	86	67	89	69	75	84	73	81	91
54006	CUSHING	82	73	56	69	77	83	68	75	72	68	87	89	66	89	70	74	83	73	81	97
54007	DEER PARK	100	91	71	87	95	101	84	92	88	84	108	110	83	110	86	90	103	90	98	118
54009	DRESSER	97	87	71	86	90	98	86	91	89	85	109	106	83	109	86	90	103	90	96	109
54011	ELLSWORTH	93	82	64	80	85	94	80	86	84	79	103	101	77	103	80	86	97	85	93	106
54013	GLENWOOD CITY	98	85	65	83	90	98	82	90	88	82	106	105	80	107	84	89	100	88	97	112
54014	HAGER CITY	109	97	75	92	102	110	90	99	95	90	116	118	88	118	92	97	110	97	107	128
54015	HAMMOND	89	101	103	103	98	97	95	94	88	95	111	111	97	114	94	84	110	93	83	103
54016	HUDSON	121	139	145	144	134	133	128	126	119	131	151	148	133	153	127	113	150	124	111	138
54017	NEW RICHMOND	90	93	89	93	92	94	89	90	87	89	108	107	89	109	88	84	105	90	85	103
54020	OSCEOLA	90	92	85	92	92	96	87	90	86	87	107	106	88	109	87	85	104	88	87	104
54021	PRESCOTT	103	116	116	117	113	112	108	108	101	108	128	127	110	131	107	97	126	106	97	120
54022	RIVER FALLS	90	90	101	94	88	91	97	91	93	95	118	111	95	116	93	88	115	95	83	101
54023	ROBERTS	102	109	102	107	108	110	100	104	97	102	121	121	101	122	101	95	119	101	98	118
54024	SAINT CROIX FALLS	87	71	51	69	76	87	74	80	80	71	96	91	68	93	73	83	89	79	91	97
54025	SOMERSET	104	117	118	119	113	112	110	109	102	110	129	128	111	131	108	97	128	107	96	120
54026	STAR PRAIRIE	101	100	89	99	102	105	94	98	94	94	116	117	93	118	94	92	112	97	97	118
54027	WILSON	106	96	74	91	101	108	88	97	93	88	113	116	87	116	91	95	108	95	105	125
54028	WOODVILLE	94	91	80	90	93	100	88	92	89	87	109	106	87	111	88	90	105	90	94	108
54082	HOULTON	123	150	158	151	146	145	135	133	124	135	157	156	143	165	136	120	157	129	119	147
54101	ABRAMS	102	92	72	88	96	103	85	94	90	85	109	111	84	111	87	91	104	91	100	119
54102	AMBERG	75	59	40	53	67	75	56	67	63	55	75	79	50	74	59	67	70	66	79	92
54103	ARMSTRONG CREEK	71	56	38	50	63	71	53	64	60	52	71	74	47	70	56	64	66	63	75	87
54104	ATHELSTANE	76	59	40	53	67	75	56	67	63	55	75	79	50	74	60	68	70	66	80	92
54106	BLACK CREEK	99	88	67	84	93	100	81	90	86	81	105	108	80	107	84	89	100	88	98	116
54107	BONDUEL	89	75	57	73	80	89	74	81	79	73	96	95	71	96	75	81	90	80	89	101
54110	BRILLION	101	89	68	86	94	102	85	93	90	84	109	110	83	111	86	92	103	91	101	118
54111	CECIL	90	75	52	70	81	88	70	81	77	70	92	96	66	93	73	79	86	79	90	107
54112	COLEMAN	79	67	50	64	72	79	65	72	70	64	85	84	62	85	66	72	79	71	80	91
54113	COMBINED LOCKS	122	119	100	117	121	124	109	116	109	110	135	137	109	137	110	108	130	112	115	141
54114	CRIVITZ	75	57	38	53	64	73	57	67	64	56	76	78	51	74	59	68	70	66	79	89
54115	DE PERE	104	113	118	115	111	113	109	108	104	109	131	127	111	133	108	101	129	107	100	120
54119	DUNBAR	75	59	40	53	67	75	56	67	63	55	75	79	50	74	59	67	69	66	79	92
54120	FENCE	83	65	44	59	73	83	62	74	70	61	83	87	55	81	66	74	77	73	88	101
54121	FLORENCE	83	65	44	59	73	82	61	74	69	61	82	86	55	81	65	74	76	73	87	101
54124	GILLETT	80	69	53	64	73	81	66	73	72	65	87	85	64	88	68	75	82	71	82	93
54125	GOODMAN	75	58	40	53	66	74	55	66	62	55	74	78	49	73	59	67	69	65	78	91
54126	GREENLEAF	106	101	86	99	104	108	95	101	96	95	118	120	94	120	96	96	114	99	102	123
54128	GRESHAM	73	62	48	62	65	73	64	68	67	62	82	77	61	81	63	69	77	67	74	80
54129	HILBERT	100	92	74	88	97	103	85	93	89	85	108	111	84	111	88	91	104	91	99	118
54130	KAUKAUNA	88	90	88	90	91	95	88	89	87	87	108	105	88	109	88	86	104	88	88	102
54135	KESHENA	60	48	45	44	51	58	50	55	56	51	68	63	47	66	51	59	65	55	62	69
54136	KIMBERLY	84	86	84	85	86	92	83	85	84	83	104	98	85	107	84	83	100	84	85	97
54137	KRAKOW	94	84	64	80	89	95	78	86	82	78	100	102	76	102	80	84	95	84	93	111
54138	LAKEWOOD	78	61	42	55	69	77	58	69	65	57	77	81	52	76	61	70	72	68	82	95
54139	LENA	83	72	55	70	76	83	69	76	74	69	89	89	67	90	70	75	84	74	83	96
54140	LITTLE CHUTE	92	94	96	96	92	96	94	93	91	94	114	109	94	115	92	88	111	93	87	104
54141	LITTLE SUAMICO	96	101	96	102	99	100	95	96	91	96	114	114	96	115	94	87	112	95	88	110
54143	MARINETTE	73	68	60	66	70	78	68	71	72	67	88	82	67	89	69	73	83	71	77	84
54149	MOUNTAIN	77	60	41	54	68	76	57	68	64	56	76	80	51	75	61	69	71	67	81	94
54150	NEOPIT	47	43	52	41	42	48	47	46	51	48	64	51	48	63	46	52	62	47	48	52
54151	NIAGARA	77	64	48	60	70	78	63	71	69	62	83	83	59	85	65	73	78	70	82	92
54153	OCONTO	81	78	69	74	80	88	75	79	79	74	97	91	76	101	77	81	92	77	85	94
54154	OCONTO FALLS	81	70	54	68	74	81	69	75	73	68	88	87	66	89	69	74	83	73	81	92
54155	ONEIDA	128	126	110	124	130	136	116	125	117	116	144	147	116	148	119	118	139	121	127	152
54156	PEMBINE	77	60	41	54	68	76	57	69	64	56	76	80	51	75	61	69	71	68	81	94
54157	PESHTIGO	78	66	50	63	71	78	65	71	70	64	85	83	62	85	66	73	80	70	80	90
54159	PORTERFIELD	82	73	56	70	77	83	68	75	72	68	87	89	66	89	70	74	83	73	81	97
54161	POUND	75	61	44	57	66	74	59	67	65	58	77	79	54	77	61	68	72	66	77	88
54162	PULASKI	94	87	71	86	90	96	83	89	86	83	105	104	82	106	84	87	100	87	93	107
54165	SEYMOUR	90	87	77	85	89	95	84	88	85	83	105	102	84	108	85	86	101	86	90	104
54166	SHAWANO	81	65	49	63	71	80	67	74	73	66	88	86	62	86	68	76	82	74	84	93
54169	SHERWOOD	104	130	138	130	127	126	116	115	107	115	135	135	123	144	118	104	135	111	103	127
54170	SHIOCTON	96	86	65	81	91	97	79	88	84	79	102	105	78	104	82	86	97	85	95	113
54171	SOBIESKI	109	115	106	117	113	112	105	107	100	108	126	126	107	127	104	96	123	105	98	123
54173	SUAMICO	117	137	138	141	133	129	123	123	113	126	144	143	129	148	123	108	143	119	106	135
54174	SURING	86	62	35	55	70	79	59	72	69	60	82	86	52	79	61	74	75	71	87	100
54175	TOWNSEND	75	59	40	53	67	75	56	67	63	55	75	79	50	74	59	67	69	66	79	92
54177	WAUSAUKEE	75	60	42	55	67	75	57	67	63	56	75	79	52	75	60	67	70	66	78	91
54180	WRIGHTSTOWN	103	107	101	107	105	106	101	103	97	101	122	122	101	123	100	94	119	102	95	118
54201	ALGOMA	79	66	49	64	70	79	66	72	71	65	86	84	63	85	67	74	81	71	81	89
54202	BAILEYS HARBOR	99	78	53	70	88	98	73	88	83	73	98	103	66	97	78	89	91	87	104	121
54204	BRUSSELS	96	84	64	80	90	97	78	87	83	78	101	104	76	103	81	86	96	85	95	113
54205	CASCO	88	76	59	74	80	88	74	81	79	74	96	95	72	97	75	81	91	79	88	100
54208	DENMARK	99	87	67	84	92	100	83	91	88	82	107	107	81	108	84	90	101	89	99	115
54209	EGG HARBOR	122	96	65	86	108	121	90	109	102	90	121	127	81	120	96	109	113	107	129	149
54210	ELLISON BAY	110	86	59	78	97	109	81	98	92	81	109	115	73	108	87	98	101	97	116	134
54212	FISH CREEK	130	102	69	92	115	129	96	116	109	95	129	135	86	127	102	116	120	114	137	158
54213	FORESTVILLE	93	83	63	78	87	94	76	85	81	76	99	101	75	101	79	83	94	82	92	109
	WISCONSIN	89	86	85	86	88	94	86	88	87	85	108	103	86	109	86	87	104	88	89	103
	UNITED STATES	100	100	100	100	100	100	100	100	100	100	100	100	100	100	100	100	100	100	100	100

POPULATION CHANGE

ZIP CODE			POPULATION			2000-2004 ANNUAL RATE		HOUSEHOLDS					FAMILIES		
#	POST OFFICE NAME	COUNTY FIPS CODE	2000	2004	2009	% Rate	State Centile	2000	2004	2009	% Annual Rate 2000-2004	2004 Average HH Size	2000	2004	% Annual Rate 2000-2004
54216	KEWAUNEE	061	6065	6277	6551	0.8	47	2310	2457	2634	1.5	2.50	1649	1727	1.1
54217	LUXEMBURG	061	6652	7159	7612	1.7	82	2344	2598	2837	2.5	2.73	1837	2013	2.2
54220	MANITOWOC	071	41190	41514	42083	0.2	23	16771	17352	18029	0.8	2.32	10786	10979	0.4
54227	MARIBEL	071	1629	1686	1721	0.8	47	563	601	629	1.6	2.80	460	486	1.3
54228	MISHICOT	071	2805	3023	3156	1.8	82	1048	1164	1247	2.5	2.60	800	877	2.2
54229	NEW FRANKEN	009	3377	3790	4147	2.8	94	1090	1266	1424	3.6	2.87	890	1020	3.3
54230	REEDSVILLE	071	4699	4791	4865	0.5	32	1680	1764	1838	1.2	2.71	1278	1326	0.9
54234	SISTER BAY	029	2039	2170	2312	1.5	74	951	1051	1159	2.4	1.98	585	634	1.9
54235	STURGEON BAY	029	17340	18034	18984	0.9	53	7278	7802	8460	1.7	2.27	4844	5120	1.3
54241	TWO RIVERS	071	15899	15966	16187	0.1	19	6409	6580	6820	0.6	2.40	4346	4406	0.3
54245	VALDERS	071	2420	2369	2372	-0.5	4	924	929	953	0.1	2.55	702	696	-0.2
54246	WASHINGTON ISLAND	029	660	668	693	0.3	26	293	303	322	0.8	2.20	199	203	0.5
54247	WHITELAW	071	2440	2536	2595	0.9	52	898	960	1007	1.6	2.64	695	734	1.3
54301	GREEN BAY	009	25942	25973	26874	0.0	16	9803	10060	10689	0.6	2.31	5888	5921	0.1
54302	GREEN BAY	009	30014	30938	32660	0.7	44	12696	13361	14400	1.2	2.28	7313	7471	0.5
54303	GREEN BAY	009	27512	27659	28899	0.1	20	12038	12426	13300	0.8	2.19	6485	6510	0.1
54304	GREEN BAY	009	30082	30541	32068	0.4	29	12737	13366	14427	1.1	2.25	8105	8279	0.5
54311	GREEN BAY	009	27836	30984	34011	2.6	93	9775	11241	12686	3.3	2.61	6756	7647	3.0
54313	GREEN BAY	009	31161	33611	36237	1.8	83	10827	12025	13294	2.5	2.79	8716	9594	2.3
54401	WAUSAU	073	30107	30065	30686	0.0	13	11808	12080	12630	0.5	2.45	7919	7986	0.2
54403	WAUSAU	073	24377	24558	25181	0.2	22	9607	9937	10456	0.8	2.38	6127	6226	0.4
54405	ABBOTSFORD	073	2934	2907	2929	-0.2	8	1138	1157	1188	0.4	2.45	785	785	0.0
54406	AMHERST	097	3198	3255	3354	0.4	31	1180	1240	1315	1.2	2.59	876	907	0.8
54407	AMHERST JUNCTION	097	1687	1666	1694	-0.3	7	635	646	674	0.4	2.58	479	479	0.0
54408	ANIWA	073	1205	1278	1337	1.4	72	431	471	505	2.1	2.71	342	370	1.9
54409	ANTIGO	067	14083	14313	14666	0.4	30	5639	5867	6154	0.9	2.40	3799	3899	0.6
54410	ARPIN	141	2249	2367	2454	1.2	65	749	820	879	2.2	2.76	574	623	2.0
54411	ATHENS	073	5341	5557	5761	0.9	54	1762	1881	1999	1.6	2.95	1413	1491	1.3
54412	AUBURNDALE	141	1912	1915	1932	0.0	17	706	731	760	0.8	2.62	547	562	0.6
54413	BABCOCK	141	387	389	392	0.1	20	157	162	168	0.7	2.40	117	119	0.4
54414	BIRNAMWOOD	115	3353	3474	3584	0.8	48	1211	1289	1361	1.5	2.68	894	939	1.2
54416	BOWLER	078	1978	2044	2106	0.8	46	678	719	758	1.4	2.82	511	534	1.0
54418	BRYANT	067	1243	1290	1331	0.9	50	457	487	515	1.5	2.65	353	372	1.2
54420	CHILI	019	1196	1306	1368	2.1	88	385	426	451	2.4	3.07	317	347	2.2
54421	COLBY	073	3157	3392	3548	1.7	81	1112	1233	1321	2.5	2.67	823	900	2.1
54422	CURTISS	019	1112	1181	1221	1.4	73	333	360	379	1.9	3.28	266	285	1.6
54423	CUSTER	097	2066	2328	2523	2.9	94	729	849	946	3.7	2.74	577	662	3.3
54424	DEERBROOK	067	1633	1684	1738	0.7	45	670	712	755	1.4	2.37	499	524	1.2
54425	DORCHESTER	019	1933	2076	2169	1.7	81	697	770	821	2.4	2.69	509	554	2.0
54426	EDGAR	073	3870	4051	4246	1.1	61	1355	1454	1563	1.7	2.78	1047	1112	1.4
54427	ELAND	073	1099	1107	1130	0.2	22	417	434	454	0.9	2.53	301	308	0.5
54428	ELCHO	067	1277	1300	1327	0.4	31	593	622	652	1.1	2.09	400	413	0.8
54430	ELTON	067	112	118	122	1.2	66	44	48	51	2.1	2.46	35	37	1.3
54433	GILMAN	119	1835	1855	1887	0.3	26	673	700	732	0.9	2.60	491	503	0.6
54435	GLEASON	069	2018	1963	1972	-0.7	2	810	812	836	0.1	2.41	590	583	-0.3
54436	GRANTON	019	2226	2250	2286	0.3	25	732	752	772	0.6	2.99	577	586	0.4
54437	GREENWOOD	019	3042	3073	3097	0.2	25	1070	1101	1125	0.7	2.76	770	783	0.4
54440	HATLEY	073	2820	2965	3089	1.2	64	1049	1141	1223	2.0	2.60	830	892	1.7
54441	HEWITT	141	664	679	689	0.5	36	232	246	258	1.4	2.76	187	198	1.4
54442	IRMA	069	1418	1483	1520	1.1	59	430	466	490	1.9	2.65	320	342	1.6
54443	JUNCTION CITY	097	2299	2306	2369	0.1	18	851	881	931	0.8	2.61	647	662	0.5
54446	LOYAL	019	3228	3261	3295	0.2	25	1093	1119	1142	0.6	2.91	834	844	0.3
54447	LUBLIN	119	543	529	528	-0.6	3	207	206	212	-0.1	2.56	150	148	-0.3
54448	MARATHON	073	4442	4542	4682	0.5	36	1607	1692	1791	1.2	2.68	1254	1303	0.9
54449	MARSHFIELD	141	26233	26893	27517	0.6	38	10817	11427	12031	1.3	2.32	6974	7260	1.0
54451	MEDFORD	119	11130	11221	11373	0.2	23	4398	4569	4769	0.9	2.43	3053	3133	0.6
54452	MERRILL	069	19491	19976	20331	0.6	38	7603	8016	8343	1.3	2.44	5423	5652	1.0
54454	MILLADORE	141	1360	1309	1306	-0.9	1	474	471	484	-0.2	2.77	377	372	-0.3
54455	MOSINEE	073	15466	16333	17081	1.3	68	5756	6253	6710	2.0	2.60	4433	4760	1.7
54456	NEILLSVILLE	019	6347	6220	6209	-0.5	4	2478	2486	2522	0.1	2.42	1652	1632	-0.3
54457	NEKOOSA	141	8701	9203	9607	1.3	70	3444	3755	4024	2.1	2.43	2555	2752	1.8
54459	OGEMA	099	1383	1391	1397	0.1	21	562	582	601	0.8	2.39	398	407	0.5
54460	OWEN	019	2541	2665	2736	1.1	63	869	928	966	1.6	2.65	622	656	1.3
54462	PEARSON	067	372	372	376	0.0	15	164	169	176	0.7	2.20	116	118	0.4
54463	PELICAN LAKE	085	655	716	770	2.1	88	292	327	359	2.7	2.19	211	233	2.4
54465	PICKEREL	067	790	789	801	0.0	13	380	391	408	0.7	2.02	270	275	0.4
54466	PITTSVILLE	141	2707	2833	2917	1.1	61	1034	1115	1182	1.8	2.46	769	821	1.6
54467	PLOVER	097	11714	12396	13001	1.3	71	4429	4844	5230	2.1	2.55	3225	3468	1.7
54469	PORT EDWARDS	141	1920	1887	1891	-0.4	5	694	695	713	0.0	2.53	511	505	-0.3
54470	RIB LAKE	119	1947	2012	2061	0.8	46	755	807	853	1.6	2.41	534	563	1.3
54471	RINGLE	073	1553	1661	1747	1.6	78	539	596	645	2.4	2.79	457	501	2.2
54473	ROSHOLT	097	2743	2928	3080	1.6	76	984	1080	1166	2.2	2.71	751	812	1.9
54474	ROTHSCHILD	073	3864	3814	3877	-0.3	7	1510	1538	1606	0.4	2.46	1098	1102	0.1
54475	RUDOLPH	141	1571	1586	1603	0.2	24	586	610	635	1.0	2.60	456	467	0.6
54476	SCHOFIELD	073	15102	16301	17248	1.8	83	5848	6479	7026	2.4	2.49	4002	4366	2.1
54479	SPENCER	019	3593	3675	3761	0.5	36	1332	1395	1460	1.1	2.63	955	983	0.7
54480	STETSONVILLE	119	1202	1200	1209	0.0	13	434	448	465	0.8	2.68	339	346	0.5
54481	STEVENS POINT	097	37946	38815	40127	0.5	36	14161	14878	15825	1.2	2.38	8401	8685	0.8
54484	STRATFORD	073	4502	4714	4907	1.1	61	1642	1774	1895	1.8	2.65	1272	1359	1.6
54485	SUMMIT LAKE	067	187	197	205	1.2	65	82	89	95	2.0	2.21	56	60	1.6
54486	TIGERTON	115	2564	2677	2784	1.0	57	1011	1080	1146	1.6	2.44	702	739	1.2
54487	TOMAHAWK	069	9943	9968	10068	0.1	17	4115	4224	4354	0.6	2.32	2869	2906	0.3
54488	UNITY	073	1139	1188	1223	1.0	57	393	422	444	1.7	2.82	312	330	1.3
54489	VESPER	141	1546	1578	1616	0.5	33	590	621	654	1.2	2.54	436	454	1.0
54490	WESTBORO	119	874	903	925	0.8	46	330	352	372	1.5	2.48	226	238	1.2
54491	WHITE LAKE	067	1634	1751	1843	1.6	79	691	758	817	2.2	2.30	491	532	1.9
54493	WILLARD	019	829	825	827	-0.1	10	336	344	351	0.6	2.40	247	250	0.3
54494	WISCONSIN RAPIDS	141	27712	27856	28197	0.1	20	10966	11337	11793	0.8	2.41	7674	7831	0.5
54495	WISCONSIN RAPIDS	141	7423	7280	7298	-0.5	4	3104	3131	3223	0.2	2.32	1974	1956	-0.2
54498	WITHEE	119	2201	2261	2303	0.6	41	772	806	832	1.0	2.80	585	604	0.8
54499	WITTENBERG	115	3060	3124	3198	0.5	33	1111	1170	1228	1.2	2.51	787	815	0.8
54501	RHINELANDER	085	20300	20819	21786	0.6	39	8145	8533	9127	1.1	2.36	5445	5632	0.8
54511	ARGONNE	041	1401	1580	1720	2.9	94	567	662	744	3.7	2.37	386	446	3.5
54512	BOULDER JUNCTION	125	798	884	975	2.4	91	370	421	476	3.1	2.10	265	298	2.8
54513	BRANTWOOD	099	473	463	460	-0.5	4	207	209	214	0.2	2.22	141	140	-0.2
	WISCONSIN					0.8					1.4	2.44			1.1
	UNITED STATES					1.2					1.3	2.58			1.1

ZIP CODE #	POST OFFICE NAME	RACE (%) White 2000	White 2004	Black 2000	Black 2004	Asian/Pacific 2000	Asian/Pacific 2004	% Hispanic Origin 2000	% Hispanic Origin 2004	2004 AGE DISTRIBUTION (%) 0-4	5-9	10-14	15-19	20-24	25-44	45-64	65-84	85+	18+	MEDIAN AGE 2004	% 2004 Males	% 2004 Females
54216	KEWAUNEE	98.6	98.4	0.3	0.3	0.2	0.3	0.5	0.6	5.8	5.9	6.6	6.8	6.1	25.9	26.9	13.0	2.9	77.4	40.6	51.2	48.8
54217	LUXEMBURG	98.9	98.8	0.1	0.1	0.2	0.2	0.5	0.5	6.9	7.4	7.7	6.5	6.2	29.5	24.3	10.0	1.5	73.8	36.3	50.7	49.3
54220	MANITOWOC	94.1	93.1	0.5	0.6	3.2	4.0	2.2	2.5	6.0	5.9	6.6	6.6	6.7	25.6	25.1	14.3	3.2	77.5	40.3	48.9	51.1
54227	MARIBEL	98.1	97.7	0.0	0.0	0.4	0.6	0.6	0.7	6.6	7.4	8.2	7.4	5.6	27.1	29.3	7.4	1.1	72.8	38.4	52.3	47.7
54228	MISHICOT	98.6	98.4	0.1	0.1	0.2	0.3	0.9	1.3	5.6	6.8	8.9	7.4	5.3	26.8	26.9	11.0	1.4	73.9	38.7	52.2	47.8
54229	NEW FRANKEN	96.9	96.5	1.5	1.7	0.4	0.5	0.6	0.7	6.3	6.6	7.5	6.8	5.0	30.7	27.5	8.7	0.8	74.9	38.0	52.3	47.7
54230	REEDSVILLE	98.5	98.2	0.0	0.0	0.2	0.2	1.0	1.2	6.0	6.4	7.4	7.2	6.3	28.4	26.6	10.3	1.5	75.7	38.0	51.7	48.3
54234	SISTER BAY	98.8	98.7	0.1	0.1	0.2	0.2	0.7	0.8	3.5	3.7	4.2	4.0	3.6	16.4	33.4	25.4	6.0	85.9	54.9	46.6	53.4
54235	STURGEON BAY	97.4	97.2	0.2	0.2	0.3	0.4	1.1	1.3	4.7	5.3	6.6	6.6	5.6	24.2	29.2	15.1	2.7	79.1	43.1	49.5	50.5
54241	TWO RIVERS	96.3	95.8	0.1	0.1	1.9	2.3	1.2	1.4	5.5	5.8	7.5	7.1	6.5	25.6	26.1	13.8	2.2	76.6	40.1	49.8	50.2
54245	VALDERS	98.7	98.6	0.0	0.0	0.2	0.2	1.0	1.1	6.3	7.1	7.7	6.8	5.6	26.1	27.7	11.2	1.4	74.5	38.6	50.6	49.4
54246	WASHINGTON ISLAND	98.8	98.7	0.0	0.0	0.3	0.5	0.2	0.2	3.6	4.2	7.8	6.3	4.2	15.0	37.4	18.4	3.1	80.7	51.0	48.7	51.4
54247	WHITELAW	98.7	98.5	0.0	0.1	0.3	0.4	0.7	0.9	6.1	6.6	7.5	7.4	6.1	27.9	27.5	9.4	1.5	75.1	38.3	51.6	48.4
54301	GREEN BAY	87.8	86.1	3.9	4.4	2.2	2.7	5.2	6.0	6.1	6.0	6.6	7.3	8.7	29.7	22.1	11.0	2.5	77.1	35.8	52.5	47.6
54302	GREEN BAY	82.1	79.3	1.4	1.5	4.3	5.3	14.0	16.2	7.5	6.7	6.7	7.2	9.8	31.5	20.2	8.9	1.6	75.3	31.7	50.2	49.8
54303	GREEN BAY	86.3	84.2	1.7	2.0	4.6	5.8	3.6	4.3	7.6	6.6	6.3	6.7	8.3	31.3	20.4	10.5	2.4	75.6	33.9	48.4	51.6
54304	GREEN BAY	90.4	89.0	0.8	1.0	2.7	3.4	2.5	3.0	6.4	6.1	6.6	6.4	7.5	28.9	23.3	12.3	2.5	77.0	37.3	48.3	51.7
54311	GREEN BAY	95.0	94.1	0.7	0.8	1.7	2.1	2.5	3.0	6.9	6.8	7.0	8.1	8.7	31.7	22.5	7.3	1.2	75.3	32.9	49.1	50.9
54313	GREEN BAY	95.3	94.7	0.3	0.4	0.9	1.1	0.9	1.1	6.9	7.2	8.4	7.6	6.7	29.1	27.6	6.0	0.5	72.4	36.1	49.8	50.2
54401	WAUSAU	88.7	86.4	0.3	0.4	9.4	11.5	0.8	1.0	6.3	6.5	7.5	7.1	6.8	27.1	24.8	12.0	2.1	75.4	37.5	49.0	51.0
54403	WAUSAU	89.8	87.7	0.6	0.7	7.8	9.7	0.9	1.0	6.0	6.0	7.1	7.2	7.0	25.8	25.0	13.0	3.1	76.5	39.0	49.0	51.0
54405	ABBOTSFORD	98.6	98.6	0.1	0.1	0.2	0.2	1.6	1.8	6.7	6.6	7.0	6.7	6.4	26.7	22.5	14.4	3.2	75.6	38.3	51.1	48.9
54406	AMHERST	98.8	98.7	0.3	0.4	0.2	0.3	0.8	1.0	6.8	7.1	7.2	6.9	5.9	27.4	27.1	9.6	2.1	74.6	38.1	51.3	48.7
54407	AMHERST JUNCTION	98.0	97.7	0.1	0.1	0.5	0.7	0.7	0.8	6.2	7.0	8.5	7.0	4.9	28.5	25.9	10.6	1.6	74.0	38.0	52.2	47.8
54408	ANIWA	96.4	95.9	0.1	0.2	0.9	1.2	0.7	0.6	6.6	6.7	8.0	7.4	5.9	28.6	25.4	10.5	1.0	74.3	37.6	53.2	46.8
54409	ANTIGO	97.5	97.3	0.2	0.2	0.3	0.4	1.0	1.2	6.2	6.0	7.2	7.1	6.3	25.4	24.2	14.2	3.3	76.1	39.5	49.2	50.8
54410	ARPIN	98.0	97.8	0.1	0.1	0.4	0.6	0.6	0.6	6.4	6.6	7.7	7.1	5.6	27.5	24.6	10.7	3.9	74.7	38.7	50.6	49.4
54411	ATHENS	98.7	98.5	0.2	0.2	0.1	0.2	1.1	1.3	8.3	8.3	8.4	7.4	6.2	28.2	22.0	10.0	1.3	70.4	34.2	50.8	49.2
54412	AUBURNDALE	99.4	99.3	0.1	0.1	0.1	0.1	0.2	0.3	5.9	7.1	7.1	6.9	6.0	30.4	23.9	11.6	1.3	75.3	37.1	52.5	47.5
54413	BABCOCK	95.6	95.1	0.5	0.8	0.3	0.5	1.3	1.5	5.7	6.4	8.0	7.2	5.1	25.7	26.7	13.9	1.3	75.3	40.2	51.7	48.3
54414	BIRNAMWOOD	96.0	95.6	0.2	0.1	0.7	0.9	0.4	0.5	6.8	6.9	7.9	7.3	6.2	28.2	23.4	11.7	1.7	73.6	37.0	51.5	48.5
54416	BOWLER	56.5	55.7	0.1	0.1	0.2	0.2	0.9	0.8	7.6	7.7	8.8	8.1	6.9	25.8	22.4	11.3	1.4	70.5	34.8	49.3	50.7
54418	BRYANT	98.7	98.5	0.1	0.2	0.2	0.2	0.3	0.4	5.6	6.1	7.7	7.4	3.6	24.1	29.2	15.0	1.4	75.7	42.4	51.6	48.4
54420	CHILI	98.1	97.7	0.0	0.0	0.8	1.1	1.0	1.2	9.8	9.1	8.6	7.7	7.3	27.0	21.3	8.4	0.9	67.8	30.5	51.6	48.4
54421	COLBY	97.5	97.2	0.1	0.2	0.3	0.4	2.3	2.7	7.2	7.0	7.2	7.5	7.0	24.9	22.8	13.2	3.3	73.9	37.7	49.4	50.6
54422	CURTISS	96.0	95.4	0.1	0.1	0.2	0.2	3.5	4.0	8.8	8.9	10.0	7.9	6.8	26.4	20.1	10.0	1.2	67.4	31.7	51.4	48.6
54423	CUSTER	98.7	98.6	0.1	0.0	0.1	0.1	0.9	1.1	5.8	6.3	7.3	6.6	5.9	28.1	29.2	9.5	1.4	76.5	39.1	52.1	47.9
54424	DEERBROOK	99.0	98.9	0.1	0.1	0.1	0.2	0.5	0.5	4.6	4.9	6.6	6.7	4.6	24.2	29.5	17.4	1.7	79.8	44.1	51.1	48.9
54425	DORCHESTER	97.8	97.5	0.1	0.1	0.1	0.1	1.9	2.2	8.7	7.2	7.5	7.1	6.9	28.2	20.8	11.4	2.2	72.3	34.9	51.0	49.0
54426	EDGAR	99.0	98.8	0.1	0.1	0.4	0.5	0.3	0.3	7.0	7.2	8.1	7.0	6.6	28.4	23.5	10.9	1.3	73.4	36.4	51.8	48.2
54427	ELAND	97.0	96.6	0.1	0.1	0.6	0.7	1.0	1.2	5.7	6.1	7.4	7.0	5.9	27.3	25.8	13.1	1.8	76.3	39.5	51.9	48.2
54428	ELCHO	98.0	97.7	0.1	0.1	0.9	1.1	0.2	0.2	3.9	4.1	5.5	4.9	4.0	21.8	30.9	22.8	2.3	83.5	49.5	50.7	49.3
54430	ELTON	98.2	97.5	0.0	0.0	0.0	0.9	0.0	0.0	5.9	5.9	8.5	11.0	3.4	24.6	28.0	11.0	1.7	71.2	39.4	50.9	49.2
54433	GILMAN	98.7	98.5	0.0	0.0	0.3	0.3	0.6	0.7	6.0	6.2	7.6	7.1	6.4	23.6	26.7	14.1	2.4	75.5	40.6	51.9	48.1
54435	GLEASON	98.5	98.3	0.2	0.2	0.3	0.4	0.6	0.7	4.8	5.6	6.8	6.9	4.9	26.3	29.1	13.8	1.7	78.2	42.0	52.4	47.6
54436	GRANTON	98.6	98.4	0.1	0.1	0.3	0.4	1.2	1.3	8.8	8.3	7.7	7.5	7.2	25.9	23.2	10.4	1.0	70.5	34.1	51.6	48.4
54437	GREENWOOD	98.6	98.4	0.1	0.1	0.3	0.3	0.8	0.9	8.3	8.0	8.3	7.4	6.6	24.4	23.0	11.9	2.0	70.8	36.0	50.8	49.2
54440	HATLEY	98.6	98.4	0.1	0.1	0.1	0.2	0.9	1.1	6.6	6.6	7.3	6.8	5.5	30.8	25.6	9.8	1.1	75.0	37.3	52.3	47.7
54441	HEWITT	99.4	99.3	0.0	0.0	0.2	0.3	0.5	0.4	6.2	6.6	7.7	7.8	5.7	28.0	28.0	8.5	1.5	74.8	39.1	49.5	50.5
54442	IRMA	89.9	89.0	4.9	5.4	0.6	0.7	2.4	2.7	4.4	4.8	7.0	19.4	4.9	20.4	27.6	11.0	0.6	66.9	36.5	59.8	40.2
54443	JUNCTION CITY	98.1	97.9	0.1	0.1	1.0	1.2	1.3	1.5	6.1	6.6	7.8	6.9	6.0	27.3	27.2	10.7	1.4	75.2	38.9	51.5	48.5
54446	LOYAL	98.9	98.8	0.2	0.2	0.1	0.2	0.9	1.0	10.1	9.2	8.5	7.3	6.7	26.1	20.1	10.4	1.6	67.7	31.8	50.8	49.2
54447	LUBLIN	99.1	99.1	0.0	0.0	0.2	0.2	0.7	0.8	6.2	6.6	7.4	6.6	5.3	24.4	27.8	13.8	1.9	75.8	40.1	53.5	46.5
54448	MARATHON	98.6	98.2	0.1	0.0	1.0	1.3	0.4	0.5	6.2	6.8	8.1	7.0	5.9	28.1	26.3	10.6	1.2	74.5	37.8	51.3	48.7
54449	MARSHFIELD	97.6	97.1	0.3	0.3	1.2	1.6	0.7	0.8	6.1	6.2	6.9	6.7	6.4	26.9	25.9	12.2	2.8	76.7	39.2	48.7	51.3
54451	MEDFORD	98.6	98.5	0.1	0.1	0.3	0.3	0.6	0.7	6.1	6.3	7.4	7.2	6.4	27.8	24.3	12.0	2.6	75.6	38.2	50.5	49.6
54452	MERRILL	98.0	97.7	0.2	0.3	0.4	0.6	0.8	0.9	6.3	6.4	7.0	7.1	6.4	27.1	24.7	12.4	2.7	75.9	38.6	49.5	50.5
54454	MILLADORE	98.4	98.2	0.0	0.0	0.6	0.7	0.5	0.6	6.8	6.8	7.3	6.9	7.3	28.8	24.7	10.4	1.2	75.1	37.2	52.8	47.2
54455	MOSINEE	98.5	98.2	0.1	0.2	0.6	0.8	0.6	0.6	6.6	6.8	7.6	6.6	5.9	29.7	26.7	9.1	1.3	74.9	37.6	50.9	49.1
54456	NEILLSVILLE	97.5	97.2	0.2	0.2	0.6	0.7	1.0	1.2	6.2	6.3	6.8	7.4	6.6	23.5	24.5	15.0	3.7	75.9	40.4	49.3	50.7
54457	NEKOOSA	95.9	95.5	0.1	0.1	0.6	0.8	1.8	2.1	5.5	5.8	7.2	6.7	5.2	23.7	27.9	16.5	1.5	77.4	42.4	50.6	49.4
54459	OGEMA	98.8	98.9	0.1	0.1	0.1	0.1	0.6	0.6	6.3	6.5	6.7	6.3	5.9	24.4	27.8	14.1	2.0	76.7	41.2	52.9	47.1
54460	OWEN	98.1	97.9	0.3	0.3	0.2	0.3	1.1	1.3	7.9	7.5	7.6	6.8	6.4	24.1	21.2	14.6	3.9	72.8	37.3	49.6	50.4
54462	PEARSON	98.9	98.9	0.0	0.0	0.3	0.3	0.3	0.3	3.0	3.2	4.8	4.3	3.2	20.7	33.9	25.0	1.9	85.8	52.5	51.9	48.1
54463	PELICAN LAKE	98.6	98.5	0.0	0.0	0.2	0.1	0.2	0.1	4.3	5.0	6.7	4.9	4.1	25.4	30.5	17.2	2.0	79.9	44.8	52.5	47.5
54465	PICKEREL	89.5	89.0	0.0	0.1	0.0	0.1	0.3	0.3	4.7	5.1	6.1	5.3	3.6	22.3	30.5	21.0	1.4	80.7	47.0	52.0	48.0
54466	PITTSVILLE	95.2	95.0	1.4	1.5	0.3	0.5	0.5	0.5	5.9	6.2	7.5	6.6	6.7	27.4	26.0	12.1	1.6	76.3	38.6	53.2	46.8
54467	PLOVER	96.9	96.4	0.4	0.4	1.1	1.3	1.2	1.4	7.2	7.1	7.4	7.4	7.8	30.0	25.6	6.8	0.6	73.4	34.5	49.9	50.1
54469	PORT EDWARDS	93.2	92.2	0.6	0.6	3.9	4.8	0.9	1.1	5.3	5.5	8.6	7.8	6.7	21.7	23.4	16.4	4.6	75.5	41.2	48.9	51.1
54470	RIB LAKE	98.9	98.7	0.1	0.1	0.4	0.5	0.6	0.7	5.2	5.7	7.6	7.2	5.8	26.3	25.4	13.8	3.1	76.6	40.0	51.6	48.4
54471	RINGLE	97.5	97.1	0.1	0.1	0.4	0.5	0.5	0.6	6.5	6.8	7.9	8.0	4.4	29.1	27.6	8.7	0.9	73.6	38.6	50.7	49.3
54473	ROSHOLT	98.4	98.2	0.2	0.2	0.2	0.2	1.7	2.1	6.2	6.3	7.7	7.3	6.0	28.1	25.4	11.2	1.9	75.3	37.9	51.7	48.3
54474	ROTHSCHILD	95.7	94.6	0.3	0.3	3.3	4.4	0.2	0.3	5.6	6.0	7.3	7.4	6.2	25.4	27.5	12.6	2.0	76.7	40.2	50.3	49.7
54475	RUDOLPH	96.8	96.2	0.3	0.3	2.2	2.7	0.7	0.8	6.4	6.6	6.6	6.5	6.0	25.2	27.6	13.6	1.6	76.9	40.2	50.1	49.9
54476	SCHOFIELD	93.8	92.2	0.3	0.4	4.2	5.6	0.8	0.9	7.6	7.2	7.6	6.4	7.6	31.4	22.2	8.7	1.3	73.6	33.9	49.8	50.3
54479	SPENCER	98.8	98.6	0.1	0.1	0.3	0.4	0.9	1.1	7.3	7.2	7.5	7.5	7.5	28.3	23.1	10.2	1.6	73.5	35.5	49.7	50.3
54480	STETSONVILLE	98.7	98.6	0.2	0.2	0.1	0.1	1.3	1.5	7.0	7.3	8.1	7.2	6.2	27.1	25.8	10.3	1.2	73.3	37.1	51.0	49.0
54481	STEVENS POINT	94.3	93.3	0.4	0.5	3.5	4.4	1.4	1.6	5.4	5.2	5.8	9.9	15.9	25.2	20.9	9.9	1.9	79.9	30.7	49.1	51.0
54484	STRATFORD	98.9	98.7	0.0	0.0	0.5	0.6	0.6	0.7	7.4	7.3	7.1	6.5	6.2	29.8	24.5	9.8	1.5	74.3	36.4	51.2	48.8
54485	SUMMIT LAKE	97.9	98.0	0.0	0.0	0.5	1.0	0.0	0.0	4.6	4.6	4.6	5.1	4.6	21.3	31.0	21.8	2.5	82.7	48.8	51.8	48.2
54486	TIGERTON	95.6	95.1	0.5	0.6	0.3	0.4	0.6	0.7	6.1	6.3	7.3	6.1	6.0	25.3	25.5	14.3	3.1	76.5	40.8	49.8	50.2
54487	TOMAHAWK	98.6	98.5	0.1	0.1	0.4	0.4	0.6	0.6	5.0	5.4	6.3	6.3	4.4	24.2	29.2	16.7	2.5	79.0	44.0	49.7	50.3
54488	UNITY	97.8	97.5	0.0	0.0	1.1	1.5	0.6	0.7	8.7	8.8	8.8	7.1	6.0	28.0	23.1	8.6	1.2	69.4	34.0	51.4	48.6
54489	VESPER	97.9	97.6	0.1	0.1	0.1	0.1	0.5	0.6	6.2	6.7	7.9	7.2	5.3	27.4	26.1	11.3	1.9	74.7	38.8	50.9	49.1
54490	WESTBORO	98.7	98.7	0.2	0.2	0.2	0.2	0.5	0.4	5.8	6.0	7.3	7.0	6.4	26.3	25.0	12.9	3.4	76.3	39.1	50.1	49.9
54491	WHITE LAKE	98.5	98.3	0.0	0.0	0.2	0.2	0.9	1.0	4.7	5.1	6.6	7.6	4.1	21.3	29.7	19.0	1.9	78.4	45.4	52.1	47.9
54493	WILLARD	97.4	97.2	0.1	0.2	0.0	0.0	0.8	0.9	6.8	7.0	7.6	6.9	6.1	23.4	28.1	12.4	1.7	74.3	40.1	51.8	48.2
54494	WISCONSIN RAPIDS	96.3	95.6	0.3	0.3	1.9	2.4	0.9	1.1	6.2	6.4	7.1	7.0	5.6	26.8	26.2	12.4	2.3	75.6	39.6	49.1	50.9
54495	WISCONSIN RAPIDS	93.6	92.6	0.2	0.3	3.2	3.9	1.6	1.9	7.0	6.9	7.2	6.6	7.1	26.4	23.2	13.6	2.1	74.9	37.0	49.1	50.9
54498	WITHEE	97.9	97.6	0.1	0.0	0.1	0.2	1.6	1.9	7.7	7.8	8.5	6.9	6.2	24.1	24.1	12.7	2.0	71.6	36.7	50.7	49.3
54499	WITTENBERG	95.1	94.7	0.9	1.0	0.2	0.2	0.7	0.8	6.5	5.9	7.6	8.1	5.6	24.7	23.1	14.7	3.9	74.4	39.2	51.3	48.7
54501	RHINELANDER	97.6	97.4	0.3	0.3	0.4	0.5	0.6	0.7	5.3	5.7	6.8	6.8	5.6	25.6	27.6	14.2	2.4	77.8	41.6	49.2	50.8
54511	ARGONNE	95.2	95.1	0.1	0.1	0.4	0.4	0.5	0.6	4.5	4.6	5.5	5.5	6.0	21.3	28.2	22.0	2.4	82.2	46.8	52.2	47.9
54512	BOULDER JUNCTION	95.6	95.7	0.0	0.0	0.1	0.1	0.5	0.5	3.3	3.9	4.6	4.4	3.5	17.8	34.2	26.1	2.3	85.5	52.6	51.1	48.9
54513	BRANTWOOD	98.9	98.7	0.2	0.2	0.2	0.2	1.3	1.3	3.5	4.1	6.5	7.6	5.0	25.1	30.5	15.6	2.4	81.4	44.0	52.1	48.0
	WISCONSIN	88.9	88.0	5.7	6.0	1.7	2.1	3.6	4.0	6.4	6.5	7.1	7.3	7.7	27.6	24.5	11.1	1.9	75.8	36.9	49.5	50.5
	UNITED STATES	75.1	73.6	12.3	12.5	3.8	4.2	12.5	14.1	6.9	6.7	7.2	7.0	7.3	28.6	23.8	10.8	1.7	75.1	36.0	49.1	50.9

ZIP CODE				2004 HOUSEHOLD INCOME DISTRIBUTION (%)					MEDIAN HOUSEHOLD INCOME					2004 HOME VALUE DISTRIBUTION (%)					
#	POST OFFICE NAME	2004 Per Capita Income	2004 HH Income Base	Less than $25,000	$25,000 to $49,999	$50,000 to $99,999	$100,000 to $149,999	$150,000 or More	2004	2009	2004 National Centile	2004 State Centile	2004 Home Value Base	Less than $50,000	$50,000 to $89,999	$90,000 to $174,999	$175,000 to $399,999	$400,000 or More	2004 Median Home Value
54216	KEWAUNEE	21074	2457	24.7	28.3	37.5	7.6	2.0	47360	52583	67	57	1988	8.1	24.1	48.0	17.2	2.6	111040
54217	LUXEMBURG	22628	2598	17.0	27.4	42.5	9.9	3.1	53988	61163	78	74	2190	6.3	10.7	50.2	28.0	4.8	140402
54220	MANITOWOC	23463	17352	24.8	31.7	34.7	6.1	2.8	44660	50674	60	48	12293	6.6	23.7	52.8	15.6	1.4	111030
54227	MARIBEL	23265	601	14.8	24.6	47.4	9.7	3.5	59373	64924	84	84	531	4.9	13.8	44.6	35.0	1.7	149821
54228	MISHICOT	22637	1164	17.3	30.9	41.6	7.7	2.5	51614	57932	75	68	985	5.1	20.0	54.9	18.2	1.8	118436
54229	NEW FRANKEN	26046	1266	9.7	22.0	46.2	16.4	5.6	65065	76243	89	93	1154	0.9	4.9	43.1	46.2	4.9	176563
54230	REEDSVILLE	22925	1764	17.1	29.1	42.8	8.6	2.5	52785	59703	77	72	1508	6.8	19.6	49.0	22.4	2.2	122232
54234	SISTER BAY	32181	1051	23.8	29.4	30.5	11.1	5.1	46603	56917	65	54	830	0.2	2.4	27.2	51.9	18.2	233465
54235	STURGEON BAY	23752	7802	27.5	32.3	28.8	8.3	3.1	40735	47342	49	33	6009	8.9	16.5	43.5	22.6	8.4	126400
54241	TWO RIVERS	22660	6580	22.8	31.4	36.9	6.4	2.5	46422	52801	65	54	5034	4.4	29.9	52.0	12.2	1.5	103932
54245	VALDERS	23932	929	17.7	26.9	44.8	7.6	3.0	54301	61210	79	75	796	11.6	11.8	45.2	29.0	2.4	136712
54246	WASHINGTON ISLAND	20054	303	36.0	28.4	29.4	5.0	1.3	34863	40222	27	7	254	2.8	12.2	35.8	39.4	9.8	172917
54247	WHITELAW	23882	960	16.6	28.5	42.7	9.4	2.8	54120	60716	79	75	832	5.9	17.8	47.8	26.6	1.9	126905
54301	GREEN BAY	25233	10060	25.6	28.9	30.6	9.4	5.5	45910	52818	64	52	6460	1.3	12.3	64.6	20.3	1.4	128676
54302	GREEN BAY	22289	13361	28.8	32.3	30.2	6.3	2.4	40719	47595	49	33	6835	12.6	17.6	56.1	12.3	1.5	110026
54303	GREEN BAY	20433	12426	29.9	35.3	29.7	4.1	1.1	38198	44726	40	22	5969	2.3	26.5	65.9	5.1	0.2	105487
54304	GREEN BAY	25206	13366	20.7	32.2	36.5	7.8	2.8	47437	54649	67	57	8592	1.7	13.0	74.3	10.7	0.2	119561
54311	GREEN BAY	26499	11241	13.3	26.1	43.4	12.5	4.7	60216	69429	85	86	7770	5.6	3.9	52.4	36.0	2.2	157931
54313	GREEN BAY	28764	12025	9.8	20.9	46.5	15.2	7.6	67864	79256	90	94	10125	0.6	2.2	52.1	41.9	3.2	167949
54401	WAUSAU	25602	12080	19.5	31.5	35.3	8.4	5.3	49009	56233	70	62	8731	5.7	22.0	52.1	17.8	2.4	113420
54403	WAUSAU	25291	9937	26.5	29.1	31.2	8.4	4.9	44584	50692	60	47	6841	3.3	20.4	59.9	14.5	2.0	114262
54405	ABBOTSFORD	19700	1157	27.7	34.6	31.6	4.3	1.8	41384	46739	51	35	884	22.0	32.9	38.1	6.0	1.0	83944
54406	AMHERST	22115	1240	20.3	30.5	38.8	7.8	2.6	49267	56961	71	63	1024	5.3	14.0	55.1	23.6	2.1	128986
54407	AMHERST JUNCTION	23979	646	18.1	31.4	38.5	7.3	4.6	50408	58253	73	65	556	6.1	15.3	52.9	22.8	2.9	123992
54408	ANIWA	20830	471	21.9	33.6	36.3	5.7	2.6	46030	52295	64	52	409	13.7	20.3	47.4	16.9	1.7	111655
54409	ANTIGO	19448	5867	33.5	32.4	28.2	4.2	1.7	36728	41208	34	14	4273	17.8	39.0	33.2	9.3	0.7	81531
54410	ARPIN	19419	820	20.7	35.1	35.5	6.5	2.2	44434	50240	60	46	678	15.5	23.9	41.6	17.3	1.8	105691
54411	ATHENS	18163	1881	22.3	30.0	39.9	5.9	2.0	48192	53625	69	59	1592	12.1	26.7	46.4	13.3	1.5	101822
54412	AUBURNDALE	21259	731	19.2	32.8	38.7	7.9	1.4	48556	55025	69	60	617	10.1	24.2	49.1	14.9	1.8	106612
54413	BABCOCK	23689	162	19.1	33.3	38.3	7.4	1.9	47644	54229	68	58	138	15.9	26.8	43.5	12.3	1.5	96250
54414	BIRNAMWOOD	19689	1289	24.2	33.9	34.1	5.6	2.2	43473	48781	57	43	1075	21.3	28.0	39.4	10.4	0.9	90904
54416	BOWLER	15390	719	31.4	35.1	29.4	2.9	1.3	37273	41721	36	17	570	24.2	29.7	35.3	9.5	1.4	85510
54418	BRYANT	19354	487	24.4	37.6	31.8	4.1	2.1	41982	46834	53	38	417	16.3	25.7	38.9	18.2	1.0	102226
54420	CHILI	14692	426	31.2	36.4	27.7	2.6	2.1	37244	41203	36	17	356	18.0	30.1	37.1	13.8	1.1	92414
54421	COLBY	18460	1233	26.3	37.6	29.9	4.1	2.1	41468	47124	51	36	996	16.8	31.0	41.6	9.5	1.1	92973
54422	CURTISS	14379	360	29.2	35.3	28.9	4.4	2.2	40144	43831	47	30	314	22.9	27.7	34.4	13.1	1.9	88824
54423	CUSTER	23662	849	13.8	27.4	45.8	9.2	3.8	56722	65645	81	80	757	5.4	10.6	51.9	28.4	3.7	142300
54424	DEERBROOK	21033	712	26.5	35.8	30.6	4.9	2.1	42041	46994	53	38	656	11.7	25.6	41.9	18.9	1.8	109500
54425	DORCHESTER	18825	770	25.7	34.7	32.3	5.2	2.1	40536	45957	48	32	622	18.2	31.4	41.6	7.2	1.6	90536
54426	EDGAR	20972	1454	20.7	31.8	38.3	6.7	2.5	47827	53238	68	58	1210	11.7	19.7	53.4	14.4	0.9	111551
54427	ELAND	20473	434	26.5	32.5	33.9	4.8	2.3	43243	49342	57	41	365	17.8	28.2	43.8	8.8	1.4	95179
54428	ELCHO	19567	622	35.5	37.1	23.5	2.6	1.3	32719	38242	20	3	512	13.7	27.7	42.2	15.0	1.4	99362
54430	ELTON	19195	48	25.0	37.5	31.3	6.3	0.0	41805	47312	52	37	40	20.0	25.0	37.5	17.5	0.0	96667
54433	GILMAN	18936	700	33.4	29.6	29.7	4.3	3.0	37461	41743	37	19	595	21.5	29.1	35.8	11.3	2.4	88939
54435	GLEASON	20524	812	26.2	32.8	34.5	5.1	1.5	43307	49255	57	42	716	10.9	22.9	45.7	18.9	1.7	111940
54436	GRANTON	15480	752	29.5	36.4	28.1	4.0	2.0	38408	42294	41	22	640	20.5	29.7	33.9	14.1	1.9	89756
54437	GREENWOOD	16792	1101	32.6	32.9	28.6	4.1	1.8	36872	41208	35	16	857	16.6	35.0	34.8	11.4	2.2	88043
54440	HATLEY	24484	1141	18.0	27.3	43.0	8.4	3.3	53632	60685	78	73	997	7.0	17.5	56.7	16.7	2.2	118061
54441	HEWITT	23828	246	13.4	27.2	45.9	8.9	4.5	55836	63346	81	79	219	1.8	19.2	55.3	22.8	0.9	122877
54442	IRMA	18875	466	21.7	32.0	39.1	6.0	1.3	46831	52138	66	55	422	10.2	19.9	48.1	20.4	1.4	114402
54443	JUNCTION CITY	24408	881	19.5	25.8	41.8	8.3	4.7	53744	62030	78	73	741	6.8	19.7	44.0	24.6	5.0	125710
54446	LOYAL	16974	1119	32.9	29.2	30.9	4.9	2.1	38552	42279	41	23	879	19.3	32.3	35.2	11.3	1.9	87769
54447	LUBLIN	16746	206	38.4	30.1	26.2	2.9	2.4	32147	36404	18	3	166	28.9	31.3	27.7	12.1	0.0	73846
54448	MARATHON	24940	1692	15.9	30.1	39.9	10.3	3.8	53406	60530	78	73	1489	8.7	14.1	51.8	23.6	1.8	124707
54449	MARSHFIELD	26176	11427	24.6	30.7	32.7	6.7	5.2	45200	51546	62	49	7847	8.6	24.7	50.5	15.1	1.2	109719
54451	MEDFORD	21829	4569	25.3	31.6	34.3	6.0	2.8	44273	50321	59	46	3548	12.1	26.2	47.6	12.7	1.3	103642
54452	MERRILL	21269	8016	26.3	28.9	36.0	7.0	1.8	45144	50735	62	49	6108	10.0	24.2	50.2	14.8	0.8	108418
54454	MILLADORE	21566	471	17.2	24.6	46.5	9.8	1.9	55468	63104	80	78	415	10.8	24.8	48.0	15.9	0.5	105322
54455	MOSINEE	25991	6253	14.6	25.7	45.5	10.9	3.4	56909	64981	82	80	5253	6.0	13.0	60.5	19.0	1.5	124255
54456	NEILLSVILLE	18942	2486	32.6	32.3	28.0	5.2	2.0	37002	41680	35	17	1860	20.1	32.7	36.4	10.2	0.7	86176
54457	NEKOOSA	23393	3755	20.3	33.5	36.6	8.0	1.6	46802	53408	66	55	3218	8.1	31.3	43.3	16.2	1.1	106126
54459	OGEMA	20954	582	31.4	37.3	25.3	3.8	2.2	36683	41655	34	14	484	26.0	28.5	32.4	10.5	2.5	83529
54460	OWEN	16071	928	34.3	33.2	27.2	3.9	1.5	35568	39579	30	10	717	29.4	31.1	29.3	8.9	1.3	74352
54462	PEARSON	19005	169	34.3	37.3	23.1	3.6	1.8	33323	38516	22	4	144	13.9	27.1	41.7	16.7	0.7	102500
54463	PELICAN LAKE	20753	327	21.7	49.2	25.7	2.5	0.9	38011	44320	39	21	278	10.4	23.7	41.0	24.1	0.7	111058
54465	PICKEREL	22035	391	33.3	38.4	23.3	3.3	1.8	34280	39826	25	7	324	13.0	23.8	44.8	17.9	0.6	109127
54466	PITTSVILLE	21107	1115	22.6	35.3	34.2	5.7	2.3	44516	50575	60	47	935	17.7	27.4	43.6	9.4	1.9	93875
54467	PLOVER	26857	4844	14.4	29.4	39.6	10.8	5.7	55619	64194	80	78	3417	8.8	6.1	60.1	23.9	1.1	138972
54469	PORT EDWARDS	23905	695	18.7	24.6	41.3	11.4	4.0	54219	62973	79	75	571	1.8	29.8	55.7	12.3	0.5	106568
54470	RIB LAKE	18522	807	31.2	33.1	30.1	4.7	0.9	39631	45366	45	27	613	17.9	32.3	41.9	7.7	0.2	89717
54471	RINGLE	24771	596	13.9	22.7	48.2	11.1	4.2	61324	68588	86	89	551	1.6	10.3	57.5	28.0	2.5	140495
54473	ROSHOLT	20794	1080	20.1	30.7	39.4	6.9	2.9	49368	56541	71	63	911	10.4	21.2	47.6	19.0	1.8	114746
54474	ROTHSCHILD	24891	1538	19.8	28.0	39.3	9.1	3.8	52053	58242	76	69	1253	1.8	23.1	60.0	14.6	0.4	111275
54475	RUDOLPH	22924	610	18.7	28.5	41.0	9.0	2.8	51992	58761	75	69	519	6.7	24.9	55.3	12.3	0.8	108903
54476	SCHOFIELD	23962	6479	19.8	30.8	38.4	8.3	2.8	49561	55957	71	63	4350	11.8	11.5	60.6	15.2	0.9	119245
54479	SPENCER	18904	1395	23.8	33.1	37.4	4.4	1.4	45508	51285	63	51	1109	16.7	33.6	41.0	7.8	0.9	89660
54480	STETSONVILLE	21248	448	19.2	34.4	35.7	7.1	3.6	47097	54026	66	56	368	14.4	22.8	50.5	10.3	1.9	103797
54481	STEVENS POINT	22742	14878	27.0	29.0	32.4	8.0	3.7	44597	51518	60	47	9466	7.2	17.8	55.4	18.2	1.4	117954
54484	STRATFORD	21545	1774	20.5	29.9	39.9	7.1	2.6	49665	55535	71	64	1469	12.9	27.0	45.5	13.6	1.1	101920
54485	SUMMIT LAKE	20733	89	33.7	33.7	27.0	3.4	2.3	36921	41936	35	16	79	8.9	22.8	45.6	19.0	3.8	115625
54486	TIGERTON	18029	1080	32.6	34.5	26.9	4.8	1.1	37079	40681	36	17	847	17.8	28.8	39.1	12.4	1.9	95182
54487	TOMAHAWK	21218	4224	28.4	32.2	31.8	5.8	1.8	41370	47046	51	35	3396	8.5	22.2	45.0	22.3	2.1	118397
54488	UNITY	17396	422	26.8	34.8	32.0	4.3	2.1	41419	45544	51	36	363	16.8	27.3	37.7	15.7	2.5	97679
54489	VESPER	20391	621	24.8	29.3	38.2	6.0	1.8	47332	53441	67	56	526	10.8	28.7	48.9	10.8	0.8	101844
54490	WESTBORO	19018	352	27.6	35.5	31.0	4.3	1.7	40793	47623	49	33	274	17.5	33.2	40.9	7.7	0.7	89259
54491	WHITE LAKE	19479	758	31.1	36.2	27.6	4.0	1.2	36015	41011	32	12	631	25.5	26.6	35.7	11.7	0.5	86029
54493	WILLARD	19273	344	30.8	34.0	29.1	4.7	1.5	37224	41490	36	17	300	15.7	25.3	44.0	13.7	1.3	103279
54494	WISCONSIN RAPIDS	24683	11337	22.5	27.1	37.4	9.1	3.9	50293	57400	72	65	9072	6.7	26.3	52.0	14.0	1.1	109270
54495	WISCONSIN RAPIDS	19922	3131	29.2	35.8	29.5	4.4	1.2	37811	43599	39	20	2055	14.0	41.0	37.0	7.7	0.3	84399
54498	WITHEE	16836	806	30.0	35.0	28.5	4.2	2.2	37286	41709	36	18	674	23.3	31.6	34.6	9.4	1.2	83265
54499	WITTENBERG	19499	1170	30.4	34.1	29.1	4.4	2.1	40155	44213	47	30	902	13.3	29.1	44.6	11.6	1.4	98023
54501	RHINELANDER	21193	8533	29.3	31.8	30.2	6.1	2.6	39865	45602	45	28	6435	10.0	21.5	45.6	20.5	2.4	115148
54511	ARGONNE	19333	662	36.7	31.1	24.6	5.1	2.4	34045	38600	24	6	585	19.8	26.7	36.2	15.2	2.1	93796
54512	BOULDER JUNCTION	25492	421	27.3	32.8	29.5	6.4	4.0	42015	48597	53	38	366	3.8	10.9	34.7	37.4	13.1	177083
54513	BRANTWOOD	20874	209	32.1	34.0	28.2	3.4	2.4	34865	40000	27	7	179	20.7	40.8	26.3	12.3	0.0	81087
	WISCONSIN	25041		22.2	28.8	35.0	9.6	4.2	48930	56561				7.0	14.9	46.8	27.8	3.6	134326
	UNITED STATES	25866		24.7	27.1	30.8	10.9	6.5	48124	56710				10.9	15.0	33.7	30.1	10.4	145905

ZIP CODE #	POST OFFICE NAME	FINANCIAL SERVICES: Auto Loan	Home Loan	Invest-ments	Retire-ment Plans	THE HOME: Home Improvements: Home Repair	Lawn & Garden	Furnishings: Comput-ers & Hard-ware	Major Appli-ances	TV, Radio, Sound Equip-ment	Furni-ture	ENTERTAINMENT: Dine out/ Carry out	Sports Equip-ment	Fees & Tickets	Toys & Games	Travel	Cable TV	PERSONAL: Apparel & Services	Auto Repairs	Health Insur-ance	Pets & Supplies
54216	KEWAUNEE	77	75	68	71	78	85	72	75	75	70	92	87	73	97	74	78	89	74	81	91
54217	LUXEMBURG	97	87	69	85	91	99	83	91	88	83	107	106	82	108	85	89	101	88	97	113
54220	MANITOWOC	78	78	76	76	79	85	77	78	78	75	96	91	77	99	78	79	93	78	81	90
54227	MARIBEL	105	93	71	88	98	105	86	95	91	86	111	114	84	113	89	94	106	93	103	123
54228	MISHICOT	94	84	64	80	89	95	77	86	82	77	100	102	76	102	80	84	95	84	93	111
54229	NEW FRANKEN	104	121	122	120	120	120	109	110	103	109	129	129	114	136	111	101	127	106	102	125
54230	REEDSVILLE	100	89	68	84	94	101	82	91	87	82	106	108	80	108	84	89	101	88	98	117
54234	SISTER BAY	111	87	59	78	98	110	82	99	93	81	110	116	73	109	87	99	102	97	117	135
54235	STURGEON BAY	87	72	54	69	78	88	72	80	78	71	94	94	67	93	73	81	88	80	91	102
54241	TWO RIVERS	80	76	68	74	78	86	75	78	78	73	95	90	75	98	76	80	91	77	83	92
54245	VALDERS	98	87	66	83	92	99	80	89	85	80	104	106	79	106	83	88	99	87	96	115
54246	WASHINGTON ISLAND	75	59	40	53	66	74	55	67	63	55	74	78	50	73	59	67	69	66	79	91
54247	WHITELAW	101	90	68	85	95	102	83	92	88	83	107	110	82	110	86	91	102	90	100	119
54301	GREEN BAY	80	88	99	87	87	92	88	86	87	87	108	100	91	111	89	85	106	87	83	94
54302	GREEN BAY	70	66	74	67	65	71	74	70	74	72	92	84	72	91	71	72	90	73	68	78
54303	GREEN BAY	61	59	66	60	59	64	64	62	65	63	81	73	64	81	63	64	78	64	61	69
54304	GREEN BAY	77	81	88	81	81	85	81	80	80	80	100	93	83	102	81	79	98	81	78	89
54311	GREEN BAY	101	105	108	109	102	103	104	101	98	104	124	121	104	123	100	93	122	102	91	113
54313	GREEN BAY	110	127	131	131	123	121	117	115	108	119	137	135	121	140	116	103	135	113	101	127
54401	WAUSAU	85	92	96	92	92	96	90	89	88	88	110	104	92	114	90	87	107	89	87	100
54403	WAUSAU	82	86	94	84	86	92	86	85	87	84	108	98	88	111	87	87	105	85	86	96
54405	ABBOTSFORD	81	64	43	60	70	79	64	72	71	63	84	84	59	83	65	74	78	71	83	93
54406	AMHERST	92	82	63	78	87	93	76	84	81	76	98	100	74	100	78	83	93	82	91	109
54407	AMHERST JUNCTION	98	89	69	85	93	100	82	90	86	82	105	107	81	108	84	88	100	88	97	116
54408	ANIWA	91	81	61	77	85	91	74	83	79	75	96	98	73	98	77	81	91	80	89	107
54409	ANTIGO	68	64	59	62	67	73	64	67	67	62	82	76	64	85	65	69	78	66	72	79
54410	ARPIN	87	76	58	73	80	87	73	80	77	72	94	93	71	95	74	79	89	78	86	99
54411	ATHENS	85	75	57	72	79	86	72	78	76	71	92	92	70	93	73	78	87	77	85	99
54412	AUBURNDALE	89	79	60	75	84	90	73	81	78	73	95	97	72	97	76	80	90	79	88	105
54413	BABCOCK	91	81	62	77	86	92	75	83	80	75	97	99	74	99	77	82	92	81	90	107
54414	BIRNAMWOOD	83	73	56	71	76	84	71	77	75	70	92	90	69	92	72	77	86	76	83	95
54416	BOWLER	67	57	48	57	59	67	59	63	63	59	77	71	57	76	59	64	72	62	68	74
54418	BRYANT	84	71	53	67	77	84	66	76	72	66	87	90	63	88	69	75	82	74	85	100
54420	CHILI	82	57	30	54	66	74	56	69	65	56	76	84	48	74	58	68	69	69	83	97
54421	COLBY	79	67	50	66	71	79	67	73	72	66	87	84	64	86	67	73	81	72	80	89
54422	CURTISS	76	64	46	62	68	75	63	70	68	62	82	81	59	81	63	69	76	68	77	87
54423	CUSTER	101	94	77	91	99	104	87	95	90	87	110	112	86	113	89	92	106	92	100	119
54424	DEERBROOK	82	69	50	64	75	82	64	74	70	64	84	87	61	85	67	73	79	72	83	98
54425	DORCHESTER	80	69	53	68	72	80	69	74	73	68	88	86	66	88	69	74	83	73	80	90
54426	EDGAR	93	82	63	79	87	94	77	85	82	77	100	101	76	102	79	84	95	83	92	109
54427	ELAND	83	73	56	70	76	83	69	76	74	69	89	89	67	90	71	75	85	74	82	95
54428	ELCHO	69	54	37	49	61	69	51	62	58	51	69	72	46	68	55	62	64	61	73	85
54430	ELTON	76	67	51	64	71	76	62	69	66	62	80	82	61	82	64	68	76	67	75	89
54433	GILMAN	80	68	50	65	72	79	66	73	71	65	85	85	63	85	67	73	80	71	80	92
54435	GLEASON	81	69	50	64	74	81	64	73	70	64	84	87	61	85	67	73	79	72	82	97
54436	GRANTON	78	61	40	59	68	75	60	69	66	59	79	82	55	79	61	68	73	68	79	91
54437	GREENWOOD	78	61	40	59	67	75	61	70	67	60	80	82	55	79	62	69	74	69	79	90
54440	HATLEY	100	92	74	88	96	102	85	93	89	85	108	110	84	111	87	90	103	90	98	118
54441	HEWITT	105	94	71	89	99	106	87	96	92	87	112	115	85	114	89	94	106	94	104	124
54442	IRMA	89	73	52	68	81	89	69	80	76	68	91	94	64	91	72	80	85	79	92	107
54443	JUNCTION CITY	101	89	68	86	94	102	85	93	90	85	110	109	83	111	87	92	104	91	101	117
54446	LOYAL	79	65	48	63	69	79	67	72	72	65	86	83	62	85	67	74	81	72	82	88
54447	LUBLIN	80	54	25	47	61	71	52	65	63	53	74	78	45	70	53	68	67	65	80	92
54448	MARATHON	103	95	78	92	99	107	90	97	94	89	115	114	89	117	92	95	109	95	103	121
54449	MARSHFIELD	87	85	85	84	86	93	85	87	87	84	107	101	85	108	86	87	103	87	88	100
54451	MEDFORD	83	74	58	70	78	85	71	77	76	70	92	90	69	93	72	78	87	76	85	97
54452	MERRILL	77	74	66	71	77	83	71	75	74	70	91	87	71	94	73	75	87	73	79	90
54454	MILLADORE	96	85	65	81	90	97	79	87	84	79	102	104	77	104	81	86	97	85	95	113
54455	MOSINEE	100	100	90	98	102	106	93	98	94	93	116	115	94	119	95	94	112	96	98	118
54456	NEILLSVILLE	77	59	40	57	65	74	61	69	68	60	81	80	56	79	62	70	74	68	80	87
54457	NEKOOSA	91	78	60	73	84	93	75	84	81	74	98	97	71	99	78	85	92	82	94	107
54459	OGEMA	90	65	37	57	73	83	62	76	72	62	85	90	54	82	64	78	78	75	92	106
54460	OWEN	70	56	40	54	61	70	58	64	63	56	76	74	53	75	58	66	70	63	74	81
54462	PEARSON	71	56	38	50	63	70	52	63	59	52	70	74	47	69	56	63	65	62	75	86
54463	PELICAN LAKE	77	60	41	55	68	76	57	69	64	56	76	80	51	75	61	69	71	68	81	94
54465	PICKEREL	75	59	40	53	67	75	56	67	63	55	75	79	50	74	59	67	70	66	79	92
54466	PITTSVILLE	85	72	53	69	77	84	70	77	75	69	91	91	67	91	71	77	85	76	85	98
54467	PLOVER	102	102	94	103	102	104	96	99	94	98	118	117	96	118	96	92	115	98	94	116
54469	PORT EDWARDS	80	91	99	86	91	99	87	87	88	85	109	97	92	116	91	91	107	85	90	95
54470	RIB LAKE	80	60	36	54	66	74	57	68	65	57	77	81	52	76	58	69	72	66	79	92
54471	RINGLE	96	108	106	107	108	109	97	100	93	97	116	117	101	122	99	92	115	96	94	115
54473	ROSHOLT	90	79	60	76	83	90	75	82	80	75	97	97	73	98	76	82	92	80	89	103
54474	ROTHSCHILD	86	90	86	87	92	97	85	87	86	83	106	101	87	112	87	87	103	85	89	102
54475	RUDOLPH	96	85	65	81	90	96	79	87	83	79	101	104	77	104	81	86	96	85	94	112
54476	SCHOFIELD	82	88	91	89	87	88	87	85	83	86	104	101	87	106	85	80	102	85	78	94
54479	SPENCER	73	70	62	67	72	78	68	71	71	67	87	82	68	90	69	72	83	70	76	84
54480	STETSONVILLE	91	81	62	77	86	92	75	83	80	75	97	99	74	99	77	82	92	81	90	107
54481	STEVENS POINT	79	77	79	77	77	82	81	79	80	78	100	94	80	100	79	79	97	81	78	90
54484	STRATFORD	91	79	61	77	84	91	76	83	81	76	98	98	74	99	78	83	93	82	90	104
54485	SUMMIT LAKE	78	61	42	55	69	77	58	69	65	57	77	81	51	76	61	70	72	68	82	95
54486	TIGERTON	74	57	38	55	63	71	58	66	64	57	76	78	52	74	59	67	70	65	77	86
54487	TOMAHAWK	81	65	47	60	71	81	64	73	71	63	85	86	59	84	66	75	79	73	85	96
54488	UNITY	77	67	52	66	71	78	66	71	70	65	85	83	64	85	66	71	80	70	77	88
54489	VESPER	83	74	56	70	78	84	68	76	73	68	88	90	67	90	70	74	84	74	82	98
54490	WESTBORO	85	63	37	57	70	78	60	72	69	61	82	85	54	80	61	73	76	70	84	98
54491	WHITE LAKE	76	60	42	55	67	75	57	68	64	56	76	79	51	75	60	68	70	66	79	92
54493	WILLARD	82	59	34	55	68	77	58	71	66	57	78	85	50	77	60	70	71	70	84	98
54494	WISCONSIN RAPIDS	87	85	79	83	87	94	83	86	85	81	104	100	83	107	84	86	100	85	89	101
54495	WISCONSIN RAPIDS	67	62	56	60	64	70	64	66	67	62	82	76	62	82	64	68	78	66	70	77
54498	WITHEE	74	63	49	59	68	76	62	69	68	61	82	80	59	83	63	71	77	67	78	86
54499	WITTENBERG	81	67	48	64	72	81	66	74	72	65	86	86	62	86	67	75	81	73	83	93
54501	RHINELANDER	77	69	60	66	73	80	68	73	72	67	88	86	66	89	70	74	83	72	80	90
54511	ARGONNE	77	60	41	55	68	77	58	69	66	57	78	81	52	76	61	70	72	68	82	93
54512	BOULDER JUNCTION	91	71	49	64	80	90	67	81	76	66	90	95	60	89	72	81	84	80	96	111
54513	BRANTWOOD	86	59	28	51	66	76	57	70	68	58	80	84	49	76	58	73	73	69	86	99
	WISCONSIN	89	86	85	86	88	94	86	88	87	85	108	103	86	109	86	87	104	88	89	103
	UNITED STATES	100	100	100	100	100	100	100	100	100	100	100	100	100	100	100	100	100	100	100	100

# POST OFFICE NAME	COUNTY FIPS CODE	POPULATION 2000	2004	2009	2000-2004 ANNUAL RATE % Rate	State Centile	HOUSEHOLDS 2000	2004	2009	% Annual Rate 2000-2004	2004 Average HH Size	FAMILIES 2000	2004	% Annual Rate 2000-2004
54514 BUTTERNUT	003	2221	2287	2321	0.7	43	910	968	1009	1.5	2.36	630	658	1.0
54515 CATAWBA	099	558	562	563	0.2	22	223	231	238	0.8	2.43	161	165	0.6
54517 CLAM LAKE	003	2	2	2	0.0	15	1	1	1	0.0	2.00	1	1	0.0
54519 CONOVER	125	1178	1250	1349	1.4	73	501	547	605	2.1	2.29	353	381	1.8
54520 CRANDON	041	4094	4065	4159	-0.2	9	1649	1686	1774	0.5	2.34	1121	1129	0.2
54521 EAGLE RIVER	125	7930	8581	9323	1.9	84	3423	3800	4234	2.5	2.20	2320	2537	2.1
54524 FIFIELD	099	700	707	708	0.2	24	298	310	320	0.9	2.28	208	214	0.7
54526 GLEN FLORA	107	890	896	899	0.2	21	341	355	366	1.0	2.52	240	246	0.6
54527 GLIDDEN	003	988	971	959	-0.4	5	419	426	432	0.4	2.28	289	289	0.0
54529 HARSHAW	085	1042	1068	1112	0.6	38	446	468	498	1.1	2.27	326	338	0.9
54530 HAWKINS	107	741	750	755	0.3	26	300	313	324	1.0	2.40	215	222	0.8
54531 HAZELHURST	085	1486	1554	1633	1.1	59	627	671	721	1.6	2.31	503	533	1.4
54534 HURLEY	051	2759	2891	3042	1.1	62	1204	1300	1406	1.8	2.14	714	758	1.4
54536 IRON BELT	051	284	286	295	0.2	22	122	126	132	0.8	2.27	86	87	0.3
54537 KENNAN	099	648	678	692	1.1	60	243	261	274	1.7	2.60	187	199	1.5
54538 LAC DU FLAMBEAU	125	2592	2747	2959	1.4	72	920	994	1093	1.8	2.74	692	740	1.6
54539 LAKE TOMAHAWK	085	1702	1767	1846	0.9	51	718	768	824	1.6	2.17	507	536	1.3
54540 LAND O LAKES	125	998	1066	1154	1.6	76	460	506	562	2.3	2.11	311	338	2.0
54541 LAONA	041	1777	1821	1887	0.6	38	632	669	713	1.4	2.56	437	457	1.1
54542 LONG LAKE	041	628	669	698	1.5	74	293	324	350	2.4	2.03	189	206	2.1
54545 MANITOWISH WATERS	125	822	878	952	1.6	76	386	423	469	2.2	2.08	266	287	1.8
54546 MELLEN	003	1761	1732	1710	-0.4	6	741	748	756	0.2	2.27	490	486	-0.2
54547 MERCER	051	1794	1840	1915	0.6	39	858	902	962	1.2	2.04	550	570	0.8
54548 MINOCQUA	085	5174	5469	5795	1.3	69	2309	2507	2721	2.0	2.17	1570	1677	1.6
54550 MONTREAL	051	1033	1061	1105	0.6	41	461	486	519	1.3	2.18	293	304	0.9
54552 PARK FALLS	099	4814	4731	4717	-0.4	5	2059	2084	2136	0.3	2.20	1338	1334	-0.1
54554 PHELPS	125	1195	1240	1320	0.9	49	495	529	578	1.6	2.27	348	366	1.2
54555 PHILLIPS	099	5572	5592	5599	0.1	18	2318	2388	2453	0.7	2.29	1532	1555	0.4
54556 PRENTICE	099	1266	1295	1307	0.5	36	527	556	577	1.3	2.33	349	362	0.9
54557 PRESQUE ISLE	125	873	959	1054	2.2	89	412	465	524	2.9	2.06	291	324	2.6
54558 SAINT GERMAIN	125	1964	2119	2305	1.8	83	909	1003	1114	2.3	2.11	644	702	2.1
54559 SAXON	051	508	515	533	0.3	28	208	217	231	1.0	2.37	155	160	0.8
54560 SAYNER	125	586	630	685	1.7	81	260	286	318	2.3	2.20	183	200	2.1
54562 THREE LAKES	085	1977	2114	2248	1.6	78	889	972	1057	2.1	2.15	618	666	1.8
54563 TONY	107	788	804	813	0.5	33	293	307	318	1.1	2.62	216	224	0.9
54564 TRIPOLI	085	470	479	491	0.5	32	218	227	238	1.0	2.11	157	161	0.6
54565 UPSON	051	61	61	63	0.0	15	28	29	30	0.8	2.10	20	20	0.0
54566 WABENO	041	1640	1725	1808	1.2	64	655	704	758	1.7	2.27	458	484	1.3
54568 WOODRUFF	125	4843	5175	5577	1.6	77	2122	2331	2575	2.2	2.20	1393	1502	1.8
54601 LA CROSSE	063	48484	48953	50272	0.2	24	19158	19836	20881	0.8	2.23	9834	9946	0.3
54603 LA CROSSE	063	14846	14803	15105	-0.1	12	6342	6482	6759	0.5	2.28	3714	3690	-0.2
54610 ALMA	011	2422	2413	2436	-0.1	11	968	992	1028	0.6	2.42	676	683	0.2
54611 ALMA CENTER	053	1034	1033	1061	0.0	14	393	402	421	0.5	2.56	284	288	0.3
54612 ARCADIA	121	4453	4394	4461	-0.3	7	1788	1810	1884	0.3	2.38	1144	1139	-0.1
54613 ARKDALE	001	1604	1690	1772	1.2	66	727	789	845	1.9	2.14	509	545	1.6
54614 BANGOR	063	3171	3203	3276	0.2	25	1166	1208	1263	0.8	2.61	898	914	0.4
54615 BLACK RIVER FALLS	053	10191	10783	11387	1.3	71	3648	3965	4296	2.0	2.45	2374	2541	1.6
54616 BLAIR	121	2481	2480	2521	0.0	14	957	980	1020	0.6	2.42	643	649	0.2
54618 CAMP DOUGLAS	057	2238	2327	2461	0.9	53	864	924	1001	1.6	2.50	618	652	1.3
54619 CASHTON	081	3497	3540	3644	0.3	27	1137	1177	1239	0.8	3.00	854	866	0.3
54621 CHASEBURG	123	1031	1239	1380	4.4	99	391	479	542	4.9	2.59	301	364	4.6
54622 COCHRANE	011	2006	2003	2019	0.0	13	843	869	901	0.7	2.30	606	617	0.4
54623 COON VALLEY	063	1995	2085	2170	1.0	58	730	783	832	1.7	2.58	532	561	1.3
54624 DE SOTO	123	1368	1420	1468	0.9	50	584	625	660	1.6	2.27	406	425	1.1
54625 DODGE	121	232	262	283	2.9	95	94	109	121	3.5	2.40	70	80	3.2
54626 EASTMAN	023	1482	1509	1549	0.4	31	553	581	613	1.2	2.60	415	430	0.8
54627 ETTRICK	121	1864	1845	1875	-0.2	8	758	771	803	0.4	2.39	530	531	0.0
54628 FERRYVILLE	023	1378	1584	1726	3.3	96	559	665	745	4.2	2.37	397	466	3.8
54629 FOUNTAIN CITY	011	2623	2820	2967	1.7	81	1070	1176	1266	2.3	2.36	720	782	2.0
54630 GALESVILLE	121	3657	3863	4034	1.3	69	1456	1578	1687	1.9	2.41	984	1052	1.6
54631 GAYS MILLS	023	2173	2236	2308	0.7	42	844	892	945	1.3	2.50	612	638	1.0
54632 GENOA	123	1008	1102	1173	2.1	88	393	439	476	2.6	2.51	284	314	2.4
54634 HILLSBORO	123	3734	3889	4019	1.0	55	1339	1412	1476	1.3	2.71	939	976	0.9
54635 HIXTON	053	1687	1694	1752	0.1	19	660	680	720	0.7	2.46	481	491	0.5
54636 HOLMEN	063	10121	10866	11468	1.7	81	3559	3921	4231	2.3	2.77	2850	3092	1.9
54638 KENDALL	081	1606	1791	1946	2.6	93	579	660	731	3.1	2.71	445	500	2.8
54639 LA FARGE	123	2337	2384	2445	0.5	33	880	914	952	0.9	2.58	608	623	0.6
54641 MATHER	057	34	36	39	1.4	71	13	14	16	1.8	2.57	9	10	2.5
54642 MELROSE	053	1869	1870	1934	0.0	15	712	726	766	0.5	2.57	507	511	0.2
54644 MINDORO	063	1287	1429	1534	2.5	92	495	562	617	3.0	2.54	384	429	2.6
54646 NECEDAH	057	3641	4018	4408	2.4	90	1370	1549	1741	2.9	2.57	984	1098	2.6
54648 NORWALK	081	1815	1905	2004	1.2	63	585	627	674	1.6	3.04	452	479	1.4
54650 ONALASKA	063	20210	21445	22459	1.4	73	7759	8457	9057	2.1	2.52	5561	5951	1.6
54651 ONTARIO	081	1097	1201	1284	2.2	88	434	482	522	2.5	2.49	308	339	2.3
54652 READSTOWN	123	772	778	791	0.2	23	311	318	327	0.5	2.45	211	212	0.1
54653 ROCKLAND	081	741	742	756	0.0	16	250	257	268	0.7	2.84	188	190	0.3
54655 SOLDIERS GROVE	023	1834	1859	1890	0.3	28	687	713	742	0.9	2.51	491	503	0.6
54656 SPARTA	081	15542	16109	16846	0.9	49	6016	6387	6830	1.4	2.45	4137	4346	1.2
54657 STEUBEN	023	113	131	142	3.5	97	39	46	52	4.0	2.85	30	35	3.7
54658 STODDARD	123	2417	2687	2898	2.5	92	947	1072	1175	3.0	2.51	694	779	2.8
54659 TAYLOR	053	1244	1294	1356	0.9	53	450	478	512	1.4	2.70	335	352	1.2
54660 TOMAH	081	14421	14831	15425	0.7	42	5597	5902	6283	1.3	2.44	3796	3941	0.9
54661 TREMPEALEAU	121	2746	2891	3012	1.2	65	1125	1215	1297	1.8	2.38	774	823	1.5
54664 VIOLA	103	1529	1547	1565	0.3	26	608	631	649	0.9	2.45	439	450	0.6
54665 VIROQUA	123	7911	8028	8205	0.4	29	3232	3345	3473	0.8	2.32	2052	2088	0.4
54666 WARRENS	053	2357	2407	2488	0.5	34	893	942	1002	1.3	2.37	669	697	1.0
54667 WESTBY	123	4672	4711	4798	0.2	23	1733	1785	1849	0.7	2.59	1268	1290	0.4
54669 WEST SALEM	063	7165	7574	7933	1.3	69	2525	2723	2910	1.8	2.68	1908	2024	1.4
54670 WILTON	081	1666	1853	2098	2.5	92	514	587	652	3.2	3.16	379	427	2.9
54701 EAU CLAIRE	035	36333	38185	40298	1.2	64	13816	14957	16254	1.9	2.28	8277	8830	1.5
54703 EAU CLAIRE	035	39681	41075	43207	0.8	48	15478	16452	17734	1.5	2.46	9421	9822	1.0
54720 ALTOONA	035	7093	7249	7575	0.5	34	2966	3116	3339	1.2	2.28	1847	1903	0.7
54721 ARKANSAW	091	1428	1464	1534	0.6	38	543	572	614	1.2	2.56	396	412	0.9
54722 AUGUSTA	035	3825	3914	4071	0.5	36	1370	1427	1514	1.0	2.70	991	1018	0.6
54723 BAY CITY	093	1315	1320	1400	0.1	18	493	508	552	0.7	2.60	373	379	0.4
WISCONSIN					0.8					1.4	2.44			1.1
UNITED STATES					1.2					1.3	2.58			1.1

ZIP CODE #	POST OFFICE NAME	RACE (%) White 2000	White 2004	Black 2000	Black 2004	Asian/Pacific 2000	Asian/Pacific 2004	% Hispanic Origin 2000	% Hispanic Origin 2004	2004 AGE DISTRIBUTION (%) 0-4	5-9	10-14	15-19	20-24	25-44	45-64	65-84	85+	18+	MEDIAN AGE 2004	% 2004 Males	% 2004 Females
54514	BUTTERNUT	98.6	98.5	0.3	0.3	0.1	0.1	0.3	0.3	4.9	5.1	5.8	7.1	6.0	22.6	30.4	15.9	2.2	79.5	44.0	51.3	48.7
54515	CATAWBA	99.1	99.3	0.0	0.0	0.0	0.0	0.2	0.2	5.5	6.1	7.3	6.1	5.2	25.4	28.3	13.9	2.3	77.2	41.5	51.8	48.2
54517	CLAM LAKE	100.0	100.0	0.0	0.0	0.0	0.0	0.0	0.0	0.0	0.0	0.0	0.0	100.0	0.0	0.0	0.0	0.0	100.0	22.5	50.0	50.0
54519	CONOVER	98.6	98.4	0.2	0.2	0.1	0.2	0.6	0.7	3.3	4.9	6.2	6.0	2.6	22.7	31.8	20.7	1.8	81.4	47.7	51.2	48.8
54520	CRANDON	85.6	84.6	0.2	0.2	0.1	0.1	0.8	1.0	6.1	6.2	7.2	6.7	5.6	23.7	24.9	17.2	2.6	76.3	41.4	48.6	51.4
54521	EAGLE RIVER	97.9	97.7	0.4	0.4	0.2	0.3	0.7	0.8	4.1	4.6	5.6	5.6	4.4	22.2	30.5	20.3	2.7	82.0	47.2	50.0	50.0
54524	FIFIELD	97.7	97.6	0.1	0.1	0.0	0.1	0.4	0.4	3.3	4.0	5.9	5.9	4.7	23.1	34.7	17.1	1.4	83.0	46.8	51.8	48.2
54526	GLEN FLORA	98.2	98.1	0.1	0.1	0.5	0.5	0.9	0.8	5.3	5.7	6.7	5.6	6.8	24.7	29.1	14.1	2.1	79.0	41.9	51.7	48.3
54527	GLIDDEN	98.5	98.6	0.0	0.0	0.1	0.1	0.3	0.3	6.3	6.0	6.5	6.9	6.2	24.8	24.9	16.2	2.3	77.0	40.9	51.5	48.5
54529	HARSHAW	98.7	98.5	0.3	0.3	0.0	0.1	0.4	0.5	3.5	4.1	6.0	5.7	3.6	23.9	34.3	17.9	1.1	82.6	47.1	52.4	47.6
54530	HAWKINS	98.3	98.1	0.1	0.1	0.4	0.4	0.9	0.8	5.3	5.9	6.9	5.6	6.8	24.8	28.3	14.3	2.1	78.4	41.4	51.9	48.1
54531	HAZELHURST	98.1	97.9	0.1	0.2	0.3	0.5	0.7	0.8	3.4	4.1	5.8	5.2	3.9	19.8	34.6	21.7	1.5	83.3	50.0	51.7	48.3
54534	HURLEY	98.0	97.8	0.0	0.0	0.2	0.3	0.8	0.9	4.3	4.4	5.8	6.2	6.3	23.8	25.2	18.4	5.7	81.9	44.5	48.1	51.9
54536	IRON BELT	98.6	98.6	0.0	0.0	0.0	0.0	0.7	0.7	5.2	5.2	7.0	6.3	5.9	21.7	30.4	16.1	2.1	78.3	44.2	49.7	50.4
54537	KENNAN	98.9	99.1	0.0	0.0	0.0	0.0	0.8	0.7	5.9	6.3	7.8	6.5	6.2	22.9	28.3	14.0	2.1	75.8	40.7	50.9	49.1
54538	LAC DU FLAMBEAU	47.5	45.0	0.2	0.2	0.0	0.0	1.4	1.5	7.2	7.2	8.4	6.7	5.2	22.8	25.4	15.5	1.7	72.8	39.9	50.2	49.8
54539	LAKE TOMAHAWK	96.1	95.6	2.4	2.7	0.2	0.3	0.7	0.8	3.4	4.0	5.8	5.4	4.0	26.7	31.2	18.0	1.5	83.1	45.4	53.1	46.9
54540	LAND O LAKES	98.1	97.9	0.0	0.0	0.2	0.3	0.6	0.8	3.9	4.4	5.1	4.8	3.9	19.7	34.2	21.5	2.5	83.4	50.3	49.9	50.1
54541	LAONA	82.8	81.5	2.8	3.1	0.2	0.3	1.7	1.9	6.3	6.0	7.0	9.1	6.5	21.9	25.0	15.7	2.6	75.7	40.0	50.3	49.8
54542	LONG LAKE	97.1	97.0	0.2	0.2	0.6	0.8	0.3	0.2	3.7	3.9	5.4	5.4	5.1	21.1	29.6	22.4	3.4	83.9	48.4	52.0	48.0
54545	MANITOWISH WATERS	96.1	95.9	0.0	0.0	0.0	0.0	1.0	1.1	2.5	3.0	4.2	3.6	4.1	16.4	36.7	27.0	2.5	87.9	54.8	50.7	49.3
54546	MELLEN	94.6	94.5	0.1	0.1	0.3	0.3	0.8	0.8	6.2	5.9	5.9	6.2	6.2	24.1	26.4	16.1	2.8	77.7	42.1	51.1	48.9
54547	MERCER	98.9	98.7	0.1	0.1	0.2	0.3	0.6	0.7	3.2	3.5	4.3	4.4	3.3	18.8	34.9	25.5	2.1	86.3	52.7	50.7	49.4
54548	MINOCQUA	93.8	93.6	0.2	0.2	0.2	0.2	1.0	1.1	4.4	4.9	5.6	5.4	4.2	20.5	31.5	21.2	2.3	81.7	48.0	50.2	49.8
54550	MONTREAL	98.0	97.9	0.0	0.0	0.2	0.2	0.9	1.0	5.8	5.7	6.2	6.6	5.9	24.5	27.1	15.4	2.8	78.3	42.1	47.9	52.1
54552	PARK FALLS	98.1	98.0	0.2	0.2	0.6	0.6	0.8	0.8	4.2	4.5	6.4	6.6	5.5	21.7	28.6	18.3	4.3	80.5	45.7	49.0	51.0
54554	PHELPS	98.1	97.8	0.2	0.2	0.3	0.4	0.8	0.9	3.3	3.9	5.3	5.5	4.7	18.8	34.1	20.7	3.7	83.9	50.0	49.9	50.1
54555	PHILLIPS	98.0	98.0	0.0	0.0	0.3	0.3	0.7	0.7	4.9	5.3	6.6	6.7	5.5	23.4	28.5	15.9	3.2	79.1	43.4	49.9	50.1
54556	PRENTICE	98.5	98.5	0.2	0.2	0.1	0.1	1.3	1.2	5.6	5.9	7.6	6.9	5.3	25.1	26.4	14.4	2.8	76.7	40.9	51.4	48.7
54557	PRESQUE ISLE	99.5	99.6	0.0	0.0	0.0	0.0	0.8	0.8	2.3	2.8	3.9	4.0	3.3	16.5	35.6	29.1	2.6	88.5	55.7	51.1	48.9
54558	SAINT GERMAIN	98.1	98.0	0.1	0.1	0.3	0.4	1.0	1.2	4.6	4.9	5.3	4.9	3.0	20.6	32.0	23.0	1.8	82.2	49.5	49.8	50.2
54559	SAXON	97.2	97.1	0.6	0.6	0.0	0.0	0.0	0.0	4.7	4.9	6.2	6.2	5.2	24.7	31.5	14.6	2.1	80.8	44.1	51.3	48.7
54560	SAYNER	98.3	98.1	0.2	0.3	0.2	0.2	0.7	0.8	4.3	4.8	4.9	4.8	3.5	19.4	33.3	23.2	1.9	82.9	50.1	50.6	49.4
54562	THREE LAKES	98.3	98.1	0.1	0.1	0.5	0.6	0.8	1.0	3.6	4.4	6.6	6.3	4.6	20.2	31.3	20.8	2.2	81.1	47.5	51.5	48.5
54563	TONY	98.9	99.0	0.1	0.1	0.1	0.1	0.4	0.5	6.3	6.6	7.3	7.2	5.9	23.5	26.5	14.8	1.9	74.5	40.3	51.0	49.0
54564	TRIPOLI	98.9	99.0	0.0	0.0	0.0	0.0	0.2	0.0	4.2	4.6	6.1	5.6	4.2	23.0	33.8	17.5	1.0	81.2	46.5	52.4	47.6
54565	UPSON	98.4	98.4	0.0	0.0	0.0	0.0	0.0	0.0	4.9	4.9	6.6	6.6	6.6	21.3	29.5	18.0	1.6	83.6	44.5	47.5	52.5
54566	WABENO	79.0	77.9	3.4	3.8	0.2	0.3	1.8	1.9	7.0	6.4	7.7	10.0	7.4	21.8	23.1	14.0	2.6	73.3	37.2	51.3	48.8
54568	WOODRUFF	92.7	92.2	0.1	0.1	0.4	0.5	1.0	1.2	4.8	5.1	6.2	5.7	3.9	22.5	28.4	20.0	3.4	80.2	46.1	48.8	51.2
54601	LA CROSSE	93.5	92.5	1.2	1.3	3.4	4.2	1.1	1.3	4.6	4.7	5.3	10.3	18.2	22.6	19.5	12.1	2.8	82.2	31.0	47.1	52.9
54603	LA CROSSE	89.4	87.6	1.8	2.1	6.3	7.8	1.0	1.1	6.4	5.9	6.5	6.9	8.4	29.0	24.8	10.7	1.4	77.1	35.9	49.5	50.5
54610	ALMA	97.9	97.7	0.3	0.3	0.3	0.4	0.9	1.1	5.5	5.8	6.7	7.1	5.4	25.2	26.4	16.1	1.8	77.5	41.7	51.3	48.7
54611	ALMA CENTER	95.9	95.5	0.1	0.1	0.1	0.2	3.1	3.6	6.6	7.0	7.4	8.0	5.8	27.9	23.3	12.4	1.7	74.2	37.4	52.1	47.9
54612	ARCADIA	98.3	98.1	0.1	0.1	0.2	0.2	2.4	2.8	6.9	6.9	7.1	5.4	5.6	29.0	23.9	12.5	2.8	75.6	38.3	50.3	49.7
54613	ARKDALE	97.9	97.8	0.3	0.3	0.2	0.2	1.4	1.6	4.0	4.3	5.2	5.1	5.0	20.4	32.3	22.3	1.5	83.4	48.9	52.2	47.8
54614	BANGOR	98.4	98.2	0.2	0.2	0.4	0.6	0.4	0.5	7.2	7.4	7.9	6.7	5.6	27.7	24.5	11.1	1.9	73.2	37.6	51.4	48.6
54615	BLACK RIVER FALLS	86.1	85.3	3.1	3.5	0.2	0.2	1.5	1.7	5.5	5.7	6.7	6.4	7.2	29.1	24.1	12.6	2.9	78.3	38.1	52.9	47.2
54616	BLAIR	98.8	98.7	0.2	0.2	0.1	0.2	1.0	1.1	6.5	6.6	7.3	5.8	5.8	24.0	23.7	16.4	4.0	76.3	40.8	49.4	50.7
54618	CAMP DOUGLAS	97.3	97.0	0.3	0.3	0.4	0.5	1.3	1.5	6.1	6.4	7.6	7.1	5.7	25.6	25.3	14.5	1.8	75.2	40.1	51.0	49.0
54619	CASHTON	98.3	98.1	0.1	0.1	0.8	1.0	1.1	1.3	10.1	9.2	8.7	7.7	7.1	24.6	20.7	10.5	1.4	67.0	31.6	50.9	49.1
54621	CHASEBURG	99.1	99.0	0.0	0.0	0.3	0.3	0.3	0.3	7.3	7.8	8.5	7.3	5.3	26.1	26.3	10.5	1.1	71.9	38.0	52.4	47.6
54622	COCHRANE	98.7	98.6	0.1	0.1	0.4	0.5	0.7	0.8	6.0	6.1	5.4	5.6	4.9	24.8	28.4	16.7	2.0	78.9	43.2	50.8	49.2
54623	COON VALLEY	98.8	98.6	0.1	0.1	0.5	0.6	0.5	0.5	6.2	6.5	7.0	6.1	5.0	26.3	26.0	13.8	3.1	76.0	40.6	49.6	50.4
54624	DE SOTO	98.2	97.8	0.1	0.1	0.2	0.3	1.2	1.5	5.5	5.9	6.0	5.4	4.4	20.3	34.9	16.1	1.6	79.4	46.5	50.4	49.6
54625	DODGE	99.1	99.2	0.0	0.0	0.4	0.4	0.0	0.0	4.2	6.1	9.2	7.6	4.2	28.2	27.9	11.8	0.8	75.2	40.2	50.8	49.2
54626	EASTMAN	98.4	98.3	0.1	0.1	0.5	0.7	0.8	0.9	6.2	7.1	8.1	6.6	5.6	24.3	28.4	12.4	1.4	74.1	40.0	51.8	48.2
54627	ETTRICK	99.1	99.0	0.1	0.1	0.2	0.2	0.4	0.5	5.7	6.0	6.7	6.5	5.2	26.2	28.8	13.0	2.1	77.7	41.5	50.4	49.6
54628	FERRYVILLE	98.3	98.0	0.4	0.5	0.2	0.3	0.7	0.9	6.2	6.5	7.3	6.2	4.9	21.4	30.6	15.0	2.0	75.9	43.3	51.4	48.6
54629	FOUNTAIN CITY	99.4	99.4	0.0	0.0	0.0	0.0	0.5	0.6	5.7	6.1	6.7	6.2	5.5	27.3	27.6	12.6	2.3	77.3	40.1	51.5	48.5
54630	GALESVILLE	98.9	98.8	0.1	0.2	0.2	0.2	0.4	0.5	6.1	6.5	7.3	7.0	5.6	26.0	26.8	12.1	2.6	75.9	40.1	49.7	50.3
54631	GAYS MILLS	98.3	98.0	0.3	0.4	0.2	0.3	1.1	1.3	5.1	5.8	7.2	6.8	5.7	22.5	31.5	13.8	1.7	77.5	42.9	50.6	49.4
54632	GENOA	98.8	98.7	0.0	0.0	0.2	0.3	0.5	0.5	7.4	7.8	7.4	6.1	5.1	25.1	28.0	12.1	1.2	73.6	39.6	51.0	49.0
54634	HILLSBORO	98.8	98.6	0.2	0.2	0.1	0.1	0.6	0.8	6.2	7.2	8.3	8.0	6.3	22.6	24.9	13.9	2.7	73.4	39.5	49.1	50.9
54635	HIXTON	97.3	97.0	0.2	0.2	0.2	0.3	1.0	1.4	6.4	6.7	6.9	6.0	4.8	26.3	27.5	13.8	1.7	76.1	40.4	52.6	47.4
54636	HOLMEN	96.1	95.2	0.2	0.3	2.5	3.3	0.7	0.8	7.6	7.9	8.4	7.0	6.6	29.6	25.4	6.9	0.7	71.6	34.5	49.9	50.1
54638	KENDALL	99.1	99.0	0.1	0.1	0.3	0.2	0.5	0.6	8.4	8.5	8.4	7.4	6.5	23.7	24.4	11.1	1.6	69.9	35.4	52.0	48.0
54639	LA FARGE	98.0	97.9	0.1	0.1	0.2	0.2	0.8	0.8	6.7	6.9	8.1	7.8	6.8	20.9	28.0	13.1	1.8	73.4	39.8	50.0	50.0
54641	MATHER	94.1	94.4	0.0	0.0	0.0	0.0	5.9	5.6	5.6	5.6	11.1	5.6	5.6	27.8	27.8	11.1	0.0	77.8	40.0	58.3	41.7
54642	MELROSE	99.0	98.9	0.1	0.1	0.2	0.2	0.3	0.4	5.5	6.3	7.4	7.2	5.2	26.8	27.0	12.9	1.7	76.1	40.7	52.5	47.5
54644	MINDORO	98.4	98.0	0.2	0.1	0.3	0.4	0.5	0.7	6.4	6.9	7.7	6.4	5.9	27.3	28.8	9.7	0.9	75.1	39.0	53.1	46.9
54646	NECEDAH	96.9	96.6	0.3	0.3	0.3	0.4	1.8	2.1	6.7	6.9	7.7	6.4	5.4	24.1	26.3	15.0	1.5	74.5	40.2	51.3	48.7
54648	NORWALK	92.7	91.8	0.1	0.1	0.2	0.3	8.6	9.8	8.5	8.2	8.5	7.3	6.8	27.7	22.5	9.1	1.4	70.3	33.2	52.4	47.6
54650	ONALASKA	95.7	94.8	0.5	0.6	2.4	3.1	0.9	1.1	7.1	7.1	7.3	6.8	6.7	29.0	26.0	8.9	1.1	74.2	35.6	48.8	51.2
54651	ONTARIO	96.8	96.6	0.1	0.1	0.2	0.2	2.4	2.7	7.2	7.5	8.6	7.2	6.4	23.2	25.9	12.3	1.8	72.0	37.5	51.0	49.0
54652	READSTOWN	99.7	99.7	0.0	0.0	0.0	0.0	0.1	0.1	6.2	6.6	8.4	6.4	5.7	23.8	25.8	14.1	3.1	74.9	40.3	51.9	48.1
54653	ROCKLAND	98.4	98.3	0.3	0.3	0.8	1.1	0.5	0.7	7.6	7.6	7.7	6.6	5.9	29.3	23.3	10.7	1.5	72.9	36.4	51.4	48.7
54655	SOLDIERS GROVE	98.4	98.2	0.1	0.1	0.1	0.2	0.9	1.2	6.0	6.0	6.2	6.9	5.8	22.9	27.2	15.4	3.6	76.9	42.4	49.4	50.6
54656	SPARTA	97.5	97.1	0.5	0.5	0.5	0.7	1.5	1.8	6.2	6.4	7.3	7.1	6.7	26.3	26.0	11.7	2.3	75.5	38.4	49.7	50.3
54657	STEUBEN	100.0	100.0	0.0	0.0	0.0	0.0	0.0	0.0	6.9	6.9	8.4	6.1	6.1	25.2	25.2	14.5	0.8	73.3	38.3	51.9	48.1
54658	STODDARD	98.9	98.8	0.0	0.0	0.3	0.3	0.3	0.3	6.1	6.6	7.0	6.2	5.6	25.7	29.0	12.6	1.3	76.6	40.7	51.1	48.9
54659	TAYLOR	98.1	98.1	0.1	0.1	0.2	0.3	0.1	0.1	7.0	7.3	7.4	7.7	6.0	25.8	26.2	11.4	1.0	73.4	37.7	51.8	48.2
54660	TOMAH	95.2	94.7	0.7	0.8	0.6	0.7	1.5	1.8	6.6	6.5	7.7	7.0	6.8	25.6	25.8	12.2	1.9	74.8	38.3	50.7	49.3
54661	TREMPEALEAU	98.8	98.6	0.1	0.1	0.2	0.3	0.6	0.7	6.0	6.5	7.3	6.1	5.1	28.8	27.6	11.5	1.2	76.4	39.4	51.2	48.8
54664	VIOLA	98.5	98.4	0.2	0.2	0.3	0.3	1.1	1.3	5.2	6.3	6.9	6.9	5.7	22.8	30.3	13.8	2.2	77.3	42.7	50.4	49.6
54665	VIROQUA	98.9	98.8	0.1	0.1	0.3	0.4	0.6	0.7	5.9	5.8	6.7	6.6	6.2	22.4	26.3	16.2	4.0	77.1	42.6	48.6	51.4
54666	WARRENS	90.0	89.4	3.0	3.4	0.2	0.2	1.6	1.7	6.2	6.1	7.4	7.3	6.8	29.8	26.1	9.2	1.1	75.8	37.1	54.3	45.7
54667	WESTBY	99.0	98.8	0.0	0.1	0.2	0.2	0.7	0.9	7.5	7.2	7.7	7.2	6.4	24.0	24.2	13.4	2.5	73.0	38.4	49.3	50.7
54669	WEST SALEM	97.8	97.4	0.4	0.5	0.7	0.9	0.5	0.7	7.6	7.7	8.3	7.2	6.0	26.4	24.7	10.1	2.1	71.7	36.7	49.7	50.3
54670	WILTON	98.1	97.8	0.0	0.0	0.1	0.1	2.9	3.5	10.7	10.0	9.0	7.5	6.3	26.2	19.5	9.3	1.5	65.7	30.0	53.3	46.7
54701	EAU CLAIRE	95.5	94.8	0.6	0.7	1.9	2.4	1.1	1.2	5.3	5.2	5.5	11.7	14.3	23.2	22.0	10.7	2.1	80.4	31.8	46.5	53.5
54703	EAU CLAIRE	92.9	91.7	0.6	0.7	4.4	5.5	0.9	1.0	6.3	6.0	6.3	6.9	14.7	27.7	21.6	9.0	1.4	77.4	31.7	49.7	50.3
54720	ALTOONA	96.0	95.5	0.4	0.5	1.1	1.4	0.8	1.0	6.8	6.4	6.8	6.5	7.2	28.3	23.2	11.5	3.3	76.1	36.7	47.8	52.2
54721	ARKANSAW	99.0	98.8	0.1	0.1	0.2	0.3	0.7	0.8	6.5	6.2	6.7	6.5	6.6	27.9	26.2	12.1	1.4	76.6	39.5	54.3	45.7
54722	AUGUSTA	97.7	97.5	0.2	0.2	0.3	0.4	1.0	1.2	7.6	7.7	9.0	7.3	5.7	25.2	22.8	12.1	2.6	70.8	36.2	49.5	50.5
54723	BAY CITY	99.2	99.1	0.1	0.1	0.1	0.1	0.8	0.9	6.4	6.7	7.0	6.0	5.6	29.6	27.6	10.0	1.1	76.2	37.3	50.9	49.1
	WISCONSIN	88.9	88.0	5.7	6.0	1.7	2.1	3.6	4.0	6.4	6.5	7.1	7.3	7.7	27.6	24.5	11.1	1.9	75.8	36.9	49.5	50.5
	UNITED STATES	75.1	73.6	12.3	12.5	3.8	4.2	12.5	14.1	6.9	6.7	7.2	7.0	7.3	28.6	23.8	10.8	1.7	75.1	36.0	49.1	50.9

#	POST OFFICE NAME	2004 Per Capita Income	2004 HH Income Base	2004 Household Income Distribution (%) Less than $25,000	$25,000 to $49,999	$50,000 to $99,999	$100,000 to $149,999	$150,000 or More	Median Household Income 2004	2009	2004 National Centile	2004 State Centile	2004 Home Value Base	2004 Home Value Distribution (%) Less than $50,000	$50,000 to $89,999	$90,000 to $174,999	$175,000 to $399,999	$400,000 or More	2004 Median Home Value
54514	BUTTERNUT	21699	968	27.5	35.1	29.9	5.1	2.5	39444	43712	44	27	787	18.0	30.8	39.0	11.3	0.9	91557
54515	CATAWBA	18274	231	30.7	37.7	25.1	5.6	0.9	36271	41617	33	12	198	29.3	35.4	28.3	5.6	1.5	70588
54517	CLAM LAKE	0	0	0.0	0.0	0.0	0.0	0.0	0	0	0	0	0	0.0	0.0	0.0	0.0	0.0	0
54519	CONOVER	21527	547	32.2	33.1	27.1	4.9	2.7	36775	42546	35	15	469	5.1	16.4	42.9	29.0	6.6	138393
54520	CRANDON	19018	1686	35.1	35.1	24.0	3.9	1.8	35207	40035	28	9	1248	15.6	24.5	44.0	14.9	1.0	103223
54521	EAGLE RIVER	21629	3800	30.5	33.5	27.8	6.1	2.1	38108	43520	40	21	3116	5.6	17.4	43.6	27.6	5.8	134053
54524	FIFIELD	22431	310	28.7	31.3	31.6	6.1	2.3	42223	48361	54	39	262	11.5	28.2	41.6	16.4	2.3	107000
54526	GLEN FLORA	16923	355	34.1	35.5	25.6	3.9	0.9	34897	39196	27	8	302	33.1	30.1	29.5	6.3	1.0	71364
54527	GLIDDEN	16606	426	42.7	35.2	19.5	1.4	1.2	28408	31643	9	1	329	43.8	34.4	20.4	1.5	0.0	56212
54529	HARSHAW	26077	468	23.3	31.8	35.7	5.3	3.9	45647	52846	63	51	421	9.3	17.1	44.4	25.4	3.8	122310
54530	HAWKINS	18003	313	33.9	36.4	24.3	4.5	1.0	35104	39346	28	8	269	32.7	30.5	29.7	6.3	0.7	71750
54531	HAZELHURST	29958	671	18.9	34.6	28.3	10.4	7.8	46700	55659	65	55	594	2.7	8.3	38.1	38.1	13.0	178333
54534	HURLEY	17522	1300	41.5	37.7	16.0	3.6	1.2	29385	32351	11	2	892	45.7	32.2	17.6	4.0	0.5	54419
54536	IRON BELT	19885	126	30.2	39.7	21.4	5.6	3.2	36462	40397	33	13	115	36.5	33.0	23.5	6.1	0.9	66250
54537	KENNAN	17872	261	32.6	35.3	24.5	5.8	1.9	36951	41950	35	16	226	25.2	25.7	37.6	11.1	0.4	88462
54538	LAC DU FLAMBEAU	16785	994	33.4	33.6	25.9	4.7	2.4	35155	40843	28	8	759	8.0	15.6	32.8	32.5	11.1	157923
54539	LAKE TOMAHAWK	27222	768	22.5	37.2	29.6	6.0	4.7	43269	51537	57	42	653	10.7	10.9	45.6	27.3	5.5	135577
54540	LAND O LAKES	23031	506	32.6	33.0	25.9	5.7	2.8	35295	41319	29	9	418	6.9	15.3	39.0	29.9	8.9	149306
54541	LAONA	18670	669	29.0	32.9	31.2	4.9	1.9	39926	44683	46	29	526	15.8	32.3	38.8	12.0	1.1	93226
54542	LONG LAKE	22052	324	36.7	34.3	23.2	4.3	1.5	33704	37909	23	6	277	28.5	26.7	33.2	9.8	1.8	80938
54545	MANITOWISH WATERS	25579	423	31.4	27.7	26.5	10.6	3.8	39873	47037	46	28	369	3.5	8.9	30.1	39.6	17.9	200568
54546	MELLEN	19331	748	36.4	33.0	25.8	3.6	1.2	34334	36857	25	7	585	42.7	26.5	23.6	7.0	0.2	60122
54547	MERCER	24372	902	31.4	37.3	24.1	5.2	2.1	35172	39283	28	9	734	9.7	18.5	38.4	29.4	4.0	124554
54548	MINOCQUA	27521	2507	26.8	28.8	32.1	7.4	5.0	44327	51153	60	46	2019	4.4	8.1	40.3	34.8	12.5	167921
54550	MONTREAL	19149	486	36.2	38.7	20.0	3.1	2.1	32233	35850	18	3	388	51.6	32.2	13.9	2.1	0.3	49130
54552	PARK FALLS	21571	2084	32.4	31.3	28.0	5.9	2.4	38443	43729	41	23	1610	19.7	28.9	37.2	12.7	1.6	92170
54554	PHELPS	20123	529	32.0	36.5	24.0	5.9	1.7	36032	41932	32	12	448	6.3	15.9	43.5	28.8	5.6	136702
54555	PHILLIPS	21003	2388	30.3	32.7	29.2	5.7	2.1	40554	45348	48	32	1874	17.1	27.6	42.5	11.9	1.0	97920
54556	PRENTICE	18588	556	37.8	28.4	28.4	3.8	1.6	33967	38384	24	6	435	24.1	37.0	32.0	6.9	0.0	78659
54557	PRESQUE ISLE	25725	465	31.0	29.0	27.7	8.6	3.7	39326	46552	44	26	405	3.7	7.9	33.6	38.5	16.3	189773
54558	SAINT GERMAIN	25107	1003	30.6	32.7	28.3	5.0	3.4	38466	43491	41	23	861	6.2	10.6	43.2	33.2	6.9	148772
54559	SAXON	20598	217	31.8	32.3	27.2	6.5	2.3	35860	39073	31	11	197	32.0	23.4	36.0	8.6	0.0	82500
54560	SAYNER	23135	286	27.6	32.9	30.4	5.6	3.5	42213	48919	54	39	249	1.6	14.1	41.8	31.3	11.2	150658
54562	THREE LAKES	22871	972	30.9	30.8	30.4	5.3	2.8	37863	43193	39	20	824	6.6	13.2	41.5	33.6	5.1	147753
54563	TONY	18208	307	32.3	32.9	29.3	3.3	2.3	38558	42356	41	23	252	19.4	31.8	32.9	15.5	0.4	88571
54564	TRIPOLI	26261	227	23.4	34.4	35.2	4.9	2.2	43635	50000	58	43	204	10.3	23.0	44.1	20.1	2.5	112195
54565	UPSON	17992	29	34.5	41.4	20.7	3.5	0.0	35393	42343	29	10	26	38.5	34.6	23.1	3.9	0.0	63333
54566	WABENO	20608	704	29.4	33.5	29.3	6.0	1.9	40361	44461	47	31	562	21.5	35.4	33.1	9.6	0.4	83036
54568	WOODRUFF	22186	2331	29.2	35.4	28.3	4.9	2.2	39618	45508	45	27	1810	11.3	12.6	50.4	22.9	2.8	123995
54601	LA CROSSE	23531	19836	31.1	31.5	26.5	6.1	4.8	38525	44582	41	23	11218	8.0	19.3	54.5	16.4	1.9	113298
54603	LA CROSSE	20116	6482	32.2	35.6	25.5	4.9	1.8	35823	41481	31	11	3743	11.9	33.3	45.9	8.0	0.8	93962
54610	ALMA	21953	992	29.3	32.2	29.5	6.3	2.7	40783	45382	49	33	746	17.4	21.5	38.2	18.0	5.0	107645
54611	ALMA CENTER	19131	402	29.9	33.3	30.1	4.0	2.7	40613	43653	48	32	324	18.5	32.1	35.8	12.0	1.5	89167
54612	ARCADIA	20813	1810	29.6	32.8	30.5	4.6	2.5	38953	43537	43	25	1329	12.0	31.8	40.0	14.7	1.7	97952
54613	ARKDALE	21066	789	34.9	36.1	23.8	3.7	1.5	33193	37285	21	4	667	21.1	31.8	35.1	11.1	0.9	86100
54614	BANGOR	21427	1208	21.0	31.0	39.1	5.8	3.1	48622	55595	70	61	998	9.9	18.7	54.9	14.2	2.2	112598
54615	BLACK RIVER FALLS	21030	3965	28.7	32.6	29.8	6.0	3.1	40593	45895	48	32	2861	15.7	26.4	45.3	11.6	1.1	99763
54616	BLAIR	18258	980	32.0	34.8	27.8	3.6	1.8	38179	42891	40	21	745	18.5	29.0	37.6	12.8	2.2	93033
54618	CAMP DOUGLAS	20680	924	25.0	32.3	37.0	4.3	1.4	43978	49074	59	45	750	16.8	29.7	39.2	12.9	1.3	94727
54619	CASHTON	14321	1177	38.2	30.8	24.1	4.5	2.3	33408	36252	22	5	914	20.6	25.8	34.8	17.6	1.2	95000
54621	CHASEBURG	20944	479	23.2	29.0	39.5	6.3	2.1	48276	53828	69	59	409	11.5	18.1	40.6	26.9	2.9	124457
54622	COCHRANE	21832	869	22.6	36.7	34.8	4.4	1.6	43292	48819	57	42	736	11.1	22.7	51.6	12.0	2.6	108466
54623	COON VALLEY	21258	783	22.2	31.0	37.2	6.4	3.2	46970	53316	66	56	656	20.7	18.5	43.9	15.4	1.5	105372
54624	DE SOTO	21997	625	29.0	32.3	31.5	5.1	2.1	40166	44860	47	30	527	26.0	23.9	32.6	16.1	1.3	90147
54625	DODGE	21076	109	26.6	33.0	33.9	5.5	0.9	43823	48309	58	44	85	10.6	17.7	43.5	25.9	2.4	126136
54626	EASTMAN	17561	581	29.3	36.8	27.2	5.0	1.7	38220	42544	40	22	485	22.5	26.6	35.5	13.0	2.5	91607
54627	ETTRICK	21306	771	24.9	33.9	33.7	5.1	2.5	44141	48932	59	45	625	13.3	21.8	44.0	20.3	0.6	108804
54628	FERRYVILLE	19439	665	33.1	34.9	24.7	4.4	3.0	35475	39842	29	10	530	23.2	26.0	32.3	16.2	2.3	91053
54629	FOUNTAIN CITY	23718	1176	24.2	33.1	33.6	5.5	3.6	43984	50000	59	45	907	9.7	22.4	47.4	18.2	2.3	112256
54630	GALESVILLE	21895	1578	26.1	31.9	33.8	5.9	2.3	44455	49377	60	46	1248	11.5	18.1	47.3	21.1	2.1	116601
54631	GAYS MILLS	18040	892	35.1	36.1	22.4	3.7	2.7	35549	39765	30	10	728	26.0	22.5	33.1	15.4	3.0	92340
54632	GENOA	20782	439	24.4	30.3	38.3	5.9	1.1	46454	51960	65	54	375	19.2	19.5	38.4	21.3	1.6	108669
54634	HILLSBORO	16773	1412	33.9	34.1	25.8	4.5	1.8	36410	40361	33	13	1096	20.3	25.6	35.2	17.1	1.9	95897
54635	HIXTON	19888	680	29.1	35.4	29.3	3.8	2.4	40111	43484	46	29	558	17.9	28.1	37.5	14.3	2.2	95000
54636	HOLMEN	21932	3921	15.2	31.5	41.1	9.1	3.2	52611	60793	76	71	3370	13.6	10.3	49.7	24.8	1.6	129745
54638	KENDALL	17632	660	31.5	34.6	28.2	3.9	1.8	36795	40364	35	15	534	16.5	23.4	38.4	18.5	3.2	108073
54639	LA FARGE	15872	914	37.4	35.8	21.4	3.8	1.5	31919	35635	18	2	729	27.3	27.6	29.2	14.5	1.4	83661
54641	MATHER	16389	14	28.6	35.7	35.7	0.0	0.0	40000	45000	46	29	12	8.3	33.3	58.3	0.0	0.0	100000
54642	MELROSE	19848	726	26.5	35.8	30.3	5.1	2.3	41497	45780	51	36	591	16.8	20.8	42.0	18.8	1.7	108701
54644	MINDORO	22315	562	21.9	30.1	38.4	6.2	3.4	48304	55467	69	60	481	11.4	18.5	46.6	19.1	4.4	117995
54646	NECEDAH	19240	1549	30.2	37.1	27.2	3.2	2.3	37351	41736	37	18	1262	19.3	32.0	39.4	8.2	1.1	88476
54648	NORWALK	16032	627	30.8	31.9	30.5	4.8	2.1	40972	45000	50	34	497	15.9	20.1	37.0	23.5	3.4	110026
54650	ONALASKA	26406	8457	17.7	27.6	39.1	11.3	4.3	53586	62678	78	73	6227	9.8	7.0	56.3	25.2	1.8	131374
54651	ONTARIO	16142	482	34.4	36.7	24.9	3.1	0.8	33843	38181	24	6	391	30.4	18.9	28.4	19.4	2.8	91389
54652	READSTOWN	17055	318	40.3	33.7	19.2	5.0	1.9	30913	35083	15	2	255	31.0	27.5	26.3	13.7	1.6	76250
54653	ROCKLAND	18831	257	22.6	32.3	37.0	5.8	2.3	46399	52581	65	54	207	12.6	19.3	50.2	15.9	1.9	111436
54655	SOLDIERS GROVE	16641	713	36.8	36.3	21.0	4.4	1.5	33038	37171	21	4	568	30.3	24.3	30.5	13.4	1.6	80370
54656	SPARTA	20646	6387	27.1	33.3	31.4	5.3	3.0	41429	46737	51	36	4693	16.5	26.0	46.0	10.5	1.1	97405
54657	STEUBEN	16378	46	26.1	37.0	34.8	2.2	0.0	40000	45000	46	29	37	27.0	16.2	35.1	18.9	2.7	102083
54658	STODDARD	23456	1072	21.6	30.3	37.6	7.2	3.3	48331	54107	69	60	892	13.2	18.1	45.7	21.8	1.2	119205
54659	TAYLOR	17376	478	28.5	38.9	25.5	4.6	2.5	37859	42754	39	20	361	24.1	28.3	30.5	14.7	2.5	86136
54660	TOMAH	20358	5902	27.2	33.1	32.0	5.6	2.2	41560	46650	52	36	4288	15.2	25.8	44.7	13.5	0.8	100143
54661	TREMPEALEAU	21810	1215	22.9	32.3	37.3	5.8	1.7	46688	51338	65	55	1013	14.0	19.0	47.9	18.3	0.9	111568
54664	VIOLA	19396	631	31.7	35.3	28.1	2.5	2.4	37276	41877	36	18	515	24.1	28.0	30.9	15.3	1.8	87000
54665	VIROQUA	18454	3345	35.4	35.1	24.0	3.2	2.2	34213	38594	25	6	2402	21.7	27.0	37.1	12.0	2.1	92026
54666	WARRENS	20310	942	25.4	34.8	34.2	4.6	1.1	41394	46594	51	35	776	18.2	23.6	41.4	15.6	1.3	104514
54667	WESTBY	17987	1785	29.1	35.7	28.5	4.7	2.0	36837	41750	35	16	1413	15.9	26.0	41.2	15.7	1.2	101526
54669	WEST SALEM	23930	2723	16.3	29.9	38.9	10.3	4.6	52866	62149	77	72	2187	14.7	11.2	50.4	21.5	2.2	123617
54670	WILTON	14272	587	34.6	34.8	23.9	3.8	3.1	36417	39631	33	13	466	17.8	31.8	31.8	15.0	3.7	90625
54701	EAU CLAIRE	26157	14957	26.0	28.8	30.0	9.2	6.0	44972	51865	61	48	9198	3.7	9.0	55.9	29.3	2.2	137633
54703	EAU CLAIRE	20386	16452	24.3	35.2	33.5	5.6	1.5	42400	49014	54	39	10440	6.7	22.5	59.1	11.1	0.6	108789
54720	ALTOONA	25241	3116	23.5	32.3	31.8	8.2	4.3	45366	51888	62	50	1996	18.2	14.8	46.3	18.5	2.3	111765
54721	ARKANSAW	20010	572	25.2	35.3	33.0	4.7	1.8	42213	47009	54	39	475	13.7	27.2	36.0	21.5	1.7	105114
54722	AUGUSTA	16943	1427	32.6	32.8	29.3	3.7	1.6	36644	41859	34	14	1129	15.2	33.0	42.1	8.3	1.4	91847
54723	BAY CITY	25659	508	14.2	24.6	47.4	11.6	2.2	59590	66360	84	85	437	9.2	8.7	47.8	31.1	3.2	144242
	WISCONSIN	25041		22.2	28.8	35.0	9.6	4.2	48930	56561				7.0	14.9	46.8	27.8	3.6	134326
	UNITED STATES	25866		24.7	27.1	30.8	10.9	6.5	48124	56710				10.9	15.0	33.7	30.1	10.4	145905

ZIP CODE		FINANCIAL SERVICES				THE HOME						ENTERTAINMENT						PERSONAL			
						Home Improvements		Furnishings													
#	POST OFFICE NAME	Auto Loan	Home Loan	Invest-ments	Retire-ment Plans	Home Repair	Lawn & Garden	Comput-ers & Hard-ware	Major Appli-ances	TV, Radio, Sound Equip-ment	Furni-ture	Dine out/ Carry out	Sports Equip-ment	Fees & Tickets	Toys & Games	Travel	Cable TV	Apparel & Services	Auto Repairs	Health Insur-ance	Pets & Supplies
54514	BUTTERNUT	77	69	59	64	74	83	67	74	73	66	89	85	66	92	70	77	84	72	83	92
54515	CATAWBA	84	56	25	48	64	73	54	68	65	55	77	81	46	72	55	70	70	67	83	96
54517	CLAM LAKE	0	0	0	0	0	0	0	0	0	0	0	0	0	0	0	0	0	0	0	0
54519	CONOVER	83	65	45	59	74	83	62	74	70	61	83	87	55	82	66	75	77	73	88	102
54520	CRANDON	75	58	40	54	65	75	58	68	65	56	77	78	51	75	60	69	71	67	80	90
54521	EAGLE RIVER	81	63	43	58	71	80	61	73	69	60	82	85	55	80	64	73	76	72	86	97
54524	FIFIELD	87	68	46	61	77	86	64	77	73	64	86	91	57	85	68	78	80	76	91	106
54526	GLEN FLORA	79	54	26	48	62	70	52	65	62	53	73	78	45	70	54	67	67	64	79	92
54527	GLIDDEN	70	48	23	42	54	62	46	57	55	47	65	69	40	62	47	60	59	57	70	81
54529	HARSHAW	101	79	54	71	89	100	74	90	84	74	100	105	67	99	79	90	93	88	106	123
54530	HAWKINS	80	54	26	48	62	71	53	66	63	53	74	79	45	71	54	67	67	65	80	93
54531	HAZELHURST	116	93	66	85	104	116	88	104	98	87	117	122	79	115	93	104	109	103	121	141
54534	HURLEY	54	49	49	47	51	58	51	53	55	50	67	61	50	68	52	57	64	54	59	63
54536	IRON BELT	77	60	41	54	68	76	57	68	64	56	76	80	51	75	60	68	71	67	81	93
54537	KENNAN	85	59	31	52	67	77	57	71	68	58	80	84	49	76	59	73	73	70	86	99
54538	LAC DU FLAMBEAU	78	61	42	55	69	77	58	70	65	57	77	81	52	76	62	70	72	69	82	95
54539	LAKE TOMAHAWK	104	81	55	73	91	103	77	92	87	76	103	108	69	101	82	93	96	91	109	126
54540	LAND O LAKES	82	65	44	58	73	82	61	73	69	60	82	86	54	81	65	74	76	72	87	100
54541	LAONA	83	65	44	59	73	82	61	74	69	61	82	86	55	81	65	74	76	73	87	101
54542	LONG LAKE	77	60	41	54	68	76	57	68	64	56	76	80	51	75	60	68	71	67	81	93
54545	MANITOWISH WATERS	90	71	48	64	80	89	67	80	75	66	89	94	60	88	71	81	83	79	95	110
54546	MELLEN	79	57	32	51	65	74	55	67	64	55	75	79	48	73	57	68	69	66	81	94
54547	MERCER	84	66	45	60	74	84	62	75	71	62	84	88	56	83	66	75	78	74	89	103
54548	MINOCQUA	98	81	60	75	89	98	78	90	85	77	102	105	71	100	81	89	95	89	102	118
54550	MONTREAL	67	53	37	51	57	67	56	62	62	54	73	70	51	71	56	64	68	61	71	75
54552	PARK FALLS	76	63	48	60	68	78	64	71	70	62	84	81	60	83	65	73	78	70	81	88
54554	PHELPS	78	62	42	56	69	78	58	70	66	57	78	82	52	77	62	70	72	69	83	96
54555	PHILLIPS	76	67	56	63	72	78	64	71	68	63	83	83	62	84	66	71	79	70	78	90
54556	PRENTICE	80	55	27	48	62	71	53	66	63	54	75	78	46	71	54	68	68	65	80	92
54557	PRESQUE ISLE	90	71	48	64	79	89	67	80	75	66	89	94	59	88	71	80	83	79	95	110
54558	SAINT GERMAIN	90	71	48	64	79	89	67	80	75	66	89	94	59	88	71	80	83	79	95	110
54559	SAXON	83	65	44	59	73	82	61	74	69	61	82	86	55	81	65	74	76	73	87	101
54560	SAYNER	86	68	46	61	76	86	64	77	72	63	86	90	57	85	68	77	80	76	91	105
54562	THREE LAKES	82	66	49	61	74	82	63	74	70	62	84	87	57	82	67	74	78	73	86	100
54563	TONY	80	65	44	61	71	78	61	71	67	61	81	85	57	81	63	70	76	69	80	94
54564	TRIPOLI	94	74	50	67	83	93	70	84	79	69	93	98	62	92	74	84	87	82	99	115
54565	UPSON	64	50	34	45	57	64	47	57	54	47	64	67	42	63	51	57	59	56	68	78
54566	WABENO	82	64	44	58	72	81	61	73	68	60	81	85	54	80	65	73	75	72	86	100
54568	WOODRUFF	82	64	43	58	71	81	63	74	71	61	83	85	56	81	65	75	77	73	87	98
54601	LA CROSSE	75	72	81	74	72	78	80	76	79	77	99	91	78	98	77	77	96	79	74	85
54603	LA CROSSE	61	62	67	63	63	67	66	64	65	63	81	75	66	83	65	64	79	65	63	71
54610	ALMA	90	67	42	64	75	86	69	80	78	67	92	93	62	89	70	82	84	79	94	103
54611	ALMA CENTER	77	65	51	65	69	77	67	72	71	66	86	82	64	85	67	72	81	70	78	85
54612	ARCADIA	76	69	58	67	72	79	67	72	71	66	87	83	67	89	69	73	82	70	78	87
54613	ARKDALE	77	60	41	54	68	76	57	68	64	56	76	80	51	75	60	68	71	67	81	93
54614	BANGOR	91	79	60	76	84	90	75	83	79	75	96	99	72	97	76	80	91	81	89	107
54615	BLACK RIVER FALLS	84	72	56	69	76	86	73	79	78	71	94	90	69	93	73	81	88	78	88	96
54616	BLAIR	75	57	36	54	63	72	59	67	66	57	78	78	53	75	59	69	71	67	79	86
54618	CAMP DOUGLAS	83	71	53	68	76	83	69	76	74	68	89	89	66	90	70	76	84	75	84	96
54619	CASHTON	72	56	38	54	61	68	56	64	62	56	74	75	51	72	57	63	69	64	72	82
54621	CHASEBURG	87	77	58	73	82	88	71	79	76	71	92	95	70	94	73	78	88	77	86	103
54622	COCHRANE	80	70	54	68	74	81	67	73	71	66	86	87	65	87	68	73	82	72	80	93
54623	COON VALLEY	90	74	53	71	79	89	74	82	81	73	97	95	69	94	75	84	90	81	93	102
54624	DE SOTO	84	67	47	61	75	84	63	75	71	63	84	88	57	84	67	75	79	74	88	102
54625	DODGE	81	72	55	69	76	82	67	74	71	67	86	88	65	88	69	73	82	72	80	96
54626	EASTMAN	80	59	35	55	68	76	57	70	65	57	77	83	50	76	60	69	71	69	83	96
54627	ETTRICK	82	73	55	69	77	82	67	75	71	67	87	89	66	89	69	73	83	73	81	96
54628	FERRYVILLE	79	61	40	55	69	77	58	70	66	57	78	83	51	77	61	70	72	69	83	96
54629	FOUNTAIN CITY	89	78	60	76	82	90	76	82	80	75	97	96	73	98	77	82	92	81	89	103
54630	GALESVILLE	82	76	64	73	79	84	71	77	74	71	91	92	70	92	73	75	87	76	82	97
54631	GAYS MILLS	80	58	33	54	67	75	57	69	65	56	76	83	49	75	59	68	70	68	82	96
54632	GENOA	84	74	55	70	79	85	68	77	73	68	89	91	66	90	71	75	84	75	84	100
54634	HILLSBORO	79	57	33	54	64	74	59	69	67	57	79	81	51	76	60	70	72	68	82	91
54635	HIXTON	81	64	44	63	70	79	65	73	71	64	85	85	60	84	65	73	79	72	82	92
54636	HOLMEN	90	91	82	90	91	93	85	88	84	86	104	104	85	105	85	82	101	87	85	104
54638	KENDALL	86	61	32	57	70	79	60	74	69	59	81	89	51	79	62	72	74	73	87	102
54639	LA FARGE	71	51	29	48	58	67	53	62	60	51	71	73	46	68	54	64	65	62	74	82
54641	MATHER	71	56	38	51	63	71	53	64	60	52	71	75	47	70	56	64	66	63	75	87
54642	MELROSE	87	68	44	65	76	83	65	77	73	65	87	92	60	86	68	75	80	75	88	103
54644	MINDORO	91	81	61	77	85	92	75	83	79	75	97	99	73	99	77	81	92	81	90	107
54646	NECEDAH	82	66	47	62	72	81	64	74	71	63	85	86	59	84	67	74	79	73	85	96
54648	NORWALK	79	64	46	63	69	78	65	72	70	64	85	84	61	84	65	72	79	71	80	89
54650	ONALASKA	94	99	96	100	98	101	95	96	92	95	115	113	96	117	95	90	112	95	91	108
54651	ONTARIO	75	51	24	45	58	66	49	61	59	50	69	74	42	66	51	63	63	61	75	87
54652	READSTOWN	68	51	33	48	56	66	56	62	63	53	74	69	50	70	55	66	67	62	74	75
54653	ROCKLAND	87	76	58	73	80	86	71	79	75	71	92	95	69	93	73	77	87	78	85	101
54655	SOLDIERS GROVE	71	52	32	50	59	68	55	63	62	53	73	73	49	70	56	66	67	63	75	81
54656	SPARTA	82	70	54	67	73	81	68	75	73	68	89	88	65	87	69	75	84	74	82	94
54657	STEUBEN	73	62	48	62	65	73	64	68	68	63	82	78	61	81	63	69	77	67	74	80
54658	STODDARD	93	81	63	79	86	94	79	86	84	78	101	101	76	102	80	85	96	84	93	107
54659	TAYLOR	84	62	35	55	68	77	59	71	68	59	81	84	53	78	60	72	74	70	84	97
54660	TOMAH	76	68	57	66	71	79	68	72	72	67	88	83	66	89	69	74	83	71	78	87
54661	TREMPEALEAU	82	71	55	69	75	83	70	76	74	69	90	88	67	90	70	76	85	74	82	93
54664	VIOLA	81	62	39	58	67	76	62	71	69	61	83	83	56	80	62	72	76	70	82	92
54665	VIROQUA	73	53	33	51	59	70	57	65	64	55	75	74	50	72	57	68	69	64	77	82
54666	WARRENS	83	66	44	63	71	80	65	74	71	64	86	87	60	85	66	74	80	73	83	95
54667	WESTBY	80	60	37	57	67	76	61	71	68	60	81	83	54	78	62	71	74	70	83	93
54669	WEST SALEM	99	94	80	92	96	102	90	95	91	90	112	111	89	113	90	92	108	93	97	114
54670	WILTON	73	59	42	58	64	72	60	67	65	59	78	77	56	77	60	67	73	66	74	83
54701	EAU CLAIRE	86	86	95	87	85	91	92	87	90	89	113	105	91	113	89	87	110	90	84	99
54703	EAU CLAIRE	69	68	72	69	68	72	73	70	72	71	89	85	72	90	71	69	87	72	68	79
54720	ALTOONA	84	83	81	83	83	88	82	84	81	82	101	97	81	100	81	80	98	84	82	95
54721	ARKANSAW	92	65	35	62	75	84	64	79	74	64	87	94	55	85	66	77	79	78	93	108
54722	AUGUSTA	76	59	39	56	65	74	61	68	67	59	80	79	55	77	61	70	74	68	80	87
54723	BAY CITY	107	95	72	90	100	108	88	97	93	88	114	116	86	116	91	96	108	95	105	126
	WISCONSIN	89	86	85	86	88	94	86	88	87	85	108	103	86	109	86	87	104	88	89	103
	UNITED STATES	100	100	100	100	100	100	100	100	100	100	100	100	100	100	100	100	100	100	100	100

# POST OFFICE NAME	COUNTY FIPS CODE	POPULATION 2000	POPULATION 2004	POPULATION 2009	2000-2004 ANNUAL RATE % Rate	2000-2004 ANNUAL RATE State Centile	HOUSEHOLDS 2000	HOUSEHOLDS 2004	HOUSEHOLDS 2009	% Annual Rate 2000-2004	2004 Average HH Size	FAMILIES 2000	FAMILIES 2004	% Annual Rate 2000-2004
54724 BLOOMER	017	6675	6819	7223	0.5	34	2598	2728	2966	1.2	2.48	1849	1915	0.8
54725 BOYCEVILLE	033	2870	3171	3499	2.4	91	1076	1214	1368	2.9	2.61	746	829	2.5
54726 BOYD	017	1971	2030	2163	0.7	43	706	747	816	1.3	2.72	539	560	0.9
54727 CADOTT	017	4552	4784	5146	1.2	64	1685	1823	2013	1.9	2.62	1282	1369	1.6
54728 CHETEK	005	6236	6526	6818	1.1	61	2532	2719	2908	1.7	2.36	1795	1899	1.3
54729 CHIPPEWA FALLS	017	27869	30134	32896	1.9	84	10983	12190	13660	2.5	2.40	7450	8174	2.2
54730 COLFAX	033	4432	4685	5048	1.3	69	1682	1817	2001	1.8	2.54	1235	1317	1.5
54731 CONRATH	107	655	680	693	0.9	51	240	255	266	1.4	2.67	177	186	1.2
54732 CORNELL	017	2749	2900	3112	1.3	67	1063	1155	1273	2.0	2.48	752	805	1.6
54733 DALLAS	005	1586	1641	1706	0.8	47	572	610	650	1.5	2.64	432	455	1.2
54734 DOWNING	033	750	901	1039	4.4	99	283	350	414	5.1	2.57	209	254	4.7
54736 DURAND	091	4049	4261	4503	1.2	65	1516	1629	1756	1.7	2.57	1060	1122	1.4
54737 EAU GALLE	033	373	372	394	-0.1	12	145	149	162	0.6	2.50	110	111	0.2
54738 ELEVA	035	2418	2524	2636	1.0	57	928	996	1065	1.7	2.52	710	753	1.4
54739 ELK MOUND	033	3849	4072	4386	1.3	70	1341	1460	1612	2.0	2.78	1075	1160	1.8
54740 ELMWOOD	093	2152	2171	2289	0.2	23	805	831	897	0.8	2.55	578	590	0.5
54741 FAIRCHILD	053	1564	1599	1659	0.5	35	538	559	592	0.9	2.77	385	394	0.6
54742 FALL CREEK	035	4198	4652	5051	2.5	91	1501	1709	1903	3.1	2.69	1158	1304	2.8
54745 HOLCOMBE	017	2130	2357	2586	2.4	91	852	968	1088	3.1	2.40	617	693	2.8
54746 HUMBIRD	019	739	730	734	-0.3	7	289	294	303	0.4	2.46	205	206	0.1
54747 INDEPENDENCE	121	2454	2547	2630	0.9	50	1020	1095	1164	1.7	2.31	664	700	1.3
54748 JIM FALLS	017	1234	1291	1379	1.1	60	456	491	539	1.8	2.63	365	389	1.5
54749 KNAPP	033	1242	1438	1639	3.5	97	468	558	652	4.2	2.58	343	402	3.8
54750 MAIDEN ROCK	093	1209	1217	1285	0.2	21	432	446	483	0.8	2.71	325	332	0.5
54751 MENOMONIE	033	23337	24560	26325	1.2	65	8172	8880	9828	2.0	2.44	4719	5035	1.5
54754 MERRILLAN	053	1567	1601	1657	0.5	34	645	678	719	1.2	2.27	441	458	0.9
54755 MONDOVI	011	6753	6987	7267	0.8	46	2542	2678	2838	1.2	2.57	1764	1841	1.0
54756 NELSON	011	942	957	970	0.4	30	394	412	428	1.1	2.32	276	284	0.7
54757 NEW AUBURN	017	2848	3162	3471	2.5	92	1095	1248	1405	3.1	2.53	788	885	2.8
54758 OSSEO	121	4775	4849	4984	0.4	29	1831	1904	2002	0.9	2.50	1308	1344	0.6
54759 PEPIN	091	1455	1524	1609	1.1	61	610	660	714	1.9	2.23	405	431	1.5
54761 PLUM CITY	093	1116	1161	1240	0.9	53	415	443	485	1.6	2.53	307	324	1.3
54762 PRAIRIE FARM	005	1207	1260	1321	1.0	57	438	468	502	1.6	2.62	315	332	1.2
54763 RIDGELAND	033	985	1060	1152	1.7	82	397	439	489	2.4	2.41	283	308	2.0
54765 SAND CREEK	033	112	113	119	0.2	23	46	48	51	1.0	2.35	34	34	0.0
54766 SHELDON	119	1630	1684	1723	0.8	46	566	601	631	1.4	2.80	419	439	1.1
54767 SPRING VALLEY	093	2906	3203	3552	2.3	90	1076	1215	1381	2.9	2.59	784	877	2.7
54768 STANLEY	017	3984	4092	4294	0.6	41	1521	1602	1723	1.2	2.51	1033	1065	0.7
54769 STOCKHOLM	091	347	352	367	0.3	28	155	162	174	1.0	2.17	107	111	0.9
54770 STRUM	121	2070	2169	2260	1.1	62	806	866	925	1.7	2.46	587	623	1.4
54771 THORP	019	3984	3970	3990	-0.1	11	1458	1476	1503	0.3	2.64	986	984	-0.1
54772 WHEELER	033	1108	1240	1377	2.7	94	409	471	537	3.4	2.63	307	348	3.0
54773 WHITEHALL	121	3405	3558	3690	1.0	58	1272	1366	1454	1.7	2.42	851	900	1.3
54801 SPOONER	129	6573	6942	7453	1.3	68	2696	2911	3196	1.8	2.34	1801	1919	1.5
54805 ALMENA	005	1728	1843	1948	1.5	75	650	712	770	2.2	2.58	498	537	1.8
54806 ASHLAND	003	12532	12457	12459	-0.1	9	4896	4969	5070	0.4	2.36	3051	3050	0.0
54810 BALSAM LAKE	095	2344	2486	2688	1.4	72	990	1080	1197	2.1	2.27	693	745	1.7
54812 BARRON	005	5314	5399	5581	0.4	30	2055	2142	2270	1.0	2.43	1384	1420	0.6
54813 BARRONETT	013	721	742	778	0.7	43	278	294	316	1.3	2.52	213	223	1.1
54814 BAYFIELD	007	2438	2536	2697	0.9	53	951	1017	1110	1.6	2.47	661	696	1.2
54817 BIRCHWOOD	129	2410	2510	2663	1.0	55	1011	1081	1173	1.6	2.32	736	777	1.3
54819 BRUCE	107	2482	2441	2435	-0.4	6	1052	1059	1080	0.2	2.31	698	691	-0.2
54820 BRULE	031	1204	1246	1297	0.8	47	466	492	521	1.3	2.53	321	333	0.9
54821 CABLE	007	1406	1462	1554	0.9	53	652	694	755	1.5	2.11	431	452	1.1
54822 CAMERON	005	3863	4084	4298	1.3	70	1498	1630	1759	2.0	2.50	1087	1166	1.7
54824 CENTURIA	095	2153	2191	2343	0.4	31	810	845	926	1.0	2.57	556	571	0.6
54826 COMSTOCK	005	762	780	814	0.6	37	309	325	347	1.2	2.38	216	224	0.9
54827 CORNUCOPIA	007	223	229	243	0.6	41	108	115	125	1.5	1.99	76	80	1.2
54828 COUDERAY	113	748	744	791	-0.1	10	297	303	331	0.5	2.43	204	206	0.2
54829 CUMBERLAND	005	5394	5472	5657	0.3	28	2212	2302	2434	0.9	2.35	1541	1580	0.6
54830 DANBURY	013	2816	2936	3068	1.0	56	1297	1388	1485	1.6	2.11	888	936	1.3
54832 DRUMMOND	007	412	431	459	1.1	60	183	195	213	1.5	2.21	121	127	1.2
54835 EXELAND	113	1020	1058	1127	0.9	49	424	451	492	1.5	2.32	296	311	1.2
54836 FOXBORO	031	1026	1063	1066	0.8	48	392	417	428	1.5	2.55	287	301	1.1
54837 FREDERIC	095	4102	4207	4451	0.6	39	1659	1749	1898	1.3	2.34	1114	1155	0.9
54838 GORDON	031	1100	1154	1166	1.1	63	480	518	536	1.8	2.16	339	359	1.4
54839 GRAND VIEW	007	314	357	398	3.1	95	142	163	186	3.3	2.19	98	112	3.2
54840 GRANTSBURG	013	4415	4671	4962	1.3	71	1756	1906	2075	2.0	2.42	1202	1286	1.6
54843 HAYWARD	113	10916	11850	12956	2.0	86	4407	4903	5487	2.5	2.37	3041	3338	2.2
54844 HERBSTER	007	241	260	282	1.8	83	116	130	145	2.7	2.00	74	81	2.2
54845 HERTEL	013	137	147	157	1.7	80	54	60	65	2.5	2.43	41	44	1.7
54846 HIGH BRIDGE	003	566	572	573	0.3	25	217	225	230	0.9	2.54	170	174	0.6
54847 IRON RIVER	007	1746	1870	2021	1.6	78	766	836	922	2.1	2.24	522	561	1.7
54848 LADYSMITH	107	6811	6770	6773	-0.1	9	2665	2714	2782	0.4	2.35	1751	1756	0.1
54849 LAKE NEBAGAMON	031	1894	1959	1971	0.8	46	750	795	819	1.4	2.39	542	568	1.1
54850 LA POINTE	003	246	251	252	0.5	33	125	130	134	0.9	1.93	89	91	0.5
54853 LUCK	095	3549	3729	4008	1.2	63	1427	1540	1697	1.8	2.37	995	1056	1.4
54854 MAPLE	031	919	891	866	-0.7	1	377	375	374	-0.1	2.38	264	257	-0.6
54855 MARENGO	003	680	689	689	0.3	27	238	246	252	0.8	2.80	181	185	0.5
54856 MASON	007	1487	1662	1840	2.7	93	572	656	744	3.3	2.53	414	469	3.0
54858 MILLTOWN	095	1486	1548	1660	1.0	55	651	700	769	1.7	2.21	410	433	1.3
54859 MINONG	129	1839	1947	2082	1.4	71	810	879	960	1.9	2.21	539	576	1.6
54862 OJIBWA	113	398	405	432	0.4	31	157	163	178	0.9	2.45	108	111	0.7
54864 POPLAR	031	1352	1366	1353	0.2	25	485	503	509	0.9	2.69	369	376	0.4
54865 PORT WING	007	503	544	591	1.9	84	235	263	294	2.7	2.07	150	165	2.3
54867 RADISSON	113	449	436	460	-0.7	2	194	193	208	-0.1	2.23	131	129	-0.4
54868 RICE LAKE	005	15345	16026	16827	1.0	58	6225	6652	7145	1.6	2.38	4128	4359	1.3
54870 SARONA	129	1391	1467	1576	1.3	66	579	627	689	1.9	2.33	420	448	1.5
54871 SHELL LAKE	129	3026	3268	3542	1.8	83	1204	1335	1483	2.5	2.38	847	925	2.1
54872 SIREN	013	2817	2852	2953	0.3	27	1166	1209	1283	0.9	2.25	754	770	0.5
54873 SOLON SPRINGS	031	2568	2675	2731	1.0	55	1103	1173	1223	1.5	2.26	740	775	1.1
54874 SOUTH RANGE	031	3378	3480	3482	0.7	43	1208	1274	1304	1.3	2.71	946	984	0.9
54875 SPRINGBROOK	129	1166	1256	1366	1.8	82	472	521	580	2.4	2.40	336	366	2.0
54876 STONE LAKE	113	1534	1619	1743	1.3	67	657	709	779	1.8	2.28	471	502	1.5
54880 SUPERIOR	031	30640	29848	29125	-0.6	3	12855	12819	12779	-0.1	2.24	7676	7511	-0.5
WISCONSIN					0.8					1.4	2.44			1.1
UNITED STATES					1.2					1.3	2.58			1.1

POPULATION COMPOSITION

WISCONSIN

54724-54880 B

ZIP CODE #	POST OFFICE NAME	RACE (%) White 2000	White 2004	Black 2000	Black 2004	Asian/Pacific 2000	Asian/Pacific 2004	% Hispanic Origin 2000	% Hispanic Origin 2004	2004 AGE DISTRIBUTION (%) 0-4	5-9	10-14	15-19	20-24	25-44	45-64	65-84	85+	18+	MEDIAN AGE 2004	% 2004 Males	% 2004 Females
54724	BLOOMER	99.2	99.1	0.0	0.0	0.1	0.1	0.4	0.5	6.4	6.6	7.4	7.2	6.8	26.3	24.6	12.5	2.4	75.1	38.1	49.9	50.1
54725	BOYCEVILLE	98.7	98.6	0.0	0.0	0.1	0.1	0.7	0.9	6.8	7.0	7.8	7.6	6.4	27.1	25.0	10.5	1.8	73.7	36.6	50.0	50.0
54726	BOYD	98.9	98.8	0.1	0.1	0.1	0.2	0.3	0.3	6.4	6.9	8.4	8.1	5.9	25.2	25.9	11.7	1.5	73.1	37.9	52.1	47.9
54727	CADOTT	98.5	98.2	0.1	0.1	0.3	0.4	0.6	0.7	6.1	6.7	7.9	7.2	6.2	26.8	26.4	11.2	1.6	74.6	38.4	51.8	48.2
54728	CHETEK	98.8	98.6	0.1	0.1	0.2	0.3	0.7	0.7	5.4	5.6	6.0	6.4	6.0	23.1	28.6	15.8	3.0	78.9	43.3	50.2	49.8
54729	CHIPPEWA FALLS	97.8	97.5	0.2	0.3	0.8	1.1	0.6	0.7	6.3	6.3	6.8	6.8	6.8	27.0	25.7	12.0	2.3	76.4	38.9	49.4	50.6
54730	COLFAX	98.7	98.4	0.1	0.1	0.4	0.5	0.6	0.7	6.0	6.2	7.5	7.0	5.8	27.1	27.1	11.3	2.0	75.8	39.4	50.4	49.6
54731	CONRATH	98.3	98.2	0.2	0.2	0.3	0.3	0.5	0.6	6.5	7.1	7.8	7.2	5.2	23.8	26.5	14.1	1.9	74.3	40.5	50.9	49.1
54732	CORNELL	98.6	98.5	0.0	0.0	0.3	0.4	0.4	0.5	6.0	6.6	8.2	7.3	5.8	25.3	25.0	13.4	2.2	74.4	39.0	50.4	49.6
54733	DALLAS	98.4	98.2	0.1	0.1	0.1	0.2	0.8	0.9	6.3	6.8	7.8	6.6	5.7	26.1	26.6	11.3	2.9	75.2	39.4	50.1	49.9
54734	DOWNING	99.2	99.2	0.0	0.0	0.1	0.1	1.6	1.9	6.6	6.7	6.3	7.3	6.6	27.2	28.0	10.0	1.4	76.0	37.5	52.3	47.7
54736	DURAND	98.9	98.7	0.1	0.1	0.3	0.4	0.4	0.4	6.8	6.7	7.6	7.2	7.8	24.4	23.8	12.7	3.0	74.2	37.6	49.5	50.5
54737	EAU GALLE	99.2	99.5	0.0	0.0	0.3	0.3	0.8	0.5	7.0	7.0	7.8	5.9	5.1	28.2	25.5	11.8	1.6	74.7	38.8	52.2	47.9
54738	ELEVA	98.7	98.6	0.1	0.1	0.4	0.5	0.7	0.9	6.3	6.9	7.6	6.7	5.3	26.6	27.7	11.4	1.6	74.7	39.6	52.1	47.9
54739	ELK MOUND	97.1	96.7	0.0	0.0	1.5	1.8	0.6	0.7	7.2	7.4	7.2	6.8	6.6	31.1	26.0	6.9	0.8	73.7	35.7	50.7	49.3
54740	ELMWOOD	98.6	98.4	0.1	0.1	0.2	0.2	0.9	1.1	6.1	6.2	7.3	6.9	6.0	26.3	24.7	13.5	3.0	76.1	39.3	49.8	50.2
54741	FAIRCHILD	95.8	95.6	0.1	0.1	0.2	0.2	2.9	3.4	7.8	7.9	8.5	7.7	5.9	25.0	23.5	11.6	2.3	70.7	36.0	51.3	48.7
54742	FALL CREEK	98.2	97.9	0.3	0.3	0.6	0.7	0.4	0.6	6.3	6.6	7.8	7.2	5.8	27.0	26.9	10.6	1.9	74.8	38.8	49.8	50.2
54745	HOLCOMBE	98.8	98.7	0.0	0.0	0.2	0.3	0.5	0.5	5.3	6.1	6.4	6.2	4.7	23.2	30.3	16.0	1.8	77.9	43.8	51.1	48.9
54746	HUMBIRD	95.9	95.6	0.3	0.3	0.1	0.1	1.9	2.2	5.8	6.0	7.0	6.6	5.9	24.1	29.3	13.7	1.6	77.3	41.7	52.3	47.7
54747	INDEPENDENCE	99.0	98.9	0.1	0.1	0.1	0.2	0.9	1.1	6.0	6.5	7.3	6.0	6.0	27.4	24.7	13.7	2.5	76.3	39.7	52.7	47.3
54748	JIM FALLS	99.1	99.0	0.1	0.1	0.1	0.1	0.1	0.1	5.8	6.4	7.4	6.4	5.7	27.6	29.4	10.4	0.9	76.4	40.1	52.5	47.5
54749	KNAPP	98.2	97.8	0.2	0.3	0.6	0.8	1.1	1.2	7.2	7.0	7.4	6.1	6.3	27.3	27.2	10.3	1.3	74.8	38.0	51.8	48.2
54750	MAIDEN ROCK	98.7	98.6	0.1	0.1	0.1	0.2	0.7	0.9	5.0	6.0	8.0	7.3	5.8	25.7	28.7	11.8	1.6	76.3	40.5	51.7	48.3
54751	MENOMONIE	94.5	93.5	0.5	0.6	3.2	4.0	0.9	1.1	5.2	4.8	5.6	11.4	20.9	23.1	18.6	8.4	2.0	80.8	26.5	50.2	49.8
54754	MERRILLAN	92.0	91.0	0.7	0.9	0.1	0.3	4.3	4.9	5.7	6.1	6.9	6.3	5.7	27.2	28.2	12.3	1.8	77.5	40.1	53.6	46.4
54755	MONDOVI	98.5	98.3	0.1	0.1	0.5	0.7	0.4	0.5	6.6	6.8	7.9	7.2	5.6	26.0	24.6	13.0	2.3	74.0	38.3	49.8	50.2
54756	NELSON	98.8	98.6	0.1	0.1	0.5	0.7	0.6	0.8	4.6	6.3	6.7	7.6	6.0	24.9	29.5	12.9	1.7	77.0	41.4	52.1	47.9
54757	NEW AUBURN	98.8	98.7	0.1	0.1	0.1	0.2	0.4	0.4	6.7	6.9	7.4	6.7	6.1	25.6	27.2	12.2	1.3	74.8	39.2	52.0	48.0
54758	OSSEO	98.1	97.9	0.1	0.1	0.3	0.4	1.1	1.2	6.6	6.7	7.6	6.6	5.4	26.2	24.7	13.6	2.7	74.8	38.9	50.1	49.9
54759	PEPIN	98.8	98.8	0.1	0.1	0.3	0.5	0.1	0.1	4.0	4.1	5.3	5.5	6.1	21.7	30.0	18.8	4.7	83.4	47.3	50.5	49.5
54761	PLUM CITY	99.5	99.5	0.0	0.0	0.0	0.0	0.3	0.3	4.9	5.3	7.2	7.6	6.3	24.6	26.1	14.8	3.3	77.4	41.9	51.5	48.5
54762	PRAIRIE FARM	99.2	99.0	0.0	0.0	0.3	0.3	1.2	1.4	6.4	6.6	6.5	6.9	5.9	26.0	26.2	12.8	2.8	75.2	39.8	50.9	49.1
54763	RIDGELAND	98.6	98.5	0.0	0.0	0.2	0.2	0.6	0.8	6.4	6.6	7.1	6.4	5.9	25.3	27.9	12.3	2.2	75.9	40.2	50.8	49.3
54765	SAND CREEK	98.2	98.2	0.0	0.0	0.0	0.9	0.0	0.0	7.1	6.2	7.1	6.2	6.2	24.8	28.3	12.4	1.8	75.2	40.3	54.0	46.0
54766	SHELDON	97.7	97.7	0.1	0.1	0.0	0.0	0.5	0.5	7.1	8.0	8.8	8.0	3.9	25.3	24.5	12.7	1.8	70.9	37.7	49.6	50.4
54767	SPRING VALLEY	98.7	98.6	0.2	0.2	0.1	0.1	0.4	0.4	6.5	6.7	7.6	7.3	6.4	26.3	26.4	10.7	2.3	74.8	38.4	50.9	49.1
54768	STANLEY	98.7	98.5	0.1	0.1	0.3	0.4	0.8	0.9	7.4	7.1	7.2	7.2	6.3	23.8	23.9	13.7	3.5	73.7	38.5	49.8	50.2
54769	STOCKHOLM	98.9	99.2	0.0	0.0	0.0	0.0	0.6	0.9	4.6	4.6	5.7	6.5	4.8	22.2	33.8	16.2	1.7	81.0	46.0	51.4	48.6
54770	STRUM	98.4	98.1	0.2	0.2	0.4	0.5	0.9	1.1	6.8	6.9	7.2	6.8	5.2	27.0	25.4	12.6	2.1	74.6	39.3	51.7	48.3
54771	THORP	99.2	99.1	0.1	0.1	0.2	0.2	0.5	0.5	8.0	7.8	8.2	7.5	6.7	23.1	22.3	13.3	3.1	71.2	36.2	49.7	50.4
54772	WHEELER	98.8	98.7	0.1	0.2	0.3	0.4	0.4	0.2	6.5	6.5	8.5	7.9	5.4	27.1	26.8	10.2	1.2	73.4	38.0	51.8	48.2
54773	WHITEHALL	99.1	98.9	0.2	0.2	0.1	0.2	0.4	0.5	5.8	6.3	7.5	6.4	5.3	26.3	26.1	13.3	3.1	76.1	40.2	50.5	49.5
54801	SPOONER	96.1	95.8	0.3	0.3	0.2	0.3	0.9	1.1	5.2	5.5	7.2	6.7	5.2	22.8	28.2	16.2	3.1	77.5	43.4	49.8	50.2
54805	ALMENA	98.6	98.4	0.1	0.1	0.1	0.1	0.7	0.9	6.3	6.6	7.6	7.0	6.0	27.8	24.7	12.7	1.4	75.2	38.2	51.7	48.4
54806	ASHLAND	86.1	85.9	0.2	0.3	0.4	0.4	1.3	1.3	6.3	6.1	6.8	8.9	8.9	24.1	23.5	12.4	2.9	76.3	36.8	48.8	51.2
54810	BALSAM LAKE	96.1	95.8	0.1	0.1	0.4	0.6	0.6	0.7	6.2	6.3	6.2	5.4	5.0	23.9	30.7	14.8	1.5	77.6	43.1	52.2	47.8
54812	BARRON	97.3	96.9	0.5	0.5	0.3	0.4	1.5	1.7	6.1	6.0	7.2	7.2	7.5	25.9	23.7	13.1	3.4	76.4	38.3	49.1	50.9
54813	BARRONETT	93.1	92.7	0.1	0.1	0.1	0.1	0.1	0.1	5.3	6.3	7.7	7.0	4.7	24.0	32.1	12.1	0.8	75.7	42.2	51.4	48.7
54814	BAYFIELD	50.6	48.5	0.2	0.2	0.0	0.0	1.5	1.6	6.8	6.7	8.4	7.3	6.4	22.8	29.3	11.0	1.3	73.1	38.7	50.0	50.0
54817	BIRCHWOOD	97.7	97.5	0.0	0.0	0.2	0.2	1.0	1.2	4.6	5.2	6.4	6.2	4.7	20.9	31.8	18.4	1.8	79.8	46.1	51.8	48.3
54819	BRUCE	98.6	98.5	0.0	0.0	0.3	0.3	0.5	0.5	4.4	5.2	6.8	6.7	4.2	22.7	29.3	18.2	2.7	79.4	45.1	50.4	49.6
54820	BRULE	97.4	97.3	0.0	0.0	0.2	0.2	0.6	0.6	6.8	7.0	7.5	6.5	4.8	24.6	29.0	12.1	1.8	74.7	40.8	51.0	49.0
54821	CABLE	99.6	99.5	0.0	0.0	0.1	0.2	0.4	0.6	3.8	4.3	5.0	4.7	3.2	18.7	35.6	22.9	1.9	83.8	50.5	51.6	48.4
54822	CAMERON	98.3	98.0	0.1	0.1	0.4	0.4	1.1	1.3	6.5	6.3	7.3	6.7	6.8	28.1	26.4	10.8	1.1	75.5	37.8	50.2	49.8
54824	CENTURIA	97.5	97.1	0.3	0.3	0.5	0.7	0.9	1.0	6.3	6.5	6.8	6.4	5.4	25.3	29.1	12.3	1.9	76.1	40.9	51.3	48.7
54826	COMSTOCK	93.2	92.7	0.0	0.1	0.3	0.3	0.8	0.8	4.7	5.0	6.9	6.7	6.2	23.3	27.8	16.9	2.4	79.1	43.0	50.5	49.5
54827	CORNUCOPIA	86.1	85.2	0.0	0.0	0.0	0.0	0.5	0.4	4.4	4.8	6.6	5.2	3.5	22.3	38.0	14.4	0.9	80.4	46.4	51.1	48.9
54828	COUDERAY	66.2	64.5	0.1	0.1	0.0	0.0	1.3	1.2	5.8	6.1	7.7	6.5	5.2	23.0	28.2	16.1	1.5	76.9	42.0	51.2	48.8
54829	CUMBERLAND	95.8	95.5	0.1	0.2	0.3	0.3	0.6	0.7	4.8	5.4	7.0	6.7	5.7	23.5	28.8	15.6	2.6	78.2	43.0	50.1	50.0
54830	DANBURY	91.5	91.1	0.5	0.6	0.1	0.2	0.5	0.5	3.6	4.0	4.4	4.4	3.7	17.3	32.9	27.5	2.0	85.1	53.3	51.2	48.8
54832	DRUMMOND	97.6	97.2	0.0	0.0	0.5	0.7	0.2	0.2	5.8	6.3	6.3	5.6	4.4	20.9	30.9	18.1	1.9	78.2	45.5	50.4	49.7
54835	EXELAND	93.4	92.9	0.7	0.9	0.5	0.6	1.5	1.6	4.6	5.0	6.3	7.5	5.3	22.3	30.0	16.8	2.2	79.4	44.4	51.8	48.2
54836	FOXBORO	98.3	98.2	0.0	0.0	0.2	0.3	0.1	0.1	4.7	6.4	7.8	6.6	4.1	28.6	30.8	9.9	1.1	76.9	40.9	53.3	46.7
54837	FREDERIC	97.2	96.9	0.1	0.1	0.3	0.4	0.5	0.6	5.3	5.6	6.4	6.9	5.5	22.3	27.4	17.2	3.3	78.2	43.7	49.8	50.2
54838	GORDON	95.5	95.1	1.6	1.8	0.3	0.3	0.5	0.5	3.6	4.3	5.6	4.2	3.5	23.5	33.7	20.5	1.4	83.8	48.4	54.6	45.4
54839	GRAND VIEW	95.9	95.5	0.3	0.6	0.6	0.6	0.0	0.3	6.4	6.7	7.6	5.9	5.6	23.0	29.1	14.3	1.4	75.9	41.6	51.3	48.7
54840	GRANTSBURG	96.7	96.4	0.3	0.4	0.3	0.3	1.2	1.4	5.8	5.9	7.3	7.4	5.9	23.2	28.7	13.4	2.5	76.5	41.3	50.6	49.5
54843	HAYWARD	81.8	80.8	0.1	0.1	0.3	0.4	0.7	0.8	6.0	6.1	6.7	6.9	5.5	22.5	28.8	15.4	2.2	76.7	42.5	49.9	50.1
54844	HERBSTER	96.7	96.5	0.4	0.4	0.0	0.0	1.2	1.5	3.9	3.9	3.9	5.8	3.9	20.8	36.2	19.2	2.7	84.6	49.2	52.3	47.7
54845	HERTEL	83.9	83.7	0.0	0.0	0.7	0.7	0.7	0.7	6.1	6.1	6.8	6.1	6.1	22.5	29.9	15.0	1.4	76.9	42.5	49.0	51.0
54846	HIGH BRIDGE	89.4	89.3	0.0	0.0	0.5	0.5	0.7	0.5	6.3	7.2	8.0	6.6	6.8	25.0	28.3	10.1	1.6	74.3	37.3	50.9	49.1
54847	IRON RIVER	96.9	96.5	0.0	0.0	0.4	0.5	0.2	0.3	6.0	6.1	6.2	5.6	4.1	21.9	30.9	17.0	2.3	78.2	45.1	51.1	48.9
54848	LADYSMITH	97.0	96.9	1.0	1.1	0.5	0.5	0.8	0.8	5.9	6.2	6.9	7.7	7.8	24.1	23.3	14.3	3.9	76.7	39.3	48.6	51.4
54849	LAKE NEBAGAMON	97.8	97.5	0.4	0.5	0.1	0.2	0.7	0.8	5.9	6.6	7.9	6.8	5.0	23.7	28.6	13.0	2.5	74.9	41.6	50.7	49.3
54850	LA POINTE	41.5	41.8	0.0	0.0	0.0	0.0	2.4	2.4	9.2	9.6	9.6	8.4	5.6	25.1	22.7	9.2	0.8	65.7	32.7	51.0	49.0
54853	LUCK	95.6	95.3	0.1	0.1	0.3	0.4	0.7	0.8	5.0	5.3	7.4	7.4	5.9	22.9	27.8	15.4	3.1	77.8	42.6	50.2	49.8
54854	MAPLE	97.2	97.1	0.0	0.0	0.2	0.2	0.9	0.9	6.5	6.9	7.5	6.6	4.8	25.5	29.0	11.8	1.5	75.0	40.6	51.1	48.9
54855	MARENGO	78.5	78.5	0.0	0.0	0.2	0.2	1.0	1.0	7.8	8.1	9.1	7.7	6.4	25.1	25.3	9.1	1.3	69.8	35.2	50.8	49.2
54856	MASON	96.2	95.7	0.4	0.5	0.4	0.5	0.3	0.4	6.0	6.4	6.9	6.1	5.6	23.4	29.5	14.5	1.6	77.0	42.1	51.6	48.4
54858	MILLTOWN	97.9	97.7	0.1	0.1	0.0	0.0	0.7	0.7	5.2	5.6	7.3	5.5	5.6	24.7	25.8	17.9	2.3	78.4	42.4	48.1	51.9
54859	MINONG	96.9	96.8	0.2	0.2	0.2	0.2	0.7	0.8	5.7	5.6	5.7	5.2	4.1	22.3	30.9	18.7	1.9	79.8	45.9	51.6	48.4
54862	OJIBWA	84.2	84.0	0.5	0.7	0.3	0.3	1.5	1.5	4.9	5.4	6.7	6.9	5.4	22.7	28.9	16.8	2.2	78.8	43.7	51.6	48.4
54864	POPLAR	97.0	96.6	0.1	0.2	0.3	0.4	0.4	0.5	6.7	7.0	7.5	7.2	5.6	25.6	28.0	10.5	1.9	74.2	39.6	50.3	49.7
54865	PORT WING	96.8	96.3	0.2	0.2	0.2	0.2	1.2	1.3	4.0	4.0	3.9	5.5	4.0	21.0	36.0	18.9	2.6	84.9	49.0	51.8	48.2
54867	RADISSON	72.4	71.6	0.0	0.0	0.0	0.0	1.3	1.2	5.1	5.7	7.8	6.4	5.5	22.9	28.2	16.5	1.8	77.8	42.5	51.6	48.4
54868	RICE LAKE	97.7	97.4	0.1	0.2	0.6	0.7	1.2	1.4	6.1	6.0	7.0	7.0	7.3	25.9	24.8	13.5	2.5	76.7	39.0	48.8	51.3
54870	SARONA	98.4	98.2	0.1	0.1	0.2	0.2	0.7	0.9	4.3	5.0	6.2	6.0	4.2	20.8	34.4	17.4	1.8	80.3	47.3	51.3	48.7
54871	SHELL LAKE	96.3	96.1	0.1	0.1	0.2	0.2	0.7	0.8	5.6	5.8	6.3	6.1	6.0	22.0	29.1	15.9	3.2	78.6	43.8	49.3	50.7
54872	SIREN	95.7	95.4	0.3	0.4	0.4	0.4	0.6	0.7	5.2	5.1	5.9	5.8	5.2	23.4	27.2	18.9	3.5	80.0	44.8	50.3	49.7
54873	SOLON SPRINGS	96.8	96.5	0.6	0.7	0.5	0.6	0.5	0.6	5.5	5.9	6.4	5.5	4.7	23.6	29.5	17.2	1.9	78.7	44.1	51.5	48.5
54874	SOUTH RANGE	97.1	96.9	0.3	0.3	0.3	0.3	0.9	1.0	5.9	6.7	8.1	7.1	5.3	26.9	28.6	10.3	1.2	74.9	39.6	50.8	49.2
54875	SPRINGBROOK	96.4	96.2	0.2	0.2	0.3	0.3	1.4	1.5	5.3	5.7	6.6	7.9	3.7	25.2	29.5	15.5	0.8	76.8	42.4	52.5	47.5
54876	STONE LAKE	75.7	75.1	0.0	0.0	0.3	0.3	0.9	0.9	5.1	5.7	6.7	6.4	4.6	21.6	30.9	17.2	1.8	78.6	44.9	51.6	48.4
54880	SUPERIOR	94.7	94.1	0.6	0.7	0.8	1.0	0.8	0.9	6.0	5.6	6.2	7.2	8.9	27.0	24.7	11.8	2.5	78.5	37.3	48.4	51.6
	WISCONSIN	88.9	88.0	5.7	6.0	1.7	2.1	3.6	4.0	6.4	6.5	7.1	7.3	7.7	27.6	24.5	11.1	1.9	75.8	36.9	49.5	50.5
	UNITED STATES	75.1	73.6	12.3	12.5	3.8	4.2	12.5	14.1	6.9	6.7	7.2	7.0	7.3	28.6	23.8	10.8	1.7	75.1	36.0	49.1	50.9

ZIP CODE #	POST OFFICE NAME	2004 Per Capita Income	2004 HH Income Base	2004 Household Income Distribution (%): Less than $25,000	$25,000 to $49,999	$50,000 to $99,999	$100,000 to $149,999	$150,000 or More	Median Household Income: 2004	2009	2004 National Centile	2004 State Centile	2004 Home Value Base	2004 Home Value Distribution (%): Less than $50,000	$50,000 to $89,999	$90,000 to $174,999	$175,000 to $399,999	$400,000 or More	2004 Median Home Value
54724	BLOOMER	21673	2728	25.3	32.1	34.3	5.7	2.6	44083	49961	59	45	2099	8.7	25.3	50.4	13.6	2.0	107698
54725	BOYCEVILLE	18480	1214	31.1	33.2	29.4	4.5	1.8	39317	44631	44	26	980	24.8	23.6	37.4	12.2	2.0	92105
54726	BOYD	16751	747	30.1	35.2	29.7	3.5	1.5	39303	43189	44	26	626	15.8	30.7	39.0	12.6	1.9	95238
54727	CADOTT	18533	1823	26.6	34.2	33.2	4.5	1.5	42406	47502	54	40	1469	14.1	25.8	46.4	12.8	1.0	104127
54728	CHETEK	21294	2719	29.4	34.2	28.0	6.2	2.2	40124	44755	47	29	2169	10.6	25.9	45.5	16.5	1.6	107424
54729	CHIPPEWA FALLS	22412	12190	23.5	32.2	34.2	7.7	2.5	44978	50471	61	48	8893	5.3	18.8	54.4	19.7	1.7	117991
54730	COLFAX	21859	1817	21.2	31.0	37.3	8.1	2.4	47975	54179	68	59	1487	11.1	19.2	48.5	19.6	1.6	117349
54731	CONRATH	16200	255	33.3	32.6	29.4	3.5	1.2	37333	41345	37	18	221	19.5	34.8	36.7	7.7	1.4	85476
54732	CORNELL	17334	1155	32.5	36.2	26.7	3.3	1.4	36446	40872	33	13	898	23.8	34.3	33.0	8.5	0.5	81205
54733	DALLAS	19545	610	25.4	36.4	28.4	7.5	2.3	39568	43447	45	27	508	21.1	27.8	34.3	15.4	1.6	91875
54734	DOWNING	20617	350	25.7	30.0	36.0	5.4	2.9	45213	50944	62	49	297	15.8	20.5	46.1	14.8	2.7	108114
54736	DURAND	20719	1629	29.8	31.5	30.0	6.8	2.0	39022	44216	43	25	1234	11.1	29.0	46.9	11.6	1.4	103405
54737	EAU GALLE	20715	149	23.5	37.6	34.2	2.7	2.0	43280	49291	57	42	122	10.7	22.1	40.2	25.4	1.6	125000
54738	ELEVA	22305	996	23.0	29.8	35.9	8.5	2.7	47487	52911	67	57	840	11.0	19.1	45.5	22.4	2.1	119521
54739	ELK MOUND	20986	1460	16.6	32.3	40.9	8.1	2.2	50757	57150	73	67	1241	8.3	16.0	54.7	19.4	1.6	121449
54740	ELMWOOD	20042	831	25.8	34.8	33.1	4.7	1.7	42215	48390	54	39	648	7.9	23.2	45.7	19.0	4.3	116136
54741	FAIRCHILD	15279	559	34.4	34.9	25.4	3.6	1.8	33385	37932	22	5	468	25.6	23.3	39.5	9.4	2.1	91613
54742	FALL CREEK	22686	1709	21.1	30.4	35.5	9.1	3.9	48807	55887	70	61	1387	7.6	16.7	50.5	22.9	2.4	122832
54745	HOLCOMBE	18731	968	33.1	31.4	29.0	5.2	1.3	36817	40566	35	15	828	15.9	29.0	34.4	18.1	2.5	100540
54746	HUMBIRD	19255	294	29.6	34.4	29.6	4.8	1.7	37950	43066	39	20	251	18.7	26.3	40.6	13.2	1.2	97353
54747	INDEPENDENCE	20336	1095	31.0	32.2	30.3	4.3	2.2	38727	42398	42	24	858	13.9	36.4	36.6	10.8	2.3	89740
54748	JIM FALLS	21124	491	21.6	31.8	37.7	6.3	2.7	47612	52835	67	57	420	10.5	19.8	48.3	19.5	1.9	113614
54749	KNAPP	22330	558	26.9	27.1	36.6	6.8	2.7	45851	51195	63	52	473	12.3	22.8	42.9	19.0	3.0	110653
54750	MAIDEN ROCK	21525	446	23.5	25.6	40.4	7.2	3.4	50641	55979	73	65	375	4.3	13.1	40.8	33.9	8.0	151894
54751	MENOMONIE	20852	8880	29.6	30.8	30.2	6.5	2.9	40929	46380	49	34	5257	12.7	14.5	52.4	19.0	1.5	121206
54754	MERRILLAN	20734	678	31.3	32.9	29.9	4.3	1.6	37332	41821	37	18	565	24.6	29.2	33.5	11.9	0.9	85426
54755	MONDOVI	19514	2678	28.3	32.6	31.9	5.3	1.9	40602	45669	48	32	2059	11.1	25.3	44.9	15.7	3.0	107893
54756	NELSON	22278	412	27.4	32.8	31.8	6.1	1.9	40991	44785	50	34	330	20.3	23.9	37.0	14.9	3.9	97917
54757	NEW AUBURN	17456	1248	28.9	38.3	27.9	3.9	1.1	37920	42637	39	20	1049	22.0	22.5	36.7	16.6	2.2	100708
54758	OSSEO	20335	1904	25.7	34.4	32.1	5.7	2.2	43338	48965	57	43	1445	11.6	27.1	44.0	15.6	1.8	104866
54759	PEPIN	21658	660	27.0	35.2	31.5	5.2	1.2	41877	47950	53	37	510	11.8	25.9	44.7	15.9	1.8	103218
54761	PLUM CITY	19855	443	26.9	33.2	31.4	5.6	2.9	42075	48018	53	38	353	9.1	21.3	47.0	17.6	5.1	117659
54762	PRAIRIE FARM	20566	468	24.6	32.3	34.4	4.9	3.9	45799	51342	63	52	384	19.8	30.7	36.7	11.5	1.3	89231
54763	RIDGELAND	21017	439	29.2	32.8	31.7	4.6	1.8	40722	45250	49	33	354	21.8	25.4	33.9	16.1	2.8	95263
54765	SAND CREEK	19537	48	29.2	33.3	31.3	6.3	0.0	41533	44298	51	36	39	15.4	25.6	43.6	15.4	0.0	107500
54766	SHELDON	15490	601	34.4	31.1	29.1	3.8	1.5	36918	40731	35	16	506	23.9	30.0	33.0	11.3	1.8	84872
54767	SPRING VALLEY	21826	1215	20.1	30.5	39.8	7.4	2.3	49502	56824	71	63	992	7.4	15.1	38.6	32.4	6.6	141732
54768	STANLEY	19129	1602	33.2	33.5	27.7	3.3	2.3	35742	39185	31	11	1222	21.5	34.5	34.9	8.2	0.9	82292
54769	STOCKHOLM	24832	162	25.3	27.8	38.3	5.6	3.1	47089	53326	66	56	134	9.0	12.7	38.1	32.8	7.5	148214
54770	STRUM	21275	866	24.4	32.6	34.9	5.9	2.3	44646	48881	60	48	701	10.7	19.8	49.8	17.1	2.6	112579
54771	THORP	16502	1476	34.5	35.4	23.4	4.5	2.2	35443	39759	29	10	1155	20.6	31.9	37.0	9.6	1.0	86935
54772	WHEELER	20879	471	27.0	33.1	32.3	5.3	2.3	43166	48298	56	41	384	15.1	19.8	44.5	17.7	2.9	112727
54773	WHITEHALL	18890	1366	30.8	32.4	30.8	4.2	1.8	38581	43063	41	23	1032	15.8	34.3	37.2	11.4	1.3	89906
54801	SPOONER	19474	2911	32.5	34.4	25.8	5.4	2.0	35707	40366	30	11	2266	14.5	27.3	40.4	15.7	2.1	100787
54805	ALMENA	20085	712	26.7	34.7	30.1	7.2	1.4	41374	45539	51	35	607	17.6	27.0	34.4	19.1	1.8	98553
54806	ASHLAND	18990	4969	34.3	34.0	26.4	3.8	1.6	35705	39655	30	11	3354	18.2	35.5	35.9	9.8	0.6	85623
54810	BALSAM LAKE	24548	1080	23.3	30.7	36.3	6.9	2.9	46192	52635	64	53	925	11.7	17.5	40.0	27.2	3.6	124914
54812	BARRON	19873	2142	29.6	34.6	29.4	5.4	1.1	39291	43862	44	26	1495	16.3	32.0	41.3	9.7	0.7	91635
54813	BARRONETT	22929	294	22.1	33.3	35.0	6.1	3.4	45264	50000	62	49	254	13.8	18.1	40.9	23.2	3.9	117553
54814	BAYFIELD	16901	1017	35.9	35.5	21.5	5.7	1.4	35262	39898	28	9	752	23.8	19.4	37.2	16.5	3.1	100197
54817	BIRCHWOOD	21790	1081	31.5	30.9	28.7	5.9	3.1	38790	43898	42	24	900	15.9	22.3	37.2	21.2	3.3	110360
54819	BRUCE	18588	1059	33.6	35.2	25.7	4.7	0.8	35180	39416	28	9	851	26.6	31.3	33.5	6.9	1.8	78810
54820	BRULE	16978	492	30.9	35.4	29.5	3.9	0.4	37382	41726	37	18	413	16.7	27.4	39.7	15.5	0.7	98448
54821	CABLE	19468	694	39.3	32.4	23.2	3.9	1.2	32009	36951	18	2	586	10.1	17.2	39.4	23.9	9.4	125893
54822	CAMERON	20629	1630	26.1	33.6	32.6	5.3	2.3	42506	48029	55	40	1279	12.7	23.2	50.2	12.5	1.4	105773
54824	CENTURIA	21528	845	25.2	29.7	34.6	7.6	3.0	45530	51611	63	51	707	11.2	15.6	45.3	24.9	3.1	123254
54826	COMSTOCK	20016	325	30.2	33.2	28.6	6.5	1.5	39859	44157	45	28	253	12.7	24.9	42.3	18.6	1.6	109593
54827	CORNUCOPIA	22322	115	29.6	32.2	32.2	6.1	0.0	40318	43304	47	31	107	14.0	22.4	42.1	20.6	0.9	110156
54828	COUDERAY	19158	303	36.0	32.7	25.7	3.6	2.0	35298	40532	29	10	240	24.2	27.5	26.7	18.3	3.3	86923
54829	CUMBERLAND	21234	2302	28.7	32.1	30.8	6.3	2.1	40996	45469	50	34	1788	15.1	24.3	40.6	17.4	2.6	105696
54830	DANBURY	21528	1388	30.0	36.9	26.8	5.3	1.0	37364	42338	37	18	1215	9.4	22.2	40.0	25.2	3.2	117724
54832	DRUMMOND	18823	195	38.5	31.8	23.6	4.1	2.1	34718	37811	26	7	161	15.5	29.2	36.7	17.4	1.2	96538
54835	EXELAND	18300	451	38.4	32.4	23.7	3.6	2.0	32654	37409	20	3	381	21.3	31.2	32.3	13.1	2.1	86481
54836	FOXBORO	20982	417	20.9	31.9	40.5	5.5	1.2	47365	53271	67	57	379	16.9	21.6	48.6	12.9	0.0	105873
54837	FREDERIC	19220	1749	34.4	31.9	27.4	4.6	1.7	36319	41161	33	12	1413	17.5	25.5	42.5	13.8	0.8	100994
54838	GORDON	22867	518	25.7	30.9	36.9	5.0	1.5	43905	49803	58	44	452	14.6	16.2	42.0	23.0	4.2	120988
54839	GRAND VIEW	18530	163	36.8	35.0	23.3	3.1	1.8	33831	37138	24	6	138	16.7	29.0	37.0	16.7	0.7	95455
54840	GRANTSBURG	21545	1906	23.9	36.7	30.9	6.4	2.2	42089	46908	53	38	1514	15.1	26.7	44.5	12.8	1.0	99690
54843	HAYWARD	21022	4903	33.0	31.0	26.9	6.0	3.1	37210	43055	36	17	3703	9.7	18.9	40.6	26.1	4.7	121870
54844	HERBSTER	22365	130	30.0	37.7	26.2	5.4	0.8	36103	42532	32	12	110	7.3	30.0	39.1	21.8	1.8	111842
54845	HERTEL	18792	60	31.7	38.3	21.7	5.0	3.3	33550	37282	23	5	50	16.0	20.0	46.0	18.0	0.0	107500
54846	HIGH BRIDGE	19070	225	32.4	35.1	26.7	3.1	2.7	36884	41115	35	16	187	18.7	44.4	28.3	8.6	0.0	77955
54847	IRON RIVER	19347	836	33.0	34.5	26.4	4.9	1.2	35169	40654	28	9	710	12.3	27.3	40.3	18.7	1.4	105943
54848	LADYSMITH	18412	2714	35.7	32.6	26.2	3.9	1.5	34754	38558	27	7	1923	20.8	36.9	34.7	7.0	0.6	82551
54849	LAKE NEBAGAMON	23078	795	21.8	30.9	36.6	8.7	2.0	47620	52570	67	58	670	14.2	18.4	43.4	20.8	3.3	118578
54850	LA POINTE	23320	130	39.2	32.3	21.5	3.1	3.9	32814	35998	20	4	95	28.4	30.5	27.4	12.6	1.1	77857
54853	LUCK	20602	1540	26.6	34.2	32.3	5.0	1.9	40648	46665	48	32	1210	11.4	21.3	45.0	20.4	1.9	113325
54854	MAPLE	18887	375	28.0	36.3	31.5	3.5	0.8	39673	43643	45	28	309	19.4	26.2	40.5	13.3	0.7	96136
54855	MARENGO	17259	246	28.9	36.2	29.3	3.3	2.4	38149	42079	40	21	202	19.8	36.6	32.2	11.4	0.0	82778
54856	MASON	17325	656	33.7	33.5	26.8	4.3	1.7	36733	40355	34	14	570	13.7	24.6	41.6	19.0	1.2	106534
54858	MILLTOWN	21911	700	34.7	25.9	31.6	6.0	1.9	38102	42829	40	21	522	17.2	22.2	42.9	15.9	1.7	103800
54859	MINONG	20480	879	34.0	35.3	24.7	3.3	2.7	36659	40838	34	14	713	21.7	26.2	31.8	15.7	4.5	93816
54862	OJIBWA	17925	163	38.0	32.5	24.5	3.1	1.8	33384	38622	22	5	135	23.0	31.9	30.4	14.1	0.7	82778
54864	POPLAR	20338	503	21.1	31.6	38.0	6.8	2.6	47682	52955	68	58	433	13.2	24.9	47.1	13.9	0.9	105891
54865	PORT WING	21673	263	29.3	37.3	27.4	4.9	1.1	36520	42221	34	13	223	6.7	30.5	39.9	21.1	1.8	111563
54867	RADISSON	20918	193	35.2	33.2	26.4	3.1	2.1	36040	40967	32	12	157	26.8	31.2	27.4	12.7	1.9	76500
54868	RICE LAKE	21578	6652	29.1	32.8	28.7	6.4	3.0	40812	45806	49	34	4724	11.9	29.7	43.5	13.0	2.0	98646
54870	SARONA	24666	627	28.6	34.5	28.6	5.6	2.9	39940	45281	46	29	537	10.4	18.6	38.2	28.1	4.7	125815
54871	SHELL LAKE	20505	1335	30.9	33.8	27.0	5.8	2.6	37551	41828	38	19	1030	15.8	26.0	37.1	18.8	2.2	101524
54872	SIREN	20332	1209	34.3	33.8	24.2	5.5	2.1	36107	39744	32	12	965	18.9	24.9	39.6	14.8	1.9	98643
54873	SOLON SPRINGS	20129	1173	32.1	31.8	29.3	5.6	1.2	37798	42221	39	20	950	15.9	22.7	43.6	16.1	1.7	107292
54874	SOUTH RANGE	20293	1274	19.9	31.6	39.7	6.6	2.1	48591	54564	69	60	1175	15.5	23.7	47.7	12.3	0.9	103457
54875	SPRINGBROOK	19528	521	26.9	41.5	25.9	3.8	1.9	38583	43488	41	24	444	15.3	23.7	38.7	17.8	4.5	108013
54876	STONE LAKE	19972	709	33.2	32.6	26.4	5.9	2.0	36731	42191	34	14	591	14.0	21.5	30.5	26.9	7.1	119542
54880	SUPERIOR	20089	12819	33.5	32.9	26.6	5.5	1.5	36787	41316	35	15	8072	18.9	31.3	39.3	9.9	0.5	89673
	WISCONSIN	25041		22.2	28.8	35.0	9.6	4.2	48930	56561				7.0	14.9	46.8	27.8	3.6	134326
	UNITED STATES	25866		24.7	27.1	30.8	10.9	6.5	48124	56710				10.9	15.0	33.7	30.1	10.4	145905

ZIP CODE #	POST OFFICE NAME	FINANCIAL SERVICES: Auto Loan	Home Loan	Investments	Retirement Plans	THE HOME: Home Improvements: Home Repair	Lawn & Garden	Furnishings: Computers & Hardware	Major Appliances	TV, Radio, Sound Equipment	Furniture	ENTERTAINMENT: Dine out/ Carry out	Sports Equipment	Fees & Tickets	Toys & Games	Travel	Cable TV	PERSONAL: Apparel & Services	Auto Repairs	Health Insurance	Pets & Supplies
54724	BLOOMER	86	72	54	69	77	86	72	79	78	70	93	91	68	93	73	81	87	78	89	98
54725	BOYCEVILLE	83	66	43	60	71	79	62	72	69	62	83	85	58	82	63	72	77	70	82	96
54726	BOYD	75	61	43	59	66	73	60	68	65	59	79	79	56	78	61	67	73	66	75	86
54727	CADOTT	78	66	49	64	70	78	65	71	69	64	84	83	62	84	66	72	79	70	79	89
54728	CHETEK	84	66	45	62	73	83	65	76	73	64	87	88	59	85	68	77	80	75	88	99
54729	CHIPPEWA FALLS	80	76	68	74	78	85	74	78	77	73	94	91	73	96	75	78	90	77	82	93
54730	COLFAX	87	79	63	77	82	88	76	82	79	75	96	96	74	97	76	80	92	80	86	100
54731	CONRATH	80	55	26	49	62	71	53	66	63	53	74	79	45	71	54	67	67	65	80	93
54732	CORNELL	70	56	39	54	60	69	58	64	63	56	75	73	53	73	58	65	70	63	73	78
54733	DALLAS	88	69	47	66	77	84	67	78	74	67	88	94	61	87	69	76	82	77	89	104
54734	DOWNING	85	76	58	72	80	86	70	78	74	70	90	92	69	92	72	76	86	75	84	100
54736	DURAND	86	70	50	67	75	86	72	79	78	70	94	91	67	91	72	81	87	78	90	98
54737	EAU GALLE	82	69	52	68	73	82	70	76	75	69	90	87	66	90	70	76	85	75	83	92
54738	ELEVA	86	79	65	78	82	89	77	82	80	76	97	95	75	99	77	81	93	80	87	99
54739	ELK MOUND	83	89	85	89	88	90	83	84	80	83	100	100	84	102	83	78	97	83	79	97
54740	ELMWOOD	82	68	49	65	73	82	69	76	75	67	90	87	65	88	69	78	84	75	86	93
54741	FAIRCHILD	70	55	37	52	60	68	56	63	62	55	74	73	51	72	57	65	68	62	73	80
54742	FALL CREEK	103	84	58	80	92	100	79	91	87	79	104	109	75	105	82	90	98	89	102	121
54745	HOLCOMBE	75	61	42	56	67	74	58	67	65	57	77	79	53	76	60	68	72	66	78	89
54746	HUMBIRD	83	61	36	58	70	78	60	72	68	60	81	87	53	80	62	71	74	71	84	98
54747	INDEPENDENCE	74	63	49	62	66	74	64	69	68	63	83	79	61	82	64	69	77	68	74	82
54748	JIM FALLS	89	79	60	75	84	90	73	81	78	73	95	97	72	97	75	80	90	79	88	105
54749	KNAPP	92	82	62	78	87	93	76	84	81	76	98	100	74	100	78	83	93	82	91	109
54750	MAIDEN ROCK	95	82	61	78	88	95	77	86	82	77	100	103	74	101	79	85	94	84	94	112
54751	MENOMONIE	81	67	63	68	69	76	77	75	79	74	97	91	71	93	73	77	92	78	77	89
54754	MERRILLAN	77	64	47	62	68	76	64	70	69	63	83	82	60	82	64	70	78	69	78	88
54755	MONDOVI	77	69	56	66	73	81	67	73	72	66	87	85	66	89	69	75	83	71	81	90
54756	NELSON	83	70	53	69	75	82	69	76	74	68	90	88	66	90	70	76	84	74	83	94
54757	NEW AUBURN	77	57	35	54	64	72	57	67	64	56	76	79	51	74	58	67	70	66	78	89
54758	OSSEO	82	69	51	66	73	82	68	75	74	67	89	87	65	88	69	76	83	74	84	93
54759	PEPIN	82	60	37	58	67	79	64	74	73	62	86	85	57	82	65	77	78	73	88	93
54761	PLUM CITY	90	66	37	62	75	84	64	78	73	64	86	94	56	85	67	76	79	77	91	107
54762	PRAIRIE FARM	86	78	61	74	82	88	72	79	76	72	93	95	71	94	74	78	88	77	85	102
54763	RIDGELAND	84	70	49	66	76	82	66	75	71	66	86	90	62	87	68	74	81	73	84	99
54765	SAND CREEK	83	58	30	55	68	76	57	71	66	57	78	86	49	76	60	69	71	70	85	99
54766	SHELDON	79	56	30	51	63	71	54	66	63	54	74	79	47	72	56	66	68	65	79	92
54767	SPRING VALLEY	90	79	62	77	84	91	76	83	81	76	98	98	74	99	77	82	93	81	90	104
54768	STANLEY	79	62	41	59	68	78	64	72	71	62	84	83	58	81	64	74	77	71	84	91
54769	STOCKHOLM	95	70	40	66	80	89	68	82	77	67	91	99	60	90	70	81	84	81	97	113
54770	STRUM	83	71	55	70	75	84	72	77	76	71	92	89	69	92	72	77	87	76	84	93
54771	THORP	73	55	36	53	61	71	57	65	64	56	76	76	51	73	58	67	70	65	77	84
54772	WHEELER	89	78	58	74	83	89	72	81	77	72	94	96	70	95	74	79	89	79	88	105
54773	WHITEHALL	74	64	49	63	67	74	64	69	67	63	82	79	61	82	64	69	77	67	74	83
54801	SPOONER	76	58	38	55	64	74	60	69	67	58	79	79	53	77	61	71	73	68	81	88
54805	ALMENA	84	70	54	66	76	84	68	77	74	67	89	89	64	88	70	77	83	76	86	98
54806	ASHLAND	68	60	57	59	62	69	63	65	66	61	81	76	60	80	63	67	77	66	70	78
54810	BALSAM LAKE	94	75	52	68	84	94	71	84	79	70	94	99	64	94	75	84	88	83	99	114
54812	BARRON	78	63	47	62	68	78	66	72	72	64	86	82	62	83	66	74	80	71	81	87
54813	BARRONETT	97	78	54	71	87	97	73	87	82	73	98	102	67	97	78	87	91	85	101	118
54814	BAYFIELD	69	58	43	54	62	67	55	63	59	56	71	73	51	69	57	61	68	62	68	80
54817	BIRCHWOOD	85	65	43	60	73	84	65	76	73	63	86	88	57	84	67	78	80	75	90	101
54819	BRUCE	74	54	32	49	60	70	55	64	63	54	74	74	48	71	56	67	68	64	77	85
54820	BRULE	73	56	37	54	62	70	56	65	62	55	74	76	50	73	57	64	68	64	74	85
54821	CABLE	70	55	37	49	61	69	51	62	58	51	69	73	46	68	55	62	64	61	73	85
54822	CAMERON	82	70	54	69	74	82	69	75	74	68	89	88	67	90	70	75	84	74	82	93
54824	CENTURIA	89	75	56	72	80	90	73	82	79	72	96	95	69	95	75	82	90	81	91	103
54826	COMSTOCK	79	62	42	57	68	78	62	71	69	60	82	82	56	80	64	73	76	70	84	92
54827	CORNUCOPIA	75	59	40	53	67	75	56	67	63	55	75	79	50	74	59	67	70	66	79	92
54828	COUDERAY	79	62	42	56	70	79	59	71	66	58	79	83	52	78	63	71	73	70	84	97
54829	CUMBERLAND	82	64	43	60	70	81	66	74	73	64	87	85	59	84	67	78	80	74	88	95
54830	DANBURY	77	60	41	55	68	76	57	69	65	56	76	80	51	75	61	69	71	68	81	94
54832	DRUMMOND	71	55	38	50	62	70	52	63	59	52	70	74	47	69	56	63	65	62	74	86
54835	EXELAND	73	56	37	51	64	72	53	64	61	53	72	76	47	71	57	65	67	63	76	88
54836	FOXBORO	94	70	42	66	79	88	68	81	76	67	90	98	60	90	70	80	83	80	95	111
54837	FREDERIC	74	57	39	54	63	74	60	68	67	58	79	77	54	76	61	71	73	67	80	85
54838	GORDON	86	66	44	60	75	84	63	76	71	62	84	89	56	83	67	76	78	75	90	104
54839	GRAND VIEW	71	53	32	49	60	68	51	62	58	50	68	73	44	67	53	61	63	61	73	85
54840	GRANTSBURG	85	71	53	67	77	85	69	77	75	68	90	90	65	90	71	77	84	76	87	100
54843	HAYWARD	85	66	44	61	73	83	64	76	72	63	86	88	58	84	67	76	79	75	88	100
54844	HERBSTER	76	59	41	54	67	75	56	68	63	56	75	79	50	74	60	68	70	67	80	92
54845	HERTEL	78	61	42	55	69	77	58	69	65	57	77	81	51	76	61	70	72	68	82	95
54846	HIGH BRIDGE	87	62	34	58	72	80	61	75	70	60	82	89	52	80	63	73	75	73	89	104
54847	IRON RIVER	74	57	37	52	65	73	54	66	62	54	73	77	48	72	58	66	67	65	78	90
54848	LADYSMITH	70	58	43	55	62	71	59	65	64	57	77	74	55	76	59	67	72	64	74	80
54849	LAKE NEBAGAMON	98	73	44	67	83	93	70	85	80	69	94	101	61	93	74	85	87	84	101	118
54850	LA POINTE	76	60	41	54	67	76	56	68	64	56	76	80	50	75	60	68	70	67	80	93
54853	LUCK	80	67	49	63	72	80	65	73	70	64	85	85	61	84	67	73	79	72	82	93
54854	MAPLE	75	58	39	57	64	72	59	67	65	58	78	79	54	76	60	67	72	66	76	86
54855	MARENGO	83	64	42	60	72	80	62	73	69	61	82	87	56	81	64	72	76	72	84	99
54856	MASON	78	56	32	52	65	73	55	67	63	54	74	81	47	73	57	66	68	66	80	93
54858	MILLTOWN	79	61	41	57	67	78	64	72	71	61	84	82	57	81	65	76	78	72	85	90
54859	MINONG	80	59	36	53	67	76	56	69	65	56	77	81	49	75	59	70	71	68	82	95
54862	OJIBWA	75	59	40	53	66	74	55	67	63	55	74	78	49	73	59	67	69	66	79	91
54864	POPLAR	94	73	48	70	81	89	71	83	78	71	93	100	64	92	73	80	87	82	94	111
54865	PORT WING	76	60	40	54	67	75	56	68	64	56	75	79	50	74	60	68	70	67	80	93
54867	RADISSON	80	62	43	56	70	79	59	71	67	58	79	83	53	78	63	71	73	70	84	97
54868	RICE LAKE	80	69	56	68	73	81	70	75	74	69	90	87	66	89	70	76	85	75	82	92
54870	SARONA	98	77	52	69	86	97	72	87	82	72	97	102	65	96	77	87	90	86	103	119
54871	SHELL LAKE	81	65	45	60	71	81	64	73	71	63	85	85	58	83	66	75	79	72	86	95
54872	SIREN	77	59	40	55	66	76	60	70	68	59	80	80	54	78	62	72	74	69	83	90
54873	SOLON SPRINGS	79	60	38	55	68	76	57	69	65	57	77	82	50	76	60	69	71	68	82	95
54874	SOUTH RANGE	88	78	61	75	82	88	74	81	77	73	94	96	71	95	75	79	90	80	87	103
54875	SPRINGBROOK	83	61	36	56	70	78	59	72	67	58	79	85	51	78	62	71	73	71	85	99
54876	STONE LAKE	77	61	41	55	68	77	57	69	65	57	77	81	51	76	61	69	71	68	81	94
54880	SUPERIOR	64	61	63	61	62	68	64	64	66	62	81	75	63	81	64	65	78	65	66	73
	WISCONSIN	89	86	85	86	88	94	86	88	87	85	108	103	86	109	86	87	104	88	89	103
	UNITED STATES	100	100	100	100	100	100	100	100	100	100	100	100	100	100	100	100	100	100	100	100

WISCONSIN

POPULATION CHANGE

A 54888-54986

ZIP CODE		POPULATION			2000-2004 ANNUAL RATE		HOUSEHOLDS					FAMILIES		
# POST OFFICE NAME	COUNTY FIPS CODE	2000	2004	2009	% Rate	State Centile	2000	2004	2009	% Annual Rate 2000-2004	2004 Average HH Size	2000	2004	% Annual Rate 2000-2004
54888 TREGO	129	1406	1541	1691	2.2	89	580	652	733	2.8	2.36	410	455	2.5
54889 TURTLE LAKE	095	2613	2717	2875	0.9	53	1080	1150	1244	1.5	2.36	719	755	1.2
54891 WASHBURN	007	3588	3690	3898	0.7	42	1435	1518	1647	1.3	2.37	979	1021	1.0
54893 WEBSTER	013	3746	3975	4212	1.4	73	1647	1795	1946	2.1	2.20	1111	1191	1.7
54895 WEYERHAEUSER	107	1072	1130	1164	1.3	66	452	493	521	2.1	2.29	320	344	1.7
54896 WINTER	113	1541	1701	1876	2.4	90	652	742	842	3.1	2.21	439	493	2.8
54901 OSHKOSH	139	37539	38214	39401	0.4	31	12982	13574	14388	1.1	2.32	6966	7124	0.5
54902 OSHKOSH	139	22602	22924	23817	0.3	28	9837	10219	10851	0.9	2.20	5946	6035	0.4
54904 OSHKOSH	139	18166	20196	21859	2.5	92	6882	7848	8693	3.1	2.52	5224	5874	2.8
54909 ALMOND	097	2298	2299	2356	0.0	15	874	906	956	0.9	2.53	641	653	0.4
54911 APPLETON	087	27639	28162	29822	0.4	32	10905	11482	12542	1.2	2.28	6586	6778	0.7
54913 APPLETON	087	9970	12849	15302	6.2	100	3443	4503	5456	6.5	2.84	2815	3620	6.1
54914 APPLETON	087	31344	32573	34685	0.9	52	12702	13544	14775	1.5	2.38	7962	8263	0.9
54915 APPLETON	015	37536	40317	44048	1.7	81	13945	15291	17070	2.2	2.61	9879	10747	2.0
54921 BANCROFT	097	1196	1263	1337	1.3	68	447	490	534	2.2	2.58	323	349	1.8
54922 BEAR CREEK	087	1463	1563	1667	1.6	77	531	586	641	2.4	2.67	422	459	2.0
54923 BERLIN	047	8602	8557	8603	-0.1	10	3387	3446	3540	0.4	2.45	2358	2370	0.1
54928 CAROLINE	115	452	445	451	-0.4	7	161	163	169	0.3	2.73	126	126	0.0
54929 CLINTONVILLE	135	9260	9299	9547	0.1	19	3717	3815	4001	0.6	2.41	2546	2582	0.3
54930 COLOMA	137	1696	1834	1995	1.9	84	612	681	760	2.6	2.56	457	503	2.3
54932 ELDORADO	039	821	868	902	1.3	70	296	323	345	2.1	2.69	245	265	1.9
54935 FOND DU LAC	039	47963	49163	50705	0.6	38	18671	19624	20767	1.2	2.38	12077	12523	0.9
54937 FOND DU LAC	039	9643	10117	10490	1.1	63	3762	4070	4337	1.9	2.45	2698	2866	1.4
54940 FREMONT	137	3701	3809	3979	0.7	43	1468	1549	1654	1.3	2.44	1090	1137	1.0
54941 GREEN LAKE	047	2855	2872	2869	0.1	21	1266	1308	1338	0.8	2.17	835	849	0.4
54942 GREENVILLE	087	4813	5762	6563	4.3	98	1590	1953	2275	5.0	2.94	1352	1643	4.7
54943 HANCOCK	137	1819	2069	2310	3.1	96	742	864	985	3.7	2.36	524	602	3.3
54944 HORTONVILLE	087	7935	8627	9356	2.0	86	2748	3072	3415	2.7	2.79	2189	2421	2.4
54945 IOLA	135	3315	3466	3606	1.1	59	1366	1464	1557	1.6	2.33	936	988	1.3
54947 LARSEN	139	2343	2435	2536	0.9	52	884	941	1001	1.5	2.59	692	728	1.2
54948 LEOPOLIS	115	370	383	396	0.8	48	146	155	163	1.4	2.46	109	114	1.1
54949 MANAWA	135	2964	3189	3371	1.7	82	1098	1207	1302	2.3	2.60	773	841	2.0
54950 MARION	135	3020	3010	3071	-0.1	11	1196	1226	1282	0.6	2.46	838	846	0.2
54952 MENASHA	015	23130	24165	25488	1.0	58	9573	10238	11033	1.6	2.34	6187	6528	1.3
54956 NEENAH	139	37966	39092	40773	0.7	43	14825	15637	16677	1.3	2.48	10477	10891	0.9
54960 NESHKORO	077	2705	2729	2902	0.2	23	1170	1207	1311	0.7	2.24	846	862	0.4
54961 NEW LONDON	135	14092	14645	15295	0.9	52	5340	5698	6094	1.5	2.52	3817	4017	1.2
54962 OGDENSBURG	135	1376	1414	1458	0.6	41	545	576	607	1.3	2.45	408	425	1.0
54963 OMRO	139	6601	6924	7267	1.1	63	2518	2711	2910	1.8	2.52	1840	1948	1.4
54964 PICKETT	139	808	867	916	1.7	80	308	340	368	2.4	2.55	242	263	2.0
54965 PINE RIVER	137	1199	1286	1399	1.7	80	478	526	585	2.3	2.44	359	391	2.0
54966 PLAINFIELD	137	2081	2223	2402	1.6	77	781	852	939	2.1	2.60	558	600	1.7
54967 POY SIPPI	137	442	468	506	1.4	71	191	207	229	1.9	2.26	139	149	1.7
54968 PRINCETON	047	3166	3291	3349	0.9	53	1261	1347	1405	1.6	2.31	848	893	1.2
54970 REDGRANITE	137	2837	3063	3344	1.8	83	1174	1298	1447	2.4	2.34	808	881	2.1
54971 RIPON	039	10478	10461	10600	0.0	13	4057	4154	4315	0.6	2.31	2640	2658	0.2
54974 ROSENDALE	039	1649	1728	1788	1.1	62	589	635	673	1.8	2.72	466	496	1.5
54977 SCANDINAVIA	135	1273	1295	1327	0.4	30	478	498	523	1.0	2.58	352	363	0.7
54978 TILLEDA	115	49	51	53	1.0	54	18	19	21	1.3	2.68	13	14	1.8
54979 VAN DYNE	039	1466	1499	1532	0.5	36	536	563	591	1.2	2.66	415	430	0.8
54981 WAUPACA	135	15286	16005	16678	1.1	61	5799	6238	6661	1.7	2.39	3965	4207	1.4
54982 WAUTOMA	137	7060	7578	8330	1.7	80	2899	3190	3592	2.3	2.30	1959	2130	2.0
54983 WEYAUWEGA	135	4794	4868	5000	0.4	29	1755	1829	1923	1.0	2.58	1273	1309	0.7
54984 WILD ROSE	137	3037	3205	3454	1.3	67	1284	1387	1528	1.8	2.27	886	944	1.5
54986 WINNECONNE	139	4568	5004	5364	2.2	89	1791	2012	2205	2.8	2.48	1358	1502	2.4
WISCONSIN					0.8					1.4	2.44			1.1
UNITED STATES					1.2					1.3	2.58			1.1

337-A

#	POST OFFICE NAME	White 2000	White 2004	Black 2000	Black 2004	Asian/Pacific 2000	Asian/Pacific 2004	% Hispanic Origin 2000	% Hispanic Origin 2004	0-4	5-9	10-14	15-19	20-24	25-44	45-64	65-84	85+	18+	MEDIAN AGE 2004	% 2004 Males	% 2004 Females
54888	TREGO	97.2	97.0	0.2	0.3	0.3	0.3	0.4	0.5	4.3	5.1	6.9	7.6	3.2	21.7	34.9	15.0	1.4	78.6	45.7	50.9	49.1
54889	TURTLE LAKE	96.6	96.5	0.1	0.1	0.2	0.2	0.9	1.0	5.8	6.0	6.7	6.8	6.4	26.0	26.5	14.0	1.8	77.1	40.5	50.4	49.6
54891	WASHBURN	92.8	92.1	0.1	0.1	0.4	0.5	0.5	0.7	4.3	5.0	7.6	8.2	6.3	21.5	32.2	11.8	3.1	77.8	43.2	48.9	51.1
54893	WEBSTER	90.3	89.7	0.4	0.4	0.5	0.6	0.7	0.8	4.7	4.9	6.0	5.4	4.7	21.6	30.4	20.3	2.1	80.9	46.8	49.5	50.5
54895	WEYERHAEUSER	98.1	98.0	0.2	0.2	0.1	0.1	1.3	1.4	3.9	4.8	6.7	6.2	4.7	22.2	31.6	17.4	2.5	80.7	45.9	51.4	48.6
54896	WINTER	93.3	93.1	2.1	2.3	0.3	0.4	1.6	1.7	5.0	4.9	4.8	5.7	4.8	22.1	31.6	19.2	1.9	81.7	46.5	53.6	46.4
54901	OSHKOSH	91.0	89.5	3.2	3.6	3.6	4.4	1.8	2.1	5.0	4.8	5.1	10.6	17.6	27.8	19.2	8.2	1.7	81.7	29.6	51.8	48.2
54902	OSHKOSH	95.7	95.0	0.6	0.7	2.2	2.7	1.6	1.8	5.4	5.3	6.4	6.3	7.1	27.9	22.9	14.8	3.9	79.0	39.6	47.8	52.2
54904	OSHKOSH	96.8	96.3	0.8	0.9	1.2	1.6	0.8	1.0	6.9	7.1	7.4	6.3	6.5	28.2	27.0	9.6	1.1	74.6	37.8	49.9	50.1
54909	ALMOND	97.2	96.8	0.1	0.1	0.4	0.4	4.7	5.7	6.3	6.6	7.5	6.7	5.9	26.3	28.1	11.4	1.2	75.1	39.5	51.6	48.4
54911	APPLETON	91.5	89.8	1.1	1.2	4.7	5.9	2.0	2.3	6.1	5.9	6.8	7.8	9.0	28.0	22.0	11.8	2.7	77.0	35.7	49.0	51.0
54913	APPLETON	97.5	96.7	0.4	0.5	0.9	1.3	0.9	1.1	7.3	7.8	8.7	7.6	6.0	28.2	27.2	6.6	0.8	71.3	36.6	51.0	49.0
54914	APPLETON	92.1	90.6	1.0	1.1	3.5	4.4	3.8	4.5	6.5	6.2	7.1	7.1	8.9	30.9	22.9	9.2	1.4	76.2	34.3	49.8	50.2
54915	APPLETON	93.4	92.4	0.6	0.7	3.3	4.1	2.7	3.0	8.0	7.7	7.9	6.9	6.9	30.9	22.5	7.9	1.3	72.0	34.1	49.2	50.8
54921	BANCROFT	96.5	95.9	0.2	0.2	0.8	1.0	3.7	4.0	5.5	6.2	7.7	7.7	6.2	26.8	27.3	11.5	1.2	75.8	38.8	51.3	48.7
54922	BEAR CREEK	97.5	96.9	0.1	0.1	0.1	0.1	3.1	3.8	6.5	6.9	8.2	6.7	6.4	29.1	24.6	10.4	1.2	74.5	37.2	52.5	47.5
54923	BERLIN	96.6	96.4	0.1	0.1	0.7	0.8	3.3	3.5	6.1	6.2	7.0	6.4	6.2	26.7	25.9	12.7	2.9	76.5	39.8	49.6	50.5
54928	CAROLINE	96.7	96.4	0.0	0.0	1.6	1.8	0.4	0.5	5.8	6.1	7.9	6.3	5.8	27.4	25.8	13.3	1.6	76.4	39.2	52.4	47.6
54929	CLINTONVILLE	97.6	97.3	0.1	0.1	0.3	0.4	1.4	1.6	5.8	5.9	7.0	7.1	6.4	25.0	25.5	14.5	2.9	76.9	40.6	49.0	51.0
54930	COLOMA	97.5	97.3	0.3	0.3	0.2	0.2	2.6	3.0	4.7	5.6	7.0	5.9	3.9	22.5	29.4	18.1	2.8	79.0	45.2	51.1	48.9
54932	ELDORADO	99.2	99.0	0.0	0.0	0.2	0.4	0.7	0.8	5.0	5.5	6.1	6.8	6.1	27.7	32.1	9.8	0.9	79.5	40.7	51.8	48.2
54935	FOND DU LAC	94.4	93.6	1.6	1.8	1.3	1.7	2.6	3.0	6.3	6.1	6.7	7.1	7.6	27.8	24.1	11.6	2.6	76.7	37.2	47.7	52.3
54937	FOND DU LAC	97.4	97.0	0.3	0.4	0.6	0.8	1.9	2.3	6.1	6.3	7.2	6.5	6.7	28.2	25.9	11.5	1.6	76.6	38.0	49.8	50.2
54940	FREMONT	98.4	98.2	0.2	0.3	0.2	0.3	0.9	1.0	5.5	6.0	6.5	6.6	5.2	25.9	30.2	12.7	1.4	77.3	42.0	51.7	48.3
54941	GREEN LAKE	98.7	98.7	0.1	0.1	0.1	0.1	1.1	1.0	4.7	5.1	5.2	5.2	4.5	22.6	32.8	17.4	2.4	81.8	46.5	50.3	49.7
54942	GREENVILLE	98.6	98.4	0.2	0.2	0.3	0.5	0.9	1.0	9.8	9.5	9.4	6.9	5.3	32.7	21.0	5.1	0.4	66.6	33.0	51.1	48.9
54943	HANCOCK	95.8	95.3	0.2	0.2	0.3	0.3	4.7	5.5	4.2	4.7	7.1	6.6	4.8	20.9	30.2	19.4	2.1	79.9	46.2	50.2	49.8
54944	HORTONVILLE	97.8	97.4	0.1	0.1	1.1	1.4	1.0	1.2	7.3	7.7	8.4	7.2	5.2	29.7	26.1	7.6	0.8	71.9	36.6	50.8	49.3
54945	IOLA	98.4	98.3	0.1	0.1	0.2	0.4	1.1	1.2	5.5	6.1	7.7	6.3	5.0	23.9	27.5	14.6	3.4	76.4	42.3	48.8	51.2
54947	LARSEN	98.7	98.4	0.2	0.2	0.1	0.1	0.8	1.1	6.1	6.7	7.0	6.5	6.1	26.9	29.4	10.9	1.5	76.0	41.0	51.7	48.3
54948	LEOPOLIS	65.4	63.7	0.0	0.0	0.5	0.5	1.1	1.0	6.8	6.8	7.8	7.8	6.5	26.9	23.2	12.5	1.6	73.4	37.1	49.4	50.7
54949	MANAWA	98.8	98.6	0.1	0.1	0.1	0.2	1.1	1.3	6.2	6.7	8.3	7.5	6.0	27.1	23.0	12.9	2.4	73.8	37.7	50.2	49.8
54950	MARION	98.6	98.5	0.1	0.1	0.6	0.8	0.4	0.5	5.6	5.8	7.4	6.6	5.8	26.3	26.2	14.3	2.1	77.2	40.5	50.2	49.8
54952	MENASHA	95.3	94.6	0.5	0.6	1.5	1.8	3.2	3.6	6.8	6.6	7.0	6.6	7.2	30.9	23.3	10.0	1.7	75.6	35.8	49.5	50.5
54956	NEENAH	96.6	96.0	0.3	0.4	1.0	1.3	1.6	1.9	6.7	6.9	7.5	7.1	6.1	29.0	25.5	9.8	1.5	74.5	37.4	49.1	50.9
54960	NESHKORO	98.2	97.9	0.2	0.2	0.6	0.7	0.8	1.0	4.4	4.6	5.0	5.2	3.9	19.9	29.6	25.6	1.8	82.6	49.4	51.3	48.7
54961	NEW LONDON	97.5	97.1	0.2	0.2	0.4	0.4	1.9	2.2	6.9	6.9	7.5	7.0	6.5	28.6	24.3	10.3	2.1	74.4	37.1	50.7	49.3
54962	OGDENSBURG	99.0	98.7	0.1	0.1	0.2	0.4	0.9	1.1	6.3	6.7	6.5	6.2	5.3	25.0	29.4	13.0	1.7	76.7	41.6	51.3	48.7
54963	OMRO	98.3	98.0	0.2	0.2	0.2	0.3	1.7	2.1	6.3	6.6	7.2	6.8	5.5	27.0	26.7	11.8	2.0	75.4	39.5	50.5	49.6
54964	PICKETT	99.1	99.1	0.0	0.0	0.1	0.1	0.3	0.2	5.3	6.1	8.1	6.7	4.3	27.8	29.3	11.3	1.2	75.8	41.4	51.2	48.8
54965	PINE RIVER	98.8	98.7	0.0	0.0	0.1	0.1	0.9	1.0	5.3	5.7	5.8	5.4	4.6	23.3	32.6	15.8	1.5	79.9	44.9	51.6	48.4
54966	PLAINFIELD	94.4	93.7	0.1	0.1	0.7	0.9	11.6	13.1	5.8	6.0	7.4	7.9	7.0	25.9	25.8	12.8	1.4	75.5	38.5	51.4	48.6
54967	POY SIPPI	98.0	97.9	0.2	0.2	0.0	0.0	1.4	1.7	5.1	6.0	7.1	4.7	4.7	25.4	29.9	14.7	2.4	78.6	43.3	50.6	49.4
54968	PRINCETON	98.5	98.4	0.4	0.4	0.1	0.1	0.8	0.8	5.1	5.3	5.8	5.8	5.4	22.4	27.1	17.9	5.2	80.3	45.1	48.5	51.5
54970	REDGRANITE	97.0	96.8	0.3	0.3	0.0	0.0	2.3	2.7	5.2	5.6	6.4	6.6	5.4	23.7	28.4	16.4	2.2	78.5	43.1	49.2	50.8
54971	RIPON	97.7	97.4	0.3	0.3	0.5	0.6	2.0	2.3	5.9	5.8	6.0	8.9	8.9	24.2	24.5	12.9	3.0	78.7	38.2	47.9	52.2
54974	ROSENDALE	99.1	99.0	0.1	0.1	0.1	0.1	0.6	0.8	6.9	7.2	7.8	6.3	6.2	28.0	26.3	10.2	1.2	74.3	37.9	50.4	49.6
54977	SCANDINAVIA	98.4	98.2	0.1	0.1	0.2	0.3	0.3	0.3	6.0	6.6	7.7	6.2	5.0	25.6	27.1	14.0	1.8	75.8	40.7	51.5	48.5
54978	TILLEDA	57.1	54.9	0.0	0.0	0.0	0.0	0.0	0.0	7.8	7.8	7.8	7.8	7.8	27.5	19.6	13.7	0.0	68.6	32.5	51.0	49.0
54979	VAN DYNE	99.5	99.4	0.0	0.0	0.2	0.3	0.5	0.6	5.1	6.4	7.3	7.0	5.0	27.4	30.2	10.8	0.9	76.7	40.8	51.2	48.8
54981	WAUPACA	97.6	97.3	0.2	0.2	0.2	0.3	1.8	2.2	5.9	6.2	7.0	6.3	5.7	24.7	25.1	16.1	3.1	76.9	41.2	50.8	49.2
54982	WAUTOMA	95.9	95.3	0.4	0.5	0.6	0.7	4.7	5.4	5.3	5.5	6.3	6.8	5.5	22.3	27.1	18.3	2.9	78.6	43.9	50.6	49.5
54983	WEYAUWEGA	98.2	98.1	0.2	0.2	0.2	0.3	0.8	0.9	6.1	6.4	7.3	6.8	5.7	26.9	25.7	12.4	2.8	75.7	39.8	50.2	49.8
54984	WILD ROSE	98.3	98.0	0.3	0.4	0.1	0.2	1.4	1.6	4.5	4.7	5.9	5.8	5.0	20.5	29.3	21.4	2.9	81.0	47.4	50.0	50.0
54986	WINNECONNE	98.9	98.8	0.1	0.1	0.1	0.2	0.5	0.5	4.8	5.7	7.2	7.3	5.6	24.7	29.5	13.4	1.9	77.6	42.3	50.7	49.3
	WISCONSIN	88.9	88.0	5.7	6.0	1.7	2.1	3.6	4.0	6.4	6.5	7.1	7.3	7.7	27.6	24.5	11.1	1.9	75.8	36.9	49.5	50.5
	UNITED STATES	75.1	73.6	12.3	12.5	3.8	4.2	12.5	14.1	6.9	6.7	7.2	7.0	7.3	28.6	23.8	10.8	1.7	75.1	36.0	49.1	50.9

WISCONSIN

INCOME

C 54888-54986

#	POST OFFICE NAME	2004 Per Capita Income	2004 HH Income Base	Less than $25,000	$25,000 to $49,999	$50,000 to $99,999	$100,000 to $149,999	$150,000 or More	2004	2009	2004 National Centile	2004 State Centile	2004 Home Value Base	Less than $50,000	$50,000 to $89,999	$90,000 to $174,999	$175,000 to $399,999	$400,000 or More	2004 Median Home Value
54888	TREGO	20341	652	29.1	35.9	28.1	4.6	2.3	39226	44608	44	26	580	12.4	19.7	42.2	22.4	3.3	115541
54889	TURTLE LAKE	20554	1150	30.4	32.5	30.0	5.5	1.7	40158	44934	47	30	881	13.2	29.3	40.5	15.6	1.5	100434
54891	WASHBURN	20636	1518	27.7	33.1	31.4	6.5	1.3	42052	46112	53	38	1208	8.5	24.3	49.5	15.6	2.1	111196
54893	WEBSTER	20515	1795	30.8	35.8	27.7	4.4	1.4	37245	41946	36	17	1511	12.4	26.1	41.0	17.9	2.7	106074
54895	WEYERHAEUSER	17363	493	33.9	40.2	21.1	3.9	1.0	32435	37447	19	3	411	22.4	28.5	35.3	11.7	2.2	88333
54896	WINTER	19736	742	36.8	33.8	23.7	4.5	1.2	33307	38679	22	4	629	17.3	29.9	37.2	14.3	1.3	94167
54901	OSHKOSH	20546	13574	27.8	32.8	30.9	6.0	2.5	40417	46289	48	31	7474	6.1	33.5	48.2	10.8	1.3	98790
54902	OSHKOSH	24733	10219	25.4	32.9	33.4	5.6	2.7	42962	49925	56	41	6665	4.1	33.8	50.4	10.2	1.6	100627
54904	OSHKOSH	28689	7848	12.3	24.3	43.3	15.3	4.8	63025	72126	87	91	6048	2.5	4.6	53.1	36.4	3.4	159729
54909	ALMOND	22478	906	22.3	32.3	36.8	5.5	3.1	46376	53366	65	53	773	14.2	22.5	45.4	16.8	1.0	107019
54911	APPLETON	25227	11482	23.2	29.9	34.5	9.1	3.3	46963	52812	66	56	7358	1.9	15.6	68.6	13.4	0.5	115780
54913	APPLETON	34578	4503	8.3	19.4	42.4	16.1	13.8	72606	84805	92	96	3915	2.6	3.1	41.8	47.0	5.6	179995
54914	APPLETON	26951	13544	17.2	30.5	37.5	10.0	4.8	51758	58843	75	69	8215	1.6	12.9	64.9	20.0	0.7	122312
54915	APPLETON	26053	15291	13.5	27.0	43.7	11.6	4.2	58829	66411	83	83	11425	1.0	8.2	69.4	20.2	1.2	130088
54921	BANCROFT	21412	490	22.7	33.1	35.7	6.3	2.2	45562	52476	63	51	399	16.5	21.6	41.9	18.1	2.0	109659
54922	BEAR CREEK	20188	586	20.1	31.7	39.9	6.8	1.4	48629	54602	70	61	500	9.4	23.0	45.2	20.4	2.0	113611
54923	BERLIN	21348	3446	22.2	35.5	35.0	4.9	2.4	44504	50056	60	47	2690	8.7	23.9	52.4	14.1	1.0	105963
54928	CAROLINE	17951	163	21.5	41.1	31.9	3.7	1.8	40222	44542	47	30	146	7.5	32.2	45.9	11.6	2.7	100962
54929	CLINTONVILLE	19647	3815	28.4	32.7	32.8	5.0	1.1	41739	47510	52	37	2842	9.8	32.4	42.3	14.7	0.8	98956
54930	COLOMA	19791	681	24.7	39.8	28.5	4.6	2.5	40397	46187	48	31	567	9.4	24.2	46.6	17.5	2.5	114375
54932	ELDORADO	31430	323	12.4	21.4	48.0	12.7	5.6	60987	68541	85	88	288	1.7	9.0	54.9	30.6	3.8	147449
54935	FOND DU LAC	23485	19624	23.3	29.5	36.3	7.3	3.6	47573	53459	67	57	13121	4.2	15.5	56.0	21.9	2.3	121662
54937	FOND DU LAC	23720	4070	19.3	28.9	42.2	7.7	1.9	50986	57898	74	67	3251	20.8	16.7	46.6	14.9	1.1	107424
54940	FREMONT	24956	1549	20.2	28.4	39.4	8.3	3.6	51057	57034	74	67	1344	5.1	13.4	48.4	30.1	3.0	141927
54941	GREEN LAKE	26093	1308	24.0	30.9	34.2	7.2	3.1	44370	48698	60	46	1060	5.7	10.1	49.4	25.6	9.3	142105
54942	GREENVILLE	25492	1953	7.9	16.5	55.9	15.9	3.7	67361	78371	90	94	1677	1.2	1.8	50.8	42.6	3.6	170070
54943	HANCOCK	20802	864	25.5	35.3	33.1	4.5	1.5	42388	47786	54	39	714	16.5	25.4	41.6	15.6	1.0	104526
54944	HORTONVILLE	26426	3072	13.1	23.4	47.1	11.7	4.7	61431	69535	86	89	2656	2.0	7.1	58.0	29.4	3.5	140903
54945	IOLA	22498	1464	24.1	33.1	33.7	7.0	2.2	43813	49593	58	44	1137	6.1	22.1	49.5	20.1	2.2	116684
54947	LARSEN	25176	941	15.3	25.8	44.7	11.9	2.2	57975	65216	83	82	862	8.4	10.8	49.5	29.6	1.7	142661
54948	LEOPOLIS	18862	155	29.0	33.6	31.6	4.5	1.3	38601	43613	41	24	129	19.4	28.7	41.9	9.3	0.8	92778
54949	MANAWA	19877	1207	24.9	30.3	36.4	7.1	1.3	43755	51360	63	51	965	9.1	28.2	45.0	17.4	0.3	103929
54950	MARION	20294	1226	27.2	34.2	31.7	5.0	2.0	40832	45612	49	34	988	8.6	31.7	45.8	12.6	1.4	101724
54952	MENASHA	25820	10238	19.3	31.6	37.3	8.8	3.1	49190	56480	70	62	6924	5.4	21.8	57.5	13.6	1.7	111476
54956	NEENAH	28876	15637	15.3	26.9	42.2	10.1	5.5	55871	64093	81	79	11708	3.7	15.4	56.8	21.5	2.6	121773
54960	NESHKORO	22753	1207	24.2	37.7	31.4	4.5	2.2	41373	47236	51	35	1067	9.2	24.3	43.2	21.8	1.5	114784
54961	NEW LONDON	22196	5698	22.6	27.5	39.7	7.9	2.4	49966	56243	72	64	4356	7.0	20.5	51.8	19.2	1.5	117539
54962	OGDENSBURG	22016	576	22.4	33.9	34.9	6.1	2.8	44569	50325	60	47	502	11.4	19.5	47.4	20.1	1.6	114844
54963	OMRO	22399	2711	19.4	30.7	40.9	6.9	2.1	49851	55843	72	64	2188	7.2	21.4	52.9	16.7	1.7	114286
54964	PICKETT	24555	340	15.3	27.4	45.9	8.2	3.2	55138	62567	80	77	294	1.7	13.6	51.7	31.6	1.4	134483
54965	PINE RIVER	22684	526	22.6	31.9	35.7	6.7	3.0	45349	50671	62	50	472	5.5	21.6	46.4	23.3	3.2	122674
54966	PLAINFIELD	19061	852	27.7	34.3	30.9	4.6	2.6	40382	43987	47	31	680	14.9	32.4	38.8	12.5	1.5	93393
54967	POY SIPPI	23110	207	26.6	29.5	34.3	7.7	1.9	43420	47631	57	43	177	5.1	30.5	44.1	19.2	1.1	108214
54968	PRINCETON	19885	1347	29.6	34.9	30.2	4.0	1.3	39061	43314	43	25	1095	9.0	28.0	42.5	17.9	2.7	107697
54970	REDGRANITE	19073	1298	30.5	35.1	29.0	4.0	1.3	37712	41539	38	19	1092	20.2	29.3	37.0	13.0	0.6	90759
54971	RIPON	22353	4154	26.2	30.3	35.4	6.1	2.0	44771	49964	61	48	2925	4.0	18.1	60.0	16.5	1.3	118375
54974	ROSENDALE	23152	635	14.7	26.9	46.9	9.3	2.2	56200	61879	81	79	550	3.1	9.6	56.4	30.0	0.9	145556
54977	SCANDINAVIA	21698	498	20.5	28.7	40.0	8.8	2.0	50451	57849	73	65	419	4.3	19.1	49.4	22.2	5.0	128664
54978	TILLEDA	17342	19	26.3	31.6	36.8	5.3	0.0	42361	42248	54	39	16	18.8	25.0	50.0	6.3	0.0	100000
54979	VAN DYNE	23991	563	12.6	22.2	54.2	9.6	1.4	60486	66707	85	87	487	2.5	9.0	51.1	34.3	3.1	149144
54981	WAUPACA	22706	6238	25.9	31.0	32.0	7.3	3.8	43930	49783	58	45	4629	6.2	16.8	51.8	21.5	3.7	120872
54982	WAUTOMA	21883	3190	28.4	35.8	28.6	4.7	2.5	39491	44668	44	27	2507	11.3	23.5	43.3	19.5	2.3	109702
54983	WEYAUWEGA	20784	1829	22.5	32.3	35.3	7.3	2.6	46463	52572	65	54	1495	6.5	23.3	50.8	18.3	1.2	114532
54984	WILD ROSE	22736	1387	29.4	36.1	26.2	5.1	3.1	37735	42532	38	19	1153	13.9	26.0	36.7	21.3	2.2	106985
54986	WINNECONNE	27126	2012	19.5	23.5	42.3	10.4	4.4	56847	63258	82	80	1654	2.5	16.8	47.3	28.9	4.5	130758
	WISCONSIN	25041		22.2	28.8	35.0	9.6	4.2	48930	56561				7.0	14.9	46.8	27.8	3.6	134326
	UNITED STATES	25866		24.7	27.1	30.8	10.9	6.5	48124	56710				10.9	15.0	33.7	30.1	10.4	145905

SPENDING POTENTIAL INDICES

# POST OFFICE NAME	Auto Loan	Home Loan	Invest- ments	Retire- ment Plans	Home Repair	Lawn & Garden	Comput- ers & Hard- ware	Major Appli- ances	TV, Radio, Sound Equip- ment	Furni- ture	Dine out/ Carry out	Sports Equip- ment	Fees & Tickets	Toys & Games	Travel	Cable TV	Apparel & Services	Auto Repairs	Health Insur- ance	Pets & Supplies
54888 TREGO	82	64	44	58	72	81	60	73	68	60	81	85	54	80	64	73	75	72	86	99
54889 TURTLE LAKE	78	64	46	61	69	78	64	72	70	63	84	83	59	82	65	73	78	71	82	90
54891 WASHBURN	80	64	49	63	71	77	65	73	71	64	85	88	60	84	66	72	79	73	81	95
54893 WEBSTER	77	60	41	54	68	76	57	68	64	56	76	80	51	75	60	69	71	67	81	93
54895 WEYERHAEUSER	68	53	35	47	59	67	50	60	57	49	67	71	44	66	53	61	62	59	71	82
54896 WINTER	75	59	40	53	66	75	56	67	63	55	75	78	50	74	59	67	69	66	79	92
54901 OSHKOSH	67	64	69	65	64	69	70	67	70	67	87	81	69	87	68	68	84	70	66	76
54902 OSHKOSH	75	75	78	73	77	84	76	77	78	74	97	88	77	100	77	80	93	76	81	87
54904 OSHKOSH	98	109	112	110	108	109	101	102	97	101	121	120	104	125	102	94	119	100	95	116
54909 ALMOND	92	79	59	76	84	92	76	84	81	75	98	99	73	99	77	83	92	82	92	106
54911 APPLETON	79	83	93	84	83	87	85	83	84	84	105	98	86	107	85	83	103	84	81	92
54913 APPLETON	141	152	147	152	152	156	138	141	133	139	167	166	144	172	140	132	164	137	136	166
54914 APPLETON	88	90	100	94	88	92	93	90	90	93	114	107	93	113	91	86	111	92	84	100
54915 APPLETON	97	103	102	106	101	102	99	98	94	100	118	115	100	119	97	90	116	97	89	109
54921 BANCROFT	88	76	59	73	80	88	73	81	78	73	95	95	71	95	75	80	90	79	88	102
54922 BEAR CREEK	86	77	58	73	81	87	71	79	75	71	92	94	70	94	73	77	87	77	85	102
54923 BERLIN	80	73	61	71	76	83	71	76	75	70	91	88	70	92	72	76	86	75	82	92
54928 CAROLINE	66	69	80	72	69	73	70	70	68	70	85	82	70	83	70	66	83	71	67	76
54929 CLINTONVILLE	76	64	47	60	68	76	63	69	69	62	82	81	60	82	64	71	77	68	79	87
54930 COLOMA	88	69	47	62	77	87	65	78	73	64	87	91	58	86	69	78	81	77	92	107
54932 ELDORADO	135	120	92	114	127	136	111	123	118	111	144	147	109	147	115	121	137	120	134	159
54935 FOND DU LAC	78	80	85	80	81	85	81	81	81	80	100	94	82	102	81	80	98	81	79	91
54937 FOND DU LAC	92	83	68	81	85	91	80	86	82	81	101	100	77	100	80	82	97	85	88	104
54940 FREMONT	98	87	66	82	92	99	80	90	86	80	104	106	77	105	83	88	98	88	98	117
54941 GREEN LAKE	95	78	55	72	85	94	73	85	80	72	96	100	67	96	77	85	90	83	97	114
54942 GREENVILLE	107	122	118	127	116	112	110	109	101	114	128	127	113	129	107	94	126	106	93	119
54943 HANCOCK	84	66	45	59	74	83	62	75	70	61	83	87	55	82	66	75	77	74	88	102
54944 HORTONVILLE	108	112	104	111	113	116	103	107	101	104	126	127	105	130	104	100	123	105	104	127
54945 IOLA	86	71	51	69	76	84	70	78	76	69	91	91	66	91	71	78	85	77	87	98
54947 LARSEN	106	92	69	86	98	106	85	96	91	85	111	114	82	112	88	94	105	93	105	125
54948 LEOPOLIS	71	62	52	62	65	73	64	68	67	63	82	77	62	81	63	68	77	67	72	79
54949 MANAWA	82	71	55	70	75	83	70	76	74	69	90	88	68	90	71	76	85	74	82	94
54950 MARION	73	69	61	67	72	79	68	71	71	67	87	82	68	89	69	72	83	70	76	84
54952 MENASHA	88	85	81	86	85	91	86	86	86	85	107	101	85	107	84	85	103	86	86	99
54956 NEENAH	99	106	109	106	105	110	102	102	100	101	124	119	104	128	103	98	121	101	99	115
54960 NESHKORO	81	70	60	67	75	82	68	76	72	67	87	89	64	86	70	74	82	75	83	96
54961 NEW LONDON	86	79	66	77	83	89	77	82	80	76	97	96	75	99	78	81	93	80	87	100
54962 OGDENSBURG	87	77	59	73	81	87	71	79	76	71	92	94	70	94	73	78	87	77	86	102
54963 OMRO	90	79	60	76	83	91	76	83	81	75	98	97	74	99	77	82	93	81	90	103
54964 PICKETT	100	89	68	85	94	101	83	92	88	83	107	109	81	109	85	90	101	89	99	118
54965 PINE RIVER	93	75	53	69	83	92	70	83	78	70	94	98	64	93	74	83	87	82	96	112
54966 PLAINFIELD	81	65	46	64	70	79	66	74	72	65	86	86	61	85	66	74	80	72	82	92
54967 POY SIPPI	85	73	53	68	78	86	68	77	73	67	88	91	64	89	70	77	83	76	87	102
54968 PRINCETON	76	62	45	59	67	76	62	69	68	61	81	80	58	80	63	71	76	68	79	87
54970 REDGRANITE	82	57	29	50	65	74	55	68	65	56	77	81	47	73	57	70	70	67	83	96
54971 RIPON	81	74	65	73	77	85	73	78	77	72	93	90	72	94	74	78	89	77	83	93
54974 ROSENDALE	101	90	68	85	95	102	83	92	88	83	107	110	81	110	86	90	102	90	100	119
54977 SCANDINAVIA	90	80	61	76	84	91	74	82	79	74	96	98	73	98	76	81	91	80	89	105
54978 TILLEDA	73	62	48	62	65	73	64	68	68	62	82	78	61	81	63	69	77	67	74	80
54979 VAN DYNE	102	91	69	87	96	103	84	93	89	84	109	111	83	111	87	92	103	91	101	120
54981 WAUPACA	91	75	54	72	81	90	74	83	81	73	97	97	69	96	75	83	90	82	93	105
54982 WAUTOMA	87	65	41	59	72	84	65	77	75	64	88	88	58	85	67	79	81	76	92	101
54983 WEYAUWEGA	86	76	60	74	80	87	73	79	77	72	94	93	71	95	74	78	89	77	85	99
54984 WILD ROSE	87	67	45	62	75	86	67	78	75	65	89	91	59	86	69	80	82	77	93	103
54986 WINNECONNE	101	96	86	95	99	106	93	98	94	92	116	115	92	117	94	95	111	96	101	117
WISCONSIN	89	86	85	86	88	94	86	88	87	85	108	103	86	109	86	87	104	88	89	103
UNITED STATES	100	100	100	100	100	100	100	100	100	100	100	100	100	100	100	100	100	100	100	100

337-D   Copyright © 2004 ESRI BIS. All rights reserved. Reproduction by any method is prohibited.

# POST OFFICE NAME	COUNTY FIPS CODE	POPULATION 2000	2004	2009	2000-2004 ANNUAL RATE % Rate	State Centile	HOUSEHOLDS 2000	2004	2009	% Annual Rate 2000-2004	2004 Average HH Size	FAMILIES 2000	2004	% Annual Rate 2000-2004
82001 CHEYENNE	021	33636	33811	34204	0.1	40	13832	14300	14821	0.8	2.21	8401	8443	0.1
82005 FE WARREN AFB	021	1055	1094	1117	0.9	71	148	163	173	2.3	3.60	146	161	2.3
82007 CHEYENNE	021	16206	16505	16819	0.4	60	6178	6497	6789	1.2	2.51	4239	4334	0.5
82009 CHEYENNE	021	27082	27994	28703	0.8	71	10395	11105	11683	1.6	2.49	7792	8152	1.1
82050 ALBIN	021	320	321	322	0.1	35	124	127	130	0.6	2.53	92	92	0.0
82051 BOSLER	001	165	172	177	1.0	73	67	72	76	1.7	2.39	47	49	1.0
82052 BUFORD	001	45	51	54	3.0	97	18	21	23	3.7	2.38	13	15	3.4
82053 BURNS	021	1065	1083	1095	0.4	58	397	413	426	0.9	2.62	303	308	0.4
82054 CARPENTER	021	634	653	665	0.7	70	210	222	231	1.3	2.94	159	165	0.9
82055 CENTENNIAL	001	275	289	297	1.2	76	134	145	153	1.9	1.99	95	99	1.0
82058 GARRETT	001	101	105	108	0.9	72	42	45	48	1.6	2.33	30	31	0.8
82063 JELM	001	81	92	98	3.0	99	44	51	57	3.5	1.80	33	37	2.7
82070 LARAMIE	001	16415	16584	16843	0.2	47	6773	7067	7403	1.0	2.14	3722	3756	0.2
82072 LARAMIE	001	14571	14710	14938	0.2	46	6051	6313	6611	1.0	2.18	2962	2976	0.1
82081 MERIDEN	021	15	15	16	0.0	32	4	4	4	0.0	3.75	3	4	7.0
82082 PINE BLUFFS	021	1594	1614	1627	0.3	51	639	664	684	0.9	2.42	464	469	0.3
82083 ROCK RIVER	001	408	418	424	0.6	67	155	164	172	1.3	2.55	109	112	0.6
82084 TIE SIDING	001	36	41	44	3.1	99	16	19	21	4.1	2.16	12	14	3.7
82190 YELLOWSTONE NATIONAL	029	539	562	586	1.0	74	275	302	328	2.2	1.86	115	116	0.2
82201 WHEATLAND	031	6475	6585	6641	0.4	58	2622	2758	2845	1.2	2.35	1832	1883	0.7
82210 CHUGWATER	031	366	373	375	0.5	62	138	144	148	1.0	2.59	105	108	0.7
82212 FORT LARAMIE	015	305	297	290	-0.6	12	147	148	149	0.2	2.01	98	97	-0.2
82213 GLENDO	031	548	547	545	0.0	26	248	255	260	0.7	2.15	164	165	0.1
82214 GUERNSEY	031	1284	1233	1219	-1.0	6	558	554	560	-0.2	2.23	355	342	-0.9
82215 HARTVILLE	031	148	148	147	0.0	32	65	67	68	0.7	2.21	43	43	0.0
82217 HAWK SPRINGS	015	154	151	148	-0.5	17	56	57	57	0.4	2.44	42	41	-0.6
82219 JAY EM	015	447	435	425	-0.7	11	169	170	171	0.1	2.56	113	111	-0.4
82221 LAGRANGE	015	505	495	485	-0.5	16	158	160	161	0.3	2.85	117	116	-0.2
82222 LANCE CREEK	027	185	180	173	-0.6	11	74	74	73	0.0	2.43	55	54	-0.4
82223 LINGLE	015	766	751	736	-0.5	17	310	313	315	0.2	2.40	227	224	-0.3
82224 LOST SPRINGS	027	2	2	2	0.0	32	1	1	1	0.0	2.00	1	1	0.0
82225 LUSK	027	1961	1889	1812	-0.9	7	826	812	795	-0.4	2.20	541	518	-1.0
82227 MANVILLE	027	172	168	161	-0.6	14	76	76	75	0.0	2.21	57	56	-0.4
82229 SHAWNEE	009	118	118	120	0.0	32	46	47	50	0.5	2.51	38	39	0.6
82240 TORRINGTON	015	9519	9423	9299	-0.2	20	3891	3987	4064	0.6	2.27	2581	2580	0.0
82242 VAN TASSELL	027	87	85	82	-0.6	14	34	34	34	0.0	2.50	25	25	0.0
82243 VETERAN	015	157	151	147	-0.9	14	59	59	59	0.0	2.54	47	46	-0.5
82244 YODER	015	691	677	664	-0.5	14	272	275	277	0.3	2.27	202	200	-0.2
82301 RAWLINS	007	9436	9362	9190	-0.2	22	3481	3577	3636	0.6	2.47	2348	2356	0.1
82310 JEFFREY CITY	013	175	178	180	0.4	58	73	77	80	1.3	2.31	54	55	0.4
82321 BAGGS	007	483	485	482	0.1	37	197	207	212	1.2	1.23	128	68	-13.8
82322 BAIROIL	037	122	120	118	-0.4	19	50	51	51	0.5	2.35	38	37	-0.6
82323 DIXON	007	253	254	252	0.1	36	112	118	121	1.2	1.14	73	29	-19.5
82325 ENCAMPMENT	007	877	846	819	-0.8	9	404	409	414	0.3	2.07	280	277	-0.3
82327 HANNA	007	1352	1294	1249	-1.0	4	546	546	549	0.0	2.37	380	371	-0.6
82329 MEDICINE BOW	007	293	260	243	-2.8	1	137	127	125	-1.8	2.05	99	89	-2.5
82331 SARATOGA	007	2311	2229	2158	-0.9	8	1001	1012	1021	0.3	2.17	651	641	-0.4
82332 SAVERY	007	94	94	94	0.0	32	38	40	41	1.2	1.25	25	14	-12.8
82334 SINCLAIR	007	441	412	393	-1.6	1	175	169	168	-0.8	2.44	126	119	-1.3
82336 WAMSUTTER	037	412	394	384	-1.1	3	160	159	160	-0.2	2.44	114	111	-0.6
82401 WORLAND	043	7519	7204	6824	-1.0	4	2944	2910	2843	-0.3	2.41	2072	2004	-0.8
82410 BASIN	003	1839	1845	1857	0.1	35	697	722	745	0.8	2.33	484	490	0.3
82411 BURLINGTON	003	610	640	659	1.1	76	176	188	197	1.6	3.40	140	147	1.2
82414 CODY	029	14009	14216	14361	0.4	55	5795	6094	6311	1.2	2.29	3976	4084	0.6
82421 DEAVER	003	607	614	619	0.3	50	230	241	249	1.1	2.55	175	179	0.5
82426 GREYBULL	003	2669	2683	2713	0.1	40	1114	1143	1180	0.6	2.35	750	751	0.0
82428 HYATTVILLE	003	105	106	107	0.2	46	46	48	49	1.0	2.21	34	35	0.7
82431 LOVELL	003	4814	4783	4806	-0.2	23	1737	1771	1822	0.5	2.66	1273	1273	0.0
82432 MANDERSON	003	442	447	451	0.3	50	169	176	181	1.0	2.53	125	127	0.4
82433 MEETEETSE	029	886	888	891	0.1	34	369	385	397	1.0	2.31	253	256	0.3
82434 OTTO	003	116	122	125	1.2	77	32	34	36	1.4	3.59	26	27	0.9
82435 POWELL	029	10497	10619	10709	0.3	50	3980	4153	4284	1.0	2.41	2756	2813	0.5
82441 SHELL	003	292	304	312	1.0	73	126	135	141	1.6	2.25	92	96	1.0
82442 TEN SLEEP	043	772	750	712	-0.7	9	335	336	330	0.1	2.23	240	235	-0.5
82443 THERMOPOLIS	017	4882	4680	4425	-1.0	5	2108	2085	2034	-0.3	2.18	1353	1304	-0.9
82501 RIVERTON	013	18246	18411	18627	0.2	44	6766	7056	7361	1.0	2.55	4733	4834	0.5
82510 ARAPAHOE	013	342	346	348	0.3	50	85	88	91	0.8	3.93	72	74	0.7
82512 CROWHEART	013	250	245	245	-0.5	16	96	97	100	0.2	2.53	66	65	-0.4
82513 DUBOIS	013	1778	1818	1842	0.5	65	817	868	909	1.4	2.09	517	533	0.7
82514 FORT WASHAKIE	013	1267	1286	1299	0.4	55	376	391	406	0.9	3.19	292	299	0.6
82516 KINNEAR	013	277	275	278	-0.2	22	106	108	113	0.4	2.55	79	79	0.0
82520 LANDER	013	11618	11641	11701	0.1	34	4487	4647	4814	0.8	2.43	3112	3149	0.3
82523 PAVILLION	013	803	853	884	1.4	81	324	357	381	2.3	2.39	250	271	1.9
82601 CASPER	025	23385	23542	23926	0.2	42	9677	9995	10431	0.8	2.26	5763	5793	0.1
82604 CASPER	025	25706	26205	26743	0.5	62	10069	10617	11168	1.3	2.42	7177	7395	0.7
82609 CASPER	025	13270	13562	13835	0.5	65	5496	5823	6128	1.4	2.31	3717	3829	0.7
82620 ALCOVA	025	28	30	31	1.6	85	14	16	17	3.2	1.81	10	11	2.3
82633 DOUGLAS	009	8160	8317	8520	0.5	62	3173	3347	3544	1.3	2.46	2283	2360	0.8
82636 EVANSVILLE	025	3540	3549	3588	0.2	42	1319	1368	1423	0.9	2.59	911	919	0.2
82637 GLENROCK	009	3774	3855	3952	0.5	64	1475	1563	1658	1.4	2.47	1089	1131	0.9
82639 KAYCEE	019	794	833	857	1.1	75	310	338	358	2.1	2.46	237	253	1.6
82642 LYSITE	013	101	103	104	0.5	63	45	47	49	1.0	2.19	33	34	0.7
82643 MIDWEST	025	602	588	589	-0.6	14	237	239	247	0.2	2.46	164	161	-0.4
82649 SHOSHONI	013	947	967	981	0.5	63	370	391	409	1.3	2.47	276	286	0.8
82701 NEWCASTLE	045	5078	5114	5158	0.2	43	1970	2060	2156	1.1	2.35	1383	1415	0.5
82710 ALADDIN	011	219	218	223	-0.1	24	89	92	98	0.8	2.36	63	64	0.4
82712 BEULAH	011	170	171	175	0.1	41	78	82	88	1.2	2.05	59	61	0.8
82714 DEVILS TOWER	011	127	141	151	2.5	96	51	59	66	3.5	2.39	38	43	3.0
82715 FOUR CORNERS	045	35	35	35	0.0	32	21	22	23	1.1	1.41	16	11	-8.4
82716 GILLETTE	005	15001	15976	17227	1.5	82	5697	6267	6976	2.3	2.51	3838	4130	1.7
82718 GILLETTE	005	15975	16934	18219	1.4	81	5535	6085	6772	2.3	2.77	4371	4722	1.8
82720 HULETT	011	1061	1055	1080	-0.1	24	413	428	456	0.8	2.46	294	298	0.3
82721 MOORCROFT	011	2426	2569	2707	1.4	79	925	1019	1115	2.3	2.52	673	727	1.8
82723 OSAGE	045	232	233	234	0.1	37	109	115	120	1.3	1.82	82	85	0.9
82725 RECLUSE	005	168	183	200	2.0	88	76	86	98	3.0	2.13	60	67	2.6
WYOMING					0.4					1.2	2.40			0.6
UNITED STATES					1.2					1.3	2.58			1.1

POPULATION COMPOSITION WYOMING
82001-82725 B

ZIP CODE #	POST OFFICE NAME	RACE (%) White 2000	White 2004	Black 2000	Black 2004	Asian/Pacific 2000	Asian/Pacific 2004	% Hispanic Origin 2000	% Hispanic Origin 2004	2004 AGE DISTRIBUTION (%) 0-4	5-9	10-14	15-19	20-24	25-44	45-64	65-84	85+	18+	MEDIAN AGE 2004	% 2004 Males	% 2004 Females
82001	CHEYENNE	87.9	87.0	3.4	3.5	1.2	1.4	10.8	11.7	6.9	6.2	6.3	6.3	9.1	31.0	21.4	11.0	1.9	77.0	34.4	50.9	49.1
82005	FE WARREN AFB	79.6	78.4	9.4	9.6	2.6	3.0	8.8	9.4	9.5	6.5	4.6	7.0	24.1	46.3	1.9	0.0	0.0	77.7	24.6	66.6	33.4
82007	CHEYENNE	83.0	82.1	3.0	3.1	0.6	0.7	20.3	21.4	8.1	7.7	8.4	7.5	7.8	30.2	21.8	8.0	0.7	71.5	32.1	50.1	49.9
82009	CHEYENNE	93.1	92.5	1.5	1.5	1.3	1.5	6.3	6.8	5.6	6.1	7.4	7.2	5.7	25.4	30.7	10.5	1.6	76.2	40.6	49.0	51.0
82050	ALBIN	95.9	95.6	0.0	0.0	0.3	0.3	4.7	4.7	5.3	6.2	9.4	8.7	4.4	27.1	26.8	10.6	1.6	72.9	38.8	52.0	48.0
82051	BOSLER	97.0	95.9	0.0	0.0	0.0	0.6	3.0	2.9	4.1	3.5	8.1	6.4	4.1	23.8	37.8	11.6	0.6	79.7	45.0	54.1	45.9
82052	BUFORD	95.6	96.1	0.0	0.0	0.0	0.0	2.2	2.0	3.9	3.9	3.9	5.9	3.9	23.5	47.1	7.8	0.0	84.3	47.1	51.0	49.0
82053	BURNS	96.2	96.0	0.0	0.0	0.4	0.5	4.3	4.7	5.7	6.4	9.2	8.2	4.8	27.3	27.3	9.8	1.2	72.9	38.4	50.9	49.1
82054	CARPENTER	96.2	96.0	0.3	0.3	0.3	0.3	5.4	5.8	5.8	6.3	8.1	7.4	6.0	26.0	27.4	11.2	1.8	74.9	39.5	49.2	50.8
82055	CENTENNIAL	96.7	96.5	0.0	0.0	0.4	0.4	2.9	3.1	4.2	3.5	7.6	5.9	3.8	23.5	39.1	11.8	0.7	80.6	45.8	54.7	45.3
82058	GARRETT	97.0	96.2	0.0	0.0	0.0	0.0	3.0	2.9	4.8	2.9	7.6	5.7	3.8	23.8	40.0	11.4	0.0	79.1	45.8	54.3	45.7
82063	JELM	96.3	96.7	0.0	0.0	0.0	0.0	2.5	2.2	4.4	5.4	4.4	5.4	2.2	22.8	44.6	10.9	0.0	81.5	47.5	51.1	48.9
82070	LARAMIE	91.9	91.1	1.0	1.1	1.5	1.8	6.6	7.1	5.0	4.7	4.7	9.8	16.9	27.4	22.0	8.3	1.3	82.6	29.4	50.5	49.5
82072	LARAMIE	90.3	89.5	1.3	1.3	2.2	2.6	8.8	9.4	5.1	3.9	4.4	10.5	27.5	24.4	17.4	6.1	0.7	83.9	24.7	52.6	47.4
82081	MERIDEN	93.3	100.0	0.0	0.0	0.0	0.0	0.0	0.0	0.0	0.0	13.3	13.3	0.0	26.7	46.7	0.0	0.0	86.7	43.8	46.7	53.3
82082	PINE BLUFFS	96.0	95.7	0.3	0.3	0.2	0.2	6.0	6.4	5.1	5.9	8.6	7.7	5.5	24.8	26.6	13.3	2.5	74.9	40.4	49.8	50.3
82083	ROCK RIVER	96.6	96.4	0.0	0.0	0.3	0.2	3.4	3.6	4.3	4.1	7.9	6.7	4.3	23.7	35.9	12.4	0.7	79.0	44.4	54.6	45.5
82084	TIE SIDING	94.4	95.1	0.0	0.0	0.0	0.0	0.0	2.4	4.9	4.9	4.9	4.9	4.9	24.4	43.9	7.3	0.0	82.9	45.6	51.2	48.8
82190	YELLOWSTONE NATIONAL	98.0	97.5	0.0	0.0	0.9	1.3	0.7	0.7	5.7	3.9	5.2	4.1	4.3	42.2	33.5	1.3	0.0	82.0	38.6	53.0	47.0
82201	WHEATLAND	96.9	97.0	0.2	0.2	0.2	0.2	5.0	5.0	5.2	5.6	7.1	7.2	5.7	23.0	29.0	14.8	2.4	77.4	42.3	49.3	50.8
82210	CHUGWATER	97.8	97.9	0.0	0.0	0.0	0.0	3.0	3.0	6.4	7.0	7.5	7.0	6.2	23.6	27.1	13.7	1.6	75.1	39.7	50.9	49.1
82212	FORT LARAMIE	97.1	97.0	0.0	0.0	0.0	0.0	3.0	3.4	5.1	5.4	7.4	7.1	4.7	20.2	33.0	15.5	1.7	77.4	45.1	50.5	49.5
82213	GLENDO	95.3	95.3	0.2	0.2	0.2	0.2	5.1	5.1	3.7	5.1	5.7	7.7	4.6	22.3	31.6	17.4	2.0	80.4	45.8	50.3	49.7
82214	GUERNSEY	92.5	92.1	0.2	0.2	0.2	0.2	7.4	7.6	6.0	6.3	6.2	7.1	5.8	21.9	31.0	13.7	2.0	77.1	42.7	50.4	49.6
82215	HARTVILLE	95.3	95.3	0.0	0.0	0.0	0.0	5.4	5.4	4.1	4.7	5.4	7.4	4.1	22.3	32.4	17.6	2.0	81.1	46.7	50.0	50.0
82217	HAWK SPRINGS	94.8	94.0	0.0	0.0	0.7	1.3	4.6	5.3	6.6	6.6	6.6	7.3	8.0	25.8	26.5	11.3	1.3	76.8	36.6	53.0	47.0
82219	JAY EM	97.1	96.8	0.0	0.0	0.2	0.2	2.9	3.2	4.8	5.3	7.1	7.4	4.6	20.7	33.1	15.4	1.6	77.7	45.1	51.3	48.7
82221	LAGRANGE	94.9	94.3	0.0	0.0	0.8	0.8	4.8	5.3	6.9	6.7	6.9	7.1	7.9	26.3	25.9	10.9	1.6	76.6	35.9	51.3	48.7
82222	LANCE CREEK	98.4	98.3	0.0	0.0	0.0	0.0	1.6	1.7	5.0	5.6	5.6	5.0	3.9	21.7	31.1	20.6	1.7	80.6	47.0	52.2	47.8
82223	LINGLE	96.6	96.5	0.0	0.0	0.1	0.1	3.1	3.5	4.9	5.2	7.1	6.8	5.6	24.6	29.8	14.7	1.3	78.6	42.2	50.2	49.8
82224	LOST SPRINGS	100.0	100.0	0.0	0.0	0.0	0.0	0.0	0.0	0.0	0.0	0.0	0.0	100.0	0.0	0.0	0.0	0.0	100.0	22.5	50.0	50.0
82225	LUSK	98.0	98.0	0.2	0.2	0.1	0.1	1.5	1.5	4.8	5.0	6.2	7.0	6.1	23.4	28.7	15.9	3.0	79.5	43.5	47.9	52.1
82227	MANVILLE	98.3	98.2	0.0	0.0	0.0	0.0	1.7	1.2	4.8	5.4	6.0	5.4	3.6	23.2	30.4	20.2	1.2	80.4	46.2	54.8	45.2
82229	SHAWNEE	94.9	94.9	0.0	0.0	0.9	0.9	3.4	3.4	4.2	6.8	9.3	7.6	5.9	23.7	33.1	9.3	0.0	74.6	40.5	52.5	47.5
82240	TORRINGTON	93.1	92.7	0.3	0.3	0.3	0.4	10.4	11.1	6.0	5.8	6.2	6.8	7.5	22.5	26.8	15.3	3.1	78.2	41.3	49.5	50.5
82242	VAN TASSELL	97.7	97.7	0.0	0.0	0.0	0.0	1.2	2.4	4.7	5.9	5.9	5.9	3.5	20.0	30.6	21.2	2.4	80.0	47.5	52.9	47.1
82243	VETERAN	98.1	98.0	0.0	0.0	0.0	0.0	2.6	3.3	4.6	5.3	6.6	8.0	5.3	24.5	29.8	14.6	1.3	78.2	42.5	53.0	47.0
82244	YODER	94.9	94.2	0.1	0.2	0.7	0.9	4.8	5.2	6.8	6.7	6.9	7.1	7.8	26.4	25.3	11.2	1.8	76.4	35.9	51.0	49.0
82301	RAWLINS	86.8	86.0	0.7	0.7	0.9	1.1	19.9	20.9	6.6	6.0	6.3	6.9	9.0	27.1	27.3	9.5	1.3	76.9	37.3	52.9	47.1
82310	JEFFREY CITY	94.3	93.8	0.0	0.0	1.1	1.1	2.9	3.4	5.1	5.1	7.3	8.4	4.5	21.9	33.2	13.5	1.1	76.4	43.7	50.0	50.0
82321	BAGGS	89.4	89.1	3.1	3.3	0.6	0.8	8.9	9.7	2.5	2.7	3.3	5.2	11.8	41.4	26.4	6.2	0.6	89.1	37.2	75.1	25.0
82322	BAIROIL	93.4	93.3	0.0	0.0	0.0	0.0	7.4	7.5	5.0	5.8	7.5	7.5	6.7	25.0	33.3	9.2	0.0	76.7	40.9	50.8	49.2
82323	DIXON	89.3	89.0	3.2	3.2	0.8	0.8	8.7	10.2	2.8	2.8	3.2	5.1	10.2	42.1	26.4	6.7	0.8	88.6	37.7	74.4	25.6
82325	ENCAMPMENT	97.8	97.6	0.0	0.0	0.6	0.7	1.5	1.5	4.7	5.0	4.1	4.9	4.4	22.9	37.8	14.7	1.5	83.5	47.3	54.0	46.0
82327	HANNA	95.0	94.5	0.4	0.5	0.2	0.2	5.3	6.0	4.9	6.6	6.9	7.3	5.6	22.6	31.3	13.9	0.9	76.7	42.6	51.3	48.7
82329	MEDICINE BOW	97.6	97.3	0.0	0.0	1.0	1.2	1.0	0.8	4.6	3.9	5.0	6.2	4.6	15.0	39.6	19.2	1.9	82.3	49.5	50.0	50.0
82331	SARATOGA	95.8	95.4	0.1	0.1	0.6	0.7	4.2	4.6	4.7	5.0	5.6	6.4	5.3	22.7	33.1	15.3	1.9	80.3	45.2	50.9	49.1
82332	SAVERY	89.4	88.3	3.2	3.2	1.1	1.1	9.6	9.6	2.1	2.1	3.2	5.3	14.9	40.4	25.5	6.4	0.0	90.4	36.5	77.7	22.3
82334	SINCLAIR	96.2	96.1	0.2	0.2	0.2	0.2	4.1	4.4	3.6	4.1	7.3	8.7	7.5	21.1	34.0	11.4	2.2	79.4	43.5	50.5	49.5
82336	WAMSUTTER	92.7	92.4	0.0	0.0	1.0	1.0	8.5	9.1	5.3	6.1	9.6	8.1	6.6	29.7	29.7	4.6	0.3	73.1	35.8	52.5	47.5
82401	WORLAND	90.0	89.2	0.1	0.1	0.8	0.9	11.9	12.7	6.1	6.4	7.5	8.2	6.0	22.9	27.2	13.5	2.4	74.6	40.2	49.4	50.7
82410	BASIN	97.2	97.2	0.1	0.1	0.2	0.2	2.2	2.2	5.2	5.8	5.5	6.0	6.1	19.0	28.1	20.3	4.1	79.5	46.9	48.7	51.3
82411	BURLINGTON	86.9	86.9	0.5	0.5	0.3	0.3	13.6	13.6	12.0	11.6	11.1	7.7	6.1	22.3	16.6	10.8	1.9	60.3	27.1	50.8	49.2
82414	CODY	96.9	96.6	0.1	0.1	0.5	0.6	2.2	2.4	5.5	5.9	6.9	7.1	5.4	23.4	31.3	12.6	1.9	77.0	42.4	48.9	51.1
82421	DEAVER	96.5	96.6	0.0	0.0	0.2	0.2	3.6	3.6	7.5	7.2	7.5	7.5	6.8	24.3	26.4	11.7	1.1	73.5	37.0	49.5	50.5
82426	GREYBULL	95.2	95.1	0.3	0.3	0.5	0.5	5.3	5.4	5.8	6.0	7.1	7.7	6.3	21.5	29.2	14.1	2.2	76.0	41.5	50.3	49.7
82428	HYATTVILLE	93.3	93.4	0.0	0.0	0.0	0.0	5.7	5.7	6.6	6.6	6.6	5.7	4.7	21.7	32.1	14.2	1.9	75.5	43.8	50.9	49.1
82431	LOVELL	93.1	93.0	0.0	0.0	0.2	0.2	7.5	7.5	7.7	7.6	8.2	7.7	6.8	21.7	23.8	13.6	2.8	71.7	36.6	50.1	50.0
82432	MANDERSON	93.7	93.7	0.0	0.0	0.5	0.5	5.2	5.2	6.3	6.5	6.5	5.6	4.9	21.7	32.2	14.5	1.8	77.4	44.0	50.6	49.4
82433	MEETEETSE	95.2	94.8	0.0	0.0	0.2	0.2	3.3	3.6	4.8	5.1	7.6	7.6	3.0	25.2	32.6	12.5	1.7	77.3	42.8	50.7	49.3
82434	OTTO	87.1	86.9	0.9	0.8	0.0	0.0	13.8	13.9	12.3	11.5	9.8	7.4	6.6	23.0	16.4	11.5	1.6	61.5	28.0	51.6	48.4
82435	POWELL	95.8	95.5	0.1	0.1	0.5	0.6	5.9	6.2	6.2	5.9	6.4	7.8	9.1	23.4	25.9	12.9	2.5	77.8	38.2	48.2	51.8
82441	SHELL	93.5	93.4	0.3	0.3	0.7	0.7	5.8	5.6	5.3	5.9	6.9	5.6	4.6	21.7	34.2	14.1	1.6	78.3	45.0	52.3	47.7
82442	TEN SLEEP	92.5	91.9	0.0	0.0	0.4	0.7	7.1	7.7	4.5	6.3	7.1	7.5	2.8	22.3	33.5	14.3	1.9	77.1	44.8	52.5	47.5
82443	THERMOPOLIS	96.0	95.7	0.4	0.4	0.3	0.3	2.4	2.6	4.8	5.0	5.8	6.5	5.6	20.2	30.9	18.3	3.0	80.1	46.3	47.9	52.1
82501	RIVERTON	76.5	75.6	0.1	0.1	0.3	0.3	5.8	6.0	7.2	7.1	7.4	7.8	7.8	24.4	25.2	11.7	1.4	73.7	36.1	49.1	50.9
82510	ARAPAHOE	25.7	25.1	0.0	0.0	0.0	0.0	4.4	4.3	9.8	10.4	10.1	9.0	9.3	22.8	21.4	6.7	0.6	64.7	26.3	51.2	48.8
82512	CROWHEART	57.6	55.9	0.0	0.0	0.4	0.4	2.4	2.5	5.7	5.3	7.8	8.2	5.3	20.8	34.7	10.6	1.6	75.9	43.4	58.0	42.0
82513	DUBOIS	95.7	95.5	0.1	0.1	0.2	0.2	1.2	1.3	3.7	4.1	5.2	5.5	4.2	21.9	36.3	17.8	1.3	83.7	47.8	50.7	49.3
82514	FORT WASHAKIE	9.9	9.3	0.1	0.1	0.0	0.0	2.8	2.6	9.6	9.3	9.7	8.7	7.9	26.5	19.8	7.5	1.1	65.9	28.6	50.0	50.0
82516	KINNEAR	75.1	74.2	0.0	0.0	0.0	0.0	2.9	2.9	4.7	6.2	7.6	6.2	4.4	21.1	34.9	13.5	1.5	77.1	44.9	50.9	49.1
82520	LANDER	80.2	79.4	0.1	0.1	0.4	0.5	3.2	3.4	5.9	6.2	7.2	7.7	6.4	23.3	28.4	13.2	1.7	75.8	40.5	49.3	50.7
82523	PAVILLION	89.3	88.8	0.1	0.1	0.1	0.1	2.5	2.7	6.5	7.0	7.3	6.1	5.2	23.8	31.2	12.2	0.8	75.4	41.4	53.1	46.9
82601	CASPER	92.4	91.9	1.3	1.3	0.5	0.6	6.4	6.9	6.9	6.2	6.5	7.7	8.8	26.8	23.9	11.2	2.1	76.4	35.4	49.3	50.7
82604	CASPER	95.8	95.5	0.4	0.4	0.3	0.3	3.4	3.7	6.4	6.4	7.4	7.2	6.6	26.5	26.6	11.9	1.2	75.5	38.2	49.9	50.1
82609	CASPER	94.6	94.2	0.7	0.7	0.8	0.9	4.9	5.3	6.2	6.1	7.0	7.5	9.0	23.9	27.5	11.8	1.0	76.3	37.8	48.4	51.6
82620	ALCOVA	96.4	100.0	0.0	0.0	0.0	0.0	0.0	0.0	6.7	6.7	6.7	6.7	6.7	26.7	33.3	6.7	0.0	80.0	37.5	50.0	50.0
82633	DOUGLAS	94.7	94.3	0.1	0.1	0.2	0.3	6.1	6.5	6.7	7.0	7.8	7.2	6.6	25.9	27.8	9.6	1.4	73.7	37.6	49.6	50.4
82636	EVANSVILLE	92.3	91.9	0.8	0.9	0.2	0.2	6.2	6.6	8.0	7.3	7.9	7.6	8.8	27.4	24.9	7.5	0.6	72.3	32.4	48.8	51.3
82637	GLENROCK	94.8	94.6	0.3	0.3	0.4	0.5	4.2	4.5	6.1	6.4	7.7	7.4	7.0	22.9	30.8	11.1	0.7	74.9	40.1	50.3	49.7
82639	KAYCEE	97.9	97.7	0.0	0.0	0.1	0.2	2.6	2.8	4.9	5.6	6.8	6.0	5.8	24.0	33.6	12.4	0.8	79.0	42.7	51.3	48.7
82642	LYSITE	94.1	94.2	0.0	0.0	1.0	1.0	3.0	2.9	4.9	5.8	6.8	8.7	3.9	21.4	33.0	14.6	1.0	75.7	44.2	49.5	50.5
82643	MIDWEST	95.5	95.2	0.3	0.3	0.2	0.2	2.2	2.2	6.0	6.6	7.3	7.5	6.3	25.7	32.8	7.0	0.9	75.5	39.2	51.0	49.0
82649	SHOSHONI	93.0	92.5	0.1	0.1	0.7	0.9	2.9	3.1	4.9	5.7	7.3	7.8	4.8	22.5	33.1	12.9	1.0	76.7	43.2	50.5	49.5
82701	NEWCASTLE	95.7	95.7	0.1	0.1	0.2	0.2	2.1	2.2	5.3	5.6	5.9	6.9	6.8	24.8	29.1	13.4	2.3	78.8	41.8	50.9	49.1
82710	ALADDIN	98.6	98.6	0.0	0.0	0.0	0.0	0.9	0.9	5.5	6.4	8.7	6.9	6.4	24.3	28.4	11.9	1.4	74.8	40.0	51.4	48.6
82712	BEULAH	97.7	98.3	0.0	0.0	0.0	0.0	0.6	0.6	4.7	5.9	6.4	6.4	5.3	20.5	33.3	16.4	1.2	77.8	45.6	50.3	49.7
82714	DEVILS TOWER	97.6	97.9	0.0	0.0	0.0	0.0	1.6	1.4	5.0	5.7	8.5	7.8	2.8	24.8	31.9	11.4	2.1	75.2	42.5	51.1	48.9
82715	FOUR CORNERS	97.1	97.1	0.0	0.0	0.0	0.0	2.9	2.9	5.7	5.7	5.7	5.7	8.6	22.9	37.1	8.6	0.0	82.9	42.5	62.9	37.1
82716	GILLETTE	95.6	95.3	0.2	0.2	0.5	0.6	4.0	4.2	7.4	7.0	7.3	7.4	9.1	28.8	25.2	6.9	0.9	73.9	32.9	51.5	48.5
82718	GILLETTE	96.3	96.0	0.1	0.1	0.4	0.4	3.3	3.5	7.7	7.4	8.4	8.5	8.3	28.6	27.2	3.7	0.2	71.1	32.3	51.0	49.0
82720	HULETT	98.5	98.4	0.2	0.2	0.1	0.1	0.9	1.0	5.4	6.2	8.6	7.1	6.1	23.9	28.8	12.2	1.7	74.9	40.6	51.9	48.2
82721	MOORCROFT	98.0	98.0	0.0	0.0	0.0	0.0	1.4	1.5	6.1	6.1	7.8	8.3	5.9	25.2	29.7	9.7	1.2	74.5	39.6	51.3	48.7
82723	OSAGE	96.6	96.1	0.4	0.4	0.0	0.0	2.6	2.2	4.3	4.7	5.6	6.9	6.4	26.6	33.9	10.7	0.9	81.6	42.6	57.1	42.9
82725	RECLUSE	98.8	99.5	0.0	0.0	0.0	0.0	1.8	1.6	4.4	5.5	6.0	7.7	7.7	25.7	35.0	8.2	0.0	79.8	41.1	50.8	49.2
	WYOMING	92.1	91.6	0.8	0.8	0.6	0.7	6.4	6.8	6.4	6.2	7.0	7.5	8.3	26.1	26.6	10.5	1.5	76.1	36.8	50.3	49.7
	UNITED STATES	75.1	73.6	12.3	12.5	3.8	4.2	12.5	14.1	6.9	6.7	7.2	7.0	7.3	28.6	23.8	10.8	1.7	75.1	36.0	49.1	50.9

#	POST OFFICE NAME	2004 Per Capita Income	2004 HH Income Base	2004 HOUSEHOLD INCOME DISTRIBUTION (%) Less than $25,000	$25,000 to $49,999	$50,000 to $99,999	$100,000 to $149,999	$150,000 or More	MEDIAN HOUSEHOLD INCOME 2004	2009	2004 National Centile	2004 State Centile	2004 Home Value Base	2004 HOME VALUE DISTRIBUTION (%) Less than $50,000	$50,000 to $89,999	$90,000 to $174,999	$175,000 to $399,999	$400,000 or More	2004 Median Home Value
82001	CHEYENNE	21330	14300	28.6	33.9	29.8	5.9	1.8	39908	46964	46	41	8728	7.1	12.7	68.3	11.5	0.3	115861
82005	FE WARREN AFB	13563	163	10.4	63.8	21.5	1.2	3.1	38067	43950	39	31	0	0.0	0.0	0.0	0.0	0.0	0
82007	CHEYENNE	17669	6497	32.0	35.7	26.9	4.6	0.9	35756	42871	31	21	4658	30.9	24.8	37.7	5.9	0.6	81275
82009	CHEYENNE	29965	11105	14.0	23.7	41.3	14.7	6.2	62685	75738	87	96	8908	3.1	3.1	48.6	41.7	3.5	167693
82050	ALBIN	21365	127	20.5	36.2	37.0	4.7	1.6	44542	52459	60	64	99	21.2	22.2	26.3	21.2	9.1	103750
82051	BOSLER	22893	72	38.9	20.8	23.6	9.7	6.9	40000	47368	46	42	53	15.1	24.5	15.1	17.0	28.3	162500
82052	BUFORD	25022	21	23.8	33.3	28.6	4.8	9.5	46113	54447	64	72	18	5.6	5.6	22.2	50.0	16.7	212500
82053	BURNS	20655	413	19.6	34.1	39.0	5.6	1.7	46645	53000	65	74	333	19.2	18.6	28.5	26.1	7.5	120259
82054	CARPENTER	17216	222	26.1	32.9	32.4	5.9	2.7	41051	48642	50	48	183	15.3	16.9	47.0	20.2	0.6	112917
82055	CENTENNIAL	28372	145	37.9	21.4	24.1	9.0	7.6	40247	48844	47	43	107	17.8	22.4	15.9	16.8	27.1	158750
82058	GARRETT	23508	45	37.8	20.0	26.7	8.9	6.7	40748	52998	49	47	33	12.1	21.2	15.2	18.2	33.3	187500
82063	JELM	35408	51	21.6	29.4	35.3	3.9	9.8	49517	59234	71	80	42	2.4	7.1	31.0	40.5	19.1	200000
82070	LARAMIE	22769	7067	36.6	26.2	27.6	6.8	2.8	36960	46239	35	27	3964	11.1	8.7	47.8	29.7	2.6	145858
82072	LARAMIE	19449	6313	42.4	26.5	22.8	6.4	1.9	30680	37932	14	6	2800	15.5	9.2	41.5	32.0	1.8	138534
82081	MERIDEN	22510	4	0.0	0.0	50.0	50.0	0.0	100000	125000	98	100	4	0.0	0.0	25.0	75.0	0.0	200000
82082	PINE BLUFFS	19984	664	29.1	33.9	29.5	4.1	3.5	39011	45827	43	36	523	15.9	22.4	49.7	10.3	1.7	100121
82083	ROCK RIVER	21047	164	37.8	22.0	23.8	9.2	7.3	40000	49392	46	42	121	21.5	24.8	18.2	14.1	21.5	112500
82084	TIE SIDING	29390	19	26.3	26.3	31.6	5.3	10.5	48601	54416	69	77	16	0.0	6.3	31.3	43.8	18.8	210000
82190	YELLOWSTONE NATIONAL	33213	302	14.2	27.8	43.7	10.6	3.6	53454	64175	78	90	17	76.5	0.0	0.0	23.5	0.0	19167
82201	WHEATLAND	21785	2758	28.3	32.2	30.1	7.2	2.2	41163	48917	50	49	2158	16.8	21.3	44.3	15.3	2.4	108738
82210	CHUGWATER	19796	144	33.3	30.6	22.2	8.3	5.6	40284	46921	47	44	115	9.6	27.8	50.4	8.7	3.5	104911
82212	FORT LARAMIE	25550	148	31.1	28.4	32.4	4.1	4.1	42359	48496	54	55	117	17.1	29.1	20.5	25.6	7.7	99000
82213	GLENDO	20457	255	47.1	24.3	17.7	6.3	4.7	26889	33287	7	2	212	29.3	25.0	17.9	23.1	4.7	83571
82214	GUERNSEY	19643	554	36.3	27.3	30.9	4.3	1.3	34223	40451	25	16	421	24.7	38.2	26.6	8.8	1.7	76029
82215	HARTVILLE	19817	67	46.3	23.9	17.9	6.0	6.0	27293	32330	8	4	56	28.6	25.0	17.9	23.2	5.4	85000
82217	HAWK SPRINGS	16416	57	38.6	31.6	22.8	7.0	0.0	32951	37963	21	14	45	6.7	26.7	24.4	24.4	17.8	121875
82219	JAY EM	20054	170	32.4	28.2	31.8	3.5	4.1	41016	48644	50	47	134	16.4	29.9	20.9	25.4	7.5	98333
82221	LAGRANGE	14283	160	40.6	30.6	23.1	5.6	0.0	32093	38394	18	11	126	7.9	26.2	23.0	25.4	17.5	122500
82222	LANCE CREEK	18074	74	37.8	32.4	21.6	8.1	0.0	31660	36360	17	9	57	21.1	17.5	15.8	14.0	31.6	147500
82223	LINGLE	21203	313	23.6	41.5	27.8	3.5	3.5	39081	45100	43	37	240	10.4	18.3	56.3	15.0	0.0	111702
82224	LOST SPRINGS	0	0	0.0	0.0	0.0	0.0	0.0	0	0	0	0	0	0.0	0.0	0.0	0.0	0.0	0
82225	LUSK	19321	812	38.4	32.0	23.0	4.9	1.6	32602	37512	20	14	596	22.3	32.4	30.4	7.6	7.4	84400
82227	MANVILLE	19888	76	39.5	31.6	21.1	7.9	0.0	31082	36906	15	7	59	20.3	20.3	15.3	15.3	28.8	142500
82229	SHAWNEE	26928	47	14.9	31.9	34.0	14.9	4.3	52593	62035	76	88	39	7.7	12.8	41.0	25.6	12.8	137500
82240	TORRINGTON	19119	3987	38.3	28.7	26.5	4.6	1.8	35781	41346	31	22	2865	17.9	27.7	42.5	9.6	2.4	95642
82242	VAN TASSELL	17585	34	38.2	32.4	20.6	8.8	0.0	31485	35000	16	8	26	19.2	15.4	11.5	15.4	38.5	225000
82243	VETERAN	16566	59	33.9	40.7	20.3	5.1	0.0	35553	40557	30	20	42	16.7	23.8	40.5	2.4	16.7	112500
82244	YODER	17698	275	38.6	31.3	23.6	5.8	0.7	33400	38752	22	15	216	7.9	25.9	23.6	25.9	16.7	122222
82301	RAWLINS	21044	3577	29.4	28.4	31.9	7.5	2.8	41886	50245	53	52	2391	19.1	35.1	37.1	8.4	0.3	86605
82310	JEFFREY CITY	22739	77	18.2	37.7	33.8	9.1	1.3	43620	50000	58	59	63	19.1	14.3	23.8	36.5	6.4	143750
82321	BAGGS	24785	207	35.3	31.9	29.5	1.9	1.5	35863	45000	31	22	165	29.7	26.1	29.7	12.1	2.4	76818
82322	BAIROIL	23707	51	19.6	25.5	45.1	9.8	0.0	52248	61481	76	87	44	36.4	31.8	13.6	13.6	4.6	70000
82323	DIXON	29250	118	33.9	31.4	29.7	2.5	2.5	37702	45665	38	29	94	30.9	25.5	26.6	13.8	3.2	76667
82325	ENCAMPMENT	26125	409	29.6	28.4	31.8	8.6	1.7	43577	51606	57	58	330	10.9	20.0	47.0	16.4	5.8	114615
82327	HANNA	21137	546	34.1	28.8	24.7	7.9	4.6	38362	46264	41	33	427	35.6	40.8	18.5	3.3	1.9	62315
82329	MEDICINE BOW	20043	127	28.4	44.1	24.4	1.6	1.6	32332	38159	19	12	104	50.0	37.5	12.5	0.0	0.0	50000
82331	SARATOGA	26352	1012	28.5	32.5	29.2	6.0	3.9	41484	49422	51	50	790	13.4	16.7	49.8	16.3	3.8	112849
82332	SAVERY	22822	40	40.0	30.0	27.5	2.5	0.0	32341	46700	19	13	32	34.4	25.0	25.0	12.5	3.1	70000
82334	SINCLAIR	23948	169	25.4	23.1	39.6	8.9	3.0	50791	56016	73	84	142	19.7	35.2	38.0	6.3	0.7	82222
82336	WAMSUTTER	26494	159	17.6	28.3	37.1	11.3	5.7	55002	62771	80	92	106	30.2	21.7	22.6	20.8	4.7	86000
82401	WORLAND	21787	2910	30.8	31.6	25.7	7.9	4.0	39823	47478	45	40	2207	12.6	25.5	46.7	13.8	1.4	101017
82410	BASIN	20099	722	31.9	33.1	26.6	6.8	1.7	37642	43106	38	29	571	24.3	27.9	37.0	10.0	0.9	87500
82411	BURLINGTON	13937	188	36.2	35.1	21.3	4.8	2.7	31741	36041	17	10	145	31.7	20.0	31.7	11.7	4.8	86875
82414	CODY	24042	6094	27.3	33.4	29.4	6.7	3.2	41526	48494	51	51	4636	9.3	8.8	45.2	31.0	5.7	145475
82421	DEAVER	19580	241	27.4	38.2	27.8	4.6	2.1	39502	45661	44	40	197	22.8	24.9	38.1	11.7	2.5	93750
82426	GREYBULL	18946	1143	33.7	36.3	23.9	4.6	1.6	35027	40337	28	18	841	20.3	29.4	32.5	15.1	2.7	90385
82428	HYATTVILLE	18774	48	39.6	33.3	20.8	4.2	2.1	31514	41711	16	9	38	15.8	18.4	44.7	18.4	2.6	109375
82431	LOVELL	17060	1771	31.7	35.6	27.2	4.1	1.4	37516	43288	38	28	1380	20.3	31.7	37.8	8.9	1.3	88042
82432	MANDERSON	18744	176	36.4	34.7	19.9	5.7	3.4	34526	40795	26	17	138	16.7	19.6	41.3	18.8	3.6	108333
82433	MEETEETSE	20612	385	29.4	40.5	21.6	7.8	0.8	35872	41554	31	24	304	15.8	21.4	36.2	17.1	9.5	110662
82434	OTTO	10553	34	35.3	38.2	23.5	2.9	0.0	32257	36502	18	12	26	26.9	26.9	30.8	11.5	3.9	85000
82435	POWELL	19877	4153	32.0	30.9	29.5	5.1	2.5	38647	45245	42	35	3087	11.4	17.7	43.7	23.3	3.9	121494
82441	SHELL	22072	135	33.3	35.6	20.7	7.4	3.0	35196	41018	28	19	106	14.2	15.1	35.9	30.2	4.7	123438
82442	TEN SLEEP	25828	336	32.4	33.0	21.4	10.4	2.7	37492	46086	37	27	241	14.1	13.7	36.9	27.0	8.3	143015
82443	THERMOPOLIS	20528	2085	35.5	30.8	25.5	6.9	1.3	35430	41603	29	19	1534	17.1	22.6	42.2	14.0	4.2	100915
82501	RIVERTON	18147	7056	34.7	33.1	24.6	5.5	2.1	36125	41814	32	25	5258	18.4	23.1	42.0	14.2	2.3	103455
82510	ARAPAHOE	8548	88	46.6	30.7	19.3	3.4	0.0	26935	31911	7	3	69	40.6	29.0	23.2	5.8	1.5	60833
82512	CROWHEART	25517	97	35.1	25.8	20.6	12.4	6.2	40571	51069	48	46	72	11.1	13.9	31.9	16.7	26.4	147917
82513	DUBOIS	25095	868	28.8	37.1	26.4	3.5	4.3	38107	45109	40	32	670	13.1	9.7	33.0	32.5	11.6	142593
82514	FORT WASHAKIE	10636	391	51.2	29.2	15.1	3.8	0.8	24259	28387	4	1	249	34.1	25.3	24.5	14.1	2.0	75750
82516	KINNEAR	20892	108	38.9	29.6	20.4	6.5	4.6	35000	41147	28	17	87	24.1	10.3	42.5	17.2	5.8	110417
82520	LANDER	22394	4647	31.3	33.1	26.0	7.1	2.6	38528	44767	41	35	3408	15.0	17.7	44.0	19.0	4.2	114593
82523	PAVILLION	21943	357	31.1	33.6	25.5	6.4	3.4	37761	43488	38	30	295	19.0	16.3	31.5	23.4	9.8	120724
82601	CASPER	22050	9995	34.1	31.1	26.1	6.5	2.2	36090	43439	32	24	6168	14.3	27.1	44.6	12.4	1.6	98709
82604	CASPER	23284	10617	23.1	31.4	33.5	8.7	3.3	45439	54110	62	71	8568	11.4	24.2	46.7	16.6	1.2	105362
82609	CASPER	27002	5823	21.8	28.7	35.2	10.1	4.3	49505	59667	71	79	4020	3.9	16.2	58.7	19.0	2.2	121772
82620	ALCOVA	31659	16	18.8	31.3	43.8	6.3	0.0	50000	54626	72	82	14	0.0	14.3	42.9	42.9	0.0	150000
82633	DOUGLAS	22360	3347	27.5	25.0	36.6	9.2	1.7	46214	54503	64	73	2588	14.6	21.1	48.4	12.6	3.3	108108
82636	EVANSVILLE	17473	1368	34.9	32.5	25.5	5.1	2.0	35871	42756	31	23	956	30.0	29.2	23.6	13.9	3.2	81111
82637	GLENROCK	21285	1563	28.0	29.4	33.6	7.7	1.3	45094	52128	61	70	1191	9.7	28.4	47.1	12.3	2.5	100232
82639	KAYCEE	23700	338	26.3	29.3	32.0	7.4	5.0	44692	53266	60	65	267	9.7	12.7	39.7	24.7	13.1	142917
82642	LYSITE	24709	47	19.2	36.2	34.0	8.5	2.1	44295	51068	59	62	38	23.7	15.8	23.7	31.6	5.3	112500
82643	MIDWEST	21386	239	25.1	31.0	34.3	8.4	1.3	44696	52728	60	65	191	45.6	15.2	18.9	18.9	1.6	67000
82649	SHOSHONI	23664	391	21.0	35.0	32.7	7.9	3.3	43367	51346	57	58	324	22.2	15.1	27.5	28.7	6.5	119853
82701	NEWCASTLE	20170	2060	32.0	32.0	27.1	7.3	1.6	36811	44242	35	26	1592	25.8	31.5	30.8	10.5	1.4	81077
82710	ALADDIN	17150	92	45.7	32.6	16.3	3.3	2.2	28157	36526	9	5	74	33.8	18.9	21.6	9.5	16.2	86000
82712	BEULAH	25601	82	31.7	22.0	32.9	11.0	2.4	43902	51452	58	60	66	9.1	10.6	47.0	21.2	12.1	125000
82714	DEVILS TOWER	23239	59	28.8	20.3	35.6	13.6	1.7	50691	64339	73	83	51	3.9	19.6	43.1	21.6	11.8	131250
82715	FOUR CORNERS	34738	22	31.8	18.2	36.4	13.6	0.0	50000	62014	72	82	19	31.6	21.1	31.6	15.8	0.0	85000
82716	GILLETTE	22436	6267	23.1	27.4	38.4	8.8	2.3	49479	57759	71	78	4198	25.6	14.8	46.0	12.6	1.0	104219
82718	GILLETTE	25827	6085	11.6	23.3	46.1	14.8	4.2	62617	73406	87	96	4876	8.9	14.6	48.9	25.6	2.0	134154
82720	HULETT	16488	428	44.2	33.6	16.1	3.3	2.8	29778	36046	12	6	344	34.3	20.4	21.5	9.9	14.0	83333
82721	MOORCROFT	21360	1019	27.3	27.2	33.1	11.1	1.4	46656	54736	65	75	848	19.0	22.2	37.4	15.9	5.5	105754
82723	OSAGE	31121	115	28.7	24.4	30.4	13.9	2.6	45578	56832	63	71	98	26.5	18.4	30.6	19.4	5.1	103846
82725	RECLUSE	31981	86	11.6	24.4	45.4	17.4	1.2	58252	69919	83	94	72	22.2	12.5	40.3	19.4	5.6	132692
	WYOMING	23508		27.1	29.5	31.9	8.2	3.3	43736	51981				14.0	17.6	44.1	19.8	4.6	116261
	UNITED STATES	25866		24.7	27.1	30.8	10.9	6.5	48124	56710				10.9	15.0	33.7	30.1	10.4	145905

ZIP CODE #	POST OFFICE NAME	FINANCIAL SERVICES: Auto Loan	FINANCIAL SERVICES: Home Loan	FINANCIAL SERVICES: Invest-ments	FINANCIAL SERVICES: Retire-ment Plans	THE HOME: Home Improvements: Home Repair	THE HOME: Home Improvements: Lawn & Garden	THE HOME: Furnishings: Comput-ers & Hard-ware	THE HOME: Furnishings: Major Appli-ances	THE HOME: Furnishings: TV, Radio, Sound Equip-ment	THE HOME: Furnishings: Furni-ture	ENTERTAINMENT: Dine out/ Carry out	ENTERTAINMENT: Sports Equip-ment	ENTERTAINMENT: Fees & Tickets	ENTERTAINMENT: Toys & Games	ENTERTAINMENT: Travel	ENTERTAINMENT: Cable TV	PERSONAL: Apparel & Services	PERSONAL: Auto Repairs	PERSONAL: Health Insur-ance	PERSONAL: Pets & Supplies
82001	CHEYENNE	66	66	71	67	66	70	69	68	68	67	85	80	68	85	68	67	83	69	66	75
82005	FE WARREN AFB	76	48	46	55	44	52	72	62	73	67	91	82	61	81	59	66	87	73	57	70
82007	CHEYENNE	67	62	54	60	63	67	62	65	63	62	78	75	59	76	61	63	75	65	65	76
82009	CHEYENNE	102	113	118	114	113	116	107	108	103	106	128	126	110	131	108	101	126	106	102	121
82050	ALBIN	98	68	36	64	79	89	67	83	78	67	91	100	58	89	70	81	83	82	99	116
82051	BOSLER	93	73	50	66	82	92	69	83	78	68	92	97	61	91	73	83	86	81	98	113
82052	BUFORD	102	81	56	74	91	101	77	92	86	77	102	107	69	101	81	91	95	90	107	124
82053	BURNS	95	71	42	67	80	89	69	82	77	68	92	99	61	91	71	81	84	81	96	113
82054	CARPENTER	87	67	42	64	75	83	64	76	72	64	86	92	58	85	67	75	79	75	88	103
82055	CENTENNIAL	96	75	51	68	85	95	71	85	80	70	95	100	63	94	76	86	88	84	101	117
82058	GARRETT	93	73	50	66	82	92	69	83	78	68	92	97	62	91	73	83	86	82	98	113
82063	JELM	108	85	58	77	96	107	80	97	91	79	107	113	72	106	85	97	100	95	114	132
82070	LARAMIE	73	59	66	62	59	65	75	69	75	71	93	86	69	88	69	70	90	75	66	79
82072	LARAMIE	59	50	60	54	49	54	66	57	64	61	81	73	61	77	59	59	78	63	53	64
82081	MERIDEN	110	136	145	136	134	132	122	121	113	121	142	142	129	151	124	109	141	117	108	134
82082	PINE BLUFFS	88	61	32	58	71	80	60	75	70	60	82	90	52	80	63	73	75	74	89	104
82083	ROCK RIVER	91	71	49	64	80	90	67	81	76	67	90	95	60	89	72	81	84	80	96	111
82084	TIE SIDING	108	84	58	76	95	107	80	96	90	79	107	112	71	105	85	96	99	94	113	131
82190	YELLOWSTONE NATIONAL	95	75	72	75	80	89	85	88	90	82	110	107	77	105	83	89	104	92	93	110
82201	WHEATLAND	90	64	37	61	73	84	66	78	75	64	88	92	57	85	67	79	81	78	93	104
82210	CHUGWATER	93	65	34	61	75	85	64	79	74	63	86	95	55	85	66	77	79	78	94	110
82212	FORT LARAMIE	93	65	34	61	75	85	64	79	74	63	86	95	55	85	66	77	79	78	94	110
82213	GLENDO	74	58	40	53	66	74	55	66	62	55	74	78	49	73	59	67	69	65	78	91
82214	GUERNSEY	71	53	35	51	58	70	59	65	66	56	77	73	52	73	58	69	70	65	77	79
82215	HARTVILLE	74	58	40	53	66	74	55	66	62	54	74	77	49	73	59	66	68	65	78	90
82217	HAWK SPRINGS	73	51	27	48	60	67	51	63	58	50	68	75	43	67	52	61	62	62	75	87
82219	JAY EM	93	65	34	61	76	85	64	79	74	63	87	95	55	85	66	77	79	78	94	110
82221	LAGRANGE	74	51	27	49	60	67	51	63	59	50	69	76	43	67	53	62	63	62	75	88
82222	LANCE CREEK	80	56	29	52	65	72	55	68	63	54	74	82	47	73	57	66	68	67	81	94
82223	LINGLE	92	64	34	61	75	84	63	78	73	63	86	95	54	84	66	77	78	77	93	109
82224	LOST SPRINGS	0	0	0	0	0	0	0	0	0	0	0	0	0	0	0	0	0	0	0	0
82225	LUSK	72	53	33	51	59	69	57	64	64	55	76	73	50	72	57	68	69	64	77	80
82227	MANVILLE	80	56	29	52	65	72	55	68	63	54	74	82	47	73	57	66	68	67	81	94
82229	SHAWNEE	104	97	83	93	101	106	92	100	94	92	115	118	88	115	93	95	110	99	103	123
82240	TORRINGTON	71	56	39	54	61	70	58	65	64	57	76	75	53	74	58	67	71	65	75	81
82242	VAN TASSELL	80	56	29	52	65	72	55	68	63	54	74	82	47	73	57	66	68	67	81	94
82243	VETERAN	76	53	28	50	62	69	52	65	60	52	71	78	45	69	54	63	65	64	77	90
82244	YODER	74	52	27	49	60	67	51	63	59	50	69	76	44	68	53	62	63	62	75	88
82301	RAWLINS	73	74	73	72	73	78	74	74	73	73	91	86	73	91	73	73	89	74	73	83
82310	JEFFREY CITY	95	66	35	63	77	87	66	81	76	65	89	98	56	87	68	79	81	80	97	113
82321	BAGGS	0	0	0	0	0	0	0	0	0	0	0	0	0	0	0	0	0	0	0	0
82322	BAIROIL	89	80	61	76	84	90	74	82	78	74	95	97	72	97	76	80	90	79	88	105
82323	DIXON	0	0	0	0	0	0	0	0	0	0	0	0	0	0	0	0	0	0	0	0
82325	ENCAMPMENT	92	72	49	65	81	91	68	82	77	67	91	96	61	90	72	82	84	80	97	112
82327	HANNA	82	66	48	63	73	82	65	75	72	64	86	86	60	85	67	75	80	73	85	96
82329	MEDICINE BOW	70	55	37	49	61	69	51	62	58	51	69	73	46	68	55	62	64	61	73	85
82331	SARATOGA	104	73	39	69	85	95	72	89	83	71	97	107	62	95	75	87	89	87	105	123
82332	SAVERY	0	0	0	0	0	0	0	0	0	0	0	0	0	0	0	0	0	0	0	0
82334	SINCLAIR	99	78	53	70	87	98	73	88	83	73	98	103	65	97	78	89	91	87	104	121
82336	WAMSUTTER	91	99	98	101	96	95	94	93	88	95	112	111	94	112	92	83	110	93	83	103
82401	WORLAND	88	68	46	65	75	86	69	79	77	68	91	92	63	89	71	80	84	78	92	101
82410	BASIN	84	60	34	57	69	79	62	73	70	60	83	86	53	80	63	74	75	72	87	98
82411	BURLINGTON	86	60	31	57	70	78	59	73	68	58	80	88	51	78	61	72	73	72	87	101
82414	CODY	85	75	65	73	80	88	75	81	79	74	96	95	72	96	76	81	91	80	88	100
82421	DEAVER	90	63	33	60	73	82	62	77	72	61	84	93	53	82	65	75	77	76	92	107
82426	GREYBULL	78	55	31	53	63	73	57	68	65	55	76	80	49	74	58	68	69	67	81	91
82428	HYATTVILLE	70	55	38	50	62	70	52	63	59	52	70	73	46	69	55	63	65	62	74	86
82431	LOVELL	79	57	32	54	65	74	58	69	66	57	78	81	50	75	59	70	71	68	82	92
82432	MANDERSON	80	63	43	57	71	80	60	72	68	59	80	84	53	79	63	72	74	71	85	97
82433	MEETEETSE	86	60	31	57	70	78	59	73	68	59	80	88	51	79	62	72	73	72	87	102
82434	OTTO	69	48	25	45	56	62	47	58	54	47	64	70	40	63	49	57	58	58	70	81
82435	POWELL	79	63	46	60	69	77	64	72	70	63	84	85	59	83	65	73	78	72	82	91
82441	SHELL	87	65	40	60	74	83	62	76	71	62	84	90	55	82	66	75	77	75	90	104
82442	TEN SLEEP	104	73	38	69	85	95	72	89	83	71	97	107	61	95	75	87	89	88	106	124
82443	THERMOPOLIS	76	56	34	53	62	73	59	68	67	57	78	78	52	75	59	70	71	67	81	87
82501	RIVERTON	71	63	54	61	66	72	63	68	66	63	81	79	60	79	64	67	77	68	72	82
82510	ARAPAHOE	54	48	37	47	49	52	46	50	47	47	58	58	43	55	46	47	56	50	50	60
82512	CROWHEART	117	81	43	77	95	106	80	99	93	79	109	120	69	107	83	97	99	98	118	138
82513	DUBOIS	89	70	48	63	79	88	66	79	75	65	88	93	59	87	70	80	82	78	94	109
82514	FORT WASHAKIE	46	43	51	40	41	47	46	44	49	47	62	50	47	61	45	51	60	46	46	51
82516	KINNEAR	96	67	35	63	78	88	66	82	76	66	90	99	57	88	69	80	82	81	98	114
82520	LANDER	89	73	54	70	79	87	73	82	79	72	95	96	67	93	74	81	89	81	91	104
82523	PAVILLION	95	66	35	63	77	86	65	81	75	65	88	97	56	87	68	79	81	80	96	113
82601	CASPER	69	70	76	70	70	74	72	71	71	71	89	83	72	90	71	70	87	72	69	79
82604	CASPER	80	83	80	81	84	88	80	82	79	79	98	95	80	100	80	79	95	81	81	94
82609	CASPER	82	90	103	91	88	93	90	87	87	89	110	102	93	112	90	85	108	88	82	95
82620	ALCOVA	99	77	53	70	87	98	73	88	82	72	98	103	65	97	78	88	91	86	104	120
82633	DOUGLAS	84	79	68	78	80	84	77	81	77	77	95	94	74	93	76	77	92	81	81	94
82636	EVANSVILLE	75	63	46	60	66	72	61	68	64	61	78	79	56	74	61	65	73	67	72	86
82637	GLENROCK	84	72	55	71	76	82	71	78	75	70	90	92	66	90	71	75	85	77	83	97
82639	KAYCEE	99	78	53	70	87	98	73	88	83	73	98	103	65	97	78	89	91	87	104	121
82642	LYSITE	98	68	36	65	80	89	68	84	78	67	91	101	58	90	70	82	83	82	100	116
82643	MIDWEST	95	66	35	63	77	87	66	81	76	65	89	98	56	87	68	79	81	80	97	113
82649	SHOSHONI	106	74	39	70	86	96	73	90	84	72	99	109	62	97	76	88	90	89	108	126
82701	NEWCASTLE	86	60	33	56	69	79	61	73	71	60	83	87	53	80	62	75	75	73	88	99
82710	ALADDIN	76	51	23	44	58	67	49	62	60	50	70	74	42	66	50	64	64	61	76	88
82712	BEULAH	96	67	35	63	78	87	66	81	76	65	89	98	56	87	68	80	81	80	97	113
82714	DEVILS TOWER	101	70	37	66	82	92	69	86	80	68	94	103	59	92	72	84	85	84	102	119
82715	FOUR CORNERS	96	67	35	63	78	87	66	82	76	65	89	98	56	88	69	80	81	81	97	114
82716	GILLETTE	84	81	74	81	80	84	80	82	79	81	99	96	78	96	78	78	95	82	79	94
82718	GILLETTE	105	111	104	114	107	106	103	104	98	107	123	122	104	121	101	92	121	103	93	116
82720	HULETT	76	51	23	44	58	67	49	62	60	50	70	74	42	66	50	64	64	61	76	88
82721	MOORCROFT	91	74	50	70	79	85	71	81	76	72	92	96	65	88	72	77	86	81	88	104
82723	OSAGE	109	76	40	72	89	99	75	93	86	74	101	112	64	99	78	91	92	91	110	129
82725	RECLUSE	109	97	74	92	103	110	90	99	95	90	116	118	88	118	92	98	110	97	108	128
	WYOMING	86	78	71	77	81	87	79	82	81	78	99	97	76	98	78	81	95	83	85	98
	UNITED STATES	100	100	100	100	100	100	100	100	100	100	100	100	100	100	100	100	100	100	100	100

WYOMING

POPULATION CHANGE

ZIP CODE		COUNTY FIPS CODE	POPULATION			2000-2004 ANNUAL RATE		HOUSEHOLDS					FAMILIES		
#	POST OFFICE NAME		2000	2004	2009	% Rate	State Centile	2000	2004	2009	% Annual Rate 2000-2004	2004 Average HH Size	2000	2004	% Annual Rate 2000-2004
82727	ROZET	005	690	757	827	2.2	90	235	268	303	3.1	2.82	201	226	2.8
82729	SUNDANCE	011	2119	2143	2195	0.3	50	838	884	943	1.3	2.32	586	605	0.8
82730	UPTON	045	1299	1276	1275	-0.4	18	524	538	560	0.6	2.37	387	391	0.2
82731	WESTON	005	179	197	215	2.3	91	69	78	88	2.9	2.53	54	60	2.5
82732	WRIGHT	005	1441	1463	1533	0.4	56	506	536	583	1.4	2.73	410	426	0.9
82801	SHERIDAN	033	22345	22629	22924	0.3	53	9425	9845	10232	1.0	2.24	5859	5956	0.4
82831	ARVADA	033	106	107	108	0.2	46	47	49	51	1.0	2.18	33	33	0.0
82832	BANNER	033	1326	1363	1385	0.7	68	598	634	660	1.4	2.15	416	429	0.7
82834	BUFFALO	019	6253	6333	6428	0.3	53	2637	2759	2879	1.1	2.26	1759	1795	0.5
82835	CLEARMONT	033	396	396	396	0.0	32	166	172	177	0.8	2.30	115	116	0.2
82836	DAYTON	033	1118	1135	1146	0.4	56	446	469	487	1.2	2.39	307	315	0.6
82838	PARKMAN	033	218	221	223	0.3	53	79	83	86	1.2	2.63	54	56	0.9
82839	RANCHESTER	033	949	951	952	0.1	34	369	383	394	0.9	2.27	269	272	0.3
82842	STORY	033	134	142	146	1.4	80	51	55	59	1.8	2.58	37	39	1.3
82844	WOLF	033	22	22	23	0.0	32	9	9	10	0.0	2.44	6	6	0.0
82901	ROCK SPRINGS	037	23877	23659	23476	-0.2	21	9217	9447	9614	0.6	2.45	6359	6374	0.1
82922	BONDURANT	035	204	226	254	2.4	94	99	114	132	3.4	1.92	70	78	2.6
82923	BOULDER	035	135	148	166	2.2	89	57	65	75	3.1	2.28	40	44	2.3
82925	CORA	035	84	93	105	2.4	94	42	48	56	3.2	1.88	30	33	2.3
82930	EVANSTON	041	13784	14110	14447	0.6	66	4770	5063	5376	1.4	2.72	3534	3678	0.9
82933	FORT BRIDGER	041	3220	3237	3286	0.1	40	1147	1210	1283	1.3	2.68	902	938	0.9
82935	GREEN RIVER	037	13017	12857	12755	-0.3	19	4611	4740	4839	0.7	2.69	3531	3561	0.2
82936	LONETREE	041	35	36	37	0.7	69	11	12	13	2.1	3.00	8	9	2.8
82937	LYMAN	041	2699	2688	2720	-0.1	25	894	934	986	1.0	2.88	701	722	0.7
82938	MC KINNON	037	193	181	175	-1.5	2	69	68	67	-0.3	2.56	57	55	-0.8
82941	PINEDALE	035	3115	3433	3850	2.3	91	1262	1438	1664	3.1	2.35	888	990	2.6
83001	JACKSON	039	13940	15148	16456	2.0	87	5754	6420	7134	2.6	2.34	3125	3372	1.8
83011	KELLY	039	143	151	162	1.3	78	64	70	77	2.1	2.16	34	36	1.4
83012	MOOSE	039	658	702	755	1.5	83	266	294	325	2.4	2.38	163	176	1.8
83013	MORAN	039	307	325	348	1.4	78	151	166	183	2.3	1.96	78	83	1.5
83014	WILSON	039	3022	3262	3531	1.8	86	1329	1478	1640	2.5	2.20	754	815	1.9
83101	KEMMERER	023	3682	3699	3888	0.1	38	1466	1535	1679	1.1	2.38	982	1000	0.4
83110	AFTON	023	4095	4364	4690	1.5	83	1336	1473	1639	2.3	2.95	1053	1139	1.9
83111	AUBURN	023	581	634	690	2.1	88	180	204	231	3.0	3.11	152	170	2.7
83112	BEDFORD	023	266	289	314	2.0	87	80	91	103	3.1	3.15	63	70	2.5
83113	BIG PINEY	035	1920	2057	2275	1.6	84	719	794	903	2.4	2.59	544	591	2.0
83114	COKEVILLE	023	913	936	985	0.6	68	306	326	356	1.5	2.87	236	247	1.1
83115	DANIEL	035	462	511	574	2.4	93	192	220	255	3.3	2.26	135	152	2.8
83118	ETNA	023	1447	1701	1925	3.9	100	573	708	837	5.1	2.40	432	523	4.6
83120	FREEDOM	023	265	301	335	3.0	99	88	105	123	4.2	2.87	70	83	4.1
83122	GROVER	023	913	1012	1111	2.5	95	327	379	434	3.5	2.66	258	293	3.0
83123	LA BARGE	023	613	624	655	0.4	59	230	244	266	1.4	2.55	161	166	0.7
83126	SMOOT	023	307	339	372	2.4	92	101	116	131	3.3	2.92	84	95	2.9
83127	THAYNE	023	1485	1659	1828	2.6	96	578	680	785	3.9	2.43	457	529	3.5
	WYOMING					0.4					1.2	2.40			0.6
	UNITED STATES					1.2					1.3	2.58			1.1

#	POST OFFICE NAME	White 2000	White 2004	Black 2000	Black 2004	Asian/Pacific 2000	Asian/Pacific 2004	% Hispanic Origin 2000	% Hispanic Origin 2004	0-4	5-9	10-14	15-19	20-24	25-44	45-64	65-84	85+	18+	MEDIAN AGE 2004	% 2004 Males	% 2004 Females
82727	ROZET	97.1	97.0	0.0	0.0	0.4	0.5	2.9	3.3	7.5	7.7	8.7	9.0	7.4	28.9	26.6	3.8	0.4	70.5	33.4	52.1	48.0
82729	SUNDANCE	97.1	96.9	0.1	0.1	0.1	0.2	0.6	0.6	4.8	5.3	6.7	6.6	5.7	21.3	29.4	17.1	3.1	78.2	44.7	49.9	50.1
82730	UPTON	96.8	96.7	0.0	0.0	0.2	0.2	1.7	1.7	6.0	6.0	5.4	7.6	7.1	20.1	31.4	14.7	1.6	78.2	43.6	49.6	50.4
82731	WESTON	96.7	97.0	0.0	0.0	0.0	0.0	2.8	3.1	7.6	7.6	8.6	8.1	7.6	27.4	27.4	5.6	0.0	70.6	33.7	52.3	47.7
82732	WRIGHT	97.5	97.3	0.0	0.0	0.1	0.1	2.6	2.9	5.7	6.0	8.3	9.9	8.3	27.7	29.1	4.7	0.3	74.0	35.7	52.4	47.6
82801	SHERIDAN	96.0	95.6	0.2	0.2	0.6	0.7	2.5	2.6	5.5	5.6	6.6	6.9	6.9	23.6	29.1	13.1	2.6	77.9	41.3	48.5	51.5
82831	ARVADA	96.2	95.3	0.0	0.0	0.0	0.9	1.9	0.9	4.7	5.6	5.6	6.5	6.5	24.3	35.5	11.2	0.0	78.5	43.3	52.3	47.7
82832	BANNER	98.4	98.3	0.1	0.1	0.2	0.2	1.5	1.6	3.7	4.2	5.5	5.5	4.6	19.4	38.8	17.1	1.3	83.2	48.6	52.5	47.5
82834	BUFFALO	96.9	96.8	0.1	0.1	0.1	0.1	2.0	2.2	5.0	5.5	6.7	6.4	5.4	20.5	31.1	16.9	2.5	78.7	45.3	49.0	51.0
82835	CLEARMONT	96.2	96.2	0.3	0.3	0.5	0.5	1.5	1.3	4.0	5.3	5.8	6.1	6.6	22.7	37.9	11.1	0.5	80.6	44.7	50.5	49.5
82836	DAYTON	94.8	94.5	0.1	0.1	0.3	0.4	3.0	3.3	4.5	5.7	8.3	8.9	3.0	23.5	33.1	11.6	1.3	75.0	42.7	49.8	50.2
82838	PARKMAN	95.0	94.1	0.0	0.0	0.5	0.5	3.2	3.2	4.5	5.4	8.1	9.1	2.7	24.0	33.5	11.3	1.4	75.6	42.8	50.2	49.8
82839	RANCHESTER	91.8	91.5	0.3	0.3	0.2	0.2	3.2	3.5	5.1	5.1	7.9	7.2	5.3	21.9	30.2	15.4	2.2	77.3	43.4	53.2	46.8
82842	STORY	97.8	97.9	0.0	0.0	0.0	0.0	1.5	1.4	4.2	4.9	6.3	5.6	4.2	20.4	37.3	15.5	1.4	80.3	47.1	51.4	48.6
82844	WOLF	95.5	100.0	0.0	0.0	0.0	0.0	0.0	0.0	4.6	9.1	9.1	9.1	0.0	27.3	36.4	4.6	0.0	77.3	40.0	45.5	54.6
82901	ROCK SPRINGS	91.6	91.0	1.0	1.0	0.9	1.0	9.0	9.6	7.0	6.6	7.3	7.6	8.7	27.6	26.1	8.1	1.1	74.6	34.4	50.1	49.9
82922	BONDURANT	98.0	97.8	0.0	0.0	0.0	0.0	2.0	1.8	4.9	5.3	5.8	5.8	4.4	23.0	34.1	14.6	2.2	79.7	45.5	48.7	51.3
82923	BOULDER	97.0	96.6	0.0	0.0	0.0	0.7	2.2	2.0	6.1	6.8	6.8	6.1	5.4	23.7	33.8	10.8	0.7	76.4	42.1	52.0	48.0
82925	CORA	97.6	97.9	0.0	0.0	0.0	0.0	2.4	2.2	5.4	5.4	5.4	6.5	4.3	23.7	32.3	15.1	2.2	78.5	44.7	49.5	50.5
82930	EVANSTON	92.9	92.4	0.1	0.2	0.4	0.5	6.6	7.1	8.6	7.8	8.1	8.8	9.1	27.1	23.6	6.1	0.7	69.7	30.8	50.3	49.7
82933	FORT BRIDGER	97.7	97.5	0.1	0.1	0.2	0.2	1.9	2.1	7.4	7.3	7.6	8.5	8.7	24.1	28.8	7.0	0.7	72.7	34.5	51.7	48.3
82935	GREEN RIVER	91.6	91.0	0.3	0.4	0.4	0.4	10.3	11.0	7.1	7.2	8.1	8.3	8.0	26.4	28.0	6.3	0.8	72.4	34.5	50.6	49.4
82936	LONETREE	97.1	100.0	0.0	0.0	0.0	0.0	0.0	0.0	5.6	5.6	5.6	11.1	5.6	22.2	44.4	0.0	0.0	80.6	40.0	52.8	47.2
82937	LYMAN	97.8	97.7	0.0	0.0	0.1	0.1	2.9	3.1	8.5	8.1	9.4	9.6	8.2	22.5	26.8	6.3	0.6	68.0	30.4	51.6	48.4
82938	MC KINNON	95.3	94.5	0.0	0.0	0.5	0.6	7.8	7.7	5.0	6.1	8.3	9.4	7.7	21.6	30.4	8.8	2.8	73.5	39.1	51.4	48.6
82941	PINEDALE	97.3	97.2	0.2	0.2	0.3	0.4	1.9	2.1	5.5	6.2	6.2	5.9	4.8	23.6	34.2	12.3	1.3	74.3	43.7	51.3	48.7
83001	JACKSON	92.4	91.8	0.2	0.2	0.6	0.7	8.1	8.7	5.0	4.9	5.3	6.3	8.0	37.4	26.1	6.3	0.7	81.1	34.7	53.3	46.7
83011	KELLY	97.2	96.7	0.0	0.0	0.7	1.3	2.1	2.0	4.6	4.6	4.6	6.0	5.3	29.8	35.8	8.0	1.3	82.1	42.1	51.7	48.3
83012	MOOSE	98.0	97.9	0.0	0.0	0.8	1.0	1.1	1.0	4.0	4.7	5.0	6.6	4.0	25.1	37.3	12.7	0.7	82.2	45.4	51.6	48.4
83013	MORAN	97.1	96.6	0.0	0.0	1.0	1.2	1.3	1.5	4.3	4.3	4.9	5.9	4.9	31.1	36.3	7.4	0.9	82.8	41.8	49.5	50.5
83014	WILSON	97.3	97.2	0.1	0.1	0.4	0.5	1.6	1.7	5.0	5.2	5.2	5.4	4.7	32.0	32.1	10.1	0.3	80.8	40.1	53.1	46.9
83101	KEMMERER	96.7	96.5	0.1	0.1	0.6	0.7	3.5	3.8	5.4	6.0	7.7	8.0	7.0	23.7	31.0	9.8	1.5	76.0	40.2	50.7	49.3
83110	AFTON	97.4	97.2	0.1	0.1	0.1	0.1	2.2	2.3	8.6	8.4	9.5	8.8	8.0	22.7	23.2	9.3	1.5	68.1	31.3	49.5	50.6
83111	AUBURN	97.1	96.9	0.0	0.0	0.2	0.2	2.1	2.4	8.4	7.9	8.7	9.3	8.8	24.0	23.2	8.8	1.0	69.6	30.3	51.3	48.7
83112	BEDFORD	97.4	96.9	0.0	0.0	0.0	0.4	1.5	1.0	7.3	7.3	9.3	8.3	8.0	22.2	24.2	12.1	1.4	70.2	35.7	50.2	49.8
83113	BIG PINEY	97.7	97.5	0.2	0.2	0.4	0.4	1.8	2.0	7.0	7.0	7.2	8.0	6.3	27.9	27.3	8.7	0.7	73.9	37.3	50.7	49.3
83114	COKEVILLE	97.3	97.0	0.3	0.3	0.2	0.3	1.6	1.7	9.0	7.3	9.2	9.0	6.5	19.2	27.5	10.0	2.4	68.3	35.8	50.1	49.9
83115	DANIEL	97.8	97.7	0.2	0.2	0.2	0.2	2.0	2.0	4.9	5.5	5.7	5.9	4.5	23.3	34.1	14.3	2.0	79.8	45.2	49.5	50.5
83118	ETNA	97.3	97.2	0.2	0.2	0.4	0.4	1.0	1.1	5.4	5.6	6.0	4.8	4.2	23.2	31.5	18.6	0.7	80.0	45.4	49.0	51.0
83120	FREEDOM	97.4	97.3	0.4	0.3	0.4	0.3	1.1	1.0	6.6	6.6	7.0	6.0	5.0	21.3	28.9	17.6	1.0	75.8	43.2	50.8	49.2
83122	GROVER	97.3	97.0	0.1	0.1	0.2	0.2	1.4	1.6	7.0	7.0	8.3	7.8	7.3	22.9	25.7	12.9	1.1	72.4	37.4	50.8	49.2
83123	LA BARGE	96.7	96.5	0.0	0.0	0.2	0.2	2.6	2.9	6.7	6.7	7.7	9.0	7.9	23.2	30.8	7.7	0.3	71.6	38.7	52.7	47.3
83126	SMOOT	97.4	97.4	0.0	0.0	0.0	0.0	2.0	2.4	9.1	8.9	10.9	10.3	8.3	23.0	21.5	7.7	0.3	64.3	28.0	49.6	50.4
83127	THAYNE	97.4	97.2	0.2	0.2	0.2	0.2	1.1	1.2	6.8	6.8	7.8	7.0	6.2	21.7	27.1	15.4	1.2	73.8	40.5	50.4	49.6
	WYOMING	92.1	91.6	0.8	0.8	0.6	0.7	6.4	6.8	6.4	6.2	7.0	7.5	8.3	26.1	26.6	10.5	1.5	76.1	36.8	50.3	49.7
	UNITED STATES	75.1	73.6	12.3	12.5	3.8	4.2	12.5	14.1	6.9	6.7	7.2	7.0	7.3	28.6	23.8	10.8	1.7	75.1	36.0	49.1	50.9

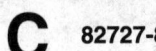

#	POST OFFICE NAME	2004 Per Capita Income	2004 HH Income Base	2004 HOUSEHOLD INCOME DISTRIBUTION (%)					MEDIAN HOUSEHOLD INCOME				2004 Home Value Base	2004 HOME VALUE DISTRIBUTION (%)					2004 Median Home Value
				Less than $25,000	$25,000 to $49,999	$50,000 to $99,999	$100,000 to $149,999	$150,000 or More	2004	2009	2004 National Centile	2004 State Centile		Less than $50,000	$50,000 to $89,999	$90,000 to $174,999	$175,000 to $399,999	$400,000 or More	
82727	ROZET	24982	268	14.6	20.9	41.8	17.9	4.9	63445	75457	87	97	241	15.4	16.2	52.3	10.0	6.2	115682
82729	SUNDANCE	23916	884	26.8	26.7	35.1	9.4	2.0	44906	55376	61	68	720	13.1	14.0	47.9	19.0	6.0	116317
82730	UPTON	22317	538	32.3	29.6	28.3	7.3	2.6	38484	47118	41	34	446	26.7	33.0	29.6	9.2	1.6	82456
82731	WESTON	24605	78	16.7	29.5	42.3	10.3	1.3	52275	60978	76	88	66	30.3	18.2	28.8	21.2	1.5	100000
82732	WRIGHT	22729	536	12.7	27.4	48.0	9.9	2.1	56081	63256	81	93	422	21.6	22.0	43.1	8.3	5.0	98710
82801	SHERIDAN	23636	9845	31.7	29.4	27.5	7.7	3.7	39444	48000	44	39	6878	10.9	16.0	44.2	24.8	4.2	121507
82831	ARVADA	25437	49	24.5	28.6	36.7	10.2	0.0	44082	53358	59	61	39	10.3	15.4	30.8	35.9	7.7	154167
82832	BANNER	27385	634	33.4	25.2	27.3	6.3	7.7	38296	49462	40	32	515	13.6	4.9	33.2	42.1	6.2	169097
82834	BUFFALO	22873	2759	29.8	32.7	28.3	5.6	3.6	39067	46430	43	37	2142	11.2	11.1	43.7	29.5	4.6	138235
82835	CLEARMONT	23760	172	27.9	29.1	32.6	9.9	0.6	41243	50356	51	50	135	9.6	13.3	31.9	35.6	9.6	160227
82836	DAYTON	21899	469	28.8	32.4	28.4	8.3	2.1	40471	51320	48	45	355	8.5	16.6	46.5	18.3	10.1	120927
82838	PARKMAN	19974	83	27.7	30.1	32.5	8.4	1.2	42999	51055	56	57	63	7.9	15.9	47.6	19.1	9.5	121094
82839	RANCHESTER	23144	383	26.6	26.6	34.7	9.1	2.9	44873	60000	61	67	293	12.6	17.1	33.8	30.0	6.5	130603
82842	STORY	27756	55	25.5	23.6	32.7	7.3	10.9	51077	61017	74	86	46	6.5	6.5	30.4	41.3	15.2	200000
82844	WOLF	11705	9	44.4	44.4	11.1	0.0	0.0	27247	40000	7	4	7	0.0	0.0	71.4	28.6	0.0	131250
82901	ROCK SPRINGS	23400	9447	22.3	26.7	37.6	11.2	2.2	50795	59887	73	85	7133	20.1	16.6	45.2	16.5	1.6	112714
82922	BONDURANT	28773	114	25.4	29.8	33.3	6.1	5.3	45000	54115	61	69	94	5.3	9.6	33.0	39.4	12.8	180556
82923	BOULDER	25029	65	26.2	32.3	27.7	9.2	4.6	44308	54473	59	63	50	6.0	6.0	42.0	34.0	12.0	162500
82925	CORA	27368	48	27.1	29.2	33.3	6.3	4.2	42374	50000	54	55	39	0.0	10.3	33.3	43.6	12.8	190625
82930	EVANSTON	20289	5063	24.4	27.0	39.0	7.5	2.2	48783	55632	70	78	3564	13.6	23.6	50.3	11.6	0.9	106129
82933	FORT BRIDGER	21738	1210	16.9	27.3	46.0	8.1	1.8	54517	60626	79	91	1014	16.9	17.7	48.2	15.7	1.6	111675
82935	GREEN RIVER	24499	4740	16.3	24.3	42.3	13.3	3.8	58603	67594	83	94	3686	14.3	12.0	53.3	18.4	2.0	122222
82936	LONETREE	18316	12	25.0	25.0	41.7	8.3	0.0	45000	61799	61	69	10	10.0	0.0	60.0	30.0	0.0	125000
82937	LYMAN	20269	934	19.8	24.3	46.8	7.9	1.2	54122	60355	79	91	780	16.7	19.5	53.5	10.1	0.3	104737
82938	MC KINNON	27280	68	10.3	25.0	47.1	14.7	2.9	65080	76708	89	99	55	0.0	3.6	49.1	38.2	9.1	171250
82941	PINEDALE	25965	1438	25.9	31.0	30.7	7.4	4.9	44786	52909	61	66	1136	7.4	8.4	36.7	35.6	12.0	168333
83001	JACKSON	39758	6420	12.6	23.3	40.0	13.8	10.4	64097	78623	88	98	3606	6.0	3.5	4.7	41.0	44.8	373633
83011	KELLY	31001	70	27.1	22.9	32.9	12.9	4.3	50000	62338	72	82	30	3.3	0.0	10.0	26.7	60.0	500000
83012	MOOSE	54760	294	22.1	18.4	29.9	11.6	18.0	60905	71633	85	95	178	2.3	0.0	3.9	15.7	78.1	1000000
83013	MORAN	31032	166	30.1	23.5	31.3	10.2	4.8	47344	56820	67	76	64	3.1	0.0	10.9	29.7	56.3	466667
83014	WILSON	103578	1478	10.8	19.6	27.3	11.3	31.0	81314	117717	95	99	1009	3.1	0.0	3.8	11.7	81.5	1000001
83101	KEMMERER	25742	1535	22.2	27.4	39.4	8.3	2.7	50253	56100	72	83	1217	19.9	27.9	47.4	4.3	0.5	92409
83110	AFTON	16831	1473	24.6	37.0	31.8	5.5	1.1	42339	48696	54	54	1231	7.2	13.6	51.9	25.4	2.0	124133
83111	AUBURN	14734	204	25.5	39.7	28.4	5.9	0.5	39366	44133	44	38	172	6.4	9.9	54.7	28.5	0.6	123214
83112	BEDFORD	16601	91	24.2	37.4	28.6	6.6	3.3	40370	45375	47	45	75	16.0	6.7	40.0	36.0	1.3	137500
83113	BIG PINEY	21182	794	21.3	34.4	33.1	8.9	2.3	44429	50923	60	63	614	19.2	24.9	39.7	13.2	2.9	101923
83114	COKEVILLE	17047	326	25.2	36.2	32.2	6.1	0.3	42376	49148	54	56	277	17.0	22.4	49.5	9.4	1.8	104647
83115	DANIEL	28616	220	26.4	30.0	31.4	6.8	5.5	44008	52175	59	60	179	5.6	10.6	34.6	36.9	12.3	172917
83118	ETNA	25899	708	15.5	32.5	38.7	10.3	3.0	51625	61093	75	86	593	6.4	5.9	34.6	47.9	5.2	181703
83120	FREEDOM	22956	105	14.3	31.4	39.1	10.5	4.8	52982	61111	77	89	89	6.7	7.9	32.6	46.1	6.7	185417
83122	GROVER	20032	379	22.7	36.9	30.6	7.7	2.1	41949	48140	53	53	315	12.1	6.7	41.9	37.1	2.2	142230
83123	LA BARGE	20957	244	23.8	29.5	36.5	7.8	2.5	46555	52434	65	73	197	33.5	21.3	32.0	10.2	3.1	80500
83126	SMOOT	15166	116	26.7	37.9	31.9	3.5	0.0	42319	47789	54	53	105	2.9	16.2	50.5	25.7	4.8	125833
83127	THAYNE	25120	680	18.1	33.4	35.3	9.0	4.3	48504	56582	69	76	571	10.3	7.2	35.9	41.0	5.6	163920
	WYOMING	23508		27.1	29.5	31.9	8.2	3.3	43736	51981				14.0	17.6	44.1	19.8	4.6	116261
	UNITED STATES	25866		24.7	27.1	30.8	10.9	6.5	48124	56710				10.9	15.0	33.7	30.1	10.4	145905

#	POST OFFICE NAME	Auto Loan	Home Loan	Invest-ments	Retire-ment Plans	Home Repair	Lawn & Garden	Comput-ers & Hard-ware	Major Appli-ances	TV, Radio, Sound Equip-ment	Furni-ture	Dine out/ Carry out	Sports Equip-ment	Fees & Tickets	Toys & Games	Travel	Cable TV	Apparel & Services	Auto Repairs	Health Insur-ance	Pets & Supplies
82727	ROZET	107	108	94	108	105	107	100	104	97	104	121	120	99	118	98	93	118	102	96	118
82729	SUNDANCE	102	71	37	67	83	93	70	87	81	70	95	105	60	93	73	85	87	86	104	121
82730	UPTON	96	67	35	63	78	87	66	82	76	65	89	98	56	87	68	80	81	80	97	114
82731	WESTON	99	90	70	86	91	96	85	92	87	87	107	107	81	103	85	87	103	91	93	111
82732	WRIGHT	87	95	95	97	92	91	90	90	85	91	107	106	91	108	88	80	105	89	79	98
82801	SHERIDAN	78	73	68	72	76	83	74	77	76	72	93	90	72	93	74	77	89	77	81	91
82831	ARVADA	100	71	38	67	82	91	70	85	80	69	94	103	60	92	72	84	86	84	101	118
82832	BANNER	100	78	53	71	88	99	74	89	84	73	99	104	66	98	79	89	92	88	105	122
82834	BUFFALO	84	67	49	64	74	84	68	77	76	67	90	89	63	88	70	79	83	76	90	97
82835	CLEARMONT	99	69	36	65	81	90	68	84	79	67	92	102	58	90	71	83	84	83	100	117
82836	DAYTON	95	66	35	63	77	87	66	81	76	65	89	98	56	87	68	79	81	80	97	113
82838	PARKMAN	95	67	35	63	78	87	66	81	76	65	89	98	56	87	68	79	81	80	97	113
82839	RANCHESTER	99	69	36	65	80	90	68	84	78	67	92	101	58	90	71	82	84	83	100	117
82842	STORY	125	93	58	86	107	120	90	109	102	89	121	129	79	119	95	108	111	108	129	150
82844	WOLF	52	36	19	34	42	47	36	44	41	35	48	53	30	47	37	43	44	44	53	61
82901	ROCK SPRINGS	85	82	76	82	83	87	82	84	81	81	101	98	80	99	81	80	97	84	83	96
82922	BONDURANT	95	75	51	67	84	95	70	85	80	70	95	99	63	93	75	85	88	84	100	116
82923	BOULDER	103	72	38	68	84	94	71	88	82	70	96	106	61	94	74	86	88	87	105	122
82925	CORA	89	69	47	63	78	88	65	79	74	65	88	92	59	87	70	79	82	78	93	108
82930	EVANSTON	81	82	78	83	80	82	80	80	77	81	97	94	79	95	78	74	94	80	74	90
82933	FORT BRIDGER	93	83	63	79	88	94	77	85	81	77	99	101	75	101	79	83	94	83	92	110
82935	GREEN RIVER	93	100	98	100	99	101	94	95	91	94	114	111	95	115	94	88	111	94	90	107
82936	LONETREE	88	78	60	74	83	89	72	80	77	72	94	96	71	96	75	79	89	78	87	104
82937	LYMAN	86	87	80	87	86	87	83	85	80	84	101	100	82	99	82	78	98	85	79	97
82938	MC KINNON	96	100	116	105	101	106	102	101	98	102	123	119	102	121	102	95	120	102	97	111
82941	PINEDALE	108	80	47	74	91	102	77	94	88	76	104	112	67	102	81	93	95	93	112	130
83001	JACKSON	134	132	142	140	129	133	135	132	130	137	165	158	133	160	130	123	161	135	120	149
83011	KELLY	110	91	67	83	101	112	85	100	94	85	112	118	78	112	90	100	105	99	116	135
83012	MOOSE	222	174	118	157	196	220	164	197	185	162	220	231	147	217	175	198	204	194	233	270
83013	MORAN	103	81	55	73	91	102	76	92	86	76	102	107	68	101	81	92	95	90	109	126
83014	WILSON	287	366	481	356	361	391	321	324	304	327	382	366	357	400	342	309	385	312	309	361
83101	KEMMERER	99	85	64	81	90	99	82	90	88	81	106	106	79	106	83	90	100	89	100	115
83110	AFTON	85	66	43	63	73	80	64	75	71	64	84	91	57	83	66	72	78	75	85	100
83111	AUBURN	83	58	30	55	67	75	57	71	66	56	77	85	49	76	59	69	70	70	84	98
83112	BEDFORD	94	67	36	63	77	87	65	81	75	65	88	97	56	87	68	79	81	79	96	112
83113	BIG PINEY	89	79	60	75	80	85	75	82	77	77	95	95	70	90	74	76	90	81	83	99
83114	COKEVILLE	88	62	32	58	72	81	61	75	70	60	82	91	52	81	63	74	75	74	90	105
83115	DANIEL	112	87	57	79	98	110	82	99	93	81	110	117	73	109	87	99	102	98	118	136
83118	ETNA	106	83	56	75	93	105	78	94	88	77	105	110	70	103	83	94	97	93	111	129
83120	FREEDOM	112	87	59	79	98	111	83	100	93	82	111	117	74	109	88	100	103	98	118	136
83122	GROVER	95	69	39	64	79	89	67	82	76	66	90	98	58	88	70	81	82	81	97	113
83123	LA BARGE	85	78	61	75	78	82	74	79	75	76	93	92	70	87	73	74	89	79	79	94
83126	SMOOT	62	68	68	69	66	65	65	64	60	65	76	76	65	77	63	57	75	64	56	70
83127	THAYNE	106	80	50	73	91	102	77	93	87	76	103	110	67	101	81	93	95	92	110	128
	WYOMING	86	78	71	77	81	87	79	82	81	78	99	97	76	98	78	81	95	83	85	98
	UNITED STATES	100	100	100	100	100	100	100	100	100	100	100	100	100	100	100	100	100	100	100	100

State Summary Data

The Community
Sourcebook
of ZIP Code
Demographics

2004
18th EDITION

POPULATION CHANGE
STATE AND U.S. TOTALS

A

STATE	State FIPS Code	POPULATION			2000-2004 ANNUAL RATE		RACE (%)					
							White		Black		Asian/Pacific	
		2000	2004	2009	% Rate	State Rank	2000	2004	2000	2004	2000	2004
ALABAMA	01	4,447,100	4,532,319	4,630,437	0.5	42	71.1	70.3	26.0	26.4	0.7	0.9
ALASKA	02	626,932	666,489	720,599	1.5	11	69.3	68.2	3.5	3.3	4.5	4.6
ARIZONA	04	5,130,632	5,746,102	6,580,726	2.7	2	75.5	74.0	3.1	3.2	1.9	2.1
ARKANSAS	05	2,673,400	2,779,891	2,914,799	0.9	22	80.0	79.3	15.7	15.8	0.8	1.0
CALIFORNIA	06	33,871,648	35,874,307	38,325,663	1.4	15	59.6	57.1	6.7	6.5	11.3	11.8
COLORADO	08	4,301,261	4,758,713	5,381,452	2.4	3	82.8	81.7	3.8	3.9	2.3	2.6
CONNECTICUT	09	3,405,565	3,475,008	3,563,632	0.5	40	81.6	80.0	9.1	9.5	2.5	3.1
DELAWARE	10	783,600	831,181	892,695	1.4	13	74.6	72.8	19.2	20.0	2.1	2.7
DISTRICT OF COLUMBIA	11	572,059	566,957	561,065	-0.2	51	30.8	31.6	60.0	57.0	2.7	3.3
FLORIDA	12	15,982,378	17,463,048	19,468,615	2.1	6	78.0	76.5	14.6	15.2	1.7	2.0
GEORGIA	13	8,186,453	9,052,085	10,256,467	2.4	4	65.1	63.4	28.7	29.4	2.2	2.5
HAWAII	15	1,211,537	1,249,329	1,289,718	0.7	33	24.3	24.4	1.8	2.1	51.0	50.4
IDAHO	16	1,293,953	1,394,540	1,520,297	1.8	9	91.0	90.3	0.4	0.5	1.0	1.2
ILLINOIS	17	12,419,293	12,802,243	13,322,810	0.7	34	73.5	71.8	15.1	15.2	3.5	4.0
INDIANA	18	6,080,485	6,286,453	6,556,095	0.8	29	87.5	86.7	8.4	8.7	1.0	1.3
IOWA	19	2,926,324	2,984,964	3,062,563	0.5	41	93.9	93.0	2.1	2.3	1.3	1.8
KANSAS	20	2,688,418	2,773,227	2,885,377	0.7	33	86.1	84.9	5.7	5.8	1.8	2.2
KENTUCKY	21	4,041,769	4,161,887	4,306,061	0.7	35	90.1	89.5	7.3	7.4	0.8	1.0
LOUISIANA	22	4,468,976	4,594,531	4,758,818	0.7	36	63.9	62.8	32.5	33.2	1.3	1.5
MAINE	23	1,274,923	1,323,312	1,383,992	0.9	24	97.0	96.6	0.5	0.6	0.7	0.9
MARYLAND	24	5,296,486	5,543,441	5,861,898	1.1	20	64.0	61.8	27.9	28.9	4.0	4.6
MASSACHUSETTS	25	6,349,097	6,448,526	6,572,355	0.4	46	84.5	82.9	5.4	5.7	3.8	4.5
MICHIGAN	26	9,938,444	10,203,863	10,543,750	0.6	37	80.2	79.2	14.2	14.4	1.8	2.3
MINNESOTA	27	4,919,479	5,215,595	5,625,678	1.4	14	89.5	88.0	3.5	4.2	2.9	3.4
MISSISSIPPI	28	2,844,658	2,918,131	3,008,345	0.6	38	61.4	60.6	36.3	36.8	0.7	0.8
MISSOURI	29	5,595,211	5,778,759	6,019,439	0.8	30	84.9	84.1	11.3	11.5	1.2	1.4
MONTANA	30	902,195	917,958	936,693	0.4	44	90.6	90.2	0.3	0.3	0.6	0.7
NEBRASKA	31	1,711,263	1,766,814	1,840,111	0.8	31	89.6	88.4	4.0	4.2	1.3	1.8
NEVADA	32	1,998,257	2,366,908	2,889,834	4.1	1	75.2	73.9	6.8	7.0	4.9	4.8
NEW HAMPSHIRE	33	1,235,786	1,316,126	1,424,122	1.5	10	96.0	95.6	0.7	0.8	1.3	1.7
NEW JERSEY	34	8,414,350	8,705,645	9,075,938	0.8	28	72.6	70.5	13.6	13.8	5.8	6.6
NEW MEXICO	35	1,819,046	1,915,323	2,040,999	1.2	17	66.8	65.8	1.9	2.0	1.1	1.3
NEW YORK	36	18,976,457	19,316,116	19,744,526	0.4	43	68.0	65.9	15.9	16.2	5.6	6.4
NORTH CAROLINA	37	8,049,313	8,701,483	9,577,600	1.9	7	72.1	71.2	21.6	21.6	1.5	1.8
NORTH DAKOTA	38	642,200	643,802	648,150	0.1	50	92.4	91.7	0.6	0.7	0.6	0.8
OHIO	39	11,353,140	11,473,289	11,634,068	0.3	48	85.0	84.1	11.5	11.8	1.2	1.6
OKLAHOMA	40	3,450,654	3,570,756	3,726,372	0.8	27	76.2	74.8	7.6	7.7	1.4	1.8
OREGON	41	3,421,399	3,581,202	3,770,744	1.1	20	86.6	85.2	1.6	1.7	3.2	3.6
PENNSYLVANIA	42	12,281,054	12,439,617	12,641,307	0.3	47	85.4	84.4	10.0	10.3	1.8	2.2
RHODE ISLAND	44	1,048,319	1,070,807	1,098,909	0.5	39	85.0	83.4	4.5	4.7	2.3	2.8
SOUTH CAROLINA	45	4,012,012	4,226,172	4,489,548	1.2	16	67.2	66.6	29.5	29.5	0.9	1.2
SOUTH DAKOTA	46	754,844	784,601	825,988	0.9	23	88.7	87.8	0.6	0.7	0.6	0.8
TENNESSEE	47	5,689,283	5,928,850	6,215,995	1.0	21	80.2	79.4	16.4	16.7	1.0	1.3
TEXAS	48	20,851,820	22,859,965	25,651,869	2.2	5	71.0	69.5	11.5	11.4	2.8	3.1
UTAH	49	2,233,169	2,413,090	2,650,538	1.8	8	89.2	88.6	0.8	0.9	2.3	2.5
VERMONT	50	608,827	630,054	657,496	0.8	27	96.8	96.4	0.5	0.6	0.9	1.1
VIRGINIA	51	7,078,515	7,510,923	8,110,520	1.4	13	72.3	70.7	19.6	19.9	3.7	4.3
WASHINGTON	53	5,894,121	6,185,300	6,495,635	1.1	18	81.8	80.6	3.2	3.3	5.9	6.3
WEST VIRGINIA	54	1,808,344	1,823,000	1,842,700	0.2	49	95.1	94.8	3.2	3.2	0.5	0.7
WISCONSIN	55	5,363,675	5,553,428	5,793,397	0.8	25	88.9	88.0	5.7	6.0	1.7	2.1
WYOMING	56	493,782	502,223	512,443	0.4	45	92.1	91.6	0.8	0.8	0.6	0.7
UNITED STATES					1.2		75.1	73.6	12.3	12.5	3.8	4.2

POPULATION COMPOSITION
STATE AND U.S. TOTALS

B

STATE	% HISPANIC ORIGIN		2004 AGE DISTRIBUTION (%)										MEDIAN AGE	% 2004 Males	% 2004 Females
	2000	2004	0-4	5-9	10-14	15-19	20-24	25-44	45-64	65-84	85+	18+	2004	2004	2004
ALABAMA	1.7	2.1	6.7	6.7	7.0	6.8	7.2	28.0	24.5	11.6	1.6	75.8	36.6	48.5	51.5
ALASKA	4.1	4.7	7.6	7.3	8.3	8.1	8.1	29.3	25.1	5.8	0.5	71.7	32.9	51.4	48.6
ARIZONA	25.3	27.9	7.6	7.1	7.3	6.9	7.5	28.1	22.1	11.9	1.5	74.0	34.8	49.9	50.2
ARKANSAS	3.3	3.8	6.9	6.7	6.9	6.8	7.3	27.3	24.1	12.2	1.8	75.7	36.7	49.0	51.0
CALIFORNIA	32.4	35.5	7.4	7.1	7.8	7.3	7.7	29.8	22.1	9.3	1.4	73.3	33.8	49.8	50.2
COLORADO	17.1	18.6	7.0	6.8	7.1	7.0	7.5	30.6	24.3	8.6	1.2	75.1	35.0	50.3	49.7
CONNECTICUT	9.4	10.5	6.4	6.7	7.1	6.9	6.3	27.5	25.4	11.7	2.2	75.8	38.5	48.5	51.5
DELAWARE	4.8	5.4	6.6	6.6	7.0	7.0	7.1	28.2	24.3	11.8	1.5	76.0	37.0	48.6	51.4
DISTRICT OF COLUMBIA	7.9	10.6	5.6	5.5	6.0	7.1	8.2	32.1	23.2	10.6	1.7	79.8	35.4	47.1	52.9
FLORIDA	16.8	19.0	6.0	5.9	6.4	6.4	6.5	26.6	24.5	15.5	2.4	78.1	40.0	48.8	51.2
GEORGIA	5.3	6.6	7.3	7.1	7.2	7.0	7.6	31.0	23.0	8.6	1.1	74.3	34.2	49.3	50.7
HAWAII	7.2	7.9	6.5	6.3	6.8	6.6	7.5	28.4	24.5	11.7	1.7	76.5	36.9	50.1	49.9
IDAHO	7.9	8.8	7.8	7.4	7.7	7.7	7.9	27.3	23.1	9.6	1.5	72.7	33.5	50.1	49.9
ILLINOIS	12.3	14.2	7.1	7.0	7.3	7.0	7.3	29.0	23.2	10.4	1.7	74.5	35.2	49.0	51.0
INDIANA	3.5	4.1	7.0	6.9	7.1	7.1	7.4	28.1	24.0	10.8	1.6	75.0	35.9	49.2	50.8
IOWA	2.8	3.2	6.5	6.5	6.9	7.2	7.6	26.4	24.2	12.3	2.4	76.0	37.2	49.2	50.8
KANSAS	7.0	8.1	7.1	7.0	7.2	7.5	7.6	27.3	23.4	10.9	2.0	74.4	35.6	49.5	50.5
KENTUCKY	1.5	1.9	6.6	6.6	6.8	6.6	7.0	28.9	24.8	11.1	1.5	76.3	36.8	49.1	50.9
LOUISIANA	2.4	2.6	7.2	7.0	7.4	7.5	7.9	28.0	23.4	10.3	1.4	74.1	34.6	48.5	51.5
MAINE	0.7	0.9	5.5	5.8	6.7	6.9	6.5	26.7	27.5	12.5	2.0	77.9	40.2	48.8	51.2
MARYLAND	4.3	5.1	6.6	6.7	7.3	6.9	6.6	29.1	25.1	10.2	1.5	75.2	37.0	48.3	51.7
MASSACHUSETTS	6.8	7.8	6.2	6.3	6.8	7.0	7.0	28.9	24.5	11.4	2.1	76.8	37.6	48.3	51.7
MICHIGAN	3.3	3.6	6.8	6.9	7.4	7.1	6.9	28.1	24.6	10.8	1.6	74.9	36.5	49.1	50.9
MINNESOTA	2.9	3.4	6.8	6.8	7.2	7.3	7.4	28.6	23.9	10.1	1.9	74.9	36.1	49.6	50.5
MISSISSIPPI	1.4	1.6	7.3	7.1	7.4	7.4	7.8	27.8	23.0	10.6	1.6	73.9	34.5	48.5	51.5
MISSOURI	2.1	2.3	6.7	6.6	7.0	7.0	7.3	27.6	24.2	11.7	1.9	75.6	36.8	48.7	51.3
MONTANA	2.0	2.2	6.1	6.2	7.1	7.5	7.2	25.5	27.0	11.7	1.9	76.2	38.5	49.9	50.1
NEBRASKA	5.5	6.4	7.0	6.9	7.2	7.3	7.6	27.5	23.5	11.2	2.1	74.8	35.7	49.4	50.6
NEVADA	19.7	22.0	7.3	6.9	7.1	6.5	7.0	29.9	23.8	10.6	1.0	74.8	35.6	50.6	49.4
NEW HAMPSHIRE	1.7	1.9	6.1	6.4	7.2	7.2	6.6	27.8	26.5	10.6	1.6	76.2	38.4	49.2	50.8
NEW JERSEY	13.3	15.0	6.6	6.7	7.1	6.5	6.3	28.8	24.6	11.5	1.9	75.6	37.7	48.6	51.4
NEW MEXICO	42.1	42.7	7.3	7.1	7.6	7.7	7.7	26.9	23.9	10.4	1.4	73.4	34.9	50.9	
NEW YORK	15.1	16.7	6.5	6.5	7.1	7.0	7.1	28.9	24.0	11.2	1.8	75.8	36.7	48.3	51.7
NORTH CAROLINA	4.7	5.9	6.7	6.6	6.8	6.7	7.1	29.8	24.2	10.8	1.4	76.2	36.2	49.2	50.8
NORTH DAKOTA	1.2	1.4	6.3	6.1	6.8	7.9	8.5	26.2	23.9	12.0	2.4	76.5	36.5	50.0	50.0
OHIO	1.9	2.1	6.7	6.6	7.1	7.0	7.1	27.5	24.7	11.6	1.8	75.6	37.0	48.6	51.4
OKLAHOMA	5.2	5.8	7.0	6.7	7.0	7.1	7.8	27.2	24.0	11.6	1.7	75.3	36.0	49.3	50.8
OREGON	8.1	9.5	6.5	6.4	6.8	6.9	7.4	27.7	25.6	11.0	1.9	76.3	36.9	49.6	50.4
PENNSYLVANIA	3.2	3.5	5.9	6.1	6.8	6.9	6.7	26.6	25.3	13.3	2.2	77.2	39.1	48.4	51.6
RHODE ISLAND	8.7	10.0	6.1	6.1	6.8	7.4	7.3	27.6	24.4	12.1	2.3	77.1	37.7	48.2	51.8
SOUTH CAROLINA	2.4	2.9	6.6	6.6	7.0	7.1	7.3	28.4	24.7	11.0	1.4	75.9	36.3	48.8	51.2
SOUTH DAKOTA	1.4	1.6	7.0	6.8	7.3	7.7	7.9	26.1	23.4	11.7	2.2	74.5	35.9	49.7	50.3
TENNESSEE	2.2	2.6	6.6	6.5	6.8	6.6	7.0	29.0	24.8	11.1	1.5	76.3	36.8	48.9	51.1
TEXAS	32.0	34.6	7.9	7.5	7.7	7.5	8.1	29.6	21.9	8.7	1.2	72.6	32.9	49.7	50.3
UTAH	9.0	10.0	9.9	8.8	8.3	8.3	9.3	29.3	17.7	7.2	1.0	68.3	27.9	50.0	50.0
VERMONT	0.9	1.0	5.5	5.9	6.9	7.5	7.2	26.5	27.5	11.2	1.8	77.5	39.1	49.1	50.9
VIRGINIA	4.7	5.7	6.5	6.6	6.9	6.9	7.0	29.7	24.9	10.1	1.4	76.2	36.6	49.1	50.9
WASHINGTON	7.5	8.6	6.7	6.6	7.1	7.0	7.6	28.7	24.9	9.8	1.6	75.4	36.1	49.7	50.3
WEST VIRGINIA	0.7	0.7	5.6	5.8	6.2	6.3	6.7	26.7	27.1	13.7	1.9	78.9	40.1	48.8	51.2
WISCONSIN	3.6	4.0	6.4	6.5	7.1	7.3	7.7	27.6	24.5	11.1	1.9	75.8	36.9	49.5	50.5
WYOMING	6.4	6.8	6.4	6.2	7.0	7.5	8.3	26.1	26.6	10.5	1.5	76.1	36.8	50.3	49.7
UNITED STATES	12.5	14.1	6.9	6.7	7.2	7.0	7.3	28.6	23.8	10.8	1.7	75.1	36.0	49.1	50.9

STATE	HOUSEHOLDS					FAMILIES			MEDIAN HOUSEHOLD INCOME		
	2000	2004	2009	% Annual Rate 2000-2004	2004 Average HH Size	2000	2004	% Annual Rate 2000-2004	2004	2009	2004 National Rank
ALABAMA	1,737,080	1,804,880	1,876,911	0.9	2.45	1,215,968	1,262,697	0.9	37,534	42,371	47
ALASKA	221,600	236,958	257,838	1.6	2.73	152,337	163,485	1.7	59,655	71,504	5
ARIZONA	1,901,327	2,133,090	2,445,631	2.7	2.64	1,287,367	1,452,416	2.9	49,168	61,784	19
ARKANSAS	1,042,696	1,094,167	1,157,262	1.1	2.47	732,261	756,246	0.8	37,742	46,417	46
CALIFORNIA	11,502,870	12,094,865	12,828,958	1.2	2.90	7,920,049	8,316,484	1.2	54,267	64,547	11
COLORADO	1,658,238	1,848,148	2,099,951	2.6	2.52	1,084,461	1,205,901	2.5	54,077	63,465	12
CONNECTICUT	1,301,670	1,340,803	1,387,811	0.7	2.51	881,170	900,068	0.5	61,358	72,202	2
DELAWARE	298,736	320,503	348,331	1.7	2.52	204,590	216,140	1.3	54,581	65,195	10
DISTRICT OF COLUMBIA	248,338	247,605	246,674	-0.1	2.15	114,166	114,067	0.0	45,445	53,484	31
FLORIDA	6,337,929	6,958,444	7,795,987	2.2	2.45	4,210,760	4,588,114	2.0	44,138	51,288	33
GEORGIA	3,006,369	3,339,872	3,798,970	2.5	2.64	2,111,647	2,318,618	2.2	50,024	60,470	17
HAWAII	403,240	424,620	446,632	1.2	2.86	287,068	297,840	0.9	55,724	64,555	8
IDAHO	469,645	513,515	566,581	2.1	2.65	335,588	361,598	1.8	42,682	49,896	37
ILLINOIS	4,591,779	4,773,156	5,001,496	0.9	2.61	3,105,513	3,186,039	0.6	52,039	60,941	14
INDIANA	2,336,306	2,460,391	2,607,848	1.2	2.48	1,602,501	1,625,811	0.3	45,964	52,146	26
IOWA	1,149,276	1,183,517	1,225,592	0.7	2.43	769,684	789,231	0.6	45,622	53,985	29
KANSAS	1,037,891	1,080,736	1,133,855	1.0	2.49	701,547	724,560	0.8	47,540	57,348	23
KENTUCKY	1,590,647	1,671,427	1,760,827	1.2	2.42	1,104,398	1,125,659	0.5	39,962	49,361	43
LOUISIANA	1,656,053	1,722,187	1,805,385	0.9	2.59	1,156,438	1,204,025	1.0	36,550	42,223	48
MAINE	518,200	552,593	592,416	1.5	2.33	340,685	364,227	1.6	40,864	45,987	40
MARYLAND	1,980,859	2,078,454	2,204,212	1.1	2.60	1,359,318	1,415,954	1.0	59,732	70,285	4
MASSACHUSETTS	2,443,580	2,507,136	2,579,843	0.6	2.48	1,576,696	1,619,058	0.6	61,110	77,759	3
MICHIGAN	3,785,661	3,944,166	4,133,985	1.0	2.52	2,575,699	2,647,042	0.6	48,729	54,505	21
MINNESOTA	1,895,127	2,030,467	2,212,062	1.6	2.50	1,255,141	1,310,874	1.0	56,724	71,660	7
MISSISSIPPI	1,046,434	1,099,244	1,157,715	1.2	2.57	747,159	777,501	0.9	34,621	39,377	50
MISSOURI	2,194,594	2,279,967	2,389,171	0.9	2.46	1,476,516	1,504,369	0.4	44,017	52,626	34
MONTANA	358,667	368,761	379,990	0.7	2.42	237,407	240,014	0.3	36,188	40,555	49
NEBRASKA	666,184	695,266	731,399	1.0	2.47	443,411	464,146	1.1	45,453	54,516	30
NEVADA	751,165	885,378	1,074,531	3.9	2.64	498,333	584,403	3.8	51,572	61,335	15
NEW HAMPSHIRE	474,606	513,433	564,311	1.9	2.49	323,651	349,064	1.8	57,516	70,005	6
NEW JERSEY	3,064,645	3,177,835	3,321,779	0.9	2.68	2,154,539	2,246,778	1.0	61,437	70,239	1
NEW MEXICO	677,971	730,075	794,343	1.8	2.57	466,515	492,708	1.3	38,669	45,233	44
NEW YORK	7,056,860	7,199,044	7,375,087	0.5	2.60	4,639,387	4,710,094	0.4	49,309	58,077	18
NORTH CAROLINA	3,132,013	3,432,329	3,827,074	2.2	2.46	2,158,869	2,329,948	1.8	43,794	50,711	35
NORTH DAKOTA	257,152	265,628	274,612	0.8	2.33	166,150	165,268	-0.1	40,503	48,701	42
OHIO	4,445,773	4,575,681	4,717,323	0.7	2.44	2,993,023	2,996,388	0.0	47,354	56,168	24
OKLAHOMA	1,342,293	1,397,158	1,466,623	1.0	2.48	921,750	956,616	0.9	38,589	46,268	45
OREGON	1,333,723	1,399,425	1,477,034	1.1	2.50	877,671	916,205	1.0	45,702	52,201	28
PENNSYLVANIA	4,777,003	4,920,131	5,077,413	0.7	2.44	3,208,388	3,286,275	0.6	46,988	57,000	25
RHODE ISLAND	408,424	420,188	434,504	0.7	2.46	265,398	271,551	0.5	48,328	57,374	22
SOUTH CAROLINA	1,533,854	1,656,028	1,800,185	1.8	2.47	1,072,822	1,125,968	1.1	42,042	49,103	39
SOUTH DAKOTA	290,245	306,669	327,756	1.3	2.47	194,330	206,165	1.4	42,239	52,729	38
TENNESSEE	2,232,905	2,361,619	2,509,099	1.3	2.45	1,547,835	1,605,714	0.9	40,531	46,137	41
TEXAS	7,393,354	8,040,131	8,956,850	2.0	2.77	5,247,794	5,730,008	2.1	45,778	54,246	27
UTAH	701,281	768,094	853,666	2.2	3.09	535,294	577,620	1.8	52,040	61,244	13
VERMONT	240,634	254,085	270,405	1.3	2.40	157,763	165,769	1.2	44,976	50,578	32
VIRGINIA	2,699,173	2,896,706	3,158,378	1.7	2.51	1,847,796	1,963,070	1.4	55,216	67,801	9
WASHINGTON	2,271,398	2,396,016	2,525,564	1.3	2.52	1,499,127	1,574,238	1.2	50,585	57,953	16
WEST VIRGINIA	736,481	756,547	779,257	0.6	2.35	504,055	498,582	-0.3	33,458	38,993	51
WISCONSIN	2,084,544	2,212,359	2,361,846	1.4	2.44	1,386,815	1,452,271	1.1	48,930	56,561	20
WYOMING	193,608	203,477	213,668	1.2	2.40	130,497	133,945	0.6	43,736	51,981	36
UNITED STATES				1.3	2.58			1.1	48,124	56,710	

INCOME
STATE AND U.S. TOTALS

D

STATE	2004 Per Capita Income	2004 HH Income Base	2004 HOUSEHOLD INCOME DISTRIBUTION (%) Less than $25,000	$25,000 to $49,999	$50,000 to $99,999	$100,000 to $149,999	$150,000 or More	2004 Home Value Base	2004 HOME VALUE DISTRIBUTION (%) Less than $50,000	$50,000 to $89,999	$90,000 to $174,999	$175,000 to $399,999	$400,000 or More	2004 Median Home Value
ALABAMA	20,998	1,804,878	34.3	28.7	26.3	7.2	3.5	1,330,034	22.7	26.7	33.4	14.6	2.7	90,917
ALASKA	27,197	236,958	17.6	24.1	35.4	15.1	7.8	154,256	9.9	7.9	33.8	43.8	4.6	171,678
ARIZONA	25,625	2,133,035	22.8	27.9	31.5	11.3	6.4	1,472,628	9.8	13.0	42.4	28.8	6.1	140,071
ARKANSAS	20,565	1,094,166	33.0	30.6	26.7	6.4	3.3	780,577	27.1	29.3	31.4	10.3	1.8	80,466
CALIFORNIA	27,293	12,094,665	21.8	24.4	30.5	13.7	9.7	7,100,604	3.3	2.7	13.3	42.9	37.9	319,678
COLORADO	28,803	1,848,125	19.1	26.9	34.1	12.5	7.5	1,273,466	4.8	4.7	28.0	49.9	12.6	203,984
CONNECTICUT	34,999	1,340,797	18.8	22.0	32.8	15.1	11.4	924,967	1.5	2.7	24.6	51.4	19.8	230,968
DELAWARE	28,477	320,503	19.6	25.7	34.1	13.2	7.3	238,378	7.3	7.1	39.1	41.1	5.4	167,398
DISTRICT OF COLUMBIA	34,983	247,596	28.5	25.6	24.7	11.1	10.1	105,869	0.6	1.8	21.7	44.7	31.2	256,143
FLORIDA	25,506	6,958,368	26.4	29.9	29.1	9.1	5.6	4,953,136	8.8	15.8	40.2	28.3	7.0	137,042
GEORGIA	26,143	3,339,856	23.6	26.3	31.4	11.6	7.0	2,323,505	12.5	17.5	39.3	24.8	6.0	125,860
HAWAII	25,763	424,610	20.1	24.4	33.2	14.5	7.9	247,950	1.5	1.9	12.2	44.3	40.1	348,617
IDAHO	21,160	513,511	26.4	31.8	30.4	7.9	3.5	381,719	9.8	16.8	49.1	20.6	3.6	122,288
ILLINOIS	27,033	4,773,056	22.1	25.9	32.9	11.9	7.3	3,339,425	7.7	12.8	34.0	36.6	8.9	162,771
INDIANA	23,565	2,460,340	24.7	29.6	32.4	9.4	3.9	1,768,436	12.3	23.5	44.9	16.9	2.4	109,048
IOWA	23,554	1,183,517	24.6	30.5	32.9	8.4	3.7	859,068	17.5	26.2	39.3	15.0	2.1	98,835
KANSAS	25,137	1,080,727	23.6	29.0	32.2	10.1	5.1	762,508	21.4	24.4	35.0	16.7	2.5	97,470
KENTUCKY	22,472	1,671,415	31.8	28.3	28.2	7.8	3.9	1,202,289	22.2	24.9	36.4	14.3	2.1	94,344
LOUISIANA	19,601	1,722,137	35.3	28.5	25.7	7.1	3.5	1,173,145	22.5	24.5	35.6	15.0	2.4	94,005
MAINE	22,411	552,589	29.6	30.7	30.0	6.5	3.2	393,486	8.5	14.0	43.9	28.6	5.1	138,610
MARYLAND	30,267	2,078,407	17.9	23.3	34.6	15.0	9.2	1,452,058	2.9	5.4	28.1	49.8	13.8	209,514
MASSACHUSETTS	33,908	2,507,120	19.9	21.2	32.0	16.1	10.9	1,592,398	0.8	1.2	14.8	55.7	27.5	282,585
MICHIGAN	25,281	3,944,122	23.8	27.4	32.3	10.9	5.5	2,925,251	10.7	16.0	40.3	28.0	5.0	134,769
MINNESOTA	29,624	2,030,465	18.6	25.2	34.9	14.0	7.4	1,538,279	6.6	9.7	36.5	40.5	6.8	168,676
MISSISSIPPI	18,480	1,099,242	36.7	30.0	24.5	5.9	2.8	794,273	29.7	30.4	28.7	9.7	1.6	75,922
MISSOURI	23,864	2,279,941	27.0	29.4	30.1	9.0	4.5	1,605,727	15.2	22.7	39.0	19.7	3.4	109,184
MONTANA	19,326	368,751	33.9	32.7	25.9	5.0	2.5	255,314	14.7	16.4	40.8	23.3	4.9	122,379
NEBRASKA	23,743	695,264	24.5	30.5	31.8	9.2	4.0	470,106	17.2	23.9	42.4	14.4	2.2	101,398
NEVADA	26,208	885,360	20.5	27.7	34.5	11.4	5.9	554,060	5.9	5.6	38.5	43.5	6.6	175,101
NEW HAMPSHIRE	29,464	513,433	17.9	24.8	36.4	13.6	7.4	361,336	4.4	5.2	30.9	50.1	9.4	196,454
NEW JERSEY	31,614	3,177,786	18.6	22.5	32.1	15.5	11.4	2,104,033	1.5	2.7	19.7	54.4	21.8	255,213
NEW MEXICO	20,647	730,055	31.7	30.6	26.4	7.4	3.8	508,150	18.9	17.7	37.6	21.5	4.4	113,735
NEW YORK	28,049	7,198,870	26.3	24.3	29.3	11.5	8.6	3,903,800	4.6	8.6	27.2	39.9	19.8	219,050
NORTH CAROLINA	23,743	3,432,329	27.0	29.8	30.1	8.5	4.7	2,391,156	14.5	20.0	39.7	21.7	4.1	115,673
NORTH DAKOTA	22,058	265,624	29.0	31.5	29.9	6.6	3.0	177,101	27.7	27.3	34.9	9.3	0.9	83,011
OHIO	25,510	4,575,660	24.6	28.1	32.2	10.1	5.0	3,191,403	9.2	18.6	47.0	22.1	3.1	121,192
OKLAHOMA	21,077	1,397,148	31.9	30.4	27.2	7.1	3.4	949,023	26.7	29.5	32.0	10.2	1.6	81,000
OREGON	24,176	1,399,424	24.9	29.7	31.4	9.2	4.8	910,922	6.4	6.5	35.2	43.4	8.6	179,540
PENNSYLVANIA	25,764	4,920,106	25.8	27.2	31.2	10.2	5.7	3,506,208	11.9	18.4	40.7	25.1	4.1	123,516
RHODE ISLAND	25,865	420,188	26.5	25.0	31.6	11.2	5.7	250,873	1.0	1.3	25.3	60.5	11.9	218,642
SOUTH CAROLINA	22,607	1,656,015	28.8	29.3	29.6	8.3	4.0	1,206,051	19.3	24.1	35.5	17.1	3.9	100,170
SOUTH DAKOTA	22,046	306,665	27.6	30.9	31.1	7.0	3.4	210,082	25.5	24.3	36.2	12.2	1.8	90,416
TENNESSEE	22,498	2,361,612	30.2	30.2	28.1	7.5	4.1	1,662,234	15.0	25.0	39.4	17.3	3.3	104,905
TEXAS	23,284	8,040,021	26.2	27.7	29.5	10.3	6.3	5,150,335	21.6	26.1	33.4	15.6	3.4	93,683
UTAH	21,907	768,090	18.7	28.9	35.1	11.8	5.5	552,580	4.3	6.7	48.5	35.1	5.4	159,338
VERMONT	23,579	254,085	25.6	30.1	32.7	7.7	3.9	182,382	5.7	9.3	47.1	32.6	5.3	151,623
VIRGINIA	30,454	2,896,691	19.8	25.2	32.5	13.6	8.9	1,992,601	6.8	10.4	35.8	36.5	10.5	166,226
WASHINGTON	26,555	2,396,001	21.6	27.8	33.4	11.4	5.9	1,586,491	4.6	5.9	31.3	45.6	12.6	195,701
WEST VIRGINIA	19,262	756,547	38.4	30.0	24.1	5.2	2.4	577,602	29.0	29.1	31.1	9.6	1.3	80,023
WISCONSIN	25,041	2,212,350	22.2	28.8	35.0	9.6	4.2	1,535,061	7.0	14.9	46.8	27.8	3.6	134,326
WYOMING	23,508	203,474	27.1	29.5	31.9	8.2	3.3	145,378	14.0	17.6	44.1	19.8	4.6	116,261
UNITED STATES	25,866		24.7	27.1	30.8	10.9	6.5		10.9	15.0	33.7	30.1	10.4	145,905

SPENDING POTENTIAL INDICES
STATE AND U.S. TOTALS

STATE	FINANCIAL SERVICES				THE HOME						ENTERTAINMENT						PERSONAL			
					Home Improvements		Furnishings													
	Auto Loan	Home Loan	Invest-ments	Retire-ment Plans	Home Repair	Lawn & Garden	Comput-ers & Hard-ware	Major Appli-ances	TV, Radio, Sound Equip-ment	Furni-ture	Dine out/ Carry out	Sports Equip-ment	Fees & Tickets	Toys & Games	Travel	Cable TV	Apparel & Services	Auto Repairs	Health Insur-ance	Pets & Supplies
ALABAMA	81	70	61	67	72	80	70	75	75	70	91	87	67	89	70	76	86	75	81	92
ALASKA	106	108	111	111	106	109	107	106	104	108	130	126	107	129	105	100	128	107	98	120
ARIZONA	97	96	98	96	95	101	96	97	95	98	119	111	95	114	95	93	116	98	95	108
ARKANSAS	81	69	57	66	72	80	69	75	74	69	90	87	65	87	69	76	85	75	82	92
CALIFORNIA	107	111	131	112	109	115	113	111	111	114	140	129	114	141	112	109	139	113	104	122
COLORADO	103	104	110	107	103	108	105	104	102	105	128	122	104	127	103	99	125	105	98	116
CONNECTICUT	116	129	153	129	127	135	127	124	124	126	156	144	132	161	128	124	154	124	119	137
DELAWARE	104	103	104	102	103	110	102	103	102	102	127	120	102	126	102	102	123	104	103	119
DISTRICT OF COLUMBIA	102	98	146	100	94	108	109	102	114	110	144	118	112	145	108	116	141	107	103	115
FLORIDA	89	87	95	86	87	96	87	89	89	89	111	100	87	107	88	90	108	90	91	101
GEORGIA	103	97	95	97	97	104	97	99	98	98	122	116	96	120	96	98	118	100	99	116
HAWAII	94	105	138	115	107	104	111	108	100	107	126	137	107	123	110	92	125	114	91	115
IDAHO	84	79	73	78	80	85	79	81	79	78	98	96	76	97	78	78	94	81	82	96
ILLINOIS	98	100	111	99	99	106	100	99	101	100	126	115	102	127	100	100	123	100	98	112
INDIANA	86	83	80	82	84	90	82	84	84	82	103	98	82	104	82	84	100	84	86	98
IOWA	87	79	73	79	82	89	80	84	83	79	102	98	78	102	80	83	97	84	84	100
KANSAS	92	87	84	87	89	95	89	91	90	88	111	106	87	110	88	89	107	91	92	105
KENTUCKY	86	74	63	71	77	85	74	80	79	74	96	94	71	95	74	81	91	80	86	98
LOUISIANA	77	69	66	67	70	77	70	73	74	70	91	84	68	88	70	75	87	74	77	87
MAINE	80	73	65	71	75	82	72	77	75	71	92	90	70	91	73	76	88	76	81	93
MARYLAND	108	114	128	115	112	119	113	111	111	114	139	129	116	140	113	109	137	112	106	124
MASSACHUSETTS	112	121	148	122	120	127	122	119	121	121	151	138	126	156	123	120	149	120	115	132
MICHIGAN	91	91	93	89	91	98	90	91	91	90	113	106	90	113	90	91	109	91	92	105
MINNESOTA	107	106	108	107	107	113	106	107	105	105	131	126	105	131	105	104	127	107	105	123
MISSISSIPPI	76	64	54	60	66	74	64	70	70	65	85	81	61	82	64	71	80	70	76	86
MISSOURI	87	82	79	80	83	90	82	85	85	82	104	99	81	103	82	85	100	85	87	100
MONTANA	72	64	57	63	66	72	65	69	68	64	83	81	62	81	65	68	79	69	72	83
NEBRASKA	88	81	77	81	83	90	83	85	84	82	104	101	80	103	82	84	100	86	87	100
NEVADA	97	98	104	100	96	101	98	98	96	100	121	113	98	119	96	93	119	99	92	109
NEW HAMPSHIRE	106	107	107	107	108	113	105	106	104	104	129	125	105	130	105	103	125	106	105	123
NEW JERSEY	110	123	153	121	120	128	120	118	119	121	150	136	125	155	123	120	149	119	114	130
NEW MEXICO	77	74	75	73	73	78	75	76	75	76	94	87	73	91	74	74	92	77	75	86
NEW YORK	95	100	134	99	98	107	103	100	105	103	133	116	105	138	104	107	131	102	99	112
NORTH CAROLINA	90	81	73	80	83	90	81	85	84	82	103	100	79	101	81	84	99	85	88	102
NORTH DAKOTA	80	69	63	69	72	79	73	76	75	71	92	90	69	90	72	75	88	77	79	90
OHIO	89	88	90	87	88	95	88	89	89	87	110	103	88	111	88	89	107	89	90	102
OKLAHOMA	79	71	65	70	73	80	73	76	76	72	93	88	70	91	72	76	88	76	79	89
OREGON	87	85	86	85	86	91	86	87	86	85	106	102	85	106	85	84	103	87	86	100
PENNSYLVANIA	89	89	93	87	90	98	89	90	91	88	112	104	89	114	90	92	109	90	92	104
RHODE ISLAND	85	91	106	90	90	96	92	90	92	91	115	104	94	117	92	91	113	91	88	99
SOUTH CAROLINA	87	78	69	75	80	87	77	82	81	78	99	95	74	96	77	82	95	82	86	99
SOUTH DAKOTA	84	74	67	74	77	84	76	80	79	75	97	94	73	95	76	79	92	81	84	95
TENNESSEE	85	76	68	73	78	85	76	80	79	76	97	94	73	96	75	81	93	80	85	97
TEXAS	94	90	91	90	89	95	92	93	92	93	115	107	90	112	90	90	112	94	89	104
UTAH	96	98	100	99	97	100	97	97	94	97	118	114	97	118	95	91	115	97	91	109
VERMONT	85	80	74	78	82	89	79	83	81	78	100	98	77	100	80	82	96	83	86	99
VIRGINIA	112	109	113	109	109	117	108	110	109	109	136	129	108	135	108	109	132	110	109	128
WASHINGTON	94	96	103	97	95	100	96	95	94	96	118	112	96	118	95	92	115	96	91	107
WEST VIRGINIA	73	60	47	57	64	72	61	67	67	60	80	78	57	78	61	69	75	67	76	84
WISCONSIN	89	86	85	86	88	94	86	88	87	85	108	103	86	109	86	87	104	88	89	103
WYOMING	86	78	71	77	81	87	79	82	81	78	99	97	76	98	78	81	95	83	85	98
UNITED STATES	100	100	100	100	100	100	100	100	100	100	100	100	100	100	100	100	100	100	100	100

Tapestry™ Data by ZIP Code

The Community
Sourcebook

2004
18th EDITION

of ZIP Code
Demographics

ZIP CODE	TOP TAPESTRY CONSUMER TYPE	% 2004 HOUSE-HOLDS	ZIP CODE	TOP TAPESTRY CONSUMER TYPE	% 2004 HOUSE-HOLDS	ZIP CODE	TOP TAPESTRY CONSUMER TYPE	% 2004 HOUSE-HOLDS
01001	24 Main Street, USA	32.8	01270	17 Green Acres	100.0	01602	24 Main Street, USA	17.4
01002	55 College Towns	35.0	01301	57 Simple Living	21.6	01603	24 Main Street, USA	21.6
01003	63 Dorms To Diplomas	100.0	01330	13 In Style	57.2	01604	24 Main Street, USA	21.1
01005	17 Green Acres	31.2	01331	32 Rustbelt Traditions	32.7	01605	60 City Dimensions	27.0
01007	06 Sophisticated Squires	32.4	01337	17 Green Acres	68.8	01606	24 Main Street, USA	45.5
01008	18 Cozy and Comfortable	92.4	01338	17 Green Acres	100.0	01607	48 Great Expectations	54.2
01010	17 Green Acres	99.6	01339	18 Cozy and Comfortable	50.6	01608	64 City Commons	43.1
01011	25 Salt of The Earth	52.7	01340	25 Salt of The Earth	97.5	01609	55 College Towns	13.8
01012	17 Green Acres	100.0	01341	07 Exurbanites	93.7	01610	60 City Dimensions	51.5
01013	60 City Dimensions	38.9	01342	18 Cozy and Comfortable	50.2	01611	24 Main Street, USA	66.4
01020	29 Rustbelt Retirees	35.2	01343	25 Salt of The Earth	100.0	01612	07 Exurbanites	50.4
01022	32 Rustbelt Traditions	45.3	01344	29 Rustbelt Retirees	84.7	01701	05 Wealthy Seaboard Suburbs	28.1
01026	31 Rural Resort Dwellers	74.7	01346	25 Salt of The Earth	100.0	01702	35 International Marketplace	22.2
01027	36 Old and Newcomers	19.9	01349	48 Great Expectations	41.5	01718	13 In Style	100.0
01028	07 Exurbanites	54.1	01350	18 Cozy and Comfortable	100.0	01719	02 Suburban Splendor	47.5
01030	18 Cozy and Comfortable	47.9	01351	17 Green Acres	65.4	01720	02 Suburban Splendor	49.3
01031	17 Green Acres	80.8	01355	17 Green Acres	99.7	01721	13 In Style	53.0
01032	17 Green Acres	100.0	01360	17 Green Acres	51.8	01730	03 Connoisseurs	44.4
01033	18 Cozy and Comfortable	77.8	01364	25 Salt of The Earth	32.6	01731	40 Military Proximity	94.3
01034	17 Green Acres	100.0	01366	14 Prosperous Empty Nesters	100.0	01740	02 Suburban Splendor	99.8
01035	14 Prosperous Empty Nesters	36.9	01367	18 Cozy and Comfortable	70.2	01741	01 Top Rung	50.8
01036	07 Exurbanites	47.5	01368	25 Salt of The Earth	99.3	01742	03 Connoisseurs	50.0
01038	14 Prosperous Empty Nesters	41.4	01370	17 Green Acres	35.1	01745	09 Urban Chic	99.2
01039	22 Metropolitans	72.1	01373	22 Metropolitans	41.6	01746	02 Suburban Splendor	45.1
01040	57 Simple Living	19.5	01375	55 College Towns	63.1	01747	06 Sophisticated Squires	40.3
01050	17 Green Acres	52.4	01376	33 Midlife Junction	28.4	01748	02 Suburban Splendor	83.6
01053	14 Prosperous Empty Nesters	60.8	01378	25 Salt of The Earth	100.0	01749	20 City Lights	30.1
01054	07 Exurbanites	99.8	01379	17 Green Acres	100.0	01752	13 In Style	25.3
01056	18 Cozy and Comfortable	47.5	01420	24 Main Street, USA	20.4	01754	13 In Style	37.9
01057	24 Main Street, USA	31.3	01430	17 Green Acres	38.9	01756	04 Boomburbs	48.9
01060	27 Metro Renters	45.0	01431	17 Green Acres	53.4	01757	13 In Style	21.4
01062	18 Cozy and Comfortable	27.4	01432	24 Main Street, USA	25.4	01760	05 Wealthy Seaboard Suburbs	30.2
01063	27 Metro Renters	100.0	01436	33 Midlife Junction	44.1	01770	01 Top Rung	79.1
01068	06 Sophisticated Squires	100.0	01440	57 Simple Living	23.0	01772	02 Suburban Splendor	38.3
01069	24 Main Street, USA	38.8	01450	06 Sophisticated Squires	48.4	01773	01 Top Rung	83.1
01070	31 Rural Resort Dwellers	99.6	01451	03 Connoisseurs	52.4	01775	02 Suburban Splendor	79.4
01071	18 Cozy and Comfortable	99.6	01452	06 Sophisticated Squires	67.6	01776	02 Suburban Splendor	57.3
01072	06 Sophisticated Squires	98.5	01453	24 Main Street, USA	25.5	01778	03 Connoisseurs	35.8
01073	17 Green Acres	52.8	01460	02 Suburban Splendor	36.5	01801	20 City Lights	38.2
01075	33 Midlife Junction	26.6	01462	07 Exurbanites	21.5	01803	05 Wealthy Seaboard Suburbs	67.4
01077	17 Green Acres	63.9	01463	06 Sophisticated Squires	40.2	01810	02 Suburban Splendor	36.6
01080	32 Rustbelt Traditions	55.2	01464	06 Sophisticated Squires	30.3	01821	10 Pleasant-Ville	35.7
01081	17 Green Acres	100.0	01468	18 Cozy and Comfortable	59.9	01824	05 Wealthy Seaboard Suburbs	51.6
01082	17 Green Acres	24.7	01469	06 Sophisticated Squires	58.5	01826	24 Main Street, USA	34.2
01084	17 Green Acres	100.0	01473	06 Sophisticated Squires	48.9	01827	02 Suburban Splendor	99.7
01085	07 Exurbanites	17.4	01474	17 Green Acres	100.0	01830	10 Pleasant-Ville	23.3
01088	17 Green Acres	100.0	01475	17 Green Acres	40.9	01832	24 Main Street, USA	23.8
01089	36 Old and Newcomers	16.9	01501	18 Cozy and Comfortable	48.1	01833	04 Boomburbs	29.3
01092	50 Heartland Communities	40.7	01503	07 Exurbanites	83.9	01834	06 Sophisticated Squires	64.8
01095	07 Exurbanites	58.9	01504	06 Sophisticated Squires	47.5	01835	24 Main Street, USA	44.3
01096	17 Green Acres	79.7	01505	13 In Style	47.9	01840	65 Social Security Set	51.0
01098	17 Green Acres	100.0	01506	49 Senior Sun Seekers	39.8	01841	58 Newest Residents	31.6
01103	65 Social Security Set	56.8	01507	06 Sophisticated Squires	81.6	01843	24 Main Street, USA	37.9
01104	32 Rustbelt Traditions	31.8	01510	24 Main Street, USA	49.5	01844	24 Main Street, USA	24.7
01105	60 City Dimensions	51.9	01515	18 Cozy and Comfortable	67.7	01845	02 Suburban Splendor	25.9
01106	07 Exurbanites	36.4	01516	06 Sophisticated Squires	61.9	01850	60 City Dimensions	42.1
01107	61 High Rise Renters	24.0	01518	24 Main Street, USA	49.1	01851	35 International Marketplace	31.8
01108	60 City Dimensions	34.1	01519	13 In Style	49.3	01852	65 Social Security Set	13.4
01109	60 City Dimensions	29.0	01520	18 Cozy and Comfortable	35.2	01854	24 Main Street, USA	32.9
01118	29 Rustbelt Retirees	34.6	01521	17 Green Acres	100.0	01860	10 Pleasant-Ville	67.5
01119	48 Great Expectations	23.7	01522	06 Sophisticated Squires	55.8	01862	10 Pleasant-Ville	52.5
01128	18 Cozy and Comfortable	82.7	01523	13 In Style	32.3	01863	13 In Style	57.9
01129	18 Cozy and Comfortable	67.3	01524	18 Cozy and Comfortable	37.0	01864	05 Wealthy Seaboard Suburbs	32.9
01151	60 City Dimensions	62.4	01527	24 Main Street, USA	27.8	01867	05 Wealthy Seaboard Suburbs	57.6
01201	18 Cozy and Comfortable	17.8	01529	24 Main Street, USA	59.1	01876	10 Pleasant-Ville	39.0
01220	50 Heartland Communities	26.6	01531	17 Green Acres	66.7	01879	06 Sophisticated Squires	37.4
01222	17 Green Acres	91.8	01532	13 In Style	23.7	01880	05 Wealthy Seaboard Suburbs	41.5
01223	31 Rural Resort Dwellers	54.9	01534	24 Main Street, USA	53.9	01886	02 Suburban Splendor	52.8
01224	17 Green Acres	100.0	01535	24 Main Street, USA	58.5	01887	06 Sophisticated Squires	42.9
01225	18 Cozy and Comfortable	99.1	01536	13 In Style	39.5	01890	03 Connoisseurs	41.7
01226	24 Main Street, USA	39.3	01537	24 Main Street, USA	70.7	01901	65 Social Security Set	90.4
01230	15 Silver and Gold	17.9	01540	18 Cozy and Comfortable	42.5	01902	24 Main Street, USA	22.3
01235	17 Green Acres	53.8	01541	07 Exurbanites	58.9	01904	10 Pleasant-Ville	60.1
01236	24 Main Street, USA	35.0	01542	24 Main Street, USA	74.9	01905	24 Main Street, USA	32.0
01237	29 Rustbelt Retirees	36.8	01543	06 Sophisticated Squires	41.1	01906	10 Pleasant-Ville	51.6
01238	33 Midlife Junction	34.8	01545	13 In Style	26.2	01907	03 Connoisseurs	21.2
01240	30 Retirement Communities	51.4	01550	24 Main Street, USA	21.4	01908	09 Urban Chic	41.1
01243	17 Green Acres	100.0	01560	24 Main Street, USA	98.2	01913	06 Sophisticated Squires	17.6
01245	31 Rural Resort Dwellers	96.7	01562	24 Main Street, USA	29.0	01915	36 Old and Newcomers	19.1
01247	33 Midlife Junction	21.6	01564	07 Exurbanites	41.4	01921	03 Connoisseurs	60.7
01253	31 Rural Resort Dwellers	54.4	01566	18 Cozy and Comfortable	36.0	01922	02 Suburban Splendor	98.2
01254	07 Exurbanites	99.7	01568	13 In Style	31.7	01923	20 City Lights	34.1
01255	31 Rural Resort Dwellers	100.0	01569	06 Sophisticated Squires	33.6	01929	09 Urban Chic	55.0
01256	25 Salt of The Earth	100.0	01570	24 Main Street, USA	27.1	01930	24 Main Street, USA	23.6
01257	31 Rural Resort Dwellers	67.6	01571	24 Main Street, USA	36.2	01938	07 Exurbanites	38.8
01258	15 Silver and Gold	100.0	01581	09 Urban Chic	31.1	01940	03 Connoisseurs	42.7
01259	17 Green Acres	84.9	01583	14 Prosperous Empty Nesters	57.7	01944	09 Urban Chic	52.6
01262	30 Retirement Communities	56.3	01585	24 Main Street, USA	27.5	01945	09 Urban Chic	36.7
01266	14 Prosperous Empty Nesters	41.6	01588	24 Main Street, USA	65.7	01949	06 Sophisticated Squires	50.3
01267	14 Prosperous Empty Nesters	26.6	01590	06 Sophisticated Squires	38.6	01950	22 Metropolitans	30.9

ZIP CODE	TOP TAPESTRY CONSUMER TYPE	% 2004 HOUSE-HOLDS	ZIP CODE	TOP TAPESTRY CONSUMER TYPE	% 2004 HOUSE-HOLDS	ZIP CODE	TOP TAPESTRY CONSUMER TYPE	% 2004 HOUSE-HOLDS
01951	09 Urban Chic	59.5	02301	60 City Dimensions	19.4	02660	15 Silver and Gold	38.2
01952	24 Main Street, USA	61.0	02302	18 Cozy and Comfortable	48.8	02664	49 Senior Sun Seekers	24.7
01960	10 Pleasant-Ville	34.9	02322	10 Pleasant-Ville	62.7	02666	31 Rural Resort Dwellers	100.0
01966	14 Prosperous Empty Nesters	29.2	02324	10 Pleasant-Ville	26.6	02667	31 Rural Resort Dwellers	100.0
01969	06 Sophisticated Squires	50.5	02325	36 Old and Newcomers	100.0	02668	07 Exurbanites	78.1
01970	20 City Lights	29.9	02330	06 Sophisticated Squires	44.0	02670	31 Rural Resort Dwellers	83.6
01982	05 Wealthy Seaboard Suburbs	37.0	02332	02 Suburban Splendor	46.3	02671	31 Rural Resort Dwellers	71.3
01983	03 Connoisseurs	58.6	02333	06 Sophisticated Squires	43.3	02673	33 Midlife Junction	50.9
01984	03 Connoisseurs	47.2	02338	06 Sophisticated Squires	35.1	02675	15 Silver and Gold	48.2
01985	02 Suburban Splendor	100.0	02339	05 Wealthy Seaboard Suburbs	47.5	02702	06 Sophisticated Squires	50.2
02019	06 Sophisticated Squires	31.6	02341	06 Sophisticated Squires	43.5	02703	24 Main Street, USA	33.9
02021	05 Wealthy Seaboard Suburbs	53.6	02343	18 Cozy and Comfortable	42.5	02713	31 Rural Resort Dwellers	100.0
02025	03 Connoisseurs	70.6	02346	24 Main Street, USA	32.1	02715	18 Cozy and Comfortable	87.7
02026	05 Wealthy Seaboard Suburbs	32.2	02347	06 Sophisticated Squires	37.3	02717	17 Green Acres	58.6
02030	01 Top Rung	84.9	02351	10 Pleasant-Ville	60.4	02718	06 Sophisticated Squires	36.3
02032	05 Wealthy Seaboard Suburbs	62.5	02356	02 Suburban Splendor	35.5	02719	18 Cozy and Comfortable	32.1
02035	02 Suburban Splendor	26.4	02357	55 College Towns	100.0	02720	60 City Dimensions	20.4
02038	04 Boomburbs	51.4	02359	06 Sophisticated Squires	32.9	02721	60 City Dimensions	32.1
02043	03 Connoisseurs	54.0	02360	06 Sophisticated Squires	24.7	02723	60 City Dimensions	32.5
02045	10 Pleasant-Ville	34.0	02364	24 Main Street, USA	32.4	02724	57 Simple Living	37.9
02048	04 Boomburbs	31.5	02367	06 Sophisticated Squires	100.0	02725	18 Cozy and Comfortable	46.5
02050	10 Pleasant-Ville	43.6	02368	10 Pleasant-Ville	54.6	02726	29 Rustbelt Retirees	43.2
02052	02 Suburban Splendor	55.6	02370	13 In Style	29.4	02738	07 Exurbanites	30.9
02053	06 Sophisticated Squires	36.9	02375	13 In Style	55.0	02739	14 Prosperous Empty Nesters	50.8
02054	13 In Style	51.5	02379	10 Pleasant-Ville	65.5	02740	60 City Dimensions	29.1
02056	02 Suburban Splendor	51.7	02382	24 Main Street, USA	45.7	02743	17 Green Acres	39.1
02061	02 Suburban Splendor	50.1	02420	03 Connoisseurs	90.3	02744	60 City Dimensions	59.0
02062	20 City Lights	46.1	02421	03 Connoisseurs	51.5	02745	60 City Dimensions	19.5
02066	05 Wealthy Seaboard Suburbs	49.5	02445	08 Laptops and Lattes	53.1	02746	60 City Dimensions	66.8
02067	02 Suburban Splendor	47.5	02446	08 Laptops and Lattes	65.8	02747	24 Main Street, USA	18.3
02071	05 Wealthy Seaboard Suburbs	100.0	02451	05 Wealthy Seaboard Suburbs	23.0	02748	07 Exurbanites	38.5
02072	10 Pleasant-Ville	43.4	02452	09 Urban Chic	34.3	02760	06 Sophisticated Squires	32.3
02081	05 Wealthy Seaboard Suburbs	54.8	02453	23 Trendsetters	51.5	02762	13 In Style	50.6
02090	03 Connoisseurs	74.7	02458	20 City Lights	23.3	02763	06 Sophisticated Squires	73.0
02093	10 Pleasant-Ville	39.2	02459	09 Urban Chic	38.7	02764	18 Cozy and Comfortable	77.6
02108	08 Laptops and Lattes	65.5	02460	09 Urban Chic	54.8	02766	13 In Style	38.2
02109	27 Metro Renters	56.8	02461	09 Urban Chic	52.8	02767	06 Sophisticated Squires	33.5
02110	08 Laptops and Lattes	96.7	02462	09 Urban Chic	93.9	02769	07 Exurbanites	50.1
02111	44 Urban Melting Pot	43.3	02464	09 Urban Chic	84.8	02770	17 Green Acres	65.9
02113	27 Metro Renters	95.6	02465	09 Urban Chic	48.2	02771	18 Cozy and Comfortable	38.4
02114	27 Metro Renters	83.5	02466	09 Urban Chic	87.0	02777	18 Cozy and Comfortable	68.2
02115	27 Metro Renters	53.6	02467	09 Urban Chic	40.0	02779	06 Sophisticated Squires	98.7
02116	08 Laptops and Lattes	68.9	02468	01 Top Rung	74.8	02780	24 Main Street, USA	46.1
02118	08 Laptops and Lattes	29.3	02472	23 Trendsetters	51.9	02790	18 Cozy and Comfortable	29.2
02119	45 City Strivers	69.1	02474	23 Trendsetters	41.4	02804	18 Cozy and Comfortable	70.6
02120	55 College Towns	40.7	02476	05 Wealthy Seaboard Suburbs	30.3	02806	07 Exurbanites	27.3
02121	45 City Strivers	85.2	02478	03 Connoisseurs	30.2	02807	09 Urban Chic	87.5
02122	20 City Lights	42.6	02481	01 Top Rung	46.3	02808	24 Main Street, USA	68.6
02124	45 City Strivers	50.7	02482	03 Connoisseurs	33.9	02809	14 Prosperous Empty Nesters	17.5
02125	45 City Strivers	35.4	02492	03 Connoisseurs	53.6	02812	17 Green Acres	100.0
02126	45 City Strivers	83.8	02493	01 Top Rung	76.5	02813	13 In Style	30.7
02127	20 City Lights	33.8	02494	09 Urban Chic	67.6	02814	17 Green Acres	68.8
02128	35 International Marketplace	51.1	02532	33 Midlife Junction	48.8	02815	06 Sophisticated Squires	77.9
02129	08 Laptops and Lattes	50.8	02535	31 Rural Resort Dwellers	96.4	02816	18 Cozy and Comfortable	29.1
02130	23 Trendsetters	50.0	02536	18 Cozy and Comfortable	34.6	02817	06 Sophisticated Squires	76.4
02131	20 City Lights	50.7	02537	07 Exurbanites	36.4	02818	02 Suburban Splendor	30.6
02132	05 Wealthy Seaboard Suburbs	29.6	02538	24 Main Street, USA	30.9	02822	06 Sophisticated Squires	76.6
02134	63 Dorms To Diplomas	42.3	02539	13 In Style	43.9	02825	07 Exurbanites	34.6
02135	27 Metro Renters	40.4	02540	15 Silver and Gold	48.3	02827	06 Sophisticated Squires	100.0
02136	20 City Lights	37.5	02542	40 Military Proximity	100.0	02828	14 Prosperous Empty Nesters	66.3
02138	27 Metro Renters	39.5	02543	15 Silver and Gold	100.0	02830	17 Green Acres	54.5
02139	23 Trendsetters	47.5	02554	09 Urban Chic	49.8	02831	07 Exurbanites	43.9
02140	08 Laptops and Lattes	44.3	02556	07 Exurbanites	57.8	02832	25 Salt of The Earth	39.0
02141	23 Trendsetters	55.2	02559	14 Prosperous Empty Nesters	62.2	02833	33 Midlife Junction	95.2
02142	27 Metro Renters	47.5	02562	13 In Style	51.1	02835	07 Exurbanites	59.4
02143	23 Trendsetters	51.1	02563	06 Sophisticated Squires	46.4	02836	17 Green Acres	100.0
02144	23 Trendsetters	61.0	02568	09 Urban Chic	46.7	02837	07 Exurbanites	75.1
02145	23 Trendsetters	44.8	02571	33 Midlife Junction	40.0	02838	24 Main Street, USA	73.2
02148	20 City Lights	48.4	02575	09 Urban Chic	100.0	02839	17 Green Acres	100.0
02149	20 City Lights	88.4	02576	49 Senior Sun Seekers	49.4	02840	22 Metropolitans	38.7
02150	35 International Marketplace	55.9	02601	33 Midlife Junction	32.0	02841	40 Military Proximity	88.9
02151	20 City Lights	48.3	02630	07 Exurbanites	40.8	02842	24 Main Street, USA	33.0
02152	20 City Lights	47.9	02631	14 Prosperous Empty Nesters	28.7	02852	07 Exurbanites	22.4
02153	23 Trendsetters	100.0	02632	14 Prosperous Empty Nesters	55.7	02857	07 Exurbanites	45.6
02155	20 City Lights	53.5	02633	15 Silver and Gold	83.9	02858	17 Green Acres	91.9
02163	27 Metro Renters	91.3	02635	15 Silver and Gold	62.5	02859	24 Main Street, USA	33.5
02169	36 Old and Newcomers	21.6	02638	15 Silver and Gold	95.1	02860	60 City Dimensions	50.2
02170	20 City Lights	51.4	02639	36 Old and Newcomers	35.7	02861	29 Rustbelt Retirees	25.3
02171	20 City Lights	48.3	02642	31 Rural Resort Dwellers	65.6	02863	60 City Dimensions	76.0
02176	05 Wealthy Seaboard Suburbs	42.0	02644	06 Sophisticated Squires	100.0	02864	18 Cozy and Comfortable	20.4
02180	20 City Lights	33.1	02645	31 Rural Resort Dwellers	71.9	02865	07 Exurbanites	25.8
02184	10 Pleasant-Ville	33.6	02646	15 Silver and Gold	64.5	02871	07 Exurbanites	43.6
02186	05 Wealthy Seaboard Suburbs	53.2	02648	17 Green Acres	43.5	02872	15 Silver and Gold	100.0
02188	10 Pleasant-Ville	36.3	02649	13 In Style	50.3	02874	06 Sophisticated Squires	34.6
02189	10 Pleasant-Ville	23.8	02650	15 Silver and Gold	100.0	02877	06 Sophisticated Squires	100.0
02190	10 Pleasant-Ville	46.2	02652	31 Rural Resort Dwellers	100.0	02878	18 Cozy and Comfortable	33.2
02191	10 Pleasant-Ville	59.1	02653	15 Silver and Gold	63.2	02879	07 Exurbanites	18.8
02199	27 Metro Renters	100.0	02655	15 Silver and Gold	63.3	02881	07 Exurbanites	60.2
02210	27 Metro Renters	81.0	02657	09 Urban Chic	59.1	02882	07 Exurbanites	18.6
02215	27 Metro Renters	59.8	02659	31 Rural Resort Dwellers	67.1	02885	48 Great Expectations	26.9

CONSUMER TYPE

02886 - 04011

ZIP CODE	TOP TAPESTRY CONSUMER TYPE	% 2004 HOUSE-HOLDS	ZIP CODE	TOP TAPESTRY CONSUMER TYPE	% 2004 HOUSE-HOLDS	ZIP CODE	TOP TAPESTRY CONSUMER TYPE	% 2004 HOUSE-HOLDS
02886	18 Cozy and Comfortable	33.7	03246	33 Midlife Junction	35.7	03770	17 Green Acres	100.0
02888	29 Rustbelt Retirees	23.4	03249	18 Cozy and Comfortable	31.2	03771	25 Salt of The Earth	100.0
02889	18 Cozy and Comfortable	43.0	03251	57 Simple Living	51.1	03773	32 Rustbelt Traditions	44.8
02891	24 Main Street, USA	23.3	03253	33 Midlife Junction	48.9	03774	50 Heartland Communities	62.0
02892	17 Green Acres	52.5	03254	31 Rural Resort Dwellers	67.2	03777	25 Salt of The Earth	100.0
02893	24 Main Street, USA	34.5	03255	31 Rural Resort Dwellers	85.4	03779	25 Salt of The Earth	99.1
02894	17 Green Acres	98.9	03256	25 Salt of The Earth	46.5	03780	46 Rooted Rural	99.6
02895	24 Main Street, USA	27.8	03257	15 Silver and Gold	78.7	03781	17 Green Acres	99.8
02896	18 Cozy and Comfortable	50.0	03258	17 Green Acres	98.8	03782	31 Rural Resort Dwellers	70.5
02898	17 Green Acres	96.3	03259	31 Rural Resort Dwellers	100.0	03784	36 Old and Newcomers	65.2
02903	65 Social Security Set	30.7	03261	26 Midland Crowd	65.7	03785	50 Heartland Communities	84.0
02904	33 Midlife Junction	16.1	03262	33 Midlife Junction	100.0	03801	22 Metropolitans	38.6
02905	38 Industrious Urban Fringe	17.4	03263	24 Main Street, USA	57.9	03809	31 Rural Resort Dwellers	71.6
02906	22 Metropolitans	24.1	03264	33 Midlife Junction	45.6	03810	31 Rural Resort Dwellers	100.0
02907	60 City Dimensions	34.6	03266	31 Rural Resort Dwellers	63.3	03811	07 Exurbanites	78.2
02908	60 City Dimensions	39.8	03268	17 Green Acres	99.3	03812	31 Rural Resort Dwellers	95.4
02909	60 City Dimensions	41.2	03269	17 Green Acres	67.2	03813	31 Rural Resort Dwellers	41.4
02910	24 Main Street, USA	33.2	03275	24 Main Street, USA	31.0	03814	31 Rural Resort Dwellers	59.1
02911	36 Old and Newcomers	21.7	03276	26 Midland Crowd	36.3	03815	17 Green Acres	100.0
02912	63 Dorms To Diplomas	100.0	03278	33 Midlife Junction	37.3	03816	31 Rural Resort Dwellers	87.2
02914	24 Main Street, USA	43.4	03279	46 Rooted Rural	99.2	03817	31 Rural Resort Dwellers	73.5
02915	29 Rustbelt Retirees	24.5	03280	31 Rural Resort Dwellers	100.0	03818	31 Rural Resort Dwellers	28.9
02916	24 Main Street, USA	36.9	03281	17 Green Acres	41.7	03819	12 Up and Coming Families	99.9
02917	18 Cozy and Comfortable	38.2	03282	25 Salt of The Earth	91.7	03820	36 Old and Newcomers	35.8
02918	55 College Towns	86.7	03284	31 Rural Resort Dwellers	100.0	03824	55 College Towns	22.6
02919	18 Cozy and Comfortable	40.2	03287	17 Green Acres	99.2	03825	17 Green Acres	57.5
02920	18 Cozy and Comfortable	22.5	03290	17 Green Acres	73.1	03826	13 In Style	71.3
02921	06 Sophisticated Squires	66.1	03301	36 Old and Newcomers	14.0	03827	17 Green Acres	66.2
03031	02 Suburban Splendor	54.5	03303	28 Aspiring Young Families	38.6	03830	31 Rural Resort Dwellers	100.0
03032	06 Sophisticated Squires	63.5	03304	06 Sophisticated Squires	99.9	03833	06 Sophisticated Squires	21.3
03033	06 Sophisticated Squires	61.5	03307	17 Green Acres	98.5	03835	32 Rustbelt Traditions	41.7
03034	06 Sophisticated Squires	66.3	03431	33 Midlife Junction	20.4	03836	31 Rural Resort Dwellers	100.0
03036	06 Sophisticated Squires	98.0	03440	24 Main Street, USA	56.3	03837	17 Green Acres	93.2
03037	17 Green Acres	98.9	03441	42 Southern Satellites	59.6	03838	31 Rural Resort Dwellers	93.3
03038	28 Aspiring Young Families	39.0	03442	24 Main Street, USA	99.8	03839	26 Midland Crowd	70.2
03042	19 Milk and Cookies	37.0	03443	17 Green Acres	100.0	03840	07 Exurbanites	51.2
03043	07 Exurbanites	99.7	03444	07 Exurbanites	100.0	03841	07 Exurbanites	78.7
03044	17 Green Acres	98.7	03445	17 Green Acres	99.7	03842	13 In Style	31.5
03045	17 Green Acres	61.2	03446	17 Green Acres	28.8	03844	07 Exurbanites	100.0
03046	06 Sophisticated Squires	100.0	03447	17 Green Acres	67.2	03845	33 Midlife Junction	74.5
03047	17 Green Acres	100.0	03448	25 Salt of The Earth	95.4	03846	31 Rural Resort Dwellers	98.1
03048	41 Crossroads	35.6	03449	14 Prosperous Empty Nesters	99.9	03848	18 Cozy and Comfortable	36.8
03049	02 Suburban Splendor	85.3	03450	17 Green Acres	100.0	03849	31 Rural Resort Dwellers	100.0
03051	06 Sophisticated Squires	55.1	03451	26 Midland Crowd	50.6	03851	26 Midland Crowd	89.3
03052	06 Sophisticated Squires	100.0	03452	18 Cozy and Comfortable	39.1	03852	25 Salt of The Earth	100.0
03053	06 Sophisticated Squires	81.6	03455	25 Salt of The Earth	47.9	03853	31 Rural Resort Dwellers	56.8
03054	06 Sophisticated Squires	68.6	03456	25 Salt of The Earth	100.0	03854	03 Connoisseurs	100.0
03055	24 Main Street, USA	36.8	03457	17 Green Acres	88.4	03855	17 Green Acres	93.0
03057	07 Exurbanites	100.0	03458	33 Midlife Junction	55.8	03856	06 Sophisticated Squires	98.9
03060	60 City Dimensions	19.7	03461	17 Green Acres	99.9	03857	28 Aspiring Young Families	40.9
03062	13 In Style	18.7	03462	07 Exurbanites	51.0	03858	06 Sophisticated Squires	38.9
03063	16 Enterprising Professionals	45.4	03464	31 Rural Resort Dwellers	99.7	03860	31 Rural Resort Dwellers	34.2
03064	07 Exurbanites	18.3	03465	25 Salt of The Earth	59.5	03862	31 Rural Resort Dwellers	41.6
03070	06 Sophisticated Squires	97.7	03466	17 Green Acres	100.0	03864	25 Salt of The Earth	54.0
03071	17 Green Acres	99.3	03467	17 Green Acres	99.4	03865	13 In Style	48.0
03076	06 Sophisticated Squires	81.9	03470	42 Southern Satellites	43.4	03867	26 Midland Crowd	17.0
03077	26 Midland Crowd	58.2	03561	50 Heartland Communities	30.0	03868	32 Rustbelt Traditions	46.9
03079	06 Sophisticated Squires	29.9	03570	50 Heartland Communities	29.6	03869	24 Main Street, USA	63.9
03082	17 Green Acres	99.6	03574	33 Midlife Junction	53.8	03870	09 Urban Chic	62.1
03084	17 Green Acres	100.0	03576	46 Rooted Rural	55.8	03872	31 Rural Resort Dwellers	58.9
03086	17 Green Acres	62.1	03579	46 Rooted Rural	100.0	03873	12 Up and Coming Families	66.6
03087	02 Suburban Splendor	54.9	03580	31 Rural Resort Dwellers	87.0	03874	26 Midland Crowd	41.1
03101	65 Social Security Set	46.5	03581	33 Midlife Junction	39.5	03875	31 Rural Resort Dwellers	100.0
03102	24 Main Street, USA	24.7	03582	50 Heartland Communities	55.3	03878	48 Great Expectations	23.2
03103	24 Main Street, USA	18.2	03583	31 Rural Resort Dwellers	100.0	03882	31 Rural Resort Dwellers	100.0
03104	24 Main Street, USA	23.9	03584	33 Midlife Junction	34.2	03883	46 Rooted Rural	89.1
03106	13 In Style	28.4	03585	25 Salt of The Earth	28.6	03884	17 Green Acres	100.0
03109	18 Cozy and Comfortable	37.3	03588	25 Salt of The Earth	80.1	03885	07 Exurbanites	57.6
03110	02 Suburban Splendor	64.0	03590	42 Southern Satellites	96.5	03886	31 Rural Resort Dwellers	51.7
03216	25 Salt of The Earth	64.6	03592	31 Rural Resort Dwellers	100.0	03887	25 Salt of The Earth	99.4
03217	33 Midlife Junction	54.1	03593	31 Rural Resort Dwellers	100.0	03890	31 Rural Resort Dwellers	100.0
03218	17 Green Acres	63.3	03598	33 Midlife Junction	27.8	03894	31 Rural Resort Dwellers	57.5
03220	26 Midland Crowd	73.0	03602	25 Salt of The Earth	61.6	03901	26 Midland Crowd	72.2
03221	17 Green Acres	94.8	03603	46 Rooted Rural	60.2	03902	14 Prosperous Empty Nesters	56.2
03222	25 Salt of The Earth	57.2	03605	25 Salt of The Earth	100.0	03903	17 Green Acres	41.0
03223	33 Midlife Junction	74.8	03607	25 Salt of The Earth	100.0	03904	28 Aspiring Young Families	30.2
03224	07 Exurbanites	96.3	03608	33 Midlife Junction	50.5	03905	14 Prosperous Empty Nesters	84.9
03225	26 Midland Crowd	54.6	03609	32 Rustbelt Traditions	100.0	03906	17 Green Acres	68.1
03226	31 Rural Resort Dwellers	96.3	03740	25 Salt of The Earth	99.7	03907	15 Silver and Gold	100.0
03227	31 Rural Resort Dwellers	100.0	03741	26 Midland Crowd	66.1	03908	17 Green Acres	29.3
03229	07 Exurbanites	63.3	03743	57 Simple Living	28.4	03909	07 Exurbanites	48.9
03230	25 Salt of The Earth	96.8	03745	17 Green Acres	96.2	04001	25 Salt of The Earth	50.6
03234	17 Green Acres	69.8	03748	13 In Style	38.7	04002	17 Green Acres	38.8
03235	57 Simple Living	29.0	03750	02 Suburban Splendor	53.0	04003	31 Rural Resort Dwellers	100.0
03237	17 Green Acres	100.0	03752	25 Salt of The Earth	100.0	04005	48 Great Expectations	23.7
03240	26 Midland Crowd	55.9	03753	14 Prosperous Empty Nesters	89.3	04006	15 Silver and Gold	100.0
03241	31 Rural Resort Dwellers	99.7	03755	09 Urban Chic	61.5	04008	26 Midland Crowd	55.3
03242	13 In Style	38.0	03765	46 Rooted Rural	100.0	04009	31 Rural Resort Dwellers	41.3
03243	25 Salt of The Earth	100.0	03766	36 Old and Newcomers	39.1	04010	31 Rural Resort Dwellers	100.0
03244	25 Salt of The Earth	27.1	03768	07 Exurbanites	44.5	04011	33 Midlife Junction	26.4

Copyright © 2004 ESRI BIS. All rights reserved. Reproduction by any method is prohibited.

ZIP CODE	TOP TAPESTRY CONSUMER TYPE	% 2004 HOUSE-HOLDS	ZIP CODE	TOP TAPESTRY CONSUMER TYPE	% 2004 HOUSE-HOLDS	ZIP CODE	TOP TAPESTRY CONSUMER TYPE	% 2004 HOUSE-HOLDS
04015	26 Midland Crowd	39.8	04266	26 Midland Crowd	100.0	04478	31 Rural Resort Dwellers	100.0
04016	31 Rural Resort Dwellers	100.0	04267	31 Rural Resort Dwellers	100.0	04479	50 Heartland Communities	57.8
04017	07 Exurbanites	100.0	04268	50 Heartland Communities	44.7	04481	46 Rooted Rural	97.4
04019	31 Rural Resort Dwellers	100.0	04270	25 Salt of The Earth	34.2	04487	46 Rooted Rural	100.0
04020	25 Salt of The Earth	100.0	04274	17 Green Acres	73.4	04488	46 Rooted Rural	100.0
04021	06 Sophisticated Squires	55.8	04275	50 Heartland Communities	100.0	04490	46 Rooted Rural	100.0
04022	31 Rural Resort Dwellers	100.0	04276	57 Simple Living	43.9	04491	46 Rooted Rural	100.0
04024	25 Salt of The Earth	100.0	04278	31 Rural Resort Dwellers	93.8	04492	46 Rooted Rural	100.0
04027	26 Midland Crowd	65.7	04280	26 Midland Crowd	100.0	04493	42 Southern Satellites	63.8
04029	31 Rural Resort Dwellers	57.2	04281	50 Heartland Communities	43.4	04495	46 Rooted Rural	100.0
04030	25 Salt of The Earth	100.0	04282	26 Midland Crowd	75.7	04496	26 Midland Crowd	96.1
04032	07 Exurbanites	28.1	04284	31 Rural Resort Dwellers	100.0	04497	46 Rooted Rural	100.0
04037	31 Rural Resort Dwellers	76.9	04285	25 Salt of The Earth	100.0	04530	48 Great Expectations	38.2
04038	17 Green Acres	36.3	04287	26 Midland Crowd	100.0	04535	25 Salt of The Earth	91.3
04039	17 Green Acres	40.2	04289	46 Rooted Rural	81.8	04537	37 Prairie Living	79.1
04040	31 Rural Resort Dwellers	56.5	04290	25 Salt of The Earth	100.0	04538	31 Rural Resort Dwellers	84.5
04041	25 Salt of The Earth	76.7	04292	25 Salt of The Earth	100.0	04539	31 Rural Resort Dwellers	100.0
04042	26 Midland Crowd	85.2	04294	50 Heartland Communities	40.7	04541	31 Rural Resort Dwellers	100.0
04043	33 Midlife Junction	27.1	04330	57 Simple Living	27.3	04543	15 Silver and Gold	54.3
04046	26 Midland Crowd	28.9	04341	31 Rural Resort Dwellers	100.0	04544	15 Silver and Gold	100.0
04047	31 Rural Resort Dwellers	100.0	04342	26 Midland Crowd	100.0	04547	31 Rural Resort Dwellers	74.1
04048	26 Midland Crowd	56.4	04344	33 Midlife Junction	87.0	04548	31 Rural Resort Dwellers	100.0
04049	26 Midland Crowd	73.5	04345	25 Salt of The Earth	33.9	04549	31 Rural Resort Dwellers	100.0
04050	37 Prairie Living	100.0	04346	50 Heartland Communities	35.5	04551	31 Rural Resort Dwellers	100.0
04051	31 Rural Resort Dwellers	100.0	04347	36 Old and Newcomers	41.0	04553	31 Rural Resort Dwellers	80.6
04055	46 Rooted Rural	62.4	04348	26 Midland Crowd	55.2	04554	15 Silver and Gold	87.0
04061	12 Up and Coming Families	66.9	04349	25 Salt of The Earth	100.0	04555	31 Rural Resort Dwellers	100.0
04062	26 Midland Crowd	33.9	04350	26 Midland Crowd	73.4	04556	31 Rural Resort Dwellers	99.2
04064	33 Midlife Junction	31.9	04351	17 Green Acres	98.1	04558	31 Rural Resort Dwellers	61.1
04066	31 Rural Resort Dwellers	100.0	04352	25 Salt of The Earth	100.0	04562	31 Rural Resort Dwellers	54.0
04068	25 Salt of The Earth	100.0	04353	26 Midland Crowd	98.5	04563	31 Rural Resort Dwellers	100.0
04069	17 Green Acres	97.3	04354	31 Rural Resort Dwellers	100.0	04564	31 Rural Resort Dwellers	99.4
04071	17 Green Acres	71.6	04355	17 Green Acres	80.3	04567	31 Rural Resort Dwellers	100.0
04072	17 Green Acres	16.2	04357	26 Midland Crowd	68.6	04568	31 Rural Resort Dwellers	100.0
04073	32 Rustbelt Traditions	21.6	04358	26 Midland Crowd	79.3	04570	15 Silver and Gold	100.0
04074	13 In Style	41.0	04360	31 Rural Resort Dwellers	79.0	04571	31 Rural Resort Dwellers	100.0
04076	25 Salt of The Earth	56.2	04363	26 Midland Crowd	100.0	04572	46 Rooted Rural	56.9
04079	31 Rural Resort Dwellers	100.0	04364	14 Prosperous Empty Nesters	42.7	04573	31 Rural Resort Dwellers	100.0
04083	24 Main Street, USA	71.8	04401	33 Midlife Junction	18.5	04574	46 Rooted Rural	97.2
04084	26 Midland Crowd	51.7	04406	31 Rural Resort Dwellers	98.1	04576	15 Silver and Gold	100.0
04085	17 Green Acres	63.5	04408	46 Rooted Rural	100.0	04578	26 Midland Crowd	34.3
04086	17 Green Acres	45.3	04410	26 Midland Crowd	100.0	04579	17 Green Acres	49.7
04087	26 Midland Crowd	57.8	04411	26 Midland Crowd	100.0	04605	31 Rural Resort Dwellers	42.2
04088	31 Rural Resort Dwellers	100.0	04412	48 Great Expectations	39.2	04606	46 Rooted Rural	100.0
04090	17 Green Acres	48.7	04413	46 Rooted Rural	100.0	04607	31 Rural Resort Dwellers	78.1
04091	25 Salt of The Earth	100.0	04414	50 Heartland Communities	99.8	04609	22 Metropolitans	39.0
04092	18 Cozy and Comfortable	21.3	04416	33 Midlife Junction	61.4	04611	37 Prairie Living	100.0
04093	17 Green Acres	58.9	04417	42 Southern Satellites	99.6	04612	31 Rural Resort Dwellers	100.0
04095	25 Salt of The Earth	99.8	04418	42 Southern Satellites	100.0	04613	31 Rural Resort Dwellers	100.0
04096	03 Connoisseurs	26.5	04419	26 Midland Crowd	100.0	04614	31 Rural Resort Dwellers	100.0
04097	07 Exurbanites	51.1	04421	15 Silver and Gold	100.0	04615	31 Rural Resort Dwellers	100.0
04101	27 Metro Renters	21.6	04422	46 Rooted Rural	100.0	04616	31 Rural Resort Dwellers	100.0
04102	24 Main Street, USA	21.2	04423	42 Southern Satellites	52.2	04617	31 Rural Resort Dwellers	100.0
04103	22 Metropolitans	29.0	04424	50 Heartland Communities	66.0	04619	50 Heartland Communities	61.9
04105	14 Prosperous Empty Nesters	24.4	04426	50 Heartland Communities	43.6	04622	46 Rooted Rural	91.5
04106	24 Main Street, USA	15.9	04427	26 Midland Crowd	55.5	04623	46 Rooted Rural	100.0
04107	07 Exurbanites	40.4	04428	33 Midlife Junction	43.3	04624	31 Rural Resort Dwellers	100.0
04108	22 Metropolitans	90.7	04429	17 Green Acres	80.9	04625	31 Rural Resort Dwellers	100.0
04109	15 Silver and Gold	100.0	04430	50 Heartland Communities	70.8	04626	37 Prairie Living	100.0
04110	07 Exurbanites	100.0	04431	31 Rural Resort Dwellers	100.0	04627	31 Rural Resort Dwellers	94.8
04210	48 Great Expectations	28.9	04434	26 Midland Crowd	100.0	04628	46 Rooted Rural	100.0
04216	31 Rural Resort Dwellers	100.0	04435	46 Rooted Rural	90.9	04630	46 Rooted Rural	100.0
04217	31 Rural Resort Dwellers	38.2	04438	26 Midland Crowd	95.7	04631	50 Heartland Communities	80.5
04219	31 Rural Resort Dwellers	91.0	04441	50 Heartland Communities	93.6	04634	46 Rooted Rural	100.0
04220	25 Salt of The Earth	100.0	04442	31 Rural Resort Dwellers	100.0	04635	37 Prairie Living	100.0
04221	46 Rooted Rural	50.5	04443	46 Rooted Rural	49.0	04640	31 Rural Resort Dwellers	100.0
04222	17 Green Acres	100.0	04444	33 Midlife Junction	32.5	04642	31 Rural Resort Dwellers	100.0
04224	25 Salt of The Earth	79.0	04448	50 Heartland Communities	78.6	04643	46 Rooted Rural	100.0
04225	25 Salt of The Earth	100.0	04449	26 Midland Crowd	100.0	04645	37 Prairie Living	100.0
04226	31 Rural Resort Dwellers	100.0	04450	26 Midland Crowd	100.0	04646	31 Rural Resort Dwellers	100.0
04228	46 Rooted Rural	100.0	04451	46 Rooted Rural	100.0	04648	46 Rooted Rural	100.0
04231	31 Rural Resort Dwellers	100.0	04453	42 Southern Satellites	80.1	04649	37 Prairie Living	100.0
04236	17 Green Acres	56.1	04454	46 Rooted Rural	100.0	04650	31 Rural Resort Dwellers	100.0
04237	31 Rural Resort Dwellers	100.0	04455	46 Rooted Rural	100.0	04652	46 Rooted Rural	58.3
04238	25 Salt of The Earth	100.0	04456	26 Midland Crowd	100.0	04653	31 Rural Resort Dwellers	100.0
04239	26 Midland Crowd	33.0	04457	50 Heartland Communities	44.2	04654	46 Rooted Rural	36.9
04240	33 Midlife Junction	13.6	04459	56 Rural Bypasses	100.0	04655	46 Rooted Rural	100.0
04250	32 Rustbelt Traditions	59.5	04460	42 Southern Satellites	92.8	04656	31 Rural Resort Dwellers	100.0
04252	32 Rustbelt Traditions	72.5	04461	26 Midland Crowd	100.0	04657	46 Rooted Rural	100.0
04253	25 Salt of The Earth	97.0	04462	50 Heartland Communities	63.1	04658	46 Rooted Rural	97.9
04254	53 Home Town	73.7	04463	50 Heartland Communities	90.3	04660	31 Rural Resort Dwellers	78.1
04255	31 Rural Resort Dwellers	100.0	04464	50 Heartland Communities	87.6	04666	46 Rooted Rural	100.0
04256	42 Southern Satellites	52.5	04468	33 Midlife Junction	27.2	04667	46 Rooted Rural	74.9
04257	50 Heartland Communities	80.7	04469	63 Dorms To Diplomas	100.0	04668	42 Southern Satellites	54.0
04258	17 Green Acres	89.9	04471	46 Rooted Rural	100.0	04669	31 Rural Resort Dwellers	100.0
04259	26 Midland Crowd	81.1	04472	25 Salt of The Earth	77.6	04671	46 Rooted Rural	100.0
04260	19 Milk and Cookies	45.3	04473	55 College Towns	61.4	04673	31 Rural Resort Dwellers	100.0
04261	31 Rural Resort Dwellers	100.0	04474	25 Salt of The Earth	82.6	04676	31 Rural Resort Dwellers	100.0
04263	25 Salt of The Earth	100.0	04475	42 Southern Satellites	100.0	04677	31 Rural Resort Dwellers	100.0
04265	25 Salt of The Earth	98.5	04476	31 Rural Resort Dwellers	99.7	04679	33 Midlife Junction	57.0

ZIP CODE	TOP TAPESTRY CONSUMER TYPE	% 2004 HOUSE-HOLDS	ZIP CODE	TOP TAPESTRY CONSUMER TYPE	% 2004 HOUSE-HOLDS	ZIP CODE	TOP TAPESTRY CONSUMER TYPE	% 2004 HOUSE-HOLDS
04680	37 Prairie Living	100.0	04943	42 Southern Satellites	90.6	05155	31 Rural Resort Dwellers	100.0
04681	37 Prairie Living	100.0	04945	50 Heartland Communities	99.5	05156	33 Midlife Junction	28.9
04683	37 Prairie Living	76.7	04947	33 Midlife Junction	100.0	05158	25 Salt of The Earth	50.3
04684	31 Rural Resort Dwellers	100.0	04949	31 Rural Resort Dwellers	100.0	05161	31 Rural Resort Dwellers	100.0
04685	37 Prairie Living	100.0	04950	50 Heartland Communities	64.5	05201	25 Salt of The Earth	17.1
04691	46 Rooted Rural	100.0	04951	46 Rooted Rural	100.0	05250	31 Rural Resort Dwellers	67.4
04693	33 Midlife Junction	100.0	04952	26 Midland Crowd	46.4	05251	31 Rural Resort Dwellers	100.0
04694	46 Rooted Rural	67.1	04953	33 Midlife Junction	40.8	05252	31 Rural Resort Dwellers	51.4
04730	50 Heartland Communities	55.5	04954	46 Rooted Rural	100.0	05253	31 Rural Resort Dwellers	100.0
04732	46 Rooted Rural	50.3	04955	37 Prairie Living	99.1	05255	33 Midlife Junction	54.0
04733	46 Rooted Rural	100.0	04956	25 Salt of The Earth	100.0	05257	33 Midlife Junction	48.5
04734	46 Rooted Rural	100.0	04957	25 Salt of The Earth	40.4	05260	25 Salt of The Earth	99.2
04735	46 Rooted Rural	96.2	04958	42 Southern Satellites	52.7	05261	25 Salt of The Earth	56.6
04736	46 Rooted Rural	41.9	04961	46 Rooted Rural	90.9	05262	17 Green Acres	40.0
04737	37 Prairie Living	100.0	04962	17 Green Acres	60.0	05301	33 Midlife Junction	17.1
04740	46 Rooted Rural	92.2	04963	48 Great Expectations	22.0	05340	31 Rural Resort Dwellers	100.0
04741	37 Prairie Living	100.0	04965	46 Rooted Rural	94.3	05341	17 Green Acres	63.2
04742	50 Heartland Communities	57.6	04966	31 Rural Resort Dwellers	70.5	05342	31 Rural Resort Dwellers	54.7
04743	50 Heartland Communities	54.8	04967	50 Heartland Communities	28.5	05343	31 Rural Resort Dwellers	100.0
04745	46 Rooted Rural	97.6	04969	26 Midland Crowd	98.3	05345	31 Rural Resort Dwellers	54.0
04746	50 Heartland Communities	97.4	04970	31 Rural Resort Dwellers	100.0	05346	26 Midland Crowd	31.0
04747	50 Heartland Communities	85.2	04971	46 Rooted Rural	54.1	05350	33 Midlife Junction	100.0
04750	32 Rustbelt Traditions	43.6	04973	25 Salt of The Earth	100.0	05351	17 Green Acres	56.0
04751	32 Rustbelt Traditions	98.7	04974	31 Rural Resort Dwellers	68.4	05352	25 Salt of The Earth	100.0
04756	50 Heartland Communities	38.7	04976	42 Southern Satellites	30.7	05353	31 Rural Resort Dwellers	100.0
04757	25 Salt of The Earth	63.5	04978	25 Salt of The Earth	100.0	05354	17 Green Acres	100.0
04758	50 Heartland Communities	100.0	04979	46 Rooted Rural	80.9	05355	31 Rural Resort Dwellers	100.0
04760	46 Rooted Rural	100.0	04981	31 Rural Resort Dwellers	43.2	05356	17 Green Acres	51.8
04761	46 Rooted Rural	89.9	04982	33 Midlife Junction	100.0	05358	31 Rural Resort Dwellers	100.0
04762	46 Rooted Rural	100.0	04983	46 Rooted Rural	73.6	05359	31 Rural Resort Dwellers	100.0
04763	50 Heartland Communities	76.2	04984	46 Rooted Rural	100.0	05360	31 Rural Resort Dwellers	100.0
04764	31 Rural Resort Dwellers	100.0	04985	50 Heartland Communities	52.4	05361	31 Rural Resort Dwellers	56.2
04765	46 Rooted Rural	80.8	04986	46 Rooted Rural	100.0	05362	17 Green Acres	100.0
04766	46 Rooted Rural	100.0	04987	46 Rooted Rural	100.0	05363	31 Rural Resort Dwellers	99.5
04768	46 Rooted Rural	100.0	04988	57 Simple Living	50.2	05401	55 College Towns	28.4
04769	30 Retirement Communities	20.9	04989	26 Midland Crowd	59.0	05403	36 Old and Newcomers	26.6
04772	46 Rooted Rural	100.0	05001	33 Midlife Junction	25.3	05404	24 Main Street, USA	34.0
04773	25 Salt of The Earth	96.3	05032	33 Midlife Junction	43.6	05405	55 College Towns	100.0
04774	50 Heartland Communities	62.9	05033	33 Midlife Junction	47.2	05440	46 Rooted Rural	100.0
04776	46 Rooted Rural	99.5	05034	31 Rural Resort Dwellers	100.0	05441	25 Salt of The Earth	99.4
04777	46 Rooted Rural	99.4	05035	31 Rural Resort Dwellers	100.0	05442	26 Midland Crowd	100.0
04779	31 Rural Resort Dwellers	100.0	05036	17 Green Acres	96.7	05443	17 Green Acres	30.8
04780	46 Rooted Rural	100.0	05037	31 Rural Resort Dwellers	100.0	05444	17 Green Acres	100.0
04781	25 Salt of The Earth	100.0	05038	37 Prairie Living	90.3	05445	07 Exurbanites	45.5
04783	31 Rural Resort Dwellers	51.0	05039	25 Salt of The Earth	100.0	05446	13 In Style	61.1
04785	50 Heartland Communities	63.0	05040	25 Salt of The Earth	67.8	05447	37 Prairie Living	100.0
04786	46 Rooted Rural	53.4	05041	33 Midlife Junction	100.0	05448	17 Green Acres	54.9
04787	46 Rooted Rural	95.0	05042	25 Salt of The Earth	100.0	05450	50 Heartland Communities	27.4
04841	33 Midlife Junction	27.0	05043	17 Green Acres	100.0	05452	13 In Style	33.3
04843	22 Metropolitans	30.3	05045	31 Rural Resort Dwellers	57.6	05454	17 Green Acres	100.0
04847	17 Green Acres	100.0	05046	25 Salt of The Earth	96.2	05455	17 Green Acres	53.8
04848	31 Rural Resort Dwellers	100.0	05048	26 Midland Crowd	45.4	05456	25 Salt of The Earth	52.7
04849	31 Rural Resort Dwellers	86.6	05051	50 Heartland Communities	100.0	05457	25 Salt of The Earth	62.7
04851	37 Prairie Living	100.0	05052	26 Midland Crowd	100.0	05458	17 Green Acres	57.9
04852	37 Prairie Living	100.0	05053	07 Exurbanites	100.0	05459	42 Southern Satellites	52.6
04853	37 Prairie Living	100.0	05055	07 Exurbanites	59.8	05461	26 Midland Crowd	57.9
04854	31 Rural Resort Dwellers	87.5	05056	31 Rural Resort Dwellers	100.0	05462	17 Green Acres	99.7
04856	31 Rural Resort Dwellers	39.6	05058	17 Green Acres	79.7	05463	31 Rural Resort Dwellers	100.0
04857	31 Rural Resort Dwellers	100.0	05060	48 Great Expectations	38.2	05464	17 Green Acres	100.0
04858	31 Rural Resort Dwellers	50.4	05061	33 Midlife Junction	75.8	05465	06 Sophisticated Squires	93.3
04859	31 Rural Resort Dwellers	100.0	05062	31 Rural Resort Dwellers	100.0	05468	17 Green Acres	53.6
04860	31 Rural Resort Dwellers	100.0	05065	26 Midland Crowd	97.3	05471	31 Rural Resort Dwellers	100.0
04861	33 Midlife Junction	85.8	05067	07 Exurbanites	100.0	05472	17 Green Acres	100.0
04862	25 Salt of The Earth	61.9	05068	36 Old and Newcomers	33.9	05473	17 Green Acres	70.8
04863	37 Prairie Living	100.0	05069	25 Salt of The Earth	61.2	05474	31 Rural Resort Dwellers	100.0
04864	26 Midland Crowd	97.5	05070	17 Green Acres	87.1	05476	50 Heartland Communities	83.5
04901	48 Great Expectations	17.5	05071	31 Rural Resort Dwellers	80.0	05477	13 In Style	47.9
04910	46 Rooted Rural	52.7	05072	17 Green Acres	100.0	05478	24 Main Street, USA	28.4
04911	42 Southern Satellites	69.5	05073	07 Exurbanites	100.0	05482	07 Exurbanites	30.2
04912	46 Rooted Rural	100.0	05075	17 Green Acres	99.9	05486	25 Salt of The Earth	100.0
04915	46 Rooted Rural	49.8	05077	25 Salt of The Earth	97.6	05486	17 Green Acres	58.4
04917	31 Rural Resort Dwellers	65.1	05079	26 Midland Crowd	97.7	05487	26 Midland Crowd	55.8
04918	31 Rural Resort Dwellers	100.0	05081	50 Heartland Communities	69.8	05488	25 Salt of The Earth	47.5
04920	50 Heartland Communities	52.9	05083	26 Midland Crowd	100.0	05489	06 Sophisticated Squires	53.9
04921	46 Rooted Rural	100.0	05084	07 Exurbanites	100.0	05491	17 Green Acres	47.4
04922	42 Southern Satellites	100.0	05086	25 Salt of The Earth	100.0	05492	26 Midland Crowd	87.7
04923	46 Rooted Rural	100.0	05089	33 Midlife Junction	32.7	05494	17 Green Acres	100.0
04924	46 Rooted Rural	100.0	05091	14 Prosperous Empty Nesters	39.0	05495	13 In Style	72.3
04925	31 Rural Resort Dwellers	100.0	05101	57 Simple Living	32.0	05602	22 Metropolitans	37.3
04927	42 Southern Satellites	97.6	05141	31 Rural Resort Dwellers	100.0	05640	17 Green Acres	100.0
04928	46 Rooted Rural	51.8	05142	31 Rural Resort Dwellers	77.4	05641	57 Simple Living	27.5
04929	42 Southern Satellites	100.0	05143	31 Rural Resort Dwellers	36.0	05647	25 Salt of The Earth	99.5
04930	50 Heartland Communities	46.5	05146	31 Rural Resort Dwellers	78.9	05648	17 Green Acres	100.0
04932	26 Midland Crowd	100.0	05148	31 Rural Resort Dwellers	100.0	05649	29 Rustbelt Retirees	78.2
04936	33 Midlife Junction	100.0	05149	31 Rural Resort Dwellers	74.7	05650	17 Green Acres	65.3
04937	26 Midland Crowd	42.0	05150	29 Rustbelt Retirees	66.7	05651	33 Midlife Junction	79.5
04938	33 Midlife Junction	42.7	05151	25 Salt of The Earth	73.0	05652	26 Midland Crowd	100.0
04939	42 Southern Satellites	100.0	05152	31 Rural Resort Dwellers	100.0	05653	26 Midland Crowd	100.0
04941	46 Rooted Rural	93.0	05153	31 Rural Resort Dwellers	58.4	05654	33 Midlife Junction	52.3
04942	46 Rooted Rural	100.0	05154	25 Salt of The Earth	100.0	05655	33 Midlife Junction	65.8

ZIP CODE	TOP TAPESTRY CONSUMER TYPE	% 2004 HOUSE-HOLDS	ZIP CODE	TOP TAPESTRY CONSUMER TYPE	% 2004 HOUSE-HOLDS	ZIP CODE	TOP TAPESTRY CONSUMER TYPE	% 2004 HOUSE-HOLDS
05656	48 Great Expectations	57.7	05871	26 Midland Crowd	60.0	06248	06 Sophisticated Squires	48.1
05658	25 Salt of The Earth	100.0	05872	46 Rooted Rural	100.0	06249	17 Green Acres	82.4
05660	17 Green Acres	61.4	05873	25 Salt of The Earth	46.4	06250	22 Metropolitans	54.0
05661	33 Midlife Junction	64.1	05874	31 Rural Resort Dwellers	100.0	06254	18 Cozy and Comfortable	98.0
05663	33 Midlife Junction	65.5	05875	31 Rural Resort Dwellers	58.5	06255	24 Main Street, USA	39.3
05666	33 Midlife Junction	100.0	05901	46 Rooted Rural	100.0	06256	41 Crossroads	51.7
05667	33 Midlife Junction	62.7	05902	42 Southern Satellites	100.0	06259	17 Green Acres	64.2
05669	25 Salt of The Earth	100.0	05903	42 Southern Satellites	100.0	06260	57 Simple Living	21.5
05672	09 Urban Chic	100.0	05904	42 Southern Satellites	100.0	06262	29 Rustbelt Retirees	100.0
05673	17 Green Acres	47.8	05905	46 Rooted Rural	100.0	06264	17 Green Acres	100.0
05674	31 Rural Resort Dwellers	58.0	05906	42 Southern Satellites	71.0	06266	18 Cozy and Comfortable	100.0
05675	25 Salt of The Earth	91.1	05907	46 Rooted Rural	100.0	06268	63 Dorms To Diplomas	25.9
05676	17 Green Acres	52.6	06001	02 Suburban Splendor	33.9	06269	55 College Towns	100.0
05677	17 Green Acres	100.0	06002	30 Retirement Communities	31.1	06277	18 Cozy and Comfortable	67.6
05679	25 Salt of The Earth	50.2	06010	24 Main Street, USA	29.0	06278	13 In Style	61.5
05680	26 Midland Crowd	100.0	06013	06 Sophisticated Squires	36.6	06279	22 Metropolitans	43.9
05681	25 Salt of The Earth	100.0	06016	24 Main Street, USA	51.5	06280	24 Main Street, USA	29.7
05682	25 Salt of The Earth	70.8	06018	33 Midlife Junction	54.2	06281	17 Green Acres	29.6
05701	33 Midlife Junction	32.8	06019	07 Exurbanites	35.2	06282	06 Sophisticated Squires	87.6
05730	25 Salt of The Earth	100.0	06021	17 Green Acres	100.0	06320	48 Great Expectations	24.7
05732	31 Rural Resort Dwellers	56.0	06023	10 Pleasant-Ville	83.2	06330	18 Cozy and Comfortable	47.1
05733	25 Salt of The Earth	40.0	06024	25 Salt of The Earth	76.2	06331	18 Cozy and Comfortable	50.2
05734	37 Prairie Living	100.0	06026	07 Exurbanites	29.0	06333	07 Exurbanites	53.0
05735	33 Midlife Junction	56.3	06027	17 Green Acres	100.0	06334	18 Cozy and Comfortable	62.0
05736	17 Green Acres	100.0	06029	13 In Style	31.4	06335	06 Sophisticated Squires	58.3
05737	17 Green Acres	100.0	06031	07 Exurbanites	68.5	06336	18 Cozy and Comfortable	100.0
05738	17 Green Acres	100.0	06032	09 Urban Chic	52.7	06339	07 Exurbanites	40.5
05739	46 Rooted Rural	100.0	06033	02 Suburban Splendor	33.8	06340	36 Old and Newcomers	28.6
05742	17 Green Acres	75.8	06035	06 Sophisticated Squires	47.8	06349	40 Military Proximity	0.0
05743	32 Rustbelt Traditions	61.2	06037	10 Pleasant-Ville	43.4	06351	17 Green Acres	41.1
05744	33 Midlife Junction	87.5	06039	09 Urban Chic	54.2	06353	33 Midlife Junction	100.0
05746	31 Rural Resort Dwellers	100.0	06040	24 Main Street, USA	17.5	06354	18 Cozy and Comfortable	38.4
05747	46 Rooted Rural	100.0	06043	13 In Style	31.8	06355	18 Cozy and Comfortable	34.3
05748	46 Rooted Rural	99.3	06051	60 City Dimensions	44.4	06357	14 Prosperous Empty Nesters	57.0
05751	13 In Style	99.0	06052	14 Prosperous Empty Nesters	23.1	06359	18 Cozy and Comfortable	58.3
05753	30 Retirement Communities	24.4	06053	60 City Dimensions	28.4	06360	48 Great Expectations	23.3
05757	31 Rural Resort Dwellers	81.1	06057	07 Exurbanites	56.2	06365	18 Cozy and Comfortable	66.4
05758	25 Salt of The Earth	99.3	06058	07 Exurbanites	48.6	06370	18 Cozy and Comfortable	67.6
05759	25 Salt of The Earth	88.2	06060	02 Suburban Splendor	89.4	06371	07 Exurbanites	38.9
05760	37 Prairie Living	72.5	06062	18 Cozy and Comfortable	38.0	06374	18 Cozy and Comfortable	35.7
05761	37 Prairie Living	76.2	06063	17 Green Acres	67.4	06375	14 Prosperous Empty Nesters	29.0
05762	31 Rural Resort Dwellers	53.9	06065	17 Green Acres	100.0	06377	17 Green Acres	60.4
05763	25 Salt of The Earth	45.0	06066	36 Old and Newcomers	26.7	06378	07 Exurbanites	39.6
05764	48 Great Expectations	36.7	06067	13 In Style	15.2	06379	18 Cozy and Comfortable	29.8
05765	29 Rustbelt Retirees	51.1	06068	15 Silver and Gold	58.1	06380	48 Great Expectations	59.5
05766	17 Green Acres	100.0	06069	07 Exurbanites	46.6	06382	18 Cozy and Comfortable	37.7
05767	33 Midlife Junction	52.9	06070	02 Suburban Splendor	48.9	06384	17 Green Acres	98.0
05769	31 Rural Resort Dwellers	82.6	06071	10 Pleasant-Ville	44.3	06385	18 Cozy and Comfortable	43.2
05770	37 Prairie Living	100.0	06073	02 Suburban Splendor	90.3	06390	09 Urban Chic	100.0
05772	31 Rural Resort Dwellers	100.0	06074	13 In Style	31.3	06401	24 Main Street, USA	47.7
05773	29 Rustbelt Retirees	41.7	06076	17 Green Acres	36.5	06403	18 Cozy and Comfortable	32.3
05774	31 Rural Resort Dwellers	100.0	06078	07 Exurbanites	53.7	06405	13 In Style	19.7
05775	37 Prairie Living	100.0	06081	13 In Style	100.0	06409	17 Green Acres	83.9
05776	31 Rural Resort Dwellers	100.0	06082	18 Cozy and Comfortable	53.1	06410	02 Suburban Splendor	24.2
05777	25 Salt of The Earth	53.5	06084	06 Sophisticated Squires	53.9	06412	10 Pleasant-Ville	40.5
05778	17 Green Acres	58.9	06085	05 Wealthy Seaboard Suburbs	35.0	06413	06 Sophisticated Squires	22.4
05819	57 Simple Living	29.7	06088	24 Main Street, USA	86.9	06415	06 Sophisticated Squires	36.6
05820	37 Prairie Living	100.0	06089	07 Exurbanites	68.2	06416	14 Prosperous Empty Nesters	17.2
05821	31 Rural Resort Dwellers	64.2	06090	05 Wealthy Seaboard Suburbs	52.4	06417	17 Green Acres	40.2
05822	50 Heartland Communities	51.6	06092	02 Suburban Splendor	79.9	06418	24 Main Street, USA	40.8
05824	42 Southern Satellites	74.1	06093	07 Exurbanites	37.5	06419	02 Suburban Splendor	49.6
05825	42 Southern Satellites	100.0	06095	18 Cozy and Comfortable	29.3	06420	06 Sophisticated Squires	100.0
05826	37 Prairie Living	97.8	06096	18 Cozy and Comfortable	65.1	06422	06 Sophisticated Squires	44.8
05827	37 Prairie Living	100.0	06098	24 Main Street, USA	44.8	06423	17 Green Acres	52.8
05828	25 Salt of The Earth	99.9	06103	27 Metro Renters	83.4	06424	13 In Style	44.6
05829	46 Rooted Rural	62.0	06105	61 High Rise Renters	30.5	06426	03 Connoisseurs	43.7
05830	32 Rustbelt Traditions	60.0	06106	60 City Dimensions	36.8	06437	07 Exurbanites	34.1
05832	31 Rural Resort Dwellers	93.1	06107	05 Wealthy Seaboard Suburbs	35.7	06438	06 Sophisticated Squires	52.3
05833	46 Rooted Rural	100.0	06108	48 Great Expectations	31.2	06441	07 Exurbanites	71.2
05836	46 Rooted Rural	78.6	06109	14 Prosperous Empty Nesters	36.5	06442	17 Green Acres	45.4
05837	46 Rooted Rural	100.0	06110	24 Main Street, USA	32.4	06443	02 Suburban Splendor	50.3
05839	31 Rural Resort Dwellers	100.0	06111	14 Prosperous Empty Nesters	24.0	06447	06 Sophisticated Squires	82.4
05841	46 Rooted Rural	100.0	06112	45 City Strivers	41.0	06450	18 Cozy and Comfortable	26.1
05842	31 Rural Resort Dwellers	55.7	06114	60 City Dimensions	45.9	06451	24 Main Street, USA	25.3
05843	50 Heartland Communities	54.9	06117	05 Wealthy Seaboard Suburbs	36.0	06455	10 Pleasant-Ville	52.2
05845	37 Prairie Living	99.5	06118	18 Cozy and Comfortable	33.2	06457	24 Main Street, USA	25.2
05846	50 Heartland Communities	92.2	06119	22 Metropolitans	20.5	06459	55 College Towns	100.0
05847	46 Rooted Rural	99.3	06120	64 City Commons	62.8	06460	10 Pleasant-Ville	20.3
05850	48 Great Expectations	100.0	06226	60 City Dimensions	27.1	06468	05 Wealthy Seaboard Suburbs	48.1
05851	50 Heartland Communities	32.4	06231	17 Green Acres	55.5	06469	13 In Style	79.9
05853	37 Prairie Living	100.0	06232	06 Sophisticated Squires	68.9	06470	02 Suburban Splendor	70.9
05855	57 Simple Living	25.6	06234	17 Green Acres	57.3	06471	10 Pleasant-Ville	56.0
05857	25 Salt of The Earth	60.2	06235	17 Green Acres	61.4	06472	07 Exurbanites	31.9
05858	46 Rooted Rural	50.3	06237	18 Cozy and Comfortable	47.1	06473	10 Pleasant-Ville	36.0
05859	42 Southern Satellites	48.5	06238	06 Sophisticated Squires	38.6	06475	14 Prosperous Empty Nesters	58.4
05860	46 Rooted Rural	46.5	06239	57 Simple Living	25.9	06477	05 Wealthy Seaboard Suburbs	70.4
05862	31 Rural Resort Dwellers	100.0	06241	25 Salt of The Earth	38.9	06478	06 Sophisticated Squires	74.2
05866	46 Rooted Rural	100.0	06242	17 Green Acres	99.8	06479	24 Main Street, USA	59.5
05867	25 Salt of The Earth	100.0	06243	18 Cozy and Comfortable	100.0	06480	24 Main Street, USA	29.2
05868	25 Salt of The Earth	91.7	06247	17 Green Acres	100.0	06481	14 Prosperous Empty Nesters	78.9

ZIP CODE	TOP TAPESTRY CONSUMER TYPE	% 2004 HOUSE-HOLDS	ZIP CODE	TOP TAPESTRY CONSUMER TYPE	% 2004 HOUSE-HOLDS	ZIP CODE	TOP TAPESTRY CONSUMER TYPE	% 2004 HOUSE-HOLDS
06482	04 Boomburbs	35.4	06897	01 Top Rung	50.5	07106	45 City Strivers	65.0
06483	24 Main Street, USA	33.2	06901	27 Metro Renters	60.4	07107	35 International Marketplace	24.4
06484	05 Wealthy Seaboard Suburbs	27.6	06902	35 International Marketplace	30.7	07108	45 City Strivers	50.1
06488	02 Suburban Splendor	31.9	06903	01 Top Rung	56.3	07109	20 City Lights	45.6
06489	07 Exurbanites	22.2	06905	05 Wealthy Seaboard Suburbs	33.0	07110	20 City Lights	45.3
06492	24 Main Street, USA	15.2	06906	23 Trendsetters	48.1	07111	45 City Strivers	71.9
06498	31 Rural Resort Dwellers	35.3	06907	05 Wealthy Seaboard Suburbs	31.7	07112	45 City Strivers	79.8
06510	27 Metro Renters	99.7	07001	10 Pleasant-Ville	22.5	07114	61 High Rise Renters	45.8
06511	27 Metro Renters	20.3	07002	20 City Lights	72.1	07201	35 International Marketplace	36.7
06512	24 Main Street, USA	27.9	07003	20 City Lights	28.4	07202	35 International Marketplace	77.5
06513	60 City Dimensions	28.8	07004	05 Wealthy Seaboard Suburbs	100.0	07203	10 Pleasant-Ville	21.8
06514	24 Main Street, USA	23.9	07005	20 City Lights	42.2	07204	20 City Lights	39.9
06515	36 Old and Newcomers	21.9	07006	03 Connoisseurs	31.5	07205	24 Main Street, USA	19.3
06516	24 Main Street, USA	21.4	07008	24 Main Street, USA	30.0	07206	47 Las Casas	48.6
06517	22 Metropolitans	31.2	07009	05 Wealthy Seaboard Suburbs	52.8	07208	35 International Marketplace	60.5
06518	16 Enterprising Professionals	22.2	07010	20 City Lights	39.5	07302	23 Trendsetters	39.7
06519	60 City Dimensions	54.5	07011	20 City Lights	47.8	07304	45 City Strivers	48.2
06524	05 Wealthy Seaboard Suburbs	53.4	07012	10 Pleasant-Ville	32.3	07305	45 City Strivers	49.8
06525	03 Connoisseurs	79.4	07013	10 Pleasant-Ville	35.5	07306	35 International Marketplace	39.1
06604	35 International Marketplace	25.0	07014	20 City Lights	50.5	07307	35 International Marketplace	88.3
06605	60 City Dimensions	35.8	07016	05 Wealthy Seaboard Suburbs	46.8	07310	27 Metro Renters	77.5
06606	24 Main Street, USA	24.2	07017	45 City Strivers	74.3	07401	03 Connoisseurs	100.0
06607	60 City Dimensions	42.2	07018	45 City Strivers	50.1	07403	10 Pleasant-Ville	66.0
06608	60 City Dimensions	35.9	07020	16 Enterprising Professionals	50.5	07405	02 Suburban Splendor	35.7
06610	60 City Dimensions	28.8	07021	01 Top Rung	73.3	07407	20 City Lights	50.3
06611	05 Wealthy Seaboard Suburbs	53.3	07022	20 City Lights	45.6	07410	05 Wealthy Seaboard Suburbs	50.0
06612	03 Connoisseurs	100.0	07023	05 Wealthy Seaboard Suburbs	100.0	07416	24 Main Street, USA	46.7
06614	10 Pleasant-Ville	36.6	07024	30 Retirement Communities	20.8	07417	01 Top Rung	73.5
06615	24 Main Street, USA	43.7	07026	20 City Lights	66.6	07418	06 Sophisticated Squires	77.1
06702	65 Social Security Set	82.7	07027	20 City Lights	83.3	07419	13 In Style	60.2
06704	60 City Dimensions	33.7	07028	02 Suburban Splendor	41.2	07420	10 Pleasant-Ville	62.9
06705	48 Great Expectations	23.7	07029	35 International Marketplace	98.5	07421	06 Sophisticated Squires	54.3
06706	32 Rustbelt Traditions	27.9	07030	27 Metro Renters	69.1	07422	06 Sophisticated Squires	80.3
06708	57 Simple Living	22.5	07031	20 City Lights	56.4	07423	03 Connoisseurs	66.1
06710	60 City Dimensions	63.4	07032	20 City Lights	48.4	07424	20 City Lights	49.3
06712	06 Sophisticated Squires	53.3	07033	10 Pleasant-Ville	77.4	07430	03 Connoisseurs	27.9
06716	18 Cozy and Comfortable	61.8	07034	16 Enterprising Professionals	50.0	07432	05 Wealthy Seaboard Suburbs	69.6
06750	33 Midlife Junction	75.5	07035	13 In Style	29.7	07435	10 Pleasant-Ville	51.3
06751	07 Exurbanites	100.0	07036	24 Main Street, USA	16.5	07436	05 Wealthy Seaboard Suburbs	57.2
06752	07 Exurbanites	62.8	07039	05 Wealthy Seaboard Suburbs	49.7	07438	06 Sophisticated Squires	78.7
06754	07 Exurbanites	54.4	07040	05 Wealthy Seaboard Suburbs	16.9	07439	18 Cozy and Comfortable	52.6
06755	06 Sophisticated Squires	69.3	07041	09 Urban Chic	36.5	07440	10 Pleasant-Ville	56.7
06756	07 Exurbanites	68.3	07042	45 City Strivers	22.3	07442	10 Pleasant-Ville	45.4
06757	33 Midlife Junction	57.0	07043	03 Connoisseurs	31.6	07444	05 Wealthy Seaboard Suburbs	60.4
06758	17 Green Acres	100.0	07044	05 Wealthy Seaboard Suburbs	31.7	07446	03 Connoisseurs	39.4
06759	14 Prosperous Empty Nesters	40.2	07045	03 Connoisseurs	64.9	07450	03 Connoisseurs	43.0
06762	07 Exurbanites	48.6	07046	01 Top Rung	64.2	07452	03 Connoisseurs	46.4
06763	17 Green Acres	99.8	07047	35 International Marketplace	37.1	07456	05 Wealthy Seaboard Suburbs	38.0
06770	24 Main Street, USA	59.7	07050	45 City Strivers	49.8	07457	10 Pleasant-Ville	100.0
06776	24 Main Street, USA	27.1	07052	05 Wealthy Seaboard Suburbs	38.8	07458	01 Top Rung	99.2
06777	31 Rural Resort Dwellers	56.1	07054	23 Trendsetters	21.3	07460	06 Sophisticated Squires	97.1
06778	07 Exurbanites	89.6	07055	35 International Marketplace	33.6	07461	06 Sophisticated Squires	55.1
06779	24 Main Street, USA	63.7	07057	20 City Lights	76.8	07462	28 Aspiring Young Families	55.4
06782	18 Cozy and Comfortable	100.0	07058	16 Enterprising Professionals	44.5	07463	05 Wealthy Seaboard Suburbs	75.0
06783	03 Connoisseurs	99.6	07059	02 Suburban Splendor	74.5	07465	06 Sophisticated Squires	39.1
06784	07 Exurbanites	61.1	07060	10 Pleasant-Ville	16.8	07470	05 Wealthy Seaboard Suburbs	44.6
06785	07 Exurbanites	85.3	07062	10 Pleasant-Ville	21.5	07480	06 Sophisticated Squires	32.7
06786	24 Main Street, USA	51.9	07063	10 Pleasant-Ville	31.7	07481	03 Connoisseurs	72.7
06787	24 Main Street, USA	53.7	07064	10 Pleasant-Ville	44.6	07501	47 Las Casas	25.7
06790	48 Great Expectations	21.4	07065	24 Main Street, USA	36.9	07502	35 International Marketplace	33.0
06791	18 Cozy and Comfortable	33.8	07066	05 Wealthy Seaboard Suburbs	45.5	07503	35 International Marketplace	40.0
06793	03 Connoisseurs	87.2	07067	10 Pleasant-Ville	76.3	07504	45 City Strivers	79.7
06794	03 Connoisseurs	52.6	07068	05 Wealthy Seaboard Suburbs	59.8	07505	61 High Rise Renters	75.2
06795	10 Pleasant-Ville	40.9	07069	03 Connoisseurs	45.2	07506	20 City Lights	59.9
06796	09 Urban Chic	59.7	07070	05 Wealthy Seaboard Suburbs	44.6	07508	21 Urban Villages	23.1
06798	07 Exurbanites	38.1	07071	20 City Lights	83.4	07512	10 Pleasant-Ville	41.0
06801	13 In Style	26.3	07072	20 City Lights	99.3	07513	47 Las Casas	45.6
06804	02 Suburban Splendor	27.4	07073	20 City Lights	92.5	07514	45 City Strivers	58.7
06807	01 Top Rung	37.3	07074	10 Pleasant-Ville	59.7	07522	47 Las Casas	37.0
06810	35 International Marketplace	38.6	07075	10 Pleasant-Ville	80.0	07524	47 Las Casas	66.9
06811	13 In Style	28.5	07076	05 Wealthy Seaboard Suburbs	32.3	07601	35 International Marketplace	20.4
06812	02 Suburban Splendor	34.1	07077	10 Pleasant-Ville	64.6	07603	10 Pleasant-Ville	58.3
06820	01 Top Rung	60.9	07078	01 Top Rung	84.4	07604	20 City Lights	48.6
06824	09 Urban Chic	27.9	07079	03 Connoisseurs	21.4	07605	11 Pacific Heights	27.8
06825	05 Wealthy Seaboard Suburbs	34.0	07080	10 Pleasant-Ville	71.0	07606	20 City Lights	99.1
06830	01 Top Rung	32.3	07081	05 Wealthy Seaboard Suburbs	30.7	07607	10 Pleasant-Ville	42.1
06831	01 Top Rung	56.3	07082	02 Suburban Splendor	44.5	07608	20 City Lights	100.0
06840	01 Top Rung	63.3	07083	10 Pleasant-Ville	58.4	07620	01 Top Rung	99.1
06850	03 Connoisseurs	17.5	07086	23 Trendsetters	44.2	07621	10 Pleasant-Ville	45.0
06851	05 Wealthy Seaboard Suburbs	30.3	07087	35 International Marketplace	46.8	07624	05 Wealthy Seaboard Suburbs	63.5
06853	03 Connoisseurs	36.3	07088	34 Family Foundations	66.7	07626	05 Wealthy Seaboard Suburbs	75.7
06854	35 International Marketplace	33.3	07090	05 Wealthy Seaboard Suburbs	21.9	07627	05 Wealthy Seaboard Suburbs	38.2
06855	20 City Lights	45.3	07092	03 Connoisseurs	71.8	07628	10 Pleasant-Ville	38.3
06870	01 Top Rung	62.1	07093	35 International Marketplace	32.7	07630	05 Wealthy Seaboard Suburbs	100.0
06877	03 Connoisseurs	49.5	07094	20 City Lights	40.3	07631	10 Pleasant-Ville	22.8
06878	01 Top Rung	55.8	07095	10 Pleasant-Ville	37.5	07632	01 Top Rung	50.2
06880	01 Top Rung	60.4	07102	65 Social Security Set	64.4	07640	03 Connoisseurs	35.0
06883	01 Top Rung	99.9	07103	64 City Commons	37.0	07641	03 Connoisseurs	75.6
06890	09 Urban Chic	61.1	07104	47 Las Casas	25.4	07642	05 Wealthy Seaboard Suburbs	65.2
06896	03 Connoisseurs	80.1	07105	35 International Marketplace	65.0	07643	20 City Lights	61.7

ZIP CODE	TOP TAPESTRY CONSUMER TYPE	% 2004 HOUSE-HOLDS	ZIP CODE	TOP TAPESTRY CONSUMER TYPE	% 2004 HOUSE-HOLDS	ZIP CODE	TOP TAPESTRY CONSUMER TYPE	% 2004 HOUSE-HOLDS
07644	20 City Lights	74.1	07871	02 Suburban Splendor	35.4	08085	04 Boomburbs	32.0
07645	09 Urban Chic	34.5	07874	06 Sophisticated Squires	55.3	08086	18 Cozy and Comfortable	39.4
07646	05 Wealthy Seaboard Suburbs	44.9	07876	05 Wealthy Seaboard Suburbs	65.8	08087	18 Cozy and Comfortable	20.8
07647	05 Wealthy Seaboard Suburbs	58.2	07882	24 Main Street, USA	33.7	08088	07 Exurbanites	26.3
07648	05 Wealthy Seaboard Suburbs	37.2	07885	10 Pleasant-Ville	25.8	08089	18 Cozy and Comfortable	57.7
07649	03 Connoisseurs	70.4	07901	01 Top Rung	23.5	08090	18 Cozy and Comfortable	35.6
07650	11 Pacific Heights	44.3	07920	01 Top Rung	26.3	08091	18 Cozy and Comfortable	73.6
07652	05 Wealthy Seaboard Suburbs	77.9	07921	16 Enterprising Professionals	80.2	08092	25 Salt of The Earth	45.1
07656	05 Wealthy Seaboard Suburbs	45.2	07922	05 Wealthy Seaboard Suburbs	46.6	08093	32 Rustbelt Traditions	52.0
07657	20 City Lights	53.5	07924	01 Top Rung	60.2	08094	19 Milk and Cookies	25.1
07660	20 City Lights	77.0	07927	05 Wealthy Seaboard Suburbs	100.0	08096	18 Cozy and Comfortable	30.0
07661	05 Wealthy Seaboard Suburbs	78.1	07928	09 Urban Chic	48.6	08097	18 Cozy and Comfortable	92.8
07662	10 Pleasant-Ville	53.8	07930	02 Suburban Splendor	71.6	08098	17 Green Acres	32.1
07663	10 Pleasant-Ville	64.1	07931	03 Connoisseurs	59.9	08102	54 Urban Rows	50.3
07666	10 Pleasant-Ville	29.2	07932	09 Urban Chic	56.8	08103	54 Urban Rows	82.9
07670	03 Connoisseurs	35.5	07933	05 Wealthy Seaboard Suburbs	61.4	08104	54 Urban Rows	60.8
07675	05 Wealthy Seaboard Suburbs	32.6	07934	03 Connoisseurs	100.0	08105	60 City Dimensions	36.6
07676	05 Wealthy Seaboard Suburbs	88.4	07935	09 Urban Chic	71.9	08106	18 Cozy and Comfortable	35.5
07677	03 Connoisseurs	75.7	07936	05 Wealthy Seaboard Suburbs	47.9	08107	36 Old and Newcomers	20.1
07701	22 Metropolitans	19.0	07940	09 Urban Chic	43.7	08108	24 Main Street, USA	28.2
07702	05 Wealthy Seaboard Suburbs	74.9	07945	03 Connoisseurs	61.9	08109	18 Cozy and Comfortable	40.2
07703	04 Boomburbs	95.9	07946	02 Suburban Splendor	58.9	08110	32 Rustbelt Traditions	28.7
07704	05 Wealthy Seaboard Suburbs	43.3	07950	05 Wealthy Seaboard Suburbs	36.5	08201	18 Cozy and Comfortable	41.3
07711	09 Urban Chic	55.4	07960	03 Connoisseurs	36.1	08202	15 Silver and Gold	95.8
07712	36 Old and Newcomers	15.4	07974	05 Wealthy Seaboard Suburbs	44.6	08203	36 Old and Newcomers	32.2
07716	13 In Style	23.4	07976	01 Top Rung	100.0	08204	29 Rustbelt Retirees	28.8
07717	09 Urban Chic	99.0	07980	20 City Lights	56.1	08205	13 In Style	23.8
07718	10 Pleasant-Ville	66.8	07981	05 Wealthy Seaboard Suburbs	100.0	08210	17 Green Acres	31.4
07719	22 Metropolitans	24.9	08002	14 Prosperous Empty Nesters	30.5	08215	17 Green Acres	27.8
07720	36 Old and Newcomers	36.6	08003	02 Suburban Splendor	38.3	08221	07 Exurbanites	28.2
07721	24 Main Street, USA	64.0	08004	24 Main Street, USA	32.7	08223	07 Exurbanites	85.1
07722	03 Connoisseurs	78.7	08005	18 Cozy and Comfortable	24.2	08225	18 Cozy and Comfortable	97.3
07723	09 Urban Chic	61.1	08007	30 Retirement Communities	46.4	08226	15 Silver and Gold	48.1
07724	05 Wealthy Seaboard Suburbs	21.0	08008	15 Silver and Gold	89.3	08230	07 Exurbanites	39.5
07726	02 Suburban Splendor	55.9	08009	18 Cozy and Comfortable	50.5	08232	51 Metro City Edge	37.6
07727	04 Boomburbs	27.3	08010	18 Cozy and Comfortable	30.6	08234	06 Sophisticated Squires	22.4
07728	02 Suburban Splendor	22.2	08012	18 Cozy and Comfortable	26.3	08241	13 In Style	100.0
07730	10 Pleasant-Ville	45.4	08015	32 Rustbelt Traditions	91.8	08242	50 Heartland Communities	51.9
07731	06 Sophisticated Squires	45.7	08015	19 Milk and Cookies	44.6	08243	15 Silver and Gold	73.0
07732	13 In Style	31.1	08016	12 Up and Coming Families	24.0	08244	24 Main Street, USA	47.3
07733	01 Top Rung	45.2	08019	17 Green Acres	91.0	08247	15 Silver and Gold	94.0
07734	24 Main Street, USA	19.8	08020	14 Prosperous Empty Nesters	42.7	08248	15 Silver and Gold	100.0
07735	18 Cozy and Comfortable	33.3	08021	52 Inner City Tenants	18.1	08251	29 Rustbelt Retirees	38.4
07737	18 Cozy and Comfortable	35.8	08022	07 Exurbanites	47.9	08260	30 Retirement Communities	29.7
07738	02 Suburban Splendor	36.9	08026	18 Cozy and Comfortable	100.0	08270	06 Sophisticated Squires	34.9
07739	03 Connoisseurs	63.4	08027	18 Cozy and Comfortable	59.8	08302	29 Rustbelt Retirees	20.0
07740	24 Main Street, USA	24.0	08028	12 Up and Coming Families	21.2	08310	34 Family Foundations	41.4
07746	02 Suburban Splendor	66.8	08029	57 Simple Living	34.8	08311	25 Salt of The Earth	99.5
07747	05 Wealthy Seaboard Suburbs	23.6	08030	32 Rustbelt Traditions	47.4	08312	32 Rustbelt Traditions	37.4
07748	05 Wealthy Seaboard Suburbs	25.1	08031	29 Rustbelt Retirees	69.3	08314	25 Salt of The Earth	57.6
07750	09 Urban Chic	34.2	08032	04 Boomburbs	77.8	08317	18 Cozy and Comfortable	100.0
07751	02 Suburban Splendor	40.2	08033	14 Prosperous Empty Nesters	24.0	08318	25 Salt of The Earth	27.7
07753	18 Cozy and Comfortable	27.4	08034	05 Wealthy Seaboard Suburbs	39.0	08319	18 Cozy and Comfortable	100.0
07755	10 Pleasant-Ville	65.1	08035	14 Prosperous Empty Nesters	30.7	08322	18 Cozy and Comfortable	34.7
07756	36 Old and Newcomers	42.6	08036	06 Sophisticated Squires	51.2	08323	18 Cozy and Comfortable	100.0
07757	05 Wealthy Seaboard Suburbs	51.4	08037	18 Cozy and Comfortable	34.0	08324	25 Salt of The Earth	100.0
07758	18 Cozy and Comfortable	36.8	08041	10 Pleasant-Ville	87.7	08326	38 Industrious Urban Fringe	100.0
07760	01 Top Rung	34.6	08043	02 Suburban Splendor	36.6	08327	25 Salt of The Earth	100.0
07762	30 Retirement Communities	27.0	08045	34 Family Foundations	70.2	08328	19 Milk and Cookies	76.4
07764	10 Pleasant-Ville	44.6	08046	34 Family Foundations	49.1	08330	28 Aspiring Young Families	39.9
07801	21 Urban Villages	38.8	08048	13 In Style	56.8	08332	18 Cozy and Comfortable	18.7
07803	10 Pleasant-Ville	46.4	08049	32 Rustbelt Traditions	47.4	08340	25 Salt of The Earth	100.0
07821	06 Sophisticated Squires	34.7	08050	12 Up and Coming Families	38.6	08341	50 Heartland Communities	76.0
07822	06 Sophisticated Squires	79.1	08051	13 In Style	28.6	08343	25 Salt of The Earth	42.2
07823	33 Midlife Junction	28.3	08052	39 Young and Restless	27.5	08344	18 Cozy and Comfortable	70.4
07825	07 Exurbanites	55.3	08053	06 Sophisticated Squires	20.2	08345	50 Heartland Communities	67.1
07826	07 Exurbanites	27.9	08054	16 Enterprising Professionals	16.4	08346	34 Family Foundations	100.0
07827	24 Main Street, USA	50.5	08055	07 Exurbanites	32.5	08349	34 Family Foundations	53.4
07828	28 Aspiring Young Families	35.5	08056	06 Sophisticated Squires	66.7	08350	25 Salt of The Earth	82.3
07830	01 Top Rung	28.3	08057	01 Top Rung	23.8	08353	17 Green Acres	100.0
07832	17 Green Acres	66.5	08059	29 Rustbelt Retirees	98.8	08360	60 City Dimensions	22.6
07834	05 Wealthy Seaboard Suburbs	33.8	08060	06 Sophisticated Squires	15.8	08361	24 Main Street, USA	23.1
07836	02 Suburban Splendor	38.8	08061	18 Cozy and Comfortable	81.7	08401	65 Social Security Set	23.0
07838	06 Sophisticated Squires	86.8	08062	07 Exurbanites	39.4	08402	14 Prosperous Empty Nesters	35.5
07840	13 In Style	42.0	08063	32 Rustbelt Traditions	75.5	08403	15 Silver and Gold	92.2
07843	06 Sophisticated Squires	55.6	08065	36 Old and Newcomers	40.5	08406	14 Prosperous Empty Nesters	24.9
07847	10 Pleasant-Ville	100.0	08066	51 Metro City Edge	28.9	08501	07 Exurbanites	38.9
07848	07 Exurbanites	50.5	08067	18 Cozy and Comfortable	100.0	08502	04 Boomburbs	68.1
07849	17 Green Acres	40.8	08068	36 Old and Newcomers	32.0	08505	06 Sophisticated Squires	28.5
07850	06 Sophisticated Squires	52.1	08069	18 Cozy and Comfortable	15.6	08510	02 Suburban Splendor	97.3
07851	18 Cozy and Comfortable	100.0	08070	29 Rustbelt Retirees	50.9	08511	06 Sophisticated Squires	100.0
07852	05 Wealthy Seaboard Suburbs	46.3	08071	18 Cozy and Comfortable	40.1	08512	02 Suburban Splendor	35.5
07853	02 Suburban Splendor	77.2	08075	18 Cozy and Comfortable	18.9	08514	07 Exurbanites	56.6
07856	13 In Style	100.0	08077	14 Prosperous Empty Nesters	35.4	08515	07 Exurbanites	100.0
07857	24 Main Street, USA	54.5	08078	29 Rustbelt Retirees	47.5	08518	24 Main Street, USA	56.8
07860	06 Sophisticated Squires	25.5	08079	62 Modest Income Homes	18.8	08520	13 In Style	36.3
07863	26 Midland Crowd	41.9	08080	06 Sophisticated Squires	49.4	08525	03 Connoisseurs	44.0
07865	10 Pleasant-Ville	32.2	08081	19 Milk and Cookies	27.5	08526	07 Exurbanites	100.0
07866	06 Sophisticated Squires	34.3	08083	18 Cozy and Comfortable	38.5	08527	06 Sophisticated Squires	36.4
07869	02 Suburban Splendor	68.2	08084	18 Cozy and Comfortable	59.7	08530	07 Exurbanites	31.9

   357

ZIP CODE	TOP TAPESTRY CONSUMER TYPE	% 2004 HOUSE-HOLDS	ZIP CODE	TOP TAPESTRY CONSUMER TYPE	% 2004 HOUSE-HOLDS	ZIP CODE	TOP TAPESTRY CONSUMER TYPE	% 2004 HOUSE-HOLDS
08533	06 Sophisticated Squires	36.3	08861	47 Las Casas	43.3	10471	30 Retirement Communities	34.3
08534	04 Boomburbs	51.4	08863	10 Pleasant-Ville	37.9	10472	61 High Rise Renters	64.9
08535	02 Suburban Splendor	100.0	08865	18 Cozy and Comfortable	18.5	10473	45 City Strivers	46.5
08536	16 Enterprising Professionals	34.3	08867	02 Suburban Splendor	54.1	10474	61 High Rise Renters	98.9
08540	09 Urban Chic	23.9	08869	20 City Lights	47.4	10475	34 Family Foundations	89.0
08542	08 Laptops and Lattes	35.9	08872	16 Enterprising Professionals	24.8	10501	02 Suburban Splendor	100.0
08544	22 Metropolitans	100.0	08873	13 In Style	31.9	10502	03 Connoisseurs	70.3
08550	02 Suburban Splendor	75.1	08876	02 Suburban Splendor	28.7	10504	01 Top Rung	74.9
08551	07 Exurbanites	39.1	08879	10 Pleasant-Ville	27.5	10505	02 Suburban Splendor	100.0
08553	09 Urban Chic	100.0	08880	24 Main Street, USA	98.9	10506	01 Top Rung	85.5
08554	32 Rustbelt Traditions	51.5	08882	10 Pleasant-Ville	49.0	10507	09 Urban Chic	30.1
08556	07 Exurbanites	100.0	08884	10 Pleasant-Ville	50.8	10509	06 Sophisticated Squires	24.2
08558	02 Suburban Splendor	93.3	08886	04 Boomburbs	58.2	10510	01 Top Rung	56.1
08559	07 Exurbanites	41.3	08887	16 Enterprising Professionals	100.0	10511	10 Pleasant-Ville	77.4
08560	05 Wealthy Seaboard Suburbs	93.3	08889	02 Suburban Splendor	43.9	10512	10 Pleasant-Ville	28.8
08562	17 Green Acres	40.4	08901	35 International Marketplace	14.4	10514	01 Top Rung	80.1
08608	60 City Dimensions	86.9	08902	13 In Style	19.5	10516	07 Exurbanites	47.7
08609	54 Urban Rows	30.5	08904	22 Metropolitans	48.8	10518	02 Suburban Splendor	100.0
08610	24 Main Street, USA	24.1	10001	27 Metro Renters	40.9	10520	09 Urban Chic	27.6
08611	48 Great Expectations	27.5	10002	44 Urban Melting Pot	44.0	10522	09 Urban Chic	36.8
08618	54 Urban Rows	20.5	10003	27 Metro Renters	52.5	10523	20 City Lights	34.3
08619	10 Pleasant-Ville	21.7	10004	27 Metro Renters	81.9	10524	03 Connoisseurs	39.4
08620	24 Main Street, USA	41.2	10005	27 Metro Renters	100.0	10526	03 Connoisseurs	100.0
08628	13 In Style	34.8	10006	27 Metro Renters	96.3	10527	02 Suburban Splendor	65.4
08629	32 Rustbelt Traditions	56.5	10007	08 Laptops and Lattes	85.7	10528	09 Urban Chic	36.9
08638	54 Urban Rows	20.6	10009	27 Metro Renters	38.6	10530	09 Urban Chic	38.2
08640	40 Military Proximity	97.8	10010	27 Metro Renters	60.6	10532	05 Wealthy Seaboard Suburbs	89.0
08641	40 Military Proximity	100.0	10011	08 Laptops and Lattes	65.8	10533	03 Connoisseurs	45.3
08648	16 Enterprising Professionals	22.3	10012	08 Laptops and Lattes	43.6	10535	05 Wealthy Seaboard Suburbs	100.0
08690	18 Cozy and Comfortable	23.7	10013	44 Urban Melting Pot	36.3	10536	02 Suburban Splendor	40.2
08691	13 In Style	48.1	10014	08 Laptops and Lattes	89.2	10537	18 Cozy and Comfortable	58.9
08701	43 The Elders	30.2	10016	27 Metro Renters	58.6	10538	09 Urban Chic	47.1
08721	18 Cozy and Comfortable	47.7	10017	27 Metro Renters	54.2	10541	05 Wealthy Seaboard Suburbs	55.8
08722	18 Cozy and Comfortable	39.2	10018	27 Metro Renters	59.5	10543	20 City Lights	34.0
08723	18 Cozy and Comfortable	18.6	10019	27 Metro Renters	51.5	10546	01 Top Rung	100.0
08724	19 Milk and Cookies	18.6	10021	08 Laptops and Lattes	65.6	10547	13 In Style	32.4
08730	09 Urban Chic	31.9	10022	08 Laptops and Lattes	72.4	10548	10 Pleasant-Ville	88.7
08731	18 Cozy and Comfortable	44.2	10023	08 Laptops and Lattes	84.2	10549	01 Top Rung	24.2
08733	32 Rustbelt Traditions	48.4	10024	08 Laptops and Lattes	81.8	10550	45 City Strivers	52.1
08734	18 Cozy and Comfortable	46.7	10025	08 Laptops and Lattes	50.8	10552	30 Retirement Communities	31.9
08735	15 Silver and Gold	100.0	10026	61 High Rise Renters	84.4	10553	45 City Strivers	60.5
08736	09 Urban Chic	36.7	10027	61 High Rise Renters	58.8	10560	03 Connoisseurs	76.0
08738	15 Silver and Gold	88.7	10028	08 Laptops and Lattes	52.8	10562	35 International Marketplace	18.8
08740	24 Main Street, USA	62.5	10029	61 High Rise Renters	73.7	10566	13 In Style	26.9
08741	14 Prosperous Empty Nesters	49.1	10030	61 High Rise Renters	75.7	10567	10 Pleasant-Ville	37.3
08742	10 Pleasant-Ville	21.0	10031	61 High Rise Renters	94.4	10570	03 Connoisseurs	28.6
08750	03 Connoisseurs	36.5	10032	61 High Rise Renters	87.2	10573	35 International Marketplace	22.7
08751	48 Great Expectations	40.0	10033	61 High Rise Renters	78.1	10576	01 Top Rung	88.3
08752	15 Silver and Gold	80.6	10034	61 High Rise Renters	68.4	10577	01 Top Rung	96.8
08753	06 Sophisticated Squires	27.1	10035	61 High Rise Renters	84.9	10578	05 Wealthy Seaboard Suburbs	100.0
08755	49 Senior Sun Seekers	36.5	10036	27 Metro Renters	53.3	10579	05 Wealthy Seaboard Suburbs	32.9
08757	43 The Elders	80.3	10037	65 Social Security Set	50.9	10580	01 Top Rung	48.8
08758	29 Rustbelt Retirees	46.2	10038	30 Retirement Communities	30.3	10583	01 Top Rung	45.1
08759	43 The Elders	84.1	10039	61 High Rise Renters	78.6	10588	05 Wealthy Seaboard Suburbs	46.9
08801	02 Suburban Splendor	72.0	10040	61 High Rise Renters	83.1	10589	43 The Elders	30.3
08802	02 Suburban Splendor	70.1	10044	22 Metropolitans	100.0	10590	03 Connoisseurs	65.6
08804	12 Up and Coming Families	37.6	10128	27 Metro Renters	36.7	10591	09 Urban Chic	32.5
08805	35 International Marketplace	31.3	10280	08 Laptops and Lattes	98.6	10594	05 Wealthy Seaboard Suburbs	81.3
08807	04 Boomburbs	25.8	10301	20 City Lights	33.4	10595	05 Wealthy Seaboard Suburbs	58.7
08809	13 In Style	41.6	10302	45 City Strivers	36.4	10597	03 Connoisseurs	51.7
08810	06 Sophisticated Squires	52.3	10303	45 City Strivers	50.5	10598	05 Wealthy Seaboard Suburbs	77.2
08812	10 Pleasant-Ville	35.9	10304	45 City Strivers	40.0	10601	36 Old and Newcomers	45.3
08816	05 Wealthy Seaboard Suburbs	25.8	10305	20 City Lights	71.0	10603	20 City Lights	30.5
08817	16 Enterprising Professionals	35.3	10306	20 City Lights	51.3	10604	20 City Lights	33.6
08820	05 Wealthy Seaboard Suburbs	28.3	10307	20 City Lights	33.3	10605	03 Connoisseurs	31.8
08822	02 Suburban Splendor	34.6	10308	10 Pleasant-Ville	57.1	10606	20 City Lights	41.5
08823	16 Enterprising Professionals	77.5	10309	05 Wealthy Seaboard Suburbs	30.5	10607	03 Connoisseurs	39.3
08824	04 Boomburbs	58.1	10310	45 City Strivers	35.3	10701	61 High Rise Renters	29.9
08825	13 In Style	34.5	10312	10 Pleasant-Ville	25.1	10703	20 City Lights	36.5
08826	07 Exurbanites	46.7	10314	10 Pleasant-Ville	36.1	10704	20 City Lights	81.4
08827	02 Suburban Splendor	51.9	10451	61 High Rise Renters	82.5	10705	35 International Marketplace	36.1
08828	12 Up and Coming Families	84.1	10452	61 High Rise Renters	100.0	10706	03 Connoisseurs	43.1
08829	06 Sophisticated Squires	34.2	10453	61 High Rise Renters	97.6	10707	05 Wealthy Seaboard Suburbs	27.2
08830	10 Pleasant-Ville	54.2	10454	61 High Rise Renters	95.5	10708	30 Retirement Communities	54.7
08831	43 The Elders	53.1	10455	61 High Rise Renters	98.4	10709	03 Connoisseurs	38.7
08832	35 International Marketplace	45.9	10456	61 High Rise Renters	94.6	10710	05 Wealthy Seaboard Suburbs	41.0
08833	02 Suburban Splendor	28.9	10457	61 High Rise Renters	99.5	10801	20 City Lights	36.4
08835	24 Main Street, USA	28.1	10458	61 High Rise Renters	87.6	10803	03 Connoisseurs	38.2
08836	02 Suburban Splendor	61.4	10459	61 High Rise Renters	83.5	10804	03 Connoisseurs	64.8
08837	36 Old and Newcomers	24.9	10460	61 High Rise Renters	86.7	10805	23 Trendsetters	29.9
08840	05 Wealthy Seaboard Suburbs	42.1	10461	20 City Lights	62.6	10901	05 Wealthy Seaboard Suburbs	21.2
08844	02 Suburban Splendor	24.0	10462	61 High Rise Renters	50.7	10913	05 Wealthy Seaboard Suburbs	82.5
08846	10 Pleasant-Ville	47.5	10463	61 High Rise Renters	36.8	10916	06 Sophisticated Squires	55.8
08848	07 Exurbanites	43.6	10464	20 City Lights	42.8	10917	13 In Style	54.7
08850	05 Wealthy Seaboard Suburbs	39.4	10465	20 City Lights	81.3	10918	06 Sophisticated Squires	37.8
08852	16 Enterprising Professionals	50.6	10466	45 City Strivers	57.9	10919	17 Green Acres	81.7
08853	02 Suburban Splendor	95.1	10467	61 High Rise Renters	55.9	10920	05 Wealthy Seaboard Suburbs	55.7
08854	10 Pleasant-Ville	24.0	10468	61 High Rise Renters	91.2	10921	06 Sophisticated Squires	44.0
08857	10 Pleasant-Ville	19.8	10469	45 City Strivers	45.2	10923	10 Pleasant-Ville	50.3
08859	10 Pleasant-Ville	27.7	10470	45 City Strivers	42.6	10924	07 Exurbanites	30.0

ZIP CODE	TOP TAPESTRY CONSUMER TYPE	% 2004 HOUSE-HOLDS	ZIP CODE	TOP TAPESTRY CONSUMER TYPE	% 2004 HOUSE-HOLDS	ZIP CODE	TOP TAPESTRY CONSUMER TYPE	% 2004 HOUSE-HOLDS
10925	24 Main Street, USA	62.8	11234	20 City Lights	49.1	11692	45 City Strivers	53.5
10926	13 In Style	89.0	11235	44 Urban Melting Pot	50.1	11693	34 Family Foundations	28.6
10927	35 International Marketplace	35.0	11236	45 City Strivers	65.5	11694	20 City Lights	24.1
10928	24 Main Street, USA	49.1	11237	58 Newest Residents	53.9	11697	14 Prosperous Empty Nesters	42.8
10930	13 In Style	35.1	11238	23 Trendsetters	50.5	11701	34 Family Foundations	21.3
10931	10 Pleasant-Ville	100.0	11239	61 High Rise Renters	100.0	11702	05 Wealthy Seaboard Suburbs	31.7
10940	24 Main Street, USA	21.7	11354	44 Urban Melting Pot	57.7	11703	10 Pleasant-Ville	91.1
10941	06 Sophisticated Squires	19.6	11355	44 Urban Melting Pot	75.6	11704	10 Pleasant-Ville	78.2
10950	06 Sophisticated Squires	26.9	11356	20 City Lights	81.1	11705	05 Wealthy Seaboard Suburbs	45.5
10952	05 Wealthy Seaboard Suburbs	43.0	11357	20 City Lights	48.9	11706	21 Urban Villages	29.1
10954	05 Wealthy Seaboard Suburbs	37.0	11358	11 Pacific Heights	34.2	11709	05 Wealthy Seaboard Suburbs	60.7
10956	05 Wealthy Seaboard Suburbs	45.5	11360	30 Retirement Communities	49.8	11710	05 Wealthy Seaboard Suburbs	50.5
10958	06 Sophisticated Squires	48.3	11361	20 City Lights	38.5	11713	06 Sophisticated Squires	30.3
10960	23 Trendsetters	34.1	11362	11 Pacific Heights	27.4	11714	10 Pleasant-Ville	47.4
10962	30 Retirement Communities	35.1	11363	11 Pacific Heights	36.0	11715	05 Wealthy Seaboard Suburbs	48.7
10963	18 Cozy and Comfortable	66.0	11364	11 Pacific Heights	48.6	11716	10 Pleasant-Ville	61.6
10964	03 Connoisseurs	53.9	11365	20 City Lights	48.1	11717	21 Urban Villages	89.9
10965	05 Wealthy Seaboard Suburbs	64.3	11366	20 City Lights	38.5	11718	05 Wealthy Seaboard Suburbs	54.1
10968	09 Urban Chic	64.9	11367	20 City Lights	27.4	11719	07 Exurbanites	58.8
10969	17 Green Acres	72.9	11368	35 International Marketplace	43.2	11720	10 Pleasant-Ville	73.8
10970	02 Suburban Splendor	22.2	11369	45 City Strivers	40.4	11721	05 Wealthy Seaboard Suburbs	55.0
10973	17 Green Acres	56.4	11370	44 Urban Melting Pot	49.0	11722	21 Urban Villages	57.3
10974	10 Pleasant-Ville	66.9	11372	44 Urban Melting Pot	67.1	11724	01 Top Rung	98.8
10975	13 In Style	100.0	11373	44 Urban Melting Pot	89.6	11725	05 Wealthy Seaboard Suburbs	76.4
10976	05 Wealthy Seaboard Suburbs	83.5	11374	44 Urban Melting Pot	73.3	11726	24 Main Street, USA	25.9
10977	05 Wealthy Seaboard Suburbs	26.4	11375	30 Retirement Communities	25.9	11727	06 Sophisticated Squires	24.9
10980	10 Pleasant-Ville	42.3	11377	44 Urban Melting Pot	75.9	11729	10 Pleasant-Ville	75.7
10983	05 Wealthy Seaboard Suburbs	97.1	11378	20 City Lights	85.4	11730	10 Pleasant-Ville	33.4
10984	10 Pleasant-Ville	51.0	11379	20 City Lights	80.3	11731	05 Wealthy Seaboard Suburbs	78.7
10985	17 Green Acres	54.2	11385	20 City Lights	30.1	11732	05 Wealthy Seaboard Suburbs	51.0
10986	05 Wealthy Seaboard Suburbs	94.6	11411	10 Pleasant-Ville	65.0	11733	02 Suburban Splendor	37.0
10987	13 In Style	70.8	11412	34 Family Foundations	68.0	11735	10 Pleasant-Ville	62.7
10989	05 Wealthy Seaboard Suburbs	63.6	11413	10 Pleasant-Ville	36.1	11738	06 Sophisticated Squires	49.8
10990	06 Sophisticated Squires	25.0	11414	20 City Lights	33.9	11740	05 Wealthy Seaboard Suburbs	28.9
10992	06 Sophisticated Squires	52.2	11415	23 Trendsetters	36.4	11741	10 Pleasant-Ville	42.0
10993	57 Simple Living	44.4	11416	35 International Marketplace	73.5	11742	13 In Style	52.1
10994	05 Wealthy Seaboard Suburbs	50.8	11417	20 City Lights	46.6	11743	09 Urban Chic	22.2
10996	40 Military Proximity	100.0	11418	35 International Marketplace	53.4	11746	05 Wealthy Seaboard Suburbs	24.2
10998	06 Sophisticated Squires	35.0	11419	35 International Marketplace	48.2	11747	05 Wealthy Seaboard Suburbs	46.0
11001	05 Wealthy Seaboard Suburbs	51.8	11420	21 Urban Villages	33.7	11749	13 In Style	36.2
11003	10 Pleasant-Ville	55.5	11421	35 International Marketplace	51.3	11751	10 Pleasant-Ville	54.8
11004	20 City Lights	60.4	11422	10 Pleasant-Ville	47.3	11752	10 Pleasant-Ville	82.6
11005	43 The Elders	94.4	11423	45 City Strivers	21.1	11753	03 Connoisseurs	77.8
11010	05 Wealthy Seaboard Suburbs	48.3	11426	05 Wealthy Seaboard Suburbs	38.9	11754	10 Pleasant-Ville	42.2
11020	01 Top Rung	55.5	11427	20 City Lights	24.1	11755	10 Pleasant-Ville	50.6
11021	22 Metropolitans	27.0	11428	10 Pleasant-Ville	40.9	11756	10 Pleasant-Ville	96.6
11023	09 Urban Chic	40.6	11429	34 Family Foundations	43.4	11757	10 Pleasant-Ville	81.0
11024	01 Top Rung	58.5	11430	45 City Strivers	89.5	11758	05 Wealthy Seaboard Suburbs	57.3
11030	01 Top Rung	73.9	11432	44 Urban Melting Pot	25.7	11762	05 Wealthy Seaboard Suburbs	85.5
11040	05 Wealthy Seaboard Suburbs	74.1	11433	45 City Strivers	57.8	11763	06 Sophisticated Squires	60.8
11042	01 Top Rung	0.0	11434	34 Family Foundations	52.7	11764	06 Sophisticated Squires	45.8
11050	03 Connoisseurs	22.1	11435	44 Urban Melting Pot	27.6	11765	01 Top Rung	84.9
11096	45 City Strivers	28.5	11436	45 City Strivers	70.7	11766	02 Suburban Splendor	36.6
11101	44 Urban Melting Pot	34.0	11501	05 Wealthy Seaboard Suburbs	37.7	11767	05 Wealthy Seaboard Suburbs	49.6
11102	44 Urban Melting Pot	52.0	11507	05 Wealthy Seaboard Suburbs	57.7	11768	03 Connoisseurs	56.2
11103	44 Urban Melting Pot	83.1	11509	65 Social Security Set	47.8	11769	10 Pleasant-Ville	46.6
11104	44 Urban Melting Pot	89.2	11510	10 Pleasant-Ville	49.0	11770	09 Urban Chic	100.0
11105	44 Urban Melting Pot	46.8	11514	05 Wealthy Seaboard Suburbs	52.7	11771	01 Top Rung	30.4
11106	44 Urban Melting Pot	59.8	11516	09 Urban Chic	27.3	11772	10 Pleasant-Ville	30.0
11201	08 Laptops and Lattes	56.4	11518	20 City Lights	39.2	11776	10 Pleasant-Ville	48.1
11203	45 City Strivers	82.5	11520	10 Pleasant-Ville	39.8	11777	09 Urban Chic	42.3
11204	44 Urban Melting Pot	90.4	11530	03 Connoisseurs	33.9	11778	24 Main Street, USA	29.8
11205	61 High Rise Renters	30.0	11542	20 City Lights	46.7	11779	10 Pleasant-Ville	53.9
11206	61 High Rise Renters	51.6	11545	05 Wealthy Seaboard Suburbs	60.0	11780	05 Wealthy Seaboard Suburbs	56.0
11207	45 City Strivers	60.5	11548	09 Urban Chic	61.2	11782	05 Wealthy Seaboard Suburbs	43.6
11208	45 City Strivers	41.2	11550	10 Pleasant-Ville	25.5	11783	05 Wealthy Seaboard Suburbs	59.0
11209	44 Urban Melting Pot	47.5	11552	05 Wealthy Seaboard Suburbs	51.3	11784	10 Pleasant-Ville	70.8
11210	45 City Strivers	49.9	11553	10 Pleasant-Ville	59.3	11786	06 Sophisticated Squires	39.6
11211	61 High Rise Renters	39.8	11554	05 Wealthy Seaboard Suburbs	48.9	11787	05 Wealthy Seaboard Suburbs	67.8
11212	45 City Strivers	46.3	11557	05 Wealthy Seaboard Suburbs	45.8	11788	05 Wealthy Seaboard Suburbs	70.6
11213	45 City Strivers	48.3	11558	05 Wealthy Seaboard Suburbs	45.4	11789	17 Green Acres	29.5
11214	44 Urban Melting Pot	86.4	11559	01 Top Rung	40.5	11790	05 Wealthy Seaboard Suburbs	65.7
11215	08 Laptops and Lattes	46.3	11560	01 Top Rung	32.2	11791	05 Wealthy Seaboard Suburbs	40.8
11216	45 City Strivers	91.0	11561	22 Metropolitans	21.8	11792	14 Prosperous Empty Nesters	48.0
11217	08 Laptops and Lattes	43.6	11563	10 Pleasant-Ville	31.3	11793	05 Wealthy Seaboard Suburbs	68.2
11218	44 Urban Melting Pot	74.9	11565	05 Wealthy Seaboard Suburbs	85.5	11794	05 Wealthy Seaboard Suburbs	100.0
11219	44 Urban Melting Pot	90.6	11566	05 Wealthy Seaboard Suburbs	58.0	11795	10 Pleasant-Ville	71.0
11220	44 Urban Melting Pot	64.2	11568	01 Top Rung	97.5	11796	10 Pleasant-Ville	85.4
11221	45 City Strivers	55.3	11570	03 Connoisseurs	24.7	11797	01 Top Rung	58.6
11222	44 Urban Melting Pot	72.3	11572	05 Wealthy Seaboard Suburbs	74.9	11798	51 Metro City Edge	38.7
11223	44 Urban Melting Pot	67.6	11575	21 Urban Villages	41.3	11801	10 Pleasant-Ville	65.3
11224	61 High Rise Renters	32.5	11576	01 Top Rung	76.4	11803	05 Wealthy Seaboard Suburbs	68.8
11225	45 City Strivers	75.0	11577	01 Top Rung	38.3	11804	05 Wealthy Seaboard Suburbs	76.2
11226	61 High Rise Renters	51.2	11579	09 Urban Chic	55.2	11901	24 Main Street, USA	28.8
11228	20 City Lights	68.1	11580	10 Pleasant-Ville	55.9	11933	33 Midlife Junction	43.3
11229	44 Urban Melting Pot	53.8	11581	05 Wealthy Seaboard Suburbs	32.1	11934	10 Pleasant-Ville	55.2
11230	44 Urban Melting Pot	77.9	11590	05 Wealthy Seaboard Suburbs	31.4	11935	14 Prosperous Empty Nesters	40.8
11231	08 Laptops and Lattes	38.0	11596	05 Wealthy Seaboard Suburbs	71.2	11937	31 Rural Resort Dwellers	30.4
11232	35 International Marketplace	47.6	11598	03 Connoisseurs	56.9	11939	31 Rural Resort Dwellers	100.0
11233	45 City Strivers	54.9	11691	45 City Strivers	32.3	11940	06 Sophisticated Squires	45.7

ZIP CODE	TOP TAPESTRY CONSUMER TYPE	% 2004 HOUSE-HOLDS	ZIP CODE	TOP TAPESTRY CONSUMER TYPE	% 2004 HOUSE-HOLDS	ZIP CODE	TOP TAPESTRY CONSUMER TYPE	% 2004 HOUSE-HOLDS
11941	03 Connoisseurs	37.4	12117	31 Rural Resort Dwellers	41.2	12424	31 Rural Resort Dwellers	100.0
11942	10 Pleasant-Ville	36.0	12118	18 Cozy and Comfortable	21.2	12427	31 Rural Resort Dwellers	79.1
11944	33 Midlife Junction	43.1	12120	46 Rooted Rural	63.5	12428	48 Great Expectations	30.4
11946	31 Rural Resort Dwellers	50.5	12121	18 Cozy and Comfortable	99.1	12430	31 Rural Resort Dwellers	61.0
11948	14 Prosperous Empty Nesters	100.0	12122	31 Rural Resort Dwellers	27.7	12431	25 Salt of The Earth	59.3
11949	04 Boomburbs	28.6	12123	18 Cozy and Comfortable	34.4	12433	14 Prosperous Empty Nesters	100.0
11950	19 Milk and Cookies	75.0	12125	31 Rural Resort Dwellers	50.3	12435	31 Rural Resort Dwellers	100.0
11951	19 Milk and Cookies	44.0	12130	25 Salt of The Earth	76.5	12439	31 Rural Resort Dwellers	100.0
11952	14 Prosperous Empty Nesters	59.6	12131	31 Rural Resort Dwellers	100.0	12440	33 Midlife Junction	48.8
11953	28 Aspiring Young Families	47.0	12134	31 Rural Resort Dwellers	57.1	12442	31 Rural Resort Dwellers	100.0
11954	31 Rural Resort Dwellers	42.2	12136	31 Rural Resort Dwellers	72.6	12443	14 Prosperous Empty Nesters	57.9
11955	36 Old and Newcomers	51.8	12137	17 Green Acres	78.8	12446	31 Rural Resort Dwellers	100.0
11957	15 Silver and Gold	97.7	12138	25 Salt of The Earth	76.7	12446	26 Midland Crowd	38.7
11958	31 Rural Resort Dwellers	100.0	12139	31 Rural Resort Dwellers	100.0	12448	09 Urban Chic	100.0
11961	43 The Elders	50.3	12140	17 Green Acres	57.0	12449	33 Midlife Junction	56.5
11963	31 Rural Resort Dwellers	39.5	12143	26 Midland Crowd	35.8	12450	31 Rural Resort Dwellers	100.0
11964	31 Rural Resort Dwellers	96.1	12144	48 Great Expectations	24.0	12451	46 Rooted Rural	50.9
11965	15 Silver and Gold	91.1	12147	25 Salt of The Earth	51.2	12454	31 Rural Resort Dwellers	100.0
11967	19 Milk and Cookies	56.4	12148	07 Exurbanites	65.3	12455	31 Rural Resort Dwellers	67.6
11968	09 Urban Chic	31.4	12149	42 Southern Satellites	29.6	12456	32 Rustbelt Traditions	100.0
11971	14 Prosperous Empty Nesters	32.1	12150	33 Midlife Junction	100.0	12457	09 Urban Chic	44.2
11976	01 Top Rung	39.0	12151	07 Exurbanites	70.0	12458	29 Rustbelt Retirees	48.2
11977	09 Urban Chic	50.6	12153	18 Cozy and Comfortable	81.6	12460	31 Rural Resort Dwellers	79.3
11978	09 Urban Chic	43.9	12154	18 Cozy and Comfortable	51.8	12461	25 Salt of The Earth	66.6
11980	18 Cozy and Comfortable	59.1	12155	46 Rooted Rural	59.7	12463	33 Midlife Junction	100.0
12007	18 Cozy and Comfortable	100.0	12156	17 Green Acres	68.5	12464	31 Rural Resort Dwellers	37.9
12008	18 Cozy and Comfortable	100.0	12157	33 Midlife Junction	45.7	12465	31 Rural Resort Dwellers	100.0
12009	13 In Style	38.6	12158	13 In Style	37.5	12466	26 Midland Crowd	45.5
12010	57 Simple Living	30.8	12159	30 Retirement Communities	26.9	12468	31 Rural Resort Dwellers	61.1
12015	31 Rural Resort Dwellers	42.9	12160	25 Salt of The Earth	70.3	12469	46 Rooted Rural	53.4
12017	31 Rural Resort Dwellers	81.5	12164	31 Rural Resort Dwellers	100.0	12470	33 Midlife Junction	100.0
12018	17 Green Acres	56.8	12165	14 Prosperous Empty Nesters	100.0	12472	33 Midlife Junction	35.0
12019	07 Exurbanites	38.7	12166	25 Salt of The Earth	58.7	12473	33 Midlife Junction	100.0
12020	12 Up and Coming Families	34.8	12167	50 Heartland Communities	66.8	12474	31 Rural Resort Dwellers	100.0
12022	25 Salt of The Earth	100.0	12168	26 Midland Crowd	98.3	12477	18 Cozy and Comfortable	29.5
12023	18 Cozy and Comfortable	55.2	12169	26 Midland Crowd	90.4	12480	50 Heartland Communities	76.1
12024	07 Exurbanites	61.3	12170	26 Midland Crowd	49.5	12481	18 Cozy and Comfortable	100.0
12025	25 Salt of The Earth	46.7	12173	26 Midland Crowd	34.2	12482	33 Midlife Junction	62.9
12027	18 Cozy and Comfortable	48.7	12175	31 Rural Resort Dwellers	100.0	12484	17 Green Acres	68.1
12028	25 Salt of The Earth	58.2	12176	33 Midlife Junction	94.6	12485	33 Midlife Junction	74.5
12029	15 Silver and Gold	50.9	12180	48 Great Expectations	16.6	12486	33 Midlife Junction	57.1
12031	25 Salt of The Earth	100.0	12182	48 Great Expectations	38.2	12487	18 Cozy and Comfortable	39.6
12032	50 Heartland Communities	57.2	12183	32 Rustbelt Traditions	38.8	12491	14 Prosperous Empty Nesters	71.2
12033	18 Cozy and Comfortable	44.4	12184	17 Green Acres	51.9	12492	31 Rural Resort Dwellers	100.0
12035	26 Midland Crowd	73.4	12185	26 Midland Crowd	40.4	12494	31 Rural Resort Dwellers	100.0
12036	31 Rural Resort Dwellers	88.3	12186	07 Exurbanites	55.5	12495	09 Urban Chic	100.0
12037	31 Rural Resort Dwellers	29.4	12187	46 Rooted Rural	73.4	12496	31 Rural Resort Dwellers	100.0
12041	18 Cozy and Comfortable	100.0	12188	13 In Style	40.1	12498	14 Prosperous Empty Nesters	44.6
12042	18 Cozy and Comfortable	62.6	12189	48 Great Expectations	30.0	12501	24 Main Street, USA	72.6
12043	33 Midlife Junction	23.9	12190	31 Rural Resort Dwellers	100.0	12502	31 Rural Resort Dwellers	79.0
12046	18 Cozy and Comfortable	94.8	12192	18 Cozy and Comfortable	32.9	12503	25 Salt of The Earth	50.1
12047	48 Great Expectations	20.4	12193	25 Salt of The Earth	80.3	12507	14 Prosperous Empty Nesters	81.3
12051	33 Midlife Junction	51.7	12194	31 Rural Resort Dwellers	100.0	12508	24 Main Street, USA	47.2
12052	18 Cozy and Comfortable	100.0	12196	18 Cozy and Comfortable	53.5	12513	29 Rustbelt Retirees	100.0
12053	17 Green Acres	46.5	12197	46 Rooted Rural	54.5	12514	07 Exurbanites	98.3
12054	14 Prosperous Empty Nesters	40.3	12198	18 Cozy and Comfortable	57.3	12515	49 Senior Sun Seekers	44.6
12056	17 Green Acres	50.2	12202	64 City Commons	27.3	12516	31 Rural Resort Dwellers	95.4
12057	25 Salt of The Earth	100.0	12203	55 College Towns	16.2	12517	31 Rural Resort Dwellers	100.0
12058	26 Midland Crowd	53.5	12204	36 Old and Newcomers	41.4	12518	13 In Style	20.9
12059	18 Cozy and Comfortable	76.6	12205	18 Cozy and Comfortable	50.7	12521	10 Pleasant-Ville	83.5
12060	31 Rural Resort Dwellers	75.2	12206	48 Great Expectations	24.7	12521	31 Rural Resort Dwellers	83.1
12061	13 In Style	30.0	12207	65 Social Security Set	56.5	12522	06 Sophisticated Squires	24.0
12062	18 Cozy and Comfortable	44.8	12208	55 College Towns	26.0	12523	31 Rural Resort Dwellers	69.0
12064	46 Rooted Rural	78.1	12209	48 Great Expectations	61.8	12524	13 In Style	31.0
12065	13 In Style	31.3	12210	27 Metro Renters	41.7	12525	26 Midland Crowd	52.8
12066	25 Salt of The Earth	74.6	12211	14 Prosperous Empty Nesters	33.5	12526	33 Midlife Junction	31.4
12067	18 Cozy and Comfortable	39.5	12302	14 Prosperous Empty Nesters	28.4	12528	24 Main Street, USA	60.9
12068	26 Midland Crowd	40.1	12303	29 Rustbelt Retirees	32.2	12529	31 Rural Resort Dwellers	93.3
12070	18 Cozy and Comfortable	65.1	12304	57 Simple Living	21.8	12531	10 Pleasant-Ville	52.7
12071	46 Rooted Rural	93.0	12305	36 Old and Newcomers	56.9	12533	06 Sophisticated Squires	48.4
12072	50 Heartland Communities	43.0	12306	32 Rustbelt Traditions	20.5	12534	29 Rustbelt Retirees	18.7
12074	18 Cozy and Comfortable	45.3	12307	60 City Dimensions	36.2	12538	18 Cozy and Comfortable	37.8
12075	25 Salt of The Earth	35.7	12308	48 Great Expectations	28.8	12542	06 Sophisticated Squires	62.8
12076	31 Rural Resort Dwellers	100.0	12309	07 Exurbanites	23.4	12542	17 Green Acres	35.0
12077	06 Sophisticated Squires	48.7	12401	33 Midlife Junction	14.9	12543	19 Milk and Cookies	53.5
12078	29 Rustbelt Retirees	30.5	12404	26 Midland Crowd	50.6	12545	33 Midlife Junction	48.6
12083	33 Midlife Junction	53.8	12405	33 Midlife Junction	77.5	12546	31 Rural Resort Dwellers	80.8
12084	16 Enterprising Professionals	48.5	12406	31 Rural Resort Dwellers	64.4	12547	17 Green Acres	100.0
12086	29 Rustbelt Retirees	57.1	12409	15 Silver and Gold	42.1	12548	26 Midland Crowd	79.5
12087	25 Salt of The Earth	54.7	12410	31 Rural Resort Dwellers	100.0	12549	06 Sophisticated Squires	45.5
12090	25 Salt of The Earth	37.5	12411	33 Midlife Junction	100.0	12550	18 Cozy and Comfortable	21.4
12092	25 Salt of The Earth	50.4	12412	18 Cozy and Comfortable	61.0	12553	24 Main Street, USA	21.6
12093	31 Rural Resort Dwellers	54.4	12413	33 Midlife Junction	50.4	12561	17 Green Acres	31.6
12094	26 Midland Crowd	90.8	12414	48 Great Expectations	26.2	12563	06 Sophisticated Squires	44.0
12095	32 Rustbelt Traditions	25.3	12416	33 Midlife Junction	93.3	12564	07 Exurbanites	38.5
12106	14 Prosperous Empty Nesters	54.8	12418	31 Rural Resort Dwellers	100.0	12566	17 Green Acres	57.3
12108	31 Rural Resort Dwellers	100.0	12419	14 Prosperous Empty Nesters	44.2	12567	17 Green Acres	54.3
12110	24 Main Street, USA	25.8	12421	31 Rural Resort Dwellers	100.0	12569	07 Exurbanites	24.5
12115	07 Exurbanites	100.0	12422	31 Rural Resort Dwellers	100.0	12570	06 Sophisticated Squires	57.7
12116	31 Rural Resort Dwellers	50.7	12423	31 Rural Resort Dwellers	99.8	12571	33 Midlife Junction	26.4

ZIP CODE	TOP TAPESTRY CONSUMER TYPE	% 2004 HOUSE-HOLDS	ZIP CODE	TOP TAPESTRY CONSUMER TYPE	% 2004 HOUSE-HOLDS	ZIP CODE	TOP TAPESTRY CONSUMER TYPE	% 2004 HOUSE-HOLDS
12572	07 Exurbanites	33.3	12834	33 Midlife Junction	45.3	12981	25 Salt of The Earth	45.2
12575	06 Sophisticated Squires	94.2	12835	32 Rustbelt Traditions	55.2	12983	33 Midlife Junction	28.4
12577	06 Sophisticated Squires	99.8	12836	31 Rural Resort Dwellers	95.5	12985	26 Midland Crowd	59.9
12578	07 Exurbanites	58.3	12837	25 Salt of The Earth	100.0	12986	57 Simple Living	40.8
12580	07 Exurbanites	64.9	12838	25 Salt of The Earth	89.8	12987	33 Midlife Junction	57.7
12581	07 Exurbanites	93.6	12839	32 Rustbelt Traditions	29.1	12989	31 Rural Resort Dwellers	100.0
12582	06 Sophisticated Squires	67.5	12842	31 Rural Resort Dwellers	100.0	12992	42 Southern Satellites	74.7
12583	22 Metropolitans	63.4	12843	46 Rooted Rural	59.1	12993	31 Rural Resort Dwellers	79.3
12585	06 Sophisticated Squires	100.0	12844	31 Rural Resort Dwellers	64.6	12996	31 Rural Resort Dwellers	63.6
12586	18 Cozy and Comfortable	26.7	12845	31 Rural Resort Dwellers	43.0	12997	33 Midlife Junction	50.0
12589	17 Green Acres	32.4	12846	46 Rooted Rural	100.0	13021	32 Rustbelt Traditions	17.0
12590	36 Old and Newcomers	21.3	12847	31 Rural Resort Dwellers	100.0	13026	25 Salt of The Earth	49.7
12592	24 Main Street, USA	97.4	12849	25 Salt of The Earth	100.0	13027	33 Midlife Junction	18.6
12594	12 Up and Coming Families	34.6	12850	26 Midland Crowd	79.5	13028	26 Midland Crowd	78.3
12601	60 City Dimensions	12.7	12851	46 Rooted Rural	100.0	13029	19 Milk and Cookies	37.8
12603	24 Main Street, USA	21.4	12852	29 Rustbelt Retirees	100.0	13030	25 Salt of The Earth	48.1
12604	22 Metropolitans	100.0	12853	31 Rural Resort Dwellers	100.0	13031	33 Midlife Junction	19.4
12701	31 Rural Resort Dwellers	25.3	12854	25 Salt of The Earth	100.0	13032	25 Salt of The Earth	48.1
12719	31 Rural Resort Dwellers	100.0	12855	50 Heartland Communities	100.0	13033	25 Salt of The Earth	66.6
12720	31 Rural Resort Dwellers	100.0	12857	46 Rooted Rural	91.6	13034	25 Salt of The Earth	89.2
12721	06 Sophisticated Squires	24.9	12858	50 Heartland Communities	100.0	13035	17 Green Acres	27.2
12723	31 Rural Resort Dwellers	98.0	12859	26 Midland Crowd	65.2	13036	26 Midland Crowd	46.6
12725	31 Rural Resort Dwellers	84.5	12860	31 Rural Resort Dwellers	100.0	13037	19 Milk and Cookies	23.2
12726	31 Rural Resort Dwellers	100.0	12861	25 Salt of The Earth	100.0	13039	12 Up and Coming Families	31.3
12727	31 Rural Resort Dwellers	100.0	12863	41 Crossroads	100.0	13040	46 Rooted Rural	54.4
12729	25 Salt of The Earth	49.8	12865	25 Salt of The Earth	53.3	13041	19 Milk and Cookies	36.9
12732	31 Rural Resort Dwellers	100.0	12866	07 Exurbanites	16.8	13042	25 Salt of The Earth	54.3
12733	57 Simple Living	62.7	12870	31 Rural Resort Dwellers	58.6	13044	25 Salt of The Earth	98.9
12734	33 Midlife Junction	61.6	12871	25 Salt of The Earth	31.5	13045	48 Great Expectations	18.1
12736	31 Rural Resort Dwellers	100.0	12872	50 Heartland Communities	100.0	13052	25 Salt of The Earth	45.7
12737	31 Rural Resort Dwellers	55.5	12873	31 Rural Resort Dwellers	91.4	13053	36 Old and Newcomers	32.3
12738	31 Rural Resort Dwellers	59.0	12878	46 Rooted Rural	100.0	13054	25 Salt of The Earth	54.2
12740	31 Rural Resort Dwellers	52.1	12883	50 Heartland Communities	29.0	13057	32 Rustbelt Traditions	30.3
12741	31 Rural Resort Dwellers	100.0	12885	46 Rooted Rural	68.1	13060	26 Midland Crowd	37.9
12742	31 Rural Resort Dwellers	100.0	12886	46 Rooted Rural	100.0	13061	17 Green Acres	80.8
12743	31 Rural Resort Dwellers	100.0	12887	25 Salt of The Earth	34.0	13063	17 Green Acres	72.5
12745	31 Rural Resort Dwellers	100.0	12901	14 Prosperous Empty Nesters	16.6	13066	03 Connoisseurs	20.5
12746	26 Midland Crowd	93.6	12903	57 Simple Living	93.6	13068	26 Midland Crowd	45.9
12747	50 Heartland Communities	24.2	12910	42 Southern Satellites	98.5	13069	26 Midland Crowd	34.0
12748	31 Rural Resort Dwellers	58.8	12911	32 Rustbelt Traditions	56.3	13071	25 Salt of The Earth	72.1
12750	31 Rural Resort Dwellers	100.0	12912	50 Heartland Communities	32.7	13072	25 Salt of The Earth	38.7
12751	33 Midlife Junction	100.0	12913	33 Midlife Junction	88.5	13073	26 Midland Crowd	53.7
12752	31 Rural Resort Dwellers	100.0	12914	56 Rural Bypasses	94.7	13074	42 Southern Satellites	64.5
12754	57 Simple Living	41.0	12916	46 Rooted Rural	53.6	13076	26 Midland Crowd	100.0
12758	33 Midlife Junction	28.3	12917	46 Rooted Rural	100.0	13077	32 Rustbelt Traditions	24.1
12759	41 Crossroads	79.1	12918	25 Salt of The Earth	59.5	13078	18 Cozy and Comfortable	17.3
12760	46 Rooted Rural	60.2	12919	50 Heartland Communities	35.2	13080	32 Rustbelt Traditions	37.9
12762	31 Rural Resort Dwellers	100.0	12920	46 Rooted Rural	54.6	13081	25 Salt of The Earth	72.7
12763	26 Midland Crowd	67.5	12921	25 Salt of The Earth	51.9	13082	26 Midland Crowd	50.1
12764	31 Rural Resort Dwellers	100.0	12922	31 Rural Resort Dwellers	100.0	13083	46 Rooted Rural	77.0
12765	17 Green Acres	38.4	12923	46 Rooted Rural	100.0	13084	18 Cozy and Comfortable	35.5
12766	31 Rural Resort Dwellers	92.8	12924	46 Rooted Rural	100.0	13088	29 Rustbelt Retirees	20.6
12768	31 Rural Resort Dwellers	57.2	12926	46 Rooted Rural	100.0	13090	19 Milk and Cookies	26.2
12770	31 Rural Resort Dwellers	100.0	12928	46 Rooted Rural	67.4	13092	26 Midland Crowd	54.3
12771	32 Rustbelt Traditions	26.3	12930	46 Rooted Rural	96.1	13101	32 Rustbelt Traditions	63.7
12775	31 Rural Resort Dwellers	100.0	12932	50 Heartland Communities	44.1	13103	26 Midland Crowd	100.0
12776	31 Rural Resort Dwellers	52.8	12934	46 Rooted Rural	72.4	13108	07 Exurbanites	24.0
12777	17 Green Acres	100.0	12935	42 Southern Satellites	42.9	13110	25 Salt of The Earth	53.5
12779	33 Midlife Junction	70.7	12936	31 Rural Resort Dwellers	100.0	13111	42 Southern Satellites	89.6
12780	26 Midland Crowd	92.0	12937	46 Rooted Rural	52.3	13112	18 Cozy and Comfortable	41.5
12782	31 Rural Resort Dwellers	100.0	12941	31 Rural Resort Dwellers	100.0	13114	26 Midland Crowd	89.3
12783	31 Rural Resort Dwellers	79.2	12942	31 Rural Resort Dwellers	98.3	13116	33 Midlife Junction	48.0
12786	31 Rural Resort Dwellers	100.0	12943	31 Rural Resort Dwellers	100.0	13118	42 Southern Satellites	28.8
12787	46 Rooted Rural	82.4	12944	32 Rustbelt Traditions	41.0	13120	32 Rustbelt Traditions	41.4
12788	26 Midland Crowd	67.7	12945	31 Rural Resort Dwellers	87.3	13122	17 Green Acres	64.8
12789	33 Midlife Junction	83.3	12946	33 Midlife Junction	64.2	13124	42 Southern Satellites	80.4
12790	32 Rustbelt Traditions	39.4	12949	46 Rooted Rural	100.0	13126	26 Midland Crowd	27.5
12791	31 Rural Resort Dwellers	98.0	12950	46 Rooted Rural	100.0	13131	26 Midland Crowd	95.4
12792	31 Rural Resort Dwellers	100.0	12952	29 Rustbelt Retirees	86.8	13132	26 Midland Crowd	97.8
12801	48 Great Expectations	51.9	12953	46 Rooted Rural	33.6	13135	26 Midland Crowd	36.4
12803	29 Rustbelt Retirees	38.8	12955	46 Rooted Rural	93.3	13136	42 Southern Satellites	52.4
12804	14 Prosperous Empty Nesters	36.0	12956	50 Heartland Communities	71.3	13140	42 Southern Satellites	45.5
12808	31 Rural Resort Dwellers	100.0	12957	46 Rooted Rural	88.5	13141	25 Salt of The Earth	72.4
12809	25 Salt of The Earth	99.8	12958	26 Midland Crowd	55.0	13142	26 Midland Crowd	38.5
12810	46 Rooted Rural	100.0	12959	42 Southern Satellites	93.4	13143	42 Southern Satellites	79.2
12812	31 Rural Resort Dwellers	100.0	12960	50 Heartland Communities	100.0	13144	42 Southern Satellites	69.0
12814	31 Rural Resort Dwellers	100.0	12961	50 Heartland Communities	100.0	13145	50 Heartland Communities	91.9
12815	31 Rural Resort Dwellers	100.0	12962	26 Midland Crowd	53.5	13146	42 Southern Satellites	90.3
12816	33 Midlife Junction	33.5	12964	29 Rustbelt Retirees	100.0	13147	25 Salt of The Earth	70.0
12817	31 Rural Resort Dwellers	91.2	12965	46 Rooted Rural	100.0	13148	33 Midlife Junction	24.5
12819	25 Salt of The Earth	100.0	12966	46 Rooted Rural	80.5	13152	07 Exurbanites	35.2
12821	42 Southern Satellites	97.3	12967	46 Rooted Rural	100.0	13155	42 Southern Satellites	94.3
12822	25 Salt of The Earth	24.6	12969	31 Rural Resort Dwellers	100.0	13156	31 Rural Resort Dwellers	46.3
12823	25 Salt of The Earth	100.0	12970	31 Rural Resort Dwellers	100.0	13158	42 Southern Satellites	51.8
12824	31 Rural Resort Dwellers	100.0	12972	26 Midland Crowd	46.3	13159	17 Green Acres	36.7
12827	25 Salt of The Earth	41.9	12973	31 Rural Resort Dwellers	100.0	13160	25 Salt of The Earth	100.0
12828	32 Rustbelt Traditions	49.2	12974	50 Heartland Communities	99.4	13164	18 Cozy and Comfortable	97.2
12831	26 Midland Crowd	53.7	12978	25 Salt of The Earth	100.0	13165	50 Heartland Communities	19.9
12832	26 Midland Crowd	32.1	12979	32 Rustbelt Traditions	36.2	13166	25 Salt of The Earth	44.8
12833	26 Midland Crowd	81.2	12980	50 Heartland Communities	82.5			

ZIP CODE	TOP TAPESTRY CONSUMER TYPE	% 2004 HOUSE-HOLDS	ZIP CODE	TOP TAPESTRY CONSUMER TYPE	% 2004 HOUSE-HOLDS	ZIP CODE	TOP TAPESTRY CONSUMER TYPE	% 2004 HOUSE-HOLDS
13167	26 Midland Crowd	75.5	13456	18 Cozy and Comfortable	63.0	13691	26 Midland Crowd	58.1
13202	64 City Commons	44.3	13459	25 Salt of The Earth	53.5	13693	31 Rural Resort Dwellers	100.0
13203	60 City Dimensions	32.8	13460	46 Rooted Rural	49.8	13694	33 Midlife Junction	80.3
13204	60 City Dimensions	36.4	13461	18 Cozy and Comfortable	61.1	13695	50 Heartland Communities	100.0
13205	57 Simple Living	16.4	13464	42 Southern Satellites	72.0	13696	46 Rooted Rural	100.0
13206	48 Great Expectations	36.2	13468	37 Prairie Living	100.0	13697	46 Rooted Rural	73.7
13207	51 Metro City Edge	25.5	13469	42 Southern Satellites	45.8	13699	63 Dorms To Diplomas	53.7
13208	60 City Dimensions	36.0	13470	42 Southern Satellites	100.0	13730	46 Rooted Rural	100.0
13209	32 Rustbelt Traditions	33.1	13471	42 Southern Satellites	98.4	13731	31 Rural Resort Dwellers	100.0
13210	55 College Towns	27.6	13473	50 Heartland Communities	43.1	13732	18 Cozy and Comfortable	49.1
13211	32 Rustbelt Traditions	51.3	13475	42 Southern Satellites	100.0	13733	46 Rooted Rural	51.8
13212	29 Rustbelt Retirees	44.6	13476	33 Midlife Junction	42.7	13734	42 Southern Satellites	53.5
13214	14 Prosperous Empty Nesters	46.6	13477	46 Rooted Rural	90.0	13736	25 Salt of The Earth	59.2
13215	18 Cozy and Comfortable	24.3	13478	25 Salt of The Earth	74.3	13739	46 Rooted Rural	77.3
13219	29 Rustbelt Retirees	50.2	13480	33 Midlife Junction	45.2	13740	31 Rural Resort Dwellers	100.0
13224	14 Prosperous Empty Nesters	26.7	13482	25 Salt of The Earth	100.0	13743	46 Rooted Rural	46.4
13244	63 Dorms To Diplomas	100.0	13483	42 Southern Satellites	71.7	13744	26 Midland Crowd	58.9
13301	50 Heartland Communities	91.7	13485	46 Rooted Rural	100.0	13746	26 Midland Crowd	58.4
13302	42 Southern Satellites	67.2	13486	46 Rooted Rural	53.9	13748	42 Southern Satellites	31.7
13303	46 Rooted Rural	38.5	13488	31 Rural Resort Dwellers	55.9	13750	46 Rooted Rural	89.8
13304	18 Cozy and Comfortable	79.0	13489	42 Southern Satellites	70.2	13751	46 Rooted Rural	100.0
13308	25 Salt of The Earth	26.1	13490	17 Green Acres	96.8	13752	31 Rural Resort Dwellers	73.7
13309	50 Heartland Communities	46.6	13491	46 Rooted Rural	89.0	13753	33 Midlife Junction	78.8
13310	46 Rooted Rural	100.0	13492	32 Rustbelt Traditions	32.0	13754	50 Heartland Communities	73.3
13314	46 Rooted Rural	100.0	13493	42 Southern Satellites	86.4	13755	50 Heartland Communities	54.9
13315	25 Salt of The Earth	62.7	13494	31 Rural Resort Dwellers	100.0	13756	46 Rooted Rural	98.8
13316	25 Salt of The Earth	52.9	13495	32 Rustbelt Traditions	57.9	13757	25 Salt of The Earth	42.0
13317	32 Rustbelt Traditions	37.1	13501	60 City Dimensions	25.7	13760	29 Rustbelt Retirees	16.4
13318	41 Crossroads	76.3	13502	29 Rustbelt Retirees	29.1	13775	33 Midlife Junction	53.2
13319	14 Prosperous Empty Nesters	57.0	13601	48 Great Expectations	19.5	13776	25 Salt of The Earth	100.0
13320	37 Prairie Living	65.7	13602	40 Military Proximity	100.0	13777	26 Midland Crowd	100.0
13322	25 Salt of The Earth	99.0	13603	40 Military Proximity	100.0	13778	33 Midlife Junction	41.2
13323	33 Midlife Junction	30.6	13605	26 Midland Crowd	28.3	13780	46 Rooted Rural	73.1
13324	46 Rooted Rural	57.8	13606	26 Midland Crowd	70.3	13782	31 Rural Resort Dwellers	100.0
13325	46 Rooted Rural	96.3	13607	31 Rural Resort Dwellers	53.4	13783	50 Heartland Communities	59.5
13326	31 Rural Resort Dwellers	33.1	13608	46 Rooted Rural	99.5	13786	31 Rural Resort Dwellers	95.7
13327	42 Southern Satellites	44.5	13611	37 Prairie Living	100.0	13787	42 Southern Satellites	59.7
13328	32 Rustbelt Traditions	73.4	13612	32 Rustbelt Traditions	36.2	13788	25 Salt of The Earth	74.1
13329	50 Heartland Communities	54.8	13613	46 Rooted Rural	68.2	13790	29 Rustbelt Retirees	20.3
13331	31 Rural Resort Dwellers	100.0	13614	46 Rooted Rural	90.0	13795	50 Heartland Communities	27.5
13332	46 Rooted Rural	94.4	13616	28 Aspiring Young Families	100.0	13796	25 Salt of The Earth	59.6
13333	37 Prairie Living	100.0	13617	33 Midlife Junction	46.4	13797	46 Rooted Rural	43.2
13334	46 Rooted Rural	49.7	13618	31 Rural Resort Dwellers	97.6	13801	46 Rooted Rural	100.0
13335	46 Rooted Rural	99.5	13619	50 Heartland Communities	23.3	13802	26 Midland Crowd	100.0
13337	31 Rural Resort Dwellers	72.8	13620	25 Salt of The Earth	73.9	13803	46 Rooted Rural	39.7
13338	31 Rural Resort Dwellers	94.8	13621	25 Salt of The Earth	59.1	13804	46 Rooted Rural	100.0
13339	50 Heartland Communities	46.8	13622	31 Rural Resort Dwellers	76.1	13806	31 Rural Resort Dwellers	100.0
13340	29 Rustbelt Retirees	23.9	13624	33 Midlife Junction	44.0	13807	46 Rooted Rural	97.7
13342	46 Rooted Rural	75.0	13625	31 Rural Resort Dwellers	58.7	13808	46 Rooted Rural	84.6
13343	46 Rooted Rural	76.9	13626	26 Midland Crowd	81.7	13809	42 Southern Satellites	42.8
13345	46 Rooted Rural	100.0	13630	46 Rooted Rural	87.3	13810	46 Rooted Rural	62.0
13346	25 Salt of The Earth	36.3	13633	46 Rooted Rural	100.0	13811	26 Midland Crowd	53.9
13348	46 Rooted Rural	76.1	13634	25 Salt of The Earth	64.4	13812	46 Rooted Rural	36.6
13350	57 Simple Living	39.3	13635	46 Rooted Rural	99.8	13813	46 Rooted Rural	91.9
13353	31 Rural Resort Dwellers	100.0	13636	37 Prairie Living	82.8	13815	46 Rooted Rural	20.9
13354	18 Cozy and Comfortable	68.2	13637	28 Aspiring Young Families	69.0	13820	55 College Towns	27.7
13355	25 Salt of The Earth	54.7	13638	32 Rustbelt Traditions	100.0	13825	42 Southern Satellites	37.4
13357	32 Rustbelt Traditions	30.2	13639	46 Rooted Rural	100.0	13826	42 Southern Satellites	100.0
13360	31 Rural Resort Dwellers	100.0	13640	31 Rural Resort Dwellers	62.7	13827	29 Rustbelt Retirees	17.5
13361	42 Southern Satellites	51.2	13642	46 Rooted Rural	29.2	13830	46 Rooted Rural	44.5
13363	42 Southern Satellites	68.8	13646	46 Rooted Rural	77.3	13832	42 Southern Satellites	96.5
13365	53 Home Town	30.3	13648	46 Rooted Rural	78.2	13833	26 Midland Crowd	26.2
13367	46 Rooted Rural	36.6	13650	31 Rural Resort Dwellers	74.0	13834	31 Rural Resort Dwellers	100.0
13368	46 Rooted Rural	55.3	13652	46 Rooted Rural	95.4	13835	41 Crossroads	53.0
13402	46 Rooted Rural	77.7	13654	46 Rooted Rural	83.8	13838	29 Rustbelt Retirees	38.5
13403	17 Green Acres	45.3	13655	51 Metro City Edge	52.2	13839	46 Rooted Rural	96.0
13406	25 Salt of The Earth	100.0	13656	26 Midland Crowd	78.6	13841	42 Southern Satellites	100.0
13407	29 Rustbelt Retirees	45.4	13658	37 Prairie Living	60.6	13842	46 Rooted Rural	100.0
13408	33 Midlife Junction	45.9	13659	26 Midland Crowd	82.2	13843	25 Salt of The Earth	45.8
13409	42 Southern Satellites	84.7	13660	46 Rooted Rural	90.6	13844	46 Rooted Rural	56.4
13411	46 Rooted Rural	53.4	13661	26 Midland Crowd	72.6	13846	37 Prairie Living	92.3
13413	14 Prosperous Empty Nesters	36.8	13662	48 Great Expectations	14.7	13849	42 Southern Satellites	49.5
13415	46 Rooted Rural	100.0	13665	46 Rooted Rural	100.0	13850	29 Rustbelt Retirees	20.0
13416	46 Rooted Rural	48.4	13666	50 Heartland Communities	89.3	13856	31 Rural Resort Dwellers	37.0
13417	30 Retirement Communities	44.1	13667	42 Southern Satellites	44.0	13859	42 Southern Satellites	100.0
13418	46 Rooted Rural	100.0	13668	32 Rustbelt Traditions	75.5	13861	14 Prosperous Empty Nesters	99.0
13420	31 Rural Resort Dwellers	100.0	13669	50 Heartland Communities	23.5	13862	26 Midland Crowd	42.4
13421	57 Simple Living	17.8	13670	50 Heartland Communities	56.2	13863	42 Southern Satellites	89.3
13424	29 Rustbelt Retirees	57.2	13672	46 Rooted Rural	67.9	13864	46 Rooted Rural	69.1
13425	32 Rustbelt Traditions	57.0	13673	28 Aspiring Young Families	46.0	13865	42 Southern Satellites	39.2
13428	46 Rooted Rural	98.8	13675	46 Rooted Rural	100.0	13901	29 Rustbelt Retirees	18.9
13431	25 Salt of The Earth	58.2	13676	55 College Towns	24.2	13903	48 Great Expectations	22.0
13433	42 Southern Satellites	50.6	13678	46 Rooted Rural	58.4	13904	32 Rustbelt Traditions	20.5
13437	42 Southern Satellites	78.1	13679	33 Midlife Junction	56.0	13905	55 College Towns	24.7
13438	32 Rustbelt Traditions	29.6	13680	46 Rooted Rural	88.9	14001	25 Salt of The Earth	40.0
13439	46 Rooted Rural	44.5	13681	46 Rooted Rural	88.9	14004	25 Salt of The Earth	28.8
13440	29 Rustbelt Retirees	22.0	13682	25 Salt of The Earth	90.9	14005	25 Salt of The Earth	48.3
13450	31 Rural Resort Dwellers	100.0	13684	46 Rooted Rural	86.7	14006	18 Cozy and Comfortable	35.6
13452	50 Heartland Communities	55.2	13685	33 Midlife Junction	66.6	14008	25 Salt of The Earth	68.2
13454	42 Southern Satellites	100.0	13687	31 Rural Resort Dwellers	100.0	14009	25 Salt of The Earth	57.7
			13690	50 Heartland Communities	100.0			

ZIP CODE	TOP TAPESTRY CONSUMER TYPE	% 2004 HOUSE-HOLDS	ZIP CODE	TOP TAPESTRY CONSUMER TYPE	% 2004 HOUSE-HOLDS	ZIP CODE	TOP TAPESTRY CONSUMER TYPE	% 2004 HOUSE-HOLDS
14011	32 Rustbelt Traditions	41.5	14215	51 Metro City Edge	42.7	14551	32 Rustbelt Traditions	57.1
14012	25 Salt of The Earth	100.0	14216	48 Great Expectations	47.9	14555	25 Salt of The Earth	99.8
14013	25 Salt of The Earth	72.1	14217	32 Rustbelt Traditions	42.0	14559	06 Sophisticated Squires	26.0
14020	48 Great Expectations	27.7	14218	57 Simple Living	33.5	14560	25 Salt of The Earth	82.9
14024	25 Salt of The Earth	79.1	14219	32 Rustbelt Traditions	29.9	14561	25 Salt of The Earth	60.0
14025	18 Cozy and Comfortable	56.1	14220	32 Rustbelt Traditions	40.7	14564	07 Exurbanites	38.2
14026	18 Cozy and Comfortable	100.0	14221	30 Retirement Communities	25.1	14568	12 Up and Coming Families	39.2
14028	29 Rustbelt Retirees	52.6	14222	22 Metropolitans	37.8	14569	25 Salt of The Earth	35.0
14030	25 Salt of The Earth	80.9	14223	29 Rustbelt Retirees	58.6	14571	25 Salt of The Earth	57.4
14031	07 Exurbanites	36.1	14224	18 Cozy and Comfortable	41.8	14572	32 Rustbelt Traditions	39.4
14032	17 Green Acres	47.6	14225	29 Rustbelt Retirees	55.3	14580	06 Sophisticated Squires	21.1
14033	17 Green Acres	57.8	14226	29 Rustbelt Retirees	26.0	14586	13 In Style	84.6
14034	42 Southern Satellites	69.7	14227	29 Rustbelt Retirees	44.3	14589	32 Rustbelt Traditions	46.6
14036	25 Salt of The Earth	48.4	14228	22 Metropolitans	28.7	14590	46 Rooted Rural	37.8
14037	17 Green Acres	67.1	14260	63 Dorms To Diplomas	0.0	14591	25 Salt of The Earth	63.6
14039	25 Salt of The Earth	100.0	14301	60 City Dimensions	16.4	14604	65 Social Security Set	89.6
14040	25 Salt of The Earth	65.2	14303	62 Modest Income Homes	37.5	14605	64 City Commons	71.6
14041	46 Rooted Rural	100.0	14304	29 Rustbelt Retirees	39.1	14606	60 City Dimensions	17.8
14042	42 Southern Satellites	40.3	14305	29 Rustbelt Retirees	30.1	14607	27 Metro Renters	53.6
14043	29 Rustbelt Retirees	55.6	14410	17 Green Acres	100.0	14608	64 City Commons	55.3
14047	18 Cozy and Comfortable	81.4	14411	25 Salt of The Earth	24.2	14609	32 Rustbelt Traditions	27.6
14048	50 Heartland Communities	27.3	14414	26 Midland Crowd	48.3	14610	27 Metro Renters	20.1
14051	02 Suburban Splendor	49.4	14415	37 Prairie Living	100.0	14611	51 Metro City Edge	24.6
14052	18 Cozy and Comfortable	37.5	14416	32 Rustbelt Traditions	41.2	14612	06 Sophisticated Squires	27.8
14054	25 Salt of The Earth	100.0	14418	46 Rooted Rural	93.9	14613	60 City Dimensions	34.1
14055	25 Salt of The Earth	100.0	14420	19 Milk and Cookies	16.1	14614	65 Social Security Set	100.0
14057	18 Cozy and Comfortable	78.9	14422	25 Salt of The Earth	32.9	14615	48 Great Expectations	26.9
14058	25 Salt of The Earth	100.0	14423	29 Rustbelt Retirees	34.2	14616	32 Rustbelt Traditions	47.0
14059	18 Cozy and Comfortable	39.8	14424	17 Green Acres	11.8	14617	18 Cozy and Comfortable	24.6
14060	50 Heartland Communities	38.0	14425	41 Crossroads	27.8	14618	36 Old and Newcomers	21.4
14062	46 Rooted Rural	62.1	14427	25 Salt of The Earth	41.8	14619	51 Metro City Edge	47.4
14063	33 Midlife Junction	42.0	14428	18 Cozy and Comfortable	46.1	14620	48 Great Expectations	21.1
14065	42 Southern Satellites	79.7	14432	57 Simple Living	24.3	14621	60 City Dimensions	26.7
14066	25 Salt of The Earth	65.5	14433	32 Rustbelt Traditions	33.6	14622	29 Rustbelt Retirees	58.3
14067	25 Salt of The Earth	51.9	14435	17 Green Acres	59.1	14623	39 Young and Restless	22.4
14068	06 Sophisticated Squires	47.3	14437	32 Rustbelt Traditions	29.9	14624	18 Cozy and Comfortable	36.6
14069	25 Salt of The Earth	66.7	14441	46 Rooted Rural	100.0	14625	07 Exurbanites	35.0
14070	50 Heartland Communities	32.3	14445	32 Rustbelt Traditions	38.1	14626	18 Cozy and Comfortable	28.0
14072	07 Exurbanites	34.7	14450	14 Prosperous Empty Nesters	23.0	14627	63 Dorms To Diplomas	100.0
14075	18 Cozy and Comfortable	31.4	14454	55 College Towns	33.4	14642	55 College Towns	100.0
14080	17 Green Acres	67.3	14456	29 Rustbelt Retirees	17.6	14701	29 Rustbelt Retirees	19.5
14081	29 Rustbelt Retirees	44.4	14462	42 Southern Satellites	100.0	14706	26 Midland Crowd	34.9
14082	25 Salt of The Earth	62.9	14464	26 Midland Crowd	57.0	14708	46 Rooted Rural	51.5
14083	17 Green Acres	100.0	14466	17 Green Acres	44.2	14709	46 Rooted Rural	99.5
14085	18 Cozy and Comfortable	61.7	14467	18 Cozy and Comfortable	97.3	14710	25 Salt of The Earth	61.2
14086	12 Up and Coming Families	26.1	14468	18 Cozy and Comfortable	42.9	14711	46 Rooted Rural	73.2
14091	25 Salt of The Earth	52.5	14469	25 Salt of The Earth	39.0	14712	31 Rural Resort Dwellers	61.1
14092	07 Exurbanites	29.2	14470	25 Salt of The Earth	39.8	14714	46 Rooted Rural	100.0
14094	48 Great Expectations	16.6	14471	25 Salt of The Earth	87.6	14715	46 Rooted Rural	34.6
14098	25 Salt of The Earth	97.4	14472	13 In Style	41.1	14716	50 Heartland Communities	57.6
14101	46 Rooted Rural	32.1	14475	25 Salt of The Earth	100.0	14717	50 Heartland Communities	52.7
14102	17 Green Acres	100.0	14476	18 Cozy and Comfortable	95.5	14718	29 Rustbelt Retirees	65.6
14103	32 Rustbelt Traditions	34.5	14477	17 Green Acres	60.6	14719	46 Rooted Rural	32.4
14105	25 Salt of The Earth	54.9	14478	25 Salt of The Earth	44.0	14721	25 Salt of The Earth	100.0
14108	32 Rustbelt Traditions	47.7	14480	33 Midlife Junction	100.0	14723	46 Rooted Rural	93.4
14109	29 Rustbelt Retirees	0.0	14481	25 Salt of The Earth	57.4	14724	37 Prairie Living	89.8
14111	29 Rustbelt Retirees	38.5	14482	18 Cozy and Comfortable	35.8	14726	37 Prairie Living	56.3
14113	25 Salt of The Earth	89.5	14485	24 Main Street, USA	57.3	14727	46 Rooted Rural	45.1
14120	32 Rustbelt Traditions	22.2	14486	25 Salt of The Earth	100.0	14728	50 Heartland Communities	44.5
14125	25 Salt of The Earth	60.7	14487	33 Midlife Junction	70.8	14729	25 Salt of The Earth	63.8
14127	18 Cozy and Comfortable	26.3	14489	53 Home Town	31.8	14731	31 Rural Resort Dwellers	88.7
14129	46 Rooted Rural	61.5	14502	17 Green Acres	27.9	14733	50 Heartland Communities	74.4
14131	18 Cozy and Comfortable	52.7	14504	49 Senior Sun Seekers	59.7	14735	50 Heartland Communities	51.3
14132	29 Rustbelt Retirees	34.5	14505	17 Green Acres	56.5	14736	25 Salt of The Earth	100.0
14134	25 Salt of The Earth	100.0	14506	02 Suburban Splendor	53.5	14737	46 Rooted Rural	34.0
14136	32 Rustbelt Traditions	39.3	14507	25 Salt of The Earth	75.0	14738	29 Rustbelt Retirees	50.5
14138	46 Rooted Rural	81.1	14510	48 Great Expectations	22.4	14739	46 Rooted Rural	52.1
14139	17 Green Acres	42.6	14512	17 Green Acres	24.6	14740	42 Southern Satellites	44.9
14141	25 Salt of The Earth	40.8	14513	48 Great Expectations	23.6	14741	46 Rooted Rural	74.8
14143	18 Cozy and Comfortable	90.1	14514	33 Midlife Junction	70.4	14743	46 Rooted Rural	63.8
14145	25 Salt of The Earth	93.5	14516	25 Salt of The Earth	42.6	14744	33 Midlife Junction	95.9
14150	29 Rustbelt Retirees	59.4	14517	32 Rustbelt Traditions	63.8	14747	42 Southern Satellites	87.2
14167	25 Salt of The Earth	99.9	14519	26 Midland Crowd	48.4	14748	25 Salt of The Earth	62.4
14170	18 Cozy and Comfortable	81.9	14521	32 Rustbelt Traditions	27.4	14750	14 Prosperous Empty Nesters	46.6
14171	25 Salt of The Earth	56.6	14522	32 Rustbelt Traditions	32.0	14753	46 Rooted Rural	54.7
14172	25 Salt of The Earth	46.3	14525	25 Salt of The Earth	66.4	14754	42 Southern Satellites	80.0
14174	18 Cozy and Comfortable	54.7	14526	07 Exurbanites	29.5	14755	50 Heartland Communities	60.0
14201	60 City Dimensions	32.9	14527	46 Rooted Rural	24.4	14757	50 Heartland Communities	32.8
14202	30 Retirement Communities	49.6	14530	32 Rustbelt Traditions	69.5	14760	57 Simple Living	17.7
14203	65 Social Security Set	83.1	14532	32 Rustbelt Traditions	52.4	14767	25 Salt of The Earth	67.3
14204	64 City Commons	37.5	14533	25 Salt of The Earth	98.8	14769	50 Heartland Communities	76.7
14206	29 Rustbelt Retirees	25.2	14534	02 Suburban Splendor	34.2	14770	25 Salt of The Earth	78.2
14207	53 Home Town	39.4	14536	46 Rooted Rural	73.1	14772	46 Rooted Rural	54.9
14208	62 Modest Income Homes	75.9	14541	25 Salt of The Earth	34.5	14775	46 Rooted Rural	55.0
14209	62 Modest Income Homes	24.1	14543	07 Exurbanites	35.5	14777	50 Heartland Communities	100.0
14210	32 Rustbelt Traditions	31.9	14544	26 Midland Crowd	43.8	14779	53 Home Town	63.2
14211	62 Modest Income Homes	38.9	14545	25 Salt of The Earth	98.3	14781	37 Prairie Living	61.4
14212	64 City Commons	29.3	14546	18 Cozy and Comfortable	44.9	14782	46 Rooted Rural	67.5
14213	60 City Dimensions	73.2	14548	32 Rustbelt Traditions	41.0	14784	42 Southern Satellites	64.1
14214	22 Metropolitans	28.1	14550	50 Heartland Communities	50.1	14787	50 Heartland Communities	68.7

ZIP CODE	TOP TAPESTRY CONSUMER TYPE	% 2004 HOUSE-HOLDS	ZIP CODE	TOP TAPESTRY CONSUMER TYPE	% 2004 HOUSE-HOLDS	ZIP CODE	TOP TAPESTRY CONSUMER TYPE	% 2004 HOUSE-HOLDS
14801	42 Southern Satellites	69.9	15026	17 Green Acres	32.7	15224	57 Simple Living	44.7
14802	55 College Towns	61.9	15027	29 Rustbelt Retirees	99.6	15225	57 Simple Living	100.0
14803	33 Midlife Junction	42.6	15030	50 Heartland Communities	80.6	15226	29 Rustbelt Retirees	56.8
14804	33 Midlife Junction	66.0	15031	29 Rustbelt Retirees	79.3	15227	29 Rustbelt Retirees	42.5
14805	26 Midland Crowd	52.7	15033	50 Heartland Communities	46.0	15228	03 Connoisseurs	30.9
14806	50 Heartland Communities	80.2	15034	29 Rustbelt Retirees	63.6	15229	32 Rustbelt Traditions	34.2
14807	46 Rooted Rural	44.4	15035	50 Heartland Communities	99.8	15232	27 Metro Renters	79.9
14808	46 Rooted Rural	100.0	15037	29 Rustbelt Retirees	66.8	15233	45 City Strivers	59.9
14809	46 Rooted Rural	59.1	15042	18 Cozy and Comfortable	38.9	15234	29 Rustbelt Retirees	37.6
14810	46 Rooted Rural	28.7	15043	26 Midland Crowd	94.9	15235	29 Rustbelt Retirees	59.5
14812	25 Salt of The Earth	43.3	15044	06 Sophisticated Squires	24.5	15236	29 Rustbelt Retirees	34.6
14813	50 Heartland Communities	50.8	15045	29 Rustbelt Retirees	52.1	15237	14 Prosperous Empty Nesters	35.8
14814	14 Prosperous Empty Nesters	51.6	15049	29 Rustbelt Retirees	100.0	15238	01 Top Rung	23.2
14815	31 Rural Resort Dwellers	36.4	15050	26 Midland Crowd	69.5	15239	18 Cozy and Comfortable	41.1
14816	33 Midlife Junction	51.9	15051	07 Exurbanites	87.3	15241	03 Connoisseurs	44.8
14817	24 Main Street, USA	56.4	15052	29 Rustbelt Retirees	55.0	15243	29 Rustbelt Retirees	28.0
14818	31 Rural Resort Dwellers	63.7	15055	33 Midlife Junction	100.0	15282	63 Dorms To Diplomas	100.0
14819	42 Southern Satellites	82.3	15056	57 Simple Living	53.5	15301	29 Rustbelt Retirees	19.3
14820	42 Southern Satellites	100.0	15057	29 Rustbelt Retirees	21.2	15310	46 Rooted Rural	74.0
14821	25 Salt of The Earth	29.5	15059	62 Modest Income Homes	27.8	15311	25 Salt of The Earth	97.9
14822	46 Rooted Rural	95.9	15060	29 Rustbelt Retirees	93.8	15312	25 Salt of The Earth	100.0
14823	50 Heartland Communities	64.9	15061	29 Rustbelt Retirees	33.5	15313	25 Salt of The Earth	92.1
14824	46 Rooted Rural	80.0	15062	29 Rustbelt Retirees	57.8	15314	50 Heartland Communities	39.8
14825	25 Salt of The Earth	54.3	15063	29 Rustbelt Retirees	78.1	15317	07 Exurbanites	24.3
14826	46 Rooted Rural	73.1	15064	24 Main Street, USA	96.7	15320	50 Heartland Communities	39.3
14830	48 Great Expectations	30.0	15065	29 Rustbelt Retirees	51.5	15321	17 Green Acres	95.8
14836	25 Salt of The Earth	58.2	15066	25 Salt of The Earth	24.4	15322	50 Heartland Communities	98.5
14837	46 Rooted Rural	48.0	15067	50 Heartland Communities	98.5	15323	25 Salt of The Earth	73.2
14838	26 Midland Crowd	60.0	15068	29 Rustbelt Retirees	35.3	15324	50 Heartland Communities	100.0
14839	46 Rooted Rural	77.7	15071	16 Enterprising Professionals	42.2	15327	56 Rural Bypasses	47.1
14840	31 Rural Resort Dwellers	92.9	15074	29 Rustbelt Retirees	30.7	15329	25 Salt of The Earth	75.2
14841	31 Rural Resort Dwellers	94.3	15076	18 Cozy and Comfortable	72.7	15330	25 Salt of The Earth	34.2
14842	25 Salt of The Earth	84.0	15077	26 Midland Crowd	100.0	15331	50 Heartland Communities	100.0
14843	53 Home Town	31.0	15078	32 Rustbelt Traditions	59.3	15332	29 Rustbelt Retirees	44.6
14845	18 Cozy and Comfortable	15.9	15083	29 Rustbelt Retirees	76.1	15333	50 Heartland Communities	66.9
14846	42 Southern Satellites	48.1	15084	29 Rustbelt Retirees	21.2	15337	46 Rooted Rural	60.9
14847	46 Rooted Rural	44.5	15085	18 Cozy and Comfortable	29.6	15338	46 Rooted Rural	58.7
14850	22 Metropolitans	26.0	15086	07 Exurbanites	86.9	15340	25 Salt of The Earth	100.0
14853	63 Dorms To Diplomas	100.0	15089	29 Rustbelt Retirees	40.4	15341	46 Rooted Rural	94.3
14855	42 Southern Satellites	95.3	15090	02 Suburban Splendor	55.1	15342	29 Rustbelt Retirees	71.0
14858	42 Southern Satellites	54.3	15101	14 Prosperous Empty Nesters	24.9	15344	46 Rooted Rural	50.3
14859	42 Southern Satellites	90.5	15102	14 Prosperous Empty Nesters	34.8	15345	50 Heartland Communities	47.0
14860	31 Rural Resort Dwellers	57.3	15104	62 Modest Income Homes	72.0	15346	50 Heartland Communities	93.2
14861	42 Southern Satellites	76.2	15106	29 Rustbelt Retirees	42.8	15349	29 Rustbelt Retirees	55.7
14864	25 Salt of The Earth	84.2	15108	18 Cozy and Comfortable	14.2	15352	56 Rural Bypasses	90.3
14865	29 Rustbelt Retirees	32.4	15110	62 Modest Income Homes	52.3	15353	42 Southern Satellites	100.0
14867	26 Midland Crowd	61.9	15112	60 City Dimensions	27.4	15357	50 Heartland Communities	57.8
14869	32 Rustbelt Traditions	71.0	15116	18 Cozy and Comfortable	44.6	15359	46 Rooted Rural	100.0
14870	33 Midlife Junction	21.6	15120	29 Rustbelt Retirees	46.7	15360	25 Salt of The Earth	86.5
14871	29 Rustbelt Retirees	28.2	15122	29 Rustbelt Retirees	66.2	15362	56 Rural Bypasses	91.7
14872	42 Southern Satellites	82.8	15126	12 Up and Coming Families	38.0	15363	50 Heartland Communities	95.1
14873	46 Rooted Rural	99.1	15129	13 In Style	24.9	15364	42 Southern Satellites	45.5
14874	46 Rooted Rural	99.0	15131	29 Rustbelt Retirees	87.9	15367	07 Exurbanites	54.4
14877	37 Prairie Living	76.0	15132	50 Heartland Communities	29.1	15370	57 Simple Living	20.4
14878	46 Rooted Rural	80.6	15133	29 Rustbelt Retirees	70.5	15376	42 Southern Satellites	50.2
14879	32 Rustbelt Traditions	39.0	15135	33 Midlife Junction	45.6	15377	25 Salt of The Earth	75.0
14880	46 Rooted Rural	75.8	15136	50 Heartland Communities	26.5	15380	46 Rooted Rural	100.0
14881	25 Salt of The Earth	100.0	15137	29 Rustbelt Retirees	57.4	15401	50 Heartland Communities	28.4
14882	33 Midlife Junction	41.2	15139	18 Cozy and Comfortable	32.5	15410	50 Heartland Communities	100.0
14883	26 Midland Crowd	62.2	15140	57 Simple Living	53.4	15411	46 Rooted Rural	100.0
14884	46 Rooted Rural	100.0	15142	14 Prosperous Empty Nesters	100.0	15412	50 Heartland Communities	98.5
14885	37 Prairie Living	100.0	15143	14 Prosperous Empty Nesters	22.5	15413	50 Heartland Communities	100.0
14886	26 Midland Crowd	29.2	15144	29 Rustbelt Retirees	65.8	15417	50 Heartland Communities	50.4
14889	50 Heartland Communities	63.7	15145	57 Simple Living	52.4	15419	55 College Towns	81.9
14891	29 Rustbelt Retirees	33.7	15146	36 Old and Newcomers	23.3	15423	29 Rustbelt Retirees	86.3
14892	46 Rooted Rural	19.3	15147	29 Rustbelt Retirees	45.3	15424	46 Rooted Rural	59.3
14894	50 Heartland Communities	44.5	15148	57 Simple Living	74.8	15425	50 Heartland Communities	24.1
14895	50 Heartland Communities	28.1	15201	57 Simple Living	31.7	15427	50 Heartland Communities	66.2
14897	46 Rooted Rural	97.4	15202	48 Great Expectations	37.4	15428	46 Rooted Rural	54.8
14898	42 Southern Satellites	80.2	15203	55 College Towns	51.4	15431	56 Rural Bypasses	61.5
14901	60 City Dimensions	21.1	15204	32 Rustbelt Traditions	28.3	15432	50 Heartland Communities	100.0
14903	29 Rustbelt Retirees	22.9	15205	33 Midlife Junction	19.8	15433	50 Heartland Communities	100.0
14904	50 Heartland Communities	20.0	15206	62 Modest Income Homes	14.0	15434	29 Rustbelt Retirees	100.0
14905	29 Rustbelt Retirees	30.4	15207	29 Rustbelt Retirees	30.7	15436	50 Heartland Communities	71.1
15001	29 Rustbelt Retirees	33.0	15208	62 Modest Income Homes	34.2	15437	25 Salt of The Earth	46.9
15003	29 Rustbelt Retirees	39.0	15209	18 Cozy and Comfortable	30.5	15438	29 Rustbelt Retirees	48.1
15005	29 Rustbelt Retirees	60.1	15210	53 Home Town	26.7	15440	42 Southern Satellites	52.3
15007	24 Main Street, USA	100.0	15211	57 Simple Living	20.1	15442	50 Heartland Communities	70.7
15009	14 Prosperous Empty Nesters	26.3	15212	57 Simple Living	24.4	15444	29 Rustbelt Retirees	100.0
15010	25 Salt of The Earth	13.8	15213	55 College Towns	30.9	15445	50 Heartland Communities	36.5
15012	29 Rustbelt Retirees	46.6	15214	29 Rustbelt Retirees	24.3	15446	56 Rural Bypasses	100.0
15014	29 Rustbelt Retirees	35.4	15215	22 Metropolitans	26.3	15450	50 Heartland Communities	100.0
15015	03 Connoisseurs	94.2	15216	48 Great Expectations	20.9	15451	56 Rural Bypasses	100.0
15017	13 In Style	26.7	15217	27 Metro Renters	20.1	15456	50 Heartland Communities	27.9
15018	18 Cozy and Comfortable	70.4	15218	22 Metropolitans	26.4	15458	50 Heartland Communities	58.4
15019	29 Rustbelt Retirees	52.1	15219	64 City Commons	31.8	15459	46 Rooted Rural	100.0
15021	29 Rustbelt Retirees	48.2	15220	36 Old and Newcomers	32.8	15461	62 Modest Income Homes	33.0
15022	29 Rustbelt Retirees	49.7	15221	62 Modest Income Homes	14.5	15462	42 Southern Satellites	96.0
15024	29 Rustbelt Retirees	46.6	15222	65 Social Security Set	68.5	15463	50 Heartland Communities	90.1
15025	50 Heartland Communities	17.4	15223	29 Rustbelt Retirees	58.2	15464	56 Rural Bypasses	50.2

ZIP CODE	TOP TAPESTRY CONSUMER TYPE	% 2004 HOUSE-HOLDS	ZIP CODE	TOP TAPESTRY CONSUMER TYPE	% 2004 HOUSE-HOLDS	ZIP CODE	TOP TAPESTRY CONSUMER TYPE	% 2004 HOUSE-HOLDS
15468	50 Heartland Communities	86.4	15697	33 Midlife Junction	75.4	15946	50 Heartland Communities	54.0
15469	56 Rural Bypasses	43.6	15698	50 Heartland Communities	100.0	15949	46 Rooted Rural	100.0
15470	46 Rooted Rural	100.0	15701	55 College Towns	25.8	15951	50 Heartland Communities	100.0
15473	29 Rustbelt Retirees	59.1	15705	63 Dorms To Diplomas	100.0	15952	25 Salt of The Earth	100.0
15474	56 Rural Bypasses	38.9	15711	46 Rooted Rural	100.0	15953	29 Rustbelt Retirees	56.0
15475	50 Heartland Communities	100.0	15713	46 Rooted Rural	100.0	15954	50 Heartland Communities	38.8
15477	50 Heartland Communities	74.2	15714	50 Heartland Communities	90.3	15955	50 Heartland Communities	56.4
15478	46 Rooted Rural	34.9	15716	56 Rural Bypasses	100.0	15956	46 Rooted Rural	35.7
15479	29 Rustbelt Retirees	87.7	15717	50 Heartland Communities	46.4	15957	46 Rooted Rural	96.4
15480	42 Southern Satellites	48.1	15720	46 Rooted Rural	100.0	15958	25 Salt of The Earth	73.1
15482	50 Heartland Communities	75.8	15721	46 Rooted Rural	100.0	15960	50 Heartland Communities	100.0
15483	50 Heartland Communities	100.0	15722	29 Rustbelt Retirees	45.0	15961	50 Heartland Communities	59.4
15486	50 Heartland Communities	63.1	15724	46 Rooted Rural	60.8	15963	50 Heartland Communities	46.6
15488	46 Rooted Rural	100.0	15725	46 Rooted Rural	82.6	16001	33 Midlife Junction	14.2
15490	25 Salt of The Earth	46.1	15728	50 Heartland Communities	48.6	16002	25 Salt of The Earth	27.9
15501	46 Rooted Rural	36.8	15729	46 Rooted Rural	100.0	16020	46 Rooted Rural	70.7
15521	42 Southern Satellites	100.0	15730	29 Rustbelt Retirees	73.2	16022	42 Southern Satellites	100.0
15522	25 Salt of The Earth	42.0	15732	42 Southern Satellites	96.6	16023	42 Southern Satellites	38.4
15530	25 Salt of The Earth	30.3	15739	25 Salt of The Earth	100.0	16025	25 Salt of The Earth	62.6
15531	25 Salt of The Earth	47.5	15742	46 Rooted Rural	73.5	16028	50 Heartland Communities	54.0
15533	42 Southern Satellites	57.0	15744	46 Rooted Rural	100.0	16030	46 Rooted Rural	100.0
15534	46 Rooted Rural	67.1	15747	46 Rooted Rural	32.6	16033	17 Green Acres	32.9
15535	46 Rooted Rural	95.5	15748	50 Heartland Communities	61.9	16034	42 Southern Satellites	80.6
15536	46 Rooted Rural	100.0	15753	56 Rural Bypasses	57.1	16036	46 Rooted Rural	97.3
15537	25 Salt of The Earth	43.1	15757	46 Rooted Rural	94.8	16037	17 Green Acres	53.1
15538	46 Rooted Rural	100.0	15758	46 Rooted Rural	100.0	16038	46 Rooted Rural	56.6
15539	42 Southern Satellites	100.0	15759	46 Rooted Rural	88.5	16040	42 Southern Satellites	65.2
15540	46 Rooted Rural	75.9	15760	46 Rooted Rural	100.0	16041	25 Salt of The Earth	47.6
15541	42 Southern Satellites	52.4	15762	50 Heartland Communities	61.8	16046	04 Boomburbs	43.1
15542	56 Rural Bypasses	51.8	15763	42 Southern Satellites	85.7	16049	46 Rooted Rural	68.1
15545	46 Rooted Rural	66.8	15764	25 Salt of The Earth	100.0	16050	42 Southern Satellites	43.2
15546	46 Rooted Rural	100.0	15765	25 Salt of The Earth	48.5	16051	25 Salt of The Earth	40.4
15550	46 Rooted Rural	61.1	15767	50 Heartland Communities	21.6	16052	26 Midland Crowd	83.7
15551	46 Rooted Rural	100.0	15770	46 Rooted Rural	100.0	16053	17 Green Acres	33.7
15552	50 Heartland Communities	40.7	15771	46 Rooted Rural	90.9	16055	25 Salt of The Earth	18.5
15554	42 Southern Satellites	74.8	15772	50 Heartland Communities	67.9	16056	33 Midlife Junction	33.0
15557	46 Rooted Rural	49.8	15773	50 Heartland Communities	99.5	16057	55 College Towns	37.0
15558	50 Heartland Communities	46.5	15774	46 Rooted Rural	40.7	16059	17 Green Acres	40.3
15559	25 Salt of The Earth	98.8	15775	50 Heartland Communities	66.5	16061	42 Southern Satellites	70.1
15562	37 Prairie Living	100.0	15776	25 Salt of The Earth	100.0	16063	30 Retirement Communities	33.8
15563	46 Rooted Rural	63.1	15777	46 Rooted Rural	100.0	16066	04 Boomburbs	51.7
15601	33 Midlife Junction	15.2	15778	46 Rooted Rural	100.0	16101	29 Rustbelt Retirees	35.5
15610	25 Salt of The Earth	44.4	15780	46 Rooted Rural	100.0	16102	25 Salt of The Earth	38.5
15611	17 Green Acres	100.0	15784	42 Southern Satellites	57.1	16105	29 Rustbelt Retirees	45.9
15612	42 Southern Satellites	72.7	15801	17 Green Acres	28.5	16110	42 Southern Satellites	79.9
15613	29 Rustbelt Retirees	28.1	15821	42 Southern Satellites	100.0	16111	42 Southern Satellites	95.9
15615	25 Salt of The Earth	100.0	15823	42 Southern Satellites	75.9	16112	29 Rustbelt Retirees	48.6
15616	25 Salt of The Earth	100.0	15824	50 Heartland Communities	49.1	16114	46 Rooted Rural	71.1
15617	18 Cozy and Comfortable	81.7	15825	50 Heartland Communities	35.9	16115	46 Rooted Rural	53.8
15618	25 Salt of The Earth	57.1	15827	50 Heartland Communities	63.7	16116	50 Heartland Communities	53.2
15620	29 Rustbelt Retirees	89.7	15828	46 Rooted Rural	63.8	16117	25 Salt of The Earth	40.3
15622	25 Salt of The Earth	72.7	15829	46 Rooted Rural	76.7	16120	42 Southern Satellites	61.4
15625	29 Rustbelt Retirees	100.0	15832	46 Rooted Rural	98.6	16121	50 Heartland Communities	46.9
15626	18 Cozy and Comfortable	40.9	15834	25 Salt of The Earth	45.8	16123	25 Salt of The Earth	100.0
15627	50 Heartland Communities	33.4	15840	25 Salt of The Earth	50.6	16124	25 Salt of The Earth	63.7
15628	46 Rooted Rural	97.9	15845	50 Heartland Communities	61.0	16125	29 Rustbelt Retirees	40.1
15631	50 Heartland Communities	100.0	15846	25 Salt of The Earth	56.2	16127	25 Salt of The Earth	42.4
15632	07 Exurbanites	40.8	15848	42 Southern Satellites	100.0	16130	46 Rooted Rural	64.3
15634	29 Rustbelt Retirees	100.0	15849	46 Rooted Rural	94.6	16131	42 Southern Satellites	82.5
15636	17 Green Acres	53.1	15851	25 Salt of The Earth	41.5	16133	25 Salt of The Earth	100.0
15637	50 Heartland Communities	53.8	15853	25 Salt of The Earth	45.3	16134	46 Rooted Rural	64.3
15639	18 Cozy and Comfortable	48.9	15856	25 Salt of The Earth	99.5	16137	25 Salt of The Earth	38.3
15641	50 Heartland Communities	100.0	15857	29 Rustbelt Retirees	47.8	16141	42 Southern Satellites	45.2
15642	18 Cozy and Comfortable	29.3	15860	46 Rooted Rural	58.2	16142	25 Salt of The Earth	65.2
15644	29 Rustbelt Retirees	29.0	15861	46 Rooted Rural	100.0	16143	42 Southern Satellites	47.1
15646	46 Rooted Rural	100.0	15864	42 Southern Satellites	99.8	16145	25 Salt of The Earth	39.1
15647	25 Salt of The Earth	56.4	15865	50 Heartland Communities	100.0	16146	53 Home Town	31.9
15650	29 Rustbelt Retirees	41.4	15868	50 Heartland Communities	58.2	16148	29 Rustbelt Retirees	25.8
15655	31 Rural Resort Dwellers	97.9	15870	25 Salt of The Earth	100.0	16150	29 Rustbelt Retirees	30.3
15656	29 Rustbelt Retirees	41.0	15901	65 Social Security Set	35.8	16153	25 Salt of The Earth	46.7
15658	31 Rural Resort Dwellers	56.5	15902	53 Home Town	31.7	16154	42 Southern Satellites	44.5
15661	29 Rustbelt Retirees	100.0	15904	29 Rustbelt Retirees	69.8	16156	25 Salt of The Earth	98.0
15663	29 Rustbelt Retirees	100.0	15905	29 Rustbelt Retirees	42.6	16157	50 Heartland Communities	73.8
15665	32 Rustbelt Traditions	88.3	15906	29 Rustbelt Retirees	43.0	16159	29 Rustbelt Retirees	52.4
15666	29 Rustbelt Retirees	31.8	15909	29 Rustbelt Retirees	52.9	16172	63 Dorms To Diplomas	100.0
15668	07 Exurbanites	58.1	15920	46 Rooted Rural	100.0	16201	25 Salt of The Earth	26.1
15670	46 Rooted Rural	42.0	15923	46 Rooted Rural	72.0	16210	46 Rooted Rural	100.0
15672	33 Midlife Junction	52.0	15924	50 Heartland Communities	99.1	16212	29 Rustbelt Retirees	100.0
15675	46 Rooted Rural	54.3	15926	50 Heartland Communities	70.4	16213	46 Rooted Rural	100.0
15677	31 Rural Resort Dwellers	76.9	15927	50 Heartland Communities	87.7	16214	55 College Towns	23.1
15678	50 Heartland Communities	100.0	15928	50 Heartland Communities	52.2	16217	50 Heartland Communities	100.0
15679	46 Rooted Rural	38.7	15931	33 Midlife Junction	29.3	16218	46 Rooted Rural	100.0
15681	46 Rooted Rural	58.2	15935	29 Rustbelt Retirees	41.6	16222	46 Rooted Rural	62.9
15683	29 Rustbelt Retirees	50.7	15936	50 Heartland Communities	61.4	16224	50 Heartland Communities	68.0
15684	46 Rooted Rural	67.8	15938	29 Rustbelt Retirees	43.7	16225	46 Rooted Rural	100.0
15686	42 Southern Satellites	59.0	15940	29 Rustbelt Retirees	54.2	16226	29 Rustbelt Retirees	30.3
15687	46 Rooted Rural	82.7	15942	29 Rustbelt Retirees	47.4	16229	25 Salt of The Earth	46.2
15688	46 Rooted Rural	100.0	15943	50 Heartland Communities	75.3	16232	25 Salt of The Earth	53.2
15690	50 Heartland Communities	52.8	15944	50 Heartland Communities	43.9	16233	25 Salt of The Earth	63.9
15692	17 Green Acres	51.6	15945	29 Rustbelt Retirees	100.0			

ZIP CODE	TOP TAPESTRY CONSUMER TYPE	% 2004 HOUSE-HOLDS	ZIP CODE	TOP TAPESTRY CONSUMER TYPE	% 2004 HOUSE-HOLDS	ZIP CODE	TOP TAPESTRY CONSUMER TYPE	% 2004 HOUSE-HOLDS
16234	25 Salt of The Earth	100.0	16601	29 Rustbelt Retirees	28.2	16844	25 Salt of The Earth	55.8
16235	25 Salt of The Earth	100.0	16602	29 Rustbelt Retirees	37.4	16845	46 Rooted Rural	100.0
16238	50 Heartland Communities	100.0	16611	25 Salt of The Earth	99.1	16852	37 Prairie Living	100.0
16239	50 Heartland Communities	100.0	16613	46 Rooted Rural	52.5	16854	32 Rustbelt Traditions	78.3
16240	46 Rooted Rural	62.5	16616	50 Heartland Communities	64.5	16858	25 Salt of The Earth	98.7
16242	50 Heartland Communities	60.2	16617	25 Salt of The Earth	52.3	16859	46 Rooted Rural	100.0
16248	50 Heartland Communities	69.2	16620	46 Rooted Rural	100.0	16860	46 Rooted Rural	47.6
16249	50 Heartland Communities	51.9	16621	42 Southern Satellites	100.0	16861	46 Rooted Rural	100.0
16254	46 Rooted Rural	68.4	16622	46 Rooted Rural	81.4	16863	46 Rooted Rural	100.0
16255	50 Heartland Communities	100.0	16623	46 Rooted Rural	100.0	16864	46 Rooted Rural	100.0
16256	42 Southern Satellites	59.9	16625	46 Rooted Rural	56.5	16865	07 Exurbanites	78.1
16258	50 Heartland Communities	47.8	16627	50 Heartland Communities	55.3	16866	46 Rooted Rural	42.2
16259	46 Rooted Rural	56.6	16630	50 Heartland Communities	55.2	16870	06 Sophisticated Squires	35.1
16260	46 Rooted Rural	59.3	16634	42 Southern Satellites	100.0	16871	46 Rooted Rural	100.0
16262	25 Salt of The Earth	72.1	16635	25 Salt of The Earth	28.6	16872	37 Prairie Living	100.0
16301	29 Rustbelt Retirees	27.5	16636	25 Salt of The Earth	57.9	16874	29 Rustbelt Retirees	54.0
16311	25 Salt of The Earth	100.0	16637	50 Heartland Communities	38.8	16875	25 Salt of The Earth	79.7
16313	46 Rooted Rural	58.0	16639	46 Rooted Rural	57.9	16877	25 Salt of The Earth	76.8
16314	25 Salt of The Earth	99.4	16640	46 Rooted Rural	85.9	16878	42 Southern Satellites	56.3
16316	46 Rooted Rural	32.0	16641	50 Heartland Communities	60.3	16879	32 Rustbelt Traditions	100.0
16317	25 Salt of The Earth	100.0	16645	50 Heartland Communities	100.0	16881	42 Southern Satellites	100.0
16319	29 Rustbelt Retirees	86.9	16646	50 Heartland Communities	67.4	16882	25 Salt of The Earth	100.0
16321	50 Heartland Communities	100.0	16647	25 Salt of The Earth	100.0	16901	46 Rooted Rural	33.1
16323	50 Heartland Communities	34.9	16648	33 Midlife Junction	26.6	16912	50 Heartland Communities	92.4
16326	25 Salt of The Earth	60.4	16650	42 Southern Satellites	99.9	16914	37 Prairie Living	54.4
16327	25 Salt of The Earth	95.0	16651	50 Heartland Communities	71.0	16915	33 Midlife Junction	37.3
16329	50 Heartland Communities	87.3	16652	25 Salt of The Earth	42.2	16917	46 Rooted Rural	97.2
16331	25 Salt of The Earth	100.0	16655	42 Southern Satellites	100.0	16920	50 Heartland Communities	99.1
16332	42 Southern Satellites	100.0	16656	42 Southern Satellites	54.2	16921	46 Rooted Rural	100.0
16333	46 Rooted Rural	89.1	16657	25 Salt of The Earth	100.0	16922	50 Heartland Communities	58.7
16334	25 Salt of The Earth	100.0	16659	25 Salt of The Earth	100.0	16923	46 Rooted Rural	89.0
16335	25 Salt of The Earth	16.4	16661	50 Heartland Communities	100.0	16925	46 Rooted Rural	82.0
16340	42 Southern Satellites	63.9	16662	25 Salt of The Earth	46.1	16926	37 Prairie Living	100.0
16341	50 Heartland Communities	52.6	16664	25 Salt of The Earth	99.0	16927	42 Southern Satellites	100.0
16342	46 Rooted Rural	97.2	16666	46 Rooted Rural	68.8	16928	50 Heartland Communities	69.4
16345	25 Salt of The Earth	100.0	16667	42 Southern Satellites	100.0	16929	42 Southern Satellites	100.0
16346	32 Rustbelt Traditions	37.3	16668	50 Heartland Communities	55.5	16930	25 Salt of The Earth	96.1
16347	50 Heartland Communities	53.3	16669	42 Southern Satellites	52.5	16932	25 Salt of The Earth	99.2
16350	42 Southern Satellites	64.7	16671	50 Heartland Communities	100.0	16933	26 Midland Crowd	19.3
16351	46 Rooted Rural	55.2	16673	25 Salt of The Earth	48.0	16935	46 Rooted Rural	93.7
16353	50 Heartland Communities	100.0	16674	42 Southern Satellites	100.0	16936	46 Rooted Rural	99.8
16354	46 Rooted Rural	31.7	16678	46 Rooted Rural	57.4	16937	42 Southern Satellites	100.0
16360	42 Southern Satellites	69.3	16679	56 Rural Bypasses	63.9	16938	46 Rooted Rural	82.8
16362	25 Salt of The Earth	79.3	16680	50 Heartland Communities	100.0	16939	46 Rooted Rural	100.0
16364	46 Rooted Rural	100.0	16683	25 Salt of The Earth	100.0	16940	46 Rooted Rural	85.7
16365	25 Salt of The Earth	23.3	16685	42 Southern Satellites	100.0	16941	42 Southern Satellites	100.0
16371	32 Rustbelt Traditions	55.0	16686	25 Salt of The Earth	33.1	16942	42 Southern Satellites	100.0
16372	46 Rooted Rural	100.0	16689	46 Rooted Rural	100.0	16943	46 Rooted Rural	100.0
16373	46 Rooted Rural	52.5	16691	46 Rooted Rural	100.0	16946	46 Rooted Rural	65.1
16374	46 Rooted Rural	98.9	16692	46 Rooted Rural	68.5	16947	50 Heartland Communities	40.7
16401	42 Southern Satellites	41.3	16693	25 Salt of The Earth	32.5	16948	46 Rooted Rural	52.3
16402	42 Southern Satellites	97.4	16695	37 Prairie Living	99.6	16950	46 Rooted Rural	54.2
16403	25 Salt of The Earth	60.7	16701	29 Rustbelt Retirees	28.6	17002	37 Prairie Living	55.9
16404	42 Southern Satellites	71.2	16720	42 Southern Satellites	64.6	17003	25 Salt of The Earth	29.2
16405	25 Salt of The Earth	60.8	16724	46 Rooted Rural	58.5	17004	46 Rooted Rural	62.5
16406	42 Southern Satellites	55.4	16726	46 Rooted Rural	78.6	17005	25 Salt of The Earth	100.0
16407	42 Southern Satellites	34.3	16727	29 Rustbelt Retirees	90.9	17006	46 Rooted Rural	100.0
16410	25 Salt of The Earth	56.9	16729	42 Southern Satellites	99.1	17007	17 Green Acres	78.3
16411	42 Southern Satellites	68.8	16731	42 Southern Satellites	58.7	17009	50 Heartland Communities	57.8
16412	55 College Towns	23.6	16732	25 Salt of The Earth	56.6	17011	14 Prosperous Empty Nesters	27.0
16415	25 Salt of The Earth	28.0	16734	46 Rooted Rural	100.0	17013	18 Cozy and Comfortable	20.8
16417	25 Salt of The Earth	34.2	16735	50 Heartland Communities	42.7	17014	42 Southern Satellites	82.4
16420	42 Southern Satellites	100.0	16738	42 Southern Satellites	61.2	17017	25 Salt of The Earth	100.0
16421	33 Midlife Junction	33.4	16740	46 Rooted Rural	83.9	17018	18 Cozy and Comfortable	81.0
16423	42 Southern Satellites	54.4	16743	42 Southern Satellites	57.4	17019	17 Green Acres	55.9
16424	46 Rooted Rural	43.1	16744	25 Salt of The Earth	56.0	17020	25 Salt of The Earth	38.1
16426	17 Green Acres	77.6	16745	42 Southern Satellites	85.7	17021	46 Rooted Rural	76.1
16428	17 Green Acres	18.6	16746	42 Southern Satellites	96.4	17022	17 Green Acres	18.0
16433	25 Salt of The Earth	66.9	16748	46 Rooted Rural	48.2	17023	25 Salt of The Earth	68.1
16434	42 Southern Satellites	99.1	16749	46 Rooted Rural	66.4	17024	25 Salt of The Earth	82.2
16435	42 Southern Satellites	70.4	16750	42 Southern Satellites	93.2	17025	18 Cozy and Comfortable	35.1
16436	25 Salt of The Earth	100.0	16801	63 Dorms To Diplomas	36.2	17026	25 Salt of The Earth	86.6
16438	25 Salt of The Earth	47.6	16802	63 Dorms To Diplomas	100.0	17028	17 Green Acres	53.0
16440	25 Salt of The Earth	100.0	16803	16 Enterprising Professionals	17.8	17029	42 Southern Satellites	100.0
16441	25 Salt of The Earth	35.0	16820	25 Salt of The Earth	100.0	17030	42 Southern Satellites	100.0
16442	17 Green Acres	61.0	16821	46 Rooted Rural	100.0	17032	25 Salt of The Earth	81.2
16443	42 Southern Satellites	74.6	16822	53 Southern Satellites	53.3	17033	14 Prosperous Empty Nesters	29.1
16444	55 College Towns	100.0	16823	25 Salt of The Earth	15.7	17034	32 Rustbelt Traditions	48.4
16501	65 Social Security Set	77.3	16827	17 Green Acres	51.6	17035	42 Southern Satellites	100.0
16502	48 Great Expectations	39.4	16828	26 Midland Crowd	35.1	17036	16 Enterprising Professionals	16.4
16503	60 City Dimensions	52.6	16829	46 Rooted Rural	100.0	17037	25 Salt of The Earth	100.0
16504	32 Rustbelt Traditions	33.1	16830	50 Heartland Communities	36.5	17038	25 Salt of The Earth	100.0
16505	30 Retirement Communities	16.2	16832	25 Salt of The Earth	100.0	17040	25 Salt of The Earth	100.0
16506	12 Up and Coming Families	16.7	16833	50 Heartland Communities	46.6	17042	29 Rustbelt Retirees	16.0
16507	60 City Dimensions	70.4	16836	42 Southern Satellites	50.1	17043	48 Great Expectations	57.8
16508	32 Rustbelt Traditions	43.8	16837	25 Salt of The Earth	100.0	17044	25 Salt of The Earth	20.9
16509	14 Prosperous Empty Nesters	19.6	16838	46 Rooted Rural	64.8	17045	25 Salt of The Earth	71.3
16510	25 Salt of The Earth	20.9	16839	46 Rooted Rural	51.4	17046	25 Salt of The Earth	23.0
16511	32 Rustbelt Traditions	25.5	16840	46 Rooted Rural	99.2	17047	37 Prairie Living	72.3
16565	30 Retirement Communities	100.0	16841	25 Salt of The Earth	47.2	17048	29 Rustbelt Retirees	32.0

ZIP CODE	TOP TAPESTRY CONSUMER TYPE	% 2004 HOUSE-HOLDS	ZIP CODE	TOP TAPESTRY CONSUMER TYPE	% 2004 HOUSE-HOLDS	ZIP CODE	TOP TAPESTRY CONSUMER TYPE	% 2004 HOUSE-HOLDS
17049	25 Salt of The Earth	97.5	17320	12 Up and Coming Families	37.7	17754	17 Green Acres	28.9
17050	07 Exurbanites	29.0	17321	17 Green Acres	98.5	17756	25 Salt of The Earth	40.5
17051	46 Rooted Rural	36.1	17322	17 Green Acres	57.5	17758	31 Rural Resort Dwellers	66.8
17052	42 Southern Satellites	63.0	17324	25 Salt of The Earth	87.2	17763	46 Rooted Rural	100.0
17053	17 Green Acres	42.5	17325	14 Prosperous Empty Nesters	19.7	17764	50 Heartland Communities	48.3
17055	36 Old and Newcomers	16.7	17327	17 Green Acres	30.4	17765	25 Salt of The Earth	53.2
17057	48 Great Expectations	19.2	17329	17 Green Acres	83.7	17768	46 Rooted Rural	100.0
17058	25 Salt of The Earth	100.0	17331	17 Green Acres	24.7	17771	25 Salt of The Earth	73.8
17059	25 Salt of The Earth	73.1	17339	17 Green Acres	76.2	17772	25 Salt of The Earth	80.6
17060	42 Southern Satellites	100.0	17340	17 Green Acres	49.8	17774	46 Rooted Rural	73.9
17061	25 Salt of The Earth	57.6	17344	32 Rustbelt Traditions	56.7	17776	25 Salt of The Earth	54.1
17062	25 Salt of The Earth	58.8	17345	25 Salt of The Earth	28.2	17777	42 Southern Satellites	40.6
17063	42 Southern Satellites	72.6	17347	42 Southern Satellites	44.8	17778	46 Rooted Rural	87.5
17065	32 Rustbelt Traditions	77.4	17349	07 Exurbanites	38.9	17779	50 Heartland Communities	33.5
17066	42 Southern Satellites	34.9	17350	26 Midland Crowd	28.7	17801	25 Salt of The Earth	29.0
17067	25 Salt of The Earth	44.5	17352	17 Green Acres	91.1	17810	25 Salt of The Earth	57.6
17068	25 Salt of The Earth	52.9	17353	25 Salt of The Earth	97.5	17812	42 Southern Satellites	100.0
17070	14 Prosperous Empty Nesters	25.3	17356	25 Salt of The Earth	39.5	17813	42 Southern Satellites	100.0
17071	46 Rooted Rural	100.0	17360	25 Salt of The Earth	49.2	17814	25 Salt of The Earth	79.2
17073	32 Rustbelt Traditions	42.6	17361	17 Green Acres	55.7	17815	25 Salt of The Earth	32.4
17074	25 Salt of The Earth	51.5	17362	25 Salt of The Earth	38.7	17820	25 Salt of The Earth	71.6
17076	25 Salt of The Earth	76.8	17363	17 Green Acres	50.3	17821	25 Salt of The Earth	26.7
17078	33 Midlife Junction	23.2	17364	25 Salt of The Earth	86.6	17823	25 Salt of The Earth	100.0
17080	25 Salt of The Earth	100.0	17365	25 Salt of The Earth	74.1	17824	14 Prosperous Empty Nesters	35.9
17082	25 Salt of The Earth	70.6	17366	42 Southern Satellites	45.8	17827	50 Heartland Communities	91.1
17084	25 Salt of The Earth	61.7	17368	32 Rustbelt Traditions	31.0	17830	25 Salt of The Earth	100.0
17086	25 Salt of The Earth	99.8	17370	26 Midland Crowd	50.4	17832	50 Heartland Communities	100.0
17087	25 Salt of The Earth	94.6	17372	25 Salt of The Earth	51.6	17834	50 Heartland Communities	65.7
17090	26 Midland Crowd	71.9	17401	52 Inner City Tenants	62.9	17835	42 Southern Satellites	100.0
17094	25 Salt of The Earth	68.4	17402	29 Rustbelt Retirees	18.6	17836	25 Salt of The Earth	100.0
17097	29 Rustbelt Retirees	100.0	17403	60 City Dimensions	13.2	17837	25 Salt of The Earth	27.2
17098	42 Southern Satellites	60.1	17404	32 Rustbelt Traditions	19.4	17841	42 Southern Satellites	55.4
17099	32 Rustbelt Traditions	67.3	17406	17 Green Acres	34.0	17842	25 Salt of The Earth	46.1
17101	65 Social Security Set	52.5	17407	18 Cozy and Comfortable	60.5	17843	25 Salt of The Earth	100.0
17102	48 Great Expectations	31.8	17501	24 Main Street, USA	65.3	17844	25 Salt of The Earth	32.4
17103	54 Urban Rows	40.3	17502	25 Salt of The Earth	99.0	17845	46 Rooted Rural	50.4
17104	64 City Commons	18.0	17505	24 Main Street, USA	34.8	17846	25 Salt of The Earth	76.2
17109	36 Old and Newcomers	34.0	17509	17 Green Acres	55.2	17847	32 Rustbelt Traditions	35.1
17110	13 In Style	37.3	17512	32 Rustbelt Traditions	24.5	17850	42 Southern Satellites	45.7
17111	13 In Style	22.6	17516	25 Salt of The Earth	48.8	17851	50 Heartland Communities	80.1
17112	18 Cozy and Comfortable	36.5	17517	17 Green Acres	55.3	17853	42 Southern Satellites	100.0
17113	32 Rustbelt Traditions	32.5	17518	25 Salt of The Earth	100.0	17855	32 Rustbelt Traditions	100.0
17201	25 Salt of The Earth	18.8	17519	25 Salt of The Earth	75.9	17856	25 Salt of The Earth	100.0
17211	46 Rooted Rural	100.0	17520	19 Milk and Cookies	43.6	17857	25 Salt of The Earth	34.1
17212	42 Southern Satellites	69.5	17522	25 Salt of The Earth	22.9	17859	17 Green Acres	47.1
17213	42 Southern Satellites	100.0	17527	17 Green Acres	43.1	17860	25 Salt of The Earth	100.0
17214	33 Midlife Junction	100.0	17529	37 Prairie Living	65.5	17864	25 Salt of The Earth	54.7
17215	42 Southern Satellites	100.0	17532	25 Salt of The Earth	56.5	17866	50 Heartland Communities	48.9
17217	25 Salt of The Earth	100.0	17535	17 Green Acres	47.4	17867	25 Salt of The Earth	100.0
17219	25 Salt of The Earth	84.8	17536	17 Green Acres	76.2	17868	18 Cozy and Comfortable	77.9
17220	25 Salt of The Earth	83.3	17538	06 Sophisticated Squires	30.6	17870	25 Salt of The Earth	29.7
17221	42 Southern Satellites	100.0	17540	17 Green Acres	37.2	17872	57 Simple Living	46.1
17222	29 Rustbelt Retirees	25.1	17543	17 Green Acres	27.4	17877	25 Salt of The Earth	100.0
17223	42 Southern Satellites	100.0	17545	17 Green Acres	27.8	17878	25 Salt of The Earth	100.0
17224	42 Southern Satellites	83.5	17547	32 Rustbelt Traditions	43.8	17881	50 Heartland Communities	81.8
17225	25 Salt of The Earth	46.7	17551	55 College Towns	27.7	17888	50 Heartland Communities	100.0
17228	42 Southern Satellites	89.4	17552	24 Main Street, USA	43.2	17889	25 Salt of The Earth	64.4
17229	46 Rooted Rural	55.6	17554	17 Green Acres	33.7	17901	29 Rustbelt Retirees	28.3
17232	42 Southern Satellites	100.0	17555	25 Salt of The Earth	67.8	17921	50 Heartland Communities	59.2
17233	42 Southern Satellites	74.4	17557	25 Salt of The Earth	43.7	17922	25 Salt of The Earth	38.6
17236	25 Salt of The Earth	49.0	17560	46 Rooted Rural	59.3	17923	50 Heartland Communities	100.0
17237	32 Rustbelt Traditions	97.9	17562	25 Salt of The Earth	74.0	17925	50 Heartland Communities	100.0
17238	25 Salt of The Earth	88.5	17563	25 Salt of The Earth	95.1	17929	32 Rustbelt Traditions	81.6
17239	42 Southern Satellites	100.0	17565	17 Green Acres	57.9	17931	29 Rustbelt Retirees	56.4
17240	25 Salt of The Earth	100.0	17566	25 Salt of The Earth	37.7	17935	50 Heartland Communities	96.0
17241	25 Salt of The Earth	65.0	17569	17 Green Acres	52.4	17938	25 Salt of The Earth	61.1
17243	42 Southern Satellites	61.5	17572	25 Salt of The Earth	48.1	17941	25 Salt of The Earth	90.3
17244	25 Salt of The Earth	100.0	17576	25 Salt of The Earth	100.0	17948	50 Heartland Communities	86.4
17246	25 Salt of The Earth	100.0	17578	17 Green Acres	42.1	17954	50 Heartland Communities	57.1
17252	25 Salt of The Earth	45.9	17579	17 Green Acres	69.5	17957	42 Southern Satellites	68.3
17255	42 Southern Satellites	100.0	17581	25 Salt of The Earth	100.0	17959	50 Heartland Communities	100.0
17257	25 Salt of The Earth	20.4	17582	25 Salt of The Earth	52.7	17960	25 Salt of The Earth	100.0
17260	46 Rooted Rural	55.1	17584	30 Retirement Communities	46.0	17961	25 Salt of The Earth	53.1
17262	42 Southern Satellites	56.7	17601	33 Midlife Junction	14.1	17963	25 Salt of The Earth	76.5
17264	46 Rooted Rural	64.2	17602	48 Great Expectations	15.8	17964	37 Prairie Living	73.4
17265	25 Salt of The Earth	98.6	17603	60 City Dimensions	14.9	17965	50 Heartland Communities	90.9
17266	25 Salt of The Earth	100.0	17701	48 Great Expectations	17.9	17967	25 Salt of The Earth	56.7
17267	42 Southern Satellites	80.7	17702	29 Rustbelt Retirees	48.5	17968	25 Salt of The Earth	100.0
17268	25 Salt of The Earth	37.6	17723	31 Rural Resort Dwellers	100.0	17970	50 Heartland Communities	100.0
17271	42 Southern Satellites	89.8	17724	46 Rooted Rural	48.6	17972	25 Salt of The Earth	26.4
17301	25 Salt of The Earth	41.0	17728	25 Salt of The Earth	47.0	17976	57 Simple Living	31.7
17302	25 Salt of The Earth	67.8	17729	46 Rooted Rural	62.5	17978	25 Salt of The Earth	100.0
17304	25 Salt of The Earth	70.2	17737	25 Salt of The Earth	44.7	17980	50 Heartland Communities	47.0
17307	25 Salt of The Earth	55.8	17740	25 Salt of The Earth	49.1	17981	50 Heartland Communities	57.8
17309	25 Salt of The Earth	72.7	17742	25 Salt of The Earth	100.0	17983	29 Rustbelt Retirees	62.5
17313	32 Rustbelt Traditions	30.9	17744	25 Salt of The Earth	51.0	17985	25 Salt of The Earth	98.5
17314	26 Midland Crowd	44.2	17745	57 Simple Living	21.9	18011	19 Milk and Cookies	42.6
17315	25 Salt of The Earth	26.0	17747	25 Salt of The Earth	100.0	18013	32 Rustbelt Traditions	24.2
17316	17 Green Acres	65.7	17751	25 Salt of The Earth	60.5	18014	17 Green Acres	33.1
17319	26 Midland Crowd	24.2	17752	25 Salt of The Earth	41.8	18015	60 City Dimensions	14.2

ZIP CODE	TOP TAPESTRY CONSUMER TYPE	% 2004 HOUSE-HOLDS	ZIP CODE	TOP TAPESTRY CONSUMER TYPE	% 2004 HOUSE-HOLDS	ZIP CODE	TOP TAPESTRY CONSUMER TYPE	% 2004 HOUSE-HOLDS
18017	29 Rustbelt Retirees	29.2	18350	31 Rural Resort Dwellers	88.3	18644	29 Rustbelt Retirees	71.5
18018	29 Rustbelt Retirees	20.3	18352	17 Green Acres	100.0	18651	50 Heartland Communities	41.3
18020	06 Sophisticated Squires	31.6	18353	17 Green Acres	86.1	18655	25 Salt of The Earth	66.9
18031	49 Senior Sun Seekers	62.4	18354	25 Salt of The Earth	63.3	18656	25 Salt of The Earth	100.0
18032	32 Rustbelt Traditions	47.7	18355	25 Salt of The Earth	96.5	18657	25 Salt of The Earth	73.7
18034	07 Exurbanites	87.6	18360	17 Green Acres	41.1	18660	25 Salt of The Earth	64.4
18035	17 Green Acres	100.0	18370	25 Salt of The Earth	100.0	18661	29 Rustbelt Retirees	33.3
18036	07 Exurbanites	63.3	18371	19 Milk and Cookies	100.0	18701	65 Social Security Set	53.9
18037	29 Rustbelt Retirees	28.3	18372	17 Green Acres	72.9	18702	50 Heartland Communities	24.6
18038	17 Green Acres	49.8	18403	29 Rustbelt Retirees	52.2	18704	29 Rustbelt Retirees	28.3
18040	06 Sophisticated Squires	59.5	18405	25 Salt of The Earth	59.2	18705	29 Rustbelt Retirees	66.5
18041	17 Green Acres	43.7	18407	29 Rustbelt Retirees	27.9	18706	29 Rustbelt Retirees	28.3
18042	32 Rustbelt Traditions	31.2	18411	14 Prosperous Empty Nesters	20.5	18707	17 Green Acres	27.4
18045	18 Cozy and Comfortable	30.3	18414	25 Salt of The Earth	47.0	18708	18 Cozy and Comfortable	34.2
18049	13 In Style	16.9	18415	31 Rural Resort Dwellers	100.0	18709	32 Rustbelt Traditions	41.1
18051	17 Green Acres	44.5	18417	46 Rooted Rural	98.7	18801	25 Salt of The Earth	42.5
18052	18 Cozy and Comfortable	20.6	18419	17 Green Acres	47.2	18810	25 Salt of The Earth	37.9
18053	17 Green Acres	100.0	18421	25 Salt of The Earth	41.8	18812	17 Green Acres	83.7
18054	17 Green Acres	44.3	18424	31 Rural Resort Dwellers	40.0	18817	25 Salt of The Earth	99.7
18055	29 Rustbelt Retirees	26.7	18425	31 Rural Resort Dwellers	100.0	18818	25 Salt of The Earth	94.2
18056	42 Southern Satellites	100.0	18426	31 Rural Resort Dwellers	100.0	18821	50 Heartland Communities	54.1
18058	25 Salt of The Earth	57.9	18427	31 Rural Resort Dwellers	91.8	18822	50 Heartland Communities	46.4
18059	12 Up and Coming Families	98.4	18428	31 Rural Resort Dwellers	57.7	18823	25 Salt of The Earth	100.0
18062	13 In Style	39.1	18430	31 Rural Resort Dwellers	100.0	18824	46 Rooted Rural	90.8
18064	18 Cozy and Comfortable	20.4	18431	25 Salt of The Earth	29.1	18825	31 Rural Resort Dwellers	100.0
18066	17 Green Acres	98.2	18433	29 Rustbelt Retirees	32.3	18826	25 Salt of The Earth	100.0
18067	29 Rustbelt Retirees	21.5	18434	29 Rustbelt Retirees	56.7	18828	25 Salt of The Earth	100.0
18069	02 Suburban Splendor	28.5	18435	31 Rural Resort Dwellers	100.0	18829	25 Salt of The Earth	100.0
18070	17 Green Acres	67.0	18436	25 Salt of The Earth	44.9	18830	25 Salt of The Earth	100.0
18071	29 Rustbelt Retirees	29.7	18437	31 Rural Resort Dwellers	100.0	18831	25 Salt of The Earth	100.0
18072	29 Rustbelt Retirees	27.5	18438	31 Rural Resort Dwellers	100.0	18832	42 Southern Satellites	70.7
18073	17 Green Acres	37.1	18439	31 Rural Resort Dwellers	100.0	18833	42 Southern Satellites	100.0
18074	17 Green Acres	87.0	18441	25 Salt of The Earth	50.9	18834	25 Salt of The Earth	72.2
18076	29 Rustbelt Retirees	33.9	18443	31 Rural Resort Dwellers	100.0	18837	25 Salt of The Earth	53.1
18077	07 Exurbanites	61.9	18444	25 Salt of The Earth	27.5	18840	50 Heartland Communities	27.1
18078	07 Exurbanites	53.7	18445	31 Rural Resort Dwellers	87.1	18842	25 Salt of The Earth	100.0
18080	17 Green Acres	20.7	18446	46 Rooted Rural	53.0	18844	25 Salt of The Earth	93.2
18087	02 Suburban Splendor	100.0	18447	29 Rustbelt Retirees	39.3	18845	46 Rooted Rural	100.0
18088	25 Salt of The Earth	32.6	18451	31 Rural Resort Dwellers	100.0	18846	25 Salt of The Earth	100.0
18091	17 Green Acres	26.4	18452	29 Rustbelt Retirees	63.2	18847	46 Rooted Rural	57.5
18092	07 Exurbanites	74.4	18453	31 Rural Resort Dwellers	100.0	18848	32 Rustbelt Traditions	30.1
18101	60 City Dimensions	88.5	18455	31 Rural Resort Dwellers	100.0	18850	25 Salt of The Earth	90.7
18102	60 City Dimensions	40.6	18456	31 Rural Resort Dwellers	56.0	18851	25 Salt of The Earth	100.0
18103	48 Great Expectations	22.0	18458	31 Rural Resort Dwellers	91.7	18853	25 Salt of The Earth	36.3
18104	14 Prosperous Empty Nesters	22.9	18460	31 Rural Resort Dwellers	100.0	18854	25 Salt of The Earth	52.9
18106	13 In Style	48.4	18461	31 Rural Resort Dwellers	100.0	18901	02 Suburban Splendor	23.0
18109	32 Rustbelt Traditions	35.4	18462	31 Rural Resort Dwellers	100.0	18913	03 Connoisseurs	100.0
18201	50 Heartland Communities	34.3	18463	25 Salt of The Earth	98.6	18914	13 In Style	32.4
18202	50 Heartland Communities	30.4	18464	31 Rural Resort Dwellers	100.0	18915	10 Pleasant-Ville	99.1
18210	31 Rural Resort Dwellers	77.1	18465	31 Rural Resort Dwellers	45.0	18917	28 Aspiring Young Families	100.0
18211	25 Salt of The Earth	98.1	18466	19 Milk and Cookies	72.6	18920	17 Green Acres	57.1
18214	25 Salt of The Earth	82.8	18469	31 Rural Resort Dwellers	99.6	18923	06 Sophisticated Squires	65.0
18216	50 Heartland Communities	43.1	18470	46 Rooted Rural	54.3	18925	03 Connoisseurs	75.0
18218	50 Heartland Communities	70.7	18472	33 Midlife Junction	39.2	18927	10 Pleasant-Ville	100.0
18219	14 Prosperous Empty Nesters	100.0	18503	65 Social Security Set	100.0	18929	04 Boomburbs	56.7
18220	50 Heartland Communities	100.0	18504	29 Rustbelt Retirees	28.8	18930	17 Green Acres	60.7
18222	25 Salt of The Earth	48.3	18505	29 Rustbelt Retirees	42.5	18932	14 Prosperous Empty Nesters	48.1
18224	50 Heartland Communities	63.5	18507	29 Rustbelt Retirees	46.7	18933	03 Connoisseurs	100.0
18229	31 Rural Resort Dwellers	30.9	18508	50 Heartland Communities	26.5	18934	02 Suburban Splendor	100.0
18232	50 Heartland Communities	78.3	18509	57 Simple Living	34.7	18936	05 Wealthy Seaboard Suburbs	100.0
18235	25 Salt of The Earth	27.3	18510	33 Midlife Junction	28.8	18938	09 Urban Chic	28.3
18237	50 Heartland Communities	57.4	18512	29 Rustbelt Retirees	81.0	18940	04 Boomburbs	22.9
18240	29 Rustbelt Retirees	51.8	18517	29 Rustbelt Retirees	50.8	18942	17 Green Acres	68.7
18245	29 Rustbelt Retirees	100.0	18518	29 Rustbelt Retirees	85.8	18944	17 Green Acres	22.2
18246	29 Rustbelt Retirees	78.6	18519	29 Rustbelt Retirees	47.9	18947	02 Suburban Splendor	46.8
18248	50 Heartland Communities	100.0	18603	50 Heartland Communities	25.1	18951	17 Green Acres	28.4
18249	17 Green Acres	34.4	18610	26 Midland Crowd	94.7	18954	02 Suburban Splendor	85.0
18250	29 Rustbelt Retirees	100.0	18612	33 Midlife Junction	26.7	18955	24 Main Street, USA	84.5
18252	50 Heartland Communities	28.5	18614	46 Rooted Rural	57.1	18960	24 Main Street, USA	16.4
18255	29 Rustbelt Retirees	57.8	18615	25 Salt of The Earth	100.0	18964	24 Main Street, USA	45.9
18301	17 Green Acres	28.7	18616	31 Rural Resort Dwellers	100.0	18966	02 Suburban Splendor	22.4
18321	17 Green Acres	100.0	18617	53 Home Town	50.9	18969	30 Retirement Communities	24.3
18322	17 Green Acres	91.6	18618	25 Salt of The Earth	61.9	18972	17 Green Acres	93.9
18324	18 Cozy and Comfortable	52.8	18619	46 Rooted Rural	100.0	18976	10 Pleasant-Ville	33.3
18325	31 Rural Resort Dwellers	54.0	18621	25 Salt of The Earth	69.1	18976	12 Up and Coming Families	23.9
18326	25 Salt of The Earth	28.8	18622	25 Salt of The Earth	100.0	18977	02 Suburban Splendor	40.9
18327	36 Old and Newcomers	68.4	18623	46 Rooted Rural	53.5	19001	18 Cozy and Comfortable	40.3
18328	19 Milk and Cookies	38.8	18624	31 Rural Resort Dwellers	93.3	19002	03 Connoisseurs	34.4
18330	17 Green Acres	86.9	18628	29 Rustbelt Retirees	100.0	19003	22 Metropolitans	29.8
18331	25 Salt of The Earth	100.0	18629	25 Salt of The Earth	100.0	19004	03 Connoisseurs	41.6
18332	25 Salt of The Earth	33.1	18630	25 Salt of The Earth	51.3	19006	03 Connoisseurs	40.1
18333	25 Salt of The Earth	78.3	18631	29 Rustbelt Retirees	86.4	19007	29 Rustbelt Retirees	21.8
18334	26 Midland Crowd	60.3	18632	46 Rooted Rural	98.8	19008	05 Wealthy Seaboard Suburbs	37.9
18336	31 Rural Resort Dwellers	40.5	18634	29 Rustbelt Retirees	38.0	19010	09 Urban Chic	18.3
18337	12 Up and Coming Families	37.2	18635	25 Salt of The Earth	51.9	19012	14 Prosperous Empty Nesters	24.2
18340	31 Rural Resort Dwellers	100.0	18636	50 Heartland Communities	56.5	19013	54 Urban Rows	67.5
18343	17 Green Acres	40.4	18640	29 Rustbelt Retirees	46.1	19014	18 Cozy and Comfortable	34.1
18344	24 Main Street, USA	82.4	18641	29 Rustbelt Retirees	75.0	19015	33 Midlife Junction	21.4
18346	31 Rural Resort Dwellers	61.2	18642	29 Rustbelt Retirees	79.7	19018	36 Old and Newcomers	21.9
18347	31 Rural Resort Dwellers	39.2	18643	50 Heartland Communities	31.2	19020	06 Sophisticated Squires	21.1

ZIP CODE	TOP TAPESTRY CONSUMER TYPE	% 2004 HOUSE-HOLDS	ZIP CODE	TOP TAPESTRY CONSUMER TYPE	% 2004 HOUSE-HOLDS	ZIP CODE	TOP TAPESTRY CONSUMER TYPE	% 2004 HOUSE-HOLDS
19021	18 Cozy and Comfortable	48.5	19149	32 Rustbelt Traditions	50.3	19602	60 City Dimensions	49.3
19022	32 Rustbelt Traditions	60.7	19150	34 Family Foundations	88.4	19604	60 City Dimensions	39.3
19023	54 Urban Rows	43.2	19151	54 Urban Rows	53.2	19605	29 Rustbelt Retirees	40.7
19025	02 Suburban Splendor	56.4	19152	29 Rustbelt Retirees	40.4	19606	06 Sophisticated Squires	15.7
19026	24 Main Street, USA	18.7	19153	34 Family Foundations	37.5	19607	29 Rustbelt Retirees	28.5
19027	52 Inner City Tenants	20.3	19154	32 Rustbelt Traditions	45.5	19608	13 In Style	22.9
19029	32 Rustbelt Traditions	82.2	19301	30 Retirement Communities	27.3	19609	29 Rustbelt Retirees	52.9
19030	18 Cozy and Comfortable	33.8	19310	17 Green Acres	53.8	19610	14 Prosperous Empty Nesters	61.7
19031	05 Wealthy Seaboard Suburbs	28.2	19311	04 Boomburbs	35.4	19611	32 Rustbelt Traditions	30.6
19032	32 Rustbelt Traditions	63.6	19312	03 Connoisseurs	47.2	19701	28 Aspiring Young Families	33.0
19033	18 Cozy and Comfortable	50.3	19317	03 Connoisseurs	57.9	19702	12 Up and Coming Families	27.1
19034	02 Suburban Splendor	27.7	19319	02 Suburban Splendor	80.8	19703	18 Cozy and Comfortable	19.9
19035	01 Top Rung	99.8	19320	17 Green Acres	19.4	19707	02 Suburban Splendor	48.9
19036	29 Rustbelt Retirees	36.7	19330	17 Green Acres	99.8	19709	04 Boomburbs	39.8
19038	18 Cozy and Comfortable	25.0	19333	09 Urban Chic	40.4	19711	13 In Style	16.9
19040	18 Cozy and Comfortable	25.1	19335	04 Boomburbs	22.3	19713	28 Aspiring Young Families	39.6
19041	03 Connoisseurs	51.9	19341	16 Enterprising Professionals	35.3	19716	63 Dorms To Diplomas	88.2
19043	29 Rustbelt Retirees	54.0	19342	05 Wealthy Seaboard Suburbs	46.1	19720	18 Cozy and Comfortable	16.8
19044	13 In Style	36.4	19343	02 Suburban Splendor	56.3	19734	17 Green Acres	71.7
19046	30 Retirement Communities	25.7	19344	17 Green Acres	36.6	19736	03 Connoisseurs	100.0
19047	02 Suburban Splendor	21.3	19348	02 Suburban Splendor	25.9	19801	54 Urban Rows	21.0
19050	32 Rustbelt Traditions	20.2	19350	02 Suburban Splendor	69.7	19802	54 Urban Rows	30.2
19053	18 Cozy and Comfortable	29.6	19352	04 Boomburbs	50.7	19803	14 Prosperous Empty Nesters	55.4
19054	18 Cozy and Comfortable	65.8	19355	13 In Style	30.1	19804	29 Rustbelt Retirees	57.9
19055	18 Cozy and Comfortable	82.1	19362	26 Midland Crowd	57.4	19805	54 Urban Rows	20.3
19056	18 Cozy and Comfortable	43.0	19363	17 Green Acres	29.7	19806	27 Metro Renters	53.3
19057	18 Cozy and Comfortable	66.6	19365	24 Main Street, USA	53.7	19807	03 Connoisseurs	58.1
19061	32 Rustbelt Traditions	22.5	19372	06 Sophisticated Squires	55.6	19808	13 In Style	16.1
19063	13 In Style	19.4	19373	02 Suburban Splendor	57.2	19809	24 Main Street, USA	26.3
19064	14 Prosperous Empty Nesters	49.3	19374	21 Urban Villages	77.2	19810	14 Prosperous Empty Nesters	42.0
19066	03 Connoisseurs	53.7	19380	02 Suburban Splendor	16.8	19901	41 Crossroads	27.7
19067	02 Suburban Splendor	24.3	19382	02 Suburban Splendor	33.4	19902	40 Military Proximity	100.0
19070	18 Cozy and Comfortable	37.8	19383	02 Suburban Splendor	78.0	19904	18 Cozy and Comfortable	12.1
19072	22 Metropolitans	38.4	19390	17 Green Acres	47.9	19930	15 Silver and Gold	100.0
19073	03 Connoisseurs	37.2	19401	36 Old and Newcomers	15.8	19931	56 Rural Bypasses	57.4
19074	18 Cozy and Comfortable	40.5	19403	07 Exurbanites	23.4	19933	53 Home Town	28.9
19075	14 Prosperous Empty Nesters	30.9	19405	29 Rustbelt Retirees	30.9	19934	18 Cozy and Comfortable	25.3
19076	24 Main Street, USA	65.2	19406	27 Metro Renters	33.2	19938	26 Midland Crowd	80.8
19078	29 Rustbelt Retirees	21.9	19422	09 Urban Chic	48.0	19939	15 Silver and Gold	29.8
19079	32 Rustbelt Traditions	50.1	19425	02 Suburban Splendor	43.8	19940	50 Heartland Communities	41.6
19081	09 Urban Chic	18.2	19426	04 Boomburbs	40.5	19941	42 Southern Satellites	64.8
19082	54 Urban Rows	20.3	19428	24 Main Street, USA	29.9	19943	26 Midland Crowd	64.4
19083	10 Pleasant-Ville	30.2	19435	17 Green Acres	100.0	19944	15 Silver and Gold	100.0
19085	01 Top Rung	77.5	19436	03 Connoisseurs	100.0	19945	46 Rooted Rural	40.3
19086	05 Wealthy Seaboard Suburbs	22.5	19438	13 In Style	48.2	19946	41 Crossroads	47.6
19087	03 Connoisseurs	34.2	19440	24 Main Street, USA	35.7	19947	26 Midland Crowd	23.5
19090	18 Cozy and Comfortable	26.4	19444	04 Boomburbs	40.1	19950	25 Salt of The Earth	84.5
19094	29 Rustbelt Retirees	37.7	19446	13 In Style	16.7	19951	46 Rooted Rural	55.7
19095	30 Retirement Communities	63.7	19453	13 In Style	61.4	19952	26 Midland Crowd	25.7
19096	03 Connoisseurs	50.9	19454	05 Wealthy Seaboard Suburbs	20.1	19953	26 Midland Crowd	97.2
19102	27 Metro Renters	100.0	19460	13 In Style	12.7	19954	26 Midland Crowd	97.1
19103	27 Metro Renters	58.9	19462	14 Prosperous Empty Nesters	25.8	19956	26 Midland Crowd	50.6
19104	63 Dorms To Diplomas	31.0	19464	32 Rustbelt Traditions	20.4	19958	31 Rural Resort Dwellers	65.5
19106	27 Metro Renters	40.6	19465	17 Green Acres	33.1	19960	26 Midland Crowd	67.1
19107	27 Metro Renters	76.5	19468	13 In Style	24.9	19962	41 Crossroads	34.2
19111	32 Rustbelt Traditions	31.0	19473	06 Sophisticated Squires	25.1	19963	33 Midlife Junction	22.3
19114	29 Rustbelt Retirees	24.8	19475	24 Main Street, USA	42.4	19964	26 Midland Crowd	73.4
19115	30 Retirement Communities	47.7	19477	03 Connoisseurs	100.0	19966	49 Senior Sun Seekers	56.0
19116	18 Cozy and Comfortable	28.1	19492	17 Green Acres	100.0	19967	31 Rural Resort Dwellers	96.3
19118	22 Metropolitans	24.1	19501	24 Main Street, USA	100.0	19968	31 Rural Resort Dwellers	28.9
19119	22 Metropolitans	26.9	19503	25 Salt of The Earth	100.0	19970	15 Silver and Gold	59.2
19120	54 Urban Rows	67.9	19504	17 Green Acres	95.8	19971	15 Silver and Gold	46.9
19121	54 Urban Rows	73.7	19505	17 Green Acres	57.1	19973	25 Salt of The Earth	26.1
19122	54 Urban Rows	61.5	19506	25 Salt of The Earth	54.3	19975	15 Silver and Gold	53.1
19123	48 Great Expectations	17.8	19507	25 Salt of The Earth	84.2	19977	26 Midland Crowd	40.7
19124	54 Urban Rows	63.6	19508	17 Green Acres	28.9	19979	42 Southern Satellites	88.0
19125	54 Urban Rows	92.1	19510	12 Up and Coming Families	50.6	20001	45 City Strivers	37.3
19126	54 Urban Rows	39.1	19512	17 Green Acres	42.3	20002	54 Urban Rows	38.6
19127	22 Metropolitans	26.3	19518	13 In Style	32.0	20003	08 Laptops and Lattes	38.1
19128	48 Great Expectations	20.8	19520	17 Green Acres	41.8	20004	27 Metro Renters	100.0
19129	27 Metro Renters	22.8	19522	17 Green Acres	44.8	20005	27 Metro Renters	98.3
19130	27 Metro Renters	38.1	19525	06 Sophisticated Squires	35.5	20006	63 Dorms To Diplomas	100.0
19131	54 Urban Rows	41.7	19526	25 Salt of The Earth	31.9	20007	08 Laptops and Lattes	62.2
19132	54 Urban Rows	93.1	19529	17 Green Acres	100.0	20008	27 Metro Renters	52.6
19133	54 Urban Rows	81.7	19530	55 College Towns	24.8	20009	27 Metro Renters	62.7
19134	54 Urban Rows	76.8	19533	17 Green Acres	49.0	20010	61 High Rise Renters	27.3
19135	32 Rustbelt Traditions	43.0	19534	17 Green Acres	63.7	20011	45 City Strivers	40.2
19136	32 Rustbelt Traditions	32.0	19539	25 Salt of The Earth	51.3	20012	20 City Lights	29.9
19137	54 Urban Rows	44.7	19540	17 Green Acres	45.4	20015	03 Connoisseurs	47.6
19138	54 Urban Rows	64.3	19541	17 Green Acres	86.3	20016	08 Laptops and Lattes	23.6
19139	54 Urban Rows	83.5	19543	24 Main Street, USA	45.3	20017	34 Family Foundations	28.9
19140	54 Urban Rows	85.0	19547	17 Green Acres	56.8	20018	34 Family Foundations	36.0
19141	54 Urban Rows	74.7	19549	25 Salt of The Earth	100.0	20019	64 City Commons	26.1
19142	54 Urban Rows	90.7	19551	32 Rustbelt Traditions	43.3	20020	64 City Commons	40.2
19143	54 Urban Rows	76.6	19555	25 Salt of The Earth	46.6	20024	27 Metro Renters	45.4
19144	54 Urban Rows	53.2	19560	29 Rustbelt Retirees	59.9	20032	45 City Strivers	38.8
19145	54 Urban Rows	56.0	19562	33 Midlife Junction	80.5	20036	27 Metro Renters	100.0
19146	54 Urban Rows	61.1	19565	29 Rustbelt Retirees	48.0	20037	27 Metro Renters	93.3
19147	27 Metro Renters	30.5	19567	32 Rustbelt Traditions	32.7	20057	63 Dorms To Diplomas	100.0
19148	54 Urban Rows	75.7	19601	60 City Dimensions	41.5	20064	63 Dorms To Diplomas	100.0

ZIP CODE	TOP TAPESTRY CONSUMER TYPE	% 2004 HOUSE-HOLDS	ZIP CODE	TOP TAPESTRY CONSUMER TYPE	% 2004 HOUSE-HOLDS	ZIP CODE	TOP TAPESTRY CONSUMER TYPE	% 2004 HOUSE-HOLDS
20105	04 Boomburbs	49.1	20678	17 Green Acres	30.5	20877	35 International Marketplace	17.7
20106	07 Exurbanites	61.0	20680	31 Rural Resort Dwellers	81.2	20878	02 Suburban Splendor	34.6
20107	04 Boomburbs	71.4	20684	14 Prosperous Empty Nesters	67.8	20879	06 Sophisticated Squires	32.9
20109	28 Aspiring Young Families	55.1	20685	12 Up and Coming Families	44.6	20882	02 Suburban Splendor	55.4
20110	28 Aspiring Young Families	16.8	20687	31 Rural Resort Dwellers	100.0	20886	16 Enterprising Professionals	18.8
20111	19 Milk and Cookies	34.1	20688	14 Prosperous Empty Nesters	58.9	20895	05 Wealthy Seaboard Suburbs	29.8
20112	04 Boomburbs	54.6	20689	07 Exurbanites	97.3	20901	10 Pleasant-Ville	27.4
20115	07 Exurbanites	60.3	20690	14 Prosperous Empty Nesters	100.0	20902	10 Pleasant-Ville	23.3
20117	09 Urban Chic	92.9	20692	14 Prosperous Empty Nesters	62.2	20903	35 International Marketplace	34.5
20119	17 Green Acres	74.4	20693	17 Green Acres	97.9	20904	39 Young and Restless	34.4
20120	02 Suburban Splendor	29.5	20695	06 Sophisticated Squires	53.2	20905	02 Suburban Splendor	37.7
20121	16 Enterprising Professionals	55.8	20701	41 Crossroads	86.7	20906	43 The Elders	17.3
20124	02 Suburban Splendor	47.8	20705	39 Young and Restless	26.2	20910	27 Metro Renters	44.5
20129	03 Connoisseurs	99.2	20706	28 Aspiring Young Families	28.4	20912	23 Trendsetters	25.4
20130	17 Green Acres	93.5	20707	28 Aspiring Young Families	21.9	21001	48 Great Expectations	23.1
20132	02 Suburban Splendor	29.3	20708	28 Aspiring Young Families	29.7	21005	40 Military Proximity	92.1
20135	17 Green Acres	66.7	20710	52 Inner City Tenants	62.6	21009	12 Up and Coming Families	48.0
20136	04 Boomburbs	96.6	20711	41 Crossroads	48.7	21010	40 Military Proximity	100.0
20137	07 Exurbanites	88.3	20712	52 Inner City Tenants	37.0	21012	06 Sophisticated Squires	25.3
20141	07 Exurbanites	73.1	20714	12 Up and Coming Families	66.8	21013	02 Suburban Splendor	39.2
20143	15 Silver and Gold	51.1	20715	10 Pleasant-Ville	45.2	21014	06 Sophisticated Squires	25.1
20144	17 Green Acres	100.0	20716	16 Enterprising Professionals	46.2	21015	04 Boomburbs	23.0
20147	04 Boomburbs	93.5	20720	06 Sophisticated Squires	48.9	21017	12 Up and Coming Families	59.5
20148	04 Boomburbs	97.2	20721	06 Sophisticated Squires	29.7	21028	07 Exurbanites	53.6
20151	02 Suburban Splendor	45.6	20722	34 Family Foundations	73.7	21029	02 Suburban Splendor	49.7
20152	04 Boomburbs	100.0	20723	12 Up and Coming Families	28.8	21030	39 Young and Restless	46.9
20155	04 Boomburbs	37.9	20724	16 Enterprising Professionals	56.4	21031	65 Social Security Set	100.0
20158	07 Exurbanites	69.7	20732	17 Green Acres	32.8	21032	07 Exurbanites	60.9
20164	06 Sophisticated Squires	21.9	20733	06 Sophisticated Squires	61.8	21034	25 Salt of The Earth	57.6
20165	04 Boomburbs	69.7	20735	06 Sophisticated Squires	67.3	21035	07 Exurbanites	54.0
20166	16 Enterprising Professionals	80.0	20736	07 Exurbanites	56.1	21036	02 Suburban Splendor	86.5
20169	07 Exurbanites	40.5	20737	28 Aspiring Young Families	35.2	21037	07 Exurbanites	35.1
20170	02 Suburban Splendor	35.8	20740	22 Metropolitans	12.6	21040	19 Milk and Cookies	26.8
20171	02 Suburban Splendor	54.2	20742	63 Dorms To Diplomas	69.8	21042	02 Suburban Splendor	57.4
20175	04 Boomburbs	40.5	20743	34 Family Foundations	33.4	21043	04 Boomburbs	28.4
20176	04 Boomburbs	31.7	20744	07 Exurbanites	23.1	21044	13 In Style	28.0
20180	07 Exurbanites	99.4	20745	52 Inner City Tenants	31.7	21045	06 Sophisticated Squires	30.0
20181	07 Exurbanites	70.6	20746	28 Aspiring Young Families	50.1	21046	16 Enterprising Professionals	66.2
20184	17 Green Acres	55.5	20747	18 Cozy and Comfortable	22.3	21047	07 Exurbanites	73.1
20186	13 In Style	38.6	20748	28 Aspiring Young Families	23.2	21048	17 Green Acres	44.8
20187	07 Exurbanites	49.3	20751	17 Green Acres	93.7	21050	13 In Style	47.7
20190	16 Enterprising Professionals	37.2	20754	07 Exurbanites	63.3	21051	07 Exurbanites	100.0
20191	09 Urban Chic	18.9	20755	40 Military Proximity	99.6	21053	06 Sophisticated Squires	50.6
20194	16 Enterprising Professionals	39.8	20758	07 Exurbanites	88.6	21054	12 Up and Coming Families	36.2
20197	03 Connoisseurs	100.0	20759	02 Suburban Splendor	100.0	21056	03 Connoisseurs	100.0
20198	09 Urban Chic	60.8	20762	40 Military Proximity	99.8	21057	14 Prosperous Empty Nesters	59.1
20601	06 Sophisticated Squires	33.9	20763	28 Aspiring Young Families	89.9	21060	18 Cozy and Comfortable	41.1
20602	28 Aspiring Young Families	24.5	20764	17 Green Acres	87.9	21061	18 Cozy and Comfortable	32.0
20603	12 Up and Coming Families	42.9	20769	06 Sophisticated Squires	47.5	21071	07 Exurbanites	100.0
20606	18 Cozy and Comfortable	66.8	20770	39 Young and Restless	32.1	21074	12 Up and Coming Families	35.3
20607	06 Sophisticated Squires	62.0	20772	06 Sophisticated Squires	30.8	21075	28 Aspiring Young Families	33.6
20608	18 Cozy and Comfortable	62.9	20774	06 Sophisticated Squires	43.7	21076	06 Sophisticated Squires	61.7
20609	31 Rural Resort Dwellers	40.8	20776	07 Exurbanites	78.9	21077	06 Sophisticated Squires	98.3
20611	07 Exurbanites	100.0	20777	02 Suburban Splendor	100.0	21078	12 Up and Coming Families	27.0
20613	10 Pleasant-Ville	53.2	20778	07 Exurbanites	57.1	21082	07 Exurbanites	52.4
20615	17 Green Acres	100.0	20779	07 Exurbanites	100.0	21084	06 Sophisticated Squires	35.4
20616	12 Up and Coming Families	52.0	20781	24 Main Street, USA	29.1	21085	18 Cozy and Comfortable	45.3
20617	07 Exurbanites	100.0	20782	52 Inner City Tenants	24.6	21087	07 Exurbanites	57.2
20618	31 Rural Resort Dwellers	80.5	20783	58 Newest Residents	19.5	21090	14 Prosperous Empty Nesters	51.5
20619	13 In Style	41.0	20784	52 Inner City Tenants	28.9	21093	14 Prosperous Empty Nesters	27.3
20620	13 In Style	63.2	20785	34 Family Foundations	21.5	21102	17 Green Acres	43.5
20621	12 Up and Coming Families	58.1	20794	31 In Style	31.0	21104	06 Sophisticated Squires	63.5
20622	06 Sophisticated Squires	85.7	20812	03 Connoisseurs	100.0	21108	02 Suburban Splendor	29.5
20623	04 Boomburbs	65.7	20814	27 Metro Renters	33.5	21111	07 Exurbanites	48.2
20624	17 Green Acres	80.1	20815	27 Metro Renters	25.1	21113	12 Up and Coming Families	40.7
20625	24 Main Street, USA	100.0	20816	03 Connoisseurs	70.2	21114	12 Up and Coming Families	32.7
20626	29 Rustbelt Retirees	100.0	20817	03 Connoisseurs	57.1	21117	16 Enterprising Professionals	42.1
20628	31 Rural Resort Dwellers	56.8	20818	03 Connoisseurs	100.0	21120	07 Exurbanites	53.7
20630	14 Prosperous Empty Nesters	67.9	20832	02 Suburban Splendor	41.1	21122	18 Cozy and Comfortable	22.2
20632	18 Cozy and Comfortable	74.7	20833	02 Suburban Splendor	92.9	21128	13 In Style	42.1
20634	12 Up and Coming Families	53.2	20837	06 Sophisticated Squires	77.8	21131	03 Connoisseurs	80.0
20636	17 Green Acres	34.3	20838	03 Connoisseurs	100.0	21132	17 Green Acres	77.9
20637	05 Wealthy Seaboard Suburbs	41.1	20839	02 Suburban Splendor	63.5	21133	18 Cozy and Comfortable	29.1
20639	06 Sophisticated Squires	68.8	20841	13 In Style	42.5	21136	13 In Style	21.0
20640	24 Main Street, USA	36.5	20842	02 Suburban Splendor	27.3	21140	02 Suburban Splendor	56.5
20645	14 Prosperous Empty Nesters	100.0	20850	05 Wealthy Seaboard Suburbs	22.0	21144	06 Sophisticated Squires	28.2
20646	07 Exurbanites	41.2	20851	10 Pleasant-Ville	64.0	21146	02 Suburban Splendor	31.9
20650	07 Exurbanites	33.0	20852	27 Metro Renters	25.7	21152	13 In Style	60.2
20653	28 Aspiring Young Families	22.4	20853	10 Pleasant-Ville	39.5	21154	17 Green Acres	59.4
20657	12 Up and Coming Families	77.7	20854	01 Top Rung	45.1	21155	07 Exurbanites	83.6
20658	18 Cozy and Comfortable	97.2	20855	02 Suburban Splendor	46.3	21156	14 Prosperous Empty Nesters	85.1
20659	17 Green Acres	45.9	20860	02 Suburban Splendor	50.5	21157	06 Sophisticated Squires	25.8
20662	25 Salt of The Earth	99.9	20861	03 Connoisseurs	75.2	21158	17 Green Acres	38.5
20664	29 Rustbelt Retirees	41.7	20862	02 Suburban Splendor	100.0	21160	18 Cozy and Comfortable	80.9
20667	24 Main Street, USA	93.2	20866	16 Enterprising Professionals	25.9	21161	07 Exurbanites	79.2
20670	40 Military Proximity	100.0	20868	07 Exurbanites	62.7	21162	18 Cozy and Comfortable	76.7
20674	14 Prosperous Empty Nesters	100.0	20871	19 Milk and Cookies	43.6	21163	02 Suburban Splendor	39.2
20675	07 Exurbanites	53.7	20872	19 Milk and Cookies	43.6	21201	27 Metro Renters	38.9
20676	17 Green Acres	49.4	20874	16 Enterprising Professionals	28.4	21202	27 Metro Renters	35.3
20677	07 Exurbanites	79.7	20876	04 Boomburbs	36.1	21204	55 College Towns	26.0

ZIP CODE	TOP TAPESTRY CONSUMER TYPE	% 2004 HOUSE-HOLDS	ZIP CODE	TOP TAPESTRY CONSUMER TYPE	% 2004 HOUSE-HOLDS	ZIP CODE	TOP TAPESTRY CONSUMER TYPE	% 2004 HOUSE-HOLDS
21205	54 Urban Rows	78.2	21659	46 Rooted Rural	80.9	21863	50 Heartland Communities	26.5
21206	32 Rustbelt Traditions	29.7	21660	17 Green Acres	56.2	21864	46 Rooted Rural	100.0
21207	34 Family Foundations	29.5	21661	31 Rural Resort Dwellers	67.1	21865	46 Rooted Rural	54.6
21208	18 Cozy and Comfortable	19.2	21662	31 Rural Resort Dwellers	100.0	21866	37 Prairie Living	100.0
21209	13 In Style	21.6	21663	15 Silver and Gold	66.3	21869	46 Rooted Rural	69.2
21210	09 Urban Chic	35.4	21665	31 Rural Resort Dwellers	100.0	21871	42 Southern Satellites	44.4
21211	48 Great Expectations	40.6	21666	07 Exurbanites	29.7	21872	46 Rooted Rural	76.1
21212	22 Metropolitans	25.8	21667	31 Rural Resort Dwellers	100.0	21874	32 Rustbelt Traditions	49.1
21213	54 Urban Rows	87.6	21668	46 Rooted Rural	66.8	21875	17 Green Acres	26.5
21214	32 Rustbelt Traditions	41.7	21669	31 Rural Resort Dwellers	100.0	21901	26 Midland Crowd	26.7
21215	54 Urban Rows	43.4	21671	31 Rural Resort Dwellers	100.0	21903	33 Midlife Junction	30.8
21216	54 Urban Rows	66.6	21672	37 Prairie Living	100.0	21904	26 Midland Crowd	38.0
21217	54 Urban Rows	40.0	21673	33 Midlife Junction	36.6	21911	17 Green Acres	35.6
21218	54 Urban Rows	32.8	21675	37 Prairie Living	100.0	21912	46 Rooted Rural	75.4
21219	18 Cozy and Comfortable	54.2	21676	31 Rural Resort Dwellers	100.0	21913	46 Rooted Rural	100.0
21220	28 Aspiring Young Families	20.3	21677	31 Rural Resort Dwellers	100.0	21914	25 Salt of The Earth	100.0
21221	29 Rustbelt Retirees	23.2	21678	31 Rural Resort Dwellers	43.2	21915	18 Cozy and Comfortable	42.8
21222	29 Rustbelt Retirees	36.5	21679	17 Green Acres	100.0	21917	17 Green Acres	86.7
21223	54 Urban Rows	79.8	21701	04 Boomburbs	12.8	21918	26 Midland Crowd	54.9
21224	54 Urban Rows	31.9	21702	13 In Style	17.8	21919	31 Rural Resort Dwellers	90.5
21225	64 City Commons	18.5	21703	28 Aspiring Young Families	39.0	21921	17 Green Acres	25.1
21226	12 Up and Coming Families	51.9	21704	17 Green Acres	29.1	22003	05 Wealthy Seaboard Suburbs	33.0
21227	18 Cozy and Comfortable	20.7	21710	14 Prosperous Empty Nesters	57.8	22015	02 Suburban Splendor	45.2
21228	13 In Style	15.2	21711	25 Salt of The Earth	100.0	22026	06 Sophisticated Squires	26.7
21229	54 Urban Rows	28.0	21713	17 Green Acres	46.6	22027	02 Suburban Splendor	83.8
21230	54 Urban Rows	25.4	21716	32 Rustbelt Traditions	51.7	22030	16 Enterprising Professionals	37.2
21231	27 Metro Renters	32.5	21718	17 Green Acres	100.0	22031	16 Enterprising Professionals	24.6
21234	29 Rustbelt Retirees	17.4	21719	26 Midland Crowd	79.7	22032	05 Wealthy Seaboard Suburbs	49.1
21236	06 Sophisticated Squires	21.5	21722	25 Salt of The Earth	58.4	22033	16 Enterprising Professionals	48.9
21237	28 Aspiring Young Families	23.4	21723	02 Suburban Splendor	100.0	22039	02 Suburban Splendor	47.2
21239	34 Family Foundations	38.1	21727	24 Main Street, USA	39.1	22041	16 Enterprising Professionals	25.1
21244	28 Aspiring Young Families	44.4	21733	17 Green Acres	79.1	22042	16 Enterprising Professionals	27.0
21250	63 Dorms To Diplomas	100.0	21737	02 Suburban Splendor	100.0	22043	16 Enterprising Professionals	34.5
21286	22 Metropolitans	19.7	21738	02 Suburban Splendor	100.0	22044	35 International Marketplace	35.8
21401	06 Sophisticated Squires	14.7	21740	48 Great Expectations	15.3	22046	09 Urban Chic	31.7
21402	40 Military Proximity	83.5	21742	14 Prosperous Empty Nesters	23.5	22060	40 Military Proximity	76.9
21403	13 In Style	23.2	21750	50 Heartland Communities	55.3	22066	01 Top Rung	59.5
21502	29 Rustbelt Retirees	39.8	21754	02 Suburban Splendor	62.6	22067	01 Top Rung	100.0
21520	46 Rooted Rural	85.5	21755	12 Up and Coming Families	44.1	22079	28 Aspiring Young Families	25.3
21521	50 Heartland Communities	83.8	21756	17 Green Acres	99.9	22101	03 Connoisseurs	52.1
21522	46 Rooted Rural	100.0	21757	17 Green Acres	65.3	22102	27 Metro Renters	41.8
21523	25 Salt of The Earth	90.6	21758	17 Green Acres	59.8	22124	01 Top Rung	35.6
21530	46 Rooted Rural	100.0	21765	02 Suburban Splendor	100.0	22134	40 Military Proximity	80.8
21531	50 Heartland Communities	62.4	21766	46 Rooted Rural	100.0	22150	10 Pleasant-Ville	34.3
21532	29 Rustbelt Retirees	30.7	21767	33 Midlife Junction	100.0	22151	05 Wealthy Seaboard Suburbs	45.4
21536	46 Rooted Rural	88.0	21769	06 Sophisticated Squires	37.9	22152	13 In Style	31.5
21538	50 Heartland Communities	100.0	21770	06 Sophisticated Squires	88.0	22153	02 Suburban Splendor	39.7
21539	50 Heartland Communities	82.9	21771	06 Sophisticated Squires	52.3	22172	24 Main Street, USA	65.8
21540	50 Heartland Communities	100.0	21773	17 Green Acres	50.5	22180	05 Wealthy Seaboard Suburbs	61.2
21541	31 Rural Resort Dwellers	90.4	21774	06 Sophisticated Squires	38.7	22181	03 Connoisseurs	38.6
21545	29 Rustbelt Retirees	45.6	21776	17 Green Acres	33.0	22182	02 Suburban Splendor	47.0
21550	33 Midlife Junction	36.4	21777	06 Sophisticated Squires	100.0	22191	28 Aspiring Young Families	35.0
21555	25 Salt of The Earth	59.8	21778	18 Cozy and Comfortable	50.4	22192	12 Up and Coming Families	23.6
21557	46 Rooted Rural	63.9	21779	17 Green Acres	100.0	22193	06 Sophisticated Squires	30.9
21561	31 Rural Resort Dwellers	56.5	21780	17 Green Acres	63.2	22201	27 Metro Renters	81.5
21562	50 Heartland Communities	89.7	21782	17 Green Acres	71.6	22202	27 Metro Renters	75.9
21601	31 Rural Resort Dwellers	18.8	21783	19 Milk and Cookies	31.3	22203	27 Metro Renters	36.5
21607	25 Salt of The Earth	99.4	21784	06 Sophisticated Squires	27.6	22204	35 International Marketplace	29.9
21610	31 Rural Resort Dwellers	100.0	21787	24 Main Street, USA	58.7	22205	05 Wealthy Seaboard Suburbs	37.7
21612	15 Silver and Gold	100.0	21788	24 Main Street, USA	44.0	22206	27 Metro Renters	50.5
21613	53 Home Town	13.5	21790	06 Sophisticated Squires	76.1	22207	03 Connoisseurs	52.9
21617	17 Green Acres	57.0	21791	17 Green Acres	47.7	22209	27 Metro Renters	80.9
21619	17 Green Acres	46.3	21793	06 Sophisticated Squires	50.9	22211	27 Metro Renters	63.5
21620	18 Cozy and Comfortable	19.4	21794	02 Suburban Splendor	100.0	22213	05 Wealthy Seaboard Suburbs	51.5
21622	31 Rural Resort Dwellers	60.3	21795	18 Cozy and Comfortable	25.2	22301	22 Metropolitans	29.7
21623	17 Green Acres	96.2	21797	02 Suburban Splendor	57.9	22302	27 Metro Renters	40.3
21625	17 Green Acres	100.0	21798	17 Green Acres	70.6	22303	36 Old and Newcomers	45.2
21626	37 Prairie Living	100.0	21801	26 Midland Crowd	14.4	22304	27 Metro Renters	21.8
21628	26 Midland Crowd	100.0	21804	33 Midlife Junction	22.0	22305	58 Newest Residents	27.5
21629	17 Green Acres	44.6	21811	15 Silver and Gold	47.5	22306	28 Aspiring Young Families	19.5
21631	46 Rooted Rural	64.7	21813	31 Rural Resort Dwellers	53.6	22307	03 Connoisseurs	31.4
21632	53 Home Town	31.0	21814	46 Rooted Rural	96.7	22308	03 Connoisseurs	44.5
21634	31 Rural Resort Dwellers	100.0	21817	46 Rooted Rural	46.3	22309	28 Aspiring Young Families	27.2
21635	18 Cozy and Comfortable	55.1	21821	37 Prairie Living	51.0	22310	16 Enterprising Professionals	35.6
21636	17 Green Acres	59.5	21822	25 Salt of The Earth	40.7	22311	39 Young and Restless	49.3
21638	31 Rural Resort Dwellers	41.7	21824	37 Prairie Living	100.0	22312	35 International Marketplace	25.4
21639	26 Midland Crowd	42.4	21826	13 In Style	31.8	22314	08 Laptops and Lattes	26.5
21640	42 Southern Satellites	77.7	21829	46 Rooted Rural	64.2	22315	16 Enterprising Professionals	43.2
21643	26 Midland Crowd	50.7	21830	18 Cozy and Comfortable	34.0	22401	39 Young and Restless	26.1
21644	25 Salt of The Earth	100.0	21835	46 Rooted Rural	100.0	22405	12 Up and Coming Families	20.9
21645	31 Rural Resort Dwellers	58.6	21837	26 Midland Crowd	38.4	22406	28 Aspiring Young Families	31.0
21647	31 Rural Resort Dwellers	100.0	21838	31 Rural Resort Dwellers	38.9	22407	12 Up and Coming Families	37.6
21648	31 Rural Resort Dwellers	100.0	21840	31 Rural Resort Dwellers	100.0	22408	12 Up and Coming Families	57.7
21649	42 Southern Satellites	81.5	21841	46 Rooted Rural	99.7	22427	29 Rustbelt Retirees	31.3
21650	25 Salt of The Earth	100.0	21842	49 Senior Sun Seekers	32.5	22432	31 Rural Resort Dwellers	100.0
21651	26 Midland Crowd	53.4	21849	26 Midland Crowd	41.5	22433	26 Midland Crowd	100.0
21654	15 Silver and Gold	63.4	21850	42 Southern Satellites	61.5	22435	46 Rooted Rural	69.0
21655	25 Salt of The Earth	78.3	21851	46 Rooted Rural	38.5	22436	46 Rooted Rural	100.0
21657	17 Green Acres	71.4	21853	26 Midland Crowd	27.7	22437	31 Rural Resort Dwellers	97.1
21658	03 Connoisseurs	40.2	21856	31 Rural Resort Dwellers	88.5	22438	46 Rooted Rural	100.0

ZIP CODE	TOP TAPESTRY CONSUMER TYPE	% 2004 HOUSE-HOLDS	ZIP CODE	TOP TAPESTRY CONSUMER TYPE	% 2004 HOUSE-HOLDS	ZIP CODE	TOP TAPESTRY CONSUMER TYPE	% 2004 HOUSE-HOLDS
22443	31 Rural Resort Dwellers	45.9	22743	25 Salt of The Earth	98.2	23055	46 Rooted Rural	100.0
22448	40 Military Proximity	100.0	22746	07 Exurbanites	72.6	23056	31 Rural Resort Dwellers	100.0
22454	29 Rustbelt Retirees	52.3	22747	31 Rural Resort Dwellers	82.7	23059	04 Boomburbs	37.1
22460	46 Rooted Rural	44.4	22749	31 Rural Resort Dwellers	100.0	23060	12 Up and Coming Families	34.3
22469	56 Rural Bypasses	49.7	22801	63 Dorms To Diplomas	17.5	23061	26 Midland Crowd	47.3
22473	31 Rural Resort Dwellers	72.0	22802	25 Salt of The Earth	16.4	23062	24 Main Street, USA	52.2
22476	46 Rooted Rural	100.0	22807	14 Prosperous Empty Nesters	100.0	23063	31 Rural Resort Dwellers	32.1
22480	15 Silver and Gold	100.0	22810	31 Rural Resort Dwellers	100.0	23065	17 Green Acres	78.9
22482	15 Silver and Gold	83.0	22811	46 Rooted Rural	91.2	23066	31 Rural Resort Dwellers	100.0
22485	26 Midland Crowd	43.4	22812	25 Salt of The Earth	50.9	23069	07 Exurbanites	38.4
22488	31 Rural Resort Dwellers	42.6	22815	25 Salt of The Earth	64.4	23070	31 Rural Resort Dwellers	100.0
22503	46 Rooted Rural	51.2	22820	46 Rooted Rural	76.1	23071	31 Rural Resort Dwellers	100.0
22504	31 Rural Resort Dwellers	100.0	22821	37 Prairie Living	38.3	23072	26 Midland Crowd	24.3
22508	15 Silver and Gold	72.7	22824	25 Salt of The Earth	53.0	23075	32 Rustbelt Traditions	59.0
22509	46 Rooted Rural	100.0	22827	42 Southern Satellites	69.5	23079	31 Rural Resort Dwellers	76.6
22511	31 Rural Resort Dwellers	99.7	22830	42 Southern Satellites	98.2	23083	26 Midland Crowd	68.3
22514	46 Rooted Rural	53.4	22831	42 Southern Satellites	82.9	23084	42 Southern Satellites	54.1
22520	56 Rural Bypasses	28.4	22832	25 Salt of The Earth	100.0	23085	46 Rooted Rural	100.0
22534	26 Midland Crowd	100.0	22834	25 Salt of The Earth	80.0	23086	26 Midland Crowd	48.5
22535	46 Rooted Rural	97.6	22835	25 Salt of The Earth	34.8	23089	17 Green Acres	40.5
22538	46 Rooted Rural	99.1	22840	17 Green Acres	58.7	23091	46 Rooted Rural	92.3
22539	15 Silver and Gold	80.4	22841	17 Green Acres	62.3	23092	31 Rural Resort Dwellers	100.0
22542	26 Midland Crowd	100.0	22842	25 Salt of The Earth	48.1	23093	50 Heartland Communities	29.6
22546	26 Midland Crowd	59.4	22843	42 Southern Satellites	42.4	23102	17 Green Acres	85.0
22553	12 Up and Coming Families	28.6	22844	33 Midlife Junction	77.8	23103	07 Exurbanites	65.5
22554	12 Up and Coming Families	40.7	22845	31 Rural Resort Dwellers	100.0	23106	26 Midland Crowd	100.0
22556	06 Sophisticated Squires	55.8	22846	25 Salt of The Earth	100.0	23109	31 Rural Resort Dwellers	100.0
22560	33 Midlife Junction	42.9	22847	25 Salt of The Earth	98.1	23110	25 Salt of The Earth	100.0
22567	26 Midland Crowd	50.8	22849	42 Southern Satellites	26.9	23111	12 Up and Coming Families	30.2
22572	50 Heartland Communities	43.2	22851	42 Southern Satellites	96.8	23112	07 Exurbanites	22.0
22576	31 Rural Resort Dwellers	70.1	22853	25 Salt of The Earth	48.3	23113	02 Suburban Splendor	63.8
22578	15 Silver and Gold	50.4	22901	39 Young and Restless	17.0	23114	04 Boomburbs	42.4
22579	31 Rural Resort Dwellers	97.3	22902	16 Enterprising Professionals	21.2	23116	06 Sophisticated Squires	31.6
22580	26 Midland Crowd	26.1	22903	63 Dorms To Diplomas	27.2	23117	31 Rural Resort Dwellers	55.8
22601	48 Great Expectations	23.5	22904	63 Dorms To Diplomas	100.0	23119	31 Rural Resort Dwellers	100.0
22602	12 Up and Coming Families	24.6	22911	12 Up and Coming Families	27.4	23120	07 Exurbanites	65.2
22603	17 Green Acres	24.2	22920	17 Green Acres	56.1	23123	46 Rooted Rural	64.0
22610	25 Salt of The Earth	67.3	22922	46 Rooted Rural	92.1	23124	06 Sophisticated Squires	55.5
22611	17 Green Acres	45.4	22923	26 Midland Crowd	39.4	23125	31 Rural Resort Dwellers	100.0
22620	25 Salt of The Earth	43.1	22931	25 Salt of The Earth	72.1	23126	46 Rooted Rural	100.0
22624	25 Salt of The Earth	33.7	22932	25 Salt of The Earth	44.9	23128	31 Rural Resort Dwellers	74.2
22625	17 Green Acres	56.5	22935	17 Green Acres	67.2	23129	07 Exurbanites	90.0
22627	17 Green Acres	100.0	22936	07 Exurbanites	33.3	23130	31 Rural Resort Dwellers	100.0
22630	24 Main Street, USA	25.1	22937	46 Rooted Rural	65.7	23138	31 Rural Resort Dwellers	100.0
22637	25 Salt of The Earth	76.7	22938	25 Salt of The Earth	47.3	23139	17 Green Acres	50.2
22639	07 Exurbanites	74.7	22939	17 Green Acres	64.8	23140	42 Southern Satellites	33.9
22640	17 Green Acres	100.0	22940	25 Salt of The Earth	38.5	23141	06 Sophisticated Squires	45.4
22641	25 Salt of The Earth	100.0	22942	25 Salt of The Earth	71.0	23146	07 Exurbanites	83.6
22642	17 Green Acres	39.9	22943	17 Green Acres	100.0	23148	46 Rooted Rural	77.2
22643	17 Green Acres	100.0	22946	25 Salt of The Earth	100.0	23149	31 Rural Resort Dwellers	74.9
22644	25 Salt of The Earth	96.0	22947	03 Connoisseurs	47.3	23150	32 Rustbelt Traditions	23.5
22645	25 Salt of The Earth	100.0	22948	25 Salt of The Earth	100.0	23153	17 Green Acres	81.5
22649	25 Salt of The Earth	100.0	22949	25 Salt of The Earth	42.9	23156	46 Rooted Rural	37.0
22650	25 Salt of The Earth	61.9	22952	17 Green Acres	41.8	23160	13 In Style	100.0
22652	31 Rural Resort Dwellers	100.0	22958	31 Rural Resort Dwellers	70.0	23161	46 Rooted Rural	100.0
22654	17 Green Acres	84.7	22959	17 Green Acres	71.2	23163	31 Rural Resort Dwellers	100.0
22655	12 Up and Coming Families	42.9	22960	25 Salt of The Earth	34.9	23168	26 Midland Crowd	85.9
22656	14 Prosperous Empty Nesters	69.1	22963	14 Prosperous Empty Nesters	58.8	23169	31 Rural Resort Dwellers	100.0
22657	25 Salt of The Earth	44.6	22964	46 Rooted Rural	100.0	23173	15 Silver and Gold	100.0
22660	25 Salt of The Earth	100.0	22967	46 Rooted Rural	78.0	23175	31 Rural Resort Dwellers	53.8
22663	31 Rural Resort Dwellers	42.4	22968	12 Up and Coming Families	68.2	23176	31 Rural Resort Dwellers	100.0
22664	33 Midlife Junction	36.0	22969	46 Rooted Rural	100.0	23177	46 Rooted Rural	88.5
22701	24 Main Street, USA	28.5	22971	32 Rustbelt Traditions	45.7	23180	31 Rural Resort Dwellers	100.0
22709	25 Salt of The Earth	100.0	22972	25 Salt of The Earth	87.7	23181	18 Cozy and Comfortable	47.6
22712	26 Midland Crowd	59.5	22973	25 Salt of The Earth	21.5	23185	15 Silver and Gold	21.5
22713	17 Green Acres	60.6	22974	17 Green Acres	53.3	23186	55 College Towns	100.0
22714	25 Salt of The Earth	67.6	22976	46 Rooted Rural	100.0	23188	13 In Style	18.7
22715	25 Salt of The Earth	100.0	22980	53 Home Town	23.8	23192	17 Green Acres	94.0
22716	31 Rural Resort Dwellers	78.8	23002	25 Salt of The Earth	46.7	23219	65 Social Security Set	49.4
22718	17 Green Acres	63.8	23004	56 Rural Bypasses	100.0	23220	55 College Towns	34.0
22720	06 Sophisticated Squires	75.2	23005	33 Midlife Junction	19.1	23221	27 Metro Renters	36.0
22722	25 Salt of The Earth	100.0	23009	12 Up and Coming Families	44.2	23222	34 Family Foundations	35.4
22724	17 Green Acres	60.7	23011	18 Cozy and Comfortable	100.0	23223	64 City Commons	20.9
22725	25 Salt of The Earth	100.0	23015	17 Green Acres	67.6	23224	51 Metro City Edge	21.1
22726	17 Green Acres	100.0	23021	31 Rural Resort Dwellers	100.0	23225	36 Old and Newcomers	16.5
22727	25 Salt of The Earth	100.0	23022	50 Heartland Communities	54.9	23226	22 Metropolitans	44.3
22728	26 Midland Crowd	42.8	23023	46 Rooted Rural	100.0	23227	22 Metropolitans	20.4
22729	25 Salt of The Earth	100.0	23024	26 Midland Crowd	66.3	23228	36 Old and Newcomers	17.2
22730	25 Salt of The Earth	100.0	23025	31 Rural Resort Dwellers	100.0	23229	03 Connoisseurs	19.6
22731	25 Salt of The Earth	100.0	23027	46 Rooted Rural	95.0	23230	52 Inner City Tenants	33.4
22732	25 Salt of The Earth	100.0	23030	42 Southern Satellites	29.3	23231	18 Cozy and Comfortable	17.5
22733	25 Salt of The Earth	61.9	23032	46 Rooted Rural	63.5	23233	04 Boomburbs	26.1
22734	26 Midland Crowd	75.6	23035	31 Rural Resort Dwellers	100.0	23234	19 Milk and Cookies	24.0
22735	17 Green Acres	57.7	23038	26 Midland Crowd	47.5	23235	14 Prosperous Empty Nesters	27.7
22736	17 Green Acres	100.0	23039	17 Green Acres	59.8	23236	19 Milk and Cookies	29.2
22737	17 Green Acres	63.4	23040	46 Rooted Rural	63.6	23237	19 Milk and Cookies	37.0
22738	25 Salt of The Earth	100.0	23043	15 Silver and Gold	74.3	23294	39 Young and Restless	52.1
22740	31 Rural Resort Dwellers	55.3	23045	31 Rural Resort Dwellers	100.0	23298	63 Dorms To Diplomas	0.0
22741	24 Main Street, USA	77.8	23047	07 Exurbanites	53.1	23301	50 Heartland Communities	72.2
22742	06 Sophisticated Squires	100.0	23050	31 Rural Resort Dwellers	54.6	23302	42 Southern Satellites	85.0

ZIP CODE	TOP TAPESTRY CONSUMER TYPE	% 2004 HOUSE-HOLDS	ZIP CODE	TOP TAPESTRY CONSUMER TYPE	% 2004 HOUSE-HOLDS	ZIP CODE	TOP TAPESTRY CONSUMER TYPE	% 2004 HOUSE-HOLDS
23306	50 Heartland Communities	53.5	23696	07 Exurbanites	100.0	23968	46 Rooted Rural	93.9
23307	46 Rooted Rural	45.3	23701	29 Rustbelt Retirees	25.7	23970	42 Southern Satellites	21.3
23308	56 Rural Bypasses	94.5	23702	51 Metro City Edge	26.8	23974	50 Heartland Communities	52.6
23310	56 Rural Bypasses	40.9	23703	52 Inner City Tenants	19.7	23976	42 Southern Satellites	90.5
23314	17 Green Acres	54.4	23704	62 Modest Income Homes	31.9	24011	48 Great Expectations	100.0
23315	25 Salt of The Earth	75.7	23707	48 Great Expectations	24.8	24012	48 Great Expectations	24.2
23320	16 Enterprising Professionals	23.8	23708	51 Metro City Edge	66.7	24013	53 Home Town	64.3
23321	12 Up and Coming Families	16.2	23709	04 Boomburbs	100.0	24014	32 Rustbelt Traditions	15.1
23322	06 Sophisticated Squires	37.4	23801	40 Military Proximity	100.0	24015	22 Metropolitans	30.1
23323	19 Milk and Cookies	38.0	23803	62 Modest Income Homes	24.3	24016	60 City Dimensions	35.1
23324	51 Metro City Edge	16.9	23805	33 Midlife Junction	22.3	24017	32 Rustbelt Traditions	25.6
23325	18 Cozy and Comfortable	30.2	23806	62 Modest Income Homes	100.0	24018	14 Prosperous Empty Nesters	27.5
23336	31 Rural Resort Dwellers	100.0	23821	46 Rooted Rural	54.5	24019	18 Cozy and Comfortable	28.8
23337	42 Southern Satellites	51.1	23824	46 Rooted Rural	36.8	24020	55 College Towns	100.0
23350	50 Heartland Communities	60.4	23827	56 Rural Bypasses	83.7	24053	42 Southern Satellites	99.9
23354	50 Heartland Communities	64.3	23828	56 Rural Bypasses	91.7	24054	42 Southern Satellites	86.8
23356	56 Rural Bypasses	100.0	23829	25 Salt of The Earth	58.6	24055	42 Southern Satellites	53.4
23357	56 Rural Bypasses	92.9	23830	56 Rural Bypasses	63.9	24059	17 Green Acres	93.0
23359	56 Rural Bypasses	79.7	23831	18 Cozy and Comfortable	19.2	24060	63 Dorms To Diplomas	40.0
23395	56 Rural Bypasses	100.0	23832	19 Milk and Cookies	32.5	24064	17 Green Acres	40.5
23404	46 Rooted Rural	100.0	23833	17 Green Acres	59.8	24065	25 Salt of The Earth	37.4
23405	46 Rooted Rural	40.6	23834	32 Rustbelt Traditions	22.0	24066	25 Salt of The Earth	61.2
23409	56 Rural Bypasses	100.0	23836	26 Midland Crowd	37.6	24067	25 Salt of The Earth	94.3
23410	46 Rooted Rural	53.9	23837	33 Midlife Junction	51.9	24069	42 Southern Satellites	100.0
23413	50 Heartland Communities	87.2	23838	06 Sophisticated Squires	26.5	24070	17 Green Acres	47.5
23415	56 Rural Bypasses	75.1	23839	46 Rooted Rural	100.0	24072	25 Salt of The Earth	76.1
23416	42 Southern Satellites	95.5	23840	25 Salt of The Earth	65.7	24073	42 Southern Satellites	15.2
23417	50 Heartland Communities	35.9	23841	25 Salt of The Earth	88.5	24076	42 Southern Satellites	100.0
23418	33 Midlife Junction	69.9	23842	18 Cozy and Comfortable	41.4	24077	46 Rooted Rural	52.7
23420	46 Rooted Rural	51.5	23843	46 Rooted Rural	73.6	24078	50 Heartland Communities	75.2
23421	56 Rural Bypasses	51.7	23844	56 Rural Bypasses	100.0	24079	46 Rooted Rural	64.0
23426	46 Rooted Rural	100.0	23845	46 Rooted Rural	100.0	24082	42 Southern Satellites	100.0
23430	25 Salt of The Earth	41.9	23846	56 Rural Bypasses	66.6	24083	07 Exurbanites	63.5
23432	07 Exurbanites	100.0	23847	56 Rural Bypasses	53.2	24084	25 Salt of The Earth	33.9
23433	07 Exurbanites	100.0	23850	25 Salt of The Earth	89.1	24085	46 Rooted Rural	91.4
23434	51 Metro City Edge	20.2	23851	33 Midlife Junction	26.4	24086	46 Rooted Rural	100.0
23435	12 Up and Coming Families	37.0	23856	56 Rural Bypasses	52.3	24087	41 Crossroads	61.4
23436	07 Exurbanites	100.0	23857	31 Rural Resort Dwellers	57.1	24088	42 Southern Satellites	56.8
23437	25 Salt of The Earth	51.7	23860	32 Rustbelt Traditions	25.0	24089	42 Southern Satellites	57.7
23438	25 Salt of The Earth	100.0	23866	25 Salt of The Earth	99.2	24090	25 Salt of The Earth	41.8
23440	37 Prairie Living	100.0	23867	56 Rural Bypasses	55.4	24091	46 Rooted Rural	68.6
23442	42 Southern Satellites	51.2	23868	56 Rural Bypasses	39.9	24092	46 Rooted Rural	37.4
23451	39 Young and Restless	20.2	23872	25 Salt of The Earth	35.3	24093	42 Southern Satellites	100.0
23452	18 Cozy and Comfortable	24.9	23874	25 Salt of The Earth	91.3	24094	46 Rooted Rural	100.0
23453	28 Aspiring Young Families	34.1	23875	19 Milk and Cookies	37.2	24095	26 Midland Crowd	43.4
23454	28 Aspiring Young Families	14.9	23876	56 Rural Bypasses	100.0	24101	25 Salt of The Earth	53.6
23455	39 Young and Restless	17.4	23878	25 Salt of The Earth	81.2	24102	42 Southern Satellites	93.7
23456	04 Boomburbs	28.2	23879	56 Rural Bypasses	100.0	24104	15 Silver and Gold	47.2
23457	17 Green Acres	100.0	23881	46 Rooted Rural	62.1	24105	42 Southern Satellites	100.0
23459	40 Military Proximity	97.7	23882	56 Rural Bypasses	76.5	24112	42 Southern Satellites	23.0
23460	40 Military Proximity	100.0	23883	46 Rooted Rural	83.3	24120	46 Rooted Rural	71.0
23461	40 Military Proximity	100.0	23885	25 Salt of The Earth	54.8	24121	15 Silver and Gold	54.0
23462	28 Aspiring Young Families	26.7	23887	31 Rural Resort Dwellers	100.0	24122	25 Salt of The Earth	54.6
23463	63 Dorms To Diplomas	100.0	23888	56 Rural Bypasses	69.4	24124	50 Heartland Communities	38.9
23464	19 Milk and Cookies	22.4	23889	46 Rooted Rural	70.5	24127	25 Salt of The Earth	62.7
23487	26 Midland Crowd	57.3	23890	56 Rural Bypasses	53.1	24128	46 Rooted Rural	58.2
23502	33 Midlife Junction	20.6	23893	56 Rural Bypasses	81.4	24131	42 Southern Satellites	100.0
23503	48 Great Expectations	26.1	23894	25 Salt of The Earth	79.3	24133	42 Southern Satellites	100.0
23504	64 City Commons	43.3	23897	46 Rooted Rural	61.8	24134	50 Heartland Communities	52.7
23505	52 Inner City Tenants	17.5	23898	25 Salt of The Earth	61.1	24136	46 Rooted Rural	59.8
23507	27 Metro Renters	51.3	23901	46 Rooted Rural	38.6	24137	42 Southern Satellites	62.8
23508	22 Metropolitans	16.8	23909	33 Midlife Junction	0.0	24138	26 Midland Crowd	51.9
23509	51 Metro City Edge	27.9	23915	46 Rooted Rural	65.5	24139	42 Southern Satellites	58.9
23510	27 Metro Renters	46.5	23917	46 Rooted Rural	36.0	24141	33 Midlife Junction	27.5
23511	40 Military Proximity	100.0	23919	49 Senior Sun Seekers	51.2	24142	63 Dorms To Diplomas	100.0
23513	32 Rustbelt Traditions	30.2	23920	56 Rural Bypasses	51.3	24147	42 Southern Satellites	59.4
23517	27 Metro Renters	60.9	23921	46 Rooted Rural	91.2	24148	42 Southern Satellites	58.9
23518	29 Rustbelt Retirees	20.2	23922	46 Rooted Rural	63.4	24149	25 Salt of The Earth	66.7
23521	40 Military Proximity	88.4	23923	46 Rooted Rural	76.3	24150	46 Rooted Rural	77.0
23523	62 Modest Income Homes	42.2	23924	56 Rural Bypasses	56.7	24151	42 Southern Satellites	24.8
23601	52 Inner City Tenants	21.5	23927	46 Rooted Rural	24.0	24153	18 Cozy and Comfortable	13.0
23602	13 In Style	22.1	23930	50 Heartland Communities	37.1	24161	31 Rural Resort Dwellers	85.5
23603	28 Aspiring Young Families	66.3	23934	46 Rooted Rural	100.0	24162	25 Salt of The Earth	56.2
23604	40 Military Proximity	100.0	23936	46 Rooted Rural	47.7	24165	42 Southern Satellites	97.3
23605	48 Great Expectations	29.4	23937	46 Rooted Rural	49.0	24167	42 Southern Satellites	97.0
23606	52 Inner City Tenants	26.2	23938	46 Rooted Rural	82.7	24168	50 Heartland Communities	100.0
23607	64 City Commons	33.8	23942	46 Rooted Rural	79.2	24171	42 Southern Satellites	52.1
23608	28 Aspiring Young Families	25.3	23944	50 Heartland Communities	53.0	24174	26 Midland Crowd	37.2
23651	40 Military Proximity	100.0	23947	46 Rooted Rural	70.9	24175	07 Exurbanites	38.0
23661	34 Family Foundations	38.2	23950	46 Rooted Rural	48.6	24176	31 Rural Resort Dwellers	82.3
23662	07 Exurbanites	47.0	23952	50 Heartland Communities	100.0	24179	18 Cozy and Comfortable	21.5
23663	32 Rustbelt Traditions	49.6	23954	46 Rooted Rural	100.0	24184	31 Rural Resort Dwellers	42.5
23664	18 Cozy and Comfortable	30.3	23958	46 Rooted Rural	36.4	24185	42 Southern Satellites	58.9
23665	40 Military Proximity	100.0	23959	42 Southern Satellites	91.5	24201	29 Rustbelt Retirees	26.5
23666	39 Young and Restless	23.6	23960	46 Rooted Rural	75.2	24202	42 Southern Satellites	49.7
23668	63 Dorms To Diplomas	100.0	23962	50 Heartland Communities	45.3	24210	33 Midlife Junction	38.9
23669	18 Cozy and Comfortable	17.7	23963	46 Rooted Rural	53.2	24211	26 Midland Crowd	34.5
23690	64 City Commons	50.7	23964	56 Rural Bypasses	78.2	24216	56 Rural Bypasses	54.2
23692	07 Exurbanites	34.2	23966	46 Rooted Rural	60.3	24217	56 Rural Bypasses	100.0
23693	04 Boomburbs	65.3	23967	42 Southern Satellites	72.4	24219	50 Heartland Communities	45.0

ZIP CODE	TOP TAPESTRY CONSUMER TYPE	% 2004 HOUSE-HOLDS	ZIP CODE	TOP TAPESTRY CONSUMER TYPE	% 2004 HOUSE-HOLDS	ZIP CODE	TOP TAPESTRY CONSUMER TYPE	% 2004 HOUSE-HOLDS
24220	56 Rural Bypasses	100.0	24442	37 Prairie Living	100.0	24649	56 Rural Bypasses	60.0
24221	46 Rooted Rural	91.4	24445	29 Rustbelt Retirees	51.3	24651	33 Midlife Junction	33.0
24224	42 Southern Satellites	40.3	24450	14 Prosperous Empty Nesters	23.9	24656	56 Rural Bypasses	100.0
24225	56 Rural Bypasses	65.5	24458	37 Prairie Living	98.1	24657	56 Rural Bypasses	100.0
24226	56 Rural Bypasses	100.0	24459	25 Salt of The Earth	97.2	24701	50 Heartland Communities	34.7
24228	56 Rural Bypasses	87.6	24460	31 Rural Resort Dwellers	96.6	24712	46 Rooted Rural	40.4
24230	56 Rural Bypasses	91.1	24464	46 Rooted Rural	100.0	24714	46 Rooted Rural	99.0
24236	42 Southern Satellites	55.6	24465	46 Rooted Rural	57.0	24715	50 Heartland Communities	99.0
24237	56 Rural Bypasses	100.0	24467	25 Salt of The Earth	60.4	24726	56 Rural Bypasses	95.6
24239	56 Rural Bypasses	100.0	24468	37 Prairie Living	100.0	24731	46 Rooted Rural	83.9
24243	56 Rural Bypasses	79.7	24471	17 Green Acres	56.7	24733	56 Rural Bypasses	84.5
24244	56 Rural Bypasses	57.3	24472	25 Salt of The Earth	52.1	24736	56 Rural Bypasses	94.7
24245	56 Rural Bypasses	87.9	24473	46 Rooted Rural	75.4	24740	50 Heartland Communities	27.7
24248	46 Rooted Rural	68.5	24477	17 Green Acres	38.4	24747	56 Rural Bypasses	67.2
24250	56 Rural Bypasses	62.6	24479	25 Salt of The Earth	56.4	24801	56 Rural Bypasses	45.9
24251	50 Heartland Communities	43.9	24482	25 Salt of The Earth	41.6	24815	56 Rural Bypasses	86.0
24256	56 Rural Bypasses	100.0	24483	42 Southern Satellites	61.3	24818	56 Rural Bypasses	100.0
24258	42 Southern Satellites	61.3	24484	31 Rural Resort Dwellers	60.5	24822	56 Rural Bypasses	100.0
24260	56 Rural Bypasses	84.1	24485	46 Rooted Rural	52.4	24823	56 Rural Bypasses	100.0
24263	50 Heartland Communities	31.8	24486	25 Salt of The Earth	68.0	24827	56 Rural Bypasses	100.0
24265	56 Rural Bypasses	61.6	24487	31 Rural Resort Dwellers	100.0	24828	56 Rural Bypasses	99.8
24266	42 Southern Satellites	34.6	24501	53 Home Town	30.3	24834	56 Rural Bypasses	100.0
24269	56 Rural Bypasses	100.0	24502	24 Main Street, USA	20.0	24839	56 Rural Bypasses	100.0
24270	42 Southern Satellites	100.0	24503	14 Prosperous Empty Nesters	21.3	24844	56 Rural Bypasses	100.0
24271	42 Southern Satellites	58.6	24504	62 Modest Income Homes	60.0	24849	50 Heartland Communities	59.3
24272	56 Rural Bypasses	100.0	24517	42 Southern Satellites	31.0	24850	56 Rural Bypasses	100.0
24273	56 Rural Bypasses	47.7	24520	42 Southern Satellites	65.8	24859	50 Heartland Communities	61.5
24277	56 Rural Bypasses	55.4	24521	25 Salt of The Earth	27.1	24860	56 Rural Bypasses	52.5
24279	46 Rooted Rural	43.0	24522	25 Salt of The Earth	40.0	24862	56 Rural Bypasses	100.0
24280	42 Southern Satellites	100.0	24523	25 Salt of The Earth	34.9	24868	62 Modest Income Homes	56.4
24281	56 Rural Bypasses	76.0	24526	25 Salt of The Earth	98.3	24869	56 Rural Bypasses	100.0
24282	56 Rural Bypasses	100.0	24527	42 Southern Satellites	99.6	24870	56 Rural Bypasses	60.2
24283	50 Heartland Communities	62.8	24528	42 Southern Satellites	48.8	24873	56 Rural Bypasses	100.0
24290	50 Heartland Communities	76.2	24529	56 Rural Bypasses	63.9	24874	50 Heartland Communities	54.3
24292	46 Rooted Rural	100.0	24530	42 Southern Satellites	59.1	24882	56 Rural Bypasses	100.0
24293	46 Rooted Rural	59.1	24531	42 Southern Satellites	36.0	24884	56 Rural Bypasses	100.0
24301	50 Heartland Communities	29.1	24534	56 Rural Bypasses	99.5	24901	33 Midlife Junction	25.6
24311	42 Southern Satellites	41.3	24536	17 Green Acres	100.0	24910	46 Rooted Rural	55.8
24312	42 Southern Satellites	73.7	24538	26 Midland Crowd	59.8	24915	31 Rural Resort Dwellers	100.0
24313	42 Southern Satellites	100.0	24539	56 Rural Bypasses	100.0	24916	46 Rooted Rural	100.0
24314	42 Southern Satellites	87.6	24540	62 Modest Income Homes	13.1	24917	46 Rooted Rural	100.0
24315	46 Rooted Rural	98.5	24541	62 Modest Income Homes	12.5	24918	42 Southern Satellites	91.6
24316	42 Southern Satellites	100.0	24549	17 Green Acres	38.0	24920	56 Rural Bypasses	96.7
24317	42 Southern Satellites	98.8	24550	42 Southern Satellites	67.0	24925	46 Rooted Rural	100.0
24318	46 Rooted Rural	73.7	24551	13 In Style	35.5	24927	31 Rural Resort Dwellers	53.7
24319	42 Southern Satellites	62.9	24553	46 Rooted Rural	47.2	24931	46 Rooted Rural	98.9
24322	46 Rooted Rural	100.0	24554	42 Southern Satellites	54.5	24934	31 Rural Resort Dwellers	81.9
24323	42 Southern Satellites	100.0	24555	50 Heartland Communities	57.4	24935	46 Rooted Rural	100.0
24324	25 Salt of The Earth	62.5	24556	17 Green Acres	62.1	24936	46 Rooted Rural	100.0
24325	42 Southern Satellites	51.0	24557	42 Southern Satellites	63.4	24938	46 Rooted Rural	100.0
24326	46 Rooted Rural	67.7	24558	42 Southern Satellites	39.8	24941	46 Rooted Rural	100.0
24328	42 Southern Satellites	68.5	24562	46 Rooted Rural	100.0	24943	46 Rooted Rural	100.0
24330	42 Southern Satellites	58.1	24563	42 Southern Satellites	100.0	24944	31 Rural Resort Dwellers	100.0
24333	42 Southern Satellites	63.9	24565	42 Southern Satellites	58.5	24945	46 Rooted Rural	70.6
24340	42 Southern Satellites	48.4	24566	42 Southern Satellites	100.0	24946	46 Rooted Rural	100.0
24343	25 Salt of The Earth	33.5	24569	42 Southern Satellites	68.7	24950	56 Rural Bypasses	100.0
24347	42 Southern Satellites	97.7	24570	25 Salt of The Earth	100.0	24951	46 Rooted Rural	100.0
24348	46 Rooted Rural	61.4	24571	42 Southern Satellites	91.6	24954	50 Heartland Communities	50.8
24350	42 Southern Satellites	40.9	24572	25 Salt of The Earth	33.3	24957	46 Rooted Rural	100.0
24351	42 Southern Satellites	100.0	24574	25 Salt of The Earth	34.5	24962	46 Rooted Rural	100.0
24352	46 Rooted Rural	54.6	24577	56 Rural Bypasses	77.9	24963	42 Southern Satellites	60.3
24354	42 Southern Satellites	49.6	24578	46 Rooted Rural	65.7	24966	46 Rooted Rural	97.9
24360	42 Southern Satellites	56.5	24579	42 Southern Satellites	73.7	24970	50 Heartland Communities	49.5
24361	42 Southern Satellites	80.9	24580	46 Rooted Rural	85.3	24974	46 Rooted Rural	100.0
24363	46 Rooted Rural	90.1	24586	42 Southern Satellites	52.7	24976	46 Rooted Rural	94.2
24366	42 Southern Satellites	84.3	24588	25 Salt of The Earth	38.2	24977	46 Rooted Rural	100.0
24368	42 Southern Satellites	63.1	24589	42 Southern Satellites	61.0	24981	46 Rooted Rural	59.9
24370	42 Southern Satellites	58.7	24590	26 Midland Crowd	24.8	24983	46 Rooted Rural	60.5
24374	42 Southern Satellites	50.4	24592	56 Rural Bypasses	25.2	24984	46 Rooted Rural	100.0
24375	42 Southern Satellites	90.8	24593	25 Salt of The Earth	71.4	24985	46 Rooted Rural	100.0
24377	42 Southern Satellites	100.0	24594	42 Southern Satellites	78.0	24986	46 Rooted Rural	58.3
24378	46 Rooted Rural	77.6	24597	42 Southern Satellites	63.7	24991	46 Rooted Rural	72.8
24380	42 Southern Satellites	43.3	24598	42 Southern Satellites	47.6	24993	46 Rooted Rural	100.0
24381	42 Southern Satellites	95.1	24599	46 Rooted Rural	55.1	25003	46 Rooted Rural	54.6
24382	42 Southern Satellites	28.6	24602	56 Rural Bypasses	92.0	25005	46 Rooted Rural	100.0
24401	17 Green Acres	15.6	24603	56 Rural Bypasses	100.0	25007	56 Rural Bypasses	97.7
24413	37 Prairie Living	100.0	24605	50 Heartland Communities	29.5	25008	56 Rural Bypasses	100.0
24416	25 Salt of The Earth	26.2	24609	46 Rooted Rural	49.3	25009	56 Rural Bypasses	100.0
24421	25 Salt of The Earth	57.2	24613	53 Home Town	47.7	25010	56 Rural Bypasses	100.0
24422	50 Heartland Communities	52.4	24614	56 Rural Bypasses	74.9	25015	50 Heartland Communities	46.9
24426	25 Salt of The Earth	25.3	24620	56 Rural Bypasses	100.0	25019	56 Rural Bypasses	95.6
24430	50 Heartland Communities	42.4	24622	56 Rural Bypasses	99.7	25021	56 Rural Bypasses	100.0
24431	41 Crossroads	65.3	24627	56 Rural Bypasses	100.0	25024	56 Rural Bypasses	100.0
24432	46 Rooted Rural	100.0	24630	46 Rooted Rural	31.8	25025	56 Rural Bypasses	57.5
24433	37 Prairie Living	100.0	24631	56 Rural Bypasses	98.4	25028	56 Rural Bypasses	100.0
24435	25 Salt of The Earth	66.0	24634	56 Rural Bypasses	100.0	25030	56 Rural Bypasses	75.9
24437	17 Green Acres	71.8	24637	42 Southern Satellites	41.3	25033	56 Rural Bypasses	69.4
24439	46 Rooted Rural	82.2	24639	56 Rural Bypasses	100.0	25035	56 Rural Bypasses	50.3
24440	46 Rooted Rural	78.4	24641	56 Rural Bypasses	53.9	25039	50 Heartland Communities	73.8
24441	42 Southern Satellites	54.4	24646	56 Rural Bypasses	100.0	25043	56 Rural Bypasses	70.5

ZIP CODE	TOP TAPESTRY CONSUMER TYPE	% 2004 HOUSE-HOLDS	ZIP CODE	TOP TAPESTRY CONSUMER TYPE	% 2004 HOUSE-HOLDS	ZIP CODE	TOP TAPESTRY CONSUMER TYPE	% 2004 HOUSE-HOLDS
25044	56 Rural Bypasses	100.0	25279	46 Rooted Rural	55.3	25670	56 Rural Bypasses	100.0
25045	56 Rural Bypasses	31.7	25281	56 Rural Bypasses	100.0	25671	56 Rural Bypasses	100.0
25046	46 Rooted Rural	100.0	25285	56 Rural Bypasses	77.9	25674	56 Rural Bypasses	100.0
25047	50 Heartland Communities	87.8	25286	42 Southern Satellites	53.6	25676	56 Rural Bypasses	100.0
25048	56 Rural Bypasses	99.1	25287	25 Salt of The Earth	77.0	25678	56 Rural Bypasses	100.0
25049	56 Rural Bypasses	100.0	25301	65 Social Security Set	86.9	25682	56 Rural Bypasses	100.0
25051	56 Rural Bypasses	100.0	25302	33 Midlife Junction	24.0	25694	56 Rural Bypasses	100.0
25053	56 Rural Bypasses	74.6	25303	14 Prosperous Empty Nesters	30.1	25699	56 Rural Bypasses	100.0
25059	56 Rural Bypasses	91.1	25304	14 Prosperous Empty Nesters	23.1	25701	55 College Towns	14.7
25060	56 Rural Bypasses	100.0	25306	50 Heartland Communities	64.7	25702	57 Simple Living	33.4
25062	56 Rural Bypasses	100.0	25309	33 Midlife Junction	32.7	25703	63 Dorms To Diplomas	43.9
25063	56 Rural Bypasses	79.8	25311	50 Heartland Communities	26.0	25704	57 Simple Living	22.4
25064	29 Rustbelt Retirees	26.5	25312	53 Home Town	21.1	25705	33 Midlife Junction	49.1
25071	46 Rooted Rural	34.0	25313	13 In Style	45.7	25755	63 Dorms To Diplomas	0.0
25075	56 Rural Bypasses	81.9	25314	07 Exurbanites	22.5	25801	50 Heartland Communities	25.5
25079	50 Heartland Communities	100.0	25315	50 Heartland Communities	77.3	25811	50 Heartland Communities	72.6
25081	56 Rural Bypasses	73.1	25320	46 Rooted Rural	43.1	25812	50 Heartland Communities	100.0
25082	46 Rooted Rural	60.4	25401	26 Midland Crowd	24.2	25813	17 Green Acres	41.7
25083	29 Rustbelt Retirees	39.6	25411	46 Rooted Rural	37.7	25817	46 Rooted Rural	95.7
25085	50 Heartland Communities	100.0	25413	26 Midland Crowd	54.9	25820	46 Rooted Rural	86.7
25088	56 Rural Bypasses	100.0	25414	26 Midland Crowd	28.2	25823	50 Heartland Communities	66.0
25093	56 Rural Bypasses	100.0	25419	26 Midland Crowd	76.1	25825	42 Southern Satellites	42.6
25103	56 Rural Bypasses	100.0	25420	26 Midland Crowd	94.2	25827	50 Heartland Communities	74.4
25106	56 Rural Bypasses	82.7	25422	42 Southern Satellites	61.4	25831	56 Rural Bypasses	97.9
25107	56 Rural Bypasses	100.0	25425	26 Midland Crowd	25.6	25832	50 Heartland Communities	52.9
25108	56 Rural Bypasses	74.7	25427	26 Midland Crowd	43.4	25837	56 Rural Bypasses	100.0
25111	56 Rural Bypasses	99.1	25428	26 Midland Crowd	92.9	25839	46 Rooted Rural	97.7
25113	56 Rural Bypasses	100.0	25430	26 Midland Crowd	41.7	25840	29 Rustbelt Retirees	33.9
25114	56 Rural Bypasses	100.0	25431	46 Rooted Rural	100.0	25841	46 Rooted Rural	100.0
25115	46 Rooted Rural	100.0	25434	50 Heartland Communities	43.4	25843	31 Rural Resort Dwellers	92.4
25118	50 Heartland Communities	100.0	25437	46 Rooted Rural	100.0	25844	46 Rooted Rural	58.4
25119	56 Rural Bypasses	100.0	25438	48 Great Expectations	24.9	25845	50 Heartland Communities	100.0
25121	56 Rural Bypasses	63.2	25442	25 Salt of The Earth	43.3	25847	50 Heartland Communities	49.9
25123	56 Rural Bypasses	54.4	25443	22 Metropolitans	68.8	25848	56 Rural Bypasses	100.0
25124	42 Southern Satellites	73.3	25444	42 Southern Satellites	64.0	25854	46 Rooted Rural	98.6
25125	56 Rural Bypasses	100.0	25446	17 Green Acres	94.1	25856	50 Heartland Communities	71.9
25130	56 Rural Bypasses	51.2	25501	56 Rural Bypasses	100.0	25857	56 Rural Bypasses	100.0
25132	56 Rural Bypasses	97.0	25502	56 Rural Bypasses	50.0	25862	56 Rural Bypasses	100.0
25133	56 Rural Bypasses	55.0	25503	46 Rooted Rural	45.9	25864	56 Rural Bypasses	100.0
25136	50 Heartland Communities	43.6	25504	29 Rustbelt Retirees	27.2	25865	56 Rural Bypasses	78.3
25140	56 Rural Bypasses	51.9	25505	26 Midland Crowd	94.9	25868	56 Rural Bypasses	56.0
25141	56 Rural Bypasses	100.0	25506	56 Rural Bypasses	97.1	25870	50 Heartland Communities	65.5
25142	56 Rural Bypasses	100.0	25508	56 Rural Bypasses	45.1	25876	56 Rural Bypasses	98.8
25143	50 Heartland Communities	22.7	25510	46 Rooted Rural	73.3	25880	33 Midlife Junction	35.2
25148	56 Rural Bypasses	100.0	25511	56 Rural Bypasses	100.0	25882	50 Heartland Communities	100.0
25150	56 Rural Bypasses	100.0	25512	56 Rural Bypasses	80.2	25901	50 Heartland Communities	55.8
25154	56 Rural Bypasses	91.9	25514	56 Rural Bypasses	72.4	25902	56 Rural Bypasses	93.3
25159	26 Midland Crowd	49.9	25515	42 Southern Satellites	84.3	25908	46 Rooted Rural	62.0
25160	56 Rural Bypasses	100.0	25517	56 Rural Bypasses	100.0	25913	56 Rural Bypasses	76.7
25161	46 Rooted Rural	100.0	25520	42 Southern Satellites	56.4	25915	56 Rural Bypasses	100.0
25164	46 Rooted Rural	95.4	25521	56 Rural Bypasses	100.0	25917	56 Rural Bypasses	53.6
25165	56 Rural Bypasses	90.3	25523	56 Rural Bypasses	39.0	25918	46 Rooted Rural	91.8
25168	29 Rustbelt Retirees	38.1	25524	56 Rural Bypasses	100.0	25920	42 Southern Satellites	70.9
25169	56 Rural Bypasses	100.0	25526	13 In Style	27.4	25922	42 Southern Satellites	65.1
25173	56 Rural Bypasses	80.6	25529	56 Rural Bypasses	100.0	25928	56 Rural Bypasses	93.2
25174	56 Rural Bypasses	100.0	25530	50 Heartland Communities	53.1	25932	56 Rural Bypasses	71.3
25177	29 Rustbelt Retirees	33.8	25534	56 Rural Bypasses	100.0	25936	56 Rural Bypasses	100.0
25180	56 Rural Bypasses	81.5	25535	46 Rooted Rural	53.9	25938	56 Rural Bypasses	49.9
25181	56 Rural Bypasses	91.8	25537	42 Southern Satellites	56.8	25951	46 Rooted Rural	40.6
25187	42 Southern Satellites	97.3	25540	56 Rural Bypasses	100.0	25958	50 Heartland Communities	100.0
25193	56 Rural Bypasses	100.0	25541	46 Rooted Rural	38.7	25962	50 Heartland Communities	62.9
25202	26 Midland Crowd	47.4	25544	56 Rural Bypasses	100.0	25965	50 Heartland Communities	97.6
25204	56 Rural Bypasses	100.0	25545	18 Cozy and Comfortable	31.9	25966	50 Heartland Communities	74.7
25209	56 Rural Bypasses	100.0	25547	50 Heartland Communities	100.0	25969	46 Rooted Rural	99.2
25213	17 Green Acres	45.5	25550	29 Rustbelt Retirees	36.9	25971	46 Rooted Rural	100.0
25214	56 Rural Bypasses	100.0	25555	42 Southern Satellites	100.0	25976	46 Rooted Rural	61.9
25231	46 Rooted Rural	100.0	25557	56 Rural Bypasses	100.0	25977	50 Heartland Communities	100.0
25234	56 Rural Bypasses	62.5	25559	26 Midland Crowd	56.1	25978	46 Rooted Rural	100.0
25235	56 Rural Bypasses	100.0	25560	18 Cozy and Comfortable	48.1	25979	46 Rooted Rural	100.0
25239	46 Rooted Rural	61.9	25564	56 Rural Bypasses	52.5	25981	56 Rural Bypasses	54.2
25241	26 Midland Crowd	96.2	25565	56 Rural Bypasses	100.0	25984	50 Heartland Communities	69.9
25243	56 Rural Bypasses	52.2	25567	56 Rural Bypasses	75.8	25985	46 Rooted Rural	90.7
25244	46 Rooted Rural	96.8	25570	56 Rural Bypasses	51.7	25986	46 Rooted Rural	100.0
25245	26 Midland Crowd	89.8	25571	56 Rural Bypasses	100.0	25989	42 Southern Satellites	66.1
25248	46 Rooted Rural	69.2	25572	56 Rural Bypasses	100.0	26003	29 Rustbelt Retirees	21.2
25251	46 Rooted Rural	71.4	25573	56 Rural Bypasses	100.0	26031	53 Home Town	34.8
25252	42 Southern Satellites	95.1	25601	50 Heartland Communities	42.6	26032	33 Midlife Junction	100.0
25253	46 Rooted Rural	39.1	25607	56 Rural Bypasses	93.7	26033	50 Heartland Communities	84.7
25259	56 Rural Bypasses	78.9	25608	56 Rural Bypasses	100.0	26034	50 Heartland Communities	46.5
25260	50 Heartland Communities	52.1	25617	56 Rural Bypasses	100.0	26035	46 Rooted Rural	81.6
25261	46 Rooted Rural	60.8	25621	56 Rural Bypasses	100.0	26036	46 Rooted Rural	59.9
25262	42 Southern Satellites	65.7	25632	56 Rural Bypasses	84.0	26037	29 Rustbelt Retirees	32.3
25264	46 Rooted Rural	100.0	25635	56 Rural Bypasses	64.1	26038	29 Rustbelt Retirees	52.1
25266	56 Rural Bypasses	98.9	25638	56 Rural Bypasses	82.6	26039	25 Salt of The Earth	57.7
25267	46 Rooted Rural	56.0	25650	56 Rural Bypasses	100.0	26040	50 Heartland Communities	100.0
25268	56 Rural Bypasses	100.0	25651	56 Rural Bypasses	100.0	26041	50 Heartland Communities	32.6
25270	46 Rooted Rural	63.5	25654	46 Rooted Rural	43.9	26047	25 Salt of The Earth	33.0
25271	50 Heartland Communities	44.3	25661	57 Simple Living	42.3	26050	56 Rural Bypasses	41.9
25275	46 Rooted Rural	99.4	25666	56 Rural Bypasses	100.0	26055	25 Salt of The Earth	53.6
25276	50 Heartland Communities	53.3	25669	56 Rural Bypasses	100.0	26059	46 Rooted Rural	65.9

ZIP CODE	TOP TAPESTRY CONSUMER TYPE	% 2004 HOUSE-HOLDS	ZIP CODE	TOP TAPESTRY CONSUMER TYPE	% 2004 HOUSE-HOLDS	ZIP CODE	TOP TAPESTRY CONSUMER TYPE	% 2004 HOUSE-HOLDS
26060	46 Rooted Rural	66.0	26332	25 Salt of The Earth	50.1	26660	46 Rooted Rural	77.0
26062	29 Rustbelt Retirees	70.4	26335	46 Rooted Rural	74.3	26662	46 Rooted Rural	100.0
26070	50 Heartland Communities	45.3	26337	46 Rooted Rural	86.6	26667	46 Rooted Rural	100.0
26101	50 Heartland Communities	33.6	26338	56 Rural Bypasses	60.1	26674	56 Rural Bypasses	67.1
26104	33 Midlife Junction	28.3	26339	46 Rooted Rural	100.0	26675	46 Rooted Rural	100.0
26105	29 Rustbelt Retirees	40.7	26342	46 Rooted Rural	54.8	26676	46 Rooted Rural	100.0
26133	25 Salt of The Earth	51.6	26343	46 Rooted Rural	67.8	26678	46 Rooted Rural	100.0
26134	50 Heartland Communities	76.0	26346	42 Southern Satellites	100.0	26679	46 Rooted Rural	100.0
26136	56 Rural Bypasses	95.0	26347	56 Rural Bypasses	62.0	26680	46 Rooted Rural	100.0
26137	46 Rooted Rural	50.9	26348	56 Rural Bypasses	100.0	26681	46 Rooted Rural	100.0
26138	46 Rooted Rural	100.0	26351	50 Heartland Communities	31.8	26684	46 Rooted Rural	100.0
26141	46 Rooted Rural	45.3	26354	50 Heartland Communities	50.8	26690	56 Rural Bypasses	50.5
26142	19 Milk and Cookies	52.7	26362	50 Heartland Communities	50.9	26691	56 Rural Bypasses	54.6
26143	46 Rooted Rural	96.7	26372	46 Rooted Rural	79.1	26704	42 Southern Satellites	71.5
26146	46 Rooted Rural	77.0	26374	46 Rooted Rural	60.2	26705	46 Rooted Rural	100.0
26147	50 Heartland Communities	93.4	26376	56 Rural Bypasses	69.9	26710	42 Southern Satellites	34.9
26148	46 Rooted Rural	100.0	26377	46 Rooted Rural	68.6	26711	42 Southern Satellites	74.7
26149	46 Rooted Rural	100.0	26378	46 Rooted Rural	47.5	26714	42 Southern Satellites	100.0
26150	26 Midland Crowd	57.6	26384	56 Rural Bypasses	86.6	26716	46 Rooted Rural	100.0
26151	50 Heartland Communities	67.6	26385	46 Rooted Rural	51.0	26717	56 Rural Bypasses	92.0
26152	46 Rooted Rural	100.0	26386	46 Rooted Rural	93.2	26719	46 Rooted Rural	95.6
26155	56 Rural Bypasses	28.7	26404	50 Heartland Communities	89.3	26720	46 Rooted Rural	99.7
26159	50 Heartland Communities	100.0	26405	46 Rooted Rural	100.0	26722	46 Rooted Rural	100.0
26160	46 Rooted Rural	100.0	26408	17 Green Acres	65.9	26726	50 Heartland Communities	40.8
26161	46 Rooted Rural	100.0	26410	56 Rural Bypasses	56.9	26731	42 Southern Satellites	52.8
26164	50 Heartland Communities	23.9	26411	46 Rooted Rural	97.0	26739	46 Rooted Rural	83.4
26167	42 Southern Satellites	61.2	26412	46 Rooted Rural	100.0	26743	25 Salt of The Earth	95.9
26169	42 Southern Satellites	86.7	26415	50 Heartland Communities	67.5	26750	53 Home Town	62.6
26170	50 Heartland Communities	44.8	26416	46 Rooted Rural	40.8	26753	25 Salt of The Earth	49.1
26173	25 Salt of The Earth	83.5	26419	50 Heartland Communities	62.5	26755	42 Southern Satellites	100.0
26175	29 Rustbelt Retirees	30.4	26421	46 Rooted Rural	100.0	26757	50 Heartland Communities	32.8
26178	46 Rooted Rural	77.8	26425	50 Heartland Communities	90.8	26761	42 Southern Satellites	73.5
26180	42 Southern Satellites	67.9	26426	46 Rooted Rural	48.3	26763	46 Rooted Rural	98.3
26181	17 Green Acres	39.9	26430	56 Rural Bypasses	100.0	26764	46 Rooted Rural	47.5
26184	25 Salt of The Earth	52.2	26431	46 Rooted Rural	53.7	26767	50 Heartland Communities	100.0
26186	46 Rooted Rural	78.4	26437	56 Rural Bypasses	73.7	26801	31 Rural Resort Dwellers	43.7
26187	29 Rustbelt Retirees	53.6	26440	56 Rural Bypasses	70.2	26802	46 Rooted Rural	77.1
26201	46 Rooted Rural	47.1	26443	50 Heartland Communities	82.2	26804	42 Southern Satellites	97.3
26202	46 Rooted Rural	100.0	26444	56 Rural Bypasses	56.8	26807	46 Rooted Rural	73.4
26203	56 Rural Bypasses	100.0	26447	46 Rooted Rural	81.7	26808	25 Salt of The Earth	64.1
26205	56 Rural Bypasses	43.4	26448	56 Rural Bypasses	98.6	26810	46 Rooted Rural	100.0
26206	56 Rural Bypasses	100.0	26451	46 Rooted Rural	57.5	26812	46 Rooted Rural	99.8
26208	56 Rural Bypasses	100.0	26452	50 Heartland Communities	51.2	26814	42 Southern Satellites	92.4
26210	46 Rooted Rural	100.0	26456	50 Heartland Communities	56.3	26815	42 Southern Satellites	100.0
26215	46 Rooted Rural	100.0	26501	33 Midlife Junction	26.3	26817	25 Salt of The Earth	88.4
26217	56 Rural Bypasses	93.7	26505	63 Dorms To Diplomas	37.7	26818	56 Rural Bypasses	100.0
26218	46 Rooted Rural	95.2	26506	63 Dorms To Diplomas	100.0	26824	46 Rooted Rural	100.0
26222	42 Southern Satellites	83.8	26508	26 Midland Crowd	36.4	26833	42 Southern Satellites	99.6
26224	46 Rooted Rural	87.8	26519	46 Rooted Rural	100.0	26836	42 Southern Satellites	44.9
26228	46 Rooted Rural	95.3	26521	46 Rooted Rural	95.5	26838	42 Southern Satellites	100.0
26230	46 Rooted Rural	80.4	26525	46 Rooted Rural	100.0	26845	42 Southern Satellites	100.0
26234	46 Rooted Rural	100.0	26529	46 Rooted Rural	100.0	26847	42 Southern Satellites	56.4
26236	46 Rooted Rural	100.0	26537	50 Heartland Communities	34.6	26851	25 Salt of The Earth	65.6
26237	56 Rural Bypasses	97.8	26541	42 Southern Satellites	95.7	26852	46 Rooted Rural	100.0
26238	46 Rooted Rural	100.0	26542	46 Rooted Rural	77.2	26855	42 Southern Satellites	100.0
26241	50 Heartland Communities	20.0	26546	41 Crossroads	100.0	26865	25 Salt of The Earth	75.3
26250	46 Rooted Rural	44.8	26547	25 Salt of The Earth	44.2	26866	46 Rooted Rural	100.0
26253	42 Southern Satellites	71.6	26554	29 Rustbelt Retirees	21.0	26884	46 Rooted Rural	98.9
26254	46 Rooted Rural	100.0	26560	50 Heartland Communities	100.0	27006	25 Salt of The Earth	28.0
26257	56 Rural Bypasses	72.0	26561	46 Rooted Rural	100.0	27007	42 Southern Satellites	58.1
26260	50 Heartland Communities	53.3	26562	50 Heartland Communities	61.8	27009	25 Salt of The Earth	64.0
26261	50 Heartland Communities	70.8	26568	46 Rooted Rural	50.5	27011	42 Southern Satellites	84.1
26263	46 Rooted Rural	97.4	26570	46 Rooted Rural	86.1	27012	02 Suburban Splendor	23.8
26264	56 Rural Bypasses	100.0	26571	50 Heartland Communities	97.7	27013	26 Midland Crowd	79.9
26266	56 Rural Bypasses	100.0	26575	56 Rural Bypasses	61.2	27016	42 Southern Satellites	71.1
26267	46 Rooted Rural	67.3	26581	46 Rooted Rural	97.9	27017	42 Southern Satellites	71.7
26268	46 Rooted Rural	80.6	26582	50 Heartland Communities	44.1	27018	42 Southern Satellites	52.9
26269	46 Rooted Rural	84.3	26585	46 Rooted Rural	60.8	27019	26 Midland Crowd	49.1
26270	46 Rooted Rural	100.0	26587	50 Heartland Communities	100.0	27020	42 Southern Satellites	100.0
26271	50 Heartland Communities	100.0	26588	50 Heartland Communities	63.8	27021	17 Green Acres	22.8
26273	46 Rooted Rural	57.3	26590	46 Rooted Rural	100.0	27022	42 Southern Satellites	68.7
26276	46 Rooted Rural	44.0	26591	50 Heartland Communities	50.8	27023	13 In Style	43.3
26278	46 Rooted Rural	100.0	26601	56 Rural Bypasses	38.2	27024	42 Southern Satellites	98.3
26280	42 Southern Satellites	51.5	26610	56 Rural Bypasses	98.6	27025	42 Southern Satellites	62.7
26282	50 Heartland Communities	73.1	26611	56 Rural Bypasses	64.6	27027	53 Home Town	46.7
26283	46 Rooted Rural	75.0	26615	42 Southern Satellites	61.6	27028	42 Southern Satellites	41.0
26287	50 Heartland Communities	62.6	26617	56 Rural Bypasses	100.0	27030	42 Southern Satellites	39.8
26288	56 Rural Bypasses	58.4	26619	42 Southern Satellites	93.6	27040	18 Cozy and Comfortable	26.0
26289	31 Rural Resort Dwellers	100.0	26621	46 Rooted Rural	100.0	27041	42 Southern Satellites	58.6
26291	46 Rooted Rural	64.9	26623	46 Rooted Rural	70.1	27042	42 Southern Satellites	100.0
26292	50 Heartland Communities	100.0	26624	46 Rooted Rural	74.7	27043	42 Southern Satellites	62.6
26293	46 Rooted Rural	90.4	26627	46 Rooted Rural	100.0	27045	25 Salt of The Earth	33.1
26294	50 Heartland Communities	61.3	26629	56 Rural Bypasses	100.0	27046	42 Southern Satellites	100.0
26296	46 Rooted Rural	99.4	26631	46 Rooted Rural	100.0	27047	42 Southern Satellites	100.0
26301	50 Heartland Communities	45.1	26636	46 Rooted Rural	58.2	27048	42 Southern Satellites	60.4
26320	46 Rooted Rural	100.0	26638	46 Rooted Rural	100.0	27050	26 Midland Crowd	29.2
26321	46 Rooted Rural	62.1	26639	56 Rural Bypasses	100.0	27051	26 Midland Crowd	77.4
26325	46 Rooted Rural	81.3	26641	46 Rooted Rural	100.0	27052	42 Southern Satellites	45.1
26327	46 Rooted Rural	100.0	26651	46 Rooted Rural	38.1	27053	42 Southern Satellites	93.8
26330	14 Prosperous Empty Nesters	24.9	26656	56 Rural Bypasses	83.0	27054	42 Southern Satellites	88.6

ZIP CODE	TOP TAPESTRY CONSUMER TYPE	% 2004 HOUSE-HOLDS	ZIP CODE	TOP TAPESTRY CONSUMER TYPE	% 2004 HOUSE-HOLDS	ZIP CODE	TOP TAPESTRY CONSUMER TYPE	% 2004 HOUSE-HOLDS
27055	42 Southern Satellites	50.9	27502	04 Boomburbs	60.9	27810	31 Rural Resort Dwellers	28.1
27101	62 Modest Income Homes	23.5	27503	07 Exurbanites	53.3	27812	56 Rural Bypasses	52.8
27103	33 Midlife Junction	15.9	27504	26 Midland Crowd	31.2	27814	15 Silver and Gold	36.8
27104	13 In Style	18.3	27505	42 Southern Satellites	42.4	27816	56 Rural Bypasses	37.1
27105	62 Modest Income Homes	15.6	27507	42 Southern Satellites	81.0	27817	42 Southern Satellites	31.3
27106	52 Inner City Tenants	15.3	27508	41 Crossroads	61.7	27818	56 Rural Bypasses	100.0
27107	17 Green Acres	16.4	27509	41 Crossroads	80.6	27820	56 Rural Bypasses	40.8
27110	62 Modest Income Homes	0.0	27510	39 Young and Restless	38.9	27821	46 Rooted Rural	100.0
27127	24 Main Street, USA	14.2	27511	04 Boomburbs	31.1	27822	42 Southern Satellites	31.5
27203	53 Home Town	28.2	27513	16 Enterprising Professionals	57.2	27823	56 Rural Bypasses	64.4
27205	42 Southern Satellites	28.8	27514	09 Urban Chic	41.4	27824	56 Rural Bypasses	100.0
27207	42 Southern Satellites	55.4	27516	16 Enterprising Professionals	31.2	27826	46 Rooted Rural	83.4
27208	46 Rooted Rural	66.2	27517	16 Enterprising Professionals	24.2	27828	56 Rural Bypasses	24.4
27209	42 Southern Satellites	80.6	27519	04 Boomburbs	100.0	27829	56 Rural Bypasses	61.5
27212	46 Rooted Rural	53.0	27520	12 Up and Coming Families	60.2	27830	42 Southern Satellites	25.1
27214	25 Salt of The Earth	26.6	27521	42 Southern Satellites	45.4	27831	56 Rural Bypasses	96.9
27215	14 Prosperous Empty Nesters	14.7	27522	26 Midland Crowd	51.2	27832	56 Rural Bypasses	51.9
27217	53 Home Town	17.9	27523	04 Boomburbs	75.5	27834	39 Young and Restless	25.7
27229	42 Southern Satellites	82.3	27524	26 Midland Crowd	44.0	27837	42 Southern Satellites	49.0
27231	46 Rooted Rural	48.3	27525	12 Up and Coming Families	24.3	27839	56 Rural Bypasses	92.4
27233	42 Southern Satellites	56.2	27526	24 Main Street, USA	31.8	27840	56 Rural Bypasses	100.0
27235	17 Green Acres	45.8	27529	12 Up and Coming Families	26.4	27842	31 Rural Resort Dwellers	94.4
27239	42 Southern Satellites	84.2	27530	26 Midland Crowd	25.5	27843	42 Southern Satellites	52.7
27242	56 Rural Bypasses	55.9	27531	40 Military Proximity	100.0	27844	56 Rural Bypasses	100.0
27243	26 Midland Crowd	68.8	27534	26 Midland Crowd	20.0	27845	56 Rural Bypasses	52.5
27244	26 Midland Crowd	22.3	27536	62 Modest Income Homes	28.2	27846	42 Southern Satellites	37.3
27248	42 Southern Satellites	81.6	27537	42 Southern Satellites	32.9	27847	56 Rural Bypasses	100.0
27249	17 Green Acres	23.2	27539	04 Boomburbs	35.6	27849	56 Rural Bypasses	100.0
27252	46 Rooted Rural	73.9	27540	12 Up and Coming Families	50.3	27850	56 Rural Bypasses	46.8
27253	26 Midland Crowd	39.9	27541	26 Midland Crowd	43.7	27851	42 Southern Satellites	66.5
27258	26 Midland Crowd	68.6	27542	46 Rooted Rural	39.5	27852	42 Southern Satellites	57.2
27260	64 City Commons	22.3	27544	42 Southern Satellites	94.2	27853	56 Rural Bypasses	100.0
27262	32 Rustbelt Traditions	15.6	27545	12 Up and Coming Families	67.0	27855	50 Heartland Communities	28.1
27263	32 Rustbelt Traditions	22.5	27546	42 Southern Satellites	22.0	27856	42 Southern Satellites	30.4
27265	12 Up and Coming Families	13.8	27549	46 Rooted Rural	32.0	27857	56 Rural Bypasses	100.0
27278	17 Green Acres	19.7	27551	31 Rural Resort Dwellers	45.7	27858	63 Dorms To Diplomas	17.0
27281	42 Southern Satellites	27.8	27553	56 Rural Bypasses	67.3	27860	46 Rooted Rural	100.0
27282	04 Boomburbs	50.5	27557	42 Southern Satellites	42.8	27862	56 Rural Bypasses	89.6
27283	25 Salt of The Earth	64.9	27559	42 Southern Satellites	43.5	27863	26 Midland Crowd	95.1
27284	13 In Style	19.9	27560	16 Enterprising Professionals	56.9	27864	26 Midland Crowd	37.8
27288	42 Southern Satellites	26.6	27562	12 Up and Coming Families	50.4	27865	46 Rooted Rural	85.2
27291	42 Southern Satellites	46.1	27563	56 Rural Bypasses	100.0	27866	56 Rural Bypasses	100.0
27292	42 Southern Satellites	26.0	27565	42 Southern Satellites	24.3	27869	50 Heartland Communities	54.4
27295	25 Salt of The Earth	38.4	27569	26 Midland Crowd	56.1	27870	56 Rural Bypasses	38.3
27298	42 Southern Satellites	52.2	27571	12 Up and Coming Families	55.3	27871	56 Rural Bypasses	80.3
27299	42 Southern Satellites	100.0	27572	26 Midland Crowd	42.1	27872	56 Rural Bypasses	100.0
27301	17 Green Acres	30.4	27573	57 Simple Living	32.6	27873	56 Rural Bypasses	100.0
27302	26 Midland Crowd	36.8	27574	25 Salt of The Earth	34.5	27874	56 Rural Bypasses	39.6
27305	42 Southern Satellites	76.6	27576	26 Midland Crowd	37.7	27875	46 Rooted Rural	100.0
27306	56 Rural Bypasses	34.5	27577	26 Midland Crowd	20.9	27876	56 Rural Bypasses	100.0
27310	06 Sophisticated Squires	44.1	27581	26 Midland Crowd	98.0	27880	42 Southern Satellites	57.8
27311	42 Southern Satellites	59.9	27583	26 Midland Crowd	85.8	27882	42 Southern Satellites	60.6
27312	17 Green Acres	29.5	27587	12 Up and Coming Families	52.2	27883	42 Southern Satellites	69.8
27313	17 Green Acres	48.2	27589	56 Rural Bypasses	87.1	27884	42 Southern Satellites	100.0
27314	42 Southern Satellites	59.8	27591	26 Midland Crowd	51.6	27885	46 Rooted Rural	84.5
27315	42 Southern Satellites	68.2	27592	12 Up and Coming Families	57.3	27886	42 Southern Satellites	26.8
27316	42 Southern Satellites	91.0	27596	26 Midland Crowd	63.8	27888	41 Crossroads	47.3
27317	42 Southern Satellites	59.4	27597	26 Midland Crowd	57.0	27889	14 Prosperous Empty Nesters	18.0
27320	42 Southern Satellites	20.4	27601	64 City Commons	42.0	27890	51 Metro City Edge	43.2
27325	42 Southern Satellites	62.1	27603	12 Up and Coming Families	32.0	27891	56 Rural Bypasses	54.5
27326	42 Southern Satellites	74.9	27604	12 Up and Coming Families	28.9	27892	26 Midland Crowd	20.4
27330	26 Midland Crowd	21.1	27605	27 Metro Renters	78.7	27893	60 City Dimensions	12.7
27332	26 Midland Crowd	28.4	27606	39 Young and Restless	34.7	27896	13 In Style	28.0
27341	42 Southern Satellites	100.0	27607	22 Metropolitans	33.8	27897	56 Rural Bypasses	100.0
27343	42 Southern Satellites	70.0	27608	22 Metropolitans	31.7	27909	26 Midland Crowd	39.2
27344	42 Southern Satellites	53.0	27609	22 Metropolitans	14.7	27910	56 Rural Bypasses	49.5
27349	26 Midland Crowd	59.4	27610	12 Up and Coming Families	19.0	27916	31 Rural Resort Dwellers	78.7
27350	42 Southern Satellites	60.6	27612	16 Enterprising Professionals	53.9	27917	56 Rural Bypasses	100.0
27355	42 Southern Satellites	83.0	27613	16 Enterprising Professionals	37.4	27919	46 Rooted Rural	100.0
27356	42 Southern Satellites	97.9	27614	02 Suburban Splendor	60.0	27921	17 Green Acres	61.0
27357	26 Midland Crowd	50.1	27615	13 In Style	31.6	27922	56 Rural Bypasses	100.0
27358	17 Green Acres	28.2	27616	12 Up and Coming Families	41.9	27923	31 Rural Resort Dwellers	85.4
27360	42 Southern Satellites	19.6	27617	04 Boomburbs	98.9	27924	56 Rural Bypasses	96.8
27370	26 Midland Crowd	41.6	27695	55 College Towns	100.0	27925	56 Rural Bypasses	58.4
27371	42 Southern Satellites	39.2	27701	64 City Commons	27.1	27926	26 Midland Crowd	53.0
27376	15 Silver and Gold	50.0	27703	12 Up and Coming Families	20.8	27927	15 Silver and Gold	100.0
27377	42 Southern Satellites	45.6	27704	48 Great Expectations	14.6	27928	56 Rural Bypasses	39.3
27379	56 Rural Bypasses	50.6	27705	39 Young and Restless	23.9	27929	17 Green Acres	96.2
27401	64 City Commons	21.7	27707	39 Young and Restless	22.7	27932	42 Southern Satellites	15.1
27403	55 College Towns	20.9	27709	33 Midlife Junction	50.0	27935	46 Rooted Rural	80.0
27405	48 Great Expectations	15.2	27712	06 Sophisticated Squires	34.7	27937	56 Rural Bypasses	68.9
27406	28 Aspiring Young Families	18.3	27713	16 Enterprising Professionals	49.6	27938	46 Rooted Rural	95.5
27407	36 Old and Newcomers	21.5	27801	51 Metro City Edge	21.8	27939	46 Rooted Rural	100.0
27408	29 Rustbelt Retirees	18.8	27803	06 Sophisticated Squires	13.8	27941	31 Rural Resort Dwellers	76.8
27409	39 Young and Restless	38.5	27804	28 Aspiring Young Families	19.3	27942	56 Rural Bypasses	100.0
27410	16 Enterprising Professionals	22.2	27805	56 Rural Bypasses	51.3	27944	49 Senior Sun Seekers	30.0
27411	55 College Towns	0.0	27806	56 Rural Bypasses	73.4	27946	46 Rooted Rural	100.0
27413	63 Dorms To Diplomas	72.2	27807	42 Southern Satellites	86.8	27947	46 Rooted Rural	72.6
27455	13 In Style	52.4	27808	31 Rural Resort Dwellers	100.0	27948	31 Rural Resort Dwellers	42.8
27501	26 Midland Crowd	81.1	27809	56 Rural Bypasses	33.7	27949	15 Silver and Gold	49.7

ZIP CODE	TOP TAPESTRY CONSUMER TYPE	% 2004 HOUSE-HOLDS	ZIP CODE	TOP TAPESTRY CONSUMER TYPE	% 2004 HOUSE-HOLDS	ZIP CODE	TOP TAPESTRY CONSUMER TYPE	% 2004 HOUSE-HOLDS
27950	26 Midland Crowd	79.7	28167	42 Southern Satellites	100.0	28395	46 Rooted Rural	66.2
27953	46 Rooted Rural	100.0	28168	42 Southern Satellites	76.9	28396	26 Midland Crowd	52.8
27954	26 Midland Crowd	71.4	28170	50 Heartland Communities	25.2	28398	56 Rural Bypasses	42.1
27956	56 Rural Bypasses	100.0	28173	04 Boomburbs	29.5	28399	56 Rural Bypasses	97.1
27957	46 Rooted Rural	61.1	28174	26 Midland Crowd	56.7	28401	62 Modest Income Homes	24.4
27958	26 Midland Crowd	55.5	28202	27 Metro Renters	56.5	28403	55 College Towns	24.3
27959	31 Rural Resort Dwellers	85.4	28203	08 Laptops and Lattes	38.2	28405	19 Milk and Cookies	22.6
27960	31 Rural Resort Dwellers	100.0	28204	27 Metro Renters	37.0	28409	07 Exurbanites	44.2
27962	56 Rural Bypasses	22.2	28205	48 Great Expectations	23.0	28411	12 Up and Coming Families	42.0
27964	26 Midland Crowd	78.2	28206	52 Inner City Tenants	28.0	28412	22 Metropolitans	26.3
27965	46 Rooted Rural	100.0	28207	03 Connoisseurs	28.9	28420	26 Midland Crowd	35.1
27966	26 Midland Crowd	74.5	28208	51 Metro City Edge	39.9	28421	46 Rooted Rural	75.7
27970	56 Rural Bypasses	39.8	28209	22 Metropolitans	42.7	28422	15 Silver and Gold	39.9
27973	46 Rooted Rural	54.5	28210	39 Young and Restless	16.4	28423	42 Southern Satellites	86.4
27974	46 Rooted Rural	100.0	28211	08 Laptops and Lattes	18.9	28425	42 Southern Satellites	48.3
27976	25 Salt of The Earth	100.0	28212	39 Young and Restless	36.0	28428	31 Rural Resort Dwellers	68.9
27978	46 Rooted Rural	100.0	28213	12 Up and Coming Families	21.0	28429	26 Midland Crowd	78.8
27979	46 Rooted Rural	64.8	28214	19 Milk and Cookies	24.2	28430	56 Rural Bypasses	77.3
27980	46 Rooted Rural	55.8	28215	12 Up and Coming Families	14.3	28431	56 Rural Bypasses	62.9
27981	26 Midland Crowd	100.0	28216	12 Up and Coming Families	27.9	28432	46 Rooted Rural	57.6
27983	56 Rural Bypasses	76.6	28217	19 Milk and Cookies	25.4	28433	56 Rural Bypasses	60.7
27986	56 Rural Bypasses	100.0	28226	16 Enterprising Professionals	13.0	28434	56 Rural Bypasses	66.9
28001	25 Salt of The Earth	26.2	28227	19 Milk and Cookies	41.2	28435	56 Rural Bypasses	74.5
28006	25 Salt of The Earth	51.4	28262	16 Enterprising Professionals	57.4	28436	42 Southern Satellites	99.3
28012	32 Rustbelt Traditions	26.1	28269	16 Enterprising Professionals	41.8	28438	56 Rural Bypasses	100.0
28016	42 Southern Satellites	41.3	28270	04 Boomburbs	20.8	28439	56 Rural Bypasses	87.9
28018	42 Southern Satellites	100.0	28273	12 Up and Coming Families	44.8	28441	56 Rural Bypasses	78.6
28020	42 Southern Satellites	62.1	28274	09 Urban Chic	100.0	28442	56 Rural Bypasses	61.1
28021	42 Southern Satellites	38.7	28277	04 Boomburbs	49.7	28443	31 Rural Resort Dwellers	42.5
28023	26 Midland Crowd	38.2	28278	12 Up and Coming Families	37.7	28444	56 Rural Bypasses	90.5
28025	26 Midland Crowd	16.1	28301	62 Modest Income Homes	25.8	28445	15 Silver and Gold	47.2
28027	12 Up and Coming Families	46.6	28303	28 Aspiring Young Families	21.6	28447	56 Rural Bypasses	69.1
28031	16 Enterprising Professionals	29.6	28304	32 Rustbelt Traditions	26.7	28448	42 Southern Satellites	84.5
28032	32 Rustbelt Traditions	66.8	28305	36 Old and Newcomers	28.2	28449	31 Rural Resort Dwellers	100.0
28033	26 Midland Crowd	53.8	28306	26 Midland Crowd	27.8	28450	31 Rural Resort Dwellers	58.3
28034	25 Salt of The Earth	22.2	28307	40 Military Proximity	96.5	28451	41 Crossroads	49.9
28036	09 Urban Chic	31.5	28308	40 Military Proximity	100.0	28452	46 Rooted Rural	100.0
28037	26 Midland Crowd	45.9	28310	40 Military Proximity	100.0	28453	42 Southern Satellites	81.8
28040	42 Southern Satellites	98.3	28311	06 Sophisticated Squires	24.6	28454	56 Rural Bypasses	50.1
28043	42 Southern Satellites	45.9	28312	26 Midland Crowd	51.1	28455	42 Southern Satellites	94.1
28052	53 Home Town	26.7	28314	39 Young and Restless	19.6	28456	42 Southern Satellites	46.3
28054	48 Great Expectations	12.8	28315	33 Midlife Junction	30.9	28457	41 Crossroads	69.5
28056	26 Midland Crowd	12.3	28318	42 Southern Satellites	100.0	28458	42 Southern Satellites	59.0
28071	42 Southern Satellites	66.0	28320	42 Southern Satellites	59.9	28460	31 Rural Resort Dwellers	69.6
28073	42 Southern Satellites	94.5	28323	41 Crossroads	84.6	28461	33 Midlife Junction	28.8
28075	06 Sophisticated Squires	66.0	28326	41 Crossroads	74.5	28462	46 Rooted Rural	45.4
28078	04 Boomburbs	36.0	28327	26 Midland Crowd	35.5	28463	56 Rural Bypasses	65.7
28079	12 Up and Coming Families	73.3	28328	42 Southern Satellites	40.8	28464	56 Rural Bypasses	63.7
28080	26 Midland Crowd	75.7	28333	41 Crossroads	65.6	28465	31 Rural Resort Dwellers	82.4
28081	53 Home Town	26.7	28334	42 Southern Satellites	26.3	28466	42 Southern Satellites	25.1
28083	53 Home Town	24.2	28337	42 Southern Satellites	29.9	28467	49 Senior Sun Seekers	54.1
28086	42 Southern Satellites	41.0	28338	56 Rural Bypasses	96.4	28468	15 Silver and Gold	87.4
28088	25 Salt of The Earth	54.8	28339	42 Southern Satellites	49.7	28469	15 Silver and Gold	36.8
28090	42 Southern Satellites	82.3	28340	56 Rural Bypasses	29.4	28470	46 Rooted Rural	51.3
28091	56 Rural Bypasses	97.4	28341	56 Rural Bypasses	54.9	28472	56 Rural Bypasses	29.0
28092	42 Southern Satellites	46.5	28343	56 Rural Bypasses	46.9	28478	42 Southern Satellites	63.1
28097	25 Salt of The Earth	100.0	28344	42 Southern Satellites	55.1	28479	26 Midland Crowd	72.4
28098	32 Rustbelt Traditions	68.8	28345	42 Southern Satellites	38.5	28480	08 Laptops and Lattes	52.0
28103	42 Southern Satellites	40.3	28347	26 Midland Crowd	68.4	28501	62 Modest Income Homes	23.3
28104	12 Up and Coming Families	28.3	28348	26 Midland Crowd	62.8	28504	33 Midlife Junction	20.7
28105	04 Boomburbs	17.3	28349	26 Midland Crowd	43.3	28508	41 Crossroads	86.7
28107	17 Green Acres	51.7	28351	42 Southern Satellites	57.0	28510	31 Rural Resort Dwellers	54.5
28110	12 Up and Coming Families	27.1	28352	26 Midland Crowd	17.7	28511	46 Rooted Rural	100.0
28112	25 Salt of The Earth	37.4	28356	42 Southern Satellites	79.5	28512	31 Rural Resort Dwellers	59.7
28114	42 Southern Satellites	67.6	28357	56 Rural Bypasses	51.1	28513	26 Midland Crowd	28.9
28115	26 Midland Crowd	31.0	28358	41 Crossroads	22.4	28515	56 Rural Bypasses	95.5
28117	07 Exurbanites	36.2	28360	41 Crossroads	53.8	28516	31 Rural Resort Dwellers	36.2
28119	56 Rural Bypasses	100.0	28363	26 Midland Crowd	87.5	28518	46 Rooted Rural	49.7
28120	25 Salt of The Earth	17.3	28364	56 Rural Bypasses	47.0	28520	37 Prairie Living	100.0
28124	25 Salt of The Earth	65.6	28365	42 Southern Satellites	63.0	28521	42 Southern Satellites	50.4
28125	26 Midland Crowd	100.0	28366	42 Southern Satellites	67.1	28523	46 Rooted Rural	49.2
28127	25 Salt of The Earth	30.4	28369	46 Rooted Rural	57.9	28525	26 Midland Crowd	61.2
28128	25 Salt of The Earth	30.5	28371	41 Crossroads	66.3	28526	56 Rural Bypasses	81.7
28129	25 Salt of The Earth	85.2	28372	42 Southern Satellites	50.6	28527	42 Southern Satellites	65.7
28133	42 Southern Satellites	100.0	28373	26 Midland Crowd	77.2	28528	31 Rural Resort Dwellers	100.0
28134	12 Up and Coming Families	38.0	28374	15 Silver and Gold	72.8	28529	46 Rooted Rural	54.0
28135	56 Rural Bypasses	52.3	28376	41 Crossroads	50.6	28530	46 Rooted Rural	44.0
28137	26 Midland Crowd	44.9	28377	41 Crossroads	49.5	28531	31 Rural Resort Dwellers	100.0
28138	26 Midland Crowd	43.1	28379	56 Rural Bypasses	30.3	28532	40 Military Proximity	31.5
28139	42 Southern Satellites	54.9	28382	42 Southern Satellites	49.2	28537	37 Prairie Living	98.9
28144	48 Great Expectations	28.8	28383	56 Rural Bypasses	62.6	28538	42 Southern Satellites	79.6
28146	26 Midland Crowd	29.1	28384	56 Rural Bypasses	29.9	28539	12 Up and Coming Families	33.9
28147	26 Midland Crowd	51.4	28385	46 Rooted Rural	43.3	28540	41 Crossroads	24.8
28150	42 Southern Satellites	32.7	28386	41 Crossroads	89.8	28543	40 Military Proximity	100.0
28152	42 Southern Satellites	39.1	28387	30 Retirement Communities	20.0	28544	40 Military Proximity	54.9
28159	32 Rustbelt Traditions	96.8	28390	41 Crossroads	50.2	28546	19 Milk and Cookies	18.9
28160	56 Rural Bypasses	57.0	28391	26 Midland Crowd	64.6	28547	40 Military Proximity	100.0
28163	25 Salt of The Earth	56.3	28392	42 Southern Satellites	71.0	28551	42 Southern Satellites	38.4
28164	26 Midland Crowd	47.0	28393	56 Rural Bypasses	61.5	28552	37 Prairie Living	100.0
28166	25 Salt of The Earth	46.3	28394	26 Midland Crowd	55.2	28553	31 Rural Resort Dwellers	100.0

ZIP CODE	TOP TAPESTRY CONSUMER TYPE	% 2004 HOUSE-HOLDS	ZIP CODE	TOP TAPESTRY CONSUMER TYPE	% 2004 HOUSE-HOLDS	ZIP CODE	TOP TAPESTRY CONSUMER TYPE	% 2004 HOUSE-HOLDS
28555	26 Midland Crowd	55.2	28702	31 Rural Resort Dwellers	71.9	29038	42 Southern Satellites	50.9
28556	31 Rural Resort Dwellers	54.7	28704	41 Crossroads	26.4	29039	41 Crossroads	77.7
28557	26 Midland Crowd	20.2	28705	42 Southern Satellites	53.9	29040	41 Crossroads	38.8
28560	26 Midland Crowd	19.5	28708	42 Southern Satellites	100.0	29042	56 Rural Bypasses	54.1
28562	14 Prosperous Empty Nesters	27.6	28709	42 Southern Satellites	86.0	29044	26 Midland Crowd	37.0
28570	26 Midland Crowd	29.8	28711	33 Midlife Junction	39.7	29045	26 Midland Crowd	54.0
28571	15 Silver and Gold	76.1	28712	46 Rooted Rural	15.6	29046	56 Rural Bypasses	100.0
28572	42 Southern Satellites	96.4	28713	46 Rooted Rural	48.1	29047	50 Heartland Communities	43.2
28573	46 Rooted Rural	74.0	28714	46 Rooted Rural	42.9	29048	56 Rural Bypasses	63.3
28574	42 Southern Satellites	37.1	28715	26 Midland Crowd	40.2	29051	56 Rural Bypasses	76.1
28577	46 Rooted Rural	100.0	28716	46 Rooted Rural	22.5	29052	34 Family Foundations	74.5
28578	41 Crossroads	59.7	28717	15 Silver and Gold	61.4	29053	41 Crossroads	96.4
28579	31 Rural Resort Dwellers	64.7	28718	31 Rural Resort Dwellers	100.0	29054	26 Midland Crowd	62.8
28580	42 Southern Satellites	56.5	28719	56 Rural Bypasses	39.9	29055	42 Southern Satellites	44.7
28581	37 Prairie Living	100.0	28721	33 Midlife Junction	37.8	29056	56 Rural Bypasses	100.0
28582	31 Rural Resort Dwellers	53.8	28722	30 Retirement Communities	32.0	29058	42 Southern Satellites	55.6
28584	31 Rural Resort Dwellers	55.0	28723	31 Rural Resort Dwellers	32.2	29059	56 Rural Bypasses	53.1
28585	46 Rooted Rural	73.8	28726	42 Southern Satellites	72.5	29061	26 Midland Crowd	32.9
28586	42 Southern Satellites	99.8	28729	49 Senior Sun Seekers	100.0	29063	12 Up and Coming Families	61.6
28587	56 Rural Bypasses	100.0	28730	17 Green Acres	71.9	29065	56 Rural Bypasses	100.0
28590	16 Enterprising Professionals	48.7	28731	15 Silver and Gold	38.1	29067	42 Southern Satellites	57.0
28594	15 Silver and Gold	100.0	28732	26 Midland Crowd	27.6	29069	56 Rural Bypasses	89.8
28601	42 Southern Satellites	18.5	28733	46 Rooted Rural	100.0	29070	26 Midland Crowd	28.4
28602	53 Home Town	17.8	28734	31 Rural Resort Dwellers	60.7	29072	12 Up and Coming Families	38.3
28604	31 Rural Resort Dwellers	76.4	28735	46 Rooted Rural	100.0	29073	26 Midland Crowd	38.6
28605	31 Rural Resort Dwellers	83.1	28736	42 Southern Satellites	97.6	29075	25 Salt of The Earth	54.6
28606	42 Southern Satellites	95.4	28739	31 Rural Resort Dwellers	18.1	29078	26 Midland Crowd	36.0
28607	55 College Towns	41.6	28740	56 Rural Bypasses	58.2	29080	56 Rural Bypasses	100.0
28608	55 College Towns	100.0	28741	15 Silver and Gold	57.0	29081	46 Rooted Rural	98.7
28609	42 Southern Satellites	71.8	28742	25 Salt of The Earth	76.2	29082	56 Rural Bypasses	86.4
28610	42 Southern Satellites	46.2	28743	56 Rural Bypasses	45.3	29101	42 Southern Satellites	57.0
28611	42 Southern Satellites	100.0	28745	15 Silver and Gold	100.0	29102	56 Rural Bypasses	39.9
28612	42 Southern Satellites	79.4	28746	31 Rural Resort Dwellers	89.1	29104	56 Rural Bypasses	97.0
28613	42 Southern Satellites	29.0	28747	42 Southern Satellites	53.6	29105	42 Southern Satellites	90.6
28615	42 Southern Satellites	58.4	28748	26 Midland Crowd	58.8	29107	56 Rural Bypasses	36.9
28617	46 Rooted Rural	96.7	28751	31 Rural Resort Dwellers	99.2	29108	42 Southern Satellites	20.1
28618	46 Rooted Rural	66.6	28752	42 Southern Satellites	60.6	29111	56 Rural Bypasses	100.0
28621	42 Southern Satellites	35.9	28753	46 Rooted Rural	46.5	29112	56 Rural Bypasses	93.9
28622	46 Rooted Rural	63.7	28754	33 Midlife Junction	34.1	29113	56 Rural Bypasses	61.8
28623	46 Rooted Rural	58.6	28756	42 Southern Satellites	90.2	29114	56 Rural Bypasses	99.5
28624	42 Southern Satellites	65.2	28761	42 Southern Satellites	91.0	29115	62 Modest Income Homes	22.3
28625	26 Midland Crowd	28.5	28762	42 Southern Satellites	68.2	29117	62 Modest Income Homes	58.1
28626	25 Salt of The Earth	55.2	28763	31 Rural Resort Dwellers	100.0	29118	41 Crossroads	22.2
28627	31 Rural Resort Dwellers	50.3	28766	56 Rural Bypasses	100.0	29123	41 Crossroads	100.0
28630	42 Southern Satellites	63.8	28768	42 Southern Satellites	35.0	29125	56 Rural Bypasses	49.6
28631	46 Rooted Rural	97.8	28771	46 Rooted Rural	50.5	29126	42 Southern Satellites	69.9
28634	42 Southern Satellites	99.1	28772	46 Rooted Rural	66.8	29127	31 Rural Resort Dwellers	43.6
28635	42 Southern Satellites	100.0	28773	31 Rural Resort Dwellers	64.2	29128	56 Rural Bypasses	73.3
28636	42 Southern Satellites	94.3	28774	31 Rural Resort Dwellers	79.7	29129	42 Southern Satellites	59.5
28637	42 Southern Satellites	82.6	28775	31 Rural Resort Dwellers	100.0	29130	56 Rural Bypasses	39.9
28638	42 Southern Satellites	60.4	28777	46 Rooted Rural	55.2	29133	56 Rural Bypasses	91.5
28640	46 Rooted Rural	36.0	28778	50 Heartland Communities	24.8	29135	56 Rural Bypasses	55.3
28642	42 Southern Satellites	53.4	28779	33 Midlife Junction	44.3	29137	56 Rural Bypasses	86.6
28643	42 Southern Satellites	59.7	28781	31 Rural Resort Dwellers	100.0	29138	42 Southern Satellites	36.6
28644	31 Rural Resort Dwellers	52.9	28782	15 Silver and Gold	59.8	29142	46 Rooted Rural	55.8
28645	42 Southern Satellites	55.7	28783	46 Rooted Rural	59.8	29145	42 Southern Satellites	100.0
28649	42 Southern Satellites	100.0	28785	31 Rural Resort Dwellers	51.6	29146	42 Southern Satellites	100.0
28650	42 Southern Satellites	52.9	28786	31 Rural Resort Dwellers	30.6	29148	56 Rural Bypasses	35.7
28651	42 Southern Satellites	72.1	28787	26 Midland Crowd	56.7	29150	62 Modest Income Homes	17.9
28654	42 Southern Satellites	46.3	28789	46 Rooted Rural	50.8	29152	40 Military Proximity	100.0
28655	42 Southern Satellites	28.8	28790	25 Salt of The Earth	67.0	29153	56 Rural Bypasses	24.8
28657	46 Rooted Rural	53.9	28791	43 The Elders	22.2	29154	41 Crossroads	24.2
28658	42 Southern Satellites	38.4	28792	42 Southern Satellites	29.5	29160	42 Southern Satellites	29.6
28659	42 Southern Satellites	53.2	28801	55 College Towns	22.3	29161	42 Southern Satellites	37.2
28660	42 Southern Satellites	54.3	28803	16 Enterprising Professionals	15.6	29162	56 Rural Bypasses	49.7
28663	37 Prairie Living	61.3	28804	14 Prosperous Empty Nesters	38.5	29163	56 Rural Bypasses	96.5
28665	42 Southern Satellites	81.3	28805	33 Midlife Junction	52.4	29164	42 Southern Satellites	52.6
28668	31 Rural Resort Dwellers	100.0	28806	33 Midlife Junction	23.3	29166	42 Southern Satellites	99.3
28669	42 Southern Satellites	100.0	28901	46 Rooted Rural	61.0	29168	41 Crossroads	54.0
28670	42 Southern Satellites	87.1	28902	31 Rural Resort Dwellers	100.0	29169	30 Retirement Communities	18.2
28672	42 Southern Satellites	100.0	28904	31 Rural Resort Dwellers	67.3	29170	26 Midland Crowd	30.8
28673	17 Green Acres	58.4	28905	42 Southern Satellites	51.5	29172	41 Crossroads	51.8
28675	50 Heartland Communities	27.8	28906	46 Rooted Rural	49.3	29175	42 Southern Satellites	100.0
28676	25 Salt of The Earth	47.8	28909	31 Rural Resort Dwellers	100.0	29178	53 Home Town	29.7
28677	26 Midland Crowd	13.8	29001	42 Southern Satellites	100.0	29180	56 Rural Bypasses	38.2
28678	42 Southern Satellites	97.2	29003	56 Rural Bypasses	41.8	29201	48 Great Expectations	27.3
28679	46 Rooted Rural	88.5	29006	42 Southern Satellites	56.7	29203	34 Family Foundations	36.3
28681	42 Southern Satellites	68.9	29009	42 Southern Satellites	99.8	29204	30 Retirement Communities	17.2
28682	15 Silver and Gold	100.0	29010	56 Rural Bypasses	57.6	29205	22 Metropolitans	38.9
28683	42 Southern Satellites	99.6	29014	56 Rural Bypasses	59.1	29206	14 Prosperous Empty Nesters	44.3
28684	31 Rural Resort Dwellers	47.6	29015	56 Rural Bypasses	99.8	29207	09 Urban Chic	92.7
28685	42 Southern Satellites	100.0	29016	26 Midland Crowd	50.9	29208	63 Dorms To Diplomas	100.0
28689	42 Southern Satellites	75.2	29018	56 Rural Bypasses	85.0	29209	13 In Style	19.0
28690	50 Heartland Communities	40.0	29020	42 Southern Satellites	21.6	29210	39 Young and Restless	52.9
28692	46 Rooted Rural	70.3	29030	46 Rooted Rural	46.7	29212	06 Sophisticated Squires	26.2
28693	46 Rooted Rural	63.9	29031	56 Rural Bypasses	82.5	29223	39 Young and Restless	12.3
28694	46 Rooted Rural	25.2	29032	42 Southern Satellites	71.6	29229	12 Up and Coming Families	47.9
28697	25 Salt of The Earth	35.6	29033	48 Great Expectations	21.7	29301	13 In Style	15.4
28698	46 Rooted Rural	67.5	29036	07 Exurbanites	65.1	29302	32 Rustbelt Traditions	16.7
28701	26 Midland Crowd	51.8	29037	42 Southern Satellites	93.3	29303	42 Southern Satellites	20.5

     379

ZIP CODE	TOP TAPESTRY CONSUMER TYPE	% 2004 HOUSE-HOLDS	ZIP CODE	TOP TAPESTRY CONSUMER TYPE	% 2004 HOUSE-HOLDS	ZIP CODE	TOP TAPESTRY CONSUMER TYPE	% 2004 HOUSE-HOLDS
29306	62 Modest Income Homes	39.3	29530	56 Rural Bypasses	51.2	29680	12 Up and Coming Families	60.6
29307	14 Prosperous Empty Nesters	18.8	29532	42 Southern Satellites	24.7	29681	04 Boomburbs	37.6
29316	12 Up and Coming Families	33.5	29536	62 Modest Income Homes	24.5	29682	26 Midland Crowd	64.4
29321	42 Southern Satellites	45.9	29540	56 Rural Bypasses	61.3	29684	42 Southern Satellites	93.3
29322	42 Southern Satellites	74.4	29541	26 Midland Crowd	33.1	29685	42 Southern Satellites	100.0
29323	42 Southern Satellites	65.6	29543	46 Rooted Rural	90.9	29686	31 Rural Resort Dwellers	52.1
29325	56 Rural Bypasses	22.5	29544	26 Midland Crowd	51.1	29687	18 Cozy and Comfortable	16.7
29330	42 Southern Satellites	61.4	29545	56 Rural Bypasses	75.9	29688	26 Midland Crowd	100.0
29332	49 Senior Sun Seekers	60.0	29546	41 Crossroads	60.4	29689	31 Rural Resort Dwellers	88.5
29334	26 Midland Crowd	21.2	29547	56 Rural Bypasses	59.9	29690	25 Salt of The Earth	30.9
29335	42 Southern Satellites	100.0	29550	42 Southern Satellites	31.7	29691	42 Southern Satellites	76.2
29340	42 Southern Satellites	54.0	29554	56 Rural Bypasses	86.5	29692	42 Southern Satellites	56.7
29341	42 Southern Satellites	24.6	29555	56 Rural Bypasses	82.4	29693	42 Southern Satellites	76.1
29349	26 Midland Crowd	34.0	29556	56 Rural Bypasses	62.9	29696	25 Salt of The Earth	48.4
29351	42 Southern Satellites	35.8	29560	56 Rural Bypasses	47.6	29697	42 Southern Satellites	52.9
29353	56 Rural Bypasses	53.2	29563	56 Rural Bypasses	74.9	29702	42 Southern Satellites	69.7
29355	42 Southern Satellites	96.1	29564	56 Rural Bypasses	100.0	29704	26 Midland Crowd	96.4
29356	50 Heartland Communities	27.7	29565	56 Rural Bypasses	49.9	29706	42 Southern Satellites	43.1
29360	42 Southern Satellites	30.4	29566	31 Rural Resort Dwellers	54.5	29708	07 Exurbanites	51.1
29365	25 Salt of The Earth	41.0	29567	56 Rural Bypasses	91.9	29709	42 Southern Satellites	87.6
29369	26 Midland Crowd	39.0	29568	41 Crossroads	40.0	29710	26 Midland Crowd	42.6
29370	56 Rural Bypasses	60.4	29569	42 Southern Satellites	34.8	29712	26 Midland Crowd	81.7
29372	50 Heartland Communities	41.9	29570	56 Rural Bypasses	100.0	29714	42 Southern Satellites	100.0
29374	42 Southern Satellites	44.5	29571	56 Rural Bypasses	35.6	29715	26 Midland Crowd	32.1
29376	25 Salt of The Earth	25.2	29572	15 Silver and Gold	31.5	29717	42 Southern Satellites	100.0
29379	42 Southern Satellites	39.4	29574	56 Rural Bypasses	71.1	29718	56 Rural Bypasses	92.3
29384	42 Southern Satellites	39.4	29575	15 Silver and Gold	34.1	29720	42 Southern Satellites	48.8
29385	25 Salt of The Earth	27.8	29576	49 Senior Sun Seekers	45.5	29726	26 Midland Crowd	67.2
29388	42 Southern Satellites	44.6	29577	36 Old and Newcomers	19.5	29727	56 Rural Bypasses	53.7
29401	08 Laptops and Lattes	32.0	29579	39 Young and Restless	56.8	29728	42 Southern Satellites	43.5
29403	62 Modest Income Homes	23.7	29580	56 Rural Bypasses	99.4	29729	26 Midland Crowd	47.9
29404	40 Military Proximity	100.0	29581	56 Rural Bypasses	78.3	29730	26 Midland Crowd	19.9
29405	62 Modest Income Homes	25.6	29582	31 Rural Resort Dwellers	31.5	29732	17 Green Acres	19.5
29406	36 Old and Newcomers	40.3	29583	46 Rooted Rural	57.5	29741	42 Southern Satellites	100.0
29407	22 Metropolitans	23.2	29584	56 Rural Bypasses	89.2	29742	42 Southern Satellites	89.7
29412	33 Midlife Junction	20.7	29585	31 Rural Resort Dwellers	56.9	29743	42 Southern Satellites	100.0
29414	28 Aspiring Young Families	32.8	29588	26 Midland Crowd	35.6	29745	26 Midland Crowd	53.9
29418	41 Crossroads	24.4	29590	56 Rural Bypasses	100.0	29801	62 Modest Income Homes	16.3
29420	12 Up and Coming Families	57.4	29591	56 Rural Bypasses	53.0	29803	07 Exurbanites	20.3
29426	56 Rural Bypasses	100.0	29592	41 Crossroads	60.7	29805	26 Midland Crowd	61.9
29429	42 Southern Satellites	34.7	29593	56 Rural Bypasses	99.2	29808	41 Crossroads	100.0
29431	46 Rooted Rural	36.6	29596	56 Rural Bypasses	55.7	29809	25 Salt of The Earth	58.6
29432	56 Rural Bypasses	99.9	29601	62 Modest Income Homes	37.2	29810	62 Modest Income Homes	36.6
29434	56 Rural Bypasses	100.0	29605	22 Metropolitans	16.2	29812	56 Rural Bypasses	34.3
29435	42 Southern Satellites	47.2	29607	39 Young and Restless	20.0	29817	56 Rural Bypasses	96.1
29436	56 Rural Bypasses	100.0	29609	33 Midlife Junction	13.0	29819	42 Southern Satellites	93.9
29437	56 Rural Bypasses	71.6	29611	53 Home Town	27.3	29821	46 Rooted Rural	66.4
29438	56 Rural Bypasses	59.6	29613	18 Cozy and Comfortable	100.0	29824	25 Salt of The Earth	37.9
29440	56 Rural Bypasses	38.4	29615	14 Prosperous Empty Nesters	22.8	29827	56 Rural Bypasses	99.4
29445	12 Up and Coming Families	27.7	29617	53 Home Town	27.2	29828	56 Rural Bypasses	100.0
29446	56 Rural Bypasses	68.1	29620	42 Southern Satellites	47.1	29829	26 Midland Crowd	30.3
29448	56 Rural Bypasses	71.5	29621	26 Midland Crowd	15.5	29831	26 Midland Crowd	48.5
29449	56 Rural Bypasses	67.0	29624	62 Modest Income Homes	40.4	29832	56 Rural Bypasses	30.2
29450	56 Rural Bypasses	93.8	29625	26 Midland Crowd	21.7	29835	56 Rural Bypasses	47.7
29451	03 Connoisseurs	77.0	29626	53 Home Town	22.4	29836	56 Rural Bypasses	100.0
29453	56 Rural Bypasses	98.7	29627	42 Southern Satellites	50.5	29838	46 Rooted Rural	100.0
29455	56 Rural Bypasses	24.6	29628	42 Southern Satellites	39.8	29840	15 Silver and Gold	99.5
29456	19 Milk and Cookies	50.2	29630	55 College Towns	40.2	29841	33 Midlife Junction	20.7
29458	46 Rooted Rural	61.1	29631	55 College Towns	40.0	29842	26 Midland Crowd	51.1
29461	26 Midland Crowd	23.5	29632	33 Midlife Junction	55.6	29843	56 Rural Bypasses	79.0
29464	13 In Style	46.7	29635	31 Rural Resort Dwellers	51.4	29845	56 Rural Bypasses	77.3
29466	04 Boomburbs	59.9	29638	42 Southern Satellites	70.4	29847	42 Southern Satellites	81.9
29468	56 Rural Bypasses	100.0	29639	33 Midlife Junction	44.8	29848	42 Southern Satellites	60.7
29469	56 Rural Bypasses	93.3	29640	26 Midland Crowd	38.3	29849	56 Rural Bypasses	100.0
29470	42 Southern Satellites	38.0	29642	26 Midland Crowd	20.8	29851	56 Rural Bypasses	68.3
29471	56 Rural Bypasses	100.0	29643	31 Rural Resort Dwellers	70.9	29853	56 Rural Bypasses	66.8
29472	56 Rural Bypasses	60.7	29644	26 Midland Crowd	51.7	29856	41 Crossroads	97.0
29474	46 Rooted Rural	43.9	29645	42 Southern Satellites	40.8	29860	26 Midland Crowd	29.1
29475	56 Rural Bypasses	54.7	29646	57 Simple Living	11.6	29902	33 Midlife Junction	39.6
29477	56 Rural Bypasses	100.0	29649	28 Aspiring Young Families	20.1	29906	41 Crossroads	43.0
29479	56 Rural Bypasses	88.0	29650	06 Sophisticated Squires	16.2	29907	12 Up and Coming Families	39.6
29481	56 Rural Bypasses	97.1	29651	26 Midland Crowd	31.6	29909	15 Silver and Gold	86.7
29482	09 Urban Chic	100.0	29653	42 Southern Satellites	70.4	29910	28 Aspiring Young Families	30.2
29483	26 Midland Crowd	24.6	29654	42 Southern Satellites	59.1	29911	56 Rural Bypasses	100.0
29485	26 Midland Crowd	19.7	29655	42 Southern Satellites	41.4	29916	56 Rural Bypasses	51.1
29487	46 Rooted Rural	51.6	29657	42 Southern Satellites	55.3	29918	56 Rural Bypasses	86.2
29488	41 Crossroads	27.3	29658	46 Rooted Rural	77.5	29920	56 Rural Bypasses	35.2
29492	12 Up and Coming Families	99.0	29659	42 Southern Satellites	100.0	29922	56 Rural Bypasses	100.0
29501	26 Midland Crowd	14.5	29661	42 Southern Satellites	91.5	29924	56 Rural Bypasses	51.3
29505	26 Midland Crowd	20.1	29662	12 Up and Coming Families	27.1	29926	15 Silver and Gold	62.4
29506	41 Crossroads	17.0	29664	31 Rural Resort Dwellers	54.4	29927	41 Crossroads	51.4
29510	56 Rural Bypasses	58.8	29666	42 Southern Satellites	44.9	29928	15 Silver and Gold	60.9
29511	42 Southern Satellites	38.0	29667	42 Southern Satellites	94.5	29929	56 Rural Bypasses	100.0
29512	56 Rural Bypasses	51.9	29669	42 Southern Satellites	38.6	29932	56 Rural Bypasses	100.0
29516	56 Rural Bypasses	100.0	29670	42 Southern Satellites	28.1	29934	56 Rural Bypasses	77.6
29518	56 Rural Bypasses	100.0	29671	42 Southern Satellites	60.3	29935	48 Great Expectations	70.1
29520	50 Heartland Communities	16.6	29672	31 Rural Resort Dwellers	33.8	29936	56 Rural Bypasses	43.5
29525	56 Rural Bypasses	82.1	29673	26 Midland Crowd	38.2	29940	56 Rural Bypasses	68.1
29526	26 Midland Crowd	39.4	29676	15 Silver and Gold	63.7	29941	56 Rural Bypasses	100.0
29527	41 Crossroads	38.4	29678	42 Southern Satellites	36.8	29943	42 Southern Satellites	53.6

ZIP CODE	TOP TAPESTRY CONSUMER TYPE	% 2004 HOUSE-HOLDS	ZIP CODE	TOP TAPESTRY CONSUMER TYPE	% 2004 HOUSE-HOLDS	ZIP CODE	TOP TAPESTRY CONSUMER TYPE	% 2004 HOUSE-HOLDS
29944	56 Rural Bypasses	57.9	30148	15 Silver and Gold	52.6	30322	63 Dorms To Diplomas	100.0
29945	56 Rural Bypasses	98.4	30149	55 College Towns	100.0	30324	27 Metro Renters	60.6
30002	22 Metropolitans	46.7	30152	12 Up and Coming Families	65.0	30326	27 Metro Renters	78.1
30004	04 Boomburbs	35.4	30153	42 Southern Satellites	52.6	30327	01 Top Rung	61.3
30005	04 Boomburbs	72.2	30157	12 Up and Coming Families	63.3	30328	16 Enterprising Professionals	27.2
30008	28 Aspiring Young Families	30.9	30161	53 Home Town	19.2	30329	27 Metro Renters	63.7
30011	12 Up and Coming Families	97.4	30165	33 Midlife Junction	32.9	30330	40 Military Proximity	100.0
30012	48 Great Expectations	27.4	30168	39 Young and Restless	24.2	30331	51 Metro City Edge	23.9
30013	28 Aspiring Young Families	22.7	30170	26 Midland Crowd	74.2	30334	27 Metro Renters	0.0
30014	26 Midland Crowd	26.5	30171	26 Midland Crowd	86.0	30336	51 Metro City Edge	87.6
30016	12 Up and Coming Families	41.1	30173	26 Midland Crowd	36.2	30337	52 Inner City Tenants	44.8
30017	12 Up and Coming Families	75.4	30175	42 Southern Satellites	47.9	30338	03 Connoisseurs	49.2
30019	12 Up and Coming Families	77.7	30176	42 Southern Satellites	60.7	30339	27 Metro Renters	44.3
30021	39 Young and Restless	37.6	30177	15 Silver and Gold	100.0	30340	39 Young and Restless	33.8
30022	04 Boomburbs	58.9	30178	26 Midland Crowd	59.3	30341	36 Old and Newcomers	18.7
30024	04 Boomburbs	83.4	30179	42 Southern Satellites	47.3	30342	23 Trendsetters	40.0
30025	26 Midland Crowd	51.4	30180	26 Midland Crowd	34.1	30344	52 Inner City Tenants	31.6
30030	22 Metropolitans	48.5	30182	42 Southern Satellites	88.5	30345	05 Wealthy Seaboard Suburbs	27.5
30032	51 Metro City Edge	33.1	30183	17 Green Acres	57.0	30346	27 Metro Renters	100.0
30033	27 Metro Renters	35.7	30184	17 Green Acres	67.1	30349	39 Young and Restless	26.2
30034	28 Aspiring Young Families	23.6	30185	26 Midland Crowd	62.4	30350	39 Young and Restless	45.4
30035	28 Aspiring Young Families	45.7	30187	17 Green Acres	77.3	30354	51 Metro City Edge	26.1
30038	28 Aspiring Young Families	25.3	30188	12 Up and Coming Families	38.0	30360	16 Enterprising Professionals	33.5
30039	06 Sophisticated Squires	61.5	30189	04 Boomburbs	51.4	30401	56 Rural Bypasses	42.3
30040	12 Up and Coming Families	52.0	30204	53 Home Town	21.5	30410	41 Crossroads	64.7
30041	06 Sophisticated Squires	34.9	30205	06 Sophisticated Squires	69.2	30411	56 Rural Bypasses	56.6
30043	12 Up and Coming Families	48.2	30206	42 Southern Satellites	63.4	30413	56 Rural Bypasses	100.0
30044	12 Up and Coming Families	44.3	30213	18 Cozy and Comfortable	25.0	30415	26 Midland Crowd	60.4
30045	12 Up and Coming Families	53.0	30214	07 Exurbanites	61.1	30417	56 Rural Bypasses	32.7
30047	06 Sophisticated Squires	36.2	30215	06 Sophisticated Squires	53.4	30420	46 Rooted Rural	52.6
30052	12 Up and Coming Families	65.9	30216	42 Southern Satellites	81.4	30421	56 Rural Bypasses	58.7
30054	17 Green Acres	44.0	30217	42 Southern Satellites	75.9	30425	56 Rural Bypasses	53.1
30055	26 Midland Crowd	69.5	30218	42 Southern Satellites	52.7	30426	56 Rural Bypasses	100.0
30056	42 Southern Satellites	57.6	30220	42 Southern Satellites	64.4	30427	41 Crossroads	23.9
30058	12 Up and Coming Families	45.9	30222	56 Rural Bypasses	86.2	30428	56 Rural Bypasses	94.2
30060	24 Main Street, USA	14.5	30223	26 Midland Crowd	16.3	30434	56 Rural Bypasses	67.1
30062	02 Suburban Splendor	34.4	30224	18 Cozy and Comfortable	23.4	30436	41 Crossroads	34.0
30064	06 Sophisticated Squires	32.7	30228	12 Up and Coming Families	32.8	30438	42 Southern Satellites	75.7
30066	06 Sophisticated Squires	55.5	30230	42 Southern Satellites	50.2	30439	56 Rural Bypasses	49.5
30067	39 Young and Restless	57.2	30233	26 Midland Crowd	44.3	30441	56 Rural Bypasses	74.9
30068	02 Suburban Splendor	49.2	30234	42 Southern Satellites	99.8	30442	56 Rural Bypasses	73.0
30069	40 Military Proximity	100.0	30236	52 Inner City Tenants	20.8	30445	33 Midlife Junction	49.2
30071	28 Aspiring Young Families	42.3	30238	12 Up and Coming Families	46.2	30446	56 Rural Bypasses	92.4
30075	02 Suburban Splendor	37.9	30241	62 Modest Income Homes	16.4	30450	56 Rural Bypasses	89.8
30076	39 Young and Restless	24.4	30248	26 Midland Crowd	60.9	30452	41 Crossroads	52.1
30078	06 Sophisticated Squires	33.0	30251	42 Southern Satellites	73.1	30453	41 Crossroads	43.4
30079	36 Old and Newcomers	28.4	30252	12 Up and Coming Families	36.0	30454	56 Rural Bypasses	69.9
30080	39 Young and Restless	39.0	30253	12 Up and Coming Families	48.6	30455	42 Southern Satellites	100.0
30082	28 Aspiring Young Families	23.9	30256	46 Rooted Rural	51.3	30456	56 Rural Bypasses	100.0
30083	39 Young and Restless	29.3	30257	26 Midland Crowd	56.8	30457	56 Rural Bypasses	100.0
30084	13 In Style	32.4	30258	26 Midland Crowd	67.3	30458	63 Dorms To Diplomas	24.7
30087	12 Up and Coming Families	25.7	30259	17 Green Acres	93.6	30461	26 Midland Crowd	29.4
30088	19 Milk and Cookies	50.2	30260	28 Aspiring Young Families	20.3	30467	56 Rural Bypasses	50.7
30092	39 Young and Restless	38.1	30263	26 Midland Crowd	22.3	30470	42 Southern Satellites	53.0
30093	28 Aspiring Young Families	44.0	30265	12 Up and Coming Families	58.0	30471	56 Rural Bypasses	92.4
30094	06 Sophisticated Squires	34.9	30268	17 Green Acres	33.4	30473	46 Rooted Rural	41.1
30096	16 Enterprising Professionals	41.5	30269	04 Boomburbs	41.8	30474	41 Crossroads	26.0
30097	04 Boomburbs	84.0	30273	19 Milk and Cookies	75.5	30477	56 Rural Bypasses	73.7
30101	12 Up and Coming Families	49.1	30274	28 Aspiring Young Families	58.3	30501	58 Newest Residents	12.2
30102	12 Up and Coming Families	43.8	30276	26 Midland Crowd	78.4	30504	52 Inner City Tenants	28.8
30103	42 Southern Satellites	38.3	30277	12 Up and Coming Families	62.4	30506	17 Green Acres	52.2
30104	42 Southern Satellites	75.0	30281	17 Green Acres	32.6	30507	42 Southern Satellites	47.3
30105	25 Salt of The Earth	50.5	30285	42 Southern Satellites	97.3	30510	42 Southern Satellites	68.2
30106	12 Up and Coming Families	31.1	30286	53 Home Town	22.2	30511	42 Southern Satellites	79.5
30107	17 Green Acres	46.1	30288	38 Industrious Urban Fringe	34.7	30512	31 Rural Resort Dwellers	62.4
30108	42 Southern Satellites	68.0	30290	07 Exurbanites	36.1	30513	31 Rural Resort Dwellers	32.1
30110	42 Southern Satellites	83.4	30291	52 Inner City Tenants	28.3	30516	42 Southern Satellites	73.5
30113	42 Southern Satellites	100.0	30292	17 Green Acres	42.6	30517	26 Midland Crowd	66.7
30114	24 Main Street, USA	18.6	30293	56 Rural Bypasses	60.1	30518	12 Up and Coming Families	44.5
30115	26 Midland Crowd	20.8	30294	19 Milk and Cookies	51.0	30519	12 Up and Coming Families	90.2
30116	26 Midland Crowd	72.1	30295	26 Midland Crowd	51.9	30520	42 Southern Satellites	68.3
30117	26 Midland Crowd	22.5	30296	28 Aspiring Young Families	45.7	30521	42 Southern Satellites	75.0
30118	63 Dorms To Diplomas	100.0	30297	52 Inner City Tenants	27.9	30522	31 Rural Resort Dwellers	97.3
30120	26 Midland Crowd	19.9	30303	27 Metro Renters	62.7	30523	25 Salt of The Earth	24.7
30121	26 Midland Crowd	45.1	30305	08 Laptops and Lattes	38.4	30525	31 Rural Resort Dwellers	27.1
30122	19 Milk and Cookies	25.5	30306	08 Laptops and Lattes	46.3	30527	25 Salt of The Earth	39.0
30124	46 Rooted Rural	57.6	30307	08 Laptops and Lattes	26.4	30528	26 Midland Crowd	45.2
30125	42 Southern Satellites	51.4	30308	27 Metro Renters	87.4	30529	26 Midland Crowd	41.4
30126	32 Rustbelt Traditions	18.0	30309	27 Metro Renters	76.9	30530	42 Southern Satellites	75.1
30127	12 Up and Coming Families	34.0	30310	34 Family Foundations	31.6	30531	42 Southern Satellites	41.2
30132	12 Up and Coming Families	45.8	30311	34 Family Foundations	34.0	30533	26 Midland Crowd	62.5
30134	12 Up and Coming Families	34.1	30312	64 City Commons	26.6	30534	26 Midland Crowd	41.0
30135	06 Sophisticated Squires	29.5	30313	27 Metro Renters	48.8	30535	42 Southern Satellites	85.3
30137	26 Midland Crowd	73.6	30314	62 Modest Income Homes	50.7	30537	42 Southern Satellites	56.4
30139	42 Southern Satellites	84.4	30315	64 City Commons	35.9	30538	42 Southern Satellites	100.0
30141	12 Up and Coming Families	65.0	30316	51 Metro City Edge	30.0	30539	42 Southern Satellites	100.0
30143	26 Midland Crowd	40.3	30317	34 Family Foundations	34.3	30540	42 Southern Satellites	70.4
30144	12 Up and Coming Families	41.9	30318	62 Modest Income Homes	21.1	30541	25 Salt of The Earth	66.6
30145	12 Up and Coming Families	37.1	30319	16 Enterprising Professionals	17.1	30542	12 Up and Coming Families	40.9
30147	42 Southern Satellites	31.3				30543	42 Southern Satellites	50.8

ZIP CODE	TOP TAPESTRY CONSUMER TYPE	% 2004 HOUSE-HOLDS	ZIP CODE	TOP TAPESTRY CONSUMER TYPE	% 2004 HOUSE-HOLDS	ZIP CODE	TOP TAPESTRY CONSUMER TYPE	% 2004 HOUSE-HOLDS
30545	31 Rural Resort Dwellers	100.0	30751	42 Southern Satellites	100.0	31076	56 Rural Bypasses	92.1
30546	31 Rural Resort Dwellers	60.4	30752	42 Southern Satellites	92.4	31077	46 Rooted Rural	57.7
30547	42 Southern Satellites	100.0	30753	42 Southern Satellites	68.8	31078	56 Rural Bypasses	73.1
30548	26 Midland Crowd	81.7	30755	42 Southern Satellites	54.9	31079	46 Rooted Rural	49.9
30549	26 Midland Crowd	73.0	30757	26 Midland Crowd	95.9	31081	46 Rooted Rural	100.0
30552	42 Southern Satellites	62.9	30802	26 Midland Crowd	72.7	31082	56 Rural Bypasses	28.7
30553	31 Rural Resort Dwellers	39.7	30803	42 Southern Satellites	98.1	31085	42 Southern Satellites	72.0
30554	42 Southern Satellites	52.0	30805	26 Midland Crowd	67.3	31087	56 Rural Bypasses	61.4
30555	50 Heartland Communities	56.1	30808	41 Crossroads	53.5	31088	12 Up and Coming Families	28.7
30557	42 Southern Satellites	94.7	30809	04 Boomburbs	56.0	31089	56 Rural Bypasses	93.0
30558	42 Southern Satellites	95.9	30810	50 Heartland Communities	50.2	31090	56 Rural Bypasses	94.4
30559	46 Rooted Rural	100.0	30813	26 Midland Crowd	49.5	31091	56 Rural Bypasses	98.2
30560	46 Rooted Rural	50.1	30814	26 Midland Crowd	98.5	31092	56 Rural Bypasses	47.7
30563	42 Southern Satellites	49.6	30815	19 Milk and Cookies	50.8	31093	32 Rustbelt Traditions	16.8
30564	26 Midland Crowd	65.1	30816	56 Rural Bypasses	61.4	31094	56 Rural Bypasses	80.0
30565	26 Midland Crowd	60.0	30817	46 Rooted Rural	48.7	31096	56 Rural Bypasses	100.0
30566	28 Aspiring Young Families	49.4	30818	42 Southern Satellites	65.7	31097	42 Southern Satellites	88.0
30567	26 Midland Crowd	61.8	30820	46 Rooted Rural	86.5	31098	40 Military Proximity	100.0
30568	42 Southern Satellites	37.2	30821	56 Rural Bypasses	100.0	31201	64 City Commons	34.3
30571	31 Rural Resort Dwellers	100.0	30822	42 Southern Satellites	70.2	31204	62 Modest Income Homes	26.1
30572	31 Rural Resort Dwellers	100.0	30823	42 Southern Satellites	80.7	31206	62 Modest Income Homes	21.9
30575	26 Midland Crowd	75.9	30824	56 Rural Bypasses	20.9	31207	63 Dorms To Diplomas	100.0
30576	31 Rural Resort Dwellers	53.6	30828	56 Rural Bypasses	78.0	31210	39 Young and Restless	16.9
30577	25 Salt of The Earth	24.4	30830	62 Modest Income Homes	24.3	31211	36 Old and Newcomers	16.3
30582	31 Rural Resort Dwellers	91.9	30833	51 Metro City Edge	28.9	31216	18 Cozy and Comfortable	41.7
30597	26 Midland Crowd	0.0	30901	62 Modest Income Homes	48.2	31217	34 Family Foundations	24.0
30601	60 City Dimensions	17.7	30904	48 Great Expectations	25.0	31220	17 Green Acres	28.4
30602	63 Dorms To Diplomas	100.0	30905	40 Military Proximity	99.5	31301	41 Crossroads	100.0
30605	55 College Towns	32.7	30906	34 Family Foundations	19.5	31302	26 Midland Crowd	60.0
30606	55 College Towns	20.7	30907	19 Milk and Cookies	22.1	31303	26 Midland Crowd	82.6
30607	26 Midland Crowd	29.2	30909	39 Young and Restless	20.4	31304	56 Rural Bypasses	100.0
30609	63 Dorms To Diplomas	100.0	30912	65 Social Security Set	73.5	31305	56 Rural Bypasses	45.4
30619	56 Rural Bypasses	49.4	31001	56 Rural Bypasses	100.0	31308	26 Midland Crowd	70.3
30620	26 Midland Crowd	69.6	31002	56 Rural Bypasses	60.0	31309	41 Crossroads	100.0
30621	17 Green Acres	48.5	31003	46 Rooted Rural	100.0	31312	26 Midland Crowd	85.7
30622	26 Midland Crowd	35.4	31005	06 Sophisticated Squires	26.7	31313	28 Aspiring Young Families	64.9
30624	42 Southern Satellites	55.0	31006	56 Rural Bypasses	56.8	31314	46 Rooted Rural	42.9
30625	25 Salt of The Earth	81.8	31007	56 Rural Bypasses	100.0	31315	40 Military Proximity	98.9
30627	42 Southern Satellites	74.1	31008	26 Midland Crowd	68.6	31316	41 Crossroads	89.2
30628	26 Midland Crowd	98.9	31009	46 Rooted Rural	55.5	31319	56 Rural Bypasses	100.0
30629	42 Southern Satellites	86.5	31011	56 Rural Bypasses	97.7	31320	41 Crossroads	45.9
30630	50 Heartland Communities	34.2	31012	56 Rural Bypasses	90.6	31321	26 Midland Crowd	50.8
30631	56 Rural Bypasses	95.9	31014	42 Southern Satellites	34.9	31322	12 Up and Coming Families	35.6
30633	42 Southern Satellites	76.9	31015	42 Southern Satellites	18.4	31323	56 Rural Bypasses	100.0
30634	42 Southern Satellites	57.0	31016	46 Rooted Rural	54.4	31324	06 Sophisticated Squires	50.7
30635	42 Southern Satellites	35.0	31017	56 Rural Bypasses	75.7	31326	12 Up and Coming Families	58.6
30641	25 Salt of The Earth	67.9	31018	56 Rural Bypasses	100.0	31327	56 Rural Bypasses	100.0
30642	15 Silver and Gold	35.9	31019	42 Southern Satellites	60.6	31328	15 Silver and Gold	77.0
30643	31 Rural Resort Dwellers	28.3	31020	56 Rural Bypasses	43.0	31329	26 Midland Crowd	90.6
30646	26 Midland Crowd	61.8	31021	26 Midland Crowd	22.9	31331	56 Rural Bypasses	44.9
30648	42 Southern Satellites	63.4	31022	25 Salt of The Earth	78.1	31401	55 College Towns	28.2
30650	26 Midland Crowd	31.5	31023	42 Southern Satellites	27.7	31404	51 Metro City Edge	26.9
30655	53 Home Town	21.4	31024	31 Rural Resort Dwellers	51.2	31405	34 Family Foundations	14.7
30656	17 Green Acres	44.4	31025	42 Southern Satellites	86.8	31406	19 Milk and Cookies	11.3
30660	56 Rural Bypasses	42.8	31027	56 Rural Bypasses	63.3	31407	32 Rustbelt Traditions	45.5
30662	42 Southern Satellites	49.2	31028	26 Midland Crowd	37.8	31408	29 Rustbelt Retirees	21.8
30663	26 Midland Crowd	59.0	31029	26 Midland Crowd	58.5	31409	40 Military Proximity	100.0
30666	26 Midland Crowd	54.2	31030	56 Rural Bypasses	26.8	31410	13 In Style	19.1
30667	46 Rooted Rural	100.0	31031	56 Rural Bypasses	46.0	31411	15 Silver and Gold	100.0
30668	56 Rural Bypasses	79.7	31032	26 Midland Crowd	51.1	31415	62 Modest Income Homes	56.0
30669	56 Rural Bypasses	95.5	31033	26 Midland Crowd	64.7	31419	16 Enterprising Professionals	20.1
30673	50 Heartland Communities	25.8	31035	56 Rural Bypasses	100.0	31501	50 Heartland Communities	25.1
30677	06 Sophisticated Squires	40.5	31036	42 Southern Satellites	26.8	31503	42 Southern Satellites	35.7
30678	31 Rural Resort Dwellers	73.9	31037	56 Rural Bypasses	88.9	31510	42 Southern Satellites	42.4
30680	26 Midland Crowd	37.9	31038	42 Southern Satellites	59.1	31512	42 Southern Satellites	80.2
30683	26 Midland Crowd	86.3	31041	56 Rural Bypasses	100.0	31513	42 Southern Satellites	55.1
30701	42 Southern Satellites	42.6	31042	56 Rural Bypasses	93.1	31516	42 Southern Satellites	34.7
30705	42 Southern Satellites	58.5	31044	56 Rural Bypasses	99.6	31518	46 Rooted Rural	70.3
30707	42 Southern Satellites	63.5	31045	56 Rural Bypasses	100.0	31519	42 Southern Satellites	75.6
30708	42 Southern Satellites	100.0	31046	26 Midland Crowd	57.6	31520	62 Modest Income Homes	22.7
30710	42 Southern Satellites	53.4	31047	17 Green Acres	44.9	31522	07 Exurbanites	36.7
30711	42 Southern Satellites	100.0	31049	56 Rural Bypasses	85.0	31523	26 Midland Crowd	67.2
30720	17 Green Acres	13.6	31050	26 Midland Crowd	61.4	31525	26 Midland Crowd	35.6
30721	42 Southern Satellites	38.4	31052	17 Green Acres	35.3	31527	15 Silver and Gold	100.0
30725	25 Salt of The Earth	47.3	31054	46 Rooted Rural	86.7	31532	42 Southern Satellites	82.8
30728	42 Southern Satellites	51.5	31055	56 Rural Bypasses	64.2	31533	42 Southern Satellites	50.0
30730	42 Southern Satellites	100.0	31057	56 Rural Bypasses	100.0	31535	41 Crossroads	48.9
30731	42 Southern Satellites	80.9	31058	41 Crossroads	40.4	31537	56 Rural Bypasses	65.9
30733	42 Southern Satellites	62.7	31060	56 Rural Bypasses	54.7	31539	42 Southern Satellites	45.2
30734	42 Southern Satellites	100.0	31061	26 Midland Crowd	19.8	31542	46 Rooted Rural	70.8
30735	42 Southern Satellites	77.4	31063	56 Rural Bypasses	44.2	31543	42 Southern Satellites	87.5
30736	26 Midland Crowd	33.2	31064	25 Salt of The Earth	47.6	31544	56 Rural Bypasses	100.0
30738	42 Southern Satellites	38.7	31065	56 Rural Bypasses	48.2	31545	41 Crossroads	33.0
30739	42 Southern Satellites	43.3	31066	46 Rooted Rural	57.2	31546	42 Southern Satellites	20.0
30740	42 Southern Satellites	28.1	31068	56 Rural Bypasses	79.6	31547	40 Military Proximity	100.0
30741	50 Heartland Communities	24.4	31069	26 Midland Crowd	22.4	31548	26 Midland Crowd	40.3
30742	33 Midlife Junction	33.2	31070	56 Rural Bypasses	89.0	31549	56 Rural Bypasses	100.0
30746	42 Southern Satellites	100.0	31071	56 Rural Bypasses	90.0	31550	46 Rooted Rural	91.0
30747	42 Southern Satellites	63.2	31072	46 Rooted Rural	51.3	31551	42 Southern Satellites	100.0
30750	26 Midland Crowd	53.7	31075	42 Southern Satellites	100.0	31552	42 Southern Satellites	98.4

ZIP CODE	TOP TAPESTRY CONSUMER TYPE	% 2004 HOUSE-HOLDS	ZIP CODE	TOP TAPESTRY CONSUMER TYPE	% 2004 HOUSE-HOLDS	ZIP CODE	TOP TAPESTRY CONSUMER TYPE	% 2004 HOUSE-HOLDS
31553	41 Crossroads	44.4	31801	56 Rural Bypasses	53.2	32136	49 Senior Sun Seekers	41.2
31554	42 Southern Satellites	68.2	31803	56 Rural Bypasses	47.0	32137	15 Silver and Gold	39.3
31555	26 Midland Crowd	55.5	31804	17 Green Acres	94.4	32139	49 Senior Sun Seekers	79.4
31557	42 Southern Satellites	52.9	31805	41 Crossroads	88.7	32140	42 Southern Satellites	86.8
31558	12 Up and Coming Families	53.9	31806	42 Southern Satellites	99.9	32141	49 Senior Sun Seekers	44.0
31560	56 Rural Bypasses	51.8	31807	17 Green Acres	93.2	32145	41 Crossroads	60.5
31561	15 Silver and Gold	100.0	31808	06 Sophisticated Squires	76.1	32148	46 Rooted Rural	40.6
31562	42 Southern Satellites	100.0	31811	50 Heartland Communities	34.5	32159	43 The Elders	70.1
31563	56 Rural Bypasses	51.0	31812	56 Rural Bypasses	100.0	32162	49 Senior Sun Seekers	76.6
31565	46 Rooted Rural	100.0	31815	50 Heartland Communities	50.1	32164	49 Senior Sun Seekers	46.0
31566	41 Crossroads	99.5	31816	50 Heartland Communities	29.3	32168	57 Simple Living	20.1
31567	42 Southern Satellites	99.7	31820	07 Exurbanites	43.6	32169	15 Silver and Gold	82.5
31568	56 Rural Bypasses	84.7	31821	56 Rural Bypasses	100.0	32174	49 Senior Sun Seekers	21.6
31569	26 Midland Crowd	70.6	31822	31 Rural Resort Dwellers	36.1	32176	15 Silver and Gold	34.8
31601	62 Modest Income Homes	24.9	31823	25 Salt of The Earth	100.0	32177	57 Simple Living	23.4
31602	28 Aspiring Young Families	22.2	31824	56 Rural Bypasses	100.0	32179	49 Senior Sun Seekers	60.3
31605	12 Up and Coming Families	23.0	31825	56 Rural Bypasses	100.0	32180	46 Rooted Rural	100.0
31606	26 Midland Crowd	45.0	31826	42 Southern Satellites	78.7	32181	49 Senior Sun Seekers	97.9
31620	42 Southern Satellites	37.8	31827	56 Rural Bypasses	100.0	32187	49 Senior Sun Seekers	74.9
31622	56 Rural Bypasses	61.7	31829	07 Exurbanites	100.0	32189	49 Senior Sun Seekers	83.1
31624	42 Southern Satellites	99.6	31830	56 Rural Bypasses	61.5	32190	46 Rooted Rural	99.0
31625	46 Rooted Rural	87.0	31831	56 Rural Bypasses	54.4	32195	26 Midland Crowd	50.6
31626	56 Rural Bypasses	82.6	31832	56 Rural Bypasses	100.0	32202	65 Social Security Set	84.3
31629	56 Rural Bypasses	100.0	31833	42 Southern Satellites	33.7	32204	65 Social Security Set	23.2
31630	42 Southern Satellites	85.9	31836	56 Rural Bypasses	100.0	32205	48 Great Expectations	19.8
31631	56 Rural Bypasses	100.0	31901	64 City Commons	28.6	32206	62 Modest Income Homes	50.0
31632	26 Midland Crowd	46.6	31903	62 Modest Income Homes	29.8	32207	32 Rustbelt Traditions	18.6
31634	56 Rural Bypasses	75.8	31904	29 Rustbelt Retirees	14.4	32208	34 Family Foundations	50.9
31635	46 Rooted Rural	27.1	31905	40 Military Proximity	98.9	32209	62 Modest Income Homes	69.8
31636	33 Midlife Junction	34.1	31906	62 Modest Income Homes	24.9	32210	32 Rustbelt Traditions	15.5
31637	56 Rural Bypasses	54.1	31907	32 Rustbelt Traditions	26.6	32211	32 Rustbelt Traditions	26.1
31638	56 Rural Bypasses	83.2	31909	19 Milk and Cookies	22.1	32212	40 Military Proximity	100.0
31639	42 Southern Satellites	31.6	32003	06 Sophisticated Squires	100.0	32215	40 Military Proximity	85.7
31641	42 Southern Satellites	76.7	32008	46 Rooted Rural	100.0	32216	52 Inner City Tenants	32.3
31642	41 Crossroads	41.2	32009	26 Midland Crowd	100.0	32217	13 In Style	32.6
31643	56 Rural Bypasses	48.5	32011	26 Midland Crowd	63.8	32218	19 Milk and Cookies	28.4
31645	41 Crossroads	84.5	32013	46 Rooted Rural	75.3	32219	34 Family Foundations	33.0
31647	41 Crossroads	32.7	32024	26 Midland Crowd	40.9	32220	41 Crossroads	44.5
31648	41 Crossroads	100.0	32025	33 Midlife Junction	37.1	32221	19 Milk and Cookies	29.0
31649	42 Southern Satellites	54.7	32033	29 Rustbelt Retirees	57.8	32222	41 Crossroads	41.4
31650	41 Crossroads	57.0	32034	26 Midland Crowd	19.6	32223	28 Aspiring Young Families	34.1
31699	41 Crossroads	100.0	32038	46 Rooted Rural	71.4	32224	16 Enterprising Professionals	45.8
31701	62 Modest Income Homes	42.1	32040	41 Crossroads	59.1	32225	12 Up and Coming Families	53.3
31704	40 Military Proximity	100.0	32043	26 Midland Crowd	24.1	32226	17 Green Acres	44.5
31705	64 City Commons	18.4	32044	41 Crossroads	75.3	32227	40 Military Proximity	100.0
31707	14 Prosperous Empty Nesters	22.3	32046	42 Southern Satellites	50.8	32233	28 Aspiring Young Families	41.7
31709	48 Great Expectations	22.0	32052	56 Rural Bypasses	59.3	32234	26 Midland Crowd	58.4
31711	46 Rooted Rural	86.1	32053	42 Southern Satellites	47.5	32244	19 Milk and Cookies	44.6
31712	56 Rural Bypasses	74.1	32054	41 Crossroads	48.0	32246	28 Aspiring Young Families	34.3
31714	46 Rooted Rural	35.5	32055	41 Crossroads	35.1	32250	13 In Style	33.5
31716	56 Rural Bypasses	52.8	32058	42 Southern Satellites	48.1	32254	51 Metro City Edge	39.1
31719	51 Metro City Edge	29.3	32059	46 Rooted Rural	100.0	32256	39 Young and Restless	52.3
31721	07 Exurbanites	29.2	32060	46 Rooted Rural	64.3	32257	28 Aspiring Young Families	39.1
31730	56 Rural Bypasses	36.1	32061	41 Crossroads	100.0	32258	04 Boomburbs	39.7
31733	17 Green Acres	54.4	32062	46 Rooted Rural	100.0	32259	04 Boomburbs	56.2
31735	31 Rural Resort Dwellers	100.0	32063	26 Midland Crowd	48.1	32266	13 In Style	58.3
31738	56 Rural Bypasses	57.5	32064	50 Heartland Communities	28.0	32277	28 Aspiring Young Families	49.5
31743	56 Rural Bypasses	43.7	32065	19 Milk and Cookies	60.7	32301	55 College Towns	34.6
31744	42 Southern Satellites	51.7	32066	46 Rooted Rural	84.0	32303	55 College Towns	26.1
31749	41 Crossroads	50.6	32068	26 Midland Crowd	35.4	32304	63 Dorms To Diplomas	66.8
31750	56 Rural Bypasses	25.7	32071	46 Rooted Rural	100.0	32305	41 Crossroads	37.8
31756	42 Southern Satellites	100.0	32073	28 Aspiring Young Families	19.2	32306	63 Dorms To Diplomas	0.0
31757	26 Midland Crowd	56.3	32080	15 Silver and Gold	43.8	32307	63 Dorms To Diplomas	0.0
31760	42 Southern Satellites	100.0	32082	13 In Style	30.5	32308	36 Old and Newcomers	21.4
31763	26 Midland Crowd	47.7	32083	19 Milk and Cookies	78.8	32309	07 Exurbanites	38.0
31764	42 Southern Satellites	45.3	32084	41 Crossroads	23.3	32310	41 Crossroads	30.1
31765	56 Rural Bypasses	58.7	32086	33 Midlife Junction	32.0	32311	26 Midland Crowd	46.8
31768	42 Southern Satellites	25.9	32087	41 Crossroads	83.5	32312	04 Boomburbs	34.0
31771	42 Southern Satellites	96.3	32091	46 Rooted Rural	26.9	32317	06 Sophisticated Squires	77.0
31772	42 Southern Satellites	96.0	32092	26 Midland Crowd	56.8	32320	46 Rooted Rural	37.1
31773	26 Midland Crowd	59.3	32094	46 Rooted Rural	100.0	32321	56 Rural Bypasses	39.8
31774	46 Rooted Rural	30.0	32095	26 Midland Crowd	70.9	32322	46 Rooted Rural	71.7
31775	56 Rural Bypasses	61.9	32096	56 Rural Bypasses	66.5	32324	50 Heartland Communities	48.8
31778	42 Southern Satellites	43.2	32097	26 Midland Crowd	88.2	32327	26 Midland Crowd	88.6
31779	46 Rooted Rural	29.7	32102	49 Senior Sun Seekers	68.5	32328	46 Rooted Rural	69.0
31780	56 Rural Bypasses	44.1	32110	26 Midland Crowd	50.4	32331	46 Rooted Rural	66.1
31781	42 Southern Satellites	91.1	32112	49 Senior Sun Seekers	52.1	32332	56 Rural Bypasses	100.0
31783	42 Southern Satellites	96.4	32113	46 Rooted Rural	46.4	32333	56 Rural Bypasses	23.5
31784	37 Prairie Living	55.0	32114	55 College Towns	21.0	32334	56 Rural Bypasses	52.8
31787	42 Southern Satellites	100.0	32117	32 Rustbelt Traditions	27.6	32336	42 Southern Satellites	47.9
31788	42 Southern Satellites	37.3	32118	36 Old and Newcomers	21.2	32340	46 Rooted Rural	35.3
31789	42 Southern Satellites	83.6	32119	36 Old and Newcomers	25.3	32343	51 Metro City Edge	83.6
31790	25 Salt of The Earth	44.4	32124	25 Salt of The Earth	94.0	32344	46 Rooted Rural	48.3
31791	26 Midland Crowd	22.6	32127	33 Midlife Junction	23.8	32346	46 Rooted Rural	82.2
31792	62 Modest Income Homes	20.6	32128	15 Silver and Gold	91.0	32347	46 Rooted Rural	41.1
31793	26 Midland Crowd	51.6	32129	49 Senior Sun Seekers	37.3	32348	46 Rooted Rural	28.6
31794	26 Midland Crowd	14.0	32130	25 Salt of The Earth	40.6	32350	46 Rooted Rural	100.0
31795	42 Southern Satellites	70.6	32131	46 Rooted Rural	36.1	32351	56 Rural Bypasses	27.6
31796	46 Rooted Rural	76.8	32132	29 Rustbelt Retirees	42.2	32352	56 Rural Bypasses	51.9
31798	46 Rooted Rural	80.3	32134	49 Senior Sun Seekers	59.6	32355	49 Senior Sun Seekers	100.0

ZIP CODE	TOP TAPESTRY CONSUMER TYPE	% 2004 HOUSE-HOLDS	ZIP CODE	TOP TAPESTRY CONSUMER TYPE	% 2004 HOUSE-HOLDS	ZIP CODE	TOP TAPESTRY CONSUMER TYPE	% 2004 HOUSE-HOLDS
32356	46 Rooted Rural	60.5	32619	46 Rooted Rural	64.0	32835	39 Young and Restless	40.1
32358	46 Rooted Rural	61.3	32621	41 Crossroads	57.8	32836	09 Urban Chic	40.1
32359	49 Senior Sun Seekers	80.2	32622	46 Rooted Rural	76.6	32837	12 Up and Coming Families	40.7
32401	62 Modest Income Homes	20.6	32625	31 Rural Resort Dwellers	100.0	32839	52 Inner City Tenants	45.3
32403	40 Military Proximity	77.0	32626	49 Senior Sun Seekers	42.4	32901	29 Rustbelt Retirees	19.0
32404	19 Milk and Cookies	16.6	32628	56 Rural Bypasses	55.9	32903	14 Prosperous Empty Nesters	55.6
32405	14 Prosperous Empty Nesters	14.3	32631	31 Rural Resort Dwellers	65.6	32904	33 Midlife Junction	25.6
32407	31 Rural Resort Dwellers	61.4	32640	46 Rooted Rural	36.5	32905	29 Rustbelt Retirees	22.3
32408	33 Midlife Junction	85.2	32641	51 Metro City Edge	48.9	32907	19 Milk and Cookies	39.0
32409	26 Midland Crowd	67.0	32643	26 Midland Crowd	42.9	32908	32 Rustbelt Traditions	58.9
32413	31 Rural Resort Dwellers	77.6	32648	46 Rooted Rural	100.0	32909	26 Midland Crowd	49.5
32420	46 Rooted Rural	61.7	32653	33 Midlife Junction	46.6	32920	33 Midlife Junction	34.2
32421	46 Rooted Rural	76.3	32656	31 Rural Resort Dwellers	38.9	32922	53 Home Town	13.9
32423	46 Rooted Rural	59.6	32666	46 Rooted Rural	47.8	32925	40 Military Proximity	95.5
32424	56 Rural Bypasses	54.0	32667	14 Prosperous Empty Nesters	28.9	32926	18 Cozy and Comfortable	13.4
32425	46 Rooted Rural	41.0	32668	46 Rooted Rural	48.5	32927	19 Milk and Cookies	72.1
32426	56 Rural Bypasses	95.9	32669	26 Midland Crowd	63.6	32931	30 Retirement Communities	24.7
32427	46 Rooted Rural	61.8	32680	49 Senior Sun Seekers	54.2	32934	13 In Style	21.6
32428	46 Rooted Rural	43.0	32686	46 Rooted Rural	67.8	32935	32 Rustbelt Traditions	22.7
32430	46 Rooted Rural	100.0	32693	46 Rooted Rural	39.3	32937	14 Prosperous Empty Nesters	45.2
32431	46 Rooted Rural	73.3	32694	46 Rooted Rural	35.6	32940	15 Silver and Gold	46.8
32433	46 Rooted Rural	36.2	32696	46 Rooted Rural	42.6	32948	41 Crossroads	61.8
32435	46 Rooted Rural	54.4	32701	36 Old and Newcomers	60.3	32949	43 The Elders	86.7
32437	46 Rooted Rural	100.0	32702	46 Rooted Rural	87.9	32950	17 Green Acres	100.0
32438	41 Crossroads	69.6	32703	12 Up and Coming Families	17.8	32951	15 Silver and Gold	83.1
32439	26 Midland Crowd	49.5	32707	13 In Style	26.0	32952	14 Prosperous Empty Nesters	25.7
32440	46 Rooted Rural	55.8	32708	06 Sophisticated Squires	31.0	32953	33 Midlife Junction	30.5
32442	46 Rooted Rural	90.7	32709	26 Midland Crowd	97.6	32955	18 Cozy and Comfortable	35.1
32443	56 Rural Bypasses	63.0	32712	06 Sophisticated Squires	22.7	32958	49 Senior Sun Seekers	47.4
32444	07 Exurbanites	26.5	32713	29 Rustbelt Retirees	26.1	32960	49 Senior Sun Seekers	23.5
32445	56 Rural Bypasses	51.8	32714	28 Aspiring Young Families	42.2	32962	43 The Elders	21.5
32446	33 Midlife Junction	29.9	32720	31 Rural Resort Dwellers	17.9	32963	15 Silver and Gold	88.5
32448	46 Rooted Rural	42.6	32724	49 Senior Sun Seekers	27.7	32966	43 The Elders	58.3
32449	46 Rooted Rural	100.0	32725	29 Rustbelt Retirees	42.3	32967	62 Modest Income Homes	28.4
32455	46 Rooted Rural	99.6	32726	33 Midlife Junction	16.8	32968	17 Green Acres	79.6
32456	31 Rural Resort Dwellers	35.3	32730	24 Main Street, USA	44.4	32976	43 The Elders	62.8
32459	31 Rural Resort Dwellers	53.1	32732	26 Midland Crowd	63.1	33004	30 Retirement Communities	39.2
32460	46 Rooted Rural	53.0	32735	49 Senior Sun Seekers	100.0	33009	30 Retirement Communities	38.0
32462	46 Rooted Rural	80.9	32736	26 Midland Crowd	43.7	33010	58 Newest Residents	43.8
32464	46 Rooted Rural	53.7	32738	19 Milk and Cookies	60.8	33012	59 Southwestern Families	33.5
32465	46 Rooted Rural	34.6	32744	32 Rustbelt Traditions	45.0	33013	59 Southwestern Families	44.0
32466	26 Midland Crowd	69.2	32746	16 Enterprising Professionals	30.5	33014	59 Southwestern Families	21.7
32501	62 Modest Income Homes	25.0	32750	06 Sophisticated Squires	27.7	33015	52 Inner City Tenants	30.2
32502	57 Simple Living	55.1	32751	36 Old and Newcomers	18.4	33016	38 Industrious Urban Fringe	61.8
32503	33 Midlife Junction	21.5	32754	29 Rustbelt Retirees	35.2	33018	21 Urban Villages	47.0
32504	14 Prosperous Empty Nesters	36.2	32757	33 Midlife Junction	22.2	33019	30 Retirement Communities	58.5
32505	51 Metro City Edge	24.6	32759	46 Rooted Rural	52.0	33020	48 Great Expectations	26.5
32506	12 Up and Coming Families	23.2	32763	43 The Elders	25.8	33021	14 Prosperous Empty Nesters	19.8
32507	17 Green Acres	16.9	32764	25 Salt of the Earth	46.7	33023	38 Industrious Urban Fringe	30.7
32508	40 Military Proximity	100.0	32765	12 Up and Coming Families	49.4	33024	38 Industrious Urban Fringe	23.4
32514	36 Old and Newcomers	32.7	32766	12 Up and Coming Families	54.8	33025	16 Enterprising Professionals	26.8
32526	26 Midland Crowd	38.1	32767	26 Midland Crowd	42.4	33026	30 Retirement Communities	31.8
32531	46 Rooted Rural	47.3	32771	07 Exurbanites	20.1	33027	43 The Elders	55.5
32533	26 Midland Crowd	33.3	32773	28 Aspiring Young Families	24.0	33028	04 Boomburbs	100.0
32534	50 Heartland Communities	41.3	32776	26 Midland Crowd	91.3	33029	04 Boomburbs	81.8
32535	56 Rural Bypasses	52.1	32778	49 Senior Sun Seekers	58.4	33030	58 Newest Residents	48.9
32536	12 Up and Coming Families	32.5	32779	07 Exurbanites	47.7	33031	07 Exurbanites	60.5
32539	26 Midland Crowd	34.4	32780	30 Retirement Communities	28.2	33032	38 Industrious Urban Fringe	45.8
32541	14 Prosperous Empty Nesters	63.5	32784	46 Rooted Rural	49.5	33033	58 Newest Residents	37.1
32542	40 Military Proximity	100.0	32789	30 Retirement Communities	16.9	33034	38 Industrious Urban Fringe	25.2
32544	40 Military Proximity	100.0	32792	36 Old and Newcomers	32.4	33035	28 Aspiring Young Families	62.1
32547	28 Aspiring Young Families	23.2	32796	29 Rustbelt Retirees	34.1	33036	15 Silver and Gold	46.5
32548	29 Rustbelt Retirees	20.7	32798	43 The Elders	90.6	33037	31 Rural Resort Dwellers	36.8
32550	15 Silver and Gold	100.0	32801	23 Trendsetters	29.3	33039	38 Industrious Urban Fringe	64.3
32561	14 Prosperous Empty Nesters	35.3	32803	22 Metropolitans	42.3	33040	23 Trendsetters	20.0
32563	07 Exurbanites	52.9	32804	22 Metropolitans	59.2	33042	31 Rural Resort Dwellers	74.6
32564	46 Rooted Rural	76.8	32805	62 Modest Income Homes	25.1	33043	31 Rural Resort Dwellers	79.3
32565	46 Rooted Rural	86.1	32806	33 Midlife Junction	22.2	33050	31 Rural Resort Dwellers	43.4
32566	26 Midland Crowd	64.2	32807	48 Great Expectations	23.5	33054	34 Family Foundations	31.2
32567	46 Rooted Rural	100.0	32808	28 Aspiring Young Families	26.6	33055	38 Industrious Urban Fringe	66.5
32568	46 Rooted Rural	100.0	32809	38 Industrious Urban Fringe	31.9	33056	34 Family Foundations	50.3
32569	19 Milk and Cookies	66.0	32810	19 Milk and Cookies	24.4	33060	24 Main Street, USA	14.6
32570	18 Cozy and Comfortable	20.4	32811	52 Inner City Tenants	40.4	33062	30 Retirement Communities	41.4
32571	26 Midland Crowd	30.4	32812	52 Inner City Tenants	16.9	33063	36 Old and Newcomers	28.1
32577	17 Green Acres	60.3	32817	28 Aspiring Young Families	31.8	33064	32 Rustbelt Traditions	16.4
32578	07 Exurbanites	38.4	32818	19 Milk and Cookies	32.3	33065	28 Aspiring Young Families	35.8
32579	14 Prosperous Empty Nesters	58.3	32819	02 Suburban Splendor	33.4	33066	43 The Elders	65.7
32580	14 Prosperous Empty Nesters	40.4	32820	41 Crossroads	82.8	33067	04 Boomburbs	51.8
32583	26 Midland Crowd	44.9	32821	22 Metropolitans	42.7	33068	19 Milk and Cookies	34.5
32601	63 Dorms To Diplomas	51.7	32822	39 Young and Restless	23.1	33069	30 Retirement Communities	50.3
32603	63 Dorms To Diplomas	68.5	32824	19 Milk and Cookies	70.2	33070	31 Rural Resort Dwellers	78.6
32605	14 Prosperous Empty Nesters	43.3	32825	28 Aspiring Young Families	39.5	33071	06 Sophisticated Squires	35.9
32606	13 In Style	47.9	32826	28 Aspiring Young Families	39.0	33073	13 In Style	54.9
32607	63 Dorms To Diplomas	49.5	32827	28 Aspiring Young Families	80.8	33076	04 Boomburbs	81.7
32608	63 Dorms To Diplomas	54.7	32828	12 Up and Coming Families	100.0	33109	65 Social Security Set	100.0
32609	51 Metro City Edge	17.1	32829	12 Up and Coming Families	43.0	33125	58 Newest Residents	35.4
32611	63 Dorms To Diplomas	100.0	32830	39 Young and Restless	92.3	33126	57 Simple Living	16.9
32615	26 Midland Crowd	58.9	32831	12 Up and Coming Families	100.0	33127	64 City Commons	22.8
32617	26 Midland Crowd	51.5	32832	07 Exurbanites	100.0	33128	58 Newest Residents	76.1
32618	26 Midland Crowd	32.7	32833	26 Midland Crowd	70.1	33129	08 Laptops and Lattes	55.5

ZIP CODE	TOP TAPESTRY CONSUMER TYPE	% 2004 HOUSE-HOLDS	ZIP CODE	TOP TAPESTRY CONSUMER TYPE	% 2004 HOUSE-HOLDS	ZIP CODE	TOP TAPESTRY CONSUMER TYPE	% 2004 HOUSE-HOLDS
33130	58 Newest Residents	61.4	33410	13 In Style	15.3	33612	52 Inner City Tenants	38.8
33131	27 Metro Renters	92.7	33411	19 Milk and Cookies	28.3	33613	52 Inner City Tenants	30.4
33132	27 Metro Renters	54.9	33412	12 Up and Coming Families	97.0	33614	52 Inner City Tenants	21.5
33133	27 Metro Renters	13.8	33413	22 Metropolitans	62.9	33615	28 Aspiring Young Families	15.3
33134	36 Old and Newcomers	24.0	33414	06 Sophisticated Squires	34.8	33616	32 Rustbelt Traditions	23.7
33135	58 Newest Residents	43.9	33415	28 Aspiring Young Families	27.5	33617	52 Inner City Tenants	28.1
33136	64 City Commons	43.8	33417	43 The Elders	44.3	33618	13 In Style	37.2
33137	58 Newest Residents	26.2	33418	15 Silver and Gold	61.3	33619	38 Industrious Urban Fringe	34.9
33138	60 City Dimensions	15.0	33426	43 The Elders	35.6	33621	40 Military Proximity	100.0
33139	27 Metro Renters	51.4	33428	30 Retirement Communities	21.1	33624	28 Aspiring Young Families	22.6
33140	30 Retirement Communities	58.1	33430	51 Metro City Edge	26.0	33625	19 Milk and Cookies	53.4
33141	36 Old and Newcomers	25.3	33431	15 Silver and Gold	20.1	33626	04 Boomburbs	67.1
33142	62 Modest Income Homes	30.1	33432	30 Retirement Communities	32.9	33629	22 Metropolitans	25.8
33143	36 Old and Newcomers	28.9	33433	15 Silver and Gold	23.5	33634	38 Industrious Urban Fringe	35.0
33144	29 Rustbelt Retirees	24.9	33434	43 The Elders	42.5	33635	12 Up and Coming Families	47.5
33145	35 International Marketplace	25.1	33435	51 Metro City Edge	23.4	33637	39 Young and Restless	54.9
33146	03 Connoisseurs	55.6	33436	43 The Elders	24.9	33647	16 Enterprising Professionals	44.6
33147	59 Southwestern Families	22.2	33437	43 The Elders	43.6	33701	36 Old and Newcomers	29.3
33149	09 Urban Chic	70.7	33438	60 City Dimensions	95.6	33702	30 Retirement Communities	17.3
33150	51 Metro City Edge	20.9	33440	41 Crossroads	35.2	33703	32 Rustbelt Traditions	30.2
33154	30 Retirement Communities	58.0	33441	39 Young and Restless	20.4	33704	22 Metropolitans	39.7
33155	10 Pleasant-Ville	18.5	33442	43 The Elders	34.8	33705	62 Modest Income Homes	19.5
33156	01 Top Rung	32.9	33444	07 Exurbanites	14.6	33706	15 Silver and Gold	65.6
33157	19 Milk and Cookies	21.2	33445	43 The Elders	18.9	33707	43 The Elders	31.2
33158	05 Wealthy Seaboard Suburbs	49.9	33446	43 The Elders	62.1	33708	15 Silver and Gold	29.4
33160	30 Retirement Communities	65.9	33455	49 Senior Sun Seekers	47.6	33709	49 Senior Sun Seekers	27.0
33161	51 Metro City Edge	27.5	33458	33 Midlife Junction	19.5	33710	29 Rustbelt Retirees	36.4
33162	38 Industrious Urban Fringe	27.0	33460	60 City Dimensions	32.2	33711	51 Metro City Edge	36.5
33165	21 Urban Villages	29.5	33461	48 Great Expectations	25.5	33712	62 Modest Income Homes	27.5
33166	24 Main Street, USA	26.6	33462	30 Retirement Communities	18.0	33713	32 Rustbelt Traditions	35.5
33167	51 Metro City Edge	37.4	33463	19 Milk and Cookies	22.4	33714	32 Rustbelt Traditions	22.2
33168	34 Family Foundations	44.4	33467	07 Exurbanites	34.4	33715	15 Silver and Gold	89.2
33169	34 Family Foundations	43.3	33469	15 Silver and Gold	56.3	33716	39 Young and Restless	53.4
33170	64 City Commons	28.7	33470	12 Up and Coming Families	77.7	33755	32 Rustbelt Traditions	20.0
33172	38 Industrious Urban Fringe	33.2	33471	49 Senior Sun Seekers	28.2	33756	29 Rustbelt Retirees	21.6
33173	36 Old and Newcomers	31.8	33476	51 Metro City Edge	67.0	33759	52 Inner City Tenants	32.3
33174	33 Midlife Junction	34.0	33477	15 Silver and Gold	84.5	33760	33 Midlife Junction	31.0
33175	21 Urban Villages	28.3	33478	06 Sophisticated Squires	83.4	33761	49 Senior Sun Seekers	31.6
33176	02 Suburban Splendor	14.7	33480	43 The Elders	47.0	33762	16 Enterprising Professionals	66.9
33177	12 Up and Coming Families	47.6	33483	15 Silver and Gold	45.8	33763	43 The Elders	54.8
33178	04 Boomburbs	40.1	33484	43 The Elders	80.0	33764	49 Senior Sun Seekers	47.7
33179	65 Social Security Set	23.5	33486	07 Exurbanites	23.8	33765	36 Old and Newcomers	31.8
33180	15 Silver and Gold	35.2	33487	15 Silver and Gold	65.7	33767	15 Silver and Gold	89.8
33181	36 Old and Newcomers	28.0	33493	51 Metro City Edge	83.2	33770	33 Midlife Junction	23.3
33182	12 Up and Coming Families	91.7	33496	15 Silver and Gold	27.3	33771	49 Senior Sun Seekers	77.2
33183	19 Milk and Cookies	32.8	33498	07 Exurbanites	70.2	33772	14 Prosperous Empty Nesters	19.0
33184	38 Industrious Urban Fringe	32.8	33510	18 Cozy and Comfortable	28.8	33773	49 Senior Sun Seekers	45.0
33185	06 Sophisticated Squires	68.9	33511	12 Up and Coming Families	27.3	33774	30 Retirement Communities	34.3
33186	06 Sophisticated Squires	27.0	33513	49 Senior Sun Seekers	58.5	33776	30 Retirement Communities	42.4
33187	12 Up and Coming Families	45.9	33514	56 Rural Bypasses	78.5	33777	33 Midlife Junction	38.0
33189	19 Milk and Cookies	24.4	33523	49 Senior Sun Seekers	28.8	33778	49 Senior Sun Seekers	54.7
33190	12 Up and Coming Families	53.3	33525	26 Midland Crowd	24.5	33781	32 Rustbelt Traditions	37.4
33193	58 Newest Residents	39.6	33527	26 Midland Crowd	36.4	33782	32 Rustbelt Traditions	34.1
33196	12 Up and Coming Families	48.7	33534	41 Crossroads	82.0	33785	13 In Style	51.3
33199	63 Dorms To Diplomas	100.0	33538	49 Senior Sun Seekers	92.8	33786	15 Silver and Gold	100.0
33301	08 Laptops and Lattes	33.0	33540	49 Senior Sun Seekers	46.1	33801	53 Home Town	22.6
33304	30 Retirement Communities	18.9	33541	49 Senior Sun Seekers	97.0	33803	33 Midlife Junction	26.0
33305	36 Old and Newcomers	35.5	33542	49 Senior Sun Seekers	55.8	33805	51 Metro City Edge	33.4
33306	09 Urban Chic	38.4	33543	12 Up and Coming Families	71.0	33809	33 Midlife Junction	56.7
33308	30 Retirement Communities	38.9	33544	12 Up and Coming Families	44.6	33810	26 Midland Crowd	37.1
33309	36 Old and Newcomers	47.2	33547	26 Midland Crowd	38.1	33811	28 Aspiring Young Families	29.1
33311	34 Family Foundations	25.8	33548	07 Exurbanites	89.4	33813	07 Exurbanites	28.6
33312	52 Inner City Tenants	14.5	33549	17 Green Acres	30.8	33815	49 Senior Sun Seekers	54.5
33313	51 Metro City Edge	26.0	33556	04 Boomburbs	36.1	33823	49 Senior Sun Seekers	34.8
33314	48 Great Expectations	25.4	33558	16 Enterprising Professionals	53.4	33825	49 Senior Sun Seekers	39.2
33315	22 Metropolitans	29.6	33559	28 Aspiring Young Families	47.7	33827	46 Rooted Rural	50.8
33316	15 Silver and Gold	27.1	33563	32 Rustbelt Traditions	15.2	33830	41 Crossroads	19.5
33317	07 Exurbanites	27.0	33565	26 Midland Crowd	56.8	33834	49 Senior Sun Seekers	29.6
33319	57 Simple Living	23.2	33566	06 Sophisticated Squires	21.1	33837	31 Rural Resort Dwellers	58.8
33321	43 The Elders	21.8	33567	41 Crossroads	42.1	33838	50 Heartland Communities	80.4
33322	43 The Elders	38.3	33569	12 Up and Coming Families	21.4	33839	46 Rooted Rural	57.3
33323	19 Milk and Cookies	45.5	33570	49 Senior Sun Seekers	49.0	33841	56 Rural Bypasses	37.4
33324	16 Enterprising Professionals	22.6	33572	07 Exurbanites	60.8	33843	41 Crossroads	24.5
33325	41 Crossroads	41.5	33573	43 The Elders	100.0	33844	49 Senior Sun Seekers	28.8
33326	04 Boomburbs	48.6	33576	26 Midland Crowd	57.8	33849	49 Senior Sun Seekers	100.0
33327	04 Boomburbs	100.0	33584	41 Crossroads	16.5	33850	32 Rustbelt Traditions	45.5
33328	06 Sophisticated Squires	23.7	33585	46 Rooted Rural	83.5	33852	49 Senior Sun Seekers	61.0
33330	02 Suburban Splendor	46.8	33592	26 Midland Crowd	44.6	33853	33 Midlife Junction	42.6
33331	04 Boomburbs	59.1	33594	04 Boomburbs	23.3	33857	49 Senior Sun Seekers	100.0
33332	04 Boomburbs	68.7	33597	46 Rooted Rural	67.2	33859	49 Senior Sun Seekers	74.4
33334	52 Inner City Tenants	32.8	33598	59 Southwestern Families	33.3	33860	26 Midland Crowd	37.6
33351	28 Aspiring Young Families	33.2	33602	08 Laptops and Lattes	22.8	33865	46 Rooted Rural	94.4
33401	30 Retirement Communities	35.7	33603	48 Great Expectations	16.9	33868	49 Senior Sun Seekers	44.7
33403	41 Crossroads	24.5	33604	32 Rustbelt Traditions	33.2	33870	46 Rooted Rural	45.2
33404	51 Metro City Edge	22.0	33605	62 Modest Income Homes	44.9	33872	49 Senior Sun Seekers	41.1
33405	38 Industrious Urban Fringe	30.0	33606	27 Metro Renters	38.1	33873	46 Rooted Rural	26.8
33406	28 Aspiring Young Families	19.7	33607	64 City Commons	14.1	33875	49 Senior Sun Seekers	79.0
33407	51 Metro City Edge	23.8	33609	36 Old and Newcomers	16.9	33876	49 Senior Sun Seekers	96.8
33408	15 Silver and Gold	28.6	33610	62 Modest Income Homes	26.3	33880	48 Great Expectations	21.5
33409	39 Young and Restless	26.6	33611	36 Old and Newcomers	25.6	33881	53 Home Town	18.5

ZIP CODE	TOP TAPESTRY CONSUMER TYPE	% 2004 HOUSE-HOLDS	ZIP CODE	TOP TAPESTRY CONSUMER TYPE	% 2004 HOUSE-HOLDS	ZIP CODE	TOP TAPESTRY CONSUMER TYPE	% 2004 HOUSE-HOLDS
33884	49 Senior Sun Seekers	26.2	34237	48 Great Expectations	26.3	34753	38 Industrious Urban Fringe	85.7
33890	42 Southern Satellites	76.4	34238	15 Silver and Gold	71.3	34756	17 Green Acres	100.0
33896	31 Rural Resort Dwellers	46.8	34239	33 Midlife Junction	19.3	34758	38 Industrious Urban Fringe	61.4
33897	49 Senior Sun Seekers	100.0	34240	07 Exurbanites	69.0	34759	19 Milk and Cookies	36.2
33898	49 Senior Sun Seekers	37.6	34241	15 Silver and Gold	48.3	34761	19 Milk and Cookies	22.0
33901	52 Inner City Tenants	22.4	34242	15 Silver and Gold	72.7	34762	49 Senior Sun Seekers	64.5
33903	43 The Elders	46.3	34243	15 Silver and Gold	35.4	34769	32 Rustbelt Traditions	31.5
33904	15 Silver and Gold	27.7	34251	17 Green Acres	42.4	34771	26 Midland Crowd	72.7
33905	29 Rustbelt Retirees	12.8	34266	49 Senior Sun Seekers	28.9	34772	26 Midland Crowd	55.0
33907	39 Young and Restless	28.6	34269	49 Senior Sun Seekers	97.3	34773	41 Crossroads	75.0
33908	49 Senior Sun Seekers	33.4	34275	15 Silver and Gold	41.4	34785	49 Senior Sun Seekers	39.9
33909	19 Milk and Cookies	38.8	34285	43 The Elders	67.8	34786	02 Suburban Splendor	83.6
33912	15 Silver and Gold	17.8	34286	12 Up and Coming Families	46.6	34787	41 Crossroads	19.4
33913	07 Exurbanites	82.4	34287	29 Rustbelt Retirees	31.3	34788	49 Senior Sun Seekers	62.3
33914	15 Silver and Gold	22.7	34288	12 Up and Coming Families	95.4	34797	49 Senior Sun Seekers	100.0
33916	39 Young and Restless	26.3	34292	15 Silver and Gold	47.9	34945	49 Senior Sun Seekers	92.3
33917	43 The Elders	33.5	34293	43 The Elders	36.1	34946	34 Family Foundations	42.3
33919	43 The Elders	23.3	34420	49 Senior Sun Seekers	49.8	34947	34 Family Foundations	20.0
33920	31 Rural Resort Dwellers	34.1	34428	15 Silver and Gold	30.4	34949	30 Retirement Communities	49.4
33921	15 Silver and Gold	63.4	34429	49 Senior Sun Seekers	40.3	34950	62 Modest Income Homes	31.9
33922	49 Senior Sun Seekers	58.1	34431	49 Senior Sun Seekers	88.6	34951	49 Senior Sun Seekers	37.6
33924	15 Silver and Gold	100.0	34432	49 Senior Sun Seekers	45.1	34952	33 Midlife Junction	29.8
33928	15 Silver and Gold	45.2	34433	49 Senior Sun Seekers	76.1	34953	26 Midland Crowd	48.2
33931	43 The Elders	41.1	34434	49 Senior Sun Seekers	89.3	34956	49 Senior Sun Seekers	36.3
33935	59 Southwestern Families	21.3	34436	49 Senior Sun Seekers	98.5	34957	43 The Elders	33.1
33936	49 Senior Sun Seekers	31.9	34442	49 Senior Sun Seekers	58.7	34972	38 Industrious Urban Fringe	32.5
33946	15 Silver and Gold	70.5	34446	49 Senior Sun Seekers	53.3	34974	49 Senior Sun Seekers	64.1
33947	15 Silver and Gold	68.0	34448	49 Senior Sun Seekers	70.2	34982	25 Salt of The Earth	46.6
33948	29 Rustbelt Retirees	49.0	34449	49 Senior Sun Seekers	99.7	34982	49 Senior Sun Seekers	34.9
33950	15 Silver and Gold	53.8	34450	49 Senior Sun Seekers	93.5	34983	32 Rustbelt Traditions	34.7
33952	49 Senior Sun Seekers	42.6	34452	49 Senior Sun Seekers	83.5	34984	32 Rustbelt Traditions	29.4
33953	43 The Elders	52.9	34453	49 Senior Sun Seekers	83.2	34986	29 Rustbelt Retirees	99.9
33954	14 Prosperous Empty Nesters	47.1	34461	15 Silver and Gold	42.7	34987	17 Green Acres	55.6
33955	49 Senior Sun Seekers	74.1	34465	43 The Elders	39.2	34988	17 Green Acres	100.0
33956	43 The Elders	46.4	34470	49 Senior Sun Seekers	29.4	34990	15 Silver and Gold	50.4
33957	15 Silver and Gold	88.1	34471	33 Midlife Junction	51.8	34994	43 The Elders	27.9
33960	49 Senior Sun Seekers	97.6	34472	49 Senior Sun Seekers	33.3	34996	43 The Elders	33.9
33971	12 Up and Coming Families	33.2	34473	49 Senior Sun Seekers	72.5	34997	15 Silver and Gold	28.2
33972	49 Senior Sun Seekers	27.0	34474	49 Senior Sun Seekers	43.3	35004	24 Main Street, USA	38.5
33980	43 The Elders	72.5	34475	53 Home Town	28.0	35005	18 Cozy and Comfortable	36.4
33981	31 Rural Resort Dwellers	39.6	34476	49 Senior Sun Seekers	56.4	35006	42 Southern Satellites	95.6
33982	49 Senior Sun Seekers	54.3	34479	26 Midland Crowd	31.7	35007	12 Up and Coming Families	70.1
33983	14 Prosperous Empty Nesters	38.5	34480	17 Green Acres	26.3	35010	42 Southern Satellites	32.5
33990	33 Midlife Junction	43.3	34481	43 The Elders	83.7	35014	56 Rural Bypasses	65.6
33991	19 Milk and Cookies	49.3	34482	49 Senior Sun Seekers	40.8	35016	42 Southern Satellites	49.8
33993	19 Milk and Cookies	30.0	34484	46 Rooted Rural	58.6	35019	42 Southern Satellites	82.1
34102	15 Silver and Gold	47.5	34488	49 Senior Sun Seekers	85.1	35020	62 Modest Income Homes	33.9
34103	15 Silver and Gold	49.4	34491	49 Senior Sun Seekers	66.8	35022	29 Rustbelt Retirees	23.3
34104	15 Silver and Gold	30.4	34498	49 Senior Sun Seekers	100.0	35023	29 Rustbelt Retirees	21.7
34105	15 Silver and Gold	41.8	34601	49 Senior Sun Seekers	24.8	35031	42 Southern Satellites	81.4
34108	15 Silver and Gold	62.9	34602	41 Crossroads	38.9	35033	42 Southern Satellites	69.0
34109	15 Silver and Gold	50.3	34604	46 Rooted Rural	32.8	35034	56 Rural Bypasses	42.5
34110	15 Silver and Gold	83.8	34606	49 Senior Sun Seekers	46.2	35035	25 Salt of The Earth	76.1
34112	43 The Elders	27.6	34607	15 Silver and Gold	76.1	35036	42 Southern Satellites	100.0
34113	43 The Elders	34.8	34608	49 Senior Sun Seekers	85.7	35040	26 Midland Crowd	63.5
34114	49 Senior Sun Seekers	44.8	34609	29 Rustbelt Retirees	38.3	35041	42 Southern Satellites	100.0
34116	38 Industrious Urban Fringe	48.9	34610	26 Midland Crowd	61.4	35042	42 Southern Satellites	26.9
34117	12 Up and Coming Families	73.4	34613	43 The Elders	64.0	35043	12 Up and Coming Families	55.5
34119	15 Silver and Gold	82.3	34614	49 Senior Sun Seekers	72.5	35044	42 Southern Satellites	41.3
34120	12 Up and Coming Families	68.2	34639	12 Up and Coming Families	38.4	35045	42 Southern Satellites	32.3
34134	15 Silver and Gold	78.2	34652	49 Senior Sun Seekers	32.7	35046	42 Southern Satellites	41.5
34135	49 Senior Sun Seekers	36.1	34653	49 Senior Sun Seekers	37.4	35049	42 Southern Satellites	80.2
34141	49 Senior Sun Seekers	99.8	34654	49 Senior Sun Seekers	32.6	35051	26 Midland Crowd	75.5
34142	58 Newest Residents	44.9	34655	15 Silver and Gold	33.8	35053	31 Rural Resort Dwellers	81.4
34145	15 Silver and Gold	87.6	34667	49 Senior Sun Seekers	79.3	35054	31 Rural Resort Dwellers	62.6
34201	15 Silver and Gold	100.0	34668	49 Senior Sun Seekers	64.4	35055	57 Simple Living	32.4
34202	04 Boomburbs	56.5	34669	49 Senior Sun Seekers	70.2	35057	42 Southern Satellites	50.5
34203	15 Silver and Gold	17.2	34677	13 In Style	38.2	35058	42 Southern Satellites	47.8
34205	57 Simple Living	21.8	34683	33 Midlife Junction	25.9	35061	50 Heartland Communities	76.2
34207	49 Senior Sun Seekers	26.2	34684	43 The Elders	22.9	35062	25 Salt of The Earth	32.0
34208	60 City Dimensions	21.2	34685	07 Exurbanites	36.3	35063	56 Rural Bypasses	71.5
34209	43 The Elders	24.0	34688	13 In Style	47.4	35064	34 Family Foundations	33.8
34210	36 Old and Newcomers	41.3	34689	33 Midlife Junction	40.4	35068	29 Rustbelt Retirees	39.5
34211	15 Silver and Gold	63.0	34690	49 Senior Sun Seekers	73.0	35071	29 Rustbelt Retirees	36.1
34212	04 Boomburbs	58.6	34691	49 Senior Sun Seekers	67.6	35072	42 Southern Satellites	55.7
34215	15 Silver and Gold	100.0	34695	13 In Style	29.2	35073	50 Heartland Communities	56.0
34217	15 Silver and Gold	70.3	34698	49 Senior Sun Seekers	23.8	35077	42 Southern Satellites	60.5
34219	31 Rural Resort Dwellers	40.5	34705	46 Rooted Rural	97.9	35078	42 Southern Satellites	100.0
34221	49 Senior Sun Seekers	51.3	34711	12 Up and Coming Families	56.3	35079	42 Southern Satellites	51.7
34222	43 The Elders	54.2	34731	49 Senior Sun Seekers	58.6	35080	12 Up and Coming Families	89.4
34223	49 Senior Sun Seekers	37.0	34734	28 Aspiring Young Families	92.2	35083	42 Southern Satellites	58.9
34224	49 Senior Sun Seekers	49.7	34736	49 Senior Sun Seekers	37.7	35085	42 Southern Satellites	96.2
34228	15 Silver and Gold	88.5	34737	14 Prosperous Empty Nesters	59.2	35087	42 Southern Satellites	54.4
34229	49 Senior Sun Seekers	44.8	34739	49 Senior Sun Seekers	67.7	35089	56 Rural Bypasses	66.0
34231	33 Midlife Junction	34.6	34741	52 Inner City Tenants	42.7	35091	42 Southern Satellites	53.3
34232	33 Midlife Junction	29.5	34743	38 Industrious Urban Fringe	77.1	35094	33 Midlife Junction	27.1
34233	49 Senior Sun Seekers	26.1	34744	19 Milk and Cookies	23.0	35096	42 Southern Satellites	42.6
34234	49 Senior Sun Seekers	26.9	34746	41 Crossroads	27.0	35098	42 Southern Satellites	80.6
34235	43 The Elders	39.2	34747	09 Urban Chic	56.2	35111	26 Midland Crowd	53.8
34236	43 The Elders	22.3	34748	49 Senior Sun Seekers	31.6	35114	12 Up and Coming Families	92.6

ZIP CODE	TOP TAPESTRY CONSUMER TYPE	% 2004 HOUSE-HOLDS	ZIP CODE	TOP TAPESTRY CONSUMER TYPE	% 2004 HOUSE-HOLDS	ZIP CODE	TOP TAPESTRY CONSUMER TYPE	% 2004 HOUSE-HOLDS
35115	12 Up and Coming Families	16.8	35475	17 Green Acres	33.4	35756	12 Up and Coming Families	49.7
35116	26 Midland Crowd	99.9	35476	33 Midlife Junction	20.9	35757	12 Up and Coming Families	59.4
35117	42 Southern Satellites	42.6	35480	46 Rooted Rural	98.2	35758	16 Enterprising Professionals	26.3
35118	29 Rustbelt Retirees	55.4	35481	56 Rural Bypasses	68.2	35759	17 Green Acres	55.6
35120	26 Midland Crowd	78.5	35487	65 Social Security Set	67.4	35760	42 Southern Satellites	78.1
35121	42 Southern Satellites	65.6	35490	26 Midland Crowd	72.6	35761	42 Southern Satellites	52.8
35124	19 Milk and Cookies	22.5	35501	42 Southern Satellites	19.4	35763	04 Boomburbs	44.8
35125	42 Southern Satellites	48.3	35503	42 Southern Satellites	56.4	35764	42 Southern Satellites	100.0
35126	19 Milk and Cookies	31.1	35504	42 Southern Satellites	47.0	35765	42 Southern Satellites	100.0
35127	18 Cozy and Comfortable	44.8	35540	42 Southern Satellites	99.3	35766	42 Southern Satellites	100.0
35128	26 Midland Crowd	28.1	35541	42 Southern Satellites	100.0	35768	42 Southern Satellites	48.1
35130	46 Rooted Rural	56.9	35542	42 Southern Satellites	100.0	35769	42 Southern Satellites	25.6
35131	42 Southern Satellites	41.8	35543	42 Southern Satellites	100.0	35771	42 Southern Satellites	100.0
35133	42 Southern Satellites	59.1	35544	56 Rural Bypasses	88.4	35772	42 Southern Satellites	80.8
35135	26 Midland Crowd	100.0	35546	42 Southern Satellites	66.5	35773	26 Midland Crowd	77.1
35136	56 Rural Bypasses	51.0	35548	42 Southern Satellites	64.7	35774	42 Southern Satellites	100.0
35143	26 Midland Crowd	46.6	35549	56 Rural Bypasses	83.0	35775	42 Southern Satellites	100.0
35146	26 Midland Crowd	51.3	35550	50 Heartland Communities	32.5	35776	42 Southern Satellites	95.8
35147	42 Southern Satellites	50.1	35552	42 Southern Satellites	100.0	35801	14 Prosperous Empty Nesters	29.9
35148	56 Rural Bypasses	53.8	35553	42 Southern Satellites	84.0	35802	14 Prosperous Empty Nesters	33.8
35150	53 Home Town	23.9	35554	42 Southern Satellites	85.1	35803	07 Exurbanites	36.7
35151	42 Southern Satellites	67.6	35555	42 Southern Satellites	49.9	35805	52 Inner City Tenants	28.8
35160	42 Southern Satellites	16.0	35563	42 Southern Satellites	65.6	35806	04 Boomburbs	36.9
35171	42 Southern Satellites	97.9	35564	42 Southern Satellites	63.8	35808	40 Military Proximity	100.0
35172	42 Southern Satellites	60.1	35565	42 Southern Satellites	70.1	35810	34 Family Foundations	29.4
35173	06 Sophisticated Squires	29.7	35570	42 Southern Satellites	89.2	35811	17 Green Acres	20.0
35175	26 Midland Crowd	62.0	35571	42 Southern Satellites	100.0	35816	52 Inner City Tenants	28.9
35176	26 Midland Crowd	62.4	35572	42 Southern Satellites	60.0	35824	16 Enterprising Professionals	97.4
35178	42 Southern Satellites	44.9	35574	42 Southern Satellites	91.9	35898	40 Military Proximity	60.0
35179	42 Southern Satellites	67.3	35575	42 Southern Satellites	100.0	35901	53 Home Town	13.4
35180	26 Midland Crowd	61.0	35576	56 Rural Bypasses	43.9	35903	25 Salt of The Earth	20.6
35183	46 Rooted Rural	100.0	35578	42 Southern Satellites	49.5	35904	50 Heartland Communities	37.6
35184	42 Southern Satellites	48.9	35579	42 Southern Satellites	46.2	35905	25 Salt of The Earth	52.0
35186	26 Midland Crowd	100.0	35580	56 Rural Bypasses	59.5	35906	17 Green Acres	53.6
35188	42 Southern Satellites	56.6	35581	42 Southern Satellites	75.3	35907	18 Cozy and Comfortable	49.6
35203	64 City Commons	67.6	35582	42 Southern Satellites	78.0	35950	42 Southern Satellites	38.5
35204	62 Modest Income Homes	65.9	35585	42 Southern Satellites	83.7	35951	42 Southern Satellites	77.0
35205	27 Metro Renters	36.7	35586	42 Southern Satellites	83.8	35952	42 Southern Satellites	81.0
35206	51 Metro City Edge	43.2	35587	56 Rural Bypasses	82.6	35953	42 Southern Satellites	42.6
35207	62 Modest Income Homes	65.0	35592	42 Southern Satellites	40.3	35954	42 Southern Satellites	57.7
35208	34 Family Foundations	48.7	35593	42 Southern Satellites	100.0	35956	42 Southern Satellites	45.3
35209	39 Young and Restless	47.0	35594	42 Southern Satellites	47.4	35957	42 Southern Satellites	46.0
35210	29 Rustbelt Retirees	16.9	35601	53 Home Town	22.6	35958	42 Southern Satellites	100.0
35211	34 Family Foundations	45.3	35603	13 In Style	34.8	35959	42 Southern Satellites	100.0
35212	64 City Commons	34.0	35610	42 Southern Satellites	100.0	35960	42 Southern Satellites	35.1
35213	09 Urban Chic	38.9	35611	26 Midland Crowd	20.0	35961	42 Southern Satellites	67.7
35214	18 Cozy and Comfortable	30.6	35613	17 Green Acres	38.8	35962	42 Southern Satellites	87.8
35215	19 Milk and Cookies	27.0	35614	42 Southern Satellites	82.7	35963	42 Southern Satellites	100.0
35216	22 Metropolitans	25.2	35616	46 Rooted Rural	64.0	35966	42 Southern Satellites	100.0
35217	53 Home Town	20.0	35618	56 Rural Bypasses	77.6	35967	42 Southern Satellites	31.2
35218	51 Metro City Edge	43.8	35619	42 Southern Satellites	100.0	35968	42 Southern Satellites	68.6
35221	34 Family Foundations	64.6	35620	42 Southern Satellites	74.4	35971	42 Southern Satellites	93.4
35222	22 Metropolitans	27.3	35621	42 Southern Satellites	94.3	35972	42 Southern Satellites	84.6
35223	01 Top Rung	34.2	35622	42 Southern Satellites	92.0	35973	42 Southern Satellites	100.0
35224	62 Modest Income Homes	30.2	35630	33 Midlife Junction	16.9	35974	42 Southern Satellites	100.0
35226	13 In Style	30.1	35633	17 Green Acres	26.4	35975	42 Southern Satellites	89.5
35228	34 Family Foundations	47.8	35634	25 Salt of The Earth	24.5	35976	33 Midlife Junction	28.6
35229	27 Metro Renters	99.0	35640	25 Salt of The Earth	38.6	35978	42 Southern Satellites	100.0
35233	63 Dorms To Diplomas	44.4	35643	42 Southern Satellites	77.6	35979	42 Southern Satellites	100.0
35234	62 Modest Income Homes	68.0	35645	17 Green Acres	39.1	35980	42 Southern Satellites	100.0
35235	19 Milk and Cookies	39.2	35646	46 Rooted Rural	40.1	35981	42 Southern Satellites	100.0
35242	02 Suburban Splendor	37.1	35647	42 Southern Satellites	100.0	35983	42 Southern Satellites	100.0
35243	22 Metropolitans	40.0	35648	46 Rooted Rural	38.2	35984	46 Rooted Rural	53.6
35244	04 Boomburbs	32.5	35650	42 Southern Satellites	71.1	35986	42 Southern Satellites	62.3
35401	55 College Towns	30.8	35651	42 Southern Satellites	85.0	35987	46 Rooted Rural	58.8
35404	33 Midlife Junction	25.3	35652	42 Southern Satellites	45.3	35988	42 Southern Satellites	100.0
35405	26 Midland Crowd	13.0	35653	56 Rural Bypasses	26.4	35989	42 Southern Satellites	97.1
35406	02 Suburban Splendor	15.3	35654	42 Southern Satellites	82.9	36003	56 Rural Bypasses	66.0
35441	56 Rural Bypasses	77.9	35660	62 Modest Income Homes	19.5	36005	46 Rooted Rural	88.3
35442	56 Rural Bypasses	76.1	35661	17 Green Acres	19.3	36006	42 Southern Satellites	81.7
35443	62 Modest Income Homes	100.0	35670	42 Southern Satellites	51.0	36009	56 Rural Bypasses	73.5
35444	42 Southern Satellites	88.0	35671	26 Midland Crowd	66.6	36010	56 Rural Bypasses	55.6
35446	46 Rooted Rural	49.4	35672	42 Southern Satellites	62.3	36013	17 Green Acres	75.3
35447	56 Rural Bypasses	70.5	35673	42 Southern Satellites	43.2	36016	56 Rural Bypasses	78.5
35452	26 Midland Crowd	65.3	35674	42 Southern Satellites	32.0	36017	56 Rural Bypasses	76.2
35453	26 Midland Crowd	47.6	35677	46 Rooted Rural	53.4	36020	42 Southern Satellites	67.0
35456	41 Crossroads	39.3	35739	42 Southern Satellites	39.1	36022	26 Midland Crowd	32.3
35457	46 Rooted Rural	100.0	35740	42 Southern Satellites	70.6	36024	42 Southern Satellites	49.5
35458	46 Rooted Rural	100.0	35741	17 Green Acres	56.4	36025	12 Up and Coming Families	46.0
35459	56 Rural Bypasses	100.0	35744	42 Southern Satellites	100.0	36026	31 Rural Resort Dwellers	48.6
35460	56 Rural Bypasses	100.0	35745	42 Southern Satellites	100.0	36027	42 Southern Satellites	43.3
35461	42 Southern Satellites	94.8	35746	42 Southern Satellites	100.0	36028	56 Rural Bypasses	90.1
35462	56 Rural Bypasses	53.6	35747	42 Southern Satellites	42.5	36029	46 Rooted Rural	92.1
35463	46 Rooted Rural	100.0	35748	26 Midland Crowd	56.7	36030	56 Rural Bypasses	57.2
35464	56 Rural Bypasses	100.0	35749	12 Up and Coming Families	36.4	36031	56 Rural Bypasses	95.1
35466	46 Rooted Rural	63.0	35750	26 Midland Crowd	42.7	36032	62 Modest Income Homes	36.0
35469	56 Rural Bypasses	89.5	35751	42 Southern Satellites	100.0	36033	56 Rural Bypasses	61.5
35470	56 Rural Bypasses	71.8	35752	42 Southern Satellites	85.1	36034	56 Rural Bypasses	49.1
35473	26 Midland Crowd	24.0	35754	42 Southern Satellites	46.4	36035	46 Rooted Rural	71.3
35474	56 Rural Bypasses	50.3	35755	31 Rural Resort Dwellers	54.7	36036	46 Rooted Rural	71.8

ZIP CODE	TOP TAPESTRY CONSUMER TYPE	% 2004 HOUSE-HOLDS	ZIP CODE	TOP TAPESTRY CONSUMER TYPE	% 2004 HOUSE-HOLDS	ZIP CODE	TOP TAPESTRY CONSUMER TYPE	% 2004 HOUSE-HOLDS
36037	56 Rural Bypasses	45.3	36343	42 Southern Satellites	54.1	36583	42 Southern Satellites	100.0
36038	46 Rooted Rural	40.4	36344	46 Rooted Rural	50.0	36584	56 Rural Bypasses	82.6
36039	56 Rural Bypasses	78.1	36345	50 Heartland Communities	36.4	36585	42 Southern Satellites	69.2
36040	56 Rural Bypasses	95.8	36346	46 Rooted Rural	42.8	36587	42 Southern Satellites	63.7
36041	56 Rural Bypasses	57.6	36349	42 Southern Satellites	70.9	36602	65 Social Security Set	64.7
36042	56 Rural Bypasses	45.2	36350	46 Rooted Rural	28.3	36603	62 Modest Income Homes	46.9
36043	46 Rooted Rural	40.1	36351	46 Rooted Rural	87.3	36604	22 Metropolitans	31.2
36046	42 Southern Satellites	47.1	36352	26 Midland Crowd	48.3	36605	51 Metro City Edge	20.4
36047	56 Rural Bypasses	42.8	36353	46 Rooted Rural	76.9	36606	48 Great Expectations	35.2
36048	56 Rural Bypasses	97.8	36360	26 Midland Crowd	21.4	36607	22 Metropolitans	23.0
36049	50 Heartland Communities	70.2	36362	40 Military Proximity	98.7	36608	36 Old and Newcomers	28.0
36051	26 Midland Crowd	54.3	36370	56 Rural Bypasses	72.0	36609	13 In Style	29.1
36052	56 Rural Bypasses	52.6	36373	56 Rural Bypasses	62.4	36610	62 Modest Income Homes	70.9
36053	56 Rural Bypasses	94.4	36374	46 Rooted Rural	88.2	36611	50 Heartland Communities	46.3
36054	26 Midland Crowd	35.8	36375	46 Rooted Rural	37.9	36612	62 Modest Income Homes	48.9
36061	56 Rural Bypasses	99.0	36376	42 Southern Satellites	90.1	36613	26 Midland Crowd	33.8
36064	34 Family Foundations	25.6	36401	56 Rural Bypasses	62.5	36615	51 Metro City Edge	100.0
36066	12 Up and Coming Families	40.8	36420	50 Heartland Communities	27.6	36617	34 Family Foundations	46.9
36067	26 Midland Crowd	33.3	36425	56 Rural Bypasses	100.0	36618	51 Metro City Edge	23.7
36069	56 Rural Bypasses	44.2	36426	42 Southern Satellites	24.1	36619	32 Rustbelt Traditions	18.1
36071	56 Rural Bypasses	39.5	36432	56 Rural Bypasses	87.0	36688	63 Dorms To Diplomas	100.0
36075	56 Rural Bypasses	86.4	36435	56 Rural Bypasses	100.0	36693	33 Midlife Junction	36.7
36078	26 Midland Crowd	23.7	36436	56 Rural Bypasses	99.3	36695	12 Up and Coming Families	34.4
36079	41 Crossroads	48.8	36441	42 Southern Satellites	83.8	36701	62 Modest Income Homes	21.5
36080	31 Rural Resort Dwellers	62.0	36442	50 Heartland Communities	53.4	36703	62 Modest Income Homes	43.5
36081	26 Midland Crowd	18.6	36444	56 Rural Bypasses	100.0	36720	56 Rural Bypasses	100.0
36082	63 Dorms To Diplomas	0.0	36445	56 Rural Bypasses	56.3	36722	56 Rural Bypasses	100.0
36083	34 Family Foundations	45.7	36446	56 Rural Bypasses	100.0	36726	62 Modest Income Homes	38.2
36088	57 Simple Living	35.9	36451	56 Rural Bypasses	66.9	36727	56 Rural Bypasses	66.2
36089	56 Rural Bypasses	82.3	36453	42 Southern Satellites	57.1	36728	56 Rural Bypasses	100.0
36091	42 Southern Satellites	67.4	36454	42 Southern Satellites	100.0	36732	62 Modest Income Homes	24.1
36092	42 Southern Satellites	37.1	36456	56 Rural Bypasses	98.0	36736	56 Rural Bypasses	100.0
36093	06 Sophisticated Squires	42.4	36460	42 Southern Satellites	35.1	36738	56 Rural Bypasses	100.0
36104	64 City Commons	42.4	36467	46 Rooted Rural	27.9	36740	56 Rural Bypasses	100.0
36105	62 Modest Income Homes	38.0	36471	56 Rural Bypasses	93.9	36742	56 Rural Bypasses	54.5
36106	22 Metropolitans	22.4	36473	42 Southern Satellites	100.0	36744	56 Rural Bypasses	72.2
36107	48 Great Expectations	39.5	36474	42 Southern Satellites	95.5	36748	56 Rural Bypasses	60.6
36108	34 Family Foundations	34.3	36475	42 Southern Satellites	63.7	36749	56 Rural Bypasses	100.0
36109	14 Prosperous Empty Nesters	25.8	36477	46 Rooted Rural	48.5	36750	42 Southern Satellites	100.0
36110	53 Home Town	29.5	36480	42 Southern Satellites	100.0	36751	62 Modest Income Homes	100.0
36111	36 Old and Newcomers	23.6	36481	56 Rural Bypasses	100.0	36752	46 Rooted Rural	100.0
36112	40 Military Proximity	100.0	36482	56 Rural Bypasses	85.4	36754	56 Rural Bypasses	100.0
36115	40 Military Proximity	100.0	36483	46 Rooted Rural	84.9	36756	56 Rural Bypasses	58.9
36116	51 Metro City Edge	16.2	36502	42 Southern Satellites	27.0	36758	56 Rural Bypasses	73.9
36117	39 Young and Restless	24.7	36505	26 Midland Crowd	100.0	36759	56 Rural Bypasses	91.0
36201	62 Modest Income Homes	33.0	36507	42 Southern Satellites	41.2	36761	56 Rural Bypasses	100.0
36203	26 Midland Crowd	36.2	36509	56 Rural Bypasses	65.1	36762	42 Southern Satellites	93.8
36205	66 Unclassified	100.0	36511	46 Rooted Rural	100.0	36765	56 Rural Bypasses	100.0
36206	32 Rustbelt Traditions	33.3	36515	42 Southern Satellites	100.0	36767	56 Rural Bypasses	100.0
36207	14 Prosperous Empty Nesters	18.5	36518	42 Southern Satellites	67.4	36768	56 Rural Bypasses	100.0
36250	26 Midland Crowd	100.0	36521	42 Southern Satellites	73.3	36769	56 Rural Bypasses	69.7
36251	42 Southern Satellites	43.2	36522	42 Southern Satellites	72.3	36773	56 Rural Bypasses	100.0
36255	42 Southern Satellites	99.5	36523	31 Rural Resort Dwellers	56.0	36775	56 Rural Bypasses	100.0
36256	42 Southern Satellites	100.0	36524	56 Rural Bypasses	99.8	36776	56 Rural Bypasses	100.0
36258	42 Southern Satellites	100.0	36525	56 Rural Bypasses	52.9	36782	46 Rooted Rural	47.1
36260	42 Southern Satellites	55.8	36526	12 Up and Coming Families	22.9	36783	56 Rural Bypasses	100.0
36262	42 Southern Satellites	100.0	36527	07 Exurbanites	88.8	36784	42 Southern Satellites	48.5
36263	42 Southern Satellites	100.0	36528	31 Rural Resort Dwellers	100.0	36785	56 Rural Bypasses	68.3
36264	42 Southern Satellites	71.3	36529	56 Rural Bypasses	63.1	36786	62 Modest Income Homes	65.1
36265	48 Great Expectations	18.2	36530	26 Midland Crowd	57.0	36790	42 Southern Satellites	100.0
36266	42 Southern Satellites	41.1	36532	14 Prosperous Empty Nesters	26.9	36792	42 Southern Satellites	88.7
36267	42 Southern Satellites	100.0	36535	46 Rooted Rural	36.2	36793	42 Southern Satellites	71.4
36268	42 Southern Satellites	83.2	36538	56 Rural Bypasses	81.8	36801	62 Modest Income Homes	16.5
36269	42 Southern Satellites	100.0	36539	42 Southern Satellites	94.6	36804	26 Midland Crowd	51.1
36271	42 Southern Satellites	63.9	36540	56 Rural Bypasses	62.4	36830	55 College Towns	23.7
36272	42 Southern Satellites	59.4	36541	42 Southern Satellites	62.6	36832	63 Dorms To Diplomas	68.9
36273	42 Southern Satellites	100.0	36542	31 Rural Resort Dwellers	62.7	36849	63 Dorms To Diplomas	100.0
36274	42 Southern Satellites	69.2	36544	42 Southern Satellites	53.3	36850	56 Rural Bypasses	67.0
36276	42 Southern Satellites	59.8	36545	56 Rural Bypasses	52.8	36852	41 Crossroads	57.5
36277	26 Midland Crowd	36.2	36548	42 Southern Satellites	94.9	36853	31 Rural Resort Dwellers	48.4
36278	42 Southern Satellites	38.7	36549	43 The Elders	70.1	36854	50 Heartland Communities	25.4
36279	42 Southern Satellites	42.0	36550	56 Rural Bypasses	58.4	36855	42 Southern Satellites	68.7
36280	42 Southern Satellites	77.8	36551	26 Midland Crowd	37.2	36856	41 Crossroads	68.2
36301	26 Midland Crowd	32.3	36553	42 Southern Satellites	53.6	36858	56 Rural Bypasses	100.0
36303	62 Modest Income Homes	19.1	36555	31 Rural Resort Dwellers	77.5	36860	56 Rural Bypasses	93.6
36305	12 Up and Coming Families	35.1	36558	42 Southern Satellites	95.6	36861	31 Rural Resort Dwellers	39.5
36310	56 Rural Bypasses	52.4	36560	56 Rural Bypasses	91.0	36862	56 Rural Bypasses	50.1
36311	56 Rural Bypasses	56.9	36561	31 Rural Resort Dwellers	40.9	36863	42 Southern Satellites	32.1
36312	42 Southern Satellites	55.1	36562	42 Southern Satellites	96.5	36866	56 Rural Bypasses	80.6
36314	42 Southern Satellites	99.1	36567	26 Midland Crowd	48.0	36867	53 Home Town	19.3
36316	56 Rural Bypasses	52.1	36569	42 Southern Satellites	70.3	36869	42 Southern Satellites	28.6
36317	56 Rural Bypasses	74.5	36571	26 Midland Crowd	28.3	36870	12 Up and Coming Families	60.4
36318	46 Rooted Rural	88.8	36572	17 Green Acres	47.0	36871	56 Rural Bypasses	68.9
36319	46 Rooted Rural	66.1	36574	26 Midland Crowd	100.0	36874	26 Midland Crowd	77.6
36320	42 Southern Satellites	54.6	36575	26 Midland Crowd	69.3	36875	42 Southern Satellites	42.9
36321	42 Southern Satellites	100.0	36576	26 Midland Crowd	68.5	36877	26 Midland Crowd	63.2
36322	26 Midland Crowd	47.4	36578	42 Southern Satellites	87.4	36879	42 Southern Satellites	53.1
36323	42 Southern Satellites	48.4	36579	42 Southern Satellites	73.4	36904	56 Rural Bypasses	68.4
36330	28 Aspiring Young Families	23.5	36580	26 Midland Crowd	61.8	36907	56 Rural Bypasses	100.0
36340	56 Rural Bypasses	48.6	36582	26 Midland Crowd	46.1	36908	46 Rooted Rural	59.0

ZIP CODE	TOP TAPESTRY CONSUMER TYPE	% 2004 HOUSE-HOLDS	ZIP CODE	TOP TAPESTRY CONSUMER TYPE	% 2004 HOUSE-HOLDS	ZIP CODE	TOP TAPESTRY CONSUMER TYPE	% 2004 HOUSE-HOLDS
36910	56 Rural Bypasses	100.0	37144	25 Salt of The Earth	54.2	37352	25 Salt of The Earth	71.2
36912	56 Rural Bypasses	100.0	37145	42 Southern Satellites	93.0	37353	42 Southern Satellites	55.8
36915	56 Rural Bypasses	100.0	37146	12 Up and Coming Families	45.7	37354	42 Southern Satellites	67.1
36916	56 Rural Bypasses	100.0	37148	25 Salt of The Earth	30.6	37355	42 Southern Satellites	30.9
36919	56 Rural Bypasses	100.0	37149	42 Southern Satellites	56.0	37356	46 Rooted Rural	54.1
36921	42 Southern Satellites	49.7	37150	42 Southern Satellites	69.0	37357	42 Southern Satellites	53.8
36922	56 Rural Bypasses	100.0	37151	42 Southern Satellites	100.0	37359	46 Rooted Rural	79.6
36925	56 Rural Bypasses	43.9	37153	12 Up and Coming Families	57.8	37360	25 Salt of The Earth	54.3
37010	17 Green Acres	53.3	37160	25 Salt of The Earth	22.6	37361	42 Southern Satellites	100.0
37012	42 Southern Satellites	70.7	37166	25 Salt of The Earth	58.8	37362	42 Southern Satellites	100.0
37013	39 Young and Restless	49.2	37167	28 Aspiring Young Families	45.9	37363	07 Exurbanites	23.8
37014	07 Exurbanites	55.5	37171	25 Salt of The Earth	100.0	37365	56 Rural Bypasses	53.7
37015	26 Midland Crowd	57.2	37172	17 Green Acres	22.0	37366	42 Southern Satellites	87.9
37016	42 Southern Satellites	91.1	37174	12 Up and Coming Families	56.0	37367	42 Southern Satellites	82.4
37018	42 Southern Satellites	98.4	37175	49 Senior Sun Seekers	50.4	37369	42 Southern Satellites	73.6
37019	25 Salt of The Earth	81.8	37178	42 Southern Satellites	70.5	37370	42 Southern Satellites	67.4
37020	25 Salt of The Earth	55.0	37179	12 Up and Coming Families	64.4	37373	25 Salt of The Earth	73.6
37022	25 Salt of The Earth	52.3	37180	42 Southern Satellites	55.3	37374	42 Southern Satellites	100.0
37023	26 Midland Crowd	60.7	37181	42 Southern Satellites	100.0	37375	14 Prosperous Empty Nesters	37.8
37025	42 Southern Satellites	52.9	37183	42 Southern Satellites	43.9	37376	56 Rural Bypasses	98.2
37026	42 Southern Satellites	100.0	37184	42 Southern Satellites	60.9	37377	07 Exurbanites	41.7
37027	02 Suburban Splendor	35.7	37185	42 Southern Satellites	39.5	37379	25 Salt of The Earth	32.4
37028	26 Midland Crowd	100.0	37186	42 Southern Satellites	84.1	37380	50 Heartland Communities	54.8
37029	26 Midland Crowd	59.8	37187	26 Midland Crowd	99.9	37381	46 Rooted Rural	35.7
37030	42 Southern Satellites	72.7	37188	12 Up and Coming Families	62.1	37383	14 Prosperous Empty Nesters	100.0
37031	26 Midland Crowd	61.2	37189	18 Cozy and Comfortable	58.6	37385	42 Southern Satellites	95.9
37032	26 Midland Crowd	57.5	37190	42 Southern Satellites	55.3	37387	56 Rural Bypasses	71.2
37033	50 Heartland Communities	55.2	37191	12 Up and Coming Families	79.5	37388	26 Midland Crowd	11.7
37034	42 Southern Satellites	49.1	37201	27 Metro Renters	55.0	37391	46 Rooted Rural	94.8
37035	26 Midland Crowd	98.6	37203	27 Metro Renters	28.3	37396	31 Rural Resort Dwellers	100.0
37036	42 Southern Satellites	54.9	37204	22 Metropolitans	39.1	37397	42 Southern Satellites	81.0
37037	25 Salt of The Earth	37.3	37205	16 Enterprising Professionals	17.0	37398	25 Salt of The Earth	30.2
37040	12 Up and Coming Families	21.4	37206	48 Great Expectations	18.6	37402	65 Social Security Set	84.2
37042	28 Aspiring Young Families	29.0	37207	51 Metro City Edge	50.6	37403	65 Social Security Set	45.5
37043	17 Green Acres	22.3	37208	62 Modest Income Homes	34.8	37404	62 Modest Income Homes	44.3
37046	25 Salt of The Earth	47.4	37209	22 Metropolitans	15.0	37405	48 Great Expectations	27.0
37047	25 Salt of The Earth	97.6	37210	65 Social Security Set	16.9	37406	62 Modest Income Homes	39.4
37048	25 Salt of The Earth	48.2	37211	16 Enterprising Professionals	19.2	37407	53 Home Town	50.4
37049	26 Midland Crowd	83.5	37212	27 Metro Renters	31.0	37408	64 City Commons	90.8
37050	46 Rooted Rural	62.9	37213	64 City Commons	100.0	37409	53 Home Town	44.1
37051	42 Southern Satellites	69.1	37214	28 Aspiring Young Families	27.6	37410	64 City Commons	49.5
37052	25 Salt of The Earth	58.4	37215	03 Connoisseurs	31.3	37411	48 Great Expectations	26.3
37055	26 Midland Crowd	39.0	37216	32 Rustbelt Traditions	40.4	37412	32 Rustbelt Traditions	25.7
37057	42 Southern Satellites	71.8	37217	39 Young and Restless	20.8	37415	29 Rustbelt Retirees	23.4
37058	46 Rooted Rural	57.9	37218	34 Family Foundations	31.8	37416	17 Green Acres	24.3
37059	42 Southern Satellites	87.3	37219	27 Metro Renters	67.4	37419	50 Heartland Communities	40.3
37060	25 Salt of The Earth	87.5	37220	14 Prosperous Empty Nesters	48.3	37421	36 Old and Newcomers	17.8
37061	42 Southern Satellites	44.2	37221	04 Boomburbs	19.9	37601	26 Midland Crowd	15.6
37062	17 Green Acres	33.3	37228	65 Social Security Set	100.0	37604	57 Simple Living	16.6
37064	04 Boomburbs	36.8	37240	63 Dorms To Diplomas	100.0	37615	26 Midland Crowd	43.8
37066	17 Green Acres	20.4	37301	42 Southern Satellites	98.0	37616	42 Southern Satellites	76.7
37067	04 Boomburbs	68.7	37302	17 Green Acres	59.6	37617	25 Salt of The Earth	22.4
37069	02 Suburban Splendor	51.5	37303	42 Southern Satellites	25.5	37618	42 Southern Satellites	53.3
37072	17 Green Acres	28.8	37305	56 Rural Bypasses	86.6	37620	42 Southern Satellites	19.9
37073	26 Midland Crowd	77.9	37306	25 Salt of The Earth	58.4	37640	46 Rooted Rural	62.3
37074	42 Southern Satellites	51.7	37307	42 Southern Satellites	100.0	37641	42 Southern Satellites	89.2
37075	13 In Style	36.7	37308	42 Southern Satellites	58.6	37642	42 Southern Satellites	74.3
37076	28 Aspiring Young Families	28.7	37309	42 Southern Satellites	100.0	37643	42 Southern Satellites	42.2
37078	42 Southern Satellites	99.7	37310	25 Salt of The Earth	65.9	37645	33 Midlife Junction	40.8
37079	42 Southern Satellites	84.6	37311	53 Home Town	21.0	37650	50 Heartland Communities	49.8
37080	26 Midland Crowd	47.0	37312	33 Midlife Junction	31.4	37656	25 Salt of The Earth	60.0
37082	12 Up and Coming Families	47.8	37313	42 Southern Satellites	100.0	37657	42 Southern Satellites	100.0
37083	42 Southern Satellites	68.1	37317	50 Heartland Communities	45.0	37658	56 Rural Bypasses	65.1
37085	12 Up and Coming Families	70.2	37318	42 Southern Satellites	52.7	37659	25 Salt of The Earth	45.3
37086	12 Up and Coming Families	75.2	37321	42 Southern Satellites	88.4	37660	50 Heartland Communities	27.0
37087	26 Midland Crowd	19.6	37322	42 Southern Satellites	100.0	37663	25 Salt of The Earth	37.5
37090	25 Salt of The Earth	36.2	37323	42 Southern Satellites	62.0	37664	50 Heartland Communities	18.5
37091	26 Midland Crowd	26.2	37324	50 Heartland Communities	34.1	37665	50 Heartland Communities	87.2
37095	42 Southern Satellites	98.3	37325	42 Southern Satellites	75.8	37680	46 Rooted Rural	100.0
37096	42 Southern Satellites	57.1	37327	42 Southern Satellites	89.9	37681	42 Southern Satellites	66.8
37097	46 Rooted Rural	74.8	37328	42 Southern Satellites	100.0	37683	56 Rural Bypasses	48.9
37098	42 Southern Satellites	93.4	37329	42 Southern Satellites	62.5	37686	25 Salt of The Earth	48.6
37101	42 Southern Satellites	98.5	37330	25 Salt of The Earth	45.7	37687	46 Rooted Rural	83.0
37110	42 Southern Satellites	27.8	37331	50 Heartland Communities	49.9	37688	46 Rooted Rural	100.0
37115	48 Great Expectations	25.2	37332	42 Southern Satellites	100.0	37690	42 Southern Satellites	75.4
37118	17 Green Acres	65.6	37333	42 Southern Satellites	99.1	37691	42 Southern Satellites	100.0
37122	06 Sophisticated Squires	40.4	37334	25 Salt of The Earth	48.7	37692	26 Midland Crowd	53.1
37127	12 Up and Coming Families	41.2	37335	42 Southern Satellites	97.7	37694	46 Rooted Rural	81.3
37128	12 Up and Coming Families	89.6	37336	17 Green Acres	39.3	37701	50 Heartland Communities	30.5
37129	26 Midland Crowd	22.3	37337	42 Southern Satellites	70.0	37705	42 Southern Satellites	31.8
37130	55 College Towns	28.5	37338	42 Southern Satellites	100.0	37708	42 Southern Satellites	81.4
37132	55 College Towns	51.4	37339	42 Southern Satellites	75.1	37709	42 Southern Satellites	100.0
37134	42 Southern Satellites	48.9	37340	56 Rural Bypasses	66.1	37710	56 Rural Bypasses	100.0
37135	06 Sophisticated Squires	63.5	37341	17 Green Acres	55.2	37711	42 Southern Satellites	100.0
37137	46 Rooted Rural	89.3	37342	42 Southern Satellites	100.0	37713	42 Southern Satellites	65.6
37138	12 Up and Coming Families	22.4	37343	06 Sophisticated Squires	16.9	37714	42 Southern Satellites	69.6
37140	46 Rooted Rural	100.0	37345	42 Southern Satellites	100.0	37715	56 Rural Bypasses	100.0
37141	25 Salt of The Earth	80.8	37347	42 Southern Satellites	47.3	37716	26 Midland Crowd	23.0
37142	25 Salt of The Earth	52.5	37348	42 Southern Satellites	90.6	37721	25 Salt of The Earth	66.4
37143	17 Green Acres	66.0	37350	03 Connoisseurs	100.0	37722	42 Southern Satellites	50.2

ZIP CODE	TOP TAPESTRY CONSUMER TYPE	% 2004 HOUSE-HOLDS	ZIP CODE	TOP TAPESTRY CONSUMER TYPE	% 2004 HOUSE-HOLDS	ZIP CODE	TOP TAPESTRY CONSUMER TYPE	% 2004 HOUSE-HOLDS
37723	42 Southern Satellites	84.1	37912	33 Midlife Junction	18.4	38225	42 Southern Satellites	65.9
37724	56 Rural Bypasses	34.9	37914	46 Rooted Rural	28.7	38226	42 Southern Satellites	100.0
37725	26 Midland Crowd	24.7	37915	64 City Commons	70.0	38229	42 Southern Satellites	98.6
37726	56 Rural Bypasses	59.3	37916	63 Dorms To Diplomas	100.0	38230	42 Southern Satellites	78.2
37727	42 Southern Satellites	50.4	37917	57 Simple Living	22.6	38231	42 Southern Satellites	96.9
37729	56 Rural Bypasses	100.0	37918	33 Midlife Junction	35.8	38232	42 Southern Satellites	100.0
37731	56 Rural Bypasses	100.0	37919	55 College Towns	18.3	38233	42 Southern Satellites	63.7
37737	42 Southern Satellites	32.4	37920	29 Rustbelt Retirees	14.4	38236	42 Southern Satellites	100.0
37738	31 Rural Resort Dwellers	71.3	37921	19 Milk and Cookies	22.1	38237	25 Salt of The Earth	31.8
37742	25 Salt of The Earth	50.4	37922	07 Exurbanites	27.5	38240	42 Southern Satellites	88.1
37743	42 Southern Satellites	34.4	37923	22 Metropolitans	37.0	38241	42 Southern Satellites	74.2
37745	42 Southern Satellites	26.5	37924	25 Salt of The Earth	33.7	38242	25 Salt of The Earth	24.9
37748	43 In Style	22.3	37931	13 In Style	26.7	38251	42 Southern Satellites	67.4
37752	46 Rooted Rural	37.9	37932	13 In Style	59.8	38253	42 Southern Satellites	87.5
37753	56 Rural Bypasses	100.0	37938	18 Cozy and Comfortable	26.9	38255	42 Southern Satellites	48.1
37754	26 Midland Crowd	49.5	38001	50 Heartland Communities	42.9	38256	49 Senior Sun Seekers	55.7
37755	42 Southern Satellites	62.1	38002	12 Up and Coming Families	38.3	38257	50 Heartland Communities	42.3
37756	56 Rural Bypasses	100.0	38004	26 Midland Crowd	62.4	38258	42 Southern Satellites	98.6
37757	42 Southern Satellites	69.4	38006	42 Southern Satellites	74.0	38259	42 Southern Satellites	98.7
37760	33 Midlife Junction	33.4	38008	56 Rural Bypasses	30.7	38260	42 Southern Satellites	83.9
37762	56 Rural Bypasses	57.3	38011	26 Midland Crowd	63.5	38261	53 Home Town	29.9
37763	26 Midland Crowd	20.7	38012	53 Home Town	27.3	38301	62 Modest Income Homes	14.0
37764	26 Midland Crowd	93.4	38015	25 Salt of The Earth	42.0	38305	12 Up and Coming Families	17.6
37765	56 Rural Bypasses	99.1	38016	04 Boomburbs	31.6	38310	42 Southern Satellites	49.6
37766	46 Rooted Rural	23.1	38017	04 Boomburbs	32.4	38311	42 Southern Satellites	100.0
37769	57 Simple Living	22.7	38018	16 Enterprising Professionals	39.3	38313	42 Southern Satellites	69.8
37770	42 Southern Satellites	100.0	38019	42 Southern Satellites	24.8	38315	42 Southern Satellites	96.5
37771	57 Simple Living	21.3	38023	26 Midland Crowd	55.6	38316	42 Southern Satellites	79.5
37772	25 Salt of The Earth	33.5	38024	42 Southern Satellites	33.6	38317	50 Heartland Communities	65.2
37774	42 Southern Satellites	26.7	38028	26 Midland Crowd	44.2	38318	42 Southern Satellites	100.0
37777	39 Young and Restless	23.6	38030	42 Southern Satellites	100.0	38320	50 Heartland Communities	35.4
37778	42 Southern Satellites	100.0	38034	42 Southern Satellites	57.1	38321	46 Rooted Rural	56.5
37779	42 Southern Satellites	71.3	38037	56 Rural Bypasses	41.8	38326	31 Rural Resort Dwellers	53.6
37801	25 Salt of The Earth	33.9	38039	56 Rural Bypasses	100.0	38327	42 Southern Satellites	100.0
37803	25 Salt of The Earth	16.6	38040	42 Southern Satellites	49.9	38328	42 Southern Satellites	73.2
37804	50 Heartland Communities	23.1	38041	56 Rural Bypasses	88.9	38329	42 Southern Satellites	80.5
37806	42 Southern Satellites	100.0	38042	56 Rural Bypasses	100.0	38330	42 Southern Satellites	65.8
37807	42 Southern Satellites	53.5	38044	42 Southern Satellites	99.8	38332	42 Southern Satellites	100.0
37809	42 Southern Satellites	100.0	38049	42 Southern Satellites	61.1	38333	46 Rooted Rural	100.0
37810	42 Southern Satellites	99.6	38052	42 Southern Satellites	69.2	38334	42 Southern Satellites	100.0
37811	42 Southern Satellites	100.0	38053	19 Milk and Cookies	15.6	38337	25 Salt of The Earth	100.0
37813	42 Southern Satellites	32.7	38057	26 Midland Crowd	40.8	38339	42 Southern Satellites	100.0
37814	53 Home Town	19.9	38058	26 Midland Crowd	70.0	38340	42 Southern Satellites	42.2
37818	42 Southern Satellites	89.9	38059	25 Salt of The Earth	37.9	38341	42 Southern Satellites	55.0
37819	56 Rural Bypasses	100.0	38060	26 Midland Crowd	74.4	38342	42 Southern Satellites	92.3
37820	42 Southern Satellites	64.4	38061	42 Southern Satellites	83.5	38343	25 Salt of The Earth	20.1
37821	42 Southern Satellites	36.5	38063	42 Southern Satellites	49.1	38344	42 Southern Satellites	54.7
37825	42 Southern Satellites	83.8	38066	25 Salt of The Earth	70.8	38345	42 Southern Satellites	100.0
37826	42 Southern Satellites	76.4	38067	56 Rural Bypasses	98.4	38347	42 Southern Satellites	100.0
37829	42 Southern Satellites	100.0	38068	56 Rural Bypasses	27.0	38348	42 Southern Satellites	77.7
37830	29 Rustbelt Retirees	22.7	38069	56 Rural Bypasses	71.7	38351	42 Southern Satellites	70.1
37840	42 Southern Satellites	39.0	38075	56 Rural Bypasses	85.9	38352	42 Southern Satellites	100.0
37841	42 Southern Satellites	66.6	38076	25 Salt of The Earth	57.8	38355	17 Green Acres	36.0
37843	42 Southern Satellites	77.4	38079	57 Simple Living	46.0	38356	25 Salt of The Earth	60.7
37846	42 Southern Satellites	100.0	38080	53 Home Town	52.5	38357	42 Southern Satellites	90.1
37847	56 Rural Bypasses	98.5	38103	27 Metro Renters	93.0	38358	53 Home Town	24.5
37848	42 Southern Satellites	100.0	38104	22 Metropolitans	31.1	38359	42 Southern Satellites	66.3
37849	33 Midlife Junction	26.3	38105	64 City Commons	39.8	38361	46 Rooted Rural	78.9
37852	56 Rural Bypasses	52.2	38106	62 Modest Income Homes	72.4	38362	26 Midland Crowd	49.8
37853	25 Salt of The Earth	42.1	38107	62 Modest Income Homes	39.8	38363	50 Heartland Communities	38.2
37854	46 Rooted Rural	34.4	38108	62 Modest Income Homes	58.3	38366	25 Salt of The Earth	60.8
37857	42 Southern Satellites	82.1	38109	34 Family Foundations	52.9	38367	42 Southern Satellites	74.8
37860	42 Southern Satellites	64.8	38111	51 Metro City Edge	20.6	38368	42 Southern Satellites	100.0
37861	42 Southern Satellites	97.2	38112	62 Modest Income Homes	30.7	38369	50 Heartland Communities	53.4
37862	33 Midlife Junction	44.0	38114	62 Modest Income Homes	45.4	38370	46 Rooted Rural	100.0
37863	26 Midland Crowd	29.1	38115	39 Young and Restless	37.6	38371	42 Southern Satellites	74.7
37865	26 Midland Crowd	65.6	38116	51 Metro City Edge	23.0	38372	42 Southern Satellites	48.1
37866	46 Rooted Rural	100.0	38117	14 Prosperous Empty Nesters	26.2	38374	42 Southern Satellites	100.0
37869	56 Rural Bypasses	78.1	38118	52 Inner City Tenants	39.1	38375	50 Heartland Communities	46.8
37870	46 Rooted Rural	68.2	38119	14 Prosperous Empty Nesters	26.4	38376	42 Southern Satellites	100.0
37871	42 Southern Satellites	39.0	38120	03 Connoisseurs	26.0	38379	42 Southern Satellites	92.5
37872	42 Southern Satellites	76.5	38122	32 Rustbelt Traditions	28.4	38380	42 Southern Satellites	91.8
37873	42 Southern Satellites	100.0	38125	12 Up and Coming Families	43.8	38381	46 Rooted Rural	58.3
37874	42 Southern Satellites	78.4	38126	64 City Commons	49.6	38382	50 Heartland Communities	42.3
37876	26 Midland Crowd	32.3	38127	51 Metro City Edge	67.4	38387	42 Southern Satellites	100.0
37877	25 Salt of The Earth	67.5	38128	51 Metro City Edge	17.3	38388	42 Southern Satellites	100.0
37878	46 Rooted Rural	62.9	38131	49 Senior Sun Seekers	100.0	38390	42 Southern Satellites	100.0
37879	42 Southern Satellites	60.4	38132	50 Heartland Communities	50.0	38391	56 Rural Bypasses	93.6
37880	42 Southern Satellites	75.3	38133	12 Up and Coming Families	51.1	38392	56 Rural Bypasses	100.0
37881	42 Southern Satellites	67.0	38134	39 Young and Restless	41.3	38401	26 Midland Crowd	18.4
37882	31 Rural Resort Dwellers	100.0	38135	06 Sophisticated Squires	54.2	38425	50 Heartland Communities	60.1
37885	42 Southern Satellites	99.9	38138	07 Exurbanites	45.6	38449	42 Southern Satellites	59.9
37886	42 Southern Satellites	39.4	38139	02 Suburban Splendor	100.0	38450	56 Rural Bypasses	51.3
37887	42 Southern Satellites	92.3	38141	19 Milk and Cookies	60.6	38451	26 Midland Crowd	82.6
37888	42 Southern Satellites	100.0	38152	55 College Towns	100.0	38452	42 Southern Satellites	100.0
37890	42 Southern Satellites	66.6	38201	42 Southern Satellites	33.2	38453	42 Southern Satellites	100.0
37891	42 Southern Satellites	77.4	38220	42 Southern Satellites	53.0	38454	42 Southern Satellites	99.7
37892	42 Southern Satellites	100.0	38221	46 Rooted Rural	50.9	38456	42 Southern Satellites	100.0
37902	65 Social Security Set	100.0	38222	49 Senior Sun Seekers	56.7	38457	42 Southern Satellites	100.0
37909	55 College Towns	40.7	38224	42 Southern Satellites	55.0	38459	42 Southern Satellites	100.0

ZIP CODE	TOP TAPESTRY CONSUMER TYPE	% 2004 HOUSE-HOLDS	ZIP CODE	TOP TAPESTRY CONSUMER TYPE	% 2004 HOUSE-HOLDS	ZIP CODE	TOP TAPESTRY CONSUMER TYPE	% 2004 HOUSE-HOLDS
38460	42 Southern Satellites	100.0	38646	62 Modest Income Homes	42.6	38876	42 Southern Satellites	100.0
38461	42 Southern Satellites	51.8	38647	56 Rural Bypasses	100.0	38878	56 Rural Bypasses	54.3
38462	42 Southern Satellites	86.3	38650	42 Southern Satellites	100.0	38901	42 Southern Satellites	16.9
38463	42 Southern Satellites	100.0	38651	17 Green Acres	99.1	38912	46 Rooted Rural	98.1
38464	42 Southern Satellites	36.4	38652	42 Southern Satellites	52.4	38913	42 Southern Satellites	79.6
38468	42 Southern Satellites	97.3	38654	12 Up and Coming Families	35.3	38914	42 Southern Satellites	82.1
38469	42 Southern Satellites	100.0	38655	55 College Towns	40.3	38915	56 Rural Bypasses	31.2
38471	42 Southern Satellites	100.0	38658	42 Southern Satellites	78.0	38916	56 Rural Bypasses	30.7
38472	46 Rooted Rural	50.4	38659	56 Rural Bypasses	98.2	38917	46 Rooted Rural	51.8
38473	42 Southern Satellites	100.0	38661	42 Southern Satellites	97.3	38920	56 Rural Bypasses	57.7
38474	42 Southern Satellites	29.7	38663	42 Southern Satellites	73.2	38921	56 Rural Bypasses	83.7
38475	42 Southern Satellites	100.0	38664	41 Crossroads	100.0	38922	56 Rural Bypasses	85.7
38476	25 Salt of The Earth	50.8	38665	42 Southern Satellites	50.5	38923	56 Rural Bypasses	52.6
38477	42 Southern Satellites	89.0	38666	56 Rural Bypasses	59.5	38924	56 Rural Bypasses	100.0
38478	42 Southern Satellites	38.3	38668	26 Midland Crowd	27.3	38925	42 Southern Satellites	50.2
38481	42 Southern Satellites	100.0	38670	51 Metro City Edge	65.9	38927	56 Rural Bypasses	100.0
38482	26 Midland Crowd	83.2	38671	28 Aspiring Young Families	26.2	38929	56 Rural Bypasses	100.0
38483	42 Southern Satellites	100.0	38672	17 Green Acres	83.6	38930	64 City Commons	23.7
38485	56 Rural Bypasses	49.0	38673	42 Southern Satellites	57.0	38940	42 Southern Satellites	72.0
38486	42 Southern Satellites	100.0	38674	42 Southern Satellites	100.0	38941	62 Modest Income Homes	65.0
38487	46 Rooted Rural	48.7	38676	51 Metro City Edge	49.1	38943	56 Rural Bypasses	100.0
38488	42 Southern Satellites	69.8	38677	26 Midland Crowd	100.0	38944	37 Prairie Living	92.4
38501	42 Southern Satellites	24.7	38680	26 Midland Crowd	78.5	38948	56 Rural Bypasses	55.0
38504	46 Rooted Rural	100.0	38683	42 Southern Satellites	69.0	38949	26 Midland Crowd	56.4
38505	63 Dorms To Diplomas	100.0	38685	56 Rural Bypasses	100.0	38950	56 Rural Bypasses	100.0
38506	25 Salt of The Earth	33.9	38701	62 Modest Income Homes	35.9	38951	56 Rural Bypasses	67.1
38541	46 Rooted Rural	65.9	38703	51 Metro City Edge	22.6	38952	56 Rural Bypasses	97.1
38542	42 Southern Satellites	75.0	38720	56 Rural Bypasses	100.0	38953	56 Rural Bypasses	100.0
38543	56 Rural Bypasses	84.3	38721	56 Rural Bypasses	60.6	38954	56 Rural Bypasses	57.4
38544	42 Southern Satellites	70.5	38725	56 Rural Bypasses	70.2	38961	56 Rural Bypasses	100.0
38545	42 Southern Satellites	83.1	38726	56 Rural Bypasses	100.0	38963	62 Modest Income Homes	79.5
38547	25 Salt of The Earth	100.0	38730	26 Midland Crowd	81.3	38964	56 Rural Bypasses	100.0
38548	46 Rooted Rural	87.9	38731	56 Rural Bypasses	100.0	38965	42 Southern Satellites	42.8
38549	46 Rooted Rural	37.4	38732	62 Modest Income Homes	23.8	38967	56 Rural Bypasses	40.0
38551	42 Southern Satellites	59.4	38733	14 Prosperous Empty Nesters	100.0	39038	62 Modest Income Homes	29.6
38552	42 Southern Satellites	100.0	38736	56 Rural Bypasses	55.6	39039	56 Rural Bypasses	92.7
38553	42 Southern Satellites	64.8	38737	56 Rural Bypasses	61.8	39040	56 Rural Bypasses	70.4
38554	42 Southern Satellites	100.0	38740	56 Rural Bypasses	76.3	39041	56 Rural Bypasses	44.2
38555	33 Midlife Junction	24.7	38744	56 Rural Bypasses	100.0	39042	26 Midland Crowd	17.8
38556	56 Rural Bypasses	35.8	38746	62 Modest Income Homes	75.9	39044	42 Southern Satellites	69.5
38558	43 The Elders	37.8	38748	62 Modest Income Homes	45.4	39045	56 Rural Bypasses	96.8
38559	42 Southern Satellites	86.5	38751	51 Metro City Edge	35.6	39046	56 Rural Bypasses	20.5
38560	42 Southern Satellites	100.0	38753	56 Rural Bypasses	61.9	39047	12 Up and Coming Families	26.7
38562	42 Southern Satellites	65.2	38754	56 Rural Bypasses	97.1	39051	56 Rural Bypasses	43.0
38563	42 Southern Satellites	73.4	38756	51 Metro City Edge	26.6	39056	28 Aspiring Young Families	13.8
38564	46 Rooted Rural	100.0	38759	56 Rural Bypasses	100.0	39057	42 Southern Satellites	96.4
38565	42 Southern Satellites	76.3	38761	51 Metro City Edge	66.9	39059	56 Rural Bypasses	24.7
38567	25 Salt of The Earth	60.6	38762	62 Modest Income Homes	63.4	39063	62 Modest Income Homes	45.2
38568	42 Southern Satellites	85.8	38769	56 Rural Bypasses	58.6	39066	51 Metro City Edge	42.8
38569	25 Salt of The Earth	63.7	38771	62 Modest Income Homes	53.8	39067	46 Rooted Rural	52.4
38570	50 Heartland Communities	53.5	38773	62 Modest Income Homes	60.7	39069	62 Modest Income Homes	55.6
38571	42 Southern Satellites	47.9	38774	62 Modest Income Homes	67.4	39071	26 Midland Crowd	97.8
38572	46 Rooted Rural	62.8	38778	62 Modest Income Homes	55.1	39073	26 Midland Crowd	66.5
38573	42 Southern Satellites	59.5	38780	42 Southern Satellites	100.0	39074	56 Rural Bypasses	73.6
38574	42 Southern Satellites	92.4	38801	51 Metro City Edge	12.0	39078	56 Rural Bypasses	78.0
38575	46 Rooted Rural	76.0	38804	42 Southern Satellites	23.9	39079	62 Modest Income Homes	68.8
38577	46 Rooted Rural	96.8	38821	42 Southern Satellites	43.5	39082	56 Rural Bypasses	100.0
38578	50 Heartland Communities	100.0	38824	42 Southern Satellites	70.9	39083	56 Rural Bypasses	28.2
38579	46 Rooted Rural	90.8	38826	42 Southern Satellites	39.2	39086	56 Rural Bypasses	89.6
38580	42 Southern Satellites	95.8	38827	42 Southern Satellites	100.0	39088	56 Rural Bypasses	100.0
38581	42 Southern Satellites	97.4	38828	42 Southern Satellites	93.5	39090	56 Rural Bypasses	26.5
38582	46 Rooted Rural	87.5	38829	42 Southern Satellites	60.1	39092	56 Rural Bypasses	56.8
38583	42 Southern Satellites	73.2	38833	42 Southern Satellites	62.4	39094	56 Rural Bypasses	100.0
38585	42 Southern Satellites	100.0	38834	42 Southern Satellites	30.4	39095	56 Rural Bypasses	67.7
38587	42 Southern Satellites	77.9	38838	42 Southern Satellites	92.8	39096	56 Rural Bypasses	100.0
38588	42 Southern Satellites	65.6	38841	42 Southern Satellites	99.7	39097	56 Rural Bypasses	100.0
38589	42 Southern Satellites	100.0	38843	42 Southern Satellites	73.0	39108	46 Rooted Rural	72.2
38601	56 Rural Bypasses	66.0	38844	42 Southern Satellites	100.0	39110	04 Boomburbs	42.0
38603	56 Rural Bypasses	90.5	38846	42 Southern Satellites	98.9	39111	56 Rural Bypasses	36.3
38606	56 Rural Bypasses	33.1	38847	42 Southern Satellites	100.0	39113	62 Modest Income Homes	42.9
38610	56 Rural Bypasses	58.4	38848	42 Southern Satellites	100.0	39114	56 Rural Bypasses	39.8
38611	42 Southern Satellites	36.8	38849	42 Southern Satellites	93.3	39116	42 Southern Satellites	98.0
38614	62 Modest Income Homes	38.0	38850	56 Rural Bypasses	70.0	39117	42 Southern Satellites	69.7
38617	62 Modest Income Homes	78.3	38851	42 Southern Satellites	55.2	39119	56 Rural Bypasses	100.0
38618	42 Southern Satellites	61.1	38852	42 Southern Satellites	35.2	39120	56 Rural Bypasses	26.2
38619	56 Rural Bypasses	75.5	38855	42 Southern Satellites	100.0	39140	56 Rural Bypasses	100.0
38620	56 Rural Bypasses	60.5	38856	42 Southern Satellites	100.0	39144	56 Rural Bypasses	99.7
38621	56 Rural Bypasses	68.1	38857	42 Southern Satellites	100.0	39145	42 Southern Satellites	60.7
38625	42 Southern Satellites	100.0	38858	42 Southern Satellites	51.3	39146	56 Rural Bypasses	97.0
38626	56 Rural Bypasses	75.3	38859	42 Southern Satellites	100.0	39149	56 Rural Bypasses	100.0
38627	42 Southern Satellites	100.0	38860	56 Rural Bypasses	44.7	39150	56 Rural Bypasses	71.2
38629	42 Southern Satellites	100.0	38862	42 Southern Satellites	55.8	39152	42 Southern Satellites	100.0
38632	26 Midland Crowd	39.8	38863	42 Southern Satellites	68.0	39153	42 Southern Satellites	84.4
38633	42 Southern Satellites	100.0	38864	42 Southern Satellites	100.0	39154	26 Midland Crowd	28.3
38635	56 Rural Bypasses	58.6	38865	42 Southern Satellites	84.2	39156	17 Green Acres	52.7
38637	28 Aspiring Young Families	33.2	38866	26 Midland Crowd	47.0	39157	39 Young and Restless	25.1
38641	26 Midland Crowd	85.0	38868	42 Southern Satellites	98.5	39159	56 Rural Bypasses	45.7
38642	56 Rural Bypasses	100.0	38870	42 Southern Satellites	100.0	39160	56 Rural Bypasses	93.3
38643	62 Modest Income Homes	60.8	38871	42 Southern Satellites	100.0	39162	46 Rooted Rural	100.0
38645	56 Rural Bypasses	92.6	38873	42 Southern Satellites	61.0	39166	56 Rural Bypasses	100.0

ZIP CODE	TOP TAPESTRY CONSUMER TYPE	% 2004 HOUSE-HOLDS	ZIP CODE	TOP TAPESTRY CONSUMER TYPE	% 2004 HOUSE-HOLDS	ZIP CODE	TOP TAPESTRY CONSUMER TYPE	% 2004 HOUSE-HOLDS
39168	56 Rural Bypasses	43.9	39466	26 Midland Crowd	29.3	39815	56 Rural Bypasses	99.3
39169	64 City Commons	41.2	39470	26 Midland Crowd	41.0	39817	56 Rural Bypasses	30.0
39170	17 Green Acres	48.1	39474	56 Rural Bypasses	89.1	39819	56 Rural Bypasses	23.7
39175	56 Rural Bypasses	40.8	39475	26 Midland Crowd	47.0	39823	56 Rural Bypasses	84.1
39176	56 Rural Bypasses	85.5	39476	42 Southern Satellites	65.4	39824	56 Rural Bypasses	100.0
39177	46 Rooted Rural	100.0	39478	56 Rural Bypasses	100.0	39825	42 Southern Satellites	97.0
39179	56 Rural Bypasses	100.0	39479	42 Southern Satellites	53.5	39826	56 Rural Bypasses	100.0
39180	33 Midlife Junction	17.9	39480	56 Rural Bypasses	52.3	39827	26 Midland Crowd	58.2
39183	51 Metro City Edge	19.3	39481	42 Southern Satellites	59.1	39828	62 Modest Income Homes	24.8
39189	56 Rural Bypasses	100.0	39482	26 Midland Crowd	72.6	39834	42 Southern Satellites	69.9
39191	42 Southern Satellites	37.9	39483	56 Rural Bypasses	74.9	39836	56 Rural Bypasses	100.0
39192	56 Rural Bypasses	51.4	39501	51 Metro City Edge	32.3	39837	46 Rooted Rural	49.9
39194	62 Modest Income Homes	33.0	39503	26 Midland Crowd	37.3	39840	56 Rural Bypasses	60.3
39201	65 Social Security Set	97.8	39507	36 Old and Newcomers	32.4	39841	56 Rural Bypasses	98.2
39202	22 Metropolitans	29.7	39520	33 Midlife Junction	32.8	39842	56 Rural Bypasses	33.1
39203	62 Modest Income Homes	66.5	39525	15 Silver and Gold	72.2	39845	56 Rural Bypasses	48.5
39204	51 Metro City Edge	32.6	39530	48 Great Expectations	14.9	39846	56 Rural Bypasses	100.0
39206	51 Metro City Edge	30.3	39531	36 Old and Newcomers	23.5	39851	56 Rural Bypasses	92.6
39208	48 Great Expectations	18.7	39532	26 Midland Crowd	56.2	39854	56 Rural Bypasses	100.0
39209	51 Metro City Edge	49.3	39534	40 Military Proximity	100.0	39859	56 Rural Bypasses	87.0
39211	14 Prosperous Empty Nesters	25.4	39540	26 Midland Crowd	34.5	39861	56 Rural Bypasses	54.6
39212	19 Milk and Cookies	34.4	39553	41 Crossroads	34.6	39862	56 Rural Bypasses	100.0
39213	62 Modest Income Homes	51.3	39556	41 Crossroads	70.5	39866	56 Rural Bypasses	100.0
39216	30 Retirement Communities	36.1	39560	32 Rustbelt Traditions	19.1	39867	56 Rural Bypasses	100.0
39218	26 Midland Crowd	75.6	39561	26 Midland Crowd	100.0	39870	56 Rural Bypasses	80.8
39232	16 Enterprising Professionals	56.5	39562	42 Southern Satellites	50.9	39877	46 Rooted Rural	100.0
39272	12 Up and Coming Families	45.2	39563	34 Family Foundations	49.9	39886	56 Rural Bypasses	100.0
39301	62 Modest Income Homes	24.4	39564	18 Cozy and Comfortable	18.6	39897	46 Rooted Rural	70.5
39305	22 Metropolitans	16.4	39565	26 Midland Crowd	100.0	40003	25 Salt of The Earth	93.1
39307	62 Modest Income Homes	21.5	39567	57 Simple Living	23.8	40004	26 Midland Crowd	29.7
39309	26 Midland Crowd	69.2	39571	31 Rural Resort Dwellers	31.0	40006	42 Southern Satellites	72.9
39320	26 Midland Crowd	100.0	39572	56 Rural Bypasses	48.5	40007	42 Southern Satellites	100.0
39322	56 Rural Bypasses	59.9	39573	26 Midland Crowd	78.5	40008	42 Southern Satellites	95.2
39323	42 Southern Satellites	99.1	39574	26 Midland Crowd	76.0	40009	42 Southern Satellites	100.0
39325	26 Midland Crowd	71.1	39576	33 Midlife Junction	60.7	40010	06 Sophisticated Squires	100.0
39326	18 Cozy and Comfortable	86.4	39577	56 Rural Bypasses	39.4	40011	25 Salt of The Earth	61.9
39327	46 Rooted Rural	55.9	39581	53 Home Town	19.0	40012	42 Southern Satellites	100.0
39328	56 Rural Bypasses	54.2	39601	42 Southern Satellites	28.3	40013	26 Midland Crowd	37.9
39330	56 Rural Bypasses	77.9	39629	42 Southern Satellites	71.1	40014	06 Sophisticated Squires	49.6
39332	42 Southern Satellites	60.1	39630	56 Rural Bypasses	100.0	40019	42 Southern Satellites	53.4
39335	26 Midland Crowd	55.1	39631	56 Rural Bypasses	81.0	40022	17 Green Acres	100.0
39336	42 Southern Satellites	98.6	39633	56 Rural Bypasses	100.0	40023	07 Exurbanites	45.7
39337	46 Rooted Rural	95.8	39638	56 Rural Bypasses	85.9	40025	03 Connoisseurs	100.0
39338	56 Rural Bypasses	100.0	39641	46 Rooted Rural	59.4	40026	06 Sophisticated Squires	71.0
39339	56 Rural Bypasses	28.2	39643	56 Rural Bypasses	81.0	40031	26 Midland Crowd	48.6
39341	56 Rural Bypasses	68.1	39645	46 Rooted Rural	46.9	40033	42 Southern Satellites	33.0
39342	51 Metro City Edge	80.7	39647	46 Rooted Rural	87.2	40036	42 Southern Satellites	100.0
39345	42 Southern Satellites	33.7	39648	56 Rural Bypasses	24.6	40037	42 Southern Satellites	98.4
39346	56 Rural Bypasses	93.5	39652	56 Rural Bypasses	81.0	40040	25 Salt of The Earth	55.9
39347	56 Rural Bypasses	100.0	39653	42 Southern Satellites	50.2	40045	42 Southern Satellites	60.5
39348	56 Rural Bypasses	100.0	39654	50 Heartland Communities	51.8	40046	26 Midland Crowd	70.1
39350	42 Southern Satellites	25.5	39656	56 Rural Bypasses	100.0	40047	26 Midland Crowd	54.5
39352	56 Rural Bypasses	100.0	39657	56 Rural Bypasses	58.5	40050	50 Heartland Communities	68.3
39354	56 Rural Bypasses	95.8	39661	56 Rural Bypasses	99.6	40051	42 Southern Satellites	88.7
39355	56 Rural Bypasses	45.2	39662	42 Southern Satellites	92.8	40052	42 Southern Satellites	100.0
39356	56 Rural Bypasses	100.0	39663	56 Rural Bypasses	100.0	40055	26 Midland Crowd	77.9
39358	56 Rural Bypasses	100.0	39664	46 Rooted Rural	57.9	40056	12 Up and Coming Families	53.7
39359	42 Southern Satellites	100.0	39665	56 Rural Bypasses	100.0	40057	42 Southern Satellites	81.4
39360	56 Rural Bypasses	97.6	39666	56 Rural Bypasses	37.6	40059	02 Suburban Splendor	50.6
39361	56 Rural Bypasses	100.0	39667	56 Rural Bypasses	58.1	40060	42 Southern Satellites	98.5
39362	56 Rural Bypasses	90.5	39668	56 Rural Bypasses	100.0	40061	25 Salt of The Earth	100.0
39363	56 Rural Bypasses	89.7	39669	56 Rural Bypasses	100.0	40062	42 Southern Satellites	100.0
39364	56 Rural Bypasses	54.8	39701	62 Modest Income Homes	48.7	40065	17 Green Acres	20.3
39365	56 Rural Bypasses	35.2	39702	26 Midland Crowd	32.1	40067	24 Main Street, USA	38.0
39366	56 Rural Bypasses	100.0	39705	17 Green Acres	22.9	40068	26 Midland Crowd	94.2
39367	56 Rural Bypasses	59.7	39710	40 Military Proximity	100.0	40069	25 Salt of The Earth	39.0
39401	62 Modest Income Homes	20.0	39730	42 Southern Satellites	32.3	40070	26 Midland Crowd	100.0
39402	13 In Style	28.5	39735	42 Southern Satellites	30.6	40071	17 Green Acres	59.1
39406	63 Dorms To Diplomas	100.0	39739	56 Rural Bypasses	82.6	40075	25 Salt of The Earth	54.9
39421	56 Rural Bypasses	99.5	39740	26 Midland Crowd	84.3	40076	17 Green Acres	49.2
39422	56 Rural Bypasses	74.4	39741	42 Southern Satellites	88.9	40077	17 Green Acres	99.2
39423	42 Southern Satellites	54.6	39743	56 Rural Bypasses	100.0	40078	42 Southern Satellites	100.0
39425	46 Rooted Rural	99.7	39744	56 Rural Bypasses	26.6	40104	46 Rooted Rural	54.9
39426	26 Midland Crowd	60.8	39745	56 Rural Bypasses	65.1	40107	42 Southern Satellites	50.4
39427	56 Rural Bypasses	100.0	39746	42 Southern Satellites	91.0	40108	26 Midland Crowd	61.5
39428	56 Rural Bypasses	48.0	39747	56 Rural Bypasses	96.9	40109	41 Crossroads	43.0
39429	46 Rooted Rural	31.4	39750	56 Rural Bypasses	52.1	40111	46 Rooted Rural	37.2
39437	42 Southern Satellites	42.4	39751	46 Rooted Rural	90.0	40115	42 Southern Satellites	100.0
39439	56 Rural Bypasses	74.2	39752	42 Southern Satellites	58.4	40117	26 Midland Crowd	63.2
39440	62 Modest Income Homes	28.4	39755	42 Southern Satellites	81.9	40118	41 Crossroads	48.7
39443	42 Southern Satellites	40.4	39756	56 Rural Bypasses	100.0	40119	42 Southern Satellites	76.9
39451	42 Southern Satellites	62.7	39759	55 College Towns	48.0	40121	40 Military Proximity	98.8
39452	42 Southern Satellites	48.6	39762	63 Dorms To Diplomas	58.3	40140	42 Southern Satellites	100.0
39455	42 Southern Satellites	32.8	39766	25 Salt of The Earth	73.5	40142	26 Midland Crowd	75.4
39456	56 Rural Bypasses	60.9	39767	42 Southern Satellites	54.4	40143	50 Heartland Communities	51.9
39459	46 Rooted Rural	82.7	39769	46 Rooted Rural	75.7	40144	46 Rooted Rural	38.0
39461	42 Southern Satellites	91.2	39772	56 Rural Bypasses	100.0	40145	42 Southern Satellites	100.0
39462	56 Rural Bypasses	49.7	39773	42 Southern Satellites	31.7	40146	46 Rooted Rural	51.5
39464	42 Southern Satellites	100.0	39776	56 Rural Bypasses	62.2	40150	25 Salt of The Earth	44.3
39465	26 Midland Crowd	42.2	39813	56 Rural Bypasses	100.0	40152	46 Rooted Rural	100.0

ZIP CODE	TOP TAPESTRY CONSUMER TYPE	% 2004 HOUSE-HOLDS	ZIP CODE	TOP TAPESTRY CONSUMER TYPE	% 2004 HOUSE-HOLDS	ZIP CODE	TOP TAPESTRY CONSUMER TYPE	% 2004 HOUSE-HOLDS
40155	41 Crossroads	61.2	40456	56 Rural Bypasses	67.3	40988	56 Rural Bypasses	100.0
40157	42 Southern Satellites	89.8	40460	56 Rural Bypasses	100.0	40995	56 Rural Bypasses	100.0
40160	19 Milk and Cookies	21.9	40461	46 Rooted Rural	29.2	40997	56 Rural Bypasses	100.0
40161	42 Southern Satellites	87.3	40464	42 Southern Satellites	69.3	40999	56 Rural Bypasses	100.0
40162	26 Midland Crowd	51.4	40468	25 Salt of The Earth	52.0	41001	17 Green Acres	29.9
40164	46 Rooted Rural	92.2	40472	50 Heartland Communities	69.2	41002	42 Southern Satellites	51.8
40165	17 Green Acres	29.0	40475	55 College Towns	16.6	41003	42 Southern Satellites	88.0
40170	46 Rooted Rural	100.0	40481	56 Rural Bypasses	100.0	41004	42 Southern Satellites	73.9
40171	46 Rooted Rural	100.0	40484	42 Southern Satellites	50.7	41005	12 Up and Coming Families	41.2
40175	26 Midland Crowd	40.8	40486	56 Rural Bypasses	61.8	41006	26 Midland Crowd	55.7
40176	42 Southern Satellites	64.0	40489	42 Southern Satellites	72.8	41007	25 Salt of The Earth	49.1
40177	53 Home Town	61.7	40502	22 Metropolitans	48.4	41008	26 Midland Crowd	31.2
40178	46 Rooted Rural	100.0	40503	33 Midlife Junction	21.7	41010	42 Southern Satellites	87.1
40202	65 Social Security Set	39.7	40504	48 Great Expectations	17.9	41011	60 City Dimensions	14.8
40203	64 City Commons	40.0	40505	32 Rustbelt Traditions	36.7	41014	48 Great Expectations	43.2
40204	48 Great Expectations	28.2	40507	55 College Towns	41.3	41015	32 Rustbelt Traditions	26.0
40205	22 Metropolitans	40.4	40508	63 Dorms To Diplomas	27.6	41016	32 Rustbelt Traditions	68.8
40206	48 Great Expectations	30.0	40509	16 Enterprising Professionals	29.9	41017	36 Old and Newcomers	15.4
40207	22 Metropolitans	40.1	40510	14 Prosperous Empty Nesters	96.6	41018	48 Great Expectations	18.0
40208	55 College Towns	32.1	40511	51 Metro City Edge	32.6	41030	41 Crossroads	54.6
40209	53 Home Town	76.0	40513	04 Boomburbs	78.7	41031	25 Salt of The Earth	45.7
40210	62 Modest Income Homes	47.1	40514	12 Up and Coming Families	50.0	41033	42 Southern Satellites	96.0
40211	62 Modest Income Homes	48.5	40515	16 Enterprising Professionals	23.4	41034	37 Prairie Living	80.4
40212	34 Family Foundations	27.6	40516	13 In Style	57.1	41035	26 Midland Crowd	50.8
40213	32 Rustbelt Traditions	26.5	40517	39 Young and Restless	47.2	41039	46 Rooted Rural	63.6
40214	48 Great Expectations	14.6	40601	29 Rustbelt Retirees	9.7	41040	26 Midland Crowd	31.3
40215	32 Rustbelt Traditions	29.6	40701	56 Rural Bypasses	28.5	41041	42 Southern Satellites	56.7
40216	29 Rustbelt Retirees	29.0	40729	56 Rural Bypasses	81.1	41042	12 Up and Coming Families	25.5
40217	32 Rustbelt Traditions	34.5	40734	56 Rural Bypasses	50.2	41043	42 Southern Satellites	78.1
40218	52 Inner City Tenants	15.7	40737	42 Southern Satellites	84.4	41044	42 Southern Satellites	100.0
40219	29 Rustbelt Retirees	19.4	40740	42 Southern Satellites	46.5	41045	26 Midland Crowd	83.1
40220	13 In Style	24.6	40741	42 Southern Satellites	21.4	41046	42 Southern Satellites	63.0
40222	36 Old and Newcomers	24.9	40744	42 Southern Satellites	47.6	41048	12 Up and Coming Families	50.6
40223	02 Suburban Splendor	17.5	40754	56 Rural Bypasses	100.0	41049	42 Southern Satellites	100.0
40228	18 Cozy and Comfortable	51.4	40759	56 Rural Bypasses	66.3	41051	12 Up and Coming Families	39.4
40229	32 Rustbelt Traditions	33.6	40763	56 Rural Bypasses	100.0	41052	26 Midland Crowd	61.9
40241	12 Up and Coming Families	25.0	40769	56 Rural Bypasses	64.5	41055	37 Prairie Living	99.2
40242	16 Enterprising Professionals	23.9	40771	56 Rural Bypasses	100.0	41056	42 Southern Satellites	20.4
40243	07 Exurbanites	25.6	40801	56 Rural Bypasses	100.0	41059	25 Salt of The Earth	37.5
40245	04 Boomburbs	46.0	40806	56 Rural Bypasses	67.8	41063	25 Salt of The Earth	46.9
40258	32 Rustbelt Traditions	44.5	40807	50 Heartland Communities	100.0	41064	46 Rooted Rural	100.0
40272	32 Rustbelt Traditions	39.8	40808	56 Rural Bypasses	100.0	41071	53 Home Town	18.1
40291	18 Cozy and Comfortable	28.6	40810	56 Rural Bypasses	100.0	41073	32 Rustbelt Traditions	37.9
40292	63 Dorms To Diplomas	0.0	40813	56 Rural Bypasses	69.9	41074	53 Home Town	44.7
40299	18 Cozy and Comfortable	15.4	40815	56 Rural Bypasses	100.0	41075	24 Main Street, USA	17.8
40311	42 Southern Satellites	43.9	40818	56 Rural Bypasses	100.0	41076	33 Midlife Junction	38.6
40312	42 Southern Satellites	56.7	40819	56 Rural Bypasses	100.0	41080	17 Green Acres	52.2
40313	41 Crossroads	37.9	40820	56 Rural Bypasses	100.0	41083	42 Southern Satellites	100.0
40316	42 Southern Satellites	100.0	40823	56 Rural Bypasses	49.0	41085	53 Home Town	99.6
40322	56 Rural Bypasses	68.5	40824	56 Rural Bypasses	100.0	41086	42 Southern Satellites	70.7
40324	12 Up and Coming Families	30.9	40826	56 Rural Bypasses	100.0	41091	04 Boomburbs	65.1
40328	42 Southern Satellites	76.2	40828	56 Rural Bypasses	100.0	41092	17 Green Acres	56.7
40330	25 Salt of The Earth	24.7	40829	56 Rural Bypasses	100.0	41093	42 Southern Satellites	100.0
40336	42 Southern Satellites	50.0	40831	56 Rural Bypasses	49.6	41094	24 Main Street, USA	30.6
40337	42 Southern Satellites	100.0	40843	56 Rural Bypasses	100.0	41095	50 Heartland Communities	50.9
40342	25 Salt of The Earth	37.3	40845	56 Rural Bypasses	100.0	41097	42 Southern Satellites	26.0
40346	56 Rural Bypasses	77.0	40847	56 Rural Bypasses	100.0	41098	42 Southern Satellites	100.0
40347	24 Main Street, USA	57.5	40855	56 Rural Bypasses	100.0	41101	50 Heartland Communities	31.2
40350	42 Southern Satellites	100.0	40858	56 Rural Bypasses	100.0	41102	29 Rustbelt Retirees	28.5
40351	42 Southern Satellites	24.4	40862	56 Rural Bypasses	100.0	41121	42 Southern Satellites	99.3
40353	25 Salt of The Earth	25.7	40863	56 Rural Bypasses	100.0	41124	56 Rural Bypasses	100.0
40355	42 Southern Satellites	48.6	40865	56 Rural Bypasses	100.0	41129	26 Midland Crowd	38.6
40356	07 Exurbanites	17.5	40868	56 Rural Bypasses	100.0	41132	56 Rural Bypasses	86.2
40358	42 Southern Satellites	100.0	40870	56 Rural Bypasses	100.0	41135	56 Rural Bypasses	99.5
40359	50 Heartland Communities	37.4	40873	50 Heartland Communities	100.0	41137	56 Rural Bypasses	100.0
40360	42 Southern Satellites	45.6	40902	56 Rural Bypasses	100.0	41139	50 Heartland Communities	50.3
40361	25 Salt of The Earth	19.4	40903	56 Rural Bypasses	100.0	41141	56 Rural Bypasses	100.0
40370	17 Green Acres	45.1	40906	56 Rural Bypasses	63.4	41143	56 Rural Bypasses	45.5
40371	46 Rooted Rural	48.8	40913	56 Rural Bypasses	100.0	41144	56 Rural Bypasses	30.7
40372	25 Salt of The Earth	87.1	40914	56 Rural Bypasses	100.0	41146	56 Rural Bypasses	100.0
40374	46 Rooted Rural	54.6	40915	26 Midland Crowd	62.6	41149	56 Rural Bypasses	100.0
40376	42 Southern Satellites	100.0	40921	56 Rural Bypasses	99.8	41159	56 Rural Bypasses	100.0
40379	42 Southern Satellites	74.6	40923	56 Rural Bypasses	99.7	41164	56 Rural Bypasses	59.5
40380	42 Southern Satellites	52.7	40927	56 Rural Bypasses	100.0	41166	56 Rural Bypasses	100.0
40383	17 Green Acres	29.2	40930	56 Rural Bypasses	100.0	41168	26 Midland Crowd	62.5
40385	42 Southern Satellites	63.8	40935	56 Rural Bypasses	100.0	41169	32 Rustbelt Traditions	30.8
40387	42 Southern Satellites	100.0	40940	56 Rural Bypasses	100.0	41171	56 Rural Bypasses	82.4
40390	28 Aspiring Young Families	45.1	40943	56 Rural Bypasses	100.0	41174	56 Rural Bypasses	99.7
40391	26 Midland Crowd	19.8	40946	56 Rural Bypasses	99.3	41175	50 Heartland Communities	46.5
40402	42 Southern Satellites	89.9	40949	56 Rural Bypasses	43.5	41179	56 Rural Bypasses	52.8
40403	26 Midland Crowd	26.0	40953	56 Rural Bypasses	100.0	41180	56 Rural Bypasses	57.1
40404	55 College Towns	100.0	40958	56 Rural Bypasses	100.0	41183	29 Rustbelt Retirees	50.6
40409	42 Southern Satellites	56.4	40962	56 Rural Bypasses	78.9	41189	42 Southern Satellites	52.2
40419	42 Southern Satellites	66.6	40964	56 Rural Bypasses	100.0	41201	56 Rural Bypasses	100.0
40422	33 Midlife Junction	30.3	40965	56 Rural Bypasses	41.5	41204	56 Rural Bypasses	100.0
40437	42 Southern Satellites	90.1	40972	56 Rural Bypasses	100.0	41214	56 Rural Bypasses	100.0
40440	42 Southern Satellites	56.7	40977	56 Rural Bypasses	67.4	41216	26 Midland Crowd	55.2
40442	56 Rural Bypasses	55.8	40979	56 Rural Bypasses	100.0	41219	56 Rural Bypasses	62.2
40444	25 Salt of The Earth	26.1	40982	56 Rural Bypasses	100.0	41222	56 Rural Bypasses	62.3
40447	56 Rural Bypasses	75.6	40983	56 Rural Bypasses	100.0	41224	56 Rural Bypasses	100.0

ZIP CODE	TOP TAPESTRY CONSUMER TYPE	% 2004 HOUSE-HOLDS	ZIP CODE	TOP TAPESTRY CONSUMER TYPE	% 2004 HOUSE-HOLDS	ZIP CODE	TOP TAPESTRY CONSUMER TYPE	% 2004 HOUSE-HOLDS
41226	42 Southern Satellites	100.0	41632	56 Rural Bypasses	100.0	42040	46 Rooted Rural	52.8
41230	50 Heartland Communities	28,6	41635	56 Rural Bypasses	77.9	42041	53 Home Town	38.1
41231	56 Rural Bypasses	100.0	41636	56 Rural Bypasses	100.0	42044	31 Rural Resort Dwellers	77.2
41232	56 Rural Bypasses	90.5	41640	56 Rural Bypasses	100.0	42045	46 Rooted Rural	74.0
41234	42 Southern Satellites	82.9	41642	42 Southern Satellites	48.0	42047	46 Rooted Rural	100.0
41238	46 Rooted Rural	70.3	41643	56 Rural Bypasses	100.0	42048	31 Rural Resort Dwellers	40.8
41240	56 Rural Bypasses	60.7	41645	56 Rural Bypasses	72.6	42049	46 Rooted Rural	89.8
41250	56 Rural Bypasses	100.0	41647	56 Rural Bypasses	100.0	42050	50 Heartland Communities	42.8
41254	56 Rural Bypasses	100.0	41649	50 Heartland Communities	32.8	42051	42 Southern Satellites	55.8
41255	56 Rural Bypasses	100.0	41650	56 Rural Bypasses	100.0	42053	46 Rooted Rural	41.7
41256	56 Rural Bypasses	76.4	41653	56 Rural Bypasses	55.7	42054	46 Rooted Rural	75.6
41257	46 Rooted Rural	100.0	41655	56 Rural Bypasses	100.0	42055	46 Rooted Rural	70.7
41260	56 Rural Bypasses	53.5	41660	56 Rural Bypasses	100.0	42056	50 Heartland Communities	51.5
41262	56 Rural Bypasses	100.0	41666	56 Rural Bypasses	100.0	42058	26 Midland Crowd	96.6
41263	56 Rural Bypasses	70.8	41701	56 Rural Bypasses	53.2	42064	50 Heartland Communities	42.0
41265	56 Rural Bypasses	50.4	41712	56 Rural Bypasses	100.0	42066	42 Southern Satellites	22.5
41267	56 Rural Bypasses	62.2	41714	56 Rural Bypasses	100.0	42069	46 Rooted Rural	84.7
41271	56 Rural Bypasses	100.0	41719	46 Rooted Rural	56.0	42071	55 College Towns	28.8
41274	56 Rural Bypasses	100.0	41721	56 Rural Bypasses	100.0	42076	49 Senior Sun Seekers	81.2
41301	56 Rural Bypasses	82.0	41722	56 Rural Bypasses	100.0	42078	46 Rooted Rural	100.0
41311	56 Rural Bypasses	83.3	41723	56 Rural Bypasses	100.0	42079	46 Rooted Rural	99.2
41314	56 Rural Bypasses	74.0	41725	56 Rural Bypasses	100.0	42081	46 Rooted Rural	96.9
41317	56 Rural Bypasses	100.0	41727	42 Southern Satellites	82.1	42082	46 Rooted Rural	80.6
41332	56 Rural Bypasses	63.0	41729	46 Rooted Rural	99.2	42083	46 Rooted Rural	100.0
41338	56 Rural Bypasses	100.0	41731	56 Rural Bypasses	100.0	42085	46 Rooted Rural	97.7
41339	56 Rural Bypasses	79.1	41735	56 Rural Bypasses	100.0	42086	26 Midland Crowd	56.1
41342	56 Rural Bypasses	100.0	41736	56 Rural Bypasses	100.0	42087	46 Rooted Rural	97.3
41348	56 Rural Bypasses	100.0	41740	56 Rural Bypasses	100.0	42088	42 Southern Satellites	89.7
41351	56 Rural Bypasses	100.0	41743	56 Rural Bypasses	100.0	42101	26 Midland Crowd	15.5
41360	56 Rural Bypasses	90.6	41745	56 Rural Bypasses	100.0	42103	17 Green Acres	26.5
41364	56 Rural Bypasses	100.0	41746	56 Rural Bypasses	100.0	42104	13 In Style	22.3
41365	56 Rural Bypasses	100.0	41749	56 Rural Bypasses	100.0	42120	42 Southern Satellites	100.0
41366	56 Rural Bypasses	100.0	41754	56 Rural Bypasses	100.0	42122	26 Midland Crowd	53.1
41367	56 Rural Bypasses	100.0	41759	56 Rural Bypasses	100.0	42123	42 Southern Satellites	81.7
41385	56 Rural Bypasses	100.0	41760	56 Rural Bypasses	100.0	42124	42 Southern Satellites	100.0
41386	56 Rural Bypasses	100.0	41763	56 Rural Bypasses	100.0	42127	46 Rooted Rural	50.4
41390	56 Rural Bypasses	100.0	41764	56 Rural Bypasses	100.0	42129	42 Southern Satellites	82.7
41397	56 Rural Bypasses	100.0	41772	56 Rural Bypasses	100.0	42130	42 Southern Satellites	100.0
41419	56 Rural Bypasses	100.0	41773	56 Rural Bypasses	100.0	42131	42 Southern Satellites	64.1
41422	56 Rural Bypasses	100.0	41774	56 Rural Bypasses	100.0	42133	42 Southern Satellites	100.0
41425	46 Rooted Rural	99.3	41775	56 Rural Bypasses	100.0	42134	42 Southern Satellites	26.7
41464	56 Rural Bypasses	100.0	41776	56 Rural Bypasses	100.0	42140	42 Southern Satellites	100.0
41465	56 Rural Bypasses	92.6	41777	56 Rural Bypasses	100.0	42141	42 Southern Satellites	22.4
41472	56 Rural Bypasses	69.6	41804	56 Rural Bypasses	91.2	42151	42 Southern Satellites	100.0
41501	56 Rural Bypasses	41.1	41812	56 Rural Bypasses	100.0	42153	42 Southern Satellites	100.0
41503	29 Rustbelt Retirees	98.0	41815	56 Rural Bypasses	100.0	42154	42 Southern Satellites	65.6
41512	56 Rural Bypasses	100.0	41817	56 Rural Bypasses	100.0	42156	42 Southern Satellites	71.9
41513	46 Rooted Rural	97.5	41819	56 Rural Bypasses	100.0	42157	37 Prairie Living	92.7
41514	56 Rural Bypasses	73.0	41821	56 Rural Bypasses	100.0	42159	25 Salt of The Earth	99.8
41519	56 Rural Bypasses	100.0	41822	56 Rural Bypasses	100.0	42160	42 Southern Satellites	46.7
41522	56 Rural Bypasses	88.3	41824	56 Rural Bypasses	100.0	42163	46 Rooted Rural	100.0
41524	56 Rural Bypasses	100.0	41825	56 Rural Bypasses	100.0	42164	42 Southern Satellites	68.6
41527	26 Midland Crowd	80.6	41826	46 Rooted Rural	57.5	42166	46 Rooted Rural	61.3
41528	56 Rural Bypasses	100.0	41828	56 Rural Bypasses	100.0	42167	42 Southern Satellites	43.9
41531	56 Rural Bypasses	95.3	41831	56 Rural Bypasses	100.0	42170	17 Green Acres	43.2
41535	46 Rooted Rural	86.6	41832	56 Rural Bypasses	50.8	42171	42 Southern Satellites	57.7
41537	56 Rural Bypasses	41.3	41833	56 Rural Bypasses	100.0	42202	42 Southern Satellites	75.4
41539	42 Southern Satellites	65.2	41834	56 Rural Bypasses	100.0	42204	37 Prairie Living	48.3
41540	56 Rural Bypasses	100.0	41835	56 Rural Bypasses	100.0	42206	42 Southern Satellites	90.9
41543	56 Rural Bypasses	98.8	41836	56 Rural Bypasses	100.0	42207	56 Rural Bypasses	81.2
41544	56 Rural Bypasses	100.0	41837	56 Rural Bypasses	100.0	42210	56 Rural Bypasses	53.8
41546	56 Rural Bypasses	100.0	41838	56 Rural Bypasses	100.0	42211	46 Rooted Rural	25.6
41548	56 Rural Bypasses	100.0	41839	56 Rural Bypasses	100.0	42214	42 Southern Satellites	71.2
41553	56 Rural Bypasses	100.0	41840	56 Rural Bypasses	100.0	42215	42 Southern Satellites	47.0
41554	56 Rural Bypasses	96.6	41843	56 Rural Bypasses	100.0	42217	42 Southern Satellites	70.7
41555	56 Rural Bypasses	100.0	41844	56 Rural Bypasses	100.0	42220	42 Southern Satellites	90.3
41557	42 Southern Satellites	65.7	41845	56 Rural Bypasses	100.0	42223	40 Military Proximity	99.3
41558	56 Rural Bypasses	100.0	41847	56 Rural Bypasses	100.0	42232	25 Salt of The Earth	85.2
41559	46 Rooted Rural	57.1	41849	56 Rural Bypasses	100.0	42234	53 Home Town	73.6
41560	42 Southern Satellites	63.8	41855	56 Rural Bypasses	100.0	42236	26 Midland Crowd	87.4
41562	56 Rural Bypasses	77.7	41858	56 Rural Bypasses	68.8	42240	62 Modest Income Homes	15.9
41563	56 Rural Bypasses	100.0	41859	56 Rural Bypasses	100.0	42252	42 Southern Satellites	100.0
41564	56 Rural Bypasses	100.0	41861	56 Rural Bypasses	100.0	42254	26 Midland Crowd	100.0
41566	56 Rural Bypasses	100.0	41862	56 Rural Bypasses	100.0	42256	42 Southern Satellites	88.7
41567	56 Rural Bypasses	60.8	42001	33 Midlife Junction	18.0	42257	42 Southern Satellites	100.0
41568	56 Rural Bypasses	100.0	42003	33 Midlife Junction	18.6	42259	46 Rooted Rural	100.0
41571	56 Rural Bypasses	100.0	42020	42 Southern Satellites	60.0	42261	42 Southern Satellites	62.5
41572	56 Rural Bypasses	100.0	42021	42 Southern Satellites	62.2	42262	40 Military Proximity	91.6
41601	46 Rooted Rural	92.5	42023	42 Southern Satellites	50.7	42265	25 Salt of The Earth	85.3
41602	56 Rural Bypasses	53.3	42024	46 Rooted Rural	98.8	42266	46 Rooted Rural	80.7
41603	56 Rural Bypasses	94.9	42025	25 Salt of The Earth	35.8	42273	46 Rooted Rural	100.0
41604	56 Rural Bypasses	100.0	42027	26 Midland Crowd	82.9	42274	26 Midland Crowd	95.4
41605	46 Rooted Rural	75.1	42028	46 Rooted Rural	100.0	42275	42 Southern Satellites	50.5
41606	56 Rural Bypasses	100.0	42029	33 Midlife Junction	36.0	42276	42 Southern Satellites	46.8
41607	26 Midland Crowd	100.0	42031	46 Rooted Rural	39.7	42280	42 Southern Satellites	100.0
41615	56 Rural Bypasses	100.0	42032	42 Southern Satellites	100.0	42285	42 Southern Satellites	100.0
41616	56 Rural Bypasses	66.7	42035	42 Southern Satellites	90.2	42286	37 Prairie Living	83.3
41622	56 Rural Bypasses	100.0	42036	42 Southern Satellites	100.0	42287	42 Southern Satellites	100.0
41630	56 Rural Bypasses	100.0	42038	50 Heartland Communities	39.1	42301	25 Salt of The Earth	13.6
41631	56 Rural Bypasses	100.0	42039	42 Southern Satellites	99.0	42303	17 Green Acres	18.7

ZIP CODE	TOP TAPESTRY CONSUMER TYPE	% 2004 HOUSE-HOLDS	ZIP CODE	TOP TAPESTRY CONSUMER TYPE	% 2004 HOUSE-HOLDS	ZIP CODE	TOP TAPESTRY CONSUMER TYPE	% 2004 HOUSE-HOLDS
42320	42 Southern Satellites	37.8	42718	25 Salt of The Earth	36.6	43125	36 Old and Newcomers	16.3
42321	42 Southern Satellites	100.0	42721	42 Southern Satellites	51.5	43128	32 Rustbelt Traditions	61.8
42323	42 Southern Satellites	99.1	42722	46 Rooted Rural	100.0	43130	48 Great Expectations	11.3
42324	42 Southern Satellites	63.8	42724	42 Southern Satellites	54.7	43135	42 Southern Satellites	33.3
42325	46 Rooted Rural	52.6	42726	42 Southern Satellites	77.1	43137	41 Crossroads	53.3
42326	42 Southern Satellites	100.0	42728	42 Southern Satellites	41.1	43138	25 Salt of The Earth	32.0
42327	46 Rooted Rural	47.4	42729	42 Southern Satellites	66.5	43140	29 Rustbelt Retirees	17.2
42328	42 Southern Satellites	89.0	42731	42 Southern Satellites	56.9	43143	32 Rustbelt Traditions	43.1
42330	42 Southern Satellites	39.3	42732	42 Southern Satellites	58.4	43145	46 Rooted Rural	60.2
42333	42 Southern Satellites	97.9	42733	42 Southern Satellites	89.6	43146	17 Green Acres	41.7
42337	56 Rural Bypasses	68.5	42735	46 Rooted Rural	100.0	43147	12 Up and Coming Families	40.9
42338	42 Southern Satellites	100.0	42740	25 Salt of The Earth	74.6	43148	17 Green Acres	57.2
42339	46 Rooted Rural	53.9	42741	46 Rooted Rural	100.0	43149	25 Salt of The Earth	87.7
42343	42 Southern Satellites	64.9	42742	42 Southern Satellites	100.0	43150	25 Salt of The Earth	54.0
42344	56 Rural Bypasses	100.0	42743	46 Rooted Rural	59.6	43152	42 Southern Satellites	56.9
42345	50 Heartland Communities	29.3	42746	42 Southern Satellites	53.3	43153	25 Salt of The Earth	91.8
42347	50 Heartland Communities	49.6	42748	26 Midland Crowd	26.3	43154	25 Salt of The Earth	88.5
42348	42 Southern Satellites	91.4	42749	50 Heartland Communities	28.3	43155	25 Salt of The Earth	93.0
42349	46 Rooted Rural	84.8	42753	42 Southern Satellites	90.0	43160	25 Salt of The Earth	28.2
42350	46 Rooted Rural	100.0	42754	42 Southern Satellites	60.7	43162	25 Salt of The Earth	29.9
42351	26 Midland Crowd	45.0	42757	42 Southern Satellites	83.1	43164	25 Salt of The Earth	66.5
42352	50 Heartland Communities	54.0	42762	42 Southern Satellites	100.0	43201	63 Dorms To Diplomas	52.6
42354	56 Rural Bypasses	100.0	42764	46 Rooted Rural	45.9	43202	55 College Towns	35.3
42355	25 Salt of The Earth	68.7	42765	42 Southern Satellites	59.5	43203	64 City Commons	23.2
42361	46 Rooted Rural	69.9	42776	42 Southern Satellites	65.1	43204	32 Rustbelt Traditions	16.4
42366	17 Green Acres	46.7	42782	42 Southern Satellites	69.1	43205	64 City Commons	19.3
42367	56 Rural Bypasses	100.0	42784	46 Rooted Rural	52.9	43206	51 Metro City Edge	32.4
42368	42 Southern Satellites	98.7	42788	25 Salt of The Earth	100.0	43207	29 Rustbelt Retirees	13.8
42369	46 Rooted Rural	100.0	43001	17 Green Acres	66.6	43209	14 Prosperous Empty Nesters	17.4
42371	46 Rooted Rural	50.9	43002	16 Enterprising Professionals	100.0	43210	55 College Towns	53.4
42372	46 Rooted Rural	72.9	43003	32 Rustbelt Traditions	55.4	43211	51 Metro City Edge	54.4
42376	26 Midland Crowd	46.9	43004	28 Aspiring Young Families	48.0	43212	22 Metropolitans	34.5
42378	42 Southern Satellites	86.5	43006	42 Southern Satellites	69.4	43213	32 Rustbelt Traditions	19.1
42404	42 Southern Satellites	58.5	43008	50 Heartland Communities	84.0	43214	22 Metropolitans	24.3
42406	25 Salt of The Earth	51.0	43009	25 Salt of The Earth	52.9	43215	27 Metro Renters	61.2
42408	50 Heartland Communities	33.5	43011	26 Midland Crowd	37.5	43217	28 Aspiring Young Families	100.0
42409	46 Rooted Rural	51.1	43013	17 Green Acres	100.0	43219	34 Family Foundations	37.5
42410	53 Home Town	49.3	43014	25 Salt of The Earth	63.5	43220	39 Young and Restless	25.0
42411	46 Rooted Rural	99.2	43015	12 Up and Coming Families	14.9	43221	14 Prosperous Empty Nesters	16.6
42413	25 Salt of The Earth	54.7	43016	16 Enterprising Professionals	58.4	43222	60 City Dimensions	54.5
42420	53 Home Town	17.7	43017	02 Suburban Splendor	32.9	43223	32 Rustbelt Traditions	27.2
42431	50 Heartland Communities	19.3	43019	25 Salt of The Earth	45.1	43224	32 Rustbelt Traditions	20.2
42436	26 Midland Crowd	87.3	43021	07 Exurbanites	38.0	43227	48 Great Expectations	28.5
42437	42 Southern Satellites	34.2	43022	22 Metropolitans	44.1	43228	28 Aspiring Young Families	28.9
42441	42 Southern Satellites	56.9	43023	07 Exurbanites	41.9	43229	39 Young and Restless	26.1
42442	56 Rural Bypasses	61.6	43025	26 Midland Crowd	25.0	43230	16 Enterprising Professionals	26.8
42445	50 Heartland Communities	43.7	43026	16 Enterprising Professionals	34.6	43231	19 Milk and Cookies	22.5
42450	53 Home Town	42.6	43028	17 Green Acres	47.5	43232	52 Inner City Tenants	16.7
42451	25 Salt of The Earth	53.2	43029	17 Green Acres	100.0	43235	16 Enterprising Professionals	40.1
42452	25 Salt of The Earth	94.8	43031	17 Green Acres	73.7	43240	16 Enterprising Professionals	100.0
42453	56 Rural Bypasses	87.4	43035	04 Boomburbs	47.8	43302	32 Rustbelt Traditions	28.5
42455	42 Southern Satellites	84.3	43037	25 Salt of The Earth	71.4	43310	25 Salt of The Earth	60.0
42456	25 Salt of The Earth	69.6	43040	12 Up and Coming Families	21.0	43311	48 Great Expectations	19.5
42458	25 Salt of The Earth	78.6	43044	25 Salt of The Earth	36.8	43314	42 Southern Satellites	52.0
42459	50 Heartland Communities	41.1	43045	17 Green Acres	91.9	43315	25 Salt of The Earth	41.1
42461	42 Southern Satellites	100.0	43046	25 Salt of The Earth	38.6	43316	32 Rustbelt Traditions	38.2
42462	42 Southern Satellites	100.0	43050	57 Simple Living	15.6	43318	25 Salt of The Earth	70.5
42464	42 Southern Satellites	51.6	43054	04 Boomburbs	41.2	43319	17 Green Acres	99.7
42501	50 Heartland Communities	30.5	43055	32 Rustbelt Traditions	19.3	43320	25 Salt of The Earth	62.5
42503	26 Midland Crowd	17.5	43056	17 Green Acres	30.2	43321	26 Midland Crowd	100.0
42516	42 Southern Satellites	100.0	43060	26 Midland Crowd	71.3	43323	25 Salt of The Earth	100.0
42518	42 Southern Satellites	58.5	43061	25 Salt of The Earth	89.4	43324	25 Salt of The Earth	55.2
42519	42 Southern Satellites	41.5	43062	17 Green Acres	41.8	43326	32 Rustbelt Traditions	26.6
42528	42 Southern Satellites	87.8	43064	17 Green Acres	32.6	43331	49 Senior Sun Seekers	31.8
42533	53 Home Town	56.3	43065	04 Boomburbs	33.4	43332	50 Heartland Communities	43.4
42539	46 Rooted Rural	39.2	43066	17 Green Acres	100.0	43333	25 Salt of The Earth	100.0
42541	42 Southern Satellites	97.5	43067	25 Salt of The Earth	47.5	43334	26 Midland Crowd	63.6
42544	46 Rooted Rural	69.6	43068	28 Aspiring Young Families	25.7	43335	25 Salt of The Earth	100.0
42553	42 Southern Satellites	79.6	43071	25 Salt of The Earth	81.7	43337	25 Salt of The Earth	94.4
42565	56 Rural Bypasses	76.4	43072	25 Salt of The Earth	92.2	43338	25 Salt of The Earth	65.9
42566	42 Southern Satellites	100.0	43074	17 Green Acres	45.8	43340	42 Southern Satellites	64.2
42567	42 Southern Satellites	74.2	43076	17 Green Acres	40.7	43341	42 Southern Satellites	85.0
42602	56 Rural Bypasses	48.9	43078	17 Green Acres	29.4	43342	25 Salt of The Earth	63.7
42603	42 Southern Satellites	89.4	43080	25 Salt of The Earth	47.1	43343	25 Salt of The Earth	100.0
42629	46 Rooted Rural	63.4	43081	16 Enterprising Professionals	31.5	43344	32 Rustbelt Traditions	53.6
42633	56 Rural Bypasses	46.2	43082	04 Boomburbs	69.7	43345	25 Salt of The Earth	99.7
42634	56 Rural Bypasses	100.0	43084	25 Salt of The Earth	98.1	43346	25 Salt of The Earth	100.0
42635	56 Rural Bypasses	100.0	43085	14 Prosperous Empty Nesters	29.2	43347	25 Salt of The Earth	95.9
42638	56 Rural Bypasses	100.0	43102	25 Salt of The Earth	64.2	43348	53 Home Town	45.8
42642	46 Rooted Rural	45.0	43103	17 Green Acres	33.4	43351	32 Rustbelt Traditions	37.2
42647	56 Rural Bypasses	100.0	43105	17 Green Acres	36.9	43356	17 Green Acres	93.2
42649	56 Rural Bypasses	100.0	43106	42 Southern Satellites	69.8	43357	17 Green Acres	47.2
42653	56 Rural Bypasses	100.0	43107	25 Salt of The Earth	93.7	43358	25 Salt of The Earth	99.3
42701	26 Midland Crowd	28.7	43110	28 Aspiring Young Families	44.7	43359	25 Salt of The Earth	100.0
42711	46 Rooted Rural	100.0	43112	07 Exurbanites	48.1	43360	26 Midland Crowd	60.3
42712	42 Southern Satellites	88.6	43113	17 Green Acres	27.0	43402	55 College Towns	23.3
42713	42 Southern Satellites	51.5	43115	42 Southern Satellites	88.3	43403	63 Dorms To Diplomas	100.0
42715	42 Southern Satellites	100.0	43116	17 Green Acres	100.0	43406	32 Rustbelt Traditions	74.7
42716	25 Salt of The Earth	76.2	43119	28 Aspiring Young Families	64.6	43407	18 Cozy and Comfortable	100.0
42717	46 Rooted Rural	63.5	43123	12 Up and Coming Families	30.1	43410	25 Salt of The Earth	43.6

ZIP CODE	TOP TAPESTRY CONSUMER TYPE	% 2004 HOUSE-HOLDS	ZIP CODE	TOP TAPESTRY CONSUMER TYPE	% 2004 HOUSE-HOLDS	ZIP CODE	TOP TAPESTRY CONSUMER TYPE	% 2004 HOUSE-HOLDS
43412	17 Green Acres	79.0	43718	25 Salt of The Earth	65.0	44004	53 Home Town	24.8
43413	25 Salt of The Earth	97.3	43719	50 Heartland Communities	73.8	44010	25 Salt of The Earth	87.4
43416	25 Salt of The Earth	67.9	43720	42 Southern Satellites	81.1	44011	07 Exurbanites	42.5
43420	32 Rustbelt Traditions	25.2	43723	50 Heartland Communities	35.2	44012	18 Cozy and Comfortable	32.0
43430	18 Cozy and Comfortable	40.7	43724	25 Salt of The Earth	36.9	44017	18 Cozy and Comfortable	40.2
43431	25 Salt of The Earth	40.8	43725	33 Midlife Junction	27.7	44021	25 Salt of The Earth	32.7
43432	25 Salt of The Earth	58.0	43727	25 Salt of The Earth	57.3	44022	03 Connoisseurs	34.7
43435	25 Salt of The Earth	83.8	43728	42 Southern Satellites	70.3	44023	07 Exurbanites	48.7
43436	31 Rural Resort Dwellers	100.0	43730	42 Southern Satellites	53.6	44024	17 Green Acres	28.0
43438	31 Rural Resort Dwellers	100.0	43731	42 Southern Satellites	60.2	44026	07 Exurbanites	100.0
43440	31 Rural Resort Dwellers	100.0	43732	25 Salt of The Earth	88.1	44028	17 Green Acres	73.9
43442	25 Salt of The Earth	91.8	43734	29 Rustbelt Retirees	67.8	44030	29 Rustbelt Retirees	20.4
43443	29 Rustbelt Retirees	70.2	43739	26 Midland Crowd	40.5	44032	25 Salt of The Earth	71.8
43445	17 Green Acres	99.3	43746	25 Salt of The Earth	59.4	44035	32 Rustbelt Traditions	20.3
43447	18 Cozy and Comfortable	51.5	43747	46 Rooted Rural	77.7	44039	18 Cozy and Comfortable	46.5
43449	25 Salt of The Earth	40.4	43748	42 Southern Satellites	93.2	44040	03 Connoisseurs	43.6
43450	17 Green Acres	58.2	43749	46 Rooted Rural	94.8	44041	53 Home Town	18.2
43451	17 Green Acres	36.3	43754	50 Heartland Communities	37.2	44044	17 Green Acres	34.3
43452	31 Rural Resort Dwellers	40.4	43755	46 Rooted Rural	100.0	44046	17 Green Acres	43.5
43456	31 Rural Resort Dwellers	100.0	43756	50 Heartland Communities	41.1	44047	25 Salt of The Earth	51.4
43457	25 Salt of The Earth	100.0	43758	46 Rooted Rural	50.7	44048	25 Salt of The Earth	65.0
43460	32 Rustbelt Traditions	29.2	43760	26 Midland Crowd	47.3	44050	17 Green Acres	45.4
43462	26 Midland Crowd	87.9	43762	33 Midlife Junction	59.6	44052	32 Rustbelt Traditions	19.8
43464	25 Salt of The Earth	79.5	43764	32 Rustbelt Traditions	30.1	44053	24 Main Street, USA	60.5
43465	49 Senior Sun Seekers	41.4	43766	56 Rural Bypasses	64.3	44054	18 Cozy and Comfortable	28.6
43466	25 Salt of The Earth	98.3	43767	25 Salt of The Earth	86.5	44055	32 Rustbelt Traditions	34.2
43469	17 Green Acres	39.6	43771	42 Southern Satellites	100.0	44056	13 In Style	35.2
43501	25 Salt of The Earth	100.0	43772	50 Heartland Communities	68.6	44057	17 Green Acres	32.4
43502	17 Green Acres	31.4	43773	25 Salt of The Earth	34.2	44060	06 Sophisticated Squires	35.0
43504	17 Green Acres	100.0	43777	42 Southern Satellites	69.0	44062	42 Southern Satellites	20.7
43506	42 Southern Satellites	23.8	43778	46 Rooted Rural	59.0	44064	17 Green Acres	99.1
43511	25 Salt of The Earth	100.0	43779	25 Salt of The Earth	53.7	44065	07 Exurbanites	70.0
43512	25 Salt of The Earth	25.3	43780	46 Rooted Rural	51.3	44067	13 In Style	28.9
43515	25 Salt of The Earth	36.7	43782	42 Southern Satellites	100.0	44070	18 Cozy and Comfortable	44.6
43516	25 Salt of The Earth	63.7	43783	25 Salt of The Earth	51.4	44072	03 Connoisseurs	87.3
43517	25 Salt of The Earth	66.1	43787	46 Rooted Rural	54.0	44074	22 Metropolitans	22.5
43518	25 Salt of The Earth	89.0	43788	42 Southern Satellites	86.2	44076	25 Salt of The Earth	45.9
43521	53 Home Town	53.1	43793	50 Heartland Communities	32.8	44077	17 Green Acres	13.4
43522	17 Green Acres	61.1	43802	42 Southern Satellites	80.4	44081	17 Green Acres	74.0
43524	25 Salt of The Earth	100.0	43804	42 Southern Satellites	62.3	44082	42 Southern Satellites	100.0
43525	17 Green Acres	100.0	43811	42 Southern Satellites	62.8	44084	17 Green Acres	62.3
43526	25 Salt of The Earth	54.1	43812	53 Home Town	31.3	44085	17 Green Acres	58.9
43527	32 Rustbelt Traditions	54.2	43821	25 Salt of The Earth	48.7	44086	17 Green Acres	60.7
43528	13 In Style	33.4	43822	42 Southern Satellites	53.7	44087	13 In Style	36.6
43532	25 Salt of The Earth	94.4	43824	42 Southern Satellites	68.8	44089	18 Cozy and Comfortable	25.0
43533	25 Salt of The Earth	100.0	43830	26 Midland Crowd	27.6	44090	17 Green Acres	45.0
43534	25 Salt of The Earth	82.3	43832	25 Salt of The Earth	26.7	44092	29 Rustbelt Retirees	70.1
43535	25 Salt of The Earth	100.0	43837	25 Salt of The Earth	64.6	44093	42 Southern Satellites	100.0
43536	25 Salt of The Earth	100.0	43840	25 Salt of The Earth	97.6	44094	30 Retirement Communities	30.8
43537	13 In Style	30.6	43843	42 Southern Satellites	42.9	44095	29 Rustbelt Retirees	30.3
43540	25 Salt of The Earth	100.0	43844	42 Southern Satellites	51.1	44099	25 Salt of The Earth	88.0
43542	06 Sophisticated Squires	65.5	43845	25 Salt of The Earth	54.1	44102	60 City Dimensions	55.6
43543	25 Salt of The Earth	34.8	43901	50 Heartland Communities	59.7	44103	62 Modest Income Homes	33.6
43545	25 Salt of The Earth	33.3	43902	46 Rooted Rural	99.1	44104	62 Modest Income Homes	43.6
43548	25 Salt of The Earth	95.1	43903	50 Heartland Communities	40.2	44105	62 Modest Income Homes	25.4
43549	25 Salt of The Earth	100.0	43906	62 Modest Income Homes	25.1	44106	27 Metro Renters	18.7
43551	04 Boomburbs	13.8	43907	50 Heartland Communities	68.2	44107	24 Main Street, USA	30.6
43554	25 Salt of The Earth	100.0	43908	42 Southern Satellites	51.9	44108	62 Modest Income Homes	51.7
43556	25 Salt of The Earth	55.7	43910	25 Salt of The Earth	60.9	44109	60 City Dimensions	31.3
43557	25 Salt of The Earth	42.8	43912	50 Heartland Communities	69.7	44110	51 Metro City Edge	33.0
43558	17 Green Acres	38.2	43913	50 Heartland Communities	100.0	44111	32 Rustbelt Traditions	31.0
43560	13 In Style	20.2	43915	29 Rustbelt Retirees	53.7	44112	51 Metro City Edge	42.3
43566	18 Cozy and Comfortable	38.4	43917	50 Heartland Communities	71.1	44113	60 City Dimensions	48.8
43567	25 Salt of The Earth	34.9	43920	53 Home Town	31.7	44114	65 Social Security Set	62.2
43569	26 Midland Crowd	56.9	43930	46 Rooted Rural	64.6	44115	64 City Commons	63.4
43570	42 Southern Satellites	50.0	43932	46 Rooted Rural	86.3	44116	14 Prosperous Empty Nesters	34.9
43571	17 Green Acres	52.5	43933	25 Salt of The Earth	69.3	44117	65 Social Security Set	46.1
43602	64 City Commons	70.2	43935	50 Heartland Communities	44.7	44118	18 Cozy and Comfortable	15.9
43604	65 Social Security Set	56.0	43938	50 Heartland Communities	51.4	44119	48 Great Expectations	36.1
43605	53 Home Town	61.7	43942	50 Heartland Communities	60.7	44120	51 Metro City Edge	22.1
43606	22 Metropolitans	14.7	43943	46 Rooted Rural	52.3	44121	18 Cozy and Comfortable	25.7
43607	62 Modest Income Homes	35.4	43944	25 Salt of The Earth	92.1	44122	30 Retirement Communities	27.0
43608	51 Metro City Edge	31.8	43945	42 Southern Satellites	65.0	44123	32 Rustbelt Traditions	57.4
43609	32 Rustbelt Traditions	33.0	43946	42 Southern Satellites	44.4	44124	30 Retirement Communities	31.6
43610	51 Metro City Edge	60.2	43947	29 Rustbelt Retirees	48.7	44125	29 Rustbelt Retirees	46.2
43611	32 Rustbelt Traditions	39.7	43950	29 Rustbelt Retirees	32.7	44126	14 Prosperous Empty Nesters	41.3
43612	32 Rustbelt Traditions	57.1	43952	29 Rustbelt Retirees	32.6	44127	60 City Dimensions	48.1
43613	32 Rustbelt Traditions	42.3	43953	29 Rustbelt Retirees	48.6	44128	34 Family Foundations	66.4
43614	36 Old and Newcomers	30.1	43963	29 Rustbelt Retirees	54.2	44129	29 Rustbelt Retirees	31.2
43615	41 Crossroads	15.0	43964	25 Salt of The Earth	25.4	44130	29 Rustbelt Retirees	32.4
43616	57 Simple Living	17.7	43968	25 Salt of The Earth	40.3	44131	14 Prosperous Empty Nesters	76.9
43617	02 Suburban Splendor	43.8	43971	50 Heartland Communities	85.4	44132	29 Rustbelt Retirees	34.0
43618	17 Green Acres	57.2	43973	46 Rooted Rural	65.5	44133	13 In Style	30.3
43619	32 Rustbelt Traditions	29.3	43976	50 Heartland Communities	59.4	44134	29 Rustbelt Retirees	45.4
43620	57 Simple Living	31.8	43977	46 Rooted Rural	76.8	44135	32 Rustbelt Traditions	44.9
43623	18 Cozy and Comfortable	16.9	43983	46 Rooted Rural	89.2	44136	06 Sophisticated Squires	44.4
43624	65 Social Security Set	86.0	43986	46 Rooted Rural	40.4	44137	32 Rustbelt Traditions	58.9
43701	53 Home Town	15.5	43988	46 Rooted Rural	59.9	44138	13 In Style	35.8
43713	50 Heartland Communities	73.5	44001	17 Green Acres	53.9	44139	02 Suburban Splendor	48.5
43716	46 Rooted Rural	75.4	44003	42 Southern Satellites	76.5	44140	07 Exurbanites	38.6

ZIP CODE	TOP TAPESTRY CONSUMER TYPE	% 2004 HOUSE-HOLDS	ZIP CODE	TOP TAPESTRY CONSUMER TYPE	% 2004 HOUSE-HOLDS	ZIP CODE	TOP TAPESTRY CONSUMER TYPE	% 2004 HOUSE-HOLDS
44141	02 Suburban Splendor	30.8	44441	42 Southern Satellites	44.4	44705	53 Home Town	54.6
44142	18 Cozy and Comfortable	44.5	44442	29 Rustbelt Retirees	93.8	44706	25 Salt of The Earth	44.9
44143	05 Wealthy Seaboard Suburbs	21.2	44443	46 Rooted Rural	71.0	44707	62 Modest Income Homes	27.4
44144	29 Rustbelt Retirees	33.8	44444	32 Rustbelt Traditions	27.0	44708	29 Rustbelt Retirees	27.5
44145	07 Exurbanites	23.8	44445	25 Salt of The Earth	66.8	44709	33 Midlife Junction	24.6
44146	36 Old and Newcomers	22.7	44446	33 Midlife Junction	36.4	44710	32 Rustbelt Traditions	33.1
44147	13 In Style	60.8	44449	25 Salt of The Earth	79.2	44714	32 Rustbelt Traditions	30.4
44149	06 Sophisticated Squires	33.5	44450	25 Salt of The Earth	86.7	44718	14 Prosperous Empty Nesters	26.7
44201	25 Salt of The Earth	48.9	44451	25 Salt of The Earth	56.8	44720	13 In Style	25.1
44202	04 Boomburbs	35.2	44452	17 Green Acres	69.6	44721	17 Green Acres	38.7
44203	29 Rustbelt Retirees	18.8	44454	26 Midland Crowd	100.0	44730	25 Salt of The Earth	95.4
44212	06 Sophisticated Squires	19.2	44455	42 Southern Satellites	55.6	44802	25 Salt of The Earth	100.0
44214	25 Salt of The Earth	84.9	44460	25 Salt of The Earth	27.5	44804	25 Salt of The Earth	64.5
44215	32 Rustbelt Traditions	75.6	44470	25 Salt of The Earth	35.7	44805	25 Salt of The Earth	21.7
44216	17 Green Acres	49.9	44471	29 Rustbelt Retirees	38.5	44807	25 Salt of The Earth	99.4
44217	42 Southern Satellites	41.7	44473	46 Rooted Rural	42.0	44811	32 Rustbelt Traditions	41.2
44221	36 Old and Newcomers	23.0	44481	25 Salt of The Earth	37.3	44813	25 Salt of The Earth	82.2
44223	13 In Style	24.7	44483	29 Rustbelt Retirees	23.1	44814	25 Salt of The Earth	49.7
44224	24 Main Street, USA	24.8	44484	14 Prosperous Empty Nesters	21.8	44817	25 Salt of The Earth	87.4
44230	17 Green Acres	36.0	44485	29 Rustbelt Retirees	20.9	44818	25 Salt of The Earth	61.4
44231	42 Southern Satellites	33.1	44490	25 Salt of The Earth	65.1	44820	25 Salt of The Earth	25.4
44233	07 Exurbanites	43.8	44491	17 Green Acres	75.3	44822	25 Salt of The Earth	87.0
44234	17 Green Acres	63.0	44502	53 Home Town	39.4	44824	18 Cozy and Comfortable	51.3
44235	17 Green Acres	100.0	44503	65 Social Security Set	100.0	44826	25 Salt of The Earth	86.9
44236	02 Suburban Splendor	47.5	44504	55 College Towns	26.1	44827	32 Rustbelt Traditions	34.2
44240	55 College Towns	25.5	44505	62 Modest Income Homes	39.7	44830	53 Home Town	27.5
44241	16 Enterprising Professionals	26.2	44506	62 Modest Income Homes	100.0	44833	25 Salt of The Earth	24.3
44243	63 Dorms To Diplomas	100.0	44507	62 Modest Income Homes	59.6	44836	25 Salt of The Earth	61.9
44253	17 Green Acres	91.1	44509	53 Home Town	33.5	44837	42 Southern Satellites	71.5
44254	17 Green Acres	35.9	44510	62 Modest Income Homes	84.3	44839	17 Green Acres	18.9
44255	17 Green Acres	57.4	44511	29 Rustbelt Retirees	45.9	44840	25 Salt of The Earth	63.8
44256	07 Exurbanites	19.6	44512	29 Rustbelt Retirees	17.6	44841	25 Salt of The Earth	93.3
44260	18 Cozy and Comfortable	37.4	44514	18 Cozy and Comfortable	25.9	44842	32 Rustbelt Traditions	23.3
44262	07 Exurbanites	68.0	44515	29 Rustbelt Retirees	27.4	44843	25 Salt of The Earth	47.8
44264	07 Exurbanites	50.7	44555	62 Modest Income Homes	100.0	44844	25 Salt of The Earth	80.3
44266	26 Midland Crowd	16.6	44601	53 Home Town	21.8	44846	17 Green Acres	56.7
44270	32 Rustbelt Traditions	47.7	44606	25 Salt of The Earth	44.6	44847	25 Salt of The Earth	78.7
44272	18 Cozy and Comfortable	41.9	44608	42 Southern Satellites	40.9	44849	25 Salt of The Earth	62.9
44273	17 Green Acres	28.7	44609	25 Salt of The Earth	69.9	44851	32 Rustbelt Traditions	27.5
44275	17 Green Acres	100.0	44611	25 Salt of The Earth	97.1	44853	25 Salt of The Earth	100.0
44276	25 Salt of The Earth	74.4	44612	06 Sophisticated Squires	34.4	44854	25 Salt of The Earth	63.8
44278	29 Rustbelt Retirees	24.5	44613	25 Salt of The Earth	94.2	44855	25 Salt of The Earth	100.0
44280	07 Exurbanites	56.4	44614	18 Cozy and Comfortable	40.1	44857	53 Home Town	15.3
44281	07 Exurbanites	15.4	44615	25 Salt of The Earth	35.9	44859	25 Salt of The Earth	98.5
44286	07 Exurbanites	95.5	44618	26 Midland Crowd	35.7	44864	25 Salt of The Earth	42.0
44287	25 Salt of The Earth	60.2	44620	25 Salt of The Earth	71.7	44865	42 Southern Satellites	67.8
44288	51 Metro City Edge	48.3	44621	50 Heartland Communities	31.8	44866	25 Salt of The Earth	100.0
44301	32 Rustbelt Traditions	49.0	44622	29 Rustbelt Retirees	21.8	44867	25 Salt of The Earth	77.9
44302	48 Great Expectations	30.5	44624	25 Salt of The Earth	38.6	44870	29 Rustbelt Retirees	17.0
44303	03 Connoisseurs	17.5	44625	25 Salt of The Earth	100.0	44875	25 Salt of The Earth	26.0
44304	63 Dorms To Diplomas	33.3	44626	25 Salt of The Earth	77.7	44878	42 Southern Satellites	48.6
44305	32 Rustbelt Traditions	74.9	44627	47 Las Casas	42.5	44880	25 Salt of The Earth	88.6
44306	32 Rustbelt Traditions	19.7	44628	42 Southern Satellites	50.4	44882	25 Salt of The Earth	41.0
44307	51 Metro City Edge	33.8	44629	25 Salt of The Earth	34.6	44883	25 Salt of The Earth	25.7
44308	65 Social Security Set	97.3	44632	17 Green Acres	60.3	44887	25 Salt of The Earth	100.0
44310	32 Rustbelt Traditions	35.1	44633	42 Southern Satellites	65.4	44889	17 Green Acres	56.7
44311	51 Metro City Edge	25.9	44634	25 Salt of The Earth	100.0	44890	25 Salt of The Earth	33.8
44312	32 Rustbelt Traditions	34.3	44637	42 Southern Satellites	65.1	44902	53 Home Town	44.5
44313	18 Cozy and Comfortable	15.1	44638	25 Salt of The Earth	54.6	44903	17 Green Acres	16.8
44314	32 Rustbelt Traditions	55.1	44641	18 Cozy and Comfortable	30.6	44904	18 Cozy and Comfortable	17.5
44319	18 Cozy and Comfortable	34.4	44643	42 Southern Satellites	37.6	44905	32 Rustbelt Traditions	26.8
44320	34 Family Foundations	42.6	44644	42 Southern Satellites	27.9	44906	50 Heartland Communities	19.1
44321	18 Cozy and Comfortable	31.3	44645	25 Salt of The Earth	59.6	44907	33 Midlife Junction	17.0
44333	03 Connoisseurs	36.6	44646	32 Rustbelt Traditions	21.3	45001	51 Metro City Edge	62.1
44401	17 Green Acres	94.6	44647	29 Rustbelt Retirees	26.9	45002	06 Sophisticated Squires	19.8
44402	18 Cozy and Comfortable	57.3	44651	25 Salt of The Earth	52.7	45003	25 Salt of The Earth	71.3
44403	46 Rooted Rural	49.0	44654	47 Las Casas	27.4	45005	32 Rustbelt Traditions	18.3
44404	25 Salt of The Earth	64.2	44656	42 Southern Satellites	59.9	45011	12 Up and Coming Families	25.5
44405	29 Rustbelt Retirees	47.8	44657	25 Salt of The Earth	67.7	45013	32 Rustbelt Traditions	20.0
44406	07 Exurbanites	34.7	44662	29 Rustbelt Retirees	40.0	45014	16 Enterprising Professionals	27.1
44408	25 Salt of The Earth	28.5	44663	25 Salt of The Earth	27.7	45015	32 Rustbelt Traditions	32.3
44410	25 Salt of The Earth	33.5	44666	17 Green Acres	66.5	45030	06 Sophisticated Squires	22.3
44411	25 Salt of The Earth	100.0	44667	25 Salt of The Earth	22.8	45034	04 Boomburbs	100.0
44412	17 Green Acres	81.9	44669	25 Salt of The Earth	100.0	45036	04 Boomburbs	18.0
44413	25 Salt of The Earth	29.8	44672	32 Rustbelt Traditions	40.9	45039	06 Sophisticated Squires	29.2
44417	25 Salt of The Earth	95.1	44675	46 Rooted Rural	36.6	45040	04 Boomburbs	61.4
44418	17 Green Acres	58.0	44676	25 Salt of The Earth	63.1	45042	17 Green Acres	21.2
44420	29 Rustbelt Retirees	29.5	44677	24 Main Street, USA	52.2	45044	32 Rustbelt Traditions	14.6
44423	46 Rooted Rural	39.8	44680	33 Midlife Junction	47.7	45050	12 Up and Coming Families	46.5
44425	29 Rustbelt Retirees	18.1	44681	25 Salt of The Earth	58.5	45052	06 Sophisticated Squires	41.0
44427	25 Salt of The Earth	78.4	44683	53 Home Town	46.2	45053	17 Green Acres	51.0
44428	25 Salt of The Earth	53.2	44685	06 Sophisticated Squires	23.5	45054	17 Green Acres	54.1
44429	32 Rustbelt Traditions	56.7	44688	42 Southern Satellites	36.8	45056	63 Dorms To Diplomas	37.5
44430	42 Southern Satellites	32.2	44689	25 Salt of The Earth	53.1	45064	17 Green Acres	87.9
44431	25 Salt of The Earth	69.3	44691	25 Salt of The Earth	21.0	45065	42 Southern Satellites	73.8
44432	42 Southern Satellites	31.8	44695	46 Rooted Rural	99.0	45066	04 Boomburbs	28.8
44436	17 Green Acres	36.9	44699	46 Rooted Rural	49.3	45067	24 Main Street, USA	47.1
44437	18 Cozy and Comfortable	36.8	44702	65 Social Security Set	91.6	45068	17 Green Acres	62.6
44438	50 Heartland Communities	45.6	44703	48 Great Expectations	56.9	45069	04 Boomburbs	39.4
44440	17 Green Acres	27.4	44704	62 Modest Income Homes	57.1	45101	41 Crossroads	59.6

ZIP CODE	TOP TAPESTRY CONSUMER TYPE	% 2004 HOUSE-HOLDS	ZIP CODE	TOP TAPESTRY CONSUMER TYPE	% 2004 HOUSE-HOLDS	ZIP CODE	TOP TAPESTRY CONSUMER TYPE	% 2004 HOUSE-HOLDS
45102	12 Up and Coming Families	28.3	45312	17 Green Acres	73.1	45622	42 Southern Satellites	96.9
45103	12 Up and Coming Families	22.8	45314	17 Green Acres	67.2	45623	42 Southern Satellites	76.0
45106	25 Salt of The Earth	21.3	45315	17 Green Acres	52.3	45628	26 Midland Crowd	36.8
45107	25 Salt of The Earth	36.5	45317	25 Salt of The Earth	100.0	45629	46 Rooted Rural	46.5
45111	18 Cozy and Comfortable	100.0	45318	32 Rustbelt Traditions	40.1	45631	26 Midland Crowd	27.5
45113	17 Green Acres	42.4	45320	32 Rustbelt Traditions	28.2	45634	42 Southern Satellites	56.9
45118	26 Midland Crowd	84.8	45321	25 Salt of The Earth	100.0	45638	29 Rustbelt Retirees	25.2
45120	26 Midland Crowd	65.0	45322	18 Cozy and Comfortable	34.2	45640	42 Southern Satellites	25.0
45121	26 Midland Crowd	34.3	45323	29 Rustbelt Retirees	29.0	45644	17 Green Acres	34.4
45122	25 Salt of The Earth	58.4	45324	32 Rustbelt Traditions	15.8	45645	42 Southern Satellites	86.9
45123	25 Salt of The Earth	40.4	45325	17 Green Acres	95.0	45646	56 Rural Bypasses	86.9
45130	42 Southern Satellites	63.6	45326	25 Salt of The Earth	100.0	45647	42 Southern Satellites	76.7
45133	25 Salt of The Earth	23.5	45327	25 Salt of The Earth	36.6	45648	56 Rural Bypasses	30.4
45135	42 Southern Satellites	59.8	45331	25 Salt of The Earth	32.3	45650	56 Rural Bypasses	100.0
45140	04 Boomburbs	32.1	45332	25 Salt of The Earth	100.0	45651	42 Southern Satellites	79.4
45142	25 Salt of The Earth	49.5	45333	25 Salt of The Earth	70.3	45652	46 Rooted Rural	40.1
45144	42 Southern Satellites	43.0	45334	25 Salt of The Earth	86.9	45653	25 Salt of The Earth	44.9
45146	26 Midland Crowd	34.6	45335	25 Salt of The Earth	41.4	45654	42 Southern Satellites	95.7
45148	42 Southern Satellites	61.3	45337	25 Salt of The Earth	78.9	45656	42 Southern Satellites	40.5
45150	18 Cozy and Comfortable	11.2	45338	25 Salt of The Earth	88.8	45657	42 Southern Satellites	82.6
45152	17 Green Acres	45.9	45339	25 Salt of The Earth	82.0	45658	42 Southern Satellites	83.9
45153	42 Southern Satellites	52.7	45340	25 Salt of The Earth	51.8	45659	56 Rural Bypasses	83.6
45154	42 Southern Satellites	31.5	45341	29 Rustbelt Retirees	45.8	45660	42 Southern Satellites	53.9
45157	26 Midland Crowd	49.1	45342	16 Enterprising Professionals	37.7	45661	42 Southern Satellites	76.9
45159	41 Crossroads	43.3	45344	32 Rustbelt Traditions	37.4	45662	53 Home Town	18.2
45160	33 Midlife Junction	82.4	45345	25 Salt of The Earth	57.7	45663	50 Heartland Communities	37.7
45162	17 Green Acres	73.1	45346	25 Salt of The Earth	100.0	45669	29 Rustbelt Retirees	29.2
45167	50 Heartland Communities	61.8	45347	25 Salt of The Earth	36.6	45671	42 Southern Satellites	99.0
45168	46 Rooted Rural	52.0	45348	37 Prairie Living	60.8	45672	42 Southern Satellites	100.0
45169	42 Southern Satellites	60.3	45356	32 Rustbelt Traditions	34.5	45673	42 Southern Satellites	100.0
45171	25 Salt of The Earth	59.1	45359	25 Salt of The Earth	64.1	45675	42 Southern Satellites	100.0
45174	03 Connoisseurs	100.0	45362	25 Salt of The Earth	76.0	45678	56 Rural Bypasses	49.9
45176	25 Salt of The Earth	43.1	45363	17 Green Acres	86.7	45679	50 Heartland Communities	42.2
45177	17 Green Acres	19.2	45365	32 Rustbelt Traditions	26.0	45680	29 Rustbelt Retirees	25.1
45202	64 City Commons	33.8	45368	25 Salt of The Earth	40.3	45681	42 Southern Satellites	57.0
45203	64 City Commons	47.3	45369	17 Green Acres	58.7	45682	42 Southern Satellites	43.7
45204	60 City Dimensions	34.3	45370	02 Suburban Splendor	42.1	45684	46 Rooted Rural	59.9
45205	48 Great Expectations	39.8	45371	24 Main Street, USA	20.0	45685	42 Southern Satellites	50.8
45206	64 City Commons	20.3	45373	32 Rustbelt Traditions	21.3	45686	42 Southern Satellites	52.4
45207	62 Modest Income Homes	27.0	45377	24 Main Street, USA	27.3	45688	56 Rural Bypasses	98.1
45208	08 Laptops and Lattes	28.1	45380	25 Salt of The Earth	84.9	45690	26 Midland Crowd	23.4
45209	22 Metropolitans	48.9	45381	25 Salt of The Earth	87.5	45692	42 Southern Satellites	39.2
45211	48 Great Expectations	27.4	45382	25 Salt of The Earth	83.6	45693	46 Rooted Rural	35.7
45212	48 Great Expectations	42.3	45383	33 Midlife Junction	35.6	45694	33 Midlife Junction	24.2
45213	51 Metro City Edge	21.8	45385	32 Rustbelt Traditions	17.7	45695	42 Southern Satellites	100.0
45214	64 City Commons	26.7	45387	22 Metropolitans	56.5	45696	56 Rural Bypasses	79.2
45215	36 Old and Newcomers	22.0	45388	25 Salt of The Earth	93.6	45697	42 Southern Satellites	62.8
45216	32 Rustbelt Traditions	30.7	45390	53 Home Town	56.9	45701	63 Dorms To Diplomas	37.4
45217	32 Rustbelt Traditions	45.9	45402	65 Social Security Set	47.6	45710	26 Midland Crowd	37.3
45218	28 Aspiring Young Families	41.7	45403	48 Great Expectations	33.2	45711	26 Midland Crowd	68.1
45219	55 College Towns	46.5	45404	53 Home Town	30.6	45714	50 Heartland Communities	39.3
45220	27 Metro Renters	30.7	45405	48 Great Expectations	34.9	45715	25 Salt of The Earth	54.2
45221	63 Dorms To Diplomas	100.0	45406	51 Metro City Edge	29.8	45723	46 Rooted Rural	99.3
45223	48 Great Expectations	42.5	45407	62 Modest Income Homes	57.4	45724	42 Southern Satellites	59.8
45224	34 Family Foundations	25.6	45408	62 Modest Income Homes	59.3	45727	42 Southern Satellites	51.4
45225	64 City Commons	50.1	45409	63 Dorms To Diplomas	16.4	45729	17 Green Acres	48.3
45226	09 Urban Chic	26.7	45410	32 Rustbelt Traditions	39.7	45732	56 Rural Bypasses	53.4
45227	32 Rustbelt Traditions	27.2	45414	32 Rustbelt Traditions	24.3	45734	46 Rooted Rural	88.4
45228	02 Suburban Splendor	100.0	45415	06 Sophisticated Squires	22.7	45735	46 Rooted Rural	87.0
45229	64 City Commons	31.5	45416	34 Family Foundations	36.9	45741	46 Rooted Rural	53.8
45230	36 Old and Newcomers	31.5	45417	62 Modest Income Homes	82.3	45742	17 Green Acres	44.8
45231	18 Cozy and Comfortable	21.3	45418	29 Rustbelt Retirees	29.1	45743	46 Rooted Rural	53.6
45232	64 City Commons	69.1	45419	55 College Towns	25.8	45744	50 Heartland Communities	56.6
45233	02 Suburban Splendor	20.4	45420	32 Rustbelt Traditions	59.2	45745	25 Salt of The Earth	42.8
45236	29 Rustbelt Retirees	23.7	45424	06 Sophisticated Squires	23.8	45746	56 Rural Bypasses	87.8
45237	57 Simple Living	19.5	45426	28 Aspiring Young Families	20.4	45750	33 Midlife Junction	17.1
45238	18 Cozy and Comfortable	19.0	45427	62 Modest Income Homes	36.2	45760	56 Rural Bypasses	46.4
45239	32 Rustbelt Traditions	26.8	45429	14 Prosperous Empty Nesters	31.8	45761	26 Midland Crowd	40.6
45240	18 Cozy and Comfortable	21.9	45430	07 Exurbanites	49.6	45764	50 Heartland Communities	27.8
45241	13 In Style	25.7	45431	07 Exurbanites	17.1	45766	26 Midland Crowd	92.4
45242	07 Exurbanites	18.1	45432	29 Rustbelt Retirees	34.3	45767	50 Heartland Communities	62.2
45243	01 Top Rung	33.3	45433	40 Military Proximity	99.2	45768	25 Salt of The Earth	74.8
45244	02 Suburban Splendor	29.1	45434	07 Exurbanites	44.5	45769	46 Rooted Rural	52.8
45245	16 Enterprising Professionals	18.0	45439	48 Great Expectations	39.9	45770	46 Rooted Rural	98.4
45246	29 Rustbelt Retirees	19.3	45440	18 Cozy and Comfortable	22.9	45771	46 Rooted Rural	62.4
45247	14 Prosperous Empty Nesters	20.4	45449	18 Cozy and Comfortable	23.1	45772	46 Rooted Rural	93.2
45248	06 Sophisticated Squires	23.0	45458	13 In Style	51.1	45773	25 Salt of The Earth	67.7
45249	02 Suburban Splendor	36.8	45459	13 In Style	30.7	45775	56 Rural Bypasses	54.6
45251	19 Milk and Cookies	32.3	45502	18 Cozy and Comfortable	35.6	45776	46 Rooted Rural	46.6
45252	13 In Style	55.0	45503	32 Rustbelt Traditions	21.2	45778	46 Rooted Rural	50.0
45255	06 Sophisticated Squires	19.4	45504	14 Prosperous Empty Nesters	12.5	45780	33 Midlife Junction	50.8
45275	41 Crossroads	100.0	45505	32 Rustbelt Traditions	29.7	45784	17 Green Acres	65.9
45302	25 Salt of The Earth	56.2	45506	34 Family Foundations	28.6	45786	46 Rooted Rural	55.1
45303	42 Southern Satellites	66.5	45601	42 Southern Satellites	17.7	45788	25 Salt of The Earth	54.5
45304	25 Salt of The Earth	44.4	45612	42 Southern Satellites	57.2	45789	42 Southern Satellites	95.2
45305	13 In Style	39.5	45613	42 Southern Satellites	100.0	45801	53 Home Town	34.7
45306	25 Salt of The Earth	74.9	45614	46 Rooted Rural	68.9	45804	53 Home Town	36.5
45308	32 Rustbelt Traditions	48.0	45616	56 Rural Bypasses	55.8	45805	29 Rustbelt Retirees	25.1
45309	18 Cozy and Comfortable	33.1	45619	46 Rooted Rural	36.0	45806	25 Salt of The Earth	27.0
45311	25 Salt of The Earth	55.3	45620	42 Southern Satellites	91.7	45807	17 Green Acres	29.9

CONSUMER TYPE

ZIP CODE	TOP TAPESTRY CONSUMER TYPE	% 2004 HOUSE-HOLDS	ZIP CODE	TOP TAPESTRY CONSUMER TYPE	% 2004 HOUSE-HOLDS	ZIP CODE	TOP TAPESTRY CONSUMER TYPE	% 2004 HOUSE-HOLDS
45810	33 Midlife Junction	28.2	46075	25 Salt of The Earth	47.2	46280	14 Prosperous Empty Nesters	31.3
45812	42 Southern Satellites	89.8	46076	42 Southern Satellites	57.7	46290	14 Prosperous Empty Nesters	74.5
45813	25 Salt of The Earth	99.9	46077	02 Suburban Splendor	36.3	46303	17 Green Acres	32.6
45814	25 Salt of The Earth	82.1	46104	25 Salt of The Earth	100.0	46304	24 Main Street, USA	25.2
45817	14 Prosperous Empty Nesters	40.6	46105	25 Salt of The Earth	53.6	46307	13 In Style	23.8
45821	42 Southern Satellites	59.3	46106	07 Exurbanites	30.5	46310	17 Green Acres	44.6
45822	25 Salt of The Earth	22.4	46107	32 Rustbelt Traditions	37.6	46311	06 Sophisticated Squires	47.7
45827	42 Southern Satellites	44.2	46110	17 Green Acres	100.0	46312	60 City Dimensions	42.3
45828	25 Salt of The Earth	45.4	46112	24 Main Street, USA	18.0	46319	18 Cozy and Comfortable	39.4
45830	25 Salt of The Earth	60.4	46113	17 Green Acres	56.8	46320	57 Simple Living	15.3
45831	42 Southern Satellites	48.1	46115	25 Salt of The Earth	60.3	46321	14 Prosperous Empty Nesters	48.0
45832	25 Salt of The Earth	100.0	46117	17 Green Acres	100.0	46322	24 Main Street, USA	31.3
45833	25 Salt of The Earth	34.4	46118	25 Salt of The Earth	58.1	46323	32 Rustbelt Traditions	59.4
45835	25 Salt of The Earth	96.8	46120	26 Midland Crowd	36.0	46324	32 Rustbelt Traditions	70.6
45836	42 Southern Satellites	71.0	46121	17 Green Acres	61.6	46327	53 Home Town	31.1
45840	48 Great Expectations	15.6	46122	17 Green Acres	50.2	46340	25 Salt of The Earth	98.4
45841	25 Salt of The Earth	90.1	46123	12 Up and Coming Families	53.3	46341	24 Main Street, USA	25.6
45843	42 Southern Satellites	63.3	46124	42 Southern Satellites	34.0	46342	18 Cozy and Comfortable	31.3
45844	25 Salt of The Earth	92.7	46126	17 Green Acres	74.6	46347	32 Rustbelt Traditions	53.1
45845	17 Green Acres	98.6	46127	25 Salt of The Earth	100.0	46348	25 Salt of The Earth	97.7
45846	25 Salt of The Earth	82.5	46128	25 Salt of The Earth	83.3	46349	25 Salt of The Earth	74.0
45849	42 Southern Satellites	86.4	46130	17 Green Acres	100.0	46350	17 Green Acres	31.2
45850	25 Salt of The Earth	100.0	46131	28 Aspiring Young Families	19.3	46356	17 Green Acres	25.8
45851	25 Salt of The Earth	74.0	46133	25 Salt of The Earth	83.1	46360	32 Rustbelt Traditions	20.3
45856	25 Salt of The Earth	48.2	46135	25 Salt of The Earth	31.4	46365	17 Green Acres	42.9
45858	42 Southern Satellites	37.2	46140	17 Green Acres	40.6	46366	42 Southern Satellites	48.4
45860	25 Salt of The Earth	82.5	46142	06 Sophisticated Squires	37.5	46368	18 Cozy and Comfortable	24.2
45862	42 Southern Satellites	58.6	46143	28 Aspiring Young Families	20.1	46371	25 Salt of The Earth	47.3
45863	25 Salt of The Earth	100.0	46147	25 Salt of The Earth	57.5	46373	06 Sophisticated Squires	58.4
45865	18 Cozy and Comfortable	47.0	46148	29 Rustbelt Retirees	49.2	46374	25 Salt of The Earth	92.3
45867	25 Salt of The Earth	98.8	46149	26 Midland Crowd	55.1	46375	07 Exurbanites	30.1
45868	25 Salt of The Earth	91.2	46150	25 Salt of The Earth	87.6	46382	25 Salt of The Earth	79.0
45869	17 Green Acres	40.7	46151	17 Green Acres	38.4	46383	17 Green Acres	28.2
45871	25 Salt of The Earth	72.3	46156	17 Green Acres	88.6	46385	07 Exurbanites	23.3
45872	32 Rustbelt Traditions	56.3	46157	25 Salt of The Earth	97.4	46390	17 Green Acres	37.6
45873	42 Southern Satellites	74.2	46158	17 Green Acres	31.3	46391	26 Midland Crowd	48.2
45874	25 Salt of The Earth	51.6	46160	25 Salt of The Earth	63.9	46392	25 Salt of The Earth	37.4
45875	25 Salt of The Earth	63.4	46161	32 Rustbelt Traditions	42.9	46394	29 Rustbelt Retirees	44.3
45877	25 Salt of The Earth	100.0	46162	17 Green Acres	100.0	46402	62 Modest Income Homes	48.7
45879	32 Rustbelt Traditions	45.5	46163	06 Sophisticated Squires	42.2	46403	51 Metro City Edge	29.2
45880	50 Heartland Communities	55.1	46164	31 Rural Resort Dwellers	42.8	46404	34 Family Foundations	47.7
45881	25 Salt of The Earth	80.0	46165	17 Green Acres	52.7	46405	32 Rustbelt Traditions	51.2
45882	25 Salt of The Earth	66.4	46166	25 Salt of The Earth	56.3	46406	34 Family Foundations	30.8
45883	25 Salt of The Earth	52.5	46167	17 Green Acres	59.1	46407	62 Modest Income Homes	49.1
45885	32 Rustbelt Traditions	37.2	46168	18 Cozy and Comfortable	28.2	46408	34 Family Foundations	31.1
45886	25 Salt of The Earth	98.6	46171	25 Salt of The Earth	93.2	46409	51 Metro City Edge	57.3
45887	25 Salt of The Earth	63.3	46172	25 Salt of The Earth	63.6	46410	24 Main Street, USA	29.6
45889	17 Green Acres	100.0	46173	25 Salt of The Earth	20.6	46501	25 Salt of The Earth	49.3
45890	25 Salt of The Earth	100.0	46175	42 Southern Satellites	91.0	46504	32 Rustbelt Traditions	55.3
45891	32 Rustbelt Traditions	34.2	46176	17 Green Acres	18.7	46506	25 Salt of The Earth	36.7
45894	25 Salt of The Earth	100.0	46180	25 Salt of The Earth	97.6	46507	42 Southern Satellites	35.6
45895	17 Green Acres	34.1	46181	17 Green Acres	55.1	46508	25 Salt of The Earth	100.0
45896	25 Salt of The Earth	58.9	46182	25 Salt of The Earth	98.9	46510	25 Salt of The Earth	79.9
45898	32 Rustbelt Traditions	64.5	46184	12 Up and Coming Families	51.0	46511	25 Salt of The Earth	43.5
46001	32 Rustbelt Traditions	37.2	46186	25 Salt of The Earth	59.1	46514	13 In Style	18.6
46011	18 Cozy and Comfortable	35.1	46201	60 City Dimensions	29.8	46516	60 City Dimensions	17.8
46012	32 Rustbelt Traditions	16.5	46202	27 Metro Renters	25.0	46517	25 Salt of The Earth	25.7
46013	50 Heartland Communities	30.7	46203	53 Home Town	42.4	46524	42 Southern Satellites	99.1
46016	53 Home Town	51.9	46204	27 Metro Renters	75.7	46526	26 Midland Crowd	20.3
46017	32 Rustbelt Traditions	50.2	46205	51 Metro City Edge	16.3	46528	17 Green Acres	33.0
46030	32 Rustbelt Traditions	40.3	46208	62 Modest Income Homes	46.4	46530	06 Sophisticated Squires	27.5
46031	26 Midland Crowd	39.6	46214	39 Young and Restless	47.2	46531	26 Midland Crowd	53.4
46032	04 Boomburbs	33.5	46216	13 In Style	88.7	46532	25 Salt of The Earth	55.8
46033	04 Boomburbs	42.1	46217	06 Sophisticated Squires	51.3	46534	25 Salt of The Earth	35.3
46034	17 Green Acres	71.7	46218	62 Modest Income Homes	28.2	46536	17 Green Acres	42.7
46035	25 Salt of The Earth	99.3	46219	32 Rustbelt Traditions	32.3	46538	25 Salt of The Earth	36.7
46036	32 Rustbelt Traditions	48.1	46220	22 Metropolitans	61.4	46539	32 Rustbelt Traditions	50.6
46038	04 Boomburbs	48.7	46221	53 Home Town	20.7	46540	17 Green Acres	61.4
46039	25 Salt of The Earth	100.0	46222	53 Home Town	33.6	46542	17 Green Acres	41.1
46040	32 Rustbelt Traditions	46.3	46224	52 Inner City Tenants	42.9	46543	17 Green Acres	40.8
46041	32 Rustbelt Traditions	22.7	46225	53 Home Town	24.7	46544	32 Rustbelt Traditions	36.8
46044	25 Salt of The Earth	47.2	46226	32 Rustbelt Traditions	21.1	46545	36 Old and Newcomers	22.9
46048	26 Midland Crowd	100.0	46227	33 Midlife Junction	14.8	46550	17 Green Acres	25.6
46049	25 Salt of The Earth	100.0	46228	12 Up and Coming Families	31.1	46552	18 Cozy and Comfortable	37.7
46050	42 Southern Satellites	53.7	46229	48 Great Expectations	27.9	46553	17 Green Acres	53.7
46051	32 Rustbelt Traditions	75.7	46231	06 Sophisticated Squires	40.0	46554	17 Green Acres	25.0
46052	17 Green Acres	30.2	46234	12 Up and Coming Families	23.1	46555	25 Salt of The Earth	82.6
46055	17 Green Acres	72.0	46235	28 Aspiring Young Families	51.5	46556	30 Retirement Communities	0.0
46056	25 Salt of The Earth	63.9	46236	12 Up and Coming Families	41.9	46561	18 Cozy and Comfortable	24.0
46057	25 Salt of The Earth	82.1	46237	12 Up and Coming Families	34.6	46562	42 Southern Satellites	41.7
46058	32 Rustbelt Traditions	54.2	46239	06 Sophisticated Squires	31.2	46563	25 Salt of The Earth	26.9
46060	12 Up and Coming Families	27.2	46240	39 Young and Restless	26.9	46565	17 Green Acres	31.6
46064	17 Green Acres	48.8	46241	32 Rustbelt Traditions	24.6	46566	25 Salt of The Earth	100.0
46065	25 Salt of The Earth	51.7	46250	39 Young and Restless	32.9	46567	25 Salt of The Earth	37.0
46068	17 Green Acres	43.3	46254	28 Aspiring Young Families	32.1	46570	25 Salt of The Earth	97.0
46069	17 Green Acres	49.3	46256	06 Sophisticated Squires	45.6	46571	42 Southern Satellites	39.2
46070	42 Southern Satellites	56.4	46259	17 Green Acres	48.0	46573	25 Salt of The Earth	33.8
46071	25 Salt of The Earth	42.3	46260	22 Metropolitans	18.0	46574	25 Salt of The Earth	34.8
46072	25 Salt of The Earth	31.1	46268	13 In Style	25.1	46580	32 Rustbelt Traditions	17.7
46074	12 Up and Coming Families	37.3	46278	04 Boomburbs	43.8	46582	26 Midland Crowd	45.2

ZIP CODE	TOP TAPESTRY CONSUMER TYPE	% 2004 HOUSE-HOLDS	ZIP CODE	TOP TAPESTRY CONSUMER TYPE	% 2004 HOUSE-HOLDS	ZIP CODE	TOP TAPESTRY CONSUMER TYPE	% 2004 HOUSE-HOLDS
46590	19 Milk and Cookies	62.3	46920	25 Salt of The Earth	90.5	47160	25 Salt of The Earth	100.0
46601	65 Social Security Set	28.2	46923	25 Salt of The Earth	72.1	47161	26 Midland Crowd	90.7
46613	53 Home Town	71.8	46926	25 Salt of The Earth	100.0	47162	25 Salt of The Earth	61.6
46614	32 Rustbelt Traditions	21.6	46928	25 Salt of The Earth	51.8	47163	25 Salt of The Earth	54.6
46615	48 Great Expectations	34.0	46929	32 Rustbelt Traditions	54.7	47164	42 Southern Satellites	55.2
46616	48 Great Expectations	41.0	46932	25 Salt of The Earth	97.1	47165	26 Midland Crowd	63.3
46617	14 Prosperous Empty Nesters	21.1	46933	32 Rustbelt Traditions	90.3	47166	26 Midland Crowd	66.2
46619	53 Home Town	28.5	46936	17 Green Acres	42.0	47167	42 Southern Satellites	51.9
46628	32 Rustbelt Traditions	19.2	46938	25 Salt of The Earth	48.9	47170	26 Midland Crowd	31.9
46635	07 Exurbanites	39.9	46939	25 Salt of The Earth	35.2	47172	17 Green Acres	18.2
46637	33 Midlife Junction	28.5	46940	25 Salt of The Earth	73.8	47174	42 Southern Satellites	100.0
46701	25 Salt of The Earth	40.2	46941	25 Salt of The Earth	99.8	47175	42 Southern Satellites	100.0
46702	25 Salt of The Earth	59.0	46947	25 Salt of The Earth	23.5	47177	26 Midland Crowd	51.1
46703	25 Salt of The Earth	16.6	46950	37 Prairie Living	64.1	47201	17 Green Acres	14.3
46705	42 Southern Satellites	79.7	46951	25 Salt of The Earth	46.5	47203	18 Cozy and Comfortable	12.8
46706	17 Green Acres	32.4	46952	53 Home Town	22.1	47220	46 Rooted Rural	43.9
46710	26 Midland Crowd	45.4	46953	53 Home Town	41.9	47223	25 Salt of The Earth	59.7
46711	37 Prairie Living	24.2	46960	46 Rooted Rural	55.1	47224	25 Salt of The Earth	57.6
46714	32 Rustbelt Traditions	20.9	46962	25 Salt of The Earth	28.8	47227	25 Salt of The Earth	79.1
46721	25 Salt of The Earth	41.6	46970	25 Salt of The Earth	32.2	47229	42 Southern Satellites	83.0
46723	26 Midland Crowd	30.6	46974	25 Salt of The Earth	76.4	47230	42 Southern Satellites	80.5
46725	17 Green Acres	36.6	46975	42 Southern Satellites	27.8	47231	42 Southern Satellites	75.9
46730	25 Salt of The Earth	97.2	46978	29 Rustbelt Retirees	48.2	47232	25 Salt of The Earth	57.5
46731	17 Green Acres	95.5	46979	17 Green Acres	53.2	47234	25 Salt of The Earth	97.5
46732	42 Southern Satellites	45.9	46982	42 Southern Satellites	79.4	47235	42 Southern Satellites	52.5
46733	25 Salt of The Earth	33.6	46985	25 Salt of The Earth	76.9	47236	25 Salt of The Earth	100.0
46737	31 Rural Resort Dwellers	41.1	46986	25 Salt of The Earth	94.2	47240	25 Salt of The Earth	37.0
46738	32 Rustbelt Traditions	45.6	46988	25 Salt of The Earth	100.0	47243	33 Midlife Junction	26.9
46740	25 Salt of The Earth	50.6	46989	17 Green Acres	29.7	47244	17 Green Acres	63.0
46741	26 Midland Crowd	37.5	46990	25 Salt of The Earth	100.0	47246	17 Green Acres	32.1
46742	25 Salt of The Earth	97.1	46991	32 Rustbelt Traditions	53.4	47250	33 Midlife Junction	29.5
46743	25 Salt of The Earth	69.1	46992	25 Salt of The Earth	37.6	47260	42 Southern Satellites	100.0
46745	17 Green Acres	100.0	46994	25 Salt of The Earth	96.2	47264	42 Southern Satellites	84.1
46746	25 Salt of The Earth	58.8	46996	25 Salt of The Earth	35.9	47265	25 Salt of The Earth	39.4
46747	25 Salt of The Earth	57.1	47001	17 Green Acres	25.7	47270	25 Salt of The Earth	100.0
46748	06 Sophisticated Squires	37.3	47003	26 Midland Crowd	73.9	47272	42 Southern Satellites	85.4
46750	32 Rustbelt Traditions	22.1	47006	17 Green Acres	58.9	47273	26 Midland Crowd	72.7
46755	32 Rustbelt Traditions	31.7	47010	25 Salt of The Earth	100.0	47274	32 Rustbelt Traditions	25.8
46759	25 Salt of The Earth	100.0	47011	42 Southern Satellites	39.7	47281	25 Salt of The Earth	62.8
46760	25 Salt of The Earth	96.3	47012	25 Salt of The Earth	63.1	47282	25 Salt of The Earth	100.0
46761	42 Southern Satellites	42.1	47016	26 Midland Crowd	47.4	47283	42 Southern Satellites	50.7
46763	17 Green Acres	85.0	47017	25 Salt of The Earth	98.6	47302	53 Home Town	51.8
46764	25 Salt of The Earth	71.0	47018	25 Salt of The Earth	61.2	47303	63 Dorms To Diplomas	22.7
46765	06 Sophisticated Squires	50.5	47020	42 Southern Satellites	93.1	47304	14 Prosperous Empty Nesters	20.6
46766	25 Salt of The Earth	100.0	47022	17 Green Acres	89.2	47305	60 City Dimensions	48.2
46767	38 Industrious Urban Fringe	47.0	47023	25 Salt of The Earth	83.3	47306	63 Dorms To Diplomas	100.0
46770	25 Salt of The Earth	41.2	47024	42 Southern Satellites	82.9	47320	25 Salt of The Earth	61.7
46772	25 Salt of The Earth	43.8	47025	06 Sophisticated Squires	43.3	47325	25 Salt of The Earth	100.0
46773	25 Salt of The Earth	59.6	47030	25 Salt of The Earth	59.8	47326	25 Salt of The Earth	54.4
46774	32 Rustbelt Traditions	34.2	47031	25 Salt of The Earth	43.4	47327	25 Salt of The Earth	49.5
46776	25 Salt of The Earth	97.4	47032	26 Midland Crowd	52.0	47330	32 Rustbelt Traditions	57.0
46777	17 Green Acres	26.0	47036	17 Green Acres	50.3	47331	25 Salt of The Earth	21.9
46779	25 Salt of The Earth	75.7	47037	25 Salt of The Earth	48.4	47334	29 Rustbelt Retirees	70.5
46781	25 Salt of The Earth	100.0	47038	26 Midland Crowd	100.0	47336	50 Heartland Communities	45.3
46783	25 Salt of The Earth	36.4	47040	17 Green Acres	33.5	47338	25 Salt of The Earth	47.5
46784	42 Southern Satellites	46.2	47041	17 Green Acres	64.6	47339	25 Salt of The Earth	100.0
46785	25 Salt of The Earth	91.2	47042	33 Midlife Junction	35.3	47340	32 Rustbelt Traditions	51.2
46787	25 Salt of The Earth	38.7	47043	46 Rooted Rural	38.6	47341	25 Salt of The Earth	56.1
46788	17 Green Acres	68.9	47060	17 Green Acres	42.4	47342	25 Salt of The Earth	48.2
46791	25 Salt of The Earth	86.4	47102	53 Home Town	43.6	47345	25 Salt of The Earth	100.0
46792	25 Salt of The Earth	76.9	47106	17 Green Acres	41.2	47346	25 Salt of The Earth	67.5
46793	25 Salt of The Earth	32.1	47108	42 Southern Satellites	99.0	47348	25 Salt of The Earth	38.5
46794	25 Salt of The Earth	82.5	47110	42 Southern Satellites	100.0	47352	25 Salt of The Earth	90.9
46795	25 Salt of The Earth	82.4	47111	26 Midland Crowd	34.6	47353	25 Salt of The Earth	23.4
46797	17 Green Acres	47.0	47112	26 Midland Crowd	29.0	47354	42 Southern Satellites	53.6
46798	17 Green Acres	38.8	47114	26 Midland Crowd	100.0	47355	25 Salt of The Earth	51.0
46802	60 City Dimensions	22.0	47115	25 Salt of The Earth	96.7	47356	25 Salt of The Earth	44.4
46803	53 Home Town	22.8	47116	42 Southern Satellites	100.0	47357	42 Southern Satellites	50.7
46804	12 Up and Coming Families	26.7	47117	25 Salt of The Earth	96.4	47358	25 Salt of The Earth	51.5
46805	32 Rustbelt Traditions	40.3	47118	42 Southern Satellites	69.3	47359	42 Southern Satellites	39.2
46806	51 Metro City Edge	48.7	47119	17 Green Acres	34.0	47360	25 Salt of The Earth	100.0
46807	32 Rustbelt Traditions	35.9	47120	42 Southern Satellites	100.0	47362	53 Home Town	25.3
46808	32 Rustbelt Traditions	24.0	47122	17 Green Acres	63.7	47368	25 Salt of The Earth	61.7
46809	32 Rustbelt Traditions	43.9	47123	42 Southern Satellites	100.0	47369	42 Southern Satellites	66.3
46814	02 Suburban Splendor	50.7	47124	17 Green Acres	64.1	47371	25 Salt of The Earth	33.0
46815	18 Cozy and Comfortable	44.6	47125	42 Southern Satellites	100.0	47373	50 Heartland Communities	35.9
46816	32 Rustbelt Traditions	34.4	47126	26 Midland Crowd	75.6	47374	53 Home Town	18.8
46818	41 Crossroads	36.4	47129	57 Simple Living	25.7	47380	42 Southern Satellites	52.4
46819	52 Inner City Tenants	25.1	47130	28 Aspiring Young Families	16.5	47381	25 Salt of The Earth	100.0
46825	32 Rustbelt Traditions	20.3	47135	25 Salt of The Earth	97.9	47382	25 Salt of The Earth	100.0
46835	06 Sophisticated Squires	16.0	47136	17 Green Acres	76.8	47383	25 Salt of The Earth	54.2
46845	06 Sophisticated Squires	34.7	47137	46 Rooted Rural	84.2	47384	25 Salt of The Earth	94.1
46901	32 Rustbelt Traditions	19.6	47138	42 Southern Satellites	53.6	47385	25 Salt of The Earth	75.2
46902	32 Rustbelt Traditions	14.3	47140	42 Southern Satellites	100.0	47386	25 Salt of The Earth	100.0
46910	25 Salt of The Earth	67.3	47141	25 Salt of The Earth	92.9	47387	25 Salt of The Earth	100.0
46911	25 Salt of The Earth	100.0	47142	25 Salt of The Earth	97.9	47390	50 Heartland Communities	38.4
46913	17 Green Acres	55.6	47143	25 Salt of The Earth	65.0	47392	25 Salt of The Earth	100.0
46914	26 Midland Crowd	53.4	47145	42 Southern Satellites	94.0	47393	25 Salt of The Earth	100.0
46917	25 Salt of The Earth	100.0	47147	25 Salt of The Earth	60.7	47394	50 Heartland Communities	41.7
46919	25 Salt of The Earth	62.8	47150	32 Rustbelt Traditions	14.1	47396	18 Cozy and Comfortable	23.5

ZIP CODE	TOP TAPESTRY CONSUMER TYPE	% 2004 HOUSE-HOLDS	ZIP CODE	TOP TAPESTRY CONSUMER TYPE	% 2004 HOUSE-HOLDS	ZIP CODE	TOP TAPESTRY CONSUMER TYPE	% 2004 HOUSE-HOLDS
47401	55 College Towns	13.9	47620	17 Green Acres	31.2	47959	42 Southern Satellites	84.1
47403	57 Simple Living	13.3	47630	06 Sophisticated Squires	21.2	47960	25 Salt of The Earth	25.3
47404	63 Dorms To Diplomas	21.1	47631	42 Salt of The Earth	43.9	47963	42 Southern Satellites	40.7
47405	63 Dorms To Diplomas	100.0	47633	25 Salt of The Earth	78.0	47967	25 Salt of The Earth	87.9
47406	63 Dorms To Diplomas	100.0	47634	25 Salt of The Earth	70.6	47968	25 Salt of The Earth	84.8
47408	63 Dorms To Diplomas	44.5	47635	25 Salt of The Earth	86.4	47970	32 Rustbelt Traditions	50.6
47421	50 Heartland Communities	27.4	47637	42 Southern Satellites	70.2	47971	25 Salt of The Earth	93.1
47424	25 Salt of The Earth	33.1	47638	17 Green Acres	68.8	47974	50 Heartland Communities	58.4
47427	42 Southern Satellites	96.6	47639	17 Green Acres	78.6	47975	25 Salt of The Earth	100.0
47429	17 Green Acres	31.8	47640	42 Southern Satellites	47.1	47977	25 Salt of The Earth	55.4
47431	42 Southern Satellites	99.0	47647	25 Salt of The Earth	100.0	47978	25 Salt of The Earth	21.0
47432	25 Salt of The Earth	35.7	47648	17 Green Acres	36.2	47980	42 Southern Satellites	46.6
47433	42 Southern Satellites	52.9	47649	25 Salt of The Earth	100.0	47981	17 Green Acres	73.7
47436	25 Salt of The Earth	88.5	47660	50 Heartland Communities	38.9	47987	42 Southern Satellites	47.6
47438	53 Home Town	57.7	47665	42 Southern Satellites	43.3	47989	25 Salt of The Earth	89.8
47441	50 Heartland Communities	49.3	47666	42 Southern Satellites	55.6	47990	32 Rustbelt Traditions	70.3
47443	46 Rooted Rural	57.1	47670	25 Salt of The Earth	25.1	47991	25 Salt of The Earth	99.5
47446	42 Southern Satellites	40.1	47708	65 Social Security Set	100.0	47992	18 Cozy and Comfortable	78.8
47448	31 Rural Resort Dwellers	43.4	47710	29 Rustbelt Retirees	20.8	47993	25 Salt of The Earth	39.9
47449	46 Rooted Rural	99.4	47711	32 Rustbelt Traditions	28.8	47994	25 Salt of The Earth	100.0
47451	50 Heartland Communities	80.6	47712	32 Rustbelt Traditions	29.2	47995	25 Salt of The Earth	52.7
47452	42 Southern Satellites	61.6	47713	62 Modest Income Homes	30.4	48001	17 Green Acres	30.7
47453	42 Southern Satellites	56.7	47714	32 Rustbelt Traditions	33.6	48002	17 Green Acres	98.8
47454	46 Rooted Rural	36.1	47715	52 Inner City Tenants	15.2	48003	06 Sophisticated Squires	30.6
47456	42 Southern Satellites	41.2	47720	17 Green Acres	44.8	48005	17 Green Acres	50.9
47459	26 Midland Crowd	67.2	47722	55 College Towns	100.0	48006	17 Green Acres	100.0
47460	26 Midland Crowd	40.9	47725	07 Exurbanites	47.7	48009	22 Metropolitans	38.6
47462	25 Salt of The Earth	64.4	47802	57 Simple Living	13.4	48014	17 Green Acres	52.1
47465	25 Salt of The Earth	79.7	47803	32 Rustbelt Traditions	18.8	48015	32 Rustbelt Traditions	34.2
47468	17 Green Acres	75.6	47804	53 Home Town	29.4	48017	18 Cozy and Comfortable	51.1
47469	42 Southern Satellites	84.3	47805	32 Rustbelt Traditions	47.2	48021	32 Rustbelt Traditions	53.8
47470	25 Salt of The Earth	50.5	47807	55 College Towns	33.5	48022	17 Green Acres	99.3
47471	50 Heartland Communities	64.3	47809	55 College Towns	100.0	48023	41 Crossroads	52.8
47501	25 Salt of The Earth	22.8	47832	42 Southern Satellites	88.3	48025	03 Connoisseurs	55.6
47512	53 Home Town	45.0	47833	42 Southern Satellites	57.5	48026	18 Cozy and Comfortable	27.0
47513	42 Southern Satellites	64.5	47834	25 Salt of The Earth	43.6	48027	17 Green Acres	100.0
47514	42 Southern Satellites	97.7	47836	46 Rooted Rural	78.1	48028	15 Silver and Gold	75.6
47515	42 Southern Satellites	72.1	47837	42 Southern Satellites	60.2	48030	32 Rustbelt Traditions	75.2
47516	42 Southern Satellites	52.4	47838	42 Southern Satellites	71.9	48032	26 Midland Crowd	44.8
47519	25 Salt of The Earth	62.1	47840	25 Salt of The Earth	99.4	48034	39 Young and Restless	19.7
47520	42 Southern Satellites	82.9	47841	50 Heartland Communities	52.7	48035	24 Main Street, USA	30.5
47521	25 Salt of The Earth	99.7	47842	50 Heartland Communities	37.3	48036	33 Midlife Junction	25.8
47522	29 Rustbelt Retirees	100.0	47846	46 Rooted Rural	94.4	48038	36 Old and Newcomers	18.2
47523	42 Southern Satellites	68.7	47847	42 Southern Satellites	60.5	48039	32 Rustbelt Traditions	27.8
47524	37 Prairie Living	100.0	47848	46 Rooted Rural	100.0	48040	18 Cozy and Comfortable	34.0
47525	25 Salt of The Earth	100.0	47849	25 Salt of The Earth	100.0	48041	17 Green Acres	62.9
47527	42 Southern Satellites	95.2	47850	50 Heartland Communities	50.8	48042	04 Boomburbs	63.0
47528	46 Rooted Rural	98.1	47854	25 Salt of The Earth	64.1	48043	32 Rustbelt Traditions	25.0
47529	37 Prairie Living	46.3	47858	25 Salt of The Earth	76.7	48044	04 Boomburbs	36.9
47531	25 Salt of The Earth	100.0	47859	25 Salt of The Earth	100.0	48045	07 Exurbanites	26.1
47532	25 Salt of The Earth	50.1	47861	25 Salt of The Earth	100.0	48047	06 Sophisticated Squires	29.6
47537	25 Salt of The Earth	74.2	47862	42 Southern Satellites	51.5	48048	41 Crossroads	55.6
47541	25 Salt of The Earth	81.9	47866	25 Salt of The Earth	100.0	48049	17 Green Acres	48.3
47542	17 Green Acres	25.4	47868	26 Midland Crowd	48.1	48050	17 Green Acres	99.7
47546	17 Green Acres	28.8	47872	50 Heartland Communities	21.1	48051	12 Up and Coming Families	41.3
47550	25 Salt of The Earth	100.0	47874	46 Rooted Rural	34.0	48054	17 Green Acres	60.5
47551	42 Southern Satellites	56.0	47879	42 Southern Satellites	37.9	48059	33 Midlife Junction	19.6
47552	17 Green Acres	88.2	47882	25 Salt of The Earth	27.0	48060	53 Home Town	14.1
47553	50 Heartland Communities	47.7	47885	25 Salt of The Earth	41.8	48062	24 Main Street, USA	50.7
47556	17 Green Acres	51.1	47901	55 College Towns	62.7	48063	26 Midland Crowd	49.0
47557	46 Rooted Rural	58.7	47904	32 Rustbelt Traditions	34.7	48064	17 Green Acres	69.9
47558	25 Salt of The Earth	86.0	47905	36 Old and Newcomers	19.8	48065	02 Suburban Splendor	27.9
47561	50 Heartland Communities	66.1	47906	63 Dorms To Diplomas	31.0	48066	32 Rustbelt Traditions	41.3
47562	42 Southern Satellites	33.5	47907	63 Dorms To Diplomas	100.0	48067	22 Metropolitans	46.8
47564	42 Southern Satellites	90.3	47909	32 Rustbelt Traditions	22.7	48069	03 Connoisseurs	48.2
47567	50 Heartland Communities	41.6	47917	37 Prairie Living	100.0	48070	05 Wealthy Seaboard Suburbs	54.7
47568	25 Salt of The Earth	98.4	47918	32 Rustbelt Traditions	38.8	48071	32 Rustbelt Traditions	33.9
47574	25 Salt of The Earth	100.0	47920	17 Green Acres	38.7	48072	18 Cozy and Comfortable	34.2
47575	25 Salt of The Earth	58.2	47921	50 Heartland Communities	86.3	48073	22 Metropolitans	42.5
47576	42 Southern Satellites	100.0	47922	17 Green Acres	68.9	48074	26 Midland Crowd	49.0
47577	25 Salt of The Earth	95.2	47923	25 Salt of The Earth	39.6	48075	36 Old and Newcomers	25.5
47578	50 Heartland Communities	97.8	47926	25 Salt of The Earth	100.0	48076	10 Pleasant-Ville	21.0
47579	17 Green Acres	88.5	47928	50 Heartland Communities	32.0	48079	17 Green Acres	40.0
47580	25 Salt of The Earth	100.0	47929	25 Salt of The Earth	55.6	48080	30 Retirement Communities	34.6
47581	42 Southern Satellites	56.2	47930	42 Southern Satellites	53.1	48081	18 Cozy and Comfortable	39.7
47585	42 Southern Satellites	100.0	47932	25 Salt of The Earth	64.8	48082	18 Cozy and Comfortable	53.6
47586	25 Salt of The Earth	28.3	47933	17 Green Acres	21.4	48083	06 Sophisticated Squires	24.9
47588	42 Southern Satellites	100.0	47940	25 Salt of The Earth	81.5	48084	27 Metro Renters	33.0
47590	42 Southern Satellites	94.8	47942	25 Salt of The Earth	100.0	48085	02 Suburban Splendor	50.2
47591	33 Midlife Junction	16.4	47943	25 Salt of The Earth	98.7	48088	18 Cozy and Comfortable	54.4
47597	37 Prairie Living	46.8	47944	32 Rustbelt Traditions	55.2	48089	32 Rustbelt Traditions	41.0
47598	42 Southern Satellites	71.2	47946	25 Salt of The Earth	58.5	48091	32 Rustbelt Traditions	22.2
47601	25 Salt of The Earth	34.7	47948	42 Southern Satellites	46.6	48092	18 Cozy and Comfortable	30.9
47610	17 Green Acres	25.3	47949	25 Salt of The Earth	69.6	48093	29 Rustbelt Retirees	25.0
47611	25 Salt of The Earth	84.2	47950	42 Southern Satellites	65.4	48094	26 Midland Crowd	26.8
47612	25 Salt of The Earth	100.0	47951	25 Salt of The Earth	65.5	48095	02 Suburban Splendor	59.9
47613	25 Salt of The Earth	95.6	47952	42 Southern Satellites	72.4	48096	17 Green Acres	100.0
47615	42 Southern Satellites	53.5	47954	25 Salt of The Earth	100.0	48097	17 Green Acres	47.5
47616	46 Rooted Rural	100.0	47955	32 Rustbelt Traditions	84.7	48098	02 Suburban Splendor	87.6
47619	25 Salt of The Earth	100.0	47957	42 Southern Satellites	91.7	48101	18 Cozy and Comfortable	50.0

ZIP CODE	TOP TAPESTRY CONSUMER TYPE	% 2004 HOUSE-HOLDS	ZIP CODE	TOP TAPESTRY CONSUMER TYPE	% 2004 HOUSE-HOLDS	ZIP CODE	TOP TAPESTRY CONSUMER TYPE	% 2004 HOUSE-HOLDS
48103	22 Metropolitans	24.0	48229	53 Home Town	67.7	48450	31 Rural Resort Dwellers	68.4
48104	63 Dorms To Diplomas	38.4	48230	09 Urban Chic	29.3	48451	17 Green Acres	18.4
48105	09 Urban Chic	18.4	48234	51 Metro City Edge	45.4	48453	25 Salt of The Earth	41.4
48108	39 Young and Restless	24.0	48235	34 Family Foundations	78.7	48454	25 Salt of The Earth	99.2
48109	63 Dorms To Diplomas	100.0	48236	05 Wealthy Seaboard Suburbs	32.8	48455	07 Exurbanites	28.4
48111	41 Crossroads	24.9	48237	18 Cozy and Comfortable	27.6	48456	37 Prairie Living	100.0
48114	02 Suburban Splendor	41.4	48238	62 Modest Income Homes	67.6	48457	25 Salt of The Earth	40.3
48116	04 Boomburbs	17.6	48239	18 Cozy and Comfortable	42.8	48458	41 Crossroads	26.3
48117	17 Green Acres	52.8	48240	32 Rustbelt Traditions	61.0	48460	25 Salt of The Earth	59.1
48118	07 Exurbanites	30.4	48301	03 Connoisseurs	66.6	48461	17 Green Acres	47.8
48120	47 Las Casas	44.0	48302	03 Connoisseurs	54.9	48462	06 Sophisticated Squires	52.8
48122	32 Rustbelt Traditions	45.7	48304	01 Top Rung	31.9	48463	17 Green Acres	43.9
48124	18 Cozy and Comfortable	38.9	48306	02 Suburban Splendor	52.6	48464	25 Salt of The Earth	78.7
48125	32 Rustbelt Traditions	61.6	48307	36 Old and Newcomers	17.3	48465	37 Prairie Living	99.7
48126	24 Main Street, USA	24.2	48309	02 Suburban Splendor	28.4	48466	25 Salt of The Earth	90.5
48127	29 Rustbelt Retirees	35.8	48310	06 Sophisticated Squires	34.6	48467	31 Rural Resort Dwellers	84.8
48128	18 Cozy and Comfortable	39.0	48312	10 Pleasant-Ville	30.0	48468	46 Rooted Rural	64.5
48130	13 In Style	27.4	48313	06 Sophisticated Squires	42.6	48469	31 Rural Resort Dwellers	100.0
48131	24 Main Street, USA	57.9	48314	04 Boomburbs	25.5	48470	37 Prairie Living	100.0
48133	18 Cozy and Comfortable	45.5	48315	02 Suburban Splendor	31.7	48471	33 Midlife Junction	51.3
48134	41 Crossroads	20.5	48316	02 Suburban Splendor	20.7	48472	25 Salt of The Earth	89.8
48135	18 Cozy and Comfortable	67.5	48317	24 Main Street, USA	23.4	48473	18 Cozy and Comfortable	34.3
48137	17 Green Acres	34.4	48320	24 Main Street, USA	42.0	48475	37 Prairie Living	51.6
48138	07 Exurbanites	38.6	48322	09 Urban Chic	37.5	48502	52 Inner City Tenants	62.6
48140	17 Green Acres	70.5	48323	03 Connoisseurs	51.8	48503	32 Rustbelt Traditions	17.0
48141	34 Family Foundations	25.2	48324	02 Suburban Splendor	50.8	48504	51 Metro City Edge	47.0
48144	17 Green Acres	58.1	48326	16 Enterprising Professionals	45.3	48505	62 Modest Income Homes	55.8
48145	17 Green Acres	48.4	48327	12 Up and Coming Families	23.1	48506	53 Home Town	30.4
48146	32 Rustbelt Traditions	62.6	48328	36 Old and Newcomers	25.2	48507	29 Rustbelt Retirees	20.0
48150	18 Cozy and Comfortable	61.3	48329	18 Cozy and Comfortable	41.8	48509	29 Rustbelt Retirees	29.4
48152	18 Cozy and Comfortable	20.1	48331	02 Suburban Splendor	33.9	48519	18 Cozy and Comfortable	34.9
48154	10 Pleasant-Ville	30.2	48334	30 Retirement Communities	24.5	48529	53 Home Town	32.3
48157	25 Salt of The Earth	50.5	48335	16 Enterprising Professionals	65.4	48532	18 Cozy and Comfortable	18.9
48158	17 Green Acres	44.2	48336	05 Wealthy Seaboard Suburbs	18.7	48601	62 Modest Income Homes	31.1
48159	17 Green Acres	70.7	48340	32 Rustbelt Traditions	24.1	48602	32 Rustbelt Traditions	26.2
48160	17 Green Acres	42.6	48341	60 City Dimensions	15.5	48603	14 Prosperous Empty Nesters	15.7
48161	41 Crossroads	21.9	48342	34 Family Foundations	31.0	48604	32 Rustbelt Traditions	41.9
48162	24 Main Street, USA	17.7	48346	07 Exurbanites	21.9	48607	62 Modest Income Homes	61.7
48164	17 Green Acres	48.2	48348	02 Suburban Splendor	44.0	48609	18 Cozy and Comfortable	47.9
48165	06 Sophisticated Squires	91.2	48350	06 Sophisticated Squires	47.8	48610	46 Rooted Rural	51.9
48166	41 Crossroads	35.5	48353	07 Exurbanites	47.3	48611	17 Green Acres	48.6
48167	03 Connoisseurs	16.8	48356	06 Sophisticated Squires	31.9	48612	46 Rooted Rural	30.8
48169	06 Sophisticated Squires	23.2	48357	41 Crossroads	47.6	48613	25 Salt of The Earth	91.2
48170	02 Suburban Splendor	20.5	48359	16 Enterprising Professionals	42.3	48614	42 Southern Satellites	62.3
48173	18 Cozy and Comfortable	43.0	48360	04 Boomburbs	63.7	48615	32 Rustbelt Traditions	48.5
48174	41 Crossroads	25.2	48362	12 Up and Coming Families	26.0	48616	25 Salt of The Earth	55.2
48176	02 Suburban Splendor	30.0	48363	02 Suburban Splendor	65.5	48617	57 Simple Living	26.0
48178	12 Up and Coming Families	21.6	48367	06 Sophisticated Squires	60.9	48618	25 Salt of The Earth	42.9
48179	17 Green Acres	36.8	48370	07 Exurbanites	46.0	48619	31 Rural Resort Dwellers	100.0
48180	32 Rustbelt Traditions	31.4	48371	06 Sophisticated Squires	32.8	48620	25 Salt of The Earth	95.5
48182	18 Cozy and Comfortable	36.3	48374	04 Boomburbs	100.0	48621	50 Heartland Communities	47.7
48183	18 Cozy and Comfortable	23.9	48375	13 In Style	68.6	48622	46 Rooted Rural	41.7
48184	32 Rustbelt Traditions	47.2	48377	13 In Style	41.2	48623	17 Green Acres	29.5
48185	18 Cozy and Comfortable	19.4	48380	02 Suburban Splendor	48.0	48624	46 Rooted Rural	27.0
48186	18 Cozy and Comfortable	28.8	48381	17 Green Acres	23.6	48625	50 Heartland Communities	32.3
48187	13 In Style	27.3	48382	06 Sophisticated Squires	43.9	48626	17 Green Acres	50.0
48188	04 Boomburbs	49.1	48383	12 Up and Coming Families	53.9	48628	25 Salt of The Earth	61.9
48189	41 Crossroads	18.2	48386	07 Exurbanites	36.4	48629	31 Rural Resort Dwellers	42.3
48191	17 Green Acres	67.0	48390	06 Sophisticated Squires	39.7	48631	26 Midland Crowd	31.6
48192	32 Rustbelt Traditions	21.0	48393	39 Young and Restless	39.6	48632	49 Senior Sun Seekers	66.1
48195	29 Rustbelt Retirees	26.8	48401	31 Rural Resort Dwellers	44.8	48634	25 Salt of The Earth	78.5
48197	39 Young and Restless	22.9	48412	17 Green Acres	100.0	48635	31 Rural Resort Dwellers	43.4
48198	32 Rustbelt Traditions	18.5	48413	25 Salt of The Earth	30.3	48636	49 Senior Sun Seekers	100.0
48201	65 Social Security Set	40.0	48414	17 Green Acres	50.3	48637	25 Salt of The Earth	91.4
48202	62 Modest Income Homes	37.4	48415	17 Green Acres	26.0	48640	26 Midland Crowd	15.0
48203	62 Modest Income Homes	41.8	48416	25 Salt of The Earth	67.0	48642	26 Midland Crowd	14.7
48204	62 Modest Income Homes	72.0	48417	25 Salt of The Earth	100.0	48647	46 Rooted Rural	38.0
48205	51 Metro City Edge	68.3	48418	17 Green Acres	68.8	48649	25 Salt of The Earth	89.5
48206	62 Modest Income Homes	67.6	48419	31 Rural Resort Dwellers	42.6	48650	25 Salt of The Earth	83.8
48207	62 Modest Income Homes	22.9	48420	18 Cozy and Comfortable	46.3	48651	49 Senior Sun Seekers	62.5
48208	62 Modest Income Homes	58.6	48421	17 Green Acres	57.2	48652	31 Rural Resort Dwellers	30.0
48209	60 City Dimensions	58.1	48422	42 Southern Satellites	44.4	48653	31 Rural Resort Dwellers	42.5
48210	60 City Dimensions	50.8	48423	39 Young and Restless	16.0	48654	31 Rural Resort Dwellers	46.0
48211	62 Modest Income Homes	70.1	48426	25 Salt of The Earth	100.0	48655	31 Rural Resort Dwellers	57.8
48212	60 City Dimensions	34.9	48427	37 Prairie Living	39.4	48656	49 Senior Sun Seekers	56.3
48213	62 Modest Income Homes	48.0	48428	06 Sophisticated Squires	48.4	48657	25 Salt of The Earth	36.3
48214	62 Modest Income Homes	54.1	48429	17 Green Acres	33.8	48658	46 Rooted Rural	38.0
48215	62 Modest Income Homes	33.7	48430	07 Exurbanites	25.7	48659	46 Rooted Rural	88.3
48216	60 City Dimensions	57.1	48432	37 Prairie Living	54.8	48661	31 Rural Resort Dwellers	39.9
48217	34 Family Foundations	53.2	48433	18 Cozy and Comfortable	24.1	48662	25 Salt of The Earth	83.1
48218	53 Home Town	41.9	48435	25 Salt of The Earth	78.7	48701	32 Rustbelt Traditions	47.9
48219	34 Family Foundations	44.6	48436	06 Sophisticated Squires	76.5	48703	31 Rural Resort Dwellers	72.0
48220	22 Metropolitans	27.7	48438	06 Sophisticated Squires	54.4	48705	49 Senior Sun Seekers	72.6
48221	34 Family Foundations	70.0	48439	07 Exurbanites	19.8	48706	29 Rustbelt Retirees	17.8
48223	51 Metro City Edge	35.7	48441	37 Prairie Living	58.0	48708	32 Rustbelt Traditions	25.6
48224	51 Metro City Edge	50.4	48442	17 Green Acres	31.1	48710	17 Green Acres	100.0
48225	18 Cozy and Comfortable	34.1	48444	17 Green Acres	49.0	48720	46 Rooted Rural	91.3
48226	65 Social Security Set	44.5	48445	50 Heartland Communities	37.3	48721	31 Rural Resort Dwellers	100.0
48227	51 Metro City Edge	50.3	48446	17 Green Acres	30.0	48722	18 Cozy and Comfortable	43.3
48228	51 Metro City Edge	56.4	48449	41 Crossroads	30.7	48723	25 Salt of The Earth	38.8

ZIP CODE	TOP TAPESTRY CONSUMER TYPE	% 2004 HOUSE-HOLDS	ZIP CODE	TOP TAPESTRY CONSUMER TYPE	% 2004 HOUSE-HOLDS	ZIP CODE	TOP TAPESTRY CONSUMER TYPE	% 2004 HOUSE-HOLDS
48725	49 Senior Sun Seekers	63.2	48875	17 Green Acres	32.8	49091	25 Salt of The Earth	26.6
48726	50 Heartland Communities	49.8	48876	41 Crossroads	42.8	49092	25 Salt of The Earth	100.0
48727	25 Salt of The Earth	100.0	48877	26 Midland Crowd	57.6	49093	53 Home Town	30.7
48728	49 Senior Sun Seekers	76.5	48878	25 Salt of The Earth	68.7	49094	32 Rustbelt Traditions	49.6
48729	25 Salt of The Earth	62.8	48879	17 Green Acres	46.5	49095	31 Rural Resort Dwellers	47.3
48730	29 Rustbelt Retirees	32.2	48880	32 Rustbelt Traditions	33.6	49096	25 Salt of The Earth	99.8
48731	50 Heartland Communities	52.0	48881	26 Midland Crowd	43.5	49097	17 Green Acres	59.9
48732	33 Midlife Junction	47.1	48883	26 Midland Crowd	67.0	49098	25 Salt of The Earth	39.6
48733	25 Salt of The Earth	100.0	48884	42 Southern Satellites	68.3	49099	25 Salt of The Earth	45.6
48734	30 Retirement Communities	32.8	48885	26 Midland Crowd	54.2	49101	26 Midland Crowd	35.1
48735	25 Salt of The Earth	86.0	48886	50 Heartland Communities	37.4	49102	26 Midland Crowd	60.7
48737	49 Senior Sun Seekers	91.3	48888	25 Salt of The Earth	60.1	49103	22 Metropolitans	25.8
48738	31 Rural Resort Dwellers	80.3	48889	25 Salt of The Earth	63.5	49104	22 Metropolitans	100.0
48739	49 Senior Sun Seekers	71.4	48890	17 Green Acres	75.1	49106	25 Salt of The Earth	52.4
48740	49 Senior Sun Seekers	60.2	48891	42 Southern Satellites	67.0	49107	25 Salt of The Earth	23.5
48741	25 Salt of The Earth	100.0	48892	26 Midland Crowd	66.9	49111	25 Salt of The Earth	60.1
48742	46 Rooted Rural	56.9	48893	25 Salt of The Earth	33.3	49112	25 Salt of The Earth	55.4
48743	49 Senior Sun Seekers	94.1	48895	07 Exurbanites	47.4	49113	25 Salt of The Earth	61.7
48744	25 Salt of The Earth	74.0	48897	25 Salt of The Earth	100.0	49116	15 Silver and Gold	100.0
48745	46 Rooted Rural	100.0	48906	48 Great Expectations	17.5	49117	25 Salt of The Earth	34.3
48746	17 Green Acres	43.7	48910	32 Rustbelt Traditions	32.3	49120	32 Rustbelt Traditions	21.1
48747	25 Salt of The Earth	98.0	48911	48 Great Expectations	25.6	49125	31 Rural Resort Dwellers	37.1
48748	49 Senior Sun Seekers	46.9	48915	48 Great Expectations	34.5	49126	46 Rooted Rural	61.3
48749	46 Rooted Rural	84.9	48915	32 Rustbelt Traditions	22.0	49127	33 Midlife Junction	30.9
48750	50 Heartland Communities	47.0	48917	13 In Style	25.3	49128	32 Rustbelt Traditions	30.7
48754	42 Southern Satellites	51.7	48933	55 College Towns	38.7	49129	15 Silver and Gold	50.5
48755	50 Heartland Communities	37.6	49001	48 Great Expectations	29.5	49130	17 Green Acres	69.9
48756	50 Heartland Communities	46.1	49002	18 Cozy and Comfortable	21.0	49201	17 Green Acres	22.8
48757	33 Midlife Junction	33.2	49004	32 Rustbelt Traditions	33.3	49202	32 Rustbelt Traditions	34.4
48759	29 Rustbelt Retirees	25.2	49006	55 College Towns	43.2	49203	32 Rustbelt Traditions	18.5
48760	25 Salt of The Earth	100.0	49007	55 College Towns	32.0	49220	31 Rural Resort Dwellers	40.7
48761	49 Senior Sun Seekers	71.0	49008	14 Prosperous Empty Nesters	13.9	49221	17 Green Acres	14.2
48762	31 Rural Resort Dwellers	45.2	49009	06 Sophisticated Squires	18.5	49224	32 Rustbelt Traditions	18.9
48763	25 Salt of The Earth	38.8	49010	26 Midland Crowd	31.1	49227	25 Salt of The Earth	96.7
48765	46 Rooted Rural	58.1	49011	25 Salt of The Earth	98.2	49228	25 Salt of The Earth	29.0
48766	46 Rooted Rural	96.8	49012	07 Exurbanites	56.5	49229	17 Green Acres	58.7
48767	25 Salt of The Earth	56.9	49013	25 Salt of The Earth	24.7	49230	17 Green Acres	33.4
48768	25 Salt of The Earth	36.2	49014	53 Home Town	24.9	49232	25 Salt of The Earth	63.6
48770	46 Rooted Rural	68.4	49015	32 Rustbelt Traditions	21.3	49233	07 Exurbanites	48.9
48801	32 Rustbelt Traditions	17.9	49017	32 Rustbelt Traditions	21.3	49234	17 Green Acres	62.3
48806	25 Salt of The Earth	55.4	49021	25 Salt of The Earth	73.3	49235	25 Salt of The Earth	98.8
48807	25 Salt of The Earth	64.4	49022	51 Metro City Edge	20.4	49236	17 Green Acres	52.6
48808	17 Green Acres	77.5	49024	36 Old and Newcomers	16.2	49237	25 Salt of The Earth	80.6
48809	32 Rustbelt Traditions	31.7	49026	26 Midland Crowd	46.7	49238	25 Salt of The Earth	88.3
48811	32 Rustbelt Traditions	35.3	49028	25 Salt of The Earth	53.0	49240	17 Green Acres	85.9
48813	17 Green Acres	33.8	49029	42 Southern Satellites	51.1	49241	25 Salt of The Earth	72.1
48815	25 Salt of The Earth	61.7	49030	25 Salt of The Earth	50.2	49242	25 Salt of The Earth	41.7
48817	25 Salt of The Earth	38.7	49031	25 Salt of The Earth	35.8	49245	42 Southern Satellites	41.1
48818	31 Rural Resort Dwellers	43.6	49032	26 Midland Crowd	37.6	49246	17 Green Acres	55.9
48819	17 Green Acres	97.2	49033	17 Green Acres	68.5	49247	25 Salt of The Earth	49.7
48820	06 Sophisticated Squires	31.2	49034	25 Salt of The Earth	79.4	49248	25 Salt of The Earth	75.4
48821	14 Prosperous Empty Nesters	46.5	49036	25 Salt of The Earth	24.4	49249	31 Rural Resort Dwellers	39.4
48822	17 Green Acres	53.1	49038	32 Rustbelt Traditions	37.7	49250	25 Salt of The Earth	58.7
48823	63 Dorms To Diplomas	32.1	49040	42 Southern Satellites	40.4	49251	32 Rustbelt Traditions	40.5
48824	63 Dorms To Diplomas	100.0	49042	25 Salt of The Earth	49.7	49252	42 Southern Satellites	51.9
48825	39 Young and Restless	94.2	49043	56 Rural Bypasses	89.1	49253	31 Rural Resort Dwellers	27.3
48827	17 Green Acres	45.5	49045	25 Salt of The Earth	35.0	49254	25 Salt of The Earth	45.8
48829	50 Heartland Communities	41.3	49046	25 Salt of The Earth	69.4	49255	42 Southern Satellites	46.7
48831	25 Salt of The Earth	44.1	49047	25 Salt of The Earth	43.2	49256	25 Salt of The Earth	53.7
48832	26 Midland Crowd	87.0	49048	32 Rustbelt Traditions	24.9	49259	26 Midland Crowd	55.0
48834	25 Salt of The Earth	56.4	49050	25 Salt of The Earth	87.3	49262	25 Salt of The Earth	100.0
48835	25 Salt of The Earth	41.1	49051	25 Salt of The Earth	63.6	49264	26 Midland Crowd	57.8
48836	17 Green Acres	36.1	49052	25 Salt of The Earth	100.0	49265	17 Green Acres	92.8
48837	07 Exurbanites	19.9	49053	41 Crossroads	27.7	49266	25 Salt of The Earth	97.2
48838	17 Green Acres	24.6	49055	25 Salt of The Earth	46.2	49267	17 Green Acres	71.0
48840	16 Enterprising Professionals	48.0	49056	42 Southern Satellites	88.8	49268	25 Salt of The Earth	56.7
48841	25 Salt of The Earth	85.3	49057	42 Southern Satellites	48.3	49269	17 Green Acres	48.7
48842	18 Cozy and Comfortable	21.9	49058	25 Salt of The Earth	39.9	49270	17 Green Acres	72.4
48843	06 Sophisticated Squires	25.7	49060	17 Green Acres	55.3	49271	25 Salt of The Earth	100.0
48845	42 Southern Satellites	83.3	49061	42 Southern Satellites	39.9	49272	17 Green Acres	75.4
48846	25 Salt of The Earth	25.2	49064	42 Southern Satellites	54.1	49274	25 Salt of The Earth	47.2
48847	25 Salt of The Earth	44.1	49065	24 Main Street, USA	23.8	49275	18 Cozy and Comfortable	100.0
48848	17 Green Acres	75.1	49066	25 Salt of The Earth	100.0	49276	17 Green Acres	100.0
48849	25 Salt of The Earth	44.1	49067	25 Salt of The Earth	74.9	49277	17 Green Acres	59.5
48850	25 Salt of The Earth	35.4	49068	25 Salt of The Earth	20.4	49279	25 Salt of The Earth	78.8
48851	25 Salt of The Earth	71.4	49070	26 Midland Crowd	63.0	49283	30 Retirement Communities	64.5
48854	17 Green Acres	22.9	49071	17 Green Acres	34.3	49284	25 Salt of The Earth	99.2
48855	06 Sophisticated Squires	57.3	49072	25 Salt of The Earth	82.2	49285	17 Green Acres	45.5
48856	46 Rooted Rural	36.2	49073	25 Salt of The Earth	34.9	49286	17 Green Acres	42.7
48857	26 Midland Crowd	50.8	49076	19 Milk and Cookies	40.3	49287	17 Green Acres	100.0
48858	55 College Towns	29.3	49078	25 Salt of The Earth	45.7	49288	42 Southern Satellites	60.8
48860	42 Southern Satellites	95.7	49079	17 Green Acres	42.4	49301	02 Suburban Splendor	72.3
48861	25 Salt of The Earth	42.0	49080	17 Green Acres	31.2	49302	06 Sophisticated Squires	76.2
48864	13 In Style	34.5	49082	25 Salt of The Earth	35.9	49303	25 Salt of The Earth	100.0
48865	26 Midland Crowd	96.0	49083	17 Green Acres	39.0	49304	49 Senior Sun Seekers	62.6
48866	32 Rustbelt Traditions	42.7	49085	36 Old and Newcomers	25.3	49305	46 Rooted Rural	72.2
48867	32 Rustbelt Traditions	21.0	49087	06 Sophisticated Squires	34.0	49306	06 Sophisticated Squires	47.5
48871	17 Green Acres	61.4	49088	17 Green Acres	54.8	49307	26 Midland Crowd	21.2
48872	17 Green Acres	30.6	49089	42 Southern Satellites	90.4	49309	46 Rooted Rural	99.6
48873	25 Salt of The Earth	67.3	49090	42 Southern Satellites	21.5	49310	25 Salt of The Earth	60.5

ZIP CODE	TOP TAPESTRY CONSUMER TYPE	% 2004 HOUSE-HOLDS	ZIP CODE	TOP TAPESTRY CONSUMER TYPE	% 2004 HOUSE-HOLDS	ZIP CODE	TOP TAPESTRY CONSUMER TYPE	% 2004 HOUSE-HOLDS
49315	17 Green Acres	40.6	49615	31 Rural Resort Dwellers	93.5	49756	49 Senior Sun Seekers	71.4
49316	13 In Style	28.8	49616	31 Rural Resort Dwellers	89.7	49757	22 Metropolitans	100.0
49318	25 Salt of The Earth	80.8	49617	31 Rural Resort Dwellers	50.2	49759	31 Rural Resort Dwellers	56.6
49319	26 Midland Crowd	38.5	49618	46 Rooted Rural	83.4	49760	31 Rural Resort Dwellers	59.9
49321	39 Young and Restless	28.4	49619	31 Rural Resort Dwellers	98.4	49762	31 Rural Resort Dwellers	100.0
49322	25 Salt of The Earth	98.1	49620	26 Midland Crowd	95.0	49765	46 Rooted Rural	47.0
49323	26 Midland Crowd	30.2	49621	17 Green Acres	51.6	49766	25 Salt of The Earth	39.8
49325	17 Green Acres	55.4	49622	31 Rural Resort Dwellers	63.5	49768	31 Rural Resort Dwellers	100.0
49326	26 Midland Crowd	47.3	49623	42 Southern Satellites	58.6	49769	26 Midland Crowd	81.9
49327	42 Southern Satellites	43.5	49625	42 Southern Satellites	76.4	49770	17 Green Acres	37.7
49328	25 Salt of The Earth	53.5	49629	31 Rural Resort Dwellers	72.5	49774	31 Rural Resort Dwellers	71.5
49329	26 Midland Crowd	89.2	49630	31 Rural Resort Dwellers	54.8	49775	15 Silver and Gold	100.0
49330	17 Green Acres	38.1	49631	46 Rooted Rural	39.8	49776	46 Rooted Rural	70.9
49331	17 Green Acres	38.9	49632	37 Prairie Living	44.7	49777	31 Rural Resort Dwellers	90.2
49332	31 Rural Resort Dwellers	42.2	49633	26 Midland Crowd	55.7	49779	50 Heartland Communities	63.3
49333	17 Green Acres	38.2	49635	15 Silver and Gold	38.3	49780	25 Salt of The Earth	59.7
49335	42 Southern Satellites	64.8	49636	15 Silver and Gold	100.0	49781	33 Midlife Junction	42.0
49337	42 Southern Satellites	29.3	49637	26 Midland Crowd	34.9	49782	31 Rural Resort Dwellers	100.0
49338	26 Midland Crowd	59.4	49638	46 Rooted Rural	92.5	49783	32 Rustbelt Traditions	30.2
49339	26 Midland Crowd	44.6	49639	42 Southern Satellites	51.5	49788	28 Aspiring Young Families	61.4
49340	46 Rooted Rural	48.9	49640	31 Rural Resort Dwellers	100.0	49792	46 Rooted Rural	100.0
49341	06 Sophisticated Squires	39.4	49642	46 Rooted Rural	54.2	49795	46 Rooted Rural	89.3
49342	46 Rooted Rural	40.3	49643	26 Midland Crowd	77.5	49799	42 Southern Satellites	53.3
49343	26 Midland Crowd	74.3	49644	49 Senior Sun Seekers	98.4	49801	29 Rustbelt Retirees	14.2
49344	25 Salt of The Earth	72.4	49645	50 Heartland Communities	47.7	49802	32 Rustbelt Traditions	38.8
49345	17 Green Acres	29.4	49646	31 Rural Resort Dwellers	36.3	49806	31 Rural Resort Dwellers	100.0
49346	26 Midland Crowd	46.3	49648	31 Rural Resort Dwellers	100.0	49807	25 Salt of The Earth	68.4
49347	25 Salt of The Earth	100.0	49649	26 Midland Crowd	89.7	49812	46 Rooted Rural	55.7
49348	26 Midland Crowd	30.7	49650	12 Up and Coming Families	55.7	49814	26 Midland Crowd	32.4
49349	42 Southern Satellites	60.6	49651	46 Rooted Rural	33.8	49815	46 Rooted Rural	100.0
49401	12 Up and Coming Families	47.3	49653	31 Rural Resort Dwellers	74.5	49816	46 Rooted Rural	61.3
49402	46 Rooted Rural	74.1	49654	15 Silver and Gold	100.0	49817	31 Rural Resort Dwellers	100.0
49403	17 Green Acres	93.2	49655	46 Rooted Rural	58.3	49818	25 Salt of The Earth	100.0
49404	17 Green Acres	58.7	49656	46 Rooted Rural	56.8	49820	31 Rural Resort Dwellers	100.0
49405	46 Rooted Rural	74.2	49657	25 Salt of The Earth	61.3	49821	46 Rooted Rural	97.3
49408	26 Midland Crowd	23.3	49659	42 Southern Satellites	53.6	49822	31 Rural Resort Dwellers	100.0
49410	46 Rooted Rural	53.6	49660	50 Heartland Communities	24.3	49825	31 Rural Resort Dwellers	95.9
49411	46 Rooted Rural	66.2	49663	26 Midland Crowd	43.9	49826	31 Rural Resort Dwellers	100.0
49412	33 Midlife Junction	36.5	49664	17 Green Acres	70.7	49827	31 Rural Resort Dwellers	100.0
49415	17 Green Acres	69.5	49665	46 Rooted Rural	70.4	49829	29 Rustbelt Retirees	19.9
49417	12 Up and Coming Families	20.4	49667	37 Prairie Living	55.6	49831	25 Salt of The Earth	71.7
49418	18 Cozy and Comfortable	22.7	49668	46 Rooted Rural	57.1	49833	46 Rooted Rural	98.3
49419	12 Up and Coming Families	60.3	49670	31 Rural Resort Dwellers	94.6	49834	46 Rooted Rural	66.1
49420	42 Southern Satellites	35.0	49675	31 Rural Resort Dwellers	86.6	49835	31 Rural Resort Dwellers	100.0
49421	42 Southern Satellites	77.3	49676	31 Rural Resort Dwellers	90.2	49836	31 Rural Resort Dwellers	67.8
49423	38 Industrious Urban Fringe	14.3	49677	25 Salt of The Earth	31.1	49837	50 Heartland Communities	29.8
49424	12 Up and Coming Families	40.1	49679	42 Southern Satellites	80.2	49838	31 Rural Resort Dwellers	100.0
49425	42 Southern Satellites	84.1	49680	26 Midland Crowd	100.0	49839	31 Rural Resort Dwellers	100.0
49426	17 Green Acres	32.4	49682	31 Rural Resort Dwellers	41.4	49840	31 Rural Resort Dwellers	96.2
49428	06 Sophisticated Squires	23.1	49683	26 Midland Crowd	35.6	49841	50 Heartland Communities	32.6
49431	31 Rural Resort Dwellers	22.2	49684	17 Green Acres	20.1	49847	46 Rooted Rural	73.8
49435	17 Green Acres	48.0	49686	33 Midlife Junction	17.3	49848	50 Heartland Communities	100.0
49436	31 Rural Resort Dwellers	100.0	49688	26 Midland Crowd	38.4	49849	53 Home Town	18.9
49437	33 Midlife Junction	21.2	49689	46 Rooted Rural	100.0	49853	31 Rural Resort Dwellers	65.9
49440	65 Social Security Set	50.2	49690	17 Green Acres	29.7	49854	50 Heartland Communities	53.6
49441	32 Rustbelt Traditions	14.8	49701	31 Rural Resort Dwellers	100.0	49855	33 Midlife Junction	21.6
49442	32 Rustbelt Traditions	23.6	49705	46 Rooted Rural	100.0	49858	42 Southern Satellites	13.6
49444	62 Modest Income Homes	22.5	49706	31 Rural Resort Dwellers	61.5	49861	31 Rural Resort Dwellers	87.7
49445	18 Cozy and Comfortable	30.3	49707	33 Midlife Junction	21.8	49862	31 Rural Resort Dwellers	36.3
49446	25 Salt of The Earth	50.5	49709	31 Rural Resort Dwellers	40.3	49866	32 Rustbelt Traditions	28.7
49448	17 Green Acres	54.2	49710	31 Rural Resort Dwellers	96.4	49868	50 Heartland Communities	63.8
49449	15 Silver and Gold	58.1	49712	31 Rural Resort Dwellers	33.5	49870	50 Heartland Communities	51.5
49450	41 Crossroads	37.2	49713	46 Rooted Rural	35.2	49873	46 Rooted Rural	100.0
49451	25 Salt of The Earth	79.1	49715	26 Midland Crowd	66.2	49874	25 Salt of The Earth	44.1
49452	42 Southern Satellites	81.2	49716	31 Rural Resort Dwellers	57.5	49876	25 Salt of The Earth	98.5
49453	33 Midlife Junction	34.6	49718	31 Rural Resort Dwellers	100.0	49878	31 Rural Resort Dwellers	76.3
49454	25 Salt of The Earth	54.0	49719	31 Rural Resort Dwellers	92.2	49879	50 Heartland Communities	98.6
49455	31 Rural Resort Dwellers	29.9	49720	31 Rural Resort Dwellers	35.3	49880	46 Rooted Rural	84.4
49456	33 Midlife Junction	23.7	49721	31 Rural Resort Dwellers	43.3	49881	46 Rooted Rural	99.4
49457	17 Green Acres	33.1	49724	26 Midland Crowd	59.5	49883	31 Rural Resort Dwellers	100.0
49459	42 Southern Satellites	88.0	49725	31 Rural Resort Dwellers	100.0	49884	25 Salt of The Earth	77.3
49460	17 Green Acres	34.8	49726	31 Rural Resort Dwellers	100.0	49885	31 Rural Resort Dwellers	51.5
49461	17 Green Acres	46.7	49727	25 Salt of The Earth	19.3	49886	46 Rooted Rural	69.7
49464	12 Up and Coming Families	34.0	49728	31 Rural Resort Dwellers	100.0	49887	46 Rooted Rural	43.0
49503	48 Great Expectations	16.0	49729	31 Rural Resort Dwellers	53.0	49891	46 Rooted Rural	100.0
49504	60 City Dimensions	29.7	49730	17 Green Acres	28.9	49892	25 Salt of The Earth	67.0
49505	48 Great Expectations	23.2	49733	31 Rural Resort Dwellers	61.5	49893	25 Salt of The Earth	75.1
49506	22 Metropolitans	16.6	49735	33 Midlife Junction	27.0	49894	50 Heartland Communities	53.0
49507	51 Metro City Edge	22.4	49736	31 Rural Resort Dwellers	100.0	49895	46 Rooted Rural	92.1
49508	28 Aspiring Young Families	25.1	49738	31 Rural Resort Dwellers	31.7	49896	46 Rooted Rural	61.0
49509	32 Rustbelt Traditions	24.1	49740	17 Green Acres	45.6	49905	50 Heartland Communities	57.4
49512	39 Young and Restless	59.9	49743	46 Rooted Rural	63.7	49908	50 Heartland Communities	74.6
49525	06 Sophisticated Squires	18.4	49744	25 Salt of The Earth	50.4	49910	49 Senior Sun Seekers	63.9
49544	39 Young and Restless	23.3	49746	31 Rural Resort Dwellers	41.3	49911	50 Heartland Communities	93.7
49546	02 Suburban Splendor	21.2	49747	25 Salt of The Earth	58.5	49912	50 Heartland Communities	52.9
49548	32 Rustbelt Traditions	34.3	49749	31 Rural Resort Dwellers	50.6	49913	50 Heartland Communities	52.5
49601	17 Green Acres	16.6	49751	31 Rural Resort Dwellers	50.9	49916	33 Midlife Junction	46.0
49612	31 Rural Resort Dwellers	79.2	49752	46 Rooted Rural	42.2	49919	46 Rooted Rural	97.7
49613	31 Rural Resort Dwellers	100.0	49753	31 Rural Resort Dwellers	54.4	49920	31 Rural Resort Dwellers	35.2
49614	31 Rural Resort Dwellers	55.1	49755	31 Rural Resort Dwellers	62.6	49921	33 Midlife Junction	100.0

ZIP CODE	TOP TAPESTRY CONSUMER TYPE	% 2004 HOUSE-HOLDS	ZIP CODE	TOP TAPESTRY CONSUMER TYPE	% 2004 HOUSE-HOLDS	ZIP CODE	TOP TAPESTRY CONSUMER TYPE	% 2004 HOUSE-HOLDS
49925	50 Heartland Communities	88.3	50112	57 Simple Living	23.4	50249	50 Heartland Communities	56.2
49927	49 Senior Sun Seekers	80.5	50115	50 Heartland Communities	66.9	50250	32 Rustbelt Traditions	47.3
49930	50 Heartland Communities	32.0	50116	42 Southern Satellites	94.6	50251	25 Salt of The Earth	80.8
49931	55 College Towns	65.9	50117	37 Prairie Living	100.0	50252	17 Green Acres	100.0
49935	50 Heartland Communities	67.7	50118	25 Salt of The Earth	100.0	50254	37 Prairie Living	94.8
49938	50 Heartland Communities	50.1	50119	42 Southern Satellites	92.8	50256	42 Southern Satellites	80.7
49945	50 Heartland Communities	63.2	50120	25 Salt of The Earth	100.0	50257	25 Salt of The Earth	89.1
49946	50 Heartland Communities	67.0	50122	29 Rustbelt Retirees	61.9	50258	37 Prairie Living	100.0
49947	31 Rural Resort Dwellers	48.3	50123	37 Prairie Living	100.0	50261	26 Midland Crowd	73.1
49948	31 Rural Resort Dwellers	60.0	50124	13 In Style	57.0	50262	46 Rooted Rural	76.2
49950	50 Heartland Communities	70.0	50125	17 Green Acres	29.8	50263	12 Up and Coming Families	75.4
49952	50 Heartland Communities	64.1	50126	29 Rustbelt Retirees	42.4	50264	46 Rooted Rural	69.1
49953	50 Heartland Communities	57.3	50127	25 Salt of The Earth	100.0	50265	16 Enterprising Professionals	25.2
49958	46 Rooted Rural	52.2	50128	37 Prairie Living	100.0	50266	36 Old and Newcomers	33.7
49962	31 Rural Resort Dwellers	100.0	50129	50 Heartland Communities	51.5	50268	50 Heartland Communities	70.2
49965	50 Heartland Communities	80.0	50130	32 Rustbelt Traditions	72.7	50271	37 Prairie Living	100.0
49967	46 Rooted Rural	44.6	50131	04 Boomburbs	64.4	50272	46 Rooted Rural	65.7
49968	50 Heartland Communities	72.2	50132	37 Prairie Living	100.0	50273	33 Midlife Junction	39.1
49969	46 Rooted Rural	61.5	50133	50 Heartland Communities	99.6	50274	37 Prairie Living	100.0
49970	46 Rooted Rural	100.0	50134	18 Cozy and Comfortable	77.4	50275	37 Prairie Living	85.0
50001	17 Green Acres	100.0	50135	25 Salt of The Earth	100.0	50276	25 Salt of The Earth	38.9
50002	50 Heartland Communities	62.7	50136	37 Prairie Living	100.0	50277	31 Rural Resort Dwellers	80.7
50003	26 Midland Crowd	30.1	50138	25 Salt of The Earth	35.2	50278	32 Rustbelt Traditions	93.1
50005	25 Salt of The Earth	85.7	50139	37 Prairie Living	62.8	50309	65 Social Security Set	87.5
50006	37 Prairie Living	100.0	50140	55 College Towns	54.1	50310	32 Rustbelt Traditions	23.3
50007	17 Green Acres	100.0	50141	25 Salt of The Earth	100.0	50311	22 Metropolitans	31.6
50008	50 Heartland Communities	76.7	50143	37 Prairie Living	100.0	50312	22 Metropolitans	13.5
50009	28 Aspiring Young Families	40.5	50144	50 Heartland Communities	86.3	50313	32 Rustbelt Traditions	57.5
50010	55 College Towns	20.2	50146	37 Prairie Living	99.5	50314	51 Metro City Edge	27.0
50011	63 Dorms To Diplomas	0.0	50147	50 Heartland Communities	94.3	50315	32 Rustbelt Traditions	44.6
50013	63 Dorms To Diplomas	0.0	50148	37 Prairie Living	100.0	50316	32 Rustbelt Traditions	42.3
50014	55 College Towns	36.8	50149	42 Southern Satellites	68.4	50317	32 Rustbelt Traditions	50.2
50020	50 Heartland Communities	75.9	50150	42 Southern Satellites	99.8	50320	28 Aspiring Young Families	46.8
50021	28 Aspiring Young Families	23.0	50151	46 Rooted Rural	89.9	50321	36 Old and Newcomers	44.7
50022	50 Heartland Communities	28.6	50152	17 Green Acres	100.0	50322	06 Sophisticated Squires	30.8
50025	50 Heartland Communities	71.4	50153	25 Salt of The Earth	96.8	50323	04 Boomburbs	100.0
50026	37 Prairie Living	100.0	50154	37 Prairie Living	100.0	50325	02 Suburban Splendor	38.5
50027	37 Prairie Living	100.0	50155	37 Prairie Living	100.0	50323	06 Sophisticated Squires	40.9
50028	32 Rustbelt Traditions	65.0	50156	32 Rustbelt Traditions	31.4	50401	32 Rustbelt Traditions	20.3
50029	37 Prairie Living	100.0	50157	25 Salt of The Earth	94.5	50420	37 Prairie Living	100.0
50033	17 Green Acres	100.0	50158	29 Rustbelt Retirees	17.3	50421	50 Heartland Communities	82.0
50034	37 Prairie Living	100.0	50161	25 Salt of The Earth	67.4	50423	50 Heartland Communities	68.5
50035	19 Milk and Cookies	57.8	50162	25 Salt of The Earth	100.0	50424	50 Heartland Communities	79.2
50036	33 Midlife Junction	50.1	50164	46 Rooted Rural	82.1	50428	33 Midlife Junction	56.0
50038	26 Midland Crowd	100.0	50165	37 Prairie Living	100.0	50430	37 Prairie Living	99.6
50039	37 Prairie Living	100.0	50166	25 Salt of The Earth	64.4	50432	37 Prairie Living	100.0
50040	37 Prairie Living	100.0	50167	25 Salt of The Earth	59.2	50433	37 Prairie Living	100.0
50041	37 Prairie Living	100.0	50168	17 Green Acres	59.0	50434	37 Prairie Living	98.0
50042	37 Prairie Living	100.0	50169	32 Rustbelt Traditions	47.0	50435	25 Salt of The Earth	82.6
50044	42 Southern Satellites	78.3	50170	25 Salt of The Earth	75.0	50436	33 Midlife Junction	36.5
50046	26 Midland Crowd	77.6	50171	25 Salt of The Earth	37.3	50438	29 Rustbelt Retirees	31.3
50047	26 Midland Crowd	36.1	50173	42 Southern Satellites	69.0	50439	37 Prairie Living	94.9
50048	37 Prairie Living	89.7	50174	42 Southern Satellites	77.2	50440	37 Prairie Living	100.0
50049	50 Heartland Communities	54.2	50201	33 Midlife Junction	44.2	50441	53 Home Town	25.6
50050	50 Heartland Communities	80.5	50206	37 Prairie Living	98.5	50444	37 Prairie Living	91.9
50051	37 Prairie Living	100.0	50207	37 Prairie Living	53.7	50446	25 Salt of The Earth	68.2
50052	50 Heartland Communities	91.3	50208	32 Rustbelt Traditions	29.4	50447	50 Heartland Communities	75.7
50054	25 Salt of The Earth	57.8	50210	25 Salt of The Earth	81.1	50448	37 Prairie Living	81.0
50055	25 Salt of The Earth	100.0	50211	19 Milk and Cookies	57.6	50449	42 Southern Satellites	93.2
50056	32 Rustbelt Traditions	69.2	50212	29 Rustbelt Retirees	39.3	50450	33 Midlife Junction	60.2
50057	25 Salt of The Earth	100.0	50213	33 Midlife Junction	41.5	50451	50 Heartland Communities	58.2
50058	29 Rustbelt Retirees	37.9	50214	17 Green Acres	100.0	50452	37 Prairie Living	100.0
50059	37 Prairie Living	100.0	50216	33 Midlife Junction	47.6	50453	25 Salt of The Earth	58.9
50060	50 Heartland Communities	68.8	50217	37 Prairie Living	96.8	50454	37 Prairie Living	100.0
50061	07 Exurbanites	37.6	50218	17 Green Acres	100.0	50455	37 Prairie Living	100.0
50062	50 Heartland Communities	78.0	50219	17 Green Acres	30.9	50456	32 Rustbelt Traditions	45.7
50063	17 Green Acres	55.9	50220	32 Rustbelt Traditions	42.4	50457	37 Prairie Living	100.0
50064	37 Prairie Living	100.0	50222	37 Prairie Living	95.5	50458	25 Salt of The Earth	57.1
50065	37 Prairie Living	94.3	50223	37 Prairie Living	100.0	50459	25 Salt of The Earth	44.2
50066	37 Prairie Living	100.0	50225	33 Midlife Junction	38.2	50460	37 Prairie Living	90.5
50067	37 Prairie Living	94.6	50226	06 Sophisticated Squires	39.0	50461	50 Heartland Communities	50.2
50068	37 Prairie Living	94.3	50227	37 Prairie Living	100.0	50464	25 Salt of The Earth	75.3
50069	26 Midland Crowd	100.0	50228	25 Salt of The Earth	93.1	50465	37 Prairie Living	100.0
50070	32 Rustbelt Traditions	45.7	50229	17 Green Acres	100.0	50466	37 Prairie Living	61.3
50071	37 Prairie Living	100.0	50230	37 Prairie Living	100.0	50467	37 Prairie Living	100.0
50072	26 Midland Crowd	64.5	50231	37 Prairie Living	100.0	50468	50 Heartland Communities	62.0
50073	17 Green Acres	100.0	50232	42 Southern Satellites	62.2	50469	32 Rustbelt Traditions	65.4
50074	31 Rural Resort Dwellers	100.0	50233	50 Heartland Communities	72.6	50470	37 Prairie Living	100.0
50075	37 Prairie Living	100.0	50234	25 Salt of The Earth	100.0	50471	37 Prairie Living	100.0
50076	37 Prairie Living	64.9	50235	37 Prairie Living	100.0	50472	50 Heartland Communities	52.4
50101	37 Prairie Living	100.0	50236	17 Green Acres	97.4	50473	37 Prairie Living	100.0
50102	37 Prairie Living	100.0	50237	17 Green Acres	70.0	50475	29 Rustbelt Retirees	61.7
50103	37 Prairie Living	100.0	50238	50 Heartland Communities	91.4	50476	37 Prairie Living	100.0
50104	37 Prairie Living	100.0	50239	37 Prairie Living	96.3	50477	37 Prairie Living	92.8
50105	26 Midland Crowd	100.0	50240	17 Green Acres	96.7	50478	37 Prairie Living	100.0
50106	32 Rustbelt Traditions	56.9	50242	17 Green Acres	90.9	50479	37 Prairie Living	96.4
50107	50 Heartland Communities	79.5	50244	18 Cozy and Comfortable	93.1	50480	37 Prairie Living	100.0
50108	37 Prairie Living	100.0	50246	37 Prairie Living	100.0	50482	31 Rural Resort Dwellers	85.6
50109	25 Salt of The Earth	42.8	50247	25 Salt of The Earth	50.4	50483	37 Prairie Living	100.0
50111	12 Up and Coming Families	76.5	50248	33 Midlife Junction	39.4	50484	37 Prairie Living	100.0

ZIP CODE	TOP TAPESTRY CONSUMER TYPE	% 2004 HOUSE-HOLDS	ZIP CODE	TOP TAPESTRY CONSUMER TYPE	% 2004 HOUSE-HOLDS	ZIP CODE	TOP TAPESTRY CONSUMER TYPE	% 2004 HOUSE-HOLDS
50501	53 Home Town	17.8	50625	50 Heartland Communities	65.0	51023	29 Rustbelt Retirees	43.9
50510	37 Prairie Living	100.0	50626	26 Midland Crowd	64.2	51024	17 Green Acres	85.1
50511	50 Heartland Communities	18.8	50627	50 Heartland Communities	58.5	51025	50 Heartland Communities	68.1
50514	50 Heartland Communities	69.4	50628	37 Prairie Living	99.2	51026	25 Salt of The Earth	91.0
50515	37 Prairie Living	100.0	50629	42 Southern Satellites	61.9	51027	37 Prairie Living	100.0
50516	25 Salt of The Earth	92.8	50630	50 Heartland Communities	52.4	51028	29 Rustbelt Retirees	68.5
50517	50 Heartland Communities	77.0	50632	32 Rustbelt Traditions	62.5	51029	37 Prairie Living	100.0
50518	37 Prairie Living	97.4	50633	37 Prairie Living	100.0	51030	17 Green Acres	82.8
50519	37 Prairie Living	100.0	50635	29 Rustbelt Retirees	74.7	51031	17 Green Acres	21.8
50520	37 Prairie Living	100.0	50636	37 Prairie Living	35.3	51033	37 Prairie Living	98.6
50521	37 Prairie Living	100.0	50638	50 Heartland Communities	31.3	51034	50 Heartland Communities	90.6
50522	50 Heartland Communities	65.4	50641	42 Southern Satellites	97.1	51035	50 Heartland Communities	68.2
50523	37 Prairie Living	100.0	50642	37 Prairie Living	100.0	51036	37 Prairie Living	100.0
50524	37 Prairie Living	100.0	50643	17 Green Acres	99.9	51037	37 Prairie Living	100.0
50525	29 Rustbelt Retirees	37.4	50644	25 Salt of The Earth	28.4	51038	25 Salt of The Earth	74.6
50527	37 Prairie Living	100.0	50645	37 Prairie Living	68.4	51039	26 Midland Crowd	71.7
50528	37 Prairie Living	100.0	50647	25 Salt of The Earth	80.0	51040	50 Heartland Communities	62.3
50529	32 Rustbelt Traditions	93.8	50648	25 Salt of The Earth	48.4	51041	33 Midlife Junction	64.6
50530	50 Heartland Communities	78.7	50649	37 Prairie Living	100.0	51044	37 Prairie Living	100.0
50531	37 Prairie Living	100.0	50650	37 Prairie Living	100.0	51046	50 Heartland Communities	67.8
50532	42 Southern Satellites	84.7	50651	32 Rustbelt Traditions	36.2	51047	37 Prairie Living	100.0
50533	50 Heartland Communities	29.7	50652	37 Prairie Living	100.0	51048	37 Prairie Living	93.8
50535	37 Prairie Living	100.0	50653	37 Prairie Living	100.0	51049	37 Prairie Living	100.0
50536	50 Heartland Communities	50.2	50654	37 Prairie Living	92.7	51050	25 Salt of The Earth	69.9
50538	50 Heartland Communities	100.0	50655	37 Prairie Living	100.0	51051	37 Prairie Living	93.8
50539	37 Prairie Living	100.0	50658	50 Heartland Communities	79.3	51052	25 Salt of The Earth	100.0
50540	50 Heartland Communities	57.9	50659	29 Rustbelt Retirees	37.9	51053	50 Heartland Communities	66.5
50541	37 Prairie Living	83.6	50660	42 Southern Satellites	59.6	51054	19 Milk and Cookies	87.9
50542	50 Heartland Communities	86.5	50662	50 Heartland Communities	42.2	51055	25 Salt of The Earth	87.7
50543	50 Heartland Communities	81.7	50665	37 Prairie Living	34.1	51056	37 Prairie Living	96.2
50544	37 Prairie Living	100.0	50666	25 Salt of The Earth	82.5	51058	50 Heartland Communities	65.6
50545	37 Prairie Living	100.0	50667	25 Salt of The Earth	100.0	51060	37 Prairie Living	100.0
50546	37 Prairie Living	100.0	50668	29 Rustbelt Retirees	58.0	51061	37 Prairie Living	100.0
50548	29 Rustbelt Retirees	37.8	50669	25 Salt of The Earth	49.4	51062	17 Green Acres	97.1
50551	37 Prairie Living	100.0	50670	32 Rustbelt Traditions	45.7	51063	50 Heartland Communities	73.8
50552	37 Prairie Living	100.0	50671	37 Prairie Living	98.2	51101	65 Social Security Set	66.8
50554	50 Heartland Communities	52.5	50672	50 Heartland Communities	91.8	51103	32 Rustbelt Traditions	31.8
50556	50 Heartland Communities	53.8	50674	37 Prairie Living	43.1	51104	18 Cozy and Comfortable	19.8
50557	50 Heartland Communities	76.4	50675	29 Rustbelt Retirees	42.1	51105	60 City Dimensions	29.0
50558	37 Prairie Living	100.0	50676	25 Salt of The Earth	44.7	51106	32 Rustbelt Traditions	39.7
50559	37 Prairie Living	100.0	50677	33 Midlife Junction	32.6	51108	32 Rustbelt Traditions	35.9
50560	37 Prairie Living	100.0	50680	50 Heartland Communities	71.6	51109	53 Home Town	28.8
50561	37 Prairie Living	84.5	50681	37 Prairie Living	100.0	51111	28 Aspiring Young Families	88.9
50562	37 Prairie Living	100.0	50682	37 Prairie Living	89.3	51201	25 Salt of The Earth	24.7
50563	50 Heartland Communities	45.2	50701	32 Rustbelt Traditions	17.8	51230	37 Prairie Living	100.0
50565	37 Prairie Living	100.0	50702	29 Rustbelt Retirees	37.0	51231	37 Prairie Living	100.0
50566	37 Prairie Living	100.0	50703	53 Home Town	46.0	51232	37 Prairie Living	100.0
50567	37 Prairie Living	100.0	50706	25 Salt of The Earth	100.0	51234	37 Prairie Living	83.0
50568	50 Heartland Communities	75.9	50707	32 Rustbelt Traditions	34.4	51235	37 Prairie Living	100.0
50569	32 Rustbelt Traditions	93.3	50801	32 Rustbelt Traditions	24.2	51237	50 Heartland Communities	65.2
50570	37 Prairie Living	100.0	50830	50 Heartland Communities	61.3	51238	37 Prairie Living	100.0
50571	37 Prairie Living	100.0	50833	50 Heartland Communities	83.7	51239	37 Prairie Living	59.1
50573	37 Prairie Living	100.0	50835	37 Prairie Living	100.0	51240	29 Rustbelt Retirees	54.1
50574	37 Prairie Living	58.1	50836	50 Heartland Communities	85.7	51241	37 Prairie Living	50.1
50575	50 Heartland Communities	77.2	50837	37 Prairie Living	100.0	51243	37 Prairie Living	100.0
50576	37 Prairie Living	100.0	50840	37 Prairie Living	97.1	51245	50 Heartland Communities	70.0
50577	37 Prairie Living	100.0	50841	50 Heartland Communities	43.2	51246	50 Heartland Communities	52.2
50578	37 Prairie Living	100.0	50843	37 Prairie Living	100.0	51247	25 Salt of The Earth	46.9
50579	50 Heartland Communities	73.5	50845	37 Prairie Living	100.0	51248	50 Heartland Communities	78.8
50581	50 Heartland Communities	79.5	50846	50 Heartland Communities	66.0	51249	50 Heartland Communities	30.9
50582	37 Prairie Living	96.8	50847	37 Prairie Living	100.0	51250	17 Green Acres	22.9
50583	50 Heartland Communities	83.8	50848	37 Prairie Living	98.3	51301	50 Heartland Communities	19.1
50585	50 Heartland Communities	69.1	50849	50 Heartland Communities	83.0	51331	31 Rural Resort Dwellers	100.0
50586	37 Prairie Living	96.6	50851	50 Heartland Communities	67.1	51333	37 Prairie Living	100.0
50588	42 Southern Satellites	37.4	50853	37 Prairie Living	100.0	51334	50 Heartland Communities	25.9
50590	50 Heartland Communities	67.2	50854	50 Heartland Communities	78.4	51338	25 Salt of The Earth	75.9
50591	37 Prairie Living	100.0	50857	37 Prairie Living	68.8	51342	50 Heartland Communities	75.9
50594	37 Prairie Living	100.0	50858	37 Prairie Living	100.0	51343	37 Prairie Living	100.0
50595	32 Rustbelt Traditions	29.8	50859	37 Prairie Living	100.0	51345	37 Prairie Living	100.0
50597	50 Heartland Communities	62.7	50860	37 Prairie Living	100.0	51346	37 Prairie Living	69.8
50598	37 Prairie Living	100.0	50861	37 Prairie Living	100.0	51347	50 Heartland Communities	78.2
50599	37 Prairie Living	100.0	50862	37 Prairie Living	100.0	51350	37 Prairie Living	100.0
50601	37 Prairie Living	52.1	50863	31 Rural Resort Dwellers	95.1	51351	33 Midlife Junction	31.6
50602	50 Heartland Communities	70.6	50864	50 Heartland Communities	73.8	51354	37 Prairie Living	100.0
50603	37 Prairie Living	100.0	51001	25 Salt of The Earth	47.8	51355	31 Rural Resort Dwellers	97.4
50604	50 Heartland Communities	67.8	51002	32 Rustbelt Traditions	73.4	51357	37 Prairie Living	100.0
50605	37 Prairie Living	100.0	51003	25 Salt of The Earth	75.3	51358	50 Heartland Communities	58.9
50606	37 Prairie Living	100.0	51004	50 Heartland Communities	70.8	51360	31 Rural Resort Dwellers	26.5
50607	37 Prairie Living	100.0	51005	29 Rustbelt Retirees	70.0	51363	31 Rural Resort Dwellers	100.0
50608	37 Prairie Living	100.0	51006	50 Heartland Communities	70.6	51364	37 Prairie Living	84.9
50609	37 Prairie Living	100.0	51007	25 Salt of The Earth	97.1	51365	37 Prairie Living	100.0
50611	37 Prairie Living	100.0	51009	37 Prairie Living	100.0	51366	37 Prairie Living	100.0
50612	33 Midlife Junction	53.5	51010	37 Prairie Living	91.1	51401	33 Midlife Junction	22.9
50613	22 Metropolitans	21.7	51012	50 Heartland Communities	48.7	51430	37 Prairie Living	100.0
50614	22 Metropolitans	100.0	51014	37 Prairie Living	100.0	51431	37 Prairie Living	100.0
50616	50 Heartland Communities	30.6	51016	50 Heartland Communities	61.5	51432	37 Prairie Living	100.0
50619	50 Heartland Communities	58.3	51018	37 Prairie Living	100.0	51433	37 Prairie Living	100.0
50621	33 Midlife Junction	73.6	51019	37 Prairie Living	98.7	51436	37 Prairie Living	100.0
50622	25 Salt of The Earth	50.4	51020	37 Prairie Living	99.2	51439	37 Prairie Living	100.0
50624	25 Salt of The Earth	88.9	51022	37 Prairie Living	100.0	51440	37 Prairie Living	100.0

ZIP CODE	TOP TAPESTRY CONSUMER TYPE	% 2004 HOUSE-HOLDS	ZIP CODE	TOP TAPESTRY CONSUMER TYPE	% 2004 HOUSE-HOLDS	ZIP CODE	TOP TAPESTRY CONSUMER TYPE	% 2004 HOUSE-HOLDS
51441	37 Prairie Living	100.0	51651	37 Prairie Living	100.0	52216	50 Heartland Communities	75.4
51442	50 Heartland Communities	31.6	51652	50 Heartland Communities	50.7	52217	37 Prairie Living	100.0
51443	50 Heartland Communities	67.6	51653	33 Midlife Junction	77.4	52218	32 Rustbelt Traditions	42.4
51444	37 Prairie Living	100.0	51654	25 Salt of The Earth	100.0	52219	25 Salt of The Earth	100.0
51445	50 Heartland Communities	58.0	51656	37 Prairie Living	100.0	52220	17 Green Acres	100.0
51446	37 Prairie Living	100.0	52001	32 Rustbelt Traditions	17.1	52221	37 Prairie Living	100.0
51447	37 Prairie Living	93.9	52002	25 Salt of The Earth	27.5	52222	37 Prairie Living	99.0
51448	37 Prairie Living	100.0	52003	17 Green Acres	20.4	52223	37 Prairie Living	72.0
51449	50 Heartland Communities	77.5	52030	25 Salt of The Earth	100.0	52224	29 Rustbelt Retirees	42.8
51450	31 Rural Resort Dwellers	42.2	52031	25 Salt of The Earth	62.6	52225	37 Prairie Living	96.0
51451	37 Prairie Living	100.0	52032	37 Prairie Living	100.0	52226	37 Prairie Living	100.0
51452	37 Prairie Living	100.0	52033	37 Prairie Living	64.4	52227	17 Green Acres	91.8
51453	37 Prairie Living	93.6	52035	37 Prairie Living	100.0	52228	17 Green Acres	58.0
51454	50 Heartland Communities	65.0	52036	37 Prairie Living	68.4	52229	37 Prairie Living	100.0
51455	50 Heartland Communities	72.7	52037	37 Prairie Living	63.7	52231	37 Prairie Living	100.0
51458	37 Prairie Living	53.8	52038	37 Prairie Living	100.0	52232	25 Salt of The Earth	85.5
51460	37 Prairie Living	100.0	52039	37 Prairie Living	34.6	52233	39 Young and Restless	28.2
51461	50 Heartland Communities	79.5	52040	32 Rustbelt Traditions	46.8	52236	17 Green Acres	100.0
51462	37 Prairie Living	99.3	52041	25 Salt of The Earth	65.6	52237	42 Southern Satellites	54.0
51463	37 Prairie Living	100.0	52042	37 Prairie Living	100.0	52240	63 Dorms To Diplomas	25.9
51465	37 Prairie Living	100.0	52043	29 Rustbelt Retirees	41.9	52241	39 Young and Restless	55.1
51466	50 Heartland Communities	74.3	52044	37 Prairie Living	100.0	52242	63 Dorms To Diplomas	100.0
51467	37 Prairie Living	100.0	52045	25 Salt of The Earth	69.1	52245	22 Metropolitans	24.9
51501	32 Rustbelt Traditions	40.4	52046	25 Salt of The Earth	70.7	52246	16 Enterprising Professionals	59.3
51503	33 Midlife Junction	16.9	52047	37 Prairie Living	100.0	52247	37 Prairie Living	37.3
51510	29 Rustbelt Retirees	31.9	52048	37 Prairie Living	100.0	52248	50 Heartland Communities	59.7
51520	37 Prairie Living	100.0	52049	50 Heartland Communities	96.8	52249	29 Rustbelt Retirees	81.4
51521	50 Heartland Communities	53.6	52050	37 Prairie Living	100.0	52251	37 Prairie Living	100.0
51523	37 Prairie Living	100.0	52052	37 Prairie Living	40.9	52253	26 Midland Crowd	73.8
51525	25 Salt of The Earth	72.6	52053	37 Prairie Living	91.2	52254	50 Heartland Communities	64.0
51526	17 Green Acres	74.6	52054	25 Salt of The Earth	83.6	52255	50 Heartland Communities	66.1
51527	37 Prairie Living	100.0	52057	32 Rustbelt Traditions	26.3	52257	25 Salt of The Earth	100.0
51528	46 Rooted Rural	62.7	52060	25 Salt of The Earth	33.9	52301	32 Rustbelt Traditions	60.5
51529	50 Heartland Communities	56.8	52064	37 Prairie Living	98.8	52302	13 In Style	25.6
51530	37 Prairie Living	100.0	52065	37 Prairie Living	100.0	52305	37 Prairie Living	91.9
51531	29 Rustbelt Retirees	95.3	52068	17 Green Acres	91.2	52306	32 Rustbelt Traditions	58.3
51532	46 Rooted Rural	75.4	52069	50 Heartland Communities	67.6	52307	17 Green Acres	100.0
51533	50 Heartland Communities	57.6	52070	46 Rooted Rural	79.4	52308	37 Prairie Living	100.0
51534	33 Midlife Junction	32.5	52071	25 Salt of The Earth	100.0	52309	46 Rooted Rural	57.2
51535	37 Prairie Living	60.0	52072	37 Prairie Living	95.9	52310	25 Salt of The Earth	31.7
51536	37 Prairie Living	65.3	52073	17 Green Acres	46.7	52313	37 Prairie Living	100.0
51537	29 Rustbelt Retirees	39.3	52074	37 Prairie Living	86.0	52314	17 Green Acres	88.6
51540	37 Prairie Living	100.0	52076	25 Salt of The Earth	56.0	52315	25 Salt of The Earth	94.2
51541	37 Prairie Living	95.2	52077	37 Prairie Living	100.0	52316	50 Heartland Communities	73.9
51542	17 Green Acres	100.0	52078	37 Prairie Living	100.0	52317	28 Aspiring Young Families	89.5
51543	37 Prairie Living	100.0	52079	37 Prairie Living	90.3	52318	12 Up and Coming Families	99.7
51544	37 Prairie Living	100.0	52101	17 Green Acres	25.6	52320	46 Rooted Rural	74.6
51545	50 Heartland Communities	97.2	52132	37 Prairie Living	100.0	52321	37 Prairie Living	89.8
51546	25 Salt of The Earth	44.8	52133	37 Prairie Living	100.0	52322	26 Midland Crowd	35.6
51548	17 Green Acres	100.0	52134	37 Prairie Living	100.0	52323	50 Heartland Communities	91.0
51549	37 Prairie Living	91.3	52135	37 Prairie Living	100.0	52324	06 Sophisticated Squires	59.4
51551	50 Heartland Communities	71.6	52136	50 Heartland Communities	50.6	52325	37 Prairie Living	75.4
51552	37 Prairie Living	97.2	52140	37 Prairie Living	85.6	52326	25 Salt of The Earth	100.0
51553	25 Salt of The Earth	87.4	52141	50 Heartland Communities	59.3	52327	24 Main Street, USA	43.8
51555	17 Green Acres	27.3	52142	50 Heartland Communities	47.8	52328	06 Sophisticated Squires	66.4
51556	37 Prairie Living	94.8	52144	37 Prairie Living	100.0	52329	25 Salt of The Earth	82.6
51557	25 Salt of The Earth	88.2	52146	31 Rural Resort Dwellers	95.4	52330	37 Prairie Living	95.3
51558	37 Prairie Living	100.0	52147	37 Prairie Living	100.0	52332	25 Salt of The Earth	100.0
51559	25 Salt of The Earth	90.7	52151	37 Prairie Living	36.6	52333	07 Exurbanites	51.3
51560	29 Rustbelt Retirees	53.3	52154	46 Rooted Rural	57.7	52334	17 Green Acres	70.1
51561	17 Green Acres	50.5	52155	37 Prairie Living	100.0	52335	25 Salt of The Earth	58.0
51562	37 Prairie Living	100.0	52156	37 Prairie Living	100.0	52336	25 Salt of The Earth	51.9
51563	25 Salt of The Earth	100.0	52157	46 Rooted Rural	54.5	52337	25 Salt of The Earth	88.3
51564	50 Heartland Communities	72.1	52158	46 Rooted Rural	100.0	52338	17 Green Acres	40.4
51565	37 Prairie Living	100.0	52159	50 Heartland Communities	72.0	52339	41 Crossroads	30.2
51566	53 Home Town	40.7	52160	46 Rooted Rural	87.4	52340	28 Aspiring Young Families	88.2
51570	37 Prairie Living	84.4	52161	37 Prairie Living	100.0	52341	17 Green Acres	99.8
51571	37 Prairie Living	77.3	52162	42 Southern Satellites	71.5	52342	50 Heartland Communities	40.1
51572	37 Prairie Living	100.0	52164	37 Prairie Living	97.6	52345	26 Midland Crowd	99.0
51573	25 Salt of The Earth	68.5	52165	37 Prairie Living	100.0	52346	37 Prairie Living	88.9
51575	17 Green Acres	100.0	52166	37 Prairie Living	100.0	52347	25 Salt of The Earth	81.8
51576	25 Salt of The Earth	51.4	52169	37 Prairie Living	100.0	52348	37 Prairie Living	100.0
51577	37 Prairie Living	100.0	52170	37 Prairie Living	93.5	52349	29 Rustbelt Retirees	28.3
51578	37 Prairie Living	100.0	52171	37 Prairie Living	93.9	52352	25 Salt of The Earth	82.1
51579	50 Heartland Communities	71.3	52172	50 Heartland Communities	43.5	52353	32 Rustbelt Traditions	35.9
51601	57 Simple Living	29.1	52175	50 Heartland Communities	57.1	52354	25 Salt of The Earth	94.8
51630	37 Prairie Living	83.9	52201	37 Prairie Living	100.0	52355	25 Salt of The Earth	66.1
51631	25 Salt of The Earth	89.0	52202	17 Green Acres	97.0	52356	50 Heartland Communities	60.5
51632	33 Midlife Junction	46.7	52203	17 Green Acres	62.7	52358	17 Green Acres	32.8
51636	37 Prairie Living	100.0	52205	32 Rustbelt Traditions	40.2	52359	37 Prairie Living	100.0
51637	25 Salt of The Earth	100.0	52206	17 Green Acres	100.0	52361	33 Midlife Junction	69.5
51638	25 Salt of The Earth	59.0	52207	46 Rooted Rural	61.6	52362	50 Heartland Communities	81.3
51639	37 Prairie Living	100.0	52208	50 Heartland Communities	38.1	52401	65 Social Security Set	37.6
51640	25 Salt of The Earth	51.9	52209	25 Salt of The Earth	99.8	52402	36 Old and Newcomers	12.8
51645	37 Prairie Living	94.4	52210	25 Salt of The Earth	97.6	52403	07 Exurbanites	23.4
51646	50 Heartland Communities	81.3	52211	25 Salt of The Earth	66.4	52404	41 Crossroads	17.8
51647	37 Prairie Living	100.0	52212	37 Prairie Living	95.3	52405	29 Rustbelt Retirees	24.1
51648	25 Salt of The Earth	100.0	52213	17 Green Acres	53.2	52411	06 Sophisticated Squires	53.4
51649	37 Prairie Living	89.2	52214	50 Heartland Communities	41.4	52501	50 Heartland Communities	20.9
51650	37 Prairie Living	99.4	52215	37 Prairie Living	59.9	52530	25 Salt of The Earth	100.0

ZIP CODE	TOP TAPESTRY CONSUMER TYPE	% 2004 HOUSE-HOLDS	ZIP CODE	TOP TAPESTRY CONSUMER TYPE	% 2004 HOUSE-HOLDS	ZIP CODE	TOP TAPESTRY CONSUMER TYPE	% 2004 HOUSE-HOLDS
52531	50 Heartland Communities	53.4	52742	33 Midlife Junction	33.8	53090	17 Green Acres	28.0
52533	37 Prairie Living	76.1	52745	17 Green Acres	63.9	53091	25 Salt of The Earth	81.9
52534	25 Salt of The Earth	100.0	52746	17 Green Acres	100.0	53092	02 Suburban Splendor	24.7
52535	46 Rooted Rural	70.3	52747	25 Salt of The Earth	50.9	53093	25 Salt of The Earth	96.9
52536	25 Salt of The Earth	97.7	52748	19 Milk and Cookies	30.4	53094	18 Cozy and Comfortable	23.0
52537	37 Prairie Living	37.9	52750	25 Salt of The Earth	59.3	53095	24 Main Street, USA	30.7
52540	37 Prairie Living	49.9	52751	25 Salt of The Earth	88.3	53097	07 Exurbanites	49.7
52542	37 Prairie Living	100.0	52753	17 Green Acres	37.0	53098	25 Salt of The Earth	19.6
52543	37 Prairie Living	78.5	52754	25 Salt of The Earth	88.0	53103	17 Green Acres	50.0
52544	50 Heartland Communities	39.0	52755	17 Green Acres	51.0	53104	17 Green Acres	72.5
52548	25 Salt of The Earth	100.0	52756	17 Green Acres	78.7	53105	17 Green Acres	38.3
52549	46 Rooted Rural	87.0	52760	25 Salt of The Earth	99.6	53108	07 Exurbanites	27.9
52550	50 Heartland Communities	81.0	52761	32 Rustbelt Traditions	32.5	53110	32 Rustbelt Traditions	21.9
52551	37 Prairie Living	66.9	52765	37 Prairie Living	100.0	53114	26 Midland Crowd	68.3
52552	37 Prairie Living	100.0	52766	25 Salt of The Earth	85.0	53115	28 Aspiring Young Families	20.1
52553	42 Southern Satellites	52.9	52768	25 Salt of The Earth	70.7	53118	24 Main Street, USA	41.3
52554	50 Heartland Communities	72.1	52769	25 Salt of The Earth	62.9	53119	06 Sophisticated Squires	59.0
52555	37 Prairie Living	92.4	52772	25 Salt of The Earth	22.2	53120	17 Green Acres	72.9
52556	37 Prairie Living	14.7	52773	26 Midland Crowd	64.8	53121	17 Green Acres	42.9
52557	22 Metropolitans	100.0	52774	25 Salt of The Earth	100.0	53122	03 Connoisseurs	42.1
52560	46 Rooted Rural	63.4	52776	32 Rustbelt Traditions	56.2	53125	14 Prosperous Empty Nesters	46.0
52561	25 Salt of The Earth	82.2	52777	50 Heartland Communities	53.9	53126	17 Green Acres	71.4
52563	50 Heartland Communities	49.7	52778	32 Rustbelt Traditions	75.7	53128	32 Rustbelt Traditions	40.4
52565	50 Heartland Communities	65.1	52801	65 Social Security Set	95.7	53129	14 Prosperous Empty Nesters	33.0
52566	25 Salt of The Earth	100.0	52802	53 Home Town	47.9	53130	18 Cozy and Comfortable	42.4
52567	25 Salt of The Earth	91.1	52803	32 Rustbelt Traditions	26.8	53132	06 Sophisticated Squires	39.6
52569	46 Rooted Rural	83.9	52804	29 Rustbelt Retirees	31.9	53137	17 Green Acres	82.6
52570	37 Prairie Living	100.0	52806	33 Midlife Junction	19.3	53139	17 Green Acres	90.9
52571	50 Heartland Communities	66.6	52807	22 Metropolitans	38.7	53140	48 Great Expectations	23.5
52572	50 Heartland Communities	70.2	53001	17 Green Acres	63.0	53142	18 Cozy and Comfortable	25.1
52573	37 Prairie Living	100.0	53002	17 Green Acres	56.4	53143	32 Rustbelt Traditions	19.2
52574	42 Southern Satellites	67.4	53004	17 Green Acres	100.0	53144	28 Aspiring Young Families	20.9
52576	37 Prairie Living	97.3	53005	07 Exurbanites	29.3	53146	18 Cozy and Comfortable	33.9
52577	33 Midlife Junction	30.5	53006	17 Green Acres	80.3	53147	31 Rural Resort Dwellers	21.8
52580	25 Salt of The Earth	92.5	53007	57 Simple Living	49.2	53149	06 Sophisticated Squires	41.1
52581	37 Prairie Living	100.0	53010	17 Green Acres	45.6	53150	06 Sophisticated Squires	33.7
52583	37 Prairie Living	97.5	53011	25 Salt of The Earth	56.5	53151	06 Sophisticated Squires	18.3
52584	37 Prairie Living	100.0	53012	13 In Style	34.4	53153	06 Sophisticated Squires	100.0
52585	37 Prairie Living	97.3	53013	17 Green Acres	100.0	53154	36 Old and Newcomers	19.1
52586	37 Prairie Living	99.1	53014	25 Salt of The Earth	80.8	53156	25 Salt of The Earth	82.7
52588	37 Prairie Living	63.6	53015	17 Green Acres	59.3	53158	06 Sophisticated Squires	27.4
52590	50 Heartland Communities	73.5	53017	07 Exurbanites	44.2	53168	17 Green Acres	32.2
52591	50 Heartland Communities	77.0	53018	02 Suburban Splendor	45.1	53170	17 Green Acres	51.5
52593	37 Prairie Living	100.0	53019	42 Southern Satellites	54.7	53172	24 Main Street, USA	29.1
52594	37 Prairie Living	81.3	53020	17 Green Acres	89.6	53177	24 Main Street, USA	40.4
52601	53 Home Town	19.2	53021	17 Green Acres	62.2	53178	17 Green Acres	57.3
52619	25 Salt of The Earth	98.1	53022	06 Sophisticated Squires	37.0	53179	26 Midland Crowd	51.4
52620	50 Heartland Communities	89.6	53023	42 Southern Satellites	52.1	53181	17 Green Acres	47.1
52621	37 Prairie Living	100.0	53024	13 In Style	25.3	53182	17 Green Acres	40.9
52623	25 Salt of The Earth	99.9	53027	24 Main Street, USA	35.3	53183	06 Sophisticated Squires	67.2
52624	25 Salt of The Earth	100.0	53029	06 Sophisticated Squires	34.0	53184	24 Main Street, USA	63.4
52625	25 Salt of The Earth	95.3	53032	32 Rustbelt Traditions	52.3	53185	06 Sophisticated Squires	40.3
52626	50 Heartland Communities	78.6	53033	07 Exurbanites	53.0	53186	24 Main Street, USA	16.1
52627	50 Heartland Communities	36.7	53034	24 Main Street, USA	100.0	53188	06 Sophisticated Squires	26.9
52630	42 Southern Satellites	64.5	53035	26 Midland Crowd	49.9	53189	06 Sophisticated Squires	36.6
52631	37 Prairie Living	100.0	53036	17 Green Acres	85.0	53190	63 Dorms To Diplomas	23.1
52632	53 Home Town	20.4	53037	12 Up and Coming Families	65.4	53191	13 In Style	43.1
52635	37 Prairie Living	94.6	53038	26 Midland Crowd	65.1	53202	27 Metro Renters	85.6
52637	25 Salt of The Earth	53.8	53039	25 Salt of The Earth	44.5	53203	27 Metro Renters	97.5
52638	42 Southern Satellites	52.5	53040	17 Green Acres	33.3	53204	60 City Dimensions	58.3
52639	46 Rooted Rural	56.6	53042	25 Salt of The Earth	35.8	53205	64 City Commons	60.9
52640	50 Heartland Communities	62.3	53044	07 Exurbanites	72.6	53206	64 City Commons	52.0
52641	48 Great Expectations	18.2	53045	07 Exurbanites	26.6	53207	32 Rustbelt Traditions	33.5
52644	25 Salt of The Earth	72.7	53046	17 Green Acres	61.7	53208	64 City Commons	26.7
52645	25 Salt of The Earth	73.8	53048	26 Midland Crowd	83.1	53209	51 Metro City Edge	45.3
52646	42 Southern Satellites	81.0	53049	25 Salt of The Earth	68.7	53210	51 Metro City Edge	31.5
52647	37 Prairie Living	100.0	53050	25 Salt of The Earth	41.2	53211	27 Metro Renters	22.3
52649	25 Salt of The Earth	88.0	53051	24 Main Street, USA	19.8	53212	64 City Commons	26.3
52650	17 Green Acres	62.3	53057	25 Salt of The Earth	67.0	53213	22 Metropolitans	48.2
52651	37 Prairie Living	100.0	53058	13 In Style	53.8	53214	48 Great Expectations	49.0
52653	25 Salt of The Earth	47.6	53059	17 Green Acres	94.2	53215	60 City Dimensions	47.7
52654	37 Prairie Living	87.0	53061	25 Salt of The Earth	76.7	53216	51 Metro City Edge	54.6
52655	32 Rustbelt Traditions	29.5	53063	17 Green Acres	66.0	53217	03 Connoisseurs	20.0
52656	29 Rustbelt Retirees	47.4	53065	17 Green Acres	100.0	53218	51 Metro City Edge	55.6
52657	37 Prairie Living	100.0	53066	07 Exurbanites	23.1	53219	29 Rustbelt Retirees	28.2
52658	25 Salt of The Earth	100.0	53069	09 Urban Chic	64.9	53220	29 Rustbelt Retirees	26.4
52659	50 Heartland Communities	66.8	53070	17 Green Acres	50.7	53221	24 Main Street, USA	28.0
52660	37 Prairie Living	81.3	53072	16 Enterprising Professionals	31.3	53222	32 Rustbelt Traditions	35.2
52701	37 Prairie Living	100.0	53073	17 Green Acres	32.4	53223	18 Cozy and Comfortable	19.1
52720	25 Salt of The Earth	74.7	53074	24 Main Street, USA	41.2	53224	19 Milk and Cookies	17.4
52721	37 Prairie Living	100.0	53075	24 Main Street, USA	54.2	53225	48 Great Expectations	23.2
52722	18 Cozy and Comfortable	14.4	53076	06 Sophisticated Squires	59.9	53226	30 Retirement Communities	26.8
52726	17 Green Acres	63.1	53078	17 Green Acres	100.0	53227	30 Retirement Communities	27.7
52727	25 Salt of The Earth	74.2	53079	25 Salt of The Earth	82.6	53228	30 Retirement Communities	27.8
52729	25 Salt of The Earth	94.6	53080	06 Sophisticated Squires	29.1	53233	63 Dorms To Diplomas	46.1
52730	29 Rustbelt Retirees	29.1	53081	32 Rustbelt Traditions	22.1	53235	24 Main Street, USA	26.7
52731	25 Salt of The Earth	85.0	53083	17 Green Acres	42.0	53402	32 Rustbelt Traditions	26.0
52732	53 Home Town	35.0	53085	24 Main Street, USA	58.6	53403	32 Rustbelt Traditions	30.4
52738	32 Rustbelt Traditions	36.0	53086	24 Main Street, USA	46.7	53404	60 City Dimensions	37.8
52739	25 Salt of The Earth	85.8	53089	06 Sophisticated Squires	38.7	53405	32 Rustbelt Traditions	48.2

ZIP CODE	TOP TAPESTRY CONSUMER TYPE	% 2004 HOUSE-HOLDS	ZIP CODE	TOP TAPESTRY CONSUMER TYPE	% 2004 HOUSE-HOLDS	ZIP CODE	TOP TAPESTRY CONSUMER TYPE	% 2004 HOUSE-HOLDS
53406	29 Rustbelt Retirees	19.5	53803	37 Prairie Living	100.0	54114	31 Rural Resort Dwellers	45.3
53502	25 Salt of The Earth	58.5	53804	50 Heartland Communities	54.8	54115	12 Up and Coming Families	28.0
53503	25 Salt of The Earth	87.7	53805	53 Home Town	28.9	54119	31 Rural Resort Dwellers	83.5
53504	25 Salt of The Earth	56.5	53806	50 Heartland Communities	67.3	54120	31 Rural Resort Dwellers	100.0
53505	17 Green Acres	100.0	53807	25 Salt of The Earth	47.2	54121	31 Rural Resort Dwellers	59.5
53506	42 Southern Satellites	69.1	53809	37 Prairie Living	48.2	54124	42 Southern Satellites	56.9
53507	17 Green Acres	98.7	53810	37 Prairie Living	100.0	54125	46 Rooted Rural	59.5
53508	24 Main Street, USA	58.7	53811	32 Rustbelt Traditions	39.1	54126	17 Green Acres	100.0
53510	50 Heartland Communities	54.5	53813	37 Prairie Living	27.1	54128	46 Rooted Rural	100.0
53511	32 Rustbelt Traditions	24.3	53816	37 Prairie Living	100.0	54129	25 Salt of The Earth	36.4
53515	24 Main Street, USA	71.6	53818	33 Midlife Junction	38.5	54130	17 Green Acres	23.8
53516	25 Salt of The Earth	52.9	53820	25 Salt of The Earth	73.6	54135	31 Rural Resort Dwellers	45.8
53517	17 Green Acres	100.0	53821	46 Rooted Rural	31.7	54136	32 Rustbelt Traditions	48.1
53518	37 Prairie Living	58.2	53825	37 Prairie Living	100.0	54137	25 Salt of The Earth	62.1
53520	32 Rustbelt Traditions	32.2	53826	37 Prairie Living	55.4	54138	31 Rural Resort Dwellers	100.0
53521	17 Green Acres	80.5	53827	37 Prairie Living	100.0	54139	25 Salt of The Earth	69.8
53522	37 Prairie Living	100.0	53901	57 Simple Living	23.8	54140	24 Main Street, USA	28.2
53523	17 Green Acres	53.7	53910	46 Rooted Rural	49.7	54141	26 Midland Crowd	68.5
53525	25 Salt of The Earth	37.9	53911	17 Green Acres	91.4	54143	50 Heartland Communities	25.3
53526	37 Prairie Living	100.0	53913	17 Green Acres	36.6	54149	31 Rural Resort Dwellers	60.1
53527	12 Up and Coming Families	74.1	53916	32 Rustbelt Traditions	26.8	54150	51 Metro City Edge	100.0
53528	12 Up and Coming Families	40.5	53919	25 Salt of The Earth	94.6	54151	32 Rustbelt Traditions	39.2
53529	17 Green Acres	98.1	53920	25 Salt of The Earth	70.2	54153	25 Salt of The Earth	33.7
53530	37 Prairie Living	39.4	53922	25 Salt of The Earth	99.2	54154	33 Midlife Junction	54.9
53531	17 Green Acres	92.1	53923	37 Prairie Living	58.0	54155	17 Green Acres	42.0
53532	06 Sophisticated Squires	35.6	53924	37 Prairie Living	94.9	54156	46 Rooted Rural	51.5
53533	32 Rustbelt Traditions	39.4	53925	24 Main Street, USA	55.2	54157	25 Salt of The Earth	57.5
53534	25 Salt of The Earth	25.8	53926	25 Salt of The Earth	85.7	54159	25 Salt of The Earth	100.0
53536	17 Green Acres	42.9	53929	25 Salt of The Earth	44.9	54161	31 Rural Resort Dwellers	46.9
53538	24 Main Street, USA	41.4	53930	26 Midland Crowd	81.8	54162	24 Main Street, USA	27.3
53541	37 Prairie Living	100.0	53932	26 Midland Crowd	66.4	54165	17 Green Acres	37.8
53543	37 Prairie Living	100.0	53933	25 Salt of The Earth	63.1	54166	25 Salt of The Earth	31.3
53544	37 Prairie Living	90.2	53934	49 Senior Sun Seekers	39.9	54169	17 Green Acres	100.0
53545	32 Rustbelt Traditions	23.0	53936	46 Rooted Rural	68.7	54170	25 Salt of The Earth	98.0
53546	28 Aspiring Young Families	18.0	53937	37 Prairie Living	100.0	54171	12 Up and Coming Families	60.0
53548	17 Green Acres	25.8	53939	25 Salt of The Earth	100.0	54173	17 Green Acres	99.5
53549	24 Main Street, USA	39.1	53941	25 Salt of The Earth	74.6	54174	46 Rooted Rural	65.5
53550	37 Prairie Living	88.4	53943	37 Prairie Living	99.0	54175	31 Rural Resort Dwellers	100.0
53551	33 Midlife Junction	24.6	53944	46 Rooted Rural	43.8	54177	46 Rooted Rural	77.4
53553	37 Prairie Living	100.0	53946	31 Rural Resort Dwellers	34.3	54180	12 Up and Coming Families	74.6
53554	37 Prairie Living	100.0	53947	31 Rural Resort Dwellers	100.0	54201	25 Salt of The Earth	30.4
53555	24 Main Street, USA	42.6	53948	46 Rooted Rural	32.7	54202	31 Rural Resort Dwellers	98.8
53556	25 Salt of The Earth	54.0	53949	50 Heartland Communities	34.0	54204	25 Salt of The Earth	91.0
53557	25 Salt of The Earth	83.0	53950	46 Rooted Rural	40.4	54205	25 Salt of The Earth	56.1
53558	06 Sophisticated Squires	53.8	53951	25 Salt of The Earth	46.5	54208	17 Green Acres	35.4
53559	26 Midland Crowd	51.7	53952	31 Rural Resort Dwellers	56.7	54209	31 Rural Resort Dwellers	100.0
53560	17 Green Acres	86.9	53954	17 Green Acres	31.0	54210	31 Rural Resort Dwellers	100.0
53561	31 Rural Resort Dwellers	48.3	53955	17 Green Acres	56.5	54212	31 Rural Resort Dwellers	100.0
53562	13 In Style	29.5	53956	25 Salt of The Earth	40.3	54213	25 Salt of The Earth	96.4
53563	17 Green Acres	42.6	53959	33 Midlife Junction	20.5	54216	50 Heartland Communities	48.4
53565	37 Prairie Living	41.1	53960	17 Green Acres	55.7	54217	25 Salt of The Earth	64.7
53566	32 Rustbelt Traditions	27.4	53961	25 Salt of The Earth	73.0	54220	17 Green Acres	17.5
53569	37 Prairie Living	100.0	53963	32 Rustbelt Traditions	46.8	54227	17 Green Acres	74.7
53570	25 Salt of The Earth	53.8	53964	31 Rural Resort Dwellers	44.8	54228	25 Salt of The Earth	100.0
53572	28 Aspiring Young Families	31.7	53965	33 Midlife Junction	37.5	54229	17 Green Acres	63.3
53573	46 Rooted Rural	59.8	53968	50 Heartland Communities	36.2	54230	25 Salt of The Earth	94.3
53574	17 Green Acres	39.7	54001	25 Salt of The Earth	37.4	54234	15 Silver and Gold	58.2
53575	06 Sophisticated Squires	35.5	54002	17 Green Acres	40.1	54235	31 Rural Resort Dwellers	18.5
53576	25 Salt of The Earth	51.0	54003	17 Green Acres	68.5	54241	32 Rustbelt Traditions	30.5
53577	37 Prairie Living	99.6	54004	37 Prairie Living	47.5	54245	25 Salt of The Earth	98.8
53578	24 Main Street, USA	39.0	54005	42 Southern Satellites	70.1	54246	31 Rural Resort Dwellers	100.0
53579	42 Southern Satellites	50.8	54006	25 Salt of The Earth	100.0	54247	25 Salt of The Earth	95.3
53580	37 Prairie Living	100.0	54007	25 Salt of The Earth	52.7	54301	52 Inner City Tenants	17.5
53581	37 Prairie Living	34.6	54009	26 Midland Crowd	55.4	54302	48 Great Expectations	28.5
53582	37 Prairie Living	87.8	54011	25 Salt of The Earth	37.4	54303	32 Rustbelt Traditions	20.7
53583	24 Main Street, USA	44.3	54013	25 Salt of The Earth	58.3	54304	29 Rustbelt Retirees	15.3
53585	25 Salt of The Earth	96.0	54014	25 Salt of The Earth	67.5	54311	12 Up and Coming Families	24.4
53586	50 Heartland Communities	56.2	54015	24 Main Street, USA	70.2	54313	12 Up and Coming Families	37.1
53587	37 Prairie Living	100.0	54016	06 Sophisticated Squires	48.8	54401	17 Green Acres	21.8
53588	33 Midlife Junction	41.0	54017	24 Main Street, USA	34.2	54403	32 Rustbelt Traditions	22.3
53589	24 Main Street, USA	28.1	54020	17 Green Acres	76.0	54405	50 Heartland Communities	36.0
53590	13 In Style	23.4	54021	13 In Style	43.5	54406	25 Salt of The Earth	70.6
53593	06 Sophisticated Squires	47.9	54022	13 In Style	25.4	54407	25 Salt of The Earth	93.8
53594	24 Main Street, USA	67.3	54023	26 Midland Crowd	47.1	54408	25 Salt of The Earth	39.9
53597	06 Sophisticated Squires	31.5	54024	25 Salt of The Earth	50.7	54409	25 Salt of The Earth	25.1
53598	13 In Style	55.1	54025	17 Green Acres	67.0	54410	25 Salt of The Earth	72.2
53703	63 Dorms To Diplomas	61.9	54026	17 Green Acres	99.1	54411	37 Prairie Living	47.9
53704	36 Old and Newcomers	22.8	54027	25 Salt of The Earth	59.8	54412	25 Salt of The Earth	71.7
53705	27 Metro Renters	35.1	54028	26 Midland Crowd	56.0	54413	25 Salt of The Earth	85.8
53706	63 Dorms To Diplomas	100.0	54082	06 Sophisticated Squires	76.1	54414	25 Salt of The Earth	79.1
53711	14 Prosperous Empty Nesters	17.4	54101	17 Green Acres	60.9	54416	46 Rooted Rural	87.1
53713	39 Young and Restless	39.7	54102	46 Rooted Rural	61.1	54418	37 Prairie Living	47.0
53714	24 Main Street, USA	17.3	54103	50 Heartland Communities	78.5	54420	37 Prairie Living	100.0
53715	63 Dorms To Diplomas	44.4	54104	46 Rooted Rural	51.7	54421	32 Rustbelt Traditions	39.8
53716	18 Cozy and Comfortable	26.0	54106	25 Salt of The Earth	82.2	54422	37 Prairie Living	97.5
53717	16 Enterprising Professionals	53.5	54107	25 Salt of The Earth	98.5	54423	17 Green Acres	90.2
53718	13 In Style	47.5	54110	25 Salt of The Earth	65.7	54424	25 Salt of The Earth	58.8
53719	16 Enterprising Professionals	83.3	54111	25 Salt of The Earth	66.7	54425	42 Southern Satellites	72.2
53726	63 Dorms To Diplomas	67.0	54112	50 Heartland Communities	41.5	54426	37 Prairie Living	40.3
53801	37 Prairie Living	100.0	54113	17 Green Acres	63.4	54427	25 Salt of The Earth	92.9

409

ZIP CODE	TOP TAPESTRY CONSUMER TYPE	% 2004 HOUSE-HOLDS	ZIP CODE	TOP TAPESTRY CONSUMER TYPE	% 2004 HOUSE-HOLDS	ZIP CODE	TOP TAPESTRY CONSUMER TYPE	% 2004 HOUSE-HOLDS
54428	31 Rural Resort Dwellers	100.0	54565	46 Rooted Rural	100.0	54761	37 Prairie Living	100.0
54430	37 Prairie Living	100.0	54566	46 Rooted Rural	94.2	54762	25 Salt of The Earth	71.2
54433	37 Prairie Living	100.0	54568	31 Rural Resort Dwellers	52.5	54763	37 Prairie Living	94.3
54435	25 Salt of The Earth	62.7	54601	55 College Towns	18.0	54765	37 Prairie Living	100.0
54436	37 Prairie Living	74.7	54603	48 Great Expectations	30.7	54766	37 Prairie Living	99.3
54437	50 Heartland Communities	47.5	54610	37 Prairie Living	48.5	54767	25 Salt of The Earth	40.4
54440	25 Salt of The Earth	88.2	54611	42 Southern Satellites	72.4	54768	50 Heartland Communities	50.6
54441	17 Green Acres	100.0	54612	37 Prairie Living	41.9	54769	31 Rural Resort Dwellers	80.2
54442	25 Salt of The Earth	89.9	54613	49 Senior Sun Seekers	42.6	54770	25 Salt of The Earth	63.5
54443	25 Salt of The Earth	56.8	54614	25 Salt of The Earth	47.2	54771	50 Heartland Communities	50.5
54446	37 Prairie Living	64.2	54615	33 Midlife Junction	30.9	54772	26 Midland Crowd	50.3
54447	37 Prairie Living	100.0	54616	50 Heartland Communities	52.4	54773	46 Rooted Rural	47.3
54448	17 Green Acres	48.6	54618	25 Salt of The Earth	44.5	54801	50 Heartland Communities	54.4
54449	25 Salt of The Earth	18.7	54619	37 Prairie Living	59.0	54805	25 Salt of The Earth	51.7
54451	26 Midland Crowd	22.3	54621	25 Salt of The Earth	96.2	54806	33 Midlife Junction	31.5
54452	32 Rustbelt Traditions	28.1	54622	25 Salt of The Earth	60.5	54810	31 Rural Resort Dwellers	86.0
54454	25 Salt of The Earth	100.0	54623	46 Rooted Rural	46.2	54812	53 Home Town	26.9
54455	17 Green Acres	33.0	54624	31 Rural Resort Dwellers	67.7	54813	25 Salt of The Earth	45.2
54456	50 Heartland Communities	48.1	54625	37 Prairie Living	100.0	54814	41 Crossroads	51.2
54457	31 Rural Resort Dwellers	35.4	54626	37 Prairie Living	100.0	54817	31 Rural Resort Dwellers	63.6
54459	46 Rooted Rural	54.1	54627	25 Salt of The Earth	97.0	54819	50 Heartland Communities	41.7
54460	37 Prairie Living	52.4	54628	37 Prairie Living	96.5	54820	46 Rooted Rural	37.8
54462	31 Rural Resort Dwellers	100.0	54629	25 Salt of The Earth	39.8	54821	31 Rural Resort Dwellers	99.4
54463	31 Rural Resort Dwellers	100.0	54630	25 Salt of The Earth	43.5	54822	32 Rustbelt Traditions	53.6
54465	31 Rural Resort Dwellers	99.5	54631	37 Prairie Living	100.0	54824	25 Salt of The Earth	67.7
54466	25 Salt of The Earth	88.2	54632	46 Rooted Rural	41.0	54826	50 Heartland Communities	43.7
54467	17 Green Acres	28.3	54634	37 Prairie Living	54.7	54827	31 Rural Resort Dwellers	100.0
54469	29 Rustbelt Retirees	63.7	54635	37 Prairie Living	93.2	54828	46 Rooted Rural	71.3
54470	50 Heartland Communities	57.6	54636	17 Green Acres	43.9	54829	50 Heartland Communities	55.8
54471	17 Green Acres	96.3	54638	37 Prairie Living	97.6	54830	31 Rural Resort Dwellers	99.9
54473	25 Salt of The Earth	37.8	54639	37 Prairie Living	50.3	54832	31 Rural Resort Dwellers	51.8
54474	29 Rustbelt Retirees	36.3	54641	46 Rooted Rural	100.0	54835	46 Rooted Rural	95.8
54475	25 Salt of The Earth	100.0	54642	37 Prairie Living	90.8	54836	25 Salt of The Earth	88.7
54476	12 Up and Coming Families	24.2	54644	25 Salt of The Earth	96.3	54837	46 Rooted Rural	38.8
54479	32 Rustbelt Traditions	37.6	54646	46 Rooted Rural	61.6	54838	31 Rural Resort Dwellers	85.3
54480	25 Salt of The Earth	98.7	54648	37 Prairie Living	60.0	54839	46 Rooted Rural	54.6
54481	17 Green Acres	20.9	54650	33 Midlife Junction	20.8	54840	25 Salt of The Earth	49.7
54484	25 Salt of The Earth	40.2	54651	46 Rooted Rural	67.0	54843	31 Rural Resort Dwellers	50.6
54485	31 Rural Resort Dwellers	100.0	54652	46 Rooted Rural	99.1	54844	31 Rural Resort Dwellers	100.0
54486	25 Salt of The Earth	50.4	54653	26 Midland Crowd	62.3	54845	37 Prairie Living	51.7
54487	31 Rural Resort Dwellers	39.8	54655	46 Rooted Rural	59.5	54846	46 Rooted Rural	98.2
54488	37 Prairie Living	100.0	54656	25 Salt of The Earth	23.0	54847	31 Rural Resort Dwellers	81.2
54489	25 Salt of The Earth	70.2	54657	37 Prairie Living	100.0	54848	50 Heartland Communities	25.6
54490	50 Heartland Communities	54.8	54658	17 Green Acres	45.1	54849	17 Green Acres	47.3
54491	46 Rooted Rural	54.6	54659	46 Rooted Rural	62.8	54850	46 Rooted Rural	100.0
54493	46 Rooted Rural	59.9	54660	25 Salt of The Earth	22.4	54853	33 Midlife Junction	40.0
54494	32 Rustbelt Traditions	29.7	54661	25 Salt of The Earth	54.2	54854	46 Rooted Rural	56.0
54495	57 Simple Living	25.0	54664	46 Rooted Rural	80.8	54855	46 Rooted Rural	65.4
54498	37 Prairie Living	56.7	54665	50 Heartland Communities	50.9	54856	37 Prairie Living	43.0
54499	25 Salt of The Earth	56.5	54666	25 Salt of The Earth	50.6	54858	50 Heartland Communities	66.7
54501	25 Salt of The Earth	20.6	54667	37 Prairie Living	45.6	54859	31 Rural Resort Dwellers	66.3
54511	31 Rural Resort Dwellers	50.5	54669	32 Rustbelt Traditions	29.6	54862	46 Rooted Rural	100.0
54512	31 Rural Resort Dwellers	95.2	54670	37 Prairie Living	100.0	54864	25 Salt of The Earth	62.2
54513	46 Rooted Rural	92.8	54701	13 In Style	22.6	54865	31 Rural Resort Dwellers	97.0
54514	50 Heartland Communities	53.1	54703	32 Rustbelt Traditions	18.6	54867	46 Rooted Rural	100.0
54515	46 Rooted Rural	77.5	54720	13 In Style	24.2	54868	33 Midlife Junction	39.1
54517	46 Rooted Rural	100.0	54721	37 Prairie Living	100.0	54870	31 Rural Resort Dwellers	96.5
54519	31 Rural Resort Dwellers	100.0	54722	50 Heartland Communities	47.4	54871	50 Heartland Communities	32.4
54520	50 Heartland Communities	55.7	54723	25 Salt of The Earth	78.5	54872	31 Rural Resort Dwellers	53.5
54521	31 Rural Resort Dwellers	87.0	54724	32 Rustbelt Traditions	32.6	54873	31 Rural Resort Dwellers	40.8
54524	31 Rural Resort Dwellers	94.2	54725	42 Southern Satellites	39.0	54874	25 Salt of The Earth	65.9
54526	46 Rooted Rural	76.9	54726	37 Prairie Living	91.4	54875	46 Rooted Rural	55.3
54527	50 Heartland Communities	87.8	54727	25 Salt of The Earth	47.4	54876	31 Rural Resort Dwellers	99.4
54529	31 Rural Resort Dwellers	98.3	54728	31 Rural Resort Dwellers	36.6	54880	33 Midlife Junction	19.7
54530	46 Rooted Rural	61.3	54729	17 Green Acres	37.9	54888	31 Rural Resort Dwellers	100.0
54531	31 Rural Resort Dwellers	93.0	54730	17 Green Acres	38.3	54889	25 Salt of The Earth	50.5
54534	50 Heartland Communities	50.5	54731	46 Rooted Rural	64.3	54891	33 Midlife Junction	36.0
54536	46 Rooted Rural	100.0	54732	50 Heartland Communities	41.6	54893	31 Rural Resort Dwellers	100.0
54537	42 Southern Satellites	69.0	54733	37 Prairie Living	75.4	54895	46 Rooted Rural	81.7
54538	31 Rural Resort Dwellers	100.0	54734	25 Salt of The Earth	88.9	54896	46 Rooted Rural	59.4
54539	31 Rural Resort Dwellers	99.5	54736	50 Heartland Communities	44.8	54901	32 Rustbelt Traditions	23.3
54540	31 Rural Resort Dwellers	100.0	54737	37 Prairie Living	93.3	54902	32 Rustbelt Traditions	34.7
54541	31 Rural Resort Dwellers	47.8	54738	25 Salt of The Earth	44.3	54904	16 Enterprising Professionals	25.5
54542	49 Senior Sun Seekers	42.0	54739	17 Green Acres	53.5	54909	25 Salt of The Earth	61.0
54545	15 Silver and Gold	74.7	54740	37 Prairie Living	57.6	54911	48 Great Expectations	20.7
54546	42 Southern Satellites	48.4	54741	46 Rooted Rural	54.4	54913	04 Boomburbs	36.4
54547	31 Rural Resort Dwellers	100.0	54742	37 Prairie Living	35.2	54914	32 Rustbelt Traditions	17.4
54548	31 Rural Resort Dwellers	75.9	54745	31 Rural Resort Dwellers	48.1	54915	12 Up and Coming Families	40.6
54550	50 Heartland Communities	87.0	54746	46 Rooted Rural	89.5	54921	25 Salt of The Earth	51.4
54552	50 Heartland Communities	38.3	54747	37 Prairie Living	55.0	54922	25 Salt of The Earth	89.4
54554	31 Rural Resort Dwellers	100.0	54748	17 Green Acres	50.9	54923	25 Salt of The Earth	54.8
54555	25 Salt of The Earth	34.5	54749	25 Salt of The Earth	72.9	54928	37 Prairie Living	100.0
54556	50 Heartland Communities	69.4	54750	37 Prairie Living	77.4	54929	25 Salt of The Earth	41.4
54557	15 Silver and Gold	52.7	54751	28 Aspiring Young Families	18.3	54930	31 Rural Resort Dwellers	97.1
54558	31 Rural Resort Dwellers	79.4	54754	46 Rooted Rural	74.2	54932	17 Green Acres	99.1
54559	46 Rooted Rural	100.0	54755	37 Prairie Living	36.6	54935	32 Rustbelt Traditions	23.0
54560	31 Rural Resort Dwellers	100.0	54756	46 Rooted Rural	53.4	54937	41 Crossroads	27.5
54562	31 Rural Resort Dwellers	100.0	54757	42 Southern Satellites	30.4	54940	25 Salt of The Earth	45.3
54563	46 Rooted Rural	68.4	54758	33 Midlife Junction	29.8	54941	31 Rural Resort Dwellers	63.2
54564	31 Rural Resort Dwellers	94.7	54759	50 Heartland Communities	67.4	54942	12 Up and Coming Families	93.5

CONSUMER TYPE

ZIP CODE	TOP TAPESTRY CONSUMER TYPE	% 2004 HOUSE-HOLDS	ZIP CODE	TOP TAPESTRY CONSUMER TYPE	% 2004 HOUSE-HOLDS	ZIP CODE	TOP TAPESTRY CONSUMER TYPE	% 2004 HOUSE-HOLDS
54943	46 Rooted Rural	52.0	55082	02 Suburban Splendor	28.4	55360	17 Green Acres	54.6
54944	17 Green Acres	70.7	55084	26 Midland Crowd	87.9	55362	12 Up and Coming Families	23.7
54945	33 Midlife Junction	52.3	55087	17 Green Acres	100.0	55363	26 Midland Crowd	93.5
54947	17 Green Acres	82.0	55088	17 Green Acres	76.8	55364	02 Suburban Splendor	22.7
54948	46 Rooted Rural	85.2	55089	17 Green Acres	52.7	55366	25 Salt of The Earth	96.7
54949	50 Heartland Communities	52.8	55092	12 Up and Coming Families	32.7	55367	37 Prairie Living	62.3
54950	25 Salt of The Earth	45.1	55101	27 Metro Renters	23.6	55368	17 Green Acres	67.6
54952	32 Rustbelt Traditions	19.3	55102	27 Metro Renters	26.3	55369	06 Sophisticated Squires	35.9
54956	32 Rustbelt Traditions	22.5	55103	52 Inner City Tenants	26.8	55370	17 Green Acres	100.0
54960	31 Rural Resort Dwellers	88.8	55104	22 Metropolitans	28.2	55371	33 Midlife Junction	26.9
54961	17 Green Acres	38.8	55105	22 Metropolitans	45.0	55372	06 Sophisticated Squires	31.3
54962	25 Salt of The Earth	95.1	55106	48 Great Expectations	22.4	55373	41 Crossroads	38.5
54963	25 Salt of The Earth	59.9	55107	48 Great Expectations	24.2	55374	12 Up and Coming Families	46.6
54964	25 Salt of The Earth	100.0	55108	39 Young and Restless	29.2	55375	12 Up and Coming Families	99.3
54965	31 Rural Resort Dwellers	75.9	55109	24 Main Street, USA	37.4	55376	12 Up and Coming Families	45.9
54966	42 Southern Satellites	55.9	55110	24 Main Street, USA	18.0	55378	04 Boomburbs	50.4
54967	25 Salt of The Earth	62.8	55112	07 Exurbanites	19.4	55379	12 Up and Coming Families	67.8
54968	25 Salt of The Earth	52.0	55113	30 Retirement Communities	23.5	55381	32 Rustbelt Traditions	55.9
54970	42 Southern Satellites	41.8	55114	36 Old and Newcomers	57.6	55382	17 Green Acres	89.7
54971	32 Rustbelt Traditions	21.6	55115	02 Suburban Splendor	30.5	55384	30 Retirement Communities	69.4
54974	25 Salt of The Earth	86.9	55116	22 Metropolitans	28.0	55385	32 Rustbelt Traditions	50.0
54977	25 Salt of The Earth	92.8	55117	36 Old and Newcomers	20.7	55386	12 Up and Coming Families	61.8
54978	46 Rooted Rural	100.0	55118	24 Main Street, USA	23.7	55387	12 Up and Coming Families	64.3
54979	25 Salt of The Earth	93.8	55119	32 Rustbelt Traditions	19.4	55388	24 Main Street, USA	49.5
54981	25 Salt of The Earth	31.8	55120	07 Exurbanites	69.4	55389	50 Heartland Communities	49.5
54982	31 Rural Resort Dwellers	40.8	55121	16 Enterprising Professionals	50.1	55390	26 Midland Crowd	81.9
54983	25 Salt of The Earth	60.9	55122	16 Enterprising Professionals	21.3	55391	02 Suburban Splendor	33.8
54984	31 Rural Resort Dwellers	61.7	55123	06 Sophisticated Squires	33.0	55395	24 Main Street, USA	71.9
54986	25 Salt of The Earth	38.9	55124	06 Sophisticated Squires	24.3	55396	37 Prairie Living	40.5
55001	02 Suburban Splendor	61.1	55125	04 Boomburbs	52.5	55397	24 Main Street, USA	71.4
55003	29 Rustbelt Retirees	57.1	55126	06 Sophisticated Squires	31.6	55398	12 Up and Coming Families	52.7
55005	06 Sophisticated Squires	41.4	55127	13 In Style	27.9	55401	27 Metro Renters	77.4
55006	32 Rustbelt Traditions	55.9	55128	12 Up and Coming Families	44.6	55402	27 Metro Renters	100.0
55007	25 Salt of The Earth	51.3	55129	04 Boomburbs	99.7	55403	27 Metro Renters	86.1
55008	17 Green Acres	39.7	55150	30 Retirement Communities	100.0	55404	52 Inner City Tenants	27.3
55009	26 Midland Crowd	39.9	55301	12 Up and Coming Families	91.0	55405	27 Metro Renters	52.2
55011	06 Sophisticated Squires	45.0	55302	17 Green Acres	49.7	55406	22 Metropolitans	38.2
55012	17 Green Acres	50.7	55303	06 Sophisticated Squires	32.8	55407	48 Great Expectations	26.9
55013	17 Green Acres	37.8	55304	06 Sophisticated Squires	49.6	55408	27 Metro Renters	51.0
55014	12 Up and Coming Families	33.6	55305	36 Old and Newcomers	23.8	55409	22 Metropolitans	45.9
55016	12 Up and Coming Families	45.0	55306	16 Enterprising Professionals	37.7	55410	22 Metropolitans	61.8
55017	25 Salt of The Earth	84.7	55307	25 Salt of The Earth	43.9	55411	51 Metro City Edge	53.4
55018	17 Green Acres	93.4	55308	12 Up and Coming Families	100.0	55412	32 Rustbelt Traditions	38.9
55019	24 Main Street, USA	51.9	55309	12 Up and Coming Families	51.5	55413	48 Great Expectations	40.1
55020	06 Sophisticated Squires	100.0	55310	50 Heartland Communities	76.9	55414	63 Dorms To Diplomas	47.3
55021	17 Green Acres	22.1	55311	04 Boomburbs	57.3	55415	65 Social Security Set	51.0
55024	12 Up and Coming Families	69.2	55312	25 Salt of The Earth	52.3	55416	22 Metropolitans	22.7
55025	06 Sophisticated Squires	33.8	55313	12 Up and Coming Families	24.9	55417	22 Metropolitans	42.4
55026	17 Green Acres	88.8	55314	25 Salt of The Earth	63.5	55418	48 Great Expectations	30.7
55027	37 Prairie Living	66.8	55315	12 Up and Coming Families	75.1	55419	22 Metropolitans	34.4
55030	25 Salt of The Earth	100.0	55316	12 Up and Coming Families	33.1	55420	18 Cozy and Comfortable	34.2
55031	17 Green Acres	100.0	55317	04 Boomburbs	47.8	55421	36 Old and Newcomers	16.9
55032	17 Green Acres	97.3	55318	04 Boomburbs	35.8	55422	18 Cozy and Comfortable	26.8
55033	24 Main Street, USA	20.4	55319	17 Green Acres	64.4	55423	18 Cozy and Comfortable	29.3
55036	31 Rural Resort Dwellers	100.0	55320	17 Green Acres	59.8	55424	03 Connoisseurs	29.9
55037	33 Midlife Junction	41.2	55321	24 Main Street, USA	37.5	55425	30 Retirement Communities	18.6
55038	12 Up and Coming Families	60.3	55322	17 Green Acres	85.3	55426	36 Old and Newcomers	18.2
55040	17 Green Acres	49.6	55324	25 Salt of The Earth	55.2	55427	13 In Style	26.1
55041	26 Midland Crowd	24.0	55325	17 Green Acres	42.5	55428	18 Cozy and Comfortable	22.8
55042	02 Suburban Splendor	64.7	55327	06 Sophisticated Squires	69.8	55429	18 Cozy and Comfortable	35.6
55043	06 Sophisticated Squires	30.3	55328	12 Up and Coming Families	47.2	55430	32 Rustbelt Traditions	38.0
55044	04 Boomburbs	54.2	55329	25 Salt of The Earth	85.9	55431	14 Prosperous Empty Nesters	31.5
55045	18 Cozy and Comfortable	30.5	55330	12 Up and Coming Families	52.4	55432	18 Cozy and Comfortable	32.7
55046	24 Main Street, USA	60.0	55331	02 Suburban Splendor	31.7	55433	24 Main Street, USA	21.0
55047	07 Exurbanites	75.4	55332	37 Prairie Living	53.7	55434	19 Milk and Cookies	28.9
55049	26 Midland Crowd	77.0	55333	50 Heartland Communities	79.5	55435	30 Retirement Communities	43.7
55051	25 Salt of The Earth	22.2	55334	50 Heartland Communities	39.7	55436	30 Retirement Communities	29.4
55052	42 Southern Satellites	54.6	55335	50 Heartland Communities	55.2	55437	14 Prosperous Empty Nesters	18.8
55053	17 Green Acres	72.4	55336	25 Salt of The Earth	58.5	55438	07 Exurbanites	24.1
55054	06 Sophisticated Squires	100.0	55337	13 In Style	32.2	55439	03 Connoisseurs	52.7
55055	24 Main Street, USA	53.4	55338	17 Green Acres	65.5	55441	13 In Style	25.5
55056	12 Up and Coming Families	38.2	55339	17 Green Acres	100.0	55442	02 Suburban Splendor	41.5
55057	22 Metropolitans	26.2	55340	06 Sophisticated Squires	64.8	55443	04 Boomburbs	25.3
55060	48 Great Expectations	14.2	55341	06 Sophisticated Squires	43.6	55444	19 Milk and Cookies	46.4
55063	25 Salt of The Earth	40.5	55342	50 Heartland Communities	68.9	55445	12 Up and Coming Families	35.5
55065	17 Green Acres	100.0	55343	39 Young and Restless	22.7	55446	04 Boomburbs	72.7
55066	33 Midlife Junction	28.0	55344	39 Young and Restless	27.9	55447	02 Suburban Splendor	31.0
55067	17 Green Acres	100.0	55345	07 Exurbanites	37.0	55448	06 Sophisticated Squires	31.5
55068	12 Up and Coming Families	36.8	55346	13 In Style	34.5	55449	12 Up and Coming Families	76.9
55069	32 Rustbelt Traditions	42.8	55347	04 Boomburbs	58.6	55454	65 Social Security Set	65.3
55070	12 Up and Coming Families	69.9	55349	17 Green Acres	56.5	55455	63 Dorms To Diplomas	100.0
55071	18 Cozy and Comfortable	52.9	55350	17 Green Acres	30.6	55602	31 Rural Resort Dwellers	99.2
55072	33 Midlife Junction	43.1	55352	12 Up and Coming Families	21.3	55603	25 Salt of The Earth	90.6
55073	06 Sophisticated Squires	58.8	55353	25 Salt of The Earth	49.7	55604	31 Rural Resort Dwellers	73.3
55074	26 Midland Crowd	66.8	55354	25 Salt of The Earth	66.1	55605	31 Rural Resort Dwellers	100.0
55075	24 Main Street, USA	55.9	55355	25 Salt of The Earth	28.7	55606	31 Rural Resort Dwellers	100.0
55076	06 Sophisticated Squires	27.1	55356	02 Suburban Splendor	41.5	55607	31 Rural Resort Dwellers	66.4
55077	39 Young and Restless	39.4	55357	06 Sophisticated Squires	63.7	55612	31 Rural Resort Dwellers	100.0
55079	06 Sophisticated Squires	55.0	55358	17 Green Acres	62.9	55613	31 Rural Resort Dwellers	100.0
55080	17 Green Acres	79.3	55359	06 Sophisticated Squires	33.4	55614	29 Rustbelt Retirees	60.0

ZIP CODE	TOP TAPESTRY CONSUMER TYPE	% 2004 HOUSE-HOLDS	ZIP CODE	TOP TAPESTRY CONSUMER TYPE	% 2004 HOUSE-HOLDS	ZIP CODE	TOP TAPESTRY CONSUMER TYPE	% 2004 HOUSE-HOLDS
55615	31 Rural Resort Dwellers	100.0	55929	37 Prairie Living	76.0	56054	37 Prairie Living	60.0
55616	31 Rural Resort Dwellers	24.2	55932	26 Midland Crowd	71.5	56055	25 Salt of The Earth	52.4
55702	25 Salt of The Earth	100.0	55933	37 Prairie Living	100.0	56057	25 Salt of The Earth	40.4
55703	31 Rural Resort Dwellers	39.2	55934	19 Milk and Cookies	55.9	56058	17 Green Acres	39.9
55704	46 Rooted Rural	95.4	55935	25 Salt of The Earth	95.8	56060	37 Prairie Living	100.0
55705	29 Rustbelt Retirees	33.2	55936	33 Midlife Junction	64.4	56062	53 Home Town	48.6
55706	50 Heartland Communities	73.9	55939	50 Heartland Communities	50.2	56063	25 Salt of The Earth	37.0
55707	25 Salt of The Earth	34.8	55940	32 Rustbelt Traditions	55.8	56065	32 Rustbelt Traditions	53.3
55709	50 Heartland Communities	37.8	55941	17 Green Acres	79.5	56068	50 Heartland Communities	82.4
55710	17 Green Acres	63.1	55943	37 Prairie Living	81.2	56069	25 Salt of The Earth	55.5
55711	26 Midland Crowd	78.1	55944	19 Milk and Cookies	28.2	56071	17 Green Acres	63.3
55712	31 Rural Resort Dwellers	100.0	55945	31 Rural Resort Dwellers	48.6	56072	50 Heartland Communities	54.5
55717	31 Rural Resort Dwellers	92.8	55946	32 Rustbelt Traditions	51.7	56073	29 Rustbelt Retirees	22.7
55718	32 Rustbelt Traditions	33.8	55947	17 Green Acres	38.6	56074	25 Salt of The Earth	64.5
55719	50 Heartland Communities	24.5	55949	33 Midlife Junction	66.5	56075	37 Prairie Living	100.0
55720	32 Rustbelt Traditions	20.9	55951	50 Heartland Communities	74.9	56078	37 Prairie Living	100.0
55721	25 Salt of The Earth	69.8	55952	25 Salt of The Earth	92.9	56080	25 Salt of The Earth	88.3
55723	31 Rural Resort Dwellers	42.0	55953	32 Rustbelt Traditions	53.2	56081	53 Home Town	41.5
55724	31 Rural Resort Dwellers	82.2	55954	50 Heartland Communities	57.8	56082	48 Great Expectations	19.1
55725	15 Silver and Gold	95.9	55955	12 Up and Coming Families	89.5	56083	37 Prairie Living	100.0
55726	46 Rooted Rural	96.0	55956	17 Green Acres	51.3	56085	37 Prairie Living	30.5
55731	50 Heartland Communities	48.1	55957	37 Prairie Living	98.6	56087	50 Heartland Communities	81.4
55732	46 Rooted Rural	52.7	55959	17 Green Acres	84.7	56088	50 Heartland Communities	66.8
55733	17 Green Acres	72.5	55960	17 Green Acres	47.8	56089	25 Salt of The Earth	93.3
55734	50 Heartland Communities	43.0	55961	37 Prairie Living	100.0	56090	37 Prairie Living	98.9
55735	31 Rural Resort Dwellers	88.6	55962	37 Prairie Living	94.8	56091	37 Prairie Living	100.0
55736	50 Heartland Communities	63.7	55963	17 Green Acres	66.1	56093	25 Salt of The Earth	23.2
55738	25 Salt of The Earth	99.1	55964	26 Midland Crowd	50.4	56096	31 Rural Resort Dwellers	36.8
55741	50 Heartland Communities	54.0	55965	37 Prairie Living	57.0	56097	50 Heartland Communities	52.5
55742	46 Rooted Rural	98.5	55967	17 Green Acres	94.9	56098	50 Heartland Communities	63.2
55744	31 Rural Resort Dwellers	21.1	55968	37 Prairie Living	100.0	56101	50 Heartland Communities	42.8
55746	50 Heartland Communities	28.8	55969	25 Salt of The Earth	89.4	56110	50 Heartland Communities	71.5
55748	50 Heartland Communities	70.9	55970	25 Salt of The Earth	76.1	56111	37 Prairie Living	100.0
55749	25 Salt of The Earth	100.0	55971	33 Midlife Junction	39.0	56113	37 Prairie Living	100.0
55750	29 Rustbelt Retirees	100.0	55972	33 Midlife Junction	60.3	56114	37 Prairie Living	100.0
55751	25 Salt of The Earth	100.0	55973	37 Prairie Living	100.0	56115	50 Heartland Communities	55.6
55752	31 Rural Resort Dwellers	78.8	55974	37 Prairie Living	100.0	56116	37 Prairie Living	100.0
55756	31 Rural Resort Dwellers	97.1	55975	33 Midlife Junction	33.5	56117	37 Prairie Living	100.0
55757	37 Prairie Living	56.0	55976	24 Main Street, USA	28.0	56118	37 Prairie Living	94.0
55760	31 Rural Resort Dwellers	72.6	55977	37 Prairie Living	100.0	56119	46 Rooted Rural	74.2
55763	31 Rural Resort Dwellers	89.0	55979	25 Salt of The Earth	78.5	56120	42 Southern Satellites	100.0
55765	46 Rooted Rural	71.7	55981	33 Midlife Junction	26.6	56121	37 Prairie Living	100.0
55766	31 Rural Resort Dwellers	100.0	55982	37 Prairie Living	100.0	56122	37 Prairie Living	100.0
55767	33 Midlife Junction	56.8	55983	25 Salt of The Earth	75.3	56123	37 Prairie Living	100.0
55768	25 Salt of The Earth	40.0	55985	32 Rustbelt Traditions	46.8	56125	37 Prairie Living	100.0
55769	50 Heartland Communities	62.5	55987	32 Rustbelt Traditions	16.8	56127	37 Prairie Living	100.0
55771	31 Rural Resort Dwellers	50.4	55990	37 Prairie Living	100.0	56128	50 Heartland Communities	54.9
55775	29 Rustbelt Retirees	52.4	55991	25 Salt of The Earth	54.4	56129	37 Prairie Living	100.0
55779	17 Green Acres	61.0	55992	33 Midlife Junction	69.7	56131	50 Heartland Communities	59.1
55780	26 Midland Crowd	100.0	56001	55 College Towns	20.9	56132	37 Prairie Living	100.0
55781	18 Cozy and Comfortable	51.6	56003	32 Rustbelt Traditions	18.8	56134	37 Prairie Living	100.0
55783	31 Rural Resort Dwellers	66.2	56007	32 Rustbelt Traditions	18.2	56136	50 Heartland Communities	63.1
55784	46 Rooted Rural	81.0	56009	25 Salt of The Earth	59.8	56137	50 Heartland Communities	75.3
55785	46 Rooted Rural	80.7	56010	37 Prairie Living	99.3	56138	37 Prairie Living	100.0
55787	31 Rural Resort Dwellers	62.1	56011	24 Main Street, USA	64.2	56139	37 Prairie Living	100.0
55790	31 Rural Resort Dwellers	54.5	56013	50 Heartland Communities	55.6	56141	37 Prairie Living	100.0
55792	29 Rustbelt Retirees	23.3	56014	50 Heartland Communities	69.8	56142	50 Heartland Communities	55.5
55793	46 Rooted Rural	92.4	56016	37 Prairie Living	59.6	56143	37 Prairie Living	26.6
55795	31 Rural Resort Dwellers	54.2	56017	25 Salt of The Earth	60.0	56144	37 Prairie Living	100.0
55797	25 Salt of The Earth	99.6	56019	37 Prairie Living	100.0	56145	37 Prairie Living	99.4
55798	46 Rooted Rural	86.9	56020	25 Salt of The Earth	100.0	56146	37 Prairie Living	100.0
55801	17 Green Acres	100.0	56021	17 Green Acres	99.6	56147	37 Prairie Living	100.0
55802	65 Social Security Set	53.0	56022	37 Prairie Living	100.0	56149	50 Heartland Communities	61.1
55803	17 Green Acres	47.5	56023	37 Prairie Living	100.0	56150	50 Heartland Communities	60.5
55804	18 Cozy and Comfortable	35.9	56024	19 Milk and Cookies	76.6	56151	37 Prairie Living	100.0
55805	55 College Towns	39.1	56025	37 Prairie Living	100.0	56152	50 Heartland Communities	58.4
55806	48 Great Expectations	39.6	56026	25 Salt of The Earth	59.7	56153	37 Prairie Living	100.0
55807	32 Rustbelt Traditions	43.5	56027	50 Heartland Communities	77.1	56155	37 Prairie Living	100.0
55808	41 Crossroads	24.1	56028	25 Salt of The Earth	74.1	56156	29 Rustbelt Retirees	48.3
55810	29 Rustbelt Retirees	33.6	56029	25 Salt of The Earth	99.2	56157	17 Green Acres	70.6
55811	29 Rustbelt Retirees	28.4	56030	37 Prairie Living	65.3	56158	37 Prairie Living	100.0
55812	22 Metropolitans	45.6	56031	50 Heartland Communities	18.2	56159	50 Heartland Communities	63.8
55901	36 Old and Newcomers	16.9	56032	37 Prairie Living	100.0	56160	37 Prairie Living	98.8
55902	02 Suburban Splendor	23.6	56033	37 Prairie Living	100.0	56161	37 Prairie Living	100.0
55904	48 Great Expectations	22.9	56034	25 Salt of The Earth	98.6	56162	37 Prairie Living	100.0
55906	06 Sophisticated Squires	18.0	56035	25 Salt of The Earth	100.0	56164	50 Heartland Communities	68.1
55909	37 Prairie Living	100.0	56036	25 Salt of The Earth	64.1	56165	37 Prairie Living	100.0
55910	37 Prairie Living	73.7	56037	25 Salt of The Earth	93.1	56166	37 Prairie Living	100.0
55912	29 Rustbelt Retirees	19.8	56039	37 Prairie Living	100.0	56167	37 Prairie Living	100.0
55917	25 Salt of The Earth	33.1	56041	37 Prairie Living	77.0	56168	37 Prairie Living	100.0
55918	32 Rustbelt Traditions	63.8	56042	37 Prairie Living	100.0	56169	37 Prairie Living	98.6
55919	25 Salt of The Earth	54.4	56043	37 Prairie Living	98.5	56170	37 Prairie Living	100.0
55920	17 Green Acres	33.8	56044	25 Salt of The Earth	69.3	56171	50 Heartland Communities	67.8
55921	32 Rustbelt Traditions	37.4	56045	37 Prairie Living	78.5	56172	50 Heartland Communities	41.7
55922	37 Prairie Living	100.0	56046	37 Prairie Living	75.0	56173	37 Prairie Living	100.0
55923	17 Green Acres	40.5	56047	37 Prairie Living	100.0	56174	37 Prairie Living	100.0
55924	42 Southern Satellites	57.5	56048	25 Salt of The Earth	60.7	56175	50 Heartland Communities	69.4
55925	17 Green Acres	96.7	56050	25 Salt of The Earth	54.2	56176	50 Heartland Communities	68.2
55926	37 Prairie Living	100.0	56051	37 Prairie Living	100.0	56178	50 Heartland Communities	56.1
55927	26 Midland Crowd	39.4	56052	25 Salt of The Earth	63.6	56180	50 Heartland Communities	66.9

ZIP CODE	TOP TAPESTRY CONSUMER TYPE	% 2004 HOUSE-HOLDS	ZIP CODE	TOP TAPESTRY CONSUMER TYPE	% 2004 HOUSE-HOLDS	ZIP CODE	TOP TAPESTRY CONSUMER TYPE	% 2004 HOUSE-HOLDS
56181	50 Heartland Communities	73.7	56315	31 Rural Resort Dwellers	78.2	56479	25 Salt of The Earth	26.0
56183	50 Heartland Communities	52.8	56316	46 Rooted Rural	81.2	56481	46 Rooted Rural	68.9
56185	37 Prairie Living	100.0	56318	25 Salt of The Earth	62.4	56482	37 Prairie Living	27.2
56186	37 Prairie Living	100.0	56319	25 Salt of The Earth	44.8	56484	31 Rural Resort Dwellers	67.1
56187	32 Rustbelt Traditions	21.0	56320	25 Salt of The Earth	50.1	56501	57 Simple Living	20.7
56201	57 Simple Living	17.5	56323	37 Prairie Living	100.0	56510	50 Heartland Communities	85.2
56207	37 Prairie Living	100.0	56324	31 Rural Resort Dwellers	70.2	56511	31 Rural Resort Dwellers	98.5
56208	50 Heartland Communities	66.0	56326	50 Heartland Communities	54.3	56514	25 Salt of The Earth	36.5
56209	50 Heartland Communities	53.4	56327	31 Rural Resort Dwellers	55.8	56515	31 Rural Resort Dwellers	90.4
56210	37 Prairie Living	53.5	56328	37 Prairie Living	100.0	56516	37 Prairie Living	98.2
56211	37 Prairie Living	100.0	56329	32 Rustbelt Traditions	35.2	56517	37 Prairie Living	97.1
56212	37 Prairie Living	100.0	56330	25 Salt of The Earth	76.2	56518	37 Prairie Living	99.4
56214	37 Prairie Living	100.0	56331	37 Prairie Living	100.0	56519	37 Prairie Living	100.0
56215	50 Heartland Communities	60.2	56332	25 Salt of The Earth	63.4	56520	32 Rustbelt Traditions	40.6
56216	37 Prairie Living	100.0	56333	37 Prairie Living	100.0	56521	37 Prairie Living	50.1
56218	37 Prairie Living	100.0	56334	37 Prairie Living	34.5	56522	37 Prairie Living	100.0
56219	50 Heartland Communities	76.9	56336	46 Rooted Rural	43.3	56523	37 Prairie Living	97.7
56220	50 Heartland Communities	69.6	56338	31 Rural Resort Dwellers	56.5	56524	37 Prairie Living	83.2
56221	50 Heartland Communities	82.8	56339	50 Heartland Communities	72.6	56525	37 Prairie Living	100.0
56222	50 Heartland Communities	56.7	56340	25 Salt of The Earth	67.6	56527	46 Rooted Rural	64.8
56223	50 Heartland Communities	64.7	56341	31 Rural Resort Dwellers	100.0	56528	31 Rural Resort Dwellers	99.7
56224	37 Prairie Living	100.0	56342	31 Rural Resort Dwellers	69.4	56529	53 Home Town	45.8
56225	50 Heartland Communities	83.9	56343	31 Rural Resort Dwellers	100.0	56531	50 Heartland Communities	64.2
56226	37 Prairie Living	100.0	56345	57 Simple Living	24.6	56533	37 Prairie Living	70.5
56227	37 Prairie Living	100.0	56347	37 Prairie Living	37.7	56534	37 Prairie Living	62.8
56228	25 Salt of The Earth	100.0	56349	37 Prairie Living	88.9	56535	50 Heartland Communities	83.3
56229	25 Salt of The Earth	67.5	56350	46 Rooted Rural	68.5	56536	37 Prairie Living	79.8
56230	37 Prairie Living	100.0	56352	37 Prairie Living	39.9	56537	50 Heartland Communities	19.4
56231	37 Prairie Living	100.0	56353	25 Salt of The Earth	32.2	56540	50 Heartland Communities	54.1
56232	50 Heartland Communities	67.7	56354	31 Rural Resort Dwellers	72.4	56542	57 Simple Living	38.5
56235	37 Prairie Living	100.0	56355	37 Prairie Living	95.8	56543	37 Prairie Living	100.0
56236	37 Prairie Living	100.0	56357	25 Salt of The Earth	100.0	56544	50 Heartland Communities	35.0
56237	37 Prairie Living	100.0	56358	26 Midland Crowd	47.0	56545	37 Prairie Living	100.0
56239	37 Prairie Living	100.0	56359	31 Rural Resort Dwellers	70.7	56546	37 Prairie Living	100.0
56240	50 Heartland Communities	78.7	56360	37 Prairie Living	50.9	56547	26 Midland Crowd	50.3
56241	29 Rustbelt Retirees	33.5	56361	37 Prairie Living	49.7	56548	50 Heartland Communities	100.0
56243	37 Prairie Living	84.1	56362	50 Heartland Communities	32.5	56549	33 Midlife Junction	62.4
56244	37 Prairie Living	100.0	56363	25 Salt of The Earth	100.0	56550	37 Prairie Living	86.7
56245	37 Prairie Living	100.0	56364	37 Prairie Living	69.4	56551	31 Rural Resort Dwellers	44.3
56248	50 Heartland Communities	73.8	56367	26 Midland Crowd	44.1	56552	25 Salt of The Earth	72.0
56249	37 Prairie Living	100.0	56368	17 Green Acres	49.3	56553	37 Prairie Living	100.0
56251	25 Salt of The Earth	69.8	56373	17 Green Acres	41.4	56554	31 Rural Resort Dwellers	54.8
56252	50 Heartland Communities	78.2	56374	17 Green Acres	39.1	56556	50 Heartland Communities	86.2
56253	37 Prairie Living	100.0	56375	17 Green Acres	100.0	56557	50 Heartland Communities	51.4
56255	37 Prairie Living	100.0	56377	12 Up and Coming Families	74.4	56560	55 College Towns	15.7
56256	50 Heartland Communities	56.0	56378	29 Rustbelt Retirees	44.1	56562	55 College Towns	100.0
56257	37 Prairie Living	100.0	56379	28 Aspiring Young Families	32.5	56563	63 Dorms To Diplomas	0.0
56258	28 Aspiring Young Families	17.8	56381	50 Heartland Communities	73.3	56565	37 Prairie Living	100.0
56260	37 Prairie Living	98.6	56382	37 Prairie Living	70.8	56566	50 Heartland Communities	54.7
56262	37 Prairie Living	100.0	56384	37 Prairie Living	100.0	56567	37 Prairie Living	57.7
56263	37 Prairie Living	100.0	56385	37 Prairie Living	100.0	56568	37 Prairie Living	100.0
56264	37 Prairie Living	40.0	56386	31 Rural Resort Dwellers	100.0	56569	46 Rooted Rural	81.4
56265	50 Heartland Communities	35.5	56387	39 Young and Restless	48.6	56570	31 Rural Resort Dwellers	64.1
56266	37 Prairie Living	57.2	56389	37 Prairie Living	100.0	56571	31 Rural Resort Dwellers	90.0
56267	33 Midlife Junction	28.8	56401	33 Midlife Junction	19.1	56572	31 Rural Resort Dwellers	31.8
56270	25 Salt of The Earth	74.1	56425	17 Green Acres	55.6	56573	50 Heartland Communities	28.7
56271	37 Prairie Living	100.0	56431	31 Rural Resort Dwellers	56.5	56574	37 Prairie Living	100.0
56273	25 Salt of The Earth	41.0	56433	31 Rural Resort Dwellers	100.0	56575	46 Rooted Rural	64.2
56274	37 Prairie Living	100.0	56434	46 Rooted Rural	100.0	56576	31 Rural Resort Dwellers	100.0
56276	37 Prairie Living	100.0	56435	31 Rural Resort Dwellers	84.4	56577	31 Rural Resort Dwellers	75.5
56277	29 Rustbelt Retirees	50.4	56437	50 Heartland Communities	74.4	56578	46 Rooted Rural	62.4
56278	50 Heartland Communities	79.2	56438	50 Heartland Communities	57.2	56579	37 Prairie Living	100.0
56279	25 Salt of The Earth	69.2	56440	50 Heartland Communities	77.1	56580	19 Milk and Cookies	56.1
56280	37 Prairie Living	100.0	56441	50 Heartland Communities	63.1	56581	50 Heartland Communities	100.0
56281	37 Prairie Living	100.0	56442	15 Silver and Gold	56.5	56583	37 Prairie Living	100.0
56282	37 Prairie Living	87.9	56443	37 Prairie Living	37.3	56584	37 Prairie Living	51.5
56283	33 Midlife Junction	24.6	56444	31 Rural Resort Dwellers	95.1	56585	50 Heartland Communities	91.9
56284	50 Heartland Communities	64.1	56446	50 Heartland Communities	69.9	56586	31 Rural Resort Dwellers	98.7
56285	37 Prairie Living	59.2	56447	31 Rural Resort Dwellers	100.0	56587	31 Rural Resort Dwellers	100.0
56287	37 Prairie Living	100.0	56448	31 Rural Resort Dwellers	100.0	56588	37 Prairie Living	84.5
56288	33 Midlife Junction	45.3	56449	25 Salt of The Earth	59.1	56589	37 Prairie Living	95.7
56289	37 Prairie Living	85.2	56450	31 Rural Resort Dwellers	100.0	56590	37 Prairie Living	100.0
56291	37 Prairie Living	100.0	56452	31 Rural Resort Dwellers	59.3	56592	46 Rooted Rural	84.1
56292	37 Prairie Living	100.0	56453	37 Prairie Living	100.0	56593	37 Prairie Living	100.0
56293	50 Heartland Communities	73.7	56455	25 Salt of The Earth	92.4	56594	37 Prairie Living	100.0
56294	37 Prairie Living	100.0	56456	31 Rural Resort Dwellers	100.0	56601	26 Midland Crowd	28.7
56295	37 Prairie Living	100.0	56458	31 Rural Resort Dwellers	100.0	56621	46 Rooted Rural	54.1
56296	50 Heartland Communities	77.1	56461	31 Rural Resort Dwellers	54.7	56623	50 Heartland Communities	56.1
56297	37 Prairie Living	100.0	56464	50 Heartland Communities	37.5	56626	46 Rooted Rural	99.4
56301	63 Dorms To Diplomas	20.4	56465	31 Rural Resort Dwellers	73.2	56627	46 Rooted Rural	99.5
56303	32 Rustbelt Traditions	21.4	56466	50 Heartland Communities	55.6	56628	31 Rural Resort Dwellers	100.0
56304	39 Young and Restless	13.1	56467	31 Rural Resort Dwellers	100.0	56629	46 Rooted Rural	100.0
56307	37 Prairie Living	27.9	56468	31 Rural Resort Dwellers	89.7	56630	46 Rooted Rural	70.4
56308	33 Midlife Junction	34.9	56469	31 Rural Resort Dwellers	89.6	56633	62 Modest Income Homes	34.8
56309	37 Prairie Living	100.0	56470	31 Rural Resort Dwellers	50.5	56634	50 Heartland Communities	73.3
56310	17 Green Acres	87.6	56472	31 Rural Resort Dwellers	47.4	56636	31 Rural Resort Dwellers	36.5
56311	37 Prairie Living	97.5	56473	31 Rural Resort Dwellers	55.4	56637	31 Rural Resort Dwellers	100.0
56312	37 Prairie Living	56.7	56474	50 Heartland Communities	42.9	56639	31 Rural Resort Dwellers	100.0
56313	25 Salt of The Earth	100.0	56475	25 Salt of The Earth	78.5	56641	31 Rural Resort Dwellers	100.0
56314	25 Salt of The Earth	77.0	56477	37 Prairie Living	50.2	56644	50 Heartland Communities	72.1

ZIP CODE	TOP TAPESTRY CONSUMER TYPE	% 2004 HOUSE-HOLDS	ZIP CODE	TOP TAPESTRY CONSUMER TYPE	% 2004 HOUSE-HOLDS	ZIP CODE	TOP TAPESTRY CONSUMER TYPE	% 2004 HOUSE-HOLDS
56646	37 Prairie Living	100.0	57021	37 Prairie Living	100.0	57248	50 Heartland Communities	68.2
56647	46 Rooted Rural	84.5	57022	33 Midlife Junction	53.3	57249	50 Heartland Communities	73.8
56649	50 Heartland Communities	33.3	57024	50 Heartland Communities	59.5	57251	37 Prairie Living	100.0
56650	46 Rooted Rural	48.8	57025	37 Prairie Living	34.7	57252	50 Heartland Communities	45.7
56651	46 Rooted Rural	93.8	57026	25 Salt of The Earth	82.4	57255	37 Prairie Living	100.0
56652	37 Prairie Living	92.5	57027	37 Prairie Living	100.0	57256	37 Prairie Living	100.0
56653	46 Rooted Rural	72.8	57028	33 Midlife Junction	58.3	57257	51 Metro City Edge	44.4
56654	46 Rooted Rural	100.0	57029	50 Heartland Communities	70.5	57258	37 Prairie Living	100.0
56655	31 Rural Resort Dwellers	71.4	57030	25 Salt of The Earth	91.2	57259	37 Prairie Living	100.0
56657	31 Rural Resort Dwellers	100.0	57031	37 Prairie Living	100.0	57260	37 Prairie Living	100.0
56659	31 Rural Resort Dwellers	87.0	57032	04 Boomburbs	54.0	57261	37 Prairie Living	100.0
56660	46 Rooted Rural	100.0	57033	19 Milk and Cookies	57.2	57262	50 Heartland Communities	40.9
56661	46 Rooted Rural	55.6	57034	37 Prairie Living	100.0	57263	37 Prairie Living	100.0
56662	31 Rural Resort Dwellers	100.0	57035	25 Salt of The Earth	85.1	57264	37 Prairie Living	100.0
56663	26 Midland Crowd	77.0	57036	37 Prairie Living	98.1	57265	37 Prairie Living	100.0
56666	51 Metro City Edge	100.0	57037	50 Heartland Communities	51.4	57266	50 Heartland Communities	75.7
56667	46 Rooted Rural	94.7	57038	25 Salt of The Earth	62.8	57268	37 Prairie Living	100.0
56668	31 Rural Resort Dwellers	100.0	57039	50 Heartland Communities	38.9	57269	37 Prairie Living	100.0
56669	31 Rural Resort Dwellers	50.3	57040	37 Prairie Living	100.0	57270	50 Heartland Communities	56.3
56670	51 Metro City Edge	100.0	57042	33 Midlife Junction	33.4	57271	37 Prairie Living	100.0
56671	51 Metro City Edge	100.0	57043	50 Heartland Communities	65.0	57272	37 Prairie Living	100.0
56672	31 Rural Resort Dwellers	100.0	57044	37 Prairie Living	100.0	57273	50 Heartland Communities	59.6
56673	42 Southern Satellites	57.5	57045	50 Heartland Communities	66.3	57274	50 Heartland Communities	61.7
56676	46 Rooted Rural	88.8	57046	37 Prairie Living	85.6	57276	37 Prairie Living	100.0
56678	26 Midland Crowd	97.8	57047	37 Prairie Living	100.0	57278	37 Prairie Living	100.0
56680	31 Rural Resort Dwellers	85.7	57048	37 Prairie Living	98.1	57279	37 Prairie Living	97.6
56681	31 Rural Resort Dwellers	100.0	57049	13 In Style	100.0	57301	33 Midlife Junction	28.9
56682	42 Southern Satellites	96.8	57050	37 Prairie Living	100.0	57311	37 Prairie Living	100.0
56683	46 Rooted Rural	100.0	57051	37 Prairie Living	100.0	57312	37 Prairie Living	100.0
56684	37 Prairie Living	100.0	57052	37 Prairie Living	99.4	57313	50 Heartland Communities	59.6
56685	46 Rooted Rural	100.0	57053	37 Prairie Living	99.5	57314	37 Prairie Living	100.0
56686	46 Rooted Rural	60.8	57054	37 Prairie Living	100.0	57315	37 Prairie Living	100.0
56688	31 Rural Resort Dwellers	100.0	57055	17 Green Acres	97.4	57317	37 Prairie Living	100.0
56701	50 Heartland Communities	40.3	57056	06 Sophisticated Squires	100.0	57319	50 Heartland Communities	68.9
56710	37 Prairie Living	100.0	57057	37 Prairie Living	100.0	57321	37 Prairie Living	100.0
56711	31 Rural Resort Dwellers	100.0	57058	50 Heartland Communities	76.4	57322	37 Prairie Living	100.0
56713	37 Prairie Living	100.0	57059	50 Heartland Communities	94.4	57323	37 Prairie Living	100.0
56714	42 Southern Satellites	62.7	57062	37 Prairie Living	100.0	57324	37 Prairie Living	100.0
56715	50 Heartland Communities	96.4	57063	37 Prairie Living	94.0	57325	33 Midlife Junction	62.5
56716	48 Great Expectations	21.4	57064	12 Up and Coming Families	97.0	57328	50 Heartland Communities	65.1
56720	37 Prairie Living	100.0	57065	37 Prairie Living	100.0	57329	37 Prairie Living	100.0
56721	28 Aspiring Young Families	29.6	57066	50 Heartland Communities	85.8	57330	37 Prairie Living	100.0
56722	37 Prairie Living	90.6	57067	37 Prairie Living	100.0	57331	37 Prairie Living	100.0
56723	37 Prairie Living	64.3	57068	25 Salt of The Earth	94.0	57332	37 Prairie Living	99.4
56724	46 Rooted Rural	100.0	57069	55 College Towns	54.7	57334	37 Prairie Living	100.0
56725	37 Prairie Living	74.7	57070	50 Heartland Communities	82.9	57335	37 Prairie Living	100.0
56726	37 Prairie Living	99.8	57071	26 Midland Crowd	64.4	57337	37 Prairie Living	100.0
56727	46 Rooted Rural	91.3	57072	37 Prairie Living	100.0	57339	64 City Commons	51.3
56728	50 Heartland Communities	66.3	57073	50 Heartland Communities	67.4	57340	37 Prairie Living	100.0
56729	37 Prairie Living	100.0	57075	31 Rural Resort Dwellers	88.8	57341	37 Prairie Living	100.0
56732	50 Heartland Communities	53.4	57076	37 Prairie Living	100.0	57342	37 Prairie Living	100.0
56733	37 Prairie Living	99.5	57077	26 Midland Crowd	79.2	57344	37 Prairie Living	100.0
56734	50 Heartland Communities	92.9	57078	26 Midland Crowd	28.3	57345	50 Heartland Communities	64.6
56735	46 Rooted Rural	63.5	57103	48 Great Expectations	23.9	57348	37 Prairie Living	100.0
56736	31 Rural Resort Dwellers	72.9	57104	48 Great Expectations	42.9	57349	50 Heartland Communities	65.1
56737	46 Rooted Rural	100.0	57105	48 Great Expectations	22.1	57350	50 Heartland Communities	29.3
56738	37 Prairie Living	55.8	57106	12 Up and Coming Families	22.4	57353	37 Prairie Living	100.0
56740	37 Prairie Living	100.0	57107	41 Crossroads	68.5	57354	37 Prairie Living	100.0
56741	31 Rural Resort Dwellers	100.0	57108	04 Boomburbs	100.0	57355	37 Prairie Living	100.0
56742	50 Heartland Communities	94.5	57110	12 Up and Coming Families	48.3	57356	50 Heartland Communities	41.9
56744	37 Prairie Living	100.0	57197	18 Cozy and Comfortable	100.0	57358	37 Prairie Living	100.0
56748	37 Prairie Living	98.8	57201	57 Simple Living	18.4	57361	51 Metro City Edge	100.0
56750	50 Heartland Communities	37.0	57212	50 Heartland Communities	54.3	57362	50 Heartland Communities	78.5
56751	25 Salt of The Earth	35.8	57213	37 Prairie Living	100.0	57363	37 Prairie Living	100.0
56754	25 Salt of The Earth	100.0	57216	46 Rooted Rural	84.1	57364	37 Prairie Living	100.0
56755	37 Prairie Living	100.0	57217	37 Prairie Living	100.0	57366	50 Heartland Communities	75.8
56756	42 Southern Satellites	100.0	57218	37 Prairie Living	100.0	57368	50 Heartland Communities	67.9
56757	50 Heartland Communities	65.8	57219	37 Prairie Living	100.0	57369	50 Heartland Communities	64.8
56758	37 Prairie Living	76.9	57220	37 Prairie Living	100.0	57370	37 Prairie Living	98.1
56759	37 Prairie Living	98.7	57221	37 Prairie Living	100.0	57371	37 Prairie Living	100.0
56760	37 Prairie Living	79.0	57223	37 Prairie Living	96.3	57373	50 Heartland Communities	58.9
56761	25 Salt of The Earth	67.7	57224	37 Prairie Living	100.0	57374	37 Prairie Living	100.0
56762	29 Rustbelt Retirees	45.9	57225	37 Prairie Living	60.7	57375	37 Prairie Living	100.0
56763	26 Midland Crowd	56.9	57226	50 Heartland Communities	76.6	57376	50 Heartland Communities	64.4
57001	50 Heartland Communities	50.1	57227	37 Prairie Living	100.0	57379	37 Prairie Living	100.0
57002	25 Salt of The Earth	76.2	57231	46 Rooted Rural	42.1	57380	50 Heartland Communities	34.8
57003	17 Green Acres	72.9	57232	37 Prairie Living	100.0	57381	37 Prairie Living	100.0
57004	33 Midlife Junction	51.3	57233	37 Prairie Living	100.0	57382	50 Heartland Communities	69.8
57005	12 Up and Coming Families	84.8	57234	46 Rooted Rural	83.2	57383	37 Prairie Living	100.0
57006	55 College Towns	30.3	57235	37 Prairie Living	100.0	57384	37 Prairie Living	100.0
57007	24 Main Street, USA	100.0	57236	37 Prairie Living	100.0	57385	37 Prairie Living	52.3
57010	37 Prairie Living	96.8	57237	37 Prairie Living	100.0	57386	37 Prairie Living	100.0
57012	50 Heartland Communities	63.0	57238	37 Prairie Living	100.0	57401	48 Great Expectations	16.4
57013	33 Midlife Junction	33.7	57239	37 Prairie Living	100.0	57420	37 Prairie Living	100.0
57014	50 Heartland Communities	75.0	57241	37 Prairie Living	100.0	57421	37 Prairie Living	100.0
57015	37 Prairie Living	95.0	57242	37 Prairie Living	100.0	57422	37 Prairie Living	100.0
57016	37 Prairie Living	93.2	57243	37 Prairie Living	100.0	57424	37 Prairie Living	100.0
57017	37 Prairie Living	100.0	57245	37 Prairie Living	100.0	57426	37 Prairie Living	100.0
57018	32 Rustbelt Traditions	53.1	57246	37 Prairie Living	100.0	57427	37 Prairie Living	100.0
57020	19 Milk and Cookies	75.7	57247	37 Prairie Living	100.0			

ZIP CODE	TOP TAPESTRY CONSUMER TYPE	% 2004 HOUSE-HOLDS	ZIP CODE	TOP TAPESTRY CONSUMER TYPE	% 2004 HOUSE-HOLDS	ZIP CODE	TOP TAPESTRY CONSUMER TYPE	% 2004 HOUSE-HOLDS
57428	37 Prairie Living	100.0	57631	37 Prairie Living	100.0	58029	37 Prairie Living	100.0
57429	37 Prairie Living	100.0	57632	37 Prairie Living	100.0	58030	37 Prairie Living	100.0
57430	50 Heartland Communities	70.2	57633	51 Metro City Edge	63.7	58031	37 Prairie Living	100.0
57432	37 Prairie Living	100.0	57634	37 Prairie Living	100.0	58032	50 Heartland Communities	85.1
57433	37 Prairie Living	100.0	57638	50 Heartland Communities	77.3	58033	37 Prairie Living	100.0
57434	37 Prairie Living	100.0	57640	37 Prairie Living	100.0	58035	37 Prairie Living	100.0
57435	37 Prairie Living	100.0	57641	37 Prairie Living	100.0	58036	25 Salt of The Earth	97.8
57436	37 Prairie Living	100.0	57642	51 Metro City Edge	82.1	58038	25 Salt of The Earth	93.9
57437	50 Heartland Communities	74.2	57644	37 Prairie Living	100.0	58040	42 Southern Satellites	79.5
57438	50 Heartland Communities	65.9	57645	37 Prairie Living	100.0	58041	37 Prairie Living	56.1
57440	37 Prairie Living	100.0	57646	37 Prairie Living	100.0	58042	06 Sophisticated Squires	57.4
57441	37 Prairie Living	100.0	57648	37 Prairie Living	100.0	58043	37 Prairie Living	100.0
57442	50 Heartland Communities	79.1	57649	37 Prairie Living	100.0	58045	50 Heartland Communities	42.3
57445	33 Midlife Junction	70.2	57650	37 Prairie Living	100.0	58046	37 Prairie Living	100.0
57446	37 Prairie Living	100.0	57651	37 Prairie Living	100.0	58047	19 Milk and Cookies	55.9
57448	37 Prairie Living	100.0	57656	46 Rooted Rural	72.4	58048	37 Prairie Living	100.0
57449	37 Prairie Living	100.0	57657	56 Rural Bypasses	76.7	58049	37 Prairie Living	100.0
57450	37 Prairie Living	100.0	57658	51 Metro City Edge	100.0	58051	32 Rustbelt Traditions	53.1
57451	37 Prairie Living	57.2	57660	37 Prairie Living	100.0	58052	25 Salt of The Earth	61.6
57452	37 Prairie Living	100.0	57701	48 Great Expectations	15.1	58053	50 Heartland Communities	60.0
57454	37 Prairie Living	100.0	57702	07 Exurbanites	33.1	58054	50 Heartland Communities	75.9
57455	37 Prairie Living	100.0	57703	19 Milk and Cookies	52.3	58056	37 Prairie Living	100.0
57456	37 Prairie Living	100.0	57706	40 Military Proximity	85.1	58057	37 Prairie Living	100.0
57457	37 Prairie Living	100.0	57714	64 City Commons	46.0	58058	37 Prairie Living	100.0
57460	37 Prairie Living	100.0	57716	51 Metro City Edge	100.0	58059	19 Milk and Cookies	53.7
57461	37 Prairie Living	100.0	57717	26 Midland Crowd	23.5	58060	37 Prairie Living	100.0
57465	37 Prairie Living	100.0	57718	26 Midland Crowd	100.0	58061	25 Salt of The Earth	75.1
57466	37 Prairie Living	100.0	57719	41 Crossroads	63.0	58062	37 Prairie Living	100.0
57467	37 Prairie Living	100.0	57720	37 Prairie Living	100.0	58063	37 Prairie Living	100.0
57468	37 Prairie Living	100.0	57722	31 Rural Resort Dwellers	100.0	58064	37 Prairie Living	100.0
57469	50 Heartland Communities	83.2	57724	37 Prairie Living	100.0	58067	37 Prairie Living	97.7
57470	37 Prairie Living	100.0	57725	25 Salt of The Earth	91.7	58068	37 Prairie Living	100.0
57471	37 Prairie Living	100.0	57730	31 Rural Resort Dwellers	80.5	58069	37 Prairie Living	100.0
57472	50 Heartland Communities	73.1	57732	33 Midlife Junction	36.7	58071	37 Prairie Living	100.0
57473	37 Prairie Living	100.0	57735	37 Prairie Living	79.9	58072	50 Heartland Communities	24.9
57474	37 Prairie Living	100.0	57736	37 Prairie Living	100.0	58075	48 Great Expectations	34.1
57475	37 Prairie Living	100.0	57737	37 Prairie Living	100.0	58076	55 College Towns	100.0
57476	37 Prairie Living	100.0	57738	31 Rural Resort Dwellers	100.0	58077	37 Prairie Living	100.0
57477	37 Prairie Living	100.0	57741	37 Prairie Living	100.0	58078	28 Aspiring Young Families	23.3
57479	37 Prairie Living	100.0	57744	31 Rural Resort Dwellers	93.7	58079	37 Prairie Living	97.0
57481	37 Prairie Living	100.0	57745	31 Rural Resort Dwellers	51.1	58081	37 Prairie Living	100.0
57501	26 Midland Crowd	27.2	57747	50 Heartland Communities	60.3	58102	36 Old and Newcomers	14.7
57520	37 Prairie Living	100.0	57748	37 Prairie Living	100.0	58103	39 Young and Restless	33.6
57521	37 Prairie Living	100.0	57750	37 Prairie Living	100.0	58104	16 Enterprising Professionals	48.3
57522	26 Midland Crowd	88.3	57751	31 Rural Resort Dwellers	72.0	58201	36 Old and Newcomers	29.2
57523	50 Heartland Communities	74.4	57752	41 Crossroads	53.2	58203	63 Dorms To Diplomas	17.9
57528	37 Prairie Living	100.0	57754	32 Rustbelt Traditions	37.2	58204	40 Military Proximity	100.0
57529	37 Prairie Living	100.0	57755	37 Prairie Living	100.0	58205	40 Military Proximity	100.0
57531	37 Prairie Living	100.0	57756	51 Metro City Edge	89.7	58210	37 Prairie Living	100.0
57532	26 Midland Crowd	84.3	57758	37 Prairie Living	100.0	58212	37 Prairie Living	100.0
57533	50 Heartland Communities	78.4	57759	31 Rural Resort Dwellers	100.0	58214	33 Midlife Junction	100.0
57534	37 Prairie Living	100.0	57760	50 Heartland Communities	61.1	58216	37 Prairie Living	100.0
57536	37 Prairie Living	71.2	57761	46 Rooted Rural	56.9	58218	37 Prairie Living	100.0
57537	37 Prairie Living	100.0	57762	37 Prairie Living	100.0	58219	37 Prairie Living	100.0
57538	37 Prairie Living	98.0	57763	31 Rural Resort Dwellers	69.3	58220	50 Heartland Communities	35.0
57540	37 Prairie Living	100.0	57766	31 Rural Resort Dwellers	100.0	58222	37 Prairie Living	98.6
57541	37 Prairie Living	100.0	57767	37 Prairie Living	100.0	58223	37 Prairie Living	100.0
57542	37 Prairie Living	100.0	57769	26 Midland Crowd	86.6	58224	37 Prairie Living	100.0
57543	50 Heartland Communities	78.3	57770	51 Metro City Edge	92.6	58225	50 Heartland Communities	79.3
57544	37 Prairie Living	93.1	57772	51 Metro City Edge	91.8	58227	37 Prairie Living	100.0
57547	37 Prairie Living	100.0	57775	37 Prairie Living	100.0	58228	26 Midland Crowd	65.8
57548	51 Metro City Edge	89.2	57777	37 Prairie Living	100.0	58229	37 Prairie Living	100.0
57551	53 Home Town	68.4	57779	37 Prairie Living	100.0	58230	37 Prairie Living	100.0
57552	37 Prairie Living	100.0	57780	37 Prairie Living	100.0	58231	37 Prairie Living	100.0
57553	37 Prairie Living	100.0	57782	31 Rural Resort Dwellers	100.0	58233	37 Prairie Living	91.6
57555	51 Metro City Edge	75.6	57783	33 Midlife Junction	22.8	58235	37 Prairie Living	100.0
57559	37 Prairie Living	100.0	57785	26 Midland Crowd	25.7	58237	50 Heartland Communities	41.2
57560	37 Prairie Living	100.0	57787	37 Prairie Living	100.0	58238	37 Prairie Living	100.0
57562	37 Prairie Living	100.0	57788	37 Prairie Living	100.0	58239	37 Prairie Living	100.0
57564	37 Prairie Living	100.0	57790	50 Heartland Communities	60.4	58240	50 Heartland Communities	76.2
57566	64 City Commons	74.5	57791	37 Prairie Living	100.0	58241	17 Green Acres	77.3
57567	46 Rooted Rural	80.4	57792	37 Prairie Living	100.0	58243	37 Prairie Living	100.0
57568	37 Prairie Living	100.0	57793	46 Rooted Rural	71.3	58244	37 Prairie Living	100.0
57569	46 Rooted Rural	88.4	57794	51 Metro City Edge	100.0	58249	37 Prairie Living	60.7
57571	37 Prairie Living	100.0	57799	33 Midlife Junction	100.0	58250	37 Prairie Living	100.0
57572	51 Metro City Edge	97.4	58004	37 Prairie Living	100.0	58251	50 Heartland Communities	65.6
57574	37 Prairie Living	100.0	58005	25 Salt of The Earth	60.4	58254	50 Heartland Communities	79.2
57576	37 Prairie Living	100.0	58006	37 Prairie Living	100.0	58255	37 Prairie Living	100.0
57577	51 Metro City Edge	63.7	58007	37 Prairie Living	100.0	58256	25 Salt of The Earth	64.4
57579	51 Metro City Edge	69.9	58008	37 Prairie Living	100.0	58257	33 Midlife Junction	85.9
57580	50 Heartland Communities	63.6	58009	37 Prairie Living	100.0	58258	26 Midland Crowd	89.1
57584	37 Prairie Living	100.0	58011	37 Prairie Living	100.0	58259	37 Prairie Living	100.0
57585	37 Prairie Living	100.0	58012	33 Midlife Junction	51.5	58260	37 Prairie Living	100.0
57601	50 Heartland Communities	46.1	58013	37 Prairie Living	100.0	58261	46 Rooted Rural	87.3
57620	37 Prairie Living	100.0	58015	37 Prairie Living	100.0	58262	37 Prairie Living	100.0
57622	64 City Commons	100.0	58016	37 Prairie Living	100.0	58265	37 Prairie Living	100.0
57623	37 Prairie Living	70.0	58017	37 Prairie Living	100.0	58266	37 Prairie Living	100.0
57625	56 Rural Bypasses	67.4	58018	37 Prairie Living	72.3	58267	50 Heartland Communities	68.1
57626	37 Prairie Living	100.0	58021	25 Salt of The Earth	92.2	58269	37 Prairie Living	100.0
57630	46 Rooted Rural	93.3	58027	50 Heartland Communities	71.3	58270	50 Heartland Communities	85.5

ZIP CODE	TOP TAPESTRY CONSUMER TYPE	% 2004 HOUSE-HOLDS	ZIP CODE	TOP TAPESTRY CONSUMER TYPE	% 2004 HOUSE-HOLDS	ZIP CODE	TOP TAPESTRY CONSUMER TYPE	% 2004 HOUSE-HOLDS
58271	25 Salt of The Earth	87.2	58461	37 Prairie Living	100.0	58647	37 Prairie Living	100.0
58272	37 Prairie Living	100.0	58463	37 Prairie Living	100.0	58649	37 Prairie Living	100.0
58273	37 Prairie Living	100.0	58464	37 Prairie Living	100.0	58650	37 Prairie Living	100.0
58274	50 Heartland Communities	74.4	58466	37 Prairie Living	100.0	58651	37 Prairie Living	100.0
58275	25 Salt of The Earth	61.8	58467	37 Prairie Living	100.0	58652	37 Prairie Living	100.0
58276	37 Prairie Living	100.0	58472	37 Prairie Living	100.0	58653	37 Prairie Living	100.0
58277	37 Prairie Living	100.0	58474	50 Heartland Communities	38.3	58654	37 Prairie Living	100.0
58278	19 Milk and Cookies	66.8	58475	37 Prairie Living	100.0	58655	37 Prairie Living	100.0
58281	37 Prairie Living	100.0	58476	37 Prairie Living	100.0	58656	37 Prairie Living	92.1
58282	50 Heartland Communities	71.3	58477	37 Prairie Living	100.0	58701	36 Old and Newcomers	19.4
58301	33 Midlife Junction	39.2	58478	37 Prairie Living	100.0	58703	48 Great Expectations	24.1
58311	37 Prairie Living	100.0	58479	37 Prairie Living	100.0	58704	40 Military Proximity	99.9
58316	64 City Commons	21.9	58480	37 Prairie Living	100.0	58705	40 Military Proximity	100.0
58317	37 Prairie Living	100.0	58481	37 Prairie Living	100.0	58707	55 College Towns	100.0
58318	50 Heartland Communities	60.5	58482	50 Heartland Communities	73.0	58710	50 Heartland Communities	62.6
58319	37 Prairie Living	100.0	58483	37 Prairie Living	100.0	58711	37 Prairie Living	100.0
58321	37 Prairie Living	100.0	58484	37 Prairie Living	100.0	58712	37 Prairie Living	100.0
58323	37 Prairie Living	100.0	58486	37 Prairie Living	100.0	58713	37 Prairie Living	100.0
58324	37 Prairie Living	100.0	58487	37 Prairie Living	100.0	58716	37 Prairie Living	100.0
58325	37 Prairie Living	100.0	58488	37 Prairie Living	100.0	58718	37 Prairie Living	99.2
58327	37 Prairie Living	99.4	58490	37 Prairie Living	100.0	58721	37 Prairie Living	100.0
58329	51 Metro City Edge	53.0	58492	37 Prairie Living	100.0	58722	19 Milk and Cookies	79.0
58330	37 Prairie Living	100.0	58494	37 Prairie Living	100.0	58723	37 Prairie Living	100.0
58331	37 Prairie Living	100.0	58495	50 Heartland Communities	80.1	58725	37 Prairie Living	100.0
58332	37 Prairie Living	92.5	58496	37 Prairie Living	100.0	58727	37 Prairie Living	100.0
58338	37 Prairie Living	100.0	58497	37 Prairie Living	100.0	58730	50 Heartland Communities	89.9
58339	37 Prairie Living	100.0	58501	33 Midlife Junction	20.4	58731	37 Prairie Living	100.0
58341	50 Heartland Communities	72.0	58503	13 In Style	26.7	58733	19 Milk and Cookies	67.1
58343	37 Prairie Living	100.0	58504	06 Sophisticated Squires	27.6	58734	37 Prairie Living	100.0
58344	50 Heartland Communities	74.5	58520	37 Prairie Living	100.0	58735	37 Prairie Living	100.0
58345	37 Prairie Living	100.0	58521	37 Prairie Living	74.2	58736	50 Heartland Communities	73.7
58346	37 Prairie Living	100.0	58523	19 Milk and Cookies	37.4	58737	37 Prairie Living	100.0
58348	50 Heartland Communities	62.6	58524	37 Prairie Living	100.0	58740	37 Prairie Living	71.3
58351	46 Rooted Rural	53.5	58529	37 Prairie Living	100.0	58741	37 Prairie Living	100.0
58352	37 Prairie Living	100.0	58530	37 Prairie Living	55.8	58744	37 Prairie Living	100.0
58353	37 Prairie Living	100.0	58531	37 Prairie Living	97.8	58746	50 Heartland Communities	53.5
58356	50 Heartland Communities	82.1	58532	37 Prairie Living	100.0	58747	37 Prairie Living	95.2
58357	51 Metro City Edge	58.2	58533	50 Heartland Communities	71.3	58748	37 Prairie Living	100.0
58361	37 Prairie Living	84.3	58535	37 Prairie Living	100.0	58750	37 Prairie Living	100.0
58362	37 Prairie Living	100.0	58538	51 Metro City Edge	82.3	58752	37 Prairie Living	100.0
58363	37 Prairie Living	100.0	58540	50 Heartland Communities	70.2	58755	37 Prairie Living	100.0
58365	37 Prairie Living	100.0	58541	37 Prairie Living	100.0	58756	37 Prairie Living	100.0
58366	50 Heartland Communities	75.9	58542	37 Prairie Living	100.0	58757	51 Metro City Edge	100.0
58367	50 Heartland Communities	49.3	58544	37 Prairie Living	100.0	58758	37 Prairie Living	100.0
58368	33 Midlife Junction	45.8	58545	19 Milk and Cookies	29.0	58759	37 Prairie Living	100.0
58369	26 Midland Crowd	100.0	58549	37 Prairie Living	92.0	58760	37 Prairie Living	100.0
58370	51 Metro City Edge	42.5	58552	50 Heartland Communities	70.6	58761	50 Heartland Communities	66.4
58372	37 Prairie Living	100.0	58554	17 Green Acres	22.7	58762	37 Prairie Living	100.0
58374	50 Heartland Communities	75.9	58558	17 Green Acres	85.0	58763	51 Metro City Edge	71.3
58377	37 Prairie Living	100.0	58559	37 Prairie Living	96.4	58765	50 Heartland Communities	82.2
58380	37 Prairie Living	96.5	58560	37 Prairie Living	56.5	58768	37 Prairie Living	84.0
58381	56 Rural Bypasses	72.1	58561	50 Heartland Communities	73.9	58769	37 Prairie Living	100.0
58382	37 Prairie Living	100.0	58562	37 Prairie Living	100.0	58770	50 Heartland Communities	76.6
58384	37 Prairie Living	100.0	58563	50 Heartland Communities	54.6	58771	37 Prairie Living	100.0
58385	37 Prairie Living	100.0	58564	37 Prairie Living	100.0	58772	37 Prairie Living	100.0
58386	37 Prairie Living	100.0	58565	37 Prairie Living	100.0	58773	37 Prairie Living	100.0
58401	33 Midlife Junction	21.1	58566	37 Prairie Living	100.0	58775	46 Rooted Rural	66.4
58405	55 College Towns	100.0	58568	37 Prairie Living	96.9	58776	37 Prairie Living	100.0
58413	50 Heartland Communities	72.7	58569	37 Prairie Living	100.0	58778	37 Prairie Living	100.0
58415	37 Prairie Living	100.0	58570	51 Metro City Edge	63.6	58779	37 Prairie Living	84.0
58416	37 Prairie Living	100.0	58571	25 Salt of The Earth	90.9	58781	37 Prairie Living	100.0
58418	37 Prairie Living	100.0	58572	17 Green Acres	53.8	58782	37 Prairie Living	100.0
58420	37 Prairie Living	100.0	58573	37 Prairie Living	100.0	58783	37 Prairie Living	96.3
58421	50 Heartland Communities	76.2	58575	50 Heartland Communities	77.5	58784	50 Heartland Communities	72.9
58422	37 Prairie Living	100.0	58576	46 Rooted Rural	81.3	58785	19 Milk and Cookies	97.2
58423	37 Prairie Living	100.0	58577	25 Salt of The Earth	35.1	58787	37 Prairie Living	100.0
58424	37 Prairie Living	100.0	58579	25 Salt of The Earth	56.2	58788	50 Heartland Communities	73.1
58425	37 Prairie Living	62.2	58580	37 Prairie Living	100.0	58789	37 Prairie Living	100.0
58426	37 Prairie Living	100.0	58581	37 Prairie Living	100.0	58790	50 Heartland Communities	83.6
58428	37 Prairie Living	100.0	58601	36 Old and Newcomers	15.2	58792	37 Prairie Living	100.0
58429	37 Prairie Living	100.0	58620	37 Prairie Living	100.0	58793	50 Heartland Communities	78.7
58430	37 Prairie Living	100.0	58621	37 Prairie Living	54.0	58794	37 Prairie Living	100.0
58431	37 Prairie Living	100.0	58622	50 Heartland Communities	72.9	58795	37 Prairie Living	100.0
58433	50 Heartland Communities	57.2	58623	37 Prairie Living	59.2	58801	33 Midlife Junction	27.9
58436	50 Heartland Communities	74.6	58625	37 Prairie Living	100.0	58830	37 Prairie Living	100.0
58438	37 Prairie Living	100.0	58626	37 Prairie Living	100.0	58831	37 Prairie Living	100.0
58439	37 Prairie Living	100.0	58627	37 Prairie Living	100.0	58833	37 Prairie Living	83.9
58440	37 Prairie Living	100.0	58630	25 Salt of The Earth	79.9	58835	37 Prairie Living	100.0
58441	37 Prairie Living	100.0	58631	50 Heartland Communities	72.5	58838	37 Prairie Living	88.9
58442	37 Prairie Living	100.0	58632	37 Prairie Living	100.0	58843	37 Prairie Living	100.0
58443	37 Prairie Living	100.0	58634	37 Prairie Living	100.0	58844	37 Prairie Living	100.0
58444	37 Prairie Living	100.0	58636	37 Prairie Living	76.4	58845	37 Prairie Living	100.0
58445	37 Prairie Living	100.0	58638	50 Heartland Communities	85.9	58847	37 Prairie Living	100.0
58448	37 Prairie Living	100.0	58639	50 Heartland Communities	68.3	58849	50 Heartland Communities	75.1
58451	37 Prairie Living	100.0	58640	37 Prairie Living	91.0	58852	50 Heartland Communities	80.2
58454	37 Prairie Living	100.0	58641	37 Prairie Living	100.0	58853	37 Prairie Living	100.0
58455	37 Prairie Living	100.0	58642	37 Prairie Living	100.0	58854	50 Heartland Communities	64.2
58456	37 Prairie Living	100.0	58643	37 Prairie Living	100.0	58856	37 Prairie Living	100.0
58458	50 Heartland Communities	82.8	58645	37 Prairie Living	100.0	59001	25 Salt of The Earth	74.3
58460	37 Prairie Living	100.0	58646	37 Prairie Living	100.0	59002	17 Green Acres	100.0

ZIP CODE	TOP TAPESTRY CONSUMER TYPE	% 2004 HOUSE-HOLDS	ZIP CODE	TOP TAPESTRY CONSUMER TYPE	% 2004 HOUSE-HOLDS	ZIP CODE	TOP TAPESTRY CONSUMER TYPE	% 2004 HOUSE-HOLDS
59003	37 Prairie Living	100.0	59258	37 Prairie Living	96.4	59483	26 Midland Crowd	80.5
59006	26 Midland Crowd	63.8	59259	37 Prairie Living	100.0	59484	56 Rural Bypasses	94.2
59007	37 Prairie Living	96.1	59260	37 Prairie Living	100.0	59486	37 Prairie Living	57.9
59008	31 Rural Resort Dwellers	81.0	59261	37 Prairie Living	100.0	59487	26 Midland Crowd	97.5
59010	37 Prairie Living	100.0	59262	37 Prairie Living	100.0	59489	37 Prairie Living	100.0
59011	37 Prairie Living	30.4	59263	37 Prairie Living	59.6	59501	33 Midlife Junction	26.0
59012	37 Prairie Living	100.0	59270	33 Midlife Junction	35.8	59520	50 Heartland Communities	40.1
59014	50 Heartland Communities	50.6	59274	37 Prairie Living	100.0	59521	51 Metro City Edge	72.3
59015	17 Green Acres	82.7	59275	37 Prairie Living	100.0	59522	50 Heartland Communities	68.6
59016	51 Metro City Edge	100.0	59276	37 Prairie Living	100.0	59523	50 Heartland Communities	37.4
59019	25 Salt of The Earth	41.7	59301	50 Heartland Communities	31.7	59524	46 Rooted Rural	92.0
59022	38 Industrious Urban Fringe	88.0	59311	37 Prairie Living	100.0	59525	37 Prairie Living	100.0
59024	37 Prairie Living	100.0	59312	37 Prairie Living	100.0	59526	51 Metro City Edge	44.3
59025	37 Prairie Living	100.0	59313	50 Heartland Communities	42.1	59527	51 Metro City Edge	100.0
59027	31 Rural Resort Dwellers	100.0	59314	37 Prairie Living	100.0	59528	37 Prairie Living	100.0
59028	31 Rural Resort Dwellers	100.0	59315	37 Prairie Living	100.0	59529	37 Prairie Living	100.0
59029	46 Rooted Rural	97.2	59316	37 Prairie Living	100.0	59530	37 Prairie Living	100.0
59030	33 Midlife Junction	53.5	59317	37 Prairie Living	100.0	59531	37 Prairie Living	100.0
59031	46 Rooted Rural	50.5	59318	37 Prairie Living	100.0	59532	37 Prairie Living	100.0
59032	37 Prairie Living	100.0	59322	37 Prairie Living	100.0	59535	37 Prairie Living	100.0
59033	37 Prairie Living	100.0	59324	37 Prairie Living	100.0	59537	37 Prairie Living	100.0
59034	50 Heartland Communities	44.7	59326	37 Prairie Living	100.0	59538	37 Prairie Living	51.8
59037	26 Midland Crowd	51.4	59327	50 Heartland Communities	34.3	59540	37 Prairie Living	100.0
59038	37 Prairie Living	100.0	59330	46 Rooted Rural	31.6	59542	37 Prairie Living	100.0
59039	37 Prairie Living	100.0	59332	37 Prairie Living	100.0	59544	37 Prairie Living	100.0
59041	37 Prairie Living	55.3	59336	37 Prairie Living	100.0	59545	37 Prairie Living	100.0
59043	51 Metro City Edge	99.9	59337	37 Prairie Living	100.0	59546	37 Prairie Living	100.0
59044	26 Midland Crowd	29.8	59338	37 Prairie Living	100.0	59601	33 Midlife Junction	14.8
59046	37 Prairie Living	74.5	59339	37 Prairie Living	100.0	59602	26 Midland Crowd	41.6
59047	33 Midlife Junction	28.0	59341	37 Prairie Living	100.0	59625	55 College Towns	100.0
59050	51 Metro City Edge	30.3	59343	37 Prairie Living	100.0	59632	41 Crossroads	46.9
59052	37 Prairie Living	82.0	59344	37 Prairie Living	100.0	59633	31 Rural Resort Dwellers	81.5
59053	37 Prairie Living	100.0	59345	37 Prairie Living	100.0	59634	07 Exurbanites	32.8
59055	37 Prairie Living	100.0	59347	19 Milk and Cookies	57.4	59635	19 Milk and Cookies	51.1
59057	17 Green Acres	65.4	59349	49 Senior Sun Seekers	79.0	59639	31 Rural Resort Dwellers	100.0
59058	37 Prairie Living	100.0	59351	37 Prairie Living	100.0	59641	37 Prairie Living	100.0
59059	37 Prairie Living	100.0	59353	50 Heartland Communities	61.0	59642	37 Prairie Living	100.0
59061	31 Rural Resort Dwellers	88.2	59354	37 Prairie Living	100.0	59643	37 Prairie Living	100.0
59062	37 Prairie Living	100.0	59401	48 Great Expectations	29.1	59644	50 Heartland Communities	63.1
59063	26 Midland Crowd	100.0	59402	40 Military Proximity	100.0	59645	37 Prairie Living	66.6
59064	37 Prairie Living	100.0	59404	07 Exurbanites	16.0	59647	37 Prairie Living	100.0
59065	31 Rural Resort Dwellers	100.0	59405	33 Midlife Junction	44.5	59648	31 Rural Resort Dwellers	100.0
59067	37 Prairie Living	100.0	59410	37 Prairie Living	99.7	59701	50 Heartland Communities	18.6
59068	33 Midlife Junction	48.4	59411	46 Rooted Rural	96.9	59711	50 Heartland Communities	41.0
59069	37 Prairie Living	100.0	59412	46 Rooted Rural	62.4	59714	28 Aspiring Young Families	54.6
59070	37 Prairie Living	100.0	59414	26 Midland Crowd	100.0	59715	55 College Towns	40.6
59071	37 Prairie Living	98.0	59416	37 Prairie Living	100.0	59717	63 Dorms To Diplomas	100.0
59072	50 Heartland Communities	54.0	59417	51 Metro City Edge	54.7	59718	22 Metropolitans	27.5
59074	37 Prairie Living	100.0	59418	37 Prairie Living	100.0	59720	31 Rural Resort Dwellers	100.0
59075	26 Midland Crowd	94.7	59419	37 Prairie Living	100.0	59721	37 Prairie Living	100.0
59076	37 Prairie Living	100.0	59420	37 Prairie Living	100.0	59722	50 Heartland Communities	45.1
59077	37 Prairie Living	100.0	59421	31 Rural Resort Dwellers	42.5	59724	37 Prairie Living	100.0
59078	37 Prairie Living	100.0	59422	50 Heartland Communities	68.4	59725	37 Prairie Living	27.5
59079	26 Midland Crowd	82.7	59424	37 Prairie Living	100.0	59727	17 Green Acres	81.4
59085	37 Prairie Living	53.3	59425	33 Midlife Junction	44.3	59729	31 Rural Resort Dwellers	99.8
59086	37 Prairie Living	98.5	59427	29 Rustbelt Retirees	23.0	59730	13 In Style	50.7
59087	37 Prairie Living	100.0	59430	37 Prairie Living	100.0	59731	37 Prairie Living	59.9
59088	46 Rooted Rural	82.1	59433	37 Prairie Living	100.0	59733	31 Rural Resort Dwellers	100.0
59089	37 Prairie Living	96.4	59434	31 Rural Resort Dwellers	83.3	59735	37 Prairie Living	100.0
59101	48 Great Expectations	23.1	59436	37 Prairie Living	100.0	59736	31 Rural Resort Dwellers	100.0
59102	33 Midlife Junction	22.8	59440	26 Midland Crowd	55.6	59739	37 Prairie Living	100.0
59105	17 Green Acres	18.3	59441	37 Prairie Living	100.0	59741	37 Prairie Living	52.1
59106	17 Green Acres	48.7	59442	37 Prairie Living	63.3	59745	37 Prairie Living	98.2
59201	50 Heartland Communities	30.8	59443	37 Prairie Living	99.7	59747	37 Prairie Living	100.0
59211	37 Prairie Living	100.0	59444	37 Prairie Living	100.0	59748	17 Green Acres	100.0
59212	37 Prairie Living	100.0	59446	37 Prairie Living	100.0	59749	37 Prairie Living	52.6
59213	37 Prairie Living	100.0	59447	37 Prairie Living	100.0	59750	17 Green Acres	100.0
59214	37 Prairie Living	100.0	59448	51 Metro City Edge	100.0	59751	37 Prairie Living	96.2
59215	50 Heartland Communities	69.5	59450	37 Prairie Living	100.0	59752	37 Prairie Living	40.0
59218	50 Heartland Communities	70.2	59451	37 Prairie Living	100.0	59754	37 Prairie Living	100.0
59219	37 Prairie Living	100.0	59452	37 Prairie Living	100.0	59755	37 Prairie Living	100.0
59221	50 Heartland Communities	54.9	59453	37 Prairie Living	100.0	59756	31 Rural Resort Dwellers	100.0
59222	37 Prairie Living	100.0	59454	56 Rural Bypasses	98.9	59758	16 Enterprising Professionals	75.3
59223	31 Rural Resort Dwellers	100.0	59456	37 Prairie Living	100.0	59759	46 Rooted Rural	47.3
59225	51 Metro City Edge	73.5	59457	50 Heartland Communities	81.0	59761	31 Rural Resort Dwellers	100.0
59226	46 Rooted Rural	71.5	59460	37 Prairie Living	100.0	59762	31 Rural Resort Dwellers	91.1
59230	50 Heartland Communities	29.6	59462	37 Prairie Living	100.0	59801	55 College Towns	49.2
59241	37 Prairie Living	100.0	59463	37 Prairie Living	100.0	59802	55 College Towns	32.4
59242	37 Prairie Living	100.0	59464	37 Prairie Living	100.0	59803	06 Sophisticated Squires	19.2
59243	37 Prairie Living	100.0	59465	37 Prairie Living	100.0	59804	33 Midlife Junction	46.5
59244	37 Prairie Living	100.0	59466	37 Prairie Living	83.3	59808	41 Crossroads	37.0
59247	37 Prairie Living	100.0	59467	37 Prairie Living	100.0	59820	17 Green Acres	53.8
59248	37 Prairie Living	66.3	59468	37 Prairie Living	83.9	59821	26 Midland Crowd	98.7
59250	37 Prairie Living	100.0	59469	37 Prairie Living	100.0	59823	31 Rural Resort Dwellers	51.6
59252	37 Prairie Living	100.0	59471	37 Prairie Living	100.0	59824	26 Midland Crowd	59.1
59253	37 Prairie Living	95.6	59472	46 Rooted Rural	86.4	59825	26 Midland Crowd	94.1
59254	50 Heartland Communities	50.1	59474	50 Heartland Communities	44.6	59826	31 Rural Resort Dwellers	100.0
59255	51 Metro City Edge	82.3	59479	37 Prairie Living	100.0	59827	31 Rural Resort Dwellers	100.0
59256	37 Prairie Living	100.0	59480	46 Rooted Rural	74.9	59828	25 Salt of The Earth	41.0
59257	37 Prairie Living	100.0	59482	37 Prairie Living	66.9	59829	31 Rural Resort Dwellers	65.7

ZIP CODE	TOP TAPESTRY CONSUMER TYPE	% 2004 HOUSE-HOLDS	ZIP CODE	TOP TAPESTRY CONSUMER TYPE	% 2004 HOUSE-HOLDS	ZIP CODE	TOP TAPESTRY CONSUMER TYPE	% 2004 HOUSE-HOLDS
59831	46 Rooted Rural	71.1	60071	17 Green Acres	54.9	60302	27 Metro Renters	25.7
59832	37 Prairie Living	79.8	60072	06 Sophisticated Squires	87.6	60304	10 Pleasant-Ville	18.1
59833	17 Green Acres	75.4	60073	19 Milk and Cookies	29.7	60305	09 Urban Chic	28.8
59834	17 Green Acres	74.2	60074	28 Aspiring Young Families	27.1	60401	18 Cozy and Comfortable	29.9
59837	37 Prairie Living	97.9	60076	05 Wealthy Seaboard Suburbs	40.4	60402	24 Main Street, USA	43.0
59840	31 Rural Resort Dwellers	38.9	60077	30 Retirement Communities	29.5	60406	24 Main Street, USA	19.0
59843	31 Rural Resort Dwellers	91.0	60081	04 Boomburbs	29.5	60407	32 Rustbelt Traditions	47.7
59844	31 Rural Resort Dwellers	100.0	60082	01 Top Rung	100.0	60408	19 Milk and Cookies	38.6
59845	50 Heartland Communities	92.2	60083	07 Exurbanites	35.8	60409	32 Rustbelt Traditions	29.9
59846	17 Green Acres	91.5	60084	06 Sophisticated Squires	29.8	60410	06 Sophisticated Squires	72.4
59847	26 Midland Crowd	71.0	60085	38 Industrious Urban Fringe	18.6	60411	32 Rustbelt Traditions	18.3
59848	50 Heartland Communities	100.0	60087	18 Cozy and Comfortable	37.7	60415	28 Aspiring Young Families	37.4
59853	31 Rural Resort Dwellers	100.0	60088	40 Military Proximity	92.6	60416	24 Main Street, USA	47.1
59854	31 Rural Resort Dwellers	100.0	60089	02 Suburban Splendor	31.5	60417	07 Exurbanites	37.5
59858	50 Heartland Communities	64.7	60090	16 Enterprising Professionals	14.7	60419	34 Family Foundations	51.4
59859	31 Rural Resort Dwellers	75.2	60091	01 Top Rung	37.0	60420	33 Midlife Junction	28.6
59860	31 Rural Resort Dwellers	40.3	60093	01 Top Rung	70.4	60421	18 Cozy and Comfortable	56.7
59864	41 Crossroads	23.2	60096	18 Cozy and Comfortable	49.1	60422	05 Wealthy Seaboard Suburbs	60.5
59865	26 Midland Crowd	41.1	60097	17 Green Acres	30.7	60423	06 Sophisticated Squires	25.1
59866	46 Rooted Rural	100.0	60098	24 Main Street, USA	29.7	60424	32 Rustbelt Traditions	44.2
59868	31 Rural Resort Dwellers	99.3	60099	12 Up and Coming Families	12.5	60425	18 Cozy and Comfortable	37.7
59870	31 Rural Resort Dwellers	44.8	60101	21 Urban Villages	19.4	60426	34 Family Foundations	48.7
59871	31 Rural Resort Dwellers	100.0	60102	04 Boomburbs	48.8	60429	34 Family Foundations	20.4
59872	31 Rural Resort Dwellers	54.3	60103	04 Boomburbs	32.7	60430	18 Cozy and Comfortable	28.3
59873	31 Rural Resort Dwellers	67.7	60104	34 Family Foundations	42.2	60431	12 Up and Coming Families	54.3
59874	31 Rural Resort Dwellers	100.0	60106	21 Urban Villages	19.8	60432	47 Las Casas	23.2
59875	31 Rural Resort Dwellers	57.6	60107	12 Up and Coming Families	41.8	60433	51 Metro City Edge	34.3
59901	26 Midland Crowd	16.7	60108	16 Enterprising Professionals	25.3	60435	36 Old and Newcomers	12.2
59910	31 Rural Resort Dwellers	84.4	60110	47 Las Casas	26.7	60436	32 Rustbelt Traditions	35.7
59911	31 Rural Resort Dwellers	95.9	60111	17 Green Acres	100.0	60437	17 Green Acres	88.0
59912	26 Midland Crowd	36.6	60112	12 Up and Coming Families	85.5	60438	18 Cozy and Comfortable	30.4
59914	31 Rural Resort Dwellers	100.0	60115	63 Dorms To Diplomas	29.9	60439	07 Exurbanites	30.5
59915	31 Rural Resort Dwellers	91.2	60118	13 In Style	34.1	60440	19 Milk and Cookies	33.5
59916	31 Rural Resort Dwellers	65.6	60119	04 Boomburbs	47.3	60441	12 Up and Coming Families	21.7
59917	31 Rural Resort Dwellers	35.4	60120	47 Las Casas	19.0	60442	06 Sophisticated Squires	57.4
59920	31 Rural Resort Dwellers	51.3	60123	12 Up and Coming Families	18.8	60443	06 Sophisticated Squires	43.6
59922	31 Rural Resort Dwellers	100.0	60126	10 Pleasant-Ville	30.5	60444	18 Cozy and Comfortable	47.6
59923	46 Rooted Rural	44.5	60129	17 Green Acres	70.7	60445	24 Main Street, USA	36.6
59925	31 Rural Resort Dwellers	72.8	60130	36 Old and Newcomers	41.6	60446	14 Prosperous Empty Nesters	22.8
59928	31 Rural Resort Dwellers	100.0	60131	21 Urban Villages	59.5	60447	06 Sophisticated Squires	57.1
59929	31 Rural Resort Dwellers	100.0	60133	06 Sophisticated Squires	21.5	60448	04 Boomburbs	34.2
59930	46 Rooted Rural	100.0	60134	04 Boomburbs	18.5	60449	17 Green Acres	69.5
59931	31 Rural Resort Dwellers	100.0	60135	24 Main Street, USA	48.4	60450	24 Main Street, USA	31.9
59932	37 Prairie Living	66.1	60136	06 Sophisticated Squires	81.9	60451	06 Sophisticated Squires	27.7
59935	31 Rural Resort Dwellers	65.0	60137	02 Suburban Splendor	23.6	60452	18 Cozy and Comfortable	33.5
59937	17 Green Acres	23.8	60139	06 Sophisticated Squires	20.7	60453	18 Cozy and Comfortable	21.8
60002	17 Green Acres	31.4	60140	07 Exurbanites	29.7	60455	18 Cozy and Comfortable	26.8
60004	05 Wealthy Seaboard Suburbs	34.6	60142	16 Enterprising Professionals	21.6	60456	32 Rustbelt Traditions	50.2
60005	05 Wealthy Seaboard Suburbs	18.5	60143	13 In Style	42.9	60457	10 Pleasant-Ville	43.9
60007	10 Pleasant-Ville	31.6	60145	12 Up and Coming Families	57.6	60458	28 Aspiring Young Families	49.3
60008	10 Pleasant-Ville	22.2	60146	24 Main Street, USA	59.8	60459	18 Cozy and Comfortable	60.6
60010	02 Suburban Splendor	34.1	60148	10 Pleasant-Ville	36.2	60460	32 Rustbelt Traditions	61.0
60012	02 Suburban Splendor	38.1	60150	18 Cozy and Comfortable	59.5	60461	07 Exurbanites	38.4
60013	04 Boomburbs	34.4	60151	06 Sophisticated Squires	38.2	60462	13 In Style	19.8
60014	06 Sophisticated Squires	25.9	60152	24 Main Street, USA	48.6	60463	05 Wealthy Seaboard Suburbs	40.6
60015	03 Connoisseurs	28.5	60153	34 Family Foundations	38.2	60464	14 Prosperous Empty Nesters	34.9
60016	10 Pleasant-Ville	21.9	60154	14 Prosperous Empty Nesters	59.7	60465	14 Prosperous Empty Nesters	25.1
60018	10 Pleasant-Ville	50.2	60155	18 Cozy and Comfortable	38.0	60466	32 Rustbelt Traditions	24.1
60020	24 Main Street, USA	39.0	60156	04 Boomburbs	52.8	60467	05 Wealthy Seaboard Suburbs	58.6
60021	06 Sophisticated Squires	37.1	60157	05 Wealthy Seaboard Suburbs	47.3	60468	17 Green Acres	46.9
60022	01 Top Rung	88.2	60160	35 International Marketplace	30.1	60469	32 Rustbelt Traditions	35.6
60025	03 Connoisseurs	26.2	60162	24 Main Street, USA	55.6	60470	25 Salt of The Earth	85.0
60029	03 Connoisseurs	100.0	60163	18 Cozy and Comfortable	50.6	60471	19 Milk and Cookies	58.7
60030	04 Boomburbs	48.1	60164	21 Urban Villages	57.3	60472	62 Modest Income Homes	68.6
60031	04 Boomburbs	52.2	60165	47 Las Casas	100.0	60473	18 Cozy and Comfortable	53.3
60033	24 Main Street, USA	46.6	60171	36 Old and Newcomers	43.6	60475	28 Aspiring Young Families	25.5
60034	24 Main Street, USA	67.6	60172	06 Sophisticated Squires	31.6	60476	29 Rustbelt Retirees	74.2
60035	01 Top Rung	33.6	60173	39 Young and Restless	41.1	60477	06 Sophisticated Squires	34.4
60037	40 Military Proximity	90.8	60174	02 Suburban Splendor	22.3	60478	19 Milk and Cookies	45.1
60040	20 City Lights	81.0	60175	02 Suburban Splendor	54.8	60479	25 Salt of The Earth	79.6
60041	17 Green Acres	56.7	60176	21 Urban Villages	48.1	60480	02 Suburban Splendor	28.9
60042	12 Up and Coming Families	92.1	60177	12 Up and Coming Families	52.6	60481	24 Main Street, USA	26.7
60043	01 Top Rung	95.4	60178	13 In Style	26.7	60482	24 Main Street, USA	53.1
60044	09 Urban Chic	60.5	60180	17 Green Acres	50.4	60490	04 Boomburbs	86.6
60045	01 Top Rung	76.7	60181	10 Pleasant-Ville	41.5	60491	06 Sophisticated Squires	49.1
60046	12 Up and Coming Families	32.8	60184	04 Boomburbs	55.8	60501	38 Industrious Urban Fringe	39.6
60047	02 Suburban Splendor	54.0	60185	06 Sophisticated Squires	24.4	60504	04 Boomburbs	65.5
60048	02 Suburban Splendor	37.0	60187	02 Suburban Splendor	32.1	60505	47 Las Casas	38.4
60050	18 Cozy and Comfortable	17.6	60188	06 Sophisticated Squires	29.5	60506	38 Industrious Urban Fringe	15.8
60051	17 Green Acres	38.4	60190	06 Sophisticated Squires	67.0	60510	06 Sophisticated Squires	22.7
60053	05 Wealthy Seaboard Suburbs	60.1	60191	10 Pleasant-Ville	24.4	60511	06 Sophisticated Squires	66.5
60056	05 Wealthy Seaboard Suburbs	35.4	60192	04 Boomburbs	100.0	60512	17 Green Acres	87.0
60060	04 Boomburbs	29.6	60193	13 In Style	42.7	60513	10 Pleasant-Ville	35.5
60061	02 Suburban Splendor	29.1	60194	13 In Style	24.3	60514	03 Connoisseurs	43.5
60062	03 Connoisseurs	36.7	60195	02 Suburban Splendor	20.0	60515	30 Retirement Communities	21.8
60064	51 Metro City Edge	29.5	60201	27 Metro Renters	32.4	60516	13 In Style	20.7
60067	02 Suburban Splendor	23.2	60202	08 Laptops and Lattes	23.4	60517	06 Sophisticated Squires	18.6
60068	05 Wealthy Seaboard Suburbs	49.3	60203	05 Wealthy Seaboard Suburbs	66.8	60518	25 Salt of The Earth	50.9
60069	01 Top Rung	36.5	60208	01 Top Rung	55.6	60520	17 Green Acres	89.8
60070	28 Aspiring Young Families	42.0	60301	27 Metro Renters	100.0	60521	01 Top Rung	39.3

ZIP CODE	TOP TAPESTRY CONSUMER TYPE	% 2004 HOUSE-HOLDS	ZIP CODE	TOP TAPESTRY CONSUMER TYPE	% 2004 HOUSE-HOLDS	ZIP CODE	TOP TAPESTRY CONSUMER TYPE	% 2004 HOUSE-HOLDS
60523	01 Top Rung	52.0	60803	57 Simple Living	21.8	61068	38 Industrious Urban Fringe	17.6
60525	03 Connoisseurs	19.7	60804	47 Las Casas	72.3	61070	37 Prairie Living	70.5
60526	10 Pleasant-Ville	27.0	60805	18 Cozy and Comfortable	39.4	61071	32 Rustbelt Traditions	32.7
60527	01 Top Rung	16.1	60827	51 Metro City Edge	37.8	61072	06 Sophisticated Squires	44.0
60530	17 Green Acres	65.5	60901	51 Metro City Edge	17.2	61073	12 Up and Coming Families	25.5
60531	25 Salt of The Earth	69.6	60911	25 Salt of The Earth	72.2	61074	50 Heartland Communities	25.0
60532	16 Enterprising Professionals	23.1	60912	46 Rooted Rural	100.0	61075	31 Rural Resort Dwellers	48.4
60534	24 Main Street, USA	98.3	60913	17 Green Acres	95.2	61078	25 Salt of The Earth	53.2
60538	06 Sophisticated Squires	35.7	60914	13 In Style	23.2	61080	12 Up and Coming Families	23.8
60540	02 Suburban Splendor	30.9	60915	32 Rustbelt Traditions	62.2	61081	32 Rustbelt Traditions	14.6
60541	17 Green Acres	100.0	60917	18 Cozy and Comfortable	100.0	61084	17 Green Acres	51.8
60542	04 Boomburbs	20.4	60918	25 Salt of The Earth	79.8	61085	37 Prairie Living	45.1
60543	12 Up and Coming Families	32.2	60919	32 Rustbelt Traditions	77.7	61087	25 Salt of The Earth	46.9
60544	04 Boomburbs	41.0	60921	50 Heartland Communities	89.3	61088	17 Green Acres	91.5
60545	17 Green Acres	46.4	60922	25 Salt of The Earth	64.5	61089	37 Prairie Living	88.4
60546	05 Wealthy Seaboard Suburbs	25.6	60924	29 Rustbelt Retirees	56.5	61101	51 Metro City Edge	25.2
60548	18 Cozy and Comfortable	27.7	60927	32 Rustbelt Traditions	59.0	61102	59 Southwestern Families	20.4
60549	17 Green Acres	81.9	60928	25 Salt of The Earth	90.4	61103	32 Rustbelt Traditions	29.4
60550	18 Cozy and Comfortable	90.9	60929	37 Prairie Living	100.0	61104	60 City Dimensions	41.6
60551	17 Green Acres	68.8	60930	37 Prairie Living	100.0	61107	29 Rustbelt Retirees	18.4
60552	17 Green Acres	52.5	60931	37 Prairie Living	74.3	61108	32 Rustbelt Traditions	23.4
60553	17 Green Acres	77.1	60934	37 Prairie Living	100.0	61109	53 Home Town	21.0
60554	06 Sophisticated Squires	41.6	60935	25 Salt of The Earth	93.4	61111	32 Rustbelt Traditions	34.0
60555	06 Sophisticated Squires	37.5	60936	29 Rustbelt Retirees	42.9	61112	13 In Style	100.0
60556	17 Green Acres	81.5	60938	50 Heartland Communities	60.5	61114	13 In Style	36.0
60558	03 Connoisseurs	55.3	60940	17 Green Acres	99.6	61115	32 Rustbelt Traditions	41.7
60559	10 Pleasant-Ville	19.8	60941	17 Green Acres	52.8	61201	29 Rustbelt Retirees	17.3
60560	12 Up and Coming Families	38.2	60942	50 Heartland Communities	41.0	61230	25 Salt of The Earth	100.0
60561	05 Wealthy Seaboard Suburbs	31.9	60946	50 Heartland Communities	73.6	61231	50 Heartland Communities	38.4
60563	16 Enterprising Professionals	49.9	60948	31 Rural Resort Dwellers	50.8	61234	29 Rustbelt Retirees	74.7
60564	04 Boomburbs	99.2	60949	42 Southern Satellites	86.0	61235	50 Heartland Communities	65.4
60565	02 Suburban Splendor	67.5	60950	26 Midland Crowd	33.2	61238	32 Rustbelt Traditions	45.4
60601	09 Urban Chic	88.9	60951	25 Salt of The Earth	71.1	61240	18 Cozy and Comfortable	31.6
60602	57 Simple Living	48.6	60952	37 Prairie Living	100.0	61241	17 Green Acres	28.2
60603	48 Great Expectations	65.0	60953	50 Heartland Communities	59.6	61242	25 Salt of The Earth	83.4
60604	01 Top Rung	62.0	60954	32 Rustbelt Traditions	28.2	61243	37 Prairie Living	100.0
60605	27 Metro Renters	73.0	60957	32 Rustbelt Traditions	33.8	61244	29 Rustbelt Retirees	41.4
60606	27 Metro Renters	47.7	60959	50 Heartland Communities	65.9	61250	25 Salt of The Earth	99.2
60607	55 College Towns	29.3	60960	50 Heartland Communities	53.5	61251	25 Salt of The Earth	100.0
60608	47 Las Casas	40.8	60961	25 Salt of The Earth	46.0	61252	32 Rustbelt Traditions	39.3
60609	58 Newest Residents	19.0	60962	37 Prairie Living	100.0	61254	17 Green Acres	26.9
60610	27 Metro Renters	49.5	60963	50 Heartland Communities	65.7	61256	18 Cozy and Comfortable	49.0
60611	08 Laptops and Lattes	53.4	60964	32 Rustbelt Traditions	25.5	61257	32 Rustbelt Traditions	57.6
60612	64 City Commons	22.8	60966	42 Southern Satellites	79.8	61259	17 Green Acres	69.5
60613	27 Metro Renters	66.7	60968	25 Salt of The Earth	93.4	61260	25 Salt of The Earth	55.4
60614	08 Laptops and Lattes	53.6	60970	50 Heartland Communities	34.8	61261	25 Salt of The Earth	100.0
60615	27 Metro Renters	50.2	60973	37 Prairie Living	100.0	61262	25 Salt of The Earth	59.5
60616	44 Urban Melting Pot	29.5	61001	31 Rural Resort Dwellers	55.7	61263	32 Rustbelt Traditions	100.0
60617	34 Family Foundations	35.2	61006	32 Rustbelt Traditions	76.8	61264	32 Rustbelt Traditions	30.9
60618	35 International Marketplace	64.6	61007	37 Prairie Living	87.9	61265	29 Rustbelt Retirees	25.3
60619	34 Family Foundations	39.1	61008	42 Southern Satellites	12.9	61270	25 Salt of The Earth	51.5
60620	34 Family Foundations	58.8	61010	06 Sophisticated Squires	45.0	61272	46 Rooted Rural	55.0
60621	64 City Commons	50.9	61011	12 Up and Coming Families	68.1	61273	17 Green Acres	34.1
60622	23 Trendsetters	52.7	61012	26 Midland Crowd	68.3	61274	37 Prairie Living	100.0
60623	47 Las Casas	53.5	61014	37 Prairie Living	83.7	61275	17 Green Acres	100.0
60624	45 City Strivers	54.6	61015	17 Green Acres	92.6	61277	29 Rustbelt Retirees	44.4
60625	35 International Marketplace	42.4	61016	06 Sophisticated Squires	48.0	61279	18 Cozy and Comfortable	75.3
60626	27 Metro Renters	44.9	61018	25 Salt of The Earth	79.5	61281	17 Green Acres	69.4
60628	34 Family Foundations	60.3	61019	17 Green Acres	58.4	61282	32 Rustbelt Traditions	38.2
60629	47 Las Casas	24.8	61020	17 Green Acres	99.6	61283	32 Rustbelt Traditions	52.4
60630	20 City Lights	65.0	61021	32 Rustbelt Traditions	27.4	61284	17 Green Acres	38.5
60631	10 Pleasant-Ville	39.1	61024	32 Rustbelt Traditions	50.3	61285	25 Salt of The Earth	89.1
60632	47 Las Casas	70.0	61025	25 Salt of The Earth	36.1	61301	48 Great Expectations	24.2
60633	29 Rustbelt Retirees	40.2	61028	50 Heartland Communities	51.3	61310	32 Rustbelt Traditions	43.9
60634	20 City Lights	31.9	61030	25 Salt of The Earth	42.3	61311	25 Salt of The Earth	90.0
60636	34 Family Foundations	28.0	61031	32 Rustbelt Traditions	71.2	61312	25 Salt of The Earth	65.0
60637	64 City Commons	32.7	61032	29 Rustbelt Retirees	14.1	61313	37 Prairie Living	100.0
60638	29 Rustbelt Retirees	27.9	61036	29 Rustbelt Retirees	29.2	61314	32 Rustbelt Traditions	88.9
60639	47 Las Casas	59.2	61038	25 Salt of The Earth	46.5	61318	25 Salt of The Earth	93.5
60640	23 Trendsetters	32.5	61039	25 Salt of The Earth	84.7	61319	25 Salt of The Earth	81.9
60641	35 International Marketplace	42.0	61041	50 Heartland Communities	51.9	61320	18 Cozy and Comfortable	79.0
60643	34 Family Foundations	56.1	61042	25 Salt of The Earth	57.5	61321	42 Southern Satellites	97.6
60644	45 City Strivers	71.9	61044	37 Prairie Living	100.0	61325	25 Salt of The Earth	71.9
60645	35 International Marketplace	24.6	61046	50 Heartland Communities	31.6	61326	25 Salt of The Earth	41.5
60646	20 City Lights	37.8	61047	25 Salt of The Earth	57.0	61327	25 Salt of The Earth	75.9
60647	35 International Marketplace	31.5	61048	25 Salt of The Earth	33.6	61329	32 Rustbelt Traditions	62.1
60649	45 City Strivers	31.4	61049	25 Salt of The Earth	62.2	61330	25 Salt of The Earth	58.8
60651	45 City Strivers	49.8	61050	37 Prairie Living	100.0	61333	37 Prairie Living	100.0
60652	18 Cozy and Comfortable	37.1	61051	25 Salt of The Earth	97.0	61334	25 Salt of The Earth	100.0
60653	64 City Commons	42.7	61052	17 Green Acres	100.0	61335	25 Salt of The Earth	70.4
60655	18 Cozy and Comfortable	51.4	61053	50 Heartland Communities	44.8	61336	25 Salt of The Earth	62.3
60656	36 Old and Newcomers	35.7	61054	32 Rustbelt Traditions	39.3	61337	25 Salt of The Earth	64.4
60657	27 Metro Renters	66.7	61060	25 Salt of The Earth	35.4	61341	32 Rustbelt Traditions	37.6
60659	44 Urban Melting Pot	35.4	61061	25 Salt of The Earth	23.9	61342	32 Rustbelt Traditions	30.7
60660	36 Old and Newcomers	32.5	61062	37 Prairie Living	50.3	61344	25 Salt of The Earth	86.3
60661	27 Metro Renters	97.2	61063	17 Green Acres	45.4	61345	25 Salt of The Earth	99.4
60706	29 Rustbelt Retirees	38.2	61064	32 Rustbelt Traditions	62.1	61346	25 Salt of The Earth	89.9
60707	20 City Lights	37.2	61065	12 Up and Coming Families	66.2	61348	50 Heartland Communities	41.4
60712	05 Wealthy Seaboard Suburbs	65.5	61067	17 Green Acres	66.1	61349	25 Salt of The Earth	85.0
60714	10 Pleasant-Ville	25.7				61350	32 Rustbelt Traditions	25.7

ZIP CODE	TOP TAPESTRY CONSUMER TYPE	% 2004 HOUSE-HOLDS	ZIP CODE	TOP TAPESTRY CONSUMER TYPE	% 2004 HOUSE-HOLDS	ZIP CODE	TOP TAPESTRY CONSUMER TYPE	% 2004 HOUSE-HOLDS
61353	25 Salt of The Earth	100.0	61525	07 Exurbanites	69.4	61772	25 Salt of The Earth	70.5
61354	29 Rustbelt Retirees	32.8	61526	17 Green Acres	89.9	61773	37 Prairie Living	100.0
61356	14 Prosperous Empty Nesters	19.9	61528	07 Exurbanites	67.9	61774	32 Rustbelt Traditions	85.7
61358	42 Southern Satellites	79.2	61529	25 Salt of The Earth	35.3	61775	37 Prairie Living	100.0
61360	18 Cozy and Comfortable	56.6	61530	29 Rustbelt Retirees	20.4	61776	18 Cozy and Comfortable	52.8
61361	29 Rustbelt Retirees	47.1	61531	29 Rustbelt Retirees	50.5	61777	25 Salt of The Earth	75.1
61362	32 Rustbelt Traditions	33.6	61532	25 Salt of The Earth	97.6	61778	46 Rooted Rural	98.5
61364	50 Heartland Communities	30.7	61533	32 Rustbelt Traditions	65.0	61790	39 Young and Restless	100.0
61367	25 Salt of The Earth	76.5	61534	17 Green Acres	48.5	61801	63 Dorms To Diplomas	38.7
61368	25 Salt of The Earth	63.8	61535	07 Exurbanites	83.8	61802	41 Crossroads	14.2
61369	50 Heartland Communities	78.5	61536	25 Salt of The Earth	62.1	61810	37 Prairie Living	100.0
61370	29 Rustbelt Retirees	63.6	61537	29 Rustbelt Retirees	58.7	61811	25 Salt of The Earth	100.0
61373	17 Green Acres	55.7	61540	29 Rustbelt Retirees	84.8	61812	37 Prairie Living	100.0
61375	25 Salt of The Earth	41.2	61542	57 Simple Living	28.1	61813	32 Rustbelt Traditions	50.2
61376	25 Salt of The Earth	50.3	61543	25 Salt of The Earth	90.0	61814	25 Salt of The Earth	68.1
61377	50 Heartland Communities	81.8	61544	46 Rooted Rural	87.1	61816	37 Prairie Living	86.7
61378	25 Salt of The Earth	86.4	61545	25 Salt of The Earth	80.9	61817	32 Rustbelt Traditions	61.9
61379	32 Rustbelt Traditions	68.0	61546	25 Salt of The Earth	83.0	61818	32 Rustbelt Traditions	77.5
61401	53 Home Town	20.4	61547	06 Sophisticated Squires	40.7	61820	63 Dorms To Diplomas	42.1
61410	25 Salt of The Earth	29.5	61548	17 Green Acres	37.8	61821	32 Rustbelt Traditions	12.2
61411	37 Prairie Living	100.0	61550	33 Midlife Junction	40.2	61822	06 Sophisticated Squires	18.0
61412	46 Rooted Rural	49.0	61552	07 Exurbanites	95.5	61830	37 Prairie Living	86.7
61413	50 Heartland Communities	70.0	61554	32 Rustbelt Traditions	27.8	61831	25 Salt of The Earth	56.4
61414	25 Salt of The Earth	87.7	61559	25 Salt of The Earth	87.3	61832	53 Home Town	30.5
61415	37 Prairie Living	41.2	61560	31 Rural Resort Dwellers	85.1	61833	50 Heartland Communities	99.4
61417	37 Prairie Living	66.4	61561	18 Cozy and Comfortable	36.5	61834	25 Salt of The Earth	23.6
61418	46 Rooted Rural	100.0	61563	14 Prosperous Empty Nesters	100.0	61839	25 Salt of The Earth	96.1
61420	50 Heartland Communities	68.3	61565	25 Salt of The Earth	67.8	61840	25 Salt of The Earth	53.0
61421	37 Prairie Living	83.3	61567	25 Salt of The Earth	100.0	61841	46 Rooted Rural	48.9
61422	32 Rustbelt Traditions	30.0	61568	17 Green Acres	72.9	61842	25 Salt of The Earth	47.2
61423	25 Salt of The Earth	100.0	61569	17 Green Acres	52.1	61843	25 Salt of The Earth	77.7
61425	46 Rooted Rural	70.9	61570	37 Prairie Living	43.2	61844	25 Salt of The Earth	92.5
61427	50 Heartland Communities	36.3	61571	18 Cozy and Comfortable	28.0	61845	25 Salt of The Earth	100.0
61428	31 Rural Resort Dwellers	80.8	61572	25 Salt of The Earth	100.0	61846	50 Heartland Communities	29.1
61431	37 Prairie Living	97.0	61602	57 Simple Living	51.5	61847	25 Salt of The Earth	88.0
61432	46 Rooted Rural	100.0	61603	32 Rustbelt Traditions	30.3	61849	25 Salt of The Earth	42.0
61433	25 Salt of The Earth	68.4	61604	32 Rustbelt Traditions	24.0	61850	25 Salt of The Earth	94.9
61434	50 Heartland Communities	55.6	61605	62 Modest Income Homes	54.6	61851	25 Salt of The Earth	100.0
61435	25 Salt of The Earth	94.2	61606	55 College Towns	55.1	61852	17 Green Acres	85.4
61436	25 Salt of The Earth	72.3	61607	29 Rustbelt Retirees	42.4	61853	06 Sophisticated Squires	28.5
61437	42 Southern Satellites	67.1	61610	32 Rustbelt Traditions	100.0	61854	32 Rustbelt Traditions	60.6
61438	37 Prairie Living	93.8	61611	29 Rustbelt Retirees	18.2	61855	37 Prairie Living	100.0
61440	37 Prairie Living	100.0	61614	22 Metropolitans	24.5	61856	14 Prosperous Empty Nesters	35.1
61441	50 Heartland Communities	60.2	61615	13 In Style	45.6	61858	41 Crossroads	33.8
61442	42 Southern Satellites	80.4	61616	32 Rustbelt Traditions	46.0	61859	19 Milk and Cookies	61.9
61443	53 Home Town	36.9	61625	55 College Towns	100.0	61862	37 Prairie Living	82.2
61447	46 Rooted Rural	72.2	61635	17 Green Acres	100.0	61863	18 Cozy and Comfortable	90.9
61448	25 Salt of The Earth	29.6	61701	48 Great Expectations	22.1	61864	18 Cozy and Comfortable	61.5
61449	37 Prairie Living	100.0	61704	16 Enterprising Professionals	23.2	61865	25 Salt of The Earth	69.7
61450	50 Heartland Communities	76.4	61720	25 Salt of The Earth	100.0	61866	48 Great Expectations	43.8
61451	25 Salt of The Earth	93.5	61721	37 Prairie Living	100.0	61870	50 Heartland Communities	69.9
61452	37 Prairie Living	100.0	61722	17 Green Acres	96.8	61872	25 Salt of The Earth	90.8
61453	37 Prairie Living	100.0	61723	32 Rustbelt Traditions	38.0	61873	12 Up and Coming Families	42.4
61454	46 Rooted Rural	90.0	61724	25 Salt of The Earth	98.0	61874	13 In Style	38.0
61455	55 College Towns	24.6	61725	17 Green Acres	74.3	61875	26 Midland Crowd	61.7
61458	50 Heartland Communities	61.5	61726	25 Salt of The Earth	36.4	61876	46 Rooted Rural	91.4
61459	25 Salt of The Earth	90.4	61727	32 Rustbelt Traditions	24.8	61877	33 Midlife Junction	54.3
61460	37 Prairie Living	96.7	61728	29 Rustbelt Retirees	72.1	61878	32 Rustbelt Traditions	84.9
61462	53 Home Town	21.4	61729	17 Green Acres	73.5	61880	33 Midlife Junction	34.5
61465	29 Rustbelt Retirees	79.2	61730	25 Salt of The Earth	90.1	61882	25 Salt of The Earth	97.9
61466	25 Salt of The Earth	97.1	61731	37 Prairie Living	100.0	61883	50 Heartland Communities	61.8
61467	25 Salt of The Earth	71.4	61732	19 Milk and Cookies	64.5	61884	17 Green Acres	97.5
61469	42 Southern Satellites	54.1	61733	25 Salt of The Earth	56.8	61910	25 Salt of The Earth	49.0
61470	37 Prairie Living	100.0	61734	32 Rustbelt Traditions	29.1	61911	42 Southern Satellites	45.8
61471	37 Prairie Living	100.0	61735	17 Green Acres	69.7	61912	25 Salt of The Earth	52.2
61472	37 Prairie Living	82.0	61736	17 Green Acres	85.3	61913	46 Rooted Rural	42.8
61473	50 Heartland Communities	36.8	61737	17 Green Acres	90.4	61914	25 Salt of The Earth	47.3
61474	42 Southern Satellites	83.4	61738	18 Cozy and Comfortable	30.5	61917	37 Prairie Living	100.0
61475	37 Prairie Living	83.3	61739	33 Midlife Junction	46.8	61919	17 Green Acres	81.3
61476	37 Prairie Living	94.9	61740	29 Rustbelt Retirees	78.8	61920	55 College Towns	21.6
61477	25 Salt of The Earth	55.6	61741	32 Rustbelt Traditions	40.6	61924	50 Heartland Communities	56.3
61478	37 Prairie Living	97.7	61742	17 Green Acres	100.0	61925	25 Salt of The Earth	64.7
61479	37 Prairie Living	82.5	61743	17 Green Acres	98.9	61928	25 Salt of The Earth	96.4
61480	46 Rooted Rural	51.2	61744	25 Salt of The Earth	63.7	61929	25 Salt of The Earth	74.9
61482	25 Salt of The Earth	89.2	61745	12 Up and Coming Families	39.7	61930	37 Prairie Living	100.0
61483	50 Heartland Communities	35.8	61747	17 Green Acres	95.6	61931	25 Salt of The Earth	85.9
61484	50 Heartland Communities	90.4	61748	12 Up and Coming Families	57.1	61932	37 Prairie Living	100.0
61485	37 Prairie Living	90.7	61749	25 Salt of The Earth	77.5	61933	50 Heartland Communities	96.1
61486	25 Salt of The Earth	50.5	61752	17 Green Acres	39.8	61937	25 Salt of The Earth	92.7
61488	32 Rustbelt Traditions	71.4	61753	18 Cozy and Comfortable	36.8	61938	32 Rustbelt Traditions	15.6
61489	25 Salt of The Earth	85.8	61754	25 Salt of The Earth	63.7	61940	37 Prairie Living	100.0
61490	50 Heartland Communities	73.0	61755	12 Up and Coming Families	55.5	61942	50 Heartland Communities	64.4
61491	50 Heartland Communities	67.4	61756	25 Salt of The Earth	70.0	61943	50 Heartland Communities	49.9
61501	50 Heartland Communities	76.8	61759	25 Salt of The Earth	100.0	61944	50 Heartland Communities	30.6
61516	25 Salt of The Earth	66.8	61760	25 Salt of The Earth	69.1	61951	50 Heartland Communities	38.1
61517	25 Salt of The Earth	46.0	61761	28 Aspiring Young Families	18.4	61953	29 Rustbelt Retirees	25.6
61519	50 Heartland Communities	100.0	61764	32 Rustbelt Traditions	27.3	61956	32 Rustbelt Traditions	56.5
61520	50 Heartland Communities	25.4	61769	25 Salt of The Earth	87.3	61957	25 Salt of The Earth	67.4
61523	17 Green Acres	33.7	61770	25 Salt of The Earth	98.7	62001	25 Salt of The Earth	96.8
61524	25 Salt of The Earth	100.0	61771	37 Prairie Living	77.1	62002	32 Rustbelt Traditions	27.6

ZIP CODE	TOP TAPESTRY CONSUMER TYPE	% 2004 HOUSE-HOLDS	ZIP CODE	TOP TAPESTRY CONSUMER TYPE	% 2004 HOUSE-HOLDS	ZIP CODE	TOP TAPESTRY CONSUMER TYPE	% 2004 HOUSE-HOLDS
62006	37 Prairie Living	94.5	62242	50 Heartland Communities	48.1	62411	25 Salt of The Earth	51.0
62009	50 Heartland Communities	99.3	62243	26 Midland Crowd	49.2	62413	25 Salt of The Earth	100.0
62010	18 Cozy and Comfortable	21.6	62244	25 Salt of The Earth	57.3	62414	42 Southern Satellites	48.9
62011	46 Rooted Rural	58.2	62245	25 Salt of The Earth	67.2	62417	50 Heartland Communities	45.4
62012	25 Salt of The Earth	48.9	62246	33 Midlife Junction	20.4	62418	50 Heartland Communities	36.3
62013	46 Rooted Rural	85.1	62248	17 Green Acres	100.0	62419	42 Southern Satellites	97.5
62014	25 Salt of The Earth	71.5	62249	17 Green Acres	35.2	62420	50 Heartland Communities	48.5
62015	37 Prairie Living	97.5	62253	46 Rooted Rural	100.0	62421	37 Prairie Living	100.0
62016	50 Heartland Communities	88.2	62254	33 Midlife Junction	72.1	62422	42 Southern Satellites	93.6
62017	50 Heartland Communities	84.0	62255	42 Southern Satellites	60.6	62423	42 Southern Satellites	88.6
62018	41 Crossroads	33.4	62257	25 Salt of The Earth	26.7	62424	25 Salt of The Earth	99.3
62019	50 Heartland Communities	53.8	62258	18 Cozy and Comfortable	27.1	62425	37 Prairie Living	95.2
62021	17 Green Acres	56.9	62260	17 Green Acres	37.4	62426	42 Southern Satellites	96.3
62022	26 Midland Crowd	84.7	62261	25 Salt of The Earth	84.3	62427	46 Rooted Rural	66.0
62024	29 Rustbelt Retirees	42.9	62262	50 Heartland Communities	51.9	62428	50 Heartland Communities	78.0
62025	17 Green Acres	23.4	62263	32 Rustbelt Traditions	20.0	62431	42 Southern Satellites	93.4
62027	46 Rooted Rural	59.2	62264	32 Rustbelt Traditions	37.2	62432	46 Rooted Rural	96.2
62028	26 Midland Crowd	66.1	62265	18 Cozy and Comfortable	44.2	62433	50 Heartland Communities	74.1
62030	25 Salt of The Earth	89.7	62268	25 Salt of The Earth	100.0	62434	25 Salt of The Earth	69.1
62031	25 Salt of The Earth	59.7	62269	13 In Style	42.2	62436	42 Southern Satellites	76.7
62032	46 Rooted Rural	94.2	62271	32 Rustbelt Traditions	47.9	62438	25 Salt of The Earth	96.3
62033	50 Heartland Communities	51.5	62272	42 Southern Satellites	65.8	62439	50 Heartland Communities	27.2
62034	13 In Style	36.7	62274	50 Heartland Communities	52.2	62440	17 Green Acres	73.9
62035	33 Midlife Junction	36.8	62275	42 Southern Satellites	64.8	62441	25 Salt of The Earth	40.0
62036	46 Rooted Rural	100.0	62277	25 Salt of The Earth	97.4	62442	42 Southern Satellites	40.4
62037	26 Midland Crowd	41.5	62278	25 Salt of The Earth	32.1	62443	42 Southern Satellites	53.1
62040	29 Rustbelt Retirees	30.2	62280	25 Salt of The Earth	59.0	62445	25 Salt of The Earth	71.7
62044	50 Heartland Communities	58.1	62281	25 Salt of The Earth	66.6	62446	46 Rooted Rural	98.2
62045	46 Rooted Rural	66.5	62284	17 Green Acres	44.4	62447	25 Salt of The Earth	77.3
62047	50 Heartland Communities	95.0	62285	26 Midland Crowd	73.9	62448	50 Heartland Communities	56.3
62048	29 Rustbelt Retirees	56.9	62286	53 Home Town	22.1	62449	50 Heartland Communities	43.1
62049	50 Heartland Communities	38.0	62288	25 Salt of The Earth	55.0	62450	50 Heartland Communities	37.3
62050	46 Rooted Rural	91.7	62293	29 Rustbelt Retirees	36.9	62451	42 Southern Satellites	57.5
62051	42 Southern Satellites	84.0	62294	28 Aspiring Young Families	30.6	62452	42 Southern Satellites	80.5
62052	50 Heartland Communities	19.7	62295	17 Green Acres	80.4	62454	50 Heartland Communities	42.3
62053	50 Heartland Communities	80.4	62297	46 Rooted Rural	35.5	62458	46 Rooted Rural	55.2
62054	46 Rooted Rural	62.0	62298	17 Green Acres	39.2	62460	46 Rooted Rural	55.3
62056	50 Heartland Communities	50.1	62301	32 Rustbelt Traditions	25.4	62461	37 Prairie Living	100.0
62060	53 Home Town	33.9	62305	25 Salt of The Earth	24.5	62462	37 Prairie Living	61.3
62061	32 Rustbelt Traditions	79.1	62311	50 Heartland Communities	89.9	62463	50 Heartland Communities	71.1
62062	19 Milk and Cookies	41.6	62312	46 Rooted Rural	43.5	62465	25 Salt of The Earth	97.8
62063	46 Rooted Rural	58.0	62313	37 Prairie Living	100.0	62466	25 Salt of The Earth	61.2
62065	50 Heartland Communities	89.4	62314	37 Prairie Living	54.0	62467	25 Salt of The Earth	95.9
62067	57 Simple Living	49.6	62316	37 Prairie Living	100.0	62468	25 Salt of The Earth	62.2
62069	50 Heartland Communities	52.1	62319	37 Prairie Living	100.0	62469	26 Midland Crowd	47.9
62070	46 Rooted Rural	97.0	62320	50 Heartland Communities	62.5	62471	50 Heartland Communities	38.7
62074	25 Salt of The Earth	59.1	62321	50 Heartland Communities	36.7	62473	26 Midland Crowd	85.7
62075	50 Heartland Communities	62.3	62323	46 Rooted Rural	97.5	62474	46 Rooted Rural	68.2
62079	25 Salt of The Earth	62.0	62324	50 Heartland Communities	62.4	62475	37 Prairie Living	57.8
62080	42 Southern Satellites	45.0	62325	37 Prairie Living	83.7	62476	42 Southern Satellites	50.3
62081	46 Rooted Rural	79.7	62326	50 Heartland Communities	62.4	62477	46 Rooted Rural	69.1
62082	53 Home Town	50.1	62330	46 Rooted Rural	71.2	62478	25 Salt of The Earth	100.0
62083	46 Rooted Rural	75.7	62334	37 Prairie Living	100.0	62479	25 Salt of The Earth	74.9
62084	32 Rustbelt Traditions	50.2	62338	25 Salt of The Earth	56.7	62480	25 Salt of The Earth	42.6
62086	46 Rooted Rural	81.8	62339	25 Salt of The Earth	54.3	62481	37 Prairie Living	97.6
62087	53 Home Town	64.5	62340	50 Heartland Communities	50.3	62501	25 Salt of The Earth	73.3
62088	32 Rustbelt Traditions	31.0	62341	25 Salt of The Earth	44.6	62510	32 Rustbelt Traditions	38.3
62090	64 City Commons	62.2	62343	37 Prairie Living	63.5	62512	25 Salt of The Earth	100.0
62091	25 Salt of The Earth	63.8	62344	37 Prairie Living	100.0	62513	25 Salt of The Earth	94.4
62092	50 Heartland Communities	76.0	62345	25 Salt of The Earth	97.3	62514	17 Green Acres	100.0
62094	50 Heartland Communities	57.4	62346	37 Prairie Living	100.0	62515	17 Green Acres	50.0
62095	32 Rustbelt Traditions	53.5	62347	25 Salt of The Earth	86.5	62517	50 Heartland Communities	100.0
62097	17 Green Acres	48.1	62348	25 Salt of The Earth	74.0	62518	25 Salt of The Earth	100.0
62201	64 City Commons	47.2	62349	25 Salt of The Earth	88.2	62520	25 Salt of The Earth	40.8
62203	34 Family Foundations	58.2	62351	25 Salt of The Earth	68.7	62521	18 Cozy and Comfortable	21.1
62204	62 Modest Income Homes	62.9	62352	46 Rooted Rural	71.2	62522	55 College Towns	17.5
62205	62 Modest Income Homes	65.8	62353	50 Heartland Communities	53.8	62523	65 Social Security Set	98.4
62206	51 Metro City Edge	51.8	62354	25 Salt of The Earth	74.6	62526	53 Home Town	20.6
62207	62 Modest Income Homes	77.5	62355	46 Rooted Rural	90.8	62530	32 Rustbelt Traditions	56.2
62208	29 Rustbelt Retirees	43.8	62356	46 Rooted Rural	97.4	62531	25 Salt of The Earth	87.8
62214	25 Salt of The Earth	61.8	62357	46 Rooted Rural	76.8	62533	25 Salt of The Earth	83.3
62215	25 Salt of The Earth	39.9	62358	46 Rooted Rural	40.8	62534	50 Heartland Communities	64.6
62217	42 Southern Satellites	99.2	62359	37 Prairie Living	100.0	62535	07 Exurbanites	100.0
62218	17 Green Acres	95.0	62360	32 Rustbelt Traditions	58.6	62536	07 Exurbanites	49.7
62220	48 Great Expectations	25.5	62361	37 Prairie Living	89.3	62538	37 Prairie Living	70.8
62221	13 In Style	23.3	62362	46 Rooted Rural	62.2	62539	32 Rustbelt Traditions	52.5
62223	29 Rustbelt Retirees	32.1	62363	50 Heartland Communities	29.5	62543	25 Salt of The Earth	100.0
62225	12 Up and Coming Families	59.7	62365	25 Salt of The Earth	100.0	62544	25 Salt of The Earth	51.0
62226	48 Great Expectations	20.2	62366	50 Heartland Communities	50.4	62545	26 Midland Crowd	52.9
62230	25 Salt of The Earth	29.0	62367	37 Prairie Living	100.0	62546	29 Rustbelt Retirees	56.6
62231	29 Rustbelt Retirees	19.8	62370	37 Prairie Living	99.6	62547	25 Salt of The Earth	100.0
62232	50 Heartland Communities	23.8	62373	37 Prairie Living	97.1	62548	29 Rustbelt Retirees	40.8
62233	50 Heartland Communities	47.8	62374	37 Prairie Living	100.0	62549	17 Green Acres	88.0
62234	33 Midlife Junction	20.9	62375	37 Prairie Living	100.0	62550	25 Salt of The Earth	40.1
62236	18 Cozy and Comfortable	80.9	62376	25 Salt of The Earth	80.0	62551	32 Rustbelt Traditions	71.8
62237	25 Salt of The Earth	40.4	62378	46 Rooted Rural	91.6	62553	25 Salt of The Earth	94.1
62238	42 Southern Satellites	83.1	62379	50 Heartland Communities	44.5	62554	25 Salt of The Earth	62.3
62239	32 Rustbelt Traditions	78.1	62380	37 Prairie Living	100.0	62555	42 Southern Satellites	89.8
62240	56 Rural Bypasses	39.4	62401	33 Midlife Junction	31.9	62556	37 Prairie Living	82.5
62241	25 Salt of The Earth	81.1	62410	25 Salt of The Earth	100.0	62557	50 Heartland Communities	54.8

ZIP CODE	TOP TAPESTRY CONSUMER TYPE	% 2004 HOUSE-HOLDS	ZIP CODE	TOP TAPESTRY CONSUMER TYPE	% 2004 HOUSE-HOLDS	ZIP CODE	TOP TAPESTRY CONSUMER TYPE	% 2004 HOUSE-HOLDS
62558	32 Rustbelt Traditions	60.9	62830	50 Heartland Communities	58.7	62948	50 Heartland Communities	44.7
62560	29 Rustbelt Retirees	67.7	62831	46 Rooted Rural	75.4	62950	50 Heartland Communities	94.7
62561	26 Midland Crowd	37.4	62832	50 Heartland Communities	54.8	62951	50 Heartland Communities	74.2
62563	07 Exurbanites	37.4	62833	25 Salt of The Earth	87.3	62952	50 Heartland Communities	61.9
62565	50 Heartland Communities	45.0	62835	46 Rooted Rural	57.1	62953	37 Prairie Living	76.1
62567	50 Heartland Communities	75.7	62836	46 Rooted Rural	100.0	62954	50 Heartland Communities	97.2
62568	50 Heartland Communities	20.3	62837	50 Heartland Communities	75.2	62955	50 Heartland Communities	82.8
62571	25 Salt of The Earth	50.8	62838	46 Rooted Rural	84.4	62956	50 Heartland Communities	81.4
62572	25 Salt of The Earth	86.8	62839	50 Heartland Communities	82.3	62957	46 Rooted Rural	96.7
62573	25 Salt of The Earth	73.6	62842	42 Southern Satellites	100.0	62958	17 Green Acres	47.2
62601	37 Prairie Living	100.0	62843	42 Southern Satellites	71.1	62959	50 Heartland Communities	17.2
62611	37 Prairie Living	76.8	62844	50 Heartland Communities	73.3	62960	50 Heartland Communities	30.1
62612	26 Midland Crowd	50.7	62845	46 Rooted Rural	96.9	62961	46 Rooted Rural	100.0
62613	17 Green Acres	60.5	62846	42 Southern Satellites	100.0	62962	31 Rural Resort Dwellers	88.6
62615	26 Midland Crowd	59.7	62849	42 Southern Satellites	42.5	62963	62 Modest Income Homes	100.0
62617	46 Rooted Rural	100.0	62850	46 Rooted Rural	67.9	62964	62 Modest Income Homes	49.4
62618	50 Heartland Communities	33.6	62851	46 Rooted Rural	64.0	62966	50 Heartland Communities	16.7
62621	25 Salt of The Earth	83.0	62853	25 Salt of The Earth	100.0	62967	46 Rooted Rural	100.0
62624	46 Rooted Rural	96.5	62854	50 Heartland Communities	56.3	62970	46 Rooted Rural	90.9
62625	17 Green Acres	49.9	62855	37 Prairie Living	100.0	62972	46 Rooted Rural	68.2
62626	33 Midlife Junction	26.4	62858	50 Heartland Communities	40.2	62974	46 Rooted Rural	61.5
62627	46 Rooted Rural	91.5	62859	50 Heartland Communities	74.4	62975	25 Salt of The Earth	52.1
62628	25 Salt of The Earth	80.6	62860	46 Rooted Rural	100.0	62976	56 Rural Bypasses	79.8
62629	12 Up and Coming Families	39.4	62862	46 Rooted Rural	97.6	62977	46 Rooted Rural	100.0
62630	46 Rooted Rural	52.6	62863	50 Heartland Communities	16.8	62979	50 Heartland Communities	55.2
62631	37 Prairie Living	100.0	62864	46 Rooted Rural	18.1	62982	50 Heartland Communities	100.0
62633	37 Prairie Living	87.2	62865	46 Rooted Rural	77.9	62983	50 Heartland Communities	92.2
62634	37 Prairie Living	67.0	62866	46 Rooted Rural	100.0	62984	50 Heartland Communities	72.9
62635	32 Rustbelt Traditions	88.9	62867	50 Heartland Communities	85.6	62985	46 Rooted Rural	100.0
62638	25 Salt of The Earth	53.7	62868	42 Southern Satellites	59.8	62987	46 Rooted Rural	100.0
62639	25 Salt of The Earth	51.0	62869	46 Rooted Rural	54.7	62988	56 Rural Bypasses	49.9
62640	50 Heartland Communities	23.1	62870	50 Heartland Communities	49.6	62990	46 Rooted Rural	41.0
62642	50 Heartland Communities	60.9	62871	37 Prairie Living	91.7	62992	56 Rural Bypasses	88.7
62643	25 Salt of The Earth	84.7	62872	26 Midland Crowd	87.8	62994	46 Rooted Rural	95.7
62644	50 Heartland Communities	55.1	62875	50 Heartland Communities	73.8	62995	46 Rooted Rural	52.5
62649	46 Rooted Rural	94.1	62877	26 Midland Crowd	47.8	62996	46 Rooted Rural	99.7
62650	14 Prosperous Empty Nesters	16.3	62878	42 Southern Satellites	92.9	62997	42 Southern Satellites	95.8
62655	46 Rooted Rural	98.4	62880	37 Prairie Living	93.3	62998	42 Southern Satellites	100.0
62656	32 Rustbelt Traditions	24.3	62881	25 Salt of The Earth	20.2	62999	50 Heartland Communities	100.0
62661	26 Midland Crowd	77.5	62882	42 Southern Satellites	39.5	63005	02 Suburban Splendor	52.1
62664	50 Heartland Communities	62.8	62883	46 Rooted Rural	83.4	63010	12 Up and Coming Families	21.8
62665	46 Rooted Rural	43.1	62884	50 Heartland Communities	56.2	63011	07 Exurbanites	23.2
62666	25 Salt of The Earth	100.0	62885	46 Rooted Rural	85.7	63012	19 Milk and Cookies	60.8
62667	25 Salt of The Earth	57.0	62886	42 Southern Satellites	61.3	63013	17 Green Acres	54.3
62668	25 Salt of The Earth	81.8	62887	25 Salt of The Earth	52.7	63014	25 Salt of The Earth	74.2
62670	33 Midlife Junction	44.4	62888	42 Southern Satellites	49.8	63015	26 Midland Crowd	89.7
62671	25 Salt of The Earth	97.0	62889	25 Salt of The Earth	76.1	63016	26 Midland Crowd	66.5
62672	46 Rooted Rural	80.4	62890	46 Rooted Rural	69.6	63017	02 Suburban Splendor	23.5
62673	37 Prairie Living	84.9	62892	25 Salt of The Earth	100.0	63019	18 Cozy and Comfortable	22.6
62674	50 Heartland Communities	52.8	62893	26 Midland Crowd	50.1	63020	26 Midland Crowd	27.2
62675	33 Midlife Junction	21.1	62894	46 Rooted Rural	70.9	63021	06 Sophisticated Squires	28.0
62677	17 Green Acres	71.6	62895	26 Midland Crowd	58.2	63023	26 Midland Crowd	59.0
62681	50 Heartland Communities	74.8	62896	50 Heartland Communities	49.2	63025	04 Boomburbs	62.2
62682	46 Rooted Rural	70.2	62897	25 Salt of The Earth	65.5	63026	06 Sophisticated Squires	31.4
62683	37 Prairie Living	100.0	62898	26 Midland Crowd	81.1	63028	26 Midland Crowd	41.2
62684	06 Sophisticated Squires	52.3	62899	25 Salt of The Earth	76.3	63030	42 Southern Satellites	83.8
62685	25 Salt of The Earth	71.4	62901	63 Dorms To Diplomas	38.4	63031	29 Rustbelt Retirees	22.9
62688	17 Green Acres	58.5	62902	55 College Towns	43.1	63033	18 Cozy and Comfortable	28.0
62690	50 Heartland Communities	41.5	62903	55 College Towns	64.2	63034	06 Sophisticated Squires	32.5
62691	50 Heartland Communities	82.2	62905	46 Rooted Rural	83.8	63036	46 Rooted Rural	94.4
62692	46 Rooted Rural	37.3	62906	50 Heartland Communities	45.0	63037	25 Salt of The Earth	65.2
62693	18 Cozy and Comfortable	91.1	62907	46 Rooted Rural	84.6	63038	04 Boomburbs	50.2
62694	50 Heartland Communities	61.3	62908	46 Rooted Rural	99.0	63039	17 Green Acres	95.3
62701	65 Social Security Set	80.1	62910	42 Southern Satellites	53.3	63040	04 Boomburbs	99.4
62702	32 Rustbelt Traditions	15.4	62912	46 Rooted Rural	95.0	63041	26 Midland Crowd	55.1
62703	32 Rustbelt Traditions	20.9	62914	62 Modest Income Homes	45.8	63042	28 Aspiring Young Families	28.7
62704	48 Great Expectations	13.5	62916	46 Rooted Rural	76.6	63043	18 Cozy and Comfortable	35.2
62707	07 Exurbanites	28.3	62918	50 Heartland Communities	41.3	63044	24 Main Street, USA	38.7
62801	53 Home Town	30.8	62918	33 Midlife Junction	39.0	63048	50 Heartland Communities	36.9
62803	37 Prairie Living	100.0	62919	46 Rooted Rural	58.3	63049	19 Milk and Cookies	38.6
62806	50 Heartland Communities	77.0	62920	46 Rooted Rural	51.9	63050	26 Midland Crowd	49.2
62807	46 Rooted Rural	59.4	62922	46 Rooted Rural	67.6	63051	26 Midland Crowd	67.9
62808	50 Heartland Communities	65.3	62923	46 Rooted Rural	100.0	63052	12 Up and Coming Families	45.0
62809	25 Salt of The Earth	69.6	62924	32 Rustbelt Traditions	68.3	63055	17 Green Acres	80.1
62810	46 Rooted Rural	90.0	62926	50 Heartland Communities	43.9	63056	25 Salt of The Earth	57.8
62812	50 Heartland Communities	53.8	62928	31 Rural Resort Dwellers	59.2	63060	26 Midland Crowd	51.7
62814	46 Rooted Rural	76.4	62930	50 Heartland Communities	51.6	63068	25 Salt of The Earth	49.6
62815	25 Salt of The Earth	100.0	62931	49 Senior Sun Seekers	79.2	63069	26 Midland Crowd	34.5
62816	46 Rooted Rural	91.0	62932	50 Heartland Communities	99.0	63070	41 Crossroads	48.1
62817	46 Rooted Rural	100.0	62933	33 Midlife Junction	100.0	63071	56 Rural Bypasses	68.4
62818	25 Salt of The Earth	79.5	62934	50 Heartland Communities	78.9	63072	26 Midland Crowd	99.1
62819	50 Heartland Communities	98.2	62935	46 Rooted Rural	63.4	63074	48 Great Expectations	36.7
62820	46 Rooted Rural	93.3	62938	46 Rooted Rural	51.8	63077	42 Southern Satellites	34.8
62821	50 Heartland Communities	49.5	62939	25 Salt of The Earth	42.9	63080	25 Salt of The Earth	34.6
62822	50 Heartland Communities	78.5	62940	50 Heartland Communities	63.5	63084	32 Rustbelt Traditions	33.1
62823	50 Heartland Communities	60.5	62941	50 Heartland Communities	72.4	63087	46 Rooted Rural	70.7
62824	46 Rooted Rural	88.9	62942	42 Southern Satellites	100.0	63088	16 Enterprising Professionals	42.5
62827	46 Rooted Rural	49.4	62943	46 Rooted Rural	91.1	63089	25 Salt of The Earth	37.2
62828	37 Prairie Living	52.2	62946	50 Heartland Communities	41.3	63090	17 Green Acres	43.6
62829	46 Rooted Rural	100.0	62947	31 Rural Resort Dwellers	78.8	63091	25 Salt of The Earth	64.5

ZIP CODE	TOP TAPESTRY CONSUMER TYPE	% 2004 HOUSE-HOLDS	ZIP CODE	TOP TAPESTRY CONSUMER TYPE	% 2004 HOUSE-HOLDS	ZIP CODE	TOP TAPESTRY CONSUMER TYPE	% 2004 HOUSE-HOLDS
63101	52 Inner City Tenants	70.2	63433	46 Rooted Rural	90.0	63654	46 Rooted Rural	100.0
63102	27 Metro Renters	96.8	63434	37 Prairie Living	100.0	63655	46 Rooted Rural	78.5
63103	65 Social Security Set	66.1	63435	53 Home Town	37.4	63656	46 Rooted Rural	85.2
63104	64 City Commons	18.8	63436	50 Heartland Communities	81.3	63660	56 Rural Bypasses	98.9
63105	08 Laptops and Lattes	50.2	63437	50 Heartland Communities	58.0	63662	42 Southern Satellites	58.5
63106	64 City Commons	67.8	63438	42 Southern Satellites	83.9	63664	42 Southern Satellites	41.2
63107	62 Modest Income Homes	67.7	63439	37 Prairie Living	70.1	63665	50 Heartland Communities	83.8
63108	27 Metro Renters	50.5	63440	42 Southern Satellites	43.5	63670	25 Salt Of The Earth	26.3
63109	32 Rustbelt Traditions	19.5	63441	42 Southern Satellites	97.2	63673	46 Rooted Rural	34.3
63110	48 Great Expectations	26.6	63443	46 Rooted Rural	84.0	63675	46 Rooted Rural	100.0
63111	60 City Dimensions	53.5	63445	50 Heartland Communities	59.3	63701	55 College Towns	19.2
63112	62 Modest Income Homes	34.9	63446	37 Prairie Living	100.0	63703	53 Home Town	25.1
63113	62 Modest Income Homes	77.6	63447	50 Heartland Communities	73.5	63730	50 Heartland Communities	57.7
63114	32 Rustbelt Traditions	53.4	63448	50 Heartland Communities	67.1	63732	25 Salt of The Earth	93.5
63115	62 Modest Income Homes	84.5	63450	50 Heartland Communities	90.3	63735	56 Rural Bypasses	73.1
63116	48 Great Expectations	30.0	63451	37 Prairie Living	100.0	63736	26 Midland Crowd	42.9
63117	22 Metropolitans	24.5	63452	50 Heartland Communities	99.1	63739	26 Midland Crowd	94.4
63118	60 City Dimensions	51.6	63453	42 Southern Satellites	100.0	63740	42 Southern Satellites	26.2
63119	30 Retirement Communities	19.9	63454	25 Salt of The Earth	61.5	63743	25 Salt of The Earth	100.0
63120	62 Modest Income Homes	73.6	63456	50 Heartland Communities	27.2	63744	46 Rooted Rural	100.0
63121	34 Family Foundations	29.3	63457	46 Rooted Rural	98.4	63747	25 Salt of The Earth	100.0
63122	14 Prosperous Empty Nesters	28.3	63458	37 Prairie Living	100.0	63748	25 Salt of The Earth	80.5
63123	29 Rustbelt Retirees	35.6	63459	37 Prairie Living	31.7	63750	46 Rooted Rural	100.0
63124	01 Top Rung	54.0	63460	37 Prairie Living	100.0	63751	42 Southern Satellites	54.6
63125	29 Rustbelt Retirees	39.4	63461	50 Heartland Communities	43.9	63755	17 Green Acres	30.1
63126	14 Prosperous Empty Nesters	54.3	63462	50 Heartland Communities	55.6	63760	46 Rooted Rural	100.0
63127	30 Retirement Communities	34.2	63463	25 Salt of The Earth	100.0	63763	46 Rooted Rural	81.9
63128	14 Prosperous Empty Nesters	43.0	63464	37 Prairie Living	100.0	63764	42 Southern Satellites	53.9
63129	06 Sophisticated Squires	32.5	63466	37 Prairie Living	96.7	63766	25 Salt of The Earth	87.5
63130	34 Family Foundations	24.9	63468	50 Heartland Communities	70.9	63769	25 Salt of The Earth	100.0
63131	03 Connoisseurs	46.8	63469	50 Heartland Communities	60.3	63770	25 Salt of The Earth	100.0
63132	03 Connoisseurs	17.4	63471	25 Salt of The Earth	100.0	63771	50 Heartland Communities	56.0
63133	62 Modest Income Homes	47.9	63472	56 Rural Bypasses	50.8	63775	50 Heartland Communities	42.5
63134	51 Metro City Edge	33.3	63473	37 Prairie Living	95.5	63780	25 Salt of The Earth	41.0
63135	32 Rustbelt Traditions	28.4	63474	46 Rooted Rural	99.2	63781	42 Southern Satellites	98.9
63136	51 Metro City Edge	37.7	63501	33 Midlife Junction	29.2	63782	42 Southern Satellites	100.0
63137	32 Rustbelt Traditions	50.8	63530	42 Southern Satellites	79.3	63783	25 Salt of The Earth	100.0
63138	52 Inner City Tenants	27.2	63531	37 Prairie Living	100.0	63785	46 Rooted Rural	99.7
63139	32 Rustbelt Traditions	37.2	63532	56 Rural Bypasses	65.2	63787	42 Southern Satellites	54.7
63140	64 City Commons	58.8	63533	37 Prairie Living	70.6	63801	53 Home Town	11.3
63141	01 Top Rung	19.9	63534	46 Rooted Rural	90.7	63821	56 Rural Bypasses	70.1
63143	48 Great Expectations	41.9	63535	37 Prairie Living	100.0	63822	53 Home Town	38.3
63144	22 Metropolitans	30.2	63536	37 Prairie Living	98.1	63823	46 Rooted Rural	61.6
63146	14 Prosperous Empty Nesters	25.5	63537	50 Heartland Communities	65.7	63825	50 Heartland Communities	46.1
63147	34 Family Foundations	49.6	63538	37 Prairie Living	100.0	63827	56 Rural Bypasses	100.0
63301	48 Great Expectations	17.7	63539	37 Prairie Living	91.9	63829	50 Heartland Communities	65.6
63303	06 Sophisticated Squires	30.9	63540	46 Rooted Rural	90.8	63830	53 Home Town	50.5
63304	12 Up and Coming Families	33.4	63541	37 Prairie Living	100.0	63833	42 Southern Satellites	87.9
63330	31 Rural Resort Dwellers	100.0	63543	37 Prairie Living	100.0	63834	37 Prairie Living	29.2
63332	17 Green Acres	53.1	63544	46 Rooted Rural	100.0	63837	56 Rural Bypasses	88.3
63333	42 Southern Satellites	91.4	63545	50 Heartland Communities	62.6	63841	50 Heartland Communities	27.2
63334	53 Home Town	23.0	63546	50 Heartland Communities	59.4	63845	53 Home Town	47.0
63336	50 Heartland Communities	50.7	63547	37 Prairie Living	97.8	63846	42 Southern Satellites	65.3
63339	42 Southern Satellites	95.0	63548	50 Heartland Communities	76.4	63848	53 Home Town	80.3
63341	07 Exurbanites	37.8	63549	50 Heartland Communities	81.0	63849	53 Home Town	70.8
63343	26 Midland Crowd	36.3	63551	46 Rooted Rural	100.0	63851	56 Rural Bypasses	36.1
63344	46 Rooted Rural	78.8	63552	50 Heartland Communities	34.1	63852	56 Rural Bypasses	71.6
63345	46 Rooted Rural	97.2	63555	50 Heartland Communities	64.9	63855	50 Heartland Communities	45.0
63347	26 Midland Crowd	62.2	63556	53 Home Town	48.1	63857	53 Home Town	41.8
63348	17 Green Acres	72.2	63557	37 Prairie Living	100.0	63862	56 Rural Bypasses	87.8
63349	42 Southern Satellites	64.7	63558	46 Rooted Rural	79.2	63863	56 Rural Bypasses	36.3
63350	50 Heartland Communities	63.3	63559	46 Rooted Rural	85.1	63866	56 Rural Bypasses	72.7
63351	50 Heartland Communities	68.6	63560	46 Rooted Rural	68.6	63867	42 Southern Satellites	60.8
63352	50 Heartland Communities	68.3	63561	50 Heartland Communities	80.0	63868	50 Heartland Communities	64.6
63353	50 Heartland Communities	71.1	63563	37 Prairie Living	100.0	63869	50 Heartland Communities	24.5
63357	17 Green Acres	56.2	63565	50 Heartland Communities	51.4	63870	53 Home Town	43.1
63359	46 Rooted Rural	56.9	63566	37 Prairie Living	52.2	63873	42 Southern Satellites	44.9
63361	53 Home Town	44.8	63567	46 Rooted Rural	100.0	63876	50 Heartland Communities	55.8
63362	26 Midland Crowd	55.5	63601	53 Home Town	26.4	63877	53 Home Town	46.2
63363	46 Rooted Rural	52.5	63620	46 Rooted Rural	100.0	63879	56 Rural Bypasses	93.8
63366	12 Up and Coming Families	47.8	63621	46 Rooted Rural	98.1	63901	53 Home Town	24.5
63367	07 Exurbanites	47.0	63622	46 Rooted Rural	52.6	63931	56 Rural Bypasses	95.7
63369	25 Salt of The Earth	67.7	63623	46 Rooted Rural	99.7	63932	46 Rooted Rural	68.3
63373	25 Salt of The Earth	100.0	63624	56 Rural Bypasses	53.0	63933	46 Rooted Rural	47.1
63376	06 Sophisticated Squires	36.6	63625	46 Rooted Rural	100.0	63934	46 Rooted Rural	71.1
63377	46 Rooted Rural	41.9	63626	42 Southern Satellites	80.0	63935	46 Rooted Rural	39.8
63379	26 Midland Crowd	42.4	63627	42 Southern Satellites	49.7	63936	42 Southern Satellites	92.1
63381	17 Green Acres	58.8	63628	42 Southern Satellites	31.4	63937	46 Rooted Rural	44.4
63382	50 Heartland Communities	52.0	63629	42 Southern Satellites	63.6	63939	46 Rooted Rural	81.3
63383	26 Midland Crowd	39.6	63630	56 Rural Bypasses	43.6	63940	56 Rural Bypasses	89.4
63384	53 Home Town	39.1	63631	46 Rooted Rural	95.8	63941	46 Rooted Rural	100.0
63385	26 Midland Crowd	35.5	63633	46 Rooted Rural	95.6	63942	46 Rooted Rural	100.0
63386	25 Salt of The Earth	100.0	63636	46 Rooted Rural	100.0	63943	56 Rural Bypasses	45.7
63388	46 Rooted Rural	99.3	63637	46 Rooted Rural	97.6	63944	46 Rooted Rural	66.9
63389	26 Midland Crowd	64.4	63638	53 Home Town	46.3	63945	26 Midland Crowd	69.2
63390	26 Midland Crowd	44.4	63640	33 Midlife Junction	34.1	63950	46 Rooted Rural	100.0
63401	53 Home Town	31.1	63645	46 Rooted Rural	49.8	63951	46 Rooted Rural	100.0
63430	37 Prairie Living	43.2	63648	42 Southern Satellites	48.2	63952	56 Rural Bypasses	84.5
63431	46 Rooted Rural	69.6	63650	50 Heartland Communities	44.1	63953	56 Rural Bypasses	67.7
63432	37 Prairie Living	100.0	63653	50 Heartland Communities	91.5	63954	56 Rural Bypasses	94.7

ZIP CODE	TOP TAPESTRY CONSUMER TYPE	% 2004 HOUSE-HOLDS	ZIP CODE	TOP TAPESTRY CONSUMER TYPE	% 2004 HOUSE-HOLDS	ZIP CODE	TOP TAPESTRY CONSUMER TYPE	% 2004 HOUSE-HOLDS
63955	46 Rooted Rural	100.0	64131	36 Old and Newcomers	20.8	64493	25 Salt of The Earth	59.6
63956	46 Rooted Rural	84.7	64132	51 Metro City Edge	52.8	64494	50 Heartland Communities	66.1
63957	50 Heartland Communities	71.2	64133	29 Rustbelt Retirees	35.1	64496	37 Prairie Living	100.0
63960	46 Rooted Rural	54.5	64134	32 Rustbelt Traditions	40.3	64497	46 Rooted Rural	82.5
63961	42 Southern Satellites	53.4	64136	18 Cozy and Comfortable	99.6	64498	37 Prairie Living	100.0
63963	46 Rooted Rural	86.4	64137	36 Old and Newcomers	21.5	64499	37 Prairie Living	98.9
63964	50 Heartland Communities	53.1	64138	18 Cozy and Comfortable	35.4	64501	53 Home Town	23.8
63965	46 Rooted Rural	45.0	64139	18 Cozy and Comfortable	77.0	64503	32 Rustbelt Traditions	37.8
63966	49 Senior Sun Seekers	96.3	64145	15 Silver and Gold	41.3	64504	50 Heartland Communities	26.8
63967	56 Rural Bypasses	37.8	64146	33 Midlife Junction	76.8	64505	32 Rustbelt Traditions	28.9
64001	37 Prairie Living	100.0	64147	64 City Commons	71.2	64506	14 Prosperous Empty Nesters	26.7
64011	26 Midland Crowd	36.9	64149	06 Sophisticated Squires	47.4	64507	32 Rustbelt Traditions	28.1
64012	26 Midland Crowd	24.8	64150	52 Inner City Tenants	63.8	64601	31 Rural Resort Dwellers	31.2
64014	19 Milk and Cookies	28.4	64151	13 In Style	34.6	64620	31 Rural Resort Dwellers	50.8
64015	06 Sophisticated Squires	46.9	64152	12 Up and Coming Families	15.4	64622	37 Prairie Living	100.0
64016	32 Rustbelt Traditions	31.8	64153	16 Enterprising Professionals	58.2	64623	37 Prairie Living	100.0
64017	42 Southern Satellites	80.4	64154	16 Enterprising Professionals	69.4	64624	50 Heartland Communities	58.3
64018	17 Green Acres	91.6	64155	12 Up and Coming Families	64.8	64625	46 Rooted Rural	97.8
64019	26 Midland Crowd	50.4	64156	41 Crossroads	73.7	64628	50 Heartland Communities	57.8
64020	50 Heartland Communities	66.5	64157	12 Up and Coming Families	100.0	64630	50 Heartland Communities	78.1
64021	50 Heartland Communities	80.7	64158	12 Up and Coming Families	98.7	64631	50 Heartland Communities	62.6
64022	33 Midlife Junction	61.2	64161	32 Rustbelt Traditions	100.0	64632	50 Heartland Communities	73.2
64024	25 Salt of The Earth	22.2	64163	41 Crossroads	87.8	64633	50 Heartland Communities	39.0
64029	12 Up and Coming Families	59.4	64164	06 Sophisticated Squires	56.6	64635	46 Rooted Rural	84.0
64030	19 Milk and Cookies	24.2	64165	06 Sophisticated Squires	100.0	64636	46 Rooted Rural	92.1
64034	12 Up and Coming Families	69.7	64166	06 Sophisticated Squires	100.0	64637	46 Rooted Rural	73.7
64035	50 Heartland Communities	70.4	64167	12 Up and Coming Families	100.0	64638	50 Heartland Communities	69.0
64036	42 Southern Satellites	100.0	64401	25 Salt of The Earth	96.3	64639	37 Prairie Living	100.0
64037	25 Salt of The Earth	38.6	64402	50 Heartland Communities	79.9	64640	37 Prairie Living	62.7
64040	25 Salt of The Earth	51.8	64421	46 Rooted Rural	100.0	64641	46 Rooted Rural	82.0
64048	17 Green Acres	43.8	64422	37 Prairie Living	94.4	64642	37 Prairie Living	83.5
64050	32 Rustbelt Traditions	27.8	64423	37 Prairie Living	100.0	64643	50 Heartland Communities	85.9
64052	29 Rustbelt Retirees	26.4	64424	50 Heartland Communities	73.2	64644	50 Heartland Communities	64.6
64053	53 Home Town	83.9	64426	37 Prairie Living	96.5	64645	50 Heartland Communities	100.0
64054	53 Home Town	54.2	64427	46 Rooted Rural	68.8	64646	50 Heartland Communities	54.3
64055	29 Rustbelt Retirees	29.7	64428	50 Heartland Communities	70.1	64647	37 Prairie Living	97.6
64056	32 Rustbelt Traditions	35.5	64429	33 Midlife Junction	24.0	64648	37 Prairie Living	39.7
64057	48 Great Expectations	30.6	64430	25 Salt of The Earth	80.8	64649	26 Midland Crowd	86.6
64058	19 Milk and Cookies	82.6	64431	50 Heartland Communities	100.0	64650	46 Rooted Rural	93.9
64060	12 Up and Coming Families	55.4	64432	37 Prairie Living	100.0	64651	46 Rooted Rural	97.5
64061	17 Green Acres	50.8	64433	37 Prairie Living	100.0	64652	37 Prairie Living	98.1
64062	17 Green Acres	59.8	64434	37 Prairie Living	99.1	64653	37 Prairie Living	98.5
64063	48 Great Expectations	28.6	64436	37 Prairie Living	87.5	64654	37 Prairie Living	100.0
64064	04 Boomburbs	27.6	64437	37 Prairie Living	67.4	64655	37 Prairie Living	100.0
64067	50 Heartland Communities	49.1	64438	37 Prairie Living	100.0	64656	50 Heartland Communities	100.0
64068	12 Up and Coming Families	22.7	64439	25 Salt of The Earth	90.9	64657	37 Prairie Living	100.0
64070	17 Green Acres	100.0	64440	25 Salt of The Earth	100.0	64658	50 Heartland Communities	42.1
64071	46 Rooted Rural	72.9	64441	37 Prairie Living	100.0	64659	37 Prairie Living	100.0
64074	25 Salt of The Earth	77.6	64442	37 Prairie Living	88.4	64660	37 Prairie Living	100.0
64075	19 Milk and Cookies	40.9	64443	25 Salt of The Earth	100.0	64661	46 Rooted Rural	82.9
64076	26 Midland Crowd	63.2	64444	25 Salt of The Earth	85.2	64664	46 Rooted Rural	100.0
64077	42 Southern Satellites	54.2	64445	50 Heartland Communities	97.8	64667	50 Heartland Communities	100.0
64078	26 Midland Crowd	42.5	64446	50 Heartland Communities	78.2	64668	50 Heartland Communities	58.7
64079	12 Up and Coming Families	21.9	64448	25 Salt of The Earth	99.4	64670	46 Rooted Rural	76.5
64080	12 Up and Coming Families	35.8	64449	42 Southern Satellites	99.0	64671	25 Salt of The Earth	56.2
64081	43 The Elders	21.4	64451	37 Prairie Living	98.8	64672	37 Prairie Living	100.0
64082	06 Sophisticated Squires	72.3	64453	37 Prairie Living	100.0	64673	37 Prairie Living	53.6
64083	12 Up and Coming Families	45.9	64454	26 Midland Crowd	64.7	64674	50 Heartland Communities	61.8
64084	25 Salt of The Earth	65.3	64455	37 Prairie Living	100.0	64676	37 Prairie Living	100.0
64085	32 Rustbelt Traditions	31.3	64456	50 Heartland Communities	72.0	64679	50 Heartland Communities	67.2
64086	12 Up and Coming Families	56.0	64457	37 Prairie Living	100.0	64681	37 Prairie Living	100.0
64088	17 Green Acres	44.4	64458	37 Prairie Living	100.0	64682	37 Prairie Living	85.0
64089	12 Up and Coming Families	50.9	64459	25 Salt of The Earth	100.0	64683	50 Heartland Communities	41.3
64093	55 College Towns	22.0	64461	42 Southern Satellites	88.8	64686	46 Rooted Rural	100.0
64096	50 Heartland Communities	72.9	64463	50 Heartland Communities	77.3	64688	37 Prairie Living	100.0
64097	50 Heartland Communities	67.0	64465	17 Green Acres	27.9	64689	37 Prairie Living	76.6
64098	33 Midlife Junction	32.4	64466	37 Prairie Living	100.0	64701	17 Green Acres	38.0
64101	27 Metro Renters	100.0	64467	46 Rooted Rural	55.4	64720	50 Heartland Communities	60.8
64105	27 Metro Renters	100.0	64468	55 College Towns	41.6	64722	46 Rooted Rural	100.0
64106	64 City Commons	23.8	64469	50 Heartland Communities	55.0	64723	46 Rooted Rural	87.5
64108	60 City Dimensions	30.3	64470	50 Heartland Communities	61.1	64724	50 Heartland Communities	87.9
64109	62 Modest Income Homes	44.9	64471	46 Rooted Rural	73.2	64725	32 Rustbelt Traditions	65.4
64110	22 Metropolitans	25.0	64473	46 Rooted Rural	65.0	64726	37 Prairie Living	94.5
64111	52 Inner City Tenants	23.1	64474	37 Prairie Living	100.0	64728	37 Prairie Living	75.9
64112	27 Metro Renters	69.6	64475	42 Southern Satellites	99.1	64730	50 Heartland Communities	31.6
64113	03 Connoisseurs	31.3	64476	37 Prairie Living	99.0	64733	46 Rooted Rural	90.3
64114	22 Metropolitans	22.1	64477	50 Heartland Communities	37.0	64734	17 Green Acres	100.0
64116	48 Great Expectations	33.9	64479	42 Southern Satellites	98.4	64735	50 Heartland Communities	33.4
64117	32 Rustbelt Traditions	56.3	64480	37 Prairie Living	100.0	64738	46 Rooted Rural	100.0
64118	29 Rustbelt Retirees	15.7	64481	50 Heartland Communities	54.8	64739	25 Salt of The Earth	77.7
64119	32 Rustbelt Traditions	40.4	64482	50 Heartland Communities	82.0	64740	46 Rooted Rural	99.3
64120	53 Home Town	91.0	64483	46 Rooted Rural	84.1	64741	46 Rooted Rural	70.3
64123	53 Home Town	68.0	64484	25 Salt of The Earth	48.2	64742	33 Midlife Junction	50.4
64124	60 City Dimensions	53.3	64485	33 Midlife Junction	40.1	64744	49 Senior Sun Seekers	21.8
64125	53 Home Town	100.0	64486	37 Prairie Living	100.0	64745	46 Rooted Rural	100.0
64126	53 Home Town	51.8	64487	37 Prairie Living	96.0	64746	25 Salt of The Earth	75.4
64127	62 Modest Income Homes	37.4	64489	37 Prairie Living	53.6	64747	25 Salt of The Earth	49.4
64128	62 Modest Income Homes	76.4	64490	25 Salt of The Earth	62.0	64748	53 Home Town	67.8
64129	32 Rustbelt Traditions	43.2	64491	50 Heartland Communities	93.1	64750	46 Rooted Rural	100.0
64130	62 Modest Income Homes	64.4	64492	25 Salt of The Earth	79.4	64752	46 Rooted Rural	68.7

ZIP CODE	TOP TAPESTRY CONSUMER TYPE	% 2004 HOUSE-HOLDS	ZIP CODE	TOP TAPESTRY CONSUMER TYPE	% 2004 HOUSE-HOLDS	ZIP CODE	TOP TAPESTRY CONSUMER TYPE	% 2004 HOUSE-HOLDS
64755	50 Heartland Communities	33.3	65072	15 Silver and Gold	80.7	65401	33 Midlife Junction	27.4
64756	46 Rooted Rural	95.9	65074	26 Midland Crowd	57.9	65409	55 College Towns	100.0
64759	37 Prairie Living	29.4	65075	37 Prairie Living	82.3	65436	46 Rooted Rural	100.0
64761	42 Southern Satellites	82.5	65076	17 Green Acres	90.9	65438	46 Rooted Rural	54.0
64762	50 Heartland Communities	50.1	65077	42 Southern Satellites	98.6	65439	46 Rooted Rural	100.0
64763	50 Heartland Communities	57.6	65078	49 Senior Sun Seekers	31.2	65440	46 Rooted Rural	100.0
64767	46 Rooted Rural	98.3	65079	15 Silver and Gold	47.7	65441	42 Southern Satellites	76.5
64769	37 Prairie Living	100.0	65080	26 Midland Crowd	100.0	65443	46 Rooted Rural	99.3
64770	37 Prairie Living	92.9	65081	50 Heartland Communities	63.1	65444	46 Rooted Rural	93.5
64771	37 Prairie Living	83.3	65082	46 Rooted Rural	88.6	65446	46 Rooted Rural	100.0
64772	50 Heartland Communities	27.5	65083	42 Southern Satellites	74.5	65449	46 Rooted Rural	90.9
64776	46 Rooted Rural	60.1	65084	50 Heartland Communities	49.0	65452	46 Rooted Rural	97.3
64778	37 Prairie Living	98.7	65085	25 Salt of The Earth	98.6	65453	50 Heartland Communities	30.8
64779	50 Heartland Communities	88.6	65101	17 Green Acres	29.6	65456	46 Rooted Rural	100.0
64780	37 Prairie Living	97.7	65109	13 In Style	24.8	65457	33 Midlife Junction	60.9
64783	46 Rooted Rural	99.7	65201	55 College Towns	28.2	65459	50 Heartland Communities	37.2
64784	46 Rooted Rural	97.6	65202	28 Aspiring Young Families	40.4	65461	46 Rooted Rural	100.0
64788	46 Rooted Rural	79.7	65203	16 Enterprising Professionals	16.8	65462	46 Rooted Rural	100.0
64790	46 Rooted Rural	100.0	65211	63 Dorms To Diplomas	100.0	65463	42 Southern Satellites	100.0
64801	53 Home Town	22.5	65215	55 College Towns	100.0	65464	46 Rooted Rural	100.0
64804	26 Midland Crowd	19.4	65216	55 College Towns	100.0	65466	46 Rooted Rural	71.6
64831	42 Southern Satellites	51.1	65230	46 Rooted Rural	60.5	65468	46 Rooted Rural	100.0
64832	26 Midland Crowd	85.5	65231	26 Midland Crowd	64.0	65470	46 Rooted Rural	47.0
64833	37 Prairie Living	100.0	65232	46 Rooted Rural	77.9	65473	40 Military Proximity	97.4
64834	17 Green Acres	35.6	65233	25 Salt of The Earth	26.3	65479	46 Rooted Rural	92.6
64835	42 Southern Satellites	100.0	65236	50 Heartland Communities	73.4	65483	46 Rooted Rural	68.7
64836	53 Home Town	29.2	65237	42 Southern Satellites	55.1	65484	46 Rooted Rural	100.0
64840	46 Rooted Rural	68.9	65239	25 Salt of The Earth	99.8	65486	46 Rooted Rural	55.3
64842	42 Southern Satellites	100.0	65240	25 Salt of The Earth	41.6	65501	46 Rooted Rural	100.0
64843	42 Southern Satellites	85.3	65243	42 Southern Satellites	62.1	65529	46 Rooted Rural	100.0
64844	42 Southern Satellites	79.1	65244	46 Rooted Rural	71.9	65534	46 Rooted Rural	78.3
64847	46 Rooted Rural	78.8	65246	50 Heartland Communities	94.0	65535	42 Southern Satellites	79.1
64848	46 Rooted Rural	50.9	65247	46 Rooted Rural	94.5	65536	42 Southern Satellites	37.3
64850	25 Salt of The Earth	22.0	65248	50 Heartland Communities	41.5	65541	46 Rooted Rural	100.0
64854	42 Southern Satellites	54.8	65250	42 Southern Satellites	99.0	65542	46 Rooted Rural	57.1
64855	26 Midland Crowd	47.6	65251	26 Midland Crowd	27.3	65543	46 Rooted Rural	100.0
64856	41 Crossroads	30.9	65254	37 Prairie Living	49.0	65548	50 Heartland Communities	58.0
64859	37 Prairie Living	49.7	65255	26 Midland Crowd	72.9	65550	50 Heartland Communities	42.5
64861	37 Prairie Living	87.6	65256	26 Midland Crowd	95.5	65552	26 Midland Crowd	59.9
64862	42 Southern Satellites	44.7	65257	50 Heartland Communities	50.3	65555	46 Rooted Rural	100.0
64863	42 Southern Satellites	100.0	65258	42 Southern Satellites	87.5	65556	46 Rooted Rural	40.0
64865	42 Southern Satellites	38.3	65259	42 Southern Satellites	41.2	65557	46 Rooted Rural	92.2
64866	42 Southern Satellites	100.0	65260	25 Salt of The Earth	94.2	65559	50 Heartland Communities	48.1
64867	42 Southern Satellites	85.1	65261	50 Heartland Communities	69.6	65560	46 Rooted Rural	52.0
64868	42 Southern Satellites	78.9	65262	26 Midland Crowd	86.1	65564	46 Rooted Rural	100.0
64870	48 Great Expectations	36.9	65263	42 Southern Satellites	49.1	65565	42 Southern Satellites	39.0
64873	42 Southern Satellites	52.9	65264	25 Salt of The Earth	84.4	65566	46 Rooted Rural	100.0
64874	42 Southern Satellites	84.3	65265	50 Heartland Communities	39.5	65567	42 Southern Satellites	74.1
65001	42 Southern Satellites	51.0	65270	53 Home Town	38.7	65570	46 Rooted Rural	100.0
65010	17 Green Acres	45.8	65274	50 Heartland Communities	69.5	65571	46 Rooted Rural	54.1
65011	37 Prairie Living	70.3	65275	37 Prairie Living	50.0	65580	46 Rooted Rural	72.9
65013	50 Heartland Communities	46.1	65276	50 Heartland Communities	43.3	65582	25 Salt of The Earth	54.2
65014	42 Southern Satellites	68.2	65279	07 Exurbanites	40.8	65583	26 Midland Crowd	29.7
65016	25 Salt of The Earth	100.0	65280	46 Rooted Rural	51.3	65584	28 Aspiring Young Families	39.6
65017	42 Southern Satellites	46.9	65281	37 Prairie Living	43.6	65586	46 Rooted Rural	68.6
65018	50 Heartland Communities	40.4	65282	25 Salt of The Earth	83.2	65588	56 Rural Bypasses	65.1
65020	31 Rural Resort Dwellers	32.2	65283	37 Prairie Living	100.0	65589	46 Rooted Rural	100.0
65023	25 Salt of The Earth	75.3	65284	50 Heartland Communities	52.3	65590	42 Southern Satellites	91.9
65024	50 Heartland Communities	75.5	65285	25 Salt of The Earth	97.4	65591	46 Rooted Rural	98.9
65025	42 Southern Satellites	75.4	65286	37 Prairie Living	100.0	65601	37 Prairie Living	52.4
65026	42 Southern Satellites	26.8	65287	17 Green Acres	100.0	65603	37 Prairie Living	100.0
65032	26 Midland Crowd	63.6	65301	53 Home Town	21.1	65604	53 Home Town	80.4
65034	46 Rooted Rural	42.2	65305	40 Military Proximity	99.8	65605	42 Southern Satellites	32.3
65035	25 Salt of The Earth	99.4	65321	37 Prairie Living	97.4	65606	46 Rooted Rural	73.5
65037	31 Rural Resort Dwellers	79.8	65322	37 Prairie Living	82.2	65608	46 Rooted Rural	58.7
65039	17 Green Acres	94.5	65323	46 Rooted Rural	98.1	65609	42 Southern Satellites	84.2
65040	26 Midland Crowd	88.7	65324	31 Rural Resort Dwellers	77.6	65610	50 Heartland Communities	41.6
65041	50 Heartland Communities	34.0	65325	50 Heartland Communities	53.8	65611	49 Senior Sun Seekers	73.1
65042	25 Salt of The Earth	100.0	65326	49 Senior Sun Seekers	76.1	65612	25 Salt of The Earth	97.0
65043	26 Midland Crowd	52.7	65329	37 Prairie Living	94.1	65613	33 Midlife Junction	41.2
65046	46 Rooted Rural	86.5	65330	50 Heartland Communities	99.0	65614	46 Rooted Rural	94.5
65047	26 Midland Crowd	69.2	65332	25 Salt of The Earth	50.4	65616	33 Midlife Junction	50.1
65048	42 Southern Satellites	66.2	65333	46 Rooted Rural	51.9	65617	26 Midland Crowd	88.2
65049	15 Silver and Gold	55.9	65334	46 Rooted Rural	59.8	65618	46 Rooted Rural	100.0
65050	42 Southern Satellites	100.0	65335	46 Rooted Rural	64.4	65619	19 Milk and Cookies	42.5
65051	25 Salt of The Earth	43.7	65336	26 Midland Crowd	28.3	65620	42 Southern Satellites	100.0
65052	31 Rural Resort Dwellers	61.9	65337	53 Home Town	54.8	65622	50 Heartland Communities	26.1
65053	17 Green Acres	74.1	65338	50 Heartland Communities	55.3	65623	42 Southern Satellites	98.9
65054	25 Salt of The Earth	100.0	65339	37 Prairie Living	100.0	65624	46 Rooted Rural	71.1
65058	25 Salt of The Earth	57.1	65340	53 Home Town	31.8	65625	46 Rooted Rural	27.9
65059	26 Midland Crowd	71.1	65344	37 Prairie Living	95.6	65626	46 Rooted Rural	57.5
65061	46 Rooted Rural	75.1	65345	25 Salt of The Earth	90.7	65627	41 Crossroads	95.0
65062	46 Rooted Rural	100.0	65347	37 Prairie Living	49.7	65629	42 Southern Satellites	79.8
65063	26 Midland Crowd	72.8	65348	46 Rooted Rural	92.9	65630	17 Green Acres	42.9
65064	26 Midland Crowd	51.9	65349	50 Heartland Communities	59.4	65631	26 Midland Crowd	67.2
65065	31 Rural Resort Dwellers	70.9	65350	32 Rustbelt Traditions	61.5	65632	46 Rooted Rural	64.5
65066	42 Southern Satellites	36.8	65351	50 Heartland Communities	58.5	65633	50 Heartland Communities	94.2
65067	42 Southern Satellites	91.3	65354	42 Southern Satellites	97.3	65634	46 Rooted Rural	95.6
65068	25 Salt of The Earth	77.5	65355	49 Senior Sun Seekers	46.8	65635	46 Rooted Rural	89.3
65069	42 Southern Satellites	65.2	65360	50 Heartland Communities	61.0	65637	46 Rooted Rural	59.7

    425

ZIP CODE	TOP TAPESTRY CONSUMER TYPE	% 2004 HOUSE-HOLDS	ZIP CODE	TOP TAPESTRY CONSUMER TYPE	% 2004 HOUSE-HOLDS	ZIP CODE	TOP TAPESTRY CONSUMER TYPE	% 2004 HOUSE-HOLDS
65638	37 Prairie Living	60.0	65769	42 Southern Satellites	93.6	66093	37 Prairie Living	100.0
65640	46 Rooted Rural	96.0	65770	25 Salt of The Earth	75.2	66094	37 Prairie Living	97.8
65641	46 Rooted Rural	46.6	65771	26 Midland Crowd	99.7	66095	46 Rooted Rural	81.9
65644	42 Southern Satellites	87.8	65772	42 Southern Satellites	98.8	66097	25 Salt of The Earth	94.0
65646	46 Rooted Rural	44.4	65773	46 Rooted Rural	76.4	66101	62 Modest Income Homes	20.7
65647	42 Southern Satellites	94.4	65774	46 Rooted Rural	90.0	66102	53 Home Town	43.0
65648	26 Midland Crowd	84.2	65775	46 Rooted Rural	24.5	66103	39 Young and Restless	39.0
65649	31 Rural Resort Dwellers	46.9	65777	46 Rooted Rural	100.0	66104	32 Rustbelt Traditions	22.1
65650	46 Rooted Rural	99.5	65778	46 Rooted Rural	100.0	66105	59 Southwestern Families	51.8
65652	42 Southern Satellites	59.3	65779	49 Senior Sun Seekers	59.2	66106	32 Rustbelt Traditions	45.3
65653	49 Senior Sun Seekers	35.6	65781	25 Salt of The Earth	51.6	66109	32 Rustbelt Traditions	34.0
65654	37 Prairie Living	100.0	65783	42 Southern Satellites	74.8	66111	41 Crossroads	30.6
65655	46 Rooted Rural	62.7	65784	46 Rooted Rural	100.0	66112	32 Rustbelt Traditions	17.7
65656	46 Rooted Rural	80.8	65785	46 Rooted Rural	52.6	66113	41 Crossroads	100.0
65657	42 Southern Satellites	100.0	65786	42 Southern Satellites	44.6	66118	66 Unclassified	100.0
65658	31 Rural Resort Dwellers	100.0	65787	31 Rural Resort Dwellers	44.0	66202	36 Old and Newcomers	29.0
65660	37 Prairie Living	100.0	65788	42 Southern Satellites	74.4	66203	24 Main Street, USA	14.3
65661	50 Heartland Communities	78.6	65789	46 Rooted Rural	82.4	66204	36 Old and Newcomers	29.1
65662	42 Southern Satellites	69.9	65790	42 Southern Satellites	79.9	66205	22 Metropolitans	30.6
65663	46 Rooted Rural	45.2	65791	50 Heartland Communities	71.7	66206	03 Connoisseurs	49.9
65666	46 Rooted Rural	70.6	65793	46 Rooted Rural	61.3	66207	14 Prosperous Empty Nesters	54.4
65667	50 Heartland Communities	35.4	65802	53 Home Town	29.5	66208	22 Metropolitans	24.7
65668	49 Senior Sun Seekers	95.7	65803	53 Home Town	31.0	66209	02 Suburban Splendor	53.4
65669	26 Midland Crowd	88.8	65804	33 Midlife Junction	21.8	66210	16 Enterprising Professionals	39.4
65672	48 Great Expectations	42.8	65806	63 Dorms To Diplomas	27.8	66211	01 Top Rung	67.1
65674	50 Heartland Communities	75.0	65807	33 Midlife Junction	12.0	66212	14 Prosperous Empty Nesters	20.6
65675	46 Rooted Rural	55.5	65809	07 Exurbanites	44.6	66213	04 Boomburbs	58.7
65676	31 Rural Resort Dwellers	82.3	65810	17 Green Acres	28.7	66214	39 Young and Restless	31.6
65679	46 Rooted Rural	85.4	66002	25 Salt of The Earth	26.4	66215	39 Young and Restless	20.5
65680	49 Senior Sun Seekers	60.8	66006	17 Green Acres	42.4	66216	18 Cozy and Comfortable	21.1
65681	31 Rural Resort Dwellers	100.0	66007	18 Cozy and Comfortable	62.5	66217	02 Suburban Splendor	59.6
65682	37 Prairie Living	54.4	66008	37 Prairie Living	100.0	66218	04 Boomburbs	63.2
65685	46 Rooted Rural	67.9	66010	37 Prairie Living	96.5	66219	16 Enterprising Professionals	39.3
65686	15 Silver and Gold	38.0	66012	48 Great Expectations	28.0	66220	02 Suburban Splendor	100.0
65688	42 Southern Satellites	100.0	66013	17 Green Acres	33.7	66221	04 Boomburbs	86.0
65689	50 Heartland Communities	59.6	66014	46 Rooted Rural	84.9	66223	04 Boomburbs	100.0
65690	46 Rooted Rural	100.0	66015	37 Prairie Living	98.1	66224	04 Boomburbs	100.0
65692	46 Rooted Rural	62.4	66016	25 Salt of The Earth	100.0	66226	04 Boomburbs	77.6
65701	46 Rooted Rural	100.0	66017	37 Prairie Living	100.0	66227	07 Exurbanites	66.5
65702	46 Rooted Rural	100.0	66018	17 Green Acres	99.9	66401	29 Rustbelt Retirees	44.0
65704	53 Home Town	44.8	66020	26 Midland Crowd	66.7	66402	19 Milk and Cookies	50.8
65705	25 Salt of The Earth	35.4	66021	19 Milk and Cookies	58.0	66403	37 Prairie Living	100.0
65706	50 Heartland Communities	32.2	66023	37 Prairie Living	69.3	66404	37 Prairie Living	100.0
65707	50 Heartland Communities	42.4	66025	28 Aspiring Young Families	39.1	66406	37 Prairie Living	100.0
65708	50 Heartland Communities	26.8	66026	17 Green Acres	68.8	66407	25 Salt of The Earth	95.1
65710	46 Rooted Rural	57.7	66027	40 Military Proximity	98.6	66408	37 Prairie Living	100.0
65711	53 Home Town	31.6	66030	12 Up and Coming Families	29.7	66409	17 Green Acres	95.1
65712	50 Heartland Communities	42.5	66032	50 Heartland Communities	51.6	66411	50 Heartland Communities	80.3
65713	42 Southern Satellites	60.7	66033	37 Prairie Living	84.5	66412	37 Prairie Living	100.0
65714	28 Aspiring Young Families	34.3	66035	50 Heartland Communities	82.2	66413	50 Heartland Communities	62.8
65715	37 Prairie Living	83.3	66039	46 Rooted Rural	70.4	66414	17 Green Acres	32.8
65717	46 Rooted Rural	93.9	66040	46 Rooted Rural	49.8	66415	50 Heartland Communities	83.8
65720	42 Southern Satellites	100.0	66041	25 Salt of The Earth	76.2	66416	37 Prairie Living	100.0
65721	12 Up and Coming Families	33.9	66042	25 Salt of The Earth	77.3	66417	37 Prairie Living	86.8
65722	42 Southern Satellites	95.8	66043	18 Cozy and Comfortable	43.8	66418	25 Salt of The Earth	100.0
65723	42 Southern Satellites	36.2	66044	63 Dorms To Diplomas	26.9	66419	37 Prairie Living	86.6
65724	49 Senior Sun Seekers	100.0	66045	63 Dorms To Diplomas	97.8	66422	25 Salt of The Earth	100.0
65725	26 Midland Crowd	48.8	66046	55 College Towns	25.4	66423	46 Rooted Rural	92.1
65727	46 Rooted Rural	100.0	66047	22 Metropolitans	30.4	66424	37 Prairie Living	100.0
65728	26 Midland Crowd	100.0	66048	48 Great Expectations	25.1	66425	37 Prairie Living	90.3
65729	31 Rural Resort Dwellers	61.0	66049	13 In Style	30.7	66427	50 Heartland Communities	73.3
65730	26 Midland Crowd	50.7	66050	26 Midland Crowd	62.1	66428	37 Prairie Living	100.0
65731	46 Rooted Rural	100.0	66052	25 Salt of The Earth	58.1	66429	25 Salt of The Earth	80.5
65732	46 Rooted Rural	96.3	66053	17 Green Acres	44.2	66431	37 Prairie Living	56.0
65733	46 Rooted Rural	98.8	66054	17 Green Acres	61.4	66432	37 Prairie Living	100.0
65734	42 Southern Satellites	74.2	66056	46 Rooted Rural	89.6	66434	50 Heartland Communities	39.6
65735	46 Rooted Rural	53.4	66058	37 Prairie Living	100.0	66436	33 Midlife Junction	25.7
65737	46 Rooted Rural	54.0	66060	37 Prairie Living	88.8	66438	37 Prairie Living	100.0
65738	26 Midland Crowd	65.3	66061	28 Aspiring Young Families	27.4	66439	50 Heartland Communities	86.7
65739	31 Rural Resort Dwellers	100.0	66062	12 Up and Coming Families	28.0	66440	25 Salt of The Earth	100.0
65740	49 Senior Sun Seekers	99.9	66064	53 Home Town	26.0	66441	33 Midlife Junction	20.7
65742	26 Midland Crowd	56.6	66066	25 Salt of The Earth	63.3	66442	40 Military Proximity	93.4
65744	46 Rooted Rural	100.0	66067	32 Rustbelt Traditions	32.1	66449	37 Prairie Living	98.4
65745	42 Southern Satellites	100.0	66070	17 Green Acres	50.7	66451	25 Salt of The Earth	86.5
65746	42 Southern Satellites	58.2	66071	17 Green Acres	45.0	66502	55 College Towns	31.1
65747	31 Rural Resort Dwellers	73.7	66072	46 Rooted Rural	91.1	66503	16 Enterprising Professionals	31.5
65752	37 Prairie Living	99.1	66073	26 Midland Crowd	67.0	66506	63 Dorms To Diplomas	100.0
65753	42 Southern Satellites	70.9	66075	46 Rooted Rural	65.1	66507	25 Salt of The Earth	77.7
65754	26 Midland Crowd	100.0	66076	46 Rooted Rural	68.1	66508	50 Heartland Communities	66.7
65755	46 Rooted Rural	100.0	66078	17 Green Acres	62.7	66509	25 Salt of The Earth	92.7
65756	42 Southern Satellites	98.7	66079	25 Salt of The Earth	100.0	66510	46 Rooted Rural	98.2
65757	26 Midland Crowd	77.2	66080	42 Southern Satellites	60.6	66512	17 Green Acres	51.6
65759	42 Southern Satellites	70.1	66083	17 Green Acres	43.4	66514	26 Midland Crowd	99.8
65760	46 Rooted Rural	100.0	66085	04 Boomburbs	38.3	66515	37 Prairie Living	100.0
65761	49 Senior Sun Seekers	81.6	66086	17 Green Acres	57.6	66516	37 Prairie Living	91.9
65762	37 Prairie Living	69.2	66087	50 Heartland Communities	42.0	66517	28 Aspiring Young Families	100.0
65764	37 Prairie Living	91.0	66088	37 Prairie Living	49.7	66518	37 Prairie Living	100.0
65766	46 Rooted Rural	97.2	66090	41 Crossroads	29.1	66520	37 Prairie Living	100.0
65767	46 Rooted Rural	100.0	66091	37 Prairie Living	51.1	66521	50 Heartland Communities	54.6
65768	37 Prairie Living	92.9	66092	26 Midland Crowd	33.6	66522	37 Prairie Living	100.0

ZIP CODE	TOP TAPESTRY CONSUMER TYPE	% 2004 HOUSE-HOLDS	ZIP CODE	TOP TAPESTRY CONSUMER TYPE	% 2004 HOUSE-HOLDS	ZIP CODE	TOP TAPESTRY CONSUMER TYPE	% 2004 HOUSE-HOLDS
66523	50 Heartland Communities	79.0	66783	50 Heartland Communities	72.7	67029	50 Heartland Communities	78.6
66524	17 Green Acres	49.1	66801	55 College Towns	12.2	67030	17 Green Acres	82.2
66526	25 Salt of The Earth	93.0	66830	37 Prairie Living	84.2	67031	25 Salt of The Earth	53.1
66527	50 Heartland Communities	100.0	66833	37 Prairie Living	93.6	67035	37 Prairie Living	100.0
66528	42 Southern Satellites	98.6	66834	37 Prairie Living	100.0	67036	37 Prairie Living	100.0
66531	37 Prairie Living	96.9	66835	25 Salt of The Earth	100.0	67037	06 Sophisticated Squires	21.0
66532	37 Prairie Living	95.7	66838	37 Prairie Living	100.0	67038	37 Prairie Living	100.0
66533	17 Green Acres	54.5	66839	50 Heartland Communities	51.5	67039	32 Rustbelt Traditions	44.9
66534	50 Heartland Communities	78.8	66840	37 Prairie Living	99.7	67042	32 Rustbelt Traditions	20.2
66535	26 Midland Crowd	100.0	66842	37 Prairie Living	100.0	67045	50 Heartland Communities	80.6
66536	25 Salt of The Earth	59.8	66843	37 Prairie Living	100.0	67047	46 Rooted Rural	81.7
66537	46 Rooted Rural	92.1	66845	50 Heartland Communities	78.2	67049	37 Prairie Living	100.0
66538	50 Heartland Communities	75.2	66846	50 Heartland Communities	49.1	67050	17 Green Acres	98.8
66539	17 Green Acres	100.0	66849	37 Prairie Living	100.0	67051	37 Prairie Living	89.8
66540	37 Prairie Living	90.6	66850	37 Prairie Living	100.0	67052	19 Milk and Cookies	38.3
66541	37 Prairie Living	100.0	66851	50 Heartland Communities	89.2	67053	25 Salt of The Earth	100.0
66542	17 Green Acres	54.9	66852	37 Prairie Living	88.5	67054	50 Heartland Communities	92.8
66543	25 Salt of The Earth	93.4	66853	46 Rooted Rural	82.5	67055	04 Boomburbs	100.0
66544	37 Prairie Living	91.2	66854	46 Rooted Rural	84.6	67056	32 Rustbelt Traditions	42.8
66546	17 Green Acres	84.3	66856	25 Salt of The Earth	88.9	67057	37 Prairie Living	100.0
66547	17 Green Acres	56.6	66857	37 Prairie Living	100.0	67058	50 Heartland Communities	77.9
66548	50 Heartland Communities	79.7	66858	37 Prairie Living	100.0	67059	37 Prairie Living	100.0
66549	46 Rooted Rural	69.5	66859	37 Prairie Living	100.0	67060	25 Salt of The Earth	35.0
66550	37 Prairie Living	100.0	66860	50 Heartland Communities	71.7	67061	37 Prairie Living	100.0
66552	37 Prairie Living	100.0	66861	25 Salt of The Earth	36.1	67062	26 Midland Crowd	52.8
66554	37 Prairie Living	59.6	66862	37 Prairie Living	100.0	67063	50 Heartland Communities	35.0
66603	48 Great Expectations	31.8	66864	25 Salt of The Earth	100.0	67065	37 Prairie Living	100.0
66604	32 Rustbelt Traditions	20.6	66865	25 Salt of The Earth	98.6	67066	37 Prairie Living	100.0
66605	53 Home Town	35.8	66866	37 Prairie Living	61.7	67067	06 Sophisticated Squires	94.1
66606	32 Rustbelt Traditions	29.2	66868	25 Salt of The Earth	77.2	67068	50 Heartland Communities	29.2
66607	60 City Dimensions	34.9	66869	50 Heartland Communities	56.6	67070	37 Prairie Living	100.0
66608	53 Home Town	49.9	66870	46 Rooted Rural	96.8	67071	37 Prairie Living	100.0
66609	26 Midland Crowd	35.1	66871	46 Rooted Rural	81.2	67072	25 Salt of The Earth	90.9
66610	07 Exurbanites	38.1	66872	50 Heartland Communities	63.7	67073	37 Prairie Living	100.0
66611	22 Metropolitans	23.2	66873	37 Prairie Living	100.0	67074	25 Salt of The Earth	75.1
66612	65 Social Security Set	32.9	66901	50 Heartland Communities	42.6	67101	17 Green Acres	55.8
66614	13 In Style	24.3	66930	37 Prairie Living	100.0	67102	37 Prairie Living	100.0
66615	12 Up and Coming Families	51.8	66932	37 Prairie Living	100.0	67103	37 Prairie Living	100.0
66616	32 Rustbelt Traditions	39.5	66933	37 Prairie Living	100.0	67104	37 Prairie Living	71.5
66617	17 Green Acres	49.9	66935	50 Heartland Communities	75.4	67105	25 Salt of The Earth	86.2
66618	17 Green Acres	73.6	66936	37 Prairie Living	100.0	67106	25 Salt of The Earth	92.9
66619	28 Aspiring Young Families	74.7	66937	37 Prairie Living	100.0	67107	33 Midlife Junction	43.7
66701	53 Home Town	33.6	66938	50 Heartland Communities	74.8	67108	25 Salt of The Earth	80.7
66710	50 Heartland Communities	68.0	66939	37 Prairie Living	100.0	67109	37 Prairie Living	100.0
66711	50 Heartland Communities	93.6	66940	37 Prairie Living	100.0	67110	19 Milk and Cookies	45.5
66712	50 Heartland Communities	95.9	66941	37 Prairie Living	100.0	67111	25 Salt of The Earth	100.0
66713	50 Heartland Communities	35.4	66942	37 Prairie Living	100.0	67112	37 Prairie Living	100.0
66714	46 Rooted Rural	50.4	66943	50 Heartland Communities	80.3	67114	26 Midland Crowd	27.3
66716	46 Rooted Rural	89.1	66944	37 Prairie Living	100.0	67117	30 Retirement Communities	100.0
66717	46 Rooted Rural	100.0	66945	37 Prairie Living	100.0	67118	25 Salt of The Earth	100.0
66720	32 Rustbelt Traditions	28.8	66946	37 Prairie Living	100.0	67119	50 Heartland Communities	76.6
66724	50 Heartland Communities	79.3	66948	37 Prairie Living	100.0	67120	17 Green Acres	78.7
66725	50 Heartland Communities	70.1	66949	50 Heartland Communities	84.9	67122	37 Prairie Living	68.6
66728	25 Salt of The Earth	100.0	66951	37 Prairie Living	100.0	67123	25 Salt of The Earth	92.8
66732	37 Prairie Living	100.0	66952	37 Prairie Living	100.0	67124	33 Midlife Junction	42.5
66733	50 Heartland Communities	55.5	66953	37 Prairie Living	91.4	67127	50 Heartland Communities	84.3
66734	37 Prairie Living	95.3	66955	37 Prairie Living	100.0	67131	25 Salt of The Earth	100.0
66735	46 Rooted Rural	93.3	66956	50 Heartland Communities	66.2	67132	25 Salt of The Earth	97.6
66736	50 Heartland Communities	73.2	66958	37 Prairie Living	98.2	67133	17 Green Acres	41.8
66738	46 Rooted Rural	92.4	66959	37 Prairie Living	100.0	67134	37 Prairie Living	100.0
66739	53 Home Town	25.2	66960	37 Prairie Living	100.0	67135	32 Rustbelt Traditions	45.7
66740	46 Rooted Rural	87.6	66961	37 Prairie Living	100.0	67137	37 Prairie Living	93.1
66743	25 Salt of The Earth	47.8	66962	37 Prairie Living	100.0	67138	37 Prairie Living	100.0
66746	37 Prairie Living	100.0	66963	37 Prairie Living	98.6	67140	37 Prairie Living	100.0
66748	50 Heartland Communities	76.4	66964	37 Prairie Living	100.0	67142	37 Prairie Living	75.0
66749	57 Simple Living	16.7	66966	37 Prairie Living	100.0	67143	37 Prairie Living	100.0
66751	42 Southern Satellites	87.4	66967	50 Heartland Communities	82.9	67144	26 Midland Crowd	100.0
66753	37 Prairie Living	91.4	66968	50 Heartland Communities	77.2	67146	25 Salt of The Earth	94.6
66754	46 Rooted Rural	100.0	66970	37 Prairie Living	100.0	67147	17 Green Acres	50.0
66755	37 Prairie Living	100.0	67001	25 Salt of The Earth	85.1	67149	26 Midland Crowd	54.9
66756	46 Rooted Rural	98.9	67002	12 Up and Coming Families	53.9	67150	37 Prairie Living	100.0
66757	42 Southern Satellites	27.2	67003	50 Heartland Communities	93.4	67151	25 Salt of The Earth	85.7
66758	37 Prairie Living	100.0	67004	50 Heartland Communities	74.7	67152	50 Heartland Communities	31.7
66759	46 Rooted Rural	65.6	67005	53 Home Town	29.8	67154	25 Salt of The Earth	76.1
66761	37 Prairie Living	100.0	67008	46 Rooted Rural	57.7	67155	37 Prairie Living	100.0
66762	55 College Towns	22.4	67009	50 Heartland Communities	69.8	67156	50 Heartland Communities	18.4
66763	50 Heartland Communities	88.7	67010	17 Green Acres	37.4	67159	37 Prairie Living	100.0
66767	46 Rooted Rural	100.0	67013	32 Rustbelt Traditions	59.9	67202	65 Social Security Set	80.1
66769	37 Prairie Living	66.7	67016	26 Midland Crowd	100.0	67203	53 Home Town	17.9
66770	25 Salt of The Earth	99.5	67017	17 Green Acres	89.6	67204	25 Salt of The Earth	17.9
66771	37 Prairie Living	93.3	67018	37 Prairie Living	100.0	67205	04 Boomburbs	50.5
66772	37 Prairie Living	100.0	67019	46 Rooted Rural	80.2	67206	14 Prosperous Empty Nesters	40.8
66773	46 Rooted Rural	74.2	67020	32 Rustbelt Traditions	65.2	67207	28 Aspiring Young Families	21.1
66775	37 Prairie Living	100.0	67021	37 Prairie Living	100.0	67208	48 Great Expectations	21.0
66776	42 Southern Satellites	74.6	67022	50 Heartland Communities	78.2	67209	12 Up and Coming Families	32.8
66777	49 Senior Sun Seekers	97.2	67023	46 Rooted Rural	94.1	67210	12 Up and Coming Families	17.5
66778	46 Rooted Rural	100.0	67024	50 Heartland Communities	62.5	67211	53 Home Town	44.8
66779	37 Prairie Living	100.0	67025	25 Salt of The Earth	73.5	67212	06 Sophisticated Squires	18.7
66780	37 Prairie Living	100.0	67026	17 Green Acres	65.9	67213	53 Home Town	62.6
66781	46 Rooted Rural	74.3	67028	37 Prairie Living	100.0	67214	62 Modest Income Homes	42.2

ZIP CODE	TOP TAPESTRY CONSUMER TYPE	% 2004 HOUSE-HOLDS	ZIP CODE	TOP TAPESTRY CONSUMER TYPE	% 2004 HOUSE-HOLDS	ZIP CODE	TOP TAPESTRY CONSUMER TYPE	% 2004 HOUSE-HOLDS
67215	19 Milk and Cookies	49.3	67487	26 Midland Crowd	82.5	67661	50 Heartland Communities	54.0
67216	41 Crossroads	28.4	67490	50 Heartland Communities	81.1	67663	50 Heartland Communities	77.7
67217	32 Rustbelt Traditions	43.2	67491	37 Prairie Living	100.0	67664	37 Prairie Living	100.0
67218	32 Rustbelt Traditions	23.7	67492	37 Prairie Living	100.0	67665	50 Heartland Communities	93.1
67219	19 Milk and Cookies	23.5	67501	53 Home Town	37.8	67669	50 Heartland Communities	79.6
67220	12 Up and Coming Families	23.2	67502	29 Rustbelt Retirees	17.2	67671	29 Rustbelt Retirees	42.2
67221	40 Military Proximity	100.0	67505	42 Southern Satellites	54.2	67672	50 Heartland Communities	64.4
67223	06 Sophisticated Squires	76.3	67510	37 Prairie Living	100.0	67673	37 Prairie Living	97.8
67226	04 Boomburbs	32.2	67511	37 Prairie Living	100.0	67675	37 Prairie Living	100.0
67227	17 Green Acres	100.0	67512	37 Prairie Living	100.0	67701	33 Midlife Junction	36.5
67228	04 Boomburbs	100.0	67513	37 Prairie Living	100.0	67730	50 Heartland Communities	75.0
67230	04 Boomburbs	40.6	67514	37 Prairie Living	100.0	67731	37 Prairie Living	100.0
67232	17 Green Acres	100.0	67516	37 Prairie Living	100.0	67732	37 Prairie Living	100.0
67235	04 Boomburbs	60.7	67518	37 Prairie Living	100.0	67733	37 Prairie Living	100.0
67301	53 Home Town	31.8	67519	37 Prairie Living	100.0	67734	37 Prairie Living	100.0
67330	50 Heartland Communities	82.3	67520	50 Heartland Communities	93.8	67735	37 Prairie Living	21.8
67332	37 Prairie Living	100.0	67521	37 Prairie Living	100.0	67736	37 Prairie Living	100.0
67333	50 Heartland Communities	75.3	67522	25 Salt of The Earth	94.8	67737	37 Prairie Living	100.0
67335	50 Heartland Communities	51.1	67523	37 Prairie Living	100.0	67738	37 Prairie Living	100.0
67336	50 Heartland Communities	85.8	67524	46 Rooted Rural	90.8	67739	37 Prairie Living	100.0
67337	50 Heartland Communities	22.2	67525	37 Prairie Living	100.0	67740	37 Prairie Living	100.0
67341	25 Salt of The Earth	100.0	67526	50 Heartland Communities	61.6	67741	37 Prairie Living	100.0
67342	25 Salt of The Earth	93.5	67529	37 Prairie Living	100.0	67743	37 Prairie Living	100.0
67344	46 Rooted Rural	67.5	67530	33 Midlife Junction	15.5	67744	37 Prairie Living	100.0
67345	37 Prairie Living	90.8	67543	25 Salt of The Earth	62.8	67745	37 Prairie Living	100.0
67346	46 Rooted Rural	93.8	67544	50 Heartland Communities	74.5	67748	50 Heartland Communities	92.5
67347	46 Rooted Rural	100.0	67545	37 Prairie Living	100.0	67749	50 Heartland Communities	55.7
67349	50 Heartland Communities	82.1	67546	50 Heartland Communities	57.7	67751	37 Prairie Living	100.0
67351	25 Salt of The Earth	100.0	67547	50 Heartland Communities	87.2	67752	37 Prairie Living	100.0
67352	50 Heartland Communities	83.4	67548	50 Heartland Communities	97.3	67753	37 Prairie Living	100.0
67353	50 Heartland Communities	93.0	67550	50 Heartland Communities	49.8	67756	50 Heartland Communities	72.2
67354	42 Southern Satellites	77.0	67552	37 Prairie Living	100.0	67757	37 Prairie Living	100.0
67355	46 Rooted Rural	100.0	67553	37 Prairie Living	100.0	67758	37 Prairie Living	100.0
67356	50 Heartland Communities	72.1	67554	50 Heartland Communities	59.4	67761	37 Prairie Living	100.0
67357	53 Home Town	35.8	67556	37 Prairie Living	100.0	67762	37 Prairie Living	100.0
67360	46 Rooted Rural	90.2	67557	37 Prairie Living	100.0	67764	37 Prairie Living	84.1
67361	50 Heartland Communities	77.1	67559	37 Prairie Living	100.0	67801	38 Industrious Urban Fringe	26.1
67401	53 Home Town	16.6	67560	37 Prairie Living	56.4	67831	37 Prairie Living	100.0
67410	50 Heartland Communities	18.2	67561	42 Southern Satellites	56.2	67834	37 Prairie Living	100.0
67416	26 Midland Crowd	76.4	67563	37 Prairie Living	100.0	67835	26 Midland Crowd	74.6
67417	37 Prairie Living	100.0	67564	37 Prairie Living	100.0	67837	37 Prairie Living	100.0
67418	37 Prairie Living	100.0	67565	50 Heartland Communities	68.0	67838	37 Prairie Living	99.8
67420	37 Prairie Living	68.7	67566	37 Prairie Living	100.0	67839	37 Prairie Living	68.9
67422	25 Salt of The Earth	94.3	67567	37 Prairie Living	100.0	67840	37 Prairie Living	100.0
67423	37 Prairie Living	100.0	67568	37 Prairie Living	100.0	67841	37 Prairie Living	100.0
67425	25 Salt of The Earth	77.6	67570	37 Prairie Living	100.0	67842	37 Prairie Living	100.0
67427	37 Prairie Living	100.0	67572	37 Prairie Living	100.0	67844	37 Prairie Living	100.0
67428	42 Southern Satellites	59.2	67573	37 Prairie Living	100.0	67846	41 Crossroads	29.2
67430	50 Heartland Communities	100.0	67574	37 Prairie Living	100.0	67849	37 Prairie Living	100.0
67431	29 Rustbelt Retirees	37.2	67575	37 Prairie Living	100.0	67850	37 Prairie Living	82.3
67432	50 Heartland Communities	51.7	67576	50 Heartland Communities	63.4	67851	19 Milk and Cookies	86.0
67436	37 Prairie Living	100.0	67578	50 Heartland Communities	85.0	67853	37 Prairie Living	100.0
67437	50 Heartland Communities	94.9	67579	33 Midlife Junction	43.1	67854	50 Heartland Communities	64.1
67438	37 Prairie Living	100.0	67581	37 Prairie Living	100.0	67855	37 Prairie Living	100.0
67439	29 Rustbelt Retirees	50.2	67583	37 Prairie Living	100.0	67857	37 Prairie Living	100.0
67441	37 Prairie Living	100.0	67584	37 Prairie Living	100.0	67859	41 Crossroads	56.1
67442	25 Salt of The Earth	83.6	67601	28 Aspiring Young Families	17.2	67860	26 Midland Crowd	76.0
67443	25 Salt of The Earth	62.8	67621	37 Prairie Living	100.0	67861	37 Prairie Living	66.3
67444	37 Prairie Living	100.0	67622	37 Prairie Living	100.0	67862	37 Prairie Living	100.0
67445	37 Prairie Living	100.0	67623	37 Prairie Living	100.0	67863	37 Prairie Living	100.0
67446	50 Heartland Communities	91.3	67625	37 Prairie Living	100.0	67864	50 Heartland Communities	84.3
67447	37 Prairie Living	100.0	67626	37 Prairie Living	100.0	67865	37 Prairie Living	100.0
67448	37 Prairie Living	86.6	67627	37 Prairie Living	100.0	67867	50 Heartland Communities	65.9
67449	50 Heartland Communities	60.9	67628	37 Prairie Living	100.0	67868	37 Prairie Living	100.0
67450	37 Prairie Living	100.0	67629	37 Prairie Living	100.0	67869	37 Prairie Living	99.1
67451	37 Prairie Living	100.0	67631	37 Prairie Living	100.0	67870	37 Prairie Living	98.4
67452	37 Prairie Living	100.0	67632	37 Prairie Living	100.0	67871	37 Prairie Living	42.7
67454	50 Heartland Communities	87.7	67634	37 Prairie Living	100.0	67876	37 Prairie Living	100.0
67455	50 Heartland Communities	45.4	67635	37 Prairie Living	100.0	67877	37 Prairie Living	60.7
67456	33 Midlife Junction	51.0	67637	32 Rustbelt Traditions	42.4	67878	37 Prairie Living	100.0
67457	37 Prairie Living	100.0	67638	37 Prairie Living	100.0	67879	37 Prairie Living	100.0
67458	37 Prairie Living	100.0	67639	37 Prairie Living	97.5	67880	26 Midland Crowd	28.6
67459	37 Prairie Living	100.0	67640	37 Prairie Living	100.0	67882	37 Prairie Living	75.2
67460	33 Midlife Junction	28.0	67642	50 Heartland Communities	84.8	67901	38 Industrious Urban Fringe	36.0
67464	37 Prairie Living	100.0	67643	37 Prairie Living	100.0	67950	26 Midland Crowd	51.8
67466	50 Heartland Communities	88.3	67644	37 Prairie Living	100.0	67951	37 Prairie Living	33.7
67467	29 Rustbelt Retirees	35.7	67645	37 Prairie Living	100.0	67952	37 Prairie Living	100.0
67468	37 Prairie Living	100.0	67646	37 Prairie Living	100.0	67953	37 Prairie Living	100.0
67470	17 Green Acres	77.0	67647	37 Prairie Living	100.0	67954	37 Prairie Living	100.0
67473	37 Prairie Living	58.1	67648	37 Prairie Living	100.0	68001	37 Prairie Living	100.0
67474	37 Prairie Living	98.0	67649	37 Prairie Living	100.0	68002	25 Salt of The Earth	66.0
67475	37 Prairie Living	100.0	67650	37 Prairie Living	100.0	68003	32 Rustbelt Traditions	37.2
67476	37 Prairie Living	100.0	67651	37 Prairie Living	100.0	68004	37 Prairie Living	100.0
67478	37 Prairie Living	100.0	67653	37 Prairie Living	100.0	68005	33 Midlife Junction	19.1
67480	25 Salt of The Earth	73.6	67654	50 Heartland Communities	87.4	68007	17 Green Acres	75.8
67481	37 Prairie Living	100.0	67656	37 Prairie Living	100.0	68008	48 Great Expectations	25.4
67482	17 Green Acres	100.0	67657	37 Prairie Living	100.0	68010	16 Enterprising Professionals	100.0
67483	37 Prairie Living	100.0	67658	37 Prairie Living	97.3	68014	37 Prairie Living	100.0
67484	37 Prairie Living	99.7	67659	37 Prairie Living	75.0	68015	25 Salt of The Earth	84.8
67485	37 Prairie Living	100.0	67660	37 Prairie Living	100.0	68017	25 Salt of The Earth	86.1

ZIP CODE	TOP TAPESTRY CONSUMER TYPE	% 2004 HOUSE-HOLDS	ZIP CODE	TOP TAPESTRY CONSUMER TYPE	% 2004 HOUSE-HOLDS	ZIP CODE	TOP TAPESTRY CONSUMER TYPE	% 2004 HOUSE-HOLDS
68018	37 Prairie Living	95.5	68322	37 Prairie Living	100.0	68452	37 Prairie Living	100.0
68019	37 Prairie Living	100.0	68323	37 Prairie Living	100.0	68453	37 Prairie Living	100.0
68020	37 Prairie Living	97.2	68324	37 Prairie Living	100.0	68454	17 Green Acres	87.5
68022	12 Up and Coming Families	35.8	68325	37 Prairie Living	100.0	68455	37 Prairie Living	97.3
68023	06 Sophisticated Squires	45.2	68326	37 Prairie Living	100.0	68456	37 Prairie Living	100.0
68025	32 Rustbelt Traditions	27.2	68327	37 Prairie Living	98.5	68457	46 Rooted Rural	89.8
68028	18 Cozy and Comfortable	34.8	68328	37 Prairie Living	100.0	68458	37 Prairie Living	87.3
68029	37 Prairie Living	100.0	68329	37 Prairie Living	100.0	68460	37 Prairie Living	100.0
68030	37 Prairie Living	98.3	68330	37 Prairie Living	100.0	68461	07 Exurbanites	68.1
68031	25 Salt of The Earth	59.7	68331	37 Prairie Living	100.0	68462	19 Milk and Cookies	76.1
68033	25 Salt of The Earth	68.7	68332	37 Prairie Living	100.0	68463	25 Salt of The Earth	68.2
68034	17 Green Acres	91.9	68333	33 Midlife Junction	49.2	68464	37 Prairie Living	97.5
68036	37 Prairie Living	100.0	68335	37 Prairie Living	100.0	68465	25 Salt of The Earth	91.8
68037	26 Midland Crowd	63.9	68336	17 Green Acres	100.0	68466	50 Heartland Communities	96.3
68038	50 Heartland Communities	73.7	68337	37 Prairie Living	95.2	68467	17 Green Acres	27.1
68039	51 Metro City Edge	83.2	68338	37 Prairie Living	100.0	68502	48 Great Expectations	37.4
68040	37 Prairie Living	100.0	68339	17 Green Acres	100.0	68503	48 Great Expectations	27.5
68041	25 Salt of The Earth	91.6	68340	37 Prairie Living	100.0	68504	48 Great Expectations	26.5
68044	26 Midland Crowd	73.2	68341	25 Salt of The Earth	77.4	68505	18 Cozy and Comfortable	22.8
68045	50 Heartland Communities	68.5	68342	37 Prairie Living	100.0	68506	13 In Style	15.2
68046	06 Sophisticated Squires	30.6	68343	37 Prairie Living	100.0	68507	32 Rustbelt Traditions	45.5
68047	29 Rustbelt Retirees	35.3	68344	37 Prairie Living	100.0	68508	55 College Towns	26.1
68048	17 Green Acres	29.7	68345	37 Prairie Living	100.0	68510	48 Great Expectations	17.6
68050	37 Prairie Living	100.0	68346	37 Prairie Living	100.0	68512	13 In Style	29.4
68055	37 Prairie Living	100.0	68347	19 Milk and Cookies	79.6	68514	17 Green Acres	86.7
68057	50 Heartland Communities	50.6	68348	37 Prairie Living	100.0	68516	04 Boomburbs	20.7
68059	07 Exurbanites	46.3	68349	37 Prairie Living	95.1	68517	17 Green Acres	81.4
68061	37 Prairie Living	100.0	68350	37 Prairie Living	100.0	68520	07 Exurbanites	89.0
68062	37 Prairie Living	100.0	68351	37 Prairie Living	100.0	68521	28 Aspiring Young Families	28.1
68064	33 Midlife Junction	37.6	68352	50 Heartland Communities	83.8	68522	28 Aspiring Young Families	51.9
68065	37 Prairie Living	74.5	68354	37 Prairie Living	100.0	68523	17 Green Acres	100.0
68066	50 Heartland Communities	46.3	68355	50 Heartland Communities	84.6	68524	28 Aspiring Young Families	66.0
68067	50 Heartland Communities	84.3	68357	37 Prairie Living	100.0	68526	07 Exurbanites	100.0
68069	25 Salt of The Earth	49.9	68358	17 Green Acres	85.7	68527	17 Green Acres	71.7
68070	37 Prairie Living	99.2	68359	29 Rustbelt Retirees	78.2	68528	12 Up and Coming Families	68.6
68071	51 Metro City Edge	90.2	68360	17 Green Acres	100.0	68531	17 Green Acres	100.0
68073	19 Milk and Cookies	81.0	68361	37 Prairie Living	61.5	68532	17 Green Acres	100.0
68102	65 Social Security Set	56.1	68362	50 Heartland Communities	100.0	68583	39 Young and Restless	100.0
68104	32 Rustbelt Traditions	42.6	68364	37 Prairie Living	100.0	68601	32 Rustbelt Traditions	29.4
68105	52 Inner City Tenants	19.3	68365	37 Prairie Living	100.0	68620	37 Prairie Living	75.4
68106	32 Rustbelt Traditions	16.8	68366	25 Salt of The Earth	91.6	68621	25 Salt of The Earth	65.1
68107	32 Rustbelt Traditions	39.1	68367	37 Prairie Living	100.0	68622	37 Prairie Living	100.0
68108	53 Home Town	34.1	68368	25 Salt of The Earth	82.2	68623	37 Prairie Living	100.0
68110	62 Modest Income Homes	42.4	68370	50 Heartland Communities	89.1	68624	37 Prairie Living	98.7
68111	51 Metro City Edge	57.3	68371	29 Rustbelt Retirees	73.0	68626	37 Prairie Living	100.0
68112	32 Rustbelt Traditions	44.1	68372	19 Milk and Cookies	53.3	68627	37 Prairie Living	100.0
68113	40 Military Proximity	99.3	68375	37 Prairie Living	79.7	68628	37 Prairie Living	100.0
68114	30 Retirement Communities	18.0	68376	50 Heartland Communities	82.8	68629	50 Heartland Communities	69.9
68116	04 Boomburbs	58.0	68377	37 Prairie Living	100.0	68631	37 Prairie Living	100.0
68117	32 Rustbelt Traditions	89.3	68378	37 Prairie Living	100.0	68632	50 Heartland Communities	75.1
68118	04 Boomburbs	52.1	68380	37 Prairie Living	100.0	68633	37 Prairie Living	100.0
68122	12 Up and Coming Families	76.7	68381	50 Heartland Communities	100.0	68635	37 Prairie Living	100.0
68123	40 Military Proximity	22.2	68401	37 Prairie Living	100.0	68636	37 Prairie Living	100.0
68124	14 Prosperous Empty Nesters	22.0	68402	17 Green Acres	100.0	68637	37 Prairie Living	100.0
68127	39 Young and Restless	40.8	68404	17 Green Acres	100.0	68638	37 Prairie Living	62.5
68128	19 Milk and Cookies	27.6	68405	33 Midlife Junction	69.2	68640	50 Heartland Communities	58.5
68130	06 Sophisticated Squires	53.2	68406	37 Prairie Living	100.0	68641	37 Prairie Living	100.0
68131	39 Young and Restless	30.0	68407	37 Prairie Living	83.5	68642	37 Prairie Living	100.0
68132	22 Metropolitans	15.6	68409	25 Salt of The Earth	76.5	68643	37 Prairie Living	100.0
68133	12 Up and Coming Families	43.5	68410	25 Salt of The Earth	35.5	68644	37 Prairie Living	98.5
68134	18 Cozy and Comfortable	28.5	68413	37 Prairie Living	96.5	68647	25 Salt of The Earth	72.3
68135	04 Boomburbs	78.1	68414	37 Prairie Living	100.0	68648	37 Prairie Living	100.0
68136	12 Up and Coming Families	61.3	68415	37 Prairie Living	100.0	68649	37 Prairie Living	59.4
68137	19 Milk and Cookies	45.9	68416	37 Prairie Living	100.0	68651	37 Prairie Living	100.0
68138	12 Up and Coming Families	46.6	68417	37 Prairie Living	100.0	68652	37 Prairie Living	100.0
68142	12 Up and Coming Families	70.9	68418	17 Green Acres	83.0	68653	37 Prairie Living	76.7
68144	07 Exurbanites	17.6	68420	50 Heartland Communities	82.0	68654	37 Prairie Living	100.0
68147	32 Rustbelt Traditions	56.2	68421	50 Heartland Communities	86.1	68655	37 Prairie Living	100.0
68152	07 Exurbanites	30.6	68422	37 Prairie Living	100.0	68658	37 Prairie Living	100.0
68154	39 Young and Restless	30.6	68423	17 Green Acres	100.0	68659	37 Prairie Living	100.0
68157	18 Cozy and Comfortable	40.6	68424	37 Prairie Living	100.0	68660	50 Heartland Communities	81.6
68164	12 Up and Coming Families	17.6	68428	17 Green Acres	100.0	68661	25 Salt of The Earth	29.9
68182	14 Prosperous Empty Nesters	0.0	68429	37 Prairie Living	100.0	68662	37 Prairie Living	100.0
68198	55 College Towns	0.0	68430	17 Green Acres	87.9	68663	37 Prairie Living	100.0
68301	37 Prairie Living	85.8	68431	37 Prairie Living	100.0	68665	37 Prairie Living	100.0
68303	37 Prairie Living	97.5	68433	37 Prairie Living	100.0	68666	50 Heartland Communities	76.9
68304	37 Prairie Living	100.0	68434	33 Midlife Junction	70.1	68667	37 Prairie Living	100.0
68305	50 Heartland Communities	45.5	68436	37 Prairie Living	100.0	68669	37 Prairie Living	100.0
68307	37 Prairie Living	99.6	68437	46 Rooted Rural	100.0	68701	48 Great Expectations	15.4
68309	50 Heartland Communities	100.0	68439	37 Prairie Living	100.0	68710	37 Prairie Living	100.0
68310	29 Rustbelt Retirees	21.2	68440	37 Prairie Living	100.0	68711	37 Prairie Living	100.0
68313	37 Prairie Living	100.0	68441	37 Prairie Living	100.0	68713	37 Prairie Living	100.0
68314	37 Prairie Living	98.3	68442	46 Rooted Rural	100.0	68714	50 Heartland Communities	66.6
68315	37 Prairie Living	98.7	68443	37 Prairie Living	100.0	68715	25 Salt of The Earth	86.5
68316	37 Prairie Living	100.0	68444	37 Prairie Living	100.0	68716	37 Prairie Living	100.0
68317	25 Salt of The Earth	47.6	68445	37 Prairie Living	100.0	68717	37 Prairie Living	100.0
68318	50 Heartland Communities	91.2	68446	29 Rustbelt Retirees	59.5	68718	50 Heartland Communities	65.5
68319	37 Prairie Living	100.0	68447	37 Prairie Living	100.0	68719	37 Prairie Living	100.0
68320	37 Prairie Living	100.0	68448	37 Prairie Living	100.0	68720	37 Prairie Living	100.0
68321	37 Prairie Living	97.8	68450	37 Prairie Living	52.2	68722	37 Prairie Living	100.0

ZIP CODE	TOP TAPESTRY CONSUMER TYPE	% 2004 HOUSEHOLDS	ZIP CODE	TOP TAPESTRY CONSUMER TYPE	% 2004 HOUSEHOLDS	ZIP CODE	TOP TAPESTRY CONSUMER TYPE	% 2004 HOUSEHOLDS
68723	37 Prairie Living	100.0	68841	37 Prairie Living	100.0	68981	37 Prairie Living	100.0
68724	37 Prairie Living	64.7	68842	37 Prairie Living	100.0	68982	37 Prairie Living	100.0
68725	37 Prairie Living	100.0	68843	37 Prairie Living	100.0	69001	50 Heartland Communities	29.1
68726	37 Prairie Living	100.0	68844	37 Prairie Living	100.0	69020	46 Rooted Rural	93.4
68727	50 Heartland Communities	74.4	68845	13 In Style	37.8	69021	37 Prairie Living	55.8
68728	37 Prairie Living	100.0	68846	37 Prairie Living	100.0	69022	50 Heartland Communities	54.3
68729	37 Prairie Living	100.0	68847	48 Great Expectations	24.0	69023	37 Prairie Living	100.0
68730	37 Prairie Living	100.0	68849	55 College Towns	100.0	69024	46 Rooted Rural	61.5
68731	38 Industrious Urban Fringe	73.8	68850	38 Industrious Urban Fringe	37.6	69025	50 Heartland Communities	84.7
68732	37 Prairie Living	100.0	68852	37 Prairie Living	100.0	69026	37 Prairie Living	100.0
68733	37 Prairie Living	60.5	68853	50 Heartland Communities	80.2	69027	37 Prairie Living	100.0
68734	37 Prairie Living	100.0	68854	37 Prairie Living	100.0	69028	37 Prairie Living	100.0
68735	37 Prairie Living	100.0	68855	37 Prairie Living	100.0	69029	37 Prairie Living	100.0
68736	37 Prairie Living	100.0	68856	37 Prairie Living	100.0	69030	37 Prairie Living	100.0
68739	50 Heartland Communities	64.3	68858	37 Prairie Living	100.0	69032	37 Prairie Living	100.0
68740	37 Prairie Living	100.0	68859	37 Prairie Living	100.0	69033	37 Prairie Living	54.1
68741	25 Salt of The Earth	62.3	68860	37 Prairie Living	100.0	69034	46 Rooted Rural	67.5
68742	37 Prairie Living	100.0	68861	17 Green Acres	100.0	69036	37 Prairie Living	100.0
68743	25 Salt of The Earth	99.2	68862	50 Heartland Communities	51.4	69037	37 Prairie Living	100.0
68745	50 Heartland Communities	67.0	68863	37 Prairie Living	100.0	69038	37 Prairie Living	100.0
68746	37 Prairie Living	100.0	68864	37 Prairie Living	100.0	69039	37 Prairie Living	78.4
68747	37 Prairie Living	100.0	68865	37 Prairie Living	100.0	69040	37 Prairie Living	100.0
68748	42 Southern Satellites	45.0	68866	37 Prairie Living	100.0	69041	37 Prairie Living	100.0
68749	37 Prairie Living	100.0	68869	50 Heartland Communities	70.6	69042	37 Prairie Living	100.0
68751	37 Prairie Living	100.0	68870	17 Green Acres	80.2	69043	37 Prairie Living	100.0
68752	37 Prairie Living	96.9	68871	37 Prairie Living	100.0	69044	50 Heartland Communities	79.9
68753	37 Prairie Living	100.0	68872	37 Prairie Living	100.0	69045	37 Prairie Living	100.0
68755	37 Prairie Living	100.0	68873	33 Midlife Junction	40.2	69046	37 Prairie Living	100.0
68756	50 Heartland Communities	48.0	68874	50 Heartland Communities	76.6	69101	53 Home Town	15.9
68757	37 Prairie Living	100.0	68875	37 Prairie Living	100.0	69120	37 Prairie Living	100.0
68758	50 Heartland Communities	86.9	68876	25 Salt of The Earth	70.0	69121	37 Prairie Living	100.0
68759	37 Prairie Living	100.0	68878	37 Prairie Living	100.0	69122	37 Prairie Living	95.4
68760	46 Rooted Rural	78.8	68879	37 Prairie Living	100.0	69123	37 Prairie Living	100.0
68761	37 Prairie Living	100.0	68881	37 Prairie Living	100.0	69125	37 Prairie Living	100.0
68763	37 Prairie Living	71.4	68882	37 Prairie Living	100.0	69127	31 Rural Resort Dwellers	83.2
68764	37 Prairie Living	100.0	68883	37 Prairie Living	99.9	69128	37 Prairie Living	100.0
68765	37 Prairie Living	100.0	68901	32 Rustbelt Traditions	23.7	69129	37 Prairie Living	100.0
68766	37 Prairie Living	100.0	68920	37 Prairie Living	56.9	69130	25 Salt of The Earth	24.5
68767	50 Heartland Communities	68.4	68922	50 Heartland Communities	86.9	69131	37 Prairie Living	100.0
68768	37 Prairie Living	100.0	68923	37 Prairie Living	100.0	69132	37 Prairie Living	100.0
68769	50 Heartland Communities	70.5	68924	37 Prairie Living	100.0	69133	37 Prairie Living	100.0
68770	37 Prairie Living	97.5	68925	37 Prairie Living	100.0	69134	37 Prairie Living	100.0
68771	37 Prairie Living	100.0	68926	50 Heartland Communities	83.2	69135	37 Prairie Living	100.0
68773	37 Prairie Living	100.0	68927	37 Prairie Living	100.0	69138	33 Midlife Junction	28.8
68774	37 Prairie Living	100.0	68928	37 Prairie Living	98.0	69140	37 Prairie Living	50.4
68776	38 Industrious Urban Fringe	21.9	68929	37 Prairie Living	94.9	69141	37 Prairie Living	100.0
68777	37 Prairie Living	100.0	68930	50 Heartland Communities	68.3	69142	37 Prairie Living	100.0
68778	37 Prairie Living	100.0	68932	37 Prairie Living	100.0	69143	25 Salt of The Earth	73.8
68779	37 Prairie Living	37.9	68933	46 Rooted Rural	86.0	69144	31 Rural Resort Dwellers	100.0
68780	37 Prairie Living	100.0	68934	37 Prairie Living	100.0	69145	50 Heartland Communities	92.3
68781	37 Prairie Living	50.5	68935	37 Prairie Living	100.0	69146	31 Rural Resort Dwellers	100.0
68783	37 Prairie Living	93.7	68936	50 Heartland Communities	83.2	69147	50 Heartland Communities	50.4
68784	50 Heartland Communities	60.1	68937	37 Prairie Living	71.3	69148	37 Prairie Living	100.0
68785	37 Prairie Living	100.0	68938	37 Prairie Living	100.0	69149	37 Prairie Living	100.0
68786	37 Prairie Living	100.0	68939	50 Heartland Communities	51.3	69150	37 Prairie Living	100.0
68787	55 College Towns	53.0	68940	37 Prairie Living	100.0	69151	37 Prairie Living	100.0
68788	50 Heartland Communities	41.3	68941	37 Prairie Living	100.0	69152	37 Prairie Living	100.0
68789	37 Prairie Living	100.0	68942	37 Prairie Living	86.6	69153	50 Heartland Communities	26.2
68790	37 Prairie Living	100.0	68943	37 Prairie Living	91.6	69154	50 Heartland Communities	78.2
68791	37 Prairie Living	100.0	68944	37 Prairie Living	99.8	69155	37 Prairie Living	95.8
68792	37 Prairie Living	100.0	68945	37 Prairie Living	100.0	69156	37 Prairie Living	100.0
68801	48 Great Expectations	21.5	68946	37 Prairie Living	100.0	69157	37 Prairie Living	100.0
68803	48 Great Expectations	19.8	68947	37 Prairie Living	100.0	69161	37 Prairie Living	100.0
68810	17 Green Acres	76.2	68948	37 Prairie Living	100.0	69162	32 Rustbelt Traditions	27.7
68812	37 Prairie Living	100.0	68949	32 Rustbelt Traditions	32.7	69163	37 Prairie Living	91.6
68813	37 Prairie Living	100.0	68950	37 Prairie Living	100.0	69165	37 Prairie Living	57.0
68814	37 Prairie Living	100.0	68952	37 Prairie Living	87.7	69166	37 Prairie Living	100.0
68815	37 Prairie Living	100.0	68954	37 Prairie Living	100.0	69167	37 Prairie Living	100.0
68816	37 Prairie Living	100.0	68955	26 Midland Crowd	78.8	69168	37 Prairie Living	100.0
68817	37 Prairie Living	100.0	68956	37 Prairie Living	100.0	69169	37 Prairie Living	95.4
68818	17 Green Acres	24.0	68957	37 Prairie Living	100.0	69170	37 Prairie Living	100.0
68819	37 Prairie Living	100.0	68958	37 Prairie Living	96.2	69201	33 Midlife Junction	39.3
68820	37 Prairie Living	100.0	68959	50 Heartland Communities	41.8	69210	37 Prairie Living	100.0
68821	37 Prairie Living	100.0	68960	37 Prairie Living	100.0	69211	37 Prairie Living	100.0
68822	50 Heartland Communities	70.4	68961	37 Prairie Living	100.0	69212	37 Prairie Living	100.0
68823	50 Heartland Communities	69.9	68964	37 Prairie Living	100.0	69214	37 Prairie Living	100.0
68824	37 Prairie Living	100.0	68966	31 Rural Resort Dwellers	85.0	69216	37 Prairie Living	100.0
68825	37 Prairie Living	100.0	68967	50 Heartland Communities	63.1	69217	37 Prairie Living	100.0
68826	50 Heartland Communities	63.5	68969	37 Prairie Living	100.0	69218	37 Prairie Living	100.0
68827	37 Prairie Living	86.1	68970	50 Heartland Communities	89.6	69221	37 Prairie Living	100.0
68828	37 Prairie Living	100.0	68971	37 Prairie Living	74.0	69301	32 Rustbelt Traditions	27.9
68831	37 Prairie Living	100.0	68972	37 Prairie Living	100.0	69331	37 Prairie Living	100.0
68832	26 Midland Crowd	56.4	68973	37 Prairie Living	100.0	69333	37 Prairie Living	100.0
68833	37 Prairie Living	100.0	68974	37 Prairie Living	100.0	69334	37 Prairie Living	40.0
68834	37 Prairie Living	100.0	68975	37 Prairie Living	87.5	69335	37 Prairie Living	100.0
68835	37 Prairie Living	100.0	68976	37 Prairie Living	100.0	69336	50 Heartland Communities	66.6
68836	42 Southern Satellites	68.2	68977	37 Prairie Living	100.0	69337	55 College Towns	52.9
68837	37 Prairie Living	100.0	68978	50 Heartland Communities	90.9	69339	50 Heartland Communities	68.6
68838	37 Prairie Living	100.0	68979	37 Prairie Living	64.7	69340	37 Prairie Living	100.0
68840	42 Southern Satellites	46.4	68980	37 Prairie Living	100.0	69341	29 Rustbelt Retirees	21.8

ZIP CODE	TOP TAPESTRY CONSUMER TYPE	% 2004 HOUSE-HOLDS	ZIP CODE	TOP TAPESTRY CONSUMER TYPE	% 2004 HOUSE-HOLDS	ZIP CODE	TOP TAPESTRY CONSUMER TYPE	% 2004 HOUSE-HOLDS
69343	37 Prairie Living	57.9	70357	56 Rural Bypasses	54.9	70581	25 Salt of The Earth	95.9
69345	37 Prairie Living	100.0	70358	46 Rooted Rural	51.7	70582	56 Rural Bypasses	29.7
69346	37 Prairie Living	100.0	70359	41 Crossroads	48.3	70583	41 Crossroads	38.3
69347	50 Heartland Communities	50.2	70360	06 Sophisticated Squires	14.7	70584	26 Midland Crowd	27.4
69348	37 Prairie Living	100.0	70363	53 Home Town	22.0	70586	62 Modest Income Homes	18.3
69350	37 Prairie Living	100.0	70364	28 Aspiring Young Families	16.1	70589	46 Rooted Rural	34.2
69351	37 Prairie Living	100.0	70372	56 Rural Bypasses	37.6	70591	50 Heartland Communities	29.1
69352	37 Prairie Living	100.0	70374	42 Southern Satellites	62.0	70592	12 Up and Coming Families	43.8
69354	37 Prairie Living	100.0	70375	42 Southern Satellites	89.5	70601	62 Modest Income Homes	29.5
69356	37 Prairie Living	53.0	70377	42 Southern Satellites	65.8	70605	07 Exurbanites	21.5
69357	37 Prairie Living	32.4	70380	42 Southern Satellites	18.1	70607	26 Midland Crowd	25.1
69358	50 Heartland Communities	54.5	70390	56 Rural Bypasses	43.2	70609	63 Dorms To Diplomas	100.0
69360	50 Heartland Communities	63.0	70392	26 Midland Crowd	47.6	70611	26 Midland Crowd	67.6
69361	48 Great Expectations	18.6	70394	56 Rural Bypasses	32.2	70615	34 Family Foundations	27.3
69366	37 Prairie Living	100.0	70395	26 Midland Crowd	66.4	70630	42 Southern Satellites	57.4
69367	37 Prairie Living	100.0	70397	37 Prairie Living	51.6	70631	56 Rural Bypasses	69.2
70001	39 Young and Restless	26.4	70401	55 College Towns	36.0	70632	46 Rooted Rural	79.9
70002	52 Inner City Tenants	21.7	70402	22 Metropolitans	0.0	70633	26 Midland Crowd	23.5
70003	18 Cozy and Comfortable	33.4	70403	26 Midland Crowd	48.1	70634	42 Southern Satellites	27.8
70005	14 Prosperous Empty Nesters	30.3	70420	26 Midland Crowd	69.2	70637	46 Rooted Rural	66.3
70006	14 Prosperous Empty Nesters	27.7	70422	56 Rural Bypasses	39.3	70639	46 Rooted Rural	100.0
70030	42 Southern Satellites	43.1	70426	56 Rural Bypasses	74.7	70643	46 Rooted Rural	100.0
70031	25 Salt of The Earth	97.8	70427	62 Modest Income Homes	38.7	70645	46 Rooted Rural	100.0
70032	29 Rustbelt Retirees	63.6	70431	26 Midland Crowd	58.8	70647	26 Midland Crowd	35.6
70036	46 Rooted Rural	100.0	70433	12 Up and Coming Families	35.4	70648	25 Salt of The Earth	26.2
70037	26 Midland Crowd	28.2	70435	17 Green Acres	52.1	70650	42 Southern Satellites	100.0
70039	41 Crossroads	54.9	70436	56 Rural Bypasses	93.3	70652	42 Southern Satellites	61.4
70040	56 Rural Bypasses	46.3	70437	26 Midland Crowd	61.5	70653	42 Southern Satellites	35.6
70041	56 Rural Bypasses	62.3	70438	46 Rooted Rural	34.2	70654	56 Rural Bypasses	100.0
70043	29 Rustbelt Retirees	26.4	70441	56 Rural Bypasses	92.1	70655	56 Rural Bypasses	38.4
70047	19 Milk and Cookies	32.3	70442	46 Rooted Rural	51.8	70656	42 Southern Satellites	44.3
70049	62 Modest Income Homes	69.0	70443	56 Rural Bypasses	55.6	70657	26 Midland Crowd	49.1
70051	56 Rural Bypasses	62.4	70444	56 Rural Bypasses	46.2	70658	46 Rooted Rural	100.0
70052	42 Southern Satellites	63.3	70445	26 Midland Crowd	48.5	70660	42 Southern Satellites	100.0
70053	48 Great Expectations	25.9	70446	56 Rural Bypasses	79.5	70661	46 Rooted Rural	58.3
70056	52 Inner City Tenants	22.9	70447	17 Green Acres	77.3	70662	42 Southern Satellites	100.0
70057	25 Salt of The Earth	48.9	70448	04 Boomburbs	39.2	70663	26 Midland Crowd	19.3
70058	19 Milk and Cookies	31.8	70449	46 Rooted Rural	42.0	70665	41 Crossroads	46.1
70062	51 Metro City Edge	24.1	70450	56 Rural Bypasses	67.8	70668	46 Rooted Rural	21.2
70065	13 In Style	12.5	70452	42 Southern Satellites	30.8	70669	26 Midland Crowd	31.2
70067	42 Southern Satellites	73.7	70453	56 Rural Bypasses	100.0	70706	26 Midland Crowd	61.6
70068	19 Milk and Cookies	38.4	70454	26 Midland Crowd	52.0	70710	26 Midland Crowd	52.1
70070	18 Cozy and Comfortable	22.8	70455	26 Midland Crowd	100.0	70711	26 Midland Crowd	65.5
70071	18 Cozy and Comfortable	33.8	70456	56 Rural Bypasses	92.0	70712	41 Crossroads	100.0
70072	19 Milk and Cookies	23.1	70458	19 Milk and Cookies	24.0	70714	51 Metro City Edge	27.7
70075	06 Sophisticated Squires	27.4	70460	19 Milk and Cookies	24.5	70715	56 Rural Bypasses	71.5
70076	56 Rural Bypasses	100.0	70461	06 Sophisticated Squires	48.8	70719	26 Midland Crowd	48.2
70079	32 Rustbelt Traditions	39.0	70462	46 Rooted Rural	58.3	70721	51 Metro City Edge	100.0
70080	26 Midland Crowd	92.2	70466	41 Crossroads	41.3	70722	56 Rural Bypasses	32.4
70081	66 Unclassified	100.0	70467	56 Rural Bypasses	100.0	70723	56 Rural Bypasses	100.0
70083	56 Rural Bypasses	81.0	70471	06 Sophisticated Squires	22.8	70725	26 Midland Crowd	100.0
70084	25 Salt of The Earth	30.4	70501	62 Modest Income Homes	39.8	70726	26 Midland Crowd	61.1
70085	41 Crossroads	38.8	70503	22 Metropolitans	20.2	70729	26 Midland Crowd	100.0
70086	56 Rural Bypasses	100.0	70504	14 Prosperous Empty Nesters	100.0	70730	26 Midland Crowd	58.1
70087	28 Aspiring Young Families	45.4	70506	28 Aspiring Young Families	28.8	70732	42 Southern Satellites	95.7
70090	42 Southern Satellites	37.9	70507	41 Crossroads	30.3	70733	26 Midland Crowd	100.0
70091	56 Rural Bypasses	100.0	70508	13 In Style	17.6	70734	41 Crossroads	68.0
70092	19 Milk and Cookies	32.3	70510	26 Midland Crowd	23.4	70736	56 Rural Bypasses	64.4
70094	53 Home Town	16.0	70512	56 Rural Bypasses	58.4	70737	26 Midland Crowd	81.0
70112	64 City Commons	63.7	70514	56 Rural Bypasses	36.8	70739	17 Green Acres	27.6
70113	64 City Commons	34.9	70515	56 Rural Bypasses	31.5	70740	56 Rural Bypasses	100.0
70114	52 Inner City Tenants	17.7	70516	26 Midland Crowd	41.9	70744	26 Midland Crowd	47.8
70115	22 Metropolitans	18.2	70517	56 Rural Bypasses	38.2	70748	56 Rural Bypasses	51.9
70116	08 Laptops and Lattes	21.1	70518	26 Midland Crowd	29.2	70749	31 Rural Resort Dwellers	55.3
70117	62 Modest Income Homes	55.2	70520	26 Midland Crowd	29.3	70750	26 Midland Crowd	100.0
70118	62 Modest Income Homes	19.4	70525	56 Rural Bypasses	40.8	70752	56 Rural Bypasses	75.4
70119	62 Modest Income Homes	18.4	70526	53 Home Town	26.8	70753	56 Rural Bypasses	100.0
70121	22 Metropolitans	19.0	70528	42 Southern Satellites	100.0	70754	26 Midland Crowd	56.6
70122	34 Family Foundations	30.6	70529	26 Midland Crowd	38.8	70755	42 Southern Satellites	80.7
70123	27 Metro Renters	18.7	70531	42 Southern Satellites	100.0	70756	56 Rural Bypasses	86.7
70124	22 Metropolitans	68.8	70532	56 Rural Bypasses	59.0	70757	56 Rural Bypasses	90.2
70125	22 Metropolitans	30.4	70533	42 Southern Satellites	61.1	70759	50 Heartland Communities	89.9
70126	34 Family Foundations	25.9	70535	50 Heartland Communities	27.4	70760	62 Modest Income Homes	38.9
70127	34 Family Foundations	27.5	70537	56 Rural Bypasses	63.4	70761	56 Rural Bypasses	100.0
70128	28 Aspiring Young Families	31.7	70538	56 Rural Bypasses	51.7	70762	26 Midland Crowd	76.5
70129	64 City Commons	41.9	70542	37 Prairie Living	43.4	70763	26 Midland Crowd	61.5
70130	27 Metro Renters	28.1	70543	56 Rural Bypasses	47.9	70764	26 Midland Crowd	28.3
70131	18 Cozy and Comfortable	20.9	70544	56 Rural Bypasses	56.8	70767	26 Midland Crowd	34.0
70301	26 Midland Crowd	20.4	70546	62 Modest Income Homes	15.1	70769	12 Up and Coming Families	55.3
70339	42 Southern Satellites	100.0	70548	50 Heartland Communities	20.6	70770	26 Midland Crowd	48.3
70341	56 Rural Bypasses	50.1	70549	56 Rural Bypasses	49.0	70772	56 Rural Bypasses	100.0
70342	56 Rural Bypasses	42.8	70552	42 Southern Satellites	71.4	70773	42 Southern Satellites	54.9
70343	17 Green Acres	47.8	70554	62 Modest Income Homes	59.1	70774	26 Midland Crowd	64.4
70344	42 Southern Satellites	47.9	70555	26 Midland Crowd	92.1	70775	26 Midland Crowd	54.0
70345	42 Southern Satellites	41.4	70559	56 Rural Bypasses	83.8	70776	26 Midland Crowd	53.2
70346	51 Metro City Edge	33.9	70560	42 Southern Satellites	18.6	70777	26 Midland Crowd	69.0
70353	56 Rural Bypasses	99.5	70563	17 Green Acres	26.2	70778	26 Midland Crowd	57.2
70354	46 Rooted Rural	61.4	70570	62 Modest Income Homes	34.7	70780	56 Rural Bypasses	100.0
70355	42 Southern Satellites	100.0	70577	56 Rural Bypasses	60.8	70783	31 Rural Resort Dwellers	51.3
70356	56 Rural Bypasses	100.0	70578	42 Southern Satellites	26.1	70785	26 Midland Crowd	95.5

ZIP CODE	TOP TAPESTRY CONSUMER TYPE	% 2004 HOUSE-HOLDS	ZIP CODE	TOP TAPESTRY CONSUMER TYPE	% 2004 HOUSE-HOLDS	ZIP CODE	TOP TAPESTRY CONSUMER TYPE	% 2004 HOUSE-HOLDS
70788	56 Rural Bypasses	69.2	71209	55 College Towns	100.0	71425	46 Rooted Rural	100.0
70789	56 Rural Bypasses	90.8	71219	46 Rooted Rural	100.0	71426	46 Rooted Rural	100.0
70791	56 Rural Bypasses	22.1	71220	62 Modest Income Homes	19.8	71427	56 Rural Bypasses	100.0
70792	56 Rural Bypasses	100.0	71222	56 Rural Bypasses	39.8	71429	46 Rooted Rural	52.6
70801	27 Metro Renters	100.0	71223	56 Rural Bypasses	92.7	71430	46 Rooted Rural	78.3
70802	62 Modest Income Homes	63.4	71225	26 Midland Crowd	100.0	71432	42 Southern Satellites	81.3
70803	63 Dorms To Diplomas	100.0	71226	56 Rural Bypasses	77.5	71433	56 Rural Bypasses	33.7
70805	51 Metro City Edge	73.3	71227	42 Southern Satellites	65.6	71435	56 Rural Bypasses	55.4
70806	57 Simple Living	19.1	71229	56 Rural Bypasses	53.9	71438	46 Rooted Rural	66.9
70807	62 Modest Income Homes	46.5	71232	56 Rural Bypasses	35.2	71439	46 Rooted Rural	99.8
70808	22 Metropolitans	23.8	71234	42 Southern Satellites	53.2	71441	46 Rooted Rural	72.5
70809	27 Metro Renters	19.8	71235	56 Rural Bypasses	35.3	71446	46 Rooted Rural	23.7
70810	02 Suburban Splendor	24.0	71237	56 Rural Bypasses	55.7	71447	56 Rural Bypasses	67.0
70811	32 Rustbelt Traditions	26.8	71238	26 Midland Crowd	61.5	71449	49 Senior Sun Seekers	25.4
70812	51 Metro City Edge	62.0	71241	42 Southern Satellites	28.1	71450	46 Rooted Rural	78.4
70813	51 Metro City Edge	100.0	71243	46 Rooted Rural	100.0	71454	56 Rural Bypasses	79.1
70814	19 Milk and Cookies	34.9	71245	55 College Towns	59.7	71455	56 Rural Bypasses	79.0
70815	14 Prosperous Empty Nesters	34.4	71250	56 Rural Bypasses	80.7	71456	56 Rural Bypasses	74.8
70816	39 Young and Restless	31.3	71251	50 Heartland Communities	39.1	71457	46 Rooted Rural	16.0
70817	06 Sophisticated Squires	31.0	71254	62 Modest Income Homes	56.9	71459	40 Military Proximity	100.0
70818	17 Green Acres	35.0	71256	56 Rural Bypasses	100.0	71461	28 Aspiring Young Families	100.0
70819	24 Main Street, USA	33.6	71259	56 Rural Bypasses	60.7	71462	46 Rooted Rural	57.7
70820	63 Dorms To Diplomas	48.2	71260	56 Rural Bypasses	60.3	71463	46 Rooted Rural	34.9
71001	56 Rural Bypasses	53.2	71261	56 Rural Bypasses	97.5	71465	42 Southern Satellites	94.6
71003	56 Rural Bypasses	100.0	71263	46 Rooted Rural	77.4	71466	42 Southern Satellites	100.0
71004	56 Rural Bypasses	54.8	71264	56 Rural Bypasses	67.7	71467	46 Rooted Rural	54.4
71006	07 Exurbanites	40.1	71266	56 Rural Bypasses	58.0	71468	46 Rooted Rural	100.0
71007	17 Green Acres	52.0	71268	56 Rural Bypasses	49.7	71469	46 Rooted Rural	64.3
71008	56 Rural Bypasses	66.8	71269	46 Rooted Rural	37.3	71472	42 Southern Satellites	99.4
71016	56 Rural Bypasses	64.8	71270	55 College Towns	29.5	71473	42 Southern Satellites	65.0
71018	56 Rural Bypasses	34.4	71275	41 Crossroads	68.1	71479	56 Rural Bypasses	53.5
71019	56 Rural Bypasses	38.5	71276	46 Rooted Rural	61.1	71483	62 Modest Income Homes	32.3
71023	46 Rooted Rural	100.0	71277	42 Southern Satellites	77.2	71485	26 Midland Crowd	82.3
71024	46 Rooted Rural	88.5	71280	32 Rustbelt Traditions	57.2	71486	56 Rural Bypasses	40.7
71027	42 Southern Satellites	87.1	71282	62 Modest Income Homes	36.6	71601	62 Modest Income Homes	32.2
71028	56 Rural Bypasses	100.0	71286	56 Rural Bypasses	50.2	71602	26 Midland Crowd	36.2
71029	56 Rural Bypasses	100.0	71291	26 Midland Crowd	22.9	71603	25 Salt of The Earth	22.7
71030	26 Midland Crowd	98.9	71292	26 Midland Crowd	23.5	71630	56 Rural Bypasses	100.0
71031	56 Rural Bypasses	64.0	71295	46 Rooted Rural	37.2	71631	56 Rural Bypasses	97.0
71032	46 Rooted Rural	82.7	71301	62 Modest Income Homes	25.3	71635	42 Southern Satellites	43.8
71033	17 Green Acres	49.2	71302	62 Modest Income Homes	48.0	71638	62 Modest Income Homes	43.4
71034	46 Rooted Rural	100.0	71303	07 Exurbanites	22.8	71639	62 Modest Income Homes	39.3
71037	26 Midland Crowd	30.8	71316	46 Rooted Rural	100.0	71640	56 Rural Bypasses	42.5
71038	56 Rural Bypasses	56.3	71322	62 Modest Income Homes	28.7	71642	42 Southern Satellites	100.0
71039	56 Rural Bypasses	73.8	71323	46 Rooted Rural	100.0	71643	62 Modest Income Homes	50.9
71040	62 Modest Income Homes	25.2	71325	62 Modest Income Homes	55.4	71644	46 Rooted Rural	41.1
71043	56 Rural Bypasses	100.0	71326	56 Rural Bypasses	90.3	71646	42 Southern Satellites	54.6
71044	56 Rural Bypasses	96.5	71327	56 Rural Bypasses	40.0	71647	56 Rural Bypasses	53.7
71045	56 Rural Bypasses	56.3	71328	26 Midland Crowd	66.7	71651	46 Rooted Rural	87.1
71046	46 Rooted Rural	65.9	71331	56 Rural Bypasses	100.0	71652	42 Southern Satellites	93.5
71047	26 Midland Crowd	67.5	71333	50 Heartland Communities	74.3	71653	56 Rural Bypasses	36.6
71048	56 Rural Bypasses	98.1	71334	62 Modest Income Homes	46.4	71654	62 Modest Income Homes	31.9
71049	46 Rooted Rural	58.1	71336	56 Rural Bypasses	53.2	71655	42 Southern Satellites	23.6
71051	46 Rooted Rural	39.6	71340	56 Rural Bypasses	53.7	71656	63 Dorms To Diplomas	100.0
71052	62 Modest Income Homes	40.7	71341	56 Rural Bypasses	58.8	71658	56 Rural Bypasses	67.4
71055	62 Modest Income Homes	20.1	71342	46 Rooted Rural	33.8	71660	42 Southern Satellites	63.3
71060	26 Midland Crowd	59.3	71343	56 Rural Bypasses	46.5	71661	56 Rural Bypasses	61.4
71061	56 Rural Bypasses	95.8	71346	62 Modest Income Homes	48.2	71662	56 Rural Bypasses	86.8
71063	56 Rural Bypasses	100.0	71350	46 Rooted Rural	42.6	71663	56 Rural Bypasses	71.3
71064	56 Rural Bypasses	64.3	71351	56 Rural Bypasses	44.4	71665	56 Rural Bypasses	37.0
71065	56 Rural Bypasses	87.1	71353	56 Rural Bypasses	42.0	71666	56 Rural Bypasses	100.0
71067	26 Midland Crowd	50.7	71354	46 Rooted Rural	75.6	71667	42 Southern Satellites	60.8
71068	56 Rural Bypasses	47.2	71355	50 Heartland Communities	49.2	71670	56 Rural Bypasses	79.7
71069	56 Rural Bypasses	79.3	71356	50 Heartland Communities	77.9	71671	50 Heartland Communities	53.9
71070	56 Rural Bypasses	74.0	71357	56 Rural Bypasses	33.2	71674	56 Rural Bypasses	91.1
71071	42 Southern Satellites	50.9	71358	56 Rural Bypasses	59.6	71675	56 Rural Bypasses	56.2
71072	46 Rooted Rural	50.3	71360	26 Midland Crowd	29.5	71676	56 Rural Bypasses	90.4
71073	46 Rooted Rural	60.3	71362	46 Rooted Rural	88.7	71677	56 Rural Bypasses	100.0
71075	50 Heartland Communities	37.9	71366	62 Modest Income Homes	81.2	71678	62 Modest Income Homes	76.1
71078	26 Midland Crowd	65.6	71367	46 Rooted Rural	55.7	71701	53 Home Town	19.5
71079	56 Rural Bypasses	100.0	71368	56 Rural Bypasses	63.6	71720	56 Rural Bypasses	72.7
71082	50 Heartland Communities	37.8	71369	56 Rural Bypasses	66.4	71722	56 Rural Bypasses	53.9
71101	62 Modest Income Homes	34.9	71371	46 Rooted Rural	43.1	71725	56 Rural Bypasses	97.9
71103	62 Modest Income Homes	70.2	71373	32 Rustbelt Traditions	38.3	71726	49 Senior Sun Seekers	52.2
71104	48 Great Expectations	26.9	71375	62 Modest Income Homes	100.0	71730	42 Southern Satellites	17.8
71105	33 Midlife Junction	26.5	71378	56 Rural Bypasses	54.3	71740	56 Rural Bypasses	74.3
71106	62 Modest Income Homes	23.0	71401	56 Rural Bypasses	95.0	71742	56 Rural Bypasses	58.6
71107	26 Midland Crowd	22.0	71403	46 Rooted Rural	81.6	71743	42 Southern Satellites	40.8
71108	51 Metro City Edge	39.4	71404	56 Rural Bypasses	71.5	71744	42 Southern Satellites	65.0
71109	62 Modest Income Homes	50.7	71406	56 Rural Bypasses	94.4	71745	56 Rural Bypasses	62.5
71110	40 Military Proximity	100.0	71407	26 Midland Crowd	97.4	71747	56 Rural Bypasses	100.0
71111	33 Midlife Junction	11.5	71409	26 Midland Crowd	64.0	71748	46 Rooted Rural	100.0
71112	32 Rustbelt Traditions	17.5	71411	56 Rural Bypasses	100.0	71749	42 Southern Satellites	79.4
71115	55 College Towns	18.2	71416	46 Rooted Rural	100.0	71751	42 Southern Satellites	59.4
71118	29 Rustbelt Retirees	21.9	71417	46 Rooted Rural	33.9	71752	46 Rooted Rural	51.7
71119	18 Cozy and Comfortable	27.2	71418	46 Rooted Rural	55.6	71753	56 Rural Bypasses	15.5
71129	52 Inner City Tenants	37.0	71419	46 Rooted Rural	65.3	71758	46 Rooted Rural	100.0
71201	22 Metropolitans	20.7	71422	56 Rural Bypasses	49.0	71762	50 Heartland Communities	52.2
71202	51 Metro City Edge	30.8	71423	46 Rooted Rural	50.7	71763	56 Rural Bypasses	53.4
71203	33 Midlife Junction	18.1	71424	46 Rooted Rural	37.2	71764	56 Rural Bypasses	52.1

ZIP CODE	TOP TAPESTRY CONSUMER TYPE	% 2004 HOUSE-HOLDS	ZIP CODE	TOP TAPESTRY CONSUMER TYPE	% 2004 HOUSE-HOLDS	ZIP CODE	TOP TAPESTRY CONSUMER TYPE	% 2004 HOUSE-HOLDS
71765	56 Rural Bypasses	52.6	72022	33 Midlife Junction	36.7	72157	46 Rooted Rural	71.0
71766	42 Southern Satellites	100.0	72023	12 Up and Coming Families	29.4	72160	50 Heartland Communities	26.2
71770	56 Rural Bypasses	59.7	72024	46 Rooted Rural	68.6	72165	46 Rooted Rural	100.0
71801	53 Home Town	26.1	72025	42 Southern Satellites	100.0	72166	37 Prairie Living	100.0
71822	42 Southern Satellites	46.1	72026	42 Southern Satellites	100.0	72167	42 Southern Satellites	75.8
71825	42 Southern Satellites	88.7	72027	46 Rooted Rural	100.0	72168	56 Rural Bypasses	90.8
71826	46 Rooted Rural	51.0	72028	46 Rooted Rural	84.0	72170	37 Prairie Living	72.7
71827	56 Rural Bypasses	54.8	72029	56 Rural Bypasses	61.8	72173	26 Midland Crowd	94.0
71828	46 Rooted Rural	100.0	72030	46 Rooted Rural	100.0	72175	56 Rural Bypasses	100.0
71831	56 Rural Bypasses	100.0	72031	46 Rooted Rural	54.5	72176	26 Midland Crowd	67.1
71832	42 Southern Satellites	49.0	72032	26 Midland Crowd	27.6	72179	46 Rooted Rural	100.0
71833	42 Southern Satellites	55.7	72034	28 Aspiring Young Families	23.0	72199	46 Rooted Rural	81.4
71834	56 Rural Bypasses	54.6	72035	63 Dorms To Diplomas	100.0	72201	39 Young and Restless	91.3
71835	46 Rooted Rural	81.0	72036	62 Modest Income Homes	49.3	72202	62 Modest Income Homes	31.8
71836	42 Southern Satellites	55.7	72038	42 Southern Satellites	82.0	72204	51 Metro City Edge	32.9
71837	42 Southern Satellites	35.4	72039	46 Rooted Rural	70.3	72205	22 Metropolitans	20.5
71838	56 Rural Bypasses	78.4	72040	46 Rooted Rural	63.9	72206	62 Modest Income Homes	29.1
71839	46 Rooted Rural	83.6	72041	56 Rural Bypasses	55.5	72207	22 Metropolitans	36.1
71841	42 Southern Satellites	92.4	72042	46 Rooted Rural	35.8	72209	51 Metro City Edge	60.8
71842	42 Southern Satellites	95.9	72044	49 Senior Sun Seekers	86.5	72210	26 Midland Crowd	34.3
71845	56 Rural Bypasses	88.4	72045	42 Southern Satellites	86.8	72211	12 Up and Coming Families	20.0
71846	42 Southern Satellites	54.8	72046	53 Home Town	24.6	72212	13 In Style	23.3
71847	42 Southern Satellites	63.6	72047	42 Southern Satellites	93.6	72223	04 Boomburbs	47.3
71851	42 Southern Satellites	63.6	72048	46 Rooted Rural	100.0	72227	13 In Style	42.5
71852	42 Southern Satellites	53.3	72051	46 Rooted Rural	100.0	72301	48 Great Expectations	22.8
71853	56 Rural Bypasses	90.4	72052	42 Southern Satellites	100.0	72310	42 Southern Satellites	100.0
71854	46 Rooted Rural	14.3	72055	46 Rooted Rural	86.8	72311	56 Rural Bypasses	100.0
71855	46 Rooted Rural	53.0	72057	42 Southern Satellites	100.0	72313	56 Rural Bypasses	100.0
71857	50 Heartland Communities	35.4	72058	26 Midland Crowd	81.0	72315	62 Modest Income Homes	19.8
71858	46 Rooted Rural	64.7	72060	46 Rooted Rural	80.3	72320	56 Rural Bypasses	100.0
71859	56 Rural Bypasses	100.0	72063	46 Rooted Rural	100.0	72321	46 Rooted Rural	100.0
71860	56 Rural Bypasses	61.2	72064	37 Prairie Living	50.4	72324	42 Southern Satellites	93.4
71861	46 Rooted Rural	64.7	72065	26 Midland Crowd	63.3	72326	42 Southern Satellites	73.4
71862	42 Southern Satellites	42.3	72066	42 Southern Satellites	100.0	72327	56 Rural Bypasses	75.5
71864	56 Rural Bypasses	56.1	72067	31 Rural Resort Dwellers	100.0	72328	56 Rural Bypasses	100.0
71865	42 Southern Satellites	100.0	72068	42 Southern Satellites	100.0	72329	42 Southern Satellites	100.0
71866	46 Rooted Rural	99.7	72069	62 Modest Income Homes	70.2	72330	56 Rural Bypasses	97.1
71901	57 Simple Living	20.6	72070	46 Rooted Rural	65.0	72331	62 Modest Income Homes	42.6
71909	43 The Elders	47.6	72072	56 Rural Bypasses	100.0	72333	62 Modest Income Homes	77.4
71913	31 Rural Resort Dwellers	20.6	72073	42 Southern Satellites	60.2	72335	62 Modest Income Homes	19.6
71921	46 Rooted Rural	61.1	72076	19 Milk and Cookies	12.9	72338	56 Rural Bypasses	100.0
71922	56 Rural Bypasses	100.0	72079	26 Midland Crowd	50.5	72339	56 Rural Bypasses	100.0
71923	46 Rooted Rural	26.9	72080	46 Rooted Rural	100.0	72340	56 Rural Bypasses	100.0
71929	46 Rooted Rural	100.0	72081	42 Southern Satellites	70.6	72341	56 Rural Bypasses	100.0
71933	46 Rooted Rural	60.6	72082	53 Home Town	78.1	72342	62 Modest Income Homes	45.6
71935	42 Southern Satellites	52.6	72083	37 Prairie Living	100.0	72346	56 Rural Bypasses	100.0
71937	56 Rural Bypasses	53.5	72084	42 Southern Satellites	100.0	72347	46 Rooted Rural	82.6
71940	46 Rooted Rural	76.7	72086	50 Heartland Communities	18.8	72348	42 Southern Satellites	38.9
71941	42 Southern Satellites	57.4	72087	26 Midland Crowd	41.8	72350	56 Rural Bypasses	95.5
71942	42 Southern Satellites	100.0	72088	43 The Elders	64.4	72351	42 Southern Satellites	100.0
71943	42 Southern Satellites	35.9	72099	40 Military Proximity	88.4	72354	56 Rural Bypasses	55.4
71944	42 Southern Satellites	76.2	72101	56 Rural Bypasses	45.7	72355	56 Rural Bypasses	62.8
71945	46 Rooted Rural	99.5	72102	42 Southern Satellites	50.7	72358	53 Home Town	50.5
71949	46 Rooted Rural	82.6	72103	26 Midland Crowd	52.4	72360	56 Rural Bypasses	38.6
71950	42 Southern Satellites	55.5	72104	50 Heartland Communities	30.1	72364	41 Crossroads	32.5
71952	42 Southern Satellites	100.0	72105	26 Midland Crowd	100.0	72365	50 Heartland Communities	39.7
71953	50 Heartland Communities	49.1	72106	42 Southern Satellites	46.5	72366	42 Southern Satellites	44.8
71956	42 Southern Satellites	97.6	72110	46 Rooted Rural	34.2	72367	56 Rural Bypasses	100.0
71957	46 Rooted Rural	35.8	72111	26 Midland Crowd	53.9	72368	56 Rural Bypasses	100.0
71958	46 Rooted Rural	88.0	72112	62 Modest Income Homes	20.4	72369	56 Rural Bypasses	65.2
71959	46 Rooted Rural	65.3	72113	12 Up and Coming Families	28.1	72370	42 Southern Satellites	30.9
71960	46 Rooted Rural	100.0	72114	64 City Commons	21.6	72372	46 Rooted Rural	51.7
71961	46 Rooted Rural	100.0	72116	14 Prosperous Empty Nesters	27.4	72373	56 Rural Bypasses	62.2
71962	46 Rooted Rural	98.8	72117	56 Rural Bypasses	39.7	72374	56 Rural Bypasses	59.9
71964	26 Midland Crowd	78.8	72118	32 Rustbelt Traditions	32.7	72376	56 Rural Bypasses	53.4
71965	46 Rooted Rural	100.0	72120	19 Milk and Cookies	22.9	72379	56 Rural Bypasses	100.0
71968	26 Midland Crowd	52.7	72121	42 Southern Satellites	79.8	72384	56 Rural Bypasses	55.8
71969	46 Rooted Rural	100.0	72122	15 Silver and Gold	40.0	72386	42 Southern Satellites	77.2
71970	46 Rooted Rural	100.0	72125	42 Southern Satellites	100.0	72390	62 Modest Income Homes	36.8
71971	37 Prairie Living	100.0	72126	50 Heartland Communities	43.9	72392	56 Rural Bypasses	100.0
71972	42 Southern Satellites	88.2	72127	56 Rural Bypasses	70.6	72394	56 Rural Bypasses	98.1
71973	56 Rural Bypasses	100.0	72128	42 Southern Satellites	73.9	72395	42 Southern Satellites	98.7
71998	63 Dorms To Diplomas	0.0	72129	42 Southern Satellites	78.8	72396	42 Southern Satellites	23.5
72001	42 Southern Satellites	100.0	72130	42 Southern Satellites	69.3	72401	26 Midland Crowd	16.0
72002	26 Midland Crowd	74.6	72131	42 Southern Satellites	67.8	72404	39 Young and Restless	26.1
72003	37 Prairie Living	62.3	72132	26 Midland Crowd	77.2	72410	37 Prairie Living	63.7
72004	56 Rural Bypasses	100.0	72133	56 Rural Bypasses	100.0	72411	42 Southern Satellites	95.5
72005	56 Rural Bypasses	100.0	72134	46 Rooted Rural	100.0	72412	42 Southern Satellites	100.0
72006	56 Rural Bypasses	34.2	72135	26 Midland Crowd	79.5	72413	56 Rural Bypasses	46.8
72007	26 Midland Crowd	91.1	72136	26 Midland Crowd	100.0	72414	46 Rooted Rural	86.2
72010	56 Rural Bypasses	33.7	72137	42 Southern Satellites	50.2	72415	42 Southern Satellites	58.4
72011	26 Midland Crowd	97.3	72140	46 Rooted Rural	100.0	72416	42 Southern Satellites	83.1
72012	26 Midland Crowd	55.3	72141	46 Rooted Rural	63.5	72417	42 Southern Satellites	100.0
72013	46 Rooted Rural	75.2	72142	46 Rooted Rural	49.3	72419	56 Rural Bypasses	90.2
72014	56 Rural Bypasses	100.0	72143	42 Southern Satellites	18.4	72421	37 Prairie Living	71.0
72015	26 Midland Crowd	34.8	72149	63 Dorms To Diplomas	100.0	72422	53 Home Town	36.7
72016	42 Southern Satellites	45.8	72150	42 Southern Satellites	48.5	72424	42 Southern Satellites	100.0
72017	56 Rural Bypasses	51.0	72152	56 Rural Bypasses	100.0	72425	42 Southern Satellites	100.0
72020	42 Southern Satellites	65.4	72153	46 Rooted Rural	48.1	72426	46 Rooted Rural	88.9
72021	53 Home Town	32.2	72156	46 Rooted Rural	100.0	72428	42 Southern Satellites	100.0

ZIP CODE	TOP TAPESTRY CONSUMER TYPE	% 2004 HOUSE-HOLDS	ZIP CODE	TOP TAPESTRY CONSUMER TYPE	% 2004 HOUSE-HOLDS	ZIP CODE	TOP TAPESTRY CONSUMER TYPE	% 2004 HOUSE-HOLDS
72429	37 Prairie Living	100.0	72581	31 Rural Resort Dwellers	73.5	72820	46 Rooted Rural	82.7
72430	46 Rooted Rural	74.7	72583	46 Rooted Rural	100.0	72821	46 Rooted Rural	49.9
72432	42 Southern Satellites	41.1	72584	46 Rooted Rural	100.0	72823	42 Southern Satellites	65.4
72433	42 Southern Satellites	34.3	72585	46 Rooted Rural	100.0	72824	42 Southern Satellites	76.3
72434	46 Rooted Rural	100.0	72587	46 Rooted Rural	100.0	72826	42 Southern Satellites	100.0
72435	42 Southern Satellites	100.0	72601	46 Rooted Rural	26.1	72827	56 Rural Bypasses	64.9
72436	42 Southern Satellites	100.0	72611	46 Rooted Rural	55.4	72828	56 Rural Bypasses	59.7
72437	56 Rural Bypasses	52.1	72616	42 Southern Satellites	61.8	72830	42 Southern Satellites	35.5
72438	53 Home Town	44.9	72617	46 Rooted Rural	100.0	72832	56 Rural Bypasses	81.4
72440	42 Southern Satellites	100.0	72619	49 Senior Sun Seekers	91.3	72833	42 Southern Satellites	39.2
72441	42 Southern Satellites	93.8	72623	46 Rooted Rural	100.0	72834	50 Heartland Communities	31.3
72442	42 Southern Satellites	100.0	72624	46 Rooted Rural	100.0	72835	46 Rooted Rural	100.0
72443	46 Rooted Rural	60.0	72626	50 Heartland Communities	78.2	72837	42 Southern Satellites	55.3
72444	42 Southern Satellites	100.0	72628	46 Rooted Rural	100.0	72838	46 Rooted Rural	71.8
72445	42 Southern Satellites	100.0	72629	46 Rooted Rural	95.0	72839	46 Rooted Rural	100.0
72447	50 Heartland Communities	75.5	72631	31 Rural Resort Dwellers	100.0	72840	42 Southern Satellites	100.0
72449	42 Southern Satellites	100.0	72632	31 Rural Resort Dwellers	66.0	72841	46 Rooted Rural	100.0
72450	42 Southern Satellites	38.2	72633	46 Rooted Rural	69.2	72842	46 Rooted Rural	80.3
72453	42 Southern Satellites	100.0	72634	50 Heartland Communities	49.1	72843	46 Rooted Rural	51.8
72454	50 Heartland Communities	63.6	72635	50 Heartland Communities	46.0	72845	42 Southern Satellites	75.1
72455	50 Heartland Communities	28.3	72638	42 Southern Satellites	91.5	72846	42 Southern Satellites	59.3
72456	42 Southern Satellites	90.6	72639	46 Rooted Rural	97.4	72847	46 Rooted Rural	65.8
72457	50 Heartland Communities	93.5	72640	46 Rooted Rural	100.0	72851	46 Rooted Rural	86.3
72458	46 Rooted Rural	61.4	72641	50 Heartland Communities	51.0	72852	46 Rooted Rural	100.0
72459	42 Southern Satellites	90.6	72642	49 Senior Sun Seekers	100.0	72853	56 Rural Bypasses	59.6
72460	46 Rooted Rural	100.0	72644	46 Rooted Rural	56.5	72854	46 Rooted Rural	100.0
72461	50 Heartland Communities	65.7	72645	46 Rooted Rural	50.4	72855	50 Heartland Communities	44.2
72464	46 Rooted Rural	100.0	72648	46 Rooted Rural	97.8	72856	42 Southern Satellites	100.0
72465	46 Rooted Rural	100.0	72650	50 Heartland Communities	62.3	72857	56 Rural Bypasses	95.9
72466	42 Southern Satellites	54.5	72651	49 Senior Sun Seekers	75.3	72858	42 Southern Satellites	73.5
72467	42 Southern Satellites	100.0	72653	49 Senior Sun Seekers	54.6	72860	56 Rural Bypasses	60.5
72469	46 Rooted Rural	53.8	72655	46 Rooted Rural	100.0	72863	42 Southern Satellites	82.5
72470	42 Southern Satellites	100.0	72658	46 Rooted Rural	96.8	72865	42 Southern Satellites	62.3
72471	56 Rural Bypasses	77.6	72660	42 Southern Satellites	100.0	72901	48 Great Expectations	38.5
72472	53 Home Town	54.8	72661	49 Senior Sun Seekers	100.0	72903	33 Midlife Junction	23.3
72473	50 Heartland Communities	50.5	72662	46 Rooted Rural	100.0	72904	53 Home Town	55.7
72476	50 Heartland Communities	81.7	72663	46 Rooted Rural	100.0	72905	26 Midland Crowd	62.5
72478	42 Southern Satellites	100.0	72666	46 Rooted Rural	100.0	72908	32 Rustbelt Traditions	24.3
72479	50 Heartland Communities	52.6	72668	49 Senior Sun Seekers	56.3	72916	28 Aspiring Young Families	49.1
72482	49 Senior Sun Seekers	55.8	72669	42 Southern Satellites	92.2	72921	26 Midland Crowd	30.0
72501	42 Southern Satellites	36.1	72670	46 Rooted Rural	100.0	72923	26 Midland Crowd	44.3
72512	43 The Elders	41.4	72675	46 Rooted Rural	77.6	72924	42 Southern Satellites	100.0
72513	50 Heartland Communities	83.7	72679	46 Rooted Rural	100.0	72926	42 Southern Satellites	78.3
72515	46 Rooted Rural	100.0	72680	46 Rooted Rural	100.0	72927	50 Heartland Communities	30.8
72517	46 Rooted Rural	100.0	72682	46 Rooted Rural	100.0	72928	46 Rooted Rural	97.2
72519	50 Heartland Communities	62.0	72683	46 Rooted Rural	100.0	72930	37 Prairie Living	55.8
72520	46 Rooted Rural	100.0	72685	46 Rooted Rural	100.0	72932	42 Southern Satellites	83.1
72521	42 Southern Satellites	66.1	72686	46 Rooted Rural	100.0	72933	25 Salt of The Earth	48.8
72522	42 Southern Satellites	88.8	72687	46 Rooted Rural	57.3	72934	46 Rooted Rural	86.8
72523	42 Southern Satellites	92.8	72701	63 Dorms To Diplomas	13.7	72936	26 Midland Crowd	80.3
72524	46 Rooted Rural	63.0	72703	39 Young and Restless	25.2	72937	42 Southern Satellites	64.8
72526	42 Southern Satellites	100.0	72704	26 Midland Crowd	36.2	72938	42 Southern Satellites	83.8
72527	25 Salt of The Earth	100.0	72712	28 Aspiring Young Families	30.1	72940	42 Southern Satellites	40.0
72528	46 Rooted Rural	100.0	72714	49 Senior Sun Seekers	44.8	72941	25 Salt of The Earth	54.1
72529	49 Senior Sun Seekers	57.8	72715	15 Silver and Gold	82.8	72943	42 Southern Satellites	100.0
72530	46 Rooted Rural	37.8	72717	46 Rooted Rural	88.3	72944	42 Southern Satellites	48.7
72531	46 Rooted Rural	58.4	72718	17 Green Acres	98.3	72946	42 Southern Satellites	70.6
72532	46 Rooted Rural	96.0	72719	26 Midland Crowd	100.0	72947	46 Rooted Rural	57.4
72533	46 Rooted Rural	100.0	72721	46 Rooted Rural	63.5	72948	46 Rooted Rural	77.7
72534	42 Southern Satellites	99.6	72722	42 Southern Satellites	73.1	72949	42 Southern Satellites	31.2
72536	46 Rooted Rural	90.4	72727	26 Midland Crowd	50.1	72950	46 Rooted Rural	97.0
72537	31 Rural Resort Dwellers	100.0	72729	46 Rooted Rural	100.0	72951	46 Rooted Rural	100.0
72538	46 Rooted Rural	94.9	72730	26 Midland Crowd	81.4	72952	42 Southern Satellites	65.0
72539	46 Rooted Rural	100.0	72732	42 Southern Satellites	62.0	72955	42 Southern Satellites	100.0
72540	46 Rooted Rural	96.5	72734	42 Southern Satellites	68.2	72956	26 Midland Crowd	22.3
72542	49 Senior Sun Seekers	47.4	72736	25 Salt of The Earth	53.6	72958	42 Southern Satellites	42.6
72543	46 Rooted Rural	30.1	72738	42 Southern Satellites	42.5	72959	46 Rooted Rural	59.2
72544	31 Rural Resort Dwellers	70.7	72739	26 Midland Crowd	65.7	73002	46 Rooted Rural	71.3
72546	46 Rooted Rural	82.1	72740	42 Southern Satellites	47.7	73003	12 Up and Coming Families	25.3
72550	42 Southern Satellites	89.3	72742	37 Prairie Living	74.1	73004	26 Midland Crowd	72.4
72553	42 Southern Satellites	100.0	72744	42 Southern Satellites	64.8	73005	53 Home Town	24.8
72554	46 Rooted Rural	66.9	72745	12 Up and Coming Families	56.3	73006	46 Rooted Rural	74.7
72555	42 Southern Satellites	53.1	72747	37 Prairie Living	78.9	73007	26 Midland Crowd	34.7
72556	50 Heartland Communities	81.0	72749	46 Rooted Rural	100.0	73008	14 Prosperous Empty Nesters	18.3
72560	46 Rooted Rural	68.4	72751	32 Rustbelt Traditions	40.0	73009	46 Rooted Rural	88.1
72561	46 Rooted Rural	94.2	72752	46 Rooted Rural	100.0	73010	26 Midland Crowd	77.0
72562	42 Southern Satellites	80.7	72753	26 Midland Crowd	30.5	73011	46 Rooted Rural	100.0
72564	46 Rooted Rural	77.6	72756	38 Industrious Urban Fringe	12.5	73013	07 Exurbanites	19.2
72565	46 Rooted Rural	100.0	72758	26 Midland Crowd	33.6	73014	37 Prairie Living	31.1
72566	46 Rooted Rural	76.0	72760	46 Rooted Rural	88.2	73015	50 Heartland Communities	56.5
72567	56 Rural Bypasses	100.0	72761	26 Midland Crowd	34.2	73016	26 Midland Crowd	100.0
72568	42 Southern Satellites	100.0	72762	26 Midland Crowd	22.9	73017	50 Heartland Communities	52.9
72569	46 Rooted Rural	73.2	72764	28 Aspiring Young Families	23.5	73018	53 Home Town	25.2
72571	42 Southern Satellites	100.0	72768	42 Southern Satellites	86.0	73020	17 Green Acres	31.2
72572	46 Rooted Rural	100.0	72769	42 Southern Satellites	100.0	73021	37 Prairie Living	100.0
72573	50 Heartland Communities	63.7	72773	42 Southern Satellites	77.0	73024	37 Prairie Living	100.0
72576	46 Rooted Rural	52.4	72774	26 Midland Crowd	75.0	73026	26 Midland Crowd	54.4
72577	37 Prairie Living	84.4	72776	46 Rooted Rural	100.0	73027	46 Rooted Rural	55.2
72578	46 Rooted Rural	100.0	72801	48 Great Expectations	43.4	73028	50 Heartland Communities	51.5
72579	42 Southern Satellites	100.0	72802	17 Green Acres	28.6	73029	50 Heartland Communities	80.0

ZIP CODE	TOP TAPESTRY CONSUMER TYPE	% 2004 HOUSE-HOLDS	ZIP CODE	TOP TAPESTRY CONSUMER TYPE	% 2004 HOUSE-HOLDS	ZIP CODE	TOP TAPESTRY CONSUMER TYPE	% 2004 HOUSE-HOLDS
73030	46 Rooted Rural	37.9	73170	12 Up and Coming Families	42.5	73647	46 Rooted Rural	100.0
73034	16 Enterprising Professionals	18.4	73173	17 Green Acres	100.0	73650	37 Prairie Living	100.0
73036	53 Home Town	23.9	73179	26 Midland Crowd	81.0	73651	50 Heartland Communities	76.9
73038	50 Heartland Communities	44.0	73401	53 Home Town	18.2	73654	37 Prairie Living	100.0
73040	50 Heartland Communities	73.6	73430	46 Rooted Rural	100.0	73655	31 Rural Resort Dwellers	100.0
73041	37 Prairie Living	100.0	73432	46 Rooted Rural	100.0	73658	37 Prairie Living	100.0
73042	46 Rooted Rural	100.0	73433	50 Heartland Communities	49.3	73659	37 Prairie Living	100.0
73043	46 Rooted Rural	100.0	73434	46 Rooted Rural	100.0	73660	37 Prairie Living	96.1
73044	26 Midland Crowd	25.7	73437	46 Rooted Rural	100.0	73661	37 Prairie Living	100.0
73045	26 Midland Crowd	89.1	73438	50 Heartland Communities	48.8	73662	50 Heartland Communities	95.4
73047	46 Rooted Rural	73.2	73439	49 Senior Sun Seekers	66.0	73663	50 Heartland Communities	64.9
73048	37 Prairie Living	59.3	73440	46 Rooted Rural	100.0	73664	37 Prairie Living	100.0
73049	50 Heartland Communities	36.0	73441	46 Rooted Rural	100.0	73666	37 Prairie Living	100.0
73051	42 Southern Satellites	44.5	73442	46 Rooted Rural	100.0	73667	37 Prairie Living	100.0
73052	50 Heartland Communities	60.0	73443	26 Midland Crowd	38.3	73668	37 Prairie Living	100.0
73053	37 Prairie Living	95.1	73444	56 Rural Bypasses	65.5	73669	50 Heartland Communities	73.4
73054	26 Midland Crowd	67.4	73446	46 Rooted Rural	48.5	73673	37 Prairie Living	76.9
73055	50 Heartland Communities	49.4	73447	42 Southern Satellites	100.0	73701	53 Home Town	62.2
73056	46 Rooted Rural	95.1	73448	50 Heartland Communities	29.7	73703	33 Midlife Junction	37.5
73057	50 Heartland Communities	67.2	73449	49 Senior Sun Seekers	53.8	73705	40 Military Proximity	0.0
73058	46 Rooted Rural	100.0	73450	46 Rooted Rural	100.0	73716	37 Prairie Living	100.0
73059	50 Heartland Communities	59.9	73453	46 Rooted Rural	74.4	73717	50 Heartland Communities	41.0
73061	26 Midland Crowd	98.0	73456	50 Heartland Communities	64.4	73718	37 Prairie Living	100.0
73062	50 Heartland Communities	72.5	73458	46 Rooted Rural	96.7	73719	37 Prairie Living	100.0
73063	46 Rooted Rural	100.0	73459	42 Southern Satellites	100.0	73720	37 Prairie Living	100.0
73064	19 Milk and Cookies	43.6	73460	50 Heartland Communities	36.8	73722	37 Prairie Living	86.0
73065	26 Midland Crowd	68.1	73461	46 Rooted Rural	100.0	73724	46 Rooted Rural	100.0
73067	46 Rooted Rural	78.4	73463	46 Rooted Rural	55.9	73726	37 Prairie Living	100.0
73068	26 Midland Crowd	50.4	73481	46 Rooted Rural	100.0	73727	37 Prairie Living	72.3
73069	55 College Towns	23.8	73488	46 Rooted Rural	100.0	73728	50 Heartland Communities	96.5
73071	55 College Towns	24.1	73501	53 Home Town	25.2	73729	37 Prairie Living	100.0
73072	22 Metropolitans	17.9	73503	40 Military Proximity	100.0	73730	37 Prairie Living	100.0
73073	46 Rooted Rural	100.0	73505	32 Rustbelt Traditions	15.1	73731	37 Prairie Living	97.6
73074	50 Heartland Communities	60.7	73507	48 Great Expectations	29.6	73733	37 Prairie Living	100.0
73075	50 Heartland Communities	31.3	73521	53 Home Town	28.4	73734	26 Midland Crowd	100.0
73077	25 Salt of The Earth	27.2	73523	40 Military Proximity	99.5	73735	37 Prairie Living	100.0
73078	17 Green Acres	74.6	73526	50 Heartland Communities	99.5	73736	37 Prairie Living	100.0
73079	25 Salt of The Earth	98.1	73527	26 Midland Crowd	83.8	73737	50 Heartland Communities	51.8
73080	26 Midland Crowd	29.2	73528	46 Rooted Rural	100.0	73738	50 Heartland Communities	77.8
73082	46 Rooted Rural	56.6	73529	46 Rooted Rural	66.3	73739	37 Prairie Living	100.0
73084	34 Family Foundations	29.6	73530	50 Heartland Communities	100.0	73741	29 Rustbelt Retirees	72.4
73086	50 Heartland Communities	51.7	73531	37 Prairie Living	100.0	73742	46 Rooted Rural	45.7
73089	26 Midland Crowd	40.0	73532	50 Heartland Communities	77.6	73744	37 Prairie Living	100.0
73090	26 Midland Crowd	100.0	73533	50 Heartland Communities	25.2	73747	37 Prairie Living	100.0
73092	46 Rooted Rural	100.0	73537	50 Heartland Communities	84.2	73749	50 Heartland Communities	95.0
73093	17 Green Acres	50.1	73538	32 Rustbelt Traditions	21.2	73750	29 Rustbelt Retirees	39.2
73095	46 Rooted Rural	100.0	73539	37 Prairie Living	100.0	73753	37 Prairie Living	78.6
73096	55 College Towns	25.5	73540	46 Rooted Rural	100.0	73754	25 Salt of The Earth	100.0
73098	50 Heartland Communities	73.0	73541	46 Rooted Rural	54.0	73755	46 Rooted Rural	100.0
73099	19 Milk and Cookies	35.7	73542	50 Heartland Communities	44.3	73756	37 Prairie Living	100.0
73102	65 Social Security Set	99.5	73543	41 Crossroads	87.7	73757	37 Prairie Living	100.0
73103	52 Inner City Tenants	33.7	73546	46 Rooted Rural	100.0	73758	37 Prairie Living	100.0
73104	64 City Commons	44.9	73547	50 Heartland Communities	63.3	73759	50 Heartland Communities	70.6
73105	62 Modest Income Homes	25.8	73548	46 Rooted Rural	100.0	73760	37 Prairie Living	100.0
73106	60 City Dimensions	45.5	73549	26 Midland Crowd	82.3	73761	37 Prairie Living	100.0
73107	48 Great Expectations	36.2	73550	50 Heartland Communities	91.9	73762	25 Salt of The Earth	70.2
73108	59 Southwestern Families	36.7	73551	37 Prairie Living	100.0	73763	37 Prairie Living	56.7
73109	53 Home Town	32.3	73552	46 Rooted Rural	84.6	73764	37 Prairie Living	100.0
73110	48 Great Expectations	25.1	73553	46 Rooted Rural	100.0	73766	37 Prairie Living	100.0
73111	62 Modest Income Homes	59.9	73554	50 Heartland Communities	74.3	73768	37 Prairie Living	100.0
73112	48 Great Expectations	18.8	73559	50 Heartland Communities	100.0	73770	37 Prairie Living	100.0
73114	51 Metro City Edge	34.9	73560	46 Rooted Rural	97.9	73771	37 Prairie Living	100.0
73115	32 Rustbelt Traditions	32.7	73561	37 Prairie Living	100.0	73772	50 Heartland Communities	38.4
73116	33 Midlife Junction	22.8	73562	42 Southern Satellites	71.1	73773	50 Heartland Communities	68.5
73117	62 Modest Income Homes	69.1	73564	50 Heartland Communities	100.0	73801	53 Home Town	23.7
73118	48 Great Expectations	30.2	73565	50 Heartland Communities	79.4	73832	37 Prairie Living	100.0
73119	53 Home Town	63.7	73566	50 Heartland Communities	100.0	73834	37 Prairie Living	100.0
73120	39 Young and Restless	26.3	73568	50 Heartland Communities	100.0	73835	37 Prairie Living	95.5
73121	14 Prosperous Empty Nesters	48.0	73569	50 Heartland Communities	100.0	73838	37 Prairie Living	100.0
73122	48 Great Expectations	27.6	73570	50 Heartland Communities	100.0	73840	37 Prairie Living	100.0
73127	52 Inner City Tenants	37.6	73571	37 Prairie Living	100.0	73841	46 Rooted Rural	100.0
73128	50 Heartland Communities	44.0	73572	50 Heartland Communities	60.3	73842	46 Rooted Rural	100.0
73129	53 Home Town	47.9	73573	46 Rooted Rural	48.3	73843	37 Prairie Living	100.0
73130	32 Rustbelt Traditions	29.8	73601	53 Home Town	38.3	73844	37 Prairie Living	100.0
73131	07 Exurbanites	69.7	73620	46 Rooted Rural	99.4	73847	37 Prairie Living	100.0
73132	52 Inner City Tenants	21.3	73622	46 Rooted Rural	100.0	73848	50 Heartland Communities	70.7
73134	16 Enterprising Professionals	52.9	73624	41 Crossroads	98.1	73851	37 Prairie Living	100.0
73135	19 Milk and Cookies	32.4	73625	37 Prairie Living	100.0	73852	46 Rooted Rural	37.7
73139	36 Old and Newcomers	19.2	73626	37 Prairie Living	90.9	73853	37 Prairie Living	100.0
73141	53 Home Town	32.1	73627	37 Prairie Living	100.0	73855	37 Prairie Living	100.0
73142	16 Enterprising Professionals	84.0	73628	50 Heartland Communities	75.5	73857	37 Prairie Living	100.0
73145	40 Military Proximity	100.0	73632	37 Prairie Living	56.0	73858	50 Heartland Communities	81.8
73149	53 Home Town	54.4	73638	37 Prairie Living	100.0	73859	50 Heartland Communities	73.0
73150	07 Exurbanites	50.3	73639	37 Prairie Living	100.0	73860	50 Heartland Communities	88.5
73151	02 Suburban Splendor	100.0	73641	50 Heartland Communities	77.4	73931	37 Prairie Living	100.0
73159	19 Milk and Cookies	27.5	73642	37 Prairie Living	100.0	73932	37 Prairie Living	68.5
73160	19 Milk and Cookies	52.5	73644	53 Home Town	32.9	73933	37 Prairie Living	55.7
73162	07 Exurbanites	21.5	73645	50 Heartland Communities	65.7	73937	37 Prairie Living	100.0
73165	17 Green Acres	71.0	73646	37 Prairie Living	100.0	73938	37 Prairie Living	99.6
73169	26 Midland Crowd	90.8				73939	55 College Towns	61.1

   435

ZIP CODE	TOP TAPESTRY CONSUMER TYPE	% 2004 HOUSE-HOLDS	ZIP CODE	TOP TAPESTRY CONSUMER TYPE	% 2004 HOUSE-HOLDS	ZIP CODE	TOP TAPESTRY CONSUMER TYPE	% 2004 HOUSE-HOLDS
73942	26 Midland Crowd	23.1	74136	39 Young and Restless	40.0	74569	46 Rooted Rural	93.6
73944	42 Southern Satellites	100.0	74137	02 Suburban Splendor	52.7	74570	46 Rooted Rural	100.0
73945	37 Prairie Living	67.7	74145	39 Young and Restless	30.0	74571	46 Rooted Rural	73.6
73946	37 Prairie Living	100.0	74146	39 Young and Restless	35.5	74572	46 Rooted Rural	55.4
73947	37 Prairie Living	100.0	74171	15 Silver and Gold	100.0	74574	46 Rooted Rural	100.0
73949	46 Rooted Rural	62.1	74301	50 Heartland Communities	63.7	74576	42 Southern Satellites	100.0
73950	37 Prairie Living	59.1	74330	26 Midland Crowd	35.1	74577	46 Rooted Rural	100.0
73951	41 Crossroads	77.4	74331	31 Rural Resort Dwellers	31.8	74578	46 Rooted Rural	54.1
74002	50 Heartland Communities	51.3	74332	46 Rooted Rural	81.6	74601	53 Home Town	43.4
74003	53 Home Town	36.4	74333	46 Rooted Rural	87.4	74604	14 Prosperous Empty Nesters	34.9
74006	33 Midlife Junction	30.1	74337	26 Midland Crowd	33.1	74630	46 Rooted Rural	100.0
74008	26 Midland Crowd	24.1	74338	42 Southern Satellites	100.0	74631	53 Home Town	41.6
74010	53 Home Town	38.4	74339	53 Home Town	98.7	74632	37 Prairie Living	100.0
74011	19 Milk and Cookies	46.8	74342	48 Southern Satellites	48.2	74633	46 Rooted Rural	86.3
74012	19 Milk and Cookies	31.4	74343	37 Prairie Living	44.2	74636	37 Prairie Living	100.0
74014	17 Green Acres	44.6	74344	49 Senior Sun Seekers	37.5	74637	50 Heartland Communities	80.0
74015	26 Midland Crowd	86.4	74346	53 Home Town	32.1	74640	37 Prairie Living	92.8
74016	26 Midland Crowd	43.4	74347	42 Southern Satellites	100.0	74641	46 Rooted Rural	100.0
74017	26 Midland Crowd	19.9	74352	42 Southern Satellites	58.7	74643	37 Prairie Living	100.0
74019	17 Green Acres	49.3	74354	50 Heartland Communities	25.7	74644	46 Rooted Rural	100.0
74020	26 Midland Crowd	36.2	74358	50 Heartland Communities	100.0	74646	37 Prairie Living	100.0
74021	32 Rustbelt Traditions	22.4	74359	42 Southern Satellites	100.0	74647	46 Rooted Rural	72.4
74022	46 Rooted Rural	60.3	74360	56 Rural Bypasses	82.9	74650	46 Rooted Rural	81.7
74023	50 Heartland Communities	54.3	74361	50 Heartland Communities	22.5	74651	46 Rooted Rural	100.0
74026	46 Rooted Rural	100.0	74363	42 Southern Satellites	41.1	74652	50 Heartland Communities	92.1
74027	46 Rooted Rural	75.8	74364	42 Southern Satellites	54.9	74653	50 Heartland Communities	67.2
74028	46 Rooted Rural	47.5	74365	42 Southern Satellites	100.0	74701	53 Home Town	33.0
74029	50 Heartland Communities	72.4	74366	56 Rural Bypasses	60.1	74723	46 Rooted Rural	100.0
74030	50 Heartland Communities	48.2	74367	31 Rural Resort Dwellers	55.7	74724	46 Rooted Rural	63.1
74032	26 Midland Crowd	69.8	74368	42 Southern Satellites	100.0	74726	46 Rooted Rural	58.2
74033	19 Milk and Cookies	50.3	74369	37 Prairie Living	58.5	74727	46 Rooted Rural	60.7
74035	50 Heartland Communities	66.8	74370	56 Rural Bypasses	32.9	74728	42 Southern Satellites	35.1
74036	26 Midland Crowd	57.8	74401	62 Modest Income Homes	19.6	74729	50 Heartland Communities	46.8
74037	12 Up and Coming Families	35.5	74403	53 Home Town	20.8	74730	50 Heartland Communities	35.0
74038	42 Southern Satellites	100.0	74421	26 Midland Crowd	60.0	74731	42 Southern Satellites	56.9
74039	42 Southern Satellites	62.4	74422	56 Rural Bypasses	65.6	74733	56 Rural Bypasses	55.0
74042	42 Southern Satellites	100.0	74423	42 Southern Satellites	100.0	74734	56 Rural Bypasses	75.8
74044	42 Southern Satellites	59.3	74425	49 Senior Sun Seekers	70.8	74735	46 Rooted Rural	100.0
74045	46 Rooted Rural	96.9	74426	49 Senior Sun Seekers	42.4	74736	46 Rooted Rural	100.0
74047	26 Midland Crowd	53.3	74427	49 Senior Sun Seekers	74.4	74738	46 Rooted Rural	100.0
74048	50 Heartland Communities	49.9	74428	46 Rooted Rural	74.4	74740	56 Rural Bypasses	100.0
74051	26 Midland Crowd	99.7	74429	26 Midland Crowd	40.2	74741	46 Rooted Rural	61.0
74053	26 Midland Crowd	100.0	74432	49 Senior Sun Seekers	43.9	74743	46 Rooted Rural	24.9
74054	46 Rooted Rural	100.0	74434	26 Midland Crowd	41.2	74745	46 Rooted Rural	38.4
74055	12 Up and Coming Families	41.6	74435	46 Rooted Rural	100.0	74748	46 Rooted Rural	95.0
74056	50 Heartland Communities	58.2	74436	46 Rooted Rural	49.3	74754	42 Southern Satellites	100.0
74058	50 Heartland Communities	59.3	74437	50 Heartland Communities	30.1	74755	46 Rooted Rural	100.0
74059	32 Rustbelt Traditions	54.5	74440	46 Rooted Rural	100.0	74756	46 Rooted Rural	100.0
74060	31 Rural Resort Dwellers	27.0	74441	46 Rooted Rural	55.0	74759	46 Rooted Rural	100.0
74061	46 Rooted Rural	50.9	74442	46 Rooted Rural	96.6	74760	46 Rooted Rural	100.0
74062	46 Rooted Rural	100.0	74445	50 Heartland Communities	44.7	74764	42 Southern Satellites	54.0
74063	26 Midland Crowd	40.1	74447	50 Heartland Communities	28.2	74766	56 Rural Bypasses	67.3
74066	26 Midland Crowd	23.1	74450	46 Rooted Rural	99.2	74801	53 Home Town	49.0
74070	32 Rustbelt Traditions	32.5	74451	31 Rural Resort Dwellers	53.6	74804	26 Midland Crowd	25.0
74072	42 Southern Satellites	100.0	74452	42 Southern Satellites	98.8	74820	33 Midlife Junction	19.5
74073	26 Midland Crowd	43.0	74454	42 Southern Satellites	42.8	74824	46 Rooted Rural	100.0
74074	55 College Towns	15.9	74455	56 Rural Bypasses	74.4	74825	25 Salt of The Earth	25.9
74075	22 Metropolitans	24.4	74457	46 Rooted Rural	51.3	74826	46 Rooted Rural	100.0
74077	63 Dorms To Diplomas	0.0	74461	49 Senior Sun Seekers	100.0	74827	46 Rooted Rural	100.0
74078	63 Dorms To Diplomas	100.0	74462	50 Heartland Communities	59.4	74829	56 Rural Bypasses	76.5
74079	50 Heartland Communities	57.0	74463	56 Rural Bypasses	100.0	74831	46 Rooted Rural	100.0
74080	26 Midland Crowd	84.5	74464	55 College Towns	20.3	74832	46 Rooted Rural	100.0
74081	42 Southern Satellites	96.7	74467	53 Home Town	19.8	74833	46 Rooted Rural	92.3
74083	42 Southern Satellites	75.1	74469	50 Heartland Communities	63.4	74834	50 Heartland Communities	45.2
74084	50 Heartland Communities	100.0	74470	46 Rooted Rural	100.0	74839	46 Rooted Rural	94.1
74085	46 Rooted Rural	38.6	74471	46 Rooted Rural	64.8	74840	25 Salt of The Earth	80.1
74103	65 Social Security Set	57.4	74472	46 Rooted Rural	100.0	74842	37 Prairie Living	100.0
74104	22 Metropolitans	45.0	74501	50 Heartland Communities	24.2	74843	37 Prairie Living	100.0
74105	36 Old and Newcomers	29.5	74523	50 Heartland Communities	52.3	74845	46 Rooted Rural	100.0
74106	62 Modest Income Homes	52.7	74525	46 Rooted Rural	52.4	74848	50 Heartland Communities	35.0
74107	32 Rustbelt Traditions	21.1	74528	46 Rooted Rural	100.0	74849	53 Home Town	52.5
74108	26 Midland Crowd	23.4	74531	46 Rooted Rural	100.0	74850	46 Rooted Rural	100.0
74110	53 Home Town	59.0	74533	46 Rooted Rural	100.0	74851	26 Midland Crowd	56.2
74112	32 Rustbelt Traditions	28.0	74534	46 Rooted Rural	99.4	74852	46 Rooted Rural	100.0
74114	03 Connoisseurs	23.7	74536	50 Heartland Communities	60.9	74854	46 Rooted Rural	52.8
74115	53 Home Town	62.4	74538	46 Rooted Rural	50.3	74855	42 Southern Satellites	32.1
74116	52 Inner City Tenants	58.4	74540	42 Southern Satellites	100.0	74856	56 Rural Bypasses	56.9
74117	25 Salt of The Earth	61.9	74543	46 Rooted Rural	100.0	74857	26 Midland Crowd	85.2
74119	30 Retirement Communities	44.1	74547	50 Heartland Communities	57.7	74859	46 Rooted Rural	37.3
74120	22 Metropolitans	27.7	74549	46 Rooted Rural	100.0	74860	46 Rooted Rural	97.5
74126	51 Metro City Edge	65.9	74552	46 Rooted Rural	99.9	74864	50 Heartland Communities	69.1
74127	53 Home Town	38.1	74553	46 Rooted Rural	100.0	74865	50 Heartland Communities	57.1
74128	32 Rustbelt Traditions	38.5	74555	46 Rooted Rural	100.0	74867	46 Rooted Rural	100.0
74129	28 Aspiring Young Families	33.6	74557	46 Rooted Rural	100.0	74868	46 Rooted Rural	45.5
74130	53 Home Town	47.5	74558	46 Rooted Rural	100.0	74869	46 Rooted Rural	100.0
74131	41 Crossroads	44.9	74560	46 Rooted Rural	100.0	74871	46 Rooted Rural	71.5
74132	19 Milk and Cookies	47.5	74561	49 Senior Sun Seekers	53.9	74872	50 Heartland Communities	56.6
74133	16 Enterprising Professionals	21.0	74562	46 Rooted Rural	100.0	74873	46 Rooted Rural	34.9
74134	28 Aspiring Young Families	65.2	74563	50 Heartland Communities	53.6	74875	46 Rooted Rural	100.0
74135	14 Prosperous Empty Nesters	31.8	74567	46 Rooted Rural	95.6	74878	46 Rooted Rural	100.0

ZIP CODE	TOP TAPESTRY CONSUMER TYPE	% 2004 HOUSE-HOLDS	ZIP CODE	TOP TAPESTRY CONSUMER TYPE	% 2004 HOUSE-HOLDS	ZIP CODE	TOP TAPESTRY CONSUMER TYPE	% 2004 HOUSE-HOLDS
74880	46 Rooted Rural	53.3	75109	26 Midland Crowd	100.0	75254	39 Young and Restless	48.9
74881	46 Rooted Rural	75.3	75110	26 Midland Crowd	15.9	75261	32 Rustbelt Traditions	100.0
74883	50 Heartland Communities	97.7	75114	19 Milk and Cookies	48.4	75287	39 Young and Restless	51.3
74884	50 Heartland Communities	39.9	75115	06 Sophisticated Squires	25.9	75401	53 Home Town	33.1
74901	53 Home Town	54.7	75116	07 Exurbanites	20.0	75402	33 Midlife Junction	28.4
74902	42 Southern Satellites	74.8	75117	46 Rooted Rural	39.8	75407	26 Midland Crowd	75.5
74930	42 Southern Satellites	50.5	75119	26 Midland Crowd	25.5	75409	26 Midland Crowd	87.3
74931	46 Rooted Rural	79.2	75124	46 Rooted Rural	36.9	75410	46 Rooted Rural	57.1
74932	46 Rooted Rural	100.0	75125	41 Crossroads	41.8	75411	46 Rooted Rural	56.3
74937	46 Rooted Rural	51.8	75126	06 Sophisticated Squires	54.0	75412	46 Rooted Rural	100.0
74939	46 Rooted Rural	100.0	75127	46 Rooted Rural	99.4	75414	26 Midland Crowd	72.6
74940	46 Rooted Rural	95.9	75134	19 Milk and Cookies	33.2	75415	46 Rooted Rural	100.0
74941	46 Rooted Rural	58.9	75135	26 Midland Crowd	65.2	75416	46 Rooted Rural	72.0
74944	46 Rooted Rural	100.0	75137	19 Milk and Cookies	33.2	75417	50 Heartland Communities	51.1
74948	46 Rooted Rural	38.0	75140	53 Home Town	25.6	75418	46 Rooted Rural	25.3
74949	46 Rooted Rural	100.0	75141	41 Crossroads	57.5	75420	46 Rooted Rural	100.0
74953	50 Heartland Communities	35.9	75142	26 Midland Crowd	65.2	75421	46 Rooted Rural	100.0
74954	42 Southern Satellites	38.8	75143	26 Midland Crowd	34.0	75422	46 Rooted Rural	100.0
74955	53 Home Town	32.7	75144	50 Heartland Communities	40.2	75423	32 Rustbelt Traditions	40.6
74956	56 Rural Bypasses	50.3	75146	28 Aspiring Young Families	36.8	75424	26 Midland Crowd	100.0
74957	56 Rural Bypasses	79.1	75147	41 Crossroads	47.5	75426	50 Heartland Communities	34.3
74959	42 Southern Satellites	59.2	75148	49 Senior Sun Seekers	30.1	75428	55 College Towns	29.9
74960	53 Home Town	32.5	75149	38 Industrious Urban Fringe	22.0	75431	46 Rooted Rural	70.2
74962	46 Rooted Rural	79.8	75150	19 Milk and Cookies	17.7	75432	46 Rooted Rural	36.3
74963	56 Rural Bypasses	67.6	75152	26 Midland Crowd	83.1	75433	46 Rooted Rural	100.0
74964	42 Southern Satellites	100.0	75153	46 Rooted Rural	100.0	75435	46 Rooted Rural	58.2
74965	42 Southern Satellites	62.4	75154	19 Milk and Cookies	30.4	75436	56 Rural Bypasses	55.4
74966	46 Rooted Rural	60.4	75155	42 Southern Satellites	100.0	75437	46 Rooted Rural	62.2
75001	16 Enterprising Professionals	38.3	75156	31 Rural Resort Dwellers	48.4	75438	46 Rooted Rural	100.0
75002	04 Boomburbs	58.2	75158	26 Midland Crowd	100.0	75439	50 Heartland Communities	81.8
75006	06 Sophisticated Squires	16.7	75159	26 Midland Crowd	36.6	75440	46 Rooted Rural	62.8
75007	06 Sophisticated Squires	26.8	75160	26 Midland Crowd	30.9	75442	26 Midland Crowd	37.6
75009	04 Boomburbs	38.1	75161	26 Midland Crowd	98.1	75446	50 Heartland Communities	38.7
75010	12 Up and Coming Families	57.4	75163	31 Rural Resort Dwellers	58.7	75447	46 Rooted Rural	69.6
75013	04 Boomburbs	90.9	75165	28 Aspiring Young Families	11.0	75448	46 Rooted Rural	100.0
75019	04 Boomburbs	53.5	75166	26 Midland Crowd	100.0	75449	50 Heartland Communities	88.0
75020	50 Heartland Communities	18.1	75167	17 Green Acres	37.8	75450	46 Rooted Rural	100.0
75021	53 Home Town	42.1	75169	46 Rooted Rural	38.3	75451	46 Rooted Rural	100.0
75022	04 Boomburbs	79.4	75172	41 Crossroads	31.2	75452	25 Salt of The Earth	38.0
75023	06 Sophisticated Squires	21.7	75173	46 Rooted Rural	81.2	75453	46 Rooted Rural	100.0
75024	16 Enterprising Professionals	60.4	75180	38 Industrious Urban Fringe	52.9	75454	26 Midland Crowd	93.0
75025	04 Boomburbs	76.3	75181	12 Up and Coming Families	71.2	75455	26 Midland Crowd	27.2
75028	04 Boomburbs	81.6	75182	07 Exurbanites	52.2	75457	46 Rooted Rural	43.9
75032	07 Exurbanites	37.3	75189	26 Midland Crowd	68.6	75459	26 Midland Crowd	45.2
75034	12 Up and Coming Families	54.3	75201	27 Metro Renters	92.6	75460	53 Home Town	30.4
75035	04 Boomburbs	64.6	75202	27 Metro Renters	99.0	75462	26 Midland Crowd	42.9
75038	39 Young and Restless	65.8	75203	58 Newest Residents	43.1	75468	46 Rooted Rural	77.2
75039	27 Metro Renters	62.1	75204	27 Metro Renters	61.2	75469	46 Rooted Rural	100.0
75040	19 Milk and Cookies	37.5	75205	01 Top Rung	35.2	75470	46 Rooted Rural	95.3
75041	38 Industrious Urban Fringe	27.8	75206	39 Young and Restless	31.9	75471	42 Southern Satellites	99.6
75042	19 Milk and Cookies	18.4	75207	62 Modest Income Homes	50.0	75472	46 Rooted Rural	100.0
75043	19 Milk and Cookies	30.7	75208	59 Southwestern Families	24.1	75473	25 Salt of The Earth	50.3
75044	19 Milk and Cookies	49.4	75209	34 Family Foundations	19.5	75474	41 Crossroads	39.7
75048	12 Up and Coming Families	38.2	75210	62 Modest Income Homes	47.4	75476	46 Rooted Rural	97.8
75050	39 Young and Restless	20.2	75211	58 Newest Residents	22.9	75477	50 Heartland Communities	70.5
75051	38 Industrious Urban Fringe	44.4	75212	59 Southwestern Families	59.8	75478	46 Rooted Rural	67.4
75052	12 Up and Coming Families	35.0	75214	22 Metropolitans	22.9	75479	25 Salt of The Earth	51.2
75056	12 Up and Coming Families	48.1	75215	62 Modest Income Homes	62.8	75480	31 Rural Resort Dwellers	85.5
75057	39 Young and Restless	41.9	75216	34 Family Foundations	39.5	75481	46 Rooted Rural	100.0
75058	26 Midland Crowd	62.1	75217	38 Industrious Urban Fringe	54.9	75482	26 Midland Crowd	19.1
75060	38 Industrious Urban Fringe	23.3	75218	14 Prosperous Empty Nesters	33.6	75486	25 Salt of The Earth	43.8
75061	58 Newest Residents	22.3	75219	27 Metro Renters	30.4	75487	46 Rooted Rural	62.6
75062	39 Young and Restless	23.3	75220	58 Newest Residents	65.5	75488	37 Prairie Living	85.7
75063	16 Enterprising Professionals	59.3	75223	59 Southwestern Families	33.2	75490	26 Midland Crowd	59.8
75065	12 Up and Coming Families	29.9	75224	38 Industrious Urban Fringe	41.0	75491	26 Midland Crowd	66.6
75067	39 Young and Restless	41.0	75225	01 Top Rung	44.7	75492	46 Rooted Rural	100.0
75068	12 Up and Coming Families	50.9	75226	27 Metro Renters	38.2	75493	26 Midland Crowd	99.1
75069	48 Great Expectations	12.2	75227	38 Industrious Urban Fringe	38.2	75494	50 Heartland Communities	42.4
75070	04 Boomburbs	84.3	75228	52 Inner City Tenants	29.0	75495	33 Midlife Junction	36.8
75071	12 Up and Coming Families	56.1	75229	03 Connoisseurs	23.4	75496	53 Home Town	46.1
75074	06 Sophisticated Squires	22.7	75230	01 Top Rung	17.6	75497	31 Rural Resort Dwellers	85.8
75075	07 Exurbanites	26.9	75231	52 Inner City Tenants	37.6	75501	62 Modest Income Homes	20.0
75076	31 Rural Resort Dwellers	32.2	75232	34 Family Foundations	45.9	75503	07 Exurbanites	28.9
75077	12 Up and Coming Families	36.8	75233	29 Rustbelt Retirees	20.6	75550	46 Rooted Rural	100.0
75078	12 Up and Coming Families	84.1	75234	38 Industrious Urban Fringe	18.3	75551	46 Rooted Rural	34.5
75080	14 Prosperous Empty Nesters	13.3	75235	58 Newest Residents	38.3	75554	46 Rooted Rural	57.1
75081	07 Exurbanites	21.0	75236	28 Aspiring Young Families	41.5	75555	46 Rooted Rural	100.0
75082	04 Boomburbs	43.6	75237	52 Inner City Tenants	80.3	75556	46 Rooted Rural	100.0
75087	04 Boomburbs	38.7	75238	39 Young and Restless	18.6	75558	26 Midland Crowd	54.0
75088	04 Boomburbs	39.1	75240	39 Young and Restless	29.9	75559	46 Rooted Rural	28.3
75089	12 Up and Coming Families	70.3	75241	34 Family Foundations	56.6	75560	46 Rooted Rural	100.0
75090	53 Home Town	26.6	75243	39 Young and Restless	59.2	75561	46 Rooted Rural	46.4
75092	36 Old and Newcomers	17.1	75244	09 Urban Chic	27.5	75563	46 Rooted Rural	57.6
75093	04 Boomburbs	27.5	75246	52 Inner City Tenants	61.5	75566	46 Rooted Rural	100.0
75094	04 Boomburbs	97.9	75247	62 Modest Income Homes	100.0	75567	46 Rooted Rural	52.8
75098	12 Up and Coming Families	51.4	75248	03 Connoisseurs	24.4	75568	50 Heartland Communities	62.8
75102	26 Midland Crowd	100.0	75249	19 Milk and Cookies	100.0	75569	53 Home Town	41.0
75103	46 Rooted Rural	53.6	75251	08 Laptops and Lattes	100.0	75570	26 Midland Crowd	24.3
75104	19 Milk and Cookies	34.6	75252	16 Enterprising Professionals	44.7	75571	50 Heartland Communities	50.2
75105	42 Southern Satellites	100.0	75253	41 Crossroads	73.5	75572	46 Rooted Rural	47.0

ZIP CODE	TOP TAPESTRY CONSUMER TYPE	% 2004 HOUSE-HOLDS	ZIP CODE	TOP TAPESTRY CONSUMER TYPE	% 2004 HOUSE-HOLDS	ZIP CODE	TOP TAPESTRY CONSUMER TYPE	% 2004 HOUSE-HOLDS
75574	46 Rooted Rural	90.3	75855	46 Rooted Rural	83.6	76066	26 Midland Crowd	64.4
75599	50 Heartland Communities	0.0	75856	46 Rooted Rural	96.3	76067	53 Home Town	24.5
75601	33 Midlife Junction	26.8	75859	26 Midland Crowd	61.9	76070	26 Midland Crowd	91.8
75602	51 Metro City Edge	18.4	75860	46 Rooted Rural	52.8	76071	26 Midland Crowd	100.0
75603	46 Rooted Rural	46.9	75861	46 Rooted Rural	44.4	76073	26 Midland Crowd	100.0
75604	41 Crossroads	14.1	75862	49 Senior Sun Seekers	54.5	76077	26 Midland Crowd	100.0
75605	26 Midland Crowd	21.1	75901	26 Midland Crowd	17.0	76078	26 Midland Crowd	100.0
75630	56 Rural Bypasses	34.7	75904	26 Midland Crowd	21.8	76082	26 Midland Crowd	92.3
75631	42 Southern Satellites	53.5	75925	46 Rooted Rural	63.9	76084	41 Crossroads	34.9
75633	50 Heartland Communities	19.3	75926	46 Rooted Rural	100.0	76085	26 Midland Crowd	96.4
75638	50 Heartland Communities	32.2	75928	56 Rural Bypasses	73.9	76086	33 Midlife Junction	44.3
75639	46 Rooted Rural	36.6	75929	46 Rooted Rural	62.7	76087	26 Midland Crowd	36.2
75640	46 Rooted Rural	54.6	75930	46 Rooted Rural	82.7	76088	26 Midland Crowd	84.0
75643	46 Rooted Rural	100.0	75931	31 Rural Resort Dwellers	67.6	76092	04 Boomburbs	56.2
75644	46 Rooted Rural	47.1	75932	49 Senior Sun Seekers	62.6	76093	42 Southern Satellites	87.3
75645	46 Rooted Rural	55.4	75933	56 Rural Bypasses	76.4	76102	27 Metro Renters	53.4
75647	46 Rooted Rural	34.8	75935	46 Rooted Rural	44.1	76103	59 Southwestern Families	20.2
75650	26 Midland Crowd	80.2	75936	46 Rooted Rural	53.1	76104	62 Modest Income Homes	60.9
75651	42 Southern Satellites	100.0	75937	46 Rooted Rural	100.0	76105	59 Southwestern Families	53.4
75652	56 Rural Bypasses	18.8	75938	46 Rooted Rural	95.2	76106	59 Southwestern Families	69.8
75654	46 Rooted Rural	36.0	75939	42 Southern Satellites	55.4	76107	22 Metropolitans	24.0
75656	46 Rooted Rural	35.0	75941	38 Industrious Urban Fringe	29.1	76108	32 Rustbelt Traditions	16.9
75657	49 Senior Sun Seekers	33.8	75943	46 Rooted Rural	100.0	76109	27 Metro Renters	19.2
75661	46 Rooted Rural	46.7	75946	56 Rural Bypasses	47.2	76110	59 Southwestern Families	36.7
75662	26 Midland Crowd	19.8	75948	49 Senior Sun Seekers	70.2	76111	38 Industrious Urban Fringe	28.7
75667	56 Rural Bypasses	77.6	75949	42 Southern Satellites	41.6	76112	52 Inner City Tenants	28.6
75668	50 Heartland Communities	39.4	75951	46 Rooted Rural	46.1	76114	53 Home Town	32.3
75669	46 Rooted Rural	59.2	75954	56 Rural Bypasses	35.9	76115	59 Southwestern Families	45.9
75670	53 Home Town	35.7	75956	46 Rooted Rural	62.8	76116	52 Inner City Tenants	35.5
75672	46 Rooted Rural	33.6	75959	49 Senior Sun Seekers	100.0	76117	32 Rustbelt Traditions	38.6
75681	56 Rural Bypasses	66.5	75960	46 Rooted Rural	42.8	76118	12 Up and Coming Families	32.3
75683	26 Midland Crowd	31.5	75961	55 College Towns	24.7	76119	62 Modest Income Homes	22.2
75684	46 Rooted Rural	44.2	75962	63 Dorms To Diplomas	100.0	76120	39 Young and Restless	76.9
75686	31 Rural Resort Dwellers	21.1	75964	38 Industrious Urban Fringe	20.1	76122	48 Great Expectations	100.0
75687	56 Rural Bypasses	67.5	75965	55 College Towns	34.6	76123	12 Up and Coming Families	60.5
75689	42 Southern Satellites	100.0	75966	56 Rural Bypasses	53.8	76126	18 Cozy and Comfortable	26.3
75691	42 Southern Satellites	73.5	75968	56 Rural Bypasses	89.2	76127	13 In Style	98.1
75692	26 Midland Crowd	63.8	75969	42 Southern Satellites	75.2	76129	63 Dorms To Diplomas	100.0
75693	17 Green Acres	27.8	75972	46 Rooted Rural	35.4	76131	12 Up and Coming Families	74.6
75701	33 Midlife Junction	16.9	75973	56 Rural Bypasses	61.3	76132	39 Young and Restless	48.1
75702	59 Southwestern Families	25.8	75974	56 Rural Bypasses	63.0	76133	29 Rustbelt Retirees	14.9
75703	36 Old and Newcomers	17.5	75975	46 Rooted Rural	66.4	76134	19 Milk and Cookies	36.6
75704	42 Southern Satellites	47.3	75976	46 Rooted Rural	100.0	76135	32 Rustbelt Traditions	26.0
75705	46 Rooted Rural	29.6	75977	56 Rural Bypasses	100.0	76137	12 Up and Coming Families	33.2
75706	42 Southern Satellites	64.1	75979	46 Rooted Rural	45.9	76140	19 Milk and Cookies	15.2
75707	26 Midland Crowd	28.4	75980	49 Senior Sun Seekers	54.4	76148	19 Milk and Cookies	75.0
75708	41 Crossroads	71.1	76001	12 Up and Coming Families	46.7	76155	39 Young and Restless	100.0
75709	26 Midland Crowd	60.9	76002	12 Up and Coming Families	84.3	76177	12 Up and Coming Families	42.6
75750	46 Rooted Rural	49.1	76006	39 Young and Restless	69.0	76179	19 Milk and Cookies	34.0
75751	14 Prosperous Empty Nesters	22.0	76008	06 Sophisticated Squires	54.8	76180	06 Sophisticated Squires	18.6
75752	46 Rooted Rural	47.2	76009	41 Crossroads	34.7	76201	55 College Towns	28.9
75754	46 Rooted Rural	82.5	76010	52 Inner City Tenants	34.8	76205	55 College Towns	26.2
75755	46 Rooted Rural	35.7	76011	39 Young and Restless	50.4	76207	39 Young and Restless	32.8
75756	46 Rooted Rural	60.5	76012	07 Exurbanites	32.7	76208	41 Crossroads	47.9
75757	26 Midland Crowd	54.1	76013	33 Midlife Junction	20.6	76209	28 Aspiring Young Families	25.9
75758	49 Senior Sun Seekers	30.5	76014	28 Aspiring Young Families	56.6	76210	12 Up and Coming Families	45.6
75760	46 Rooted Rural	100.0	76015	39 Young and Restless	21.0	76225	46 Rooted Rural	52.3
75762	17 Green Acres	55.0	76016	06 Sophisticated Squires	35.6	76226	02 Suburban Splendor	89.0
75763	49 Senior Sun Seekers	41.2	76017	12 Up and Coming Families	25.4	76227	17 Green Acres	63.6
75765	15 Silver and Gold	33.2	76018	12 Up and Coming Families	58.9	76228	37 Prairie Living	100.0
75766	53 Home Town	26.4	76019	22 Metropolitans	100.0	76230	50 Heartland Communities	41.5
75770	46 Rooted Rural	66.7	76020	26 Midland Crowd	40.3	76233	25 Salt of The Earth	68.8
75771	26 Midland Crowd	33.7	76021	06 Sophisticated Squires	31.9	76234	26 Midland Crowd	63.3
75773	31 Rural Resort Dwellers	33.5	76022	36 Old and Newcomers	35.9	76238	25 Salt of The Earth	100.0
75778	46 Rooted Rural	46.8	76023	26 Midland Crowd	99.5	76239	46 Rooted Rural	84.9
75783	31 Rural Resort Dwellers	58.2	76028	17 Green Acres	37.5	76240	53 Home Town	16.4
75784	46 Rooted Rural	100.0	76031	26 Midland Crowd	33.4	76245	49 Senior Sun Seekers	68.9
75785	46 Rooted Rural	73.2	76033	53 Home Town	14.8	76247	26 Midland Crowd	59.9
75789	42 Southern Satellites	31.6	76034	02 Suburban Splendor	66.1	76248	04 Boomburbs	50.3
75790	46 Rooted Rural	45.6	76035	26 Midland Crowd	100.0	76249	19 Milk and Cookies	50.8
75791	26 Midland Crowd	25.8	76036	04 Boomburbs	23.4	76250	25 Salt of The Earth	100.0
75792	26 Midland Crowd	71.8	76039	16 Enterprising Professionals	30.2	76251	46 Rooted Rural	100.0
75798	33 Midlife Junction	100.0	76040	39 Young and Restless	29.2	76252	25 Salt of The Earth	100.0
75799	16 Enterprising Professionals	100.0	76041	42 Southern Satellites	81.0	76255	50 Heartland Communities	43.3
75801	48 Great Expectations	19.4	76043	26 Midland Crowd	77.5	76258	26 Midland Crowd	40.5
75803	26 Midland Crowd	25.3	76044	26 Midland Crowd	93.2	76259	26 Midland Crowd	55.7
75831	46 Rooted Rural	53.9	76048	46 Rooted Rural	24.7	76261	46 Rooted Rural	100.0
75833	46 Rooted Rural	87.4	76049	26 Midland Crowd	38.5	76262	02 Suburban Splendor	36.0
75835	46 Rooted Rural	40.7	76050	17 Green Acres	43.2	76263	25 Salt of The Earth	100.0
75838	46 Rooted Rural	100.0	76051	16 Enterprising Professionals	20.7	76264	46 Rooted Rural	72.4
75839	46 Rooted Rural	73.7	76052	04 Boomburbs	54.3	76265	31 Rural Resort Dwellers	58.2
75840	46 Rooted Rural	35.9	76053	29 Rustbelt Retirees	24.0	76266	17 Green Acres	36.9
75844	46 Rooted Rural	69.7	76054	06 Sophisticated Squires	44.5	76270	46 Rooted Rural	56.6
75845	53 Home Town	46.7	76055	26 Midland Crowd	50.6	76271	26 Midland Crowd	80.8
75846	41 Crossroads	50.8	76058	41 Crossroads	52.0	76272	26 Midland Crowd	50.5
75847	46 Rooted Rural	63.4	76059	41 Crossroads	44.1	76273	26 Midland Crowd	38.0
75850	46 Rooted Rural	100.0	76060	28 Aspiring Young Families	31.9	76301	53 Home Town	34.1
75851	46 Rooted Rural	64.6	76063	12 Up and Coming Families	18.2	76302	52 Inner City Tenants	38.6
75852	46 Rooted Rural	65.7	76064	26 Midland Crowd	65.2	76305	46 Rooted Rural	29.3
75853	46 Rooted Rural	100.0	76065	12 Up and Coming Families	19.7	76306	19 Milk and Cookies	27.8

ZIP CODE	TOP TAPESTRY CONSUMER TYPE	% 2004 HOUSE-HOLDS	ZIP CODE	TOP TAPESTRY CONSUMER TYPE	% 2004 HOUSE-HOLDS	ZIP CODE	TOP TAPESTRY CONSUMER TYPE	% 2004 HOUSE-HOLDS
76308	32 Rustbelt Traditions	15.9	76548	12 Up and Coming Families	37.6	76841	31 Rural Resort Dwellers	100.0
76309	53 Home Town	29.8	76549	12 Up and Coming Families	20.7	76842	37 Prairie Living	100.0
76310	19 Milk and Cookies	25.7	76550	53 Home Town	31.3	76844	50 Heartland Communities	62.5
76311	40 Military Proximity	100.0	76554	26 Midland Crowd	74.0	76845	37 Prairie Living	100.0
76351	50 Heartland Communities	42.8	76556	46 Rooted Rural	100.0	76848	31 Rural Resort Dwellers	100.0
76354	53 Home Town	29.4	76557	26 Midland Crowd	48.3	76849	50 Heartland Communities	53.2
76357	37 Prairie Living	98.5	76559	41 Crossroads	99.9	76852	37 Prairie Living	100.0
76360	50 Heartland Communities	60.3	76561	42 Southern Satellites	96.2	76853	50 Heartland Communities	56.0
76363	37 Prairie Living	100.0	76565	31 Rural Resort Dwellers	100.0	76854	31 Rural Resort Dwellers	100.0
76364	37 Prairie Living	100.0	76566	25 Salt of The Earth	90.9	76856	37 Prairie Living	41.9
76365	46 Rooted Rural	20.2	76567	25 Salt of The Earth	34.6	76857	49 Senior Sun Seekers	66.4
76366	37 Prairie Living	36.4	76569	50 Heartland Communities	52.4	76858	37 Prairie Living	100.0
76367	29 Rustbelt Retirees	19.6	76570	46 Rooted Rural	41.9	76859	50 Heartland Communities	47.0
76371	50 Heartland Communities	79.2	76571	17 Green Acres	51.7	76861	46 Rooted Rural	66.2
76372	46 Rooted Rural	94.3	76574	38 Industrious Urban Fringe	16.5	76862	37 Prairie Living	100.0
76373	37 Prairie Living	100.0	76577	37 Prairie Living	60.9	76864	37 Prairie Living	99.8
76374	57 Simple Living	29.1	76578	42 Southern Satellites	53.5	76865	37 Prairie Living	100.0
76377	46 Rooted Rural	57.6	76579	26 Midland Crowd	100.0	76866	37 Prairie Living	100.0
76379	37 Prairie Living	100.0	76621	46 Rooted Rural	52.2	76869	37 Prairie Living	100.0
76380	50 Heartland Communities	57.7	76622	46 Rooted Rural	98.5	76870	37 Prairie Living	100.0
76384	50 Heartland Communities	37.2	76624	26 Midland Crowd	73.8	76871	37 Prairie Living	99.4
76388	37 Prairie Living	100.0	76626	50 Heartland Communities	59.1	76872	31 Rural Resort Dwellers	71.3
76389	37 Prairie Living	97.4	76627	46 Rooted Rural	46.9	76873	37 Prairie Living	100.0
76401	33 Midlife Junction	21.2	76629	50 Heartland Communities	65.4	76874	31 Rural Resort Dwellers	83.3
76424	53 Home Town	45.0	76630	26 Midland Crowd	100.0	76875	37 Prairie Living	100.0
76426	38 Industrious Urban Fringe	37.4	76631	46 Rooted Rural	100.0	76877	50 Heartland Communities	73.2
76427	46 Rooted Rural	100.0	76632	46 Rooted Rural	62.5	76878	53 Home Town	41.5
76429	37 Prairie Living	51.5	76633	26 Midland Crowd	38.9	76880	37 Prairie Living	100.0
76430	46 Rooted Rural	43.5	76634	31 Rural Resort Dwellers	48.0	76882	37 Prairie Living	100.0
76431	42 Southern Satellites	76.4	76635	53 Home Town	57.0	76883	31 Rural Resort Dwellers	100.0
76432	46 Rooted Rural	93.5	76636	26 Midland Crowd	100.0	76884	37 Prairie Living	100.0
76433	31 Rural Resort Dwellers	48.9	76637	31 Rural Resort Dwellers	100.0	76885	31 Rural Resort Dwellers	100.0
76435	37 Prairie Living	94.1	76638	17 Green Acres	70.0	76887	37 Prairie Living	87.3
76436	46 Rooted Rural	99.6	76639	46 Rooted Rural	100.0	76888	37 Prairie Living	100.0
76437	50 Heartland Communities	37.3	76640	26 Midland Crowd	90.0	76890	46 Rooted Rural	99.7
76442	50 Heartland Communities	47.8	76641	42 Southern Satellites	38.3	76901	48 Great Expectations	22.4
76443	46 Rooted Rural	60.1	76642	46 Rooted Rural	42.9	76903	59 Southwestern Families	32.1
76444	37 Prairie Living	46.1	76643	19 Milk and Cookies	34.2	76904	33 Midlife Junction	13.5
76445	46 Rooted Rural	68.1	76645	53 Home Town	30.6	76905	38 Industrious Urban Fringe	33.3
76446	37 Prairie Living	39.2	76648	46 Rooted Rural	55.8	76908	40 Military Proximity	98.0
76448	50 Heartland Communities	56.0	76649	31 Rural Resort Dwellers	100.0	76909	63 Dorms To Diplomas	100.0
76449	46 Rooted Rural	35.4	76651	26 Midland Crowd	67.0	76930	37 Prairie Living	100.0
76450	46 Rooted Rural	29.8	76652	46 Rooted Rural	100.0	76932	42 Southern Satellites	29.0
76453	31 Rural Resort Dwellers	100.0	76653	50 Heartland Communities	57.7	76933	50 Heartland Communities	70.2
76454	50 Heartland Communities	46.3	76655	26 Midland Crowd	46.6	76934	46 Rooted Rural	100.0
76455	37 Prairie Living	64.2	76656	46 Rooted Rural	70.2	76935	31 Rural Resort Dwellers	99.3
76457	37 Prairie Living	45.2	76657	26 Midland Crowd	34.4	76936	59 Southwestern Families	42.0
76458	37 Prairie Living	32.7	76660	46 Rooted Rural	100.0	76937	37 Prairie Living	100.0
76459	46 Rooted Rural	100.0	76661	50 Heartland Communities	70.3	76940	37 Prairie Living	100.0
76460	37 Prairie Living	100.0	76664	50 Heartland Communities	73.4	76941	46 Rooted Rural	51.9
76462	46 Rooted Rural	64.5	76665	50 Heartland Communities	54.9	76943	59 Southwestern Families	44.3
76463	31 Rural Resort Dwellers	100.0	76666	46 Rooted Rural	100.0	76945	50 Heartland Communities	60.0
76464	46 Rooted Rural	93.3	76667	46 Rooted Rural	38.3	76949	31 Rural Resort Dwellers	100.0
76470	50 Heartland Communities	69.6	76670	56 Rural Bypasses	65.4	76950	37 Prairie Living	33.5
76471	50 Heartland Communities	45.1	76671	49 Senior Sun Seekers	58.3	76951	46 Rooted Rural	77.7
76472	31 Rural Resort Dwellers	100.0	76673	46 Rooted Rural	100.0	76955	37 Prairie Living	100.0
76474	37 Prairie Living	100.0	76676	46 Rooted Rural	100.0	77002	27 Metro Renters	72.9
76475	50 Heartland Communities	77.7	76678	46 Rooted Rural	100.0	77003	59 Southwestern Families	43.3
76476	26 Midland Crowd	52.9	76679	46 Rooted Rural	100.0	77004	62 Modest Income Homes	23.5
76483	50 Heartland Communities	72.4	76680	46 Rooted Rural	100.0	77005	01 Top Rung	34.5
76484	31 Rural Resort Dwellers	100.0	76681	46 Rooted Rural	98.9	77006	27 Metro Renters	70.3
76486	46 Rooted Rural	87.9	76682	46 Rooted Rural	59.3	77007	59 Southwestern Families	20.6
76487	26 Midland Crowd	92.0	76687	31 Rural Resort Dwellers	71.4	77008	22 Metropolitans	32.8
76490	42 Southern Satellites	100.0	76689	17 Green Acres	25.5	77009	59 Southwestern Families	47.4
76491	37 Prairie Living	100.0	76690	46 Rooted Rural	100.0	77010	65 Social Security Set	100.0
76501	26 Midland Crowd	20.3	76691	50 Heartland Communities	38.9	77011	59 Southwestern Families	85.4
76502	13 In Style	18.3	76692	46 Rooted Rural	43.4	77012	59 Southwestern Families	69.2
76504	53 Home Town	27.9	76693	50 Heartland Communities	52.2	77013	58 Newest Residents	42.0
76511	50 Heartland Communities	41.1	76701	36 Old and Newcomers	49.5	77014	12 Up and Coming Families	39.3
76513	26 Midland Crowd	16.9	76704	62 Modest Income Homes	47.8	77015	28 Aspiring Young Families	20.1
76518	46 Rooted Rural	100.0	76705	53 Home Town	23.4	77016	34 Family Foundations	37.0
76519	37 Prairie Living	100.0	76706	63 Dorms To Diplomas	36.7	77017	58 Newest Residents	36.5
76520	53 Home Town	36.2	76707	53 Home Town	36.0	77018	32 Rustbelt Traditions	24.7
76522	28 Aspiring Young Families	22.4	76708	53 Home Town	18.5	77019	08 Laptops and Lattes	35.0
76523	26 Midland Crowd	99.8	76710	14 Prosperous Empty Nesters	15.3	77020	59 Southwestern Families	56.5
76524	26 Midland Crowd	100.0	76711	53 Home Town	65.0	77021	62 Modest Income Homes	56.5
76525	31 Rural Resort Dwellers	100.0	76712	28 Aspiring Young Families	20.7	77022	59 Southwestern Families	57.2
76526	46 Rooted Rural	100.0	76801	53 Home Town	25.7	77023	59 Southwestern Families	45.4
76527	26 Midland Crowd	78.0	76802	46 Rooted Rural	60.1	77024	01 Top Rung	29.7
76528	50 Heartland Communities	40.2	76820	37 Prairie Living	100.0	77025	27 Metro Renters	30.8
76530	37 Prairie Living	34.9	76821	50 Heartland Communities	58.8	77026	62 Modest Income Homes	72.4
76531	50 Heartland Communities	49.4	76823	46 Rooted Rural	32.6	77027	27 Metro Renters	45.4
76534	53 Home Town	47.8	76825	50 Heartland Communities	45.4	77028	62 Modest Income Homes	65.5
76537	26 Midland Crowd	100.0	76827	31 Rural Resort Dwellers	100.0	77029	59 Southwestern Families	41.4
76538	37 Prairie Living	82.9	76828	37 Prairie Living	100.0	77030	27 Metro Renters	41.1
76539	26 Midland Crowd	100.0	76831	31 Rural Resort Dwellers	91.5	77031	52 Inner City Tenants	29.6
76541	52 Inner City Tenants	53.1	76832	37 Prairie Living	100.0	77032	38 Industrious Urban Fringe	39.6
76542	12 Up and Coming Families	31.3	76834	50 Heartland Communities	56.0	77033	34 Family Foundations	50.6
76543	40 Military Proximity	25.0	76836	37 Prairie Living	100.0	77034	38 Industrious Urban Fringe	24.8
76544	40 Military Proximity	99.9	76837	50 Heartland Communities	79.7	77035	52 Inner City Tenants	32.6

ZIP CODE	TOP TAPESTRY CONSUMER TYPE	% 2004 HOUSE-HOLDS	ZIP CODE	TOP TAPESTRY CONSUMER TYPE	% 2004 HOUSE-HOLDS	ZIP CODE	TOP TAPESTRY CONSUMER TYPE	% 2004 HOUSE-HOLDS
77036	52 Inner City Tenants	46.3	77364	49 Senior Sun Seekers	70.1	77545	12 Up and Coming Families	53.6
77037	38 Industrious Urban Fringe	76.6	77365	41 Crossroads	63.6	77546	12 Up and Coming Families	27.7
77038	38 Industrious Urban Fringe	39.4	77371	46 Rooted Rural	31.8	77547	59 Southwestern Families	65.4
77039	38 Industrious Urban Fringe	61.9	77372	41 Crossroads	61.9	77550	48 Great Expectations	21.6
77040	19 Milk and Cookies	27.0	77373	19 Milk and Cookies	65.7	77551	14 Prosperous Empty Nesters	18.7
77041	19 Milk and Cookies	43.4	77375	12 Up and Coming Families	36.5	77554	15 Silver and Gold	34.7
77042	39 Young and Restless	64.2	77377	12 Up and Coming Families	46.8	77560	56 Rural Bypasses	100.0
77043	28 Aspiring Young Families	30.3	77378	41 Crossroads	61.1	77562	26 Midland Crowd	37.7
77044	41 Crossroads	28.2	77379	02 Suburban Splendor	30.1	77563	07 Exurbanites	26.1
77045	38 Industrious Urban Fringe	34.0	77380	16 Enterprising Professionals	31.9	77564	42 Southern Satellites	61.8
77046	09 Urban Chic	100.0	77381	04 Boomburbs	31.6	77565	09 Urban Chic	28.8
77047	34 Family Foundations	58.9	77382	04 Boomburbs	99.8	77566	06 Sophisticated Squires	21.6
77048	34 Family Foundations	41.5	77384	06 Sophisticated Squires	52.7	77568	29 Rustbelt Retirees	19.5
77049	38 Industrious Urban Fringe	88.4	77385	12 Up and Coming Families	30.9	77571	19 Milk and Cookies	39.1
77050	34 Family Foundations	41.2	77386	12 Up and Coming Families	59.1	77573	04 Boomburbs	24.3
77051	62 Modest Income Homes	67.2	77388	19 Milk and Cookies	25.7	77575	56 Rural Bypasses	32.4
77053	38 Industrious Urban Fringe	37.0	77389	12 Up and Coming Families	33.4	77577	26 Midland Crowd	55.8
77054	39 Young and Restless	61.6	77396	41 Crossroads	27.3	77578	26 Midland Crowd	40.5
77055	58 Newest Residents	34.6	77401	09 Urban Chic	36.7	77581	12 Up and Coming Families	33.3
77056	27 Metro Renters	52.5	77414	52 Inner City Tenants	21.3	77583	41 Crossroads	33.4
77057	27 Metro Renters	33.4	77417	26 Midland Crowd	68.3	77584	12 Up and Coming Families	56.1
77058	39 Young and Restless	62.2	77418	17 Green Acres	23.5	77585	56 Rural Bypasses	57.3
77059	02 Suburban Splendor	51.5	77419	46 Rooted Rural	100.0	77586	36 Old and Newcomers	20.0
77060	52 Inner City Tenants	36.8	77420	56 Rural Bypasses	56.8	77587	38 Industrious Urban Fringe	47.9
77061	52 Inner City Tenants	26.5	77422	26 Midland Crowd	22.5	77590	32 Rustbelt Traditions	27.1
77062	04 Boomburbs	25.9	77423	26 Midland Crowd	44.0	77591	34 Family Foundations	33.2
77063	27 Metro Renters	38.6	77426	31 Rural Resort Dwellers	35.4	77597	26 Midland Crowd	52.6
77064	19 Milk and Cookies	27.8	77429	04 Boomburbs	55.7	77598	39 Young and Restless	66.1
77065	12 Up and Coming Families	32.7	77430	17 Green Acres	39.9	77611	26 Midland Crowd	47.9
77066	19 Milk and Cookies	30.9	77432	42 Southern Satellites	100.0	77612	42 Southern Satellites	87.7
77067	52 Inner City Tenants	34.2	77433	04 Boomburbs	62.3	77614	42 Southern Satellites	100.0
77068	13 In Style	60.2	77434	59 Southwestern Families	37.7	77616	42 Southern Satellites	100.0
77069	13 In Style	33.3	77435	25 Salt of The Earth	39.8	77619	29 Rustbelt Retirees	35.3
77070	07 Exurbanites	24.3	77437	59 Southwestern Families	14.3	77622	26 Midland Crowd	98.1
77071	19 Milk and Cookies	38.3	77440	46 Rooted Rural	100.0	77624	46 Rooted Rural	100.0
77072	38 Industrious Urban Fringe	33.3	77441	03 Connoisseurs	57.7	77625	26 Midland Crowd	35.2
77073	28 Aspiring Young Families	33.6	77442	46 Rooted Rural	51.1	77627	32 Rustbelt Traditions	27.7
77074	58 Newest Residents	28.5	77444	26 Midland Crowd	43.2	77630	53 Home Town	15.0
77075	38 Industrious Urban Fringe	44.1	77445	41 Crossroads	28.3	77632	17 Green Acres	29.2
77076	59 Southwestern Families	52.8	77447	26 Midland Crowd	67.4	77640	62 Modest Income Homes	49.8
77077	39 Young and Restless	35.4	77449	12 Up and Coming Families	51.4	77642	59 Southwestern Families	15.3
77078	51 Metro City Edge	40.5	77450	04 Boomburbs	47.0	77650	31 Rural Resort Dwellers	84.6
77079	03 Connoisseurs	30.6	77455	37 Prairie Living	59.1	77651	18 Cozy and Comfortable	30.2
77080	58 Newest Residents	32.5	77456	25 Salt of The Earth	51.2	77656	42 Southern Satellites	33.4
77081	58 Newest Residents	58.3	77457	31 Rural Resort Dwellers	79.3	77657	26 Midland Crowd	84.1
77082	39 Young and Restless	44.5	77458	46 Rooted Rural	100.0	77659	07 Exurbanites	41.7
77083	19 Milk and Cookies	42.7	77459	04 Boomburbs	56.2	77660	56 Rural Bypasses	86.6
77084	19 Milk and Cookies	32.5	77461	26 Midland Crowd	55.0	77662	26 Midland Crowd	43.9
77085	19 Milk and Cookies	47.3	77465	59 Southwestern Families	34.1	77664	46 Rooted Rural	98.4
77086	38 Industrious Urban Fringe	56.8	77468	42 Southern Satellites	100.0	77665	42 Southern Satellites	28.1
77087	59 Southwestern Families	35.3	77469	06 Sophisticated Squires	20.8	77701	62 Modest Income Homes	53.2
77088	38 Industrious Urban Fringe	17.0	77471	59 Southwestern Families	26.6	77702	48 Great Expectations	75.2
77089	06 Sophisticated Squires	23.7	77474	26 Midland Crowd	34.9	77703	62 Modest Income Homes	39.8
77090	39 Young and Restless	48.8	77477	16 Enterprising Professionals	40.6	77705	51 Metro City Edge	24.9
77091	52 Inner City Tenants	30.6	77478	19 Milk and Cookies	25.8	77706	07 Exurbanites	26.1
77092	52 Inner City Tenants	44.1	77479	04 Boomburbs	53.0	77707	19 Milk and Cookies	19.4
77093	59 Southwestern Families	88.9	77480	42 Southern Satellites	22.6	77708	51 Metro City Edge	43.3
77094	04 Boomburbs	94.9	77482	56 Rural Bypasses	37.7	77710	52 Inner City Tenants	100.0
77095	04 Boomburbs	34.1	77483	37 Prairie Living	100.0	77713	26 Midland Crowd	32.9
77096	14 Prosperous Empty Nesters	20.7	77484	26 Midland Crowd	44.5	77801	55 College Towns	39.5
77098	27 Metro Renters	58.0	77485	46 Rooted Rural	40.9	77802	12 Up and Coming Families	19.8
77099	19 Milk and Cookies	29.9	77486	33 Midlife Junction	49.2	77803	38 Industrious Urban Fringe	27.4
77301	41 Crossroads	18.1	77488	46 Rooted Rural	14.6	77807	41 Crossroads	49.8
77302	41 Crossroads	40.8	77489	19 Milk and Cookies	79.3	77808	26 Midland Crowd	67.1
77303	26 Midland Crowd	57.8	77494	04 Boomburbs	76.6	77830	46 Rooted Rural	63.0
77304	28 Aspiring Young Families	25.4	77502	38 Industrious Urban Fringe	40.7	77831	46 Rooted Rural	100.0
77306	41 Crossroads	61.5	77503	38 Industrious Urban Fringe	58.5	77833	33 Midlife Junction	25.0
77316	26 Midland Crowd	89.6	77504	19 Milk and Cookies	31.5	77835	37 Prairie Living	46.8
77318	26 Midland Crowd	59.0	77505	04 Boomburbs	45.1	77836	46 Rooted Rural	40.3
77320	26 Midland Crowd	21.0	77506	58 Newest Residents	34.5	77837	50 Heartland Communities	53.1
77327	26 Midland Crowd	33.1	77507	02 Suburban Splendor	100.0	77840	63 Dorms To Diplomas	76.0
77328	41 Crossroads	33.2	77510	26 Midland Crowd	64.7	77845	22 Metropolitans	15.0
77331	49 Senior Sun Seekers	37.9	77511	26 Midland Crowd	24.7	77850	46 Rooted Rural	100.0
77335	49 Senior Sun Seekers	51.7	77514	56 Rural Bypasses	42.2	77853	56 Rural Bypasses	94.6
77336	19 Milk and Cookies	43.9	77515	41 Crossroads	22.1	77856	46 Rooted Rural	77.8
77338	19 Milk and Cookies	41.5	77517	26 Midland Crowd	61.4	77859	42 Southern Satellites	34.6
77339	06 Sophisticated Squires	28.7	77518	41 Crossroads	48.3	77861	46 Rooted Rural	100.0
77340	63 Dorms To Diplomas	23.2	77519	41 Crossroads	100.0	77864	50 Heartland Communities	33.8
77345	02 Suburban Splendor	36.2	77520	59 Southwestern Families	18.6	77865	46 Rooted Rural	100.0
77346	12 Up and Coming Families	41.0	77521	19 Milk and Cookies	18.1	77868	33 Midlife Junction	24.8
77351	49 Senior Sun Seekers	45.9	77530	19 Milk and Cookies	33.0	77871	46 Rooted Rural	50.1
77354	12 Up and Coming Families	39.7	77531	38 Industrious Urban Fringe	31.0	77872	46 Rooted Rural	98.9
77355	06 Sophisticated Squires	32.9	77532	17 Green Acres	21.8	77873	46 Rooted Rural	70.8
77356	14 Prosperous Empty Nesters	39.9	77534	25 Salt of The Earth	46.0	77879	46 Rooted Rural	44.0
77357	41 Crossroads	83.1	77535	41 Crossroads	43.4	77880	46 Rooted Rural	100.0
77358	56 Rural Bypasses	30.8	77536	06 Sophisticated Squires	39.2	77901	59 Southwestern Families	22.9
77359	46 Rooted Rural	72.5	77538	26 Midland Crowd	87.0	77904	17 Green Acres	17.0
77360	49 Senior Sun Seekers	100.0	77539	13 In Style	15.0	77905	26 Midland Crowd	42.3
77362	26 Midland Crowd	86.7	77541	38 Industrious Urban Fringe	29.7	77951	59 Southwestern Families	66.4
77363	42 Southern Satellites	63.8				77954	56 Rural Bypasses	26.5

ZIP CODE	TOP TAPESTRY CONSUMER TYPE	% 2004 HOUSE-HOLDS	ZIP CODE	TOP TAPESTRY CONSUMER TYPE	% 2004 HOUSE-HOLDS	ZIP CODE	TOP TAPESTRY CONSUMER TYPE	% 2004 HOUSE-HOLDS
77957	53 Home Town	31.0	78154	12 Up and Coming Families	37.6	78379	46 Rooted Rural	100.0
77962	46 Rooted Rural	100.0	78155	26 Midland Crowd	37.0	78380	59 Southwestern Families	59.4
77963	37 Prairie Living	26.0	78159	56 Rural Bypasses	100.0	78382	31 Rural Resort Dwellers	34.5
77964	46 Rooted Rural	73.3	78160	46 Rooted Rural	76.6	78383	49 Senior Sun Seekers	52.7
77968	17 Green Acres	61.6	78161	26 Midland Crowd	94.6	78384	59 Southwestern Families	100.0
77971	46 Rooted Rural	38.1	78163	07 Exurbanites	100.0	78385	59 Southwestern Families	100.0
77974	37 Prairie Living	100.0	78164	46 Rooted Rural	73.8	78387	59 Southwestern Families	48.0
77975	46 Rooted Rural	74.5	78201	59 Southwestern Families	42.7	78389	56 Rural Bypasses	83.7
77979	25 Salt of The Earth	29.2	78202	62 Modest Income Homes	75.6	78390	59 Southwestern Families	37.8
77983	42 Southern Satellites	45.9	78203	59 Southwestern Families	66.6	78391	37 Prairie Living	64.6
77984	50 Heartland Communities	54.8	78204	59 Southwestern Families	85.5	78393	46 Rooted Rural	64.3
77990	46 Rooted Rural	100.0	78205	65 Social Security Set	96.3	78401	65 Social Security Set	24.9
77994	46 Rooted Rural	98.6	78207	59 Southwestern Families	84.1	78402	30 Retirement Communities	99.6
77995	46 Rooted Rural	35.6	78208	60 City Dimensions	45.3	78404	59 Southwestern Families	33.0
78002	59 Southwestern Families	42.3	78209	14 Prosperous Empty Nesters	17.2	78405	59 Southwestern Families	94.9
78003	26 Midland Crowd	35.1	78210	59 Southwestern Families	63.9	78406	59 Southwestern Families	100.0
78004	07 Exurbanites	100.0	78211	59 Southwestern Families	99.7	78407	59 Southwestern Families	48.4
78005	46 Rooted Rural	100.0	78212	48 Great Expectations	17.7	78408	59 Southwestern Families	62.4
78006	07 Exurbanites	54.3	78213	39 Young and Restless	25.7	78409	59 Southwestern Families	66.1
78007	46 Rooted Rural	65.5	78214	59 Southwestern Families	85.8	78410	19 Milk and Cookies	37.0
78008	46 Rooted Rural	100.0	78215	52 Inner City Tenants	41.4	78411	32 Rustbelt Traditions	25.6
78009	26 Midland Crowd	63.9	78216	52 Inner City Tenants	21.4	78412	36 Old and Newcomers	20.1
78010	41 Crossroads	37.0	78217	36 Old and Newcomers	22.9	78413	19 Milk and Cookies	21.3
78011	59 Southwestern Families	57.0	78218	52 Inner City Tenants	16.0	78414	28 Aspiring Young Families	25.8
78013	31 Rural Resort Dwellers	46.0	78219	62 Modest Income Homes	19.3	78415	59 Southwestern Families	32.0
78014	59 Southwestern Families	48.2	78220	62 Modest Income Homes	46.3	78416	59 Southwestern Families	86.7
78015	03 Connoisseurs	68.1	78221	59 Southwestern Families	64.8	78417	59 Southwestern Families	50.6
78016	56 Rural Bypasses	37.4	78222	41 Crossroads	28.2	78418	07 Exurbanites	29.9
78017	59 Southwestern Families	50.4	78223	59 Southwestern Families	22.2	78419	40 Military Proximity	100.0
78019	59 Southwestern Families	100.0	78224	59 Southwestern Families	34.2	78501	59 Southwestern Families	33.2
78021	46 Rooted Rural	100.0	78225	59 Southwestern Families	100.0	78503	59 Southwestern Families	62.2
78022	46 Rooted Rural	50.7	78226	59 Southwestern Families	67.0	78504	19 Milk and Cookies	20.2
78023	07 Exurbanites	58.8	78227	59 Southwestern Families	37.3	78516	59 Southwestern Families	63.8
78024	31 Rural Resort Dwellers	97.5	78228	59 Southwestern Families	37.4	78520	59 Southwestern Families	56.7
78025	15 Silver and Gold	32.6	78229	39 Young and Restless	61.0	78521	59 Southwestern Families	68.3
78026	41 Crossroads	60.8	78230	22 Metropolitans	16.0	78526	59 Southwestern Families	37.4
78027	31 Rural Resort Dwellers	100.0	78231	16 Enterprising Professionals	48.3	78536	56 Rural Bypasses	100.0
78028	46 Rooted Rural	17.3	78232	16 Enterprising Professionals	23.2	78537	59 Southwestern Families	91.5
78039	26 Midland Crowd	97.8	78233	19 Milk and Cookies	41.0	78538	59 Southwestern Families	100.0
78040	59 Southwestern Families	91.8	78234	40 Military Proximity	99.2	78539	59 Southwestern Families	47.6
78041	59 Southwestern Families	34.4	78235	40 Military Proximity	80.0	78541	59 Southwestern Families	76.7
78043	59 Southwestern Families	59.0	78236	40 Military Proximity	81.4	78547	59 Southwestern Families	100.0
78045	12 Up and Coming Families	39.0	78237	59 Southwestern Families	100.0	78548	59 Southwestern Families	100.0
78046	59 Southwestern Families	77.7	78238	36 Old and Newcomers	18.1	78549	59 Southwestern Families	100.0
78052	26 Midland Crowd	42.6	78239	19 Milk and Cookies	17.0	78550	59 Southwestern Families	44.3
78055	31 Rural Resort Dwellers	53.6	78240	39 Young and Restless	40.7	78552	59 Southwestern Families	27.1
78056	17 Green Acres	61.5	78242	59 Southwestern Families	55.9	78557	59 Southwestern Families	100.0
78057	46 Rooted Rural	100.0	78244	19 Milk and Cookies	58.3	78559	59 Southwestern Families	51.7
78058	31 Rural Resort Dwellers	100.0	78245	19 Milk and Cookies	64.5	78560	59 Southwestern Families	93.4
78059	41 Crossroads	72.5	78247	12 Up and Coming Families	42.5	78563	56 Rural Bypasses	91.3
78061	59 Southwestern Families	72.2	78248	04 Boomburbs	45.1	78566	59 Southwestern Families	61.6
78063	31 Rural Resort Dwellers	44.6	78249	12 Up and Coming Families	31.3	78569	59 Southwestern Families	99.8
78064	26 Midland Crowd	55.0	78250	19 Milk and Cookies	72.8	78570	59 Southwestern Families	92.1
78065	59 Southwestern Families	43.5	78251	28 Aspiring Young Families	36.7	78572	59 Southwestern Families	64.8
78066	17 Green Acres	98.4	78252	59 Southwestern Families	31.5	78574	59 Southwestern Families	77.2
78067	59 Southwestern Families	100.0	78253	12 Up and Coming Families	92.9	78575	59 Southwestern Families	61.0
78069	38 Industrious Urban Fringe	38.5	78254	12 Up and Coming Families	48.2	78577	59 Southwestern Families	62.3
78070	07 Exurbanites	53.0	78255	07 Exurbanites	46.8	78578	59 Southwestern Families	31.6
78071	42 Southern Satellites	41.7	78256	39 Young and Restless	64.4	78580	59 Southwestern Families	89.7
78072	46 Rooted Rural	75.0	78257	03 Connoisseurs	99.5	78582	59 Southwestern Families	97.1
78073	41 Crossroads	66.3	78258	04 Boomburbs	64.4	78583	59 Southwestern Families	89.0
78074	31 Rural Resort Dwellers	100.0	78259	04 Boomburbs	91.7	78584	59 Southwestern Families	100.0
78075	42 Southern Satellites	100.0	78260	07 Exurbanites	100.0	78586	59 Southwestern Families	71.6
78076	59 Southwestern Families	63.8	78261	02 Suburban Splendor	100.0	78588	56 Rural Bypasses	100.0
78101	26 Midland Crowd	57.1	78263	26 Midland Crowd	44.2	78589	59 Southwestern Families	75.0
78102	59 Southwestern Families	25.2	78264	41 Crossroads	99.5	78590	46 Rooted Rural	76.2
78108	06 Sophisticated Squires	31.6	78266	07 Exurbanites	99.3	78591	59 Southwestern Families	50.6
78109	19 Milk and Cookies	54.4	78332	59 Southwestern Families	55.1	78593	59 Southwestern Families	87.3
78111	46 Rooted Rural	100.0	78336	41 Crossroads	29.1	78594	59 Southwestern Families	100.0
78112	41 Crossroads	64.1	78338	59 Southwestern Families	100.0	78595	59 Southwestern Families	100.0
78113	46 Rooted Rural	94.4	78340	46 Rooted Rural	100.0	78596	59 Southwestern Families	58.5
78114	26 Midland Crowd	61.4	78343	38 Industrious Urban Fringe	44.4	78597	15 Silver and Gold	100.0
78116	46 Rooted Rural	100.0	78344	59 Southwestern Families	100.0	78598	46 Rooted Rural	100.0
78117	46 Rooted Rural	100.0	78349	59 Southwestern Families	74.0	78602	26 Midland Crowd	56.8
78118	59 Southwestern Families	44.5	78353	56 Rural Bypasses	100.0	78605	26 Midland Crowd	47.9
78119	46 Rooted Rural	31.3	78355	59 Southwestern Families	77.9	78606	31 Rural Resort Dwellers	58.2
78121	26 Midland Crowd	68.9	78357	59 Southwestern Families	84.3	78607	31 Rural Resort Dwellers	61.9
78122	46 Rooted Rural	100.0	78360	59 Southwestern Families	100.0	78608	26 Midland Crowd	100.0
78123	31 Rural Resort Dwellers	55.0	78361	59 Southwestern Families	82.6	78609	15 Silver and Gold	85.8
78124	26 Midland Crowd	83.7	78362	28 Aspiring Young Families	30.2	78610	06 Sophisticated Squires	47.8
78130	26 Midland Crowd	21.2	78363	28 Aspiring Young Families	19.5	78611	31 Rural Resort Dwellers	35.4
78132	07 Exurbanites	47.2	78368	59 Southwestern Families	43.2	78612	26 Midland Crowd	76.5
78133	31 Rural Resort Dwellers	59.2	78369	59 Southwestern Families	100.0	78613	12 Up and Coming Families	61.1
78140	59 Southwestern Families	75.3	78370	59 Southwestern Families	58.3	78614	37 Prairie Living	81.3
78141	46 Rooted Rural	100.0	78372	26 Midland Crowd	37.1	78615	25 Salt of The Earth	53.8
78147	42 Southern Satellites	67.3	78373	31 Rural Resort Dwellers	93.3	78616	26 Midland Crowd	100.0
78148	06 Sophisticated Squires	24.5	78374	12 Up and Coming Families	23.5	78617	41 Crossroads	71.6
78150	40 Military Proximity	99.4	78375	59 Southwestern Families	41.7	78618	31 Rural Resort Dwellers	100.0
78151	50 Heartland Communities	66.3	78376	59 Southwestern Families	97.3	78619	07 Exurbanites	58.5
78152	17 Green Acres	79.4	78377	50 Heartland Communities	56.8	78620	04 Boomburbs	33.8

ZIP CODE	TOP TAPESTRY CONSUMER TYPE	% 2004 HOUSE-HOLDS	ZIP CODE	TOP TAPESTRY CONSUMER TYPE	% 2004 HOUSE-HOLDS	ZIP CODE	TOP TAPESTRY CONSUMER TYPE	% 2004 HOUSE-HOLDS
78621	26 Midland Crowd	55.8	78833	56 Rural Bypasses	52.5	79086	37 Prairie Living	62.8
78623	26 Midland Crowd	94.3	78834	59 Southwestern Families	50.4	79087	37 Prairie Living	100.0
78624	31 Rural Resort Dwellers	40.3	78837	46 Rooted Rural	99.6	79088	50 Heartland Communities	28.4
78626	12 Up and Coming Families	31.3	78838	31 Rural Resort Dwellers	92.3	79092	46 Rooted Rural	72.7
78628	15 Silver and Gold	31.4	78839	59 Southwestern Families	99.6	79094	37 Prairie Living	100.0
78629	46 Rooted Rural	21.6	78840	59 Southwestern Families	55.4	79095	37 Prairie Living	39.0
78631	31 Rural Resort Dwellers	86.4	78843	40 Military Proximity	100.0	79096	46 Rooted Rural	74.7
78632	46 Rooted Rural	100.0	78850	46 Rooted Rural	100.0	79097	25 Salt of The Earth	98.3
78634	12 Up and Coming Families	42.2	78851	50 Heartland Communities	41.9	79098	37 Prairie Living	100.0
78635	31 Rural Resort Dwellers	100.0	78852	59 Southwestern Families	80.2	79101	57 Simple Living	51.0
78636	31 Rural Resort Dwellers	59.0	78861	46 Rooted Rural	29.0	79102	48 Great Expectations	21.0
78638	46 Rooted Rural	50.6	78870	46 Rooted Rural	100.0	79103	32 Rustbelt Traditions	47.9
78639	49 Senior Sun Seekers	83.6	78872	59 Southwestern Families	100.0	79104	59 Southwestern Families	49.8
78640	41 Crossroads	40.5	78873	31 Rural Resort Dwellers	68.3	79106	53 Home Town	22.7
78641	12 Up and Coming Families	59.8	78877	56 Rural Bypasses	73.2	79107	59 Southwestern Families	24.2
78642	26 Midland Crowd	67.0	78879	31 Rural Resort Dwellers	100.0	79108	26 Midland Crowd	34.7
78643	31 Rural Resort Dwellers	25.7	78880	59 Southwestern Families	66.1	79109	39 Young and Restless	12.4
78644	26 Midland Crowd	22.9	78881	46 Rooted Rural	46.7	79110	32 Rustbelt Traditions	36.2
78645	30 Retirement Communities	27.0	78883	26 Midland Crowd	90.9	79111	28 Aspiring Young Families	84.8
78648	53 Home Town	33.7	78884	31 Rural Resort Dwellers	100.0	79118	41 Crossroads	48.8
78650	46 Rooted Rural	73.4	78885	31 Rural Resort Dwellers	100.0	79119	26 Midland Crowd	43.4
78652	06 Sophisticated Squires	79.9	78886	46 Rooted Rural	98.4	79121	07 Exurbanites	23.5
78653	26 Midland Crowd	70.6	78931	46 Rooted Rural	100.0	79124	07 Exurbanites	40.3
78654	46 Rooted Rural	27.4	78932	31 Rural Resort Dwellers	89.5	79201	50 Heartland Communities	53.5
78655	26 Midland Crowd	66.4	78933	46 Rooted Rural	41.0	79220	37 Prairie Living	100.0
78656	41 Crossroads	60.1	78934	46 Rooted Rural	43.3	79225	50 Heartland Communities	85.3
78657	15 Silver and Gold	63.9	78935	31 Rural Resort Dwellers	100.0	79226	50 Heartland Communities	62.3
78659	26 Midland Crowd	79.1	78938	37 Prairie Living	100.0	79227	50 Heartland Communities	64.3
78660	12 Up and Coming Families	70.1	78940	46 Rooted Rural	45.7	79229	37 Prairie Living	100.0
78662	26 Midland Crowd	82.8	78941	56 Rural Bypasses	57.7	79230	37 Prairie Living	100.0
78663	31 Rural Resort Dwellers	100.0	78942	38 Industrious Urban Fringe	22.9	79234	37 Prairie Living	100.0
78664	12 Up and Coming Families	42.8	78944	46 Rooted Rural	78.8	79235	59 Southwestern Families	50.3
78666	55 College Towns	23.1	78945	37 Prairie Living	31.7	79237	37 Prairie Living	100.0
78669	07 Exurbanites	64.6	78946	56 Rural Bypasses	46.2	79239	37 Prairie Living	100.0
78671	31 Rural Resort Dwellers	100.0	78947	26 Midland Crowd	69.1	79241	50 Heartland Communities	43.2
78672	49 Senior Sun Seekers	97.7	78948	46 Rooted Rural	54.1	79243	37 Prairie Living	100.0
78675	37 Prairie Living	100.0	78949	46 Rooted Rural	84.5	79244	50 Heartland Communities	71.4
78676	31 Rural Resort Dwellers	40.5	78950	46 Rooted Rural	42.8	79245	50 Heartland Communities	99.9
78677	37 Prairie Living	100.0	78953	46 Rooted Rural	62.7	79247	37 Prairie Living	100.0
78681	04 Boomburbs	36.3	78954	31 Rural Resort Dwellers	58.9	79248	50 Heartland Communities	62.0
78701	27 Metro Renters	53.8	78956	50 Heartland Communities	44.8	79250	50 Heartland Communities	54.1
78702	59 Southwestern Families	46.3	78957	46 Rooted Rural	38.8	79251	37 Prairie Living	100.0
78703	08 Laptops and Lattes	29.5	78959	56 Rural Bypasses	90.1	79252	50 Heartland Communities	55.2
78704	39 Young and Restless	18.1	78962	50 Heartland Communities	29.5	79255	37 Prairie Living	100.0
78705	63 Dorms To Diplomas	73.8	78963	25 Salt of The Earth	69.3	79256	37 Prairie Living	100.0
78712	63 Dorms To Diplomas	0.0	79001	37 Prairie Living	100.0	79257	37 Prairie Living	100.0
78717	04 Boomburbs	92.8	79005	38 Industrious Urban Fringe	87.0	79259	37 Prairie Living	100.0
78719	38 Industrious Urban Fringe	99.8	79007	53 Home Town	30.5	79261	37 Prairie Living	86.1
78721	34 Family Foundations	34.0	79009	59 Southwestern Families	59.1	79311	37 Prairie Living	47.2
78722	27 Metro Renters	26.1	79011	37 Prairie Living	100.0	79312	37 Prairie Living	99.5
78723	32 Rustbelt Traditions	24.2	79014	46 Rooted Rural	29.1	79313	50 Heartland Communities	100.0
78724	38 Industrious Urban Fringe	55.5	79015	55 College Towns	39.5	79316	37 Prairie Living	34.5
78725	19 Milk and Cookies	78.7	79016	55 College Towns	0.0	79320	37 Prairie Living	100.0
78726	04 Boomburbs	89.9	79018	37 Prairie Living	100.0	79322	50 Heartland Communities	51.2
78727	39 Young and Restless	31.9	79019	37 Prairie Living	64.5	79323	38 Industrious Urban Fringe	22.8
78728	16 Enterprising Professionals	46.3	79022	37 Prairie Living	24.9	79324	37 Prairie Living	100.0
78729	12 Up and Coming Families	38.8	79027	37 Prairie Living	42.2	79325	37 Prairie Living	68.8
78730	09 Urban Chic	89.1	79029	38 Industrious Urban Fringe	22.7	79326	37 Prairie Living	100.0
78731	03 Connoisseurs	30.5	79031	59 Southwestern Families	79.7	79329	33 Midlife Junction	32.0
78732	04 Boomburbs	100.0	79034	37 Prairie Living	100.0	79331	59 Southwestern Families	38.7
78733	04 Boomburbs	52.3	79035	37 Prairie Living	45.0	79336	59 Southwestern Families	22.2
78734	07 Exurbanites	53.5	79036	46 Rooted Rural	67.6	79339	50 Heartland Communities	39.4
78735	16 Enterprising Professionals	49.4	79039	37 Prairie Living	95.9	79342	37 Prairie Living	100.0
78736	06 Sophisticated Squires	47.1	79040	37 Prairie Living	100.0	79343	56 Rural Bypasses	74.4
78737	07 Exurbanites	55.8	79041	50 Heartland Communities	40.8	79344	37 Prairie Living	100.0
78738	03 Connoisseurs	48.4	79042	37 Prairie Living	100.0	79345	37 Prairie Living	100.0
78739	04 Boomburbs	89.5	79043	59 Southwestern Families	92.1	79346	37 Prairie Living	75.8
78741	39 Young and Restless	57.7	79044	37 Prairie Living	100.0	79347	50 Heartland Communities	33.1
78742	41 Crossroads	100.0	79045	59 Southwestern Families	49.1	79351	59 Southwestern Families	76.2
78744	38 Industrious Urban Fringe	59.7	79046	37 Prairie Living	100.0	79353	37 Prairie Living	100.0
78745	28 Aspiring Young Families	14.2	79052	56 Rural Bypasses	53.9	79355	37 Prairie Living	100.0
78746	01 Top Rung	24.1	79056	37 Prairie Living	100.0	79356	50 Heartland Communities	41.6
78747	07 Exurbanites	42.9	79057	50 Heartland Communities	100.0	79357	50 Heartland Communities	61.2
78748	12 Up and Coming Families	46.8	79058	26 Midland Crowd	91.1	79358	37 Prairie Living	100.0
78749	04 Boomburbs	31.7	79059	37 Prairie Living	100.0	79359	59 Southwestern Families	50.0
78750	02 Suburban Splendor	28.5	79061	37 Prairie Living	100.0	79360	37 Prairie Living	26.9
78751	27 Metro Renters	43.3	79062	37 Prairie Living	100.0	79363	26 Midland Crowd	68.3
78752	52 Inner City Tenants	35.7	79063	37 Prairie Living	100.0	79364	50 Heartland Communities	39.2
78753	52 Inner City Tenants	37.2	79064	46 Rooted Rural	41.1	79366	25 Salt of The Earth	100.0
78754	39 Young and Restless	43.1	79065	50 Heartland Communities	32.7	79370	50 Heartland Communities	87.6
78756	27 Metro Renters	25.7	79068	18 Cozy and Comfortable	49.9	79371	50 Heartland Communities	93.8
78757	22 Metropolitans	39.2	79070	37 Prairie Living	35.5	79373	37 Prairie Living	69.5
78758	39 Young and Restless	37.4	79072	59 Southwestern Families	28.9	79376	37 Prairie Living	100.0
78759	16 Enterprising Professionals	27.2	79079	50 Heartland Communities	81.0	79377	37 Prairie Living	100.0
78801	59 Southwestern Families	41.7	79080	46 Rooted Rural	100.0	79379	46 Rooted Rural	78.3
78827	59 Southwestern Families	100.0	79081	37 Prairie Living	52.7	79381	38 Industrious Urban Fringe	55.6
78828	31 Rural Resort Dwellers	100.0	79082	37 Prairie Living	96.9	79382	26 Midland Crowd	60.0
78829	59 Southwestern Families	100.0	79083	32 Rustbelt Traditions	42.5	79401	55 College Towns	41.5
78830	59 Southwestern Families	95.5	79084	37 Prairie Living	100.0	79403	62 Modest Income Homes	29.8
78832	49 Senior Sun Seekers	51.8	79085	42 Southern Satellites	100.0	79404	59 Southwestern Families	41.6

ZIP CODE	TOP TAPESTRY CONSUMER TYPE	% 2004 HOUSE-HOLDS	ZIP CODE	TOP TAPESTRY CONSUMER TYPE	% 2004 HOUSE-HOLDS	ZIP CODE	TOP TAPESTRY CONSUMER TYPE	% 2004 HOUSE-HOLDS
79407	55 College Towns	18.9	79754	37 Prairie Living	100.0	80111	02 Suburban Splendor	37.4
79409	63 Dorms To Diplomas	100.0	79755	46 Rooted Rural	62.7	80112	02 Suburban Splendor	29.3
79410	55 College Towns	55.9	79756	46 Rooted Rural	26.0	80113	36 Old and Newcomers	25.8
79411	48 Great Expectations	29.6	79758	25 Salt of The Earth	52.1	80116	03 Connoisseurs	47.0
79412	48 Great Expectations	25.6	79761	59 Southwestern Families	29.8	80117	17 Green Acres	61.3
79413	33 Midlife Junction	25.3	79762	38 Industrious Urban Fringe	11.3	80118	04 Boomburbs	44.7
79414	48 Great Expectations	31.4	79763	59 Southwestern Families	31.8	80120	13 In Style	16.9
79415	59 Southwestern Families	41.2	79764	41 Crossroads	53.9	80121	10 Pleasant-Ville	20.6
79416	55 College Towns	30.3	79765	07 Exurbanites	35.8	80122	02 Suburban Splendor	23.8
79423	12 Up and Coming Families	20.8	79766	41 Crossroads	44.3	80123	06 Sophisticated Squires	16.6
79424	06 Sophisticated Squires	18.8	79772	59 Southwestern Families	61.9	80124	04 Boomburbs	61.3
79501	50 Heartland Communities	59.4	79777	56 Rural Bypasses	100.0	80125	12 Up and Coming Families	59.9
79502	50 Heartland Communities	50.0	79781	42 Southern Satellites	100.0	80126	04 Boomburbs	56.2
79503	50 Heartland Communities	88.6	79782	46 Rooted Rural	38.7	80127	02 Suburban Splendor	23.8
79504	46 Rooted Rural	59.7	79783	37 Prairie Living	100.0	80128	06 Sophisticated Squires	31.9
79506	50 Heartland Communities	54.4	79789	26 Midland Crowd	100.0	80129	04 Boomburbs	91.5
79508	17 Green Acres	100.0	79821	59 Southwestern Families	92.7	80130	04 Boomburbs	84.0
79510	46 Rooted Rural	52.3	79830	33 Midlife Junction	39.9	80132	02 Suburban Splendor	66.8
79511	25 Salt of The Earth	45.7	79832	33 Midlife Junction	75.0	80133	17 Green Acres	42.1
79512	50 Heartland Communities	32.4	79834	46 Rooted Rural	92.2	80134	04 Boomburbs	49.7
79517	37 Prairie Living	100.0	79835	59 Southwestern Families	78.4	80135	02 Suburban Splendor	31.9
79518	37 Prairie Living	100.0	79836	59 Southwestern Families	75.8	80136	17 Green Acres	69.3
79519	46 Rooted Rural	100.0	79837	46 Rooted Rural	96.2	80137	26 Midland Crowd	72.7
79520	50 Heartland Communities	97.1	79839	59 Southwestern Families	100.0	80138	04 Boomburbs	56.8
79521	50 Heartland Communities	65.7	79842	46 Rooted Rural	99.6	80202	27 Metro Renters	47.8
79525	26 Midland Crowd	90.8	79843	59 Southwestern Families	31.6	80203	27 Metro Renters	96.3
79526	46 Rooted Rural	82.8	79845	59 Southwestern Families	100.0	80204	27 Metro Renters	15.4
79527	37 Prairie Living	99.1	79847	46 Rooted Rural	89.7	80205	60 City Dimensions	14.7
79528	50 Heartland Communities	78.3	79849	59 Southwestern Families	100.0	80206	27 Metro Renters	54.1
79529	50 Heartland Communities	100.0	79851	41 Crossroads	100.0	80207	34 Family Foundations	32.0
79530	46 Rooted Rural	99.6	79852	46 Rooted Rural	100.0	80208	63 Dorms To Diplomas	67.5
79532	50 Heartland Communities	99.1	79854	37 Prairie Living	100.0	80209	27 Metro Renters	36.1
79533	46 Rooted Rural	95.4	79855	59 Southwestern Families	61.1	80210	22 Metropolitans	45.8
79534	37 Prairie Living	100.0	79901	59 Southwestern Families	38.7	80211	22 Metropolitans	28.2
79535	37 Prairie Living	84.4	79902	59 Southwestern Families	24.3	80212	22 Metropolitans	48.4
79536	50 Heartland Communities	39.3	79903	59 Southwestern Families	57.8	80214	52 Inner City Tenants	31.4
79537	50 Heartland Communities	100.0	79904	59 Southwestern Families	38.8	80215	36 Old and Newcomers	37.5
79538	46 Rooted Rural	100.0	79905	59 Southwestern Families	90.9	80216	38 Industrious Urban Fringe	44.0
79539	37 Prairie Living	100.0	79906	40 Military Proximity	91.5	80218	27 Metro Renters	83.5
79540	37 Prairie Living	100.0	79907	59 Southwestern Families	56.2	80219	38 Industrious Urban Fringe	35.4
79541	46 Rooted Rural	46.9	79908	40 Military Proximity	100.0	80220	22 Metropolitans	22.2
79543	50 Heartland Communities	53.0	79912	04 Boomburbs	18.4	80221	24 Main Street, USA	30.0
79544	37 Prairie Living	100.0	79915	59 Southwestern Families	60.4	80222	36 Old and Newcomers	32.4
79545	50 Heartland Communities	38.8	79916	59 Southwestern Families	100.0	80223	38 Industrious Urban Fringe	24.2
79546	50 Heartland Communities	74.7	79918	40 Military Proximity	0.0	80224	36 Old and Newcomers	21.3
79547	50 Heartland Communities	70.4	79922	02 Suburban Splendor	35.3	80226	10 Pleasant-Ville	23.3
79548	37 Prairie Living	100.0	79924	38 Industrious Urban Fringe	25.2	80227	13 In Style	23.0
79549	59 Southwestern Families	16.4	79925	29 Rustbelt Retirees	24.2	80228	39 Young and Restless	26.3
79553	50 Heartland Communities	75.9	79927	59 Southwestern Families	97.1	80229	28 Aspiring Young Families	17.8
79556	53 Home Town	30.2	79928	59 Southwestern Families	68.7	80230	52 Inner City Tenants	53.0
79560	37 Prairie Living	86.4	79930	59 Southwestern Families	55.2	80231	39 Young and Restless	35.3
79561	46 Rooted Rural	100.0	79932	07 Exurbanites	32.8	80232	18 Cozy and Comfortable	19.7
79562	25 Salt of The Earth	55.2	79934	12 Up and Coming Families	31.4	80233	18 Cozy and Comfortable	27.5
79563	41 Crossroads	94.5	79935	28 Aspiring Young Families	22.1	80234	39 Young and Restless	24.9
79565	31 Rural Resort Dwellers	100.0	79936	19 Milk and Cookies	36.7	80235	16 Enterprising Professionals	27.1
79566	37 Prairie Living	62.2	79938	38 Industrious Urban Fringe	43.2	80236	13 In Style	22.8
79567	50 Heartland Communities	31.6	79968	55 College Towns	100.0	80237	36 Old and Newcomers	18.8
79601	55 College Towns	33.6	80002	52 Inner City Tenants	31.1	80239	12 Up and Coming Families	28.7
79602	53 Home Town	24.8	80003	13 In Style	21.3	80241	04 Boomburbs	31.9
79603	53 Home Town	30.7	80004	13 In Style	20.9	80246	39 Young and Restless	66.5
79605	53 Home Town	15.0	80005	06 Sophisticated Squires	34.2	80247	39 Young and Restless	53.9
79606	39 Young and Restless	23.2	80007	04 Boomburbs	73.2	80249	12 Up and Coming Families	76.7
79607	40 Military Proximity	100.0	80010	58 Newest Residents	43.9	80260	41 Crossroads	36.3
79697	48 Great Expectations	100.0	80011	18 Cozy and Comfortable	22.5	80262	27 Metro Renters	0.0
79698	55 College Towns	100.0	80012	28 Aspiring Young Families	27.4	80301	16 Enterprising Professionals	29.7
79699	55 College Towns	100.0	80013	12 Up and Coming Families	36.8	80302	63 Dorms To Diplomas	43.9
79701	59 Southwestern Families	40.6	80014	13 In Style	29.2	80303	09 Urban Chic	33.8
79703	38 Industrious Urban Fringe	29.6	80015	04 Boomburbs	26.4	80304	09 Urban Chic	30.1
79705	14 Prosperous Empty Nesters	31.5	80016	02 Suburban Splendor	46.4	80305	09 Urban Chic	43.9
79706	26 Midland Crowd	39.3	80017	28 Aspiring Young Families	34.9	80309	63 Dorms To Diplomas	0.0
79707	13 In Style	12.8	80018	12 Up and Coming Families	70.4	80401	03 Connoisseurs	21.6
79713	37 Prairie Living	100.0	80019	17 Green Acres	100.0	80403	07 Exurbanites	33.3
79714	59 Southwestern Families	23.0	80020	04 Boomburbs	24.7	80421	17 Green Acres	89.6
79718	59 Southwestern Families	100.0	80021	06 Sophisticated Squires	24.6	80422	22 Metropolitans	100.0
79719	56 Rural Bypasses	100.0	80022	38 Industrious Urban Fringe	64.8	80423	37 Prairie Living	96.0
79720	53 Home Town	17.9	80026	04 Boomburbs	27.8	80424	16 Enterprising Professionals	64.9
79730	46 Rooted Rural	100.0	80027	16 Enterprising Professionals	28.2	80428	17 Green Acres	100.0
79731	59 Southwestern Families	48.4	80030	24 Main Street, USA	40.7	80430	37 Prairie Living	100.0
79734	46 Rooted Rural	53.8	80031	13 In Style	24.0	80433	02 Suburban Splendor	70.9
79735	56 Rural Bypasses	35.9	80033	33 Midlife Junction	24.0	80435	16 Enterprising Professionals	37.6
79738	37 Prairie Living	100.0	80101	37 Prairie Living	100.0	80439	07 Exurbanites	24.0
79739	37 Prairie Living	100.0	80102	19 Milk and Cookies	50.1	80440	17 Green Acres	56.3
79741	46 Rooted Rural	100.0	80103	26 Midland Crowd	53.5	80446	17 Green Acres	40.6
79742	50 Heartland Communities	100.0	80104	13 In Style	41.6	80447	31 Rural Resort Dwellers	92.2
79743	46 Rooted Rural	100.0	80105	46 Rooted Rural	60.6	80449	31 Rural Resort Dwellers	99.0
79744	42 Southern Satellites	54.3	80106	04 Boomburbs	64.6	80452	33 Midlife Junction	31.7
79745	50 Heartland Communities	26.3	80107	06 Sophisticated Squires	85.5	80455	22 Metropolitans	87.0
79748	37 Prairie Living	100.0	80108	02 Suburban Splendor	34.2	80456	31 Rural Resort Dwellers	100.0
79749	37 Prairie Living	100.0	80109	04 Boomburbs	79.1	80459	26 Midland Crowd	80.0
79752	46 Rooted Rural	32.2	80110	24 Main Street, USA	25.1	80461	33 Midlife Junction	24.6

ZIP CODE	TOP TAPESTRY CONSUMER TYPE	% 2004 HOUSE-HOLDS	ZIP CODE	TOP TAPESTRY CONSUMER TYPE	% 2004 HOUSE-HOLDS	ZIP CODE	TOP TAPESTRY CONSUMER TYPE	% 2004 HOUSE-HOLDS
80463	37 Prairie Living	65.4	80754	37 Prairie Living	100.0	81054	50 Heartland Communities	47.6
80465	06 Sophisticated Squires	36.0	80755	37 Prairie Living	100.0	81055	33 Midlife Junction	67.3
80466	22 Metropolitans	54.1	80757	37 Prairie Living	100.0	81057	37 Prairie Living	100.0
80467	26 Midland Crowd	57.7	80758	46 Rooted Rural	36.9	81058	46 Rooted Rural	88.2
80468	17 Green Acres	100.0	80759	37 Prairie Living	52.4	81059	37 Prairie Living	80.8
80470	07 Exurbanites	67.5	80801	37 Prairie Living	100.0	81062	37 Prairie Living	99.5
80479	37 Prairie Living	100.0	80802	37 Prairie Living	100.0	81063	50 Heartland Communities	73.7
80480	46 Rooted Rural	56.3	80804	37 Prairie Living	100.0	81064	37 Prairie Living	100.0
80481	22 Metropolitans	70.9	80805	37 Prairie Living	100.0	81067	59 Southwestern Families	27.3
80487	09 Urban Chic	37.9	80807	46 Rooted Rural	32.9	81069	31 Rural Resort Dwellers	100.0
80498	16 Enterprising Professionals	88.2	80808	26 Midland Crowd	81.7	81071	37 Prairie Living	100.0
80501	12 Up and Coming Families	16.2	80809	31 Rural Resort Dwellers	63.5	81073	50 Heartland Communities	77.1
80503	02 Suburban Splendor	40.9	80810	37 Prairie Living	100.0	81076	37 Prairie Living	100.0
80504	07 Exurbanites	24.5	80812	37 Prairie Living	100.0	81081	37 Prairie Living	97.1
80510	31 Rural Resort Dwellers	100.0	80813	33 Midlife Junction	67.6	81082	50 Heartland Communities	30.8
80512	31 Rural Resort Dwellers	35.4	80814	17 Green Acres	64.4	81084	37 Prairie Living	100.0
80513	06 Sophisticated Squires	20.5	80815	50 Heartland Communities	70.5	81087	37 Prairie Living	100.0
80514	41 Crossroads	74.3	80816	31 Rural Resort Dwellers	50.4	81089	50 Heartland Communities	54.3
80515	31 Rural Resort Dwellers	99.8	80817	12 Up and Coming Families	36.2	81090	37 Prairie Living	100.0
80516	04 Boomburbs	50.9	80818	37 Prairie Living	86.0	81091	31 Rural Resort Dwellers	87.7
80517	31 Rural Resort Dwellers	69.0	80820	31 Rural Resort Dwellers	100.0	81092	37 Prairie Living	100.0
80521	55 College Towns	35.8	80821	50 Heartland Communities	73.0	81101	26 Midland Crowd	17.4
80523	63 Dorms To Diplomas	100.0	80822	37 Prairie Living	100.0	81102	55 College Towns	100.0
80524	41 Crossroads	18.1	80823	37 Prairie Living	100.0	81120	56 Rural Bypasses	80.9
80525	04 Boomburbs	12.2	80824	37 Prairie Living	100.0	81121	31 Rural Resort Dwellers	100.0
80526	13 In Style	15.2	80825	37 Prairie Living	100.0	81122	26 Midland Crowd	36.1
80528	04 Boomburbs	82.6	80827	31 Rural Resort Dwellers	92.1	81123	46 Rooted Rural	100.0
80530	12 Up and Coming Families	69.4	80828	33 Midlife Junction	80.0	81125	38 Industrious Urban Fringe	41.1
80534	12 Up and Coming Families	89.0	80829	22 Metropolitans	71.3	81130	31 Rural Resort Dwellers	100.0
80535	17 Green Acres	55.1	80830	37 Prairie Living	100.0	81132	37 Prairie Living	38.5
80536	07 Exurbanites	72.0	80831	17 Green Acres	41.7	81133	46 Rooted Rural	100.0
80537	28 Aspiring Young Families	15.0	80832	26 Midland Crowd	70.9	81136	37 Prairie Living	84.7
80538	12 Up and Coming Families	18.9	80833	26 Midland Crowd	57.7	81137	26 Midland Crowd	32.9
80540	07 Exurbanites	69.9	80834	37 Prairie Living	100.0	81140	46 Rooted Rural	93.8
80542	12 Up and Coming Families	91.5	80835	37 Prairie Living	98.0	81143	31 Rural Resort Dwellers	67.2
80543	38 Industrious Urban Fringe	80.9	80836	37 Prairie Living	100.0	81144	46 Rooted Rural	25.0
80545	15 Silver and Gold	83.3	80840	40 Military Proximity	100.0	81146	37 Prairie Living	56.5
80549	19 Milk and Cookies	43.9	80861	37 Prairie Living	100.0	81147	31 Rural Resort Dwellers	100.0
80550	12 Up and Coming Families	72.4	80863	06 Sophisticated Squires	56.8	81149	46 Rooted Rural	64.0
80601	12 Up and Coming Families	26.4	80864	26 Midland Crowd	100.0	81151	56 Rural Bypasses	43.2
80602	12 Up and Coming Families	50.7	80903	22 Metropolitans	22.1	81152	46 Rooted Rural	100.0
80603	17 Green Acres	56.8	80904	48 Great Expectations	18.7	81153	56 Rural Bypasses	95.9
80610	26 Midland Crowd	60.1	80905	24 Main Street, USA	34.9	81154	31 Rural Resort Dwellers	99.9
80611	37 Prairie Living	100.0	80906	36 Old and Newcomers	21.0	81155	31 Rural Resort Dwellers	100.0
80612	26 Midland Crowd	80.6	80907	28 Aspiring Young Families	19.9	81201	31 Rural Resort Dwellers	46.7
80615	17 Green Acres	72.4	80908	02 Suburban Splendor	59.0	81210	31 Rural Resort Dwellers	52.1
80620	19 Milk and Cookies	28.1	80909	52 Inner City Tenants	25.4	81211	31 Rural Resort Dwellers	55.3
80621	38 Industrious Urban Fringe	35.1	80910	52 Inner City Tenants	18.3	81212	33 Midlife Junction	45.2
80624	17 Green Acres	73.8	80911	19 Milk and Cookies	39.1	81220	31 Rural Resort Dwellers	100.0
80631	41 Crossroads	18.2	80913	40 Military Proximity	99.1	81223	31 Rural Resort Dwellers	100.0
80634	13 In Style	22.2	80914	40 Military Proximity	100.0	81226	08 Laptops and Lattes	40.6
80639	63 Dorms To Diplomas	100.0	80915	28 Aspiring Young Families	25.3	81226	26 Midland Crowd	41.5
80640	17 Green Acres	95.5	80916	19 Milk and Cookies	32.6	81228	41 Crossroads	63.0
80642	26 Midland Crowd	53.5	80917	19 Milk and Cookies	20.0	81230	22 Metropolitans	27.9
80643	17 Green Acres	61.5	80918	12 Up and Coming Families	28.5	81231	31 Rural Resort Dwellers	63.6
80644	26 Midland Crowd	66.5	80919	04 Boomburbs	20.6	81233	31 Rural Resort Dwellers	100.0
80645	25 Salt of The Earth	33.3	80920	04 Boomburbs	50.1	81235	31 Rural Resort Dwellers	100.0
80648	26 Midland Crowd	100.0	80921	07 Exurbanites	84.4	81236	15 Silver and Gold	100.0
80649	37 Prairie Living	87.2	80922	12 Up and Coming Families	93.0	81239	31 Rural Resort Dwellers	100.0
80650	25 Salt of The Earth	56.9	80925	12 Up and Coming Families	81.4	81240	26 Midland Crowd	68.1
80651	26 Midland Crowd	44.0	80926	02 Suburban Splendor	58.5	81241	31 Rural Resort Dwellers	100.0
80652	37 Prairie Living	90.8	80928	26 Midland Crowd	76.1	81243	31 Rural Resort Dwellers	100.0
80653	37 Prairie Living	91.5	80929	12 Up and Coming Families	53.2	81251	41 Crossroads	100.0
80654	37 Prairie Living	57.3	80930	12 Up and Coming Families	100.0	81252	31 Rural Resort Dwellers	100.0
80701	50 Heartland Communities	20.2	81001	53 Home Town	12.7	81253	31 Rural Resort Dwellers	98.1
80705	42 Southern Satellites	100.0	81003	57 Simple Living	18.6	81301	22 Metropolitans	24.7
80720	50 Heartland Communities	70.0	81004	32 Rustbelt Traditions	30.2	81303	13 In Style	41.1
80721	37 Prairie Living	100.0	81005	29 Rustbelt Retirees	29.9	81320	22 Metropolitans	56.0
80722	37 Prairie Living	100.0	81006	18 Cozy and Comfortable	19.0	81321	48 Great Expectations	18.9
80723	50 Heartland Communities	25.1	81007	26 Midland Crowd	27.8	81323	31 Rural Resort Dwellers	73.0
80726	37 Prairie Living	100.0	81008	14 Prosperous Empty Nesters	33.1	81324	46 Rooted Rural	100.0
80727	37 Prairie Living	100.0	81019	31 Rural Resort Dwellers	100.0	81325	26 Midland Crowd	100.0
80728	37 Prairie Living	100.0	81020	49 Senior Sun Seekers	94.5	81326	26 Midland Crowd	78.9
80729	37 Prairie Living	98.6	81021	37 Prairie Living	100.0	81327	37 Prairie Living	69.5
80731	37 Prairie Living	100.0	81022	46 Rooted Rural	68.0	81328	33 Midlife Junction	57.0
80733	37 Prairie Living	100.0	81023	31 Rural Resort Dwellers	100.0	81331	37 Prairie Living	100.0
80734	37 Prairie Living	73.2	81025	46 Rooted Rural	79.4	81334	59 Southwestern Families	44.5
80735	37 Prairie Living	100.0	81027	37 Prairie Living	100.0	81335	37 Prairie Living	100.0
80736	37 Prairie Living	100.0	81029	37 Prairie Living	100.0	81401	31 Rural Resort Dwellers	32.7
80737	50 Heartland Communities	83.3	81036	50 Heartland Communities	83.3	81410	46 Rooted Rural	82.5
80740	37 Prairie Living	100.0	81039	50 Heartland Communities	87.3	81411	46 Rooted Rural	100.0
80741	37 Prairie Living	100.0	81040	31 Rural Resort Dwellers	100.0	81413	49 Senior Sun Seekers	58.5
80742	37 Prairie Living	100.0	81041	59 Southwestern Families	85.8	81415	37 Prairie Living	85.5
80743	37 Prairie Living	100.0	81043	37 Prairie Living	100.0	81416	25 Salt of The Earth	25.8
80744	37 Prairie Living	99.6	81044	37 Prairie Living	100.0	81418	31 Rural Resort Dwellers	83.1
80745	37 Prairie Living	100.0	81045	37 Prairie Living	100.0	81419	31 Rural Resort Dwellers	70.4
80747	37 Prairie Living	100.0	81047	37 Prairie Living	99.2	81422	46 Rooted Rural	100.0
80749	37 Prairie Living	100.0	81049	37 Prairie Living	100.0	81423	26 Midland Crowd	99.6
80750	37 Prairie Living	99.0	81050	33 Midlife Junction	18.7	81424	46 Rooted Rural	100.0
80751	33 Midlife Junction	17.6	81052	53 Home Town	16.5	81425	38 Industrious Urban Fringe	36.4

ZIP CODE	TOP TAPESTRY CONSUMER TYPE	% 2004 HOUSE-HOLDS	ZIP CODE	TOP TAPESTRY CONSUMER TYPE	% 2004 HOUSE-HOLDS	ZIP CODE	TOP TAPESTRY CONSUMER TYPE	% 2004 HOUSE-HOLDS
81426	09 Urban Chic	75.9	82327	46 Rooted Rural	94.3	83120	31 Rural Resort Dwellers	93.3
81427	31 Rural Resort Dwellers	100.0	82329	49 Senior Sun Seekers	98.4	83122	26 Midland Crowd	68.1
81428	31 Rural Resort Dwellers	41.7	82331	46 Rooted Rural	50.1	83123	26 Midland Crowd	100.0
81430	09 Urban Chic	100.0	82332	37 Prairie Living	100.0	83126	26 Midland Crowd	99.1
81431	46 Rooted Rural	100.0	82334	26 Midland Crowd	100.0	83127	31 Rural Resort Dwellers	66.5
81432	31 Rural Resort Dwellers	56.3	82336	26 Midland Crowd	99.4	83201	32 Rustbelt Traditions	17.5
81433	31 Rural Resort Dwellers	100.0	82401	50 Heartland Communities	27.2	83202	17 Green Acres	18.7
81434	31 Rural Resort Dwellers	100.0	82410	29 Rustbelt Retirees	61.9	83203	26 Midland Crowd	100.0
81435	08 Laptops and Lattes	65.9	82411	37 Prairie Living	97.9	83204	48 Great Expectations	28.5
81501	33 Midlife Junction	25.2	82414	33 Midlife Junction	29.4	83209	14 Prosperous Empty Nesters	100.0
81503	07 Exurbanites	22.4	82421	37 Prairie Living	85.1	83210	37 Prairie Living	35.8
81504	18 Cozy and Comfortable	24.1	82426	50 Heartland Communities	75.7	83211	41 Crossroads	51.8
81505	14 Prosperous Empty Nesters	24.9	82428	37 Prairie Living	100.0	83212	37 Prairie Living	100.0
81506	30 Retirement Communities	38.2	82431	50 Heartland Communities	33.1	83213	46 Rooted Rural	52.4
81520	28 Aspiring Young Families	49.6	82432	37 Prairie Living	94.3	83214	37 Prairie Living	100.0
81521	26 Midland Crowd	38.1	82433	37 Prairie Living	92.7	83217	37 Prairie Living	100.0
81522	17 Green Acres	100.0	82434	37 Prairie Living	100.0	83220	46 Rooted Rural	95.1
81524	37 Prairie Living	96.6	82435	33 Midlife Junction	20.3	83221	26 Midland Crowd	27.0
81525	37 Prairie Living	100.0	82441	37 Prairie Living	100.0	83226	37 Prairie Living	53.4
81526	33 Midlife Junction	52.1	82442	31 Rural Resort Dwellers	99.7	83227	31 Rural Resort Dwellers	100.0
81527	17 Green Acres	100.0	82443	31 Rural Resort Dwellers	36.1	83228	37 Prairie Living	100.0
81601	09 Urban Chic	22.6	82501	41 Crossroads	12.5	83230	26 Midland Crowd	100.0
81610	46 Rooted Rural	100.0	82510	56 Rural Bypasses	73.9	83232	37 Prairie Living	100.0
81611	08 Laptops and Lattes	53.0	82512	37 Prairie Living	100.0	83234	37 Prairie Living	99.1
81621	16 Enterprising Professionals	33.0	82513	31 Rural Resort Dwellers	99.3	83235	49 Senior Sun Seekers	92.0
81623	12 Up and Coming Families	30.0	82514	51 Metro City Edge	96.7	83236	26 Midland Crowd	46.3
81624	31 Rural Resort Dwellers	100.0	82516	37 Prairie Living	55.6	83237	25 Salt of The Earth	79.1
81625	19 Milk and Cookies	19.1	82520	33 Midlife Junction	45.7	83238	37 Prairie Living	89.2
81630	31 Rural Resort Dwellers	88.4	82523	37 Prairie Living	96.9	83241	37 Prairie Living	100.0
81631	12 Up and Coming Families	57.1	82601	32 Rustbelt Traditions	12.1	83243	37 Prairie Living	100.0
81633	46 Rooted Rural	100.0	82604	19 Milk and Cookies	16.5	83244	37 Prairie Living	100.0
81635	31 Rural Resort Dwellers	79.9	82609	33 Midlife Junction	16.3	83245	25 Salt of The Earth	80.9
81637	12 Up and Coming Families	87.6	82620	31 Rural Resort Dwellers	81.3	83246	46 Rooted Rural	100.0
81638	37 Prairie Living	100.0	82633	17 Green Acres	18.8	83250	25 Salt of The Earth	78.2
81639	26 Midland Crowd	45.6	82636	41 Crossroads	63.5	83251	31 Rural Resort Dwellers	97.9
81640	37 Prairie Living	78.2	82637	33 Midlife Junction	37.8	83252	37 Prairie Living	64.7
81641	17 Green Acres	37.7	82639	37 Prairie Living	97.6	83253	49 Senior Sun Seekers	100.0
81642	31 Rural Resort Dwellers	100.0	82642	31 Rural Resort Dwellers	100.0	83254	50 Heartland Communities	36.8
81643	31 Rural Resort Dwellers	100.0	82643	26 Midland Crowd	100.0	83255	37 Prairie Living	82.5
81647	12 Up and Coming Families	66.9	82649	31 Rural Resort Dwellers	75.2	83261	46 Rooted Rural	65.4
81648	19 Milk and Cookies	54.4	82701	50 Heartland Communities	50.6	83262	26 Midland Crowd	69.9
81650	28 Aspiring Young Families	39.6	82710	37 Prairie Living	100.0	83263	25 Salt of The Earth	33.8
81652	26 Midland Crowd	68.2	82712	37 Prairie Living	100.0	83271	37 Prairie Living	100.0
81653	17 Green Acres	100.0	82714	31 Rural Resort Dwellers	100.0	83272	31 Rural Resort Dwellers	84.9
81654	09 Urban Chic	52.4	82715	31 Rural Resort Dwellers	100.0	83274	25 Salt of The Earth	33.7
81657	16 Enterprising Professionals	45.5	82716	26 Midland Crowd	34.6	83276	26 Midland Crowd	40.6
82001	48 Great Expectations	20.7	82718	06 Sophisticated Squires	30.1	83278	31 Rural Resort Dwellers	92.9
82005	40 Military Proximity	99.4	82720	37 Prairie Living	99.5	83283	37 Prairie Living	100.0
82007	41 Crossroads	50.7	82721	26 Midland Crowd	55.2	83285	31 Rural Resort Dwellers	61.7
82009	07 Exurbanites	22.9	82723	31 Rural Resort Dwellers	100.0	83286	37 Prairie Living	100.0
82050	37 Prairie Living	100.0	82725	26 Midland Crowd	100.0	83287	31 Rural Resort Dwellers	100.0
82051	31 Rural Resort Dwellers	100.0	82727	26 Midland Crowd	53.7	83301	32 Rustbelt Traditions	15.5
82052	31 Rural Resort Dwellers	90.5	82729	25 Salt of The Earth	64.0	83302	37 Prairie Living	100.0
82053	37 Prairie Living	74.3	82730	46 Rooted Rural	98.5	83313	24 Main Street, USA	32.6
82054	37 Prairie Living	60.4	82731	26 Midland Crowd	100.0	83314	37 Prairie Living	100.0
82055	31 Rural Resort Dwellers	100.0	82732	26 Midland Crowd	100.0	83316	37 Prairie Living	50.5
82058	31 Rural Resort Dwellers	100.0	82801	57 Simple Living	20.0	83318	37 Prairie Living	25.5
82063	31 Rural Resort Dwellers	100.0	82831	37 Prairie Living	93.9	83320	37 Prairie Living	98.5
82070	22 Metropolitans	28.5	82832	31 Rural Resort Dwellers	91.6	83321	37 Prairie Living	100.0
82072	55 College Towns	45.4	82834	31 Rural Resort Dwellers	25.2	83322	31 Rural Resort Dwellers	100.0
82081	07 Exurbanites	100.0	82835	37 Prairie Living	98.8	83323	37 Prairie Living	99.7
82082	37 Prairie Living	100.0	82836	31 Rural Resort Dwellers	99.8	83324	26 Midland Crowd	92.6
82083	31 Rural Resort Dwellers	77.4	82838	31 Rural Resort Dwellers	100.0	83325	37 Prairie Living	100.0
82084	31 Rural Resort Dwellers	100.0	82839	31 Rural Resort Dwellers	100.0	83327	31 Rural Resort Dwellers	100.0
82190	13 In Style	50.7	82842	31 Rural Resort Dwellers	60.0	83328	50 Heartland Communities	23.5
82201	25 Salt of The Earth	31.2	82844	31 Rural Resort Dwellers	100.0	83330	50 Heartland Communities	64.3
82210	37 Prairie Living	100.0	82901	26 Midland Crowd	20.9	83332	31 Rural Resort Dwellers	48.9
82212	31 Rural Resort Dwellers	100.0	82922	31 Rural Resort Dwellers	100.0	83333	09 Urban Chic	36.1
82213	31 Rural Resort Dwellers	100.0	82923	31 Rural Resort Dwellers	100.0	83334	41 Crossroads	53.2
82214	46 Rooted Rural	94.2	82925	31 Rural Resort Dwellers	100.0	83335	37 Prairie Living	100.0
82215	31 Rural Resort Dwellers	100.0	82930	28 Aspiring Young Families	22.7	83336	42 Southern Satellites	36.8
82217	37 Prairie Living	100.0	82933	26 Midland Crowd	99.9	83338	37 Prairie Living	24.9
82219	31 Rural Resort Dwellers	98.8	82935	17 Green Acres	26.4	83340	08 Laptops and Lattes	41.8
82221	37 Prairie Living	100.0	82936	26 Midland Crowd	100.0	83341	26 Midland Crowd	34.6
82222	37 Prairie Living	100.0	82937	26 Midland Crowd	100.0	83342	37 Prairie Living	100.0
82223	37 Prairie Living	100.0	82938	17 Green Acres	100.0	83343	37 Prairie Living	60.6
82224	37 Prairie Living	100.0	82941	31 Rural Resort Dwellers	100.0	83344	37 Prairie Living	100.0
82225	50 Heartland Communities	78.7	83001	16 Enterprising Professionals	31.1	83346	37 Prairie Living	100.0
82227	37 Prairie Living	100.0	83011	22 Metropolitans	88.6	83347	37 Prairie Living	50.2
82229	37 Prairie Living	100.0	83012	31 Rural Resort Dwellers	53.7	83348	37 Prairie Living	100.0
82240	33 Midlife Junction	25.6	83013	22 Metropolitans	100.0	83349	37 Prairie Living	100.0
82242	37 Prairie Living	100.0	83014	09 Urban Chic	90.2	83350	37 Prairie Living	36.3
82243	37 Prairie Living	100.0	83101	26 Midland Crowd	79.7	83352	37 Prairie Living	47.9
82244	37 Prairie Living	99.6	83110	25 Salt of The Earth	63.1	83355	26 Midland Crowd	57.6
82301	32 Rustbelt Traditions	17.4	83111	26 Midland Crowd	100.0	83401	25 Salt of The Earth	11.8
82310	31 Rural Resort Dwellers	100.0	83112	26 Midland Crowd	85.7	83402	48 Great Expectations	15.3
82321	37 Prairie Living	100.0	83113	26 Midland Crowd	89.5	83404	07 Exurbanites	34.9
82322	26 Midland Crowd	100.0	83114	25 Salt of The Earth	100.0	83406	12 Up and Coming Families	46.5
82323	37 Prairie Living	100.0	83115	31 Rural Resort Dwellers	100.0	83420	37 Prairie Living	89.7
82325	31 Rural Resort Dwellers	100.0	83118	31 Rural Resort Dwellers	100.0	83422	26 Midland Crowd	66.2

ZIP CODE	TOP TAPESTRY CONSUMER TYPE	% 2004 HOUSE-HOLDS	ZIP CODE	TOP TAPESTRY CONSUMER TYPE	% 2004 HOUSE-HOLDS	ZIP CODE	TOP TAPESTRY CONSUMER TYPE	% 2004 HOUSE-HOLDS
83423	42 Southern Satellites	100.0	83655	46 Rooted Rural	44.8	84031	46 Rooted Rural	100.0
83424	37 Prairie Living	100.0	83657	37 Prairie Living	100.0	84032	12 Up and Coming Families	39.2
83425	37 Prairie Living	100.0	83660	37 Prairie Living	27.6	84033	17 Green Acres	100.0
83428	31 Rural Resort Dwellers	100.0	83661	25 Salt of The Earth	35.5	84035	26 Midland Crowd	100.0
83429	31 Rural Resort Dwellers	100.0	83669	12 Up and Coming Families	64.6	84036	17 Green Acres	64.6
83431	37 Prairie Living	100.0	83670	37 Prairie Living	100.0	84037	07 Exurbanites	32.3
83434	25 Salt of The Earth	64.5	83672	25 Salt of The Earth	24.1	84038	31 Rural Resort Dwellers	92.0
83435	37 Prairie Living	100.0	83676	59 Southwestern Families	34.3	84039	26 Midland Crowd	98.2
83436	42 Southern Satellites	88.9	83677	31 Rural Resort Dwellers	100.0	84040	06 Sophisticated Squires	37.9
83440	63 Dorms To Diplomas	29.5	83686	12 Up and Coming Families	48.4	84041	12 Up and Coming Families	32.4
83442	26 Midland Crowd	52.0	83687	12 Up and Coming Families	45.9	84042	04 Boomburbs	45.5
83443	37 Prairie Living	50.8	83702	22 Metropolitans	31.9	84043	12 Up and Coming Families	62.2
83444	26 Midland Crowd	97.6	83703	13 In Style	22.6	84044	19 Milk and Cookies	35.6
83445	46 Rooted Rural	41.1	83704	28 Aspiring Young Families	26.4	84046	31 Rural Resort Dwellers	100.0
83446	31 Rural Resort Dwellers	100.0	83705	48 Great Expectations	43.5	84047	39 Young and Restless	22.8
83448	19 Milk and Cookies	57.0	83706	09 Urban Chic	16.9	84049	17 Green Acres	100.0
83449	31 Rural Resort Dwellers	96.7	83709	12 Up and Coming Families	18.8	84050	17 Green Acres	66.5
83450	37 Prairie Living	100.0	83712	36 Old and Newcomers	40.9	84051	46 Rooted Rural	100.0
83451	42 Southern Satellites	100.0	83713	04 Boomburbs	31.3	84052	37 Prairie Living	76.3
83452	37 Prairie Living	94.2	83714	12 Up and Coming Families	45.9	84053	25 Salt of The Earth	100.0
83455	12 Up and Coming Families	99.3	83716	12 Up and Coming Families	69.6	84054	13 In Style	35.3
83460	63 Dorms To Diplomas	0.0	83725	63 Dorms To Diplomas	0.0	84056	40 Military Proximity	100.0
83462	31 Rural Resort Dwellers	100.0	83801	26 Midland Crowd	67.1	84057	28 Aspiring Young Families	23.6
83463	31 Rural Resort Dwellers	100.0	83802	31 Rural Resort Dwellers	100.0	84058	28 Aspiring Young Families	25.2
83464	37 Prairie Living	100.0	83803	31 Rural Resort Dwellers	100.0	84060	16 Enterprising Professionals	43.0
83466	31 Rural Resort Dwellers	100.0	83804	46 Rooted Rural	100.0	84061	17 Green Acres	77.8
83467	31 Rural Resort Dwellers	50.3	83805	46 Rooted Rural	43.2	84062	12 Up and Coming Families	29.9
83469	31 Rural Resort Dwellers	100.0	83809	31 Rural Resort Dwellers	100.0	84063	56 Rural Bypasses	100.0
83501	33 Midlife Junction	18.9	83810	46 Rooted Rural	100.0	84064	37 Prairie Living	100.0
83520	25 Salt of The Earth	100.0	83811	31 Rural Resort Dwellers	100.0	84065	12 Up and Coming Families	65.8
83522	33 Midlife Junction	55.9	83812	31 Rural Resort Dwellers	100.0	84066	26 Midland Crowd	78.2
83523	37 Prairie Living	88.1	83813	31 Rural Resort Dwellers	99.3	84067	12 Up and Coming Families	42.1
83524	46 Rooted Rural	43.2	83814	48 Great Expectations	22.9	84069	25 Salt of The Earth	81.4
83525	31 Rural Resort Dwellers	100.0	83815	26 Midland Crowd	43.0	84070	28 Aspiring Young Families	31.1
83526	37 Prairie Living	85.7	83821	31 Rural Resort Dwellers	100.0	84071	26 Midland Crowd	70.3
83530	31 Rural Resort Dwellers	43.6	83822	46 Rooted Rural	96.6	84072	46 Rooted Rural	100.0
83533	37 Prairie Living	100.0	83823	25 Salt of The Earth	52.5	84073	46 Rooted Rural	53.2
83535	46 Rooted Rural	72.7	83824	46 Rooted Rural	100.0	84074	12 Up and Coming Families	57.7
83536	50 Heartland Communities	46.3	83827	31 Rural Resort Dwellers	100.0	84075	12 Up and Coming Families	51.7
83537	37 Prairie Living	96.7	83830	46 Rooted Rural	100.0	84076	26 Midland Crowd	100.0
83539	31 Rural Resort Dwellers	39.1	83832	37 Prairie Living	92.2	84078	26 Midland Crowd	33.2
83540	26 Midland Crowd	69.6	83833	31 Rural Resort Dwellers	92.5	84080	25 Salt of The Earth	100.0
83541	31 Rural Resort Dwellers	51.1	83834	46 Rooted Rural	100.0	84082	17 Green Acres	98.1
83542	31 Rural Resort Dwellers	100.0	83835	26 Midland Crowd	56.5	84083	58 Newest Residents	70.6
83543	37 Prairie Living	100.0	83836	31 Rural Resort Dwellers	100.0	84084	12 Up and Coming Families	37.5
83544	46 Rooted Rural	50.7	83837	50 Heartland Communities	57.4	84085	56 Rural Bypasses	61.1
83545	37 Prairie Living	79.6	83839	46 Rooted Rural	76.9	84086	37 Prairie Living	100.0
83546	46 Rooted Rural	93.2	83842	46 Rooted Rural	72.5	84087	12 Up and Coming Families	37.4
83547	31 Rural Resort Dwellers	100.0	83843	55 College Towns	26.5	84088	12 Up and Coming Families	58.8
83548	37 Prairie Living	52.2	83845	26 Midland Crowd	52.9	84092	02 Suburban Splendor	61.3
83549	31 Rural Resort Dwellers	100.0	83846	50 Heartland Communities	100.0	84093	06 Sophisticated Squires	50.5
83553	46 Rooted Rural	46.5	83847	17 Green Acres	36.7	84094	06 Sophisticated Squires	44.4
83554	31 Rural Resort Dwellers	100.0	83848	31 Rural Resort Dwellers	100.0	84095	04 Boomburbs	40.0
83555	31 Rural Resort Dwellers	100.0	83850	46 Rooted Rural	51.2	84097	06 Sophisticated Squires	46.2
83601	31 Rural Resort Dwellers	100.0	83851	26 Midland Crowd	39.9	84098	09 Urban Chic	59.5
83604	37 Prairie Living	100.0	83853	37 Prairie Living	100.0	84101	27 Metro Renters	51.8
83605	41 Crossroads	21.3	83854	26 Midland Crowd	67.6	84102	55 College Towns	39.8
83607	26 Midland Crowd	44.9	83855	50 Heartland Communities	59.2	84103	27 Metro Renters	29.7
83610	37 Prairie Living	100.0	83856	31 Rural Resort Dwellers	41.5	84104	38 Industrious Urban Fringe	66.4
83611	31 Rural Resort Dwellers	100.0	83857	46 Rooted Rural	87.7	84105	22 Metropolitans	70.5
83612	31 Rural Resort Dwellers	50.7	83858	26 Midland Crowd	94.4	84106	24 Main Street, USA	20.8
83615	31 Rural Resort Dwellers	100.0	83860	26 Midland Crowd	56.7	84107	28 Aspiring Young Families	19.0
83616	06 Sophisticated Squires	34.8	83861	46 Rooted Rural	47.8	84108	22 Metropolitans	26.2
83617	25 Salt of The Earth	22.9	83864	31 Rural Resort Dwellers	26.0	84109	05 Wealthy Seaboard Suburbs	26.5
83619	42 Southern Satellites	33.7	83868	50 Heartland Communities	86.6	84111	27 Metro Renters	27.3
83622	31 Rural Resort Dwellers	98.2	83869	26 Midland Crowd	51.6	84112	01 Top Rung	62.3
83623	46 Rooted Rural	77.1	83870	46 Rooted Rural	100.0	84113	63 Dorms To Diplomas	97.8
83624	42 Southern Satellites	55.4	83871	17 Green Acres	94.7	84115	52 Inner City Tenants	44.6
83626	26 Midland Crowd	85.5	83872	17 Green Acres	99.2	84116	38 Industrious Urban Fringe	19.8
83627	37 Prairie Living	86.8	83873	46 Rooted Rural	22.3	84117	36 Old and Newcomers	21.7
83628	53 Home Town	38.6	83876	31 Rural Resort Dwellers	63.6	84118	19 Milk and Cookies	38.0
83629	46 Rooted Rural	100.0	84001	37 Prairie Living	100.0	84119	38 Industrious Urban Fringe	16.8
83631	31 Rural Resort Dwellers	92.6	84003	24 Main Street, USA	24.1	84120	19 Milk and Cookies	36.8
83632	31 Rural Resort Dwellers	100.0	84004	04 Boomburbs	70.2	84121	07 Exurbanites	23.8
83633	37 Prairie Living	100.0	84006	18 Cozy and Comfortable	100.0	84123	39 Young and Restless	18.5
83634	12 Up and Coming Families	51.4	84007	25 Salt of The Earth	43.7	84124	05 Wealthy Seaboard Suburbs	24.6
83636	26 Midland Crowd	100.0	84010	24 Main Street, USA	20.9	84128	19 Milk and Cookies	54.1
83637	31 Rural Resort Dwellers	100.0	84013	12 Up and Coming Families	45.4	84302	32 Rustbelt Traditions	22.0
83638	31 Rural Resort Dwellers	100.0	84014	06 Sophisticated Squires	33.6	84305	25 Salt of The Earth	98.7
83639	37 Prairie Living	52.0	84015	12 Up and Coming Families	44.9	84306	17 Green Acres	60.1
83641	26 Midland Crowd	93.4	84017	17 Green Acres	53.4	84307	25 Salt of The Earth	77.7
83642	12 Up and Coming Families	61.0	84018	07 Exurbanites	100.0	84308	37 Prairie Living	98.5
83643	31 Rural Resort Dwellers	100.0	84020	04 Boomburbs	52.5	84309	17 Green Acres	100.0
83644	26 Midland Crowd	38.6	84021	46 Rooted Rural	51.5	84310	06 Sophisticated Squires	92.7
83645	37 Prairie Living	99.7	84022	19 Milk and Cookies	92.5	84311	25 Salt of The Earth	85.2
83647	26 Midland Crowd	33.8	84023	31 Rural Resort Dwellers	100.0	84312	25 Salt of The Earth	71.7
83648	40 Military Proximity	93.9	84025	06 Sophisticated Squires	31.0	84313	37 Prairie Living	100.0
83650	37 Prairie Living	100.0	84026	56 Rural Bypasses	59.5	84314	17 Green Acres	65.9
83651	48 Great Expectations	24.3	84028	31 Rural Resort Dwellers	100.0	84315	17 Green Acres	76.8
83654	31 Rural Resort Dwellers	56.3	84029	26 Midland Crowd	27.3	84317	06 Sophisticated Squires	60.5

ZIP CODE	TOP TAPESTRY CONSUMER TYPE	% 2004 HOUSE-HOLDS	ZIP CODE	TOP TAPESTRY CONSUMER TYPE	% 2004 HOUSE-HOLDS	ZIP CODE	TOP TAPESTRY CONSUMER TYPE	% 2004 HOUSE-HOLDS
84318	17 Green Acres	73.9	84753	42 Southern Satellites	88.9	85247	62 Modest Income Homes	33.0
84319	12 Up and Coming Families	44.0	84754	46 Rooted Rural	85.3	85248	04 Boomburbs	43.7
84320	25 Salt of The Earth	80.1	84755	46 Rooted Rural	88.9	85249	43 The Elders	38.4
84321	55 College Towns	23.3	84756	42 Southern Satellites	91.3	85250	22 Metropolitans	30.4
84322	63 Dorms To Diplomas	100.0	84757	31 Rural Resort Dwellers	100.0	85251	36 Old and Newcomers	23.0
84324	17 Green Acres	97.3	84758	46 Rooted Rural	93.2	85253	01 Top Rung	74.2
84325	17 Green Acres	96.3	84759	31 Rural Resort Dwellers	78.6	85254	07 Exurbanites	28.9
84328	17 Green Acres	100.0	84760	31 Rural Resort Dwellers	100.0	85255	03 Connoisseurs	48.4
84329	37 Prairie Living	100.0	84761	46 Rooted Rural	99.1	85256	56 Rural Bypasses	87.3
84330	17 Green Acres	100.0	84765	25 Salt of The Earth	44.8	85257	36 Old and Newcomers	16.0
84331	17 Green Acres	100.0	84766	25 Salt of The Earth	100.0	85258	09 Urban Chic	33.4
84332	06 Sophisticated Squires	38.6	84770	28 Aspiring Young Families	26.0	85259	16 Enterprising Professionals	33.9
84333	25 Salt of The Earth	99.1	84772	46 Rooted Rural	55.9	85260	16 Enterprising Professionals	30.2
84335	17 Green Acres	49.1	84773	31 Rural Resort Dwellers	100.0	85262	03 Connoisseurs	69.5
84336	26 Midland Crowd	96.2	84775	31 Rural Resort Dwellers	100.0	85263	15 Silver and Gold	97.6
84337	17 Green Acres	35.1	84780	49 Senior Sun Seekers	43.4	85264	38 Industrious Urban Fringe	83.0
84338	37 Prairie Living	99.4	84781	31 Rural Resort Dwellers	100.0	85268	15 Silver and Gold	28.6
84339	17 Green Acres	87.8	84782	31 Rural Resort Dwellers	98.5	85272	59 Southwestern Families	100.0
84340	17 Green Acres	99.9	84783	12 Up and Coming Families	55.0	85273	50 Heartland Communities	85.5
84341	39 Young and Restless	37.0	84790	15 Silver and Gold	26.5	85281	39 Young and Restless	28.0
84401	60 City Dimensions	22.6	85003	65 Social Security Set	41.1	85282	28 Aspiring Young Families	19.5
84403	07 Exurbanites	20.5	85004	65 Social Security Set	21.3	85283	39 Young and Restless	19.8
84404	26 Midland Crowd	16.0	85006	58 Newest Residents	51.4	85284	02 Suburban Splendor	46.0
84405	17 Green Acres	12.5	85007	58 Newest Residents	30.7	85287	22 Metropolitans	88.9
84408	14 Prosperous Empty Nesters	100.0	85008	58 Newest Residents	23.0	85292	56 Rural Bypasses	34.8
84414	06 Sophisticated Squires	39.0	85009	59 Southwestern Families	40.5	85296	04 Boomburbs	53.6
84501	26 Midland Crowd	19.5	85012	09 Urban Chic	23.4	85297	12 Up and Coming Families	72.0
84510	59 Southwestern Families	99.7	85013	36 Old and Newcomers	21.2	85301	52 Inner City Tenants	30.5
84511	26 Midland Crowd	79.8	85014	36 Old and Newcomers	30.1	85302	19 Milk and Cookies	31.8
84520	50 Heartland Communities	100.0	85015	52 Inner City Tenants	43.4	85303	19 Milk and Cookies	29.3
84523	25 Salt of The Earth	51.5	85016	36 Old and Newcomers	18.4	85304	19 Milk and Cookies	30.0
84525	42 Southern Satellites	87.8	85017	38 Industrious Urban Fringe	38.5	85305	12 Up and Coming Families	97.6
84526	50 Heartland Communities	51.6	85018	52 Inner City Tenants	13.7	85306	19 Milk and Cookies	44.2
84528	26 Midland Crowd	49.2	85019	58 Newest Residents	24.1	85307	12 Up and Coming Families	43.2
84531	59 Southwestern Families	98.3	85020	36 Old and Newcomers	10.1	85308	12 Up and Coming Families	21.9
84532	33 Midlife Junction	41.9	85021	39 Young and Restless	22.0	85309	40 Military Proximity	0.0
84533	41 Crossroads	100.0	85022	07 Exurbanites	19.7	85310	04 Boomburbs	52.2
84535	25 Salt of The Earth	36.7	85023	39 Young and Restless	17.5	85321	49 Senior Sun Seekers	69.7
84536	59 Southwestern Families	100.0	85024	19 Milk and Cookies	29.7	85322	41 Crossroads	100.0
84540	26 Midland Crowd	99.0	85027	19 Milk and Cookies	34.5	85323	12 Up and Coming Families	48.1
84542	26 Midland Crowd	100.0	85028	07 Exurbanites	26.9	85324	49 Senior Sun Seekers	100.0
84601	12 Up and Coming Families	30.8	85029	39 Young and Restless	15.5	85326	26 Midland Crowd	28.8
84604	63 Dorms To Diplomas	32.9	85031	38 Industrious Urban Fringe	76.0	85328	41 Crossroads	100.0
84606	63 Dorms To Diplomas	41.3	85032	19 Milk and Cookies	24.9	85331	04 Boomburbs	30.9
84621	37 Prairie Living	100.0	85033	38 Industrious Urban Fringe	67.1	85332	49 Senior Sun Seekers	71.6
84622	25 Salt of The Earth	90.1	85034	59 Southwestern Families	35.8	85333	59 Southwestern Families	100.0
84624	37 Prairie Living	39.9	85035	38 Industrious Urban Fringe	68.5	85335	38 Industrious Urban Fringe	43.3
84627	55 College Towns	52.9	85037	12 Up and Coming Families	41.9	85337	56 Rural Bypasses	100.0
84628	41 Crossroads	100.0	85040	58 Newest Residents	33.6	85338	12 Up and Coming Families	40.5
84629	31 Rural Resort Dwellers	41.6	85041	59 Southwestern Families	38.2	85339	17 Green Acres	28.9
84630	37 Prairie Living	100.0	85042	38 Industrious Urban Fringe	30.6	85340	15 Silver and Gold	30.5
84631	37 Prairie Living	48.6	85043	38 Industrious Urban Fringe	39.0	85342	46 Rooted Rural	54.3
84634	33 Midlife Junction	87.2	85044	16 Enterprising Professionals	25.9	85343	41 Crossroads	100.0
84635	25 Salt of The Earth	81.4	85045	04 Boomburbs	100.0	85344	49 Senior Sun Seekers	49.8
84642	33 Midlife Junction	74.9	85048	04 Boomburbs	64.2	85345	19 Milk and Cookies	28.9
84645	26 Midland Crowd	100.0	85050	12 Up and Coming Families	43.6	85347	59 Southwestern Families	55.3
84647	25 Salt of The Earth	51.8	85051	18 Cozy and Comfortable	25.9	85348	49 Senior Sun Seekers	100.0
84648	26 Midland Crowd	72.7	85053	18 Cozy and Comfortable	23.7	85350	59 Southwestern Families	71.3
84650	37 Prairie Living	100.0	85054	16 Enterprising Professionals	99.6	85351	43 The Elders	98.0
84651	12 Up and Coming Families	35.3	85085	04 Boomburbs	70.7	85353	38 Industrious Urban Fringe	38.8
84653	17 Green Acres	64.4	85086	06 Sophisticated Squires	60.0	85354	41 Crossroads	91.0
84654	25 Salt of The Earth	52.2	85087	17 Green Acres	75.3	85355	06 Sophisticated Squires	99.9
84655	12 Up and Coming Families	56.4	85201	28 Aspiring Young Families	24.9	85356	49 Senior Sun Seekers	63.7
84660	12 Up and Coming Families	31.7	85202	39 Young and Restless	28.3	85361	46 Rooted Rural	95.1
84663	17 Green Acres	18.1	85203	13 In Style	23.2	85362	31 Rural Resort Dwellers	62.5
84664	06 Sophisticated Squires	54.4	85204	19 Milk and Cookies	25.9	85363	57 Simple Living	73.0
84701	25 Salt of The Earth	22.7	85205	43 The Elders	29.6	85364	59 Southwestern Families	21.0
84710	31 Rural Resort Dwellers	100.0	85206	43 The Elders	46.9	85365	59 Southwestern Families	37.5
84712	31 Rural Resort Dwellers	100.0	85207	19 Milk and Cookies	27.1	85367	43 The Elders	57.4
84713	37 Prairie Living	79.9	85208	49 Senior Sun Seekers	30.5	85373	43 The Elders	74.5
84714	42 Southern Satellites	78.3	85210	52 Inner City Tenants	26.9	85374	43 The Elders	36.8
84716	26 Midland Crowd	100.0	85212	12 Up and Coming Families	89.1	85375	43 The Elders	100.0
84717	31 Rural Resort Dwellers	100.0	85213	06 Sophisticated Squires	31.8	85379	12 Up and Coming Families	75.0
84719	31 Rural Resort Dwellers	100.0	85215	43 The Elders	33.1	85381	06 Sophisticated Squires	34.9
84720	17 Green Acres	17.8	85218	15 Silver and Gold	63.3	85382	12 Up and Coming Families	46.3
84722	25 Salt of The Earth	70.4	85219	49 Senior Sun Seekers	45.4	85383	04 Boomburbs	50.3
84726	26 Midland Crowd	60.7	85220	49 Senior Sun Seekers	56.7	85387	43 The Elders	57.3
84728	53 Home Town	100.0	85222	41 Crossroads	17.6	85390	49 Senior Sun Seekers	62.1
84729	46 Rooted Rural	99.2	85224	19 Milk and Cookies	31.8	85501	50 Heartland Communities	29.4
84731	37 Prairie Living	83.7	85225	12 Up and Coming Families	31.5	85530	59 Southwestern Families	100.0
84734	46 Rooted Rural	42.2	85226	04 Boomburbs	26.8	85533	46 Rooted Rural	98.7
84737	26 Midland Crowd	43.9	85228	38 Industrious Urban Fringe	17.6	85534	42 Southern Satellites	46.5
84738	26 Midland Crowd	82.6	85231	59 Southwestern Families	34.5	85535	46 Rooted Rural	100.0
84739	25 Salt of The Earth	100.0	85232	59 Southwestern Families	59.4	85539	49 Senior Sun Seekers	24.4
84741	31 Rural Resort Dwellers	48.2	85233	12 Up and Coming Families	43.2	85540	19 Milk and Cookies	64.0
84743	37 Prairie Living	100.0	85234	12 Up and Coming Families	31.7	85541	31 Rural Resort Dwellers	31.3
84745	26 Midland Crowd	76.7	85236	12 Up and Coming Families	68.9	85542	59 Southwestern Families	88.1
84747	37 Prairie Living	100.0	85237	29 Rustbelt Retirees	45.0	85543	46 Rooted Rural	69.5
84750	37 Prairie Living	100.0	85239	41 Crossroads	74.6	85544	31 Rural Resort Dwellers	57.1
84751	37 Prairie Living	63.8	85242	26 Midland Crowd	49.2	85545	49 Senior Sun Seekers	100.0

ZIP CODE	TOP TAPESTRY CONSUMER TYPE	% 2004 HOUSE-HOLDS	ZIP CODE	TOP TAPESTRY CONSUMER TYPE	% 2004 HOUSE-HOLDS	ZIP CODE	TOP TAPESTRY CONSUMER TYPE	% 2004 HOUSE-HOLDS
85546	41 Crossroads	29.0	86042	59 Southwestern Families	100.0	87059	07 Exurbanites	46.6
85550	59 Southwestern Families	100.0	86043	56 Rural Bypasses	94.8	87060	26 Midland Crowd	100.0
85552	26 Midland Crowd	51.0	86044	29 Rustbelt Retirees	42.1	87062	41 Crossroads	94.9
85601	49 Senior Sun Seekers	100.0	86045	51 Metro City Edge	32.0	87063	46 Rooted Rural	100.0
85602	49 Senior Sun Seekers	34.9	86046	31 Rural Resort Dwellers	22.1	87068	07 Exurbanites	30.1
85603	50 Heartland Communities	69.9	86047	59 Southwestern Families	36.6	87083	14 Prosperous Empty Nesters	100.0
85606	49 Senior Sun Seekers	100.0	86053	59 Southwestern Families	98.1	87102	59 Southwestern Families	32.3
85607	59 Southwestern Families	56.6	86054	59 Southwestern Families	100.0	87104	33 Midlife Junction	27.1
85610	46 Rooted Rural	66.3	86301	14 Prosperous Empty Nesters	28.4	87105	38 Industrious Urban Fringe	36.3
85611	15 Silver and Gold	74.1	86303	15 Silver and Gold	43.2	87106	22 Metropolitans	40.9
85613	40 Military Proximity	99.8	86305	15 Silver and Gold	46.9	87107	33 Midlife Junction	25.6
85614	43 The Elders	77.0	86314	33 Midlife Junction	26.3	87108	52 Inner City Tenants	17.7
85615	26 Midland Crowd	53.6	86320	41 Crossroads	95.6	87109	36 Old and Newcomers	18.8
85616	46 Rooted Rural	61.2	86321	41 Crossroads	100.0	87110	14 Prosperous Empty Nesters	18.0
85617	49 Senior Sun Seekers	100.0	86322	49 Senior Sun Seekers	60.1	87111	36 Old and Newcomers	22.2
85618	59 Southwestern Families	51.4	86323	26 Midland Crowd	41.6	87112	32 Rustbelt Traditions	14.3
85619	07 Exurbanites	70.4	86324	49 Senior Sun Seekers	35.8	87113	12 Up and Coming Families	39.8
85621	59 Southwestern Families	69.7	86325	31 Rural Resort Dwellers	87.1	87114	12 Up and Coming Families	26.7
85623	46 Rooted Rural	70.8	86326	33 Midlife Junction	30.5	87116	40 Military Proximity	100.0
85624	49 Senior Sun Seekers	89.4	86327	15 Silver and Gold	47.6	87117	40 Military Proximity	100.0
85625	49 Senior Sun Seekers	100.0	86332	49 Senior Sun Seekers	68.7	87118	40 Military Proximity	100.0
85629	26 Midland Crowd	35.2	86333	49 Senior Sun Seekers	98.8	87120	12 Up and Coming Families	35.8
85630	49 Senior Sun Seekers	99.6	86334	26 Midland Crowd	80.4	87121	38 Industrious Urban Fringe	53.3
85631	38 Industrious Urban Fringe	29.4	86335	49 Senior Sun Seekers	94.2	87122	04 Boomburbs	41.7
85632	46 Rooted Rural	80.3	86336	15 Silver and Gold	62.7	87123	28 Aspiring Young Families	16.3
85634	51 Metro City Edge	44.1	86337	49 Senior Sun Seekers	99.6	87124	19 Milk and Cookies	42.1
85635	33 Midlife Junction	22.3	86343	31 Rural Resort Dwellers	86.8	87131	65 Social Security Set	98.4
85637	15 Silver and Gold	89.6	86351	15 Silver and Gold	100.0	87144	12 Up and Coming Families	68.9
85638	49 Senior Sun Seekers	97.6	86401	49 Senior Sun Seekers	31.5	87301	59 Southwestern Families	30.7
85640	46 Rooted Rural	61.0	86403	49 Senior Sun Seekers	31.0	87310	56 Rural Bypasses	100.0
85641	17 Green Acres	49.5	86404	31 Rural Resort Dwellers	51.1	87312	59 Southwestern Families	62.6
85643	46 Rooted Rural	41.9	86406	49 Senior Sun Seekers	31.6	87313	59 Southwestern Families	49.8
85645	49 Senior Sun Seekers	31.5	86413	49 Senior Sun Seekers	85.6	87315	46 Rooted Rural	78.9
85648	38 Industrious Urban Fringe	51.6	86426	33 Midlife Junction	77.1	87320	59 Southwestern Families	100.0
85650	07 Exurbanites	33.3	86429	33 Midlife Junction	76.3	87321	46 Rooted Rural	87.9
85653	41 Crossroads	29.9	86432	41 Crossroads	100.0	87323	41 Crossroads	50.8
85701	48 Great Expectations	19.9	86434	51 Metro City Edge	76.2	87325	59 Southwestern Families	41.5
85704	30 Retirement Communities	29.7	86435	59 Southwestern Families	100.0	87327	56 Rural Bypasses	81.2
85705	52 Inner City Tenants	34.9	86436	49 Senior Sun Seekers	100.0	87328	59 Southwestern Families	84.8
85706	38 Industrious Urban Fringe	29.3	86440	31 Rural Resort Dwellers	56.1	87401	41 Crossroads	30.8
85707	40 Military Proximity	99.9	86441	49 Senior Sun Seekers	100.0	87402	07 Exurbanites	23.9
85709	29 Rustbelt Retirees	100.0	86442	49 Senior Sun Seekers	62.4	87410	26 Midland Crowd	54.3
85710	33 Midlife Junction	18.6	86444	49 Senior Sun Seekers	100.0	87412	26 Midland Crowd	57.8
85711	52 Inner City Tenants	20.7	86502	59 Southwestern Families	65.8	87413	41 Crossroads	51.0
85712	52 Inner City Tenants	21.4	86503	59 Southwestern Families	79.7	87415	26 Midland Crowd	100.0
85713	59 Southwestern Families	32.9	86505	59 Southwestern Families	47.6	87416	26 Midland Crowd	100.0
85714	59 Southwestern Families	58.6	86507	59 Southwestern Families	100.0	87417	19 Milk and Cookies	63.7
85715	13 In Style	38.4	86510	59 Southwestern Families	100.0	87418	26 Midland Crowd	100.0
85716	52 Inner City Tenants	31.7	86514	59 Southwestern Families	100.0	87419	31 Rural Resort Dwellers	61.8
85718	03 Connoisseurs	27.4	86535	59 Southwestern Families	100.0	87420	51 Metro City Edge	41.9
85719	55 College Towns	32.5	86538	51 Metro City Edge	48.5	87421	26 Midland Crowd	53.7
85721	63 Dorms To Diplomas	100.0	86556	59 Southwestern Families	97.5	87501	09 Urban Chic	28.7
85730	19 Milk and Cookies	30.8	87001	59 Southwestern Families	87.8	87505	09 Urban Chic	23.4
85735	26 Midland Crowd	66.4	87002	26 Midland Crowd	26.9	87506	03 Connoisseurs	18.2
85736	41 Crossroads	77.9	87004	41 Crossroads	40.5	87507	41 Crossroads	43.6
85737	15 Silver and Gold	44.9	87005	46 Rooted Rural	57.7	87508	07 Exurbanites	61.2
85739	15 Silver and Gold	51.3	87006	41 Crossroads	82.6	87510	26 Midland Crowd	99.7
85741	19 Milk and Cookies	43.1	87007	51 Metro City Edge	77.0	87513	31 Rural Resort Dwellers	78.1
85742	12 Up and Coming Families	35.4	87008	07 Exurbanites	100.0	87514	31 Rural Resort Dwellers	100.0
85743	12 Up and Coming Families	55.3	87009	46 Rooted Rural	100.0	87520	31 Rural Resort Dwellers	100.0
85745	07 Exurbanites	21.9	87010	17 Green Acres	88.0	87521	46 Rooted Rural	74.8
85746	38 Industrious Urban Fringe	26.0	87012	46 Rooted Rural	100.0	87522	26 Midland Crowd	74.7
85747	12 Up and Coming Families	78.2	87013	56 Rural Bypasses	53.7	87524	31 Rural Resort Dwellers	66.1
85748	07 Exurbanites	33.7	87014	56 Rural Bypasses	33.4	87527	46 Rooted Rural	100.0
85749	07 Exurbanites	59.7	87015	12 Up and Coming Families	58.1	87528	51 Metro City Edge	77.9
85750	03 Connoisseurs	19.5	87016	46 Rooted Rural	100.0	87530	26 Midland Crowd	99.7
85901	31 Rural Resort Dwellers	32.7	87017	59 Southwestern Families	76.2	87531	41 Crossroads	58.5
85920	31 Rural Resort Dwellers	100.0	87018	31 Rural Resort Dwellers	70.2	87532	41 Crossroads	34.3
85922	46 Rooted Rural	100.0	87020	46 Rooted Rural	22.4	87535	26 Midland Crowd	76.7
85924	49 Senior Sun Seekers	82.2	87023	41 Crossroads	57.0	87537	41 Crossroads	55.2
85925	26 Midland Crowd	52.7	87024	59 Southwestern Families	79.8	87539	26 Midland Crowd	100.0
85928	31 Rural Resort Dwellers	100.0	87025	31 Rural Resort Dwellers	99.4	87540	07 Exurbanites	49.1
85929	31 Rural Resort Dwellers	100.0	87026	59 Southwestern Families	86.7	87544	13 In Style	23.3
85935	31 Rural Resort Dwellers	54.7	87027	31 Rural Resort Dwellers	100.0	87549	46 Rooted Rural	100.0
85936	46 Rooted Rural	45.0	87028	46 Rooted Rural	100.0	87552	41 Crossroads	54.6
85937	26 Midland Crowd	74.4	87029	46 Rooted Rural	98.4	87553	56 Rural Bypasses	76.5
85938	26 Midland Crowd	57.1	87031	26 Midland Crowd	39.0	87556	56 Rural Bypasses	37.7
86001	63 Dorms To Diplomas	19.3	87035	41 Crossroads	58.8	87557	26 Midland Crowd	36.1
86004	07 Exurbanites	14.9	87036	50 Heartland Communities	78.0	87560	56 Rural Bypasses	58.9
86021	26 Midland Crowd	88.2	87041	38 Industrious Urban Fringe	65.4	87564	31 Rural Resort Dwellers	85.7
86022	46 Rooted Rural	84.6	87042	26 Midland Crowd	76.8	87565	26 Midland Crowd	92.5
86025	26 Midland Crowd	37.8	87043	03 Connoisseurs	44.1	87566	41 Crossroads	71.3
86030	59 Southwestern Families	100.0	87044	31 Rural Resort Dwellers	69.3	87567	26 Midland Crowd	100.0
86033	41 Crossroads	58.0	87045	56 Rural Bypasses	95.1	87571	26 Midland Crowd	43.4
86034	59 Southwestern Families	78.2	87046	66 Unclassified	100.0	87573	31 Rural Resort Dwellers	100.0
86035	59 Southwestern Families	85.4	87047	17 Green Acres	48.8	87575	31 Rural Resort Dwellers	77.0
86036	26 Midland Crowd	88.4	87048	07 Exurbanites	41.5	87579	46 Rooted Rural	50.8
86038	31 Rural Resort Dwellers	100.0	87052	56 Rural Bypasses	74.5	87580	31 Rural Resort Dwellers	100.0
86039	59 Southwestern Families	100.0	87053	38 Industrious Urban Fringe	60.2	87581	26 Midland Crowd	97.3
86040	41 Crossroads	36.1	87056	17 Green Acres	56.4	87701	41 Crossroads	17.6

ZIP CODE	TOP TAPESTRY CONSUMER TYPE	% 2004 HOUSE-HOLDS	ZIP CODE	TOP TAPESTRY CONSUMER TYPE	% 2004 HOUSE-HOLDS	ZIP CODE	TOP TAPESTRY CONSUMER TYPE	% 2004 HOUSE-HOLDS
87711	56 Rural Bypasses	100.0	88203	50 Heartland Communities	24.2	89061	31 Rural Resort Dwellers	100.0
87713	46 Rooted Rural	74.2	88210	59 Southwestern Families	16.1	89074	06 Sophisticated Squires	19.9
87714	31 Rural Resort Dwellers	68.2	88213	37 Prairie Living	100.0	89084	37 Prairie Living	100.0
87715	46 Rooted Rural	64.7	88220	26 Midland Crowd	12.8	89101	58 Newest Residents	34.2
87718	31 Rural Resort Dwellers	100.0	88230	56 Rural Bypasses	36.0	89102	28 Aspiring Young Families	16.7
87722	46 Rooted Rural	100.0	88231	50 Heartland Communities	29.9	89103	39 Young and Restless	30.8
87724	56 Rural Bypasses	100.0	88232	59 Southwestern Families	70.4	89104	65 Social Security Set	16.7
87728	37 Prairie Living	100.0	88240	59 Southwestern Families	26.5	89106	52 Inner City Tenants	24.9
87729	37 Prairie Living	100.0	88242	26 Midland Crowd	58.0	89107	18 Cozy and Comfortable	18.2
87730	37 Prairie Living	100.0	88250	26 Midland Crowd	94.7	89108	52 Inner City Tenants	22.6
87731	41 Crossroads	55.6	88252	50 Heartland Communities	37.3	89109	52 Inner City Tenants	54.1
87732	56 Rural Bypasses	67.0	88253	41 Crossroads	76.7	89110	38 Industrious Urban Fringe	22.2
87733	37 Prairie Living	100.0	88256	56 Rural Bypasses	100.0	89113	16 Enterprising Professionals	74.4
87734	46 Rooted Rural	100.0	88260	59 Southwestern Families	34.0	89115	52 Inner City Tenants	25.8
87740	50 Heartland Communities	19.3	88264	46 Rooted Rural	100.0	89117	16 Enterprising Professionals	26.9
87742	31 Rural Resort Dwellers	100.0	88265	46 Rooted Rural	100.0	89118	39 Young and Restless	52.3
87743	37 Prairie Living	100.0	88267	46 Rooted Rural	53.4	89119	52 Inner City Tenants	40.3
87745	31 Rural Resort Dwellers	100.0	88301	50 Heartland Communities	87.2	89120	36 Old and Newcomers	26.9
87746	37 Prairie Living	100.0	88310	26 Midland Crowd	19.7	89121	52 Inner City Tenants	12.3
87747	50 Heartland Communities	71.0	88314	46 Rooted Rural	100.0	89122	49 Senior Sun Seekers	21.5
87750	46 Rooted Rural	100.0	88316	46 Rooted Rural	70.1	89123	12 Up and Coming Families	34.9
87752	46 Rooted Rural	100.0	88317	31 Rural Resort Dwellers	74.2	89124	07 Exurbanites	26.9
87801	41 Crossroads	31.7	88318	37 Prairie Living	100.0	89128	28 Aspiring Young Families	17.3
87820	31 Rural Resort Dwellers	100.0	88321	46 Rooted Rural	100.0	89129	12 Up and Coming Families	49.0
87821	31 Rural Resort Dwellers	100.0	88324	31 Rural Resort Dwellers	100.0	89130	12 Up and Coming Families	38.8
87823	46 Rooted Rural	81.9	88330	40 Military Proximity	100.0	89131	12 Up and Coming Families	78.2
87825	46 Rooted Rural	36.9	88336	46 Rooted Rural	100.0	89134	43 The Elders	49.2
87827	31 Rural Resort Dwellers	100.0	88337	46 Rooted Rural	38.0	89135	13 In Style	100.0
87828	46 Rooted Rural	100.0	88339	31 Rural Resort Dwellers	100.0	89139	07 Exurbanites	54.1
87829	31 Rural Resort Dwellers	100.0	88340	51 Metro City Edge	100.0	89141	26 Midland Crowd	100.0
87830	31 Rural Resort Dwellers	100.0	88341	31 Rural Resort Dwellers	87.7	89142	12 Up and Coming Families	35.0
87831	46 Rooted Rural	88.0	88343	46 Rooted Rural	100.0	89143	12 Up and Coming Families	100.0
87901	49 Senior Sun Seekers	82.0	88344	31 Rural Resort Dwellers	56.3	89144	07 Exurbanites	36.7
87930	49 Senior Sun Seekers	100.0	88345	31 Rural Resort Dwellers	59.2	89145	19 Milk and Cookies	22.9
87931	49 Senior Sun Seekers	100.0	88346	41 Crossroads	50.5	89146	36 Old and Newcomers	23.2
87933	49 Senior Sun Seekers	100.0	88347	31 Rural Resort Dwellers	100.0	89147	13 In Style	32.5
87936	59 Southwestern Families	100.0	88348	46 Rooted Rural	100.0	89148	13 In Style	100.0
87937	59 Southwestern Families	100.0	88351	46 Rooted Rural	100.0	89149	07 Exurbanites	47.6
87940	59 Southwestern Families	100.0	88352	46 Rooted Rural	77.7	89154	65 Social Security Set	100.0
87941	59 Southwestern Families	100.0	88353	50 Heartland Communities	100.0	89156	12 Up and Coming Families	22.4
87942	49 Senior Sun Seekers	100.0	88354	31 Rural Resort Dwellers	100.0	89191	40 Military Proximity	100.0
87943	49 Senior Sun Seekers	100.0	88401	50 Heartland Communities	35.1	89301	50 Heartland Communities	33.9
88001	41 Crossroads	14.6	88410	37 Prairie Living	100.0	89310	49 Senior Sun Seekers	96.2
88002	40 Military Proximity	100.0	88411	46 Rooted Rural	100.0	89311	46 Rooted Rural	100.0
88005	33 Midlife Junction	21.5	88414	37 Prairie Living	100.0	89316	26 Midland Crowd	55.8
88007	26 Midland Crowd	36.0	88415	50 Heartland Communities	87.1	89317	26 Midland Crowd	99.3
88008	07 Exurbanites	40.5	88416	49 Senior Sun Seekers	100.0	89403	26 Midland Crowd	93.9
88011	22 Metropolitans	34.1	88417	46 Rooted Rural	100.0	89404	17 Green Acres	98.5
88012	41 Crossroads	66.3	88418	37 Prairie Living	100.0	89405	41 Crossroads	91.3
88020	46 Rooted Rural	100.0	88419	37 Prairie Living	100.0	89406	17 Green Acres	23.0
88021	59 Southwestern Families	76.5	88421	49 Senior Sun Seekers	100.0	89408	26 Midland Crowd	40.6
88022	41 Crossroads	92.1	88422	37 Prairie Living	100.0	89409	50 Heartland Communities	100.0
88023	59 Southwestern Families	29.9	88424	37 Prairie Living	100.0	89410	07 Exurbanites	38.2
88025	46 Rooted Rural	100.0	88426	46 Rooted Rural	100.0	89412	42 Southern Satellites	84.7
88026	56 Rural Bypasses	47.9	88427	37 Prairie Living	100.0	89413	15 Silver and Gold	53.1
88030	56 Rural Bypasses	27.4	88430	46 Rooted Rural	100.0	89414	26 Midland Crowd	100.0
88039	31 Rural Resort Dwellers	100.0	88431	49 Senior Sun Seekers	100.0	89415	49 Senior Sun Seekers	37.6
88041	46 Rooted Rural	98.4	88434	46 Rooted Rural	97.5	89418	26 Midland Crowd	100.0
88042	49 Senior Sun Seekers	100.0	88435	56 Rural Bypasses	38.8	89419	26 Midland Crowd	38.6
88043	50 Heartland Communities	70.6	88436	37 Prairie Living	100.0	89420	49 Senior Sun Seekers	100.0
88044	59 Southwestern Families	57.6	88437	37 Prairie Living	100.0	89423	07 Exurbanites	53.8
88045	42 Southern Satellites	38.1	88439	49 Senior Sun Seekers	100.0	89424	41 Crossroads	100.0
88047	41 Crossroads	43.0	89001	46 Rooted Rural	100.0	89425	37 Prairie Living	58.8
88048	59 Southwestern Families	100.0	89005	14 Prosperous Empty Nesters	39.6	89426	37 Prairie Living	93.8
88049	46 Rooted Rural	99.8	89008	50 Heartland Communities	87.3	89427	53 Home Town	100.0
88061	33 Midlife Junction	25.3	89011	15 Silver and Gold	100.0	89429	26 Midland Crowd	53.7
88063	59 Southwestern Families	100.0	89012	16 Enterprising Professionals	35.1	89430	31 Rural Resort Dwellers	58.0
88072	59 Southwestern Families	100.0	89013	49 Senior Sun Seekers	100.0	89431	52 Inner City Tenants	19.2
88081	59 Southwestern Families	57.2	89014	13 In Style	23.9	89433	41 Crossroads	40.4
88101	53 Home Town	14.7	89015	12 Up and Coming Families	26.2	89434	06 Sophisticated Squires	21.6
88103	40 Military Proximity	100.0	89017	46 Rooted Rural	100.0	89436	12 Up and Coming Families	43.2
88112	37 Prairie Living	100.0	89018	41 Crossroads	84.2	89440	17 Green Acres	91.3
88113	37 Prairie Living	100.0	89019	26 Midland Crowd	91.0	89442	41 Crossroads	100.0
88114	37 Prairie Living	100.0	89020	33 Midlife Junction	49.0	89444	49 Senior Sun Seekers	63.3
88116	37 Prairie Living	95.3	89027	15 Silver and Gold	36.2	89445	26 Midland Crowd	36.2
88118	37 Prairie Living	100.0	89029	36 Old and Newcomers	82.9	89447	49 Senior Sun Seekers	43.7
88119	50 Heartland Communities	67.6	89030	38 Industrious Urban Fringe	42.6	89451	09 Urban Chic	29.8
88120	37 Prairie Living	100.0	89031	12 Up and Coming Families	82.9	89460	19 Milk and Cookies	26.2
88121	37 Prairie Living	100.0	89032	12 Up and Coming Families	69.3	89501	65 Social Security Set	76.7
88123	37 Prairie Living	100.0	89033	37 Prairie Living	100.0	89502	52 Inner City Tenants	18.2
88124	50 Heartland Communities	66.6	89040	31 Rural Resort Dwellers	25.8	89503	18 Cozy and Comfortable	24.2
88125	37 Prairie Living	100.0	89041	49 Senior Sun Seekers	72.9	89506	28 Aspiring Young Families	24.6
88126	37 Prairie Living	100.0	89043	31 Rural Resort Dwellers	54.0	89509	03 Connoisseurs	17.5
88130	37 Prairie Living	17.3	89045	41 Crossroads	100.0	89510	07 Exurbanites	75.1
88132	37 Prairie Living	100.0	89046	49 Senior Sun Seekers	100.0	89511	07 Exurbanites	31.3
88133	37 Prairie Living	100.0	89047	41 Crossroads	99.2	89512	52 Inner City Tenants	36.3
88134	37 Prairie Living	92.3	89048	49 Senior Sun Seekers	51.7	89521	13 In Style	20.6
88135	56 Rural Bypasses	71.3	89049	26 Midland Crowd	31.4	89523	12 Up and Coming Families	60.0
88136	37 Prairie Living	97.9	89052	13 In Style	43.8	89701	36 Old and Newcomers	15.9
88201	14 Prosperous Empty Nesters	24.5	89060	49 Senior Sun Seekers	90.5	89703	33 Midlife Junction	28.6

ZIP CODE	TOP TAPESTRY CONSUMER TYPE	% 2004 HOUSE-HOLDS	ZIP CODE	TOP TAPESTRY CONSUMER TYPE	% 2004 HOUSE-HOLDS	ZIP CODE	TOP TAPESTRY CONSUMER TYPE	% 2004 HOUSE-HOLDS
89704	06 Sophisticated Squires	54.0	90245	09 Urban Chic	75.5	91001	10 Pleasant-Ville	21.0
89705	18 Cozy and Comfortable	72.5	90247	35 International Marketplace	43.4	91006	11 Pacific Heights	29.1
89706	28 Aspiring Young Families	28.3	90248	10 Pleasant-Ville	19.5	91007	11 Pacific Heights	34.1
89801	12 Up and Coming Families	29.0	90249	10 Pleasant-Ville	25.6	91010	21 Urban Villages	26.7
89815	12 Up and Coming Families	66.1	90250	35 International Marketplace	36.6	91011	01 Top Rung	69.3
89820	26 Midland Crowd	62.4	90254	08 Laptops and Lattes	77.6	91016	35 International Marketplace	42.8
89821	46 Rooted Rural	100.0	90255	47 Las Casas	65.9	91020	23 Trendsetters	47.0
89822	26 Midland Crowd	59.5	90260	35 International Marketplace	82.0	91024	09 Urban Chic	69.4
89823	41 Crossroads	69.0	90262	47 Las Casas	70.1	91030	23 Trendsetters	49.5
89825	41 Crossroads	86.3	90263	01 Top Rung	100.0	91040	10 Pleasant-Ville	36.2
89831	51 Metro City Edge	75.3	90265	01 Top Rung	58.3	91042	05 Wealthy Seaboard Suburbs	26.0
89833	26 Midland Crowd	100.0	90266	01 Top Rung	41.2	91101	27 Metro Renters	62.1
89834	37 Prairie Living	100.0	90270	47 Las Casas	100.0	91103	58 Newest Residents	20.7
89835	41 Crossroads	72.6	90272	01 Top Rung	83.0	91104	09 Urban Chic	31.4
90001	47 Las Casas	94.8	90274	01 Top Rung	75.6	91105	03 Connoisseurs	35.9
90002	47 Las Casas	65.2	90275	01 Top Rung	39.2	91106	27 Metro Renters	23.4
90003	47 Las Casas	89.5	90277	08 Laptops and Lattes	43.3	91107	23 Trendsetters	30.7
90004	58 Newest Residents	45.3	90278	09 Urban Chic	46.6	91108	01 Top Rung	89.9
90005	58 Newest Residents	70.2	90280	47 Las Casas	72.8	91123	08 Laptops and Lattes	100.0
90006	58 Newest Residents	71.7	90290	09 Urban Chic	59.2	91201	35 International Marketplace	54.5
90007	63 Dorms To Diplomas	31.0	90291	23 Trendsetters	40.2	91202	20 City Lights	26.1
90008	45 City Strivers	26.1	90292	27 Metro Renters	42.7	91203	35 International Marketplace	70.2
90010	65 Social Security Set	40.3	90293	27 Metro Renters	46.8	91204	35 International Marketplace	49.7
90011	47 Las Casas	90.5	90301	35 International Marketplace	30.1	91205	35 International Marketplace	49.0
90012	65 Social Security Set	33.4	90302	52 Inner City Tenants	24.3	91206	44 Urban Melting Pot	34.7
90013	47 Las Casas	90.2	90303	47 Las Casas	42.6	91207	03 Connoisseurs	58.3
90014	65 Social Security Set	99.3	90304	47 Las Casas	77.0	91208	03 Connoisseurs	38.9
90015	58 Newest Residents	77.9	90305	34 Family Foundations	50.6	91214	05 Wealthy Seaboard Suburbs	31.3
90016	45 City Strivers	28.4	90401	08 Laptops and Lattes	29.5	91301	02 Suburban Splendor	48.8
90017	58 Newest Residents	99.8	90402	01 Top Rung	60.7	91302	01 Top Rung	56.2
90018	35 International Marketplace	29.2	90403	08 Laptops and Lattes	57.5	91303	35 International Marketplace	25.5
90019	35 International Marketplace	33.1	90404	23 Trendsetters	78.7	91304	35 International Marketplace	31.4
90020	58 Newest Residents	26.0	90405	08 Laptops and Lattes	56.4	91306	35 International Marketplace	40.1
90021	65 Social Security Set	50.4	90501	11 Pacific Heights	28.7	91307	10 Pleasant-Ville	37.8
90022	47 Las Casas	87.3	90502	11 Pacific Heights	50.5	91311	13 In Style	21.2
90023	47 Las Casas	88.6	90503	23 Trendsetters	37.1	91316	30 Retirement Communities	36.5
90024	08 Laptops and Lattes	44.6	90504	11 Pacific Heights	45.2	91320	02 Suburban Splendor	24.2
90025	27 Metro Renters	50.4	90505	09 Urban Chic	28.2	91321	13 In Style	29.5
90026	35 International Marketplace	46.7	90601	21 Urban Villages	17.7	91324	23 Trendsetters	15.6
90027	23 Trendsetters	33.8	90602	47 Las Casas	18.6	91325	23 Trendsetters	33.1
90028	27 Metro Renters	31.8	90603	10 Pleasant-Ville	57.0	91326	03 Connoisseurs	31.6
90029	58 Newest Residents	56.1	90604	10 Pleasant-Ville	32.6	91330	55 College Towns	100.0
90031	47 Las Casas	66.2	90605	21 Urban Villages	51.2	91331	47 Las Casas	49.5
90032	47 Las Casas	51.0	90606	21 Urban Villages	69.4	91335	21 Urban Villages	31.9
90033	47 Las Casas	63.7	90620	10 Pleasant-Ville	36.3	91340	47 Las Casas	52.2
90034	23 Trendsetters	26.5	90621	35 International Marketplace	38.2	91342	21 Urban Villages	50.4
90035	23 Trendsetters	61.3	90623	05 Wealthy Seaboard Suburbs	40.7	91343	58 Newest Residents	39.9
90036	27 Metro Renters	31.1	90630	05 Wealthy Seaboard Suburbs	29.0	91344	10 Pleasant-Ville	38.7
90037	47 Las Casas	54.5	90631	10 Pleasant-Ville	17.6	91345	10 Pleasant-Ville	41.8
90038	58 Newest Residents	63.5	90638	10 Pleasant-Ville	47.8	91350	06 Sophisticated Squires	35.0
90039	35 International Marketplace	23.6	90639	30 Retirement Communities	100.0	91351	06 Sophisticated Squires	29.8
90040	47 Las Casas	59.0	90640	21 Urban Villages	22.5	91352	47 Las Casas	45.4
90041	35 International Marketplace	22.3	90650	21 Urban Villages	70.3	91354	04 Boomburbs	65.5
90042	35 International Marketplace	25.9	90660	21 Urban Villages	79.4	91355	04 Boomburbs	17.0
90043	45 City Strivers	29.8	90670	21 Urban Villages	75.2	91356	36 Old and Newcomers	31.5
90044	47 Las Casas	41.1	90680	35 International Marketplace	48.7	91360	05 Wealthy Seaboard Suburbs	22.3
90045	23 Trendsetters	18.4	90701	21 Urban Villages	29.5	91361	09 Urban Chic	37.2
90046	27 Metro Renters	50.1	90703	11 Pacific Heights	60.3	91362	02 Suburban Splendor	28.5
90047	34 Family Foundations	48.1	90704	35 International Marketplace	59.2	91364	09 Urban Chic	46.9
90048	08 Laptops and Lattes	54.6	90706	35 International Marketplace	46.7	91367	05 Wealthy Seaboard Suburbs	26.2
90049	01 Top Rung	43.5	90710	35 International Marketplace	37.3	91371	39 Young and Restless	100.0
90056	03 Connoisseurs	44.3	90712	10 Pleasant-Ville	82.5	91377	02 Suburban Splendor	75.5
90057	58 Newest Residents	74.4	90713	10 Pleasant-Ville	87.4	91381	04 Boomburbs	68.9
90058	58 Newest Residents	52.2	90715	35 International Marketplace	33.2	91384	04 Boomburbs	61.9
90059	47 Las Casas	46.8	90716	47 Las Casas	64.4	91387	06 Sophisticated Squires	28.1
90061	47 Las Casas	66.3	90717	20 City Lights	29.3	91390	06 Sophisticated Squires	38.6
90062	45 City Strivers	64.9	90720	03 Connoisseurs	29.7	91401	35 International Marketplace	38.6
90063	47 Las Casas	97.5	90723	47 Las Casas	37.3	91402	58 Newest Residents	48.4
90064	23 Trendsetters	29.6	90731	35 International Marketplace	27.8	91403	23 Trendsetters	52.6
90065	47 Las Casas	25.6	90732	05 Wealthy Seaboard Suburbs	25.6	91405	35 International Marketplace	69.3
90066	23 Trendsetters	40.2	90740	43 The Elders	46.2	91406	35 International Marketplace	50.2
90067	08 Laptops and Lattes	100.0	90742	08 Laptops and Lattes	85.8	91411	35 International Marketplace	22.0
90068	08 Laptops and Lattes	41.9	90743	09 Urban Chic	100.0	91423	23 Trendsetters	33.2
90069	27 Metro Renters	66.2	90744	47 Las Casas	54.1	91436	01 Top Rung	49.3
90071	66 Unclassified	100.0	90745	21 Urban Villages	48.3	91501	23 Trendsetters	25.6
90077	01 Top Rung	100.0	90746	10 Pleasant-Ville	39.3	91502	35 International Marketplace	60.5
90089	63 Dorms To Diplomas	100.0	90747	34 Family Foundations	100.0	91504	05 Wealthy Seaboard Suburbs	21.0
90095	27 Metro Renters	100.0	90755	16 Enterprising Professionals	38.7	91505	20 City Lights	27.8
90201	47 Las Casas	96.6	90802	27 Metro Renters	32.7	91506	20 City Lights	32.7
90210	01 Top Rung	71.3	90803	08 Laptops and Lattes	31.1	91522	23 Trendsetters	100.0
90211	08 Laptops and Lattes	56.0	90804	58 Newest Residents	25.5	91601	23 Trendsetters	22.8
90212	08 Laptops and Lattes	94.1	90805	35 International Marketplace	33.6	91602	23 Trendsetters	56.5
90220	47 Las Casas	34.9	90806	35 International Marketplace	34.0	91604	09 Urban Chic	34.0
90221	47 Las Casas	83.9	90807	10 Pleasant-Ville	12.9	91605	58 Newest Residents	34.2
90222	47 Las Casas	55.5	90808	10 Pleasant-Ville	41.3	91606	35 International Marketplace	39.0
90230	22 Metropolitans	29.8	90810	21 Urban Villages	59.9	91607	23 Trendsetters	58.5
90232	23 Trendsetters	22.9	90813	58 Newest Residents	78.4	91701	06 Sophisticated Squires	26.2
90240	10 Pleasant-Ville	24.6	90814	23 Trendsetters	51.5	91702	21 Urban Villages	36.9
90241	35 International Marketplace	38.5	90815	05 Wealthy Seaboard Suburbs	55.6	91706	21 Urban Villages	51.9
90242	21 Urban Villages	43.3	90840	63 Dorms To Diplomas	100.0	91709	04 Boomburbs	48.5

ZIP CODE	TOP TAPESTRY CONSUMER TYPE	% 2004 HOUSE-HOLDS	ZIP CODE	TOP TAPESTRY CONSUMER TYPE	% 2004 HOUSE-HOLDS	ZIP CODE	TOP TAPESTRY CONSUMER TYPE	% 2004 HOUSE-HOLDS
91710	06 Sophisticated Squires	25.8	92064	06 Sophisticated Squires	30.8	92280	49 Senior Sun Seekers	66.7
91711	05 Wealthy Seaboard Suburbs	30.4	92065	06 Sophisticated Squires	26.7	92281	59 Southwestern Families	94.9
91722	21 Urban Villages	58.7	92066	31 Rural Resort Dwellers	99.4	92282	49 Senior Sun Seekers	60.1
91723	35 International Marketplace	50.8	92067	01 Top Rung	100.0	92283	56 Rural Bypasses	57.0
91724	13 In Style	30.1	92069	43 The Elders	14.5	92284	49 Senior Sun Seekers	30.1
91730	28 Aspiring Young Families	37.8	92070	46 Rooted Rural	61.0	92285	49 Senior Sun Seekers	78.5
91731	47 Las Casas	46.2	92071	06 Sophisticated Squires	24.9	92301	38 Industrious Urban Fringe	61.8
91732	47 Las Casas	48.6	92075	09 Urban Chic	47.4	92304	31 Rural Resort Dwellers	88.9
91733	47 Las Casas	72.9	92078	12 Up and Coming Families	40.2	92305	17 Green Acres	92.1
91737	06 Sophisticated Squires	68.7	92081	06 Sophisticated Squires	21.9	92307	13 In Style	15.1
91739	12 Up and Coming Families	37.4	92082	07 Exurbanites	45.0	92308	38 Industrious Urban Fringe	15.3
91740	10 Pleasant-Ville	50.5	92083	28 Aspiring Young Families	26.0	92309	41 Crossroads	96.1
91741	05 Wealthy Seaboard Suburbs	32.4	92084	10 Pleasant-Ville	18.1	92310	40 Military Proximity	100.0
91744	21 Urban Villages	73.4	92086	31 Rural Resort Dwellers	94.3	92311	32 Rustbelt Traditions	36.5
91745	11 Pacific Heights	41.5	92091	01 Top Rung	100.0	92313	16 Enterprising Professionals	19.0
91746	21 Urban Villages	84.5	92101	27 Metro Renters	41.4	92314	31 Rural Resort Dwellers	50.0
91748	11 Pacific Heights	43.8	92102	47 Las Casas	29.0	92315	31 Rural Resort Dwellers	64.9
91750	49 Senior Sun Seekers	21.7	92103	27 Metro Renters	57.9	92316	38 Industrious Urban Fringe	45.6
91752	57 Simple Living	31.2	92104	52 Inner City Tenants	26.6	92317	07 Exurbanites	100.0
91754	11 Pacific Heights	52.5	92105	58 Newest Residents	48.5	92320	49 Senior Sun Seekers	28.6
91755	35 International Marketplace	37.5	92106	09 Urban Chic	47.0	92321	07 Exurbanites	52.4
91759	07 Exurbanites	85.8	92107	23 Trendsetters	33.4	92322	19 Milk and Cookies	57.5
91761	19 Milk and Cookies	21.8	92108	39 Young and Restless	50.3	92324	38 Industrious Urban Fringe	38.6
91762	21 Urban Villages	16.0	92109	27 Metro Renters	50.9	92325	18 Cozy and Comfortable	27.4
91763	21 Urban Villages	46.5	92110	22 Metropolitans	19.8	92327	50 Heartland Communities	69.6
91764	47 Las Casas	21.0	92111	35 International Marketplace	18.0	92328	49 Senior Sun Seekers	100.0
91765	11 Pacific Heights	37.6	92113	47 Las Casas	61.0	92332	31 Rural Resort Dwellers	79.4
91766	47 Las Casas	50.4	92114	21 Urban Villages	39.6	92335	38 Industrious Urban Fringe	29.7
91767	21 Urban Villages	40.9	92115	55 College Towns	18.8	92336	12 Up and Coming Families	31.9
91768	47 Las Casas	43.8	92116	52 Inner City Tenants	33.1	92337	12 Up and Coming Families	45.9
91770	21 Urban Villages	45.4	92117	20 City Lights	20.8	92338	49 Senior Sun Seekers	80.8
91773	10 Pleasant-Ville	27.2	92118	09 Urban Chic	36.6	92339	22 Metropolitans	77.7
91775	11 Pacific Heights	35.0	92119	05 Wealthy Seaboard Suburbs	28.9	92342	14 Prosperous Empty Nesters	93.8
91776	35 International Marketplace	53.1	92120	14 Prosperous Empty Nesters	18.7	92345	19 Milk and Cookies	24.9
91780	11 Pacific Heights	73.7	92121	04 Boomburbs	53.0	92346	06 Sophisticated Squires	16.2
91784	02 Suburban Splendor	37.5	92122	27 Metro Renters	46.6	92347	46 Rooted Rural	91.3
91786	52 Inner City Tenants	30.3	92123	16 Enterprising Professionals	26.8	92350	23 Trendsetters	78.6
91789	11 Pacific Heights	46.3	92124	16 Enterprising Professionals	27.9	92352	07 Exurbanites	92.2
91790	21 Urban Villages	61.9	92126	06 Sophisticated Squires	19.4	92354	36 Old and Newcomers	27.6
91791	11 Pacific Heights	24.1	92127	16 Enterprising Professionals	29.3	92356	46 Rooted Rural	81.4
91792	21 Urban Villages	37.9	92128	04 Boomburbs	39.6	92358	31 Rural Resort Dwellers	95.1
91801	35 International Marketplace	46.9	92129	02 Suburban Splendor	39.4	92359	24 Main Street, USA	57.9
91803	35 International Marketplace	48.7	92130	04 Boomburbs	38.0	92363	49 Senior Sun Seekers	27.8
91901	07 Exurbanites	39.2	92131	02 Suburban Splendor	37.6	92364	41 Crossroads	65.2
91902	09 Urban Chic	27.9	92133	40 Military Proximity	100.0	92365	49 Senior Sun Seekers	42.5
91905	31 Rural Resort Dwellers	95.5	92134	66 Unclassified	0.0	92368	53 Home Town	100.0
91906	26 Midland Crowd	96.5	92135	40 Military Proximity	100.0	92371	26 Midland Crowd	73.3
91910	52 Inner City Tenants	14.0	92136	40 Military Proximity	100.0	92372	17 Green Acres	52.5
91911	21 Urban Villages	24.2	92139	21 Urban Villages	27.1	92373	36 Old and Newcomers	20.1
91913	04 Boomburbs	40.1	92140	40 Military Proximity	100.0	92374	06 Sophisticated Squires	14.5
91914	12 Up and Coming Families	54.0	92145	40 Military Proximity	100.0	92376	38 Industrious Urban Fringe	32.8
91915	04 Boomburbs	51.0	92154	21 Urban Villages	41.8	92377	12 Up and Coming Families	47.5
91916	26 Midland Crowd	92.6	92173	58 Newest Residents	37.0	92382	07 Exurbanites	85.9
91917	31 Rural Resort Dwellers	99.6	92182	63 Dorms To Diplomas	100.0	92384	49 Senior Sun Seekers	100.0
91932	52 Inner City Tenants	28.4	92201	58 Newest Residents	22.6	92385	13 In Style	66.5
91934	50 Heartland Communities	100.0	92203	43 The Elders	78.1	92389	49 Senior Sun Seekers	100.0
91935	02 Suburban Splendor	58.0	92210	15 Silver and Gold	84.8	92392	19 Milk and Cookies	29.8
91941	36 Old and Newcomers	34.6	92211	15 Silver and Gold	51.6	92394	38 Industrious Urban Fringe	49.6
91942	36 Old and Newcomers	33.0	92220	38 Industrious Urban Fringe	32.7	92397	13 In Style	87.1
91945	24 Main Street, USA	27.4	92223	24 Main Street, USA	30.0	92399	49 Senior Sun Seekers	12.8
91950	21 Urban Villages	25.8	92225	38 Industrious Urban Fringe	39.2	92401	58 Newest Residents	98.5
91962	07 Exurbanites	76.3	92227	59 Southwestern Families	29.7	92404	38 Industrious Urban Fringe	16.7
91963	26 Midland Crowd	83.0	92230	51 Metro City Edge	54.9	92405	38 Industrious Urban Fringe	24.7
91977	28 Aspiring Young Families	15.6	92231	59 Southwestern Families	58.3	92407	38 Industrious Urban Fringe	20.7
91978	13 In Style	42.4	92233	38 Industrious Urban Fringe	39.1	92408	52 Inner City Tenants	23.6
91980	26 Midland Crowd	100.0	92234	12 Up and Coming Families	23.1	92410	58 Newest Residents	37.8
92003	14 Prosperous Empty Nesters	64.2	92236	47 Las Casas	42.5	92411	59 Southwestern Families	57.3
92004	31 Rural Resort Dwellers	80.5	92239	29 Rustbelt Retirees	43.7	92501	38 Industrious Urban Fringe	34.4
92007	08 Laptops and Lattes	39.8	92240	52 Inner City Tenants	18.3	92503	38 Industrious Urban Fringe	15.5
92008	09 Urban Chic	29.6	92241	49 Senior Sun Seekers	88.2	92504	24 Main Street, USA	24.7
92009	09 Urban Chic	34.8	92242	49 Senior Sun Seekers	100.0	92505	21 Urban Villages	26.9
92014	01 Top Rung	45.9	92243	59 Southwestern Families	24.5	92506	02 Suburban Splendor	17.9
92019	13 In Style	26.2	92249	59 Southwestern Families	88.8	92507	16 Enterprising Professionals	18.0
92020	52 Inner City Tenants	39.0	92250	38 Industrious Urban Fringe	44.1	92508	04 Boomburbs	60.1
92021	28 Aspiring Young Families	21.5	92251	12 Up and Coming Families	42.9	92509	38 Industrious Urban Fringe	29.0
92024	02 Suburban Splendor	20.8	92252	50 Heartland Communities	43.4	92518	43 The Elders	100.0
92025	58 Newest Residents	14.5	92253	15 Silver and Gold	32.1	92521	63 Dorms To Diplomas	100.0
92026	14 Prosperous Empty Nesters	14.2	92254	47 Las Casas	100.0	92530	12 Up and Coming Families	21.6
92027	21 Urban Villages	16.5	92256	33 Midlife Junction	86.0	92532	17 Green Acres	65.6
92028	07 Exurbanites	29.7	92257	43 The Elders	98.5	92536	31 Rural Resort Dwellers	84.5
92029	03 Connoisseurs	29.1	92259	49 Senior Sun Seekers	100.0	92539	49 Senior Sun Seekers	43.9
92036	31 Rural Resort Dwellers	85.3	92260	15 Silver and Gold	28.0	92543	49 Senior Sun Seekers	23.5
92037	01 Top Rung	29.9	92262	30 Retirement Communities	18.6	92544	49 Senior Sun Seekers	19.5
92040	28 Aspiring Young Families	18.5	92264	15 Silver and Gold	50.1	92545	49 Senior Sun Seekers	35.6
92054	28 Aspiring Young Families	16.0	92267	49 Senior Sun Seekers	100.0	92548	49 Senior Sun Seekers	51.1
92055	40 Military Proximity	100.0	92270	15 Silver and Gold	47.4	92549	31 Rural Resort Dwellers	100.0
92056	06 Sophisticated Squires	25.5	92274	58 Newest Residents	35.4	92551	12 Up and Coming Families	51.4
92057	21 Urban Villages	14.5	92276	49 Senior Sun Seekers	67.6	92553	19 Milk and Cookies	33.0
92059	26 Midland Crowd	83.8	92277	52 Inner City Tenants	32.8	92555	06 Sophisticated Squires	48.5
92061	38 Industrious Urban Fringe	78.4	92278	40 Military Proximity	100.0	92557	19 Milk and Cookies	40.2

451

ZIP CODE	TOP TAPESTRY CONSUMER TYPE	% 2004 HOUSE-HOLDS	ZIP CODE	TOP TAPESTRY CONSUMER TYPE	% 2004 HOUSE-HOLDS	ZIP CODE	TOP TAPESTRY CONSUMER TYPE	% 2004 HOUSE-HOLDS
92561	31 Rural Resort Dwellers	90.9	92868	35 International Marketplace	24.9	93283	49 Senior Sun Seekers	100.0
92562	14 Prosperous Empty Nesters	24.3	92869	03 Connoisseurs	19.5	93285	49 Senior Sun Seekers	97.7
92563	06 Sophisticated Squires	38.1	92870	05 Wealthy Seaboard Suburbs	25.5	93286	59 Southwestern Families	39.2
92567	26 Midland Crowd	31.9	92879	12 Up and Coming Families	35.9	93287	31 Rural Resort Dwellers	100.0
92570	38 Industrious Urban Fringe	50.7	92880	04 Boomburbs	23.8	93291	38 Industrious Urban Fringe	27.8
92571	38 Industrious Urban Fringe	81.3	92881	04 Boomburbs	63.7	93292	19 Milk and Cookies	30.7
92582	46 Rooted Rural	49.1	92882	04 Boomburbs	26.6	93301	33 Midlife Junction	21.0
92583	49 Senior Sun Seekers	24.7	92883	12 Up and Coming Families	84.2	93304	38 Industrious Urban Fringe	50.2
92584	12 Up and Coming Families	38.9	92886	05 Wealthy Seaboard Suburbs	19.2	93305	58 Newest Residents	42.6
92585	33 Midlife Junction	33.8	92887	02 Suburban Splendor	59.3	93306	38 Industrious Urban Fringe	27.1
92586	43 The Elders	73.4	93001	28 Aspiring Young Families	17.4	93307	38 Industrious Urban Fringe	52.8
92587	07 Exurbanites	45.5	93003	36 Old and Newcomers	18.5	93308	60 City Dimensions	12.3
92590	28 Aspiring Young Families	87.7	93004	13 In Style	27.8	93309	28 Aspiring Young Families	23.2
92591	06 Sophisticated Squires	19.3	93010	05 Wealthy Seaboard Suburbs	27.1	93311	13 In Style	35.8
92592	04 Boomburbs	62.1	93012	04 Boomburbs	25.8	93312	12 Up and Coming Families	64.6
92595	26 Midland Crowd	36.7	93013	24 Main Street, USA	17.5	93313	12 Up and Coming Families	63.7
92596	12 Up and Coming Families	62.8	93015	21 Urban Villages	49.4	93314	06 Sophisticated Squires	81.6
92602	04 Boomburbs	100.0	93021	02 Suburban Splendor	38.0	93401	55 College Towns	32.1
92603	03 Connoisseurs	69.2	93022	10 Pleasant-Ville	45.7	93402	10 Pleasant-Ville	22.3
92604	02 Suburban Splendor	31.7	93023	09 Urban Chic	33.2	93405	63 Dorms To Diplomas	37.8
92606	16 Enterprising Professionals	54.7	93030	21 Urban Villages	29.9	93407	63 Dorms To Diplomas	100.0
92610	04 Boomburbs	78.9	93033	21 Urban Villages	57.6	93420	33 Midlife Junction	26.0
92612	27 Metro Renters	16.3	93035	09 Urban Chic	27.2	93422	07 Exurbanites	29.7
92614	02 Suburban Splendor	43.9	93036	13 In Style	19.0	93426	26 Midland Crowd	57.8
92618	16 Enterprising Professionals	95.0	93041	35 International Marketplace	24.4	93427	33 Midlife Junction	37.4
92620	02 Suburban Splendor	43.6	93042	40 Military Proximity	100.0	93428	15 Silver and Gold	97.0
92624	09 Urban Chic	31.4	93043	40 Military Proximity	100.0	93429	59 Southwestern Families	100.0
92625	01 Top Rung	54.1	93060	47 Las Casas	28.7	93430	31 Rural Resort Dwellers	91.5
92626	39 Young and Restless	25.8	93063	06 Sophisticated Squires	20.7	93432	17 Green Acres	44.9
92627	23 Trendsetters	27.7	93065	10 Pleasant-Ville	20.9	93433	13 In Style	33.2
92629	09 Urban Chic	46.1	93066	03 Connoisseurs	45.5	93434	21 Urban Villages	56.2
92630	02 Suburban Splendor	23.7	93067	09 Urban Chic	100.0	93436	18 Cozy and Comfortable	17.0
92646	05 Wealthy Seaboard Suburbs	30.2	93101	23 Trendsetters	43.2	93437	40 Military Proximity	99.5
92647	05 Wealthy Seaboard Suburbs	25.3	93103	35 International Marketplace	22.6	93441	07 Exurbanites	65.1
92648	08 Laptops and Lattes	18.5	93105	09 Urban Chic	30.1	93442	15 Silver and Gold	29.5
92649	05 Wealthy Seaboard Suburbs	17.6	93106	63 Dorms To Diplomas	98.8	93444	17 Green Acres	33.7
92651	09 Urban Chic	29.0	93108	01 Top Rung	57.3	93445	49 Senior Sun Seekers	30.1
92653	43 The Elders	48.3	93109	09 Urban Chic	53.0	93446	33 Midlife Junction	19.3
92655	11 Pacific Heights	68.3	93110	09 Urban Chic	45.1	93449	09 Urban Chic	61.0
92656	04 Boomburbs	47.8	93111	03 Connoisseurs	29.9	93450	26 Midland Crowd	100.0
92657	01 Top Rung	58.5	93117	63 Dorms To Diplomas	28.7	93451	17 Green Acres	47.4
92660	01 Top Rung	37.0	93202	38 Industrious Urban Fringe	100.0	93452	31 Rural Resort Dwellers	76.2
92661	08 Laptops and Lattes	73.3	93203	47 Las Casas	61.3	93453	17 Green Acres	42.7
92662	08 Laptops and Lattes	86.1	93204	38 Industrious Urban Fringe	32.4	93454	24 Main Street, USA	18.3
92663	08 Laptops and Lattes	27.9	93205	49 Senior Sun Seekers	100.0	93455	10 Pleasant-Ville	28.0
92672	23 Trendsetters	24.3	93206	59 Southwestern Families	64.9	93458	47 Las Casas	24.9
92673	04 Boomburbs	26.5	93207	37 Prairie Living	49.6	93460	07 Exurbanites	33.1
92675	01 Top Rung	15.5	93210	38 Industrious Urban Fringe	35.0	93461	38 Industrious Urban Fringe	67.1
92676	09 Urban Chic	44.7	93212	38 Industrious Urban Fringe	60.3	93463	03 Connoisseurs	24.5
92677	02 Suburban Splendor	32.5	93215	38 Industrious Urban Fringe	32.3	93465	31 Rural Resort Dwellers	24.3
92679	04 Boomburbs	41.2	93219	59 Southwestern Families	70.1	93501	48 Great Expectations	28.2
92683	11 Pacific Heights	27.1	93221	24 Main Street, USA	35.0	93505	26 Midland Crowd	53.9
92688	04 Boomburbs	46.2	93223	38 Industrious Urban Fringe	58.8	93510	07 Exurbanites	68.3
92691	05 Wealthy Seaboard Suburbs	27.7	93224	42 Southern Satellites	72.8	93512	31 Rural Resort Dwellers	100.0
92692	02 Suburban Splendor	24.5	93225	26 Midland Crowd	56.5	93513	33 Midlife Junction	100.0
92694	01 Top Rung	100.0	93226	31 Rural Resort Dwellers	100.0	93514	07 Exurbanites	42.3
92697	63 Dorms To Diplomas	58.4	93230	38 Industrious Urban Fringe	18.2	93516	50 Heartland Communities	48.6
92701	58 Newest Residents	55.8	93234	47 Las Casas	60.3	93517	31 Rural Resort Dwellers	100.0
92703	47 Las Casas	54.9	93235	38 Industrious Urban Fringe	66.9	93518	49 Senior Sun Seekers	54.0
92704	21 Urban Villages	29.3	93238	49 Senior Sun Seekers	100.0	93519	49 Senior Sun Seekers	97.3
92705	03 Connoisseurs	22.2	93239	59 Southwestern Families	87.9	93523	40 Military Proximity	80.1
92706	35 International Marketplace	17.2	93240	49 Senior Sun Seekers	100.0	93524	14 Prosperous Empty Nesters	42.9
92707	47 Las Casas	32.4	93241	47 Las Casas	91.0	93526	33 Midlife Junction	100.0
92708	05 Wealthy Seaboard Suburbs	38.5	93242	38 Industrious Urban Fringe	58.1	93527	46 Rooted Rural	46.5
92780	35 International Marketplace	24.9	93243	26 Midland Crowd	64.9	93528	49 Senior Sun Seekers	100.0
92782	16 Enterprising Professionals	73.0	93244	07 Exurbanites	77.4	93529	31 Rural Resort Dwellers	100.0
92801	35 International Marketplace	45.0	93245	12 Up and Coming Families	22.0	93531	07 Exurbanites	68.8
92802	35 International Marketplace	24.6	93247	38 Industrious Urban Fringe	25.2	93532	19 Milk and Cookies	84.1
92804	35 International Marketplace	52.6	93249	47 Las Casas	100.0	93534	52 Inner City Tenants	19.2
92805	21 Urban Villages	30.2	93250	59 Southwestern Families	66.1	93535	19 Milk and Cookies	34.7
92806	35 International Marketplace	17.4	93251	42 Southern Satellites	100.0	93536	13 In Style	16.6
92807	03 Connoisseurs	16.8	93252	56 Rural Bypasses	66.8	93541	31 Rural Resort Dwellers	100.0
92808	04 Boomburbs	65.7	93254	37 Prairie Living	100.0	93543	19 Milk and Cookies	71.9
92821	05 Wealthy Seaboard Suburbs	13.4	93255	49 Senior Sun Seekers	100.0	93544	31 Rural Resort Dwellers	67.3
92823	13 In Style	52.3	93256	59 Southwestern Families	85.0	93545	50 Heartland Communities	43.7
92831	39 Young and Restless	25.6	93257	38 Industrious Urban Fringe	19.8	93546	09 Urban Chic	65.9
92832	21 Urban Villages	22.3	93260	31 Rural Resort Dwellers	91.8	93550	38 Industrious Urban Fringe	39.2
92833	21 Urban Villages	16.7	93262	31 Rural Resort Dwellers	100.0	93551	06 Sophisticated Squires	46.3
92835	03 Connoisseurs	20.8	93263	38 Industrious Urban Fringe	43.3	93552	12 Up and Coming Families	34.0
92840	35 International Marketplace	34.2	93265	31 Rural Resort Dwellers	51.4	93553	25 Salt of The Earth	79.2
92841	35 International Marketplace	37.6	93266	38 Industrious Urban Fringe	90.3	93554	49 Senior Sun Seekers	100.0
92843	21 Urban Villages	53.9	93267	59 Southwestern Families	64.8	93555	19 Milk and Cookies	17.0
92844	35 International Marketplace	40.9	93268	53 Home Town	35.9	93560	26 Midland Crowd	32.1
92845	05 Wealthy Seaboard Suburbs	57.8	93270	38 Industrious Urban Fringe	41.5	93561	07 Exurbanites	21.9
92860	10 Pleasant-Ville	30.9	93271	31 Rural Resort Dwellers	82.6	93562	53 Home Town	98.3
92861	01 Top Rung	70.3	93272	38 Industrious Urban Fringe	96.7	93563	31 Rural Resort Dwellers	100.0
92862	04 Boomburbs	85.7	93274	38 Industrious Urban Fringe	44.6	93591	38 Industrious Urban Fringe	62.8
92865	10 Pleasant-Ville	28.6	93276	42 Southern Satellites	77.4	93601	31 Rural Resort Dwellers	100.0
92866	36 Old and Newcomers	17.8	93277	28 Aspiring Young Families	13.9	93602	46 Rooted Rural	44.8
92867	10 Pleasant-Ville	21.0	93280	38 Industrious Urban Fringe	52.6	93604	31 Rural Resort Dwellers	100.0

ZIP CODE	TOP TAPESTRY CONSUMER TYPE	% 2004 HOUSE-HOLDS	ZIP CODE	TOP TAPESTRY CONSUMER TYPE	% 2004 HOUSE-HOLDS	ZIP CODE	TOP TAPESTRY CONSUMER TYPE	% 2004 HOUSE-HOLDS
93608	47 Las Casas	76.2	94024	01 Top Rung	87.9	94542	09 Urban Chic	40.5
93609	38 Industrious Urban Fringe	77.9	94025	08 Laptops and Lattes	38.2	94544	35 International Marketplace	33.9
93610	38 Industrious Urban Fringe	32.6	94027	01 Top Rung	94.7	94545	10 Pleasant-Ville	28.2
93611	07 Exurbanites	31.3	94028	01 Top Rung	83.6	94546	05 Wealthy Seaboard Suburbs	34.8
93612	52 Inner City Tenants	28.1	94030	05 Wealthy Seaboard Suburbs	40.4	94547	11 Pacific Heights	39.4
93614	31 Rural Resort Dwellers	56.3	94035	40 Military Proximity	100.0	94548	25 Salt of The Earth	100.0
93615	47 Las Casas	45.4	94038	02 Suburban Splendor	72.0	94549	03 Connoisseurs	36.1
93616	59 Southwestern Families	50.0	94040	27 Metro Renters	31.1	94550	02 Suburban Splendor	21.3
93618	38 Industrious Urban Fringe	41.4	94041	23 Trendsetters	41.8	94551	06 Sophisticated Squires	28.7
93620	38 Industrious Urban Fringe	73.0	94043	23 Trendsetters	54.6	94552	02 Suburban Splendor	70.6
93621	31 Rural Resort Dwellers	100.0	94044	11 Pacific Heights	26.5	94553	13 In Style	26.0
93622	38 Industrious Urban Fringe	31.5	94060	09 Urban Chic	100.0	94555	11 Pacific Heights	38.0
93623	28 Aspiring Young Families	91.2	94061	23 Trendsetters	48.0	94556	03 Connoisseurs	71.3
93625	21 Urban Villages	37.3	94062	01 Top Rung	38.6	94558	03 Connoisseurs	17.1
93626	49 Senior Sun Seekers	43.4	94063	35 International Marketplace	28.4	94559	35 International Marketplace	32.1
93627	47 Las Casas	100.0	94065	08 Laptops and Lattes	47.0	94560	11 Pacific Heights	32.3
93630	47 Las Casas	40.5	94066	11 Pacific Heights	21.9	94561	12 Up and Coming Families	32.3
93631	26 Midland Crowd	23.9	94070	09 Urban Chic	40.4	94563	01 Top Rung	59.2
93633	31 Rural Resort Dwellers	54.0	94074	09 Urban Chic	100.0	94564	05 Wealthy Seaboard Suburbs	29.0
93635	12 Up and Coming Families	29.6	94080	11 Pacific Heights	50.9	94565	38 Industrious Urban Fringe	17.2
93637	24 Main Street, USA	15.6	94085	16 Enterprising Professionals	68.0	94566	02 Suburban Splendor	27.0
93638	58 Newest Residents	24.6	94086	16 Enterprising Professionals	33.0	94567	26 Midland Crowd	51.4
93640	47 Las Casas	66.0	94087	09 Urban Chic	28.3	94568	16 Enterprising Professionals	38.0
93641	31 Rural Resort Dwellers	52.6	94089	11 Pacific Heights	29.8	94569	14 Prosperous Empty Nesters	100.0
93643	31 Rural Resort Dwellers	100.0	94102	65 Social Security Set	44.4	94571	31 Rural Resort Dwellers	30.7
93644	31 Rural Resort Dwellers	36.6	94103	23 Trendsetters	44.8	94572	06 Sophisticated Squires	27.1
93645	31 Rural Resort Dwellers	100.0	94104	65 Social Security Set	100.0	94574	09 Urban Chic	35.0
93646	47 Las Casas	59.9	94105	08 Laptops and Lattes	99.9	94576	09 Urban Chic	100.0
93647	59 Southwestern Families	48.8	94107	08 Laptops and Lattes	52.0	94577	20 City Lights	30.8
93648	47 Las Casas	49.6	94108	65 Social Security Set	41.1	94578	35 International Marketplace	26.8
93650	59 Southwestern Families	33.5	94109	27 Metro Renters	46.6	94579	10 Pleasant-Ville	40.8
93651	17 Green Acres	100.0	94110	23 Trendsetters	41.0	94580	10 Pleasant-Ville	62.2
93652	21 Urban Villages	92.5	94111	08 Laptops and Lattes	48.9	94583	02 Suburban Splendor	44.0
93653	31 Rural Resort Dwellers	87.2	94112	11 Pacific Heights	91.3	94585	19 Milk and Cookies	36.0
93654	38 Industrious Urban Fringe	19.0	94114	08 Laptops and Lattes	94.6	94586	05 Wealthy Seaboard Suburbs	61.0
93656	38 Industrious Urban Fringe	73.2	94115	08 Laptops and Lattes	59.0	94587	11 Pacific Heights	54.6
93657	38 Industrious Urban Fringe	16.6	94116	11 Pacific Heights	79.3	94588	02 Suburban Splendor	39.4
93660	47 Las Casas	64.7	94117	08 Laptops and Lattes	72.6	94589	10 Pleasant-Ville	20.4
93662	38 Industrious Urban Fringe	35.2	94118	08 Laptops and Lattes	52.3	94590	35 International Marketplace	17.7
93664	15 Silver and Gold	36.4	94121	11 Pacific Heights	37.7	94591	06 Sophisticated Squires	18.7
93667	17 Green Acres	73.3	94122	11 Pacific Heights	47.8	94592	63 Dorms To Diplomas	100.0
93668	38 Industrious Urban Fringe	58.7	94123	08 Laptops and Lattes	95.7	94595	43 The Elders	64.3
93669	31 Rural Resort Dwellers	100.0	94124	11 Pacific Heights	35.9	94596	27 Metro Renters	36.5
93675	46 Rooted Rural	66.8	94127	09 Urban Chic	53.3	94597	09 Urban Chic	27.4
93701	58 Newest Residents	73.5	94129	08 Laptops and Lattes	97.4	94598	03 Connoisseurs	39.8
93702	59 Southwestern Families	44.5	94130	39 Young and Restless	100.0	94599	49 Senior Sun Seekers	50.2
93703	38 Industrious Urban Fringe	35.5	94131	08 Laptops and Lattes	45.7	94601	35 International Marketplace	42.9
93704	33 Midlife Junction	23.7	94132	11 Pacific Heights	35.5	94602	35 International Marketplace	29.6
93705	38 Industrious Urban Fringe	35.6	94133	08 Laptops and Lattes	40.0	94603	47 Las Casas	25.3
93706	59 Southwestern Families	26.8	94134	11 Pacific Heights	93.3	94605	45 City Strivers	28.1
93710	52 Inner City Tenants	27.3	94158	27 Metro Renters	100.0	94606	35 International Marketplace	46.6
93711	07 Exurbanites	20.9	94301	01 Top Rung	39.7	94607	65 Social Security Set	27.7
93720	04 Boomburbs	35.3	94303	21 Urban Villages	21.1	94608	45 City Strivers	42.9
93721	65 Social Security Set	36.2	94304	27 Metro Renters	72.7	94609	23 Trendsetters	65.2
93722	12 Up and Coming Families	30.9	94305	63 Dorms To Diplomas	73.1	94610	27 Metro Renters	55.3
93725	59 Southwestern Families	41.1	94306	09 Urban Chic	44.6	94611	27 Metro Renters	33.5
93726	55 College Towns	24.3	94401	23 Trendsetters	26.6	94612	65 Social Security Set	54.4
93727	52 Inner City Tenants	18.4	94402	09 Urban Chic	34.2	94613	55 College Towns	81.3
93728	38 Industrious Urban Fringe	32.6	94403	09 Urban Chic	33.7	94618	08 Laptops and Lattes	32.8
93740	63 Dorms To Diplomas	0.0	94404	09 Urban Chic	40.5	94619	35 International Marketplace	29.7
93741	22 Metropolitans	100.0	94501	23 Trendsetters	46.0	94621	47 Las Casas	38.2
93901	20 City Lights	50.4	94502	03 Connoisseurs	35.2	94702	23 Trendsetters	47.0
93905	47 Las Casas	79.4	94503	06 Sophisticated Squires	46.4	94703	23 Trendsetters	84.7
93906	35 International Marketplace	46.1	94506	01 Top Rung	48.6	94704	63 Dorms To Diplomas	68.4
93907	07 Exurbanites	33.3	94507	01 Top Rung	72.9	94705	08 Laptops and Lattes	41.6
93908	03 Connoisseurs	40.8	94508	09 Urban Chic	68.3	94706	09 Urban Chic	35.9
93920	09 Urban Chic	84.6	94509	24 Main Street, USA	18.3	94707	03 Connoisseurs	49.3
93923	15 Silver and Gold	66.6	94510	13 In Style	32.5	94708	03 Connoisseurs	77.5
93924	09 Urban Chic	53.4	94512	18 Cozy and Comfortable	100.0	94709	08 Laptops and Lattes	53.3
93925	21 Urban Villages	100.0	94513	04 Boomburbs	55.8	94710	23 Trendsetters	72.6
93926	47 Las Casas	39.3	94514	07 Exurbanites	86.3	94720	63 Dorms To Diplomas	100.0
93927	47 Las Casas	71.7	94515	50 Heartland Communities	22.9	94801	47 Las Casas	23.9
93930	47 Las Casas	57.9	94517	02 Suburban Splendor	61.0	94803	13 In Style	40.4
93932	26 Midland Crowd	66.4	94518	05 Wealthy Seaboard Suburbs	23.9	94804	45 City Strivers	16.7
93933	35 International Marketplace	22.1	94519	10 Pleasant-Ville	57.4	94805	05 Wealthy Seaboard Suburbs	30.7
93940	23 Trendsetters	43.9	94520	52 Inner City Tenants	20.0	94806	21 Urban Villages	24.6
93943	23 Trendsetters	81.8	94521	05 Wealthy Seaboard Suburbs	23.6	94901	23 Trendsetters	33.6
93950	09 Urban Chic	64.5	94523	05 Wealthy Seaboard Suburbs	25.5	94903	09 Urban Chic	32.1
93953	15 Silver and Gold	54.1	94525	20 City Lights	32.4	94904	01 Top Rung	45.8
93955	35 International Marketplace	33.4	94526	03 Connoisseurs	32.2	94920	01 Top Rung	74.0
93960	47 Las Casas	48.4	94528	03 Connoisseurs	100.0	94922	15 Silver and Gold	100.0
94002	08 Laptops and Lattes	30.3	94530	05 Wealthy Seaboard Suburbs	29.3	94923	15 Silver and Gold	66.2
94005	09 Urban Chic	100.0	94531	04 Boomburbs	87.4	94924	09 Urban Chic	100.0
94010	01 Top Rung	30.7	94533	24 Main Street, USA	23.0	94925	09 Urban Chic	68.6
94014	11 Pacific Heights	83.9	94534	02 Suburban Splendor	21.4	94928	28 Aspiring Young Families	19.5
94015	11 Pacific Heights	63.5	94535	40 Military Proximity	100.0	94929	31 Rural Resort Dwellers	100.0
94019	09 Urban Chic	75.9	94536	11 Pacific Heights	35.4	94930	09 Urban Chic	100.0
94020	09 Urban Chic	99.3	94538	11 Pacific Heights	40.6	94931	28 Aspiring Young Families	35.9
94021	09 Urban Chic	100.0	94539	02 Suburban Splendor	44.8	94933	09 Urban Chic	100.0
94022	01 Top Rung	81.8	94541	35 International Marketplace	37.1	94937	15 Silver and Gold	57.4

ZIP CODE	TOP TAPESTRY CONSUMER TYPE	% 2004 HOUSE-HOLDS	ZIP CODE	TOP TAPESTRY CONSUMER TYPE	% 2004 HOUSE-HOLDS	ZIP CODE	TOP TAPESTRY CONSUMER TYPE	% 2004 HOUSE-HOLDS
94938	09 Urban Chic	100.0	95207	24 Main Street, USA	16.7	95404	03 Connoisseurs	21.0
94939	09 Urban Chic	43.3	95209	18 Cozy and Comfortable	23.4	95405	24 Main Street, USA	19.3
94940	37 Prairie Living	100.0	95210	19 Milk and Cookies	19.4	95407	21 Urban Villages	31.2
94941	01 Top Rung	42.2	95211	63 Dorms To Diplomas	100.0	95409	43 The Elders	24.1
94945	23 Trendsetters	24.8	95212	14 Prosperous Empty Nesters	42.2	95410	15 Silver and Gold	98.6
94946	01 Top Rung	74.2	95215	38 Industrious Urban Fringe	42.1	95412	15 Silver and Gold	100.0
94947	09 Urban Chic	31.0	95219	13 In Style	22.6	95415	46 Rooted Rural	68.9
94949	09 Urban Chic	59.2	95220	17 Green Acres	25.9	95417	31 Rural Resort Dwellers	46.8
94951	31 Rural Resort Dwellers	38.3	95222	31 Rural Resort Dwellers	62.5	95420	31 Rural Resort Dwellers	100.0
94952	09 Urban Chic	47.8	95223	31 Rural Resort Dwellers	56.5	95421	31 Rural Resort Dwellers	85.1
94954	10 Pleasant-Ville	32.1	95228	31 Rural Resort Dwellers	98.5	95422	49 Senior Sun Seekers	64.4
94956	09 Urban Chic	100.0	95230	25 Salt of The Earth	47.2	95423	49 Senior Sun Seekers	68.2
94960	09 Urban Chic	72.0	95231	24 Main Street, USA	29.5	95425	46 Rooted Rural	29.3
94963	09 Urban Chic	100.0	95232	31 Rural Resort Dwellers	100.0	95427	31 Rural Resort Dwellers	98.5
94964	18 Cozy and Comfortable	52.2	95236	10 Pleasant-Ville	34.6	95428	46 Rooted Rural	78.0
94965	08 Laptops and Lattes	69.1	95237	26 Midland Crowd	54.0	95429	31 Rural Resort Dwellers	100.0
94970	09 Urban Chic	100.0	95240	24 Main Street, USA	16.6	95432	15 Silver and Gold	100.0
94971	09 Urban Chic	61.2	95242	13 In Style	22.0	95436	22 Metropolitans	26.3
94972	03 Connoisseurs	100.0	95245	31 Rural Resort Dwellers	93.8	95437	31 Rural Resort Dwellers	41.4
94973	09 Urban Chic	100.0	95246	31 Rural Resort Dwellers	71.8	95439	13 In Style	67.6
95002	21 Urban Villages	100.0	95247	15 Silver and Gold	32.3	95441	17 Green Acres	57.3
95003	09 Urban Chic	52.2	95249	49 Senior Sun Seekers	41.8	95442	09 Urban Chic	70.6
95004	06 Sophisticated Squires	45.0	95251	31 Rural Resort Dwellers	100.0	95443	49 Senior Sun Seekers	100.0
95005	09 Urban Chic	73.5	95252	17 Green Acres	51.8	95444	17 Green Acres	85.9
95006	09 Urban Chic	100.0	95255	31 Rural Resort Dwellers	41.9	95445	31 Rural Resort Dwellers	99.9
95008	23 Trendsetters	43.4	95257	31 Rural Resort Dwellers	100.0	95446	22 Metropolitans	47.0
95010	36 Old and Newcomers	42.7	95258	19 Milk and Cookies	58.3	95448	09 Urban Chic	24.6
95012	47 Las Casas	60.0	95301	38 Industrious Urban Fringe	29.4	95449	38 Industrious Urban Fringe	53.3
95013	17 Green Acres	60.0	95303	37 Prairie Living	96.8	95450	31 Rural Resort Dwellers	100.0
95014	01 Top Rung	27.0	95304	26 Midland Crowd	30.0	95451	31 Rural Resort Dwellers	44.9
95017	09 Urban Chic	100.0	95306	31 Rural Resort Dwellers	99.8	95452	07 Exurbanites	51.1
95018	09 Urban Chic	51.3	95307	38 Industrious Urban Fringe	32.4	95453	31 Rural Resort Dwellers	33.0
95019	47 Las Casas	27.3	95309	31 Rural Resort Dwellers	100.0	95454	46 Rooted Rural	93.1
95020	06 Sophisticated Squires	17.0	95310	49 Senior Sun Seekers	54.4	95456	15 Silver and Gold	75.0
95023	04 Boomburbs	21.0	95311	31 Rural Resort Dwellers	63.2	95457	31 Rural Resort Dwellers	36.8
95030	01 Top Rung	62.9	95313	37 Prairie Living	40.2	95458	49 Senior Sun Seekers	96.7
95032	09 Urban Chic	39.3	95315	38 Industrious Urban Fringe	80.3	95459	31 Rural Resort Dwellers	100.0
95033	03 Connoisseurs	38.7	95316	19 Milk and Cookies	28.8	95460	15 Silver and Gold	82.0
95035	11 Pacific Heights	60.7	95317	38 Industrious Urban Fringe	56.5	95461	17 Green Acres	54.4
95037	02 Suburban Splendor	35.3	95318	28 Aspiring Young Families	90.2	95462	22 Metropolitans	61.0
95039	47 Las Casas	43.6	95320	17 Green Acres	30.6	95464	49 Senior Sun Seekers	98.7
95043	37 Prairie Living	99.7	95321	15 Silver and Gold	82.5	95465	09 Urban Chic	82.9
95045	24 Main Street, USA	51.2	95322	25 Salt of The Earth	31.0	95466	31 Rural Resort Dwellers	64.8
95046	03 Connoisseurs	49.4	95323	37 Prairie Living	100.0	95468	31 Rural Resort Dwellers	100.0
95050	23 Trendsetters	36.7	95324	25 Salt of The Earth	34.4	95469	17 Green Acres	64.5
95051	11 Pacific Heights	28.2	95326	17 Green Acres	35.9	95470	26 Midland Crowd	50.0
95053	55 College Towns	0.0	95327	33 Midlife Junction	35.4	95472	09 Urban Chic	57.7
95054	16 Enterprising Professionals	61.2	95329	31 Rural Resort Dwellers	98.2	95476	09 Urban Chic	20.8
95060	09 Urban Chic	50.6	95330	21 Urban Villages	65.6	95480	15 Silver and Gold	100.0
95062	09 Urban Chic	33.7	95333	38 Industrious Urban Fringe	41.8	95482	24 Main Street, USA	22.6
95064	63 Dorms To Diplomas	100.0	95334	47 Las Casas	56.0	95485	46 Rooted Rural	49.6
95065	30 Retirement Communities	25.0	95335	31 Rural Resort Dwellers	100.0	95488	31 Rural Resort Dwellers	100.0
95066	09 Urban Chic	56.4	95336	24 Main Street, USA	26.2	95490	31 Rural Resort Dwellers	23.5
95070	01 Top Rung	85.3	95337	06 Sophisticated Squires	25.7	95492	12 Up and Coming Families	27.0
95073	09 Urban Chic	51.8	95338	31 Rural Resort Dwellers	79.8	95493	31 Rural Resort Dwellers	100.0
95076	21 Urban Villages	27.5	95340	38 Industrious Urban Fringe	15.3	95494	37 Prairie Living	65.7
95110	35 International Marketplace	42.5	95345	31 Rural Resort Dwellers	100.0	95497	15 Silver and Gold	100.0
95111	11 Pacific Heights	27.8	95346	31 Rural Resort Dwellers	99.8	95501	33 Midlife Junction	31.8
95112	35 International Marketplace	35.0	95348	52 Inner City Tenants	23.8	95503	18 Cozy and Comfortable	21.6
95113	65 Social Security Set	76.0	95350	24 Main Street, USA	27.9	95511	37 Prairie Living	100.0
95116	35 International Marketplace	35.7	95351	38 Industrious Urban Fringe	45.0	95514	37 Prairie Living	98.0
95117	23 Trendsetters	49.7	95354	38 Industrious Urban Fringe	21.7	95519	33 Midlife Junction	22.5
95118	05 Wealthy Seaboard Suburbs	29.9	95355	24 Main Street, USA	17.8	95521	55 College Towns	43.7
95119	11 Pacific Heights	33.5	95356	28 Aspiring Young Families	25.0	95524	07 Exurbanites	84.5
95120	02 Suburban Splendor	41.6	95357	12 Up and Coming Families	37.1	95525	07 Exurbanites	66.9
95121	11 Pacific Heights	65.3	95358	38 Industrious Urban Fringe	36.6	95526	46 Rooted Rural	74.7
95122	21 Urban Villages	51.3	95360	38 Industrious Urban Fringe	59.9	95527	46 Rooted Rural	82.3
95123	06 Sophisticated Squires	22.1	95361	38 Industrious Urban Fringe	18.6	95528	25 Salt of The Earth	68.8
95124	09 Urban Chic	38.9	95363	38 Industrious Urban Fringe	39.6	95531	48 Great Expectations	19.2
95125	09 Urban Chic	39.8	95364	31 Rural Resort Dwellers	100.0	95536	37 Prairie Living	64.1
95126	23 Trendsetters	46.7	95366	19 Milk and Cookies	33.6	95540	53 Home Town	14.9
95127	21 Urban Villages	42.2	95367	38 Industrious Urban Fringe	34.5	95542	33 Midlife Junction	40.6
95128	23 Trendsetters	39.4	95368	12 Up and Coming Families	74.4	95543	31 Rural Resort Dwellers	100.0
95129	09 Urban Chic	27.2	95369	38 Industrious Urban Fringe	65.5	95546	51 Metro City Edge	82.9
95130	23 Trendsetters	33.0	95370	49 Senior Sun Seekers	15.8	95547	17 Green Acres	98.1
95131	11 Pacific Heights	42.5	95372	18 Cozy and Comfortable	87.1	95548	49 Senior Sun Seekers	100.0
95132	11 Pacific Heights	90.1	95374	26 Midland Crowd	92.5	95549	07 Exurbanites	55.6
95133	11 Pacific Heights	57.2	95376	04 Boomburbs	24.3	95550	07 Exurbanites	72.6
95134	08 Laptops and Lattes	43.2	95377	04 Boomburbs	80.2	95551	37 Prairie Living	99.2
95135	15 Silver and Gold	40.9	95379	17 Green Acres	34.8	95552	49 Senior Sun Seekers	100.0
95136	16 Enterprising Professionals	43.5	95380	38 Industrious Urban Fringe	25.6	95554	31 Rural Resort Dwellers	66.5
95138	04 Boomburbs	54.3	95382	12 Up and Coming Families	18.1	95555	31 Rural Resort Dwellers	100.0
95139	06 Sophisticated Squires	59.2	95383	31 Rural Resort Dwellers	78.4	95556	46 Rooted Rural	100.0
95140	03 Connoisseurs	64.2	95385	38 Industrious Urban Fringe	65.2	95558	37 Prairie Living	100.0
95148	11 Pacific Heights	69.8	95386	38 Industrious Urban Fringe	47.1	95560	31 Rural Resort Dwellers	99.0
95202	65 Social Security Set	54.8	95388	38 Industrious Urban Fringe	57.4	95562	53 Home Town	39.7
95203	24 Main Street, USA	18.6	95389	28 Aspiring Young Families	100.0	95563	31 Rural Resort Dwellers	100.0
95204	32 Rustbelt Traditions	19.5	95391	17 Green Acres	79.3	95564	48 Great Expectations	100.0
95205	38 Industrious Urban Fringe	50.8	95401	28 Aspiring Young Families	12.8	95565	25 Salt of The Earth	100.0
95206	38 Industrious Urban Fringe	30.4	95403	13 In Style	20.4	95567	49 Senior Sun Seekers	58.8

ZIP CODE	TOP TAPESTRY CONSUMER TYPE	% 2004 HOUSE- HOLDS	ZIP CODE	TOP TAPESTRY CONSUMER TYPE	% 2004 HOUSE- HOLDS	ZIP CODE	TOP TAPESTRY CONSUMER TYPE	% 2004 HOUSE- HOLDS
95568	31 Rural Resort Dwellers	100.0	95721	14 Prosperous Empty Nesters	60.0	95973	36 Old and Newcomers	17.7
95569	33 Midlife Junction	63.1	95722	07 Exurbanites	96.1	95975	31 Rural Resort Dwellers	99.2
95570	31 Rural Resort Dwellers	69.7	95724	31 Rural Resort Dwellers	100.0	95977	07 Exurbanites	45.0
95573	31 Rural Resort Dwellers	99.6	95726	17 Green Acres	39.3	95979	49 Senior Sun Seekers	92.8
95585	37 Prairie Living	65.4	95728	31 Rural Resort Dwellers	100.0	95981	31 Rural Resort Dwellers	100.0
95587	37 Prairie Living	76.8	95742	49 Senior Sun Seekers	93.7	95982	25 Salt of The Earth	57.9
95589	31 Rural Resort Dwellers	87.5	95746	04 Boomburbs	32.4	95983	46 Rooted Rural	70.0
95595	46 Rooted Rural	41.1	95747	12 Up and Coming Families	40.9	95984	46 Rooted Rural	100.0
95602	07 Exurbanites	50.2	95758	12 Up and Coming Families	60.7	95987	38 Industrious Urban Fringe	83.0
95603	07 Exurbanites	31.9	95762	02 Suburban Splendor	51.7	95988	25 Salt of The Earth	18.9
95605	38 Industrious Urban Fringe	51.1	95765	04 Boomburbs	97.8	95991	48 Great Expectations	18.8
95606	07 Exurbanites	76.0	95776	12 Up and Coming Families	37.7	95993	17 Green Acres	31.6
95607	37 Prairie Living	70.5	95814	27 Metro Renters	26.4	96001	07 Exurbanites	25.9
95608	13 In Style	24.8	95815	60 City Dimensions	23.1	96002	17 Green Acres	26.0
95610	13 In Style	20.0	95816	27 Metro Renters	50.6	96003	33 Midlife Junction	18.8
95612	37 Prairie Living	100.0	95817	22 Metropolitans	27.5	96006	46 Rooted Rural	100.0
95614	07 Exurbanites	97.9	95818	22 Metropolitans	22.6	96007	46 Rooted Rural	21.1
95615	37 Prairie Living	100.0	95819	22 Metropolitans	50.3	96008	31 Rural Resort Dwellers	68.2
95616	55 College Towns	22.6	95820	38 Industrious Urban Fringe	32.4	96010	31 Rural Resort Dwellers	100.0
95618	03 Connoisseurs	73.1	95821	36 Old and Newcomers	36.4	96013	50 Heartland Communities	59.3
95619	29 Rustbelt Retirees	66.6	95822	34 Family Foundations	16.8	96014	46 Rooted Rural	100.0
95620	12 Up and Coming Families	35.5	95823	38 Industrious Urban Fringe	22.4	96015	46 Rooted Rural	91.9
95621	28 Aspiring Young Families	18.1	95824	38 Industrious Urban Fringe	38.0	96016	31 Rural Resort Dwellers	90.9
95623	31 Rural Resort Dwellers	52.1	95825	39 Young and Restless	38.9	96019	50 Heartland Communities	46.4
95624	12 Up and Coming Families	25.6	95826	28 Aspiring Young Families	28.0	96020	46 Rooted Rural	60.2
95626	19 Milk and Cookies	43.1	95827	19 Milk and Cookies	25.5	96021	46 Rooted Rural	39.7
95627	38 Industrious Urban Fringe	51.9	95828	19 Milk and Cookies	27.5	96022	31 Rural Resort Dwellers	28.0
95628	07 Exurbanites	19.2	95829	12 Up and Coming Families	79.3	96023	46 Rooted Rural	100.0
95629	31 Rural Resort Dwellers	100.0	95830	02 Suburban Splendor	63.7	96024	46 Rooted Rural	100.0
95630	04 Boomburbs	46.3	95831	13 In Style	37.1	96025	50 Heartland Communities	49.8
95631	17 Green Acres	71.8	95832	38 Industrious Urban Fringe	96.1	96027	31 Rural Resort Dwellers	72.7
95632	12 Up and Coming Families	29.2	95833	28 Aspiring Young Families	54.2	96028	46 Rooted Rural	48.9
95633	07 Exurbanites	32.4	95834	39 Young and Restless	34.8	96031	31 Rural Resort Dwellers	100.0
95634	31 Rural Resort Dwellers	63.0	95835	12 Up and Coming Families	97.7	96032	31 Rural Resort Dwellers	100.0
95635	14 Prosperous Empty Nesters	84.6	95836	46 Rooted Rural	70.6	96033	31 Rural Resort Dwellers	93.2
95636	31 Rural Resort Dwellers	100.0	95837	09 Urban Chic	84.5	96034	46 Rooted Rural	83.6
95637	07 Exurbanites	54.3	95838	51 Metro City Edge	36.9	96035	46 Rooted Rural	62.0
95638	07 Exurbanites	54.4	95841	52 Inner City Tenants	35.1	96038	46 Rooted Rural	85.0
95640	26 Midland Crowd	52.4	95842	28 Aspiring Young Families	29.0	96039	49 Senior Sun Seekers	58.1
95641	31 Rural Resort Dwellers	88.6	95843	12 Up and Coming Families	58.5	96040	49 Senior Sun Seekers	75.0
95642	14 Prosperous Empty Nesters	26.5	95864	14 Prosperous Empty Nesters	24.3	96041	46 Rooted Rural	87.9
95645	50 Heartland Communities	49.5	95901	38 Industrious Urban Fringe	22.1	96044	49 Senior Sun Seekers	61.9
95648	28 Aspiring Young Families	31.8	95903	40 Military Proximity	100.0	96046	31 Rural Resort Dwellers	100.0
95650	07 Exurbanites	37.9	95910	31 Rural Resort Dwellers	100.0	96047	46 Rooted Rural	63.3
95651	17 Green Acres	73.6	95912	38 Industrious Urban Fringe	77.5	96048	31 Rural Resort Dwellers	100.0
95652	52 Inner City Tenants	53.0	95914	31 Rural Resort Dwellers	100.0	96050	31 Rural Resort Dwellers	83.5
95653	38 Industrious Urban Fringe	94.5	95915	46 Rooted Rural	100.0	96051	31 Rural Resort Dwellers	100.0
95655	61 High Rise Renters	100.0	95916	31 Rural Resort Dwellers	70.7	96052	31 Rural Resort Dwellers	91.1
95658	07 Exurbanites	43.6	95917	38 Industrious Urban Fringe	63.8	96054	46 Rooted Rural	87.8
95659	37 Prairie Living	100.0	95918	31 Rural Resort Dwellers	97.0	96055	46 Rooted Rural	100.0
95660	32 Rustbelt Traditions	22.9	95919	46 Rooted Rural	57.9	96056	46 Rooted Rural	66.8
95661	16 Enterprising Professionals	31.5	95920	37 Prairie Living	100.0	96057	31 Rural Resort Dwellers	100.0
95662	06 Sophisticated Squires	20.9	95922	31 Rural Resort Dwellers	100.0	96058	46 Rooted Rural	83.5
95663	07 Exurbanites	85.3	95923	15 Silver and Gold	100.0	96059	31 Rural Resort Dwellers	100.0
95664	07 Exurbanites	99.0	95925	46 Rooted Rural	55.4	96062	31 Rural Resort Dwellers	100.0
95665	31 Rural Resort Dwellers	56.6	95926	63 Dorms To Diplomas	22.3	96063	31 Rural Resort Dwellers	100.0
95666	31 Rural Resort Dwellers	71.6	95928	63 Dorms To Diplomas	14.0	96064	31 Rural Resort Dwellers	50.8
95667	07 Exurbanites	37.4	95932	38 Industrious Urban Fringe	57.1	96065	31 Rural Resort Dwellers	93.6
95668	46 Rooted Rural	64.8	95934	46 Rooted Rural	100.0	96067	31 Rural Resort Dwellers	52.3
95669	31 Rural Resort Dwellers	47.0	95935	31 Rural Resort Dwellers	73.4	96069	31 Rural Resort Dwellers	100.0
95670	28 Aspiring Young Families	14.5	95936	31 Rural Resort Dwellers	100.0	96071	31 Rural Resort Dwellers	50.6
95672	07 Exurbanites	97.3	95937	46 Rooted Rural	84.8	96073	07 Exurbanites	52.5
95673	18 Cozy and Comfortable	31.1	95938	07 Exurbanites	48.6	96075	31 Rural Resort Dwellers	100.0
95674	37 Prairie Living	100.0	95939	37 Prairie Living	100.0	96076	46 Rooted Rural	67.3
95677	07 Exurbanites	24.7	95941	49 Senior Sun Seekers	80.5	96080	57 Simple Living	19.7
95678	13 In Style	30.4	95942	07 Exurbanites	64.7	96085	31 Rural Resort Dwellers	100.0
95679	37 Prairie Living	90.9	95943	37 Prairie Living	91.8	96086	31 Rural Resort Dwellers	100.0
95681	17 Green Acres	61.1	95944	31 Rural Resort Dwellers	100.0	96087	33 Midlife Junction	100.0
95682	07 Exurbanites	47.3	95945	33 Midlife Junction	18.2	96088	31 Rural Resort Dwellers	100.0
95683	07 Exurbanites	89.4	95946	15 Silver and Gold	59.2	96091	31 Rural Resort Dwellers	100.0
95684	07 Exurbanites	41.5	95947	50 Heartland Communities	49.6	96093	33 Midlife Junction	79.5
95685	33 Midlife Junction	45.8	95948	37 Prairie Living	36.2	96094	31 Rural Resort Dwellers	54.0
95687	06 Sophisticated Squires	21.7	95949	07 Exurbanites	29.3	96096	31 Rural Resort Dwellers	100.0
95688	07 Exurbanites	32.8	95951	59 Southwestern Families	89.5	96097	57 Simple Living	40.2
95689	31 Rural Resort Dwellers	58.6	95953	38 Industrious Urban Fringe	79.9	96101	50 Heartland Communities	30.3
95690	37 Prairie Living	33.0	95954	49 Senior Sun Seekers	91.4	96103	15 Silver and Gold	88.4
95691	13 In Style	19.7	95955	37 Prairie Living	100.0	96104	37 Prairie Living	67.6
95692	38 Industrious Urban Fringe	43.1	95956	31 Rural Resort Dwellers	100.0	96105	31 Rural Resort Dwellers	100.0
95693	07 Exurbanites	97.2	95957	50 Heartland Communities	46.8	96106	15 Silver and Gold	100.0
95694	19 Milk and Cookies	30.3	95959	07 Exurbanites	46.5	96107	31 Rural Resort Dwellers	71.4
95695	35 International Marketplace	14.0	95960	31 Rural Resort Dwellers	100.0	96108	31 Rural Resort Dwellers	91.3
95698	37 Prairie Living	64.8	95961	38 Industrious Urban Fringe	45.2	96109	46 Rooted Rural	100.0
95701	31 Rural Resort Dwellers	73.1	95963	37 Prairie Living	25.3	96111	31 Rural Resort Dwellers	100.0
95703	31 Rural Resort Dwellers	77.6	95965	46 Rooted Rural	17.8	96112	50 Heartland Communities	100.0
95709	31 Rural Resort Dwellers	60.5	95966	49 Senior Sun Seekers	16.8	96113	46 Rooted Rural	76.3
95713	07 Exurbanites	45.0	95968	56 Rural Bypasses	72.7	96114	17 Green Acres	58.3
95714	07 Exurbanites	80.9	95969	49 Senior Sun Seekers	22.0	96115	50 Heartland Communities	100.0
95715	31 Rural Resort Dwellers	100.0	95970	37 Prairie Living	100.0	96116	31 Rural Resort Dwellers	100.0
95717	17 Green Acres	78.0	95971	31 Rural Resort Dwellers	21.7	96117	26 Midland Crowd	98.6
95720	31 Rural Resort Dwellers	58.8	95972	49 Senior Sun Seekers	100.0	96118	31 Rural Resort Dwellers	43.9

ZIP CODE	TOP TAPESTRY CONSUMER TYPE	% 2004 HOUSE-HOLDS	ZIP CODE	TOP TAPESTRY CONSUMER TYPE	% 2004 HOUSE-HOLDS	ZIP CODE	TOP TAPESTRY CONSUMER TYPE	% 2004 HOUSE-HOLDS
96119	46 Rooted Rural	100.0	96790	09 Urban Chic	100.0	97114	26 Midland Crowd	53.0
96120	17 Green Acres	52.3	96791	11 Pacific Heights	56.7	97115	17 Green Acres	90.3
96121	46 Rooted Rural	100.0	96792	21 Urban Villages	44.6	97116	17 Green Acres	41.0
96122	46 Rooted Rural	55.9	96793	11 Pacific Heights	58.6	97117	17 Green Acres	93.3
96123	46 Rooted Rural	100.0	96795	11 Pacific Heights	22.1	97119	17 Green Acres	94.8
96124	31 Rural Resort Dwellers	100.0	96796	11 Pacific Heights	93.4	97121	24 Main Street, USA	100.0
96125	31 Rural Resort Dwellers	100.0	96797	11 Pacific Heights	42.4	97122	31 Rural Resort Dwellers	100.0
96126	31 Rural Resort Dwellers	100.0	96813	36 Old and Newcomers	29.9	97123	12 Up and Coming Families	29.4
96128	26 Midland Crowd	100.0	96814	30 Retirement Communities	36.8	97124	39 Young and Restless	24.2
96130	26 Midland Crowd	31.7	96815	36 Old and Newcomers	55.2	97125	17 Green Acres	100.0
96132	46 Rooted Rural	100.0	96816	11 Pacific Heights	76.8	97127	26 Midland Crowd	100.0
96133	33 Midlife Junction	70.7	96817	44 Urban Melting Pot	40.8	97128	24 Main Street, USA	25.6
96134	53 Home Town	55.8	96818	40 Military Proximity	39.9	97131	31 Rural Resort Dwellers	74.9
96135	31 Rural Resort Dwellers	100.0	96819	11 Pacific Heights	63.9	97132	17 Green Acres	29.5
96136	26 Midland Crowd	100.0	96821	03 Connoisseurs	46.7	97133	17 Green Acres	51.0
96137	15 Silver and Gold	88.6	96822	36 Old and Newcomers	36.5	97136	31 Rural Resort Dwellers	72.3
96140	09 Urban Chic	100.0	96825	09 Urban Chic	28.0	97137	26 Midland Crowd	57.9
96141	32 Rustbelt Traditions	85.9	96826	36 Old and Newcomers	52.5	97138	33 Midlife Junction	48.5
96142	13 In Style	53.8	96844	55 College Towns	100.0	97140	12 Up and Coming Families	50.7
96143	35 International Marketplace	50.8	96853	40 Military Proximity	100.0	97141	31 Rural Resort Dwellers	23.3
96145	09 Urban Chic	53.8	96858	44 Urban Melting Pot	64.7	97144	17 Green Acres	100.0
96146	08 Laptops and Lattes	100.0	96860	40 Military Proximity	100.0	97145	15 Silver and Gold	78.3
96148	13 In Style	75.0	96862	40 Military Proximity	100.0	97146	26 Midland Crowd	38.3
96150	36 Old and Newcomers	12.9	96863	40 Military Proximity	100.0	97148	17 Green Acres	49.7
96161	06 Sophisticated Squires	25.1	97001	31 Rural Resort Dwellers	98.5	97149	15 Silver and Gold	100.0
96162	31 Rural Resort Dwellers	90.5	97002	26 Midland Crowd	26.7	97201	27 Metro Renters	62.9
96701	11 Pacific Heights	35.9	97004	17 Green Acres	68.5	97202	22 Metropolitans	33.7
96704	11 Pacific Heights	28.5	97005	36 Old and Newcomers	35.9	97203	24 Main Street, USA	50.9
96705	21 Urban Villages	51.3	97006	16 Enterprising Professionals	34.8	97204	65 Social Security Set	100.0
96706	12 Up and Coming Families	39.3	97007	04 Boomburbs	21.9	97205	65 Social Security Set	52.8
96707	04 Boomburbs	26.2	97008	06 Sophisticated Squires	23.3	97206	24 Main Street, USA	67.2
96708	09 Urban Chic	81.2	97009	27 Metro Renters	67.2	97209	27 Metro Renters	81.9
96710	33 Midlife Junction	100.0	97011	31 Rural Resort Dwellers	88.5	97210	27 Metro Renters	51.9
96712	09 Urban Chic	59.8	97013	24 Main Street, USA	18.0	97211	24 Main Street, USA	42.4
96713	31 Rural Resort Dwellers	60.6	97014	26 Midland Crowd	87.6	97212	05 Wealthy Seaboard Suburbs	28.1
96716	10 Pleasant-Ville	39.7	97015	13 In Style	24.6	97213	24 Main Street, USA	29.2
96717	21 Urban Villages	41.7	97016	25 Salt of The Earth	39.0	97214	27 Metro Renters	44.9
96718	50 Heartland Communities	100.0	97017	17 Green Acres	100.0	97215	22 Metropolitans	50.2
96719	10 Pleasant-Ville	56.1	97018	17 Green Acres	100.0	97216	24 Main Street, USA	59.3
96720	14 Prosperous Empty Nesters	15.4	97019	17 Green Acres	95.0	97217	24 Main Street, USA	51.9
96722	09 Urban Chic	86.3	97021	46 Rooted Rural	92.1	97218	24 Main Street, USA	70.8
96725	09 Urban Chic	91.4	97022	17 Green Acres	44.8	97219	22 Metropolitans	23.6
96727	31 Rural Resort Dwellers	30.5	97023	17 Green Acres	55.1	97220	24 Main Street, USA	45.1
96728	50 Heartland Communities	94.2	97024	17 Green Acres	28.2	97221	22 Metropolitans	37.1
96729	25 Salt of The Earth	65.1	97026	38 Industrious Urban Fringe	56.0	97222	24 Main Street, USA	47.9
96730	09 Urban Chic	92.7	97027	17 Green Acres	38.7	97223	13 In Style	36.9
96731	34 Family Foundations	57.3	97028	13 In Style	100.0	97224	36 Old and Newcomers	19.1
96732	11 Pacific Heights	48.3	97029	37 Prairie Living	100.0	97225	16 Enterprising Professionals	27.8
96734	05 Wealthy Seaboard Suburbs	34.1	97030	28 Aspiring Young Families	20.3	97227	52 Inner City Tenants	21.9
96738	13 In Style	98.6	97031	37 Prairie Living	16.2	97229	04 Boomburbs	30.0
96740	13 In Style	26.8	97032	26 Midland Crowd	40.3	97230	24 Main Street, USA	25.0
96741	07 Exurbanites	46.1	97033	37 Prairie Living	100.0	97231	07 Exurbanites	50.7
96742	65 Social Security Set	100.0	97034	03 Connoisseurs	39.8	97232	27 Metro Renters	65.7
96743	09 Urban Chic	47.4	97035	16 Enterprising Professionals	33.6	97233	24 Main Street, USA	51.6
96744	11 Pacific Heights	54.7	97037	31 Rural Resort Dwellers	35.0	97236	24 Main Street, USA	48.4
96746	13 In Style	35.6	97038	26 Midland Crowd	40.6	97239	27 Metro Renters	35.0
96747	38 Industrious Urban Fringe	100.0	97039	37 Prairie Living	72.9	97266	24 Main Street, USA	43.1
96748	31 Rural Resort Dwellers	42.8	97040	26 Midland Crowd	100.0	97267	24 Main Street, USA	18.5
96749	24 Main Street, USA	77.9	97041	25 Salt of The Earth	41.8	97301	48 Great Expectations	18.7
96750	14 Prosperous Empty Nesters	69.7	97042	17 Green Acres	55.7	97302	36 Old and Newcomers	21.5
96752	18 Cozy and Comfortable	36.6	97045	13 In Style	28.5	97303	24 Main Street, USA	20.4
96753	28 Aspiring Young Families	29.7	97048	25 Salt of The Earth	45.3	97304	07 Exurbanites	41.5
96754	20 City Lights	64.3	97049	13 In Style	61.7	97305	52 Inner City Tenants	25.4
96755	10 Pleasant-Ville	53.5	97050	46 Rooted Rural	100.0	97306	13 In Style	37.3
96756	20 City Lights	42.6	97051	24 Main Street, USA	50.9	97321	07 Exurbanites	31.8
96757	25 Salt of The Earth	100.0	97053	17 Green Acres	46.8	97322	28 Aspiring Young Families	16.9
96760	26 Midland Crowd	80.0	97054	17 Green Acres	50.1	97324	37 Prairie Living	69.9
96761	11 Pacific Heights	30.1	97055	17 Green Acres	43.6	97325	26 Midland Crowd	59.3
96762	09 Urban Chic	52.5	97056	25 Salt of The Earth	32.0	97326	17 Green Acres	60.4
96763	24 Main Street, USA	65.9	97057	31 Rural Resort Dwellers	100.0	97327	25 Salt of The Earth	57.9
96764	25 Salt of The Earth	81.5	97058	33 Midlife Junction	18.9	97329	25 Salt of The Earth	100.0
96766	11 Pacific Heights	40.0	97060	12 Up and Coming Families	24.6	97330	16 Enterprising Professionals	15.6
96768	19 Milk and Cookies	40.3	97062	39 Young and Restless	23.1	97331	63 Dorms To Diplomas	100.0
96769	21 Urban Villages	80.5	97063	49 Senior Sun Seekers	99.8	97333	63 Dorms To Diplomas	20.8
96770	33 Midlife Junction	100.0	97064	26 Midland Crowd	63.1	97338	17 Green Acres	25.6
96771	26 Midland Crowd	68.3	97065	46 Rooted Rural	99.6	97341	31 Rural Resort Dwellers	65.1
96772	31 Rural Resort Dwellers	82.4	97067	31 Rural Resort Dwellers	98.1	97342	31 Rural Resort Dwellers	84.8
96773	18 Cozy and Comfortable	88.9	97068	02 Suburban Splendor	40.7	97343	37 Prairie Living	98.2
96774	18 Cozy and Comfortable	93.3	97070	16 Enterprising Professionals	48.5	97344	26 Midland Crowd	78.5
96776	34 Family Foundations	46.8	97071	47 Las Casas	23.8	97345	25 Salt of The Earth	92.1
96777	50 Heartland Communities	100.0	97080	06 Sophisticated Squires	37.9	97346	46 Rooted Rural	68.1
96778	46 Rooted Rural	60.0	97101	17 Green Acres	46.4	97347	26 Midland Crowd	69.6
96779	10 Pleasant-Ville	77.6	97103	33 Midlife Junction	20.2	97348	25 Salt of The Earth	69.2
96780	18 Cozy and Comfortable	100.0	97106	17 Green Acres	93.9	97350	31 Rural Resort Dwellers	100.0
96781	29 Rustbelt Retirees	87.7	97107	31 Rural Resort Dwellers	100.0	97351	41 Crossroads	36.2
96782	11 Pacific Heights	45.3	97108	46 Rooted Rural	98.3	97352	26 Midland Crowd	33.2
96783	33 Midlife Junction	60.6	97109	17 Green Acres	100.0	97355	25 Salt of The Earth	19.3
96785	33 Midlife Junction	50.6	97111	25 Salt of The Earth	67.8	97357	26 Midland Crowd	97.0
96786	40 Military Proximity	38.6	97112	31 Rural Resort Dwellers	75.7	97358	25 Salt of The Earth	90.1
96789	11 Pacific Heights	33.9	97113	12 Up and Coming Families	35.7	97360	25 Salt of The Earth	55.6

ZIP CODE	TOP TAPESTRY CONSUMER TYPE	% 2004 HOUSE-HOLDS	ZIP CODE	TOP TAPESTRY CONSUMER TYPE	% 2004 HOUSE-HOLDS	ZIP CODE	TOP TAPESTRY CONSUMER TYPE	% 2004 HOUSE-HOLDS
97361	55 College Towns	42.3	97487	26 Midland Crowd	50.7	97828	31 Rural Resort Dwellers	35.7
97362	30 Retirement Communities	29.7	97488	31 Rural Resort Dwellers	100.0	97830	31 Rural Resort Dwellers	99.6
97364	31 Rural Resort Dwellers	100.0	97489	31 Rural Resort Dwellers	73.6	97833	37 Prairie Living	83.5
97365	31 Rural Resort Dwellers	22.2	97490	26 Midland Crowd	52.9	97834	49 Senior Sun Seekers	55.4
97366	31 Rural Resort Dwellers	100.0	97492	25 Salt of The Earth	94.8	97835	37 Prairie Living	98.7
97367	31 Rural Resort Dwellers	45.7	97493	31 Rural Resort Dwellers	100.0	97836	37 Prairie Living	47.7
97368	31 Rural Resort Dwellers	94.8	97496	53 Home Town	32.6	97837	31 Rural Resort Dwellers	81.8
97370	07 Exurbanites	38.1	97497	46 Rooted Rural	58.2	97838	41 Crossroads	21.3
97371	37 Prairie Living	48.6	97498	31 Rural Resort Dwellers	100.0	97839	37 Prairie Living	100.0
97374	25 Salt of The Earth	46.9	97499	42 Southern Satellites	59.3	97840	31 Rural Resort Dwellers	100.0
97375	17 Green Acres	100.0	97501	26 Midland Crowd	20.9	97841	37 Prairie Living	100.0
97376	31 Rural Resort Dwellers	96.6	97502	26 Midland Crowd	32.2	97842	31 Rural Resort Dwellers	100.0
97377	37 Prairie Living	64.1	97503	41 Crossroads	44.0	97843	37 Prairie Living	100.0
97378	24 Main Street, USA	50.4	97504	07 Exurbanites	22.4	97844	41 Crossroads	62.8
97380	26 Midland Crowd	96.1	97520	22 Metropolitans	38.5	97845	46 Rooted Rural	43.3
97381	24 Main Street, USA	54.1	97522	46 Rooted Rural	93.5	97846	31 Rural Resort Dwellers	56.3
97383	28 Aspiring Young Families	30.2	97523	46 Rooted Rural	27.3	97848	46 Rooted Rural	100.0
97385	17 Green Acres	95.3	97524	26 Midland Crowd	60.8	97850	33 Midlife Junction	21.4
97386	50 Heartland Communities	31.7	97525	46 Rooted Rural	39.5	97856	37 Prairie Living	100.0
97389	26 Midland Crowd	75.6	97526	31 Rural Resort Dwellers	28.4	97857	46 Rooted Rural	91.4
97390	15 Silver and Gold	62.7	97527	31 Rural Resort Dwellers	48.6	97862	46 Rooted Rural	28.7
97391	26 Midland Crowd	27.2	97530	31 Rural Resort Dwellers	84.0	97864	37 Prairie Living	99.4
97392	07 Exurbanites	51.7	97531	46 Rooted Rural	43.2	97865	46 Rooted Rural	100.0
97394	31 Rural Resort Dwellers	51.0	97532	31 Rural Resort Dwellers	99.5	97867	46 Rooted Rural	89.1
97396	26 Midland Crowd	42.4	97534	46 Rooted Rural	100.0	97868	46 Rooted Rural	81.5
97401	63 Dorms To Diplomas	25.5	97535	49 Senior Sun Seekers	76.2	97869	46 Rooted Rural	99.7
97402	28 Aspiring Young Families	15.1	97536	31 Rural Resort Dwellers	81.7	97870	49 Senior Sun Seekers	63.4
97403	55 College Towns	29.7	97537	31 Rural Resort Dwellers	70.4	97873	46 Rooted Rural	99.3
97404	18 Cozy and Comfortable	29.4	97538	46 Rooted Rural	76.2	97874	31 Rural Resort Dwellers	100.0
97405	07 Exurbanites	27.3	97539	49 Senior Sun Seekers	78.5	97875	26 Midland Crowd	39.5
97406	31 Rural Resort Dwellers	100.0	97540	33 Midlife Junction	49.7	97876	31 Rural Resort Dwellers	63.0
97408	13 In Style	29.6	97541	31 Rural Resort Dwellers	51.1	97877	31 Rural Resort Dwellers	73.3
97410	31 Rural Resort Dwellers	81.4	97543	31 Rural Resort Dwellers	70.2	97882	26 Midland Crowd	34.2
97411	31 Rural Resort Dwellers	61.1	97544	31 Rural Resort Dwellers	87.3	97883	46 Rooted Rural	50.6
97412	37 Prairie Living	100.0	97601	48 Great Expectations	28.4	97884	31 Rural Resort Dwellers	100.0
97413	31 Rural Resort Dwellers	100.0	97603	26 Midland Crowd	14.1	97885	46 Rooted Rural	66.6
97414	46 Rooted Rural	100.0	97620	37 Prairie Living	100.0	97886	46 Rooted Rural	81.3
97415	49 Senior Sun Seekers	43.7	97621	46 Rooted Rural	100.0	97901	37 Prairie Living	100.0
97416	46 Rooted Rural	71.6	97623	26 Midland Crowd	39.7	97903	37 Prairie Living	100.0
97417	50 Heartland Communities	76.1	97624	46 Rooted Rural	42.0	97904	37 Prairie Living	100.0
97419	25 Salt of The Earth	58.6	97625	26 Midland Crowd	93.3	97906	37 Prairie Living	100.0
97420	33 Midlife Junction	21.8	97627	26 Midland Crowd	52.0	97907	50 Heartland Communities	83.9
97423	33 Midlife Junction	28.8	97630	50 Heartland Communities	33.5	97908	37 Prairie Living	100.0
97424	50 Heartland Communities	24.0	97632	38 Industrious Urban Fringe	55.6	97909	37 Prairie Living	100.0
97426	24 Main Street, USA	20.6	97633	46 Rooted Rural	72.1	97910	37 Prairie Living	100.0
97427	25 Salt of The Earth	100.0	97635	46 Rooted Rural	100.0	97911	37 Prairie Living	100.0
97429	31 Rural Resort Dwellers	53.5	97636	37 Prairie Living	100.0	97913	37 Prairie Living	38.6
97430	37 Prairie Living	59.7	97637	37 Prairie Living	98.4	97914	33 Midlife Junction	16.0
97431	26 Midland Crowd	57.7	97638	46 Rooted Rural	99.3	97917	37 Prairie Living	100.0
97434	46 Rooted Rural	66.9	97639	46 Rooted Rural	100.0	97918	37 Prairie Living	39.1
97435	46 Rooted Rural	89.0	97640	37 Prairie Living	100.0	97920	37 Prairie Living	100.0
97436	46 Rooted Rural	54.9	97701	07 Exurbanites	17.9	98001	07 Sophisticated Squires	34.9
97437	46 Rooted Rural	62.0	97702	26 Midland Crowd	19.2	98002	24 Main Street, USA	16.8
97438	17 Green Acres	79.9	97707	31 Rural Resort Dwellers	60.9	98003	39 Young and Restless	20.3
97439	49 Senior Sun Seekers	56.0	97710	37 Prairie Living	100.0	98004	09 Urban Chic	17.2
97441	31 Rural Resort Dwellers	100.0	97711	37 Prairie Living	100.0	98005	16 Enterprising Professionals	32.5
97442	46 Rooted Rural	61.8	97712	07 Exurbanites	75.0	98006	02 Suburban Splendor	29.4
97443	17 Green Acres	59.7	97720	50 Heartland Communities	59.3	98007	39 Young and Restless	30.6
97444	31 Rural Resort Dwellers	70.8	97721	37 Prairie Living	100.0	98008	05 Wealthy Seaboard Suburbs	44.8
97446	26 Midland Crowd	68.4	97730	31 Rural Resort Dwellers	100.0	98010	06 Sophisticated Squires	34.5
97447	31 Rural Resort Dwellers	44.1	97731	46 Rooted Rural	48.4	98011	13 In Style	29.1
97448	24 Main Street, USA	22.2	97733	49 Senior Sun Seekers	50.1	98012	16 Enterprising Professionals	33.4
97449	49 Senior Sun Seekers	86.0	97734	26 Midland Crowd	67.4	98014	06 Sophisticated Squires	57.1
97450	31 Rural Resort Dwellers	100.0	97735	46 Rooted Rural	100.0	98019	04 Boomburbs	57.0
97451	17 Green Acres	93.1	97737	49 Senior Sun Seekers	100.0	98020	30 Retirement Communities	30.9
97452	26 Midland Crowd	67.1	97738	25 Salt of The Earth	69.9	98021	06 Sophisticated Squires	33.2
97453	31 Rural Resort Dwellers	93.9	97739	49 Senior Sun Seekers	54.8	98022	24 Main Street, USA	22.2
97454	17 Green Acres	82.2	97741	26 Midland Crowd	38.9	98023	16 Enterprising Professionals	18.5
97455	07 Exurbanites	82.0	97750	31 Rural Resort Dwellers	100.0	98024	17 Green Acres	58.2
97456	26 Midland Crowd	56.0	97751	37 Prairie Living	100.0	98026	10 Pleasant-Ville	15.2
97457	46 Rooted Rural	34.1	97752	37 Prairie Living	100.0	98027	02 Suburban Splendor	28.5
97458	46 Rooted Rural	43.9	97753	17 Green Acres	100.0	98028	36 Old and Newcomers	23.6
97459	33 Midlife Junction	50.9	97754	53 Home Town	28.4	98029	04 Boomburbs	59.8
97461	25 Salt of The Earth	63.8	97756	26 Midland Crowd	30.7	98030	12 Up and Coming Families	22.3
97462	46 Rooted Rural	47.9	97758	17 Green Acres	72.5	98031	06 Sophisticated Squires	30.6
97463	46 Rooted Rural	56.5	97759	31 Rural Resort Dwellers	49.2	98032	16 Enterprising Professionals	19.8
97465	31 Rural Resort Dwellers	54.7	97760	31 Rural Resort Dwellers	72.4	98033	09 Urban Chic	27.6
97466	46 Rooted Rural	100.0	97761	51 Metro City Edge	100.0	98034	13 In Style	25.2
97467	49 Senior Sun Seekers	65.8	97801	48 Great Expectations	28.1	98036	06 Sophisticated Squires	25.0
97469	46 Rooted Rural	63.5	97810	26 Midland Crowd	63.3	98037	39 Young and Restless	19.7
97470	14 Prosperous Empty Nesters	13.9	97812	37 Prairie Living	100.0	98038	06 Sophisticated Squires	26.7
97473	31 Rural Resort Dwellers	100.0	97813	37 Prairie Living	60.3	98039	01 Top Rung	99.5
97476	31 Rural Resort Dwellers	100.0	97814	50 Heartland Communities	36.5	98040	01 Top Rung	46.4
97477	48 Great Expectations	27.2	97818	41 Crossroads	36.3	98042	06 Sophisticated Squires	25.1
97478	17 Green Acres	20.7	97820	26 Midland Crowd	100.0	98043	28 Aspiring Young Families	33.9
97479	50 Heartland Communities	40.1	97823	37 Prairie Living	100.0	98045	06 Sophisticated Squires	36.0
97480	50 Heartland Communities	87.9	97824	31 Rural Resort Dwellers	89.4	98047	24 Main Street, USA	34.4
97481	25 Salt of The Earth	100.0	97825	46 Rooted Rural	100.0	98051	17 Green Acres	45.3
97484	31 Rural Resort Dwellers	100.0	97826	46 Rooted Rural	81.0	98052	16 Enterprising Professionals	37.0
97486	31 Rural Resort Dwellers	100.0	97827	46 Rooted Rural	48.1	98053	02 Suburban Splendor	75.3

457

ZIP CODE	TOP TAPESTRY CONSUMER TYPE	% 2004 HOUSE-HOLDS	ZIP CODE	TOP TAPESTRY CONSUMER TYPE	% 2004 HOUSE-HOLDS	ZIP CODE	TOP TAPESTRY CONSUMER TYPE	% 2004 HOUSE-HOLDS
98055	36 Old and Newcomers	29.5	98277	26 Midland Crowd	13.6	98443	17 Green Acres	48.3
98056	13 In Style	17.4	98278	40 Military Proximity	98.3	98444	52 Inner City Tenants	28.8
98058	06 Sophisticated Squires	23.2	98279	15 Silver and Gold	77.2	98445	18 Cozy and Comfortable	31.7
98059	16 Enterprising Professionals	20.0	98281	31 Rural Resort Dwellers	100.0	98446	18 Cozy and Comfortable	30.4
98065	10 Pleasant-Ville	23.9	98282	31 Rural Resort Dwellers	47.2	98447	29 Rustbelt Retirees	100.0
98070	07 Exurbanites	43.8	98283	26 Midland Crowd	51.8	98465	36 Old and Newcomers	31.6
98072	02 Suburban Splendor	37.5	98284	26 Midland Crowd	41.5	98466	36 Old and Newcomers	19.6
98074	02 Suburban Splendor	51.0	98288	31 Rural Resort Dwellers	100.0	98467	07 Exurbanites	30.0
98075	02 Suburban Splendor	46.1	98290	06 Sophisticated Squires	36.7	98498	14 Prosperous Empty Nesters	22.5
98077	02 Suburban Splendor	66.5	98292	17 Green Acres	49.0	98499	52 Inner City Tenants	42.6
98092	06 Sophisticated Squires	27.4	98294	24 Main Street, USA	26.4	98501	07 Exurbanites	14.2
98101	27 Metro Renters	91.3	98295	26 Midland Crowd	63.9	98502	13 In Style	18.7
98102	27 Metro Renters	82.1	98296	04 Boomburbs	44.8	98503	28 Aspiring Young Families	31.5
98103	23 Trendsetters	33.7	98303	15 Silver and Gold	100.0	98505	13 In Style	100.0
98104	65 Social Security Set	61.6	98304	31 Rural Resort Dwellers	100.0	98506	36 Old and Newcomers	29.5
98105	63 Dorms To Diplomas	34.7	98305	46 Rooted Rural	100.0	98512	13 In Style	28.1
98106	35 International Marketplace	21.4	98310	57 Simple Living	23.3	98513	19 Milk and Cookies	22.8
98107	23 Trendsetters	41.6	98311	28 Aspiring Young Families	29.3	98516	07 Exurbanites	26.1
98108	11 Pacific Heights	34.0	98312	33 Midlife Junction	26.6	98520	53 Home Town	14.9
98109	27 Metro Renters	52.0	98315	40 Military Proximity	97.8	98524	15 Silver and Gold	43.7
98110	03 Connoisseurs	46.2	98320	31 Rural Resort Dwellers	100.0	98526	46 Rooted Rural	100.0
98112	03 Connoisseurs	21.9	98321	26 Midland Crowd	43.1	98528	31 Rural Resort Dwellers	44.7
98115	22 Metropolitans	37.9	98323	12 Up and Coming Families	85.7	98531	48 Great Expectations	23.0
98116	09 Urban Chic	37.4	98325	26 Midland Crowd	58.6	98532	26 Midland Crowd	24.4
98117	22 Metropolitans	34.0	98326	49 Senior Sun Seekers	74.1	98533	49 Senior Sun Seekers	77.0
98118	35 International Marketplace	29.2	98327	12 Up and Coming Families	95.9	98535	31 Rural Resort Dwellers	100.0
98119	27 Metro Renters	53.7	98328	17 Green Acres	58.0	98536	31 Rural Resort Dwellers	100.0
98121	27 Metro Renters	95.7	98329	26 Midland Crowd	42.1	98537	25 Salt of The Earth	59.8
98122	27 Metro Renters	53.4	98330	31 Rural Resort Dwellers	91.1	98538	25 Salt of The Earth	82.8
98125	22 Metropolitans	26.7	98331	46 Rooted Rural	51.5	98541	26 Midland Crowd	24.2
98126	22 Metropolitans	19.9	98332	07 Exurbanites	53.2	98542	46 Rooted Rural	100.0
98133	36 Old and Newcomers	29.3	98333	07 Exurbanites	100.0	98546	15 Silver and Gold	50.7
98134	27 Metro Renters	92.4	98335	07 Exurbanites	42.0	98547	31 Rural Resort Dwellers	93.2
98136	09 Urban Chic	38.5	98336	46 Rooted Rural	98.6	98548	49 Senior Sun Seekers	46.9
98144	44 Urban Melting Pot	14.0	98337	48 Great Expectations	63.4	98550	32 Rustbelt Traditions	34.1
98146	35 International Marketplace	25.1	98338	26 Midland Crowd	38.3	98552	46 Rooted Rural	100.0
98148	36 Old and Newcomers	47.8	98339	26 Midland Crowd	72.0	98555	49 Senior Sun Seekers	100.0
98155	10 Pleasant-Ville	28.8	98340	15 Silver and Gold	89.4	98557	50 Heartland Communities	39.4
98158	52 Inner City Tenants	100.0	98342	12 Up and Coming Families	60.3	98560	31 Rural Resort Dwellers	100.0
98166	36 Old and Newcomers	18.3	98345	17 Green Acres	100.0	98562	31 Rural Resort Dwellers	100.0
98168	24 Main Street, USA	38.8	98346	13 In Style	41.2	98563	17 Green Acres	34.0
98177	05 Wealthy Seaboard Suburbs	27.5	98349	31 Rural Resort Dwellers	58.4	98564	31 Rural Resort Dwellers	65.6
98178	10 Pleasant-Ville	25.8	98351	26 Midland Crowd	74.4	98568	26 Midland Crowd	84.4
98188	52 Inner City Tenants	21.6	98354	18 Cozy and Comfortable	30.7	98569	31 Rural Resort Dwellers	71.7
98195	63 Dorms To Diplomas	0.0	98355	31 Rural Resort Dwellers	78.0	98570	46 Rooted Rural	70.2
98198	52 Inner City Tenants	18.9	98356	50 Heartland Communities	57.3	98571	31 Rural Resort Dwellers	100.0
98199	23 Trendsetters	24.2	98358	15 Silver and Gold	100.0	98572	46 Rooted Rural	95.2
98201	24 Main Street, USA	26.9	98359	17 Green Acres	60.4	98575	46 Rooted Rural	100.0
98203	24 Main Street, USA	28.7	98360	12 Up and Coming Families	51.7	98576	26 Midland Crowd	65.4
98204	28 Aspiring Young Families	32.9	98361	31 Rural Resort Dwellers	100.0	98577	25 Salt of The Earth	37.4
98205	12 Up and Coming Families	55.0	98362	33 Midlife Junction	30.6	98579	26 Midland Crowd	78.1
98208	06 Sophisticated Squires	25.3	98363	33 Midlife Junction	25.5	98580	26 Midland Crowd	69.2
98220	37 Prairie Living	75.7	98365	15 Silver and Gold	96.3	98581	49 Senior Sun Seekers	100.0
98221	17 Green Acres	21.9	98366	24 Main Street, USA	23.8	98582	46 Rooted Rural	98.6
98223	17 Green Acres	35.8	98367	17 Green Acres	40.9	98584	26 Midland Crowd	19.7
98224	31 Rural Resort Dwellers	100.0	98368	31 Rural Resort Dwellers	34.0	98585	31 Rural Resort Dwellers	45.3
98225	24 Main Street, USA	19.9	98370	17 Green Acres	32.1	98586	50 Heartland Communities	97.9
98226	36 Old and Newcomers	24.6	98371	17 Green Acres	20.7	98587	46 Rooted Rural	100.0
98229	13 In Style	46.4	98372	36 Old and Newcomers	15.3	98588	31 Rural Resort Dwellers	55.0
98230	31 Rural Resort Dwellers	33.3	98373	06 Sophisticated Squires	22.2	98589	26 Midland Crowd	69.0
98232	07 Exurbanites	62.0	98374	06 Sophisticated Squires	45.0	98590	50 Heartland Communities	64.0
98233	24 Main Street, USA	33.1	98375	26 Midland Crowd	28.5	98591	46 Rooted Rural	95.4
98236	31 Rural Resort Dwellers	61.1	98376	31 Rural Resort Dwellers	90.9	98592	31 Rural Resort Dwellers	98.7
98237	26 Midland Crowd	74.6	98377	49 Senior Sun Seekers	40.9	98593	26 Midland Crowd	77.3
98239	31 Rural Resort Dwellers	51.5	98380	17 Green Acres	51.2	98595	31 Rural Resort Dwellers	51.1
98240	17 Green Acres	57.9	98381	26 Midland Crowd	41.4	98596	26 Midland Crowd	74.7
98241	50 Heartland Communities	68.4	98382	15 Silver and Gold	33.9	98597	26 Midland Crowd	80.9
98244	17 Green Acres	64.2	98383	39 Young and Restless	30.0	98601	26 Midland Crowd	76.7
98245	31 Rural Resort Dwellers	97.0	98387	12 Up and Coming Families	35.0	98602	31 Rural Resort Dwellers	87.3
98247	26 Midland Crowd	49.2	98388	13 In Style	50.4	98603	26 Midland Crowd	73.8
98248	17 Green Acres	32.7	98390	12 Up and Coming Families	29.4	98604	12 Up and Coming Families	31.1
98249	31 Rural Resort Dwellers	98.0	98392	26 Midland Crowd	55.9	98605	17 Green Acres	82.5
98250	15 Silver and Gold	47.6	98394	31 Rural Resort Dwellers	74.9	98606	07 Exurbanites	37.7
98251	26 Midland Crowd	44.4	98402	65 Social Security Set	82.0	98607	04 Boomburbs	35.3
98252	26 Midland Crowd	41.2	98403	22 Metropolitans	28.9	98610	41 Crossroads	57.0
98253	15 Silver and Gold	67.0	98404	38 Industrious Urban Fringe	23.3	98611	25 Salt of The Earth	44.0
98257	15 Silver and Gold	55.0	98405	24 Main Street, USA	23.0	98612	31 Rural Resort Dwellers	63.4
98258	12 Up and Coming Families	34.7	98406	22 Metropolitans	17.8	98613	37 Prairie Living	90.4
98260	31 Rural Resort Dwellers	70.1	98407	24 Main Street, USA	23.4	98616	26 Midland Crowd	100.0
98261	31 Rural Resort Dwellers	54.6	98408	32 Rustbelt Traditions	53.9	98617	46 Rooted Rural	93.4
98262	31 Rural Resort Dwellers	100.0	98409	48 Great Expectations	30.5	98619	46 Rooted Rural	100.0
98264	17 Green Acres	42.0	98416	55 College Towns	100.0	98620	33 Midlife Junction	21.9
98266	41 Crossroads	88.2	98418	48 Great Expectations	56.9	98621	31 Rural Resort Dwellers	93.7
98267	31 Rural Resort Dwellers	91.2	98421	37 Prairie Living	100.0	98624	31 Rural Resort Dwellers	100.0
98270	12 Up and Coming Families	30.5	98422	16 Enterprising Professionals	26.1	98625	17 Green Acres	38.0
98271	17 Green Acres	23.9	98424	52 Inner City Tenants	53.3	98626	17 Green Acres	18.4
98272	12 Up and Coming Families	24.1	98430	52 Inner City Tenants	100.0	98628	26 Midland Crowd	88.3
98273	24 Main Street, USA	18.3	98433	40 Military Proximity	99.8	98629	26 Midland Crowd	36.3
98274	24 Main Street, USA	59.1	98438	40 Military Proximity	100.0	98631	31 Rural Resort Dwellers	71.8
98275	02 Suburban Splendor	23.6	98439	52 Inner City Tenants	54.6	98632	17 Green Acres	18.6

ZIP CODE	TOP TAPESTRY CONSUMER TYPE	% 2004 HOUSE-HOLDS	ZIP CODE	TOP TAPESTRY CONSUMER TYPE	% 2004 HOUSE-HOLDS	ZIP CODE	TOP TAPESTRY CONSUMER TYPE	% 2004 HOUSE-HOLDS
98635	46 Rooted Rural	40.2	99011	40 Military Proximity	99.9	99224	07 Exurbanites	15.6
98638	31 Rural Resort Dwellers	100.0	99012	46 Rooted Rural	55.5	99251	14 Prosperous Empty Nesters	100.0
98640	49 Senior Sun Seekers	100.0	99013	26 Midland Crowd	46.0	99301	58 Newest Residents	19.1
98642	07 Exurbanites	55.3	99016	32 Rustbelt Traditions	25.2	99320	26 Midland Crowd	32.2
98643	31 Rural Resort Dwellers	100.0	99017	37 Prairie Living	100.0	99321	38 Industrious Urban Fringe	100.0
98645	26 Midland Crowd	59.1	99018	46 Rooted Rural	78.8	99322	37 Prairie Living	100.0
98647	46 Rooted Rural	98.1	99019	12 Up and Coming Families	66.8	99323	17 Green Acres	100.0
98648	26 Midland Crowd	30.9	99021	26 Midland Crowd	35.9	99324	33 Midlife Junction	37.3
98649	25 Salt of The Earth	91.5	99022	24 Main Street, USA	25.5	99326	38 Industrious Urban Fringe	82.6
98650	31 Rural Resort Dwellers	100.0	99023	07 Exurbanites	92.0	99328	46 Rooted Rural	33.2
98651	17 Green Acres	100.0	99025	19 Milk and Cookies	40.7	99330	26 Midland Crowd	100.0
98660	24 Main Street, USA	28.2	99026	17 Green Acres	42.0	99336	28 Aspiring Young Families	17.2
98661	24 Main Street, USA	22.3	99027	17 Green Acres	58.4	99337	26 Midland Crowd	31.2
98662	36 Old and Newcomers	18.3	99029	37 Prairie Living	46.5	99338	06 Sophisticated Squires	49.0
98663	48 Great Expectations	31.6	99030	25 Salt of The Earth	76.1	99341	46 Rooted Rural	74.8
98664	24 Main Street, USA	31.6	99031	37 Prairie Living	61.2	99343	38 Industrious Urban Fringe	66.7
98665	57 Simple Living	16.2	99032	37 Prairie Living	100.0	99344	41 Crossroads	27.4
98671	17 Green Acres	52.9	99033	50 Heartland Communities	92.6	99347	50 Heartland Communities	64.9
98672	17 Green Acres	38.4	99034	26 Midland Crowd	82.1	99348	38 Industrious Urban Fringe	100.0
98674	17 Green Acres	54.0	99036	07 Exurbanites	95.4	99349	38 Industrious Urban Fringe	100.0
98675	26 Midland Crowd	70.2	99037	06 Sophisticated Squires	30.7	99350	26 Midland Crowd	30.6
98682	12 Up and Coming Families	50.7	99040	51 Metro City Edge	70.8	99352	07 Exurbanites	20.4
98683	12 Up and Coming Families	21.5	99101	25 Salt of The Earth	34.7	99353	12 Up and Coming Families	40.3
98684	28 Aspiring Young Families	29.6	99103	37 Prairie Living	98.0	99356	37 Prairie Living	100.0
98685	06 Sophisticated Squires	26.6	99105	37 Prairie Living	100.0	99357	47 Las Casas	46.2
98686	13 In Style	23.8	99107	31 Rural Resort Dwellers	100.0	99360	25 Salt of The Earth	64.0
98801	07 Exurbanites	19.7	99109	31 Rural Resort Dwellers	30.6	99361	46 Rooted Rural	58.3
98802	26 Midland Crowd	21.6	99110	26 Midland Crowd	61.3	99362	14 Prosperous Empty Nesters	15.9
98812	47 Las Casas	34.4	99111	33 Midlife Junction	31.1	99371	37 Prairie Living	100.0
98813	42 Southern Satellites	38.7	99113	37 Prairie Living	98.1	99401	25 Salt of The Earth	67.9
98814	31 Rural Resort Dwellers	100.0	99114	33 Midlife Junction	26.4	99402	25 Salt of The Earth	74.8
98815	26 Midland Crowd	30.4	99115	49 Senior Sun Seekers	74.0	99403	33 Midlife Junction	18.5
98816	33 Midlife Junction	39.8	99116	29 Rustbelt Retirees	23.8	99501	52 Inner City Tenants	39.3
98822	26 Midland Crowd	92.8	99117	31 Rural Resort Dwellers	99.7	99502	06 Sophisticated Squires	26.1
98823	26 Midland Crowd	56.2	99118	31 Rural Resort Dwellers	68.7	99503	52 Inner City Tenants	24.0
98826	31 Rural Resort Dwellers	64.6	99119	31 Rural Resort Dwellers	52.5	99504	28 Aspiring Young Families	24.0
98827	37 Prairie Living	71.5	99121	31 Rural Resort Dwellers	100.0	99505	40 Military Proximity	100.0
98828	26 Midland Crowd	72.6	99122	33 Midlife Junction	55.6	99506	40 Military Proximity	100.0
98830	37 Prairie Living	100.0	99123	31 Rural Resort Dwellers	100.0	99507	28 Aspiring Young Families	35.1
98831	31 Rural Resort Dwellers	50.2	99125	29 Rustbelt Retirees	54.4	99508	52 Inner City Tenants	24.2
98832	37 Prairie Living	99.6	99126	46 Rooted Rural	79.9	99515	06 Sophisticated Squires	29.3
98833	15 Silver and Gold	99.2	99128	37 Prairie Living	84.9	99516	02 Suburban Splendor	60.4
98834	31 Rural Resort Dwellers	90.2	99129	26 Midland Crowd	66.8	99517	28 Aspiring Young Families	25.7
98837	17 Green Acres	18.0	99130	37 Prairie Living	97.0	99518	28 Aspiring Young Families	46.2
98840	46 Rooted Rural	39.0	99131	31 Rural Resort Dwellers	100.0	99540	07 Exurbanites	100.0
98841	26 Midland Crowd	32.0	99133	50 Heartland Communities	75.4	99546	19 Milk and Cookies	100.0
98843	38 Industrious Urban Fringe	57.0	99134	37 Prairie Living	100.0	99547	19 Milk and Cookies	100.0
98844	31 Rural Resort Dwellers	24.8	99135	31 Rural Resort Dwellers	100.0	99549	19 Milk and Cookies	100.0
98845	37 Prairie Living	100.0	99136	37 Prairie Living	100.0	99551	59 Southwestern Families	100.0
98846	46 Rooted Rural	99.6	99137	31 Rural Resort Dwellers	100.0	99553	48 Great Expectations	100.0
98847	26 Midland Crowd	54.0	99138	46 Rooted Rural	98.0	99554	38 Industrious Urban Fringe	100.0
98848	47 Las Casas	20.4	99139	31 Rural Resort Dwellers	65.5	99555	38 Industrious Urban Fringe	100.0
98849	46 Rooted Rural	75.6	99140	50 Heartland Communities	91.7	99556	37 Prairie Living	52.9
98850	41 Crossroads	80.7	99141	31 Rural Resort Dwellers	37.3	99557	56 Rural Bypasses	97.8
98851	46 Rooted Rural	52.6	99143	37 Prairie Living	99.1	99558	51 Metro City Edge	100.0
98852	36 Old and Newcomers	100.0	99147	31 Rural Resort Dwellers	100.0	99559	59 Southwestern Families	32.0
98855	46 Rooted Rural	74.8	99148	31 Rural Resort Dwellers	78.8	99561	59 Southwestern Families	100.0
98856	31 Rural Resort Dwellers	61.9	99150	46 Rooted Rural	64.9	99563	51 Metro City Edge	100.0
98857	38 Industrious Urban Fringe	63.7	99153	50 Heartland Communities	72.3	99564	19 Milk and Cookies	100.0
98858	25 Salt of The Earth	61.6	99156	31 Rural Resort Dwellers	72.6	99565	19 Milk and Cookies	100.0
98859	31 Rural Resort Dwellers	100.0	99157	31 Rural Resort Dwellers	100.0	99567	06 Sophisticated Squires	66.8
98862	31 Rural Resort Dwellers	99.0	99158	37 Prairie Living	100.0	99568	31 Rural Resort Dwellers	100.0
98901	58 Newest Residents	13.4	99159	29 Rustbelt Retirees	75.7	99569	38 Industrious Urban Fringe	100.0
98902	57 Simple Living	15.3	99161	33 Midlife Junction	70.5	99571	48 Great Expectations	51.6
98903	17 Green Acres	25.8	99163	63 Dorms To Diplomas	41.4	99572	31 Rural Resort Dwellers	100.0
98908	14 Prosperous Empty Nesters	17.6	99164	63 Dorms To Diplomas	100.0	99573	31 Rural Resort Dwellers	72.5
98922	31 Rural Resort Dwellers	45.8	99166	31 Rural Resort Dwellers	53.8	99574	13 In Style	54.3
98923	26 Midland Crowd	81.3	99167	25 Salt of The Earth	49.0	99575	56 Rural Bypasses	100.0
98926	63 Dorms To Diplomas	22.2	99169	50 Heartland Communities	45.2	99576	13 In Style	56.7
98930	38 Industrious Urban Fringe	59.4	99170	37 Prairie Living	100.0	99577	06 Sophisticated Squires	51.0
98932	38 Industrious Urban Fringe	65.9	99171	29 Rustbelt Retirees	73.7	99578	59 Southwestern Families	100.0
98933	38 Industrious Urban Fringe	63.9	99173	46 Rooted Rural	81.4	99579	19 Milk and Cookies	100.0
98935	59 Southwestern Families	49.4	99176	37 Prairie Living	90.8	99580	38 Industrious Urban Fringe	100.0
98936	26 Midland Crowd	51.7	99179	37 Prairie Living	100.0	99583	48 Great Expectations	100.0
98937	26 Midland Crowd	40.5	99180	46 Rooted Rural	60.1	99584	51 Metro City Edge	100.0
98938	38 Industrious Urban Fringe	49.0	99181	46 Rooted Rural	49.9	99585	51 Metro City Edge	100.0
98942	17 Green Acres	58.8	99185	50 Heartland Communities	74.7	99586	31 Rural Resort Dwellers	100.0
98944	38 Industrious Urban Fringe	46.6	99201	48 Great Expectations	37.6	99587	22 Metropolitans	48.6
98946	17 Green Acres	56.3	99202	48 Great Expectations	22.8	99588	31 Rural Resort Dwellers	73.4
98947	38 Industrious Urban Fringe	65.5	99203	30 Retirement Communities	19.9	99589	59 Southwestern Families	100.0
98948	38 Industrious Urban Fringe	50.0	99204	55 College Towns	22.9	99591	19 Milk and Cookies	100.0
98951	59 Southwestern Families	31.1	99205	32 Rustbelt Traditions	36.3	99602	51 Metro City Edge	100.0
98952	38 Industrious Urban Fringe	76.2	99206	33 Midlife Junction	20.7	99603	13 In Style	34.2
98953	37 Prairie Living	36.6	99207	48 Great Expectations	57.3	99604	51 Metro City Edge	100.0
99003	17 Green Acres	55.9	99208	06 Sophisticated Squires	15.5	99606	26 Midland Crowd	100.0
99004	55 College Towns	46.2	99212	48 Great Expectations	33.0	99607	38 Industrious Urban Fringe	100.0
99005	07 Exurbanites	60.4	99216	11 Cozy and Comfortable	18.1	99610	31 Rural Resort Dwellers	100.0
99006	26 Midland Crowd	54.6	99217	32 Rustbelt Traditions	17.5	99611	26 Midland Crowd	26.8
99008	37 Prairie Living	84.9	99218	36 Old and Newcomers	22.7	99612	24 Main Street, USA	100.0
99009	26 Midland Crowd	96.3	99223	30 Retirement Communities	19.5	99613	13 In Style	86.7

ZIP CODE	TOP TAPESTRY CONSUMER TYPE	% 2004 HOUSE-HOLDS	ZIP CODE	TOP TAPESTRY CONSUMER TYPE	% 2004 HOUSE-HOLDS	ZIP CODE	TOP TAPESTRY CONSUMER TYPE	% 2004 HOUSE-HOLDS
99614	59 Southwestern Families	100.0	99768	51 Metro City Edge	100.0			
99615	13 In Style	30.8	99769	59 Southwestern Families	100.0			
99620	38 Industrious Urban Fringe	100.0	99771	19 Milk and Cookies	80.0			
99622	59 Southwestern Families	100.0	99772	51 Metro City Edge	100.0			
99625	26 Midland Crowd	100.0	99773	51 Metro City Edge	100.0			
99626	38 Industrious Urban Fringe	100.0	99777	62 Modest Income Homes	100.0			
99627	33 Midlife Junction	100.0	99778	51 Metro City Edge	100.0			
99628	38 Industrious Urban Fringe	100.0	99780	26 Midland Crowd	62.1			
99630	59 Southwestern Families	100.0	99781	51 Metro City Edge	100.0			
99631	31 Rural Resort Dwellers	100.0	99782	38 Industrious Urban Fringe	100.0			
99632	51 Metro City Edge	83.5	99783	51 Metro City Edge	100.0			
99636	38 Industrious Urban Fringe	100.0	99784	51 Metro City Edge	100.0			
99638	19 Milk and Cookies	100.0	99785	51 Metro City Edge	100.0			
99639	31 Rural Resort Dwellers	100.0	99786	51 Metro City Edge	100.0			
99640	26 Midland Crowd	100.0	99788	51 Metro City Edge	100.0			
99645	17 Green Acres	23.5	99789	66 Unclassified	100.0			
99647	26 Midland Crowd	100.0	99801	13 In Style	26.2			
99648	19 Milk and Cookies	100.0	99820	26 Midland Crowd	100.0			
99649	19 Milk and Cookies	100.0	99824	16 Enterprising Professionals	100.0			
99654	26 Midland Crowd	22.7	99825	31 Rural Resort Dwellers	100.0			
99655	59 Southwestern Families	100.0	99826	31 Rural Resort Dwellers	100.0			
99656	56 Rural Bypasses	100.0	99827	31 Rural Resort Dwellers	59.7			
99658	51 Metro City Edge	100.0	99829	26 Midland Crowd	83.6			
99659	51 Metro City Edge	100.0	99833	26 Midland Crowd	67.6			
99660	19 Milk and Cookies	100.0	99835	13 In Style	65.6			
99661	24 Main Street, USA	100.0	99840	22 Metropolitans	100.0			
99662	51 Metro City Edge	100.0	99901	24 Main Street, USA	26.9			
99664	22 Metropolitans	55.1	99903	31 Rural Resort Dwellers	100.0			
99667	31 Rural Resort Dwellers	100.0	99919	26 Midland Crowd	100.0			
99668	56 Rural Bypasses	100.0	99921	41 Crossroads	83.2			
99669	17 Green Acres	27.7	99922	25 Salt of The Earth	100.0			
99670	13 In Style	100.0	99923	31 Rural Resort Dwellers	100.0			
99671	51 Metro City Edge	100.0	99925	41 Crossroads	100.0			
99672	26 Midland Crowd	72.4	99926	26 Midland Crowd	54.9			
99676	31 Rural Resort Dwellers	100.0	99927	37 Prairie Living	100.0			
99679	59 Southwestern Families	100.0	99929	31 Rural Resort Dwellers	60.5			
99681	59 Southwestern Families	100.0	99950	37 Prairie Living	52.4			
99682	51 Metro City Edge	100.0						
99683	31 Rural Resort Dwellers	100.0						
99684	19 Milk and Cookies	100.0						
99685	16 Enterprising Professionals	100.0						
99686	06 Sophisticated Squires	45.8						
99687	26 Midland Crowd	68.5						
99688	31 Rural Resort Dwellers	79.6						
99689	26 Midland Crowd	100.0						
99691	33 Midlife Junction	100.0						
99701	36 Old and Newcomers	24.4						
99702	40 Military Proximity	100.0						
99703	40 Military Proximity	100.0						
99704	31 Rural Resort Dwellers	100.0						
99705	19 Milk and Cookies	39.4						
99709	28 Aspiring Young Families	23.4						
99712	06 Sophisticated Squires	63.4						
99714	19 Milk and Cookies	76.3						
99722	51 Metro City Edge	100.0						
99723	19 Milk and Cookies	67.5						
99724	51 Metro City Edge	100.0						
99726	62 Modest Income Homes	100.0						
99727	51 Metro City Edge	100.0						
99729	13 In Style	100.0						
99730	50 Heartland Communities	100.0						
99733	50 Heartland Communities	100.0						
99734	66 Unclassified	100.0						
99736	51 Metro City Edge	100.0						
99737	26 Midland Crowd	44.8						
99739	51 Metro City Edge	100.0						
99740	50 Heartland Communities	95.7						
99741	51 Metro City Edge	100.0						
99742	59 Southwestern Families	100.0						
99743	13 In Style	91.6						
99744	13 In Style	100.0						
99745	51 Metro City Edge	100.0						
99746	51 Metro City Edge	100.0						
99747	19 Milk and Cookies	100.0						
99748	51 Metro City Edge	100.0						
99749	38 Industrious Urban Fringe	58.0						
99750	38 Industrious Urban Fringe	100.0						
99751	51 Metro City Edge	100.0						
99752	45 City Strivers	42.4						
99753	51 Metro City Edge	100.0						
99755	13 In Style	75.0						
99756	31 Rural Resort Dwellers	96.6						
99757	33 Midlife Junction	100.0						
99758	62 Modest Income Homes	96.0						
99760	31 Rural Resort Dwellers	100.0						
99762	28 Aspiring Young Families	55.1						
99763	51 Metro City Edge	100.0						
99765	19 Milk and Cookies	62.2						
99766	38 Industrious Urban Fringe	100.0						
99767	62 Modest Income Homes	100.0						

Business Data by ZIP Code

The Community
Sourcebook
of ZIP Code
Demographics

2004
18th EDITION

ZIP CODE	2004 Total Firms	2004 Total Employ-ees	TOP INDUSTRY RANKED on 2004 EMPLOYMENT
01002	988	16352	Educational Services
01003	23	1303	Unclassified Establishments
01004	9	56	Other Information Services
01005	183	1178	Educational Services
01007	333	2303	Transit & Grnd Pass. Transport
01008	37	291	Accommodation
01009	20	133	Warehousing and Storage
01010	134	1014	Miscellaneous Store Retailers
01011	53	129	Exec., Legis., & Other Support
01012	35	164	Educational Services
01013	598	5344	Exec., Legis., & Other Support
01014	1	13	Special Trade Contractors
01020	828	8905	Food Svcs & Drinking Places
01021	4	13	Administrative & Support Svcs
01022	76	3481	Paper Manufacturing
01026	43	190	Support Act. for Transport.
01027	630	4834	Plastics & Rubber Products Mfg
01028	766	9274	Miscellaneous Manufacturing
01029	15	100	Accommodation
01030	322	1865	Educational Services
01031	42	197	Educational Services
01032	28	122	Accommodation
01033	219	851	Educational Services
01034	51	224	Accommodation
01035	428	4280	Food Svcs & Drinking Places
01036	179	797	Nursing & Resid. Care Facilit.
01037	40	300	Relig., Grant, Civic, Prof Org
01038	114	2223	Merch. Wholesalers,Nondur. Gds
01039	59	293	Relig., Grant, Civic, Prof Org
01040	1451	20397	Educational Services
01041	7	111	Food Svcs & Drinking Places
01050	77	375	Educational Services
01053	49	1212	Hospitals
01054	48	190	Textile Mills
01056	680	5639	Educational Services
01057	270	1283	Educational Services
01059	2	12	Support Act. for Transport.
01060	1442	14123	Educational Services
01061	13	20	Prof., Scientific, & Tech Svcs
01062	329	2025	Relig., Grant, Civic, Prof Org
01063	8	126	Other Information Services
01066	9	43	Construction of Buildings
01068	51	252	Educational Services
01069	472	6083	Hospitals
01070	22	40	Miscellaneous Manufacturing
01071	45	278	Chemical Manufacturing
01072	49	166	Educational Services
01073	185	1004	Food and Beverage Stores
01074	13	52	Food Svcs & Drinking Places
01075	437	6049	Educational Services
01077	361	2583	Food Svcs & Drinking Places
01079	25	244	Paper Manufacturing
01080	87	357	Machinery Manufacturing
01081	44	157	Educational Services
01082	371	2628	Hospitals
01083	90	514	Machinery Manufacturing
01084	5	25	Repair and Maintenance
01085	1390	15601	Educational Services
01086	12	79	Administrative & Support Svcs
01088	29	248	Plastics & Rubber Products Mfg
01089	1636	16185	Food Svcs & Drinking Places
01090	11	24	Merch. Wholesalers,Nondur. Gds
01092	35	787	Textile Mills
01093	43	235	Food Svcs & Drinking Places
01094	8	32	Wood Product Manufacturing
01095	512	3739	Educational Services
01096	111	529	Educational Services
01097	3	3	Construction of Buildings
01098	50	235	Transit & Grnd Pass. Transport
01101	13	561	Postal Service
01103	1169	10674	Prof., Scientific, & Tech Svcs
01104	827	17434	Hospitals
01105	570	7861	Justice, Pubic Order/Safety
01106	431	3447	Educational Services
01107	270	3148	Ambulatory Health Care Svcs
01108	534	3769	Educational Services
01109	598	6740	Educational Services
01111	2	5020	Insurance Carriers & Related
01115	105	1253	Prof., Scientific, & Tech Svcs
01116	6	6	Prof., Scientific, & Tech Svcs
01118	245	1797	Ambulatory Health Care Svcs
01119	237	3037	Educational Services
01128	70	650	Educational Services
01129	283	3203	General Merchandise Stores
01133	1	150	Insurance Carriers & Related
01138	8	13	Construction of Buildings
01139	1	1	Special Trade Contractors
01144	51	1001	Accommodation
01151	310	2118	Chemical Manufacturing
01152	2	3004	Postal Service
01199	27	12999	Hospitals
01201	2107	24671	Chemical Manufacturing
01202	15	39	Prof., Scientific, & Tech Svcs
01220	298	2304	Mining (Except Oil and Gas)
01222	22	76	Wood Product Manufacturing
01223	79	411	Educational Services
01224	5	28	Plastics & Rubber Products Mfg
01225	86	503	Educational Services
01226	193	2573	Paper Manufacturing
01227	1	6	Construction of Buildings
01229	5	16	Food Svcs & Drinking Places
01230	769	5059	Educational Services
01235	76	492	Transit & Grnd Pass. Transport
01236	64	557	Paper Manufacturing
01237	216	2253	Accommodation
01238	410	3152	Food Svcs & Drinking Places
01240	361	4991	Accommodation
01242	20	86	Special Trade Contractors
01243	16	29	Exec., Legis., & Other Support
01244	12	43	Educational Services
01245	38	134	Hospitals
01247	654	6221	Hospitals
01252	12	37	Food Svcs & Drinking Places
01253	53	283	Accommodation
01254	65	212	Food and Beverage Stores
01255	31	131	Nursing & Resid. Care Facilit.
01256	16	92	Educational Services
01257	210	963	Plastics & Rubber Products Mfg
01258	46	490	Accommodation
01259	20	29	Food and Beverage Stores
01260	10	503	Paper Manufacturing
01262	158	1221	Educational Services
01263	1	110	Relig., Grant, Civic, Prof Org
01264	10	42	Justice, Pubic Order/Safety
01266	96	522	Accommodation
01267	343	4002	Educational Services
01270	23	77	Justice, Pubic Order/Safety
01301	1023	10342	Hospitals
01302	6	19	Sportg Gds,Hobby,Book, & Music
01330	71	248	Educational Services
01331	470	4214	Fabricated Metal Product Mfg
01337	85	416	Merch. Wholesalers,Nondur. Gds
01338	15	109	Transit & Grnd Pass. Transport
01339	62	413	Accommodation
01340	46	218	Textile Mills
01341	51	130	Educational Services
01342	65	936	Educational Services
01343	1	5	Exec., Legis., & Other Support
01344	23	113	Justice, Pubic Order/Safety
01346	18	35	Exec., Legis., & Other Support
01347	3	5	Exec., Legis., & Other Support
01349	32	295	Prof., Scientific, & Tech Svcs
01350	5	5	Postal Service
01351	76	256	Educational Services
01355	36	160	Educational Services
01360	103	1174	Educational Services
01364	311	2287	Educational Services
01366	62	329	Educational Services
01367	22	67	Educational Services
01368	39	96	Educational Services
01370	265	1011	Educational Services
01373	269	4593	Miscellaneous Store Retailers
01375	103	598	Heavy & Civil Eng. Construct'N
01376	249	2851	Educational Services
01378	21	114	Educational Services
01379	35	196	Educational Services
01380	2	2	Support Act. for Transport.
01420	1493	15623	Ambulatory Health Care Svcs
01430	188	938	Educational Services
01431	105	310	Educational Services
01432	453	5356	Hospitals
01436	67	733	Educational Services
01438	26	227	Bldg Matl & Garden Eqpmt Dlrs
01440	773	8720	Educational Services
01441	1	1500	Computer & Electronic Prod Mfg
01450	331	1946	Educational Services
01451	225	1182	Ambulatory Health Care Svcs
01452	115	411	Justice, Pubic Order/Safety
01453	1644	18570	Plastics & Rubber Products Mfg
01460	478	4923	Computer & Electronic Prod Mfg
01462	347	2606	Bldg Matl & Garden Eqpmt Dlrs
01463	360	1498	Educational Services
01464	183	1691	Exec., Legis., & Other Support
01467	12	92	Relig., Grant, Civic, Prof Org
01468	119	533	Prof., Scientific, & Tech Svcs
01469	204	2489	Plastics & Rubber Products Mfg
01471	1	850	Merch. Wholesalers,Nondur. Gds
01472	14	260	Paper Manufacturing
01473	246	1769	Plastics & Rubber Products Mfg
01474	52	169	Transit & Grnd Pass. Transport
01475	292	1954	Educational Services
01477	5	134	Miscellaneous Manufacturing
01501	838	9644	Food Svcs & Drinking Places
01503	118	481	Justice, Pubic Order/Safety
01504	205	901	Food and Beverage Stores
01505	153	789	Food Svcs & Drinking Places
01506	94	411	Educational Services
01507	394	2514	Educational Services
01508	14	109	Justice, Pubic Order/Safety
01509	4	3	Furn. & Home Furnishgs Stores
01510	464	5244	Plastics & Rubber Products Mfg
01515	88	531	Accommodation
01516	197	874	Educational Services
01518	133	897	Educational Services
01519	192	945	Educational Services
01520	463	3241	Nursing & Resid. Care Facilit.
01521	42	156	Educational Services
01522	44	213	Computer & Electronic Prod Mfg
01523	172	1421	Educational Services
01524	206	1433	Merch. Wholesalers,Nondur. Gds
01525	21	187	Food Svcs & Drinking Places
01526	15	40	Educational Services
01527	428	3494	Nursing & Resid. Care Facilit.
01529	50	162	Justice, Pubic Order/Safety
01531	37	193	Justice, Pubic Order/Safety
01532	721	5266	Prof., Scientific, & Tech Svcs
01534	133	1007	Nursing & Resid. Care Facilit.
01535	158	1450	Educational Services
01536	226	2557	Fabricated Metal Product Mfg
01537	90	746	Merch. Wholesalers,Durable Gds
01538	30	182	Food Svcs & Drinking Places
01540	369	2873	Fabricated Metal Product Mfg
01541	116	1290	Accommodation
01542	50	229	Fabricated Metal Product Mfg
01543	170	1074	Educational Services
01545	1171	11757	Computer & Electronic Prod Mfg
01546	1	0	Postal Service
01550	569	6937	Fabricated Metal Product Mfg
01560	75	285	Elect'l Eqpmt, App, & Comp Mfg
01561	30	362	Educational Services
01562	409	3888	Unclassified Establishments
01564	291	2761	Real Estate
01566	347	4083	Food Svcs & Drinking Places
01568	233	1287	Educational Services
01569	427	2804	Food and Beverage Stores
01570	630	5803	Food Svcs & Drinking Places
01571	248	2156	Miscellaneous Manufacturing
01580	3	0	Real Estate
01581	1169	17954	Securities/Commodity Contracts
01582	3	2002	Utilities
01583	371	3979	Justice, Pubic Order/Safety
01585	126	838	Relig., Grant, Civic, Prof Org
01588	286	3731	Computer & Electronic Prod Mfg
01590	287	1817	Food Svcs & Drinking Places
01602	464	3923	Educational Services
01603	668	6711	General Merchandise Stores
01604	1181	11089	Food Svcs & Drinking Places
01605	846	15834	Hospitals
01606	701	12611	Nonmetallic Mineral Prod. Mfg
01607	236	2972	Special Trade Contractors
01608	1112	18194	Ambulatory Health Care Svcs
01609	978	7558	Educational Services
01610	625	8266	Educational Services
01611	49	203	Educational Services
01612	115	679	Educational Services
01613	14	53	Social Assistance
01614	22	131	Exec., Legis., & Other Support
01653	5	4012	Insurance Carriers & Related
01655	65	6946	Educational Services
01701	1397	16131	General Merchandise Stores
01702	1637	22465	Miscellaneous Store Retailers
01703	10	23	Special Trade Contractors
01704	5	16	Waste Managmt & Remediat'n Svc
01705	9	18	Special Trade Contractors
01718	5	7	Special Trade Contractors
01719	185	1478	Miscellaneous Manufacturing
01720	1036	8516	Prof., Scientific, & Tech Svcs
01721	620	4091	Computer & Electronic Prod Mfg
01730	715	18206	Computer & Electronic Prod Mfg
01731	11	849	Nat'l Security & Int'l Affairs
01740	176	2299	Computer & Electronic Prod Mfg
01741	180	982	Educational Services
01742	1253	9799	Prof., Scientific, & Tech Svcs
01745	25	116	Prof., Scientific, & Tech Svcs
01746	617	4233	Prof., Scientific, & Tech Svcs
01747	197	2009	Utilities
01748	471	8962	Computer & Electronic Prod Mfg
01749	775	7388	Fabricated Metal Product Mfg
01752	1893	28323	Computer & Electronic Prod Mfg
01754	422	4492	Prof., Scientific, & Tech Svcs

ZIP CODE	2004 Total Firms	2004 Total Employ-ees	TOP INDUSTRY RANKED on 2004 EMPLOYMENT	ZIP CODE	2004 Total Firms	2004 Total Employ-ees	TOP INDUSTRY RANKED on 2004 EMPLOYMENT	ZIP CODE	2004 Total Firms	2004 Total Employ-ees	TOP INDUSTRY RANKED on 2004 EMPLOYMENT
01756	241	1249	Food Svcs & Drinking Places	02020	6	20	Exec., Legis., & Other Support	02187	1	2	Relig., Grant, Civic, Prof Org
01757	1224	15980	Computer & Electronic Prod Mfg	02021	1176	17438	Merch. Wholesalers,Durable Gds	02188	456	3782	Nursing & Resid. Care Facilit.
01760	1781	18822	Prof., Scientific, & Tech Svcs	02025	450	2641	Educational Services	02189	581	5356	Special Trade Contractors
01770	144	665	Heavy & Civil Eng. Construct'N	02026	1157	11480	Food Svcs & Drinking Places	02190	636	7138	Hospitals
01772	406	8666	Miscellaneous Manufacturing	02027	17	31	Merch. Wholesalers,Nondur. Gds	02191	207	1308	Food Svcs & Drinking Places
01773	244	1293	Educational Services	02030	138	961	Educational Services	02199	210	7695	Prof., Scientific, & Tech Svcs
01775	283	1765	Exec., Legis., & Other Support	02032	128	2027	Miscellaneous Manufacturing	02201	14	2246	Exec., Legis., & Other Support
01776	755	5938	Educational Services	02035	725	6952	Prof., Scientific, & Tech Svcs	02203	21	744	Admin. Human Resource Programs
01778	457	3445	Food Svcs & Drinking Places	02038	1061	11591	Educational Services	02205	12	83	Exec., Legis., & Other Support
01784	7	208	Relig., Grant, Civic, Prof Org	02040	3	2	Prof., Scientific, & Tech Svcs	02208	1	1	Miscellaneous Manufacturing
01801	2490	34116	Prof., Scientific, & Tech Svcs	02041	5	212	Relig., Grant, Civic, Prof Org	02210	1109	25106	Prof., Scientific, & Tech Svcs
01803	1709	22238	Computer & Electronic Prod Mfg	02043	1222	13558	Prof., Scientific, & Tech Svcs	02215	944	31566	Educational Services
01805	17	8639	Ambulatory Health Care Svcs	02045	314	1411	Food Svcs & Drinking Places	02222	30	551	Exec., Legis., & Other Support
01810	1422	24119	Computer & Electronic Prod Mfg	02047	5	15	Nat'l Security & Int'l Affairs	02228	2	352	Postal Service
01821	868	16078	Computer & Electronic Prod Mfg	02048	715	9600	Merch. Wholesalers,Durable Gds	02238	14	40	Publishing Industries
01822	1	1	Special Trade Contractors	02050	895	5937	Exec., Legis., & Other Support	02269	9	74	Administrative & Support Svcs
01824	1199	13157	Computer & Electronic Prod Mfg	02051	11	24	Relig., Grant, Civic, Prof Org	02284	1	0	Prof., Scientific, & Tech Svcs
01826	803	3932	Food Svcs & Drinking Places	02052	454	3954	Educational Services	02301	2285	27071	Hospitals
01827	78	297	Accommodation	02053	421	3284	Electronics & Appliance Stores	02302	618	8180	Hospitals
01830	1042	11814	Special Trade Contractors	02054	336	2382	Food and Beverage Stores	02303	11	26	Social Assistance
01831	8	28	Administrative & Support Svcs	02056	265	2446	Ambulatory Health Care Svcs	02304	2	1	Merch. Wholesalers,Durable Gds
01832	517	4163	Educational Services	02059	6	4	Postal Service	02305	5	43	Administrative & Support Svcs
01833	306	2179	Merch. Wholesalers,Durable Gds	02060	3	290	Amusement, Gambling,& Recreat.	02322	325	5954	Fabricated Metal Product Mfg
01834	177	809	Exec., Legis., & Other Support	02061	718	7271	Nonstore Retailers	02324	661	4575	Food Svcs & Drinking Places
01835	387	5196	Merch. Wholesalers,Durable Gds	02062	1762	21624	Hospitals	02325	3	957	Educational Services
01840	830	7761	Educational Services	02065	1	99	Repair and Maintenance	02327	14	92	Transit & Grnd Pass. Transport
01841	641	9879	Textile Product Mills	02066	620	3418	Food Svcs & Drinking Places	02330	330	1905	Perform'g Arts, Spec. Sports
01843	658	9804	Ambulatory Health Care Svcs	02067	474	3559	Educational Services	02331	12	20	Construction of Buildings
01844	1370	12504	Hospitals	02070	8	8	General Merchandise Stores	02332	575	3209	Educational Services
01845	1133	16436	Computer & Electronic Prod Mfg	02071	20	332	Fabricated Metal Product Mfg	02333	396	2077	Educational Services
01850	203	1740	Educational Services	02072	1300	12335	Ambulatory Health Care Svcs	02334	7	25	Accommodation
01851	719	7292	Food Svcs & Drinking Places	02081	875	6329	Educational Services	02337	2	1	Postal Service
01852	1524	14495	Hospitals	02090	595	9352	Computer & Electronic Prod Mfg	02338	177	1096	Food Svcs & Drinking Places
01853	13	15	Special Trade Contractors	02093	537	4829	Clothing & Cloth'g Acc. Stores	02339	987	6932	Educational Services
01854	448	7386	Educational Services	02101	1	4	Administrative & Support Svcs	02341	307	1938	Food Svcs & Drinking Places
01860	181	995	Educational Services	02108	2375	30134	Prof., Scientific, & Tech Svcs	02343	388	2799	Special Trade Contractors
01862	489	8251	Merch. Wholesalers,Durable Gds	02109	2226	27700	Prof., Scientific, & Tech Svcs	02345	51	216	Relig., Grant, Civic, Prof Org
01863	381	2845	Food Svcs & Drinking Places	02110	2316	40879	Prof., Scientific, & Tech Svcs	02346	832	6911	Food Svcs & Drinking Places
01864	612	4726	Food Svcs & Drinking Places	02111	1380	27529	Hospitals	02347	387	2717	Admin. Enviro. Quality Progrms
01865	4	11	Postal Service	02112	3	30	Social Assistance	02349	1	500	Food Manufacturing
01866	2	7	Special Trade Contractors	02113	289	1436	Food Svcs & Drinking Places	02350	2	2	Postal Service
01867	788	6015	Prof., Scientific, & Tech Svcs	02114	1279	34712	Hospitals	02351	519	3954	Food Svcs & Drinking Places
01876	1006	12166	Prof., Scientific, & Tech Svcs	02115	969	31533	Hospitals	02355	10	45	Social Assistance
01879	483	3532	Educational Services	02116	2919	52845	Prof., Scientific, & Tech Svcs	02356	370	3183	Food and Beverage Stores
01880	1392	12644	Prof., Scientific, & Tech Svcs	02117	11	28	Prof., Scientific, & Tech Svcs	02357	2	583	Educational Services
01885	8	40	Personal and Laundry Services	02118	1194	30733	Hospitals	02358	5	24	Unclassified Establishments
01886	839	8430	Prof., Scientific, & Tech Svcs	02119	819	8338	Hospitals	02359	777	4297	Food Svcs & Drinking Places
01887	911	21284	Computer & Electronic Prod Mfg	02120	237	5587	Justice, Pubic Order/Safety	02360	2133	19700	Nursing & Resid. Care Facilit.
01888	9	13	Special Trade Contractors	02121	405	2497	Educational Services	02361	4	8	Merch. Wholesalers,Durable Gds
01889	2	3	Credit Intermediation & Relatd	02122	769	7937	Bldg Matl & Garden Eqpmt Dlrs	02362	11	55	Waste Managmt & Remediat'n Svc
01890	884	8156	Hospitals	02123	3	6	Motion Pict. & Sound Recording	02364	638	5378	Food Svcs & Drinking Places
01901	451	7502	Print'g & Related Supp't Act's	02124	989	7893	Hospitals	02366	19	200	Justice, Pubic Order/Safety
01902	732	4665	Educational Services	02125	651	8268	Educational Services	02367	114	302	Merch. Wholesalers,Durable Gds
01903	5	4	Merch. Wholesalers,Durable Gds	02126	466	2271	Educational Services	02368	886	8377	Food Svcs & Drinking Places
01904	450	4446	Hospitals	02127	1063	12223	Merch. Wholesalers,Nondur. Gds	02370	775	6778	Ambulatory Health Care Svcs
01905	555	11956	Transportation Equipment Mfg	02128	1123	14250	Support Act. for Transport.	02375	630	5634	Prof., Scientific, & Tech Svcs
01906	986	8790	Food Svcs & Drinking Places	02129	686	12128	Heavy & Civil Eng. Construct'N	02379	495	6475	Merch. Wholesalers,Nondur. Gds
01907	483	3940	Food Svcs & Drinking Places	02130	1068	13174	Hospitals	02381	3	16	General Merchandise Stores
01908	78	462	Food Svcs & Drinking Places	02131	691	5199	Nursing & Resid. Care Facilit.	02382	445	3259	Food Svcs & Drinking Places
01913	622	4358	Educational Services	02132	786	7456	Hospitals	02420	771	5826	Prof., Scientific, & Tech Svcs
01915	1788	18578	Hospitals	02133	41	752	Exec., Legis., & Other Support	02421	701	14160	Prof., Scientific, & Tech Svcs
01921	136	560	Educational Services	02134	809	8706	Broadcasting	02445	834	6480	Educational Services
01922	81	625	Educational Services	02135	1146	15933	Hospitals	02446	1409	8579	Ambulatory Health Care Svcs
01923	1570	22054	Social Assistance	02136	729	5780	Merch. Wholesalers,Nondur. Gds	02447	3	7	Food Svcs & Drinking Places
01929	248	1810	Food Svcs & Drinking Places	02137	3	27	Rail Transportation	02451	1289	25812	Prof., Scientific, & Tech Svcs
01930	1503	11500	Computer & Electronic Prod Mfg	02138	2250	32131	Educational Services	02452	494	6795	Educational Services
01931	10	24	Motion Pict. & Sound Recording	02139	1645	50898	Educational Services	02453	1266	10667	Miscellaneous Manufacturing
01936	17	5	Bldg Matl & Garden Eqpmt Dlrs	02140	813	6324	Food Svcs & Drinking Places	02454	14	37	Prof., Scientific, & Tech Svcs
01937	4	7	Prof., Scientific, & Tech Svcs	02141	668	9432	Relig., Grant, Civic, Prof Org	02456	3	2	Administrative & Support Svcs
01938	649	4367	Publishing Industries	02142	398	12459	Prof., Scientific, & Tech Svcs	02457	2	2	Accommodation
01940	434	3488	Prof., Scientific, & Tech Svcs	02143	1026	10637	Merch. Wholesalers,Nondur. Gds	02458	700	7659	Prof., Scientific, & Tech Svcs
01944	278	1653	Educational Services	02144	651	4211	Prof., Scientific, & Tech Svcs	02459	1265	8810	Educational Services
01945	953	5772	Educational Services	02145	541	4738	Bldg Matl & Garden Eqpmt Dlrs	02460	397	2911	Educational Services
01949	403	3990	Publishing Industries	02148	1705	15551	Administrative & Support Svcs	02461	346	2859	Food Svcs & Drinking Places
01950	1283	10619	Hospitals	02149	1214	12379	Print'g & Related Supp't Act's	02462	172	3815	Hospitals
01951	185	967	Merch. Wholesalers,Durable Gds	02150	1045	13384	Merch. Wholesalers,Nondur. Gds	02464	342	3446	Ambulatory Health Care Svcs
01952	508	3082	Food Svcs & Drinking Places	02151	1193	7507	Food Svcs & Drinking Places	02465	402	3122	Justice, Pubic Order/Safety
01960	1941	21399	Food Svcs & Drinking Places	02152	525	2808	Utilities	02466	270	3542	Prof., Scientific, & Tech Svcs
01961	7	10	Merch. Wholesalers,Durable Gds	02153	1	0	Special Trade Contractors	02467	578	7624	Educational Services
01965	7	324	Educational Services	02155	1758	15582	Prof., Scientific, & Tech Svcs	02468	150	628	Educational Services
01966	426	1788	Food Svcs & Drinking Places	02156	5	4	Prof., Scientific, & Tech Svcs	02471	13	39	Food Svcs & Drinking Places
01969	323	2201	Food and Beverage Stores	02163	12	759	Educational Services	02472	1430	20527	Wood Product Manufacturing
01970	1849	29377	Hospitals	02169	2259	28052	Ambulatory Health Care Svcs	02474	689	3033	Ambulatory Health Care Svcs
01971	1	0	Rental and Leasing Services	02170	378	2212	Food Svcs & Drinking Places	02475	1	3	Prof., Scientific, & Tech Svcs
01982	242	1632	Educational Services	02171	482	7039	Securities/Commodity Contracts	02476	579	3843	Food Svcs & Drinking Places
01983	395	2331	Educational Services	02176	867	8792	Couriers and Messengers	02478	899	4447	Ambulatory Health Care Svcs
01984	111	791	Educational Services	02180	932	7565	Educational Services	02479	4	2	Merch. Wholesalers,Durable Gds
01985	115	432	Social Assistance	02184	1893	22477	Ambulatory Health Care Svcs	02481	1117	9957	Educational Services
02018	7	92	Fabricated Metal Product Mfg	02185	7	18	Administrative & Support Svcs	02482	693	4925	Educational Services
02019	505	4383	Food Svcs & Drinking Places	02186	647	5551	Educational Services	02492	781	5737	Social Assistance

ZIP CODE	2004 Total Firms	2004 Total Employ-ees	TOP INDUSTRY RANKED on 2004 EMPLOYMENT	ZIP CODE	2004 Total Firms	2004 Total Employ-ees	TOP INDUSTRY RANKED on 2004 EMPLOYMENT	ZIP CODE	2004 Total Firms	2004 Total Employ-ees	TOP INDUSTRY RANKED on 2004 EMPLOYMENT
02493	367	4400	Ambulatory Health Care Svcs	02742	3	2	Elect'l Eqpmt, App, & Comp Mfg	02896	373	2928	Nursing & Resid. Care Facilit.
02494	841	14137	Telecommunications	02743	287	1344	Construction of Buildings	02898	106	1025	Amusement, Gambling,& Recreat.
02532	545	3519	Educational Services	02744	299	2392	Textile Mills	02901	4	3	Ambulatory Health Care Svcs
02534	100	604	Merch. Wholesalers,Nondur. Gds	02745	681	10213	Machinery Manufacturing	02902	5	9	Other Information Services
02535	133	520	Exec., Legis., & Other Support	02746	556	4510	Transit & Grnd Pass. Transport	02903	2297	35106	Educational Services
02536	574	2765	Bldg Matl & Garden Eqpmt Dlrs	02747	846	10680	Educational Services	02904	1151	15955	Ambulatory Health Care Svcs
02537	184	1228	Educational Services	02748	329	5649	Merch. Wholesalers,Durable Gds	02905	804	13405	Hospitals
02538	153	1720	Food Svcs & Drinking Places	02760	955	8229	General Merchandise Stores	02906	1067	8935	Ambulatory Health Care Svcs
02539	556	3134	Food Svcs & Drinking Places	02761	4	11	Administrative & Support Svcs	02907	796	10723	Miscellaneous Manufacturing
02540	1012	8356	Ambulatory Health Care Svcs	02762	334	2711	Miscellaneous Manufacturing	02908	800	15447	Exec., Legis., & Other Support
02541	13	18	Personal and Laundry Services	02763	138	2142	Miscellaneous Manufacturing	02909	916	6392	Miscellaneous Manufacturing
02542	23	1026	Nat'l Security & Int'l Affairs	02764	84	718	Fabricated Metal Product Mfg	02910	949	8248	Food Svcs & Drinking Places
02543	88	1690	Scenic & Sightseeing Transport	02766	466	4613	Wholesale Elec. Mrkts & Agents	02911	374	2146	Miscellaneous Manufacturing
02552	8	41	Accommodation	02767	635	8725	Miscellaneous Manufacturing	02912	25	3692	Educational Services
02553	27	72	Food Svcs & Drinking Places	02768	11	19	Construction of Buildings	02914	988	11346	Miscellaneous Manufacturing
02554	1130	6469	Food Svcs & Drinking Places	02769	338	1633	Educational Services	02915	447	4631	Hospitals
02556	179	1272	Accommodation	02770	146	975	Food Manufacturing	02916	323	4032	Miscellaneous Manufacturing
02557	380	1611	Food Svcs & Drinking Places	02771	715	7438	Food Svcs & Drinking Places	02917	577	7696	Administrative & Support Svcs
02558	63	266	Justice, Pubic Order/Safety	02777	601	4583	Food Svcs & Drinking Places	02918	3	1256	Educational Services
02559	203	1030	Fabricated Metal Product Mfg	02779	129	566	Educational Services	02919	1298	10969	Insurance Carriers & Related
02561	86	553	Miscellaneous Store Retailers	02780	1742	22169	Exec., Legis., & Other Support	02920	1535	19515	Miscellaneous Manufacturing
02562	128	853	Social Assistance	02790	511	2995	Special Trade Contractors	02921	221	3786	Fabricated Metal Product Mfg
02563	676	4184	Food Svcs & Drinking Places	02791	15	70	Repair and Maintenance	02940	8	19	Administrative & Support Svcs
02564	18	22	Special Trade Contractors	02801	7	67	Food Svcs & Drinking Places	03031	694	5793	Accommodation
02568	682	3405	Food Svcs & Drinking Places	02802	5	33	Perform'g Arts, Spec. Sports	03032	184	1162	Special Trade Contractors
02571	599	5285	Merch. Wholesalers,Durable Gds	02804	70	441	Miscellaneous Manufacturing	03033	158	654	Educational Services
02574	34	142	Nursing & Resid. Care Facilit.	02806	434	2907	Educational Services	03034	171	782	Construction of Buildings
02575	173	578	Educational Services	02807	227	1433	Accommodation	03036	157	400	Educational Services
02576	91	825	Merch. Wholesalers,Durable Gds	02808	35	314	Textile Mills	03037	121	499	Educational Services
02584	9	216	Air Transportation	02809	685	6147	Educational Services	03038	996	7952	Educational Services
02601	2071	19990	Food Svcs & Drinking Places	02812	20	106	Justice, Pubic Order/Safety	03041	13	32	Social Assistance
02630	222	919	Exec., Legis., & Other Support	02813	280	1116	Food Svcs & Drinking Places	03042	218	1184	Food Svcs & Drinking Places
02631	485	3448	Accommodation	02814	197	1129	Educational Services	03043	47	128	Amusement, Gambling,& Recreat.
02632	391	1952	Real Estate	02815	5	27	Educational Services	03044	87	481	Educational Services
02633	547	2632	Food Svcs & Drinking Places	02816	799	6432	Food Svcs & Drinking Places	03045	446	3149	Exec., Legis., & Other Support
02634	2	1	Real Estate	02817	173	4669	Prof., Scientific, & Tech Svcs	03046	65	190	Educational Services
02635	142	497	Construction of Buildings	02818	889	8425	Food Svcs & Drinking Places	03047	57	664	Social Assistance
02637	12	35	Food Svcs & Drinking Places	02822	161	970	Accommodation	03048	127	630	Food Svcs & Drinking Places
02638	260	806	Food Svcs & Drinking Places	02823	61	426	Machinery Manufacturing	03049	301	2383	Educational Services
02639	219	1307	Food Svcs & Drinking Places	02824	6	69	Food Svcs & Drinking Places	03051	905	9519	Computer & Electronic Prod Mfg
02641	57	224	Amusement, Gambling,& Recreat.	02825	118	442	Educational Services	03052	133	631	Educational Services
02642	221	1003	Food Svcs & Drinking Places	02826	16	156	Textile Mills	03053	1071	10398	Educational Services
02643	44	154	Food and Beverage Stores	02827	29	151	Educational Services	03054	953	11765	Securities/Commodity Contracts
02644	47	275	Educational Services	02828	304	2745	Food Svcs & Drinking Places	03055	702	6646	Primary Metal Manufacturing
02645	503	3072	Educational Services	02829	20	195	Nursing & Resid. Care Facilit.	03057	58	157	Educational Services
02646	177	727	Food Svcs & Drinking Places	02830	166	1096	Educational Services	03060	1977	22089	Hospitals
02647	14	82	Relig., Grant, Civic, Prof Org	02831	75	578	Prof., Scientific, & Tech Svcs	03061	14	130	Transit & Grnd Pass. Transport
02648	296	1057	Educational Services	02832	112	844	Miscellaneous Manufacturing	03062	548	8050	Ambulatory Health Care Svcs
02649	663	4184	Food Svcs & Drinking Places	02833	53	119	Justice, Pubic Order/Safety	03063	853	10900	Food Svcs & Drinking Places
02650	39	440	Ambulatory Health Care Svcs	02835	223	1203	Educational Services	03064	417	3356	Computer & Electronic Prod Mfg
02651	80	521	Educational Services	02836	8	23	Textile Mills	03070	161	555	Educational Services
02652	84	349	Accommodation	02837	141	561	Educational Services	03071	174	997	Special Trade Contractors
02653	798	5076	Food Svcs & Drinking Places	02838	59	513	Nursing & Resid. Care Facilit.	03073	6	56	Computer & Electronic Prod Mfg
02655	380	1672	Relig., Grant, Civic, Prof Org	02839	21	158	Primary Metal Manufacturing	03076	375	2102	Educational Services
02657	677	3233	Food Svcs & Drinking Places	02840	1707	13125	Food Svcs & Drinking Places	03077	286	2919	General Merchandise Stores
02659	71	245	Special Trade Contractors	02841	27	2425	Administrative & Support Svcs	03079	1693	18095	Food Svcs & Drinking Places
02660	366	2236	Nursing & Resid. Care Facilit.	02842	972	9560	Prof., Scientific, & Tech Svcs	03082	54	125	Special Trade Contractors
02661	18	68	Food Svcs & Drinking Places	02852	1013	10814	Transportation Equipment Mfg	03084	59	199	Educational Services
02662	23	59	Real Estate	02857	263	1520	Educational Services	03086	212	1782	Prof., Scientific, & Tech Svcs
02663	25	156	Food Svcs & Drinking Places	02858	12	58	Justice, Pubic Order/Safety	03087	330	2052	Educational Services
02664	596	4814	Accommodation	02859	128	1538	Hospitals	03101	1332	13240	Prof., Scientific, & Tech Svcs
02666	103	298	Justice, Pubic Order/Safety	02860	1486	20824	Hospitals	03102	745	7877	Hospitals
02667	281	1175	Food Svcs & Drinking Places	02861	612	9593	Prof., Scientific, & Tech Svcs	03103	1575	26689	Ambulatory Health Care Svcs
02668	174	1212	Educational Services	02862	5	37	Social Assistance	03104	935	8773	Ambulatory Health Care Svcs
02669	25	65	Amusement, Gambling,& Recreat.	02863	391	4456	Textile Mills	03105	13	48	Social Assistance
02670	145	704	Food Svcs & Drinking Places	02864	777	7331	Educational Services	03106	623	7530	Educational Services
02671	100	343	Food Svcs & Drinking Places	02865	675	11368	Insurance Carriers & Related	03108	14	37	Merch. Wholesalers,Durable Gds
02672	7	19	Real Estate	02871	606	5865	Special Trade Contractors	03109	413	4716	Merch. Wholesalers,Durable Gds
02673	371	2841	Food Svcs & Drinking Places	02872	12	17	Exec., Legis., & Other Support	03110	1149	10954	Prof., Scientific, & Tech Svcs
02675	303	1346	Food Svcs & Drinking Places	02873	5	179	Accommodation	03215	50	468	Accommodation
02702	106	582	Food Svcs & Drinking Places	02874	91	230	Food Svcs & Drinking Places	03216	104	550	Educational Services
02703	1294	20265	Computer & Electronic Prod Mfg	02875	4	207	Textile Mills	03217	128	892	Wood Product Manufacturing
02712	10	104	Computer & Electronic Prod Mfg	02876	42	560	Plastics & Rubber Products Mfg	03218	27	70	Administrative & Support Svcs
02713	5	17	Amusement, Gambling,& Recreat.	02877	6	33	Administrative & Support Svcs	03220	330	2436	Food and Beverage Stores
02714	28	9	Truck Transportation	02878	527	2647	Educational Services	03221	119	390	Educational Services
02715	132	1147	Merch. Wholesalers,Durable Gds	02879	953	7323	Food Svcs & Drinking Places	03222	287	2790	Miscellaneous Manufacturing
02717	214	1307	Educational Services	02880	7	9	Prof., Scientific, & Tech Svcs	03223	227	853	Educational Services
02718	98	669	Educational Services	02881	88	3093	Educational Services	03224	81	296	Museums, Hist. Sites,& Similar
02719	632	5794	Food Svcs & Drinking Places	02882	591	4542	Food Svcs & Drinking Places	03225	68	456	Wood Product Manufacturing
02720	1254	16611	Educational Services	02883	4	4	Bldg Matl & Garden Eqpmt Dlrs	03226	99	573	Food Svcs & Drinking Places
02721	1038	10715	Ambulatory Health Care Svcs	02885	517	4339	Food Svcs & Drinking Places	03227	57	160	Educational Services
02722	46	487	Postal Service	02886	2094	32215	Support Act. for Transport.	03229	243	1586	Merch. Wholesalers,Nondur. Gds
02723	430	3346	Textile Product Mills	02887	12	31	Administrative & Support Svcs	03230	45	232	Accommodation
02724	395	4654	Textile Mills	02888	941	9280	Food Svcs & Drinking Places	03231	3	3	Postal Service
02725	79	1416	Utilities	02889	644	4074	Educational Services	03233	10	33	Prof., Scientific, & Tech Svcs
02726	414	3186	Food Svcs & Drinking Places	02891	1175	8695	Food Svcs & Drinking Places	03234	184	1101	Broadcasting
02738	263	1971	Computer & Electronic Prod Mfg	02892	119	1843	Utilities	03235	341	3161	Fabricated Metal Product Mfg
02739	307	1587	Educational Services	02893	769	6270	Food Svcs & Drinking Places	03237	68	156	Heavy & Civil Eng. Construct'N
02740	1758	18083	Exec., Legis., & Other Support	02894	19	477	Educational Services	03238	1	180	Admin. Human Resource Programs
02741	1	1	Transit & Grnd Pass. Transport	02895	1157	17691	Merch. Wholesalers,Durable Gds	03240	31	73	Justice, Pubic Order/Safety

BUSINESS DATA

ZIP CODE	2004 Total Firms	2004 Total Employ-ees	TOP INDUSTRY RANKED on 2004 EMPLOYMENT
03241	35	105	Relig., Grant, Civic, Prof Org
03242	218	1967	Educational Services
03243	34	86	Educational Services
03244	313	2409	Merch. Wholesalers,Durable Gds
03245	90	487	Educational Services
03246	1107	11133	Hospitals
03247	11	19	Prof., Scientific, & Tech Svcs
03249	435	3750	Food Svcs & Drinking Places
03251	200	3084	Accommodation
03252	5	15	Truck Transportation
03253	447	3344	Food Svcs & Drinking Places
03254	201	1322	Educational Services
03255	69	291	Food Svcs & Drinking Places
03256	99	687	Educational Services
03257	405	3590	Nursing & Resid. Care Facilit.
03258	133	599	Food Svcs & Drinking Places
03259	16	31	Prof., Scientific, & Tech Svcs
03260	27	246	Machinery Manufacturing
03261	191	894	Food Svcs & Drinking Places
03262	82	438	Accommodation
03263	157	1388	Unclassified Establishments
03264	423	3502	Miscellaneous Store Retailers
03266	95	488	Accommodation
03268	46	88	Special Trade Contractors
03269	89	437	Educational Services
03272	6	5	Construction of Buildings
03273	14	20	Nursing & Resid. Care Facilit.
03275	387	3198	Prof., Scientific, & Tech Svcs
03276	441	4721	Clothing & Cloth'g Acc. Stores
03278	146	837	Elect'l Eqpmt, App, & Comp Mfg
03279	29	122	Accommodation
03280	36	93	Exec., Legis., & Other Support
03281	321	1276	Educational Services
03282	32	296	Wood Product Manufacturing
03284	37	159	Food Manufacturing
03287	58	238	Relig., Grant, Civic, Prof Org
03289	19	137	Justice, Pubic Order/Safety
03290	81	305	Educational Services
03291	7	25	Support Act. for Transport.
03293	21	103	Accommodation
03301	2528	35267	Hospitals
03302	17	43	Relig., Grant, Civic, Prof Org
03303	337	2709	Exec., Legis., & Other Support
03304	346	3546	Motor Vehicle & Parts Dealers
03307	169	2000	Perform'g Arts, Spec. Sports
03431	1428	17425	Insurance Carriers & Related
03440	119	483	Educational Services
03441	12	68	Special Trade Contractors
03442	45	398	Paper Manufacturing
03443	34	380	Merch. Wholesalers,Nondur. Gds
03444	73	463	Educational Services
03445	26	43	Construction of Buildings
03446	229	1545	Educational Services
03447	87	513	Construction of Buildings
03448	24	103	Chemical Manufacturing
03449	77	267	Construction of Buildings
03450	31	153	Justice, Pubic Order/Safety
03451	98	1176	Plastics & Rubber Products Mfg
03452	250	2446	Elect'l Eqpmt, App, & Comp Mfg
03455	104	376	Special Trade Contractors
03456	22	97	Computer & Electronic Prod Mfg
03457	17	33	Exec., Legis., & Other Support
03458	508	5216	Hospitals
03461	197	2132	Educational Services
03462	58	373	Administrative & Support Svcs
03464	26	138	Wood Product Manufacturing
03465	78	527	Textile Mills
03466	39	236	Bldg Matl & Garden Eqpmt Dlrs
03467	62	552	Nursing & Resid. Care Facilit.
03468	1	0	Relig., Grant, Civic, Prof Org
03469	26	150	Miscellaneous Manufacturing
03470	158	812	Educational Services
03561	532	4206	Prof., Scientific, & Tech Svcs
03570	404	4562	Paper Manufacturing
03574	128	586	Educational Services
03575	10	442	Accommodation
03576	202	2136	Accommodation
03579	45	151	Food and Beverage Stores
03580	117	1151	Museums, Hist. Sites,& Similar
03581	242	2077	Motor Vehicle & Parts Dealers
03582	84	806	Paper Manufacturing
03583	50	244	Amusement, Gambling,& Recreat.
03584	253	1739	Hospitals
03585	145	1003	Miscellaneous Manufacturing
03588	45	249	Exec., Legis., & Other Support
03590	41	127	Educational Services
03592	77	327	Accommodation
03593	7	11	Accommodation
03595	66	256	Accommodation
03597	40	158	General Merchandise Stores
03598	154	780	Educational Services
03601	20	21	Crop Production
03602	94	416	Educational Services
03603	199	1552	Elect'l Eqpmt, App, & Comp Mfg
03604	2	4	Educational Services
03605	34	133	Exec., Legis., & Other Support
03607	7	24	Merch. Wholesalers,Durable Gds
03608	150	1050	Food and Beverage Stores
03609	34	220	Paper Manufacturing
03740	23	109	Wood Product Manufacturing
03741	96	530	Educational Services
03743	708	6207	Educational Services
03745	32	161	Special Trade Contractors
03746	9	15	Food and Beverage Stores
03748	131	728	Admin. of Economic Programs
03749	7	20	Merch. Wholesalers,Durable Gds
03750	20	75	Prof., Scientific, & Tech Svcs
03751	19	81	Special Trade Contractors
03752	27	48	Bldg Matl & Garden Eqpmt Dlrs
03753	108	353	Educational Services
03754	10	120	Textile Mills
03755	347	8545	Educational Services
03756	30	6297	Ambulatory Health Care Svcs
03765	22	185	Educational Services
03766	588	6691	Hospitals
03768	83	456	Educational Services
03769	4	59	Accommodation
03770	28	268	Educational Services
03771	24	87	Merch. Wholesalers,Nondur. Gds
03773	399	5041	Fabricated Metal Product Mfg
03774	91	1056	Merch. Wholesalers,Durable Gds
03777	61	182	Accommodation
03779	25	313	Accommodation
03780	7	10	Special Trade Contractors
03781	51	226	Merch. Wholesalers,Durable Gds
03782	164	586	Educational Services
03784	430	4747	Food Svcs & Drinking Places
03785	153	1022	Ambulatory Health Care Svcs
03801	2697	31545	Relig., Grant, Civic, Prof Org
03802	23	76	Rental and Leasing Services
03804	1	5	Relig., Grant, Civic, Prof Org
03805	1	45	Sportg Gds,Hobby,Book, & Music
03809	151	823	Educational Services
03810	46	270	Accommodation
03811	152	866	Construction of Buildings
03812	104	752	Accommodation
03813	129	964	Food and Beverage Stores
03814	109	950	Educational Services
03815	12	103	Educational Services
03816	27	156	Relig., Grant, Civic, Prof Org
03817	37	116	Accommodation
03818	431	2357	Educational Services
03819	60	199	Educational Services
03820	1319	12985	Food Svcs & Drinking Places
03821	13	17	Administrative & Support Svcs
03824	427	6532	Educational Services
03825	230	1059	Educational Services
03826	73	466	Food and Beverage Stores
03827	105	416	Special Trade Contractors
03830	25	68	Food Svcs & Drinking Places
03832	17	90	Accommodation
03833	1000	9242	Educational Services
03835	218	973	Heavy & Civil Eng. Construct'N
03836	68	274	Accommodation
03837	35	339	Accommodation
03838	64	713	Amusement, Gambling,& Recreat.
03839	94	530	Prof., Scientific, & Tech Svcs
03840	248	1713	Food Svcs & Drinking Places
03841	282	2724	Motor Vehicle & Parts Dealers
03842	882	6640	Food Svcs & Drinking Places
03843	11	11	Prof., Scientific, & Tech Svcs
03844	158	886	Administrative & Support Svcs
03845	60	317	Clothing & Cloth'g Acc. Stores
03846	86	904	Accommodation
03847	3	7	Accommodation
03848	268	1785	Educational Services
03849	59	322	Accommodation
03850	20	62	Heavy & Civil Eng. Construct'N
03851	93	491	Plastics & Rubber Products Mfg
03852	15	20	Repair and Maintenance
03853	16	86	Plastics & Rubber Products Mfg
03854	34	183	Exec., Legis., & Other Support
03855	75	294	Food Svcs & Drinking Places
03856	71	912	Transportation Equipment Mfg
03857	220	1449	Educational Services
03858	94	449	Educational Services
03859	7	10	Nonmetallic Mineral Prod. Mfg
03860	550	5237	Accommodation
03862	394	1889	Motor Vehicle & Parts Dealers
03864	181	1091	Nursing & Resid. Care Facilit.
03865	587	4464	Educational Services
03866	3	7	Miscellaneous Store Retailers
03867	881	7857	Hospitals
03868	144	1406	Computer & Electronic Prod Mfg
03869	74	416	Computer & Electronic Prod Mfg
03870	264	1102	Food Svcs & Drinking Places
03871	33	168	Amusement, Gambling,& Recreat.
03872	126	457	Educational Services
03873	101	318	Educational Services
03874	418	5781	Utilities
03875	14	45	Bldg Matl & Garden Eqpmt Dlrs
03878	462	4633	Educational Services
03882	18	33	Social Assistance
03883	9	39	Educational Services
03884	33	106	Construction of Buildings
03885	326	3514	Leather & Allied Product Mfg
03886	139	681	Food Svcs & Drinking Places
03887	69	284	Wood Product Manufacturing
03890	38	551	Accommodation
03894	513	3531	Accommodation
03896	37	199	Food and Beverage Stores
03897	1	0	Special Trade Contractors
03901	144	1027	Leather & Allied Product Mfg
03902	86	373	Food Svcs & Drinking Places
03903	228	1135	Prof., Scientific, & Tech Svcs
03904	496	4044	Food Svcs & Drinking Places
03905	38	153	Educational Services
03906	132	1205	Furniture & Related Prod. Mfg
03907	255	2543	Food Svcs & Drinking Places
03908	156	867	Educational Services
03909	659	4937	Hospitals
03910	15	93	Food Svcs & Drinking Places
03911	14	159	Accommodation
04001	34	139	Food Svcs & Drinking Places
04002	194	1061	Justice, Pubic Order/Safety
04003	15	147	Food Svcs & Drinking Places
04004	34	155	Telecommunications
04005	1033	10869	Hospitals
04006	14	68	Food and Beverage Stores
04007	1	0	Motion Pict. & Sound Recording
04008	74	269	Miscellaneous Manufacturing
04009	293	1848	Accommodation
04010	46	88	Accommodation
04011	1061	10956	Social Assistance
04014	5	31	Prof., Scientific, & Tech Svcs
04015	92	1004	Amusement, Gambling,& Recreat.
04016	20	237	Justice, Pubic Order/Safety
04017	25	106	Accommodation
04019	3	2	Other Information Services
04020	78	398	Ambulatory Health Care Svcs
04021	152	1124	Educational Services
04022	42	241	Accommodation
04024	20	109	Merch. Wholesalers,Durable Gds
04027	97	479	Educational Services
04028	3	0	Postal Service
04029	55	193	Educational Services
04030	89	627	Educational Services
04032	441	4056	Leather & Allied Product Mfg
04033	3	0	Sportg Gds,Hobby,Book, & Music
04037	209	1811	Administrative & Support Svcs
04038	492	4179	Educational Services
04039	377	1774	Educational Services
04040	97	568	Accommodation
04041	31	215	Educational Services
04042	137	647	Educational Services
04043	714	4618	Food Svcs & Drinking Places
04046	475	2410	Accommodation
04047	55	356	Accommodation
04048	97	424	Educational Services
04049	87	230	Educational Services
04050	14	44	General Merchandise Stores
04051	49	206	Amusement, Gambling,& Recreat.
04054	20	142	Food Svcs & Drinking Places
04055	177	1400	Educational Services
04056	9	15	Museums, Hist. Sites,& Similar
04057	12	80	Educational Services
04061	30	56	Heavy & Civil Eng. Construct'N
04062	721	5186	Educational Services
04063	10	82	Educational Services
04064	368	2191	Accommodation
04066	18	47	Construction of Buildings
04068	35	196	Computer & Electronic Prod Mfg
04069	35	135	Educational Services
04070	10	27	Personal and Laundry Services
04071	186	1398	Computer & Electronic Prod Mfg
04072	720	6439	Ambulatory Health Care Svcs
04073	733	8524	Plastics & Rubber Products Mfg
04074	983	11649	Food and Beverage Stores
04075	13	74	Educational Services
04076	72	184	Educational Services

ZIP CODE	2004 Total Firms	2004 Total Employ-ees	TOP INDUSTRY RANKED on 2004 EMPLOYMENT
04077	20	189	Accommodation
04078	15	114	Food and Beverage Stores
04079	124	343	Food Svcs & Drinking Places
04082	3	7	Wood Product Manufacturing
04083	157	935	Educational Services
04084	208	1964	Educational Services
04085	28	116	Accommodation
04086	309	2750	Educational Services
04087	101	755	Educational Services
04088	50	428	Accommodation
04090	502	3495	Food Svcs & Drinking Places
04091	18	73	Justice, Pubic Order/Safety
04092	746	9472	Miscellaneous Manufacturing
04093	242	1143	Educational Services
04094	10	486	Paper Manufacturing
04095	12	45	Justice, Pubic Order/Safety
04096	493	3215	Educational Services
04097	110	416	Special Trade Contractors
04098	7	18	Relig., Grant, Civic, Prof Org
04101	2891	32024	Prof., Scientific, & Tech Svcs
04102	843	23033	Hospitals
04103	1304	14600	Educational Services
04104	30	107	Insurance Carriers & Related
04105	559	4522	Educational Services
04106	1414	20546	Food Svcs & Drinking Places
04107	248	1433	Educational Services
04108	39	128	Food and Beverage Stores
04109	3	61	Food Svcs & Drinking Places
04110	16	68	Social Assistance
04112	13	22	Merch. Wholesalers,Nondur. Gds
04116	9	26	Administrative & Support Svcs
04122	1	8	Credit Intermediation & Relatd
04210	1101	15906	Food Svcs & Drinking Places
04212	3	2	Leather & Allied Product Mfg
04216	27	239	Wood Product Manufacturing
04217	262	4026	Accommodation
04219	47	118	Educational Services
04220	67	330	Telecommunications
04221	36	220	Accommodation
04222	63	201	Educational Services
04223	2	32	Rail Transportation
04224	81	641	Wood Product Manufacturing
04225	3	17	Food Svcs & Drinking Places
04226	3	5	Special Trade Contractors
04227	5	28	Merch. Wholesalers,Durable Gds
04228	8	12	Bldg Matl & Garden Eqpmt Dlrs
04230	3	2	Miscellaneous Manufacturing
04231	14	21	Food and Beverage Stores
04234	21	110	Social Assistance
04236	124	464	Educational Services
04237	10	7	Accommodation
04238	19	157	Educational Services
04239	137	2345	Paper Manufacturing
04240	1520	20575	Administrative & Support Svcs
04241	4	5	Special Trade Contractors
04243	2	3	Prof., Scientific, & Tech Svcs
04250	130	1075	Print'g & Related Supp't Act's
04252	158	1120	Educational Services
04253	55	217	Justice, Pubic Order/Safety
04254	125	817	Food and Beverage Stores
04255	31	109	Wood Product Manufacturing
04256	100	628	Educational Services
04257	124	819	Educational Services
04258	48	218	Educational Services
04259	104	779	Educational Services
04260	192	784	Educational Services
04261	16	300	Accommodation
04262	5	8	Motor Vehicle & Parts Dealers
04263	53	452	Wholesale Elec. Mrkts & Agents
04265	36	317	Textile Mills
04266	12	37	Crop Production
04267	5	47	Wood Product Manufacturing
04268	250	2100	Hospitals
04270	184	2229	General Merchandise Stores
04271	24	28	Sportg Gds,Hobby,Book, & Music
04274	131	1441	Accommodation
04275	18	32	Furn. & Home Furnishgs Stores
04276	275	1813	Hospitals
04278	2	3	Food Svcs & Drinking Places
04280	129	776	Educational Services
04281	199	2097	Educational Services
04282	191	1447	Educational Services
04284	29	81	Educational Services
04285	35	139	Accommodation
04286	7	7	Crop Production
04287	29	113	Educational Services
04288	4	23	Food Manufacturing
04289	55	338	Nursing & Resid. Care Facilit.
04290	25	78	Educational Services
04291	5	5	Real Estate

ZIP CODE	2004 Total Firms	2004 Total Employ-ees	TOP INDUSTRY RANKED on 2004 EMPLOYMENT
04292	17	130	Educational Services
04294	131	963	Miscellaneous Manufacturing
04330	1553	24403	Hospitals
04332	4	17	Administrative & Support Svcs
04333	119	6502	Admin. of Economic Programs
04336	1	0	Utilities
04338	1	1	Relig., Grant, Civic, Prof Org
04341	11	90	Nursing & Resid. Care Facilit.
04342	29	126	Miscellaneous Store Retailers
04343	22	44	Merch. Wholesalers,Durable Gds
04344	111	671	Construction of Buildings
04345	410	3288	Educational Services
04346	38	228	Food and Beverage Stores
04347	169	1141	Food Svcs & Drinking Places
04348	74	370	Educational Services
04349	29	257	Educational Services
04350	82	281	Educational Services
04351	118	609	Relig., Grant, Civic, Prof Org
04352	49	109	Educational Services
04353	43	212	Educational Services
04354	30	93	Educational Services
04355	65	397	Educational Services
04357	101	651	Educational Services
04358	140	594	Educational Services
04359	6	67	Educational Services
04360	21	46	Justice, Pubic Order/Safety
04363	46	163	Educational Services
04364	304	2083	Merch. Wholesalers,Nondur. Gds
04401	2698	36165	Hospitals
04402	17	71	Justice, Pubic Order/Safety
04406	20	55	Social Assistance
04408	9	30	Telecommunications
04410	23	55	Wood Product Manufacturing
04411	27	192	Relig., Grant, Civic, Prof Org
04412	516	5703	Relig., Grant, Civic, Prof Org
04413	6	8	Heavy & Civil Eng. Construct'N
04414	32	122	Educational Services
04415	7	26	Relig., Grant, Civic, Prof Org
04416	216	2162	Paper Manufacturing
04417	10	13	Exec., Legis., & Other Support
04418	16	62	Truck Transportation
04419	64	420	Educational Services
04420	2	194	Educational Services
04421	54	313	Accommodation
04422	34	223	Justice, Pubic Order/Safety
04423	2	23	Merch. Wholesalers,Durable Gds
04424	49	358	Educational Services
04426	257	2334	Hospitals
04427	72	391	Educational Services
04428	73	437	Relig., Grant, Civic, Prof Org
04429	135	706	Motor Vehicle & Parts Dealers
04430	68	385	Educational Services
04431	10	34	Crop Production
04434	27	92	Educational Services
04435	27	93	Merch. Wholesalers,Nondur. Gds
04438	17	47	Special Trade Contractors
04441	148	844	Nursing & Resid. Care Facilit.
04442	17	67	Accommodation
04443	87	1455	Miscellaneous Manufacturing
04444	299	2139	Educational Services
04448	52	270	Nursing & Resid. Care Facilit.
04449	25	50	Food and Beverage Stores
04450	32	158	Wood Product Manufacturing
04451	12	72	Forestry and Logging
04453	13	34	Food Svcs & Drinking Places
04455	33	187	Educational Services
04456	42	116	Educational Services
04457	264	3343	Paper Manufacturing
04459	29	97	Wood Product Manufacturing
04460	44	308	Food Svcs & Drinking Places
04461	42	308	Educational Services
04462	226	3480	Paper Manufacturing
04463	92	881	Educational Services
04464	28	148	Furniture & Related Prod. Mfg
04467	6	15	Educational Services
04468	281	3252	Paper Manufacturing
04469	14	2745	Educational Services
04471	6	40	Forestry and Logging
04472	53	476	Transit & Grnd Pass. Transport
04473	194	1926	Credit Intermediation & Relatd
04474	102	444	Merch. Wholesalers,Durable Gds
04475	6	6	General Merchandise Stores
04476	27	190	Nursing & Resid. Care Facilit.
04478	38	165	Accommodation
04479	32	172	Construction of Buildings
04481	23	105	Administrative & Support Svcs
04485	7	14	Admin. of Economic Programs
04487	12	47	Educational Services
04488	21	73	Nursing & Resid. Care Facilit.
04489	10	330	Heavy & Civil Eng. Construct'N

ZIP CODE	2004 Total Firms	2004 Total Employ-ees	TOP INDUSTRY RANKED on 2004 EMPLOYMENT
04490	10	236	Unclassified Establishments
04491	10	24	Educational Services
04492	5	85	Forestry and Logging
04493	67	208	Educational Services
04495	12	95	Merch. Wholesalers,Durable Gds
04496	95	341	Educational Services
04497	7	47	Paper Manufacturing
04530	580	4801	Educational Services
04535	22	39	Construction of Buildings
04537	136	471	Special Trade Contractors
04538	293	2359	Accommodation
04539	63	136	Special Trade Contractors
04541	4	3	Postal Service
04543	326	2862	Hospitals
04544	30	294	Transportation Equipment Mfg
04547	30	145	Fabricated Metal Product Mfg
04548	41	249	Food Svcs & Drinking Places
04551	41	163	Social Assistance
04553	148	582	Educational Services
04554	71	221	Justice, Pubic Order/Safety
04555	62	231	Isps, Web Search Portals
04556	77	297	Food Svcs & Drinking Places
04558	15	92	Educational Services
04562	74	255	Food Svcs & Drinking Places
04563	23	58	Nursing & Resid. Care Facilit.
04564	30	196	Fabricated Metal Product Mfg
04565	7	116	Accommodation
04567	1	0	Food and Beverage Stores
04568	41	123	Food Manufacturing
04570	2	10	Food and Beverage Stores
04571	6	28	Food and Beverage Stores
04572	200	1502	Educational Services
04573	30	61	Merch. Wholesalers,Nondur. Gds
04574	55	153	Educational Services
04575	9	143	Admin. of Housing Programs
04576	43	215	Accommodation
04578	283	1576	Food Svcs & Drinking Places
04579	93	409	Food Svcs & Drinking Places
04605	895	6896	Social Assistance
04606	25	59	Educational Services
04607	62	304	Educational Services
04609	501	5257	Prof., Scientific, & Tech Svcs
04611	21	65	Educational Services
04612	19	95	Food Manufacturing
04613	7	14	Food and Beverage Stores
04614	224	1390	Hospitals
04615	2	2	Prof., Scientific, & Tech Svcs
04616	41	238	Transportation Equipment Mfg
04617	41	141	Accommodation
04619	268	2372	Food Svcs & Drinking Places
04622	64	303	Food Manufacturing
04623	49	256	Real Estate
04624	5	18	Transportation Equipment Mfg
04625	10	31	Scenic & Sightseeing Transport
04626	13	221	Nat'l Security & Int'l Affairs
04627	76	421	Nursing & Resid. Care Facilit.
04628	20	34	Administrative & Support Svcs
04629	1	1	Prof., Scientific, & Tech Svcs
04630	50	484	Nat'l Security & Int'l Affairs
04631	95	587	Educational Services
04634	50	143	Merch. Wholesalers,Nondur. Gds
04635	7	5	Food and Beverage Stores
04637	15	30	Accommodation
04640	89	1196	Merch. Wholesalers,Nondur. Gds
04642	6	40	Accommodation
04643	37	849	Miscellaneous Manufacturing
04644	9	227	Food Svcs & Drinking Places
04645	7	11	General Merchandise Stores
04646	8	50	Food Svcs & Drinking Places
04648	30	104	Food Svcs & Drinking Places
04649	84	313	Food and Beverage Stores
04650	11	66	Accommodation
04652	70	640	Educational Services
04653	34	213	Amusement, Gambling,& Recreat.
04654	262	2272	Hospitals
04655	26	220	Unclassified Establishments
04656	3	16	Transportation Equipment Mfg
04657	7	11	Construction of Buildings
04658	85	918	Food and Beverage Stores
04660	83	486	Accommodation
04662	87	451	Special Trade Contractors
04664	49	210	Educational Services
04666	40	129	Educational Services
04667	26	163	Educational Services
04668	46	511	Educational Services
04669	13	684	Food Manufacturing
04671	11	31	Educational Services
04672	4	44	Prof., Scientific, & Tech Svcs
04673	4	9	Real Estate
04674	9	28	Construction of Buildings

BUSINESS DATA

ZIP CODE	2004 Total Firms	2004 Total Employees	TOP INDUSTRY RANKED on 2004 EMPLOYMENT	ZIP CODE	2004 Total Firms	2004 Total Employees	TOP INDUSTRY RANKED on 2004 EMPLOYMENT	ZIP CODE	2004 Total Firms	2004 Total Employees	TOP INDUSTRY RANKED on 2004 EMPLOYMENT
04675	13	104	Miscellaneous Store Retailers	04922	22	58	Prof., Scientific, & Tech Svcs	05060	238	2032	Hospitals
04676	37	123	Educational Services	04923	16	24	Merch. Wholesalers,Nondur. Gds	05061	29	437	Educational Services
04677	15	33	Sportg Gds,Hobby,Book, & Music	04924	46	127	Educational Services	05062	23	46	Educational Services
04679	208	1604	Transportation Equipment Mfg	04925	8	77	Motor Vehicle & Parts Dealers	05065	49	281	Educational Services
04680	35	116	Transportation Equipment Mfg	04926	28	112	Bldg Matl & Garden Eqpmt Dlrs	05067	16	72	Educational Services
04681	74	333	Amusement, Gambling,& Recreat.	04927	60	599	Machinery Manufacturing	05068	118	771	Educational Services
04683	7	83	Accommodation	04928	75	238	Prof., Scientific, & Tech Svcs	05069	17	66	Nonmetallic Mineral Prod. Mfg
04684	33	200	Construction of Buildings	04929	19	169	Wood Product Manufacturing	05070	19	60	Educational Services
04685	36	66	Educational Services	04930	162	1058	Educational Services	05071	16	83	Food Svcs & Drinking Places
04686	5	86	Crop Production	04932	37	104	Relig., Grant, Civic, Prof Org	05072	17	39	Crop Production
04691	15	51	Food Manufacturing	04933	2	9	Food and Beverage Stores	05073	13	68	Construction of Buildings
04693	36	519	Nat'l Security & Int'l Affairs	04935	14	29	Perform'g Arts, Spec. Sports	05074	34	181	Educational Services
04694	80	1134	Paper Manufacturing	04936	24	171	Relig., Grant, Civic, Prof Org	05075	30	157	Accommodation
04730	527	4759	Hospitals	04937	247	2030	Educational Services	05076	6	10	Print'g & Related Supp't Act's
04732	84	645	Wood Product Manufacturing	04938	491	3861	Hospitals	05077	31	153	Educational Services
04733	6	11	Educational Services	04939	12	33	Educational Services	05079	15	60	Educational Services
04734	22	37	Truck Transportation	04940	12	27	Merch. Wholesalers,Durable Gds	05081	47	492	Educational Services
04735	28	170	Accommodation	04941	36	56	Special Trade Contractors	05083	10	48	Educational Services
04736	491	4323	Hospitals	04942	31	218	Miscellaneous Manufacturing	05084	11	41	Special Trade Contractors
04738	3	4	Bldg Matl & Garden Eqpmt Dlrs	04943	73	254	Educational Services	05085	9	6	Special Trade Contractors
04739	52	545	Relig., Grant, Civic, Prof Org	04944	9	334	Educational Services	05086	13	38	General Merchandise Stores
04740	36	953	Food Manufacturing	04945	91	618	Forestry and Logging	05088	51	273	Special Trade Contractors
04742	120	702	Educational Services	04947	159	1281	Accommodation	05089	218	1484	Hospitals
04743	275	3618	Merch. Wholesalers,Durable Gds	04949	49	198	Print'g & Related Supp't Act's	05091	374	2258	Food Svcs & Drinking Places
04744	9	142	Ambulatory Health Care Svcs	04950	178	1007	Educational Services	05101	271	2213	Educational Services
04745	42	366	Educational Services	04951	23	81	Nonmetallic Mineral Prod. Mfg	05141	5	4	General Merchandise Stores
04746	17	43	Hospitals	04952	47	167	Merch. Wholesalers,Nondur. Gds	05142	44	259	Plastics & Rubber Products Mfg
04747	71	481	Educational Services	04953	206	1567	Food and Beverage Stores	05143	288	1277	Other Information Services
04750	85	655	Administrative & Support Svcs	04954	13	17	Miscellaneous Manufacturing	05144	1	0	Exec., Legis., & Other Support
04751	2	309	Nat'l Security & Int'l Affairs	04955	37	90	Educational Services	05146	46	203	Accommodation
04756	203	2483	Paper Manufacturing	04956	24	127	Wood Product Manufacturing	05148	56	338	Educational Services
04757	58	272	Construction of Buildings	04957	138	873	Leather & Allied Product Mfg	05149	303	3045	Accommodation
04758	82	626	Nursing & Resid. Care Facilit.	04958	66	342	Educational Services	05150	72	827	Prof., Scientific, & Tech Svcs
04759	5	21	Exec., Legis., & Other Support	04961	34	107	Wood Product Manufacturing	05151	56	141	Educational Services
04760	27	71	Food Manufacturing	04962	23	67	Computer & Electronic Prod Mfg	05152	10	85	Accommodation
04761	14	159	Wood Product Manufacturing	04963	224	1614	Educational Services	05153	42	268	Food and Beverage Stores
04762	17	59	Crop Production	04964	24	123	Food Svcs & Drinking Places	05154	54	335	Educational Services
04763	26	243	Wood Product Manufacturing	04965	63	571	General Merchandise Stores	05155	39	1496	Accommodation
04764	4	16	Miscellaneous Store Retailers	04966	65	281	Educational Services	05156	491	3854	Educational Services
04765	87	321	Nursing & Resid. Care Facilit.	04967	181	2744	Merch. Wholesalers,Durable Gds	05158	77	574	Educational Services
04766	10	22	Exec., Legis., & Other Support	04969	33	191	Nursing & Resid. Care Facilit.	05159	8	54	Fabricated Metal Product Mfg
04768	19	99	Wood Product Manufacturing	04970	150	636	Accommodation	05161	27	151	General Merchandise Stores
04769	644	7722	Hospitals	04971	43	121	Educational Services	05201	865	10091	Educational Services
04770	1	1	Support Activities: Agr./For.	04972	1	1	Special Trade Contractors	05250	141	763	Plastics & Rubber Products Mfg
04772	34	174	Merch. Wholesalers,Nondur. Gds	04973	28	239	Wood Product Manufacturing	05251	101	508	Relig., Grant, Civic, Prof Org
04773	9	36	Truck Transportation	04974	139	761	Educational Services	05252	20	43	Plastics & Rubber Products Mfg
04774	30	114	Justice, Pubic Order/Safety	04975	6	94	Administrative & Support Svcs	05253	32	156	Special Trade Contractors
04775	1	0	Postal Service	04976	571	7341	Prof., Scientific, & Tech Svcs	05254	159	1278	Accommodation
04776	31	142	Justice, Pubic Order/Safety	04978	30	140	Accommodation	05255	481	2850	Food Svcs & Drinking Places
04777	15	152	Educational Services	04979	58	392	Wood Product Manufacturing	05257	89	782	Merch. Wholesalers,Durable Gds
04779	16	44	Food Svcs & Drinking Places	04981	52	127	Educational Services	05260	5	6	Merch. Wholesalers,Nondur. Gds
04780	14	31	Accommodation	04982	46	293	Wood Product Manufacturing	05261	64	304	Justice, Pubic Order/Safety
04781	10	35	Educational Services	04983	65	502	Wood Product Manufacturing	05262	103	530	Bldg Matl & Garden Eqpmt Dlrs
04783	15	41	Food Svcs & Drinking Places	04984	7	12	Furniture & Related Prod. Mfg	05301	1227	12828	Merch. Wholesalers,Nondur. Gds
04785	98	841	Nursing & Resid. Care Facilit.	04985	24	247	Motor Vehicle & Parts Dealers	05302	10	45	Construction of Buildings
04786	50	263	Educational Services	04986	61	297	Educational Services	05303	2	5	Relig., Grant, Civic, Prof Org
04787	8	69	Crop Production	04987	39	84	Food and Beverage Stores	05340	37	196	Administrative & Support Svcs
04788	1	0	Special Trade Contractors	04988	124	611	Educational Services	05341	27	69	Educational Services
04841	691	6072	Food Svcs & Drinking Places	04989	83	488	Wood Product Manufacturing	05342	37	124	Educational Services
04843	442	3186	Food Svcs & Drinking Places	04992	14	127	Special Trade Contractors	05343	43	125	Construction of Buildings
04846	14	69	Social Assistance	05001	475	4104	Hospitals	05344	35	208	Educational Services
04847	42	204	Accommodation	05009	4	10	Credit Intermediation & Relatd	05345	82	401	Justice, Pubic Order/Safety
04848	41	147	Educational Services	05030	46	224	Educational Services	05346	166	1081	Educational Services
04849	176	715	Food Svcs & Drinking Places	05031	36	139	Accommodation	05350	23	58	Administrative & Support Svcs
04850	6	20	Broadcasting	05032	114	1012	Plastics & Rubber Products Mfg	05351	5	14	Bldg Matl & Garden Eqpmt Dlrs
04851	2	2	Postal Service	05033	171	1297	Educational Services	05352	24	119	Wood Product Manufacturing
04852	9	72	Accommodation	05034	40	263	Administrative & Support Svcs	05353	78	708	Hospitals
04853	22	91	Educational Services	05035	24	120	Food Svcs & Drinking Places	05354	50	917	Utilities
04854	41	161	Heavy & Civil Eng. Construct'N	05036	29	132	Special Trade Contractors	05355	24	48	Educational Services
04855	11	73	Construction of Buildings	05037	37	467	Accommodation	05356	129	3352	Accommodation
04856	316	3707	Hospitals	05038	84	331	Fabricated Metal Product Mfg	05357	6	12	Amusement, Gambling,& Recreat.
04857	22	25	Heavy & Civil Eng. Construct'N	05039	18	25	Publishing Industries	05358	11	27	Educational Services
04858	42	138	Food and Beverage Stores	05040	28	98	Educational Services	05359	16	48	Accommodation
04859	18	107	Food and Beverage Stores	05041	9	32	Merch. Wholesalers,Durable Gds	05360	13	16	Food and Beverage Stores
04860	33	215	Merch. Wholesalers,Nondur. Gds	05042	23	63	Prof., Scientific, & Tech Svcs	05361	22	119	Educational Services
04861	166	1421	Justice, Pubic Order/Safety	05043	33	312	Furniture & Related Prod. Mfg	05362	18	36	Prof., Scientific, & Tech Svcs
04862	136	541	Educational Services	05045	98	826	Accommodation	05363	219	1038	Food Svcs & Drinking Places
04863	69	289	Educational Services	05046	42	109	Justice, Pubic Order/Safety	05401	2098	26772	Hospitals
04864	163	695	Justice, Pubic Order/Safety	05047	83	190	Construction of Buildings	05402	11	26	Special Trade Contractors
04865	19	129	Construction of Buildings	05048	88	354	Educational Services	05403	1205	15743	Food Svcs & Drinking Places
04901	1181	17114	Ambulatory Health Care Svcs	05049	5	12	Food Svcs & Drinking Places	05404	236	2890	Social Assistance
04903	6	31	Food Svcs & Drinking Places	05050	4	10	Bldg Matl & Garden Eqpmt Dlrs	05405	21	366	Ambulatory Health Care Svcs
04910	56	178	Educational Services	05051	32	155	Educational Services	05406	16	39	Administrative & Support Svcs
04911	47	161	Heavy & Civil Eng. Construct'N	05052	15	67	Machinery Manufacturing	05407	1	1	Prof., Scientific, & Tech Svcs
04912	28	143	Forestry and Logging	05053	22	52	Publishing Industries	05439	1	5	Relig., Grant, Civic, Prof Org
04915	569	5042	Food and Beverage Stores	05054	6	49	Bldg Matl & Garden Eqpmt Dlrs	05440	80	302	Educational Services
04917	76	718	Nonmetallic Mineral Prod. Mfg	05055	198	889	Merch. Wholesalers,Nondur. Gds	05441	17	80	Educational Services
04918	23	191	Food Svcs & Drinking Places	05056	38	377	Accommodation	05442	5	12	Educational Services
04920	76	408	Unclassified Establishments	05058	12	104	Accommodation	05443	263	1312	Educational Services
04921	48	135	Educational Services	05059	89	842	Amusement, Gambling,& Recreat.	05444	77	279	Educational Services

ZIP CODE	2004 Total Firms	2004 Total Employ-ees	TOP INDUSTRY RANKED on 2004 EMPLOYMENT	ZIP CODE	2004 Total Firms	2004 Total Employ-ees	TOP INDUSTRY RANKED on 2004 EMPLOYMENT	ZIP CODE	2004 Total Firms	2004 Total Employ-ees	TOP INDUSTRY RANKED on 2004 EMPLOYMENT
05445	132	470	Educational Services	05702	9	6	Miscellaneous Store Retailers	05901	1	28	Accommodation
05446	730	8296	Ambulatory Health Care Svcs	05730	15	19	General Merchandise Stores	05902	9	709	Furniture & Related Prod. Mfg
05447	7	11	General Merchandise Stores	05731	17	53	Accommodation	05903	32	150	Educational Services
05448	20	58	Special Trade Contractors	05732	55	219	Ambulatory Health Care Svcs	05904	10	31	Educational Services
05449	1	1	Perform'g Arts, Spec. Sports	05733	254	1587	Educational Services	05905	26	49	Merch. Wholesalers,Durable Gds
05450	172	1015	Food Svcs & Drinking Places	05734	42	142	Educational Services	05906	25	106	Print'g & Related Supp't Act's
05451	13	39	Administrative & Support Svcs	05735	123	1029	Educational Services	05907	19	49	Prof., Scientific, & Tech Svcs
05452	834	13572	Computer & Electronic Prod Mfg	05736	37	142	Merch. Wholesalers,Durable Gds	06001	1148	8318	Food Svcs & Drinking Places
05453	6	6	Prof., Scientific, & Tech Svcs	05737	22	93	Accommodation	06002	1216	14323	Transportation Equipment Mfg
05454	101	611	Educational Services	05738	47	222	Accommodation	06006	1	6	Administrative & Support Svcs
05455	26	97	Educational Services	05739	71	344	Educational Services	06010	2112	19893	Fabricated Metal Product Mfg
05456	51	246	Food and Beverage Stores	05740	12	57	Merch. Wholesalers,Nondur. Gds	06011	5	3	Computer & Electronic Prod Mfg
05457	44	138	Exec., Legis., & Other Support	05741	2	3	General Merchandise Stores	06013	250	1049	Educational Services
05458	64	182	Educational Services	05742	13	36	Administrative & Support Svcs	06016	92	1019	Merch. Wholesalers,Nondur. Gds
05459	51	275	Educational Services	05743	165	1000	Educational Services	06018	235	1929	Merch. Wholesalers,Durable Gds
05460	14	277	Accommodation	05744	16	63	Special Trade Contractors	06019	607	3098	Educational Services
05461	155	945	Educational Services	05745	7	135	Furniture & Related Prod. Mfg	06021	20	216	Social Assistance
05462	59	166	Educational Services	05746	4	9	Accommodation	06023	87	1013	Motor Vehicle & Parts Dealers
05463	18	50	Relig., Grant, Civic, Prof Org	05747	13	57	Wood Product Manufacturing	06024	16	148	Accommodation
05464	104	1020	Accommodation	05748	21	147	Wood Product Manufacturing	06025	10	165	Fabricated Metal Product Mfg
05465	155	778	Educational Services	05750	16	67	Nursing & Resid. Care Facilit.	06026	299	3878	Nat'l Security & Int'l Affairs
05466	10	208	Prof., Scientific, & Tech Svcs	05751	233	3999	Accommodation	06027	47	169	Educational Services
05468	341	2661	Food Manufacturing	05753	674	7925	Educational Services	06028	4	6	Postal Service
05469	24	56	Educational Services	05757	39	113	Justice, Pubic Order/Safety	06029	404	2335	Educational Services
05470	16	50	Construction of Buildings	05758	38	115	Educational Services	06030	11	38	Ambulatory Health Care Svcs
05471	37	124	Food Svcs & Drinking Places	05759	100	940	Prof., Scientific, & Tech Svcs	06031	54	370	Educational Services
05472	84	478	Transit & Grnd Pass. Transport	05760	69	200	Construction of Buildings	06032	1565	25089	Ambulatory Health Care Svcs
05473	28	98	Food and Beverage Stores	05761	52	199	Fabricated Metal Product Mfg	06033	1717	14038	Prof., Scientific, & Tech Svcs
05474	45	272	Accommodation	05762	24	133	Wood Product Manufacturing	06034	2	2	Merch. Wholesalers,Nondur. Gds
05476	86	632	Merch. Wholesalers,Nondur. Gds	05763	115	522	Educational Services	06035	353	1914	Educational Services
05477	190	899	Educational Services	05764	131	813	Educational Services	06037	950	11069	Managmt of Companies & Enterp.
05478	738	6642	Hospitals	05765	42	228	Educational Services	06039	140	1600	Educational Services
05479	2	0	Relig., Grant, Civic, Prof Org	05766	9	38	Educational Services	06040	2408	27122	Ambulatory Health Care Svcs
05481	13	75	Truck Transportation	05767	68	376	Support Activities: Agr./For.	06043	185	1151	Educational Services
05482	408	3271	Nursing & Resid. Care Facilit.	05768	10	26	Relig., Grant, Civic, Prof Org	06045	5	6	Administrative & Support Svcs
05483	37	142	Educational Services	05769	36	263	Accommodation	06050	12	186	Postal Service
05485	9	177	Paper Manufacturing	05770	56	355	Merch. Wholesalers,Nondur. Gds	06051	1132	11800	Fabricated Metal Product Mfg
05486	87	384	Accommodation	05772	23	113	Miscellaneous Manufacturing	06052	316	6055	Hospitals
05487	32	133	Educational Services	05773	106	407	Educational Services	06053	554	6934	Educational Services
05488	265	2567	Educational Services	05774	28	105	Educational Services	06057	226	2029	Nonstore Retailers
05489	69	207	Relig., Grant, Civic, Prof Org	05775	20	243	Repair and Maintenance	06058	111	311	Social Assistance
05490	5	16	Construction of Buildings	05776	12	35	Elect'l Eqpmt, App, & Comp Mfg	06059	8	5	Special Trade Contractors
05491	248	2311	Motor Vehicle & Parts Dealers	05777	120	572	Educational Services	06060	28	150	Accommodation
05492	13	40	Educational Services	05778	21	45	Crop Production	06061	15	66	Merch. Wholesalers,Nondur. Gds
05494	46	223	Truck Transportation	05819	669	6659	Educational Services	06062	873	9598	Special Trade Contractors
05495	833	9230	Special Trade Contractors	05820	21	71	Educational Services	06063	104	446	Food Svcs & Drinking Places
05601	15	37	Exec., Legis., & Other Support	05821	50	198	Administrative & Support Svcs	06064	5	6	Postal Service
05602	1099	10243	Ambulatory Health Care Svcs	05822	102	537	Nursing & Resid. Care Facilit.	06065	24	55	Accommodation
05603	1	0	Exec., Legis., & Other Support	05823	4	4	Food and Beverage Stores	06066	1166	10220	Food Svcs & Drinking Places
05604	1	15	Securities/Commodity Contracts	05824	39	193	Educational Services	06067	992	13215	General Merchandise Stores
05609	16	394	Exec., Legis., & Other Support	05825	16	92	Educational Services	06068	158	804	Nursing & Resid. Care Facilit.
05620	15	391	Admin. Human Resource Programs	05826	29	137	Educational Services	06069	207	1345	Hospitals
05633	22	335	Exec., Legis., & Other Support	05827	17	194	Accommodation	06070	754	6833	Nursing & Resid. Care Facilit.
05640	1	3	Food and Beverage Stores	05828	82	354	Educational Services	06071	313	1520	Justice, Pubic Order/Safety
05641	910	8904	Transportation Equipment Mfg	05829	160	1167	Food and Beverage Stores	06072	12	34	Fabricated Metal Product Mfg
05647	44	563	Animal Production	05830	54	483	Machinery Manufacturing	06073	154	696	Educational Services
05648	18	35	Furn. & Home Furnishgs Stores	05832	36	344	Accommodation	06074	1188	11960	Prof., Scientific, & Tech Svcs
05649	24	128	Educational Services	05833	7	93	Educational Services	06075	26	14	Prof., Scientific, & Tech Svcs
05650	16	37	General Merchandise Stores	05836	22	55	Merch. Wholesalers,Nondur. Gds	06076	422	4557	Hospitals
05651	82	416	Wood Product Manufacturing	05837	5	9	Educational Services	06077	3	2	Merch. Wholesalers,Durable Gds
05652	19	59	Educational Services	05838	4	7	Furn. & Home Furnishgs Stores	06078	397	3383	Justice, Pubic Order/Safety
05653	9	15	Food and Beverage Stores	05839	22	132	Nursing & Resid. Care Facilit.	06079	1	1	Postal Service
05654	22	540	Mining (Except Oil and Gas)	05840	3	20	Heavy & Civil Eng. Construct'N	06081	31	116	Educational Services
05655	93	691	Educational Services	05841	31	320	Accommodation	06082	1551	19869	Insurance Carriers & Related
05656	117	777	Educational Services	05842	10	15	Food and Beverage Stores	06083	8	9	Insurance Carriers & Related
05657	15	65	General Merchandise Stores	05843	147	709	Educational Services	06084	429	3242	Educational Services
05658	61	100	Accommodation	05845	41	184	Educational Services	06085	214	1327	Educational Services
05660	76	233	Hospitals	05846	73	233	Educational Services	06088	467	4756	Food Svcs & Drinking Places
05661	405	3570	Hospitals	05847	22	89	Educational Services	06089	116	4422	Insurance Carriers & Related
05662	4	42	Wood Product Manufacturing	05848	12	91	Petroleum & Coal Products Mfg	06090	22	30	Crop Production
05663	219	1986	Educational Services	05849	40	106	Furniture & Related Prod. Mfg	06091	13	28	Justice, Pubic Order/Safety
05664	5	19	Accommodation	05850	10	178	Educational Services	06092	116	960	Motor Vehicle & Parts Dealers
05665	8	38	Administrative & Support Svcs	05851	250	2116	Educational Services	06093	60	563	Educational Services
05666	4	13	Food and Beverage Stores	05853	18	48	Educational Services	06094	4	4	Administrative & Support Svcs
05667	69	578	Educational Services	05855	491	4973	Social Assistance	06095	1082	19136	Machinery Manufacturing
05669	26	51	Educational Services	05857	25	134	Miscellaneous Store Retailers	06096	628	12000	Transportation Equipment Mfg
05670	34	284	Food Svcs & Drinking Places	05858	6	16	Food and Beverage Stores	06098	521	4111	Educational Services
05671	32	1790	Admin. Human Resource Programs	05859	60	566	Accommodation	06101	6	12	Postal Service
05672	507	4708	Accommodation	05860	101	1118	Furn. & Home Furnishgs Stores	06102	3	306	Insurance Carriers & Related
05673	348	1598	Food Svcs & Drinking Places	05861	3	3	Forestry and Logging	06103	1344	18901	Prof., Scientific, & Tech Svcs
05674	143	1141	Amusement, Gambling,& Recreat.	05862	23	102	Educational Services	06105	853	14276	Insurance Carriers & Related
05675	29	86	Special Trade Contractors	05863	9	58	Postal Service	06106	1870	22652	Exec., Legis., & Other Support
05676	310	2847	Food and Beverage Stores	05866	10	32	Educational Services	06107	1051	6972	Food Svcs & Drinking Places
05677	80	311	Amusement, Gambling,& Recreat.	05867	19	120	Educational Services	06108	1330	15706	Unclassified Establishments
05678	19	201	Nonmetallic Mineral Prod. Mfg	05868	24	70	Justice, Pubic Order/Safety	06109	1086	8247	Prof., Scientific, & Tech Svcs
05679	88	517	Educational Services	05871	46	129	Educational Services	06110	707	8715	Fabricated Metal Product Mfg
05680	43	177	Educational Services	05872	14	46	Educational Services	06111	1378	18923	Heavy & Civil Eng. Construct'N
05681	14	40	Educational Services	05873	29	70	Educational Services	06112	420	4378	Educational Services
05682	22	68	Educational Services	05874	20	62	Chemical Manufacturing	06114	871	8835	Educational Services
05701	1629	17656	Wood Product Manufacturing	05875	7	46	Sportg Gds,Hobby,Book, & Music	06115	22	6600	Hospitals

BUSINESS DATA

ZIP CODE	2004 Total Firms	2004 Total Employ-ees	TOP INDUSTRY RANKED on 2004 EMPLOYMENT	ZIP CODE	2004 Total Firms	2004 Total Employ-ees	TOP INDUSTRY RANKED on 2004 EMPLOYMENT	ZIP CODE	2004 Total Firms	2004 Total Employ-ees	TOP INDUSTRY RANKED on 2004 EMPLOYMENT
06117	427	10473	Ambulatory Health Care Svcs	06378	368	1520	Food Svcs & Drinking Places	06605	679	6514	Social Assistance
06118	449	14050	Transportation Equipment Mfg	06379	268	2140	Machinery Manufacturing	06606	1279	9625	Hospitals
06119	530	3210	Educational Services	06380	81	502	Special Trade Contractors	06607	348	3160	Merch. Wholesalers,Durable Gds
06120	518	7791	Justice, Pubic Order/Safety	06382	281	3270	Justice, Pubic Order/Safety	06608	393	3006	Exec., Legis., & Other Support
06123	1	0	Repair and Maintenance	06383	4	443	Paper Manufacturing	06610	588	8794	Hospitals
06127	3	11	Insurance Carriers & Related	06384	70	272	Educational Services	06611	1436	13956	Ambulatory Health Care Svcs
06128	1	3	Construction of Buildings	06385	711	9447	Utilities	06612	231	750	Educational Services
06129	3	2	Animal Production	06387	24	820	Primary Metal Manufacturing	06614	939	7848	Merch. Wholesalers,Durable Gds
06131	5	5	Administrative & Support Svcs	06388	2	1	Construction of Buildings	06615	1106	11074	Prof., Scientific, & Tech Svcs
06132	1	2	Prof., Scientific, & Tech Svcs	06389	13	133	Justice, Pubic Order/Safety	06702	715	7551	Justice, Pubic Order/Safety
06133	2	1	Administrative & Support Svcs	06390	61	199	Construction of Buildings	06703	1	1	Miscellaneous Store Retailers
06134	9	26	Social Assistance	06401	606	4562	Relig., Grant, Civic, Prof Org	06704	591	4700	Food Svcs & Drinking Places
06137	3	12	Repair and Maintenance	06403	160	795	Merch. Wholesalers,Durable Gds	06705	791	7693	Nursing & Resid. Care Facilit.
06138	1	0	Special Trade Contractors	06404	4	3	Personal and Laundry Services	06706	517	4932	Food Svcs & Drinking Places
06143	1	2	Unclassified Establishments	06405	1754	14594	Food Svcs & Drinking Places	06708	1097	12036	Ambulatory Health Care Svcs
06144	2	6	Special Trade Contractors	06409	94	754	Prof., Scientific, & Tech Svcs	06710	178	1211	Fabricated Metal Product Mfg
06145	1	0	Merch. Wholesalers,Nondur. Gds	06410	1268	12639	Merch. Wholesalers,Nondur. Gds	06712	345	1903	Prof., Scientific, & Tech Svcs
06147	2	2	Waste Managmt & Remediat'n Svc	06412	221	2032	Elect'l Eqpmt, App, & Comp Mfg	06716	558	3161	Fabricated Metal Product Mfg
06152	1	200	Insurance Carriers & Related	06413	646	4468	Chemical Manufacturing	06720	1	0	Relig., Grant, Civic, Prof Org
06154	2	5000	Insurance Carriers & Related	06414	12	232	Relig., Grant, Civic, Prof Org	06721	2	0	Repair and Maintenance
06156	5	10003	Insurance Carriers & Related	06415	481	4554	Prof., Scientific, & Tech Svcs	06722	2	0	Special Trade Contractors
06183	2	4070	Insurance Carriers & Related	06416	595	6066	Food Svcs & Drinking Places	06724	1	1	Insurance Carriers & Related
06226	659	16501	Educational Services	06417	248	1534	Educational Services	06749	2	18	Special Trade Contractors
06230	4	13	Merch. Wholesalers,Durable Gds	06418	499	5250	Hospitals	06750	103	793	Transportation Equipment Mfg
06231	37	112	Ambulatory Health Care Svcs	06419	190	528	Educational Services	06751	179	640	Hospitals
06232	82	327	Educational Services	06420	127	601	Bldg Matl & Garden Eqpmt Dlrs	06752	83	288	Prof., Scientific, & Tech Svcs
06233	6	6	Ambulatory Health Care Svcs	06422	257	2019	Fabricated Metal Product Mfg	06753	46	60	Administrative & Support Svcs
06234	165	1045	Nursing & Resid. Care Facilit.	06423	203	606	Food Svcs & Drinking Places	06754	76	184	Bldg Matl & Garden Eqpmt Dlrs
06235	77	341	Educational Services	06424	423	1755	Educational Services	06755	36	157	Wood Product Manufacturing
06237	176	1231	Educational Services	06426	464	2803	Ambulatory Health Care Svcs	06756	130	429	Relig., Grant, Civic, Prof Org
06238	291	1225	Educational Services	06437	1124	7353	Ambulatory Health Care Svcs	06757	239	1989	Educational Services
06239	541	4558	Educational Services	06438	191	700	Relig., Grant, Civic, Prof Org	06758	5	65	Accommodation
06241	170	4664	Merch. Wholesalers,Nondur. Gds	06439	8	29	Construction of Buildings	06759	477	2975	Educational Services
06242	71	488	Transportation Equipment Mfg	06440	7	19	Food Svcs & Drinking Places	06762	330	2761	Amusement, Gambling,& Recreat.
06243	10	24	Accommodation	06441	130	769	Educational Services	06763	91	284	Food Svcs & Drinking Places
06244	3	22	Furniture & Related Prod. Mfg	06442	52	403	Other Information Services	06770	836	7456	Educational Services
06246	8	18	Repair and Maintenance	06443	909	5452	Educational Services	06776	1388	10179	Paper Manufacturing
06247	69	274	Educational Services	06444	14	39	Special Trade Contractors	06777	147	573	Food Svcs & Drinking Places
06248	195	1167	Educational Services	06447	227	1328	Insurance Carriers & Related	06778	22	49	Educational Services
06249	165	1126	Chemical Manufacturing	06450	1190	13207	Nursing & Resid. Care Facilit.	06779	170	930	Educational Services
06250	158	1518	Ambulatory Health Care Svcs	06451	765	8134	General Merchandise Stores	06781	21	81	Amusement, Gambling,& Recreat.
06251	3	9	Merch. Wholesalers,Nondur. Gds	06455	218	1688	Computer & Electronic Prod Mfg	06782	123	480	Nursing & Resid. Care Facilit.
06254	117	1351	Food Manufacturing	06456	7	11	Relig., Grant, Civic, Prof Org	06783	109	217	Exec., Legis., & Other Support
06255	96	834	Educational Services	06457	2003	23988	Ambulatory Health Care Svcs	06784	129	307	Educational Services
06256	105	1554	General Merchandise Stores	06459	5	32	Other Information Services	06785	14	61	Educational Services
06258	45	413	Educational Services	06460	2844	26968	Food Svcs & Drinking Places	06786	269	1890	Fabricated Metal Product Mfg
06259	118	1146	Food Manufacturing	06467	54	731	Nonmetallic Mineral Prod. Mfg	06787	391	3219	Fabricated Metal Product Mfg
06260	562	6052	Hospitals	06468	977	6375	Merch. Wholesalers,Durable Gds	06790	1601	16860	Educational Services
06262	16	85	Miscellaneous Store Retailers	06469	103	893	Accommodation	06791	175	709	Administrative & Support Svcs
06263	9	261	Computer & Electronic Prod Mfg	06470	882	6576	Prof., Scientific, & Tech Svcs	06793	72	407	Educational Services
06264	44	142	Merch. Wholesalers,Durable Gds	06471	401	2450	Nursing & Resid. Care Facilit.	06794	118	568	Transit & Grnd Pass. Transport
06265	1	6	Repair and Maintenance	06472	149	1543	Computer & Electronic Prod Mfg	06795	673	7621	Computer & Electronic Prod Mfg
06266	27	481	Plastics & Rubber Products Mfg	06473	1346	16088	Miscellaneous Manufacturing	06796	55	269	Justice, Pubic Order/Safety
06267	15	126	Social Assistance	06475	1042	7062	Food Svcs & Drinking Places	06798	633	2781	Food Svcs & Drinking Places
06268	322	2450	Educational Services	06477	799	7594	Food Svcs & Drinking Places	06801	922	6675	Educational Services
06269	12	5182	Educational Services	06478	390	2137	Special Trade Contractors	06804	1004	6660	Social Assistance
06277	135	716	Paper Manufacturing	06479	276	2858	Nursing & Resid. Care Facilit.	06807	343	1443	Transit & Grnd Pass. Transport
06278	129	545	Accommodation	06480	407	2901	Paper Manufacturing	06810	2883	86451	Prof., Scientific, & Tech Svcs
06279	158	912	Food Svcs & Drinking Places	06481	17	131	Plastics & Rubber Products Mfg	06811	1129	8552	Educational Services
06280	113	557	Nursing & Resid. Care Facilit.	06482	266	1568	Prof., Scientific, & Tech Svcs	06812	377	1636	Educational Services
06281	234	1533	Educational Services	06483	551	3922	Merch. Wholesalers,Durable Gds	06813	13	31	Special Trade Contractors
06282	15	144	Social Assistance	06484	1528	16548	Prof., Scientific, & Tech Svcs	06816	3	1130	Prof., Scientific, & Tech Svcs
06320	1344	12171	Educational Services	06487	2	5	Relig., Grant, Civic, Prof Org	06817	1	6	Support Act. for Transport.
06330	72	532	Paper Manufacturing	06488	851	5789	Nursing & Resid. Care Facilit.	06820	1027	8009	Prof., Scientific, & Tech Svcs
06331	105	499	Educational Services	06489	1214	10758	Food Svcs & Drinking Places	06824	1770	12375	Educational Services
06332	35	215	Educational Services	06491	7	169	Wood Product Manufacturing	06825	984	12174	Educational Services
06333	251	1986	Justice, Pubic Order/Safety	06492	2097	24688	Chemical Manufacturing	06828	2	717	Computer & Electronic Prod Mfg
06334	91	699	Merch. Wholesalers,Nondur. Gds	06498	374	3048	Fabricated Metal Product Mfg	06829	48	155	Justice, Pubic Order/Safety
06335	163	1072	Educational Services	06503	1	2	Ambulatory Health Care Svcs	06830	2594	21597	Securities/Commodity Contracts
06336	5	120	Miscellaneous Manufacturing	06504	1	30	Ambulatory Health Care Svcs	06831	599	4967	Prof., Scientific, & Tech Svcs
06339	173	13246	Accommodation	06506	4	7	Prof., Scientific, & Tech Svcs	06836	6	6	Miscellaneous Manufacturing
06340	1028	14151	Chemical Manufacturing	06508	1	1	Relig., Grant, Civic, Prof Org	06838	5	17	Construction of Buildings
06349	12	135	Computer & Electronic Prod Mfg	06510	1145	17803	Ambulatory Health Care Svcs	06840	1042	6299	Educational Services
06350	1	0	Relig., Grant, Civic, Prof Org	06511	2209	32859	Educational Services	06850	910	10278	Ambulatory Health Care Svcs
06351	383	2791	Educational Services	06512	860	6857	Food Svcs & Drinking Places	06851	1756	16490	Prof., Scientific, & Tech Svcs
06353	40	110	Repair and Maintenance	06513	715	6170	Transit & Grnd Pass. Transport	06852	9	198	Chemical Manufacturing
06354	96	837	Miscellaneous Store Retailers	06514	928	8063	Educational Services	06853	180	773	Educational Services
06355	783	6303	Food Svcs & Drinking Places	06515	460	6134	Educational Services	06854	1358	14308	Computer & Electronic Prod Mfg
06357	378	4068	Justice, Pubic Order/Safety	06516	1583	17410	Merch. Wholesalers,Nondur. Gds	06855	427	3731	Computer & Electronic Prod Mfg
06359	160	1850	Prof., Scientific, & Tech Svcs	06517	468	4467	Relig., Grant, Civic, Prof Org	06856	6	48	Merch. Wholesalers,Nondur. Gds
06360	1483	14754	Educational Services	06518	852	4376	Ambulatory Health Care Svcs	06857	1	600	Merch. Wholesalers,Durable Gds
06365	149	746	Motor Vehicle & Parts Dealers	06519	524	7295	Ambulatory Health Care Svcs	06859	1	0	Miscellaneous Manufacturing
06370	123	837	Educational Services	06520	2	3	Ambulatory Health Care Svcs	06870	370	2377	Accommodation
06371	491	2690	Educational Services	06524	207	1132	Educational Services	06875	8	5	Administrative & Support Svcs
06372	17	47	Other Information Services	06525	458	3775	Social Assistance	06876	9	30	Social Assistance
06373	13	116	Educational Services	06530	2	1	Real Estate	06877	1352	9410	Chemical Manufacturing
06374	351	2769	Perform'g Arts, Spec. Sports	06534	2	0	Special Trade Contractors	06878	229	1639	Educational Services
06375	63	477	Relig., Grant, Civic, Prof Org	06601	5	8	Transit & Grnd Pass. Transport	06880	2761	17585	Prof., Scientific, & Tech Svcs
06376	4	8	Exec., Legis., & Other Support	06602	4	6	Credit Intermediation & Relatd	06881	11	59	Paper Manufacturing
06377	65	248	Clothing & Cloth'g Acc. Stores	06604	1515	16537	Justice, Pubic Order/Safety	06883	309	1416	Educational Services

ZIP CODE	2004 Total Firms	2004 Total Employees	TOP INDUSTRY RANKED on 2004 EMPLOYMENT
06890	311	2425	Prof., Scientific, & Tech Svcs
06896	356	4792	Special Trade Contractors
06897	1138	10085	Prof., Scientific, & Tech Svcs
06901	1432	20289	Prof., Scientific, & Tech Svcs
06902	2858	30840	Prof., Scientific, & Tech Svcs
06903	441	2027	Educational Services
06904	5	12	Insurance Carriers & Related
06905	1443	10306	Prof., Scientific, & Tech Svcs
06906	481	2831	Special Trade Contractors
06907	458	3060	Computer & Electronic Prod Mfg
06910	2	6	Postal Service
06921	2	141	Paper Manufacturing
06922	1	3	Credit Intermediation & Relatd
06926	2	1217	Administrative & Support Svcs
06927	3	300	Credit Intermediation & Relatd
07001	407	7424	Motor Vehicle & Parts Dealers
07002	1802	16072	Educational Services
07003	1774	13868	Prof., Scientific, & Tech Svcs
07004	1755	22399	Prof., Scientific, & Tech Svcs
07005	720	5308	Special Trade Contractors
07006	1393	11422	Educational Services
07007	10	43	Special Trade Contractors
07008	456	9271	Food and Beverage Stores
07009	462	5607	Hospitals
07010	613	2684	Food Svcs & Drinking Places
07011	1292	8491	Food and Beverage Stores
07012	470	5865	Bldg Matl & Garden Eqpmt Dlrs
07013	1192	8446	Ambulatory Health Care Svcs
07014	253	4993	Computer & Electronic Prod Mfg
07015	4	9	Administrative & Support Svcs
07016	1133	13296	Unclassified Establishments
07017	634	8308	Exec., Legis., & Other Support
07018	851	10243	Hospitals
07019	2	0	Heavy & Civil Eng. Construct'N
07020	420	4248	Prof., Scientific, & Tech Svcs
07021	30	187	Educational Services
07022	465	3439	Waste Managmt & Remediat'n Svc
07023	267	1451	Special Trade Contractors
07024	1712	11400	Prof., Scientific, & Tech Svcs
07026	906	7115	Special Trade Contractors
07027	259	2546	Food and Beverage Stores
07028	158	1088	Educational Services
07029	519	4257	Food Manufacturing
07030	1621	11259	Food Svcs & Drinking Places
07031	435	3399	Rental and Leasing Services
07032	1314	14277	Truck Transportation
07033	651	10449	Merch. Wholesalers,Nondur. Gds
07034	207	820	Educational Services
07035	354	3511	Nursing & Resid. Care Facilit.
07036	1791	21584	Merch. Wholesalers,Nondur. Gds
07039	1682	18053	Ambulatory Health Care Svcs
07040	878	5497	Educational Services
07041	738	4723	Ambulatory Health Care Svcs
07042	1634	10383	Educational Services
07043	502	3870	Special Trade Contractors
07044	744	4445	Prof., Scientific, & Tech Svcs
07045	477	2861	Prof., Scientific, & Tech Svcs
07046	235	2769	Prof., Scientific, & Tech Svcs
07047	1595	15739	Clothing & Cloth'g Acc. Stores
07050	1024	8318	Relig., Grant, Civic, Prof Org
07051	5	16	Administrative & Support Svcs
07052	1785	14454	Ambulatory Health Care Svcs
07054	1993	35698	Prof., Scientific, & Tech Svcs
07055	1933	16913	Hospitals
07057	300	2091	Apparel Manufacturing
07058	313	5023	Merch. Wholesalers,Durable Gds
07059	612	8301	Insurance Carriers & Related
07060	1477	10991	Hospitals
07061	4	9	Prof., Scientific, & Tech Svcs
07062	281	4811	Prof., Scientific, & Tech Svcs
07063	139	2011	Broadcasting
07064	57	584	Nonmetallic Mineral Prod. Mfg
07065	1091	11240	Truck Transportation
07066	779	7116	Prof., Scientific, & Tech Svcs
07067	338	1621	Educational Services
07068	429	8946	Isps, Web Search Portals
07069	426	4241	General Merchandise Stores
07070	722	5272	Telecommunications
07071	792	9183	Prof., Scientific, & Tech Svcs
07072	557	11386	Merch. Wholesalers,Nondur. Gds
07073	495	10925	Perform'g Arts, Spec. Sports
07074	276	4990	Merch. Wholesalers,Durable Gds
07075	204	2891	Merch. Wholesalers,Durable Gds
07076	753	5424	Educational Services
07077	31	303	Educational Services
07078	548	8669	Clothing & Cloth'g Acc. Stores
07079	764	4685	Educational Services
07080	1329	16343	Merch. Wholesalers,Durable Gds
07081	1020	10141	Prof., Scientific, & Tech Svcs
07082	132	849	Paper Manufacturing

ZIP CODE	2004 Total Firms	2004 Total Employees	TOP INDUSTRY RANKED on 2004 EMPLOYMENT
07083	2567	26374	Educational Services
07086	285	8388	Securities/Commodity Contracts
07087	2131	11349	Educational Services
07088	120	1391	Bldg Matl & Garden Eqpmt Dlrs
07090	1486	9423	Prof., Scientific, & Tech Svcs
07091	13	74	Prof., Scientific, & Tech Svcs
07092	460	4939	Ambulatory Health Care Svcs
07093	1641	7594	Educational Services
07094	1148	23740	Elect'l Eqpmt, App, & Comp Mfg
07095	1182	13744	Prof., Scientific, & Tech Svcs
07096	7	46	Administrative & Support Svcs
07097	4	406	Relig., Grant, Civic, Prof Org
07099	5	42	Relig., Grant, Civic, Prof Org
07101	6	41	Admin. of Economic Programs
07102	2132	35588	Prof., Scientific, & Tech Svcs
07103	810	18130	Exec., Legis., & Other Support
07104	983	9550	Educational Services
07105	1953	22401	Insurance Carriers & Related
07106	364	3017	Merch. Wholesalers,Durable Gds
07107	644	6012	Relig., Grant, Civic, Prof Org
07108	422	3055	Educational Services
07109	1012	9017	Relig., Grant, Civic, Prof Org
07110	1000	10295	Merch. Wholesalers,Nondur. Gds
07111	1368	11144	Exec., Legis., & Other Support
07112	479	2691	Educational Services
07114	915	26017	Air Transportation
07188	1	0	Special Trade Contractors
07201	1658	18325	Justice, Pubic Order/Safety
07202	814	7564	Educational Services
07203	590	4525	Educational Services
07204	412	2487	Miscellaneous Store Retailers
07205	747	6230	Merch. Wholesalers,Durable Gds
07206	572	5420	Merch. Wholesalers,Nondur. Gds
07207	10	92	Administrative & Support Svcs
07208	761	6671	Food Manufacturing
07302	1254	17798	Prof., Scientific, & Tech Svcs
07303	2	1	Food and Beverage Stores
07304	912	9178	Hospitals
07305	994	13599	Educational Services
07306	1917	21002	Educational Services
07307	789	4189	Educational Services
07310	312	5281	Securities/Commodity Contracts
07311	21	432	Other Information Services
07399	4	3525	Securities/Commodity Contracts
07401	245	3781	Miscellaneous Manufacturing
07403	281	1606	Accommodation
07405	805	4676	Educational Services
07407	651	6622	Paper Manufacturing
07410	1392	11944	Food Manufacturing
07416	394	2280	Educational Services
07417	381	5911	Chemical Manufacturing
07418	47	119	Special Trade Contractors
07419	363	1645	Plastics & Rubber Products Mfg
07420	119	1484	Nursing & Resid. Care Facilit.
07421	250	799	Food and Beverage Stores
07422	129	209	Relig., Grant, Civic, Prof Org
07423	204	1105	Educational Services
07424	1164	10539	Prof., Scientific, & Tech Svcs
07428	37	423	Accommodation
07430	722	11461	Administrative & Support Svcs
07432	485	3261	Educational Services
07435	230	774	Ambulatory Health Care Svcs
07436	470	6154	Prof., Scientific, & Tech Svcs
07438	320	2243	Educational Services
07439	91	308	Educational Services
07440	174	789	Plastics & Rubber Products Mfg
07442	540	2977	Securities/Commodity Contracts
07444	476	4646	Hospitals
07446	815	8338	Merch. Wholesalers,Durable Gds
07450	1349	8141	Ambulatory Health Care Svcs
07451	7	13	Transit & Grnd Pass. Transport
07452	422	3907	Educational Services
07456	417	2424	Accommodation
07457	250	3279	Repair and Maintenance
07458	350	5010	Publishing Industries
07460	81	233	Exec., Legis., & Other Support
07461	747	3368	Educational Services
07462	488	2997	Educational Services
07463	403	2777	Educational Services
07465	139	995	Relig., Grant, Civic, Prof Org
07470	2561	32532	Educational Services
07474	22	37	Administrative & Support Svcs
07480	565	3002	Educational Services
07481	603	4891	Nursing & Resid. Care Facilit.
07495	30	611	Accommodation
07501	874	6677	Justice, Pubic Order/Safety
07502	245	1326	Administrative & Support Svcs
07503	714	9882	Hospitals
07504	236	1278	Food and Beverage Stores
07505	751	9583	Exec., Legis., & Other Support

ZIP CODE	2004 Total Firms	2004 Total Employees	TOP INDUSTRY RANKED on 2004 EMPLOYMENT
07506	813	6281	Educational Services
07507	7	12	Administrative & Support Svcs
07508	682	4033	Educational Services
07509	3	2	Construction of Buildings
07510	3	1204	Postal Service
07511	6	8	Real Estate
07512	841	13741	Administrative & Support Svcs
07513	269	1671	Repair and Maintenance
07514	386	4603	Ambulatory Health Care Svcs
07522	313	1825	Educational Services
07524	376	2943	Textile Mills
07538	1	4	Merch. Wholesalers,Nondur. Gds
07543	2	0	Special Trade Contractors
07601	3745	37528	Hospitals
07602	6	35	Transit & Grnd Pass. Transport
07603	235	1135	Educational Services
07604	633	4598	Prof., Scientific, & Tech Svcs
07605	285	2425	Chemical Manufacturing
07606	331	5258	Merch. Wholesalers,Durable Gds
07607	335	3448	Miscellaneous Manufacturing
07608	179	6238	Ambulatory Health Care Svcs
07620	42	323	Amusement, Gambling,& Recreat.
07621	736	4641	Educational Services
07624	494	3213	Food and Beverage Stores
07626	250	1771	Educational Services
07627	82	562	Educational Services
07628	430	1724	Educational Services
07630	289	2316	Nursing & Resid. Care Facilit.
07631	1650	14237	Hospitals
07632	655	7227	Food Manufacturing
07640	104	695	Utilities
07641	89	606	Educational Services
07642	352	3121	Transit & Grnd Pass. Transport
07643	416	3447	Exec., Legis., & Other Support
07644	706	4977	Educational Services
07645	437	7771	Prof., Scientific, & Tech Svcs
07646	317	2087	Educational Services
07647	294	4552	Machinery Manufacturing
07648	217	2299	Beverage & Tobacco Product Mfg
07649	530	3338	Prof., Scientific, & Tech Svcs
07650	679	3208	Educational Services
07652	2226	35301	General Merchandise Stores
07653	14	73	Merch. Wholesalers,Durable Gds
07656	471	4451	Computer & Electronic Prod Mfg
07657	588	4634	Chemical Manufacturing
07660	362	3718	Merch. Wholesalers,Durable Gds
07661	370	2546	Educational Services
07662	445	4184	Prof., Scientific, & Tech Svcs
07663	703	8867	Merch. Wholesalers,Durable Gds
07666	1606	13696	Ambulatory Health Care Svcs
07670	512	3683	Prof., Scientific, & Tech Svcs
07675	1275	9096	Hospitals
07676	236	1215	Food Svcs & Drinking Places
07677	250	3749	Transportation Equipment Mfg
07701	2171	15838	Prof., Scientific, & Tech Svcs
07702	669	5410	Prof., Scientific, & Tech Svcs
07703	33	485	Hospitals
07704	245	894	Educational Services
07710	15	47	Educational Services
07711	122	395	Food Svcs & Drinking Places
07712	1612	9986	Educational Services
07716	412	1836	Nursing & Resid. Care Facilit.
07717	132	583	Educational Services
07718	163	827	Special Trade Contractors
07719	1213	8179	Food Svcs & Drinking Places
07720	202	723	Food Svcs & Drinking Places
07721	87	1103	Educational Services
07722	422	2652	Food and Beverage Stores
07723	142	843	Amusement, Gambling,& Recreat.
07724	1279	14432	Prof., Scientific, & Tech Svcs
07726	1714	15723	Administrative & Support Svcs
07727	589	5800	Educational Services
07728	2862	29593	Exec., Legis., & Other Support
07730	716	5791	Food Svcs & Drinking Places
07731	1239	8009	Administrative & Support Svcs
07732	210	1458	Food Svcs & Drinking Places
07733	622	11824	Motor Vehicle & Parts Dealers
07734	289	1842	Educational Services
07735	706	5194	Food Svcs & Drinking Places
07737	97	836	Transit & Grnd Pass. Transport
07738	197	2401	Educational Services
07739	352	2241	Educational Services
07740	1142	10239	Ambulatory Health Care Svcs
07746	591	4137	Prof., Scientific, & Tech Svcs
07747	1255	7500	Food Svcs & Drinking Places
07748	929	7369	Educational Services
07750	142	582	Food Svcs & Drinking Places
07751	548	3189	Hospitals
07752	15	33	Construction of Buildings
07753	1300	16725	Hospitals

BUSINESS DATA

ZIP CODE	2004 Total Firms	2004 Total Employees	TOP INDUSTRY RANKED on 2004 EMPLOYMENT	ZIP CODE	2004 Total Firms	2004 Total Employees	TOP INDUSTRY RANKED on 2004 EMPLOYMENT	ZIP CODE	2004 Total Firms	2004 Total Employees	TOP INDUSTRY RANKED on 2004 EMPLOYMENT
07754	9	26	Merch. Wholesalers,Durable Gds	07962	9	71	Social Assistance	08089	106	505	Special Trade Contractors
07755	392	2993	Food Svcs & Drinking Places	07963	11	13	Construction of Buildings	08090	162	703	Food Svcs & Drinking Places
07756	156	776	Nursing & Resid. Care Facilit.	07970	40	266	Administrative & Support Svcs	08091	489	5474	Merch. Wholesalers,Durable Gds
07757	180	2087	Perform'g Arts, Spec. Sports	07974	436	13161	Chemical Manufacturing	08092	159	839	Merch. Wholesalers,Durable Gds
07758	96	745	Educational Services	07976	47	243	Real Estate	08093	310	4251	Relig., Grant, Civic, Prof Org
07760	365	2671	Food Svcs & Drinking Places	07977	71	817	Hospitals	08094	995	7014	Educational Services
07762	523	3094	Accommodation	07978	50	332	Real Estate	08095	63	1475	Relig., Grant, Civic, Prof Org
07763	19	97	Merch. Wholesalers,Durable Gds	07979	41	109	Educational Services	08096	1649	17265	Food Svcs & Drinking Places
07764	432	4776	Educational Services	07980	154	1167	Food and Beverage Stores	08097	166	1271	Food Svcs & Drinking Places
07765	5	106	Social Assistance	07981	564	12593	Prof., Scientific, & Tech Svcs	08098	375	2964	Construction of Buildings
07799	4	195	Relig., Grant, Civic, Prof Org	07999	2	950	Relig., Grant, Civic, Prof Org	08099	6	17	Special Trade Contractors
07801	1035	12562	Fabricated Metal Product Mfg	08001	42	252	Educational Services	08101	2	0	Relig., Grant, Civic, Prof Org
07802	1	2	Special Trade Contractors	08002	1445	18985	Food Svcs & Drinking Places	08102	353	5543	Educational Services
07803	129	667	Exec., Legis., & Other Support	08003	1293	13655	Managmt of Companies & Enterp.	08103	703	13228	Hospitals
07806	15	167	Prof., Scientific, & Tech Svcs	08004	302	1779	Educational Services	08104	436	4476	Educational Services
07820	42	323	Relig., Grant, Civic, Prof Org	08005	523	2181	Food Svcs & Drinking Places	08105	411	3293	Educational Services
07821	320	1692	Nursing & Resid. Care Facilit.	08006	76	440	Merch. Wholesalers,Nondur. Gds	08106	325	1866	General Merchandise Stores
07822	118	610	Justice, Pubic Order/Safety	08007	172	1526	Paper Manufacturing	08107	330	1773	Educational Services
07823	412	3274	Chemical Manufacturing	08008	908	6041	Food Svcs & Drinking Places	08108	777	5699	Prof., Scientific, & Tech Svcs
07825	529	2207	Educational Services	08009	688	6117	Relig., Grant, Civic, Prof Org	08109	977	9958	Print'g & Related Supp't Act's
07826	374	2015	Insurance Carriers & Related	08010	250	1542	Food and Beverage Stores	08110	820	13553	Beverage & Tobacco Product Mfg
07827	165	659	Food and Beverage Stores	08011	4	16	Special Trade Contractors	08201	489	3973	Educational Services
07828	390	5383	Merch. Wholesalers,Nondur. Gds	08012	1503	16896	Motor Vehicle & Parts Dealers	08202	284	2038	Food Svcs & Drinking Places
07829	15	69	Fabricated Metal Product Mfg	08014	32	968	Computer & Electronic Prod Mfg	08203	344	3068	Educational Services
07830	332	1257	Educational Services	08015	272	3029	Hospitals	08204	1027	8097	Food Svcs & Drinking Places
07831	5	53	Construction of Buildings	08016	1113	14229	General Merchandise Stores	08205	562	4210	Hospitals
07832	169	880	Gasoline Stations	08018	41	393	Educational Services	08210	919	10039	Exec., Legis., & Other Support
07833	13	284	Waste Managmt & Remediat'n Svc	08019	28	122	Merch. Wholesalers,Nondur. Gds	08212	21	107	Museums, Hist. Sites,& Similar
07834	1086	9526	Hospitals	08020	73	475	Exec., Legis., & Other Support	08213	18	543	Transit & Grnd Pass. Transport
07836	489	4913	Prof., Scientific, & Tech Svcs	08021	982	7337	Food Svcs & Drinking Places	08214	43	513	Educational Services
07837	3	3	Special Trade Contractors	08022	219	1187	Merch. Wholesalers,Durable Gds	08215	458	2432	Relig., Grant, Civic, Prof Org
07838	136	795	Administrative & Support Svcs	08023	23	1585	Chemical Manufacturing	08217	30	154	Support Act. for Transport.
07839	10	15	Repair and Maintenance	08025	5	19	Food and Beverage Stores	08218	7	12	Merch. Wholesalers,Nondur. Gds
07840	1308	10522	Food Manufacturing	08026	174	1455	Electronics & Appliance Stores	08219	38	148	Air Transportation
07842	11	52	Educational Services	08027	122	1511	Relig., Grant, Civic, Prof Org	08220	5	61	Food Svcs & Drinking Places
07843	240	1385	Educational Services	08028	630	5965	Educational Services	08221	464	3100	Nursing & Resid. Care Facilit.
07844	68	307	Real Estate	08029	101	729	Administrative & Support Svcs	08223	301	1654	Food Svcs & Drinking Places
07845	18	60	Food Svcs & Drinking Places	08030	434	3364	Educational Services	08224	22	166	Justice, Pubic Order/Safety
07846	17	71	Educational Services	08031	375	5638	Postal Service	08225	672	7008	Exec., Legis., & Other Support
07847	157	1108	Bldg Matl & Garden Eqpmt Dlrs	08032	8	121	Plastics & Rubber Products Mfg	08226	1112	6617	Food Svcs & Drinking Places
07848	239	1287	Amusement, Gambling,& Recreat.	08033	1093	5781	Prof., Scientific, & Tech Svcs	08230	244	2047	Accommodation
07849	328	1624	Food Svcs & Drinking Places	08034	1404	11643	Prof., Scientific, & Tech Svcs	08231	14	35	Museums, Hist. Sites,& Similar
07850	212	1090	Print'g & Related Supp't Act's	08035	429	2316	Prof., Scientific, & Tech Svcs	08232	797	7822	Educational Services
07851	21	155	Educational Services	08036	233	1584	Special Trade Contractors	08234	1202	13128	Food Svcs & Drinking Places
07852	267	2316	Food Svcs & Drinking Places	08037	1054	11942	Hospitals	08240	64	3010	Hospitals
07853	412	1853	Educational Services	08038	16	2288	Utilities	08241	40	205	Admin. Enviro. Quality Progrms
07855	10	56	Exec., Legis., & Other Support	08039	21	135	Educational Services	08242	261	2111	Food Svcs & Drinking Places
07856	183	1185	Prof., Scientific, & Tech Svcs	08041	44	224	Educational Services	08243	256	1625	Food Svcs & Drinking Places
07857	159	911	Food and Beverage Stores	08042	9	13	Repair and Maintenance	08244	648	6261	Hospitals
07860	1557	10723	Exec., Legis., & Other Support	08043	1379	13954	Prof., Scientific, & Tech Svcs	08245	16	303	Social Assistance
07863	121	745	Exec., Legis., & Other Support	08045	87	1106	Bldg Matl & Garden Eqpmt Dlrs	08246	20	47	Bldg Matl & Garden Eqpmt Dlrs
07865	96	987	Nat'l Security & Int'l Affairs	08046	448	6397	Ambulatory Health Care Svcs	08247	228	1093	Clothing & Cloth'g Acc. Stores
07866	1135	11472	Educational Services	08048	314	4187	Merch. Wholesalers,Durable Gds	08248	15	214	Food Svcs & Drinking Places
07869	892	8130	Educational Services	08049	130	839	Educational Services	08250	44	188	Exec., Legis., & Other Support
07870	11	27	Relig., Grant, Civic, Prof Org	08050	846	7669	Food and Beverage Stores	08251	190	897	Food Svcs & Drinking Places
07871	1105	5843	Educational Services	08051	225	1555	Educational Services	08252	17	31	Social Assistance
07874	301	2098	Educational Services	08052	571	5998	Food Svcs & Drinking Places	08260	1437	9567	Food Svcs & Drinking Places
07875	39	296	Accommodation	08053	1924	17911	Prof., Scientific, & Tech Svcs	08270	217	2358	Exec., Legis., & Other Support
07876	480	3663	Educational Services	08054	1784	26588	Prof., Scientific, & Tech Svcs	08302	1428	13076	Exec., Legis., & Other Support
07877	10	85	Transit & Grnd Pass. Transport	08055	1058	9244	Educational Services	08310	84	1087	Miscellaneous Manufacturing
07878	24	119	Food and Beverage Stores	08056	79	807	Special Trade Contractors	08311	68	834	Merch. Wholesalers,Nondur. Gds
07879	25	129	Accommodation	08057	1334	16714	Computer & Electronic Prod Mfg	08312	177	1687	Exec., Legis., & Other Support
07880	5	5	Gasoline Stations	08059	200	1602	Educational Services	08313	8	18	Fabricated Metal Product Mfg
07881	3	17	Relig., Grant, Civic, Prof Org	08060	878	15036	Hospitals	08314	8	571	Justice, Pubic Order/Safety
07882	631	4526	Educational Services	08061	31	176	Relig., Grant, Civic, Prof Org	08315	12	6	Food Svcs & Drinking Places
07885	317	4756	Administrative & Support Svcs	08062	332	1879	Educational Services	08316	12	128	Food and Beverage Stores
07901	1288	12718	Hospitals	08063	49	332	Educational Services	08317	40	167	Special Trade Contractors
07902	10	88	Relig., Grant, Civic, Prof Org	08064	13	72	Exec., Legis., & Other Support	08318	404	2620	Educational Services
07920	600	5003	Relig., Grant, Civic, Prof Org	08065	224	1909	Educational Services	08319	33	116	Educational Services
07921	348	5718	Telecommunications	08066	324	5645	Petroleum & Coal Products Mfg	08320	19	55	Social Assistance
07922	521	5748	Educational Services	08067	61	712	Crop Production	08321	13	35	Food Svcs & Drinking Places
07924	523	2904	Food and Beverage Stores	08068	178	3232	Educational Services	08322	250	1473	Educational Services
07926	28	406	Educational Services	08069	382	2894	Educational Services	08323	26	103	Educational Services
07927	236	4144	Prof., Scientific, & Tech Svcs	08070	417	3135	Educational Services	08324	11	15	Merch. Wholesalers,Durable Gds
07928	731	5305	Educational Services	08071	439	2840	Relig., Grant, Civic, Prof Org	08326	54	435	Textile Mills
07930	693	3920	Food and Beverage Stores	08072	19	145	Educational Services	08327	21	594	Justice, Pubic Order/Safety
07931	139	909	Relig., Grant, Civic, Prof Org	08073	26	657	Machinery Manufacturing	08328	70	452	Food and Beverage Stores
07932	731	11923	Prof., Scientific, & Tech Svcs	08074	23	218	Merch. Wholesalers,Nondur. Gds	08329	11	88	Mining (Except Oil and Gas)
07933	118	713	Health & Personal Care Stores	08075	808	7188	Educational Services	08330	839	9716	Educational Services
07934	92	684	Educational Services	08077	843	8128	Isps, Web Search Portals	08332	895	10020	Educational Services
07935	38	117	Prof., Scientific, & Tech Svcs	08078	298	3508	Ambulatory Health Care Svcs	08340	28	90	Special Trade Contractors
07936	812	13963	Chemical Manufacturing	08079	446	4668	Plastics & Rubber Products Mfg	08341	48	252	Educational Services
07938	25	639	Insurance Carriers & Related	08080	1014	14308	Ambulatory Health Care Svcs	08342	16	34	Social Assistance
07939	9	47	Amusement, Gambling,& Recreat.	08081	511	3792	Educational Services	08343	104	618	Educational Services
07940	746	6972	Educational Services	08083	271	1744	Educational Services	08344	189	1132	Primary Metal Manufacturing
07945	391	2235	Food Svcs & Drinking Places	08084	260	3148	Hospitals	08345	28	199	Educational Services
07946	189	722	Mining (Except Oil and Gas)	08085	471	6501	Merch. Wholesalers,Durable Gds	08346	19	42	Social Assistance
07950	576	10657	Merch. Wholesalers,Nondur. Gds	08086	195	3832	Fabricated Metal Product Mfg	08347	18	322	Food Manufacturing
07960	2995	34939	Prof., Scientific, & Tech Svcs	08087	644	4502	Transportation Equipment Mfg	08348	9	134	Educational Services
07961	17	225	Accommodation	08088	624	3849	Educational Services	08349	71	626	Educational Services

ZIP CODE	2004 Total Firms	2004 Total Employ-ees	TOP INDUSTRY RANKED on 2004 EMPLOYMENT	ZIP CODE	2004 Total Firms	2004 Total Employ-ees	TOP INDUSTRY RANKED on 2004 EMPLOYMENT	ZIP CODE	2004 Total Firms	2004 Total Employ-ees	TOP INDUSTRY RANKED on 2004 EMPLOYMENT
08350	25	163	Educational Services	08755	1281	12972	Hospitals	10014	2534	22452	Prof., Scientific, & Tech Svcs
08352	23	219	Food Manufacturing	08757	285	5817	Heavy & Civil Eng. Construct'N	10016	8389	79208	Prof., Scientific, & Tech Svcs
08353	23	217	Merch. Wholesalers,Nondur. Gds	08758	188	1008	Relig., Grant, Civic, Prof Org	10017	6347	106598	Prof., Scientific, & Tech Svcs
08360	2153	21513	Nonmetallic Mineral Prod. Mfg	08759	489	5208	Nursing & Resid. Care Facilit.	10018	8489	76472	Apparel Manufacturing
08361	373	5660	Exec., Legis., & Other Support	08801	252	2432	Prof., Scientific, & Tech Svcs	10019	6071	119990	Prof., Scientific, & Tech Svcs
08362	9	14	Special Trade Contractors	08802	168	802	Educational Services	10020	752	32370	Publishing Industries
08401	1807	58986	Accommodation	08803	12	39	Justice, Pubic Order/Safety	10021	7403	69329	Hospitals
08402	319	1855	Food Svcs & Drinking Places	08804	111	554	Paper Manufacturing	10022	8704	116726	Prof., Scientific, & Tech Svcs
08403	62	338	Ambulatory Health Care Svcs	08805	512	3138	Educational Services	10023	2734	26228	Food Svcs & Drinking Places
08404	11	31	Special Trade Contractors	08807	1437	32236	Merch. Wholesalers,Nondur. Gds	10024	2470	16219	Food Svcs & Drinking Places
08406	403	1970	Food and Beverage Stores	08808	27	304	Merch. Wholesalers,Nondur. Gds	10025	2214	13783	Educational Services
08501	230	1273	Fabricated Metal Product Mfg	08809	655	8893	Prof., Scientific, & Tech Svcs	10026	470	2392	Educational Services
08502	271	2202	Hospitals	08810	291	6383	Merch. Wholesalers,Nondur. Gds	10027	1427	14508	Educational Services
08504	10	27	Social Assistance	08812	731	4638	Food Svcs & Drinking Places	10028	2457	14627	Exec., Legis., & Other Support
08505	583	6223	Exec., Legis., & Other Support	08816	2108	21253	Prof., Scientific, & Tech Svcs	10029	1517	28436	Hospitals
08510	67	552	Food Svcs & Drinking Places	08817	1467	25238	Exec., Legis., & Other Support	10030	405	2719	Educational Services
08511	47	293	Accommodation	08818	19	59	Special Trade Contractors	10031	829	5612	Educational Services
08512	548	7636	Chemical Manufacturing	08820	1067	8081	Ambulatory Health Care Svcs	10032	1212	45126	Hospitals
08514	135	773	Bldg Matl & Garden Eqpmt Dlrs	08821	11	167	Machinery Manufacturing	10033	1129	6516	Educational Services
08515	27	107	Special Trade Contractors	08822	1954	13778	Hospitals	10034	672	3317	Educational Services
08518	130	1439	Merch. Wholesalers,Durable Gds	08823	158	1117	Food and Beverage Stores	10035	831	13004	Exec., Legis., & Other Support
08520	921	9631	Publishing Industries	08824	226	1156	Educational Services	10036	8067	108580	Prof., Scientific, & Tech Svcs
08525	297	1462	Prof., Scientific, & Tech Svcs	08825	324	1579	Educational Services	10037	300	1979	Real Estate
08526	12	63	Bldg Matl & Garden Eqpmt Dlrs	08826	199	1312	Exec., Legis., & Other Support	10038	2925	40819	Justice, Pubic Order/Safety
08527	1094	10231	Amusement, Gambling,& Recreat.	08827	244	1484	Food Svcs & Drinking Places	10039	260	1624	Educational Services
08528	76	640	Mining (Except Oil and Gas)	08828	35	124	Justice, Pubic Order/Safety	10040	607	4066	Ambulatory Health Care Svcs
08530	503	2501	Food Svcs & Drinking Places	08829	153	712	Educational Services	10041	28	1772	Securities/Commodity Contracts
08533	160	778	Food and Beverage Stores	08830	787	10001	Prof., Scientific, & Tech Svcs	10043	1	25	Credit Intermediation & Relatd
08534	626	6985	Chemical Manufacturing	08831	891	11155	Sportg Gds,Hobby,Book, & Music	10044	101	3560	Exec., Legis., & Other Support
08535	52	250	Exec., Legis., & Other Support	08832	48	886	Truck Transportation	10045	3	3015	Credit Intermediation & Relatd
08536	379	6093	Funds, Trusts, & Other Finance	08833	530	3331	Insurance Carriers & Related	10055	17	2566	Insurance Carriers & Related
08540	2807	49881	Prof., Scientific, & Tech Svcs	08834	1	1	Postal Service	10069	24	51	Personal and Laundry Services
08542	644	5038	Credit Intermediation & Relatd	08835	329	2448	Merch. Wholesalers,Durable Gds	10080	3	15043	Securities/Commodity Contracts
08543	9	16	Prof., Scientific, & Tech Svcs	08836	168	863	Educational Services	10095	1	0	Prof., Scientific, & Tech Svcs
08544	8	161	Hospitals	08837	1267	24266	Prof., Scientific, & Tech Svcs	10103	96	1842	Prof., Scientific, & Tech Svcs
08550	470	3794	Educational Services	08840	929	5557	Prof., Scientific, & Tech Svcs	10104	57	8305	Insurance Carriers & Related
08551	222	1369	Administrative & Support Svcs	08844	1293	9369	Educational Services	10105	41	7181	Prof., Scientific, & Tech Svcs
08553	64	305	Prof., Scientific, & Tech Svcs	08846	745	5932	Bldg Matl & Garden Eqpmt Dlrs	10106	109	1839	Prof., Scientific, & Tech Svcs
08554	64	651	Food and Beverage Stores	08848	294	1407	Paper Manufacturing	10107	297	1048	Prof., Scientific, & Tech Svcs
08555	32	103	Educational Services	08850	307	1877	Bldg Matl & Garden Eqpmt Dlrs	10108	1	2	Relig., Grant, Civic, Prof Org
08556	27	63	Food Svcs & Drinking Places	08852	407	12683	Publishing Industries	10110	181	1514	Prof., Scientific, & Tech Svcs
08557	28	441	Educational Services	08853	112	336	Educational Services	10111	202	2008	Securities/Commodity Contracts
08558	290	5623	Publishing Industries	08854	1295	27351	Prof., Scientific, & Tech Svcs	10112	139	4296	Prof., Scientific, & Tech Svcs
08559	157	441	Food Svcs & Drinking Places	08855	6	14	Personal and Laundry Services	10113	3	3	Wholesale Elec. Mrkts & Agents
08560	89	476	Educational Services	08857	925	9866	Hospitals	10115	73	1303	Relig., Grant, Civic, Prof Org
08561	70	477	Special Trade Contractors	08858	80	868	Publishing Industries	10116	9	51	Prof., Scientific, & Tech Svcs
08562	189	1249	Food Svcs & Drinking Places	08859	317	2465	Educational Services	10118	849	5107	Prof., Scientific, & Tech Svcs
08603	1	0	Relig., Grant, Civic, Prof Org	08861	1283	12235	Hospitals	10119	326	5134	Prof., Scientific, & Tech Svcs
08604	1	0	Broadcasting	08863	269	1616	Chemical Manufacturing	10120	101	1842	Clothing & Cloth'g Acc. Stores
08607	2	13	Administrative & Support Svcs	08865	1185	12628	Hospitals	10121	139	2076	Prof., Scientific, & Tech Svcs
08608	666	15284	Exec., Legis., & Other Support	08867	209	1080	Crop Production	10122	196	1255	Prof., Scientific, & Tech Svcs
08609	368	4812	Educational Services	08868	11	93	Educational Services	10123	311	3260	Accommodation
08610	780	4672	Educational Services	08869	400	7643	Prof., Scientific, & Tech Svcs	10128	2464	14766	Educational Services
08611	736	22573	Justice, Pubic Order/Safety	08870	12	31	Educational Services	10150	8	8	Electronics & Appliance Stores
08618	837	15365	Admin. of Economic Programs	08871	1	0	Special Trade Contractors	10151	63	806	Publishing Industries
08619	1205	12357	Admin. Human Resource Programs	08872	465	3630	Justice, Pubic Order/Safety	10152	138	753	Prof., Scientific, & Tech Svcs
08620	253	2228	Exec., Legis., & Other Support	08873	1603	22447	Electronics & Appliance Stores	10153	87	3405	Securities/Commodity Contracts
08625	9	385	Admin. Human Resource Programs	08875	7	25	Special Trade Contractors	10154	50	5061	Prof., Scientific, & Tech Svcs
08628	485	11257	Justice, Pubic Order/Safety	08876	1720	19185	Prof., Scientific, & Tech Svcs	10155	161	904	Prof., Scientific, & Tech Svcs
08629	158	2263	Hospitals	08878	7	82	Insurance Carriers & Related	10156	5	24	Prof., Scientific, & Tech Svcs
08638	896	10521	Hospitals	08879	555	6148	Relig., Grant, Civic, Prof Org	10158	55	2285	Securities/Commodity Contracts
08640	37	317	Nat'l Security & Int'l Affairs	08880	101	562	Educational Services	10159	4	8	Prof., Scientific, & Tech Svcs
08641	48	4284	Nat'l Security & Int'l Affairs	08882	472	2056	Special Trade Contractors	10162	32	52	Food Svcs & Drinking Places
08648	1441	16848	Prof., Scientific, & Tech Svcs	08884	228	1548	Paper Manufacturing	10163	7	20	Prof., Scientific, & Tech Svcs
08650	13	72	Relig., Grant, Civic, Prof Org	08885	15	47	Social Assistance	10165	661	3740	Prof., Scientific, & Tech Svcs
08690	606	6184	Educational Services	08886	113	624	Repair and Maintenance	10166	175	6476	Prof., Scientific, & Tech Svcs
08691	445	5002	Food Svcs & Drinking Places	08887	37	648	Food Svcs & Drinking Places	10167	135	1836	Credit Intermediation & Relatd
08701	2047	23964	Educational Services	08888	96	957	Prof., Scientific, & Tech Svcs	10168	221	1805	Prof., Scientific, & Tech Svcs
08720	38	414	Nursing & Resid. Care Facilit.	08889	450	5140	Chemical Manufacturing	10169	384	3303	Prof., Scientific, & Tech Svcs
08721	559	4461	Educational Services	08890	7	79	Unclassified Establishments	10170	366	3045	Administrative & Support Svcs
08722	215	961	Food Svcs & Drinking Places	08899	5	41	Relig., Grant, Civic, Prof Org	10171	27	2792	Credit Intermediation & Relatd
08723	1264	9451	Food Svcs & Drinking Places	08901	1838	21539	Hospitals	10172	46	788	Food Manufacturing
08724	1063	8577	Hospitals	08902	1116	18795	Fabricated Metal Product Mfg	10173	70	633	Administrative & Support Svcs
08730	262	1091	Food Svcs & Drinking Places	08903	2	2	Prof., Scientific, & Tech Svcs	10174	181	2241	Prof., Scientific, & Tech Svcs
08731	638	3943	Prof., Scientific, & Tech Svcs	08904	556	2895	Educational Services	10175	166	1068	Prof., Scientific, & Tech Svcs
08732	67	293	Educational Services	08906	4	9	Prof., Scientific, & Tech Svcs	10176	123	933	Prof., Scientific, & Tech Svcs
08733	155	1058	Food Svcs & Drinking Places	08933	1	2000	Chemical Manufacturing	10177	61	1014	Prof., Scientific, & Tech Svcs
08734	228	1556	Food and Beverage Stores	10001	10020	92502	Prof., Scientific, & Tech Svcs	10178	64	13834	Credit Intermediation & Relatd
08735	195	950	Food Svcs & Drinking Places	10002	2762	20250	Hospitals	10179	9	6049	Securities/Commodity Contracts
08736	901	5863	Amusement, Gambling,& Recreat.	10003	5055	69034	Ambulatory Health Care Svcs	10185	3	3	Motion Pict. & Sound Recording
08738	55	167	Real Estate	10004	1625	29876	Securities/Commodity Contracts	10199	9	7504	Postal Service
08739	23	130	Food and Beverage Stores	10005	1711	28458	Credit Intermediation & Relatd	10260	1	0	Ambulatory Health Care Svcs
08740	36	100	Educational Services	10006	963	13939	Prof., Scientific, & Tech Svcs	10270	15	5257	Insurance Carriers & Related
08741	72	268	Educational Services	10007	2124	25547	Prof., Scientific, & Tech Svcs	10271	110	5326	Justice, Pubic Order/Safety
08742	1489	9585	Food Svcs & Drinking Places	10008	7	6	Print'g & Related Supp't Act's	10272	1	8	Administrative & Support Svcs
08750	313	1953	Ambulatory Health Care Svcs	10009	1291	5981	Food Svcs & Drinking Places	10274	3	15	Publishing Industries
08751	280	2454	Amusement, Gambling,& Recreat.	10010	4295	56063	Prof., Scientific, & Tech Svcs	10278	57	1927	Admin. of Economic Programs
08752	126	884	Food Svcs & Drinking Places	10011	4884	52540	Educational Services	10279	130	1093	Prof., Scientific, & Tech Svcs
08753	2794	22821	Food Svcs & Drinking Places	10012	3425	24696	Prof., Scientific, & Tech Svcs	10280	203	914	Food Svcs & Drinking Places
08754	32	622	Educational Services	10013	5814	46934	Justice, Pubic Order/Safety	10281	70	4911	Prof., Scientific, & Tech Svcs

10282 - 11360 BUSINESS DATA

ZIP CODE	2004 Total Firms	2004 Total Employees	TOP INDUSTRY RANKED on 2004 EMPLOYMENT	ZIP CODE	2004 Total Firms	2004 Total Employees	TOP INDUSTRY RANKED on 2004 EMPLOYMENT	ZIP CODE	2004 Total Firms	2004 Total Employees	TOP INDUSTRY RANKED on 2004 EMPLOYMENT
10282	79	833	Educational Services	10570	621	5071	Publishing Industries	10982	62	607	Hospitals
10285	9	6093	Securities/Commodity Contracts	10573	1634	12513	Ambulatory Health Care Svcs	10983	199	1227	Merch. Wholesalers,Durable Gds
10286	3	2010	Managmt of Companies & Enterp.	10576	230	898	Food and Beverage Stores	10984	61	1011	Admin. Human Resource Programs
10292	1	40	Securities/Commodity Contracts	10577	301	9304	Educational Services	10985	17	44	Heavy & Civil Eng. Construct'N
10301	1115	9717	Educational Services	10578	42	317	Nursing & Resid. Care Facilit.	10986	46	119	Construction of Buildings
10302	593	4486	Relig., Grant, Civic, Prof Org	10579	229	1026	Educational Services	10987	150	1305	Administrative & Support Svcs
10303	514	5117	Bldg Matl & Garden Eqpmt Dlrs	10580	753	7664	Relig., Grant, Civic, Prof Org	10988	29	81	Print'g & Related Supp't Act's
10304	899	8675	Relig., Grant, Civic, Prof Org	10583	1717	10942	Ambulatory Health Care Svcs	10989	280	2572	Prof., Scientific, & Tech Svcs
10305	1040	12479	Hospitals	10587	18	19	Prof., Scientific, & Tech Svcs	10990	1015	5935	Educational Services
10306	1373	9186	Food Svcs & Drinking Places	10588	92	741	Educational Services	10992	289	2012	Educational Services
10307	284	1082	Educational Services	10589	320	5945	Publishing Industries	10993	151	1102	Food and Beverage Stores
10308	472	2254	Educational Services	10590	203	751	Educational Services	10994	633	7803	Educational Services
10309	814	4696	Educational Services	10591	1281	15370	Transportation Equipment Mfg	10996	62	1157	Hospitals
10310	748	7289	Ambulatory Health Care Svcs	10594	340	2082	Food and Beverage Stores	10998	60	124	Unclassified Establishments
10311	21	139	Prof., Scientific, & Tech Svcs	10595	458	10936	Exec., Legis., & Other Support	11001	808	5264	Prof., Scientific, & Tech Svcs
10312	1028	5482	Educational Services	10596	50	195	Educational Services	11002	6	10	Electronics & Appliance Stores
10314	2126	19854	Educational Services	10597	18	10	Prof., Scientific, & Tech Svcs	11003	857	8622	Perform'g Arts, Spec. Sports
10451	1220	20239	Hospitals	10598	1003	9651	Prof., Scientific, & Tech Svcs	11004	257	1570	Educational Services
10452	1077	7630	Educational Services	10601	2241	21811	Prof., Scientific, & Tech Svcs	11005	40	579	Merch. Wholesalers,Durable Gds
10453	998	6549	Educational Services	10602	5	6	Support Act. for Transport.	11010	778	4378	Food Svcs & Drinking Places
10454	802	8059	Educational Services	10603	729	5432	Educational Services	11020	109	1112	Educational Services
10455	980	8341	Educational Services	10604	826	14165	Credit Intermediation & Relatd	11021	2332	12609	Prof., Scientific, & Tech Svcs
10456	934	7770	Educational Services	10605	917	10069	Hospitals	11022	2	1	Prof., Scientific, & Tech Svcs
10457	1183	9984	Educational Services	10606	666	5489	Prof., Scientific, & Tech Svcs	11023	375	8308	Hospitals
10458	1526	18230	Educational Services	10607	381	3275	Food Svcs & Drinking Places	11024	159	1371	Relig., Grant, Civic, Prof Org
10459	848	5081	Educational Services	10610	4	9	Transit & Grnd Pass. Transport	11030	972	11473	Ambulatory Health Care Svcs
10460	826	8049	Educational Services	10701	1848	17225	Hospitals	11040	1547	14946	Social Assistance
10461	1901	25197	Hospitals	10702	4	7	Relig., Grant, Civic, Prof Org	11042	506	8773	Prof., Scientific, & Tech Svcs
10462	1619	9283	Educational Services	10703	386	4733	Hospitals	11050	1376	15648	Prof., Scientific, & Tech Svcs
10463	1274	9948	Nursing & Resid. Care Facilit.	10704	1177	6945	Food Svcs & Drinking Places	11096	372	3308	Ambulatory Health Care Svcs
10464	211	1154	Food Svcs & Drinking Places	10705	757	4039	Food Manufacturing	11101	3512	52345	Special Trade Contractors
10465	642	5141	Educational Services	10706	377	2842	Educational Services	11102	875	5536	Hospitals
10466	1128	8691	Hospitals	10707	378	1894	Relig., Grant, Civic, Prof Org	11103	1426	6479	Educational Services
10467	1793	12844	Hospitals	10708	709	5234	Hospitals	11104	682	5234	Social Assistance
10468	1059	12691	Educational Services	10709	402	2559	Educational Services	11105	1100	7123	Miscellaneous Manufacturing
10469	1122	8841	Nursing & Resid. Care Facilit.	10710	894	6702	Food Svcs & Drinking Places	11106	1250	8112	Educational Services
10470	409	2150	Educational Services	10801	1981	13214	Educational Services	11109	15	101	Educational Services
10471	460	5688	Nursing & Resid. Care Facilit.	10802	4	5	Perform'g Arts, Spec. Sports	11201	3362	44860	Educational Services
10472	792	4020	Educational Services	10803	534	3291	Computer & Electronic Prod Mfg	11202	6	16	Administrative & Support Svcs
10473	525	7134	Broadcasting	10804	376	2170	Educational Services	11203	1497	22172	Educational Services
10474	836	10378	Merch. Wholesalers,Nondur. Gds	10805	312	3503	Relig., Grant, Civic, Prof Org	11204	2130	11229	Educational Services
10475	537	7567	Nursing & Resid. Care Facilit.	10901	1020	10663	Educational Services	11205	1238	11923	Educational Services
10501	23	52	Prof., Scientific, & Tech Svcs	10910	3	26	Real Estate	11206	1456	15572	Ambulatory Health Care Svcs
10502	343	2059	Educational Services	10911	8	210	Museums, Hist. Sites,& Similar	11207	1416	22941	Prof., Scientific, & Tech Svcs
10503	6	113	Relig., Grant, Civic, Prof Org	10912	7	23	Food Svcs & Drinking Places	11208	1181	11982	Educational Services
10504	527	5341	Computer & Electronic Prod Mfg	10913	235	2499	Prof., Scientific, & Tech Svcs	11209	2158	14201	Hospitals
10505	52	209	Food Svcs & Drinking Places	10914	31	79	Social Assistance	11210	1299	6853	Educational Services
10506	316	2275	Educational Services	10915	33	117	Merch. Wholesalers,Durable Gds	11211	3436	18140	Educational Services
10507	453	6417	Insurance Carriers & Related	10916	110	888	Relig., Grant, Civic, Prof Org	11212	1221	9235	Educational Services
10509	1006	6834	Educational Services	10917	343	3426	Miscellaneous Store Retailers	11213	1092	10808	Hospitals
10510	468	3912	Educational Services	10918	424	3255	Educational Services	11214	1810	11247	Educational Services
10511	105	1442	Admin. of Economic Programs	10919	58	495	Social Assistance	11215	2177	17612	Hospitals
10512	810	5975	Hospitals	10920	333	2903	Exec., Legis., & Other Support	11216	1241	6675	Social Assistance
10514	401	2716	Educational Services	10921	281	1506	Food and Beverage Stores	11217	1428	12004	Exec., Legis., & Other Support
10516	307	1712	Accommodation	10922	16	98	Accommodation	11218	1802	7206	Educational Services
10517	19	109	Educational Services	10923	225	1135	Food and Beverage Stores	11219	3131	14529	Educational Services
10518	89	470	Educational Services	10924	839	9964	Justice, Pubic Order/Safety	11220	2033	16678	Hospitals
10519	51	206	Special Trade Contractors	10925	146	498	Educational Services	11221	901	8491	Truck Transportation
10520	529	2816	Nursing & Resid. Care Facilit.	10926	143	1166	Prof., Scientific, & Tech Svcs	11222	1762	16408	Fabricated Metal Product Mfg
10522	477	5174	Educational Services	10927	345	2893	Textile Product Mills	11223	2079	10421	Educational Services
10523	893	10333	Administrative & Support Svcs	10928	198	873	Food Svcs & Drinking Places	11224	684	6127	Nursing & Resid. Care Facilit.
10524	144	913	Relig., Grant, Civic, Prof Org	10930	162	445	Ambulatory Health Care Svcs	11225	1081	5345	Educational Services
10526	66	452	Motor Vehicle & Parts Dealers	10931	44	567	Food Svcs & Drinking Places	11226	1812	8750	Educational Services
10527	25	230	Accommodation	10932	13	14	Merch. Wholesalers,Nondur. Gds	11228	784	5386	Hospitals
10528	538	5206	Credit Intermediation & Relatd	10933	14	15	Real Estate	11229	1981	10145	Educational Services
10530	603	3575	Ambulatory Health Care Svcs	10940	1824	17488	Social Assistance	11230	2195	11083	Educational Services
10532	460	6019	Prof., Scientific, & Tech Svcs	10941	539	8611	Insurance Carriers & Related	11231	1142	8335	Transit & Grnd Pass. Transport
10533	315	2060	Prof., Scientific, & Tech Svcs	10950	970	5830	Educational Services	11232	1431	13464	Merch. Wholesalers,Nondur. Gds
10535	99	1151	Personal and Laundry Services	10952	976	4772	Educational Services	11233	750	4217	Educational Services
10536	482	2644	Hospitals	10953	25	81	Justice, Pubic Order/Safety	11234	2077	14349	Ambulatory Health Care Svcs
10537	15	18	Postal Service	10954	1216	10173	Food Svcs & Drinking Places	11235	2125	16457	Hospitals
10538	849	4383	Food Svcs & Drinking Places	10956	1484	8977	Prof., Scientific, & Tech Svcs	11236	1488	9562	Educational Services
10540	51	736	Educational Services	10958	125	746	Motor Vehicle & Parts Dealers	11237	1082	9827	Hospitals
10541	785	3845	Educational Services	10959	7	8	Prof., Scientific, & Tech Svcs	11238	1126	8272	Hospitals
10542	19	117	Social Assistance	10960	950	6383	Hospitals	11239	101	1697	Food Svcs & Drinking Places
10543	1169	8943	Educational Services	10962	338	8600	Telecommunications	11241	119	633	Prof., Scientific, & Tech Svcs
10545	3	5	Postal Service	10963	105	788	Justice, Pubic Order/Safety	11242	301	873	Prof., Scientific, & Tech Svcs
10546	93	703	Special Trade Contractors	10964	47	1000	Educational Services	11243	63	300	Ambulatory Health Care Svcs
10547	240	2303	General Merchandise Stores	10965	633	4562	Prof., Scientific, & Tech Svcs	11248	1	0	Prof., Scientific, & Tech Svcs
10548	115	1032	Educational Services	10968	133	516	Food Svcs & Drinking Places	11252	3	4	Educational Services
10549	1322	9037	Ambulatory Health Care Svcs	10969	102	570	Merch. Wholesalers,Nondur. Gds	11256	5	553	Relig., Grant, Civic, Prof Org
10550	1739	11698	Merch. Wholesalers,Durable Gds	10970	488	11589	Hospitals	11351	7	4524	Prof., Scientific, & Tech Svcs
10551	2	2	Relig., Grant, Civic, Prof Org	10973	123	1326	Educational Services	11352	2	52	Perform'g Arts, Spec. Sports
10552	387	4875	Nursing & Resid. Care Facilit.	10974	120	602	Nonstore Retailers	11354	2656	16939	Nursing & Resid. Care Facilit.
10553	254	2347	Unclassified Establishments	10975	15	55	Motor Vehicle & Parts Dealers	11355	1601	11164	Ambulatory Health Care Svcs
10558	1	20	Credit Intermediation & Relatd	10976	46	749	Educational Services	11356	721	6675	Social Assistance
10560	162	795	Educational Services	10977	1500	9901	Educational Services	11357	920	4581	Educational Services
10562	941	6578	Justice, Pubic Order/Safety	10979	13	2	Special Trade Contractors	11358	1176	4644	Educational Services
10566	954	6377	Ambulatory Health Care Svcs	10980	431	2896	Nonmetallic Mineral Prod. Mfg	11359	11	73	Clothing & Cloth'g Acc. Stores
10567	482	3947	Hospitals	10981	49	144	Elect'l Eqpmt, App, & Comp Mfg	11360	338	2897	Hospitals

ZIP CODE	2004 Total Firms	2004 Total Employ-ees	TOP INDUSTRY RANKED on 2004 EMPLOYMENT
11361	1118	6906	Educational Services
11362	503	4143	Educational Services
11363	160	506	Relig., Grant, Civic, Prof Org
11364	514	4078	Educational Services
11365	585	5451	Educational Services
11366	473	2809	Hospitals
11367	708	3764	Educational Services
11368	1798	9823	Educational Services
11369	322	3906	Accommodation
11370	313	4979	Transit & Grnd Pass. Transport
11371	92	1768	Rental and Leasing Services
11372	2063	8194	Food Svcs & Drinking Places
11373	1588	17779	Hospitals
11374	1144	8409	Real Estate
11375	2372	14104	Ambulatory Health Care Svcs
11377	1908	13980	Educational Services
11378	1168	12153	Special Trade Contractors
11379	674	3788	Educational Services
11385	2388	15295	Educational Services
11386	1	1	Merch. Wholesalers,Durable Gds
11411	267	1136	Educational Services
11412	569	2274	Educational Services
11413	688	4288	Educational Services
11414	527	4407	Real Estate
11415	595	3657	Justice, Pubic Order/Safety
11416	560	3768	Educational Services
11417	558	3150	Educational Services
11418	936	8385	Hospitals
11419	940	3662	Food and Beverage Stores
11420	536	4588	Perform'g Arts, Spec. Sports
11421	589	2287	Ambulatory Health Care Svcs
11422	436	2357	Educational Services
11423	527	3178	Educational Services
11424	21	156	Exec., Legis., & Other Support
11425	2	503	Admin. Human Resource Programs
11426	326	2445	Hospitals
11427	238	1822	Educational Services
11428	493	2521	Real Estate
11429	335	2037	Relig., Grant, Civic, Prof Org
11430	373	10492	Support Act. for Transport.
11431	1	50	Support Act. for Transport.
11432	1957	17581	Educational Services
11433	608	6087	Educational Services
11434	1439	11968	Support Act. for Transport.
11435	1155	8875	Rail Transportation
11436	156	1274	Accommodation
11501	1824	22555	Prof., Scientific, & Tech Svcs
11507	277	1764	Educational Services
11509	72	649	Relig., Grant, Civic, Prof Org
11510	1001	6953	Educational Services
11514	481	4998	Prof., Scientific, & Tech Svcs
11516	598	3090	Ambulatory Health Care Svcs
11518	282	4988	Repair and Maintenance
11520	1478	12699	Educational Services
11530	2343	30326	Prof., Scientific, & Tech Svcs
11531	1	1	Personal and Laundry Services
11535	9	105	Food Svcs & Drinking Places
11542	1182	9699	Hospitals
11545	465	3445	Prof., Scientific, & Tech Svcs
11547	24	173	Food Svcs & Drinking Places
11548	236	7516	Educational Services
11549	8	2681	Educational Services
11550	1618	13232	Motor Vehicle & Parts Dealers
11551	1	3	Social Assistance
11552	826	4903	Administrative & Support Svcs
11553	714	9150	Educational Services
11554	1063	11845	Hospitals
11555	15	55	Social Assistance
11556	65	1311	Prof., Scientific, & Tech Svcs
11557	530	2903	Educational Services
11558	384	2537	Food Svcs & Drinking Places
11559	473	3736	Food Svcs & Drinking Places
11560	316	2396	Educational Services
11561	977	5917	Educational Services
11563	1071	7223	Insurance Carriers & Related
11565	218	1029	Educational Services
11566	1133	7577	Educational Services
11568	98	2221	Educational Services
11569	51	339	Museums, Hist. Sites,& Similar
11570	1525	12208	Hospitals
11571	5	6	Construction of Buildings
11572	1242	20458	Educational Services
11575	221	1721	Educational Services
11576	549	3999	Motor Vehicle & Parts Dealers
11577	578	3690	Educational Services
11579	249	1016	Educational Services
11580	1266	10098	Hospitals
11581	698	5626	Clothing & Cloth'g Acc. Stores
11582	8	33	Prof., Scientific, & Tech Svcs
11590	1840	21410	Food Svcs & Drinking Places
11596	448	2568	Food Svcs & Drinking Places
11598	450	2538	Food Svcs & Drinking Places
11599	3	801	Postal Service
11691	790	7867	Hospitals
11692	143	1751	Nursing & Resid. Care Facilit.
11693	201	1380	Food Manufacturing
11694	443	2900	Educational Services
11697	57	240	Relig., Grant, Civic, Prof Org
11701	1007	10568	Hospitals
11702	716	4568	Ambulatory Health Care Svcs
11703	367	2847	Educational Services
11704	1274	10434	Educational Services
11705	250	1817	Merch. Wholesalers,Nondur. Gds
11706	2045	23428	Ambulatory Health Care Svcs
11709	140	837	Food Svcs & Drinking Places
11710	1274	6395	Educational Services
11713	291	2312	Educational Services
11714	640	12644	Computer & Electronic Prod Mfg
11715	165	727	Educational Services
11716	1401	15124	Merch. Wholesalers,Durable Gds
11717	952	10563	Educational Services
11718	117	487	Special Trade Contractors
11719	128	1489	Nursing & Resid. Care Facilit.
11720	688	5803	Educational Services
11721	165	745	Relig., Grant, Civic, Prof Org
11722	623	7300	Educational Services
11724	110	910	Educational Services
11725	1410	11771	Prof., Scientific, & Tech Svcs
11726	614	5154	Transit & Grnd Pass. Transport
11727	537	3018	Justice, Pubic Order/Safety
11729	1608	12238	Prof., Scientific, & Tech Svcs
11730	512	3406	Prof., Scientific, & Tech Svcs
11731	964	5760	Educational Services
11732	146	1199	Relig., Grant, Civic, Prof Org
11733	748	5608	Educational Services
11735	2168	23462	Prof., Scientific, & Tech Svcs
11738	398	2229	Food Svcs & Drinking Places
11739	56	250	Prof., Scientific, & Tech Svcs
11740	284	3183	Computer & Electronic Prod Mfg
11741	939	6944	Educational Services
11742	330	4906	Computer & Electronic Prod Mfg
11743	2480	16125	Ambulatory Health Care Svcs
11746	1956	15103	Educational Services
11747	1437	26621	Prof., Scientific, & Tech Svcs
11749	441	9051	Publishing Industries
11751	534	4005	Educational Services
11752	215	1216	Educational Services
11753	916	9927	Prof., Scientific, & Tech Svcs
11754	470	5431	Hospitals
11755	386	3363	Clothing & Cloth'g Acc. Stores
11756	983	7778	Educational Services
11757	1383	10260	Educational Services
11758	1757	11688	Educational Services
11762	438	2598	Food and Beverage Stores
11763	838	6500	Merch. Wholesalers,Durable Gds
11764	364	1665	Educational Services
11765	21	191	Educational Services
11766	341	1180	Exec., Legis., & Other Support
11767	343	2349	Nursing & Resid. Care Facilit.
11768	834	4742	Educational Services
11769	321	4098	Educational Services
11770	84	565	Food Svcs & Drinking Places
11771	526	3231	Exec., Legis., & Other Support
11772	1741	13878	Hospitals
11776	840	6668	Ambulatory Health Care Svcs
11777	641	7471	Hospitals
11778	406	1924	Food Svcs & Drinking Places
11779	1841	19549	Educational Services
11780	532	4044	Nursing & Resid. Care Facilit.
11782	797	4285	Educational Services
11783	533	3145	Educational Services
11784	576	4423	Educational Services
11786	130	1224	Educational Services
11787	1752	13828	Ambulatory Health Care Svcs
11788	1442	28525	Prof., Scientific, & Tech Svcs
11789	97	237	Special Trade Contractors
11790	517	3453	Ambulatory Health Care Svcs
11791	1184	12980	Computer & Electronic Prod Mfg
11792	251	1537	Social Assistance
11793	907	6083	Food Svcs & Drinking Places
11794	117	11441	Educational Services
11795	629	7891	Ambulatory Health Care Svcs
11796	96	745	Educational Services
11797	535	12120	Insurance Carriers & Related
11798	276	2394	Educational Services
11801	2221	21686	Prof., Scientific, & Tech Svcs
11802	5	17	Administrative & Support Svcs
11803	1534	15150	Merch. Wholesalers,Durable Gds
11804	108	969	Exec., Legis., & Other Support
11855	1	0	Prof., Scientific, & Tech Svcs
11901	1444	13920	Educational Services
11930	173	880	Food Svcs & Drinking Places
11931	62	311	Merch. Wholesalers,Durable Gds
11932	370	2473	Bldg Matl & Garden Eqpmt Dlrs
11933	170	1819	Amusement, Gambling,& Recreat.
11934	347	2191	Educational Services
11935	192	1088	Educational Services
11937	1013	6118	Food Svcs & Drinking Places
11939	22	40	Accommodation
11940	182	645	Nursing & Resid. Care Facilit.
11941	117	926	Educational Services
11942	152	635	Food Svcs & Drinking Places
11944	278	1826	Miscellaneous Store Retailers
11946	573	3019	Food Svcs & Drinking Places
11947	72	336	Exec., Legis., & Other Support
11948	21	167	Bldg Matl & Garden Eqpmt Dlrs
11949	237	820	Educational Services
11950	239	662	Food Svcs & Drinking Places
11951	177	895	Educational Services
11952	284	1703	Educational Services
11953	344	3317	Educational Services
11954	367	2311	Accommodation
11955	99	503	Educational Services
11956	13	55	Food Svcs & Drinking Places
11957	30	90	Educational Services
11958	58	286	Administrative & Support Svcs
11959	133	729	Special Trade Contractors
11960	29	66	Educational Services
11961	159	784	Educational Services
11962	30	142	Amusement, Gambling,& Recreat.
11963	460	2083	Food Svcs & Drinking Places
11964	160	605	Justice, Pubic Order/Safety
11965	46	305	Accommodation
11967	543	4096	Health & Personal Care Stores
11968	1266	9381	Educational Services
11969	19	322	Relig., Grant, Civic, Prof Org
11970	14	18	Amusement, Gambling,& Recreat.
11971	346	1908	Exec., Legis., & Other Support
11972	62	285	Educational Services
11973	8	96	Hospitals
11975	103	584	Ambulatory Health Care Svcs
11976	167	634	Food Svcs & Drinking Places
11977	118	641	Nursing & Resid. Care Facilit.
11978	442	3843	Food Svcs & Drinking Places
11980	220	6898	Justice, Pubic Order/Safety
12007	8	31	Nonmetallic Mineral Prod. Mfg
12008	17	83	Justice, Pubic Order/Safety
12009	231	1130	Educational Services
12010	1016	11052	Hospitals
12015	105	528	Primary Metal Manufacturing
12016	1	1	Food Svcs & Drinking Places
12017	21	25	Prof., Scientific, & Tech Svcs
12018	137	988	Educational Services
12019	271	1457	Educational Services
12020	892	10658	Exec., Legis., & Other Support
12022	44	305	Educational Services
12023	61	440	Educational Services
12024	4	3	Postal Service
12025	175	590	Furniture & Related Prod. Mfg
12027	178	1158	Educational Services
12028	14	28	Administrative & Support Svcs
12029	91	748	Social Assistance
12031	8	12	Exec., Legis., & Other Support
12032	40	118	Educational Services
12033	284	2501	Educational Services
12035	29	175	Justice, Pubic Order/Safety
12036	7	5	Food and Beverage Stores
12037	308	1755	Educational Services
12040	4	90	Educational Services
12041	20	59	Educational Services
12042	14	37	Food Svcs & Drinking Places
12043	382	3559	Educational Services
12045	22	156	Food Svcs & Drinking Places
12046	20	48	Special Trade Contractors
12047	496	5760	Ambulatory Health Care Svcs
12050	4	11	Special Trade Contractors
12051	173	1990	Justice, Pubic Order/Safety
12052	38	179	Ambulatory Health Care Svcs
12053	80	443	Educational Services
12054	532	3832	Educational Services
12055	1	1	Clothing & Cloth'g Acc. Stores
12056	93	545	Justice, Pubic Order/Safety
12057	36	196	Machinery Manufacturing
12058	20	55	Food Svcs & Drinking Places
12059	21	69	Food Svcs & Drinking Places
12060	44	95	Prof., Scientific, & Tech Svcs
12061	351	3226	Educational Services
12062	23	51	Bldg Matl & Garden Eqpmt Dlrs
12063	12	27	Administrative & Support Svcs
12064	7	17	Postal Service

ZIP CODE	2004 Total Firms	2004 Total Employ-ees	TOP INDUSTRY RANKED on 2004 EMPLOYMENT	ZIP CODE	2004 Total Firms	2004 Total Employ-ees	TOP INDUSTRY RANKED on 2004 EMPLOYMENT	ZIP CODE	2004 Total Firms	2004 Total Employ-ees	TOP INDUSTRY RANKED on 2004 EMPLOYMENT
12065	1574	14053	Food Svcs & Drinking Places	12189	343	4764	Nat'l Security & Int'l Affairs	12443	88	395	Food and Beverage Stores
12066	43	141	Justice, Pubic Order/Safety	12190	38	87	Gasoline Stations	12444	14	29	Administrative & Support Svcs
12067	46	792	Nonmetallic Mineral Prod. Mfg	12192	92	433	Food Svcs & Drinking Places	12446	140	736	Accommodation
12068	150	1449	Educational Services	12193	56	311	Fabricated Metal Product Mfg	12448	8	12	Nursing & Resid. Care Facilit.
12069	4	16	Museums, Hist. Sites,& Similar	12194	11	4	Postal Service	12449	110	1404	Nursing & Resid. Care Facilit.
12070	25	150	Amusement, Gambling,& Recreat.	12195	20	407	Educational Services	12450	5	4	Merch. Wholesalers,Durable Gds
12071	9	9	Prof., Scientific, & Tech Svcs	12196	85	472	Food and Beverage Stores	12451	37	206	Justice, Pubic Order/Safety
12072	98	980	Justice, Pubic Order/Safety	12197	70	246	Educational Services	12452	13	28	Heavy & Civil Eng. Construct'N
12073	7	7	Relig., Grant, Civic, Prof Org	12198	168	1484	Educational Services	12453	14	101	Food Svcs & Drinking Places
12074	93	674	Educational Services	12201	5	15	Merch. Wholesalers,Nondur. Gds	12454	5	8	Exec., Legis., & Other Support
12075	129	1018	Nursing & Resid. Care Facilit.	12202	326	3785	Educational Services	12455	232	1156	Hospitals
12076	33	272	Accommodation	12203	1219	18084	Food Svcs & Drinking Places	12456	14	122	Nonmetallic Mineral Prod. Mfg
12077	197	2116	Insurance Carriers & Related	12204	406	11305	Ambulatory Health Care Svcs	12457	44	405	Accommodation
12078	835	7897	Hospitals	12205	2486	32915	Food Svcs & Drinking Places	12458	44	1301	Justice, Pubic Order/Safety
12082	18	113	Museums, Hist. Sites,& Similar	12206	858	12088	Elect'l Eqpmt, App, & Comp Mfg	12459	8	14	Relig., Grant, Civic, Prof Org
12083	156	927	Accommodation	12207	969	15186	Credit Intermediation & Relatd	12460	11	18	Chemical Manufacturing
12084	231	2762	Amusement, Gambling,& Recreat.	12208	605	32445	Hospitals	12461	35	81	Educational Services
12085	44	1363	Educational Services	12209	179	1710	Nursing & Resid. Care Facilit.	12463	37	119	Accommodation
12086	27	206	Justice, Pubic Order/Safety	12210	665	8808	Admin. Human Resource Programs	12464	95	328	Food Svcs & Drinking Places
12087	22	101	Admin. of Economic Programs	12211	391	13055	Insurance Carriers & Related	12465	23	77	Justice, Pubic Order/Safety
12089	13	69	Educational Services	12212	4	17	Relig., Grant, Civic, Prof Org	12466	112	1043	Educational Services
12090	214	1610	Nursing & Resid. Care Facilit.	12220	3	3	Miscellaneous Store Retailers	12468	45	140	Food and Beverage Stores
12092	35	342	Museums, Hist. Sites,& Similar	12222	10	4229	Educational Services	12469	13	23	Food Svcs & Drinking Places
12093	30	109	Educational Services	12223	97	8459	Admin. of Economic Programs	12470	11	34	Food Svcs & Drinking Places
12094	29	34	Postal Service	12224	10	24	Publishing Industries	12471	11	95	Justice, Pubic Order/Safety
12095	728	8124	Exec., Legis., & Other Support	12225	2	42	Exec., Legis., & Other Support	12472	99	469	Food Svcs & Drinking Places
12106	176	650	Prof., Scientific, & Tech Svcs	12226	30	2681	Justice, Pubic Order/Safety	12473	24	131	Accommodation
12107	10	44	Exec., Legis., & Other Support	12227	2	14	Relig., Grant, Civic, Prof Org	12474	62	304	Food Manufacturing
12108	71	197	Exec., Legis., & Other Support	12228	1	0	Exec., Legis., & Other Support	12475	12	82	Nonstore Retailers
12110	1355	21345	Ambulatory Health Care Svcs	12229	1	3	Ambulatory Health Care Svcs	12477	640	3044	Educational Services
12115	10	22	Bldg Matl & Garden Eqpmt Dlrs	12230	11	1108	Other Information Services	12480	33	94	Justice, Pubic Order/Safety
12116	26	28	Exec., Legis., & Other Support	12231	1	500	Exec., Legis., & Other Support	12481	91	365	Exec., Legis., & Other Support
12117	132	699	Educational Services	12232	4	62	Admin. of Economic Programs	12482	17	159	Justice, Pubic Order/Safety
12118	334	3380	Nursing & Resid. Care Facilit.	12236	6	4519	Exec., Legis., & Other Support	12483	8	206	Accommodation
12120	7	111	Exec., Legis., & Other Support	12237	5	324	Ambulatory Health Care Svcs	12484	143	1361	Educational Services
12121	37	199	Special Trade Contractors	12239	3	548	Exec., Legis., & Other Support	12485	104	549	Accommodation
12122	224	844	Educational Services	12240	7	1793	Admin. Human Resource Programs	12486	30	142	Transit & Grnd Pass. Transport
12123	154	883	Educational Services	12246	1	10	Heavy & Civil Eng. Construct'N	12487	41	842	Relig., Grant, Civic, Prof Org
12124	25	229	Food Svcs & Drinking Places	12247	2	1614	Exec., Legis., & Other Support	12489	29	102	Heavy & Civil Eng. Construct'N
12125	121	661	Merch. Wholesalers,Nondur. Gds	12248	1	0	Exec., Legis., & Other Support	12490	6	33	Waste Managmt & Remediat'n Svc
12128	13	31	Justice, Pubic Order/Safety	12249	1	15	Justice, Pubic Order/Safety	12491	86	468	Sportg Gds,Hobby,Book, & Music
12130	40	81	Special Trade Contractors	12260	9	34	Heavy & Civil Eng. Construct'N	12492	9	8	Wood Product Manufacturing
12131	10	64	Museums, Hist. Sites,& Similar	12288	1	1700	Postal Service	12493	16	253	Educational Services
12132	20	52	Construction of Buildings	12301	3	1	Prof., Scientific, & Tech Svcs	12494	21	70	Exec., Legis., & Other Support
12133	12	159	Paper Manufacturing	12302	799	9473	Nat'l Security & Int'l Affairs	12495	8	19	Prof., Scientific, & Tech Svcs
12134	174	812	Educational Services	12303	732	7034	Educational Services	12496	146	1122	Accommodation
12136	45	259	Prof., Scientific, & Tech Svcs	12304	607	7986	Hospitals	12498	342	1682	Machinery Manufacturing
12137	27	325	Food Svcs & Drinking Places	12305	700	8941	Prof., Scientific, & Tech Svcs	12501	149	1118	Educational Services
12138	49	306	Textile Mills	12306	743	6932	Food and Beverage Stores	12502	55	265	Paper Manufacturing
12139	23	70	Exec., Legis., & Other Support	12307	184	1786	Justice, Pubic Order/Safety	12503	30	73	Crop Production
12140	32	306	Justice, Pubic Order/Safety	12308	394	6647	Hospitals	12504	3	51	Museums, Hist. Sites,& Similar
12141	4	9	Other Information Services	12309	640	9977	Prof., Scientific, & Tech Svcs	12506	5	16	Food Svcs & Drinking Places
12143	247	1880	Nonmetallic Mineral Prod. Mfg	12325	2	0	Merch. Wholesalers,Nondur. Gds	12507	5	0	Rental and Leasing Services
12144	597	6721	Administrative & Support Svcs	12345	2	4806	Machinery Manufacturing	12508	535	4910	Justice, Pubic Order/Safety
12147	25	185	Relig., Grant, Civic, Prof Org	12401	2289	25118	Ambulatory Health Care Svcs	12510	10	40	Special Trade Contractors
12148	88	546	Relig., Grant, Civic, Prof Org	12402	5	5	Heavy & Civil Eng. Construct'N	12511	11	34	Social Assistance
12149	58	263	Educational Services	12404	98	386	Miscellaneous Manufacturing	12512	9	5	Postal Service
12150	33	642	Chemical Manufacturing	12405	14	73	Accommodation	12513	50	336	Social Assistance
12151	51	240	Justice, Pubic Order/Safety	12406	63	203	Relig., Grant, Civic, Prof Org	12514	59	134	Educational Services
12153	25	42	Exec., Legis., & Other Support	12407	15	65	Truck Transportation	12515	39	166	Crop Production
12154	77	442	Educational Services	12409	31	140	Food Svcs & Drinking Places	12516	87	208	Miscellaneous Manufacturing
12155	40	312	Educational Services	12410	18	44	Accommodation	12517	24	72	Prof., Scientific, & Tech Svcs
12156	22	422	Merch. Wholesalers,Nondur. Gds	12411	14	37	Construction of Buildings	12518	246	1566	Hospitals
12157	238	2121	Educational Services	12412	40	729	Educational Services	12520	93	503	Educational Services
12158	121	1190	Chemical Manufacturing	12413	165	1066	Educational Services	12521	56	740	Educational Services
12159	176	1231	Social Assistance	12414	547	4234	Nursing & Resid. Care Facilit.	12522	142	1262	Educational Services
12160	13	28	Real Estate	12416	4	27	Isps, Web Search Portals	12523	38	103	Accommodation
12161	16	222	Nonmetallic Mineral Prod. Mfg	12417	12	24	Amusement, Gambling,& Recreat.	12524	786	8226	Food Svcs & Drinking Places
12164	63	473	Accommodation	12418	6	6	Postal Service	12525	101	427	Food Svcs & Drinking Places
12165	38	104	Bldg Matl & Garden Eqpmt Dlrs	12419	11	152	Educational Services	12526	170	2365	Hospitals
12166	19	146	Bldg Matl & Garden Eqpmt Dlrs	12420	8	50	Justice, Pubic Order/Safety	12527	19	439	Prof., Scientific, & Tech Svcs
12167	131	1198	Relig., Grant, Civic, Prof Org	12421	5	2	Prof., Scientific, & Tech Svcs	12528	426	10224	Accommodation
12168	69	225	Fabricated Metal Product Mfg	12422	14	82	Educational Services	12529	136	610	Accommodation
12169	10	14	Merch. Wholesalers,Durable Gds	12423	56	195	Accommodation	12530	5	10	Real Estate
12170	87	617	Educational Services	12424	7	55	Relig., Grant, Civic, Prof Org	12531	55	393	Nursing & Resid. Care Facilit.
12172	10	116	Justice, Pubic Order/Safety	12427	14	61	Miscellaneous Manufacturing	12533	758	12980	Computer & Electronic Prod Mfg
12173	52	176	Textile Product Mills	12428	299	4082	Accommodation	12534	946	8219	Ambulatory Health Care Svcs
12174	15	25	Special Trade Contractors	12429	21	82	Relig., Grant, Civic, Prof Org	12537	12	37	Real Estate
12175	46	180	Justice, Pubic Order/Safety	12430	57	200	Accommodation	12538	504	3698	Educational Services
12176	3	55	Fabricated Metal Product Mfg	12431	37	209	Justice, Pubic Order/Safety	12540	264	2100	Educational Services
12177	19	23	Special Trade Contractors	12432	15	45	Heavy & Civil Eng. Construct'N	12541	34	304	Nursing & Resid. Care Facilit.
12180	1761	21736	Educational Services	12433	13	48	Unclassified Establishments	12542	187	1074	Educational Services
12181	5	18	Elect'l Eqpmt, App, & Comp Mfg	12434	39	218	Educational Services	12543	69	845	Truck Transportation
12182	322	2701	Educational Services	12435	12	66	Accommodation	12544	12	225	Social Assistance
12183	96	1000	Paper Manufacturing	12436	31	77	Exec., Legis., & Other Support	12545	320	2355	Educational Services
12184	240	1652	Nursing & Resid. Care Facilit.	12438	7	18	Wood Product Manufacturing	12546	201	1038	Justice, Pubic Order/Safety
12185	33	74	Special Trade Contractors	12439	32	189	Accommodation	12547	89	729	Merch. Wholesalers,Nondur. Gds
12186	194	1993	Educational Services	12440	89	501	Accommodation	12548	53	356	Exec., Legis., & Other Support
12187	18	47	Fabricated Metal Product Mfg	12441	5	461	Accommodation	12549	460	3588	Miscellaneous Manufacturing
12188	215	3448	Chemical Manufacturing	12442	107	1569	Administrative & Support Svcs	12550	2275	22131	Educational Services

BUSINESS DATA 12551 - 13065

ZIP CODE	2004 Total Firms	2004 Total Employ-ees	TOP INDUSTRY RANKED on 2004 EMPLOYMENT	ZIP CODE	2004 Total Firms	2004 Total Employ-ees	TOP INDUSTRY RANKED on 2004 EMPLOYMENT	ZIP CODE	2004 Total Firms	2004 Total Employ-ees	TOP INDUSTRY RANKED on 2004 EMPLOYMENT
12551	2	0	Administrative & Support Svcs	12787	15	33	Forestry and Logging	12926	46	259	Justice, Pubic Order/Safety
12552	2	1	Heavy & Civil Eng. Construct'N	12788	78	230	Social Assistance	12927	19	121	Justice, Pubic Order/Safety
12553	865	8040	Educational Services	12789	91	383	Personal and Laundry Services	12928	86	374	Exec., Legis., & Other Support
12555	6	850	Postal Service	12790	169	1221	Accommodation	12929	50	187	Educational Services
12561	698	7844	Educational Services	12791	27	124	Transit & Grnd Pass. Transport	12930	13	20	Motor Vehicle & Parts Dealers
12563	266	1764	Social Assistance	12792	15	19	Food Svcs & Drinking Places	12932	142	1743	Relig., Grant, Civic, Prof Org
12564	323	2764	Educational Services	12801	910	12142	Hospitals	12933	9	25	Food and Beverage Stores
12565	53	579	Plastics & Rubber Products Mfg	12803	268	2399	Educational Services	12934	13	20	Exec., Legis., & Other Support
12566	328	1871	Educational Services	12804	1059	11473	Food Svcs & Drinking Places	12935	35	450	Educational Services
12567	184	850	Educational Services	12808	8	10	General Merchandise Stores	12936	33	97	Food Svcs & Drinking Places
12568	33	590	Relig., Grant, Civic, Prof Org	12809	80	1186	Miscellaneous Manufacturing	12937	48	1040	Educational Services
12569	325	1976	Justice, Pubic Order/Safety	12810	12	61	Justice, Pubic Order/Safety	12939	12	14	Special Trade Contractors
12570	132	490	Educational Services	12811	9	8	Postal Service	12941	37	200	Wood Product Manufacturing
12571	545	2307	Educational Services	12812	27	122	Accommodation	12942	46	102	Accommodation
12572	594	4217	Relig., Grant, Civic, Prof Org	12814	146	1466	Administrative & Support Svcs	12943	38	321	Relig., Grant, Civic, Prof Org
12574	12	21	Special Trade Contractors	12815	54	518	Relig., Grant, Civic, Prof Org	12944	163	887	Social Assistance
12575	53	459	Administrative & Support Svcs	12816	184	1058	Educational Services	12945	26	93	Admin. of Economic Programs
12577	54	295	Justice, Pubic Order/Safety	12817	158	545	Food Svcs & Drinking Places	12946	486	5295	Accommodation
12578	74	366	Justice, Pubic Order/Safety	12819	1	7	Real Estate	12949	9	7	Merch. Wholesalers,Durable Gds
12580	97	802	Educational Services	12820	14	92	Justice, Pubic Order/Safety	12950	21	79	Exec., Legis., & Other Support
12581	101	318	Miscellaneous Manufacturing	12821	8	27	Motor Vehicle & Parts Dealers	12952	11	14	Gasoline Stations
12582	93	1114	Justice, Pubic Order/Safety	12822	157	1346	Paper Manufacturing	12953	657	7776	Justice, Pubic Order/Safety
12583	72	146	Food Svcs & Drinking Places	12823	5	23	Fabricated Metal Product Mfg	12955	6	55	Accommodation
12584	67	1025	Food and Beverage Stores	12824	37	174	Accommodation	12956	28	370	Exec., Legis., & Other Support
12585	28	222	Accommodation	12827	98	309	Forestry and Logging	12957	36	198	Food Svcs & Drinking Places
12586	343	2313	Food and Beverage Stores	12828	254	2435	Exec., Legis., & Other Support	12958	61	207	Educational Services
12588	13	19	Motor Vehicle & Parts Dealers	12831	249	1577	Merch. Wholesalers,Durable Gds	12959	25	37	Food and Beverage Stores
12589	274	2348	Justice, Pubic Order/Safety	12832	195	2413	Furniture & Related Prod. Mfg	12960	10	35	Exec., Legis., & Other Support
12590	1068	7483	Educational Services	12833	75	210	Educational Services	12961	2	2	Food Svcs & Drinking Places
12592	35	3639	Admin. Human Resource Programs	12834	268	1821	Nonmetallic Mineral Prod. Mfg	12962	76	541	Nat'l Security & Int'l Affairs
12594	111	932	Exec., Legis., & Other Support	12835	70	181	Exec., Legis., & Other Support	12965	34	155	Miscellaneous Manufacturing
12601	2123	28913	Hospitals	12836	37	72	Exec., Legis., & Other Support	12966	38	126	Justice, Pubic Order/Safety
12602	6	14	Social Assistance	12837	14	46	Justice, Pubic Order/Safety	12967	16	184	Merch. Wholesalers,Nondur. Gds
12603	1389	12802	Educational Services	12838	26	218	Educational Services	12969	5	28	Justice, Pubic Order/Safety
12604	4	26	Educational Services	12839	344	2663	Educational Services	12970	15	230	Educational Services
12701	740	5886	Ambulatory Health Care Svcs	12841	6	2	Postal Service	12972	127	1186	Educational Services
12719	67	377	Accommodation	12842	120	497	Exec., Legis., & Other Support	12973	7	16	Exec., Legis., & Other Support
12720	20	266	Perform'g Arts, Spec. Sports	12843	18	28	Motor Vehicle & Parts Dealers	12974	94	690	Exec., Legis., & Other Support
12721	144	467	Food Svcs & Drinking Places	12844	13	156	Accommodation	12975	7	40	Water Transportation
12722	9	108	Accommodation	12845	598	5748	Accommodation	12976	2	3	Prof., Scientific, & Tech Svcs
12723	93	1072	Accommodation	12846	133	612	Educational Services	12977	30	1014	Justice, Pubic Order/Safety
12724	10	34	Electronics & Appliance Stores	12847	96	577	Accommodation	12978	5	16	Food and Beverage Stores
12725	10	35	Exec., Legis., & Other Support	12848	2	27	Justice, Pubic Order/Safety	12979	105	3001	Chemical Manufacturing
12726	41	115	Special Trade Contractors	12849	21	151	Nonmetallic Mineral Prod. Mfg	12980	35	125	Educational Services
12727	6	3	Special Trade Contractors	12850	38	163	Accommodation	12981	44	282	Educational Services
12729	37	202	Educational Services	12851	21	34	Heavy & Civil Eng. Construct'N	12983	471	3977	Educational Services
12732	34	286	Educational Services	12852	35	102	Educational Services	12985	13	106	Exec., Legis., & Other Support
12733	46	340	Educational Services	12853	133	1497	Accommodation	12986	250	3280	Exec., Legis., & Other Support
12734	66	381	Merch. Wholesalers,Nondur. Gds	12854	10	41	Social Assistance	12987	15	18	Ambulatory Health Care Svcs
12736	7	10	Exec., Legis., & Other Support	12855	12	30	Accommodation	12989	16	46	Exec., Legis., & Other Support
12737	43	544	Accommodation	12856	10	125	Accommodation	12992	44	177	Justice, Pubic Order/Safety
12738	10	27	Prof., Scientific, & Tech Svcs	12857	24	102	Educational Services	12993	108	694	Accommodation
12740	52	324	Justice, Pubic Order/Safety	12858	4	135	Accommodation	12995	1	0	Construction of Buildings
12741	9	10	Special Trade Contractors	12859	26	106	Justice, Pubic Order/Safety	12996	78	754	Textile Mills
12742	16	905	Hospitals	12860	35	501	Educational Services	12997	91	733	Accommodation
12743	6	12	Relig., Grant, Civic, Prof Org	12861	13	159	Justice, Pubic Order/Safety	12998	3	3	Electronics & Appliance Stores
12745	7	51	Exec., Legis., & Other Support	12862	6	38	Bldg Matl & Garden Eqpmt Dlrs	13020	3	3	Postal Service
12746	32	659	Social Assistance	12863	10	102	Paper Manufacturing	13021	1674	17479	Educational Services
12747	47	252	Ambulatory Health Care Svcs	12864	8	33	Accommodation	13022	19	157	General Merchandise Stores
12748	112	695	Educational Services	12865	89	805	Educational Services	13024	2	7	Justice, Pubic Order/Safety
12749	34	100	Justice, Pubic Order/Safety	12866	1825	21584	Food Svcs & Drinking Places	13026	50	549	Nonmetallic Mineral Prod. Mfg
12750	8	26	Admin. of Economic Programs	12870	123	474	Justice, Pubic Order/Safety	13027	734	8361	Merch. Wholesalers,Nondur. Gds
12751	28	1030	Amusement, Gambling,& Recreat.	12871	106	783	Educational Services	13028	17	184	Merch. Wholesalers,Durable Gds
12752	14	35	Merch. Wholesalers,Nondur. Gds	12872	7	10	Accommodation	13029	227	1157	Food Svcs & Drinking Places
12754	444	3569	Nursing & Resid. Care Facilit.	12873	9	34	Merch. Wholesalers,Durable Gds	13030	95	412	Amusement, Gambling,& Recreat.
12758	147	507	Food and Beverage Stores	12874	10	57	Repair and Maintenance	13031	476	3907	Educational Services
12759	67	1035	Relig., Grant, Civic, Prof Org	12878	25	141	Accommodation	13032	328	2780	Plastics & Rubber Products Mfg
12760	13	68	Miscellaneous Manufacturing	12879	2	5	Forestry and Logging	13033	123	948	Educational Services
12762	23	141	Merch. Wholesalers,Nondur. Gds	12883	259	2638	Paper Manufacturing	13034	28	105	Educational Services
12763	24	120	Telecommunications	12884	8	12	Exec., Legis., & Other Support	13035	391	2816	Educational Services
12764	105	574	Bldg Matl & Garden Eqpmt Dlrs	12885	248	2060	Accommodation	13036	327	1834	Educational Services
12765	17	180	Accommodation	12886	18	45	Bldg Matl & Garden Eqpmt Dlrs	13037	262	2260	Primary Metal Manufacturing
12766	13	11	Postal Service	12887	131	888	Educational Services	13039	481	5110	Food Svcs & Drinking Places
12767	2	3	Postal Service	12901	1628	24419	Ambulatory Health Care Svcs	13040	73	363	Educational Services
12768	35	548	Accommodation	12903	56	561	Administrative & Support Svcs	13041	227	1844	General Merchandise Stores
12769	4	6	Support Activities: Agr./For.	12910	30	74	Exec., Legis., & Other Support	13042	34	123	Educational Services
12770	15	46	Real Estate	12911	2	41	Miscellaneous Store Retailers	13043	7	58	Heavy & Civil Eng. Construct'N
12771	599	4152	Chemical Manufacturing	12912	90	306	Relig., Grant, Civic, Prof Org	13044	64	247	Food and Beverage Stores
12775	78	656	Insurance Carriers & Related	12913	25	67	Educational Services	13045	1206	17529	Educational Services
12776	131	807	Accommodation	12914	15	53	Unclassified Establishments	13051	7	7	Postal Service
12777	26	161	Truck Transportation	12915	9	24	Special Trade Contractors	13052	46	346	Educational Services
12778	13	13	Electronics & Appliance Stores	12916	40	331	Educational Services	13053	166	1685	Educational Services
12779	139	1633	Accommodation	12917	26	94	Nonmetallic Mineral Prod. Mfg	13054	30	146	Educational Services
12780	53	229	Accommodation	12918	25	120	Justice, Pubic Order/Safety	13057	1275	27058	Machinery Manufacturing
12781	13	315	Support Activities: Agr./For.	12919	222	2428	Prof., Scientific, & Tech Svcs	13060	126	1138	Plastics & Rubber Products Mfg
12782	4	3	Exec., Legis., & Other Support	12920	70	480	Educational Services	13061	23	131	Justice, Pubic Order/Safety
12783	51	224	Justice, Pubic Order/Safety	12921	76	814	Educational Services	13062	11	36	Food and Beverage Stores
12784	10	7	Heavy & Civil Eng. Construct'N	12922	6	11	Food and Beverage Stores	13063	49	629	Educational Services
12785	23	48	Nursing & Resid. Care Facilit.	12923	14	18	Exec., Legis., & Other Support	13064	48	173	Relig., Grant, Civic, Prof Org
12786	67	241	Justice, Pubic Order/Safety	12924	8	72	Educational Services	13065	8	3	Postal Service

 Copyright © 2004 ESRI BIS. All rights reserved. Reproduction by any method is prohibited.

ZIP CODE	2004 Total Firms	2004 Total Employ-ees	TOP INDUSTRY RANKED on 2004 EMPLOYMENT	ZIP CODE	2004 Total Firms	2004 Total Employ-ees	TOP INDUSTRY RANKED on 2004 EMPLOYMENT	ZIP CODE	2004 Total Firms	2004 Total Employ-ees	TOP INDUSTRY RANKED on 2004 EMPLOYMENT
13066	637	5040	Food and Beverage Stores	13218	5	38	Postal Service	13439	133	707	Educational Services
13068	92	702	Relig., Grant, Civic, Prof Org	13219	557	5471	Food Svcs & Drinking Places	13440	1427	17377	Justice, Pubic Order/Safety
13069	868	9205	Relig., Grant, Civic, Prof Org	13220	24	872	Postal Service	13441	48	537	Support Act. for Transport.
13071	20	72	Food and Beverage Stores	13221	3	8	Credit Intermediation & Relatd	13442	1	2	Ambulatory Health Care Svcs
13072	28	176	Justice, Pubic Order/Safety	13224	321	3670	Food Svcs & Drinking Places	13450	5	5	Postal Service
13073	155	885	Educational Services	13244	34	4428	Educational Services	13452	128	1156	Educational Services
13074	108	1010	Educational Services	13261	26	219	Exec., Legis., & Other Support	13454	18	59	Educational Services
13076	49	157	Justice, Pubic Order/Safety	13290	179	3073	Clothing & Cloth'g Acc. Stores	13455	14	287	Wood Product Manufacturing
13077	198	1358	Educational Services	13301	12	40	Admin. of Economic Programs	13456	79	919	Educational Services
13078	239	2393	Nursing & Resid. Care Facilit.	13302	30	124	Educational Services	13457	8	18	Accommodation
13080	102	1009	Educational Services	13303	12	47	Accommodation	13459	84	967	Merch. Wholesalers,Durable Gds
13081	40	141	Fabricated Metal Product Mfg	13304	118	638	Ambulatory Health Care Svcs	13460	175	1412	Educational Services
13082	83	583	Fabricated Metal Product Mfg	13305	23	439	Educational Services	13461	94	3491	Miscellaneous Manufacturing
13083	52	163	Transit & Grnd Pass. Transport	13308	55	904	Furniture & Related Prod. Mfg	13464	24	74	Wood Product Manufacturing
13084	161	1260	Educational Services	13309	244	1929	Furn. & Home Furnishgs Stores	13465	2	7	Food Svcs & Drinking Places
13087	10	57	Administrative & Support Svcs	13310	34	216	Miscellaneous Store Retailers	13468	18	30	Prof., Scientific, & Tech Svcs
13088	1047	15750	Computer & Electronic Prod Mfg	13312	14	67	Accommodation	13469	21	141	Justice, Pubic Order/Safety
13089	5	6	Prof., Scientific, & Tech Svcs	13313	24	54	Food and Beverage Stores	13470	9	47	Justice, Pubic Order/Safety
13090	701	7550	Educational Services	13314	28	111	Educational Services	13471	40	308	Exec., Legis., & Other Support
13092	46	291	Crop Production	13315	19	70	Insurance Carriers & Related	13472	21	92	Food Svcs & Drinking Places
13093	4	763	Exec., Legis., & Other Support	13316	184	1730	Primary Metal Manufacturing	13473	36	500	Educational Services
13101	48	530	Educational Services	13317	146	1573	Food Manufacturing	13475	10	39	Computer & Electronic Prod Mfg
13102	16	42	Educational Services	13318	15	26	Food and Beverage Stores	13476	164	1177	Perform'g Arts, Spec. Sports
13103	9	9	Heavy & Civil Eng. Construct'N	13319	45	277	Transportation Equipment Mfg	13477	26	54	Special Trade Contractors
13104	574	4201	Furn. & Home Furnishgs Stores	13320	67	640	Educational Services	13478	70	5865	Accommodation
13107	6	59	Food and Beverage Stores	13321	20	117	Ambulatory Health Care Svcs	13479	21	167	Food Svcs & Drinking Places
13108	232	1402	Educational Services	13322	30	277	Primary Metal Manufacturing	13480	122	704	Educational Services
13110	57	95	Food Svcs & Drinking Places	13323	353	3093	Educational Services	13482	2	3	Computer & Electronic Prod Mfg
13111	30	51	Bldg Matl & Garden Eqpmt Dlrs	13324	42	83	Forestry and Logging	13483	6	8	General Merchandise Stores
13112	31	58	Accommodation	13325	30	91	Educational Services	13484	5	8	Food Svcs & Drinking Places
13113	8	12	Real Estate	13326	457	8170	Hospitals	13485	11	30	Merch. Wholesalers,Nondur. Gds
13114	164	2029	Educational Services	13327	78	211	Food Svcs & Drinking Places	13486	25	78	Accommodation
13115	27	322	Educational Services	13328	29	75	Construction of Buildings	13488	7	15	Truck Transportation
13116	78	669	Support Act. for Transport.	13329	107	904	Educational Services	13489	15	77	Educational Services
13117	15	30	Food and Beverage Stores	13331	39	113	Accommodation	13490	68	1037	Educational Services
13118	165	964	Special Trade Contractors	13332	76	251	Relig., Grant, Civic, Prof Org	13491	83	494	Educational Services
13119	4	32	Justice, Pubic Order/Safety	13333	9	24	Accommodation	13492	288	1932	Transportation Equipment Mfg
13120	81	715	Educational Services	13334	24	65	Exec., Legis., & Other Support	13493	50	584	Primary Metal Manufacturing
13121	14	25	Exec., Legis., & Other Support	13335	50	1469	Insurance Carriers & Related	13494	15	93	Accommodation
13122	41	120	Special Trade Contractors	13337	44	182	Heavy & Civil Eng. Construct'N	13495	181	1675	Motor Vehicle & Parts Dealers
13123	10	33	Food and Beverage Stores	13338	56	266	Food Svcs & Drinking Places	13501	1240	17943	Educational Services
13124	1	1	Construction of Buildings	13339	173	759	Educational Services	13502	1349	22720	Educational Services
13126	1102	11983	Educational Services	13340	175	1716	Food Manufacturing	13503	7	13	Merch. Wholesalers,Durable Gds
13131	88	1149	Educational Services	13341	5	32	Machinery Manufacturing	13504	6	509	Postal Service
13132	51	99	Administrative & Support Svcs	13342	7	30	Accommodation	13505	1	1	Administrative & Support Svcs
13134	6	8	Heavy & Civil Eng. Construct'N	13343	32	151	Educational Services	13601	1845	23469	Nursing & Resid. Care Facilit.
13135	286	1462	Educational Services	13345	5	12	Heavy & Civil Eng. Construct'N	13602	27	784	Nat'l Security & Int'l Affairs
13136	10	13	Repair and Maintenance	13346	194	1561	Hospitals	13603	17	89	Construction of Buildings
13137	6	157	Food Manufacturing	13348	35	177	Justice, Pubic Order/Safety	13605	142	1323	Educational Services
13138	19	92	Justice, Pubic Order/Safety	13350	516	5875	Exec., Legis., & Other Support	13606	69	668	Educational Services
13139	12	67	Educational Services	13352	3	4	Postal Service	13607	213	2112	Accommodation
13140	153	790	Educational Services	13353	7	17	Support Act. for Transport.	13608	25	90	Special Trade Contractors
13141	24	304	Transportation Equipment Mfg	13354	70	793	Educational Services	13611	20	145	Educational Services
13142	338	2319	Machinery Manufacturing	13355	12	26	Nursing & Resid. Care Facilit.	13612	57	237	Educational Services
13143	67	575	Educational Services	13357	236	2997	Fabricated Metal Product Mfg	13613	45	253	Educational Services
13144	28	53	Food and Beverage Stores	13360	87	293	Accommodation	13614	12	74	Justice, Pubic Order/Safety
13145	89	433	Educational Services	13361	10	45	Mining (Except Oil and Gas)	13615	36	270	Paper Manufacturing
13146	93	285	Educational Services	13362	7	34	Special Trade Contractors	13616	19	303	Educational Services
13147	35	99	Crop Production	13363	40	159	Exec., Legis., & Other Support	13617	456	6848	Educational Services
13148	379	3482	Machinery Manufacturing	13364	12	61	Educational Services	13618	92	769	Justice, Pubic Order/Safety
13152	446	3377	Miscellaneous Manufacturing	13365	269	3116	Hospitals	13619	246	2255	Hospitals
13153	13	804	Elect'l Eqpmt, App, & Comp Mfg	13367	462	4138	Hospitals	13620	36	126	Special Trade Contractors
13154	2	5	Relig., Grant, Civic, Prof Org	13368	60	237	Paper Manufacturing	13621	6	16	Food and Beverage Stores
13155	32	282	Educational Services	13401	4	23	Amusement, Gambling,& Recreat.	13622	66	221	Educational Services
13156	35	289	Museums, Hist. Sites,& Similar	13402	71	228	Educational Services	13623	8	11	Motor Vehicle & Parts Dealers
13157	49	594	Food Svcs & Drinking Places	13403	195	3792	Justice, Pubic Order/Safety	13624	238	1175	Food Svcs & Drinking Places
13158	35	271	Accommodation	13404	11	41	Exec., Legis., & Other Support	13625	34	266	Special Trade Contractors
13159	195	1210	Educational Services	13406	35	112	Food Svcs & Drinking Places	13626	40	224	Educational Services
13160	76	602	Educational Services	13407	128	833	Educational Services	13627	6	16	Insurance Carriers & Related
13162	17	95	Food Svcs & Drinking Places	13408	119	1375	Educational Services	13628	8	14	Credit Intermediation & Relatd
13163	63	671	Admin. Human Resource Programs	13409	60	443	Educational Services	13630	45	181	Educational Services
13164	65	337	Food Svcs & Drinking Places	13410	23	143	Ambulatory Health Care Svcs	13631	6	33	Truck Transportation
13165	514	5466	Exec., Legis., & Other Support	13411	137	1198	Insurance Carriers & Related	13632	15	20	Food and Beverage Stores
13166	152	837	Educational Services	13413	856	13044	Hospitals	13633	3	11	Merch. Wholesalers,Durable Gds
13167	78	286	Motor Vehicle & Parts Dealers	13415	2	2	Postal Service	13634	89	673	Educational Services
13201	7	10	Perform'g Arts, Spec. Sports	13416	87	445	Educational Services	13635	38	75	Repair and Maintenance
13202	1801	39118	Admin. Human Resource Programs	13417	139	1585	Educational Services	13636	15	36	Exec., Legis., & Other Support
13203	640	9492	Ambulatory Health Care Svcs	13418	8	5	Construction of Buildings	13637	79	424	Educational Services
13204	1059	15355	Exec., Legis., & Other Support	13420	202	1231	Exec., Legis., & Other Support	13638	21	126	Construction of Buildings
13205	429	5682	Nursing & Resid. Care Facilit.	13421	568	8658	Miscellaneous Manufacturing	13639	3	0	Postal Service
13206	1019	9016	Merch. Wholesalers,Durable Gds	13424	122	5756	Justice, Pubic Order/Safety	13640	24	209	Museums, Hist. Sites,& Similar
13207	229	1537	Educational Services	13425	50	427	Miscellaneous Manufacturing	13641	8	78	Food Svcs & Drinking Places
13208	753	6552	Nonmetallic Mineral Prod. Mfg	13426	12	29	Educational Services	13642	324	3572	Educational Services
13209	533	5312	Food Svcs & Drinking Places	13428	62	529	Nursing & Resid. Care Facilit.	13643	16	81	Justice, Pubic Order/Safety
13210	978	22342	Hospitals	13431	64	476	Educational Services	13645	7	45	Mining (Except Oil and Gas)
13211	397	4802	Educational Services	13433	45	136	Educational Services	13646	106	303	Educational Services
13212	987	10695	Food Svcs & Drinking Places	13435	12	50	Justice, Pubic Order/Safety	13647	8	60	Justice, Pubic Order/Safety
13214	614	9603	Food Svcs & Drinking Places	13436	31	83	Accommodation	13648	61	548	Educational Services
13215	383	3911	Hospitals	13437	21	41	Food Svcs & Drinking Places	13649	6	10	Prof., Scientific, & Tech Svcs
13217	10	134	Postal Service	13438	85	416	Educational Services	13650	54	225	Food Svcs & Drinking Places

ZIP CODE	2004 Total Firms	2004 Total Employees	TOP INDUSTRY RANKED on 2004 EMPLOYMENT	ZIP CODE	2004 Total Firms	2004 Total Employees	TOP INDUSTRY RANKED on 2004 EMPLOYMENT	ZIP CODE	2004 Total Firms	2004 Total Employees	TOP INDUSTRY RANKED on 2004 EMPLOYMENT
13651	19	80	Real Estate	13802	43	225	Educational Services	14059	270	3575	Transportation Equipment Mfg
13652	46	81	Exec., Legis., & Other Support	13803	135	856	Educational Services	14060	5	1	Personal and Laundry Services
13654	69	671	Food Manufacturing	13804	33	186	Accommodation	14061	9	30	Exec., Legis., & Other Support
13655	103	1197	Educational Services	13806	10	42	Exec., Legis., & Other Support	14062	53	320	Educational Services
13656	46	423	Merch. Wholesalers,Nondur. Gds	13807	53	318	Educational Services	14063	519	4399	Educational Services
13657	1	1	Special Trade Contractors	13808	72	382	Educational Services	14065	16	94	Wood Product Manufacturing
13658	43	350	Educational Services	13809	35	106	Merch. Wholesalers,Durable Gds	14066	26	556	Educational Services
13659	14	23	Exec., Legis., & Other Support	13810	14	32	Bldg Matl & Garden Eqpmt Dlrs	14067	130	789	Justice, Pubic Order/Safety
13660	45	174	Educational Services	13811	106	577	Educational Services	14068	168	3486	Credit Intermediation & Relatd
13661	27	82	Educational Services	13812	63	453	Support Act. for Transport.	14069	21	599	Accommodation
13662	678	8231	Primary Metal Manufacturing	13813	19	97	Wood Product Manufacturing	14070	201	2885	Justice, Pubic Order/Safety
13664	36	203	Educational Services	13814	13	49	Educational Services	14072	394	5300	Chemical Manufacturing
13665	14	35	Merch. Wholesalers,Nondur. Gds	13815	802	10343	Exec., Legis., & Other Support	14075	1170	13258	Food Svcs & Drinking Places
13666	5	10	Heavy & Civil Eng. Construct'N	13820	1081	12351	Educational Services	14080	121	704	Educational Services
13667	64	289	Paper Manufacturing	13825	82	786	Educational Services	14081	114	977	Food Svcs & Drinking Places
13668	89	995	Educational Services	13826	3	1	Relig., Grant, Civic, Prof Org	14082	25	156	Accommodation
13669	561	6692	Hospitals	13827	560	8960	Computer & Electronic Prod Mfg	14083	7	21	Food Svcs & Drinking Places
13670	10	29	Food and Beverage Stores	13830	157	921	Nursing & Resid. Care Facilit.	14085	74	349	Relig., Grant, Civic, Prof Org
13671	1	0	Justice, Pubic Order/Safety	13832	13	29	Social Assistance	14086	622	9945	Relig., Grant, Civic, Prof Org
13672	26	286	Educational Services	13833	68	298	Bldg Matl & Garden Eqpmt Dlrs	14091	13	53	Justice, Pubic Order/Safety
13673	47	444	Educational Services	13834	11	54	Wood Product Manufacturing	14092	347	3578	Hospitals
13674	9	31	Merch. Wholesalers,Nondur. Gds	13835	18	101	Justice, Pubic Order/Safety	14094	1595	20798	Transportation Equipment Mfg
13675	7	6	Postal Service	13838	300	4643	Print'g & Related Supp't Act's	14095	3	1	Administrative & Support Svcs
13676	529	6541	Educational Services	13839	33	312	Educational Services	14098	59	486	Educational Services
13677	2	1	Heavy & Civil Eng. Construct'N	13840	4	5	Food Svcs & Drinking Places	14101	39	438	Exec., Legis., & Other Support
13678	7	10	Food Svcs & Drinking Places	13841	18	79	Relig., Grant, Civic, Prof Org	14102	31	58	Exec., Legis., & Other Support
13679	37	181	Justice, Pubic Order/Safety	13842	18	277	Educational Services	14103	358	3518	Hospitals
13680	11	79	Social Assistance	13843	41	230	Educational Services	14105	131	1113	Educational Services
13681	14	22	Relig., Grant, Civic, Prof Org	13844	12	146	Justice, Pubic Order/Safety	14107	6	490	Waste Managmt & Remediat'n Svc
13682	15	115	Justice, Pubic Order/Safety	13845	21	175	Educational Services	14108	134	1256	Hospitals
13683	20	98	Gasoline Stations	13846	9	30	Educational Services	14109	4	464	Educational Services
13684	32	337	Educational Services	13847	10	90	Justice, Pubic Order/Safety	14110	13	78	Food and Beverage Stores
13685	81	503	Food Svcs & Drinking Places	13848	1	2	Postal Service	14111	103	771	Educational Services
13687	9	40	Forestry and Logging	13849	130	607	Wood Product Manufacturing	14112	6	50	Social Assistance
13690	42	321	Educational Services	13850	905	12960	Food Svcs & Drinking Places	14113	16	122	Bldg Matl & Garden Eqpmt Dlrs
13691	59	349	Exec., Legis., & Other Support	13851	2	0	Real Estate	14120	1098	9594	Educational Services
13692	13	32	Construction of Buildings	13856	320	1911	Exec., Legis., & Other Support	14125	82	1089	Nonmetallic Mineral Prod. Mfg
13693	17	91	Justice, Pubic Order/Safety	13859	5	33	Justice, Pubic Order/Safety	14126	36	155	Food Svcs & Drinking Places
13694	59	236	Construction of Buildings	13860	6	14	Food and Beverage Stores	14127	1012	13717	Educational Services
13695	5	28	Educational Services	13861	28	145	Special Trade Contractors	14129	15	199	Exec., Legis., & Other Support
13696	5	2	Bldg Matl & Garden Eqpmt Dlrs	13862	136	1292	Educational Services	14130	18	91	Exec., Legis., & Other Support
13697	42	109	Exec., Legis., & Other Support	13863	9	11	Ambulatory Health Care Svcs	14131	102	429	Transit & Grnd Pass. Transport
13730	112	594	Educational Services	13864	12	25	Special Trade Contractors	14132	164	2860	Other Information Services
13731	87	235	Educational Services	13865	170	643	Educational Services	14133	7	60	Exec., Legis., & Other Support
13732	178	1371	Food Svcs & Drinking Places	13901	1177	14347	Prof., Scientific, & Tech Svcs	14134	17	384	Social Assistance
13733	196	858	Chemical Manufacturing	13902	31	4632	Educational Services	14135	29	120	Justice, Pubic Order/Safety
13734	20	27	Nonmetallic Mineral Prod. Mfg	13903	439	8474	Hospitals	14136	145	1103	Food Manufacturing
13736	40	88	Merch. Wholesalers,Durable Gds	13904	311	4301	Merch. Wholesalers,Nondur. Gds	14138	47	475	Educational Services
13737	1	3	Sportg Gds,Hobby,Book, & Music	13905	923	13789	Educational Services	14139	32	260	Educational Services
13738	1	10	Merch. Wholesalers,Durable Gds	14001	192	2872	Educational Services	14140	5	83	Justice, Pubic Order/Safety
13739	16	52	Food and Beverage Stores	14004	270	3703	Justice, Pubic Order/Safety	14141	338	3769	Educational Services
13740	28	58	Prof., Scientific, & Tech Svcs	14005	39	322	Educational Services	14143	29	208	Food Svcs & Drinking Places
13743	105	615	Educational Services	14006	234	2929	Educational Services	14144	4	135	Educational Services
13744	26	80	Wood Product Manufacturing	14008	22	69	Crop Production	14145	30	190	Food Svcs & Drinking Places
13745	29	215	Fabricated Metal Product Mfg	14009	215	2659	Transportation Equipment Mfg	14150	1320	18721	Ambulatory Health Care Svcs
13746	47	300	Educational Services	14010	2	5	Rental and Leasing Services	14151	3	8	Relig., Grant, Civic, Prof Org
13747	12	232	Electronics & Appliance Stores	14011	164	2746	Justice, Pubic Order/Safety	14167	29	143	Amusement, Gambling,& Recreat.
13748	120	3411	Merch. Wholesalers,Nondur. Gds	14012	68	786	Educational Services	14168	3	8	Food and Beverage Stores
13749	1	1	Postal Service	14013	23	60	Special Trade Contractors	14169	13	142	Justice, Pubic Order/Safety
13750	33	166	Educational Services	14020	1105	12537	Food Svcs & Drinking Places	14170	49	334	Justice, Pubic Order/Safety
13751	16	23	Exec., Legis., & Other Support	14021	3	15	Social Assistance	14171	52	786	Prof., Scientific, & Tech Svcs
13752	18	21	Administrative & Support Svcs	14024	29	101	Crop Production	14172	114	886	Food Svcs & Drinking Places
13753	327	2915	Educational Services	14025	87	327	Food Svcs & Drinking Places	14173	28	287	Educational Services
13754	199	1374	Educational Services	14026	61	599	Special Trade Contractors	14174	149	776	Educational Services
13755	89	444	Justice, Pubic Order/Safety	14027	16	81	Justice, Pubic Order/Safety	14201	301	4005	Nursing & Resid. Care Facilit.
13756	23	62	Mining (Except Oil and Gas)	14028	22	198	Warehousing and Storage	14202	1406	23718	Exec., Legis., & Other Support
13757	14	64	Justice, Pubic Order/Safety	14029	4	10	Exec., Legis., & Other Support	14203	680	18994	Hospitals
13758	6	32	Justice, Pubic Order/Safety	14030	42	279	Food Svcs & Drinking Places	14204	289	4009	Educational Services
13760	1305	12049	Educational Services	14031	381	4884	Educational Services	14205	4	45	Construction of Buildings
13761	1	14	Perform'g Arts, Spec. Sports	14032	156	828	Special Trade Contractors	14206	683	8324	Transit & Grnd Pass. Transport
13762	1	7	Administrative & Support Svcs	14033	55	230	Educational Services	14207	750	14433	Transportation Equipment Mfg
13763	1	1	Social Assistance	14034	51	1069	Justice, Pubic Order/Safety	14208	182	3026	Educational Services
13774	9	26	Forestry and Logging	14035	3	3	Food Svcs & Drinking Places	14209	428	12161	Educational Services
13775	66	180	Educational Services	14036	115	3537	Amusement, Gambling,& Recreat.	14210	398	5276	Merch. Wholesalers,Durable Gds
13776	42	287	Educational Services	14037	14	200	Accommodation	14211	461	4011	Educational Services
13777	14	63	Food Svcs & Drinking Places	14038	8	40	Special Trade Contractors	14212	323	2462	Food and Beverage Stores
13778	221	2348	Machinery Manufacturing	14039	4	9	Mining (Except Oil and Gas)	14213	390	6681	Hospitals
13780	31	79	Educational Services	14040	49	437	Perform'g Arts, Spec. Sports	14214	539	7585	Hospitals
13782	38	210	Miscellaneous Store Retailers	14041	4	4	Postal Service	14215	686	12954	Hospitals
13783	195	1249	Miscellaneous Manufacturing	14042	69	413	Accommodation	14216	616	4288	Food Svcs & Drinking Places
13784	10	64	Justice, Pubic Order/Safety	14043	841	11363	Food Svcs & Drinking Places	14217	731	8120	Hospitals
13786	14	50	Food and Beverage Stores	14047	146	836	Food and Beverage Stores	14218	504	5418	Relig., Grant, Civic, Prof Org
13787	92	498	Educational Services	14048	535	6578	Merch. Wholesalers,Nondur. Gds	14219	495	7839	Transportation Equipment Mfg
13788	42	585	Chemical Manufacturing	14051	358	2385	Educational Services	14220	436	4461	Educational Services
13790	819	11529	Ambulatory Health Care Svcs	14052	578	7286	Merch. Wholesalers,Durable Gds	14221	2675	36483	Ambulatory Health Care Svcs
13794	7	6	Nonmetallic Mineral Prod. Mfg	14054	25	75	Nonmetallic Mineral Prod. Mfg	14222	416	4835	Educational Services
13795	122	3235	Utilities	14055	19	77	Exec., Legis., & Other Support	14223	455	5086	Educational Services
13796	30	168	Educational Services	14056	38	154	Educational Services	14224	1187	15098	Exec., Legis., & Other Support
13797	39	99	Museums, Hist. Sites,& Similar	14057	183	2188	Educational Services	14225	1381	22246	Food Svcs & Drinking Places
13801	24	80	Justice, Pubic Order/Safety	14058	71	839	Merch. Wholesalers,Nondur. Gds	14226	1388	16144	Food Svcs & Drinking Places

BUSINESS DATA

ZIP CODE	2004 Total Firms	2004 Total Employ-ees	TOP INDUSTRY RANKED on 2004 EMPLOYMENT	ZIP CODE	2004 Total Firms	2004 Total Employ-ees	TOP INDUSTRY RANKED on 2004 EMPLOYMENT	ZIP CODE	2004 Total Firms	2004 Total Employ-ees	TOP INDUSTRY RANKED on 2004 EMPLOYMENT
14227	562	8628	Nursing & Resid. Care Facilit.	14532	193	1337	Fabricated Metal Product Mfg	14719	66	481	Educational Services
14228	629	12665	Prof., Scientific, & Tech Svcs	14533	35	369	Chemical Manufacturing	14720	21	139	Educational Services
14231	14	59	Prof., Scientific, & Tech Svcs	14534	1169	9986	Prof., Scientific, & Tech Svcs	14721	9	30	Food Svcs & Drinking Places
14240	5	1002	Postal Service	14536	17	96	Accommodation	14722	51	509	Museums, Hist. Sites,& Similar
14241	1	60	Postal Service	14537	7	81	Truck Transportation	14723	44	233	Merch. Wholesalers,Nondur. Gds
14260	15	1288	Educational Services	14538	13	31	Food Svcs & Drinking Places	14724	86	1335	Accommodation
14261	3	53	Relig., Grant, Civic, Prof Org	14539	13	258	Educational Services	14726	17	51	Merch. Wholesalers,Durable Gds
14263	15	4146	Hospitals	14541	49	204	Educational Services	14727	170	1402	Food Manufacturing
14301	620	5546	Hospitals	14542	12	15	Exec., Legis., & Other Support	14728	29	153	Accommodation
14302	1	160	Support Act. for Transport.	14543	121	1027	Educational Services	14729	17	48	Food Svcs & Drinking Places
14303	334	5942	Accommodation	14544	76	549	Educational Services	14730	9	26	Relig., Grant, Civic, Prof Org
14304	1084	13958	Food Svcs & Drinking Places	14545	4	4	Sportg Gds,Hobby,Book, & Music	14731	165	2299	Real Estate
14305	399	3483	Educational Services	14546	156	2335	Merch. Wholesalers,Durable Gds	14732	24	75	Merch. Wholesalers,Durable Gds
14410	4	2	Miscellaneous Manufacturing	14547	16	55	Merch. Wholesalers,Nondur. Gds	14733	230	3314	Transportation Equipment Mfg
14411	475	5629	Justice, Pubic Order/Safety	14548	96	1031	Educational Services	14735	88	482	Educational Services
14413	13	59	Merch. Wholesalers,Nondur. Gds	14549	5	32	Accommodation	14736	58	134	Accommodation
14414	268	3044	Merch. Wholesalers,Nondur. Gds	14550	47	390	Food and Beverage Stores	14737	127	605	Educational Services
14415	8	10	Crop Production	14551	239	2325	Educational Services	14738	108	773	Educational Services
14416	114	853	Educational Services	14555	57	220	Amusement, Gambling,& Recreat.	14739	58	488	Merch. Wholesalers,Nondur. Gds
14418	41	146	Educational Services	14556	6	8	Amusement, Gambling,& Recreat.	14740	33	648	Nursing & Resid. Care Facilit.
14420	621	7818	Educational Services	14557	4	52	Justice, Pubic Order/Safety	14741	40	263	Crop Production
14422	42	268	Merch. Wholesalers,Durable Gds	14558	3	8	Amusement, Gambling,& Recreat.	14742	8	160	Nursing & Resid. Care Facilit.
14423	159	1842	Prof., Scientific, & Tech Svcs	14559	562	4842	Educational Services	14743	30	180	Educational Services
14424	1254	16717	Nursing & Resid. Care Facilit.	14560	50	121	Exec., Legis., & Other Support	14744	32	285	Nursing & Resid. Care Facilit.
14425	237	3005	Electronics & Appliance Stores	14561	78	344	Educational Services	14745	9	15	Exec., Legis., & Other Support
14427	71	636	Accommodation	14563	11	63	Special Trade Contractors	14747	43	183	Educational Services
14428	174	1071	Educational Services	14564	780	9136	General Merchandise Stores	14748	11	64	Food Svcs & Drinking Places
14429	7	6	Exec., Legis., & Other Support	14568	106	787	Educational Services	14750	313	3899	Merch. Wholesalers,Durable Gds
14430	12	44	Exec., Legis., & Other Support	14569	339	5276	Food Svcs & Drinking Places	14751	8	44	Food and Beverage Stores
14432	209	2950	Hospitals	14571	29	140	Merch. Wholesalers,Nondur. Gds	14752	18	20	Relig., Grant, Civic, Prof Org
14433	115	1111	Construction of Buildings	14572	152	2001	Educational Services	14753	42	161	Gasoline Stations
14435	42	391	Admin. Enviro. Quality Progrms	14580	1351	12400	Ambulatory Health Care Svcs	14754	13	29	Prof., Scientific, & Tech Svcs
14437	394	2894	Hospitals	14585	21	85	Heavy & Civil Eng. Construct'N	14755	103	1147	Justice, Pubic Order/Safety
14441	15	80	Justice, Pubic Order/Safety	14586	127	2746	Transportation Equipment Mfg	14756	7	131	Museums, Hist. Sites,& Similar
14443	9	371	Miscellaneous Manufacturing	14588	10	429	Exec., Legis., & Other Support	14757	274	3381	Justice, Pubic Order/Safety
14445	421	3706	Educational Services	14589	225	1792	Educational Services	14758	2	3	Relig., Grant, Civic, Prof Org
14449	8	27	Special Trade Contractors	14590	200	2044	Educational Services	14760	998	14737	Machinery Manufacturing
14450	1328	14663	Electronics & Appliance Stores	14591	51	488	Primary Metal Manufacturing	14766	7	10	Heavy & Civil Eng. Construct'N
14452	4	35	Amusement, Gambling,& Recreat.	14592	17	138	Forestry and Logging	14767	43	231	Educational Services
14453	27	679	Merch. Wholesalers,Durable Gds	14602	6	71	Prof., Scientific, & Tech Svcs	14769	27	51	Crop Production
14454	392	4625	Educational Services	14603	14	51	Postal Service	14770	92	572	Food Svcs & Drinking Places
14456	856	9952	Hospitals	14604	712	16546	Prof., Scientific, & Tech Svcs	14772	113	1081	Educational Services
14461	38	223	Construction of Buildings	14605	421	7143	Educational Services	14774	10	54	Educational Services
14462	23	32	Exec., Legis., & Other Support	14606	921	17497	Transportation Equipment Mfg	14775	69	365	Educational Services
14463	20	105	Merch. Wholesalers,Nondur. Gds	14607	1210	11528	Ambulatory Health Care Svcs	14777	37	184	Educational Services
14464	144	710	Food and Beverage Stores	14608	441	5064	Educational Services	14778	7	573	Educational Services
14466	55	235	Justice, Pubic Order/Safety	14609	990	9180	Miscellaneous Manufacturing	14779	290	3072	Educational Services
14467	268	4290	Justice, Pubic Order/Safety	14610	503	7739	Computer & Electronic Prod Mfg	14781	86	401	Educational Services
14468	366	2132	Educational Services	14611	665	10777	Health & Personal Care Stores	14782	60	525	Educational Services
14469	213	1158	Educational Services	14612	613	5628	Educational Services	14783	22	117	Justice, Pubic Order/Safety
14470	139	945	Educational Services	14613	271	3188	Educational Services	14784	22	44	Relig., Grant, Civic, Prof Org
14471	169	1223	Educational Services	14614	904	15942	Exec., Legis., & Other Support	14785	19	96	Exec., Legis., & Other Support
14472	273	2166	Educational Services	14615	475	5665	Food Svcs & Drinking Places	14786	5	19	Prof., Scientific, & Tech Svcs
14475	13	26	Construction of Buildings	14616	503	3696	Food and Beverage Stores	14787	309	2011	Ambulatory Health Care Svcs
14476	34	547	Educational Services	14617	499	3712	Educational Services	14788	13	147	Furn. & Home Furnishgs Stores
14477	18	34	Food Svcs & Drinking Places	14618	1270	12868	Ambulatory Health Care Svcs	14801	154	820	Educational Services
14478	16	316	Educational Services	14619	175	1065	Educational Services	14802	85	1642	Educational Services
14479	7	15	Merch. Wholesalers,Nondur. Gds	14620	755	18522	Hospitals	14803	52	315	Nonmetallic Mineral Prod. Mfg
14480	102	556	Food Svcs & Drinking Places	14621	878	9985	Nursing & Resid. Care Facilit.	14804	38	298	Educational Services
14481	55	576	Food Manufacturing	14622	423	4061	Amusement, Gambling,& Recreat.	14805	16	19	Accommodation
14482	282	2398	Nonmetallic Mineral Prod. Mfg	14623	1828	34169	Prof., Scientific, & Tech Svcs	14806	76	376	Educational Services
14485	132	905	Educational Services	14624	1393	20199	Food and Beverage Stores	14807	67	537	Food Manufacturing
14486	4	17	Bldg Matl & Garden Eqpmt Dlrs	14625	572	7785	Isps, Web Search Portals	14808	17	59	Merch. Wholesalers,Durable Gds
14487	146	841	Educational Services	14626	1069	13827	Hospitals	14809	78	479	Educational Services
14488	1	0	Relig., Grant, Civic, Prof Org	14627	8	171	Other Information Services	14810	541	7941	Relig., Grant, Civic, Prof Org
14489	302	3162	Exec., Legis., & Other Support	14642	110	3958	Ambulatory Health Care Svcs	14812	41	317	Justice, Pubic Order/Safety
14502	312	3018	Plastics & Rubber Products Mfg	14643	3	1	Personal and Laundry Services	14813	129	1223	Admin. Human Resource Programs
14504	48	367	Plastics & Rubber Products Mfg	14644	1	15	Prof., Scientific, & Tech Svcs	14814	115	1027	Miscellaneous Manufacturing
14505	139	1017	Food Manufacturing	14646	1	500	Computer & Electronic Prod Mfg	14815	12	64	Educational Services
14506	107	649	Relig., Grant, Civic, Prof Org	14647	6	1237	Insurance Carriers & Related	14816	15	35	Educational Services
14507	56	189	Merch. Wholesalers,Nondur. Gds	14649	1	312	Managmt of Companies & Enterp.	14817	45	241	Social Assistance
14508	5	43	Justice, Pubic Order/Safety	14650	5	2563	Machinery Manufacturing	14818	58	164	Exec., Legis., & Other Support
14510	198	1938	Admin. Human Resource Programs	14652	6	30	Miscellaneous Manufacturing	14819	7	13	Exec., Legis., & Other Support
14511	28	343	Museums, Hist. Sites,& Similar	14653	2	5	Ambulatory Health Care Svcs	14820	5	30	Heavy & Civil Eng. Construct'N
14512	220	822	Food Svcs & Drinking Places	14692	24	2325	Postal Service	14821	67	753	Merch. Wholesalers,Nondur. Gds
14513	575	10419	Social Assistance	14694	2	652	Print'g & Related Supp't Act's	14822	36	110	Educational Services
14514	112	761	Food and Beverage Stores	14701	1751	24262	Furniture & Related Prod. Mfg	14823	116	683	Educational Services
14515	8	26	Administrative & Support Svcs	14702	4	4	Exec., Legis., & Other Support	14824	18	160	Bldg Matl & Garden Eqpmt Dlrs
14516	56	437	Educational Services	14706	170	1218	Educational Services	14825	23	139	Justice, Pubic Order/Safety
14517	102	726	Educational Services	14707	8	11	Heavy & Civil Eng. Construct'N	14826	58	241	Educational Services
14518	4	276	Miscellaneous Manufacturing	14708	1	0	Relig., Grant, Civic, Prof Org	14827	12	35	Heavy & Civil Eng. Construct'N
14519	331	1870	Food Svcs & Drinking Places	14709	55	287	Justice, Pubic Order/Safety	14830	770	7333	Educational Services
14520	11	407	Educational Services	14710	97	573	Educational Services	14831	4	1707	Prof., Scientific, & Tech Svcs
14521	130	550	Food Svcs & Drinking Places	14711	44	187	Educational Services	14836	15	163	Educational Services
14522	304	2769	Miscellaneous Manufacturing	14712	116	934	Food Svcs & Drinking Places	14837	176	1025	Educational Services
14525	72	958	Educational Services	14714	6	17	Social Assistance	14838	24	104	Unclassified Establishments
14526	545	4081	Food and Beverage Stores	14715	81	400	Justice, Pubic Order/Safety	14839	25	32	Heavy & Civil Eng. Construct'N
14527	602	4906	Hospitals	14716	87	417	Educational Services	14840	167	1121	Educational Services
14529	6	15	Food Svcs & Drinking Places	14717	17	17	Admin. Enviro. Quality Progrms	14841	47	152	Beverage & Tobacco Product Mfg
14530	198	1975	Food Svcs & Drinking Places	14718	72	479	Educational Services	14842	26	80	Accommodation

ZIP CODE	2004 Total Firms	2004 Total Employees	TOP INDUSTRY RANKED on 2004 EMPLOYMENT	ZIP CODE	2004 Total Firms	2004 Total Employees	TOP INDUSTRY RANKED on 2004 EMPLOYMENT	ZIP CODE	2004 Total Firms	2004 Total Employees	TOP INDUSTRY RANKED on 2004 EMPLOYMENT
14843	561	7566	Real Estate	15050	55	278	Educational Services	15222	2199	48017	Prof., Scientific, & Tech Svcs
14844	2	40	Miscellaneous Store Retailers	15051	33	1320	Miscellaneous Manufacturing	15223	312	2374	Food Svcs & Drinking Places
14845	802	11079	Merch. Wholesalers,Durable Gds	15052	65	353	Food Svcs & Drinking Places	15224	518	6149	Hospitals
14846	14	46	Bldg Matl & Garden Eqpmt Dlrs	15053	2	6	Construction of Buildings	15225	124	2071	Chemical Manufacturing
14847	89	547	Educational Services	15054	9	120	Primary Metal Manufacturing	15226	375	3591	Food Svcs & Drinking Places
14850	2464	30537	Educational Services	15055	56	1412	Merch. Wholesalers,Durable Gds	15227	614	3727	Educational Services
14851	6	77	Relig., Grant, Civic, Prof Org	15056	107	1736	Primary Metal Manufacturing	15228	646	4021	Educational Services
14852	2	1	Administrative & Support Svcs	15057	224	1467	Educational Services	15229	351	3164	Educational Services
14853	65	1745	Educational Services	15059	154	1218	Primary Metal Manufacturing	15230	6	33	Social Assistance
14854	11	21	Nursing & Resid. Care Facilit.	15060	29	195	Amusement, Gambling,& Recreat.	15231	84	1782	Food Svcs & Drinking Places
14855	25	163	Educational Services	15061	588	7284	Chemical Manufacturing	15232	489	7214	Hospitals
14856	9	66	Food Svcs & Drinking Places	15062	285	2153	Primary Metal Manufacturing	15233	329	6535	Hospitals
14857	9	64	Educational Services	15063	390	4956	Hospitals	15234	628	4415	Food and Beverage Stores
14858	23	82	Exec., Legis., & Other Support	15064	38	313	Exec., Legis., & Other Support	15235	1230	10493	Food Svcs & Drinking Places
14859	9	23	Food Svcs & Drinking Places	15065	438	4620	Hospitals	15236	1097	12723	Hospitals
14860	41	192	Beverage & Tobacco Product Mfg	15066	437	2796	Social Assistance	15237	2071	19433	Food Svcs & Drinking Places
14861	21	46	Bldg Matl & Garden Eqpmt Dlrs	15067	62	352	Nonmetallic Mineral Prod. Mfg	15238	875	14788	Food and Beverage Stores
14863	5	5	Support Activities: Agr./For.	15068	1374	12449	Primary Metal Manufacturing	15239	605	4772	Food Svcs & Drinking Places
14864	32	92	Exec., Legis., & Other Support	15069	2	47	Administrative & Support Svcs	15240	7	1033	Hospitals
14865	118	1076	Hospitals	15071	292	2831	Food Svcs & Drinking Places	15241	826	6451	Educational Services
14867	90	350	Waste Managmt & Remediat'n Svc	15072	6	5	Merch. Wholesalers,Nondur. Gds	15242	8	17	Construction of Buildings
14869	58	337	Educational Services	15074	363	3581	Social Assistance	15243	243	3164	Hospitals
14870	269	4182	Machinery Manufacturing	15075	5	8	Relig., Grant, Civic, Prof Org	15244	4	11	Administrative & Support Svcs
14871	79	457	Nonmetallic Mineral Prod. Mfg	15076	55	371	Educational Services	15253	1	0	Insurance Carriers & Related
14872	16	34	Food and Beverage Stores	15077	9	66	Mining (Except Oil and Gas)	15258	5	77	Securities/Commodity Contracts
14873	91	482	Bldg Matl & Garden Eqpmt Dlrs	15078	22	143	Fabricated Metal Product Mfg	15259	4	8076	Credit Intermediation & Relatd
14874	26	29	Exec., Legis., & Other Support	15081	18	65	Support Act. for Transport.	15260	15	9098	Educational Services
14876	7	19	Exec., Legis., & Other Support	15082	10	14	Heavy & Civil Eng. Construct'N	15261	24	210	Ambulatory Health Care Svcs
14877	9	13	Heavy & Civil Eng. Construct'N	15083	35	75	Special Trade Contractors	15272	1	1300	Chemical Manufacturing
14878	17	43	Pipeline Transportation	15084	363	2355	Truck Transportation	15275	148	5796	Merch. Wholesalers,Durable Gds
14879	37	193	Educational Services	15085	218	1213	Heavy & Civil Eng. Construct'N	15276	57	864	Prof., Scientific, & Tech Svcs
14880	34	203	Educational Services	15086	169	8254	Telecommunications	15290	4	14	Postal Service
14881	21	83	Educational Services	15087	16	27	Fabricated Metal Product Mfg	15301	2201	24395	Food Svcs & Drinking Places
14882	135	1016	Food and Beverage Stores	15088	49	594	Merch. Wholesalers,Nondur. Gds	15310	7	18	Educational Services
14883	113	587	Educational Services	15089	221	971	Nonstore Retailers	15311	22	36	Merch. Wholesalers,Durable Gds
14884	8	556	Accommodation	15090	1000	7006	Prof., Scientific, & Tech Svcs	15312	74	389	Educational Services
14885	27	174	Educational Services	15091	11	80	Motor Vehicle & Parts Dealers	15313	25	192	Ambulatory Health Care Svcs
14886	287	1183	Justice, Pubic Order/Safety	15095	1	40	Special Trade Contractors	15314	176	1504	Mining (Except Oil and Gas)
14887	9	59	Accommodation	15096	1	3	Prof., Scientific, & Tech Svcs	15315	17	71	Educational Services
14889	36	250	Educational Services	15101	658	5314	Chemical Manufacturing	15316	7	144	Fabricated Metal Product Mfg
14891	284	2624	Educational Services	15102	1039	8037	Food Svcs & Drinking Places	15317	1537	15187	Prof., Scientific, & Tech Svcs
14892	242	2499	Ambulatory Health Care Svcs	15104	240	2816	Hospitals	15320	214	1069	Educational Services
14893	21	25	Machinery Manufacturing	15106	922	7311	Prof., Scientific, & Tech Svcs	15321	72	252	Primary Metal Manufacturing
14894	36	122	Electronics & Appliance Stores	15108	1401	20121	Prof., Scientific, & Tech Svcs	15322	34	122	Nursing & Resid. Care Facilit.
14895	415	5345	Machinery Manufacturing	15110	181	1226	Textile Product Mills	15323	130	925	Educational Services
14897	32	94	Educational Services	15112	113	542	Relig., Grant, Civic, Prof Org	15324	16	232	Relig., Grant, Civic, Prof Org
14898	40	132	Food and Beverage Stores	15116	371	2620	Food and Beverage Stores	15325	5	21	Justice, Pubic Order/Safety
14901	834	13127	Hospitals	15120	625	4868	Food Svcs & Drinking Places	15327	23	81	Merch. Wholesalers,Durable Gds
14902	3	10	Social Assistance	15122	570	9690	Primary Metal Manufacturing	15329	40	234	Social Assistance
14903	386	6063	Transportation Equipment Mfg	15123	146	1477	Clothing & Cloth'g Acc. Stores	15330	168	3366	Heavy & Civil Eng. Construct'N
14904	385	3747	Educational Services	15126	224	1737	Educational Services	15331	23	64	Educational Services
14905	203	2698	Hospitals	15127	33	210	Food and Beverage Stores	15332	199	1312	Food and Beverage Stores
15001	939	6728	Securities/Commodity Contracts	15129	185	897	Educational Services	15333	71	496	Educational Services
15003	536	3684	Primary Metal Manufacturing	15131	377	2573	Ambulatory Health Care Svcs	15334	7	30	Nonmetallic Mineral Prod. Mfg
15004	13	62	Wood Product Manufacturing	15132	849	9662	Hospitals	15336	6	6	Miscellaneous Store Retailers
15005	204	1568	Ambulatory Health Care Svcs	15133	97	586	Educational Services	15337	32	74	Educational Services
15006	6	28	Fabricated Metal Product Mfg	15134	4	27	Social Assistance	15338	54	313	Educational Services
15007	41	225	Motor Vehicle & Parts Dealers	15135	88	699	Relig., Grant, Civic, Prof Org	15339	6	77	Merch. Wholesalers,Nondur. Gds
15009	684	10777	Hospitals	15136	809	6917	Hospitals	15340	81	272	Food Svcs & Drinking Places
15010	1044	8347	Educational Services	15137	417	4307	General Merchandise Stores	15341	14	16	Special Trade Contractors
15012	654	5475	Food Svcs & Drinking Places	15139	370	3698	Nursing & Resid. Care Facilit.	15342	137	1811	Machinery Manufacturing
15014	95	2424	Primary Metal Manufacturing	15140	93	377	Exec., Legis., & Other Support	15344	54	431	Apparel Manufacturing
15015	28	210	Educational Services	15142	39	340	Amusement, Gambling,& Recreat.	15345	55	86	Relig., Grant, Civic, Prof Org
15017	818	9783	Prof., Scientific, & Tech Svcs	15143	759	6438	Hospitals	15346	12	24	Exec., Legis., & Other Support
15018	22	141	Machinery Manufacturing	15144	171	1572	Chemical Manufacturing	15347	70	1045	Perform'g Arts, Spec. Sports
15019	20	37	Food and Beverage Stores	15145	234	1815	Special Trade Contractors	15348	17	55	Food and Beverage Stores
15020	9	105	Chemical Manufacturing	15146	1671	19829	Food Svcs & Drinking Places	15349	66	561	Miscellaneous Manufacturing
15021	246	2263	Perform'g Arts, Spec. Sports	15147	406	3617	Nursing & Resid. Care Facilit.	15350	10	28	Educational Services
15022	487	3730	Educational Services	15148	122	1248	Transportation Equipment Mfg	15351	8	39	Justice, Pubic Order/Safety
15024	256	3291	Prof., Scientific, & Tech Svcs	15201	607	6912	Special Trade Contractors	15352	27	58	Justice, Pubic Order/Safety
15025	462	3741	Educational Services	15202	608	4306	Hospitals	15353	5	23	Justice, Pubic Order/Safety
15026	78	712	Support Act. for Transport.	15203	748	8589	Food Svcs & Drinking Places	15357	59	499	Relig., Grant, Civic, Prof Org
15027	58	305	Food Svcs & Drinking Places	15204	142	756	Special Trade Contractors	15358	25	129	Food and Beverage Stores
15028	2	2	Postal Service	15205	1144	18086	Prof., Scientific, & Tech Svcs	15359	22	90	Ambulatory Health Care Svcs
15030	56	650	Bldg Matl & Garden Eqpmt Dlrs	15206	1030	12497	Prof., Scientific, & Tech Svcs	15360	69	160	Food Svcs & Drinking Places
15031	26	299	Construction of Buildings	15207	209	1601	Nursing & Resid. Care Facilit.	15361	2	1	Repair and Maintenance
15032	11	33	Relig., Grant, Civic, Prof Org	15208	297	2596	Educational Services	15362	11	28	Special Trade Contractors
15033	191	1347	Fabricated Metal Product Mfg	15209	350	2510	Transit & Grnd Pass. Transport	15363	19	128	Social Assistance
15034	86	589	Transit & Grnd Pass. Transport	15210	570	2802	Educational Services	15364	12	59	Fabricated Metal Product Mfg
15035	80	433	Ambulatory Health Care Svcs	15211	197	1337	Food Svcs & Drinking Places	15365	9	27	Special Trade Contractors
15036	2	1	Postal Service	15212	1051	11178	Ambulatory Health Care Svcs	15366	2	2	Postal Service
15037	346	2380	Educational Services	15213	1143	52833	Hospitals	15367	93	393	Transit & Grnd Pass. Transport
15038	12	46	Merch. Wholesalers,Nondur. Gds	15214	175	1478	Educational Services	15368	8	16	Social Assistance
15042	144	1380	Prof., Scientific, & Tech Svcs	15215	553	4462	Hospitals	15370	669	5999	Justice, Pubic Order/Safety
15043	42	246	Support Act. for Transport.	15216	723	4991	Food Svcs & Drinking Places	15376	39	124	Chemical Manufacturing
15044	684	5950	Truck Transportation	15217	812	7030	Food Svcs & Drinking Places	15377	19	426	Mining (Except Oil and Gas)
15045	130	614	Merch. Wholesalers,Durable Gds	15218	434	3278	Educational Services	15378	6	18	Print'g & Related Supp't Act's
15046	64	446	Fabricated Metal Product Mfg	15219	2321	47868	Prof., Scientific, & Tech Svcs	15379	6	8	Securities/Commodity Contracts
15047	8	42	Special Trade Contractors	15220	1061	14232	Prof., Scientific, & Tech Svcs	15380	23	113	Special Trade Contractors
15049	18	366	Relig., Grant, Civic, Prof Org	15221	935	7086	Educational Services	15401	1752	17465	Food Svcs & Drinking Places

ZIP CODE	2004 Total Firms	2004 Total Employees	TOP INDUSTRY RANKED on 2004 EMPLOYMENT	ZIP CODE	2004 Total Firms	2004 Total Employees	TOP INDUSTRY RANKED on 2004 EMPLOYMENT	ZIP CODE	2004 Total Firms	2004 Total Employees	TOP INDUSTRY RANKED on 2004 EMPLOYMENT
15410	7	30	Mining (Except Oil and Gas)	15544	4	4	Postal Service	15691	7	21	Fabricated Metal Product Mfg
15411	32	101	Wood Product Manufacturing	15545	75	284	Educational Services	15692	20	43	Administrative & Support Svcs
15412	13	274	Primary Metal Manufacturing	15546	11	16	Relig., Grant, Civic, Prof Org	15693	15	70	Relig., Grant, Civic, Prof Org
15413	10	28	Fabricated Metal Product Mfg	15547	42	330	Accommodation	15695	5	20	Food and Beverage Stores
15415	6	48	Mining (Except Oil and Gas)	15548	4	7	Merch. Wholesalers,Durable Gds	15696	38	309	Prof., Scientific, & Tech Svcs
15416	1	2	Relig., Grant, Civic, Prof Org	15549	3	3	Food Svcs & Drinking Places	15697	204	1454	Computer & Electronic Prod Mfg
15417	308	1983	Hospitals	15550	50	204	Merch. Wholesalers,Durable Gds	15698	39	117	Machinery Manufacturing
15419	113	1183	Educational Services	15551	11	50	Merch. Wholesalers,Durable Gds	15701	1585	17023	Food Svcs & Drinking Places
15420	5	11	Sportg Gds,Hobby,Book, & Music	15552	192	1528	Apparel Manufacturing	15705	6	2282	Educational Services
15421	20	76	Museums, Hist. Sites,& Similar	15553	4	9	Relig., Grant, Civic, Prof Org	15710	6	4	Gasoline Stations
15422	1	2	Postal Service	15554	67	255	Educational Services	15711	11	70	Justice, Pubic Order/Safety
15423	51	564	Educational Services	15555	1	1	Repair and Maintenance	15712	1	2	Food and Beverage Stores
15424	77	417	Educational Services	15557	128	1095	Educational Services	15713	3	4	Merch. Wholesalers,Durable Gds
15425	715	6034	Nonmetallic Mineral Prod. Mfg	15558	61	379	Truck Transportation	15714	226	1214	Educational Services
15427	19	36	Relig., Grant, Civic, Prof Org	15559	68	156	Museums, Hist. Sites,& Similar	15715	31	169	Machinery Manufacturing
15428	35	164	Food Svcs & Drinking Places	15560	15	90	Educational Services	15716	26	195	Special Trade Contractors
15429	4	13	Food Svcs & Drinking Places	15561	7	20	Educational Services	15717	386	3042	Primary Metal Manufacturing
15430	3	7	Motor Vehicle & Parts Dealers	15562	23	170	Heavy & Civil Eng. Construct'N	15720	14	16	Motor Vehicle & Parts Dealers
15431	105	648	Ambulatory Health Care Svcs	15563	109	747	Fabricated Metal Product Mfg	15721	11	20	Wood Product Manufacturing
15432	16	58	Electronics & Appliance Stores	15564	2	4	Electronics & Appliance Stores	15722	104	507	Educational Services
15433	13	63	Educational Services	15565	5	27	Primary Metal Manufacturing	15723	1	0	Postal Service
15434	8	48	Nursing & Resid. Care Facilit.	15601	2917	30606	Food Svcs & Drinking Places	15724	65	283	Relig., Grant, Civic, Prof Org
15435	16	26	Repair and Maintenance	15606	1	9	Credit Intermediation & Relatd	15725	28	67	Unclassified Establishments
15436	97	401	Food and Beverage Stores	15610	100	438	Food Svcs & Drinking Places	15727	1	2	Postal Service
15437	91	1303	Accommodation	15611	27	250	Motor Vehicle & Parts Dealers	15728	135	847	Educational Services
15438	51	138	Nursing & Resid. Care Facilit.	15612	12	158	Educational Services	15729	30	411	Educational Services
15440	3	1	Postal Service	15613	385	2215	Machinery Manufacturing	15730	7	26	Museums, Hist. Sites,& Similar
15442	53	636	Prof., Scientific, & Tech Svcs	15615	6	12	Construction of Buildings	15731	4	16	Waste Managmt & Remediat'n Svc
15443	1	2	Postal Service	15616	7	42	Bldg Matl & Garden Eqpmt Dlrs	15732	33	83	Educational Services
15444	14	20	Administrative & Support Svcs	15617	13	23	Food Svcs & Drinking Places	15733	6	23	Nursing & Resid. Care Facilit.
15445	115	750	Ambulatory Health Care Svcs	15618	91	732	Primary Metal Manufacturing	15734	13	214	Nonmetallic Mineral Prod. Mfg
15446	25	75	Telecommunications	15619	12	60	Scenic & Sightseeing Transport	15736	57	377	Educational Services
15447	6	40	Amusement, Gambling,& Recreat.	15620	29	132	Crop Production	15737	16	56	Construction of Buildings
15448	3	4	Postal Service	15621	8	22	Merch. Wholesalers,Durable Gds	15738	4	8	Ambulatory Health Care Svcs
15449	2	3	Postal Service	15622	58	1428	Accommodation	15739	6	0	Food and Beverage Stores
15450	7	111	Justice, Pubic Order/Safety	15623	13	109	Educational Services	15741	4	5	Clothing & Cloth'g Acc. Stores
15451	11	46	Mining (Except Oil and Gas)	15624	15	160	Food Svcs & Drinking Places	15742	19	80	Nursing & Resid. Care Facilit.
15454	3	2	Postal Service	15625	8	32	Repair and Maintenance	15744	7	49	Nonmetallic Mineral Prod. Mfg
15455	8	15	Relig., Grant, Civic, Prof Org	15626	227	1965	Food Svcs & Drinking Places	15745	9	13	Relig., Grant, Civic, Prof Org
15456	72	868	Social Assistance	15627	185	948	Educational Services	15746	14	239	Relig., Grant, Civic, Prof Org
15458	77	363	Educational Services	15628	77	359	Food Svcs & Drinking Places	15747	41	243	Educational Services
15459	78	563	Nursing & Resid. Care Facilit.	15629	17	36	Relig., Grant, Civic, Prof Org	15748	199	1751	Machinery Manufacturing
15460	1	1	Postal Service	15631	23	136	Merch. Wholesalers,Nondur. Gds	15750	4	13	Merch. Wholesalers,Durable Gds
15461	154	1071	Machinery Manufacturing	15632	299	3365	Relig., Grant, Civic, Prof Org	15752	3	8	Transit & Grnd Pass. Transport
15462	20	73	Educational Services	15633	8	52	Machinery Manufacturing	15753	11	10	Merch. Wholesalers,Durable Gds
15463	6	10	Construction of Buildings	15634	13	33	Food Svcs & Drinking Places	15754	10	68	Computer & Electronic Prod Mfg
15464	38	345	Transit & Grnd Pass. Transport	15635	6	6	Repair and Maintenance	15756	5	6	Food Svcs & Drinking Places
15465	21	171	Merch. Wholesalers,Durable Gds	15636	107	702	Exec., Legis., & Other Support	15757	56	268	Educational Services
15466	8	47	Chemical Manufacturing	15637	85	461	Educational Services	15758	2	0	Postal Service
15467	2	4	Construction of Buildings	15638	7	9	Relig., Grant, Civic, Prof Org	15759	76	428	Educational Services
15468	55	263	Justice, Pubic Order/Safety	15639	47	242	Food Svcs & Drinking Places	15760	3	4	Special Trade Contractors
15469	53	201	Educational Services	15640	2	2	Postal Service	15761	2	31	Special Trade Contractors
15470	33	411	Motor Vehicle & Parts Dealers	15641	7	53	Primary Metal Manufacturing	15762	22	167	Wood Product Manufacturing
15472	7	40	Repair and Maintenance	15642	1367	12026	Food Svcs & Drinking Places	15764	5	33	Special Trade Contractors
15473	135	877	Educational Services	15644	639	5103	Hospitals	15765	62	410	Bldg Matl & Garden Eqpmt Dlrs
15474	67	381	Nonmetallic Mineral Prod. Mfg	15646	42	150	Relig., Grant, Civic, Prof Org	15767	669	5186	Fabricated Metal Product Mfg
15475	61	210	Food Manufacturing	15647	11	35	Fabricated Metal Product Mfg	15770	8	49	Prof., Scientific, & Tech Svcs
15476	3	1	Postal Service	15650	1217	14058	Hospitals	15771	27	149	Merch. Wholesalers,Nondur. Gds
15477	28	137	Paper Manufacturing	15655	28	171	Special Trade Contractors	15772	29	133	Nursing & Resid. Care Facilit.
15478	140	843	Merch. Wholesalers,Durable Gds	15656	358	4955	Primary Metal Manufacturing	15773	14	94	Special Trade Contractors
15479	63	1168	Sportg Gds,Hobby,Book, & Music	15658	459	3130	Amusement, Gambling,& Recreat.	15774	97	470	Heavy & Civil Eng. Construct'N
15480	38	179	Administrative & Support Svcs	15660	5	118	Merch. Wholesalers,Durable Gds	15775	12	29	Isps, Web Search Portals
15482	19	92	Food Svcs & Drinking Places	15661	36	260	Primary Metal Manufacturing	15777	8	8	Food Svcs & Drinking Places
15483	9	67	Justice, Pubic Order/Safety	15662	3	7	Waste Managmt & Remediat'n Svc	15778	3	13	Bldg Matl & Garden Eqpmt Dlrs
15484	4	7	Truck Transportation	15663	21	164	Relig., Grant, Civic, Prof Org	15779	11	608	Hospitals
15485	1	2	Relig., Grant, Civic, Prof Org	15664	15	179	Merch. Wholesalers,Durable Gds	15780	7	45	Justice, Pubic Order/Safety
15486	46	159	Special Trade Contractors	15665	59	225	Chemical Manufacturing	15781	4	4	Postal Service
15488	11	34	Textile Product Mills	15666	714	7702	Prof., Scientific, & Tech Svcs	15783	4	11	Relig., Grant, Civic, Prof Org
15489	6	4	Postal Service	15668	586	5989	Ambulatory Health Care Svcs	15784	4	3	Repair and Maintenance
15490	17	62	Merch. Wholesalers,Durable Gds	15670	159	749	Educational Services	15801	1129	15262	Ambulatory Health Care Svcs
15492	3	0	Special Trade Contractors	15671	13	46	Educational Services	15821	9	33	Food and Beverage Stores
15501	1139	12700	Food Svcs & Drinking Places	15672	153	2309	Food and Beverage Stores	15822	3	2	Miscellaneous Store Retailers
15502	9	314	Accommodation	15673	45	297	Food and Beverage Stores	15823	29	235	Machinery Manufacturing
15510	1	550	Justice, Pubic Order/Safety	15674	50	418	Apparel Manufacturing	15824	201	1891	Machinery Manufacturing
15520	4	3	Postal Service	15675	25	263	Merch. Wholesalers,Nondur. Gds	15825	568	5653	Merch. Wholesalers,Durable Gds
15521	68	476	Plastics & Rubber Products Mfg	15676	43	159	Justice, Pubic Order/Safety	15827	8	46	Insurance Carriers & Related
15522	766	7211	Miscellaneous Manufacturing	15677	17	116	Relig., Grant, Civic, Prof Org	15828	18	53	Accommodation
15530	160	1250	Food Manufacturing	15678	20	76	Fabricated Metal Product Mfg	15829	36	122	Administrative & Support Svcs
15531	139	795	Accommodation	15679	95	629	Educational Services	15831	3	5	Relig., Grant, Civic, Prof Org
15532	4	14	Bldg Matl & Garden Eqpmt Dlrs	15680	11	55	Educational Services	15832	14	20	Miscellaneous Store Retailers
15533	99	1027	Food Svcs & Drinking Places	15681	160	1364	Fabricated Metal Product Mfg	15834	257	2169	Primary Metal Manufacturing
15534	15	20	Postal Service	15682	8	129	Real Estate	15840	85	598	Chemical Manufacturing
15535	40	87	Bldg Matl & Garden Eqpmt Dlrs	15683	288	3090	Paper Manufacturing	15841	11	29	Ambulatory Health Care Svcs
15536	12	60	Wood Product Manufacturing	15684	24	59	Relig., Grant, Civic, Prof Org	15845	127	1217	Paper Manufacturing
15537	382	2944	Wood Product Manufacturing	15685	11	14	Relig., Grant, Civic, Prof Org	15846	97	848	Fabricated Metal Product Mfg
15538	11	11	Special Trade Contractors	15686	38	379	Educational Services	15847	5	10	Construction of Buildings
15539	24	96	Crop Production	15687	59	220	Personal and Laundry Services	15848	21	86	Utilities
15540	8	186	Mining (Except Oil and Gas)	15688	14	180	Special Trade Contractors	15849	46	351	Mining (Except Oil and Gas)
15541	96	605	Nonstore Retailers	15689	9	58	Relig., Grant, Civic, Prof Org	15851	207	1203	Educational Services
15542	20	56	Social Assistance	15690	319	2417	Relig., Grant, Civic, Prof Org	15853	361	3980	Exec., Legis., & Other Support

ZIP CODE	2004 Total Firms	2004 Total Employees	TOP INDUSTRY RANKED on 2004 EMPLOYMENT	ZIP CODE	2004 Total Firms	2004 Total Employees	TOP INDUSTRY RANKED on 2004 EMPLOYMENT	ZIP CODE	2004 Total Firms	2004 Total Employees	TOP INDUSTRY RANKED on 2004 EMPLOYMENT
15856	22	49	Furn. & Home Furnishgs Stores	16061	91	911	Administrative & Support Svcs	16262	109	1075	Food Manufacturing
15857	709	9936	Chemical Manufacturing	16063	423	4501	Prof., Scientific, & Tech Svcs	16263	11	37	Relig., Grant, Civic, Prof Org
15860	39	140	Food Svcs & Drinking Places	16066	1076	13371	Nursing & Resid. Care Facilit.	16301	582	6631	Support Act. for Transport.
15861	7	9	Postal Service	16101	1699	16489	Food Svcs & Drinking Places	16311	28	186	Support Activities for Mining
15863	8	14	Bldg Matl & Garden Eqpmt Dlrs	16102	170	1077	Transportation Equipment Mfg	16312	4	2	Gasoline Stations
15864	53	311	Prof., Scientific, & Tech Svcs	16103	5	24	Fabricated Metal Product Mfg	16313	57	419	Justice, Pubic Order/Safety
15865	54	283	Primary Metal Manufacturing	16105	580	8032	Nursing & Resid. Care Facilit.	16314	228	1356	Plastics & Rubber Products Mfg
15866	4	7	Food Manufacturing	16107	3	19	Machinery Manufacturing	16316	259	1556	Amusement, Gambling,& Recreat.
15868	57	138	Educational Services	16108	3	300	Prof., Scientific, & Tech Svcs	16317	45	212	Repair and Maintenance
15870	40	200	Fabricated Metal Product Mfg	16110	9	43	Fabricated Metal Product Mfg	16319	95	879	Food Svcs & Drinking Places
15901	599	7636	Hospitals	16111	25	64	Food and Beverage Stores	16321	5	19	Food Svcs & Drinking Places
15902	344	2668	Relig., Grant, Civic, Prof Org	16112	63	435	Educational Services	16322	7	93	Merch. Wholesalers,Durable Gds
15904	926	13207	Food Svcs & Drinking Places	16113	11	108	Accommodation	16323	754	10188	Relig., Grant, Civic, Prof Org
15905	664	12029	Hospitals	16114	22	31	Exec., Legis., & Other Support	16326	23	114	Credit Intermediation & Relatd
15906	272	2181	Merch. Wholesalers,Durable Gds	16115	110	1089	Wood Product Manufacturing	16327	78	341	Educational Services
15907	2	0	Prof., Scientific, & Tech Svcs	16116	69	159	Truck Transportation	16328	8	15	Food Svcs & Drinking Places
15909	166	733	Transportation Equipment Mfg	16117	658	6688	Real Estate	16329	6	35	Support Activities: Agr./For.
15920	30	258	Educational Services	16120	57	266	Construction of Buildings	16331	6	43	Food Manufacturing
15921	27	77	Miscellaneous Manufacturing	16121	209	2105	Hospitals	16332	3	4	Construction of Buildings
15922	12	39	Relig., Grant, Civic, Prof Org	16123	58	1030	Plastics & Rubber Products Mfg	16333	18	52	Relig., Grant, Civic, Prof Org
15923	51	206	Educational Services	16124	60	225	Nonmetallic Mineral Prod. Mfg	16334	14	129	Wood Product Manufacturing
15924	24	175	Educational Services	16125	622	8035	Primary Metal Manufacturing	16335	1584	19234	Machinery Manufacturing
15925	5	4	Relig., Grant, Civic, Prof Org	16127	602	6796	Educational Services	16340	45	205	Merch. Wholesalers,Durable Gds
15926	86	337	Nonstore Retailers	16130	105	507	Computer & Electronic Prod Mfg	16341	64	319	Primary Metal Manufacturing
15927	15	96	Utilities	16131	23	87	Nonmetallic Mineral Prod. Mfg	16342	44	172	Fabricated Metal Product Mfg
15928	58	662	Educational Services	16132	32	151	Amusement, Gambling,& Recreat.	16343	29	263	Truck Transportation
15929	5	6	Postal Service	16133	40	185	Support Activities for Mining	16344	18	44	Fabricated Metal Product Mfg
15930	7	40	Nonstore Retailers	16134	119	671	Educational Services	16345	87	402	Educational Services
15931	617	7165	Exec., Legis., & Other Support	16136	38	534	Primary Metal Manufacturing	16346	190	1121	Educational Services
15934	16	102	Machinery Manufacturing	16137	540	5482	Food Svcs & Drinking Places	16347	85	603	Elect'l Eqpmt, App, & Comp Mfg
15935	85	376	Administrative & Support Svcs	16140	14	36	Relig., Grant, Civic, Prof Org	16350	83	351	Justice, Pubic Order/Safety
15936	51	216	Relig., Grant, Civic, Prof Org	16141	33	140	Heavy & Civil Eng. Construct'N	16351	60	270	Wood Product Manufacturing
15937	16	65	Educational Services	16142	194	1273	Food Manufacturing	16352	6	25	Food Svcs & Drinking Places
15938	57	215	Educational Services	16143	62	335	Miscellaneous Manufacturing	16353	155	844	Educational Services
15940	48	864	Educational Services	16145	157	630	Bldg Matl & Garden Eqpmt Dlrs	16354	515	3899	Educational Services
15942	36	252	Truck Transportation	16146	628	7870	Hospitals	16360	65	448	Administrative & Support Svcs
15943	101	511	Educational Services	16148	838	9257	Food Svcs & Drinking Places	16361	12	63	Repair and Maintenance
15944	92	863	Utilities	16150	257	1731	Merch. Wholesalers,Nondur. Gds	16362	30	48	Educational Services
15945	7	22	Food Svcs & Drinking Places	16151	7	4	Postal Service	16364	31	62	Bldg Matl & Garden Eqpmt Dlrs
15946	188	1118	Justice, Pubic Order/Safety	16153	96	331	Educational Services	16365	921	11345	Hospitals
15948	10	20	Mining (Except Oil and Gas)	16154	85	424	Primary Metal Manufacturing	16366	1	700	Clothing & Cloth'g Acc. Stores
15949	56	152	Construction of Buildings	16155	6	23	Publishing Industries	16370	8	19	Bldg Matl & Garden Eqpmt Dlrs
15951	28	135	Justice, Pubic Order/Safety	16156	103	517	Waste Managmt & Remediat'n Svc	16371	125	985	Relig., Grant, Civic, Prof Org
15952	43	203	Repair and Maintenance	16157	102	717	Nonmetallic Mineral Prod. Mfg	16372	20	77	Food and Beverage Stores
15953	2	1	Social Assistance	16159	155	1966	Truck Transportation	16373	145	743	Construction of Buildings
15954	52	409	Truck Transportation	16160	24	85	Administrative & Support Svcs	16374	46	193	Waste Managmt & Remediat'n Svc
15955	59	270	Educational Services	16161	48	1164	Primary Metal Manufacturing	16375	5	3	Postal Service
15956	65	359	Apparel Manufacturing	16172	2	357	Educational Services	16388	1	175	Administrative & Support Svcs
15957	18	65	Heavy & Civil Eng. Construct'N	16201	919	8791	Hospitals	16401	151	760	Food Svcs & Drinking Places
15958	48	293	Wood Product Manufacturing	16210	20	99	Merch. Wholesalers,Durable Gds	16402	22	164	Relig., Grant, Civic, Prof Org
15959	17	51	Merch. Wholesalers,Durable Gds	16211	2	4	Merch. Wholesalers,Durable Gds	16403	154	1186	Merch. Wholesalers,Nondur. Gds
15960	17	32	Relig., Grant, Civic, Prof Org	16212	10	26	Food Svcs & Drinking Places	16404	80	215	Bldg Matl & Garden Eqpmt Dlrs
15961	17	46	Relig., Grant, Civic, Prof Org	16213	8	12	Relig., Grant, Civic, Prof Org	16405	20	81	Justice, Pubic Order/Safety
15962	13	49	Food Svcs & Drinking Places	16214	621	6539	Educational Services	16406	117	752	Nursing & Resid. Care Facilit.
15963	328	2942	Ambulatory Health Care Svcs	16217	25	214	Accommodation	16407	470	4570	Plastics & Rubber Products Mfg
16001	2030	20250	Hospitals	16218	40	210	Transit & Grnd Pass. Transport	16410	34	225	Food Svcs & Drinking Places
16002	521	4033	Merch. Wholesalers,Durable Gds	16220	7	37	Food Svcs & Drinking Places	16411	31	189	Plastics & Rubber Products Mfg
16003	7	12	Administrative & Support Svcs	16221	2	0	Postal Service	16412	358	2944	Food Svcs & Drinking Places
16020	32	92	Mining (Except Oil and Gas)	16222	49	199	Wood Product Manufacturing	16413	4	6	Clothing & Cloth'g Acc. Stores
16022	12	48	Educational Services	16223	8	25	Truck Transportation	16415	284	3917	Computer & Electronic Prod Mfg
16023	114	1755	Fabricated Metal Product Mfg	16224	33	237	Miscellaneous Manufacturing	16416	7	33	Wood Product Manufacturing
16024	14	86	Machinery Manufacturing	16225	3	1	General Merchandise Stores	16417	314	2670	Nursing & Resid. Care Facilit.
16025	163	714	Nursing & Resid. Care Facilit.	16226	302	2470	Nonmetallic Mineral Prod. Mfg	16420	15	56	Accommodation
16027	17	75	Administrative & Support Svcs	16228	5	28	Justice, Pubic Order/Safety	16421	59	690	Plastics & Rubber Products Mfg
16028	85	400	Justice, Pubic Order/Safety	16229	182	1919	Machinery Manufacturing	16422	18	84	Transit & Grnd Pass. Transport
16029	33	951	Computer & Electronic Prod Mfg	16230	20	121	Truck Transportation	16423	88	873	Plastics & Rubber Products Mfg
16030	19	155	Motor Vehicle & Parts Dealers	16232	165	1508	Educational Services	16424	195	1094	Plastics & Rubber Products Mfg
16033	223	1297	Merch. Wholesalers,Nondur. Gds	16233	42	278	Furniture & Related Prod. Mfg	16426	122	934	Fabricated Metal Product Mfg
16034	57	300	Heavy & Civil Eng. Construct'N	16234	6	11	Utilities	16427	5	22	Educational Services
16035	7	6	Relig., Grant, Civic, Prof Org	16235	37	94	Food Svcs & Drinking Places	16428	425	4047	Food Manufacturing
16036	22	1707	Educational Services	16236	13	56	Justice, Pubic Order/Safety	16430	7	119	Accommodation
16037	201	2017	Merch. Wholesalers,Nondur. Gds	16238	13	25	Heavy & Civil Eng. Construct'N	16433	197	2218	Machinery Manufacturing
16038	134	867	Food Svcs & Drinking Places	16239	89	509	Nursing & Resid. Care Facilit.	16434	63	329	Wood Product Manufacturing
16039	5	11	Relig., Grant, Civic, Prof Org	16240	28	87	Food and Beverage Stores	16435	64	134	Exec., Legis., & Other Support
16040	16	33	Construction of Buildings	16242	200	1084	Educational Services	16436	11	44	Food Svcs & Drinking Places
16041	47	469	Merch. Wholesalers,Nondur. Gds	16244	13	52	Food and Beverage Stores	16438	265	2224	Merch. Wholesalers,Nondur. Gds
16045	65	2258	Primary Metal Manufacturing	16245	5	5	Personal and Laundry Services	16440	14	45	Amusement, Gambling,& Recreat.
16046	411	3969	Food Svcs & Drinking Places	16246	14	99	Justice, Pubic Order/Safety	16441	313	1781	Merch. Wholesalers,Nondur. Gds
16048	5	143	Justice, Pubic Order/Safety	16248	86	415	Educational Services	16442	66	261	Justice, Pubic Order/Safety
16049	75	482	Bldg Matl & Garden Eqpmt Dlrs	16249	63	290	Educational Services	16443	45	133	Food Svcs & Drinking Places
16050	57	774	Chemical Manufacturing	16250	7	41	Bldg Matl & Garden Eqpmt Dlrs	16444	5	929	Educational Services
16051	145	1354	Repair and Maintenance	16253	2	5	Motor Vehicle & Parts Dealers	16475	1	500	Justice, Pubic Order/Safety
16052	102	429	Educational Services	16254	178	1876	Wood Product Manufacturing	16501	838	11893	Exec., Legis., & Other Support
16053	100	350	Accommodation	16255	60	436	Nursing & Resid. Care Facilit.	16502	474	5937	Fabricated Metal Product Mfg
16054	10	20	Utilities	16256	20	61	Beverage & Tobacco Product Mfg	16503	422	4639	Relig., Grant, Civic, Prof Org
16055	250	1802	Bldg Matl & Garden Eqpmt Dlrs	16257	1	2	Food Svcs & Drinking Places	16504	278	3432	Hospitals
16056	241	2281	Machinery Manufacturing	16258	51	592	Construction of Buildings	16505	965	10977	Machinery Manufacturing
16057	378	2231	Educational Services	16259	41	58	Special Trade Contractors	16506	845	10524	Miscellaneous Manufacturing
16058	2	1	Relig., Grant, Civic, Prof Org	16260	5	87	Postal Service	16507	336	5649	Educational Services
16059	266	1531	Fabricated Metal Product Mfg	16261	1	0	Postal Service	16508	670	6482	Prof., Scientific, & Tech Svcs

BUSINESS DATA

ZIP CODE	2004 Total Firms	2004 Total Employees	TOP INDUSTRY RANKED on 2004 EMPLOYMENT	ZIP CODE	2004 Total Firms	2004 Total Employees	TOP INDUSTRY RANKED on 2004 EMPLOYMENT	ZIP CODE	2004 Total Firms	2004 Total Employees	TOP INDUSTRY RANKED on 2004 EMPLOYMENT
16509	916	13354	Food Svcs & Drinking Places	16720	50	240	Fabricated Metal Product Mfg	16922	131	693	Primary Metal Manufacturing
16510	592	6816	Food and Beverage Stores	16724	8	53	Merch. Wholesalers,Nondur. Gds	16923	52	157	Food and Beverage Stores
16511	244	2648	Merch. Wholesalers,Nondur. Gds	16725	10	77	Truck Transportation	16925	80	245	Fabricated Metal Product Mfg
16512	10	7	Insurance Carriers & Related	16726	12	87	Exec., Legis., & Other Support	16926	20	167	Educational Services
16514	5	5	Administrative & Support Svcs	16727	9	33	Unclassified Establishments	16927	32	140	Social Assistance
16515	1	300	Postal Service	16728	1	1	General Merchandise Stores	16928	47	160	Justice, Pubic Order/Safety
16522	1	50	Credit Intermediation & Relatd	16729	29	232	Educational Services	16929	74	196	Food and Beverage Stores
16530	1	2500	Insurance Carriers & Related	16730	6	66	Special Trade Contractors	16930	70	325	Educational Services
16531	2	25	Special Trade Contractors	16731	77	613	Furn. & Home Furnishgs Stores	16932	27	96	Special Trade Contractors
16534	2	150	Publishing Industries	16732	4	11	Special Trade Contractors	16933	375	3652	Educational Services
16541	3	700	Educational Services	16733	4	5	Exec., Legis., & Other Support	16935	53	261	Food Manufacturing
16544	10	2718	Hospitals	16734	6	9	Exec., Legis., & Other Support	16936	62	232	Food and Beverage Stores
16546	4	421	Educational Services	16735	300	2247	Merch. Wholesalers,Durable Gds	16937	3	14	Prof., Scientific, & Tech Svcs
16550	11	3150	Other Information Services	16738	55	443	Primary Metal Manufacturing	16938	39	83	Food Svcs & Drinking Places
16553	1	600	Credit Intermediation & Relatd	16740	77	401	Wood Product Manufacturing	16939	11	38	Relig., Grant, Civic, Prof Org
16563	3	507	Educational Services	16743	180	1593	Nonmetallic Mineral Prod. Mfg	16940	13	37	Special Trade Contractors
16565	167	2297	Clothing & Cloth'g Acc. Stores	16744	10	6	Bldg Matl & Garden Eqpmt Dlrs	16941	3	1	Relig., Grant, Civic, Prof Org
16601	1021	14835	Ambulatory Health Care Svcs	16745	12	26	Repair and Maintenance	16942	20	59	Food and Beverage Stores
16602	1602	19042	Food Svcs & Drinking Places	16746	37	239	Admin. Human Resource Programs	16943	16	29	Utilities
16603	8	23	Administrative & Support Svcs	16748	114	792	Merch. Wholesalers,Durable Gds	16945	14	20	Gasoline Stations
16611	91	739	Paper Manufacturing	16749	210	1712	Nursing & Resid. Care Facilit.	16946	84	444	Educational Services
16613	30	194	Relig., Grant, Civic, Prof Org	16750	9	45	Food and Beverage Stores	16947	278	2355	Paper Manufacturing
16616	1	40	Wood Product Manufacturing	16801	1890	22857	Food Svcs & Drinking Places	16948	72	502	Educational Services
16617	128	874	Educational Services	16802	44	1393	Other Information Services	16950	126	891	Leather & Allied Product Mfg
16619	9	8	Utilities	16803	524	10543	Accommodation	17001	17	33	Construction of Buildings
16620	11	25	Waste Managmt & Remediat'n Svc	16804	9	17	Ambulatory Health Care Svcs	17002	24	270	Bldg Matl & Garden Eqpmt Dlrs
16621	15	43	Ambulatory Health Care Svcs	16805	4	7	Special Trade Contractors	17003	331	3112	Educational Services
16622	6	9	Machinery Manufacturing	16820	25	47	Wood Product Manufacturing	17004	175	2106	Machinery Manufacturing
16623	16	64	Educational Services	16821	14	171	Educational Services	17005	28	46	Special Trade Contractors
16624	5	14	Special Trade Contractors	16822	49	609	Merch. Wholesalers,Durable Gds	17006	34	139	Educational Services
16625	134	1566	Print'g & Related Supp't Act's	16823	802	8044	Justice, Pubic Order/Safety	17007	115	679	Educational Services
16627	72	225	Food and Beverage Stores	16825	19	429	Truck Transportation	17008	4	11	Relig., Grant, Civic, Prof Org
16629	3	30	Educational Services	16826	18	85	Educational Services	17009	129	2405	Primary Metal Manufacturing
16630	192	2014	Justice, Pubic Order/Safety	16827	144	841	Educational Services	17010	29	178	Nursing & Resid. Care Facilit.
16631	13	66	Motor Vehicle & Parts Dealers	16828	178	1353	Hospitals	17011	1625	23623	Prof., Scientific, & Tech Svcs
16633	4	43	Educational Services	16829	14	186	Fabricated Metal Product Mfg	17013	2020	26894	Truck Transportation
16634	8	14	Merch. Wholesalers,Durable Gds	16830	833	9531	Hospitals	17014	5	2	Repair and Maintenance
16635	512	5741	Food Svcs & Drinking Places	16832	12	58	Museums, Hist. Sites,& Similar	17016	28	451	Nursing & Resid. Care Facilit.
16636	17	44	Special Trade Contractors	16833	170	1328	Nursing & Resid. Care Facilit.	17017	50	211	Construction of Buildings
16637	72	381	Food Svcs & Drinking Places	16834	7	27	Animal Production	17018	114	318	Educational Services
16638	1	0	Relig., Grant, Civic, Prof Org	16835	9	17	Exec., Legis., & Other Support	17019	504	3134	Construction of Buildings
16639	24	188	Primary Metal Manufacturing	16836	28	79	Relig., Grant, Civic, Prof Org	17020	252	1712	Educational Services
16640	16	301	Educational Services	16837	2	1	Administrative & Support Svcs	17021	35	83	Utilities
16641	64	305	Educational Services	16838	60	153	Special Trade Contractors	17022	773	8319	Nursing & Resid. Care Facilit.
16644	14	53	Wood Product Manufacturing	16839	7	17	Food Svcs & Drinking Places	17023	181	1370	Fabricated Metal Product Mfg
16645	8	152	Furniture & Related Prod. Mfg	16840	12	59	Admin. Enviro. Quality Progrms	17024	53	324	Educational Services
16646	72	691	Hospitals	16841	96	441	Admin. Enviro. Quality Progrms	17025	354	2285	Food Svcs & Drinking Places
16647	21	141	Amusement, Gambling,& Recreat.	16843	25	347	Machinery Manufacturing	17026	100	1642	Food Manufacturing
16648	599	7466	Nursing & Resid. Care Facilit.	16844	35	93	Special Trade Contractors	17027	9	669	Educational Services
16650	45	250	Waste Managmt & Remediat'n Svc	16845	25	103	Mining (Except Oil and Gas)	17028	141	2157	Perform'g Arts, Spec. Sports
16651	111	1148	Justice, Pubic Order/Safety	16847	27	306	Food and Beverage Stores	17029	10	82	Nursing & Resid. Care Facilit.
16652	711	6286	Justice, Pubic Order/Safety	16848	14	146	Gasoline Stations	17030	53	633	Fabricated Metal Product Mfg
16654	3	650	Justice, Pubic Order/Safety	16849	6	13	Relig., Grant, Civic, Prof Org	17032	237	1463	Educational Services
16655	24	123	Construction of Buildings	16850	5	10	Accommodation	17033	714	15238	Food Manufacturing
16656	41	148	Nonmetallic Mineral Prod. Mfg	16851	57	145	Food Svcs & Drinking Places	17034	81	344	Food Svcs & Drinking Places
16657	39	305	Scenic & Sightseeing Transport	16852	3	69	Relig., Grant, Civic, Prof Org	17035	16	43	Educational Services
16659	22	119	Educational Services	16853	83	889	Plastics & Rubber Products Mfg	17036	480	3681	Food Svcs & Drinking Places
16660	10	15	Exec., Legis., & Other Support	16854	66	172	Relig., Grant, Civic, Prof Org	17037	32	102	Apparel Manufacturing
16661	22	129	Apparel Manufacturing	16855	10	15	Motor Vehicle & Parts Dealers	17038	185	1906	Merch. Wholesalers,Durable Gds
16662	204	2172	Leather & Allied Product Mfg	16856	6	48	Sportg Gds,Hobby,Book, & Music	17039	4	5	Postal Service
16663	3	2	Postal Service	16858	71	194	Truck Transportation	17040	72	218	Heavy & Civil Eng. Construct'N
16664	48	202	Heavy & Civil Eng. Construct'N	16859	10	28	Food Svcs & Drinking Places	17041	5	54	Food Svcs & Drinking Places
16665	33	142	Special Trade Contractors	16860	4	8	Construction of Buildings	17042	1573	18325	Hospitals
16666	89	301	Educational Services	16861	3	5	Exec., Legis., & Other Support	17043	616	5171	Food Svcs & Drinking Places
16667	34	80	Food Svcs & Drinking Places	16863	11	28	Machinery Manufacturing	17044	870	10335	Hospitals
16668	137	713	Educational Services	16865	33	90	Administrative & Support Svcs	17045	97	479	Wood Product Manufacturing
16669	65	214	Relig., Grant, Civic, Prof Org	16866	461	4267	Justice, Pubic Order/Safety	17046	707	5242	Merch. Wholesalers,Durable Gds
16670	1	1	Prof., Scientific, & Tech Svcs	16868	26	250	Special Trade Contractors	17047	94	488	Educational Services
16671	22	26	Repair and Maintenance	16870	146	557	Unclassified Establishments	17048	126	834	Machinery Manufacturing
16672	10	54	Petroleum & Coal Products Mfg	16871	2	5	Exec., Legis., & Other Support	17049	105	483	Construction of Buildings
16673	197	2758	Paper Manufacturing	16872	25	73	Educational Services	17050	988	13334	Food Svcs & Drinking Places
16674	11	38	Educational Services	16873	7	15	Heavy & Civil Eng. Construct'N	17051	116	779	Educational Services
16675	6	7	Special Trade Contractors	16874	69	285	Food Svcs & Drinking Places	17052	25	179	Mining (Except Oil and Gas)
16677	8	17	Motor Vehicle & Parts Dealers	16875	128	832	Computer & Electronic Prod Mfg	17053	134	622	Merch. Wholesalers,Nondur. Gds
16678	106	922	Leather & Allied Product Mfg	16876	8	70	Educational Services	17054	4	21	Administrative & Support Svcs
16679	12	10	Postal Service	16877	41	102	Prof., Scientific, & Tech Svcs	17055	1111	19209	Ambulatory Health Care Svcs
16680	18	43	Merch. Wholesalers,Nondur. Gds	16878	29	126	Heavy & Civil Eng. Construct'N	17056	16	89	Construction of Buildings
16681	5	6	Machinery Manufacturing	16879	21	24	Construction of Buildings	17057	607	11438	Nat'l Security & Int'l Affairs
16682	1	1	Museums, Hist. Sites,& Similar	16881	62	2695	Merch. Wholesalers,Durable Gds	17058	44	370	Relig., Grant, Civic, Prof Org
16683	19	137	Animal Production	16882	8	29	Accommodation	17059	392	3752	Food Manufacturing
16684	27	1525	Amusement, Gambling,& Recreat.	16901	684	5350	Hospitals	17060	28	150	Educational Services
16685	3	8	Prof., Scientific, & Tech Svcs	16910	6	16	Construction of Buildings	17061	275	2553	Machinery Manufacturing
16686	411	3854	Ambulatory Health Care Svcs	16911	4	27	Forestry and Logging	17062	114	589	Educational Services
16689	16	233	Food Svcs & Drinking Places	16912	86	2073	Fabricated Metal Product Mfg	17063	86	413	Furniture & Related Prod. Mfg
16691	6	1	Postal Service	16914	40	139	Transit & Grnd Pass. Transport	17064	42	1019	Social Assistance
16692	18	208	Educational Services	16915	405	2779	Elect'l Eqpmt, App, & Comp Mfg	17065	117	1015	Computer & Electronic Prod Mfg
16693	113	893	Paper Manufacturing	16917	61	184	Food Svcs & Drinking Places	17066	194	1542	Fabricated Metal Product Mfg
16694	6	17	Special Trade Contractors	16918	1	0	Postal Service	17067	437	4780	Nursing & Resid. Care Facilit.
16695	44	175	Merch. Wholesalers,Nondur. Gds	16920	79	743	Plastics & Rubber Products Mfg	17068	184	1075	Justice, Pubic Order/Safety
16701	812	10139	Repair and Maintenance	16921	28	84	Food Svcs & Drinking Places	17069	8	19	Food Svcs & Drinking Places

ZIP CODE	2004 Total Firms	2004 Total Employees	TOP INDUSTRY RANKED on 2004 EMPLOYMENT	ZIP CODE	2004 Total Firms	2004 Total Employees	TOP INDUSTRY RANKED on 2004 EMPLOYMENT	ZIP CODE	2004 Total Firms	2004 Total Employees	TOP INDUSTRY RANKED on 2004 EMPLOYMENT
17070	577	4193	Food Svcs & Drinking Places	17267	86	439	Educational Services	17537	10	34	Relig., Grant, Civic, Prof Org
17071	1	1	Postal Service	17268	873	7412	Machinery Manufacturing	17538	195	2244	Educational Services
17072	34	414	Truck Transportation	17270	5	4	Merch. Wholesalers,Nondur. Gds	17540	384	5246	Plastics & Rubber Products Mfg
17073	94	417	Furniture & Related Prod. Mfg	17271	19	224	Educational Services	17543	1151	13378	Chemical Manufacturing
17074	287	1513	Food Svcs & Drinking Places	17272	9	27	Food Manufacturing	17545	878	9642	Merch. Wholesalers,Durable Gds
17075	6	8	Food and Beverage Stores	17301	114	734	Nursing & Resid. Care Facilit.	17547	150	2412	Chemical Manufacturing
17076	11	69	Truck Transportation	17302	52	89	Special Trade Contractors	17549	2	0	Postal Service
17077	17	409	Waste Managmt & Remediat'n Svc	17303	25	124	Educational Services	17550	26	183	Justice, Pubic Order/Safety
17078	527	4226	Prof., Scientific, & Tech Svcs	17304	55	614	Food Manufacturing	17551	201	2400	Educational Services
17080	15	55	Food Svcs & Drinking Places	17306	23	248	Justice, Pubic Order/Safety	17552	459	5036	Food Svcs & Drinking Places
17081	15	127	Justice, Pubic Order/Safety	17307	185	1435	Food Manufacturing	17554	156	1737	Prof., Scientific, & Tech Svcs
17082	99	289	Special Trade Contractors	17309	53	244	Educational Services	17555	136	1053	Nursing & Resid. Care Facilit.
17083	18	137	Textile Product Mills	17310	11	111	Educational Services	17557	636	10259	Machinery Manufacturing
17084	129	1092	Miscellaneous Manufacturing	17311	12	43	Insurance Carriers & Related	17560	93	1021	Relig., Grant, Civic, Prof Org
17085	1	0	Relig., Grant, Civic, Prof Org	17312	4	51	Food and Beverage Stores	17562	153	1267	Bldg Matl & Garden Eqpmt Dlrs
17086	90	300	Relig., Grant, Civic, Prof Org	17313	255	2139	Fabricated Metal Product Mfg	17563	85	306	Construction of Buildings
17087	76	664	Elect'l Eqpmt, App, & Comp Mfg	17314	120	580	Repair and Maintenance	17564	3	19	Furn. & Home Furnishgs Stores
17088	65	670	Furniture & Related Prod. Mfg	17315	431	2921	Justice, Pubic Order/Safety	17565	61	173	Educational Services
17090	130	493	Educational Services	17316	189	1550	Computer & Electronic Prod Mfg	17566	423	3445	Food and Beverage Stores
17093	27	310	Educational Services	17317	17	158	Educational Services	17567	42	583	Merch. Wholesalers,Durable Gds
17094	69	860	Furniture & Related Prod. Mfg	17318	66	1712	Computer & Electronic Prod Mfg	17568	11	137	Bldg Matl & Garden Eqpmt Dlrs
17097	19	71	Merch. Wholesalers,Nondur. Gds	17319	238	1229	Special Trade Contractors	17569	161	465	Special Trade Contractors
17098	70	330	Machinery Manufacturing	17320	191	1324	Print'g & Related Supp't Act's	17570	15	604	Food Manufacturing
17099	43	228	Social Assistance	17321	47	305	Educational Services	17572	144	1325	Food Svcs & Drinking Places
17101	1014	21890	Exec., Legis., & Other Support	17322	95	427	Plastics & Rubber Products Mfg	17575	10	79	Justice, Pubic Order/Safety
17102	386	3162	Relig., Grant, Civic, Prof Org	17323	8	19	Justice, Pubic Order/Safety	17576	26	492	Food Svcs & Drinking Places
17103	389	3968	Hospitals	17324	79	1232	Food Manufacturing	17578	184	1075	Special Trade Contractors
17104	512	9663	Admin. of Economic Programs	17325	1473	14575	Educational Services	17579	227	1341	Rail Transportation
17105	7	437	Amusement, Gambling,& Recreat.	17327	218	1846	Chemical Manufacturing	17580	9	53	Special Trade Contractors
17106	8	104	Transit & Grnd Pass. Transport	17329	46	138	Educational Services	17581	62	528	Special Trade Contractors
17107	2	2005	Truck Transportation	17331	1810	23103	Food Svcs & Drinking Places	17582	48	280	Educational Services
17108	11	217	Prof., Scientific, & Tech Svcs	17337	1	1	Postal Service	17583	1	0	Justice, Pubic Order/Safety
17109	879	10594	Food Svcs & Drinking Places	17339	199	1581	Educational Services	17584	313	2688	Nursing & Resid. Care Facilit.
17110	1095	20645	Hospitals	17340	327	2576	Furniture & Related Prod. Mfg	17585	8	54	Amusement, Gambling,& Recreat.
17111	1114	16417	Food Svcs & Drinking Places	17342	28	257	Food and Beverage Stores	17601	2678	40925	Print'g & Related Supp't Act's
17112	1273	25699	Ambulatory Health Care Svcs	17343	10	13	Merch. Wholesalers,Nondur. Gds	17602	1860	29908	Exec., Legis., & Other Support
17113	295	1873	Educational Services	17344	85	693	Merch. Wholesalers,Nondur. Gds	17603	2282	26092	Wood Product Manufacturing
17120	83	4900	Admin. of Economic Programs	17345	183	1766	Educational Services	17604	15	840	Postal Service
17121	1	155	Social Assistance	17347	82	830	Fabricated Metal Product Mfg	17605	2	14	Administrative & Support Svcs
17124	2	438	Admin. of Economic Programs	17349	182	1202	Wood Product Manufacturing	17606	3	140	Educational Services
17125	1	10	Exec., Legis., & Other Support	17350	392	4214	Food Manufacturing	17608	8	37	Social Assistance
17128	1	1500	Exec., Legis., & Other Support	17352	32	107	Prof., Scientific, & Tech Svcs	17701	2136	30433	Educational Services
17177	2	4	Credit Intermediation & Relatd	17353	63	555	Food Manufacturing	17702	327	1989	Food Svcs & Drinking Places
17201	2239	21535	Food Svcs & Drinking Places	17354	1	0	Justice, Pubic Order/Safety	17703	1	1	Prof., Scientific, & Tech Svcs
17210	2	1	Merch. Wholesalers,Durable Gds	17355	9	17	Machinery Manufacturing	17720	8	7	Construction of Buildings
17211	7	13	General Merchandise Stores	17356	563	5076	Furniture & Related Prod. Mfg	17721	57	469	Wood Product Manufacturing
17212	13	18	Exec., Legis., & Other Support	17358	4	49	Heavy & Civil Eng. Construct'N	17723	3	1	Clothing & Cloth'g Acc. Stores
17213	8	15	Credit Intermediation & Relatd	17360	81	265	Administrative & Support Svcs	17724	224	1510	Plastics & Rubber Products Mfg
17214	62	385	Nonmetallic Mineral Prod. Mfg	17361	297	2275	Food Svcs & Drinking Places	17726	7	14	Repair and Maintenance
17215	6	8	Food Manufacturing	17362	259	1213	Relig., Grant, Civic, Prof Org	17727	4	5	Accommodation
17217	17	14	Merch. Wholesalers,Nondur. Gds	17363	192	1429	Wood Product Manufacturing	17728	125	686	Amusement, Gambling,& Recreat.
17219	10	18	Food Manufacturing	17364	95	1122	Furn. & Home Furnishgs Stores	17729	9	8	Food Svcs & Drinking Places
17220	22	67	Exec., Legis., & Other Support	17365	83	510	Primary Metal Manufacturing	17730	19	54	Waste Managmt & Remediat'n Svc
17221	19	145	Justice, Pubic Order/Safety	17366	77	202	Educational Services	17731	36	126	Relig., Grant, Civic, Prof Org
17222	198	1550	Miscellaneous Store Retailers	17368	166	1162	Primary Metal Manufacturing	17735	5	5	Relig., Grant, Civic, Prof Org
17223	19	292	Exec., Legis., & Other Support	17370	94	936	Special Trade Contractors	17737	198	1086	Educational Services
17224	61	286	Wood Product Manufacturing	17371	21	97	Justice, Pubic Order/Safety	17738	3	5	Food Svcs & Drinking Places
17225	577	7081	Food and Beverage Stores	17372	118	470	Educational Services	17739	5	3	Food Svcs & Drinking Places
17228	23	58	Educational Services	17401	452	5450	Social Assistance	17740	403	2960	Educational Services
17229	31	243	Construction of Buildings	17402	1817	33109	Food Svcs & Drinking Places	17742	8	55	Educational Services
17231	10	21	Exec., Legis., & Other Support	17403	1602	33130	Ambulatory Health Care Svcs	17744	79	302	Food Svcs & Drinking Places
17232	4	17	Educational Services	17404	1765	24626	Food Svcs & Drinking Places	17745	686	4792	Nat'l Security & Int'l Affairs
17233	287	4518	Machinery Manufacturing	17405	5	54	Relig., Grant, Civic, Prof Org	17747	65	340	Educational Services
17235	31	320	Justice, Pubic Order/Safety	17406	224	2434	Fabricated Metal Product Mfg	17748	31	1489	Miscellaneous Manufacturing
17236	254	2735	Accommodation	17407	51	231	Furn. & Home Furnishgs Stores	17749	9	18	Other Information Services
17237	25	380	Educational Services	17501	173	1139	Food Svcs & Drinking Places	17750	7	68	Amusement, Gambling,& Recreat.
17238	41	352	Justice, Pubic Order/Safety	17502	68	307	Special Trade Contractors	17751	263	2741	General Merchandise Stores
17239	5	6	Prof., Scientific, & Tech Svcs	17503	4	8	Ambulatory Health Care Svcs	17752	148	2256	Furniture & Related Prod. Mfg
17240	71	219	Food Svcs & Drinking Places	17504	5	5	Postal Service	17754	516	6020	Exec., Legis., & Other Support
17241	316	1710	Administrative & Support Svcs	17505	117	1194	Food Svcs & Drinking Places	17756	519	6895	Machinery Manufacturing
17243	66	450	Nursing & Resid. Care Facilit.	17506	41	602	Managmt of Companies & Enterp.	17758	44	118	Food and Beverage Stores
17244	55	165	Special Trade Contractors	17507	36	680	Special Trade Contractors	17759	6	10	Exec., Legis., & Other Support
17246	10	38	Merch. Wholesalers,Durable Gds	17508	62	611	Special Trade Contractors	17760	17	148	Justice, Pubic Order/Safety
17247	12	458	Nursing & Resid. Care Facilit.	17509	126	737	Nursing & Resid. Care Facilit.	17762	16	124	Justice, Pubic Order/Safety
17249	16	139	Apparel Manufacturing	17512	464	5119	Merch. Wholesalers,Durable Gds	17763	16	61	Wood Product Manufacturing
17250	3	32	Heavy & Civil Eng. Construct'N	17516	105	865	Food Manufacturing	17764	108	509	Educational Services
17251	6	51	Relig., Grant, Civic, Prof Org	17517	446	7057	Prof., Scientific, & Tech Svcs	17765	25	47	Relig., Grant, Civic, Prof Org
17252	100	509	Special Trade Contractors	17518	19	66	Prof., Scientific, & Tech Svcs	17767	2	13	Merch. Wholesalers,Durable Gds
17253	8	8	Insurance Carriers & Related	17519	140	1716	Food and Beverage Stores	17768	9	36	Wood Product Manufacturing
17254	20	90	Educational Services	17520	186	3065	Truck Transportation	17769	5	14	Sportg Gds,Hobby,Book, & Music
17255	43	209	Special Trade Contractors	17521	6	34	Merch. Wholesalers,Durable Gds	17771	54	348	Administrative & Support Svcs
17256	2	2	Postal Service	17522	1298	16643	Hospitals	17772	71	526	Educational Services
17257	671	8073	Educational Services	17527	250	1599	Food Svcs & Drinking Places	17773	3	15	Admin. Enviro. Quality Progrms
17260	32	73	Nursing & Resid. Care Facilit.	17528	12	16	Prof., Scientific, & Tech Svcs	17774	18	70	Food Svcs & Drinking Places
17261	11	736	Nursing & Resid. Care Facilit.	17529	119	625	Special Trade Contractors	17776	14	78	Mining (Except Oil and Gas)
17262	30	132	Food Svcs & Drinking Places	17532	63	319	Transit & Grnd Pass. Transport	17777	170	1080	Nursing & Resid. Care Facilit.
17263	17	32	Credit Intermediation & Relatd	17533	7	23	Apparel Manufacturing	17778	1	1	Accommodation
17264	59	245	Educational Services	17534	104	1121	Food Svcs & Drinking Places	17779	27	157	Miscellaneous Store Retailers
17265	10	15	Special Trade Contractors	17535	78	320	Educational Services	17801	720	6864	Hospitals
17266	20	72	Special Trade Contractors	17536	57	191	Bldg Matl & Garden Eqpmt Dlrs	17810	47	475	Relig., Grant, Civic, Prof Org

BUSINESS DATA

ZIP CODE	2004 Total Firms	2004 Total Employees	TOP INDUSTRY RANKED on 2004 EMPLOYMENT	ZIP CODE	2004 Total Firms	2004 Total Employees	TOP INDUSTRY RANKED on 2004 EMPLOYMENT	ZIP CODE	2004 Total Firms	2004 Total Employees	TOP INDUSTRY RANKED on 2004 EMPLOYMENT
17812	84	394	Educational Services	17964	20	95	Nursing & Resid. Care Facilit.	18201	1328	11797	Hospitals
17813	60	224	Relig., Grant, Civic, Prof Org	17965	62	216	Truck Transportation	18202	509	10642	Paper Manufacturing
17814	168	913	Primary Metal Manufacturing	17966	2	13	Justice, Pubic Order/Safety	18210	81	283	Relig., Grant, Civic, Prof Org
17815	1195	12827	Food Svcs & Drinking Places	17967	68	767	Plastics & Rubber Products Mfg	18211	35	152	Mining (Except Oil and Gas)
17820	150	1215	Educational Services	17968	10	118	Merch. Wholesalers,Nondur. Gds	18212	6	7	Food and Beverage Stores
17821	647	6237	Hospitals	17970	151	1512	General Merchandise Stores	18214	50	209	Furniture & Related Prod. Mfg
17822	14	8159	Hospitals	17972	443	5242	Educational Services	18216	30	201	Prof., Scientific, & Tech Svcs
17823	39	121	Support Act. for Transport.	17974	3	82	Relig., Grant, Civic, Prof Org	18218	55	597	Hospitals
17824	142	1616	Merch. Wholesalers,Nondur. Gds	17976	258	1542	Nursing & Resid. Care Facilit.	18219	113	471	Relig., Grant, Civic, Prof Org
17827	26	122	Furniture & Related Prod. Mfg	17978	11	54	Food Manufacturing	18220	11	433	Furniture & Related Prod. Mfg
17829	11	42	Special Trade Contractors	17979	10	90	Transportation Equipment Mfg	18221	9	37	Perform'g Arts, Spec. Sports
17830	98	451	Educational Services	17980	128	699	Educational Services	18222	227	1475	Educational Services
17831	44	563	General Merchandise Stores	17981	104	761	Warehousing and Storage	18223	4	65	Nonstore Retailers
17832	12	40	Mining (Except Oil and Gas)	17982	11	46	Prof., Scientific, & Tech Svcs	18224	168	950	Food Manufacturing
17833	23	1964	Furniture & Related Prod. Mfg	17983	62	309	Educational Services	18225	15	32	Food and Beverage Stores
17834	110	335	Nursing & Resid. Care Facilit.	17985	19	58	Special Trade Contractors	18229	392	2548	Relig., Grant, Civic, Prof Org
17835	21	471	Admin. Human Resource Programs	18002	40	42	Administrative & Support Svcs	18230	2	0	Postal Service
17836	3	29	Educational Services	18010	2	2	Repair and Maintenance	18231	7	19	Fabricated Metal Product Mfg
17837	924	10269	Educational Services	18011	83	484	Primary Metal Manufacturing	18232	157	935	Justice, Pubic Order/Safety
17839	3	9	Food and Beverage Stores	18012	2	1	Personal and Laundry Services	18234	10	41	Nonstore Retailers
17840	6	17	Construction of Buildings	18013	570	3356	Apparel Manufacturing	18235	739	6513	Hospitals
17841	86	208	Justice, Pubic Order/Safety	18014	388	3064	Administrative & Support Svcs	18237	130	938	Beverage & Tobacco Product Mfg
17842	265	1820	Construction of Buildings	18015	782	9972	Hospitals	18239	12	23	Gasoline Stations
17844	425	2933	Wood Product Manufacturing	18016	10	258	Postal Service	18240	127	1792	Motor Vehicle & Parts Dealers
17845	59	296	Justice, Pubic Order/Safety	18017	1257	23965	Hospitals	18241	34	64	Justice, Pubic Order/Safety
17846	132	790	Educational Services	18018	1500	11615	Educational Services	18242	6	4	Postal Service
17847	433	6103	Food Manufacturing	18020	583	5343	Educational Services	18244	15	74	Truck Transportation
17850	36	220	Food and Beverage Stores	18025	1	2000	Administrative & Support Svcs	18245	6	6	Postal Service
17851	305	1852	Educational Services	18030	28	169	Nonmetallic Mineral Prod. Mfg	18246	10	42	Nursing & Resid. Care Facilit.
17853	105	506	Wood Product Manufacturing	18031	111	2212	Telecommunications	18247	9	27	Relig., Grant, Civic, Prof Org
17855	33	308	Educational Services	18032	232	1329	Educational Services	18248	23	73	Accommodation
17856	82	1130	Fabricated Metal Product Mfg	18034	154	1943	Educational Services	18249	100	500	Educational Services
17857	283	3501	Food Manufacturing	18035	20	69	Relig., Grant, Civic, Prof Org	18250	68	266	Justice, Pubic Order/Safety
17858	11	22	Merch. Wholesalers,Nondur. Gds	18036	384	2251	Elect'l Eqpmt, App, & Comp Mfg	18251	33	107	Bldg Matl & Garden Eqpmt Dlrs
17859	95	266	Support Act. for Transport.	18037	178	925	Food and Beverage Stores	18252	516	3672	Chemical Manufacturing
17860	64	1145	Transportation Equipment Mfg	18038	50	149	Machinery Manufacturing	18254	18	35	Food and Beverage Stores
17861	8	64	Food Manufacturing	18039	16	20	Miscellaneous Store Retailers	18255	126	1048	Accommodation
17862	19	144	Educational Services	18040	297	4243	Merch. Wholesalers,Nondur. Gds	18256	10	46	Justice, Pubic Order/Safety
17864	47	200	Merch. Wholesalers,Durable Gds	18041	150	2782	Furniture & Related Prod. Mfg	18301	1014	8795	Hospitals
17865	6	10	Repair and Maintenance	18042	1621	12937	Hospitals	18320	25	212	Accommodation
17866	198	3242	Justice, Pubic Order/Safety	18043	5	29	Construction of Buildings	18321	103	630	Gasoline Stations
17867	8	20	Relig., Grant, Civic, Prof Org	18044	8	47	Administrative & Support Svcs	18322	335	1606	Food and Beverage Stores
17868	32	761	Chemical Manufacturing	18045	832	9369	Food Svcs & Drinking Places	18323	9	347	Accommodation
17870	628	7957	Exec., Legis., & Other Support	18046	13	585	Merch. Wholesalers,Nondur. Gds	18324	95	2724	Accommodation
17872	467	2274	Food and Beverage Stores	18049	702	4829	Motor Vehicle & Parts Dealers	18325	93	316	Accommodation
17876	85	582	Food Svcs & Drinking Places	18051	112	1224	Warehousing and Storage	18326	150	1077	Miscellaneous Manufacturing
17877	6	8	Miscellaneous Store Retailers	18052	1048	11992	Food Svcs & Drinking Places	18327	60	827	Computer & Electronic Prod Mfg
17878	35	153	Nursing & Resid. Care Facilit.	18053	46	84	Repair and Maintenance	18328	190	810	Educational Services
17880	1	2	Postal Service	18054	116	758	Fabricated Metal Product Mfg	18330	129	660	Nursing & Resid. Care Facilit.
17881	52	160	Educational Services	18055	349	2077	Educational Services	18331	71	259	Motor Vehicle & Parts Dealers
17882	5	1	Relig., Grant, Civic, Prof Org	18056	27	135	Justice, Pubic Order/Safety	18332	47	279	Accommodation
17883	13	48	Administrative & Support Svcs	18058	134	745	Educational Services	18333	74	375	Food Svcs & Drinking Places
17884	19	50	Merch. Wholesalers,Nondur. Gds	18059	31	152	Ambulatory Health Care Svcs	18334	42	176	Perform'g Arts, Spec. Sports
17885	7	16	Accommodation	18060	3	52	Justice, Pubic Order/Safety	18335	141	856	Accommodation
17886	26	228	Credit Intermediation & Relatd	18062	305	4536	Transportation Equipment Mfg	18336	183	1148	Accommodation
17887	16	96	Truck Transportation	18063	34	101	Transit & Grnd Pass. Transport	18337	640	3865	Exec., Legis., & Other Support
17888	10	11	Postal Service	18064	740	6870	Nursing & Resid. Care Facilit.	18340	6	9	Prof., Scientific, & Tech Svcs
17889	82	572	Mining (Except Oil and Gas)	18065	22	130	Credit Intermediation & Relatd	18341	10	45	Prof., Scientific, & Tech Svcs
17901	1157	14053	Ambulatory Health Care Svcs	18066	172	909	Educational Services	18342	72	420	Transportation Equipment Mfg
17920	6	6	Repair and Maintenance	18067	454	2775	Educational Services	18343	110	666	Food Manufacturing
17921	228	2228	Machinery Manufacturing	18068	3	6	Relig., Grant, Civic, Prof Org	18344	355	3226	General Merchandise Stores
17922	79	729	Plastics & Rubber Products Mfg	18069	181	1685	Educational Services	18346	100	820	Truck Transportation
17923	12	36	Truck Transportation	18070	36	140	Food Svcs & Drinking Places	18347	138	523	Heavy & Civil Eng. Construct'N
17925	6	7	Relig., Grant, Civic, Prof Org	18071	379	2569	Merch. Wholesalers,Durable Gds	18349	9	305	Accommodation
17929	64	1870	Primary Metal Manufacturing	18072	225	1724	Waste Managmt & Remediat'n Svc	18350	104	520	Educational Services
17930	11	15	Merch. Wholesalers,Durable Gds	18073	274	1867	Repair and Maintenance	18351	34	62	Ambulatory Health Care Svcs
17931	313	3104	Justice, Pubic Order/Safety	18074	92	359	Machinery Manufacturing	18352	43	147	Food Svcs & Drinking Places
17932	1	558	Justice, Pubic Order/Safety	18076	83	742	Food and Beverage Stores	18353	230	551	Prof., Scientific, & Tech Svcs
17933	20	129	Educational Services	18077	73	136	Food Svcs & Drinking Places	18354	81	293	Educational Services
17934	8	43	Merch. Wholesalers,Durable Gds	18078	180	1773	Educational Services	18355	49	184	Food Svcs & Drinking Places
17935	50	199	Ambulatory Health Care Svcs	18079	10	19	Merch. Wholesalers,Durable Gds	18356	34	865	Accommodation
17936	16	30	Exec., Legis., & Other Support	18080	276	1138	Merch. Wholesalers,Durable Gds	18357	4	253	Accommodation
17938	65	661	Fabricated Metal Product Mfg	18081	39	80	Construction of Buildings	18360	1602	11615	Food Svcs & Drinking Places
17941	28	319	Merch. Wholesalers,Nondur. Gds	18083	56	517	Nonmetallic Mineral Prod. Mfg	18370	51	1991	Chemical Manufacturing
17942	10	17	Special Trade Contractors	18084	24	100	Prof., Scientific, & Tech Svcs	18371	6	125	Food Svcs & Drinking Places
17943	12	29	Food and Beverage Stores	18085	25	161	Furniture & Related Prod. Mfg	18372	381	3739	Truck Transportation
17944	15	44	Educational Services	18086	5	23	Food Manufacturing	18403	255	2356	Educational Services
17945	7	7	Food Manufacturing	18087	118	966	Food and Beverage Stores	18405	65	533	Accommodation
17946	5	4	Support Act. for Transport.	18088	221	2066	Apparel Manufacturing	18407	545	3848	Hospitals
17948	188	722	Merch. Wholesalers,Durable Gds	18091	295	1761	Food Svcs & Drinking Places	18410	24	81	Food Svcs & Drinking Places
17949	9	15	Wholesale Elec. Mrkts & Agents	18092	83	321	Merch. Wholesalers,Nondur. Gds	18411	992	10335	Prof., Scientific, & Tech Svcs
17951	13	924	Educational Services	18098	1	1400	Publishing Industries	18413	67	248	Merch. Wholesalers,Durable Gds
17952	5	5	Postal Service	18101	476	5433	Managmt of Companies & Enterp.	18414	176	691	Special Trade Contractors
17953	16	97	Relig., Grant, Civic, Prof Org	18102	1352	10707	Hospitals	18415	30	141	Educational Services
17954	181	1306	Justice, Pubic Order/Safety	18103	1426	24459	Hospitals	18416	22	74	Educational Services
17957	9	251	Justice, Pubic Order/Safety	18104	1630	20005	Amusement, Gambling,& Recreat.	18417	36	135	Justice, Pubic Order/Safety
17959	41	93	Special Trade Contractors	18105	10	70	Relig., Grant, Civic, Prof Org	18419	130	1014	Educational Services
17960	110	875	Justice, Pubic Order/Safety	18106	490	8507	Merch. Wholesalers,Durable Gds	18420	27	60	Transit & Grnd Pass. Transport
17961	305	2859	Nursing & Resid. Care Facilit.	18109	951	16067	Computer & Electronic Prod Mfg	18421	131	992	Merch. Wholesalers,Durable Gds
17963	278	2247	Textile Product Mills	18195	38	5133	Chemical Manufacturing	18424	142	668	Nursing & Resid. Care Facilit.

ZIP CODE	2004 Total Firms	2004 Total Employees	TOP INDUSTRY RANKED on 2004 EMPLOYMENT
18425	32	150	Accommodation
18426	141	550	Special Trade Contractors
18427	183	969	Food Svcs & Drinking Places
18428	484	3660	Accommodation
18430	2	4	Food Svcs & Drinking Places
18431	878	6150	Hospitals
18433	195	1017	Educational Services
18434	118	748	Print'g & Related Supp't Act's
18435	28	152	Accommodation
18436	298	1352	Educational Services
18437	21	100	Accommodation
18438	44	347	Accommodation
18439	29	305	Accommodation
18440	24	141	Educational Services
18441	10	20	Motor Vehicle & Parts Dealers
18443	7	5	Postal Service
18444	318	1789	Nursing & Resid. Care Facilit.
18445	86	458	Nursing & Resid. Care Facilit.
18446	143	396	Mining (Except Oil and Gas)
18447	400	2754	Ambulatory Health Care Svcs
18448	2	2317	Computer & Electronic Prod Mfg
18449	4	4	Food Svcs & Drinking Places
18451	34	112	Bldg Matl & Garden Eqpmt Dlrs
18452	196	1724	Warehousing and Storage
18453	36	64	Food and Beverage Stores
18454	7	73	Unclassified Establishments
18455	13	174	Accommodation
18456	16	54	Wood Product Manufacturing
18457	22	38	Telecommunications
18458	89	258	Educational Services
18459	27	266	Miscellaneous Manufacturing
18460	17	214	Accommodation
18461	21	262	Accommodation
18462	11	18	Special Trade Contractors
18463	22	60	Administrative & Support Svcs
18464	46	196	Accommodation
18465	44	180	Accommodation
18466	187	4317	Nat'l Security & Int'l Affairs
18469	13	33	Accommodation
18470	79	132	Accommodation
18471	42	204	Relig., Grant, Civic, Prof Org
18472	139	1456	Justice, Pubic Order/Safety
18473	23	219	Apparel Manufacturing
18501	6	18	Merch. Wholesalers,Nondur. Gds
18502	1	1	Educational Services
18503	899	10574	Exec., Legis., & Other Support
18504	565	3807	Food and Beverage Stores
18505	610	7259	Relig., Grant, Civic, Prof Org
18507	261	4664	General Merchandise Stores
18508	579	8885	Ambulatory Health Care Svcs
18509	561	6673	Educational Services
18510	414	11591	Hospitals
18512	604	8525	Publishing Industries
18515	2	750	Prof., Scientific, & Tech Svcs
18517	210	3127	Truck Transportation
18518	302	2483	Textile Mills
18519	286	2972	General Merchandise Stores
18601	7	8	Fabricated Metal Product Mfg
18602	21	96	Amusement, Gambling,& Recreat.
18603	713	6542	Food Manufacturing
18610	170	1232	Accommodation
18611	5	13	Real Estate
18612	596	5756	Print'g & Related Supp't Act's
18614	162	562	Food and Beverage Stores
18615	68	151	Educational Services
18616	54	313	Nursing & Resid. Care Facilit.
18617	30	54	Food and Beverage Stores
18618	109	370	Food Svcs & Drinking Places
18619	15	94	Accommodation
18621	147	586	Food Svcs & Drinking Places
18622	13	313	Merch. Wholesalers,Nondur. Gds
18623	96	318	Bldg Matl & Garden Eqpmt Dlrs
18624	38	646	Accommodation
18625	44	317	Prof., Scientific, & Tech Svcs
18626	47	411	Nursing & Resid. Care Facilit.
18627	30	371	Educational Services
18628	8	128	Educational Services
18629	66	2776	Merch. Wholesalers,Nondur. Gds
18630	95	429	Warehousing and Storage
18631	31	315	Food Svcs & Drinking Places
18632	17	58	Educational Services
18634	420	2612	Educational Services
18635	102	521	Truck Transportation
18636	35	51	Food and Beverage Stores
18640	776	12030	Nonmetallic Mineral Prod. Mfg
18641	216	1485	Food Svcs & Drinking Places
18642	120	1075	Miscellaneous Manufacturing
18643	446	4277	Motor Vehicle & Parts Dealers
18644	337	1939	Fabricated Metal Product Mfg
18651	288	1505	Educational Services
18653	3	54	Prof., Scientific, & Tech Svcs
18654	5	9	Telecommunications
18655	178	734	Educational Services
18656	98	316	Heavy & Civil Eng. Construct'N
18657	661	4785	Ambulatory Health Care Svcs
18660	74	127	Relig., Grant, Civic, Prof Org
18661	184	1761	Exec., Legis., & Other Support
18701	592	7463	Prof., Scientific, & Tech Svcs
18702	1780	22325	Food Svcs & Drinking Places
18703	11	24	Relig., Grant, Civic, Prof Org
18704	1524	12121	Ambulatory Health Care Svcs
18705	460	3266	Ambulatory Health Care Svcs
18706	506	7388	Credit Intermediation & Relatd
18707	457	4538	Computer & Electronic Prod Mfg
18708	289	1910	Personal and Laundry Services
18709	173	1189	Food Svcs & Drinking Places
18711	85	10244	Justice, Pubic Order/Safety
18764	8	4337	Hospitals
18765	2	918	Hospitals
18766	3	440	Educational Services
18801	423	2534	Justice, Pubic Order/Safety
18810	180	1256	Educational Services
18812	29	71	Special Trade Contractors
18813	13	46	Accommodation
18814	7	61	Waste Managmt & Remediat'n Svc
18815	10	71	Accommodation
18816	12	230	Educational Services
18817	27	100	Educational Services
18818	40	184	Educational Services
18820	8	81	Justice, Pubic Order/Safety
18821	69	273	Food Svcs & Drinking Places
18822	129	583	Computer & Electronic Prod Mfg
18823	24	101	Food Svcs & Drinking Places
18824	47	54	Merch. Wholesalers,Nondur. Gds
18825	13	18	Repair and Maintenance
18826	79	674	Educational Services
18827	7	37	Computer & Electronic Prod Mfg
18828	16	23	Food Svcs & Drinking Places
18829	27	55	Food and Beverage Stores
18830	32	72	Miscellaneous Store Retailers
18831	30	112	Merch. Wholesalers,Nondur. Gds
18832	64	208	Truck Transportation
18833	56	153	Food Manufacturing
18834	166	751	Food Svcs & Drinking Places
18837	92	201	Educational Services
18840	456	8945	Hospitals
18842	13	38	Wood Product Manufacturing
18843	25	153	Apparel Manufacturing
18844	43	80	Mining (Except Oil and Gas)
18845	9	25	Food Svcs & Drinking Places
18846	12	8	Exec., Legis., & Other Support
18847	166	1176	Hospitals
18848	530	6721	Primary Metal Manufacturing
18850	77	226	Educational Services
18851	13	14	Special Trade Contractors
18853	183	2104	Food Manufacturing
18854	120	592	Food Svcs & Drinking Places
18901	2635	24631	Justice, Pubic Order/Safety
18910	26	113	Ambulatory Health Care Svcs
18911	6	26	Repair and Maintenance
18912	208	940	Special Trade Contractors
18913	26	47	Food Svcs & Drinking Places
18914	554	4426	Print'g & Related Supp't Act's
18915	199	3104	Motor Vehicle & Parts Dealers
18916	25	848	Merch. Wholesalers,Durable Gds
18917	160	619	Food Svcs & Drinking Places
18918	5	19	Amusement, Gambling,& Recreat.
18920	38	76	Accommodation
18921	17	33	Repair and Maintenance
18922	11	23	Relig., Grant, Civic, Prof Org
18923	49	252	Ambulatory Health Care Svcs
18924	26	792	Motor Vehicle & Parts Dealers
18925	107	420	Amusement, Gambling,& Recreat.
18926	10	15	Administrative & Support Svcs
18927	72	185	Special Trade Contractors
18928	42	180	Prof., Scientific, & Tech Svcs
18929	242	1480	Educational Services
18930	90	299	Educational Services
18931	146	1122	Real Estate
18932	54	272	Food Svcs & Drinking Places
18933	11	100	Nonmetallic Mineral Prod. Mfg
18934	22	61	Prof., Scientific, & Tech Svcs
18935	6	28	Isps, Web Search Portals
18936	363	5030	Food Svcs & Drinking Places
18938	714	3534	Food Svcs & Drinking Places
18940	1278	11678	Educational Services
18942	188	989	Special Trade Contractors
18943	23	197	Merch. Wholesalers,Durable Gds
18944	617	4112	Educational Services
18946	25	239	Nursing & Resid. Care Facilit.
18947	237	1425	Special Trade Contractors
18949	151	1341	Chemical Manufacturing
18950	33	214	Sportg Gds,Hobby,Book, & Music
18951	1473	12655	Food Svcs & Drinking Places
18953	21	23	Transportation Equipment Mfg
18954	410	2208	Food Svcs & Drinking Places
18955	43	333	Construction of Buildings
18956	15	158	Mining (Except Oil and Gas)
18957	8	19	Special Trade Contractors
18958	12	26	Merch. Wholesalers,Durable Gds
18960	387	4790	Hospitals
18962	41	139	Merch. Wholesalers,Durable Gds
18963	64	194	Educational Services
18964	560	8233	Food Manufacturing
18966	1371	9660	Prof., Scientific, & Tech Svcs
18968	7	15	Miscellaneous Manufacturing
18969	389	5168	Miscellaneous Manufacturing
18970	34	338	Fabricated Metal Product Mfg
18971	18	97	Truck Transportation
18972	84	220	Accommodation
18974	1584	18940	Prof., Scientific, & Tech Svcs
18976	560	5924	Food and Beverage Stores
18977	156	689	Prof., Scientific, & Tech Svcs
18979	13	38	Merch. Wholesalers,Durable Gds
18980	52	113	Social Assistance
19001	677	9090	Hospitals
19002	1157	8849	Prof., Scientific, & Tech Svcs
19003	903	7353	Justice, Pubic Order/Safety
19004	1224	14326	Ambulatory Health Care Svcs
19006	1191	11100	Ambulatory Health Care Svcs
19007	1149	15929	Chemical Manufacturing
19008	796	9293	Prof., Scientific, & Tech Svcs
19009	34	294	Educational Services
19010	1043	11555	Hospitals
19012	291	1020	Amusement, Gambling,& Recreat.
19013	961	14661	Hospitals
19014	714	7360	Fabricated Metal Product Mfg
19015	356	2728	Food and Beverage Stores
19016	1	8	Fabricated Metal Product Mfg
19017	86	173	Construction of Buildings
19018	521	4564	Bldg Matl & Garden Eqpmt Dlrs
19020	2182	26684	Food Svcs & Drinking Places
19021	242	3014	Prof., Scientific, & Tech Svcs
19022	176	2279	Prof., Scientific, & Tech Svcs
19023	536	5594	Hospitals
19025	216	2125	Securities/Commodity Contracts
19026	692	5878	Hospitals
19027	741	4948	Hospitals
19028	67	774	Food and Beverage Stores
19029	215	2116	Accommodation
19030	569	9227	General Merchandise Stores
19031	306	2516	Nursing & Resid. Care Facilit.
19032	265	2829	Food Svcs & Drinking Places
19033	293	2745	Food and Beverage Stores
19034	613	9751	Prof., Scientific, & Tech Svcs
19035	123	1067	Relig., Grant, Civic, Prof Org
19036	288	1818	Food and Beverage Stores
19037	5	1134	Nursing & Resid. Care Facilit.
19038	1208	8839	Educational Services
19039	18	62	Real Estate
19040	850	6175	Insurance Carriers & Related
19041	261	3115	Educational Services
19043	160	5697	Rental and Leasing Services
19044	918	20446	Prof., Scientific, & Tech Svcs
19046	1473	12643	Prof., Scientific, & Tech Svcs
19047	1824	26037	Ambulatory Health Care Svcs
19050	692	4813	Special Trade Contractors
19052	13	216	Plastics & Rubber Products Mfg
19053	1474	14595	Prof., Scientific, & Tech Svcs
19054	295	1761	Educational Services
19055	178	1000	Educational Services
19056	395	3447	Administrative & Support Svcs
19057	663	5539	Publishing Industries
19058	7	23	Administrative & Support Svcs
19061	736	5868	Plastics & Rubber Products Mfg
19063	2089	18549	Prof., Scientific, & Tech Svcs
19064	975	10102	Food Svcs & Drinking Places
19066	119	879	Educational Services
19067	1832	12755	Prof., Scientific, & Tech Svcs
19070	176	927	Special Trade Contractors
19072	487	2177	Prof., Scientific, & Tech Svcs
19073	795	8175	Administrative & Support Svcs
19074	126	569	Educational Services
19075	228	1035	Special Trade Contractors
19076	194	1424	Educational Services
19078	284	2293	Hospitals
19079	293	2760	Prof., Scientific, & Tech Svcs
19081	275	1935	Educational Services
19082	1192	7622	Food and Beverage Stores
19083	1043	5882	Ambulatory Health Care Svcs

BUSINESS DATA

ZIP CODE	2004 Total Firms	2004 Total Employees	TOP INDUSTRY RANKED on 2004 EMPLOYMENT	ZIP CODE	2004 Total Firms	2004 Total Employees	TOP INDUSTRY RANKED on 2004 EMPLOYMENT	ZIP CODE	2004 Total Firms	2004 Total Employees	TOP INDUSTRY RANKED on 2004 EMPLOYMENT
19085	137	780	Other Information Services	19354	9	26	Special Trade Contractors	19522	441	3378	Educational Services
19086	152	844	Nursing & Resid. Care Facilit.	19355	1394	32416	Securities/Commodity Contracts	19523	14	76	Educational Services
19087	1852	36793	Merch. Wholesalers,Nondur. Gds	19357	23	81	Food Svcs & Drinking Places	19525	400	2415	Food and Beverage Stores
19089	1	0	Prof., Scientific, & Tech Svcs	19358	8	44	Paper Manufacturing	19526	402	4236	Prof., Scientific, & Tech Svcs
19090	1231	18201	Nat'l Security & Int'l Affairs	19360	35	94	Support Act. for Transport.	19529	87	333	Relig., Grant, Civic, Prof Org
19091	4	1558	Miscellaneous Store Retailers	19362	98	903	Food Manufacturing	19530	469	4053	Educational Services
19094	118	608	Food Svcs & Drinking Places	19363	485	2987	Educational Services	19533	265	4846	Exec., Legis., & Other Support
19095	211	2670	Educational Services	19365	233	1038	Food Svcs & Drinking Places	19534	61	474	Crop Production
19096	420	5522	Hospitals	19366	6	10	Postal Service	19535	8	10	Waste Managmt & Remediat'n Svc
19101	8	24	Isps, Web Search Portals	19367	13	49	Merch. Wholesalers,Nondur. Gds	19536	17	4134	Elect'l Eqpmt, App, & Comp Mfg
19102	2196	32750	Prof., Scientific, & Tech Svcs	19369	27	147	Food Svcs & Drinking Places	19538	23	46	Miscellaneous Manufacturing
19103	4160	65871	Prof., Scientific, & Tech Svcs	19371	2	5	Miscellaneous Store Retailers	19539	106	485	Food and Beverage Stores
19104	1691	39009	Hospitals	19372	136	1319	Food and Beverage Stores	19540	314	1693	Prof., Scientific, & Tech Svcs
19105	3	13	Motion Pict. & Sound Recording	19373	41	189	Social Assistance	19541	47	181	Special Trade Contractors
19106	2046	24991	Prof., Scientific, & Tech Svcs	19374	84	1091	Crop Production	19542	7	7	Administrative & Support Svcs
19107	2695	38063	Ambulatory Health Care Svcs	19375	49	143	Merch. Wholesalers,Durable Gds	19543	320	3351	Transportation Equipment Mfg
19108	34	447	Publishing Industries	19376	20	120	Amusement, Gambling,& Recreat.	19544	13	83	Merch. Wholesalers,Durable Gds
19109	77	2141	Credit Intermediation & Relatd	19380	1984	22416	Prof., Scientific, & Tech Svcs	19545	28	244	Food Svcs & Drinking Places
19110	106	805	Justice, Pubic Order/Safety	19381	9	70	Social Assistance	19547	188	1347	Educational Services
19111	1146	11408	Hospitals	19382	1807	16672	Prof., Scientific, & Tech Svcs	19548	15	93	Fabricated Metal Product Mfg
19112	42	413	Support Act. for Transport.	19383	4	48	Other Information Services	19549	11	134	Rail Transportation
19113	72	1643	Nat'l Security & Int'l Affairs	19390	345	3101	Hospitals	19550	21	153	Relig., Grant, Civic, Prof Org
19114	738	14862	Hospitals	19395	47	328	Educational Services	19551	159	2717	Food and Beverage Stores
19115	929	8087	Ambulatory Health Care Svcs	19399	16	1309	Postal Service	19554	31	215	Food Svcs & Drinking Places
19116	772	9788	Food Svcs & Drinking Places	19401	1853	20449	Hospitals	19555	125	1324	Primary Metal Manufacturing
19118	633	5565	Hospitals	19403	1387	15795	Educational Services	19559	20	358	Primary Metal Manufacturing
19119	539	3430	Nursing & Resid. Care Facilit.	19404	18	2114	Exec., Legis., & Other Support	19560	258	2974	General Merchandise Stores
19120	1121	6016	Educational Services	19405	278	1617	Waste Managmt & Remediat'n Svc	19562	109	1761	Relig., Grant, Civic, Prof Org
19121	658	3682	Educational Services	19406	2063	40117	Computer & Electronic Prod Mfg	19564	13	100	Food Svcs & Drinking Places
19122	484	11422	Educational Services	19407	6	302	Educational Services	19565	180	2063	Hospitals
19123	882	10709	Administrative & Support Svcs	19408	3	15	Special Trade Contractors	19567	140	1467	Textile Product Mills
19124	1537	19850	Transportation Equipment Mfg	19409	13	42	Administrative & Support Svcs	19601	1267	15313	Primary Metal Manufacturing
19125	705	6198	Educational Services	19420	2	2	Postal Service	19602	497	5079	Educational Services
19126	253	2087	Nursing & Resid. Care Facilit.	19421	8	32	Exec., Legis., & Other Support	19603	7	9	Prof., Scientific, & Tech Svcs
19127	355	3354	Food Svcs & Drinking Places	19422	993	13045	Prof., Scientific, & Tech Svcs	19604	403	5675	Hospitals
19128	899	8233	Hospitals	19423	18	78	Heavy & Civil Eng. Construct'N	19605	1008	16533	Merch. Wholesalers,Durable Gds
19129	283	7900	Hospitals	19424	1	2	Other Information Services	19606	856	10016	General Merchandise Stores
19130	904	11958	Educational Services	19425	278	1548	Food and Beverage Stores	19607	759	9790	Prof., Scientific, & Tech Svcs
19131	937	12044	Educational Services	19426	924	7522	Justice, Pubic Order/Safety	19608	554	6171	Miscellaneous Manufacturing
19132	787	7152	Special Trade Contractors	19428	1353	20831	Hospitals	19609	311	2476	Educational Services
19133	673	4305	Educational Services	19430	13	39	Food Svcs & Drinking Places	19610	1081	21285	Merch. Wholesalers,Nondur. Gds
19134	1449	16025	Hospitals	19432	16	448	Educational Services	19611	448	13208	Ambulatory Health Care Svcs
19135	940	5309	Food Svcs & Drinking Places	19435	26	412	Nursing & Resid. Care Facilit.	19612	13	423	Postal Service
19136	894	8097	Food Svcs & Drinking Places	19436	19	342	Nursing & Resid. Care Facilit.	19701	761	6488	Admin. of Economic Programs
19137	340	3884	Transit & Grnd Pass. Transport	19437	28	181	Nursing & Resid. Care Facilit.	19702	1136	12789	Food Svcs & Drinking Places
19138	491	2536	Educational Services	19438	509	7572	Food Manufacturing	19703	440	3748	Chemical Manufacturing
19139	1014	5572	Educational Services	19440	498	8939	Food Manufacturing	19706	114	2148	Petroleum & Coal Products Mfg
19140	1178	11850	Hospitals	19442	73	732	Petroleum & Coal Products Mfg	19707	552	3483	Nursing & Resid. Care Facilit.
19141	717	8955	Hospitals	19443	83	1352	Merch. Wholesalers,Durable Gds	19708	2	7	Administrative & Support Svcs
19142	559	2823	Educational Services	19444	328	2505	Prof., Scientific, & Tech Svcs	19709	626	4152	Food Svcs & Drinking Places
19143	953	6581	Hospitals	19446	1600	14789	Educational Services	19710	18	145	Accommodation
19144	1215	10499	Educational Services	19450	38	201	Prof., Scientific, & Tech Svcs	19711	1593	14959	Food Svcs & Drinking Places
19145	1025	11514	Exec., Legis., & Other Support	19451	14	514	Plastics & Rubber Products Mfg	19712	1	650	Health & Personal Care Stores
19146	908	7741	Hospitals	19453	36	157	Prof., Scientific, & Tech Svcs	19713	1000	14811	Securities/Commodity Contracts
19147	1617	9070	Food Svcs & Drinking Places	19454	884	9670	Food Svcs & Drinking Places	19714	21	300	Prof., Scientific, & Tech Svcs
19148	1483	13209	Merch. Wholesalers,Nondur. Gds	19456	119	2746	Securities/Commodity Contracts	19715	3	6	Publishing Industries
19149	956	7024	Food Svcs & Drinking Places	19457	30	342	Sportg Gds,Hobby,Book, & Music	19716	22	3668	Educational Services
19150	468	2795	Food and Beverage Stores	19460	1264	10006	Hospitals	19717	1	20	Sportg Gds,Hobby,Book, & Music
19151	582	2922	Educational Services	19462	992	14786	Prof., Scientific, & Tech Svcs	19718	24	6345	Hospitals
19152	742	6778	Hospitals	19464	1787	16905	Educational Services	19720	1965	37610	Credit Intermediation & Relatd
19153	505	29414	Support Act. for Transport.	19465	454	3073	Food Svcs & Drinking Places	19730	44	355	Justice, Pubic Order/Safety
19154	709	14864	Food Svcs & Drinking Places	19468	739	5567	Nursing & Resid. Care Facilit.	19731	9	25	Food Svcs & Drinking Places
19181	1	500	Insurance Carriers & Related	19470	19	79	Textile Product Mills	19732	8	27	Securities/Commodity Contracts
19192	3	8500	Insurance Carriers & Related	19472	22	48	Food Manufacturing	19733	24	162	Motor Vehicle & Parts Dealers
19301	764	6639	Ambulatory Health Care Svcs	19473	281	2218	Educational Services	19734	163	497	Food and Beverage Stores
19310	75	1134	Educational Services	19474	251	2683	Special Trade Contractors	19735	3	600	Museums, Hist. Sites,& Similar
19311	220	2317	Crop Production	19475	283	1491	Truck Transportation	19736	30	222	Special Trade Contractors
19312	492	7136	Social Assistance	19477	217	4226	Ambulatory Health Care Svcs	19801	2917	28250	Prof., Scientific, & Tech Svcs
19316	8	14	Special Trade Contractors	19478	15	196	Accommodation	19802	730	6542	Educational Services
19317	521	3580	Prof., Scientific, & Tech Svcs	19480	126	834	Special Trade Contractors	19803	1115	18862	Chemical Manufacturing
19318	8	134	Nursing & Resid. Care Facilit.	19481	31	118	Social Assistance	19804	925	12463	Transportation Equipment Mfg
19319	12	63	Administrative & Support Svcs	19482	9	9052	Prof., Scientific, & Tech Svcs	19805	1122	11804	Hospitals
19320	1031	8922	Primary Metal Manufacturing	19484	4	5	Administrative & Support Svcs	19806	583	4945	Prof., Scientific, & Tech Svcs
19330	113	400	Construction of Buildings	19486	48	1032	Health & Personal Care Stores	19807	358	3797	Prof., Scientific, & Tech Svcs
19331	112	2797	Fabricated Metal Product Mfg	19490	96	993	Chemical Manufacturing	19808	1517	14186	Food Svcs & Drinking Places
19333	264	2774	Real Estate	19492	40	311	Special Trade Contractors	19809	552	8020	Securities/Commodity Contracts
19335	1215	9292	Educational Services	19501	77	699	Apparel Manufacturing	19810	927	11858	Nonstore Retailers
19339	2	1004	Insurance Carriers & Related	19503	54	582	Textile Mills	19850	11	31	Support Act. for Transport.
19341	1563	22438	Prof., Scientific, & Tech Svcs	19504	132	376	Educational Services	19880	2	3	Ambulatory Health Care Svcs
19342	372	3881	Isps, Web Search Portals	19505	127	659	Food Svcs & Drinking Places	19884	2	4801	Managmt of Companies & Enterp.
19343	240	1059	Special Trade Contractors	19506	175	1016	Accommodation	19898	1	3	Ambulatory Health Care Svcs
19344	265	2086	Nursing & Resid. Care Facilit.	19507	134	899	Nonmetallic Mineral Prod. Mfg	19899	10	19	Prof., Scientific, & Tech Svcs
19345	5	837	Educational Services	19508	443	2605	Educational Services	19901	1789	27432	Miscellaneous Manufacturing
19346	6	43	Plastics & Rubber Products Mfg	19510	130	2263	Crop Production	19902	37	7566	Nat'l Security & Int'l Affairs
19347	29	130	Educational Services	19511	19	62	Food Svcs & Drinking Places	19903	13	83	Admin. of Economic Programs
19348	938	9261	Crop Production	19512	659	5996	Primary Metal Manufacturing	19904	1111	10860	Ambulatory Health Care Svcs
19350	155	1032	Crop Production	19516	12	82	Electronics & Appliance Stores	19930	281	2292	Real Estate
19351	10	24	Bldg Matl & Garden Eqpmt Dlrs	19518	373	2560	Prof., Scientific, & Tech Svcs	19931	18	47	Administrative & Support Svcs
19352	60	785	Educational Services	19519	8	9	Repair and Maintenance	19933	243	1805	Educational Services
19353	17	18	Ambulatory Health Care Svcs	19520	208	2078	Merch. Wholesalers,Nondur. Gds	19934	335	2392	Educational Services

ZIP CODE	2004 Total Firms	2004 Total Employees	TOP INDUSTRY RANKED on 2004 EMPLOYMENT	ZIP CODE	2004 Total Firms	2004 Total Employees	TOP INDUSTRY RANKED on 2004 EMPLOYMENT	ZIP CODE	2004 Total Firms	2004 Total Employees	TOP INDUSTRY RANKED on 2004 EMPLOYMENT
19936	26	314	Chemical Manufacturing	20107	35	121	Educational Services	20241	4	6	Ambulatory Health Care Svcs
19938	117	1031	Miscellaneous Manufacturing	20108	32	113	Administrative & Support Svcs	20242	5	587	Admin. Enviro. Quality Progrms
19939	150	609	Bldg Matl & Garden Eqpmt Dlrs	20109	1298	18502	Food Svcs & Drinking Places	20245	1	630	Admin. Enviro. Quality Progrms
19940	229	1526	Food Svcs & Drinking Places	20110	2041	21874	Prof., Scientific, & Tech Svcs	20250	16	2138	Support Activities: Agr./For.
19941	35	183	Relig., Grant, Civic, Prof Org	20111	706	5798	Special Trade Contractors	20260	8	3008	Postal Service
19943	229	959	Educational Services	20112	391	1736	Educational Services	20301	6	3	Ambulatory Health Care Svcs
19944	107	935	Food Svcs & Drinking Places	20113	3	24	Administrative & Support Svcs	20303	1	150	Prof., Scientific, & Tech Svcs
19945	164	780	Educational Services	20115	274	1388	Educational Services	20306	24	1174	Ambulatory Health Care Svcs
19946	86	695	Merch. Wholesalers,Durable Gds	20116	2	12	Special Trade Contractors	20307	21	171	Special Trade Contractors
19947	924	10220	Exec., Legis., & Other Support	20117	381	1566	Educational Services	20310	1	0	Relig., Grant, Civic, Prof Org
19950	186	1118	Plastics & Rubber Products Mfg	20118	10	25	Perform'g Arts, Spec. Sports	20317	7	1020	Nursing & Resid. Care Facilit.
19951	61	940	Merch. Wholesalers,Nondur. Gds	20119	104	509	Construction of Buildings	20319	10	76	Food Svcs & Drinking Places
19952	293	2510	Food Svcs & Drinking Places	20120	581	3364	Educational Services	20330	4	6	Ambulatory Health Care Svcs
19953	90	297	Special Trade Contractors	20121	548	4454	Food Svcs & Drinking Places	20350	1	0	Nat'l Security & Int'l Affairs
19954	35	134	Support Act. for Transport.	20122	26	114	Nonstore Retailers	20373	7	124	Nat'l Security & Int'l Affairs
19955	20	145	Fabricated Metal Product Mfg	20124	321	2057	Educational Services	20374	28	173	Relig., Grant, Civic, Prof Org
19956	501	2596	Educational Services	20128	9	15	Food and Beverage Stores	20375	5	270	Prof., Scientific, & Tech Svcs
19958	1017	7235	Hospitals	20129	23	56	Prof., Scientific, & Tech Svcs	20390	2	1506	Nat'l Security & Int'l Affairs
19960	103	444	Relig., Grant, Civic, Prof Org	20130	16	72	Amusement, Gambling,& Recreat.	20392	4	14	Administrative & Support Svcs
19961	10	71	Waste Managmt & Remediat'n Svc	20131	14	55	Justice, Pubic Order/Safety	20393	2	400	Nat'l Security & Int'l Affairs
19962	72	187	Educational Services	20132	562	2974	Educational Services	20401	3	10	Credit Intermediation & Relatd
19963	850	8766	Food Manufacturing	20134	12	44	Transit & Grnd Pass. Transport	20403	1	9	Sportg Gds,Hobby,Book, & Music
19964	29	88	Merch. Wholesalers,Durable Gds	20135	68	170	Construction of Buildings	20405	7	170	Exec., Legis., & Other Support
19966	659	6767	Crop Production	20136	152	1626	Perform'g Arts, Spec. Sports	20407	1	0	Exec., Legis., & Other Support
19967	41	146	Food and Beverage Stores	20137	48	103	Administrative & Support Svcs	20408	7	457	Exec., Legis., & Other Support
19968	302	1290	Special Trade Contractors	20138	31	133	Construction of Buildings	20410	7	60	Special Trade Contractors
19969	12	52	Bldg Matl & Garden Eqpmt Dlrs	20139	8	16	Special Trade Contractors	20415	4	30	Other Information Services
19970	405	1983	Food Svcs & Drinking Places	20140	8	11	Prof., Scientific, & Tech Svcs	20418	12	225	Relig., Grant, Civic, Prof Org
19971	1312	9885	Food Svcs & Drinking Places	20141	95	390	Construction of Buildings	20419	1	150	Admin. of Economic Programs
19973	919	10394	Chemical Manufacturing	20142	7	18	Postal Service	20420	5	56	Ambulatory Health Care Svcs
19975	371	5336	Food Manufacturing	20143	36	214	Administrative & Support Svcs	20422	26	1998	Hospitals
19977	485	5198	Hospitals	20144	34	102	Special Trade Contractors	20424	1	0	Admin. of Economic Programs
19979	15	36	Prof., Scientific, & Tech Svcs	20146	11	23	Relig., Grant, Civic, Prof Org	20426	5	55	Administrative & Support Svcs
19980	25	354	Educational Services	20147	797	6856	Prof., Scientific, & Tech Svcs	20427	1	70	Admin. of Economic Programs
20001	2389	41913	Transit & Grnd Pass. Transport	20148	81	428	Educational Services	20429	3	26	Other Information Services
20002	2348	24512	Educational Services	20151	1666	29275	Prof., Scientific, & Tech Svcs	20431	4	4002	Securities/Commodity Contracts
20003	1511	12951	Relig., Grant, Civic, Prof Org	20152	239	2603	Administrative & Support Svcs	20433	7	10283	Credit Intermediation & Relatd
20004	1852	25728	Prof., Scientific, & Tech Svcs	20153	17	160	Insurance Carriers & Related	20439	16	307	Exec., Legis., & Other Support
20005	3540	45551	Prof., Scientific, & Tech Svcs	20155	293	3305	Special Trade Contractors	20441	2	18	Relig., Grant, Civic, Prof Org
20006	2952	31140	Prof., Scientific, & Tech Svcs	20156	6	519	Construction of Buildings	20442	7	80	Justice, Pubic Order/Safety
20007	2446	30147	Prof., Scientific, & Tech Svcs	20158	87	242	Educational Services	20444	1	8	Admin. Enviro. Quality Progrms
20008	1271	12992	Nat'l Security & Int'l Affairs	20159	5	11	Social Assistance	20447	1	900	Admin. Human Resource Programs
20009	2348	16842	Relig., Grant, Civic, Prof Org	20160	11	9	Relig., Grant, Civic, Prof Org	20451	2	251	Nat'l Security & Int'l Affairs
20010	755	13515	Hospitals	20164	1205	9451	Educational Services	20463	1	0	Exec., Legis., & Other Support
20011	1441	9747	Educational Services	20165	613	4540	Food Svcs & Drinking Places	20472	1	1900	Justice, Pubic Order/Safety
20012	596	2994	Prof., Scientific, & Tech Svcs	20166	1214	22174	Special Trade Contractors	20500	13	48	Ambulatory Health Care Svcs
20013	11	11	Relig., Grant, Civic, Prof Org	20167	16	314	Special Trade Contractors	20503	1	0	Unclassified Establishments
20015	693	5914	Food Svcs & Drinking Places	20168	2	32	Special Trade Contractors	20506	1	25	Other Information Services
20016	1587	20203	Educational Services	20169	334	1486	Special Trade Contractors	20507	1	0	Admin. Human Resource Programs
20017	609	7130	Hospitals	20170	1715	14517	Prof., Scientific, & Tech Svcs	20510	12	159	Relig., Grant, Civic, Prof Org
20018	723	6191	Heavy & Civil Eng. Construct'N	20171	864	15128	Isps, Web Search Portals	20515	20	264	Exec., Legis., & Other Support
20019	786	6655	Educational Services	20172	19	52	Administrative & Support Svcs	20520	11	66	Prof., Scientific, & Tech Svcs
20020	885	6730	Educational Services	20175	1095	8885	Prof., Scientific, & Tech Svcs	20521	1	1	Merch. Wholesalers,Nondur. Gds
20024	697	16846	Justice, Pubic Order/Safety	20176	1132	11551	Hospitals	20522	1	1	Construction of Buildings
20026	2	20	Transit & Grnd Pass. Transport	20177	17	78	Educational Services	20523	7	6	Clothing & Cloth'g Acc. Stores
20027	4	4	Prof., Scientific, & Tech Svcs	20178	3	8	Special Trade Contractors	20526	4	563	Nat'l Security & Int'l Affairs
20030	2	17	Motion Pict. & Sound Recording	20180	150	471	Special Trade Contractors	20527	1	215	Exec., Legis., & Other Support
20032	546	12022	Admin. Human Resource Programs	20181	188	955	Special Trade Contractors	20528	1	0	Nat'l Security & Int'l Affairs
20033	1	0	Prof., Scientific, & Tech Svcs	20182	4	104	Merch. Wholesalers,Durable Gds	20530	11	86	Other Information Services
20035	5	31	Prof., Scientific, & Tech Svcs	20184	45	186	Heavy & Civil Eng. Construct'N	20531	1	0	Exec., Legis., & Other Support
20036	4972	55987	Prof., Scientific, & Tech Svcs	20185	4	4	Real Estate	20534	7	27	Administrative & Support Svcs
20037	1552	30956	Publishing Industries	20186	1087	9625	Food Svcs & Drinking Places	20535	2	0	Miscellaneous Store Retailers
20038	2	7	Relig., Grant, Civic, Prof Org	20187	365	2670	Special Trade Contractors	20536	2	0	Prof., Scientific, & Tech Svcs
20039	4	3	Sportg Gds,Hobby,Book, & Music	20188	13	36	Prof., Scientific, & Tech Svcs	20540	7	100	Nonstore Retailers
20040	4	4	Relig., Grant, Civic, Prof Org	20190	1443	24901	Prof., Scientific, & Tech Svcs	20541	1	45	Relig., Grant, Civic, Prof Org
20041	96	634	Food Svcs & Drinking Places	20191	1067	16832	Prof., Scientific, & Tech Svcs	20542	2	117	Other Information Services
20043	3	16	Social Assistance	20192	7	3126	Admin. Enviro. Quality Progrms	20543	7	356	Exec., Legis., & Other Support
20044	8	570	Justice, Pubic Order/Safety	20193	1	400	Credit Intermediation & Relatd	20546	1	5	Credit Intermediation & Relatd
20045	226	1490	Other Information Services	20194	170	1151	Food Svcs & Drinking Places	20547	5	408	Nat'l Security & Int'l Affairs
20049	4	1646	Relig., Grant, Civic, Prof Org	20195	8	10	Administrative & Support Svcs	20548	7	5691	Publishing Industries
20050	22	135	Credit Intermediation & Relatd	20197	54	185	Educational Services	20551	4	1778	Monetary Auth. - Central Bank
20052	1	9527	Educational Services	20198	117	487	Merch. Wholesalers,Durable Gds	20552	6	20	Exec., Legis., & Other Support
20056	6	23	Prof., Scientific, & Tech Svcs	20201	11	2716	Admin. Human Resource Programs	20553	3	3035	Other Information Services
20057	13	6707	Educational Services	20202	5	97	Miscellaneous Store Retailers	20554	2	3	Other Information Services
20059	11	4890	Educational Services	20204	1	11	Other Information Services	20560	41	6843	Museums, Hist. Sites,& Similar
20060	23	2511	Hospitals	20210	10	168	Nat'l Security & Int'l Affairs	20565	3	1935	Prof., Scientific, & Tech Svcs
20062	4	358	Relig., Grant, Civic, Prof Org	20212	2	1	Administrative & Support Svcs	20566	7	1925	Perform'g Arts, Spec. Sports
20064	14	3013	Educational Services	20216	2	0	Broadcasting	20571	1	408	Credit Intermediation & Relatd
20065	2	1600	Insurance Carriers & Related	20217	32	496	Justice, Pubic Order/Safety	20573	1	125	Admin. of Economic Programs
20066	3	3554	Postal Service	20219	2	431	Exec., Legis., & Other Support	20576	2	55	Exec., Legis., & Other Support
20068	1	1000	Managmt of Companies & Enterp.	20220	6	43	Credit Intermediation & Relatd	20577	2	32	Heavy & Civil Eng. Construct'N
20071	3	2853	Publishing Industries	20223	1	0	Justice, Pubic Order/Safety	20579	1	7	Nat'l Security & Int'l Affairs
20073	1	50	Managmt of Companies & Enterp.	20224	11	121	Administrative & Support Svcs	20580	3	25	Administrative & Support Svcs
20076	1	2000	Insurance Carriers & Related	20226	1	0	Justice, Pubic Order/Safety	20585	10	179	Construction of Buildings
20080	3	99	Managmt of Companies & Enterp.	20228	2	1800	Securities/Commodity Contracts	20590	11	393	Admin. of Economic Programs
20090	6	4	Prof., Scientific, & Tech Svcs	20229	2	12	Credit Intermediation & Relatd	20591	2	4	Personal and Laundry Services
20091	1	1	Prof., Scientific, & Tech Svcs	20230	13	3719	Admin. of Economic Programs	20593	9	55	Food Svcs & Drinking Places
20101	41	370	Support Act. for Transport.	20233	2	0	Other Information Services	20594	2	363	Admin. of Economic Programs
20105	91	321	Educational Services	20239	2	31	Prof., Scientific, & Tech Svcs	20601	1028	8538	Food Svcs & Drinking Places
20106	88	173	Food and Beverage Stores	20240	12	49	Special Trade Contractors	20602	645	6579	Prof., Scientific, & Tech Svcs

BUSINESS DATA

ZIP CODE	2004 Total Firms	2004 Total Employees	TOP INDUSTRY RANKED on 2004 EMPLOYMENT	ZIP CODE	2004 Total Firms	2004 Total Employees	TOP INDUSTRY RANKED on 2004 EMPLOYMENT	ZIP CODE	2004 Total Firms	2004 Total Employees	TOP INDUSTRY RANKED on 2004 EMPLOYMENT
20603	535	6941	General Merchandise Stores	20732	171	1195	Food Svcs & Drinking Places	20876	386	9681	Computer & Electronic Prod Mfg
20604	21	95	Special Trade Contractors	20733	57	178	Food Svcs & Drinking Places	20877	2176	19657	Prof., Scientific, & Tech Svcs
20606	4	4	Postal Service	20735	1225	12027	Special Trade Contractors	20878	1283	14318	Food Svcs & Drinking Places
20607	165	1990	Construction of Buildings	20736	267	1873	Educational Services	20879	1351	14568	Special Trade Contractors
20608	14	245	Utilities	20737	456	3944	Computer & Electronic Prod Mfg	20880	21	50	Electronics & Appliance Stores
20609	28	70	Food and Beverage Stores	20738	11	67	Food and Beverage Stores	20882	314	1656	Administrative & Support Svcs
20610	14	143	Justice, Pubic Order/Safety	20740	1010	10537	Food Svcs & Drinking Places	20883	3	17	Special Trade Contractors
20611	27	103	Relig., Grant, Civic, Prof Org	20741	5	21	Transit & Grnd Pass. Transport	20884	5	15	Administrative & Support Svcs
20612	14	34	Motor Vehicle & Parts Dealers	20742	27	1678	Educational Services	20885	9	72	Social Assistance
20613	239	1361	Educational Services	20743	1262	10760	Special Trade Contractors	20886	457	3170	Educational Services
20615	12	84	Food Svcs & Drinking Places	20744	1009	5907	Educational Services	20889	48	4542	Nat'l Security & Int'l Affairs
20616	124	892	Food and Beverage Stores	20745	805	6651	Educational Services	20891	3	2	Transit & Grnd Pass. Transport
20617	26	208	Educational Services	20746	659	5644	Prof., Scientific, & Tech Svcs	20892	115	4972	Prof., Scientific, & Tech Svcs
20618	20	164	Administrative & Support Svcs	20747	1044	10255	Educational Services	20894	1	500	Other Information Services
20619	352	3541	Food Svcs & Drinking Places	20748	1238	9017	Motor Vehicle & Parts Dealers	20895	1129	9117	Food Svcs & Drinking Places
20620	45	181	Special Trade Contractors	20749	11	26	Prof., Scientific, & Tech Svcs	20896	39	158	Educational Services
20621	21	122	Educational Services	20750	6	19	Publishing Industries	20898	9	1245	Postal Service
20622	173	1680	Nursing & Resid. Care Facilit.	20751	148	667	Food Svcs & Drinking Places	20899	4	6595	Miscellaneous Manufacturing
20623	48	520	Educational Services	20752	1	1	Prof., Scientific, & Tech Svcs	20901	818	5210	Educational Services
20624	33	98	Merch. Wholesalers,Durable Gds	20753	6	6	Special Trade Contractors	20902	1438	10193	Educational Services
20625	18	95	Food Svcs & Drinking Places	20754	309	1886	Food and Beverage Stores	20903	373	3140	Relig., Grant, Civic, Prof Org
20626	12	31	Amusement, Gambling,& Recreat.	20755	77	1252	Educational Services	20904	1267	11832	Motor Vehicle & Parts Dealers
20627	11	14	Special Trade Contractors	20757	9	12	Couriers and Messengers	20905	357	1717	Educational Services
20628	10	32	Merch. Wholesalers,Durable Gds	20758	23	99	Accommodation	20906	1057	7868	Educational Services
20629	10	46	Special Trade Contractors	20759	70	401	Educational Services	20907	6	10	Wholesale Elec. Mrkts & Agents
20630	7	22	Amusement, Gambling,& Recreat.	20762	75	3087	Hospitals	20908	1	0	Transit & Grnd Pass. Transport
20632	14	68	Special Trade Contractors	20763	156	2278	Merch. Wholesalers,Durable Gds	20910	2864	27190	Prof., Scientific, & Tech Svcs
20634	83	555	Educational Services	20764	86	259	Relig., Grant, Civic, Prof Org	20911	1	0	Prof., Scientific, & Tech Svcs
20635	5	21	Educational Services	20765	50	262	Food Svcs & Drinking Places	20912	770	6069	Hospitals
20636	238	4076	Relig., Grant, Civic, Prof Org	20768	3	9	Administrative & Support Svcs	20913	3	9	Special Trade Contractors
20637	141	844	Social Assistance	20769	129	783	Prof., Scientific, & Tech Svcs	20914	11	25	Prof., Scientific, & Tech Svcs
20639	314	1366	Educational Services	20770	965	24589	Space Research and Technology	20915	16	54	Administrative & Support Svcs
20640	189	1181	Educational Services	20771	6	20643	Computer & Electronic Prod Mfg	20916	16	30	Publishing Industries
20643	2	1	Food and Beverage Stores	20772	1286	11770	Special Trade Contractors	20918	4	1	Prof., Scientific, & Tech Svcs
20645	11	122	Food Svcs & Drinking Places	20773	11	29	Motion Pict. & Sound Recording	21001	713	7654	Prof., Scientific, & Tech Svcs
20646	689	8851	Educational Services	20774	1053	18770	Educational Services	21005	52	820	Credit Intermediation & Relatd
20650	476	5143	Hospitals	20775	8	18	Special Trade Contractors	21009	424	3427	Prof., Scientific, & Tech Svcs
20653	590	7735	Prof., Scientific, & Tech Svcs	20776	78	403	Educational Services	21010	17	263	Repair and Maintenance
20656	14	154	Educational Services	20777	117	311	Special Trade Contractors	21012	501	2964	Educational Services
20657	264	1393	Educational Services	20778	86	315	Administrative & Support Svcs	21013	104	564	Transit & Grnd Pass. Transport
20658	20	142	Educational Services	20779	48	306	Heavy & Civil Eng. Construct'N	21014	1885	15158	Food Svcs & Drinking Places
20659	423	1775	Special Trade Contractors	20781	773	8425	Special Trade Contractors	21015	630	4585	Food Svcs & Drinking Places
20660	3	127	Educational Services	20782	660	6779	Prof., Scientific, & Tech Svcs	21017	138	3602	Social Assistance
20661	2	2	Personal and Laundry Services	20783	801	6439	Nat'l Security & Int'l Affairs	21018	4	20	Special Trade Contractors
20662	30	161	Educational Services	20784	500	3767	Educational Services	21020	6	9	Construction of Buildings
20664	69	508	Food Svcs & Drinking Places	20785	1106	25090	Beverage & Tobacco Product Mfg	21022	25	645	Educational Services
20667	12	88	Educational Services	20787	3	5	Truck Transportation	21023	25	475	Heavy & Civil Eng. Construct'N
20670	44	1742	Support Act. for Transport.	20788	1	3	Electronics & Appliance Stores	21027	12	18	Relig., Grant, Civic, Prof Org
20674	25	226	Educational Services	20790	3	4024	Postal Service	21028	151	824	Heavy & Civil Eng. Construct'N
20675	29	271	Educational Services	20791	5	9	Insurance Carriers & Related	21029	316	2313	Motor Vehicle & Parts Dealers
20676	57	345	Educational Services	20792	2	0	Nonstore Retailers	21030	1230	17114	Prof., Scientific, & Tech Svcs
20677	51	201	Transit & Grnd Pass. Transport	20794	673	12423	Merch. Wholesalers,Nondur. Gds	21031	197	7558	Food Manufacturing
20678	774	8243	Hospitals	20812	24	105	Educational Services	21032	178	2648	Hospitals
20680	43	173	Educational Services	20813	5	10	Administrative & Support Svcs	21034	120	506	Wood Product Manufacturing
20682	3	44	Accommodation	20814	3370	36576	Prof., Scientific, & Tech Svcs	21035	202	1310	Bldg Matl & Garden Eqpmt Dlrs
20684	32	1250	Nat'l Security & Int'l Affairs	20815	1153	16617	Insurance Carriers & Related	21036	74	279	Special Trade Contractors
20685	117	1361	Insurance Carriers & Related	20816	551	3499	Food and Beverage Stores	21037	684	4235	Educational Services
20686	24	48	Food Svcs & Drinking Places	20817	1530	17284	Accommodation	21040	537	4866	Food Svcs & Drinking Places
20687	7	48	Museums, Hist. Sites,& Similar	20818	91	303	Prof., Scientific, & Tech Svcs	21041	15	54	Transit & Grnd Pass. Transport
20688	218	2632	Food Svcs & Drinking Places	20824	7	16	Prof., Scientific, & Tech Svcs	21042	1267	8650	Educational Services
20689	46	263	Special Trade Contractors	20825	7	13	Special Trade Contractors	21043	1082	8677	Food Svcs & Drinking Places
20690	13	102	Educational Services	20827	14	200	Utilities	21044	1752	15692	Educational Services
20692	40	66	Construction of Buildings	20830	14	110	Administrative & Support Svcs	21045	1496	17801	Prof., Scientific, & Tech Svcs
20693	19	29	Justice, Pubic Order/Safety	20832	780	6116	Hospitals	21046	924	19055	Prof., Scientific, & Tech Svcs
20695	262	1975	Special Trade Contractors	20833	158	523	Administrative & Support Svcs	21047	482	3075	Special Trade Contractors
20701	135	3241	Prof., Scientific, & Tech Svcs	20837	217	1110	Educational Services	21048	338	2144	Special Trade Contractors
20703	12	254	Securities/Commodity Contracts	20838	14	40	Special Trade Contractors	21050	483	4276	Special Trade Contractors
20704	8	16	Heavy & Civil Eng. Construct'N	20839	15	156	Educational Services	21051	47	69	Relig., Grant, Civic, Prof Org
20705	1545	23970	Special Trade Contractors	20841	119	325	Special Trade Contractors	21052	9	573	Hospitals
20706	1395	17209	Prof., Scientific, & Tech Svcs	20842	93	507	Prof., Scientific, & Tech Svcs	21053	55	239	Educational Services
20707	1753	15547	Food Svcs & Drinking Places	20847	6	7	Prof., Scientific, & Tech Svcs	21054	357	3096	Food Svcs & Drinking Places
20708	319	2298	Educational Services	20848	7	43	Truck Transportation	21056	12	25	Amusement, Gambling,& Recreat.
20709	2	12	Clothing & Cloth'g Acc. Stores	20849	18	87	Machinery Manufacturing	21057	125	791	Machinery Manufacturing
20710	284	2406	Special Trade Contractors	20850	3521	46558	Prof., Scientific, & Tech Svcs	21060	579	7738	Exec., Legis., & Other Support
20711	150	947	Educational Services	20851	234	1700	Educational Services	21061	2216	21730	Food Svcs & Drinking Places
20712	163	870	Educational Services	20852	2968	37415	Prof., Scientific, & Tech Svcs	21062	2	13	Food Svcs & Drinking Places
20714	129	357	Food Svcs & Drinking Places	20853	483	2362	Educational Services	21071	51	517	Food Svcs & Drinking Places
20715	722	4969	Educational Services	20854	1250	9853	Publishing Industries	21074	479	4490	Educational Services
20716	789	6051	Food Svcs & Drinking Places	20855	620	7236	Prof., Scientific, & Tech Svcs	21075	749	8406	Merch. Wholesalers,Durable Gds
20717	4	19	Administrative & Support Svcs	20857	3	3	Ambulatory Health Care Svcs	21076	720	12873	Prof., Scientific, & Tech Svcs
20718	15	30	Construction of Buildings	20859	12	51	Special Trade Contractors	21077	27	606	Machinery Manufacturing
20719	1	1	Administrative & Support Svcs	20860	79	1251	Nursing & Resid. Care Facilit.	21078	613	5506	Hospitals
20720	286	1266	Administrative & Support Svcs	20861	128	305	Food Svcs & Drinking Places	21082	29	98	Educational Services
20721	370	2645	Nursing & Resid. Care Facilit.	20862	17	53	Administrative & Support Svcs	21084	276	1206	Educational Services
20722	243	1855	Special Trade Contractors	20866	409	3162	Prof., Scientific, & Tech Svcs	21085	386	2919	Educational Services
20723	481	10858	Educational Services	20868	38	246	Administrative & Support Svcs	21087	165	699	Educational Services
20724	263	4185	Perform'g Arts, Spec. Sports	20871	190	2707	Telecommunications	21088	2	19	Bldg Matl & Garden Eqpmt Dlrs
20725	14	54	Relig., Grant, Civic, Prof Org	20872	439	2453	Educational Services	21090	555	9745	Prof., Scientific, & Tech Svcs
20726	4	5	Nonstore Retailers	20874	1037	7237	Educational Services	21092	18	78	Relig., Grant, Civic, Prof Org
20731	2	8	Justice, Pubic Order/Safety	20875	16	30	Support Act. for Transport.	21093	2064	22012	Ambulatory Health Care Svcs

ZIP CODE	2004 Total Firms	2004 Total Employees	TOP INDUSTRY RANKED on 2004 EMPLOYMENT	ZIP CODE	2004 Total Firms	2004 Total Employees	TOP INDUSTRY RANKED on 2004 EMPLOYMENT	ZIP CODE	2004 Total Firms	2004 Total Employees	TOP INDUSTRY RANKED on 2004 EMPLOYMENT
21094	16	35	Prof., Scientific, & Tech Svcs	21411	2	403	Exec., Legis., & Other Support	21678	58	507	Accommodation
21102	255	1346	Transit & Grnd Pass. Transport	21501	10	128	Exec., Legis., & Other Support	21679	36	440	Educational Services
21104	93	885	Construction of Buildings	21502	2062	23784	Hospitals	21701	2274	24890	Relig., Grant, Civic, Prof Org
21105	12	285	Relig., Grant, Civic, Prof Org	21503	2	1	Postal Service	21702	1092	18465	Nat'l Security & Int'l Affairs
21106	17	51	Food and Beverage Stores	21504	4	64	Nonmetallic Mineral Prod. Mfg	21703	726	16046	Prof., Scientific, & Tech Svcs
21108	684	6953	Administrative & Support Svcs	21505	1	1	Sportg Gds,Hobby,Book, & Music	21704	701	10675	Food Svcs & Drinking Places
21111	197	1067	Food Svcs & Drinking Places	21520	99	716	Educational Services	21705	20	26	Prof., Scientific, & Tech Svcs
21113	499	5158	Plastics & Rubber Products Mfg	21521	24	160	Mining (Except Oil and Gas)	21710	68	302	Nursing & Resid. Care Facilit.
21114	793	7053	Food Svcs & Drinking Places	21522	11	10	Educational Services	21711	13	46	Gasoline Stations
21117	1916	25430	Insurance Carriers & Related	21523	8	74	Credit Intermediation & Relatd	21713	218	1640	Nursing & Resid. Care Facilit.
21120	201	981	Educational Services	21524	17	72	Food and Beverage Stores	21714	21	164	Nursing & Resid. Care Facilit.
21122	1523	8911	Food Svcs & Drinking Places	21528	4	70	Merch. Wholesalers,Durable Gds	21715	3	7	Wood Product Manufacturing
21123	7	18	Administrative & Support Svcs	21529	21	75	Special Trade Contractors	21716	137	854	Educational Services
21128	152	635	Educational Services	21530	55	334	Museums, Hist. Sites,& Similar	21717	31	124	Merch. Wholesalers,Durable Gds
21130	10	1825	Health & Personal Care Stores	21531	74	306	Educational Services	21718	11	11	Waste Managmt & Remediat'n Svc
21131	252	1651	Relig., Grant, Civic, Prof Org	21532	380	3551	Educational Services	21719	33	151	Educational Services
21132	64	330	Educational Services	21536	168	1595	Food and Beverage Stores	21720	3	8	Construction of Buildings
21133	806	6266	Hospitals	21538	20	43	Educational Services	21721	2	2	Furn. & Home Furnishgs Stores
21136	1020	7142	Food Svcs & Drinking Places	21539	77	459	Educational Services	21722	124	718	Special Trade Contractors
21139	3	30	Social Assistance	21540	8	1437	Merch. Wholesalers,Nondur. Gds	21723	19	34	Transit & Grnd Pass. Transport
21140	61	229	Food Svcs & Drinking Places	21541	168	1321	Accommodation	21727	155	2086	Educational Services
21144	369	2979	Merch. Wholesalers,Nondur. Gds	21542	17	47	Social Assistance	21733	16	65	Special Trade Contractors
21146	1080	6573	Educational Services	21543	6	24	Special Trade Contractors	21734	17	125	Justice, Pubic Order/Safety
21150	9	15	Administrative & Support Svcs	21545	37	200	Educational Services	21737	57	639	Educational Services
21152	156	3359	Nursing & Resid. Care Facilit.	21550	808	7473	Exec., Legis., & Other Support	21738	96	534	Educational Services
21153	51	756	Educational Services	21555	34	99	Educational Services	21740	2698	36456	Food Svcs & Drinking Places
21154	153	805	Educational Services	21556	6	20	Miscellaneous Store Retailers	21741	6	15	Chemical Manufacturing
21155	83	353	Food Svcs & Drinking Places	21557	31	57	Repair and Maintenance	21742	758	14356	Isps, Web Search Portals
21156	12	24	Relig., Grant, Civic, Prof Org	21560	3	26	Justice, Pubic Order/Safety	21746	5	1205	Justice, Pubic Order/Safety
21157	1991	21404	Exec., Legis., & Other Support	21561	61	237	Exec., Legis., & Other Support	21750	180	2054	Merch. Wholesalers,Durable Gds
21158	348	2420	Exec., Legis., & Other Support	21562	104	843	Nursing & Resid. Care Facilit.	21754	203	1883	Construction of Buildings
21160	96	607	Food and Beverage Stores	21601	1689	14885	Hospitals	21755	142	467	Educational Services
21161	148	574	Special Trade Contractors	21607	13	135	Fabricated Metal Product Mfg	21756	72	123	Prof., Scientific, & Tech Svcs
21162	244	2728	Special Trade Contractors	21609	6	5	Support Act. for Transport.	21757	74	344	Educational Services
21163	117	435	Real Estate	21610	15	74	Relig., Grant, Civic, Prof Org	21758	85	363	Food Svcs & Drinking Places
21201	2366	57283	Ambulatory Health Care Svcs	21612	21	45	Relig., Grant, Civic, Prof Org	21759	1	1	Repair and Maintenance
21202	2513	44476	Prof., Scientific, & Tech Svcs	21613	964	10896	Machinery Manufacturing	21762	37	120	Educational Services
21203	14	33	Merch. Wholesalers,Durable Gds	21617	406	2909	Educational Services	21765	29	254	Educational Services
21204	2403	29472	Hospitals	21619	283	1341	Food Svcs & Drinking Places	21766	18	38	Food and Beverage Stores
21205	543	8236	Educational Services	21620	836	6298	Educational Services	21767	27	120	Merch. Wholesalers,Nondur. Gds
21206	801	6390	Educational Services	21622	22	70	Educational Services	21769	303	1371	Educational Services
21207	969	7713	Educational Services	21623	61	266	Justice, Pubic Order/Safety	21770	143	618	Educational Services
21208	1723	11855	Ambulatory Health Care Svcs	21624	10	22	Special Trade Contractors	21771	800	4853	Food Svcs & Drinking Places
21209	643	5300	Prof., Scientific, & Tech Svcs	21625	72	777	Food Manufacturing	21773	176	813	Special Trade Contractors
21210	464	4136	Educational Services	21626	5	21	Food and Beverage Stores	21774	210	1040	Educational Services
21211	813	10167	Special Trade Contractors	21627	2	1	Postal Service	21775	4	13	Repair and Maintenance
21212	791	4986	Educational Services	21628	15	128	Justice, Pubic Order/Safety	21776	155	917	Wholesale Elec. Mrkts & Agents
21213	565	4748	Educational Services	21629	463	3272	Nursing & Resid. Care Facilit.	21777	19	496	Fabricated Metal Product Mfg
21214	553	3449	Educational Services	21631	63	235	Relig., Grant, Civic, Prof Org	21778	19	89	Nonmetallic Mineral Prod. Mfg
21215	1855	22917	Ambulatory Health Care Svcs	21632	246	2614	Merch. Wholesalers,Nondur. Gds	21779	19	40	Prof., Scientific, & Tech Svcs
21216	500	3453	Educational Services	21634	21	190	Food Manufacturing	21780	25	86	Educational Services
21217	916	6653	Educational Services	21635	79	325	Justice, Pubic Order/Safety	21781	6	70	Educational Services
21218	1597	15433	Hospitals	21636	38	117	Special Trade Contractors	21782	89	406	Museums, Hist. Sites,& Similar
21219	234	2902	Transportation Equipment Mfg	21638	189	1579	Food Svcs & Drinking Places	21783	214	1488	Educational Services
21220	986	7499	Transportation Equipment Mfg	21639	121	575	Educational Services	21784	1156	9032	Hospitals
21221	1053	9118	Educational Services	21640	14	109	Special Trade Contractors	21787	277	1532	Food Svcs & Drinking Places
21222	1381	12961	Educational Services	21641	16	19	Credit Intermediation & Relatd	21788	369	3503	Construction of Buildings
21223	916	8066	Hospitals	21643	140	1661	Food Manufacturing	21790	3	5	Food Svcs & Drinking Places
21224	2074	30670	Transportation Equipment Mfg	21644	3	10	Machinery Manufacturing	21791	145	1214	Credit Intermediation & Relatd
21225	770	6775	Hospitals	21645	38	417	Bldg Matl & Garden Eqpmt Dlrs	21792	1	0	Construction of Buildings
21226	429	7780	Chemical Manufacturing	21647	14	74	Food Manufacturing	21793	279	2423	Chemical Manufacturing
21227	1181	18850	Ambulatory Health Care Svcs	21648	10	50	Nursing & Resid. Care Facilit.	21794	73	415	Educational Services
21228	1695	23149	Nursing & Resid. Care Facilit.	21649	25	101	Special Trade Contractors	21795	268	6063	Leather & Allied Product Mfg
21229	807	9543	Hospitals	21650	11	72	Food and Beverage Stores	21797	223	1483	Administrative & Support Svcs
21230	1418	18558	Merch. Wholesalers,Durable Gds	21651	99	464	Justice, Pubic Order/Safety	21798	81	723	Wood Product Manufacturing
21231	727	5726	Prof., Scientific, & Tech Svcs	21652	10	17	Construction of Buildings	21801	1892	20931	Food Svcs & Drinking Places
21233	2	15	Postal Service	21653	7	18	Amusement, Gambling,& Recreat.	21802	24	112	Administrative & Support Svcs
21234	1553	11591	Educational Services	21654	90	471	Food Svcs & Drinking Places	21803	8	19	Wholesale Elec. Mrkts & Agents
21235	8	79	Credit Intermediation & Relatd	21655	152	856	Motor Vehicle & Parts Dealers	21804	1124	13023	Educational Services
21236	1385	16004	Food Svcs & Drinking Places	21656	1	2	Wood Product Manufacturing	21810	7	3	Postal Service
21237	1042	15444	Hospitals	21657	35	174	Merch. Wholesalers,Durable Gds	21811	915	6901	Hospitals
21239	312	4154	Hospitals	21658	243	1536	Food Manufacturing	21813	129	894	Relig., Grant, Civic, Prof Org
21240	82	13442	Computer & Electronic Prod Mfg	21659	23	109	Accommodation	21814	9	25	Food and Beverage Stores
21241	2	6	Credit Intermediation & Relatd	21660	111	1494	Prof., Scientific, & Tech Svcs	21817	231	2225	Hospitals
21244	914	17315	Admin. Human Resource Programs	21661	156	885	Relig., Grant, Civic, Prof Org	21821	20	40	Educational Services
21250	2	75	Other Information Services	21662	29	33	Administrative & Support Svcs	21822	48	338	Heavy & Civil Eng. Construct'N
21251	5	830	Educational Services	21663	293	1781	Food Svcs & Drinking Places	21824	15	46	Administrative & Support Svcs
21252	9	3359	Educational Services	21664	25	145	Food and Beverage Stores	21826	146	1041	Food Svcs & Drinking Places
21281	1	1	Merch. Wholesalers,Durable Gds	21665	10	23	Food and Beverage Stores	21829	13	16	Merch. Wholesalers,Nondur. Gds
21282	12	32	Food Svcs & Drinking Places	21666	590	3630	Food Svcs & Drinking Places	21830	94	558	Fabricated Metal Product Mfg
21284	12	22	Special Trade Contractors	21667	18	58	Administrative & Support Svcs	21835	14	172	Food Manufacturing
21285	13	43	Postal Service	21668	51	344	Educational Services	21836	3	5	Postal Service
21286	1161	16994	Prof., Scientific, & Tech Svcs	21669	17	108	Justice, Pubic Order/Safety	21837	56	317	Educational Services
21287	100	10226	Hospitals	21670	3	2	Postal Service	21838	38	184	Educational Services
21290	1	2	Food Svcs & Drinking Places	21671	56	267	Accommodation	21840	6	110	Food Manufacturing
21401	4268	45236	Prof., Scientific, & Tech Svcs	21672	8	11	Food and Beverage Stores	21841	27	291	Educational Services
21402	34	3443	Educational Services	21673	105	455	Justice, Pubic Order/Safety	21842	1775	19371	Food Svcs & Drinking Places
21403	1037	6320	Educational Services	21675	5	72	Justice, Pubic Order/Safety	21843	18	58	Construction of Buildings
21404	11	7	Real Estate	21676	15	18	Furn. & Home Furnishgs Stores	21849	87	257	Special Trade Contractors
21405	17	12	Prof., Scientific, & Tech Svcs	21677	8	27	Merch. Wholesalers,Nondur. Gds	21850	77	377	Special Trade Contractors

ZIP CODE	2004 Total Firms	2004 Total Employ-ees	TOP INDUSTRY RANKED on 2004 EMPLOYMENT	ZIP CODE	2004 Total Firms	2004 Total Employ-ees	TOP INDUSTRY RANKED on 2004 EMPLOYMENT	ZIP CODE	2004 Total Firms	2004 Total Employ-ees	TOP INDUSTRY RANKED on 2004 EMPLOYMENT
21851	350	3569	Wholesale Elec. Mrkts & Agents	22210	11	96	Postal Service	22554	1025	9858	Exec., Legis., & Other Support
21852	5	8	Forestry and Logging	22211	27	379	Relig., Grant, Civic, Prof Org	22555	21	48	Heavy & Civil Eng. Construct'N
21853	303	2169	Educational Services	22213	50	754	Publishing Industries	22556	244	2139	Educational Services
21856	38	202	Relig., Grant, Civic, Prof Org	22214	9	211	General Merchandise Stores	22558	1	4	Other Information Services
21857	2	0	Crop Production	22216	1	2	Prof., Scientific, & Tech Svcs	22560	474	4659	Transportation Equipment Mfg
21861	42	190	Wood Product Manufacturing	22219	1	1	Merch. Wholesalers,Durable Gds	22565	22	133	Merch. Wholesalers,Durable Gds
21862	13	1132	Food Manufacturing	22227	1	7	Rental and Leasing Services	22567	50	210	Educational Services
21863	214	1565	Exec., Legis., & Other Support	22230	2	1206	Admin. Human Resource Programs	22570	4	29	Heavy & Civil Eng. Construct'N
21864	14	21	Social Assistance	22301	446	3129	Admin. Human Resource Programs	22572	356	2675	Educational Services
21865	12	7	Relig., Grant, Civic, Prof Org	22302	575	7121	Prof., Scientific, & Tech Svcs	22576	43	183	Merch. Wholesalers,Nondur. Gds
21866	6	49	Justice, Pubic Order/Safety	22303	342	3086	Prof., Scientific, & Tech Svcs	22577	4	9	Special Trade Contractors
21867	9	31	Museums, Hist. Sites,& Similar	22304	1472	20450	Ambulatory Health Care Svcs	22578	152	633	Relig., Grant, Civic, Prof Org
21869	39	62	Educational Services	22305	297	2753	Food Svcs & Drinking Places	22579	14	32	Prof., Scientific, & Tech Svcs
21871	75	1667	Justice, Pubic Order/Safety	22306	779	7877	Hospitals	22580	78	359	Prof., Scientific, & Tech Svcs
21872	29	107	Special Trade Contractors	22307	209	1734	Educational Services	22581	2	8	Wood Product Manufacturing
21874	60	415	Insurance Carriers & Related	22308	206	1230	Educational Services	22601	1918	25357	Educational Services
21875	153	931	Educational Services	22309	724	4429	Educational Services	22602	572	6321	Food Svcs & Drinking Places
21901	498	4063	Food Svcs & Drinking Places	22310	873	7065	Prof., Scientific, & Tech Svcs	22603	454	6681	Plastics & Rubber Products Mfg
21902	17	1506	Hospitals	22311	287	6104	Educational Services	22604	26	56	Social Assistance
21903	168	1519	Educational Services	22312	899	10667	Administrative & Support Svcs	22610	42	116	Nursing & Resid. Care Facilit.
21904	152	848	Justice, Pubic Order/Safety	22313	9	7	Special Trade Contractors	22611	384	2729	Print'g & Related Supp't Act's
21911	351	1940	Food Svcs & Drinking Places	22314	3942	42201	Prof., Scientific, & Tech Svcs	22620	82	320	Educational Services
21912	33	195	Merch. Wholesalers,Nondur. Gds	22315	334	3908	General Merchandise Stores	22623	7	4	Relig., Grant, Civic, Prof Org
21913	53	213	Bldg Matl & Garden Eqpmt Dlrs	22320	6	8	Postal Service	22624	65	829	Special Trade Contractors
21914	19	87	Educational Services	22331	8	161	Heavy & Civil Eng. Construct'N	22625	56	253	Educational Services
21915	136	1007	Food Svcs & Drinking Places	22332	5	27	Relig., Grant, Civic, Prof Org	22626	3	2	Food and Beverage Stores
21916	6	53	Educational Services	22401	1892	19847	Hospitals	22627	37	166	Food Svcs & Drinking Places
21917	49	290	Social Assistance	22402	8	17	Prof., Scientific, & Tech Svcs	22630	1227	8721	Educational Services
21918	82	279	Educational Services	22403	4	13	Merch. Wholesalers,Nondur. Gds	22637	43	133	Mining (Except Oil and Gas)
21919	46	170	Accommodation	22404	20	35	Merch. Wholesalers,Durable Gds	22639	21	90	Animal Production
21920	6	65	Nonmetallic Mineral Prod. Mfg	22405	653	5578	Educational Services	22640	10	20	Beverage & Tobacco Product Mfg
21921	1427	15990	Educational Services	22406	433	5258	Merch. Wholesalers,Nondur. Gds	22641	10	17	Special Trade Contractors
21922	9	89	Prof., Scientific, & Tech Svcs	22407	1097	9814	Food Svcs & Drinking Places	22642	53	179	Beverage & Tobacco Product Mfg
21930	21	243	Amusement, Gambling,& Recreat.	22408	944	10016	Special Trade Contractors	22643	14	20	Crop Production
22003	2019	14800	Educational Services	22412	2	4003	Insurance Carriers & Related	22644	58	100	Nursing & Resid. Care Facilit.
22009	15	21	Print'g & Related Supp't Act's	22427	184	1248	Justice, Pubic Order/Safety	22645	96	835	Educational Services
22015	942	6699	Food Svcs & Drinking Places	22430	1	2	Postal Service	22646	24	147	Relig., Grant, Civic, Prof Org
22026	524	3819	Food Svcs & Drinking Places	22432	59	359	Ambulatory Health Care Svcs	22649	2	0	Relig., Grant, Civic, Prof Org
22027	77	499	Educational Services	22433	4	17	Merch. Wholesalers,Durable Gds	22650	18	64	Educational Services
22030	3324	34574	Prof., Scientific, & Tech Svcs	22435	146	726	Transportation Equipment Mfg	22652	42	75	Special Trade Contractors
22031	1957	19542	Prof., Scientific, & Tech Svcs	22436	6	3	Postal Service	22654	13	26	Accommodation
22032	508	9046	Relig., Grant, Civic, Prof Org	22437	17	41	Crop Production	22655	328	1866	Food Svcs & Drinking Places
22033	1086	24203	Prof., Scientific, & Tech Svcs	22438	10	56	Accommodation	22656	46	664	Heavy & Civil Eng. Construct'N
22035	70	4125	Heavy & Civil Eng. Construct'N	22442	7	29	Amusement, Gambling,& Recreat.	22657	291	4067	Transportation Equipment Mfg
22037	1	5000	Utilities	22443	249	1350	Food and Beverage Stores	22660	48	219	Food Svcs & Drinking Places
22038	8	17	Special Trade Contractors	22446	7	16	Admin. of Economic Programs	22663	57	243	Justice, Pubic Order/Safety
22039	360	1600	Educational Services	22448	68	1489	Prof., Scientific, & Tech Svcs	22664	504	3844	Hospitals
22040	7	54	Justice, Pubic Order/Safety	22451	2	2	Administrative & Support Svcs	22701	1114	10159	Educational Services
22041	1041	10829	Prof., Scientific, & Tech Svcs	22454	28	62	Construction of Buildings	22709	11	81	Nursing & Resid. Care Facilit.
22042	1027	28358	Prof., Scientific, & Tech Svcs	22460	47	157	Nursing & Resid. Care Facilit.	22711	5	8	Special Trade Contractors
22043	677	5478	Educational Services	22463	6	30	Mining (Except Oil and Gas)	22712	177	1195	Educational Services
22044	666	4518	Ambulatory Health Care Svcs	22469	49	225	Educational Services	22713	21	260	Prof., Scientific, & Tech Svcs
22046	1269	8633	Ambulatory Health Care Svcs	22471	23	11	Construction of Buildings	22714	42	227	Justice, Pubic Order/Safety
22060	95	1281	Nursing & Resid. Care Facilit.	22472	7	382	Justice, Pubic Order/Safety	22715	17	26	Fabricated Metal Product Mfg
22066	650	2599	Prof., Scientific, & Tech Svcs	22473	188	660	Educational Services	22716	16	21	Relig., Grant, Civic, Prof Org
22079	998	10378	Special Trade Contractors	22476	4	5	Food and Beverage Stores	22718	14	416	Bldg Matl & Garden Eqpmt Dlrs
22101	1707	11474	Prof., Scientific, & Tech Svcs	22480	80	716	Accommodation	22719	4	8	Food and Beverage Stores
22102	1844	48305	Prof., Scientific, & Tech Svcs	22481	3	14	Special Trade Contractors	22720	17	42	Prof., Scientific, & Tech Svcs
22103	3	1	Prof., Scientific, & Tech Svcs	22482	363	2686	Hospitals	22721	3	0	Postal Service
22106	5	20	Credit Intermediation & Relatd	22485	519	3853	Prof., Scientific, & Tech Svcs	22722	7	6	Special Trade Contractors
22116	28	216	Perform'g Arts, Spec. Sports	22488	40	555	Wood Product Manufacturing	22723	7	12	Accommodation
22121	16	394	Food Svcs & Drinking Places	22501	32	85	Construction of Buildings	22724	31	53	Amusement, Gambling,& Recreat.
22122	36	790	Prof., Scientific, & Tech Svcs	22503	156	572	Educational Services	22725	7	28	Food Svcs & Drinking Places
22124	421	2282	Prof., Scientific, & Tech Svcs	22504	11	18	Special Trade Contractors	22726	15	192	Ambulatory Health Care Svcs
22125	151	425	Miscellaneous Store Retailers	22507	30	93	Nonmetallic Mineral Prod. Mfg	22727	265	1994	Nonstore Retailers
22134	128	1260	Educational Services	22508	182	892	Food Svcs & Drinking Places	22728	80	534	Machinery Manufacturing
22135	2	1003	Educational Services	22509	4	0	Postal Service	22729	14	345	Justice, Pubic Order/Safety
22150	1543	15627	Food Svcs & Drinking Places	22511	53	347	Merch. Wholesalers,Nondur. Gds	22730	6	1	General Merchandise Stores
22151	599	8896	Prof., Scientific, & Tech Svcs	22513	1	0	Postal Service	22731	7	42	Food and Beverage Stores
22152	592	4497	Educational Services	22514	58	625	Educational Services	22732	9	22	Merch. Wholesalers,Nondur. Gds
22153	600	5940	Unclassified Establishments	22517	5	16	Waste Managmt & Remediat'n Svc	22733	31	216	Crop Production
22172	165	977	Educational Services	22520	228	1264	Educational Services	22734	110	607	Paper Manufacturing
22180	1326	12737	Credit Intermediation & Relatd	22523	2	0	Postal Service	22735	26	56	Special Trade Contractors
22181	219	1163	Educational Services	22524	12	55	Merch. Wholesalers,Nondur. Gds	22736	9	89	Social Assistance
22182	1944	21207	Prof., Scientific, & Tech Svcs	22526	1	10	Special Trade Contractors	22737	46	125	Special Trade Contractors
22183	13	43	Administrative & Support Svcs	22528	1	0	Postal Service	22738	28	93	Accommodation
22191	1241	12933	Motor Vehicle & Parts Dealers	22529	3	2	Postal Service	22739	2	1	Postal Service
22192	1620	17043	Food Svcs & Drinking Places	22530	4	3	Postal Service	22740	70	138	Miscellaneous Store Retailers
22193	851	6021	Educational Services	22534	39	64	Special Trade Contractors	22741	9	88	Crop Production
22194	12	118	Food Svcs & Drinking Places	22535	29	106	Justice, Pubic Order/Safety	22742	29	148	Unclassified Establishments
22195	15	47	Administrative & Support Svcs	22538	6	33	Accommodation	22743	7	84	Accommodation
22199	4	19	Truck Transportation	22539	110	676	Food Manufacturing	22746	11	18	Special Trade Contractors
22201	1697	17757	Prof., Scientific, & Tech Svcs	22542	38	108	Special Trade Contractors	22747	136	645	Educational Services
22202	1254	24055	Prof., Scientific, & Tech Svcs	22544	2	0	Postal Service	22748	16	41	Food and Beverage Stores
22203	806	11879	Prof., Scientific, & Tech Svcs	22545	4	3	Postal Service	22749	8	21	Crop Production
22204	988	7433	Educational Services	22546	188	2378	Food Svcs & Drinking Places	22801	1915	24270	Food Svcs & Drinking Places
22205	384	4195	Relig., Grant, Civic, Prof Org	22547	5	129	Relig., Grant, Civic, Prof Org	22802	675	9690	Print'g & Related Supp't Act's
22206	427	4433	Educational Services	22548	4	19	Fishing, Hunting and Trapping	22803	10	14	Motor Vehicle & Parts Dealers
22207	889	7590	Educational Services	22552	6	54	Wood Product Manufacturing	22807	8	2429	Educational Services
22209	937	15030	Prof., Scientific, & Tech Svcs	22553	609	4644	Educational Services	22810	52	355	Bldg Matl & Garden Eqpmt Dlrs

BUSINESS DATA 22811 - 23410

ZIP CODE	2004 Total Firms	2004 Total Employees	TOP INDUSTRY RANKED on 2004 EMPLOYMENT	ZIP CODE	2004 Total Firms	2004 Total Employees	TOP INDUSTRY RANKED on 2004 EMPLOYMENT	ZIP CODE	2004 Total Firms	2004 Total Employees	TOP INDUSTRY RANKED on 2004 EMPLOYMENT
22811	14	103	Justice, Pubic Order/Safety	23030	174	1119	Educational Services	23178	8	26	Food and Beverage Stores
22812	201	3918	Food Manufacturing	23031	2	65	Educational Services	23180	7	27	Justice, Pubic Order/Safety
22815	235	2000	Apparel Manufacturing	23032	13	29	Food and Beverage Stores	23181	237	1560	Wood Product Manufacturing
22820	10	7	Special Trade Contractors	23035	31	179	Textile Mills	23183	30	120	Prof., Scientific, & Tech Svcs
22821	175	2318	Merch. Wholesalers,Nondur. Gds	23038	24	82	Pipeline Transportation	23184	7	22	Social Assistance
22824	236	2948	Food Manufacturing	23039	29	117	Educational Services	23185	1915	32227	Prof., Scientific, & Tech Svcs
22827	302	3232	Merch. Wholesalers,Nondur. Gds	23040	132	734	Educational Services	23186	3	4828	Educational Services
22830	35	101	Educational Services	23043	150	585	Amusement, Gambling,& Recreat.	23187	23	108	Relig., Grant, Civic, Prof Org
22831	21	1535	Merch. Wholesalers,Nondur. Gds	23045	4	6	Relig., Grant, Civic, Prof Org	23188	1086	10526	Hospitals
22832	24	26	Accommodation	23047	79	6575	Amusement, Gambling,& Recreat.	23190	6	17	Food and Beverage Stores
22833	3	5	Food and Beverage Stores	23050	13	19	Insurance Carriers & Related	23192	135	560	Educational Services
22834	34	141	Educational Services	23055	75	734	Furniture & Related Prod. Mfg	23218	8	36	Exec., Legis., & Other Support
22835	552	4501	Accommodation	23056	9	27	Admin. of Economic Programs	23219	1909	49185	Exec., Legis., & Other Support
22840	86	850	Accommodation	23058	13	36	Heavy & Civil Eng. Construct'N	23220	1384	16923	Food Svcs & Drinking Places
22841	97	1165	Special Trade Contractors	23059	609	10190	Bldg Matl & Garden Eqpmt Dlrs	23221	540	6208	Exec., Legis., & Other Support
22842	211	1248	Merch. Wholesalers,Nondur. Gds	23060	964	20299	Credit Intermediation & Relatd	23222	543	4281	Educational Services
22843	40	146	Educational Services	23061	687	6141	Hospitals	23223	961	8864	Educational Services
22844	227	1663	Primary Metal Manufacturing	23062	93	807	Educational Services	23224	1263	12350	Administrative & Support Svcs
22845	10	26	Relig., Grant, Civic, Prof Org	23063	197	1320	Justice, Pubic Order/Safety	23225	1320	15096	Hospitals
22846	39	397	Educational Services	23064	8	55	Accommodation	23226	1043	11631	Hospitals
22847	41	316	Educational Services	23065	24	59	Prof., Scientific, & Tech Svcs	23227	645	8012	Nursing & Resid. Care Facilit.
22848	3	5	Insurance Carriers & Related	23066	9	90	Museums, Hist. Sites,& Similar	23228	1314	15727	Special Trade Contractors
22849	134	1199	Elect'l Eqpmt, App, & Comp Mfg	23067	2	55	Educational Services	23229	1096	9876	Hospitals
22850	20	13	Repair and Maintenance	23068	5	5	Special Trade Contractors	23230	2050	32568	Prof., Scientific, & Tech Svcs
22851	139	735	Wood Product Manufacturing	23069	151	3071	Exec., Legis., & Other Support	23231	887	11555	Chemical Manufacturing
22853	126	2256	Food Manufacturing	23070	10	88	Merch. Wholesalers,Nondur. Gds	23232	4	2217	Postal Service
22901	1601	37451	Educational Services	23071	59	296	Amusement, Gambling,& Recreat.	23233	1355	11300	Electronics & Appliance Stores
22902	1838	14292	Prof., Scientific, & Tech Svcs	23072	359	2048	Food and Beverage Stores	23234	758	18942	Merch. Wholesalers,Nondur. Gds
22903	1673	16716	Food Svcs & Drinking Places	23075	209	1232	Educational Services	23235	1975	22184	Justice, Pubic Order/Safety
22904	16	426	Educational Services	23076	24	88	Nat'l Security & Int'l Affairs	23236	956	9207	Prof., Scientific, & Tech Svcs
22905	7	18	Transit & Grnd Pass. Transport	23079	8	14	Perform'g Arts, Spec. Sports	23237	560	6825	Merch. Wholesalers,Durable Gds
22906	22	63	Special Trade Contractors	23081	3	31	Exec., Legis., & Other Support	23238	11	1019	Furn. & Home Furnishgs Stores
22908	204	8713	Hospitals	23083	53	391	Food and Beverage Stores	23240	19	232	Nat'l Security & Int'l Affairs
22909	2	1505	Insurance Carriers & Related	23084	27	47	Relig., Grant, Civic, Prof Org	23242	10	19	Merch. Wholesalers,Durable Gds
22911	568	8106	Elect'l Eqpmt, App, & Comp Mfg	23085	50	238	Educational Services	23249	8	1083	Hospitals
22920	109	411	Educational Services	23086	154	1310	Educational Services	23250	40	856	Admin. of Economic Programs
22922	56	424	Utilities	23089	72	277	Heavy & Civil Eng. Construct'N	23255	7	13	Transit & Grnd Pass. Transport
22923	89	218	Special Trade Contractors	23090	30	570	Furn. & Home Furnishgs Stores	23260	7	70	Administrative & Support Svcs
22924	6	81	Merch. Wholesalers,Nondur. Gds	23091	2	1	Merch. Wholesalers,Durable Gds	23261	4	5	Prof., Scientific, & Tech Svcs
22931	15	126	Wholesale Elec. Mrkts & Agents	23092	24	175	Nursing & Resid. Care Facilit.	23269	3	9	Credit Intermediation & Relatd
22932	200	1125	Educational Services	23093	381	2711	Educational Services	23280	1	0	Food and Beverage Stores
22935	16	84	Educational Services	23101	2	24	Miscellaneous Store Retailers	23284	30	9197	Educational Services
22936	115	581	Merch. Wholesalers,Durable Gds	23102	45	184	Food Svcs & Drinking Places	23285	1	8	Insurance Carriers & Related
22937	23	81	Educational Services	23103	175	939	Merch. Wholesalers,Durable Gds	23288	1	2	Prof., Scientific, & Tech Svcs
22938	31	95	Administrative & Support Svcs	23105	3	6	Food and Beverage Stores	23294	1008	11018	Food Svcs & Drinking Places
22939	229	4511	Hospitals	23106	32	82	Food and Beverage Stores	23297	9	2329	Exec., Legis., & Other Support
22940	40	131	Construction of Buildings	23107	2	35	Food Manufacturing	23298	111	9433	Ambulatory Health Care Svcs
22942	180	2317	Plastics & Rubber Products Mfg	23109	240	2925	Prof., Scientific, & Tech Svcs	23301	137	2413	Food Manufacturing
22943	24	35	Real Estate	23110	25	148	Educational Services	23302	2	4	Administrative & Support Svcs
22945	20	76	Food Svcs & Drinking Places	23111	1091	9128	Food Svcs & Drinking Places	23303	20	115	Justice, Pubic Order/Safety
22946	9	24	Admin. of Economic Programs	23112	1178	10430	Food Svcs & Drinking Places	23304	1	2	Postal Service
22947	128	502	Accommodation	23113	873	7703	Food Svcs & Drinking Places	23306	87	391	Merch. Wholesalers,Nondur. Gds
22948	9	27	Electronics & Appliance Stores	23114	210	1455	Educational Services	23307	9	26	Merch. Wholesalers,Nondur. Gds
22949	155	866	Educational Services	23115	15	114	Wood Product Manufacturing	23308	25	44	Personal and Laundry Services
22952	53	376	Special Trade Contractors	23116	522	7111	Managmt of Companies & Enterp.	23310	198	1600	Merch. Wholesalers,Durable Gds
22954	1	2	General Merchandise Stores	23117	200	986	Educational Services	23313	2	7	Furn. & Home Furnishgs Stores
22957	6	40	Museums, Hist. Sites,& Similar	23119	4	6	Special Trade Contractors	23314	122	517	Educational Services
22958	110	823	Accommodation	23120	90	307	Educational Services	23315	28	102	Educational Services
22959	42	276	Wood Product Manufacturing	23123	33	201	Relig., Grant, Civic, Prof Org	23316	42	488	Merch. Wholesalers,Nondur. Gds
22960	507	3942	Furniture & Related Prod. Mfg	23124	72	833	Educational Services	23320	2556	39832	Special Trade Contractors
22963	326	1495	Educational Services	23125	8	7	Accommodation	23321	839	9944	Food Svcs & Drinking Places
22964	27	128	Crop Production	23126	8	26	Ambulatory Health Care Svcs	23322	1052	10656	Justice, Pubic Order/Safety
22965	8	8	Special Trade Contractors	23127	4	11	Food and Beverage Stores	23323	792	9297	Educational Services
22967	51	161	Accommodation	23128	20	34	Food and Beverage Stores	23324	537	5754	Special Trade Contractors
22968	250	1235	Food Svcs & Drinking Places	23129	50	326	Merch. Wholesalers,Durable Gds	23325	238	2032	Educational Services
22969	22	26	Miscellaneous Store Retailers	23130	6	8	Construction of Buildings	23326	1	0	Nat'l Security & Int'l Affairs
22971	22	75	Admin. of Economic Programs	23131	18	66	Repair and Maintenance	23327	7	15	Machinery Manufacturing
22972	11	88	Nonmetallic Mineral Prod. Mfg	23138	12	41	Bldg Matl & Garden Eqpmt Dlrs	23328	13	26	Prof., Scientific, & Tech Svcs
22973	205	1108	Educational Services	23139	604	3313	Educational Services	23336	275	1442	Accommodation
22974	101	616	Special Trade Contractors	23140	132	841	Truck Transportation	23337	17	1372	Space Research and Technology
22976	8	73	Crop Production	23141	153	809	Food and Beverage Stores	23341	7	38	Merch. Wholesalers,Nondur. Gds
22980	1136	11826	Chemical Manufacturing	23146	116	908	Special Trade Contractors	23347	80	441	Justice, Pubic Order/Safety
22987	4	5	Food and Beverage Stores	23147	3	2	Postal Service	23350	177	1979	Merch. Wholesalers,Nondur. Gds
22989	2	200	Educational Services	23148	30	139	Educational Services	23354	15	46	Ambulatory Health Care Svcs
23001	3	4	Merch. Wholesalers,Nondur. Gds	23149	182	1305	Educational Services	23356	13	55	Justice, Pubic Order/Safety
23002	366	1763	Educational Services	23150	357	6395	Computer & Electronic Prod Mfg	23357	7	519	Merch. Wholesalers,Nondur. Gds
23003	1	2	Postal Service	23153	14	28	General Merchandise Stores	23358	3	27	Food Manufacturing
23004	27	474	Merch. Wholesalers,Durable Gds	23154	4	0	Oil and Gas Extraction	23359	19	40	Relig., Grant, Civic, Prof Org
23005	1401	15371	Special Trade Contractors	23156	32	154	Educational Services	23389	4	5	Food and Beverage Stores
23009	131	558	Ambulatory Health Care Svcs	23160	4	323	Justice, Pubic Order/Safety	23395	14	80	Accommodation
23011	23	70	Merch. Wholesalers,Durable Gds	23161	5	45	Relig., Grant, Civic, Prof Org	23397	29	444	Exec., Legis., & Other Support
23014	1	175	Justice, Pubic Order/Safety	23162	6	5	Food and Beverage Stores	23398	4	11	Accommodation
23015	66	340	Special Trade Contractors	23163	4	5	Relig., Grant, Civic, Prof Org	23399	1	0	Relig., Grant, Civic, Prof Org
23018	7	29	Merch. Wholesalers,Nondur. Gds	23168	160	1316	Nonmetallic Mineral Prod. Mfg	23401	17	62	Bldg Matl & Garden Eqpmt Dlrs
23021	3	0	Postal Service	23169	53	222	Special Trade Contractors	23404	6	25	Bldg Matl & Garden Eqpmt Dlrs
23022	10	8	Personal and Laundry Services	23170	1	4	Publishing Industries	23405	18	127	Educational Services
23023	5	36	Educational Services	23173	7	1442	Educational Services	23407	13	565	Merch. Wholesalers,Nondur. Gds
23024	86	229	Justice, Pubic Order/Safety	23175	142	533	Merch. Wholesalers,Nondur. Gds	23408	3	3	Miscellaneous Store Retailers
23025	4	5	Special Trade Contractors	23176	7	18	Special Trade Contractors	23409	6	24	Bldg Matl & Garden Eqpmt Dlrs
23027	24	69	Relig., Grant, Civic, Prof Org	23177	22	124	Transportation Equipment Mfg	23410	71	518	Educational Services

BUSINESS DATA

ZIP CODE	2004 Total Firms	2004 Total Employees	TOP INDUSTRY RANKED on 2004 EMPLOYMENT	ZIP CODE	2004 Total Firms	2004 Total Employees	TOP INDUSTRY RANKED on 2004 EMPLOYMENT	ZIP CODE	2004 Total Firms	2004 Total Employees	TOP INDUSTRY RANKED on 2004 EMPLOYMENT
23412	2	3	Special Trade Contractors	23665	64	790	Nat'l Security & Int'l Affairs	23934	11	16	Food Svcs & Drinking Places
23413	73	1147	Hospitals	23666	1701	23076	Food Svcs & Drinking Places	23936	226	1594	Justice, Pubic Order/Safety
23414	14	122	Nursing & Resid. Care Facilit.	23667	1	1271	Hospitals	23937	66	824	Textile Mills
23415	64	323	Justice, Pubic Order/Safety	23668	2	32	Other Information Services	23938	11	7	Food and Beverage Stores
23416	34	371	Educational Services	23669	1197	11001	Administrative & Support Svcs	23939	9	72	Repair and Maintenance
23417	178	803	Nursing & Resid. Care Facilit.	23670	5	218	Postal Service	23941	1	0	Relig., Grant, Civic, Prof Org
23418	129	1120	Educational Services	23681	3	5145	Space Research and Technology	23942	14	47	Admin. of Economic Programs
23419	4	10	Food and Beverage Stores	23690	81	471	Admin. Enviro. Quality Progrms	23943	18	80	Justice, Pubic Order/Safety
23420	47	200	Educational Services	23691	2	37	Credit Intermediation & Relatd	23944	161	1199	Nonmetallic Mineral Prod. Mfg
23421	121	720	Educational Services	23692	689	4909	Educational Services	23947	172	1150	Educational Services
23422	12	18	Special Trade Contractors	23693	546	4254	Food Svcs & Drinking Places	23950	118	813	Textile Product Mills
23423	9	35	Accommodation	23696	70	419	Special Trade Contractors	23952	28	120	Justice, Pubic Order/Safety
23424	2	4	Motor Vehicle & Parts Dealers	23701	602	5727	Educational Services	23954	22	64	Food and Beverage Stores
23426	8	52	Food Manufacturing	23702	241	2679	Merch. Wholesalers,Durable Gds	23955	25	291	Educational Services
23427	9	32	Merch. Wholesalers,Nondur. Gds	23703	461	5527	Educational Services	23958	47	94	Merch. Wholesalers,Durable Gds
23429	4	5	Repair and Maintenance	23704	854	10283	Nursing & Resid. Care Facilit.	23959	20	94	Educational Services
23430	492	8712	Food and Beverage Stores	23705	5	37	Social Assistance	23960	38	54	Special Trade Contractors
23431	1	3	Heavy & Civil Eng. Construct'N	23707	497	7840	Hospitals	23962	8	14	Museums, Hist. Sites,& Similar
23432	34	142	Justice, Pubic Order/Safety	23708	9	33	Ambulatory Health Care Svcs	23963	11	51	Justice, Pubic Order/Safety
23433	22	117	Bldg Matl & Garden Eqpmt Dlrs	23709	15	4128	Nat'l Security & Int'l Affairs	23964	26	155	Merch. Wholesalers,Durable Gds
23434	1384	19400	Exec., Legis., & Other Support	23801	45	393	Food and Beverage Stores	23966	36	87	Construction of Buildings
23435	257	2851	Food Svcs & Drinking Places	23803	1407	12974	Ambulatory Health Care Svcs	23967	10	93	Wood Product Manufacturing
23436	9	25	Utilities	23804	2	3	Prof., Scientific, & Tech Svcs	23968	22	194	Educational Services
23437	69	255	Educational Services	23805	542	5415	Food Svcs & Drinking Places	23970	541	5707	General Merchandise Stores
23438	36	171	Merch. Wholesalers,Durable Gds	23806	4	1098	Educational Services	23974	131	689	Educational Services
23439	4	6	Construction of Buildings	23821	40	374	Other Information Services	23976	15	266	Wood Product Manufacturing
23440	31	109	Educational Services	23824	325	2364	Nat'l Security & Int'l Affairs	24003	1	0	Heavy & Civil Eng. Construct'N
23441	32	220	Merch. Wholesalers,Nondur. Gds	23827	45	537	Textile Mills	24005	1	5	Special Trade Contractors
23442	45	1633	Merch. Wholesalers,Nondur. Gds	23828	12	31	Special Trade Contractors	24011	739	6872	Prof., Scientific, & Tech Svcs
23443	2	6	Accommodation	23829	40	513	Justice, Pubic Order/Safety	24012	1532	23454	Motor Vehicle & Parts Dealers
23450	16	102	Special Trade Contractors	23830	25	146	Justice, Pubic Order/Safety	24013	288	4792	Hospitals
23451	2045	18201	Food Svcs & Drinking Places	23831	821	6903	Food Svcs & Drinking Places	24014	1022	13141	Ambulatory Health Care Svcs
23452	2725	40141	Motor Vehicle & Parts Dealers	23832	629	11520	Exec., Legis., & Other Support	24015	499	4619	Educational Services
23453	433	5234	Educational Services	23833	29	185	Justice, Pubic Order/Safety	24016	875	13869	Hospitals
23454	1783	18523	Hospitals	23834	1129	13639	Food Svcs & Drinking Places	24017	626	6208	Special Trade Contractors
23455	1335	15454	Food Svcs & Drinking Places	23836	300	6575	Merch. Wholesalers,Durable Gds	24018	1382	10892	Insurance Carriers & Related
23456	890	10805	Exec., Legis., & Other Support	23837	151	1322	Educational Services	24019	847	22207	Credit Intermediation & Relatd
23457	91	473	Crop Production	23838	158	462	Special Trade Contractors	24020	1	0	Postal Service
23458	1	6	Construction of Buildings	23839	24	252	Educational Services	24022	3	13	Relig., Grant, Civic, Prof Org
23459	8	26	Relig., Grant, Civic, Prof Org	23840	28	58	Nursing & Resid. Care Facilit.	24023	1	2	Prof., Scientific, & Tech Svcs
23460	23	327	Nat'l Security & Int'l Affairs	23841	149	1081	Educational Services	24025	2	0	Merch. Wholesalers,Durable Gds
23461	7	48	Credit Intermediation & Relatd	23842	84	1324	Food and Beverage Stores	24028	1	0	Administrative & Support Svcs
23462	2554	28137	Prof., Scientific, & Tech Svcs	23843	9	51	Justice, Pubic Order/Safety	24033	2	13	Ambulatory Health Care Svcs
23463	3	1543	Broadcasting	23844	8	23	Food Svcs & Drinking Places	24034	1	23	Museums, Hist. Sites,& Similar
23464	1461	12089	Educational Services	23845	22	38	Forestry and Logging	24035	1	2	Waste Managmt & Remediat'n Svc
23466	14	70	Administrative & Support Svcs	23846	8	8	Construction of Buildings	24038	1	3	Special Trade Contractors
23467	8	98	Merch. Wholesalers,Nondur. Gds	23847	577	5721	Food Manufacturing	24042	1	900	Rail Transportation
23471	15	48	Scenic & Sightseeing Transport	23850	13	17	Truck Transportation	24053	50	306	Ambulatory Health Care Svcs
23480	22	89	Accommodation	23851	558	6918	Paper Manufacturing	24054	106	716	Furniture & Related Prod. Mfg
23482	1	1	Relig., Grant, Civic, Prof Org	23856	19	99	Mining (Except Oil and Gas)	24055	343	3152	Furniture & Related Prod. Mfg
23483	3	39	Food Svcs & Drinking Places	23857	31	242	Forestry and Logging	24058	4	2	Real Estate
23486	8	36	Merch. Wholesalers,Nondur. Gds	23860	825	9624	Chemical Manufacturing	24059	28	55	Educational Services
23487	148	983	Educational Services	23866	55	204	Food and Beverage Stores	24060	1247	12156	Food Svcs & Drinking Places
23488	3	0	Postal Service	23867	65	1642	Wholesale Elec. Mrkts & Agents	24061	21	7728	Educational Services
23501	18	1045	Postal Service	23868	291	2689	Educational Services	24062	9	25	Ambulatory Health Care Svcs
23502	1663	28668	Prof., Scientific, & Tech Svcs	23870	1	900	Justice, Pubic Order/Safety	24063	7	38	Social Assistance
23503	323	2972	Educational Services	23872	76	519	Beverage & Tobacco Product Mfg	24064	99	418	Mining (Except Oil and Gas)
23504	468	6120	Educational Services	23873	1	1	Postal Service	24065	151	575	Wood Product Manufacturing
23505	663	7887	Hospitals	23874	26	171	Educational Services	24066	151	666	Plastics & Rubber Products Mfg
23507	219	10148	Hospitals	23875	244	2436	Educational Services	24067	36	231	Special Trade Contractors
23508	352	3239	Educational Services	23876	10	10	Truck Transportation	24068	14	39	Special Trade Contractors
23509	246	2625	Educational Services	23878	34	126	Educational Services	24069	31	87	Nonmetallic Mineral Prod. Mfg
23510	1371	20308	Prof., Scientific, & Tech Svcs	23879	20	255	Wood Product Manufacturing	24070	25	393	Hospitals
23511	63	871	Nat'l Security & Int'l Affairs	23881	18	76	Forestry and Logging	24072	18	67	Educational Services
23513	659	8270	Relig., Grant, Civic, Prof Org	23882	90	512	Ambulatory Health Care Svcs	24073	1284	13020	Food Svcs & Drinking Places
23514	5	11	Postal Service	23883	114	1444	Utilities	24076	29	137	Prof., Scientific, & Tech Svcs
23515	1	3	Rental and Leasing Services	23884	11	120	Educational Services	24077	56	715	Merch. Wholesalers,Durable Gds
23517	577	5939	Food Svcs & Drinking Places	23885	44	208	Special Trade Contractors	24078	320	1955	Food Svcs & Drinking Places
23518	800	6658	Food Svcs & Drinking Places	23887	14	29	Food and Beverage Stores	24079	26	58	Heavy & Civil Eng. Construct'N
23521	29	1364	Nat'l Security & Int'l Affairs	23888	85	492	Food Svcs & Drinking Places	24082	11	60	Educational Services
23523	185	4757	Transportation Equipment Mfg	23889	8	87	Relig., Grant, Civic, Prof Org	24083	159	1092	Food and Beverage Stores
23529	2	3000	Educational Services	23890	169	1071	Nursing & Resid. Care Facilit.	24084	359	6038	Transportation Equipment Mfg
23541	5	23	Construction of Buildings	23891	2	0	Ambulatory Health Care Svcs	24085	35	312	Machinery Manufacturing
23551	2	3	Administrative & Support Svcs	23893	4	12	Real Estate	24086	5	3	Postal Service
23601	1050	8980	Administrative & Support Svcs	23894	3	13	Forestry and Logging	24087	75	523	Educational Services
23602	1185	14378	Food Svcs & Drinking Places	23897	14	19	Special Trade Contractors	24088	93	648	Educational Services
23603	90	2949	Merch. Wholesalers,Durable Gds	23898	29	115	Educational Services	24089	72	1201	Textile Mills
23604	38	672	Prof., Scientific, & Tech Svcs	23899	17	39	Wood Product Manufacturing	24090	157	1384	Exec., Legis., & Other Support
23605	470	3953	Educational Services	23901	777	6527	Food Svcs & Drinking Places	24091	338	1755	Miscellaneous Manufacturing
23606	1395	16225	Prof., Scientific, & Tech Svcs	23909	3	630	Educational Services	24092	65	214	Educational Services
23607	827	27087	Transportation Equipment Mfg	23915	20	188	Justice, Pubic Order/Safety	24093	17	273	Machinery Manufacturing
23608	918	7223	Educational Services	23917	113	1058	Exec., Legis., & Other Support	24094	3	8	Special Trade Contractors
23609	5	2	Electronics & Appliance Stores	23919	113	474	Food Svcs & Drinking Places	24095	70	142	Educational Services
23612	5	9	Administrative & Support Svcs	23920	62	249	Textile Mills	24101	130	541	Food and Beverage Stores
23630	5	11	Motion Pict. & Sound Recording	23921	100	499	Educational Services	24102	34	138	Chemical Manufacturing
23651	13	35	Other Information Services	23922	74	1360	Justice, Pubic Order/Safety	24104	80	336	Educational Services
23661	529	10145	Hospitals	23923	105	554	Educational Services	24105	10	6	Food Manufacturing
23662	286	1876	Educational Services	23924	240	2059	Administrative & Support Svcs	24111	9	8	Repair and Maintenance
23663	257	2477	Educational Services	23927	261	1379	Food Svcs & Drinking Places	24112	1646	19161	Furniture & Related Prod. Mfg
23664	128	351	Social Assistance	23930	196	1040	Utilities	24113	1	0	Relig., Grant, Civic, Prof Org

ZIP CODE	2004 Total Firms	2004 Total Employ-ees	TOP INDUSTRY RANKED on 2004 EMPLOYMENT	ZIP CODE	2004 Total Firms	2004 Total Employ-ees	TOP INDUSTRY RANKED on 2004 EMPLOYMENT	ZIP CODE	2004 Total Firms	2004 Total Employ-ees	TOP INDUSTRY RANKED on 2004 EMPLOYMENT
24114	3	10	Justice, Pubic Order/Safety	24290	112	905	Health & Personal Care Stores	24501	1345	21399	Hospitals
24115	3	0	Plastics & Rubber Products Mfg	24292	11	79	Justice, Pubic Order/Safety	24502	1496	18035	Food Svcs & Drinking Places
24120	67	801	Chemical Manufacturing	24293	437	3644	Educational Services	24503	436	5354	Hospitals
24121	387	1875	Educational Services	24301	505	5945	Furn. & Home Furnishgs Stores	24504	572	7496	Prof., Scientific, & Tech Svcs
24122	53	242	Nursing & Resid. Care Facilit.	24311	54	2314	Transportation Equipment Mfg	24505	6	13	Broadcasting
24124	123	1649	Chemical Manufacturing	24312	40	80	Mining (Except Oil and Gas)	24506	11	338	Postal Service
24126	9	13	Relig., Grant, Civic, Prof Org	24313	6	22	Food and Beverage Stores	24513	1	1500	Nonstore Retailers
24127	129	539	Educational Services	24314	20	167	Nursing & Resid. Care Facilit.	24514	1	100	Relig., Grant, Civic, Prof Org
24128	35	107	Construction of Buildings	24315	96	1342	Justice, Pubic Order/Safety	24517	299	3439	Textile Mills
24129	3	57	Machinery Manufacturing	24316	4	14	Food and Beverage Stores	24520	34	291	Perform'g Arts, Spec. Sports
24130	6	3	Nonstore Retailers	24317	95	414	Educational Services	24521	377	2982	Machinery Manufacturing
24131	8	15	Food and Beverage Stores	24318	6	8	Postal Service	24522	363	3265	Furniture & Related Prod. Mfg
24132	1	2	Postal Service	24319	175	1918	Heavy & Civil Eng. Construct'N	24523	832	6724	Ambulatory Health Care Svcs
24133	55	310	Justice, Pubic Order/Safety	24322	2	4	Social Assistance	24526	44	664	Paper Manufacturing
24134	260	1713	Hospitals	24323	9	17	Repair and Maintenance	24527	74	1952	Sportg Gds,Hobby,Book, & Music
24136	111	476	Accommodation	24324	36	74	Educational Services	24528	173	1545	Textile Mills
24137	54	223	Amusement, Gambling,& Recreat.	24325	15	50	Justice, Pubic Order/Safety	24529	42	124	Crop Production
24138	18	137	Food and Beverage Stores	24326	22	64	Educational Services	24530	19	32	Heavy & Civil Eng. Construct'N
24139	11	11	Food and Beverage Stores	24327	6	243	Educational Services	24531	368	3895	Exec., Legis., & Other Support
24141	731	7944	Prof., Scientific, & Tech Svcs	24328	66	327	Accommodation	24533	2	2	Postal Service
24142	4	1466	Educational Services	24330	66	255	Educational Services	24534	33	285	Textile Mills
24143	5	59	Nursing & Resid. Care Facilit.	24333	689	8655	Furniture & Related Prod. Mfg	24535	2	0	Administrative & Support Svcs
24146	2	0	Postal Service	24340	131	630	Educational Services	24536	3	10	Forestry and Logging
24147	60	389	Nursing & Resid. Care Facilit.	24343	424	5543	Exec., Legis., & Other Support	24538	96	618	Truck Transportation
24148	227	2360	Food and Beverage Stores	24347	23	235	Accommodation	24539	5	9	General Merchandise Stores
24149	65	381	Educational Services	24348	184	1532	Miscellaneous Manufacturing	24540	1347	13701	Beverage & Tobacco Product Mfg
24150	15	273	Nonmetallic Mineral Prod. Mfg	24350	14	22	Merch. Wholesalers,Durable Gds	24541	1319	17877	Textile Product Mills
24151	837	8084	Wood Product Manufacturing	24351	10	41	Food Svcs & Drinking Places	24543	8	16	Construction of Buildings
24153	1770	26337	Hospitals	24352	24	188	Nursing & Resid. Care Facilit.	24549	68	288	Educational Services
24156	1	900	Electronics & Appliance Stores	24354	633	8151	Wood Product Manufacturing	24550	109	442	Relig., Grant, Civic, Prof Org
24161	13	13	Administrative & Support Svcs	24360	142	956	Gasoline Stations	24551	598	5109	Prof., Scientific, & Tech Svcs
24162	67	264	Merch. Wholesalers,Durable Gds	24361	86	414	Educational Services	24553	37	396	Fabricated Metal Product Mfg
24165	39	257	Ambulatory Health Care Svcs	24363	32	200	Educational Services	24554	67	428	Merch. Wholesalers,Durable Gds
24167	4	7	Truck Transportation	24366	38	260	Special Trade Contractors	24555	55	1276	Furn. & Home Furnishgs Stores
24168	26	1529	Furniture & Related Prod. Mfg	24368	128	1102	Warehousing and Storage	24556	68	251	Food Manufacturing
24171	346	3466	Textile Mills	24370	141	853	Plastics & Rubber Products Mfg	24557	263	1935	Construction of Buildings
24174	38	146	Educational Services	24374	11	74	Educational Services	24558	272	1416	Justice, Pubic Order/Safety
24175	240	1885	Food Svcs & Drinking Places	24375	24	119	Educational Services	24562	1	2	Administrative & Support Svcs
24176	38	137	Heavy & Civil Eng. Construct'N	24377	2	1	Relig., Grant, Civic, Prof Org	24563	145	2044	Textile Mills
24177	5	171	Transportation Equipment Mfg	24378	27	108	Support Activities: Agr./For.	24565	22	73	Wood Product Manufacturing
24178	3	3	Merch. Wholesalers,Durable Gds	24380	65	200	Educational Services	24566	17	13	Postal Service
24179	644	4351	Textile Mills	24381	87	443	Educational Services	24569	22	51	Wood Product Manufacturing
24184	122	463	Educational Services	24382	854	8583	Food Svcs & Drinking Places	24570	2	3	Prof., Scientific, & Tech Svcs
24185	31	297	Merch. Wholesalers,Durable Gds	24401	1529	16218	Food Svcs & Drinking Places	24571	45	69	Food and Beverage Stores
24201	831	10283	Food Svcs & Drinking Places	24402	5	6	Real Estate	24572	485	4902	Hospitals
24202	413	6138	Food Svcs & Drinking Places	24411	4	5	Relig., Grant, Civic, Prof Org	24574	77	456	Educational Services
24203	5	11	Waste Managmt & Remediat'n Svc	24412	2	1	Postal Service	24576	8	107	Educational Services
24209	3	6	Special Trade Contractors	24413	20	128	Computer & Electronic Prod Mfg	24577	87	348	Educational Services
24210	1048	10134	Food Svcs & Drinking Places	24415	3	4	Prof., Scientific, & Tech Svcs	24578	60	478	Food Svcs & Drinking Places
24211	250	1247	Social Assistance	24416	290	2627	Transportation Equipment Mfg	24579	29	326	Justice, Pubic Order/Safety
24212	4	55	Administrative & Support Svcs	24421	85	253	Educational Services	24580	13	33	Relig., Grant, Civic, Prof Org
24215	2	18	Merch. Wholesalers,Durable Gds	24422	233	1774	Nursing & Resid. Care Facilit.	24581	2	2	Miscellaneous Store Retailers
24216	89	451	Educational Services	24426	638	8010	Paper Manufacturing	24586	116	768	Educational Services
24217	6	23	Truck Transportation	24430	37	589	Justice, Pubic Order/Safety	24588	319	2086	Educational Services
24218	8	52	Educational Services	24431	26	118	Miscellaneous Store Retailers	24589	50	322	Educational Services
24219	375	3367	Educational Services	24432	10	30	Support Activities: Agr./For.	24590	217	844	Textile Product Mills
24220	9	105	Educational Services	24433	2	2	Special Trade Contractors	24592	881	8555	Educational Services
24221	8	14	Crop Production	24435	63	506	Miscellaneous Manufacturing	24593	31	80	Repair and Maintenance
24224	110	760	Educational Services	24437	17	185	Educational Services	24594	33	124	Merch. Wholesalers,Durable Gds
24225	25	247	Utilities	24438	2	1	Utilities	24595	7	382	Educational Services
24226	38	182	Educational Services	24439	31	683	Accommodation	24597	18	97	Merch. Wholesalers,Nondur. Gds
24228	233	1647	Food and Beverage Stores	24440	37	224	Justice, Pubic Order/Safety	24598	42	141	Truck Transportation
24230	275	1766	Merch. Wholesalers,Durable Gds	24441	111	938	Plastics & Rubber Products Mfg	24599	4	6	Heavy & Civil Eng. Construct'N
24236	117	780	Machinery Manufacturing	24442	5	2	Food and Beverage Stores	24601	2	21	Mining (Except Oil and Gas)
24237	24	123	Justice, Pubic Order/Safety	24445	162	1941	Accommodation	24602	3	7	Postal Service
24239	10	65	Ambulatory Health Care Svcs	24448	14	294	Plastics & Rubber Products Mfg	24603	29	195	Merch. Wholesalers,Durable Gds
24243	47	219	Educational Services	24450	854	7905	Educational Services	24604	5	91	Mining (Except Oil and Gas)
24244	138	1589	Nursing & Resid. Care Facilit.	24457	45	1469	Hospitals	24605	391	5048	General Merchandise Stores
24245	25	104	Ambulatory Health Care Svcs	24458	28	104	Relig., Grant, Civic, Prof Org	24606	6	44	Educational Services
24246	6	6	Waste Managmt & Remediat'n Svc	24459	22	34	Administrative & Support Svcs	24607	12	140	Accommodation
24248	72	366	Educational Services	24460	55	300	Museums, Hist. Sites,& Similar	24608	1	0	Accommodation
24250	13	58	Educational Services	24463	8	34	Admin. of Economic Programs	24609	189	1922	General Merchandise Stores
24251	271	1676	Educational Services	24464	9	21	Accommodation	24612	23	67	Food Svcs & Drinking Places
24256	91	397	Food and Beverage Stores	24465	150	566	Educational Services	24613	13	54	Truck Transportation
24258	13	75	Educational Services	24467	51	348	Merch. Wholesalers,Durable Gds	24614	367	3385	Hospitals
24260	117	732	Educational Services	24468	2	4	Prof., Scientific, & Tech Svcs	24618	5	29	Food Svcs & Drinking Places
24263	182	1406	Educational Services	24469	11	19	Repair and Maintenance	24619	1	0	Postal Service
24265	16	134	Mining (Except Oil and Gas)	24471	27	73	Social Assistance	24620	46	194	Educational Services
24266	410	3546	Transportation Equipment Mfg	24472	59	486	Gasoline Stations	24622	9	7	Postal Service
24269	9	46	Food and Beverage Stores	24473	18	70	Accommodation	24624	16	76	Admin. Enviro. Quality Progrms
24270	11	15	Social Assistance	24474	7	10	Social Assistance	24627	3	395	Mining (Except Oil and Gas)
24271	45	239	Educational Services	24476	10	19	Repair and Maintenance	24628	18	120	Mining (Except Oil and Gas)
24272	17	269	Construction of Buildings	24477	242	4701	Warehousing and Storage	24630	155	1093	Food Svcs & Drinking Places
24273	455	6168	Mining (Except Oil and Gas)	24479	29	167	Educational Services	24631	82	526	Merch. Wholesalers,Durable Gds
24277	271	1943	Social Assistance	24482	226	4515	Exec., Legis., & Other Support	24634	5	43	Educational Services
24279	151	661	Educational Services	24483	16	94	Exec., Legis., & Other Support	24635	32	105	Educational Services
24280	39	332	Special Trade Contractors	24484	87	305	Exec., Legis., & Other Support	24637	68	1370	General Merchandise Stores
24281	58	449	Miscellaneous Manufacturing	24485	7	12	Food and Beverage Stores	24639	35	147	Educational Services
24282	25	423	Mining (Except Oil and Gas)	24486	132	1470	Truck Transportation	24640	2	4	Merch. Wholesalers,Durable Gds
24283	117	1326	Furniture & Related Prod. Mfg	24487	16	28	Telecommunications	24641	405	3302	Hospitals

BUSINESS DATA

ZIP CODE	2004 Total Firms	2004 Total Employees	TOP INDUSTRY RANKED on 2004 EMPLOYMENT	ZIP CODE	2004 Total Firms	2004 Total Employees	TOP INDUSTRY RANKED on 2004 EMPLOYMENT	ZIP CODE	2004 Total Firms	2004 Total Employees	TOP INDUSTRY RANKED on 2004 EMPLOYMENT
24646	4	364	Mining (Except Oil and Gas)	24902	23	187	Machinery Manufacturing	25102	8	35	Justice, Pubic Order/Safety
24649	33	250	Mining (Except Oil and Gas)	24910	87	319	Educational Services	25103	7	32	Bldg Matl & Garden Eqpmt Dlrs
24651	315	2725	Educational Services	24915	18	30	Accommodation	25106	24	85	Special Trade Contractors
24656	109	1405	Merch. Wholesalers,Durable Gds	24916	13	20	Construction of Buildings	25107	12	67	Mining (Except Oil and Gas)
24657	11	64	Truck Transportation	24917	2	2	Truck Transportation	25108	4	19	Educational Services
24658	4	4	Relig., Grant, Civic, Prof Org	24918	17	44	Justice, Pubic Order/Safety	25109	6	33	Educational Services
24701	1050	9767	Hospitals	24920	18	323	Merch. Wholesalers,Durable Gds	25110	5	4	Merch. Wholesalers,Nondur. Gds
24712	50	594	Educational Services	24924	17	175	Hospitals	25111	4	29	Repair and Maintenance
24714	2	9	Wood Product Manufacturing	24925	21	160	Accommodation	25112	35	2320	Chemical Manufacturing
24715	17	58	Justice, Pubic Order/Safety	24927	10	153	Museums, Hist. Sites,& Similar	25113	26	157	Nursing & Resid. Care Facilit.
24716	7	34	Educational Services	24931	20	94	Ambulatory Health Care Svcs	25114	15	63	Justice, Pubic Order/Safety
24719	2	2	Postal Service	24934	10	85	Educational Services	25118	12	27	Fabricated Metal Product Mfg
24724	4	4	Food and Beverage Stores	24935	12	30	Merch. Wholesalers,Nondur. Gds	25119	6	15	Utilities
24726	8	128	Fabricated Metal Product Mfg	24936	3	26	Mining (Except Oil and Gas)	25121	9	15	Repair and Maintenance
24729	1	0	Postal Service	24938	38	133	Educational Services	25123	20	71	Educational Services
24731	7	14	Food and Beverage Stores	24941	21	51	Food and Beverage Stores	25124	8	21	Postal Service
24732	3	8	Relig., Grant, Civic, Prof Org	24944	20	139	Educational Services	25125	12	50	Petroleum & Coal Products Mfg
24733	12	47	Repair and Maintenance	24945	15	24	Credit Intermediation & Relatd	25126	9	59	Admin. Enviro. Quality Progrms
24736	16	177	Educational Services	24946	43	273	Justice, Pubic Order/Safety	25130	172	1374	Educational Services
24737	10	45	Educational Services	24951	25	267	Nursing & Resid. Care Facilit.	25132	2	2	Food and Beverage Stores
24738	1	2	Food and Beverage Stores	24954	200	1144	Food and Beverage Stores	25133	10	19	Food and Beverage Stores
24739	10	60	Educational Services	24957	8	39	Special Trade Contractors	25134	6	24	Educational Services
24740	1225	12749	Hospitals	24961	6	29	Support Activities: Agr./For.	25136	149	1220	Educational Services
24747	10	68	Educational Services	24962	5	7	General Merchandise Stores	25139	12	39	Admin. of Economic Programs
24751	2	7	Ambulatory Health Care Svcs	24963	90	279	Educational Services	25140	16	349	Special Trade Contractors
24801	244	1916	Hospitals	24966	16	167	Prof., Scientific, & Tech Svcs	25141	3	18	Wood Product Manufacturing
24808	9	28	Educational Services	24970	159	1955	Hospitals	25142	8	22	Educational Services
24811	3	28	Educational Services	24974	2	5	Forestry and Logging	25143	401	4744	General Merchandise Stores
24813	5	22	Educational Services	24976	15	39	Prof., Scientific, & Tech Svcs	25147	4	0	Mining (Except Oil and Gas)
24815	8	29	Educational Services	24977	7	85	Wood Product Manufacturing	25148	4	9	Personal and Laundry Services
24816	5	54	Educational Services	24981	15	79	Bldg Matl & Garden Eqpmt Dlrs	25149	2	3	Postal Service
24817	33	145	Educational Services	24983	110	442	Admin. Human Resource Programs	25150	3	2	Heavy & Civil Eng. Construct'N
24818	20	260	Construction of Buildings	24985	4	3	Heavy & Civil Eng. Construct'N	25152	8	7	Food and Beverage Stores
24820	2	2	Postal Service	24986	187	2110	Accommodation	25154	10	13	Wholesale Elec. Mrkts & Agents
24821	6	27	Social Assistance	24991	13	84	Waste Managmt & Remediat'n Svc	25156	18	63	Merch. Wholesalers,Nondur. Gds
24822	3	53	Educational Services	24993	3	6	Beverage & Tobacco Product Mfg	25159	129	2082	Merch. Wholesalers,Nondur. Gds
24823	8	17	Justice, Pubic Order/Safety	25002	21	360	Machinery Manufacturing	25160	2	7	Fabricated Metal Product Mfg
24824	8	37	Justice, Pubic Order/Safety	25003	82	354	Food and Beverage Stores	25161	9	24	Miscellaneous Store Retailers
24825	1	1	Postal Service	25004	1	2	Food and Beverage Stores	25162	12	107	Educational Services
24826	6	5	Support Act. for Transport.	25005	11	97	Construction of Buildings	25164	9	21	Utilities
24827	17	50	Educational Services	25007	6	9	Insurance Carriers & Related	25165	19	98	Justice, Pubic Order/Safety
24828	11	18	Merch. Wholesalers,Durable Gds	25008	1	1	Merch. Wholesalers,Nondur. Gds	25168	32	181	Admin. of Economic Programs
24829	4	10	Relig., Grant, Civic, Prof Org	25009	8	44	Educational Services	25169	4	7	Special Trade Contractors
24830	2	2	Postal Service	25010	4	14	Food and Beverage Stores	25173	12	15	Construction of Buildings
24831	2	6	Utilities	25011	8	18	Utilities	25174	7	60	Admin. Human Resource Programs
24834	1	3	Relig., Grant, Civic, Prof Org	25015	137	2302	Chemical Manufacturing	25177	784	7580	Motor Vehicle & Parts Dealers
24836	29	515	Nursing & Resid. Care Facilit.	25019	12	562	Mining (Except Oil and Gas)	25181	29	534	Mining (Except Oil and Gas)
24839	27	128	Educational Services	25021	6	13	Broadcasting	25183	2	3	Postal Service
24842	2	2	Postal Service	25022	1	2	Postal Service	25185	2	379	Justice, Pubic Order/Safety
24843	1	2	Postal Service	25024	5	32	Truck Transportation	25186	57	493	Food Svcs & Drinking Places
24844	79	469	Educational Services	25025	2	0	Ambulatory Health Care Svcs	25187	12	63	Wood Product Manufacturing
24845	10	12	Truck Transportation	25026	7	21	Furn. & Home Furnishgs Stores	25193	16	622	Mining (Except Oil and Gas)
24846	4	4	Postal Service	25028	7	108	Mining (Except Oil and Gas)	25201	4	17	Educational Services
24847	6	31	Relig., Grant, Civic, Prof Org	25030	5	15	Educational Services	25202	18	81	Educational Services
24848	1	2	Postal Service	25031	7	48	Prof., Scientific, & Tech Svcs	25203	9	48	Miscellaneous Store Retailers
24849	8	77	Special Trade Contractors	25033	36	806	Repair and Maintenance	25204	3	3	Postal Service
24850	8	15	Food and Beverage Stores	25035	41	354	Merch. Wholesalers,Durable Gds	25205	11	60	Admin. of Economic Programs
24851	26	74	Wood Product Manufacturing	25036	9	34	Miscellaneous Store Retailers	25206	16	108	Educational Services
24852	11	50	Justice, Pubic Order/Safety	25039	27	213	Justice, Pubic Order/Safety	25208	24	1286	Mining (Except Oil and Gas)
24853	25	169	Educational Services	25040	11	21	Repair and Maintenance	25209	69	891	Mining (Except Oil and Gas)
24854	7	19	Administrative & Support Svcs	25043	145	844	Educational Services	25211	2	5	Construction of Buildings
24855	1	0	Relig., Grant, Civic, Prof Org	25044	6	32	Educational Services	25213	195	1521	Educational Services
24857	7	16	Special Trade Contractors	25045	126	638	Educational Services	25214	10	58	Repair and Maintenance
24859	2	13	Utilities	25047	6	8	Food and Beverage Stores	25234	33	281	Heavy & Civil Eng. Construct'N
24860	15	115	Relig., Grant, Civic, Prof Org	25048	3	8	Educational Services	25235	6	4	Bldg Matl & Garden Eqpmt Dlrs
24861	9	49	Educational Services	25049	11	159	Educational Services	25239	20	78	Educational Services
24862	3	6	Food Svcs & Drinking Places	25051	1	2	Postal Service	25241	19	89	Construction of Buildings
24866	7	41	Food and Beverage Stores	25053	153	1361	Food Svcs & Drinking Places	25243	10	44	Justice, Pubic Order/Safety
24867	8	125	Nursing & Resid. Care Facilit.	25054	4	135	Mining (Except Oil and Gas)	25244	2	3	Construction of Buildings
24868	56	251	Ambulatory Health Care Svcs	25057	2	1	Utilities	25245	8	16	Construction of Buildings
24870	147	799	Food Svcs & Drinking Places	25059	17	131	Bldg Matl & Garden Eqpmt Dlrs	25247	8	10	Special Trade Contractors
24871	3	5	Mining (Except Oil and Gas)	25060	4	9	Miscellaneous Store Retailers	25248	39	120	Educational Services
24872	6	31	Food Svcs & Drinking Places	25061	5	23	Nonstore Retailers	25251	7	66	Educational Services
24873	5	8	Special Trade Contractors	25062	2	3	General Merchandise Stores	25252	7	36	Educational Services
24874	178	1739	Fabricated Metal Product Mfg	25063	9	18	Merch. Wholesalers,Durable Gds	25253	8	36	Exec., Legis., & Other Support
24878	2	8	Prof., Scientific, & Tech Svcs	25064	393	3361	Educational Services	25259	6	3	Postal Service
24879	10	26	Construction of Buildings	25067	30	78	Educational Services	25260	64	653	General Merchandise Stores
24880	9	53	Mining (Except Oil and Gas)	25070	79	645	Fabricated Metal Product Mfg	25261	7	10	Postal Service
24881	9	42	Wood Product Manufacturing	25071	240	1463	Food Svcs & Drinking Places	25262	26	308	Truck Transportation
24882	2	4	Postal Service	25075	8	341	Mining (Except Oil and Gas)	25264	6	7	Food and Beverage Stores
24884	3	8	Food and Beverage Stores	25076	4	4	Postal Service	25265	54	485	Utilities
24888	6	25	Mining (Except Oil and Gas)	25079	2	2	Postal Service	25266	15	74	Justice, Pubic Order/Safety
24892	90	329	Educational Services	25081	9	90	Educational Services	25267	8	51	Textile Product Mills
24894	3	2	Postal Service	25082	18	68	Food Svcs & Drinking Places	25268	4	3	Food and Beverage Stores
24895	6	42	Social Assistance	25083	12	64	Food Svcs & Drinking Places	25270	17	128	Bldg Matl & Garden Eqpmt Dlrs
24896	1	0	Support Activities for Mining	25085	53	272	Food and Beverage Stores	25271	463	4424	Ambulatory Health Care Svcs
24897	1	1	Postal Service	25086	28	228	Nursing & Resid. Care Facilit.	25275	22	190	Heavy & Civil Eng. Construct'N
24898	3	1	Motor Vehicle & Parts Dealers	25088	3	3	Relig., Grant, Civic, Prof Org	25276	327	2904	Food Svcs & Drinking Places
24899	4	6	Ambulatory Health Care Svcs	25090	6	18	Accommodation	25279	6	13	Construction of Buildings
24901	656	5578	Educational Services	25093	1	2	Postal Service	25285	7	24	Educational Services

ZIP CODE	2004 Total Firms	2004 Total Employees	TOP INDUSTRY RANKED on 2004 EMPLOYMENT	ZIP CODE	2004 Total Firms	2004 Total Employees	TOP INDUSTRY RANKED on 2004 EMPLOYMENT	ZIP CODE	2004 Total Firms	2004 Total Employees	TOP INDUSTRY RANKED on 2004 EMPLOYMENT
25286	25	122	Educational Services	25550	384	3195	Hospitals	25832	93	791	Personal and Laundry Services
25287	10	533	Support Act. for Transport.	25555	25	325	Merch. Wholesalers,Durable Gds	25833	1	2	Special Trade Contractors
25301	1699	20282	Prof., Scientific, & Tech Svcs	25557	13	57	Educational Services	25836	10	14	Merch. Wholesalers,Durable Gds
25302	700	6851	Hospitals	25559	36	152	Educational Services	25837	4	6	Special Trade Contractors
25303	422	5610	Transportation Equipment Mfg	25560	225	1946	Prof., Scientific, & Tech Svcs	25839	13	88	Educational Services
25304	574	10683	Hospitals	25562	5	5	Personal and Laundry Services	25840	244	1544	Food Svcs & Drinking Places
25305	130	5449	Exec., Legis., & Other Support	25564	10	8	Heavy & Civil Eng. Construct'N	25841	22	422	Accommodation
25306	141	955	Mining (Except Oil and Gas)	25565	8	67	Mining (Except Oil and Gas)	25843	22	152	Sportg Gds,Hobby,Book, & Music
25309	526	9071	Hospitals	25567	12	17	Special Trade Contractors	25844	43	274	Food and Beverage Stores
25311	472	7003	Merch. Wholesalers,Durable Gds	25569	36	149	Food Svcs & Drinking Places	25845	11	34	Educational Services
25312	459	4928	Motor Vehicle & Parts Dealers	25570	195	1875	Exec., Legis., & Other Support	25846	14	184	Admin. Enviro. Quality Progrms
25313	490	4802	Food Svcs & Drinking Places	25571	54	211	Food and Beverage Stores	25847	24	145	Waste Managmt & Remediat'n Svc
25314	335	2139	Relig., Grant, Civic, Prof Org	25573	17	84	Petroleum & Coal Products Mfg	25848	4	8	Utilities
25315	126	806	Food and Beverage Stores	25601	481	5021	Hospitals	25849	8	59	Social Assistance
25317	1	0	Exec., Legis., & Other Support	25606	13	88	Educational Services	25851	6	22	Motor Vehicle & Parts Dealers
25320	120	990	Transportation Equipment Mfg	25607	11	68	Justice, Pubic Order/Safety	25853	3	2	Postal Service
25321	2	4	Prof., Scientific, & Tech Svcs	25608	10	31	Educational Services	25854	35	409	Administrative & Support Svcs
25324	1	0	Prof., Scientific, & Tech Svcs	25611	6	6	Support Act. for Transport.	25855	11	273	Ambulatory Health Care Svcs
25326	1	2	Support Activities for Mining	25612	4	6	Relig., Grant, Civic, Prof Org	25859	2	2	Postal Service
25327	2	5	Prof., Scientific, & Tech Svcs	25614	8	58	Food and Beverage Stores	25860	2	3	Repair and Maintenance
25329	2	2	Telecommunications	25617	15	30	Machinery Manufacturing	25862	21	455	Scenic & Sightseeing Transport
25330	1	2	Insurance Carriers & Related	25621	136	846	Nonstore Retailers	25864	3	11	Fabricated Metal Product Mfg
25332	1	4	Miscellaneous Store Retailers	25624	8	43	Justice, Pubic Order/Safety	25865	14	74	Machinery Manufacturing
25337	1	2	Prof., Scientific, & Tech Svcs	25625	43	598	Mining (Except Oil and Gas)	25866	11	61	Ambulatory Health Care Svcs
25339	5	30	Administrative & Support Svcs	25628	15	34	Ambulatory Health Care Svcs	25868	14	91	Educational Services
25356	5	31	Waste Managmt & Remediat'n Svc	25630	6	10	Social Assistance	25870	6	36	Relig., Grant, Civic, Prof Org
25357	1	9	Administrative & Support Svcs	25632	21	612	Merch. Wholesalers,Durable Gds	25871	35	577	Relig., Grant, Civic, Prof Org
25358	1	3	Special Trade Contractors	25634	11	80	Merch. Wholesalers,Durable Gds	25873	25	127	Educational Services
25360	3	3	Prof., Scientific, & Tech Svcs	25635	106	609	Educational Services	25875	2	1	Special Trade Contractors
25361	2	1	Insurance Carriers & Related	25636	6	46	Utilities	25876	6	15	Educational Services
25362	8	13	Electronics & Appliance Stores	25637	25	279	Food and Beverage Stores	25878	19	51	Social Assistance
25364	6	15	Prof., Scientific, & Tech Svcs	25638	21	104	Educational Services	25879	6	8	Utilities
25365	4	1	Relig., Grant, Civic, Prof Org	25639	8	128	Rail Transportation	25880	227	1700	General Merchandise Stores
25375	1	1	Prof., Scientific, & Tech Svcs	25644	7	50	Mining (Except Oil and Gas)	25882	95	587	Food and Beverage Stores
25387	34	289	Food Svcs & Drinking Places	25646	43	244	Motor Vehicle & Parts Dealers	25901	457	4197	Ambulatory Health Care Svcs
25389	129	1590	Food Svcs & Drinking Places	25647	21	53	Construction of Buildings	25902	2	5	Administrative & Support Svcs
25396	1	1200	Telecommunications	25649	24	68	Educational Services	25904	12	19	Merch. Wholesalers,Durable Gds
25401	1793	19596	Hospitals	25650	9	13	Petroleum & Coal Products Mfg	25906	11	20	Fabricated Metal Product Mfg
25402	10	861	Ambulatory Health Care Svcs	25651	18	250	Mining (Except Oil and Gas)	25907	1	0	Relig., Grant, Civic, Prof Org
25411	393	3082	Accommodation	25652	26	158	Merch. Wholesalers,Durable Gds	25908	2	0	Postal Service
25413	104	503	Educational Services	25653	40	248	Merch. Wholesalers,Durable Gds	25909	27	156	Relig., Grant, Civic, Prof Org
25414	627	5912	Food Svcs & Drinking Places	25654	7	339	Mining (Except Oil and Gas)	25911	7	42	Machinery Manufacturing
25419	118	702	Chemical Manufacturing	25661	330	2465	Hospitals	25913	7	17	Utilities
25420	28	99	Educational Services	25665	6	8	Food and Beverage Stores	25915	9	38	Administrative & Support Svcs
25421	4	2	Special Trade Contractors	25666	6	5	Forestry and Logging	25916	2	0	Merch. Wholesalers,Durable Gds
25422	18	74	Prof., Scientific, & Tech Svcs	25667	14	79	Hospitals	25917	26	151	Ambulatory Health Care Svcs
25423	10	259	Paper Manufacturing	25669	18	122	Educational Services	25918	85	352	Educational Services
25425	161	1188	Museums, Hist. Sites,& Similar	25670	93	534	Educational Services	25919	9	13	Repair and Maintenance
25427	214	1191	Educational Services	25671	20	315	Mining (Except Oil and Gas)	25920	11	131	Prof., Scientific, & Tech Svcs
25428	236	1762	Food and Beverage Stores	25672	6	19	Relig., Grant, Civic, Prof Org	25921	96	799	Food and Beverage Stores
25430	111	2984	Machinery Manufacturing	25674	74	419	Truck Transportation	25922	11	52	Educational Services
25431	10	50	Justice, Pubic Order/Safety	25676	35	383	Mining (Except Oil and Gas)	25927	16	83	Educational Services
25432	5	84	Mining (Except Oil and Gas)	25678	54	221	Educational Services	25928	4	4	Merch. Wholesalers,Durable Gds
25434	37	169	Justice, Pubic Order/Safety	25682	5	40	Mining (Except Oil and Gas)	25931	2	0	Relig., Grant, Civic, Prof Org
25437	3	1	Administrative & Support Svcs	25685	20	1009	Mining (Except Oil and Gas)	25932	12	51	Educational Services
25438	144	2243	Prof., Scientific, & Tech Svcs	25686	3	4	Real Estate	25934	2	9	Special Trade Contractors
25440	2	0	Construction of Buildings	25687	4	4	Unclassified Establishments	25936	3	3	Scenic & Sightseeing Transport
25441	8	41	Food Svcs & Drinking Places	25688	14	48	Nonmetallic Mineral Prod. Mfg	25938	7	22	Support Act. for Transport.
25442	15	180	Educational Services	25690	10	66	Wood Product Manufacturing	25942	2	4	Perform'g Arts, Spec. Sports
25443	255	2561	Educational Services	25691	3	3	Merch. Wholesalers,Durable Gds	25951	269	1860	Rail Transportation
25444	14	59	Educational Services	25692	14	41	Truck Transportation	25958	13	56	Educational Services
25446	19	110	Wood Product Manufacturing	25694	3	1	Mining (Except Oil and Gas)	25962	167	1146	Relig., Grant, Civic, Prof Org
25501	12	28	Forestry and Logging	25696	19	170	Special Trade Contractors	25966	3	23	Waste Managmt & Remediat'n Svc
25502	17	469	Merch. Wholesalers,Nondur. Gds	25701	1487	19133	Ambulatory Health Care Svcs	25967	5	4	Fabricated Metal Product Mfg
25503	9	83	Educational Services	25702	278	5345	Hospitals	25969	15	82	Motor Vehicle & Parts Dealers
25504	597	6402	Food Svcs & Drinking Places	25703	235	4840	Relig., Grant, Civic, Prof Org	25971	14	61	Educational Services
25505	5	21	Special Trade Contractors	25704	421	6268	Hospitals	25972	2	2	Postal Service
25506	62	320	Educational Services	25705	438	6743	Primary Metal Manufacturing	25976	35	124	Educational Services
25507	97	1026	Plastics & Rubber Products Mfg	25708	4	16	Social Assistance	25977	1	10	Accommodation
25508	241	1602	Food and Beverage Stores	25711	1	2	Isps, Web Search Portals	25978	21	85	Wood Product Manufacturing
25510	62	371	Fabricated Metal Product Mfg	25718	2	2	Special Trade Contractors	25979	21	156	Food Svcs & Drinking Places
25511	15	105	Justice, Pubic Order/Safety	25726	1	400	Special Trade Contractors	25981	17	101	Wholesale Elec. Mrkts & Agents
25512	21	560	Mining (Except Oil and Gas)	25755	8	1507	Educational Services	25984	66	290	Admin. Human Resource Programs
25514	63	446	Educational Services	25773	2	6	Relig., Grant, Civic, Prof Org	25985	14	24	Justice, Pubic Order/Safety
25515	29	500	Support Act. for Transport.	25775	1	4	Administrative & Support Svcs	25986	4	28	Construction of Buildings
25517	11	44	Educational Services	25801	1790	19452	Hospitals	25989	8	13	Merch. Wholesalers,Durable Gds
25520	7	13	Wood Product Manufacturing	25802	9	42	Mining (Except Oil and Gas)	26003	2070	30354	Hospitals
25521	23	144	Educational Services	25810	5	4	Postal Service	26030	16	199	Fabricated Metal Product Mfg
25523	137	1252	Ambulatory Health Care Svcs	25811	3	6	Food and Beverage Stores	26031	55	636	Food Svcs & Drinking Places
25524	48	264	Educational Services	25812	67	354	Accommodation	26032	21	101	Relig., Grant, Civic, Prof Org
25526	717	5601	Food Svcs & Drinking Places	25813	223	2010	Food Svcs & Drinking Places	26033	81	466	Nursing & Resid. Care Facilit.
25529	21	52	Bldg Matl & Garden Eqpmt Dlrs	25816	3	32	Relig., Grant, Civic, Prof Org	26034	157	3742	Accommodation
25530	172	1555	Merch. Wholesalers,Nondur. Gds	25817	10	62	Machinery Manufacturing	26035	31	141	Waste Managmt & Remediat'n Svc
25534	2	0	Postal Service	25818	36	261	Special Trade Contractors	26036	6	416	Mining (Except Oil and Gas)
25535	85	409	Motor Vehicle & Parts Dealers	25820	6	17	Gasoline Stations	26037	207	1660	Nursing & Resid. Care Facilit.
25537	30	372	Food and Beverage Stores	25823	34	193	Educational Services	26038	94	1192	Hospitals
25540	5	9	Heavy & Civil Eng. Construct'N	25825	30	94	Construction of Buildings	26039	9	625	Nonstore Retailers
25541	236	1926	Food and Beverage Stores	25826	2	2	Postal Service	26040	41	283	Ambulatory Health Care Svcs
25545	71	601	Educational Services	25827	106	514	Educational Services	26041	474	4025	Food Svcs & Drinking Places
25547	23	135	Special Trade Contractors	25831	22	139	Construction of Buildings	26047	124	1470	Educational Services

BUSINESS DATA

ZIP CODE	2004 Total Firms	2004 Total Employees	TOP INDUSTRY RANKED on 2004 EMPLOYMENT	ZIP CODE	2004 Total Firms	2004 Total Employees	TOP INDUSTRY RANKED on 2004 EMPLOYMENT	ZIP CODE	2004 Total Firms	2004 Total Employees	TOP INDUSTRY RANKED on 2004 EMPLOYMENT
26050	62	2197	Nonmetallic Mineral Prod. Mfg	26288	133	816	Hospitals	26537	291	2857	Educational Services
26055	26	208	Chemical Manufacturing	26289	1	4	Special Trade Contractors	26541	18	156	Mining (Except Oil and Gas)
26056	13	136	Educational Services	26291	22	167	Merch. Wholesalers,Durable Gds	26542	52	271	Waste Managmt & Remediat'n Svc
26058	5	62	Truck Transportation	26292	45	301	Nursing & Resid. Care Facilit.	26543	9	86	Educational Services
26059	139	1284	Plastics & Rubber Products Mfg	26293	14	74	Food Svcs & Drinking Places	26544	6	34	Construction of Buildings
26060	35	289	Electronics & Appliance Stores	26294	14	57	Justice, Pubic Order/Safety	26546	11	37	Relig., Grant, Civic, Prof Org
26062	805	8581	Hospitals	26296	1	1	Justice, Pubic Order/Safety	26547	61	452	Paper Manufacturing
26070	277	2207	Educational Services	26298	3	4	Food and Beverage Stores	26554	1620	15859	Educational Services
26074	17	688	Petroleum & Coal Products Mfg	26301	1376	17702	Hospitals	26555	5	49	Merch. Wholesalers,Durable Gds
26075	6	55	Justice, Pubic Order/Safety	26302	21	165	Heavy & Civil Eng. Construct'N	26559	16	30	Relig., Grant, Civic, Prof Org
26101	1876	22037	Hospitals	26306	2	3000	Justice, Pubic Order/Safety	26560	3	1	Personal and Laundry Services
26102	9	49	Utilities	26320	16	46	Unclassified Establishments	26561	1	0	Postal Service
26103	2	28	Merch. Wholesalers,Durable Gds	26321	5	13	Educational Services	26562	9	22	Real Estate
26104	446	4125	Educational Services	26323	33	339	Elect'l Eqpmt, App, & Comp Mfg	26563	4	9	Educational Services
26105	505	5209	General Merchandise Stores	26325	3	2	Food and Beverage Stores	26566	2	4	Prof., Scientific, & Tech Svcs
26106	3	8	Credit Intermediation & Relatd	26327	1	0	Accommodation	26568	12	42	Food Svcs & Drinking Places
26120	1	850	Prof., Scientific, & Tech Svcs	26330	757	7110	Food Svcs & Drinking Places	26570	61	896	Merch. Wholesalers,Durable Gds
26133	16	37	Admin. Enviro. Quality Progrms	26332	8	29	Admin. of Economic Programs	26571	49	346	Educational Services
26134	40	396	Ambulatory Health Care Svcs	26334	4	12	Educational Services	26572	1	2	Postal Service
26136	10	37	Oil and Gas Extraction	26335	35	150	Admin. Enviro. Quality Progrms	26574	14	80	Utilities
26137	13	29	Ambulatory Health Care Svcs	26337	36	123	Museums, Hist. Sites,& Similar	26575	44	132	Food Svcs & Drinking Places
26141	4	35	Wood Product Manufacturing	26338	4	5	Food and Beverage Stores	26576	5	12	Warehousing and Storage
26142	25	267	Special Trade Contractors	26339	4	5	Food Svcs & Drinking Places	26578	6	11	Merch. Wholesalers,Durable Gds
26143	124	674	Educational Services	26342	4	1	Food and Beverage Stores	26581	8	24	Relig., Grant, Civic, Prof Org
26146	22	193	Primary Metal Manufacturing	26343	1	0	Prof., Scientific, & Tech Svcs	26582	127	1763	Mining (Except Oil and Gas)
26147	127	804	Ambulatory Health Care Svcs	26346	53	386	Educational Services	26585	10	51	Educational Services
26148	3	5	Wood Product Manufacturing	26347	24	80	Educational Services	26586	4	2	Construction of Buildings
26149	73	383	Food and Beverage Stores	26348	7	16	Forestry and Logging	26587	6	45	Wood Product Manufacturing
26150	135	1637	Food Svcs & Drinking Places	26349	2	2	Postal Service	26588	39	123	Educational Services
26151	8	27	Exec., Legis., & Other Support	26351	189	1635	Educational Services	26590	12	95	Mining (Except Oil and Gas)
26155	422	4376	Merch. Wholesalers,Nondur. Gds	26354	321	2918	Educational Services	26591	31	110	Nursing & Resid. Care Facilit.
26159	78	512	Fabricated Metal Product Mfg	26361	4	23	Merch. Wholesalers,Nondur. Gds	26601	238	1819	Educational Services
26160	8	10	Special Trade Contractors	26362	148	818	Transportation Equipment Mfg	26610	26	148	Heavy & Civil Eng. Construct'N
26161	4	18	Mining (Except Oil and Gas)	26366	6	285	Utilities	26611	4	3	Merch. Wholesalers,Durable Gds
26164	232	3972	Primary Metal Manufacturing	26369	13	212	Miscellaneous Manufacturing	26615	2	1	Forestry and Logging
26167	16	103	Educational Services	26372	8	25	Support Activities: Agr./For.	26617	2	2	Gasoline Stations
26169	13	19	Pipeline Transportation	26374	11	45	Construction of Buildings	26619	6	11	Prof., Scientific, & Tech Svcs
26170	186	1150	Food Svcs & Drinking Places	26376	5	21	Wood Product Manufacturing	26621	29	86	Educational Services
26173	2	4	Special Trade Contractors	26377	7	40	Wood Product Manufacturing	26623	14	69	Educational Services
26175	111	808	Educational Services	26378	92	844	Nursing & Resid. Care Facilit.	26624	162	1084	Food and Beverage Stores
26178	17	95	Transportation Equipment Mfg	26384	6	4	Furn. & Home Furnishgs Stores	26627	9	58	Merch. Wholesalers,Durable Gds
26180	29	197	Social Assistance	26385	58	321	Educational Services	26629	8	80	Motor Vehicle & Parts Dealers
26181	73	3344	Chemical Manufacturing	26386	37	184	Educational Services	26636	5	9	Relig., Grant, Civic, Prof Org
26184	31	251	Nonmetallic Mineral Prod. Mfg	26404	9	126	Construction of Buildings	26639	2	2	Postal Service
26186	6	24	Justice, Pubic Order/Safety	26405	10	127	Construction of Buildings	26641	2	4	Electronics & Appliance Stores
26187	175	2112	Nonmetallic Mineral Prod. Mfg	26408	46	446	Administrative & Support Svcs	26651	533	4569	General Merchandise Stores
26201	756	7233	Educational Services	26410	21	106	Ambulatory Health Care Svcs	26656	10	86	Justice, Pubic Order/Safety
26202	12	191	Computer & Electronic Prod Mfg	26411	9	14	Postal Service	26660	10	25	Gasoline Stations
26203	4	27	Truck Transportation	26412	1	4	Postal Service	26662	11	50	Food Svcs & Drinking Places
26205	101	770	Wood Product Manufacturing	26415	92	1493	Fabricated Metal Product Mfg	26667	11	275	Mining (Except Oil and Gas)
26206	80	705	Mining (Except Oil and Gas)	26416	278	2216	Educational Services	26671	4	39	Machinery Manufacturing
26208	8	64	Ambulatory Health Care Svcs	26419	38	297	Utilities	26674	2	0	Relig., Grant, Civic, Prof Org
26209	46	2944	Accommodation	26421	3	5	Postal Service	26675	1	6	Food and Beverage Stores
26210	5	5	Special Trade Contractors	26422	10	15	Utilities	26676	9	13	Mining (Except Oil and Gas)
26217	12	25	Educational Services	26424	7	14	Administrative & Support Svcs	26678	24	65	Educational Services
26218	24	127	Educational Services	26425	29	139	Educational Services	26679	33	200	Food and Beverage Stores
26222	17	71	Wood Product Manufacturing	26426	128	1254	Educational Services	26680	4	6	Food Svcs & Drinking Places
26224	6	13	Ambulatory Health Care Svcs	26430	11	79	Nonstore Retailers	26681	31	140	Educational Services
26228	3	107	Wood Product Manufacturing	26431	186	1394	Educational Services	26690	4	4	Prof., Scientific, & Tech Svcs
26229	6	131	Heavy & Civil Eng. Construct'N	26434	2	13	Justice, Pubic Order/Safety	26691	6	10	Machinery Manufacturing
26230	6	16	Educational Services	26435	1	4	Food and Beverage Stores	26704	85	342	Personal and Laundry Services
26234	30	127	Ambulatory Health Care Svcs	26436	11	102	Educational Services	26705	19	76	Justice, Pubic Order/Safety
26236	2	20	Accommodation	26437	15	30	Pipeline Transportation	26707	13	10	Credit Intermediation & Relatd
26237	7	13	Mining (Except Oil and Gas)	26438	4	29	Justice, Pubic Order/Safety	26710	38	162	Justice, Pubic Order/Safety
26238	10	83	Mining (Except Oil and Gas)	26440	10	26	Special Trade Contractors	26711	70	355	Justice, Pubic Order/Safety
26241	845	8381	Educational Services	26443	5	30	Educational Services	26714	2	0	Postal Service
26250	115	758	Nursing & Resid. Care Facilit.	26444	56	391	Merch. Wholesalers,Durable Gds	26716	17	46	Wood Product Manufacturing
26253	59	1264	Wood Product Manufacturing	26447	21	105	Justice, Pubic Order/Safety	26717	15	71	Educational Services
26254	11	20	Accommodation	26448	9	43	Justice, Pubic Order/Safety	26719	76	343	Nursing & Resid. Care Facilit.
26257	8	34	Educational Services	26451	22	144	Educational Services	26720	7	11	Food and Beverage Stores
26259	20	272	Merch. Wholesalers,Durable Gds	26452	360	3067	Educational Services	26722	8	48	Wood Product Manufacturing
26260	121	1450	Accommodation	26456	122	638	Exec., Legis., & Other Support	26726	487	4955	Chemical Manufacturing
26261	124	868	Nursing & Resid. Care Facilit.	26461	1	0	Food Svcs & Drinking Places	26731	3	8	Support Act. for Transport.
26263	8	26	Food Svcs & Drinking Places	26463	3	6	Utilities	26739	29	225	Petroleum & Coal Products Mfg
26264	18	53	Wood Product Manufacturing	26501	725	7349	General Merchandise Stores	26743	23	82	Admin. of Economic Programs
26266	8	65	Educational Services	26502	1	1	Real Estate	26750	38	128	Justice, Pubic Order/Safety
26267	9	17	Special Trade Contractors	26504	9	74	Fabricated Metal Product Mfg	26753	115	656	Educational Services
26268	2	0	Postal Service	26505	1525	17824	Food Svcs & Drinking Places	26755	7	14	Educational Services
26269	7	155	Educational Services	26506	95	11242	Ambulatory Health Care Svcs	26757	341	3032	Educational Services
26270	31	103	Educational Services	26507	22	127	Museums, Hist. Sites,& Similar	26761	6	19	Miscellaneous Store Retailers
26271	7	142	Wood Product Manufacturing	26508	566	5823	Merch. Wholesalers,Durable Gds	26763	25	85	Educational Services
26273	17	57	Merch. Wholesalers,Durable Gds	26519	34	261	Truck Transportation	26764	98	756	Hospitals
26275	10	22	Food and Beverage Stores	26520	23	159	Social Assistance	26767	22	82	Motor Vehicle & Parts Dealers
26276	4	1	Postal Service	26521	27	218	Educational Services	26801	55	327	Educational Services
26278	5	3	Paper Manufacturing	26524	2	0	Postal Service	26802	29	89	Support Activities: Agr./For.
26280	47	362	Wood Product Manufacturing	26525	125	978	Construction of Buildings	26804	4	46	Educational Services
26282	3	11	Mining (Except Oil and Gas)	26527	5	25	Justice, Pubic Order/Safety	26807	156	1027	Nursing & Resid. Care Facilit.
26283	5	12	Postal Service	26529	26	68	Construction of Buildings	26808	9	636	Accommodation
26285	6	25	Merch. Wholesalers,Durable Gds	26531	19	2051	Mining (Except Oil and Gas)	26810	27	65	Telecommunications
26287	143	1181	Exec., Legis., & Other Support	26534	19	109	Special Trade Contractors	26812	57	108	Museums, Hist. Sites,& Similar

ZIP CODE	2004 Total Firms	2004 Total Employ-ees	TOP INDUSTRY RANKED on 2004 EMPLOYMENT	ZIP CODE	2004 Total Firms	2004 Total Employ-ees	TOP INDUSTRY RANKED on 2004 EMPLOYMENT	ZIP CODE	2004 Total Firms	2004 Total Employ-ees	TOP INDUSTRY RANKED on 2004 EMPLOYMENT
26814	8	117	Nonmetallic Mineral Prod. Mfg	27231	30	30	Special Trade Contractors	27415	8	31	Construction of Buildings
26815	11	225	Nat'l Security & Int'l Affairs	27233	84	469	Prof., Scientific, & Tech Svcs	27416	10	18	Special Trade Contractors
26817	7	10	General Merchandise Stores	27235	111	1681	Special Trade Contractors	27417	8	16	Construction of Buildings
26818	9	27	Crop Production	27239	302	1695	Educational Services	27419	18	33	Construction of Buildings
26823	5	42	Justice, Pubic Order/Safety	27242	41	332	Exec., Legis., & Other Support	27420	5	19	Relig., Grant, Civic, Prof Org
26824	1	2	Miscellaneous Store Retailers	27243	69	214	Accommodation	27425	3	2	Miscellaneous Store Retailers
26833	34	191	Justice, Pubic Order/Safety	27244	206	2111	Educational Services	27427	2	1	Securities/Commodity Contracts
26836	257	5996	Food Manufacturing	27247	8	58	Furniture & Related Prod. Mfg	27429	10	23	Construction of Buildings
26838	2	7	Social Assistance	27248	102	733	Textile Mills	27435	4	11	Miscellaneous Store Retailers
26845	5	18	Educational Services	27249	243	1312	Educational Services	27438	8	16	Construction of Buildings
26847	316	2854	Hospitals	27252	67	275	Apparel Manufacturing	27455	451	3850	Ambulatory Health Care Svcs
26851	60	263	Special Trade Contractors	27253	864	8217	Educational Services	27495	4	765	Postal Service
26852	7	20	Construction of Buildings	27256	6	14	Support Act. for Transport.	27498	1	6	Prof., Scientific, & Tech Svcs
26855	8	16	Heavy & Civil Eng. Construct'N	27258	175	1655	Plastics & Rubber Products Mfg	27501	403	2030	Educational Services
26865	10	63	Accommodation	27259	12	48	Educational Services	27502	798	4452	Educational Services
26866	20	59	Sportg Gds,Hobby,Book, & Music	27260	1936	21234	Furniture & Related Prod. Mfg	27503	88	244	Educational Services
26884	7	31	Real Estate	27261	13	108	Electronics & Appliance Stores	27504	525	3943	Warehousing and Storage
26886	2	4	Relig., Grant, Civic, Prof Org	27262	1706	16284	Ambulatory Health Care Svcs	27505	121	350	Educational Services
27006	308	1985	Nursing & Resid. Care Facilit.	27263	1315	14272	Furniture & Related Prod. Mfg	27506	28	993	Educational Services
27007	48	89	Accommodation	27264	3	1	Repair and Maintenance	27507	17	37	Justice, Pubic Order/Safety
27009	43	242	Utilities	27265	1182	10639	Educational Services	27508	59	774	Educational Services
27010	6	21	Construction of Buildings	27278	883	5968	Educational Services	27509	123	4099	Hospitals
27011	134	706	Educational Services	27281	45	140	Accommodation	27510	479	3452	Food Svcs & Drinking Places
27012	725	6208	Food Svcs & Drinking Places	27282	439	4341	Furn. & Home Furnishgs Stores	27511	2773	26466	Food Svcs & Drinking Places
27013	121	3883	Miscellaneous Manufacturing	27283	53	144	Bldg Matl & Garden Eqpmt Dlrs	27512	37	74	Prof., Scientific, & Tech Svcs
27014	43	405	Apparel Manufacturing	27284	1501	14765	Food Svcs & Drinking Places	27513	1078	18333	Administrative & Support Svcs
27016	110	1943	Exec., Legis., & Other Support	27285	10	47	Miscellaneous Store Retailers	27514	1537	19125	Hospitals
27017	353	3546	Merch. Wholesalers,Nondur. Gds	27288	1024	11436	Textile Mills	27515	17	34	Prof., Scientific, & Tech Svcs
27018	173	873	Educational Services	27289	4	14	Special Trade Contractors	27516	741	6262	Food Svcs & Drinking Places
27019	57	161	Educational Services	27291	38	104	Special Trade Contractors	27517	538	5343	Prof., Scientific, & Tech Svcs
27020	113	619	Textile Mills	27292	1740	18215	Furniture & Related Prod. Mfg	27519	273	5237	Publishing Industries
27021	465	3369	Food Svcs & Drinking Places	27293	2	0	Waste Managmt & Remediat'n Svc	27520	1050	9327	Chemical Manufacturing
27022	29	109	Educational Services	27294	1	150	Nonstore Retailers	27521	130	588	Educational Services
27023	229	1450	Educational Services	27295	871	7981	Fabricated Metal Product Mfg	27522	314	3229	Telecommunications
27024	55	351	Bldg Matl & Garden Eqpmt Dlrs	27298	340	2313	Furniture & Related Prod. Mfg	27523	259	2198	Bldg Matl & Garden Eqpmt Dlrs
27025	448	4351	Textile Mills	27299	61	492	Bldg Matl & Garden Eqpmt Dlrs	27524	240	1082	Educational Services
27027	124	1157	Textile Mills	27301	168	3050	Nonstore Retailers	27525	225	1936	Other Information Services
27028	821	7996	Apparel Manufacturing	27302	708	8224	Elect'l Eqpmt, App, & Comp Mfg	27526	966	6611	Educational Services
27030	1696	18170	Apparel Manufacturing	27305	29	16	Gasoline Stations	27529	1559	13360	Food Svcs & Drinking Places
27031	4	22	Food and Beverage Stores	27306	208	1413	Merch. Wholesalers,Durable Gds	27530	1482	16309	Ambulatory Health Care Svcs
27040	160	811	Furn. & Home Furnishgs Stores	27310	137	447	Educational Services	27531	32	169	Food Svcs & Drinking Places
27041	294	1804	Textile Mills	27311	54	167	Mining (Except Oil and Gas)	27532	3	15	Perform'g Arts, Spec. Sports
27042	16	529	Merch. Wholesalers,Durable Gds	27312	596	3647	Educational Services	27533	5	1154	Hospitals
27043	115	291	Educational Services	27313	134	993	Furniture & Related Prod. Mfg	27534	1205	14032	Food Svcs & Drinking Places
27045	222	2882	Prof., Scientific, & Tech Svcs	27314	21	212	Clothing & Cloth'g Acc. Stores	27536	1087	10304	Food Svcs & Drinking Places
27046	45	137	Educational Services	27315	50	354	Construction of Buildings	27537	434	4460	Educational Services
27047	30	166	Truck Transportation	27316	255	2784	Textile Mills	27539	332	3482	Computer & Electronic Prod Mfg
27048	175	1120	Textile Mills	27317	502	5427	Furniture & Related Prod. Mfg	27540	330	2151	Exec., Legis., & Other Support
27049	4	38	Justice, Pubic Order/Safety	27320	1260	12010	Educational Services	27541	68	169	Educational Services
27050	57	333	Educational Services	27323	1	3	Social Assistance	27542	230	1910	Merch. Wholesalers,Durable Gds
27051	163	1110	Repair and Maintenance	27325	199	1070	Educational Services	27543	3	6	Prof., Scientific, & Tech Svcs
27052	280	1816	Miscellaneous Store Retailers	27326	55	226	Educational Services	27544	63	394	Educational Services
27053	65	352	Bldg Matl & Garden Eqpmt Dlrs	27330	1539	15619	Machinery Manufacturing	27545	485	4060	Elect'l Eqpmt, App, & Comp Mfg
27054	44	252	Educational Services	27331	7	7	Insurance Carriers & Related	27546	501	5025	Justice, Pubic Order/Safety
27055	519	6231	Textile Mills	27332	630	6806	Fabricated Metal Product Mfg	27549	690	5384	Educational Services
27101	1762	30383	Beverage & Tobacco Product Mfg	27340	18	21	Real Estate	27551	25	69	Forestry and Logging
27102	4	18	Personal and Laundry Services	27341	195	1026	Furniture & Related Prod. Mfg	27552	11	41	Ambulatory Health Care Svcs
27103	2350	34863	Hospitals	27342	5	68	Educational Services	27553	35	609	Unclassified Establishments
27104	734	6645	Food Svcs & Drinking Places	27343	36	160	Educational Services	27555	19	107	Educational Services
27105	1205	21508	Miscellaneous Store Retailers	27344	675	7686	Merch. Wholesalers,Nondur. Gds	27556	15	165	Educational Services
27106	1238	13241	Educational Services	27349	77	228	Educational Services	27557	135	1256	Wood Product Manufacturing
27107	939	8517	Merch. Wholesalers,Durable Gds	27350	159	822	Furniture & Related Prod. Mfg	27559	60	1489	Paper Manufacturing
27108	2	7	Administrative & Support Svcs	27351	33	63	Relig., Grant, Civic, Prof Org	27560	805	17134	Prof., Scientific, & Tech Svcs
27109	1	45	Educational Services	27355	82	389	Furniture & Related Prod. Mfg	27562	49	190	Special Trade Contractors
27110	3	521	Educational Services	27356	97	2374	Apparel Manufacturing	27563	110	678	Repair and Maintenance
27113	7	17	Special Trade Contractors	27357	181	1338	Construction of Buildings	27565	816	9691	Chemical Manufacturing
27114	9	28	Bldg Matl & Garden Eqpmt Dlrs	27358	294	1035	Educational Services	27568	28	245	Educational Services
27115	2	5	Admin. of Economic Programs	27359	15	959	Machinery Manufacturing	27569	150	803	Apparel Manufacturing
27116	3	84	Electronics & Appliance Stores	27360	1796	15948	Furniture & Related Prod. Mfg	27570	3	18	Paper Manufacturing
27117	3	9	Prof., Scientific, & Tech Svcs	27361	10	37	Construction of Buildings	27571	90	740	Prof., Scientific, & Tech Svcs
27120	2	45	Administrative & Support Svcs	27370	345	2089	Educational Services	27572	126	271	Special Trade Contractors
27127	741	7180	Educational Services	27371	386	3870	Textile Product Mills	27573	803	8953	Textile Mills
27130	1	3	Insurance Carriers & Related	27373	2	2	Postal Service	27574	247	1076	Wood Product Manufacturing
27157	56	27791	Ambulatory Health Care Svcs	27374	76	827	Special Trade Contractors	27576	438	3309	Food Svcs & Drinking Places
27201	7	30	Special Trade Contractors	27375	50	1350	Justice, Pubic Order/Safety	27577	1103	12696	Computer & Electronic Prod Mfg
27202	3	4	Postal Service	27376	298	1793	Amusement, Gambling,& Recreat.	27581	33	65	Administrative & Support Svcs
27203	1478	17750	Apparel Manufacturing	27377	107	1893	Machinery Manufacturing	27582	18	118	Educational Services
27204	8	37	Social Assistance	27379	254	1795	Educational Services	27583	107	1668	Construction of Buildings
27205	804	11410	Furniture & Related Prod. Mfg	27401	1900	30544	Prof., Scientific, & Tech Svcs	27584	6	16	Food Svcs & Drinking Places
27207	80	405	Educational Services	27402	6	8	Special Trade Contractors	27586	6	29	Bldg Matl & Garden Eqpmt Dlrs
27208	52	119	Educational Services	27403	915	8058	Food Svcs & Drinking Places	27587	1117	6908	Educational Services
27209	148	2602	Apparel Manufacturing	27404	17	27	Prof., Scientific, & Tech Svcs	27588	9	26	Special Trade Contractors
27212	43	416	Justice, Pubic Order/Safety	27405	1613	14672	Food Svcs & Drinking Places	27589	312	2112	Educational Services
27213	16	33	Repair and Maintenance	27406	1691	18748	Merch. Wholesalers,Durable Gds	27591	477	3732	Elect'l Eqpmt, App, & Comp Mfg
27214	169	1690	Educational Services	27407	2459	28616	Food Svcs & Drinking Places	27592	154	499	Educational Services
27215	2115	27115	Food Svcs & Drinking Places	27408	1519	16372	Food Svcs & Drinking Places	27593	16	131	Educational Services
27216	5	11	Relig., Grant, Civic, Prof Org	27409	1314	32156	Administrative & Support Svcs	27594	10	33	Educational Services
27217	1034	9608	Textile Mills	27410	1275	16997	Food and Beverage Stores	27596	289	3022	Miscellaneous Manufacturing
27229	111	1552	Furniture & Related Prod. Mfg	27411	2	4	Museums, Hist. Sites,& Similar	27597	541	4217	Merch. Wholesalers,Nondur. Gds
27230	1	1	Special Trade Contractors	27412	9	1924	Ambulatory Health Care Svcs	27599	111	19582	Educational Services

BUSINESS DATA

ZIP CODE	2004 Total Firms	2004 Total Employees	TOP INDUSTRY RANKED on 2004 EMPLOYMENT	ZIP CODE	2004 Total Firms	2004 Total Employees	TOP INDUSTRY RANKED on 2004 EMPLOYMENT	ZIP CODE	2004 Total Firms	2004 Total Employees	TOP INDUSTRY RANKED on 2004 EMPLOYMENT
27601	1362	23274	Justice, Pubic Order/Safety	27844	44	201	Ambulatory Health Care Svcs	27958	183	1000	Food Svcs & Drinking Places
27602	3	78	Exec., Legis., & Other Support	27845	140	1206	Justice, Pubic Order/Safety	27959	496	4009	Food Svcs & Drinking Places
27603	2077	26154	Exec., Legis., & Other Support	27846	71	574	Textile Mills	27960	133	711	Food Svcs & Drinking Places
27604	1835	24529	Food Svcs & Drinking Places	27847	16	151	Educational Services	27962	392	4370	Paper Manufacturing
27605	565	7069	Social Assistance	27849	57	2808	Food Manufacturing	27964	55	262	Bldg Matl & Garden Eqpmt Dlrs
27606	1162	13229	Prof., Scientific, & Tech Svcs	27850	246	1134	Educational Services	27965	23	126	Educational Services
27607	1193	18347	Hospitals	27851	94	426	Educational Services	27966	102	378	Administrative & Support Svcs
27608	507	3340	Relig., Grant, Civic, Prof Org	27852	62	211	Ambulatory Health Care Svcs	27967	11	85	Educational Services
27609	2625	25341	Prof., Scientific, & Tech Svcs	27853	8	34	Support Activities: Agr./For.	27968	47	203	Food Svcs & Drinking Places
27610	1283	19452	Hospitals	27854	3	3	Food and Beverage Stores	27969	3	6	Relig., Grant, Civic, Prof Org
27611	12	19	Administrative & Support Svcs	27855	209	1584	Educational Services	27970	84	410	Wood Product Manufacturing
27612	1774	19115	Food Svcs & Drinking Places	27856	451	4230	Educational Services	27972	17	56	Real Estate
27613	803	5795	Food Svcs & Drinking Places	27857	40	71	Food and Beverage Stores	27973	29	87	Crop Production
27614	351	2052	Educational Services	27858	1756	20075	Educational Services	27974	29	75	Repair and Maintenance
27615	2096	16957	Prof., Scientific, & Tech Svcs	27860	108	532	Truck Transportation	27976	57	140	Justice, Pubic Order/Safety
27616	1051	10110	Motor Vehicle & Parts Dealers	27861	5	2	Postal Service	27978	13	68	Educational Services
27617	454	6849	Prof., Scientific, & Tech Svcs	27862	9	72	Educational Services	27979	57	268	Educational Services
27619	19	43	Special Trade Contractors	27863	144	661	Educational Services	27980	48	165	Educational Services
27620	4	8	Miscellaneous Store Retailers	27864	118	1054	Educational Services	27981	98	8880	Food Manufacturing
27622	8	20	Merch. Wholesalers,Durable Gds	27865	74	415	Educational Services	27982	18	114	Food Svcs & Drinking Places
27623	54	1273	Rental and Leasing Services	27866	12	155	Heavy & Civil Eng. Construct'N	27983	357	2819	Educational Services
27624	28	67	Administrative & Support Svcs	27867	5	29	Nursing & Resid. Care Facilit.	27985	17	187	Educational Services
27627	8	17	Food and Beverage Stores	27868	19	109	Educational Services	27986	87	557	Justice, Pubic Order/Safety
27628	7	20	Rental and Leasing Services	27869	94	613	Nursing & Resid. Care Facilit.	28001	1363	13291	Food Svcs & Drinking Places
27629	13	37	Special Trade Contractors	27870	1011	9748	Food Svcs & Drinking Places	28002	6	14	Administrative & Support Svcs
27636	6	5	Special Trade Contractors	27871	153	1198	Merch. Wholesalers,Nondur. Gds	28006	20	60	Special Trade Contractors
27656	1	900	Insurance Carriers & Related	27872	17	48	Food and Beverage Stores	28007	42	322	Chemical Manufacturing
27658	6	8	Motion Pict. & Sound Recording	27873	15	25	Food and Beverage Stores	28009	52	827	Primary Metal Manufacturing
27661	5	11	Special Trade Contractors	27874	204	1222	Educational Services	28010	4	79	Relig., Grant, Civic, Prof Org
27675	12	37	Administrative & Support Svcs	27875	13	26	Sportg Gds,Hobby,Book, & Music	28012	629	5378	Educational Services
27676	3	9	Nonstore Retailers	27876	50	286	Wood Product Manufacturing	28016	335	1774	Educational Services
27695	14	10699	Educational Services	27877	12	442	Merch. Wholesalers,Nondur. Gds	28017	41	641	Educational Services
27697	5	7	Exec., Legis., & Other Support	27878	90	396	Food Svcs & Drinking Places	28018	102	776	Educational Services
27699	4	127	Admin. Human Resource Programs	27879	9	20	Special Trade Contractors	28019	13	14	Relig., Grant, Civic, Prof Org
27701	1443	13446	Prof., Scientific, & Tech Svcs	27880	52	690	Bldg Matl & Garden Eqpmt Dlrs	28020	48	127	Educational Services
27702	11	24	Prof., Scientific, & Tech Svcs	27881	6	8	General Merchandise Stores	28021	407	3096	Furniture & Related Prod. Mfg
27703	1141	12195	Educational Services	27882	201	2123	Merch. Wholesalers,Nondur. Gds	28023	418	3279	Educational Services
27704	1075	12438	Hospitals	27883	76	433	Merch. Wholesalers,Nondur. Gds	28024	12	777	Textile Product Mills
27705	1595	18448	Ambulatory Health Care Svcs	27884	39	129	Educational Services	28025	1917	18296	Hospitals
27707	1620	14975	Educational Services	27885	110	510	Exec., Legis., & Other Support	28026	7	12	Construction of Buildings
27708	23	23231	Educational Services	27886	788	10574	Textile Mills	28027	1391	20282	Beverage & Tobacco Product Mfg
27709	197	26838	Electronics & Appliance Stores	27887	9	594	Exec., Legis., & Other Support	28031	1122	7243	Food Svcs & Drinking Places
27710	157	12464	Educational Services	27888	48	89	Merch. Wholesalers,Nondur. Gds	28032	74	652	Educational Services
27711	9	1057	Admin. Enviro. Quality Progrms	27889	1359	11001	Educational Services	28033	32	203	Utilities
27712	319	3206	Educational Services	27890	152	1623	Educational Services	28034	448	2748	Educational Services
27713	1260	12511	Prof., Scientific, & Tech Svcs	27891	123	1689	Machinery Manufacturing	28036	416	3450	Educational Services
27715	15	55	Educational Services	27892	683	5371	Educational Services	28037	701	3798	Wood Product Manufacturing
27717	9	29	Administrative & Support Svcs	27893	1754	26551	Motor Vehicle & Parts Dealers	28038	6	9	Admin. Enviro. Quality Progrms
27722	11	19	Merch. Wholesalers,Durable Gds	27894	4	19	Museums, Hist. Sites,& Similar	28039	22	421	Educational Services
27801	550	5604	Educational Services	27895	4	7	Administrative & Support Svcs	28040	117	434	Educational Services
27802	10	122	Exec., Legis., & Other Support	27896	419	3737	Food Svcs & Drinking Places	28041	38	166	Educational Services
27803	560	3860	Merch. Wholesalers,Durable Gds	27897	50	330	Social Assistance	28042	31	249	Educational Services
27804	1904	25228	Food Svcs & Drinking Places	27906	2	4	Bldg Matl & Garden Eqpmt Dlrs	28043	972	9065	Plastics & Rubber Products Mfg
27805	89	382	Food and Beverage Stores	27907	1	1	Justice, Pubic Order/Safety	28052	1409	13660	Educational Services
27806	102	1594	Chemical Manufacturing	27909	1545	16338	Nat'l Security & Int'l Affairs	28053	5	37	Construction of Buildings
27807	137	843	Educational Services	27910	577	6194	Hospitals	28054	1623	21736	Hospitals
27808	91	395	Fabricated Metal Product Mfg	27915	108	615	Food Svcs & Drinking Places	28055	4	8	Insurance Carriers & Related
27809	148	2391	Merch. Wholesalers,Nondur. Gds	27916	10	7	Isps, Web Search Portals	28056	670	6570	General Merchandise Stores
27810	246	1289	Hospitals	27917	24	404	Educational Services	28070	24	108	Securities/Commodity Contracts
27811	8	34	Social Assistance	27919	25	39	Merch. Wholesalers,Nondur. Gds	28071	51	515	Heavy & Civil Eng. Construct'N
27812	82	513	Educational Services	27920	136	614	Accommodation	28072	89	891	Credit Intermediation & Relatd
27813	28	151	Special Trade Contractors	27921	107	732	Educational Services	28073	93	2257	Merch. Wholesalers,Durable Gds
27814	33	70	Crop Production	27922	28	252	Merch. Wholesalers,Nondur. Gds	28074	2	2	Miscellaneous Manufacturing
27816	54	145	Miscellaneous Manufacturing	27923	61	167	Food Svcs & Drinking Places	28075	352	2510	Plastics & Rubber Products Mfg
27817	149	766	Educational Services	27924	67	233	Educational Services	28076	17	344	Textile Mills
27818	18	48	Nursing & Resid. Care Facilit.	27925	181	1237	Crop Production	28077	10	25	Furn. & Home Furnishgs Stores
27819	19	61	Justice, Pubic Order/Safety	27926	22	82	Prof., Scientific, & Tech Svcs	28078	1264	12150	Food Svcs & Drinking Places
27820	77	567	Ambulatory Health Care Svcs	27927	213	1224	Food Svcs & Drinking Places	28079	649	4952	Special Trade Contractors
27821	12	25	Food and Beverage Stores	27928	85	407	Merch. Wholesalers,Nondur. Gds	28080	99	1182	Fabricated Metal Product Mfg
27822	212	1849	Print'g & Related Supp't Act's	27929	66	485	Justice, Pubic Order/Safety	28081	544	2975	Special Trade Contractors
27823	202	1626	Bldg Matl & Garden Eqpmt Dlrs	27930	1	2	Relig., Grant, Civic, Prof Org	28082	1	0	Support Act. for Transport.
27824	61	322	Merch. Wholesalers,Nondur. Gds	27932	562	5614	Hospitals	28083	843	5532	General Merchandise Stores
27825	12	127	Social Assistance	27935	23	55	Food Svcs & Drinking Places	28086	738	7879	Transportation Equipment Mfg
27826	38	237	Support Activities: Agr./For.	27936	67	180	Sportg Gds,Hobby,Book, & Music	28088	84	654	Educational Services
27827	16	10	Relig., Grant, Civic, Prof Org	27937	46	213	Educational Services	28089	32	95	Educational Services
27828	353	4383	Repair and Maintenance	27938	96	753	Educational Services	28090	160	776	Educational Services
27829	48	130	Social Assistance	27939	105	415	Food Svcs & Drinking Places	28091	61	631	Repair and Maintenance
27830	121	655	Educational Services	27941	60	236	Special Trade Contractors	28092	1257	13565	Textile Mills
27831	44	240	Educational Services	27942	20	81	Construction of Buildings	28093	5	10	Admin. Human Resource Programs
27832	73	567	Educational Services	27943	91	554	Admin. of Economic Programs	28097	164	833	Food Svcs & Drinking Places
27833	6	33	Insurance Carriers & Related	27944	358	1905	Exec., Legis., & Other Support	28098	147	1347	Motor Vehicle & Parts Dealers
27834	1991	31099	Hospitals	27946	21	77	Merch. Wholesalers,Nondur. Gds	28101	23	1862	Textile Mills
27835	10	43	Relig., Grant, Civic, Prof Org	27947	33	122	Special Trade Contractors	28102	6	14	Relig., Grant, Civic, Prof Org
27836	3	11	Furn. & Home Furnishgs Stores	27948	768	4339	Food Svcs & Drinking Places	28103	263	2744	Merch. Wholesalers,Nondur. Gds
27837	87	252	Educational Services	27949	741	4684	Food Svcs & Drinking Places	28104	508	3885	Special Trade Contractors
27839	143	2149	Exec., Legis., & Other Support	27950	33	162	Special Trade Contractors	28105	1418	16103	Food Svcs & Drinking Places
27840	29	104	Educational Services	27953	38	258	Exec., Legis., & Other Support	28106	26	73	Administrative & Support Svcs
27841	6	6	Special Trade Contractors	27954	443	2889	Educational Services	28107	188	1125	Special Trade Contractors
27842	29	100	Real Estate	27956	15	91	Educational Services	28108	24	93	Construction of Buildings
27843	20	88	Relig., Grant, Civic, Prof Org	27957	32	261	Educational Services	28109	6	82	Educational Services

ZIP CODE	2004 Total Firms	2004 Total Employ-ees	TOP INDUSTRY RANKED on 2004 EMPLOYMENT	ZIP CODE	2004 Total Firms	2004 Total Employ-ees	TOP INDUSTRY RANKED on 2004 EMPLOYMENT	ZIP CODE	2004 Total Firms	2004 Total Employ-ees	TOP INDUSTRY RANKED on 2004 EMPLOYMENT
28110	1627	21781	Special Trade Contractors	28278	179	1972	Machinery Manufacturing	28393	45	297	Food Manufacturing
28111	18	74	Heavy & Civil Eng. Construct'N	28280	45	520	Prof., Scientific, & Tech Svcs	28394	167	641	Educational Services
28112	767	8779	Merch. Wholesalers,Nondur. Gds	28281	57	815	Telecommunications	28395	53	259	Educational Services
28114	108	870	Repair and Maintenance	28282	32	1409	Credit Intermediation & Relatd	28396	71	5402	Textile Mills
28115	1057	8228	Educational Services	28284	27	267	Prof., Scientific, & Tech Svcs	28398	292	2960	Wholesale Elec. Mrkts & Agents
28117	1097	8804	Food Svcs & Drinking Places	28285	11	411	Real Estate	28399	43	123	Crop Production
28119	67	729	Repair and Maintenance	28287	29	555	Construction of Buildings	28401	2135	25127	Hospitals
28120	468	5774	Transportation Equipment Mfg	28297	6	13	Insurance Carriers & Related	28402	12	57	Exec., Legis., & Other Support
28123	5	21	Repair and Maintenance	28299	7	9	Prof., Scientific, & Tech Svcs	28403	2933	26483	Food Svcs & Drinking Places
28124	192	1273	Educational Services	28301	1462	17245	Exec., Legis., & Other Support	28404	9	25	Bldg Matl & Garden Eqpmt Dlrs
28125	51	366	Educational Services	28302	10	44	Admin. of Economic Programs	28405	1405	13922	Elect'l Eqpmt, App, & Comp Mfg
28126	7	14	Electronics & Appliance Stores	28303	1807	18125	Educational Services	28406	18	38	Special Trade Contractors
28127	158	903	Educational Services	28304	1107	13871	Ambulatory Health Care Svcs	28408	8	21	Perform'g Arts, Spec. Sports
28128	226	1955	Plastics & Rubber Products Mfg	28305	385	2801	Ambulatory Health Care Svcs	28409	418	1527	Educational Services
28129	191	1289	Educational Services	28306	1023	14028	Fabricated Metal Product Mfg	28411	544	2860	Food Svcs & Drinking Places
28130	8	29	Merch. Wholesalers,Nondur. Gds	28307	91	1889	Educational Services	28412	880	8258	Food Svcs & Drinking Places
28133	67	432	Wood Product Manufacturing	28308	29	211	Prof., Scientific, & Tech Svcs	28420	72	248	Furn. & Home Furnishgs Stores
28134	743	9526	General Merchandise Stores	28309	8	13	Insurance Carriers & Related	28421	38	124	Construction of Buildings
28135	75	862	Fabricated Metal Product Mfg	28310	33	960	Personal and Laundry Services	28422	192	1205	Exec., Legis., & Other Support
28136	22	95	Justice, Pubic Order/Safety	28311	593	7764	Motor Vehicle & Parts Dealers	28423	51	146	Forestry and Logging
28137	81	1188	Wood Product Manufacturing	28312	433	5307	Merch. Wholesalers,Durable Gds	28424	16	333	Justice, Pubic Order/Safety
28138	214	2200	Wood Product Manufacturing	28314	670	7417	Food Svcs & Drinking Places	28425	403	4011	Justice, Pubic Order/Safety
28139	680	6889	Hospitals	28315	566	5417	Food Svcs & Drinking Places	28428	374	1789	Food Svcs & Drinking Places
28144	1329	16733	Ambulatory Health Care Svcs	28318	94	280	Merch. Wholesalers,Durable Gds	28429	213	1727	Chemical Manufacturing
28145	10	35	Special Trade Contractors	28319	2	3	Postal Service	28430	33	186	Educational Services
28146	458	5036	Educational Services	28320	227	1015	Special Trade Contractors	28431	238	1241	Ambulatory Health Care Svcs
28147	666	8871	Food Svcs & Drinking Places	28323	51	256	Educational Services	28432	20	31	Repair and Maintenance
28150	1268	14157	Bldg Matl & Garden Eqpmt Dlrs	28325	15	36	Special Trade Contractors	28433	137	526	Educational Services
28151	7	13	Administrative & Support Svcs	28326	153	806	Educational Services	28434	37	114	Crop Production
28152	832	8925	Educational Services	28327	449	2741	Educational Services	28435	34	181	Administrative & Support Svcs
28159	114	892	Educational Services	28328	1204	11005	Educational Services	28436	56	252	Plastics & Rubber Products Mfg
28160	269	5378	Textile Mills	28329	8	51	Justice, Pubic Order/Safety	28438	31	166	Relig., Grant, Civic, Prof Org
28163	71	697	Merch. Wholesalers,Durable Gds	28330	8	296	Paper Manufacturing	28439	107	409	Construction of Buildings
28164	313	2035	Fabricated Metal Product Mfg	28331	1	2	Postal Service	28441	114	740	Apparel Manufacturing
28166	224	2028	Furniture & Related Prod. Mfg	28332	43	301	Educational Services	28442	36	183	Educational Services
28167	36	126	Special Trade Contractors	28333	132	1316	Crop Production	28443	408	1780	Educational Services
28168	168	1043	Educational Services	28334	1153	10733	Elect'l Eqpmt, App, & Comp Mfg	28444	85	462	Truck Transportation
28169	12	56	Justice, Pubic Order/Safety	28335	4	4	Special Trade Contractors	28445	352	1754	Food Svcs & Drinking Places
28170	540	4783	Hospitals	28337	630	5037	Ambulatory Health Care Svcs	28446	2	32	Waste Managmt & Remediat'n Svc
28173	453	2088	Relig., Grant, Civic, Prof Org	28338	151	874	Textile Mills	28447	30	111	Crop Production
28174	125	990	Educational Services	28339	233	1726	Educational Services	28448	25	48	Wood Product Manufacturing
28201	1	0	Accommodation	28340	279	1760	Educational Services	28449	69	265	Food Svcs & Drinking Places
28202	1363	39731	Prof., Scientific, & Tech Svcs	28341	133	1214	Food Manufacturing	28450	69	765	Nursing & Resid. Care Facilit.
28203	1601	14559	Food Svcs & Drinking Places	28342	17	118	Nursing & Resid. Care Facilit.	28451	428	8190	Chemical Manufacturing
28204	1127	9966	Prof., Scientific, & Tech Svcs	28343	34	92	Educational Services	28452	24	52	Special Trade Contractors
28205	2150	13933	Food Svcs & Drinking Places	28344	52	288	Food Manufacturing	28453	88	304	Crop Production
28206	975	14764	Merch. Wholesalers,Durable Gds	28345	394	3516	Educational Services	28454	37	76	Crop Production
28207	518	11858	Social Assistance	28347	24	517	Exec., Legis., & Other Support	28455	38	94	Justice, Pubic Order/Safety
28208	1779	25641	Merch. Wholesalers,Durable Gds	28348	530	5660	Merch. Wholesalers,Durable Gds	28456	91	1930	Merch. Wholesalers,Nondur. Gds
28209	1078	9733	Prof., Scientific, & Tech Svcs	28349	254	3363	Merch. Wholesalers,Durable Gds	28457	147	866	Chemical Manufacturing
28210	1225	11032	Educational Services	28350	13	65	Food and Beverage Stores	28458	215	2486	Food Manufacturing
28211	1360	15800	Ambulatory Health Care Svcs	28351	96	1235	Textile Product Mills	28459	82	589	Telecommunications
28212	1248	11484	Motor Vehicle & Parts Dealers	28352	985	10712	Textile Mills	28460	232	1002	Food Svcs & Drinking Places
28213	934	8477	Food Svcs & Drinking Places	28353	2	4	Crop Production	28461	698	8028	Utilities
28214	595	7020	Truck Transportation	28355	10	64	Mining (Except Oil and Gas)	28462	374	1983	Hospitals
28215	758	6719	Nursing & Resid. Care Facilit.	28356	78	348	Special Trade Contractors	28463	300	1650	Educational Services
28216	1006	11506	Educational Services	28357	31	147	Construction of Buildings	28464	34	571	Food Manufacturing
28217	2177	31283	Prof., Scientific, & Tech Svcs	28358	1677	19446	Hospitals	28465	267	1070	Relig., Grant, Civic, Prof Org
28218	9	30	Real Estate	28359	4	10	Food Manufacturing	28466	475	2925	Food Svcs & Drinking Places
28219	6	100	Postal Service	28360	239	3524	Admin. Human Resource Programs	28467	232	1729	Amusement, Gambling,& Recreat.
28220	10	430	Bldg Matl & Garden Eqpmt Dlrs	28361	6	758	Hospitals	28468	149	1458	Amusement, Gambling,& Recreat.
28221	8	295	Print'g & Related Supp't Act's	28362	3	41	Machinery Manufacturing	28469	319	1421	Food Svcs & Drinking Places
28222	15	28	Construction of Buildings	28363	25	404	Heavy & Civil Eng. Construct'N	28470	504	3855	General Merchandise Stores
28223	5	2342	Educational Services	28364	290	3515	Food Manufacturing	28472	1121	10395	Exec., Legis., & Other Support
28224	9	26	Publishing Industries	28365	513	6663	Food and Beverage Stores	28478	94	473	Apparel Manufacturing
28226	1303	9792	Food Svcs & Drinking Places	28366	170	1551	Machinery Manufacturing	28479	58	405	Nursing & Resid. Care Facilit.
28227	1288	9160	Motor Vehicle & Parts Dealers	28367	10	27	Wood Product Manufacturing	28480	199	2052	Food Svcs & Drinking Places
28228	2	1	Relig., Grant, Civic, Prof Org	28368	43	112	Educational Services	28501	950	9448	Hospitals
28229	10	25	Prof., Scientific, & Tech Svcs	28369	36	159	Educational Services	28502	3	14	Exec., Legis., & Other Support
28230	3	8	Social Assistance	28370	15	245	Special Trade Contractors	28503	3	3	Nonstore Retailers
28231	4	11	Insurance Carriers & Related	28371	96	486	Educational Services	28504	856	12803	Hospitals
28232	3	26	Ambulatory Health Care Svcs	28372	339	4253	Ambulatory Health Care Svcs	28508	28	102	Educational Services
28233	5	9	Administrative & Support Svcs	28373	64	440	Wood Product Manufacturing	28509	23	137	Social Assistance
28234	3	7	Motor Vehicle & Parts Dealers	28374	586	14028	Ambulatory Health Care Svcs	28510	46	826	Accommodation
28235	3	16	Prof., Scientific, & Tech Svcs	28375	8	9	Relig., Grant, Civic, Prof Org	28511	23	178	Food Manufacturing
28236	5	20	Special Trade Contractors	28376	694	5681	Merch. Wholesalers,Nondur. Gds	28512	317	2269	Accommodation
28237	5	14	Truck Transportation	28377	307	2199	Apparel Manufacturing	28513	294	2923	Administrative & Support Svcs
28241	13	73	Nonstore Retailers	28378	1	1	Postal Service	28515	166	1172	Educational Services
28242	1	1	Other Information Services	28379	1057	10923	Textile Mills	28516	628	4835	Wood Product Manufacturing
28244	33	1006	Administrative & Support Svcs	28380	1	6	Relig., Grant, Civic, Prof Org	28518	242	1440	Educational Services
28246	17	502	Prof., Scientific, & Tech Svcs	28382	233	1317	Plastics & Rubber Products Mfg	28519	55	291	Educational Services
28247	27	79	Prof., Scientific, & Tech Svcs	28383	181	1119	Educational Services	28520	15	120	Admin. of Economic Programs
28256	4	28	Transit & Grnd Pass. Transport	28384	241	1745	Educational Services	28521	49	194	Educational Services
28262	974	14089	Food Svcs & Drinking Places	28385	79	386	Educational Services	28522	8	36	Educational Services
28266	4	7	Administrative & Support Svcs	28386	64	229	Educational Services	28523	58	297	Educational Services
28269	1181	19493	Truck Transportation	28387	1005	7755	Food Svcs & Drinking Places	28524	16	57	Food Manufacturing
28270	706	4405	Educational Services	28388	14	30	Ambulatory Health Care Svcs	28525	47	270	Merch. Wholesalers,Nondur. Gds
28271	11	40	Transit & Grnd Pass. Transport	28390	527	2924	Food Svcs & Drinking Places	28526	54	144	Crop Production
28273	1232	37840	Merch. Wholesalers,Durable Gds	28391	98	516	Educational Services	28527	22	28	Food and Beverage Stores
28277	1165	11196	Food Svcs & Drinking Places	28392	44	4801	Food Manufacturing	28528	6	9	Transportation Equipment Mfg

ZIP CODE	2004 Total Firms	2004 Total Employees	TOP INDUSTRY RANKED on 2004 EMPLOYMENT
28529	60	617	Nursing & Resid. Care Facilit.
28530	178	858	Educational Services
28531	61	252	Food Svcs & Drinking Places
28532	656	4029	Educational Services
28533	33	4375	Repair and Maintenance
28537	5	30	Nat'l Security & Int'l Affairs
28538	38	161	Merch. Wholesalers,Durable Gds
28539	164	573	Transportation Equipment Mfg
28540	1529	10973	Educational Services
28541	4	14	Prof., Scientific, & Tech Svcs
28542	11	25	Exec., Legis., & Other Support
28543	7	86	Special Trade Contractors
28544	81	470	Food Svcs & Drinking Places
28545	4	16	Telecommunications
28546	1252	15511	Food Svcs & Drinking Places
28547	30	1847	Hospitals
28551	309	2599	Special Trade Contractors
28552	9	12	Food Manufacturing
28553	24	27	Transportation Equipment Mfg
28554	18	563	Exec., Legis., & Other Support
28555	132	493	Educational Services
28556	24	89	Transportation Equipment Mfg
28557	1300	10642	Food Svcs & Drinking Places
28560	1185	12480	Hospitals
28561	8	30	Ambulatory Health Care Svcs
28562	1379	13034	Ambulatory Health Care Svcs
28563	9	36	Merch. Wholesalers,Nondur. Gds
28564	2	1	Prof., Scientific, & Tech Svcs
28570	475	2762	Educational Services
28571	132	713	Merch. Wholesalers,Nondur. Gds
28572	184	719	Food and Beverage Stores
28573	83	558	Ambulatory Health Care Svcs
28574	269	1208	Educational Services
28575	44	309	Food Svcs & Drinking Places
28577	17	244	Nursing & Resid. Care Facilit.
28578	74	299	Educational Services
28579	23	100	Educational Services
28580	315	2364	Educational Services
28581	11	16	Merch. Wholesalers,Nondur. Gds
28582	13	22	Prof., Scientific, & Tech Svcs
28583	12	34	Relig., Grant, Civic, Prof Org
28584	407	2244	Educational Services
28585	148	821	Exec., Legis., & Other Support
28586	205	1706	Paper Manufacturing
28587	13	100	Merch. Wholesalers,Nondur. Gds
28589	9	16	Heavy & Civil Eng. Construct'N
28590	436	4452	Educational Services
28594	112	1051	Real Estate
28601	2154	25599	Furniture & Related Prod. Mfg
28602	1999	30415	Hospitals
28603	25	171	Motor Vehicle & Parts Dealers
28604	597	5600	Relig., Grant, Civic, Prof Org
28605	380	3654	Food Svcs & Drinking Places
28606	32	100	Educational Services
28607	1576	14626	Food Svcs & Drinking Places
28608	7	2030	Educational Services
28609	111	951	Educational Services
28610	214	5589	Telecommunications
28611	15	105	Educational Services
28612	197	1579	Furniture & Related Prod. Mfg
28613	688	11562	Furniture & Related Prod. Mfg
28615	38	90	Bldg Matl & Garden Eqpmt Dlrs
28616	19	203	Relig., Grant, Civic, Prof Org
28617	51	231	Food Svcs & Drinking Places
28618	47	435	Social Assistance
28619	45	638	Furniture & Related Prod. Mfg
28621	579	7535	Hospitals
28622	55	176	Truck Transportation
28623	38	230	Miscellaneous Store Retailers
28624	42	153	Accommodation
28625	1064	17625	Repair and Maintenance
28626	70	142	Educational Services
28627	30	220	Accommodation
28628	24	52	Justice, Pubic Order/Safety
28629	14	102	Food Svcs & Drinking Places
28630	482	4533	Apparel Manufacturing
28631	17	61	Bldg Matl & Garden Eqpmt Dlrs
28633	1	400	Furniture & Related Prod. Mfg
28634	122	561	Wood Product Manufacturing
28635	73	445	Educational Services
28636	89	912	Furniture & Related Prod. Mfg
28637	137	2122	Apparel Manufacturing
28638	347	4320	Educational Services
28640	276	3736	Textile Mills
28641	7	12	Construction of Buildings
28642	224	1382	Food Svcs & Drinking Places
28643	85	454	Computer & Electronic Prod Mfg
28644	57	164	Accommodation
28645	1543	20719	Furniture & Related Prod. Mfg
28646	71	1384	Hospitals
28647	9	21	Food Svcs & Drinking Places
28649	16	20	Food and Beverage Stores
28650	312	4070	Furniture & Related Prod. Mfg
28651	124	613	Educational Services
28652	3	2	Postal Service
28653	1	2	Prof., Scientific, & Tech Svcs
28654	72	181	Educational Services
28655	1928	22551	Furniture & Related Prod. Mfg
28657	394	3423	Miscellaneous Store Retailers
28658	967	10974	Furniture & Related Prod. Mfg
28659	1002	9374	Furniture & Related Prod. Mfg
28660	32	266	Educational Services
28661	7	77	Paper Manufacturing
28662	21	190	Bldg Matl & Garden Eqpmt Dlrs
28663	20	91	Educational Services
28664	8	111	Nonmetallic Mineral Prod. Mfg
28665	44	40	Relig., Grant, Civic, Prof Org
28666	12	257	Educational Services
28667	7	19	Exec., Legis., & Other Support
28668	20	330	Relig., Grant, Civic, Prof Org
28669	75	584	Fabricated Metal Product Mfg
28670	85	413	Educational Services
28671	64	841	Miscellaneous Manufacturing
28672	9	14	Motor Vehicle & Parts Dealers
28673	88	366	Educational Services
28675	415	2628	Ambulatory Health Care Svcs
28676	98	407	Special Trade Contractors
28677	1595	16976	Hospitals
28678	97	715	Paper Manufacturing
28679	61	192	Educational Services
28680	6	8	Miscellaneous Store Retailers
28681	729	7943	Furniture & Related Prod. Mfg
28682	33	83	Motor Vehicle & Parts Dealers
28683	24	63	Merch. Wholesalers,Nondur. Gds
28684	33	58	Amusement, Gambling,& Recreat.
28685	38	119	Educational Services
28687	8	4	Construction of Buildings
28688	5	257	Textile Mills
28689	59	506	Bldg Matl & Garden Eqpmt Dlrs
28690	305	4853	Textile Mills
28691	5	56	General Merchandise Stores
28692	132	397	Special Trade Contractors
28693	49	264	Educational Services
28694	497	3915	Telecommunications
28697	761	10588	Bldg Matl & Garden Eqpmt Dlrs
28698	42	198	Construction of Buildings
28699	2	51	Educational Services
28701	37	94	Prof., Scientific, & Tech Svcs
28702	11	25	Accommodation
28704	735	7838	Machinery Manufacturing
28705	179	989	Educational Services
28707	7	95	Accommodation
28708	17	19	Merch. Wholesalers,Nondur. Gds
28709	52	233	Elect'l Eqpmt, App, & Comp Mfg
28710	12	23	Real Estate
28711	495	5009	Exec., Legis., & Other Support
28712	975	7049	Accommodation
28713	458	3420	Sportg Gds,Hobby,Book, & Music
28714	551	3759	Textile Mills
28715	497	3604	Educational Services
28716	420	4230	Paper Manufacturing
28717	343	2030	Unclassified Establishments
28718	49	227	Accommodation
28719	387	6683	Amusement, Gambling,& Recreat.
28720	34	192	Unclassified Establishments
28721	276	3962	Ambulatory Health Care Svcs
28722	279	2400	Hospitals
28723	129	1817	Educational Services
28724	9	29	Special Trade Contractors
28725	62	414	Food Svcs & Drinking Places
28726	85	833	Paper Manufacturing
28727	16	97	Food and Beverage Stores
28728	25	749	Prof., Scientific, & Tech Svcs
28729	85	548	Food and Beverage Stores
28730	214	1038	Computer & Electronic Prod Mfg
28731	213	2122	Food Svcs & Drinking Places
28732	490	8109	Transportation Equipment Mfg
28733	11	112	Justice, Pubic Order/Safety
28734	1254	9582	Food Svcs & Drinking Places
28735	6	5	Postal Service
28736	39	191	Special Trade Contractors
28737	11	48	Heavy & Civil Eng. Construct'N
28738	3	3	Real Estate
28739	485	3650	Accommodation
28740	15	49	Educational Services
28741	439	2304	Food Svcs & Drinking Places
28742	187	924	Accommodation
28743	76	401	Machinery Manufacturing
28744	11	38	Special Trade Contractors
28745	19	137	Food Svcs & Drinking Places
28746	164	1114	Amusement, Gambling,& Recreat.
28747	105	661	Real Estate
28748	215	655	Educational Services
28749	13	201	Accommodation
28750	15	175	Textile Mills
28751	234	1667	Accommodation
28752	1081	14778	Merch. Wholesalers,Durable Gds
28753	263	1985	Exec., Legis., & Other Support
28754	201	1971	Elect'l Eqpmt, App, & Comp Mfg
28755	32	436	Apparel Manufacturing
28756	72	587	Repair and Maintenance
28757	14	373	Other Information Services
28758	21	896	Nonmetallic Mineral Prod. Mfg
28760	15	248	Textile Product Mills
28761	103	747	Nursing & Resid. Care Facilit.
28762	163	2626	Textile Product Mills
28763	32	66	Support Activities: Agr./For.
28765	3	8	Sportg Gds,Hobby,Book, & Music
28766	26	101	Heavy & Civil Eng. Construct'N
28768	228	2325	Paper Manufacturing
28770	10	83	Relig., Grant, Civic, Prof Org
28771	299	2515	Furniture & Related Prod. Mfg
28772	94	994	Textile Mills
28773	138	472	Nursing & Resid. Care Facilit.
28774	48	410	Heavy & Civil Eng. Construct'N
28775	24	49	Relig., Grant, Civic, Prof Org
28776	20	464	Machinery Manufacturing
28777	514	5123	Furniture & Related Prod. Mfg
28778	251	3731	Textile Mills
28779	731	7012	Hospitals
28781	30	106	Educational Services
28782	329	1610	Nursing & Resid. Care Facilit.
28783	16	69	Bldg Matl & Garden Eqpmt Dlrs
28784	23	646	Accommodation
28785	129	719	Merch. Wholesalers,Durable Gds
28786	1183	8724	Food Svcs & Drinking Places
28787	406	3690	Computer & Electronic Prod Mfg
28788	8	136	Miscellaneous Manufacturing
28789	115	575	Educational Services
28790	40	116	Construction of Buildings
28791	507	5528	Hospitals
28792	1695	14336	Food Svcs & Drinking Places
28793	13	28	Special Trade Contractors
28801	2338	21474	Ambulatory Health Care Svcs
28802	20	44	Prof., Scientific, & Tech Svcs
28803	1322	15776	Ambulatory Health Care Svcs
28804	654	7151	Accommodation
28805	738	8953	Food Svcs & Drinking Places
28806	1466	15793	Food Svcs & Drinking Places
28810	3	104	Clothing & Cloth'g Acc. Stores
28813	6	24	Motion Pict. & Sound Recording
28814	9	35	Publishing Industries
28815	7	16	Special Trade Contractors
28816	13	31	Heavy & Civil Eng. Construct'N
28901	263	1842	Food Svcs & Drinking Places
28902	27	109	Educational Services
28903	1	1	Postal Service
28904	382	1901	Food Svcs & Drinking Places
28905	51	758	Textile Mills
28906	820	6550	Hospitals
28909	21	46	Fabricated Metal Product Mfg
29001	54	213	Merch. Wholesalers,Durable Gds
29002	7	50	Merch. Wholesalers,Durable Gds
29003	302	2641	Educational Services
29006	332	3655	Food Manufacturing
29009	97	771	Textile Mills
29010	424	3758	Justice, Pubic Order/Safety
29014	28	51	Relig., Grant, Civic, Prof Org
29015	20	71	Educational Services
29016	319	2701	Fabricated Metal Product Mfg
29018	100	617	Educational Services
29020	1105	7816	Hospitals
29030	75	267	Bldg Matl & Garden Eqpmt Dlrs
29031	26	782	Textile Mills
29032	44	533	Wood Product Manufacturing
29033	481	4998	Food Svcs & Drinking Places
29036	413	2799	Special Trade Contractors
29037	15	29	Paper Manufacturing
29038	43	191	Educational Services
29039	42	315	Educational Services
29040	123	504	Relig., Grant, Civic, Prof Org
29041	11	9	Food and Beverage Stores
29042	171	1664	Educational Services
29044	146	1400	Paper Manufacturing
29045	301	2898	Administrative & Support Svcs
29046	6	86	Educational Services
29047	109	1077	Food and Beverage Stores
29048	126	709	Motor Vehicle & Parts Dealers
29051	27	104	Crop Production
29052	34	96	Educational Services

ZIP CODE	2004 Total Firms	2004 Total Employ-ees	TOP INDUSTRY RANKED on 2004 EMPLOYMENT	ZIP CODE	2004 Total Firms	2004 Total Employ-ees	TOP INDUSTRY RANKED on 2004 EMPLOYMENT	ZIP CODE	2004 Total Firms	2004 Total Employ-ees	TOP INDUSTRY RANKED on 2004 EMPLOYMENT
29053	222	1434	Merch. Wholesalers,Durable Gds	29216	2	19	Admin. of Economic Programs	29431	100	318	Justice, Pubic Order/Safety
29054	168	1104	Educational Services	29220	6	53	Ambulatory Health Care Svcs	29432	61	279	Educational Services
29055	166	512	Educational Services	29221	11	20	Prof., Scientific, & Tech Svcs	29433	7	89	Utilities
29056	83	476	Educational Services	29223	1714	15348	Food Svcs & Drinking Places	29434	23	77	Exec., Legis., & Other Support
29058	113	615	Repair and Maintenance	29224	10	21	Special Trade Contractors	29435	92	312	Social Assistance
29059	226	1509	Educational Services	29229	385	4489	Educational Services	29436	89	526	Truck Transportation
29061	184	1445	Elect'l Eqpmt, App, & Comp Mfg	29230	2	10	Perform'g Arts, Spec. Sports	29437	39	462	Educational Services
29062	5	8	Merch. Wholesalers,Durable Gds	29240	2	1	Prof., Scientific, & Tech Svcs	29438	161	605	Food Svcs & Drinking Places
29063	844	5039	Food Svcs & Drinking Places	29250	7	14	Prof., Scientific, & Tech Svcs	29439	79	351	Accommodation
29065	16	162	Administrative & Support Svcs	29260	5	34	Relig., Grant, Civic, Prof Org	29440	1337	11711	Educational Services
29067	275	1211	Educational Services	29290	6	6	Prof., Scientific, & Tech Svcs	29442	3	2	Scenic & Sightseeing Transport
29069	113	601	Educational Services	29301	1186	13172	Food Svcs & Drinking Places	29445	793	9651	Educational Services
29070	313	1731	Repair and Maintenance	29302	929	9763	Nonmetallic Mineral Prod. Mfg	29446	51	122	Justice, Pubic Order/Safety
29071	12	17	Administrative & Support Svcs	29303	1275	27298	Hospitals	29447	2	0	Postal Service
29072	1572	14870	Food Svcs & Drinking Places	29304	12	55	Prof., Scientific, & Tech Svcs	29448	74	977	Truck Transportation
29073	679	5033	Educational Services	29305	1	4	Administrative & Support Svcs	29449	210	1279	Fabricated Metal Product Mfg
29074	8	39	Accommodation	29306	911	10866	Exec., Legis., & Other Support	29450	77	2095	Primary Metal Manufacturing
29075	40	195	Heavy & Civil Eng. Construct'N	29307	628	9371	Hospitals	29451	196	1690	Accommodation
29078	415	4130	Food Svcs & Drinking Places	29316	461	3067	Educational Services	29452	16	21	Food Svcs & Drinking Places
29079	5	51	Food Svcs & Drinking Places	29318	1	1	Administrative & Support Svcs	29453	36	279	Relig., Grant, Civic, Prof Org
29080	85	382	Relig., Grant, Civic, Prof Org	29319	1	400	Food Svcs & Drinking Places	29455	594	5552	Accommodation
29081	65	158	Educational Services	29320	5	37	Justice, Pubic Order/Safety	29456	323	3268	Social Assistance
29082	20	31	Food and Beverage Stores	29321	42	266	Merch. Wholesalers,Nondur. Gds	29457	7	13	Scenic & Sightseeing Transport
29101	85	1928	Merch. Wholesalers,Durable Gds	29322	131	542	Educational Services	29458	117	456	Educational Services
29102	822	5488	Food Svcs & Drinking Places	29323	350	1700	Educational Services	29461	1065	9440	Educational Services
29104	55	184	Furniture & Related Prod. Mfg	29324	5	7	Administrative & Support Svcs	29464	2387	18957	Food Svcs & Drinking Places
29105	38	359	Merch. Wholesalers,Nondur. Gds	29325	495	6948	Social Assistance	29465	25	96	Prof., Scientific, & Tech Svcs
29106	1	0	Social Assistance	29329	6	43	Justice, Pubic Order/Safety	29466	335	1623	Educational Services
29107	59	402	Chemical Manufacturing	29330	185	1390	Fabricated Metal Product Mfg	29468	56	270	Admin. of Economic Programs
29108	852	9921	Food Manufacturing	29331	3	4	Relig., Grant, Civic, Prof Org	29469	18	42	Utilities
29111	31	159	Educational Services	29332	54	111	Justice, Pubic Order/Safety	29470	126	892	Special Trade Contractors
29112	127	462	Educational Services	29333	11	81	Justice, Pubic Order/Safety	29471	30	60	Special Trade Contractors
29113	48	153	Bldg Matl & Garden Eqpmt Dlrs	29334	425	9120	Paper Manufacturing	29472	157	1333	Unclassified Establishments
29114	77	605	Furniture & Related Prod. Mfg	29335	85	1209	Textile Mills	29474	34	70	Relig., Grant, Civic, Prof Org
29115	1549	19243	Educational Services	29336	5	21	Relig., Grant, Civic, Prof Org	29475	48	165	Relig., Grant, Civic, Prof Org
29116	6	20	Relig., Grant, Civic, Prof Org	29338	1	2	Postal Service	29476	3	406	Miscellaneous Store Retailers
29117	2	52	Educational Services	29340	592	6714	Merch. Wholesalers,Nondur. Gds	29477	336	2826	Exec., Legis., & Other Support
29118	403	6223	Hospitals	29341	719	9196	Fabricated Metal Product Mfg	29479	255	1743	Educational Services
29122	7	37	Ambulatory Health Care Svcs	29342	3	7	Insurance Carriers & Related	29481	40	83	Heavy & Civil Eng. Construct'N
29123	91	542	Educational Services	29346	6	47	Educational Services	29482	70	465	Food Svcs & Drinking Places
29125	102	263	Educational Services	29348	13	443	Wood Product Manufacturing	29483	1628	15420	Food Svcs & Drinking Places
29126	37	155	Educational Services	29349	567	4244	Primary Metal Manufacturing	29484	11	63	Construction of Buildings
29127	180	1283	Wood Product Manufacturing	29351	41	126	Educational Services	29485	824	7880	Ambulatory Health Care Svcs
29128	74	554	Justice, Pubic Order/Safety	29353	93	600	Unclassified Establishments	29487	51	184	Accommodation
29129	86	291	Educational Services	29355	19	170	Miscellaneous Manufacturing	29488	1086	9502	Educational Services
29130	132	865	Nursing & Resid. Care Facilit.	29356	309	2556	Textile Product Mills	29492	305	3418	Furn. & Home Furnishgs Stores
29132	2	2	Postal Service	29360	845	7616	Fabricated Metal Product Mfg	29493	10	121	Wood Product Manufacturing
29133	26	355	Wood Product Manufacturing	29364	12	46	Educational Services	29501	2532	28992	Food Svcs & Drinking Places
29135	326	2308	Educational Services	29365	243	2881	Textile Product Mills	29502	9	11	Administrative & Support Svcs
29137	47	197	Relig., Grant, Civic, Prof Org	29368	18	91	Educational Services	29504	8	14	Special Trade Contractors
29138	366	2827	Apparel Manufacturing	29369	144	834	Educational Services	29505	683	7031	Hospitals
29142	259	1933	Food Svcs & Drinking Places	29370	16	41	Unclassified Establishments	29506	695	10467	Ambulatory Health Care Svcs
29143	5	81	Crop Production	29372	101	557	Educational Services	29510	314	2286	Primary Metal Manufacturing
29145	11	39	Merch. Wholesalers,Durable Gds	29373	8	53	Textile Product Mills	29511	166	762	Educational Services
29146	39	151	Wood Product Manufacturing	29374	50	187	Educational Services	29512	635	6736	Machinery Manufacturing
29147	4	36	Exec., Legis., & Other Support	29375	14	65	Educational Services	29516	22	212	Educational Services
29148	234	1687	Miscellaneous Manufacturing	29376	237	2325	Educational Services	29518	47	158	Educational Services
29150	2201	25195	Food and Beverage Stores	29377	8	68	Plastics & Rubber Products Mfg	29519	3	27	Educational Services
29151	6	605	Fabricated Metal Product Mfg	29378	8	33	Relig., Grant, Civic, Prof Org	29520	589	6087	Fabricated Metal Product Mfg
29152	55	400	Educational Services	29379	733	6649	Fabricated Metal Product Mfg	29525	62	248	Merch. Wholesalers,Durable Gds
29153	437	6086	Textile Product Mills	29384	72	170	Food Svcs & Drinking Places	29526	1765	23851	Relig., Grant, Civic, Prof Org
29154	566	5548	Relig., Grant, Civic, Prof Org	29385	140	1631	Textile Product Mills	29527	384	2146	Educational Services
29160	171	814	Educational Services	29386	3	57	Paper Manufacturing	29528	9	14	Special Trade Contractors
29161	246	1316	Transportation Equipment Mfg	29388	335	2159	Educational Services	29530	92	238	Educational Services
29162	136	1030	Justice, Pubic Order/Safety	29395	1	13	Miscellaneous Store Retailers	29532	741	6135	Educational Services
29163	36	124	Educational Services	29401	1788	18290	Food Svcs & Drinking Places	29536	674	7128	Textile Mills
29164	149	488	Educational Services	29402	10	50	Special Trade Contractors	29540	77	1012	Primary Metal Manufacturing
29166	27	490	Merch. Wholesalers,Nondur. Gds	29403	1048	18071	Educational Services	29541	139	1499	Justice, Pubic Order/Safety
29168	60	124	Educational Services	29404	30	146	Educational Services	29543	10	109	Nursing & Resid. Care Facilit.
29169	1435	18008	Hospitals	29405	1565	23677	Special Trade Contractors	29544	82	193	Educational Services
29170	548	6936	Educational Services	29406	1872	27667	Food Svcs & Drinking Places	29545	27	166	Educational Services
29171	4	10	Administrative & Support Svcs	29407	2281	20098	Food Svcs & Drinking Places	29546	44	268	Educational Services
29172	237	4050	Truck Transportation	29409	4	49	Other Information Services	29547	42	213	Textile Mills
29175	9	11	Social Assistance	29410	1	6	Insurance Carriers & Related	29550	1044	11176	Paper Manufacturing
29177	10	762	Nursing & Resid. Care Facilit.	29412	947	7068	Food Svcs & Drinking Places	29551	5	82	Prof., Scientific, & Tech Svcs
29178	97	887	Apparel Manufacturing	29413	7	16	Scenic & Sightseeing Transport	29554	285	3010	Furn. & Home Furnishgs Stores
29180	536	5043	Transportation Equipment Mfg	29414	563	5184	Hospitals	29555	196	1868	Chemical Manufacturing
29201	3159	57920	Food Svcs & Drinking Places	29415	1	0	Special Trade Contractors	29556	669	5588	Educational Services
29202	15	690	Plastics & Rubber Products Mfg	29416	5	27	Administrative & Support Svcs	29560	620	5765	Plastics & Rubber Products Mfg
29203	1375	23164	Hospitals	29417	7	6	Administrative & Support Svcs	29563	81	471	Textile Product Mills
29204	1086	11693	Hospitals	29418	1227	16938	Transportation Equipment Mfg	29564	24	129	Textile Product Mills
29205	1083	7750	Food Svcs & Drinking Places	29419	6	22	Credit Intermediation & Relatd	29565	153	1004	Merch. Wholesalers,Nondur. Gds
29206	778	6108	Food Svcs & Drinking Places	29420	219	2234	Educational Services	29566	627	3268	Food Svcs & Drinking Places
29207	50	1263	Special Trade Contractors	29422	10	41	Administrative & Support Svcs	29567	15	52	Social Assistance
29208	35	5461	Educational Services	29423	8	21	Special Trade Contractors	29568	259	827	Amusement, Gambling,& Recreat.
29209	891	10978	Hospitals	29424	2	1146	Educational Services	29569	566	5310	Amusement, Gambling,& Recreat.
29210	1821	31565	Justice, Pubic Order/Safety	29425	46	9947	Educational Services	29570	95	299	Educational Services
29211	3	11	Admin. of Economic Programs	29426	21	52	Special Trade Contractors	29571	594	5423	Repair and Maintenance
29212	1044	13773	Justice, Pubic Order/Safety	29429	69	202	Administrative & Support Svcs	29572	775	9967	Food Svcs & Drinking Places
29215	1	100	Telecommunications	29430	4	3	Construction of Buildings	29573	3	28	Nursing & Resid. Care Facilit.

29574 - 30056 BUSINESS DATA

ZIP CODE	2004 Total Firms	2004 Total Employees	TOP INDUSTRY RANKED on 2004 EMPLOYMENT	ZIP CODE	2004 Total Firms	2004 Total Employees	TOP INDUSTRY RANKED on 2004 EMPLOYMENT	ZIP CODE	2004 Total Firms	2004 Total Employees	TOP INDUSTRY RANKED on 2004 EMPLOYMENT
29574	438	3872	Hospitals	29676	92	500	Unclassified Establishments	29856	32	49	Special Trade Contractors
29575	927	7657	Insurance Carriers & Related	29677	13	1391	Plastics & Rubber Products Mfg	29860	169	1525	Truck Transportation
29576	1052	6819	Food Svcs & Drinking Places	29678	1015	8456	Food Svcs & Drinking Places	29861	5	4	Social Assistance
29577	2799	31604	Food Svcs & Drinking Places	29679	1	1	Relig., Grant, Civic, Prof Org	29901	25	116	Miscellaneous Store Retailers
29578	20	35	Special Trade Contractors	29680	325	3333	Food Svcs & Drinking Places	29902	986	8173	Hospitals
29579	566	5642	Amusement, Gambling,& Recreat.	29681	936	14727	Computer & Electronic Prod Mfg	29903	3	25	Unclassified Establishments
29580	20	74	Educational Services	29682	65	348	Educational Services	29904	10	60	Educational Services
29581	94	602	Furniture & Related Prod. Mfg	29683	9	355	Textile Mills	29905	15	77	Amusement, Gambling,& Recreat.
29582	1304	8604	Food Svcs & Drinking Places	29684	75	789	Chemical Manufacturing	29906	676	5181	Food Svcs & Drinking Places
29583	135	1081	Textile Mills	29685	26	39	Real Estate	29907	395	2856	Educational Services
29584	52	129	Educational Services	29686	13	101	Educational Services	29909	139	1116	Amusement, Gambling,& Recreat.
29585	713	4544	Amusement, Gambling,& Recreat.	29687	891	5686	Educational Services	29910	1181	7147	Amusement, Gambling,& Recreat.
29587	11	19	Special Trade Contractors	29688	8	385	Educational Services	29911	24	148	Relig., Grant, Civic, Prof Org
29588	826	4089	Educational Services	29689	61	189	Special Trade Contractors	29912	10	33	Fishing, Hunting and Trapping
29589	6	41	Merch. Wholesalers,Durable Gds	29690	485	4506	Food Svcs & Drinking Places	29914	4	5	Construction of Buildings
29590	61	256	Educational Services	29691	399	3042	Fabricated Metal Product Mfg	29915	12	399	Accommodation
29591	139	661	Merch. Wholesalers,Nondur. Gds	29692	124	1123	Textile Product Mills	29916	10	12	Food and Beverage Stores
29592	11	15	Textile Mills	29693	356	3890	Merch. Wholesalers,Durable Gds	29918	190	1366	Educational Services
29593	45	1698	Textile Mills	29695	1	5	Prof., Scientific, & Tech Svcs	29920	219	1189	Prof., Scientific, & Tech Svcs
29594	5	52	Paper Manufacturing	29696	121	1822	Computer & Electronic Prod Mfg	29921	12	54	Chemical Manufacturing
29596	35	538	Textile Mills	29697	263	3442	Unclassified Establishments	29922	24	41	Social Assistance
29597	3	1	Nonstore Retailers	29702	216	2097	Textile Mills	29923	6	9	Social Assistance
29598	2	5	Special Trade Contractors	29703	4	204	Textile Mills	29924	367	2729	Paper Manufacturing
29601	1945	23414	Prof., Scientific, & Tech Svcs	29704	50	1622	Paper Manufacturing	29925	41	140	Special Trade Contractors
29602	10	777	Postal Service	29706	843	8346	Textile Product Mills	29926	1473	10511	Food Svcs & Drinking Places
29603	1	4	Miscellaneous Store Retailers	29708	524	5937	Prof., Scientific, & Tech Svcs	29927	297	2014	General Merchandise Stores
29604	8	38	Prof., Scientific, & Tech Svcs	29709	337	1779	Exec., Legis., & Other Support	29928	1804	14271	Food Svcs & Drinking Places
29605	1321	21777	Hospitals	29710	690	4857	Educational Services	29929	28	50	Merch. Wholesalers,Nondur. Gds
29606	17	98	Postal Service	29712	100	89	Food and Beverage Stores	29931	8	28	Educational Services
29607	2988	48275	Prof., Scientific, & Tech Svcs	29714	65	1340	Textile Product Mills	29932	12	64	Forestry and Logging
29608	12	40	Food Svcs & Drinking Places	29715	697	7639	Fabricated Metal Product Mfg	29933	2	10	Merch. Wholesalers,Durable Gds
29609	1308	11165	Food Svcs & Drinking Places	29716	14	22	Administrative & Support Svcs	29934	15	55	Forestry and Logging
29610	3	46	Postal Service	29717	27	124	Educational Services	29935	183	1573	Special Trade Contractors
29611	928	9103	Textile Product Mills	29718	166	593	Nat'l Security & Int'l Affairs	29936	490	3071	Special Trade Contractors
29612	2	1	Food Svcs & Drinking Places	29720	1716	16789	Textile Product Mills	29938	47	136	Administrative & Support Svcs
29613	5	55	Other Information Services	29721	9	23	Insurance Carriers & Related	29939	2	3	Food and Beverage Stores
29614	3	3	Administrative & Support Svcs	29724	5	26	Justice, Pubic Order/Safety	29940	58	424	Educational Services
29615	1689	29824	Machinery Manufacturing	29726	23	60	Mining (Except Oil and Gas)	29941	17	83	Museums, Hist. Sites,& Similar
29616	18	72	Postal Service	29727	26	39	Fabricated Metal Product Mfg	29943	10	13	Support Activities: Agr./For.
29617	460	3748	Educational Services	29728	403	4203	General Merchandise Stores	29944	137	881	Educational Services
29620	511	5632	Repair and Maintenance	29729	129	1777	Nonmetallic Mineral Prod. Mfg	29945	128	800	Food Svcs & Drinking Places
29621	1694	23051	Hospitals	29730	2034	21953	Educational Services	30002	149	1344	Textile Product Mills
29622	9	19	Special Trade Contractors	29731	9	500	Exec., Legis., & Other Support	30003	5	34	Prof., Scientific, & Tech Svcs
29623	4	6	Merch. Wholesalers,Durable Gds	29732	1707	14759	Ambulatory Health Care Svcs	30004	3040	32129	Food Svcs & Drinking Places
29624	819	7443	Chemical Manufacturing	29734	2	22	Relig., Grant, Civic, Prof Org	30005	1165	17938	Miscellaneous Manufacturing
29625	674	7324	Plastics & Rubber Products Mfg	29741	53	193	Educational Services	30006	13	76	Administrative & Support Svcs
29626	241	4560	Elect'l Eqpmt, App, & Comp Mfg	29742	46	91	Food Svcs & Drinking Places	30007	14	43	Furniture & Related Prod. Mfg
29627	401	3071	Fabricated Metal Product Mfg	29743	21	56	Justice, Pubic Order/Safety	30008	581	3915	Exec., Legis., & Other Support
29628	78	1561	Textile Mills	29744	8	140	Nonmetallic Mineral Prod. Mfg	30009	12	46	Prof., Scientific, & Tech Svcs
29630	187	2196	Paper Manufacturing	29745	709	6509	Justice, Pubic Order/Safety	30010	14	50	Repair and Maintenance
29631	487	6405	Textile Mills	29801	1263	27449	Utilities	30011	175	2042	Warehousing and Storage
29632	1	0	Unclassified Establishments	29802	9	157	Exec., Legis., & Other Support	30012	1226	13136	Elect'l Eqpmt, App, & Comp Mfg
29633	5	247	Other Information Services	29803	954	9037	Food Svcs & Drinking Places	30013	1113	11526	Food Svcs & Drinking Places
29634	7	263	Food Svcs & Drinking Places	29804	2	4	Construction of Buildings	30014	1435	14990	Educational Services
29635	24	103	Accommodation	29805	99	1658	Merch. Wholesalers,Durable Gds	30015	7	14	Food and Beverage Stores
29636	9	31	Machinery Manufacturing	29808	1	14000	Prof., Scientific, & Tech Svcs	30016	522	2258	Food and Beverage Stores
29638	55	329	Wood Product Manufacturing	29809	93	463	Support Activities: Agr./For.	30017	294	1657	Bldg Matl & Garden Eqpmt Dlrs
29639	47	405	Educational Services	29810	239	1507	Wood Product Manufacturing	30018	13	35	Food and Beverage Stores
29640	1108	9592	Food Svcs & Drinking Places	29812	536	5002	Exec., Legis., & Other Support	30019	587	4674	Educational Services
29641	6	212	Plastics & Rubber Products Mfg	29813	3	2	Repair and Maintenance	30021	377	2777	Educational Services
29642	486	4275	Nursing & Resid. Care Facilit.	29816	31	143	Special Trade Contractors	30022	1941	20730	Food Svcs & Drinking Places
29643	74	394	Special Trade Contractors	29817	128	1137	Machinery Manufacturing	30023	8	15	Prof., Scientific, & Tech Svcs
29644	403	7666	Computer & Electronic Prod Mfg	29819	29	114	Heavy & Civil Eng. Construct'N	30024	1676	16868	Merch. Wholesalers,Durable Gds
29645	169	829	Educational Services	29821	29	37	Transportation Equipment Mfg	30025	211	2552	Merch. Wholesalers,Nondur. Gds
29646	970	11174	Educational Services	29822	29	354	Food and Beverage Stores	30026	4	1723	Postal Service
29647	2	355	Nonstore Retailers	29824	270	2170	Exec., Legis., & Other Support	30028	19	27	Construction of Buildings
29648	7	5	Merch. Wholesalers,Nondur. Gds	29826	18	14	Personal and Laundry Services	30030	1294	14745	Exec., Legis., & Other Support
29649	1142	13946	Food Svcs & Drinking Places	29827	129	1641	Justice, Pubic Order/Safety	30031	11	43	Administrative & Support Svcs
29650	1071	11536	Food Svcs & Drinking Places	29828	27	129	Educational Services	30032	1557	14882	Justice, Pubic Order/Safety
29651	999	12613	Transportation Equipment Mfg	29829	134	2062	Textile Product Mills	30033	1070	14896	Hospitals
29652	7	19	Administrative & Support Svcs	29831	78	1828	Paper Manufacturing	30034	1023	9903	Educational Services
29653	114	1067	Repair and Maintenance	29832	199	1961	Repair and Maintenance	30035	855	9475	General Merchandise Stores
29654	228	2564	Transportation Equipment Mfg	29834	25	247	Mining (Except Oil and Gas)	30036	11	21	Ambulatory Health Care Svcs
29655	133	617	Educational Services	29835	263	2350	Justice, Pubic Order/Safety	30037	9	28	Special Trade Contractors
29656	3	44	Educational Services	29836	14	284	Chemical Manufacturing	30038	610	4061	Educational Services
29657	246	2342	Transportation Equipment Mfg	29838	10	53	Construction of Buildings	30039	667	4866	Educational Services
29658	11	111	Motor Vehicle & Parts Dealers	29839	7	22	Relig., Grant, Civic, Prof Org	30040	2128	15141	Food and Beverage Stores
29659	11	36	Relig., Grant, Civic, Prof Org	29840	6	10	Merch. Wholesalers,Durable Gds	30041	1122	7763	Food Svcs & Drinking Places
29661	112	736	Textile Mills	29841	838	6241	Food Svcs & Drinking Places	30042	11	112	Waste Managmt & Remediat'n Svc
29662	518	4649	Food and Beverage Stores	29842	182	1553	Special Trade Contractors	30043	1604	16076	Educational Services
29664	32	202	Accommodation	29843	25	98	Wood Product Manufacturing	30044	1217	7823	Educational Services
29665	3	4	Postal Service	29844	2	4	Food and Beverage Stores	30045	2433	34406	Hospitals
29666	141	893	Educational Services	29845	33	66	Museums, Hist. Sites,& Similar	30046	13	34	Social Assistance
29667	10	17	Exec., Legis., & Other Support	29846	2	2	Bldg Matl & Garden Eqpmt Dlrs	30047	1696	12270	Educational Services
29669	240	1606	Educational Services	29847	83	964	Miscellaneous Manufacturing	30048	13	64	Special Trade Contractors
29670	298	2556	Educational Services	29848	26	10	Postal Service	30049	4	3	Insurance Carriers & Related
29671	552	4518	Educational Services	29849	15	448	Textile Mills	30052	1181	7243	Educational Services
29672	270	3490	Hospitals	29850	5	9	Relig., Grant, Civic, Prof Org	30054	192	783	Special Trade Contractors
29673	668	6706	Fabricated Metal Product Mfg	29851	136	734	Educational Services	30055	65	541	Textile Mills
29675	4	126	Administrative & Support Svcs	29853	209	2417	Machinery Manufacturing	30056	37	123	Heavy & Civil Eng. Construct'N

ZIP CODE	2004 Total Firms	2004 Total Employees	TOP INDUSTRY RANKED on 2004 EMPLOYMENT	ZIP CODE	2004 Total Firms	2004 Total Employees	TOP INDUSTRY RANKED on 2004 EMPLOYMENT	ZIP CODE	2004 Total Firms	2004 Total Employees	TOP INDUSTRY RANKED on 2004 EMPLOYMENT
30058	1081	7984	Educational Services	30160	1	3	Personal and Laundry Services	30304	3	86	Credit Intermediation & Relatd
30060	2650	29590	Hospitals	30161	1533	17386	Educational Services	30305	2285	22814	Food Svcs & Drinking Places
30061	18	64	Administrative & Support Svcs	30162	6	38	Social Assistance	30306	692	5644	Food Svcs & Drinking Places
30062	2819	19819	Educational Services	30164	2	2	Administrative & Support Svcs	30307	519	3826	Food Svcs & Drinking Places
30064	1178	8446	Food Svcs & Drinking Places	30165	1350	18744	Hospitals	30308	1195	24492	Prof., Scientific, & Tech Svcs
30065	13	24	Prof., Scientific, & Tech Svcs	30168	720	9964	Amusement, Gambling,& Recreat.	30309	2036	34929	Prof., Scientific, & Tech Svcs
30066	2225	16988	Food Svcs & Drinking Places	30169	4	10	Perform'g Arts, Spec. Sports	30310	914	6428	Educational Services
30067	2263	22773	Computer & Electronic Prod Mfg	30170	56	217	Educational Services	30311	706	4365	Educational Services
30068	1215	8753	Educational Services	30171	39	196	Transportation Equipment Mfg	30312	680	7437	Hospitals
30069	18	1482	Nat'l Security & Int'l Affairs	30172	10	705	Textile Mills	30313	197	2266	Admin. of Economic Programs
30070	22	428	Textile Mills	30173	79	213	Educational Services	30314	394	4802	Educational Services
30071	1936	34102	Merch. Wholesalers,Durable Gds	30175	92	329	Chemical Manufacturing	30315	851	14914	Perform'g Arts, Spec. Sports
30072	13	21	Exec., Legis., & Other Support	30176	247	2331	Fabricated Metal Product Mfg	30316	892	9977	Educational Services
30074	5	5	Prof., Scientific, & Tech Svcs	30177	25	359	Nonmetallic Mineral Prod. Mfg	30317	265	1664	Educational Services
30075	2273	12750	Educational Services	30178	48	171	Food Svcs & Drinking Places	30318	2148	29502	Merch. Wholesalers,Nondur. Gds
30076	2340	22624	Ambulatory Health Care Svcs	30179	200	1007	Educational Services	30319	774	11676	Furn. & Home Furnishgs Stores
30077	18	43	Computer & Electronic Prod Mfg	30180	680	7546	Personal and Laundry Services	30320	115	4784	Food Svcs & Drinking Places
30078	1391	11437	Food Svcs & Drinking Places	30182	45	294	Perform'g Arts, Spec. Sports	30321	5	6	Prof., Scientific, & Tech Svcs
30079	146	2236	Administrative & Support Svcs	30183	82	531	Educational Services	30322	102	14649	Hospitals
30080	2276	21663	Food Svcs & Drinking Places	30184	95	499	Accommodation	30324	1171	11814	Food Svcs & Drinking Places
30081	18	37	Special Trade Contractors	30185	80	336	Educational Services	30325	11	63	Personal and Laundry Services
30082	490	7177	Prof., Scientific, & Tech Svcs	30187	166	804	Merch. Wholesalers,Durable Gds	30326	1182	23128	Prof., Scientific, & Tech Svcs
30083	1484	11644	Educational Services	30188	1640	9156	Food Svcs & Drinking Places	30327	632	8297	Educational Services
30084	2302	26794	Ambulatory Health Care Svcs	30189	1211	7569	Educational Services	30328	2529	28360	Prof., Scientific, & Tech Svcs
30085	12	47	Special Trade Contractors	30204	419	3059	Educational Services	30329	1328	23964	Admin. Human Resource Programs
30086	15	46	Administrative & Support Svcs	30205	61	118	Construction of Buildings	30330	13	103	Electronics & Appliance Stores
30087	942	7208	Food Svcs & Drinking Places	30206	36	84	Real Estate	30331	953	12242	Chemical Manufacturing
30088	444	1896	Educational Services	30212	1	0	Relig., Grant, Civic, Prof Org	30332	5	3201	Educational Services
30090	32	379	Exec., Legis., & Other Support	30213	525	5620	Educational Services	30333	2	8	Administrative & Support Svcs
30091	4	8	Electronics & Appliance Stores	30214	1662	13552	Food Svcs & Drinking Places	30334	236	11051	Exec., Legis., & Other Support
30092	1463	20946	Prof., Scientific, & Tech Svcs	30215	482	2534	Special Trade Contractors	30336	736	17218	Merch. Wholesalers,Durable Gds
30093	1595	16976	Merch. Wholesalers,Durable Gds	30216	32	81	Relig., Grant, Civic, Prof Org	30337	535	9316	Accommodation
30094	675	4836	Educational Services	30217	217	3231	Unclassified Establishments	30338	1613	15085	Educational Services
30095	7	24	Prof., Scientific, & Tech Svcs	30218	46	146	Transportation Equipment Mfg	30339	2485	44556	Prof., Scientific, & Tech Svcs
30096	2360	33261	Food Svcs & Drinking Places	30220	68	244	Special Trade Contractors	30340	1753	15847	Administrative & Support Svcs
30097	940	14090	Miscellaneous Manufacturing	30222	150	1023	Wood Product Manufacturing	30341	2103	19162	Prof., Scientific, & Tech Svcs
30098	2	2007	Insurance Carriers & Related	30223	1212	10969	Food Svcs & Drinking Places	30342	1812	22787	Hospitals
30099	1	1600	Insurance Carriers & Related	30224	675	8282	Hospitals	30343	1	5	Perform'g Arts, Spec. Sports
30101	1102	6293	Special Trade Contractors	30228	404	3185	Educational Services	30344	1098	9391	Educational Services
30102	707	3675	Administrative & Support Svcs	30229	14	23	Truck Transportation	30345	782	8919	Prof., Scientific, & Tech Svcs
30103	300	2035	Educational Services	30230	171	1120	Textile Product Mills	30346	512	13036	Accommodation
30104	47	132	Construction of Buildings	30233	561	4498	Exec., Legis., & Other Support	30347	1	1	Support Act. for Transport.
30105	43	683	Textile Product Mills	30234	22	61	Prof., Scientific, & Tech Svcs	30349	1504	14134	Food Svcs & Drinking Places
30106	726	9595	Hospitals	30236	1675	17248	Relig., Grant, Civic, Prof Org	30350	1055	9907	Prof., Scientific, & Tech Svcs
30107	277	2048	Fabricated Metal Product Mfg	30237	5	27	Exec., Legis., & Other Support	30354	635	38742	Air Transportation
30108	229	2142	Apparel Manufacturing	30238	341	1954	Educational Services	30355	20	77	Prof., Scientific, & Tech Svcs
30109	1	1	Administrative & Support Svcs	30240	1203	17030	Hospitals	30356	15	43	Securities/Commodity Contracts
30110	404	3185	Administrative & Support Svcs	30241	749	7782	Food Svcs & Drinking Places	30357	7	11	Special Trade Contractors
30111	3	3	Construction of Buildings	30248	359	2123	Paper Manufacturing	30358	10	31	Prof., Scientific, & Tech Svcs
30112	4	19	Insurance Carriers & Related	30250	9	64	Heavy & Civil Eng. Construct'N	30359	12	23	Prof., Scientific, & Tech Svcs
30113	162	982	Educational Services	30251	61	391	Merch. Wholesalers,Durable Gds	30360	522	9957	Relig., Grant, Civic, Prof Org
30114	1211	11914	Food Svcs & Drinking Places	30252	333	1387	Food and Beverage Stores	30361	205	2863	Insurance Carriers & Related
30115	710	5502	Food Manufacturing	30253	1344	16131	Food Svcs & Drinking Places	30362	4	10	Construction of Buildings
30116	378	3110	Educational Services	30256	22	112	Social Assistance	30364	2	1	Merch. Wholesalers,Nondur. Gds
30117	1646	16634	Hospitals	30257	64	340	Repair and Maintenance	30366	5	33	Special Trade Contractors
30118	2	880	Educational Services	30258	40	408	Textile Mills	30369	3	2007	Postal Service
30119	3	1522	Merch. Wholesalers,Durable Gds	30259	54	186	Educational Services	30375	2	5002	Telecommunications
30120	1588	15124	Educational Services	30260	1041	15251	Food Svcs & Drinking Places	30377	6	18	Heavy & Civil Eng. Construct'N
30121	606	7757	Food Svcs & Drinking Places	30263	1676	13608	Merch. Wholesalers,Durable Gds	30401	637	5720	Educational Services
30122	699	8075	Bldg Matl & Garden Eqpmt Dlrs	30264	5	6	Repair and Maintenance	30410	32	228	Educational Services
30123	4	9	Justice, Pubic Order/Safety	30265	634	10117	Food Svcs & Drinking Places	30411	84	765	Justice, Pubic Order/Safety
30124	83	440	Educational Services	30266	16	68	Prof., Scientific, & Tech Svcs	30412	5	8	Repair and Maintenance
30125	714	5781	Furniture & Related Prod. Mfg	30268	243	1435	Nonmetallic Mineral Prod. Mfg	30413	34	66	Administrative & Support Svcs
30126	1017	7957	Educational Services	30269	1149	14364	Computer & Electronic Prod Mfg	30414	11	84	Educational Services
30127	989	6247	Educational Services	30271	2	9	Waste Managmt & Remediat'n Svc	30415	195	1074	Educational Services
30129	4	22	Merch. Wholesalers,Durable Gds	30272	2	4	Postal Service	30417	372	3890	Food Manufacturing
30132	847	4368	Educational Services	30273	145	773	Educational Services	30420	51	122	Food and Beverage Stores
30133	7	15	Construction of Buildings	30274	1094	9099	Hospitals	30421	38	226	Crop Production
30134	1406	10282	Food Svcs & Drinking Places	30275	3	2	Postal Service	30423	6	12	Food and Beverage Stores
30135	1418	10572	Food Svcs & Drinking Places	30276	175	805	Repair and Maintenance	30424	6	313	Textile Mills
30137	27	428	Chemical Manufacturing	30277	268	1325	Educational Services	30425	17	64	Merch. Wholesalers,Nondur. Gds
30138	1	2	Postal Service	30281	1695	14065	Food Svcs & Drinking Places	30426	19	38	Crop Production
30139	95	483	Textile Product Mills	30284	22	107	Construction of Buildings	30427	327	3923	Crop Production
30140	3	45	Plastics & Rubber Products Mfg	30285	11	766	Print'g & Related Supp't Act's	30428	95	444	Educational Services
30141	619	5060	Food Svcs & Drinking Places	30286	898	7141	Educational Services	30429	24	190	Wood Product Manufacturing
30142	36	158	Truck Transportation	30287	2	3	Repair and Maintenance	30434	268	2235	Machinery Manufacturing
30143	758	5728	Educational Services	30288	218	6186	Truck Transportation	30436	365	2817	Merch. Wholesalers,Nondur. Gds
30144	2338	31377	Food Svcs & Drinking Places	30289	22	57	Bldg Matl & Garden Eqpmt Dlrs	30438	4	16	Exec., Legis., & Other Support
30145	85	273	Educational Services	30290	260	2107	Heavy & Civil Eng. Construct'N	30439	407	2760	Food Svcs & Drinking Places
30146	6	25	Publishing Industries	30291	471	5307	Motor Vehicle & Parts Dealers	30441	67	288	Food Svcs & Drinking Places
30147	86	533	Educational Services	30292	61	216	Amusement, Gambling,& Recreat.	30442	253	2505	Wood Product Manufacturing
30148	60	279	Nonmetallic Mineral Prod. Mfg	30293	78	467	Educational Services	30445	107	725	Educational Services
30149	4	25	Other Information Services	30294	458	4386	Truck Transportation	30446	40	102	Telecommunications
30150	9	164	Educational Services	30295	205	1228	Educational Services	30447	3	9	Administrative & Support Svcs
30151	24	49	Telecommunications	30296	286	1011	Educational Services	30448	6	23	Social Assistance
30152	804	7412	Educational Services	30297	1040	16048	General Merchandise Stores	30449	8	17	Wood Product Manufacturing
30153	376	3151	Food Manufacturing	30298	2	6	Truck Transportation	30450	86	619	Educational Services
30154	4	13	Elect'l Eqpmt, App, & Comp Mfg	30301	9	15	Administrative & Support Svcs	30451	6	109	Nursing & Resid. Care Facilit.
30156	18	129	Sportg Gds,Hobby,Book, & Music	30302	5	13	Social Assistance	30452	54	181	Wood Product Manufacturing
30157	429	3068	Educational Services	30303	3158	57496	Prof., Scientific, & Tech Svcs	30453	221	1443	Educational Services

BUSINESS DATA

ZIP CODE	2004 Total Firms	2004 Total Employ-ees	TOP INDUSTRY RANKED on 2004 EMPLOYMENT	ZIP CODE	2004 Total Firms	2004 Total Employ-ees	TOP INDUSTRY RANKED on 2004 EMPLOYMENT	ZIP CODE	2004 Total Firms	2004 Total Employ-ees	TOP INDUSTRY RANKED on 2004 EMPLOYMENT
30454	8	4	Heavy & Civil Eng. Construct'N	30606	1673	16828	Hospitals	30812	5	1574	Hospitals
30455	15	27	Merch. Wholesalers,Durable Gds	30607	311	3064	Elect'l Eqpmt, App, & Comp Mfg	30813	341	4582	Justice, Pubic Order/Safety
30456	52	277	Apparel Manufacturing	30608	4	16	Administrative & Support Svcs	30814	184	1020	Educational Services
30457	223	1196	Textile Mills	30609	1	0	Unclassified Establishments	30815	498	2658	Educational Services
30458	1698	15063	Food Svcs & Drinking Places	30619	22	82	Administrative & Support Svcs	30816	27	225	Nursing & Resid. Care Facilit.
30459	12	36	Exec., Legis., & Other Support	30620	77	831	Food Manufacturing	30817	355	1436	Educational Services
30460	3	1869	Educational Services	30621	76	457	Nursing & Resid. Care Facilit.	30818	13	26	Special Trade Contractors
30461	294	1827	Special Trade Contractors	30622	490	4783	Merch. Wholesalers,Durable Gds	30819	3	12	Merch. Wholesalers,Durable Gds
30464	19	893	Merch. Wholesalers,Nondur. Gds	30623	7	9	Relig., Grant, Civic, Prof Org	30820	20	56	Merch. Wholesalers,Durable Gds
30467	512	3432	Fabricated Metal Product Mfg	30624	74	340	Food and Beverage Stores	30821	19	19	Motor Vehicle & Parts Dealers
30470	12	25	Crop Production	30625	44	94	Prof., Scientific, & Tech Svcs	30822	9	5	Food and Beverage Stores
30471	124	598	Educational Services	30627	28	89	Nonmetallic Mineral Prod. Mfg	30823	37	79	Merch. Wholesalers,Nondur. Gds
30473	57	366	Crop Production	30628	97	603	Wood Product Manufacturing	30824	732	7395	Motor Vehicle & Parts Dealers
30474	904	9035	General Merchandise Stores	30629	99	603	Nursing & Resid. Care Facilit.	30828	158	1166	Educational Services
30475	1	0	Relig., Grant, Civic, Prof Org	30630	110	509	Nursing & Resid. Care Facilit.	30830	518	5310	Ambulatory Health Care Svcs
30477	88	978	Wood Product Manufacturing	30631	90	316	Educational Services	30833	175	2005	Food and Beverage Stores
30501	2528	32020	Hospitals	30633	222	1414	Educational Services	30901	1596	25948	Hospitals
30502	2	4	Prof., Scientific, & Tech Svcs	30634	50	138	Nonmetallic Mineral Prod. Mfg	30903	7	10	Nonstore Retailers
30503	10	203	Administrative & Support Svcs	30635	835	6627	Merch. Wholesalers,Durable Gds	30904	1049	11859	Hospitals
30504	521	7438	General Merchandise Stores	30638	3	13	Bldg Matl & Garden Eqpmt Dlrs	30905	90	1693	Unclassified Establishments
30506	600	2453	Educational Services	30639	17	133	Sportg Gds,Hobby,Book, & Music	30906	1590	20048	Educational Services
30507	428	5500	Food Manufacturing	30641	25	77	Heavy & Civil Eng. Construct'N	30907	2190	18041	Food Svcs & Drinking Places
30510	119	2992	Repair and Maintenance	30642	403	3196	Real Estate	30909	1807	20799	Food Svcs & Drinking Places
30511	141	957	Nursing & Resid. Care Facilit.	30643	742	5718	Transportation Equipment Mfg	30911	33	3096	Exec., Legis., & Other Support
30512	1073	5222	Educational Services	30645	11	28	Ambulatory Health Care Svcs	30912	36	405	Ambulatory Health Care Svcs
30513	840	5021	Food Svcs & Drinking Places	30646	123	532	Food and Beverage Stores	30914	3	9	Special Trade Contractors
30514	14	38	Social Assistance	30647	34	121	Educational Services	30916	3	5	Food and Beverage Stores
30515	14	36	Special Trade Contractors	30648	111	678	Educational Services	30917	8	12	Repair and Maintenance
30516	48	204	Educational Services	30650	575	5184	Food Svcs & Drinking Places	30919	8	16	Ambulatory Health Care Svcs
30517	185	3461	Merch. Wholesalers,Durable Gds	30655	783	6709	Educational Services	31001	64	641	Justice, Pubic Order/Safety
30518	1621	12751	Food Svcs & Drinking Places	30656	184	1058	Apparel Manufacturing	31002	54	410	Merch. Wholesalers,Durable Gds
30519	750	7399	Food Svcs & Drinking Places	30660	38	147	Crop Production	31003	7	21	Credit Intermediation & Relatd
30520	92	250	Wood Product Manufacturing	30662	340	3395	Hospitals	31004	14	78	Special Trade Contractors
30521	174	1460	Truck Transportation	30663	83	329	Merch. Wholesalers,Durable Gds	31005	114	918	Food and Beverage Stores
30522	28	59	Educational Services	30664	4	9	Merch. Wholesalers,Nondur. Gds	31006	243	1387	Educational Services
30523	656	3721	Fabricated Metal Product Mfg	30665	10	47	Educational Services	31007	28	263	Nursing & Resid. Care Facilit.
30525	514	3394	Accommodation	30666	129	684	Administrative & Support Svcs	31008	370	2557	Food Svcs & Drinking Places
30527	115	393	Food Svcs & Drinking Places	30667	15	57	Construction of Buildings	31009	39	59	Furn. & Home Furnishgs Stores
30528	970	5514	Educational Services	30668	65	185	Merch. Wholesalers,Nondur. Gds	31010	3	2	Relig., Grant, Civic, Prof Org
30529	629	5651	Food Svcs & Drinking Places	30669	99	469	Nursing & Resid. Care Facilit.	31011	17	123	Relig., Grant, Civic, Prof Org
30530	93	501	Wood Product Manufacturing	30671	11	23	Crop Production	31012	35	37	Exec., Legis., & Other Support
30531	645	5958	Miscellaneous Manufacturing	30673	515	3563	Merch. Wholesalers,Durable Gds	31013	5	134	Nonmetallic Mineral Prod. Mfg
30533	971	6328	Educational Services	30677	569	4070	Educational Services	31014	407	3762	Merch. Wholesalers,Durable Gds
30534	878	4937	Food Svcs & Drinking Places	30678	31	70	Forestry and Logging	31015	930	8878	Food Svcs & Drinking Places
30535	191	1713	Hospitals	30680	997	9560	Educational Services	31016	37	67	Administrative & Support Svcs
30537	110	723	Accommodation	30683	115	880	Exec., Legis., & Other Support	31017	34	69	Justice, Pubic Order/Safety
30538	96	753	Educational Services	30701	1421	18749	Textile Product Mills	31018	27	563	Justice, Pubic Order/Safety
30539	17	485	General Merchandise Stores	30703	3	3	Elect'l Eqpmt, App, & Comp Mfg	31019	56	129	Crop Production
30540	1185	7846	Food Manufacturing	30705	764	11781	Textile Product Mills	31020	40	812	Nonmetallic Mineral Prod. Mfg
30541	21	36	Relig., Grant, Civic, Prof Org	30707	306	3291	Textile Mills	31021	1419	14715	Ambulatory Health Care Svcs
30542	527	4746	Food Manufacturing	30708	3	11	Mining (Except Oil and Gas)	31022	43	470	Wood Product Manufacturing
30543	43	143	Heavy & Civil Eng. Construct'N	30710	73	278	Educational Services	31023	577	5142	Educational Services
30544	5	3	Relig., Grant, Civic, Prof Org	30711	28	86	Other Information Services	31024	755	6001	Wood Product Manufacturing
30545	250	1379	Accommodation	30719	3	3	Personal and Laundry Services	31025	23	67	Merch. Wholesalers,Durable Gds
30546	461	2135	Educational Services	30720	1615	21604	Textile Product Mills	31027	253	3683	Textile Product Mills
30547	151	693	Educational Services	30721	1742	21996	Textile Product Mills	31028	199	1506	Food Svcs & Drinking Places
30548	177	846	Special Trade Contractors	30722	11	67	Social Assistance	31029	513	3845	Educational Services
30549	526	3181	Educational Services	30724	20	124	Textile Product Mills	31030	520	6282	Transportation Equipment Mfg
30552	40	95	Food Svcs & Drinking Places	30725	78	652	Textile Mills	31031	148	1716	Mining (Except Oil and Gas)
30553	359	2859	Textile Mills	30726	3	4	Merch. Wholesalers,Durable Gds	31032	358	2197	Educational Services
30554	117	404	Educational Services	30728	772	10653	General Merchandise Stores	31033	33	45	Relig., Grant, Civic, Prof Org
30555	86	313	Food Svcs & Drinking Places	30730	30	205	Apparel Manufacturing	31034	12	1500	Justice, Pubic Order/Safety
30557	50	101	Relig., Grant, Civic, Prof Org	30731	57	737	Apparel Manufacturing	31035	28	89	Transit & Grnd Pass. Transport
30558	94	321	Educational Services	30732	7	45	Unclassified Establishments	31036	428	2880	Justice, Pubic Order/Safety
30559	98	185	Educational Services	30733	23	134	Educational Services	31037	56	349	Bldg Matl & Garden Eqpmt Dlrs
30560	145	314	Educational Services	30734	26	130	Chemical Manufacturing	31038	14	31	Exec., Legis., & Other Support
30562	45	245	Accommodation	30735	74	489	Furn. & Home Furnishgs Stores	31039	5	2	Miscellaneous Store Retailers
30563	102	561	Educational Services	30736	831	6554	Furn. & Home Furnishgs Stores	31040	5	56	Social Assistance
30564	100	1789	Food Manufacturing	30738	86	385	Repair and Maintenance	31041	16	103	Nursing & Resid. Care Facilit.
30565	62	216	Special Trade Contractors	30739	102	557	Justice, Pubic Order/Safety	31042	85	1079	Admin. Human Resource Programs
30566	247	3499	Educational Services	30740	105	492	Educational Services	31044	130	874	Educational Services
30567	95	3204	Food Manufacturing	30741	600	3964	Educational Services	31045	2	0	Postal Service
30568	42	1523	Apparel Manufacturing	30742	499	7048	Hospitals	31046	71	964	Utilities
30571	109	325	Special Trade Contractors	30746	24	793	Textile Product Mills	31047	56	1357	Food Manufacturing
30572	47	153	Educational Services	30747	491	4000	Educational Services	31049	35	84	Construction of Buildings
30573	24	199	Relig., Grant, Civic, Prof Org	30750	45	485	Educational Services	31050	9	105	Justice, Pubic Order/Safety
30575	40	438	Food Manufacturing	30751	6	67	Wood Product Manufacturing	31051	6	25	Support Activities: Agr./For.
30576	56	330	Educational Services	30752	371	2779	Educational Services	31052	150	578	Relig., Grant, Civic, Prof Org
30577	875	9345	Textile Mills	30753	132	3490	Textile Mills	31054	77	998	Bldg Matl & Garden Eqpmt Dlrs
30580	10	28	Special Trade Contractors	30755	148	1290	Truck Transportation	31055	258	3423	Machinery Manufacturing
30581	10	26	Heavy & Civil Eng. Construct'N	30756	10	27	Relig., Grant, Civic, Prof Org	31057	42	177	Nursing & Resid. Care Facilit.
30582	173	966	Accommodation	30757	34	255	Hospitals	31058	10	47	Waste Managmt & Remediat'n Svc
30597	1	345	Educational Services	30802	171	1132	Justice, Pubic Order/Safety	31059	5	28	Exec., Legis., & Other Support
30598	3	258	Educational Services	30803	12	55	Apparel Manufacturing	31060	46	185	Bldg Matl & Garden Eqpmt Dlrs
30599	1	430	Merch. Wholesalers,Nondur. Gds	30805	53	192	Educational Services	31061	1437	15525	Educational Services
30601	1017	14488	Food Manufacturing	30806	2	3	Postal Service	31062	8	4234	Hospitals
30602	52	9852	Educational Services	30807	6	163	Wood Product Manufacturing	31063	267	1821	Food Manufacturing
30603	6	12	Administrative & Support Svcs	30808	71	519	Bldg Matl & Garden Eqpmt Dlrs	31064	261	1831	Wood Product Manufacturing
30604	8	15	Social Assistance	30809	767	8407	Educational Services	31065	20	44	Nursing & Resid. Care Facilit.
30605	904	7537	Prof., Scientific, & Tech Svcs	30810	63	278	Social Assistance	31066	13	41	Merch. Wholesalers,Nondur. Gds

ZIP CODE	2004 Total Firms	2004 Total Employ-ees	TOP INDUSTRY RANKED on 2004 EMPLOYMENT	ZIP CODE	2004 Total Firms	2004 Total Employ-ees	TOP INDUSTRY RANKED on 2004 EMPLOYMENT	ZIP CODE	2004 Total Firms	2004 Total Employ-ees	TOP INDUSTRY RANKED on 2004 EMPLOYMENT
31067	9	74	Nursing & Resid. Care Facilit.	31405	1533	18158	Hospitals	31639	388	3438	Textile Mills
31068	102	1336	Paper Manufacturing	31406	2037	19579	Food Svcs & Drinking Places	31641	23	25	Fishing, Hunting and Trapping
31069	713	7368	Food Manufacturing	31407	176	2774	Food Manufacturing	31642	149	1268	Textile Product Mills
31070	35	312	Educational Services	31408	860	26147	Educational Services	31643	335	2722	Nursing & Resid. Care Facilit.
31071	25	123	Nursing & Resid. Care Facilit.	31409	18	132	Ambulatory Health Care Svcs	31645	44	139	Food Svcs & Drinking Places
31072	19	60	Merch. Wholesalers,Durable Gds	31410	515	3167	Food Svcs & Drinking Places	31647	64	385	Chemical Manufacturing
31075	58	442	Educational Services	31411	152	1136	Relig., Grant, Civic, Prof Org	31648	30	167	Educational Services
31076	97	753	Utilities	31412	6	44	Construction of Buildings	31649	15	28	Gasoline Stations
31077	33	77	Merch. Wholesalers,Durable Gds	31414	2	3	Amusement, Gambling,& Recreat.	31650	75	639	Merch. Wholesalers,Durable Gds
31078	210	1013	Educational Services	31415	393	7781	Paper Manufacturing	31698	6	896	Educational Services
31079	109	640	Educational Services	31416	15	93	Nat'l Security & Int'l Affairs	31699	36	660	Hospitals
31081	1	1	Postal Service	31418	7	22	Exec., Legis., & Other Support	31701	1709	24412	Ambulatory Health Care Svcs
31082	528	6795	Mining (Except Oil and Gas)	31419	912	14243	Hospitals	31702	4	16	Relig., Grant, Civic, Prof Org
31083	8	15	Administrative & Support Svcs	31420	11	62	Social Assistance	31703	3	4	Repair and Maintenance
31085	22	245	Merch. Wholesalers,Nondur. Gds	31421	8	459	Accommodation	31704	13	75	Special Trade Contractors
31086	6	46	Wood Product Manufacturing	31422	7	182	General Merchandise Stores	31705	823	12874	Motor Vehicle & Parts Dealers
31087	230	1260	Educational Services	31501	1111	9676	Hospitals	31706	3	1	Educational Services
31088	1020	9984	Educational Services	31502	5	17	Social Assistance	31707	1453	17201	General Merchandise Stores
31089	98	1050	Admin. of Economic Programs	31503	496	6099	Wood Product Manufacturing	31708	11	16	Prof., Scientific, & Tech Svcs
31090	30	194	Nursing & Resid. Care Facilit.	31510	481	3141	Hospitals	31709	873	9902	Transportation Equipment Mfg
31091	107	1095	Justice, Pubic Order/Safety	31512	36	182	Educational Services	31710	4	487	Prof., Scientific, & Tech Svcs
31092	258	2195	Merch. Wholesalers,Nondur. Gds	31513	691	5208	Educational Services	31711	25	294	Nonmetallic Mineral Prod. Mfg
31093	1122	11344	Hospitals	31515	1	1	Real Estate	31712	30	117	Bldg Matl & Garden Eqpmt Dlrs
31094	22	30	Construction of Buildings	31516	418	2615	Educational Services	31714	290	2490	Administrative & Support Svcs
31095	5	6	Real Estate	31518	21	94	Sportg Gds,Hobby,Book, & Music	31716	43	293	Educational Services
31096	212	1353	Apparel Manufacturing	31519	77	304	Educational Services	31719	201	2966	Elect'l Eqpmt, App, & Comp Mfg
31097	31	55	Food Svcs & Drinking Places	31520	1765	18312	Ambulatory Health Care Svcs	31720	17	52	Justice, Pubic Order/Safety
31098	97	21270	Nat'l Security & Int'l Affairs	31521	11	32	Food Svcs & Drinking Places	31721	249	1472	Relig., Grant, Civic, Prof Org
31099	1	0	Personal and Laundry Services	31522	1041	8251	Accommodation	31722	12	55	Machinery Manufacturing
31106	1	3	Prof., Scientific, & Tech Svcs	31523	324	2073	Food Svcs & Drinking Places	31727	2	5	Merch. Wholesalers,Durable Gds
31107	7	19	Unclassified Establishments	31524	10	214	Unclassified Establishments	31730	449	5033	Food Manufacturing
31119	8	26	Prof., Scientific, & Tech Svcs	31525	719	10300	Justice, Pubic Order/Safety	31733	34	134	Relig., Grant, Civic, Prof Org
31126	4	15	Administrative & Support Svcs	31527	81	1904	Accommodation	31735	30	184	Merch. Wholesalers,Durable Gds
31131	5	6	Construction of Buildings	31532	15	35	Wood Product Manufacturing	31738	49	503	Merch. Wholesalers,Durable Gds
31139	7	12	Prof., Scientific, & Tech Svcs	31533	1008	11329	Merch. Wholesalers,Nondur. Gds	31739	1	2	Insurance Carriers & Related
31141	8	8	Credit Intermediation & Relatd	31534	2	2	Merch. Wholesalers,Nondur. Gds	31743	11	27	Animal Production
31145	8	22	Miscellaneous Manufacturing	31535	199	3185	Transportation Equipment Mfg	31744	72	410	Bldg Matl & Garden Eqpmt Dlrs
31146	3	11	Electronics & Appliance Stores	31537	305	1863	Educational Services	31747	9	46	Merch. Wholesalers,Durable Gds
31150	2	6	Administrative & Support Svcs	31539	486	4964	Plastics & Rubber Products Mfg	31749	38	129	Merch. Wholesalers,Nondur. Gds
31156	1	1	Prof., Scientific, & Tech Svcs	31542	78	365	Special Trade Contractors	31750	693	8013	Transportation Equipment Mfg
31201	1476	13997	Ambulatory Health Care Svcs	31543	68	187	Food and Beverage Stores	31753	18	92	Educational Services
31202	2	6	Administrative & Support Svcs	31544	20	77	Special Trade Contractors	31756	13	54	Educational Services
31203	2	2	Repair and Maintenance	31545	613	6528	Paper Manufacturing	31757	296	2837	Prof., Scientific, & Tech Svcs
31204	1198	9522	Educational Services	31546	203	1172	Educational Services	31758	2	15	Social Assistance
31205	2	2	Couriers and Messengers	31547	38	9783	Nat'l Security & Int'l Affairs	31760	12	57	Truck Transportation
31206	1268	15603	Food Svcs & Drinking Places	31548	689	5035	Food Svcs & Drinking Places	31763	501	4014	Educational Services
31207	9	1488	Educational Services	31549	57	301	Nursing & Resid. Care Facilit.	31764	65	144	Telecommunications
31208	10	276	Justice, Pubic Order/Safety	31550	22	157	Educational Services	31765	56	231	Nonmetallic Mineral Prod. Mfg
31209	5	11	Motion Pict. & Sound Recording	31551	15	58	Truck Transportation	31768	1002	10042	Apparel Manufacturing
31210	1181	14629	Food Svcs & Drinking Places	31552	14	46	Chemical Manufacturing	31769	4	6	Food and Beverage Stores
31211	448	4218	Educational Services	31553	238	1441	Educational Services	31771	70	1038	Merch. Wholesalers,Nondur. Gds
31212	3	15	Miscellaneous Store Retailers	31554	89	1059	Textile Mills	31772	12	36	Personal and Laundry Services
31213	4	683	Postal Service	31555	48	239	Justice, Pubic Order/Safety	31773	67	427	Chemical Manufacturing
31216	347	4731	Transportation Equipment Mfg	31556	7	16	Merch. Wholesalers,Durable Gds	31774	239	2066	Ambulatory Health Care Svcs
31217	417	8939	Beverage & Tobacco Product Mfg	31557	91	506	Special Trade Contractors	31775	77	736	Crop Production
31220	205	1707	Exec., Legis., & Other Support	31558	650	5566	Paper Manufacturing	31776	9	41	Merch. Wholesalers,Nondur. Gds
31221	2	2	Isps, Web Search Portals	31560	73	264	Furniture & Related Prod. Mfg	31778	52	118	Food and Beverage Stores
31295	3	2540	Insurance Carriers & Related	31561	13	1953	Accommodation	31779	243	1960	Justice, Pubic Order/Safety
31297	17	1140	Air Transportation	31562	27	65	Educational Services	31780	62	328	Nursing & Resid. Care Facilit.
31301	36	153	Real Estate	31563	27	89	Educational Services	31781	39	107	Exec., Legis., & Other Support
31302	133	549	Special Trade Contractors	31564	7	27	Merch. Wholesalers,Nondur. Gds	31782	5	20	Merch. Wholesalers,Durable Gds
31303	16	103	Administrative & Support Svcs	31565	35	101	Special Trade Contractors	31783	14	84	Amusement, Gambling,& Recreat.
31304	14	61	Food Manufacturing	31566	84	199	Educational Services	31784	12	39	Merch. Wholesalers,Nondur. Gds
31305	311	1610	Food Svcs & Drinking Places	31567	10	87	Educational Services	31787	34	180	Food and Beverage Stores
31307	14	64	Nonmetallic Mineral Prod. Mfg	31568	12	23	Food and Beverage Stores	31788	257	3241	General Merchandise Stores
31308	125	356	Food and Beverage Stores	31569	218	1580	Exec., Legis., & Other Support	31789	19	71	Social Assistance
31309	18	61	Special Trade Contractors	31598	9	16	Social Assistance	31790	46	270	Apparel Manufacturing
31310	7	9	Prof., Scientific, & Tech Svcs	31599	1	357	Justice, Pubic Order/Safety	31791	464	3405	Educational Services
31312	141	747	Educational Services	31601	1858	20945	Merch. Wholesalers,Durable Gds	31792	1440	16234	Hospitals
31313	1162	9335	Educational Services	31602	1265	12761	Ambulatory Health Care Svcs	31793	251	4182	Apparel Manufacturing
31314	49	20391	Nat'l Security & Int'l Affairs	31603	9	67	Unclassified Establishments	31794	1467	16640	Exec., Legis., & Other Support
31315	23	1471	Hospitals	31604	8	14	Educational Services	31795	41	197	Crop Production
31316	139	748	Educational Services	31605	230	1065	Educational Services	31796	38	92	Merch. Wholesalers,Nondur. Gds
31318	7	135	Wood Product Manufacturing	31606	73	179	Special Trade Contractors	31798	9	27	Repair and Maintenance
31319	11	16	Special Trade Contractors	31620	432	4310	Food Svcs & Drinking Places	31799	6	7	Miscellaneous Store Retailers
31320	238	1278	Relig., Grant, Civic, Prof Org	31622	37	336	Wood Product Manufacturing	31801	16	74	Justice, Pubic Order/Safety
31321	229	996	Educational Services	31623	3	8	Food and Beverage Stores	31803	172	2482	Food Manufacturing
31322	355	3656	General Merchandise Stores	31624	6	15	Food and Beverage Stores	31804	94	288	Educational Services
31323	38	968	Chemical Manufacturing	31625	5	22	Merch. Wholesalers,Nondur. Gds	31805	66	350	Educational Services
31324	538	3001	Food Svcs & Drinking Places	31626	64	158	Merch. Wholesalers,Nondur. Gds	31806	118	1345	Wood Product Manufacturing
31326	418	4204	Paper Manufacturing	31627	15	140	Merch. Wholesalers,Nondur. Gds	31807	33	238	Educational Services
31327	16	31	Admin. Enviro. Quality Progrms	31629	13	40	Merch. Wholesalers,Durable Gds	31808	108	679	Heavy & Civil Eng. Construct'N
31328	207	1050	Food Svcs & Drinking Places	31630	8	203	Construction of Buildings	31810	32	34	Relig., Grant, Civic, Prof Org
31329	263	1941	Educational Services	31631	23	110	Merch. Wholesalers,Durable Gds	31811	165	1148	Educational Services
31331	156	359	Food and Beverage Stores	31632	145	1149	Educational Services	31812	10	65	Nonmetallic Mineral Prod. Mfg
31333	23	183	Truck Transportation	31634	236	2350	Fabricated Metal Product Mfg	31814	2	1	Paper Manufacturing
31401	1903	17866	Food Svcs & Drinking Places	31635	178	1237	Hospitals	31815	93	397	Educational Services
31402	10	556	Postal Service	31636	333	2910	Food Svcs & Drinking Places	31816	254	2365	Miscellaneous Manufacturing
31403	4	6	Administrative & Support Svcs	31637	59	122	Crop Production	31820	93	2225	Transportation Equipment Mfg
31404	851	13180	Hospitals	31638	33	164	Educational Services	31821	5	56	Elect'l Eqpmt, App, & Comp Mfg

ZIP CODE	2004 Total Firms	2004 Total Employees	TOP INDUSTRY RANKED on 2004 EMPLOYMENT	ZIP CODE	2004 Total Firms	2004 Total Employees	TOP INDUSTRY RANKED on 2004 EMPLOYMENT	ZIP CODE	2004 Total Firms	2004 Total Employees	TOP INDUSTRY RANKED on 2004 EMPLOYMENT
31822	183	1795	Accommodation	32116	1	1	Special Trade Contractors	32237	4	7	Bldg Matl & Garden Eqpmt Dlrs
31823	16	1333	Merch. Wholesalers,Nondur. Gds	32117	1390	11700	Special Trade Contractors	32238	7	9	Support Act. for Transport.
31824	54	305	Bldg Matl & Garden Eqpmt Dlrs	32118	1176	10001	Accommodation	32239	20	82	Administrative & Support Svcs
31825	88	704	Wood Product Manufacturing	32119	931	6525	Food Svcs & Drinking Places	32240	9	21	Prof., Scientific, & Tech Svcs
31826	19	54	Bldg Matl & Garden Eqpmt Dlrs	32120	6	13	Administrative & Support Svcs	32241	36	68	Administrative & Support Svcs
31827	88	764	Admin. Human Resource Programs	32121	1	1	Administrative & Support Svcs	32244	658	7224	Motor Vehicle & Parts Dealers
31829	12	23	Relig., Grant, Civic, Prof Org	32122	3	2	Waste Managmt & Remediat'n Svc	32245	10	31	Electronics & Appliance Stores
31830	102	1834	Exec., Legis., & Other Support	32123	3	5	Special Trade Contractors	32246	1050	8904	Credit Intermediation & Relatd
31831	64	312	Nursing & Resid. Care Facilit.	32124	211	3833	Justice, Pubic Order/Safety	32247	11	39	Special Trade Contractors
31832	5	30	Food and Beverage Stores	32125	5	5	Administrative & Support Svcs	32250	1721	15547	Construction of Buildings
31833	275	3176	Textile Product Mills	32126	1	0	Transit & Grnd Pass. Transport	32254	1150	21293	Merch. Wholesalers,Nondur. Gds
31836	19	34	Justice, Pubic Order/Safety	32127	1064	7639	Food Svcs & Drinking Places	32255	6	12	Relig., Grant, Civic, Prof Org
31901	1340	23183	Hospitals	32128	268	1363	Food and Beverage Stores	32256	2203	47152	Administrative & Support Svcs
31902	6	11	Exec., Legis., & Other Support	32129	475	3777	Educational Services	32257	1502	11726	Food Svcs & Drinking Places
31903	551	3888	Educational Services	32130	145	1202	Computer & Electronic Prod Mfg	32258	257	3973	Nursing & Resid. Care Facilit.
31904	1689	20359	Prof., Scientific, & Tech Svcs	32131	171	1081	Justice, Pubic Order/Safety	32259	498	3215	Educational Services
31905	122	34173	Nat'l Security & Int'l Affairs	32132	414	2114	Exec., Legis., & Other Support	32260	16	41	Construction of Buildings
31906	705	5758	Educational Services	32133	4	4	Heavy & Civil Eng. Construct'N	32266	279	1751	Educational Services
31907	1071	12532	Food Svcs & Drinking Places	32134	189	495	Food and Beverage Stores	32277	420	2863	Educational Services
31908	17	54	Construction of Buildings	32135	15	43	Heavy & Civil Eng. Construct'N	32301	2579	23718	Prof., Scientific, & Tech Svcs
31909	937	12910	Food Svcs & Drinking Places	32136	297	1878	Motor Vehicle & Parts Dealers	32302	18	37	Prof., Scientific, & Tech Svcs
31914	2	1	Special Trade Contractors	32137	911	6104	Food Svcs & Drinking Places	32303	2295	19787	Food Svcs & Drinking Places
31917	6	12	Rental and Leasing Services	32138	12	72	General Merchandise Stores	32304	1098	16785	Perform'g Arts, Spec. Sports
31995	2	5	Clothing & Cloth'g Acc. Stores	32139	24	39	Accommodation	32305	516	2492	Educational Services
31999	1	1600	Insurance Carriers & Related	32140	30	62	Food and Beverage Stores	32306	22	584	Relig., Grant, Civic, Prof Org
32003	337	3562	Food Svcs & Drinking Places	32141	331	1691	Transportation Equipment Mfg	32307	8	2428	Educational Services
32004	14	54	Educational Services	32145	169	750	Social Assistance	32308	1770	18597	Ambulatory Health Care Svcs
32006	3	7	Repair and Maintenance	32147	34	215	Truck Transportation	32309	806	4489	Food and Beverage Stores
32007	9	37	Special Trade Contractors	32148	190	902	Educational Services	32310	430	4166	Support Act. for Transport.
32008	184	877	Bldg Matl & Garden Eqpmt Dlrs	32149	1	41	Merch. Wholesalers,Durable Gds	32311	268	2617	General Merchandise Stores
32009	21	57	Educational Services	32157	4	11	Food Svcs & Drinking Places	32312	824	5510	Educational Services
32011	338	1896	Food Svcs & Drinking Places	32158	25	33	Administrative & Support Svcs	32313	5	4	Credit Intermediation & Relatd
32013	3	7	Construction of Buildings	32159	724	8198	Nursing & Resid. Care Facilit.	32314	12	24	Special Trade Contractors
32024	165	810	Educational Services	32160	4	21	Merch. Wholesalers,Durable Gds	32315	12	56	Administrative & Support Svcs
32025	663	8721	Hospitals	32162	60	715	Special Trade Contractors	32316	3	57	Social Assistance
32026	1	3	Ambulatory Health Care Svcs	32164	208	2995	Prof., Scientific, & Tech Svcs	32317	192	1145	Educational Services
32030	2	6	Special Trade Contractors	32168	1175	6236	Food Svcs & Drinking Places	32318	5	10	Administrative & Support Svcs
32033	73	517	Merch. Wholesalers,Nondur. Gds	32169	457	2787	Food Svcs & Drinking Places	32320	333	1588	Exec., Legis., & Other Support
32034	1365	12233	Accommodation	32170	19	47	Construction of Buildings	32321	165	1445	Justice, Pubic Order/Safety
32035	13	46	Exec., Legis., & Other Support	32173	9	30	Nonmetallic Mineral Prod. Mfg	32322	185	742	Real Estate
32038	92	348	Educational Services	32174	2030	17300	Ambulatory Health Care Svcs	32323	9	12	Utilities
32040	92	484	Educational Services	32175	12	35	Special Trade Contractors	32324	156	5330	Hospitals
32041	4	43	Justice, Pubic Order/Safety	32176	597	3971	Food Svcs & Drinking Places	32326	11	24	Merch. Wholesalers,Durable Gds
32042	3	2	Postal Service	32177	1341	13264	Bldg Matl & Garden Eqpmt Dlrs	32327	577	3765	Educational Services
32043	606	8176	Justice, Pubic Order/Safety	32178	12	21	Social Assistance	32328	286	1159	Real Estate
32044	29	114	Educational Services	32179	197	592	Administrative & Support Svcs	32329	1	2	Accommodation
32046	207	1040	Educational Services	32180	144	1676	Merch. Wholesalers,Nondur. Gds	32330	24	131	Educational Services
32050	7	16	Prof., Scientific, & Tech Svcs	32181	63	155	Computer & Electronic Prod Mfg	32331	84	542	Social Assistance
32052	245	1865	Justice, Pubic Order/Safety	32182	28	105	Accommodation	32332	45	98	Exec., Legis., & Other Support
32053	63	208	Educational Services	32183	5	4	Special Trade Contractors	32333	325	2029	Wood Product Manufacturing
32054	213	3442	Hospitals	32185	2	1	Clothing & Cloth'g Acc. Stores	32334	51	612	Heavy & Civil Eng. Construct'N
32055	1217	11670	Hospitals	32187	77	314	Educational Services	32336	28	96	Food Svcs & Drinking Places
32056	22	54	Exec., Legis., & Other Support	32189	64	165	Special Trade Contractors	32337	9	59	Motor Vehicle & Parts Dealers
32058	63	497	Justice, Pubic Order/Safety	32190	32	340	Merch. Wholesalers,Nondur. Gds	32340	481	4289	Food Manufacturing
32059	50	150	Motor Vehicle & Parts Dealers	32192	25	48	Food and Beverage Stores	32343	58	729	Bldg Matl & Garden Eqpmt Dlrs
32060	381	4121	Merch. Wholesalers,Nondur. Gds	32193	51	158	Health & Personal Care Stores	32344	485	2857	Justice, Pubic Order/Safety
32061	3	4	Special Trade Contractors	32195	118	624	Support Activities: Agr./For.	32345	2	3	Real Estate
32062	31	160	Bldg Matl & Garden Eqpmt Dlrs	32201	8	28	Chemical Manufacturing	32346	101	431	Food Svcs & Drinking Places
32063	461	4673	Hospitals	32202	1244	26565	Prof., Scientific, & Tech Svcs	32347	481	3175	Justice, Pubic Order/Safety
32064	504	4812	Nursing & Resid. Care Facilit.	32203	13	2024	Postal Service	32348	320	3663	Paper Manufacturing
32065	530	3550	Food Svcs & Drinking Places	32204	928	21697	Hospitals	32350	19	46	Educational Services
32066	188	1113	Merch. Wholesalers,Nondur. Gds	32205	1162	12068	Educational Services	32351	770	7947	Merch. Wholesalers,Nondur. Gds
32067	19	90	Prof., Scientific, & Tech Svcs	32206	877	9389	Merch. Wholesalers,Durable Gds	32352	79	618	Administrative & Support Svcs
32068	616	5673	Furn. & Home Furnishgs Stores	32207	2562	28959	Hospitals	32353	4	15	Admin. Human Resource Programs
32071	37	126	Crop Production	32208	905	6022	Educational Services	32355	40	163	Petroleum & Coal Products Mfg
32072	9	42	Support Activities: Agr./For.	32209	838	13134	Ambulatory Health Care Svcs	32356	4	9	Accommodation
32073	1927	17844	Food Svcs & Drinking Places	32210	2036	13660	Food Svcs & Drinking Places	32357	4	3	Food and Beverage Stores
32079	35	177	Nursing & Resid. Care Facilit.	32211	1387	10405	Educational Services	32358	59	159	Prof., Scientific, & Tech Svcs
32080	807	4182	Food Svcs & Drinking Places	32212	64	1041	Nat'l Security & Int'l Affairs	32359	80	272	Food Svcs & Drinking Places
32082	1040	8165	Accommodation	32214	3	2504	Hospitals	32360	7	7	Food and Beverage Stores
32083	26	265	Furn. & Home Furnishgs Stores	32215	2	4	Exec., Legis., & Other Support	32361	1	2	Postal Service
32084	1995	15705	Educational Services	32216	2130	25984	Ambulatory Health Care Svcs	32362	18	100	Food and Beverage Stores
32085	24	96	Special Trade Contractors	32217	1038	6576	Educational Services	32399	167	22738	Exec., Legis., & Other Support
32086	1090	9268	Insurance Carriers & Related	32218	1212	16546	Beverage & Tobacco Product Mfg	32401	1771	18666	Educational Services
32087	64	814	Justice, Pubic Order/Safety	32219	321	3593	Merch. Wholesalers,Durable Gds	32402	6	10	Prof., Scientific, & Tech Svcs
32091	691	6822	Justice, Pubic Order/Safety	32220	277	3027	Merch. Wholesalers,Durable Gds	32403	62	1549	Ambulatory Health Care Svcs
32092	295	2283	Food Svcs & Drinking Places	32221	362	2986	Educational Services	32404	782	5763	Food Svcs & Drinking Places
32094	61	139	Merch. Wholesalers,Nondur. Gds	32222	61	185	Amusement, Gambling,& Recreat.	32405	1666	17922	Food Svcs & Drinking Places
32095	244	1847	Educational Services	32223	694	5518	Food Svcs & Drinking Places	32406	1	5	Special Trade Contractors
32096	89	1411	Chemical Manufacturing	32224	530	11159	Ambulatory Health Care Svcs	32407	674	6139	Food Svcs & Drinking Places
32097	372	2970	Justice, Pubic Order/Safety	32225	1525	14699	Food Svcs & Drinking Places	32408	678	4631	Food Svcs & Drinking Places
32099	5	10	Food Svcs & Drinking Places	32226	248	5969	Transportation Equipment Mfg	32409	152	904	Educational Services
32102	104	388	Food Svcs & Drinking Places	32227	1	1	Unclassified Establishments	32410	53	210	Food Svcs & Drinking Places
32105	8	180	Merch. Wholesalers,Nondur. Gds	32228	30	952	Special Trade Contractors	32412	1	1	Support Act. for Transport.
32110	528	3583	Special Trade Contractors	32229	4	115	Admin. of Economic Programs	32413	555	3540	Food Svcs & Drinking Places
32111	5	12	Administrative & Support Svcs	32232	1	1	Prof., Scientific, & Tech Svcs	32417	5	13	Construction of Buildings
32112	193	1669	Bldg Matl & Garden Eqpmt Dlrs	32233	675	8633	Postal Service	32420	44	112	Educational Services
32113	180	819	Educational Services	32234	142	1379	Fabricated Metal Product Mfg	32421	69	700	Truck Transportation
32114	2419	37588	Hospitals	32235	15	25	Administrative & Support Svcs	32422	3	3	Postal Service
32115	8	20	Relig., Grant, Civic, Prof Org	32236	15	22	Administrative & Support Svcs	32423	19	28	Crop Production

ZIP CODE	2004 Total Firms	2004 Total Employees	TOP INDUSTRY RANKED on 2004 EMPLOYMENT	ZIP CODE	2004 Total Firms	2004 Total Employees	TOP INDUSTRY RANKED on 2004 EMPLOYMENT	ZIP CODE	2004 Total Firms	2004 Total Employees	TOP INDUSTRY RANKED on 2004 EMPLOYMENT
32424	408	3184	Justice, Pubic Order/Safety	32588	11	24	Administrative & Support Svcs	32750	2474	16341	Merch. Wholesalers,Durable Gds
32425	395	3017	Justice, Pubic Order/Safety	32591	9	121	Petroleum & Coal Products Mfg	32751	1699	17028	Prof., Scientific, & Tech Svcs
32426	22	65	Food and Beverage Stores	32601	1625	16772	Exec., Legis., & Other Support	32752	15	31	Special Trade Contractors
32427	27	112	Justice, Pubic Order/Safety	32602	12	84	Exec., Legis., & Other Support	32753	1	4	Construction of Buildings
32428	528	5066	Repair and Maintenance	32603	103	845	Food Svcs & Drinking Places	32754	193	911	Educational Services
32430	23	99	Construction of Buildings	32604	8	19	Clothing & Cloth'g Acc. Stores	32756	14	25	Real Estate
32431	105	405	Educational Services	32605	743	8883	Ambulatory Health Care Svcs	32757	1079	8164	Nursing & Resid. Care Facilit.
32432	2	5	Merch. Wholesalers,Durable Gds	32606	878	8256	Food and Beverage Stores	32759	86	245	Fabricated Metal Product Mfg
32433	474	3640	Justice, Pubic Order/Safety	32607	665	5539	Food Svcs & Drinking Places	32762	28	99	Administrative & Support Svcs
32434	2	9	Food and Beverage Stores	32608	923	15510	Food Svcs & Drinking Places	32763	1066	8139	Food Svcs & Drinking Places
32435	267	2731	Ambulatory Health Care Svcs	32609	1050	12146	Hospitals	32764	112	430	Educational Services
32437	19	167	Perform'g Arts, Spec. Sports	32610	73	3026	Ambulatory Health Care Svcs	32765	1600	10682	Food Svcs & Drinking Places
32438	36	114	Social Assistance	32611	41	1315	Other Information Services	32766	143	325	Educational Services
32439	246	1275	Educational Services	32614	11	43	Special Trade Contractors	32767	49	191	Educational Services
32440	194	1318	Educational Services	32615	452	4810	Merch. Wholesalers,Durable Gds	32768	17	105	Merch. Wholesalers,Nondur. Gds
32442	69	193	Educational Services	32616	9	25	Special Trade Contractors	32771	1982	19898	Rental and Leasing Services
32443	40	86	Food and Beverage Stores	32617	140	455	Educational Services	32772	7	8	Social Assistance
32444	458	4451	Credit Intermediation & Relatd	32618	130	464	Machinery Manufacturing	32773	1034	10281	Educational Services
32445	42	250	Educational Services	32619	77	503	Animal Production	32774	8	21	Other Information Services
32446	681	7400	Educational Services	32621	164	1497	Educational Services	32775	15	86	Support Activities: Agr./For.
32447	7	24	Administrative & Support Svcs	32622	36	123	Special Trade Contractors	32776	236	1048	Bldg Matl & Garden Eqpmt Dlrs
32448	346	3292	General Merchandise Stores	32625	127	473	Food Svcs & Drinking Places	32777	6	318	Construction of Buildings
32449	11	20	Administrative & Support Svcs	32626	434	2934	General Merchandise Stores	32778	965	7675	Justice, Pubic Order/Safety
32452	3	2	Postal Service	32627	8	26	Special Trade Contractors	32779	1040	6793	Insurance Carriers & Related
32454	33	65	Bldg Matl & Garden Eqpmt Dlrs	32628	207	1907	Justice, Pubic Order/Safety	32780	1317	12049	Justice, Pubic Order/Safety
32455	79	436	Educational Services	32631	10	28	Crop Production	32781	8	14	Relig., Grant, Civic, Prof Org
32456	561	2870	Telecommunications	32633	1	1	Postal Service	32782	4	9	Special Trade Contractors
32459	894	4202	Food Svcs & Drinking Places	32634	13	46	Crop Production	32783	5	9	Administrative & Support Svcs
32460	109	1020	Justice, Pubic Order/Safety	32635	4	20	Administrative & Support Svcs	32784	400	1644	Educational Services
32461	2	9	Personal and Laundry Services	32639	9	53	Nonmetallic Mineral Prod. Mfg	32789	3135	21973	Prof., Scientific, & Tech Svcs
32462	80	417	Educational Services	32640	219	1433	Wood Product Manufacturing	32790	25	79	Nonstore Retailers
32463	7	17	Food and Beverage Stores	32641	251	3885	Educational Services	32791	29	79	Administrative & Support Svcs
32464	58	101	Food and Beverage Stores	32643	358	2102	Prof., Scientific, & Tech Svcs	32792	2351	18309	Food Svcs & Drinking Places
32465	203	1407	Justice, Pubic Order/Safety	32644	8	10	Furn. & Home Furnishgs Stores	32793	7	27	Merch. Wholesalers,Durable Gds
32466	87	352	Educational Services	32648	17	46	Amusement, Gambling,& Recreat.	32794	28	116	Social Assistance
32501	1242	17751	Hospitals	32653	342	3831	Special Trade Contractors	32795	27	76	Prof., Scientific, & Tech Svcs
32502	902	10454	Prof., Scientific, & Tech Svcs	32654	1	2	Personal and Laundry Services	32796	698	6968	Hospitals
32503	1411	13678	Educational Services	32655	5	3	Publishing Industries	32798	92	770	Merch. Wholesalers,Durable Gds
32504	1428	17322	Ambulatory Health Care Svcs	32656	315	1807	Food Svcs & Drinking Places	32799	1	2	Credit Intermediation & Relatd
32505	1404	11991	Motor Vehicle & Parts Dealers	32658	16	33	Administrative & Support Svcs	32801	2456	36084	Prof., Scientific, & Tech Svcs
32506	782	5734	General Merchandise Stores	32662	3	2	Motor Vehicle & Parts Dealers	32802	16	42	Administrative & Support Svcs
32507	955	6163	Food Svcs & Drinking Places	32663	8	85	Merch. Wholesalers,Nondur. Gds	32803	2504	35395	Hospitals
32508	119	17610	Nat'l Security & Int'l Affairs	32664	74	103	Crop Production	32804	1752	16859	Ambulatory Health Care Svcs
32509	12	191	Justice, Pubic Order/Safety	32666	170	699	Accommodation	32805	1377	15476	Exec., Legis., & Other Support
32511	13	4205	Nat'l Security & Int'l Affairs	32667	126	470	Crop Production	32806	1619	35791	Hospitals
32512	15	110	Ambulatory Health Care Svcs	32668	92	324	Support Activities: Agr./For.	32807	1499	10799	Merch. Wholesalers,Durable Gds
32513	5	8	Special Trade Contractors	32669	312	2129	Educational Services	32808	1689	16425	Merch. Wholesalers,Nondur. Gds
32514	975	17905	Hospitals	32680	135	572	Heavy & Civil Eng. Construct'N	32809	2456	31443	Food Svcs & Drinking Places
32516	6	4	Educational Services	32681	23	161	Repair and Maintenance	32810	1228	14245	Administrative & Support Svcs
32520	2	407	Utilities	32683	7	24	Social Assistance	32811	1105	37634	Administrative & Support Svcs
32522	5	13	Exec., Legis., & Other Support	32686	151	855	Prof., Scientific, & Tech Svcs	32812	632	5177	Food and Beverage Stores
32523	2	8	Publishing Industries	32692	20	52	Food Svcs & Drinking Places	32814	20	122	Prof., Scientific, & Tech Svcs
32524	13	19	Administrative & Support Svcs	32693	289	3225	Justice, Pubic Order/Safety	32815	10	8	Transportation Equipment Mfg
32526	665	4461	Food Svcs & Drinking Places	32694	77	249	Food Svcs & Drinking Places	32816	30	4654	Educational Services
32530	20	130	Educational Services	32696	397	2413	Motor Vehicle & Parts Dealers	32817	862	7594	Food Svcs & Drinking Places
32531	150	515	Educational Services	32697	16	265	Mining (Except Oil and Gas)	32818	704	5169	Food Svcs & Drinking Places
32533	525	8121	Chemical Manufacturing	32701	1572	13572	Ambulatory Health Care Svcs	32819	2498	46019	Food Svcs & Drinking Places
32534	690	6742	Fabricated Metal Product Mfg	32702	69	527	Nursing & Resid. Care Facilit.	32820	138	984	Support Act. for Transport.
32535	132	1090	Justice, Pubic Order/Safety	32703	1819	18288	Special Trade Contractors	32821	503	20884	Accommodation
32536	888	5997	Food Svcs & Drinking Places	32704	23	59	Ambulatory Health Care Svcs	32822	1175	12378	Food Svcs & Drinking Places
32537	6	105	Wood Product Manufacturing	32706	13	36	Sportg Gds,Hobby,Book,& Music	32824	845	13061	Merch. Wholesalers,Durable Gds
32538	10	26	Justice, Pubic Order/Safety	32707	1518	9901	Food Svcs & Drinking Places	32825	512	3108	Educational Services
32539	389	3361	Hospitals	32708	1080	5384	Food Svcs & Drinking Places	32826	398	7466	Plastics & Rubber Products Mfg
32540	19	60	Heavy & Civil Eng. Construct'N	32709	65	226	Food and Beverage Stores	32827	196	6111	Educational Services
32541	1659	11720	Food Svcs & Drinking Places	32710	1	6	Administrative & Support Svcs	32828	429	3277	Food Svcs & Drinking Places
32542	89	2855	Hospitals	32712	804	4603	Educational Services	32829	80	847	Admin. Enviro. Quality Progrms
32544	42	360	Special Trade Contractors	32713	476	2446	Special Trade Contractors	32830	232	31606	Accommodation
32547	1504	9941	Hospitals	32714	2125	17262	Food Svcs & Drinking Places	32831	5	923	Exec., Legis., & Other Support
32548	1792	15640	Food Svcs & Drinking Places	32715	16	30	General Merchandise Stores	32832	59	514	Relig., Grant, Civic, Prof Org
32549	18	67	Prof., Scientific, & Tech Svcs	32716	17	48	Special Trade Contractors	32833	85	250	Construction of Buildings
32550	626	6241	Accommodation	32718	12	41	Merch. Wholesalers,Durable Gds	32835	698	4704	Food Svcs & Drinking Places
32559	1	5	Special Trade Contractors	32719	7	15	Prof., Scientific, & Tech Svcs	32836	318	6852	Accommodation
32560	7	32	Special Trade Contractors	32720	1661	13172	Exec., Legis., & Other Support	32837	1283	13330	Administrative & Support Svcs
32561	623	4599	Food Svcs & Drinking Places	32721	18	44	Administrative & Support Svcs	32839	830	8183	Justice, Pubic Order/Safety
32562	14	40	Ambulatory Health Care Svcs	32722	2	3	Construction of Buildings	32853	12	33	Relig., Grant, Civic, Prof Org
32563	796	4388	Food Svcs & Drinking Places	32724	849	8792	Miscellaneous Manufacturing	32854	19	102	Nonstore Retailers
32564	58	170	Merch. Wholesalers,Durable Gds	32725	1044	4979	Educational Services	32855	3	8	Prof., Scientific, & Tech Svcs
32565	227	1349	Educational Services	32726	961	5849	Food Svcs & Drinking Places	32856	18	35	Administrative & Support Svcs
32566	894	3520	Food Svcs & Drinking Places	32727	15	26	Construction of Buildings	32857	5	7	Special Trade Contractors
32567	102	338	Educational Services	32728	13	37	Administrative & Support Svcs	32858	5	23	Administrative & Support Svcs
32568	71	385	Wood Product Manufacturing	32730	333	2629	Food Svcs & Drinking Places	32859	14	36	Administrative & Support Svcs
32569	546	3481	Food Svcs & Drinking Places	32732	139	390	Special Trade Contractors	32860	16	32	Truck Transportation
32570	1016	7514	Educational Services	32733	27	87	Special Trade Contractors	32861	12	53	Administrative & Support Svcs
32571	816	4445	General Merchandise Stores	32735	40	104	Real Estate	32862	12	2040	Postal Service
32572	11	32	Special Trade Contractors	32736	226	1033	Merch. Wholesalers,Nondur. Gds	32867	10	25	Special Trade Contractors
32577	105	333	Special Trade Contractors	32738	437	1830	Educational Services	32868	16	60	Administrative & Support Svcs
32578	1034	7692	Food Svcs & Drinking Places	32739	11	28	Special Trade Contractors	32869	12	34	Personal and Laundry Services
32579	360	2501	Justice, Pubic Order/Safety	32744	145	436	Special Trade Contractors	32872	9	45	Transit & Grnd Pass. Transport
32580	174	1778	Special Trade Contractors	32746	1415	19630	Prof., Scientific, & Tech Svcs	32877	16	81	Special Trade Contractors
32583	542	3481	Justice, Pubic Order/Safety	32747	4	218	Construction of Buildings	32878	10	32	Electronics & Appliance Stores

BUSINESS DATA

ZIP CODE	2004 Total Firms	2004 Total Employ-ees	TOP INDUSTRY RANKED on 2004 EMPLOYMENT	ZIP CODE	2004 Total Firms	2004 Total Employ-ees	TOP INDUSTRY RANKED on 2004 EMPLOYMENT	ZIP CODE	2004 Total Firms	2004 Total Employ-ees	TOP INDUSTRY RANKED on 2004 EMPLOYMENT
32887	2	1001	Publishing Industries	33039	17	162	Nat'l Security & Int'l Affairs	33169	1581	19708	Administrative & Support Svcs
32893	1	40	Exec., Legis., & Other Support	33040	2819	22128	Food Svcs & Drinking Places	33170	279	2989	Merch. Wholesalers,Nondur. Gds
32899	12	2651	Space Research and Technology	33041	15	34	Unclassified Establishments	33172	2397	36920	Justice, Pubic Order/Safety
32901	2190	22426	Hospitals	33042	274	1071	Accommodation	33173	1213	8715	Ambulatory Health Care Svcs
32902	12	19	Real Estate	33043	355	1560	Relig., Grant, Civic, Prof Org	33174	800	4070	Food Svcs & Drinking Places
32903	516	2682	Accommodation	33045	13	23	Special Trade Contractors	33175	1045	8851	Ambulatory Health Care Svcs
32904	1419	16323	Transportation Equipment Mfg	33050	971	5631	Accommodation	33176	2372	25881	Ambulatory Health Care Svcs
32905	1058	10316	Computer & Electronic Prod Mfg	33051	50	192	Food Svcs & Drinking Places	33177	512	4519	Food and Beverage Stores
32906	5	8	Nursing & Resid. Care Facilit.	33052	4	5	Motor Vehicle & Parts Dealers	33178	1532	26932	Administrative & Support Svcs
32907	592	5006	Exec., Legis., & Other Support	33054	1358	12491	Educational Services	33179	1064	8647	Credit Intermediation & Relatd
32908	70	458	Educational Services	33055	384	2673	Educational Services	33180	1854	17162	Real Estate
32909	396	2065	Educational Services	33056	637	5161	Educational Services	33181	1124	13408	Motion Pict. & Sound Recording
32910	7	17	Administrative & Support Svcs	33060	1777	10953	Relig., Grant, Civic, Prof Org	33182	87	595	Educational Services
32911	4	12	Construction of Buildings	33061	14	16	Prof., Scientific, & Tech Svcs	33183	665	7266	Credit Intermediation & Relatd
32912	8	19	Prof., Scientific, & Tech Svcs	33062	1488	8644	Food Svcs & Drinking Places	33184	363	2435	Food and Beverage Stores
32919	1	430	Computer & Electronic Prod Mfg	33063	1764	12611	Educational Services	33185	198	1722	Educational Services
32920	593	4960	Prof., Scientific, & Tech Svcs	33064	2545	22451	Administrative & Support Svcs	33186	3132	17891	Food Svcs & Drinking Places
32922	1300	8173	Educational Services	33065	2365	16839	Prof., Scientific, & Tech Svcs	33187	259	2297	Merch. Wholesalers,Nondur. Gds
32923	11	40	Relig., Grant, Civic, Prof Org	33066	135	888	Educational Services	33189	457	4233	General Merchandise Stores
32924	4	4	Construction of Buildings	33067	659	3938	General Merchandise Stores	33190	37	545	Ambulatory Health Care Svcs
32925	50	3266	Nat'l Security & Int'l Affairs	33068	743	9679	Prof., Scientific, & Tech Svcs	33193	246	1464	Educational Services
32926	701	4854	Special Trade Contractors	33069	2471	28814	Special Trade Contractors	33194	24	667	Accommodation
32927	506	2836	Justice, Pubic Order/Safety	33070	439	2389	Food and Beverage Stores	33196	453	4581	Merch. Wholesalers,Durable Gds
32931	1011	7155	Food Svcs & Drinking Places	33071	1230	10695	Food Svcs & Drinking Places	33197	14	30	Administrative & Support Svcs
32932	14	814	Administrative & Support Svcs	33072	4	13	Prof., Scientific, & Tech Svcs	33199	5	421	Other Information Services
32934	579	4752	Merch. Wholesalers,Durable Gds	33073	946	8328	Motor Vehicle & Parts Dealers	33231	1	1	Paper Manufacturing
32935	1983	12490	Food Svcs & Drinking Places	33074	6	7	Special Trade Contractors	33233	7	19	Prof., Scientific, & Tech Svcs
32936	17	29	Prof., Scientific, & Tech Svcs	33075	12	52	Administrative & Support Svcs	33234	2	5	Elect'l Eqpmt, App, & Comp Mfg
32937	1110	6088	Food Svcs & Drinking Places	33076	577	3926	Educational Services	33239	4	21	Special Trade Contractors
32940	980	9126	Food Svcs & Drinking Places	33077	12	36	Nonmetallic Mineral Prod. Mfg	33242	5	38	Beverage & Tobacco Product Mfg
32941	17	37	Isps, Web Search Portals	33081	15	32	Ambulatory Health Care Svcs	33243	14	25	Prof., Scientific, & Tech Svcs
32948	99	1140	Merch. Wholesalers,Nondur. Gds	33082	20	49	Merch. Wholesalers,Durable Gds	33245	7	18	Prof., Scientific, & Tech Svcs
32949	84	236	Prof., Scientific, & Tech Svcs	33083	6	22	Administrative & Support Svcs	33247	4	3	Special Trade Contractors
32950	145	786	Heavy & Civil Eng. Construct'N	33084	16	27	Merch. Wholesalers,Durable Gds	33255	4	10	Merch. Wholesalers,Durable Gds
32951	337	1181	Food and Beverage Stores	33090	19	55	Administrative & Support Svcs	33256	30	94	Administrative & Support Svcs
32952	870	6986	General Merchandise Stores	33092	9	35	Special Trade Contractors	33257	9	17	Social Assistance
32953	978	7313	Motor Vehicle & Parts Dealers	33093	9	14	Prof., Scientific, & Tech Svcs	33261	7	47	Bldg Matl & Garden Eqpmt Dlrs
32954	15	36	Merch. Wholesalers,Durable Gds	33097	5	23	Prof., Scientific, & Tech Svcs	33265	23	66	Merch. Wholesalers,Durable Gds
32955	1045	12602	Hospitals	33101	14	43	Real Estate	33266	7	14	Special Trade Contractors
32956	11	14	Administrative & Support Svcs	33102	1	21	Ambulatory Health Care Svcs	33269	12	34	Transit & Grnd Pass. Transport
32957	15	36	Miscellaneous Store Retailers	33109	118	185	Real Estate	33280	6	31	Prof., Scientific, & Tech Svcs
32958	880	5866	Food and Beverage Stores	33112	5	21	Merch. Wholesalers,Durable Gds	33283	24	79	Personal and Laundry Services
32959	12	261	Justice, Pubic Order/Safety	33114	19	40	Publishing Industries	33296	6	22	Administrative & Support Svcs
32960	2405	18861	Hospitals	33116	20	114	Prof., Scientific, & Tech Svcs	33299	7	414	Food Svcs & Drinking Places
32961	21	92	Administrative & Support Svcs	33119	5	5	Publishing Industries	33301	2131	25350	Prof., Scientific, & Tech Svcs
32962	631	3697	Special Trade Contractors	33122	1492	14364	Merch. Wholesalers,Durable Gds	33302	8	92	Air Transportation
32963	818	5470	Relig., Grant, Civic, Prof Org	33124	5	226	Educational Services	33303	5	10	Special Trade Contractors
32964	11	30	Prof., Scientific, & Tech Svcs	33125	1281	10275	Hospitals	33304	1474	10180	Motor Vehicle & Parts Dealers
32965	9	26	Couriers and Messengers	33126	2452	32062	Administrative & Support Svcs	33305	620	4611	Food Svcs & Drinking Places
32966	544	6730	General Merchandise Stores	33127	1135	10562	Merch. Wholesalers,Durable Gds	33306	851	5034	Food Svcs & Drinking Places
32967	466	3229	Merch. Wholesalers,Nondur. Gds	33128	364	7602	Exec., Legis., & Other Support	33307	12	32	Real Estate
32968	284	1875	Food Manufacturing	33129	420	2014	Real Estate	33308	2072	15450	Hospitals
32969	5	17	Special Trade Contractors	33130	1241	15681	Ambulatory Health Care Svcs	33309	3127	36864	Administrative & Support Svcs
32970	39	1002	Merch. Wholesalers,Nondur. Gds	33131	2743	27624	Prof., Scientific, & Tech Svcs	33310	15	37	Real Estate
32971	6	14	Furniture & Related Prod. Mfg	33132	1293	17055	Educational Services	33311	2795	20545	Ambulatory Health Care Svcs
32976	184	888	Food and Beverage Stores	33133	1659	16202	Prof., Scientific, & Tech Svcs	33312	2019	16244	Prof., Scientific, & Tech Svcs
32978	3	29	Special Trade Contractors	33134	3702	27682	Prof., Scientific, & Tech Svcs	33313	1454	12109	Ambulatory Health Care Svcs
33001	23	83	Real Estate	33135	1587	7294	Ambulatory Health Care Svcs	33314	1574	11191	Educational Services
33002	3	2	Support Activities: Agr./For.	33136	542	22381	Hospitals	33315	968	11131	Support Act. for Transport.
33004	1117	8968	Amusement, Gambling,& Recreat.	33137	1137	12260	Miscellaneous Manufacturing	33316	2038	24563	Hospitals
33008	6	21	Fabricated Metal Product Mfg	33138	1373	7077	Merch. Wholesalers,Durable Gds	33317	1550	12629	Motor Vehicle & Parts Dealers
33009	1893	13274	Food Svcs & Drinking Places	33139	2810	27562	Food Svcs & Drinking Places	33318	21	135	Transit & Grnd Pass. Transport
33010	1922	14506	Broadcasting	33140	1121	9578	Accommodation	33319	1271	6946	Food Svcs & Drinking Places
33011	4	5	Administrative & Support Svcs	33141	923	5040	Accommodation	33320	8	18	Administrative & Support Svcs
33012	2700	17453	Ambulatory Health Care Svcs	33142	2763	30721	Admin. of Economic Programs	33321	1109	7187	Ambulatory Health Care Svcs
33013	1056	8701	Hospitals	33143	1842	13485	Ambulatory Health Care Svcs	33322	973	7974	Telecommunications
33014	1810	23562	Miscellaneous Manufacturing	33144	1690	9020	Food Svcs & Drinking Places	33323	826	11967	Telecommunications
33015	874	7282	Educational Services	33145	1159	6413	Prof., Scientific, & Tech Svcs	33324	2071	19711	Food Svcs & Drinking Places
33016	2239	17091	Merch. Wholesalers,Durable Gds	33146	1132	10619	Prof., Scientific, & Tech Svcs	33325	697	5872	Prof., Scientific, & Tech Svcs
33017	8	38	Real Estate	33147	1288	11630	Educational Services	33326	1115	8135	Food Svcs & Drinking Places
33018	637	4538	Educational Services	33149	586	5067	Accommodation	33327	237	629	Educational Services
33019	514	2426	Food Svcs & Drinking Places	33150	697	6922	Hospitals	33328	927	6060	Educational Services
33020	2617	18281	Prof., Scientific, & Tech Svcs	33151	2	3	Postal Service	33329	23	91	Scenic & Sightseeing Transport
33021	2419	21625	Hospitals	33152	14	2073	Postal Service	33330	491	3346	Food and Beverage Stores
33022	13	198	Postal Service	33153	5	24	Special Trade Contractors	33331	513	5721	Ambulatory Health Care Svcs
33023	2174	11927	Special Trade Contractors	33154	742	5409	Accommodation	33332	181	1749	Justice, Pubic Order/Safety
33024	2190	15258	Food Svcs & Drinking Places	33155	2950	16885	Prof., Scientific, & Tech Svcs	33334	2320	16166	Special Trade Contractors
33025	772	12401	Merch. Wholesalers,Durable Gds	33156	2014	16564	Prof., Scientific, & Tech Svcs	33335	15	60	Administrative & Support Svcs
33026	965	8239	General Merchandise Stores	33157	2084	15831	Managmt of Companies & Enterp.	33337	2	4700	Administrative & Support Svcs
33027	595	6220	Food Svcs & Drinking Places	33158	87	448	Relig., Grant, Civic, Prof Org	33338	9	113	Motion Pict. & Sound Recording
33028	375	3829	Hospitals	33159	63	1955	Support Act. for Transport.	33339	9	10	Prof., Scientific, & Tech Svcs
33029	632	4171	Educational Services	33160	1222	9689	Food Svcs & Drinking Places	33345	16	101	Postal Service
33030	1117	9415	Educational Services	33161	1315	9792	Educational Services	33346	3	5	Real Estate
33031	253	2402	Merch. Wholesalers,Nondur. Gds	33162	1856	11635	Educational Services	33348	1	0	Postal Service
33032	461	3584	Educational Services	33163	4	13	Merch. Wholesalers,Durable Gds	33349	4	41	Administrative & Support Svcs
33033	381	3203	Educational Services	33164	6	7	Furniture & Related Prod. Mfg	33351	2084	14675	Ambulatory Health Care Svcs
33034	382	5333	General Merchandise Stores	33165	1618	9646	Educational Services	33355	26	38	Merch. Wholesalers,Durable Gds
33035	31	533	Nursing & Resid. Care Facilit.	33166	5731	46758	Merch. Wholesalers,Durable Gds	33359	4	7	Prof., Scientific, & Tech Svcs
33036	540	3779	Accommodation	33167	342	4947	Merch. Wholesalers,Nondur. Gds	33388	132	1142	Clothing & Cloth'g Acc. Stores
33037	1020	13079	Credit Intermediation & Relatd	33168	657	4154	Food and Beverage Stores	33394	103	1491	Prof., Scientific, & Tech Svcs

ZIP CODE	2004 Total Firms	2004 Total Employees	TOP INDUSTRY RANKED on 2004 EMPLOYMENT
33401	2909	29240	Prof., Scientific, & Tech Svcs
33402	8	23	Truck Transportation
33403	1006	6443	Motor Vehicle & Parts Dealers
33404	1595	17381	Special Trade Contractors
33405	1193	8363	Prof., Scientific, & Tech Svcs
33406	1200	14006	Justice, Pubic Order/Safety
33407	1720	25850	Insurance Carriers & Related
33408	1540	11164	Managmt of Companies & Enterp.
33409	2259	19254	Food Svcs & Drinking Places
33410	1969	19254	Ambulatory Health Care Svcs
33411	1758	18147	Merch. Wholesalers,Durable Gds
33412	389	1872	Amusement, Gambling,& Recreat.
33413	356	3365	Merch. Wholesalers,Durable Gds
33414	1545	9793	Food Svcs & Drinking Places
33415	1053	8633	Motor Vehicle & Parts Dealers
33416	41	1269	Relig., Grant, Civic, Prof Org
33417	594	3513	Nursing & Resid. Care Facilit.
33418	594	4962	Accommodation
33419	7	16	Heavy & Civil Eng. Construct'N
33420	31	104	Special Trade Contractors
33421	15	26	Construction of Buildings
33422	10	31	Administrative & Support Svcs
33424	12	45	Special Trade Contractors
33425	11	90	Support Activities: Agr./For.
33426	1418	14441	Hospitals
33427	18	106	Telecommunications
33428	1058	7945	Relig., Grant, Civic, Prof Org
33429	13	38	Real Estate
33430	698	8737	Merch. Wholesalers,Nondur. Gds
33431	3176	32169	Prof., Scientific, & Tech Svcs
33432	2875	19328	Accommodation
33433	1252	9880	Nursing & Resid. Care Facilit.
33434	974	7224	Food Svcs & Drinking Places
33435	1300	7919	Exec., Legis., & Other Support
33436	761	5272	General Merchandise Stores
33437	696	4611	Administrative & Support Svcs
33438	27	381	Educational Services
33439	1	250	Food Manufacturing
33440	582	5109	Food Manufacturing
33441	1718	11469	Food Svcs & Drinking Places
33442	1440	19878	Credit Intermediation & Relatd
33443	15	31	Personal and Laundry Services
33444	1049	8610	Food Svcs & Drinking Places
33445	871	10458	Miscellaneous Store Retailers
33446	448	4644	Administrative & Support Svcs
33447	10	31	Special Trade Contractors
33448	1	4	Merch. Wholesalers,Durable Gds
33454	16	47	Health & Personal Care Stores
33455	330	2810	Educational Services
33458	2184	14797	Nursing & Resid. Care Facilit.
33459	7	14	Crop Production
33460	1227	6385	Educational Services
33461	1265	11272	Educational Services
33462	964	9679	Hospitals
33463	1188	8008	Food Svcs & Drinking Places
33464	1	500	Publishing Industries
33465	10	82	Social Assistance
33466	11	18	Administrative & Support Svcs
33467	1300	7586	Food Svcs & Drinking Places
33468	37	79	Administrative & Support Svcs
33469	767	3344	Prof., Scientific, & Tech Svcs
33470	730	4113	Hospitals
33471	209	1256	Exec., Legis., & Other Support
33474	18	44	Prof., Scientific, & Tech Svcs
33475	11	25	Administrative & Support Svcs
33476	169	1048	Educational Services
33477	707	5379	Food Svcs & Drinking Places
33478	392	3535	Transportation Equipment Mfg
33480	1194	13776	Accommodation
33481	23	90	Prof., Scientific, & Tech Svcs
33482	12	35	Publishing Industries
33483	1669	9712	Food Svcs & Drinking Places
33484	791	6309	Hospitals
33486	779	6521	Ambulatory Health Care Svcs
33487	1639	19592	Prof., Scientific, & Tech Svcs
33488	4	10	Administrative & Support Svcs
33493	94	1535	Social Assistance
33496	388	3943	Relig., Grant, Civic, Prof Org
33497	18	39	Prof., Scientific, & Tech Svcs
33498	466	2152	Food Svcs & Drinking Places
33499	1	385	Nonstore Retailers
33503	13	32	Exec., Legis., & Other Support
33508	10	22	Transit & Grnd Pass. Transport
33509	43	123	Special Trade Contractors
33510	421	3209	Educational Services
33511	2307	21317	Food Svcs & Drinking Places
33513	488	3823	Justice, Pubic Order/Safety
33514	41	205	Food Manufacturing
33521	31	216	Special Trade Contractors
33523	469	5174	Food Manufacturing
33524	11	57	Mining (Except Oil and Gas)
33525	710	5679	Justice, Pubic Order/Safety
33526	10	17	Support Act. for Transport.
33527	217	2372	Merch. Wholesalers,Nondur. Gds
33530	1	15	Perform'g Arts, Spec. Sports
33534	193	1372	Educational Services
33537	19	53	Relig., Grant, Civic, Prof Org
33538	150	540	Bldg Matl & Garden Eqpmt Dlrs
33539	6	9	Food Svcs & Drinking Places
33540	136	737	Waste Managmt & Remediat'n Svc
33541	392	4156	Hospitals
33542	767	4994	Ambulatory Health Care Svcs
33543	387	3849	Accommodation
33544	217	908	Educational Services
33547	154	1437	Merch. Wholesalers,Nondur. Gds
33548	223	946	Food and Beverage Stores
33549	670	4116	Food and Beverage Stores
33550	11	23	Special Trade Contractors
33556	563	3189	Special Trade Contractors
33558	209	1292	Amusement, Gambling,& Recreat.
33559	192	964	Educational Services
33563	1228	14037	Merch. Wholesalers,Nondur. Gds
33564	3	5	Administrative & Support Svcs
33565	208	1120	Educational Services
33566	395	6470	Food Manufacturing
33567	176	1207	Educational Services
33568	21	43	Construction of Buildings
33569	763	7883	Food and Beverage Stores
33570	404	3315	Justice, Pubic Order/Safety
33571	3	12	Administrative & Support Svcs
33572	269	1967	Merch. Wholesalers,Nondur. Gds
33573	306	4351	Nursing & Resid. Care Facilit.
33574	15	647	Educational Services
33575	4	9	Merch. Wholesalers,Nondur. Gds
33576	133	873	Food Svcs & Drinking Places
33583	9	24	Personal and Laundry Services
33584	500	7487	Furn. & Home Furnishgs Stores
33585	49	499	Utilities
33586	16	804	Merch. Wholesalers,Nondur. Gds
33587	2	3	Miscellaneous Store Retailers
33592	277	1814	Truck Transportation
33593	12	23	Heavy & Civil Eng. Construct'N
33594	677	5221	Food and Beverage Stores
33595	15	30	Administrative & Support Svcs
33597	140	545	Educational Services
33598	173	1411	Crop Production
33601	11	225	Social Assistance
33602	1857	27885	Prof., Scientific, & Tech Svcs
33603	684	5703	Educational Services
33604	1240	7118	Food and Beverage Stores
33605	1147	17161	Justice, Pubic Order/Safety
33606	1453	16683	Hospitals
33607	2405	41978	Hospitals
33608	1	8	Educational Services
33609	1980	18969	Prof., Scientific, & Tech Svcs
33610	1456	23518	Educational Services
33611	952	8386	Food and Beverage Stores
33612	1993	30809	Hospitals
33613	901	10429	Hospitals
33614	1943	18955	Motor Vehicle & Parts Dealers
33615	863	8028	Relig., Grant, Civic, Prof Org
33616	144	1988	Admin. Human Resource Programs
33617	1187	9442	Food Svcs & Drinking Places
33618	1791	13535	Food Svcs & Drinking Places
33619	2037	36292	Merch. Wholesalers,Durable Gds
33620	19	4408	Educational Services
33621	32	1118	Hospitals
33622	20	156	Food Svcs & Drinking Places
33623	10	147	Personal and Laundry Services
33624	775	6607	Administrative & Support Svcs
33625	558	5629	Food Svcs & Drinking Places
33626	456	5691	Administrative & Support Svcs
33629	1071	6447	Prof., Scientific, & Tech Svcs
33630	4	137	Postal Service
33634	1542	26519	Credit Intermediation & Relatd
33635	185	1125	Prof., Scientific, & Tech Svcs
33637	355	9095	Isps, Web Search Portals
33647	667	7707	Insurance Carriers & Related
33655	1	7	Repair and Maintenance
33660	1	0	Couriers and Messengers
33672	5	7	Isps, Web Search Portals
33673	1	0	Merch. Wholesalers,Durable Gds
33674	8	11	Credit Intermediation & Relatd
33675	3	35	Primary Metal Manufacturing
33677	3	8	Credit Intermediation & Relatd
33679	15	32	Prof., Scientific, & Tech Svcs
33680	4	21	Merch. Wholesalers,Durable Gds
33681	12	23	Administrative & Support Svcs
33682	14	12	Isps, Web Search Portals
33684	16	35	Special Trade Contractors
33685	19	46	Administrative & Support Svcs
33687	23	93	Special Trade Contractors
33688	44	240	Motor Vehicle & Parts Dealers
33689	3	6	Special Trade Contractors
33690	2	0	Special Trade Contractors
33694	10	55	Perform'g Arts, Spec. Sports
33697	1	1	Educational Services
33701	1748	18773	Ambulatory Health Care Svcs
33702	984	8593	Food Svcs & Drinking Places
33703	452	2960	Food Svcs & Drinking Places
33704	600	3828	Food and Beverage Stores
33705	611	7445	Hospitals
33706	917	7787	Accommodation
33707	978	8774	Credit Intermediation & Relatd
33708	786	7261	Hospitals
33709	779	8869	Social Assistance
33710	1467	11949	Food Svcs & Drinking Places
33711	603	6559	Educational Services
33712	555	4517	Educational Services
33713	1328	11859	Exec., Legis., & Other Support
33714	725	5005	Motor Vehicle & Parts Dealers
33715	193	845	Real Estate
33716	396	27515	Computer & Electronic Prod Mfg
33729	1	0	Electronics & Appliance Stores
33730	2	1400	Postal Service
33731	17	70	Prof., Scientific, & Tech Svcs
33732	14	45	Personal and Laundry Services
33733	18	54	Administrative & Support Svcs
33734	12	19	Administrative & Support Svcs
33736	4	11	Electronics & Appliance Stores
33737	3	9	Electronics & Appliance Stores
33738	5	13	Animal Production
33740	8	9	Publishing Industries
33741	2	6	Administrative & Support Svcs
33742	14	17	Publishing Industries
33743	23	41	Administrative & Support Svcs
33744	4	29	Credit Intermediation & Relatd
33747	6	16	Prof., Scientific, & Tech Svcs
33755	1080	7271	Prof., Scientific, & Tech Svcs
33756	1802	16929	Hospitals
33757	15	66	Social Assistance
33758	36	83	Administrative & Support Svcs
33759	685	8163	Construction of Buildings
33760	753	14694	Merch. Wholesalers,Durable Gds
33761	1208	10064	Food Svcs & Drinking Places
33762	1097	16014	Special Trade Contractors
33763	473	4392	Food Svcs & Drinking Places
33764	997	13976	Nonstore Retailers
33765	1353	13775	Educational Services
33766	16	20	Prof., Scientific, & Tech Svcs
33767	533	5325	Accommodation
33770	1070	11802	Ambulatory Health Care Svcs
33771	1141	10845	Food Svcs & Drinking Places
33772	809	7074	Nursing & Resid. Care Facilit.
33773	814	12703	Educational Services
33774	542	5498	Social Assistance
33775	24	50	Prof., Scientific, & Tech Svcs
33776	234	1647	Educational Services
33777	532	9193	Health & Personal Care Stores
33778	424	8116	Justice, Pubic Order/Safety
33779	24	58	Repair and Maintenance
33780	15	59	Special Trade Contractors
33781	1485	18208	Real Estate
33782	450	4929	Machinery Manufacturing
33784	5	3	Special Trade Contractors
33785	269	1595	Food Svcs & Drinking Places
33786	20	81	Exec., Legis., & Other Support
33801	1974	19819	Insurance Carriers & Related
33802	10	29	Special Trade Contractors
33803	1261	11407	Food Svcs & Drinking Places
33804	22	38	Merch. Wholesalers,Durable Gds
33805	597	8070	Ambulatory Health Care Svcs
33806	10	28	Administrative & Support Svcs
33807	39	75	Administrative & Support Svcs
33809	967	10083	General Merchandise Stores
33810	522	2797	Educational Services
33811	563	4732	Food and Beverage Stores
33813	1392	9499	Food Svcs & Drinking Places
33815	584	9220	Motor Vehicle & Parts Dealers
33820	16	119	Educational Services
33823	887	8863	Truck Transportation
33825	806	5287	Educational Services
33826	6	7	Relig., Grant, Civic, Prof Org
33827	51	218	Educational Services
33830	1070	16496	Justice, Pubic Order/Safety
33831	6	15	Social Assistance
33834	140	1078	Food Manufacturing
33835	9	7	Relig., Grant, Civic, Prof Org
33836	6	5	Merch. Wholesalers,Nondur. Gds
33837	302	2313	Hospitals

BUSINESS DATA

ZIP CODE	2004 Total Firms	2004 Total Employ-ees	TOP INDUSTRY RANKED on 2004 EMPLOYMENT	ZIP CODE	2004 Total Firms	2004 Total Employ-ees	TOP INDUSTRY RANKED on 2004 EMPLOYMENT	ZIP CODE	2004 Total Firms	2004 Total Employ-ees	TOP INDUSTRY RANKED on 2004 EMPLOYMENT
33838	187	1913	Support Activities: Agr./For.	33960	32	209	Prof., Scientific, & Tech Svcs	34270	13	35	Special Trade Contractors
33839	73	592	Educational Services	33965	3	758	Educational Services	34272	4	23	Relig., Grant, Civic, Prof Org
33840	27	274	Merch. Wholesalers,Nondur. Gds	33970	13	24	Transit & Grnd Pass. Transport	34274	9	27	Merch. Wholesalers,Durable Gds
33841	250	2467	Merch. Wholesalers,Nondur. Gds	33971	268	2607	General Merchandise Stores	34275	518	5269	Plastics & Rubber Products Mfg
33843	262	1969	Merch. Wholesalers,Nondur. Gds	33972	164	565	Amusement, Gambling,& Recreat.	34276	31	58	Special Trade Contractors
33844	932	7093	Accommodation	33975	7	51	Exec., Legis., & Other Support	34277	21	36	Merch. Wholesalers,Durable Gds
33845	5	22	Special Trade Contractors	33980	558	4699	Nursing & Resid. Care Facilit.	34278	10	42	Administrative & Support Svcs
33846	30	153	Educational Services	33981	118	319	Educational Services	34280	9	11	Special Trade Contractors
33847	7	16	Food and Beverage Stores	33982	243	1781	Support Activities: Agr./For.	34281	2	3	Ambulatory Health Care Svcs
33848	16	41	Special Trade Contractors	33983	149	862	Special Trade Contractors	34282	10	240	Heavy & Civil Eng. Construct'N
33849	15	187	General Merchandise Stores	33990	1334	14149	Perform'g Arts, Spec. Sports	34284	22	67	Heavy & Civil Eng. Construct'N
33850	150	1497	Beverage & Tobacco Product Mfg	33991	292	2324	Nursing & Resid. Care Facilit.	34285	1475	12024	Food Svcs & Drinking Places
33851	51	264	Merch. Wholesalers,Durable Gds	33993	141	599	Educational Services	34286	160	529	Educational Services
33852	802	4490	Food and Beverage Stores	33994	11	31	Special Trade Contractors	34287	520	2467	Food Svcs & Drinking Places
33853	687	6957	Food Manufacturing	34101	38	103	Merch. Wholesalers,Durable Gds	34288	37	337	Educational Services
33854	2	17	Real Estate	34102	2210	20430	Hospitals	34289	37	387	Prof., Scientific, & Tech Svcs
33855	22	53	Heavy & Civil Eng. Construct'N	34103	1385	11220	Real Estate	34292	429	3023	Nursing & Resid. Care Facilit.
33856	5	39	Food Svcs & Drinking Places	34104	1845	16567	Special Trade Contractors	34293	957	6479	General Merchandise Stores
33857	52	351	Crop Production	34105	298	4403	Nursing & Resid. Care Facilit.	34295	14	32	Special Trade Contractors
33858	16	29	Special Trade Contractors	34106	18	68	Waste Managmt & Remediat'n Svc	34420	901	4875	Educational Services
33859	312	3304	General Merchandise Stores	34107	8	53	Merch. Wholesalers,Durable Gds	34421	33	46	Special Trade Contractors
33860	482	5035	Merch. Wholesalers,Nondur. Gds	34108	966	7573	Accommodation	34423	12	16	Prof., Scientific, & Tech Svcs
33862	8	8	Special Trade Contractors	34109	1865	14116	Special Trade Contractors	34428	418	4092	Utilities
33863	3	15	Miscellaneous Store Retailers	34110	969	9033	Nursing & Resid. Care Facilit.	34429	874	5758	Food Svcs & Drinking Places
33865	18	103	Merch. Wholesalers,Durable Gds	34112	1158	9561	Exec., Legis., & Other Support	34430	10	34	Administrative & Support Svcs
33867	4	130	Accommodation	34113	431	4421	Food and Beverage Stores	34431	168	623	Educational Services
33868	176	1373	Justice, Pubic Order/Safety	34114	272	3050	Support Activities: Agr./For.	34432	434	2780	General Merchandise Stores
33870	1545	12102	Food Svcs & Drinking Places	34116	962	3941	Educational Services	34433	115	411	Educational Services
33871	9	20	Social Assistance	34117	323	1083	Special Trade Contractors	34434	122	510	Educational Services
33872	212	1943	Hospitals	34119	574	3700	Amusement, Gambling,& Recreat.	34436	207	570	Educational Services
33873	576	4679	Educational Services	34120	500	3850	Merch. Wholesalers,Nondur. Gds	34442	401	1754	Prof., Scientific, & Tech Svcs
33875	220	1288	Accommodation	34133	26	76	Administrative & Support Svcs	34445	11	49	Nonmetallic Mineral Prod. Mfg
33876	183	929	Food Svcs & Drinking Places	34134	980	7627	Food Svcs & Drinking Places	34446	415	1533	Food Svcs & Drinking Places
33877	19	673	Support Activities: Agr./For.	34135	1436	10458	Special Trade Contractors	34447	20	19	Construction of Buildings
33880	1547	12565	Food Svcs & Drinking Places	34136	6	37	Truck Transportation	34448	442	3052	Transportation Equipment Mfg
33881	1057	12005	Hospitals	34137	9	38	Justice, Pubic Order/Safety	34449	126	510	Heavy & Civil Eng. Construct'N
33882	10	32	Heavy & Civil Eng. Construct'N	34138	17	31	Food and Beverage Stores	34450	707	4315	Food Svcs & Drinking Places
33883	16	41	Publishing Industries	34139	76	421	Accommodation	34451	14	14	Administrative & Support Svcs
33884	554	4489	Nursing & Resid. Care Facilit.	34140	21	122	Food Svcs & Drinking Places	34452	264	2828	Hospitals
33885	2	0	Prof., Scientific, & Tech Svcs	34141	18	71	Social Assistance	34453	473	2578	General Merchandise Stores
33888	1	1776	Insurance Carriers & Related	34142	510	6143	Crop Production	34460	6	11	Construction of Buildings
33890	137	804	Merch. Wholesalers,Nondur. Gds	34143	1	10	Social Assistance	34461	447	3822	Educational Services
33896	68	695	Prof., Scientific, & Tech Svcs	34145	1150	6741	Accommodation	34464	4	5	Special Trade Contractors
33897	114	1007	Administrative & Support Svcs	34146	20	87	Special Trade Contractors	34465	318	1291	Ambulatory Health Care Svcs
33898	269	2366	General Merchandise Stores	34201	68	593	Food Svcs & Drinking Places	34470	1672	12396	Food Svcs & Drinking Places
33901	2419	31703	Hospitals	34202	292	2574	Heavy & Civil Eng. Construct'N	34471	1221	11089	Ambulatory Health Care Svcs
33902	12	13	Special Trade Contractors	34203	945	9491	General Merchandise Stores	34472	433	3347	Computer & Electronic Prod Mfg
33903	1118	7671	Food Svcs & Drinking Places	34204	15	59	Miscellaneous Store Retailers	34473	205	891	Food Svcs & Drinking Places
33904	1768	8715	Prof., Scientific, & Tech Svcs	34205	1694	13058	Prof., Scientific, & Tech Svcs	34474	1680	27566	Food Svcs & Drinking Places
33905	931	9358	Special Trade Contractors	34206	12	18	Unclassified Establishments	34475	930	9934	Justice, Pubic Order/Safety
33906	22	31	Construction of Buildings	34207	1114	8420	Food Svcs & Drinking Places	34476	337	993	Real Estate
33907	1950	17243	Food Svcs & Drinking Places	34208	930	11550	Ambulatory Health Care Svcs	34477	10	67	Construction of Buildings
33908	1424	14167	Social Assistance	34209	914	8715	Ambulatory Health Care Svcs	34478	46	407	Postal Service
33909	473	2690	Special Trade Contractors	34210	498	5863	Food Svcs & Drinking Places	34479	391	1617	Special Trade Contractors
33910	20	53	Real Estate	34211	70	615	Merch. Wholesalers,Nondur. Gds	34480	517	2036	Special Trade Contractors
33911	11	17	Prof., Scientific, & Tech Svcs	34212	96	656	Educational Services	34481	329	2525	Nursing & Resid. Care Facilit.
33912	2119	20610	Special Trade Contractors	34215	47	291	Food Svcs & Drinking Places	34482	599	4291	Support Activities: Agr./For.
33913	315	5111	Other Information Services	34216	80	585	Food Svcs & Drinking Places	34483	6	30	Special Trade Contractors
33914	646	3125	Food and Beverage Stores	34217	337	1909	Food Svcs & Drinking Places	34484	97	373	Special Trade Contractors
33915	22	37	Special Trade Contractors	34218	8	11	Transit & Grnd Pass. Transport	34487	4	5	Postal Service
33916	979	9929	Special Trade Contractors	34219	163	1073	Crop Production	34488	335	1608	Museums, Hist. Sites,& Similar
33917	644	3097	Bldg Matl & Garden Eqpmt Dlrs	34220	5	136	Merch. Wholesalers,Nondur. Gds	34489	17	29	Special Trade Contractors
33918	10	111	Administrative & Support Svcs	34221	951	9883	Merch. Wholesalers,Nondur. Gds	34491	542	3097	Heavy & Civil Eng. Construct'N
33919	1426	8490	Educational Services	34222	340	2404	Food Svcs & Drinking Places	34492	7	22	Administrative & Support Svcs
33920	148	714	Crop Production	34223	952	5475	Food Svcs & Drinking Places	34498	23	118	Relig., Grant, Civic, Prof Org
33921	185	1182	Accommodation	34224	573	2884	Food Svcs & Drinking Places	34601	1226	9682	Hospitals
33922	182	595	Merch. Wholesalers,Nondur. Gds	34228	348	3215	Food Svcs & Drinking Places	34602	149	2583	General Merchandise Stores
33924	81	1421	Accommodation	34229	259	981	Educational Services	34603	3	5	Special Trade Contractors
33927	1	2	Relig., Grant, Civic, Prof Org	34230	52	128	Credit Intermediation & Relatd	34604	251	2157	Special Trade Contractors
33928	434	3340	Food and Beverage Stores	34231	2032	12599	Food Svcs & Drinking Places	34605	6	7	Prof., Scientific, & Tech Svcs
33930	29	602	Support Activities: Agr./For.	34232	1259	9853	Food Svcs & Drinking Places	34606	986	6814	Food Svcs & Drinking Places
33931	765	4416	Food Svcs & Drinking Places	34233	1142	10542	Food Svcs & Drinking Places	34607	210	631	Food Svcs & Drinking Places
33932	6	8	Insurance Carriers & Related	34234	952	7225	Educational Services	34608	353	1679	Nursing & Resid. Care Facilit.
33935	628	5165	Support Activities: Agr./For.	34235	253	1811	Nursing & Resid. Care Facilit.	34609	714	4180	Food and Beverage Stores
33936	640	3586	Food and Beverage Stores	34236	2516	17330	Prof., Scientific, & Tech Svcs	34610	193	965	Heavy & Civil Eng. Construct'N
33938	15	27	Transit & Grnd Pass. Transport	34237	955	10906	Justice, Pubic Order/Safety	34611	12	24	Special Trade Contractors
33944	15	85	Prof., Scientific, & Tech Svcs	34238	578	5820	Nursing & Resid. Care Facilit.	34613	640	5594	Hospitals
33945	16	54	Accommodation	34239	1278	16319	Ambulatory Health Care Svcs	34614	92	323	Amusement, Gambling,& Recreat.
33946	93	737	Accommodation	34240	757	8110	Special Trade Contractors	34636	5	11	Special Trade Contractors
33947	93	729	Amusement, Gambling,& Recreat.	34241	240	1770	Special Trade Contractors	34639	643	4512	Educational Services
33948	667	8753	Ambulatory Health Care Svcs	34242	438	2547	Real Estate	34652	1734	10547	Ambulatory Health Care Svcs
33949	20	39	Prof., Scientific, & Tech Svcs	34243	1398	17999	Transportation Equipment Mfg	34653	722	5393	Nursing & Resid. Care Facilit.
33950	1202	9267	Hospitals	34250	18	165	Support Act. for Transport.	34654	477	4509	Prof., Scientific, & Tech Svcs
33951	27	72	Special Trade Contractors	34251	141	460	Crop Production	34655	564	4119	General Merchandise Stores
33952	1395	8199	Ambulatory Health Care Svcs	34264	7	27	Special Trade Contractors	34656	16	62	Transit & Grnd Pass. Transport
33953	372	2052	Ambulatory Health Care Svcs	34265	5	4	Special Trade Contractors	34660	6	24	Administrative & Support Svcs
33954	307	2164	Personal and Laundry Services	34266	877	8692	Support Activities: Agr./For.	34661	11	43	Justice, Pubic Order/Safety
33955	138	1142	Justice, Pubic Order/Safety	34267	10	51	Special Trade Contractors	34667	1363	9367	Ambulatory Health Care Svcs
33956	145	685	Food and Beverage Stores	34268	17	87	Social Assistance	34668	1442	10789	Food Svcs & Drinking Places
33957	619	3685	Food Svcs & Drinking Places	34269	68	352	Amusement, Gambling,& Recreat.	34669	384	1907	Educational Services

ZIP CODE	2004 Total Firms	2004 Total Employees	TOP INDUSTRY RANKED on 2004 EMPLOYMENT
34673	10	32	Administrative & Support Svcs
34674	13	25	Insurance Carriers & Related
34677	872	7748	Special Trade Contractors
34679	3	3	Postal Service
34680	19	150	Educational Services
34681	18	23	Prof., Scientific, & Tech Svcs
34682	27	69	Administrative & Support Svcs
34683	785	4450	Educational Services
34684	1119	10848	Nursing & Resid. Care Facilit.
34685	308	1973	Food Svcs & Drinking Places
34688	132	783	Educational Services
34689	1419	9547	Nursing & Resid. Care Facilit.
34690	315	1501	Food and Beverage Stores
34691	451	2602	Food Svcs & Drinking Places
34695	537	3665	Personal and Laundry Services
34697	19	43	Prof., Scientific, & Tech Svcs
34698	1357	15089	Hospitals
34705	76	480	Nonmetallic Mineral Prod. Mfg
34711	1715	10903	Food Svcs & Drinking Places
34712	21	25	Administrative & Support Svcs
34713	1	2	Transit & Grnd Pass. Transport
34729	3	3	Relig., Grant, Civic, Prof Org
34731	347	1691	Special Trade Contractors
34734	42	211	Personal and Laundry Services
34736	342	2340	Merch. Wholesalers,Nondur. Gds
34737	89	711	Accommodation
34739	35	159	Administrative & Support Svcs
34740	2	4	Nonstore Retailers
34741	2082	15047	Food Svcs & Drinking Places
34742	13	29	Administrative & Support Svcs
34743	381	1734	Educational Services
34744	1721	11641	Educational Services
34745	13	19	Prof., Scientific, & Tech Svcs
34746	1179	12740	Accommodation
34747	617	9751	Accommodation
34748	1765	16947	Hospitals
34749	15	24	Administrative & Support Svcs
34753	87	404	Educational Services
34755	87	416	Special Trade Contractors
34756	102	325	Educational Services
34758	173	2223	Merch. Wholesalers,Nondur. Gds
34759	160	1165	Food and Beverage Stores
34760	36	301	Bldg Matl & Garden Eqpmt Dlrs
34761	1042	10482	Merch. Wholesalers,Durable Gds
34762	41	659	Waste Managmt & Remediat'n Svc
34769	945	6336	Food Svcs & Drinking Places
34770	25	70	Special Trade Contractors
34771	303	959	Food and Beverage Stores
34772	267	927	Nursing & Resid. Care Facilit.
34773	49	240	Animal Production
34777	8	20	General Merchandise Stores
34778	2	4	Construction of Buildings
34785	430	3722	Admin. Human Resource Programs
34786	428	1824	Real Estate
34787	1292	10073	Special Trade Contractors
34788	530	4820	Food Svcs & Drinking Places
34789	3	5	Special Trade Contractors
34797	36	94	Prof., Scientific, & Tech Svcs
34945	242	3852	Support Activities: Agr./For.
34946	336	3167	Transportation Equipment Mfg
34947	475	4665	Educational Services
34948	7	14	Social Assistance
34949	180	1002	Food Svcs & Drinking Places
34950	1128	8151	Educational Services
34951	256	1623	Food and Beverage Stores
34952	1135	10507	Ambulatory Health Care Svcs
34953	353	1045	Special Trade Contractors
34954	6	8	Fabricated Metal Product Mfg
34956	205	2114	Justice, Pubic Order/Safety
34957	934	6786	Food Svcs & Drinking Places
34958	8	12	Special Trade Contractors
34972	811	5906	Animal Production
34973	8	26	Animal Production
34974	675	4312	Food Svcs & Drinking Places
34979	9	18	Perform'g Arts, Spec. Sports
34981	193	5557	Educational Services
34982	1057	9162	Exec., Legis., & Other Support
34983	362	1767	Educational Services
34984	331	1716	Justice, Pubic Order/Safety
34985	13	33	Ambulatory Health Care Svcs
34986	280	2684	Food Svcs & Drinking Places
34987	45	295	Merch. Wholesalers,Nondur. Gds
34988	4	4	Health & Personal Care Stores
34990	748	5751	Truck Transportation
34991	20	28	Special Trade Contractors
34992	11	28	Bldg Matl & Garden Eqpmt Dlrs
34994	2317	19307	Hospitals
34995	21	30	Social Assistance
34996	492	5890	Exec., Legis., & Other Support
34997	1226	9842	Food Svcs & Drinking Places
35004	233	2120	Merch. Wholesalers,Durable Gds
35005	150	1224	Educational Services
35006	55	179	Justice, Pubic Order/Safety
35007	699	12705	Credit Intermediation & Relatd
35010	887	7794	Nursing & Resid. Care Facilit.
35011	4	7	Relig., Grant, Civic, Prof Org
35013	4	4	Postal Service
35014	52	274	Educational Services
35015	1	2	Postal Service
35016	617	4703	Elect'l Eqpmt, App, & Comp Mfg
35019	42	479	Bldg Matl & Garden Eqpmt Dlrs
35020	1195	10132	Food and Beverage Stores
35022	610	8115	Hospitals
35023	628	5125	Exec., Legis., & Other Support
35031	169	1943	Food Manufacturing
35032	5	6	Machinery Manufacturing
35033	43	441	Machinery Manufacturing
35034	94	910	Clothing & Cloth'g Acc. Stores
35035	29	220	Merch. Wholesalers,Durable Gds
35036	14	20	Justice, Pubic Order/Safety
35038	1	2	Postal Service
35040	320	3087	Nonstore Retailers
35041	2	1	Special Trade Contractors
35042	227	1455	Nursing & Resid. Care Facilit.
35043	161	828	Educational Services
35044	269	3351	Forestry and Logging
35045	701	4966	General Merchandise Stores
35046	82	726	Miscellaneous Manufacturing
35048	15	140	Educational Services
35049	91	518	Educational Services
35051	328	3042	Textile Mills
35052	4	252	Nursing & Resid. Care Facilit.
35053	35	66	Motor Vehicle & Parts Dealers
35054	96	363	Educational Services
35055	1337	14896	General Merchandise Stores
35056	4	5	Administrative & Support Svcs
35057	242	1507	Transportation Equipment Mfg
35058	299	3585	Hospitals
35060	8	51	Merch. Wholesalers,Durable Gds
35061	49	551	Truck Transportation
35062	158	1068	Food Svcs & Drinking Places
35063	33	100	Merch. Wholesalers,Nondur. Gds
35064	430	7177	Primary Metal Manufacturing
35068	179	1366	Food Svcs & Drinking Places
35070	19	75	Construction of Buildings
35071	537	4162	Food Svcs & Drinking Places
35072	99	788	Furniture & Related Prod. Mfg
35073	94	512	Special Trade Contractors
35074	14	111	Food and Beverage Stores
35077	326	2991	Educational Services
35078	94	428	Special Trade Contractors
35079	71	455	Educational Services
35080	255	2216	Machinery Manufacturing
35082	4	5	Postal Service
35083	70	697	Merch. Wholesalers,Nondur. Gds
35085	143	928	Educational Services
35087	45	239	Admin. of Economic Programs
35089	30	90	Fishing, Hunting and Trapping
35091	33	93	Repair and Maintenance
35094	429	3975	Furniture & Related Prod. Mfg
35096	206	1467	Food Svcs & Drinking Places
35097	45	350	Educational Services
35098	15	29	Educational Services
35111	192	1434	Educational Services
35112	15	45	Special Trade Contractors
35114	37	237	Educational Services
35115	340	2956	Educational Services
35116	69	408	Educational Services
35117	83	440	Electronics & Appliance Stores
35118	70	236	Mining (Except Oil and Gas)
35119	3	6	Administrative & Support Svcs
35120	123	596	Educational Services
35121	613	4627	Educational Services
35123	9	41	Special Trade Contractors
35124	1330	13304	Merch. Wholesalers,Durable Gds
35125	519	4832	Fabricated Metal Product Mfg
35126	411	2670	Educational Services
35127	137	1021	Nursing & Resid. Care Facilit.
35128	244	1674	Credit Intermediation & Relatd
35130	41	207	Educational Services
35131	88	541	Nonmetallic Mineral Prod. Mfg
35133	55	220	Fabricated Metal Product Mfg
35135	40	166	Accommodation
35136	76	596	Textile Mills
35137	14	458	Merch. Wholesalers,Durable Gds
35139	4	8	Special Trade Contractors
35142	2	1	Postal Service
35143	47	238	Wood Product Manufacturing
35146	206	1567	Justice, Pubic Order/Safety
35147	59	261	Special Trade Contractors
35148	185	1551	General Merchandise Stores
35149	14	265	Truck Transportation
35150	850	7243	Hospitals
35151	110	1276	Chemical Manufacturing
35160	906	9375	Educational Services
35161	4	138	Educational Services
35171	70	632	Wood Product Manufacturing
35172	41	188	Waste Managmt & Remediat'n Svc
35173	532	6447	Food Svcs & Drinking Places
35175	118	468	Heavy & Civil Eng. Construct'N
35176	18	42	Fabricated Metal Product Mfg
35178	57	646	Fabricated Metal Product Mfg
35179	150	1288	Truck Transportation
35180	295	1880	Relig., Grant, Civic, Prof Org
35181	1	1	Postal Service
35182	4	8	Utilities
35183	10	84	Educational Services
35184	86	249	Educational Services
35185	15	99	Wood Product Manufacturing
35186	55	400	Prof., Scientific, & Tech Svcs
35187	8	17	Relig., Grant, Civic, Prof Org
35188	101	495	Educational Services
35201	6	261	Merch. Wholesalers,Durable Gds
35202	6	33	Social Assistance
35203	1583	26774	Prof., Scientific, & Tech Svcs
35204	446	5048	Exec., Legis., & Other Support
35205	1036	17754	Hospitals
35206	494	4084	Food Svcs & Drinking Places
35207	280	5537	Primary Metal Manufacturing
35208	394	2721	Food Svcs & Drinking Places
35209	2494	33728	Hospitals
35210	972	16670	General Merchandise Stores
35211	625	10866	Administrative & Support Svcs
35212	353	4259	Primary Metal Manufacturing
35213	395	6227	Hospitals
35214	457	5204	Truck Transportation
35215	1063	11260	Furniture & Related Prod. Mfg
35216	1653	14169	Food Svcs & Drinking Places
35217	586	10325	Merch. Wholesalers,Durable Gds
35218	284	2068	Educational Services
35219	4	65	Rental and Leasing Services
35220	7	11	Merch. Wholesalers,Durable Gds
35221	109	1320	Educational Services
35222	660	10047	Special Trade Contractors
35223	702	6578	Insurance Carriers & Related
35224	117	807	Special Trade Contractors
35226	508	2871	Educational Services
35228	234	1825	Educational Services
35229	6	1065	Educational Services
35231	4	5	Relig., Grant, Civic, Prof Org
35232	2	7	Exec., Legis., & Other Support
35233	907	21310	Ambulatory Health Care Svcs
35234	281	7307	Hospitals
35235	522	6522	Hospitals
35236	8	13	Administrative & Support Svcs
35238	15	51	Food Svcs & Drinking Places
35242	1301	16935	Food Svcs & Drinking Places
35243	986	13950	Prof., Scientific, & Tech Svcs
35244	1376	19541	Insurance Carriers & Related
35246	1	2	Prof., Scientific, & Tech Svcs
35249	23	6521	Hospitals
35253	5	24	Mining (Except Oil and Gas)
35254	1	350	Educational Services
35255	3	15	Administrative & Support Svcs
35259	4	5	Repair and Maintenance
35260	6	27	Insurance Carriers & Related
35261	8	40	Administrative & Support Svcs
35266	7	8	Prof., Scientific, & Tech Svcs
35285	6	59	Administrative & Support Svcs
35294	41	11418	Educational Services
35401	1850	34446	Educational Services
35402	4	5	Electronics & Appliance Stores
35403	4	11	Ambulatory Health Care Svcs
35404	621	8304	Hospitals
35405	917	11544	Food Svcs & Drinking Places
35406	300	4080	Prof., Scientific, & Tech Svcs
35407	4	12	Repair and Maintenance
35440	3	2	Construction of Buildings
35441	18	81	Educational Services
35442	182	1320	Wood Product Manufacturing
35443	31	144	Educational Services
35444	98	2118	Mining (Except Oil and Gas)
35446	29	98	Educational Services
35447	159	1253	Hospitals
35448	2	5	Food and Beverage Stores
35449	1	1	Postal Service
35452	55	179	Educational Services
35453	229	2196	Miscellaneous Manufacturing
35456	52	297	Special Trade Contractors
35457	7	17	Construction of Buildings

ZIP CODE	2004 Total Firms	2004 Total Employees	TOP INDUSTRY RANKED on 2004 EMPLOYMENT	ZIP CODE	2004 Total Firms	2004 Total Employees	TOP INDUSTRY RANKED on 2004 EMPLOYMENT	ZIP CODE	2004 Total Firms	2004 Total Employees	TOP INDUSTRY RANKED on 2004 EMPLOYMENT
35458	5	12	Food and Beverage Stores	35640	703	5609	Machinery Manufacturing	35956	125	801	Truck Transportation
35459	19	168	Waste Managmt & Remediat'n Svc	35643	59	228	Justice, Pubic Order/Safety	35957	586	8013	Food Manufacturing
35460	15	175	Wood Product Manufacturing	35645	267	1358	Educational Services	35958	75	256	Educational Services
35461	30	31	Computer & Electronic Prod Mfg	35646	99	668	Educational Services	35959	103	409	Educational Services
35462	240	1800	Hospitals	35647	11	115	Educational Services	35960	526	3552	Clothing & Cloth'g Acc. Stores
35463	18	61	Educational Services	35648	74	702	Apparel Manufacturing	35961	127	1662	Food Manufacturing
35464	15	50	Social Assistance	35649	9	67	Food Svcs & Drinking Places	35962	125	966	Nursing & Resid. Care Facilit.
35466	132	634	Educational Services	35650	463	3036	Food Svcs & Drinking Places	35963	16	25	Food and Beverage Stores
35469	7	15	Heavy & Civil Eng. Construct'N	35651	18	92	Educational Services	35964	25	175	Educational Services
35470	261	1974	Educational Services	35652	263	1141	Food Svcs & Drinking Places	35966	76	190	Food and Beverage Stores
35471	1	85	Merch. Wholesalers,Durable Gds	35653	510	4840	Ambulatory Health Care Svcs	35967	801	10836	Apparel Manufacturing
35473	263	1678	Administrative & Support Svcs	35654	149	889	Merch. Wholesalers,Nondur. Gds	35968	226	4011	Apparel Manufacturing
35474	130	1004	Paper Manufacturing	35660	476	4398	Ambulatory Health Care Svcs	35971	137	859	Educational Services
35475	133	890	Educational Services	35661	824	8795	Food Svcs & Drinking Places	35972	10	65	Accommodation
35476	695	7009	Food Svcs & Drinking Places	35662	4	86	Relig., Grant, Civic, Prof Org	35973	37	128	Educational Services
35477	13	49	Educational Services	35670	125	619	Educational Services	35974	87	522	Educational Services
35478	6	86	Special Trade Contractors	35671	72	4109	Transportation Equipment Mfg	35975	10	11	Food and Beverage Stores
35480	16	22	Utilities	35672	113	570	Relig., Grant, Civic, Prof Org	35976	824	9108	Food Manufacturing
35481	138	834	Apparel Manufacturing	35673	156	1374	Special Trade Contractors	35978	166	815	Apparel Manufacturing
35482	3	1	Real Estate	35674	571	5733	Educational Services	35979	41	239	Relig., Grant, Civic, Prof Org
35486	4	31	Educational Services	35677	25	101	Educational Services	35980	42	182	Educational Services
35487	25	707	Prof., Scientific, & Tech Svcs	35739	161	827	Justice, Pubic Order/Safety	35981	77	553	Educational Services
35490	61	2346	Transportation Equipment Mfg	35740	88	1912	Textile Product Mills	35983	95	783	Apparel Manufacturing
35491	2	3	Fishing, Hunting and Trapping	35741	77	511	Fabricated Metal Product Mfg	35984	61	592	Accommodation
35501	1050	9936	Hospitals	35742	7	310	Justice, Pubic Order/Safety	35986	333	2365	Educational Services
35502	7	24	Social Assistance	35744	33	119	Admin. of Economic Programs	35987	53	427	Fabricated Metal Product Mfg
35503	244	1290	Educational Services	35745	2	0	Fishing, Hunting and Trapping	35988	47	346	Merch. Wholesalers,Nondur. Gds
35504	231	1478	Nursing & Resid. Care Facilit.	35746	6	16	Gasoline Stations	35989	63	730	Furn. & Home Furnishgs Stores
35540	96	800	Construction of Buildings	35747	131	678	Educational Services	35990	18	97	Educational Services
35541	81	391	Educational Services	35748	146	715	Educational Services	36003	56	361	Miscellaneous Manufacturing
35542	13	20	Exec., Legis., & Other Support	35749	175	957	Educational Services	36005	27	144	Educational Services
35543	41	282	Merch. Wholesalers,Durable Gds	35750	280	1162	Educational Services	36006	26	121	Educational Services
35544	19	47	Construction of Buildings	35751	7	14	Construction of Buildings	36008	2	8	Food Manufacturing
35545	13	237	Merch. Wholesalers,Durable Gds	35752	56	267	Food Manufacturing	36009	56	402	Waste Managmt & Remediat'n Svc
35546	78	781	Mining (Except Oil and Gas)	35754	135	626	Computer & Electronic Prod Mfg	36010	155	1498	Apparel Manufacturing
35548	41	183	Educational Services	35755	16	73	Accommodation	36013	5	54	Educational Services
35549	118	643	Educational Services	35756	118	2187	Prof., Scientific, & Tech Svcs	36015	5	479	Wood Product Manufacturing
35550	86	575	Nursing & Resid. Care Facilit.	35757	121	682	Bldg Matl & Garden Eqpmt Dlrs	36016	166	1156	Justice, Pubic Order/Safety
35551	4	55	Animal Production	35758	1142	10354	Food Svcs & Drinking Places	36017	61	437	Justice, Pubic Order/Safety
35552	22	88	Justice, Pubic Order/Safety	35759	146	986	Food and Beverage Stores	36020	12	139	Nonmetallic Mineral Prod. Mfg
35553	196	2189	Fabricated Metal Product Mfg	35760	120	542	Educational Services	36022	113	664	Educational Services
35554	20	89	Mining (Except Oil and Gas)	35761	140	471	Educational Services	36024	167	1122	Furniture & Related Prod. Mfg
35555	474	3863	Apparel Manufacturing	35762	2	4	Postal Service	36025	61	824	Justice, Pubic Order/Safety
35559	9	10	Primary Metal Manufacturing	35763	189	1152	Food and Beverage Stores	36026	17	47	Amusement, Gambling,& Recreat.
35560	7	39	Educational Services	35764	21	114	Merch. Wholesalers,Nondur. Gds	36027	779	8627	Wood Product Manufacturing
35563	141	1077	Wood Product Manufacturing	35765	72	287	Educational Services	36028	23	268	Apparel Manufacturing
35564	58	1228	Apparel Manufacturing	35766	3	23	Educational Services	36029	21	19	Merch. Wholesalers,Nondur. Gds
35565	509	6033	Furniture & Related Prod. Mfg	35767	3	2	Postal Service	36030	10	9	Administrative & Support Svcs
35570	454	3677	Wood Product Manufacturing	35768	712	6992	Textile Product Mills	36031	5	3	Crop Production
35571	18	45	Merch. Wholesalers,Durable Gds	35769	261	2366	Textile Product Mills	36032	75	911	Clothing & Cloth'g Acc. Stores
35572	16	27	Food and Beverage Stores	35771	104	399	Educational Services	36033	118	707	Hospitals
35573	6	12	Food and Beverage Stores	35772	162	1348	Furn. & Home Furnishgs Stores	36034	13	10	Food Svcs & Drinking Places
35574	30	92	Truck Transportation	35773	172	526	Educational Services	36035	47	249	Educational Services
35575	38	416	Wood Product Manufacturing	35774	4	153	Educational Services	36036	31	81	Educational Services
35576	78	701	Wood Product Manufacturing	35775	12	21	Relig., Grant, Civic, Prof Org	36037	569	5192	Food Svcs & Drinking Places
35577	7	6	Forestry and Logging	35776	57	201	Educational Services	36038	15	36	Food and Beverage Stores
35578	56	221	Educational Services	35801	2692	27951	Ambulatory Health Care Svcs	36039	5	32	Computer & Electronic Prod Mfg
35579	58	295	Educational Services	35802	779	6950	Prof., Scientific, & Tech Svcs	36040	165	965	Exec., Legis., & Other Support
35580	78	449	Mining (Except Oil and Gas)	35803	483	7759	Computer & Electronic Prod Mfg	36041	43	340	Truck Transportation
35581	89	586	Educational Services	35804	26	88	Prof., Scientific, & Tech Svcs	36042	14	21	Relig., Grant, Civic, Prof Org
35582	182	2413	Motor Vehicle & Parts Dealers	35805	1089	21176	Computer & Electronic Prod Mfg	36043	78	791	Computer & Electronic Prod Mfg
35584	14	104	Educational Services	35806	796	13939	Prof., Scientific, & Tech Svcs	36045	2	3	Food and Beverage Stores
35585	31	84	Heavy & Civil Eng. Construct'N	35807	3	21	Educational Services	36046	33	50	Food and Beverage Stores
35586	135	1560	Transportation Equipment Mfg	35808	5	35	Special Trade Contractors	36047	29	96	Merch. Wholesalers,Durable Gds
35587	15	47	Educational Services	35809	4	31	Special Trade Contractors	36048	42	257	Wood Product Manufacturing
35592	252	2851	Machinery Manufacturing	35810	672	6269	Educational Services	36049	246	1940	Food Manufacturing
35593	25	102	Educational Services	35811	657	8684	Computer & Electronic Prod Mfg	36051	37	126	Educational Services
35594	344	2673	Machinery Manufacturing	35812	4	39	Construction of Buildings	36052	14	40	Administrative & Support Svcs
35601	2333	28871	Food Svcs & Drinking Places	35813	1	300	Postal Service	36053	42	95	Educational Services
35602	6	28	Miscellaneous Store Retailers	35814	9	129	Administrative & Support Svcs	36054	389	2469	Food and Beverage Stores
35603	684	7185	Relig., Grant, Civic, Prof Org	35815	20	30	Prof., Scientific, & Tech Svcs	36057	15	1423	Social Assistance
35609	1	9	Prof., Scientific, & Tech Svcs	35816	947	10083	Food Svcs & Drinking Places	36062	2	101	Bldg Matl & Garden Eqpmt Dlrs
35610	31	128	Educational Services	35824	157	9571	Computer & Electronic Prod Mfg	36064	101	427	Special Trade Contractors
35611	1129	10886	Food and Beverage Stores	35893	3	450	Credit Intermediation & Relatd	36065	20	70	General Merchandise Stores
35612	3	3	Merch. Wholesalers,Durable Gds	35894	1	20	Print'g & Related Supp't Act's	36066	388	3656	General Merchandise Stores
35613	209	1942	Miscellaneous Manufacturing	35896	4	431	Educational Services	36067	832	6460	Paper Manufacturing
35614	77	395	Educational Services	35898	48	577	Administrative & Support Svcs	36068	3	6	Publishing Industries
35615	8	45	Support Activities: Agr./For.	35899	4	27	Broadcasting	36069	85	420	Justice, Pubic Order/Safety
35616	126	732	Chemical Manufacturing	35901	1332	10906	Food Svcs & Drinking Places	36071	12	20	Food and Beverage Stores
35617	2	1	Postal Service	35902	6	23	Social Assistance	36072	4	5	Administrative & Support Svcs
35618	81	2295	Paper Manufacturing	35903	554	10258	Motor Vehicle & Parts Dealers	36075	58	741	Perform'g Arts, Spec. Sports
35619	75	413	Educational Services	35904	385	4011	Transportation Equipment Mfg	36078	383	3556	Computer & Electronic Prod Mfg
35620	115	772	Merch. Wholesalers,Nondur. Gds	35905	166	1390	Special Trade Contractors	36079	134	2401	Truck Transportation
35621	66	301	Educational Services	35906	494	4377	Food Svcs & Drinking Places	36080	30	52	Construction of Buildings
35622	108	996	Nursing & Resid. Care Facilit.	35907	127	618	Educational Services	36081	712	6453	Wood Product Manufacturing
35630	1932	23285	Food Svcs & Drinking Places	35950	858	9209	Food Manufacturing	36082	4	588	Educational Services
35631	3	8	Administrative & Support Svcs	35951	180	1748	Paper Manufacturing	36083	387	4087	Hospitals
35632	5	600	Educational Services	35952	171	720	Food Svcs & Drinking Places	36087	2	4	Postal Service
35633	296	2341	Furniture & Related Prod. Mfg	35953	183	1031	Educational Services	36088	62	1333	Educational Services
35634	212	1513	Wood Product Manufacturing	35954	366	3609	Food Svcs & Drinking Places	36089	329	9971	General Merchandise Stores

ZIP CODE	2004 Total Firms	2004 Total Employees	TOP INDUSTRY RANKED on 2004 EMPLOYMENT	ZIP CODE	2004 Total Firms	2004 Total Employees	TOP INDUSTRY RANKED on 2004 EMPLOYMENT	ZIP CODE	2004 Total Firms	2004 Total Employees	TOP INDUSTRY RANKED on 2004 EMPLOYMENT
36091	50	176	Educational Services	36353	36	72	Forestry and Logging	36561	639	4207	Food Svcs & Drinking Places
36092	611	4421	Educational Services	36360	777	5584	Ambulatory Health Care Svcs	36562	19	77	Educational Services
36093	128	457	Special Trade Contractors	36361	4	9	Admin. of Economic Programs	36564	22	565	Accommodation
36101	1	5	Administrative & Support Svcs	36362	60	1142	Educational Services	36567	462	3054	Food Svcs & Drinking Places
36102	4	34	Exec., Legis., & Other Support	36370	9	13	Special Trade Contractors	36568	10	48	Justice, Pubic Order/Safety
36104	1705	24988	Justice, Pubic Order/Safety	36371	15	124	Merch. Wholesalers,Durable Gds	36569	14	22	Relig., Grant, Civic, Prof Org
36105	391	4257	Fabricated Metal Product Mfg	36373	11	65	Support Activities: Agr./For.	36571	636	5793	General Merchandise Stores
36106	856	9667	Ambulatory Health Care Svcs	36374	9	54	Educational Services	36572	103	961	Educational Services
36107	426	3903	Food Svcs & Drinking Places	36375	155	982	Miscellaneous Manufacturing	36574	41	207	Truck Transportation
36108	729	13176	Nat'l Security & Int'l Affairs	36376	43	421	Fabricated Metal Product Mfg	36575	345	2301	Educational Services
36109	731	11840	Elect'l Eqpmt, App, & Comp Mfg	36401	362	3214	Truck Transportation	36576	86	282	Heavy & Civil Eng. Construct'N
36110	346	5735	Exec., Legis., & Other Support	36420	867	6986	Utilities	36577	6	31	Justice, Pubic Order/Safety
36111	254	2478	Educational Services	36425	30	258	Wood Product Manufacturing	36578	30	278	Mining (Except Oil and Gas)
36112	37	1224	Hospitals	36426	701	6337	Paper Manufacturing	36579	36	100	Food Svcs & Drinking Places
36113	1	40	Construction of Buildings	36427	10	18	Justice, Pubic Order/Safety	36580	196	1086	Utilities
36114	13	92	Nat'l Security & Int'l Affairs	36429	5	59	Forestry and Logging	36581	4	28	Forestry and Logging
36115	1	0	Other Information Services	36432	62	378	Bldg Matl & Garden Eqpmt Dlrs	36582	760	9463	Chemical Manufacturing
36116	1146	19183	Hospitals	36435	5	10	Postal Service	36583	13	15	Relig., Grant, Civic, Prof Org
36117	1858	20572	Food Svcs & Drinking Places	36436	6	14	Merch. Wholesalers,Durable Gds	36584	13	6	Heavy & Civil Eng. Construct'N
36119	3	500	Postal Service	36439	41	189	Educational Services	36585	15	34	Food Svcs & Drinking Places
36120	3	3	Educational Services	36441	153	991	Construction of Buildings	36587	125	465	Educational Services
36121	2	3	Administrative & Support Svcs	36442	177	709	Repair and Maintenance	36590	2	3	Merch. Wholesalers,Durable Gds
36123	7	31	Postal Service	36444	19	38	Justice, Pubic Order/Safety	36601	13	115	Personal and Laundry Services
36124	10	17	Special Trade Contractors	36445	103	798	Furniture & Related Prod. Mfg	36602	793	9865	Prof., Scientific, & Tech Svcs
36125	1	1	Merch. Wholesalers,Durable Gds	36446	17	401	Wood Product Manufacturing	36603	372	5464	Admin. Human Resource Programs
36130	91	4470	Exec., Legis., & Other Support	36449	1	1	Relig., Grant, Civic, Prof Org	36604	445	5423	Hospitals
36131	13	704	Exec., Legis., & Other Support	36451	269	1763	Exec., Legis., & Other Support	36605	446	3780	Educational Services
36201	1213	12056	Fabricated Metal Product Mfg	36453	45	199	Truck Transportation	36606	1428	16473	Motor Vehicle & Parts Dealers
36202	4	4	Food and Beverage Stores	36454	3	3	Food and Beverage Stores	36607	561	9333	Hospitals
36203	905	9241	Food Svcs & Drinking Places	36455	16	56	Educational Services	36608	1610	20635	Ambulatory Health Care Svcs
36205	29	267	Educational Services	36456	35	139	Educational Services	36609	1093	11703	Prof., Scientific, & Tech Svcs
36206	345	2853	Primary Metal Manufacturing	36457	1	0	Postal Service	36610	392	7167	Fabricated Metal Product Mfg
36207	603	9728	Hospitals	36458	9	96	Bldg Matl & Garden Eqpmt Dlrs	36611	159	1922	Chemical Manufacturing
36250	139	934	Educational Services	36460	579	4968	Ambulatory Health Care Svcs	36612	153	1305	Prof., Scientific, & Tech Svcs
36251	215	3186	Furniture & Related Prod. Mfg	36461	4	4	Merch. Wholesalers,Durable Gds	36613	191	1357	Educational Services
36253	9	68	Credit Intermediation & Relatd	36462	2	25	Miscellaneous Store Retailers	36615	83	3231	Computer & Electronic Prod Mfg
36254	4	11	Insurance Carriers & Related	36467	370	4652	Merch. Wholesalers,Durable Gds	36616	7	112	Electronics & Appliance Stores
36255	12	54	Educational Services	36470	11	971	Paper Manufacturing	36617	269	4912	Hospitals
36256	21	128	Educational Services	36471	31	390	Wood Product Manufacturing	36618	360	4092	Merch. Wholesalers,Durable Gds
36257	3	3	Special Trade Contractors	36473	4	3	Truck Transportation	36619	520	6238	General Merchandise Stores
36258	25	183	Social Assistance	36474	39	257	Educational Services	36621	1	100	Credit Intermediation & Relatd
36260	82	1017	Furniture & Related Prod. Mfg	36475	35	91	Educational Services	36622	1	600	Credit Intermediation & Relatd
36261	3	2	Motor Vehicle & Parts Dealers	36476	8	36	Merch. Wholesalers,Durable Gds	36625	1	75	Prof., Scientific, & Tech Svcs
36262	21	80	Educational Services	36477	125	633	Educational Services	36633	4	30	Exec., Legis., & Other Support
36263	11	17	Special Trade Contractors	36480	50	143	Educational Services	36652	4	19	Merch. Wholesalers,Nondur. Gds
36264	281	2567	Apparel Manufacturing	36481	19	35	Merch. Wholesalers,Durable Gds	36660	7	19	Construction of Buildings
36265	480	4974	Educational Services	36482	15	18	Forestry and Logging	36670	5	8	Administrative & Support Svcs
36266	167	1320	Plastics & Rubber Products Mfg	36483	8	14	Food and Beverage Stores	36671	1	5	Construction of Buildings
36267	6	99	Heavy & Civil Eng. Construct'N	36502	645	6044	Truck Transportation	36685	9	23	Special Trade Contractors
36268	84	470	Educational Services	36505	27	274	Chemical Manufacturing	36688	30	326	Ambulatory Health Care Svcs
36269	8	5	Repair and Maintenance	36507	672	7927	Exec., Legis., & Other Support	36689	5	21	Real Estate
36271	105	527	Educational Services	36509	169	2033	Transportation Equipment Mfg	36691	12	50	Social Assistance
36272	323	3675	Textile Product Mills	36511	41	351	Merch. Wholesalers,Nondur. Gds	36693	776	9702	Rental and Leasing Services
36273	65	404	Merch. Wholesalers,Durable Gds	36512	11	331	Merch. Wholesalers,Nondur. Gds	36695	717	7081	Food Svcs & Drinking Places
36274	468	3609	Textile Mills	36513	12	37	Wood Product Manufacturing	36701	1064	9271	Hospitals
36275	3	55	Educational Services	36515	2	2	Food and Beverage Stores	36702	8	80	Utilities
36276	64	1512	Fabricated Metal Product Mfg	36518	217	1258	Hospitals	36703	441	7030	Paper Manufacturing
36277	62	339	Educational Services	36521	45	210	Construction of Buildings	36720	13	45	Educational Services
36278	199	1091	Exec., Legis., & Other Support	36522	209	1508	Educational Services	36721	1	1	Relig., Grant, Civic, Prof Org
36279	36	229	Relig., Grant, Civic, Prof Org	36523	74	780	Petroleum & Coal Products Mfg	36722	12	3	Relig., Grant, Civic, Prof Org
36280	74	237	Educational Services	36524	51	187	Educational Services	36723	3	6	Food and Beverage Stores
36301	1604	17043	Hospitals	36525	64	648	Truck Transportation	36726	278	1847	Educational Services
36302	12	128	Postal Service	36526	929	8466	Food Svcs & Drinking Places	36727	2	2	Postal Service
36303	1877	25466	Exec., Legis., & Other Support	36527	283	2175	Special Trade Contractors	36728	12	53	Prof., Scientific, & Tech Svcs
36304	1	8	Merch. Wholesalers,Durable Gds	36528	84	548	Museums, Hist. Sites,& Similar	36732	558	7468	Nonmetallic Mineral Prod. Mfg
36305	344	5043	Hospitals	36529	4	4	Postal Service	36736	29	120	Educational Services
36310	254	2732	Repair and Maintenance	36530	225	1488	Truck Transportation	36738	24	81	Crop Production
36311	48	274	Petroleum & Coal Products Mfg	36532	1090	6795	Ambulatory Health Care Svcs	36740	21	140	Crop Production
36312	148	1518	Truck Transportation	36533	9	18	Administrative & Support Svcs	36741	1	2	Postal Service
36313	5	24	Merch. Wholesalers,Durable Gds	36535	1313	10005	Food Svcs & Drinking Places	36742	44	101	Construction of Buildings
36314	6	21	Ambulatory Health Care Svcs	36536	16	38	Isps, Web Search Portals	36744	255	2436	Food Manufacturing
36316	25	91	Merch. Wholesalers,Nondur. Gds	36538	5	3	Postal Service	36745	1	1	Postal Service
36317	7	7	Food Svcs & Drinking Places	36539	16	80	Educational Services	36748	201	1719	Wood Product Manufacturing
36318	12	19	Educational Services	36540	4	16	Food and Beverage Stores	36749	11	15	Support Act. for Transport.
36319	56	1776	Utilities	36541	171	1073	Food Svcs & Drinking Places	36750	87	701	Paper Manufacturing
36320	78	625	Merch. Wholesalers,Nondur. Gds	36542	919	6899	Real Estate	36751	10	23	Truck Transportation
36321	32	364	Food Manufacturing	36543	14	121	Merch. Wholesalers,Nondur. Gds	36752	56	217	Warehousing and Storage
36322	308	1857	Food Svcs & Drinking Places	36544	127	1576	Educational Services	36753	3	28	Wood Product Manufacturing
36323	245	2039	Apparel Manufacturing	36545	414	4105	Paper Manufacturing	36754	6	6	Prof., Scientific, & Tech Svcs
36330	1037	10615	Educational Services	36547	25	65	Prof., Scientific, & Tech Svcs	36756	234	2082	Educational Services
36331	5	10	Special Trade Contractors	36548	25	288	Utilities	36758	20	252	Miscellaneous Store Retailers
36340	316	3089	Merch. Wholesalers,Durable Gds	36549	123	392	Relig., Grant, Civic, Prof Org	36759	31	48	Food Manufacturing
36343	35	75	Justice, Pubic Order/Safety	36550	6	9	Food and Beverage Stores	36761	23	192	Merch. Wholesalers,Durable Gds
36344	152	980	Exec., Legis., & Other Support	36551	234	2097	Merch. Wholesalers,Nondur. Gds	36762	1	1	Postal Service
36345	219	1398	Educational Services	36553	70	3132	Chemical Manufacturing	36763	6	4	Postal Service
36346	13	138	Educational Services	36555	59	157	Food Svcs & Drinking Places	36764	8	67	Merch. Wholesalers,Durable Gds
36349	15	57	Prof., Scientific, & Tech Svcs	36556	5	7	Personal and Laundry Services	36765	14	103	Educational Services
36350	116	971	Real Estate	36558	94	332	Educational Services	36766	5	6	Food Svcs & Drinking Places
36351	75	568	Ambulatory Health Care Svcs	36559	25	208	Nursing & Resid. Care Facilit.	36767	35	188	Educational Services
36352	119	453	Educational Services	36560	78	1109	Hospitals	36768	32	117	Bldg Matl & Garden Eqpmt Dlrs

BUSINESS DATA

ZIP CODE	2004 Total Firms	2004 Total Employees	TOP INDUSTRY RANKED on 2004 EMPLOYMENT	ZIP CODE	2004 Total Firms	2004 Total Employees	TOP INDUSTRY RANKED on 2004 EMPLOYMENT	ZIP CODE	2004 Total Firms	2004 Total Employees	TOP INDUSTRY RANKED on 2004 EMPLOYMENT
36769	84	1477	Paper Manufacturing	37049	68	318	Educational Services	37181	26	49	Wood Product Manufacturing
36773	10	18	Food and Beverage Stores	37050	37	1020	Utilities	37183	69	364	Educational Services
36775	26	60	Educational Services	37051	26	64	Relig., Grant, Civic, Prof Org	37184	95	435	Educational Services
36776	18	93	Primary Metal Manufacturing	37052	45	300	Educational Services	37185	414	2921	Food Svcs & Drinking Places
36782	41	194	Educational Services	37055	1143	12879	Ambulatory Health Care Svcs	37186	235	1452	Wood Product Manufacturing
36783	40	80	Educational Services	37056	2	2	Merch. Wholesalers,Durable Gds	37187	146	1026	Transportation Equipment Mfg
36784	371	3409	Apparel Manufacturing	37057	10	12	Postal Service	37188	346	2957	Food Svcs & Drinking Places
36785	32	118	Petroleum & Coal Products Mfg	37058	257	1552	Educational Services	37189	98	1156	Merch. Wholesalers,Durable Gds
36786	97	706	Food Manufacturing	37059	25	59	Accommodation	37190	353	1962	Motor Vehicle & Parts Dealers
36790	6	14	Forestry and Logging	37060	57	339	Educational Services	37191	55	296	Educational Services
36792	14	126	Educational Services	37061	250	1470	Social Assistance	37201	668	12366	Justice, Pubic Order/Safety
36793	6	61	Fabricated Metal Product Mfg	37062	228	1715	Elect'l Eqpmt, App, & Comp Mfg	37202	12	184	Postal Service
36801	1183	13767	Hospitals	37063	1	0	Justice, Pubic Order/Safety	37203	3052	43160	Ambulatory Health Care Svcs
36803	9	21	Merch. Wholesalers,Nondur. Gds	37064	1807	14558	Food Svcs & Drinking Places	37204	1115	13467	Prof., Scientific, & Tech Svcs
36804	290	4427	Plastics & Rubber Products Mfg	37065	14	43	Ambulatory Health Care Svcs	37205	951	13930	Ambulatory Health Care Svcs
36830	1196	16873	Educational Services	37066	1372	14796	Educational Services	37206	631	5659	Exec., Legis., & Other Support
36831	10	17	Special Trade Contractors	37067	1211	16697	Food Svcs & Drinking Places	37207	1154	10437	Educational Services
36832	356	4037	Food Svcs & Drinking Places	37068	15	25	Administrative & Support Svcs	37208	651	6801	Educational Services
36849	27	598	Other Information Services	37069	266	1456	Educational Services	37209	1285	18075	Educational Services
36850	51	291	Relig., Grant, Civic, Prof Org	37070	14	29	Special Trade Contractors	37210	1546	26236	Merch. Wholesalers,Durable Gds
36851	8	766	Paper Manufacturing	37071	5	19	Relig., Grant, Civic, Prof Org	37211	2605	26655	Food Svcs & Drinking Places
36852	27	214	Gasoline Stations	37072	1161	10541	Food Svcs & Drinking Places	37212	1031	10438	Hospitals
36853	369	2267	Nursing & Resid. Care Facilit.	37073	194	1105	Educational Services	37213	88	1644	Merch. Wholesalers,Durable Gds
36854	447	4684	Textile Mills	37074	221	1475	Educational Services	37214	1500	27215	Accommodation
36855	18	58	Educational Services	37075	1534	11295	Food Svcs & Drinking Places	37215	1186	10774	Food Svcs & Drinking Places
36856	44	153	Machinery Manufacturing	37076	872	9082	Prof., Scientific, & Tech Svcs	37216	443	3113	Educational Services
36858	16	35	Justice, Pubic Order/Safety	37077	14	25	Motion Pict. & Sound Recording	37217	1299	14954	Transportation Equipment Mfg
36859	1	2	Utilities	37078	44	343	Food Svcs & Drinking Places	37218	409	5198	Nursing & Resid. Care Facilit.
36860	59	163	Educational Services	37079	35	104	Special Trade Contractors	37219	539	9963	Prof., Scientific, & Tech Svcs
36861	47	150	Special Trade Contractors	37080	194	965	Special Trade Contractors	37220	245	1931	Admin. of Economic Programs
36862	248	2707	Truck Transportation	37082	151	895	Educational Services	37221	858	5244	Food Svcs & Drinking Places
36863	422	3184	Textile Mills	37083	497	3618	General Merchandise Stores	37222	11	36	Prof., Scientific, & Tech Svcs
36865	9	56	Educational Services	37085	41	201	Educational Services	37224	3	4	Prof., Scientific, & Tech Svcs
36866	70	416	Educational Services	37086	399	10334	Machinery Manufacturing	37227	1	1	Transit & Grnd Pass. Transport
36867	920	7274	Food Svcs & Drinking Places	37087	1522	16993	Food Svcs & Drinking Places	37228	262	6297	Insurance Carriers & Related
36868	5	4	Special Trade Contractors	37088	4	14	Prof., Scientific, & Tech Svcs	37229	16	59	Repair and Maintenance
36869	258	2269	Nonmetallic Mineral Prod. Mfg	37089	1	0	Merch. Wholesalers,Durable Gds	37230	2	6	Postal Service
36870	228	1087	Food and Beverage Stores	37090	332	6312	Computer & Electronic Prod Mfg	37232	164	16454	Hospitals
36871	30	186	Transportation Equipment Mfg	37091	712	8536	Miscellaneous Manufacturing	37234	4	1623	Sportg Gds,Hobby,Book, & Music
36874	75	346	Educational Services	37095	57	185	Educational Services	37236	9	3041	Hospitals
36875	75	402	Educational Services	37096	220	1715	Transportation Equipment Mfg	37238	43	695	Prof., Scientific, & Tech Svcs
36877	174	1251	Educational Services	37097	84	542	Merch. Wholesalers,Durable Gds	37240	4	283	Other Information Services
36879	20	39	Merch. Wholesalers,Nondur. Gds	37098	112	451	Educational Services	37242	14	1293	Exec., Legis., & Other Support
36901	3	15	Social Assistance	37101	125	598	Educational Services	37243	344	11259	Admin. Human Resource Programs
36904	286	1482	Educational Services	37110	1529	12047	Ambulatory Health Care Svcs	37246	2	12	Credit Intermediation & Relatd
36907	33	86	Educational Services	37111	2	8	Social Assistance	37247	17	754	Admin. Human Resource Programs
36908	128	435	Educational Services	37115	1249	15408	Hospitals	37250	1	4	Credit Intermediation & Relatd
36910	5	89	Wood Product Manufacturing	37116	12	29	Special Trade Contractors	37301	92	330	Educational Services
36912	53	114	Educational Services	37118	36	129	Relig., Grant, Civic, Prof Org	37302	60	163	Educational Services
36913	5	48	Oil and Gas Extraction	37121	8	27	Administrative & Support Svcs	37303	1143	14363	Transportation Equipment Mfg
36915	15	12	Relig., Grant, Civic, Prof Org	37122	465	6732	Heavy & Civil Eng. Construct'N	37305	36	58	Relig., Grant, Civic, Prof Org
36916	54	416	Construction of Buildings	37127	265	5016	Relig., Grant, Civic, Prof Org	37306	46	159	Justice, Pubic Order/Safety
36919	65	220	Wood Product Manufacturing	37128	371	2429	Educational Services	37307	185	1036	Motor Vehicle & Parts Dealers
36921	26	99	Educational Services	37129	1954	20459	Food Svcs & Drinking Places	37308	19	86	Educational Services
36922	8	6	Postal Service	37130	1540	15001	Hospitals	37309	45	1215	Paper Manufacturing
36925	129	1153	Wood Product Manufacturing	37131	3	1106	Insurance Carriers & Related	37310	127	2002	Chemical Manufacturing
37010	43	178	Social Assistance	37132	5	2012	Educational Services	37311	1515	17938	Merch. Wholesalers,Nondur. Gds
37011	10	15	Prof., Scientific, & Tech Svcs	37133	20	83	Miscellaneous Manufacturing	37312	987	12942	Food Svcs & Drinking Places
37012	69	377	Clothing & Cloth'g Acc. Stores	37134	127	1733	Chemical Manufacturing	37313	57	436	Educational Services
37013	1070	11874	Food Svcs & Drinking Places	37135	130	756	Special Trade Contractors	37314	12	60	Justice, Pubic Order/Safety
37014	48	126	Motor Vehicle & Parts Dealers	37136	16	15	Food and Beverage Stores	37315	40	843	Educational Services
37015	431	5072	Elect'l Eqpmt, App, & Comp Mfg	37137	28	196	Relig., Grant, Civic, Prof Org	37316	4	71	Clothing & Cloth'g Acc. Stores
37016	27	76	Bldg Matl & Garden Eqpmt Dlrs	37138	445	3557	Chemical Manufacturing	37317	109	617	Hospitals
37018	29	55	Special Trade Contractors	37140	10	324	Exec., Legis., & Other Support	37318	56	278	Educational Services
37019	28	219	Heavy & Civil Eng. Construct'N	37141	18	54	Textile Product Mills	37320	15	18	Prof., Scientific, & Tech Svcs
37020	91	372	Merch. Wholesalers,Nondur. Gds	37142	19	147	Nursing & Resid. Care Facilit.	37321	630	8413	Furn. & Home Furnishgs Stores
37022	76	197	Educational Services	37143	74	281	Educational Services	37322	202	1796	Furn. & Home Furnishgs Stores
37023	19	131	Educational Services	37144	58	177	Educational Services	37323	447	3526	Chemical Manufacturing
37024	25	58	Special Trade Contractors	37145	24	69	Wood Product Manufacturing	37324	193	2448	Transportation Equipment Mfg
37025	81	276	Special Trade Contractors	37146	128	839	Educational Services	37325	25	54	Exec., Legis., & Other Support
37026	21	104	Truck Transportation	37148	460	6432	Fabricated Metal Product Mfg	37326	64	670	Motor Vehicle & Parts Dealers
37027	2209	27942	Hospitals	37149	30	133	Social Assistance	37327	452	2912	Machinery Manufacturing
37028	10	93	Justice, Pubic Order/Safety	37150	155	971	Apparel Manufacturing	37328	26	161	Wood Product Manufacturing
37029	89	746	Accommodation	37151	11	28	Social Assistance	37329	109	509	Educational Services
37030	377	2790	Hospitals	37152	14	85	Nursing & Resid. Care Facilit.	37330	98	450	Fabricated Metal Product Mfg
37031	25	64	Relig., Grant, Civic, Prof Org	37153	64	208	Educational Services	37331	263	3795	Nonmetallic Mineral Prod. Mfg
37032	39	199	Educational Services	37155	1	3	Postal Service	37332	44	189	Educational Services
37033	346	2302	Educational Services	37160	1148	19687	Amusement, Gambling,& Recreat.	37333	7	44	Bldg Matl & Garden Eqpmt Dlrs
37034	134	623	Educational Services	37161	4	464	Miscellaneous Manufacturing	37334	868	7289	Electronics & Appliance Stores
37035	32	112	Educational Services	37162	5	12	Heavy & Civil Eng. Construct'N	37335	37	109	Educational Services
37036	138	851	Justice, Pubic Order/Safety	37165	1	4	Food and Beverage Stores	37336	57	169	Special Trade Contractors
37037	85	388	Administrative & Support Svcs	37166	561	5293	Transportation Equipment Mfg	37337	15	29	Mining (Except Oil and Gas)
37040	1819	24268	Food Svcs & Drinking Places	37167	1118	10903	Food Svcs & Drinking Places	37338	27	135	Educational Services
37041	4	240	Merch. Wholesalers,Nondur. Gds	37171	8	7	Heavy & Civil Eng. Construct'N	37339	66	494	Educational Services
37042	867	6051	Educational Services	37172	1021	13617	Elect'l Eqpmt, App, & Comp Mfg	37340	17	108	Transportation Equipment Mfg
37043	807	7658	Hospitals	37174	235	9657	Transportation Equipment Mfg	37341	188	841	Educational Services
37044	4	706	Perform'g Arts, Spec. Sports	37175	9	45	Wood Product Manufacturing	37342	54	228	Educational Services
37046	80	195	Merch. Wholesalers,Nondur. Gds	37178	49	210	Educational Services	37343	1161	10449	Food Svcs & Drinking Places
37047	45	333	Educational Services	37179	99	355	Educational Services	37345	71	411	Wood Product Manufacturing
37048	47	160	Fabricated Metal Product Mfg	37180	31	173	Educational Services	37347	401	3035	Food Svcs & Drinking Places

ZIP CODE	2004 Total Firms	2004 Total Employees	TOP INDUSTRY RANKED on 2004 EMPLOYMENT	ZIP CODE	2004 Total Firms	2004 Total Employees	TOP INDUSTRY RANKED on 2004 EMPLOYMENT	ZIP CODE	2004 Total Firms	2004 Total Employees	TOP INDUSTRY RANKED on 2004 EMPLOYMENT
37348	18	49	Crop Production	37680	10	69	Wood Product Manufacturing	37845	11	336	Exec., Legis., & Other Support
37350	51	249	Exec., Legis., & Other Support	37681	85	473	Educational Services	37846	30	100	Educational Services
37351	5	11	Amusement, Gambling,& Recreat.	37682	12	229	Educational Services	37847	46	326	Transportation Equipment Mfg
37352	128	965	Beverage & Tobacco Product Mfg	37683	426	3826	Administrative & Support Svcs	37848	6	13	Real Estate
37353	85	527	Exec., Legis., & Other Support	37684	14	292	Unclassified Establishments	37849	581	4631	Apparel Manufacturing
37354	515	3254	General Merchandise Stores	37686	173	2134	Fabricated Metal Product Mfg	37852	44	162	Educational Services
37355	835	8445	Transportation Equipment Mfg	37687	96	446	Educational Services	37853	72	824	Textile Product Mills
37356	173	1027	Food Svcs & Drinking Places	37688	22	139	Relig., Grant, Civic, Prof Org	37854	312	3214	General Merchandise Stores
37357	151	3269	Machinery Manufacturing	37690	44	323	Machinery Manufacturing	37857	625	6171	Transportation Equipment Mfg
37359	5	9	Relig., Grant, Civic, Prof Org	37691	18	30	Food Svcs & Drinking Places	37860	66	1994	Transportation Equipment Mfg
37360	30	101	Beverage & Tobacco Product Mfg	37692	103	991	Merch. Wholesalers,Nondur. Gds	37861	205	1239	Educational Services
37361	36	302	Motor Vehicle & Parts Dealers	37694	44	137	Mining (Except Oil and Gas)	37862	1288	11728	Food Svcs & Drinking Places
37362	38	118	Educational Services	37701	585	11728	Primary Metal Manufacturing	37863	822	8697	Accommodation
37363	530	8700	Food Manufacturing	37705	89	652	Wood Product Manufacturing	37864	7	14	Prof., Scientific, & Tech Svcs
37364	2	2	General Merchandise Stores	37707	5	8	Food and Beverage Stores	37865	348	1832	Educational Services
37365	42	108	Educational Services	37708	163	1413	Merch. Wholesalers,Durable Gds	37866	16	50	Educational Services
37366	21	93	Special Trade Contractors	37709	51	200	Food and Beverage Stores	37867	1	1	Relig., Grant, Civic, Prof Org
37367	402	2538	Justice, Pubic Order/Safety	37710	27	121	Mining (Except Oil and Gas)	37868	3	9	Other Information Services
37369	17	133	Construction of Buildings	37711	99	1515	Wood Product Manufacturing	37869	172	1133	Elect'l Eqpmt, App, & Comp Mfg
37370	72	225	Educational Services	37713	14	37	Miscellaneous Store Retailers	37870	53	156	Educational Services
37371	1	1	Credit Intermediation & Relatd	37714	84	1204	Food Manufacturing	37871	157	822	Educational Services
37373	60	256	Fabricated Metal Product Mfg	37715	23	252	Nonstore Retailers	37872	47	359	Textile Product Mills
37374	9	60	Merch. Wholesalers,Durable Gds	37716	814	8356	Educational Services	37873	98	1798	Relig., Grant, Civic, Prof Org
37375	77	480	Food Svcs & Drinking Places	37717	1	4	Real Estate	37874	511	4204	Nonmetallic Mineral Prod. Mfg
37376	8	57	Mining (Except Oil and Gas)	37719	7	92	Educational Services	37876	516	3302	Food Svcs & Drinking Places
37377	332	1870	Nursing & Resid. Care Facilit.	37721	166	651	Educational Services	37877	113	959	Hospitals
37378	9	44	Merch. Wholesalers,Durable Gds	37722	78	427	Educational Services	37878	11	28	Museums, Hist. Sites,& Similar
37379	454	3629	Utilities	37723	28	284	Mining (Except Oil and Gas)	37879	245	2138	Hospitals
37380	233	2475	Furn. & Home Furnishgs Stores	37724	80	250	Educational Services	37880	43	186	Food Svcs & Drinking Places
37381	202	1290	Nursing & Resid. Care Facilit.	37725	378	3366	Food Svcs & Drinking Places	37881	32	78	Bldg Matl & Garden Eqpmt Dlrs
37382	4	17	Warehousing and Storage	37726	33	87	Educational Services	37882	174	821	Accommodation
37383	5	654	Educational Services	37727	22	49	Educational Services	37885	128	3523	Transportation Equipment Mfg
37384	3	2	Insurance Carriers & Related	37729	14	79	Educational Services	37886	77	309	Accommodation
37385	171	810	Educational Services	37731	7	26	Educational Services	37887	228	1634	Justice, Pubic Order/Safety
37387	161	593	Educational Services	37732	7	10	Food and Beverage Stores	37888	37	239	Educational Services
37388	1120	11748	Food Svcs & Drinking Places	37733	8	32	Museums, Hist. Sites,& Similar	37890	176	1735	Truck Transportation
37389	5	3541	Exec., Legis., & Other Support	37737	120	435	Educational Services	37891	43	340	Furniture & Related Prod. Mfg
37391	27	75	Educational Services	37738	970	7918	Accommodation	37892	61	280	Merch. Wholesalers,Durable Gds
37394	14	41	Bldg Matl & Garden Eqpmt Dlrs	37742	83	360	Educational Services	37901	20	111	Rental and Leasing Services
37396	2	1	Postal Service	37743	704	7471	Educational Services	37902	818	12432	Justice, Pubic Order/Safety
37397	174	738	Educational Services	37744	6	26	Exec., Legis., & Other Support	37909	459	7223	Ambulatory Health Care Svcs
37398	642	6616	Plastics & Rubber Products Mfg	37745	996	12384	Educational Services	37912	793	8465	Food Svcs & Drinking Places
37401	5	7	Special Trade Contractors	37748	583	5145	Educational Services	37914	650	10660	Transportation Equipment Mfg
37402	1010	18421	Insurance Carriers & Related	37752	141	1197	Educational Services	37915	207	4131	Justice, Pubic Order/Safety
37403	510	11083	Hospitals	37753	18	130	Motor Vehicle & Parts Dealers	37916	399	10655	Hospitals
37404	771	12136	Hospitals	37754	73	317	Special Trade Contractors	37917	1543	16557	Hospitals
37405	797	8466	Machinery Manufacturing	37755	75	339	Utilities	37918	1366	10776	Exec., Legis., & Other Support
37406	603	11151	Merch. Wholesalers,Durable Gds	37756	152	1379	Educational Services	37919	2488	26519	Food Svcs & Drinking Places
37407	461	5983	Special Trade Contractors	37757	274	2797	Merch. Wholesalers,Durable Gds	37920	1287	16559	Hospitals
37408	374	6447	Food Manufacturing	37760	466	5080	Educational Services	37921	1079	15007	Merch. Wholesalers,Durable Gds
37409	154	1375	Health & Personal Care Stores	37762	162	1431	Hospitals	37922	2476	21836	Food Svcs & Drinking Places
37410	116	1763	Merch. Wholesalers,Durable Gds	37763	424	3343	Educational Services	37923	1485	13351	Prof., Scientific, & Tech Svcs
37411	747	5738	Food Svcs & Drinking Places	37764	175	1338	Food Svcs & Drinking Places	37924	534	6900	General Merchandise Stores
37412	872	6327	Food Svcs & Drinking Places	37765	1	1	Repair and Maintenance	37927	6	4	Prof., Scientific, & Tech Svcs
37414	8	37	Heavy & Civil Eng. Construct'N	37766	641	4452	Nursing & Resid. Care Facilit.	37928	10	13	Administrative & Support Svcs
37415	860	7485	Chemical Manufacturing	37769	167	1190	Food Svcs & Drinking Places	37929	63	1148	Prof., Scientific, & Tech Svcs
37416	525	5116	Prof., Scientific, & Tech Svcs	37770	34	73	Merch. Wholesalers,Nondur. Gds	37930	18	33	Prof., Scientific, & Tech Svcs
37419	217	2968	Truck Transportation	37771	580	5592	Food Svcs & Drinking Places	37931	432	3664	Construction of Buildings
37421	2489	32532	Food Svcs & Drinking Places	37772	217	1193	Food Svcs & Drinking Places	37932	622	9064	Prof., Scientific, & Tech Svcs
37422	13	21	Prof., Scientific, & Tech Svcs	37774	478	6040	Transportation Equipment Mfg	37933	18	28	Administrative & Support Svcs
37424	5	14	Repair and Maintenance	37777	309	3071	Hospitals	37938	325	1691	Educational Services
37450	72	675	Prof., Scientific, & Tech Svcs	37778	4	6	Warehousing and Storage	37939	9	43	Social Assistance
37601	1588	22082	Food Svcs & Drinking Places	37779	49	390	Nonmetallic Mineral Prod. Mfg	37940	8	10	Merch. Wholesalers,Durable Gds
37602	14	47	Special Trade Contractors	37801	954	11221	Transportation Equipment Mfg	37950	10	22	Merch. Wholesalers,Durable Gds
37604	1570	22044	Hospitals	37802	8	24	Perform'g Arts, Spec. Sports	37996	27	10011	Educational Services
37605	6	18	Administrative & Support Svcs	37803	409	2144	Educational Services	37997	1	8	Credit Intermediation & Relatd
37614	17	2031	Educational Services	37804	1021	10037	Social Assistance	37998	2	430	Educational Services
37615	509	6764	Isps, Web Search Portals	37806	77	489	Social Assistance	38001	259	1647	Computer & Electronic Prod Mfg
37616	60	1518	Paper Manufacturing	37807	323	2003	Educational Services	38002	440	4721	Hospitals
37617	510	4293	Educational Services	37809	25	567	Construction of Buildings	38004	157	855	Food Svcs & Drinking Places
37618	260	1197	Special Trade Contractors	37810	16	84	Educational Services	38006	144	1541	Food Manufacturing
37620	1498	20912	Nursing & Resid. Care Facilit.	37811	39	261	Truck Transportation	38007	3	2	Food and Beverage Stores
37621	7	218	Postal Service	37813	729	13059	Paper Manufacturing	38008	465	3613	Hospitals
37625	3	12	Educational Services	37814	1315	14289	Food Svcs & Drinking Places	38010	2	3	Chemical Manufacturing
37640	75	254	Wood Product Manufacturing	37816	1	0	Special Trade Contractors	38011	114	970	Educational Services
37641	113	568	Educational Services	37818	92	804	Educational Services	38012	603	5792	Plastics & Rubber Products Mfg
37642	218	2639	Nonmetallic Mineral Prod. Mfg	37819	8	35	Food and Beverage Stores	38014	6	24	Administrative & Support Svcs
37643	1102	10756	Textile Mills	37820	91	712	Mining (Except Oil and Gas)	38015	41	404	Special Trade Contractors
37644	1	3	Special Trade Contractors	37821	790	8084	Food Svcs & Drinking Places	38016	634	6617	Administrative & Support Svcs
37645	97	450	Food Svcs & Drinking Places	37822	2	7	Prof., Scientific, & Tech Svcs	38017	1211	12396	Special Trade Contractors
37650	395	4251	Chemical Manufacturing	37824	3	10	Miscellaneous Store Retailers	38018	916	8021	Administrative & Support Svcs
37656	65	324	Justice, Pubic Order/Safety	37825	200	4584	Furniture & Related Prod. Mfg	38019	748	7003	Print'g & Related Supp't Act's
37657	11	16	Wood Product Manufacturing	37826	71	647	Apparel Manufacturing	38021	5	40	Support Activities: Agr./For.
37658	98	419	Educational Services	37828	54	390	Paper Manufacturing	38023	35	320	Educational Services
37659	543	3051	Educational Services	37829	26	85	Educational Services	38024	1250	12680	Print'g & Related Supp't Act's
37660	1921	28929	Hospitals	37830	1409	27729	Prof., Scientific, & Tech Svcs	38025	5	8	Justice, Pubic Order/Safety
37662	2	1	Transit & Grnd Pass. Transport	37831	14	177	Relig., Grant, Civic, Prof Org	38027	14	57	Prof., Scientific, & Tech Svcs
37663	471	5450	Construction of Buildings	37840	272	1378	Educational Services	38028	103	384	Construction of Buildings
37664	679	8001	Relig., Grant, Civic, Prof Org	37841	475	4324	Wood Product Manufacturing	38029	7	17	Relig., Grant, Civic, Prof Org
37665	96	413	Food Svcs & Drinking Places	37843	37	128	Educational Services	38030	15	55	Educational Services

ZIP CODE	2004 Total Firms	2004 Total Employees	TOP INDUSTRY RANKED on 2004 EMPLOYMENT	ZIP CODE	2004 Total Firms	2004 Total Employees	TOP INDUSTRY RANKED on 2004 EMPLOYMENT	ZIP CODE	2004 Total Firms	2004 Total Employees	TOP INDUSTRY RANKED on 2004 EMPLOYMENT
38034	64	247	Plastics & Rubber Products Mfg	38220	62	286	Machinery Manufacturing	38382	407	3495	Merch. Wholesalers,Durable Gds
38036	24	406	Plastics & Rubber Products Mfg	38221	72	214	Educational Services	38387	2	2	Personal and Laundry Services
38037	21	73	Justice, Pubic Order/Safety	38222	75	535	Accommodation	38388	36	329	Food Svcs & Drinking Places
38039	69	583	Plastics & Rubber Products Mfg	38223	2	6	Merch. Wholesalers,Nondur. Gds	38389	4	5	Exec., Legis., & Other Support
38040	180	901	Educational Services	38224	28	128	Educational Services	38390	6	14	Food and Beverage Stores
38041	54	286	Apparel Manufacturing	38225	304	2160	Exec., Legis., & Other Support	38391	27	381	Educational Services
38042	18	37	Unclassified Establishments	38226	7	16	Personal and Laundry Services	38392	18	43	Real Estate
38044	19	126	Merch. Wholesalers,Nondur. Gds	38229	84	655	Mining (Except Oil and Gas)	38393	1	0	Postal Service
38045	1	1	Food and Beverage Stores	38230	103	828	Machinery Manufacturing	38401	2004	19622	Educational Services
38046	2	6	Administrative & Support Svcs	38231	51	788	Merch. Wholesalers,Durable Gds	38402	5	16	Special Trade Contractors
38048	4	39	Educational Services	38232	51	175	Educational Services	38425	87	1264	Administrative & Support Svcs
38049	76	467	Administrative & Support Svcs	38233	73	632	Transportation Equipment Mfg	38449	108	779	Wood Product Manufacturing
38050	51	169	Construction of Buildings	38235	17	99	Educational Services	38450	112	785	Wood Product Manufacturing
38052	103	497	Educational Services	38236	6	21	Justice, Pubic Order/Safety	38451	45	170	Educational Services
38053	385	3864	General Merchandise Stores	38237	488	5727	Educational Services	38452	15	25	Forestry and Logging
38054	1	0	Nat'l Security & Int'l Affairs	38240	40	206	Apparel Manufacturing	38453	2	1	Food and Beverage Stores
38057	76	618	Primary Metal Manufacturing	38241	17	56	Food Svcs & Drinking Places	38454	11	16	Special Trade Contractors
38058	221	1040	Educational Services	38242	941	9538	Plastics & Rubber Products Mfg	38455	28	103	Educational Services
38059	192	2873	Merch. Wholesalers,Nondur. Gds	38251	82	348	Truck Transportation	38456	80	279	Educational Services
38060	117	509	Food Svcs & Drinking Places	38253	16	84	Bldg Matl & Garden Eqpmt Dlrs	38457	15	34	Justice, Pubic Order/Safety
38061	11	51	Wood Product Manufacturing	38254	12	29	Food Svcs & Drinking Places	38459	12	55	Credit Intermediation & Relatd
38063	522	5868	Fabricated Metal Product Mfg	38255	78	384	Educational Services	38460	16	24	Relig., Grant, Civic, Prof Org
38066	59	521	Food Manufacturing	38256	49	240	Accommodation	38461	20	114	Educational Services
38067	21	55	Relig., Grant, Civic, Prof Org	38257	127	856	Special Trade Contractors	38462	355	2589	Plastics & Rubber Products Mfg
38068	450	2727	Educational Services	38258	42	177	Educational Services	38463	40	233	Fabricated Metal Product Mfg
38069	51	164	Gasoline Stations	38259	29	110	Educational Services	38464	966	10810	Machinery Manufacturing
38070	3	3	Food and Beverage Stores	38260	83	460	Wood Product Manufacturing	38468	110	446	Food Svcs & Drinking Places
38071	4	7	Relig., Grant, Civic, Prof Org	38261	836	10377	Motor Vehicle & Parts Dealers	38469	152	867	Educational Services
38075	110	942	Exec., Legis., & Other Support	38271	8	30	Merch. Wholesalers,Nondur. Gds	38471	11	17	Administrative & Support Svcs
38076	9	10	Special Trade Contractors	38281	3	10	Exec., Legis., & Other Support	38472	61	174	Educational Services
38077	7	17	Merch. Wholesalers,Nondur. Gds	38301	1758	31960	Ambulatory Health Care Svcs	38473	33	96	Educational Services
38079	152	2220	Justice, Pubic Order/Safety	38302	8	252	Construction of Buildings	38474	216	1798	Educational Services
38080	72	356	Nursing & Resid. Care Facilit.	38303	2	3	Construction of Buildings	38475	6	58	Wood Product Manufacturing
38083	2	4	Special Trade Contractors	38305	2077	25221	Food Svcs & Drinking Places	38476	9	15	Special Trade Contractors
38088	25	115	Administrative & Support Svcs	38308	5	34	Special Trade Contractors	38477	23	44	Wood Product Manufacturing
38101	39	357	Truck Transportation	38310	217	2539	Plastics & Rubber Products Mfg	38478	744	7622	Fabricated Metal Product Mfg
38103	1893	36115	Prof., Scientific, & Tech Svcs	38311	7	27	Waste Managmt & Remediat'n Svc	38481	46	256	Merch. Wholesalers,Durable Gds
38104	1552	22933	Hospitals	38313	26	99	Educational Services	38482	26	115	Educational Services
38105	394	9502	Hospitals	38315	70	324	Admin. of Economic Programs	38483	76	307	Educational Services
38106	821	7847	Educational Services	38316	96	391	Educational Services	38485	358	2628	Merch. Wholesalers,Durable Gds
38107	473	4457	Educational Services	38317	66	534	Educational Services	38486	12	33	Forestry and Logging
38108	439	6098	Textile Product Mills	38318	8	7	Postal Service	38487	19	41	Construction of Buildings
38109	979	10375	Truck Transportation	38320	486	3711	Food Svcs & Drinking Places	38488	38	126	Educational Services
38111	1265	11579	Relig., Grant, Civic, Prof Org	38321	38	122	Bldg Matl & Garden Eqpmt Dlrs	38501	1931	18632	Food Svcs & Drinking Places
38112	728	9220	Administrative & Support Svcs	38324	8	20	Wood Product Manufacturing	38502	6	15	Relig., Grant, Civic, Prof Org
38113	68	2317	Heavy & Civil Eng. Construct'N	38326	126	551	Food Svcs & Drinking Places	38503	11	36	Merch. Wholesalers,Durable Gds
38114	791	7615	Educational Services	38327	42	184	Heavy & Civil Eng. Construct'N	38504	23	70	Educational Services
38115	1591	18483	Food Svcs & Drinking Places	38328	11	10	Personal and Laundry Services	38505	3	1432	Educational Services
38116	1621	20558	Truck Transportation	38329	150	666	Exec., Legis., & Other Support	38506	599	7539	Motor Vehicle & Parts Dealers
38117	1549	16024	Food Svcs & Drinking Places	38330	120	992	Merch. Wholesalers,Nondur. Gds	38541	21	115	Educational Services
38118	2265	46982	Merch. Wholesalers,Durable Gds	38332	17	41	Apparel Manufacturing	38543	9	17	Forestry and Logging
38119	1444	15181	Ambulatory Health Care Svcs	38333	5	24	Museums, Hist. Sites,& Similar	38544	166	544	Educational Services
38120	673	18428	Hospitals	38334	24	48	Wood Product Manufacturing	38545	20	68	Exec., Legis., & Other Support
38122	878	7451	Food Svcs & Drinking Places	38336	1	0	Postal Service	38547	18	52	Special Trade Contractors
38124	2	25	Prof., Scientific, & Tech Svcs	38337	20	55	Educational Services	38548	4	5	Merch. Wholesalers,Nondur. Gds
38125	597	8283	General Merchandise Stores	38338	14	101	Repair and Maintenance	38549	196	1170	Merch. Wholesalers,Durable Gds
38126	313	4550	Social Assistance	38339	12	17	Motor Vehicle & Parts Dealers	38550	1	6	Plastics & Rubber Products Mfg
38127	772	6830	Educational Services	38340	444	2820	Educational Services	38551	239	1718	Transportation Equipment Mfg
38128	1032	10433	Motor Vehicle & Parts Dealers	38341	43	292	Gasoline Stations	38552	18	18	Repair and Maintenance
38130	3	3	Truck Transportation	38342	42	80	Food and Beverage Stores	38553	98	422	Textile Product Mills
38131	71	1690	Administrative & Support Svcs	38343	548	5975	Elect'l Eqpmt, App, & Comp Mfg	38554	18	54	Educational Services
38132	141	3180	Miscellaneous Manufacturing	38344	375	3719	Heavy & Civil Eng. Construct'N	38555	1190	12337	Hospitals
38133	1046	15004	Food Svcs & Drinking Places	38345	21	104	Educational Services	38556	530	3516	Ambulatory Health Care Svcs
38134	2012	25632	Exec., Legis., & Other Support	38347	9	59	Truck Transportation	38557	10	34	Merch. Wholesalers,Nondur. Gds
38135	261	2161	Educational Services	38348	14	68	Nat'l Security & Int'l Affairs	38558	62	884	Exec., Legis., & Other Support
38136	2	1149	Postal Service	38351	719	7546	Transportation Equipment Mfg	38559	40	135	Educational Services
38137	153	3169	Credit Intermediation & Relatd	38352	5	19	Bldg Matl & Garden Eqpmt Dlrs	38560	8	30	Prof., Scientific, & Tech Svcs
38138	1287	11779	Ambulatory Health Care Svcs	38355	78	363	Educational Services	38562	273	1839	Transportation Equipment Mfg
38139	178	1094	Educational Services	38356	45	77	Special Trade Contractors	38563	122	2424	Transportation Equipment Mfg
38141	407	6786	Merch. Wholesalers,Durable Gds	38357	45	112	Educational Services	38564	14	15	Postal Service
38146	3	3211	Hospitals	38358	430	5979	Fabricated Metal Product Mfg	38565	20	61	Educational Services
38152	19	410	Accommodation	38359	20	84	Apparel Manufacturing	38567	15	34	Merch. Wholesalers,Nondur. Gds
38157	118	749	Prof., Scientific, & Tech Svcs	38361	9	17	Special Trade Contractors	38568	11	65	Educational Services
38161	4	137	Justice, Pubic Order/Safety	38362	20	71	Merch. Wholesalers,Durable Gds	38569	9	68	Admin. Enviro. Quality Progrms
38163	8	26	Ambulatory Health Care Svcs	38363	336	2246	Prof., Scientific, & Tech Svcs	38570	546	5104	Furniture & Related Prod. Mfg
38168	7	29	Special Trade Contractors	38365	19	112	Plastics & Rubber Products Mfg	38571	340	1440	Food Svcs & Drinking Places
38173	2	2	Miscellaneous Store Retailers	38366	48	342	Social Assistance	38572	182	1056	Educational Services
38174	4	14	Credit Intermediation & Relatd	38367	42	281	Apparel Manufacturing	38573	20	53	Relig., Grant, Civic, Prof Org
38175	11	21	Administrative & Support Svcs	38368	26	126	Educational Services	38574	192	2517	Food Manufacturing
38177	14	23	Construction of Buildings	38369	96	287	Educational Services	38575	38	212	Wood Product Manufacturing
38181	5	24	Administrative & Support Svcs	38370	18	36	Truck Transportation	38577	18	62	Bldg Matl & Garden Eqpmt Dlrs
38182	4	11	Securities/Commodity Contracts	38371	25	30	Administrative & Support Svcs	38578	29	239	Special Trade Contractors
38183	21	58	Prof., Scientific, & Tech Svcs	38372	769	6822	Educational Services	38579	12	75	Accommodation
38184	7	35	Merch. Wholesalers,Nondur. Gds	38374	79	299	Apparel Manufacturing	38580	63	195	Educational Services
38186	4	5	Merch. Wholesalers,Durable Gds	38375	453	4163	Elect'l Eqpmt, App, & Comp Mfg	38581	109	720	Truck Transportation
38187	7	23	Prof., Scientific, & Tech Svcs	38376	36	154	Paper Manufacturing	38582	34	204	Food Svcs & Drinking Places
38190	7	22	Truck Transportation	38378	3	4	Food and Beverage Stores	38583	846	7270	Merch. Wholesalers,Durable Gds
38193	1	700	Computer & Electronic Prod Mfg	38379	22	101	Merch. Wholesalers,Durable Gds	38585	128	572	Nursing & Resid. Care Facilit.
38197	1	5000	Paper Manufacturing	38380	7	10	Machinery Manufacturing	38587	27	54	Educational Services
38201	344	3295	Furniture & Related Prod. Mfg	38381	40	598	Chemical Manufacturing	38588	15	99	Wood Product Manufacturing

ZIP CODE	2004 Total Firms	2004 Total Employees	TOP INDUSTRY RANKED on 2004 EMPLOYMENT
38589	2	7	Administrative & Support Svcs
38601	17	99	Educational Services
38602	4	30	Accommodation
38603	141	787	Merch. Wholesalers,Durable Gds
38606	841	7707	Miscellaneous Manufacturing
38609	5	77	Support Activities: Agr./For.
38610	62	1267	Furniture & Related Prod. Mfg
38611	251	1388	Educational Services
38614	977	11121	Relig., Grant, Civic, Prof Org
38617	9	26	Social Assistance
38618	178	1075	Educational Services
38619	91	475	Educational Services
38620	19	70	Exec., Legis., & Other Support
38621	52	322	Plastics & Rubber Products Mfg
38622	10	20	Warehousing and Storage
38623	2	1	Postal Service
38625	11	71	Furniture & Related Prod. Mfg
38626	12	47	Food Svcs & Drinking Places
38627	11	39	Construction of Buildings
38628	1	1	Food and Beverage Stores
38629	29	270	Educational Services
38630	2	18	Support Activities: Agr./For.
38631	31	271	Petroleum & Coal Products Mfg
38632	572	4004	Justice, Pubic Order/Safety
38633	29	286	Furniture & Related Prod. Mfg
38635	542	4327	Educational Services
38637	389	4484	Food Svcs & Drinking Places
38638	17	88	Educational Services
38639	31	197	Food Manufacturing
38641	33	109	Special Trade Contractors
38642	17	93	Crop Production
38643	35	226	Truck Transportation
38644	24	939	Accommodation
38645	26	367	Support Activities: Agr./For.
38646	210	1414	Educational Services
38647	6	6	Crop Production
38649	12	68	Motor Vehicle & Parts Dealers
38650	55	326	Educational Services
38651	81	531	Exec., Legis., & Other Support
38652	680	9331	Machinery Manufacturing
38654	973	11206	Food Svcs & Drinking Places
38655	1367	13814	Food Svcs & Drinking Places
38658	20	98	Educational Services
38659	62	316	Educational Services
38661	22	103	Gasoline Stations
38663	481	4405	Furniture & Related Prod. Mfg
38664	92	10413	Accommodation
38665	21	98	Educational Services
38666	203	1707	Textile Product Mills
38668	526	5523	Furniture & Related Prod. Mfg
38669	2	10	Support Activities: Agr./For.
38670	19	88	Merch. Wholesalers,Durable Gds
38671	1103	12038	General Merchandise Stores
38672	69	699	Educational Services
38673	9	96	Unclassified Establishments
38674	11	75	Merch. Wholesalers,Nondur. Gds
38676	361	2786	Sportg Gds,Hobby,Book, & Music
38677	24	322	Educational Services
38679	9	52	Justice, Pubic Order/Safety
38680	68	413	Construction of Buildings
38683	105	647	Elect'l Eqpmt, App, & Comp Mfg
38685	16	45	Justice, Pubic Order/Safety
38686	1	100	Relig., Grant, Civic, Prof Org
38701	1271	11750	Educational Services
38702	8	76	Merch. Wholesalers,Durable Gds
38703	585	7351	Hospitals
38704	2	4	Merch. Wholesalers,Durable Gds
38720	7	14	Postal Service
38721	25	122	Educational Services
38722	19	135	Educational Services
38723	10	180	Educational Services
38725	31	168	Educational Services
38726	6	10	Food and Beverage Stores
38730	52	329	Miscellaneous Manufacturing
38731	1	24	Support Activities: Agr./For.
38732	813	7453	Merch. Wholesalers,Durable Gds
38733	2	681	Educational Services
38736	6	8	Postal Service
38737	100	1666	Justice, Pubic Order/Safety
38738	3	381	Justice, Pubic Order/Safety
38739	7	73	Relig., Grant, Civic, Prof Org
38740	10	153	Nursing & Resid. Care Facilit.
38744	32	63	Educational Services
38745	3	8	Crop Production
38746	15	81	Support Activities: Agr./For.
38748	133	1311	Food Manufacturing
38751	515	4864	Merch. Wholesalers,Nondur. Gds
38753	74	446	Food Manufacturing
38754	55	858	Food Manufacturing
38756	272	1620	Furn. & Home Furnishgs Stores
38758	1	2	Crop Production
38759	33	186	Crop Production
38760	12	23	Social Assistance
38761	52	647	Educational Services
38762	76	419	Ambulatory Health Care Svcs
38764	15	24	Exec., Legis., & Other Support
38767	1	2	Postal Service
38768	1	0	Postal Service
38769	80	883	Repair and Maintenance
38771	110	868	Apparel Manufacturing
38772	7	525	Crop Production
38773	89	450	Educational Services
38774	83	451	Educational Services
38776	20	630	Admin. of Economic Programs
38778	42	235	Crop Production
38780	2	3	Postal Service
38781	3	5	Exec., Legis., & Other Support
38782	1	20	Support Activities: Agr./For.
38801	1715	15919	Ambulatory Health Care Svcs
38802	7	24	Unclassified Establishments
38803	7	20	Broadcasting
38804	1220	17559	Plastics & Rubber Products Mfg
38820	3	8	Miscellaneous Store Retailers
38821	570	4732	Furniture & Related Prod. Mfg
38824	244	1839	Furniture & Related Prod. Mfg
38825	3	6	Relig., Grant, Civic, Prof Org
38826	90	1611	Furniture & Related Prod. Mfg
38827	140	1496	Furniture & Related Prod. Mfg
38828	31	123	Educational Services
38829	638	6993	Computer & Electronic Prod Mfg
38833	66	714	Truck Transportation
38834	1304	13846	Hospitals
38835	5	6	Special Trade Contractors
38838	23	123	Merch. Wholesalers,Durable Gds
38839	16	33	Nonstore Retailers
38841	71	2384	Furniture & Related Prod. Mfg
38843	522	3694	Educational Services
38844	6	37	Waste Managmt & Remediat'n Svc
38846	23	58	Relig., Grant, Civic, Prof Org
38847	57	507	Apparel Manufacturing
38848	3	5	Postal Service
38849	82	1037	Furniture & Related Prod. Mfg
38850	81	781	Furniture & Related Prod. Mfg
38851	418	4592	Furniture & Related Prod. Mfg
38852	389	2945	Nursing & Resid. Care Facilit.
38854	1	0	Relig., Grant, Civic, Prof Org
38855	113	346	Educational Services
38856	30	403	Apparel Manufacturing
38857	44	409	Educational Services
38858	138	1500	Furniture & Related Prod. Mfg
38859	11	54	Educational Services
38860	217	1595	Furniture & Related Prod. Mfg
38862	39	200	Merch. Wholesalers,Durable Gds
38863	666	7696	Furniture & Related Prod. Mfg
38864	16	108	Food and Beverage Stores
38865	74	364	Truck Transportation
38866	240	2117	Furniture & Related Prod. Mfg
38868	131	1198	Furniture & Related Prod. Mfg
38869	37	480	Furniture & Related Prod. Mfg
38870	78	314	Educational Services
38871	15	142	Nursing & Resid. Care Facilit.
38873	69	419	Educational Services
38874	4	205	Ambulatory Health Care Svcs
38876	29	195	Miscellaneous Store Retailers
38877	5	36	Exec., Legis., & Other Support
38878	77	334	Merch. Wholesalers,Nondur. Gds
38879	132	4953	Furniture & Related Prod. Mfg
38880	4	69	Educational Services
38901	981	11429	Real Estate
38902	5	4	Special Trade Contractors
38913	6	10	Food Svcs & Drinking Places
38914	12	54	Relig., Grant, Civic, Prof Org
38915	216	1531	Furniture & Related Prod. Mfg
38916	227	1909	Hospitals
38917	72	214	Educational Services
38920	7	16	Construction of Buildings
38921	209	1351	Educational Services
38922	108	592	Educational Services
38923	7	25	Special Trade Contractors
38924	8	25	Construction of Buildings
38925	36	127	Educational Services
38926	5	49	Bldg Matl & Garden Eqpmt Dlrs
38927	10	24	Truck Transportation
38928	7	56	Social Assistance
38929	13	32	Truck Transportation
38930	1237	14635	Hospitals
38935	1	3	Justice, Pubic Order/Safety
38940	17	41	Food and Beverage Stores
38941	97	1508	Educational Services
38943	4	10	Food Svcs & Drinking Places
38944	20	111	Support Activities: Agr./For.
38945	1	28	Support Activities: Agr./For.
38946	9	47	Support Activities: Agr./For.
38947	24	190	Educational Services
38948	40	116	Food Svcs & Drinking Places
38950	5	4	Furniture & Related Prod. Mfg
38951	56	171	Justice, Pubic Order/Safety
38952	17	287	Animal Production
38953	5	14	Mining (Except Oil and Gas)
38954	12	48	Support Activities: Agr./For.
38955	3	1	Furn. & Home Furnishgs Stores
38957	66	392	Educational Services
38958	1	3	Air Transportation
38959	1	2	Postal Service
38960	1	75	Unclassified Establishments
38961	10	92	Gasoline Stations
38962	2	4	Food and Beverage Stores
38963	43	198	Unclassified Establishments
38964	4	40	Crop Production
38965	288	2679	Transportation Equipment Mfg
38966	32	145	Educational Services
38967	342	2789	Transportation Equipment Mfg
39038	282	1720	Food Manufacturing
39039	59	225	Support Activities: Agr./For.
39040	62	260	Educational Services
39041	82	529	Educational Services
39042	879	7011	Hospitals
39043	10	23	Administrative & Support Svcs
39044	18	28	Merch. Wholesalers,Nondur. Gds
39045	11	101	Educational Services
39046	732	6423	Educational Services
39047	627	3633	General Merchandise Stores
39051	502	6878	Food Manufacturing
39054	18	184	Crop Production
39056	707	8084	Transportation Equipment Mfg
39057	21	66	Admin. Human Resource Programs
39058	1	10	Broadcasting
39059	299	2312	Elect'l Eqpmt, App, & Comp Mfg
39060	3	11	Prof., Scientific, & Tech Svcs
39061	2	1	Postal Service
39062	15	42	Relig., Grant, Civic, Prof Org
39063	148	1120	Educational Services
39066	85	803	Merch. Wholesalers,Nondur. Gds
39067	24	76	Educational Services
39069	192	1125	Educational Services
39071	159	1159	Administrative & Support Svcs
39073	376	2245	Educational Services
39074	529	7534	Merch. Wholesalers,Nondur. Gds
39077	11	309	Chemical Manufacturing
39078	26	98	Merch. Wholesalers,Durable Gds
39079	41	414	Educational Services
39080	20	27	Exec., Legis., & Other Support
39082	11	27	Relig., Grant, Civic, Prof Org
39083	380	3942	Food Manufacturing
39086	30	112	Merch. Wholesalers,Durable Gds
39087	4	6	Wholesale Elec. Mrkts & Agents
39088	31	135	Support Activities: Agr./For.
39090	634	5409	Hospitals
39092	55	406	Educational Services
39094	38	140	Clothing & Cloth'g Acc. Stores
39095	274	2066	Hospitals
39096	22	922	Educational Services
39097	49	127	Crop Production
39098	3	1	Postal Service
39107	6	31	Educational Services
39108	28	100	Educational Services
39109	9	68	Educational Services
39110	751	6998	Educational Services
39111	407	6982	Food Svcs & Drinking Places
39112	2	10	Plastics & Rubber Products Mfg
39113	24	82	Social Assistance
39114	363	2119	Educational Services
39115	4	18	Support Activities: Agr./For.
39116	49	191	Educational Services
39117	227	2537	Food Manufacturing
39119	94	610	Heavy & Civil Eng. Construct'N
39120	1591	13062	Educational Services
39121	5	13	Justice, Pubic Order/Safety
39122	3	5	Insurance Carriers & Related
39130	12	21	Special Trade Contractors
39140	63	300	Special Trade Contractors
39144	17	23	Crop Production
39145	130	1231	Transportation Equipment Mfg
39146	56	214	Food Svcs & Drinking Places
39148	3	305	Educational Services
39149	18	119	Educational Services
39150	289	2089	Educational Services
39151	12	200	Transportation Equipment Mfg
39152	6	30	Support Activities: Agr./For.
39153	143	1250	Educational Services

39154 - 39837 BUSINESS DATA

ZIP CODE	2004 Total Firms	2004 Total Employees	TOP INDUSTRY RANKED on 2004 EMPLOYMENT	ZIP CODE	2004 Total Firms	2004 Total Employees	TOP INDUSTRY RANKED on 2004 EMPLOYMENT	ZIP CODE	2004 Total Firms	2004 Total Employees	TOP INDUSTRY RANKED on 2004 EMPLOYMENT
39154	228	4691	Prof., Scientific, & Tech Svcs	39352	7	14	Truck Transportation	39569	1	5	Special Trade Contractors
39156	15	464	Paper Manufacturing	39354	27	79	Nat'l Security & Int'l Affairs	39571	433	2413	Construction of Buildings
39157	1556	14543	Food Svcs & Drinking Places	39355	316	2684	Educational Services	39572	42	287	Chemical Manufacturing
39158	15	34	Real Estate	39356	15	33	Construction of Buildings	39573	62	562	Educational Services
39159	186	1130	Educational Services	39358	37	396	Educational Services	39574	177	781	Educational Services
39160	23	53	Educational Services	39359	41	931	Food Manufacturing	39576	301	1643	General Merchandise Stores
39161	1	1	Other Information Services	39360	74	192	Ambulatory Health Care Svcs	39577	411	2906	Wood Product Manufacturing
39162	3	5	Food and Beverage Stores	39361	53	310	Wood Product Manufacturing	39581	380	7571	Hospitals
39163	2	3	Postal Service	39362	54	181	Forestry and Logging	39595	1	13	Social Assistance
39165	5	21	Special Trade Contractors	39363	31	993	Textile Mills	39601	1127	10804	Educational Services
39166	7	21	Motor Vehicle & Parts Dealers	39364	48	231	Bldg Matl & Garden Eqpmt Dlrs	39602	2	1	Motion Pict. & Sound Recording
39167	12	84	Miscellaneous Store Retailers	39365	157	1422	Hospitals	39603	3	4	Prof., Scientific, & Tech Svcs
39168	135	1676	Wood Product Manufacturing	39366	7	23	Merch. Wholesalers,Durable Gds	39629	82	323	Educational Services
39169	83	402	Educational Services	39367	610	6082	Special Trade Contractors	39630	64	478	Support Act. for Transport.
39170	158	575	Educational Services	39401	2003	24668	Hospitals	39631	113	795	Nursing & Resid. Care Facilit.
39171	3	5	Food and Beverage Stores	39402	1506	14823	Food Svcs & Drinking Places	39632	3	62	Relig., Grant, Civic, Prof Org
39173	4	3	Postal Service	39403	3	12	Petroleum & Coal Products Mfg	39633	30	80	Merch. Wholesalers,Durable Gds
39174	9	42	Food Svcs & Drinking Places	39404	13	30	Special Trade Contractors	39635	15	720	Food Manufacturing
39175	104	645	Educational Services	39406	4	12	Ambulatory Health Care Svcs	39638	115	745	Wood Product Manufacturing
39176	78	368	Nursing & Resid. Care Facilit.	39421	102	593	Educational Services	39641	38	142	Construction of Buildings
39177	6	28	Crop Production	39422	281	4025	Food Manufacturing	39643	18	48	Social Assistance
39179	11	66	Educational Services	39423	51	467	Wood Product Manufacturing	39645	176	1110	Educational Services
39180	1247	19475	Accommodation	39425	43	220	Educational Services	39647	20	53	Wood Product Manufacturing
39181	3	20	Social Assistance	39426	134	615	Educational Services	39648	1127	10730	Food and Beverage Stores
39182	2	15	Social Assistance	39427	22	41	Educational Services	39649	4	64	Admin. of Economic Programs
39183	607	6038	Ambulatory Health Care Svcs	39428	359	4427	Food Manufacturing	39652	225	1744	Wood Product Manufacturing
39189	67	361	Educational Services	39429	785	7106	General Merchandise Stores	39653	164	998	Educational Services
39190	4	20	Museums, Hist. Sites,& Similar	39436	3	8	Food and Beverage Stores	39654	277	2014	Paper Manufacturing
39191	96	699	Educational Services	39437	324	4233	Educational Services	39656	10	13	Relig., Grant, Civic, Prof Org
39192	31	104	Relig., Grant, Civic, Prof Org	39439	144	905	Educational Services	39657	60	226	Forestry and Logging
39193	9	3520	Hospitals	39440	1435	20921	Food Manufacturing	39661	30	84	Educational Services
39194	691	6839	Chemical Manufacturing	39441	6	42	Crop Production	39662	14	97	Prof., Scientific, & Tech Svcs
39201	1258	21126	Exec., Legis., & Other Support	39442	3	22	Forestry and Logging	39663	44	491	Bldg Matl & Garden Eqpmt Dlrs
39202	822	14988	Hospitals	39443	395	2879	Educational Services	39664	26	36	Relig., Grant, Civic, Prof Org
39203	298	2416	Educational Services	39451	210	1093	Educational Services	39665	7	22	Broadcasting
39204	1011	13255	Hospitals	39452	634	3904	Educational Services	39666	217	1360	Educational Services
39205	4	8	Insurance Carriers & Related	39455	183	1410	Merch. Wholesalers,Durable Gds	39667	386	2252	Educational Services
39206	1134	9507	Food Svcs & Drinking Places	39456	29	69	Educational Services	39668	11	30	Pipeline Transportation
39207	3	1	Repair and Maintenance	39457	11	30	Waste Managmt & Remediat'n Svc	39669	205	1214	Educational Services
39208	1055	11853	Justice, Pubic Order/Safety	39459	61	588	Truck Transportation	39701	1044	11363	Educational Services
39209	1145	12326	Educational Services	39460	3	4	Food and Beverage Stores	39702	711	7441	Plastics & Rubber Products Mfg
39210	4	297	Educational Services	39461	9	30	Forestry and Logging	39703	3	20	Exec., Legis., & Other Support
39211	1145	13291	Food Svcs & Drinking Places	39462	92	585	Wood Product Manufacturing	39704	2	17	Construction of Buildings
39212	614	3945	Educational Services	39463	11	36	Merch. Wholesalers,Durable Gds	39705	713	8213	General Merchandise Stores
39213	726	9173	Utilities	39464	24	41	Fabricated Metal Product Mfg	39710	37	234	Justice, Pubic Order/Safety
39215	4	1	Real Estate	39465	491	2667	Food Svcs & Drinking Places	39730	476	3715	Chemical Manufacturing
39216	827	25666	Hospitals	39466	991	6110	Educational Services	39735	219	1336	Educational Services
39217	4	9	Unclassified Establishments	39470	380	2628	Exec., Legis., & Other Support	39736	28	289	Rail Transportation
39218	382	6113	Truck Transportation	39474	285	1724	Educational Services	39737	7	14	Leather & Allied Product Mfg
39225	2	2	Prof., Scientific, & Tech Svcs	39475	284	2289	Exec., Legis., & Other Support	39739	68	4865	Ambulatory Health Care Svcs
39232	808	12119	Hospitals	39476	195	1450	Apparel Manufacturing	39740	89	382	Educational Services
39236	16	33	Prof., Scientific, & Tech Svcs	39477	34	319	Truck Transportation	39741	7	11	Postal Service
39269	16	285	Justice, Pubic Order/Safety	39478	34	200	Wood Product Manufacturing	39743	49	135	Educational Services
39272	384	4161	Machinery Manufacturing	39479	96	519	Educational Services	39744	235	1777	Nursing & Resid. Care Facilit.
39282	8	17	Special Trade Contractors	39480	54	145	Justice, Pubic Order/Safety	39745	16	1284	Construction of Buildings
39283	1	0	Administrative & Support Svcs	39481	26	100	Educational Services	39746	69	935	Chemical Manufacturing
39286	5	15	Ambulatory Health Care Svcs	39482	135	640	Educational Services	39747	42	228	Educational Services
39288	8	260	Merch. Wholesalers,Nondur. Gds	39483	90	527	Educational Services	39750	71	348	Educational Services
39289	2	1	Prof., Scientific, & Tech Svcs	39501	1558	16821	Food Svcs & Drinking Places	39751	14	35	Food and Beverage Stores
39296	8	22	Relig., Grant, Civic, Prof Org	39502	7	72	Unclassified Establishments	39752	47	339	Educational Services
39298	1	10	Truck Transportation	39503	1444	15274	Food Svcs & Drinking Places	39753	14	762	Educational Services
39301	1937	27212	Hospitals	39505	5	7	Construction of Buildings	39754	5	63	Educational Services
39302	5	23	Credit Intermediation & Relatd	39506	9	11	Prof., Scientific, & Tech Svcs	39755	12	74	Educational Services
39303	6	14	Construction of Buildings	39507	909	8143	Hospitals	39756	20	235	Transportation Equipment Mfg
39304	1	3	Insurance Carriers & Related	39520	768	6264	Food Svcs & Drinking Places	39759	1294	12638	Educational Services
39305	506	3991	Educational Services	39521	5	5	Insurance Carriers & Related	39760	3	502	Hospitals
39307	533	8752	Educational Services	39522	1	6	Other Information Services	39762	156	6628	Educational Services
39309	39	712	Support Act. for Transport.	39525	184	876	Food Svcs & Drinking Places	39766	43	96	Special Trade Contractors
39320	33	64	Utilities	39529	19	1495	Nat'l Security & Int'l Affairs	39767	10	51	Truck Transportation
39322	33	261	Relig., Grant, Civic, Prof Org	39530	808	17906	Amusement, Gambling,& Recreat.	39769	49	115	Educational Services
39323	18	22	Merch. Wholesalers,Durable Gds	39531	907	13433	Hospitals	39771	10	92	Exec., Legis., & Other Support
39324	7	28	Exec., Legis., & Other Support	39532	610	3324	Ambulatory Health Care Svcs	39772	31	160	Educational Services
39325	91	523	Educational Services	39533	10	53	Social Assistance	39773	738	8418	Food Manufacturing
39326	11	23	Sportg Gds,Hobby,Book, & Music	39534	66	970	Securities/Commodity Contracts	39776	29	122	Furniture & Related Prod. Mfg
39327	140	1328	Educational Services	39535	4	6	Administrative & Support Svcs	39813	91	487	Hospitals
39328	185	1042	Educational Services	39540	374	3228	General Merchandise Stores	39815	46	478	Chemical Manufacturing
39330	63	355	Educational Services	39552	19	62	Admin. of Economic Programs	39817	539	5543	Furn. & Home Furnishgs Stores
39332	46	135	Miscellaneous Store Retailers	39553	565	4224	Educational Services	39818	6	3	Bldg Matl & Garden Eqpmt Dlrs
39335	30	81	Food and Beverage Stores	39555	57	578	Educational Services	39819	419	3997	Food and Beverage Stores
39336	10	102	Gasoline Stations	39556	127	779	Educational Services	39823	476	3004	Educational Services
39337	22	44	Food and Beverage Stores	39558	8	60	Merch. Wholesalers,Nondur. Gds	39824	6	23	Crop Production
39338	32	66	Relig., Grant, Civic, Prof Org	39560	540	4692	Educational Services	39825	27	67	Repair and Maintenance
39339	565	5838	Merch. Wholesalers,Durable Gds	39561	20	122	Telecommunications	39826	13	47	Nursing & Resid. Care Facilit.
39341	302	2514	Educational Services	39562	223	1119	Construction of Buildings	39827	74	422	Bldg Matl & Garden Eqpmt Dlrs
39342	44	317	Nursing & Resid. Care Facilit.	39563	509	4770	Educational Services	39828	660	5621	Educational Services
39345	272	3801	Furn. & Home Furnishgs Stores	39564	1145	8224	Food Svcs & Drinking Places	39829	15	30	Real Estate
39346	60	265	Apparel Manufacturing	39565	236	1188	Educational Services	39832	17	820	Paper Manufacturing
39347	20	46	Chemical Manufacturing	39566	5	7	Special Trade Contractors	39834	51	257	Transportation Equipment Mfg
39348	7	13	Exec., Legis., & Other Support	39567	935	17275	Transportation Equipment Mfg	39836	8	12	Crop Production
39350	854	11507	Exec., Legis., & Other Support	39568	8	18	Justice, Pubic Order/Safety	39837	265	1451	Hospitals

ZIP CODE	2004 Total Firms	2004 Total Employees	TOP INDUSTRY RANKED on 2004 EMPLOYMENT	ZIP CODE	2004 Total Firms	2004 Total Employees	TOP INDUSTRY RANKED on 2004 EMPLOYMENT	ZIP CODE	2004 Total Firms	2004 Total Employees	TOP INDUSTRY RANKED on 2004 EMPLOYMENT
39840	253	1919	Educational Services	40150	84	464	Gasoline Stations	40351	777	9085	Educational Services
39841	22	172	Food and Beverage Stores	40152	43	179	Educational Services	40353	826	8122	Food Manufacturing
39842	327	2290	Educational Services	40153	10	23	Relig., Grant, Civic, Prof Org	40355	15	60	Construction of Buildings
39845	363	2730	Crop Production	40155	44	225	Food Svcs & Drinking Places	40356	1148	11767	Special Trade Contractors
39846	88	665	Apparel Manufacturing	40157	33	64	Educational Services	40357	14	51	Educational Services
39851	94	623	Educational Services	40160	764	5734	Food Svcs & Drinking Places	40358	6	122	Construction of Buildings
39852	1	2	Postal Service	40161	5	10	Bldg Matl & Garden Eqpmt Dlrs	40359	214	1471	Educational Services
39854	73	324	Educational Services	40162	48	195	Educational Services	40360	198	1513	Apparel Manufacturing
39859	30	62	Special Trade Contractors	40164	1	0	Administrative & Support Svcs	40361	606	5900	Educational Services
39861	24	104	Forestry and Logging	40165	811	7444	Publishing Industries	40363	3	70	Relig., Grant, Civic, Prof Org
39862	47	104	Crop Production	40170	12	20	Construction of Buildings	40370	36	49	Special Trade Contractors
39866	34	159	Machinery Manufacturing	40171	2	2	Merch. Wholesalers,Durable Gds	40371	65	217	Educational Services
39867	4	20	Forestry and Logging	40175	223	915	Educational Services	40372	48	112	Miscellaneous Store Retailers
39870	90	406	Exec., Legis., & Other Support	40176	16	25	Construction of Buildings	40374	28	181	Construction of Buildings
39877	21	48	Food Svcs & Drinking Places	40177	49	201	Educational Services	40376	22	186	Accommodation
39885	23	71	Crop Production	40178	10	14	Food and Beverage Stores	40379	63	226	Fabricated Metal Product Mfg
39886	56	258	Machinery Manufacturing	40201	20	86	Special Trade Contractors	40380	259	1719	Educational Services
39897	71	381	Social Assistance	40202	2329	69030	Ambulatory Health Care Svcs	40383	768	7406	Print'g & Related Supp't Act's
39901	4	11	Prof., Scientific, & Tech Svcs	40203	952	18482	Relig., Grant, Civic, Prof Org	40385	42	188	Educational Services
40003	26	115	Food Manufacturing	40204	791	8642	Food Svcs & Drinking Places	40387	26	37	Food and Beverage Stores
40004	1009	11140	Transportation Equipment Mfg	40205	850	10931	Educational Services	40390	110	1471	Educational Services
40006	105	548	Educational Services	40206	810	11276	Food Manufacturing	40391	1179	13556	Utilities
40007	4	31	Special Trade Contractors	40207	2049	25633	Hospitals	40392	5	11	Isps, Web Search Portals
40008	75	242	Educational Services	40208	444	6122	Educational Services	40402	105	1390	Computer & Electronic Prod Mfg
40009	12	27	Special Trade Contractors	40209	244	11002	Educational Services	40403	645	6846	Machinery Manufacturing
40010	62	1233	Educational Services	40210	303	7602	Beverage & Tobacco Product Mfg	40404	2	586	Educational Services
40011	49	258	Educational Services	40211	619	6597	Educational Services	40405	1	2	Postal Service
40012	18	66	Educational Services	40212	264	2868	Educational Services	40409	64	359	Nursing & Resid. Care Facilit.
40013	62	295	Educational Services	40213	996	24980	Couriers and Messengers	40410	10	71	Special Trade Contractors
40014	483	2463	Educational Services	40214	958	12012	Special Trade Contractors	40419	63	240	Educational Services
40018	2	13	Administrative & Support Svcs	40215	358	4355	Hospitals	40422	1089	14615	Elect'l Eqpmt, App, & Comp Mfg
40019	143	1337	Textile Product Mills	40216	1094	13039	Chemical Manufacturing	40423	6	13	Special Trade Contractors
40020	7	10	Merch. Wholesalers,Durable Gds	40217	428	5637	Hospitals	40434	21	77	Heavy & Civil Eng. Construct'N
40022	23	30	Food Manufacturing	40218	1332	17530	Personal and Laundry Services	40437	61	276	Educational Services
40023	54	222	Special Trade Contractors	40219	1097	14136	Food Svcs & Drinking Places	40440	52	325	Machinery Manufacturing
40025	2	3	Postal Service	40220	845	9326	Food Svcs & Drinking Places	40442	7	14	Food and Beverage Stores
40026	84	647	Educational Services	40221	1	7	Support Act. for Transport.	40444	350	2435	Social Assistance
40027	5	198	Food Svcs & Drinking Places	40222	1440	16633	Food Svcs & Drinking Places	40445	16	21	Relig., Grant, Civic, Prof Org
40031	564	6920	Justice, Pubic Order/Safety	40223	1076	17981	Insurance Carriers & Related	40447	225	1855	Educational Services
40033	443	5135	Fabricated Metal Product Mfg	40224	1	0	Relig., Grant, Civic, Prof Org	40448	9	58	Educational Services
40036	6	62	Mining (Except Oil and Gas)	40225	5	1503	Repair and Maintenance	40452	3	0	Construction of Buildings
40037	43	342	Nursing & Resid. Care Facilit.	40228	353	3560	Special Trade Contractors	40456	328	2786	Educational Services
40040	15	39	Justice, Pubic Order/Safety	40229	476	4853	Food Svcs & Drinking Places	40460	1	0	Relig., Grant, Civic, Prof Org
40041	4	259	Nursing & Resid. Care Facilit.	40231	2	156	Postal Service	40461	43	149	Educational Services
40045	48	333	Fabricated Metal Product Mfg	40232	10	69	Construction of Buildings	40464	8	21	Food and Beverage Stores
40046	26	32	Educational Services	40233	2	10	Perform'g Arts, Spec. Sports	40468	47	483	Relig., Grant, Civic, Prof Org
40047	331	2153	Educational Services	40241	612	14473	Transportation Equipment Mfg	40472	44	213	Wood Product Manufacturing
40048	8	121	Relig., Grant, Civic, Prof Org	40242	207	1420	Educational Services	40473	16	368	Amusement, Gambling,& Recreat.
40049	1	100	Hospitals	40243	718	5319	Food Svcs & Drinking Places	40475	1609	17763	Educational Services
40050	107	727	Educational Services	40245	342	3395	Merch. Wholesalers,Nondur. Gds	40476	5	3	Merch. Wholesalers,Durable Gds
40051	109	1079	Food and Beverage Stores	40250	14	34	Special Trade Contractors	40481	31	129	Educational Services
40052	10	23	Prof., Scientific, & Tech Svcs	40251	1	2	Administrative & Support Svcs	40484	338	2973	Merch. Wholesalers,Durable Gds
40055	24	74	Petroleum & Coal Products Mfg	40252	9	51	Merch. Wholesalers,Durable Gds	40486	34	338	Food and Beverage Stores
40056	81	524	Nursing & Resid. Care Facilit.	40253	8	44	Administrative & Support Svcs	40488	3	2	Sportg Gds,Hobby,Book, & Music
40057	41	181	Educational Services	40255	7	9	Construction of Buildings	40489	50	298	Educational Services
40058	10	24	Merch. Wholesalers,Durable Gds	40256	1	3	Relig., Grant, Civic, Prof Org	40492	3	5	General Merchandise Stores
40059	373	1580	Food Svcs & Drinking Places	40257	6	9	Administrative & Support Svcs	40495	1	1	Relig., Grant, Civic, Prof Org
40060	15	27	Food and Beverage Stores	40258	545	7293	Food Svcs & Drinking Places	40502	861	8383	Hospitals
40061	1	3	Crop Production	40259	7	23	Administrative & Support Svcs	40503	1906	21185	Food Svcs & Drinking Places
40062	2	5	Special Trade Contractors	40261	3	11	Administrative & Support Svcs	40504	1057	15491	Hospitals
40063	2	157	Justice, Pubic Order/Safety	40268	2	2	Construction of Buildings	40505	1272	13033	Special Trade Contractors
40065	900	9685	Merch. Wholesalers,Nondur. Gds	40269	12	26	Administrative & Support Svcs	40507	1161	12341	Prof., Scientific, & Tech Svcs
40066	9	38	Special Trade Contractors	40270	1	7	Merch. Wholesalers,Durable Gds	40508	868	9908	Hospitals
40067	141	1763	Fabricated Metal Product Mfg	40272	578	5291	Educational Services	40509	1284	18525	Food Svcs & Drinking Places
40068	36	319	Unclassified Establishments	40280	7	697	Educational Services	40510	152	2745	Food Svcs & Drinking Places
40069	287	2184	Transportation Equipment Mfg	40291	570	3679	Food Svcs & Drinking Places	40511	981	27728	Machinery Manufacturing
40070	26	132	Truck Transportation	40292	17	2875	Educational Services	40512	1	0	Special Trade Contractors
40071	260	1116	Educational Services	40299	1786	24352	Merch. Wholesalers,Durable Gds	40513	283	2978	Food Svcs & Drinking Places
40075	6	13	Truck Transportation	40310	26	117	Justice, Pubic Order/Safety	40514	108	657	Food and Beverage Stores
40076	34	173	Educational Services	40311	174	1186	Nursing & Resid. Care Facilit.	40515	306	2346	Food Svcs & Drinking Places
40077	13	25	Repair and Maintenance	40312	132	808	Apparel Manufacturing	40516	60	466	Nonmetallic Mineral Prod. Mfg
40078	29	136	Educational Services	40313	22	62	Educational Services	40517	784	5927	Educational Services
40104	29	167	Mining (Except Oil and Gas)	40316	7	66	Educational Services	40522	9	15	Merch. Wholesalers,Durable Gds
40107	34	210	Beverage & Tobacco Product Mfg	40317	3	28	Justice, Pubic Order/Safety	40523	6	8	Special Trade Contractors
40108	462	2776	Chemical Manufacturing	40319	2	2	Postal Service	40524	11	40	Special Trade Contractors
40109	78	491	Heavy & Civil Eng. Construct'N	40320	3	60	Waste Managmt & Remediat'n Svc	40533	1	0	Truck Transportation
40110	7	480	Beverage & Tobacco Product Mfg	40322	147	781	Social Assistance	40536	71	4335	Hospitals
40111	48	156	Educational Services	40324	1082	11456	Food Svcs & Drinking Places	40544	3	3	Prof., Scientific, & Tech Svcs
40115	15	33	Educational Services	40328	15	24	Food and Beverage Stores	40546	2	60	Relig., Grant, Civic, Prof Org
40117	59	207	Educational Services	40330	637	6218	Transportation Equipment Mfg	40555	12	30	Administrative & Support Svcs
40118	143	1187	Educational Services	40334	2	50	Nursing & Resid. Care Facilit.	40575	1	5	Crop Production
40119	37	224	Accommodation	40336	333	2403	Educational Services	40577	2	1	Prof., Scientific, & Tech Svcs
40121	107	1767	Hospitals	40337	72	292	Wood Product Manufacturing	40579	1	0	Food Svcs & Drinking Places
40129	5	47	Food Svcs & Drinking Places	40339	3	12	Miscellaneous Manufacturing	40583	2	9	Special Trade Contractors
40140	12	35	Food Svcs & Drinking Places	40340	7	17	Special Trade Contractors	40588	9	18	Construction of Buildings
40142	37	34	Heavy & Civil Eng. Construct'N	40342	479	4140	Educational Services	40591	3	7	Construction of Buildings
40143	264	1777	Hospitals	40346	17	158	Machinery Manufacturing	40601	2091	39947	Admin. Human Resource Programs
40144	38	241	Educational Services	40347	130	1007	Support Activities: Agr./For.	40602	8	43	Justice, Pubic Order/Safety
40145	7	5	Food and Beverage Stores	40348	32	338	Machinery Manufacturing	40603	1	2	Administrative & Support Svcs
40146	128	514	Relig., Grant, Civic, Prof Org	40350	1	1	Personal and Laundry Services	40604	3	4	Real Estate

BUSINESS DATA

ZIP CODE	2004 Total Firms	2004 Total Employees	TOP INDUSTRY RANKED on 2004 EMPLOYMENT	ZIP CODE	2004 Total Firms	2004 Total Employees	TOP INDUSTRY RANKED on 2004 EMPLOYMENT	ZIP CODE	2004 Total Firms	2004 Total Employees	TOP INDUSTRY RANKED on 2004 EMPLOYMENT
40621	7	403	Admin. Human Resource Programs	40999	1	1	Repair and Maintenance	41179	204	1357	Educational Services
40622	12	2392	Exec., Legis., & Other Support	41001	388	3558	Food Manufacturing	41180	9	30	Justice, Pubic Order/Safety
40701	1169	11660	Hospitals	41002	83	533	Plastics & Rubber Products Mfg	41181	5	24	Food Manufacturing
40702	3	10	Insurance Carriers & Related	41003	25	68	Justice, Pubic Order/Safety	41183	27	175	Special Trade Contractors
40724	1	0	Justice, Pubic Order/Safety	41004	107	496	Educational Services	41189	42	155	Educational Services
40729	108	892	Food and Beverage Stores	41005	420	3826	Exec., Legis., & Other Support	41203	17	19	Repair and Maintenance
40730	1	1	Motor Vehicle & Parts Dealers	41006	89	1132	Nonmetallic Mineral Prod. Mfg	41204	9	24	Justice, Pubic Order/Safety
40734	62	999	Wood Product Manufacturing	41007	35	240	Relig., Grant, Civic, Prof Org	41214	14	998	Unclassified Establishments
40737	9	23	Construction of Buildings	41008	399	4769	Chemical Manufacturing	41216	10	57	Merch. Wholesalers,Durable Gds
40740	44	249	Wood Product Manufacturing	41010	35	111	Gasoline Stations	41219	27	77	Educational Services
40741	1141	11970	Food Manufacturing	41011	1377	13208	Food Svcs & Drinking Places	41222	64	414	Social Assistance
40743	10	101	Credit Intermediation & Relatd	41012	2	2	Administrative & Support Svcs	41224	219	1572	Mining (Except Oil and Gas)
40744	338	3747	Isps, Web Search Portals	41014	165	1653	Ambulatory Health Care Svcs	41226	2	4	Special Trade Contractors
40745	1	3	Exec., Legis., & Other Support	41015	420	4049	Educational Services	41230	385	2546	Educational Services
40754	1	2	Mining (Except Oil and Gas)	41016	119	644	Educational Services	41231	16	69	Mining (Except Oil and Gas)
40755	4	20	Relig., Grant, Civic, Prof Org	41017	1141	18449	Hospitals	41232	23	79	Gasoline Stations
40759	16	114	Educational Services	41018	816	11770	Prof., Scientific, & Tech Svcs	41234	8	10	Prof., Scientific, & Tech Svcs
40763	7	30	Merch. Wholesalers,Durable Gds	41022	11	24	Heavy & Civil Eng. Construct'N	41238	20	32	Food and Beverage Stores
40769	441	4836	Educational Services	41030	91	535	Relig., Grant, Civic, Prof Org	41240	539	5046	Food Svcs & Drinking Places
40771	17	60	Justice, Pubic Order/Safety	41031	518	5099	Chemical Manufacturing	41250	13	306	Mining (Except Oil and Gas)
40801	4	23	Social Assistance	41033	17	42	Merch. Wholesalers,Durable Gds	41254	8	15	Special Trade Contractors
40803	4	9	Truck Transportation	41034	11	45	Fabricated Metal Product Mfg	41255	9	17	Truck Transportation
40806	82	463	Exec., Legis., & Other Support	41035	242	2390	General Merchandise Stores	41256	66	325	Telecommunications
40807	17	84	Exec., Legis., & Other Support	41039	35	101	Educational Services	41257	4	5	Merch. Wholesalers,Nondur. Gds
40808	6	9	Prof., Scientific, & Tech Svcs	41040	213	1275	Educational Services	41260	11	140	Exec., Legis., & Other Support
40810	30	176	Mining (Except Oil and Gas)	41041	355	2607	Educational Services	41262	12	70	Food and Beverage Stores
40813	4	4	Postal Service	41042	2024	32041	Food Svcs & Drinking Places	41263	5	35	Special Trade Contractors
40815	14	106	Educational Services	41043	24	73	Truck Transportation	41264	9	38	Truck Transportation
40816	2	52	Mining (Except Oil and Gas)	41044	16	54	Food Svcs & Drinking Places	41265	24	769	Heavy & Civil Eng. Construct'N
40818	5	2	Mining (Except Oil and Gas)	41045	46	734	Primary Metal Manufacturing	41267	51	267	Educational Services
40819	7	27	Truck Transportation	41046	30	87	Motor Vehicle & Parts Dealers	41268	10	51	Justice, Pubic Order/Safety
40820	4	7	Support Activities: Agr./For.	41048	310	11758	Support Act. for Transport.	41271	3	51	Educational Services
40823	161	1445	Educational Services	41049	16	62	Educational Services	41274	19	100	Educational Services
40824	7	19	Heavy & Civil Eng. Construct'N	41051	324	2189	Educational Services	41301	200	1080	Educational Services
40826	4	42	Educational Services	41052	8	19	Nursing & Resid. Care Facilit.	41311	236	1912	Educational Services
40827	7	12	Food and Beverage Stores	41053	9	13	Special Trade Contractors	41313	4	69	Educational Services
40828	91	866	Mining (Except Oil and Gas)	41054	3	10	Food and Beverage Stores	41314	159	1142	Educational Services
40829	11	265	Petroleum & Coal Products Mfg	41055	31	78	Relig., Grant, Civic, Prof Org	41317	4	10	Prof., Scientific, & Tech Svcs
40830	4	33	Mining (Except Oil and Gas)	41056	686	8689	Machinery Manufacturing	41332	28	261	Textile Product Mills
40831	407	4007	Hospitals	41059	56	231	Merch. Wholesalers,Durable Gds	41333	1	1	Repair and Maintenance
40840	16	316	Mining (Except Oil and Gas)	41061	1	2	Relig., Grant, Civic, Prof Org	41338	3	3	Food and Beverage Stores
40843	7	602	Mining (Except Oil and Gas)	41062	1	2	Postal Service	41339	361	3075	Educational Services
40844	8	59	Educational Services	41063	30	121	Educational Services	41342	1	0	Bldg Matl & Garden Eqpmt Dlrs
40845	7	8	Food and Beverage Stores	41064	64	195	Nursing & Resid. Care Facilit.	41344	1	1	Postal Service
40847	3	36	Educational Services	41065	1	0	Postal Service	41348	13	101	Educational Services
40849	4	10	Special Trade Contractors	41071	738	7149	Food Svcs & Drinking Places	41352	5	13	Merch. Wholesalers,Nondur. Gds
40854	24	172	Rail Transportation	41073	182	1615	Food Svcs & Drinking Places	41360	10	104	Social Assistance
40855	21	102	Ambulatory Health Care Svcs	41074	111	982	Educational Services	41364	1	1	Food and Beverage Stores
40856	4	3	Support Activities: Agr./For.	41075	413	4402	Hospitals	41365	9	39	Educational Services
40858	4	9	Food and Beverage Stores	41076	417	5821	Food Svcs & Drinking Places	41366	2	21	Educational Services
40862	7	54	Mining (Except Oil and Gas)	41080	31	93	Merch. Wholesalers,Durable Gds	41367	2	2	Postal Service
40863	5	172	Mining (Except Oil and Gas)	41081	2	12	Merch. Wholesalers,Nondur. Gds	41368	1	2	Food and Beverage Stores
40865	6	28	Support Activities: Agr./For.	41083	7	26	Nursing & Resid. Care Facilit.	41385	6	45	Educational Services
40868	20	23	Food Svcs & Drinking Places	41085	30	243	Special Trade Contractors	41386	4	5	Repair and Maintenance
40870	11	59	Fabricated Metal Product Mfg	41086	26	170	Perform'g Arts, Spec. Sports	41390	1	0	Broadcasting
40873	27	100	Educational Services	41091	184	913	Educational Services	41397	2	22	Support Act. for Transport.
40874	5	6	Support Act. for Transport.	41092	43	280	Educational Services	41408	5	40	Educational Services
40902	8	27	Furn. & Home Furnishgs Stores	41093	22	122	Wood Product Manufacturing	41413	4	63	Publishing Industries
40903	9	77	Educational Services	41094	325	3240	Food Svcs & Drinking Places	41419	1	0	Postal Service
40906	458	3802	Educational Services	41095	147	1248	Transportation Equipment Mfg	41421	1	0	Unclassified Establishments
40913	13	256	Accommodation	41096	18	34	Food and Beverage Stores	41422	1	0	Postal Service
40914	11	27	Food and Beverage Stores	41097	217	1527	Educational Services	41425	26	64	Educational Services
40915	11	23	Bldg Matl & Garden Eqpmt Dlrs	41098	7	15	Rail Transportation	41426	4	5	Postal Service
40921	6	14	Truck Transportation	41099	5	2198	Educational Services	41433	1	0	Postal Service
40923	7	17	Social Assistance	41101	1263	19420	Hospitals	41451	2	2	Personal and Laundry Services
40927	3	128	Nonstore Retailers	41102	596	6439	Educational Services	41464	7	36	Justice, Pubic Order/Safety
40930	8	64	Educational Services	41105	5	28	Social Assistance	41465	401	2607	Educational Services
40932	3	8	General Merchandise Stores	41121	17	111	Educational Services	41472	350	2878	Justice, Pubic Order/Safety
40935	31	118	Educational Services	41124	25	127	Educational Services	41477	4	48	Educational Services
40939	6	109	Educational Services	41128	2	6	Furn. & Home Furnishgs Stores	41501	1271	13373	Mining (Except Oil and Gas)
40940	9	73	Relig., Grant, Civic, Prof Org	41129	272	2401	Chemical Manufacturing	41502	8	30	Justice, Pubic Order/Safety
40941	13	90	Ambulatory Health Care Svcs	41132	1	1	Postal Service	41503	142	1952	Hospitals
40943	11	92	Educational Services	41137	5	9	Prof., Scientific, & Tech Svcs	41512	11	44	Food and Beverage Stores
40944	1	1	Postal Service	41139	189	1255	Food Svcs & Drinking Places	41513	13	62	Admin. of Economic Programs
40949	16	36	Heavy & Civil Eng. Construct'N	41141	40	194	Educational Services	41514	95	686	Educational Services
40953	7	7	Construction of Buildings	41142	2	3	Postal Service	41517	5	40	Educational Services
40955	2	16	Mining (Except Oil and Gas)	41143	491	4495	Food Manufacturing	41519	11	25	Heavy & Civil Eng. Construct'N
40958	3	3	Postal Service	41144	303	2385	Educational Services	41520	15	121	Educational Services
40962	528	3753	Educational Services	41146	4	18	Nonmetallic Mineral Prod. Mfg	41522	145	674	Educational Services
40964	1	2	Postal Service	41149	9	45	Educational Services	41524	43	378	Mining (Except Oil and Gas)
40965	673	6913	General Merchandise Stores	41159	7	22	Oil and Gas Extraction	41526	1	18	Food Svcs & Drinking Places
40972	20	247	Educational Services	41160	2	2	Postal Service	41527	8	17	Print'g & Related Supp't Act's
40977	253	2225	Educational Services	41164	258	2062	Educational Services	41528	29	82	Mining (Except Oil and Gas)
40979	4	3	Special Trade Contractors	41166	11	28	Relig., Grant, Civic, Prof Org	41531	6	3	Motor Vehicle & Parts Dealers
40981	1	1	Relig., Grant, Civic, Prof Org	41168	35	416	Social Assistance	41534	2	2	Postal Service
40982	2	2	Postal Service	41169	211	1971	Transportation Equipment Mfg	41535	7	4	Truck Transportation
40983	2	3	Special Trade Contractors	41171	134	714	Educational Services	41537	109	692	Hospitals
40988	10	113	Educational Services	41173	2	2	Truck Transportation	41538	4	4	Sportg Gds,Hobby,Book, & Music
40995	1	2	Postal Service	41174	10	67	Administrative & Support Svcs	41539	32	1195	Mining (Except Oil and Gas)
40997	4	7	Social Assistance	41175	149	933	Nonmetallic Mineral Prod. Mfg	41540	5	147	Educational Services

ZIP CODE	2004 Total Firms	2004 Total Employ-ees	TOP INDUSTRY RANKED on 2004 EMPLOYMENT	ZIP CODE	2004 Total Firms	2004 Total Employ-ees	TOP INDUSTRY RANKED on 2004 EMPLOYMENT	ZIP CODE	2004 Total Firms	2004 Total Employ-ees	TOP INDUSTRY RANKED on 2004 EMPLOYMENT
41542	3	8	Social Assistance	41775	6	22	Accommodation	42101	2083	34115	Merch. Wholesalers,Durable Gds
41543	7	14	Merch. Wholesalers,Nondur. Gds	41776	40	158	Mining (Except Oil and Gas)	42102	18	25	Insurance Carriers & Related
41544	22	43	Repair and Maintenance	41777	13	37	Educational Services	42103	470	4419	Apparel Manufacturing
41546	3	2	Administrative & Support Svcs	41778	3	7	Social Assistance	42104	994	12010	Food Svcs & Drinking Places
41547	5	33	Educational Services	41804	12	31	Gasoline Stations	42120	34	97	Crop Production
41548	23	71	Food and Beverage Stores	41810	4	13	Publishing Industries	42122	54	166	Educational Services
41549	3	211	Mining (Except Oil and Gas)	41812	8	185	Mining (Except Oil and Gas)	42123	15	8	Food and Beverage Stores
41553	63	635	Mining (Except Oil and Gas)	41815	12	89	Construction of Buildings	42124	1	1	Food and Beverage Stores
41554	11	58	Educational Services	41817	13	56	Repair and Maintenance	42127	253	1784	Food Svcs & Drinking Places
41555	6	77	Educational Services	41819	5	17	Nonmetallic Mineral Prod. Mfg	42128	1	7	Prof., Scientific, & Tech Svcs
41557	21	40	Special Trade Contractors	41821	2	3	Educational Services	42129	258	2147	Computer & Electronic Prod Mfg
41558	12	220	Mining (Except Oil and Gas)	41822	240	1362	Educational Services	42130	2	2	Miscellaneous Store Retailers
41559	22	112	Justice, Pubic Order/Safety	41824	34	206	Gasoline Stations	42131	2	1	Securities/Commodity Contracts
41560	24	247	Justice, Pubic Order/Safety	41825	4	3	Furn. & Home Furnishgs Stores	42133	42	147	Nonstore Retailers
41561	2	2	Personal and Laundry Services	41826	12	49	Justice, Pubic Order/Safety	42134	621	6468	Food Svcs & Drinking Places
41562	28	303	Rail Transportation	41828	28	393	Mining (Except Oil and Gas)	42135	2	3	Justice, Pubic Order/Safety
41563	5	6	Gasoline Stations	41831	25	338	Mining (Except Oil and Gas)	42140	52	306	Educational Services
41564	19	1107	Mining (Except Oil and Gas)	41832	4	71	Educational Services	42141	1264	15428	Print'g & Related Supp't Act's
41566	6	93	Unclassified Establishments	41833	2	13	Educational Services	42142	3	4	Special Trade Contractors
41567	17	56	Special Trade Contractors	41834	13	83	Educational Services	42151	3	6	Food Svcs & Drinking Places
41568	5	6	Relig., Grant, Civic, Prof Org	41835	4	17	Educational Services	42152	19	103	Educational Services
41571	8	17	Exec., Legis., & Other Support	41836	15	123	Special Trade Contractors	42153	3	2	Postal Service
41572	102	513	Mining (Except Oil and Gas)	41837	16	57	Justice, Pubic Order/Safety	42154	19	42	Merch. Wholesalers,Nondur. Gds
41601	93	619	Educational Services	41838	6	31	Mining (Except Oil and Gas)	42156	23	251	Museums, Hist. Sites,& Similar
41602	15	74	Justice, Pubic Order/Safety	41839	22	695	Mining (Except Oil and Gas)	42157	10	13	Repair and Maintenance
41603	26	80	Merch. Wholesalers,Durable Gds	41840	69	336	Educational Services	42159	10	185	Merch. Wholesalers,Nondur. Gds
41604	6	25	Mining (Except Oil and Gas)	41843	16	94	Mining (Except Oil and Gas)	42160	47	267	Accommodation
41605	61	342	Prof., Scientific, & Tech Svcs	41844	21	323	Educational Services	42163	1	0	Justice, Pubic Order/Safety
41606	14	71	Educational Services	41845	2	1	Merch. Wholesalers,Durable Gds	42164	463	3858	Elect'l Eqpmt, App, & Comp Mfg
41607	4	4	Special Trade Contractors	41847	21	118	Mining (Except Oil and Gas)	42166	51	173	Electronics & Appliance Stores
41612	17	39	Food and Beverage Stores	41848	3	27	Mining (Except Oil and Gas)	42167	328	3046	Primary Metal Manufacturing
41615	9	109	Prof., Scientific, & Tech Svcs	41849	2	3	Postal Service	42170	30	563	Truck Transportation
41616	11	46	Justice, Pubic Order/Safety	41855	3	9	Repair and Maintenance	42171	110	533	Educational Services
41619	5	13	Motor Vehicle & Parts Dealers	41858	400	4445	Mining (Except Oil and Gas)	42201	1	7	Ambulatory Health Care Svcs
41621	4	6	Special Trade Contractors	41859	3	32	Mining (Except Oil and Gas)	42202	67	454	Apparel Manufacturing
41622	12	222	Educational Services	41861	2	16	Mining (Except Oil and Gas)	42204	14	26	Merch. Wholesalers,Nondur. Gds
41630	28	112	Justice, Pubic Order/Safety	41862	23	145	Mining (Except Oil and Gas)	42206	122	953	Apparel Manufacturing
41631	31	205	Educational Services	42001	1584	17798	Food Svcs & Drinking Places	42207	26	61	Construction of Buildings
41632	5	47	Educational Services	42002	13	121	Heavy & Civil Eng. Construct'N	42210	146	915	Educational Services
41635	90	300	Print'g & Related Supp't Act's	42003	1500	17337	Hospitals	42211	423	3677	Transportation Equipment Mfg
41636	12	151	Educational Services	42020	25	114	Transportation Equipment Mfg	42214	17	19	Clothing & Cloth'g Acc. Stores
41640	12	74	Support Activities for Mining	42021	38	163	Wood Product Manufacturing	42215	14	25	Relig., Grant, Civic, Prof Org
41642	45	397	Transportation Equipment Mfg	42022	11	15	Bldg Matl & Garden Eqpmt Dlrs	42216	2	1	Personal and Laundry Services
41643	10	87	Nursing & Resid. Care Facilit.	42023	117	586	Educational Services	42217	76	262	Educational Services
41645	25	66	Petroleum & Coal Products Mfg	42024	56	115	Fabricated Metal Product Mfg	42220	215	1810	Apparel Manufacturing
41647	59	368	Ambulatory Health Care Svcs	42025	693	4529	Food Svcs & Drinking Places	42221	3	8	Museums, Hist. Sites,& Similar
41649	146	1106	Hospitals	42027	39	131	Special Trade Contractors	42223	105	25570	Exec., Legis., & Other Support
41650	9	11	Food and Beverage Stores	42028	17	79	Educational Services	42232	16	20	Food and Beverage Stores
41651	15	55	Social Assistance	42029	255	4439	Chemical Manufacturing	42234	100	700	Merch. Wholesalers,Nondur. Gds
41653	729	6803	Educational Services	42031	143	925	Educational Services	42236	17	154	Educational Services
41655	9	62	Mining (Except Oil and Gas)	42032	9	108	Transportation Equipment Mfg	42240	1751	20387	Hospitals
41659	48	299	Prof., Scientific, & Tech Svcs	42033	2	4	Postal Service	42241	7	35	Social Assistance
41660	5	15	Food and Beverage Stores	42035	32	154	Bldg Matl & Garden Eqpmt Dlrs	42251	2	0	Crop Production
41663	1	0	Postal Service	42036	13	20	Special Trade Contractors	42252	3	22	Educational Services
41666	29	67	Mining (Except Oil and Gas)	42037	3	4	Food and Beverage Stores	42254	9	8	Postal Service
41667	8	13	Heavy & Civil Eng. Construct'N	42038	230	1375	Justice, Pubic Order/Safety	42256	86	445	Educational Services
41669	31	396	Justice, Pubic Order/Safety	42039	32	85	Educational Services	42257	4	6	Sportg Gds,Hobby,Book, & Music
41701	866	8487	Educational Services	42040	32	50	Justice, Pubic Order/Safety	42259	23	453	Museums, Hist. Sites,& Similar
41702	9	48	Heavy & Civil Eng. Construct'N	42041	239	2584	Transportation Equipment Mfg	42261	316	2388	Educational Services
41712	7	52	Educational Services	42044	71	537	Accommodation	42262	188	1107	Food Svcs & Drinking Places
41713	4	10	Special Trade Contractors	42045	101	1282	Mining (Except Oil and Gas)	42265	17	81	Educational Services
41714	9	22	Educational Services	42047	7	6	Crop Production	42266	62	256	Nursing & Resid. Care Facilit.
41719	20	49	Motor Vehicle & Parts Dealers	42048	89	464	Accommodation	42273	11	13	Sportg Gds,Hobby,Book, & Music
41721	22	366	Accommodation	42049	59	131	Miscellaneous Store Retailers	42274	30	69	Special Trade Contractors
41722	27	82	Justice, Pubic Order/Safety	42050	141	874	Educational Services	42275	7	18	Wood Product Manufacturing
41723	10	60	Educational Services	42051	55	1382	Merch. Wholesalers,Nondur. Gds	42276	673	6847	Primary Metal Manufacturing
41725	10	12	Motor Vehicle & Parts Dealers	42053	132	494	Prof., Scientific, & Tech Svcs	42280	3	7	Animal Production
41727	19	984	Prof., Scientific, & Tech Svcs	42054	14	15	Merch. Wholesalers,Nondur. Gds	42283	5	34	Relig., Grant, Civic, Prof Org
41729	15	114	Educational Services	42055	74	499	Nursing & Resid. Care Facilit.	42285	7	73	Educational Services
41731	21	398	Mining (Except Oil and Gas)	42056	129	577	Nursing & Resid. Care Facilit.	42286	33	65	Warehousing and Storage
41735	3	4	Mining (Except Oil and Gas)	42058	47	434	Special Trade Contractors	42287	1	0	Construction of Buildings
41736	2	38	Educational Services	42060	8	35	Justice, Pubic Order/Safety	42301	1515	21218	Food Svcs & Drinking Places
41739	4	5	Motor Vehicle & Parts Dealers	42061	12	92	Educational Services	42302	6	11	Real Estate
41740	14	145	Accommodation	42063	5	33	Justice, Pubic Order/Safety	42303	1516	19548	Hospitals
41743	9	18	Construction of Buildings	42064	275	2319	Hospitals	42320	243	2113	General Merchandise Stores
41745	5	9	Food Svcs & Drinking Places	42066	937	9675	Merch. Wholesalers,Durable Gds	42321	1	2	Relig., Grant, Civic, Prof Org
41746	13	82	Educational Services	42069	22	71	Justice, Pubic Order/Safety	42322	12	63	Machinery Manufacturing
41747	2	1	Relig., Grant, Civic, Prof Org	42070	11	30	Truck Transportation	42323	23	153	Educational Services
41749	230	1576	Hospitals	42071	1188	13847	Educational Services	42324	11	37	Educational Services
41751	18	137	Machinery Manufacturing	42076	23	28	Food and Beverage Stores	42325	35	182	Merch. Wholesalers,Nondur. Gds
41754	3	13	Mining (Except Oil and Gas)	42078	83	454	Hospitals	42326	5	5	Motor Vehicle & Parts Dealers
41759	10	51	Wholesale Elec. Mrkts & Agents	42079	33	80	Machinery Manufacturing	42327	141	845	Educational Services
41760	4	15	Gasoline Stations	42081	100	485	Mining (Except Oil and Gas)	42328	23	301	Utilities
41762	5	9	Forestry and Logging	42082	33	130	Educational Services	42330	340	3427	General Merchandise Stores
41763	6	46	Nonstore Retailers	42083	4	3	Food and Beverage Stores	42332	4	5	Postal Service
41764	16	116	Mining (Except Oil and Gas)	42084	2	5	Food and Beverage Stores	42333	13	104	Educational Services
41766	7	3	Postal Service	42085	18	30	Relig., Grant, Civic, Prof Org	42334	2	4	Relig., Grant, Civic, Prof Org
41772	6	31	Educational Services	42086	97	894	Admin. Enviro. Quality Progrms	42337	55	632	Admin. Enviro. Quality Progrms
41773	39	200	Mining (Except Oil and Gas)	42087	129	1239	Paper Manufacturing	42338	9	36	Prof., Scientific, & Tech Svcs
41774	33	288	Mining (Except Oil and Gas)	42088	57	228	Educational Services	42339	17	51	Accommodation

BUSINESS DATA

ZIP CODE	2004 Total Firms	2004 Total Employees	TOP INDUSTRY RANKED on 2004 EMPLOYMENT	ZIP CODE	2004 Total Firms	2004 Total Employees	TOP INDUSTRY RANKED on 2004 EMPLOYMENT	ZIP CODE	2004 Total Firms	2004 Total Employees	TOP INDUSTRY RANKED on 2004 EMPLOYMENT
42343	44	589	Furniture & Related Prod. Mfg	42713	41	112	Educational Services	43072	153	2257	Transportation Equipment Mfg
42344	15	165	Merch. Wholesalers,Nondur. Gds	42715	5	8	Wood Product Manufacturing	43073	12	220	Educational Services
42345	390	4042	Hospitals	42716	36	115	Educational Services	43074	396	3167	Transportation Equipment Mfg
42347	231	2131	Educational Services	42717	239	1769	Hospitals	43076	155	826	Educational Services
42348	135	3084	Transportation Equipment Mfg	42718	959	7976	Bldg Matl & Garden Eqpmt Dlrs	43077	2	9	Special Trade Contractors
42349	14	70	Relig., Grant, Civic, Prof Org	42721	92	466	Unclassified Establishments	43078	884	9326	Motor Vehicle & Parts Dealers
42350	27	113	Food Svcs & Drinking Places	42722	17	21	Utilities	43080	137	856	Educational Services
42351	89	1819	Primary Metal Manufacturing	42724	77	643	Educational Services	43081	1982	21906	Educational Services
42352	70	451	Fabricated Metal Product Mfg	42726	124	483	Educational Services	43082	498	5985	Prof., Scientific, & Tech Svcs
42354	7	30	Primary Metal Manufacturing	42728	522	4571	Educational Services	43083	3	3	Relig., Grant, Civic, Prof Org
42355	34	155	Special Trade Contractors	42729	18	57	Justice, Pubic Order/Safety	43084	12	29	Exec., Legis., & Other Support
42356	3	90	Relig., Grant, Civic, Prof Org	42731	4	8	Rental and Leasing Services	43085	1556	15420	Prof., Scientific, & Tech Svcs
42361	5	10	Crop Production	42732	19	155	Educational Services	43086	26	488	Administrative & Support Svcs
42364	3	7	Relig., Grant, Civic, Prof Org	42733	17	28	Bldg Matl & Garden Eqpmt Dlrs	43101	7	10	Credit Intermediation & Relatd
42366	71	801	Fabricated Metal Product Mfg	42735	10	27	Mining (Except Oil and Gas)	43102	75	518	Fabricated Metal Product Mfg
42367	42	366	Ambulatory Health Care Svcs	42740	51	429	Social Assistance	43103	219	1871	Chemical Manufacturing
42368	8	10	General Merchandise Stores	42741	7	12	Motor Vehicle & Parts Dealers	43105	205	1134	Educational Services
42369	4	31	Justice, Pubic Order/Safety	42742	1	0	Postal Service	43106	25	142	Educational Services
42370	4	28	Justice, Pubic Order/Safety	42743	285	1676	Educational Services	43107	77	766	Miscellaneous Manufacturing
42371	6	20	Special Trade Contractors	42746	39	85	Educational Services	43109	24	353	Special Trade Contractors
42372	42	176	Educational Services	42748	295	2195	Clothing & Cloth'g Acc. Stores	43110	601	5156	Transportation Equipment Mfg
42374	2	102	Wood Product Manufacturing	42749	196	2616	Plastics & Rubber Products Mfg	43111	6	71	Ambulatory Health Care Svcs
42375	8	45	Justice, Pubic Order/Safety	42753	6	35	Educational Services	43112	169	1244	Educational Services
42376	94	549	Credit Intermediation & Relatd	42754	545	6616	Food Svcs & Drinking Places	43113	966	11171	Miscellaneous Manufacturing
42378	59	308	Educational Services	42755	3	1	Social Assistance	43115	28	122	Relig., Grant, Civic, Prof Org
42402	3	1	Relig., Grant, Civic, Prof Org	42757	58	178	Educational Services	43116	23	152	Justice, Pubic Order/Safety
42404	64	797	Mining (Except Oil and Gas)	42758	8	34	Educational Services	43117	4	13	Merch. Wholesalers,Nondur. Gds
42406	39	205	Educational Services	42759	7	104	Apparel Manufacturing	43119	252	1468	Educational Services
42408	150	1352	Social Assistance	42762	7	66	Wood Product Manufacturing	43123	1424	17553	Merch. Wholesalers,Durable Gds
42409	89	591	Exec., Legis., & Other Support	42764	12	19	Relig., Grant, Civic, Prof Org	43125	414	8929	Prof., Scientific, & Tech Svcs
42410	40	223	Educational Services	42765	240	1744	Furn. & Home Furnishgs Stores	43126	34	73	Educational Services
42411	38	207	Nonmetallic Mineral Prod. Mfg	42776	47	353	Gasoline Stations	43127	4	52	Wood Product Manufacturing
42413	56	574	Merch. Wholesalers,Nondur. Gds	42782	12	53	Educational Services	43128	194	1586	Clothing & Cloth'g Acc. Stores
42419	7	19	Food Svcs & Drinking Places	42783	1	22	Wood Product Manufacturing	43130	2104	22233	Food Svcs & Drinking Places
42420	1405	16595	Hospitals	42784	45	177	Special Trade Contractors	43135	92	454	Wood Product Manufacturing
42431	1310	16246	Hospitals	42788	6	15	Relig., Grant, Civic, Prof Org	43136	21	174	Exec., Legis., & Other Support
42436	13	166	Unclassified Establishments	43001	56	244	Amusement, Gambling,& Recreat.	43137	139	1393	Plastics & Rubber Products Mfg
42437	308	2949	Transportation Equipment Mfg	43002	5	174	Merch. Wholesalers,Durable Gds	43138	730	6027	Food Svcs & Drinking Places
42440	34	157	Food Svcs & Drinking Places	43003	62	423	Accommodation	43140	634	6482	Justice, Pubic Order/Safety
42441	46	476	Mining (Except Oil and Gas)	43004	213	3525	Publishing Industries	43142	10	135	Food Svcs & Drinking Places
42442	81	428	Educational Services	43005	12	175	Educational Services	43143	155	1744	Fabricated Metal Product Mfg
42444	10	29	Food Svcs & Drinking Places	43006	7	58	Accommodation	43144	12	15	Personal and Laundry Services
42445	452	3755	Special Trade Contractors	43007	4	11	Food Svcs & Drinking Places	43145	44	153	Educational Services
42450	143	1424	Mining (Except Oil and Gas)	43008	39	276	Food Svcs & Drinking Places	43146	141	1367	Justice, Pubic Order/Safety
42451	8	31	Fabricated Metal Product Mfg	43009	28	83	Amusement, Gambling,& Recreat.	43147	723	5843	Food Svcs & Drinking Places
42452	39	1760	Food Manufacturing	43010	10	50	Justice, Pubic Order/Safety	43148	39	110	Educational Services
42453	14	36	Justice, Pubic Order/Safety	43011	126	758	Educational Services	43149	56	114	Accommodation
42455	87	772	Apparel Manufacturing	43013	48	293	Merch. Wholesalers,Nondur. Gds	43150	41	176	Educational Services
42456	24	103	Educational Services	43014	114	620	Accommodation	43151	13	78	Truck Transportation
42457	4	5	Postal Service	43015	1475	15082	Educational Services	43152	19	77	Accommodation
42458	11	59	Educational Services	43016	785	10963	Food Svcs & Drinking Places	43153	17	51	Crop Production
42459	149	729	Electronics & Appliance Stores	43017	1827	26694	Prof., Scientific, & Tech Svcs	43154	40	161	Educational Services
42460	6	17	Food Svcs & Drinking Places	43018	18	72	Merch. Wholesalers,Durable Gds	43155	65	383	Educational Services
42461	29	225	Educational Services	43019	198	1408	Construction of Buildings	43156	9	39	Food and Beverage Stores
42462	23	434	Mining (Except Oil and Gas)	43021	151	723	Special Trade Contractors	43157	10	30	Special Trade Contractors
42463	6	13	Merch. Wholesalers,Durable Gds	43022	66	859	Educational Services	43158	10	59	Educational Services
42464	28	116	Bldg Matl & Garden Eqpmt Dlrs	43023	403	3278	Educational Services	43160	860	8313	Plastics & Rubber Products Mfg
42501	1131	11879	Food Svcs & Drinking Places	43025	261	4793	Plastics & Rubber Products Mfg	43162	209	1938	Transportation Equipment Mfg
42502	8	65	Merch. Wholesalers,Durable Gds	43026	1399	17920	Prof., Scientific, & Tech Svcs	43164	49	370	Educational Services
42503	605	6432	Ambulatory Health Care Svcs	43027	7	30	Pipeline Transportation	43201	916	19150	Miscellaneous Manufacturing
42516	5	25	Educational Services	43028	93	463	Educational Services	43202	542	5239	Educational Services
42518	67	316	Special Trade Contractors	43029	8	64	Relig., Grant, Civic, Prof Org	43203	275	1693	Educational Services
42519	93	794	Wood Product Manufacturing	43030	9	338	Admin. of Economic Programs	43204	1051	10072	Prof., Scientific, & Tech Svcs
42528	22	731	Wood Product Manufacturing	43031	316	2641	Merch. Wholesalers,Nondur. Gds	43205	588	9018	Hospitals
42533	16	122	Motor Vehicle & Parts Dealers	43032	5	7	Food and Beverage Stores	43206	684	5455	Insurance Carriers & Related
42539	385	2628	Ambulatory Health Care Svcs	43033	26	115	Educational Services	43207	1285	24723	Justice, Pubic Order/Safety
42541	9	81	Merch. Wholesalers,Durable Gds	43035	476	5994	Merch. Wholesalers,Durable Gds	43209	788	6639	Educational Services
42544	98	341	Food Svcs & Drinking Places	43036	7	19	Educational Services	43210	188	44152	Educational Services
42553	113	410	Educational Services	43037	20	125	Justice, Pubic Order/Safety	43211	512	5453	Educational Services
42558	3	19	Justice, Pubic Order/Safety	43040	924	20052	Transportation Equipment Mfg	43212	1195	14560	Food Svcs & Drinking Places
42564	3	4	Real Estate	43044	106	546	Educational Services	43213	1461	22225	Nat'l Security & Int'l Affairs
42565	14	58	Educational Services	43045	42	219	Educational Services	43214	1263	20502	Hospitals
42566	11	26	Food and Beverage Stores	43046	109	577	Gasoline Stations	43215	3940	89048	Prof., Scientific, & Tech Svcs
42567	81	523	Merch. Wholesalers,Durable Gds	43047	2	4	Food and Beverage Stores	43216	15	2024	Postal Service
42602	345	3602	Food Manufacturing	43048	3	4	Heavy & Civil Eng. Construct'N	43217	54	1059	Merch. Wholesalers,Durable Gds
42603	7	21	Crop Production	43050	1251	13692	Merch. Wholesalers,Durable Gds	43218	3	9	Sportg Gds,Hobby,Book, & Music
42629	220	2346	Apparel Manufacturing	43054	407	3725	Clothing & Cloth'g Acc. Stores	43219	1439	27189	Food Svcs & Drinking Places
42631	6	9	Food and Beverage Stores	43055	2143	21171	Educational Services	43220	1212	12744	Isps, Web Search Portals
42633	526	5430	Educational Services	43056	658	8159	Food Svcs & Drinking Places	43221	913	7249	Ambulatory Health Care Svcs
42634	23	125	Justice, Pubic Order/Safety	43058	16	77	Special Trade Contractors	43222	272	10810	Prof., Scientific, & Tech Svcs
42635	91	707	Educational Services	43060	58	267	Educational Services	43223	756	12420	Admin. of Economic Programs
42638	8	14	Merch. Wholesalers,Nondur. Gds	43061	86	377	Educational Services	43224	790	10404	General Merchandise Stores
42642	561	3494	Merch. Wholesalers,Durable Gds	43062	611	4296	Special Trade Contractors	43226	2	1	Bldg Matl & Garden Eqpmt Dlrs
42647	83	1968	Transportation Equipment Mfg	43064	440	4378	Food Svcs & Drinking Places	43227	437	4406	Motor Vehicle & Parts Dealers
42649	13	48	Merch. Wholesalers,Durable Gds	43065	812	5449	Prof., Scientific, & Tech Svcs	43228	1704	38985	Prof., Scientific, & Tech Svcs
42653	230	1903	Hospitals	43066	31	131	Educational Services	43229	1765	38844	Justice, Pubic Order/Safety
42701	1891	24594	Transportation Equipment Mfg	43067	38	292	Merch. Wholesalers,Nondur. Gds	43230	1436	26242	Clothing & Cloth'g Acc. Stores
42702	12	64	Social Assistance	43068	1405	15955	Clothing & Cloth'g Acc. Stores	43231	839	9179	Nursing & Resid. Care Facilit.
42711	2	4	Animal Production	43070	16	168	Fabricated Metal Product Mfg	43232	1093	14747	General Merchandise Stores
42712	29	58	Merch. Wholesalers,Durable Gds	43071	84	321	Special Trade Contractors	43234	7	19	Special Trade Contractors

ZIP CODE	2004 Total Firms	2004 Total Employees	TOP INDUSTRY RANKED on 2004 EMPLOYMENT	ZIP CODE	2004 Total Firms	2004 Total Employees	TOP INDUSTRY RANKED on 2004 EMPLOYMENT	ZIP CODE	2004 Total Firms	2004 Total Employees	TOP INDUSTRY RANKED on 2004 EMPLOYMENT
43235	1543	19573	Food Svcs & Drinking Places	43501	16	30	Relig., Grant, Civic, Prof Org	43723	179	2784	Plastics & Rubber Products Mfg
43236	1	5	Real Estate	43502	354	10201	Furniture & Related Prod. Mfg	43724	257	2450	Primary Metal Manufacturing
43240	380	8186	Food Svcs & Drinking Places	43504	22	158	Justice, Pubic Order/Safety	43725	1042	10664	Nursing & Resid. Care Facilit.
43301	11	45	Social Assistance	43505	13	73	Construction of Buildings	43727	15	34	Food Manufacturing
43302	1900	23480	Elect'l Eqpmt, App, & Comp Mfg	43506	699	10162	Plastics & Rubber Products Mfg	43728	26	60	Special Trade Contractors
43310	71	301	Mining (Except Oil and Gas)	43511	18	120	Educational Services	43730	47	229	Educational Services
43311	864	11179	Merch. Wholesalers,Durable Gds	43512	1189	16633	Primary Metal Manufacturing	43731	119	861	Primary Metal Manufacturing
43314	59	397	Nonmetallic Mineral Prod. Mfg	43515	248	1834	Fabricated Metal Product Mfg	43732	30	247	Museums, Hist. Sites,& Similar
43315	118	1195	Transportation Equipment Mfg	43516	105	839	Transportation Equipment Mfg	43733	3	153	Prof., Scientific, & Tech Svcs
43316	175	2403	Plastics & Rubber Products Mfg	43517	126	1745	Fabricated Metal Product Mfg	43734	47	266	Educational Services
43317	23	96	Nursing & Resid. Care Facilit.	43518	83	839	Transportation Equipment Mfg	43735	9	66	Amusement, Gambling,& Recreat.
43318	78	352	Plastics & Rubber Products Mfg	43519	8	17	Special Trade Contractors	43736	3	17	Justice, Pubic Order/Safety
43319	43	1861	Merch. Wholesalers,Durable Gds	43520	4	2	Prof., Scientific, & Tech Svcs	43738	10	4	Postal Service
43320	33	155	Heavy & Civil Eng. Construct'N	43521	81	630	Miscellaneous Manufacturing	43739	35	263	Justice, Pubic Order/Safety
43321	9	68	Nursing & Resid. Care Facilit.	43522	122	695	Food Svcs & Drinking Places	43740	16	31	Waste Managmt & Remediat'n Svc
43322	22	104	Educational Services	43523	5	12	Merch. Wholesalers,Nondur. Gds	43746	22	83	Educational Services
43323	18	200	Crop Production	43524	46	317	Educational Services	43747	12	23	Crop Production
43324	73	413	Merch. Wholesalers,Durable Gds	43525	17	51	Educational Services	43748	45	217	Plastics & Rubber Products Mfg
43325	9	84	Educational Services	43526	190	2100	Fabricated Metal Product Mfg	43749	39	251	Accommodation
43326	562	6894	Exec., Legis., & Other Support	43527	60	338	Educational Services	43750	2	6	Construction of Buildings
43330	7	23	Bldg Matl & Garden Eqpmt Dlrs	43528	758	10325	Food Svcs & Drinking Places	43752	4	8	Utilities
43331	123	752	Nursing & Resid. Care Facilit.	43529	9	60	Educational Services	43754	22	99	Merch. Wholesalers,Durable Gds
43332	59	338	Fabricated Metal Product Mfg	43530	3	3	Relig., Grant, Civic, Prof Org	43755	45	269	Educational Services
43333	18	281	Educational Services	43531	6	7	Food and Beverage Stores	43756	248	2121	Fabricated Metal Product Mfg
43334	106	516	Food Svcs & Drinking Places	43532	96	859	Exec., Legis., & Other Support	43757	3	8	Food and Beverage Stores
43335	1	175	Merch. Wholesalers,Nondur. Gds	43533	51	305	Transportation Equipment Mfg	43758	71	553	Wood Product Manufacturing
43336	4	38	Administrative & Support Svcs	43534	47	213	Educational Services	43759	26	157	Merch. Wholesalers,Durable Gds
43337	26	228	Educational Services	43535	18	147	Special Trade Contractors	43760	14	114	Merch. Wholesalers,Nondur. Gds
43338	383	2948	Justice, Pubic Order/Safety	43536	12	18	Bldg Matl & Garden Eqpmt Dlrs	43761	2	3	Food and Beverage Stores
43340	45	391	Merch. Wholesalers,Nondur. Gds	43537	1137	18689	Prof., Scientific, & Tech Svcs	43762	139	1242	Warehousing and Storage
43341	15	59	Repair and Maintenance	43540	40	545	Transportation Equipment Mfg	43764	330	3554	Transportation Equipment Mfg
43342	74	271	Educational Services	43541	3	6	Bldg Matl & Garden Eqpmt Dlrs	43766	21	69	Justice, Pubic Order/Safety
43343	25	152	Primary Metal Manufacturing	43542	89	509	Special Trade Contractors	43767	42	305	Miscellaneous Manufacturing
43344	137	753	Educational Services	43543	249	2948	Fabricated Metal Product Mfg	43768	24	114	Educational Services
43345	16	57	Educational Services	43545	635	7513	Food Manufacturing	43771	47	160	Educational Services
43346	4	29	Justice, Pubic Order/Safety	43547	16	68	Justice, Pubic Order/Safety	43772	29	71	Food and Beverage Stores
43347	29	88	Construction of Buildings	43548	18	46	Warehousing and Storage	43773	62	221	Merch. Wholesalers,Nondur. Gds
43348	120	1571	Transportation Equipment Mfg	43549	34	153	Merch. Wholesalers,Nondur. Gds	43777	85	559	Nonmetallic Mineral Prod. Mfg
43349	17	100	Educational Services	43550	4	20	Food Manufacturing	43778	24	63	Repair and Maintenance
43350	12	231	Educational Services	43551	1232	17590	Transportation Equipment Mfg	43779	22	148	Educational Services
43351	498	9166	Merch. Wholesalers,Durable Gds	43552	11	26	Prof., Scientific, & Tech Svcs	43780	43	244	Educational Services
43356	51	296	Food Svcs & Drinking Places	43553	31	240	Educational Services	43782	28	189	Chemical Manufacturing
43357	154	1399	Educational Services	43554	92	867	Fabricated Metal Product Mfg	43783	121	585	Nursing & Resid. Care Facilit.
43358	53	182	Merch. Wholesalers,Nondur. Gds	43555	10	551	Fabricated Metal Product Mfg	43786	4	3	Food Svcs & Drinking Places
43359	20	57	Special Trade Contractors	43556	66	428	Educational Services	43787	65	158	Educational Services
43360	25	112	Accommodation	43557	95	1256	Justice, Pubic Order/Safety	43788	21	39	Pipeline Transportation
43402	1211	15673	Food Svcs & Drinking Places	43558	400	5573	Air Transportation	43789	2	2	Repair and Maintenance
43403	15	469	Other Information Services	43560	1114	12326	Hospitals	43791	3	7	Repair and Maintenance
43406	42	420	Plastics & Rubber Products Mfg	43565	17	97	Educational Services	43793	273	1724	Exec., Legis., & Other Support
43407	10	42	Educational Services	43566	211	2623	Nonmetallic Mineral Prod. Mfg	43802	24	97	Educational Services
43408	10	55	Mining (Except Oil and Gas)	43567	547	6324	Hospitals	43803	3	10	Merch. Wholesalers,Durable Gds
43410	282	6743	Elect'l Eqpmt, App, & Comp Mfg	43569	64	437	Food Manufacturing	43804	68	605	Plastics & Rubber Products Mfg
43412	64	362	Educational Services	43570	113	1131	Transportation Equipment Mfg	43805	1	0	Postal Service
43413	28	179	Miscellaneous Store Retailers	43571	176	1607	Educational Services	43811	23	500	Utilities
43414	5	122	Merch. Wholesalers,Durable Gds	43601	2	305	Postal Service	43812	917	11107	Textile Product Mills
43416	91	1365	Primary Metal Manufacturing	43602	224	3538	Social Assistance	43821	164	859	Educational Services
43420	1338	15773	Plastics & Rubber Products Mfg	43604	720	11549	Prof., Scientific, & Tech Svcs	43822	78	862	Museums, Hist. Sites,& Similar
43430	146	1632	Food Svcs & Drinking Places	43605	565	7214	Special Trade Contractors	43824	28	128	Educational Services
43431	118	1031	Machinery Manufacturing	43606	982	13060	Educational Services	43830	79	457	Truck Transportation
43432	19	96	Educational Services	43607	603	8252	Educational Services	43832	251	2499	Plastics & Rubber Products Mfg
43433	6	496	Nonmetallic Mineral Prod. Mfg	43608	371	14247	Hospitals	43836	4	6	Truck Transportation
43434	3	3	Postal Service	43609	474	4209	Educational Services	43837	21	264	Furniture & Related Prod. Mfg
43435	27	192	Social Assistance	43610	96	5632	Transportation Equipment Mfg	43840	23	136	Nonmetallic Mineral Prod. Mfg
43436	2	13	Beverage & Tobacco Product Mfg	43611	393	4976	Nonmetallic Mineral Prod. Mfg	43842	3	5	Postal Service
43437	8	8	Justice, Pubic Order/Safety	43612	1227	23427	Repair and Maintenance	43843	10	27	Bldg Matl & Garden Eqpmt Dlrs
43438	38	181	Accommodation	43613	815	7134	Educational Services	43844	102	481	Educational Services
43439	4	10	Food Svcs & Drinking Places	43614	966	25253	Ambulatory Health Care Svcs	43845	121	782	Nursing & Resid. Care Facilit.
43440	232	1647	Food Svcs & Drinking Places	43615	1365	15213	Motor Vehicle & Parts Dealers	43901	46	237	Relig., Grant, Civic, Prof Org
43441	4	44	Educational Services	43616	625	10410	Hospitals	43902	3	503	Petroleum & Coal Products Mfg
43442	21	81	Educational Services	43617	475	4374	Prof., Scientific, & Tech Svcs	43903	50	149	Food Svcs & Drinking Places
43443	52	273	Plastics & Rubber Products Mfg	43618	57	353	Educational Services	43905	4	6	Miscellaneous Store Retailers
43445	15	61	Special Trade Contractors	43619	368	6303	Prof., Scientific, & Tech Svcs	43906	310	2496	Hospitals
43446	13	10	Accommodation	43620	138	1829	Social Assistance	43907	283	2255	Merch. Wholesalers,Durable Gds
43447	110	1451	Truck Transportation	43623	1208	12565	Food Svcs & Drinking Places	43908	43	314	Bldg Matl & Garden Eqpmt Dlrs
43449	291	2052	Exec., Legis., & Other Support	43624	643	12400	Justice, Pubic Order/Safety	43909	5	27	Merch. Wholesalers,Durable Gds
43450	108	1124	Transportation Equipment Mfg	43635	11	29	Prof., Scientific, & Tech Svcs	43910	51	325	Relig., Grant, Civic, Prof Org
43451	39	349	Truck Transportation	43659	2	1218	Wood Product Manufacturing	43912	209	1728	Food Svcs & Drinking Places
43452	874	7144	Food Svcs & Drinking Places	43660	4	7	Other Information Services	43913	52	592	Utilities
43456	116	692	Food Svcs & Drinking Places	43697	6	10	Transportation Equipment Mfg	43914	3	9	Educational Services
43457	30	137	Educational Services	43701	2447	29938	Hospitals	43915	33	129	Credit Intermediation & Relatd
43458	6	64	Truck Transportation	43702	7	15	Social Assistance	43916	15	82	Food and Beverage Stores
43460	205	2491	Food Svcs & Drinking Places	43711	6	12	Special Trade Contractors	43917	72	384	Construction of Buildings
43462	13	29	Fabricated Metal Product Mfg	43713	261	1932	Hospitals	43920	913	9763	Real Estate
43463	24	121	Exec., Legis., & Other Support	43716	53	570	Mining (Except Oil and Gas)	43925	13	68	Amusement, Gambling,& Recreat.
43464	22	131	Merch. Wholesalers,Durable Gds	43717	16	94	Exec., Legis., & Other Support	43926	13	79	Construction of Buildings
43465	112	3021	Bldg Matl & Garden Eqpmt Dlrs	43718	76	634	Educational Services	43927	4	6	Merch. Wholesalers,Durable Gds
43466	57	331	Prof., Scientific, & Tech Svcs	43719	76	341	Paper Manufacturing	43928	3	35	Social Assistance
43467	6	26	Mining (Except Oil and Gas)	43720	19	55	Bldg Matl & Garden Eqpmt Dlrs	43930	11	110	Educational Services
43468	13	477	Relig., Grant, Civic, Prof Org	43721	6	22	Special Trade Contractors	43931	16	2508	Primary Metal Manufacturing
43469	97	618	Prof., Scientific, & Tech Svcs	43722	14	46	Food Svcs & Drinking Places	43932	12	67	Educational Services

BUSINESS DATA

ZIP CODE	2004 Total Firms	2004 Total Employees	TOP INDUSTRY RANKED on 2004 EMPLOYMENT	ZIP CODE	2004 Total Firms	2004 Total Employees	TOP INDUSTRY RANKED on 2004 EMPLOYMENT	ZIP CODE	2004 Total Firms	2004 Total Employees	TOP INDUSTRY RANKED on 2004 EMPLOYMENT
43933	11	20	Postal Service	44088	4	44	Food Svcs & Drinking Places	44256	2340	23645	Food Svcs & Drinking Places
43934	16	74	Educational Services	44089	522	3354	Food Svcs & Drinking Places	44258	13	36	Special Trade Contractors
43935	364	3362	Hospitals	44090	338	3689	Plastics & Rubber Products Mfg	44260	346	3725	Warehousing and Storage
43937	4	4	Postal Service	44092	725	10096	Merch. Wholesalers,Nondur. Gds	44262	121	1045	Special Trade Contractors
43938	132	969	Educational Services	44093	25	102	Justice, Pubic Order/Safety	44264	148	1584	Primary Metal Manufacturing
43939	20	109	Justice, Pubic Order/Safety	44094	1999	19168	Fabricated Metal Product Mfg	44265	31	522	Transportation Equipment Mfg
43940	7	7	Construction of Buildings	44095	944	8835	Food Svcs & Drinking Places	44266	1090	12102	Hospitals
43941	2	0	Postal Service	44096	16	59	Furn. & Home Furnishgs Stores	44270	212	2080	Chemical Manufacturing
43942	74	324	Justice, Pubic Order/Safety	44099	37	110	Special Trade Contractors	44272	193	1506	Educational Services
43943	43	321	Educational Services	44101	19	257	Relig., Grant, Civic, Prof Org	44273	228	1853	Food Svcs & Drinking Places
43944	64	273	Educational Services	44102	1241	12547	Fabricated Metal Product Mfg	44274	32	565	Plastics & Rubber Products Mfg
43945	56	229	Educational Services	44103	1138	12390	Fabricated Metal Product Mfg	44275	72	329	Fabricated Metal Product Mfg
43946	54	172	Truck Transportation	44104	628	6541	Educational Services	44276	43	272	Merch. Wholesalers,Durable Gds
43947	130	1289	Transportation Equipment Mfg	44105	1146	18541	Primary Metal Manufacturing	44278	637	7292	Educational Services
43948	41	104	Personal and Laundry Services	44106	1032	22264	Hospitals	44280	185	4156	Miscellaneous Manufacturing
43950	807	11128	Food Svcs & Drinking Places	44107	1723	14193	Food Svcs & Drinking Places	44281	883	9097	Food Svcs & Drinking Places
43951	9	27	Justice, Pubic Order/Safety	44108	520	4708	Educational Services	44282	16	47	Special Trade Contractors
43952	1128	16645	Hospitals	44109	1296	15572	Relig., Grant, Civic, Prof Org	44285	5	14	Accommodation
43953	418	2784	Food Svcs & Drinking Places	44110	651	6044	Machinery Manufacturing	44286	348	4979	Truck Transportation
43961	21	309	Construction of Buildings	44111	1286	15427	Justice, Pubic Order/Safety	44287	129	974	Educational Services
43962	6	526	Nonmetallic Mineral Prod. Mfg	44112	694	7780	Hospitals	44288	90	678	Educational Services
43963	47	258	Relig., Grant, Civic, Prof Org	44113	2512	30152	Prof., Scientific, & Tech Svcs	44301	402	3775	Transit & Grnd Pass. Transport
43964	248	1881	Chemical Manufacturing	44114	2359	59766	Exec., Legis., & Other Support	44302	172	1817	Ambulatory Health Care Svcs
43967	4	21	Repair and Maintenance	44115	1389	47561	Credit Intermediation & Relatd	44303	345	3132	Nursing & Resid. Care Facilit.
43968	194	1384	Nonmetallic Mineral Prod. Mfg	44116	1235	9417	Food Svcs & Drinking Places	44304	304	13094	Hospitals
43971	49	680	Primary Metal Manufacturing	44117	392	9309	Machinery Manufacturing	44305	538	6675	Merch. Wholesalers,Durable Gds
43972	6	16	Merch. Wholesalers,Durable Gds	44118	1411	10584	Educational Services	44306	647	8501	Educational Services
43973	51	368	Print'g & Related Supp't Act's	44119	500	4215	Hospitals	44307	242	4695	Social Assistance
43974	10	68	Justice, Pubic Order/Safety	44120	1028	7057	Educational Services	44308	861	18033	Justice, Pubic Order/Safety
43976	59	300	Nursing & Resid. Care Facilit.	44121	973	6485	Ambulatory Health Care Svcs	44309	7	1124	Postal Service
43977	54	176	Prof., Scientific, & Tech Svcs	44122	3101	32354	Nursing & Resid. Care Facilit.	44310	958	14019	Hospitals
43981	11	50	Justice, Pubic Order/Safety	44123	378	3103	Educational Services	44311	509	8019	Prof., Scientific, & Tech Svcs
43983	12	24	Food Svcs & Drinking Places	44124	1754	22142	Prof., Scientific, & Tech Svcs	44312	1023	9771	Food Svcs & Drinking Places
43985	7	26	Justice, Pubic Order/Safety	44125	1213	22148	Merch. Wholesalers,Durable Gds	44313	929	8892	Sportg Gds,Hobby,Book, & Music
43986	41	234	Educational Services	44126	581	4386	Prof., Scientific, & Tech Svcs	44314	464	3800	Educational Services
43988	70	251	Motor Vehicle & Parts Dealers	44127	307	4809	Computer & Electronic Prod Mfg	44315	1	650	Prof., Scientific, & Tech Svcs
44001	652	6356	Merch. Wholesalers,Durable Gds	44128	1399	16391	Merch. Wholesalers,Durable Gds	44316	2	6000	Prof., Scientific, & Tech Svcs
44003	179	2104	Plastics & Rubber Products Mfg	44129	1135	12665	Hospitals	44317	3	667	Motor Vehicle & Parts Dealers
44004	1456	16695	Plastics & Rubber Products Mfg	44130	2173	37264	Educational Services	44319	1011	9305	Food Svcs & Drinking Places
44005	3	32	Social Assistance	44131	1618	23534	Insurance Carriers & Related	44320	559	5029	Ambulatory Health Care Svcs
44010	86	1301	Miscellaneous Manufacturing	44132	497	4440	Ambulatory Health Care Svcs	44321	406	4775	Food Svcs & Drinking Places
44011	546	5754	Merch. Wholesalers,Durable Gds	44133	1050	8454	Merch. Wholesalers,Nondur. Gds	44322	58	1211	General Merchandise Stores
44012	550	8209	Transportation Equipment Mfg	44134	936	7948	Food Svcs & Drinking Places	44325	5	4146	Educational Services
44017	692	9984	Educational Services	44135	865	20413	Space Research and Technology	44326	1	5	Isps, Web Search Portals
44021	259	2101	Plastics & Rubber Products Mfg	44136	1121	12596	Food Svcs & Drinking Places	44328	6	14	Other Information Services
44022	750	5106	Educational Services	44137	682	7469	Educational Services	44333	1542	19113	Food Svcs & Drinking Places
44023	738	5469	Plastics & Rubber Products Mfg	44138	413	2929	Nursing & Resid. Care Facilit.	44334	18	60	Prof., Scientific, & Tech Svcs
44024	932	9530	Hospitals	44139	1335	23745	Food Manufacturing	44372	2	6	Social Assistance
44026	555	4377	Educational Services	44140	358	2233	Educational Services	44401	67	330	Educational Services
44028	289	1791	Amusement, Gambling,& Recreat.	44141	682	10172	Hospitals	44402	75	464	Educational Services
44030	493	4708	Educational Services	44142	643	15626	Wholesale Elec. Mrkts & Agents	44403	147	1206	Construction of Buildings
44032	29	125	Plastics & Rubber Products Mfg	44143	1009	16912	Insurance Carriers & Related	44404	15	68	Bldg Matl & Garden Eqpmt Dlrs
44033	6	45	Educational Services	44144	496	10520	Miscellaneous Store Retailers	44405	158	990	Educational Services
44035	2594	35928	Food Svcs & Drinking Places	44145	1846	20344	Food Svcs & Drinking Places	44406	826	5704	Food Svcs & Drinking Places
44036	10	16	Construction of Buildings	44146	1568	25808	Fabricated Metal Product Mfg	44408	463	4299	Food Svcs & Drinking Places
44039	645	5380	Educational Services	44147	625	6492	Prof., Scientific, & Tech Svcs	44410	545	3537	Educational Services
44040	84	671	Educational Services	44149	465	7198	Fabricated Metal Product Mfg	44411	42	302	Food Svcs & Drinking Places
44041	609	4366	Hospitals	44181	5	305	Postal Service	44412	59	404	Educational Services
44044	346	1971	Educational Services	44195	126	11741	Ambulatory Health Care Svcs	44413	263	2047	Educational Services
44045	37	605	Food Svcs & Drinking Places	44199	25	649	Justice, Pubic Order/Safety	44416	10	51	Ambulatory Health Care Svcs
44046	42	205	Nursing & Resid. Care Facilit.	44201	98	314	Educational Services	44417	19	108	Justice, Pubic Order/Safety
44047	375	4231	Exec., Legis., & Other Support	44202	651	10908	Amusement, Gambling,& Recreat.	44418	24	138	Nursing & Resid. Care Facilit.
44048	100	3670	Merch. Wholesalers,Durable Gds	44203	1352	15289	Prof., Scientific, & Tech Svcs	44420	578	4594	Merch. Wholesalers,Durable Gds
44049	10	11	Miscellaneous Store Retailers	44210	24	314	Prof., Scientific, & Tech Svcs	44422	12	88	Educational Services
44050	171	1528	Special Trade Contractors	44211	4	0	Motor Vehicle & Parts Dealers	44423	55	324	Educational Services
44052	793	7753	Educational Services	44212	908	8242	Food Svcs & Drinking Places	44424	18	137	Perform'g Arts, Spec. Sports
44053	558	7013	Transportation Equipment Mfg	44214	124	929	Clothing & Cloth'g Acc. Stores	44425	510	3684	Merch. Wholesalers,Durable Gds
44054	259	2583	Food Svcs & Drinking Places	44215	27	127	Food Svcs & Drinking Places	44427	37	233	Social Assistance
44055	463	7485	Primary Metal Manufacturing	44216	141	554	Merch. Wholesalers,Durable Gds	44428	105	931	Fabricated Metal Product Mfg
44056	488	7038	Food Svcs & Drinking Places	44217	99	470	Educational Services	44429	88	407	Ambulatory Health Care Svcs
44057	616	4765	Nursing & Resid. Care Facilit.	44221	957	10104	Food Svcs & Drinking Places	44430	65	561	Educational Services
44060	2761	33546	Food Svcs & Drinking Places	44222	2	4	Merch. Wholesalers,Durable Gds	44431	157	713	Machinery Manufacturing
44061	12	61	Relig., Grant, Civic, Prof Org	44223	654	7051	Hospitals	44432	462	3921	Educational Services
44062	396	5690	Plastics & Rubber Products Mfg	44224	1056	12430	Food Svcs & Drinking Places	44436	123	991	Primary Metal Manufacturing
44064	54	210	Special Trade Contractors	44230	223	1448	Educational Services	44437	71	459	Primary Metal Manufacturing
44065	268	2631	Repair and Maintenance	44231	239	2032	Food Svcs & Drinking Places	44438	87	739	Nursing & Resid. Care Facilit.
44067	567	4720	Hospitals	44232	39	476	Motor Vehicle & Parts Dealers	44439	11	205	Plastics & Rubber Products Mfg
44068	45	1020	Chemical Manufacturing	44233	216	1083	Amusement, Gambling,& Recreat.	44440	110	1883	Nursing & Resid. Care Facilit.
44070	1327	15121	Food Svcs & Drinking Places	44234	67	770	Educational Services	44441	37	161	Nonmetallic Mineral Prod. Mfg
44072	180	669	Educational Services	44235	22	42	Truck Transportation	44442	116	584	Educational Services
44074	389	5052	Educational Services	44236	1158	10706	Food Svcs & Drinking Places	44443	88	534	Food Svcs & Drinking Places
44076	157	2367	Furniture & Related Prod. Mfg	44240	1287	13670	Food Svcs & Drinking Places	44444	285	1992	Food Svcs & Drinking Places
44077	1847	21079	Ambulatory Health Care Svcs	44241	426	6743	Food Svcs & Drinking Places	44445	75	528	Nonmetallic Mineral Prod. Mfg
44080	38	250	Plastics & Rubber Products Mfg	44242	17	3706	Educational Services	44446	982	10912	Food Svcs & Drinking Places
44081	260	3704	Utilities	44243	1	5	Construction of Buildings	44449	31	65	Exec., Legis., & Other Support
44082	37	111	Educational Services	44250	15	93	Educational Services	44450	44	263	Educational Services
44084	88	485	Hospitals	44251	26	1501	Insurance Carriers & Related	44451	198	2325	Prof., Scientific, & Tech Svcs
44085	56	166	Ambulatory Health Care Svcs	44253	95	315	Food Svcs & Drinking Places	44452	249	2762	Nursing & Resid. Care Facilit.
44086	62	782	Nonmetallic Mineral Prod. Mfg	44254	190	1536	Hospitals	44453	10	34	Merch. Wholesalers,Nondur. Gds
44087	1049	17606	Transportation Equipment Mfg	44255	276	2263	Plastics & Rubber Products Mfg	44454	34	154	Mining (Except Oil and Gas)

ZIP CODE	2004 Total Firms	2004 Total Employees	TOP INDUSTRY RANKED on 2004 EMPLOYMENT
44455	49	306	Prof., Scientific, & Tech Svcs
44460	1035	11320	Fabricated Metal Product Mfg
44470	51	265	Educational Services
44471	297	2655	Primary Metal Manufacturing
44473	143	1367	Plastics & Rubber Products Mfg
44481	569	16847	Transportation Equipment Mfg
44482	4	4	Merch. Wholesalers,Durable Gds
44483	1132	16409	Hospitals
44484	853	8872	Ambulatory Health Care Svcs
44485	320	3072	Primary Metal Manufacturing
44490	24	121	Fabricated Metal Product Mfg
44491	35	147	Educational Services
44492	6	34	Educational Services
44493	7	30	Justice, Pubic Order/Safety
44501	9	868	Postal Service
44502	521	6161	Merch. Wholesalers,Nondur. Gds
44503	454	7570	Exec., Legis., & Other Support
44504	217	10375	Hospitals
44505	844	10062	Real Estate
44506	116	791	Social Assistance
44507	258	2080	Educational Services
44509	446	4622	Nursing & Resid. Care Facilit.
44510	80	1340	Special Trade Contractors
44511	326	2286	Social Assistance
44512	2148	24315	Food Svcs & Drinking Places
44513	9	13	Administrative & Support Svcs
44514	743	6826	Food Svcs & Drinking Places
44515	1053	13791	Food Svcs & Drinking Places
44555	13	1230	Educational Services
44601	1381	17162	Food and Beverage Stores
44606	164	1661	Exec., Legis., & Other Support
44607	3	4	Food and Beverage Stores
44608	73	487	Merch. Wholesalers,Durable Gds
44609	99	659	Educational Services
44610	137	1565	Plastics & Rubber Products Mfg
44611	30	240	Fabricated Metal Product Mfg
44612	139	1451	Miscellaneous Manufacturing
44613	61	859	Food Manufacturing
44614	360	2877	Educational Services
44615	445	3370	Exec., Legis., & Other Support
44617	17	365	Bldg Matl & Garden Eqpmt Dlrs
44618	174	2106	Fabricated Metal Product Mfg
44619	21	96	Educational Services
44620	31	103	Food Svcs & Drinking Places
44621	100	922	Hospitals
44622	786	9247	Hospitals
44624	67	469	Primary Metal Manufacturing
44625	28	114	Educational Services
44626	76	448	Construction of Buildings
44627	77	565	Plastics & Rubber Products Mfg
44628	21	110	Mining (Except Oil and Gas)
44629	68	477	Prof., Scientific, & Tech Svcs
44630	19	108	Justice, Pubic Order/Safety
44631	2	1	Relig., Grant, Civic, Prof Org
44632	456	4640	Sportg Gds,Hobby,Book, & Music
44633	71	1214	Plastics & Rubber Products Mfg
44634	47	175	Miscellaneous Manufacturing
44636	62	916	Food Manufacturing
44637	67	750	Plastics & Rubber Products Mfg
44638	28	124	Accommodation
44639	4	7	Relig., Grant, Civic, Prof Org
44640	1	0	Justice, Pubic Order/Safety
44641	516	4647	Special Trade Contractors
44643	102	628	Educational Services
44644	131	963	Educational Services
44645	50	219	Food and Beverage Stores
44646	1360	15977	Hospitals
44647	440	6049	Food Manufacturing
44648	6	13	Broadcasting
44650	2	4	Administrative & Support Svcs
44651	18	60	Machinery Manufacturing
44652	8	36	Chemical Manufacturing
44653	25	445	Plastics & Rubber Products Mfg
44654	659	5839	Bldg Matl & Garden Eqpmt Dlrs
44656	76	491	Educational Services
44657	346	4018	Primary Metal Manufacturing
44659	32	345	Plastics & Rubber Products Mfg
44660	13	814	Bldg Matl & Garden Eqpmt Dlrs
44661	15	91	Educational Services
44662	231	2130	Food Manufacturing
44663	1073	11775	Food Svcs & Drinking Places
44665	14	26	Relig., Grant, Civic, Prof Org
44666	61	329	Accommodation
44667	510	6812	Food Manufacturing
44669	37	155	Truck Transportation
44670	14	43	Justice, Pubic Order/Safety
44671	7	17	Food Manufacturing
44672	170	1945	Miscellaneous Manufacturing
44675	40	222	Relig., Grant, Civic, Prof Org
44676	135	920	Elect'l Eqpmt, App, & Comp Mfg

ZIP CODE	2004 Total Firms	2004 Total Employees	TOP INDUSTRY RANKED on 2004 EMPLOYMENT
44677	121	1079	Educational Services
44678	3	4	Food Svcs & Drinking Places
44680	143	1392	Ambulatory Health Care Svcs
44681	285	2611	Food Svcs & Drinking Places
44682	24	89	Educational Services
44683	292	2383	Food Svcs & Drinking Places
44685	576	5720	Educational Services
44687	42	822	Nursing & Resid. Care Facilit.
44688	105	789	Food Svcs & Drinking Places
44689	36	427	Food Manufacturing
44690	39	1077	Food Manufacturing
44691	1897	27709	Educational Services
44693	5	48	Accommodation
44695	37	496	Wood Product Manufacturing
44697	21	145	Food Svcs & Drinking Places
44699	18	44	Wood Product Manufacturing
44702	716	9837	Justice, Pubic Order/Safety
44703	198	1477	Special Trade Contractors
44704	126	1330	Primary Metal Manufacturing
44705	551	7932	Food Manufacturing
44706	545	15798	Fabricated Metal Product Mfg
44707	512	6634	Merch. Wholesalers,Durable Gds
44708	1010	10937	Hospitals
44709	574	4734	Food Svcs & Drinking Places
44710	179	6151	Ambulatory Health Care Svcs
44711	11	28	Perform'g Arts, Spec. Sports
44714	218	1327	Nursing & Resid. Care Facilit.
44718	1381	14417	Food Svcs & Drinking Places
44720	1928	27536	Elect'l Eqpmt, App, & Comp Mfg
44721	256	1839	Educational Services
44730	172	1444	Plastics & Rubber Products Mfg
44735	13	32	Special Trade Contractors
44750	1	99	Sportg Gds,Hobby,Book, & Music
44767	4	900	Nonstore Retailers
44802	19	288	Construction of Buildings
44804	36	249	Educational Services
44805	1194	15263	Educational Services
44807	88	571	Educational Services
44809	26	144	Educational Services
44811	473	5558	Rail Transportation
44813	198	1634	Food Svcs & Drinking Places
44814	73	436	Special Trade Contractors
44815	36	316	Heavy & Civil Eng. Construct'N
44816	35	423	Merch. Wholesalers,Durable Gds
44817	28	215	Educational Services
44818	61	323	Food Svcs & Drinking Places
44820	760	8740	Fabricated Metal Product Mfg
44822	74	436	Educational Services
44824	115	645	Educational Services
44825	8	37	Educational Services
44826	32	147	Educational Services
44827	208	2018	Bldg Matl & Garden Eqpmt Dlrs
44828	7	166	Relig., Grant, Civic, Prof Org
44830	618	6226	Fabricated Metal Product Mfg
44833	614	5352	Computer & Electronic Prod Mfg
44836	60	881	Nursing & Resid. Care Facilit.
44837	89	893	Machinery Manufacturing
44838	20	98	Educational Services
44839	379	5391	Relig., Grant, Civic, Prof Org
44840	67	277	Educational Services
44841	14	89	Educational Services
44842	262	2116	Educational Services
44843	67	296	Educational Services
44844	24	150	Accommodation
44845	2	2	Relig., Grant, Civic, Prof Org
44846	180	2094	Machinery Manufacturing
44847	115	1436	Administrative & Support Svcs
44848	9	38	Educational Services
44849	48	279	Food Manufacturing
44850	15	74	Merch. Wholesalers,Durable Gds
44851	160	1538	Miscellaneous Manufacturing
44853	34	514	Food Manufacturing
44854	66	749	Print'g & Related Supp't Act's
44855	30	93	Crop Production
44856	6	39	Educational Services
44857	939	11638	Furniture & Related Prod. Mfg
44859	39	165	Elect'l Eqpmt, App, & Comp Mfg
44860	3	2	Repair and Maintenance
44861	17	216	Educational Services
44862	57	533	General Merchandise Stores
44864	93	1560	Fabricated Metal Product Mfg
44865	92	500	Merch. Wholesalers,Nondur. Gds
44866	40	122	Educational Services
44867	43	169	Administrative & Support Svcs
44870	2009	40878	Amusement, Gambling,& Recreat.
44871	11	27	Social Assistance
44874	16	27	Social Assistance
44875	456	5885	Merch. Wholesalers,Durable Gds
44878	61	302	Bldg Matl & Garden Eqpmt Dlrs
44880	40	269	Educational Services

ZIP CODE	2004 Total Firms	2004 Total Employees	TOP INDUSTRY RANKED on 2004 EMPLOYMENT
44881	5	29	Educational Services
44882	79	675	Plastics & Rubber Products Mfg
44883	1081	12584	Educational Services
44887	27	70	Educational Services
44888	2	1606	Print'g & Related Supp't Act's
44889	131	435	Food Svcs & Drinking Places
44890	323	5562	Machinery Manufacturing
44901	8	480	Postal Service
44902	688	7277	Prof., Scientific, & Tech Svcs
44903	659	12100	Hospitals
44904	345	3424	Transportation Equipment Mfg
44905	506	4163	Educational Services
44906	931	15889	Transportation Equipment Mfg
44907	553	5993	Computer & Electronic Prod Mfg
45001	30	146	Educational Services
45002	398	3158	Special Trade Contractors
45003	38	240	Accommodation
45004	3	38	Justice, Pubic Order/Safety
45005	905	10773	Food Svcs & Drinking Places
45011	1637	20000	Educational Services
45012	2	4	Administrative & Support Svcs
45013	1109	9351	Food Svcs & Drinking Places
45014	1698	25242	Insurance Carriers & Related
45015	361	4413	Merch. Wholesalers,Durable Gds
45018	7	30	Nonmetallic Mineral Prod. Mfg
45030	582	7408	Merch. Wholesalers,Durable Gds
45032	8	30	Fabricated Metal Product Mfg
45033	7	86	Justice, Pubic Order/Safety
45034	19	5069	Amusement, Gambling,& Recreat.
45036	1191	12314	Exec., Legis., & Other Support
45039	317	2252	Computer & Electronic Prod Mfg
45040	1169	26679	Credit Intermediation & Relatd
45041	30	204	Special Trade Contractors
45042	849	7637	Educational Services
45044	1439	13724	Hospitals
45050	307	3947	Plastics & Rubber Products Mfg
45051	3	25	Social Assistance
45052	91	1134	Chemical Manufacturing
45053	62	192	Special Trade Contractors
45054	36	293	Social Assistance
45055	7	61	Machinery Manufacturing
45056	615	6550	Food Svcs & Drinking Places
45061	27	218	Nonmetallic Mineral Prod. Mfg
45062	18	132	Educational Services
45063	20	68	Computer & Electronic Prod Mfg
45064	28	161	Nursing & Resid. Care Facilit.
45065	62	419	Merch. Wholesalers,Durable Gds
45066	566	5621	Food Svcs & Drinking Places
45067	211	1772	Beverage & Tobacco Product Mfg
45068	311	1642	Food Svcs & Drinking Places
45069	1596	18146	Food Svcs & Drinking Places
45070	15	51	Educational Services
45071	9	18	Construction of Buildings
45101	68	523	Special Trade Contractors
45102	516	3477	Food Svcs & Drinking Places
45103	798	13937	Merch. Wholesalers,Durable Gds
45105	1	0	Postal Service
45106	260	1800	Merch. Wholesalers,Durable Gds
45107	240	2321	Transportation Equipment Mfg
45110	4	36	Gasoline Stations
45111	12	112	Exec., Legis., & Other Support
45112	6	7	Relig., Grant, Civic, Prof Org
45113	68	351	Educational Services
45114	3	2	Sportg Gds,Hobby,Book, & Music
45115	2	4	Food and Beverage Stores
45118	99	530	Educational Services
45119	3	4	Food and Beverage Stores
45120	59	526	Educational Services
45121	348	3111	Educational Services
45122	220	1024	Educational Services
45123	264	2331	Motor Vehicle & Parts Dealers
45130	65	256	Educational Services
45131	13	71	Food Svcs & Drinking Places
45132	10	15	Truck Transportation
45133	825	7667	Educational Services
45135	83	654	Miscellaneous Manufacturing
45138	7	82	Educational Services
45140	1077	11427	Administrative & Support Svcs
45142	94	359	Educational Services
45144	124	954	Utilities
45145	4	5	Special Trade Contractors
45146	21	34	Exec., Legis., & Other Support
45147	17	225	Prof., Scientific, & Tech Svcs
45148	25	57	Insurance Carriers & Related
45150	1198	13681	Food Svcs & Drinking Places
45152	195	1181	Educational Services
45153	39	180	Justice, Pubic Order/Safety
45154	217	2189	Educational Services
45155	17	101	Educational Services
45156	2	2	Postal Service

ZIP CODE	2004 Total Firms	2004 Total Employ-ees	TOP INDUSTRY RANKED on 2004 EMPLOYMENT	ZIP CODE	2004 Total Firms	2004 Total Employ-ees	TOP INDUSTRY RANKED on 2004 EMPLOYMENT	ZIP CODE	2004 Total Firms	2004 Total Employ-ees	TOP INDUSTRY RANKED on 2004 EMPLOYMENT
45157	209	1129	Educational Services	45318	207	1772	Relig., Grant, Civic, Prof Org	45432	601	6030	Prof., Scientific, & Tech Svcs
45158	20	266	Educational Services	45319	19	229	Nonmetallic Mineral Prod. Mfg	45433	106	1425	Nat'l Security & Int'l Affairs
45159	68	625	Plastics & Rubber Products Mfg	45320	578	7317	Hospitals	45434	278	3426	Transportation Equipment Mfg
45160	48	365	Educational Services	45321	25	72	Plastics & Rubber Products Mfg	45435	13	447	Other Information Services
45162	59	395	Food Manufacturing	45322	540	5191	Food Svcs & Drinking Places	45437	4	14	Publishing Industries
45164	12	12	Construction of Buildings	45323	141	1842	Miscellaneous Store Retailers	45439	739	17649	Machinery Manufacturing
45166	3	2	Perform'g Arts, Spec. Sports	45324	1002	13234	Food Svcs & Drinking Places	45440	421	6243	Nonstore Retailers
45167	118	980	Nursing & Resid. Care Facilit.	45325	75	274	Justice, Pubic Order/Safety	45441	5	18	Personal and Laundry Services
45168	51	201	Educational Services	45326	23	553	Merch. Wholesalers,Durable Gds	45449	570	8347	Machinery Manufacturing
45169	137	1474	Transportation Equipment Mfg	45327	249	1665	Educational Services	45458	756	6413	Food Svcs & Drinking Places
45171	133	804	Educational Services	45328	21	209	Machinery Manufacturing	45459	2050	22532	Food Svcs & Drinking Places
45172	8	45	Justice, Pubic Order/Safety	45330	27	110	Relig., Grant, Civic, Prof Org	45463	1	79	Paper Manufacturing
45174	60	236	Insurance Carriers & Related	45331	1047	13890	Hospitals	45469	11	2970	Educational Services
45176	174	1365	Miscellaneous Manufacturing	45332	20	122	Educational Services	45475	7	29	Truck Transportation
45177	959	20038	Air Transportation	45333	23	167	Educational Services	45479	2	3500	Prof., Scientific, & Tech Svcs
45201	4	12	Isps, Web Search Portals	45334	89	1729	Plastics & Rubber Products Mfg	45490	2	38	Transit & Grnd Pass. Transport
45202	3503	85381	Chemical Manufacturing	45335	145	1074	Educational Services	45501	16	279	Postal Service
45203	304	7673	Rail Transportation	45336	6	61	Food Svcs & Drinking Places	45502	685	9235	Transportation Equipment Mfg
45204	194	4013	Exec., Legis., & Other Support	45337	41	139	Heavy & Civil Eng. Construct'N	45503	878	10203	Transportation Equipment Mfg
45205	316	2246	Educational Services	45338	138	1831	Food Manufacturing	45504	862	17598	Insurance Carriers & Related
45206	755	11148	Hospitals	45339	27	86	Food Svcs & Drinking Places	45505	697	8178	Hospitals
45207	159	2277	Educational Services	45340	12	29	Construction of Buildings	45506	361	4211	Fabricated Metal Product Mfg
45208	719	5933	Food Svcs & Drinking Places	45341	66	288	Special Trade Contractors	45601	1824	22499	Educational Services
45209	547	8104	Food Svcs & Drinking Places	45342	970	20561	Prof., Scientific, & Tech Svcs	45612	118	644	Educational Services
45211	1023	10000	Food Svcs & Drinking Places	45343	5	9	Miscellaneous Store Retailers	45613	78	540	Educational Services
45212	795	12250	Administrative & Support Svcs	45344	449	4037	Bldg Matl & Garden Eqpmt Dlrs	45614	63	927	Nonmetallic Mineral Prod. Mfg
45213	353	4819	General Merchandise Stores	45345	145	905	Educational Services	45616	19	55	Bldg Matl & Garden Eqpmt Dlrs
45214	524	6327	Educational Services	45346	68	521	Transportation Equipment Mfg	45617	5	2	Postal Service
45215	1351	25355	Transportation Equipment Mfg	45347	120	1030	Educational Services	45618	5	12	Merch. Wholesalers,Nondur. Gds
45216	450	5318	Social Assistance	45348	16	60	Food and Beverage Stores	45619	181	942	Educational Services
45217	227	3864	Chemical Manufacturing	45349	26	48	Relig., Grant, Civic, Prof Org	45620	39	686	Utilities
45218	86	679	Educational Services	45350	15	115	Justice, Pubic Order/Safety	45621	15	65	Educational Services
45219	712	11948	Hospitals	45351	13	129	Food Manufacturing	45622	12	68	Merch. Wholesalers,Durable Gds
45220	372	8241	Hospitals	45352	11	27	Relig., Grant, Civic, Prof Org	45623	35	138	Educational Services
45221	17	8974	Educational Services	45353	4	36	Educational Services	45624	3	10	Merch. Wholesalers,Nondur. Gds
45222	2	10	Postal Service	45354	22	85	Educational Services	45628	103	539	Miscellaneous Manufacturing
45223	518	4967	Educational Services	45356	1015	12187	Machinery Manufacturing	45629	58	690	Merch. Wholesalers,Nondur. Gds
45224	449	3881	Nursing & Resid. Care Facilit.	45358	18	60	Educational Services	45630	9	35	Amusement, Gambling,& Recreat.
45225	277	4932	Food Manufacturing	45359	62	242	Educational Services	45631	748	9113	Exec., Legis., & Other Support
45226	385	5510	Admin. Human Resource Programs	45360	14	96	Food Svcs & Drinking Places	45633	6	2	Food and Beverage Stores
45227	838	9719	Educational Services	45361	8	10	Relig., Grant, Civic, Prof Org	45634	45	831	Merch. Wholesalers,Durable Gds
45228	33	316	Amusement, Gambling,& Recreat.	45362	17	159	Food and Beverage Stores	45636	3	15	Merch. Wholesalers,Durable Gds
45229	501	8844	Relig., Grant, Civic, Prof Org	45363	36	1126	Bldg Matl & Garden Eqpmt Dlrs	45638	697	5913	Relig., Grant, Civic, Prof Org
45230	699	5022	Ambulatory Health Care Svcs	45365	1099	20848	Machinery Manufacturing	45640	698	7706	Food Manufacturing
45231	1070	9325	Educational Services	45368	103	1091	Transportation Equipment Mfg	45642	1	1	Repair and Maintenance
45232	194	4974	Merch. Wholesalers,Nondur. Gds	45369	54	431	Administrative & Support Svcs	45643	1	2	Postal Service
45233	318	3537	Educational Services	45370	68	277	Special Trade Contractors	45644	63	333	Educational Services
45234	1	0	Postal Service	45371	601	7510	Prof., Scientific, & Tech Svcs	45645	35	138	Special Trade Contractors
45235	3	4	Food Svcs & Drinking Places	45372	18	49	Print'g & Related Supp't Act's	45646	18	224	Educational Services
45236	1421	16551	Food Svcs & Drinking Places	45373	1304	21249	Ambulatory Health Care Svcs	45647	45	139	Educational Services
45237	850	12175	Merch. Wholesalers,Durable Gds	45374	1	1300	Machinery Manufacturing	45648	219	1754	Educational Services
45238	1097	10937	Food Svcs & Drinking Places	45377	624	11525	Transportation Equipment Mfg	45650	3	3	Special Trade Contractors
45239	702	7262	Hospitals	45378	12	65	Justice, Pubic Order/Safety	45651	227	1726	Educational Services
45240	777	11838	Food Svcs & Drinking Places	45380	214	2502	Miscellaneous Manufacturing	45652	52	712	Educational Services
45241	1676	30347	Prof., Scientific, & Tech Svcs	45381	129	798	Educational Services	45653	98	2123	Ambulatory Health Care Svcs
45242	2528	44432	Computer & Electronic Prod Mfg	45382	34	86	Support Act. for Transport.	45654	18	66	Truck Transportation
45243	447	3776	Relig., Grant, Civic, Prof Org	45383	196	1404	Educational Services	45656	143	989	Petroleum & Coal Products Mfg
45244	655	7093	Machinery Manufacturing	45384	10	383	Educational Services	45657	30	74	Wood Product Manufacturing
45245	745	9891	Food Svcs & Drinking Places	45385	1156	14033	Food and Beverage Stores	45658	16	141	Utilities
45246	1719	37200	Food Svcs & Drinking Places	45387	261	2912	Educational Services	45659	29	163	Hospitals
45247	611	4299	Food Svcs & Drinking Places	45388	13	75	Food Manufacturing	45660	205	1674	Wood Product Manufacturing
45248	477	4847	Educational Services	45389	21	43	Food Svcs & Drinking Places	45661	227	3956	Chemical Manufacturing
45249	734	11016	Food Svcs & Drinking Places	45390	97	775	Educational Services	45662	1420	17700	Ambulatory Health Care Svcs
45250	4	2	Prof., Scientific, & Tech Svcs	45401	13	1543	Postal Service	45663	144	938	Educational Services
45251	635	8399	Food Svcs & Drinking Places	45402	1638	26450	Justice, Pubic Order/Safety	45669	211	1304	Ambulatory Health Care Svcs
45252	85	1349	Other Information Services	45403	506	5527	Fabricated Metal Product Mfg	45671	6	50	Justice, Pubic Order/Safety
45253	6	13	Special Trade Contractors	45404	658	15089	Fabricated Metal Product Mfg	45672	18	30	Merch. Wholesalers,Nondur. Gds
45254	6	17	Administrative & Support Svcs	45405	528	4827	Food Svcs & Drinking Places	45673	13	231	Educational Services
45255	841	14259	Relig., Grant, Civic, Prof Org	45406	554	6417	Hospitals	45674	60	795	Educational Services
45258	8	15	Real Estate	45407	236	1565	Machinery Manufacturing	45677	2	4	Rental and Leasing Services
45262	3	27	Administrative & Support Svcs	45408	279	5582	Print'g & Related Supp't Act's	45678	8	33	Merch. Wholesalers,Durable Gds
45263	4	2042	Managmt of Companies & Enterp.	45409	423	9658	Hospitals	45679	74	466	Educational Services
45267	70	5863	Hospitals	45410	337	3119	Real Estate	45680	309	4125	General Merchandise Stores
45275	36	1096	Wholesale Elec. Mrkts & Agents	45413	2	3	Print'g & Related Supp't Act's	45681	16	48	Educational Services
45301	11	256	Bldg Matl & Garden Eqpmt Dlrs	45414	1291	17546	Food Svcs & Drinking Places	45682	47	246	Educational Services
45302	93	3590	Machinery Manufacturing	45415	503	4710	Ambulatory Health Care Svcs	45683	1	25	Construction of Buildings
45303	68	563	Educational Services	45416	136	1456	Nursing & Resid. Care Facilit.	45684	18	57	Food and Beverage Stores
45304	196	1034	Educational Services	45417	211	1192	Relig., Grant, Civic, Prof Org	45685	11	49	Merch. Wholesalers,Durable Gds
45305	263	1360	Food Svcs & Drinking Places	45418	149	1776	Justice, Pubic Order/Safety	45686	38	202	Support Act. for Transport.
45306	77	595	Plastics & Rubber Products Mfg	45419	440	3419	Educational Services	45687	2	92	Social Assistance
45307	11	17	Relig., Grant, Civic, Prof Org	45420	649	8250	Transportation Equipment Mfg	45688	3	6	Food and Beverage Stores
45308	84	668	Truck Transportation	45422	48	2768	Exec., Legis., & Other Support	45690	505	7239	Furniture & Related Prod. Mfg
45309	335	3997	Transportation Equipment Mfg	45423	66	1959	Credit Intermediation & Relatd	45692	274	2928	Merch. Wholesalers,Nondur. Gds
45310	13	120	Waste Managmt & Remediat'n Svc	45424	1214	14804	Food Svcs & Drinking Places	45693	377	2517	Exec., Legis., & Other Support
45311	134	886	Educational Services	45426	419	5742	Educational Services	45694	374	2764	Food Svcs & Drinking Places
45312	34	221	Educational Services	45427	255	1892	Food Svcs & Drinking Places	45695	12	61	Educational Services
45314	87	967	Educational Services	45428	9	1562	Hospitals	45696	8	195	Educational Services
45315	158	2078	Educational Services	45429	1093	9609	Ambulatory Health Care Svcs	45697	90	605	Relig., Grant, Civic, Prof Org
45316	7	31	Food Svcs & Drinking Places	45430	163	2255	Prof., Scientific, & Tech Svcs	45698	11	74	Educational Services
45317	15	68	Merch. Wholesalers,Durable Gds	45431	787	9655	General Merchandise Stores	45699	1	10	Other Information Services

ZIP CODE	2004 Total Firms	2004 Total Employees	TOP INDUSTRY RANKED on 2004 EMPLOYMENT	ZIP CODE	2004 Total Firms	2004 Total Employees	TOP INDUSTRY RANKED on 2004 EMPLOYMENT	ZIP CODE	2004 Total Firms	2004 Total Employees	TOP INDUSTRY RANKED on 2004 EMPLOYMENT
45701	1176	14853	Educational Services	45853	78	1066	Unclassified Establishments	46077	693	5114	Food and Beverage Stores
45710	130	622	Educational Services	45854	21	38	Food Svcs & Drinking Places	46082	13	30	Construction of Buildings
45711	29	145	Educational Services	45855	4	52	Merch. Wholesalers,Nondur. Gds	46102	9	56	Justice, Pubic Order/Safety
45712	31	180	Merch. Wholesalers,Durable Gds	45856	143	1241	Educational Services	46103	11	71	Educational Services
45713	17	112	Justice, Pubic Order/Safety	45858	87	1680	Food Manufacturing	46104	13	84	Machinery Manufacturing
45714	363	2572	Merch. Wholesalers,Nondur. Gds	45859	9	19	Food Svcs & Drinking Places	46105	65	294	Educational Services
45715	132	843	Educational Services	45860	54	569	Waste Managmt & Remediat'n Svc	46106	121	718	Special Trade Contractors
45716	5	23	Food and Beverage Stores	45861	7	20	Food and Beverage Stores	46107	316	8128	Hospitals
45719	23	158	Educational Services	45862	36	233	Merch. Wholesalers,Nondur. Gds	46110	12	116	Heavy & Civil Eng. Construct'N
45720	17	72	Construction of Buildings	45863	41	233	Exec., Legis., & Other Support	46111	20	145	Merch. Wholesalers,Durable Gds
45723	84	460	Nursing & Resid. Care Facilit.	45864	13	176	Educational Services	46112	728	5888	Food Svcs & Drinking Places
45724	13	20	Educational Services	45865	176	3423	Machinery Manufacturing	46113	124	880	Food Svcs & Drinking Places
45727	11	192	Nonstore Retailers	45866	9	15	Food Svcs & Drinking Places	46115	42	209	Paper Manufacturing
45729	12	89	Support Activities for Mining	45867	24	143	Educational Services	46117	12	184	Educational Services
45732	106	565	Educational Services	45868	15	32	Furn. & Home Furnishgs Stores	46118	129	788	Waste Managmt & Remediat'n Svc
45734	13	58	Educational Services	45869	130	4409	Machinery Manufacturing	46120	230	1325	Food Svcs & Drinking Places
45735	26	47	Special Trade Contractors	45870	4	26	Miscellaneous Manufacturing	46121	68	191	Merch. Wholesalers,Durable Gds
45739	3	16	Food and Beverage Stores	45871	75	412	Wood Product Manufacturing	46122	485	4624	Hospitals
45740	10	45	Justice, Pubic Order/Safety	45872	130	1796	Transportation Equipment Mfg	46123	692	7524	Food Svcs & Drinking Places
45741	8	11	Food and Beverage Stores	45873	107	822	Food and Beverage Stores	46124	345	4471	Wood Product Manufacturing
45742	54	522	Chemical Manufacturing	45874	46	235	Plastics & Rubber Products Mfg	46125	12	114	Educational Services
45743	14	87	Special Trade Contractors	45875	442	5914	Computer & Electronic Prod Mfg	46126	90	463	Educational Services
45744	68	452	Truck Transportation	45876	88	868	Machinery Manufacturing	46127	10	78	Educational Services
45745	19	52	Educational Services	45877	85	736	Nursing & Resid. Care Facilit.	46128	43	168	Educational Services
45746	10	106	Wood Product Manufacturing	45879	280	2429	Educational Services	46129	5	9	Chemical Manufacturing
45750	1456	18948	Educational Services	45880	78	560	Nonmetallic Mineral Prod. Mfg	46130	42	150	Special Trade Contractors
45760	145	1057	Educational Services	45881	26	337	Educational Services	46131	1002	12623	Transportation Equipment Mfg
45761	29	66	Merch. Wholesalers,Durable Gds	45882	85	988	Truck Transportation	46133	25	97	Justice, Pubic Order/Safety
45764	249	2832	Educational Services	45883	102	1355	Food Manufacturing	46135	668	9375	Justice, Pubic Order/Safety
45766	22	79	Educational Services	45884	5	6	Bldg Matl & Garden Eqpmt Dlrs	46140	1118	13337	Transportation Equipment Mfg
45767	65	262	Educational Services	45885	466	5647	Motor Vehicle & Parts Dealers	46142	1249	11095	Food Svcs & Drinking Places
45768	46	203	Food and Beverage Stores	45886	11	29	Warehousing and Storage	46143	769	8961	Food Svcs & Drinking Places
45769	263	1868	Food Svcs & Drinking Places	45887	124	1471	Transportation Equipment Mfg	46144	7	16	Merch. Wholesalers,Durable Gds
45770	12	50	Merch. Wholesalers,Durable Gds	45888	17	52	Motor Vehicle & Parts Dealers	46146	8	31	Furniture & Related Prod. Mfg
45771	72	379	Educational Services	45889	24	227	Educational Services	46147	67	230	Educational Services
45772	29	301	Educational Services	45890	20	113	Educational Services	46148	168	1216	Nursing & Resid. Care Facilit.
45773	23	196	Support Activities for Mining	45891	674	9592	Fabricated Metal Product Mfg	46149	58	235	Educational Services
45775	34	105	Justice, Pubic Order/Safety	45893	11	11	Telecommunications	46150	14	30	Heavy & Civil Eng. Construct'N
45776	18	49	Educational Services	45894	12	83	Fabricated Metal Product Mfg	46151	934	9073	Educational Services
45778	20	249	Educational Services	45895	701	5332	Food Svcs & Drinking Places	46154	13	106	Special Trade Contractors
45779	22	73	Educational Services	45896	57	370	Educational Services	46155	6	40	Educational Services
45780	108	953	Nursing & Resid. Care Facilit.	45897	6	12	Bldg Matl & Garden Eqpmt Dlrs	46156	51	304	Machinery Manufacturing
45782	16	86	Relig., Grant, Civic, Prof Org	45898	32	170	Food Svcs & Drinking Places	46157	59	376	Educational Services
45783	23	106	Food and Beverage Stores	45899	7	16	Other Information Services	46158	668	6638	Ambulatory Health Care Svcs
45784	41	286	Educational Services	46001	333	2315	Educational Services	46160	169	858	Apparel Manufacturing
45786	65	1005	Utilities	46011	305	3581	Ambulatory Health Care Svcs	46161	82	895	Miscellaneous Manufacturing
45787	5	6	Prof., Scientific, & Tech Svcs	46012	556	5333	Food Svcs & Drinking Places	46162	8	10	Food and Beverage Stores
45788	18	51	Repair and Maintenance	46013	530	7455	Food Svcs & Drinking Places	46163	216	1210	Educational Services
45789	2	3	Food and Beverage Stores	46014	1	0	Special Trade Contractors	46164	65	227	Educational Services
45801	1069	20088	Transportation Equipment Mfg	46015	7	215	Unclassified Establishments	46165	40	211	Educational Services
45802	7	72	Special Trade Contractors	46016	1117	11489	Ambulatory Health Care Svcs	46166	38	93	Educational Services
45804	687	11149	Food Svcs & Drinking Places	46017	168	1223	Exec., Legis., & Other Support	46167	112	522	Food Svcs & Drinking Places
45805	880	10123	Food Svcs & Drinking Places	46018	4	14	Administrative & Support Svcs	46168	814	13391	Utilities
45806	309	2550	Educational Services	46030	81	622	Educational Services	46170	4	4	Perform'g Arts, Spec. Sports
45807	359	2793	Fabricated Metal Product Mfg	46031	49	224	Bldg Matl & Garden Eqpmt Dlrs	46171	32	178	Bldg Matl & Garden Eqpmt Dlrs
45808	21	54	Justice, Pubic Order/Safety	46032	2072	30798	Insurance Carriers & Related	46172	88	431	Educational Services
45809	13	62	Educational Services	46033	382	3467	Educational Services	46173	489	4276	Fabricated Metal Product Mfg
45810	163	1745	Educational Services	46034	196	828	Food Svcs & Drinking Places	46175	13	64	Fabricated Metal Product Mfg
45812	45	133	Educational Services	46035	47	104	Justice, Pubic Order/Safety	46176	991	13263	Nonmetallic Mineral Prod. Mfg
45813	102	954	Nonmetallic Mineral Prod. Mfg	46036	391	4299	Transportation Equipment Mfg	46180	32	100	Support Act. for Transport.
45814	59	406	Prof., Scientific, & Tech Svcs	46038	1302	16526	Credit Intermediation & Relatd	46181	130	687	Educational Services
45815	2	0	Repair and Maintenance	46039	14	28	Bldg Matl & Garden Eqpmt Dlrs	46182	53	381	Educational Services
45816	9	14	Relig., Grant, Civic, Prof Org	46040	223	1252	Educational Services	46183	13	80	Educational Services
45817	228	4189	Educational Services	46041	818	12659	Merch. Wholesalers,Nondur. Gds	46184	281	1953	Educational Services
45819	18	51	Educational Services	46044	57	468	Educational Services	46186	27	57	Machinery Manufacturing
45820	19	61	Chemical Manufacturing	46045	6	19	Wood Product Manufacturing	46201	761	12032	Nonstore Retailers
45821	27	112	Food Svcs & Drinking Places	46047	5	26	Food Manufacturing	46202	1444	53252	Educational Services
45822	774	7332	Food Svcs & Drinking Places	46048	21	52	Justice, Pubic Order/Safety	46203	1108	13088	Merch. Wholesalers,Durable Gds
45826	13	103	Food Svcs & Drinking Places	46049	23	32	Merch. Wholesalers,Nondur. Gds	46204	2364	51079	Prof., Scientific, & Tech Svcs
45827	54	192	Nursing & Resid. Care Facilit.	46050	47	142	Wood Product Manufacturing	46205	931	11757	Administrative & Support Svcs
45828	228	2571	Hospitals	46051	84	664	Nonmetallic Mineral Prod. Mfg	46206	21	447	Ambulatory Health Care Svcs
45830	159	805	Educational Services	46052	795	7795	Food Svcs & Drinking Places	46207	1	50	Special Trade Contractors
45831	96	727	Educational Services	46055	132	602	Special Trade Contractors	46208	707	8707	Educational Services
45832	55	506	Educational Services	46056	42	145	Wood Product Manufacturing	46214	491	7034	Ambulatory Health Care Svcs
45833	374	4054	Food Manufacturing	46057	46	206	Educational Services	46216	164	1898	Prof., Scientific, & Tech Svcs
45835	9	104	Educational Services	46058	66	314	Nursing & Resid. Care Facilit.	46217	610	7807	Special Trade Contractors
45836	44	155	Plastics & Rubber Products Mfg	46060	1549	15292	Food Svcs & Drinking Places	46218	882	10196	Special Trade Contractors
45837	6	9	Merch. Wholesalers,Durable Gds	46061	12	21	Special Trade Contractors	46219	1491	32847	Merch. Wholesalers,Durable Gds
45838	1	13	Warehousing and Storage	46063	10	557	Food Manufacturing	46220	2093	14220	Food Svcs & Drinking Places
45839	7	20	Social Assistance	46064	351	3486	Justice, Pubic Order/Safety	46221	496	7501	Educational Services
45840	2282	35980	Food Svcs & Drinking Places	46065	99	527	Educational Services	46222	946	15195	Transportation Equipment Mfg
45841	15	52	Relig., Grant, Civic, Prof Org	46067	4	14	Merch. Wholesalers,Durable Gds	46224	671	7363	Food Svcs & Drinking Places
45843	72	641	Transportation Equipment Mfg	46068	67	398	Educational Services	46225	563	18734	Merch. Wholesalers,Nondur. Gds
45844	106	423	Educational Services	46069	170	1092	Fabricated Metal Product Mfg	46226	1136	11954	Educational Services
45845	101	858	Merch. Wholesalers,Durable Gds	46070	47	209	Merch. Wholesalers,Durable Gds	46227	1710	17653	Food Svcs & Drinking Places
45846	165	1753	Primary Metal Manufacturing	46071	111	723	Educational Services	46228	193	889	Educational Services
45848	32	338	Hospitals	46072	481	3879	Hospitals	46229	709	9333	General Merchandise Stores
45849	34	108	Educational Services	46074	465	4758	Special Trade Contractors	46230	10	16	Administrative & Support Svcs
45850	63	311	Justice, Pubic Order/Safety	46075	128	826	Merch. Wholesalers,Durable Gds	46231	150	6204	Special Trade Contractors
45851	18	342	Plastics & Rubber Products Mfg	46076	44	202	Fabricated Metal Product Mfg	46234	318	3031	Heavy & Civil Eng. Construct'N

BUSINESS DATA

ZIP CODE	2004 Total Firms	2004 Total Employ-ees	TOP INDUSTRY RANKED on 2004 EMPLOYMENT	ZIP CODE	2004 Total Firms	2004 Total Employ-ees	TOP INDUSTRY RANKED on 2004 EMPLOYMENT	ZIP CODE	2004 Total Firms	2004 Total Employ-ees	TOP INDUSTRY RANKED on 2004 EMPLOYMENT
46235	161	2848	Sportg Gds,Hobby,Book, & Music	46501	114	885	Educational Services	46741	84	1609	Plastics & Rubber Products Mfg
46236	491	3985	Educational Services	46502	16	104	Special Trade Contractors	46742	101	1061	Machinery Manufacturing
46237	583	6573	Food Svcs & Drinking Places	46504	88	701	Fabricated Metal Product Mfg	46743	60	433	Special Trade Contractors
46239	412	5128	Merch. Wholesalers,Durable Gds	46506	294	4165	Fabricated Metal Product Mfg	46745	35	285	Prof., Scientific, & Tech Svcs
46240	1742	24772	Prof., Scientific, & Tech Svcs	46507	257	5300	Transportation Equipment Mfg	46746	131	1425	Food Manufacturing
46241	1323	30387	Machinery Manufacturing	46508	12	58	Fabricated Metal Product Mfg	46747	41	259	Fabricated Metal Product Mfg
46242	5	12	Accommodation	46510	49	157	Waste Managmt & Remediat'n Svc	46748	103	632	Educational Services
46244	3	5	Prof., Scientific, & Tech Svcs	46511	149	1309	Educational Services	46750	918	12313	Computer & Electronic Prod Mfg
46247	8	22	Special Trade Contractors	46513	4	64	Educational Services	46755	596	9764	Plastics & Rubber Products Mfg
46249	8	276	Prof., Scientific, & Tech Svcs	46514	1532	29488	Fabricated Metal Product Mfg	46759	8	21	Crop Production
46250	1572	22798	Food Svcs & Drinking Places	46515	17	227	Postal Service	46760	26	77	Fabricated Metal Product Mfg
46251	2	61	Construction of Buildings	46516	1449	20955	Transportation Equipment Mfg	46761	376	3544	Educational Services
46253	11	13	Real Estate	46517	747	12297	Merch. Wholesalers,Durable Gds	46763	40	480	Fabricated Metal Product Mfg
46254	979	12342	Food Svcs & Drinking Places	46524	48	296	Miscellaneous Store Retailers	46764	37	215	Computer & Electronic Prod Mfg
46255	1	0	Credit Intermediation & Relatd	46526	1104	18182	General Merchandise Stores	46765	126	603	Social Assistance
46256	742	14029	Managmt of Companies & Enterp.	46527	9	107	Paper Manufacturing	46766	17	31	Special Trade Contractors
46259	135	1038	Educational Services	46528	500	8642	Transportation Equipment Mfg	46767	244	4016	Plastics & Rubber Products Mfg
46260	939	23349	Ambulatory Health Care Svcs	46530	619	5905	Admin. of Economic Programs	46769	3	7	Special Trade Contractors
46268	1691	32286	Prof., Scientific, & Tech Svcs	46531	19	63	Gasoline Stations	46770	82	482	Bldg Matl & Garden Eqpmt Dlrs
46277	1	7	Ambulatory Health Care Svcs	46532	59	422	Educational Services	46771	10	30	Accommodation
46278	457	10080	Merch. Wholesalers,Durable Gds	46534	442	3144	Fabricated Metal Product Mfg	46772	44	960	Educational Services
46280	235	2584	Merch. Wholesalers,Durable Gds	46536	115	630	Educational Services	46773	89	685	Transportation Equipment Mfg
46282	47	2723	Insurance Carriers & Related	46537	31	247	Food Svcs & Drinking Places	46774	463	5011	Fabricated Metal Product Mfg
46285	11	6065	Merch. Wholesalers,Nondur. Gds	46538	136	640	Food Svcs & Drinking Places	46776	69	743	Transportation Equipment Mfg
46290	154	3144	Merch. Wholesalers,Durable Gds	46539	85	678	Fabricated Metal Product Mfg	46777	153	1655	Computer & Electronic Prod Mfg
46298	2	0	Postal Service	46540	336	7167	Merch. Wholesalers,Durable Gds	46778	5	7	Postal Service
46301	19	23	Food and Beverage Stores	46542	137	4111	Machinery Manufacturing	46779	38	128	Educational Services
46302	4	50	Educational Services	46543	64	602	Transportation Equipment Mfg	46780	2	4	Sportg Gds,Hobby,Book, & Music
46303	279	1587	Food Svcs & Drinking Places	46544	870	13085	Food and Beverage Stores	46781	20	198	Educational Services
46304	931	14113	Primary Metal Manufacturing	46545	1504	21469	Food Svcs & Drinking Places	46782	6	5	Merch. Wholesalers,Nondur. Gds
46307	1405	15592	Hospitals	46546	7	11	Prof., Scientific, & Tech Svcs	46783	143	3903	Transportation Equipment Mfg
46308	11	52	Print'g & Related Supp't Act's	46550	415	8392	Wood Product Manufacturing	46784	70	368	Educational Services
46310	446	2071	Food Svcs & Drinking Places	46552	173	2171	Relig., Grant, Civic, Prof Org	46785	29	702	Fabricated Metal Product Mfg
46311	390	3109	Nursing & Resid. Care Facilit.	46553	135	2611	Bldg Matl & Garden Eqpmt Dlrs	46786	17	314	Special Trade Contractors
46312	804	12828	Primary Metal Manufacturing	46554	100	653	Primary Metal Manufacturing	46787	119	1354	Miscellaneous Store Retailers
46319	568	5090	Food Svcs & Drinking Places	46555	182	1206	Machinery Manufacturing	46788	45	201	Machinery Manufacturing
46320	670	11693	Health & Personal Care Stores	46556	48	5935	Educational Services	46789	20	58	Credit Intermediation & Relatd
46321	853	16409	Prof., Scientific, & Tech Svcs	46561	309	2096	Relig., Grant, Civic, Prof Org	46791	19	245	Truck Transportation
46322	1019	9306	Food and Beverage Stores	46562	150	963	Primary Metal Manufacturing	46792	141	713	Food Svcs & Drinking Places
46323	419	4154	Educational Services	46563	992	11775	Food Svcs & Drinking Places	46793	116	1544	Fabricated Metal Product Mfg
46324	511	4007	Educational Services	46565	258	2264	Transportation Equipment Mfg	46794	27	189	Machinery Manufacturing
46325	3	12	Social Assistance	46566	6	3	Food and Beverage Stores	46795	121	620	Elect'l Eqpmt, App, & Comp Mfg
46327	235	3523	Primary Metal Manufacturing	46567	428	4166	Relig., Grant, Civic, Prof Org	46796	15	175	Machinery Manufacturing
46340	33	114	Food Svcs & Drinking Places	46570	18	142	Fabricated Metal Product Mfg	46797	115	2487	Plastics & Rubber Products Mfg
46341	256	1430	Food Svcs & Drinking Places	46571	126	2955	Transportation Equipment Mfg	46798	26	142	Waste Managmt & Remediat'n Svc
46342	849	7658	Hospitals	46572	4	3	Food and Beverage Stores	46799	23	57	Merch. Wholesalers,Durable Gds
46345	40	871	Fabricated Metal Product Mfg	46573	150	4596	Transportation Equipment Mfg	46802	1159	22092	Elect'l Eqpmt, App, & Comp Mfg
46346	24	118	Educational Services	46574	226	2028	Bldg Matl & Garden Eqpmt Dlrs	46803	581	13443	Primary Metal Manufacturing
46347	124	722	Merch. Wholesalers,Durable Gds	46580	1141	18934	Miscellaneous Manufacturing	46804	1252	23378	Hospitals
46348	37	138	Educational Services	46581	10	21	Social Assistance	46805	1209	21222	Hospitals
46349	67	211	Special Trade Contractors	46582	290	5452	Miscellaneous Manufacturing	46806	447	3842	Social Assistance
46350	1446	16148	Primary Metal Manufacturing	46590	101	850	Educational Services	46807	337	4147	Prof., Scientific, & Tech Svcs
46352	8	32	Relig., Grant, Civic, Prof Org	46595	14	78	Merch. Wholesalers,Durable Gds	46808	929	18705	Transportation Equipment Mfg
46355	2	6	Fabricated Metal Product Mfg	46601	1223	18785	Hospitals	46809	525	10848	Machinery Manufacturing
46356	416	3694	Transportation Equipment Mfg	46604	3	0	Insurance Carriers & Related	46814	149	1429	Educational Services
46360	1853	24230	Amusement, Gambling,& Recreat.	46613	327	3103	Food Svcs & Drinking Places	46815	660	5162	Educational Services
46361	19	78	Other Information Services	46614	787	8565	Food Svcs & Drinking Places	46816	269	2478	Educational Services
46365	11	16	Crop Production	46615	409	4414	Prof., Scientific, & Tech Svcs	46818	571	10420	Miscellaneous Manufacturing
46366	168	944	Educational Services	46616	101	726	Educational Services	46819	88	1019	Educational Services
46368	1026	11340	Primary Metal Manufacturing	46617	458	8009	Ambulatory Health Care Svcs	46825	1287	16659	Food Svcs & Drinking Places
46371	86	668	Food Svcs & Drinking Places	46619	476	6111	Merch. Wholesalers,Durable Gds	46835	448	4724	Other Information Services
46372	58	205	Educational Services	46624	9	56	Administrative & Support Svcs	46845	284	1722	Educational Services
46373	285	2011	Educational Services	46626	3	1110	Publishing Industries	46850	2	1	Prof., Scientific, & Tech Svcs
46374	20	240	Nursing & Resid. Care Facilit.	46628	776	14899	Transportation Equipment Mfg	46852	1	0	Educational Services
46375	766	9121	Food Svcs & Drinking Places	46629	23	51	Relig., Grant, Civic, Prof Org	46853	1	0	Social Assistance
46376	18	93	Miscellaneous Manufacturing	46634	7	12	Administrative & Support Svcs	46854	1	15	Administrative & Support Svcs
46377	9	31	Administrative & Support Svcs	46635	248	2639	Nursing & Resid. Care Facilit.	46856	1	0	Relig., Grant, Civic, Prof Org
46379	3	7	Food Svcs & Drinking Places	46637	537	5844	Food Svcs & Drinking Places	46857	1	30	Miscellaneous Manufacturing
46380	2	32	Fabricated Metal Product Mfg	46660	6	93	Relig., Grant, Civic, Prof Org	46858	2	6	Perform'g Arts, Spec. Sports
46381	8	18	Food Manufacturing	46680	8	28	Special Trade Contractors	46863	3	3	Miscellaneous Manufacturing
46382	39	293	Educational Services	46701	219	2788	Transportation Equipment Mfg	46864	1	1	Perform'g Arts, Spec. Sports
46383	1906	19587	Hospitals	46702	53	373	Transportation Equipment Mfg	46865	1	0	Administrative & Support Svcs
46384	25	42	Special Trade Contractors	46703	915	8793	Food Svcs & Drinking Places	46866	1	0	Prof., Scientific, & Tech Svcs
46385	796	5620	Educational Services	46704	22	65	Educational Services	46868	2	4	Educational Services
46390	77	536	Food Svcs & Drinking Places	46705	69	1138	Transportation Equipment Mfg	46869	1	0	Special Trade Contractors
46391	106	3090	Justice, Pubic Order/Safety	46706	736	11456	Primary Metal Manufacturing	46885	9	12	Administrative & Support Svcs
46392	135	930	Educational Services	46710	134	1719	Plastics & Rubber Products Mfg	46895	5	26	Perform'g Arts, Spec. Sports
46393	22	81	Justice, Pubic Order/Safety	46711	273	3842	Prof., Scientific, & Tech Svcs	46896	3	8	Heavy & Civil Eng. Construct'N
46394	298	3951	Petroleum & Coal Products Mfg	46713	8	6	Special Trade Contractors	46898	12	22	Special Trade Contractors
46401	2	8	Exec., Legis., & Other Support	46714	630	8846	Merch. Wholesalers,Nondur. Gds	46899	4	11	Waste Managmt & Remediat'n Svc
46402	401	14410	Primary Metal Manufacturing	46721	154	2687	Fabricated Metal Product Mfg	46901	1473	16516	Food Svcs & Drinking Places
46403	295	2180	Educational Services	46723	181	1856	Transportation Equipment Mfg	46902	1244	25767	Computer & Electronic Prod Mfg
46404	324	2733	Educational Services	46725	768	7769	Transportation Equipment Mfg	46903	5	5	Transit & Grnd Pass. Transport
46405	288	1956	Food Svcs & Drinking Places	46730	32	134	Food and Beverage Stores	46904	7	16	Administrative & Support Svcs
46406	286	3305	Miscellaneous Manufacturing	46731	21	100	Construction of Buildings	46910	83	648	Wood Product Manufacturing
46407	331	2696	Educational Services	46732	65	296	Elect'l Eqpmt, App, & Comp Mfg	46911	28	143	Relig., Grant, Civic, Prof Org
46408	526	5079	Educational Services	46733	738	8522	Transportation Equipment Mfg	46912	1	1	Merch. Wholesalers,Durable Gds
46409	216	1625	Educational Services	46737	312	3841	Primary Metal Manufacturing	46913	21	32	Special Trade Contractors
46410	2153	30136	Food Svcs & Drinking Places	46738	204	2794	Educational Services	46914	63	342	Educational Services
46411	13	31	Construction of Buildings	46740	76	916	Food Manufacturing	46915	37	249	Justice, Pubic Order/Safety

ZIP CODE	2004 Total Firms	2004 Total Employees	TOP INDUSTRY RANKED on 2004 EMPLOYMENT	ZIP CODE	2004 Total Firms	2004 Total Employees	TOP INDUSTRY RANKED on 2004 EMPLOYMENT	ZIP CODE	2004 Total Firms	2004 Total Employees	TOP INDUSTRY RANKED on 2004 EMPLOYMENT
46916	9	15	Justice, Pubic Order/Safety	47102	164	1344	Food Manufacturing	47304	892	11283	Transportation Equipment Mfg
46917	72	266	Bldg Matl & Garden Eqpmt Dlrs	47104	1	0	Accommodation	47305	454	5663	Justice, Pubic Order/Safety
46919	80	484	Educational Services	47106	107	1211	Wood Product Manufacturing	47306	25	2135	Educational Services
46920	26	41	Food Manufacturing	47107	2	7	Relig., Grant, Civic, Prof Org	47307	2	0	Special Trade Contractors
46922	3	6	Food and Beverage Stores	47108	61	494	Chemical Manufacturing	47308	9	14	Special Trade Contractors
46923	306	3495	Food and Beverage Stores	47110	13	53	Educational Services	47320	99	893	Food Svcs & Drinking Places
46926	43	329	Educational Services	47111	301	2279	Hospitals	47322	2	0	Relig., Grant, Civic, Prof Org
46928	152	848	Educational Services	47112	671	7885	Food Manufacturing	47324	6	20	Warehousing and Storage
46929	156	920	Educational Services	47114	7	6	Credit Intermediation & Relatd	47325	10	21	Administrative & Support Svcs
46930	6	5	Special Trade Contractors	47115	23	100	Furniture & Related Prod. Mfg	47326	26	269	Food Svcs & Drinking Places
46931	25	239	Educational Services	47116	18	90	Educational Services	47327	194	1447	Furniture & Related Prod. Mfg
46932	86	293	Educational Services	47117	53	193	Educational Services	47330	161	936	Nursing & Resid. Care Facilit.
46933	168	1787	Merch. Wholesalers,Durable Gds	47118	111	485	Exec., Legis., & Other Support	47331	866	11724	Merch. Wholesalers,Durable Gds
46936	129	881	Nursing & Resid. Care Facilit.	47119	258	2076	Food Svcs & Drinking Places	47334	128	1137	Food Svcs & Drinking Places
46937	3	5	Relig., Grant, Civic, Prof Org	47120	19	71	Fabricated Metal Product Mfg	47335	24	48	Special Trade Contractors
46938	64	264	Educational Services	47122	188	983	Repair and Maintenance	47336	111	1389	Nonmetallic Mineral Prod. Mfg
46939	53	325	Fabricated Metal Product Mfg	47123	2	1	Relig., Grant, Civic, Prof Org	47337	11	36	Truck Transportation
46940	50	366	Nursing & Resid. Care Facilit.	47124	78	339	Educational Services	47338	74	429	Paper Manufacturing
46941	26	76	Special Trade Contractors	47125	32	56	Truck Transportation	47339	15	46	Merch. Wholesalers,Nondur. Gds
46942	2	2	Food Svcs & Drinking Places	47126	82	406	Educational Services	47340	74	245	Food and Beverage Stores
46943	15	176	Truck Transportation	47129	844	12142	Food Svcs & Drinking Places	47341	42	256	Educational Services
46945	11	15	Merch. Wholesalers,Nondur. Gds	47130	1415	20292	Hospitals	47342	74	562	Educational Services
46946	2	2	Postal Service	47131	14	31	Special Trade Contractors	47344	7	8	Truck Transportation
46947	1058	16006	Food Manufacturing	47135	20	48	Museums, Hist. Sites,& Similar	47345	28	59	Prof., Scientific, & Tech Svcs
46950	11	24	Unclassified Establishments	47136	62	292	Educational Services	47346	156	1077	Educational Services
46951	26	98	Construction of Buildings	47137	49	437	Nonmetallic Mineral Prod. Mfg	47348	339	3217	Paper Manufacturing
46952	955	12118	Ambulatory Health Care Svcs	47138	72	223	Educational Services	47351	9	58	Educational Services
46953	786	12529	Merch. Wholesalers,Durable Gds	47139	2	2	Relig., Grant, Civic, Prof Org	47352	27	34	Relig., Grant, Civic, Prof Org
46957	20	175	Merch. Wholesalers,Durable Gds	47140	82	501	Educational Services	47353	224	1287	Educational Services
46958	18	64	Furn. & Home Furnishgs Stores	47141	14	31	Special Trade Contractors	47354	27	65	Administrative & Support Svcs
46959	6	22	Fabricated Metal Product Mfg	47142	18	220	Wood Product Manufacturing	47355	97	823	Miscellaneous Manufacturing
46960	38	120	Educational Services	47143	50	385	Gasoline Stations	47356	141	1164	Educational Services
46961	3	3	Relig., Grant, Civic, Prof Org	47145	39	146	Educational Services	47357	20	73	Justice, Pubic Order/Safety
46962	347	3794	Nursing & Resid. Care Facilit.	47146	6	29	Relig., Grant, Civic, Prof Org	47358	32	337	Educational Services
46965	4	77	Plastics & Rubber Products Mfg	47147	21	73	Merch. Wholesalers,Durable Gds	47359	119	840	Fabricated Metal Product Mfg
46967	6	6	Miscellaneous Store Retailers	47150	1762	26238	Educational Services	47360	23	32	Credit Intermediation & Relatd
46968	1	0	Postal Service	47151	7	12	Real Estate	47361	26	108	Justice, Pubic Order/Safety
46970	780	9290	Food Svcs & Drinking Places	47160	9	23	Educational Services	47362	985	10621	Transportation Equipment Mfg
46971	11	162	Construction of Buildings	47161	76	504	Furniture & Related Prod. Mfg	47366	10	87	Gasoline Stations
46974	33	89	Repair and Maintenance	47162	35	246	Educational Services	47367	4	46	Warehousing and Storage
46975	700	5722	Fabricated Metal Product Mfg	47163	20	72	Nonmetallic Mineral Prod. Mfg	47368	56	451	Educational Services
46977	7	3	Merch. Wholesalers,Durable Gds	47164	77	454	Merch. Wholesalers,Durable Gds	47369	37	127	Special Trade Contractors
46978	51	326	Educational Services	47165	121	603	Educational Services	47370	9	26	Educational Services
46979	101	750	Educational Services	47166	48	417	Educational Services	47371	507	5023	Food Manufacturing
46980	1	2	Relig., Grant, Civic, Prof Org	47167	639	5264	Furniture & Related Prod. Mfg	47373	56	199	Justice, Pubic Order/Safety
46982	76	549	Furniture & Related Prod. Mfg	47170	620	5903	Plastics & Rubber Products Mfg	47374	1986	28395	Food Svcs & Drinking Places
46984	14	26	Food Svcs & Drinking Places	47172	370	4265	Truck Transportation	47375	10	13	Real Estate
46985	45	140	Merch. Wholesalers,Nondur. Gds	47174	5	8	Nonstore Retailers	47380	38	333	Wood Product Manufacturing
46986	63	396	Truck Transportation	47175	21	44	Wood Product Manufacturing	47381	3	3	Miscellaneous Store Retailers
46987	35	158	Educational Services	47177	27	146	Accommodation	47382	14	127	Machinery Manufacturing
46988	21	108	Crop Production	47201	1833	26565	Hospitals	47383	55	398	Educational Services
46989	86	1051	Educational Services	47202	10	29	Administrative & Support Svcs	47384	31	151	Primary Metal Manufacturing
46990	19	128	Machinery Manufacturing	47203	473	4319	Educational Services	47385	51	851	Miscellaneous Manufacturing
46991	38	342	Food and Beverage Stores	47220	255	1775	Educational Services	47386	14	39	Truck Transportation
46992	747	8822	Plastics & Rubber Products Mfg	47223	37	1401	Hospitals	47387	22	133	Educational Services
46994	68	435	Educational Services	47224	19	56	Justice, Pubic Order/Safety	47388	15	61	Repair and Maintenance
46995	6	12	Administrative & Support Svcs	47225	5	36	Justice, Pubic Order/Safety	47390	202	2867	Transportation Equipment Mfg
46996	352	3321	Educational Services	47226	5	6	Support Act. for Transport.	47392	4	6	Food and Beverage Stores
46998	4	26	Justice, Pubic Order/Safety	47227	25	120	Educational Services	47393	23	51	Justice, Pubic Order/Safety
47001	387	3347	General Merchandise Stores	47228	4	1	Special Trade Contractors	47394	376	3379	Nonmetallic Mineral Prod. Mfg
47003	23	43	Miscellaneous Store Retailers	47229	86	802	Miscellaneous Manufacturing	47396	177	1907	Educational Services
47006	488	5903	Miscellaneous Manufacturing	47230	27	98	Wood Product Manufacturing	47401	1160	14316	Administrative & Support Svcs
47010	7	32	Credit Intermediation & Relatd	47231	32	140	Justice, Pubic Order/Safety	47402	24	36	Miscellaneous Manufacturing
47011	22	44	Administrative & Support Svcs	47232	45	163	Construction of Buildings	47403	808	9173	Special Trade Contractors
47012	350	3061	Educational Services	47234	24	44	Construction of Buildings	47404	1585	18061	Food Svcs & Drinking Places
47016	16	73	Educational Services	47235	25	65	Educational Services	47405	49	3249	Other Information Services
47017	31	73	Justice, Pubic Order/Safety	47236	3	31	Administrative & Support Svcs	47406	32	382	Relig., Grant, Civic, Prof Org
47018	143	729	Nursing & Resid. Care Facilit.	47240	875	12816	Transportation Equipment Mfg	47407	15	72	Furniture & Related Prod. Mfg
47019	11	31	Merch. Wholesalers,Durable Gds	47243	118	1241	Educational Services	47408	479	4443	Food Svcs & Drinking Places
47020	22	1169	Amusement, Gambling, & Recreat.	47244	11	36	Justice, Pubic Order/Safety	47420	9	48	Relig., Grant, Civic, Prof Org
47021	8	28	Credit Intermediation & Relatd	47245	4	52	Merch. Wholesalers,Durable Gds	47421	1081	13341	Merch. Wholesalers,Durable Gds
47022	43	195	Educational Services	47246	120	781	Nursing & Resid. Care Facilit.	47424	315	1859	Educational Services
47023	34	68	Nonmetallic Mineral Prod. Mfg	47247	8	46	Electronics & Appliance Stores	47426	8	13	Fabricated Metal Product Mfg
47024	57	203	Educational Services	47249	3	3	Relig., Grant, Civic, Prof Org	47427	15	30	Wood Product Manufacturing
47025	748	11061	Amusement, Gambling,& Recreat.	47250	1054	12984	Transportation Equipment Mfg	47429	200	1602	Miscellaneous Manufacturing
47030	71	157	Food Svcs & Drinking Places	47260	53	253	Educational Services	47430	1	1	Postal Service
47031	138	762	Educational Services	47261	2	42	Justice, Pubic Order/Safety	47431	17	35	Special Trade Contractors
47032	69	366	Construction of Buildings	47263	10	29	Truck Transportation	47432	168	1436	Accommodation
47033	3	7	Relig., Grant, Civic, Prof Org	47264	17	81	Waste Managmt & Remediat'n Svc	47433	94	398	Nursing & Resid. Care Facilit.
47034	23	158	Wood Product Manufacturing	47265	667	6912	Transportation Equipment Mfg	47434	7	7	Relig., Grant, Civic, Prof Org
47035	3	23	Miscellaneous Store Retailers	47270	14	23	Relig., Grant, Civic, Prof Org	47435	4	72	Apparel Manufacturing
47036	35	191	Food Svcs & Drinking Places	47272	51	150	Food and Beverage Stores	47436	15	83	Educational Services
47037	138	857	Educational Services	47273	28	122	Educational Services	47437	5	13	Fabricated Metal Product Mfg
47038	23	175	Motor Vehicle & Parts Dealers	47274	1152	17424	Transportation Equipment Mfg	47438	114	752	Educational Services
47039	2	2	Miscellaneous Store Retailers	47280	24	238	Educational Services	47439	1	0	Postal Service
47040	186	800	Educational Services	47281	28	104	Admin. Enviro. Quality Progrms	47441	396	3509	Food Svcs & Drinking Places
47041	159	1407	Print'g & Related Supp't Act's	47282	47	129	Exec., Legis., & Other Support	47443	42	220	Nursing & Resid. Care Facilit.
47042	218	1578	Justice, Pubic Order/Safety	47283	93	441	Bldg Matl & Garden Eqpmt Dlrs	47446	335	3173	Fabricated Metal Product Mfg
47043	194	928	Educational Services	47302	714	10076	Machinery Manufacturing	47448	557	3210	Accommodation
47060	148	751	Relig., Grant, Civic, Prof Org	47303	1019	13490	Hospitals	47449	18	106	Food Manufacturing

BUSINESS DATA

ZIP CODE	2004 Total Firms	2004 Total Employees	TOP INDUSTRY RANKED on 2004 EMPLOYMENT
47451	47	277	Educational Services
47452	140	2187	Furniture & Related Prod. Mfg
47453	16	61	Justice, Pubic Order/Safety
47454	369	3103	Accommodation
47455	9	50	Educational Services
47456	23	46	Food and Beverage Stores
47457	1	2	Bldg Matl & Garden Eqpmt Dlrs
47458	14	12	Furniture & Related Prod. Mfg
47459	77	154	Food Svcs & Drinking Places
47460	409	3327	Miscellaneous Manufacturing
47462	52	334	Plastics & Rubber Products Mfg
47463	18	75	Educational Services
47464	11	73	Educational Services
47465	55	434	Educational Services
47467	1	0	Postal Service
47468	28	108	Educational Services
47469	63	299	Food and Beverage Stores
47470	23	31	Truck Transportation
47471	88	534	Elect'l Eqpmt, App, & Comp Mfg
47501	634	7300	Food Manufacturing
47512	142	1083	Educational Services
47513	61	275	Accommodation
47514	4	3	Food Svcs & Drinking Places
47515	18	24	Food Manufacturing
47516	28	118	Educational Services
47519	21	158	Fabricated Metal Product Mfg
47520	102	644	Fabricated Metal Product Mfg
47521	34	170	Relig., Grant, Civic, Prof Org
47522	22	5759	Nat'l Security & Int'l Affairs
47523	132	1477	Plastics & Rubber Products Mfg
47524	11	42	Food and Beverage Stores
47525	13	46	Exec., Legis., & Other Support
47527	65	562	Food and Beverage Stores
47528	20	183	Educational Services
47529	40	287	Educational Services
47531	15	24	Special Trade Contractors
47532	162	2593	Furniture & Related Prod. Mfg
47535	17	111	Relig., Grant, Civic, Prof Org
47536	6	38	Wood Product Manufacturing
47537	15	27	Support Activities: Agr./For.
47541	50	306	Animal Production
47542	367	4670	Furniture & Related Prod. Mfg
47545	18	316	Prof., Scientific, & Tech Svcs
47546	1066	16663	Furniture & Related Prod. Mfg
47547	11	17	Administrative & Support Svcs
47549	7	2085	Furniture & Related Prod. Mfg
47550	21	225	Construction of Buildings
47551	14	307	Educational Services
47552	7	28	Museums, Hist. Sites,& Similar
47553	302	1843	Food Svcs & Drinking Places
47556	7	52	Food Svcs & Drinking Places
47557	38	173	Mining (Except Oil and Gas)
47558	152	1386	Construction of Buildings
47561	41	440	Food and Beverage Stores
47562	169	854	Clothing & Cloth'g Acc. Stores
47564	34	228	Warehousing and Storage
47567	252	2412	Utilities
47568	42	81	Merch. Wholesalers,Nondur. Gds
47573	1	0	Relig., Grant, Civic, Prof Org
47574	6	28	Accommodation
47575	38	483	Furniture & Related Prod. Mfg
47576	10	78	Wood Product Manufacturing
47577	41	564	Educational Services
47578	27	49	Food and Beverage Stores
47579	83	1597	Amusement, Gambling,& Recreat.
47580	7	27	Bldg Matl & Garden Eqpmt Dlrs
47581	134	1202	Nonmetallic Mineral Prod. Mfg
47584	5	3	Special Trade Contractors
47585	10	28	Administrative & Support Svcs
47586	453	4531	Primary Metal Manufacturing
47588	29	353	Merch. Wholesalers,Durable Gds
47590	8	18	Waste Managmt & Remediat'n Svc
47591	1165	15664	Hospitals
47596	6	16	Crop Production
47597	21	66	Justice, Pubic Order/Safety
47598	72	347	Educational Services
47601	480	3836	Ambulatory Health Care Svcs
47610	123	1101	Computer & Electronic Prod Mfg
47611	50	214	Exec., Legis., & Other Support
47612	30	101	Special Trade Contractors
47613	69	352	Machinery Manufacturing
47614	1	2	Postal Service
47615	31	267	Transportation Equipment Mfg
47616	19	24	Crop Production
47617	10	16	Food and Beverage Stores
47618	2	4	Transit & Grnd Pass. Transport
47619	42	258	Educational Services
47620	457	6033	Plastics & Rubber Products Mfg
47629	7	10	Utilities
47630	753	7914	Primary Metal Manufacturing
47631	100	773	Food Svcs & Drinking Places
47633	104	775	Educational Services
47634	32	102	Educational Services
47635	256	1976	Utilities
47637	24	55	Educational Services
47638	61	274	Educational Services
47639	146	1177	Gasoline Stations
47640	20	47	Utilities
47647	2	1	Personal and Laundry Services
47648	144	835	Prof., Scientific, & Tech Svcs
47649	35	362	Mining (Except Oil and Gas)
47654	10	71	Educational Services
47660	158	1413	Mining (Except Oil and Gas)
47665	69	372	Nursing & Resid. Care Facilit.
47666	36	133	Administrative & Support Svcs
47670	586	11149	Transportation Equipment Mfg
47683	3	3	Postal Service
47701	1	0	Merch. Wholesalers,Durable Gds
47706	1	1	Sportg Gds,Hobby,Book, & Music
47708	611	10658	Exec., Legis., & Other Support
47710	870	11020	Ambulatory Health Care Svcs
47711	1174	18726	General Merchandise Stores
47712	656	10079	Educational Services
47713	391	8526	Ambulatory Health Care Svcs
47714	850	11870	Hospitals
47715	1524	21022	Food Svcs & Drinking Places
47716	13	15	Nonstore Retailers
47719	4	507	Administrative & Support Svcs
47720	331	3522	Broadcasting
47721	1	2500	Food Manufacturing
47722	1	506	Educational Services
47724	5	7	Special Trade Contractors
47725	373	6716	Plastics & Rubber Products Mfg
47727	2	5001	Elect'l Eqpmt, App, & Comp Mfg
47728	5	10	Special Trade Contractors
47730	2	3	Administrative & Support Svcs
47731	1	19	Social Assistance
47744	2	550	Managmt of Companies & Enterp.
47747	4	2626	Hospitals
47801	5	9	Perform'g Arts, Spec. Sports
47802	1298	16950	Food Svcs & Drinking Places
47803	532	6349	Nat'l Security & Int'l Affairs
47804	403	9719	Hospitals
47805	235	2567	Plastics & Rubber Products Mfg
47807	972	9711	Food Svcs & Drinking Places
47808	4	5	Social Assistance
47809	8	2098	Educational Services
47811	2	2607	Sportg Gds,Hobby,Book, & Music
47830	6	45	Justice, Pubic Order/Safety
47831	3	4	Postal Service
47832	39	589	Plastics & Rubber Products Mfg
47833	20	44	Construction of Buildings
47834	676	5857	Transportation Equipment Mfg
47836	9	8	Truck Transportation
47837	19	89	Wood Product Manufacturing
47838	60	281	Educational Services
47840	33	162	Gasoline Stations
47841	90	377	Educational Services
47842	284	3472	Merch. Wholesalers,Nondur. Gds
47845	2	2	Repair and Maintenance
47846	13	21	Warehousing and Storage
47847	36	121	Construction of Buildings
47848	46	152	Machinery Manufacturing
47849	10	33	Support Act. for Transport.
47850	60	370	Broadcasting
47851	6	85	Plastics & Rubber Products Mfg
47852	3	2	Postal Service
47853	10	24	Machinery Manufacturing
47854	21	306	Special Trade Contractors
47855	21	82	Educational Services
47856	1	0	Postal Service
47857	8	35	Educational Services
47858	7	36	Mining (Except Oil and Gas)
47859	30	405	Educational Services
47860	7	22	Justice, Pubic Order/Safety
47861	12	29	Relig., Grant, Civic, Prof Org
47862	46	396	Educational Services
47863	4	11	Food and Beverage Stores
47864	1	0	Relig., Grant, Civic, Prof Org
47865	3	0	Utilities
47866	15	277	Mining (Except Oil and Gas)
47868	43	70	Support Act. for Transport.
47869	5	11	Food and Beverage Stores
47870	4	18	Justice, Pubic Order/Safety
47871	23	108	Educational Services
47872	315	2424	Exec., Legis., & Other Support
47874	64	281	Educational Services
47875	8	13	Miscellaneous Store Retailers
47876	12	317	Relig., Grant, Civic, Prof Org
47878	12	63	Justice, Pubic Order/Safety
47879	63	269	Truck Transportation
47880	5	23	Justice, Pubic Order/Safety
47881	8	52	Educational Services
47882	350	2801	Food Svcs & Drinking Places
47884	7	59	Nonmetallic Mineral Prod. Mfg
47885	187	1357	Educational Services
47901	612	5370	Credit Intermediation & Relatd
47902	4	53	Securities/Commodity Contracts
47903	9	17	Truck Transportation
47904	733	14007	Hospitals
47905	1422	23694	Transportation Equipment Mfg
47906	960	11036	Food Svcs & Drinking Places
47907	34	651	Other Information Services
47909	489	7908	Machinery Manufacturing
47916	4	1	Postal Service
47917	11	36	Utilities
47918	220	2348	Primary Metal Manufacturing
47920	56	296	Educational Services
47921	43	210	Merch. Wholesalers,Nondur. Gds
47922	65	403	Merch. Wholesalers,Nondur. Gds
47923	114	530	Educational Services
47924	9	12	Merch. Wholesalers,Nondur. Gds
47925	13	42	Educational Services
47926	27	148	Merch. Wholesalers,Nondur. Gds
47928	75	585	Paper Manufacturing
47929	21	100	Educational Services
47930	29	138	Wood Product Manufacturing
47932	223	1748	Food Svcs & Drinking Places
47933	1045	14506	Print'g & Related Supp't Act's
47940	38	173	Nat'l Security & Int'l Affairs
47941	27	161	Educational Services
47942	25	100	Truck Transportation
47943	17	134	Animal Production
47944	173	1100	Food Svcs & Drinking Places
47946	96	793	Merch. Wholesalers,Nondur. Gds
47948	59	412	Plastics & Rubber Products Mfg
47949	45	100	Unclassified Establishments
47950	13	34	Special Trade Contractors
47951	145	1477	Plastics & Rubber Products Mfg
47952	64	186	Miscellaneous Manufacturing
47954	59	314	Social Assistance
47955	55	511	Educational Services
47957	49	176	Exec., Legis., & Other Support
47958	7	26	Repair and Maintenance
47959	107	537	Educational Services
47960	727	7104	Accommodation
47962	2	51	Elect'l Eqpmt, App, & Comp Mfg
47963	93	717	Computer & Electronic Prod Mfg
47964	10	3	Postal Service
47965	27	123	Educational Services
47966	48	794	Fabricated Metal Product Mfg
47967	29	203	Food and Beverage Stores
47968	25	107	Educational Services
47969	8	19	Warehousing and Storage
47970	67	416	Miscellaneous Manufacturing
47971	54	348	Plastics & Rubber Products Mfg
47974	23	124	Truck Transportation
47975	22	111	Other Information Services
47977	130	1283	Fabricated Metal Product Mfg
47978	527	4258	Food Svcs & Drinking Places
47980	57	441	Food and Beverage Stores
47981	34	82	Merch. Wholesalers,Nondur. Gds
47982	5	16	Chemical Manufacturing
47983	9	15	Food and Beverage Stores
47986	3	16	Merch. Wholesalers,Nondur. Gds
47987	130	2234	Transportation Equipment Mfg
47988	3	8	Food and Beverage Stores
47989	50	187	Educational Services
47990	45	124	Personal and Laundry Services
47991	46	402	Fabricated Metal Product Mfg
47992	41	68	Bldg Matl & Garden Eqpmt Dlrs
47993	153	1140	Fabricated Metal Product Mfg
47994	23	64	Administrative & Support Svcs
47995	71	631	Fabricated Metal Product Mfg
47996	10	10	Real Estate
47997	7	17	Bldg Matl & Garden Eqpmt Dlrs
48001	373	2178	Food Svcs & Drinking Places
48002	63	155	Relig., Grant, Civic, Prof Org
48003	212	1568	Educational Services
48004	4	20	Special Trade Contractors
48005	192	1342	Educational Services
48006	63	207	Fabricated Metal Product Mfg
48009	2060	13111	Prof., Scientific, & Tech Svcs
48012	18	203	Postal Service
48014	155	655	Educational Services
48015	344	6318	Fabricated Metal Product Mfg
48017	571	3482	Food Svcs & Drinking Places
48021	1032	7555	Food Svcs & Drinking Places
48022	88	306	Credit Intermediation & Relatd
48023	183	1244	Educational Services

ZIP CODE	2004 Total Firms	2004 Total Employ-ees	TOP INDUSTRY RANKED on 2004 EMPLOYMENT	ZIP CODE	2004 Total Firms	2004 Total Employ-ees	TOP INDUSTRY RANKED on 2004 EMPLOYMENT	ZIP CODE	2004 Total Firms	2004 Total Employ-ees	TOP INDUSTRY RANKED on 2004 EMPLOYMENT
48025	1058	7970	Prof., Scientific, & Tech Svcs	48133	182	1355	Machinery Manufacturing	48239	1138	13831	Machinery Manufacturing
48026	772	8477	Machinery Manufacturing	48134	456	6912	Transportation Equipment Mfg	48240	530	3403	Educational Services
48027	52	129	Construction of Buildings	48135	874	7944	Hospitals	48242	80	3984	Food Svcs & Drinking Places
48028	50	203	Relig., Grant, Civic, Prof Org	48136	8	23	Administrative & Support Svcs	48243	135	12137	Transportation Equipment Mfg
48030	580	4219	Educational Services	48137	130	468	Crop Production	48244	3	9	Transit & Grnd Pass. Transport
48032	60	168	Prof., Scientific, & Tech Svcs	48138	277	1508	Relig., Grant, Civic, Prof Org	48265	1	65	Prof., Scientific, & Tech Svcs
48034	2639	37430	Prof., Scientific, & Tech Svcs	48139	79	934	Fabricated Metal Product Mfg	48301	541	3630	Food Svcs & Drinking Places
48035	1135	10588	Food Svcs & Drinking Places	48140	90	428	Educational Services	48302	819	8148	Prof., Scientific, & Tech Svcs
48036	957	8925	Repair and Maintenance	48141	516	3592	Nat'l Security & Int'l Affairs	48303	8	28	Prof., Scientific, & Tech Svcs
48037	14	595	Postal Service	48143	28	132	Educational Services	48304	860	12104	Educational Services
48038	1287	13144	Hospitals	48144	281	1801	Food Svcs & Drinking Places	48306	489	3192	Educational Services
48039	370	2657	Fabricated Metal Product Mfg	48145	79	278	Amusement, Gambling,& Recreat.	48307	1854	20545	Ambulatory Health Care Svcs
48040	366	4752	Plastics & Rubber Products Mfg	48146	782	7054	Food Svcs & Drinking Places	48308	27	240	Postal Service
48041	127	722	Machinery Manufacturing	48150	2290	37060	Merch. Wholesalers,Durable Gds	48309	1101	18574	Machinery Manufacturing
48042	440	3673	Amusement, Gambling,& Recreat.	48151	8	44	Unclassified Establishments	48310	1036	9944	Ambulatory Health Care Svcs
48043	1250	14799	Ambulatory Health Care Svcs	48152	1917	22446	Prof., Scientific, & Tech Svcs	48311	8	2	Merch. Wholesalers,Durable Gds
48044	545	3838	Educational Services	48153	9	28	Special Trade Contractors	48312	891	23199	Transportation Equipment Mfg
48045	716	5664	Food Svcs & Drinking Places	48154	1201	11135	Hospitals	48313	853	11204	Food Svcs & Drinking Places
48046	12	59	Relig., Grant, Civic, Prof Org	48157	33	145	Food Svcs & Drinking Places	48314	723	10710	Transportation Equipment Mfg
48047	888	6485	Food Svcs & Drinking Places	48158	283	2347	Plastics & Rubber Products Mfg	48315	804	11423	Food Svcs & Drinking Places
48048	164	1375	Justice, Pubic Order/Safety	48159	63	171	Food Svcs & Drinking Places	48316	593	6082	Educational Services
48049	99	350	Special Trade Contractors	48160	408	3114	Educational Services	48317	1099	9816	Food Svcs & Drinking Places
48050	55	312	Bldg Matl & Garden Eqpmt Dlrs	48161	1069	10884	Educational Services	48318	18	16	Prof., Scientific, & Tech Svcs
48051	553	9269	Transportation Equipment Mfg	48162	931	14889	Hospitals	48320	363	2411	Personal and Laundry Services
48054	197	2050	Utilities	48164	247	1599	Educational Services	48321	3	1	Insurance Carriers & Related
48059	638	5258	Food Svcs & Drinking Places	48165	198	2079	Merch. Wholesalers,Durable Gds	48322	1361	10377	Ambulatory Health Care Svcs
48060	1895	23229	Hospitals	48166	184	2397	Prof., Scientific, & Tech Svcs	48323	378	3501	Educational Services
48061	2	1	Prof., Scientific, & Tech Svcs	48167	1228	11753	Food and Beverage Stores	48324	203	1547	Amusement, Gambling,& Recreat.
48062	385	2518	Food Svcs & Drinking Places	48169	464	2304	Educational Services	48325	8	86	Accommodation
48063	76	272	Furniture & Related Prod. Mfg	48170	2204	31367	Transportation Equipment Mfg	48326	1391	36740	Transportation Equipment Mfg
48064	95	538	Special Trade Contractors	48173	242	1476	Educational Services	48327	843	5651	Food Svcs & Drinking Places
48065	504	6838	Machinery Manufacturing	48174	1168	25026	Transportation Equipment Mfg	48328	1201	11641	Educational Services
48066	1807	22643	Food Svcs & Drinking Places	48175	8	8	Administrative & Support Svcs	48329	914	8163	Merch. Wholesalers,Durable Gds
48067	1434	11205	Food Svcs & Drinking Places	48176	793	8961	Plastics & Rubber Products Mfg	48330	23	11	Bldg Matl & Garden Eqpmt Dlrs
48068	15	39	Miscellaneous Manufacturing	48177	4	4	Postal Service	48331	808	11877	Prof., Scientific, & Tech Svcs
48069	92	280	Prof., Scientific, & Tech Svcs	48178	759	4135	Food Svcs & Drinking Places	48332	17	16	Prof., Scientific, & Tech Svcs
48070	218	722	Ambulatory Health Care Svcs	48179	58	319	Educational Services	48333	10	233	Postal Service
48071	1640	22099	Merch. Wholesalers,Durable Gds	48180	1851	24398	Food Svcs & Drinking Places	48334	2001	18412	Prof., Scientific, & Tech Svcs
48072	618	3716	Food Svcs & Drinking Places	48182	474	3443	Educational Services	48335	961	14185	Merch. Wholesalers,Durable Gds
48073	1176	24846	Hospitals	48183	1246	16421	Transportation Equipment Mfg	48336	1463	12886	Hospitals
48074	293	1710	Food Svcs & Drinking Places	48184	708	11990	Wholesale Elec. Mrkts & Agents	48340	535	6452	Prof., Scientific, & Tech Svcs
48075	2792	28734	Prof., Scientific, & Tech Svcs	48185	1472	16822	Food Svcs & Drinking Places	48341	872	18409	Hospitals
48076	1961	17301	Prof., Scientific, & Tech Svcs	48186	626	5149	Educational Services	48342	776	10471	Transportation Equipment Mfg
48079	452	4702	Plastics & Rubber Products Mfg	48187	1350	12060	Food Svcs & Drinking Places	48343	7	645	Postal Service
48080	1071	8058	Food Svcs & Drinking Places	48188	511	5066	Wholesale Elec. Mrkts & Agents	48346	981	6959	Food Svcs & Drinking Places
48081	686	4949	Ambulatory Health Care Svcs	48189	431	4108	Educational Services	48347	16	86	Prof., Scientific, & Tech Svcs
48082	334	3233	Furniture & Related Prod. Mfg	48190	8	31	Justice, Pubic Order/Safety	48348	483	2792	Educational Services
48083	2344	29954	Prof., Scientific, & Tech Svcs	48191	69	242	Food and Beverage Stores	48350	196	878	Educational Services
48084	2064	37317	Prof., Scientific, & Tech Svcs	48192	1465	14147	Ambulatory Health Care Svcs	48353	287	2145	Food Svcs & Drinking Places
48085	718	18752	Hospitals	48195	907	11158	Food Svcs & Drinking Places	48356	217	1073	Food Svcs & Drinking Places
48088	499	5792	Educational Services	48197	1607	23888	Hospitals	48357	387	2365	Educational Services
48089	1302	22158	Fabricated Metal Product Mfg	48198	884	15878	Transportation Equipment Mfg	48359	318	9315	Transportation Equipment Mfg
48090	10	392	Postal Service	48201	836	49957	Hospitals	48360	293	2707	Educational Services
48091	998	19013	Transportation Equipment Mfg	48202	811	28187	Educational Services	48361	9	12	Administrative & Support Svcs
48092	910	16980	Nat'l Security & Int'l Affairs	48203	947	8149	Prof., Scientific, & Tech Svcs	48362	503	2942	Food Svcs & Drinking Places
48093	871	18457	Transportation Equipment Mfg	48204	673	5002	Educational Services	48363	112	703	Managmt of Companies & Enterp.
48094	350	1606	Educational Services	48205	772	3874	Food Svcs & Drinking Places	48366	1	2	Postal Service
48095	228	1549	Food Svcs & Drinking Places	48206	320	1820	Relig., Grant, Civic, Prof Org	48367	134	615	Transportation Equipment Mfg
48096	110	483	Educational Services	48207	1090	15211	Relig., Grant, Civic, Prof Org	48370	46	362	Food Svcs & Drinking Places
48097	183	1042	Nursing & Resid. Care Facilit.	48208	394	3693	Educational Services	48371	747	5348	Fabricated Metal Product Mfg
48098	738	14187	Prof., Scientific, & Tech Svcs	48209	750	8073	Truck Transportation	48374	253	2999	Educational Services
48099	19	309	Postal Service	48210	608	6546	Nonmetallic Mineral Prod. Mfg	48375	1368	15517	Food Svcs & Drinking Places
48101	680	6861	Postal Service	48211	377	9757	Transportation Equipment Mfg	48376	15	92	Postal Service
48103	2317	20019	Food Svcs & Drinking Places	48212	995	13539	Transportation Equipment Mfg	48377	599	9428	General Merchandise Stores
48104	2881	25894	Food Svcs & Drinking Places	48213	627	4531	Educational Services	48380	159	5352	Transportation Equipment Mfg
48105	1127	14172	Prof., Scientific, & Tech Svcs	48214	562	7450	Hospitals	48381	645	4106	Food Svcs & Drinking Places
48106	28	147	Personal and Laundry Services	48215	384	7834	Transportation Equipment Mfg	48382	636	4304	Hospitals
48107	13	62	Accommodation	48216	431	5795	Publishing Industries	48383	216	1289	Educational Services
48108	1477	20964	Prof., Scientific, & Tech Svcs	48217	201	2250	Merch. Wholesalers,Nondur. Gds	48386	435	2862	Food and Beverage Stores
48109	279	51357	Educational Services	48218	199	1951	Educational Services	48387	6	5	Postal Service
48110	2	3	Food and Beverage Stores	48219	1134	7930	Educational Services	48390	1156	12997	Educational Services
48111	980	12271	Fabricated Metal Product Mfg	48220	1142	11733	Miscellaneous Manufacturing	48393	763	12887	Merch. Wholesalers,Durable Gds
48112	7	16	Transit & Grnd Pass. Transport	48221	987	5726	Educational Services	48401	28	55	Clothing & Cloth'g Acc. Stores
48113	10	47	Repair and Maintenance	48222	1	20	Prof., Scientific, & Tech Svcs	48410	2	7	Bldg Matl & Garden Eqpmt Dlrs
48114	717	4348	Educational Services	48223	559	3959	Machinery Manufacturing	48411	7	22	Fabricated Metal Product Mfg
48115	3	5	Print'g & Related Supp't Act's	48224	871	4758	Educational Services	48412	99	566	Educational Services
48116	1513	15031	Food and Beverage Stores	48225	465	4617	General Merchandise Stores	48413	541	5345	Machinery Manufacturing
48117	255	2101	Educational Services	48226	2419	58892	Prof., Scientific, & Tech Svcs	48414	50	167	Administrative & Support Svcs
48118	576	7068	Ambulatory Health Care Svcs	48227	1133	10088	Transportation Equipment Mfg	48415	393	3283	Food Svcs & Drinking Places
48120	235	8481	Primary Metal Manufacturing	48228	1094	8748	Educational Services	48416	170	887	Machinery Manufacturing
48121	4	6	Transportation Equipment Mfg	48229	191	1266	Fabricated Metal Product Mfg	48417	50	162	Educational Services
48122	246	2787	Fabricated Metal Product Mfg	48230	615	5082	Hospitals	48418	103	769	Educational Services
48123	6	9	Administrative & Support Svcs	48231	4	1	Real Estate	48419	73	317	Accommodation
48124	1280	25572	Hospitals	48232	6	122	Merch. Wholesalers,Durable Gds	48420	683	4138	Food Svcs & Drinking Places
48125	413	3469	Food Svcs & Drinking Places	48233	3	12	Relig., Grant, Civic, Prof Org	48421	137	437	Special Trade Contractors
48126	1790	30548	Transportation Equipment Mfg	48234	918	13407	Transportation Equipment Mfg	48422	207	1415	Educational Services
48127	922	6380	Food Svcs & Drinking Places	48235	1175	9120	Hospitals	48423	805	5410	Food Svcs & Drinking Places
48128	241	3524	Educational Services	48236	1208	16450	Hospitals	48426	17	46	Merch. Wholesalers,Durable Gds
48130	532	5080	Electronics & Appliance Stores	48237	1272	11335	Merch. Wholesalers,Durable Gds	48427	129	1553	Plastics & Rubber Products Mfg
48131	232	2432	Food Svcs & Drinking Places	48238	799	6236	Educational Services	48428	161	610	Educational Services

BUSINESS DATA

ZIP CODE	2004 Total Firms	2004 Total Employees	TOP INDUSTRY RANKED on 2004 EMPLOYMENT	ZIP CODE	2004 Total Firms	2004 Total Employees	TOP INDUSTRY RANKED on 2004 EMPLOYMENT	ZIP CODE	2004 Total Firms	2004 Total Employees	TOP INDUSTRY RANKED on 2004 EMPLOYMENT
48429	278	2043	Nonmetallic Mineral Prod. Mfg	48631	171	1215	Construction of Buildings	48809	329	2379	Educational Services
48430	1311	10330	Food Svcs & Drinking Places	48632	69	260	Social Assistance	48811	160	1819	Justice, Pubic Order/Safety
48432	11	15	Bldg Matl & Garden Eqpmt Dlrs	48633	15	74	Pipeline Transportation	48812	8	25	Food Manufacturing
48433	715	4990	Educational Services	48634	136	697	Amusement, Gambling,& Recreat.	48813	693	6493	Food Svcs & Drinking Places
48434	4	3	Repair and Maintenance	48635	42	140	Accommodation	48815	49	190	Fabricated Metal Product Mfg
48435	36	114	Social Assistance	48636	25	65	Food Svcs & Drinking Places	48816	6	10	Warehousing and Storage
48436	55	182	Educational Services	48637	101	555	Machinery Manufacturing	48817	201	2369	Health & Personal Care Stores
48437	49	262	Food Svcs & Drinking Places	48640	1584	14197	Educational Services	48818	93	242	Educational Services
48438	179	1722	Nursing & Resid. Care Facilit.	48641	14	73	Special Trade Contractors	48819	64	184	Merch. Wholesalers,Durable Gds
48439	1229	15029	Hospitals	48642	780	8997	Special Trade Contractors	48820	424	2399	Food Svcs & Drinking Places
48440	42	209	Prof., Scientific, & Tech Svcs	48647	261	1171	Machinery Manufacturing	48821	160	1609	Exec., Legis., & Other Support
48441	185	1217	Hospitals	48649	46	164	Educational Services	48822	58	193	Educational Services
48442	653	3948	Educational Services	48650	273	2345	Merch. Wholesalers,Nondur. Gds	48823	1639	17753	Food Svcs & Drinking Places
48444	441	4259	Food Manufacturing	48651	188	990	Exec., Legis., & Other Support	48824	83	11345	Educational Services
48445	46	246	Educational Services	48652	26	65	Special Trade Contractors	48825	6	194	Food Manufacturing
48446	1389	14138	Hospitals	48653	412	2636	Educational Services	48826	16	33	Perform'g Arts, Spec. Sports
48449	79	381	Waste Managmt & Remediat'n Svc	48654	149	966	Nursing & Resid. Care Facilit.	48827	403	3242	Educational Services
48450	227	1484	Fabricated Metal Product Mfg	48655	195	1285	Educational Services	48829	174	1427	Fabricated Metal Product Mfg
48451	322	1538	Educational Services	48656	130	556	Food and Beverage Stores	48830	2	1	Prof., Scientific, & Tech Svcs
48453	285	1467	Fabricated Metal Product Mfg	48657	243	1332	Educational Services	48831	101	999	Transportation Equipment Mfg
48454	23	68	Special Trade Contractors	48658	297	3178	Justice, Pubic Order/Safety	48832	29	53	Furn. & Home Furnishgs Stores
48455	304	1369	Plastics & Rubber Products Mfg	48659	73	449	Nursing & Resid. Care Facilit.	48833	3	12	Unclassified Establishments
48456	30	91	Bldg Matl & Garden Eqpmt Dlrs	48661	692	5224	Food Svcs & Drinking Places	48834	29	77	Educational Services
48457	225	1150	Educational Services	48662	30	66	Relig., Grant, Civic, Prof Org	48835	86	468	Educational Services
48458	524	3631	Educational Services	48667	3	68	Merch. Wholesalers,Nondur. Gds	48836	445	2722	Transportation Equipment Mfg
48460	64	651	Educational Services	48670	18	2172	Hospitals	48837	564	3716	Educational Services
48461	210	1210	Educational Services	48674	7	2959	Miscellaneous Manufacturing	48838	745	9043	Elect'l Eqpmt, App, & Comp Mfg
48462	428	2072	Food Svcs & Drinking Places	48686	2	1285	Fabricated Metal Product Mfg	48840	364	1769	Educational Services
48463	126	437	Food Svcs & Drinking Places	48701	34	114	Educational Services	48841	19	33	Miscellaneous Store Retailers
48464	35	76	Food and Beverage Stores	48703	142	625	Food and Beverage Stores	48842	577	4416	Special Trade Contractors
48465	19	64	Construction of Buildings	48705	13	16	Relig., Grant, Civic, Prof Org	48843	1633	16354	Educational Services
48466	40	329	Educational Services	48706	1621	16731	Food Svcs & Drinking Places	48844	16	34	Real Estate
48467	136	534	Food Svcs & Drinking Places	48707	2	24	Prof., Scientific, & Tech Svcs	48845	19	76	Educational Services
48468	51	190	Animal Production	48708	1212	12872	Hospitals	48846	589	7483	Justice, Pubic Order/Safety
48469	90	329	Accommodation	48710	5	635	Educational Services	48847	278	2060	Educational Services
48470	23	73	Relig., Grant, Civic, Prof Org	48720	46	183	Fabricated Metal Product Mfg	48848	159	720	Educational Services
48471	417	3232	Food Svcs & Drinking Places	48721	15	31	Special Trade Contractors	48849	207	1159	Food and Beverage Stores
48472	50	122	Merch. Wholesalers,Durable Gds	48722	174	2163	Food Svcs & Drinking Places	48850	189	1423	Hospitals
48473	478	3197	Relig., Grant, Civic, Prof Org	48723	604	6713	Exec., Legis., & Other Support	48851	34	64	Fabricated Metal Product Mfg
48475	96	459	Plastics & Rubber Products Mfg	48724	31	379	Food Manufacturing	48852	14	58	Merch. Wholesalers,Durable Gds
48476	27	125	Bldg Matl & Garden Eqpmt Dlrs	48725	133	680	Food Svcs & Drinking Places	48853	24	48	Food and Beverage Stores
48501	4	9	Repair and Maintenance	48726	253	2413	Motor Vehicle & Parts Dealers	48854	713	7602	Plastics & Rubber Products Mfg
48502	560	8188	Justice, Pubic Order/Safety	48727	30	245	Machinery Manufacturing	48855	417	2552	Transportation Equipment Mfg
48503	1063	14175	Hospitals	48728	13	28	Food and Beverage Stores	48856	33	224	Educational Services
48504	916	8184	Educational Services	48729	18	28	Construction of Buildings	48857	81	317	Educational Services
48505	659	4936	Educational Services	48730	309	2113	Transportation Equipment Mfg	48858	1679	23304	Accommodation
48506	798	13159	Transportation Equipment Mfg	48731	68	1733	Transportation Equipment Mfg	48859	6	343	Other Information Services
48507	1857	22404	Food Svcs & Drinking Places	48732	288	3572	Food Svcs & Drinking Places	48860	24	143	Food and Beverage Stores
48509	536	5087	Food Svcs & Drinking Places	48733	47	288	Educational Services	48861	44	181	Furn. & Home Furnishgs Stores
48519	207	2144	Food and Beverage Stores	48734	394	6539	Food Svcs & Drinking Places	48862	4	4	Food and Beverage Stores
48529	471	3502	Food Svcs & Drinking Places	48735	25	88	Educational Services	48863	2	1	Special Trade Contractors
48531	2	9	Administrative & Support Svcs	48736	3	2	Gasoline Stations	48864	1268	13549	Food Svcs & Drinking Places
48532	958	10339	Ambulatory Health Care Svcs	48737	59	217	Educational Services	48865	35	266	Hospitals
48550	4	7101	Prof., Scientific, & Tech Svcs	48738	32	132	Food Svcs & Drinking Places	48866	113	782	Nursing & Resid. Care Facilit.
48551	1	3000	Motor Vehicle & Parts Dealers	48739	180	923	Educational Services	48867	1143	11340	Hospitals
48552	1	0	Transportation Equipment Mfg	48740	170	688	Fabricated Metal Product Mfg	48870	3	0	Credit Intermediation & Relatd
48553	1	3500	Special Trade Contractors	48741	69	374	Educational Services	48871	42	180	Social Assistance
48554	1	1029	Transportation Equipment Mfg	48742	108	867	Educational Services	48872	237	1113	Educational Services
48555	1	2	Relig., Grant, Civic, Prof Org	48743	8	28	Food Svcs & Drinking Places	48873	37	411	Educational Services
48556	1	3999	Transportation Equipment Mfg	48744	109	696	Educational Services	48874	5	11	Bldg Matl & Garden Eqpmt Dlrs
48557	1	3	Ambulatory Health Care Svcs	48745	36	74	Miscellaneous Store Retailers	48875	298	2201	Transportation Equipment Mfg
48601	1117	28059	Transportation Equipment Mfg	48746	265	1399	Print'g & Related Supp't Act's	48876	91	587	Educational Services
48602	1085	16758	Hospitals	48747	34	110	Nonmetallic Mineral Prod. Mfg	48877	54	143	Special Trade Contractors
48603	1602	15229	Ambulatory Health Care Svcs	48748	47	297	Nonmetallic Mineral Prod. Mfg	48878	63	572	Prof., Scientific, & Tech Svcs
48604	752	11845	Food Svcs & Drinking Places	48749	75	626	Fabricated Metal Product Mfg	48879	670	6669	Educational Services
48605	3	6	Perform'g Arts, Spec. Sports	48750	505	3356	Transportation Equipment Mfg	48880	269	1931	Wood Product Manufacturing
48607	296	3859	Exec., Legis., & Other Support	48754	27	106	Educational Services	48881	123	1074	Merch. Wholesalers,Nondur. Gds
48608	8	10	Educational Services	48755	196	2071	Primary Metal Manufacturing	48882	10	66	Educational Services
48609	425	3458	Food and Beverage Stores	48756	105	386	Relig., Grant, Civic, Prof Org	48883	150	745	Educational Services
48610	59	176	Merch. Wholesalers,Durable Gds	48757	131	1221	Educational Services	48884	119	751	Hospitals
48611	234	1373	Educational Services	48758	10	63	Food Svcs & Drinking Places	48885	17	272	Educational Services
48612	231	1448	Machinery Manufacturing	48759	140	1066	Food Manufacturing	48886	79	158	Utilities
48613	10	14	Heavy & Civil Eng. Construct'N	48760	17	30	Merch. Wholesalers,Durable Gds	48888	261	1904	Exec., Legis., & Other Support
48614	33	108	General Merchandise Stores	48761	22	43	Wood Product Manufacturing	48889	25	60	Merch. Wholesalers,Durable Gds
48615	75	626	Educational Services	48762	58	133	Amusement, Gambling,& Recreat.	48890	67	385	Primary Metal Manufacturing
48616	303	2094	Food Svcs & Drinking Places	48763	304	2838	Hospitals	48891	78	382	Educational Services
48617	467	3472	Food Svcs & Drinking Places	48764	1	1	Construction of Buildings	48892	153	802	Educational Services
48618	165	1446	Plastics & Rubber Products Mfg	48765	23	45	Food and Beverage Stores	48893	119	865	Machinery Manufacturing
48619	19	62	Admin. Human Resource Programs	48766	37	212	Educational Services	48894	48	214	Special Trade Contractors
48620	14	38	Relig., Grant, Civic, Prof Org	48767	56	264	Crop Production	48895	476	2776	Food Svcs & Drinking Places
48621	77	518	Transportation Equipment Mfg	48768	261	2332	Educational Services	48896	18	703	Machinery Manufacturing
48622	188	1273	Plastics & Rubber Products Mfg	48769	2	33	Amusement, Gambling,& Recreat.	48897	42	159	Educational Services
48623	385	2816	Special Trade Contractors	48770	73	476	Educational Services	48901	5	37	Social Assistance
48624	579	4224	Ambulatory Health Care Svcs	48787	1	500	Insurance Carriers & Related	48906	1151	14172	Social Assistance
48625	473	2389	Educational Services	48801	568	7791	Machinery Manufacturing	48908	11	20	Prof., Scientific, & Tech Svcs
48626	173	1271	Computer & Electronic Prod Mfg	48804	6	20	Administrative & Support Svcs	48909	56	381	Admin. of Economic Programs
48627	12	61	Amusement, Gambling,& Recreat.	48805	8	11	Hospitals	48910	1089	16348	Hospitals
48628	50	293	Machinery Manufacturing	48806	44	182	Nursing & Resid. Care Facilit.	48911	1054	12199	Food Svcs & Drinking Places
48629	537	3228	Food Svcs & Drinking Places	48807	20	40	Repair and Maintenance	48912	1153	17503	Hospitals
48630	10	49	Bldg Matl & Garden Eqpmt Dlrs	48808	115	510	Educational Services	48913	32	625	Exec., Legis., & Other Support

BUSINESS DATA

48915 - 49449

ZIP CODE	2004 Total Firms	2004 Total Employ-ees	TOP INDUSTRY RANKED on 2004 EMPLOYMENT	ZIP CODE	2004 Total Firms	2004 Total Employ-ees	TOP INDUSTRY RANKED on 2004 EMPLOYMENT	ZIP CODE	2004 Total Firms	2004 Total Employ-ees	TOP INDUSTRY RANKED on 2004 EMPLOYMENT
48915	188	1702	Relig., Grant, Civic, Prof Org	49091	848	9455	Educational Services	49288	49	199	Educational Services
48917	1603	25470	Insurance Carriers & Related	49092	85	592	Transportation Equipment Mfg	49289	7	77	Chemical Manufacturing
48918	8	931	Exec., Legis., & Other Support	49093	731	8327	Transportation Equipment Mfg	49301	442	2497	Construction of Buildings
48919	1	310	Publishing Industries	49094	141	717	Fabricated Metal Product Mfg	49302	158	1326	Merch. Wholesalers,Durable Gds
48921	4	3240	Transportation Equipment Mfg	49095	46	119	Special Trade Contractors	49303	29	146	Merch. Wholesalers,Nondur. Gds
48922	7	840	Exec., Legis., & Other Support	49096	69	251	Educational Services	49304	271	1796	Ambulatory Health Care Svcs
48924	3	810	Postal Service	49097	304	2730	Plastics & Rubber Products Mfg	49305	68	226	Educational Services
48933	997	25937	Exec., Legis., & Other Support	49098	224	1703	Hospitals	49306	222	2412	Accommodation
48951	2	1225	Insurance Carriers & Related	49099	201	1480	Fabricated Metal Product Mfg	49307	782	8043	Food Svcs & Drinking Places
49001	1071	14238	Merch. Wholesalers,Nondur. Gds	49101	125	486	Machinery Manufacturing	49309	33	86	Other Information Services
49002	1094	14953	Food Svcs & Drinking Places	49102	41	815	Nursing & Resid. Care Facilit.	49310	76	398	Food Svcs & Drinking Places
49003	10	92	Administrative & Support Svcs	49103	429	3940	Educational Services	49311	5	37	Truck Transportation
49004	371	3842	Furniture & Related Prod. Mfg	49104	9	192	Relig., Grant, Civic, Prof Org	49312	10	29	Food and Beverage Stores
49005	3	6	Miscellaneous Store Retailers	49106	238	3431	Utilities	49314	10	83	Merch. Wholesalers,Durable Gds
49006	503	5514	Educational Services	49107	331	2343	Fabricated Metal Product Mfg	49315	608	8145	Food and Beverage Stores
49007	1221	17211	Hospitals	49111	128	758	Primary Metal Manufacturing	49316	563	5049	Insurance Carriers & Related
49008	652	14362	Educational Services	49112	252	2137	Transportation Equipment Mfg	49317	7	49	Food Svcs & Drinking Places
49009	1170	13359	Food Svcs & Drinking Places	49113	52	279	Fabricated Metal Product Mfg	49318	42	254	Elect'l Eqpmt, App, & Comp Mfg
49010	659	8163	Miscellaneous Manufacturing	49115	6	19	Real Estate	49319	364	2686	Food Svcs & Drinking Places
49011	78	466	Food Manufacturing	49116	21	101	Amusement, Gambling,& Recreat.	49320	9	27	Food and Beverage Stores
49012	151	790	Social Assistance	49117	373	2286	Food Svcs & Drinking Places	49321	590	7467	Food Svcs & Drinking Places
49013	224	1445	Educational Services	49119	19	245	Prof., Scientific, & Tech Svcs	49322	20	28	Special Trade Contractors
49014	627	8370	Merch. Wholesalers,Nondur. Gds	49120	1319	11962	Educational Services	49323	185	879	Special Trade Contractors
49015	1662	24029	Transportation Equipment Mfg	49125	101	662	Gasoline Stations	49325	44	150	Wood Product Manufacturing
49016	14	418	Postal Service	49126	44	234	Primary Metal Manufacturing	49326	48	188	Accommodation
49017	1129	13756	Hospitals	49127	388	3724	Food Svcs & Drinking Places	49327	189	1842	Merch. Wholesalers,Nondur. Gds
49019	8	12	Prof., Scientific, & Tech Svcs	49128	200	1176	Educational Services	49328	102	492	Bldg Matl & Garden Eqpmt Dlrs
49020	5	10	Food Svcs & Drinking Places	49129	57	344	Food Svcs & Drinking Places	49329	225	1187	Educational Services
49021	132	612	Educational Services	49130	59	251	Fabricated Metal Product Mfg	49330	113	933	Special Trade Contractors
49022	1406	17901	Educational Services	49201	1573	17732	Ambulatory Health Care Svcs	49331	508	3835	Fabricated Metal Product Mfg
49023	5	43	Prof., Scientific, & Tech Svcs	49202	1190	15598	Food Svcs & Drinking Places	49332	106	393	Educational Services
49024	978	10504	General Merchandise Stores	49203	1213	11619	Educational Services	49333	257	1904	Educational Services
49026	86	481	Educational Services	49204	4	7	Waste Managmt & Remediat'n Svc	49335	10	53	Educational Services
49027	6	6	Food and Beverage Stores	49220	105	678	Educational Services	49336	62	378	Educational Services
49028	154	1415	Fabricated Metal Product Mfg	49221	1533	20776	Educational Services	49337	363	2472	Transportation Equipment Mfg
49029	32	76	Justice, Pubic Order/Safety	49224	450	4311	Educational Services	49338	59	270	Unclassified Establishments
49030	70	242	Plastics & Rubber Products Mfg	49227	44	140	Repair and Maintenance	49339	39	176	Amusement, Gambling,& Recreat.
49031	285	2345	Exec., Legis., & Other Support	49228	248	1965	Miscellaneous Manufacturing	49340	115	1355	Educational Services
49032	182	2160	Educational Services	49229	76	219	Educational Services	49341	989	5651	Educational Services
49033	25	44	Special Trade Contractors	49230	383	1828	Food Svcs & Drinking Places	49342	26	46	Accommodation
49034	70	390	Educational Services	49232	65	265	Educational Services	49343	121	421	Special Trade Contractors
49035	4	13	Bldg Matl & Garden Eqpmt Dlrs	49233	65	314	Motor Vehicle & Parts Dealers	49344	86	382	Food and Beverage Stores
49036	1070	10482	Food Svcs & Drinking Places	49234	105	513	Fabricated Metal Product Mfg	49345	445	4147	Educational Services
49038	363	2669	Food Svcs & Drinking Places	49235	52	129	Merch. Wholesalers,Durable Gds	49346	114	604	Food and Beverage Stores
49039	2	5	Accommodation	49236	189	1864	Nonmetallic Mineral Prod. Mfg	49347	34	93	Ambulatory Health Care Svcs
49040	105	873	Machinery Manufacturing	49237	110	678	Educational Services	49348	420	4451	Educational Services
49041	31	120	Food Svcs & Drinking Places	49238	63	294	Educational Services	49349	244	1747	Educational Services
49042	149	1276	Fabricated Metal Product Mfg	49239	4	25	Justice, Pubic Order/Safety	49351	2	2500	Leather & Allied Product Mfg
49043	62	489	Educational Services	49240	228	1117	Nursing & Resid. Care Facilit.	49355	6	524	Nonstore Retailers
49045	169	1018	Merch. Wholesalers,Durable Gds	49241	68	197	Educational Services	49401	311	5182	Educational Services
49046	208	928	Educational Services	49242	722	7206	Educational Services	49402	33	44	Food Svcs & Drinking Places
49047	582	5953	Primary Metal Manufacturing	49245	144	1414	Special Trade Contractors	49403	66	475	Crop Production
49048	931	14169	Hospitals	49246	96	574	Educational Services	49404	322	3983	Transportation Equipment Mfg
49050	42	114	Repair and Maintenance	49247	221	1569	Fabricated Metal Product Mfg	49405	36	306	Educational Services
49051	44	151	Educational Services	49248	28	75	Food and Beverage Stores	49406	130	701	Food Svcs & Drinking Places
49052	24	115	Animal Production	49249	58	157	Accommodation	49408	261	1345	Crop Production
49053	191	1844	Fabricated Metal Product Mfg	49250	281	2682	Plastics & Rubber Products Mfg	49409	39	329	Food and Beverage Stores
49055	180	1324	Crop Production	49251	183	974	Fabricated Metal Product Mfg	49410	34	114	Wood Product Manufacturing
49056	65	284	Crop Production	49252	119	2271	Transportation Equipment Mfg	49411	35	345	Print'g & Related Supp't Act's
49057	206	1734	Educational Services	49253	93	320	Motor Vehicle & Parts Dealers	49412	553	6754	Food Manufacturing
49058	723	7216	Plastics & Rubber Products Mfg	49254	161	1146	Educational Services	49415	243	1298	Educational Services
49060	52	368	Educational Services	49255	24	79	Crop Production	49416	8	9	Food and Beverage Stores
49061	43	296	Accommodation	49256	137	896	Relig., Grant, Civic, Prof Org	49417	1533	17045	Educational Services
49062	3	6	Food and Beverage Stores	49257	6	9	Food and Beverage Stores	49418	1266	15636	Food Svcs & Drinking Places
49063	3	1	Relig., Grant, Civic, Prof Org	49258	4	31	Fabricated Metal Product Mfg	49419	208	1274	Educational Services
49064	104	1160	Educational Services	49259	65	205	Textile Product Mills	49420	338	3209	Exec., Legis., & Other Support
49065	156	1464	Food Manufacturing	49261	69	504	Educational Services	49421	134	605	Educational Services
49066	19	57	Exec., Legis., & Other Support	49262	57	288	Educational Services	49422	6	14	Prof., Scientific, & Tech Svcs
49067	114	538	Educational Services	49263	5	24	Exec., Legis., & Other Support	49423	2153	38709	Merch. Wholesalers,Durable Gds
49068	758	8575	Transportation Equipment Mfg	49264	34	277	Social Assistance	49424	1681	19111	Food Svcs & Drinking Places
49070	94	529	Educational Services	49265	186	1021	Educational Services	49425	77	476	Educational Services
49071	248	2430	Plastics & Rubber Products Mfg	49266	67	188	Fabricated Metal Product Mfg	49426	787	6653	Educational Services
49072	108	1289	Transportation Equipment Mfg	49267	144	1187	Amusement, Gambling,& Recreat.	49427	7	0	Print'g & Related Supp't Act's
49073	120	614	Food Svcs & Drinking Places	49268	23	45	Construction of Buildings	49428	802	7082	Food and Beverage Stores
49074	6	15	Real Estate	49269	158	1498	Transportation Equipment Mfg	49429	8	46	Special Trade Contractors
49075	14	55	Merch. Wholesalers,Nondur. Gds	49270	144	781	Educational Services	49430	3	74	Nursing & Resid. Care Facilit.
49076	104	739	Educational Services	49271	72	275	Educational Services	49431	953	9339	Food Svcs & Drinking Places
49077	57	198	Food Svcs & Drinking Places	49272	49	134	Exec., Legis., & Other Support	49434	7	167	Amusement, Gambling,& Recreat.
49078	272	3653	Fabricated Metal Product Mfg	49274	91	709	Fabricated Metal Product Mfg	49435	129	797	Bldg Matl & Garden Eqpmt Dlrs
49079	576	5273	Merch. Wholesalers,Nondur. Gds	49275	2	4	Waste Managmt & Remediat'n Svc	49436	75	556	Food Svcs & Drinking Places
49080	508	5287	Food Manufacturing	49276	28	80	Special Trade Contractors	49437	231	1464	Chemical Manufacturing
49081	16	61	Ambulatory Health Care Svcs	49277	69	229	Merch. Wholesalers,Nondur. Gds	49440	300	3556	Exec., Legis., & Other Support
49082	174	1400	Miscellaneous Manufacturing	49279	21	252	Educational Services	49441	1318	14528	Food Svcs & Drinking Places
49083	301	7154	Administrative & Support Svcs	49281	10	61	Fabricated Metal Product Mfg	49442	1213	15693	Educational Services
49084	4	28	Merch. Wholesalers,Nondur. Gds	49282	30	171	Accommodation	49443	6	10	Prof., Scientific, & Tech Svcs
49085	1336	14214	Hospitals	49283	100	1210	Other Information Services	49444	1217	12224	Food Svcs & Drinking Places
49087	228	1686	Food Svcs & Drinking Places	49284	92	452	Educational Services	49445	629	5100	Food and Beverage Stores
49088	78	364	Crop Production	49285	200	968	Educational Services	49446	74	554	Food Manufacturing
49089	24	46	Educational Services	49286	546	7578	Machinery Manufacturing	49448	124	632	Special Trade Contractors
49090	838	7950	Food Svcs & Drinking Places	49287	56	182	Food Svcs & Drinking Places	49449	171	800	Food Svcs & Drinking Places

BUSINESS DATA

ZIP CODE	2004 Total Firms	2004 Total Employees	TOP INDUSTRY RANKED on 2004 EMPLOYMENT	ZIP CODE	2004 Total Firms	2004 Total Employees	TOP INDUSTRY RANKED on 2004 EMPLOYMENT	ZIP CODE	2004 Total Firms	2004 Total Employees	TOP INDUSTRY RANKED on 2004 EMPLOYMENT
49450	66	257	Educational Services	49674	11	44	Special Trade Contractors	49805	9	36	Real Estate
49451	153	1119	Educational Services	49675	84	356	Educational Services	49806	32	68	Accommodation
49452	48	706	Primary Metal Manufacturing	49676	105	262	Special Trade Contractors	49807	70	388	Relig., Grant, Civic, Prof Org
49453	307	1569	Food Svcs & Drinking Places	49677	313	3406	Food Manufacturing	49808	25	325	Accommodation
49454	178	968	Educational Services	49679	24	68	Food and Beverage Stores	49812	38	190	Wood Product Manufacturing
49455	216	1876	Merch. Wholesalers,Nondur. Gds	49680	55	231	Support Activities for Mining	49814	44	184	Sportg Gds,Hobby,Book, & Music
49456	570	6194	Furniture & Related Prod. Mfg	49682	308	1854	Amusement, Gambling,& Recreat.	49815	21	85	Forestry and Logging
49457	164	904	Accommodation	49683	47	427	Accommodation	49816	50	168	Accommodation
49458	15	55	Food Svcs & Drinking Places	49684	2810	28845	Hospitals	49817	18	91	Educational Services
49459	42	664	Merch. Wholesalers,Nondur. Gds	49685	23	43	Administrative & Support Svcs	49818	15	70	Crop Production
49460	251	1472	Bldg Matl & Garden Eqpmt Dlrs	49686	2160	19916	Educational Services	49819	2	13	Educational Services
49461	362	3086	Transportation Equipment Mfg	49688	60	322	Broadcasting	49820	71	180	Accommodation
49464	781	13095	Furniture & Related Prod. Mfg	49689	107	307	Food and Beverage Stores	49821	28	93	Ambulatory Health Care Svcs
49468	8	51	Administrative & Support Svcs	49690	330	2282	Amusement, Gambling,& Recreat.	49822	11	10	Food Svcs & Drinking Places
49501	34	44	Unclassified Establishments	49696	12	19	Isps, Web Search Portals	49825	15	108	Educational Services
49502	4	21	Real Estate	49701	254	1926	Food Svcs & Drinking Places	49826	8	20	Special Trade Contractors
49503	2785	45704	Ambulatory Health Care Svcs	49705	8	176	Fabricated Metal Product Mfg	49827	40	176	Educational Services
49504	1269	14582	Prof., Scientific, & Tech Svcs	49706	163	679	Special Trade Contractors	49829	1103	12354	Paper Manufacturing
49505	789	12043	Machinery Manufacturing	49707	1218	12164	Hospitals	49831	27	106	Educational Services
49506	932	11798	Hospitals	49709	190	849	Real Estate	49833	15	25	Food and Beverage Stores
49507	918	10480	Transportation Equipment Mfg	49710	21	29	Accommodation	49834	6	16	Food and Beverage Stores
49508	1230	13985	Merch. Wholesalers,Durable Gds	49711	3	13	Motor Vehicle & Parts Dealers	49835	34	83	Museums, Hist. Sites,& Similar
49509	1597	22026	Food Svcs & Drinking Places	49712	423	2573	Food Svcs & Drinking Places	49836	27	75	Construction of Buildings
49510	4	5	Isps, Web Search Portals	49713	82	345	Accommodation	49837	336	2124	Food Svcs & Drinking Places
49512	1557	41629	Motor Vehicle & Parts Dealers	49715	38	400	Educational Services	49838	25	68	Food Svcs & Drinking Places
49514	10	20	Administrative & Support Svcs	49716	40	77	Amusement, Gambling,& Recreat.	49839	49	143	Educational Services
49515	8	9	Special Trade Contractors	49717	2	2	Postal Service	49840	35	175	Mining (Except Oil and Gas)
49516	6	6	Administrative & Support Svcs	49718	30	80	Construction of Buildings	49841	214	1294	Educational Services
49518	12	20	Motion Pict. & Sound Recording	49719	136	845	Educational Services	49845	10	773	Accommodation
49525	1207	12738	Educational Services	49720	660	6047	Food Svcs & Drinking Places	49847	27	226	Fabricated Metal Product Mfg
49530	3	226	Miscellaneous Store Retailers	49721	770	5384	General Merchandise Stores	49848	8	35	Merch. Wholesalers,Durable Gds
49544	1294	26551	Food and Beverage Stores	49722	24	67	Construction of Buildings	49849	412	3522	Food Svcs & Drinking Places
49546	2037	23073	Ambulatory Health Care Svcs	49723	5	45	Food Svcs & Drinking Places	49852	6	12	Food and Beverage Stores
49548	1472	27867	Transportation Equipment Mfg	49724	34	131	Utilities	49853	39	136	Accommodation
49560	2	30	Relig., Grant, Civic, Prof Org	49725	61	244	Utilities	49854	372	2740	Exec., Legis., & Other Support
49601	1122	14161	Plastics & Rubber Products Mfg	49726	111	590	Accommodation	49855	1599	18480	Hospitals
49610	37	768	Food Svcs & Drinking Places	49727	269	2081	Primary Metal Manufacturing	49858	531	5803	Hospitals
49611	18	20	Merch. Wholesalers,Durable Gds	49728	19	51	Food Svcs & Drinking Places	49861	37	142	Justice, Pubic Order/Safety
49612	55	186	Bldg Matl & Garden Eqpmt Dlrs	49729	63	276	Food Svcs & Drinking Places	49862	320	2873	Justice, Pubic Order/Safety
49613	44	95	Accommodation	49730	83	262	Wood Product Manufacturing	49863	4	11	Merch. Wholesalers,Durable Gds
49614	127	650	Merch. Wholesalers,Nondur. Gds	49733	45	178	Wood Product Manufacturing	49864	3	7	Amusement, Gambling,& Recreat.
49615	312	2442	Accommodation	49734	9	16	Administrative & Support Svcs	49866	277	2308	Educational Services
49616	125	841	Miscellaneous Manufacturing	49735	1291	11957	Food Svcs & Drinking Places	49868	329	2520	Hospitals
49617	229	861	Food Svcs & Drinking Places	49736	24	52	Exec., Legis., & Other Support	49870	170	1125	Educational Services
49618	13	98	Exec., Legis., & Other Support	49738	536	5095	Ambulatory Health Care Svcs	49871	15	732	Mining (Except Oil and Gas)
49619	37	384	Educational Services	49739	1	100	Nat'l Security & Int'l Affairs	49872	9	22	Food and Beverage Stores
49620	79	286	Educational Services	49740	586	6132	Accommodation	49873	3	8	Food Svcs & Drinking Places
49621	108	240	Special Trade Contractors	49743	16	40	Food Manufacturing	49874	44	577	Nursing & Resid. Care Facilit.
49622	134	940	Apparel Manufacturing	49744	24	82	Truck Transportation	49876	49	825	Merch. Wholesalers,Durable Gds
49623	18	47	Food Svcs & Drinking Places	49745	35	149	Sportg Gds,Hobby,Book, & Music	49877	2	2	Food Svcs & Drinking Places
49625	49	225	Bldg Matl & Garden Eqpmt Dlrs	49746	152	1198	Fabricated Metal Product Mfg	49878	105	556	Wood Product Manufacturing
49626	3	3	Postal Service	49747	72	205	Real Estate	49879	47	200	Educational Services
49627	23	44	Food and Beverage Stores	49748	16	41	Accommodation	49880	23	135	Educational Services
49628	18	67	Food Svcs & Drinking Places	49749	279	1163	Food Svcs & Drinking Places	49881	16	296	Wood Product Manufacturing
49629	253	1296	Food Svcs & Drinking Places	49751	52	302	Educational Services	49883	19	78	Food Svcs & Drinking Places
49630	99	436	Admin. of Economic Programs	49752	39	90	Exec., Legis., & Other Support	49884	23	134	Justice, Pubic Order/Safety
49631	222	2589	Transportation Equipment Mfg	49753	53	192	Educational Services	49885	55	130	Construction of Buildings
49632	43	193	Electronics & Appliance Stores	49755	51	228	Administrative & Support Svcs	49886	23	196	Forestry and Logging
49633	88	360	Educational Services	49756	178	1093	Food Svcs & Drinking Places	49887	113	734	Nursing & Resid. Care Facilit.
49634	8	392	Paper Manufacturing	49757	180	2070	Accommodation	49891	43	78	Food Svcs & Drinking Places
49635	228	1777	Merch. Wholesalers,Nondur. Gds	49759	55	215	Relig., Grant, Civic, Prof Org	49892	46	137	Miscellaneous Store Retailers
49636	132	603	Food Svcs & Drinking Places	49760	29	98	Support Activities: Agr./For.	49893	38	90	Food and Beverage Stores
49637	97	1267	Food Manufacturing	49761	4	8	Amusement, Gambling,& Recreat.	49894	24	223	Rail Transportation
49638	21	51	Merch. Wholesalers,Durable Gds	49762	48	169	Food Svcs & Drinking Places	49895	42	146	Accommodation
49639	35	137	Amusement, Gambling,& Recreat.	49764	14	31	Motor Vehicle & Parts Dealers	49896	29	325	Educational Services
49640	114	527	Special Trade Contractors	49765	177	1039	Relig., Grant, Civic, Prof Org	49901	15	59	Fabricated Metal Product Mfg
49642	17	72	Transit & Grnd Pass. Transport	49766	75	370	Relig., Grant, Civic, Prof Org	49902	6	10	Exec., Legis., & Other Support
49643	202	1133	Educational Services	49768	61	312	Accommodation	49903	12	140	Wood Product Manufacturing
49644	61	220	Food Svcs & Drinking Places	49769	80	487	Educational Services	49905	36	160	Special Trade Contractors
49645	78	451	Repair and Maintenance	49770	1487	13109	Hospitals	49908	153	1728	Amusement, Gambling,& Recreat.
49646	485	4464	Special Trade Contractors	49774	66	350	Educational Services	49910	32	139	Educational Services
49648	56	541	Food Manufacturing	49775	15	20	Real Estate	49911	146	1118	Educational Services
49649	232	853	Educational Services	49776	65	342	Relig., Grant, Civic, Prof Org	49912	61	209	Food Svcs & Drinking Places
49650	94	277	Amusement, Gambling,& Recreat.	49777	43	84	Real Estate	49913	386	2566	Hospitals
49651	334	1824	Fabricated Metal Product Mfg	49779	311	1942	Transportation Equipment Mfg	49915	42	197	Clothing & Cloth'g Acc. Stores
49653	108	401	Food Svcs & Drinking Places	49780	62	360	Educational Services	49916	90	367	Educational Services
49654	101	1020	Food Svcs & Drinking Places	49781	339	2876	Accommodation	49917	4	1	Food Svcs & Drinking Places
49655	70	555	Educational Services	49782	104	292	Food Svcs & Drinking Places	49918	38	269	Food Svcs & Drinking Places
49656	36	124	Accommodation	49783	1005	10661	Accommodation	49919	18	67	Relig., Grant, Civic, Prof Org
49657	128	863	Educational Services	49788	75	2035	Exec., Legis., & Other Support	49920	241	1489	Nursing & Resid. Care Facilit.
49659	232	1652	Transportation Equipment Mfg	49790	4	6	Administrative & Support Svcs	49921	5	8	Bldg Matl & Garden Eqpmt Dlrs
49660	730	8797	Accommodation	49791	9	15	Food and Beverage Stores	49922	30	226	Wood Product Manufacturing
49663	152	671	Educational Services	49792	8	22	Wood Product Manufacturing	49925	34	244	Educational Services
49664	94	442	Educational Services	49793	24	42	Accommodation	49927	12	43	Relig., Grant, Civic, Prof Org
49665	144	643	Educational Services	49795	80	571	Primary Metal Manufacturing	49929	7	12	Motor Vehicle & Parts Dealers
49666	9	19	Postal Service	49796	42	143	Amusement, Gambling,& Recreat.	49930	305	2326	Educational Services
49667	23	94	Construction of Buildings	49797	25	94	Food Svcs & Drinking Places	49931	499	6025	Educational Services
49668	142	666	Educational Services	49799	86	280	Educational Services	49934	18	107	Nursing & Resid. Care Facilit.
49670	127	786	Hospitals	49801	873	8555	Hospitals	49935	348	2531	Educational Services
49673	17	74	Food Svcs & Drinking Places	49802	276	3642	Primary Metal Manufacturing	49938	453	3690	Educational Services

ZIP CODE	2004 Total Firms	2004 Total Employees	TOP INDUSTRY RANKED on 2004 EMPLOYMENT	ZIP CODE	2004 Total Firms	2004 Total Employees	TOP INDUSTRY RANKED on 2004 EMPLOYMENT	ZIP CODE	2004 Total Firms	2004 Total Employees	TOP INDUSTRY RANKED on 2004 EMPLOYMENT
49945	84	421	Educational Services	50106	42	239	Educational Services	50235	18	85	Educational Services
49946	238	1999	Educational Services	50107	46	313	Educational Services	50236	40	294	Merch. Wholesalers,Nondur. Gds
49947	35	249	Justice, Pubic Order/Safety	50108	13	26	Justice, Pubic Order/Safety	50237	57	473	Educational Services
49948	25	96	Accommodation	50109	54	672	Truck Transportation	50238	29	127	Educational Services
49950	45	230	Prof., Scientific, & Tech Svcs	50110	6	53	Ambulatory Health Care Svcs	50239	9	21	Unclassified Establishments
49952	3	5	Food and Beverage Stores	50111	221	2417	Machinery Manufacturing	50240	60	238	Insurance Carriers & Related
49953	219	1676	Merch. Wholesalers,Nondur. Gds	50112	456	5854	Educational Services	50241	14	28	Special Trade Contractors
49955	14	144	Educational Services	50115	211	1529	Educational Services	50242	13	34	Justice, Pubic Order/Safety
49958	25	97	Construction of Buildings	50116	4	19	Waste Managmt & Remediat'n Svc	50243	4	18	Exec., Legis., & Other Support
49959	13	30	Food Svcs & Drinking Places	50117	9	27	Food Svcs & Drinking Places	50244	53	411	Prof., Scientific, & Tech Svcs
49960	9	16	Other Information Services	50118	14	89	Educational Services	50246	42	137	Justice, Pubic Order/Safety
49961	8	28	Wood Product Manufacturing	50119	9	45	Nonmetallic Mineral Prod. Mfg	50247	78	406	Educational Services
49962	12	35	Justice, Pubic Order/Safety	50120	14	20	Crop Production	50248	208	2021	Fabricated Metal Product Mfg
49963	35	409	Wood Product Manufacturing	50122	80	335	Nursing & Resid. Care Facilit.	50249	80	344	Nursing & Resid. Care Facilit.
49964	16	34	Special Trade Contractors	50123	43	183	Merch. Wholesalers,Nondur. Gds	50250	115	747	Food Svcs & Drinking Places
49965	30	80	Wood Product Manufacturing	50124	118	584	Educational Services	50251	90	795	Educational Services
49967	24	103	Exec., Legis., & Other Support	50125	614	5954	Educational Services	50252	3	5	Truck Transportation
49968	99	976	Accommodation	50126	403	3577	Merch. Wholesalers,Durable Gds	50254	6	19	Crop Production
49969	66	1062	Accommodation	50127	3	3	Postal Service	50255	3	55	Educational Services
49970	7	24	Food and Beverage Stores	50128	4	7	Food and Beverage Stores	50256	13	49	Waste Managmt & Remediat'n Svc
49971	30	198	Merch. Wholesalers,Durable Gds	50129	395	2342	Food Svcs & Drinking Places	50257	41	199	Educational Services
50001	5	9	Personal and Laundry Services	50130	66	357	Educational Services	50258	41	173	Crop Production
50002	88	776	Construction of Buildings	50131	469	8173	Bldg Matl & Garden Eqpmt Dlrs	50259	5	6	Mining (Except Oil and Gas)
50003	242	2044	Fabricated Metal Product Mfg	50132	15	25	Relig., Grant, Civic, Prof Org	50261	42	259	Educational Services
50005	31	136	Fabricated Metal Product Mfg	50133	17	57	Justice, Pubic Order/Safety	50262	10	38	Justice, Pubic Order/Safety
50006	49	375	Mining (Except Oil and Gas)	50134	29	145	Food and Beverage Stores	50263	212	1934	Educational Services
50007	18	148	Educational Services	50135	54	382	Transportation Equipment Mfg	50264	8	17	Merch. Wholesalers,Nondur. Gds
50008	24	65	Justice, Pubic Order/Safety	50136	28	83	Fabricated Metal Product Mfg	50265	1124	11863	Insurance Carriers & Related
50009	372	8068	Amusement, Gambling,& Recreat.	50137	12	17	Merch. Wholesalers,Durable Gds	50266	1314	24980	Credit Intermediation & Relatd
50010	1445	21178	Food Svcs & Drinking Places	50138	433	4897	Hospitals	50268	24	55	Food and Beverage Stores
50011	30	12571	Educational Services	50139	28	117	Merch. Wholesalers,Nondur. Gds	50269	10	18	Merch. Wholesalers,Durable Gds
50012	1	70	Broadcasting	50140	99	1323	Educational Services	50271	38	241	Food Svcs & Drinking Places
50013	2	5	Amusement, Gambling,& Recreat.	50141	32	79	Educational Services	50272	4	2	Food Svcs & Drinking Places
50014	474	3509	Food Svcs & Drinking Places	50142	28	251	Heavy & Civil Eng. Construct'N	50273	347	2632	Food Svcs & Drinking Places
50020	77	388	Educational Services	50143	20	60	Crop Production	50274	16	34	Postal Service
50021	1059	13464	Educational Services	50144	128	959	Educational Services	50275	13	15	Food Svcs & Drinking Places
50022	518	4919	Fabricated Metal Product Mfg	50145	4	75	Educational Services	50276	64	1720	Social Assistance
50025	243	1548	Educational Services	50146	7	9	Postal Service	50277	23	57	Merch. Wholesalers,Nondur. Gds
50026	19	42	Prof., Scientific, & Tech Svcs	50147	27	76	Educational Services	50278	56	198	Nursing & Resid. Care Facilit.
50027	15	24	Unclassified Establishments	50148	14	12	Merch. Wholesalers,Nondur. Gds	50301	6	43	Relig., Grant, Civic, Prof Org
50028	59	340	Unclassified Establishments	50149	20	101	Transportation Equipment Mfg	50302	2	1	Relig., Grant, Civic, Prof Org
50029	34	161	Nursing & Resid. Care Facilit.	50150	26	59	Food Svcs & Drinking Places	50303	1	0	Relig., Grant, Civic, Prof Org
50031	6	23	Rail Transportation	50151	27	135	Elect'l Eqpmt, App, & Comp Mfg	50304	1	2	Prof., Scientific, & Tech Svcs
50032	8	16	Special Trade Contractors	50152	5	17	Relig., Grant, Civic, Prof Org	50306	4	1	Prof., Scientific, & Tech Svcs
50033	9	28	Food and Beverage Stores	50153	39	160	Truck Transportation	50309	1739	40888	Hospitals
50034	18	179	Educational Services	50154	18	56	Educational Services	50310	1017	7700	Food Svcs & Drinking Places
50035	78	611	Educational Services	50155	9	25	Merch. Wholesalers,Nondur. Gds	50311	549	5218	Educational Services
50036	669	6509	Food and Beverage Stores	50156	119	650	Nursing & Resid. Care Facilit.	50312	698	6532	Educational Services
50038	6	48	Special Trade Contractors	50157	30	198	Chemical Manufacturing	50313	967	16143	Plastics & Rubber Products Mfg
50039	22	53	Exec., Legis., & Other Support	50158	1239	19109	Merch. Wholesalers,Durable Gds	50314	466	13130	Hospitals
50040	20	77	Educational Services	50160	20	200	Educational Services	50315	853	10304	Nonstore Retailers
50041	7	204	Merch. Wholesalers,Nondur. Gds	50161	48	219	Educational Services	50316	438	6242	Hospitals
50042	17	33	Support Activities: Agr./For.	50162	30	84	Heavy & Civil Eng. Construct'N	50317	884	10678	Food Manufacturing
50044	22	183	Educational Services	50163	35	112	Educational Services	50318	1	1200	Postal Service
50046	29	83	Educational Services	50164	34	130	Educational Services	50319	158	8286	Admin. Human Resource Programs
50047	126	1131	Educational Services	50165	4	11	Food Svcs & Drinking Places	50320	330	2835	Food Svcs & Drinking Places
50048	60	164	Construction of Buildings	50166	31	102	Educational Services	50321	363	10785	Nat'l Security & Int'l Affairs
50049	300	4403	Food and Beverage Stores	50167	41	95	Educational Services	50322	1672	18718	Food Svcs & Drinking Places
50050	41	94	Educational Services	50168	21	70	Educational Services	50323	90	1820	Credit Intermediation & Relatd
50051	13	26	Educational Services	50169	56	620	Educational Services	50325	888	10082	Food Svcs & Drinking Places
50052	8	14	Warehousing and Storage	50170	83	455	Educational Services	50327	211	1894	Food Svcs & Drinking Places
50054	81	561	Educational Services	50171	181	1541	Transportation Equipment Mfg	50333	4	15	Administrative & Support Svcs
50055	21	68	Educational Services	50173	13	70	Food Svcs & Drinking Places	50391	5	1107	Insurance Carriers & Related
50056	43	168	Educational Services	50174	30	195	Transportation Equipment Mfg	50392	4	10019	Securities/Commodity Contracts
50057	7	25	Merch. Wholesalers,Nondur. Gds	50201	301	2755	Food Manufacturing	50393	1	0	Administrative & Support Svcs
50058	72	469	Bldg Matl & Garden Eqpmt Dlrs	50206	22	58	Machinery Manufacturing	50398	14	1211	Insurance Carriers & Related
50059	3	1	Repair and Maintenance	50207	83	517	Educational Services	50401	1542	22039	Ambulatory Health Care Svcs
50060	162	1435	Educational Services	50208	759	10486	Elect'l Eqpmt, App, & Comp Mfg	50402	10	37	Social Assistance
50061	46	130	Heavy & Civil Eng. Construct'N	50210	30	94	Fabricated Metal Product Mfg	50420	22	62	Bldg Matl & Garden Eqpmt Dlrs
50062	8	43	Educational Services	50211	190	1091	Educational Services	50421	159	1849	Fabricated Metal Product Mfg
50063	51	536	Animal Production	50212	142	533	Educational Services	50423	148	1098	Food Manufacturing
50064	5	19	Warehousing and Storage	50213	343	3592	Accommodation	50424	95	492	Educational Services
50065	14	38	Justice, Pubic Order/Safety	50214	16	48	Food Manufacturing	50426	8	24	Merch. Wholesalers,Nondur. Gds
50066	6	7	Warehousing and Storage	50216	179	927	Insurance Carriers & Related	50427	3	13	Merch. Wholesalers,Durable Gds
50067	14	48	Food Svcs & Drinking Places	50217	39	119	Machinery Manufacturing	50428	564	4533	Food Svcs & Drinking Places
50068	5	11	Prof., Scientific, & Tech Svcs	50218	4	4	Special Trade Contractors	50430	31	112	Educational Services
50069	27	143	Educational Services	50219	539	10232	Fabricated Metal Product Mfg	50431	18	26	Repair and Maintenance
50070	39	173	Fabricated Metal Product Mfg	50220	315	4875	Food Manufacturing	50432	18	67	Educational Services
50071	52	209	Educational Services	50222	8	12	Postal Service	50433	13	13	Warehousing and Storage
50072	63	394	Educational Services	50223	11	12	Postal Service	50434	27	106	Special Trade Contractors
50073	19	49	Special Trade Contractors	50225	80	470	Educational Services	50435	40	116	Merch. Wholesalers,Durable Gds
50074	11	11	Unclassified Establishments	50226	76	483	Amusement, Gambling,& Recreat.	50436	302	5376	Transportation Equipment Mfg
50075	43	191	Justice, Pubic Order/Safety	50227	4	4	Postal Service	50438	226	1892	Machinery Manufacturing
50076	78	473	Educational Services	50228	52	305	Educational Services	50439	10	75	Animal Production
50078	7	23	Educational Services	50229	21	62	Construction of Buildings	50440	31	98	Justice, Pubic Order/Safety
50101	3	4	Crop Production	50230	56	386	Educational Services	50441	311	2219	Merch. Wholesalers,Nondur. Gds
50102	5	2	Personal and Laundry Services	50231	12	25	Merch. Wholesalers,Nondur. Gds	50444	26	83	Justice, Pubic Order/Safety
50103	7	56	Educational Services	50232	16	22	Fabricated Metal Product Mfg	50446	23	74	Warehousing and Storage
50104	7	23	Merch. Wholesalers,Nondur. Gds	50233	26	210	Educational Services	50447	69	534	Transportation Equipment Mfg
50105	37	187	Educational Services	50234	7	14	Exec., Legis., & Other Support	50448	28	63	Justice, Pubic Order/Safety

ZIP CODE	2004 Total Firms	2004 Total Employees	TOP INDUSTRY RANKED on 2004 EMPLOYMENT
50449	32	95	Merch. Wholesalers,Durable Gds
50450	190	2570	Motor Vehicle & Parts Dealers
50451	25	47	Motor Vehicle & Parts Dealers
50452	48	419	Educational Services
50453	30	65	Merch. Wholesalers,Nondur. Gds
50454	4	8	Warehousing and Storage
50455	19	71	Fabricated Metal Product Mfg
50456	60	376	Educational Services
50457	16	24	Merch. Wholesalers,Nondur. Gds
50458	106	406	Nursing & Resid. Care Facilit.
50459	162	1376	Plastics & Rubber Products Mfg
50460	7	8	Relig., Grant, Civic, Prof Org
50461	281	2217	Textile Mills
50464	31	60	Justice, Pubic Order/Safety
50465	33	92	Warehousing and Storage
50466	88	463	Transportation Equipment Mfg
50467	8	12	Social Assistance
50468	74	440	Educational Services
50469	73	398	Educational Services
50470	15	34	Food Manufacturing
50471	40	96	Animal Production
50472	103	692	Educational Services
50473	16	15	Educational Services
50475	80	701	Machinery Manufacturing
50476	42	213	Nursing & Resid. Care Facilit.
50477	16	40	Animal Production
50478	55	317	Merch. Wholesalers,Durable Gds
50479	32	167	Machinery Manufacturing
50480	52	272	Educational Services
50481	1	4	Relig., Grant, Civic, Prof Org
50482	47	307	Accommodation
50483	36	135	Merch. Wholesalers,Nondur. Gds
50484	33	76	Educational Services
50501	1574	16704	Ambulatory Health Care Svcs
50510	54	411	Educational Services
50511	457	4191	Machinery Manufacturing
50514	86	869	Fabricated Metal Product Mfg
50515	20	27	Food and Beverage Stores
50516	28	57	Construction of Buildings
50517	72	381	Nursing & Resid. Care Facilit.
50518	14	91	Educational Services
50519	28	119	Educational Services
50520	7	34	Merch. Wholesalers,Durable Gds
50521	10	258	Educational Services
50522	45	251	Social Assistance
50523	30	111	Educational Services
50524	27	49	Merch. Wholesalers,Nondur. Gds
50525	226	2045	Educational Services
50526	2	139	Publishing Industries
50527	8	16	Truck Transportation
50528	17	74	Educational Services
50529	46	203	Educational Services
50530	89	399	Unclassified Establishments
50531	8	31	Unclassified Establishments
50532	35	113	Truck Transportation
50533	165	1318	Nursing & Resid. Care Facilit.
50535	45	139	Educational Services
50536	273	2219	Educational Services
50538	31	246	Warehousing and Storage
50539	36	119	Educational Services
50540	40	191	Nursing & Resid. Care Facilit.
50541	41	177	Educational Services
50542	57	330	Relig., Grant, Civic, Prof Org
50543	92	401	Merch. Wholesalers,Nondur. Gds
50544	29	96	Merch. Wholesalers,Durable Gds
50545	5	15	Relig., Grant, Civic, Prof Org
50546	15	88	Telecommunications
50548	357	3445	Machinery Manufacturing
50551	9	10	Special Trade Contractors
50552	9	27	Warehousing and Storage
50554	103	889	Machinery Manufacturing
50556	20	44	Credit Intermediation & Relatd
50557	34	96	Relig., Grant, Civic, Prof Org
50558	30	105	Special Trade Contractors
50559	22	46	Warehousing and Storage
50560	35	121	Educational Services
50561	26	135	Food Manufacturing
50562	35	174	Educational Services
50563	112	520	Relig., Grant, Civic, Prof Org
50565	19	138	Merch. Wholesalers,Nondur. Gds
50566	24	88	Warehousing and Storage
50567	15	31	Special Trade Contractors
50568	52	350	Nursing & Resid. Care Facilit.
50569	21	50	Special Trade Contractors
50570	10	38	Warehousing and Storage
50571	29	97	Educational Services
50573	10	13	Merch. Wholesalers,Nondur. Gds
50574	178	1177	Educational Services
50575	42	244	Nursing & Resid. Care Facilit.
50576	20	43	Credit Intermediation & Relatd

ZIP CODE	2004 Total Firms	2004 Total Employees	TOP INDUSTRY RANKED on 2004 EMPLOYMENT
50577	21	79	Bldg Matl & Garden Eqpmt Dlrs
50578	40	106	Educational Services
50579	154	947	Exec., Legis., & Other Support
50581	45	225	Educational Services
50582	11	54	Special Trade Contractors
50583	234	1424	Educational Services
50585	75	500	Educational Services
50586	13	18	Warehousing and Storage
50588	624	8023	Food Manufacturing
50590	56	234	Educational Services
50591	12	24	Perform'g Arts, Spec. Sports
50592	4	8	Food Svcs & Drinking Places
50593	6	7	Special Trade Contractors
50594	26	55	Merch. Wholesalers,Nondur. Gds
50595	426	8072	Elect'l Eqpmt, App, & Comp Mfg
50597	107	738	Warehousing and Storage
50598	40	144	Food Manufacturing
50599	17	43	Merch. Wholesalers,Durable Gds
50601	120	734	Educational Services
50602	118	867	Educational Services
50603	27	45	Special Trade Contractors
50604	68	460	Educational Services
50605	7	12	Postal Service
50606	31	341	Educational Services
50607	32	53	Warehousing and Storage
50608	5	13	Bldg Matl & Garden Eqpmt Dlrs
50609	24	119	Warehousing and Storage
50611	17	55	Justice, Pubic Order/Safety
50612	4	23	Relig., Grant, Civic, Prof Org
50613	1232	17056	Educational Services
50614	3	153	Perform'g Arts, Spec. Sports
50616	488	5020	Social Assistance
50619	86	428	Educational Services
50620	1	4	Merch. Wholesalers,Nondur. Gds
50621	74	753	Educational Services
50622	107	582	Special Trade Contractors
50623	8	16	Special Trade Contractors
50624	47	451	Educational Services
50625	57	235	Nursing & Resid. Care Facilit.
50626	53	248	Educational Services
50627	217	1842	Educational Services
50628	50	259	Nursing & Resid. Care Facilit.
50629	77	302	Educational Services
50630	72	739	Food Manufacturing
50631	14	58	Justice, Pubic Order/Safety
50632	39	157	Educational Services
50633	12	39	Food Svcs & Drinking Places
50634	24	121	Educational Services
50635	63	291	Educational Services
50636	98	488	Educational Services
50638	204	1428	Plastics & Rubber Products Mfg
50641	55	235	Food Svcs & Drinking Places
50642	22	86	Bldg Matl & Garden Eqpmt Dlrs
50643	111	739	Motor Vehicle & Parts Dealers
50644	420	3702	Hospitals
50645	46	116	Truck Transportation
50647	56	361	Fabricated Metal Product Mfg
50648	170	908	Educational Services
50649	11	36	Bldg Matl & Garden Eqpmt Dlrs
50650	33	114	Food Svcs & Drinking Places
50651	153	685	Educational Services
50652	13	18	Merch. Wholesalers,Nondur. Gds
50653	22	33	Food Svcs & Drinking Places
50654	19	31	Food Svcs & Drinking Places
50655	32	137	Educational Services
50657	5	24	Machinery Manufacturing
50658	97	462	Educational Services
50659	324	3053	Fabricated Metal Product Mfg
50660	38	198	Educational Services
50662	346	3125	Food Svcs & Drinking Places
50664	13	29	Merch. Wholesalers,Nondur. Gds
50665	106	483	Food Svcs & Drinking Places
50666	37	146	Educational Services
50667	16	83	Mining (Except Oil and Gas)
50668	64	215	Educational Services
50669	98	746	Construction of Buildings
50670	66	517	Machinery Manufacturing
50671	15	42	Crop Production
50672	21	122	Unclassified Establishments
50673	5	4	Relig., Grant, Civic, Prof Org
50674	176	1056	Transportation Equipment Mfg
50675	120	887	Transportation Equipment Mfg
50676	93	418	Educational Services
50677	511	6656	Insurance Carriers & Related
50680	51	258	Educational Services
50681	14	35	Special Trade Contractors
50682	72	677	Plastics & Rubber Products Mfg
50701	940	21549	Merch. Wholesalers,Durable Gds
50702	848	14232	Hospitals
50703	816	17381	Food Manufacturing

ZIP CODE	2004 Total Firms	2004 Total Employees	TOP INDUSTRY RANKED on 2004 EMPLOYMENT
50704	18	44	Administrative & Support Svcs
50706	24	133	Construction of Buildings
50707	185	1389	Food Svcs & Drinking Places
50799	1	130	Electronics & Appliance Stores
50801	484	5303	Machinery Manufacturing
50830	61	495	Educational Services
50831	9	6	Gasoline Stations
50833	156	868	Educational Services
50835	5	12	Bldg Matl & Garden Eqpmt Dlrs
50836	14	53	Justice, Pubic Order/Safety
50837	19	55	Educational Services
50839	2	2	Food Svcs & Drinking Places
50840	32	225	Food and Beverage Stores
50841	218	1245	Educational Services
50842	3	8	Food Svcs & Drinking Places
50843	37	111	Educational Services
50845	18	107	Educational Services
50846	47	235	Nursing & Resid. Care Facilit.
50847	7	9	Machinery Manufacturing
50848	3	0	Animal Production
50849	185	1741	Nonmetallic Mineral Prod. Mfg
50851	111	907	Merch. Wholesalers,Nondur. Gds
50853	51	273	Educational Services
50854	183	1213	Nursing & Resid. Care Facilit.
50857	13	36	Prof., Scientific, & Tech Svcs
50858	24	91	Educational Services
50859	21	44	Educational Services
50860	7	11	Motor Vehicle & Parts Dealers
50861	4	2	Postal Service
50862	3	3	General Merchandise Stores
50863	10	8	Crop Production
50864	111	609	Educational Services
51001	99	666	Educational Services
51002	85	429	Educational Services
51003	85	384	Construction of Buildings
51004	53	162	Food Svcs & Drinking Places
51005	80	429	Educational Services
51006	56	238	Nursing & Resid. Care Facilit.
51007	19	73	Educational Services
51008	15	52	Merch. Wholesalers,Nondur. Gds
51009	13	34	Merch. Wholesalers,Nondur. Gds
51010	25	60	Educational Services
51012	393	4228	Food Manufacturing
51014	22	93	Educational Services
51015	1	1	Heavy & Civil Eng. Construct'N
51016	56	254	Nursing & Resid. Care Facilit.
51018	18	96	Educational Services
51019	37	132	Merch. Wholesalers,Nondur. Gds
51020	32	201	Merch. Wholesalers,Nondur. Gds
51022	38	109	Educational Services
51023	159	1337	Educational Services
51024	57	455	Educational Services
51025	112	932	Plastics & Rubber Products Mfg
51026	51	139	Merch. Wholesalers,Nondur. Gds
51027	56	241	Special Trade Contractors
51028	90	467	Educational Services
51029	12	37	Merch. Wholesalers,Nondur. Gds
51030	50	404	Machinery Manufacturing
51031	562	5393	Food Svcs & Drinking Places
51033	19	20	Merch. Wholesalers,Nondur. Gds
51034	128	665	Educational Services
51035	101	630	Textile Product Mills
51036	40	126	Animal Production
51037	14	31	Special Trade Contractors
51038	41	155	Construction of Buildings
51039	87	426	Educational Services
51040	248	1941	Amusement, Gambling,& Recreat.
51041	310	3545	Food Manufacturing
51044	16	58	Justice, Pubic Order/Safety
51045	8	31	Merch. Wholesalers,Nondur. Gds
51046	84	562	Educational Services
51047	42	94	Nursing & Resid. Care Facilit.
51048	28	91	Educational Services
51049	27	62	Food Manufacturing
51050	152	704	Educational Services
51051	6	29	Warehousing and Storage
51052	35	142	Construction of Buildings
51053	73	417	Educational Services
51054	136	2825	Telecommunications
51055	60	960	Food Svcs & Drinking Places
51056	20	56	Food and Beverage Stores
51058	62	195	Educational Services
51060	33	200	Bldg Matl & Garden Eqpmt Dlrs
51061	21	68	Educational Services
51062	13	33	Unclassified Establishments
51063	32	400	Nursing & Resid. Care Facilit.
51101	823	12462	Nursing & Resid. Care Facilit.
51102	21	106	Social Assistance
51103	420	4780	Food Svcs & Drinking Places
51104	463	7381	Hospitals

ZIP CODE	2004 Total Firms	2004 Total Employ-ees	TOP INDUSTRY RANKED on 2004 EMPLOYMENT	ZIP CODE	2004 Total Firms	2004 Total Employ-ees	TOP INDUSTRY RANKED on 2004 EMPLOYMENT	ZIP CODE	2004 Total Firms	2004 Total Employ-ees	TOP INDUSTRY RANKED on 2004 EMPLOYMENT
51105	402	5885	Administrative & Support Svcs	51527	37	97	Construction of Buildings	52052	179	1587	Relig., Grant, Civic, Prof Org
51106	872	13326	Food Manufacturing	51528	42	154	Educational Services	52053	33	101	Merch. Wholesalers,Durable Gds
51108	156	931	Food Manufacturing	51529	93	549	Educational Services	52054	42	165	Justice, Pubic Order/Safety
51109	75	454	Food Svcs & Drinking Places	51530	41	126	Nursing & Resid. Care Facilit.	52056	13	58	Merch. Wholesalers,Nondur. Gds
51111	83	2342	Food Manufacturing	51531	85	417	Relig., Grant, Civic, Prof Org	52057	415	4219	Educational Services
51201	326	4738	Ambulatory Health Care Svcs	51532	28	80	Educational Services	52060	447	3703	Furn. & Home Furnishgs Stores
51230	15	49	Crop Production	51533	48	126	Truck Transportation	52064	43	209	Educational Services
51231	17	50	Special Trade Contractors	51534	279	2833	Social Assistance	52065	37	161	Bldg Matl & Garden Eqpmt Dlrs
51232	35	123	Food Svcs & Drinking Places	51535	119	622	Educational Services	52066	1	3	Gasoline Stations
51234	47	566	Machinery Manufacturing	51536	16	69	Warehousing and Storage	52068	95	1785	Miscellaneous Manufacturing
51235	52	167	Bldg Matl & Garden Eqpmt Dlrs	51537	433	4065	Nonstore Retailers	52069	104	608	Educational Services
51237	93	621	Machinery Manufacturing	51540	11	68	Educational Services	52070	43	253	Elect'l Eqpmt, App, & Comp Mfg
51238	73	557	Plastics & Rubber Products Mfg	51541	16	33	Merch. Wholesalers,Nondur. Gds	52071	12	56	Food Svcs & Drinking Places
51239	135	1066	Food and Beverage Stores	51542	15	99	Accommodation	52072	14	58	Nursing & Resid. Care Facilit.
51240	89	558	Educational Services	51543	35	91	Truck Transportation	52073	34	140	Accommodation
51241	70	467	Food Manufacturing	51544	36	130	Educational Services	52074	8	15	Food Svcs & Drinking Places
51242	21	77	Merch. Wholesalers,Nondur. Gds	51545	8	18	Accommodation	52075	13	30	Chemical Manufacturing
51243	32	161	Educational Services	51546	150	948	Merch. Wholesalers,Nondur. Gds	52076	110	549	Nursing & Resid. Care Facilit.
51244	6	11	Special Trade Contractors	51548	10	84	Truck Transportation	52077	19	62	Crop Production
51245	96	476	Hospitals	51549	18	57	Merch. Wholesalers,Durable Gds	52078	25	102	Merch. Wholesalers,Nondur. Gds
51246	211	1462	Educational Services	51550	3	6	Food Svcs & Drinking Places	52079	22	49	Special Trade Contractors
51247	209	2565	Fabricated Metal Product Mfg	51551	60	578	Educational Services	52101	651	7984	Fabricated Metal Product Mfg
51248	114	609	Food and Beverage Stores	51552	18	72	Food Svcs & Drinking Places	52132	68	701	Educational Services
51249	200	1922	Paper Manufacturing	51553	37	137	Relig., Grant, Civic, Prof Org	52133	13	14	Relig., Grant, Civic, Prof Org
51250	403	5228	Educational Services	51554	5	28	Food Svcs & Drinking Places	52134	17	56	Food and Beverage Stores
51301	809	8426	Merch. Wholesalers,Durable Gds	51555	215	1568	Food Svcs & Drinking Places	52135	52	189	Merch. Wholesalers,Nondur. Gds
51331	137	1134	Food Svcs & Drinking Places	51556	13	30	Warehousing and Storage	52136	290	4973	Miscellaneous Manufacturing
51333	12	31	Crop Production	51557	32	195	Educational Services	52140	19	110	Accommodation
51334	369	3459	Educational Services	51558	42	123	Educational Services	52141	40	258	Food and Beverage Stores
51338	49	425	Broadcasting	51559	53	327	Educational Services	52142	90	602	Educational Services
51340	7	34	Furn. & Home Furnishgs Stores	51560	103	1180	Merch. Wholesalers,Nondur. Gds	52144	65	196	Truck Transportation
51341	9	60	Educational Services	51561	35	198	Motor Vehicle & Parts Dealers	52146	54	149	Unclassified Establishments
51342	67	444	Relig., Grant, Civic, Prof Org	51562	22	233	Truck Transportation	52147	23	72	Food Svcs & Drinking Places
51343	5	13	Crop Production	51563	19	28	Truck Transportation	52151	104	962	Miscellaneous Manufacturing
51344	7	118	Educational Services	51564	25	36	Insurance Carriers & Related	52154	36	126	Construction of Buildings
51345	15	162	Merch. Wholesalers,Durable Gds	51565	13	65	Food Svcs & Drinking Places	52155	47	177	Heavy & Civil Eng. Construct'N
51346	116	650	Nursing & Resid. Care Facilit.	51566	392	4693	Nonstore Retailers	52156	27	159	Food Manufacturing
51347	67	383	Primary Metal Manufacturing	51570	45	276	Educational Services	52157	61	329	Nursing & Resid. Care Facilit.
51350	18	150	Construction of Buildings	51571	11	17	Food Svcs & Drinking Places	52158	21	928	Food Svcs & Drinking Places
51351	221	2218	Furniture & Related Prod. Mfg	51572	24	57	Exec., Legis., & Other Support	52159	125	806	Merch. Wholesalers,Durable Gds
51354	49	183	Warehousing and Storage	51573	67	135	Educational Services	52160	42	155	Justice, Pubic Order/Safety
51355	89	1007	Food Svcs & Drinking Places	51575	34	259	Educational Services	52161	91	848	Heavy & Civil Eng. Construct'N
51357	47	248	Educational Services	51576	42	504	Merch. Wholesalers,Durable Gds	52162	192	2074	Merch. Wholesalers,Nondur. Gds
51358	77	370	Educational Services	51577	113	423	Educational Services	52163	23	110	Food Manufacturing
51360	536	4311	Transportation Equipment Mfg	51578	13	14	Special Trade Contractors	52164	9	10	Prof., Scientific, & Tech Svcs
51363	12	54	Merch. Wholesalers,Nondur. Gds	51579	109	633	Educational Services	52165	37	117	Merch. Wholesalers,Nondur. Gds
51364	37	175	Telecommunications	51601	360	3840	Fabricated Metal Product Mfg	52166	11	45	Food Svcs & Drinking Places
51365	24	209	Social Assistance	51630	5	5	Postal Service	52168	25	127	Accommodation
51366	28	39	Truck Transportation	51631	14	73	Transportation Equipment Mfg	52169	10	19	Food and Beverage Stores
51401	754	7704	Insurance Carriers & Related	51632	327	3287	Fabricated Metal Product Mfg	52170	29	49	Educational Services
51430	50	258	Warehousing and Storage	51636	22	61	Bldg Matl & Garden Eqpmt Dlrs	52171	35	327	Merch. Wholesalers,Nondur. Gds
51431	27	107	Educational Services	51637	8	126	Educational Services	52172	339	2446	Fabricated Metal Product Mfg
51432	7	75	Amusement, Gambling,& Recreat.	51638	50	247	Educational Services	52175	179	1943	Transportation Equipment Mfg
51433	21	65	Food Svcs & Drinking Places	51639	26	149	Educational Services	52201	32	204	Food Svcs & Drinking Places
51436	55	259	Transportation Equipment Mfg	51640	90	801	Food Manufacturing	52202	42	261	Educational Services
51439	46	187	Educational Services	51645	8	13	Justice, Pubic Order/Safety	52203	126	1057	Food Svcs & Drinking Places
51440	18	74	Justice, Pubic Order/Safety	51646	38	185	Truck Transportation	52204	1	3000	Elect'l Eqpmt, App, & Comp Mfg
51441	5	11	Food Svcs & Drinking Places	51647	10	17	Warehousing and Storage	52205	291	2660	Justice, Pubic Order/Safety
51442	498	6002	Food Manufacturing	51648	18	120	Gasoline Stations	52206	60	257	Clothing & Cloth'g Acc. Stores
51443	68	350	Educational Services	51649	12	30	Credit Intermediation & Relatd	52207	21	29	Food and Beverage Stores
51444	21	87	Construction of Buildings	51650	11	30	Exec., Legis., & Other Support	52208	129	790	Educational Services
51445	207	2008	Merch. Wholesalers,Durable Gds	51651	4	4	Merch. Wholesalers,Nondur. Gds	52209	78	300	Merch. Wholesalers,Nondur. Gds
51446	38	188	Educational Services	51652	105	666	Educational Services	52210	18	52	Primary Metal Manufacturing
51447	9	5	Food Svcs & Drinking Places	51653	50	353	Educational Services	52211	141	936	Educational Services
51448	36	57	Merch. Wholesalers,Nondur. Gds	51654	13	26	Mining (Except Oil and Gas)	52212	14	25	Merch. Wholesalers,Nondur. Gds
51449	118	1209	Relig., Grant, Civic, Prof Org	51656	3	12	Social Assistance	52213	114	697	Motor Vehicle & Parts Dealers
51450	108	822	Educational Services	52001	1560	29667	Ambulatory Health Care Svcs	52214	95	532	Educational Services
51451	8	9	Warehousing and Storage	52002	636	9933	Food Svcs & Drinking Places	52215	25	61	Justice, Pubic Order/Safety
51452	15	42	Food and Beverage Stores	52003	559	8840	Administrative & Support Svcs	52216	83	340	Nursing & Resid. Care Facilit.
51453	36	198	Educational Services	52004	28	114	Administrative & Support Svcs	52217	34	60	Merch. Wholesalers,Nondur. Gds
51454	81	328	Educational Services	52030	21	82	Educational Services	52218	36	184	Educational Services
51455	127	981	Ambulatory Health Care Svcs	52031	195	1311	Miscellaneous Manufacturing	52219	9	30	Food Svcs & Drinking Places
51458	116	460	Educational Services	52032	32	97	Justice, Pubic Order/Safety	52220	13	39	Relig., Grant, Civic, Prof Org
51459	5	79	Merch. Wholesalers,Nondur. Gds	52033	166	1251	Bldg Matl & Garden Eqpmt Dlrs	52221	8	13	Special Trade Contractors
51460	6	8	Credit Intermediation & Relatd	52035	27	137	Educational Services	52222	41	64	Special Trade Contractors
51461	52	298	Educational Services	52036	4	36	Exec., Legis., & Other Support	52223	61	456	Machinery Manufacturing
51462	49	276	Merch. Wholesalers,Nondur. Gds	52037	24	107	Educational Services	52224	119	530	Educational Services
51463	42	111	Merch. Wholesalers,Nondur. Gds	52038	13	42	Sportg Gds,Hobby,Book, & Music	52225	15	37	Exec., Legis., & Other Support
51465	29	82	Educational Services	52039	21	100	Truck Transportation	52226	8	9	Repair and Maintenance
51466	90	454	Nursing & Resid. Care Facilit.	52040	295	3056	Food Svcs & Drinking Places	52227	65	242	Special Trade Contractors
51467	42	191	Educational Services	52041	44	250	Machinery Manufacturing	52228	82	313	Special Trade Contractors
51501	984	16166	Accommodation	52042	77	468	Nursing & Resid. Care Facilit.	52229	31	64	Exec., Legis., & Other Support
51502	7	7	Administrative & Support Svcs	52043	209	1692	Educational Services	52231	12	38	Warehousing and Storage
51503	1085	15015	Educational Services	52044	4	7	Prof., Scientific, & Tech Svcs	52232	7	9	Credit Intermediation & Relatd
51510	92	1245	Truck Transportation	52045	58	502	Educational Services	52233	305	4221	Prof., Scientific, & Tech Svcs
51520	5	76	Food Manufacturing	52046	70	870	Educational Services	52235	35	225	Merch. Wholesalers,Nondur. Gds
51521	118	750	Educational Services	52047	26	30	Personal and Laundry Services	52236	24	95	Food Svcs & Drinking Places
51523	14	43	Warehousing and Storage	52048	14	20	Food Svcs & Drinking Places	52237	51	321	Food Manufacturing
51525	40	180	Educational Services	52049	75	397	Educational Services	52240	1552	16802	Food Svcs & Drinking Places
51526	53	367	Heavy & Civil Eng. Construct'N	52050	19	42	Relig., Grant, Civic, Prof Org	52241	774	9720	Food Svcs & Drinking Places

52242 - 53060 BUSINESS DATA

ZIP CODE	2004 Total Firms	2004 Total Employ-ees	TOP INDUSTRY RANKED on 2004 EMPLOYMENT	ZIP CODE	2004 Total Firms	2004 Total Employ-ees	TOP INDUSTRY RANKED on 2004 EMPLOYMENT	ZIP CODE	2004 Total Firms	2004 Total Employ-ees	TOP INDUSTRY RANKED on 2004 EMPLOYMENT
52242	125	29275	Educational Services	52540	59	117	Merch. Wholesalers,Nondur. Gds	52738	135	1918	Food Manufacturing
52243	2	1204	Prof., Scientific, & Tech Svcs	52542	22	92	Educational Services	52739	20	49	Merch. Wholesalers,Nondur. Gds
52244	35	391	Prof., Scientific, & Tech Svcs	52543	5	6	Special Trade Contractors	52742	337	3267	Miscellaneous Manufacturing
52245	393	5925	Hospitals	52544	425	4184	Merch. Wholesalers,Nondur. Gds	52745	31	53	Fabricated Metal Product Mfg
52246	450	6250	Hospitals	52548	4	6	Merch. Wholesalers,Nondur. Gds	52746	25	69	Educational Services
52247	296	1650	Plastics & Rubber Products Mfg	52549	13	35	Educational Services	52747	110	754	Educational Services
52248	77	452	Merch. Wholesalers,Nondur. Gds	52550	12	24	Food and Beverage Stores	52748	282	2939	Print'g & Related Supp't Act's
52249	53	243	Nursing & Resid. Care Facilit.	52551	25	86	Educational Services	52749	9	18	Special Trade Contractors
52251	24	50	Justice, Pubic Order/Safety	52552	20	49	Food Svcs & Drinking Places	52750	23	152	Educational Services
52252	2	9	Furn. & Home Furnishgs Stores	52553	64	1148	Food Manufacturing	52751	45	133	Relig., Grant, Civic, Prof Org
52253	98	454	Merch. Wholesalers,Durable Gds	52554	41	223	Educational Services	52752	13	45	Gasoline Stations
52254	44	195	Administrative & Support Svcs	52555	4	1	Exec., Legis., & Other Support	52753	126	723	Educational Services
52255	47	158	Educational Services	52556	856	6823	Machinery Manufacturing	52754	31	311	Educational Services
52257	9	6	Administrative & Support Svcs	52557	4	362	Educational Services	52755	56	331	Educational Services
52301	175	1308	Publishing Industries	52560	14	27	Relig., Grant, Civic, Prof Org	52756	59	219	Educational Services
52302	933	8650	Food and Beverage Stores	52561	37	207	Real Estate	52757	23	58	Heavy & Civil Eng. Construct'N
52305	27	47	Food Manufacturing	52562	3	5	Bldg Matl & Garden Eqpmt Dlrs	52758	14	27	Motor Vehicle & Parts Dealers
52306	56	154	Educational Services	52563	45	90	Bldg Matl & Garden Eqpmt Dlrs	52760	11	309	Machinery Manufacturing
52307	24	88	Educational Services	52565	171	1373	Elect'l Eqpmt, App, & Comp Mfg	52761	1146	15672	Miscellaneous Manufacturing
52308	21	85	Educational Services	52566	3	3	General Merchandise Stores	52765	17	80	Accommodation
52309	13	24	Food Svcs & Drinking Places	52567	22	76	Educational Services	52766	24	80	Food Svcs & Drinking Places
52310	327	2600	Plastics & Rubber Products Mfg	52568	5	21	Food and Beverage Stores	52767	19	153	Amusement, Gambling,& Recreat.
52312	11	1	Merch. Wholesalers,Nondur. Gds	52569	13	29	Sportg Gds,Hobby,Book, & Music	52768	42	212	Fabricated Metal Product Mfg
52313	17	40	Merch. Wholesalers,Nondur. Gds	52570	24	126	Merch. Wholesalers,Durable Gds	52769	22	86	Justice, Pubic Order/Safety
52314	191	1497	Educational Services	52571	67	340	Educational Services	52772	297	1762	Prof., Scientific, & Tech Svcs
52315	48	149	Educational Services	52572	43	205	Educational Services	52773	81	959	Gasoline Stations
52316	76	417	Educational Services	52573	10	11	Unclassified Establishments	52774	10	71	Educational Services
52317	278	2747	Plastics & Rubber Products Mfg	52574	20	70	Mining (Except Oil and Gas)	52776	205	2460	Food Manufacturing
52318	41	544	Food and Beverage Stores	52576	18	47	Waste Managmt & Remediat'n Svc	52777	62	220	Nursing & Resid. Care Facilit.
52319	6	674	Hospitals	52577	714	6642	Food Svcs & Drinking Places	52778	140	1613	Fabricated Metal Product Mfg
52320	57	291	Educational Services	52580	21	305	Educational Services	52801	379	8147	Exec., Legis., & Other Support
52321	29	86	Educational Services	52581	13	24	Special Trade Contractors	52802	420	6003	Merch. Wholesalers,Durable Gds
52322	70	212	Educational Services	52583	10	26	Bldg Matl & Garden Eqpmt Dlrs	52803	742	9087	Hospitals
52323	34	63	Educational Services	52584	20	35	Publishing Industries	52804	560	9896	Hospitals
52324	69	823	Special Trade Contractors	52585	42	170	Truck Transportation	52805	4	4	Prof., Scientific, & Tech Svcs
52325	11	15	Relig., Grant, Civic, Prof Org	52586	11	23	Construction of Buildings	52806	976	17111	Food Svcs & Drinking Places
52326	22	104	Educational Services	52588	5	13	Mining (Except Oil and Gas)	52807	848	11211	Food Svcs & Drinking Places
52327	84	452	Educational Services	52590	37	243	Educational Services	52808	9	61	Merch. Wholesalers,Nondur. Gds
52328	32	110	Social Assistance	52591	195	1329	Educational Services	52809	9	29	Administrative & Support Svcs
52329	28	120	Merch. Wholesalers,Durable Gds	52593	3	5	Special Trade Contractors	53001	65	293	Food Manufacturing
52330	25	76	Food Svcs & Drinking Places	52594	4	4	Postal Service	53002	88	1250	Fabricated Metal Product Mfg
52332	65	194	Telecommunications	52595	5	29	Social Assistance	53003	26	135	Special Trade Contractors
52333	153	585	Special Trade Contractors	52601	1298	15464	Food Svcs & Drinking Places	53004	105	1009	Food Manufacturing
52334	16	128	Construction of Buildings	52619	19	29	Exec., Legis., & Other Support	53005	1982	22749	Prof., Scientific, & Tech Svcs
52335	35	74	Unclassified Establishments	52620	50	244	Machinery Manufacturing	53006	56	926	Merch. Wholesalers,Durable Gds
52336	81	308	Educational Services	52621	26	92	Educational Services	53007	271	4109	Merch. Wholesalers,Durable Gds
52337	33	274	Educational Services	52623	86	500	Educational Services	53008	18	59	Special Trade Contractors
52338	96	280	Construction of Buildings	52624	20	83	Educational Services	53010	247	1650	Educational Services
52339	164	1340	Food Manufacturing	52625	104	668	Educational Services	53011	43	141	Educational Services
52340	41	122	Educational Services	52626	53	187	Educational Services	53012	768	6418	Educational Services
52341	27	73	Heavy & Civil Eng. Construct'N	52627	590	7357	Rail Transportation	53013	90	722	Primary Metal Manufacturing
52342	165	1275	Justice, Pubic Order/Safety	52630	14	24	Unclassified Establishments	53014	336	4136	Food Manufacturing
52344	11	33	Merch. Wholesalers,Nondur. Gds	52631	29	239	Machinery Manufacturing	53015	74	1058	Educational Services
52345	46	277	Administrative & Support Svcs	52632	668	8018	Plastics & Rubber Products Mfg	53016	16	540	Food Manufacturing
52346	75	300	Educational Services	52635	29	85	Educational Services	53017	77	283	Educational Services
52347	96	978	Machinery Manufacturing	52637	120	973	Truck Transportation	53018	373	3378	Food Svcs & Drinking Places
52348	2	4	Motor Vehicle & Parts Dealers	52638	18	1027	Fabricated Metal Product Mfg	53019	75	801	Truck Transportation
52349	376	2475	Educational Services	52639	40	296	Administrative & Support Svcs	53020	136	1335	Accommodation
52350	2	0	Postal Service	52640	66	390	Educational Services	53021	136	1134	Educational Services
52351	32	246	Truck Transportation	52641	561	9102	Merch. Wholesalers,Durable Gds	53022	716	11618	Relig., Grant, Civic, Prof Org
52352	36	178	Educational Services	52644	25	70	Warehousing and Storage	53023	33	135	Construction of Buildings
52353	466	4428	Primary Metal Manufacturing	52645	97	535	Educational Services	53024	599	7398	Primary Metal Manufacturing
52354	12	18	Credit Intermediation & Relatd	52646	25	106	Merch. Wholesalers,Nondur. Gds	53026	11	94	Motor Vehicle & Parts Dealers
52355	5	7	Exec., Legis., & Other Support	52647	17	84	Construction of Buildings	53027	650	9006	Fabricated Metal Product Mfg
52356	138	944	Health & Personal Care Stores	52648	5	110	Managmt of Companies & Enterp.	53029	812	7267	Educational Services
52358	164	1040	Educational Services	52649	27	60	Educational Services	53031	8	23	Bldg Matl & Garden Eqpmt Dlrs
52359	15	28	Warehousing and Storage	52650	24	259	Nonmetallic Mineral Prod. Mfg	53032	181	3121	Machinery Manufacturing
52361	244	3548	Crop Production	52651	33	103	Educational Services	53033	140	813	Food Svcs & Drinking Places
52362	71	344	Truck Transportation	52652	6	10	Relig., Grant, Civic, Prof Org	53034	69	666	Fabricated Metal Product Mfg
52401	748	13423	Isps, Web Search Portals	52653	171	1117	Exec., Legis., & Other Support	53035	70	446	Fabricated Metal Product Mfg
52402	1794	27931	Ambulatory Health Care Svcs	52654	84	367	Educational Services	53036	97	914	Machinery Manufacturing
52403	525	6056	Hospitals	52655	302	6078	Hospitals	53037	270	3844	Merch. Wholesalers,Nondur. Gds
52404	1572	28377	Educational Services	52656	100	697	Relig., Grant, Civic, Prof Org	53038	201	2394	Ambulatory Health Care Svcs
52405	471	5336	Food and Beverage Stores	52657	5	36	Educational Services	53039	192	2455	Nursing & Resid. Care Facilit.
52406	27	44	Administrative & Support Svcs	52658	34	265	Truck Transportation	53040	238	2633	Fabricated Metal Product Mfg
52407	1	2	Prof., Scientific, & Tech Svcs	52659	67	540	Educational Services	53042	243	2262	Machinery Manufacturing
52408	6	17	Prof., Scientific, & Tech Svcs	52660	14	48	Truck Transportation	53044	79	9849	Fabricated Metal Product Mfg
52409	5	15	Special Trade Contractors	52701	11	23	Truck Transportation	53045	1057	14171	Food Svcs & Drinking Places
52410	13	36	Merch. Wholesalers,Durable Gds	52720	23	152	Food Manufacturing	53046	92	864	Chemical Manufacturing
52411	97	1083	Insurance Carriers & Related	52721	29	142	Educational Services	53047	12	40	Credit Intermediation & Relatd
52498	3	11	Ambulatory Health Care Svcs	52722	1137	17313	Merch. Wholesalers,Durable Gds	53048	115	2732	Print'g & Related Supp't Act's
52499	3	450	Insurance Carriers & Related	52726	105	634	Truck Transportation	53049	73	426	Food Svcs & Drinking Places
52501	1244	17076	Food Manufacturing	52727	6	3	Postal Service	53050	246	4732	Fabricated Metal Product Mfg
52530	41	119	Social Assistance	52728	36	341	Merch. Wholesalers,Durable Gds	53051	1584	31394	General Merchandise Stores
52531	300	2226	Nursing & Resid. Care Facilit.	52729	38	115	Educational Services	53052	12	32	Wholesale Elec. Mrkts & Agents
52533	38	100	Truck Transportation	52730	133	7024	Relig., Grant, Civic, Prof Org	53056	29	256	Chemical Manufacturing
52534	9	26	Food and Beverage Stores	52731	25	341	Relig., Grant, Civic, Prof Org	53057	62	434	Educational Services
52535	35	92	Pipeline Transportation	52732	1163	15348	Ambulatory Health Care Svcs	53058	97	782	Plastics & Rubber Products Mfg
52536	21	140	Educational Services	52733	5	15	Primary Metal Manufacturing	53059	52	195	Educational Services
52537	344	2046	Hospitals	52737	7	7	Exec., Legis., & Other Support	53060	26	207	Special Trade Contractors

ZIP CODE	2004 Total Firms	2004 Total Employees	TOP INDUSTRY RANKED on 2004 EMPLOYMENT
53061	177	2715	Machinery Manufacturing
53063	53	466	Truck Transportation
53064	30	287	Exec., Legis., & Other Support
53065	64	320	Educational Services
53066	1144	14632	Motor Vehicle & Parts Dealers
53069	56	363	Food Svcs & Drinking Places
53070	142	1097	Special Trade Contractors
53072	992	25456	Print'g & Related Supp't Act's
53073	546	7101	Food Manufacturing
53074	507	5512	Food Svcs & Drinking Places
53075	128	1668	Print'g & Related Supp't Act's
53076	151	1750	Machinery Manufacturing
53078	39	175	Merch. Wholesalers,Durable Gds
53079	37	297	Food Manufacturing
53080	209	2790	Primary Metal Manufacturing
53081	1656	26806	Ambulatory Health Care Svcs
53082	6	52	Credit Intermediation & Relatd
53083	469	7402	Elect'l Eqpmt, App, & Comp Mfg
53085	332	3783	Bldg Matl & Garden Eqpmt Dlrs
53086	285	5301	Truck Transportation
53088	33	221	Special Trade Contractors
53089	444	5644	Print'g & Related Supp't Act's
53090	424	3096	Prof., Scientific, & Tech Svcs
53091	49	243	Merch. Wholesalers,Durable Gds
53092	1366	15918	Merch. Wholesalers,Durable Gds
53093	35	294	Food and Beverage Stores
53094	811	9794	Social Assistance
53095	1265	15828	Food Svcs & Drinking Places
53097	204	2722	Educational Services
53098	239	2694	Nursing & Resid. Care Facilit.
53099	6	30	Food Svcs & Drinking Places
53101	6	92	Educational Services
53102	1	2	Administrative & Support Svcs
53103	203	1179	Special Trade Contractors
53104	169	1601	Computer & Electronic Prod Mfg
53105	1048	10278	Ambulatory Health Care Svcs
53108	154	1325	Merch. Wholesalers,Durable Gds
53109	4	4	Real Estate
53110	531	8059	Transportation Equipment Mfg
53114	103	1372	Food Manufacturing
53115	722	6652	Food Svcs & Drinking Places
53118	162	1317	Nursing & Resid. Care Facilit.
53119	147	1027	Elect'l Eqpmt, App, & Comp Mfg
53120	323	2893	Primary Metal Manufacturing
53121	801	8356	Hospitals
53122	385	2630	Prof., Scientific, & Tech Svcs
53125	84	988	Accommodation
53126	251	2201	Food Manufacturing
53127	46	235	Food Svcs & Drinking Places
53128	183	773	Educational Services
53129	458	6936	General Merchandise Stores
53130	459	3712	Food Svcs & Drinking Places
53132	823	10217	Machinery Manufacturing
53137	40	257	Computer & Electronic Prod Mfg
53138	11	42	Fabricated Metal Product Mfg
53139	75	335	Educational Services
53140	948	11647	Relig., Grant, Civic, Prof Org
53141	18	64	Social Assistance
53142	881	10438	Food Svcs & Drinking Places
53143	554	6084	Hospitals
53144	696	12596	Machinery Manufacturing
53146	222	1910	Educational Services
53147	970	9413	Accommodation
53148	14	38	Food Svcs & Drinking Places
53149	540	4869	Educational Services
53150	678	5550	Educational Services
53151	1153	20362	Prof., Scientific, & Tech Svcs
53152	8	54	Construction of Buildings
53153	95	760	Elect'l Eqpmt, App, & Comp Mfg
53154	801	15790	Transportation Equipment Mfg
53156	121	1128	Chemical Manufacturing
53157	21	77	Justice, Pubic Order/Safety
53158	321	6064	Fabricated Metal Product Mfg
53159	6	10	Food Svcs & Drinking Places
53167	33	238	Transportation Equipment Mfg
53168	223	1420	Educational Services
53170	64	496	Merch. Wholesalers,Nondur. Gds
53171	27	56	Exec., Legis., & Other Support
53172	431	4575	Machinery Manufacturing
53176	3	3	Amusement, Gambling,& Recreat.
53177	350	7193	Merch. Wholesalers,Durable Gds
53178	89	388	Relig., Grant, Civic, Prof Org
53179	90	410	Wood Product Manufacturing
53181	220	1283	Food Svcs & Drinking Places
53182	309	2760	Admin. Human Resource Programs
53183	125	734	Educational Services
53184	218	2308	Transportation Equipment Mfg
53185	494	3560	Educational Services
53186	1902	26235	Prof., Scientific, & Tech Svcs
53187	15	101	Merch. Wholesalers,Nondur. Gds

ZIP CODE	2004 Total Firms	2004 Total Employees	TOP INDUSTRY RANKED on 2004 EMPLOYMENT
53188	1155	22831	Hospitals
53189	592	5584	Elect'l Eqpmt, App, & Comp Mfg
53190	532	5889	Educational Services
53191	131	712	Educational Services
53192	46	670	Educational Services
53194	2	5	Ambulatory Health Care Svcs
53195	16	72	Merch. Wholesalers,Durable Gds
53201	31	270	Administrative & Support Svcs
53202	2558	44859	Prof., Scientific, & Tech Svcs
53203	682	18286	Insurance Carriers & Related
53204	1065	15235	Merch. Wholesalers,Durable Gds
53205	279	3087	Educational Services
53206	508	2308	Educational Services
53207	1106	20682	Support Act. for Transport.
53208	878	11100	Beverage & Tobacco Product Mfg
53209	1437	22278	Ambulatory Health Care Svcs
53210	730	6472	Hospitals
53211	991	21719	Hospitals
53212	1106	13380	Social Assistance
53213	896	8200	Educational Services
53214	1430	23886	Machinery Manufacturing
53215	1226	19670	Ambulatory Health Care Svcs
53216	742	8869	Transportation Equipment Mfg
53217	1319	13706	Educational Services
53218	742	6913	Nat'l Security & Int'l Affairs
53219	746	7367	Prof., Scientific, & Tech Svcs
53220	712	7712	Food Svcs & Drinking Places
53221	822	10427	Food Svcs & Drinking Places
53222	775	14348	General Merchandise Stores
53223	919	16978	Miscellaneous Manufacturing
53224	458	13054	Isps, Web Search Portals
53225	535	9475	Nursing & Resid. Care Facilit.
53226	1762	32424	Hospitals
53227	1018	14405	Ambulatory Health Care Svcs
53228	349	3492	Social Assistance
53233	658	21692	Educational Services
53234	8	6	Real Estate
53235	249	3452	Miscellaneous Manufacturing
53237	12	8	Perform'g Arts, Spec. Sports
53263	1	20	General Merchandise Stores
53295	10	2619	Hospitals
53401	5	7	Motor Vehicle & Parts Dealers
53402	737	5356	Educational Services
53403	1242	17448	Chemical Manufacturing
53404	487	7761	Administrative & Support Svcs
53405	607	8477	Educational Services
53406	922	13967	Food Svcs & Drinking Places
53408	12	22	Special Trade Contractors
53501	12	17	Food Svcs & Drinking Places
53502	73	456	Fabricated Metal Product Mfg
53503	59	244	Special Trade Contractors
53504	66	248	Educational Services
53505	10	26	Amusement, Gambling,& Recreat.
53506	27	30	Food Svcs & Drinking Places
53507	55	348	Educational Services
53508	147	1072	Educational Services
53510	58	329	Educational Services
53511	1430	15323	Educational Services
53512	7	37	Administrative & Support Svcs
53515	89	636	Clothing & Cloth'g Acc. Stores
53516	72	302	Educational Services
53517	60	293	Food Manufacturing
53518	69	166	Telecommunications
53520	238	1951	Transportation Equipment Mfg
53521	84	267	Educational Services
53522	41	336	Primary Metal Manufacturing
53523	214	1181	Educational Services
53525	140	1209	Educational Services
53526	35	159	Merch. Wholesalers,Durable Gds
53527	251	2218	Merch. Wholesalers,Nondur. Gds
53528	184	2051	Nonstore Retailers
53529	59	281	Plastics & Rubber Products Mfg
53530	239	1816	Educational Services
53531	113	1468	Fabricated Metal Product Mfg
53532	393	4482	Prof., Scientific, & Tech Svcs
53533	389	3573	Ambulatory Health Care Svcs
53534	307	2544	Educational Services
53535	4	4	Credit Intermediation & Relatd
53536	246	2517	Transportation Equipment Mfg
53537	40	297	Truck Transportation
53538	729	10267	Food Manufacturing
53540	6	20	Bldg Matl & Garden Eqpmt Dlrs
53541	25	72	Educational Services
53542	4	18	Food Svcs & Drinking Places
53543	74	425	Construction of Buildings
53544	34	128	Educational Services
53545	1376	16882	Food Svcs & Drinking Places
53546	797	23292	Transportation Equipment Mfg
53547	13	47	Exec., Legis., & Other Support
53548	629	9132	Ambulatory Health Care Svcs

ZIP CODE	2004 Total Firms	2004 Total Employees	TOP INDUSTRY RANKED on 2004 EMPLOYMENT
53549	420	6488	Food Manufacturing
53550	44	246	Educational Services
53551	289	2901	Elect'l Eqpmt, App, & Comp Mfg
53553	15	30	Food and Beverage Stores
53554	43	335	Educational Services
53555	267	1851	Educational Services
53556	51	170	Truck Transportation
53557	20	143	Truck Transportation
53558	313	2398	Educational Services
53559	137	742	Educational Services
53560	136	1870	Educational Services
53561	42	226	Accommodation
53562	1026	11001	Prof., Scientific, & Tech Svcs
53563	343	3041	Truck Transportation
53565	206	1500	Social Assistance
53566	839	10556	Nonstore Retailers
53569	43	160	Food Svcs & Drinking Places
53570	97	554	Merch. Wholesalers,Nondur. Gds
53571	8	22	Food Svcs & Drinking Places
53572	351	2273	Food and Beverage Stores
53573	102	653	Machinery Manufacturing
53574	183	1178	Food Svcs & Drinking Places
53575	383	2879	Educational Services
53576	57	368	Educational Services
53577	56	369	Construction of Buildings
53578	204	2052	Hospitals
53579	61	179	Warehousing and Storage
53580	13	52	Construction of Buildings
53581	557	5423	Elect'l Eqpmt, App, & Comp Mfg
53582	42	146	Food Svcs & Drinking Places
53583	230	2405	Motor Vehicle & Parts Dealers
53584	5	4	Heavy & Civil Eng. Construct'N
53585	74	376	Wood Product Manufacturing
53586	82	422	Educational Services
53587	62	292	Educational Services
53588	239	2626	Nonmetallic Mineral Prod. Mfg
53589	619	6481	Transportation Equipment Mfg
53590	874	9212	Food Svcs & Drinking Places
53593	594	4504	Nursing & Resid. Care Facilit.
53594	153	2159	Transportation Equipment Mfg
53595	1	4000	Clothing & Cloth'g Acc. Stores
53597	534	5845	Prof., Scientific, & Tech Svcs
53598	81	2315	Health & Personal Care Stores
53599	6	12	Health & Personal Care Stores
53701	13	36	Relig., Grant, Civic, Prof Org
53702	197	16610	Exec., Legis., & Other Support
53703	2116	26507	Prof., Scientific, & Tech Svcs
53704	1760	33004	Merch. Wholesalers,Nondur. Gds
53705	862	12943	Insurance Carriers & Related
53706	129	12665	Educational Services
53707	12	100	Admin. Human Resource Programs
53708	12	17	Exec., Legis., & Other Support
53711	1223	14738	Prof., Scientific, & Tech Svcs
53713	1063	26716	Insurance Carriers & Related
53714	449	6467	Postal Service
53715	476	10903	Hospitals
53716	988	9217	Educational Services
53717	426	9540	Prof., Scientific, & Tech Svcs
53718	513	10073	Admin. of Economic Programs
53719	1429	15444	Prof., Scientific, & Tech Svcs
53725	2	3	Special Trade Contractors
53726	106	1842	Educational Services
53744	19	92	Food Svcs & Drinking Places
53778	1	325	Nonstore Retailers
53783	1	2000	Prof., Scientific, & Tech Svcs
53784	3	360	Isps, Web Search Portals
53788	1	340	Utilities
53792	64	11160	Ambulatory Health Care Svcs
53801	27	68	Accommodation
53802	12	35	Food Manufacturing
53803	43	179	Educational Services
53804	68	324	Merch. Wholesalers,Nondur. Gds
53805	242	2016	Elect'l Eqpmt, App, & Comp Mfg
53806	95	497	Support Act. for Transport.
53807	165	1023	Nursing & Resid. Care Facilit.
53808	58	703	Nonstore Retailers
53809	190	1936	Elect'l Eqpmt, App, & Comp Mfg
53810	14	68	Justice, Pubic Order/Safety
53811	92	543	Educational Services
53812	40	219	Repair and Maintenance
53813	374	3089	Nursing & Resid. Care Facilit.
53816	25	92	Justice, Pubic Order/Safety
53817	14	236	Educational Services
53818	529	5639	Educational Services
53820	90	324	Educational Services
53821	486	6345	Prof., Scientific, & Tech Svcs
53824	1	150	Relig., Grant, Civic, Prof Org
53825	13	23	Bldg Matl & Garden Eqpmt Dlrs
53826	41	220	Educational Services
53827	7	11	Food Svcs & Drinking Places

BUSINESS DATA

ZIP CODE	2004 Total Firms	2004 Total Employ-ees	TOP INDUSTRY RANKED on 2004 EMPLOYMENT	ZIP CODE	2004 Total Firms	2004 Total Employ-ees	TOP INDUSTRY RANKED on 2004 EMPLOYMENT	ZIP CODE	2004 Total Firms	2004 Total Employ-ees	TOP INDUSTRY RANKED on 2004 EMPLOYMENT
53901	713	9307	Merch. Wholesalers,Durable Gds	54123	24	106	Special Trade Contractors	54409	696	6480	Food Svcs & Drinking Places
53910	148	1344	Paper Manufacturing	54124	117	1236	Educational Services	54410	37	401	Truck Transportation
53911	53	348	Prof., Scientific, & Tech Svcs	54125	35	381	Forestry and Logging	54411	125	693	Educational Services
53913	885	11781	Plastics & Rubber Products Mfg	54126	116	424	Merch. Wholesalers,Durable Gds	54412	61	471	Educational Services
53916	903	10744	Social Assistance	54127	4	7	Special Trade Contractors	54413	12	98	Merch. Wholesalers,Nondur. Gds
53919	59	276	Educational Services	54128	59	298	Food Svcs & Drinking Places	54414	85	425	Special Trade Contractors
53920	20	89	Construction of Buildings	54129	113	550	Food Manufacturing	54415	7	534	Truck Transportation
53922	29	139	Truck Transportation	54130	727	8832	Paper Manufacturing	54416	59	1037	Amusement, Gambling,& Recreat.
53923	60	799	Food Manufacturing	54131	3	79	Educational Services	54417	12	878	Paper Manufacturing
53924	40	253	Educational Services	54135	114	2571	Exec., Legis., & Other Support	54418	24	147	Wood Product Manufacturing
53925	326	2990	Food Manufacturing	54136	200	3579	Paper Manufacturing	54420	32	145	Merch. Wholesalers,Nondur. Gds
53926	27	123	Construction of Buildings	54137	27	109	Educational Services	54421	107	1223	Educational Services
53927	5	7	Accommodation	54138	101	508	Furniture & Related Prod. Mfg	54422	34	314	Food Manufacturing
53928	9	7	Merch. Wholesalers,Nondur. Gds	54139	98	439	Educational Services	54423	66	177	Support Activities: Agr./For.
53929	110	1068	Educational Services	54140	260	4299	Merch. Wholesalers,Nondur. Gds	54424	45	163	Administrative & Support Svcs
53930	40	323	Construction of Buildings	54141	65	215	Food Svcs & Drinking Places	54425	79	1014	Wood Product Manufacturing
53931	12	387	Food Manufacturing	54143	758	10774	Transportation Equipment Mfg	54426	95	670	Educational Services
53932	71	1161	Truck Transportation	54149	61	264	Food Svcs & Drinking Places	54427	31	53	Food Svcs & Drinking Places
53933	126	1350	Motor Vehicle & Parts Dealers	54150	15	467	Wood Product Manufacturing	54428	62	404	Educational Services
53934	180	1313	Hospitals	54151	162	1039	Educational Services	54429	21	43	Educational Services
53935	21	99	Truck Transportation	54152	14	75	Paper Manufacturing	54430	4	44	Accommodation
53936	29	99	Credit Intermediation & Relatd	54153	314	2891	Repair and Maintenance	54433	74	471	Educational Services
53937	29	188	Truck Transportation	54154	220	2032	Hospitals	54434	6	38	Justice, Pubic Order/Safety
53939	16	43	Construction of Buildings	54155	165	1418	Exec., Legis., & Other Support	54435	51	132	Truck Transportation
53940	89	1983	Accommodation	54156	66	480	Bldg Matl & Garden Eqpmt Dlrs	54436	52	306	Educational Services
53941	95	320	Bldg Matl & Garden Eqpmt Dlrs	54157	214	2680	Nursing & Resid. Care Facilit.	54437	103	987	Food Manufacturing
53942	10	21	Merch. Wholesalers,Nondur. Gds	54159	27	112	Wood Product Manufacturing	54439	2	1	Relig., Grant, Civic, Prof Org
53943	33	119	Special Trade Contractors	54160	12	58	Machinery Manufacturing	54440	84	398	Special Trade Contractors
53944	63	287	Wood Product Manufacturing	54161	77	523	Machinery Manufacturing	54441	16	78	Wood Product Manufacturing
53946	153	1095	Nursing & Resid. Care Facilit.	54162	290	2867	Transportation Equipment Mfg	54442	25	92	Relig., Grant, Civic, Prof Org
53947	13	29	Food Svcs & Drinking Places	54165	222	2091	Food Svcs & Drinking Places	54443	56	265	Truck Transportation
53948	369	3987	Ambulatory Health Care Svcs	54166	846	8032	Food Svcs & Drinking Places	54446	96	694	Educational Services
53949	241	1549	Wood Product Manufacturing	54169	75	411	Food Svcs & Drinking Places	54447	20	58	Justice, Pubic Order/Safety
53950	156	1322	Fabricated Metal Product Mfg	54170	66	330	Educational Services	54448	149	1892	Food Manufacturing
53951	58	268	Sportg Gds,Hobby,Book, & Music	54171	55	155	Educational Services	54449	1094	23914	Ambulatory Health Care Svcs
53952	118	732	Justice, Pubic Order/Safety	54173	122	484	Special Trade Contractors	54450	20	214	Wood Product Manufacturing
53953	13	23	Merch. Wholesalers,Durable Gds	54174	109	770	Educational Services	54451	535	6808	Merch. Wholesalers,Nondur. Gds
53954	185	1132	Computer & Electronic Prod Mfg	54175	48	155	Food Svcs & Drinking Places	54452	677	9383	Fabricated Metal Product Mfg
53955	186	1038	Food Svcs & Drinking Places	54177	121	823	Educational Services	54454	32	210	Food and Beverage Stores
53956	139	1137	Machinery Manufacturing	54180	83	472	Educational Services	54455	557	6899	Bldg Matl & Garden Eqpmt Dlrs
53958	1	0	Nonstore Retailers	54182	3	43	Merch. Wholesalers,Nondur. Gds	54456	330	3310	Exec., Legis., & Other Support
53959	489	6680	Primary Metal Manufacturing	54201	252	2166	Wood Product Manufacturing	54457	292	1931	Amusement, Gambling,& Recreat.
53960	105	423	Educational Services	54202	113	519	Accommodation	54458	12	38	Accommodation
53961	20	45	Merch. Wholesalers,Durable Gds	54204	68	409	Educational Services	54459	38	166	Wood Product Manufacturing
53962	20	349	Relig., Grant, Civic, Prof Org	54205	81	353	Food Svcs & Drinking Places	54460	79	952	Nursing & Resid. Care Facilit.
53963	401	5035	Justice, Pubic Order/Safety	54207	12	40	Amusement, Gambling,& Recreat.	54462	9	34	Food Svcs & Drinking Places
53964	144	1648	Food Manufacturing	54208	201	1737	Crop Production	54463	41	72	Accommodation
53965	699	8793	Accommodation	54209	152	1068	Accommodation	54464	5	12	Food Svcs & Drinking Places
53968	66	241	Educational Services	54210	76	360	Food Svcs & Drinking Places	54465	37	69	Food Svcs & Drinking Places
53969	19	291	Nursing & Resid. Care Facilit.	54211	98	337	Accommodation	54466	101	567	Educational Services
54001	380	3562	Heavy & Civil Eng. Construct'N	54212	183	1214	Food Svcs & Drinking Places	54467	450	5510	Food Manufacturing
54002	294	3168	Bldg Matl & Garden Eqpmt Dlrs	54213	34	134	Food Svcs & Drinking Places	54469	56	1434	Paper Manufacturing
54003	21	110	Print'g & Related Supp't Act's	54214	17	82	Construction of Buildings	54470	76	527	Nursing & Resid. Care Facilit.
54004	61	293	Educational Services	54215	8	51	Food Svcs & Drinking Places	54471	39	176	Educational Services
54005	151	1009	Educational Services	54216	260	1826	Fabricated Metal Product Mfg	54473	88	442	Educational Services
54006	39	120	Justice, Pubic Order/Safety	54217	216	1762	Construction of Buildings	54474	141	3060	Paper Manufacturing
54007	34	73	Bldg Matl & Garden Eqpmt Dlrs	54220	1635	21766	Hospitals	54475	53	295	Justice, Pubic Order/Safety
54009	84	977	Accommodation	54221	6	15	Special Trade Contractors	54476	671	9569	Machinery Manufacturing
54010	7	24	Food Svcs & Drinking Places	54226	3	8	Construction of Buildings	54479	119	1597	Food Manufacturing
54011	273	2355	Exec., Legis., & Other Support	54227	58	251	Food Svcs & Drinking Places	54480	46	219	Relig., Grant, Civic, Prof Org
54013	113	846	Educational Services	54228	98	804	Accommodation	54481	1576	24631	Insurance Carriers & Related
54014	66	585	Fabricated Metal Product Mfg	54229	116	519	Miscellaneous Manufacturing	54484	129	1530	Food Svcs & Drinking Places
54015	80	843	Educational Services	54230	117	739	Merch. Wholesalers,Nondur. Gds	54485	20	48	Accommodation
54016	1088	9405	Food Svcs & Drinking Places	54232	44	430	Machinery Manufacturing	54486	82	435	Educational Services
54017	609	5738	Machinery Manufacturing	54234	259	1566	Food Svcs & Drinking Places	54487	519	3955	Paper Manufacturing
54020	256	2877	Transportation Equipment Mfg	54235	1089	10187	Food Svcs & Drinking Places	54488	35	122	Crop Production
54021	194	1334	Food Svcs & Drinking Places	54240	10	15	Food Svcs & Drinking Places	54489	58	574	Merch. Wholesalers,Durable Gds
54022	645	5969	Educational Services	54241	438	5667	Miscellaneous Manufacturing	54490	25	160	Accommodation
54023	93	664	Merch. Wholesalers,Durable Gds	54245	94	996	Educational Services	54491	60	281	Accommodation
54024	274	2855	Hospitals	54246	74	386	Accommodation	54492	1	300	Sportg Gds,Hobby,Book, & Music
54025	222	1648	Food Svcs & Drinking Places	54247	47	159	Food Svcs & Drinking Places	54493	21	78	Food Manufacturing
54026	67	100	Food Svcs & Drinking Places	54301	1302	23670	Hospitals	54494	1205	11867	Educational Services
54027	32	317	Food Manufacturing	54302	1033	13638	Paper Manufacturing	54495	387	5998	Paper Manufacturing
54028	110	994	Elect'l Eqpmt, App, & Comp Mfg	54303	1311	23265	Educational Services	54498	60	148	Merch. Wholesalers,Durable Gds
54082	33	140	Special Trade Contractors	54304	1709	30211	Paper Manufacturing	54499	156	1726	Educational Services
54101	84	470	Food Svcs & Drinking Places	54305	9	20	Perform'g Arts, Spec. Sports	54501	1233	12783	Nursing & Resid. Care Facilit.
54102	30	77	Food Svcs & Drinking Places	54306	2	0	Isps, Web Search Portals	54511	61	144	Wood Product Manufacturing
54103	18	41	General Merchandise Stores	54307	20	51	Special Trade Contractors	54512	136	544	Accommodation
54104	37	115	Relig., Grant, Civic, Prof Org	54308	5	9	Construction of Buildings	54513	9	49	Forestry and Logging
54106	119	489	Special Trade Contractors	54311	796	12765	Hospitals	54514	65	363	Wood Product Manufacturing
54107	160	896	Educational Services	54313	875	13668	Amusement, Gambling,& Recreat.	54515	23	64	Educational Services
54110	161	3182	Primary Metal Manufacturing	54324	4	16	Administrative & Support Svcs	54517	18	113	Special Trade Contractors
54111	63	219	Food Svcs & Drinking Places	54344	1	0	Funds, Trusts, & Other Finance	54519	79	160	Construction of Buildings
54112	98	738	Educational Services	54401	1385	33876	Insurance Carriers & Related	54520	305	1622	Exec., Legis., & Other Support
54113	46	1129	Paper Manufacturing	54402	17	97	Merch. Wholesalers,Nondur. Gds	54521	700	4159	Food and Beverage Stores
54114	303	1854	Educational Services	54403	1045	12964	Nursing & Resid. Care Facilit.	54524	25	152	Motor Vehicle & Parts Dealers
54115	1207	15111	Special Trade Contractors	54405	162	1695	Food Svcs & Drinking Places	54525	6	10	Administrative & Support Svcs
54119	10	51	Food Svcs & Drinking Places	54406	142	807	Educational Services	54526	31	125	Print'g & Related Supp't Act's
54120	9	39	Justice, Pubic Order/Safety	54407	43	277	Print'g & Related Supp't Act's	54527	39	245	Educational Services
54121	193	1213	Educational Services	54408	37	105	Special Trade Contractors	54529	43	119	Amusement, Gambling,& Recreat.

ZIP CODE	2004 Total Firms	2004 Total Employees	TOP INDUSTRY RANKED on 2004 EMPLOYMENT	ZIP CODE	2004 Total Firms	2004 Total Employees	TOP INDUSTRY RANKED on 2004 EMPLOYMENT	ZIP CODE	2004 Total Firms	2004 Total Employees	TOP INDUSTRY RANKED on 2004 EMPLOYMENT
54530	29	729	Bldg Matl & Garden Eqpmt Dlrs	54670	53	266	Truck Transportation	54848	349	4282	Fabricated Metal Product Mfg
54531	85	274	Food Svcs & Drinking Places	54701	1986	26570	Food Svcs & Drinking Places	54849	62	209	Other Information Services
54532	2	1	Accommodation	54702	18	50	Merch. Wholesalers,Durable Gds	54850	80	223	Accommodation
54534	208	1901	Food Svcs & Drinking Places	54703	1289	29536	Ambulatory Health Care Svcs	54853	189	1222	Wood Product Manufacturing
54536	5	81	Construction of Buildings	54720	264	2251	Prof., Scientific, & Tech Svcs	54854	35	401	Educational Services
54537	16	44	Justice, Pubic Order/Safety	54721	35	114	Educational Services	54855	26	89	Special Trade Contractors
54538	103	739	Accommodation	54722	108	799	Food Manufacturing	54856	56	183	Accommodation
54539	77	144	Justice, Pubic Order/Safety	54723	50	133	Bldg Matl & Garden Eqpmt Dlrs	54857	13	42	Food Svcs & Drinking Places
54540	130	727	Wood Product Manufacturing	54724	272	1993	Ambulatory Health Care Svcs	54858	84	394	Food and Beverage Stores
54541	77	849	Educational Services	54725	80	558	Educational Services	54859	124	1153	Food Manufacturing
54542	29	118	Wood Product Manufacturing	54726	50	169	Educational Services	54861	46	632	Accommodation
54543	7	28	Accommodation	54727	141	1171	Educational Services	54862	13	14	Repair and Maintenance
54545	129	496	Accommodation	54728	285	1922	Food and Beverage Stores	54864	42	312	Merch. Wholesalers,Nondur. Gds
54546	66	753	Wood Product Manufacturing	54729	1213	19737	Electronics & Appliance Stores	54865	41	258	Educational Services
54547	161	611	Wood Product Manufacturing	54730	129	708	Educational Services	54867	36	126	Wood Product Manufacturing
54548	624	3960	Food Svcs & Drinking Places	54731	22	51	Food and Beverage Stores	54868	863	9943	Fabricated Metal Product Mfg
54550	18	76	Accommodation	54732	125	713	Educational Services	54870	57	137	Accommodation
54552	299	2972	Paper Manufacturing	54733	50	268	Telecommunications	54871	178	1659	Exec., Legis., & Other Support
54554	77	401	Nursing & Resid. Care Facilit.	54734	19	89	Merch. Wholesalers,Durable Gds	54872	252	1684	Educational Services
54555	393	3424	Machinery Manufacturing	54735	20	156	Food Svcs & Drinking Places	54873	180	720	Educational Services
54556	87	878	Machinery Manufacturing	54736	257	1917	Repair and Maintenance	54874	72	280	Nursing & Resid. Care Facilit.
54557	82	210	Food Svcs & Drinking Places	54737	24	129	Exec., Legis., & Other Support	54875	31	88	Wood Product Manufacturing
54558	164	735	Food Svcs & Drinking Places	54738	93	370	Electronics & Appliance Stores	54876	90	224	Food Svcs & Drinking Places
54559	23	28	Food Svcs & Drinking Places	54739	96	489	Educational Services	54880	1395	15445	Food Svcs & Drinking Places
54560	54	209	Accommodation	54740	67	577	Educational Services	54888	82	266	Food Svcs & Drinking Places
54561	6	10	Accommodation	54741	30	224	Nursing & Resid. Care Facilit.	54889	121	2038	Amusement, Gambling,& Recreat.
54562	177	845	Accommodation	54742	126	686	Special Trade Contractors	54890	4	3	Food Svcs & Drinking Places
54563	17	94	Educational Services	54743	8	72	Educational Services	54891	180	876	Exec., Legis., & Other Support
54564	15	73	Justice, Pubic Order/Safety	54745	74	446	Food Svcs & Drinking Places	54893	187	1256	Amusement, Gambling,& Recreat.
54565	9	149	Accommodation	54746	12	32	Animal Production	54895	56	228	Waste Managmt & Remediat'n Svc
54566	77	635	Amusement, Gambling,& Recreat.	54747	122	785	Educational Services	54896	123	476	Educational Services
54568	356	2926	Prof., Scientific, & Tech Svcs	54748	26	239	Food Manufacturing	54901	1243	17781	Educational Services
54601	1922	44563	Prof., Scientific, & Tech Svcs	54749	30	154	Special Trade Contractors	54902	889	14942	Relig., Grant, Civic, Prof Org
54602	21	68	Social Assistance	54750	35	159	Nonmetallic Mineral Prod. Mfg	54903	18	123	Miscellaneous Manufacturing
54603	752	10450	Food Svcs & Drinking Places	54751	915	13264	Educational Services	54904	586	8479	Hospitals
54610	137	764	Utilities	54754	55	321	Food Svcs & Drinking Places	54909	78	399	Educational Services
54611	46	206	Food Manufacturing	54755	293	1796	Truck Transportation	54911	1465	22686	Insurance Carriers & Related
54612	179	4565	Furniture & Related Prod. Mfg	54756	42	156	Food Svcs & Drinking Places	54912	20	91	Computer & Electronic Prod Mfg
54613	49	119	Educational Services	54757	122	389	Educational Services	54913	732	10117	General Merchandise Stores
54614	85	781	Wood Product Manufacturing	54758	174	1699	Food Svcs & Drinking Places	54914	1586	26398	Merch. Wholesalers,Durable Gds
54615	499	5142	Exec., Legis., & Other Support	54759	71	391	Educational Services	54915	811	10194	Hospitals
54616	86	761	Educational Services	54760	32	159	Nursing & Resid. Care Facilit.	54919	2	1924	Insurance Carriers & Related
54618	81	475	Nat'l Security & Int'l Affairs	54761	52	259	Nursing & Resid. Care Facilit.	54921	52	281	Merch. Wholesalers,Nondur. Gds
54619	109	529	Educational Services	54762	60	384	Educational Services	54922	41	188	Justice, Pubic Order/Safety
54620	5	3	Merch. Wholesalers,Durable Gds	54763	59	348	Merch. Wholesalers,Durable Gds	54923	397	4268	Hospitals
54621	36	152	Merch. Wholesalers,Nondur. Gds	54764	2	0	Food and Beverage Stores	54926	5	8	Food Svcs & Drinking Places
54622	97	413	Food Manufacturing	54765	16	48	Motor Vehicle & Parts Dealers	54927	4	26	Food Svcs & Drinking Places
54623	80	317	Food Svcs & Drinking Places	54766	51	156	Merch. Wholesalers,Durable Gds	54928	10	20	Relig., Grant, Civic, Prof Org
54624	84	450	Educational Services	54767	111	790	Educational Services	54929	385	3456	Transportation Equipment Mfg
54625	12	85	Merch. Wholesalers,Nondur. Gds	54768	163	1062	Hospitals	54930	100	461	Paper Manufacturing
54626	30	59	Exec., Legis., & Other Support	54769	21	79	Accommodation	54931	31	173	Merch. Wholesalers,Durable Gds
54627	63	373	Miscellaneous Manufacturing	54770	71	370	Ambulatory Health Care Svcs	54932	32	100	Animal Production
54628	37	119	Accommodation	54771	188	1216	Educational Services	54933	21	100	Furniture & Related Prod. Mfg
54629	91	744	Educational Services	54772	32	86	Construction of Buildings	54934	5	4	Food Svcs & Drinking Places
54630	140	1308	Machinery Manufacturing	54773	142	1631	Furniture & Related Prod. Mfg	54935	1903	28246	Machinery Manufacturing
54631	82	400	Crop Production	54801	468	2727	Hospitals	54936	7	8	Prof., Scientific, & Tech Svcs
54632	51	216	Utilities	54805	60	442	Food Manufacturing	54937	435	7411	Unclassified Establishments
54634	160	1070	Relig., Grant, Civic, Prof Org	54806	661	6623	Educational Services	54940	138	541	Food Svcs & Drinking Places
54635	79	312	Merch. Wholesalers,Nondur. Gds	54810	158	763	Furniture & Related Prod. Mfg	54941	221	1836	Accommodation
54636	291	2392	Educational Services	54812	269	2206	Hospitals	54942	215	2224	Special Trade Contractors
54637	11	23	Nursing & Resid. Care Facilit.	54813	31	120	Fabricated Metal Product Mfg	54943	66	194	Crop Production
54638	55	148	Educational Services	54814	224	1480	Exec., Legis., & Other Support	54944	250	1489	Educational Services
54639	112	532	Merch. Wholesalers,Nondur. Gds	54816	10	12	Rental and Leasing Services	54945	144	876	Educational Services
54640	1	1	Accommodation	54817	112	747	Wood Product Manufacturing	54946	7	1611	Hospitals
54641	5	6	Merch. Wholesalers,Nondur. Gds	54818	5	15	Crop Production	54947	52	268	Merch. Wholesalers,Nondur. Gds
54642	54	283	Educational Services	54819	110	672	Educational Services	54948	10	21	Special Trade Contractors
54643	8	32	Prof., Scientific, & Tech Svcs	54820	53	207	Exec., Legis., & Other Support	54949	157	1285	Merch. Wholesalers,Nondur. Gds
54644	33	127	Accommodation	54821	172	729	Accommodation	54950	138	1221	Wood Product Manufacturing
54645	6	12	Food and Beverage Stores	54822	167	768	Educational Services	54952	733	14515	Ambulatory Health Care Svcs
54646	131	1180	Miscellaneous Manufacturing	54824	61	301	Merch. Wholesalers,Durable Gds	54956	1402	28124	Paper Manufacturing
54648	55	225	Merch. Wholesalers,Nondur. Gds	54826	24	90	Food and Beverage Stores	54957	9	26	Exec., Legis., & Other Support
54649	15	118	Justice, Pubic Order/Safety	54827	21	81	Food Svcs & Drinking Places	54960	86	225	Food Svcs & Drinking Places
54650	752	9881	Food Svcs & Drinking Places	54828	20	48	Food Svcs & Drinking Places	54961	500	6996	Food Manufacturing
54651	56	361	Educational Services	54829	253	2168	Food Manufacturing	54962	40	57	Merch. Wholesalers,Durable Gds
54652	36	110	Food Svcs & Drinking Places	54830	122	694	Amusement, Gambling,& Recreat.	54963	186	1380	Educational Services
54653	16	128	Special Trade Contractors	54832	52	185	Educational Services	54964	26	70	Construction of Buildings
54654	17	117	Educational Services	54834	4	4	Accommodation	54965	17	29	Educational Services
54655	80	501	Educational Services	54835	40	81	Special Trade Contractors	54966	137	1000	Crop Production
54656	692	6125	Exec., Legis., & Other Support	54836	21	29	Special Trade Contractors	54967	34	86	Educational Services
54657	8	10	Food Svcs & Drinking Places	54837	197	1254	Nursing & Resid. Care Facilit.	54968	163	824	Construction of Buildings
54658	92	277	Food Svcs & Drinking Places	54838	58	158	Justice, Pubic Order/Safety	54969	17	87	Educational Services
54659	40	199	Nonmetallic Mineral Prod. Mfg	54839	22	31	Exec., Legis., & Other Support	54970	86	482	Merch. Wholesalers,Durable Gds
54660	630	8531	Hospitals	54840	202	1934	Machinery Manufacturing	54971	504	7923	Elect'l Eqpmt, App, & Comp Mfg
54661	90	488	Food Svcs & Drinking Places	54841	20	115	Accommodation	54974	48	439	Administrative & Support Svcs
54662	3	6	Real Estate	54842	13	43	Justice, Pubic Order/Safety	54975	1	1	Relig., Grant, Civic, Prof Org
54664	83	505	Merch. Wholesalers,Durable Gds	54843	942	6725	Accommodation	54976	6	4	Furniture & Related Prod. Mfg
54665	498	4496	General Merchandise Stores	54844	24	48	Bldg Matl & Garden Eqpmt Dlrs	54977	38	140	Truck Transportation
54666	80	469	Accommodation	54845	13	61	Construction of Buildings	54978	13	37	Bldg Matl & Garden Eqpmt Dlrs
54667	201	1363	Educational Services	54846	7	36	Special Trade Contractors	54979	54	194	Food Svcs & Drinking Places
54669	260	2756	Nursing & Resid. Care Facilit.	54847	193	694	Machinery Manufacturing	54980	6	3	Food Svcs & Drinking Places

ZIP CODE	2004 Total Firms	2004 Total Employees	TOP INDUSTRY RANKED on 2004 EMPLOYMENT	ZIP CODE	2004 Total Firms	2004 Total Employees	TOP INDUSTRY RANKED on 2004 EMPLOYMENT	ZIP CODE	2004 Total Firms	2004 Total Employees	TOP INDUSTRY RANKED on 2004 EMPLOYMENT
54981	762	8113	Primary Metal Manufacturing	55113	2062	35667	Food Svcs & Drinking Places	55369	1360	17404	Food Svcs & Drinking Places
54982	337	2806	Social Assistance	55114	693	10357	Prof., Scientific, & Tech Svcs	55370	29	245	Furniture & Related Prod. Mfg
54983	187	1500	Plastics & Rubber Products Mfg	55115	146	1182	Educational Services	55371	451	5598	Furniture & Related Prod. Mfg
54984	134	969	Accommodation	55116	637	9010	Transportation Equipment Mfg	55372	739	8435	Amusement, Gambling,& Recreat.
54985	15	1452	Hospitals	55117	958	13116	Special Trade Contractors	55373	171	1408	Educational Services
54986	157	1481	Educational Services	55118	826	10124	Food Svcs & Drinking Places	55374	474	6112	Food Svcs & Drinking Places
54990	1	600	Prof., Scientific, & Tech Svcs	55119	509	5679	Educational Services	55375	90	593	Educational Services
55001	109	475	Heavy & Civil Eng. Construct'N	55120	313	6872	Insurance Carriers & Related	55376	289	2162	Merch. Wholesalers,Nondur. Gds
55003	70	6000	Fabricated Metal Product Mfg	55121	791	22181	Prof., Scientific, & Tech Svcs	55377	6	39	Merch. Wholesalers,Nondur. Gds
55005	76	394	Fabricated Metal Product Mfg	55122	858	11348	Insurance Carriers & Related	55378	563	5776	Merch. Wholesalers,Durable Gds
55006	108	798	Educational Services	55123	365	15418	Prof., Scientific, & Tech Svcs	55379	997	14535	Merch. Wholesalers,Durable Gds
55007	34	61	Food and Beverage Stores	55124	1093	12065	Food Svcs & Drinking Places	55380	3	6	Relig., Grant, Civic, Prof Org
55008	535	6826	Hospitals	55125	1116	17035	Insurance Carriers & Related	55381	53	250	Educational Services
55009	366	3694	Merch. Wholesalers,Durable Gds	55126	801	12398	Prof., Scientific, & Tech Svcs	55382	107	244	Food Svcs & Drinking Places
55010	1	10	Credit Intermediation & Relatd	55127	326	4736	Administrative & Support Svcs	55384	92	1268	Food Svcs & Drinking Places
55011	214	935	Special Trade Contractors	55128	651	6813	Food Svcs & Drinking Places	55385	33	190	Merch. Wholesalers,Nondur. Gds
55012	95	1553	Relig., Grant, Civic, Prof Org	55129	133	826	Educational Services	55386	130	849	Computer & Electronic Prod Mfg
55013	177	1569	Ambulatory Health Care Svcs	55133	1	2	Other Information Services	55387	363	3914	Hospitals
55014	462	5003	Justice, Pubic Order/Safety	55144	14	13297	Chemical Manufacturing	55388	173	1126	Educational Services
55016	494	5689	Educational Services	55146	3	1202	Exec., Legis., & Other Support	55389	92	429	Special Trade Contractors
55017	13	76	Merch. Wholesalers,Nondur. Gds	55150	23	139	Food Svcs & Drinking Places	55390	77	310	Relig., Grant, Civic, Prof Org
55018	27	156	Merch. Wholesalers,Nondur. Gds	55155	134	7630	Admin. Enviro. Quality Progrms	55391	1044	12436	Warehousing and Storage
55019	73	485	Administrative & Support Svcs	55164	3	37	Postal Service	55392	11	42	Support Act. for Transport.
55020	69	351	Amusement, Gambling,& Recreat.	55165	1	8	Perform'g Arts, Spec. Sports	55395	148	1792	Relig., Grant, Civic, Prof Org
55021	1010	12403	Food Manufacturing	55175	4	23	Social Assistance	55396	128	881	Administrative & Support Svcs
55024	475	4358	Educational Services	55191	1	6	Transit & Grnd Pass. Transport	55397	44	1581	Prof., Scientific, & Tech Svcs
55025	820	7627	Educational Services	55301	219	2082	Clothing & Cloth'g Acc. Stores	55398	302	1344	Bldg Matl & Garden Eqpmt Dlrs
55026	13	117	Accommodation	55302	357	2177	Educational Services	55401	1328	14538	Prof., Scientific, & Tech Svcs
55027	105	569	Warehousing and Storage	55303	1475	18256	Machinery Manufacturing	55402	2276	45408	Prof., Scientific, & Tech Svcs
55029	12	36	Food Svcs & Drinking Places	55304	840	6685	Special Trade Contractors	55403	919	15394	Food Svcs & Drinking Places
55030	23	59	Food Svcs & Drinking Places	55305	1058	23302	Ambulatory Health Care Svcs	55404	840	18571	Hospitals
55031	63	407	Merch. Wholesalers,Durable Gds	55306	626	7874	Computer & Electronic Prod Mfg	55405	638	5902	Educational Services
55032	79	306	Construction of Buildings	55307	124	1126	Food Manufacturing	55406	1007	10225	Educational Services
55033	991	10922	Miscellaneous Store Retailers	55308	247	2161	Utilities	55407	832	12258	Hospitals
55036	2	3	Food and Beverage Stores	55309	380	2260	Food Svcs & Drinking Places	55408	1266	9328	Food Svcs & Drinking Places
55037	197	3221	Accommodation	55310	90	709	Educational Services	55409	472	4338	Prof., Scientific, & Tech Svcs
55038	276	2394	Print'g & Related Supp't Act's	55311	420	4269	Miscellaneous Manufacturing	55410	507	2784	Educational Services
55040	264	1317	Food Svcs & Drinking Places	55312	49	190	Educational Services	55411	719	10700	Educational Services
55041	314	3703	Primary Metal Manufacturing	55313	747	7559	Educational Services	55412	314	2564	Educational Services
55042	256	1910	Ambulatory Health Care Svcs	55314	52	582	Food Manufacturing	55413	838	23196	Couriers and Messengers
55043	114	480	Heavy & Civil Eng. Construct'N	55315	95	326	Special Trade Contractors	55414	1108	14637	Food Svcs & Drinking Places
55044	992	10002	Educational Services	55316	317	2880	Educational Services	55415	587	13575	Justice, Pubic Order/Safety
55045	230	1368	Plastics & Rubber Products Mfg	55317	589	13667	Administrative & Support Svcs	55416	1752	21454	Prof., Scientific, & Tech Svcs
55046	131	702	Administrative & Support Svcs	55318	783	11071	Plastics & Rubber Products Mfg	55417	384	5195	Hospitals
55047	95	259	Accommodation	55319	105	542	Merch. Wholesalers,Durable Gds	55418	806	9040	Special Trade Contractors
55049	101	1104	General Merchandise Stores	55320	133	1047	Gasoline Stations	55419	428	4878	Miscellaneous Store Retailers
55051	411	3921	Plastics & Rubber Products Mfg	55321	220	1745	Motor Vehicle & Parts Dealers	55420	1117	15683	Machinery Manufacturing
55052	74	557	Accommodation	55322	74	242	Special Trade Contractors	55421	690	9069	Food Svcs & Drinking Places
55053	38	428	Merch. Wholesalers,Nondur. Gds	55323	2	3	Prof., Scientific, & Tech Svcs	55422	927	20154	Hospitals
55054	24	130	Special Trade Contractors	55324	33	111	Personal and Laundry Services	55423	949	12858	Electronics & Appliance Stores
55055	143	2136	Merch. Wholesalers,Nondur. Gds	55325	154	901	Miscellaneous Manufacturing	55424	307	2268	Educational Services
55056	379	3516	Educational Services	55327	83	378	Educational Services	55425	1038	28970	Ambulatory Health Care Svcs
55057	706	8124	Educational Services	55328	299	2495	Sportg Gds,Hobby,Book, & Music	55426	1099	19667	Food Manufacturing
55060	1137	18006	Fabricated Metal Product Mfg	55329	93	807	Educational Services	55427	926	13496	Prof., Scientific, & Tech Svcs
55063	347	2846	Food Svcs & Drinking Places	55330	1056	10388	Food Svcs & Drinking Places	55428	951	18911	Nursing & Resid. Care Facilit.
55065	32	227	Educational Services	55331	739	4801	Food Svcs & Drinking Places	55429	526	5817	Motor Vehicle & Parts Dealers
55066	882	10866	Ambulatory Health Care Svcs	55332	105	623	Nursing & Resid. Care Facilit.	55430	636	8925	Food Svcs & Drinking Places
55067	4	8	Machinery Manufacturing	55333	35	182	Nursing & Resid. Care Facilit.	55431	1031	17709	Merch. Wholesalers,Durable Gds
55068	438	4926	Educational Services	55334	158	1477	Food Manufacturing	55432	1264	37630	Prof., Scientific, & Tech Svcs
55069	156	1572	Plastics & Rubber Products Mfg	55335	76	293	Educational Services	55433	901	14440	Educational Services
55070	134	817	Food Svcs & Drinking Places	55336	314	4632	Food Manufacturing	55434	695	7245	Food Svcs & Drinking Places
55071	117	1221	Petroleum & Coal Products Mfg	55337	1995	23247	Food Svcs & Drinking Places	55435	1760	31687	Hospitals
55072	128	1494	Justice, Pubic Order/Safety	55338	34	100	Merch. Wholesalers,Nondur. Gds	55436	323	3445	Fabricated Metal Product Mfg
55073	100	305	Educational Services	55339	21	157	Heavy & Civil Eng. Construct'N	55437	585	12944	Credit Intermediation & Relatd
55074	44	528	Heavy & Civil Eng. Construct'N	55340	270	3858	Transportation Equipment Mfg	55438	319	5119	Prof., Scientific, & Tech Svcs
55075	544	5935	Educational Services	55341	63	389	Educational Services	55439	940	14435	Prof., Scientific, & Tech Svcs
55076	363	4688	Educational Services	55342	106	706	Computer & Electronic Prod Mfg	55440	10	80	Prof., Scientific, & Tech Svcs
55077	241	4700	Relig., Grant, Civic, Prof Org	55343	1350	25497	Prof., Scientific, & Tech Svcs	55441	959	18792	Prof., Scientific, & Tech Svcs
55079	122	581	Prof., Scientific, & Tech Svcs	55344	1469	33320	Computer & Electronic Prod Mfg	55442	284	10301	Insurance Carriers & Related
55080	54	201	Primary Metal Manufacturing	55345	674	7394	Educational Services	55443	532	3739	Food Svcs & Drinking Places
55082	1326	13752	Food Svcs & Drinking Places	55346	363	2825	Educational Services	55444	203	875	Food Svcs & Drinking Places
55084	80	640	Accommodation	55347	337	3024	Educational Services	55445	377	8772	Prof., Scientific, & Tech Svcs
55085	16	105	Credit Intermediation & Relatd	55349	138	1352	Special Trade Contractors	55446	219	3085	Merch. Wholesalers,Nondur. Gds
55087	7	22	Nursing & Resid. Care Facilit.	55350	945	12316	Computer & Electronic Prod Mfg	55447	845	13780	Merch. Wholesalers,Durable Gds
55088	41	154	Construction of Buildings	55352	168	1824	Educational Services	55448	475	6369	Food Svcs & Drinking Places
55089	48	1294	Utilities	55353	133	797	Educational Services	55449	614	7087	Special Trade Contractors
55090	33	176	Construction of Buildings	55354	86	725	Construction of Buildings	55450	67	2633	Support Act. for Transport.
55092	252	3469	Social Assistance	55355	424	4506	Food Svcs & Drinking Places	55454	259	11787	Ambulatory Health Care Svcs
55101	1651	29509	Prof., Scientific, & Tech Svcs	55356	269	2194	Special Trade Contractors	55455	227	36797	Educational Services
55102	1143	26972	Hospitals	55357	105	774	Special Trade Contractors	55458	15	57	Relig., Grant, Civic, Prof Org
55103	510	6087	Social Assistance	55358	221	2021	Utilities	55474	3	22	Securities/Commodity Contracts
55104	2008	20329	Special Trade Contractors	55359	277	2249	Prof., Scientific, & Tech Svcs	55479	3	12	Crop Production
55105	795	8635	Educational Services	55360	47	163	Educational Services	55487	110	6190	Exec., Legis., & Other Support
55106	918	8475	Educational Services	55361	1	0	Furn. & Home Furnishgs Stores	55488	3	2846	Publishing Industries
55107	548	11986	Broadcasting	55362	555	6318	Food Svcs & Drinking Places	55601	27	126	Accommodation
55108	486	13676	Educational Services	55363	82	419	Wood Product Manufacturing	55602	6	14	Prof., Scientific, & Tech Svcs
55109	1267	18194	Food Svcs & Drinking Places	55364	404	1833	Administrative & Support Svcs	55603	28	116	Educational Services
55110	1373	19536	Educational Services	55366	11	15	Food and Beverage Stores	55604	309	2004	Accommodation
55111	99	3718	Support Act. for Transport.	55367	28	88	Food and Beverage Stores	55605	35	310	Exec., Legis., & Other Support
55112	1080	21161	Prof., Scientific, & Tech Svcs	55368	114	1306	Food Manufacturing	55606	12	31	Museums, Hist. Sites,& Similar

ZIP CODE	2004 Total Firms	2004 Total Employees	TOP INDUSTRY RANKED on 2004 EMPLOYMENT	ZIP CODE	2004 Total Firms	2004 Total Employees	TOP INDUSTRY RANKED on 2004 EMPLOYMENT	ZIP CODE	2004 Total Firms	2004 Total Employees	TOP INDUSTRY RANKED on 2004 EMPLOYMENT
55607	12	18	Accommodation	55812	303	2699	Food Svcs & Drinking Places	56021	32	145	Food and Beverage Stores
55609	12	60	Amusement, Gambling,& Recreat.	55814	1	130	Justice, Pubic Order/Safety	56022	8	25	Chemical Manufacturing
55612	46	692	Accommodation	55815	3	25	Administrative & Support Svcs	56023	29	98	Educational Services
55613	11	109	Utilities	55816	17	101	Prof., Scientific, & Tech Svcs	56024	57	267	Educational Services
55614	105	991	Mining (Except Oil and Gas)	55901	1461	20119	Food Svcs & Drinking Places	56025	38	111	Truck Transportation
55615	37	333	Accommodation	55902	923	16910	Hospitals	56026	50	316	Educational Services
55616	335	3190	Machinery Manufacturing	55903	51	157	Insurance Carriers & Related	56027	48	224	Social Assistance
55701	1	4	Food and Beverage Stores	55904	1088	14386	Food Svcs & Drinking Places	56028	63	321	Food Svcs & Drinking Places
55702	9	18	Food Svcs & Drinking Places	55905	31	324	Ambulatory Health Care Svcs	56029	29	133	Educational Services
55703	14	51	Machinery Manufacturing	55906	532	4653	Educational Services	56030	3	18	Utilities
55704	30	144	Educational Services	55909	67	696	Educational Services	56031	692	8047	Food Svcs & Drinking Places
55705	129	767	Hospitals	55910	50	268	Animal Production	56032	22	76	Bldg Matl & Garden Eqpmt Dlrs
55706	81	479	Educational Services	55912	1021	14184	Merch. Wholesalers,Nondur. Gds	56033	28	61	Exec., Legis., & Other Support
55707	75	441	Educational Services	55917	157	873	Educational Services	56034	12	16	Animal Production
55708	53	359	Accommodation	55918	33	219	Unclassified Establishments	56035	26	188	Wood Product Manufacturing
55709	87	314	Educational Services	55919	20	32	Food and Beverage Stores	56036	53	315	Merch. Wholesalers,Durable Gds
55710	33	112	Unclassified Establishments	55920	143	940	Educational Services	56037	47	235	Educational Services
55711	20	66	Nursing & Resid. Care Facilit.	55921	230	2111	Social Assistance	56039	27	209	Educational Services
55712	9	66	Prof., Scientific, & Tech Svcs	55922	35	67	Food Svcs & Drinking Places	56041	52	214	Chemical Manufacturing
55713	40	322	Educational Services	55923	157	1295	Nursing & Resid. Care Facilit.	56042	35	82	Machinery Manufacturing
55716	14	55	Motor Vehicle & Parts Dealers	55924	42	136	Motor Vehicle & Parts Dealers	56043	27	144	Machinery Manufacturing
55717	9	87	Special Trade Contractors	55925	37	165	Miscellaneous Manufacturing	56044	61	182	Construction of Buildings
55718	157	1849	Accommodation	55926	25	155	Food Svcs & Drinking Places	56045	35	138	Prof., Scientific, & Tech Svcs
55719	197	1699	Relig., Grant, Civic, Prof Org	55927	145	1236	Educational Services	56046	11	54	Bldg Matl & Garden Eqpmt Dlrs
55720	608	7237	Paper Manufacturing	55929	20	95	Heavy & Civil Eng. Construct'N	56047	7	12	Special Trade Contractors
55721	87	653	Utilities	55931	25	147	Truck Transportation	56048	132	762	Educational Services
55722	56	337	Educational Services	55932	58	443	Educational Services	56050	32	273	Plastics & Rubber Products Mfg
55723	152	1123	Wood Product Manufacturing	55933	13	55	Merch. Wholesalers,Nondur. Gds	56051	37	157	Educational Services
55724	31	190	Food Svcs & Drinking Places	55934	90	528	Educational Services	56052	17	44	Construction of Buildings
55725	22	100	Scenic & Sightseeing Transport	55935	25	249	Fabricated Metal Product Mfg	56054	35	134	Relig., Grant, Civic, Prof Org
55726	34	219	Educational Services	55936	87	470	Nursing & Resid. Care Facilit.	56055	140	998	Machinery Manufacturing
55731	412	3019	Accommodation	55939	143	659	Nursing & Resid. Care Facilit.	56056	9	70	Chemical Manufacturing
55732	34	119	Justice, Pubic Order/Safety	55940	108	934	Educational Services	56057	165	1732	Exec., Legis., & Other Support
55733	96	537	Educational Services	55941	66	180	Educational Services	56058	224	2942	Primary Metal Manufacturing
55734	212	1752	Nursing & Resid. Care Facilit.	55942	2	0	Relig., Grant, Civic, Prof Org	56060	24	87	Justice, Pubic Order/Safety
55735	54	270	Food Svcs & Drinking Places	55943	144	652	Telecommunications	56062	149	1403	Food Manufacturing
55736	78	384	Educational Services	55944	227	1665	Educational Services	56063	99	354	Special Trade Contractors
55738	13	696	Mining (Except Oil and Gas)	55945	44	186	Merch. Wholesalers,Nondur. Gds	56065	121	937	Educational Services
55741	101	479	Transit & Grnd Pass. Transport	55946	110	786	Furniture & Related Prod. Mfg	56068	57	201	Educational Services
55742	9	13	Food and Beverage Stores	55947	284	1974	Educational Services	56069	149	1829	Food Manufacturing
55744	1125	11438	Paper Manufacturing	55949	137	471	Relig., Grant, Civic, Prof Org	56071	352	3761	Fabricated Metal Product Mfg
55745	1	200	Prof., Scientific, & Tech Svcs	55950	8	34	Educational Services	56072	92	600	Nursing & Resid. Care Facilit.
55746	850	9761	Mining (Except Oil and Gas)	55951	80	431	Merch. Wholesalers,Durable Gds	56073	872	10468	Food Manufacturing
55748	47	200	Educational Services	55952	107	1599	Prof., Scientific, & Tech Svcs	56074	62	406	Educational Services
55749	3	3	Accommodation	55953	29	169	Educational Services	56075	4	18	Educational Services
55750	50	270	Utilities	55954	91	411	Educational Services	56078	18	37	Food and Beverage Stores
55751	28	234	Rail Transportation	55955	93	403	Food Svcs & Drinking Places	56080	32	249	Educational Services
55752	11	15	Special Trade Contractors	55956	68	231	Educational Services	56081	268	2880	Food Manufacturing
55753	38	729	Primary Metal Manufacturing	55957	31	47	Food and Beverage Stores	56082	359	6367	Hospitals
55756	11	34	Food and Beverage Stores	55959	48	274	Transit & Grnd Pass. Transport	56083	51	152	Special Trade Contractors
55757	17	77	Nonstore Retailers	55960	73	289	Food Svcs & Drinking Places	56084	4	6	Truck Transportation
55758	7	17	Social Assistance	55961	20	131	Nursing & Resid. Care Facilit.	56085	287	2576	Miscellaneous Manufacturing
55760	179	1123	Educational Services	55962	35	119	Educational Services	56087	181	1279	Machinery Manufacturing
55763	12	37	Construction of Buildings	55963	172	1209	Food and Beverage Stores	56088	97	749	Educational Services
55764	23	45	Educational Services	55964	173	1247	Educational Services	56089	13	18	Credit Intermediation & Relatd
55765	26	90	Furn. & Home Furnishgs Stores	55965	161	1394	Exec., Legis., & Other Support	56090	38	98	Food and Beverage Stores
55766	1	5	Exec., Legis., & Other Support	55967	34	156	Food Svcs & Drinking Places	56091	24	99	Educational Services
55767	199	1741	Justice, Pubic Order/Safety	55968	2	1	Truck Transportation	56093	479	6854	Print'g & Related Supp't Act's
55768	74	2117	Primary Metal Manufacturing	55969	42	139	Food and Beverage Stores	56096	144	990	Educational Services
55769	94	450	Educational Services	55970	30	157	Educational Services	56097	193	1391	Food Manufacturing
55771	109	518	Educational Services	55971	142	1331	Transportation Equipment Mfg	56098	128	818	Nursing & Resid. Care Facilit.
55772	5	49	Ambulatory Health Care Svcs	55972	167	1191	Educational Services	56101	355	3099	Machinery Manufacturing
55775	24	66	Amusement, Gambling,& Recreat.	55973	20	67	Unclassified Establishments	56110	100	559	Educational Services
55779	88	591	Educational Services	55974	142	1054	Transportation Equipment Mfg	56111	14	23	Credit Intermediation & Relatd
55780	11	97	Relig., Grant, Civic, Prof Org	55975	172	1022	Educational Services	56113	5	10	Food Svcs & Drinking Places
55781	15	63	Food Svcs & Drinking Places	55976	196	1238	Miscellaneous Manufacturing	56114	15	37	Miscellaneous Store Retailers
55782	11	100	Prof., Scientific, & Tech Svcs	55977	5	4	Food Svcs & Drinking Places	56115	60	287	Nursing & Resid. Care Facilit.
55783	50	200	Exec., Legis., & Other Support	55979	16	56	Food Svcs & Drinking Places	56116	15	62	Amusement, Gambling,& Recreat.
55784	2	22	Gasoline Stations	55981	225	2237	Educational Services	56117	9	12	Heavy & Civil Eng. Construct'N
55785	11	19	Construction of Buildings	55982	17	114	Gasoline Stations	56118	18	227	Chemical Manufacturing
55786	5	76	Exec., Legis., & Other Support	55983	80	359	Educational Services	56119	18	60	Educational Services
55787	9	13	Construction of Buildings	55985	66	300	Educational Services	56120	36	151	Educational Services
55790	123	904	Amusement, Gambling,& Recreat.	55987	1423	22302	Educational Services	56121	24	40	Repair and Maintenance
55791	2	35	Justice, Pubic Order/Safety	55988	7	123	Primary Metal Manufacturing	56122	37	411	Food Manufacturing
55792	758	7926	Hospitals	55990	50	156	Motor Vehicle & Parts Dealers	56123	30	104	Food Svcs & Drinking Places
55793	15	36	Amusement, Gambling,& Recreat.	55991	42	140	Transit & Grnd Pass. Transport	56125	5	22	Warehousing and Storage
55795	49	369	Educational Services	55992	226	1852	Merch. Wholesalers,Nondur. Gds	56127	28	175	Nonmetallic Mineral Prod. Mfg
55796	6	22	Construction of Buildings	56001	2083	30913	Food Svcs & Drinking Places	56128	101	752	Plastics & Rubber Products Mfg
55797	30	160	Educational Services	56002	21	46	Truck Transportation	56129	35	228	Educational Services
55798	19	106	Nursing & Resid. Care Facilit.	56003	409	6494	Print'g & Related Supp't Act's	56131	86	612	Nursing & Resid. Care Facilit.
55801	11	2	Real Estate	56007	973	12648	Hospitals	56132	15	36	Food Svcs & Drinking Places
55802	1254	18682	Utilities	56009	46	233	Educational Services	56134	12	25	Credit Intermediation & Relatd
55803	470	2074	Food and Beverage Stores	56010	51	215	Merch. Wholesalers,Nondur. Gds	56136	77	412	Nursing & Resid. Care Facilit.
55804	321	2031	Nursing & Resid. Care Facilit.	56011	119	1035	Relig., Grant, Civic, Prof Org	56137	47	231	Nursing & Resid. Care Facilit.
55805	371	23669	Ambulatory Health Care Svcs	56013	380	3250	Educational Services	56138	33	220	Nursing & Resid. Care Facilit.
55806	403	3475	Social Assistance	56014	47	117	Animal Production	56139	20	36	Justice, Pubic Order/Safety
55807	461	4961	Special Trade Contractors	56016	46	160	Food and Beverage Stores	56140	4	16	Food Svcs & Drinking Places
55808	103	647	Primary Metal Manufacturing	56017	39	251	Educational Services	56141	10	16	Merch. Wholesalers,Nondur. Gds
55810	216	2080	Exec., Legis., & Other Support	56019	43	143	Educational Services	56142	79	317	Exec., Legis., & Other Support
55811	1083	16468	Educational Services	56020	16	76	Food and Beverage Stores	56143	258	2499	Educational Services

BUSINESS DATA

ZIP CODE	2004 Total Firms	2004 Total Employ-ees	TOP INDUSTRY RANKED on 2004 EMPLOYMENT	ZIP CODE	2004 Total Firms	2004 Total Employ-ees	TOP INDUSTRY RANKED on 2004 EMPLOYMENT	ZIP CODE	2004 Total Firms	2004 Total Employ-ees	TOP INDUSTRY RANKED on 2004 EMPLOYMENT
56144	37	145	Educational Services	56273	224	1408	Educational Services	56381	134	908	Nursing & Resid. Care Facilit.
56145	27	126	Educational Services	56274	13	37	Isps, Web Search Portals	56382	51	290	Truck Transportation
56146	2	3	Warehousing and Storage	56276	20	48	Admin. Enviro. Quality Progrms	56384	53	336	Educational Services
56147	5	3	Warehousing and Storage	56277	230	1606	Bldg Matl & Garden Eqpmt Dlrs	56385	31	180	Machinery Manufacturing
56149	99	391	Educational Services	56278	216	1471	Educational Services	56386	26	72	Accommodation
56150	120	766	Nursing & Resid. Care Facilit.	56279	52	126	Animal Production	56387	433	6440	Food Svcs & Drinking Places
56151	41	122	Merch. Wholesalers,Durable Gds	56280	15	47	Administrative & Support Svcs	56389	4	9	Relig., Grant, Civic, Prof Org
56152	66	544	Warehousing and Storage	56281	38	542	Heavy & Civil Eng. Construct'N	56396	2	235	Accommodation
56153	17	61	Personal and Laundry Services	56282	50	277	Educational Services	56401	1388	14303	Nursing & Resid. Care Facilit.
56155	28	85	Special Trade Contractors	56283	400	3631	Educational Services	56425	344	5147	Food Svcs & Drinking Places
56156	315	3032	Nursing & Resid. Care Facilit.	56284	104	1603	Food Manufacturing	56430	1	9	Exec., Legis., & Other Support
56157	12	61	Educational Services	56285	49	294	Fabricated Metal Product Mfg	56431	422	3297	Ambulatory Health Care Svcs
56158	10	34	Nursing & Resid. Care Facilit.	56287	5	10	Food Svcs & Drinking Places	56433	59	154	Social Assistance
56159	118	1201	Educational Services	56288	242	1295	Food Svcs & Drinking Places	56434	12	21	Food Svcs & Drinking Places
56160	11	24	Credit Intermediation & Relatd	56289	35	56	Relig., Grant, Civic, Prof Org	56435	110	471	Nursing & Resid. Care Facilit.
56161	17	62	Educational Services	56291	9	40	Food Svcs & Drinking Places	56436	7	16	Accommodation
56162	16	62	Food Svcs & Drinking Places	56292	39	93	Repair and Maintenance	56437	32	231	Educational Services
56164	345	3067	Ambulatory Health Care Svcs	56293	77	611	Wood Product Manufacturing	56438	77	492	Food Manufacturing
56165	7	28	Transit & Grnd Pass. Transport	56294	11	42	Food Svcs & Drinking Places	56440	70	356	Real Estate
56166	8	30	Nursing & Resid. Care Facilit.	56295	18	52	Admin. Enviro. Quality Progrms	56441	175	1863	Hospitals
56167	22	486	Food Manufacturing	56296	159	955	Educational Services	56442	257	969	Food Svcs & Drinking Places
56168	18	41	Special Trade Contractors	56297	39	272	Furniture & Related Prod. Mfg	56443	62	161	Accommodation
56169	32	129	Educational Services	56301	1662	23779	Food Svcs & Drinking Places	56444	133	1508	Accommodation
56170	36	109	Educational Services	56302	32	49	Prof., Scientific, & Tech Svcs	56446	78	316	Educational Services
56171	87	370	Educational Services	56303	872	19349	Hospitals	56447	82	263	Food Svcs & Drinking Places
56172	225	1776	Educational Services	56304	488	8129	Print'g & Related Supp't Act's	56448	25	46	Special Trade Contractors
56173	8	11	Relig., Grant, Civic, Prof Org	56307	197	1432	Nursing & Resid. Care Facilit.	56449	13	99	Special Trade Contractors
56174	21	44	Truck Transportation	56308	1360	13776	Food Svcs & Drinking Places	56450	66	389	Food Svcs & Drinking Places
56175	162	962	Educational Services	56309	79	494	Educational Services	56452	189	642	Food Svcs & Drinking Places
56176	61	358	Nursing & Resid. Care Facilit.	56310	141	717	Bldg Matl & Garden Eqpmt Dlrs	56453	13	21	Food Svcs & Drinking Places
56177	4	1	Merch. Wholesalers,Nondur. Gds	56311	46	561	Educational Services	56455	47	324	Plastics & Rubber Products Mfg
56178	106	847	Hospitals	56312	92	596	Nursing & Resid. Care Facilit.	56456	10	88	Fabricated Metal Product Mfg
56180	58	173	Educational Services	56313	9	23	Repair and Maintenance	56458	15	54	Accommodation
56181	54	194	Educational Services	56314	25	64	Truck Transportation	56461	95	266	Special Trade Contractors
56183	64	355	Educational Services	56315	107	406	Educational Services	56464	154	645	Bldg Matl & Garden Eqpmt Dlrs
56185	29	73	Warehousing and Storage	56316	75	475	Food Manufacturing	56465	103	936	Fabricated Metal Product Mfg
56186	15	34	Relig., Grant, Civic, Prof Org	56317	8	54	Merch. Wholesalers,Nondur. Gds	56466	107	943	Food Manufacturing
56187	648	8668	Food Manufacturing	56318	24	129	Accommodation	56467	90	388	Educational Services
56201	1162	19298	Food Manufacturing	56319	54	185	Educational Services	56468	265	1809	Accommodation
56207	14	53	Educational Services	56320	219	3682	Nonmetallic Mineral Prod. Mfg	56469	35	108	Machinery Manufacturing
56208	140	1220	Justice, Pubic Order/Safety	56321	15	674	Educational Services	56470	667	5040	Food Manufacturing
56209	88	534	Educational Services	56323	29	131	Educational Services	56472	402	3219	Amusement, Gambling,& Recreat.
56210	1	1	Merch. Wholesalers,Nondur. Gds	56324	59	231	Miscellaneous Manufacturing	56473	100	671	Educational Services
56211	26	66	Educational Services	56325	18	142	Construction of Buildings	56474	267	1256	Nursing & Resid. Care Facilit.
56212	39	156	Bldg Matl & Garden Eqpmt Dlrs	56326	86	346	Nursing & Resid. Care Facilit.	56475	58	257	Food and Beverage Stores
56214	37	204	Nursing & Resid. Care Facilit.	56327	22	34	Prof., Scientific, & Tech Svcs	56477	104	545	Educational Services
56215	279	2319	Merch. Wholesalers,Durable Gds	56328	5	15	Merch. Wholesalers,Nondur. Gds	56478	2	2	Bldg Matl & Garden Eqpmt Dlrs
56216	29	164	Machinery Manufacturing	56329	219	2114	Exec., Legis., & Other Support	56479	217	1983	Hospitals
56218	21	42	Merch. Wholesalers,Nondur. Gds	56330	34	304	Wood Product Manufacturing	56481	76	334	Educational Services
56219	55	295	Educational Services	56331	79	326	Food Svcs & Drinking Places	56482	405	4357	Educational Services
56220	149	1107	Nursing & Resid. Care Facilit.	56332	78	207	Construction of Buildings	56484	389	2628	Amusement, Gambling,& Recreat.
56221	49	222	Educational Services	56333	12	29	Food Svcs & Drinking Places	56501	962	9704	Food Svcs & Drinking Places
56222	114	849	Educational Services	56334	304	2944	Educational Services	56502	9	55	Amusement, Gambling,& Recreat.
56223	75	529	Educational Services	56335	16	59	Food Manufacturing	56510	194	1205	Educational Services
56224	20	48	Utilities	56336	71	265	Miscellaneous Manufacturing	56511	60	525	Fabricated Metal Product Mfg
56225	38	285	Relig., Grant, Civic, Prof Org	56338	20	57	Food Svcs & Drinking Places	56514	145	723	Educational Services
56226	12	52	Wholesale Elec. Mrkts & Agents	56339	80	391	Nursing & Resid. Care Facilit.	56515	166	784	Nursing & Resid. Care Facilit.
56227	8	10	Construction of Buildings	56340	51	927	Educational Services	56516	10	38	Food Svcs & Drinking Places
56228	46	306	Fabricated Metal Product Mfg	56341	5	8	Food and Beverage Stores	56517	16	39	Food Svcs & Drinking Places
56229	71	824	Furniture & Related Prod. Mfg	56342	144	761	Educational Services	56518	15	32	Relig., Grant, Civic, Prof Org
56230	41	212	Educational Services	56343	36	266	Accommodation	56519	19	70	Educational Services
56231	17	88	Merch. Wholesalers,Durable Gds	56344	1	2	Food Manufacturing	56520	192	1898	Nursing & Resid. Care Facilit.
56232	138	1365	Ambulatory Health Care Svcs	56345	645	7874	Transportation Equipment Mfg	56521	51	198	Accommodation
56235	26	76	Bldg Matl & Garden Eqpmt Dlrs	56347	290	3094	Food Manufacturing	56522	14	88	Educational Services
56236	19	23	Chemical Manufacturing	56349	39	97	Machinery Manufacturing	56523	28	121	Educational Services
56237	27	115	Merch. Wholesalers,Nondur. Gds	56350	14	31	Food Svcs & Drinking Places	56524	20	58	Accommodation
56239	16	47	Merch. Wholesalers,Nondur. Gds	56352	255	2851	Food Manufacturing	56525	12	25	Merch. Wholesalers,Nondur. Gds
56240	55	363	Nursing & Resid. Care Facilit.	56353	263	2322	Educational Services	56527	24	99	Educational Services
56241	251	2161	Educational Services	56354	60	199	Bldg Matl & Garden Eqpmt Dlrs	56528	71	201	Accommodation
56243	50	297	Educational Services	56355	23	105	Furniture & Related Prod. Mfg	56529	90	959	General Merchandise Stores
56244	76	407	Merch. Wholesalers,Durable Gds	56356	15	53	Nursing & Resid. Care Facilit.	56531	149	722	Ambulatory Health Care Svcs
56245	16	78	Warehousing and Storage	56357	11	28	Furniture & Related Prod. Mfg	56533	12	21	Food and Beverage Stores
56248	54	174	Educational Services	56358	63	434	Educational Services	56534	37	133	Special Trade Contractors
56249	13	12	Food and Beverage Stores	56359	139	2274	Educational Services	56535	76	494	Nursing & Resid. Care Facilit.
56251	38	189	Administrative & Support Svcs	56360	168	768	Educational Services	56536	27	87	Merch. Wholesalers,Durable Gds
56252	60	391	Educational Services	56361	128	648	Nursing & Resid. Care Facilit.	56537	903	11209	Hospitals
56253	38	178	Nonmetallic Mineral Prod. Mfg	56362	333	2344	Hospitals	56538	6	22	Social Assistance
56255	24	110	Merch. Wholesalers,Durable Gds	56363	14	63	Merch. Wholesalers,Nondur. Gds	56540	124	589	Nursing & Resid. Care Facilit.
56256	181	1144	Nursing & Resid. Care Facilit.	56364	176	960	Nursing & Resid. Care Facilit.	56541	9	24	Relig., Grant, Civic, Prof Org
56257	33	61	Merch. Wholesalers,Nondur. Gds	56367	162	1138	Merch. Wholesalers,Nondur. Gds	56542	191	1334	Hospitals
56258	803	10472	Food Manufacturing	56368	160	629	Food Svcs & Drinking Places	56543	10	41	Crop Production
56260	37	207	Miscellaneous Store Retailers	56369	22	113	Educational Services	56544	135	957	Educational Services
56262	41	171	Educational Services	56371	2	2	Relig., Grant, Civic, Prof Org	56545	38	139	Educational Services
56263	24	86	Educational Services	56373	72	465	Educational Services	56546	14	27	Special Trade Contractors
56264	91	843	Educational Services	56374	221	1838	Educational Services	56547	81	471	Educational Services
56265	428	4470	Food Svcs & Drinking Places	56375	29	154	Transit & Grnd Pass. Transport	56548	44	330	Nursing & Resid. Care Facilit.
56266	84	494	Educational Services	56376	25	119	Waste Managmt & Remediat'n Svc	56549	125	871	Machinery Manufacturing
56267	387	4188	Educational Services	56377	226	3495	Paper Manufacturing	56550	27	140	Educational Services
56270	48	1272	Credit Intermediation & Relatd	56378	376	3325	Educational Services	56551	105	525	Nursing & Resid. Care Facilit.
56271	65	312	Merch. Wholesalers,Nondur. Gds	56379	521	6203	Plastics & Rubber Products Mfg	56552	19	32	Merch. Wholesalers,Nondur. Gds

ZIP CODE	2004 Total Firms	2004 Total Employees	TOP INDUSTRY RANKED on 2004 EMPLOYMENT
56553	8	11	Warehousing and Storage
56554	105	525	Educational Services
56556	78	303	Nursing & Resid. Care Facilit.
56557	181	1292	Educational Services
56560	1134	12713	Food Svcs & Drinking Places
56561	11	43	Social Assistance
56562	5	730	Educational Services
56563	4	736	Educational Services
56565	3	8	Merch. Wholesalers,Nondur. Gds
56566	16	133	Admin. Human Resource Programs
56567	152	1657	Transportation Equipment Mfg
56568	8	33	Warehousing and Storage
56569	32	262	Ambulatory Health Care Svcs
56570	46	96	Accommodation
56571	100	477	Administrative & Support Svcs
56572	225	1990	Food Manufacturing
56573	390	3377	Food Manufacturing
56574	10	34	Warehousing and Storage
56575	23	78	Educational Services
56576	37	63	Prof., Scientific, & Tech Svcs
56577	2	2	Miscellaneous Store Retailers
56578	18	41	Accommodation
56579	46	258	Educational Services
56580	32	93	Construction of Buildings
56581	20	72	Justice, Pubic Order/Safety
56583	12	16	Crop Production
56584	75	555	Nursing & Resid. Care Facilit.
56585	50	385	Educational Services
56586	78	377	Educational Services
56587	83	253	Special Trade Contractors
56588	19	22	Special Trade Contractors
56589	70	370	Educational Services
56590	28	70	Crop Production
56591	13	381	Exec., Legis., & Other Support
56592	32	115	Merch. Wholesalers,Durable Gds
56593	12	22	Food and Beverage Stores
56594	24	74	Merch. Wholesalers,Nondur. Gds
56601	1512	15990	Accommodation
56619	25	45	Special Trade Contractors
56621	246	2150	Miscellaneous Manufacturing
56623	251	1522	Accommodation
56626	27	199	Educational Services
56627	28	118	Wood Product Manufacturing
56628	75	813	Hospitals
56629	7	12	Food Svcs & Drinking Places
56630	165	1269	Furn. & Home Furnishgs Stores
56631	1	0	Postal Service
56633	200	2442	Amusement, Gambling,& Recreat.
56634	74	519	Nursing & Resid. Care Facilit.
56636	243	1842	Relig., Grant, Civic, Prof Org
56637	13	53	Educational Services
56639	20	34	Food Svcs & Drinking Places
56641	25	40	Accommodation
56644	47	238	Educational Services
56646	20	93	Support Activities: Agr./For.
56647	24	42	Accommodation
56649	498	4783	Paper Manufacturing
56650	58	221	Educational Services
56651	25	33	Merch. Wholesalers,Durable Gds
56652	16	24	Food Svcs & Drinking Places
56653	58	323	Nursing & Resid. Care Facilit.
56654	5	5	Repair and Maintenance
56655	153	463	Accommodation
56657	27	116	Exec., Legis., & Other Support
56659	8	7	Accommodation
56660	13	34	Transportation Equipment Mfg
56661	72	323	Educational Services
56662	34	97	Food Svcs & Drinking Places
56663	9	18	Accommodation
56666	14	111	Educational Services
56667	18	17	Merch. Wholesalers,Nondur. Gds
56668	23	101	Miscellaneous Manufacturing
56669	42	77	Accommodation
56670	20	111	Exec., Legis., & Other Support
56671	62	1037	Educational Services
56672	128	565	Educational Services
56673	18	53	Accommodation
56676	54	156	Special Trade Contractors
56678	40	263	Wood Product Manufacturing
56679	16	35	Food Svcs & Drinking Places
56680	11	8	Accommodation
56681	29	65	Accommodation
56683	22	69	Wood Product Manufacturing
56684	11	29	Merch. Wholesalers,Durable Gds
56685	11	14	Food Svcs & Drinking Places
56686	49	144	Warehousing and Storage
56687	6	9	Bldg Matl & Garden Eqpmt Dlrs
56688	4	7	Construction of Buildings
56701	557	8324	Electronics & Appliance Stores
56710	20	41	Warehousing and Storage

ZIP CODE	2004 Total Firms	2004 Total Employees	TOP INDUSTRY RANKED on 2004 EMPLOYMENT
56711	4	21	Accommodation
56713	51	323	Educational Services
56714	45	212	Relig., Grant, Civic, Prof Org
56715	22	167	Chemical Manufacturing
56716	436	5447	Hospitals
56720	7	11	Crop Production
56721	365	3913	Food Manufacturing
56722	10	21	Transit & Grnd Pass. Transport
56723	32	86	Educational Services
56724	6	10	Air Transportation
56725	26	142	Educational Services
56726	82	470	Educational Services
56727	39	241	Fabricated Metal Product Mfg
56728	127	844	Exec., Legis., & Other Support
56729	8	28	Merch. Wholesalers,Durable Gds
56731	7	15	Utilities
56732	82	485	Educational Services
56733	30	122	Educational Services
56734	27	72	Museums, Hist. Sites,& Similar
56735	34	92	Educational Services
56736	59	236	Food Svcs & Drinking Places
56737	43	222	Educational Services
56738	60	436	Educational Services
56740	5	9	Rail Transportation
56741	1	2	Accommodation
56742	37	223	Relig., Grant, Civic, Prof Org
56744	32	179	Special Trade Contractors
56748	27	109	Educational Services
56750	143	1008	Educational Services
56751	320	4362	Transportation Equipment Mfg
56754	25	97	Merch. Wholesalers,Durable Gds
56755	12	42	Relig., Grant, Civic, Prof Org
56756	7	14	Ambulatory Health Care Svcs
56757	67	400	Educational Services
56758	11	14	Food Svcs & Drinking Places
56759	9	15	Food and Beverage Stores
56760	15	64	Educational Services
56761	24	48	Support Activities: Agr./For.
56762	164	1174	Educational Services
56763	177	1549	Amusement, Gambling,& Recreat.
57001	44	519	Educational Services
57002	29	53	Crop Production
57003	47	298	Educational Services
57004	183	1206	Educational Services
57005	269	2192	Educational Services
57006	904	12065	Miscellaneous Manufacturing
57007	7	1926	Educational Services
57010	10	43	Food Svcs & Drinking Places
57012	49	300	Educational Services
57013	192	1853	Fabricated Metal Product Mfg
57014	52	286	Nursing & Resid. Care Facilit.
57015	33	153	Petroleum & Coal Products Mfg
57016	21	126	Educational Services
57017	34	423	Elect'l Eqpmt, App, & Comp Mfg
57018	46	294	Educational Services
57020	35	98	Construction of Buildings
57021	16	21	Exec., Legis., & Other Support
57022	173	1239	Nursing & Resid. Care Facilit.
57024	16	52	Educational Services
57025	117	932	Educational Services
57026	72	351	Animal Production
57027	4	11	Perform'g Arts, Spec. Sports
57028	162	1563	Accommodation
57029	108	826	Hospitals
57030	92	577	Educational Services
57031	30	561	Food and Beverage Stores
57032	79	790	Furniture & Related Prod. Mfg
57033	121	506	Educational Services
57034	22	112	Nursing & Resid. Care Facilit.
57035	46	193	Educational Services
57036	46	199	Justice, Pubic Order/Safety
57037	54	333	Truck Transportation
57038	44	167	Special Trade Contractors
57039	124	691	Machinery Manufacturing
57040	12	64	Construction of Buildings
57041	6	186	Transportation Equipment Mfg
57042	379	4088	Educational Services
57043	68	438	Nursing & Resid. Care Facilit.
57044	12	41	Food Svcs & Drinking Places
57045	66	389	Nursing & Resid. Care Facilit.
57046	15	48	Heavy & Civil Eng. Construct'N
57047	10	7	Warehousing and Storage
57048	30	188	Relig., Grant, Civic, Prof Org
57049	226	4477	Food Manufacturing
57050	7	14	Food Svcs & Drinking Places
57051	15	58	Educational Services
57052	24	97	Crop Production
57053	139	553	Educational Services
57054	12	67	Educational Services
57055	29	91	Educational Services

ZIP CODE	2004 Total Firms	2004 Total Employees	TOP INDUSTRY RANKED on 2004 EMPLOYMENT
57056	3	9	Gasoline Stations
57057	5	44	Educational Services
57058	116	812	Machinery Manufacturing
57059	76	506	Educational Services
57061	11	18	Warehousing and Storage
57062	69	738	Justice, Pubic Order/Safety
57063	37	135	Justice, Pubic Order/Safety
57064	159	898	Educational Services
57065	9	26	Truck Transportation
57066	122	599	Relig., Grant, Civic, Prof Org
57067	8	120	Relig., Grant, Civic, Prof Org
57068	42	153	Educational Services
57069	414	4656	Educational Services
57070	63	417	Ambulatory Health Care Svcs
57071	83	494	Food Manufacturing
57072	18	35	Food Svcs & Drinking Places
57073	32	166	Relig., Grant, Civic, Prof Org
57075	26	113	Oil and Gas Extraction
57076	15	79	Animal Production
57077	34	156	Motor Vehicle & Parts Dealers
57078	973	12266	Prof., Scientific, & Tech Svcs
57101	44	90	Relig., Grant, Civic, Prof Org
57103	853	11231	Food Manufacturing
57104	2060	35200	Isps, Web Search Portals
57105	1373	28160	Hospitals
57106	985	13537	Food Svcs & Drinking Places
57107	246	4828	Merch. Wholesalers,Durable Gds
57108	361	3681	Ambulatory Health Care Svcs
57109	34	80	Administrative & Support Svcs
57110	263	2312	Food and Beverage Stores
57117	1	0	Prof., Scientific, & Tech Svcs
57118	11	34	Special Trade Contractors
57193	3	452	Insurance Carriers & Related
57197	7	439	Educational Services
57198	5	1106	Admin. Enviro. Quality Progrms
57201	1285	14719	Computer & Electronic Prod Mfg
57212	89	606	Repair and Maintenance
57213	22	35	Educational Services
57214	8	39	Justice, Pubic Order/Safety
57216	42	573	Food and Beverage Stores
57217	14	25	Truck Transportation
57218	17	30	Insurance Carriers & Related
57219	31	202	Educational Services
57220	28	134	Food Manufacturing
57221	29	151	Nursing & Resid. Care Facilit.
57223	40	250	Educational Services
57224	17	61	Relig., Grant, Civic, Prof Org
57225	131	637	Educational Services
57226	144	1221	Educational Services
57227	16	48	Food Svcs & Drinking Places
57231	126	779	Miscellaneous Manufacturing
57232	15	38	Food Svcs & Drinking Places
57233	8	13	Truck Transportation
57234	63	274	Nursing & Resid. Care Facilit.
57235	19	76	Educational Services
57236	9	29	Miscellaneous Manufacturing
57237	45	153	Merch. Wholesalers,Durable Gds
57238	20	48	Animal Production
57239	7	22	Accommodation
57241	58	302	Educational Services
57242	10	28	Fabricated Metal Product Mfg
57243	16	85	Educational Services
57245	8	17	Educational Services
57246	4	27	Warehousing and Storage
57247	9	29	Museums, Hist. Sites,& Similar
57248	40	147	Bldg Matl & Garden Eqpmt Dlrs
57249	58	390	Educational Services
57251	4	27	Nonmetallic Mineral Prod. Mfg
57252	307	2864	Merch. Wholesalers,Durable Gds
57255	35	108	Telecommunications
57256	1	1	Relig., Grant, Civic, Prof Org
57257	11	25	Food and Beverage Stores
57258	8	52	Support Activities: Agr./For.
57259	19	85	Educational Services
57260	55	463	Securities/Commodity Contracts
57261	20	150	Educational Services
57262	300	2214	Educational Services
57263	21	70	Educational Services
57264	14	25	Merch. Wholesalers,Durable Gds
57265	4	3	Bldg Matl & Garden Eqpmt Dlrs
57266	17	125	Educational Services
57268	34	115	Merch. Wholesalers,Nondur. Gds
57269	4	5	Merch. Wholesalers,Durable Gds
57270	22	111	Animal Production
57271	8	8	Warehousing and Storage
57272	6	17	Warehousing and Storage
57273	58	226	Educational Services
57274	194	1287	Educational Services
57276	67	295	Educational Services
57278	36	224	Educational Services

BUSINESS DATA

ZIP CODE	2004 Total Firms	2004 Total Employ-ees	TOP INDUSTRY RANKED on 2004 EMPLOYMENT	ZIP CODE	2004 Total Firms	2004 Total Employ-ees	TOP INDUSTRY RANKED on 2004 EMPLOYMENT	ZIP CODE	2004 Total Firms	2004 Total Employ-ees	TOP INDUSTRY RANKED on 2004 EMPLOYMENT
57279	35	269	Educational Services	57454	23	92	Educational Services	57656	60	270	Educational Services
57301	949	11699	Educational Services	57455	9	13	Postal Service	57657	2	4	Animal Production
57311	65	316	Crop Production	57456	59	161	Educational Services	57658	4	32	Educational Services
57312	24	594	Merch. Wholesalers,Nondur. Gds	57457	6	27	Justice, Pubic Order/Safety	57660	3	5	Merch. Wholesalers,Nondur. Gds
57313	105	476	Educational Services	57460	6	13	Food Svcs & Drinking Places	57661	3	9	Ambulatory Health Care Svcs
57314	25	190	Educational Services	57461	19	122	Educational Services	57701	2253	35510	Hospitals
57315	65	262	Educational Services	57465	11	24	Crop Production	57702	1408	14215	Administrative & Support Svcs
57317	35	209	Educational Services	57466	11	38	Crop Production	57703	361	3842	Electronics & Appliance Stores
57319	55	252	Nursing & Resid. Care Facilit.	57467	22	68	Justice, Pubic Order/Safety	57706	33	5225	Nat'l Security & Int'l Affairs
57321	26	62	Justice, Pubic Order/Safety	57468	10	29	Merch. Wholesalers,Nondur. Gds	57709	61	285	Perform'g Arts, Spec. Sports
57322	10	42	Crop Production	57469	203	1777	Exec., Legis., & Other Support	57714	6	119	Educational Services
57323	12	24	Food Svcs & Drinking Places	57470	2	2	Merch. Wholesalers,Nondur. Gds	57716	8	102	Educational Services
57324	8	18	Merch. Wholesalers,Nondur. Gds	57471	37	177	Educational Services	57717	281	1927	Educational Services
57325	289	1934	Educational Services	57472	82	386	Nursing & Resid. Care Facilit.	57718	159	858	Special Trade Contractors
57328	78	584	Merch. Wholesalers,Nondur. Gds	57473	6	8	Merch. Wholesalers,Durable Gds	57719	112	765	Educational Services
57329	5	8	Merch. Wholesalers,Nondur. Gds	57474	12	53	Educational Services	57720	81	317	Educational Services
57330	31	82	Educational Services	57475	15	47	Justice, Pubic Order/Safety	57722	8	25	Exec., Legis., & Other Support
57331	16	61	Construction of Buildings	57476	28	126	Educational Services	57724	14	92	Relig., Grant, Civic, Prof Org
57332	45	126	Educational Services	57477	13	46	Justice, Pubic Order/Safety	57725	4	19	Merch. Wholesalers,Durable Gds
57334	29	127	Educational Services	57479	19	158	Educational Services	57730	230	2687	Accommodation
57335	16	61	Educational Services	57481	11	246	General Merchandise Stores	57732	182	2391	Amusement, Gambling,& Recreat.
57337	11	18	Merch. Wholesalers,Nondur. Gds	57501	1064	11980	Exec., Legis., & Other Support	57735	33	163	Educational Services
57339	67	588	Exec., Legis., & Other Support	57520	10	24	Educational Services	57737	3	9	Educational Services
57340	4	10	Credit Intermediation & Relatd	57521	6	6	Food and Beverage Stores	57738	6	4	Educational Services
57341	17	18	Exec., Legis., & Other Support	57522	24	81	Utilities	57741	10	39	Support Activities: Agr./For.
57342	20	58	Educational Services	57523	94	450	Educational Services	57744	52	176	Educational Services
57344	10	25	Construction of Buildings	57528	32	146	Educational Services	57745	145	1078	Accommodation
57345	103	610	Educational Services	57529	13	42	Amusement, Gambling,& Recreat.	57747	187	1665	Hospitals
57346	6	454	Educational Services	57531	16	33	Amusement, Gambling,& Recreat.	57748	2	67	Educational Services
57348	21	54	Educational Services	57532	161	1294	Educational Services	57750	15	220	Museums, Hist. Sites,& Similar
57349	103	582	Educational Services	57533	141	782	Hospitals	57751	92	837	Accommodation
57350	722	6326	Food Svcs & Drinking Places	57534	3	2	Prof., Scientific, & Tech Svcs	57752	27	640	Educational Services
57353	24	213	Crop Production	57536	32	93	Educational Services	57754	116	902	Accommodation
57354	7	27	Warehousing and Storage	57537	10	16	Exec., Legis., & Other Support	57755	5	7	Animal Production
57355	80	431	Crop Production	57538	11	14	Food and Beverage Stores	57756	15	180	Educational Services
57356	89	817	Accommodation	57540	4	16	Construction of Buildings	57758	6	6	Educational Services
57358	2	5	Repair and Maintenance	57541	3	19	Support Activities: Agr./For.	57759	7	134	Support Activities: Agr./For.
57359	44	157	Nursing & Resid. Care Facilit.	57543	96	493	Educational Services	57760	43	334	Educational Services
57361	11	303	Educational Services	57544	57	253	Exec., Legis., & Other Support	57761	23	175	Nursing & Resid. Care Facilit.
57362	175	1104	Educational Services	57547	4	3	Educational Services	57762	3	3	Postal Service
57363	33	110	Educational Services	57548	68	737	Exec., Legis., & Other Support	57763	14	61	Educational Services
57364	11	29	Educational Services	57551	78	535	Educational Services	57764	15	112	Educational Services
57365	23	401	Accommodation	57552	22	82	Educational Services	57766	4	12	Exec., Legis., & Other Support
57366	107	818	Hospitals	57553	7	4	Educational Services	57767	3	1	Special Trade Contractors
57367	20	148	Admin. Enviro. Quality Progrms	57555	122	1277	Educational Services	57769	94	427	Merch. Wholesalers,Durable Gds
57368	92	363	Educational Services	57559	84	498	Accommodation	57770	169	2493	Exec., Legis., & Other Support
57369	185	986	Hospitals	57560	6	18	Educational Services	57772	25	306	Educational Services
57370	28	42	Special Trade Contractors	57562	2	4	Unclassified Establishments	57773	4	12	Food Svcs & Drinking Places
57371	11	10	Postal Service	57563	3	9	Educational Services	57775	4	5	Educational Services
57373	12	28	Warehousing and Storage	57564	96	458	Educational Services	57777	2	3	Repair and Maintenance
57374	20	55	Nonmetallic Mineral Prod. Mfg	57566	12	81	Educational Services	57779	11	70	Merch. Wholesalers,Nondur. Gds
57375	42	138	Educational Services	57567	94	735	Nursing & Resid. Care Facilit.	57780	6	6	Postal Service
57376	43	249	Relig., Grant, Civic, Prof Org	57568	68	298	Educational Services	57782	1	0	Postal Service
57379	2	0	Animal Production	57569	22	75	Special Trade Contractors	57783	555	5533	Credit Intermediation & Relatd
57380	149	1202	Educational Services	57570	80	2230	Exec., Legis., & Other Support	57785	352	2622	Educational Services
57381	35	124	Machinery Manufacturing	57571	2	1	Repair and Maintenance	57787	8	36	Food Manufacturing
57382	103	611	Educational Services	57572	25	367	Educational Services	57788	4	53	Educational Services
57383	44	214	Nursing & Resid. Care Facilit.	57574	1	0	Postal Service	57790	70	824	Health & Personal Care Stores
57384	23	204	Educational Services	57576	11	38	Gasoline Stations	57791	3	9	Merch. Wholesalers,Durable Gds
57385	97	633	Nonmetallic Mineral Prod. Mfg	57577	11	235	Educational Services	57792	2	1	Food and Beverage Stores
57386	8	28	Warehousing and Storage	57579	70	514	Educational Services	57793	42	254	Wood Product Manufacturing
57401	1438	17977	Hospitals	57580	315	2274	Nursing & Resid. Care Facilit.	57794	5	5	Postal Service
57402	7	11	Special Trade Contractors	57584	10	21	Educational Services	57799	2	321	Educational Services
57420	5	9	Sportg Gds,Hobby,Book, & Music	57585	11	21	Educational Services	58001	11	70	Wood Product Manufacturing
57421	6	27	Animal Production	57601	267	2114	Food and Beverage Stores	58002	2	2	Telecommunications
57422	12	29	Fabricated Metal Product Mfg	57620	74	240	Educational Services	58004	8	38	Crop Production
57424	7	11	Merch. Wholesalers,Nondur. Gds	57621	8	29	Educational Services	58005	7	8	Special Trade Contractors
57426	2	21	Educational Services	57622	5	19	Educational Services	58006	33	230	Nursing & Resid. Care Facilit.
57427	19	101	Utilities	57623	57	308	Educational Services	58007	7	18	Warehousing and Storage
57428	55	319	Nursing & Resid. Care Facilit.	57625	216	2619	Exec., Legis., & Other Support	58008	10	17	Merch. Wholesalers,Nondur. Gds
57429	4	11	Construction of Buildings	57626	83	377	Educational Services	58009	1	1	Construction of Buildings
57430	151	1128	Merch. Wholesalers,Nondur. Gds	57630	1	0	Postal Service	58011	31	79	Truck Transportation
57432	31	77	Justice, Pubic Order/Safety	57631	22	29	Accommodation	58012	107	679	Educational Services
57433	27	75	Justice, Pubic Order/Safety	57632	57	219	Merch. Wholesalers,Nondur. Gds	58013	11	17	Admin. Enviro. Quality Progrms
57434	19	87	Justice, Pubic Order/Safety	57633	41	197	Educational Services	58015	14	36	Justice, Pubic Order/Safety
57435	14	56	Educational Services	57634	3	3	Food and Beverage Stores	58016	15	94	Truck Transportation
57436	28	121	Educational Services	57636	3	4	Support Act. for Transport.	58017	22	31	Crop Production
57437	82	507	Educational Services	57638	133	822	Miscellaneous Manufacturing	58018	17	82	Educational Services
57438	101	522	Ambulatory Health Care Svcs	57639	2	7	Educational Services	58021	14	44	Administrative & Support Svcs
57439	4	27	Merch. Wholesalers,Durable Gds	57640	8	19	Educational Services	58027	83	648	Food Manufacturing
57440	12	100	Crop Production	57641	35	186	Educational Services	58029	5	28	Justice, Pubic Order/Safety
57441	16	53	Educational Services	57642	83	615	Educational Services	58030	27	228	Merch. Wholesalers,Nondur. Gds
57442	141	809	Real Estate	57644	13	14	Animal Production	58031	11	20	Bldg Matl & Garden Eqpmt Dlrs
57445	106	529	Educational Services	57645	6	13	Postal Service	58032	72	378	Fabricated Metal Product Mfg
57446	32	130	Food and Beverage Stores	57646	20	46	Exec., Legis., & Other Support	58033	24	68	Accommodation
57448	20	88	Nursing & Resid. Care Facilit.	57648	31	201	Food Manufacturing	58035	22	104	Educational Services
57449	10	11	Postal Service	57649	13	28	Relig., Grant, Civic, Prof Org	58036	6	9	Postal Service
57450	58	369	Exec., Legis., & Other Support	57650	1	2	Insurance Carriers & Related	58038	17	147	Food Manufacturing
57451	100	704	Crop Production	57651	10	18	Educational Services	58040	43	257	Print'g & Related Supp't Act's
57452	11	37	Educational Services	57652	14	118	Educational Services	58041	87	896	Accommodation

ZIP CODE	2004 Total Firms	2004 Total Employees	TOP INDUSTRY RANKED on 2004 EMPLOYMENT
58042	41	164	Special Trade Contractors
58043	10	14	Crop Production
58045	123	994	Food Manufacturing
58046	36	182	Special Trade Contractors
58047	57	223	Amusement, Gambling,& Recreat.
58048	35	217	Educational Services
58049	17	56	Justice, Pubic Order/Safety
58051	55	398	Educational Services
58052	23	42	Relig., Grant, Civic, Prof Org
58053	76	303	Educational Services
58054	152	1254	Nursing & Resid. Care Facilit.
58056	8	17	Warehousing and Storage
58057	3	5	Special Trade Contractors
58058	9	37	Educational Services
58059	26	130	Truck Transportation
58060	67	352	Educational Services
58061	27	68	Merch. Wholesalers,Nondur. Gds
58062	7	10	Telecommunications
58063	8	44	Justice, Pubic Order/Safety
58064	28	162	Educational Services
58065	2	4	Warehousing and Storage
58067	23	62	Construction of Buildings
58068	18	39	Educational Services
58069	4	5	Special Trade Contractors
58071	22	131	Food Svcs & Drinking Places
58072	488	4617	Educational Services
58075	457	5686	Computer & Electronic Prod Mfg
58076	4	365	Educational Services
58077	28	43	Postal Service
58078	700	6293	Educational Services
58079	23	52	Construction of Buildings
58081	38	145	Educational Services
58102	1627	29890	Educational Services
58103	2428	34715	Food Svcs & Drinking Places
58104	499	5187	Merch. Wholesalers,Durable Gds
58105	11	55	Admin. Human Resource Programs
58106	33	124	Isps, Web Search Portals
58107	23	110	Administrative & Support Svcs
58108	7	68	Air Transportation
58109	8	8	Special Trade Contractors
58121	3	2007	Insurance Carriers & Related
58122	12	8413	Educational Services
58124	2	329	Managmt of Companies & Enterp.
58126	5	22	Prof., Scientific, & Tech Svcs
58201	1375	26932	Ambulatory Health Care Svcs
58202	17	562	Unclassified Establishments
58203	785	12841	Educational Services
58204	14	196	Educational Services
58205	30	182	Food Svcs & Drinking Places
58206	6	6	Ambulatory Health Care Svcs
58208	19	76	Broadcasting
58210	17	78	Justice, Pubic Order/Safety
58212	34	143	Nursing & Resid. Care Facilit.
58214	10	28	Merch. Wholesalers,Nondur. Gds
58216	10	30	Publishing Industries
58218	20	172	Merch. Wholesalers,Nondur. Gds
58219	2	3	Repair and Maintenance
58220	215	1370	Nursing & Resid. Care Facilit.
58222	30	101	Crop Production
58223	10	63	Merch. Wholesalers,Durable Gds
58224	4	7	Warehousing and Storage
58225	81	606	Food Manufacturing
58227	46	133	Educational Services
58228	38	238	Food Svcs & Drinking Places
58229	6	13	Warehousing and Storage
58230	69	385	Educational Services
58231	30	194	Merch. Wholesalers,Durable Gds
58233	21	71	Merch. Wholesalers,Nondur. Gds
58235	20	85	Crop Production
58236	3	7	Merch. Wholesalers,Nondur. Gds
58237	354	3297	Miscellaneous Manufacturing
58238	6	12	Crop Production
58239	8	14	Food and Beverage Stores
58240	45	298	Nursing & Resid. Care Facilit.
58241	10	14	Merch. Wholesalers,Nondur. Gds
58243	49	243	Crop Production
58244	9	102	Educational Services
58249	236	1268	Educational Services
58250	19	68	Educational Services
58251	93	578	Merch. Wholesalers,Nondur. Gds
58254	53	355	Hospitals
58255	1	2	Exec., Legis., & Other Support
58256	25	131	Educational Services
58257	131	1005	Educational Services
58258	5	41	Special Trade Contractors
58259	32	152	Miscellaneous Manufacturing
58260	14	178	Construction of Buildings
58261	64	456	Truck Transportation
58262	14	53	Nursing & Resid. Care Facilit.
58265	39	208	Educational Services
58266	14	14	Crop Production
58267	65	595	Nursing & Resid. Care Facilit.
58269	18	103	Nursing & Resid. Care Facilit.
58270	138	854	Nursing & Resid. Care Facilit.
58271	66	952	Transportation Equipment Mfg
58272	23	56	Educational Services
58273	14	67	Justice, Pubic Order/Safety
58274	38	132	Merch. Wholesalers,Nondur. Gds
58275	16	44	Warehousing and Storage
58276	37	152	Educational Services
58277	7	12	Warehousing and Storage
58278	47	212	Educational Services
58281	9	14	Food Svcs & Drinking Places
58282	98	598	Crop Production
58301	620	5795	Educational Services
58310	2	9	Warehousing and Storage
58311	5	7	Chemical Manufacturing
58313	7	8	Merch. Wholesalers,Nondur. Gds
58316	101	4359	Exec., Legis., & Other Support
58317	19	64	Warehousing and Storage
58318	288	2133	Accommodation
58319	1	6	Warehousing and Storage
58321	13	10	Warehousing and Storage
58323	5	23	Merch. Wholesalers,Nondur. Gds
58324	126	780	Food Manufacturing
58325	9	23	Warehousing and Storage
58327	13	33	Warehousing and Storage
58329	70	857	Computer & Electronic Prod Mfg
58330	21	103	Educational Services
58331	12	49	Justice, Pubic Order/Safety
58332	15	31	Merch. Wholesalers,Nondur. Gds
58335	64	1101	Relig., Grant, Civic, Prof Org
58338	15	27	Merch. Wholesalers,Nondur. Gds
58339	5	13	Merch. Wholesalers,Nondur. Gds
58341	193	1088	Relig., Grant, Civic, Prof Org
58343	1	2	Postal Service
58344	85	388	Educational Services
58345	11	10	Merch. Wholesalers,Nondur. Gds
58346	37	180	Educational Services
58348	49	290	Prof., Scientific, & Tech Svcs
58351	41	129	Educational Services
58352	38	182	Educational Services
58353	4	13	Crop Production
58355	10	28	Justice, Pubic Order/Safety
58356	127	740	Relig., Grant, Civic, Prof Org
58357	8	28	Educational Services
58359	1	0	Postal Service
58361	12	26	Food Svcs & Drinking Places
58362	4	2	Merch. Wholesalers,Durable Gds
58363	2	2	Warehousing and Storage
58365	32	143	Educational Services
58366	51	324	Educational Services
58367	152	1016	Hospitals
58368	257	1612	Hospitals
58369	23	81	Educational Services
58370	16	492	Accommodation
58372	12	30	Support Activities: Agr./For.
58374	24	103	Educational Services
58377	17	37	Educational Services
58379	8	51	Social Assistance
58380	32	106	Merch. Wholesalers,Nondur. Gds
58381	13	111	Educational Services
58382	9	15	Postal Service
58384	37	61	Crop Production
58385	11	69	Educational Services
58386	7	20	Merch. Wholesalers,Nondur. Gds
58401	862	9409	Hospitals
58402	11	65	Relig., Grant, Civic, Prof Org
58405	1	150	Educational Services
58413	87	508	Educational Services
58415	3	10	Merch. Wholesalers,Nondur. Gds
58416	55	150	Accommodation
58418	41	61	Crop Production
58420	13	30	Educational Services
58421	224	1709	Food Manufacturing
58422	17	26	Crop Production
58423	15	24	Crop Production
58424	41	118	Construction of Buildings
58425	183	910	Nursing & Resid. Care Facilit.
58426	8	18	Merch. Wholesalers,Nondur. Gds
58428	11	66	Accommodation
58429	15	37	Accommodation
58430	1	1	Postal Service
58431	10	8	Prof., Scientific, & Tech Svcs
58433	85	649	Crop Production
58436	131	799	Educational Services
58438	68	380	Merch. Wholesalers,Nondur. Gds
58439	11	38	Animal Production
58440	21	34	Food Svcs & Drinking Places
58441	21	194	Unclassified Establishments
58442	36	138	Educational Services
58443	24	52	Crop Production
58444	18	53	Educational Services
58445	17	29	Crop Production
58448	33	91	Warehousing and Storage
58451	31	57	Crop Production
58452	3	3	Postal Service
58454	18	36	Relig., Grant, Civic, Prof Org
58455	13	85	Justice, Pubic Order/Safety
58456	48	142	Relig., Grant, Civic, Prof Org
58458	116	828	Educational Services
58460	11	38	Elect'l Eqpmt, App, & Comp Mfg
58461	28	61	Educational Services
58463	66	307	Construction of Buildings
58464	30	84	Social Assistance
58466	18	48	Educational Services
58467	81	259	Crop Production
58472	24	41	Crop Production
58474	187	1179	Nursing & Resid. Care Facilit.
58475	12	39	Educational Services
58476	28	79	Crop Production
58477	4	13	Educational Services
58478	15	24	Food Svcs & Drinking Places
58479	11	60	Educational Services
58480	15	31	Merch. Wholesalers,Nondur. Gds
58481	13	91	Food Manufacturing
58482	82	448	Nursing & Resid. Care Facilit.
58483	26	50	Exec., Legis., & Other Support
58484	6	19	Relig., Grant, Civic, Prof Org
58486	35	79	Educational Services
58487	25	67	Educational Services
58488	15	45	Educational Services
58490	17	35	Educational Services
58492	26	93	Educational Services
58494	19	47	Educational Services
58495	93	691	Nursing & Resid. Care Facilit.
58496	36	67	Crop Production
58497	26	88	Educational Services
58501	1714	22795	Ambulatory Health Care Svcs
58502	26	36	Prof., Scientific, & Tech Svcs
58503	591	7151	Food Svcs & Drinking Places
58504	1165	14624	Food Svcs & Drinking Places
58505	100	2912	Exec., Legis., & Other Support
58506	5	80	Textile Product Mills
58507	4	7	Construction of Buildings
58520	11	29	Educational Services
58521	16	34	Crop Production
58523	187	2817	Oil and Gas Extraction
58524	7	8	Postal Service
58528	6	45	Educational Services
58529	48	184	Educational Services
58530	70	621	Utilities
58531	11	31	Admin. Enviro. Quality Progrms
58532	9	15	Prof., Scientific, & Tech Svcs
58533	60	318	Hospitals
58535	28	137	Educational Services
58538	79	1723	Exec., Legis., & Other Support
58540	129	903	Educational Services
58541	15	56	Justice, Pubic Order/Safety
58542	13	25	Food Svcs & Drinking Places
58544	30	151	Educational Services
58545	152	1029	Educational Services
58549	11	17	Machinery Manufacturing
58552	124	932	Educational Services
58554	817	7850	Food Svcs & Drinking Places
58558	19	79	Nonmetallic Mineral Prod. Mfg
58559	13	13	Postal Service
58560	4	16	Admin. Enviro. Quality Progrms
58561	71	436	Educational Services
58562	28	94	Educational Services
58563	63	453	Educational Services
58564	2	64	Relig., Grant, Civic, Prof Org
58565	18	141	Admin. Enviro. Quality Progrms
58566	10	12	Support Activities: Agr./For.
58568	14	54	Educational Services
58569	4	6	Food Svcs & Drinking Places
58570	9	48	Educational Services
58571	46	349	Utilities
58572	16	56	Educational Services
58573	36	255	Nursing & Resid. Care Facilit.
58575	55	235	Hospitals
58576	47	758	Mining (Except Oil and Gas)
58577	99	648	Educational Services
58579	38	216	Educational Services
58580	15	21	Postal Service
58581	20	47	Educational Services
58601	1143	10316	Food Svcs & Drinking Places
58602	10	24	Social Assistance
58620	31	32	Exec., Legis., & Other Support
58621	140	606	Merch. Wholesalers,Durable Gds

BUSINESS DATA

ZIP CODE	2004 Total Firms	2004 Total Employees	TOP INDUSTRY RANKED on 2004 EMPLOYMENT	ZIP CODE	2004 Total Firms	2004 Total Employees	TOP INDUSTRY RANKED on 2004 EMPLOYMENT	ZIP CODE	2004 Total Firms	2004 Total Employees	TOP INDUSTRY RANKED on 2004 EMPLOYMENT
58622	94	522	Pipeline Transportation	58794	4	15	Support Activities for Mining	59102	2333	20659	Food Svcs & Drinking Places
58623	212	1316	Educational Services	58795	24	44	Educational Services	59103	26	59	Ambulatory Health Care Svcs
58625	11	17	Educational Services	58801	1063	8610	Support Activities for Mining	59104	42	58	Insurance Carriers & Related
58626	13	26	Justice, Pubic Order/Safety	58802	20	16	Educational Services	59105	797	5107	Food Svcs & Drinking Places
58627	7	24	Educational Services	58830	14	22	Justice, Pubic Order/Safety	59106	213	1496	Heavy & Civil Eng. Construct'N
58630	10	18	Administrative & Support Svcs	58831	20	76	Educational Services	59107	21	45	Construction of Buildings
58631	65	431	Nursing & Resid. Care Facilit.	58833	9	11	Postal Service	59108	18	89	Administrative & Support Svcs
58632	17	48	Educational Services	58835	21	45	Oil and Gas Extraction	59201	257	1786	Hospitals
58634	20	54	Utilities	58838	4	23	Construction of Buildings	59211	6	12	Postal Service
58636	46	147	Educational Services	58843	18	64	Justice, Pubic Order/Safety	59212	16	53	Educational Services
58638	62	252	Nonmetallic Mineral Prod. Mfg	58844	13	24	Warehousing and Storage	59213	15	115	Educational Services
58639	167	893	Hospitals	58845	30	100	Educational Services	59214	5	7	Animal Production
58640	87	583	Ambulatory Health Care Svcs	58847	23	90	Special Trade Contractors	59215	115	785	Educational Services
58641	5	2	Animal Production	58849	58	375	Merch. Wholesalers,Durable Gds	59217	3	5	Miscellaneous Manufacturing
58642	21	46	Exec., Legis., & Other Support	58852	126	782	Educational Services	59218	69	350	Nursing & Resid. Care Facilit.
58643	11	51	Merch. Wholesalers,Durable Gds	58853	22	215	Educational Services	59219	11	18	Special Trade Contractors
58645	87	694	Unclassified Establishments	58854	199	874	Educational Services	59221	55	203	Educational Services
58646	86	402	Nursing & Resid. Care Facilit.	58856	9	19	Warehousing and Storage	59222	16	29	Educational Services
58647	56	267	Educational Services	59001	109	305	Educational Services	59223	26	78	Admin. Enviro. Quality Progrms
58649	25	58	Justice, Pubic Order/Safety	59002	1	4	Food Svcs & Drinking Places	59225	26	181	Educational Services
58650	35	89	Educational Services	59003	40	201	Educational Services	59226	19	48	Food Svcs & Drinking Places
58651	28	95	Educational Services	59006	16	71	Food Svcs & Drinking Places	59230	331	2253	Hospitals
58652	55	238	Relig., Grant, Civic, Prof Org	59007	4	6	Food Manufacturing	59231	7	6	Transportation Equipment Mfg
58653	36	188	Educational Services	59008	25	58	Educational Services	59240	3	0	Postal Service
58654	6	90	Social Assistance	59010	6	10	Animal Production	59241	20	46	Educational Services
58655	31	110	Educational Services	59011	269	1071	Nursing & Resid. Care Facilit.	59242	8	45	Educational Services
58656	14	52	Warehousing and Storage	59012	10	14	Animal Production	59243	15	56	Educational Services
58701	1608	19598	Hospitals	59013	11	23	Construction of Buildings	59244	3	2	Special Trade Contractors
58702	24	26	Exec., Legis., & Other Support	59014	74	271	Furniture & Related Prod. Mfg	59247	23	101	Educational Services
58703	550	5263	Unclassified Establishments	59015	16	78	Educational Services	59248	30	96	Educational Services
58704	16	214	Educational Services	59016	15	214	Educational Services	59250	22	103	Educational Services
58705	45	911	Administrative & Support Svcs	59018	32	195	Unclassified Establishments	59252	12	43	Educational Services
58707	2	501	Educational Services	59019	187	1323	Miscellaneous Manufacturing	59253	10	42	Educational Services
58710	26	83	Educational Services	59020	30	116	Food Svcs & Drinking Places	59254	202	1096	Hospitals
58711	17	30	Food Svcs & Drinking Places	59022	57	1264	Exec., Legis., & Other Support	59255	125	1742	Educational Services
58712	7	19	Heavy & Civil Eng. Construct'N	59024	17	49	Educational Services	59256	14	20	Nat'l Security & Int'l Affairs
58713	2	2	Construction of Buildings	59025	21	406	Mining (Except Oil and Gas)	59257	3	5	Postal Service
58716	7	12	Special Trade Contractors	59026	6	19	Educational Services	59258	10	19	Animal Production
58718	59	276	Construction of Buildings	59027	47	296	Merch. Wholesalers,Durable Gds	59259	27	86	Educational Services
58721	70	239	Justice, Pubic Order/Safety	59028	28	42	Food Svcs & Drinking Places	59260	14	15	Gasoline Stations
58722	48	174	Educational Services	59029	20	124	Educational Services	59261	26	166	Educational Services
58723	13	18	Relig., Grant, Civic, Prof Org	59030	110	833	Educational Services	59262	15	61	Educational Services
58725	18	43	Exec., Legis., & Other Support	59031	5	22	Museums, Hist. Sites,& Similar	59263	130	594	Telecommunications
58727	15	73	Exec., Legis., & Other Support	59032	22	59	Educational Services	59270	482	3674	Unclassified Establishments
58730	118	622	Nursing & Resid. Care Facilit.	59033	7	10	Bldg Matl & Garden Eqpmt Dlrs	59273	3	3	Animal Production
58731	13	16	Food and Beverage Stores	59034	264	1470	Food Svcs & Drinking Places	59274	12	21	Crop Production
58733	14	76	Educational Services	59035	23	83	Admin. Enviro. Quality Progrms	59275	26	91	Educational Services
58734	15	28	Plastics & Rubber Products Mfg	59036	107	488	Hospitals	59276	4	5	Warehousing and Storage
58735	3	2	Food Svcs & Drinking Places	59037	57	210	Utilities	59301	670	4887	Hospitals
58736	39	121	Educational Services	59038	50	141	Educational Services	59311	16	16	Support Activities: Agr./For.
58737	14	16	Warehousing and Storage	59039	4	10	Food Svcs & Drinking Places	59312	5	2	Postal Service
58740	39	163	Educational Services	59041	66	203	Educational Services	59313	208	989	Ambulatory Health Care Svcs
58741	35	131	Educational Services	59043	101	943	Exec., Legis., & Other Support	59314	3	6	Educational Services
58744	13	20	Rail Transportation	59044	338	2851	Rail Transportation	59315	8	12	Food and Beverage Stores
58746	116	842	Merch. Wholesalers,Durable Gds	59046	22	64	Educational Services	59316	2	1	Prof., Scientific, & Tech Svcs
58747	1	1	Postal Service	59047	776	4167	Food Svcs & Drinking Places	59317	131	420	Educational Services
58748	8	10	Bldg Matl & Garden Eqpmt Dlrs	59050	25	211	Educational Services	59318	4	4	Construction of Buildings
58750	30	79	Merch. Wholesalers,Nondur. Gds	59052	17	572	Mining (Except Oil and Gas)	59322	3	6	Merch. Wholesalers,Nondur. Gds
58752	32	118	Educational Services	59053	16	152	Animal Production	59323	106	1663	Educational Services
58755	6	11	Oil and Gas Extraction	59054	18	72	Animal Production	59324	72	300	Nursing & Resid. Care Facilit.
58756	18	69	Educational Services	59055	8	13	Educational Services	59326	10	20	Justice, Pubic Order/Safety
58757	21	122	Educational Services	59057	19	32	Prof., Scientific, & Tech Svcs	59327	180	882	Nursing & Resid. Care Facilit.
58758	11	15	Repair and Maintenance	59058	2	3	Educational Services	59330	440	3390	Educational Services
58759	28	94	Educational Services	59059	7	16	Animal Production	59332	5	5	Educational Services
58760	13	33	Bldg Matl & Garden Eqpmt Dlrs	59061	13	844	Mining (Except Oil and Gas)	59336	12	33	Justice, Pubic Order/Safety
58761	108	655	Administrative & Support Svcs	59062	1	1	Educational Services	59337	81	317	Educational Services
58762	30	99	Machinery Manufacturing	59063	35	152	Educational Services	59338	5	20	Educational Services
58763	219	2091	Exec., Legis., & Other Support	59064	5	7	Postal Service	59339	9	16	Animal Production
58765	28	96	Nursing & Resid. Care Facilit.	59065	19	213	Accommodation	59343	3	1	Food Manufacturing
58768	6	11	Truck Transportation	59066	13	127	Educational Services	59344	15	58	Educational Services
58769	4	11	Food Svcs & Drinking Places	59067	11	43	Educational Services	59345	2	4	Animal Production
58770	64	274	Educational Services	59068	341	1648	Accommodation	59347	9	33	Educational Services
58771	23	76	Merch. Wholesalers,Nondur. Gds	59069	17	32	Accommodation	59349	76	224	Nursing & Resid. Care Facilit.
58772	25	76	Prof., Scientific, & Tech Svcs	59070	32	62	Educational Services	59351	7	9	Support Activities: Agr./For.
58773	44	133	Educational Services	59071	11	28	Food Svcs & Drinking Places	59353	63	216	Educational Services
58775	19	180	Educational Services	59072	207	921	Hospitals	59354	1	0	Relig., Grant, Civic, Prof Org
58776	14	26	Support Activities: Agr./For.	59074	27	121	Animal Production	59401	1019	7903	Prof., Scientific, & Tech Svcs
58778	4	12	Justice, Pubic Order/Safety	59075	6	49	Educational Services	59402	38	3457	Nat'l Security & Int'l Affairs
58779	18	31	Merch. Wholesalers,Nondur. Gds	59077	7	12	Educational Services	59403	22	86	Social Assistance
58781	31	107	Educational Services	59078	3	7	Postal Service	59404	765	7100	General Merchandise Stores
58782	34	106	Educational Services	59079	67	251	Educational Services	59405	1336	14634	Hospitals
58783	20	39	Crop Production	59081	4	16	Accommodation	59406	11	17	Relig., Grant, Civic, Prof Org
58784	166	735	Nursing & Resid. Care Facilit.	59082	1	0	Postal Service	59410	66	187	Educational Services
58785	26	175	Educational Services	59084	2	5	Animal Production	59411	12	25	Educational Services
58787	13	36	Justice, Pubic Order/Safety	59085	5	18	Animal Production	59412	64	253	Educational Services
58788	70	392	Bldg Matl & Garden Eqpmt Dlrs	59086	32	77	Educational Services	59414	95	787	Broadcasting
58789	20	80	Admin. Enviro. Quality Progrms	59087	36	84	Educational Services	59416	17	63	Educational Services
58790	72	464	Nursing & Resid. Care Facilit.	59088	53	197	Educational Services	59417	239	5207	Exec., Legis., & Other Support
58792	6	46	Bldg Matl & Garden Eqpmt Dlrs	59089	4	36	Animal Production	59418	1	0	Postal Service
58793	63	344	Relig., Grant, Civic, Prof Org	59101	3098	33450	Hospitals	59419	6	21	Educational Services

ZIP CODE	2004 Total Firms	2004 Total Employees	TOP INDUSTRY RANKED on 2004 EMPLOYMENT	ZIP CODE	2004 Total Firms	2004 Total Employees	TOP INDUSTRY RANKED on 2004 EMPLOYMENT	ZIP CODE	2004 Total Firms	2004 Total Employees	TOP INDUSTRY RANKED on 2004 EMPLOYMENT
59420	20	108	Support Activities: Agr./For.	59642	3	4	Postal Service	59854	36	82	Support Activities: Agr./For.
59421	50	277	Educational Services	59643	5	41	Special Trade Contractors	59855	73	1057	Exec., Legis., & Other Support
59422	211	1113	Animal Production	59644	195	918	Food Svcs & Drinking Places	59856	10	96	Food Svcs & Drinking Places
59424	2	5	Repair and Maintenance	59645	110	490	Animal Production	59858	81	401	Prof., Scientific, & Tech Svcs
59425	248	1332	Hospitals	59647	3	1	Construction of Buildings	59859	164	981	Ambulatory Health Care Svcs
59427	298	1936	Educational Services	59648	37	139	Scenic & Sightseeing Transport	59860	636	3605	Ambulatory Health Care Svcs
59430	33	158	Educational Services	59701	1626	17800	Special Trade Contractors	59863	13	34	Food Svcs & Drinking Places
59432	17	24	Educational Services	59702	9	7	Health & Personal Care Stores	59864	364	2102	Hospitals
59433	29	126	Educational Services	59703	8	21	Museums, Hist. Sites,& Similar	59865	151	818	Exec., Legis., & Other Support
59434	38	405	Accommodation	59710	26	58	Wood Product Manufacturing	59866	41	337	Wood Product Manufacturing
59435	10	25	Oil and Gas Extraction	59711	419	2787	Accommodation	59867	5	18	Admin. of Economic Programs
59436	111	809	Educational Services	59713	18	28	Educational Services	59868	170	693	Wood Product Manufacturing
59440	3	12	Waste Managmt & Remediat'n Svc	59714	653	3836	Food Svcs & Drinking Places	59870	340	1764	Educational Services
59442	160	724	Nursing & Resid. Care Facilit.	59715	2286	15857	Ambulatory Health Care Svcs	59871	9	26	Exec., Legis., & Other Support
59443	21	46	Educational Services	59716	241	1677	Accommodation	59872	133	738	Educational Services
59444	17	32	Relig., Grant, Civic, Prof Org	59717	16	315	Ambulatory Health Care Svcs	59873	220	1161	Educational Services
59445	1	1	Warehousing and Storage	59718	1102	7563	Food Svcs & Drinking Places	59874	53	192	Support Activities: Agr./For.
59446	30	147	Educational Services	59719	18	23	Special Trade Contractors	59875	169	819	Wood Product Manufacturing
59447	14	51	Educational Services	59720	32	118	Mining (Except Oil and Gas)	59901	2953	23395	Food Svcs & Drinking Places
59448	13	240	Educational Services	59721	10	26	Educational Services	59903	56	124	Construction of Buildings
59450	16	45	Educational Services	59722	227	2067	Justice, Pubic Order/Safety	59904	35	94	Relig., Grant, Civic, Prof Org
59451	8	22	Food Manufacturing	59724	7	22	Animal Production	59910	13	36	Relig., Grant, Civic, Prof Org
59452	28	115	Educational Services	59725	526	2918	Educational Services	59911	531	2310	Food Svcs & Drinking Places
59453	13	37	Educational Services	59727	12	9	Motor Vehicle & Parts Dealers	59912	530	3706	Merch. Wholesalers,Durable Gds
59454	22	58	Merch. Wholesalers,Durable Gds	59728	17	48	Construction of Buildings	59913	28	72	Food Svcs & Drinking Places
59456	10	22	Crop Production	59729	256	699	Accommodation	59914	9	26	Beverage & Tobacco Product Mfg
59457	589	3695	Hospitals	59730	110	667	Accommodation	59915	16	32	Exec., Legis., & Other Support
59460	21	48	Motor Vehicle & Parts Dealers	59731	6	10	Educational Services	59916	4	24	Accommodation
59461	2	1	Repair and Maintenance	59732	4	6	Educational Services	59917	345	1220	Educational Services
59462	8	26	Prof., Scientific, & Tech Svcs	59733	7	39	Accommodation	59918	26	203	Wood Product Manufacturing
59463	7	12	Accommodation	59735	18	60	Educational Services	59919	38	182	Support Activities: Agr./For.
59464	17	86	Food Svcs & Drinking Places	59736	28	75	Unclassified Establishments	59920	23	58	Educational Services
59465	11	109	Accommodation	59739	35	97	Educational Services	59921	1	0	Postal Service
59466	17	80	Special Trade Contractors	59740	27	37	Food Svcs & Drinking Places	59922	114	623	Relig., Grant, Civic, Prof Org
59467	13	161	Animal Production	59741	162	782	Food Svcs & Drinking Places	59923	603	3835	Support Activities: Agr./For.
59468	23	76	Educational Services	59743	14	34	Food Svcs & Drinking Places	59925	37	172	Educational Services
59469	13	27	Justice, Pubic Order/Safety	59745	13	92	Truck Transportation	59926	12	42	Accommodation
59471	18	68	Educational Services	59746	11	25	Accommodation	59927	21	60	Merch. Wholesalers,Durable Gds
59472	13	228	Animal Production	59747	17	23	Animal Production	59928	3	3	General Merchandise Stores
59474	254	1536	Hospitals	59748	6	93	Educational Services	59929	7	15	Accommodation
59477	20	102	Educational Services	59749	115	428	Educational Services	59930	22	47	Furn. & Home Furnishgs Stores
59479	61	318	Support Activities: Agr./For.	59750	10	250	Miscellaneous Manufacturing	59931	10	32	Accommodation
59480	10	42	Justice, Pubic Order/Safety	59751	5	5	Social Assistance	59932	51	218	Educational Services
59482	51	203	Educational Services	59752	152	1805	Perform'g Arts, Spec. Sports	59933	2	0	Postal Service
59483	20	81	Special Trade Contractors	59754	79	305	Miscellaneous Manufacturing	59934	13	49	Support Activities: Agr./For.
59484	29	248	Prof., Scientific, & Tech Svcs	59755	62	243	Exec., Legis., & Other Support	59935	157	687	Health & Personal Care Stores
59485	16	84	Animal Production	59756	13	328	Hospitals	59936	40	633	Accommodation
59486	61	741	Construction of Buildings	59758	305	1794	Accommodation	59937	872	4960	Food Svcs & Drinking Places
59487	33	123	Educational Services	59759	176	584	Educational Services	60001	1	2	Machinery Manufacturing
59489	26	65	Educational Services	59760	10	47	Educational Services	60002	915	5574	Food Svcs & Drinking Places
59501	673	5680	Hospitals	59761	39	111	Support Activities: Agr./For.	60004	2015	22310	Telecommunications
59520	105	361	Educational Services	59762	34	95	Support Activities: Agr./For.	60005	1891	29303	Air Transportation
59521	44	1246	Exec., Legis., & Other Support	59771	52	109	Perform'g Arts, Spec. Sports	60006	13	40	Nonmetallic Mineral Prod. Mfg
59522	133	723	Unclassified Establishments	59772	27	29	Administrative & Support Svcs	60007	3058	49401	Merch. Wholesalers,Durable Gds
59523	217	791	Educational Services	59773	6	19	Special Trade Contractors	60008	1113	20528	Isps, Web Search Portals
59524	22	63	Educational Services	59801	1936	15452	Food Svcs & Drinking Places	60009	7	62	Fabricated Metal Product Mfg
59525	18	92	Relig., Grant, Civic, Prof Org	59802	1182	11649	Social Assistance	60010	2316	18535	Insurance Carriers & Related
59526	75	829	Exec., Legis., & Other Support	59803	340	1214	Educational Services	60011	29	131	Heavy & Civil Eng. Construct'N
59527	24	251	Educational Services	59804	305	4180	Hospitals	60012	299	5268	Fabricated Metal Product Mfg
59528	20	40	Merch. Wholesalers,Nondur. Gds	59806	63	209	Nonmetallic Mineral Prod. Mfg	60013	836	7300	Machinery Manufacturing
59529	10	18	Crop Production	59807	21	51	Prof., Scientific, & Tech Svcs	60014	2138	21484	Food Svcs & Drinking Places
59530	10	50	Justice, Pubic Order/Safety	59808	780	10915	Food Svcs & Drinking Places	60015	1557	25180	Prof., Scientific, & Tech Svcs
59531	35	94	Educational Services	59812	29	1846	Educational Services	60016	1602	20053	Educational Services
59532	6	26	Educational Services	59820	36	144	Educational Services	60017	8	22	Transit & Grnd Pass. Transport
59535	9	5	Educational Services	59821	85	269	Educational Services	60018	1854	38154	Prof., Scientific, & Tech Svcs
59537	8	39	Unclassified Establishments	59823	63	194	Educational Services	60020	393	2528	Food Svcs & Drinking Places
59538	225	1137	Food Svcs & Drinking Places	59824	60	278	Educational Services	60021	195	1313	Food Svcs & Drinking Places
59540	37	126	Educational Services	59825	69	155	Educational Services	60022	331	2319	Museums, Hist. Sites,& Similar
59542	25	97	Educational Services	59826	60	162	Support Activities: Agr./For.	60025	2227	24418	Prof., Scientific, & Tech Svcs
59544	11	76	Educational Services	59827	12	31	Food Svcs & Drinking Places	60026	1	75	Nat'l Security & Int'l Affairs
59545	8	6	Relig., Grant, Civic, Prof Org	59828	143	663	Educational Services	60029	12	196	Relig., Grant, Civic, Prof Org
59546	10	36	Prof., Scientific, & Tech Svcs	59829	131	683	Educational Services	60030	1136	9712	Educational Services
59547	6	15	Educational Services	59830	6	12	Food Svcs & Drinking Places	60031	1560	21605	Amusement, Gambling,& Recreat.
59601	2399	26016	Exec., Legis., & Other Support	59831	16	42	Construction of Buildings	60033	490	4005	Bldg Matl & Garden Eqpmt Dlrs
59602	506	2966	Food Svcs & Drinking Places	59832	54	172	Educational Services	60034	102	918	Machinery Manufacturing
59604	27	19	Administrative & Support Svcs	59833	147	675	Educational Services	60035	1904	15056	Hospitals
59620	7	442	Admin. Enviro. Quality Progrms	59834	66	344	Educational Services	60037	10	77	Nat'l Security & Int'l Affairs
59623	7	410	Exec., Legis., & Other Support	59835	2	2	Construction of Buildings	60039	23	64	Administrative & Support Svcs
59624	17	14	Administrative & Support Svcs	59837	12	59	Wood Product Manufacturing	60040	215	1553	Food Svcs & Drinking Places
59625	2	217	Educational Services	59840	952	5804	Nursing & Resid. Care Facilit.	60041	271	1505	Educational Services
59626	2	25	Admin. of Housing Programs	59841	4	15	Educational Services	60042	216	1303	Merch. Wholesalers,Durable Gds
59631	11	17	Food Svcs & Drinking Places	59842	8	37	Accommodation	60043	91	449	Educational Services
59632	100	855	Exec., Legis., & Other Support	59843	17	22	Animal Production	60044	725	7171	Prof., Scientific, & Tech Svcs
59633	6	6	Educational Services	59844	21	78	Fabricated Metal Product Mfg	60045	1179	17277	Merch. Wholesalers,Durable Gds
59634	101	542	Food Svcs & Drinking Places	59845	73	336	Educational Services	60046	812	4321	Relig., Grant, Civic, Prof Org
59635	137	941	Primary Metal Manufacturing	59846	24	62	Food Svcs & Drinking Places	60047	1548	15426	Support Act. for Transport.
59636	11	846	Ambulatory Health Care Svcs	59847	166	757	Educational Services	60048	1891	22656	Hospitals
59638	10	211	Mining (Except Oil and Gas)	59848	3	7	Food and Beverage Stores	60049	6	3055	Insurance Carriers & Related
59639	122	496	Food Manufacturing	59851	24	111	Food and Beverage Stores	60050	1525	17235	Hospitals
59640	5	45	Accommodation	59853	46	173	Educational Services	60051	382	1884	Special Trade Contractors

BUSINESS DATA

ZIP CODE	2004 Total Firms	2004 Total Employ-ees	TOP INDUSTRY RANKED on 2004 EMPLOYMENT	ZIP CODE	2004 Total Firms	2004 Total Employ-ees	TOP INDUSTRY RANKED on 2004 EMPLOYMENT	ZIP CODE	2004 Total Firms	2004 Total Employ-ees	TOP INDUSTRY RANKED on 2004 EMPLOYMENT
60053	905	13441	Chemical Manufacturing	60170	15	338	Educational Services	60463	800	8699	Hospitals
60056	1672	22355	Administrative & Support Svcs	60171	348	4748	Educational Services	60464	247	2120	Educational Services
60060	1430	14378	Educational Services	60172	1000	7261	Prof., Scientific, & Tech Svcs	60465	528	5290	Educational Services
60061	951	19062	Merch. Wholesalers,Durable Gds	60173	2040	40747	Prof., Scientific, & Tech Svcs	60466	521	7803	Educational Services
60062	3630	40151	Insurance Carriers & Related	60174	1918	24068	Food Svcs & Drinking Places	60467	449	3322	Ambulatory Health Care Svcs
60064	349	25496	Merch. Wholesalers,Nondur. Gds	60175	505	3127	Exec., Legis., & Other Support	60468	209	1365	Educational Services
60065	39	78	Repair and Maintenance	60176	475	9817	Food Svcs & Drinking Places	60469	149	1217	Special Trade Contractors
60067	1675	14070	Educational Services	60177	553	5244	Plastics & Rubber Products Mfg	60470	29	95	Nonmetallic Mineral Prod. Mfg
60068	1674	14398	Ambulatory Health Care Svcs	60178	778	7696	Chemical Manufacturing	60471	233	1873	Food Svcs & Drinking Places
60069	385	13548	Administrative & Support Svcs	60179	2	5002	General Merchandise Stores	60472	103	1289	Educational Services
60070	395	4943	Credit Intermediation & Relatd	60180	96	1010	Electronics & Appliance Stores	60473	954	12334	Educational Services
60071	245	2514	Computer & Electronic Prod Mfg	60181	1734	21101	Administrative & Support Svcs	60474	23	132	Food and Beverage Stores
60072	66	908	Fabricated Metal Product Mfg	60183	29	200	Educational Services	60475	282	1565	Educational Services
60073	915	7537	Educational Services	60184	76	216	Insurance Carriers & Related	60476	99	1106	Heavy & Civil Eng. Construct'N
60074	920	7355	Educational Services	60185	1278	15894	Special Trade Contractors	60477	1471	17102	Food Svcs & Drinking Places
60075	13	234	Construction of Buildings	60186	8	50	Construction of Buildings	60478	259	1644	Educational Services
60076	1413	14733	Miscellaneous Manufacturing	60187	2416	23244	Educational Services	60479	22	55	Merch. Wholesalers,Nondur. Gds
60077	1752	25991	Prof., Scientific, & Tech Svcs	60188	1295	20091	Merch. Wholesalers,Durable Gds	60480	150	754	Food Svcs & Drinking Places
60078	20	38	Electronics & Appliance Stores	60189	31	71	Prof., Scientific, & Tech Svcs	60481	422	2424	Special Trade Contractors
60079	10	30	Amusement, Gambling,& Recreat.	60190	334	4873	Hospitals	60482	344	2067	Credit Intermediation & Relatd
60081	324	3471	Elect'l Eqpmt, App, & Comp Mfg	60191	893	12235	Merch. Wholesalers,Durable Gds	60490	203	2264	Food Svcs & Drinking Places
60082	5	46	Other Information Services	60192	77	1935	Credit Intermediation & Relatd	60491	396	3102	Food Svcs & Drinking Places
60083	146	1068	Administrative & Support Svcs	60193	1151	13389	Ambulatory Health Care Svcs	60499	5	5	Unclassified Establishments
60084	767	8022	Administrative & Support Svcs	60194	871	11485	Hospitals	60501	352	3618	Educational Services
60085	2101	29812	Exec., Legis., & Other Support	60195	983	11446	Food Svcs & Drinking Places	60504	1482	22507	Food Svcs & Drinking Places
60087	527	5674	Computer & Electronic Prod Mfg	60196	19	3481	Insurance Carriers & Related	60505	1076	9963	Educational Services
60088	61	1213	Unclassified Establishments	60201	2408	30633	Hospitals	60506	1600	23477	Amusement, Gambling,& Recreat.
60089	1415	15306	Prof., Scientific, & Tech Svcs	60202	1050	10119	Hospitals	60507	10	26	Merch. Wholesalers,Durable Gds
60090	1436	22751	Food Svcs & Drinking Places	60203	89	476	Administrative & Support Svcs	60510	1200	16397	Exec., Legis., & Other Support
60091	1209	7891	Educational Services	60204	16	70	Educational Services	60511	82	426	Funds, Trusts, & Other Finance
60093	1572	11074	Educational Services	60208	19	433	Other Information Services	60512	39	270	Merch. Wholesalers,Nondur. Gds
60095	2	0	Nonstore Retailers	60301	604	4391	Prof., Scientific, & Tech Svcs	60513	563	4224	Museums, Hist. Sites,& Similar
60096	160	836	Food Svcs & Drinking Places	60302	1383	10542	Hospitals	60514	311	1926	Credit Intermediation & Relatd
60097	189	554	Food and Beverage Stores	60303	10	24	Miscellaneous Store Retailers	60515	2222	34791	Prof., Scientific, & Tech Svcs
60098	1270	13227	Educational Services	60304	498	3321	Hospitals	60516	719	4738	Educational Services
60099	700	6702	Educational Services	60305	406	3645	Educational Services	60517	749	9657	Prof., Scientific, & Tech Svcs
60101	1926	24153	Merch. Wholesalers,Durable Gds	60401	188	1142	Machinery Manufacturing	60518	118	476	Educational Services
60102	886	6402	Educational Services	60402	1371	12212	Hospitals	60519	7	9	Real Estate
60103	769	4368	Educational Services	60406	669	9916	Hospitals	60520	102	446	Educational Services
60104	505	7337	Transportation Equipment Mfg	60407	37	204	Museums, Hist. Sites,& Similar	60521	1335	9214	Ambulatory Health Care Svcs
60106	1610	20328	Merch. Wholesalers,Durable Gds	60408	125	771	Educational Services	60522	28	71	Prof., Scientific, & Tech Svcs
60107	670	6712	Educational Services	60409	1016	10109	Food Svcs & Drinking Places	60523	1859	33311	Prof., Scientific, & Tech Svcs
60108	1202	13891	General Merchandise Stores	60410	261	4225	Oil and Gas Extraction	60525	1660	20585	Food Svcs & Drinking Places
60109	33	463	Educational Services	60411	1841	22178	Truck Transportation	60526	265	2860	Educational Services
60110	519	4883	Educational Services	60412	3	7	Personal and Laundry Services	60527	1449	16583	Prof., Scientific, & Tech Svcs
60111	15	17	Postal Service	60415	518	6872	Truck Transportation	60530	22	103	Machinery Manufacturing
60112	69	384	Fabricated Metal Product Mfg	60416	242	1710	Construction of Buildings	60531	57	324	Educational Services
60113	20	110	Admin. of Economic Programs	60417	498	3596	Educational Services	60532	1373	17690	Prof., Scientific, & Tech Svcs
60115	1280	14783	Food Svcs & Drinking Places	60419	446	4697	Educational Services	60534	329	2488	Merch. Wholesalers,Durable Gds
60118	988	9094	General Merchandise Stores	60420	214	2851	Print'g & Related Supp't Act's	60536	7	34	Bldg Matl & Garden Eqpmt Dlrs
60119	388	2601	Electronics & Appliance Stores	60421	93	881	Chemical Manufacturing	60537	15	42	Truck Transportation
60120	1228	16476	Hospitals	60422	311	2682	Educational Services	60538	419	5588	Merch. Wholesalers,Durable Gds
60121	20	148	Social Assistance	60423	1029	8366	Food Svcs & Drinking Places	60539	5	617	Relig., Grant, Civic, Prof Org
60123	2049	26988	Fabricated Metal Product Mfg	60424	65	426	Food Manufacturing	60540	2346	24343	Food Svcs & Drinking Places
60126	2089	27461	Ambulatory Health Care Svcs	60425	213	2468	Prof., Scientific, & Tech Svcs	60541	96	518	Educational Services
60129	12	15	Crop Production	60426	1169	13272	Administrative & Support Svcs	60542	369	4177	Food Svcs & Drinking Places
60130	556	6224	Food Manufacturing	60429	445	4861	Hospitals	60543	690	5251	Educational Services
60131	1110	21577	Fabricated Metal Product Mfg	60430	933	8420	Food Svcs & Drinking Places	60544	1447	11049	Educational Services
60133	570	6234	Administrative & Support Svcs	60431	813	7459	Educational Services	60545	269	2504	General Merchandise Stores
60134	1405	13080	Ambulatory Health Care Svcs	60432	902	11322	Justice, Pubic Order/Safety	60546	654	5867	Food and Beverage Stores
60135	205	1749	Computer & Electronic Prod Mfg	60433	377	5268	Justice, Pubic Order/Safety	60548	440	3166	Educational Services
60136	146	1023	Special Trade Contractors	60434	22	1348	Justice, Pubic Order/Safety	60549	23	524	Educational Services
60137	1545	15618	Educational Services	60435	2205	24655	Ambulatory Health Care Svcs	60550	62	413	Nursing & Resid. Care Facilit.
60138	17	46	Administrative & Support Svcs	60436	563	11612	Amusement, Gambling,& Recreat.	60551	107	645	Accommodation
60139	688	10456	Merch. Wholesalers,Durable Gds	60437	10	12	Special Trade Contractors	60552	129	773	Educational Services
60140	287	2551	Primary Metal Manufacturing	60438	1049	11355	Food Svcs & Drinking Places	60553	28	68	Merch. Wholesalers,Nondur. Gds
60141	10	25	Ambulatory Health Care Svcs	60439	825	12434	Prof., Scientific, & Tech Svcs	60554	295	2441	Educational Services
60142	467	4899	Educational Services	60440	1148	13796	Prof., Scientific, & Tech Svcs	60555	617	8423	Petroleum & Coal Products Mfg
60143	756	19319	Merch. Wholesalers,Durable Gds	60441	860	7506	Justice, Pubic Order/Safety	60556	80	523	Crop Production
60144	21	84	Prof., Scientific, & Tech Svcs	60442	219	1076	Educational Services	60557	11	102	Nonmetallic Mineral Prod. Mfg
60145	67	414	Unclassified Establishments	60443	705	7777	Food Svcs & Drinking Places	60558	352	2042	Educational Services
60146	91	737	Merch. Wholesalers,Nondur. Gds	60444	68	329	Educational Services	60559	1232	11247	Food Svcs & Drinking Places
60147	16	61	Fabricated Metal Product Mfg	60445	857	10216	Food Svcs & Drinking Places	60560	549	3939	Food Svcs & Drinking Places
60148	2304	25410	Food Svcs & Drinking Places	60446	663	8898	Educational Services	60561	598	5191	Food Svcs & Drinking Places
60150	61	529	Educational Services	60447	252	1903	Educational Services	60563	2327	32341	Computer & Electronic Prod Mfg
60151	153	1164	Educational Services	60448	916	6615	Machinery Manufacturing	60564	887	6317	Educational Services
60152	457	4002	Merch. Wholesalers,Durable Gds	60449	251	1384	Food Svcs & Drinking Places	60565	680	3684	Educational Services
60153	712	14377	Educational Services	60450	935	8572	Chemical Manufacturing	60566	14	327	Social Assistance
60154	784	7091	Prof., Scientific, & Tech Svcs	60451	975	6225	Educational Services	60567	35	59	Miscellaneous Store Retailers
60155	430	10811	Merch. Wholesalers,Durable Gds	60452	671	7097	Hospitals	60572	1	1150	Telecommunications
60156	511	3593	Food Svcs & Drinking Places	60453	1925	21706	Hospitals	60598	5	12	Wholesale Elec. Mrkts & Agents
60157	81	590	Relig., Grant, Civic, Prof Org	60454	18	58	Administrative & Support Svcs	60601	3270	69966	Prof., Scientific, & Tech Svcs
60159	7	18	Prof., Scientific, & Tech Svcs	60455	842	11055	Fabricated Metal Product Mfg	60602	3163	38128	Prof., Scientific, & Tech Svcs
60160	1129	19416	Hospitals	60456	56	490	Justice, Pubic Order/Safety	60603	2297	47837	Prof., Scientific, & Tech Svcs
60161	6	9	Repair and Maintenance	60457	439	2644	Food Svcs & Drinking Places	60604	1666	41160	Insurance Carriers & Related
60162	456	6956	Repair and Maintenance	60458	223	1285	Educational Services	60605	1336	19636	Securities/Commodity Contracts
60163	145	1411	Food Manufacturing	60459	549	5496	Educational Services	60606	3338	79723	Prof., Scientific, & Tech Svcs
60164	431	9667	Food Manufacturing	60460	41	149	Educational Services	60607	2062	35836	Postal Service
60165	150	741	Food Svcs & Drinking Places	60461	325	3523	Health & Personal Care Stores	60608	1969	41913	Exec., Legis., & Other Support
60168	15	112	Administrative & Support Svcs	60462	1826	21357	Food Svcs & Drinking Places	60609	1648	30406	Food Manufacturing

ZIP CODE	2004 Total Firms	2004 Total Employees	TOP INDUSTRY RANKED on 2004 EMPLOYMENT	ZIP CODE	2004 Total Firms	2004 Total Employees	TOP INDUSTRY RANKED on 2004 EMPLOYMENT	ZIP CODE	2004 Total Firms	2004 Total Employees	TOP INDUSTRY RANKED on 2004 EMPLOYMENT
60610	3830	46961	Food Svcs & Drinking Places	60939	3	25	Warehousing and Storage	61081	883	11681	Fabricated Metal Product Mfg
60611	4252	78040	Prof., Scientific, & Tech Svcs	60940	102	855	Plastics & Rubber Products Mfg	61084	76	443	Educational Services
60612	1523	45408	Hospitals	60941	88	778	Educational Services	61085	205	1372	Transportation Equipment Mfg
60613	1524	11545	Educational Services	60942	271	2196	Educational Services	61087	109	610	Elect'l Eqpmt, App, & Comp Mfg
60614	2918	26911	Food Svcs & Drinking Places	60944	35	270	Educational Services	61088	124	854	Food Svcs & Drinking Places
60615	1000	6733	Educational Services	60945	16	51	Rail Transportation	61089	26	184	Computer & Electronic Prod Mfg
60616	1634	25205	Hospitals	60946	22	142	Educational Services	61091	5	10	Nonmetallic Mineral Prod. Mfg
60617	1644	14638	Educational Services	60948	48	321	Merch. Wholesalers,Nondur. Gds	61101	810	11301	Exec., Legis., & Other Support
60618	2758	21189	Educational Services	60949	23	69	Warehousing and Storage	61102	493	4596	Educational Services
60619	1627	9916	Educational Services	60950	343	4214	Support Act. for Transport.	61103	698	14074	Ambulatory Health Care Svcs
60620	1450	11165	Educational Services	60951	25	30	Motor Vehicle & Parts Dealers	61104	1138	16859	Fabricated Metal Product Mfg
60621	638	6101	Educational Services	60952	28	91	Merch. Wholesalers,Durable Gds	61105	4	3	Special Trade Contractors
60622	3024	34239	Hospitals	60953	107	588	Educational Services	61107	1073	11401	Ambulatory Health Care Svcs
60623	1631	15108	Educational Services	60954	263	3011	Merch. Wholesalers,Nondur. Gds	61108	1665	23222	Transportation Equipment Mfg
60624	811	8934	Educational Services	60955	85	596	Bldg Matl & Garden Eqpmt Dlrs	61109	973	14082	Fabricated Metal Product Mfg
60625	1844	14997	Educational Services	60956	6	13	Warehousing and Storage	61110	10	19	Social Assistance
60626	1008	14465	Educational Services	60957	274	2142	Nursing & Resid. Care Facilit.	61111	1153	14593	Transportation Equipment Mfg
60628	1473	14370	Educational Services	60959	48	252	Nursing & Resid. Care Facilit.	61112	195	2255	Clothing & Cloth'g Acc. Stores
60629	1396	14660	Food Manufacturing	60960	25	44	Food and Beverage Stores	61114	414	4849	Relig., Grant, Civic, Prof Org
60630	1569	12444	Justice, Pubic Order/Safety	60961	21	95	Educational Services	61115	587	5787	Educational Services
60631	1343	16545	Accommodation	60962	35	138	Repair and Maintenance	61125	11	824	Postal Service
60632	1602	23409	Merch. Wholesalers,Durable Gds	60963	81	395	Food Manufacturing	61126	6	5	Motor Vehicle & Parts Dealers
60633	278	5654	Wholesale Elec. Mrkts & Agents	60964	194	929	Educational Services	61130	2	4	Administrative & Support Svcs
60634	1875	13875	Educational Services	60966	54	227	Nursing & Resid. Care Facilit.	61132	11	23	Real Estate
60636	856	11996	Admin. Enviro. Quality Progrms	60967	10	72	Postal Service	61201	1426	22896	Ambulatory Health Care Svcs
60637	910	25903	Educational Services	60968	8	54	Educational Services	61204	6	9	Special Trade Contractors
60638	1504	24899	Prof., Scientific, & Tech Svcs	60969	7	61	Wood Product Manufacturing	61230	31	174	Justice, Pubic Order/Safety
60639	2074	17867	Fabricated Metal Product Mfg	60970	451	3429	Hospitals	61231	300	1992	Nursing & Resid. Care Facilit.
60640	2213	20532	Educational Services	60973	29	97	Relig., Grant, Civic, Prof Org	61232	32	146	Food Svcs & Drinking Places
60641	1951	14992	Educational Services	60974	11	28	Educational Services	61233	21	52	Food and Beverage Stores
60643	1384	8787	Educational Services	61001	48	269	Food Svcs & Drinking Places	61234	71	360	Educational Services
60644	861	8947	Educational Services	61006	69	728	Food Manufacturing	61235	74	338	Relig., Grant, Civic, Prof Org
60645	805	4838	Educational Services	61007	20	45	Crop Production	61236	5	7	Special Trade Contractors
60646	1161	8936	Prof., Scientific, & Tech Svcs	61008	910	12107	Transportation Equipment Mfg	61237	14	70	Food Manufacturing
60647	2415	18018	Food Svcs & Drinking Places	61010	192	2438	Fabricated Metal Product Mfg	61238	199	1084	Justice, Pubic Order/Safety
60649	981	8611	Hospitals	61011	61	298	Educational Services	61239	32	133	Exec., Legis., & Other Support
60651	1148	8726	Educational Services	61012	40	225	Fabricated Metal Product Mfg	61240	158	1136	Nursing & Resid. Care Facilit.
60652	770	8487	Educational Services	61013	22	1934	Relig., Grant, Civic, Prof Org	61241	176	693	Food Svcs & Drinking Places
60653	603	5340	Educational Services	61014	47	295	Machinery Manufacturing	61242	43	657	Chemical Manufacturing
60654	693	7625	Insurance Carriers & Related	61015	22	83	Prof., Scientific, & Tech Svcs	61243	13	68	Food Svcs & Drinking Places
60655	476	3521	Educational Services	61016	138	1296	Amusement, Gambling,& Recreat.	61244	613	12642	Machinery Manufacturing
60656	567	5361	Merch. Wholesalers,Durable Gds	61018	34	305	Educational Services	61250	101	434	Educational Services
60657	2500	25392	Hospitals	61019	72	330	Relig., Grant, Civic, Prof Org	61251	6	9	Postal Service
60659	1741	9531	Educational Services	61020	49	234	Support Act. for Transport.	61252	174	1670	Machinery Manufacturing
60660	1012	5436	Educational Services	61021	940	12171	Bldg Matl & Garden Eqpmt Dlrs	61254	554	4453	Food Svcs & Drinking Places
60661	882	22405	Prof., Scientific, & Tech Svcs	61024	104	626	Nursing & Resid. Care Facilit.	61256	37	201	Educational Services
60664	4	4	Prof., Scientific, & Tech Svcs	61025	147	1466	Educational Services	61257	48	2797	Merch. Wholesalers,Nondur. Gds
60666	189	11202	Support Act. for Transport.	61027	6	10	Administrative & Support Svcs	61258	10	30	Merch. Wholesalers,Durable Gds
60670	92	1254	Managmt of Companies & Enterp.	61028	122	454	Nursing & Resid. Care Facilit.	61259	15	48	Educational Services
60680	17	76	Prof., Scientific, & Tech Svcs	61030	95	404	Educational Services	61260	27	154	Educational Services
60681	2	5	Ambulatory Health Care Svcs	61031	59	294	Nursing & Resid. Care Facilit.	61261	26	130	Merch. Wholesalers,Nondur. Gds
60688	2	100	Air Transportation	61032	1502	17994	Elect'l Eqpmt, App, & Comp Mfg	61262	16	49	Food Manufacturing
60690	13	32	Special Trade Contractors	61036	562	4716	Accommodation	61263	16	60	Educational Services
60693	1	100	Merch. Wholesalers,Durable Gds	61037	7	27	Educational Services	61264	402	5106	Wholesale Elec. Mrkts & Agents
60697	1	0	Credit Intermediation & Relatd	61038	45	182	Truck Transportation	61265	2142	28722	Ambulatory Health Care Svcs
60701	2	10	Construction of Buildings	61039	32	128	Credit Intermediation & Relatd	61266	14	39	Special Trade Contractors
60706	797	9153	Food Svcs & Drinking Places	61041	58	228	Educational Services	61270	302	2680	Computer & Electronic Prod Mfg
60707	972	9662	Food Svcs & Drinking Places	61042	19	66	Bldg Matl & Garden Eqpmt Dlrs	61272	30	164	Educational Services
60712	847	10051	Prof., Scientific, & Tech Svcs	61043	3	17	Managmt of Companies & Enterp.	61273	117	651	Educational Services
60714	1466	24985	Social Assistance	61044	9	6	Merch. Wholesalers,Nondur. Gds	61274	17	107	Justice, Pubic Order/Safety
60803	873	13544	Merch. Wholesalers,Durable Gds	61046	130	908	Relig., Grant, Civic, Prof Org	61275	89	508	Educational Services
60804	1458	15354	Educational Services	61047	42	189	Justice, Pubic Order/Safety	61276	11	18	Prof., Scientific, & Tech Svcs
60805	851	8156	Hospitals	61048	201	1831	Merch. Wholesalers,Nondur. Gds	61277	117	1159	Nursing & Resid. Care Facilit.
60827	476	3982	Educational Services	61049	8	172	Machinery Manufacturing	61278	27	98	Food Svcs & Drinking Places
60901	1584	19583	Other Information Services	61050	19	46	Crop Production	61279	40	120	Educational Services
60910	39	119	Educational Services	61051	82	485	Educational Services	61281	52	250	Educational Services
60911	50	481	Motor Vehicle & Parts Dealers	61052	31	119	Food Svcs & Drinking Places	61282	211	2932	Hospitals
60912	22	57	Special Trade Contractors	61053	193	884	Relig., Grant, Civic, Prof Org	61283	45	264	Educational Services
60913	50	163	Educational Services	61054	131	2506	Print'g & Related Supp't Act's	61284	45	546	Educational Services
60914	801	8156	Food Svcs & Drinking Places	61057	4	118	Social Assistance	61285	64	292	Food Svcs & Drinking Places
60915	593	6585	Merch. Wholesalers,Nondur. Gds	61058	4	2	Food Svcs & Drinking Places	61299	7	197	Construction of Buildings
60917	13	33	Relig., Grant, Civic, Prof Org	61059	7	11	Special Trade Contractors	61301	500	4898	Educational Services
60918	35	151	Pipeline Transportation	61060	48	296	Educational Services	61310	144	1029	Food Manufacturing
60919	11	50	Bldg Matl & Garden Eqpmt Dlrs	61061	404	2840	Machinery Manufacturing	61311	6	21	Warehousing and Storage
60920	6	16	Credit Intermediation & Relatd	61062	73	369	Bldg Matl & Garden Eqpmt Dlrs	61312	10	33	Justice, Pubic Order/Safety
60921	63	429	Primary Metal Manufacturing	61063	146	841	Justice, Pubic Order/Safety	61313	15	131	Nonmetallic Mineral Prod. Mfg
60922	66	243	Educational Services	61064	136	1782	Special Trade Contractors	61314	29	155	Unclassified Establishments
60924	111	441	Educational Services	61065	134	747	Food and Beverage Stores	61315	13	25	Educational Services
60926	6	4	Relig., Grant, Civic, Prof Org	61067	23	36	Chemical Manufacturing	61316	11	41	Truck Transportation
60927	79	426	Educational Services	61068	619	6447	Food and Beverage Stores	61317	13	87	Food Svcs & Drinking Places
60928	39	193	Educational Services	61070	33	118	Food and Beverage Stores	61318	26	56	Admin. of Economic Programs
60929	43	177	Justice, Pubic Order/Safety	61071	498	4273	Food Svcs & Drinking Places	61319	36	192	Educational Services
60930	24	243	Nursing & Resid. Care Facilit.	61072	250	2810	Educational Services	61320	10	26	Food Svcs & Drinking Places
60931	19	254	Educational Services	61073	474	2994	Food Svcs & Drinking Places	61321	11	34	Justice, Pubic Order/Safety
60932	7	23	Construction of Buildings	61074	248	2929	Nat'l Security & Int'l Affairs	61322	41	169	Educational Services
60933	12	44	Justice, Pubic Order/Safety	61075	45	154	Educational Services	61323	6	48	Miscellaneous Manufacturing
60934	5	8	Postal Service	61077	18	202	Fabricated Metal Product Mfg	61324	2	2	Postal Service
60935	19	96	Food Svcs & Drinking Places	61078	71	251	Food Svcs & Drinking Places	61325	33	241	Special Trade Contractors
60936	251	2372	Nursing & Resid. Care Facilit.	61079	11	99	Justice, Pubic Order/Safety	61326	84	674	Miscellaneous Store Retailers
60938	135	894	Food Svcs & Drinking Places	61080	381	4159	Machinery Manufacturing	61327	70	380	Chemical Manufacturing

BUSINESS DATA

ZIP CODE	2004 Total Firms	2004 Total Employ-ees	TOP INDUSTRY RANKED on 2004 EMPLOYMENT	ZIP CODE	2004 Total Firms	2004 Total Employ-ees	TOP INDUSTRY RANKED on 2004 EMPLOYMENT	ZIP CODE	2004 Total Firms	2004 Total Employ-ees	TOP INDUSTRY RANKED on 2004 EMPLOYMENT
61328	3	5	Warehousing and Storage	61462	500	5209	Food Manufacturing	61635	2	9	Rental and Leasing Services
61329	51	321	Plastics & Rubber Products Mfg	61465	58	138	Pipeline Transportation	61636	13	101	Ambulatory Health Care Svcs
61330	45	183	Educational Services	61466	8	10	Relig., Grant, Civic, Prof Org	61637	12	8402	Hospitals
61331	2	3	Insurance Carriers & Related	61467	47	208	Educational Services	61641	1	0	Primary Metal Manufacturing
61332	15	58	Justice, Pubic Order/Safety	61469	91	295	Exec., Legis., & Other Support	61643	4	678	Publishing Industries
61333	15	23	Warehousing and Storage	61470	19	125	Nursing & Resid. Care Facilit.	61650	1	0	Prof., Scientific, & Tech Svcs
61334	32	222	Food Svcs & Drinking Places	61471	13	33	Credit Intermediation & Relatd	61651	1	5	Transit & Grnd Pass. Transport
61335	42	3051	Bldg Matl & Garden Eqpmt Dlrs	61472	13	24	Print'g & Related Supp't Act's	61652	2	12	Special Trade Contractors
61336	14	40	Relig., Grant, Civic, Prof Org	61473	77	390	Educational Services	61653	1	1	Print'g & Related Supp't Act's
61337	17	111	Educational Services	61474	9	57	Food Svcs & Drinking Places	61701	1925	26048	Food Svcs & Drinking Places
61338	26	228	Educational Services	61475	14	96	Educational Services	61702	37	92	Administrative & Support Svcs
61340	16	261	Fabricated Metal Product Mfg	61476	11	28	Waste Managmt & Remediat'n Svc	61704	1230	14587	Food Svcs & Drinking Places
61341	276	1825	Nat'l Security & Int'l Affairs	61477	18	34	Wood Product Manufacturing	61709	1	2200	Insurance Carriers & Related
61342	408	4402	Food Manufacturing	61478	7	78	Bldg Matl & Garden Eqpmt Dlrs	61710	3	10809	Insurance Carriers & Related
61344	10	32	Truck Transportation	61479	5	127	Merch. Wholesalers,Nondur. Gds	61720	9	29	Food Svcs & Drinking Places
61345	36	304	Machinery Manufacturing	61480	75	441	Educational Services	61721	18	48	Merch. Wholesalers,Durable Gds
61346	2	3	Postal Service	61482	28	119	Educational Services	61722	19	35	Educational Services
61348	153	1998	Educational Services	61483	88	510	Nursing & Resid. Care Facilit.	61723	84	419	Truck Transportation
61349	41	214	Educational Services	61484	36	140	Primary Metal Manufacturing	61724	18	25	Personal and Laundry Services
61350	1202	13123	Educational Services	61485	35	99	Accommodation	61725	48	156	Food Svcs & Drinking Places
61353	55	162	Educational Services	61486	77	352	Educational Services	61726	117	867	Special Trade Contractors
61354	673	8458	Food Svcs & Drinking Places	61488	33	153	Justice, Pubic Order/Safety	61727	419	3480	Food Svcs & Drinking Places
61356	695	6748	Merch. Wholesalers,Durable Gds	61489	37	173	Educational Services	61728	56	302	Educational Services
61358	14	40	Justice, Pubic Order/Safety	61490	70	282	Food Svcs & Drinking Places	61729	38	187	Repair and Maintenance
61359	9	16	Crop Production	61491	103	547	Educational Services	61730	12	35	Exec., Legis., & Other Support
61360	148	828	Educational Services	61501	92	399	Educational Services	61731	11	108	Relig., Grant, Civic, Prof Org
61361	70	256	Food and Beverage Stores	61516	28	99	Educational Services	61732	43	120	Educational Services
61362	216	2476	Hospitals	61517	88	778	Machinery Manufacturing	61733	30	203	Construction of Buildings
61363	11	36	Justice, Pubic Order/Safety	61519	6	4	Postal Service	61734	83	483	Educational Services
61364	708	7223	Machinery Manufacturing	61520	584	5165	Educational Services	61735	17	54	Exec., Legis., & Other Support
61367	42	300	Accommodation	61523	323	2089	Food Svcs & Drinking Places	61736	49	344	Educational Services
61368	55	145	Food Svcs & Drinking Places	61524	6	39	Justice, Pubic Order/Safety	61737	16	27	Merch. Wholesalers,Durable Gds
61369	66	977	Food Manufacturing	61525	122	662	Educational Services	61738	208	1755	Fabricated Metal Product Mfg
61370	52	374	Accommodation	61526	19	170	Chemical Manufacturing	61739	249	1511	Food and Beverage Stores
61371	11	43	Food Svcs & Drinking Places	61528	63	408	Print'g & Related Supp't Act's	61740	63	508	Educational Services
61372	12	67	Mining (Except Oil and Gas)	61529	99	539	Educational Services	61741	89	541	Educational Services
61373	111	821	Accommodation	61530	245	2689	Educational Services	61742	58	877	Merch. Wholesalers,Durable Gds
61374	13	50	Merch. Wholesalers,Nondur. Gds	61531	123	774	Food and Beverage Stores	61743	12	98	Merch. Wholesalers,Nondur. Gds
61375	34	263	Educational Services	61532	12	40	Construction of Buildings	61744	91	580	Food Manufacturing
61376	99	569	Nursing & Resid. Care Facilit.	61533	80	340	Educational Services	61745	103	496	Construction of Buildings
61377	59	632	Food Manufacturing	61534	35	181	Educational Services	61747	53	504	Hospitals
61378	16	42	Credit Intermediation & Relatd	61535	39	125	Perform'g Arts, Spec. Sports	61748	63	284	Museums, Hist. Sites,& Similar
61379	49	180	Justice, Pubic Order/Safety	61536	83	485	Educational Services	61749	21	57	Justice, Pubic Order/Safety
61401	1459	21007	Miscellaneous Manufacturing	61537	143	1171	Merch. Wholesalers,Nondur. Gds	61750	5	14	Exec., Legis., & Other Support
61402	1	6	Administrative & Support Svcs	61539	7	22	Merch. Wholesalers,Nondur. Gds	61751	3	4	Food Svcs & Drinking Places
61410	94	521	Educational Services	61540	154	922	Food Svcs & Drinking Places	61752	139	873	Food Svcs & Drinking Places
61411	27	54	Bldg Matl & Garden Eqpmt Dlrs	61541	10	51	Truck Transportation	61753	103	469	Plastics & Rubber Products Mfg
61412	58	274	Educational Services	61542	159	967	Educational Services	61754	61	386	Gasoline Stations
61413	36	155	Educational Services	61543	6	21	Food Svcs & Drinking Places	61755	107	461	Educational Services
61414	46	122	Justice, Pubic Order/Safety	61544	21	219	Educational Services	61756	65	377	Educational Services
61415	67	301	Nursing & Resid. Care Facilit.	61545	21	110	Accommodation	61758	3	14	Food Svcs & Drinking Places
61416	2	1	Postal Service	61546	108	503	Educational Services	61759	70	386	Food Svcs & Drinking Places
61417	6	13	Bldg Matl & Garden Eqpmt Dlrs	61547	71	1110	Relig., Grant, Civic, Prof Org	61760	108	910	Fabricated Metal Product Mfg
61418	40	358	Educational Services	61548	283	2262	Educational Services	61761	1104	17960	Social Assistance
61419	31	149	Museums, Hist. Sites,& Similar	61550	683	9595	Truck Transportation	61764	635	7922	Justice, Pubic Order/Safety
61420	54	124	Bldg Matl & Garden Eqpmt Dlrs	61552	35	759	Plastics & Rubber Products Mfg	61769	19	67	Educational Services
61421	61	253	Educational Services	61553	11	58	Food Svcs & Drinking Places	61770	44	101	Repair and Maintenance
61422	150	1215	Fabricated Metal Product Mfg	61554	1321	14789	Food Svcs & Drinking Places	61771	18	71	Amusement, Gambling,& Recreat.
61423	19	55	Fabricated Metal Product Mfg	61555	3	9	Social Assistance	61772	17	19	Food and Beverage Stores
61424	8	17	Construction of Buildings	61559	89	697	Food Manufacturing	61773	29	87	Justice, Pubic Order/Safety
61425	16	56	Food and Beverage Stores	61560	21	42	Food Svcs & Drinking Places	61774	30	240	Educational Services
61426	2	3	Postal Service	61561	120	948	Special Trade Contractors	61775	11	29	Crop Production
61427	71	396	Educational Services	61562	8	25	Food Svcs & Drinking Places	61776	33	145	Educational Services
61428	33	119	Relig., Grant, Civic, Prof Org	61563	15	49	Justice, Pubic Order/Safety	61777	30	77	Special Trade Contractors
61430	13	57	Educational Services	61564	25	147	Educational Services	61778	14	31	Merch. Wholesalers,Nondur. Gds
61431	14	27	Justice, Pubic Order/Safety	61565	27	123	Educational Services	61790	9	3334	Educational Services
61432	33	115	Fabricated Metal Product Mfg	61567	12	89	Exec., Legis., & Other Support	61801	758	25529	Educational Services
61433	5	14	Warehousing and Storage	61568	163	1473	Petroleum & Coal Products Mfg	61802	642	8924	Food and Beverage Stores
61434	126	964	Fabricated Metal Product Mfg	61569	24	98	Special Trade Contractors	61803	10	15	Prof., Scientific, & Tech Svcs
61435	3	4	Insurance Carriers & Related	61570	68	296	Educational Services	61810	11	73	Chemical Manufacturing
61436	20	44	Justice, Pubic Order/Safety	61571	530	4762	Educational Services	61811	10	15	Postal Service
61437	35	297	Warehousing and Storage	61572	47	122	Educational Services	61812	8	78	Educational Services
61438	27	122	Bldg Matl & Garden Eqpmt Dlrs	61601	18	604	Postal Service	61813	77	523	Transportation Equipment Mfg
61439	6	3	Postal Service	61602	894	19450	Educational Services	61814	40	224	Educational Services
61440	27	200	Mining (Except Oil and Gas)	61603	674	11120	Educational Services	61815	11	41	Construction of Buildings
61441	26	75	Justice, Pubic Order/Safety	61604	961	9498	Justice, Pubic Order/Safety	61816	17	81	Educational Services
61442	32	169	Primary Metal Manufacturing	61605	357	3839	Educational Services	61817	76	449	Educational Services
61443	588	6334	Educational Services	61606	259	2958	Educational Services	61818	52	337	Educational Services
61447	35	83	Justice, Pubic Order/Safety	61607	409	4326	Administrative & Support Svcs	61820	1965	38576	Educational Services
61448	128	925	Nursing & Resid. Care Facilit.	61610	134	834	Educational Services	61821	843	10010	Merch. Wholesalers,Nondur. Gds
61449	21	84	Administrative & Support Svcs	61611	967	13463	Educational Services	61822	571	10060	Food Svcs & Drinking Places
61450	87	438	Nursing & Resid. Care Facilit.	61612	17	42	Ambulatory Health Care Svcs	61824	5	8	Prof., Scientific, & Tech Svcs
61451	8	11	Relig., Grant, Civic, Prof Org	61613	96	1356	General Merchandise Stores	61825	3	2	Administrative & Support Svcs
61452	9	16	Warehousing and Storage	61614	1335	14516	Ambulatory Health Care Svcs	61826	16	61	Administrative & Support Svcs
61453	14	17	Postal Service	61615	1060	15989	Food Svcs & Drinking Places	61830	23	56	Merch. Wholesalers,Nondur. Gds
61454	18	56	Ambulatory Health Care Svcs	61616	334	2264	Food Svcs & Drinking Places	61831	6	9	Relig., Grant, Civic, Prof Org
61455	896	12665	Ambulatory Health Care Svcs	61625	7	77	Other Information Services	61832	1712	22940	Social Assistance
61458	29	85	Justice, Pubic Order/Safety	61629	3	2753	Machinery Manufacturing	61833	80	695	Construction of Buildings
61459	9	21	Justice, Pubic Order/Safety	61633	1	68	Insurance Carriers & Related	61834	297	7579	Merch. Wholesalers,Nondur. Gds
61460	6	132	Amusement, Gambling,& Recreat.	61634	1	204	Insurance Carriers & Related	61839	24	122	Educational Services

ZIP CODE	2004 Total Firms	2004 Total Employ-ees	TOP INDUSTRY RANKED on 2004 EMPLOYMENT	ZIP CODE	2004 Total Firms	2004 Total Employ-ees	TOP INDUSTRY RANKED on 2004 EMPLOYMENT	ZIP CODE	2004 Total Firms	2004 Total Employ-ees	TOP INDUSTRY RANKED on 2004 EMPLOYMENT
61840	16	105	Warehousing and Storage	62031	22	83	Construction of Buildings	62246	404	3437	Exec., Legis., & Other Support
61841	52	226	Bldg Matl & Garden Eqpmt Dlrs	62032	25	105	Truck Transportation	62247	1	0	Postal Service
61842	153	762	Educational Services	62033	174	958	Merch. Wholesalers,Durable Gds	62248	19	83	Truck Transportation
61843	70	531	Fabricated Metal Product Mfg	62034	367	3217	Ambulatory Health Care Svcs	62249	580	6966	Elect'l Eqpmt, App, & Comp Mfg
61844	30	152	Educational Services	62035	470	4053	Nursing & Resid. Care Facilit.	62250	27	141	Managmt of Companies & Enterp.
61845	13	14	Repair and Maintenance	62036	11	23	Water Transportation	62252	4	27	Justice, Pubic Order/Safety
61846	115	584	Educational Services	62037	104	720	Amusement, Gambling,& Recreat.	62253	34	87	Merch. Wholesalers,Durable Gds
61847	48	305	Nursing & Resid. Care Facilit.	62040	1408	13532	Food Svcs & Drinking Places	62254	181	1356	Educational Services
61848	10	41	Food Manufacturing	62044	77	450	Educational Services	62255	17	73	Special Trade Contractors
61849	64	231	Justice, Pubic Order/Safety	62045	12	72	Justice, Pubic Order/Safety	62256	12	47	Food Svcs & Drinking Places
61850	7	1	Postal Service	62046	46	370	Merch. Wholesalers,Durable Gds	62257	97	535	Fabricated Metal Product Mfg
61851	16	81	Bldg Matl & Garden Eqpmt Dlrs	62047	114	616	Food Svcs & Drinking Places	62258	235	1732	Educational Services
61852	5	28	Justice, Pubic Order/Safety	62048	68	830	Merch. Wholesalers,Durable Gds	62259	4	1082	Justice, Pubic Order/Safety
61853	325	1993	Educational Services	62049	364	2901	Justice, Pubic Order/Safety	62260	211	1228	Special Trade Contractors
61854	53	286	Bldg Matl & Garden Eqpmt Dlrs	62050	12	28	Administrative & Support Svcs	62261	9	25	Water Transportation
61855	3	6	Truck Transportation	62051	31	85	Truck Transportation	62262	40	255	Educational Services
61856	354	2098	Ambulatory Health Care Svcs	62052	527	4186	Food Svcs & Drinking Places	62263	322	3551	Transportation Equipment Mfg
61857	6	4	Postal Service	62053	20	88	Exec., Legis., & Other Support	62264	111	758	Educational Services
61858	94	524	Food Svcs & Drinking Places	62054	12	19	Crop Production	62265	106	733	Nursing & Resid. Care Facilit.
61859	37	199	Food Svcs & Drinking Places	62056	506	5393	Food Svcs & Drinking Places	62266	6	10	Utilities
61862	16	61	Food Svcs & Drinking Places	62058	34	131	Educational Services	62268	25	54	Educational Services
61863	17	190	Justice, Pubic Order/Safety	62059	38	459	Food Svcs & Drinking Places	62269	901	8239	Food Svcs & Drinking Places
61864	44	248	Educational Services	62060	180	1563	Truck Transportation	62271	75	632	Educational Services
61865	29	102	Bldg Matl & Garden Eqpmt Dlrs	62061	47	113	Motor Vehicle & Parts Dealers	62272	50	180	Food Svcs & Drinking Places
61866	489	8253	Transportation Equipment Mfg	62062	212	2363	Hospitals	62273	13	29	Merch. Wholesalers,Nondur. Gds
61870	38	170	Construction of Buildings	62063	34	84	Educational Services	62274	272	2725	Computer & Electronic Prod Mfg
61871	19	96	Educational Services	62065	5	9	Sportg Gds,Hobby,Book, & Music	62275	74	242	Food Svcs & Drinking Places
61872	24	77	Fabricated Metal Product Mfg	62067	39	111	Educational Services	62277	41	143	Educational Services
61873	130	559	Educational Services	62069	96	634	Paper Manufacturing	62278	300	2117	Educational Services
61874	201	1882	General Merchandise Stores	62070	4	7	Food Svcs & Drinking Places	62279	6	5	Postal Service
61875	23	92	Special Trade Contractors	62071	12	141	Food Manufacturing	62280	8	60	Mining (Except Oil and Gas)
61876	34	345	Educational Services	62074	28	75	Justice, Pubic Order/Safety	62281	49	325	Educational Services
61877	45	162	Merch. Wholesalers,Nondur. Gds	62075	149	833	Educational Services	62282	28	163	Truck Transportation
61878	43	209	Bldg Matl & Garden Eqpmt Dlrs	62076	2	2	Postal Service	62284	15	30	Special Trade Contractors
61880	86	664	Bldg Matl & Garden Eqpmt Dlrs	62077	11	16	Food Svcs & Drinking Places	62285	67	397	Nursing & Resid. Care Facilit.
61882	25	107	Educational Services	62078	5	2	Exec., Legis., & Other Support	62286	327	2687	Primary Metal Manufacturing
61883	124	715	Educational Services	62079	14	107	Educational Services	62288	122	2159	Food Manufacturing
61884	20	34	Prof., Scientific, & Tech Svcs	62080	71	408	Educational Services	62289	16	40	Educational Services
61910	199	1933	Merch. Wholesalers,Durable Gds	62081	7	20	Bldg Matl & Garden Eqpmt Dlrs	62292	20	77	Justice, Pubic Order/Safety
61911	248	2122	Furniture & Related Prod. Mfg	62082	88	603	Exec., Legis., & Other Support	62293	144	907	Educational Services
61912	39	123	Furn. & Home Furnishgs Stores	62083	13	21	Warehousing and Storage	62294	355	2271	Food Svcs & Drinking Places
61913	63	302	Educational Services	62084	50	348	Educational Services	62295	31	294	Educational Services
61914	67	335	Educational Services	62085	3	13	Exec., Legis., & Other Support	62297	6	12	Relig., Grant, Civic, Prof Org
61917	13	24	Food and Beverage Stores	62086	23	73	Educational Services	62298	550	3732	General Merchandise Stores
61919	16	50	Administrative & Support Svcs	62087	54	375	Repair and Maintenance	62301	1827	21512	Hospitals
61920	879	14091	Publishing Industries	62088	235	1783	Educational Services	62305	584	8545	Merch. Wholesalers,Nondur. Gds
61924	76	489	Nursing & Resid. Care Facilit.	62089	27	77	Food Svcs & Drinking Places	62306	6	11	Prof., Scientific, & Tech Svcs
61925	21	97	Construction of Buildings	62090	42	308	Educational Services	62311	61	213	Educational Services
61928	19	55	Warehousing and Storage	62091	8	21	Bldg Matl & Garden Eqpmt Dlrs	62312	89	566	Educational Services
61929	32	98	Justice, Pubic Order/Safety	62092	114	742	Educational Services	62313	9	11	Warehousing and Storage
61930	18	92	Construction of Buildings	62093	9	24	Construction of Buildings	62314	12	23	Support Activities: Agr./For.
61931	29	81	Educational Services	62094	41	158	Truck Transportation	62316	29	170	Educational Services
61932	20	105	Educational Services	62095	381	5155	Petroleum & Coal Products Mfg	62319	6	12	Support Activities: Agr./For.
61933	53	983	Support Activities: Agr./For.	62097	59	166	Educational Services	62320	96	687	Educational Services
61936	10	12	Special Trade Contractors	62098	3	2	Exec., Legis., & Other Support	62321	261	1531	Hospitals
61937	67	341	Educational Services	62201	453	6405	Prof., Scientific, & Tech Svcs	62323	10	9	Administrative & Support Svcs
61938	1132	14361	Print'g & Related Supp't Act's	62202	1	0	Rail Transportation	62324	46	107	Food Svcs & Drinking Places
61940	8	25	Justice, Pubic Order/Safety	62203	185	1403	Ambulatory Health Care Svcs	62325	10	33	Merch. Wholesalers,Nondur. Gds
61941	3	2	Postal Service	62204	138	1233	Chemical Manufacturing	62326	88	350	Educational Services
61942	50	242	Nursing & Resid. Care Facilit.	62205	261	2249	Transportation Equipment Mfg	62329	6	24	Merch. Wholesalers,Nondur. Gds
61943	91	441	Educational Services	62206	432	5864	Primary Metal Manufacturing	62330	70	260	Educational Services
61944	580	5857	Bldg Matl & Garden Eqpmt Dlrs	62207	202	1374	Hospitals	62334	7	27	Merch. Wholesalers,Nondur. Gds
61949	7	15	Warehousing and Storage	62208	942	10798	Food Svcs & Drinking Places	62336	9	37	Merch. Wholesalers,Nondur. Gds
61951	323	2706	Machinery Manufacturing	62214	38	207	Food Manufacturing	62338	26	47	Construction of Buildings
61953	359	2374	Food Svcs & Drinking Places	62215	56	529	Special Trade Contractors	62339	58	344	Telecommunications
61955	8	34	Justice, Pubic Order/Safety	62216	41	378	Nursing & Resid. Care Facilit.	62340	68	282	Educational Services
61956	97	545	Educational Services	62217	31	184	Merch. Wholesalers,Durable Gds	62341	136	1003	Heavy & Civil Eng. Construct'N
61957	67	356	Educational Services	62218	36	112	Educational Services	62343	26	91	Educational Services
62001	52	300	Nursing & Resid. Care Facilit.	62219	31	145	Merch. Wholesalers,Durable Gds	62344	4	5	Construction of Buildings
62002	1499	16868	Hospitals	62220	1092	13740	Hospitals	62345	12	31	Merch. Wholesalers,Nondur. Gds
62006	15	80	Justice, Pubic Order/Safety	62221	481	4160	Educational Services	62346	9	19	Warehousing and Storage
62009	53	271	Educational Services	62222	7	9	Insurance Carriers & Related	62347	42	287	Educational Services
62010	300	2188	Food Svcs & Drinking Places	62223	524	5546	Administrative & Support Svcs	62348	8	31	Special Trade Contractors
62011	7	16	Sportg Gds,Hobby,Book, & Music	62225	85	4156	Nat'l Security & Int'l Affairs	62349	19	30	Food and Beverage Stores
62012	151	699	Educational Services	62226	1074	12127	Hospitals	62351	70	435	Relig., Grant, Civic, Prof Org
62013	27	121	Educational Services	62230	292	3003	Food Svcs & Drinking Places	62352	19	27	Repair and Maintenance
62014	98	589	Educational Services	62231	339	2773	Food Svcs & Drinking Places	62353	204	3094	Merch. Wholesalers,Nondur. Gds
62015	22	42	Special Trade Contractors	62232	186	1503	Food Svcs & Drinking Places	62354	110	599	Accommodation
62016	173	1046	Hospitals	62233	263	2821	Admin. Human Resource Programs	62355	23	55	Accommodation
62017	34	391	Construction of Buildings	62234	1103	9392	Food Svcs & Drinking Places	62356	23	56	Exec., Legis., & Other Support
62018	71	282	Food Svcs & Drinking Places	62236	482	3205	Food Svcs & Drinking Places	62357	5	7	Accommodation
62019	15	18	Food and Beverage Stores	62237	76	338	Nursing & Resid. Care Facilit.	62358	22	92	Justice, Pubic Order/Safety
62021	21	84	Merch. Wholesalers,Durable Gds	62238	18	48	Special Trade Contractors	62359	9	43	Support Activities: Agr./For.
62022	21	58	Educational Services	62239	115	807	Educational Services	62360	50	285	Educational Services
62023	2	0	Postal Service	62240	47	285	Water Transportation	62361	18	50	Food and Beverage Stores
62024	397	3140	Special Trade Contractors	62241	22	34	Exec., Legis., & Other Support	62362	19	88	Educational Services
62025	1135	9870	Prof., Scientific, & Tech Svcs	62242	65	226	Educational Services	62363	360	2807	Food Svcs & Drinking Places
62026	6	94	Broadcasting	62243	185	1781	Relig., Grant, Civic, Prof Org	62365	14	32	Food and Beverage Stores
62027	14	13	Postal Service	62244	24	28	Construction of Buildings	62366	58	269	Educational Services
62028	20	289	Educational Services	62245	64	337	Merch. Wholesalers,Nondur. Gds	62367	37	127	Educational Services

ZIP CODE	2004 Total Firms	2004 Total Employ-ees	TOP INDUSTRY RANKED on 2004 EMPLOYMENT	ZIP CODE	2004 Total Firms	2004 Total Employ-ees	TOP INDUSTRY RANKED on 2004 EMPLOYMENT	ZIP CODE	2004 Total Firms	2004 Total Employ-ees	TOP INDUSTRY RANKED on 2004 EMPLOYMENT
62370	17	74	Food Svcs & Drinking Places	62535	207	2509	Food Svcs & Drinking Places	62694	140	1110	Heavy & Civil Eng. Construct'N
62373	4	9	Bldg Matl & Garden Eqpmt Dlrs	62536	22	130	Administrative & Support Svcs	62695	13	41	Merch. Wholesalers,Durable Gds
62374	10	25	Accommodation	62537	17	83	Merch. Wholesalers,Durable Gds	62701	660	11905	Exec., Legis., & Other Support
62375	8	61	Bldg Matl & Garden Eqpmt Dlrs	62538	12	37	Warehousing and Storage	62702	1397	25301	Exec., Legis., & Other Support
62376	45	186	Warehousing and Storage	62539	49	469	Chemical Manufacturing	62703	1660	23211	Ambulatory Health Care Svcs
62378	24	97	Educational Services	62540	44	313	Utilities	62704	2127	23293	Admin. Human Resource Programs
62379	87	336	Educational Services	62541	5	13	Warehousing and Storage	62705	4	5	Merch. Wholesalers,Durable Gds
62380	9	34	Justice, Pubic Order/Safety	62543	25	61	Food Svcs & Drinking Places	62706	50	1997	Exec., Legis., & Other Support
62401	1200	16969	Print'g & Related Supp't Act's	62544	70	365	Nursing & Resid. Care Facilit.	62707	830	10067	Nat'l Security & Int'l Affairs
62410	18	107	Special Trade Contractors	62545	27	106	Fabricated Metal Product Mfg	62708	4	7	Relig., Grant, Civic, Prof Org
62411	177	1228	Educational Services	62546	73	316	Educational Services	62713	1	1200	Insurance Carriers & Related
62413	11	28	Warehousing and Storage	62547	31	99	Educational Services	62756	17	836	Exec., Legis., & Other Support
62414	49	139	Educational Services	62548	113	764	Educational Services	62761	2	4	Admin. Human Resource Programs
62417	99	746	Merch. Wholesalers,Nondur. Gds	62549	187	1610	Nonmetallic Mineral Prod. Mfg	62764	14	1537	Exec., Legis., & Other Support
62418	47	315	Truck Transportation	62550	111	580	Educational Services	62769	3	3856	Hospitals
62419	4	3	Postal Service	62551	23	169	Educational Services	62777	1	10	Educational Services
62420	237	1764	Food Svcs & Drinking Places	62553	11	24	Merch. Wholesalers,Nondur. Gds	62781	15	269	Ambulatory Health Care Svcs
62421	22	42	Fabricated Metal Product Mfg	62554	28	258	Educational Services	62791	14	66	Administrative & Support Svcs
62422	39	247	Educational Services	62555	12	22	Merch. Wholesalers,Nondur. Gds	62794	4	63	Admin. of Economic Programs
62423	10	10	Food and Beverage Stores	62556	13	20	Warehousing and Storage	62801	949	10418	Educational Services
62424	59	475	Educational Services	62557	328	2647	Construction of Buildings	62803	37	326	Social Assistance
62425	14	31	Truck Transportation	62558	100	456	Educational Services	62805	4	12	Miscellaneous Manufacturing
62426	26	78	Justice, Pubic Order/Safety	62560	96	482	Educational Services	62806	173	1767	Transportation Equipment Mfg
62427	38	327	Primary Metal Manufacturing	62561	124	706	Machinery Manufacturing	62807	20	65	Fabricated Metal Product Mfg
62428	126	721	Machinery Manufacturing	62563	171	890	Administrative & Support Svcs	62808	35	143	Educational Services
62431	22	117	Educational Services	62565	417	6001	Prof., Scientific, & Tech Svcs	62809	3	4	Accommodation
62432	14	32	Educational Services	62567	46	280	Bldg Matl & Garden Eqpmt Dlrs	62810	27	74	Educational Services
62433	36	277	Educational Services	62568	697	5633	Hospitals	62811	8	17	Warehousing and Storage
62434	13	38	Bldg Matl & Garden Eqpmt Dlrs	62570	9	18	Support Activities: Agr./For.	62812	577	4242	Transportation Equipment Mfg
62435	2	1	Relig., Grant, Civic, Prof Org	62571	37	102	Educational Services	62814	48	217	Educational Services
62436	4	6	Postal Service	62572	8	11	Administrative & Support Svcs	62815	10	30	Merch. Wholesalers,Nondur. Gds
62438	6	15	Telecommunications	62573	51	346	Educational Services	62816	19	75	Special Trade Contractors
62439	370	3876	Insurance Carriers & Related	62601	17	60	Educational Services	62817	15	28	Merch. Wholesalers,Nondur. Gds
62440	25	77	Educational Services	62610	10	46	Merch. Wholesalers,Durable Gds	62818	23	52	Justice, Pubic Order/Safety
62441	277	2492	Computer & Electronic Prod Mfg	62611	36	123	Merch. Wholesalers,Durable Gds	62819	13	40	Relig., Grant, Civic, Prof Org
62442	96	653	Educational Services	62612	91	408	Educational Services	62820	7	28	Food Manufacturing
62443	16	41	Construction of Buildings	62613	98	502	Educational Services	62821	419	3374	Nursing & Resid. Care Facilit.
62444	4	25	Mining (Except Oil and Gas)	62615	156	1240	Computer & Electronic Prod Mfg	62822	102	609	Educational Services
62445	31	105	Special Trade Contractors	62617	24	78	Justice, Pubic Order/Safety	62823	62	302	Nursing & Resid. Care Facilit.
62446	25	71	Educational Services	62618	275	3873	Food Manufacturing	62824	81	372	Merch. Wholesalers,Durable Gds
62447	99	672	Apparel Manufacturing	62621	47	248	Educational Services	62825	5	8	Food Svcs & Drinking Places
62448	302	2186	Educational Services	62622	4	30	Merch. Wholesalers,Nondur. Gds	62827	68	283	Special Trade Contractors
62449	130	537	Educational Services	62624	15	42	Unclassified Establishments	62828	36	144	Telecommunications
62450	647	7728	Merch. Wholesalers,Durable Gds	62625	23	255	Special Trade Contractors	62829	6	8	Bldg Matl & Garden Eqpmt Dlrs
62451	87	361	Educational Services	62626	450	4519	Truck Transportation	62830	52	194	Food Svcs & Drinking Places
62452	5	12	Special Trade Contractors	62627	54	137	Educational Services	62831	20	84	Accommodation
62454	496	5735	Food Manufacturing	62628	24	85	Credit Intermediation & Relatd	62832	381	2910	Food Svcs & Drinking Places
62458	97	628	Crop Production	62629	246	1334	Educational Services	62833	5	2	Relig., Grant, Civic, Prof Org
62459	18	189	Educational Services	62630	20	35	Truck Transportation	62834	1	0	Exec., Legis., & Other Support
62460	28	119	Merch. Wholesalers,Nondur. Gds	62631	12	117	Educational Services	62835	42	221	Nursing & Resid. Care Facilit.
62461	25	121	Machinery Manufacturing	62633	28	194	Food Manufacturing	62836	16	61	Educational Services
62462	38	111	Educational Services	62634	32	377	Mining (Except Oil and Gas)	62837	446	3998	Transportation Equipment Mfg
62463	47	183	Merch. Wholesalers,Nondur. Gds	62635	29	116	Educational Services	62838	61	359	Food Manufacturing
62464	1	0	Postal Service	62638	43	240	Food Svcs & Drinking Places	62839	376	3083	Nursing & Resid. Care Facilit.
62465	33	204	Educational Services	62639	4	15	Merch. Wholesalers,Nondur. Gds	62840	2	53	Broadcasting
62466	93	1337	Truck Transportation	62640	120	855	Educational Services	62841	6	15	Exec., Legis., & Other Support
62467	88	1588	Furniture & Related Prod. Mfg	62642	32	194	Educational Services	62842	24	60	Educational Services
62468	109	552	Educational Services	62643	13	57	Justice, Pubic Order/Safety	62843	3	8	Warehousing and Storage
62469	9	15	Fabricated Metal Product Mfg	62644	293	2417	Primary Metal Manufacturing	62844	116	655	Educational Services
62471	475	5358	Justice, Pubic Order/Safety	62649	18	34	Truck Transportation	62846	28	707	Educational Services
62473	31	64	Relig., Grant, Civic, Prof Org	62650	1201	14925	Educational Services	62848	30	89	Educational Services
62474	30	56	Warehousing and Storage	62651	1	0	Special Trade Contractors	62849	41	121	Educational Services
62475	4	18	Support Act. for Transport.	62655	19	84	Bldg Matl & Garden Eqpmt Dlrs	62850	17	50	Educational Services
62476	63	929	Machinery Manufacturing	62656	786	8034	Educational Services	62851	8	17	Support Activities: Agr./For.
62477	34	98	Merch. Wholesalers,Durable Gds	62660	4	1	Relig., Grant, Civic, Prof Org	62852	6	6	Postal Service
62478	6	5	Miscellaneous Store Retailers	62661	36	80	Motor Vehicle & Parts Dealers	62853	21	71	Justice, Pubic Order/Safety
62479	17	41	Wood Product Manufacturing	62663	9	13	Special Trade Contractors	62854	47	213	Educational Services
62480	26	68	Justice, Pubic Order/Safety	62664	117	858	Educational Services	62855	2	2	Postal Service
62481	8	19	Merch. Wholesalers,Durable Gds	62665	61	647	Chemical Manufacturing	62856	9	33	Educational Services
62501	73	439	Educational Services	62666	20	91	Educational Services	62857	1	7	Oil and Gas Extraction
62510	85	1179	Machinery Manufacturing	62667	16	36	Credit Intermediation & Relatd	62858	180	718	Educational Services
62512	14	18	Bldg Matl & Garden Eqpmt Dlrs	62668	39	121	Educational Services	62859	263	1185	Nursing & Resid. Care Facilit.
62513	65	384	Educational Services	62670	97	475	Educational Services	62860	12	14	Special Trade Contractors
62514	6	9	Merch. Wholesalers,Durable Gds	62671	18	55	Bldg Matl & Garden Eqpmt Dlrs	62861	1	1	Postal Service
62515	31	292	Educational Services	62672	10	11	Merch. Wholesalers,Durable Gds	62862	15	32	Educational Services
62517	7	9	Prof., Scientific, & Tech Svcs	62673	20	38	Justice, Pubic Order/Safety	62863	489	3953	Fabricated Metal Product Mfg
62518	14	30	Warehousing and Storage	62674	44	262	Educational Services	62864	1496	15471	Motor Vehicle & Parts Dealers
62519	7	21	Justice, Pubic Order/Safety	62675	254	1694	Educational Services	62865	45	201	Educational Services
62520	27	61	Truck Transportation	62677	74	389	Educational Services	62866	2	2	Postal Service
62521	1143	12549	Hospitals	62681	289	2007	Construction of Buildings	62867	14	26	Bldg Matl & Garden Eqpmt Dlrs
62522	462	4234	Fabricated Metal Product Mfg	62682	24	101	Justice, Pubic Order/Safety	62868	63	353	Educational Services
62523	547	5716	Justice, Pubic Order/Safety	62683	6	7	Merch. Wholesalers,Nondur. Gds	62869	103	601	Educational Services
62524	8	12	Administrative & Support Svcs	62684	100	742	Food Svcs & Drinking Places	62870	73	346	Nursing & Resid. Care Facilit.
62525	6	15	Real Estate	62685	56	152	Chemical Manufacturing	62871	22	48	Merch. Wholesalers,Nondur. Gds
62526	1427	25495	Food Manufacturing	62688	26	61	Educational Services	62872	22	63	Educational Services
62530	51	287	Food Svcs & Drinking Places	62689	11	23	Electronics & Appliance Stores	62874	6	12	Food Svcs & Drinking Places
62531	51	256	Educational Services	62690	188	1475	Educational Services	62875	42	147	Educational Services
62532	12	60	Petroleum & Coal Products Mfg	62691	155	933	Bldg Matl & Garden Eqpmt Dlrs	62876	6	9	Educational Services
62533	52	460	Mining (Except Oil and Gas)	62692	88	447	Educational Services	62877	17	43	Warehousing and Storage
62534	44	372	Accommodation	62693	48	494	Nonstore Retailers	62878	3	2	Postal Service

ZIP CODE	2004 Total Firms	2004 Total Employees	TOP INDUSTRY RANKED on 2004 EMPLOYMENT	ZIP CODE	2004 Total Firms	2004 Total Employees	TOP INDUSTRY RANKED on 2004 EMPLOYMENT	ZIP CODE	2004 Total Firms	2004 Total Employees	TOP INDUSTRY RANKED on 2004 EMPLOYMENT
62879	3	1	Relig., Grant, Civic, Prof Org	62983	40	130	Special Trade Contractors	63112	401	3358	Hospitals
62880	37	190	Food and Beverage Stores	62984	93	427	Truck Transportation	63113	442	3059	Educational Services
62881	597	6106	Truck Transportation	62985	27	69	Educational Services	63114	1284	12977	Special Trade Contractors
62882	74	403	Educational Services	62987	25	26	Special Trade Contractors	63115	500	4190	Social Assistance
62883	6	16	Mining (Except Oil and Gas)	62988	49	237	Merch. Wholesalers, Durable Gds	63116	775	6116	Food Svcs & Drinking Places
62884	97	801	Mining (Except Oil and Gas)	62990	10	46	Ambulatory Health Care Svcs	63117	1005	10781	Hospitals
62885	17	29	Support Activities: Agr./For.	62992	50	578	Admin. Human Resource Programs	63118	881	9154	Ambulatory Health Care Svcs
62886	4	7	Wood Product Manufacturing	62993	1	0	Relig., Grant, Civic, Prof Org	63119	1537	15168	Educational Services
62887	16	27	Crop Production	62994	21	57	Educational Services	63120	267	4185	Machinery Manufacturing
62888	46	214	Machinery Manufacturing	62995	201	2112	Justice, Pubic Order/Safety	63121	568	4630	Educational Services
62889	16	66	Educational Services	62996	9	13	Merch. Wholesalers, Nondur. Gds	63122	1796	18710	Educational Services
62890	73	216	Educational Services	62997	17	48	Exec., Legis., & Other Support	63123	1235	12847	Food Svcs & Drinking Places
62891	11	30	Exec., Legis., & Other Support	62998	19	366	Merch. Wholesalers, Nondur. Gds	63124	509	7753	Educational Services
62892	10	84	Wood Product Manufacturing	62999	56	352	Educational Services	63125	971	11941	Hospitals
62893	16	23	Merch. Wholesalers, Durable Gds	63001	5	20	Heavy & Civil Eng. Construct'N	63126	867	8254	Food Svcs & Drinking Places
62894	18	115	Educational Services	63005	886	11662	Prof., Scientific, & Tech Svcs	63127	524	8583	Prof., Scientific, & Tech Svcs
62895	86	508	Educational Services	63006	36	106	Administrative & Support Svcs	63128	942	14444	Hospitals
62896	532	3992	Transportation Equipment Mfg	63010	1014	9852	Food Svcs & Drinking Places	63129	1234	10103	Food Svcs & Drinking Places
62897	32	237	Accommodation	63011	1947	19523	Credit Intermediation & Relatd	63130	838	9330	Educational Services
62898	33	216	Educational Services	63012	156	895	Furn. & Home Furnishgs Stores	63131	1327	21097	Hospitals
62899	58	396	Elect'l Eqpmt, App, & Comp Mfg	63013	43	169	Merch. Wholesalers, Durable Gds	63132	1289	29856	Broadcasting
62901	1158	19545	Educational Services	63014	19	43	Construction of Buildings	63133	331	4622	Transportation Equipment Mfg
62902	113	613	Food and Beverage Stores	63015	14	64	Educational Services	63134	484	8689	Accommodation
62903	77	475	Prof., Scientific, & Tech Svcs	63016	169	856	Nursing & Resid. Care Facilit.	63135	486	4124	Educational Services
62905	19	173	Merch. Wholesalers, Nondur. Gds	63017	2032	28545	Hospitals	63136	1160	12604	Hospitals
62906	399	2805	Food Svcs & Drinking Places	63019	275	1820	Food Svcs & Drinking Places	63137	278	3773	Exec., Legis., & Other Support
62907	58	253	Mining (Except Oil and Gas)	63020	496	3333	Educational Services	63138	333	3326	Educational Services
62908	15	33	Justice, Pubic Order/Safety	63021	866	7256	Educational Services	63139	791	10979	Food Svcs & Drinking Places
62909	4	13	Miscellaneous Store Retailers	63022	20	17	Construction of Buildings	63140	45	323	Relig., Grant, Civic, Prof Org
62910	54	166	Educational Services	63023	62	252	Educational Services	63141	2417	38351	Hospitals
62912	33	120	Educational Services	63024	4	6	Prof., Scientific, & Tech Svcs	63143	533	5569	Merch. Wholesalers, Durable Gds
62914	226	1622	Water Transportation	63025	432	4125	Machinery Manufacturing	63144	836	10410	Prof., Scientific, & Tech Svcs
62915	24	46	Mining (Except Oil and Gas)	63026	1535	25139	Transportation Equipment Mfg	63145	31	2545	Food Svcs & Drinking Places
62916	31	274	Educational Services	63028	840	8766	Ambulatory Health Care Svcs	63146	1357	21215	Prof., Scientific, & Tech Svcs
62917	72	322	Nursing & Resid. Care Facilit.	63030	2	1	Relig., Grant, Civic, Prof Org	63147	452	8244	Truck Transportation
62918	329	2170	Broadcasting	63031	1140	10117	Educational Services	63151	26	58	Prof., Scientific, & Tech Svcs
62919	43	304	Nonmetallic Mineral Prod. Mfg	63032	12	38	Prof., Scientific, & Tech Svcs	63155	5	5550	Postal Service
62920	90	671	Educational Services	63033	1002	9641	Food Svcs & Drinking Places	63156	6	17	Personal and Laundry Services
62921	8	7	Relig., Grant, Civic, Prof Org	63034	269	2057	General Merchandise Stores	63157	2	3	Administrative & Support Svcs
62922	61	160	Educational Services	63036	12	69	Accommodation	63158	3	1	Merch. Wholesalers, Nondur. Gds
62923	16	71	Merch. Wholesalers, Durable Gds	63037	133	877	Machinery Manufacturing	63163	3	7	Insurance Carriers & Related
62924	58	310	Waste Managmt & Remediat'n Svc	63038	122	976	Educational Services	63164	2	1900	Food Manufacturing
62926	54	320	Educational Services	63039	26	132	Merch. Wholesalers, Nondur. Gds	63166	12	18	Merch. Wholesalers, Nondur. Gds
62927	8	19	Merch. Wholesalers, Durable Gds	63040	204	1285	Food and Beverage Stores	63169	1	1	Insurance Carriers & Related
62928	19	39	Utilities	63041	5	8	Bldg Matl & Garden Eqpmt Dlrs	63177	4	10	Miscellaneous Store Retailers
62930	243	2037	Food and Beverage Stores	63042	774	22344	Transportation Equipment Mfg	63178	3	2	Miscellaneous Store Retailers
62931	62	265	Educational Services	63043	1088	19545	Merch. Wholesalers, Durable Gds	63188	20	71	Prof., Scientific, & Tech Svcs
62932	35	162	Educational Services	63044	1147	23833	Machinery Manufacturing	63199	1	80	Postal Service
62933	51	430	Nursing & Resid. Care Facilit.	63045	315	11958	Insurance Carriers & Related	63301	1986	20867	Prof., Scientific, & Tech Svcs
62934	40	291	Unclassified Establishments	63047	5	14	Special Trade Contractors	63302	21	31	Social Assistance
62935	71	1120	Mining (Except Oil and Gas)	63048	119	1316	Primary Metal Manufacturing	63303	1019	10358	Food Svcs & Drinking Places
62938	124	760	Social Assistance	63049	423	2954	Food Svcs & Drinking Places	63304	1098	9673	Educational Services
62939	93	603	Educational Services	63050	433	3709	Exec., Legis., & Other Support	63330	7	16	Admin. Enviro. Quality Progrms
62940	8	15	Special Trade Contractors	63051	285	1735	Educational Services	63332	58	200	Museums, Hist. Sites, & Similar
62941	21	221	Merch. Wholesalers, Durable Gds	63052	466	3007	Educational Services	63333	28	70	Educational Services
62942	18	67	Educational Services	63053	22	109	Food Svcs & Drinking Places	63334	339	2564	Justice, Pubic Order/Safety
62943	19	37	Accommodation	63055	59	363	Prof., Scientific, & Tech Svcs	63336	78	634	Educational Services
62946	690	5612	Educational Services	63056	29	52	Construction of Buildings	63338	7	15	Prof., Scientific, & Tech Svcs
62947	14	150	Mining (Except Oil and Gas)	63057	5	167	Publishing Industries	63339	21	57	Merch. Wholesalers, Durable Gds
62948	509	4797	Elect'l Eqpmt, App, & Comp Mfg	63060	39	158	Educational Services	63341	77	350	Special Trade Contractors
62949	22	37	Merch. Wholesalers, Durable Gds	63065	10	195	Nursing & Resid. Care Facilit.	63342	17	154	Fabricated Metal Product Mfg
62950	15	24	Food Svcs & Drinking Places	63066	2	7	Special Trade Contractors	63343	137	713	Educational Services
62951	193	989	Special Trade Contractors	63068	201	1822	Merch. Wholesalers, Durable Gds	63344	50	171	Educational Services
62952	130	552	Educational Services	63069	484	4958	Merch. Wholesalers, Durable Gds	63345	17	22	Telecommunications
62953	14	386	Utilities	63070	147	1783	Nonmetallic Mineral Prod. Mfg	63346	5	23	Utilities
62954	25	431	Educational Services	63071	21	121	Educational Services	63347	37	128	Special Trade Contractors
62955	1	1	Personal and Laundry Services	63072	39	161	Bldg Matl & Garden Eqpmt Dlrs	63348	114	586	Repair and Maintenance
62956	36	464	Exec., Legis., & Other Support	63073	10	227	Relig., Grant, Civic, Prof Org	63349	49	242	Animal Production
62957	34	96	Food Svcs & Drinking Places	63074	629	6848	General Merchandise Stores	63350	21	162	Mining (Except Oil and Gas)
62958	58	315	Accommodation	63077	414	3383	Machinery Manufacturing	63351	76	621	Repair and Maintenance
62959	1433	14122	Food Svcs & Drinking Places	63079	14	104	Museums, Hist. Sites, & Similar	63352	38	256	Educational Services
62960	481	5357	Amusement, Gambling, & Recreat.	63080	592	5336	Food Svcs & Drinking Places	63353	249	2129	Educational Services
62961	4	7	Exec., Legis., & Other Support	63084	648	6163	Educational Services	63357	105	793	Relig., Grant, Civic, Prof Org
62962	5	29	Administrative & Support Svcs	63087	13	32	Administrative & Support Svcs	63359	35	60	Crop Production
62963	35	239	Merch. Wholesalers, Nondur. Gds	63088	341	2533	Food Svcs & Drinking Places	63361	261	1289	Warehousing and Storage
62964	78	357	Educational Services	63089	133	683	Special Trade Contractors	63362	102	639	Educational Services
62965	3	4	Miscellaneous Store Retailers	63090	1037	11575	Relig., Grant, Civic, Prof Org	63363	93	590	Fabricated Metal Product Mfg
62966	663	5444	Educational Services	63091	43	238	Waste Managmt & Remediat'n Svc	63365	55	95	Nonmetallic Mineral Prod. Mfg
62967	10	10	Utilities	63099	4	3200	Educational Services	63366	1715	15190	Food Svcs & Drinking Places
62969	44	185	Educational Services	63101	917	23431	Credit Intermediation & Relatd	63367	344	1997	Hospitals
62970	25	181	Construction of Buildings	63102	743	18468	Prof., Scientific, & Tech Svcs	63369	52	240	Wood Product Manufacturing
62971	2	3	Postal Service	63103	1041	35512	Educational Services	63370	8	6	Postal Service
62972	21	145	Accommodation	63104	816	14200	Educational Services	63373	33	81	Amusement, Gambling, & Recreat.
62973	3	2	Food and Beverage Stores	63105	2041	27992	Prof., Scientific, & Tech Svcs	63376	1929	21736	Food Svcs & Drinking Places
62974	29	64	Educational Services	63106	381	7273	Hospitals	63377	71	321	Educational Services
62975	7	29	Bldg Matl & Garden Eqpmt Dlrs	63107	307	2332	Educational Services	63378	4	9	Food Svcs & Drinking Places
62976	18	51	Relig., Grant, Civic, Prof Org	63108	1234	12560	Food Svcs & Drinking Places	63379	652	6033	Primary Metal Manufacturing
62977	21	136	Truck Transportation	63109	840	5256	Ambulatory Health Care Svcs	63381	7	8	Unclassified Establishments
62979	72	279	Food Manufacturing	63110	1089	28402	Educational Services	63382	163	1101	Mining (Except Oil and Gas)
62982	71	549	Nursing & Resid. Care Facilit.	63111	482	5184	Food Manufacturing	63383	580	4021	Fabricated Metal Product Mfg

BUSINESS DATA

ZIP CODE	2004 Total Firms	2004 Total Employees	TOP INDUSTRY RANKED on 2004 EMPLOYMENT	ZIP CODE	2004 Total Firms	2004 Total Employees	TOP INDUSTRY RANKED on 2004 EMPLOYMENT	ZIP CODE	2004 Total Firms	2004 Total Employees	TOP INDUSTRY RANKED on 2004 EMPLOYMENT
63384	69	368	Educational Services	63628	356	1798	Educational Services	63845	186	1326	Educational Services
63385	804	9886	Transportation Equipment Mfg	63629	42	492	Mining (Except Oil and Gas)	63846	38	202	Educational Services
63386	21	81	Wood Product Manufacturing	63630	57	235	Educational Services	63847	2	2	Postal Service
63387	8	12	Prof., Scientific, & Tech Svcs	63631	44	186	Educational Services	63848	52	400	Educational Services
63388	22	113	Educational Services	63632	4	21	Justice, Pubic Order/Safety	63849	2	8	Merch. Wholesalers,Durable Gds
63389	127	575	Educational Services	63633	35	190	Exec., Legis., & Other Support	63850	1	1	Postal Service
63390	204	1798	Furniture & Related Prod. Mfg	63636	9	12	Special Trade Contractors	63851	213	2358	Hospitals
63401	1018	12523	Merch. Wholesalers,Nondur. Gds	63637	24	90	Justice, Pubic Order/Safety	63852	38	152	Educational Services
63430	12	74	Food and Beverage Stores	63638	147	938	Machinery Manufacturing	63853	8	37	Merch. Wholesalers,Durable Gds
63431	5	21	Miscellaneous Store Retailers	63640	1044	11879	Hospitals	63855	37	226	Truck Transportation
63432	10	21	Food Svcs & Drinking Places	63645	464	3682	Ambulatory Health Care Svcs	63857	659	5603	Elect'l Eqpmt, App, & Comp Mfg
63434	32	160	Educational Services	63648	24	24	Food and Beverage Stores	63860	5	20	Merch. Wholesalers,Nondur. Gds
63435	168	1284	Educational Services	63650	224	940	Relig., Grant, Civic, Prof Org	63862	58	282	Relig., Grant, Civic, Prof Org
63436	46	428	Educational Services	63651	4	2	Postal Service	63863	346	2557	Transportation Equipment Mfg
63437	82	335	Nursing & Resid. Care Facilit.	63653	31	78	Educational Services	63866	34	291	Food Manufacturing
63438	9	8	Food and Beverage Stores	63654	42	364	Educational Services	63867	35	426	Gasoline Stations
63439	4	8	Unclassified Establishments	63655	35	95	Educational Services	63868	28	156	Furniture & Related Prod. Mfg
63440	60	372	Educational Services	63656	9	31	Museums, Hist. Sites,& Similar	63869	215	2520	Primary Metal Manufacturing
63441	25	98	Educational Services	63660	43	590	Justice, Pubic Order/Safety	63870	38	116	Machinery Manufacturing
63442	3	35	Wood Product Manufacturing	63661	1	0	Relig., Grant, Civic, Prof Org	63873	206	2401	Transportation Equipment Mfg
63443	11	19	Merch. Wholesalers,Durable Gds	63662	44	241	Educational Services	63874	18	125	Educational Services
63445	199	1170	Relig., Grant, Civic, Prof Org	63663	48	253	Food Svcs & Drinking Places	63875	1	0	Postal Service
63446	28	48	Amusement, Gambling,& Recreat.	63664	450	3248	Accommodation	63876	77	523	Nursing & Resid. Care Facilit.
63447	62	328	Nursing & Resid. Care Facilit.	63665	8	13	Relig., Grant, Civic, Prof Org	63877	128	875	Truck Transportation
63448	56	420	Primary Metal Manufacturing	63666	3	13	Bldg Matl & Garden Eqpmt Dlrs	63878	1	2	Postal Service
63450	3	5	Postal Service	63670	496	5691	Nonmetallic Mineral Prod. Mfg	63879	25	81	Justice, Pubic Order/Safety
63451	15	19	Postal Service	63673	45	141	Nursing & Resid. Care Facilit.	63880	3	8	Support Activities: Agr./For.
63452	46	229	Nursing & Resid. Care Facilit.	63674	4	8	Special Trade Contractors	63881	2	3	Crop Production
63453	9	35	Educational Services	63675	3	1	Relig., Grant, Civic, Prof Org	63882	19	102	Amusement, Gambling,& Recreat.
63454	19	46	Isps, Web Search Portals	63701	1294	13929	Hospitals	63901	1592	18118	Hospitals
63456	199	1623	Primary Metal Manufacturing	63702	18	181	Plastics & Rubber Products Mfg	63902	8	18	Special Trade Contractors
63457	39	176	Exec., Legis., & Other Support	63703	1055	16125	Ambulatory Health Care Svcs	63931	3	3	Administrative & Support Svcs
63458	10	99	Accommodation	63730	126	983	Truck Transportation	63932	36	242	Educational Services
63459	128	645	Textile Product Mills	63732	30	170	Educational Services	63933	120	734	Educational Services
63460	17	92	Wood Product Manufacturing	63735	36	115	Educational Services	63934	3	13	Wood Product Manufacturing
63461	257	2407	Chemical Manufacturing	63736	108	991	Educational Services	63935	414	2486	Educational Services
63462	93	404	Plastics & Rubber Products Mfg	63737	2	5	Heavy & Civil Eng. Construct'N	63936	35	652	Miscellaneous Store Retailers
63463	23	87	Educational Services	63738	2	3	Repair and Maintenance	63937	71	551	Educational Services
63464	8	7	Repair and Maintenance	63739	7	18	Museums, Hist. Sites,& Similar	63938	2	3	Postal Service
63465	10	55	Educational Services	63740	144	984	Educational Services	63939	45	114	Special Trade Contractors
63466	3	2	Miscellaneous Store Retailers	63742	6	18	Beverage & Tobacco Product Mfg	63940	28	146	Educational Services
63467	3	13	Admin. Enviro. Quality Progrms	63743	4	7	Nonmetallic Mineral Prod. Mfg	63941	7	28	Nursing & Resid. Care Facilit.
63468	143	836	Relig., Grant, Civic, Prof Org	63744	30	152	Educational Services	63942	8	36	Educational Services
63469	64	429	Educational Services	63745	8	17	Food and Beverage Stores	63943	31	126	Social Assistance
63471	63	300	Food and Beverage Stores	63746	4	15	Educational Services	63944	96	394	Educational Services
63472	20	63	Merch. Wholesalers,Nondur. Gds	63747	6	15	Merch. Wholesalers,Nondur. Gds	63945	20	49	Educational Services
63473	11	17	Wood Product Manufacturing	63748	26	205	Wood Product Manufacturing	63950	4	8	Truck Transportation
63474	31	85	Educational Services	63750	2	4	Administrative & Support Svcs	63951	3	24	Justice, Pubic Order/Safety
63501	952	10492	Educational Services	63751	16	47	Special Trade Contractors	63952	10	14	Merch. Wholesalers,Nondur. Gds
63530	37	101	Educational Services	63752	5	26	Miscellaneous Manufacturing	63953	52	231	Educational Services
63531	18	16	Merch. Wholesalers,Nondur. Gds	63755	808	9280	Paper Manufacturing	63954	54	270	Educational Services
63532	53	177	Food Svcs & Drinking Places	63758	15	66	Bldg Matl & Garden Eqpmt Dlrs	63955	9	7	Special Trade Contractors
63533	23	51	Justice, Pubic Order/Safety	63760	6	62	Educational Services	63956	27	97	Relig., Grant, Civic, Prof Org
63534	30	57	Educational Services	63763	1	1	Postal Service	63957	267	1991	Educational Services
63535	4	5	Bldg Matl & Garden Eqpmt Dlrs	63764	227	1409	Nursing & Resid. Care Facilit.	63960	116	628	Educational Services
63536	25	53	Merch. Wholesalers,Nondur. Gds	63766	22	44	Educational Services	63961	53	165	Educational Services
63537	144	860	Educational Services	63767	16	111	Transportation Equipment Mfg	63962	3	4	Repair and Maintenance
63538	7	8	Food Svcs & Drinking Places	63769	23	173	Educational Services	63963	1	8	Mining (Except Oil and Gas)
63539	18	31	Animal Production	63770	9	52	Truck Transportation	63964	15	40	Food and Beverage Stores
63540	1	0	Postal Service	63771	74	478	Educational Services	63965	212	1095	Accommodation
63541	7	20	Publishing Industries	63772	1	1	Relig., Grant, Civic, Prof Org	63966	73	236	Admin. Enviro. Quality Progrms
63543	12	44	Educational Services	63774	3	5	Merch. Wholesalers,Durable Gds	63967	45	186	Support Activities: Agr./For.
63544	19	25	Support Activities: Agr./For.	63775	607	8740	Transportation Equipment Mfg	64001	33	184	Educational Services
63545	45	283	Educational Services	63776	2	900	Food Manufacturing	64011	53	360	Merch. Wholesalers,Durable Gds
63546	28	66	Food Svcs & Drinking Places	63779	11	42	Food Svcs & Drinking Places	64012	795	6130	Food and Beverage Stores
63547	21	59	Telecommunications	63780	217	1990	Truck Transportation	64013	23	65	Motion Pict. & Sound Recording
63548	79	400	Food and Beverage Stores	63781	22	141	Merch. Wholesalers,Nondur. Gds	64014	623	7859	Food Svcs & Drinking Places
63549	86	381	Educational Services	63782	1	1	Postal Service	64015	1111	7480	Educational Services
63551	7	6	Motor Vehicle & Parts Dealers	63783	4	16	Social Assistance	64016	101	540	Merch. Wholesalers,Durable Gds
63552	432	4113	Nursing & Resid. Care Facilit.	63784	9	16	Food and Beverage Stores	64017	6	4	Postal Service
63555	233	1474	Nursing & Resid. Care Facilit.	63785	13	39	Construction of Buildings	64018	19	85	Educational Services
63556	186	2481	Food Manufacturing	63787	18	115	Educational Services	64019	45	250	Educational Services
63557	16	16	Pipeline Transportation	63801	1331	13105	Food Svcs & Drinking Places	64020	168	1303	Food Manufacturing
63558	35	174	Educational Services	63820	3	11	Support Activities: Agr./For.	64021	30	55	Merch. Wholesalers,Nondur. Gds
63559	29	170	Educational Services	63821	26	83	Warehousing and Storage	64022	5	6	Special Trade Contractors
63560	3	2	Postal Service	63822	122	509	Crop Production	64024	478	4313	Educational Services
63561	38	307	Educational Services	63823	37	199	Nursing & Resid. Care Facilit.	64028	10	23	Credit Intermediation & Relatd
63563	23	87	Food Manufacturing	63824	3	3	Postal Service	64029	274	2934	Transportation Equipment Mfg
63565	225	1100	Educational Services	63825	141	1050	Educational Services	64030	876	10700	Special Trade Contractors
63566	12	39	Prof., Scientific, & Tech Svcs	63826	4	8	Ambulatory Health Care Svcs	64034	149	735	Fabricated Metal Product Mfg
63567	8	32	Merch. Wholesalers,Nondur. Gds	63827	14	55	Utilities	64035	26	100	Educational Services
63601	651	6152	Educational Services	63828	1	1	Postal Service	64036	19	72	Securities/Commodity Contracts
63620	44	478	Primary Metal Manufacturing	63829	37	195	Educational Services	64037	366	2742	Exec., Legis., & Other Support
63621	59	227	Relig., Grant, Civic, Prof Org	63830	317	2644	Amusement, Gambling,& Recreat.	64040	207	969	Educational Services
63622	24	58	Educational Services	63833	4	11	Merch. Wholesalers,Nondur. Gds	64048	88	231	Educational Services
63623	26	182	Educational Services	63834	285	2109	Educational Services	64050	914	9086	Hospitals
63624	95	467	Educational Services	63837	32	259	Educational Services	64051	13	40	Unclassified Establishments
63625	16	87	Social Assistance	63839	15	168	Educational Services	64052	379	2473	Educational Services
63626	9	18	Construction of Buildings	63840	12	98	Educational Services	64053	113	612	Educational Services
63627	77	392	Merch. Wholesalers,Durable Gds	63841	708	6228	Food Manufacturing	64054	116	717	Food Svcs & Drinking Places

ZIP CODE	2004 Total Firms	2004 Total Employ-ees	TOP INDUSTRY RANKED on 2004 EMPLOYMENT	ZIP CODE	2004 Total Firms	2004 Total Employ-ees	TOP INDUSTRY RANKED on 2004 EMPLOYMENT	ZIP CODE	2004 Total Firms	2004 Total Employ-ees	TOP INDUSTRY RANKED on 2004 EMPLOYMENT
64055	1528	14131	Food Svcs & Drinking Places	64166	1	3	Prof., Scientific, & Tech Svcs	64622	11	10	Rail Transportation
64056	271	4284	Insurance Carriers & Related	64167	5	31	Special Trade Contractors	64623	18	93	Educational Services
64057	525	6415	Food Svcs & Drinking Places	64168	2	1	Repair and Maintenance	64624	59	316	Educational Services
64058	117	1085	Educational Services	64171	15	20	Social Assistance	64625	18	126	Educational Services
64060	365	2570	Food Svcs & Drinking Places	64188	18	19	Administrative & Support Svcs	64628	314	2816	Merch. Wholesalers,Durable Gds
64061	52	877	Primary Metal Manufacturing	64190	5	3	Waste Managmt & Remediat'n Svc	64630	19	23	Warehousing and Storage
64062	119	836	Educational Services	64192	77	418	Clothing & Cloth'g Acc. Stores	64631	37	108	Educational Services
64063	1131	7603	Food Svcs & Drinking Places	64195	2	23	Administrative & Support Svcs	64632	26	88	Educational Services
64064	374	3501	Food Svcs & Drinking Places	64197	1	1100	Nat'l Security & Int'l Affairs	64633	302	1955	Social Assistance
64065	8	771	Educational Services	64401	24	53	Mining (Except Oil and Gas)	64635	13	48	Educational Services
64066	9	14	Merch. Wholesalers,Nondur. Gds	64402	169	785	Educational Services	64636	13	26	Educational Services
64067	289	1961	Educational Services	64420	7	24	Food Svcs & Drinking Places	64637	20	60	Justice, Pubic Order/Safety
64068	1220	21316	Transportation Equipment Mfg	64421	19	83	Crop Production	64638	14	30	Mining (Except Oil and Gas)
64069	16	33	Waste Managmt & Remediat'n Svc	64422	4	15	Furniture & Related Prod. Mfg	64639	2	1	Postal Service
64070	69	307	Educational Services	64423	29	69	Educational Services	64640	178	1121	Educational Services
64071	23	39	Justice, Pubic Order/Safety	64424	314	2535	Nursing & Resid. Care Facilit.	64641	28	88	Educational Services
64072	7	29	Educational Services	64426	9	19	Credit Intermediation & Relatd	64642	27	83	Educational Services
64073	4	25	Bldg Matl & Garden Eqpmt Dlrs	64427	9	31	Food and Beverage Stores	64643	27	86	Food Manufacturing
64074	15	22	Credit Intermediation & Relatd	64428	43	236	Educational Services	64644	133	614	Educational Services
64075	269	1993	Food Svcs & Drinking Places	64429	478	4354	Justice, Pubic Order/Safety	64645	7	27	Justice, Pubic Order/Safety
64076	312	1978	Educational Services	64430	14	38	Chemical Manufacturing	64646	9	29	Educational Services
64077	45	298	Plastics & Rubber Products Mfg	64431	15	22	Bldg Matl & Garden Eqpmt Dlrs	64647	14	42	Educational Services
64078	150	1372	Educational Services	64432	2	3	Repair and Maintenance	64648	104	341	Educational Services
64079	369	2595	Educational Services	64433	5	155	Relig., Grant, Civic, Prof Org	64649	12	15	Furn. & Home Furnishgs Stores
64080	293	2077	Unclassified Establishments	64434	13	92	Educational Services	64650	48	126	Exec., Legis., & Other Support
64081	518	8489	Food Svcs & Drinking Places	64436	14	46	Educational Services	64651	27	42	Museums, Hist. Sites,& Similar
64082	148	1061	Machinery Manufacturing	64437	46	175	Accommodation	64652	19	64	Educational Services
64083	292	2424	General Merchandise Stores	64438	5	2	Postal Service	64653	43	133	Exec., Legis., & Other Support
64084	23	49	Mining (Except Oil and Gas)	64439	45	204	Educational Services	64654	5	1	Food Svcs & Drinking Places
64085	346	2614	Exec., Legis., & Other Support	64440	9	57	Heavy & Civil Eng. Construct'N	64655	9	22	Merch. Wholesalers,Nondur. Gds
64086	553	7379	Food Svcs & Drinking Places	64441	6	4	Postal Service	64656	7	42	Educational Services
64088	19	30	Construction of Buildings	64442	52	315	Educational Services	64657	4	3	Nonmetallic Mineral Prod. Mfg
64089	315	2112	Hospitals	64443	25	96	Paper Manufacturing	64658	138	2320	Print'g & Related Supp't Act's
64090	11	41	Educational Services	64444	31	117	Food Svcs & Drinking Places	64659	39	114	Educational Services
64092	4	51	Accommodation	64445	12	30	Merch. Wholesalers,Nondur. Gds	64660	24	71	Educational Services
64093	981	9202	Personal and Laundry Services	64446	71	305	Hospitals	64661	41	146	Educational Services
64096	56	320	Exec., Legis., & Other Support	64447	1	0	Relig., Grant, Civic, Prof Org	64664	6	6	Construction of Buildings
64097	49	271	Educational Services	64448	23	368	Educational Services	64667	23	70	Educational Services
64098	141	966	Accommodation	64449	6	9	Relig., Grant, Civic, Prof Org	64668	44	179	Educational Services
64101	116	1541	Plastics & Rubber Products Mfg	64451	31	162	Merch. Wholesalers,Durable Gds	64670	50	178	Educational Services
64102	115	1791	Fabricated Metal Product Mfg	64453	11	26	Food Svcs & Drinking Places	64671	44	299	Educational Services
64105	786	26055	Isps, Web Search Portals	64454	82	396	Relig., Grant, Civic, Prof Org	64672	5	9	Postal Service
64106	962	34280	Educational Services	64455	22	76	Educational Services	64673	151	822	Educational Services
64108	1321	36796	Miscellaneous Store Retailers	64456	94	511	Educational Services	64674	27	104	Educational Services
64109	297	2225	Educational Services	64457	8	49	Educational Services	64676	6	23	Credit Intermediation & Relatd
64110	498	7985	Educational Services	64458	7	15	Support Activities: Agr./For.	64679	28	69	Plastics & Rubber Products Mfg
64111	1628	24574	Hospitals	64459	11	47	Educational Services	64680	5	24	Educational Services
64112	737	11276	Food Svcs & Drinking Places	64461	31	189	Educational Services	64681	12	30	Justice, Pubic Order/Safety
64113	340	1823	Food Svcs & Drinking Places	64463	74	360	Educational Services	64682	16	126	Educational Services
64114	1300	17682	Prof., Scientific, & Tech Svcs	64465	110	700	Educational Services	64683	455	3599	Food Manufacturing
64116	1249	21836	Amusement, Gambling,& Recreat.	64466	27	337	Animal Production	64686	8	60	Nonmetallic Mineral Prod. Mfg
64117	272	4650	Electronics & Appliance Stores	64467	3	4	Truck Transportation	64688	4	6	Postal Service
64118	1061	9150	Food Svcs & Drinking Places	64468	656	7781	Educational Services	64689	21	135	Educational Services
64119	793	6550	Food Svcs & Drinking Places	64469	116	574	Educational Services	64701	669	6295	Food Svcs & Drinking Places
64120	460	13771	Merch. Wholesalers,Durable Gds	64470	138	711	Educational Services	64720	100	437	Educational Services
64123	125	1526	Museums, Hist. Sites,& Similar	64471	21	29	Merch. Wholesalers,Durable Gds	64722	14	141	Educational Services
64124	221	1650	Educational Services	64473	108	512	Educational Services	64723	21	52	Miscellaneous Manufacturing
64125	71	650	Paper Manufacturing	64474	22	79	Educational Services	64724	94	600	Educational Services
64126	200	2560	Fabricated Metal Product Mfg	64475	11	69	Educational Services	64725	60	297	Educational Services
64127	520	5859	Educational Services	64476	13	51	Educational Services	64726	15	15	Food Svcs & Drinking Places
64128	263	3773	Hospitals	64477	156	1149	Educational Services	64728	13	108	Educational Services
64129	322	6796	Amusement, Gambling,& Recreat.	64479	31	160	Educational Services	64730	381	2810	Food Svcs & Drinking Places
64130	418	5490	Educational Services	64480	5	11	Special Trade Contractors	64733	32	102	Educational Services
64131	848	13746	Ambulatory Health Care Svcs	64481	39	110	Educational Services	64734	44	318	Educational Services
64132	368	4294	Ambulatory Health Care Svcs	64482	201	1228	Educational Services	64735	716	6452	Hospitals
64133	1231	11693	Food Svcs & Drinking Places	64483	14	142	Educational Services	64738	36	136	Food Svcs & Drinking Places
64134	460	3297	Educational Services	64484	31	109	Educational Services	64739	23	280	Educational Services
64136	59	724	Food Svcs & Drinking Places	64485	273	1655	Educational Services	64740	42	78	Educational Services
64137	203	4014	Prof., Scientific, & Tech Svcs	64486	25	44	Merch. Wholesalers,Nondur. Gds	64741	16	108	Merch. Wholesalers,Nondur. Gds
64138	514	5243	Educational Services	64487	23	46	Merch. Wholesalers,Nondur. Gds	64742	68	242	Educational Services
64139	31	1156	Hospitals	64489	93	708	Educational Services	64743	13	45	Educational Services
64141	19	35	Prof., Scientific, & Tech Svcs	64490	60	163	Educational Services	64744	348	1929	Hospitals
64145	190	4113	Food Svcs & Drinking Places	64491	140	830	Educational Services	64745	5	22	Justice, Pubic Order/Safety
64146	25	76	Prof., Scientific, & Tech Svcs	64492	21	40	Prof., Scientific, & Tech Svcs	64746	40	108	Pipeline Transportation
64147	30	526	Bldg Matl & Garden Eqpmt Dlrs	64493	10	18	Accommodation	64747	93	297	Food and Beverage Stores
64148	12	32	Special Trade Contractors	64494	18	67	Educational Services	64748	58	344	Educational Services
64149	14	35	Special Trade Contractors	64496	10	32	Crop Production	64750	5	13	Warehousing and Storage
64150	276	4020	Amusement, Gambling,& Recreat.	64497	7	12	Repair and Maintenance	64752	25	141	Educational Services
64151	516	4011	Food Svcs & Drinking Places	64498	14	33	Special Trade Contractors	64755	79	485	Educational Services
64152	574	3469	Educational Services	64499	5	4	Special Trade Contractors	64756	11	25	Justice, Pubic Order/Safety
64153	415	19351	Support Act. for Transport.	64501	815	13191	Hospitals	64759	375	3431	Furniture & Related Prod. Mfg
64154	173	2988	Food Svcs & Drinking Places	64502	4	3	Administrative & Support Svcs	64761	37	142	Educational Services
64155	415	4479	General Merchandise Stores	64503	386	6195	Paper Manufacturing	64762	57	216	Educational Services
64156	23	176	Educational Services	64504	318	3802	Food Manufacturing	64763	52	257	Nursing & Resid. Care Facilit.
64157	72	965	Food Svcs & Drinking Places	64505	263	2173	Educational Services	64765	4	14	Warehousing and Storage
64158	32	853	General Merchandise Stores	64506	1127	15982	Hospitals	64766	1	1	Personal and Laundry Services
64161	131	9997	Amusement, Gambling,& Recreat.	64507	438	6898	Prof., Scientific, & Tech Svcs	64767	16	21	Utilities
64163	25	899	Relig., Grant, Civic, Prof Org	64508	7	15	Unclassified Establishments	64769	15	52	Machinery Manufacturing
64164	7	75	Educational Services	64601	676	6210	Merch. Wholesalers,Durable Gds	64770	39	134	Educational Services
64165	4	28	Rental and Leasing Services	64620	8	17	Food and Beverage Stores	64771	9	12	Construction of Buildings

64772 - 65613 BUSINESS DATA

ZIP CODE	2004 Total Firms	2004 Total Employ-ees	TOP INDUSTRY RANKED on 2004 EMPLOYMENT	ZIP CODE	2004 Total Firms	2004 Total Employ-ees	TOP INDUSTRY RANKED on 2004 EMPLOYMENT	ZIP CODE	2004 Total Firms	2004 Total Employ-ees	TOP INDUSTRY RANKED on 2004 EMPLOYMENT
64772	722	6097	Hospitals	65067	10	7	Crop Production	65336	161	935	Food Svcs & Drinking Places
64776	160	1238	Social Assistance	65068	17	75	Educational Services	65337	47	228	Educational Services
64778	15	35	Furn. & Home Furnishgs Stores	65069	27	90	Warehousing and Storage	65338	129	528	Educational Services
64779	115	392	Educational Services	65072	51	205	Special Trade Contractors	65339	22	111	Educational Services
64780	23	92	Food Manufacturing	65074	77	438	Educational Services	65340	667	7649	Exec., Legis., & Other Support
64781	6	29	Educational Services	65075	37	248	Nursing & Resid. Care Facilit.	65344	12	35	Educational Services
64783	20	83	Educational Services	65076	17	43	Relig., Grant, Civic, Prof Org	65345	2	5	Bldg Matl & Garden Eqpmt Dlrs
64784	46	196	Educational Services	65077	17	35	Accommodation	65347	17	30	Food Svcs & Drinking Places
64788	53	122	Credit Intermediation & Relatd	65078	112	624	Educational Services	65348	38	209	Educational Services
64790	21	109	Educational Services	65079	387	1468	Food Svcs & Drinking Places	65349	109	774	Machinery Manufacturing
64801	1893	20803	Educational Services	65080	24	55	Special Trade Contractors	65350	26	185	Educational Services
64802	15	18	Administrative & Support Svcs	65081	145	1318	Justice, Pubic Order/Safety	65351	103	513	Educational Services
64803	13	61	Repair and Maintenance	65082	64	363	Relig., Grant, Civic, Prof Org	65354	16	50	Food Svcs & Drinking Places
64804	1596	26793	Hospitals	65083	6	6	Special Trade Contractors	65355	515	2413	Food Svcs & Drinking Places
64830	20	61	Justice, Pubic Order/Safety	65084	340	2371	Fabricated Metal Product Mfg	65360	182	1075	Educational Services
64831	247	1349	Educational Services	65085	48	310	Transportation Equipment Mfg	65401	1356	15749	Educational Services
64832	20	31	Food and Beverage Stores	65101	1579	30206	Exec., Legis., & Other Support	65402	13	54	Waste Managmt & Remediat'n Svc
64833	13	78	Animal Production	65102	7	38	Prof., Scientific, & Tech Svcs	65409	9	1078	Educational Services
64834	144	869	Educational Services	65103	1	50	Admin. Human Resource Programs	65436	2	0	Relig., Grant, Civic, Prof Org
64835	38	269	Furniture & Related Prod. Mfg	65109	1652	23151	Food Svcs & Drinking Places	65438	74	468	Furn. & Home Furnishgs Stores
64836	829	9096	Food and Beverage Stores	65110	6	66	Merch. Wholesalers,Durable Gds	65439	8	63	Mining (Except Oil and Gas)
64840	99	400	Educational Services	65201	1985	29591	Ambulatory Health Care Svcs	65440	11	444	Mining (Except Oil and Gas)
64841	18	450	Truck Transportation	65202	1098	13130	Special Trade Contractors	65441	142	987	Apparel Manufacturing
64842	26	52	Wood Product Manufacturing	65203	1667	17791	Food Svcs & Drinking Places	65443	5	4	General Merchandise Stores
64843	75	437	Personal and Laundry Services	65205	51	98	Special Trade Contractors	65444	17	24	Special Trade Contractors
64844	134	439	Educational Services	65211	49	9170	Educational Services	65446	19	21	Prof., Scientific, & Tech Svcs
64847	24	30	Exec., Legis., & Other Support	65212	56	7015	Hospitals	65449	10	27	Accommodation
64848	17	130	Merch. Wholesalers,Nondur. Gds	65215	1	25	Educational Services	65452	120	577	Educational Services
64849	2	3	Postal Service	65216	1	276	Educational Services	65453	382	3703	Gasoline Stations
64850	896	10795	Furn. & Home Furnishgs Stores	65217	1	900	Insurance Carriers & Related	65456	12	20	Fabricated Metal Product Mfg
64854	89	2054	Food Manufacturing	65218	1	1200	Insurance Carriers & Related	65457	6	10	Waste Managmt & Remediat'n Svc
64855	41	112	Relig., Grant, Civic, Prof Org	65230	21	30	Nursing & Resid. Care Facilit.	65459	205	779	Educational Services
64856	198	879	Food Manufacturing	65231	103	408	Repair and Maintenance	65461	6	8	Motor Vehicle & Parts Dealers
64857	9	8	Exec., Legis., & Other Support	65232	6	6	Postal Service	65462	26	92	Educational Services
64858	9	29	Educational Services	65233	528	6293	Administrative & Support Svcs	65463	22	19	Special Trade Contractors
64859	9	15	Special Trade Contractors	65236	83	460	Educational Services	65464	6	7	Bldg Matl & Garden Eqpmt Dlrs
64861	28	116	Educational Services	65237	35	141	Educational Services	65466	124	591	Educational Services
64862	122	733	Educational Services	65239	28	113	Educational Services	65468	2	3	Repair and Maintenance
64863	55	1136	Food Manufacturing	65240	217	1349	Educational Services	65470	14	37	Educational Services
64864	6	8	Postal Service	65243	13	31	Warehousing and Storage	65473	119	2775	Nonstore Retailers
64865	195	935	Educational Services	65244	27	405	Utilities	65479	4	8	Support Activities: Agr./For.
64866	33	80	Bldg Matl & Garden Eqpmt Dlrs	65246	4	4	Bldg Matl & Garden Eqpmt Dlrs	65483	337	2419	General Merchandise Stores
64867	20	94	Educational Services	65247	20	53	Heavy & Civil Eng. Construct'N	65484	2	3	Support Activities: Agr./For.
64868	12	38	Electronics & Appliance Stores	65248	236	1240	Educational Services	65486	127	728	Educational Services
64869	3	6	Chemical Manufacturing	65250	11	14	Crop Production	65501	8	36	Justice, Pubic Order/Safety
64870	373	3373	Machinery Manufacturing	65251	736	6574	Educational Services	65529	2	5	Special Trade Contractors
64873	11	16	Special Trade Contractors	65254	85	587	Textile Product Mills	65532	1	1	Postal Service
64874	59	239	Educational Services	65255	76	468	Educational Services	65534	15	297	Educational Services
65001	16	35	Food Svcs & Drinking Places	65256	47	238	Educational Services	65535	35	107	Motor Vehicle & Parts Dealers
65010	146	979	Educational Services	65257	37	177	Educational Services	65536	1326	13132	Transportation Equipment Mfg
65011	43	114	Food Svcs & Drinking Places	65258	11	22	Social Assistance	65541	5	5	Crop Production
65013	125	606	Educational Services	65259	111	433	Educational Services	65542	161	881	Utilities
65014	63	268	Miscellaneous Manufacturing	65260	16	22	Merch. Wholesalers,Durable Gds	65543	2	3	General Merchandise Stores
65016	16	44	Food Svcs & Drinking Places	65261	61	325	Justice, Pubic Order/Safety	65546	1	2	Postal Service
65017	27	65	Special Trade Contractors	65262	56	975	Food Svcs & Drinking Places	65548	243	1949	Machinery Manufacturing
65018	300	2237	Food and Beverage Stores	65263	52	176	Educational Services	65550	71	298	Educational Services
65020	919	6877	Educational Services	65264	40	132	Credit Intermediation & Relatd	65552	29	186	Educational Services
65023	41	89	Special Trade Contractors	65265	738	7090	Hospitals	65555	27	122	Merch. Wholesalers,Durable Gds
65024	39	212	Apparel Manufacturing	65270	809	8726	Rental and Leasing Services	65556	174	926	Educational Services
65025	11	34	Educational Services	65274	59	349	Educational Services	65557	15	42	Relig., Grant, Civic, Prof Org
65026	532	4114	Elect'l Eqpmt, App, & Comp Mfg	65275	177	945	Educational Services	65559	338	2013	Relig., Grant, Civic, Prof Org
65031	1	2	Postal Service	65276	63	376	Educational Services	65560	595	4652	Merch. Wholesalers,Nondur. Gds
65032	39	411	Educational Services	65278	5	44	Educational Services	65564	2	1	Miscellaneous Manufacturing
65034	12	20	Merch. Wholesalers,Nondur. Gds	65279	76	395	Beverage & Tobacco Product Mfg	65565	299	1444	Educational Services
65035	55	597	Wood Product Manufacturing	65280	2	7	Postal Service	65566	80	1075	Mining (Except Oil and Gas)
65036	2	4	Admin. Enviro. Quality Progrms	65281	215	999	Educational Services	65567	42	376	Educational Services
65037	283	1111	Food Svcs & Drinking Places	65282	2	1	Postal Service	65570	12	61	Educational Services
65038	61	422	Nursing & Resid. Care Facilit.	65283	18	46	Museums, Hist. Sites,& Similar	65571	93	393	Educational Services
65039	54	204	Amusement, Gambling,& Recreat.	65284	67	369	Educational Services	65572	3	25	Educational Services
65040	10	24	Relig., Grant, Civic, Prof Org	65285	14	27	Chemical Manufacturing	65580	15	79	Air Transportation
65041	354	2058	Educational Services	65286	7	8	Merch. Wholesalers,Nondur. Gds	65582	131	748	Merch. Wholesalers,Nondur. Gds
65042	9	12	Merch. Wholesalers,Durable Gds	65287	3	5	Postal Service	65583	334	2113	Educational Services
65043	177	869	Food Svcs & Drinking Places	65299	1	10	Relig., Grant, Civic, Prof Org	65584	467	3307	Food Svcs & Drinking Places
65046	38	132	Educational Services	65301	1516	15532	Food Svcs & Drinking Places	65586	3	3	Merch. Wholesalers,Durable Gds
65047	58	454	Educational Services	65302	12	22	Social Assistance	65588	94	615	Apparel Manufacturing
65048	3	3	Merch. Wholesalers,Nondur. Gds	65305	40	6321	Nat'l Security & Int'l Affairs	65589	3	1	Postal Service
65049	653	3975	Food Svcs & Drinking Places	65320	25	88	Perform'g Arts, Spec. Sports	65590	21	56	Relig., Grant, Civic, Prof Org
65050	14	43	Educational Services	65321	21	63	Justice, Pubic Order/Safety	65591	23	54	Prof., Scientific, & Tech Svcs
65051	218	1432	Educational Services	65322	41	65	Special Trade Contractors	65601	19	15	Sportg Gds,Hobby,Book, & Music
65052	98	679	Amusement, Gambling,& Recreat.	65323	26	112	Educational Services	65603	5	7	Fabricated Metal Product Mfg
65053	33	114	Merch. Wholesalers,Nondur. Gds	65324	78	297	Educational Services	65604	133	618	Educational Services
65054	26	92	Merch. Wholesalers,Nondur. Gds	65325	147	704	Educational Services	65605	434	3635	Heavy & Civil Eng. Construct'N
65058	34	232	Food Manufacturing	65326	33	134	Justice, Pubic Order/Safety	65606	137	604	Nursing & Resid. Care Facilit.
65059	30	562	Educational Services	65327	16	49	Relig., Grant, Civic, Prof Org	65607	1	2	Amusement, Gambling,& Recreat.
65061	25	39	Food Svcs & Drinking Places	65329	12	12	Postal Service	65608	385	2349	Merch. Wholesalers,Durable Gds
65062	7	38	Bldg Matl & Garden Eqpmt Dlrs	65330	22	66	Truck Transportation	65609	20	94	Educational Services
65063	81	448	Educational Services	65332	31	90	Educational Services	65610	109	545	Educational Services
65064	12	15	Special Trade Contractors	65333	15	76	Educational Services	65611	62	221	Educational Services
65065	879	8792	Accommodation	65334	17	115	Educational Services	65612	21	176	Gasoline Stations
65066	311	2827	Print'g & Related Supp't Act's	65335	10	13	Warehousing and Storage	65613	832	7437	Food Svcs & Drinking Places

ZIP CODE	2004 Total Firms	2004 Total Employ-ees	TOP INDUSTRY RANKED on 2004 EMPLOYMENT	ZIP CODE	2004 Total Firms	2004 Total Employ-ees	TOP INDUSTRY RANKED on 2004 EMPLOYMENT	ZIP CODE	2004 Total Firms	2004 Total Employ-ees	TOP INDUSTRY RANKED on 2004 EMPLOYMENT
65614	20	60	Educational Services	65734	97	685	Educational Services	66044	1576	16523	Prof., Scientific, & Tech Svcs
65615	28	125	Administrative & Support Svcs	65735	2	5	Postal Service	66045	40	3655	Educational Services
65616	1922	23224	Accommodation	65737	479	2447	General Merchandise Stores	66046	733	11375	Administrative & Support Svcs
65617	32	165	Forestry and Logging	65738	430	3068	General Merchandise Stores	66047	407	3668	Relig., Grant, Civic, Prof Org
65618	3	3	Primary Metal Manufacturing	65739	41	617	Accommodation	66048	1129	11428	Hospitals
65619	127	701	Special Trade Contractors	65740	62	129	Accommodation	66049	665	7112	Food Svcs & Drinking Places
65620	5	3	Bldg Matl & Garden Eqpmt Dlrs	65741	2	46	Amusement, Gambling,& Recreat.	66050	55	188	Educational Services
65622	381	2484	Merch. Wholesalers,Nondur. Gds	65742	337	1489	Educational Services	66051	19	48	Relig., Grant, Civic, Prof Org
65623	18	885	Food Manufacturing	65744	3	14	Educational Services	66052	33	206	Crop Production
65624	64	165	Special Trade Contractors	65745	46	158	Food and Beverage Stores	66053	258	1761	Food Svcs & Drinking Places
65625	377	4380	Elect'l Eqpmt, App, & Comp Mfg	65746	174	1424	Transportation Equipment Mfg	66054	59	420	Educational Services
65626	29	148	Relig., Grant, Civic, Prof Org	65747	225	751	Food Svcs & Drinking Places	66056	130	499	Exec., Legis., & Other Support
65627	14	78	Prof., Scientific, & Tech Svcs	65752	4	7	Rail Transportation	66058	12	14	Motor Vehicle & Parts Dealers
65629	3	36	Educational Services	65753	83	410	Educational Services	66060	43	151	Educational Services
65630	5	34	Real Estate	65754	26	165	Educational Services	66061	1799	23825	Exec., Legis., & Other Support
65631	66	304	Educational Services	65755	11	25	Merch. Wholesalers,Nondur. Gds	66062	1791	22326	Food Svcs & Drinking Places
65632	70	394	Educational Services	65756	15	63	Construction of Buildings	66063	25	60	Administrative & Support Svcs
65633	134	704	Educational Services	65757	185	2146	Truck Transportation	66064	183	1658	Hospitals
65634	15	36	Justice, Pubic Order/Safety	65759	26	90	Educational Services	66066	145	1007	Educational Services
65635	16	105	Educational Services	65760	19	40	Accommodation	66067	722	7420	Merch. Wholesalers,Durable Gds
65636	8	15	Merch. Wholesalers,Nondur. Gds	65761	66	322	Educational Services	66070	45	179	Food Svcs & Drinking Places
65637	33	186	Educational Services	65762	9	51	Educational Services	66071	512	3883	Educational Services
65638	12	14	Waste Managmt & Remediat'n Svc	65764	11	12	Special Trade Contractors	66072	27	143	Educational Services
65640	8	12	Postal Service	65765	3	4	Food and Beverage Stores	66073	81	414	Educational Services
65641	64	184	Food Svcs & Drinking Places	65766	1	2	Amusement, Gambling,& Recreat.	66075	131	544	Justice, Pubic Order/Safety
65644	37	95	Personal and Laundry Services	65767	65	513	Educational Services	66076	43	217	Educational Services
65645	3	1	Special Trade Contractors	65768	7	13	Special Trade Contractors	66077	3	1	Repair and Maintenance
65646	42	131	Educational Services	65769	61	307	Food Manufacturing	66078	12	33	Food and Beverage Stores
65647	41	251	Educational Services	65770	52	203	Justice, Pubic Order/Safety	66079	17	110	Motor Vehicle & Parts Dealers
65648	129	590	Educational Services	65771	46	133	Administrative & Support Svcs	66080	23	202	Educational Services
65649	46	190	Educational Services	65772	44	313	Educational Services	66083	174	1224	Educational Services
65650	14	32	Motor Vehicle & Parts Dealers	65773	19	19	Special Trade Contractors	66085	259	2166	Educational Services
65652	79	381	Educational Services	65774	30	166	Educational Services	66086	214	1266	Educational Services
65653	283	1694	Educational Services	65775	1285	11843	Hospitals	66087	105	499	Exec., Legis., & Other Support
65654	7	22	Relig., Grant, Civic, Prof Org	65777	13	26	Relig., Grant, Civic, Prof Org	66088	108	530	Educational Services
65655	180	1069	Educational Services	65778	23	160	Educational Services	66090	114	599	Educational Services
65656	129	572	Educational Services	65779	78	295	Educational Services	66091	10	37	Utilities
65657	1	0	Relig., Grant, Civic, Prof Org	65781	201	1007	Educational Services	66092	80	534	Educational Services
65658	34	162	Motor Vehicle & Parts Dealers	65783	6	9	Food and Beverage Stores	66093	16	43	Educational Services
65660	2	4	Prof., Scientific, & Tech Svcs	65784	3	5	Accommodation	66094	22	253	Amusement, Gambling,& Recreat.
65661	148	1124	Merch. Wholesalers,Nondur. Gds	65785	301	1240	Educational Services	66095	24	43	Food and Beverage Stores
65662	27	75	Nursing & Resid. Care Facilit.	65786	59	309	Educational Services	66097	32	163	Hospitals
65663	51	248	Educational Services	65787	20	58	Furn. & Home Furnishgs Stores	66101	661	11646	Exec., Legis., & Other Support
65664	24	29	Miscellaneous Store Retailers	65788	15	31	Justice, Pubic Order/Safety	66102	810	7894	Hospitals
65666	3	4	Repair and Maintenance	65789	43	398	Machinery Manufacturing	66103	511	4603	Special Trade Contractors
65667	132	570	Educational Services	65790	5	14	Postal Service	66104	325	2583	Educational Services
65668	127	589	Nursing & Resid. Care Facilit.	65791	233	1132	Educational Services	66105	359	5829	Merch. Wholesalers,Durable Gds
65669	64	172	Educational Services	65793	235	2055	Transit & Grnd Pass. Transport	66106	687	9885	Merch. Wholesalers,Nondur. Gds
65672	329	2150	Food Svcs & Drinking Places	65801	44	884	Postal Service	66109	269	2858	Relig., Grant, Civic, Prof Org
65673	4	4	Prof., Scientific, & Tech Svcs	65802	2009	43186	Hospitals	66110	2	4	Special Trade Contractors
65674	111	556	Educational Services	65803	1692	30003	Truck Transportation	66111	320	5665	Truck Transportation
65675	16	81	Educational Services	65804	3079	41513	Hospitals	66112	471	6077	Hospitals
65676	21	38	Accommodation	65805	1	2	Special Trade Contractors	66113	2	2	Prof., Scientific, & Tech Svcs
65679	79	222	Educational Services	65806	830	10555	Food Manufacturing	66115	159	9214	Transportation Equipment Mfg
65680	25	75	Exec., Legis., & Other Support	65807	1989	31010	Hospitals	66117	1	1	Real Estate
65681	89	263	Accommodation	65808	33	56	Prof., Scientific, & Tech Svcs	66118	55	1057	Rental and Leasing Services
65682	81	647	Nursing & Resid. Care Facilit.	65809	232	1577	Insurance Carriers & Related	66119	2	38	Bldg Matl & Garden Eqpmt Dlrs
65685	14	58	Educational Services	65810	365	1904	Food and Beverage Stores	66160	60	5846	Hospitals
65686	267	1555	Accommodation	65814	18	34	Merch. Wholesalers,Nondur. Gds	66201	18	142	Insurance Carriers & Related
65688	5	93	Merch. Wholesalers,Durable Gds	66002	589	6519	Educational Services	66202	1218	14624	Insurance Carriers & Related
65689	210	1822	Truck Transportation	66006	223	1400	Educational Services	66203	841	8912	Credit Intermediation & Relatd
65690	5	6	Motor Vehicle & Parts Dealers	66007	135	826	Educational Services	66204	869	10222	Hospitals
65692	27	213	Wood Product Manufacturing	66008	15	95	Educational Services	66205	594	6250	Broadcasting
65702	10	16	Wood Product Manufacturing	66010	24	62	Food Svcs & Drinking Places	66206	342	2582	Ambulatory Health Care Svcs
65704	133	882	Transportation Equipment Mfg	66012	366	2740	Food Svcs & Drinking Places	66207	517	3201	Educational Services
65705	116	790	Educational Services	66013	65	354	Heavy & Civil Eng. Construct'N	66208	659	6018	Insurance Carriers & Related
65706	532	3561	Food Svcs & Drinking Places	66014	11	22	Merch. Wholesalers,Durable Gds	66209	491	6813	Ambulatory Health Care Svcs
65707	86	343	Educational Services	66015	27	68	Educational Services	66210	1410	22172	Prof., Scientific, & Tech Svcs
65708	553	8524	Primary Metal Manufacturing	66016	6	17	Educational Services	66211	967	17041	Prof., Scientific, & Tech Svcs
65710	27	245	Educational Services	66017	15	66	Educational Services	66212	1527	14313	Food Svcs & Drinking Places
65711	359	2225	General Merchandise Stores	66018	154	1726	Plastics & Rubber Products Mfg	66213	767	7946	Food Svcs & Drinking Places
65712	383	3868	Truck Transportation	66019	2	1	Postal Service	66214	929	15395	Prof., Scientific, & Tech Svcs
65713	33	233	Educational Services	66020	37	178	Educational Services	66215	1557	22474	Merch. Wholesalers,Durable Gds
65714	872	5561	Administrative & Support Svcs	66021	38	139	Educational Services	66216	631	4894	Food and Beverage Stores
65715	3	5	Merch. Wholesalers,Nondur. Gds	66023	44	216	Educational Services	66217	190	5793	Waste Managmt & Remediat'n Svc
65717	63	356	Educational Services	66024	48	581	Miscellaneous Manufacturing	66218	103	840	Special Trade Contractors
65720	7	18	Food Manufacturing	66025	172	1068	Educational Services	66219	371	11069	Print'g & Related Supp't Act's
65721	782	6055	Merch. Wholesalers,Durable Gds	66026	16	39	Educational Services	66220	50	209	Amusement, Gambling,& Recreat.
65722	17	103	Truck Transportation	66027	58	3515	Exec., Legis., & Other Support	66221	187	1966	Food and Beverage Stores
65723	80	313	Educational Services	66030	268	2340	Educational Services	66222	7	16	Perform'g Arts, Spec. Sports
65724	54	126	Food Svcs & Drinking Places	66031	48	1938	Food Manufacturing	66223	462	4129	Food Svcs & Drinking Places
65725	81	428	Educational Services	66032	276	1857	Food Svcs & Drinking Places	66224	106	1668	Repair and Maintenance
65726	3	254	Educational Services	66033	21	109	Fabricated Metal Product Mfg	66225	27	43	Construction of Buildings
65727	12	12	Food and Beverage Stores	66035	61	369	Educational Services	66226	149	1565	Special Trade Contractors
65728	1	0	Postal Service	66036	10	62	Educational Services	66227	119	2120	Special Trade Contractors
65729	12	46	Justice, Pubic Order/Safety	66039	14	99	Educational Services	66250	3	9	Nonstore Retailers
65730	3	9	Accommodation	66040	136	961	Utilities	66251	7	2817	Telecommunications
65731	3	6	Exec., Legis., & Other Support	66041	22	47	Warehousing and Storage	66282	12	21	Bldg Matl & Garden Eqpmt Dlrs
65732	25	68	Utilities	66042	9	38	Administrative & Support Svcs	66283	19	65	Administrative & Support Svcs
65733	20	54	Justice, Pubic Order/Safety	66043	175	2285	Justice, Pubic Order/Safety	66285	26	60	Merch. Wholesalers,Durable Gds

BUSINESS DATA

ZIP CODE	2004 Total Firms	2004 Total Employ-ees	TOP INDUSTRY RANKED on 2004 EMPLOYMENT	ZIP CODE	2004 Total Firms	2004 Total Employ-ees	TOP INDUSTRY RANKED on 2004 EMPLOYMENT	ZIP CODE	2004 Total Firms	2004 Total Employ-ees	TOP INDUSTRY RANKED on 2004 EMPLOYMENT
66286	4	5	Prof., Scientific, & Tech Svcs	66610	102	419	Educational Services	66857	25	141	Warehousing and Storage
66401	92	399	Educational Services	66611	562	6110	Motor Vehicle & Parts Dealers	66858	24	38	Credit Intermediation & Relatd
66402	51	412	Justice, Pubic Order/Safety	66612	463	13535	Exec., Legis., & Other Support	66859	16	132	Educational Services
66403	40	131	Educational Services	66614	936	7696	Prof., Scientific, & Tech Svcs	66860	84	339	Educational Services
66404	15	86	Educational Services	66615	121	2021	Prof., Scientific, & Tech Svcs	66861	198	1435	Nursing & Resid. Care Facilit.
66406	35	225	Social Assistance	66616	108	789	Educational Services	66862	7	6	Crop Production
66407	17	124	Repair and Maintenance	66617	182	1111	Educational Services	66863	2	2	Postal Service
66408	22	225	Food Manufacturing	66618	242	5519	Motor Vehicle & Parts Dealers	66864	9	77	Educational Services
66409	43	167	Educational Services	66619	144	2752	Nat'l Security & Int'l Affairs	66865	33	195	Educational Services
66411	52	374	Nonmetallic Mineral Prod. Mfg	66620	8	431	Nat'l Security & Int'l Affairs	66866	60	394	Nursing & Resid. Care Facilit.
66412	9	28	Insurance Carriers & Related	66621	11	712	Educational Services	66868	21	75	Educational Services
66413	64	287	Educational Services	66622	6	311	Exec., Legis., & Other Support	66869	41	183	Transit & Grnd Pass. Transport
66414	61	339	Educational Services	66624	2	450	Postal Service	66870	6	22	Oil and Gas Extraction
66415	45	184	Nursing & Resid. Care Facilit.	66629	1	2500	Insurance Carriers & Related	66871	76	272	Educational Services
66416	12	21	Justice, Pubic Order/Safety	66636	1	0	Insurance Carriers & Related	66872	44	93	Educational Services
66417	15	75	Exec., Legis., & Other Support	66667	8	22	Perform'g Arts, Spec. Sports	66873	15	38	Justice, Pubic Order/Safety
66418	12	40	Educational Services	66675	5	9	Bldg Matl & Garden Eqpmt Dlrs	66901	401	3227	Educational Services
66419	13	16	Motor Vehicle & Parts Dealers	66683	11	85	Justice, Pubic Order/Safety	66930	7	6	Gasoline Stations
66420	2	0	Postal Service	66701	598	6160	Merch. Wholesalers,Nondur. Gds	66932	10	20	Warehousing and Storage
66422	12	30	Educational Services	66710	31	99	Educational Services	66933	20	47	Justice, Pubic Order/Safety
66423	56	220	Educational Services	66711	19	36	Exec., Legis., & Other Support	66935	217	1523	Hospitals
66424	34	122	Educational Services	66712	86	346	Educational Services	66936	18	92	Justice, Pubic Order/Safety
66425	39	64	Justice, Pubic Order/Safety	66713	215	1933	Paper Manufacturing	66937	40	181	Educational Services
66426	2	1	Gasoline Stations	66714	7	30	Oil and Gas Extraction	66938	65	327	Nursing & Resid. Care Facilit.
66427	79	328	Nursing & Resid. Care Facilit.	66716	25	64	Food Svcs & Drinking Places	66939	35	209	Educational Services
66428	17	36	Truck Transportation	66717	17	129	Educational Services	66940	18	82	Educational Services
66429	21	171	Special Trade Contractors	66720	612	6837	Educational Services	66941	10	35	Educational Services
66431	23	53	Educational Services	66724	31	232	Educational Services	66942	6	25	Justice, Pubic Order/Safety
66432	17	15	Pipeline Transportation	66725	367	2340	Print'g & Related Supp't Act's	66943	36	163	Social Assistance
66434	328	2021	Educational Services	66728	7	10	Waste Managmt & Remediat'n Svc	66944	18	80	Educational Services
66436	332	2111	Educational Services	66732	8	10	Merch. Wholesalers,Nondur. Gds	66945	52	320	Hospitals
66438	20	126	Prof., Scientific, & Tech Svcs	66733	130	744	Exec., Legis., & Other Support	66946	3	11	Support Activities: Agr./For.
66439	158	986	Hospitals	66734	17	20	Museums, Hist. Sites,& Similar	66948	20	83	Nursing & Resid. Care Facilit.
66440	38	151	Educational Services	66735	9	7	Relig., Grant, Civic, Prof Org	66949	38	120	Educational Services
66441	905	8430	Food Svcs & Drinking Places	66736	242	1380	Educational Services	66951	50	221	Nursing & Resid. Care Facilit.
66442	91	14246	Nat'l Security & Int'l Affairs	66738	12	23	Mining (Except Oil and Gas)	66952	25	53	Merch. Wholesalers,Nondur. Gds
66449	25	90	Nursing & Resid. Care Facilit.	66739	146	1488	Chemical Manufacturing	66953	46	340	Nursing & Resid. Care Facilit.
66451	122	764	Educational Services	66740	23	140	Computer & Electronic Prod Mfg	66955	9	80	Personal and Laundry Services
66501	5	12	Relig., Grant, Civic, Prof Org	66741	2	186	Warehousing and Storage	66956	105	656	Exec., Legis., & Other Support
66502	1647	18608	Food Svcs & Drinking Places	66742	20	99	Heavy & Civil Eng. Construct'N	66958	15	68	Educational Services
66503	272	2878	Prof., Scientific, & Tech Svcs	66743	271	2760	Educational Services	66959	14	26	Credit Intermediation & Relatd
66505	17	76	Social Assistance	66746	17	24	Merch. Wholesalers,Nondur. Gds	66960	6	5	Postal Service
66506	26	3924	Educational Services	66748	121	853	Hospitals	66961	5	6	Merch. Wholesalers,Nondur. Gds
66507	24	123	Fabricated Metal Product Mfg	66749	432	4269	Plastics & Rubber Products Mfg	66962	22	47	Food Manufacturing
66508	315	2948	Transportation Equipment Mfg	66751	34	127	Bldg Matl & Garden Eqpmt Dlrs	66963	13	37	Miscellaneous Store Retailers
66509	64	1342	Accommodation	66753	34	92	Educational Services	66964	16	33	Truck Transportation
66510	41	186	Educational Services	66754	4	2	Food and Beverage Stores	66966	33	113	Educational Services
66512	99	517	Educational Services	66755	45	303	Educational Services	66967	176	1134	Transportation Equipment Mfg
66514	35	82	Amusement, Gambling,& Recreat.	66756	24	72	Food Svcs & Drinking Places	66968	143	767	Educational Services
66515	15	23	Warehousing and Storage	66757	175	2257	Transportation Equipment Mfg	66970	7	8	Museums, Hist. Sites,& Similar
66516	9	33	Gasoline Stations	66758	8	15	Justice, Pubic Order/Safety	67001	42	270	Educational Services
66517	32	125	Educational Services	66759	1	0	Postal Service	67002	343	2931	Educational Services
66518	7	5	Warehousing and Storage	66760	1	8	Administrative & Support Svcs	67003	200	1363	Educational Services
66520	23	67	Educational Services	66761	10	54	Gasoline Stations	67004	49	185	Educational Services
66521	100	777	Hospitals	66762	1031	12669	Educational Services	67005	667	5556	Support Act. for Transport.
66522	2	8	Waste Managmt & Remediat'n Svc	66763	120	1096	Food Manufacturing	67008	12	49	Justice, Pubic Order/Safety
66523	179	1113	Wood Product Manufacturing	66767	25	135	Nursing & Resid. Care Facilit.	67009	52	360	Educational Services
66524	74	291	Nursing & Resid. Care Facilit.	66769	14	17	Postal Service	67010	443	2790	Educational Services
66526	29	87	Educational Services	66770	39	628	Educational Services	67012	3	3	Repair and Maintenance
66527	16	142	Educational Services	66771	53	506	Nursing & Resid. Care Facilit.	67013	86	485	Educational Services
66528	18	33	Educational Services	66772	16	27	Special Trade Contractors	67016	10	65	Educational Services
66531	48	287	Educational Services	66773	25	154	Fabricated Metal Product Mfg	67017	55	306	Educational Services
66532	33	74	Food and Beverage Stores	66775	10	20	Truck Transportation	67018	6	9	Warehousing and Storage
66533	65	347	Educational Services	66776	42	160	Food Svcs & Drinking Places	67019	35	64	Exec., Legis., & Other Support
66534	198	2289	Machinery Manufacturing	66777	30	95	Unclassified Establishments	67020	67	329	Educational Services
66535	42	185	Educational Services	66778	5	151	Merch. Wholesalers,Durable Gds	67021	10	23	Repair and Maintenance
66536	151	1204	Utilities	66779	25	139	Educational Services	67022	109	494	Educational Services
66537	34	128	Educational Services	66780	20	38	Construction of Buildings	67023	9	8	Animal Production
66538	254	1984	Miscellaneous Manufacturing	66781	37	148	Nonmetallic Mineral Prod. Mfg	67024	53	280	Educational Services
66539	72	331	Educational Services	66782	10	14	Museums, Hist. Sites,& Similar	67025	116	802	Educational Services
66540	15	27	Relig., Grant, Civic, Prof Org	66783	147	707	Educational Services	67026	152	762	Educational Services
66541	27	109	Nursing & Resid. Care Facilit.	66801	1204	14761	Food Manufacturing	67028	16	14	Warehousing and Storage
66542	76	734	Educational Services	66830	12	43	Educational Services	67029	112	381	Hospitals
66543	12	71	Admin. Enviro. Quality Progrms	66833	27	83	Educational Services	67030	74	476	Educational Services
66544	24	52	Justice, Pubic Order/Safety	66834	35	145	Special Trade Contractors	67031	83	418	Educational Services
66546	31	169	Educational Services	66835	49	159	Educational Services	67035	54	298	Nursing & Resid. Care Facilit.
66547	331	2462	Machinery Manufacturing	66838	10	20	Food Manufacturing	67036	11	26	Warehousing and Storage
66548	61	405	Transportation Equipment Mfg	66839	239	1761	Exec., Legis., & Other Support	67037	649	4863	Educational Services
66549	73	385	Justice, Pubic Order/Safety	66840	29	72	Justice, Pubic Order/Safety	67038	24	110	Nursing & Resid. Care Facilit.
66550	19	68	Educational Services	66842	20	49	Food and Beverage Stores	67039	66	344	Educational Services
66552	19	43	Relig., Grant, Civic, Prof Org	66843	9	46	Mining (Except Oil and Gas)	67041	8	49	Educational Services
66554	19	106	Educational Services	66845	103	445	Educational Services	67042	751	8555	Educational Services
66601	17	36	Special Trade Contractors	66846	242	1517	Educational Services	67045	248	1280	Hospitals
66603	630	8370	Admin. Human Resource Programs	66849	24	55	Animal Production	67047	23	124	Fishing, Hunting and Trapping
66604	1119	15880	Hospitals	66850	6	52	Accommodation	67049	6	4	Credit Intermediation & Relatd
66605	339	2071	Educational Services	66851	37	241	Educational Services	67050	41	233	Educational Services
66606	479	5600	Ambulatory Health Care Svcs	66852	32	145	Furniture & Related Prod. Mfg	67051	17	41	Justice, Pubic Order/Safety
66607	287	5981	Justice, Pubic Order/Safety	66853	22	66	Educational Services	67052	193	2448	Educational Services
66608	420	3790	Food Svcs & Drinking Places	66854	31	214	Nursing & Resid. Care Facilit.	67053	37	259	Relig., Grant, Civic, Prof Org
66609	287	4540	Print'g & Related Supp't Act's	66856	60	394	Food Svcs & Drinking Places	67054	140	652	Hospitals

ZIP CODE	2004 Total Firms	2004 Total Employees	TOP INDUSTRY RANKED on 2004 EMPLOYMENT	ZIP CODE	2004 Total Firms	2004 Total Employees	TOP INDUSTRY RANKED on 2004 EMPLOYMENT	ZIP CODE	2004 Total Firms	2004 Total Employees	TOP INDUSTRY RANKED on 2004 EMPLOYMENT
67056	137	1313	Hospitals	67277	29	84	Prof., Scientific, & Tech Svcs	67505	137	1668	Nursing & Resid. Care Facilit.
67057	26	64	Food Svcs & Drinking Places	67278	31	60	Prof., Scientific, & Tech Svcs	67510	13	13	Warehousing and Storage
67058	139	805	Hospitals	67301	732	6943	Hospitals	67511	14	33	Justice, Pubic Order/Safety
67059	38	213	Educational Services	67330	77	435	Educational Services	67512	13	58	Pipeline Transportation
67060	283	2164	Educational Services	67332	19	100	Warehousing and Storage	67513	11	11	Warehousing and Storage
67061	18	14	Credit Intermediation & Relatd	67333	134	1217	Plastics & Rubber Products Mfg	67514	33	93	Food Svcs & Drinking Places
67062	148	2310	Machinery Manufacturing	67334	3	4	Postal Service	67515	5	2	Warehousing and Storage
67063	184	1587	Educational Services	67335	135	1043	Plastics & Rubber Products Mfg	67516	38	110	Educational Services
67065	12	24	Warehousing and Storage	67336	84	441	Educational Services	67518	11	8	Warehousing and Storage
67066	19	75	Food Manufacturing	67337	656	7764	Nursing & Resid. Care Facilit.	67519	14	19	Warehousing and Storage
67067	60	315	Special Trade Contractors	67340	18	32	Food Svcs & Drinking Places	67520	25	70	Warehousing and Storage
67068	272	1493	Educational Services	67341	4	10	Support Activities: Agr./For.	67521	9	32	Merch. Wholesalers,Durable Gds
67070	112	434	Educational Services	67342	44	163	Educational Services	67522	65	552	Educational Services
67071	9	4	Prof., Scientific, & Tech Svcs	67344	26	37	Nursing & Resid. Care Facilit.	67523	28	99	Educational Services
67072	8	25	Justice, Pubic Order/Safety	67345	8	11	Food Svcs & Drinking Places	67524	34	238	Repair and Maintenance
67073	12	36	Fabricated Metal Product Mfg	67346	16	54	Transportation Equipment Mfg	67525	72	298	Special Trade Contractors
67074	45	315	Educational Services	67347	15	44	Special Trade Contractors	67526	163	720	Educational Services
67101	109	1125	Educational Services	67349	77	305	Nursing & Resid. Care Facilit.	67529	8	27	Justice, Pubic Order/Safety
67102	1	0	Relig., Grant, Civic, Prof Org	67351	11	18	Furn. & Home Furnishgs Stores	67530	1149	11246	Educational Services
67103	20	35	Merch. Wholesalers,Durable Gds	67352	27	66	Educational Services	67543	68	441	Educational Services
67104	195	1287	Nonmetallic Mineral Prod. Mfg	67353	40	168	Nursing & Resid. Care Facilit.	67544	164	1102	Merch. Wholesalers,Durable Gds
67105	5	9	Crop Production	67354	31	88	Educational Services	67545	14	70	Food Manufacturing
67106	20	30	Crop Production	67355	7	9	Merch. Wholesalers,Durable Gds	67546	85	488	Nursing & Resid. Care Facilit.
67107	149	1340	Machinery Manufacturing	67356	147	824	Justice, Pubic Order/Safety	67547	135	592	Exec., Legis., & Other Support
67108	48	257	Nursing & Resid. Care Facilit.	67357	554	7902	Hospitals	67548	129	812	Exec., Legis., & Other Support
67109	30	176	Educational Services	67360	5	21	Ambulatory Health Care Svcs	67550	295	3638	Ambulatory Health Care Svcs
67110	198	1163	Educational Services	67361	155	839	Educational Services	67552	43	334	Machinery Manufacturing
67111	8	5	Postal Service	67363	2	6	Motor Vehicle & Parts Dealers	67553	8	9	Food Manufacturing
67112	16	27	Insurance Carriers & Related	67364	11	48	Educational Services	67554	240	1769	Food and Beverage Stores
67114	925	10675	Prof., Scientific, & Tech Svcs	67401	2405	28289	Food Manufacturing	67556	22	63	Educational Services
67117	39	413	Educational Services	67402	18	28	Prof., Scientific, & Tech Svcs	67557	43	240	Social Assistance
67118	38	299	Primary Metal Manufacturing	67410	560	3656	General Merchandise Stores	67559	2	2	Warehousing and Storage
67119	61	264	Educational Services	67416	38	101	Nonmetallic Mineral Prod. Mfg	67560	192	907	Hospitals
67120	20	61	Oil and Gas Extraction	67417	7	7	Food Svcs & Drinking Places	67561	59	252	Educational Services
67122	4	4	Merch. Wholesalers,Durable Gds	67418	18	31	Justice, Pubic Order/Safety	67563	16	70	Educational Services
67123	30	133	Educational Services	67420	304	2718	Exec., Legis., & Other Support	67564	11	10	Postal Service
67124	555	4272	Hospitals	67422	54	197	Educational Services	67565	35	96	Educational Services
67127	45	208	Nursing & Resid. Care Facilit.	67423	16	35	Merch. Wholesalers,Nondur. Gds	67566	18	44	Educational Services
67131	10	9	Motor Vehicle & Parts Dealers	67425	21	53	Educational Services	67567	19	76	Animal Production
67132	12	97	Educational Services	67427	29	121	Petroleum & Coal Products Mfg	67568	13	8	Postal Service
67133	146	811	Educational Services	67428	72	270	Relig., Grant, Civic, Prof Org	67570	41	228	Educational Services
67134	26	47	Construction of Buildings	67430	47	184	Educational Services	67572	47	275	Hospitals
67135	80	412	Educational Services	67431	75	427	Educational Services	67573	10	7	Merch. Wholesalers,Durable Gds
67137	35	128	Educational Services	67432	356	2703	Machinery Manufacturing	67574	15	54	Educational Services
67138	24	44	Educational Services	67436	38	71	Merch. Wholesalers,Nondur. Gds	67575	30	152	Merch. Wholesalers,Durable Gds
67140	36	124	Educational Services	67437	97	469	Nursing & Resid. Care Facilit.	67576	150	655	Exec., Legis., & Other Support
67142	16	53	Special Trade Contractors	67438	20	85	Machinery Manufacturing	67578	91	500	Educational Services
67143	10	24	Nonmetallic Mineral Prod. Mfg	67439	199	1833	Nursing & Resid. Care Facilit.	67579	130	844	Educational Services
67144	58	387	Educational Services	67441	36	197	Nursing & Resid. Care Facilit.	67581	25	79	Educational Services
67146	53	246	Educational Services	67442	7	10	Animal Production	67583	45	208	Educational Services
67147	263	2252	Ambulatory Health Care Svcs	67443	70	284	Educational Services	67584	32	114	Educational Services
67149	28	138	Fabricated Metal Product Mfg	67444	22	49	Fabricated Metal Product Mfg	67585	16	175	Food Svcs & Drinking Places
67150	2	2	Repair and Maintenance	67445	37	172	Nursing & Resid. Care Facilit.	67601	1355	13998	Educational Services
67151	19	64	Educational Services	67446	49	162	Telecommunications	67621	29	133	Educational Services
67152	459	3788	Prof., Scientific, & Tech Svcs	67447	10	29	Educational Services	67622	25	137	Educational Services
67154	50	270	Nursing & Resid. Care Facilit.	67448	45	269	Educational Services	67623	16	64	Educational Services
67155	13	19	Postal Service	67449	176	1056	Special Trade Contractors	67625	14	15	Credit Intermediation & Relatd
67156	700	6713	Educational Services	67450	37	102	Educational Services	67626	14	63	Broadcasting
67159	22	60	Educational Services	67451	41	148	Educational Services	67627	3	0	Postal Service
67201	38	119	Social Assistance	67452	19	36	Credit Intermediation & Relatd	67628	5	5	Warehousing and Storage
67202	1435	18462	Prof., Scientific, & Tech Svcs	67454	24	199	Mining (Except Oil and Gas)	67629	5	6	Machinery Manufacturing
67203	1345	14094	Justice, Pubic Order/Safety	67455	153	728	Hospitals	67631	10	17	Merch. Wholesalers,Durable Gds
67204	429	2275	Educational Services	67456	192	1406	Educational Services	67632	24	39	Educational Services
67205	425	4211	Food Svcs & Drinking Places	67457	50	219	Nursing & Resid. Care Facilit.	67634	19	30	Sportg Gds,Hobby,Book, & Music
67206	737	27648	Transportation Equipment Mfg	67458	19	69	Food Svcs & Drinking Places	67635	6	12	Miscellaneous Store Retailers
67207	925	10630	Food Svcs & Drinking Places	67459	11	57	Machinery Manufacturing	67637	128	592	Ambulatory Health Care Svcs
67208	813	7712	Ambulatory Health Care Svcs	67460	802	9216	Plastics & Rubber Products Mfg	67638	14	19	Warehousing and Storage
67209	821	22734	Transportation Equipment Mfg	67464	45	228	Relig., Grant, Civic, Prof Org	67639	5	144	Educational Services
67210	166	22558	Transportation Equipment Mfg	67466	49	154	Educational Services	67640	39	75	Special Trade Contractors
67211	1096	10022	Educational Services	67467	166	1101	Relig., Grant, Civic, Prof Org	67642	215	950	Hospitals
67212	1005	7727	Food Svcs & Drinking Places	67468	13	56	Educational Services	67643	23	80	Educational Services
67213	933	12663	Fabricated Metal Product Mfg	67470	12	47	Administrative & Support Svcs	67644	17	88	Accommodation
67214	1230	17916	Hospitals	67473	150	968	Ambulatory Health Care Svcs	67645	32	285	Electronics & Appliance Stores
67215	127	3776	Merch. Wholesalers,Nondur. Gds	67474	7	20	Truck Transportation	67646	63	221	Educational Services
67216	603	5827	Food Svcs & Drinking Places	67475	12	21	Animal Production	67647	25	156	Crop Production
67217	585	9041	Educational Services	67476	8	18	Credit Intermediation & Relatd	67648	50	253	Machinery Manufacturing
67218	645	25357	Transportation Equipment Mfg	67478	7	7	Food Svcs & Drinking Places	67649	29	88	Educational Services
67219	444	8446	Sportg Gds,Hobby,Book, & Music	67480	44	707	Elect'l Eqpmt, App, & Comp Mfg	67650	29	87	Educational Services
67220	226	5865	Chemical Manufacturing	67481	48	237	Educational Services	67651	40	155	Educational Services
67221	16	105	Educational Services	67482	12	32	Warehousing and Storage	67653	13	19	Chemical Manufacturing
67223	5	12	Administrative & Support Svcs	67483	13	57	Merch. Wholesalers,Nondur. Gds	67654	281	2078	Justice, Pubic Order/Safety
67226	556	9557	Food Svcs & Drinking Places	67484	43	124	Educational Services	67656	8	12	Merch. Wholesalers,Nondur. Gds
67227	6	207	Telecommunications	67485	32	210	Machinery Manufacturing	67657	36	152	Educational Services
67228	11	131	Special Trade Contractors	67487	47	229	Educational Services	67658	10	20	Fabricated Metal Product Mfg
67230	77	205	Relig., Grant, Civic, Prof Org	67490	86	380	Educational Services	67659	12	25	Animal Production
67232	3	5	Construction of Buildings	67491	18	95	Educational Services	67660	2	4	Repair and Maintenance
67235	103	426	Relig., Grant, Civic, Prof Org	67492	16	30	Special Trade Contractors	67661	250	1640	Petroleum & Coal Products Mfg
67260	14	2228	Educational Services	67501	1581	18363	Justice, Pubic Order/Safety	67663	182	1091	Miscellaneous Store Retailers
67275	9	30	Administrative & Support Svcs	67502	520	7203	Hospitals	67664	15	31	Truck Transportation
67276	2	1200	Postal Service	67504	9	42	Machinery Manufacturing	67665	399	2082	Food Svcs & Drinking Places

BUSINESS DATA

ZIP CODE	2004 Total Firms	2004 Total Employ-ees	TOP INDUSTRY RANKED on 2004 EMPLOYMENT	ZIP CODE	2004 Total Firms	2004 Total Employ-ees	TOP INDUSTRY RANKED on 2004 EMPLOYMENT	ZIP CODE	2004 Total Firms	2004 Total Employ-ees	TOP INDUSTRY RANKED on 2004 EMPLOYMENT
67667	4	9	Repair and Maintenance	68016	11	31	Special Trade Contractors	68182	7	3087	Educational Services
67669	156	803	Exec., Legis., & Other Support	68017	35	224	Furn. & Home Furnishgs Stores	68183	58	1053	Exec., Legis., & Other Support
67671	87	539	Relig., Grant, Civic, Prof Org	68018	12	27	Crop Production	68197	15	585	Isps, Web Search Portals
67672	227	1229	Hospitals	68019	18	44	Exec., Legis., & Other Support	68198	70	7948	Hospitals
67673	8	4	Gasoline Stations	68020	41	130	Food Svcs & Drinking Places	68301	55	343	Nursing & Resid. Care Facilit.
67674	1	0	Warehousing and Storage	68022	294	2076	Educational Services	68303	10	10	Postal Service
67675	13	17	Justice, Pubic Order/Safety	68023	73	570	Plastics & Rubber Products Mfg	68304	2	5	Merch. Wholesalers,Nondur. Gds
67701	491	3313	Educational Services	68025	1154	14788	Hospitals	68305	275	2133	Machinery Manufacturing
67730	150	725	Relig., Grant, Civic, Prof Org	68026	2	10	Administrative & Support Svcs	68307	15	42	Food Svcs & Drinking Places
67731	55	138	Educational Services	68028	267	1849	Amusement, Gambling,& Recreat.	68309	5	6	Warehousing and Storage
67732	35	142	Educational Services	68029	26	60	Machinery Manufacturing	68310	799	7514	Educational Services
67733	6	5	Merch. Wholesalers,Durable Gds	68030	27	113	Educational Services	68313	23	55	Special Trade Contractors
67734	8	22	Truck Transportation	68031	91	480	Educational Services	68314	7	24	Food Svcs & Drinking Places
67735	388	2640	Educational Services	68033	14	114	Educational Services	68315	13	25	Heavy & Civil Eng. Construct'N
67736	43	89	Exec., Legis., & Other Support	68034	18	15	Special Trade Contractors	68316	15	52	Educational Services
67737	48	243	Educational Services	68036	14	23	Crop Production	68317	50	167	Educational Services
67738	44	188	Warehousing and Storage	68037	71	876	Accommodation	68318	21	118	Educational Services
67739	16	44	Educational Services	68038	68	456	Relig., Grant, Civic, Prof Org	68319	28	128	Educational Services
67740	156	796	Hospitals	68039	37	749	Exec., Legis., & Other Support	68320	6	41	Justice, Pubic Order/Safety
67741	20	46	Exec., Legis., & Other Support	68040	12	25	Credit Intermediation & Relatd	68321	19	979	Chemical Manufacturing
67743	10	18	Warehousing and Storage	68041	44	566	Educational Services	68322	36	210	Educational Services
67744	7	11	Administrative & Support Svcs	68042	5	11	Exec., Legis., & Other Support	68323	10	22	Postal Service
67745	27	63	Educational Services	68044	21	84	Educational Services	68324	10	35	Warehousing and Storage
67747	4	10	Truck Transportation	68045	101	695	Educational Services	68325	19	62	Merch. Wholesalers,Durable Gds
67748	222	1564	Educational Services	68046	608	6266	Prof., Scientific, & Tech Svcs	68326	16	41	Warehousing and Storage
67749	199	1025	Nursing & Resid. Care Facilit.	68047	106	1002	Machinery Manufacturing	68327	26	111	Educational Services
67751	23	40	Merch. Wholesalers,Nondur. Gds	68048	357	2289	Educational Services	68328	16	31	Repair and Maintenance
67752	119	786	Hospitals	68050	21	83	Educational Services	68329	20	150	Educational Services
67753	36	134	Animal Production	68055	11	21	Educational Services	68330	13	24	Merch. Wholesalers,Nondur. Gds
67756	178	757	Educational Services	68056	1	49	Social Assistance	68331	25	61	Construction of Buildings
67757	34	72	Educational Services	68057	78	546	Educational Services	68332	2	4	Special Trade Contractors
67758	134	543	Nursing & Resid. Care Facilit.	68058	5	5	Postal Service	68333	290	4399	Food Manufacturing
67761	15	19	Animal Production	68059	99	377	Educational Services	68335	35	127	Educational Services
67762	22	42	Educational Services	68061	144	682	Educational Services	68336	12	28	Nonstore Retailers
67764	40	122	Educational Services	68062	7	67	Machinery Manufacturing	68337	20	79	Educational Services
67801	1248	16288	Food Manufacturing	68063	29	103	Educational Services	68338	16	88	Educational Services
67831	141	649	Educational Services	68064	114	2986	Primary Metal Manufacturing	68339	30	135	Food Svcs & Drinking Places
67834	61	356	Educational Services	68065	37	153	Educational Services	68340	57	679	Machinery Manufacturing
67835	187	1068	Educational Services	68066	295	2349	Educational Services	68341	36	1452	Merch. Wholesalers,Durable Gds
67836	17	73	Animal Production	68067	49	223	Exec., Legis., & Other Support	68342	29	226	Educational Services
67837	51	154	Educational Services	68068	5	14	Special Trade Contractors	68343	29	178	Warehousing and Storage
67838	45	174	Educational Services	68069	84	741	Merch. Wholesalers,Nondur. Gds	68344	15	17	Furniture & Related Prod. Mfg
67839	160	806	Educational Services	68070	25	108	Food Svcs & Drinking Places	68345	12	36	Mining (Except Oil and Gas)
67840	14	9	Special Trade Contractors	68071	54	976	Exec., Legis., & Other Support	68346	9	23	Construction of Buildings
67841	16	46	Educational Services	68072	5	28	Justice, Pubic Order/Safety	68347	40	176	Educational Services
67842	27	125	Animal Production	68073	51	266	Educational Services	68348	13	37	Construction of Buildings
67844	56	255	Educational Services	68101	6	28	Special Trade Contractors	68349	44	165	Merch. Wholesalers,Nondur. Gds
67846	1586	15180	Educational Services	68102	1057	25827	Food Manufacturing	68350	5	224	Nonmetallic Mineral Prod. Mfg
67849	29	86	Educational Services	68103	14	38	Construction of Buildings	68351	48	295	Heavy & Civil Eng. Construct'N
67850	24	160	Merch. Wholesalers,Nondur. Gds	68104	625	4604	Social Assistance	68352	321	2179	Hospitals
67851	69	3622	Food Manufacturing	68105	460	12586	Hospitals	68354	49	244	Educational Services
67853	49	279	Educational Services	68106	655	7447	Real Estate	68355	335	2065	Educational Services
67854	96	423	Hospitals	68107	759	10725	Food Manufacturing	68357	20	41	Special Trade Contractors
67855	168	680	Animal Production	68108	407	5590	Postal Service	68358	43	731	Educational Services
67857	19	24	Oil and Gas Extraction	68109	1	1	Administrative & Support Svcs	68359	71	472	Hospitals
67859	21	171	Educational Services	68110	375	7212	Merch. Wholesalers,Durable Gds	68360	15	25	Food Svcs & Drinking Places
67860	195	1052	Educational Services	68111	375	4090	Educational Services	68361	196	1510	Educational Services
67861	199	871	Animal Production	68112	282	3591	Machinery Manufacturing	68362	3	11	Food Svcs & Drinking Places
67862	20	46	Warehousing and Storage	68113	60	1395	Hospitals	68364	13	24	Merch. Wholesalers,Nondur. Gds
67863	26	64	Food Manufacturing	68114	1664	34833	Wholesale Elec. Mrkts & Agents	68365	19	52	Crop Production
67864	165	752	Educational Services	68116	205	1772	Food Svcs & Drinking Places	68366	43	292	Warehousing and Storage
67865	54	362	Educational Services	68117	443	8200	Motor Vehicle & Parts Dealers	68367	18	30	Food and Beverage Stores
67867	82	571	Educational Services	68118	109	876	Educational Services	68368	17	128	Utilities
67868	9	24	Support Activities: Agr./For.	68119	7	54	Air Transportation	68370	179	1131	Nursing & Resid. Care Facilit.
67869	70	376	Warehousing and Storage	68122	193	4865	Hospitals	68371	118	658	Hospitals
67870	106	667	Animal Production	68123	349	4834	Food Svcs & Drinking Places	68372	50	240	Social Assistance
67871	372	2217	Animal Production	68124	691	12377	Hospitals	68375	11	25	Food Svcs & Drinking Places
67876	45	263	Educational Services	68127	1372	23331	Merch. Wholesalers,Durable Gds	68376	73	459	Nursing & Resid. Care Facilit.
67877	160	905	Educational Services	68128	402	6140	Food Svcs & Drinking Places	68377	21	65	Construction of Buildings
67878	207	1052	Animal Production	68130	405	4233	Food Svcs & Drinking Places	68378	24	121	Educational Services
67879	170	793	Animal Production	68131	613	18284	Insurance Carriers & Related	68380	5	48	Educational Services
67880	474	3782	Educational Services	68132	401	3604	Broadcasting	68381	9	9	Postal Service
67882	14	239	Merch. Wholesalers,Nondur. Gds	68133	56	245	Educational Services	68382	4	5	Food Svcs & Drinking Places
67901	1058	8375	Educational Services	68134	1136	10957	Food Svcs & Drinking Places	68401	30	130	Merch. Wholesalers,Nondur. Gds
67905	10	41	Justice, Pubic Order/Safety	68135	160	1150	Educational Services	68402	25	150	Educational Services
67950	204	1215	Hospitals	68136	101	623	Special Trade Contractors	68403	7	10	Educational Services
67951	319	1670	Educational Services	68137	1387	25770	Merch. Wholesalers,Durable Gds	68404	21	75	Special Trade Contractors
67952	42	161	Educational Services	68138	316	7982	Truck Transportation	68405	106	1053	Educational Services
67953	14	50	Utilities	68139	22	59	Special Trade Contractors	68406	21	97	Food Svcs & Drinking Places
67954	46	810	Crop Production	68142	22	88	Amusement, Gambling,& Recreat.	68407	22	109	Educational Services
68001	4	6	Educational Services	68144	1733	17620	Food Svcs & Drinking Places	68409	32	217	Educational Services
68002	76	440	Educational Services	68145	16	46	Prof., Scientific, & Tech Svcs	68410	476	4479	Merch. Wholesalers,Durable Gds
68003	174	1276	Museums, Hist. Sites,& Similar	68147	127	917	Educational Services	68413	23	112	Educational Services
68004	56	265	Educational Services	68152	163	1949	Merch. Wholesalers,Durable Gds	68414	7	6	Food and Beverage Stores
68005	789	11727	Securities/Commodity Contracts	68154	1097	18880	Prof., Scientific, & Tech Svcs	68415	32	147	Educational Services
68007	97	472	Heavy & Civil Eng. Construct'N	68157	44	494	Educational Services	68416	12	45	Animal Production
68008	526	5532	Nursing & Resid. Care Facilit.	68164	616	10343	Administrative & Support Svcs	68417	8	25	Construction of Buildings
68010	20	320	Postal Service	68175	1	0	Insurance Carriers & Related	68418	37	126	Educational Services
68014	8	15	Food Svcs & Drinking Places	68178	20	3194	Educational Services	68419	13	23	Special Trade Contractors
68015	28	181	Educational Services	68179	2	1855	Rail Transportation	68420	84	458	Food Manufacturing

ZIP CODE	2004 Total Firms	2004 Total Employ-ees	TOP INDUSTRY RANKED on 2004 EMPLOYMENT	ZIP CODE	2004 Total Firms	2004 Total Employ-ees	TOP INDUSTRY RANKED on 2004 EMPLOYMENT	ZIP CODE	2004 Total Firms	2004 Total Employ-ees	TOP INDUSTRY RANKED on 2004 EMPLOYMENT
68421	22	249	Sportg Gds,Hobby,Book, & Music	68644	32	721	Merch. Wholesalers,Durable Gds	68788	274	2390	Food Manufacturing
68422	25	84	Special Trade Contractors	68647	21	105	Educational Services	68789	8	18	Credit Intermediation & Relatd
68423	23	77	Special Trade Contractors	68648	13	28	Educational Services	68790	27	148	Educational Services
68424	35	329	Warehousing and Storage	68649	101	550	Educational Services	68791	141	770	Educational Services
68428	30	254	Educational Services	68651	103	537	Nursing & Resid. Care Facilit.	68792	21	92	Educational Services
68429	8	7	Warehousing and Storage	68652	51	158	Educational Services	68801	1151	14438	Food Manufacturing
68430	45	229	Motor Vehicle & Parts Dealers	68653	29	149	Nonmetallic Mineral Prod. Mfg	68802	13	62	Nonmetallic Mineral Prod. Mfg
68431	12	28	Admin. of Economic Programs	68654	31	164	Educational Services	68803	1032	15912	Hospitals
68433	9	32	Animal Production	68655	4	14	Unclassified Establishments	68810	38	550	Plastics & Rubber Products Mfg
68434	375	3908	Educational Services	68658	24	80	Educational Services	68812	13	76	Educational Services
68436	43	230	Educational Services	68659	3	12	Truck Transportation	68813	29	58	Animal Production
68437	10	28	Museums, Hist. Sites,& Similar	68660	65	383	Warehousing and Storage	68814	53	158	Educational Services
68438	7	27	Exec., Legis., & Other Support	68661	229	3728	Food Manufacturing	68815	42	164	Educational Services
68439	8	9	Postal Service	68662	46	361	Merch. Wholesalers,Nondur. Gds	68816	8	20	Credit Intermediation & Relatd
68440	5	9	Food Svcs & Drinking Places	68663	36	142	Educational Services	68817	16	35	Credit Intermediation & Relatd
68441	5	13	Special Trade Contractors	68664	24	369	Machinery Manufacturing	68818	383	3029	Educational Services
68442	23	117	Educational Services	68665	63	339	Educational Services	68820	9	32	Special Trade Contractors
68443	40	170	Educational Services	68666	97	424	Nursing & Resid. Care Facilit.	68821	25	30	Exec., Legis., & Other Support
68444	10	14	Educational Services	68667	6	8	Food Svcs & Drinking Places	68822	354	2615	Miscellaneous Manufacturing
68445	9	27	Credit Intermediation & Relatd	68669	13	28	Machinery Manufacturing	68823	181	889	Nursing & Resid. Care Facilit.
68446	142	1270	Merch. Wholesalers,Nondur. Gds	68701	1373	23699	Ambulatory Health Care Svcs	68824	49	307	Educational Services
68447	21	70	Educational Services	68702	11	37	Credit Intermediation & Relatd	68825	53	301	Educational Services
68448	20	42	Crop Production	68710	32	134	Educational Services	68826	209	1477	Educational Services
68450	165	1216	Merch. Wholesalers,Nondur. Gds	68711	6	4	Educational Services	68827	29	123	Heavy & Civil Eng. Construct'N
68452	3	23	Justice, Pubic Order/Safety	68713	158	1029	Educational Services	68828	6	5	Ambulatory Health Care Svcs
68453	12	19	Merch. Wholesalers,Nondur. Gds	68714	124	570	Educational Services	68831	34	57	Relig., Grant, Civic, Prof Org
68454	19	81	Construction of Buildings	68715	48	517	Educational Services	68832	82	456	Prof., Scientific, & Tech Svcs
68455	23	32	Repair and Maintenance	68716	61	351	Nursing & Resid. Care Facilit.	68833	27	66	Educational Services
68456	41	432	Educational Services	68717	10	25	Credit Intermediation & Relatd	68834	12	39	Animal Production
68457	13	21	Merch. Wholesalers,Durable Gds	68718	124	689	Merch. Wholesalers,Nondur. Gds	68835	18	75	Educational Services
68458	7	13	Special Trade Contractors	68719	14	19	Credit Intermediation & Relatd	68836	66	220	Merch. Wholesalers,Durable Gds
68460	32	161	Machinery Manufacturing	68720	24	71	Merch. Wholesalers,Nondur. Gds	68837	5	12	Crop Production
68461	22	134	Administrative & Support Svcs	68722	53	230	Nursing & Resid. Care Facilit.	68838	12	72	Truck Transportation
68462	102	1788	Machinery Manufacturing	68723	21	37	Merch. Wholesalers,Nondur. Gds	68840	108	1289	Food Manufacturing
68463	92	616	Educational Services	68724	37	105	Exec., Legis., & Other Support	68841	37	146	Educational Services
68464	26	48	Exec., Legis., & Other Support	68725	37	85	Educational Services	68842	58	206	Educational Services
68465	105	559	Nursing & Resid. Care Facilit.	68726	55	207	Food Manufacturing	68843	70	182	Educational Services
68466	75	406	Educational Services	68727	54	276	Educational Services	68844	9	15	Food Svcs & Drinking Places
68467	549	6664	Food Svcs & Drinking Places	68728	12	35	Nursing & Resid. Care Facilit.	68845	425	5050	Educational Services
68501	25	754	Postal Service	68729	113	687	Educational Services	68846	14	37	Educational Services
68502	741	10511	Hospitals	68730	89	378	Educational Services	68847	1267	17454	Machinery Manufacturing
68503	325	3692	Admin. of Economic Programs	68731	78	520	Exec., Legis., & Other Support	68848	13	30	Special Trade Contractors
68504	838	12233	Motor Vehicle & Parts Dealers	68732	14	19	Merch. Wholesalers,Nondur. Gds	68849	9	141	Nonstore Retailers
68505	508	5291	General Merchandise Stores	68733	42	283	Educational Services	68850	504	7239	Food Manufacturing
68506	1009	13004	Hospitals	68734	8	24	Merch. Wholesalers,Nondur. Gds	68852	17	117	Merch. Wholesalers,Nondur. Gds
68507	419	6732	Ambulatory Health Care Svcs	68735	62	247	Educational Services	68853	105	512	Educational Services
68508	1604	32035	Admin. Human Resource Programs	68736	21	48	Warehousing and Storage	68854	30	102	Accommodation
68509	7	84	Exec., Legis., & Other Support	68738	1	6	Food Svcs & Drinking Places	68855	17	24	Educational Services
68510	1068	18447	Insurance Carriers & Related	68739	232	1491	Food Manufacturing	68856	32	150	Educational Services
68512	254	3727	Merch. Wholesalers,Durable Gds	68740	31	72	Credit Intermediation & Relatd	68858	16	100	Animal Production
68514	11	150	Motor Vehicle & Parts Dealers	68741	12	20	Truck Transportation	68859	29	154	Justice, Pubic Order/Safety
68516	1145	11040	Food Svcs & Drinking Places	68742	12	30	Educational Services	68860	22	81	Justice, Pubic Order/Safety
68517	21	596	Chemical Manufacturing	68743	37	131	Broadcasting	68861	10	143	Truck Transportation
68520	35	527	Fabricated Metal Product Mfg	68745	89	557	Educational Services	68862	245	1166	Hospitals
68521	649	11762	Prof., Scientific, & Tech Svcs	68746	35	117	Educational Services	68863	48	238	Educational Services
68522	160	3012	Elect'l Eqpmt, App, & Comp Mfg	68747	3	25	Merch. Wholesalers,Durable Gds	68864	35	155	Educational Services
68523	30	133	Bldg Matl & Garden Eqpmt Dlrs	68748	110	2229	Food Manufacturing	68865	37	88	Bldg Matl & Garden Eqpmt Dlrs
68524	97	6369	Transportation Equipment Mfg	68749	2	1	Merch. Wholesalers,Nondur. Gds	68866	39	165	Educational Services
68526	39	282	Real Estate	68751	11	24	Gasoline Stations	68869	112	730	Food Manufacturing
68527	20	78	Special Trade Contractors	68752	26	57	Exec., Legis., & Other Support	68870	18	45	Educational Services
68528	226	3312	Truck Transportation	68753	4	2	Educational Services	68871	8	6	Food Svcs & Drinking Places
68529	4	23	Special Trade Contractors	68755	16	30	Food Svcs & Drinking Places	68872	15	52	Educational Services
68531	1	1	Waste Managmt & Remediat'n Svc	68756	176	1209	Educational Services	68873	145	1004	Hospitals
68532	11	19	Construction of Buildings	68757	24	47	Educational Services	68874	61	264	Educational Services
68542	23	49	Merch. Wholesalers,Durable Gds	68758	60	381	Educational Services	68875	40	126	Educational Services
68583	18	823	Educational Services	68759	15	26	Educational Services	68876	75	344	Educational Services
68588	31	6614	Educational Services	68760	72	537	Exec., Legis., & Other Support	68878	24	119	Educational Services
68601	1255	17397	Educational Services	68761	17	57	Justice, Pubic Order/Safety	68879	38	82	Educational Services
68602	6	10	Construction of Buildings	68763	377	2393	Merch. Wholesalers,Nondur. Gds	68881	5	15	Merch. Wholesalers,Nondur. Gds
68620	194	1470	Educational Services	68764	54	188	Educational Services	68882	22	98	Educational Services
68621	13	33	Miscellaneous Store Retailers	68765	78	516	Hospitals	68883	93	638	Nursing & Resid. Care Facilit.
68622	43	260	Merch. Wholesalers,Nondur. Gds	68766	26	61	Educational Services	68901	1297	14066	Hospitals
68623	10	20	Warehousing and Storage	68767	160	604	Educational Services	68902	8	22	Administrative & Support Svcs
68624	25	83	Educational Services	68768	28	119	Warehousing and Storage	68920	129	628	Nursing & Resid. Care Facilit.
68626	27	181	Merch. Wholesalers,Nondur. Gds	68769	106	704	Ambulatory Health Care Svcs	68922	111	786	Support Activities: Agr./For.
68627	44	129	Educational Services	68770	84	378	Nursing & Resid. Care Facilit.	68923	8	7	Special Trade Contractors
68628	51	177	Construction of Buildings	68771	74	303	Educational Services	68924	50	499	Social Assistance
68629	53	500	Educational Services	68773	12	35	Animal Production	68925	13	23	Heavy & Civil Eng. Construct'N
68631	18	53	Merch. Wholesalers,Nondur. Gds	68774	5	5	Personal and Laundry Services	68926	58	229	Nursing & Resid. Care Facilit.
68632	197	1712	Nursing & Resid. Care Facilit.	68776	484	5335	Insurance Carriers & Related	68927	57	304	Nursing & Resid. Care Facilit.
68633	68	481	Nursing & Resid. Care Facilit.	68777	61	257	Educational Services	68928	16	71	Merch. Wholesalers,Durable Gds
68634	14	49	Educational Services	68778	66	116	Educational Services	68929	6	7	Merch. Wholesalers,Nondur. Gds
68635	15	39	Educational Services	68779	137	658	Nursing & Resid. Care Facilit.	68930	70	362	Educational Services
68636	90	359	Educational Services	68780	63	326	Nursing & Resid. Care Facilit.	68932	31	165	Nursing & Resid. Care Facilit.
68637	17	90	Merch. Wholesalers,Nondur. Gds	68781	73	440	Educational Services	68933	71	573	Exec., Legis., & Other Support
68638	111	502	Nursing & Resid. Care Facilit.	68783	60	339	Nursing & Resid. Care Facilit.	68934	11	42	Merch. Wholesalers,Durable Gds
68640	79	371	Nursing & Resid. Care Facilit.	68784	81	1148	Merch. Wholesalers,Nondur. Gds	68935	48	195	Nursing & Resid. Care Facilit.
68641	50	234	Educational Services	68785	6	3	Food Svcs & Drinking Places	68936	9	183	Warehousing and Storage
68642	78	429	Merch. Wholesalers,Nondur. Gds	68786	73	315	Nursing & Resid. Care Facilit.	68937	102	383	Educational Services
68643	47	242	Educational Services	68787	310	3402	Educational Services	68938	32	164	Educational Services

BUSINESS DATA

ZIP CODE	2004 Total Firms	2004 Total Employ-ees	TOP INDUSTRY RANKED on 2004 EMPLOYMENT	ZIP CODE	2004 Total Firms	2004 Total Employ-ees	TOP INDUSTRY RANKED on 2004 EMPLOYMENT	ZIP CODE	2004 Total Firms	2004 Total Employ-ees	TOP INDUSTRY RANKED on 2004 EMPLOYMENT
68939	111	509	Hospitals	69149	42	110	Educational Services	70056	994	8637	Hospitals
68940	15	115	Warehousing and Storage	69150	41	129	Educational Services	70057	122	3495	Chemical Manufacturing
68941	23	56	Crop Production	69151	28	120	Accommodation	70058	1296	17207	Special Trade Contractors
68942	23	77	Food and Beverage Stores	69152	86	354	Amusement, Gambling,& Recreat.	70059	7	61	Administrative & Support Svcs
68943	14	40	Truck Transportation	69153	451	3280	Food Svcs & Drinking Places	70062	1537	14452	Special Trade Contractors
68944	39	249	Nursing & Resid. Care Facilit.	69154	92	421	Hospitals	70063	10	26	Administrative & Support Svcs
68945	10	38	Animal Production	69155	58	373	Food Svcs & Drinking Places	70064	6	22	Transit & Grnd Pass. Transport
68946	6	5	Warehousing and Storage	69156	30	117	Educational Services	70065	1087	10397	Food Svcs & Drinking Places
68947	27	106	Educational Services	69157	7	16	Credit Intermediation & Relatd	70067	75	792	Transportation Equipment Mfg
68948	29	67	Securities/Commodity Contracts	69160	1	220	Sportg Gds,Hobby,Book, & Music	70068	899	9353	Food Svcs & Drinking Places
68949	400	4260	Miscellaneous Manufacturing	69161	7	6	Construction of Buildings	70069	3	2	Rental and Leasing Services
68950	17	35	Crop Production	69162	483	4139	Sportg Gds,Hobby,Book, & Music	70070	304	3353	Chemical Manufacturing
68952	6	15	Nursing & Resid. Care Facilit.	69163	48	182	Educational Services	70071	132	989	Hospitals
68954	6	35	Prof., Scientific, & Tech Svcs	69165	82	692	Utilities	70072	1334	12848	Hospitals
68955	50	291	Merch. Wholesalers,Nondur. Gds	69166	73	240	Educational Services	70073	5	6	Construction of Buildings
68956	40	271	Nursing & Resid. Care Facilit.	69167	30	62	Educational Services	70075	155	1825	Food and Beverage Stores
68957	33	220	Relig., Grant, Civic, Prof Org	69168	24	73	Educational Services	70076	10	253	Chemical Manufacturing
68958	35	124	Educational Services	69169	53	209	Educational Services	70078	16	536	Petroleum & Coal Products Mfg
68959	240	1485	Food Svcs & Drinking Places	69170	22	98	Animal Production	70079	124	885	Educational Services
68960	7	10	Merch. Wholesalers,Nondur. Gds	69171	2	5	Animal Production	70080	49	302	Educational Services
68961	52	325	Educational Services	69201	323	1781	Educational Services	70081	1	2	Postal Service
68964	6	8	Warehousing and Storage	69210	211	1318	Educational Services	70082	22	184	Justice, Pubic Order/Safety
68966	38	133	Educational Services	69211	15	47	Educational Services	70083	121	1488	Exec., Legis., & Other Support
68967	79	290	Educational Services	69212	10	16	Educational Services	70084	215	3157	Special Trade Contractors
68969	3	4	Warehousing and Storage	69214	18	36	Relig., Grant, Civic, Prof Org	70085	111	718	Educational Services
68970	133	684	Educational Services	69216	13	49	Educational Services	70086	58	496	Educational Services
68971	33	123	Food Svcs & Drinking Places	69217	29	98	Accommodation	70087	226	4382	Merch. Wholesalers,Durable Gds
68972	6	10	Postal Service	69218	23	75	Exec., Legis., & Other Support	70090	164	1193	Credit Intermediation & Relatd
68973	28	99	Educational Services	69219	3	6	Support Activities: Agr./For.	70091	108	821	Special Trade Contractors
68974	18	41	Chemical Manufacturing	69220	5	16	Motor Vehicle & Parts Dealers	70092	100	535	Food Svcs & Drinking Places
68975	3	4	Warehousing and Storage	69221	18	36	Animal Production	70094	556	13553	Transportation Equipment Mfg
68976	7	9	Crop Production	69301	490	4039	Plastics & Rubber Products Mfg	70096	2	5	Prof., Scientific, & Tech Svcs
68977	15	42	Publishing Industries	69331	4	5	Crop Production	70112	1411	47939	Hospitals
68978	193	1091	Hospitals	69333	29	75	Animal Production	70113	527	12023	Postal Service
68979	121	790	Educational Services	69334	79	382	Educational Services	70114	663	6694	Ambulatory Health Care Svcs
68980	18	89	Educational Services	69335	4	3	Postal Service	70115	1470	15501	Ambulatory Health Care Svcs
68981	9	14	Merch. Wholesalers,Nondur. Gds	69336	152	1121	Educational Services	70116	853	5945	Food Svcs & Drinking Places
68982	40	151	Educational Services	69337	396	3007	Educational Services	70117	962	7869	Educational Services
69001	578	5169	Food Svcs & Drinking Places	69339	110	592	Museums, Hist. Sites,& Similar	70118	981	15794	Educational Services
69020	27	111	Educational Services	69340	6	19	Animal Production	70119	2090	24516	Justice, Pubic Order/Safety
69021	145	656	Educational Services	69341	435	4086	Merch. Wholesalers,Durable Gds	70121	673	17428	Hospitals
69022	128	796	Hospitals	69343	176	1153	Educational Services	70122	727	7542	Educational Services
69023	15	51	Crop Production	69345	23	149	Educational Services	70123	1724	25285	Merch. Wholesalers,Durable Gds
69024	37	214	Educational Services	69346	40	108	Educational Services	70124	586	8821	Food Svcs & Drinking Places
69025	94	436	Educational Services	69347	67	270	Nursing & Resid. Care Facilit.	70125	601	8924	Educational Services
69026	10	38	Merch. Wholesalers,Nondur. Gds	69348	88	344	Educational Services	70126	866	10541	Educational Services
69027	10	29	Construction of Buildings	69350	71	216	Justice, Pubic Order/Safety	70127	1030	9446	Hospitals
69028	60	214	Educational Services	69351	10	17	Food Svcs & Drinking Places	70128	207	3282	Hospitals
69029	20	100	Educational Services	69352	23	225	Merch. Wholesalers,Durable Gds	70129	299	7584	Space Research and Technology
69030	25	60	Crop Production	69353	1	1	Motor Vehicle & Parts Dealers	70130	2546	40656	Accommodation
69032	38	178	Educational Services	69354	2	2	Educational Services	70131	377	2867	Nursing & Resid. Care Facilit.
69033	214	1256	Food Manufacturing	69355	7	9	Bldg Matl & Garden Eqpmt Dlrs	70139	54	2821	Special Trade Contractors
69034	48	198	Educational Services	69356	55	291	Educational Services	70141	5	144	Rental and Leasing Services
69036	4	9	Postal Service	69357	136	654	Educational Services	70142	6	26	Food Svcs & Drinking Places
69037	5	61	Postal Service	69358	86	484	Merch. Wholesalers,Nondur. Gds	70143	2	1230	Support Act. for Transport.
69038	34	231	Air Transportation	69360	110	513	Educational Services	70146	7	115	Administrative & Support Svcs
69039	6	4	Postal Service	69361	1150	11498	Hospitals	70148	3	3062	Educational Services
69040	40	228	Relig., Grant, Civic, Prof Org	69363	9	7	Electronics & Appliance Stores	70149	1	15	Nat'l Security & Int'l Affairs
69041	8	15	Bldg Matl & Garden Eqpmt Dlrs	69365	13	35	Food and Beverage Stores	70150	2	7	Couriers and Messengers
69042	8	17	Exec., Legis., & Other Support	69366	31	63	Animal Production	70151	2	2	Special Trade Contractors
69043	37	167	Construction of Buildings	69367	5	7	Educational Services	70152	2	2	Relig., Grant, Civic, Prof Org
69044	65	296	Nursing & Resid. Care Facilit.	70001	1609	15582	Prof., Scientific, & Tech Svcs	70156	4	16	Credit Intermediation & Relatd
69045	84	347	Educational Services	70002	2438	28801	Prof., Scientific, & Tech Svcs	70157	1	6	Social Assistance
69046	10	17	Merch. Wholesalers,Nondur. Gds	70003	887	9223	Educational Services	70160	1	5	Prof., Scientific, & Tech Svcs
69101	1323	11814	Food Svcs & Drinking Places	70004	13	21	Prof., Scientific, & Tech Svcs	70163	106	1774	Prof., Scientific, & Tech Svcs
69103	10	47	Food Svcs & Drinking Places	70005	1060	8652	Food Svcs & Drinking Places	70165	2	506	Exec., Legis., & Other Support
69120	68	275	Educational Services	70006	1227	11661	Hospitals	70170	116	1620	Prof., Scientific, & Tech Svcs
69121	41	92	Animal Production	70009	8	30	Administrative & Support Svcs	70172	3	11	Prof., Scientific, & Tech Svcs
69122	39	321	Educational Services	70010	5	11	Heavy & Civil Eng. Construct'N	70174	4	49	Isps, Web Search Portals
69123	40	130	Educational Services	70011	11	27	Prof., Scientific, & Tech Svcs	70175	8	9	Prof., Scientific, & Tech Svcs
69125	17	49	Animal Production	70030	62	572	Support Act. for Transport.	70176	1	0	Personal and Laundry Services
69127	33	151	Amusement, Gambling,& Recreat.	70031	16	150	Warehousing and Storage	70177	6	41	Relig., Grant, Civic, Prof Org
69128	18	19	Prof., Scientific, & Tech Svcs	70032	232	1806	Food Manufacturing	70179	2	3	Merch. Wholesalers,Durable Gds
69129	100	482	Educational Services	70033	14	82	Administrative & Support Svcs	70181	3	3	Motion Pict. & Sound Recording
69130	280	2752	Transportation Equipment Mfg	70036	20	43	Amusement, Gambling,& Recreat.	70182	2	3	Special Trade Contractors
69131	37	125	Educational Services	70037	604	8033	Special Trade Contractors	70183	11	57	Waste Managmt & Remediat'n Svc
69132	5	5	Crop Production	70038	13	167	Educational Services	70184	10	22	Merch. Wholesalers,Durable Gds
69133	25	63	Educational Services	70039	147	1500	General Merchandise Stores	70185	8	15	Administrative & Support Svcs
69134	26	124	Merch. Wholesalers,Nondur. Gds	70040	36	543	Unclassified Establishments	70186	2	1	Special Trade Contractors
69135	2	2	Educational Services	70041	236	1525	Repair and Maintenance	70187	7	28	Motor Vehicle & Parts Dealers
69138	246	1986	Machinery Manufacturing	70043	1099	10836	Hospitals	70189	1	1	Nonstore Retailers
69140	151	964	Nursing & Resid. Care Facilit.	70044	9	48	Prof., Scientific, & Tech Svcs	70301	1314	12185	Educational Services
69141	19	178	Fabricated Metal Product Mfg	70047	243	2697	Educational Services	70302	3	4	Special Trade Contractors
69142	21	90	Support Activities: Agr./For.	70049	61	319	Educational Services	70310	1	1300	Educational Services
69143	59	388	Educational Services	70050	12	59	Food and Beverage Stores	70339	136	785	Construction of Buildings
69144	15	43	Food Svcs & Drinking Places	70051	46	716	Petroleum & Coal Products Mfg	70340	25	1212	Pipeline Transportation
69145	250	1714	Merch. Wholesalers,Durable Gds	70052	90	1737	Chemical Manufacturing	70341	43	363	Food Manufacturing
69146	21	41	Accommodation	70053	1191	13901	Administrative & Support Svcs	70342	120	1156	Scenic & Sightseeing Transport
69147	43	111	Nursing & Resid. Care Facilit.	70054	3	3	Construction of Buildings	70343	97	598	Support Act. for Transport.
69148	13	69	Food and Beverage Stores	70055	8	40	Lessrs of Nonfin. Intang.	70344	147	827	Educational Services

ZIP CODE	2004 Total Firms	2004 Total Employ-ees	TOP INDUSTRY RANKED on 2004 EMPLOYMENT	ZIP CODE	2004 Total Firms	2004 Total Employ-ees	TOP INDUSTRY RANKED on 2004 EMPLOYMENT	ZIP CODE	2004 Total Firms	2004 Total Employ-ees	TOP INDUSTRY RANKED on 2004 EMPLOYMENT
70345	343	3195	General Merchandise Stores	70519	4	150	Prof., Scientific, & Tech Svcs	70659	48	371	Educational Services
70346	372	3375	Educational Services	70520	358	2650	Perform'g Arts, Spec. Sports	70660	16	48	Forestry and Logging
70352	3	6	Amusement, Gambling,& Recreat.	70521	7	62	Food Svcs & Drinking Places	70661	35	198	Educational Services
70353	66	536	Merch. Wholesalers,Nondur. Gds	70522	42	552	Chemical Manufacturing	70662	11	33	Food and Beverage Stores
70354	173	1795	Scenic & Sightseeing Transport	70523	34	1195	Amusement, Gambling,& Recreat.	70663	943	9184	Food Svcs & Drinking Places
70355	6	15	Social Assistance	70524	10	37	Educational Services	70664	4	2	Special Trade Contractors
70356	64	791	Transportation Equipment Mfg	70525	245	1556	Educational Services	70665	270	4746	Unclassified Establishments
70357	277	2662	Special Trade Contractors	70526	813	7330	Educational Services	70668	149	1938	Perform'g Arts, Spec. Sports
70358	135	970	Food Svcs & Drinking Places	70527	3	24	Exec., Legis., & Other Support	70669	354	9762	Accommodation
70359	117	739	Special Trade Contractors	70528	95	706	Educational Services	70704	1	3	Administrative & Support Svcs
70360	1864	19568	Food Svcs & Drinking Places	70529	208	1452	Educational Services	70706	209	1258	Educational Services
70361	11	24	Social Assistance	70531	25	150	Gasoline Stations	70707	2	1	Admin. Human Resource Programs
70363	1003	18125	Ambulatory Health Care Svcs	70532	73	463	Exec., Legis., & Other Support	70710	76	869	Unclassified Establishments
70364	926	7661	Food Svcs & Drinking Places	70533	127	609	Educational Services	70711	113	558	Educational Services
70371	1	3	Admin. of Economic Programs	70534	14	48	Educational Services	70712	4	1771	Justice, Pubic Order/Safety
70372	62	312	Educational Services	70535	736	5176	Educational Services	70714	456	4549	Justice, Pubic Order/Safety
70373	153	1220	Transportation Equipment Mfg	70537	10	80	Special Trade Contractors	70715	26	373	Plastics & Rubber Products Mfg
70374	260	2744	Fabricated Metal Product Mfg	70538	543	4826	Educational Services	70718	1	20	Admin. of Economic Programs
70375	23	119	Food Svcs & Drinking Places	70540	3	14	Merch. Wholesalers,Durable Gds	70719	69	985	Transportation Equipment Mfg
70377	76	301	Educational Services	70541	61	406	Educational Services	70721	13	311	Chemical Manufacturing
70380	1279	23094	Prof., Scientific, & Tech Svcs	70542	109	526	Educational Services	70722	255	1443	Educational Services
70381	4	8	Special Trade Contractors	70543	75	587	Educational Services	70723	139	3386	Exec., Legis., & Other Support
70390	174	1479	Educational Services	70544	249	2097	Food Manufacturing	70725	29	417	Support Act. for Transport.
70391	41	334	Food Manufacturing	70546	656	5724	Food Svcs & Drinking Places	70726	1261	7607	Food Svcs & Drinking Places
70392	231	1482	Merch. Wholesalers,Durable Gds	70548	354	2164	Educational Services	70727	3	8	Special Trade Contractors
70393	19	151	Food and Beverage Stores	70549	123	571	Merch. Wholesalers,Nondur. Gds	70728	1	10	Special Trade Contractors
70394	338	2854	Educational Services	70550	35	112	Educational Services	70729	25	107	Nonmetallic Mineral Prod. Mfg
70395	105	827	Educational Services	70551	25	127	Educational Services	70730	50	110	Relig., Grant, Civic, Prof Org
70397	26	123	Educational Services	70552	59	387	Transportation Equipment Mfg	70732	11	62	Exec., Legis., & Other Support
70401	901	9780	Exec., Legis., & Other Support	70554	202	1622	Hospitals	70733	45	173	Educational Services
70402	4	54	Other Information Services	70555	140	820	Special Trade Contractors	70734	126	4672	Merch. Wholesalers,Nondur. Gds
70403	976	10309	Hospitals	70556	17	107	Food Manufacturing	70736	3	3	Animal Production
70404	5	20	Social Assistance	70558	11	49	Food and Beverage Stores	70737	1370	12552	Food Svcs & Drinking Places
70420	201	1031	Educational Services	70559	28	166	Educational Services	70738	5	6	Merch. Wholesalers,Durable Gds
70421	8	14	Administrative & Support Svcs	70560	1819	21167	Special Trade Contractors	70739	199	1814	Social Assistance
70422	501	4062	Justice, Pubic Order/Safety	70562	9	131	Motor Vehicle & Parts Dealers	70740	42	229	Gasoline Stations
70426	74	722	Justice, Pubic Order/Safety	70563	400	2860	Hospitals	70743	4	13	Bldg Matl & Garden Eqpmt Dlrs
70427	737	7391	Paper Manufacturing	70569	8	13	Oil and Gas Extraction	70744	71	764	Transportation Equipment Mfg
70431	91	283	Educational Services	70570	1362	12318	General Merchandise Stores	70747	20	52	Food and Beverage Stores
70433	1933	17701	Hospitals	70571	3	1	Insurance Carriers & Related	70748	166	2611	Hospitals
70434	29	102	Heavy & Civil Eng. Construct'N	70575	4	3	Food and Beverage Stores	70749	23	58	Utilities
70435	311	1372	Special Trade Contractors	70576	38	283	Nursing & Resid. Care Facilit.	70750	69	887	Wholesale Elec. Mrkts & Agents
70436	8	56	Merch. Wholesalers,Durable Gds	70577	128	697	Food Svcs & Drinking Places	70752	27	249	Food Manufacturing
70437	232	709	Educational Services	70578	445	3269	Educational Services	70753	26	91	Support Activities: Agr./For.
70438	573	3777	Educational Services	70580	2	5	Food and Beverage Stores	70754	201	1499	Justice, Pubic Order/Safety
70441	169	1310	Educational Services	70581	19	71	Merch. Wholesalers,Nondur. Gds	70755	69	418	Nonmetallic Mineral Prod. Mfg
70442	13	17	Construction of Buildings	70582	507	4469	Justice, Pubic Order/Safety	70756	17	91	Repair and Maintenance
70443	164	1244	Exec., Legis., & Other Support	70583	421	4071	Fabricated Metal Product Mfg	70757	71	335	Educational Services
70444	230	1465	Educational Services	70584	127	643	Educational Services	70759	37	336	Justice, Pubic Order/Safety
70445	217	2060	Bldg Matl & Garden Eqpmt Dlrs	70585	34	75	Special Trade Contractors	70760	382	3582	Prof., Scientific, & Tech Svcs
70446	77	470	Educational Services	70586	694	4983	Educational Services	70761	14	75	Computer & Electronic Prod Mfg
70447	221	1280	Transportation Equipment Mfg	70589	89	481	Educational Services	70762	19	26	Furniture & Related Prod. Mfg
70448	895	6996	Amusement, Gambling,& Recreat.	70591	153	1028	Nursing & Resid. Care Facilit.	70763	56	391	Fabricated Metal Product Mfg
70449	48	187	Educational Services	70592	225	2358	Special Trade Contractors	70764	604	5930	Justice, Pubic Order/Safety
70450	29	151	Educational Services	70596	6	6	Administrative & Support Svcs	70765	3	3	Repair and Maintenance
70451	27	412	Wood Product Manufacturing	70598	11	36	Ambulatory Health Care Svcs	70767	622	7642	Special Trade Contractors
70452	244	1253	Educational Services	70601	2440	26904	Hospitals	70769	710	5155	Fabricated Metal Product Mfg
70453	20	43	Administrative & Support Svcs	70602	5	21	Special Trade Contractors	70770	32	215	Educational Services
70454	535	3495	Educational Services	70605	861	9058	Educational Services	70772	20	71	Justice, Pubic Order/Safety
70455	40	245	Food and Beverage Stores	70606	7	14	Rental and Leasing Services	70773	14	35	Educational Services
70456	77	478	Motor Vehicle & Parts Dealers	70607	547	5682	Food Svcs & Drinking Places	70774	162	1096	Educational Services
70458	1893	13794	Food Svcs & Drinking Places	70609	6	88	Educational Services	70775	343	3078	Paper Manufacturing
70459	28	82	Special Trade Contractors	70611	360	2042	Educational Services	70776	101	3590	Chemical Manufacturing
70460	614	7113	General Merchandise Stores	70612	2	6	Administrative & Support Svcs	70777	51	374	Machinery Manufacturing
70461	618	5871	Hospitals	70615	415	7709	Justice, Pubic Order/Safety	70778	69	411	Food Svcs & Drinking Places
70462	119	481	Educational Services	70629	53	424	Credit Intermediation & Relatd	70780	12	90	Transportation Equipment Mfg
70463	13	29	Justice, Pubic Order/Safety	70630	19	114	Educational Services	70782	15	70	Educational Services
70464	9	6	Support Act. for Transport.	70631	253	2438	Prof., Scientific, & Tech Svcs	70783	24	58	Amusement, Gambling,& Recreat.
70465	19	54	Social Assistance	70632	53	230	Rental and Leasing Services	70784	4	5	Postal Service
70466	108	459	Construction of Buildings	70633	247	1929	Justice, Pubic Order/Safety	70785	358	3043	Fabricated Metal Product Mfg
70469	4	14	Waste Managmt & Remediat'n Svc	70634	799	7615	Paper Manufacturing	70786	2	4	Postal Service
70470	25	38	Merch. Wholesalers,Durable Gds	70637	20	29	Accommodation	70787	1	2	Accommodation
70471	1163	8609	Food Svcs & Drinking Places	70638	37	88	Educational Services	70788	95	716	Educational Services
70501	1816	16620	Prof., Scientific, & Tech Svcs	70639	13	69	Educational Services	70789	20	14	Exec., Legis., & Other Support
70502	2	1	Prof., Scientific, & Tech Svcs	70640	11	49	Educational Services	70791	591	6102	Merch. Wholesalers,Nondur. Gds
70503	2252	22565	Ambulatory Health Care Svcs	70643	36	286	Special Trade Contractors	70801	341	4039	Justice, Pubic Order/Safety
70504	8	99	Educational Services	70644	3	58	Educational Services	70802	1470	28514	Exec., Legis., & Other Support
70505	11	17	Administrative & Support Svcs	70645	57	461	Administrative & Support Svcs	70803	69	1237	Exec., Legis., & Other Support
70506	1661	20998	Hospitals	70646	13	28	Food Svcs & Drinking Places	70804	9	97	Justice, Pubic Order/Safety
70507	459	5840	Motor Vehicle & Parts Dealers	70647	158	905	Educational Services	70805	976	14404	Petroleum & Coal Products Mfg
70508	1930	22429	Prof., Scientific, & Tech Svcs	70648	253	1575	Educational Services	70806	2281	26212	Hospitals
70509	10	59	Nursing & Resid. Care Facilit.	70650	18	96	Educational Services	70807	397	5591	Justice, Pubic Order/Safety
70510	959	8577	Food Manufacturing	70651	4	5	Postal Service	70808	1454	20729	Ambulatory Health Care Svcs
70512	125	945	Educational Services	70652	31	264	Educational Services	70809	2119	26704	Prof., Scientific, & Tech Svcs
70513	6	418	Merch. Wholesalers,Nondur. Gds	70653	70	433	Educational Services	70810	961	13990	Administrative & Support Svcs
70514	64	391	Fabricated Metal Product Mfg	70654	4	9	Rental and Leasing Services	70811	223	1602	Educational Services
70515	96	545	Justice, Pubic Order/Safety	70655	126	753	Justice, Pubic Order/Safety	70812	67	599	Educational Services
70516	13	66	Educational Services	70656	62	255	Educational Services	70813	11	2064	Educational Services
70517	660	5199	Educational Services	70657	61	133	Construction of Buildings	70814	566	6261	Museums, Hist. Sites,& Similar
70518	667	9749	Special Trade Contractors	70658	23	91	Educational Services	70815	1411	16654	General Merchandise Stores

ZIP CODE	2004 Total Firms	2004 Total Employ-ees	TOP INDUSTRY RANKED on 2004 EMPLOYMENT	ZIP CODE	2004 Total Firms	2004 Total Employ-ees	TOP INDUSTRY RANKED on 2004 EMPLOYMENT	ZIP CODE	2004 Total Firms	2004 Total Employ-ees	TOP INDUSTRY RANKED on 2004 EMPLOYMENT
70816	2144	20102	Prof., Scientific, & Tech Svcs	71119	178	1369	Merch. Wholesalers,Durable Gds	71329	3	8	Truck Transportation
70817	763	6463	Special Trade Contractors	71129	482	9965	Machinery Manufacturing	71330	5	6	Postal Service
70818	273	1746	Food and Beverage Stores	71130	1	1	Relig., Grant, Civic, Prof Org	71331	20	77	Educational Services
70819	136	973	Motor Vehicle & Parts Dealers	71133	7	11	Special Trade Contractors	71333	8	45	Construction of Buildings
70820	167	2218	Food Svcs & Drinking Places	71134	2	8	Nursing & Resid. Care Facilit.	71334	330	2411	Hospitals
70821	10	32	Administrative & Support Svcs	71135	7	11	Administrative & Support Svcs	71336	39	180	Support Activities: Agr./For.
70825	32	813	Prof., Scientific, & Tech Svcs	71136	3	6	Insurance Carriers & Related	71339	10	25	Merch. Wholesalers,Nondur. Gds
70826	1	6	Educational Services	71137	1	1	Construction of Buildings	71340	58	449	Justice, Pubic Order/Safety
70827	83	330	Prof., Scientific, & Tech Svcs	71138	5	3	Machinery Manufacturing	71341	56	442	Food Manufacturing
70835	3	3	Administrative & Support Svcs	71148	2	0	Truck Transportation	71342	361	2539	Hospitals
70836	150	2402	Clothing & Cloth'g Acc. Stores	71149	3	5	Electronics & Appliance Stores	71343	284	1552	Educational Services
70837	2	1	Special Trade Contractors	71162	1	0	Relig., Grant, Civic, Prof Org	71345	4	62	Educational Services
70874	1	10	Administrative & Support Svcs	71166	1	1	Health & Personal Care Stores	71346	106	765	Nursing & Resid. Care Facilit.
70879	13	22	Perform'g Arts, Spec. Sports	71171	1	0	Administrative & Support Svcs	71348	1	2	Postal Service
70884	5	14	Relig., Grant, Civic, Prof Org	71172	5	6	Truck Transportation	71350	116	913	Educational Services
70893	2	16	Isps, Web Search Portals	71201	2370	21453	Hospitals	71351	477	3982	Justice, Pubic Order/Safety
70895	5	17	Warehousing and Storage	71202	633	7121	Exec., Legis., & Other Support	71353	56	268	Merch. Wholesalers,Durable Gds
70896	3	4	Educational Services	71203	1095	14376	Food Svcs & Drinking Places	71354	39	198	Crop Production
70898	8	20	Construction of Buildings	71207	4	8	Publishing Industries	71355	50	293	Educational Services
71001	248	2658	Food Manufacturing	71208	2	2405	Insurance Carriers & Related	71356	15	450	Wood Product Manufacturing
71002	3	3	Postal Service	71209	4	1352	Educational Services	71357	94	597	Educational Services
71003	32	186	Educational Services	71210	1	2	Relig., Grant, Civic, Prof Org	71358	23	213	Merch. Wholesalers,Nondur. Gds
71004	25	206	Educational Services	71211	5	33	Administrative & Support Svcs	71360	1191	15160	Hospitals
71006	202	1279	Justice, Pubic Order/Safety	71213	1	1	Prof., Scientific, & Tech Svcs	71361	5	20	Prof., Scientific, & Tech Svcs
71007	13	75	Special Trade Contractors	71218	3	1	Relig., Grant, Civic, Prof Org	71362	35	297	Educational Services
71008	26	130	Educational Services	71219	20	136	Educational Services	71363	5	7	Admin. Enviro. Quality Progrms
71009	74	400	Chemical Manufacturing	71220	863	7406	Paper Manufacturing	71366	115	632	Justice, Pubic Order/Safety
71016	37	179	Educational Services	71221	2	16	Exec., Legis., & Other Support	71367	17	30	Justice, Pubic Order/Safety
71018	54	252	Oil and Gas Extraction	71222	105	819	Hospitals	71368	50	235	Educational Services
71019	323	2501	Hospitals	71223	39	105	Crop Production	71369	80	644	Apparel Manufacturing
71021	55	396	Machinery Manufacturing	71225	120	662	Educational Services	71371	28	79	Admin. of Economic Programs
71023	53	210	Educational Services	71226	61	192	Educational Services	71373	330	2694	Justice, Pubic Order/Safety
71024	16	106	Educational Services	71227	77	459	Merch. Wholesalers,Nondur. Gds	71375	53	277	Support Activities: Agr./For.
71025	1	3	Truck Transportation	71229	41	140	Electronics & Appliance Stores	71377	3	13	Merch. Wholesalers,Nondur. Gds
71027	24	41	Fabricated Metal Product Mfg	71230	38	178	Support Activities: Agr./For.	71378	64	841	Food Manufacturing
71028	49	203	Educational Services	71232	256	2245	Social Assistance	71401	7	9	Food and Beverage Stores
71029	24	40	Merch. Wholesalers,Nondur. Gds	71233	16	84	Food Svcs & Drinking Places	71403	48	239	Educational Services
71030	21	90	Motor Vehicle & Parts Dealers	71234	75	258	Nonmetallic Mineral Prod. Mfg	71404	13	80	Educational Services
71031	13	129	Special Trade Contractors	71235	84	322	Educational Services	71405	6	3	Insurance Carriers & Related
71032	46	117	Prof., Scientific, & Tech Svcs	71237	44	228	Educational Services	71406	12	23	Educational Services
71033	100	653	Truck Transportation	71238	43	87	Construction of Buildings	71407	11	68	Support Activities: Agr./For.
71034	17	73	Educational Services	71240	3	54	Support Activities for Mining	71409	154	571	Support Activities: Agr./For.
71037	325	1703	Educational Services	71241	415	4234	Food Manufacturing	71410	9	11	Special Trade Contractors
71038	158	899	Educational Services	71242	9	58	Educational Services	71411	64	731	Chemical Manufacturing
71039	24	31	Relig., Grant, Civic, Prof Org	71243	17	78	Support Activities: Agr./For.	71414	10	30	Food Svcs & Drinking Places
71040	379	3751	Justice, Pubic Order/Safety	71245	97	1341	Educational Services	71415	14	103	Nat'l Security & Int'l Affairs
71043	19	74	Educational Services	71247	48	292	Merch. Wholesalers,Nondur. Gds	71416	27	89	Educational Services
71044	20	39	Food and Beverage Stores	71249	3	7	Relig., Grant, Civic, Prof Org	71417	149	1041	Merch. Wholesalers,Durable Gds
71045	7	59	Nonmetallic Mineral Prod. Mfg	71250	21	55	Crop Production	71418	285	2113	Food and Beverage Stores
71046	19	16	Relig., Grant, Civic, Prof Org	71251	346	2271	Educational Services	71419	37	111	Educational Services
71047	171	1193	Educational Services	71253	16	100	Educational Services	71422	43	201	Educational Services
71048	19	138	Justice, Pubic Order/Safety	71254	280	1901	Justice, Pubic Order/Safety	71423	82	467	Educational Services
71049	115	616	Educational Services	71256	8	151	Paper Manufacturing	71424	10	75	Educational Services
71050	3	0	Support Activities for Mining	71259	77	407	Ambulatory Health Care Svcs	71425	3	20	Food Svcs & Drinking Places
71051	30	84	Special Trade Contractors	71260	73	255	Hospitals	71426	6	26	Construction of Buildings
71052	473	4054	Paper Manufacturing	71261	88	628	Nursing & Resid. Care Facilit.	71427	1	1	Relig., Grant, Civic, Prof Org
71055	898	6962	Special Trade Contractors	71263	299	2508	Nursing & Resid. Care Facilit.	71428	1	3	Merch. Wholesalers,Durable Gds
71060	50	164	Support Activities for Mining	71264	26	66	Crop Production	71429	86	1743	Paper Manufacturing
71061	67	350	Oil and Gas Extraction	71266	34	194	Merch. Wholesalers,Nondur. Gds	71430	102	569	Bldg Matl & Garden Eqpmt Dlrs
71063	22	92	Educational Services	71268	44	207	Educational Services	71432	21	74	Educational Services
71064	127	408	Nursing & Resid. Care Facilit.	71269	440	2836	Educational Services	71433	102	511	Educational Services
71065	49	165	Nursing & Resid. Care Facilit.	71270	1262	14508	Educational Services	71435	56	285	Justice, Pubic Order/Safety
71066	6	5	Food and Beverage Stores	71272	2	29	Other Information Services	71438	31	166	Nursing & Resid. Care Facilit.
71067	34	297	Petroleum & Coal Products Mfg	71273	2	4	Administrative & Support Svcs	71439	29	165	Educational Services
71068	112	620	Ambulatory Health Care Svcs	71275	41	772	Nonmetallic Mineral Prod. Mfg	71440	8	27	Food and Beverage Stores
71069	21	66	Educational Services	71276	10	81	Bldg Matl & Garden Eqpmt Dlrs	71441	5	25	Educational Services
71070	48	182	Forestry and Logging	71277	31	77	Educational Services	71446	926	7325	Educational Services
71071	65	468	Plastics & Rubber Products Mfg	71279	11	82	Educational Services	71447	21	592	Wood Product Manufacturing
71072	19	46	Food Svcs & Drinking Places	71280	105	838	Chemical Manufacturing	71448	3	18	Merch. Wholesalers,Durable Gds
71073	73	782	Special Trade Contractors	71281	11	18	Waste Managmt & Remediat'n Svc	71449	519	3173	Food and Beverage Stores
71075	327	2737	Paper Manufacturing	71282	458	3517	Justice, Pubic Order/Safety	71450	22	104	Educational Services
71078	76	401	Educational Services	71286	20	85	Educational Services	71452	4	11	Crop Production
71079	7	53	Educational Services	71291	1499	13561	Ambulatory Health Care Svcs	71454	55	168	Educational Services
71080	12	112	Paper Manufacturing	71292	635	7966	Paper Manufacturing	71455	5	13	Merch. Wholesalers,Durable Gds
71082	214	1511	Educational Services	71294	6	6	Food Svcs & Drinking Places	71456	24	88	Relig., Grant, Civic, Prof Org
71101	1624	25453	Hospitals	71295	486	4010	Educational Services	71457	1153	10132	Food Svcs & Drinking Places
71102	3	818	Postal Service	71301	1831	25353	Hospitals	71458	1	0	Food and Beverage Stores
71103	563	21451	Educational Services	71302	438	5434	Educational Services	71459	88	2083	Exec., Legis., & Other Support
71104	650	6328	Administrative & Support Svcs	71303	965	9967	Food Svcs & Drinking Places	71460	3	55	Educational Services
71105	1261	12552	Motor Vehicle & Parts Dealers	71306	1	18	Special Trade Contractors	71461	29	111	Motor Vehicle & Parts Dealers
71106	1173	11894	Educational Services	71307	2	1	Electronics & Appliance Stores	71462	16	85	Educational Services
71107	980	11302	Administrative & Support Svcs	71315	5	15	Insurance Carriers & Related	71463	304	2755	Hospitals
71108	564	4692	Personal and Laundry Services	71320	3	4	Admin. of Economic Programs	71465	110	642	Hospitals
71109	686	6784	Nonmetallic Mineral Prod. Mfg	71322	282	1912	Educational Services	71466	6	8	Food and Beverage Stores
71110	35	10780	Nat'l Security & Int'l Affairs	71323	10	99	Nursing & Resid. Care Facilit.	71467	71	668	Wood Product Manufacturing
71111	1650	21384	Amusement, Gambling,& Recreat.	71324	6	23	Exec., Legis., & Other Support	71468	14	98	Educational Services
71112	678	6051	Food Svcs & Drinking Places	71325	38	680	Hospitals	71469	47	196	Construction of Buildings
71113	2	4	Transit & Grnd Pass. Transport	71326	23	122	Educational Services	71472	1	2	Relig., Grant, Civic, Prof Org
71115	252	6670	Hospitals	71327	94	982	Justice, Pubic Order/Safety	71473	12	43	Bldg Matl & Garden Eqpmt Dlrs
71118	776	10473	Hospitals	71328	88	341	Educational Services	71474	18	95	Educational Services

ZIP CODE	2004 Total Firms	2004 Total Employ-ees	TOP INDUSTRY RANKED on 2004 EMPLOYMENT	ZIP CODE	2004 Total Firms	2004 Total Employ-ees	TOP INDUSTRY RANKED on 2004 EMPLOYMENT	ZIP CODE	2004 Total Firms	2004 Total Employ-ees	TOP INDUSTRY RANKED on 2004 EMPLOYMENT
71475	2	25	Justice, Pubic Order/Safety	71831	5	8	Fishing, Hunting and Trapping	72021	303	1965	Apparel Manufacturing
71477	10	31	Food Svcs & Drinking Places	71832	424	5317	Merch. Wholesalers,Nondur. Gds	72022	476	5349	Bldg Matl & Garden Eqpmt Dlrs
71479	40	142	Support Activities for Mining	71833	102	1027	Wood Product Manufacturing	72023	765	5671	Educational Services
71480	19	390	Wood Product Manufacturing	71834	29	200	Educational Services	72024	145	837	Educational Services
71483	456	3790	Justice, Pubic Order/Safety	71835	19	104	Educational Services	72025	20	95	Educational Services
71485	52	277	Exec., Legis., & Other Support	71836	102	535	Educational Services	72026	5	6	Special Trade Contractors
71486	134	1013	Merch. Wholesalers,Durable Gds	71837	84	613	Educational Services	72027	22	218	Educational Services
71496	2	2	Relig., Grant, Civic, Prof Org	71838	28	41	Educational Services	72028	22	86	Educational Services
71497	5	725	Educational Services	71839	18	36	Food Svcs & Drinking Places	72029	130	571	Educational Services
71601	1213	12215	Educational Services	71840	5	25	Merch. Wholesalers,Durable Gds	72030	12	15	Relig., Grant, Civic, Prof Org
71602	446	6738	Food Manufacturing	71841	24	190	Special Trade Contractors	72031	422	2697	Educational Services
71603	968	9319	Hospitals	71842	52	285	Educational Services	72032	1543	17576	Food Svcs & Drinking Places
71611	9	110	Special Trade Contractors	71844	1	0	Relig., Grant, Civic, Prof Org	72033	13	100	Merch. Wholesalers,Durable Gds
71613	6	19	Administrative & Support Svcs	71845	154	778	Educational Services	72034	822	7948	Furniture & Related Prod. Mfg
71630	37	597	Paper Manufacturing	71846	79	277	Educational Services	72035	5	251	Food Svcs & Drinking Places
71631	13	27	Justice, Pubic Order/Safety	71847	1	0	Postal Service	72036	32	165	Educational Services
71635	583	4803	Relig., Grant, Civic, Prof Org	71851	67	346	Educational Services	72037	8	41	Support Activities: Agr./For.
71638	141	1214	Educational Services	71852	483	8043	Food Manufacturing	72038	3	2	Miscellaneous Store Retailers
71639	356	2624	General Merchandise Stores	71853	4	6	Crop Production	72039	57	287	Social Assistance
71640	148	893	Apparel Manufacturing	71854	1127	12504	Plastics & Rubber Products Mfg	72040	123	717	Educational Services
71642	16	120	Educational Services	71855	9	11	Crop Production	72041	52	250	Educational Services
71643	54	161	Educational Services	71857	257	2182	Bldg Matl & Garden Eqpmt Dlrs	72042	276	2135	Leather & Allied Product Mfg
71644	35	881	Exec., Legis., & Other Support	71858	47	272	Educational Services	72043	7	53	Justice, Pubic Order/Safety
71646	230	1402	Educational Services	71859	12	72	Educational Services	72044	13	36	Publishing Industries
71647	101	524	Educational Services	71860	127	831	Furniture & Related Prod. Mfg	72045	20	83	Special Trade Contractors
71651	4	10	Museums, Hist. Sites,& Similar	71861	42	170	Educational Services	72046	153	653	Educational Services
71652	38	277	Educational Services	71862	24	125	Fabricated Metal Product Mfg	72047	15	51	Educational Services
71653	288	2164	Prof., Scientific, & Tech Svcs	71864	3	0	Postal Service	72048	3	2	Sportg Gds,Hobby,Book, & Music
71654	248	1826	Educational Services	71865	7	33	Merch. Wholesalers,Durable Gds	72051	31	114	Educational Services
71655	705	5720	Educational Services	71866	26	82	Educational Services	72052	5	21	Motor Vehicle & Parts Dealers
71656	4	309	Educational Services	71901	1659	15906	Food Svcs & Drinking Places	72053	12	147	Nursing & Resid. Care Facilit.
71657	2	1	Exec., Legis., & Other Support	71902	5	7	Amusement, Gambling,& Recreat.	72055	40	201	Educational Services
71658	13	44	Justice, Pubic Order/Safety	71903	7	17	Personal and Laundry Services	72057	10	3	Support Act. for Transport.
71659	4	12	Crop Production	71909	452	2255	Food Svcs & Drinking Places	72058	309	1661	Educational Services
71660	12	30	Relig., Grant, Civic, Prof Org	71910	4	7	Food Svcs & Drinking Places	72059	2	2	General Merchandise Stores
71661	9	60	Credit Intermediation & Relatd	71913	2061	17539	Food Svcs & Drinking Places	72060	14	48	Amusement, Gambling,& Recreat.
71662	5	40	General Merchandise Stores	71914	7	5	Heavy & Civil Eng. Construct'N	72061	11	181	Educational Services
71663	40	351	Merch. Wholesalers,Nondur. Gds	71920	2	0	Special Trade Contractors	72063	17	163	Educational Services
71665	200	1124	Educational Services	71921	83	740	Wood Product Manufacturing	72064	120	539	Educational Services
71666	2	11	Prof., Scientific, & Tech Svcs	71922	9	53	Forestry and Logging	72065	67	155	Special Trade Contractors
71667	264	2130	Apparel Manufacturing	71923	679	6813	Food Manufacturing	72066	5	16	Food Svcs & Drinking Places
71670	44	235	Wood Product Manufacturing	71929	127	905	Educational Services	72067	160	636	Educational Services
71671	394	3379	Wood Product Manufacturing	71932	1	0	Relig., Grant, Civic, Prof Org	72068	9	27	Justice, Pubic Order/Safety
71674	24	61	Crop Production	71933	24	44	Prof., Scientific, & Tech Svcs	72069	54	210	Educational Services
71675	24	112	Fabricated Metal Product Mfg	71935	14	16	Accommodation	72070	16	23	Postal Service
71676	37	97	Educational Services	71937	43	286	Educational Services	72072	13	22	Food and Beverage Stores
71677	4	34	Support Activities: Agr./For.	71940	48	173	Educational Services	72073	20	94	Educational Services
71678	5	7	Relig., Grant, Civic, Prof Org	71941	38	132	Educational Services	72074	4	11	Relig., Grant, Civic, Prof Org
71701	937	8565	Educational Services	71942	8	18	Motor Vehicle & Parts Dealers	72075	5	2	Postal Service
71711	2	0	Relig., Grant, Civic, Prof Org	71943	240	1818	Wood Product Manufacturing	72076	939	8338	Educational Services
71720	66	659	Merch. Wholesalers,Durable Gds	71944	17	70	Food Manufacturing	72078	9	26	Special Trade Contractors
71721	6	127	Wood Product Manufacturing	71945	48	426	Wood Product Manufacturing	72079	15	701	Exec., Legis., & Other Support
71722	7	22	Museums, Hist. Sites,& Similar	71949	56	328	Educational Services	72080	5	12	Crop Production
71724	23	140	Merch. Wholesalers,Durable Gds	71950	47	239	Educational Services	72081	139	852	Nursing & Resid. Care Facilit.
71725	26	140	Wood Product Manufacturing	71952	3	4	Food and Beverage Stores	72082	42	478	Furniture & Related Prod. Mfg
71726	37	73	Educational Services	71953	745	4975	Apparel Manufacturing	72083	11	44	Sportg Gds,Hobby,Book, & Music
71728	2	0	Postal Service	71956	34	458	Wood Product Manufacturing	72084	23	333	Merch. Wholesalers,Durable Gds
71730	1761	19025	Food Manufacturing	71957	222	1508	Accommodation	72085	3	2	Personal and Laundry Services
71731	2	0	Relig., Grant, Civic, Prof Org	71958	143	864	Educational Services	72086	365	3509	Fabricated Metal Product Mfg
71740	46	440	Paper Manufacturing	71959	14	41	Justice, Pubic Order/Safety	72087	29	113	Food and Beverage Stores
71742	342	2584	Bldg Matl & Garden Eqpmt Dlrs	71960	40	170	Educational Services	72088	94	785	Relig., Grant, Civic, Prof Org
71743	124	731	Relig., Grant, Civic, Prof Org	71961	19	74	Educational Services	72089	9	21	Merch. Wholesalers,Nondur. Gds
71744	158	1122	Chemical Manufacturing	71962	11	10	Postal Service	72099	32	315	Merch. Wholesalers,Nondur. Gds
71745	16	35	Truck Transportation	71964	88	732	Educational Services	72101	126	1053	Print'g & Related Supp't Act's
71747	33	378	Wood Product Manufacturing	71965	14	45	Repair and Maintenance	72102	31	170	Educational Services
71748	1	0	Relig., Grant, Civic, Prof Org	71968	108	668	Bldg Matl & Garden Eqpmt Dlrs	72103	240	1956	Rental and Leasing Services
71749	82	495	Educational Services	71969	2	3	Crop Production	72104	747	6417	Educational Services
71750	1	7	Food Svcs & Drinking Places	71970	11	13	Accommodation	72105	16	243	Primary Metal Manufacturing
71751	19	28	Accommodation	71971	17	43	Educational Services	72106	126	877	Construction of Buildings
71752	30	129	Educational Services	71972	5	32	Educational Services	72107	10	188	Construction of Buildings
71753	927	8735	Merch. Wholesalers,Durable Gds	71973	48	823	Merch. Wholesalers,Nondur. Gds	72108	3	25	Animal Production
71754	3	2	Special Trade Contractors	71998	1	375	Educational Services	72110	650	5508	Forestry and Logging
71758	24	140	Educational Services	71999	2	17	Other Information Services	72111	15	61	Educational Services
71759	28	105	Waste Managmt & Remediat'n Svc	72001	8	6	Construction of Buildings	72112	559	4577	Hospitals
71762	110	656	Educational Services	72002	184	1384	Social Assistance	72113	559	7020	Prof., Scientific, & Tech Svcs
71763	42	185	Wood Product Manufacturing	72003	10	14	Air Transportation	72114	863	12981	Hospitals
71764	84	288	Educational Services	72004	59	354	Educational Services	72115	8	18	Administrative & Support Svcs
71765	75	385	Educational Services	72005	6	6	Merch. Wholesalers,Nondur. Gds	72116	1029	8867	Food Svcs & Drinking Places
71766	13	15	Admin. of Economic Programs	72006	147	1039	Ambulatory Health Care Svcs	72117	760	12819	Truck Transportation
71768	4	1	Oil and Gas Extraction	72007	56	151	Relig., Grant, Civic, Prof Org	72118	700	4969	Educational Services
71770	68	465	Wood Product Manufacturing	72010	209	1126	Educational Services	72120	825	5602	Educational Services
71772	2	2	Postal Service	72011	63	945	Merch. Wholesalers,Durable Gds	72121	59	647	Educational Services
71801	805	9095	Food Manufacturing	72012	329	2050	Educational Services	72122	30	107	Wood Product Manufacturing
71802	7	17	Museums, Hist. Sites,& Similar	72013	36	213	Educational Services	72123	13	55	Bldg Matl & Garden Eqpmt Dlrs
71820	4	1	Food and Beverage Stores	72014	4	18	Support Activities: Agr./For.	72124	7	8	Special Trade Contractors
71822	391	3895	Paper Manufacturing	72015	1471	12180	Food Svcs & Drinking Places	72125	27	95	Nonstore Retailers
71823	1	1	Food and Beverage Stores	72016	57	107	Educational Services	72126	190	919	Educational Services
71825	26	212	Educational Services	72017	17	29	Food and Beverage Stores	72127	52	448	Merch. Wholesalers,Durable Gds
71826	52	320	Educational Services	72018	14	28	Heavy & Civil Eng. Construct'N	72128	14	85	Educational Services
71827	7	12	Postal Service	72020	85	235	Educational Services	72129	32	102	Food Svcs & Drinking Places

72130 - 72635 BUSINESS DATA

ZIP CODE	2004 Total Firms	2004 Total Employ-ees	TOP INDUSTRY RANKED on 2004 EMPLOYMENT	ZIP CODE	2004 Total Firms	2004 Total Employ-ees	TOP INDUSTRY RANKED on 2004 EMPLOYMENT	ZIP CODE	2004 Total Firms	2004 Total Employ-ees	TOP INDUSTRY RANKED on 2004 EMPLOYMENT
72130	18	15	Food and Beverage Stores	72342	366	2631	Educational Services	72466	23	32	Food and Beverage Stores
72131	116	557	Educational Services	72346	18	49	Food and Beverage Stores	72467	10	2289	Educational Services
72132	74	558	Utilities	72347	35	128	Support Activities: Agr./For.	72469	18	126	Educational Services
72133	5	3	Food Svcs & Drinking Places	72348	102	508	Educational Services	72470	12	35	Warehousing and Storage
72134	13	66	Justice, Pubic Order/Safety	72350	28	90	Support Activities: Agr./For.	72471	31	147	Educational Services
72135	111	171	Heavy & Civil Eng. Construct'N	72351	27	122	Educational Services	72472	318	2921	Educational Services
72136	16	29	Food Manufacturing	72352	2	1	Relig., Grant, Civic, Prof Org	72473	80	508	Educational Services
72137	77	389	Educational Services	72353	2	1	Postal Service	72474	1	2	Relig., Grant, Civic, Prof Org
72139	8	15	Fabricated Metal Product Mfg	72354	105	498	Educational Services	72475	35	189	Food Manufacturing
72140	10	31	Justice, Pubic Order/Safety	72355	32	82	Merch. Wholesalers,Durable Gds	72476	379	3399	Nursing & Resid. Care Facilit.
72141	17	94	Educational Services	72358	41	276	Justice, Pubic Order/Safety	72478	5	117	Relig., Grant, Civic, Prof Org
72142	67	146	Educational Services	72359	15	54	Educational Services	72479	119	448	Educational Services
72143	1442	15172	Hospitals	72360	289	1784	Educational Services	72482	24	102	Educational Services
72145	11	32	Construction of Buildings	72364	315	1963	Merch. Wholesalers,Durable Gds	72501	1221	15322	Food Manufacturing
72149	7	811	Educational Services	72365	151	1325	Transportation Equipment Mfg	72503	2	7	Motion Pict. & Sound Recording
72150	415	2891	Merch. Wholesalers,Durable Gds	72366	106	554	Educational Services	72512	84	409	Nursing & Resid. Care Facilit.
72152	20	79	Support Activities: Agr./For.	72367	5	6	Food and Beverage Stores	72513	202	1273	General Merchandise Stores
72153	91	340	Educational Services	72368	29	41	Food and Beverage Stores	72515	1	2	Postal Service
72156	11	22	Truck Transportation	72369	3	4	Food and Beverage Stores	72517	10	81	Educational Services
72157	13	29	Heavy & Civil Eng. Construct'N	72370	370	4632	Merch. Wholesalers,Nondur. Gds	72519	111	701	Educational Services
72160	566	5084	Machinery Manufacturing	72372	56	174	Educational Services	72520	7	6	Special Trade Contractors
72164	1	2	Postal Service	72373	63	298	Educational Services	72521	121	673	Educational Services
72165	4	5	Food and Beverage Stores	72374	13	37	Merch. Wholesalers,Durable Gds	72522	10	122	Educational Services
72166	13	26	Sportg Gds,Hobby,Book, & Music	72376	35	233	Bldg Matl & Garden Eqpmt Dlrs	72523	31	150	Educational Services
72167	9	10	Postal Service	72377	3	4	Postal Service	72524	12	79	Merch. Wholesalers,Nondur. Gds
72168	5	212	Justice, Pubic Order/Safety	72379	3	1	Relig., Grant, Civic, Prof Org	72525	1	2	Special Trade Contractors
72169	6	6	Crop Production	72383	3	26	Support Activities: Agr./For.	72526	7	84	Educational Services
72170	4	6	Accommodation	72384	39	171	Educational Services	72527	6	13	Crop Production
72173	138	628	Educational Services	72386	43	197	Educational Services	72528	7	6	Utilities
72175	18	35	Air Transportation	72387	4	22	Educational Services	72529	88	503	Hospitals
72176	53	237	Educational Services	72389	3	5	Ambulatory Health Care Svcs	72530	37	213	Accommodation
72178	2	17	Electronics & Appliance Stores	72390	372	2702	Educational Services	72531	13	19	Food Svcs & Drinking Places
72179	5	58	Educational Services	72391	3	6	Food Manufacturing	72532	37	144	Special Trade Contractors
72180	5	1	Postal Service	72392	27	229	Merch. Wholesalers,Nondur. Gds	72533	10	38	Food Svcs & Drinking Places
72181	7	15	Food and Beverage Stores	72394	16	43	Truck Transportation	72534	15	121	Educational Services
72182	6	11	Admin. Enviro. Quality Progrms	72395	43	373	Educational Services	72536	25	76	Bldg Matl & Garden Eqpmt Dlrs
72183	21	293	Justice, Pubic Order/Safety	72396	551	3577	Educational Services	72537	39	74	Food Svcs & Drinking Places
72190	10	10	Prof., Scientific, & Tech Svcs	72401	2705	31433	Ambulatory Health Care Svcs	72538	5	14	Food and Beverage Stores
72199	7	527	Nat'l Security & Int'l Affairs	72402	6	21	Unclassified Establishments	72539	14	52	Educational Services
72201	1706	30043	Exec., Legis., & Other Support	72403	11	25	Waste Managmt & Remediat'n Svc	72540	5	68	Merch. Wholesalers,Durable Gds
72202	872	19112	Electronics & Appliance Stores	72404	525	5302	Educational Services	72542	385	1712	Educational Services
72203	18	58	Exec., Legis., & Other Support	72410	7	29	Justice, Pubic Order/Safety	72543	738	5675	Chemical Manufacturing
72204	1238	14746	Educational Services	72411	42	387	Educational Services	72544	28	69	Food Svcs & Drinking Places
72205	1667	53238	Hospitals	72412	5	7	Food and Beverage Stores	72546	4	20	Repair and Maintenance
72206	1005	12195	Truck Transportation	72413	12	64	Educational Services	72550	16	29	Justice, Pubic Order/Safety
72207	508	3663	Social Assistance	72414	11	13	Machinery Manufacturing	72553	3	2	Machinery Manufacturing
72209	1305	21738	Admin. of Economic Programs	72415	44	261	Educational Services	72554	107	452	Educational Services
72210	359	2212	Special Trade Contractors	72416	89	415	Elect'l Eqpmt, App, & Comp Mfg	72555	3	3	Utilities
72211	1234	13969	Food Svcs & Drinking Places	72417	66	337	Educational Services	72556	214	1500	Educational Services
72212	521	7188	Isps, Web Search Portals	72419	51	282	Computer & Electronic Prod Mfg	72560	565	3715	Food Svcs & Drinking Places
72214	4	7	Administrative & Support Svcs	72421	16	71	Support Activities: Agr./For.	72561	23	192	Educational Services
72215	11	81	Amusement, Gambling,& Recreat.	72422	211	2530	Furniture & Related Prod. Mfg	72562	63	138	Food and Beverage Stores
72216	5	6	Special Trade Contractors	72424	1	0	Merch. Wholesalers,Nondur. Gds	72564	14	28	Educational Services
72217	5	2	Prof., Scientific, & Tech Svcs	72425	16	120	Educational Services	72565	16	28	Crop Production
72219	8	10	Special Trade Contractors	72426	22	100	Support Activities: Agr./For.	72566	14	26	Exec., Legis., & Other Support
72221	20	25	Prof., Scientific, & Tech Svcs	72427	3	4	Food and Beverage Stores	72567	15	35	Justice, Pubic Order/Safety
72222	2	1	Administrative & Support Svcs	72428	10	12	Food and Beverage Stores	72568	46	168	Food Svcs & Drinking Places
72223	425	4024	Rental and Leasing Services	72429	31	66	Support Activities: Agr./For.	72569	3	19	Educational Services
72225	13	18	Prof., Scientific, & Tech Svcs	72430	4	4	Merch. Wholesalers,Nondur. Gds	72571	4	2	Merch. Wholesalers,Nondur. Gds
72227	433	3166	Food Svcs & Drinking Places	72431	20	36	Educational Services	72572	9	8	Relig., Grant, Civic, Prof Org
72231	7	169	Relig., Grant, Civic, Prof Org	72432	214	1339	Educational Services	72573	5	10	Nursing & Resid. Care Facilit.
72260	2	4	Prof., Scientific, & Tech Svcs	72433	92	598	Educational Services	72575	2	4	Postal Service
72295	2	2	Rental and Leasing Services	72434	76	322	Educational Services	72576	193	1525	Ambulatory Health Care Svcs
72301	1139	14583	Truck Transportation	72435	14	62	Bldg Matl & Garden Eqpmt Dlrs	72577	8	153	Nursing & Resid. Care Facilit.
72303	6	19	Museums, Hist. Sites,& Similar	72436	4	12	Food and Beverage Stores	72578	1	0	Postal Service
72310	13	1033	Fabricated Metal Product Mfg	72437	94	485	Educational Services	72579	19	160	Educational Services
72311	6	27	Administrative & Support Svcs	72438	88	340	Educational Services	72581	25	80	Relig., Grant, Civic, Prof Org
72312	9	145	Educational Services	72439	4	23	Food and Beverage Stores	72583	26	222	Educational Services
72313	6	9	Special Trade Contractors	72440	21	186	Educational Services	72584	11	91	Educational Services
72315	1027	11739	Primary Metal Manufacturing	72441	6	19	Utilities	72585	3	7	Special Trade Contractors
72316	7	20	Special Trade Contractors	72442	162	958	Machinery Manufacturing	72587	3	6	Bldg Matl & Garden Eqpmt Dlrs
72320	6	396	Justice, Pubic Order/Safety	72443	57	507	Miscellaneous Manufacturing	72601	1564	13632	Merch. Wholesalers,Nondur. Gds
72321	7	76	Educational Services	72444	38	225	Educational Services	72602	14	36	Machinery Manufacturing
72322	14	96	Support Activities: Agr./For.	72445	3	9	Air Transportation	72611	64	290	Educational Services
72324	52	369	Educational Services	72447	83	523	Plastics & Rubber Products Mfg	72613	3	4	Transit & Grnd Pass. Transport
72325	4	25	Crop Production	72449	3	5	Food and Beverage Stores	72615	10	107	Food Manufacturing
72326	47	329	Plastics & Rubber Products Mfg	72450	1212	14090	Transportation Equipment Mfg	72616	455	4835	Food Manufacturing
72327	47	260	Support Activities: Agr./For.	72451	2	10	Merch. Wholesalers,Durable Gds	72617	7	18	Animal Production
72328	3	6	Crop Production	72453	3	7	Postal Service	72619	146	502	Amusement, Gambling,& Recreat.
72329	2	49	Crop Production	72454	234	2232	Furniture & Related Prod. Mfg	72623	7	9	Construction of Buildings
72330	14	36	Educational Services	72455	482	4496	Wood Product Manufacturing	72624	15	12	Food and Beverage Stores
72331	92	523	Gasoline Stations	72456	21	52	Wood Product Manufacturing	72626	54	233	Educational Services
72332	6	28	Educational Services	72457	23	89	Educational Services	72628	27	164	Educational Services
72333	63	238	Educational Services	72458	12	25	Museums, Hist. Sites,& Similar	72629	10	26	Construction of Buildings
72335	812	7083	Educational Services	72459	31	96	Construction of Buildings	72630	31	42	Amusement, Gambling,& Recreat.
72336	5	4	Special Trade Contractors	72460	12	62	Educational Services	72631	178	516	Accommodation
72338	3	13	Wholesale Elec. Mrkts & Agents	72461	119	764	Apparel Manufacturing	72632	676	3239	Accommodation
72339	4	12	Justice, Pubic Order/Safety	72462	14	23	Food and Beverage Stores	72633	27	90	Educational Services
72340	1	0	Relig., Grant, Civic, Prof Org	72464	4	7	Warehousing and Storage	72634	253	3517	Repair and Maintenance
72341	4	15	Justice, Pubic Order/Safety	72465	4	11	Prof., Scientific, & Tech Svcs	72635	133	978	Apparel Manufacturing

ZIP CODE	2004 Total Firms	2004 Total Employees	TOP INDUSTRY RANKED on 2004 EMPLOYMENT
72636	4	5	Accommodation
72638	183	2480	Food Manufacturing
72639	7	35	Accommodation
72640	9	10	Accommodation
72641	180	950	Educational Services
72642	71	297	Accommodation
72644	104	382	Educational Services
72645	49	165	Educational Services
72648	19	34	Ambulatory Health Care Svcs
72650	214	1281	Educational Services
72651	75	351	Transportation Equipment Mfg
72653	1415	11866	Merch. Wholesalers,Durable Gds
72654	17	50	Telecommunications
72655	16	79	Educational Services
72658	57	263	Educational Services
72660	12	21	Accommodation
72661	21	36	Accommodation
72662	89	275	Educational Services
72663	7	9	Construction of Buildings
72666	16	38	Food and Beverage Stores
72668	12	26	Heavy & Civil Eng. Construct'N
72669	4	46	Merch. Wholesalers,Durable Gds
72670	15	24	Accommodation
72672	32	39	Wood Product Manufacturing
72675	49	185	Wood Product Manufacturing
72677	23	76	Justice, Pubic Order/Safety
72679	2	27	Support Activities: Agr./For.
72680	29	97	Educational Services
72682	27	287	Educational Services
72683	6	7	Utilities
72685	45	150	Educational Services
72686	10	30	Educational Services
72687	307	1617	Merch. Wholesalers,Nondur. Gds
72701	1625	19532	Educational Services
72702	20	43	Administrative & Support Svcs
72703	1655	17438	Hospitals
72704	310	2833	General Merchandise Stores
72711	10	53	Heavy & Civil Eng. Construct'N
72712	1507	17773	General Merchandise Stores
72714	238	1544	Relig., Grant, Civic, Prof Org
72715	76	242	Relig., Grant, Civic, Prof Org
72716	1	8600	General Merchandise Stores
72717	12	19	Food Manufacturing
72718	30	104	Justice, Pubic Order/Safety
72719	68	373	Apparel Manufacturing
72721	6	22	Wood Product Manufacturing
72722	79	638	Educational Services
72727	74	324	Educational Services
72728	26	890	Truck Transportation
72729	5	11	Food Svcs & Drinking Places
72730	203	858	Educational Services
72732	95	307	Special Trade Contractors
72733	8	18	Food Svcs & Drinking Places
72734	191	2371	Food Manufacturing
72735	11	35	Food and Beverage Stores
72736	193	1346	Hospitals
72737	20	216	Educational Services
72738	51	165	Nonstore Retailers
72739	19	175	Special Trade Contractors
72740	354	2608	Food Manufacturing
72741	17	298	Hospitals
72742	32	140	Educational Services
72744	187	1071	Merch. Wholesalers,Durable Gds
72745	308	4405	Truck Transportation
72747	10	11	Food and Beverage Stores
72749	14	24	Relig., Grant, Civic, Prof Org
72751	112	622	Educational Services
72752	8	17	Justice, Pubic Order/Safety
72753	224	1033	Educational Services
72756	1603	17244	Food Svcs & Drinking Places
72757	17	66	Nonmetallic Mineral Prod. Mfg
72758	451	4086	Educational Services
72760	20	143	Educational Services
72761	731	8183	Plastics & Rubber Products Mfg
72762	885	12456	Ambulatory Health Care Svcs
72764	1758	21222	Food Manufacturing
72765	13	36	Special Trade Contractors
72766	8	36	Administrative & Support Svcs
72768	27	139	Justice, Pubic Order/Safety
72769	15	76	Animal Production
72770	34	305	Food Svcs & Drinking Places
72773	10	49	Wood Product Manufacturing
72774	110	409	Educational Services
72776	5	16	Forestry and Logging
72801	1115	9634	Educational Services
72802	663	10556	Utilities
72811	14	48	Social Assistance
72812	2	120	Support Activities: Agr./For.
72820	1	1	Special Trade Contractors
72821	59	288	Educational Services

ZIP CODE	2004 Total Firms	2004 Total Employees	TOP INDUSTRY RANKED on 2004 EMPLOYMENT
72823	173	1018	Educational Services
72824	36	95	Educational Services
72826	5	5	Exec., Legis., & Other Support
72827	4	6	Truck Transportation
72828	6	76	Educational Services
72829	20	74	Fabricated Metal Product Mfg
72830	688	7933	Merch. Wholesalers,Nondur. Gds
72832	27	70	Educational Services
72833	231	2163	Food Manufacturing
72834	284	1801	Food Svcs & Drinking Places
72835	10	71	Merch. Wholesalers,Durable Gds
72837	146	788	Educational Services
72838	7	37	Crop Production
72839	5	3	Special Trade Contractors
72840	25	90	Educational Services
72841	5	15	Personal and Laundry Services
72842	39	138	Educational Services
72843	39	304	Educational Services
72845	37	397	Wood Product Manufacturing
72846	68	296	Educational Services
72847	43	118	Educational Services
72851	15	47	Food and Beverage Stores
72852	8	82	Educational Services
72853	66	528	Educational Services
72854	17	23	Wood Product Manufacturing
72855	298	1910	Educational Services
72856	17	17	Miscellaneous Store Retailers
72857	71	327	Social Assistance
72858	62	432	Educational Services
72860	15	43	Support Activities: Agr./For.
72863	57	212	Educational Services
72865	38	499	Machinery Manufacturing
72901	2011	21648	Hospitals
72902	13	48	Paper Manufacturing
72903	1328	18570	Food Svcs & Drinking Places
72904	485	10095	Merch. Wholesalers,Nondur. Gds
72905	18	1112	Nat'l Security & Int'l Affairs
72906	4	17	Special Trade Contractors
72908	450	9623	Elect'l Eqpmt, App, & Comp Mfg
72913	5	13	Administrative & Support Svcs
72914	2	4	Administrative & Support Svcs
72916	196	3075	Fabricated Metal Product Mfg
72917	15	20	Special Trade Contractors
72918	11	26	Special Trade Contractors
72919	2	622	Nursing & Resid. Care Facilit.
72921	307	2434	Educational Services
72923	128	1088	Hospitals
72926	16	46	Gasoline Stations
72927	274	2713	Food Manufacturing
72928	20	224	Educational Services
72930	8	33	Social Assistance
72932	36	201	Educational Services
72933	146	785	Furniture & Related Prod. Mfg
72934	7	21	Wood Product Manufacturing
72935	9	13	Relig., Grant, Civic, Prof Org
72936	388	2089	Educational Services
72937	62	186	Educational Services
72938	29	195	Educational Services
72940	43	110	Social Assistance
72941	92	536	Educational Services
72943	43	220	Educational Services
72944	75	573	Wood Product Manufacturing
72945	13	40	Chemical Manufacturing
72946	72	471	Educational Services
72947	98	599	Educational Services
72948	7	13	Food and Beverage Stores
72949	359	3176	Merch. Wholesalers,Nondur. Gds
72950	8	13	Museums, Hist. Sites,& Similar
72951	43	107	Furniture & Related Prod. Mfg
72952	27	56	Construction of Buildings
72955	4	3	Postal Service
72956	1188	11482	Merch. Wholesalers,Nondur. Gds
72957	4	8	Special Trade Contractors
72958	300	2880	Merch. Wholesalers,Nondur. Gds
72959	45	168	Educational Services
73001	6	5	Food and Beverage Stores
73002	29	176	Educational Services
73003	822	4113	Educational Services
73004	21	164	Educational Services
73005	431	3299	Utilities
73006	114	622	Educational Services
73007	61	172	Accommodation
73008	760	5411	Educational Services
73009	60	392	Utilities
73010	263	1655	Educational Services
73011	12	18	Construction of Buildings
73013	1238	11359	Food Svcs & Drinking Places
73014	52	403	Food Svcs & Drinking Places
73015	167	822	Exec., Legis., & Other Support
73016	42	288	Educational Services

ZIP CODE	2004 Total Firms	2004 Total Employees	TOP INDUSTRY RANKED on 2004 EMPLOYMENT
73017	54	226	Educational Services
73018	1035	10131	Fabricated Metal Product Mfg
73019	31	7868	Educational Services
73020	377	1882	Educational Services
73021	18	51	Museums, Hist. Sites,& Similar
73022	17	395	Amusement, Gambling,& Recreat.
73023	9	20	Social Assistance
73024	32	278	Nursing & Resid. Care Facilit.
73026	177	1151	Amusement, Gambling,& Recreat.
73027	24	137	Educational Services
73028	126	509	Educational Services
73029	78	402	Educational Services
73030	210	1271	Museums, Hist. Sites,& Similar
73031	29	227	Educational Services
73032	16	54	Ambulatory Health Care Svcs
73033	43	155	Merch. Wholesalers,Durable Gds
73034	1586	11930	Administrative & Support Svcs
73036	728	7393	Educational Services
73038	80	264	Educational Services
73040	100	272	Educational Services
73041	15	72	Truck Transportation
73042	27	107	Educational Services
73043	4	9	Relig., Grant, Civic, Prof Org
73044	738	5164	Educational Services
73045	218	1461	Educational Services
73047	186	999	Justice, Pubic Order/Safety
73048	90	389	Educational Services
73049	119	636	Educational Services
73050	22	481	Educational Services
73051	139	1268	Exec., Legis., & Other Support
73052	279	2078	Special Trade Contractors
73053	45	203	Educational Services
73054	86	299	Educational Services
73055	312	1647	Nursing & Resid. Care Facilit.
73056	14	45	Gasoline Stations
73057	78	533	Educational Services
73058	10	13	Justice, Pubic Order/Safety
73059	90	307	Educational Services
73061	40	193	Educational Services
73062	56	207	Educational Services
73063	15	54	Educational Services
73064	482	3089	Educational Services
73065	281	1516	Educational Services
73066	23	121	Educational Services
73067	27	320	Special Trade Contractors
73068	260	1523	Educational Services
73069	1930	16587	Food Svcs & Drinking Places
73070	62	345	Relig., Grant, Civic, Prof Org
73071	660	9430	Hospitals
73072	1008	9499	Food Svcs & Drinking Places
73073	17	149	Educational Services
73074	22	112	Educational Services
73075	493	4301	Exec., Legis., & Other Support
73077	347	3157	Machinery Manufacturing
73078	166	878	Special Trade Contractors
73079	12	71	Educational Services
73080	436	2368	Food Svcs & Drinking Places
73082	91	521	Educational Services
73083	67	117	Administrative & Support Svcs
73084	144	1078	Hospitals
73085	15	41	Special Trade Contractors
73086	444	2876	Educational Services
73089	222	1666	Animal Production
73090	23	191	Educational Services
73092	43	135	Educational Services
73093	83	846	Educational Services
73095	42	479	Educational Services
73096	588	4377	Educational Services
73097	20	76	Special Trade Contractors
73098	128	831	Merch. Wholesalers,Durable Gds
73099	1168	8256	Food Svcs & Drinking Places
73101	26	62	Special Trade Contractors
73102	1394	29912	Exec., Legis., & Other Support
73103	445	4060	Ambulatory Health Care Svcs
73104	375	15560	Hospitals
73105	701	18207	Exec., Legis., & Other Support
73106	817	7275	Educational Services
73107	1131	16893	Administrative & Support Svcs
73108	845	14816	Couriers and Messengers
73109	1124	9780	Hospitals
73110	1143	14794	Educational Services
73111	438	7015	Admin. of Economic Programs
73112	2469	21496	Ambulatory Health Care Svcs
73113	20	45	Special Trade Contractors
73114	668	10559	Motor Vehicle & Parts Dealers
73115	592	5817	Miscellaneous Store Retailers
73116	1789	14874	Insurance Carriers & Related
73117	298	7751	Educational Services
73118	1428	15949	Prof., Scientific, & Tech Svcs
73119	780	5840	Educational Services

ZIP CODE	2004 Total Firms	2004 Total Employ-ees	TOP INDUSTRY RANKED on 2004 EMPLOYMENT	ZIP CODE	2004 Total Firms	2004 Total Employ-ees	TOP INDUSTRY RANKED on 2004 EMPLOYMENT	ZIP CODE	2004 Total Firms	2004 Total Employ-ees	TOP INDUSTRY RANKED on 2004 EMPLOYMENT
73120	1448	14547	Hospitals	73520	6	15	Unclassified Establishments	73722	27	119	Educational Services
73121	127	1177	Truck Transportation	73521	931	8022	Educational Services	73724	100	336	Educational Services
73122	436	3049	Educational Services	73522	7	38	Prof., Scientific, & Tech Svcs	73726	29	91	Utilities
73123	28	102	Transit & Grnd Pass. Transport	73523	16	4853	Nat'l Security & Int'l Affairs	73727	7	43	Merch. Wholesalers,Durable Gds
73125	3	14	Relig., Grant, Civic, Prof Org	73526	58	222	Educational Services	73728	134	732	Exec., Legis., & Other Support
73126	5	103	Ambulatory Health Care Svcs	73527	92	662	Bldg Matl & Garden Eqpmt Dlrs	73729	30	60	Food and Beverage Stores
73127	1159	16044	Merch. Wholesalers,Durable Gds	73528	29	179	Food and Beverage Stores	73730	37	168	Educational Services
73128	403	9463	Machinery Manufacturing	73529	146	689	Educational Services	73731	14	47	Warehousing and Storage
73129	1000	11837	Food and Beverage Stores	73530	21	126	Educational Services	73733	8	27	Justice, Pubic Order/Safety
73130	428	3103	Food and Beverage Stores	73531	10	20	Miscellaneous Store Retailers	73734	42	209	Heavy & Civil Eng. Construct'N
73131	126	2909	Amusement, Gambling,& Recreat.	73532	30	331	Nonmetallic Mineral Prod. Mfg	73735	23	160	Educational Services
73132	944	8776	Food Svcs & Drinking Places	73533	1299	10719	Social Assistance	73736	6	14	Postal Service
73134	424	7492	General Merchandise Stores	73534	21	98	Educational Services	73737	257	1502	Nursing & Resid. Care Facilit.
73135	279	4781	Transportation Equipment Mfg	73537	31	84	Educational Services	73738	53	252	Educational Services
73136	4	2	Administrative & Support Svcs	73538	133	689	Educational Services	73739	25	51	Justice, Pubic Order/Safety
73137	12	58	Rental and Leasing Services	73539	4	5	Crop Production	73741	52	698	Exec., Legis., & Other Support
73139	798	7261	Food Svcs & Drinking Places	73540	8	7	Social Assistance	73742	205	2083	Truck Transportation
73140	13	29	Construction of Buildings	73541	62	407	Educational Services	73743	6	19	Educational Services
73141	199	1869	Hospitals	73542	278	1410	Educational Services	73744	6	24	Justice, Pubic Order/Safety
73142	178	1670	Educational Services	73543	17	180	Educational Services	73746	9	13	Credit Intermediation & Relatd
73143	8	85	Credit Intermediation & Relatd	73544	11	35	Support Activities: Agr./For.	73747	9	9	Merch. Wholesalers,Nondur. Gds
73144	11	18	Prof., Scientific, & Tech Svcs	73546	53	170	Educational Services	73749	46	116	Educational Services
73145	39	22713	Transportation Equipment Mfg	73547	53	476	Justice, Pubic Order/Safety	73750	395	3229	Telecommunications
73146	10	63	Special Trade Contractors	73548	14	139	Truck Transportation	73753	23	270	Petroleum & Coal Products Mfg
73147	11	90	Nonstore Retailers	73549	7	4	Food Svcs & Drinking Places	73754	50	316	Educational Services
73148	6	11	Administrative & Support Svcs	73550	151	872	Nursing & Resid. Care Facilit.	73755	35	72	Special Trade Contractors
73149	476	5981	General Merchandise Stores	73551	2	10	Warehousing and Storage	73756	17	57	Justice, Pubic Order/Safety
73150	114	1088	Relig., Grant, Civic, Prof Org	73552	22	148	Educational Services	73757	6	9	Relig., Grant, Civic, Prof Org
73151	10	26	Special Trade Contractors	73554	197	1185	Truck Transportation	73758	18	70	Justice, Pubic Order/Safety
73152	3	8	Admin. of Economic Programs	73555	5	132	Justice, Pubic Order/Safety	73759	116	562	Oil and Gas Extraction
73153	25	126	Clothing & Cloth'g Acc. Stores	73556	8	32	Support Activities: Agr./For.	73760	23	82	Exec., Legis., & Other Support
73154	18	30	Prof., Scientific, & Tech Svcs	73557	26	118	Food Svcs & Drinking Places	73761	19	71	Justice, Pubic Order/Safety
73155	8	25	Truck Transportation	73559	18	60	Educational Services	73762	93	908	Machinery Manufacturing
73156	26	66	Securities/Commodity Contracts	73560	16	75	Educational Services	73763	131	652	Hospitals
73157	18	69	Print'g & Related Supp't Act's	73561	1	2	Merch. Wholesalers,Durable Gds	73764	11	92	Educational Services
73159	711	6796	Food Svcs & Drinking Places	73562	25	135	Educational Services	73766	62	306	Educational Services
73160	1271	13342	Administrative & Support Svcs	73564	27	88	Mining (Except Oil and Gas)	73768	63	498	Special Trade Contractors
73162	477	3047	Food Svcs & Drinking Places	73565	53	283	Educational Services	73770	4	303	Nonmetallic Mineral Prod. Mfg
73165	69	245	Special Trade Contractors	73566	81	381	Educational Services	73771	35	144	Nursing & Resid. Care Facilit.
73169	59	9324	Admin. of Economic Programs	73567	26	130	Educational Services	73772	292	1800	Justice, Pubic Order/Safety
73170	431	2867	Educational Services	73568	58	256	Educational Services	73773	45	275	Educational Services
73172	27	56	Administrative & Support Svcs	73569	24	78	Merch. Wholesalers,Durable Gds	73801	971	7896	Support Activities for Mining
73173	73	802	Truck Transportation	73570	51	241	Educational Services	73802	8	17	Support Activities for Mining
73178	1	0	Special Trade Contractors	73571	6	5	Food Svcs & Drinking Places	73832	95	311	Exec., Legis., & Other Support
73179	225	7179	Sportg Gds,Hobby,Book, & Music	73572	149	616	Educational Services	73834	125	736	Educational Services
73189	30	54	Real Estate	73573	136	990	Wood Product Manufacturing	73835	17	63	Special Trade Contractors
73190	4	15	Ambulatory Health Care Svcs	73601	563	4854	Food Manufacturing	73838	17	40	Exec., Legis., & Other Support
73195	2	0	Postal Service	73620	40	220	Exec., Legis., & Other Support	73840	27	109	Educational Services
73401	1741	21139	Miscellaneous Store Retailers	73622	14	55	Nonmetallic Mineral Prod. Mfg	73841	29	430	Exec., Legis., & Other Support
73402	18	131	Heavy & Civil Eng. Construct'N	73624	66	573	Educational Services	73842	50	207	Educational Services
73403	4	5	Construction of Buildings	73625	18	112	Educational Services	73843	37	138	Educational Services
73425	13	265	Special Trade Contractors	73626	41	204	Educational Services	73844	17	42	Exec., Legis., & Other Support
73430	21	272	Educational Services	73627	19	55	Educational Services	73847	5	46	Support Act. for Transport.
73432	25	688	Transportation Equipment Mfg	73628	126	656	Educational Services	73848	122	564	Educational Services
73433	81	394	Educational Services	73632	233	1220	Educational Services	73851	7	14	Special Trade Contractors
73434	10	13	Special Trade Contractors	73638	7	34	Justice, Pubic Order/Safety	73852	81	443	Educational Services
73435	15	154	Educational Services	73639	29	86	Educational Services	73853	13	55	Educational Services
73436	12	20	Transportation Equipment Mfg	73641	26	52	Exec., Legis., & Other Support	73855	3	4	Postal Service
73437	4	4	Postal Service	73642	12	25	Crop Production	73857	18	57	Educational Services
73438	147	940	Special Trade Contractors	73644	785	6201	Special Trade Contractors	73858	119	602	Hospitals
73439	306	1274	Educational Services	73645	79	335	Educational Services	73859	78	461	Educational Services
73440	5	12	Construction of Buildings	73646	8	18	Repair and Maintenance	73860	107	606	Educational Services
73441	2	5	Miscellaneous Store Retailers	73647	23	86	Social Assistance	73901	11	10	Construction of Buildings
73442	10	14	Oil and Gas Extraction	73648	7	26	Construction of Buildings	73931	30	84	Educational Services
73443	189	863	Electronics & Appliance Stores	73650	33	221	Educational Services	73932	175	847	Special Trade Contractors
73444	9	12	Food and Beverage Stores	73651	255	1846	Miscellaneous Manufacturing	73933	155	579	Hospitals
73446	355	3554	Merch. Wholesalers,Durable Gds	73654	69	235	Educational Services	73937	15	70	Educational Services
73447	17	79	Fabricated Metal Product Mfg	73655	42	191	Merch. Wholesalers,Nondur. Gds	73938	34	114	Educational Services
73448	219	1707	Food Manufacturing	73658	27	101	Utilities	73939	48	372	Educational Services
73449	47	303	Waste Managmt & Remediat'n Svc	73659	13	27	Justice, Pubic Order/Safety	73942	721	7165	Crop Production
73450	28	62	Justice, Pubic Order/Safety	73660	32	146	Educational Services	73944	28	79	Educational Services
73453	12	30	Merch. Wholesalers,Durable Gds	73661	23	70	Warehousing and Storage	73945	133	707	Educational Services
73455	16	101	Food Manufacturing	73662	218	1367	Justice, Pubic Order/Safety	73946	13	18	Merch. Wholesalers,Nondur. Gds
73456	97	366	Educational Services	73663	100	506	Hospitals	73947	33	120	Credit Intermediation & Relatd
73458	46	339	Fabricated Metal Product Mfg	73664	58	213	Educational Services	73949	81	756	Crop Production
73459	33	705	Amusement, Gambling,& Recreat.	73666	18	37	Educational Services	73950	63	283	Educational Services
73460	254	1990	Educational Services	73667	67	239	Justice, Pubic Order/Safety	73951	28	105	Educational Services
73461	25	138	Transportation Equipment Mfg	73668	4	12	Food Svcs & Drinking Places	74001	13	43	Educational Services
73463	106	641	Educational Services	73669	92	476	Prof., Scientific, & Tech Svcs	74002	77	517	Merch. Wholesalers,Nondur. Gds
73476	2	9	Support Activities for Mining	73673	12	44	Support Activities: Agr./For.	74003	813	9457	Wholesale Elec. Mrkts & Agents
73481	82	368	Special Trade Contractors	73701	1331	11851	Hospitals	74004	5	676	Petroleum & Coal Products Mfg
73487	7	5	Postal Service	73702	12	51	Exec., Legis., & Other Support	74005	8	8	Special Trade Contractors
73488	1	2	Postal Service	73703	969	8870	Food Svcs & Drinking Places	74006	948	8436	Food Svcs & Drinking Places
73491	98	553	Educational Services	73705	14	333	Isps, Web Search Portals	74008	567	3454	Educational Services
73501	1513	12472	Prof., Scientific, & Tech Svcs	73706	6	38	Special Trade Contractors	74010	361	1827	Educational Services
73502	22	150	Exec., Legis., & Other Support	73716	28	74	Educational Services	74011	385	2678	Food Svcs & Drinking Places
73503	108	2743	Hospitals	73717	404	2709	Educational Services	74012	1749	18938	Educational Services
73505	1224	16367	Educational Services	73718	33	123	Support Activities: Agr./For.	74013	37	69	Special Trade Contractors
73506	8	21	Special Trade Contractors	73719	13	13	Animal Production	74014	352	2398	Machinery Manufacturing
73507	483	2940	Educational Services	73720	10	24	Gasoline Stations	74015	394	4666	Fabricated Metal Product Mfg

ZIP CODE	2004 Total Firms	2004 Total Employees	TOP INDUSTRY RANKED on 2004 EMPLOYMENT
74016	148	777	Social Assistance
74017	1101	9909	Educational Services
74018	20	40	Relig., Grant, Civic, Prof Org
74019	199	1884	Fabricated Metal Product Mfg
74020	267	1426	Educational Services
74021	315	1374	Educational Services
74022	41	171	Educational Services
74023	509	3740	Educational Services
74026	56	253	Educational Services
74027	23	70	Unclassified Establishments
74028	52	245	Educational Services
74029	212	1477	Educational Services
74030	192	1241	Educational Services
74031	16	198	Educational Services
74032	39	200	Educational Services
74033	189	1263	Educational Services
74034	6	10	Food and Beverage Stores
74035	144	1163	Justice, Pubic Order/Safety
74036	170	765	Educational Services
74037	489	2811	Paper Manufacturing
74038	36	100	Educational Services
74039	40	303	Computer & Electronic Prod Mfg
74041	54	306	Educational Services
74042	17	22	Exec., Legis., & Other Support
74043	12	41	Educational Services
74044	224	1238	Educational Services
74045	9	16	Exec., Legis., & Other Support
74046	4	9	Educational Services
74047	85	502	Educational Services
74048	268	1671	Educational Services
74050	6	11	Repair and Maintenance
74051	50	213	Utilities
74052	47	309	Educational Services
74053	115	544	Educational Services
74054	11	24	Oil and Gas Extraction
74055	871	7120	General Merchandise Stores
74056	358	1930	Exec., Legis., & Other Support
74058	225	1337	Educational Services
74059	144	904	Educational Services
74060	16	169	Educational Services
74061	38	339	Educational Services
74062	22	245	Educational Services
74063	919	8928	Primary Metal Manufacturing
74066	1039	9997	Social Assistance
74067	14	25	Special Trade Contractors
74068	7	6	Postal Service
74070	360	1921	Educational Services
74071	6	6	Prof., Scientific, & Tech Svcs
74072	58	718	Educational Services
74073	109	445	Educational Services
74074	1333	11521	Food Svcs & Drinking Places
74075	567	8270	Food Svcs & Drinking Places
74076	16	102	Prof., Scientific, & Tech Svcs
74077	1	2	Educational Services
74078	116	11609	Educational Services
74079	201	1722	Truck Transportation
74080	52	380	Computer & Electronic Prod Mfg
74081	16	65	Justice, Pubic Order/Safety
74082	3	3	Merch. Wholesalers,Durable Gds
74083	27	76	Construction of Buildings
74084	30	125	Educational Services
74085	72	363	Educational Services
74101	41	17	Administrative & Support Svcs
74102	2	10	Administrative & Support Svcs
74103	993	12599	Prof., Scientific, & Tech Svcs
74104	890	15855	Hospitals
74105	1623	8264	Food Svcs & Drinking Places
74106	382	3326	Educational Services
74107	832	12602	Machinery Manufacturing
74108	132	545	Special Trade Contractors
74110	416	4543	Primary Metal Manufacturing
74112	972	8634	General Merchandise Stores
74114	669	5778	Educational Services
74115	1025	10970	Fabricated Metal Product Mfg
74116	554	10905	Transportation Equipment Mfg
74117	28	4579	Computer & Electronic Prod Mfg
74119	756	9844	Insurance Carriers & Related
74120	625	9574	Justice, Pubic Order/Safety
74126	230	954	Educational Services
74127	414	6263	Hospitals
74128	362	3819	Special Trade Contractors
74129	567	4889	Food Svcs & Drinking Places
74130	39	199	Educational Services
74131	164	2915	Fabricated Metal Product Mfg
74132	180	1961	Support Act. for Transport.
74133	1685	21463	Food Svcs & Drinking Places
74134	265	5931	Credit Intermediation & Relatd
74135	1737	15491	Food Svcs & Drinking Places
74136	1865	27593	Ambulatory Health Care Svcs
74137	639	6404	Food Svcs & Drinking Places

ZIP CODE	2004 Total Firms	2004 Total Employees	TOP INDUSTRY RANKED on 2004 EMPLOYMENT
74145	1928	18965	Merch. Wholesalers,Durable Gds
74146	1284	18536	Administrative & Support Svcs
74147	25	52	Special Trade Contractors
74148	5	6	Truck Transportation
74149	2	0	Special Trade Contractors
74150	9	29	Administrative & Support Svcs
74152	16	28	Sportg Gds,Hobby,Book, & Music
74153	18	52	Truck Transportation
74155	20	991	Personal and Laundry Services
74156	2	1	Special Trade Contractors
74157	14	41	Merch. Wholesalers,Durable Gds
74158	18	34	Special Trade Contractors
74159	18	87	Electronics & Appliance Stores
74169	13	31	Telecommunications
74170	45	210	Administrative & Support Svcs
74171	6	1082	Educational Services
74172	22	7082	Pipeline Transportation
74186	1	12	Truck Transportation
74301	528	5543	Personal and Laundry Services
74330	88	410	Educational Services
74331	221	1317	Accommodation
74332	54	363	Gasoline Stations
74333	30	132	Educational Services
74335	5	5	Postal Service
74337	211	1378	Utilities
74338	87	351	Educational Services
74339	91	650	Educational Services
74340	69	152	Perform'g Arts, Spec. Sports
74342	14	37	Amusement, Gambling,& Recreat.
74343	91	515	Educational Services
74344	841	4716	Food Svcs & Drinking Places
74345	16	32	Administrative & Support Svcs
74346	287	2261	Exec., Legis., & Other Support
74347	105	615	Educational Services
74349	105	353	Educational Services
74350	94	373	Food Svcs & Drinking Places
74352	207	1228	Fabricated Metal Product Mfg
74354	772	9266	Relig., Grant, Civic, Prof Org
74355	4	4	Special Trade Contractors
74358	15	154	Leather & Allied Product Mfg
74359	15	240	Educational Services
74360	46	322	Educational Services
74361	714	8548	Machinery Manufacturing
74362	25	238	Nonmetallic Mineral Prod. Mfg
74363	50	365	Relig., Grant, Civic, Prof Org
74364	33	165	Animal Production
74365	155	841	Educational Services
74366	38	227	Crop Production
74367	9	20	Support Activities: Agr./For.
74368	7	36	Educational Services
74369	73	306	Educational Services
74370	86	373	Educational Services
74401	1260	12484	Hospitals
74402	15	28	Food and Beverage Stores
74403	995	12078	Paper Manufacturing
74421	125	583	Educational Services
74422	20	84	Educational Services
74423	25	91	Educational Services
74425	25	129	Educational Services
74426	305	1812	Educational Services
74427	52	175	Food Svcs & Drinking Places
74428	19	74	Educational Services
74429	344	1799	Educational Services
74430	31	338	Social Assistance
74431	21	162	Educational Services
74432	460	2365	Ambulatory Health Care Svcs
74434	221	1651	Administrative & Support Svcs
74435	121	513	Educational Services
74436	120	538	Food and Beverage Stores
74437	404	3032	Nonmetallic Mineral Prod. Mfg
74438	13	42	Justice, Pubic Order/Safety
74441	88	865	Bldg Matl & Garden Eqpmt Dlrs
74442	27	156	Educational Services
74444	3	7	Educational Services
74445	83	337	Educational Services
74446	27	175	Educational Services
74447	768	6551	Exec., Legis., & Other Support
74450	19	111	Educational Services
74451	78	912	Merch. Wholesalers,Nondur. Gds
74452	25	114	Educational Services
74454	52	376	Educational Services
74455	70	263	Educational Services
74456	6	103	Educational Services
74457	6	10	Heavy & Civil Eng. Construct'N
74458	3	2	Postal Service
74459	1	0	Exec., Legis., & Other Support
74460	14	99	Educational Services
74461	5	27	Educational Services
74462	343	2586	Ambulatory Health Care Svcs
74463	14	383	Justice, Pubic Order/Safety

ZIP CODE	2004 Total Firms	2004 Total Employees	TOP INDUSTRY RANKED on 2004 EMPLOYMENT
74464	1090	9876	Justice, Pubic Order/Safety
74465	15	281	Social Assistance
74467	485	3521	Prof., Scientific, & Tech Svcs
74468	8	48	Educational Services
74469	98	746	Educational Services
74470	52	279	Educational Services
74471	16	195	Social Assistance
74472	18	60	Educational Services
74477	5	6	Special Trade Contractors
74501	1327	12541	Bldg Matl & Garden Eqpmt Dlrs
74502	9	34	Heavy & Civil Eng. Construct'N
74521	15	53	Educational Services
74522	9	45	Waste Managmt & Remediat'n Svc
74523	358	1974	Hospitals
74525	417	4453	Credit Intermediation & Relatd
74528	3	2	Postal Service
74529	3	6	Educational Services
74530	6	10	Justice, Pubic Order/Safety
74531	32	110	Educational Services
74533	19	159	Educational Services
74534	2	13	Miscellaneous Store Retailers
74535	9	19	Merch. Wholesalers,Nondur. Gds
74536	112	394	Educational Services
74538	191	1350	Hospitals
74540	3	4	Prof., Scientific, & Tech Svcs
74543	6	8	Animal Production
74545	6	33	Special Trade Contractors
74546	28	195	Educational Services
74547	105	743	Educational Services
74549	5	5	Social Assistance
74552	29	165	Utilities
74553	48	206	Educational Services
74554	58	313	Food Svcs & Drinking Places
74555	15	161	Educational Services
74556	10	22	Repair and Maintenance
74557	8	33	Educational Services
74558	19	60	Bldg Matl & Garden Eqpmt Dlrs
74559	5	150	Educational Services
74560	17	124	Educational Services
74561	76	320	Educational Services
74562	25	128	Educational Services
74563	55	197	Educational Services
74565	28	250	Educational Services
74567	2	2	Prof., Scientific, & Tech Svcs
74569	38	491	Justice, Pubic Order/Safety
74570	29	166	Educational Services
74571	171	1201	Educational Services
74572	18	143	Educational Services
74574	22	66	Educational Services
74576	1	2	Postal Service
74577	8	112	Educational Services
74578	300	2303	Educational Services
74601	1271	15647	Pipeline Transportation
74602	18	175	Clothing & Cloth'g Acc. Stores
74604	259	1194	Nursing & Resid. Care Facilit.
74630	37	360	Nursing & Resid. Care Facilit.
74631	338	2698	Apparel Manufacturing
74632	27	147	Food Svcs & Drinking Places
74633	11	10	Postal Service
74636	6	24	Educational Services
74637	86	520	Educational Services
74640	13	29	Warehousing and Storage
74641	25	49	Educational Services
74643	27	113	Educational Services
74644	8	14	Animal Production
74646	4	9	Administrative & Support Svcs
74647	163	1003	Amusement, Gambling,& Recreat.
74650	18	33	Merch. Wholesalers,Durable Gds
74651	25	270	Educational Services
74652	57	240	Educational Services
74653	169	1318	Educational Services
74701	1332	10865	Educational Services
74702	8	34	Social Assistance
74720	22	134	Educational Services
74721	5	2	Nursing & Resid. Care Facilit.
74722	15	156	Educational Services
74723	31	123	Educational Services
74724	5	5	Postal Service
74726	52	254	Educational Services
74727	56	314	Educational Services
74728	505	5914	Food Manufacturing
74729	89	350	Educational Services
74730	96	611	Educational Services
74731	34	72	Food Svcs & Drinking Places
74733	90	464	Educational Services
74734	22	127	Educational Services
74735	36	301	Educational Services
74736	17	33	Food and Beverage Stores
74737	5	3	Special Trade Contractors
74738	14	84	Educational Services

BUSINESS DATA

ZIP CODE	2004 Total Firms	2004 Total Employ-ees	TOP INDUSTRY RANKED on 2004 EMPLOYMENT	ZIP CODE	2004 Total Firms	2004 Total Employ-ees	TOP INDUSTRY RANKED on 2004 EMPLOYMENT	ZIP CODE	2004 Total Firms	2004 Total Employ-ees	TOP INDUSTRY RANKED on 2004 EMPLOYMENT
74740	42	356	Educational Services	74956	45	156	Educational Services	75103	710	4153	Food Svcs & Drinking Places
74741	23	145	Animal Production	74957	34	320	Educational Services	75104	1015	7502	Food Svcs & Drinking Places
74743	507	4047	General Merchandise Stores	74959	171	1152	Educational Services	75105	3	7	Repair and Maintenance
74745	560	3968	Educational Services	74960	387	3892	Food Manufacturing	75106	27	48	Prof., Scientific, & Tech Svcs
74747	6	3	Relig., Grant, Civic, Prof Org	74962	128	713	Educational Services	75109	141	2639	Nonmetallic Mineral Prod. Mfg
74748	8	9	Merch. Wholesalers,Nondur. Gds	74963	8	23	Educational Services	75110	1386	11886	Educational Services
74750	16	38	Food and Beverage Stores	74964	58	291	Educational Services	75114	118	706	Educational Services
74752	4	8	Miscellaneous Store Retailers	74965	117	1179	Elect'l Eqpmt, App, & Comp Mfg	75115	1485	10250	Food Svcs & Drinking Places
74753	3	5	Postal Service	74966	82	459	Educational Services	75116	982	5897	Food Svcs & Drinking Places
74754	11	12	Relig., Grant, Civic, Prof Org	75001	2328	27533	Prof., Scientific, & Tech Svcs	75117	149	656	Educational Services
74755	8	16	Justice, Pubic Order/Safety	75002	960	6037	Educational Services	75118	1	1	Postal Service
74756	19	89	Mining (Except Oil and Gas)	75006	2855	39917	Merch. Wholesalers,Durable Gds	75119	856	9856	Fabricated Metal Product Mfg
74759	24	140	Educational Services	75007	1113	10286	Food Svcs & Drinking Places	75120	6	8	Clothing & Cloth'g Acc. Stores
74760	1	1	Postal Service	75009	209	1042	Heavy & Civil Eng. Construct'N	75121	9	46	Merch. Wholesalers,Durable Gds
74761	5	16	Educational Services	75010	283	3598	Hospitals	75123	25	29	Special Trade Contractors
74764	170	735	Educational Services	75011	47	124	Truck Transportation	75124	106	353	Educational Services
74766	56	799	Wood Product Manufacturing	75013	698	8115	Administrative & Support Svcs	75125	158	1192	Educational Services
74801	972	7670	Educational Services	75014	7	74	Merch. Wholesalers,Nondur. Gds	75126	552	3426	Paper Manufacturing
74802	9	61	Administrative & Support Svcs	75015	19	83	Special Trade Contractors	75127	23	268	Educational Services
74804	791	8801	Food Svcs & Drinking Places	75016	4	5	Prof., Scientific, & Tech Svcs	75132	35	58	Merch. Wholesalers,Durable Gds
74818	6	32	Truck Transportation	75017	11	27	Administrative & Support Svcs	75134	292	2641	Plastics & Rubber Products Mfg
74820	1404	14081	Educational Services	75019	896	10630	Food and Beverage Stores	75135	140	556	Educational Services
74821	21	51	Exec., Legis., & Other Support	75020	1103	10612	Hospitals	75137	560	7470	Furniture & Related Prod. Mfg
74824	27	108	Educational Services	75021	274	1303	Miscellaneous Store Retailers	75138	21	30	Real Estate
74825	68	321	Educational Services	75022	359	2586	Food Svcs & Drinking Places	75140	235	1855	Educational Services
74826	24	150	Educational Services	75023	1350	8214	Food Svcs & Drinking Places	75141	163	2140	Waste Managmt & Remediat'n Svc
74827	10	23	Construction of Buildings	75024	622	29833	Prof., Scientific, & Tech Svcs	75142	623	3569	Educational Services
74829	39	135	Educational Services	75025	504	2062	Educational Services	75143	483	1904	Educational Services
74830	16	130	Educational Services	75026	23	43	Special Trade Contractors	75144	99	437	Educational Services
74831	13	27	Educational Services	75027	22	91	Special Trade Contractors	75146	555	4622	General Merchandise Stores
74832	31	157	Educational Services	75028	852	7119	Educational Services	75147	283	1807	Educational Services
74833	13	34	Transportation Equipment Mfg	75029	22	195	Administrative & Support Svcs	75148	238	1591	Educational Services
74834	324	2519	Insurance Carriers & Related	75030	30	98	Repair and Maintenance	75149	1534	17164	Food Svcs & Drinking Places
74836	12	37	Animal Production	75032	434	2938	Educational Services	75150	2337	22801	Food Svcs & Drinking Places
74837	27	115	Educational Services	75034	1583	14148	Food Svcs & Drinking Places	75151	5	15	Food Svcs & Drinking Places
74839	30	87	Educational Services	75035	339	1684	Educational Services	75152	76	452	Educational Services
74840	27	181	Educational Services	75038	896	24245	Telecommunications	75153	14	40	Gasoline Stations
74842	26	155	Educational Services	75039	632	15640	Prof., Scientific, & Tech Svcs	75154	658	3338	Educational Services
74843	8	34	Truck Transportation	75040	1325	11646	Educational Services	75155	58	359	Educational Services
74844	10	37	Merch. Wholesalers,Nondur. Gds	75041	1428	16817	Merch. Wholesalers,Durable Gds	75156	468	2387	Food Svcs & Drinking Places
74845	26	111	Food Svcs & Drinking Places	75042	1414	15221	Fabricated Metal Product Mfg	75157	10	6	Bldg Matl & Garden Eqpmt Dlrs
74848	345	1892	Educational Services	75043	1164	7035	Educational Services	75158	73	448	Educational Services
74849	93	599	Ambulatory Health Care Svcs	75044	557	3240	Prof., Scientific, & Tech Svcs	75159	484	2660	Special Trade Contractors
74850	7	10	Nursing & Resid. Care Facilit.	75045	16	25	Merch. Wholesalers,Durable Gds	75160	1031	10397	Hospitals
74851	157	1084	Educational Services	75046	16	17	Prof., Scientific, & Tech Svcs	75161	93	807	Telecommunications
74852	33	134	Educational Services	75047	6	6	Prof., Scientific, & Tech Svcs	75163	71	264	Educational Services
74854	59	179	Nursing & Resid. Care Facilit.	75048	238	922	Food Svcs & Drinking Places	75164	3	5	Food and Beverage Stores
74855	93	568	Educational Services	75049	26	92	Administrative & Support Svcs	75165	1273	14138	Educational Services
74856	26	271	Mining (Except Oil and Gas)	75050	2346	31191	Merch. Wholesalers,Durable Gds	75166	23	75	Food Svcs & Drinking Places
74857	88	279	Relig., Grant, Civic, Prof Org	75051	1191	13984	Transportation Equipment Mfg	75167	108	922	Admin. of Economic Programs
74859	261	1567	Apparel Manufacturing	75052	1028	9314	Food Svcs & Drinking Places	75168	10	8	Construction of Buildings
74860	30	164	Educational Services	75053	32	88	Miscellaneous Manufacturing	75169	399	2143	Educational Services
74864	166	852	Nursing & Resid. Care Facilit.	75054	15	28	Prof., Scientific, & Tech Svcs	75172	65	762	Truck Transportation
74865	27	156	Educational Services	75056	752	6136	Prof., Scientific, & Tech Svcs	75173	78	562	Educational Services
74866	12	31	Special Trade Contractors	75057	977	13877	Merch. Wholesalers,Durable Gds	75180	576	4374	Special Trade Contractors
74867	25	133	Educational Services	75058	66	436	Nursing & Resid. Care Facilit.	75181	311	1243	Heavy & Civil Eng. Construct'N
74868	566	4804	Apparel Manufacturing	75060	1074	10342	Merch. Wholesalers,Durable Gds	75182	179	2076	Merch. Wholesalers,Durable Gds
74869	14	12	Accommodation	75061	1806	18108	Hospitals	75185	21	440	Relig., Grant, Civic, Prof Org
74871	69	361	Educational Services	75062	1903	27426	Motor Vehicle & Parts Dealers	75187	8	22	Administrative & Support Svcs
74872	114	613	Educational Services	75063	1063	21380	Prof., Scientific, & Tech Svcs	75189	348	1641	Educational Services
74873	252	1394	Educational Services	75065	316	2319	Telecommunications	75201	2736	51902	Prof., Scientific, & Tech Svcs
74875	29	57	Justice, Pubic Order/Safety	75067	1670	16982	Food Svcs & Drinking Places	75202	1170	17374	Prof., Scientific, & Tech Svcs
74878	36	115	Educational Services	75068	263	1443	Educational Services	75203	661	8604	Hospitals
74880	63	409	Educational Services	75069	1543	14759	Exec., Legis., & Other Support	75204	1703	15682	Prof., Scientific, & Tech Svcs
74881	79	520	Educational Services	75070	934	8599	Food Svcs & Drinking Places	75205	1379	9622	Prof., Scientific, & Tech Svcs
74883	107	619	Educational Services	75071	416	5864	Computer & Electronic Prod Mfg	75206	2450	16381	Food Svcs & Drinking Places
74884	289	2215	Exec., Legis., & Other Support	75074	2466	25697	Educational Services	75207	2170	27350	Accommodation
74901	65	312	Educational Services	75075	2001	20417	Food Svcs & Drinking Places	75208	1709	9837	Ambulatory Health Care Svcs
74902	149	1367	Heavy & Civil Eng. Construct'N	75076	320	1524	Educational Services	75209	890	10060	Motor Vehicle & Parts Dealers
74930	26	141	Educational Services	75077	630	4175	Educational Services	75210	230	2153	Food Svcs & Drinking Places
74931	7	66	Educational Services	75078	166	753	Educational Services	75211	1155	12499	Transportation Equipment Mfg
74932	34	220	Educational Services	75080	2613	26036	Educational Services	75212	756	11787	Merch. Wholesalers,Durable Gds
74935	6	28	Educational Services	75081	2612	22328	Merch. Wholesalers,Durable Gds	75214	1056	6379	Nursing & Resid. Care Facilit.
74936	17	60	Educational Services	75082	321	12017	Prof., Scientific, & Tech Svcs	75215	863	9912	Food Manufacturing
74937	161	744	Educational Services	75083	45	155	Transit & Grnd Pass. Transport	75216	1162	5748	Hospitals
74939	18	245	Justice, Pubic Order/Safety	75085	24	63	Special Trade Contractors	75217	1370	8784	Food and Beverage Stores
74940	34	205	Educational Services	75086	45	91	Administrative & Support Svcs	75218	991	6638	Hospitals
74941	59	268	Educational Services	75087	1179	8196	Food Svcs & Drinking Places	75219	2040	17285	Prof., Scientific, & Tech Svcs
74942	9	71	Educational Services	75088	855	6547	Food Svcs & Drinking Places	75220	2340	29480	Food Svcs & Drinking Places
74943	2	2	Postal Service	75089	188	1005	Educational Services	75221	19	30	Clothing & Cloth'g Acc. Stores
74944	34	101	Educational Services	75090	1639	16415	Food Svcs & Drinking Places	75222	23	20	Prof., Scientific, & Tech Svcs
74945	9	49	Educational Services	75091	12	56	Merch. Wholesalers,Durable Gds	75223	448	3638	Merch. Wholesalers,Durable Gds
74946	20	148	Merch. Wholesalers,Nondur. Gds	75092	584	5447	Hospitals	75224	934	4931	Food Svcs & Drinking Places
74947	4	22	Educational Services	75093	2150	23636	Food Svcs & Drinking Places	75225	2057	16704	Prof., Scientific, & Tech Svcs
74948	211	1564	Truck Transportation	75094	182	825	Food and Beverage Stores	75226	763	6075	Food Svcs & Drinking Places
74949	12	42	Support Activities: Agr./For.	75097	8	14	Furniture & Related Prod. Mfg	75227	955	7667	Special Trade Contractors
74951	65	305	Educational Services	75098	727	7030	Transportation Equipment Mfg	75228	1600	11136	Food Svcs & Drinking Places
74953	666	5583	Educational Services	75099	3	7	Nonstore Retailers	75229	2731	26450	Special Trade Contractors
74954	146	1786	Educational Services	75101	10	25	Bldg Matl & Garden Eqpmt Dlrs	75230	1789	17945	Prof., Scientific, & Tech Svcs
74955	583	4961	Educational Services	75102	8	12	Print'g & Related Supp't Act's	75231	2306	23263	Prof., Scientific, & Tech Svcs

ZIP CODE	2004 Total Firms	2004 Total Employees	TOP INDUSTRY RANKED on 2004 EMPLOYMENT	ZIP CODE	2004 Total Firms	2004 Total Employees	TOP INDUSTRY RANKED on 2004 EMPLOYMENT	ZIP CODE	2004 Total Firms	2004 Total Employees	TOP INDUSTRY RANKED on 2004 EMPLOYMENT
75232	494	2827	Educational Services	75440	262	1090	Food Svcs & Drinking Places	75633	729	5665	Food Manufacturing
75233	286	2278	Special Trade Contractors	75441	2	9	Credit Intermediation & Relatd	75636	4	3	Special Trade Contractors
75234	2224	33438	Prof., Scientific, & Tech Svcs	75442	236	1252	Educational Services	75637	3	20	Justice, Pubic Order/Safety
75235	1358	38986	Hospitals	75443	3	7	Prof., Scientific, & Tech Svcs	75638	223	1437	Educational Services
75236	294	8539	Merch. Wholesalers,Nondur. Gds	75444	23	62	Relig., Grant, Civic, Prof Org	75639	57	225	Special Trade Contractors
75237	800	11968	General Merchandise Stores	75446	126	537	Nursing & Resid. Care Facilit.	75640	65	461	Educational Services
75238	1531	15456	Special Trade Contractors	75447	17	172	Educational Services	75641	5	49	Machinery Manufacturing
75240	2554	30010	Prof., Scientific, & Tech Svcs	75448	13	23	Motor Vehicle & Parts Dealers	75642	33	389	Educational Services
75241	431	4470	Truck Transportation	75449	41	145	Educational Services	75643	28	226	Special Trade Contractors
75242	45	564	Admin. Enviro. Quality Progrms	75450	4	8	Construction of Buildings	75644	581	3608	Educational Services
75243	2681	29342	Computer & Electronic Prod Mfg	75451	19	66	Truck Transportation	75645	106	270	Educational Services
75244	1628	22057	Prof., Scientific, & Tech Svcs	75452	105	731	Educational Services	75647	440	3381	Educational Services
75246	320	8469	Hospitals	75453	71	298	Educational Services	75650	154	802	Mining (Except Oil and Gas)
75247	1785	41721	Administrative & Support Svcs	75454	111	719	Bldg Matl & Garden Eqpmt Dlrs	75651	52	371	Educational Services
75248	1899	12419	Prof., Scientific, & Tech Svcs	75455	1252	12109	Food Manufacturing	75652	609	4958	Justice, Pubic Order/Safety
75249	82	332	Food and Beverage Stores	75456	7	7	Special Trade Contractors	75653	10	20	Social Assistance
75250	4	1	Prof., Scientific, & Tech Svcs	75457	309	2200	Educational Services	75654	360	2451	General Merchandise Stores
75251	537	8734	Prof., Scientific, & Tech Svcs	75458	13	70	Educational Services	75656	162	1119	Nursing & Resid. Care Facilit.
75252	1196	9070	Prof., Scientific, & Tech Svcs	75459	117	677	Fabricated Metal Product Mfg	75657	404	2100	Educational Services
75253	255	1184	Special Trade Contractors	75460	1532	14969	Food Manufacturing	75658	2	0	Postal Service
75254	1511	17632	Food Svcs & Drinking Places	75461	5	11	Electronics & Appliance Stores	75659	5	77	Special Trade Contractors
75258	730	2109	Merch. Wholesalers,Durable Gds	75462	375	2666	General Merchandise Stores	75660	5	39	Administrative & Support Svcs
75260	3	3015	Postal Service	75468	12	82	Educational Services	75661	77	270	Educational Services
75261	206	37298	Air Transportation	75469	19	10	Motor Vehicle & Parts Dealers	75662	1110	11627	Educational Services
75263	1	2	Prof., Scientific, & Tech Svcs	75470	2	0	Electronics & Appliance Stores	75663	10	21	Special Trade Contractors
75265	2	0	Credit Intermediation & Relatd	75471	24	32	Relig., Grant, Civic, Prof Org	75666	4	7	Rental and Leasing Services
75266	1	0	Insurance Carriers & Related	75472	92	232	Primary Metal Manufacturing	75667	42	236	Educational Services
75270	146	4063	Prof., Scientific, & Tech Svcs	75473	77	312	Heavy & Civil Eng. Construct'N	75668	99	3727	Special Trade Contractors
75275	8	1944	Educational Services	75474	393	1902	Educational Services	75669	3	1	Sportg Gds,Hobby,Book, & Music
75283	1	0	Lessrs of Nonfin. Intang.	75475	3	5	Postal Service	75670	1153	9268	Educational Services
75285	1	0	Special Trade Contractors	75476	18	33	Food Svcs & Drinking Places	75671	11	25	Administrative & Support Svcs
75287	910	6219	Food Svcs & Drinking Places	75477	24	125	Educational Services	75672	472	4471	Merch. Wholesalers,Nondur. Gds
75301	9	3	Prof., Scientific, & Tech Svcs	75478	13	21	Food and Beverage Stores	75680	20	59	Utilities
75313	2	2	Prof., Scientific, & Tech Svcs	75479	53	336	Nursing & Resid. Care Facilit.	75681	88	308	Educational Services
75315	2	1	Construction of Buildings	75480	47	128	Construction of Buildings	75682	31	478	Educational Services
75336	4	26	Special Trade Contractors	75481	11	63	Educational Services	75683	124	711	Educational Services
75339	6	2	Truck Transportation	75482	1163	10132	Merch. Wholesalers,Nondur. Gds	75684	146	742	Petroleum & Coal Products Mfg
75342	1	2	Prof., Scientific, & Tech Svcs	75483	7	27	Merch. Wholesalers,Nondur. Gds	75685	9	24	Construction of Buildings
75354	5	13	Construction of Buildings	75485	7	13	Utilities	75686	499	3106	Food Manufacturing
75355	14	32	Truck Transportation	75486	31	276	Transportation Equipment Mfg	75687	18	312	Educational Services
75356	8	11	Utilities	75487	51	283	Oil and Gas Extraction	75688	9	435	Elect'l Eqpmt, App, & Comp Mfg
75357	6	9	Special Trade Contractors	75488	15	99	Crop Production	75689	25	84	Support Activities for Mining
75359	6	39	Social Assistance	75489	50	419	Educational Services	75691	117	1566	Utilities
75360	13	20	Sportg Gds,Hobby,Book, & Music	75490	54	375	Educational Services	75692	153	847	Transportation Equipment Mfg
75367	19	98	Educational Services	75491	143	562	Educational Services	75693	192	1633	Educational Services
75370	26	109	Transit & Grnd Pass. Transport	75492	12	14	Exec., Legis., & Other Support	75694	6	23	Oil and Gas Extraction
75371	1	2	Publishing Industries	75493	29	282	Mining (Except Oil and Gas)	75701	2119	27998	Hospitals
75372	12	20	Prof., Scientific, & Tech Svcs	75494	486	2827	Exec., Legis., & Other Support	75702	1831	19737	Exec., Legis., & Other Support
75374	22	31	Administrative & Support Svcs	75495	216	1119	Educational Services	75703	1539	13312	Food Svcs & Drinking Places
75376	18	29	Credit Intermediation & Relatd	75496	84	601	Print'g & Related Supp't Act's	75704	227	1610	Educational Services
75378	5	9	Transit & Grnd Pass. Transport	75497	104	379	Food Svcs & Drinking Places	75705	45	238	Special Trade Contractors
75379	27	55	Prof., Scientific, & Tech Svcs	75501	1518	14804	Hospitals	75706	221	6274	Prof., Scientific, & Tech Svcs
75380	20	99	Transportation Equipment Mfg	75503	1222	13783	Hospitals	75707	427	5605	Machinery Manufacturing
75381	24	49	Special Trade Contractors	75504	32	287	Bldg Matl & Garden Eqpmt Dlrs	75708	305	4533	Hospitals
75382	15	24	Prof., Scientific, & Tech Svcs	75505	8	7	Special Trade Contractors	75709	161	2032	Motor Vehicle & Parts Dealers
75390	75	10906	Ambulatory Health Care Svcs	75507	4	21	Construction of Buildings	75710	8	10	Support Activities: Agr./For.
75398	2	0	Postal Service	75550	15	145	Wood Product Manufacturing	75711	26	39	Special Trade Contractors
75401	831	7121	Hospitals	75551	534	4779	Relig., Grant, Civic, Prof Org	75712	4	5	Ambulatory Health Care Svcs
75402	743	11641	Transportation Equipment Mfg	75554	37	235	Educational Services	75713	25	150	Justice, Pubic Order/Safety
75403	7	73	Merch. Wholesalers,Nondur. Gds	75555	18	34	Bldg Matl & Garden Eqpmt Dlrs	75750	98	537	Educational Services
75404	4	19	Special Trade Contractors	75556	27	123	Educational Services	75751	1067	9276	Ambulatory Health Care Svcs
75407	237	1001	Educational Services	75558	26	382	Machinery Manufacturing	75752	145	582	Motor Vehicle & Parts Dealers
75409	137	1241	Merch. Wholesalers,Durable Gds	75559	157	929	Educational Services	75754	134	756	Bldg Matl & Garden Eqpmt Dlrs
75410	132	649	Educational Services	75560	27	134	Utilities	75755	206	1232	Sportg Gds,Hobby,Book, & Music
75411	19	23	Truck Transportation	75561	134	547	Educational Services	75756	114	605	Educational Services
75412	10	22	Merch. Wholesalers,Durable Gds	75562	5	14	Merch. Wholesalers,Durable Gds	75757	256	1111	Educational Services
75413	8	10	Relig., Grant, Civic, Prof Org	75563	219	1183	Educational Services	75758	219	837	Food and Beverage Stores
75414	92	386	Educational Services	75564	2	12	Support Activities for Mining	75759	8	20	Food and Beverage Stores
75415	5	2	Electronics & Appliance Stores	75565	9	92	Educational Services	75760	65	315	Educational Services
75416	90	291	Educational Services	75566	20	38	Educational Services	75762	249	780	Food and Beverage Stores
75417	81	475	Educational Services	75567	67	270	Educational Services	75763	211	986	Educational Services
75418	593	5352	Hospitals	75568	90	379	Transportation Equipment Mfg	75764	5	12	Relig., Grant, Civic, Prof Org
75420	16	15	Special Trade Contractors	75569	95	862	Fabricated Metal Product Mfg	75765	260	1330	Educational Services
75421	13	49	Utilities	75570	363	2925	Exec., Legis., & Other Support	75766	943	9796	General Merchandise Stores
75422	60	390	Educational Services	75571	82	493	Educational Services	75770	56	179	Educational Services
75423	55	172	Educational Services	75572	107	669	Educational Services	75771	533	3247	Educational Services
75424	65	320	Educational Services	75573	47	388	Educational Services	75772	25	37	Museums, Hist. Sites,& Similar
75425	6	7	Food and Beverage Stores	75574	29	264	Educational Services	75773	565	2942	General Merchandise Stores
75426	284	2099	Fabricated Metal Product Mfg	75599	1	14	Other Information Services	75778	81	215	Educational Services
75428	386	3625	Educational Services	75601	1552	13188	Hospitals	75779	25	192	Educational Services
75429	10	63	Other Information Services	75602	655	7472	Educational Services	75780	44	555	Bldg Matl & Garden Eqpmt Dlrs
75431	55	405	Transit & Grnd Pass. Transport	75603	238	4752	Chemical Manufacturing	75782	27	103	Petroleum & Coal Products Mfg
75432	176	1074	Transportation Equipment Mfg	75604	1522	11530	Special Trade Contractors	75783	391	2130	Educational Services
75433	72	331	Educational Services	75605	1161	11936	Food Svcs & Drinking Places	75784	13	148	Bldg Matl & Garden Eqpmt Dlrs
75434	5	3	Utilities	75606	14	112	Motor Vehicle & Parts Dealers	75785	299	3481	Hospitals
75435	48	180	Nursing & Resid. Care Facilit.	75607	10	65	Truck Transportation	75788	4	15	Justice, Pubic Order/Safety
75436	53	200	Educational Services	75608	14	29	Administrative & Support Svcs	75789	202	2279	Bldg Matl & Garden Eqpmt Dlrs
75437	7	17	Truck Transportation	75615	6	5	Special Trade Contractors	75790	175	1372	Accommodation
75438	12	52	Educational Services	75630	88	265	Educational Services	75791	400	2390	Educational Services
75439	18	63	Educational Services	75631	61	520	Educational Services	75792	89	410	Educational Services

BUSINESS DATA

ZIP CODE	2004 Total Firms	2004 Total Employ-ees	TOP INDUSTRY RANKED on 2004 EMPLOYMENT	ZIP CODE	2004 Total Firms	2004 Total Employ-ees	TOP INDUSTRY RANKED on 2004 EMPLOYMENT	ZIP CODE	2004 Total Firms	2004 Total Employ-ees	TOP INDUSTRY RANKED on 2004 EMPLOYMENT
75798	2	800	Educational Services	76010	1639	14695	Ambulatory Health Care Svcs	76132	905	12188	Food Svcs & Drinking Places
75799	1	575	Educational Services	76011	2277	38249	Prof., Scientific, & Tech Svcs	76133	1184	8414	Educational Services
75801	1111	10121	Hospitals	76012	1120	9317	Hospitals	76134	355	7460	Miscellaneous Manufacturing
75802	9	23	Special Trade Contractors	76013	1950	13414	Educational Services	76135	565	4390	Food Svcs & Drinking Places
75803	224	2622	General Merchandise Stores	76014	407	3606	Educational Services	76136	15	41	Administrative & Support Svcs
75831	226	1525	Construction of Buildings	76015	1370	12630	Food Svcs & Drinking Places	76137	731	13031	Food Svcs & Drinking Places
75832	15	252	Educational Services	76016	757	4519	Educational Services	76140	778	9991	Merch. Wholesalers,Durable Gds
75833	186	821	Educational Services	76017	1029	12953	Food Svcs & Drinking Places	76147	18	30	Prof., Scientific, & Tech Svcs
75834	2	0	Postal Service	76018	379	4181	Educational Services	76148	660	4959	Food Svcs & Drinking Places
75835	544	4134	Educational Services	76019	5	4083	Educational Services	76155	97	8206	Air Transportation
75838	21	45	Heavy & Civil Eng. Construct'N	76020	735	4451	Educational Services	76161	24	53	Isps, Web Search Portals
75839	123	599	Educational Services	76021	1238	10081	Food Svcs & Drinking Places	76162	5	4	Prof., Scientific, & Tech Svcs
75840	471	2742	Food Svcs & Drinking Places	76022	564	5689	Relig., Grant, Civic, Prof Org	76163	18	19	Special Trade Contractors
75844	157	1002	Fabricated Metal Product Mfg	76023	168	802	Special Trade Contractors	76164	5	6	Support Activities for Mining
75845	130	623	Educational Services	76028	1533	11884	Food Svcs & Drinking Places	76177	163	5236	Merch. Wholesalers,Durable Gds
75846	134	1925	Primary Metal Manufacturing	76031	496	4061	Transportation Equipment Mfg	76179	675	5980	Educational Services
75847	31	252	Educational Services	76033	1174	10591	Food Svcs & Drinking Places	76180	1919	19755	Food Svcs & Drinking Places
75848	9	13	Special Trade Contractors	76034	735	5163	Educational Services	76181	4	4	Prof., Scientific, & Tech Svcs
75849	13	233	Educational Services	76035	49	262	Chemical Manufacturing	76182	34	36	Prof., Scientific, & Tech Svcs
75850	27	65	Food and Beverage Stores	76036	409	2830	Educational Services	76185	28	45	Administrative & Support Svcs
75851	47	856	Justice, Pubic Order/Safety	76039	429	5412	Electronics & Appliance Stores	76196	14	474	Exec., Legis., & Other Support
75852	19	717	Justice, Pubic Order/Safety	76040	868	8336	Merch. Wholesalers,Durable Gds	76201	1638	16281	Educational Services
75853	42	64	Relig., Grant, Civic, Prof Org	76041	5	5	Special Trade Contractors	76202	27	36	Administrative & Support Svcs
75855	59	213	Construction of Buildings	76043	342	3483	Utilities	76203	5	253	Other Information Services
75856	12	29	Nonmetallic Mineral Prod. Mfg	76044	92	573	Educational Services	76204	4	5	Couriers and Messengers
75858	7	5	Food and Beverage Stores	76048	1005	6629	Food Svcs & Drinking Places	76205	877	11171	Justice, Pubic Order/Safety
75859	66	173	Special Trade Contractors	76049	727	3111	Motor Vehicle & Parts Dealers	76206	14	41	Special Trade Contractors
75860	196	1389	Justice, Pubic Order/Safety	76050	144	871	Educational Services	76207	237	4132	Transportation Equipment Mfg
75861	45	2962	Justice, Pubic Order/Safety	76051	1878	18189	Food Svcs & Drinking Places	76208	226	3234	Merch. Wholesalers,Durable Gds
75862	307	1707	Educational Services	76052	142	1004	Rail Transportation	76209	441	3346	Educational Services
75865	4	34	Relig., Grant, Civic, Prof Org	76053	1389	17956	Transportation Equipment Mfg	76210	445	8514	Computer & Electronic Prod Mfg
75901	1634	14321	Educational Services	76054	629	5752	Food Svcs & Drinking Places	76225	93	367	Educational Services
75902	8	62	Educational Services	76055	79	401	Waste Managmt & Remediat'n Svc	76226	226	1043	Educational Services
75903	2	0	Special Trade Contractors	76058	311	1963	Educational Services	76227	286	1169	Food Svcs & Drinking Places
75904	1091	13157	Hospitals	76059	106	1046	Educational Services	76228	26	120	Educational Services
75915	16	26	Special Trade Contractors	76060	449	3023	Special Trade Contractors	76230	540	3026	Ambulatory Health Care Svcs
75925	112	702	Educational Services	76061	11	67	Educational Services	76233	81	517	Educational Services
75926	37	200	Educational Services	76063	1332	11706	Merch. Wholesalers,Durable Gds	76234	719	5747	Hospitals
75928	22	147	Wood Product Manufacturing	76064	47	325	Educational Services	76238	11	151	Educational Services
75929	44	132	Educational Services	76065	618	5652	Primary Metal Manufacturing	76239	24	67	Educational Services
75930	21	78	Heavy & Civil Eng. Construct'N	76066	77	458	Educational Services	76240	1330	11014	Educational Services
75931	50	215	Educational Services	76067	855	7134	Educational Services	76241	13	24	Prof., Scientific, & Tech Svcs
75932	65	260	Educational Services	76068	4	13	Social Assistance	76244	14	35	Real Estate
75933	12	19	Food and Beverage Stores	76070	11	40	Animal Production	76245	70	232	Amusement, Gambling,& Recreat.
75934	6	612	Wood Product Manufacturing	76071	74	773	Relig., Grant, Civic, Prof Org	76246	5	8	Relig., Grant, Civic, Prof Org
75935	647	5906	Food Manufacturing	76073	67	414	Educational Services	76247	199	2607	Educational Services
75936	24	243	Relig., Grant, Civic, Prof Org	76077	13	39	Special Trade Contractors	76248	960	8652	Heavy & Civil Eng. Construct'N
75937	33	121	Educational Services	76078	129	1080	Educational Services	76249	125	538	Food Svcs & Drinking Places
75938	60	184	Educational Services	76082	376	1542	Educational Services	76250	26	234	Food Svcs & Drinking Places
75939	141	1335	Educational Services	76084	82	792	Unclassified Establishments	76251	49	182	Justice, Pubic Order/Safety
75941	192	2754	Forestry and Logging	76085	103	333	Special Trade Contractors	76252	179	1221	Food Svcs & Drinking Places
75942	3	4	Machinery Manufacturing	76086	1321	9758	Food Svcs & Drinking Places	76253	13	73	Special Trade Contractors
75943	23	97	Educational Services	76087	554	3296	Motor Vehicle & Parts Dealers	76255	263	1404	Educational Services
75944	33	95	Educational Services	76088	213	727	Special Trade Contractors	76258	257	1796	Educational Services
75946	108	552	Educational Services	76092	1174	12354	Administrative & Support Svcs	76259	64	236	Merch. Wholesalers,Durable Gds
75947	2	1	Postal Service	76093	65	412	Educational Services	76261	8	13	Educational Services
75948	285	1598	Ambulatory Health Care Svcs	76094	13	21	Prof., Scientific, & Tech Svcs	76262	581	4616	Motor Vehicle & Parts Dealers
75949	143	749	Educational Services	76095	25	63	Special Trade Contractors	76263	12	21	Construction of Buildings
75951	983	6938	Accommodation	76096	17	31	Perform'g Arts, Spec. Sports	76264	27	93	Educational Services
75954	74	525	Educational Services	76097	19	31	Prof., Scientific, & Tech Svcs	76265	60	235	Educational Services
75956	273	1188	Food and Beverage Stores	76098	17	41	Special Trade Contractors	76266	308	2478	Exec., Legis., & Other Support
75958	6	61	Educational Services	76099	34	99	Special Trade Contractors	76267	10	84	Educational Services
75959	46	109	Relig., Grant, Civic, Prof Org	76101	26	17	Other Information Services	76268	11	50	Educational Services
75960	10	11	Utilities	76102	2161	40014	Prof., Scientific, & Tech Svcs	76270	24	61	Special Trade Contractors
75961	942	8565	Food Manufacturing	76103	484	3858	Educational Services	76271	46	198	Food Svcs & Drinking Places
75962	10	1434	Educational Services	76104	1378	28400	Hospitals	76272	109	1022	Truck Transportation
75963	8	31	Special Trade Contractors	76105	518	4084	Educational Services	76273	259	1461	Educational Services
75964	570	5290	Telecommunications	76106	1564	17925	Food Svcs & Drinking Places	76301	1623	14999	Hospitals
75965	599	5807	Food Svcs & Drinking Places	76107	2286	24500	Ambulatory Health Care Svcs	76302	479	5153	Ambulatory Health Care Svcs
75966	212	1251	Educational Services	76108	653	16884	Ambulatory Health Care Svcs	76305	197	2447	Machinery Manufacturing
75968	65	525	Bldg Matl & Garden Eqpmt Dlrs	76109	859	9106	Insurance Carriers & Related	76306	524	4801	Educational Services
75969	69	1654	Educational Services	76110	1001	9072	Fabricated Metal Product Mfg	76307	6	5	Prof., Scientific, & Tech Svcs
75972	286	1894	Educational Services	76111	1012	9929	Merch. Wholesalers,Durable Gds	76308	1199	12668	Hospitals
75973	53	312	Educational Services	76112	1177	7203	Educational Services	76309	424	2576	Educational Services
75974	67	338	Educational Services	76113	4	2	Prof., Scientific, & Tech Svcs	76310	432	4507	Nonmetallic Mineral Prod. Mfg
75975	123	474	Educational Services	76114	715	4950	Educational Services	76311	71	724	Nat'l Security & Int'l Affairs
75976	49	302	Educational Services	76115	571	4521	Food Svcs & Drinking Places	76351	126	626	Educational Services
75977	8	21	Construction of Buildings	76116	2098	16011	Food Svcs & Drinking Places	76352	7	18	Utilities
75978	10	198	Educational Services	76117	1397	13238	Special Trade Contractors	76354	321	2094	Educational Services
75979	407	2314	Nursing & Resid. Care Facilit.	76118	651	7667	Prof., Scientific, & Tech Svcs	76357	15	91	Educational Services
75980	64	195	Educational Services	76119	1048	12017	Educational Services	76360	162	1055	Machinery Manufacturing
75990	1	3	Justice, Pubic Order/Safety	76120	270	3468	Merch. Wholesalers,Durable Gds	76363	9	62	Educational Services
76001	499	4368	Merch. Wholesalers,Durable Gds	76121	19	91	Food Svcs & Drinking Places	76364	11	84	Educational Services
76002	136	598	Educational Services	76122	1	1	Repair and Maintenance	76365	245	1196	Educational Services
76003	43	101	Special Trade Contractors	76123	134	810	Educational Services	76366	70	259	Educational Services
76004	48	124	Publishing Industries	76124	13	34	Publishing Industries	76367	306	2310	Paper Manufacturing
76006	692	7031	Prof., Scientific, & Tech Svcs	76126	461	3122	Food Svcs & Drinking Places	76369	15	27	Educational Services
76007	4	1	Administrative & Support Svcs	76127	28	611	Relig., Grant, Civic, Prof Org	76370	14	51	Justice, Pubic Order/Safety
76008	326	1486	Educational Services	76129	7	1612	Educational Services	76371	100	462	Educational Services
76009	406	2497	Merch. Wholesalers,Durable Gds	76131	190	7727	Rail Transportation	76372	38	200	Educational Services

ZIP CODE	2004 Total Firms	2004 Total Employees	TOP INDUSTRY RANKED on 2004 EMPLOYMENT
76373	8	5	Postal Service
76374	221	1926	Merch. Wholesalers,Nondur. Gds
76377	18	204	Educational Services
76379	24	53	Merch. Wholesalers,Nondur. Gds
76380	195	1298	Ambulatory Health Care Svcs
76384	620	5143	Hospitals
76385	1	2	Accommodation
76388	12	15	Support Activities: Agr./For.
76389	65	401	Educational Services
76401	1173	8676	Food Svcs & Drinking Places
76402	3	931	Educational Services
76424	555	2508	Educational Services
76426	473	4082	Oil and Gas Extraction
76427	24	131	Educational Services
76429	4	5	Food and Beverage Stores
76430	189	840	Educational Services
76431	87	728	Special Trade Contractors
76432	27	193	Educational Services
76433	34	75	Justice, Pubic Order/Safety
76435	25	94	Machinery Manufacturing
76436	11	9	Animal Production
76437	245	1242	Educational Services
76439	4	33	Amusement, Gambling,& Recreat.
76442	405	2865	Animal Production
76443	105	339	Educational Services
76444	235	1266	Merch. Wholesalers,Nondur. Gds
76445	20	24	Relig., Grant, Civic, Prof Org
76446	272	1382	Educational Services
76448	422	2947	Primary Metal Manufacturing
76449	178	1515	Social Assistance
76450	855	4485	Educational Services
76452	3	1	Animal Production
76453	46	200	Educational Services
76454	84	930	Merch. Wholesalers,Nondur. Gds
76455	30	140	Educational Services
76457	151	736	Educational Services
76458	330	1517	Educational Services
76459	3	14	Merch. Wholesalers,Durable Gds
76460	30	71	Truck Transportation
76461	6	84	Educational Services
76462	78	199	Educational Services
76463	19	105	Food Svcs & Drinking Places
76464	15	49	Educational Services
76465	6	20	Educational Services
76466	20	52	Justice, Pubic Order/Safety
76467	7	18	Animal Production
76468	31	55	Food and Beverage Stores
76469	8	18	Food and Beverage Stores
76470	158	757	Educational Services
76471	46	171	Nursing & Resid. Care Facilit.
76472	56	303	Educational Services
76474	14	43	Educational Services
76475	58	273	Educational Services
76476	72	303	Educational Services
76481	33	47	Prof., Scientific, & Tech Svcs
76483	90	376	Educational Services
76484	59	329	Justice, Pubic Order/Safety
76485	9	61	Educational Services
76486	31	223	Educational Services
76487	40	187	Educational Services
76490	5	3	Bldg Matl & Garden Eqpmt Dlrs
76491	23	74	Educational Services
76501	639	7209	Merch. Wholesalers,Durable Gds
76502	761	7808	Food Svcs & Drinking Places
76503	15	36	Special Trade Contractors
76504	1235	27458	Hospitals
76505	12	14	Special Trade Contractors
76508	11	2246	Ambulatory Health Care Svcs
76511	74	582	Educational Services
76513	1054	9042	Exec., Legis., & Other Support
76518	24	147	Educational Services
76519	11	23	Relig., Grant, Civic, Prof Org
76520	384	2312	Furniture & Related Prod. Mfg
76522	828	5661	Educational Services
76523	7	7	Special Trade Contractors
76524	58	505	Educational Services
76525	57	218	Educational Services
76526	4	1	Postal Service
76527	116	660	Educational Services
76528	544	3928	Exec., Legis., & Other Support
76530	63	364	Educational Services
76531	315	1969	Educational Services
76533	11	30	Special Trade Contractors
76534	61	476	Educational Services
76537	85	666	Educational Services
76538	28	91	Educational Services
76539	62	154	Construction of Buildings
76540	8	15	Administrative & Support Svcs
76541	1223	7667	Food Svcs & Drinking Places
76542	593	4651	Educational Services

ZIP CODE	2004 Total Firms	2004 Total Employees	TOP INDUSTRY RANKED on 2004 EMPLOYMENT
76543	793	8429	Educational Services
76544	222	5403	Unclassified Establishments
76547	8	26	Special Trade Contractors
76548	475	3569	Ambulatory Health Care Svcs
76549	232	3792	Educational Services
76550	578	3199	Educational Services
76554	45	236	Educational Services
76556	32	238	Educational Services
76557	105	497	Educational Services
76558	3	5	Construction of Buildings
76559	59	449	Educational Services
76561	19	114	Educational Services
76564	5	7	Merch. Wholesalers,Nondur. Gds
76565	10	7	Insurance Carriers & Related
76566	8	20	Merch. Wholesalers,Durable Gds
76567	403	3622	Merch. Wholesalers,Durable Gds
76569	68	548	Educational Services
76570	94	381	Educational Services
76571	311	1126	Educational Services
76573	4	98	Merch. Wholesalers,Nondur. Gds
76574	656	5413	Miscellaneous Manufacturing
76577	82	257	Educational Services
76578	27	227	Educational Services
76579	89	719	Primary Metal Manufacturing
76598	1	315	Exec., Legis., & Other Support
76599	2	31	Relig., Grant, Civic, Prof Org
76621	19	208	Educational Services
76622	12	78	Educational Services
76623	22	156	Merch. Wholesalers,Nondur. Gds
76624	55	356	Educational Services
76626	37	346	Educational Services
76627	38	144	Educational Services
76628	4	4	Utilities
76629	86	448	Educational Services
76630	32	150	Motor Vehicle & Parts Dealers
76631	12	55	Educational Services
76632	28	191	Educational Services
76633	111	446	Educational Services
76634	339	2060	Nursing & Resid. Care Facilit.
76635	42	413	Primary Metal Manufacturing
76636	30	194	Educational Services
76637	34	90	Educational Services
76638	58	253	Special Trade Contractors
76639	39	245	Educational Services
76640	134	721	Merch. Wholesalers,Durable Gds
76641	24	160	Educational Services
76642	285	1943	Educational Services
76643	293	2777	Insurance Carriers & Related
76644	3	5	Relig., Grant, Civic, Prof Org
76645	673	5504	Educational Services
76648	87	407	Educational Services
76649	26	123	Accommodation
76650	6	0	Crop Production
76651	92	691	Educational Services
76652	25	156	Educational Services
76653	40	265	Mining (Except Oil and Gas)
76654	17	23	Relig., Grant, Civic, Prof Org
76655	206	877	Educational Services
76656	59	241	Educational Services
76657	254	2781	Special Trade Contractors
76660	25	77	Food Manufacturing
76661	352	3080	Justice, Pubic Order/Safety
76664	99	596	Educational Services
76665	186	954	Educational Services
76666	4	16	Support Activities: Agr./For.
76667	515	5267	Educational Services
76670	29	97	Educational Services
76671	35	90	Educational Services
76673	15	55	Educational Services
76675	3	4	Real Estate
76676	5	33	Educational Services
76678	10	28	Educational Services
76679	24	31	Admin. Enviro. Quality Progrms
76680	10	43	Merch. Wholesalers,Durable Gds
76681	13	49	Exec., Legis., & Other Support
76682	57	281	Educational Services
76684	8	71	Unclassified Establishments
76685	3	0	Animal Production
76686	10	22	Mining (Except Oil and Gas)
76687	36	72	Heavy & Civil Eng. Construct'N
76689	92	533	Educational Services
76690	29	69	Educational Services
76691	259	1566	Educational Services
76692	325	2066	Educational Services
76693	55	409	Fabricated Metal Product Mfg
76701	837	9671	Justice, Pubic Order/Safety
76702	26	552	Postal Service
76703	15	11	Administrative & Support Svcs
76704	263	3951	Heavy & Civil Eng. Construct'N
76705	755	9104	Transportation Equipment Mfg

ZIP CODE	2004 Total Firms	2004 Total Employees	TOP INDUSTRY RANKED on 2004 EMPLOYMENT
76706	901	7828	Food Svcs & Drinking Places
76707	308	3660	Nat'l Security & Int'l Affairs
76708	499	7150	Hospitals
76710	1975	20176	Food Svcs & Drinking Places
76711	208	3856	Hospitals
76712	1043	20115	Administrative & Support Svcs
76714	13	19	Construction of Buildings
76715	2	2	Prof., Scientific, & Tech Svcs
76716	3	5	Construction of Buildings
76798	3	1912	Educational Services
76799	2	19	Exec., Legis., & Other Support
76801	1142	12004	Fabricated Metal Product Mfg
76802	240	1756	Educational Services
76804	9	37	Social Assistance
76820	1	1	Nonstore Retailers
76821	300	1759	Fabricated Metal Product Mfg
76823	81	554	Educational Services
76824	18	47	Construction of Buildings
76825	396	2793	Merch. Wholesalers,Nondur. Gds
76827	4	41	Educational Services
76828	16	18	Support Activities: Agr./For.
76831	3	7	Food and Beverage Stores
76832	48	140	Educational Services
76834	362	1796	Educational Services
76836	10	4	Support Activities: Agr./For.
76837	96	809	Justice, Pubic Order/Safety
76841	2	11	Animal Production
76842	7	23	Mining (Except Oil and Gas)
76844	209	1128	Relig., Grant, Civic, Prof Org
76845	6	8	Prof., Scientific, & Tech Svcs
76848	3	2	Special Trade Contractors
76849	263	1456	Educational Services
76852	11	36	Educational Services
76853	45	271	Educational Services
76854	11	13	Animal Production
76855	2	1	Personal and Laundry Services
76856	237	757	Food Svcs & Drinking Places
76857	32	165	Educational Services
76858	18	26	Merch. Wholesalers,Nondur. Gds
76859	145	591	Educational Services
76861	45	316	Animal Production
76862	10	24	Utilities
76864	46	113	Educational Services
76865	5	14	Support Activities: Agr./For.
76866	41	171	Educational Services
76869	4	4	Postal Service
76870	20	59	Educational Services
76871	43	114	Educational Services
76872	29	67	Educational Services
76873	4	5	Animal Production
76874	2	15	Bldg Matl & Garden Eqpmt Dlrs
76875	19	132	Food Manufacturing
76877	316	1661	Merch. Wholesalers,Nondur. Gds
76878	95	353	Educational Services
76880	18	72	Justice, Pubic Order/Safety
76882	9	44	Educational Services
76883	3	3	Animal Production
76884	18	103	Educational Services
76885	4	9	Food and Beverage Stores
76886	8	75	Educational Services
76887	21	153	Merch. Wholesalers,Durable Gds
76888	5	89	Exec., Legis., & Other Support
76890	24	84	Educational Services
76901	906	6606	Food Svcs & Drinking Places
76902	7	26	Social Assistance
76903	1886	16995	Ambulatory Health Care Svcs
76904	1143	10128	Food Svcs & Drinking Places
76905	165	2583	Miscellaneous Manufacturing
76906	7	27	Sportg Gds,Hobby,Book, & Music
76908	28	494	Nat'l Security & Int'l Affairs
76909	2	16	Ambulatory Health Care Svcs
76930	8	29	Justice, Pubic Order/Safety
76932	185	1216	Educational Services
76933	60	385	Educational Services
76934	16	31	Miscellaneous Manufacturing
76935	39	209	Educational Services
76936	146	774	Educational Services
76937	19	20	Support Activities: Agr./For.
76939	2	5	Support Activities for Mining
76940	6	16	Machinery Manufacturing
76941	69	363	Educational Services
76943	261	1174	Special Trade Contractors
76945	94	372	Educational Services
76949	5	18	Petroleum & Coal Products Mfg
76950	287	1657	Special Trade Contractors
76951	83	376	Educational Services
76953	1	0	Relig., Grant, Civic, Prof Org
76955	10	31	Merch. Wholesalers,Nondur. Gds
76957	12	123	Educational Services
76958	15	122	Educational Services

BUSINESS DATA

ZIP CODE	2004 Total Firms	2004 Total Employ-ees	TOP INDUSTRY RANKED on 2004 EMPLOYMENT	ZIP CODE	2004 Total Firms	2004 Total Employ-ees	TOP INDUSTRY RANKED on 2004 EMPLOYMENT	ZIP CODE	2004 Total Firms	2004 Total Employ-ees	TOP INDUSTRY RANKED on 2004 EMPLOYMENT
77001	48	105	Prof., Scientific, & Tech Svcs	77091	872	7228	Food Manufacturing	77325	37	118	Prof., Scientific, & Tech Svcs
77002	4205	103708	Prof., Scientific, & Tech Svcs	77092	2826	32298	Merch. Wholesalers,Durable Gds	77326	2	1	Relig., Grant, Civic, Prof Org
77003	662	10442	Food Manufacturing	77093	1151	8201	Special Trade Contractors	77327	816	5528	Educational Services
77004	1442	18123	Educational Services	77094	260	2784	Support Activities for Mining	77328	165	655	Special Trade Contractors
77005	1336	14323	Educational Services	77095	950	9685	Educational Services	77331	253	1362	Educational Services
77006	1558	10509	Food Svcs & Drinking Places	77096	1063	14264	Justice, Pubic Order/Safety	77332	5	58	Educational Services
77007	1765	19356	Prof., Scientific, & Tech Svcs	77098	2230	20243	Prof., Scientific, & Tech Svcs	77333	12	19	Food and Beverage Stores
77008	2235	20653	Prof., Scientific, & Tech Svcs	77099	1369	9812	Motor Vehicle & Parts Dealers	77334	5	7	Relig., Grant, Civic, Prof Org
77009	1190	9208	Educational Services	77201	1	80	Postal Service	77335	83	316	Educational Services
77010	380	8894	Prof., Scientific, & Tech Svcs	77204	7	278	Prof., Scientific, & Tech Svcs	77336	199	938	Relig., Grant, Civic, Prof Org
77011	735	6832	Machinery Manufacturing	77205	5	6	Transportation Equipment Mfg	77338	1595	16407	Food Svcs & Drinking Places
77012	423	7370	Relig., Grant, Civic, Prof Org	77206	9	15	Special Trade Contractors	77339	1338	11033	Educational Services
77013	351	5733	Truck Transportation	77207	12	16	Transit & Grnd Pass. Transport	77340	1168	16588	Exec., Legis., & Other Support
77014	824	4891	Prof., Scientific, & Tech Svcs	77208	6	3	General Merchandise Stores	77341	1	1	Prof., Scientific, & Tech Svcs
77015	1543	17828	Machinery Manufacturing	77210	4	36	Unclassified Establishments	77342	12	7	Special Trade Contractors
77016	574	3125	Educational Services	77213	7	7	Real Estate	77345	280	1983	Food and Beverage Stores
77017	993	9671	Educational Services	77215	12	33	Repair and Maintenance	77346	704	4898	Educational Services
77018	1406	13455	Special Trade Contractors	77217	2	14	Merch. Wholesalers,Durable Gds	77347	36	72	Special Trade Contractors
77019	1016	13243	Insurance Carriers & Related	77218	17	49	Prof., Scientific, & Tech Svcs	77350	13	141	Educational Services
77020	868	11468	Merch. Wholesalers,Durable Gds	77219	18	27	Prof., Scientific, & Tech Svcs	77351	1138	8208	Exec., Legis., & Other Support
77021	877	7132	Personal and Laundry Services	77220	3	6	Wholesale Elec. Mrkts & Agents	77353	6	9	Special Trade Contractors
77022	1138	11003	Admin. Human Resource Programs	77221	5	1	Miscellaneous Store Retailers	77354	582	3151	Educational Services
77023	835	15401	Administrative & Support Svcs	77222	8	9	Administrative & Support Svcs	77355	373	1619	Educational Services
77024	3342	31426	Prof., Scientific, & Tech Svcs	77223	6	8	Miscellaneous Manufacturing	77356	623	3884	Amusement, Gambling,& Recreat.
77025	806	7315	Food Svcs & Drinking Places	77224	6	12	Miscellaneous Manufacturing	77357	374	2419	Educational Services
77026	614	6162	Merch. Wholesalers,Durable Gds	77225	3	6	Credit Intermediation & Relatd	77358	108	887	Relig., Grant, Civic, Prof Org
77027	2900	29567	Prof., Scientific, & Tech Svcs	77227	21	64	Merch. Wholesalers,Durable Gds	77359	49	86	Justice, Pubic Order/Safety
77028	575	5122	Merch. Wholesalers,Durable Gds	77228	5	1	Prof., Scientific, & Tech Svcs	77360	204	619	Educational Services
77029	1077	15938	Merch. Wholesalers,Durable Gds	77229	6	9	Prof., Scientific, & Tech Svcs	77362	175	600	Special Trade Contractors
77030	1199	63348	Hospitals	77230	5	6	Real Estate	77363	78	3750	Perform'g Arts, Spec. Sports
77031	439	3046	Prof., Scientific, & Tech Svcs	77231	14	22	Merch. Wholesalers,Durable Gds	77364	38	81	Construction of Buildings
77032	1057	23575	Special Trade Contractors	77233	5	6	Prof., Scientific, & Tech Svcs	77365	537	3633	General Merchandise Stores
77033	477	3075	Educational Services	77234	5	10	Special Trade Contractors	77367	26	123	Food and Beverage Stores
77034	1068	10640	Food Svcs & Drinking Places	77235	10	7	Prof., Scientific, & Tech Svcs	77368	9	26	Insurance Carriers & Related
77035	1016	6584	Food and Beverage Stores	77236	4	10	Truck Transportation	77369	13	54	Justice, Pubic Order/Safety
77036	4324	22956	Prof., Scientific, & Tech Svcs	77237	2	5	Truck Transportation	77371	139	806	Educational Services
77037	984	7511	Motor Vehicle & Parts Dealers	77238	5	6	Merch. Wholesalers,Durable Gds	77372	255	1339	Educational Services
77038	391	2992	Educational Services	77240	8	23	Prof., Scientific, & Tech Svcs	77373	900	6102	Educational Services
77039	688	9260	Fabricated Metal Product Mfg	77241	7	22	Merch. Wholesalers,Durable Gds	77374	5	11	Special Trade Contractors
77040	1829	33487	Prof., Scientific, & Tech Svcs	77242	34	110	Real Estate	77375	1220	11022	Prof., Scientific, & Tech Svcs
77041	1934	33420	Merch. Wholesalers,Durable Gds	77243	8	9	Prof., Scientific, & Tech Svcs	77376	5	4	Repair and Maintenance
77042	2464	34674	Prof., Scientific, & Tech Svcs	77244	15	133	Prof., Scientific, & Tech Svcs	77377	440	2269	Food Svcs & Drinking Places
77043	1397	18642	Merch. Wholesalers,Durable Gds	77245	11	51	Managmt of Companies & Enterp.	77378	320	2524	Educational Services
77044	263	2397	Support Act. for Transport.	77248	4	3	Prof., Scientific, & Tech Svcs	77379	1657	10004	Educational Services
77045	690	5295	Educational Services	77249	4	11	Nonstore Retailers	77380	1816	20015	Food Svcs & Drinking Places
77046	481	13336	Pipeline Transportation	77251	24	2118	Oil and Gas Extraction	77381	530	8511	Prof., Scientific, & Tech Svcs
77047	317	3703	Special Trade Contractors	77252	11	8	Motor Vehicle & Parts Dealers	77382	204	1102	Food Svcs & Drinking Places
77048	217	2463	Educational Services	77253	8	18	Relig., Grant, Civic, Prof Org	77383	29	78	Construction of Buildings
77049	399	5469	Educational Services	77254	18	58	Miscellaneous Store Retailers	77384	199	2755	Educational Services
77050	84	1234	Heavy & Civil Eng. Construct'N	77255	11	23	Prof., Scientific, & Tech Svcs	77385	528	3719	Educational Services
77051	441	3439	Fabricated Metal Product Mfg	77256	7	43	Real Estate	77386	583	2857	Food Svcs & Drinking Places
77052	3	2	Prof., Scientific, & Tech Svcs	77257	27	106	Transit & Grnd Pass. Transport	77387	42	92	Administrative & Support Svcs
77053	275	1489	Food and Beverage Stores	77258	16	20	Prof., Scientific, & Tech Svcs	77388	791	5083	Special Trade Contractors
77054	1308	25257	Ambulatory Health Care Svcs	77259	16	52	Truck Transportation	77389	273	1689	Administrative & Support Svcs
77055	2753	26554	Merch. Wholesalers,Durable Gds	77261	1	50	Merch. Wholesalers,Durable Gds	77391	20	52	Perform'g Arts, Spec. Sports
77056	3376	59157	Prof., Scientific, & Tech Svcs	77262	1	4	Credit Intermediation & Relatd	77393	17	22	Prof., Scientific, & Tech Svcs
77057	4219	29225	Food Svcs & Drinking Places	77263	22	110	Prof., Scientific, & Tech Svcs	77396	530	5131	Justice, Pubic Order/Safety
77058	1681	23576	Space Research and Technology	77265	7	10	Real Estate	77399	3	112	Prof., Scientific, & Tech Svcs
77059	141	4586	Computer & Electronic Prod Mfg	77266	17	42	Prof., Scientific, & Tech Svcs	77401	1162	9503	Gasoline Stations
77060	2014	21108	Prof., Scientific, & Tech Svcs	77267	19	21	Prof., Scientific, & Tech Svcs	77402	31	103	Merch. Wholesalers,Durable Gds
77061	753	8999	Merch. Wholesalers,Durable Gds	77268	17	23	Special Trade Contractors	77404	5	33	Merch. Wholesalers,Durable Gds
77062	497	3695	Educational Services	77269	33	47	Real Estate	77406	13	44	Merch. Wholesalers,Nondur. Gds
77063	2309	16288	Prof., Scientific, & Tech Svcs	77270	18	45	Nonstore Retailers	77410	28	82	Prof., Scientific, & Tech Svcs
77064	763	9488	Perform'g Arts, Spec. Sports	77271	17	37	Isps, Web Search Portals	77411	19	39	Support Act. for Transport.
77065	947	10134	Food Svcs & Drinking Places	77272	15	44	Personal and Laundry Services	77412	11	146	Educational Services
77066	509	3956	Construction of Buildings	77273	9	95	Construction of Buildings	77413	113	104	Electronics & Appliance Stores
77067	482	7491	Merch. Wholesalers,Durable Gds	77274	10	24	Insurance Carriers & Related	77414	1125	7873	Educational Services
77068	854	11435	Electronics & Appliance Stores	77275	10	22	Merch. Wholesalers,Durable Gds	77415	7	4	Postal Service
77069	1141	7493	Food Svcs & Drinking Places	77277	30	40	Prof., Scientific, & Tech Svcs	77417	30	576	Fabricated Metal Product Mfg
77070	1906	15660	Food Svcs & Drinking Places	77279	15	36	Isps, Web Search Portals	77418	426	2872	Educational Services
77071	554	2812	Repair and Maintenance	77280	18	45	Administrative & Support Svcs	77419	56	171	Educational Services
77072	1351	8199	Prof., Scientific, & Tech Svcs	77282	20	98	Administrative & Support Svcs	77420	75	324	Educational Services
77073	597	9149	Special Trade Contractors	77284	28	75	Administrative & Support Svcs	77422	398	1736	Educational Services
77074	2235	25332	Hospitals	77287	6	11	Special Trade Contractors	77423	292	3209	Merch. Wholesalers,Durable Gds
77075	689	8791	Merch. Wholesalers,Durable Gds	77288	7	16	Relig., Grant, Civic, Prof Org	77426	54	248	Food and Beverage Stores
77076	843	6555	Hospitals	77289	18	26	Prof., Scientific, & Tech Svcs	77428	3	4	Relig., Grant, Civic, Prof Org
77077	1958	16614	Prof., Scientific, & Tech Svcs	77290	7	16	Administrative & Support Svcs	77429	1002	6320	Educational Services
77078	139	2383	Educational Services	77291	1	3	Special Trade Contractors	77430	49	164	Merch. Wholesalers,Nondur. Gds
77079	2198	22306	Prof., Scientific, & Tech Svcs	77292	25	43	Prof., Scientific, & Tech Svcs	77431	1	0	Postal Service
77080	1238	9023	Educational Services	77293	11	196	Administrative & Support Svcs	77432	7	31	Support Activities: Agr./For.
77081	2028	15483	Prof., Scientific, & Tech Svcs	77301	1766	13815	Food Svcs & Drinking Places	77433	229	1367	Educational Services
77082	1143	9489	Prof., Scientific, & Tech Svcs	77302	206	814	Educational Services	77434	192	1040	Hospitals
77083	1059	6366	Educational Services	77303	373	2856	Special Trade Contractors	77435	144	1196	Furniture & Related Prod. Mfg
77084	2207	19899	Prof., Scientific, & Tech Svcs	77304	866	10548	Hospitals	77436	6	2	Postal Service
77085	158	689	Educational Services	77305	41	87	Merch. Wholesalers,Durable Gds	77437	826	6705	Special Trade Contractors
77086	519	6154	Machinery Manufacturing	77306	158	1294	Educational Services	77440	11	371	Educational Services
77087	1398	15944	Prof., Scientific, & Tech Svcs	77315	2	5	Credit Intermediation & Relatd	77441	72	303	Educational Services
77088	708	4158	Educational Services	77316	167	668	Special Trade Contractors	77442	41	255	Merch. Wholesalers,Durable Gds
77089	787	8070	Hospitals	77318	213	1242	Special Trade Contractors	77443	12	46	Bldg Matl & Garden Eqpmt Dlrs
77090	1475	17219	Hospitals	77320	481	5545	Justice, Pubic Order/Safety	77444	13	69	Truck Transportation

ZIP CODE	2004 Total Firms	2004 Total Employ-ees	TOP INDUSTRY RANKED on 2004 EMPLOYMENT	ZIP CODE	2004 Total Firms	2004 Total Employ-ees	TOP INDUSTRY RANKED on 2004 EMPLOYMENT	ZIP CODE	2004 Total Firms	2004 Total Employ-ees	TOP INDUSTRY RANKED on 2004 EMPLOYMENT
77445	387	2819	Prof., Scientific, & Tech Svcs	77560	23	70	Food and Beverage Stores	77836	387	2182	Primary Metal Manufacturing
77446	53	1840	Educational Services	77561	49	461	Educational Services	77837	66	295	Educational Services
77447	121	903	Utilities	77562	217	1589	Educational Services	77840	1239	14546	Food Svcs & Drinking Places
77448	22	130	Chemical Manufacturing	77563	249	925	Educational Services	77841	2	2	Merch. Wholesalers,Durable Gds
77449	566	4537	Educational Services	77564	26	135	Educational Services	77842	18	42	Merch. Wholesalers,Durable Gds
77450	1477	10186	Food Svcs & Drinking Places	77565	395	22621	Food Svcs & Drinking Places	77843	25	8440	Educational Services
77451	18	109	Educational Services	77566	1023	8835	Food Svcs & Drinking Places	77844	2	1	Miscellaneous Manufacturing
77452	4	11	Machinery Manufacturing	77568	553	6372	Chemical Manufacturing	77845	824	8752	Prof., Scientific, & Tech Svcs
77453	6	104	Miscellaneous Manufacturing	77571	1028	15216	Chemical Manufacturing	77850	2	4	Prof., Scientific, & Tech Svcs
77454	6	24	Crop Production	77572	15	31	Administrative & Support Svcs	77852	21	76	Oil and Gas Extraction
77455	55	456	Educational Services	77573	1327	10500	Educational Services	77853	42	164	Special Trade Contractors
77456	31	176	Pipeline Transportation	77574	17	75	Nonstore Retailers	77855	9	24	Merch. Wholesalers,Nondur. Gds
77457	56	181	Food Svcs & Drinking Places	77575	612	4408	General Merchandise Stores	77856	161	894	Educational Services
77458	8	37	Food Svcs & Drinking Places	77577	35	140	Chemical Manufacturing	77857	10	76	Educational Services
77459	758	4863	Educational Services	77578	256	1377	Educational Services	77859	289	1876	Food Svcs & Drinking Places
77460	7	23	Educational Services	77580	118	1461	Chemical Manufacturing	77861	41	232	Educational Services
77461	225	1189	Educational Services	77581	1290	10471	Educational Services	77862	22	31	Special Trade Contractors
77463	27	1392	Petroleum & Coal Products Mfg	77582	28	160	Nonmetallic Mineral Prod. Mfg	77863	12	47	Food and Beverage Stores
77464	19	106	Educational Services	77583	224	2950	Exec., Legis., & Other Support	77864	388	2756	Crop Production
77465	241	1266	Educational Services	77584	554	4010	Food Svcs & Drinking Places	77865	43	78	Food and Beverage Stores
77466	15	83	Fabricated Metal Product Mfg	77585	23	186	Educational Services	77866	7	13	Merch. Wholesalers,Nondur. Gds
77467	6	96	Admin. of Economic Programs	77586	612	4878	Food Svcs & Drinking Places	77867	4	39	Educational Services
77468	3	2	Postal Service	77587	657	4522	Educational Services	77868	545	5636	Educational Services
77469	1408	12473	Educational Services	77588	12	103	Heavy & Civil Eng. Construct'N	77870	6	21	Food and Beverage Stores
77470	6	30	Justice, Pubic Order/Safety	77590	1074	12798	Petroleum & Coal Products Mfg	77871	107	299	Food Svcs & Drinking Places
77471	1166	9992	Educational Services	77591	335	3914	Hospitals	77872	36	111	Educational Services
77473	14	124	Merch. Wholesalers,Durable Gds	77592	8	15	Special Trade Contractors	77873	28	104	Educational Services
77474	464	4134	Merch. Wholesalers,Durable Gds	77597	34	116	Motor Vehicle & Parts Dealers	77875	3	15	Food and Beverage Stores
77475	20	105	Utilities	77598	1103	12652	Food Svcs & Drinking Places	77876	18	56	Unclassified Establishments
77476	89	406	Elect'l Eqpmt, App, & Comp Mfg	77611	330	1921	Educational Services	77878	53	485	Oil and Gas Extraction
77477	1855	26675	Plastics & Rubber Products Mfg	77612	203	1893	Educational Services	77879	118	683	Educational Services
77478	1978	31012	Special Trade Contractors	77613	40	284	Educational Services	77880	29	60	Museums, Hist. Sites,& Similar
77479	922	8397	Educational Services	77614	71	343	Educational Services	77881	5	17	Construction of Buildings
77480	174	937	Educational Services	77615	44	1605	Paper Manufacturing	77882	5	21	Support Activities: Agr./For.
77481	12	75	Merch. Wholesalers,Nondur. Gds	77616	13	43	Educational Services	77901	2226	22480	Educational Services
77482	52	440	Educational Services	77617	31	55	Accommodation	77902	8	3	Plastics & Rubber Products Mfg
77483	14	132	Administrative & Support Svcs	77619	424	3225	Food Svcs & Drinking Places	77903	14	18	Special Trade Contractors
77484	360	2065	Educational Services	77622	46	236	Educational Services	77904	992	9384	Food Svcs & Drinking Places
77485	76	279	Educational Services	77623	32	97	Educational Services	77905	379	3493	Merch. Wholesalers,Durable Gds
77486	261	1554	Educational Services	77624	14	81	Bldg Matl & Garden Eqpmt Dlrs	77950	7	22	Admin. Enviro. Quality Progrms
77487	38	71	Merch. Wholesalers,Durable Gds	77625	289	1553	Special Trade Contractors	77951	38	257	Educational Services
77488	629	4480	Educational Services	77626	79	267	Educational Services	77954	440	3745	Exec., Legis., & Other Support
77489	592	3210	Educational Services	77627	1072	8037	Food Svcs & Drinking Places	77957	384	2185	Food Svcs & Drinking Places
77491	26	54	Administrative & Support Svcs	77629	35	82	Merch. Wholesalers,Durable Gds	77960	4	7	Miscellaneous Store Retailers
77492	14	79	Food Svcs & Drinking Places	77630	1211	12268	Educational Services	77962	147	928	Educational Services
77493	589	3686	Educational Services	77631	5	8	Credit Intermediation & Relatd	77963	269	1125	Educational Services
77494	633	6311	Educational Services	77632	402	2922	Paper Manufacturing	77964	381	2572	Educational Services
77496	23	43	Construction of Buildings	77639	17	145	Merch. Wholesalers,Durable Gds	77967	1	1	Postal Service
77497	24	75	Prof., Scientific, & Tech Svcs	77640	665	8771	Educational Services	77968	40	170	Educational Services
77501	6	19	Administrative & Support Svcs	77641	1	0	Special Trade Contractors	77969	2	1	Food and Beverage Stores
77502	1103	9128	Educational Services	77642	1092	12080	Hospitals	77970	26	76	Educational Services
77503	549	6372	Chemical Manufacturing	77643	3	2	Special Trade Contractors	77971	27	2687	Paper Manufacturing
77504	856	8603	Ambulatory Health Care Svcs	77650	170	598	Food Svcs & Drinking Places	77973	6	3	Food Svcs & Drinking Places
77505	695	8492	Educational Services	77651	358	3947	Chemical Manufacturing	77974	9	69	Educational Services
77506	815	10369	Educational Services	77655	55	559	Special Trade Contractors	77975	93	454	Relig., Grant, Civic, Prof Org
77507	78	4352	Chemical Manufacturing	77656	561	3996	Educational Services	77976	12	233	Utilities
77508	13	44	Special Trade Contractors	77657	488	2258	Food Svcs & Drinking Places	77977	10	74	Educational Services
77510	340	1871	Educational Services	77659	158	758	Educational Services	77978	62	3894	Chemical Manufacturing
77511	1259	12496	Educational Services	77660	38	117	Educational Services	77979	668	5516	Ambulatory Health Care Svcs
77512	9	20	Special Trade Contractors	77661	16	53	Heavy & Civil Eng. Construct'N	77982	106	349	Food Svcs & Drinking Places
77514	251	1601	Exec., Legis., & Other Support	77662	905	6197	Educational Services	77983	89	1424	Chemical Manufacturing
77515	1015	9944	Exec., Legis., & Other Support	77663	35	156	Accommodation	77984	184	2538	Fabricated Metal Product Mfg
77516	7	15	Amusement, Gambling,& Recreat.	77664	50	404	Educational Services	77986	3	1	Postal Service
77517	85	246	Special Trade Contractors	77665	259	1715	Food Svcs & Drinking Places	77987	9	28	Educational Services
77518	178	680	Food Svcs & Drinking Places	77670	4	14	Special Trade Contractors	77988	19	75	Special Trade Contractors
77519	31	127	Wood Product Manufacturing	77701	1471	18845	Hospitals	77989	7	24	Pipeline Transportation
77520	1422	13371	Educational Services	77702	534	7464	Hospitals	77990	30	187	Educational Services
77521	1098	13501	Food Svcs & Drinking Places	77703	421	3530	Educational Services	77991	19	176	Educational Services
77522	20	113	Special Trade Contractors	77704	6	28	Administrative & Support Svcs	77993	4	12	Food Svcs & Drinking Places
77530	675	8402	Chemical Manufacturing	77705	962	15320	Educational Services	77994	26	55	Educational Services
77531	584	6157	Special Trade Contractors	77706	1297	12379	Amusement, Gambling,& Recreat.	77995	351	3361	Leather & Allied Product Mfg
77532	485	2994	Educational Services	77707	847	9533	Ambulatory Health Care Svcs	78001	24	27	Animal Production
77533	25	116	Food and Beverage Stores	77708	328	3056	Food Svcs & Drinking Places	78002	90	368	Merch. Wholesalers,Nondur. Gds
77534	67	421	Educational Services	77710	2	25	Publishing Industries	78003	457	2080	Educational Services
77535	475	3727	Justice, Pubic Order/Safety	77713	249	2547	Motor Vehicle & Parts Dealers	78004	16	25	Animal Production
77536	822	10558	Chemical Manufacturing	77720	11	48	Pipeline Transportation	78005	16	74	Bldg Matl & Garden Eqpmt Dlrs
77538	26	136	Educational Services	77725	2	3	Miscellaneous Store Retailers	78006	1161	7920	Food Svcs & Drinking Places
77539	739	4756	Educational Services	77726	24	69	Special Trade Contractors	78007	4	7	Food and Beverage Stores
77541	767	14751	Chemical Manufacturing	77801	396	3302	Fabricated Metal Product Mfg	78008	18	70	Animal Production
77542	7	5	Construction of Buildings	77802	1132	13198	Hospitals	78009	247	1322	Food Svcs & Drinking Places
77545	102	727	Museums, Hist. Sites,& Similar	77803	978	8850	Food Manufacturing	78010	119	594	Educational Services
77546	1415	11139	Food Svcs & Drinking Places	77805	27	60	Special Trade Contractors	78011	50	355	Educational Services
77547	169	2623	Educational Services	77806	4	3	Merch. Wholesalers,Durable Gds	78012	13	294	Utilities
77549	25	31	Prof., Scientific, & Tech Svcs	77807	143	2568	Heavy & Civil Eng. Construct'N	78013	261	897	Educational Services
77550	1539	16034	Insurance Carriers & Related	77808	347	1998	Special Trade Contractors	78014	215	1096	Educational Services
77551	738	6053	Food Svcs & Drinking Places	77830	96	565	Educational Services	78015	114	507	Relig., Grant, Civic, Prof Org
77552	15	18	Administrative & Support Svcs	77831	46	94	Justice, Pubic Order/Safety	78016	294	1636	Educational Services
77553	9	334	Educational Services	77833	1317	15073	Educational Services	78017	126	1141	Justice, Pubic Order/Safety
77554	479	3605	Accommodation	77834	16	39	Special Trade Contractors	78019	31	429	Pipeline Transportation
77555	43	2753	Hospitals	77835	77	305	Educational Services	78021	16	10	Truck Transportation

BUSINESS DATA

ZIP CODE	2004 Total Firms	2004 Total Employ-ees	TOP INDUSTRY RANKED on 2004 EMPLOYMENT	ZIP CODE	2004 Total Firms	2004 Total Employ-ees	TOP INDUSTRY RANKED on 2004 EMPLOYMENT	ZIP CODE	2004 Total Firms	2004 Total Employ-ees	TOP INDUSTRY RANKED on 2004 EMPLOYMENT
78022	239	984	Food Svcs & Drinking Places	78207	1457	29550	Hospitals	78357	160	1204	Special Trade Contractors
78023	407	2879	Special Trade Contractors	78208	134	1678	Educational Services	78358	91	327	Food Svcs & Drinking Places
78024	95	794	Accommodation	78209	2643	19865	Food Svcs & Drinking Places	78359	43	727	Chemical Manufacturing
78025	242	1051	Educational Services	78210	769	6499	Educational Services	78360	1	2	Crop Production
78026	214	1468	Ambulatory Health Care Svcs	78211	703	5672	Educational Services	78361	235	1283	Educational Services
78027	20	46	Fishing, Hunting and Trapping	78212	1946	18376	Educational Services	78362	252	3420	Fabricated Metal Product Mfg
78028	2117	16463	Hospitals	78213	1358	9055	Educational Services	78363	1004	8609	Educational Services
78029	47	128	Administrative & Support Svcs	78214	573	5013	Educational Services	78364	4	48	Support Act. for Transport.
78039	48	215	Educational Services	78215	435	5541	Ambulatory Health Care Svcs	78368	257	1602	Educational Services
78040	1819	14135	Educational Services	78216	4271	48888	Prof., Scientific, & Tech Svcs	78369	51	127	Oil and Gas Extraction
78041	2593	27928	Educational Services	78217	2643	25078	Prof., Scientific, & Tech Svcs	78370	75	361	Food Svcs & Drinking Places
78042	4	37	Animal Production	78218	1256	15204	Food Svcs & Drinking Places	78371	6	55	Educational Services
78043	777	6325	Educational Services	78219	854	20431	Merch. Wholesalers,Durable Gds	78372	113	476	Educational Services
78044	12	139	Truck Transportation	78220	430	4403	Educational Services	78373	421	2419	Real Estate
78045	1377	14016	Support Act. for Transport.	78221	901	9214	Nonmetallic Mineral Prod. Mfg	78374	397	2659	Educational Services
78046	328	3922	Educational Services	78222	473	5431	Machinery Manufacturing	78375	122	721	Educational Services
78050	10	73	Educational Services	78223	879	26184	Admin. of Economic Programs	78376	5	26	Educational Services
78052	170	1131	Educational Services	78224	496	7837	Educational Services	78377	256	1558	Special Trade Contractors
78054	6	36	Social Assistance	78225	220	1580	Food Svcs & Drinking Places	78379	82	367	Food Svcs & Drinking Places
78055	82	296	Educational Services	78226	192	2871	Computer & Electronic Prod Mfg	78380	541	4193	Educational Services
78056	15	82	Food Svcs & Drinking Places	78227	940	13496	Prof., Scientific, & Tech Svcs	78381	13	37	Prof., Scientific, & Tech Svcs
78057	9	23	Machinery Manufacturing	78228	1394	11084	Educational Services	78382	1012	4940	Educational Services
78058	45	143	Amusement, Gambling,& Recreat.	78229	1963	35915	Hospitals	78383	50	230	Telecommunications
78059	56	475	Educational Services	78230	1895	19549	Food Svcs & Drinking Places	78384	146	1610	Educational Services
78060	3	17	Food Svcs & Drinking Places	78231	226	1321	Social Assistance	78385	16	110	Animal Production
78061	369	2346	Educational Services	78232	1863	16384	Food Svcs & Drinking Places	78387	363	2110	Social Assistance
78062	2	8	Merch. Wholesalers,Durable Gds	78233	1121	9977	Special Trade Contractors	78389	35	266	Educational Services
78063	222	514	Educational Services	78234	94	2910	Hospitals	78390	129	769	Hospitals
78064	505	3631	Educational Services	78235	37	415	Ambulatory Health Care Svcs	78391	7	38	Warehousing and Storage
78065	135	671	Educational Services	78236	113	12118	Ambulatory Health Care Svcs	78393	85	483	Educational Services
78066	15	20	Mining (Except Oil and Gas)	78237	703	5653	Educational Services	78401	1108	14145	Justice, Pubic Order/Safety
78067	17	65	Educational Services	78238	1676	23506	Prof., Scientific, & Tech Svcs	78402	79	1062	Amusement, Gambling,& Recreat.
78069	79	552	Educational Services	78239	413	3545	Nursing & Resid. Care Facilit.	78403	16	102	Construction of Buildings
78070	253	1157	Educational Services	78240	938	8607	Ambulatory Health Care Svcs	78404	796	8173	Hospitals
78071	157	1112	Petroleum & Coal Products Mfg	78242	186	1514	Educational Services	78405	768	12812	Hospitals
78072	74	255	Educational Services	78243	2	29	Repair and Maintenance	78406	83	1360	Support Act. for Transport.
78073	121	665	Food Svcs & Drinking Places	78244	260	2547	Educational Services	78407	96	2843	Petroleum & Coal Products Mfg
78074	12	34	Justice, Pubic Order/Safety	78245	304	5351	Credit Intermediation & Relatd	78408	786	8575	Merch. Wholesalers,Durable Gds
78075	5	23	Food and Beverage Stores	78246	22	40	Prof., Scientific, & Tech Svcs	78409	303	7731	Construction of Buildings
78076	409	2926	Educational Services	78247	1059	11886	Educational Services	78410	750	6192	Educational Services
78101	164	508	Food Svcs & Drinking Places	78248	275	1235	Food and Beverage Stores	78411	2038	21002	Food Svcs & Drinking Places
78102	807	8322	Exec., Legis., & Other Support	78249	884	21006	Administrative & Support Svcs	78412	1107	8516	Hospitals
78104	3	4	Heavy & Civil Eng. Construct'N	78250	786	6193	Educational Services	78413	956	6070	Food Svcs & Drinking Places
78107	7	9	Administrative & Support Svcs	78251	528	10754	Amusement, Gambling,& Recreat.	78414	376	2690	Ambulatory Health Care Svcs
78108	183	1300	Educational Services	78252	71	1587	Merch. Wholesalers,Nondur. Gds	78415	1287	12985	Administrative & Support Svcs
78109	382	3453	Educational Services	78253	157	883	Educational Services	78416	308	5079	Educational Services
78112	87	547	Merch. Wholesalers,Durable Gds	78254	288	1812	General Merchandise Stores	78417	162	1904	Food Svcs & Drinking Places
78113	53	189	Food and Beverage Stores	78255	162	588	Personal and Laundry Services	78418	839	4727	Food Svcs & Drinking Places
78114	493	3127	Educational Services	78256	63	509	Special Trade Contractors	78419	32	455	Support Act. for Transport.
78115	9	12	Food and Beverage Stores	78257	228	3766	Merch. Wholesalers,Durable Gds	78426	5	18	Special Trade Contractors
78116	8	22	Justice, Pubic Order/Safety	78258	919	7774	Ambulatory Health Care Svcs	78427	20	53	Social Assistance
78117	6	12	Elect'l Eqpmt, App, & Comp Mfg	78259	205	2525	Publishing Industries	78460	4	7	Special Trade Contractors
78118	192	1180	Educational Services	78260	71	314	Educational Services	78463	5	16	Prof., Scientific, & Tech Svcs
78119	227	2431	Justice, Pubic Order/Safety	78261	20	125	Food Svcs & Drinking Places	78465	3	7	Rental and Leasing Services
78121	168	973	Educational Services	78263	176	2151	Educational Services	78466	10	18	Heavy & Civil Eng. Construct'N
78122	12	4	Sportg Gds,Hobby,Book, & Music	78264	152	430	Special Trade Contractors	78467	11	24	Administrative & Support Svcs
78123	70	770	Nonmetallic Mineral Prod. Mfg	78265	31	36	Administrative & Support Svcs	78468	22	52	Miscellaneous Store Retailers
78124	114	617	Special Trade Contractors	78266	251	2630	Special Trade Contractors	78469	12	32	Merch. Wholesalers,Nondur. Gds
78125	4	1	Food and Beverage Stores	78268	28	55	Rental and Leasing Services	78470	54	474	Prof., Scientific, & Tech Svcs
78130	2225	22024	Food Svcs & Drinking Places	78269	39	123	Prof., Scientific, & Tech Svcs	78471	100	705	Prof., Scientific, & Tech Svcs
78131	24	60	Prof., Scientific, & Tech Svcs	78270	40	183	Administrative & Support Svcs	78472	7	42	Administrative & Support Svcs
78132	416	4120	Merch. Wholesalers,Durable Gds	78278	37	66	Prof., Scientific, & Tech Svcs	78473	75	241	Prof., Scientific, & Tech Svcs
78133	614	1705	Relig., Grant, Civic, Prof Org	78279	26	45	Administrative & Support Svcs	78475	98	563	Support Activities for Mining
78135	1	512	Print'g & Related Supp't Act's	78280	12	17	Administrative & Support Svcs	78476	97	465	Prof., Scientific, & Tech Svcs
78140	89	559	Food Manufacturing	78283	2	2	Prof., Scientific, & Tech Svcs	78477	80	498	Credit Intermediation & Relatd
78141	16	96	Relig., Grant, Civic, Prof Org	78284	46	8713	Educational Services	78478	49	954	Administrative & Support Svcs
78142	4	2	Special Trade Contractors	78288	12	13045	Insurance Carriers & Related	78480	8	100	Museums, Hist. Sites,& Similar
78144	5	6	Prof., Scientific, & Tech Svcs	78291	3	6	Personal and Laundry Services	78501	3307	27353	Educational Services
78145	10	40	Educational Services	78292	1	0	Motion Pict. & Sound Recording	78502	30	81	Unclassified Establishments
78146	29	199	Nursing & Resid. Care Facilit.	78293	5	13	Administrative & Support Svcs	78503	1008	17900	Hospitals
78147	65	601	Relig., Grant, Civic, Prof Org	78297	3	3	Prof., Scientific, & Tech Svcs	78504	1552	15605	Administrative & Support Svcs
78148	642	6237	Nonstore Retailers	78299	1	2	Prof., Scientific, & Tech Svcs	78505	2	0	Special Trade Contractors
78150	51	757	Merch. Wholesalers,Durable Gds	78330	33	283	Educational Services	78516	409	3339	Educational Services
78151	44	223	Educational Services	78332	1160	13142	Support Activities for Mining	78520	2092	20150	Educational Services
78152	50	100	Special Trade Contractors	78333	3	5	Special Trade Contractors	78521	2189	23670	Educational Services
78154	696	7779	Food Svcs & Drinking Places	78335	4	5	Prof., Scientific, & Tech Svcs	78522	2	0	Special Trade Contractors
78155	1614	15062	Transportation Equipment Mfg	78336	503	4399	Miscellaneous Manufacturing	78523	8	20	Social Assistance
78156	10	23	Relig., Grant, Civic, Prof Org	78339	20	270	Educational Services	78526	585	6578	Food Svcs & Drinking Places
78159	29	85	Merch. Wholesalers,Durable Gds	78340	11	24	Food Svcs & Drinking Places	78535	27	168	Educational Services
78160	108	444	Educational Services	78341	61	379	Support Activities for Mining	78536	6	34	Petroleum & Coal Products Mfg
78161	16	18	Food and Beverage Stores	78342	12	258	Educational Services	78537	473	4386	Educational Services
78162	10	31	Prof., Scientific, & Tech Svcs	78343	94	439	Exec., Legis., & Other Support	78538	106	1531	Educational Services
78163	348	1083	Educational Services	78344	20	181	Educational Services	78539	1809	19570	Educational Services
78164	157	725	Special Trade Contractors	78347	7	13	Crop Production	78540	17	193	Special Trade Contractors
78201	1766	13813	Food Svcs & Drinking Places	78349	21	40	Exec., Legis., & Other Support	78541	480	7436	Educational Services
78202	280	2535	Educational Services	78350	3	3	Food and Beverage Stores	78543	164	1251	Educational Services
78203	155	1453	Food Manufacturing	78351	17	238	Educational Services	78545	30	111	Prof., Scientific, & Tech Svcs
78204	535	7238	Food and Beverage Stores	78352	10	42	Merch. Wholesalers,Durable Gds	78547	12	117	Educational Services
78205	1952	31915	Prof., Scientific, & Tech Svcs	78353	35	96	Animal Production	78548	20	240	Educational Services
78206	17	181	Justice, Pubic Order/Safety	78355	299	1948	Educational Services	78549	14	90	Educational Services

ZIP CODE	2004 Total Firms	2004 Total Employees	TOP INDUSTRY RANKED on 2004 EMPLOYMENT
78550	2431	25874	Hospitals
78551	9	9	Real Estate
78552	603	6583	General Merchandise Stores
78553	11	26	Construction of Buildings
78557	490	7725	Miscellaneous Store Retailers
78558	16	52	Food and Beverage Stores
78559	212	1416	Educational Services
78560	70	1308	Educational Services
78561	19	83	Educational Services
78562	21	392	Educational Services
78563	15	63	Animal Production
78564	7	24	Petroleum & Coal Products Mfg
78565	4	2	Food and Beverage Stores
78566	238	2054	Educational Services
78567	25	3071	Unclassified Establishments
78568	1	2	Postal Service
78569	62	308	Crop Production
78570	470	4427	Educational Services
78572	2033	17830	Educational Services
78573	12	39	Machinery Manufacturing
78574	225	2108	Educational Services
78575	65	410	Accommodation
78576	32	140	Administrative & Support Svcs
78577	1789	18063	Prof., Scientific, & Tech Svcs
78578	378	2237	Food Svcs & Drinking Places
78579	67	1406	Paper Manufacturing
78580	312	2562	Administrative & Support Svcs
78582	665	5826	Educational Services
78583	122	741	Educational Services
78584	335	1979	Educational Services
78585	2	7	Food and Beverage Stores
78586	863	8077	Educational Services
78588	43	271	Educational Services
78589	519	3197	Educational Services
78590	18	118	Educational Services
78591	7	12	Animal Production
78592	11	119	Educational Services
78593	51	771	Educational Services
78594	17	114	Machinery Manufacturing
78595	50	528	Ambulatory Health Care Svcs
78596	1210	15410	Educational Services
78597	435	3816	Accommodation
78598	45	124	Support Act. for Transport.
78599	3	41	Special Trade Contractors
78602	987	6344	Ambulatory Health Care Svcs
78604	7	9	Food and Beverage Stores
78605	124	587	Relig., Grant, Civic, Prof Org
78606	245	1011	Educational Services
78607	4	4	Food and Beverage Stores
78608	15	28	Heavy & Civil Eng. Construct'N
78609	115	380	Relig., Grant, Civic, Prof Org
78610	450	4195	Educational Services
78611	613	3257	Accommodation
78612	130	508	Educational Services
78613	1278	9206	Food Svcs & Drinking Places
78614	26	86	Telecommunications
78615	35	115	Educational Services
78616	57	130	Heavy & Civil Eng. Construct'N
78617	245	2865	Educational Services
78618	18	45	Justice, Pubic Order/Safety
78619	54	162	Nursing & Resid. Care Facilit.
78620	486	2223	Educational Services
78621	414	2168	Educational Services
78622	20	29	Food and Beverage Stores
78623	19	51	Accommodation
78624	1256	7708	Food Svcs & Drinking Places
78626	964	9974	Exec., Legis., & Other Support
78627	26	203	Mining (Except Oil and Gas)
78628	856	5792	Educational Services
78629	542	4302	Merch. Wholesalers,Nondur. Gds
78630	30	55	Construction of Buildings
78631	78	267	Educational Services
78632	35	98	Merch. Wholesalers,Nondur. Gds
78634	233	1502	Special Trade Contractors
78635	2	7	Heavy & Civil Eng. Construct'N
78636	230	1569	Utilities
78638	63	144	Construction of Buildings
78639	327	1338	Nursing & Resid. Care Facilit.
78640	339	2054	Educational Services
78641	647	3443	Educational Services
78642	275	1255	Educational Services
78643	393	2122	Hospitals
78644	585	3752	Educational Services
78645	359	1536	Amusement, Gambling,& Recreat.
78646	18	22	Administrative & Support Svcs
78648	336	1877	Educational Services
78650	24	73	Educational Services
78651	3	1	Food and Beverage Stores
78652	186	1274	Special Trade Contractors
78653	290	1572	Special Trade Contractors

ZIP CODE	2004 Total Firms	2004 Total Employees	TOP INDUSTRY RANKED on 2004 EMPLOYMENT
78654	1148	7106	Food Svcs & Drinking Places
78655	53	134	Special Trade Contractors
78656	36	183	Plastics & Rubber Products Mfg
78657	161	732	Real Estate
78659	37	107	Special Trade Contractors
78660	1055	7562	Special Trade Contractors
78661	14	195	Educational Services
78662	31	100	Educational Services
78663	30	80	Prof., Scientific, & Tech Svcs
78664	1681	16455	General Merchandise Stores
78666	2298	25168	Food Svcs & Drinking Places
78667	29	62	Social Assistance
78669	295	737	Amusement, Gambling,& Recreat.
78670	9	90	Unclassified Establishments
78671	54	235	Social Assistance
78672	34	113	Justice, Pubic Order/Safety
78673	3	17	Food Svcs & Drinking Places
78674	7	10	Food and Beverage Stores
78675	13	64	Justice, Pubic Order/Safety
78676	679	2453	Educational Services
78677	1	0	Postal Service
78680	37	67	Special Trade Contractors
78681	1121	10070	Food Svcs & Drinking Places
78682	1	21000	Electronics & Appliance Stores
78683	7	20	Special Trade Contractors
78691	25	76	Special Trade Contractors
78701	4195	57264	Prof., Scientific, & Tech Svcs
78702	1229	10562	Educational Services
78703	1242	13331	Nat'l Security & Int'l Affairs
78704	2794	29514	Food Svcs & Drinking Places
78705	1235	15889	Hospitals
78708	30	195	Administrative & Support Svcs
78709	56	132	Administrative & Support Svcs
78710	2	800	Postal Service
78711	21	689	Exec., Legis., & Other Support
78712	53	26233	Educational Services
78713	9	50	Clothing & Cloth'g Acc. Stores
78714	30	51	Administrative & Support Svcs
78715	32	126	Administrative & Support Svcs
78716	52	170	Relig., Grant, Civic, Prof Org
78717	265	2567	Merch. Wholesalers,Durable Gds
78718	7	19	Truck Transportation
78719	106	7462	Support Act. for Transport.
78720	75	142	Administrative & Support Svcs
78721	228	5695	Computer & Electronic Prod Mfg
78722	263	2418	Food Svcs & Drinking Places
78723	833	6918	Educational Services
78724	246	5483	Computer & Electronic Prod Mfg
78725	40	1826	Computer & Electronic Prod Mfg
78726	241	3738	Machinery Manufacturing
78727	640	5463	Admin. Human Resource Programs
78728	870	12057	Miscellaneous Manufacturing
78729	715	6561	Insurance Carriers & Related
78730	233	2697	Insurance Carriers & Related
78731	1671	12689	Prof., Scientific, & Tech Svcs
78732	126	1024	Food Svcs & Drinking Places
78733	214	1379	Food and Beverage Stores
78734	931	5302	Administrative & Support Svcs
78735	734	11612	Computer & Electronic Prod Mfg
78736	293	1346	Special Trade Contractors
78737	354	4389	Administrative & Support Svcs
78738	384	2339	Prof., Scientific, & Tech Svcs
78739	141	540	Educational Services
78741	841	14136	Computer & Electronic Prod Mfg
78742	45	1134	Wood Product Manufacturing
78744	763	10689	Merch. Wholesalers,Durable Gds
78745	1866	17834	Food Svcs & Drinking Places
78746	2836	23166	Prof., Scientific, & Tech Svcs
78747	150	623	Relig., Grant, Civic, Prof Org
78748	827	4863	Educational Services
78749	475	4808	Amusement, Gambling,& Recreat.
78750	1342	8428	Food Svcs & Drinking Places
78751	698	11394	Admin. Human Resource Programs
78752	1137	18244	Justice, Pubic Order/Safety
78753	1280	20965	Admin. Enviro. Quality Progrms
78754	497	11210	Computer & Electronic Prod Mfg
78755	46	110	Prof., Scientific, & Tech Svcs
78756	887	8047	Admin. Human Resource Programs
78757	1651	12385	Food Svcs & Drinking Places
78758	1912	23959	Administrative & Support Svcs
78759	2893	29996	Prof., Scientific, & Tech Svcs
78760	18	171	Social Assistance
78761	13	85	Relig., Grant, Civic, Prof Org
78762	4	31	Securities/Commodity Contracts
78763	37	64	Publishing Industries
78764	24	59	Personal and Laundry Services
78765	24	50	Ambulatory Health Care Svcs
78766	34	48	Prof., Scientific, & Tech Svcs
78767	50	91	Prof., Scientific, & Tech Svcs
78768	26	51	Administrative & Support Svcs

ZIP CODE	2004 Total Firms	2004 Total Employees	TOP INDUSTRY RANKED on 2004 EMPLOYMENT
78773	1	1	Exec., Legis., & Other Support
78779	1	180	Exec., Legis., & Other Support
78801	885	7634	Educational Services
78802	11	7	Special Trade Contractors
78827	17	35	Exec., Legis., & Other Support
78828	33	101	Educational Services
78829	30	142	Educational Services
78830	19	163	Special Trade Contractors
78832	126	569	Exec., Legis., & Other Support
78833	98	366	Exec., Legis., & Other Support
78834	288	2448	Social Assistance
78836	10	13	Animal Production
78837	43	188	Animal Production
78838	36	124	Accommodation
78839	221	1993	Food Manufacturing
78840	1432	12075	Educational Services
78841	4	22	Exec., Legis., & Other Support
78842	3	41	Museums, Hist. Sites,& Similar
78843	38	2081	Nat'l Security & Int'l Affairs
78850	49	257	Educational Services
78851	10	12	Animal Production
78852	1274	10505	Educational Services
78853	4	3	Repair and Maintenance
78860	3	34	Nat'l Security & Int'l Affairs
78861	453	3438	Exec., Legis., & Other Support
78870	22	174	Educational Services
78871	24	15	Prof., Scientific, & Tech Svcs
78872	41	218	Educational Services
78873	160	607	Educational Services
78877	86	247	Exec., Legis., & Other Support
78879	14	29	Accommodation
78880	147	544	Educational Services
78881	81	267	Educational Services
78883	8	6	Accommodation
78884	118	338	Relig., Grant, Civic, Prof Org
78885	20	25	Museums, Hist. Sites,& Similar
78886	8	11	Food Manufacturing
78931	6	6	Clothing & Cloth'g Acc. Stores
78932	42	167	Educational Services
78933	32	73	Merch. Wholesalers,Durable Gds
78934	434	3032	Food Svcs & Drinking Places
78935	18	393	Machinery Manufacturing
78938	12	27	Food and Beverage Stores
78940	85	217	Educational Services
78941	146	933	Merch. Wholesalers,Nondur. Gds
78942	507	4081	Exec., Legis., & Other Support
78943	3	2	Sportg Gds,Hobby,Book, & Music
78944	61	258	Merch. Wholesalers,Nondur. Gds
78945	634	4029	Utilities
78946	20	25	Food Svcs & Drinking Places
78947	113	536	Educational Services
78948	10	55	Food Svcs & Drinking Places
78949	7	23	Miscellaneous Manufacturing
78950	72	218	Amusement, Gambling,& Recreat.
78951	3	1	Postal Service
78952	17	41	Real Estate
78953	24	36	Clothing & Cloth'g Acc. Stores
78954	76	200	Food Svcs & Drinking Places
78956	303	2197	Transportation Equipment Mfg
78957	304	1776	Educational Services
78959	56	709	Food Manufacturing
78960	10	62	Accommodation
78961	20	19	Food Svcs & Drinking Places
78962	222	1564	Machinery Manufacturing
78963	21	24	Unclassified Establishments
79001	18	71	Educational Services
79003	11	47	Educational Services
79005	71	555	Food Manufacturing
79007	779	8107	Petroleum & Coal Products Mfg
79009	27	247	Educational Services
79010	16	322	Animal Production
79011	6	52	Educational Services
79012	25	446	Educational Services
79013	45	5260	Food Manufacturing
79014	271	1463	Special Trade Contractors
79015	559	2833	Food Svcs & Drinking Places
79016	4	717	Educational Services
79018	24	140	Educational Services
79019	80	483	Educational Services
79021	18	131	Educational Services
79022	581	3901	Crop Production
79024	31	123	Educational Services
79025	16	105	Food Manufacturing
79027	277	1703	Educational Services
79029	601	4400	Educational Services
79031	57	589	Educational Services
79032	10	33	Support Activities: Agr./For.
79033	7	39	Warehousing and Storage
79034	40	138	Educational Services
79035	202	3169	Food Manufacturing

BUSINESS DATA

ZIP CODE	2004 Total Firms	2004 Total Employees	TOP INDUSTRY RANKED on 2004 EMPLOYMENT	ZIP CODE	2004 Total Firms	2004 Total Employees	TOP INDUSTRY RANKED on 2004 EMPLOYMENT	ZIP CODE	2004 Total Firms	2004 Total Employees	TOP INDUSTRY RANKED on 2004 EMPLOYMENT
79036	117	711	Educational Services	79250	54	312	Educational Services	79510	273	1149	Educational Services
79039	56	238	Educational Services	79251	5	7	Food Manufacturing	79511	64	437	Educational Services
79040	89	695	Utilities	79252	203	1063	Nonmetallic Mineral Prod. Mfg	79512	299	2245	Exec., Legis., & Other Support
79041	82	385	Educational Services	79255	40	121	Credit Intermediation & Relatd	79516	1	1	Postal Service
79042	42	275	Educational Services	79256	24	86	Plastics & Rubber Products Mfg	79517	8	6	Food Svcs & Drinking Places
79043	58	320	Educational Services	79257	60	206	Educational Services	79518	6	2	Animal Production
79044	24	163	Animal Production	79258	3	16	Crop Production	79519	2	3	Animal Production
79045	738	6285	Food Manufacturing	79259	3	2	Prof., Scientific, & Tech Svcs	79520	135	1007	Special Trade Contractors
79046	29	75	Educational Services	79261	35	158	Educational Services	79521	223	1044	Educational Services
79051	5	7	Crop Production	79311	109	453	Justice, Pubic Order/Safety	79525	77	466	Educational Services
79052	41	221	Educational Services	79312	34	187	Educational Services	79526	18	86	Educational Services
79053	23	243	Educational Services	79313	35	174	Educational Services	79527	29	213	Educational Services
79054	25	100	Educational Services	79314	4	2	Merch. Wholesalers,Nondur. Gds	79528	64	232	Nursing & Resid. Care Facilit.
79056	12	40	Exec., Legis., & Other Support	79316	456	3187	Educational Services	79529	82	502	Educational Services
79057	79	337	Educational Services	79320	6	2	Clothing & Cloth'g Acc. Stores	79530	28	153	Educational Services
79058	7	88	Petroleum & Coal Products Mfg	79322	126	644	Hospitals	79532	18	115	Educational Services
79059	46	145	Educational Services	79323	303	2179	Special Trade Contractors	79533	20	158	Mining (Except Oil and Gas)
79061	14	68	Educational Services	79324	2	4	Support Activities: Agr./For.	79534	3	8	Merch. Wholesalers,Nondur. Gds
79062	5	36	Educational Services	79325	127	839	Educational Services	79535	8	168	Nonmetallic Mineral Prod. Mfg
79063	31	94	Educational Services	79326	4	6	Merch. Wholesalers,Nondur. Gds	79536	160	1244	Educational Services
79064	138	977	Educational Services	79329	99	447	Educational Services	79537	13	14	Animal Production
79065	1017	8175	Educational Services	79330	3	9	Food Svcs & Drinking Places	79538	7	60	Educational Services
79066	16	56	Exec., Legis., & Other Support	79331	567	3934	Justice, Pubic Order/Safety	79539	3	6	Support Activities: Agr./For.
79068	133	718	Educational Services	79336	668	6264	Educational Services	79540	2	2	Food and Beverage Stores
79070	505	3518	Special Trade Contractors	79338	1	1	Prof., Scientific, & Tech Svcs	79541	11	22	Exec., Legis., & Other Support
79072	1200	12031	Food Manufacturing	79339	310	2243	Textile Mills	79543	64	417	Educational Services
79073	7	24	Justice, Pubic Order/Safety	79342	25	264	Educational Services	79544	18	98	Educational Services
79077	2	2	Food and Beverage Stores	79343	52	381	Educational Services	79545	73	401	Educational Services
79078	10	54	Exec., Legis., & Other Support	79344	9	78	Educational Services	79546	98	818	Educational Services
79079	185	1012	Educational Services	79345	23	233	Educational Services	79547	30	144	Educational Services
79080	30	142	Pipeline Transportation	79346	118	649	Educational Services	79548	2	3	Relig., Grant, Civic, Prof Org
79081	221	1251	Nursing & Resid. Care Facilit.	79347	378	2592	Educational Services	79549	713	6131	Special Trade Contractors
79082	22	148	Merch. Wholesalers,Nondur. Gds	79350	26	372	Educational Services	79550	6	19	Social Assistance
79083	89	464	Educational Services	79351	73	323	Educational Services	79553	212	1213	Educational Services
79084	158	673	Educational Services	79353	3	21	Educational Services	79556	655	4586	Educational Services
79085	10	131	Animal Production	79355	131	578	Educational Services	79560	5	6	Exec., Legis., & Other Support
79086	83	1446	Petroleum & Coal Products Mfg	79356	260	1213	Special Trade Contractors	79561	24	123	Educational Services
79087	53	208	Educational Services	79357	94	429	Educational Services	79562	94	422	Educational Services
79088	262	2199	Educational Services	79358	38	183	Educational Services	79563	67	886	Heavy & Civil Eng. Construct'N
79091	20	19	Amusement, Gambling,& Recreat.	79359	112	745	Educational Services	79565	22	180	Educational Services
79092	83	411	Educational Services	79360	468	3175	Educational Services	79566	14	40	Food Svcs & Drinking Places
79093	3	11	Warehousing and Storage	79363	93	460	Educational Services	79567	162	791	Fabricated Metal Product Mfg
79094	2	5	Animal Production	79364	277	1609	Educational Services	79601	1570	16898	Hospitals
79095	161	956	Educational Services	79366	22	48	Justice, Pubic Order/Safety	79602	1164	11067	Construction of Buildings
79096	116	635	Educational Services	79367	25	194	Educational Services	79603	767	6054	Educational Services
79097	47	160	Heavy & Civil Eng. Construct'N	79369	6	53	Educational Services	79604	25	39	Special Trade Contractors
79098	17	77	Animal Production	79370	128	659	Educational Services	79605	1363	9898	Food Svcs & Drinking Places
79101	1264	14779	Nursing & Resid. Care Facilit.	79371	53	362	Educational Services	79606	709	7952	Food Svcs & Drinking Places
79102	535	5154	Educational Services	79372	76	653	Special Trade Contractors	79607	46	733	Hospitals
79103	268	4439	General Merchandise Stores	79373	117	834	Electronics & Appliance Stores	79608	17	30	Special Trade Contractors
79104	235	1696	Relig., Grant, Civic, Prof Org	79376	9	27	Oil and Gas Extraction	79697	2	268	Educational Services
79105	32	51	Special Trade Contractors	79377	20	110	Special Trade Contractors	79698	1	16	Other Information Services
79106	1479	19205	Ambulatory Health Care Svcs	79378	8	87	Educational Services	79699	4	888	Educational Services
79107	799	8407	Educational Services	79379	28	189	Educational Services	79701	3097	21605	Special Trade Contractors
79108	296	5110	Chemical Manufacturing	79380	7	78	Educational Services	79702	29	27	Special Trade Contractors
79109	2584	15734	Food Svcs & Drinking Places	79381	23	182	Educational Services	79703	632	6680	Hospitals
79110	605	5206	Plastics & Rubber Products Mfg	79382	172	1209	Educational Services	79704	10	33	Oil and Gas Extraction
79111	52	1271	Support Act. for Transport.	79383	34	70	Educational Services	79705	1337	11636	Educational Services
79114	26	39	Administrative & Support Svcs	79401	1167	14512	Exec., Legis., & Other Support	79706	645	7124	Special Trade Contractors
79116	10	24	Administrative & Support Svcs	79402	1	430	Postal Service	79707	475	4910	Food Svcs & Drinking Places
79117	2	3	Postal Service	79403	450	6193	Merch. Wholesalers,Durable Gds	79708	17	25	Prof., Scientific, & Tech Svcs
79118	565	6118	Merch. Wholesalers,Nondur. Gds	79404	719	14064	Warehousing and Storage	79710	13	17	Prof., Scientific, & Tech Svcs
79119	256	2745	General Merchandise Stores	79406	1	0	Unclassified Establishments	79711	19	414	Broadcasting
79120	16	621	Administrative & Support Svcs	79407	582	6363	Relig., Grant, Civic, Prof Org	79712	1	0	Food and Beverage Stores
79121	259	2965	General Merchandise Stores	79408	21	39	Relig., Grant, Civic, Prof Org	79713	32	126	Support Activities: Agr./For.
79124	277	2273	Food Svcs & Drinking Places	79409	26	8385	Educational Services	79714	541	4349	Special Trade Contractors
79159	13	16	Merch. Wholesalers,Durable Gds	79410	862	11926	Hospitals	79718	32	169	Educational Services
79187	5	4151	Food Manufacturing	79411	292	2122	Educational Services	79719	8	16	Chemical Manufacturing
79201	334	2259	Admin. of Economic Programs	79412	496	4735	Telecommunications	79720	1193	10991	Hospitals
79220	6	37	Educational Services	79413	736	7103	Educational Services	79721	6	16	Construction of Buildings
79221	2	61	Merch. Wholesalers,Nondur. Gds	79414	723	7093	Food Svcs & Drinking Places	79730	17	140	Utilities
79223	5	1	Machinery Manufacturing	79415	487	6872	Ambulatory Health Care Svcs	79731	206	1439	Special Trade Contractors
79225	41	158	Educational Services	79416	468	4723	Relig., Grant, Civic, Prof Org	79733	16	154	Educational Services
79226	199	916	Educational Services	79423	1278	10723	Food Svcs & Drinking Places	79734	152	1350	Merch. Wholesalers,Nondur. Gds
79227	105	366	Educational Services	79424	1297	10777	Food Svcs & Drinking Places	79735	566	4231	Food Svcs & Drinking Places
79229	30	97	Animal Production	79430	21	480	Ambulatory Health Care Svcs	79738	33	190	Educational Services
79230	6	25	Support Activities: Agr./For.	79452	6	67	Postal Service	79739	61	360	Educational Services
79231	4	32	Support Activities: Agr./For.	79453	19	74	Heavy & Civil Eng. Construct'N	79740	3	54	Utilities
79233	14	31	Food and Beverage Stores	79457	2	17	Exec., Legis., & Other Support	79741	42	408	Oil and Gas Extraction
79234	10	5	Support Activities: Agr./For.	79464	19	92	Postal Service	79742	33	124	Educational Services
79235	211	1236	Educational Services	79490	9	45	Postal Service	79743	21	139	Educational Services
79236	24	107	Animal Production	79493	27	108	Administrative & Support Svcs	79744	92	594	Educational Services
79237	19	94	Animal Production	79499	4	5	Ambulatory Health Care Svcs	79745	286	1721	Special Trade Contractors
79239	5	55	Support Activities: Agr./For.	79501	182	1456	Motor Vehicle & Parts Dealers	79748	10	32	Relig., Grant, Civic, Prof Org
79241	101	470	Educational Services	79502	111	568	Educational Services	79749	21	112	Educational Services
79243	8	23	Justice, Pubic Order/Safety	79503	6	17	Educational Services	79752	118	831	Educational Services
79244	67	192	Educational Services	79504	117	632	Exec., Legis., & Other Support	79754	16	16	Exec., Legis., & Other Support
79245	161	721	Educational Services	79505	18	39	Educational Services	79755	26	198	Utilities
79247	7	7	Exec., Legis., & Other Support	79506	28	82	Educational Services	79756	434	2654	Educational Services
79248	104	492	Educational Services	79508	69	309	Special Trade Contractors	79758	39	73	Food and Beverage Stores

ZIP CODE	2004 Total Firms	2004 Total Employees	TOP INDUSTRY RANKED on 2004 EMPLOYMENT
79759	1	0	Unclassified Establishments
79760	10	139	Accommodation
79761	1785	16154	Hospitals
79762	1317	11286	Food Svcs & Drinking Places
79763	682	6110	Merch. Wholesalers,Durable Gds
79764	817	7033	Merch. Wholesalers,Durable Gds
79765	412	4456	Transportation Equipment Mfg
79766	138	2447	Chemical Manufacturing
79768	14	17	Special Trade Contractors
79769	3	6	Merch. Wholesalers,Nondur. Gds
79770	8	26	Special Trade Contractors
79772	430	4717	Food and Beverage Stores
79776	8	49	Truck Transportation
79777	17	319	Educational Services
79778	66	255	Educational Services
79780	5	18	Machinery Manufacturing
79781	45	126	Exec., Legis., & Other Support
79782	155	972	Educational Services
79783	3	11	Food Manufacturing
79785	10	20	Justice, Pubic Order/Safety
79786	3	8	Museums, Hist. Sites,& Similar
79788	20	124	Merch. Wholesalers,Nondur. Gds
79789	42	397	Educational Services
79821	193	2193	Primary Metal Manufacturing
79830	516	2489	Food Svcs & Drinking Places
79831	5	6	Animal Production
79832	2	404	Educational Services
79834	17	206	Museums, Hist. Sites,& Similar
79835	253	1816	Educational Services
79836	117	1085	Educational Services
79837	49	207	Educational Services
79838	159	2191	Apparel Manufacturing
79839	36	220	Educational Services
79842	63	207	Accommodation
79843	230	1015	Merch. Wholesalers,Nondur. Gds
79845	200	831	Educational Services
79847	29	68	Animal Production
79848	143	287	Educational Services
79849	81	727	Educational Services
79851	57	249	Educational Services
79852	95	497	Accommodation
79853	24	140	Educational Services
79854	8	24	Educational Services
79855	188	997	Accommodation
79901	1704	23988	Exec., Legis., & Other Support
79902	1626	17123	Hospitals
79903	927	7347	Unclassified Establishments
79904	613	4187	Educational Services
79905	1063	16280	Educational Services
79906	188	7826	Computer & Electronic Prod Mfg
79907	1066	11709	Educational Services
79908	11	406	Justice, Pubic Order/Safety
79910	1	0	Postal Service
79912	2247	22505	Food Svcs & Drinking Places
79913	43	82	Ambulatory Health Care Svcs
79914	6	21	Special Trade Contractors
79915	1209	12823	Primary Metal Manufacturing
79916	45	372	Relig., Grant, Civic, Prof Org
79918	5	21	Food and Beverage Stores
79920	16	2199	Hospitals
79922	326	3192	Primary Metal Manufacturing
79923	7	6	Special Trade Contractors
79924	963	11194	Educational Services
79925	2517	29186	Food Svcs & Drinking Places
79926	4	29	Prof., Scientific, & Tech Svcs
79927	599	8432	Apparel Manufacturing
79928	282	3253	Truck Transportation
79929	3	4	Administrative & Support Svcs
79930	455	3815	Educational Services
79931	1	3	Personal and Laundry Services
79932	501	4061	Food Svcs & Drinking Places
79934	77	983	Nonmetallic Mineral Prod. Mfg
79935	746	8054	Electronics & Appliance Stores
79936	1984	22370	Food Svcs & Drinking Places
79937	14	37	Real Estate
79938	325	3224	Personal and Laundry Services
79942	1	1	Prof., Scientific, & Tech Svcs
79943	1	0	Personal and Laundry Services
79946	1	0	Prof., Scientific, & Tech Svcs
79948	2	25	Social Assistance
79950	1	1	Prof., Scientific, & Tech Svcs
79954	1	2	Social Assistance
79968	13	3867	Educational Services
79995	1	5	Telecommunications
79996	9	11	Administrative & Support Svcs
79997	7	10	Isps, Web Search Portals
80001	27	78	Administrative & Support Svcs
80002	1343	11540	Food Svcs & Drinking Places
80003	970	8192	Food Svcs & Drinking Places
80004	640	4803	Educational Services

ZIP CODE	2004 Total Firms	2004 Total Employees	TOP INDUSTRY RANKED on 2004 EMPLOYMENT
80005	408	2524	Educational Services
80006	21	86	Administrative & Support Svcs
80007	140	1496	Machinery Manufacturing
80010	876	5782	Educational Services
80011	1603	34921	Nat'l Security & Int'l Affairs
80012	1337	17923	Food Svcs & Drinking Places
80013	711	4902	Educational Services
80014	1938	19381	Food Svcs & Drinking Places
80015	1046	6548	Educational Services
80016	311	3475	Transportation Equipment Mfg
80017	352	2192	Postal Service
80018	46	127	Waste Managmt & Remediat'n Svc
80019	13	167	Personal and Laundry Services
80020	1551	14233	Furniture & Related Prod. Mfg
80021	971	17031	Telecommunications
80022	1211	20677	Merch. Wholesalers,Durable Gds
80024	1	12	Pipeline Transportation
80025	9	10	Amusement, Gambling,& Recreat.
80026	827	6532	Educational Services
80027	1066	16008	Electronics & Appliance Stores
80030	624	3822	Educational Services
80031	919	8748	Educational Services
80033	1809	20516	Ambulatory Health Care Svcs
80034	18	38	Prof., Scientific, & Tech Svcs
80035	8	42	Administrative & Support Svcs
80036	9	26	Social Assistance
80038	27	122	Publishing Industries
80040	7	28	Real Estate
80041	5	9	Administrative & Support Svcs
80042	5	7	Credit Intermediation & Relatd
80044	17	43	Administrative & Support Svcs
80046	39	87	Administrative & Support Svcs
80047	21	35	Administrative & Support Svcs
80101	20	93	Justice, Pubic Order/Safety
80102	149	475	Gasoline Stations
80103	101	405	Educational Services
80104	946	6683	Exec., Legis., & Other Support
80105	53	158	Educational Services
80106	97	465	Accommodation
80107	438	1404	Educational Services
80108	356	2416	Amusement, Gambling,& Recreat.
80109	328	3063	Justice, Pubic Order/Safety
80110	1961	20212	Special Trade Contractors
80111	2832	33162	Insurance Carriers & Related
80112	3005	44911	Prof., Scientific, & Tech Svcs
80113	960	9054	Hospitals
80116	187	837	Special Trade Contractors
80117	133	528	Educational Services
80118	119	589	Nursing & Resid. Care Facilit.
80120	1563	17189	Educational Services
80121	471	3999	Motor Vehicle & Parts Dealers
80122	1198	13515	Motion Pict. & Sound Recording
80123	1347	13986	Food Svcs & Drinking Places
80124	675	10071	Food Svcs & Drinking Places
80125	355	12205	Ambulatory Health Care Svcs
80126	640	5240	Food Svcs & Drinking Places
80127	1075	14926	Computer & Electronic Prod Mfg
80128	631	3236	Educational Services
80129	600	5100	Food Svcs & Drinking Places
80130	171	1681	Educational Services
80131	15	282	Construction of Buildings
80132	622	3210	Merch. Wholesalers,Durable Gds
80133	101	422	Prof., Scientific, & Tech Svcs
80134	1207	8102	Educational Services
80135	171	1200	Special Trade Contractors
80136	170	642	Educational Services
80137	67	704	Unclassified Establishments
80138	521	2443	Educational Services
80150	13	43	Administrative & Support Svcs
80151	8	51	Educational Services
80155	23	43	Administrative & Support Svcs
80160	34	94	Special Trade Contractors
80161	21	54	Special Trade Contractors
80162	29	80	Special Trade Contractors
80163	30	138	Administrative & Support Svcs
80201	17	10	Personal and Laundry Services
80202	3975	52693	Prof., Scientific, & Tech Svcs
80203	1819	21988	Prof., Scientific, & Tech Svcs
80204	1690	35132	Hospitals
80205	1123	10551	Ambulatory Health Care Svcs
80206	2002	15000	Food Svcs & Drinking Places
80207	502	6401	Air Transportation
80208	2	5	Ambulatory Health Care Svcs
80209	1232	8138	Plastics & Rubber Products Mfg
80210	1547	12967	Educational Services
80211	1336	11134	Educational Services
80212	590	4472	Miscellaneous Store Retailers
80214	1104	10139	Administrative & Support Svcs
80215	1251	15943	Merch. Wholesalers,Durable Gds
80216	1930	35420	Merch. Wholesalers,Durable Gds

ZIP CODE	2004 Total Firms	2004 Total Employees	TOP INDUSTRY RANKED on 2004 EMPLOYMENT
80217	7	18	Truck Transportation
80218	961	20412	Hospitals
80219	1058	6858	Educational Services
80220	904	8798	Ambulatory Health Care Svcs
80221	976	13149	Educational Services
80222	2067	17663	Prof., Scientific, & Tech Svcs
80223	1417	21292	Administrative & Support Svcs
80224	733	5235	Ambulatory Health Care Svcs
80225	14	68	Construction of Buildings
80226	1176	10637	Food Svcs & Drinking Places
80227	931	6405	Educational Services
80228	1164	11165	Prof., Scientific, & Tech Svcs
80229	1029	13669	Educational Services
80230	120	1887	Ambulatory Health Care Svcs
80231	1224	10388	Administrative & Support Svcs
80232	572	3594	Food Svcs & Drinking Places
80233	888	8212	Food Svcs & Drinking Places
80234	852	14267	Computer & Electronic Prod Mfg
80235	310	4128	Prof., Scientific, & Tech Svcs
80236	179	2196	Educational Services
80237	896	13468	Prof., Scientific, & Tech Svcs
80238	71	1448	Special Trade Contractors
80239	945	18556	Justice, Pubic Order/Safety
80241	311	3091	Merch. Wholesalers,Nondur. Gds
80246	935	12781	Admin. Human Resource Programs
80247	229	1704	Ambulatory Health Care Svcs
80248	7	7	Isps, Web Search Portals
80249	214	6984	Relig., Grant, Civic, Prof Org
80250	23	89	Administrative & Support Svcs
80260	557	4829	Food Svcs & Drinking Places
80262	67	7470	Educational Services
80264	63	664	Prof., Scientific, & Tech Svcs
80265	55	1086	Food Svcs & Drinking Places
80266	5	2206	Postal Service
80273	1	0	Insurance Carriers & Related
80274	3	14	Food Svcs & Drinking Places
80280	4	604	Exec., Legis., & Other Support
80290	71	795	Prof., Scientific, & Tech Svcs
80293	90	317	Prof., Scientific, & Tech Svcs
80294	18	474	Justice, Pubic Order/Safety
80295	2	0	Telecommunications
80299	1	0	Postal Service
80301	2330	32965	Merch. Wholesalers,Durable Gds
80302	2611	21734	Educational Services
80303	1195	8679	Prof., Scientific, & Tech Svcs
80304	927	10178	Hospitals
80305	509	7945	Exec., Legis., & Other Support
80306	52	87	Prof., Scientific, & Tech Svcs
80307	13	28	Prof., Scientific, & Tech Svcs
80308	57	136	Administrative & Support Svcs
80309	37	1286	Other Information Services
80310	1	9	Relig., Grant, Civic, Prof Org
80401	2106	26067	Beverage & Tobacco Product Mfg
80402	19	36	Special Trade Contractors
80403	454	9049	Exec., Legis., & Other Support
80419	4	118	Exec., Legis., & Other Support
80420	36	51	Food Svcs & Drinking Places
80421	308	920	Educational Services
80422	52	3379	Amusement, Gambling,& Recreat.
80423	14	40	Accommodation
80424	1010	8070	Accommodation
80425	11	18	Support Activities: Agr./For.
80426	1	1	Postal Service
80427	68	695	Accommodation
80428	18	192	Accommodation
80430	5	13	Support Activities: Agr./For.
80432	6	7	Social Assistance
80433	397	1487	Food and Beverage Stores
80434	5	11	Animal Production
80435	543	6354	Accommodation
80436	20	111	Exec., Legis., & Other Support
80437	55	76	Special Trade Contractors
80438	30	81	Food Svcs & Drinking Places
80439	1449	5860	Prof., Scientific, & Tech Svcs
80440	230	697	Educational Services
80442	218	932	Amusement, Gambling,& Recreat.
80443	660	3588	Food Svcs & Drinking Places
80444	129	1100	Accommodation
80446	392	1979	Social Assistance
80447	206	905	Amusement, Gambling,& Recreat.
80448	7	80	Accommodation
80449	35	116	Construction of Buildings
80451	52	440	Exec., Legis., & Other Support
80452	254	1575	Accommodation
80453	12	18	Administrative & Support Svcs
80454	42	183	Accommodation
80455	19	43	Educational Services
80456	19	31	Animal Production
80457	38	293	Bldg Matl & Garden Eqpmt Dlrs
80459	168	898	Educational Services

BUSINESS DATA

ZIP CODE	2004 Total Firms	2004 Total Employees	TOP INDUSTRY RANKED on 2004 EMPLOYMENT	ZIP CODE	2004 Total Firms	2004 Total Employees	TOP INDUSTRY RANKED on 2004 EMPLOYMENT	ZIP CODE	2004 Total Firms	2004 Total Employees	TOP INDUSTRY RANKED on 2004 EMPLOYMENT
80461	380	1844	Educational Services	80649	8	20	Crop Production	80915	898	9760	Special Trade Contractors
80463	12	32	Amusement, Gambling,& Recreat.	80650	33	125	Educational Services	80916	545	6823	Computer & Electronic Prod Mfg
80465	367	1362	Food Svcs & Drinking Places	80651	135	964	Support Activities for Mining	80917	686	5166	Ambulatory Health Care Svcs
80466	155	1070	Accommodation	80652	42	313	Warehousing and Storage	80918	2221	16465	Educational Services
80467	91	711	Mining (Except Oil and Gas)	80653	28	157	Support Activities: Agr./For.	80919	781	12472	Prof., Scientific, & Tech Svcs
80468	16	95	Special Trade Contractors	80654	110	615	Animal Production	80920	1156	20141	Prof., Scientific, & Tech Svcs
80469	6	12	Special Trade Contractors	80701	744	7854	Food Manufacturing	80921	233	3621	Educational Services
80470	188	552	Educational Services	80705	11	18	Heavy & Civil Eng. Construct'N	80922	239	2428	Food Svcs & Drinking Places
80471	4	5	Postal Service	80720	161	857	Food Manufacturing	80925	36	191	Food Manufacturing
80473	6	14	Accommodation	80721	12	46	Warehousing and Storage	80926	37	68	Food Svcs & Drinking Places
80474	19	63	Special Trade Contractors	80722	18	65	Food Svcs & Drinking Places	80928	15	49	Educational Services
80475	10	34	Accommodation	80723	276	2032	Nursing & Resid. Care Facilit.	80929	23	52	Merch. Wholesalers,Durable Gds
80476	15	54	Rail Transportation	80726	22	111	Justice, Pubic Order/Safety	80930	19	50	Administrative & Support Svcs
80477	56	104	Special Trade Contractors	80727	19	48	Merch. Wholesalers,Nondur. Gds	80931	9	38	Administrative & Support Svcs
80478	62	366	Accommodation	80728	40	142	Warehousing and Storage	80932	19	30	Waste Managmt & Remediat'n Svc
80479	4	10	Waste Managmt & Remediat'n Svc	80729	28	106	Crop Production	80933	15	24	Relig., Grant, Civic, Prof Org
80480	127	560	Educational Services	80731	95	458	Educational Services	80934	14	21	Construction of Buildings
80481	13	67	Accommodation	80733	12	154	Insurance Carriers & Related	80935	20	118	Prof., Scientific, & Tech Svcs
80482	261	1977	Food Svcs & Drinking Places	80734	171	757	Hospitals	80936	28	44	Special Trade Contractors
80483	33	111	Educational Services	80735	36	126	Educational Services	80937	8	16	Construction of Buildings
80487	1566	14313	Accommodation	80736	17	176	Animal Production	80949	26	60	Prof., Scientific, & Tech Svcs
80488	22	19	Special Trade Contractors	80737	133	676	Hospitals	80960	10	26	Administrative & Support Svcs
80497	2	50	Amusement, Gambling,& Recreat.	80740	5	8	Crop Production	80962	21	114	Special Trade Contractors
80498	476	3220	Food Svcs & Drinking Places	80741	28	315	Unclassified Establishments	80970	15	26	Special Trade Contractors
80501	2910	25461	Food Svcs & Drinking Places	80742	20	83	Educational Services	81001	698	9140	Machinery Manufacturing
80502	30	67	Special Trade Contractors	80743	33	273	Educational Services	81002	9	8	Relig., Grant, Civic, Prof Org
80503	633	7410	Computer & Electronic Prod Mfg	80744	26	95	Food Manufacturing	81003	1425	16230	Hospitals
80504	523	5367	Merch. Wholesalers,Nondur. Gds	80745	4	6	Special Trade Contractors	81004	829	11823	Ambulatory Health Care Svcs
80510	47	169	Accommodation	80746	4	9	Warehousing and Storage	81005	663	5793	Food Svcs & Drinking Places
80511	3	45	Accommodation	80747	22	141	Educational Services	81006	440	3337	Food Svcs & Drinking Places
80512	92	330	Accommodation	80749	15	37	Educational Services	81007	556	3249	Special Trade Contractors
80513	401	2304	Wood Product Manufacturing	80750	12	32	Utilities	81008	689	8811	Food Svcs & Drinking Places
80514	59	206	Motor Vehicle & Parts Dealers	80751	869	6615	Food Svcs & Drinking Places	81019	89	219	Food Svcs & Drinking Places
80515	25	146	Miscellaneous Store Retailers	80754	13	23	Miscellaneous Store Retailers	81020	30	117	Food Svcs & Drinking Places
80516	348	1994	Special Trade Contractors	80755	3	6	Crop Production	81021	1	2	Animal Production
80517	977	5733	Accommodation	80757	13	46	Educational Services	81022	34	170	Food and Beverage Stores
80520	36	106	Amusement, Gambling,& Recreat.	80758	250	1497	Exec., Legis., & Other Support	81023	36	142	Construction of Buildings
80521	934	16955	Educational Services	80759	286	1889	Crop Production	81024	5	7	Fabricated Metal Product Mfg
80522	42	252	Admin. Human Resource Programs	80801	19	79	Educational Services	81025	25	80	Repair and Maintenance
80523	24	401	Other Information Services	80802	7	13	Exec., Legis., & Other Support	81027	3	20	Educational Services
80524	2757	22779	Hospitals	80804	26	50	Admin. of Economic Programs	81029	17	54	Educational Services
80525	2473	26638	Food Svcs & Drinking Places	80805	12	68	Crop Production	81030	12	48	Educational Services
80526	1016	6463	Educational Services	80807	333	1925	Food Svcs & Drinking Places	81033	9	347	Justice, Pubic Order/Safety
80527	48	294	Special Trade Contractors	80808	173	787	Educational Services	81036	96	526	Hospitals
80528	261	3724	Miscellaneous Manufacturing	80809	71	358	Administrative & Support Svcs	81038	3	598	Hospitals
80530	87	568	Merch. Wholesalers,Nondur. Gds	80810	123	786	Educational Services	81039	91	457	Educational Services
80532	11	36	Accommodation	80812	15	59	Justice, Pubic Order/Safety	81040	18	110	Administrative & Support Svcs
80533	13	14	Heavy & Civil Eng. Construct'N	80813	120	2379	Amusement, Gambling,& Recreat.	81041	17	143	Educational Services
80534	182	922	Heavy & Civil Eng. Construct'N	80814	120	435	Educational Services	81043	4	3	Support Activities: Agr./For.
80535	102	718	Special Trade Contractors	80815	84	377	Merch. Wholesalers,Nondur. Gds	81044	6	19	Admin. Enviro. Quality Progrms
80536	59	125	Special Trade Contractors	80816	71	210	Other Information Services	81045	11	16	Exec., Legis., & Other Support
80537	1947	13020	Special Trade Contractors	80817	374	3680	General Merchandise Stores	81046	3	94	Educational Services
80538	1240	11837	Food Svcs & Drinking Places	80818	20	38	Exec., Legis., & Other Support	81047	91	507	Educational Services
80539	23	42	Merch. Wholesalers,Durable Gds	80819	32	163	Relig., Grant, Civic, Prof Org	81049	15	45	Educational Services
80540	190	709	Food Svcs & Drinking Places	80820	17	30	Prof., Scientific, & Tech Svcs	81050	557	4837	Hospitals
80541	8	19	Special Trade Contractors	80821	78	400	Hospitals	81052	617	4852	Transportation Equipment Mfg
80542	68	296	Educational Services	80822	26	76	Educational Services	81054	168	1036	Justice, Pubic Order/Safety
80543	70	339	Educational Services	80823	16	40	Educational Services	81055	132	548	Accommodation
80544	70	174	Special Trade Contractors	80824	22	64	Relig., Grant, Civic, Prof Org	81057	18	123	Educational Services
80545	42	137	Amusement, Gambling,& Recreat.	80825	46	125	Educational Services	81058	40	230	Educational Services
80546	11	15	Exec., Legis., & Other Support	80827	36	249	Social Assistance	81062	14	229	Justice, Pubic Order/Safety
80547	16	143	Educational Services	80828	218	1757	Justice, Pubic Order/Safety	81063	101	580	Educational Services
80549	201	1172	Miscellaneous Store Retailers	80829	300	1351	Food Svcs & Drinking Places	81064	15	74	Educational Services
80550	544	5661	Machinery Manufacturing	80830	8	14	Animal Production	81067	226	1431	Educational Services
80601	887	8865	Special Trade Contractors	80831	233	1110	Educational Services	81069	66	346	Construction of Buildings
80602	110	449	Educational Services	80832	22	211	Relig., Grant, Civic, Prof Org	81071	42	98	Educational Services
80603	204	1560	Special Trade Contractors	80833	18	94	Educational Services	81073	154	789	Hospitals
80610	105	375	Educational Services	80834	36	80	Educational Services	81076	12	20	Wood Product Manufacturing
80611	26	61	Educational Services	80835	60	316	Educational Services	81077	27	133	Educational Services
80612	13	56	Unclassified Establishments	80836	79	416	Motor Vehicle & Parts Dealers	81081	2	0	Wood Product Manufacturing
80614	29	61	Insurance Carriers & Related	80840	53	1407	Hospitals	81082	703	4405	Educational Services
80615	188	1021	Machinery Manufacturing	80860	25	342	Mining (Except Oil and Gas)	81084	11	15	Air Transportation
80620	241	2034	Food Svcs & Drinking Places	80861	15	23	Educational Services	81087	7	66	Educational Services
80621	338	3399	Educational Services	80862	3	5	Animal Production	81089	272	2449	Nursing & Resid. Care Facilit.
80622	13	32	Educational Services	80863	593	3352	Educational Services	81090	60	342	Educational Services
80623	24	164	Educational Services	80864	16	52	Educational Services	81091	32	246	Construction of Buildings
80624	17	30	Special Trade Contractors	80866	22	47	Special Trade Contractors	81092	36	173	Educational Services
80631	2080	26999	Ambulatory Health Care Svcs	80901	40	53	Relig., Grant, Civic, Prof Org	81101	858	6916	Educational Services
80632	10	12	Prof., Scientific, & Tech Svcs	80903	2781	26514	Ambulatory Health Care Svcs	81102	1	9	Other Information Services
80633	14	37	Prof., Scientific, & Tech Svcs	80904	1020	7107	Food Svcs & Drinking Places	81120	90	502	Nonmetallic Mineral Prod. Mfg
80634	1372	13823	Food Svcs & Drinking Places	80905	311	3355	General Merchandise Stores	81121	36	71	Museums, Hist. Sites,& Similar
80638	1	4	Credit Intermediation & Relatd	80906	1688	23073	Computer & Electronic Prod Mfg	81122	435	1396	Special Trade Contractors
80639	13	5193	Educational Services	80907	1858	27686	Hospitals	81123	37	225	Educational Services
80640	230	5139	Truck Transportation	80908	364	1812	Merch. Wholesalers,Durable Gds	81124	8	11	Relig., Grant, Civic, Prof Org
80642	88	620	Merch. Wholesalers,Nondur. Gds	80909	2354	24484	Educational Services	81125	150	1129	Merch. Wholesalers,Nondur. Gds
80643	94	458	Educational Services	80910	713	8119	Educational Services	81126	1	0	Postal Service
80644	69	741	Educational Services	80911	438	3313	Educational Services	81127	9	25	Merch. Wholesalers,Durable Gds
80645	146	1005	Food Svcs & Drinking Places	80912	1	4800	Nat'l Security & Int'l Affairs	81128	12	15	Animal Production
80646	17	162	Truck Transportation	80913	93	1145	Prof., Scientific, & Tech Svcs	81129	14	136	Unclassified Establishments
80648	30	86	Prof., Scientific, & Tech Svcs	80914	42	14717	Nat'l Security & Int'l Affairs	81130	114	342	Accommodation

ZIP CODE	2004 Total Firms	2004 Total Employees	TOP INDUSTRY RANKED on 2004 EMPLOYMENT	ZIP CODE	2004 Total Firms	2004 Total Employees	TOP INDUSTRY RANKED on 2004 EMPLOYMENT	ZIP CODE	2004 Total Firms	2004 Total Employees	TOP INDUSTRY RANKED on 2004 EMPLOYMENT
81131	82	141	Relig., Grant, Civic, Prof Org	81433	137	374	Food Svcs & Drinking Places	82223	52	148	Utilities
81132	160	864	Exec., Legis., & Other Support	81434	26	637	Merch. Wholesalers,Durable Gds	82225	156	674	Educational Services
81133	32	173	Crop Production	81435	761	4541	Accommodation	82227	2	13	Gasoline Stations
81134	1	1	Food Svcs & Drinking Places	81501	2244	27604	Educational Services	82229	4	2	Food and Beverage Stores
81136	21	135	Merch. Wholesalers,Durable Gds	81502	51	131	Special Trade Contractors	82240	510	3795	Educational Services
81137	275	1753	Exec., Legis., & Other Support	81503	652	3575	Administrative & Support Svcs	82242	1	1	Animal Production
81138	2	0	Sportg Gds,Hobby,Book, & Music	81504	483	3385	Special Trade Contractors	82243	4	3	Special Trade Contractors
81140	92	458	Educational Services	81505	1014	11222	Food Svcs & Drinking Places	82244	19	74	Educational Services
81141	33	115	Educational Services	81506	502	5816	Ambulatory Health Care Svcs	82301	484	4032	Justice, Pubic Order/Safety
81143	27	91	Educational Services	81520	266	1646	Food Svcs & Drinking Places	82310	8	12	Primary Metal Manufacturing
81144	427	2898	Merch. Wholesalers,Nondur. Gds	81521	351	2638	Nursing & Resid. Care Facilit.	82321	68	194	Special Trade Contractors
81146	29	164	Educational Services	81522	15	21	Educational Services	82322	12	60	Oil and Gas Extraction
81147	1145	4161	Accommodation	81523	10	23	Animal Production	82323	9	24	Animal Production
81148	8	15	Food Svcs & Drinking Places	81524	41	190	Truck Transportation	82324	24	48	Support Act. for Transport.
81149	71	395	Exec., Legis., & Other Support	81525	18	32	Heavy & Civil Eng. Construct'N	82325	59	247	Animal Production
81151	20	115	Educational Services	81526	206	1122	Food and Beverage Stores	82327	48	399	Mining (Except Oil and Gas)
81152	75	378	Educational Services	81527	44	82	Construction of Buildings	82329	35	76	Food Manufacturing
81153	2	2	Personal and Laundry Services	81601	1296	10691	Special Trade Contractors	82331	218	1048	Wood Product Manufacturing
81154	125	453	Food Svcs & Drinking Places	81602	40	63	Construction of Buildings	82332	11	47	Animal Production
81155	11	17	Food and Beverage Stores	81610	24	49	Food and Beverage Stores	82334	19	132	Food Svcs & Drinking Places
81157	5	6	Rental and Leasing Services	81611	1558	11204	Accommodation	82335	2	12	Gasoline Stations
81201	781	3918	Food Svcs & Drinking Places	81612	77	86	Prof., Scientific, & Tech Svcs	82336	44	527	Special Trade Contractors
81210	17	151	Accommodation	81615	227	3081	Food Svcs & Drinking Places	82401	529	3899	Educational Services
81211	490	2826	Justice, Pubic Order/Safety	81620	865	11527	Accommodation	82410	138	894	Ambulatory Health Care Svcs
81212	1225	10907	Justice, Pubic Order/Safety	81621	579	3540	Educational Services	82411	28	112	Educational Services
81215	10	83	Relig., Grant, Civic, Prof Org	81623	924	4454	Special Trade Contractors	82412	26	128	Educational Services
81220	20	47	Social Assistance	81624	73	540	Miscellaneous Store Retailers	82414	1234	7709	Accommodation
81221	5	7	Sportg Gds,Hobby,Book, & Music	81625	618	4286	Food Svcs & Drinking Places	82420	37	168	Construction of Buildings
81222	12	25	Accommodation	81626	8	9	Real Estate	82421	17	52	Educational Services
81223	50	216	Educational Services	81630	30	85	Educational Services	82422	5	0	Animal Production
81224	478	3925	Accommodation	81631	531	3741	Exec., Legis., & Other Support	82423	17	44	Nonmetallic Mineral Prod. Mfg
81225	6	115	Accommodation	81632	604	4455	Accommodation	82426	176	1041	Mining (Except Oil and Gas)
81226	259	1284	Educational Services	81635	147	851	Educational Services	82428	11	30	Animal Production
81227	1	350	Accommodation	81636	2	1	Prof., Scientific, & Tech Svcs	82430	5	22	Pipeline Transportation
81228	2	9	Postal Service	81637	282	1566	Special Trade Contractors	82431	227	1810	Educational Services
81230	638	4349	Educational Services	81638	7	8	Amusement, Gambling,& Recreat.	82432	17	61	Educational Services
81232	3	6	Accommodation	81639	116	805	Educational Services	82433	83	177	Educational Services
81233	30	58	Postal Service	81640	18	35	Food Svcs & Drinking Places	82434	3	12	Special Trade Contractors
81235	140	384	Accommodation	81641	265	1677	Mining (Except Oil and Gas)	82435	550	3794	Educational Services
81236	41	215	Accommodation	81642	2	0	Support Activities: Agr./For.	82440	12	38	Beverage & Tobacco Product Mfg
81237	2	4	Accommodation	81643	36	312	Accommodation	82441	26	103	Prof., Scientific, & Tech Svcs
81239	3	6	Miscellaneous Manufacturing	81645	144	864	Special Trade Contractors	82442	90	334	Accommodation
81240	181	742	Miscellaneous Manufacturing	81646	4	3	Bldg Matl & Garden Eqpmt Dlrs	82443	368	1969	Educational Services
81241	10	79	Educational Services	81647	205	935	Educational Services	82450	10	17	Educational Services
81242	49	180	Bldg Matl & Garden Eqpmt Dlrs	81648	173	1544	Educational Services	82501	962	6922	Educational Services
81243	5	70	Accommodation	81649	19	22	Educational Services	82510	18	250	Educational Services
81244	7	10	Special Trade Contractors	81650	531	3644	Construction of Buildings	82512	16	21	Animal Production
81248	7	9	Food Svcs & Drinking Places	81652	208	584	Special Trade Contractors	82513	275	949	Food Svcs & Drinking Places
81251	15	21	Accommodation	81653	10	68	Animal Production	82514	76	1021	Exec., Legis., & Other Support
81252	259	942	Educational Services	81654	82	279	Relig., Grant, Civic, Prof Org	82515	12	68	Food Svcs & Drinking Places
81253	15	20	Special Trade Contractors	81655	31	605	Special Trade Contractors	82516	16	31	Food Svcs & Drinking Places
81301	2509	18407	Accommodation	81656	38	182	Administrative & Support Svcs	82520	767	6227	Exec., Legis., & Other Support
81302	118	226	Special Trade Contractors	81657	830	10938	Accommodation	82523	34	258	Educational Services
81303	638	9196	Special Trade Contractors	81658	59	296	Food Svcs & Drinking Places	82524	8	126	Educational Services
81320	12	21	Wholesale Elec. Mrkts & Agents	82001	2004	22086	Hospitals	82601	2229	17301	Hospitals
81321	1012	6866	Food Svcs & Drinking Places	82003	58	113	Administrative & Support Svcs	82602	23	29	Waste Managmt & Remediat'n Svc
81323	250	969	Unclassified Establishments	82005	35	402	Hospitals	82604	884	7575	Special Trade Contractors
81324	81	321	Exec., Legis., & Other Support	82007	433	6196	Educational Services	82605	5	9	Construction of Buildings
81325	5	22	Educational Services	82009	790	10674	Nat'l Security & Int'l Affairs	82609	479	5362	General Merchandise Stores
81326	84	241	Mining (Except Oil and Gas)	82050	22	60	Educational Services	82615	1	4	Mining (Except Oil and Gas)
81327	24	39	Food Svcs & Drinking Places	82051	3	6	Exec., Legis., & Other Support	82620	18	90	Accommodation
81328	218	1084	Heavy & Civil Eng. Construct'N	82052	2	2	Support Activities: Agr./For.	82630	1	0	Special Trade Contractors
81329	20	14	Exec., Legis., & Other Support	82053	53	225	Gasoline Stations	82633	461	3003	Food Svcs & Drinking Places
81330	5	470	Museums, Hist. Sites,& Similar	82054	22	52	Educational Services	82635	16	74	Special Trade Contractors
81331	26	43	Telecommunications	82055	24	104	Accommodation	82636	105	1160	Special Trade Contractors
81332	38	101	Support Activities: Agr./For.	82058	1	0	Accommodation	82637	157	1057	Utilities
81334	28	838	Amusement, Gambling,& Recreat.	82059	8	79	Construction of Buildings	82638	1	2	Food Svcs & Drinking Places
81335	14	13	Special Trade Contractors	82060	5	4	Amusement, Gambling,& Recreat.	82639	50	156	Educational Services
81401	1725	11182	Food and Beverage Stores	82061	1	1	Educational Services	82640	5	49	Special Trade Contractors
81402	18	996	Administrative & Support Svcs	82063	7	50	Accommodation	82642	12	58	Oil and Gas Extraction
81410	52	177	Food and Beverage Stores	82070	948	7453	Food Svcs & Drinking Places	82643	25	142	Educational Services
81411	4	5	Animal Production	82071	18	375	Other Information Services	82644	113	1004	Miscellaneous Manufacturing
81413	255	828	Educational Services	82072	433	9225	Educational Services	82648	6	9	Educational Services
81414	14	19	Miscellaneous Store Retailers	82073	13	34	Construction of Buildings	82649	64	576	Educational Services
81415	89	237	Food Svcs & Drinking Places	82081	2	7	Crop Production	82701	288	1573	Educational Services
81416	672	4660	Ambulatory Health Care Svcs	82082	98	515	Educational Services	82710	3	7	Food and Beverage Stores
81418	55	177	Nursing & Resid. Care Facilit.	82083	32	130	Educational Services	82711	2	3	Animal Production
81419	253	800	Food and Beverage Stores	82084	5	8	Food and Beverage Stores	82712	4	7	Food and Beverage Stores
81420	3	6	Accommodation	82190	44	3245	Accommodation	82714	8	32	General Merchandise Stores
81422	50	171	Food Svcs & Drinking Places	82201	393	2625	Utilities	82716	1005	9781	Special Trade Contractors
81423	140	479	Educational Services	82210	31	122	Educational Services	82717	23	58	Ambulatory Health Care Svcs
81424	73	445	Utilities	82212	21	79	Museums, Hist. Sites,& Similar	82718	762	8600	Mining (Except Oil and Gas)
81425	137	879	Crop Production	82213	24	130	Amusement, Gambling,& Recreat.	82720	58	348	Wood Product Manufacturing
81426	3	5	Scenic & Sightseeing Transport	82214	76	394	Educational Services	82721	96	454	Truck Transportation
81427	187	732	Accommodation	82215	4	5	Museums, Hist. Sites,& Similar	82723	14	52	Oil and Gas Extraction
81428	250	1138	Mining (Except Oil and Gas)	82217	9	19	Merch. Wholesalers,Nondur. Gds	82725	5	20	Educational Services
81429	9	46	Admin. Enviro. Quality Progrms	82218	1	0	Postal Service	82727	24	95	Educational Services
81430	21	39	Construction of Buildings	82219	2	2	Furn. & Home Furnishgs Stores	82729	157	972	Nursing & Resid. Care Facilit.
81431	10	33	Amusement, Gambling,& Recreat.	82221	23	64	Relig., Grant, Civic, Prof Org	82730	65	303	Educational Services
81432	224	817	Educational Services	82222	9	21	Construction of Buildings	82731	2	15	Educational Services

ZIP CODE	2004 Total Firms	2004 Total Employees	TOP INDUSTRY RANKED on 2004 EMPLOYMENT	ZIP CODE	2004 Total Firms	2004 Total Employees	TOP INDUSTRY RANKED on 2004 EMPLOYMENT	ZIP CODE	2004 Total Firms	2004 Total Employees	TOP INDUSTRY RANKED on 2004 EMPLOYMENT
82732	68	2912	Mining (Except Oil and Gas)	83244	17	42	Animal Production	83445	240	1941	Justice, Pubic Order/Safety
82801	1436	11396	Educational Services	83245	43	310	Accommodation	83446	6	13	Food Svcs & Drinking Places
82831	17	25	Utilities	83246	68	274	Accommodation	83448	48	506	Educational Services
82832	14	42	Prof., Scientific, & Tech Svcs	83250	47	201	Gasoline Stations	83449	21	74	Support Activities: Agr./For.
82833	31	133	Educational Services	83251	73	226	Ambulatory Health Care Svcs	83450	64	314	Educational Services
82834	460	2623	Accommodation	83252	168	834	Educational Services	83451	23	80	Truck Transportation
82835	16	114	Educational Services	83253	20	13	Animal Production	83452	38	95	Merch. Wholesalers,Nondur. Gds
82836	36	116	Educational Services	83254	213	1392	Insurance Carriers & Related	83454	18	184	Machinery Manufacturing
82837	4	4	Animal Production	83255	11	49	Nursing & Resid. Care Facilit.	83455	100	322	Special Trade Contractors
82838	7	13	Animal Production	83256	3	10	Special Trade Contractors	83460	2	1490	Educational Services
82839	52	311	Educational Services	83261	26	103	Educational Services	83462	15	21	Special Trade Contractors
82842	36	130	Food Svcs & Drinking Places	83262	24	89	Crop Production	83463	6	8	Amusement, Gambling,& Recreat.
82844	1	80	Educational Services	83263	311	2076	Educational Services	83464	20	112	Educational Services
82845	1	3	Sportg Gds,Hobby,Book, & Music	83271	23	271	Telecommunications	83465	4	15	Scenic & Sightseeing Transport
82901	1280	12077	Special Trade Contractors	83272	8	14	Accommodation	83466	18	125	Support Activities: Agr./For.
82902	15	23	Admin. of Economic Programs	83274	228	1583	Food Manufacturing	83467	456	2383	Admin. Enviro. Quality Progrms
82922	17	38	Food and Beverage Stores	83276	252	2325	Chemical Manufacturing	83468	4	9	Educational Services
82923	34	207	Special Trade Contractors	83277	6	16	Exec., Legis., & Other Support	83469	1	1	General Merchandise Stores
82925	14	47	Animal Production	83278	63	399	Accommodation	83501	1761	17850	Food Svcs & Drinking Places
82929	3	440	Accommodation	83281	4	6	Animal Production	83520	12	170	Admin. Enviro. Quality Progrms
82930	738	6466	Hospitals	83283	5	22	Educational Services	83522	115	726	Hospitals
82931	5	5	Ambulatory Health Care Svcs	83285	6	21	Mining (Except Oil and Gas)	83523	46	285	Educational Services
82932	36	125	Special Trade Contractors	83286	19	34	Special Trade Contractors	83524	26	119	Educational Services
82933	34	160	Repair and Maintenance	83287	12	27	Amusement, Gambling,& Recreat.	83525	36	232	Support Activities: Agr./For.
82934	11	46	Educational Services	83301	2578	24708	Food Svcs & Drinking Places	83526	13	44	Furniture & Related Prod. Mfg
82935	512	6678	Chemical Manufacturing	83302	8	14	Animal Production	83530	357	1949	Nursing & Resid. Care Facilit.
82936	4	3	Health & Personal Care Stores	83303	35	290	Museums, Hist. Sites,& Similar	83531	6	25	Miscellaneous Store Retailers
82937	150	894	Construction of Buildings	83311	33	166	Accommodation	83533	3	5	Food Manufacturing
82938	7	26	Construction of Buildings	83312	9	26	Relig., Grant, Civic, Prof Org	83535	29	85	Educational Services
82939	98	788	Telecommunications	83313	211	1064	Special Trade Contractors	83536	191	930	Wood Product Manufacturing
82941	390	1934	Educational Services	83314	32	192	Food and Beverage Stores	83537	59	207	Food Manufacturing
82942	9	881	Mining (Except Oil and Gas)	83316	359	2731	Crop Production	83539	103	517	Wood Product Manufacturing
82943	17	214	Repair and Maintenance	83318	936	7982	Merch. Wholesalers,Nondur. Gds	83540	56	616	Educational Services
82944	3	5	Postal Service	83320	31	124	Educational Services	83541	19	47	Crop Production
82945	10	20	Exec., Legis., & Other Support	83321	22	147	Educational Services	83542	8	16	Accommodation
83001	1648	11770	Food Svcs & Drinking Places	83323	40	235	Animal Production	83543	54	268	Educational Services
83002	39	69	Special Trade Contractors	83324	28	126	Educational Services	83544	329	2298	Hospitals
83011	7	69	Educational Services	83325	35	240	Gasoline Stations	83545	17	41	Bldg Matl & Garden Eqpmt Dlrs
83012	24	556	Museums, Hist. Sites,& Similar	83327	61	229	Educational Services	83546	52	211	Forestry and Logging
83013	34	1787	Accommodation	83328	155	913	Exec., Legis., & Other Support	83547	6	46	Motor Vehicle & Parts Dealers
83014	131	842	Amusement, Gambling,& Recreat.	83330	287	2084	Educational Services	83548	3	10	Merch. Wholesalers,Nondur. Gds
83025	55	1263	Accommodation	83332	110	448	Educational Services	83549	86	353	Food Svcs & Drinking Places
83101	182	1871	Mining (Except Oil and Gas)	83333	635	3657	Prof., Scientific, & Tech Svcs	83552	13	32	Prof., Scientific, & Tech Svcs
83110	274	1652	Educational Services	83334	43	290	Social Assistance	83553	45	187	Educational Services
83111	3	5	Admin. Enviro. Quality Progrms	83335	62	351	Educational Services	83554	29	104	Exec., Legis., & Other Support
83112	14	15	Special Trade Contractors	83336	127	1301	Merch. Wholesalers,Nondur. Gds	83555	15	31	Food Svcs & Drinking Places
83113	184	902	Special Trade Contractors	83337	1	0	Fabricated Metal Product Mfg	83601	6	29	Support Activities: Agr./For.
83114	52	220	Gasoline Stations	83338	678	5496	Truck Transportation	83602	8	38	Motor Vehicle & Parts Dealers
83115	31	64	Special Trade Contractors	83340	992	6020	Food Svcs & Drinking Places	83604	34	131	Educational Services
83116	40	283	Ambulatory Health Care Svcs	83341	156	839	Nursing & Resid. Care Facilit.	83605	1121	13303	Justice, Pubic Order/Safety
83118	28	117	Construction of Buildings	83342	42	248	Educational Services	83606	15	94	Administrative & Support Svcs
83120	26	60	Fabricated Metal Product Mfg	83343	6	47	Wholesale Elec. Mrkts & Agents	83607	377	2718	Educational Services
83121	1	2	Postal Service	83344	43	363	Crop Production	83610	62	320	Educational Services
83122	5	7	Amusement, Gambling,& Recreat.	83346	54	402	Mining (Except Oil and Gas)	83611	187	854	Support Activities: Agr./For.
83123	66	386	Special Trade Contractors	83347	141	2345	Wholesale Elec. Mrkts & Agents	83612	111	541	Support Activities: Agr./For.
83124	4	15	Merch. Wholesalers,Durable Gds	83348	8	77	Animal Production	83615	70	136	Food Svcs & Drinking Places
83126	7	12	Prof., Scientific, & Tech Svcs	83349	23	136	Food Manufacturing	83616	621	3675	Educational Services
83127	127	639	Real Estate	83350	513	4010	Educational Services	83617	529	3190	Relig., Grant, Civic, Prof Org
83128	91	344	Accommodation	83352	117	971	Heavy & Civil Eng. Construct'N	83619	301	2227	Merch. Wholesalers,Durable Gds
83201	1642	16882	Food Svcs & Drinking Places	83353	92	1260	Accommodation	83622	112	434	Support Activities: Agr./For.
83202	492	5093	General Merchandise Stores	83354	3	10	Real Estate	83623	91	761	Merch. Wholesalers,Nondur. Gds
83203	39	1136	Exec., Legis., & Other Support	83355	207	1148	Animal Production	83624	56	469	Merch. Wholesalers,Nondur. Gds
83204	600	6154	Administrative & Support Svcs	83401	1309	10542	Educational Services	83626	29	192	Educational Services
83205	7	28	Administrative & Support Svcs	83402	1341	14594	Chemical Manufacturing	83627	20	129	Crop Production
83206	5	14	Construction of Buildings	83403	20	97	Construction of Buildings	83628	151	1007	Educational Services
83209	12	1686	Educational Services	83404	826	9453	Hospitals	83629	60	332	Educational Services
83210	146	1152	Crop Production	83405	12	46	Museums, Hist. Sites,& Similar	83630	2	7	Mining (Except Oil and Gas)
83211	276	2324	Food Manufacturing	83406	220	2441	General Merchandise Stores	83631	56	244	Support Activities: Agr./For.
83212	7	20	Educational Services	83414	13	38	Accommodation	83632	13	19	Food Svcs & Drinking Places
83213	123	560	Hospitals	83415	2	33	Ambulatory Health Care Svcs	83633	5	26	Support Activities: Agr./For.
83214	15	111	Educational Services	83420	134	542	Educational Services	83634	283	1697	Educational Services
83215	1	3	Gasoline Stations	83421	3	9	Sportg Gds,Hobby,Book, & Music	83635	7	33	Construction of Buildings
83217	24	103	Educational Services	83422	291	1389	Electronics & Appliance Stores	83636	5	13	Truck Transportation
83218	5	13	Truck Transportation	83423	65	666	Food Manufacturing	83637	9	40	Support Activities: Agr./For.
83220	1	4	Construction of Buildings	83424	5	9	Amusement, Gambling,& Recreat.	83638	539	3124	Support Activities: Agr./For.
83221	832	8320	Educational Services	83425	31	557	Crop Production	83639	101	507	Educational Services
83223	5	11	Wood Product Manufacturing	83427	29	88	Educational Services	83641	78	318	Educational Services
83226	241	921	Bldg Matl & Garden Eqpmt Dlrs	83428	27	91	Educational Services	83642	1864	18948	Food Svcs & Drinking Places
83227	22	176	Mining (Except Oil and Gas)	83429	89	409	Accommodation	83643	1	0	Telecommunications
83228	9	20	Food Manufacturing	83431	26	669	Food Manufacturing	83644	161	589	Educational Services
83232	15	95	Educational Services	83433	13	82	Accommodation	83645	25	104	Educational Services
83233	3	5	Animal Production	83434	31	187	Merch. Wholesalers,Nondur. Gds	83647	661	3646	Food Svcs & Drinking Places
83234	39	192	Gasoline Stations	83435	17	122	Crop Production	83648	42	5289	Nat'l Security & Int'l Affairs
83235	5	8	Crop Production	83436	23	235	Merch. Wholesalers,Nondur. Gds	83650	22	224	Exec., Legis., & Other Support
83236	39	635	Food Manufacturing	83438	7	9	Special Trade Contractors	83651	1214	8500	Food Svcs & Drinking Places
83237	18	136	Merch. Wholesalers,Nondur. Gds	83440	825	7507	Prof., Scientific, & Tech Svcs	83652	3	4	Miscellaneous Manufacturing
83238	4	5	Truck Transportation	83441	1	726	Print'g & Related Supp't Act's	83653	17	47	Social Assistance
83239	10	24	Educational Services	83442	396	2317	Merch. Wholesalers,Nondur. Gds	83654	66	499	Forestry and Logging
83241	77	388	Fabricated Metal Product Mfg	83443	66	528	Food Manufacturing	83655	131	521	Educational Services
83243	8	11	Truck Transportation	83444	43	139	Educational Services	83656	21	166	Educational Services

ZIP CODE	2004 Total Firms	2004 Total Employees	TOP INDUSTRY RANKED on 2004 EMPLOYMENT	ZIP CODE	2004 Total Firms	2004 Total Employees	TOP INDUSTRY RANKED on 2004 EMPLOYMENT	ZIP CODE	2004 Total Firms	2004 Total Employees	TOP INDUSTRY RANKED on 2004 EMPLOYMENT
83657	8	40	Forestry and Logging	83869	94	297	Educational Services	84094	579	5105	Educational Services
83660	172	1019	Merch. Wholesalers,Nondur. Gds	83870	11	23	Unclassified Establishments	84095	734	7524	Merch. Wholesalers,Durable Gds
83661	381	2678	Food and Beverage Stores	83871	76	334	Educational Services	84097	807	8376	Food Svcs & Drinking Places
83666	5	10	Food Svcs & Drinking Places	83872	9	18	Construction of Buildings	84098	598	4832	Accommodation
83669	106	393	Bldg Matl & Garden Eqpmt Dlrs	83873	155	834	Mining (Except Oil and Gas)	84101	1367	20298	Food Svcs & Drinking Places
83670	14	45	Support Activities: Agr./For.	83874	5	8	Exec., Legis., & Other Support	84102	911	12674	Food Svcs & Drinking Places
83672	352	2695	Food and Beverage Stores	83876	37	506	Amusement, Gambling,& Recreat.	84103	468	9988	Admin. Human Resource Programs
83676	88	1096	Food Manufacturing	83877	37	85	Construction of Buildings	84104	1331	29537	Merch. Wholesalers,Durable Gds
83680	31	79	Construction of Buildings	84001	44	272	Oil and Gas Extraction	84105	572	3307	Educational Services
83686	741	6279	Ambulatory Health Care Svcs	84002	1	0	Prof., Scientific, & Tech Svcs	84106	1363	11544	Food Svcs & Drinking Places
83687	863	11985	Merch. Wholesalers,Nondur. Gds	84003	1099	11374	Educational Services	84107	2625	33990	Motor Vehicle & Parts Dealers
83701	39	71	Prof., Scientific, & Tech Svcs	84004	186	1534	Chemical Manufacturing	84108	473	6837	Prof., Scientific, & Tech Svcs
83702	2606	27126	Prof., Scientific, & Tech Svcs	84006	17	259	Mining (Except Oil and Gas)	84109	698	5782	Prof., Scientific, & Tech Svcs
83703	480	4442	Admin. of Economic Programs	84007	8	30	Relig., Grant, Civic, Prof Org	84110	19	24	Museums, Hist. Sites,& Similar
83704	2008	22330	Food Svcs & Drinking Places	84010	1528	13397	Food Svcs & Drinking Places	84111	1902	25685	Prof., Scientific, & Tech Svcs
83705	1367	17105	Nat'l Security & Int'l Affairs	84011	16	173	Real Estate	84112	63	4818	Admin. Human Resource Programs
83706	1389	21229	Hospitals	84013	16	37	Educational Services	84113	37	3797	Hospitals
83707	39	80	Perform'g Arts, Spec. Sports	84014	413	4478	Special Trade Contractors	84114	42	1140	Exec., Legis., & Other Support
83708	3	1	Credit Intermediation & Relatd	84015	906	11087	Educational Services	84115	2489	30543	Merch. Wholesalers,Durable Gds
83709	1386	12405	Food Svcs & Drinking Places	84016	21	2684	Computer & Electronic Prod Mfg	84116	736	23017	Merch. Wholesalers,Durable Gds
83711	26	79	Fabricated Metal Product Mfg	84017	159	1095	Exec., Legis., & Other Support	84117	1247	8861	Food Svcs & Drinking Places
83712	290	6584	Hospitals	84020	1096	11478	Plastics & Rubber Products Mfg	84118	947	9103	Educational Services
83713	700	6266	Educational Services	84021	147	796	Justice, Pubic Order/Safety	84119	1860	39205	Couriers and Messengers
83714	1168	13984	Electronics & Appliance Stores	84022	27	259	Prof., Scientific, & Tech Svcs	84120	731	24579	Truck Transportation
83715	8	3	Telecommunications	84023	27	265	Postal Service	84121	1548	13461	Food Svcs & Drinking Places
83716	313	15808	Computer & Electronic Prod Mfg	84024	2	21	Food Svcs & Drinking Places	84122	14	953	Food Svcs & Drinking Places
83717	6	2	Miscellaneous Store Retailers	84025	311	2948	Justice, Pubic Order/Safety	84123	1053	18094	Sportg Gds,Hobby,Book, & Music
83719	35	113	Merch. Wholesalers,Durable Gds	84026	46	413	Exec., Legis., & Other Support	84124	688	6449	Hospitals
83720	21	401	Exec., Legis., & Other Support	84027	19	60	Sportg Gds,Hobby,Book,& Music	84125	3	1	Bldg Matl & Garden Eqpmt Dlrs
83724	11	186	Exec., Legis., & Other Support	84028	88	533	Food and Beverage Stores	84126	2	5	Prof., Scientific, & Tech Svcs
83725	16	2211	Educational Services	84029	141	1270	Food and Beverage Stores	84127	7	33	Administrative & Support Svcs
83728	6	836	Paper Manufacturing	84031	8	28	Food Svcs & Drinking Places	84128	160	1747	Apparel Manufacturing
83729	3	612	Construction of Buildings	84032	627	3682	Food Svcs & Drinking Places	84130	1	2	Credit Intermediation & Relatd
83735	7	349	Admin. of Economic Programs	84033	9	79	Prof., Scientific, & Tech Svcs	84132	101	6085	Hospitals
83801	125	1033	Amusement, Gambling,& Recreat.	84034	16	46	Exec., Legis., & Other Support	84133	21	350	Prof., Scientific, & Tech Svcs
83802	8	59	Exec., Legis., & Other Support	84035	20	152	Educational Services	84134	5	33	Exec., Legis., & Other Support
83803	42	232	Nat'l Security & Int'l Affairs	84036	186	730	Educational Services	84138	20	287	Admin. Enviro. Quality Progrms
83804	22	117	Amusement, Gambling,& Recreat.	84037	591	4465	Educational Services	84143	33	8172	Hospitals
83805	452	2955	Educational Services	84038	18	58	Educational Services	84144	128	2010	General Merchandise Stores
83806	15	37	Educational Services	84039	19	81	Educational Services	84147	5	11	Publishing Industries
83808	8	13	Accommodation	84040	200	1159	Educational Services	84148	8	2030	Hospitals
83809	9	18	Construction of Buildings	84041	1403	17935	Food Svcs & Drinking Places	84150	18	654	Food Svcs & Drinking Places
83810	39	168	Forestry and Logging	84042	370	5589	Electronics & Appliance Stores	84151	3	3	Construction of Buildings
83811	64	170	Educational Services	84043	646	5880	Food Svcs & Drinking Places	84152	25	353	Prof., Scientific, & Tech Svcs
83812	6	11	Exec., Legis., & Other Support	84044	288	5258	Computer & Electronic Prod Mfg	84157	24	52	Bldg Matl & Garden Eqpmt Dlrs
83813	30	70	Educational Services	84046	46	227	Amusement, Gambling,& Recreat.	84158	19	33	Transit & Grnd Pass. Transport
83814	1989	20854	Social Assistance	84047	1703	15570	Food Svcs & Drinking Places	84165	6	18	Construction of Buildings
83815	914	10010	Special Trade Contractors	84049	131	927	Accommodation	84170	12	28	Special Trade Contractors
83816	40	66	Administrative & Support Svcs	84050	246	1474	Fabricated Metal Product Mfg	84171	20	40	Administrative & Support Svcs
83821	24	70	Admin. Enviro. Quality Progrms	84051	8	29	Accommodation	84180	48	1146	Prof., Scientific, & Tech Svcs
83822	65	419	Wood Product Manufacturing	84052	26	216	Oil and Gas Extraction	84184	4	182	Credit Intermediation & Relatd
83823	42	110	Educational Services	84053	16	53	Educational Services	84190	66	2960	Exec., Legis., & Other Support
83824	4	39	Educational Services	84054	454	7176	Merch. Wholesalers,Nondur. Gds	84199	3	9	Postal Service
83825	7	9	Miscellaneous Manufacturing	84055	39	107	Educational Services	84201	3	42	Food Svcs & Drinking Places
83826	13	45	Prof., Scientific, & Tech Svcs	84056	61	720	Hospitals	84301	18	79	Educational Services
83827	15	41	Administrative & Support Svcs	84057	1323	11962	Prof., Scientific, & Tech Svcs	84302	760	8387	Transportation Equipment Mfg
83830	19	95	Nonmetallic Mineral Prod. Mfg	84058	1018	13988	Educational Services	84304	2	5	Food Manufacturing
83832	43	284	Educational Services	84059	21	83	Prof., Scientific, & Tech Svcs	84305	8	7	Special Trade Contractors
83833	41	243	Accommodation	84060	1197	12874	Accommodation	84306	5	43	Truck Transportation
83834	8	53	Accommodation	84061	15	35	Merch. Wholesalers,Durable Gds	84307	28	1933	Computer & Electronic Prod Mfg
83835	802	4347	Special Trade Contractors	84062	632	4123	Educational Services	84308	2	9	Motor Vehicle & Parts Dealers
83836	48	193	Accommodation	84063	13	23	Mining (Except Oil and Gas)	84309	5	26	Special Trade Contractors
83837	225	2108	Accommodation	84064	53	219	Educational Services	84310	98	791	Accommodation
83839	38	152	Special Trade Contractors	84065	801	5092	Special Trade Contractors	84311	14	36	Special Trade Contractors
83840	25	96	Wood Product Manufacturing	84066	498	3688	Educational Services	84312	54	343	Educational Services
83841	12	182	Wood Product Manufacturing	84067	544	5624	Prof., Scientific, & Tech Svcs	84314	19	120	Social Assistance
83842	2	5	Food and Beverage Stores	84068	24	85	Food Svcs & Drinking Places	84315	53	177	Construction of Buildings
83843	1016	10827	Educational Services	84069	11	54	Electronics & Appliance Stores	84316	5	18	Exec., Legis., & Other Support
83844	4	87	Publishing Industries	84070	1734	22746	Isps, Web Search Portals	84317	69	843	Rental and Leasing Services
83845	29	239	Wood Product Manufacturing	84071	11	18	Exec., Legis., & Other Support	84318	77	579	Sportg Gds,Hobby,Book, & Music
83846	33	292	Mining (Except Oil and Gas)	84072	14	86	Educational Services	84319	146	1213	Truck Transportation
83847	32	323	Relig., Grant, Civic, Prof Org	84073	8	17	Special Trade Contractors	84320	59	675	Plastics & Rubber Products Mfg
83848	13	115	Accommodation	84074	828	7749	Food Svcs & Drinking Places	84321	1395	18904	Miscellaneous Manufacturing
83849	72	329	Prof., Scientific, & Tech Svcs	84075	157	1763	Special Trade Contractors	84322	19	5378	Educational Services
83850	98	457	Relig., Grant, Civic, Prof Org	84076	4	9	Animal Production	84323	15	66	Insurance Carriers & Related
83851	73	574	Exec., Legis., & Other Support	84078	1165	7659	Special Trade Contractors	84324	15	30	Special Trade Contractors
83852	77	395	Food Svcs & Drinking Places	84079	1	5	Administrative & Support Svcs	84325	25	68	Ambulatory Health Care Svcs
83853	10	77	Merch. Wholesalers,Nondur. Gds	84080	9	12	Educational Services	84326	25	140	Educational Services
83854	1067	8468	Food Svcs & Drinking Places	84082	15	32	Special Trade Contractors	84327	11	17	Relig., Grant, Civic, Prof Org
83855	85	404	Educational Services	84083	100	408	Educational Services	84328	34	58	Food Svcs & Drinking Places
83856	257	1672	Wood Product Manufacturing	84084	572	4132	Food Svcs & Drinking Places	84329	1	9	Educational Services
83857	22	213	Wood Product Manufacturing	84085	9	20	Food and Beverage Stores	84330	12	447	Primary Metal Manufacturing
83858	337	1769	Educational Services	84086	13	32	Support Activities: Agr./For.	84331	2	2	Fabricated Metal Product Mfg
83860	161	533	Ambulatory Health Care Svcs	84087	270	2391	Special Trade Contractors	84332	119	833	Prof., Scientific, & Tech Svcs
83861	320	2466	Wood Product Manufacturing	84088	1206	15300	Educational Services	84333	66	1012	Food Manufacturing
83864	1312	9462	Accommodation	84089	7	67	Perform'g Arts, Spec. Sports	84334	10	18	Admin. of Economic Programs
83865	2	3	Administrative & Support Svcs	84090	23	53	Transit & Grnd Pass. Transport	84335	217	1954	Merch. Wholesalers,Nondur. Gds
83866	7	24	Merch. Wholesalers,Durable Gds	84091	25	64	Construction of Buildings	84336	14	78	Gasoline Stations
83867	10	114	Relig., Grant, Civic, Prof Org	84092	479	4520	Prof., Scientific, & Tech Svcs	84337	340	3680	Furn. & Home Furnishgs Stores
83868	28	271	Administrative & Support Svcs	84093	498	2650	Educational Services	84338	9	54	Merch. Wholesalers,Nondur. Gds

BUSINESS DATA

ZIP CODE	2004 Total Firms	2004 Total Employees	TOP INDUSTRY RANKED on 2004 EMPLOYMENT	ZIP CODE	2004 Total Firms	2004 Total Employees	TOP INDUSTRY RANKED on 2004 EMPLOYMENT	ZIP CODE	2004 Total Firms	2004 Total Employees	TOP INDUSTRY RANKED on 2004 EMPLOYMENT
84339	79	649	Accommodation	84712	13	36	Accommodation	85023	704	9617	Motor Vehicle & Parts Dealers
84340	62	454	Food and Beverage Stores	84713	217	1286	Food Svcs & Drinking Places	85024	383	4067	Special Trade Contractors
84341	726	9638	Hospitals	84714	25	232	Utilities	85025	13	378	Justice, Pubic Order/Safety
84401	1897	21921	Food Svcs & Drinking Places	84715	32	249	Educational Services	85026	3	25	Postal Service
84402	10	24	Ambulatory Health Care Svcs	84716	24	130	Educational Services	85027	1620	27335	Special Trade Contractors
84403	983	15883	Hospitals	84717	8	728	Accommodation	85028	1025	6722	Real Estate
84404	1072	13787	Educational Services	84718	15	83	Relig., Grant, Civic, Prof Org	85029	1293	15075	Insurance Carriers & Related
84405	904	17961	Transportation Equipment Mfg	84719	40	92	Real Estate	85030	3	34	Truck Transportation
84407	5	44	Merch. Wholesalers,Durable Gds	84720	1280	11736	Educational Services	85031	479	9482	Exec., Legis., & Other Support
84408	11	2042	Educational Services	84721	10	15	Credit Intermediation & Relatd	85032	2498	19144	Food Svcs & Drinking Places
84409	12	25	Administrative & Support Svcs	84722	4	3	Utilities	85033	666	6343	Educational Services
84412	9	43	Administrative & Support Svcs	84723	20	59	Educational Services	85034	1493	46270	Support Act. for Transport.
84414	314	2281	Personal and Laundry Services	84724	25	128	Merch. Wholesalers,Durable Gds	85035	255	4250	General Merchandise Stores
84415	5	13	Construction of Buildings	84725	41	273	Relig., Grant, Civic, Prof Org	85036	4	53	Social Assistance
84501	734	6837	Educational Services	84726	73	354	Telecommunications	85037	256	2320	Food and Beverage Stores
84510	1	0	Relig., Grant, Civic, Prof Org	84728	16	51	Repair and Maintenance	85040	1829	34239	Merch. Wholesalers,Durable Gds
84511	203	1444	Educational Services	84729	15	35	Accommodation	85041	406	4055	Educational Services
84512	32	147	Miscellaneous Store Retailers	84730	6	11	Admin. Enviro. Quality Progrms	85042	458	4951	Educational Services
84513	157	736	Exec., Legis., & Other Support	84731	1	0	Relig., Grant, Civic, Prof Org	85043	685	20944	Truck Transportation
84515	1	2	Unclassified Establishments	84733	3	5	Bldg Matl & Garden Eqpmt Dlrs	85044	1036	13085	Food Svcs & Drinking Places
84516	5	6	Bldg Matl & Garden Eqpmt Dlrs	84734	30	133	Food Svcs & Drinking Places	85045	31	122	Amusement, Gambling,& Recreat.
84518	21	107	Truck Transportation	84735	17	47	Utilities	85046	40	104	Administrative & Support Svcs
84520	37	206	Waste Managmt & Remediat'n Svc	84736	3	2	Social Assistance	85048	673	4438	Food Svcs & Drinking Places
84521	12	27	Nursing & Resid. Care Facilit.	84737	373	3284	Merch. Wholesalers,Durable Gds	85050	373	3183	Food Svcs & Drinking Places
84522	16	105	Mining (Except Oil and Gas)	84738	88	653	Accommodation	85051	1167	9528	Food Svcs & Drinking Places
84523	45	247	Relig., Grant, Civic, Prof Org	84739	12	19	Food and Beverage Stores	85053	751	7391	Food Svcs & Drinking Places
84525	91	684	Telecommunications	84740	23	62	Educational Services	85054	79	1559	Hospitals
84526	145	815	Mining (Except Oil and Gas)	84741	322	1927	Accommodation	85060	29	54	Food and Beverage Stores
84528	103	1764	Mining (Except Oil and Gas)	84742	4	2	Real Estate	85061	5	17	Merch. Wholesalers,Durable Gds
84530	16	78	Wood Product Manufacturing	84743	3	4	Nonmetallic Mineral Prod. Mfg	85063	10	9	Special Trade Contractors
84531	13	92	Educational Services	84744	9	158	Educational Services	85064	45	209	Special Trade Contractors
84532	735	4142	Food Svcs & Drinking Places	84745	61	478	Unclassified Establishments	85066	9	32	Construction of Buildings
84533	17	429	Amusement, Gambling,& Recreat.	84746	23	35	Exec., Legis., & Other Support	85067	18	53	Relig., Grant, Civic, Prof Org
84534	30	328	Educational Services	84747	58	464	Hospitals	85068	43	184	Prof., Scientific, & Tech Svcs
84535	171	1058	Educational Services	84749	6	17	Wood Product Manufacturing	85069	33	50	Merch. Wholesalers,Durable Gds
84536	18	271	Accommodation	84750	24	92	Educational Services	85070	7	18	Merch. Wholesalers,Durable Gds
84537	33	334	Prof., Scientific, & Tech Svcs	84751	83	834	Animal Production	85071	18	43	Special Trade Contractors
84539	13	162	Educational Services	84752	22	71	Educational Services	85072	2	400	Petroleum & Coal Products Mfg
84540	5	14	Admin. of Economic Programs	84753	1	0	General Merchandise Stores	85073	20	75	Relig., Grant, Civic, Prof Org
84542	51	634	Mining (Except Oil and Gas)	84754	67	259	Educational Services	85074	2	6	Isps, Web Search Portals
84601	1117	11810	Food Svcs & Drinking Places	84755	15	165	Accommodation	85075	2	3	Construction of Buildings
84602	4	180	Other Information Services	84756	9	17	Crop Production	85076	24	52	Construction of Buildings
84603	13	60	Special Trade Contractors	84757	25	46	Special Trade Contractors	85078	27	54	Insurance Carriers & Related
84604	1310	17477	Hospitals	84758	31	90	Educational Services	85079	9	36	Perform'g Arts, Spec. Sports
84605	3	4	Administrative & Support Svcs	84759	185	949	Hospitals	85080	50	185	Administrative & Support Svcs
84606	574	10209	Publishing Industries	84760	7	7	Special Trade Contractors	85082	15	48	Telecommunications
84620	28	233	Truck Transportation	84761	133	579	Exec., Legis., & Other Support	85085	77	295	Special Trade Contractors
84621	3	4	Special Trade Contractors	84762	31	116	Construction of Buildings	85086	386	2115	Justice, Pubic Order/Safety
84622	38	104	Merch. Wholesalers,Nondur. Gds	84763	11	9	Accommodation	85087	97	396	Special Trade Contractors
84623	8	32	Animal Production	84764	8	977	Accommodation	85201	1385	13980	Hospitals
84624	278	2164	Utilities	84765	94	394	Merch. Wholesalers,Nondur. Gds	85202	1354	18756	Hospitals
84626	14	74	Merch. Wholesalers,Nondur. Gds	84766	2	8	Museums, Hist. Sites,& Similar	85203	1030	6784	Food Svcs & Drinking Places
84627	195	1897	Educational Services	84767	85	781	Accommodation	85204	1416	12624	Food Svcs & Drinking Places
84628	30	80	Educational Services	84770	2092	16872	Food Svcs & Drinking Places	85205	1021	7039	Food Svcs & Drinking Places
84629	70	324	Telecommunications	84771	26	72	Administrative & Support Svcs	85206	1123	13269	Hospitals
84630	6	64	Miscellaneous Manufacturing	84772	5	63	Food Svcs & Drinking Places	85207	608	3505	Educational Services
84631	191	1519	Food and Beverage Stores	84773	9	29	Accommodation	85208	518	5647	Prof., Scientific, & Tech Svcs
84632	21	59	Educational Services	84774	18	64	Social Assistance	85210	2062	23560	Special Trade Contractors
84633	11	80	Educational Services	84775	53	267	Accommodation	85211	30	122	Merch. Wholesalers,Nondur. Gds
84634	108	1235	Justice, Pubic Order/Safety	84776	42	218	Accommodation	85212	220	2189	Special Trade Contractors
84635	9	25	Merch. Wholesalers,Durable Gds	84779	9	22	Accommodation	85213	637	4476	Educational Services
84636	13	22	Bldg Matl & Garden Eqpmt Dlrs	84780	295	2289	General Merchandise Stores	85214	21	54	Sportg Gds,Hobby,Book, & Music
84637	13	16	Special Trade Contractors	84781	8	16	Accommodation	85215	509	9826	Transportation Equipment Mfg
84638	4	87	Bldg Matl & Garden Eqpmt Dlrs	84782	24	85	Mining (Except Oil and Gas)	85216	26	83	Prof., Scientific, & Tech Svcs
84639	9	43	Animal Production	84783	15	38	Machinery Manufacturing	85217	7	11	Special Trade Contractors
84640	4	3	Animal Production	84784	64	639	Special Trade Contractors	85218	205	1341	Amusement, Gambling,& Recreat.
84642	163	813	Nat'l Security & Int'l Affairs	84790	961	9207	Food Svcs & Drinking Places	85219	335	1777	Educational Services
84643	13	73	Nursing & Resid. Care Facilit.	84791	6	31	Administrative & Support Svcs	85220	781	5006	Food Svcs & Drinking Places
84644	10	21	Gasoline Stations	85001	7	20	Transit & Grnd Pass. Transport	85221	3	0	Relig., Grant, Civic, Prof Org
84645	19	146	Furniture & Related Prod. Mfg	85002	5	10	Administrative & Support Svcs	85222	1299	12543	Food Svcs & Drinking Places
84646	50	794	Food Manufacturing	85003	951	19112	Justice, Pubic Order/Safety	85223	81	219	Amusement, Gambling,& Recreat.
84647	172	1123	Educational Services	85004	1731	31847	Prof., Scientific, & Tech Svcs	85224	1278	16729	Computer & Electronic Prod Mfg
84648	256	2235	Prof., Scientific, & Tech Svcs	85005	6	9	Transit & Grnd Pass. Transport	85225	1679	17051	Exec., Legis., & Other Support
84649	13	17	Construction of Buildings	85006	905	14816	Hospitals	85226	1371	28611	Prof., Scientific, & Tech Svcs
84651	473	4728	Relig., Grant, Civic, Prof Org	85007	857	20314	Exec., Legis., & Other Support	85227	2	7	Administrative & Support Svcs
84652	17	169	Nonmetallic Mineral Prod. Mfg	85008	1264	15264	Hospitals	85228	300	2867	Other Information Services
84653	125	1027	Chemical Manufacturing	85009	1938	39952	Admin. of Economic Programs	85230	15	32	Special Trade Contractors
84654	142	1627	Truck Transportation	85010	5	19	Administrative & Support Svcs	85231	227	2109	Educational Services
84655	100	634	Merch. Wholesalers,Nondur. Gds	85011	20	75	Administrative & Support Svcs	85232	239	5021	Justice, Pubic Order/Safety
84656	5	14	Support Act. for Transport.	85012	1710	21058	Prof., Scientific, & Tech Svcs	85233	1004	13842	Special Trade Contractors
84657	11	46	Animal Production	85013	979	13825	Ambulatory Health Care Svcs	85234	1132	7696	Educational Services
84660	756	7205	Educational Services	85014	1606	15068	Motor Vehicle & Parts Dealers	85235	27	1837	Primary Metal Manufacturing
84662	21	83	Educational Services	85015	1324	11369	Hospitals	85236	140	801	Educational Services
84663	659	9346	Merch. Wholesalers,Nondur. Gds	85016	3090	35182	Food Svcs & Drinking Places	85237	80	745	Relig., Grant, Civic, Prof Org
84664	147	618	Construction of Buildings	85017	1256	12392	Merch. Wholesalers,Durable Gds	85239	163	2181	Amusement, Gambling,& Recreat.
84665	11	55	Amusement, Gambling,& Recreat.	85018	1930	16619	Prof., Scientific, & Tech Svcs	85241	18	140	Justice, Pubic Order/Safety
84667	9	67	Construction of Buildings	85019	546	7521	Special Trade Contractors	85242	374	3651	Transportation Equipment Mfg
84701	516	4202	Food Svcs & Drinking Places	85020	1502	16832	Hospitals	85244	31	71	Merch. Wholesalers,Durable Gds
84710	4	14	Special Trade Contractors	85021	1439	18108	Prof., Scientific, & Tech Svcs	85245	4	63	Animal Production
84711	10	30	Miscellaneous Manufacturing	85022	1073	8947	Food Svcs & Drinking Places	85246	35	65	Administrative & Support Svcs

ZIP CODE	2004 Total Firms	2004 Total Employees	TOP INDUSTRY RANKED on 2004 EMPLOYMENT
85247	139	1482	Exec., Legis., & Other Support
85248	650	8805	Computer & Electronic Prod Mfg
85249	321	1939	Construction of Buildings
85250	703	6473	Food Svcs & Drinking Places
85251	3445	40665	Prof., Scientific, & Tech Svcs
85252	57	260	Perform'g Arts, Spec. Sports
85253	849	10511	Accommodation
85254	1894	17074	Food Svcs & Drinking Places
85255	1120	10124	Personal and Laundry Services
85256	79	2956	Educational Services
85257	795	11922	Telecommunications
85258	1771	15538	Accommodation
85259	423	2642	Food and Beverage Stores
85260	3349	31593	Food Svcs & Drinking Places
85261	33	126	Prof., Scientific, & Tech Svcs
85262	408	4353	Accommodation
85263	21	229	Heavy & Civil Eng. Construct'N
85264	41	413	Exec., Legis., & Other Support
85267	54	242	Special Trade Contractors
85268	833	4253	Food Svcs & Drinking Places
85269	21	65	Bldg Matl & Garden Eqpmt Dlrs
85271	23	151	Motion Pict. & Sound Recording
85272	57	720	Prof., Scientific, & Tech Svcs
85273	95	472	Educational Services
85274	22	42	Prof., Scientific, & Tech Svcs
85275	18	53	Prof., Scientific, & Tech Svcs
85277	24	145	Special Trade Contractors
85278	5	9	Special Trade Contractors
85280	20	30	Personal and Laundry Services
85281	2887	37136	Computer & Electronic Prod Mfg
85282	2893	33623	Prof., Scientific, & Tech Svcs
85283	1424	16003	Food Svcs & Drinking Places
85284	944	17942	Food Svcs & Drinking Places
85285	37	131	Administrative & Support Svcs
85287	28	7096	Educational Services
85290	1	12	Accommodation
85291	4	13	Special Trade Contractors
85292	34	210	Educational Services
85296	606	4706	Educational Services
85297	154	647	Construction of Buildings
85299	55	149	Ambulatory Health Care Svcs
85301	2059	22208	Special Trade Contractors
85302	643	6510	Bldg Matl & Garden Eqpmt Dlrs
85303	300	3375	Special Trade Contractors
85304	358	2765	Educational Services
85305	99	1126	General Merchandise Stores
85306	764	8832	Hospitals
85307	132	1852	Merch. Wholesalers,Durable Gds
85308	1595	18006	Food Svcs & Drinking Places
85309	36	1154	Hospitals
85310	292	2191	Special Trade Contractors
85311	16	32	Merch. Wholesalers,Nondur. Gds
85312	26	141	Administrative & Support Svcs
85318	56	166	Special Trade Contractors
85320	27	681	Crop Production
85321	186	684	Educational Services
85322	13	67	Support Activities: Agr./For.
85323	525	5330	Educational Services
85324	95	388	Food Svcs & Drinking Places
85325	14	65	Crop Production
85326	322	2859	Educational Services
85327	30	51	Prof., Scientific, & Tech Svcs
85328	4	20	Crop Production
85329	19	1383	Support Activities: Agr./For.
85331	738	3756	Food Svcs & Drinking Places
85332	43	116	Crop Production
85333	13	121	Accommodation
85334	61	480	Educational Services
85335	199	1671	Educational Services
85336	9	395	Support Activities: Agr./For.
85337	89	940	Educational Services
85338	545	8828	Food Svcs & Drinking Places
85339	135	1197	Educational Services
85340	267	2635	Accommodation
85341	9	103	Food and Beverage Stores
85342	28	49	Educational Services
85343	6	122	Educational Services
85344	505	4285	Exec., Legis., & Other Support
85345	953	11493	Special Trade Contractors
85346	206	707	Food Svcs & Drinking Places
85347	26	242	Crop Production
85348	79	292	Educational Services
85349	240	2673	Justice, Pubic Order/Safety
85350	208	2614	Educational Services
85351	724	13123	Hospitals
85352	17	64	Support Activities: Agr./For.
85353	259	5627	Food and Beverage Stores
85354	38	288	Gasoline Stations
85355	70	920	Crop Production
85356	95	749	Animal Production
85357	17	76	Educational Services
85358	11	9	Bldg Matl & Garden Eqpmt Dlrs
85359	1	1	Electronics & Appliance Stores
85360	22	108	Food Svcs & Drinking Places
85361	29	174	Educational Services
85362	46	105	Food Svcs & Drinking Places
85363	164	1219	Nursing & Resid. Care Facilit.
85364	2188	22944	Educational Services
85365	1017	18255	Merch. Wholesalers,Nondur. Gds
85366	30	113	Food Manufacturing
85367	275	1961	Crop Production
85369	18	7747	Nat'l Security & Int'l Affairs
85371	18	96	Real Estate
85372	11	18	Construction of Buildings
85373	163	1413	Relig., Grant, Civic, Prof Org
85374	574	5982	Food Svcs & Drinking Places
85375	403	5138	Hospitals
85376	2	2	Prof., Scientific, & Tech Svcs
85377	341	1787	Accommodation
85379	36	280	Wood Product Manufacturing
85380	16	35	Administrative & Support Svcs
85381	498	5144	Nursing & Resid. Care Facilit.
85382	578	8646	Motor Vehicle & Parts Dealers
85383	146	574	Special Trade Contractors
85385	13	51	Truck Transportation
85387	33	121	Administrative & Support Svcs
85390	497	3385	Nursing & Resid. Care Facilit.
85501	547	4254	Food Svcs & Drinking Places
85502	3	3	Nonstore Retailers
85530	3	24	Waste Managmt & Remediat'n Svc
85531	11	17	Real Estate
85532	37	1369	Mining (Except Oil and Gas)
85533	100	442	Exec., Legis., & Other Support
85534	91	301	Educational Services
85535	1	4	Administrative & Support Svcs
85536	14	90	Educational Services
85539	119	696	Food and Beverage Stores
85540	58	3344	Mining (Except Oil and Gas)
85541	986	6519	Food Svcs & Drinking Places
85542	11	238	Exec., Legis., & Other Support
85543	67	276	Educational Services
85544	131	438	Food Svcs & Drinking Places
85545	35	108	Accommodation
85546	602	5529	Justice, Pubic Order/Safety
85547	24	49	Special Trade Contractors
85548	1	2	Construction of Buildings
85550	101	1264	Exec., Legis., & Other Support
85551	13	48	Educational Services
85552	129	1906	Educational Services
85553	57	164	Food Svcs & Drinking Places
85554	27	125	Support Activities: Agr./For.
85601	17	66	Justice, Pubic Order/Safety
85602	368	2502	Food Svcs & Drinking Places
85603	435	2779	Justice, Pubic Order/Safety
85605	31	158	Food and Beverage Stores
85606	33	239	Utilities
85607	510	5045	Justice, Pubic Order/Safety
85608	3	16	Social Assistance
85609	8	39	Mining (Except Oil and Gas)
85610	51	236	Educational Services
85611	13	89	Support Activities: Agr./For.
85613	52	455	Accommodation
85614	334	4266	Mining (Except Oil and Gas)
85615	140	508	Special Trade Contractors
85616	128	490	Special Trade Contractors
85617	23	67	Educational Services
85618	44	267	Educational Services
85619	21	128	Accommodation
85620	15	90	Amusement, Gambling,& Recreat.
85621	1177	10993	Food and Beverage Stores
85622	3	6	Prof., Scientific, & Tech Svcs
85623	88	411	Motor Vehicle & Parts Dealers
85624	66	321	Educational Services
85625	121	329	Educational Services
85626	9	33	Educational Services
85627	2	16	Educational Services
85628	4	12	Food and Beverage Stores
85629	79	1547	Primary Metal Manufacturing
85630	41	212	Educational Services
85631	68	514	Educational Services
85632	44	322	Gasoline Stations
85633	11	64	Admin. Enviro. Quality Progrms
85634	104	3696	Exec., Legis., & Other Support
85635	1331	12909	Food Svcs & Drinking Places
85636	27	129	Ambulatory Health Care Svcs
85637	90	316	Gasoline Stations
85638	163	608	Miscellaneous Store Retailers
85639	3	13	Relig., Grant, Civic, Prof Org
85640	24	94	Educational Services
85641	109	589	Educational Services
85643	362	2826	Merch. Wholesalers,Nondur. Gds
85644	4	29	Admin. Enviro. Quality Progrms
85645	27	188	Food Svcs & Drinking Places
85646	75	334	Miscellaneous Store Retailers
85648	208	1741	Food and Beverage Stores
85650	224	1349	Special Trade Contractors
85652	19	32	Prof., Scientific, & Tech Svcs
85653	229	2376	Amusement, Gambling,& Recreat.
85654	7	40	Truck Transportation
85670	3	3	Prof., Scientific, & Tech Svcs
85701	1155	15378	Exec., Legis., & Other Support
85702	16	27	Prof., Scientific, & Tech Svcs
85703	22	55	Construction of Buildings
85704	1345	12388	Ambulatory Health Care Svcs
85705	2966	32408	Motor Vehicle & Parts Dealers
85706	1119	35436	Transportation Equipment Mfg
85707	60	448	Clothing & Cloth'g Acc. Stores
85708	8	147	Educational Services
85709	25	961	Educational Services
85710	1695	17001	Food Svcs & Drinking Places
85711	2266	25729	Food Svcs & Drinking Places
85712	2117	22142	Ambulatory Health Care Svcs
85713	1481	21820	Educational Services
85714	885	15799	Exec., Legis., & Other Support
85715	711	6303	Food Svcs & Drinking Places
85716	1528	12143	Food Svcs & Drinking Places
85717	23	16	Special Trade Contractors
85718	925	7680	Food Svcs & Drinking Places
85719	1920	29044	Educational Services
85721	23	12703	Educational Services
85722	1	10	Publishing Industries
85723	6	1214	Hospitals
85724	81	3786	Hospitals
85725	1	0	Prof., Scientific, & Tech Svcs
85726	15	20	Relig., Grant, Civic, Prof Org
85728	34	69	Construction of Buildings
85730	407	3700	Administrative & Support Svcs
85731	32	81	Special Trade Contractors
85732	40	156	Social Assistance
85733	25	141	Perform'g Arts, Spec. Sports
85734	7	18	Construction of Buildings
85735	120	827	Amusement, Gambling,& Recreat.
85736	30	148	Educational Services
85737	500	5579	Accommodation
85738	11	17	Special Trade Contractors
85739	269	2295	Food Svcs & Drinking Places
85740	34	64	Support Act. for Transport.
85741	952	10961	General Merchandise Stores
85742	225	1963	Educational Services
85743	334	4365	Food Svcs & Drinking Places
85744	2	2	Credit Intermediation & Relatd
85745	816	12686	Hospitals
85746	407	5201	Exec., Legis., & Other Support
85747	167	1915	Prof., Scientific, & Tech Svcs
85748	201	1573	Educational Services
85749	452	2317	Educational Services
85750	393	3274	Accommodation
85751	46	74	Administrative & Support Svcs
85752	28	83	Special Trade Contractors
85754	12	14	Construction of Buildings
85901	825	6522	Ambulatory Health Care Svcs
85902	22	56	Special Trade Contractors
85911	21	304	Educational Services
85912	6	23	Justice, Pubic Order/Safety
85920	40	165	Support Activities: Agr./For.
85922	3	2	Educational Services
85923	7	37	Justice, Pubic Order/Safety
85924	30	114	Educational Services
85925	134	612	Educational Services
85926	9	63	Educational Services
85927	39	119	Accommodation
85928	92	449	Educational Services
85929	351	2134	Educational Services
85930	13	73	Educational Services
85931	17	41	Food and Beverage Stores
85932	8	42	Forestry and Logging
85933	121	457	Unclassified Establishments
85934	9	10	Construction of Buildings
85935	354	2182	Accommodation
85936	181	983	Justice, Pubic Order/Safety
85937	278	2384	Paper Manufacturing
85938	183	1433	Utilities
85939	111	684	Heavy & Civil Eng. Construct'N
85940	22	55	Educational Services
85941	128	3442	Exec., Legis., & Other Support
85942	4	9	Other Information Services
86001	1939	21300	Food Svcs & Drinking Places
86002	40	37	Prof., Scientific, & Tech Svcs
86003	43	96	Special Trade Contractors
86004	1613	14334	Food Svcs & Drinking Places

BUSINESS DATA

ZIP CODE	2004 Total Firms	2004 Total Employ-ees	TOP INDUSTRY RANKED on 2004 EMPLOYMENT	ZIP CODE	2004 Total Firms	2004 Total Employ-ees	TOP INDUSTRY RANKED on 2004 EMPLOYMENT	ZIP CODE	2004 Total Firms	2004 Total Employ-ees	TOP INDUSTRY RANKED on 2004 EMPLOYMENT
86011	14	2371	Educational Services	86445	3	10	Amusement, Gambling,& Recreat.	87113	656	15302	Computer & Electronic Prod Mfg
86015	18	301	Gasoline Stations	86446	7	8	Utilities	87114	1195	10174	Food Svcs & Drinking Places
86016	5	25	Accommodation	86502	19	145	Educational Services	87116	6	87	Educational Services
86017	44	236	Amusement, Gambling,& Recreat.	86503	192	2628	Educational Services	87117	67	1745	Nat'l Security & Int'l Affairs
86018	22	55	Educational Services	86504	96	1387	Utilities	87118	3	50	Educational Services
86020	17	318	Accommodation	86505	73	1809	Educational Services	87119	9	89	Educational Services
86021	118	927	Educational Services	86506	12	91	Miscellaneous Store Retailers	87120	992	6117	Food Svcs & Drinking Places
86022	81	492	Accommodation	86507	7	90	Educational Services	87121	739	7689	Truck Transportation
86023	99	2629	Accommodation	86508	10	58	Food and Beverage Stores	87122	265	1228	Educational Services
86024	26	153	Exec., Legis., & Other Support	86510	21	415	Educational Services	87123	1047	9160	Food Svcs & Drinking Places
86025	322	3856	Exec., Legis., & Other Support	86511	24	423	Educational Services	87124	1215	11725	Prof., Scientific, & Tech Svcs
86028	3	155	Museums, Hist. Sites,& Similar	86512	72	576	Educational Services	87125	27	105	Social Assistance
86029	6	78	Educational Services	86514	28	388	Educational Services	87131	65	13704	Educational Services
86030	13	26	Exec., Legis., & Other Support	86515	319	1845	Justice, Pubic Order/Safety	87144	212	2114	Nonstore Retailers
86031	6	39	Merch. Wholesalers,Durable Gds	86520	1	0	Exec., Legis., & Other Support	87153	6	12	Construction of Buildings
86032	35	508	Utilities	86535	7	7	Relig., Grant, Civic, Prof Org	87154	16	23	Prof., Scientific, & Tech Svcs
86033	113	2522	Educational Services	86538	15	331	Educational Services	87174	38	122	Furniture & Related Prod. Mfg
86034	51	1341	Educational Services	86540	3	43	Educational Services	87176	29	35	Prof., Scientific, & Tech Svcs
86035	21	268	Educational Services	86544	10	61	Educational Services	87181	20	51	Special Trade Contractors
86036	15	201	Scenic & Sightseeing Transport	86545	7	169	Educational Services	87184	5	18	Special Trade Contractors
86038	16	250	Accommodation	86547	2	34	Educational Services	87185	5	8	Admin. Enviro. Quality Progrms
86039	38	666	Exec., Legis., & Other Support	86556	13	441	Educational Services	87187	5	17	Prof., Scientific, & Tech Svcs
86040	445	5717	Administrative & Support Svcs	87001	46	260	Food Svcs & Drinking Places	87190	23	55	Administrative & Support Svcs
86042	21	107	Exec., Legis., & Other Support	87002	601	5307	Educational Services	87191	28	92	Nursing & Resid. Care Facilit.
86043	26	186	Exec., Legis., & Other Support	87004	325	3589	Amusement, Gambling,& Recreat.	87192	52	88	Prof., Scientific, & Tech Svcs
86044	6	116	Educational Services	87005	8	61	Educational Services	87193	42	74	Real Estate
86045	183	2387	Educational Services	87006	8	12	Special Trade Contractors	87194	14	18	Administrative & Support Svcs
86046	283	2134	Accommodation	87007	13	376	Amusement, Gambling,& Recreat.	87195	13	21	Publishing Industries
86047	465	4177	Justice, Pubic Order/Safety	87008	119	365	Food Svcs & Drinking Places	87196	25	61	Admin. Human Resource Programs
86052	1	0	Unclassified Establishments	87010	56	114	Food Svcs & Drinking Places	87197	15	40	Food Manufacturing
86053	9	94	Educational Services	87011	2	3	Animal Production	87198	27	44	Sportg Gds,Hobby,Book, & Music
86054	15	177	Educational Services	87012	9	53	Exec., Legis., & Other Support	87199	66	103	Construction of Buildings
86301	1629	15890	Educational Services	87013	139	939	Educational Services	87301	1323	14455	Hospitals
86302	33	71	Special Trade Contractors	87014	9	50	Educational Services	87305	17	89	Museums, Hist. Sites,& Similar
86303	725	3793	Prof., Scientific, & Tech Svcs	87015	192	865	Health & Personal Care Stores	87310	3	71	Relig., Grant, Civic, Prof Org
86304	32	62	Administrative & Support Svcs	87016	91	770	Administrative & Support Svcs	87311	12	170	Educational Services
86305	674	4815	Exec., Legis., & Other Support	87017	16	206	Educational Services	87312	8	50	Miscellaneous Manufacturing
86312	29	151	Relig., Grant, Civic, Prof Org	87018	6	27	Exec., Legis., & Other Support	87313	124	1268	Educational Services
86313	4	595	Hospitals	87020	491	4758	Educational Services	87315	9	13	Animal Production
86314	1081	7895	Food Svcs & Drinking Places	87021	111	968	Justice, Pubic Order/Safety	87316	21	539	Educational Services
86320	58	344	Mining (Except Oil and Gas)	87022	36	693	Relig., Grant, Civic, Prof Org	87317	15	125	Merch. Wholesalers,Durable Gds
86321	50	755	Mining (Except Oil and Gas)	87023	5	8	Special Trade Contractors	87319	6	18	Educational Services
86322	480	2817	Exec., Legis., & Other Support	87024	39	496	Educational Services	87321	62	420	Exec., Legis., & Other Support
86323	506	2618	Educational Services	87025	67	267	Construction of Buildings	87322	6	102	Educational Services
86324	107	1173	Nonmetallic Mineral Prod. Mfg	87026	62	1229	Exec., Legis., & Other Support	87323	61	605	Educational Services
86325	110	504	Special Trade Contractors	87027	1	2	Utilities	87325	44	361	Educational Services
86326	1105	6927	Food Svcs & Drinking Places	87028	1	0	Relig., Grant, Civic, Prof Org	87326	24	186	Educational Services
86327	162	852	Special Trade Contractors	87029	17	68	Special Trade Contractors	87327	108	2155	Exec., Legis., & Other Support
86329	53	101	Merch. Wholesalers,Nondur. Gds	87031	736	5960	Educational Services	87328	27	301	Educational Services
86331	103	267	Miscellaneous Store Retailers	87032	16	28	Administrative & Support Svcs	87347	5	372	Gasoline Stations
86332	24	78	Educational Services	87034	20	190	Educational Services	87357	27	795	Educational Services
86333	138	745	Educational Services	87035	239	1641	Food Svcs & Drinking Places	87364	1	2	Relig., Grant, Civic, Prof Org
86334	44	108	Relig., Grant, Civic, Prof Org	87036	74	291	Educational Services	87365	4	33	Educational Services
86335	74	387	Educational Services	87037	5	14	Special Trade Contractors	87375	6	22	Exec., Legis., & Other Support
86336	1402	8005	Accommodation	87038	5	84	Educational Services	87401	2294	22966	Special Trade Contractors
86337	90	287	Educational Services	87040	3	19	Construction of Buildings	87402	555	6931	Food Svcs & Drinking Places
86338	16	39	Relig., Grant, Civic, Prof Org	87041	8	33	Admin. Enviro. Quality Progrms	87410	505	4287	Special Trade Contractors
86339	37	49	Construction of Buildings	87042	63	230	Educational Services	87412	12	42	Justice, Pubic Order/Safety
86340	15	17	Miscellaneous Store Retailers	87043	96	276	Merch. Wholesalers,Nondur. Gds	87413	378	3830	Heavy & Civil Eng. Construct'N
86341	11	34	Publishing Industries	87044	8	5	Beverage & Tobacco Product Mfg	87415	71	383	Truck Transportation
86342	28	70	Food Svcs & Drinking Places	87045	14	195	Paper Manufacturing	87416	35	2251	Utilities
86343	9	25	Support Activities: Agr./For.	87046	2	2	Gasoline Stations	87417	141	955	Educational Services
86351	320	2097	Accommodation	87047	80	382	Educational Services	87418	16	198	Mining (Except Oil and Gas)
86401	1698	14730	Educational Services	87048	281	950	Food Svcs & Drinking Places	87419	21	141	Museums, Hist. Sites,& Similar
86402	19	51	Social Assistance	87049	15	43	Educational Services	87420	206	1832	Educational Services
86403	1917	14019	Food Svcs & Drinking Places	87051	5	6	Food Svcs & Drinking Places	87421	31	1895	Utilities
86404	278	1371	Special Trade Contractors	87052	7	48	Gasoline Stations	87455	19	283	Educational Services
86405	51	121	Special Trade Contractors	87053	34	54	Food and Beverage Stores	87461	6	25	Educational Services
86406	358	1639	Special Trade Contractors	87056	10	29	Heavy & Civil Eng. Construct'N	87499	41	249	Food and Beverage Stores
86411	3	15	Animal Production	87059	234	936	Educational Services	87501	2557	19013	Food Svcs & Drinking Places
86412	2	3	Bldg Matl & Garden Eqpmt Dlrs	87060	3	3	Heavy & Civil Eng. Construct'N	87502	65	157	Special Trade Contractors
86413	171	950	Truck Transportation	87061	11	31	Nonstore Retailers	87503	8	194	Exec., Legis., & Other Support
86426	373	1938	Food Svcs & Drinking Places	87062	15	23	General Merchandise Stores	87504	81	129	Prof., Scientific, & Tech Svcs
86427	8	47	Administrative & Support Svcs	87063	4	18	Food Svcs & Drinking Places	87505	2892	28847	Admin. Human Resource Programs
86429	177	1104	Accommodation	87068	168	837	Food Svcs & Drinking Places	87506	271	3338	Prof., Scientific, & Tech Svcs
86430	11	19	Special Trade Contractors	87070	7	77	Miscellaneous Store Retailers	87507	1713	13610	Food Svcs & Drinking Places
86431	15	24	Accommodation	87072	6	83	Relig., Grant, Civic, Prof Org	87508	474	2430	Educational Services
86432	43	194	Educational Services	87083	9	66	Amusement, Gambling,& Recreat.	87509	1	1	Special Trade Contractors
86433	32	68	Miscellaneous Store Retailers	87101	5	58	Postal Service	87510	36	165	Accommodation
86434	46	616	Exec., Legis., & Other Support	87102	2390	32832	Exec., Legis., & Other Support	87511	19	230	Educational Services
86435	13	31	Exec., Legis., & Other Support	87103	13	19	Prof., Scientific, & Tech Svcs	87512	3	5	Exec., Legis., & Other Support
86436	58	196	Food Svcs & Drinking Places	87104	627	4529	Food Svcs & Drinking Places	87513	17	41	Administrative & Support Svcs
86437	3	1	Repair and Maintenance	87105	1038	9312	Educational Services	87514	43	96	Food Svcs & Drinking Places
86438	13	274	Transportation Equipment Mfg	87106	1387	35296	Ambulatory Health Care Svcs	87515	9	26	Support Activities: Agr./For.
86439	12	52	Relig., Grant, Civic, Prof Org	87107	2460	29138	Special Trade Contractors	87516	3	3	Construction of Buildings
86440	210	794	Educational Services	87108	1608	18358	Hospitals	87517	6	14	Machinery Manufacturing
86441	59	208	Educational Services	87109	2579	31082	Food Svcs & Drinking Places	87518	2	2	Prof., Scientific, & Tech Svcs
86442	1089	7782	General Merchandise Stores	87110	3535	30897	Prof., Scientific, & Tech Svcs	87519	6	33	Justice, Pubic Order/Safety
86443	3	90	Museums, Hist. Sites,& Similar	87111	1715	12280	Food Svcs & Drinking Places	87520	159	588	Accommodation
86444	43	135	Museums, Hist. Sites,& Similar	87112	1956	12483	Food Svcs & Drinking Places	87521	21	33	Justice, Pubic Order/Safety

ZIP CODE	2004 Total Firms	2004 Total Employees	TOP INDUSTRY RANKED on 2004 EMPLOYMENT
87522	42	223	Food Svcs & Drinking Places
87523	6	26	Educational Services
87524	14	131	Accommodation
87525	43	935	Accommodation
87527	15	31	Educational Services
87528	82	1857	Exec., Legis., & Other Support
87529	84	236	Amusement, Gambling,& Recreat.
87530	21	333	Educational Services
87531	15	81	Relig., Grant, Civic, Prof Org
87532	784	6901	Educational Services
87533	7	40	Exec., Legis., & Other Support
87535	29	332	Other Information Services
87537	21	60	Heavy & Civil Eng. Construct'N
87539	2	5	Forestry and Logging
87540	34	91	Administrative & Support Svcs
87544	711	13832	Exec., Legis., & Other Support
87545	3	76	Other Information Services
87548	1	5	Special Trade Contractors
87549	27	222	Educational Services
87551	20	110	Textile Mills
87552	116	653	Educational Services
87553	44	439	Educational Services
87556	109	319	Educational Services
87557	109	351	Food Svcs & Drinking Places
87558	142	981	Accommodation
87560	21	107	Educational Services
87562	14	23	Furniture & Related Prod. Mfg
87564	7	21	Relig., Grant, Civic, Prof Org
87565	7	9	Accommodation
87566	41	874	Amusement, Gambling,& Recreat.
87567	22	102	Educational Services
87569	4	2	Truck Transportation
87571	1344	11795	Credit Intermediation & Relatd
87573	5	90	Accommodation
87574	23	76	Food Svcs & Drinking Places
87575	54	360	Educational Services
87577	12	89	Mining (Except Oil and Gas)
87578	17	69	Justice, Pubic Order/Safety
87579	6	75	Accommodation
87580	1	2	Accommodation
87581	4	8	Merch. Wholesalers,Durable Gds
87582	51	165	Nonmetallic Mineral Prod. Mfg
87583	5	6	Museums, Hist. Sites,& Similar
87592	19	56	Heavy & Civil Eng. Construct'N
87594	8	9	Special Trade Contractors
87701	814	8007	Educational Services
87710	222	1493	Accommodation
87711	23	49	Educational Services
87712	5	43	Ambulatory Health Care Svcs
87713	4	10	Apparel Manufacturing
87714	74	1212	Social Assistance
87715	9	22	Social Assistance
87718	64	175	Educational Services
87722	8	12	Construction of Buildings
87723	4	3	Construction of Buildings
87724	2	3	Real Estate
87728	16	48	Educational Services
87729	2	2	Miscellaneous Store Retailers
87730	1	0	Postal Service
87731	4	105	Educational Services
87732	92	791	Educational Services
87733	34	111	Exec., Legis., & Other Support
87734	10	10	Animal Production
87736	1	0	Postal Service
87740	451	3265	Food Svcs & Drinking Places
87742	9	75	Amusement, Gambling,& Recreat.
87743	32	76	Educational Services
87745	9	15	Construction of Buildings
87746	2	2	Accommodation
87747	85	704	Educational Services
87749	5	21	Prof., Scientific, & Tech Svcs
87750	1	86	Nursing & Resid. Care Facilit.
87752	28	87	Educational Services
87753	6	16	Museums, Hist. Sites,& Similar
87801	432	4347	Educational Services
87820	3	4	Wood Product Manufacturing
87821	44	138	Support Activities: Agr./For.
87823	19	67	Food Svcs & Drinking Places
87824	11	74	Exec., Legis., & Other Support
87825	86	475	Educational Services
87827	21	53	Justice, Pubic Order/Safety
87828	8	4	Food and Beverage Stores
87829	51	200	Educational Services
87830	86	304	Educational Services
87831	5	15	Admin. Enviro. Quality Progrms
87832	20	61	Admin. Enviro. Quality Progrms
87901	454	2610	Nursing & Resid. Care Facilit.
87930	14	237	Food Manufacturing
87931	17	77	Construction of Buildings
87933	2	4	Postal Service
87935	91	288	Accommodation
87936	9	40	Educational Services
87937	111	804	Animal Production
87939	2	0	Justice, Pubic Order/Safety
87940	9	87	Merch. Wholesalers,Nondur. Gds
87941	10	15	Merch. Wholesalers,Nondur. Gds
87942	32	83	Exec., Legis., & Other Support
87943	10	25	Exec., Legis., & Other Support
88001	1533	15835	Educational Services
88002	18	198	Educational Services
88003	17	3122	Educational Services
88004	23	189	Telecommunications
88005	1178	17221	Prof., Scientific, & Tech Svcs
88006	15	44	Administrative & Support Svcs
88007	341	3991	Educational Services
88008	84	858	Plastics & Rubber Products Mfg
88009	6	5	Amusement, Gambling,& Recreat.
88011	612	7935	Hospitals
88012	191	2035	Space Research and Technology
88020	40	435	Educational Services
88021	73	1081	Educational Services
88022	33	136	Construction of Buildings
88023	85	430	Educational Services
88024	3	79	Merch. Wholesalers,Nondur. Gds
88025	10	12	Animal Production
88026	27	122	Educational Services
88027	4	42	Utilities
88028	35	106	Educational Services
88029	49	545	Merch. Wholesalers,Nondur. Gds
88030	685	7449	Food Manufacturing
88031	5	20	Exec., Legis., & Other Support
88032	11	21	Food and Beverage Stores
88033	8	48	Special Trade Contractors
88034	4	10	Animal Production
88036	7	448	Nursing & Resid. Care Facilit.
88038	19	28	Animal Production
88039	35	75	Food Svcs & Drinking Places
88040	7	9	Heavy & Civil Eng. Construct'N
88041	13	275	Mining (Except Oil and Gas)
88042	21	68	Support Activities: Agr./For.
88043	20	101	Educational Services
88044	38	426	Food and Beverage Stores
88045	221	1138	Food Svcs & Drinking Places
88046	83	486	Food Svcs & Drinking Places
88047	80	731	Merch. Wholesalers,Nondur. Gds
88048	39	588	Animal Production
88049	38	38	Construction of Buildings
88051	4	9	Animal Production
88052	10	21	Bldg Matl & Garden Eqpmt Dlrs
88053	7	30	Food Svcs & Drinking Places
88054	8	261	Merch. Wholesalers,Nondur. Gds
88055	3	14	Relig., Grant, Civic, Prof Org
88056	15	51	Miscellaneous Store Retailers
88058	10	77	Educational Services
88061	880	7310	Educational Services
88062	9	18	Construction of Buildings
88063	57	1715	Special Trade Contractors
88065	18	645	Mining (Except Oil and Gas)
88072	22	92	Gasoline Stations
88081	48	366	Educational Services
88101	1695	13176	Educational Services
88102	14	55	Relig., Grant, Civic, Prof Org
88103	34	536	Hospitals
88112	8	6	General Merchandise Stores
88113	6	3	Bldg Matl & Garden Eqpmt Dlrs
88114	4	11	Special Trade Contractors
88115	17	69	Educational Services
88116	31	88	Educational Services
88118	13	23	Animal Production
88119	133	585	Educational Services
88120	13	63	Educational Services
88121	12	157	Educational Services
88122	1	1	Food Svcs & Drinking Places
88124	43	186	Educational Services
88125	7	4	Oil and Gas Extraction
88126	1	1	Food and Beverage Stores
88130	545	4220	Educational Services
88132	2	18	Animal Production
88134	1	6	Mining (Except Oil and Gas)
88135	68	323	Educational Services
88136	4	6	Merch. Wholesalers,Nondur. Gds
88201	1256	10898	Food Svcs & Drinking Places
88202	28	84	Admin. of Economic Programs
88203	820	8343	Educational Services
88210	627	6169	Special Trade Contractors
88211	2	4	Exec., Legis., & Other Support
88213	7	5	Crop Production
88220	1264	11157	Food Svcs & Drinking Places
88221	5	10	Social Assistance
88230	92	732	Merch. Wholesalers,Nondur. Gds
88231	137	1231	Heavy & Civil Eng. Construct'N
88232	39	361	Educational Services
88240	1618	14488	Special Trade Contractors
88241	16	34	Special Trade Contractors
88242	79	211	Educational Services
88250	15	15	Educational Services
88252	95	463	Utilities
88253	40	171	Educational Services
88254	19	24	Oil and Gas Extraction
88255	39	343	Truck Transportation
88256	39	163	Educational Services
88260	457	3656	Special Trade Contractors
88262	6	14	Animal Production
88263	2	3	Utilities
88264	23	83	Utilities
88265	13	67	Utilities
88267	77	262	Educational Services
88268	4	202	Accommodation
88301	113	476	Educational Services
88310	1362	10327	Educational Services
88311	15	33	Special Trade Contractors
88312	99	405	Amusement, Gambling,& Recreat.
88314	3	4	Administrative & Support Svcs
88316	126	473	Educational Services
88317	149	648	Accommodation
88318	43	108	Educational Services
88321	15	76	Merch. Wholesalers,Durable Gds
88323	3	38	Justice, Pubic Order/Safety
88324	2	7	Miscellaneous Store Retailers
88325	24	49	Unclassified Establishments
88330	62	971	Nat'l Security & Int'l Affairs
88336	35	164	Educational Services
88337	44	193	Educational Services
88338	9	33	Museums, Hist. Sites,& Similar
88339	57	86	Support Activities: Agr./For.
88340	41	2151	Exec., Legis., & Other Support
88341	12	19	Construction of Buildings
88342	3	3	Postal Service
88343	6	46	Support Activities: Agr./For.
88344	7	8	Animal Production
88345	872	4827	Food Svcs & Drinking Places
88346	141	1525	Perform'g Arts, Spec. Sports
88347	7	118	Accommodation
88348	8	18	Miscellaneous Store Retailers
88349	5	93	Prof., Scientific, & Tech Svcs
88350	30	109	Justice, Pubic Order/Safety
88351	8	17	Food Svcs & Drinking Places
88352	156	688	Educational Services
88353	51	2677	Repair and Maintenance
88354	9	13	Food Svcs & Drinking Places
88355	7	21	Special Trade Contractors
88401	421	2620	Food Svcs & Drinking Places
88410	9	25	Support Activities: Agr./For.
88411	2	2	Crop Production
88414	6	3	Accommodation
88415	189	1079	Educational Services
88416	25	64	Amusement, Gambling,& Recreat.
88417	4	16	Animal Production
88418	28	150	Educational Services
88419	19	22	Animal Production
88422	2	2	Animal Production
88424	4	1	Exec., Legis., & Other Support
88426	97	328	Educational Services
88427	3	27	Justice, Pubic Order/Safety
88430	18	29	Heavy & Civil Eng. Construct'N
88431	4	35	Animal Production
88433	4	0	Crop Production
88434	36	188	Gasoline Stations
88435	232	1850	Justice, Pubic Order/Safety
88436	3	35	Justice, Pubic Order/Safety
88437	1	6	Museums, Hist. Sites,& Similar
88439	3	0	Animal Production
89001	57	236	Educational Services
89003	74	593	Accommodation
89004	13	94	Food Svcs & Drinking Places
89005	707	4864	Accommodation
89006	13	26	Special Trade Contractors
89007	22	109	Educational Services
89008	91	433	Exec., Legis., & Other Support
89009	20	67	Construction of Buildings
89010	9	62	Educational Services
89011	40	1400	Food Svcs & Drinking Places
89012	250	1313	Food Svcs & Drinking Places
89013	34	100	Educational Services
89014	1521	17701	Food Svcs & Drinking Places
89015	1608	19260	Exec., Legis., & Other Support
89016	16	70	Truck Transportation
89017	8	32	Accommodation
89018	34	516	Justice, Pubic Order/Safety
89019	147	10712	Accommodation

BUSINESS DATA

ZIP CODE	2004 Total Firms	2004 Total Employ-ees	TOP INDUSTRY RANKED on 2004 EMPLOYMENT	ZIP CODE	2004 Total Firms	2004 Total Employ-ees	TOP INDUSTRY RANKED on 2004 EMPLOYMENT	ZIP CODE	2004 Total Firms	2004 Total Employ-ees	TOP INDUSTRY RANKED on 2004 EMPLOYMENT
89020	40	198	Mining (Except Oil and Gas)	89191	50	9423	Nat'l Security & Int'l Affairs	89815	201	879	Educational Services
89021	79	335	Educational Services	89193	36	87	Administrative & Support Svcs	89820	198	1362	Educational Services
89022	5	9	Accommodation	89199	2	3	Food Svcs & Drinking Places	89821	17	449	Mining (Except Oil and Gas)
89023	1	0	Prof., Scientific, & Tech Svcs	89301	355	2998	Justice, Pubic Order/Safety	89822	87	636	Construction of Buildings
89024	12	26	Special Trade Contractors	89310	64	146	Exec., Legis., & Other Support	89823	6	11	Animal Production
89025	53	822	Utilities	89311	13	97	Museums, Hist. Sites,& Similar	89824	3	7	Animal Production
89027	437	4724	Accommodation	89314	11	25	Admin. Human Resource Programs	89825	45	1879	Accommodation
89028	6	15	Transit & Grnd Pass. Transport	89315	3	18	Exec., Legis., & Other Support	89826	10	40	Support Activities: Agr./For.
89029	286	16661	Accommodation	89316	92	492	Construction of Buildings	89828	26	72	Educational Services
89030	1299	32070	Admin. of Economic Programs	89317	10	51	Food and Beverage Stores	89830	7	8	Educational Services
89031	412	7709	General Merchandise Stores	89318	23	67	Educational Services	89831	11	20	Food Svcs & Drinking Places
89032	537	12455	Exec., Legis., & Other Support	89319	4	31	Mining (Except Oil and Gas)	89832	42	319	Exec., Legis., & Other Support
89033	11	65	Administrative & Support Svcs	89402	151	931	Accommodation	89833	19	37	Animal Production
89036	10	90	Justice, Pubic Order/Safety	89403	196	1239	Educational Services	89834	13	119	Animal Production
89039	6	49	Amusement, Gambling,& Recreat.	89404	2	3	Educational Services	89835	120	710	Food Svcs & Drinking Places
89040	170	877	Educational Services	89405	9	248	Nonmetallic Mineral Prod. Mfg	89883	101	3078	Amusement, Gambling,& Recreat.
89041	7	42	Special Trade Contractors	89406	1069	7102	Educational Services	90001	1282	10425	Educational Services
89042	41	202	Educational Services	89407	12	54	Publishing Industries	90002	456	3071	Educational Services
89043	70	227	Justice, Pubic Order/Safety	89408	349	2536	Food Svcs & Drinking Places	90003	1516	7917	Educational Services
89045	39	191	Educational Services	89409	22	126	Mining (Except Oil and Gas)	90004	1496	8154	Educational Services
89046	31	289	Amusement, Gambling,& Recreat.	89410	734	3767	Food and Beverage Stores	90005	1177	7150	Educational Services
89047	16	67	Mining (Except Oil and Gas)	89411	63	307	Amusement, Gambling,& Recreat.	90006	2072	8873	Food Svcs & Drinking Places
89048	685	3408	Educational Services	89412	16	72	Educational Services	90007	1500	14567	Educational Services
89049	217	1294	Accommodation	89413	35	135	Food and Beverage Stores	90008	1214	5137	Educational Services
89052	685	5422	Food Svcs & Drinking Places	89414	10	1508	Mining (Except Oil and Gas)	90009	25	48	Transit & Grnd Pass. Transport
89053	13	421	Prof., Scientific, & Tech Svcs	89415	177	1704	Prof., Scientific, & Tech Svcs	90010	3666	24691	Prof., Scientific, & Tech Svcs
89060	162	857	Justice, Pubic Order/Safety	89418	15	359	Mining (Except Oil and Gas)	90011	1540	11123	Educational Services
89061	37	141	Amusement, Gambling,& Recreat.	89419	184	1471	Mining (Except Oil and Gas)	90012	2215	47226	Exec., Legis., & Other Support
89074	1009	9469	Real Estate	89420	3	6	Special Trade Contractors	90013	2264	14514	Utilities
89084	4	4	Prof., Scientific, & Tech Svcs	89421	13	108	Food Svcs & Drinking Places	90014	4428	16072	Heavy & Civil Eng. Construct'N
89101	2512	38746	Accommodation	89422	14	16	Food and Beverage Stores	90015	4339	26238	Relig., Grant, Civic, Prof Org
89102	4114	36886	Hospitals	89423	678	6078	Elect'l Eqpmt, App, & Comp Mfg	90016	1140	9961	Food and Beverage Stores
89103	2893	32810	Accommodation	89424	12	137	Exec., Legis., & Other Support	90017	2265	32418	Prof., Scientific, & Tech Svcs
89104	2565	21352	Food Svcs & Drinking Places	89425	10	29	Machinery Manufacturing	90018	1030	6149	Nursing & Resid. Care Facilit.
89106	1135	14722	Ambulatory Health Care Svcs	89426	5	9	Educational Services	90019	1626	8477	Educational Services
89107	1181	15296	Food Svcs & Drinking Places	89427	23	203	Social Assistance	90020	1098	6501	Admin. Human Resource Programs
89108	1308	8403	Food Svcs & Drinking Places	89428	6	25	Justice, Pubic Order/Safety	90021	2074	21302	Merch. Wholesalers,Nondur. Gds
89109	4129	139484	Accommodation	89429	149	913	Support Act. for Transport.	90022	1816	15618	Educational Services
89110	995	5833	Food Svcs & Drinking Places	89430	33	111	Educational Services	90023	1657	25248	Merch. Wholesalers,Nondur. Gds
89111	13	153	Merch. Wholesalers,Nondur. Gds	89431	2409	29458	Special Trade Contractors	90024	1984	50707	Educational Services
89112	17	60	Administrative & Support Svcs	89432	39	83	Social Assistance	90025	3955	26494	Prof., Scientific, & Tech Svcs
89113	193	1053	Educational Services	89433	170	831	Educational Services	90026	1339	10862	Educational Services
89114	17	47	Perform'g Arts, Spec. Sports	89434	425	7551	Merch. Wholesalers,Durable Gds	90027	1694	21716	Ambulatory Health Care Svcs
89115	1138	11217	Special Trade Contractors	89435	12	21	Special Trade Contractors	90028	2701	22420	Motion Pict. & Sound Recording
89116	21	99	Transit & Grnd Pass. Transport	89436	325	1829	Educational Services	90029	1162	5585	Educational Services
89117	1852	15312	Ambulatory Health Care Svcs	89438	8	757	Mining (Except Oil and Gas)	90030	2	0	Nonstore Retailers
89118	2075	32665	Special Trade Contractors	89439	89	1874	Nonstore Retailers	90031	827	8131	Educational Services
89119	3171	52281	Accommodation	89440	172	542	Food Svcs & Drinking Places	90032	596	6403	Educational Services
89120	1538	13589	Administrative & Support Svcs	89442	28	94	Educational Services	90033	1011	14173	Educational Services
89121	2182	17538	Food Svcs & Drinking Places	89444	53	198	Prof., Scientific, & Tech Svcs	90034	1581	12606	Hospitals
89122	368	7899	Accommodation	89445	607	4606	Accommodation	90035	1418	8589	Personal and Laundry Services
89123	1697	8671	Food Svcs & Drinking Places	89446	6	6	Construction of Buildings	90036	2625	19557	Prof., Scientific, & Tech Svcs
89124	70	1314	Prof., Scientific, & Tech Svcs	89447	340	2611	Justice, Pubic Order/Safety	90037	1042	5922	Educational Services
89125	10	17	Publishing Industries	89448	213	1487	Administrative & Support Svcs	90038	1404	14683	Motion Pict. & Sound Recording
89126	34	96	Administrative & Support Svcs	89449	477	10818	Accommodation	90039	910	9225	Museums, Hist. Sites,& Similar
89127	5	7	Relig., Grant, Civic, Prof Org	89450	41	54	Prof., Scientific, & Tech Svcs	90040	1493	38840	Merch. Wholesalers,Durable Gds
89128	1571	13258	Ambulatory Health Care Svcs	89451	728	4377	Accommodation	90041	967	7023	Educational Services
89129	694	4008	Food Svcs & Drinking Places	89452	22	32	Construction of Buildings	90042	1013	4864	Educational Services
89130	1102	8868	Prof., Scientific, & Tech Svcs	89460	279	1204	Educational Services	90043	1090	4749	Educational Services
89131	300	1060	Food Svcs & Drinking Places	89501	993	18073	Accommodation	90044	1075	8170	Educational Services
89132	5	26	Unclassified Establishments	89502	4475	51992	Accommodation	90045	3021	41058	Food Svcs & Drinking Places
89133	65	265	Special Trade Contractors	89503	1032	12822	Hospitals	90046	2353	10604	Food Svcs & Drinking Places
89134	455	2795	Ambulatory Health Care Svcs	89504	9	63	Managmt of Companies & Enterp.	90047	1069	5980	Educational Services
89135	238	1950	Administrative & Support Svcs	89505	17	75	Administrative & Support Svcs	90048	2979	21919	Ambulatory Health Care Svcs
89136	3	4	Isps, Web Search Portals	89506	579	6759	Educational Services	90049	1584	10849	Educational Services
89137	27	39	Miscellaneous Store Retailers	89507	19	40	Postal Service	90050	6	19	Couriers and Messengers
89138	13	101	Food Svcs & Drinking Places	89509	1807	11084	Prof., Scientific, & Tech Svcs	90051	5	9	Sportg Gds,Hobby,Book, & Music
89139	192	3298	Accommodation	89510	66	140	Animal Production	90052	5	127	Postal Service
89141	98	359	Amusement, Gambling,& Recreat.	89511	1155	9606	Prof., Scientific, & Tech Svcs	90053	4	4	Real Estate
89142	208	1334	Educational Services	89512	709	10627	Educational Services	90054	1	7	Couriers and Messengers
89143	50	80	Special Trade Contractors	89513	27	34	Special Trade Contractors	90056	174	2230	Motor Vehicle & Parts Dealers
89144	336	6278	Hospitals	89515	26	30	Personal and Laundry Services	90057	1631	8424	Ambulatory Health Care Svcs
89145	668	8960	Accommodation	89520	2	30	Justice, Pubic Order/Safety	90058	1729	39822	Merch. Wholesalers,Nondur. Gds
89146	2226	18583	Prof., Scientific, & Tech Svcs	89521	395	10702	Accommodation	90059	483	12670	Exec., Legis., & Other Support
89147	754	4979	Food and Beverage Stores	89523	333	2471	Educational Services	90060	1	1	Social Assistance
89148	117	625	Educational Services	89533	14	48	Repair and Maintenance	90061	667	8027	Educational Services
89149	266	1950	General Merchandise Stores	89557	25	410	Ambulatory Health Care Svcs	90062	438	2260	Justice, Pubic Order/Safety
89150	113	716	Credit Intermediation & Relatd	89570	22	125	Construction of Buildings	90063	816	8618	Justice, Pubic Order/Safety
89151	1	10	Miscellaneous Manufacturing	89595	11	210	Food Svcs & Drinking Places	90064	2371	25629	Broadcasting
89152	1	800	Telecommunications	89701	1597	20055	Exec., Legis., & Other Support	90065	948	8871	Educational Services
89154	15	409	Food Svcs & Drinking Places	89702	48	88	Special Trade Contractors	90066	1602	14141	Prof., Scientific, & Tech Svcs
89155	30	583	Exec., Legis., & Other Support	89703	760	4033	Hospitals	90067	2002	27122	Prof., Scientific, & Tech Svcs
89156	278	1570	Educational Services	89704	106	325	Food Svcs & Drinking Places	90068	657	4429	Motor Vehicle & Parts Dealers
89160	3	6	Administrative & Support Svcs	89705	105	1404	General Merchandise Stores	90069	2053	14474	Food Svcs & Drinking Places
89162	5	28	Special Trade Contractors	89706	1481	9556	Transportation Equipment Mfg	90070	1	1	Construction of Buildings
89163	1	0	Credit Intermediation & Relatd	89713	4	1503	Social Assistance	90071	1226	32467	Prof., Scientific, & Tech Svcs
89170	17	66	Perform'g Arts, Spec. Sports	89721	16	42	Administrative & Support Svcs	90072	4	7	Postal Service
89173	10	19	Heavy & Civil Eng. Construct'N	89801	1368	13860	Mining (Except Oil and Gas)	90073	22	4072	Hospitals
89180	20	56	Administrative & Support Svcs	89802	3	5	Merch. Wholesalers,Durable Gds	90075	4	0	Wholesale Elec. Mrkts & Agents
89185	1	10	Hospitals	89803	18	56	Construction of Buildings	90076	2	0	Construction of Buildings

ZIP CODE	2004 Total Firms	2004 Total Employees	TOP INDUSTRY RANKED on 2004 EMPLOYMENT
90077	179	1898	Educational Services
90078	22	79	Clothing & Cloth'g Acc. Stores
90079	658	1912	Apparel Manufacturing
90081	2	19	Isps, Web Search Portals
90083	5	10	Publishing Industries
90086	5	17	Ambulatory Health Care Svcs
90089	89	15596	Educational Services
90091	2	0	Construction of Buildings
90093	8	12	Prof., Scientific, & Tech Svcs
90094	1	17	Real Estate
90095	194	4761	Ambulatory Health Care Svcs
90201	1730	16278	Educational Services
90202	1	4	Motion Pict. & Sound Recording
90209	36	76	Prof., Scientific, & Tech Svcs
90210	3350	21019	Accommodation
90211	1891	9409	Ambulatory Health Care Svcs
90212	2170	13649	Prof., Scientific, & Tech Svcs
90213	29	58	Prof., Scientific, & Tech Svcs
90220	1158	20638	Merch. Wholesalers,Durable Gds
90221	1291	14679	Merch. Wholesalers,Durable Gds
90222	434	4196	Educational Services
90223	3	7	Truck Transportation
90224	1	0	Social Assistance
90230	1603	15671	Educational Services
90231	26	37	Transit & Grnd Pass. Transport
90232	1518	16721	Motion Pict. & Sound Recording
90239	10	22	Truck Transportation
90240	801	4173	Real Estate
90241	1814	19750	Beverage & Tobacco Product Mfg
90242	666	13223	Ambulatory Health Care Svcs
90245	1637	34585	Prof., Scientific, & Tech Svcs
90247	1458	11465	Amusement, Gambling,& Recreat.
90248	2180	32864	Merch. Wholesalers,Durable Gds
90249	1476	12067	Fabricated Metal Product Mfg
90250	2299	17068	Educational Services
90251	14	33	Motion Pict. & Sound Recording
90254	1149	5699	Food Svcs & Drinking Places
90255	2132	15447	Educational Services
90260	918	6189	Educational Services
90261	5	807	Admin. of Economic Programs
90262	1209	9773	Educational Services
90263	3	1028	Educational Services
90264	28	70	Electronics & Appliance Stores
90265	1264	6353	Food Svcs & Drinking Places
90266	1862	12542	Food Svcs & Drinking Places
90267	24	34	Waste Managmt & Remediat'n Svc
90270	447	2955	Educational Services
90272	902	4547	Food Svcs & Drinking Places
90274	1221	6958	Educational Services
90275	749	3967	Educational Services
90277	2023	10281	Food Svcs & Drinking Places
90278	1095	17540	Computer & Electronic Prod Mfg
90280	1985	19735	Educational Services
90290	235	782	Accommodation
90291	1282	6949	Food Svcs & Drinking Places
90292	1554	13179	Food Svcs & Drinking Places
90293	325	1739	Waste Managmt & Remediat'n Svc
90294	25	34	Merch. Wholesalers,Durable Gds
90295	41	269	Prof., Scientific, & Tech Svcs
90296	6	12	Special Trade Contractors
90301	2094	20373	Hospitals
90302	786	5582	Prof., Scientific, & Tech Svcs
90303	490	4289	Amusement, Gambling,& Recreat.
90304	608	3878	Educational Services
90305	320	1703	Perform'g Arts, Spec. Sports
90306	2	0	Transit & Grnd Pass. Transport
90307	1	1	Perform'g Arts, Spec. Sports
90308	2	7	Repair and Maintenance
90309	5	50	Transit & Grnd Pass. Transport
90310	5	6	Nonstore Retailers
90311	2	6	Credit Intermediation & Relatd
90312	2	10	Exec., Legis., & Other Support
90401	2232	22206	Prof., Scientific, & Tech Svcs
90402	235	839	Food Svcs & Drinking Places
90403	1253	7515	Food Svcs & Drinking Places
90404	1858	21905	Hospitals
90405	1840	12814	Educational Services
90406	24	40	Merch. Wholesalers,Nondur. Gds
90408	10	16	Educational Services
90409	14	26	Isps, Web Search Portals
90410	1	10	Motion Pict. & Sound Recording
90501	2415	26763	Wholesale Elec. Mrkts & Agents
90502	803	11482	Merch. Wholesalers,Durable Gds
90503	2381	29915	Hospitals
90504	824	9728	Motor Vehicle & Parts Dealers
90505	3034	27349	Merch. Wholesalers,Durable Gds
90506	2	2050	Educational Services
90507	6	34	Heavy & Civil Eng. Construct'N
90508	10	66	Special Trade Contractors
90510	22	42	Prof., Scientific, & Tech Svcs
90601	854	11576	Merch. Wholesalers,Durable Gds
90602	927	7478	Hospitals
90603	586	4391	Food Svcs & Drinking Places
90604	377	2163	Educational Services
90605	871	7686	Educational Services
90606	681	5297	Educational Services
90607	13	11	Prof., Scientific, & Tech Svcs
90608	18	53	Social Assistance
90609	14	40	Waste Managmt & Remediat'n Svc
90620	1106	14797	Food Svcs & Drinking Places
90621	1430	11584	Justice, Pubic Order/Safety
90622	16	31	Insurance Carriers & Related
90623	386	5125	Isps, Web Search Portals
90630	1591	19142	Insurance Carriers & Related
90631	2037	15006	Food Svcs & Drinking Places
90632	16	46	Truck Transportation
90633	12	30	Heavy & Civil Eng. Construct'N
90637	21	53	Merch. Wholesalers,Nondur. Gds
90638	1206	15678	Merch. Wholesalers,Durable Gds
90639	1	0	Educational Services
90640	2231	25543	Food Manufacturing
90650	1887	20275	Educational Services
90651	7	7	Administrative & Support Svcs
90660	1278	12736	Merch. Wholesalers,Durable Gds
90661	2	0	Special Trade Contractors
90670	2955	45973	Merch. Wholesalers,Durable Gds
90680	1094	6531	Food Svcs & Drinking Places
90701	727	3934	Food Svcs & Drinking Places
90702	10	58	Isps, Web Search Portals
90703	1687	23838	Motor Vehicle & Parts Dealers
90704	388	2446	Food Svcs & Drinking Places
90706	1914	11551	Educational Services
90707	13	15	Unclassified Establishments
90710	652	7180	Hospitals
90711	8	13	Merch. Wholesalers,Durable Gds
90712	834	10746	Food Svcs & Drinking Places
90713	411	3107	Educational Services
90714	13	182	Postal Service
90715	170	1151	Educational Services
90716	305	3612	Amusement, Gambling,& Recreat.
90717	928	4064	Food Svcs & Drinking Places
90720	1470	12865	Hospitals
90721	9	19	Administrative & Support Svcs
90723	1685	14402	Merch. Wholesalers,Durable Gds
90731	1892	12992	Educational Services
90732	446	3768	Hospitals
90733	18	33	Administrative & Support Svcs
90734	14	12	Chemical Manufacturing
90740	886	9028	Transportation Equipment Mfg
90742	80	366	Food Svcs & Drinking Places
90743	9	35	Food Svcs & Drinking Places
90744	1400	10815	Educational Services
90745	1265	15731	Motor Vehicle & Parts Dealers
90746	950	10756	Merch. Wholesalers,Durable Gds
90747	8	63	Relig., Grant, Civic, Prof Org
90748	10	26	Heavy & Civil Eng. Construct'N
90749	15	38	Educational Services
90755	1040	11687	Merch. Wholesalers,Durable Gds
90801	13	19	Educational Services
90802	1898	22569	Justice, Pubic Order/Safety
90803	1367	7955	Food Svcs & Drinking Places
90804	1169	8630	Hospitals
90805	1461	12686	Educational Services
90806	1289	20622	Hospitals
90807	1421	10300	Prof., Scientific, & Tech Svcs
90808	905	8397	Educational Services
90809	21	36	Insurance Carriers & Related
90810	674	12638	Merch. Wholesalers,Durable Gds
90813	1393	11401	Ambulatory Health Care Svcs
90814	321	1601	Educational Services
90815	891	13383	Merch. Wholesalers,Durable Gds
90822	20	709	Ambulatory Health Care Svcs
90831	124	1020	Accommodation
90832	3	8	Food and Beverage Stores
90840	13	608	Food Svcs & Drinking Places
90844	2	300	Publishing Industries
90845	1	0	Miscellaneous Store Retailers
90846	2	7205	Transportation Equipment Mfg
90853	16	9	Clothing & Cloth'g Acc. Stores
91001	806	3954	Educational Services
91003	14	65	Food Svcs & Drinking Places
91006	1728	13355	Prof., Scientific, & Tech Svcs
91007	1161	11123	Perform'g Arts, Spec. Sports
91009	7	15	Miscellaneous Store Retailers
91010	653	8055	Hospitals
91011	755	4909	Educational Services
91012	21	53	Prof., Scientific, & Tech Svcs
91016	1691	16150	Food Svcs & Drinking Places
91017	17	58	Perform'g Arts, Spec. Sports
91020	490	2644	Administrative & Support Svcs
91021	10	47	Special Trade Contractors
91023	4	10	Isps, Web Search Portals
91024	446	1893	Relig., Grant, Civic, Prof Org
91025	12	30	Miscellaneous Manufacturing
91030	993	5571	Educational Services
91031	18	78	Crop Production
91040	489	2590	Educational Services
91041	20	35	Special Trade Contractors
91042	566	2367	Educational Services
91043	8	67	Waste Managmt & Remediat'n Svc
91046	28	45	Nursing & Resid. Care Facilit.
91066	22	56	Special Trade Contractors
91077	7	24	Prof., Scientific, & Tech Svcs
91101	2857	22297	Prof., Scientific, & Tech Svcs
91102	15	809	Print'g & Related Supp't Act's
91103	760	8500	Educational Services
91104	1044	3984	Educational Services
91105	1312	16122	Hospitals
91106	1007	6231	Prof., Scientific, & Tech Svcs
91107	1645	14381	Food Svcs & Drinking Places
91108	460	2611	Real Estate
91109	27	6339	Ambulatory Health Care Svcs
91114	6	61	Educational Services
91115	9	46	Social Assistance
91116	9	20	Educational Services
91117	10	26	Prof., Scientific, & Tech Svcs
91118	2	7	Merch. Wholesalers,Durable Gds
91121	1	600	Health & Personal Care Stores
91123	3	120	Relig., Grant, Civic, Prof Org
91124	4	2016	Prof., Scientific, & Tech Svcs
91125	12	3982	Relig., Grant, Civic, Prof Org
91182	1	3	Prof., Scientific, & Tech Svcs
91188	3	1506	Ambulatory Health Care Svcs
91201	929	11091	Prof., Scientific, & Tech Svcs
91202	681	3314	Educational Services
91203	1524	17532	Prof., Scientific, & Tech Svcs
91204	1497	13014	Hospitals
91205	1363	6578	Educational Services
91206	793	8184	Hospitals
91207	182	733	Prof., Scientific, & Tech Svcs
91208	535	3956	Educational Services
91209	26	59	Insurance Carriers & Related
91210	258	3143	Clothing & Cloth'g Acc. Stores
91214	1023	4814	Educational Services
91221	14	8522	Perform'g Arts, Spec. Sports
91222	16	191	Insurance Carriers & Related
91224	13	29	Special Trade Contractors
91225	10	6	Truck Transportation
91226	15	20	Transit & Grnd Pass. Transport
91301	1675	14187	Special Trade Contractors
91302	1379	11401	Prof., Scientific, & Tech Svcs
91303	1842	11450	Food Svcs & Drinking Places
91304	1293	11194	Special Trade Contractors
91305	3	5	Prof., Scientific, & Tech Svcs
91306	745	3452	Educational Services
91307	698	5774	Hospitals
91308	33	59	Telecommunications
91309	18	48	Administrative & Support Svcs
91310	10	20	Administrative & Support Svcs
91311	3103	35831	Merch. Wholesalers,Durable Gds
91313	38	160	Construction of Buildings
91316	1366	9108	Real Estate
91319	21	63	Administrative & Support Svcs
91320	1325	13298	Miscellaneous Manufacturing
91321	1476	8636	Educational Services
91322	31	58	Prof., Scientific, & Tech Svcs
91324	2460	17476	Food Svcs & Drinking Places
91325	972	11279	Chemical Manufacturing
91326	450	3039	Food Svcs & Drinking Places
91327	27	62	Relig., Grant, Civic, Prof Org
91328	16	182	Telecommunications
91329	3	4000	Computer & Electronic Prod Mfg
91330	13	2918	Educational Services
91331	1610	14616	Educational Services
91333	1	0	Special Trade Contractors
91334	2	3	Educational Services
91335	2247	11744	Educational Services
91337	17	44	Relig., Grant, Civic, Prof Org
91340	1232	12671	Educational Services
91341	8	105	Special Trade Contractors
91342	1480	21437	Miscellaneous Manufacturing
91343	928	10328	Motor Vehicle & Parts Dealers
91344	1520	9814	Educational Services
91345	578	6662	Hospitals
91346	13	66	Prof., Scientific, & Tech Svcs
91350	1102	6037	Educational Services
91351	1228	6862	Educational Services
91352	2094	21429	Merch. Wholesalers,Durable Gds
91353	12	71	Machinery Manufacturing
91354	141	914	Educational Services

BUSINESS DATA

ZIP CODE	2004 Total Firms	2004 Total Employ-ees	TOP INDUSTRY RANKED on 2004 EMPLOYMENT	ZIP CODE	2004 Total Firms	2004 Total Employ-ees	TOP INDUSTRY RANKED on 2004 EMPLOYMENT	ZIP CODE	2004 Total Firms	2004 Total Employ-ees	TOP INDUSTRY RANKED on 2004 EMPLOYMENT
91355	2325	37185	Amusement, Gambling,& Recreat.	91737	316	2994	Educational Services	92022	29	80	Support Activities: Agr./For.
91356	2253	12754	Ambulatory Health Care Svcs	91739	327	4084	Educational Services	92023	72	144	Prof., Scientific, & Tech Svcs
91357	42	147	Administrative & Support Svcs	91740	1259	7723	Food Svcs & Drinking Places	92024	3229	18660	Food Svcs & Drinking Places
91358	19	38	Clothing & Cloth'g Acc. Stores	91741	732	6352	Educational Services	92025	3094	26793	Ambulatory Health Care Svcs
91359	57	148	Prof., Scientific, & Tech Svcs	91743	24	133	Food Svcs & Drinking Places	92026	673	4942	Educational Services
91360	2049	17197	Insurance Carriers & Related	91744	1363	12997	Educational Services	92027	794	6401	Educational Services
91361	1485	11854	Prof., Scientific, & Tech Svcs	91745	1496	14771	Merch. Wholesalers,Nondur. Gds	92028	1604	9870	Merch. Wholesalers,Nondur. Gds
91362	2191	20539	Insurance Carriers & Related	91746	1230	18880	Fabricated Metal Product Mfg	92029	1379	15808	Special Trade Contractors
91363	2	650	Insurance Carriers & Related	91747	15	278	Postal Service	92030	27	54	Administrative & Support Svcs
91364	2686	16390	Prof., Scientific, & Tech Svcs	91748	2136	22086	Food Svcs & Drinking Places	92033	50	107	Special Trade Contractors
91365	42	77	Administrative & Support Svcs	91750	1003	8381	Educational Services	92036	278	1290	Accommodation
91367	2324	27436	Insurance Carriers & Related	91752	527	6965	Merch. Wholesalers,Durable Gds	92037	3275	27942	Prof., Scientific, & Tech Svcs
91371	5	78	Amusement, Gambling,& Recreat.	91754	1613	63468	Isps, Web Search Portals	92038	72	146	Relig., Grant, Civic, Prof Org
91372	32	122	Construction of Buildings	91755	443	2849	Credit Intermediation & Relatd	92039	11	10	Isps, Web Search Portals
91376	38	156	Prof., Scientific, & Tech Svcs	91759	16	73	Support Activities: Agr./For.	92040	1115	8976	Amusement, Gambling,& Recreat.
91377	173	1022	Educational Services	91761	2627	51774	Admin. of Economic Programs	92046	32	160	Chemical Manufacturing
91380	68	124	Construction of Buildings	91762	1782	11137	Educational Services	92049	15	51	Administrative & Support Svcs
91381	328	3600	Food Svcs & Drinking Places	91763	1488	13671	General Merchandise Stores	92051	17	58	Heavy & Civil Eng. Construct'N
91383	4	11	Food Svcs & Drinking Places	91764	1187	14329	Food Svcs & Drinking Places	92052	31	59	Social Assistance
91384	294	1555	Food Svcs & Drinking Places	91765	1336	10861	Prof., Scientific, & Tech Svcs	92054	2747	18844	Food Svcs & Drinking Places
91385	18	122	Merch. Wholesalers,Durable Gds	91766	1544	16021	Educational Services	92055	50	2231	Hospitals
91386	21	62	Prof., Scientific, & Tech Svcs	91767	1320	13732	Hospitals	92056	966	12103	Hospitals
91387	430	2105	Special Trade Contractors	91768	868	19192	Educational Services	92057	428	4303	Educational Services
91390	307	1146	Educational Services	91769	9	190	Postal Service	92058	4	4	Insurance Carriers & Related
91392	27	69	Administrative & Support Svcs	91770	1496	22672	Managmt of Companies & Enterp.	92059	27	194	Relig., Grant, Civic, Prof Org
91393	16	28	Ambulatory Health Care Svcs	91773	1452	16586	Special Trade Contractors	92060	22	123	Educational Services
91394	32	92	Special Trade Contractors	91775	252	1520	Educational Services	92061	100	655	Merch. Wholesalers,Nondur. Gds
91395	6	48	Transit & Grnd Pass. Transport	91776	1808	11077	Ambulatory Health Care Svcs	92064	2155	22959	Special Trade Contractors
91396	11	27	Prof., Scientific, & Tech Svcs	91778	7	24	Prof., Scientific, & Tech Svcs	92065	1215	6488	Educational Services
91401	1564	12327	Educational Services	91780	867	4791	Educational Services	92066	9	20	Chemical Manufacturing
91402	1287	8190	Food Svcs & Drinking Places	91784	344	1631	Educational Services	92067	86	224	Prof., Scientific, & Tech Svcs
91403	1840	11910	Prof., Scientific, & Tech Svcs	91785	44	121	Transit & Grnd Pass. Transport	92068	8	8	Clothing & Cloth'g Acc. Stores
91404	5	10	Prof., Scientific, & Tech Svcs	91786	3271	22141	Food Svcs & Drinking Places	92069	2527	23586	Educational Services
91405	1691	13798	Ambulatory Health Care Svcs	91788	18	116	Postal Service	92070	48	253	Food Manufacturing
91406	2868	26446	Merch. Wholesalers,Durable Gds	91789	1821	16998	Educational Services	92071	1745	14341	Food Svcs & Drinking Places
91407	6	11	Chemical Manufacturing	91790	1335	13506	Ambulatory Health Care Svcs	92072	37	338	Unclassified Establishments
91408	11	62	Administrative & Support Svcs	91791	717	6726	Food Svcs & Drinking Places	92074	36	71	Special Trade Contractors
91409	29	49	Relig., Grant, Civic, Prof Org	91792	311	1368	Food Svcs & Drinking Places	92075	1303	6998	Food Svcs & Drinking Places
91411	1269	9526	Prof., Scientific, & Tech Svcs	91793	15	175	Postal Service	92078	231	1874	Special Trade Contractors
91412	8	20	Special Trade Contractors	91801	1782	11337	Food Svcs & Drinking Places	92079	39	79	Special Trade Contractors
91413	41	109	Administrative & Support Svcs	91802	13	283	Postal Service	92081	1233	16716	Miscellaneous Manufacturing
91416	38	98	Prof., Scientific, & Tech Svcs	91803	979	10122	Heavy & Civil Eng. Construct'N	92082	580	2506	Educational Services
91423	1534	9355	Food Svcs & Drinking Places	91901	582	4790	Amusement, Gambling,& Recreat.	92083	1400	9052	Educational Services
91426	29	58	Educational Services	91902	457	2409	Food Svcs & Drinking Places	92084	1486	8188	Educational Services
91436	2799	16039	Prof., Scientific, & Tech Svcs	91903	33	62	Special Trade Contractors	92085	65	126	Chemical Manufacturing
91501	225	1091	Educational Services	91905	53	204	Nat'l Security & Int'l Affairs	92086	42	397	Accommodation
91502	1789	16206	Food Svcs & Drinking Places	91906	71	881	Amusement, Gambling,& Recreat.	92088	45	75	Special Trade Contractors
91503	7	9	Administrative & Support Svcs	91908	32	157	Prof., Scientific, & Tech Svcs	92091	480	3466	Accommodation
91504	724	10933	Prof., Scientific, & Tech Svcs	91909	12	25	Special Trade Contractors	92093	54	1195	Other Information Services
91505	2000	25905	Other Information Services	91910	2605	25859	Transportation Equipment Mfg	92096	5	476	Educational Services
91506	1068	7165	Administrative & Support Svcs	91911	2313	16939	Educational Services	92101	5736	68998	Prof., Scientific, & Tech Svcs
91507	14	29	Electronics & Appliance Stores	91912	30	45	Administrative & Support Svcs	92102	900	9080	Educational Services
91508	12	21	Administrative & Support Svcs	91913	164	892	Educational Services	92103	2735	24021	Hospitals
91510	26	115	Motion Pict. & Sound Recording	91914	102	1591	Prof., Scientific, & Tech Svcs	92104	1146	5612	Food Svcs & Drinking Places
91521	4	6020	Motion Pict. & Sound Recording	91915	104	773	Educational Services	92105	1072	6568	Educational Services
91522	5	244	Motion Pict. & Sound Recording	91916	50	166	Educational Services	92106	733	5388	Food Svcs & Drinking Places
91523	7	1244	Broadcasting	91917	26	56	Relig., Grant, Civic, Prof Org	92107	905	3389	Food Svcs & Drinking Places
91601	1894	9037	Motion Pict. & Sound Recording	91921	5	10	Securities/Commodity Contracts	92108	3339	55718	Educational Services
91602	780	4696	Food Svcs & Drinking Places	91931	13	31	Heavy & Civil Eng. Construct'N	92109	2310	20274	Amusement, Gambling,& Recreat.
91603	7	12	Motion Pict. & Sound Recording	91932	466	2773	Educational Services	92110	2447	27310	Food Svcs & Drinking Places
91604	1995	10653	Food Svcs & Drinking Places	91933	9	19	Bldg Matl & Garden Eqpmt Dlrs	92111	3299	37815	Administrative & Support Svcs
91605	2482	18751	Merch. Wholesalers,Durable Gds	91934	32	141	Relig., Grant, Civic, Prof Org	92112	23	65	Personal and Laundry Services
91606	1138	7977	Educational Services	91935	228	833	Educational Services	92113	878	12039	Merch. Wholesalers,Durable Gds
91607	877	5736	Administrative & Support Svcs	91941	2261	10935	Prof., Scientific, & Tech Svcs	92114	470	3401	Educational Services
91608	130	2931	Food Svcs & Drinking Places	91942	1073	12312	Hospitals	92115	1480	8183	Educational Services
91609	4	35	Clothing & Cloth'g Acc. Stores	91943	13	24	Miscellaneous Store Retailers	92116	796	2868	Educational Services
91610	4	5	Motion Pict. & Sound Recording	91944	36	156	Administrative & Support Svcs	92117	1511	10340	Educational Services
91614	21	88	Publishing Industries	91945	750	6695	Administrative & Support Svcs	92118	828	7671	Accommodation
91615	3	3	Prof., Scientific, & Tech Svcs	91946	10	26	Administrative & Support Svcs	92119	354	1811	Educational Services
91616	5	2	Merch. Wholesalers,Durable Gds	91948	11	32	Justice, Pubic Order/Safety	92120	1433	17960	Ambulatory Health Care Svcs
91617	6	13	Prof., Scientific, & Tech Svcs	91950	2285	20595	Motor Vehicle & Parts Dealers	92121	3253	72426	Prof., Scientific, & Tech Svcs
91618	6	19	Relig., Grant, Civic, Prof Org	91951	2	12	Prof., Scientific, & Tech Svcs	92122	1339	13475	Prof., Scientific, & Tech Svcs
91701	734	4725	Educational Services	91962	58	217	Educational Services	92123	2238	64674	Hospitals
91702	1261	15781	Educational Services	91963	20	59	Educational Services	92124	360	2400	Educational Services
91706	2057	24118	Ambulatory Health Care Svcs	91976	16	35	Construction of Buildings	92126	2532	21980	Food Svcs & Drinking Places
91708	40	273	Postal Service	91977	1027	6814	Educational Services	92127	711	16944	Electronics & Appliance Stores
91709	989	5889	Educational Services	91978	253	1435	Construction of Buildings	92128	1627	16521	Food Svcs & Drinking Places
91710	2948	35235	Merch. Wholesalers,Durable Gds	91979	20	43	Utilities	92129	740	4275	Educational Services
91711	1266	13879	Educational Services	91980	74	296	Relig., Grant, Civic, Prof Org	92130	1156	9998	Prof., Scientific, & Tech Svcs
91715	17	956	Postal Service	92003	210	1177	Merch. Wholesalers,Nondur. Gds	92131	812	10673	Prof., Scientific, & Tech Svcs
91722	799	7606	Food Svcs & Drinking Places	92004	199	1099	Accommodation	92132	6	720	Nat'l Security & Int'l Affairs
91723	1512	11757	Ambulatory Health Care Svcs	92007	386	1986	Food Svcs & Drinking Places	92134	33	5469	Hospitals
91724	659	5405	Educational Services	92008	3105	31488	Prof., Scientific, & Tech Svcs	92135	40	36322	Nat'l Security & Int'l Affairs
91729	63	265	Postal Service	92009	1475	14193	Accommodation	92136	28	43332	Nat'l Security & Int'l Affairs
91730	3405	33198	Food Svcs & Drinking Places	92013	25	109	Isps, Web Search Portals	92137	9	8	Food Svcs & Drinking Places
91731	1584	16940	Motor Vehicle & Parts Dealers	92014	1099	8376	Food Svcs & Drinking Places	92138	62	112	Truck Transportation
91732	948	6490	Educational Services	92018	76	133	Special Trade Contractors	92139	177	1615	Educational Services
91733	2561	19583	Merch. Wholesalers,Durable Gds	92019	844	9464	Educational Services	92140	12	7084	Nat'l Security & Int'l Affairs
91734	5	128	Postal Service	92020	3118	29102	Educational Services	92142	22	53	Prof., Scientific, & Tech Svcs
91735	1	0	Credit Intermediation & Relatd	92021	1760	11816	Food Svcs & Drinking Places	92143	4	2	Motor Vehicle & Parts Dealers

ZIP CODE	2004 Total Firms	2004 Total Employees	TOP INDUSTRY RANKED on 2004 EMPLOYMENT	ZIP CODE	2004 Total Firms	2004 Total Employees	TOP INDUSTRY RANKED on 2004 EMPLOYMENT	ZIP CODE	2004 Total Firms	2004 Total Employees	TOP INDUSTRY RANKED on 2004 EMPLOYMENT
92145	21	1228	Nat'l Security & Int'l Affairs	92280	2	18	Gasoline Stations	92415	84	7961	Justice, Pubic Order/Safety
92147	8	2556	Exec., Legis., & Other Support	92281	47	350	Educational Services	92418	36	1141	Exec., Legis., & Other Support
92149	6	13	Transit & Grnd Pass. Transport	92282	18	218	Educational Services	92423	12	27	Merch. Wholesalers,Durable Gds
92150	31	72	Special Trade Contractors	92283	36	351	Exec., Legis., & Other Support	92427	21	86	Ambulatory Health Care Svcs
92152	7	73	Exec., Legis., & Other Support	92284	911	5378	Food Svcs & Drinking Places	92501	1606	17347	Hospitals
92153	4	16	Support Act. for Transport.	92285	44	124	Relig., Grant, Civic, Prof Org	92502	22	60	Administrative & Support Svcs
92154	1758	16160	Merch. Wholesalers,Durable Gds	92286	31	55	Special Trade Contractors	92503	2528	22169	Educational Services
92155	7	99	Nat'l Security & Int'l Affairs	92301	272	3900	Truck Transportation	92504	1285	15408	Motor Vehicle & Parts Dealers
92158	3	80	Prof., Scientific, & Tech Svcs	92304	4	4	Merch. Wholesalers,Nondur. Gds	92505	697	4545	Food Svcs & Drinking Places
92159	34	69	Real Estate	92305	36	158	Accommodation	92506	1846	14792	Educational Services
92160	12	149	Unclassified Establishments	92307	864	5357	Hospitals	92507	1940	24689	Merch. Wholesalers,Durable Gds
92161	10	1826	Ambulatory Health Care Svcs	92308	568	3400	Educational Services	92508	515	3164	Credit Intermediation & Relatd
92162	5	6	Construction of Buildings	92309	54	568	Food Svcs & Drinking Places	92509	1276	12875	Educational Services
92163	23	24	Ambulatory Health Care Svcs	92310	56	556	Educational Services	92513	20	39	Merch. Wholesalers,Durable Gds
92164	16	22	Waste Managmt & Remediat'n Svc	92311	994	8076	Food Svcs & Drinking Places	92514	17	22	Waste Managmt & Remediat'n Svc
92165	7	8	Special Trade Contractors	92312	6	24	Administrative & Support Svcs	92515	8	20	Miscellaneous Store Retailers
92166	24	28	Prof., Scientific, & Tech Svcs	92313	369	3074	Educational Services	92516	29	71	Merch. Wholesalers,Durable Gds
92167	23	92	Special Trade Contractors	92314	366	1074	Ambulatory Health Care Svcs	92517	29	68	Food Svcs & Drinking Places
92168	13	85	Administrative & Support Svcs	92315	827	6489	Accommodation	92518	42	803	Relig., Grant, Civic, Prof Org
92169	45	94	Prof., Scientific, & Tech Svcs	92316	681	6981	Truck Transportation	92519	10	8	Special Trade Contractors
92170	2	1	Merch. Wholesalers,Durable Gds	92317	147	878	Food Svcs & Drinking Places	92521	7	3168	Museums, Hist. Sites,& Similar
92171	13	62	Administrative & Support Svcs	92318	7	9	Isps, Web Search Portals	92522	13	57	Exec., Legis., & Other Support
92172	19	76	Administrative & Support Svcs	92320	211	1145	Food Svcs & Drinking Places	92530	1154	6948	Educational Services
92173	745	5247	Educational Services	92321	55	362	Administrative & Support Svcs	92531	18	28	Truck Transportation
92174	4	8	Sportg Gds,Hobby,Book, & Music	92322	33	82	Merch. Wholesalers,Durable Gds	92532	143	6217	Support Act. for Transport.
92175	29	103	Bldg Matl & Garden Eqpmt Dlrs	92324	1467	12810	Educational Services	92536	52	171	Accommodation
92176	14	28	Merch. Wholesalers,Durable Gds	92325	366	1463	Food Svcs & Drinking Places	92539	117	586	Amusement, Gambling,& Recreat.
92177	39	114	Administrative & Support Svcs	92326	10	38	Relig., Grant, Civic, Prof Org	92543	1254	9416	Hospitals
92178	31	446	Perform'g Arts, Spec. Sports	92327	27	124	Merch. Wholesalers,Durable Gds	92544	695	4111	Educational Services
92179	5	1206	Justice, Pubic Order/Safety	92328	17	664	Accommodation	92545	486	5983	Food Svcs & Drinking Places
92182	30	1040	Personal and Laundry Services	92329	16	22	Special Trade Contractors	92546	18	36	Real Estate
92190	15	48	Administrative & Support Svcs	92332	3	7	Fabricated Metal Product Mfg	92548	68	146	Special Trade Contractors
92191	10	18	Merch. Wholesalers,Durable Gds	92333	34	169	Accommodation	92549	282	1167	Educational Services
92192	44	87	Prof., Scientific, & Tech Svcs	92334	28	43	Special Trade Contractors	92551	109	1825	Educational Services
92193	18	115	Administrative & Support Svcs	92335	2465	23775	Real Estate	92552	16	55	Relig., Grant, Civic, Prof Org
92194	2	1	Insurance Carriers & Related	92336	529	3796	Educational Services	92553	1695	11984	Food Svcs & Drinking Places
92195	11	23	Electronics & Appliance Stores	92337	790	13592	Truck Transportation	92554	6	80	Administrative & Support Svcs
92196	15	112	Relig., Grant, Civic, Prof Org	92338	6	57	Food and Beverage Stores	92555	136	4611	Hospitals
92198	29	42	Prof., Scientific, & Tech Svcs	92339	29	177	Accommodation	92556	24	27	Administrative & Support Svcs
92199	3	13	Food Svcs & Drinking Places	92340	36	73	Special Trade Contractors	92557	519	3844	Educational Services
92201	1746	14765	Educational Services	92341	25	114	Accommodation	92561	58	247	Educational Services
92202	10	18	Special Trade Contractors	92342	109	532	Food Svcs & Drinking Places	92562	1409	9105	Ambulatory Health Care Svcs
92203	56	1994	Amusement, Gambling,& Recreat.	92345	2002	11723	Educational Services	92563	365	2227	Food Svcs & Drinking Places
92210	256	3379	Accommodation	92346	855	7045	Amusement, Gambling,& Recreat.	92564	25	53	Special Trade Contractors
92211	980	9297	Administrative & Support Svcs	92347	24	133	Educational Services	92567	136	980	Special Trade Contractors
92220	697	5522	Food Svcs & Drinking Places	92350	6	366	Educational Services	92570	757	6021	Educational Services
92222	1	2	Postal Service	92352	516	2431	Educational Services	92571	386	6141	Transportation Equipment Mfg
92223	597	5336	Motor Vehicle & Parts Dealers	92354	494	13779	Hospitals	92572	3	4	Isps, Web Search Portals
92225	592	5153	Justice, Pubic Order/Safety	92356	137	894	Nonmetallic Mineral Prod. Mfg	92581	13	23	Prof., Scientific, & Tech Svcs
92226	5	9	Merch. Wholesalers,Durable Gds	92357	9	1452	Hospitals	92582	146	956	Nursing & Resid. Care Facilit.
92227	719	8866	Administrative & Support Svcs	92358	28	268	Accommodation	92583	528	4023	Educational Services
92230	170	3240	Amusement, Gambling,& Recreat.	92359	193	1210	Furniture & Related Prod. Mfg	92584	316	2055	Educational Services
92231	992	7045	Educational Services	92363	302	1869	Food Svcs & Drinking Places	92585	144	1412	Hospitals
92232	4	8	Rental and Leasing Services	92364	4	25	Food and Beverage Stores	92586	428	2284	Nursing & Resid. Care Facilit.
92233	96	2823	Justice, Pubic Order/Safety	92365	60	256	Educational Services	92587	373	1599	Special Trade Contractors
92234	1540	11086	Motor Vehicle & Parts Dealers	92366	3	143	Mining (Except Oil and Gas)	92589	55	106	Special Trade Contractors
92235	25	54	Special Trade Contractors	92368	27	317	Merch. Wholesalers,Nondur. Gds	92590	2293	14506	Prof., Scientific, & Tech Svcs
92236	435	6091	Utilities	92369	13	166	Admin. Enviro. Quality Progrms	92591	1052	14078	Miscellaneous Manufacturing
92239	26	213	Unclassified Establishments	92371	273	1776	Educational Services	92592	654	7386	Amusement, Gambling,& Recreat.
92240	496	2639	Educational Services	92372	59	190	Educational Services	92593	35	159	Food Svcs & Drinking Places
92241	100	392	Motor Vehicle & Parts Dealers	92373	1720	17623	Ambulatory Health Care Svcs	92595	393	2482	Educational Services
92242	42	166	Accommodation	92374	999	10626	Educational Services	92596	108	493	Educational Services
92243	1768	19761	Merch. Wholesalers,Nondur. Gds	92375	19	18	Prof., Scientific, & Tech Svcs	92599	2	2550	Nonstore Retailers
92244	15	131	Administrative & Support Svcs	92376	1551	11096	Educational Services	92602	220	4647	Food Svcs & Drinking Places
92249	36	355	Utilities	92377	272	2563	Educational Services	92603	17	23	Construction of Buildings
92250	204	3450	Support Activities: Agr./For.	92378	65	287	Bldg Matl & Garden Eqpmt Dlrs	92604	1241	7991	Food Svcs & Drinking Places
92251	254	3102	Educational Services	92382	216	1527	Accommodation	92605	18	31	Prof., Scientific, & Tech Svcs
92252	208	2509	Ambulatory Health Care Svcs	92384	18	66	Educational Services	92606	894	15621	Computer & Electronic Prod Mfg
92253	708	7440	Accommodation	92385	31	97	Social Assistance	92607	47	281	Postal Service
92254	70	490	Merch. Wholesalers,Nondur. Gds	92386	31	49	Food and Beverage Stores	92609	46	64	Credit Intermediation & Relatd
92255	41	107	Special Trade Contractors	92389	11	33	Administrative & Support Svcs	92610	352	7149	Merch. Wholesalers,Durable Gds
92256	99	253	Special Trade Contractors	92391	80	365	Educational Services	92612	2536	25811	Prof., Scientific, & Tech Svcs
92257	58	222	Animal Production	92392	2548	23439	Educational Services	92614	2446	38054	Prof., Scientific, & Tech Svcs
92258	88	545	Merch. Wholesalers,Durable Gds	92393	31	43	Special Trade Contractors	92615	32	53	Real Estate
92259	17	46	Truck Transportation	92394	200	1850	Truck Transportation	92616	22	51	Special Trade Contractors
92260	2549	21091	Food Svcs & Drinking Places	92397	174	831	Food Svcs & Drinking Places	92618	2304	45958	Prof., Scientific, & Tech Svcs
92261	66	163	Special Trade Contractors	92398	58	408	Educational Services	92619	28	47	Merch. Wholesalers,Durable Gds
92262	2197	16561	Food Svcs & Drinking Places	92399	1239	6504	Educational Services	92620	400	2269	Educational Services
92263	111	322	Merch. Wholesalers,Nondur. Gds	92401	581	6993	Admin. of Economic Programs	92623	31	711	Postal Service
92264	898	6208	Accommodation	92402	9	19	Real Estate	92624	373	1673	Administrative & Support Svcs
92266	19	29	Food Svcs & Drinking Places	92403	1	1200	Postal Service	92625	696	3483	Food Svcs & Drinking Places
92267	17	162	Accommodation	92404	1077	7210	Educational Services	92626	3850	52570	Prof., Scientific, & Tech Svcs
92268	20	41	Food Svcs & Drinking Places	92405	547	4014	Educational Services	92627	3588	19080	Food Svcs & Drinking Places
92270	854	11700	Ambulatory Health Care Svcs	92406	17	29	Construction of Buildings	92628	44	99	Administrative & Support Svcs
92273	18	161	Educational Services	92407	717	8473	Educational Services	92629	1358	7995	Food Svcs & Drinking Places
92274	204	4136	Merch. Wholesalers,Nondur. Gds	92408	1702	20784	Food Svcs & Drinking Places	92630	2773	20393	Food Svcs & Drinking Places
92275	29	416	Justice, Pubic Order/Safety	92410	1179	9552	Educational Services	92646	1143	6635	Educational Services
92276	221	2415	Special Trade Contractors	92411	405	5476	Ambulatory Health Care Svcs	92647	2724	29086	Transportation Equipment Mfg
92277	413	3333	Publishing Industries	92412	11	22	Perform'g Arts, Spec. Sports	92648	2175	12643	Food Svcs & Drinking Places
92278	13	550	Hospitals	92413	12	13	Prof., Scientific, & Tech Svcs	92649	1762	15178	Merch. Wholesalers,Durable Gds

BUSINESS DATA

ZIP CODE	2004 Total Firms	2004 Total Employ-ees	TOP INDUSTRY RANKED on 2004 EMPLOYMENT	ZIP CODE	2004 Total Firms	2004 Total Employ-ees	TOP INDUSTRY RANKED on 2004 EMPLOYMENT	ZIP CODE	2004 Total Firms	2004 Total Employ-ees	TOP INDUSTRY RANKED on 2004 EMPLOYMENT
92650	3	26	Relig., Grant, Civic, Prof Org	92865	1607	15850	Special Trade Contractors	93216	6	24	Truck Transportation
92651	2157	10518	Food Svcs & Drinking Places	92866	866	4852	Prof., Scientific, & Tech Svcs	93218	35	139	Crop Production
92652	61	138	Special Trade Contractors	92867	2864	19479	Food Svcs & Drinking Places	93219	98	540	Educational Services
92653	3411	23742	Ambulatory Health Care Svcs	92868	2177	38329	Hospitals	93220	16	4904	Beverage & Tobacco Product Mfg
92654	23	326	Postal Service	92869	872	5745	Educational Services	93221	454	4104	Merch. Wholesalers,Nondur. Gds
92655	169	556	Educational Services	92870	1969	13500	Food Svcs & Drinking Places	93222	10	23	Prof., Scientific, & Tech Svcs
92656	1259	9548	Prof., Scientific, & Tech Svcs	92871	25	119	Postal Service	93223	148	1418	Educational Services
92657	85	496	Educational Services	92877	17	43	Special Trade Contractors	93224	30	442	Oil and Gas Extraction
92658	44	371	Postal Service	92878	53	184	Postal Service	93225	265	808	Accommodation
92659	48	86	Prof., Scientific, & Tech Svcs	92879	1787	18523	Food Svcs & Drinking Places	93226	17	100	Relig., Grant, Civic, Prof Org
92660	4811	44841	Prof., Scientific, & Tech Svcs	92880	1014	14566	Merch. Wholesalers,Durable Gds	93227	41	299	Merch. Wholesalers,Nondur. Gds
92661	168	887	Food Svcs & Drinking Places	92881	539	6210	Educational Services	93230	1794	19890	Food Manufacturing
92662	168	459	Food Svcs & Drinking Places	92882	1573	13618	Educational Services	93232	14	36	Construction of Buildings
92663	2013	14560	Hospitals	92883	190	2536	Special Trade Contractors	93234	136	1182	Merch. Wholesalers,Nondur. Gds
92672	1843	7840	Food Svcs & Drinking Places	92885	28	163	Postal Service	93235	73	529	Merch. Wholesalers,Nondur. Gds
92673	911	7176	Miscellaneous Manufacturing	92886	1340	7535	Food Svcs & Drinking Places	93238	121	694	Food Svcs & Drinking Places
92674	51	623	Merch. Wholesalers,Nondur. Gds	92887	702	6237	Food Svcs & Drinking Places	93239	45	449	Food Svcs & Drinking Places
92675	1979	13250	Ambulatory Health Care Svcs	92899	1	0	Postal Service	93240	326	2266	Justice, Pubic Order/Safety
92676	88	247	Educational Services	93001	1998	14088	Food Svcs & Drinking Places	93241	251	2020	Ambulatory Health Care Svcs
92677	2335	13606	Food Svcs & Drinking Places	93002	47	147	Administrative & Support Svcs	93242	57	322	Educational Services
92678	14	40	Postal Service	93003	4002	34947	Prof., Scientific, & Tech Svcs	93243	125	1265	Repair and Maintenance
92679	587	2033	Amusement, Gambling,& Recreat.	93004	615	2794	Educational Services	93244	23	154	Educational Services
92683	3657	20059	Educational Services	93005	16	30	Heavy & Civil Eng. Construct'N	93245	587	14868	Nat'l Security & Int'l Affairs
92684	22	80	Special Trade Contractors	93006	46	76	Bldg Matl & Garden Eqpmt Dlrs	93247	352	3643	Merch. Wholesalers,Nondur. Gds
92685	7	142	Postal Service	93007	15	30	Special Trade Contractors	93249	62	3271	Crop Production
92688	1192	10725	Food Svcs & Drinking Places	93009	77	3765	Exec., Legis., & Other Support	93250	177	3114	Merch. Wholesalers,Nondur. Gds
92690	49	322	Postal Service	93010	2008	14592	Food Svcs & Drinking Places	93251	31	369	Construction of Buildings
92691	2409	20312	Prof., Scientific, & Tech Svcs	93011	47	249	Insurance Carriers & Related	93252	46	318	Oil and Gas Extraction
92692	1138	6734	Real Estate	93012	835	17286	Computer & Electronic Prod Mfg	93254	44	382	Crop Production
92693	22	39	Relig., Grant, Civic, Prof Org	93013	757	6511	Merch. Wholesalers,Nondur. Gds	93255	8	12	Gasoline Stations
92694	91	213	Miscellaneous Store Retailers	93014	13	45	Special Trade Contractors	93256	108	732	Food Manufacturing
92697	36	9212	Educational Services	93015	430	2776	Merch. Wholesalers,Nondur. Gds	93257	1823	18439	Hospitals
92698	2	11	Credit Intermediation & Relatd	93016	9	48	Animal Production	93258	17	47	Truck Transportation
92701	2177	21864	Exec., Legis., & Other Support	93020	18	78	Real Estate	93260	8	28	Educational Services
92702	5	16	Postal Service	93021	1092	12186	Computer & Electronic Prod Mfg	93261	22	188	Educational Services
92703	1207	8268	Exec., Legis., & Other Support	93022	226	467	Nursing & Resid. Care Facilit.	93262	12	202	Accommodation
92704	2454	28529	Educational Services	93023	1027	6536	Educational Services	93263	368	3316	Support Act. for Transport.
92705	4432	52057	Merch. Wholesalers,Durable Gds	93024	28	68	Prof., Scientific, & Tech Svcs	93265	160	741	Support Activities: Agr./For.
92706	904	7969	Educational Services	93030	2048	24008	Merch. Wholesalers,Nondur. Gds	93266	41	421	Crop Production
92707	1409	18534	Prof., Scientific, & Tech Svcs	93031	25	39	Administrative & Support Svcs	93267	95	878	Merch. Wholesalers,Nondur. Gds
92708	2733	23504	Hospitals	93032	2	3	Waste Managmt & Remediat'n Svc	93268	447	4723	Educational Services
92711	22	65	Social Assistance	93033	990	10763	Educational Services	93270	99	1050	Support Activities: Agr./For.
92712	1	0	Administrative & Support Svcs	93034	7	12	Miscellaneous Store Retailers	93271	141	556	Food Svcs & Drinking Places
92728	21	29	Merch. Wholesalers,Durable Gds	93035	423	1839	Food Svcs & Drinking Places	93272	106	1000	Animal Production
92735	5	16	Special Trade Contractors	93036	1249	13684	Food Svcs & Drinking Places	93274	1785	14594	Educational Services
92780	3880	30412	Prof., Scientific, & Tech Svcs	93040	41	205	Merch. Wholesalers,Nondur. Gds	93275	17	49	Heavy & Civil Eng. Construct'N
92781	57	244	Postal Service	93041	382	2594	Food Svcs & Drinking Places	93276	9	823	Support Activities for Mining
92782	299	3774	Motor Vehicle & Parts Dealers	93042	19	5083	Nat'l Security & Int'l Affairs	93277	1693	15359	Educational Services
92799	23	36	Food Svcs & Drinking Places	93043	9	9835	Nat'l Security & Int'l Affairs	93278	28	402	Paper Manufacturing
92801	2458	23788	Special Trade Contractors	93044	13	37	Truck Transportation	93279	30	59	Nursing & Resid. Care Facilit.
92802	996	13691	Accommodation	93060	875	7959	Administrative & Support Svcs	93280	383	3619	Bldg Matl & Garden Eqpmt Dlrs
92803	20	46	Electronics & Appliance Stores	93061	6	17	Support Activities: Agr./For.	93282	4	4	Administrative & Support Svcs
92804	1817	9831	Educational Services	93062	39	247	Relig., Grant, Civic, Prof Org	93283	31	174	Educational Services
92805	2333	25613	Educational Services	93063	1436	9971	Food Svcs & Drinking Places	93285	81	213	Real Estate
92806	2805	42955	Ambulatory Health Care Svcs	93064	2	70	Accommodation	93286	198	3531	Support Activities: Agr./For.
92807	2094	23292	Merch. Wholesalers,Durable Gds	93065	2931	23810	Ambulatory Health Care Svcs	93287	6	15	Justice, Pubic Order/Safety
92808	461	4072	Credit Intermediation & Relatd	93066	173	1796	Crop Production	93290	7	35	Nursing & Resid. Care Facilit.
92809	6	6	Prof., Scientific, & Tech Svcs	93067	77	288	Food Svcs & Drinking Places	93291	1918	23053	Hospitals
92811	12	36	Prof., Scientific, & Tech Svcs	93094	13	40	Special Trade Contractors	93292	1119	9886	Merch. Wholesalers,Nondur. Gds
92812	12	14	Prof., Scientific, & Tech Svcs	93101	3766	24392	Food Svcs & Drinking Places	93301	2573	22144	Ambulatory Health Care Svcs
92814	10	20	Special Trade Contractors	93102	26	116	Relig., Grant, Civic, Prof Org	93302	19	55	Administrative & Support Svcs
92815	8	10	Perform'g Arts, Spec. Sports	93103	927	8062	Special Trade Contractors	93303	11	12	Prof., Scientific, & Tech Svcs
92816	4	8	Special Trade Contractors	93105	1566	14389	Ambulatory Health Care Svcs	93304	1291	9329	Educational Services
92817	34	51	Merch. Wholesalers,Durable Gds	93106	11	8325	Educational Services	93305	935	7612	Hospitals
92821	2792	33949	Food Svcs & Drinking Places	93107	1	59	Food Svcs & Drinking Places	93306	991	7398	Educational Services
92822	33	63	Administrative & Support Svcs	93108	711	5059	Accommodation	93307	1290	14616	Admin. Human Resource Programs
92823	61	1215	Heavy & Civil Eng. Construct'N	93109	305	3590	Educational Services	93308	2044	26783	Special Trade Contractors
92825	2	16	Transit & Grnd Pass. Transport	93110	463	6386	Insurance Carriers & Related	93309	2406	20814	Food Svcs & Drinking Places
92831	2055	21888	Educational Services	93111	706	5435	Prof., Scientific, & Tech Svcs	93311	454	5837	Insurance Carriers & Related
92832	1265	11494	Educational Services	93116	20	48	Truck Transportation	93312	746	4784	Food Svcs & Drinking Places
92833	1120	9178	Computer & Electronic Prod Mfg	93117	1603	19034	Prof., Scientific, & Tech Svcs	93313	931	10451	Motor Vehicle & Parts Dealers
92834	20	306	Postal Service	93118	9	36	Administrative & Support Svcs	93314	383	3948	Merch. Wholesalers,Nondur. Gds
92835	890	14291	Hospitals	93120	20	18	Prof., Scientific, & Tech Svcs	93380	26	76	Special Trade Contractors
92836	6	3	Prof., Scientific, & Tech Svcs	93121	16	55	Truck Transportation	93384	37	52	Special Trade Contractors
92837	11	16	Administrative & Support Svcs	93130	60	130	Perform'g Arts, Spec. Sports	93385	8	9	Special Trade Contractors
92838	25	42	Special Trade Contractors	93140	29	69	Special Trade Contractors	93386	19	68	Amusement, Gambling,& Recreat.
92840	1359	9284	Educational Services	93150	31	56	Prof., Scientific, & Tech Svcs	93387	1	2	Construction of Buildings
92841	1203	14915	Fabricated Metal Product Mfg	93160	29	40	Electronics & Appliance Stores	93388	9	7	Special Trade Contractors
92842	44	118	Waste Managmt & Remediat'n Svc	93190	19	17	Merch. Wholesalers,Nondur. Gds	93389	36	52	Special Trade Contractors
92843	1978	13277	Educational Services	93201	16	69	Educational Services	93390	23	53	Special Trade Contractors
92844	876	3967	Food Svcs & Drinking Places	93202	62	326	Educational Services	93401	3233	26630	Prof., Scientific, & Tech Svcs
92845	384	2263	Educational Services	93203	231	2827	Merch. Wholesalers,Nondur. Gds	93402	602	1800	Prof., Scientific, & Tech Svcs
92846	11	44	Postal Service	93204	137	748	Educational Services	93403	51	824	Educational Services
92856	25	68	Special Trade Contractors	93205	20	50	Heavy & Civil Eng. Construct'N	93405	613	6630	Food Svcs & Drinking Places
92857	15	68	Construction of Buildings	93206	109	1500	Merch. Wholesalers,Nondur. Gds	93406	91	231	Prof., Scientific, & Tech Svcs
92859	29	10121	Administrative & Support Svcs	93207	15	66	Exec., Legis., & Other Support	93407	16	3930	Educational Services
92860	867	8835	Educational Services	93208	5	11	Accommodation	93408	38	825	Exec., Legis., & Other Support
92861	190	894	Educational Services	93210	366	5390	Merch. Wholesalers,Nondur. Gds	93409	2	203	Hospitals
92862	1	0	Relig., Grant, Civic, Prof Org	93212	240	4523	Justice, Pubic Order/Safety	93412	33	36	Special Trade Contractors
92863	45	424	Postal Service	93215	775	8215	Merch. Wholesalers,Nondur. Gds	93420	1423	7623	Educational Services

ZIP CODE	2004 Total Firms	2004 Total Employ-ees	TOP INDUSTRY RANKED on 2004 EMPLOYMENT	ZIP CODE	2004 Total Firms	2004 Total Employ-ees	TOP INDUSTRY RANKED on 2004 EMPLOYMENT	ZIP CODE	2004 Total Firms	2004 Total Employ-ees	TOP INDUSTRY RANKED on 2004 EMPLOYMENT
93421	46	49	Construction of Buildings	93590	34	63	Special Trade Contractors	93740	18	2675	Isps, Web Search Portals
93422	1556	9715	Hospitals	93591	124	482	Educational Services	93741	1	2533	Educational Services
93423	56	82	Special Trade Contractors	93601	73	155	Educational Services	93744	17	20	Administrative & Support Svcs
93424	90	1675	Utilities	93602	159	752	Amusement, Gambling,& Recreat.	93745	3	2	Special Trade Contractors
93426	40	266	Accommodation	93603	14	46	Accommodation	93747	25	59	Merch. Wholesalers,Durable Gds
93427	331	2287	Food Svcs & Drinking Places	93604	74	786	Accommodation	93750	3	232	Admin. Human Resource Programs
93428	549	1875	Food Svcs & Drinking Places	93605	12	44	Educational Services	93755	34	327	Relig., Grant, Civic, Prof Org
93429	7	43	Food Svcs & Drinking Places	93606	16	36	Merch. Wholesalers,Nondur. Gds	93761	1	15	Relig., Grant, Civic, Prof Org
93430	167	473	Food Svcs & Drinking Places	93607	4	1	Animal Production	93771	1	2	Truck Transportation
93432	36	102	Food Svcs & Drinking Places	93608	23	223	Animal Production	93772	1	0	Prof., Scientific, & Tech Svcs
93433	664	3314	Food Svcs & Drinking Places	93609	125	858	Crop Production	93773	1	1	Unclassified Establishments
93434	123	1426	Support Activities: Agr./For.	93610	375	4000	Justice, Pubic Order/Safety	93774	1	0	Administrative & Support Svcs
93435	11	20	Beverage & Tobacco Product Mfg	93611	1095	9301	Educational Services	93775	2	2	Merch. Wholesalers,Durable Gds
93436	1327	10338	Educational Services	93612	1913	14856	Merch. Wholesalers,Durable Gds	93776	4	4	Merch. Wholesalers,Nondur. Gds
93437	51	573	Educational Services	93613	66	127	Prof., Scientific, & Tech Svcs	93777	2	3	Special Trade Contractors
93438	16	33	Special Trade Contractors	93614	378	1013	Educational Services	93779	2	2	Insurance Carriers & Related
93440	54	258	Animal Production	93615	81	1461	Merch. Wholesalers,Nondur. Gds	93780	1	450	General Merchandise Stores
93441	129	750	Beverage & Tobacco Product Mfg	93616	39	1339	Merch. Wholesalers,Nondur. Gds	93790	3	2	Support Act. for Transport.
93442	764	4021	Food Svcs & Drinking Places	93618	611	7572	Merch. Wholesalers,Nondur. Gds	93791	4	4	Prof., Scientific, & Tech Svcs
93443	30	40	Relig., Grant, Civic, Prof Org	93620	208	1414	Educational Services	93792	2	4	Clothing & Cloth'g Acc. Stores
93444	471	2266	Miscellaneous Store Retailers	93621	19	174	Educational Services	93793	4	38	Administrative & Support Svcs
93445	168	740	Truck Transportation	93622	247	3414	Merch. Wholesalers,Nondur. Gds	93794	9	7	Construction of Buildings
93446	1998	13639	Food Svcs & Drinking Places	93623	25	418	Accommodation	93901	2672	31980	Merch. Wholesalers,Nondur. Gds
93447	84	132	Prof., Scientific, & Tech Svcs	93624	37	2288	Administrative & Support Svcs	93902	46	91	Social Assistance
93448	43	79	Prof., Scientific, & Tech Svcs	93625	195	2813	Administrative & Support Svcs	93905	699	5397	Educational Services
93449	559	3759	Food Svcs & Drinking Places	93626	53	481	Exec., Legis., & Other Support	93906	1080	11768	Educational Services
93450	26	263	Special Trade Contractors	93627	9	85	Merch. Wholesalers,Nondur. Gds	93907	640	7054	General Merchandise Stores
93451	107	3486	Nat'l Security & Int'l Affairs	93628	5	8	Accommodation	93908	462	5639	Merch. Wholesalers,Nondur. Gds
93452	49	971	Exec., Legis., & Other Support	93630	380	2627	Support Activities: Agr./For.	93912	43	64	Special Trade Contractors
93453	137	374	Educational Services	93631	442	4966	Merch. Wholesalers,Nondur. Gds	93915	7	5	Construction of Buildings
93454	1812	16611	Food Svcs & Drinking Places	93633	9	652	Museums, Hist. Sites,& Similar	93920	84	1197	Accommodation
93455	1250	11514	Merch. Wholesalers,Durable Gds	93634	15	607	Accommodation	93921	116	251	Prof., Scientific, & Tech Svcs
93456	51	383	Food and Beverage Stores	93635	831	7061	Educational Services	93922	92	152	Administrative & Support Svcs
93457	25	26	Special Trade Contractors	93637	1045	13241	Food Manufacturing	93923	1688	10366	Food Svcs & Drinking Places
93458	832	8172	Administrative & Support Svcs	93638	976	9815	Ambulatory Health Care Svcs	93924	410	1479	Accommodation
93460	359	1969	Amusement, Gambling,& Recreat.	93639	12	30	Truck Transportation	93925	34	266	Crop Production
93461	38	529	Administrative & Support Svcs	93640	163	3890	Merch. Wholesalers,Nondur. Gds	93926	181	3197	Administrative & Support Svcs
93463	726	3956	Accommodation	93641	20	116	Educational Services	93927	256	5028	Administrative & Support Svcs
93464	19	30	Prof., Scientific, & Tech Svcs	93642	1	15	Accommodation	93928	2	7	Relig., Grant, Civic, Prof Org
93465	439	2400	Hospitals	93643	136	333	Educational Services	93930	455	4435	Food Manufacturing
93483	19	25	Special Trade Contractors	93644	925	4106	Food Svcs & Drinking Places	93932	14	60	Educational Services
93501	224	2133	Transportation Equipment Mfg	93645	21	201	Bldg Matl & Garden Eqpmt Dlrs	93933	617	3849	Relig., Grant, Civic, Prof Org
93502	1	0	Relig., Grant, Civic, Prof Org	93646	137	1360	Merch. Wholesalers,Nondur. Gds	93940	3306	27071	Hospitals
93504	2	3	Prof., Scientific, & Tech Svcs	93647	157	1506	Merch. Wholesalers,Nondur. Gds	93942	75	131	Social Assistance
93505	200	875	Educational Services	93648	153	1338	Merch. Wholesalers,Nondur. Gds	93943	14	1447	Nat'l Security & Int'l Affairs
93510	259	1242	Educational Services	93649	1	0	Isps, Web Search Portals	93944	12	23	Other Information Services
93512	14	31	Educational Services	93650	170	2352	Nonstore Retailers	93950	898	5155	Educational Services
93513	60	262	Educational Services	93651	67	351	Educational Services	93953	129	2564	Accommodation
93514	821	5281	Food Svcs & Drinking Places	93652	12	467	Administrative & Support Svcs	93954	16	197	Crop Production
93515	12	27	Unclassified Establishments	93653	41	166	Prof., Scientific, & Tech Svcs	93955	1044	7543	Motor Vehicle & Parts Dealers
93516	75	1489	Mining (Except Oil and Gas)	93654	695	10506	Merch. Wholesalers,Nondur. Gds	93960	242	2803	Merch. Wholesalers,Nondur. Gds
93517	128	1158	Heavy & Civil Eng. Construct'N	93656	112	782	Educational Services	93962	20	283	Merch. Wholesalers,Nondur. Gds
93518	31	72	Educational Services	93657	694	6642	Educational Services	94002	979	8361	Educational Services
93519	2	5	Educational Services	93660	75	609	Crop Production	94005	356	7953	Merch. Wholesalers,Durable Gds
93522	2	1	Postal Service	93661	3	3	Animal Production	94010	3007	23758	Prof., Scientific, & Tech Svcs
93523	44	1795	Space Research and Technology	93662	691	7916	Food and Beverage Stores	94011	57	118	Unclassified Establishments
93524	34	16225	Nat'l Security & Int'l Affairs	93664	93	429	Accommodation	94013	1	20	Food Manufacturing
93526	74	798	Exec., Legis., & Other Support	93665	10	167	Food Manufacturing	94014	1000	10915	Motor Vehicle & Parts Dealers
93527	69	317	Support Act. for Transport.	93666	13	123	Merch. Wholesalers,Nondur. Gds	94015	1200	12345	Ambulatory Health Care Svcs
93528	8	15	Utilities	93667	50	321	Educational Services	94016	1	5	Personal and Laundry Services
93529	84	492	Accommodation	93668	42	448	Educational Services	94017	11	17	Administrative & Support Svcs
93530	4	30	Heavy & Civil Eng. Construct'N	93669	7	142	Accommodation	94018	43	72	Prof., Scientific, & Tech Svcs
93531	13	28	Prof., Scientific, & Tech Svcs	93670	5	11	Educational Services	94019	928	5886	Merch. Wholesalers,Nondur. Gds
93532	63	387	Accommodation	93673	17	281	Merch. Wholesalers,Nondur. Gds	94020	72	397	Educational Services
93534	2281	21527	Hospitals	93675	65	151	Perform'g Arts, Spec. Sports	94021	10	72	Accommodation
93535	795	7927	Educational Services	93701	475	2747	Educational Services	94022	1388	6339	Prof., Scientific, & Tech Svcs
93536	862	8285	Educational Services	93702	796	6179	Educational Services	94023	37	68	Merch. Wholesalers,Durable Gds
93539	34	324	Relig., Grant, Civic, Prof Org	93703	990	7881	Educational Services	94024	451	2324	Educational Services
93541	61	336	Support Activities: Agr./For.	93704	1154	8426	Educational Services	94025	2359	33077	Admin. Enviro. Quality Progrms
93542	1	7	Merch. Wholesalers,Durable Gds	93705	554	3149	Educational Services	94026	54	101	Prof., Scientific, & Tech Svcs
93543	256	1225	Educational Services	93706	1077	16300	Animal Production	94027	121	1320	Educational Services
93544	19	57	Amusement, Gambling,& Recreat.	93707	6	4	Electronics & Appliance Stores	94028	212	1284	Prof., Scientific, & Tech Svcs
93545	122	719	Educational Services	93708	4	2	Isps, Web Search Portals	94030	810	5912	Accommodation
93546	810	7404	Accommodation	93709	2	1	Prof., Scientific, & Tech Svcs	94035	20	183	Credit Intermediation & Relatd
93549	25	529	Unclassified Establishments	93710	2055	17887	Food Svcs & Drinking Places	94037	67	254	Educational Services
93550	1827	11511	Educational Services	93711	2019	16772	Prof., Scientific, & Tech Svcs	94038	127	470	Hospitals
93551	904	9130	Food Svcs & Drinking Places	93712	1	0	Real Estate	94039	19	49	Electronics & Appliance Stores
93552	235	1797	Educational Services	93714	4	2	Special Trade Contractors	94040	1353	13009	Hospitals
93553	58	181	Educational Services	93715	1	0	Hospitals	94041	597	5984	Electronics & Appliance Stores
93554	10	48	Mining (Except Oil and Gas)	93717	1	0	Administrative & Support Svcs	94042	18	22	Real Estate
93555	996	20767	Nat'l Security & Int'l Affairs	93718	1	0	Special Trade Contractors	94043	1543	27011	Electronics & Appliance Stores
93556	16	70	Prof., Scientific, & Tech Svcs	93720	1630	13766	Ambulatory Health Care Svcs	94044	1022	4427	Food Svcs & Drinking Places
93558	2	0	Postal Service	93721	1390	29262	Hospitals	94060	93	924	Crop Production
93560	292	1022	Food Svcs & Drinking Places	93722	1836	14439	Educational Services	94061	714	4250	Educational Services
93561	780	3825	Food Svcs & Drinking Places	93724	1	0	Justice, Pubic Order/Safety	94062	829	4083	Ambulatory Health Care Svcs
93562	58	1993	Chemical Manufacturing	93725	705	13149	Merch. Wholesalers,Durable Gds	94063	2803	29532	Prof., Scientific, & Tech Svcs
93563	8	147	Relig., Grant, Civic, Prof Org	93726	1476	10862	Food Svcs & Drinking Places	94064	41	51	Heavy & Civil Eng. Construct'N
93581	27	72	Relig., Grant, Civic, Prof Org	93727	1965	20136	Special Trade Contractors	94065	316	16156	Publishing Industries
93584	12	20	Special Trade Contractors	93728	701	4044	Food Svcs & Drinking Places	94066	1280	9087	Food Svcs & Drinking Places
93586	21	21	Administrative & Support Svcs	93729	65	118	Administrative & Support Svcs	94070	2361	16113	Prof., Scientific, & Tech Svcs

ZIP CODE	2004 Total Firms	2004 Total Employees	TOP INDUSTRY RANKED on 2004 EMPLOYMENT	ZIP CODE	2004 Total Firms	2004 Total Employees	TOP INDUSTRY RANKED on 2004 EMPLOYMENT	ZIP CODE	2004 Total Firms	2004 Total Employees	TOP INDUSTRY RANKED on 2004 EMPLOYMENT
94074	9	23	Computer & Electronic Prod Mfg	94534	948	11297	Food Svcs & Drinking Places	94708	146	484	Educational Services
94080	3095	39647	Merch. Wholesalers,Nondur. Gds	94535	144	14305	Nat'l Security & Int'l Affairs	94709	448	3109	Educational Services
94083	31	70	Repair and Maintenance	94536	1547	7844	Educational Services	94710	1414	16372	Chemical Manufacturing
94085	893	25564	Computer & Electronic Prod Mfg	94537	33	62	Administrative & Support Svcs	94712	11	26	Prof., Scientific, & Tech Svcs
94086	1113	13444	Computer & Electronic Prod Mfg	94538	3525	52862	Computer & Electronic Prod Mfg	94720	84	11978	Educational Services
94087	1597	10776	Motor Vehicle & Parts Dealers	94539	1378	16690	Computer & Electronic Prod Mfg	94801	696	6283	Prof., Scientific, & Tech Svcs
94088	21	91	Exec., Legis., & Other Support	94540	21	33	Administrative & Support Svcs	94802	4	10	Transit & Grnd Pass. Transport
94089	693	26594	Merch. Wholesalers,Durable Gds	94541	2122	12345	General Merchandise Stores	94803	687	2789	Educational Services
94102	2932	42523	Prof., Scientific, & Tech Svcs	94542	116	1951	Educational Services	94804	1324	14120	Exec., Legis., & Other Support
94103	4342	46131	Prof., Scientific, & Tech Svcs	94543	12	15	Special Trade Contractors	94805	401	2524	Admin. Human Resource Programs
94104	2656	25939	Prof., Scientific, & Tech Svcs	94544	1773	21330	Special Trade Contractors	94806	1219	11757	Hospitals
94105	2494	65375	Prof., Scientific, & Tech Svcs	94545	2302	33694	Hospitals	94807	8	17	Special Trade Contractors
94107	2484	22413	Prof., Scientific, & Tech Svcs	94546	1384	8654	Hospitals	94808	6	10	Relig., Grant, Civic, Prof Org
94108	2557	22715	Securities/Commodity Contracts	94547	246	2719	Computer & Electronic Prod Mfg	94820	20	49	Special Trade Contractors
94109	3072	27630	Beverage & Tobacco Product Mfg	94548	25	133	Educational Services	94901	4385	21245	Prof., Scientific, & Tech Svcs
94110	3143	21298	Hospitals	94549	1728	8967	Prof., Scientific, & Tech Svcs	94903	2085	14977	Prof., Scientific, & Tech Svcs
94111	3124	49220	Prof., Scientific, & Tech Svcs	94550	1736	16489	Prof., Scientific, & Tech Svcs	94904	768	6461	Hospitals
94112	1512	8832	Educational Services	94551	1349	18520	Prof., Scientific, & Tech Svcs	94912	69	255	Motion Pict. & Sound Recording
94114	1392	6400	Food Svcs & Drinking Places	94552	187	862	Educational Services	94913	20	37	Administrative & Support Svcs
94115	2139	23813	Hospitals	94553	1993	19071	Exec., Legis., & Other Support	94914	23	22	Prof., Scientific, & Tech Svcs
94116	906	6276	Hospitals	94555	307	4190	Computer & Electronic Prod Mfg	94915	37	78	Prof., Scientific, & Tech Svcs
94117	1141	8878	Museums, Hist. Sites,& Similar	94556	501	4112	Educational Services	94920	660	2419	Food Svcs & Drinking Places
94118	2159	14136	Hospitals	94557	5	6	Prof., Scientific, & Tech Svcs	94922	29	39	Accommodation
94119	19	81	Administrative & Support Svcs	94558	2911	31642	Accommodation	94923	122	1061	Food Svcs & Drinking Places
94120	1	7	Other Information Services	94559	1906	15030	Health & Personal Care Stores	94924	109	398	Food Svcs & Drinking Places
94121	978	5312	Hospitals	94560	1455	17376	General Merchandise Stores	94925	892	5968	General Merchandise Stores
94122	2010	18965	Ambulatory Health Care Svcs	94561	568	7722	Repair and Maintenance	94926	2	805	Insurance Carriers & Related
94123	1548	7732	Food Svcs & Drinking Places	94562	39	454	Beverage & Tobacco Product Mfg	94927	30	80	Administrative & Support Svcs
94124	1972	22976	Special Trade Contractors	94563	856	3877	Educational Services	94928	1518	15289	Computer & Electronic Prod Mfg
94125	9	124	Support Act. for Transport.	94564	776	4988	Food Svcs & Drinking Places	94929	16	65	Motor Vehicle & Parts Dealers
94126	15	68	Exec., Legis., & Other Support	94565	1534	12712	Educational Services	94930	382	1450	Food Svcs & Drinking Places
94127	681	5764	Administrative & Support Svcs	94566	2018	13878	Prof., Scientific, & Tech Svcs	94931	615	3147	Special Trade Contractors
94128	110	3469	Rental and Leasing Services	94567	31	105	Educational Services	94933	39	82	Relig., Grant, Civic, Prof Org
94129	73	1578	Prof., Scientific, & Tech Svcs	94568	1565	14215	Food Svcs & Drinking Places	94937	66	253	Prof., Scientific, & Tech Svcs
94130	32	461	Educational Services	94569	7	15	Merch. Wholesalers,Durable Gds	94938	42	77	Publishing Industries
94131	517	1885	Educational Services	94570	14	30	Prof., Scientific, & Tech Svcs	94939	572	3075	Prof., Scientific, & Tech Svcs
94132	613	12001	Educational Services	94571	316	1576	Food Svcs & Drinking Places	94940	29	78	Relig., Grant, Civic, Prof Org
94133	1998	16287	Food Svcs & Drinking Places	94572	168	1280	Oil and Gas Extraction	94941	2106	8498	Prof., Scientific, & Tech Svcs
94134	577	3374	Educational Services	94573	45	932	Beverage & Tobacco Product Mfg	94942	81	117	Prof., Scientific, & Tech Svcs
94140	8	10	Prof., Scientific, & Tech Svcs	94574	1010	7546	Beverage & Tobacco Product Mfg	94945	1378	8967	Prof., Scientific, & Tech Svcs
94141	14	34	Relig., Grant, Civic, Prof Org	94576	43	182	Ambulatory Health Care Svcs	94946	51	473	Motion Pict. & Sound Recording
94142	21	133	Perform'g Arts, Spec. Sports	94577	2637	34222	Merch. Wholesalers,Durable Gds	94947	637	3712	Electronics & Appliance Stores
94143	27	664	Hospitals	94578	1050	8192	Educational Services	94948	85	141	Prof., Scientific, & Tech Svcs
94146	16	14	Bldg Matl & Garden Eqpmt Dlrs	94579	249	2199	General Merchandise Stores	94949	1135	7577	Administrative & Support Svcs
94147	28	87	Prof., Scientific, & Tech Svcs	94580	459	3937	Educational Services	94950	18	68	Accommodation
94158	99	1568	Truck Transportation	94581	70	142	Special Trade Contractors	94951	140	451	Merch. Wholesalers,Nondur. Gds
94159	20	23	Prof., Scientific, & Tech Svcs	94583	2387	22468	Prof., Scientific, & Tech Svcs	94952	2377	14367	Nat'l Security & Int'l Affairs
94164	20	38	Print'g & Related Supp't Act's	94585	587	3266	Food Svcs & Drinking Places	94953	38	65	Relig., Grant, Civic, Prof Org
94188	30	76	Special Trade Contractors	94586	75	1062	Merch. Wholesalers,Nondur. Gds	94954	1101	13866	Prof., Scientific, & Tech Svcs
94301	1754	14034	Prof., Scientific, & Tech Svcs	94587	1382	16500	Merch. Wholesalers,Durable Gds	94955	24	48	Ambulatory Health Care Svcs
94302	42	51	Prof., Scientific, & Tech Svcs	94588	1730	32631	Prof., Scientific, & Tech Svcs	94956	205	873	Exec., Legis., & Other Support
94303	1142	15028	Computer & Electronic Prod Mfg	94589	533	10197	Hospitals	94957	111	563	Educational Services
94304	596	34878	Hospitals	94590	2039	11244	Educational Services	94960	820	3898	Educational Services
94305	92	10617	Educational Services	94591	931	7064	Food Svcs & Drinking Places	94963	32	257	Educational Services
94306	1351	10699	Prof., Scientific, & Tech Svcs	94592	69	1141	Support Activities: Agr./For.	94964	8	15	Social Assistance
94309	5	2	Transportation Equipment Mfg	94595	491	3836	Real Estate	94965	1538	6046	Prof., Scientific, & Tech Svcs
94401	1952	9472	Ambulatory Health Care Svcs	94596	3792	25686	Prof., Scientific, & Tech Svcs	94966	65	165	Relig., Grant, Civic, Prof Org
94402	1316	14899	Credit Intermediation & Relatd	94597	769	7587	Prof., Scientific, & Tech Svcs	94970	67	356	Food Svcs & Drinking Places
94403	1786	20130	Securities/Commodity Contracts	94598	1159	12447	Hospitals	94971	42	148	Educational Services
94404	1071	15343	Merch. Wholesalers,Durable Gds	94599	230	2516	Hospitals	94972	23	42	Miscellaneous Manufacturing
94497	1	450	Postal Service	94601	1418	10388	Ambulatory Health Care Svcs	94973	81	137	Justice, Pubic Order/Safety
94501	2431	18331	Educational Services	94602	797	5447	Hospitals	94975	33	36	Special Trade Contractors
94502	259	3273	Prof., Scientific, & Tech Svcs	94603	513	4419	Merch. Wholesalers,Durable Gds	94976	32	56	Construction of Buildings
94503	349	2805	Special Trade Contractors	94604	24	42	Prof., Scientific, & Tech Svcs	94977	33	37	Prof., Scientific, & Tech Svcs
94506	462	2443	Prof., Scientific, & Tech Svcs	94605	799	4561	Educational Services	94978	35	41	Special Trade Contractors
94507	535	2765	Prof., Scientific, & Tech Svcs	94606	983	7073	Educational Services	94979	46	315	Prof., Scientific, & Tech Svcs
94508	130	2775	Educational Services	94607	2114	30428	Prof., Scientific, & Tech Svcs	94998	1	3000	Insurance Carriers & Related
94509	2091	15513	General Merchandise Stores	94608	1808	18165	Prof., Scientific, & Tech Svcs	94999	1	0	Postal Service
94510	1613	13134	Prof., Scientific, & Tech Svcs	94609	1271	9780	Hospitals	95001	85	157	Special Trade Contractors
94511	111	374	Amusement, Gambling,& Recreat.	94610	1063	5414	Administrative & Support Svcs	95002	66	2406	Administrative & Support Svcs
94512	6	44	Prof., Scientific, & Tech Svcs	94611	1429	8288	Educational Services	95003	1346	6848	Food Svcs & Drinking Places
94513	1110	7041	Educational Services	94612	3334	28986	Prof., Scientific, & Tech Svcs	95004	97	504	Merch. Wholesalers,Nondur. Gds
94514	291	1691	Special Trade Contractors	94613	8	73	Educational Services	95005	253	612	Prof., Scientific, & Tech Svcs
94515	522	2844	Accommodation	94614	13	20	Unclassified Establishments	95006	395	1480	Accommodation
94516	7	18	Educational Services	94615	3	0	Postal Service	95007	26	105	Food Svcs & Drinking Places
94517	356	1325	Food and Beverage Stores	94618	605	4495	Educational Services	95008	3411	24117	Food Svcs & Drinking Places
94518	618	4598	Educational Services	94619	490	2646	Educational Services	95009	28	73	Construction of Buildings
94519	540	3076	Educational Services	94620	19	21	Construction of Buildings	95010	985	7597	Food Svcs & Drinking Places
94520	3385	35572	Prof., Scientific, & Tech Svcs	94621	1476	17772	Prof., Scientific, & Tech Svcs	95011	33	41	Special Trade Contractors
94521	772	5324	Educational Services	94623	9	35	Prof., Scientific, & Tech Svcs	95012	275	2266	Merch. Wholesalers,Nondur. Gds
94522	21	52	Administrative & Support Svcs	94626	7	67	Support Act. for Transport.	95013	21	57	Special Trade Contractors
94523	1562	12070	Food Svcs & Drinking Places	94661	7	18	Prof., Scientific, & Tech Svcs	95014	2071	27563	Computer & Electronic Prod Mfg
94524	25	162	Relig., Grant, Civic, Prof Org	94662	7	6	Relig., Grant, Civic, Prof Org	95015	40	128	Administrative & Support Svcs
94525	122	1157	Credit Intermediation & Relatd	94701	29	72	Social Assistance	95017	39	583	Nonmetallic Mineral Prod. Mfg
94526	1713	9161	Educational Services	94702	591	2863	Educational Services	95018	426	1553	Educational Services
94527	20	26	Administrative & Support Svcs	94703	494	2310	Relig., Grant, Civic, Prof Org	95019	247	1496	Ambulatory Health Care Svcs
94528	17	105	Relig., Grant, Civic, Prof Org	94704	1715	12101	Food Svcs & Drinking Places	95020	1968	17910	Educational Services
94530	824	5275	Educational Services	94705	836	7545	Hospitals	95021	14	20	Print'g & Related Supp't Act's
94531	420	3089	Food Svcs & Drinking Places	94706	907	3541	Ambulatory Health Care Svcs	95023	1553	14684	Food and Beverage Stores
94533	2581	22943	Educational Services	94707	694	2531	Food and Beverage Stores	95024	28	45	Relig., Grant, Civic, Prof Org

ZIP CODE	2004 Total Firms	2004 Total Employees	TOP INDUSTRY RANKED on 2004 EMPLOYMENT	ZIP CODE	2004 Total Firms	2004 Total Employees	TOP INDUSTRY RANKED on 2004 EMPLOYMENT	ZIP CODE	2004 Total Firms	2004 Total Employees	TOP INDUSTRY RANKED on 2004 EMPLOYMENT
95030	1072	6186	Food Svcs & Drinking Places	95201	18	12	Prof., Scientific, & Tech Svcs	95346	49	208	Support Activities: Agr./For.
95031	52	137	Prof., Scientific, & Tech Svcs	95202	943	16221	Special Trade Contractors	95347	2	141	Utilities
95032	1314	12088	Hospitals	95203	529	6862	Hospitals	95348	672	9690	Educational Services
95033	274	757	Educational Services	95204	914	10326	Hospitals	95350	2338	23101	Educational Services
95035	2461	47102	Computer & Electronic Prod Mfg	95205	1437	13140	Food Manufacturing	95351	1295	12691	Educational Services
95036	9	13	Relig., Grant, Civic, Prof Org	95206	856	17111	Educational Services	95352	36	102	Isps, Web Search Portals
95037	1644	16104	Miscellaneous Manufacturing	95207	2288	17896	Food Svcs & Drinking Places	95353	45	103	Clothing & Cloth'g Acc. Stores
95038	33	58	Special Trade Contractors	95208	17	159	Postal Service	95354	1921	22809	Beverage & Tobacco Product Mfg
95039	96	1566	Merch. Wholesalers,Nondur. Gds	95209	389	3155	Nursing & Resid. Care Facilit.	95355	1249	14080	Hospitals
95041	18	319	Other Information Services	95210	544	5992	Ambulatory Health Care Svcs	95356	1119	12866	Motor Vehicle & Parts Dealers
95042	2	2	Bldg Matl & Garden Eqpmt Dlrs	95211	13	1055	Educational Services	95357	311	4932	Food Manufacturing
95043	33	138	Beverage & Tobacco Product Mfg	95212	185	3227	Motor Vehicle & Parts Dealers	95358	600	8569	Exec., Legis., & Other Support
95044	5	10	Insurance Carriers & Related	95213	11	18	Heavy & Civil Eng. Construct'N	95360	228	1945	Food Manufacturing
95045	174	1171	Merch. Wholesalers,Nondur. Gds	95215	610	10702	Justice, Pubic Order/Safety	95361	1142	9134	Food Manufacturing
95046	233	1506	Food Manufacturing	95219	477	4573	Food Svcs & Drinking Places	95363	432	4176	Food Manufacturing
95050	2414	30157	Computer & Electronic Prod Mfg	95220	154	1429	Beverage & Tobacco Product Mfg	95364	23	756	Accommodation
95051	1428	19986	Computer & Electronic Prod Mfg	95221	70	328	Special Trade Contractors	95365	57	506	Educational Services
95052	18	64	Merch. Wholesalers,Durable Gds	95222	322	2060	Educational Services	95366	368	3720	Educational Services
95053	2	1209	Educational Services	95223	361	1646	Accommodation	95367	375	2384	Educational Services
95054	2097	58492	Computer & Electronic Prod Mfg	95224	40	115	Educational Services	95368	214	1470	Educational Services
95055	19	29	Isps, Web Search Portals	95225	20	38	Bldg Matl & Garden Eqpmt Dlrs	95369	23	120	Educational Services
95056	4	8	Educational Services	95226	2	1	Postal Service	95370	1775	12647	Hospitals
95060	3210	28689	Exec., Legis., & Other Support	95227	39	154	Merch. Wholesalers,Nondur. Gds	95372	47	210	Educational Services
95061	79	180	Educational Services	95228	114	466	Heavy & Civil Eng. Construct'N	95373	7	7	Truck Transportation
95062	2212	10599	Ambulatory Health Care Svcs	95229	26	71	Construction of Buildings	95374	39	294	Animal Production
95063	86	71	Prof., Scientific, & Tech Svcs	95230	19	176	Bldg Matl & Garden Eqpmt Dlrs	95375	11	85	Utilities
95064	21	5323	Educational Services	95231	137	4888	Hospitals	95376	1490	10640	Educational Services
95065	422	4179	Hospitals	95232	17	10	Relig., Grant, Civic, Prof Org	95377	231	3314	Prof., Scientific, & Tech Svcs
95066	905	7311	Computer & Electronic Prod Mfg	95233	19	65	Support Activities: Agr./For.	95378	29	73	Special Trade Contractors
95067	30	56	Prof., Scientific, & Tech Svcs	95234	16	76	Merch. Wholesalers,Nondur. Gds	95379	102	479	Educational Services
95070	967	6119	Educational Services	95236	105	1582	Merch. Wholesalers,Nondur. Gds	95380	1646	18423	Food Manufacturing
95071	10	26	Motion Pict. & Sound Recording	95237	140	732	Food and Beverage Stores	95381	45	119	Administrative & Support Svcs
95073	774	3381	Food Svcs & Drinking Places	95240	2186	22031	Food Manufacturing	95382	600	6804	Educational Services
95075	31	74	Food Svcs & Drinking Places	95241	37	116	Special Trade Contractors	95383	236	794	Food and Beverage Stores
95076	2733	24987	Merch. Wholesalers,Nondur. Gds	95242	636	7853	Hospitals	95385	28	92	Food Svcs & Drinking Places
95077	27	284	Crop Production	95245	62	158	Special Trade Contractors	95386	196	1133	Food and Beverage Stores
95101	13	3	Food Svcs & Drinking Places	95246	42	170	Food and Beverage Stores	95387	53	590	Food Svcs & Drinking Places
95103	9	15	Administrative & Support Svcs	95247	280	1064	Beverage & Tobacco Product Mfg	95388	147	763	Educational Services
95108	1	0	Administrative & Support Svcs	95248	11	37	Educational Services	95389	43	194	Accommodation
95109	10	17	Special Trade Contractors	95249	365	2445	Prof., Scientific, & Tech Svcs	95391	9	35	Fabricated Metal Product Mfg
95110	1507	26319	Prof., Scientific, & Tech Svcs	95250	8	15	Beverage & Tobacco Product Mfg	95401	2378	21847	Educational Services
95111	863	5377	Educational Services	95251	22	114	Administrative & Support Svcs	95402	140	828	Relig., Grant, Civic, Prof Org
95112	3994	41160	Special Trade Contractors	95252	281	1191	Educational Services	95403	2407	24060	Prof., Scientific, & Tech Svcs
95113	1389	15898	Prof., Scientific, & Tech Svcs	95253	14	34	Special Trade Contractors	95404	2801	14024	Prof., Scientific, & Tech Svcs
95116	1155	7269	Ambulatory Health Care Svcs	95254	24	71	Amusement, Gambling,& Recreat.	95405	1017	11257	Hospitals
95117	639	3432	Motor Vehicle & Parts Dealers	95255	98	190	Educational Services	95406	49	165	Special Trade Contractors
95118	931	6707	Food Svcs & Drinking Places	95257	16	25	Accommodation	95407	1370	15840	Motor Vehicle & Parts Dealers
95119	425	8479	Hospitals	95258	63	357	Amusement, Gambling,& Recreat.	95409	757	3439	Nursing & Resid. Care Facilit.
95120	744	3959	Educational Services	95267	29	82	Social Assistance	95410	56	194	Accommodation
95121	443	3865	Educational Services	95269	33	75	Administrative & Support Svcs	95412	15	69	Educational Services
95122	1231	9955	Educational Services	95290	4	23	Telecommunications	95415	86	488	Educational Services
95123	1673	10585	Food Svcs & Drinking Places	95296	1	18	Relig., Grant, Civic, Prof Org	95416	33	80	Food Svcs & Drinking Places
95124	1296	11619	Hospitals	95301	710	5666	Educational Services	95417	7	511	Merch. Wholesalers,Durable Gds
95125	2299	14909	Relig., Grant, Civic, Prof Org	95303	31	613	Support Activities: Agr./For.	95418	14	125	Merch. Wholesalers,Durable Gds
95126	1652	13466	Prof., Scientific, & Tech Svcs	95304	606	7038	Justice, Pubic Order/Safety	95419	10	22	Support Act. for Transport.
95127	940	5175	Educational Services	95305	26	113	Bldg Matl & Garden Eqpmt Dlrs	95420	21	27	Food Svcs & Drinking Places
95128	2031	18144	Hospitals	95306	33	71	Educational Services	95421	39	157	Accommodation
95129	1502	11487	Food Svcs & Drinking Places	95307	881	6975	Educational Services	95422	501	2873	Hospitals
95130	218	1482	Educational Services	95309	9	303	Food Manufacturing	95423	115	994	Crop Production
95131	1446	32167	Computer & Electronic Prod Mfg	95310	88	577	Scenic & Sightseeing Transport	95424	5	13	Special Trade Contractors
95132	531	3470	Educational Services	95311	78	182	Educational Services	95425	384	2444	Wood Product Manufacturing
95133	626	11102	Special Trade Contractors	95312	12	65	Educational Services	95426	77	190	Educational Services
95134	450	41666	Computer & Electronic Prod Mfg	95313	67	494	Merch. Wholesalers,Nondur. Gds	95427	17	55	Fabricated Metal Product Mfg
95135	227	1970	Educational Services	95314	1	4	Accommodation	95428	85	374	Exec., Legis., & Other Support
95136	518	6911	Motor Vehicle & Parts Dealers	95315	120	597	Educational Services	95430	30	90	Accommodation
95138	195	6367	Computer & Electronic Prod Mfg	95316	147	777	Merch. Wholesalers,Durable Gds	95431	7	2823	Exec., Legis., & Other Support
95139	94	569	Administrative & Support Svcs	95317	20	174	Justice, Pubic Order/Safety	95432	32	126	Accommodation
95140	15	34	Museums, Hist. Sites,& Similar	95318	23	273	Accommodation	95433	27	51	Utilities
95141	6	1632	Electronics & Appliance Stores	95319	59	481	Educational Services	95435	7	166	Merch. Wholesalers,Nondur. Gds
95148	507	3355	Educational Services	95320	362	3224	Food Manufacturing	95436	273	890	Educational Services
95150	41	59	Administrative & Support Svcs	95321	227	971	Accommodation	95437	1002	6143	Accommodation
95151	11	24	Miscellaneous Manufacturing	95322	248	2616	Support Activities: Agr./For.	95439	50	664	Beverage & Tobacco Product Mfg
95152	18	52	Heavy & Civil Eng. Construct'N	95323	25	398	Merch. Wholesalers,Nondur. Gds	95441	121	1251	Beverage & Tobacco Product Mfg
95153	31	104	Administrative & Support Svcs	95324	210	1448	Food Manufacturing	95442	167	880	Beverage & Tobacco Product Mfg
95154	28	53	Special Trade Contractors	95325	1	1	Miscellaneous Store Retailers	95443	10	22	Support Act. for Transport.
95155	13	48	Sportg Gds,Hobby,Book, & Music	95326	238	2283	Merch. Wholesalers,Nondur. Gds	95444	58	258	Beverage & Tobacco Product Mfg
95156	12	19	Funds, Trusts, & Other Finance	95327	264	2190	Justice, Pubic Order/Safety	95445	209	755	Accommodation
95157	12	14	Merch. Wholesalers,Durable Gds	95328	31	379	Merch. Wholesalers,Nondur. Gds	95446	275	1557	Beverage & Tobacco Product Mfg
95158	27	45	Prof., Scientific, & Tech Svcs	95329	67	338	Educational Services	95448	1296	8326	Beverage & Tobacco Product Mfg
95159	37	144	Special Trade Contractors	95330	209	4866	Construction of Buildings	95449	86	1442	Beverage & Tobacco Product Mfg
95160	25	72	Administrative & Support Svcs	95333	56	909	Merch. Wholesalers,Nondur. Gds	95450	24	158	Accommodation
95161	14	9	Administrative & Support Svcs	95334	235	6318	Food Manufacturing	95451	386	2543	Accommodation
95164	7	10	Ambulatory Health Care Svcs	95335	25	131	Accommodation	95452	94	687	Beverage & Tobacco Product Mfg
95170	12	20	Administrative & Support Svcs	95336	1069	8963	Educational Services	95453	912	5734	Ambulatory Health Care Svcs
95172	5	18	Administrative & Support Svcs	95337	482	6302	Special Trade Contractors	95454	107	616	Educational Services
95173	8	36	Construction of Buildings	95338	653	3106	Exec., Legis., & Other Support	95456	41	342	Accommodation
95190	1	1600	Publishing Industries	95340	2002	19207	Educational Services	95457	172	1064	Educational Services
95191	1	0	Prof., Scientific, & Tech Svcs	95341	20	45	Merch. Wholesalers,Durable Gds	95458	73	259	Construction of Buildings
95192	4	3006	Educational Services	95344	24	57	Administrative & Support Svcs	95459	14	79	Forestry and Logging
95193	1	7000	Computer & Electronic Prod Mfg	95345	28	63	Accommodation	95460	344	1464	Accommodation

BUSINESS DATA

ZIP CODE	2004 Total Firms	2004 Total Employees	TOP INDUSTRY RANKED on 2004 EMPLOYMENT	ZIP CODE	2004 Total Firms	2004 Total Employees	TOP INDUSTRY RANKED on 2004 EMPLOYMENT	ZIP CODE	2004 Total Firms	2004 Total Employees	TOP INDUSTRY RANKED on 2004 EMPLOYMENT
95461	332	1608	Food Svcs & Drinking Places	95616	1919	33857	Educational Services	95728	72	2644	Accommodation
95462	64	208	Relig., Grant, Civic, Prof Org	95617	67	116	Prof., Scientific, & Tech Svcs	95735	10	757	Accommodation
95463	10	23	Wood Product Manufacturing	95618	17	91	Amusement, Gambling,& Recreat.	95736	32	196	Educational Services
95464	78	253	Relig., Grant, Civic, Prof Org	95619	336	1626	Electronics & Appliance Stores	95741	29	64	Publishing Industries
95465	164	841	Accommodation	95620	647	5765	Food Svcs & Drinking Places	95742	1202	14503	Special Trade Contractors
95466	67	427	Beverage & Tobacco Product Mfg	95621	666	3717	Food Svcs & Drinking Places	95746	507	2702	Educational Services
95468	112	378	Educational Services	95623	161	545	Educational Services	95747	409	13859	Electronics & Appliance Stores
95469	58	481	Crop Production	95624	1518	10917	Food Svcs & Drinking Places	95758	1100	9248	Computer & Electronic Prod Mfg
95470	195	1058	Amusement, Gambling,& Recreat.	95625	15	19	Food Svcs & Drinking Places	95759	39	75	Administrative & Support Svcs
95471	1	2	Prof., Scientific, & Tech Svcs	95626	117	493	Special Trade Contractors	95762	857	8348	Publishing Industries
95472	1791	7582	Educational Services	95627	71	1039	Beverage & Tobacco Product Mfg	95763	56	131	Administrative & Support Svcs
95473	80	119	Prof., Scientific, & Tech Svcs	95628	2026	8397	Prof., Scientific, & Tech Svcs	95765	381	5740	Merch. Wholesalers,Durable Gds
95476	2059	11864	Food Svcs & Drinking Places	95629	21	16	Merch. Wholesalers,Nondur. Gds	95776	626	11374	Food Manufacturing
95480	2	1	General Merchandise Stores	95630	2118	22693	Computer & Electronic Prod Mfg	95798	4	2	Prof., Scientific, & Tech Svcs
95481	11	19	Food Svcs & Drinking Places	95631	227	964	Educational Services	95812	34	237	Insurance Carriers & Related
95482	2001	15018	Educational Services	95632	591	4369	Educational Services	95813	9	117	Postal Service
95485	101	794	Food Svcs & Drinking Places	95633	72	187	Educational Services	95814	4328	77772	Admin. Human Resource Programs
95486	4	4	Postal Service	95634	168	735	Educational Services	95815	1945	22261	Food Svcs & Drinking Places
95487	6	86	Construction of Buildings	95635	26	126	Admin. Enviro. Quality Progrms	95816	1651	16842	Ambulatory Health Care Svcs
95488	13	29	Accommodation	95636	14	43	Accommodation	95817	402	22048	Ambulatory Health Care Svcs
95490	633	3727	Educational Services	95637	3	0	Crop Production	95818	812	5535	Prof., Scientific, & Tech Svcs
95492	852	5522	Special Trade Contractors	95638	50	154	Educational Services	95819	837	11647	Hospitals
95493	1	6	Special Trade Contractors	95639	8	13	Food Svcs & Drinking Places	95820	996	12514	Relig., Grant, Civic, Prof Org
95494	4	6	Unclassified Establishments	95640	202	2731	Justice, Pubic Order/Safety	95821	1870	9495	Educational Services
95497	33	232	Accommodation	95641	141	738	Crop Production	95822	1101	9874	Educational Services
95501	2042	19562	Food Svcs & Drinking Places	95642	708	7181	Amusement, Gambling,& Recreat.	95823	2097	14518	Educational Services
95502	66	210	Ambulatory Health Care Svcs	95645	38	264	Animal Production	95824	600	5283	Food Manufacturing
95503	560	5078	Educational Services	95646	31	805	Accommodation	95825	3078	28138	Hospitals
95511	6	11	Amusement, Gambling,& Recreat.	95648	635	5133	Special Trade Contractors	95826	1521	16259	Special Trade Contractors
95514	3	21	Educational Services	95650	595	4632	Special Trade Contractors	95827	1327	12897	Prof., Scientific, & Tech Svcs
95518	42	49	Construction of Buildings	95651	43	295	Scenic & Sightseeing Transport	95828	1282	12261	Special Trade Contractors
95519	452	2472	Food Svcs & Drinking Places	95652	92	1399	Special Trade Contractors	95829	339	2654	Educational Services
95521	1086	8378	Food Svcs & Drinking Places	95653	18	143	Crop Production	95830	13	212	Waste Managmt & Remediat'n Svc
95524	44	182	Educational Services	95654	8	244	Wood Product Manufacturing	95831	725	4216	Educational Services
95525	71	749	Amusement, Gambling,& Recreat.	95655	72	615	Justice, Pubic Order/Safety	95832	99	1036	Educational Services
95526	27	130	Exec., Legis., & Other Support	95656	20	52	Beverage & Tobacco Product Mfg	95833	748	7927	Prof., Scientific, & Tech Svcs
95527	9	27	Educational Services	95658	289	1366	Special Trade Contractors	95834	666	13002	Merch. Wholesalers,Durable Gds
95528	18	47	Educational Services	95659	31	172	Educational Services	95835	127	304	Prof., Scientific, & Tech Svcs
95531	867	5609	Educational Services	95660	1136	8455	Special Trade Contractors	95836	3	32	Air Transportation
95532	2	3	Ambulatory Health Care Svcs	95661	2252	22600	Ambulatory Health Care Svcs	95837	46	4407	Support Act. for Transport.
95534	8	11	Prof., Scientific, & Tech Svcs	95662	1102	4714	Educational Services	95838	675	7793	Special Trade Contractors
95536	147	533	Food Svcs & Drinking Places	95663	78	333	Special Trade Contractors	95841	1264	10667	Educational Services
95537	18	133	Chemical Manufacturing	95664	24	41	Food Svcs & Drinking Places	95842	496	3190	Educational Services
95540	567	4258	Educational Services	95665	228	936	Broadcasting	95843	438	2420	Educational Services
95542	204	1015	Accommodation	95666	225	709	Accommodation	95851	2	4	Social Assistance
95543	19	102	Support Activities: Agr./For.	95667	2062	13117	Hospitals	95852	6	2	Real Estate
95545	6	6	Educational Services	95668	46	645	Merch. Wholesalers,Nondur. Gds	95853	3	4	Administrative & Support Svcs
95546	87	572	Ambulatory Health Care Svcs	95669	120	473	Beverage & Tobacco Product Mfg	95860	39	470	Amusement, Gambling,& Recreat.
95547	25	180	Truck Transportation	95670	1908	20864	Computer & Electronic Prod Mfg	95864	655	4280	Educational Services
95548	61	306	Food Svcs & Drinking Places	95671	2	205	Justice, Pubic Order/Safety	95865	25	35	Admin. Enviro. Quality Progrms
95549	28	37	Educational Services	95672	82	300	Educational Services	95866	22	42	Administrative & Support Svcs
95550	9	407	Forestry and Logging	95673	423	2641	Motor Vehicle & Parts Dealers	95901	1216	12898	Hospitals
95551	35	162	Educational Services	95674	24	233	Merch. Wholesalers,Nondur. Gds	95903	36	416	Educational Services
95552	14	55	Educational Services	95675	7	18	Justice, Pubic Order/Safety	95910	8	26	Mining (Except Oil and Gas)
95553	29	118	Educational Services	95676	31	230	Animal Production	95912	106	1089	Truck Transportation
95554	20	76	Admin. Enviro. Quality Progrms	95677	1005	8567	Educational Services	95913	17	80	Crop Production
95555	32	120	Food Svcs & Drinking Places	95678	1656	14132	Food Svcs & Drinking Places	95914	24	73	Educational Services
95556	27	111	Support Activities: Agr./For.	95680	2	1	Postal Service	95915	2	4	Accommodation
95558	28	81	Educational Services	95681	20	110	Merch. Wholesalers,Durable Gds	95916	29	101	Educational Services
95559	7	17	Bldg Matl & Garden Eqpmt Dlrs	95682	1236	6066	Food Svcs & Drinking Places	95917	86	524	Educational Services
95560	111	587	Food and Beverage Stores	95683	195	865	Amusement, Gambling,& Recreat.	95918	43	141	Educational Services
95562	70	283	Educational Services	95684	84	289	Educational Services	95919	58	143	Ambulatory Health Care Svcs
95563	9	42	Food and Beverage Stores	95685	330	1481	Accommodation	95920	14	60	Administrative & Support Svcs
95564	14	77	Heavy & Civil Eng. Construct'N	95686	30	98	Educational Services	95922	25	178	Support Activities: Agr./For.
95565	20	240	Educational Services	95687	1173	12227	Exec., Legis., & Other Support	95923	13	29	Accommodation
95567	75	646	Merch. Wholesalers,Nondur. Gds	95688	1740	13284	Merch. Wholesalers,Nondur. Gds	95924	38	67	Administrative & Support Svcs
95568	12	33	Educational Services	95689	53	68	Prof., Scientific, & Tech Svcs	95925	12	71	Educational Services
95569	11	267	Wood Product Manufacturing	95690	163	959	Merch. Wholesalers,Nondur. Gds	95926	2061	18075	Hospitals
95570	116	902	Prof., Scientific, & Tech Svcs	95691	1236	16000	Merch. Wholesalers,Nondur. Gds	95927	137	199	Administrative & Support Svcs
95571	16	103	Admin. Enviro. Quality Progrms	95692	94	704	Educational Services	95928	2092	19061	Food Svcs & Drinking Places
95573	105	518	Support Activities: Agr./For.	95693	182	360	Educational Services	95929	10	120	Educational Services
95585	25	121	Educational Services	95694	269	2341	Food and Beverage Stores	95930	12	29	Educational Services
95587	12	28	Special Trade Contractors	95695	1487	11678	Hospitals	95932	466	3492	Amusement, Gambling,& Recreat.
95589	46	148	Accommodation	95696	61	160	Special Trade Contractors	95934	19	50	Support Act. for Transport.
95595	6	14	Educational Services	95697	17	369	Merch. Wholesalers,Nondur. Gds	95935	15	86	Educational Services
95601	19	43	Food Svcs & Drinking Places	95698	8	43	Administrative & Support Svcs	95936	60	266	Justice, Pubic Order/Safety
95602	647	5563	Computer & Electronic Prod Mfg	95699	5	11	Accommodation	95937	138	310	Gasoline Stations
95603	2294	21095	Administrative & Support Svcs	95701	39	110	Educational Services	95938	164	1203	Educational Services
95604	86	265	Miscellaneous Manufacturing	95703	48	78	Special Trade Contractors	95939	24	108	Educational Services
95605	237	4339	Justice, Pubic Order/Safety	95709	145	861	Exec., Legis., & Other Support	95941	9	35	Museums, Hist. Sites,& Similar
95606	3	8	Justice, Pubic Order/Safety	95712	19	50	Accommodation	95942	51	83	Educational Services
95607	5	1	Construction of Buildings	95713	252	1166	Educational Services	95943	40	375	Relig., Grant, Civic, Prof Org
95608	2117	15590	Educational Services	95714	14	68	Justice, Pubic Order/Safety	95944	5	8	Social Assistance
95609	53	82	Prof., Scientific, & Tech Svcs	95715	13	57	Accommodation	95945	2221	13599	Ambulatory Health Care Svcs
95610	1908	12140	Food Svcs & Drinking Places	95717	4	10	Prof., Scientific, & Tech Svcs	95946	388	1170	Educational Services
95611	35	28	Prof., Scientific, & Tech Svcs	95720	15	27	Personal and Laundry Services	95947	103	402	Hospitals
95612	54	364	Ambulatory Health Care Svcs	95721	1	0	Accommodation	95948	405	3926	Food Manufacturing
95613	41	222	Scenic & Sightseeing Transport	95722	198	501	Educational Services	95949	827	3636	Educational Services
95614	88	355	Educational Services	95724	12	864	Accommodation	95950	24	144	Animal Production
95615	47	1126	Merch. Wholesalers,Nondur. Gds	95726	217	1172	Food Svcs & Drinking Places	95951	46	385	Educational Services

ZIP CODE	2004 Total Firms	2004 Total Employ-ees	TOP INDUSTRY RANKED on 2004 EMPLOYMENT	ZIP CODE	2004 Total Firms	2004 Total Employ-ees	TOP INDUSTRY RANKED on 2004 EMPLOYMENT	ZIP CODE	2004 Total Firms	2004 Total Employ-ees	TOP INDUSTRY RANKED on 2004 EMPLOYMENT
95953	172	1750	Merch. Wholesalers,Nondur. Gds	96068	2	1	Postal Service	96715	4	0	Special Trade Contractors
95954	245	730	Educational Services	96069	22	69	Educational Services	96716	134	507	Food Svcs & Drinking Places
95955	57	462	Food Manufacturing	96070	3	70	Accommodation	96717	68	348	Nursing & Resid. Care Facilit.
95956	16	43	Accommodation	96071	13	32	Food Svcs & Drinking Places	96718	8	178	Accommodation
95957	30	137	Support Activities: Agr./For.	96073	213	892	Educational Services	96719	62	210	Food and Beverage Stores
95958	9	45	Food Manufacturing	96074	11	115	Support Activities: Agr./For.	96720	2601	22124	Food Svcs & Drinking Places
95959	1288	5617	Educational Services	96075	7	47	Justice, Pubic Order/Safety	96721	36	63	Administrative & Support Svcs
95960	40	94	Educational Services	96076	5	5	Food and Beverage Stores	96722	130	1959	Accommodation
95961	71	414	Educational Services	96078	6	6	Repair and Maintenance	96725	104	332	Construction of Buildings
95962	65	362	Beverage & Tobacco Product Mfg	96079	7	31	Transportation Equipment Mfg	96726	65	139	Crop Production
95963	549	3099	Educational Services	96080	1327	12285	General Merchandise Stores	96727	184	747	Educational Services
95965	922	7392	Educational Services	96084	11	39	Ambulatory Health Care Svcs	96728	27	48	Food Svcs & Drinking Places
95966	853	6393	Hospitals	96085	3	6	Exec., Legis., & Other Support	96729	35	345	Educational Services
95967	44	72	Merch. Wholesalers,Durable Gds	96086	7	19	Educational Services	96730	26	194	Animal Production
95968	32	77	Educational Services	96087	40	147	Educational Services	96731	74	1797	Accommodation
95969	1365	7289	Hospitals	96088	136	439	Educational Services	96732	1308	15906	Merch. Wholesalers,Nondur. Gds
95970	27	144	Educational Services	96089	13	20	Nursing & Resid. Care Facilit.	96733	52	113	Relig., Grant, Civic, Prof Org
95971	489	3346	Educational Services	96090	7	9	Relig., Grant, Civic, Prof Org	96734	1456	9950	Ambulatory Health Care Svcs
95972	3	3	Construction of Buildings	96091	15	143	Accommodation	96737	38	136	Relig., Grant, Civic, Prof Org
95973	1135	8009	Ambulatory Health Care Svcs	96092	23	116	Animal Production	96738	214	3135	Accommodation
95974	26	237	Food Manufacturing	96093	378	2491	Justice, Pubic Order/Safety	96739	31	65	Special Trade Contractors
95975	57	105	Prof., Scientific, & Tech Svcs	96094	232	1712	Educational Services	96740	2153	13499	Food Svcs & Drinking Places
95977	39	84	Postal Service	96095	3	9	Amusement, Gambling,& Recreat.	96741	151	578	Food Svcs & Drinking Places
95978	10	11	Educational Services	96096	23	146	Educational Services	96742	10	63	Exec., Legis., & Other Support
95979	22	164	Support Activities: Agr./For.	96097	709	5468	Food Svcs & Drinking Places	96743	734	6883	Accommodation
95980	4	3	Educational Services	96099	52	135	Prof., Scientific, & Tech Svcs	96744	1270	9524	Educational Services
95981	13	60	Merch. Wholesalers,Durable Gds	96101	342	2371	Hospitals	96745	182	692	Rental and Leasing Services
95982	57	435	Educational Services	96103	171	692	Food Svcs & Drinking Places	96746	811	4660	Accommodation
95983	18	44	Animal Production	96104	80	257	Hospitals	96747	13	334	Food Manufacturing
95984	8	7	Food and Beverage Stores	96105	15	38	Forestry and Logging	96748	228	1364	Food and Beverage Stores
95986	12	64	Relig., Grant, Civic, Prof Org	96106	22	160	Accommodation	96749	282	2118	Crop Production
95987	188	1665	Food Svcs & Drinking Places	96107	44	142	Educational Services	96750	278	1686	Hospitals
95988	466	3964	Exec., Legis., & Other Support	96108	6	31	Justice, Pubic Order/Safety	96751	9	13	Merch. Wholesalers,Nondur. Gds
95991	1752	13708	Hospitals	96109	33	91	Educational Services	96752	60	419	Crop Production
95992	29	68	Social Assistance	96110	7	14	Animal Production	96753	1479	11774	Accommodation
95993	729	7319	Food Manufacturing	96112	6	7	Ambulatory Health Care Svcs	96754	197	589	Educational Services
96001	2285	19682	Ambulatory Health Care Svcs	96113	44	744	Nat'l Security & Int'l Affairs	96755	144	525	Educational Services
96002	1997	14148	Food Svcs & Drinking Places	96114	67	246	Educational Services	96756	323	3771	Accommodation
96003	1382	14104	Educational Services	96115	5	4	Construction of Buildings	96757	36	193	Educational Services
96006	21	150	Exec., Legis., & Other Support	96116	14	37	Justice, Pubic Order/Safety	96759	9	872	Merch. Wholesalers,Durable Gds
96007	850	5034	Educational Services	96117	8	74	Educational Services	96760	44	273	Merch. Wholesalers,Nondur. Gds
96008	54	201	Educational Services	96118	74	406	Educational Services	96761	1469	16746	Accommodation
96009	54	329	Educational Services	96119	2	3	Postal Service	96762	66	1875	Museums, Hist. Sites,& Similar
96010	12	78	Support Activities: Agr./For.	96120	66	357	Exec., Legis., & Other Support	96763	122	2125	Accommodation
96011	7	12	Educational Services	96121	12	21	Utilities	96764	19	128	Educational Services
96013	227	1317	Merch. Wholesalers,Durable Gds	96122	260	1131	Ambulatory Health Care Svcs	96765	52	171	Bldg Matl & Garden Eqpmt Dlrs
96014	14	25	Truck Transportation	96123	5	25	Admin. Enviro. Quality Progrms	96766	1308	12926	Food Svcs & Drinking Places
96015	15	70	Educational Services	96124	13	19	Food Svcs & Drinking Places	96767	15	37	Construction of Buildings
96016	15	100	Truck Transportation	96125	28	116	Accommodation	96768	580	2496	Educational Services
96017	12	52	Educational Services	96126	26	132	Exec., Legis., & Other Support	96769	4	11	Unclassified Establishments
96019	272	1774	Educational Services	96127	1	0	Other Information Services	96770	23	360	Animal Production
96020	243	1375	Wood Product Manufacturing	96128	18	65	Support Activities: Agr./For.	96771	71	152	Crop Production
96021	448	3917	Wood Product Manufacturing	96129	33	87	Admin. of Economic Programs	96772	103	317	Educational Services
96022	346	1553	Educational Services	96130	843	6060	Educational Services	96773	1	2	Postal Service
96023	61	347	Educational Services	96132	3	8	Educational Services	96774	4	3	Special Trade Contractors
96024	17	57	Educational Services	96133	13	42	Support Activities: Agr./For.	96776	32	137	Educational Services
96025	121	903	Rail Transportation	96134	125	822	Merch. Wholesalers,Nondur. Gds	96777	42	215	Educational Services
96027	161	505	Educational Services	96135	7	33	Justice, Pubic Order/Safety	96778	202	1061	Educational Services
96028	114	725	Hospitals	96136	2	35	Utilities	96779	195	1145	Food Svcs & Drinking Places
96029	5	9	Educational Services	96137	216	622	Educational Services	96780	9	16	General Merchandise Stores
96031	6	13	Educational Services	96140	110	473	Food Svcs & Drinking Places	96781	94	200	Educational Services
96032	161	503	Educational Services	96141	60	501	Accommodation	96782	722	7330	Food Svcs & Drinking Places
96033	16	70	Educational Services	96142	89	281	Construction of Buildings	96783	14	37	Utilities
96034	11	30	Heavy & Civil Eng. Construct'N	96143	318	955	Food Svcs & Drinking Places	96784	64	516	Heavy & Civil Eng. Construct'N
96035	47	329	Educational Services	96145	771	4231	Food Svcs & Drinking Places	96785	82	315	Accommodation
96037	11	31	Food and Beverage Stores	96146	123	3262	Accommodation	96786	490	4402	Educational Services
96038	20	110	Nursing & Resid. Care Facilit.	96148	120	570	Food Svcs & Drinking Places	96788	26	33	Administrative & Support Svcs
96039	89	369	Support Activities: Agr./For.	96150	1863	14470	Accommodation	96789	487	4799	Food Svcs & Drinking Places
96040	18	55	Support Activities: Agr./For.	96151	50	78	Repair and Maintenance	96790	289	1114	Nursing & Resid. Care Facilit.
96041	105	519	Educational Services	96152	7	15	Construction of Buildings	96791	105	657	Educational Services
96044	34	174	Animal Production	96154	6	19	Construction of Buildings	96792	505	4810	Educational Services
96046	9	39	Support Activities: Agr./For.	96155	11	13	Transit & Grnd Pass. Transport	96793	1598	11770	Ambulatory Health Care Svcs
96047	25	54	Educational Services	96156	16	26	Construction of Buildings	96795	179	1422	Food Svcs & Drinking Places
96048	19	71	Support Activities: Agr./For.	96157	5	7	Insurance Carriers & Related	96796	104	1064	Educational Services
96049	58	382	Postal Service	96158	52	64	Motion Pict. & Sound Recording	96797	1260	13300	Food Svcs & Drinking Places
96050	33	69	Exec., Legis., & Other Support	96160	111	264	Accommodation	96801	6	65	Prof., Scientific, & Tech Svcs
96051	54	266	Accommodation	96161	1357	9010	Food Svcs & Drinking Places	96802	1	4	Special Trade Contractors
96052	63	168	Educational Services	96162	59	81	Special Trade Contractors	96803	1	2	Personal and Laundry Services
96054	9	15	Postal Service	96701	1521	16132	Food Svcs & Drinking Places	96804	1	0	Special Trade Contractors
96055	129	503	Food and Beverage Stores	96703	25	63	Special Trade Contractors	96805	6	3	Prof., Scientific, & Tech Svcs
96056	57	181	Educational Services	96704	146	883	Crop Production	96806	6	15	Administrative & Support Svcs
96057	78	511	Wood Product Manufacturing	96705	43	642	Crop Production	96807	5	16	Special Trade Contractors
96058	38	243	Admin. of Economic Programs	96706	322	4142	Hospitals	96808	6	7	Real Estate
96059	15	70	Educational Services	96707	526	8917	Food Svcs & Drinking Places	96809	5	9	Construction of Buildings
96061	5	19	Accommodation	96708	287	757	Educational Services	96810	1	0	Administrative & Support Svcs
96062	40	96	Educational Services	96709	20	57	Merch. Wholesalers,Durable Gds	96811	2	1	Merch. Wholesalers,Durable Gds
96063	6	30	Food Svcs & Drinking Places	96710	9	49	Crop Production	96812	12	10	Prof., Scientific, & Tech Svcs
96064	110	336	Educational Services	96712	302	1743	Food Svcs & Drinking Places	96813	4407	56507	Prof., Scientific, & Tech Svcs
96065	9	17	Educational Services	96713	94	783	Accommodation	96814	3076	28140	Food Svcs & Drinking Places
96067	584	3117	Hospitals	96714	225	809	Food Svcs & Drinking Places	96815	2166	33045	Accommodation

ZIP CODE	2004 Total Firms	2004 Total Employees	TOP INDUSTRY RANKED on 2004 EMPLOYMENT
96816	1598	13482	Educational Services
96817	2696	29848	Hospitals
96818	398	4668	Educational Services
96819	2613	40388	Special Trade Contractors
96820	34	244	Rental and Leasing Services
96821	285	1468	Educational Services
96822	557	5201	Educational Services
96823	57	78	Prof., Scientific, & Tech Svcs
96824	29	61	Prof., Scientific, & Tech Svcs
96825	595	3582	Food Svcs & Drinking Places
96826	1291	10232	Hospitals
96827	13	31	Publishing Industries
96828	18	29	Special Trade Contractors
96830	56	91	Prof., Scientific, & Tech Svcs
96835	30	90	Administrative & Support Svcs
96836	9	7	Social Assistance
96837	11	8	Prof., Scientific, & Tech Svcs
96839	46	49	Special Trade Contractors
96841	1	0	Telecommunications
96848	4	184	Relig., Grant, Civic, Prof Org
96850	42	588	Justice, Pubic Order/Safety
96853	44	558	Nat'l Security & Int'l Affairs
96854	11	25	Nat'l Security & Int'l Affairs
96857	36	24056	Nat'l Security & Int'l Affairs
96858	17	93	Justice, Pubic Order/Safety
96859	17	2925	Hospitals
96860	40	269	Food Svcs & Drinking Places
96861	10	34	Electronics & Appliance Stores
96862	12	307	Nat'l Security & Int'l Affairs
96863	29	245	Food Svcs & Drinking Places
97001	1	0	Unclassified Establishments
97002	303	2495	Merch. Wholesalers,Nondur. Gds
97004	164	606	Miscellaneous Store Retailers
97005	2080	26676	Leather & Allied Product Mfg
97006	1342	15795	Food Svcs & Drinking Places
97007	981	5035	Educational Services
97008	746	9259	Credit Intermediation & Relatd
97009	455	4547	Merch. Wholesalers,Nondur. Gds
97010	5	3	Ambulatory Health Care Svcs
97011	27	36	Merch. Wholesalers,Durable Gds
97013	832	5921	Merch. Wholesalers,Nondur. Gds
97014	60	699	Special Trade Contractors
97015	1455	24619	Hospitals
97016	195	2245	Paper Manufacturing
97017	99	292	Educational Services
97018	34	183	Educational Services
97019	76	417	Accommodation
97020	27	229	Special Trade Contractors
97021	43	233	Support Activities: Agr./For.
97022	71	342	Primary Metal Manufacturing
97023	360	1613	Educational Services
97024	159	3748	Food Manufacturing
97026	75	423	Educational Services
97027	306	2558	Motor Vehicle & Parts Dealers
97028	41	1395	Accommodation
97029	18	53	Educational Services
97030	1576	10803	Food Svcs & Drinking Places
97031	1155	8677	Merch. Wholesalers,Nondur. Gds
97032	154	1279	Merch. Wholesalers,Nondur. Gds
97033	4	2	Postal Service
97034	714	4044	Educational Services
97035	1643	13179	Prof., Scientific, & Tech Svcs
97036	22	492	Educational Services
97037	71	473	Educational Services
97038	573	2713	Merch. Wholesalers,Durable Gds
97039	46	130	Educational Services
97040	39	74	Educational Services
97041	115	1291	Accommodation
97042	105	317	Computer & Electronic Prod Mfg
97044	20	62	Machinery Manufacturing
97045	1807	12463	Educational Services
97048	195	919	Nonmetallic Mineral Prod. Mfg
97049	29	91	Food Svcs & Drinking Places
97050	21	64	Food Svcs & Drinking Places
97051	597	4991	Paper Manufacturing
97053	69	324	Plastics & Rubber Products Mfg
97054	29	172	Chemical Manufacturing
97055	538	3460	Food Svcs & Drinking Places
97056	350	2251	Food Svcs & Drinking Places
97057	1	3	Accommodation
97058	1025	8000	Food Svcs & Drinking Places
97060	532	6494	Truck Transportation
97062	1175	15268	Merch. Wholesalers,Durable Gds
97063	66	137	Special Trade Contractors
97064	133	478	Educational Services
97065	46	236	Food Svcs & Drinking Places
97067	119	649	Accommodation
97068	714	13959	Merch. Wholesalers,Durable Gds
97070	807	13395	Publishing Industries
97071	807	9717	Food and Beverage Stores

ZIP CODE	2004 Total Firms	2004 Total Employees	TOP INDUSTRY RANKED on 2004 EMPLOYMENT
97075	51	119	Special Trade Contractors
97077	4	2110	Computer & Electronic Prod Mfg
97080	496	4129	Educational Services
97101	92	435	Educational Services
97102	10	14	Educational Services
97103	952	5920	Food Svcs & Drinking Places
97106	147	655	Educational Services
97107	46	420	Food Manufacturing
97108	16	50	Educational Services
97109	10	22	Educational Services
97110	240	1273	Accommodation
97111	104	581	Food and Beverage Stores
97112	93	254	Educational Services
97113	257	3358	Merch. Wholesalers,Nondur. Gds
97114	125	1502	Merch. Wholesalers,Nondur. Gds
97115	120	540	Food Svcs & Drinking Places
97116	656	5579	Educational Services
97117	20	72	Food Svcs & Drinking Places
97118	85	474	Food Svcs & Drinking Places
97119	125	894	Wood Product Manufacturing
97121	40	420	Food Manufacturing
97122	19	76	Support Activities: Agr./For.
97123	1539	13171	Hospitals
97124	1178	24815	Prof., Scientific, & Tech Svcs
97125	2	20	Food Svcs & Drinking Places
97127	59	190	Educational Services
97128	1338	12749	Educational Services
97130	111	290	Food Svcs & Drinking Places
97131	151	393	Amusement, Gambling,& Recreat.
97132	944	8370	Educational Services
97133	134	1187	Amusement, Gambling,& Recreat.
97134	11	34	Food Svcs & Drinking Places
97135	81	282	Food Svcs & Drinking Places
97136	115	463	Accommodation
97137	88	889	Crop Production
97138	754	4211	Food Svcs & Drinking Places
97140	593	4355	Bldg Matl & Garden Eqpmt Dlrs
97141	803	5643	Exec., Legis., & Other Support
97143	12	16	Accommodation
97144	4	7	Food Svcs & Drinking Places
97145	13	131	Food Svcs & Drinking Places
97146	302	2570	General Merchandise Stores
97147	46	152	Nursing & Resid. Care Facilit.
97148	94	768	Merch. Wholesalers,Nondur. Gds
97149	33	83	Real Estate
97201	1133	20361	Educational Services
97202	1498	18449	Transit & Grnd Pass. Transport
97203	669	12229	Primary Metal Manufacturing
97204	2234	34016	Prof., Scientific, & Tech Svcs
97205	1621	15021	Prof., Scientific, & Tech Svcs
97206	1173	8431	Primary Metal Manufacturing
97207	52	87	Merch. Wholesalers,Nondur. Gds
97208	47	3053	Postal Service
97209	1646	16932	Prof., Scientific, & Tech Svcs
97210	1285	25574	Hospitals
97211	947	11106	Food Svcs & Drinking Places
97212	713	3790	Educational Services
97213	1191	13002	Hospitals
97214	2275	21723	Educational Services
97215	420	2455	Nursing & Resid. Care Facilit.
97216	660	7341	Hospitals
97217	1433	23874	Transportation Equipment Mfg
97218	621	8021	Merch. Wholesalers,Durable Gds
97219	1761	11878	Educational Services
97220	1649	17533	Food Svcs & Drinking Places
97221	511	3161	Prof., Scientific, & Tech Svcs
97222	1207	13827	Merch. Wholesalers,Nondur. Gds
97223	2595	24089	Prof., Scientific, & Tech Svcs
97224	905	12269	Prof., Scientific, & Tech Svcs
97225	1414	9653	Ambulatory Health Care Svcs
97227	409	12946	Hospitals
97228	32	36	Prof., Scientific, & Tech Svcs
97229	728	6235	Merch. Wholesalers,Nondur. Gds
97230	1085	17629	Transportation Equipment Mfg
97231	144	763	Merch. Wholesalers,Nondur. Gds
97232	1644	21556	Admin. of Economic Programs
97233	720	5268	Food Svcs & Drinking Places
97236	719	4249	Educational Services
97238	18	195	Postal Service
97239	1068	29107	Hospitals
97240	10	11	Truck Transportation
97242	17	36	Prof., Scientific, & Tech Svcs
97258	72	431	Prof., Scientific, & Tech Svcs
97266	1314	12526	Food Svcs & Drinking Places
97267	742	6068	Administrative & Support Svcs
97268	20	63	Real Estate
97269	27	30	Merch. Wholesalers,Durable Gds
97280	70	105	Special Trade Contractors
97281	69	122	Prof., Scientific, & Tech Svcs
97282	22	32	Prof., Scientific, & Tech Svcs

ZIP CODE	2004 Total Firms	2004 Total Employees	TOP INDUSTRY RANKED on 2004 EMPLOYMENT
97283	10	20	Construction of Buildings
97286	15	19	Truck Transportation
97290	30	95	Administrative & Support Svcs
97291	23	39	Administrative & Support Svcs
97292	29	109	Transit & Grnd Pass. Transport
97293	28	51	Social Assistance
97294	42	69	Educational Services
97296	14	154	Truck Transportation
97298	35	57	Prof., Scientific, & Tech Svcs
97301	2861	32713	Hospitals
97302	1873	18356	Prof., Scientific, & Tech Svcs
97303	1524	15248	Food Svcs & Drinking Places
97304	535	4369	Food Manufacturing
97305	814	9615	Educational Services
97306	345	2376	Food Svcs & Drinking Places
97307	29	61	Merch. Wholesalers,Durable Gds
97308	29	45	Prof., Scientific, & Tech Svcs
97309	42	108	Construction of Buildings
97310	94	9544	Admin. Human Resource Programs
97311	3	2	Food Svcs & Drinking Places
97312	1	850	Insurance Carriers & Related
97313	1	560	Insurance Carriers & Related
97314	1	500	Admin. of Economic Programs
97321	1172	12251	Educational Services
97322	912	10071	Food Manufacturing
97324	58	108	Support Activities: Agr./For.
97325	130	742	Wood Product Manufacturing
97326	21	125	Transit & Grnd Pass. Transport
97327	96	286	Justice, Pubic Order/Safety
97329	4	55	Wood Product Manufacturing
97330	1547	14568	Ambulatory Health Care Svcs
97331	21	5098	Educational Services
97333	821	7340	Exec., Legis., & Other Support
97335	11	14	Merch. Wholesalers,Nondur. Gds
97336	5	39	Educational Services
97338	594	4308	Food Svcs & Drinking Places
97339	51	98	Construction of Buildings
97341	164	574	Accommodation
97342	32	220	Support Activities: Agr./For.
97343	13	40	Educational Services
97344	20	89	Justice, Pubic Order/Safety
97345	17	48	Admin. Enviro. Quality Progrms
97346	30	87	Educational Services
97347	48	194	Ambulatory Health Care Svcs
97348	76	1256	Paper Manufacturing
97350	10	30	Food Svcs & Drinking Places
97351	233	2014	Educational Services
97352	106	726	Merch. Wholesalers,Nondur. Gds
97355	893	6099	Hospitals
97357	8	13	Food and Beverage Stores
97358	91	927	Wood Product Manufacturing
97359	2	11	Justice, Pubic Order/Safety
97360	65	275	Educational Services
97361	207	2343	Educational Services
97362	154	2284	Crop Production
97364	14	19	Special Trade Contractors
97365	1022	7529	Food Svcs & Drinking Places
97366	122	414	Nonstore Retailers
97367	789	5463	Amusement, Gambling,& Recreat.
97368	90	293	Relig., Grant, Civic, Prof Org
97369	12	134	Accommodation
97370	378	1974	Wood Product Manufacturing
97371	48	488	Relig., Grant, Civic, Prof Org
97372	8	7	Food and Beverage Stores
97373	3	55	Educational Services
97374	174	857	Wood Product Manufacturing
97375	34	82	Special Trade Contractors
97376	47	93	Miscellaneous Store Retailers
97377	34	99	Crop Production
97378	181	2078	Justice, Pubic Order/Safety
97380	44	282	Exec., Legis., & Other Support
97381	579	4015	Educational Services
97383	436	8500	Food Manufacturing
97384	10	53	Wood Product Manufacturing
97385	90	743	Nursing & Resid. Care Facilit.
97386	384	2438	Educational Services
97388	67	516	Accommodation
97389	112	1221	Merch. Wholesalers,Nondur. Gds
97390	21	52	Forestry and Logging
97391	184	1412	Paper Manufacturing
97392	109	724	Educational Services
97394	329	989	Food and Beverage Stores
97396	99	2425	Amusement, Gambling,& Recreat.
97401	3629	92342	Securities/Commodity Contracts
97402	2630	30019	Merch. Wholesalers,Durable Gds
97403	301	7150	Educational Services
97404	640	4096	Food Svcs & Drinking Places
97405	1015	8822	Educational Services
97406	15	58	Food and Beverage Stores
97407	3	2	Textile Product Mills

ZIP CODE	2004 Total Firms	2004 Total Employ-ees	TOP INDUSTRY RANKED on 2004 EMPLOYMENT	ZIP CODE	2004 Total Firms	2004 Total Employ-ees	TOP INDUSTRY RANKED on 2004 EMPLOYMENT	ZIP CODE	2004 Total Firms	2004 Total Employ-ees	TOP INDUSTRY RANKED on 2004 EMPLOYMENT
97408	337	7657	Transportation Equipment Mfg	97528	48	112	Administrative & Support Svcs	97837	5	6	Forestry and Logging
97409	7	35	Bldg Matl & Garden Eqpmt Dlrs	97530	333	1214	Food Svcs & Drinking Places	97838	946	10534	Motor Vehicle & Parts Dealers
97410	19	86	Food Svcs & Drinking Places	97531	22	74	Transportation Equipment Mfg	97839	22	81	Merch. Wholesalers,Durable Gds
97411	424	2258	Accommodation	97532	96	534	Motor Vehicle & Parts Dealers	97840	7	19	Scenic & Sightseeing Transport
97412	20	68	Educational Services	97533	6	8	Prof., Scientific, & Tech Svcs	97841	19	113	Educational Services
97413	60	352	Accommodation	97534	18	30	Food Svcs & Drinking Places	97842	10	37	Support Activities: Agr./For.
97414	8	36	Wood Product Manufacturing	97535	200	1045	Merch. Wholesalers,Nondur. Gds	97843	25	108	Educational Services
97415	788	4401	Wood Product Manufacturing	97536	45	259	Admin. of Economic Programs	97844	54	313	Educational Services
97416	22	150	Forestry and Logging	97537	229	909	Educational Services	97845	227	1548	Wood Product Manufacturing
97417	129	1598	Amusement, Gambling,& Recreat.	97538	59	141	Food and Beverage Stores	97846	146	679	Accommodation
97419	32	81	Accommodation	97539	139	464	Food Svcs & Drinking Places	97848	8	36	Crop Production
97420	1185	11004	Educational Services	97540	242	1330	Nonmetallic Mineral Prod. Mfg	97850	994	8579	Educational Services
97423	310	1762	Wood Product Manufacturing	97541	31	117	Admin. Enviro. Quality Progrms	97856	24	68	Educational Services
97424	610	4071	Food Svcs & Drinking Places	97543	22	29	Special Trade Contractors	97857	20	91	Transit & Grnd Pass. Transport
97425	15	96	Accommodation	97544	66	190	Chemical Manufacturing	97859	5	8	Museums, Hist. Sites,& Similar
97426	283	1633	Food Manufacturing	97601	1150	10801	Wood Product Manufacturing	97862	376	3414	Food Manufacturing
97427	4	2	Special Trade Contractors	97602	6	14	Special Trade Contractors	97864	15	60	Educational Services
97428	3	9	Merch. Wholesalers,Nondur. Gds	97603	1095	9155	Food Svcs & Drinking Places	97865	44	145	Educational Services
97429	33	233	Wood Product Manufacturing	97604	5	11	Justice, Pubic Order/Safety	97867	29	134	Educational Services
97430	14	38	Forestry and Logging	97620	6	19	Educational Services	97868	63	324	Merch. Wholesalers,Durable Gds
97431	48	218	Forestry and Logging	97621	6	8	Prof., Scientific, & Tech Svcs	97869	63	443	Wood Product Manufacturing
97432	10	38	Truck Transportation	97622	19	96	Admin. of Economic Programs	97870	42	67	Bldg Matl & Garden Eqpmt Dlrs
97434	7	30	Educational Services	97623	60	264	Educational Services	97873	9	19	Animal Production
97435	112	791	Merch. Wholesalers,Durable Gds	97624	104	1018	Relig., Grant, Civic, Prof Org	97874	29	59	Educational Services
97436	40	290	Exec., Legis., & Other Support	97625	6	12	Food Svcs & Drinking Places	97875	72	264	Educational Services
97437	51	256	Educational Services	97626	14	21	Accommodation	97876	16	26	Crop Production
97438	28	245	Educational Services	97627	22	74	Educational Services	97877	31	41	Accommodation
97439	678	4278	Food Svcs & Drinking Places	97630	356	1847	Wood Product Manufacturing	97880	23	91	Support Activities: Agr./For.
97440	54	172	Crop Production	97632	43	273	Social Assistance	97882	141	1106	Merch. Wholesalers,Nondur. Gds
97441	17	54	Educational Services	97633	78	490	Merch. Wholesalers,Nondur. Gds	97883	79	222	Food Svcs & Drinking Places
97442	79	838	Bldg Matl & Garden Eqpmt Dlrs	97634	7	8	Construction of Buildings	97884	19	98	Educational Services
97443	67	554	Educational Services	97635	12	52	Forestry and Logging	97885	58	290	Educational Services
97444	389	1867	Accommodation	97636	26	116	Exec., Legis., & Other Support	97886	29	1763	Food Manufacturing
97446	132	1349	Truck Transportation	97637	4	11	Educational Services	97901	19	117	Educational Services
97447	25	133	Exec., Legis., & Other Support	97638	27	105	Educational Services	97902	2	6	Educational Services
97448	427	4132	Transportation Equipment Mfg	97639	11	79	Merch. Wholesalers,Durable Gds	97903	6	8	Food and Beverage Stores
97449	58	191	Accommodation	97640	11	23	Accommodation	97904	12	19	Animal Production
97450	25	71	Educational Services	97641	45	125	Food Svcs & Drinking Places	97905	10	149	Nonmetallic Mineral Prod. Mfg
97451	14	32	Beverage & Tobacco Product Mfg	97701	3613	24853	Ambulatory Health Care Svcs	97906	9	28	Educational Services
97452	44	332	Educational Services	97702	1592	12847	Accommodation	97907	21	109	Admin. of Economic Programs
97453	34	218	Wood Product Manufacturing	97707	267	2823	Accommodation	97908	6	11	Animal Production
97454	43	147	Educational Services	97708	112	220	Special Trade Contractors	97909	2	4	Animal Production
97455	81	313	Educational Services	97709	55	81	Accommodation	97910	38	87	Educational Services
97456	89	545	Miscellaneous Store Retailers	97710	6	28	Animal Production	97911	11	11	Food Svcs & Drinking Places
97457	305	1856	Relig., Grant, Civic, Prof Org	97711	2	3	Educational Services	97913	162	1716	Food Manufacturing
97458	160	809	Educational Services	97712	6	12	Heavy & Civil Eng. Construct'N	97914	880	8031	Food Manufacturing
97459	655	4879	Accommodation	97720	311	1623	Exec., Legis., & Other Support	97917	1	0	Fishing, Hunting and Trapping
97461	20	243	Wood Product Manufacturing	97721	5	91	Admin. Enviro. Quality Progrms	97918	181	1284	Educational Services
97462	103	467	Gasoline Stations	97722	7	16	Animal Production	97920	2	4	Food and Beverage Stores
97463	137	999	Support Activities: Agr./For.	97730	20	57	Accommodation	98001	1063	27915	Transportation Equipment Mfg
97464	6	10	Prof., Scientific, & Tech Svcs	97731	35	228	Sportg Gds,Hobby,Book, & Music	98002	1344	12953	Motor Vehicle & Parts Dealers
97465	149	498	Utilities	97732	10	79	Educational Services	98003	2162	21794	Food Svcs & Drinking Places
97466	32	184	Educational Services	97733	23	209	Support Activities: Agr./For.	98004	3817	42539	Prof., Scientific, & Tech Svcs
97467	335	1769	Food Svcs & Drinking Places	97734	61	624	Transportation Equipment Mfg	98005	1888	21801	Prof., Scientific, & Tech Svcs
97469	76	1265	Wood Product Manufacturing	97735	7	4	Animal Production	98006	882	8283	Food Svcs & Drinking Places
97470	2470	24235	Wood Product Manufacturing	97736	8	34	Admin. Enviro. Quality Progrms	98007	954	10236	Educational Services
97473	7	19	Food Svcs & Drinking Places	97737	27	93	Educational Services	98008	460	3811	Educational Services
97476	12	14	Unclassified Establishments	97738	61	745	Transportation Equipment Mfg	98009	43	81	Educational Services
97477	1468	14633	Food Svcs & Drinking Places	97739	326	1612	Relig., Grant, Civic, Prof Org	98010	117	435	Educational Services
97478	625	4943	Educational Services	97741	455	3969	Wood Product Manufacturing	98011	875	8229	Educational Services
97479	389	1966	Food Svcs & Drinking Places	97750	27	63	Educational Services	98012	876	6406	Food Svcs & Drinking Places
97480	7	65	Wood Product Manufacturing	97751	9	80	Admin. of Economic Programs	98013	11	9	Prof., Scientific, & Tech Svcs
97481	15	41	Educational Services	97752	4	13	Animal Production	98014	185	1089	Educational Services
97482	4	3	Miscellaneous Store Retailers	97753	55	121	Heavy & Civil Eng. Construct'N	98015	26	126	Educational Services
97484	13	80	Exec., Legis., & Other Support	97754	632	5685	Motor Vehicle & Parts Dealers	98019	287	1442	Food and Beverage Stores
97486	23	58	Merch. Wholesalers,Nondur. Gds	97756	1371	8430	Food Svcs & Drinking Places	98020	814	4914	Food Svcs & Drinking Places
97487	233	985	Food Svcs & Drinking Places	97758	5	9	Sportg Gds,Hobby,Book, & Music	98021	540	7065	Prof., Scientific, & Tech Svcs
97488	43	290	Educational Services	97759	455	2926	Accommodation	98022	757	6039	Educational Services
97489	40	89	Miscellaneous Store Retailers	97760	156	560	Truck Transportation	98023	454	3752	Educational Services
97490	6	4	Miscellaneous Manufacturing	97761	63	1149	Amusement, Gambling,& Recreat.	98024	191	757	Educational Services
97491	5	15	Food Manufacturing	97801	1121	13080	Exec., Legis., & Other Support	98025	6	17	Fabricated Metal Product Mfg
97492	9	239	Admin. of Economic Programs	97810	15	88	Admin. of Economic Programs	98026	857	7084	Hospitals
97493	17	25	Accommodation	97812	51	406	Support Act. for Transport.	98027	1401	11951	General Merchandise Stores
97494	4	41	Merch. Wholesalers,Durable Gds	97813	43	153	Educational Services	98028	484	3500	Amusement, Gambling,& Recreat.
97495	32	135	Educational Services	97814	692	4821	Food and Beverage Stores	98029	227	3487	Merch. Wholesalers,Durable Gds
97496	179	1119	Educational Services	97817	3	2	Food Svcs & Drinking Places	98030	653	5560	Educational Services
97497	48	118	Educational Services	97818	139	2071	Food Manufacturing	98031	596	5402	Educational Services
97498	156	563	Accommodation	97819	3	5	Animal Production	98032	2499	47907	Transportation Equipment Mfg
97499	63	272	Educational Services	97820	73	393	Forestry and Logging	98033	1843	15787	Prof., Scientific, & Tech Svcs
97501	2482	22760	Merch. Wholesalers,Nondur. Gds	97823	125	326	Educational Services	98034	1399	14194	Ambulatory Health Care Svcs
97502	936	7263	Truck Transportation	97824	38	121	Other Information Services	98035	17	72	Couriers and Messengers
97503	354	4959	Wood Product Manufacturing	97825	17	81	Special Trade Contractors	98036	1844	15436	Educational Services
97504	2062	19513	Ambulatory Health Care Svcs	97826	31	209	Crop Production	98037	1349	12029	General Merchandise Stores
97520	1559	9602	Food Svcs & Drinking Places	97827	91	654	Merch. Wholesalers,Durable Gds	98038	568	3674	Educational Services
97522	27	113	Educational Services	97828	284	1257	Educational Services	98039	42	314	Educational Services
97523	298	1490	Educational Services	97830	71	190	Accommodation	98040	835	5673	Educational Services
97524	295	1715	Merch. Wholesalers,Durable Gds	97833	32	121	Support Activities: Agr./For.	98041	35	120	Real Estate
97525	137	594	Heavy & Civil Eng. Construct'N	97834	105	346	Educational Services	98042	701	4266	Educational Services
97526	2048	14893	Food Svcs & Drinking Places	97835	26	144	Educational Services	98043	502	5363	Insurance Carriers & Related
97527	900	5774	Educational Services	97836	148	761	Ambulatory Health Care Svcs	98045	568	3037	Food Svcs & Drinking Places

BUSINESS DATA

ZIP CODE	2004 Total Firms	2004 Total Employees	TOP INDUSTRY RANKED on 2004 EMPLOYMENT	ZIP CODE	2004 Total Firms	2004 Total Employees	TOP INDUSTRY RANKED on 2004 EMPLOYMENT	ZIP CODE	2004 Total Firms	2004 Total Employees	TOP INDUSTRY RANKED on 2004 EMPLOYMENT
98046	33	105	Administrative & Support Svcs	98206	20	107	Social Assistance	98330	14	20	Food Svcs & Drinking Places
98047	160	1603	Truck Transportation	98207	3	9	Nat'l Security & Int'l Affairs	98331	290	1811	Hospitals
98050	42	380	Merch. Wholesalers,Durable Gds	98208	1139	8937	Food Svcs & Drinking Places	98332	394	3470	Justice, Pubic Order/Safety
98051	62	318	Educational Services	98213	25	34	Administrative & Support Svcs	98333	61	157	Museums, Hist. Sites,& Similar
98052	2607	54131	Publishing Industries	98220	27	92	Educational Services	98335	1344	7188	Food Svcs & Drinking Places
98053	270	1620	Educational Services	98221	995	7534	Food Svcs & Drinking Places	98336	16	60	Educational Services
98054	6	8	Construction of Buildings	98222	6	10	Amusement, Gambling,& Recreat.	98337	372	3810	Educational Services
98055	1875	26989	Motor Vehicle & Parts Dealers	98223	1244	10876	Transportation Equipment Mfg	98338	356	1577	Educational Services
98056	413	3250	Educational Services	98224	6	13	Ambulatory Health Care Svcs	98339	211	856	Food Svcs & Drinking Places
98057	18	71	Food Svcs & Drinking Places	98225	2946	28366	Social Assistance	98340	59	148	Miscellaneous Store Retailers
98058	469	3299	Educational Services	98226	1472	17213	Food Svcs & Drinking Places	98342	23	97	Special Trade Contractors
98059	433	3034	Food and Beverage Stores	98227	71	129	Social Assistance	98343	6	4	Food Svcs & Drinking Places
98061	9	8	Prof., Scientific, & Tech Svcs	98228	43	65	Special Trade Contractors	98344	9	11	Food Svcs & Drinking Places
98062	3	4	Construction of Buildings	98229	627	5142	Educational Services	98345	19	293	Computer & Electronic Prod Mfg
98063	27	99	Special Trade Contractors	98230	475	4160	Merch. Wholesalers,Nondur. Gds	98346	341	1579	Educational Services
98064	21	21	Administrative & Support Svcs	98231	9	23	Special Trade Contractors	98348	4	15	Utilities
98065	230	2440	Relig., Grant, Civic, Prof Org	98232	129	1143	Amusement, Gambling,& Recreat.	98349	111	403	Educational Services
98068	26	470	Educational Services	98233	904	9115	Motor Vehicle & Parts Dealers	98350	17	206	Relig., Grant, Civic, Prof Org
98070	543	2598	Miscellaneous Manufacturing	98235	18	78	Educational Services	98351	13	126	Merch. Wholesalers,Nondur. Gds
98071	33	125	Special Trade Contractors	98236	339	814	Food and Beverage Stores	98352	1	400	Sportg Gds,Hobby,Book, & Music
98072	1507	17298	Special Trade Contractors	98237	116	434	Forestry and Logging	98353	14	45	Food Svcs & Drinking Places
98073	48	130	Special Trade Contractors	98238	17	80	Food Svcs & Drinking Places	98354	214	1949	Food Svcs & Drinking Places
98074	328	1922	Educational Services	98239	338	2666	Hospitals	98355	22	64	Justice, Pubic Order/Safety
98075	231	1361	Educational Services	98240	73	627	Crop Production	98356	148	1071	Wood Product Manufacturing
98077	175	993	Educational Services	98241	78	583	Educational Services	98357	46	378	Social Assistance
98082	31	88	Transit & Grnd Pass. Transport	98243	24	73	Accommodation	98358	25	47	Museums, Hist. Sites,& Similar
98083	55	240	Educational Services	98244	96	686	Amusement, Gambling,& Recreat.	98359	85	261	Educational Services
98089	16	38	Administrative & Support Svcs	98245	359	1707	Accommodation	98360	188	1452	Educational Services
98092	339	3080	Educational Services	98247	235	1524	Educational Services	98361	59	223	Food Svcs & Drinking Places
98093	27	26	Administrative & Support Svcs	98248	638	5839	Primary Metal Manufacturing	98362	1389	10010	Food Svcs & Drinking Places
98101	4389	59535	Prof., Scientific, & Tech Svcs	98249	328	1423	Transportation Equipment Mfg	98363	325	2429	Paper Manufacturing
98102	923	7681	Prof., Scientific, & Tech Svcs	98250	829	3508	Accommodation	98364	19	49	Merch. Wholesalers,Nondur. Gds
98103	2253	15407	Food Svcs & Drinking Places	98251	77	312	Educational Services	98365	123	436	Accommodation
98104	3146	47280	Prof., Scientific, & Tech Svcs	98252	186	1115	Educational Services	98366	1168	9193	Exec., Legis., & Other Support
98105	1528	13768	Hospitals	98253	36	57	Accommodation	98367	385	3113	Educational Services
98106	508	10248	Educational Services	98255	14	62	Exec., Legis., & Other Support	98368	1195	5750	Food Svcs & Drinking Places
98107	1580	15098	Hospitals	98256	18	71	Accommodation	98370	1188	7602	Motor Vehicle & Parts Dealers
98108	1721	32619	Educational Services	98257	260	1644	Support Act. for Transport.	98371	788	7283	Motor Vehicle & Parts Dealers
98109	2080	27145	Prof., Scientific, & Tech Svcs	98258	472	2344	Educational Services	98372	609	14159	Educational Services
98110	1327	5817	Prof., Scientific, & Tech Svcs	98259	4	11	Unclassified Establishments	98373	1032	8101	Food Svcs & Drinking Places
98111	32	89	Administrative & Support Svcs	98260	440	1717	Educational Services	98374	314	3665	Educational Services
98112	841	4725	Food Svcs & Drinking Places	98261	193	621	Educational Services	98375	320	3163	Special Trade Contractors
98113	13	14	Electronics & Appliance Stores	98262	38	80	Social Assistance	98376	99	341	Educational Services
98114	9	6	Scenic & Sightseeing Transport	98263	13	69	Educational Services	98377	77	615	Wood Product Manufacturing
98115	1590	9154	Food Svcs & Drinking Places	98264	698	6516	Crop Production	98380	85	204	Special Trade Contractors
98116	923	5084	Food Svcs & Drinking Places	98266	54	182	Educational Services	98381	23	67	Accommodation
98117	723	3946	Prof., Scientific, & Tech Svcs	98267	22	176	Accommodation	98382	1152	5798	Educational Services
98118	1068	8538	Merch. Wholesalers,Nondur. Gds	98270	1112	7512	Food Svcs & Drinking Places	98383	1289	10037	Food Svcs & Drinking Places
98119	1120	13647	Administrative & Support Svcs	98271	394	5958	Amusement, Gambling,& Recreat.	98384	9	24	Administrative & Support Svcs
98121	1444	19401	Prof., Scientific, & Tech Svcs	98272	887	7765	Justice, Pubic Order/Safety	98385	23	127	Wood Product Manufacturing
98122	1684	22178	Hospitals	98273	1606	15175	Exec., Legis., & Other Support	98386	7	11	Administrative & Support Svcs
98124	28	50	Mining (Except Oil and Gas)	98274	297	3986	Hospitals	98387	544	3896	Educational Services
98125	1513	10896	Motor Vehicle & Parts Dealers	98275	679	5875	Fabricated Metal Product Mfg	98388	79	502	Educational Services
98126	393	4190	Hospitals	98276	15	30	Repair and Maintenance	98390	1197	9761	Special Trade Contractors
98127	29	42	Prof., Scientific, & Tech Svcs	98277	1053	16712	Nat'l Security & Int'l Affairs	98392	64	747	Amusement, Gambling,& Recreat.
98133	1665	19376	Hospitals	98278	18	2072	Hospitals	98393	8	11	Special Trade Contractors
98134	986	25813	Merch. Wholesalers,Durable Gds	98279	24	131	Miscellaneous Store Retailers	98394	34	128	Educational Services
98136	349	1695	Food Svcs & Drinking Places	98280	63	125	Accommodation	98395	11	33	Postal Service
98138	15	56	Transit & Grnd Pass. Transport	98281	108	353	Food Svcs & Drinking Places	98396	12	87	Educational Services
98139	24	127	Exec., Legis., & Other Support	98282	247	780	Educational Services	98401	15	28	Miscellaneous Store Retailers
98141	6	2	Social Assistance	98283	22	65	Food Svcs & Drinking Places	98402	1386	15705	Prof., Scientific, & Tech Svcs
98144	863	9915	Social Assistance	98284	592	6525	Ambulatory Health Care Svcs	98403	304	2439	Wholesale Elec. Mrkts & Agents
98145	20	26	Prof., Scientific, & Tech Svcs	98286	12	75	Merch. Wholesalers,Durable Gds	98404	372	4021	Relig., Grant, Civic, Prof Org
98146	369	2160	Educational Services	98287	10	12	Food and Beverage Stores	98405	991	25997	Ambulatory Health Care Svcs
98148	501	3751	Educational Services	98288	26	696	Accommodation	98406	612	4620	Nursing & Resid. Care Facilit.
98154	178	1777	Prof., Scientific, & Tech Svcs	98290	986	6046	Educational Services	98407	420	2498	Food Svcs & Drinking Places
98155	774	6007	Administrative & Support Svcs	98291	33	219	Waste Managmt & Remediat'n Svc	98408	400	3730	Food Svcs & Drinking Places
98158	101	24113	Support Act. for Transport.	98292	657	3851	Educational Services	98409	1599	21563	General Merchandise Stores
98160	7	6	Prof., Scientific, & Tech Svcs	98293	12	37	Wood Product Manufacturing	98411	18	33	Prof., Scientific, & Tech Svcs
98161	19	891	Insurance Carriers & Related	98294	205	913	Educational Services	98412	5	33	Administrative & Support Svcs
98164	54	1005	Justice, Pubic Order/Safety	98295	89	556	Food Svcs & Drinking Places	98413	1	0	Postal Service
98165	30	48	Construction of Buildings	98296	440	2734	Special Trade Contractors	98415	5	7	Merch. Wholesalers,Nondur. Gds
98166	993	6719	Hospitals	98303	30	138	Relig., Grant, Civic, Prof Org	98416	1	750	Educational Services
98168	1003	13978	Transportation Equipment Mfg	98304	46	247	Accommodation	98418	247	1928	Ambulatory Health Care Svcs
98174	24	324	Admin. of Economic Programs	98305	28	147	Merch. Wholesalers,Durable Gds	98421	430	13669	Amusement, Gambling,& Recreat.
98175	16	109	Social Assistance	98310	685	6932	Hospitals	98422	261	2083	Wood Product Manufacturing
98177	348	1557	Educational Services	98311	363	2863	Educational Services	98424	735	12248	Fabricated Metal Product Mfg
98178	262	2132	Educational Services	98312	855	8367	Hospitals	98430	8	531	Nat'l Security & Int'l Affairs
98181	7	1527	General Merchandise Stores	98314	25	170	Exec., Legis., & Other Support	98431	15	3098	Hospitals
98185	2	1202	Insurance Carriers & Related	98315	24	517	General Merchandise Stores	98433	111	1243	Educational Services
98188	1768	24127	Food Svcs & Drinking Places	98320	53	220	Accommodation	98438	39	537	Relig., Grant, Civic, Prof Org
98191	4	0	Construction of Buildings	98321	278	2456	Social Assistance	98439	32	533	General Merchandise Stores
98194	9	19	Transit & Grnd Pass. Transport	98322	10	48	Special Trade Contractors	98442	2	3	Heavy & Civil Eng. Construct'N
98195	131	32032	Educational Services	98323	12	42	Educational Services	98443	112	803	Construction of Buildings
98198	813	8882	Administrative & Support Svcs	98324	21	39	Truck Transportation	98444	930	6758	Food Svcs & Drinking Places
98199	662	3794	Food Svcs & Drinking Places	98325	69	843	Merch. Wholesalers,Nondur. Gds	98445	359	3308	Administrative & Support Svcs
98201	1917	26338	Exec., Legis., & Other Support	98326	44	574	Justice, Pubic Order/Safety	98446	205	1832	Educational Services
98203	720	11277	Computer & Electronic Prod Mfg	98327	35	1337	Insurance Carriers & Related	98447	47	1243	Other Information Services
98204	985	39170	Transportation Equipment Mfg	98328	293	1240	Educational Services	98464	16	54	Support Act. for Transport.
98205	327	2744	Merch. Wholesalers,Durable Gds	98329	119	537	Social Assistance	98465	123	1241	Social Assistance

ZIP CODE	2004 Total Firms	2004 Total Employ-ees	TOP INDUSTRY RANKED on 2004 EMPLOYMENT	ZIP CODE	2004 Total Firms	2004 Total Employ-ees	TOP INDUSTRY RANKED on 2004 EMPLOYMENT	ZIP CODE	2004 Total Firms	2004 Total Employ-ees	TOP INDUSTRY RANKED on 2004 EMPLOYMENT
98466	1000	7193	Educational Services	98609	1	1	General Merchandise Stores	98851	76	447	Educational Services
98467	163	1127	Nursing & Resid. Care Facilit.	98610	69	457	Forestry and Logging	98852	3	11	Accommodation
98492	1	0	Special Trade Contractors	98611	246	1265	Educational Services	98853	3	5	Merch. Wholesalers,Nondur. Gds
98493	3	1037	Hospitals	98612	145	705	Forestry and Logging	98855	202	1257	Educational Services
98497	3	6	Perform'g Arts, Spec. Sports	98613	8	26	Educational Services	98856	210	736	Exec., Legis., & Other Support
98498	392	5621	Hospitals	98614	41	119	Food Manufacturing	98857	104	1181	Merch. Wholesalers,Nondur. Gds
98499	1852	18042	Administrative & Support Svcs	98616	9	48	Support Activities: Agr./For.	98858	74	408	Educational Services
98501	2204	29999	Exec., Legis., & Other Support	98617	33	130	Heavy & Civil Eng. Construct'N	98859	6	21	Merch. Wholesalers,Durable Gds
98502	1258	11921	Exec., Legis., & Other Support	98619	24	174	Forestry and Logging	98860	15	40	Educational Services
98503	1012	10849	Admin. Enviro. Quality Progrms	98620	354	1972	Exec., Legis., & Other Support	98862	213	1084	Accommodation
98504	225	3726	Admin. of Economic Programs	98621	9	43	Justice, Pubic Order/Safety	98901	1216	13683	Food Svcs & Drinking Places
98505	3	616	Educational Services	98623	11	20	Motor Vehicle & Parts Dealers	98902	1983	24177	Merch. Wholesalers,Nondur. Gds
98506	861	8102	Hospitals	98624	129	850	Merch. Wholesalers,Nondur. Gds	98903	703	9106	Merch. Wholesalers,Nondur. Gds
98507	50	154	Construction of Buildings	98625	171	1304	Educational Services	98904	1	1	Prof., Scientific, & Tech Svcs
98508	28	170	Social Assistance	98626	685	6621	Food Manufacturing	98907	20	45	Construction of Buildings
98509	39	84	Administrative & Support Svcs	98628	18	54	Educational Services	98908	894	6353	Merch. Wholesalers,Nondur. Gds
98511	7	18	Prof., Scientific, & Tech Svcs	98629	152	910	Food Svcs & Drinking Places	98909	25	58	Truck Transportation
98512	676	5857	Educational Services	98631	297	1243	Food Svcs & Drinking Places	98920	1	1	Postal Service
98513	234	1864	Merch. Wholesalers,Nondur. Gds	98632	1877	22594	Paper Manufacturing	98921	5	79	Relig., Grant, Civic, Prof Org
98516	555	5149	Food Svcs & Drinking Places	98635	67	143	Educational Services	98922	334	1692	Food Svcs & Drinking Places
98520	1068	9623	Ambulatory Health Care Svcs	98637	19	144	Unclassified Establishments	98923	32	315	Educational Services
98522	2	1	Administrative & Support Svcs	98638	76	476	Exec., Legis., & Other Support	98925	30	107	Accommodation
98524	51	231	Food Svcs & Drinking Places	98639	30	196	Admin. Enviro. Quality Progrms	98926	1236	7979	Food Svcs & Drinking Places
98526	29	235	Fabricated Metal Product Mfg	98640	144	546	Food and Beverage Stores	98930	320	3209	Merch. Wholesalers,Nondur. Gds
98527	11	24	Merch. Wholesalers,Nondur. Gds	98641	7	39	Museums, Hist. Sites,& Similar	98932	82	838	Merch. Wholesalers,Nondur. Gds
98528	346	1539	Educational Services	98642	411	2055	Merch. Wholesalers,Nondur. Gds	98933	35	457	Crop Production
98530	9	12	Food Svcs & Drinking Places	98643	20	33	Telecommunications	98934	44	120	Educational Services
98531	1075	10525	Utilities	98644	61	215	Food Svcs & Drinking Places	98935	57	624	Merch. Wholesalers,Nondur. Gds
98532	1064	10997	Food Svcs & Drinking Places	98645	20	61	Support Activities: Agr./For.	98936	88	800	Wood Product Manufacturing
98533	16	44	Merch. Wholesalers,Durable Gds	98647	19	61	Accommodation	98937	153	1409	Accommodation
98535	23	63	Accommodation	98648	209	1158	Other Information Services	98938	31	505	Merch. Wholesalers,Nondur. Gds
98536	7	18	Exec., Legis., & Other Support	98649	32	415	Educational Services	98939	9	55	Bldg Matl & Garden Eqpmt Dlrs
98537	61	589	Forestry and Logging	98650	47	145	Exec., Legis., & Other Support	98940	13	15	Real Estate
98538	12	85	Miscellaneous Store Retailers	98651	22	57	Exec., Legis., & Other Support	98941	80	284	Special Trade Contractors
98539	5	5	Food and Beverage Stores	98660	1134	12045	Prof., Scientific, & Tech Svcs	98942	405	3595	Food Manufacturing
98540	2	2	Special Trade Contractors	98661	1519	15670	Educational Services	98943	4	8	Repair and Maintenance
98541	318	1476	Educational Services	98662	1202	11880	Food Svcs & Drinking Places	98944	728	7658	Food Manufacturing
98542	27	86	Forestry and Logging	98663	538	3925	Ambulatory Health Care Svcs	98946	34	113	Educational Services
98544	3	5	Miscellaneous Store Retailers	98664	357	3471	Ambulatory Health Care Svcs	98947	40	504	Merch. Wholesalers,Nondur. Gds
98546	41	114	Educational Services	98665	1059	7223	Food Svcs & Drinking Places	98948	341	4358	Food Manufacturing
98547	60	164	Food Svcs & Drinking Places	98666	26	80	Prof., Scientific, & Tech Svcs	98950	14	1125	Crop Production
98548	80	248	Food Svcs & Drinking Places	98668	36	67	Administrative & Support Svcs	98951	254	3358	Merch. Wholesalers,Nondur. Gds
98550	388	3158	Educational Services	98670	1	0	Construction of Buildings	98952	40	914	Educational Services
98552	17	49	Wood Product Manufacturing	98671	393	3000	Wood Product Manufacturing	98953	175	1422	Crop Production
98554	7	14	Educational Services	98672	249	1095	Educational Services	99001	162	1755	Prof., Scientific, & Tech Svcs
98555	19	61	Food and Beverage Stores	98673	14	106	Rail Transportation	99003	82	472	Educational Services
98556	7	142	Justice, Pubic Order/Safety	98674	397	3606	Merch. Wholesalers,Nondur. Gds	99004	329	3513	Educational Services
98557	75	980	Wood Product Manufacturing	98675	106	423	Special Trade Contractors	99005	111	413	Educational Services
98558	25	189	Nursing & Resid. Care Facilit.	98682	771	6603	Computer & Electronic Prod Mfg	99006	323	1560	Educational Services
98559	5	6	Postal Service	98683	583	4581	Ambulatory Health Care Svcs	99008	11	37	Merch. Wholesalers,Nondur. Gds
98560	2	7	Food and Beverage Stores	98684	687	6864	Food Svcs & Drinking Places	99009	62	185	Bldg Matl & Garden Eqpmt Dlrs
98561	9	139	Educational Services	98685	424	2465	Educational Services	99011	46	5448	Nat'l Security & Int'l Affairs
98562	12	82	Accommodation	98686	364	2700	Food Svcs & Drinking Places	99012	43	213	Nursing & Resid. Care Facilit.
98563	312	2031	Justice, Pubic Order/Safety	98687	17	19	Relig., Grant, Civic, Prof Org	99013	8	33	Mining (Except Oil and Gas)
98564	103	480	Educational Services	98801	1955	22619	Merch. Wholesalers,Nondur. Gds	99014	9	42	Motor Vehicle & Parts Dealers
98565	37	209	Educational Services	98802	792	5654	Educational Services	99016	169	1058	Nursing & Resid. Care Facilit.
98566	4	9	Truck Transportation	98807	55	87	Construction of Buildings	99017	5	18	Educational Services
98568	47	366	Educational Services	98811	1	2	Postal Service	99018	10	24	Credit Intermediation & Relatd
98569	305	1568	Accommodation	98812	180	3823	Merch. Wholesalers,Nondur. Gds	99019	204	4135	Merch. Wholesalers,Durable Gds
98570	110	389	Educational Services	98813	58	311	Educational Services	99020	3	4	Special Trade Contractors
98571	33	108	Nat'l Security & Int'l Affairs	98814	14	33	Accommodation	99021	195	1221	Educational Services
98572	31	387	Forestry and Logging	98815	261	1570	Special Trade Contractors	99022	130	1905	Hospitals
98575	13	179	Accommodation	98816	391	3082	Merch. Wholesalers,Nondur. Gds	99023	11	62	Nonmetallic Mineral Prod. Mfg
98576	127	521	Educational Services	98817	6	5	Bldg Matl & Garden Eqpmt Dlrs	99025	80	334	Educational Services
98577	248	1309	Wood Product Manufacturing	98819	15	36	Food Svcs & Drinking Places	99026	118	584	Educational Services
98579	266	1870	Food Svcs & Drinking Places	98821	20	108	Warehousing and Storage	99027	110	445	Food Svcs & Drinking Places
98580	132	917	Merch. Wholesalers,Nondur. Gds	98822	64	361	Educational Services	99029	38	285	Educational Services
98581	9	12	Unclassified Establishments	98823	430	2845	Educational Services	99030	39	378	Educational Services
98582	38	90	Miscellaneous Store Retailers	98824	9	59	Food Manufacturing	99031	44	317	Educational Services
98583	19	66	Forestry and Logging	98826	451	2388	Accommodation	99032	33	199	Educational Services
98584	1133	9742	Social Assistance	98827	13	16	Food and Beverage Stores	99033	57	354	Educational Services
98585	19	91	Exec., Legis., & Other Support	98828	44	572	Merch. Wholesalers,Durable Gds	99034	5	10	Fabricated Metal Product Mfg
98586	189	1174	Justice, Pubic Order/Safety	98829	16	94	Crop Production	99036	30	60	Exec., Legis., & Other Support
98587	20	636	Social Assistance	98830	20	96	Admin. of Economic Programs	99037	339	2980	Educational Services
98588	25	30	Accommodation	98831	125	825	Amusement, Gambling,& Recreat.	99039	7	8	Bldg Matl & Garden Eqpmt Dlrs
98589	223	768	Educational Services	98832	6	6	Merch. Wholesalers,Nondur. Gds	99040	33	440	Exec., Legis., & Other Support
98590	15	229	Amusement, Gambling,& Recreat.	98833	16	106	Accommodation	99101	28	453	Merch. Wholesalers,Durable Gds
98591	145	622	Educational Services	98834	6	12	Fabricated Metal Product Mfg	99102	5	7	Exec., Legis., & Other Support
98592	63	268	Accommodation	98836	12	168	Support Activities: Agr./For.	99103	26	83	Merch. Wholesalers,Nondur. Gds
98593	24	81	Educational Services	98837	1424	14117	Educational Services	99104	2	4	Warehousing and Storage
98595	181	1430	Repair and Maintenance	98840	289	1974	Justice, Pubic Order/Safety	99105	4	8	Educational Services
98596	164	677	Educational Services	98841	426	2836	Food Svcs & Drinking Places	99109	225	1389	Hospitals
98597	561	3338	Educational Services	98843	41	907	Merch. Wholesalers,Nondur. Gds	99110	25	47	Food Svcs & Drinking Places
98601	89	238	Educational Services	98844	197	1169	Warehousing and Storage	99111	270	2431	Merch. Wholesalers,Nondur. Gds
98602	4	3	Construction of Buildings	98845	4	9	Educational Services	99113	34	124	Educational Services
98603	30	122	Forestry and Logging	98846	46	443	Educational Services	99114	619	5296	Machinery Manufacturing
98604	751	4033	Educational Services	98847	51	907	Support Activities: Agr./For.	99115	66	290	Accommodation
98605	95	1416	Merch. Wholesalers,Nondur. Gds	98848	331	4777	Food Manufacturing	99116	61	408	Exec., Legis., & Other Support
98606	192	826	Educational Services	98849	21	190	Merch. Wholesalers,Nondur. Gds	99117	20	82	Educational Services
98607	509	5658	Paper Manufacturing	98850	30	139	Educational Services	99118	27	161	Social Assistance

BUSINESS DATA

ZIP CODE	2004 Total Firms	2004 Total Employ-ees	TOP INDUSTRY RANKED on 2004 EMPLOYMENT	ZIP CODE	2004 Total Firms	2004 Total Employ-ees	TOP INDUSTRY RANKED on 2004 EMPLOYMENT	ZIP CODE	2004 Total Firms	2004 Total Employ-ees	TOP INDUSTRY RANKED on 2004 EMPLOYMENT
99119	18	67	Educational Services	99335	14	96	Justice, Pubic Order/Safety	99591	17	55	Exec., Legis., & Other Support
99121	9	10	Food and Beverage Stores	99336	2247	21950	Food Svcs & Drinking Places	99599	1	30	Postal Service
99122	191	1304	Hospitals	99337	261	2396	Educational Services	99602	14	34	Relig., Grant, Civic, Prof Org
99123	32	84	Admin. of Economic Programs	99338	120	695	Educational Services	99603	910	3663	Hospitals
99124	7	11	Food and Beverage Stores	99341	58	316	Food and Beverage Stores	99604	38	207	Educational Services
99125	45	145	Educational Services	99343	65	554	Merch. Wholesalers,Nondur. Gds	99605	15	19	Educational Services
99126	5	20	Construction of Buildings	99344	453	6345	Merch. Wholesalers,Nondur. Gds	99606	43	162	Relig., Grant, Civic, Prof Org
99128	9	28	Food Manufacturing	99345	22	582	Beverage & Tobacco Product Mfg	99607	15	31	Educational Services
99129	11	21	Gasoline Stations	99346	6	60	Crop Production	99608	6	7	Utilities
99130	34	153	Educational Services	99347	142	768	Hospitals	99609	17	100	Exec., Legis., & Other Support
99131	3	7	Educational Services	99348	37	1431	Crop Production	99610	68	226	Forestry and Logging
99133	109	1017	Admin. Enviro. Quality Progrms	99349	134	1801	Crop Production	99611	799	5765	Food Svcs & Drinking Places
99134	34	113	Educational Services	99350	405	4041	Food Manufacturing	99612	44	546	Food Manufacturing
99135	16	51	Educational Services	99352	1498	16083	Prof., Scientific, & Tech Svcs	99613	127	810	Food Manufacturing
99136	4	68	Educational Services	99353	152	812	Special Trade Contractors	99614	15	110	Educational Services
99137	23	135	Educational Services	99356	13	206	Waste Managmt & Remediat'n Svc	99615	807	6262	Food Manufacturing
99138	35	283	Exec., Legis., & Other Support	99357	110	763	Educational Services	99619	7	438	Nat'l Security & Int'l Affairs
99139	27	128	Educational Services	99359	16	93	Admin. Enviro. Quality Progrms	99620	28	113	Educational Services
99140	44	86	Exec., Legis., & Other Support	99360	46	188	Educational Services	99621	29	130	Educational Services
99141	161	1143	Wood Product Manufacturing	99361	73	209	Educational Services	99622	20	88	Educational Services
99143	58	104	Merch. Wholesalers,Nondur. Gds	99362	1701	16740	Hospitals	99624	10	206	Merch. Wholesalers,Nondur. Gds
99146	3	11	Exec., Legis., & Other Support	99363	12	2223	Food Manufacturing	99625	14	28	Exec., Legis., & Other Support
99147	4	9	Wood Product Manufacturing	99371	26	95	Educational Services	99626	4	16	Educational Services
99148	66	284	Accommodation	99401	14	21	Food Svcs & Drinking Places	99627	58	211	Educational Services
99149	6	9	Merch. Wholesalers,Nondur. Gds	99402	68	247	Educational Services	99628	15	58	Educational Services
99150	11	31	Relig., Grant, Civic, Prof Org	99403	627	4534	Food Svcs & Drinking Places	99629	14	21	Couriers and Messengers
99151	4	7	Machinery Manufacturing	99501	2805	27279	Prof., Scientific, & Tech Svcs	99630	20	72	Food and Beverage Stores
99152	3	11	Food and Beverage Stores	99502	741	13837	Support Act. for Transport.	99631	28	124	Relig., Grant, Civic, Prof Org
99153	30	129	Utilities	99503	2748	28319	Prof., Scientific, & Tech Svcs	99632	26	200	Educational Services
99154	1	0	Personal and Laundry Services	99504	902	4511	Food Svcs & Drinking Places	99633	107	1615	Food and Beverage Stores
99155	49	647	Exec., Legis., & Other Support	99505	46	4648	Nat'l Security & Int'l Affairs	99634	15	59	Educational Services
99156	290	1966	Educational Services	99506	100	1624	Hospitals	99635	63	474	Food Manufacturing
99157	33	178	Educational Services	99507	1115	9627	Food Svcs & Drinking Places	99636	15	101	Educational Services
99158	29	190	Educational Services	99508	1205	15756	Hospitals	99637	27	192	Educational Services
99159	90	529	Educational Services	99509	40	100	Construction of Buildings	99638	5	2	Postal Service
99160	6	38	Educational Services	99510	28	67	Prof., Scientific, & Tech Svcs	99639	109	375	Food Manufacturing
99161	37	118	Educational Services	99511	78	180	Special Trade Contractors	99640	16	34	Educational Services
99163	637	5481	Food Svcs & Drinking Places	99512	2	47	Other Information Services	99641	18	150	Educational Services
99164	10	6332	Educational Services	99513	32	1393	Justice, Pubic Order/Safety	99643	17	54	Relig., Grant, Civic, Prof Org
99165	3	16	Credit Intermediation & Relatd	99514	26	91	Ambulatory Health Care Svcs	99644	14	31	Ambulatory Health Care Svcs
99166	188	1069	Educational Services	99515	1364	9278	General Merchandise Stores	99645	1095	6742	Educational Services
99167	6	13	Health & Personal Care Stores	99516	337	1427	Educational Services	99647	12	24	Exec., Legis., & Other Support
99169	185	949	Educational Services	99517	446	3639	Accommodation	99648	12	17	Educational Services
99170	51	321	Justice, Pubic Order/Safety	99518	1279	12386	Merch. Wholesalers,Durable Gds	99649	9	16	Exec., Legis., & Other Support
99171	74	166	Merch. Wholesalers,Nondur. Gds	99519	24	268	Admin. of Economic Programs	99650	16	71	Educational Services
99173	27	163	Educational Services	99520	15	20	Special Trade Contractors	99651	8	19	Exec., Legis., & Other Support
99174	6	17	Educational Services	99521	21	55	Personal and Laundry Services	99652	174	690	Administrative & Support Svcs
99176	2	22	Exec., Legis., & Other Support	99522	36	87	Construction of Buildings	99653	17	63	Relig., Grant, Civic, Prof Org
99179	40	81	Construction of Buildings	99523	44	100	Administrative & Support Svcs	99654	1711	9059	Food Svcs & Drinking Places
99180	9	101	Wood Product Manufacturing	99524	39	70	Special Trade Contractors	99655	24	217	Educational Services
99181	67	233	Educational Services	99540	15	86	Food Svcs & Drinking Places	99656	9	6	Forestry and Logging
99185	99	451	Educational Services	99547	12	44	Merch. Wholesalers,Nondur. Gds	99657	10	48	Educational Services
99201	2163	25663	Prof., Scientific, & Tech Svcs	99548	7	29	Exec., Legis., & Other Support	99658	53	238	Educational Services
99202	1666	20013	Ambulatory Health Care Svcs	99549	13	27	Exec., Legis., & Other Support	99659	17	85	Educational Services
99203	343	2119	Educational Services	99550	23	60	Exec., Legis., & Other Support	99660	38	188	Educational Services
99204	562	13191	Hospitals	99551	20	151	Educational Services	99661	56	759	Food Manufacturing
99205	1086	9715	Educational Services	99552	17	103	Educational Services	99662	20	67	Educational Services
99206	1517	13640	Administrative & Support Svcs	99553	15	842	Food Manufacturing	99663	60	166	Relig., Grant, Civic, Prof Org
99207	1089	10233	Food Svcs & Drinking Places	99554	24	159	Educational Services	99664	422	2853	Food Manufacturing
99208	900	9661	Food Svcs & Drinking Places	99555	18	59	Relig., Grant, Civic, Prof Org	99665	11	26	Educational Services
99209	31	50	Administrative & Support Svcs	99556	103	291	Accommodation	99666	15	46	Educational Services
99210	23	29	Special Trade Contractors	99557	52	135	Relig., Grant, Civic, Prof Org	99667	13	38	Relig., Grant, Civic, Prof Org
99211	7	5	Merch. Wholesalers,Durable Gds	99558	14	43	Exec., Legis., & Other Support	99668	10	5	Educational Services
99212	1126	14106	Merch. Wholesalers,Durable Gds	99559	366	3353	Relig., Grant, Civic, Prof Org	99669	1120	7590	Educational Services
99213	10	13	Merch. Wholesalers,Durable Gds	99561	17	87	Educational Services	99670	15	43	Food and Beverage Stores
99214	42	76	Miscellaneous Store Retailers	99563	26	195	Educational Services	99671	13	134	Educational Services
99215	3	3	Waste Managmt & Remediat'n Svc	99564	17	306	Food Manufacturing	99672	129	376	Special Trade Contractors
99216	907	15199	Merch. Wholesalers,Durable Gds	99565	12	24	Educational Services	99674	41	165	Relig., Grant, Civic, Prof Org
99217	552	5461	Merch. Wholesalers,Nondur. Gds	99566	17	37	Relig., Grant, Civic, Prof Org	99675	7	10	Exec., Legis., & Other Support
99218	658	6020	Food Svcs & Drinking Places	99567	246	1263	Perform'g Arts, Spec. Sports	99676	183	937	Accommodation
99219	10	135	Rental and Leasing Services	99568	14	24	Amusement, Gambling,& Recreat.	99677	7	16	Educational Services
99220	25	33	Prof., Scientific, & Tech Svcs	99569	9	34	Food Manufacturing	99678	36	114	Educational Services
99223	592	4269	Food Svcs & Drinking Places	99571	29	62	Air Transportation	99679	12	91	Social Assistance
99224	406	7786	Educational Services	99572	43	355	Relig., Grant, Civic, Prof Org	99680	17	87	Educational Services
99228	35	68	Prof., Scientific, & Tech Svcs	99573	72	334	Relig., Grant, Civic, Prof Org	99681	16	94	Educational Services
99252	1	700	Utilities	99574	265	1862	Food Manufacturing	99682	22	111	Exec., Legis., & Other Support
99258	5	1216	Educational Services	99575	10	14	Educational Services	99683	28	66	Relig., Grant, Civic, Prof Org
99260	64	815	Justice, Pubic Order/Safety	99576	253	1617	Hospitals	99684	52	237	Educational Services
99301	1548	20421	Food Manufacturing	99577	801	3469	Food Svcs & Drinking Places	99685	123	779	Food Manufacturing
99302	21	18	Special Trade Contractors	99578	13	54	Educational Services	99686	384	3415	Relig., Grant, Civic, Prof Org
99320	130	1180	Merch. Wholesalers,Nondur. Gds	99579	15	272	Food Manufacturing	99687	79	172	Construction of Buildings
99321	9	13	Food and Beverage Stores	99580	8	30	Prof., Scientific, & Tech Svcs	99688	112	275	Accommodation
99322	12	35	Educational Services	99581	41	167	Educational Services	99689	80	402	Relig., Grant, Civic, Prof Org
99323	56	883	Food and Beverage Stores	99583	9	32	Food Manufacturing	99690	11	33	Educational Services
99324	156	1527	Educational Services	99585	17	71	Educational Services	99691	6	4	Exec., Legis., & Other Support
99326	103	1665	Educational Services	99586	40	117	Ambulatory Health Care Svcs	99692	113	2589	Food Manufacturing
99328	208	1257	Accommodation	99587	144	1081	Accommodation	99693	42	195	Food Manufacturing
99329	6	14	Educational Services	99588	185	894	Relig., Grant, Civic, Prof Org	99694	47	202	Educational Services
99330	23	222	Crop Production	99589	19	89	Educational Services	99695	4	6	Amusement, Gambling,& Recreat.
99333	1	2	Postal Service	99590	11	48	Educational Services	99697	2	21	Animal Production

ZIP CODE	2004 Total Firms	2004 Total Employees	TOP INDUSTRY RANKED on 2004 EMPLOYMENT	ZIP CODE	2004 Total Firms	2004 Total Employees	TOP INDUSTRY RANKED on 2004 EMPLOYMENT	ZIP CODE	2004 Total Firms	2004 Total Employees	TOP INDUSTRY RANKED on 2004 EMPLOYMENT
99701	2064	18246	Relig., Grant, Civic, Prof Org	99830	47	323	Food Manufacturing				
99702	33	363	Educational Services	99832	30	94	Food Manufacturing				
99703	48	6280	Exec., Legis., & Other Support	99833	333	2478	Food Manufacturing				
99704	6	12	General Merchandise Stores	99835	703	5489	Hospitals				
99705	569	2669	Petroleum & Coal Products Mfg	99836	8	22	Scenic & Sightseeing Transport				
99706	23	33	Special Trade Contractors	99840	219	1364	Administrative & Support Svcs				
99707	62	165	Transit & Grnd Pass. Transport	99841	10	46	Support Activities: Agr./For.				
99708	76	203	Relig., Grant, Civic, Prof Org	99850	1	50	Forestry and Logging				
99709	1093	11382	Educational Services	99901	1110	8862	Food Manufacturing				
99710	9	10	Administrative & Support Svcs	99903	1	2	Relig., Grant, Civic, Prof Org				
99711	11	9	Special Trade Contractors	99918	18	27	Educational Services				
99712	275	755	Educational Services	99919	46	142	Support Activities: Agr./For.				
99714	39	170	Accommodation	99921	169	830	Educational Services				
99716	8	9	Prof., Scientific, & Tech Svcs	99922	24	98	Educational Services				
99720	6	29	Exec., Legis., & Other Support	99923	1	0	Relig., Grant, Civic, Prof Org				
99721	25	62	Museums, Hist. Sites,& Similar	99925	72	321	Bldg Matl & Garden Eqpmt Dlrs				
99722	9	27	Exec., Legis., & Other Support	99926	77	736	Food Manufacturing				
99723	179	2347	Exec., Legis., & Other Support	99927	5	6	Amusement, Gambling,& Recreat.				
99724	6	19	Educational Services	99928	25	38	Construction of Buildings				
99725	19	59	Food Svcs & Drinking Places	99929	197	1164	Educational Services				
99726	18	52	Relig., Grant, Civic, Prof Org	99950	12	33	Food and Beverage Stores				
99727	14	56	Educational Services								
99729	29	93	Relig., Grant, Civic, Prof Org								
99730	10	34	Accommodation								
99733	6	14	Exec., Legis., & Other Support								
99734	79	1011	Special Trade Contractors								
99736	14	36	Educational Services								
99737	218	1216	Nat'l Security & Int'l Affairs								
99738	26	47	Museums, Hist. Sites,& Similar								
99739	16	84	Educational Services								
99740	42	225	Exec., Legis., & Other Support								
99741	50	204	Exec., Legis., & Other Support								
99742	30	185	Exec., Legis., & Other Support								
99743	98	609	Accommodation								
99744	17	37	Educational Services								
99745	9	22	Educational Services								
99746	14	39	Educational Services								
99747	31	104	Exec., Legis., & Other Support								
99748	14	48	Educational Services								
99749	27	96	Educational Services								
99750	10	43	Educational Services								
99751	14	32	Educational Services								
99752	158	2339	Relig., Grant, Civic, Prof Org								
99753	15	56	Educational Services								
99754	12	17	Exec., Legis., & Other Support								
99755	46	1316	Accommodation								
99756	13	24	Educational Services								
99757	4	4	Relig., Grant, Civic, Prof Org								
99758	16	50	Educational Services								
99759	23	66	Exec., Legis., & Other Support								
99760	55	205	Educational Services								
99761	16	70	Relig., Grant, Civic, Prof Org								
99762	287	2141	Hospitals								
99763	20	91	Educational Services								
99764	19	98	Justice, Pubic Order/Safety								
99765	16	61	Educational Services								
99766	27	246	Relig., Grant, Civic, Prof Org								
99767	6	5	Utilities								
99768	11	40	Educational Services								
99769	24	110	Educational Services								
99770	24	124	Educational Services								
99771	14	55	Educational Services								
99772	23	132	Educational Services								
99773	12	50	Educational Services								
99774	10	18	Exec., Legis., & Other Support								
99775	12	104	Museums, Hist. Sites,& Similar								
99776	2	10	Social Assistance								
99777	21	114	Exec., Legis., & Other Support								
99778	20	75	Educational Services								
99779	6	19	Relig., Grant, Civic, Prof Org								
99780	171	609	Accommodation								
99781	11	42	Educational Services								
99782	26	141	Educational Services								
99783	12	42	Educational Services								
99784	7	39	Exec., Legis., & Other Support								
99785	9	33	Educational Services								
99786	14	40	Educational Services								
99788	7	24	Justice, Pubic Order/Safety								
99789	26	136	Exec., Legis., & Other Support								
99791	24	121	Exec., Legis., & Other Support								
99801	2047	18797	Exec., Legis., & Other Support								
99802	35	77	Transit & Grnd Pass. Transport								
99803	41	97	Construction of Buildings								
99820	33	313	Amusement, Gambling,& Recreat.								
99821	18	48	Food Manufacturing								
99824	58	415	Admin. Enviro. Quality Progrms								
99825	17	52	Relig., Grant, Civic, Prof Org								
99826	66	485	Air Transportation								
99827	283	1133	Food Svcs & Drinking Places								
99829	75	503	Educational Services								

Appendices

The Community
Sourcebook
of ZIP Code
Demographics

2004
18th EDITION

Appendix I:
Non-Residential ZIP Codes
by State

The Community
Sourcebook

2004
18th EDITION

of **ZIP** Code
Demographics

ALABAMA   **ALABAMA**

Point ZIP Code		Enclosing Residential ZIP Code		Point ZIP Code		Enclosing Residential ZIP Code	
ZIP	Post Office Name	ZIP	Post Office Name	ZIP	Post Office Name	ZIP	Post Office Name
35011	ALEXANDER CITY	35010	ALEXANDER CITY	35609	DECATUR	35601	DECATUR
35013	ALLGOOD	35121	ONEONTA	35612	ATHENS	35611	ATHENS
35015	ALTON	35210	BIRMINGHAM	35615	BELLE MINA	35671	TANNER
35021	BESSEMER	35020	BESSEMER	35617	CLOVERDALE	35633	FLORENCE
35032	BON AIR	35044	CHILDERSBURG	35631	FLORENCE	35630	FLORENCE
35038	BURNWELL	35130	QUINTON	35632	FLORENCE	35630	FLORENCE
35048	CLAY	35173	TRUSSVILLE	35649	MOORESVILLE	35758	MADISON
35052	COOK SPRINGS	35128	PELL CITY	35662	MUSCLE SHOALS	35661	MUSCLE SHOALS
35056	CULLMAN	35055	CULLMAN	35699	DECATUR	35601	DECATUR
35060	DOCENA	35005	ADAMSVILLE	35742	CAPSHAW	35749	HARVEST
35070	GARDEN CITY	35077	HANCEVILLE	35762	NORMAL	35810	HUNTSVILLE
35074	GREEN POND	35111	MC CALLA	35767	RYLAND	35811	HUNTSVILLE
35082	HOLLINS	35072	GOODWATER	35804	HUNTSVILLE	35801	HUNTSVILLE
35097	LOCUST FORK	35049	CLEVELAND	35807	HUNTSVILLE	35805	HUNTSVILLE
35112	MARGARET	35120	ODENVILLE	35809	HUNTSVILLE	35805	HUNTSVILLE
35119	NEW CASTLE	35071	GARDENDALE	35812	HUNTSVILLE	35824	HUNTSVILLE
35123	PALMERDALE	35126	PINSON	35813	HUNTSVILLE	35824	HUNTSVILLE
35137	SAGINAW	35007	ALABASTER	35814	HUNTSVILLE	35816	HUNTSVILLE
35139	SAYRE	35071	GARDENDALE	35815	HUNTSVILLE	35802	HUNTSVILLE
35142	SHANNON	35022	BESSEMER	35893	HUNTSVILLE	35805	HUNTSVILLE
35144	SILURIA	35007	ALABASTER	35894	HUNTSVILLE	35824	HUNTSVILLE
35149	SYCAMORE	35150	SYLACAUGA	35896	HUNTSVILLE	35824	HUNTSVILLE
35161	TALLADEGA	35160	TALLADEGA	35897	HUNTSVILLE	35805	HUNTSVILLE
35181	WATSON	35117	MOUNT OLIVE	35899	HUNTSVILLE	35816	HUNTSVILLE
35182	WATTSVILLE	35125	PELL CITY	35902	GADSDEN	35901	GADSDEN
35185	WESTOVER	35147	STERRETT	35964	DOUGLAS	35980	HORTON
35187	WILTON	35035	BRIERFIELD	35990	WALNUT GROVE	35952	ALTOONA
35201	BIRMINGHAM	35203	BIRMINGHAM	36008	BOOTH	36067	PRATTVILLE
35202	BIRMINGHAM	35207	BIRMINGHAM	36015	CHAPMAN	36033	GEORGIANA
35219	BIRMINGHAM	35209	BIRMINGHAM	36045	KENT	36078	TALLASSEE
35220	BIRMINGHAM	35215	BIRMINGHAM	36057	MOUNT MEIGS	36064	PIKE ROAD
35225	BIRMINGHAM	35203	BIRMINGHAM	36062	PETREY	36049	LUVERNE
35230	BIRMINGHAM	35203	BIRMINGHAM	36065	PINE LEVEL	36069	RAMER
35231	BIRMINGHAM	35214	BIRMINGHAM	36068	PRATTVILLE	36067	PRATTVILLE
35232	BIRMINGHAM	35212	BIRMINGHAM	36072	EUFAULA	36027	EUFAULA
35236	BIRMINGHAM	35244	BIRMINGHAM	36087	TUSKEGEE INSTITUTE	36088	TUSKEGEE INSTITUTE
35237	BIRMINGHAM	35207	BIRMINGHAM	36101	MONTGOMERY	36104	MONTGOMERY
35238	BIRMINGHAM	35242	BIRMINGHAM	36102	MONTGOMERY	36104	MONTGOMERY
35240	BIRMINGHAM	35203	BIRMINGHAM	36103	MONTGOMERY	36104	MONTGOMERY
35245	BIRMINGHAM	35203	BIRMINGHAM	36114	MONTGOMERY	36117	MONTGOMERY
35246	BIRMINGHAM	35203	BIRMINGHAM	36118	MONTGOMERY	36115	MONTGOMERY
35249	BIRMINGHAM	35233	BIRMINGHAM	36119	MONTGOMERY	36117	MONTGOMERY
35253	BIRMINGHAM	35223	BIRMINGHAM	36120	MONTGOMERY	36111	MONTGOMERY
35255	BIRMINGHAM	35205	BIRMINGHAM	36121	MONTGOMERY	36117	MONTGOMERY
35259	BIRMINGHAM	35209	BIRMINGHAM	36123	MONTGOMERY	36106	MONTGOMERY
35260	BIRMINGHAM	35226	BIRMINGHAM	36124	MONTGOMERY	36117	MONTGOMERY
35261	BIRMINGHAM	35206	BIRMINGHAM	36125	MONTGOMERY	36105	MONTGOMERY
35266	BIRMINGHAM	35216	BIRMINGHAM	36130	MONTGOMERY	36104	MONTGOMERY
35277	BIRMINGHAM	35203	BIRMINGHAM	36131	MONTGOMERY	36104	MONTGOMERY
35278	BIRMINGHAM	35209	BIRMINGHAM	36132	MONTGOMERY	36117	MONTGOMERY
35279	BIRMINGHAM	35211	BIRMINGHAM	36133	MONTGOMERY	36104	MONTGOMERY
35280	BIRMINGHAM	35203	BIRMINGHAM	36135	MONTGOMERY	36104	MONTGOMERY
35281	BIRMINGHAM	35203	BIRMINGHAM	36140	MONTGOMERY	36104	MONTGOMERY
35282	BIRMINGHAM	35205	BIRMINGHAM	36141	MONTGOMERY	36117	MONTGOMERY
35283	BIRMINGHAM	35203	BIRMINGHAM	36142	MONTGOMERY	36104	MONTGOMERY
35285	BIRMINGHAM	35234	BIRMINGHAM	36177	MONTGOMERY	36104	MONTGOMERY
35286	BIRMINGHAM	35216	BIRMINGHAM	36191	MONTGOMERY	36116	MONTGOMERY
35287	BIRMINGHAM	35203	BIRMINGHAM	36202	ANNISTON	36207	ANNISTON
35288	BIRMINGHAM	35203	BIRMINGHAM	36204	ANNISTON	36207	ANNISTON
35289	BIRMINGHAM	35209	BIRMINGHAM	36253	BYNUM	36260	EASTABOGA
35290	BIRMINGHAM	35212	BIRMINGHAM	36254	CHOCCOLOCCO	36207	ANNISTON
35291	BIRMINGHAM	35203	BIRMINGHAM	36257	DE ARMANVILLE	36207	ANNISTON
35292	BIRMINGHAM	35203	BIRMINGHAM	36261	EDWARDSVILLE	36264	HEFLIN
35293	BIRMINGHAM	35209	BIRMINGHAM	36275	SPRING GARDEN	35960	CENTRE
35294	BIRMINGHAM	35233	BIRMINGHAM	36302	DOTHAN	36303	DOTHAN
35295	BIRMINGHAM	35233	BIRMINGHAM	36304	DOTHAN	36303	DOTHAN
35296	BIRMINGHAM	35226	BIRMINGHAM	36313	BELLWOOD	36322	DALEVILLE
35297	BIRMINGHAM	35213	BIRMINGHAM	36331	ENTERPRISE	36330	ENTERPRISE
35298	BIRMINGHAM	35205	BIRMINGHAM	36361	OZARK	36360	OZARK
35299	BIRMINGHAM	35203	BIRMINGHAM	36371	PINCKARD	36350	MIDLAND CITY
35402	TUSCALOOSA	35401	TUSCALOOSA	36427	BREWTON	36426	BREWTON
35403	TUSCALOOSA	35401	TUSCALOOSA	36429	BROOKLYN	36401	EVERGREEN
35407	TUSCALOOSA	35405	TUSCALOOSA	36439	EXCEL	36460	MONROEVILLE
35440	ABERNANT	35490	VANCE	36449	GOODWAY	36502	ATMORE
35448	CLINTON	35462	EUTAW	36455	LOCKHART	36442	FLORALA
35449	COALING	35453	COTTONDALE	36457	MEGARGEL	36445	FRISCO CITY
35468	KELLERMAN	35490	VANCE	36458	MEXIA	36445	FRISCO CITY
35471	MC SHAN	35461	ETHELSVILLE	36461	MONROEVILLE	36460	MONROEVILLE
35477	PANOLA	35464	GAINESVILLE	36462	MONROEVILLE	36460	MONROEVILLE
35478	PETERSON	35490	VANCE	36470	PERDUE HILL	36460	MONROEVILLE
35482	SAMANTHA	35475	NORTHPORT	36476	RIVER FALLS	36420	ANDALUSIA
35485	TUSCALOOSA	35401	TUSCALOOSA	36503	ATMORE	36502	ATMORE
35486	TUSCALOOSA	35487	TUSCALOOSA	36504	ATMORE	36502	ATMORE
35491	WEST GREENE	35462	EUTAW	36512	BUCKS	36560	MOUNT VERNON
35502	JASPER	35501	JASPER	36513	CALVERT	36553	MC INTOSH
35545	BELK	35555	FAYETTE	36533	FAIRHOPE	36532	FAIRHOPE
35551	DELMAR	35565	HALEYVILLE	36536	FOLEY	36535	FOLEY
35559	GLEN ALLEN	35594	WINFIELD	36543	HUXFORD	36502	ATMORE
35560	GOODSPRINGS	35580	PARRISH	36547	GULF SHORES	36542	GULF SHORES
35573	KANSAS	35549	CARBON HILL	36556	MALCOLM	36553	MC INTOSH
35577	NATURAL BRIDGE	35575	LYNN	36559	MONTROSE	36526	DAPHNE
35584	SIPSEY	35063	EMPIRE	36564	POINT CLEAR	36532	FAIRHOPE
35602	DECATUR	35601	DECATUR	36568	SAINT ELMO	36544	IRVINGTON

Appendix I — NONRESIDENTIAL ZIP CODES

ALABAMA   **ARIZONA**

Point ZIP Code	Post Office Name	Enclosing Residential ZIP Code	Post Office Name	Point ZIP Code	Post Office Name	Enclosing Residential ZIP Code	Post Office Name
36577	SPANISH FORT	36526	DAPHNE	99779	TETLIN	99780	TOK
36581	SUNFLOWER	36585	WAGARVILLE	99791	ATQASUK	99723	BARROW
36590	THEODORE	36582	THEODORE	99802	JUNEAU	99801	JUNEAU
36601	MOBILE	36602	MOBILE	99803	JUNEAU	99801	JUNEAU
36616	MOBILE	36606	MOBILE	99811	JUNEAU	99801	JUNEAU
36621	MOBILE	36602	MOBILE	99821	AUKE BAY	99801	JUNEAU
36622	MOBILE	36602	MOBILE	99830	KAKE	99833	PETERSBURG
36625	MOBILE	36602	MOBILE	99832	PELICAN	99829	HOONAH
36628	MOBILE	36602	MOBILE	99836	PORT ALEXANDER	99835	SITKA
36633	MOBILE	36602	MOBILE	99841	TENAKEE SPRINGS	99829	HOONAH
36640	MOBILE	36603	MOBILE	99850	JUNEAU	99801	JUNEAU
36652	MOBILE	36602	MOBILE	99918	COFFMAN COVE	99901	KETCHIKAN
36660	MOBILE	36606	MOBILE	99928	WARD COVE	99901	KETCHIKAN
36663	MOBILE	36613	EIGHT MILE	85001	PHOENIX	85003	PHOENIX
36670	MOBILE	36607	MOBILE	85002	PHOENIX	85003	PHOENIX
36671	MOBILE	36611	MOBILE	85005	PHOENIX	85009	PHOENIX
36675	MOBILE	36602	MOBILE	85010	PHOENIX	85008	PHOENIX
36685	MOBILE	36608	MOBILE	85011	PHOENIX	85014	PHOENIX
36689	MOBILE	36608	MOBILE	85025	PHOENIX	85003	PHOENIX
36691	MOBILE	36609	MOBILE	85026	PHOENIX	85008	PHOENIX
36702	SELMA	36701	SELMA	85030	PHOENIX	85003	PHOENIX
36721	ANNEMANIE	36722	ARLINGTON	85036	PHOENIX	85008	PHOENIX
36723	BOYKIN	36720	ALBERTA	85038	PHOENIX	85008	PHOENIX
36741	FURMAN	36768	PINE APPLE	85046	PHOENIX	85032	PHOENIX
36745	JEFFERSON	36732	DEMOPOLIS	85055	PHOENIX	85008	PHOENIX
36753	MC WILLIAMS	36768	PINE APPLE	85060	PHOENIX	85018	PHOENIX
36763	MYRTLEWOOD	36748	LINDEN	85061	PHOENIX	85017	PHOENIX
36764	NANAFALIA	36782	SWEET WATER	85062	PHOENIX	85008	PHOENIX
36766	OAK HILL	36768	PINE APPLE	85063	PHOENIX	85031	PHOENIX
36802	OPELIKA	36801	OPELIKA	85064	PHOENIX	85033	PHOENIX
36803	OPELIKA	36801	OPELIKA	85065	PHOENIX	85034	PHOENIX
36831	AUBURN	36830	AUBURN	85066	PHOENIX	85040	PHOENIX
36851	COTTONTON	36871	PITTSVIEW	85067	PHOENIX	85013	PHOENIX
36859	HOLY TRINITY	36871	PITTSVIEW	85068	PHOENIX	85020	PHOENIX
36865	LOACHAPOKA	36830	AUBURN	85069	PHOENIX	85021	PHOENIX
36868	PHENIX CITY	36867	PHENIX CITY	85070	PHOENIX	85247	SACATON
36872	VALLEY	36854	VALLEY	85071	PHOENIX	85029	PHOENIX
36901	BELLAMY	36925	YORK	85072	PHOENIX	85008	PHOENIX
36906	CROMWELL	36912	LISMAN	85073	PHOENIX	85004	PHOENIX
36913	MELVIN	36908	GILBERTOWN	85074	PHOENIX	85034	PHOENIX
99509	ANCHORAGE	99503	ANCHORAGE	85075	PHOENIX	85033	PHOENIX
99510	ANCHORAGE	99501	ANCHORAGE	85076	PHOENIX	85044	PHOENIX
99511	ANCHORAGE	99515	ANCHORAGE	85078	PHOENIX	85020	PHOENIX
99512	ANCHORAGE	99508	ANCHORAGE	85079	PHOENIX	85017	PHOENIX
99513	ANCHORAGE	99501	ANCHORAGE	85080	PHOENIX	85018	PHOENIX
99514	ANCHORAGE	99508	ANCHORAGE	85082	PHOENIX	85008	PHOENIX
99519	ANCHORAGE	99502	ANCHORAGE	85098	PHOENIX	85008	PHOENIX
99520	ANCHORAGE	99501	ANCHORAGE	85099	PHOENIX	85008	PHOENIX
99521	ANCHORAGE	99504	ANCHORAGE	85211	MESA	85201	MESA
99522	ANCHORAGE	99502	ANCHORAGE	85214	MESA	85201	MESA
99523	ANCHORAGE	99507	ANCHORAGE	85216	MESA	85206	MESA
99524	ANCHORAGE	99502	ANCHORAGE	85217	APACHE JUNCTION	85220	APACHE JUNCTION
99548	CHIGNIK LAKE	99564	CHIGNIK	85221	BAPCHULE	85222	CASA GRANDE
99550	PORT LIONS	99615	KODIAK	85223	ARIZONA CITY	85222	CASA GRANDE
99566	CHITINA	99573	COPPER CENTER	85227	CHANDLER HEIGHTS	85242	QUEEN CREEK
99599	ANCHORAGE	99503	ANCHORAGE	85230	CASA GRANDE	85222	CASA GRANDE
99605	HOPE	99631	MOOSE PASS	85235	HAYDEN	85292	WINKELMAN
99608	KARLUK	99615	KODIAK	85241	PICACHO	85231	ELOY
99609	KASIGLUK	99559	BETHEL	85244	CHANDLER	85225	CHANDLER
99619	KODIAK	99615	KODIAK	85245	RED ROCK	85653	MARANA
99624	LARSEN BAY	99615	KODIAK	85246	CHANDLER	85224	CHANDLER
99629	WASILLA	99654	WASILLA	85252	SCOTTSDALE	85251	SCOTTSDALE
99635	NIKISKI	99611	KENAI	85261	SCOTTSDALE	85251	SCOTTSDALE
99637	TOKSOOK BAY	99681	TUNUNAK	85266	SCOTTSDALE	85251	SCOTTSDALE
99641	NUNAPITCHUK	99559	BETHEL	85267	SCOTTSDALE	85260	SCOTTSDALE
99643	OLD HARBOR	99615	KODIAK	85269	FOUNTAIN HILLS	85268	FOUNTAIN HILLS
99644	OUZINKIE	99615	KODIAK	85271	SCOTTSDALE	85257	SCOTTSDALE
99652	BIG LAKE	99687	WASILLA	85274	MESA	85202	MESA
99663	SELDOVIA	99603	HOMER	85275	MESA	85213	MESA
99666	NUNAM IQUA	99554	ALAKANUK	85277	MESA	85215	MESA
99674	SUTTON	99645	PALMER	85278	APACHE JUNCTION	85220	APACHE JUNCTION
99675	TAKOTNA	99627	MC GRATH	85279	FLORENCE	85232	FLORENCE
99677	TATITLEK	99686	VALDEZ	85280	TEMPE	85282	TEMPE
99678	TOGIAK	99576	DILLINGHAM	85285	TEMPE	85282	TEMPE
99680	TUNTUTULIAK	99559	BETHEL	85290	TORTILLA FLAT	85264	FORT MCDOWELL
99690	NIGHTMUTE	99559	BETHEL	85291	VALLEY FARMS	85228	COOLIDGE
99693	WHITTIER	99686	VALDEZ	85299	GILBERT	85296	GILBERT
99694	HOUSTON	99688	WILLOW	85311	GLENDALE	85301	GLENDALE
99695	ANCHORAGE	99502	ANCHORAGE	85312	GLENDALE	85306	GLENDALE
99697	KODIAK	99615	KODIAK	85318	GLENDALE	85301	GLENDALE
99706	FAIRBANKS	99709	FAIRBANKS	85320	AGUILA	85390	WICKENBURG
99707	FAIRBANKS	99701	FAIRBANKS	85325	BOUSE	85344	PARKER
99708	FAIRBANKS	99709	FAIRBANKS	85327	CAVE CREEK	85331	CAVE CREEK
99710	FAIRBANKS	99712	FAIRBANKS	85329	CASHION	85323	AVONDALE
99711	FAIRBANKS	99705	NORTH POLE	85334	EHRENBERG	85328	CIBOLA
99716	TWO RIVERS	99709	FAIRBANKS	85336	GADSDEN	85350	SOMERTON
99725	ESTER	99709	FAIRBANKS	85346	QUARTZSITE	85344	PARKER
99732	CHICKEN	99780	TOK	85349	SAN LUIS	85350	SOMERTON
99738	EAGLE	99780	TOK	85352	TACNA	85356	WELLTON
99754	KOYUKUK	99765	NULATO	85357	WENDEN	85348	SALOME
99764	NORTHWAY	99780	TOK	85358	WICKENBURG	85390	WICKENBURG
99775	FAIRBANKS	99709	FAIRBANKS	85359	QUARTZSITE	85344	PARKER
99776	TANACROSS	99780	TOK	85360	WIKIEUP	86406	LAKE HAVASU CITY

ARIZONA   **ARKANSAS**

Point ZIP Code		Enclosing Residential ZIP Code		Point ZIP Code		Enclosing Residential ZIP Code	
ZIP	Post Office Name	ZIP	Post Office Name	ZIP	Post Office Name	ZIP	Post Office Name
85366	YUMA	85364	YUMA	86339	SEDONA	86336	SEDONA
85369	YUMA	85364	YUMA	86340	SEDONA	86336	SEDONA
85371	POSTON	85344	PARKER	86341	SEDONA	86351	SEDONA
85372	SUN CITY	85373	SUN CITY	86342	LAKE MONTEZUMA	86335	RIMROCK
85376	SUN CITY WEST	85375	SUN CITY WEST	86402	KINGMAN	86401	KINGMAN
85377	CAREFREE	85331	CAVE CREEK	86405	LAKE HAVASU CITY	86403	LAKE HAVASU CITY
85378	SURPRISE	85374	SURPRISE	86411	HACKBERRY	86401	KINGMAN
85380	PEORIA	85345	PEORIA	86412	HUALAPAI	86401	KINGMAN
85385	PEORIA	85345	PEORIA	86427	FORT MOHAVE	86426	FORT MOHAVE
85502	GLOBE	85501	GLOBE	86430	BULLHEAD CITY	86429	BULLHEAD CITY
85531	CENTRAL	85552	THATCHER	86431	CHLORIDE	86401	KINGMAN
85532	CLAYPOOL	85539	MIAMI	86433	OATMAN	86442	BULLHEAD CITY
85536	FORT THOMAS	85535	EDEN	86437	VALENTINE	86401	KINGMAN
85547	PAYSON	85541	PAYSON	86438	YUCCA	86442	BULLHEAD CITY
85548	SAFFORD	85546	SAFFORD	86439	BULLHEAD CITY	86442	BULLHEAD CITY
85551	SOLOMON	85546	SAFFORD	86443	TEMPLE BAR MARINA	86444	MEADVIEW
85553	TONTO BASIN	85541	PAYSON	86445	WILLOW BEACH	86441	DOLAN SPRINGS
85554	YOUNG	85541	PAYSON	86446	MOHAVE VALLEY	86442	BULLHEAD CITY
85605	BOWIE	85632	SAN SIMON	86504	FORT DEFIANCE	86505	GANADO
85608	DOUGLAS	85607	DOUGLAS	86506	HOUCK	86505	GANADO
85609	DRAGOON	85606	COCHISE	86508	LUPTON	86505	GANADO
85620	NACO	85603	BISBEE	86511	SAINT MICHAELS	86505	GANADO
85622	GREEN VALLEY	85614	GREEN VALLEY	86512	SANDERS	86502	CHAMBERS
85626	PIRTLEVILLE	85607	DOUGLAS	86515	WINDOW ROCK	86505	GANADO
85627	POMERENE	85602	BENSON	86520	BLUE GAP	86510	PINON
85628	NOGALES	85621	NOGALES	86540	NAZLINI	86503	CHINLE
85633	SASABE	85736	TUCSON	86544	RED VALLEY	86514	TEEC NOS POS
85636	SIERRA VISTA	85635	SIERRA VISTA	86545	ROCK POINT	86514	TEEC NOS POS
85639	TOPAWA	85634	SELLS	86547	ROUND ROCK	86538	MANY FARMS
85644	WILLCOX	85643	WILLCOX	71611	PINE BLUFF	71601	PINE BLUFF
85646	TUBAC	85640	TUMACACORI	71612	WHITE HALL	71602	WHITE HALL
85652	CORTARO	85741	TUCSON	71613	PINE BLUFF	71603	PINE BLUFF
85654	RILLITO	85653	MARANA	71657	MONTICELLO	71655	MONTICELLO
85655	DOUGLAS	85607	DOUGLAS	71659	MOSCOW	71644	GRADY
85662	NOGALES	85621	NOGALES	71711	CAMDEN	71701	CAMDEN
85670	FORT HUACHUCA	85635	SIERRA VISTA	71721	BEIRNE	71743	GURDON
85702	TUCSON	85701	TUCSON	71724	CALION	71730	EL DORADO
85703	TUCSON	85705	TUCSON	71728	CURTIS	71743	GURDON
85717	TUCSON	85719	TUCSON	71731	EL DORADO	71730	EL DORADO
85722	TUCSON	85719	TUCSON	71750	LAWSON	71730	EL DORADO
85723	TUCSON	85713	TUCSON	71754	MAGNOLIA	71753	MAGNOLIA
85724	TUCSON	85719	TUCSON	71759	NORPHLET	71730	EL DORADO
85725	TUCSON	85713	TUCSON	71768	URBANA	71730	EL DORADO
85726	TUCSON	85713	TUCSON	71772	WHELEN SPRINGS	71743	GURDON
85728	TUCSON	85718	TUCSON	71802	HOPE	71801	HOPE
85731	TUCSON	85710	TUCSON	71820	ALLEENE	71822	ASHDOWN
85732	TUCSON	85711	TUCSON	71823	BEN LOMOND	71846	LOCKESBURG
85733	TUCSON	85719	TUCSON	71840	GENOA	71837	FOUKE
85734	TUCSON	85706	TUCSON	71844	LANEBURG	71835	EMMET
85738	CATALINA	85704	TUCSON	71902	HOT SPRINGS NATIONAL	71901	HOT SPRINGS NATIONAL
85740	TUCSON	85704	TUCSON	71903	HOT SPRINGS NATIONAL	71901	HOT SPRINGS NATIONAL
85744	TUCSON	85747	TUCSON	71910	HOT SPRINGS VILLAGE	71909	HOT SPRINGS VILLAGE
85751	TUCSON	85715	TUCSON	71914	HOT SPRINGS NATIONAL	71913	HOT SPRINGS NATIONAL
85752	TUCSON	85741	TUCSON	71920	ALPINE	71921	AMITY
85754	TUCSON	85745	TUCSON	71932	BOARD CAMP	71953	MENA
85775	TUCSON	85711	TUCSON	72018	BENTON	72015	BENTON
85902	SHOW LOW	85901	SHOW LOW	72033	CONWAY	72032	CONWAY
85911	CIBECUE	85901	SHOW LOW	72037	COY	72046	ENGLAND
85912	WHITE MOUNTAIN LAKE	85901	SHOW LOW	72043	DIAZ	72112	NEWPORT
85923	CLAY SPRINGS	85901	SHOW LOW	72053	COLLEGE STATION	72206	LITTLE ROCK
85926	FORT APACHE	85901	SHOW LOW	72059	GREGORY	72006	AUGUSTA
85927	GREER	85925	EAGAR	72061	GUY	72058	GREENBRIER
85930	MCNARY	85901	SHOW LOW	72074	HUNTER	72036	COTTON PLANT
85931	FOREST LAKES	86336	SEDONA	72075	JACKSONPORT	72112	NEWPORT
85932	NUTRIOSO	85925	EAGAR	72078	JACKSONVILLE	72076	JACKSONVILLE
85933	OVERGAARD	85928	HEBER	72085	LETONA	72143	SEARCY
85934	PINEDALE	85901	SHOW LOW	72089	BRYANT	72022	BRYANT
85939	TAYLOR	85937	SNOWFLAKE	72107	MENIFEE	72127	PLUMERVILLE
85940	VERNON	85938	SPRINGERVILLE	72108	MONROE	72021	BRINKLEY
85941	WHITERIVER	85901	SHOW LOW	72115	NORTH LITTLE ROCK	72114	NORTH LITTLE ROCK
85942	WOODRUFF	86025	HOLBROOK	72119	NORTH LITTLE ROCK	72114	NORTH LITTLE ROCK
86002	FLAGSTAFF	86001	FLAGSTAFF	72123	PATTERSON	72101	MC CRORY
86003	FLAGSTAFF	86001	FLAGSTAFF	72124	NORTH LITTLE ROCK	72120	SHERWOOD
86011	FLAGSTAFF	86001	FLAGSTAFF	72139	RUSSELL	72010	BALD KNOB
86015	BELLEMONT	86001	FLAGSTAFF	72145	SEARCY	72143	SEARCY
86016	GRAY MOUNTAIN	86001	FLAGSTAFF	72164	SWEET HOME	72206	LITTLE ROCK
86017	MUNDS PARK	86336	SEDONA	72169	TUPELO	72112	NEWPORT
86018	PARKS	86046	WILLIAMS	72178	WEST POINT	72143	SEARCY
86020	CAMERON	86045	TUBA CITY	72180	WOODSON	72065	HENSLEY
86023	GRAND CANYON	86046	WILLIAMS	72181	WOOSTER	72058	GREENBRIER
86028	PETRIFIED FOREST NAT	86025	HOLBROOK	72182	WRIGHT	72168	TUCKER
86029	SUN VALLEY	86025	HOLBROOK	72183	WRIGHTSVILLE	72206	LITTLE ROCK
86031	INDIAN WELLS	86047	WINSLOW	72189	MC CRORY	72101	MC CRORY
86032	JOSEPH CITY	86047	WINSLOW	72190	NORTH LITTLE ROCK	72116	NORTH LITTLE ROCK
86052	NORTH RIM	86022	FREDONIA	72198	NORTH LITTLE ROCK	72114	NORTH LITTLE ROCK
86302	PRESCOTT	86305	PRESCOTT	72203	LITTLE ROCK	72202	LITTLE ROCK
86304	PRESCOTT	86305	PRESCOTT	72214	LITTLE ROCK	72204	LITTLE ROCK
86312	PRESCOTT VALLEY	86314	PRESCOTT VALLEY	72215	LITTLE ROCK	72205	LITTLE ROCK
86313	PRESCOTT	86301	PRESCOTT	72216	LITTLE ROCK	72206	LITTLE ROCK
86329	HUMBOLDT	86327	DEWEY	72217	LITTLE ROCK	72207	LITTLE ROCK
86330	IRON SPRINGS	86305	PRESCOTT	72219	LITTLE ROCK	72209	LITTLE ROCK
86331	JEROME	86324	CLARKDALE	72221	LITTLE ROCK	72211	LITTLE ROCK
86338	SKULL VALLEY	86305	PRESCOTT	72222	LITTLE ROCK	72212	LITTLE ROCK

ARKANSAS

Point ZIP Code	Post Office Name	Enclosing Residential ZIP Code	Post Office Name
72225	LITTLE ROCK	72205	LITTLE ROCK
72231	LITTLE ROCK	72117	NORTH LITTLE ROCK
72260	LITTLE ROCK	72202	LITTLE ROCK
72295	LITTLE ROCK	72202	LITTLE ROCK
72303	WEST MEMPHIS	72301	WEST MEMPHIS
72312	BARTON	72355	LEXA
72316	BLYTHEVILLE	72315	BLYTHEVILLE
72319	GOSNELL	72315	BLYTHEVILLE
72322	CALDWELL	72326	COLT
72325	CLARKEDALE	72384	TURRELL
72332	EDMONDSON	72376	PROCTOR
72336	FORREST CITY	72335	FORREST CITY
72352	LA GRANGE	72355	LEXA
72353	LAMBROOK	72333	ELAINE
72359	MADISON	72335	FORREST CITY
72377	RIVERVALE	72365	MARKED TREE
72383	TURNER	72366	MARVELL
72387	VANNDALE	72396	WYNNE
72389	WABASH	72369	ONEIDA
72391	WEST RIDGE	72428	ETOWAH
72402	JONESBORO	72401	JONESBORO
72403	JONESBORO	72401	JONESBORO
72427	EGYPT	72421	CASH
72431	GRUBBS	72112	NEWPORT
72439	LIGHT	72401	JONESBORO
72451	PARAGOULD	72450	PARAGOULD
72462	REYNO	72413	BIGGERS
72474	WALCOTT	72450	PARAGOULD
72475	WALDENBURG	72429	FISHER
72503	BATESVILLE	72501	BATESVILLE
72525	CHEROKEE VILLAGE	72529	CHEROKEE VILLAGE
72545	HEBER SPRINGS	72543	HEBER SPRINGS
72575	SALADO	72501	BATESVILLE
72602	HARRISON	72601	HARRISON
72613	BEAVER	72632	EUREKA SPRINGS
72615	BERGMAN	72601	HARRISON
72630	DIAMOND CITY	72644	LEAD HILL
72636	GILBERT	72675	SAINT JOE
72654	MOUNTAIN HOME	72653	MOUNTAIN HOME
72657	TIMBO	72680	TIMBO
72672	PYATT	72687	YELLVILLE
72677	SUMMIT	72687	YELLVILLE
72702	FAYETTEVILLE	72701	FAYETTEVILLE
72711	AVOCA	72756	ROGERS
72716	BENTONVILLE	72712	BENTONVILLE
72728	ELM SPRINGS	72762	SPRINGDALE
72733	GATEWAY	72732	GARFIELD
72735	GOSHEN	72703	FAYETTEVILLE
72737	GREENLAND	72701	FAYETTEVILLE
72741	JOHNSON	72704	FAYETTEVILLE
72757	ROGERS	72756	ROGERS
72765	SPRINGDALE	72764	SPRINGDALE
72766	SPRINGDALE	72764	SPRINGDALE
72770	TONTITOWN	72762	SPRINGDALE
72811	RUSSELLVILLE	72801	RUSSELLVILLE
72812	RUSSELLVILLE	72802	RUSSELLVILLE
72829	CENTERVILLE	72834	DARDANELLE
72902	FORT SMITH	72903	FORT SMITH
72906	FORT SMITH	72903	FORT SMITH
72913	FORT SMITH	72903	FORT SMITH
72914	FORT SMITH	72904	FORT SMITH
72917	FORT SMITH	72903	FORT SMITH
72918	FORT SMITH	72908	FORT SMITH
72919	FORT SMITH	72903	FORT SMITH
72935	DYER	72921	ALMA
72945	MIDLAND	72940	HUNTINGTON
72957	VAN BUREN	72956	VAN BUREN
90009	LOS ANGELES	90045	LOS ANGELES
90030	LOS ANGELES	90012	LOS ANGELES
90050	LOS ANGELES	90042	LOS ANGELES
90051	LOS ANGELES	90012	LOS ANGELES
90052	LOS ANGELES	90001	LOS ANGELES
90053	LOS ANGELES	90012	LOS ANGELES
90054	LOS ANGELES	90012	LOS ANGELES
90055	LOS ANGELES	90017	LOS ANGELES
90060	LOS ANGELES	90012	LOS ANGELES
90070	LOS ANGELES	90010	LOS ANGELES
90072	LOS ANGELES	90028	LOS ANGELES
90074	LOS ANGELES	90071	LOS ANGELES
90075	LOS ANGELES	90020	LOS ANGELES
90076	LOS ANGELES	90020	LOS ANGELES
90078	LOS ANGELES	90028	LOS ANGELES
90079	LOS ANGELES	90015	LOS ANGELES
90080	LOS ANGELES	90045	LOS ANGELES
90081	LOS ANGELES	90017	LOS ANGELES
90082	LOS ANGELES	90037	LOS ANGELES
90083	LOS ANGELES	90045	LOS ANGELES
90084	LOS ANGELES	90017	LOS ANGELES
90086	LOS ANGELES	90012	LOS ANGELES
90087	LOS ANGELES	90012	LOS ANGELES
90088	LOS ANGELES	90017	LOS ANGELES
90091	LOS ANGELES	90040	LOS ANGELES
90093	LOS ANGELES	90028	LOS ANGELES

CALIFORNIA

Point ZIP Code	Post Office Name	Enclosing Residential ZIP Code	Post Office Name
90094	LOS ANGELES	90066	LOS ANGELES
90096	LOS ANGELES	90017	LOS ANGELES
90101	LOS ANGELES	90021	BELL
90102	LOS ANGELES	90023	LOS ANGELES
90103	LOS ANGELES	90201	BELL
90174	LOS ANGELES	90001	LOS ANGELES
90185	LOS ANGELES	90001	LOS ANGELES
90189	LOS ANGELES	90045	LOS ANGELES
90202	BELL GARDENS	90201	BELL
90209	BEVERLY HILLS	90210	BEVERLY HILLS
90213	BEVERLY HILLS	90210	BEVERLY HILLS
90223	COMPTON	90220	COMPTON
90224	COMPTON	90221	COMPTON
90231	CULVER CITY	90230	CULVER CITY
90233	CULVER CITY	90230	CULVER CITY
90239	DOWNEY	90241	DOWNEY
90251	HAWTHORNE	90250	HAWTHORNE
90261	LAWNDALE	90260	LAWNDALE
90264	MALIBU	90265	MALIBU
90267	MANHATTAN BEACH	90266	MANHATTAN BEACH
90294	VENICE	90291	VENICE
90295	MARINA DEL REY	90292	MARINA DEL REY
90296	PLAYA DEL REY	90293	PLAYA DEL REY
90306	INGLEWOOD	90301	INGLEWOOD
90307	INGLEWOOD	90301	INGLEWOOD
90308	INGLEWOOD	90301	INGLEWOOD
90309	INGLEWOOD	90302	INGLEWOOD
90310	INGLEWOOD	90250	HAWTHORNE
90311	INGLEWOOD	90066	LOS ANGELES
90312	INGLEWOOD	90066	LOS ANGELES
90313	INGLEWOOD	90301	INGLEWOOD
90397	INGLEWOOD	90066	LOS ANGELES
90398	INGLEWOOD	90302	INGLEWOOD
90406	SANTA MONICA	90401	SANTA MONICA
90407	SANTA MONICA	90401	SANTA MONICA
90408	SANTA MONICA	90403	SANTA MONICA
90409	SANTA MONICA	90405	SANTA MONICA
90410	SANTA MONICA	90401	SANTA MONICA
90411	SANTA MONICA	90401	SANTA MONICA
90507	TORRANCE	90501	TORRANCE
90508	TORRANCE	90501	TORRANCE
90509	TORRANCE	90503	TORRANCE
90510	TORRANCE	90503	TORRANCE
90607	WHITTIER	90605	WHITTIER
90608	WHITTIER	90601	WHITTIER
90609	WHITTIER	90603	WHITTIER
90610	WHITTIER	90606	WHITTIER
90622	BUENA PARK	90620	BUENA PARK
90624	BUENA PARK	90621	BUENA PARK
90632	LA HABRA	90631	LA HABRA
90633	LA HABRA	90631	LA HABRA
90637	LA MIRADA	90638	LA MIRADA
90651	NORWALK	90650	NORWALK
90652	NORWALK	90650	NORWALK
90659	NORWALK	90650	NORWALK
90661	PICO RIVERA	90660	PICO RIVERA
90662	PICO RIVERA	90660	PICO RIVERA
90665	PICO RIVERA	90660	PICO RIVERA
90702	ARTESIA	90701	ARTESIA
90707	BELLFLOWER	90706	BELLFLOWER
90711	LAKEWOOD	90712	LAKEWOOD
90714	LAKEWOOD	90712	LAKEWOOD
90721	LOS ALAMITOS	90720	LOS ALAMITOS
90733	SAN PEDRO	90731	SAN PEDRO
90734	SAN PEDRO	90275	RANCHO PALOS VERDES
90748	WILMINGTON	90744	WILMINGTON
90749	CARSON	90745	CARSON
90801	LONG BEACH	90802	LONG BEACH
90809	LONG BEACH	90815	LONG BEACH
90831	LONG BEACH	90802	LONG BEACH
90832	LONG BEACH	90802	LONG BEACH
90833	LONG BEACH	90802	LONG BEACH
90834	LONG BEACH	90802	LONG BEACH
90835	LONG BEACH	90802	LONG BEACH
90842	LONG BEACH	90807	LONG BEACH
90844	LONG BEACH	90802	LONG BEACH
90845	LONG BEACH	90802	LONG BEACH
90846	LONG BEACH	90808	LONG BEACH
90847	LONG BEACH	90807	LONG BEACH
90848	LONG BEACH	90807	LONG BEACH
90853	LONG BEACH	90803	LONG BEACH
90888	LONG BEACH	90815	LONG BEACH
90899	LONG BEACH	90802	LONG BEACH
91003	ALTADENA	91001	ALTADENA
91009	DUARTE	91010	DUARTE
91012	LA CANADA FLINTRIDGE	91011	LA CANADA FLINTRIDGE
91017	MONROVIA	91016	MONROVIA
91021	MONTROSE	91020	MONTROSE
91023	MOUNT WILSON	91011	LA CANADA FLINTRIDGE
91025	SIERRA MADRE	91024	SIERRA MADRE
91031	SOUTH PASADENA	91030	SOUTH PASADENA
91041	SUNLAND	91040	SUNLAND
91043	TUJUNGA	91042	TUJUNGA

CALIFORNIA   **CALIFORNIA**

Point ZIP Code		Enclosing Residential ZIP Code		Point ZIP Code		Enclosing Residential ZIP Code	
ZIP	Post Office Name	ZIP	Post Office Name	ZIP	Post Office Name	ZIP	Post Office Name
91046	VERDUGO CITY	91214	LA CRESCENTA	91614	STUDIO CITY	91604	STUDIO CITY
91066	ARCADIA	91006	ARCADIA	91615	NORTH HOLLYWOOD	91605	NORTH HOLLYWOOD
91077	ARCADIA	91007	ARCADIA	91616	NORTH HOLLYWOOD	91606	NORTH HOLLYWOOD
91102	PASADENA	91103	PASADENA	91617	VALLEY VILLAGE	91607	VALLEY VILLAGE
91109	PASADENA	91103	PASADENA	91708	CHINO	91710	CHINO
91110	PASADENA	91103	PASADENA	91715	CITY OF INDUSTRY	91745	HACIENDA HEIGHTS
91114	PASADENA	91104	PASADENA	91716	CITY OF INDUSTRY	91745	HACIENDA HEIGHTS
91115	PASADENA	91105	PASADENA	91729	RANCHO CUCAMONGA	91730	RANCHO CUCAMONGA
91116	PASADENA	91106	PASADENA	91734	EL MONTE	91731	EL MONTE
91117	PASADENA	91107	PASADENA	91735	EL MONTE	91731	EL MONTE
91118	SAN MARINO	91108	SAN MARINO	91743	GUASTI	91761	ONTARIO
91121	PASADENA	91107	PASADENA	91747	LA PUENTE	91744	LA PUENTE
91124	PASADENA	91103	PASADENA	91749	LA PUENTE	91745	HACIENDA HEIGHTS
91125	PASADENA	91106	PASADENA	91756	MONTEREY PARK	91754	MONTEREY PARK
91126	PASADENA	91106	PASADENA	91758	ONTARIO	91761	ONTARIO
91129	PASADENA	91123	PASADENA	91769	POMONA	91768	POMONA
91131	PASADENA	91108	SAN MARINO	91771	ROSEMEAD	91770	ROSEMEAD
91175	PASADENA	91105	PASADENA	91772	ROSEMEAD	91770	ROSEMEAD
91182	PASADENA	91101	PASADENA	91778	SAN GABRIEL	91776	SAN GABRIEL
91184	PASADENA	91105	PASADENA	91785	UPLAND	91786	UPLAND
91185	PASADENA	91801	ALHAMBRA	91788	WALNUT	91789	WALNUT
91186	PASADENA	91107	PASADENA	91793	WEST COVINA	91790	WEST COVINA
91187	PASADENA	91801	ALHAMBRA	91795	WALNUT	91789	WALNUT
91188	PASADENA	91101	PASADENA	91798	ONTARIO	91761	ONTARIO
91189	PASADENA	91105	PASADENA	91802	ALHAMBRA	91801	ALHAMBRA
91191	PASADENA	91108	SAN MARINO	91804	ALHAMBRA	91801	ALHAMBRA
91209	GLENDALE	91205	GLENDALE	91896	ALHAMBRA	91801	ALHAMBRA
91210	GLENDALE	91204	GLENDALE	91903	ALPINE	91901	ALPINE
91221	GLENDALE	91201	GLENDALE	91908	BONITA	91902	BONITA
91222	GLENDALE	91202	GLENDALE	91909	CHULA VISTA	91911	CHULA VISTA
91224	LA CRESCENTA	91214	LA CRESCENTA	91912	CHULA VISTA	91910	CHULA VISTA
91225	GLENDALE	91205	GLENDALE	91921	CHULA VISTA	91915	CHULA VISTA
91226	GLENDALE	91206	GLENDALE	91931	GUATAY	91916	DESCANSO
91305	CANOGA PARK	91303	CANOGA PARK	91933	IMPERIAL BEACH	91932	IMPERIAL BEACH
91308	WEST HILLS	91307	WEST HILLS	91943	LA MESA	91942	LA MESA
91309	CANOGA PARK	91303	CANOGA PARK	91944	LA MESA	91941	LA MESA
91310	CASTAIC	91384	CASTAIC	91946	LEMON GROVE	91945	LEMON GROVE
91312	CHATSWORTH	91311	CHATSWORTH	91947	LINCOLN ACRES	91950	NATIONAL CITY
91313	CHATSWORTH	91311	CHATSWORTH	91948	MOUNT LAGUNA	91962	PINE VALLEY
91319	NEWBURY PARK	91320	NEWBURY PARK	91951	NATIONAL CITY	91950	NATIONAL CITY
91322	NEWHALL	91321	NEWHALL	91976	SPRING VALLEY	91977	SPRING VALLEY
91327	NORTHRIDGE	91326	NORTHRIDGE	91979	SPRING VALLEY	91977	SPRING VALLEY
91328	NORTHRIDGE	91324	NORTHRIDGE	91987	TECATE	91980	TECATE
91329	NORTHRIDGE	91343	NORTH HILLS	92013	CARLSBAD	92009	CARLSBAD
91333	PACOIMA	91331	PACOIMA	92018	CARLSBAD	92008	CARLSBAD
91334	PACOIMA	91331	PACOIMA	92022	EL CAJON	92020	EL CAJON
91337	RESEDA	91335	RESEDA	92023	ENCINITAS	92024	ENCINITAS
91341	SAN FERNANDO	91340	SAN FERNANDO	92030	ESCONDIDO	92027	ESCONDIDO
91346	MISSION HILLS	91345	MISSION HILLS	92033	ESCONDIDO	92025	ESCONDIDO
91353	SUN VALLEY	91352	SUN VALLEY	92038	LA JOLLA	92037	LA JOLLA
91357	TARZANA	91356	TARZANA	92039	LA JOLLA	92037	LA JOLLA
91358	THOUSAND OAKS	91360	THOUSAND OAKS	92046	ESCONDIDO	92025	ESCONDIDO
91359	WESTLAKE VILLAGE	91362	THOUSAND OAKS	92049	OCEANSIDE	92054	OCEANSIDE
91363	WESTLAKE VILLAGE	91361	WESTLAKE VILLAGE	92051	OCEANSIDE	92054	OCEANSIDE
91365	WOODLAND HILLS	91367	WOODLAND HILLS	92052	OCEANSIDE	92054	OCEANSIDE
91372	CALABASAS	91302	CALABASAS	92058	OCEANSIDE	92056	OCEANSIDE
91376	AGOURA HILLS	91301	AGOURA HILLS	92060	PALOMAR MOUNTAIN	92059	PALA
91380	SANTA CLARITA	91355	VALENCIA	92068	SAN LUIS REY	92054	OCEANSIDE
91383	SANTA CLARITA	91355	VALENCIA	92072	SANTEE	92071	SANTEE
91385	VALENCIA	91355	VALENCIA	92074	POWAY	92064	POWAY
91386	CANYON COUNTRY	91350	SANTA CLARITA	92079	SAN MARCOS	92069	SAN MARCOS
91388	VAN NUYS	91405	VAN NUYS	92085	VISTA	92083	VISTA
91392	SYLMAR	91342	SYLMAR	92088	FALLBROOK	92028	FALLBROOK
91393	NORTH HILLS	91343	NORTH HILLS	92090	EL CAJON	92020	EL CAJON
91394	GRANADA HILLS	91326	NORTHRIDGE	92092	LA JOLLA	92037	LA JOLLA
91395	MISSION HILLS	91345	MISSION HILLS	92093	LA JOLLA	92037	LA JOLLA
91396	WINNETKA	91306	WINNETKA	92112	SAN DIEGO	92101	SAN DIEGO
91399	WOODLAND HILLS	91302	CALABASAS	92132	SAN DIEGO	92101	SAN DIEGO
91404	VAN NUYS	91411	VAN NUYS	92137	SAN DIEGO	92110	SAN DIEGO
91407	VAN NUYS	91411	VAN NUYS	92138	SAN DIEGO	92110	SAN DIEGO
91408	VAN NUYS	91411	VAN NUYS	92142	SAN DIEGO	92124	SAN DIEGO
91409	VAN NUYS	91406	VAN NUYS	92143	SAN YSIDRO	92173	SAN YSIDRO
91410	VAN NUYS	91406	VAN NUYS	92147	SAN DIEGO	92133	SAN DIEGO
91412	PANORAMA CITY	91402	PANORAMA CITY	92149	SAN DIEGO	92139	SAN DIEGO
91413	SHERMAN OAKS	91403	SHERMAN OAKS	92150	SAN DIEGO	92128	SAN DIEGO
91416	ENCINO	91316	ENCINO	92153	SAN DIEGO	92154	SAN DIEGO
91426	ENCINO	91316	ENCINO	92158	SAN DIEGO	92154	SAN DIEGO
91470	VAN NUYS	91406	VAN NUYS	92159	SAN DIEGO	92119	SAN DIEGO
91482	VAN NUYS	91406	VAN NUYS	92160	SAN DIEGO	92120	SAN DIEGO
91495	SHERMAN OAKS	91403	SHERMAN OAKS	92161	SAN DIEGO	92037	LA JOLLA
91496	VAN NUYS	91403	SHERMAN OAKS	92162	SAN DIEGO	92102	SAN DIEGO
91497	VAN NUYS	91411	VAN NUYS	92163	SAN DIEGO	92103	SAN DIEGO
91499	VAN NUYS	91405	VAN NUYS	92164	SAN DIEGO	92104	SAN DIEGO
91503	BURBANK	91502	BURBANK	92165	SAN DIEGO	92105	SAN DIEGO
91507	BURBANK	91505	BURBANK	92166	SAN DIEGO	92106	SAN DIEGO
91508	BURBANK	91504	BURBANK	92167	SAN DIEGO	92107	SAN DIEGO
91510	BURBANK	91505	BURBANK	92168	SAN DIEGO	92108	SAN DIEGO
91526	BURBANK	91505	BURBANK	92169	SAN DIEGO	92109	SAN DIEGO
91603	NORTH HOLLYWOOD	91601	NORTH HOLLYWOOD	92170	SAN DIEGO	92113	SAN DIEGO
91609	NORTH HOLLYWOOD	91606	NORTH HOLLYWOOD	92171	SAN DIEGO	92111	SAN DIEGO
91610	TOLUCA LAKE	91602	NORTH HOLLYWOOD	92172	SAN DIEGO	92129	SAN DIEGO
91611	NORTH HOLLYWOOD	91606	NORTH HOLLYWOOD	92174	SAN DIEGO	92102	SAN DIEGO
91612	NORTH HOLLYWOOD	91606	NORTH HOLLYWOOD	92175	SAN DIEGO	92115	SAN DIEGO

CALIFORNIA **CALIFORNIA**

Point ZIP Code		Enclosing Residential ZIP Code		Point ZIP Code		Enclosing Residential ZIP Code	
ZIP	Post Office Name	ZIP	Post Office Name	ZIP	Post Office Name	ZIP	Post Office Name
92176	SAN DIEGO	92116	SAN DIEGO	92654	LAGUNA HILLS	92653	LAGUNA HILLS
92177	SAN DIEGO	92117	SAN DIEGO	92658	NEWPORT BEACH	92660	NEWPORT BEACH
92178	CORONADO	92118	CORONADO	92659	NEWPORT BEACH	92663	NEWPORT BEACH
92179	SAN DIEGO	92154	SAN DIEGO	92674	SAN CLEMENTE	92673	SAN CLEMENTE
92184	SAN DIEGO	92101	SAN DIEGO	92678	TRABUCO CANYON	92679	TRABUCO CANYON
92186	SAN DIEGO	92110	SAN DIEGO	92684	WESTMINSTER	92683	WESTMINSTER
92187	SAN DIEGO	92101	SAN DIEGO	92685	WESTMINSTER	92683	WESTMINSTER
92190	SAN DIEGO	92120	SAN DIEGO	92690	MISSION VIEJO	92691	MISSION VIEJO
92191	SAN DIEGO	92126	SAN DIEGO	92693	SAN JUAN CAPISTRANO	92675	SAN JUAN CAPISTRANO
92192	SAN DIEGO	92122	SAN DIEGO	92698	ALISO VIEJO	92612	IRVINE
92193	SAN DIEGO	92123	SAN DIEGO	92702	SANTA ANA	92701	SANTA ANA
92194	SAN DIEGO	92123	SAN DIEGO	92711	SANTA ANA	92701	SANTA ANA
92195	SAN DIEGO	92115	SAN DIEGO	92712	SANTA ANA	92701	SANTA ANA
92196	SAN DIEGO	92126	SAN DIEGO	92725	SANTA ANA	92707	SANTA ANA
92197	SAN DIEGO	92128	SAN DIEGO	92728	FOUNTAIN VALLEY	92708	FOUNTAIN VALLEY
92198	SAN DIEGO	92128	SAN DIEGO	92735	SANTA ANA	92705	SANTA ANA
92199	SAN DIEGO	92128	SAN DIEGO	92781	TUSTIN	92780	TUSTIN
92202	INDIO	92201	INDIO	92799	SANTA ANA	92704	SANTA ANA
92222	BARD	92283	WINTERHAVEN	92803	ANAHEIM	92801	ANAHEIM
92226	BLYTHE	92225	BLYTHE	92809	ANAHEIM	92807	ANAHEIM
92232	CALEXICO	92231	CALEXICO	92811	ATWOOD	92870	PLACENTIA
92235	CATHEDRAL CITY	92234	CATHEDRAL CITY	92812	ANAHEIM	92802	ANAHEIM
92244	EL CENTRO	92243	EL CENTRO	92814	ANAHEIM	92804	ANAHEIM
92255	PALM DESERT	92260	PALM DESERT	92815	ANAHEIM	92802	ANAHEIM
92258	NORTH PALM SPRINGS	92240	DESERT HOT SPRINGS	92816	ANAHEIM	92806	ANAHEIM
92261	PALM DESERT	92260	PALM DESERT	92817	ANAHEIM	92807	ANAHEIM
92263	PALM SPRINGS	92262	PALM SPRINGS	92822	BREA	92821	BREA
92266	PALO VERDE	92283	WINTERHAVEN	92825	ANAHEIM	92805	ANAHEIM
92268	PIONEERTOWN	92284	YUCCA VALLEY	92834	FULLERTON	92831	FULLERTON
92273	SEELEY	92243	EL CENTRO	92836	FULLERTON	92832	FULLERTON
92275	SALTON CITY	92274	THERMAL	92837	FULLERTON	92833	FULLERTON
92286	YUCCA VALLEY	92284	YUCCA VALLEY	92838	FULLERTON	92835	FULLERTON
92292	PALM SPRINGS	92262	PALM SPRINGS	92842	GARDEN GROVE	92840	GARDEN GROVE
92312	BARSTOW	92311	BARSTOW	92846	GARDEN GROVE	92845	GARDEN GROVE
92318	BRYN MAWR	92354	LOMA LINDA	92850	ANAHEIM	92801	ANAHEIM
92323	CIMA	92364	NIPTON	92856	ORANGE	92866	ORANGE
92326	CREST PARK	92407	SAN BERNARDINO	92857	ORANGE	92865	ORANGE
92329	PHELAN	92371	PHELAN	92859	ORANGE	92869	ORANGE
92333	FAWNSKIN	92314	BIG BEAR CITY	92863	ORANGE	92867	ORANGE
92334	FONTANA	92335	FONTANA	92864	ORANGE	92867	ORANGE
92340	HESPERIA	92345	HESPERIA	92871	PLACENTIA	92870	PLACENTIA
92341	GREEN VALLEY LAKE	92314	BIG BEAR CITY	92877	CORONA	92881	CORONA
92357	LOMA LINDA	92354	LOMA LINDA	92878	CORONA	92882	CORONA
92366	MOUNTAIN PASS	92364	NIPTON	92885	YORBA LINDA	92886	YORBA LINDA
92369	PATTON	92346	HIGHLAND	92899	ANAHEIM	92807	ANAHEIM
92375	REDLANDS	92373	REDLANDS	93002	VENTURA	93001	VENTURA
92378	RIMFOREST	92407	SAN BERNARDINO	93005	VENTURA	93003	VENTURA
92386	SUGARLOAF	92314	BIG BEAR CITY	93006	VENTURA	93003	VENTURA
92391	TWIN PEAKS	92407	SAN BERNARDINO	93007	VENTURA	93003	VENTURA
92393	VICTORVILLE	92392	VICTORVILLE	93009	VENTURA	93003	VENTURA
92398	YERMO	92365	NEWBERRY SPRINGS	93011	CAMARILLO	93010	CAMARILLO
92402	SAN BERNARDINO	92401	SAN BERNARDINO	93014	CARPINTERIA	93013	CARPINTERIA
92403	SAN BERNARDINO	92401	SAN BERNARDINO	93016	FILLMORE	93015	FILLMORE
92406	SAN BERNARDINO	92405	SAN BERNARDINO	93020	MOORPARK	93021	MOORPARK
92412	SAN BERNARDINO	92401	SAN BERNARDINO	93024	OJAI	93023	OJAI
92413	SAN BERNARDINO	92404	SAN BERNARDINO	93031	OXNARD	93036	OXNARD
92414	SAN BERNARDINO	92404	SAN BERNARDINO	93032	OXNARD	93036	OXNARD
92415	SAN BERNARDINO	92404	SAN BERNARDINO	93034	OXNARD	93033	OXNARD
92418	SAN BERNARDINO	92401	SAN BERNARDINO	93040	PIRU	93015	FILLMORE
92420	SAN BERNARDINO	92407	SAN BERNARDINO	93044	PORT HUENEME	93043	PORT HUENEME CBC BAS
92423	SAN BERNARDINO	92408	SAN BERNARDINO	93061	SANTA PAULA	93060	SANTA PAULA
92424	SAN BERNARDINO	92404	SAN BERNARDINO	93062	SIMI VALLEY	93065	SIMI VALLEY
92427	SAN BERNARDINO	92407	SAN BERNARDINO	93064	BRANDEIS	93063	SIMI VALLEY
92502	RIVERSIDE	92501	RIVERSIDE	93094	SIMI VALLEY	93065	SIMI VALLEY
92513	RIVERSIDE	92503	RIVERSIDE	93099	SIMI VALLEY	93063	SIMI VALLEY
92514	RIVERSIDE	92504	RIVERSIDE	93102	SANTA BARBARA	93101	SANTA BARBARA
92515	RIVERSIDE	92503	RIVERSIDE	93107	SANTA BARBARA	93117	GOLETA
92516	RIVERSIDE	92506	RIVERSIDE	93116	GOLETA	93117	GOLETA
92517	RIVERSIDE	92507	RIVERSIDE	93118	GOLETA	93117	GOLETA
92519	RIVERSIDE	92509	RIVERSIDE	93120	SANTA BARBARA	93101	SANTA BARBARA
92522	RIVERSIDE	92501	RIVERSIDE	93121	SANTA BARBARA	93101	SANTA BARBARA
92531	LAKE ELSINORE	92530	LAKE ELSINORE	93130	SANTA BARBARA	93105	SANTA BARBARA
92546	HEMET	92543	HEMET	93140	SANTA BARBARA	93103	SANTA BARBARA
92552	MORENO VALLEY	92553	MORENO VALLEY	93150	SANTA BARBARA	93108	SANTA BARBARA
92554	MORENO VALLEY	92553	MORENO VALLEY	93160	SANTA BARBARA	93111	SANTA BARBARA
92556	MORENO VALLEY	92553	MORENO VALLEY	93190	SANTA BARBARA	93101	SANTA BARBARA
92564	MURRIETA	92562	MURRIETA	93199	GOLETA	93117	GOLETA
92572	PERRIS	92570	PERRIS	93201	ALPAUGH	93219	EARLIMART
92581	SAN JACINTO	92583	SAN JACINTO	93208	CAMP NELSON	93265	SPRINGVILLE
92589	TEMECULA	92591	TEMECULA	93216	DELANO	93215	DELANO
92593	TEMECULA	92590	TEMECULA	93218	DUCOR	93270	TERRA BELLA
92599	PERRIS	92571	PERRIS	93220	EDISON	93307	BAKERSFIELD
92605	HUNTINGTON BEACH	92647	HUNTINGTON BEACH	93222	FRAZIER PARK	93225	FRAZIER PARK
92607	LAGUNA NIGUEL	92677	LAGUNA NIGUEL	93227	GOSHEN	93291	VISALIA
92609	EL TORO	92630	LAKE FOREST	93232	HANFORD	93230	HANFORD
92615	HUNTINGTON BEACH	92646	HUNTINGTON BEACH	93237	KAWEAH	93271	THREE RIVERS
92616	IRVINE	92612	IRVINE	93246	LEMOORE	93245	LEMOORE
92619	IRVINE	92618	IRVINE	93258	PORTERVILLE	93257	PORTERVILLE
92623	IRVINE	92614	IRVINE	93261	RICHGROVE	93219	EARLIMART
92628	COSTA MESA	92626	COSTA MESA	93275	TULARE	93274	TULARE
92637	LAGUNA HILLS	92653	LAGUNA HILLS	93278	VISALIA	93277	VISALIA
92650	EAST IRVINE	92618	IRVINE	93279	VISALIA	93277	VISALIA
92652	LAGUNA BEACH	92651	LAGUNA BEACH	93282	WAUKENA	93212	CORCORAN

CALIFORNIA   **CALIFORNIA**

Point ZIP Code		Enclosing Residential ZIP Code		Point ZIP Code		Enclosing Residential ZIP Code	
ZIP	Post Office Name	ZIP	Post Office Name	ZIP	Post Office Name	ZIP	Post Office Name
93290	VISALIA	93277	VISALIA	93779	FRESNO	93706	FRESNO
93302	BAKERSFIELD	93308	BAKERSFIELD	93780	FRESNO	93720	FRESNO
93303	BAKERSFIELD	93308	BAKERSFIELD	93784	FRESNO	93726	FRESNO
93380	BAKERSFIELD	93308	BAKERSFIELD	93786	FRESNO	93706	FRESNO
93383	BAKERSFIELD	93313	BAKERSFIELD	93790	FRESNO	93705	FRESNO
93384	BAKERSFIELD	93304	BAKERSFIELD	93791	FRESNO	93705	FRESNO
93385	BAKERSFIELD	93304	BAKERSFIELD	93792	FRESNO	93705	FRESNO
93386	BAKERSFIELD	93306	BAKERSFIELD	93793	FRESNO	93705	FRESNO
93387	BAKERSFIELD	93304	BAKERSFIELD	93794	FRESNO	93705	FRESNO
93388	BAKERSFIELD	93308	BAKERSFIELD	93844	FRESNO	93727	FRESNO
93389	BAKERSFIELD	93309	BAKERSFIELD	93888	FRESNO	93727	FRESNO
93390	BAKERSFIELD	93311	BAKERSFIELD	93902	SALINAS	93901	SALINAS
93403	SAN LUIS OBISPO	93401	SAN LUIS OBISPO	93912	SALINAS	93907	SALINAS
93406	SAN LUIS OBISPO	93401	SAN LUIS OBISPO	93915	SALINAS	93905	SALINAS
93408	SAN LUIS OBISPO	93401	SAN LUIS OBISPO	93921	CARMEL BY THE SEA	93923	CARMEL
93409	SAN LUIS OBISPO	93405	SAN LUIS OBISPO	93922	CARMEL	93923	CARMEL
93410	SAN LUIS OBISPO	93407	SAN LUIS OBISPO	93928	JOLON	93932	LOCKWOOD
93412	LOS OSOS	93402	LOS OSOS	93942	MONTEREY	93940	MONTEREY
93421	ARROYO GRANDE	93445	OCEANO	93944	MONTEREY	93940	MONTEREY
93423	ATASCADERO	93422	ATASCADERO	93954	SAN LUCAS	93930	KING CITY
93424	AVILA BEACH	93401	SAN LUIS OBISPO	93962	SPRECKELS	93908	SALINAS
93435	HARMONY	93430	CAYUCOS	94003	BELMONT	94002	BELMONT
93438	LOMPOC	93436	LOMPOC	94011	BURLINGAME	94010	BURLINGAME
93440	LOS ALAMOS	93455	SANTA MARIA	94012	BURLINGAME	94010	BURLINGAME
93443	MORRO BAY	93442	MORRO BAY	94013	DALY CITY	94014	DALY CITY
93447	PASO ROBLES	93446	PASO ROBLES	94016	DALY CITY	94014	DALY CITY
93448	PISMO BEACH	93449	PISMO BEACH	94017	DALY CITY	94015	DALY CITY
93456	SANTA MARIA	93454	SANTA MARIA	94018	EL GRANADA	94019	HALF MOON BAY
93457	SANTA MARIA	93455	SANTA MARIA	94023	LOS ALTOS	94022	LOS ALTOS
93464	SOLVANG	93463	SOLVANG	94026	MENLO PARK	94025	MENLO PARK
93483	GROVER BEACH	93433	GROVER BEACH	94029	MENLO PARK	94025	MENLO PARK
93502	MOJAVE	93501	MOJAVE	94031	MILLBRAE	94030	MILLBRAE
93504	CALIFORNIA CITY	93505	CALIFORNIA CITY	94037	MONTARA	94038	MOSS BEACH
93515	BISHOP	93514	BISHOP	94039	MOUNTAIN VIEW	94043	MOUNTAIN VIEW
93522	DARWIN	93555	RIDGECREST	94042	MOUNTAIN VIEW	94041	MOUNTAIN VIEW
93530	KEELER	93545	LONE PINE	94045	PACIFICA	94044	PACIFICA
93539	LANCASTER	93534	LANCASTER	94059	REDWOOD CITY	94063	REDWOOD CITY
93542	LITTLE LAKE	93555	RIDGECREST	94064	REDWOOD CITY	94063	REDWOOD CITY
93549	OLANCHA	93555	RIDGECREST	94067	SAN BRUNO	94066	SAN BRUNO
93556	RIDGECREST	93555	RIDGECREST	94071	SAN CARLOS	94070	SAN CARLOS
93558	RED MOUNTAIN	93555	RIDGECREST	94083	SOUTH SAN FRANCISCO	94080	SOUTH SAN FRANCISCO
93581	TEHACHAPI	93561	TEHACHAPI	94088	SUNNYVALE	94085	SUNNYVALE
93584	LANCASTER	93534	LANCASTER	94090	SUNNYVALE	94087	SUNNYVALE
93586	LANCASTER	93536	LANCASTER	94099	SOUTH SAN FRANCISCO	94124	SAN FRANCISCO
93590	PALMDALE	93550	PALMDALE	94101	SAN FRANCISCO	94102	SAN FRANCISCO
93592	TRONA	93562	TRONA	94106	SAN FRANCISCO	94105	SAN FRANCISCO
93596	BORON	93516	BORON	94119	SAN FRANCISCO	94105	SAN FRANCISCO
93599	PALMDALE	93550	PALMDALE	94120	SAN FRANCISCO	94104	SAN FRANCISCO
93603	BADGER	93641	MIRAMONTE	94126	SAN FRANCISCO	94111	SAN FRANCISCO
93605	BIG CREEK	93664	SHAVER LAKE	94135	SAN FRANCISCO	94109	SAN FRANCISCO
93606	BIOLA	93722	FRESNO	94136	SAN FRANCISCO	94124	SAN FRANCISCO
93607	BURREL	93656	RIVERDALE	94137	SAN FRANCISCO	94104	SAN FRANCISCO
93613	CLOVIS	93612	CLOVIS	94138	SAN FRANCISCO	94104	SAN FRANCISCO
93624	FIVE POINTS	93234	HURON	94139	SAN FRANCISCO	94104	SAN FRANCISCO
93628	HUME	93633	KINGS CANYON NATIONA	94140	SAN FRANCISCO	94109	SAN FRANCISCO
93634	LAKESHORE	93664	SHAVER LAKE	94141	SAN FRANCISCO	94103	SAN FRANCISCO
93639	MADERA	93638	MADERA	94142	SAN FRANCISCO	94103	SAN FRANCISCO
93642	MONO HOT SPRINGS	93664	SHAVER LAKE	94143	SAN FRANCISCO	94117	SAN FRANCISCO
93649	PIEDRA	93654	REEDLEY	94144	SAN FRANCISCO	94118	SAN FRANCISCO
93661	SANTA RITA PARK	93620	DOS PALOS	94145	SAN FRANCISCO	94104	SAN FRANCISCO
93665	SOUTH DOS PALOS	93620	DOS PALOS	94146	SAN FRANCISCO	94114	SAN FRANCISCO
93666	SULTANA	93618	DINUBA	94147	SAN FRANCISCO	94123	SAN FRANCISCO
93670	YETTEM	93615	CUTLER	94150	SAN FRANCISCO	94105	SAN FRANCISCO
93673	TRAVER	93631	KINGSBURG	94151	SAN FRANCISCO	94105	SAN FRANCISCO
93707	FRESNO	93721	FRESNO	94152	SAN FRANCISCO	94105	SAN FRANCISCO
93708	FRESNO	93721	FRESNO	94155	SAN FRANCISCO	94124	SAN FRANCISCO
93709	FRESNO	93721	FRESNO	94156	SAN FRANCISCO	94104	SAN FRANCISCO
93712	FRESNO	93721	FRESNO	94159	SAN FRANCISCO	94118	SAN FRANCISCO
93714	FRESNO	93721	FRESNO	94160	SAN FRANCISCO	94124	SAN FRANCISCO
93715	FRESNO	93721	FRESNO	94161	SAN FRANCISCO	94111	SAN FRANCISCO
93716	FRESNO	93721	FRESNO	94162	SAN FRANCISCO	94104	SAN FRANCISCO
93717	FRESNO	93721	FRESNO	94163	SAN FRANCISCO	94104	SAN FRANCISCO
93718	FRESNO	93721	FRESNO	94164	SAN FRANCISCO	94109	SAN FRANCISCO
93724	FRESNO	93721	FRESNO	94165	SAN FRANCISCO	94112	SAN FRANCISCO
93729	FRESNO	93720	FRESNO	94166	SAN FRANCISCO	94114	SAN FRANCISCO
93744	FRESNO	93728	FRESNO	94168	SAN FRANCISCO	94121	SAN FRANCISCO
93745	FRESNO	93725	FRESNO	94169	SAN FRANCISCO	94127	SAN FRANCISCO
93747	FRESNO	93727	FRESNO	94170	SAN FRANCISCO	94134	SAN FRANCISCO
93750	FRESNO	93702	FRESNO	94172	SAN FRANCISCO	94122	SAN FRANCISCO
93755	FRESNO	93704	FRESNO	94175	SAN FRANCISCO	94102	SAN FRANCISCO
93760	FRESNO	93721	FRESNO	94177	SAN FRANCISCO	94105	SAN FRANCISCO
93761	FRESNO	93701	FRESNO	94188	SAN FRANCISCO	94124	SAN FRANCISCO
93762	FRESNO	93706	FRESNO	94199	SAN FRANCISCO	94105	SAN FRANCISCO
93764	FRESNO	93721	FRESNO	94203	SACRAMENTO	95814	SACRAMENTO
93765	FRESNO	93705	FRESNO	94204	SACRAMENTO	95815	SACRAMENTO
93771	FRESNO	93706	FRESNO	94205	SACRAMENTO	95823	SACRAMENTO
93772	FRESNO	93706	FRESNO	94206	SACRAMENTO	95823	SACRAMENTO
93773	FRESNO	93706	FRESNO	94207	SACRAMENTO	95814	SACRAMENTO
93774	FRESNO	93706	FRESNO	94208	SACRAMENTO	95814	SACRAMENTO
93775	FRESNO	93706	FRESNO	94209	SACRAMENTO	95814	SACRAMENTO
93776	FRESNO	93706	FRESNO	94211	SACRAMENTO	95814	SACRAMENTO
93777	FRESNO	93706	FRESNO	94229	SACRAMENTO	95814	SACRAMENTO
93778	FRESNO	93706	FRESNO	94230	SACRAMENTO	95823	SACRAMENTO

CALIFORNIA   **CALIFORNIA**

Point ZIP Code		Enclosing Residential ZIP Code		Point ZIP Code		Enclosing Residential ZIP Code	
ZIP	Post Office Name	ZIP	Post Office Name	ZIP	Post Office Name	ZIP	Post Office Name
94232	SACRAMENTO	95818	SACRAMENTO	94712	BERKELEY	94704	BERKELEY
94234	SACRAMENTO	95814	SACRAMENTO	94802	RICHMOND	94801	RICHMOND
94235	SACRAMENTO	95814	SACRAMENTO	94807	RICHMOND	94801	RICHMOND
94236	SACRAMENTO	95814	SACRAMENTO	94808	RICHMOND	94804	RICHMOND
94237	SACRAMENTO	95814	SACRAMENTO	94820	EL SOBRANTE	94803	EL SOBRANTE
94239	SACRAMENTO	95818	SACRAMENTO	94850	RICHMOND	94804	RICHMOND
94240	SACRAMENTO	95814	SACRAMENTO	94875	RICHMOND	94801	RICHMOND
94243	SACRAMENTO	95814	SACRAMENTO	94912	SAN RAFAEL	94903	SAN RAFAEL
94244	SACRAMENTO	95814	SACRAMENTO	94913	SAN RAFAEL	94903	SAN RAFAEL
94246	SACRAMENTO	95691	WEST SACRAMENTO	94914	KENTFIELD	94903	SAN RAFAEL
94247	SACRAMENTO	95823	SACRAMENTO	94915	SAN RAFAEL	94901	SAN RAFAEL
94248	SACRAMENTO	95814	SACRAMENTO	94926	COTATI	94928	ROHNERT PARK
94249	SACRAMENTO	95816	SACRAMENTO	94927	ROHNERT PARK	94928	ROHNERT PARK
94250	SACRAMENTO	95814	SACRAMENTO	94942	MILL VALLEY	94941	MILL VALLEY
94252	SACRAMENTO	95814	SACRAMENTO	94948	NOVATO	94947	NOVATO
94254	SACRAMENTO	95823	SACRAMENTO	94950	OLEMA	94946	NICASIO
94256	SACRAMENTO	95823	SACRAMENTO	94953	PETALUMA	94952	PETALUMA
94257	SACRAMENTO	95814	SACRAMENTO	94955	PETALUMA	94952	PETALUMA
94258	SACRAMENTO	95814	SACRAMENTO	94957	ROSS	94960	SAN ANSELMO
94259	SACRAMENTO	95818	SACRAMENTO	94966	SAUSALITO	94965	SAUSALITO
94261	SACRAMENTO	95814	SACRAMENTO	94974	SAN QUENTIN	94964	SAN QUENTIN
94262	SACRAMENTO	95823	SACRAMENTO	94975	PETALUMA	94952	PETALUMA
94263	SACRAMENTO	95814	SACRAMENTO	94976	CORTE MADERA	94925	CORTE MADERA
94267	SACRAMENTO	95815	SACRAMENTO	94977	LARKSPUR	94939	LARKSPUR
94268	SACRAMENTO	95814	SACRAMENTO	94978	FAIRFAX	94930	FAIRFAX
94269	SACRAMENTO	95814	SACRAMENTO	94979	SAN ANSELMO	94960	SAN ANSELMO
94271	SACRAMENTO	95814	SACRAMENTO	94998	NOVATO	94945	NOVATO
94273	SACRAMENTO	95814	SACRAMENTO	94999	PETALUMA	94954	PETALUMA
94274	SACRAMENTO	95814	SACRAMENTO	95001	APTOS	95003	APTOS
94277	SACRAMENTO	95814	SACRAMENTO	95007	BROOKDALE	95005	BEN LOMOND
94278	SACRAMENTO	95814	SACRAMENTO	95009	CAMPBELL	95008	CAMPBELL
94279	SACRAMENTO	95814	SACRAMENTO	95011	CAMPBELL	95008	CAMPBELL
94280	SACRAMENTO	95822	SACRAMENTO	95015	CUPERTINO	95014	CUPERTINO
94282	SACRAMENTO	95823	SACRAMENTO	95021	GILROY	95020	GILROY
94283	SACRAMENTO	95823	SACRAMENTO	95024	HOLLISTER	95023	HOLLISTER
94284	SACRAMENTO	95818	SACRAMENTO	95026	HOLY CITY	95033	LOS GATOS
94285	SACRAMENTO	95818	SACRAMENTO	95031	LOS GATOS	95030	LOS GATOS
94286	SACRAMENTO	95818	SACRAMENTO	95036	MILPITAS	95035	MILPITAS
94287	SACRAMENTO	95814	SACRAMENTO	95038	MORGAN HILL	95037	MORGAN HILL
94288	SACRAMENTO	95814	SACRAMENTO	95041	MOUNT HERMON	95018	FELTON
94289	SACRAMENTO	95814	SACRAMENTO	95042	NEW ALMADEN	95120	SAN JOSE
94290	SACRAMENTO	95818	SACRAMENTO	95044	REDWOOD ESTATES	95033	LOS GATOS
94291	SACRAMENTO	95818	SACRAMENTO	95052	SANTA CLARA	95050	SANTA CLARA
94293	SACRAMENTO	95818	SACRAMENTO	95055	SANTA CLARA	95051	SANTA CLARA
94294	SACRAMENTO	95818	SACRAMENTO	95056	SANTA CLARA	95054	SANTA CLARA
94295	SACRAMENTO	95814	SACRAMENTO	95061	SANTA CRUZ	95060	SANTA CRUZ
94296	SACRAMENTO	95814	SACRAMENTO	95063	SANTA CRUZ	95062	SANTA CRUZ
94297	SACRAMENTO	95818	SACRAMENTO	95067	SCOTTS VALLEY	95066	SCOTTS VALLEY
94298	SACRAMENTO	95814	SACRAMENTO	95071	SARATOGA	95070	SARATOGA
94302	PALO ALTO	94303	PALO ALTO	95075	TRES PINOS	95023	HOLLISTER
94307	PALO ALTO	94303	PALO ALTO	95077	WATSONVILLE	95076	WATSONVILLE
94308	PALO ALTO	94303	PALO ALTO	95101	SAN JOSE	95131	SAN JOSE
94309	PALO ALTO	94305	STANFORD	95102	SAN JOSE	95131	SAN JOSE
94310	PALO ALTO	94306	PALO ALTO	95103	SAN JOSE	95113	SAN JOSE
94405	SAN MATEO	94401	SAN MATEO	95106	SAN JOSE	95113	SAN JOSE
94406	SAN MATEO	94402	SAN MATEO	95108	SAN JOSE	95113	SAN JOSE
94407	SAN MATEO	94403	SAN MATEO	95109	SAN JOSE	95113	SAN JOSE
94408	SAN MATEO	94404	SAN MATEO	95114	SAN JOSE	95113	SAN JOSE
94409	SAN MATEO	94402	SAN MATEO	95115	SAN JOSE	95113	SAN JOSE
94497	SAN MATEO	94403	SAN MATEO	95137	SAN JOSE	95125	SAN JOSE
94511	BETHEL ISLAND	94561	OAKLEY	95142	SAN JOSE	95125	SAN JOSE
94516	CANYON	94563	ORINDA	95150	SAN JOSE	95131	SAN JOSE
94522	CONCORD	94520	CONCORD	95151	SAN JOSE	95121	SAN JOSE
94524	CONCORD	94520	CONCORD	95152	SAN JOSE	95132	SAN JOSE
94527	CONCORD	94520	CONCORD	95153	SAN JOSE	95123	SAN JOSE
94529	CONCORD	94520	CONCORD	95154	SAN JOSE	95124	SAN JOSE
94537	FREMONT	94536	FREMONT	95155	SAN JOSE	95125	SAN JOSE
94540	HAYWARD	94544	HAYWARD	95156	SAN JOSE	95116	SAN JOSE
94543	HAYWARD	94541	HAYWARD	95157	SAN JOSE	95130	SAN JOSE
94557	HAYWARD	94544	HAYWARD	95158	SAN JOSE	95118	SAN JOSE
94562	OAKVILLE	94574	SAINT HELENA	95159	SAN JOSE	95128	SAN JOSE
94570	MORAGA	94556	MORAGA	95160	SAN JOSE	95120	SAN JOSE
94573	RUTHERFORD	94574	SAINT HELENA	95161	SAN JOSE	95131	SAN JOSE
94575	MORAGA	94556	MORAGA	95164	SAN JOSE	95134	SAN JOSE
94581	NAPA	94558	NAPA	95170	SAN JOSE	95129	SAN JOSE
94604	OAKLAND	94612	OAKLAND	95172	SAN JOSE	95113	SAN JOSE
94614	OAKLAND	94621	OAKLAND	95173	SAN JOSE	95122	SAN JOSE
94615	OAKLAND	94607	OAKLAND	95190	SAN JOSE	95112	SAN JOSE
94617	OAKLAND	94607	OAKLAND	95191	SAN JOSE	95126	SAN JOSE
94620	PIEDMONT	94601	OAKLAND	95193	SAN JOSE	95123	SAN JOSE
94622	OAKLAND	94577	SAN LEANDRO	95194	SAN JOSE	95110	SAN JOSE
94623	OAKLAND	94607	OAKLAND	95196	SAN JOSE	95113	SAN JOSE
94624	OAKLAND	94603	OAKLAND	95201	STOCKTON	95206	STOCKTON
94625	OAKLAND	94607	OAKLAND	95208	STOCKTON	95206	STOCKTON
94626	OAKLAND	94607	OAKLAND	95213	STOCKTON	95206	STOCKTON
94643	OAKLAND	94612	OAKLAND	95221	ALTAVILLE	95222	ANGELS CAMP
94649	OAKLAND	94612	OAKLAND	95224	AVERY	95223	ARNOLD
94659	OAKLAND	94612	OAKLAND	95225	BURSON	95252	VALLEY SPRINGS
94660	OAKLAND	94607	OAKLAND	95226	CAMPO SECO	95252	VALLEY SPRINGS
94661	OAKLAND	94611	OAKLAND	95227	CLEMENTS	95220	ACAMPO
94662	EMERYVILLE	94608	EMERYVILLE	95229	DOUGLAS FLAT	95251	VALLECITO
94666	OAKLAND	94612	OAKLAND	95233	HATHAWAY PINES	95223	ARNOLD
94701	BERKELEY	94704	BERKELEY	95234	HOLT	95206	STOCKTON

CALIFORNIA   **CALIFORNIA**

Point ZIP Code		Enclosing Residential ZIP Code		Point ZIP Code		Enclosing Residential ZIP Code	
ZIP	Post Office Name	ZIP	Post Office Name	ZIP	Post Office Name	ZIP	Post Office Name
95241	LODI	95240	LODI	95899	SACRAMENTO	95691	WEST SACRAMENTO
95248	RAIL ROAD FLAT	95245	MOKELUMNE HILL	95913	ARTOIS	95963	ORLAND
95250	SHEEP RANCH	95249	SAN ANDREAS	95924	CEDAR RIDGE	95945	GRASS VALLEY
95253	VICTOR	95240	LODI	95927	CHICO	95926	CHICO
95254	WALLACE	95252	VALLEY SPRINGS	95929	CHICO	95928	CHICO
95267	STOCKTON	95207	STOCKTON	95930	CLIPPER MILLS	95941	FORBESTOWN
95269	STOCKTON	95207	STOCKTON	95940	FEATHER FALLS	95965	OROVILLE
95290	STOCKTON	95203	STOCKTON	95950	GRIMES	95912	ARBUCKLE
95296	LYOTH	95206	STOCKTON	95958	NELSON	95965	OROVILLE
95297	STOCKTON	95204	STOCKTON	95967	PARADISE	95969	PARADISE
95298	STOCKTON	95206	STOCKTON	95974	RICHVALE	95965	OROVILLE
95305	BIG OAK FLAT	95321	GROVELAND	95976	CHICO	95973	CHICO
95312	CRESSEY	95388	WINTON	95978	STIRLING CITY	95954	MAGALIA
95314	DARDANELLE	95364	PINECREST	95980	STORRIE	95915	BELDEN
95319	EMPIRE	95357	MODESTO	95986	WASHINGTON	95959	NEVADA CITY
95328	KEYES	95307	CERES	95992	YUBA CITY	95991	YUBA CITY
95341	MERCED	95340	MERCED	96009	BIEBER	96056	MCARTHUR
95344	MERCED	95340	MERCED	96011	BIG BEND	96065	MONTGOMERY CREEK
95347	MOCCASIN	95321	GROVELAND	96017	CASTELLA	96051	LAKEHEAD
95352	MODESTO	95350	MODESTO	96029	FLOURNOY	96021	CORNING
95353	MODESTO	95354	MODESTO	96037	GREENVIEW	96032	FORT JONES
95365	PLANADA	95340	MERCED	96049	REDDING	96002	REDDING
95373	STANDARD	95370	SONORA	96061	MILL CREEK	96063	MINERAL
95375	STRAWBERRY	95335	LONG BARN	96068	NUBIEBER	96056	MCARTHUR
95378	TRACY	95376	TRACY	96070	OBRIEN	96051	LAKEHEAD
95381	TURLOCK	95380	TURLOCK	96074	PASKENTA	96021	CORNING
95387	WESTLEY	95363	PATTERSON	96078	PROBERTA	96035	GERBER
95402	SANTA ROSA	95404	SANTA ROSA	96079	SHASTA LAKE	96019	SHASTA LAKE
95406	SANTA ROSA	95401	SANTA ROSA	96084	ROUND MOUNTAIN	96065	MONTGOMERY CREEK
95408	SANTA ROSA	95407	SANTA ROSA	96089	SHASTA LAKE	96003	REDDING
95416	BOYES HOT SPRINGS	95476	SONOMA	96090	TEHAMA	96035	GERBER
95418	CALPELLA	95482	UKIAH	96092	VINA	96021	CORNING
95419	CAMP MEEKER	95472	SEBASTOPOL	96095	WHISKEYTOWN	96033	FRENCH GULCH
95424	CLEARLAKE PARK	95422	CLEARLAKE	96099	REDDING	96001	REDDING
95426	COBB	95461	MIDDLETOWN	96110	EAGLEVILLE	96104	CEDARVILLE
95430	DUNCANS MILLS	95472	SEBASTOPOL	96127	SUSANVILLE	96130	SUSANVILLE
95431	ELDRIDGE	95442	GLEN ELLEN	96129	BECKWOURTH	96122	PORTOLA
95433	EL VERANO	95476	SONOMA	96151	SOUTH LAKE TAHOE	96150	SOUTH LAKE TAHOE
95435	FINLEY	95453	LAKEPORT	96152	SOUTH LAKE TAHOE	96150	SOUTH LAKE TAHOE
95463	NAVARRO	95466	PHILO	96154	SOUTH LAKE TAHOE	96150	SOUTH LAKE TAHOE
95471	RIO NIDO	95446	GUERNEVILLE	96155	SOUTH LAKE TAHOE	96150	SOUTH LAKE TAHOE
95473	SEBASTOPOL	95472	SEBASTOPOL	96156	SOUTH LAKE TAHOE	96150	SOUTH LAKE TAHOE
95481	TALMAGE	95482	UKIAH	96157	SOUTH LAKE TAHOE	96150	SOUTH LAKE TAHOE
95486	VILLA GRANDE	95421	CAZADERO	96158	SOUTH LAKE TAHOE	96150	SOUTH LAKE TAHOE
95487	VINEBURG	95476	SONOMA	96160	TRUCKEE	96161	TRUCKEE
95502	EUREKA	95501	EUREKA	96201	APO	00000	NO ENCLOSING ZIP
95518	ARCATA	95521	ARCATA	96202	APO	00000	NO ENCLOSING ZIP
95532	CRESCENT CITY	95531	CRESCENT CITY	96203	APO	00000	NO ENCLOSING ZIP
95534	CUTTEN	95503	EUREKA	96204	APO	00000	NO ENCLOSING ZIP
95537	FIELDS LANDING	95503	EUREKA	96205	APO	00000	NO ENCLOSING ZIP
95538	FORT DICK	95531	CRESCENT CITY	96206	APO	00000	NO ENCLOSING ZIP
95545	HONEYDEW	95542	GARBERVILLE	96207	APO	00000	NO ENCLOSING ZIP
95553	MIRANDA	95554	MYERS FLAT	96208	APO	00000	NO ENCLOSING ZIP
95559	PHILLIPSVILLE	95554	MYERS FLAT	96212	APO	00000	NO ENCLOSING ZIP
95571	WEOTT	95569	REDCREST	96213	APO	00000	NO ENCLOSING ZIP
95601	AMADOR CITY	95685	SUTTER CREEK	96214	APO	00000	NO ENCLOSING ZIP
95604	AUBURN	95603	AUBURN	96215	APO	00000	NO ENCLOSING ZIP
95609	CARMICHAEL	95608	CARMICHAEL	96217	APO	00000	NO ENCLOSING ZIP
95611	CITRUS HEIGHTS	95621	CITRUS HEIGHTS	96218	APO	00000	NO ENCLOSING ZIP
95613	COLOMA	95667	PLACERVILLE	96219	APO	00000	NO ENCLOSING ZIP
95617	DAVIS	95616	DAVIS	96220	APO	00000	NO ENCLOSING ZIP
95625	ELMIRA	95687	VACAVILLE	96221	APO	00000	NO ENCLOSING ZIP
95639	HOOD	95758	ELK GROVE	96224	APO	00000	NO ENCLOSING ZIP
95646	KIRKWOOD	95666	PIONEER	96251	APO	00000	NO ENCLOSING ZIP
95654	MARTELL	95642	JACKSON	96257	APO	00000	NO ENCLOSING ZIP
95656	MOUNT AUKUM	95684	SOMERSET	96258	APO	00000	NO ENCLOSING ZIP
95671	REPRESA	95673	RIO LINDA	96259	APO	00000	NO ENCLOSING ZIP
95675	RIVER PINES	95669	PLYMOUTH	96260	APO	00000	NO ENCLOSING ZIP
95676	ROBBINS	95645	KNIGHTS LANDING	96262	APO	00000	NO ENCLOSING ZIP
95680	RYDE	95690	WALNUT GROVE	96264	APO	00000	NO ENCLOSING ZIP
95686	THORNTON	95242	LODI	96266	APO	00000	NO ENCLOSING ZIP
95696	VACAVILLE	95688	VACAVILLE	96267	APO	00000	NO ENCLOSING ZIP
95697	YOLO	95695	WOODLAND	96269	FPO	00000	NO ENCLOSING ZIP
95699	DRYTOWN	95685	SUTTER CREEK	96271	APO	00000	NO ENCLOSING ZIP
95712	CHICAGO PARK	95945	GRASS VALLEY	96275	APO	00000	NO ENCLOSING ZIP
95736	WEIMAR	95713	COLFAX	96276	APO	00000	NO ENCLOSING ZIP
95741	RANCHO CORDOVA	95670	RANCHO CORDOVA	96278	APO	00000	NO ENCLOSING ZIP
95759	ELK GROVE	95624	ELK GROVE	96283	APO	00000	NO ENCLOSING ZIP
95763	FOLSOM	95630	FOLSOM	96284	APO	00000	NO ENCLOSING ZIP
95798	WEST SACRAMENTO	95691	WEST SACRAMENTO	96297	APO	00000	NO ENCLOSING ZIP
95799	WEST SACRAMENTO	95691	WEST SACRAMENTO	96306	FPO	00000	NO ENCLOSING ZIP
95812	SACRAMENTO	95814	SACRAMENTO	96309	FPO	00000	NO ENCLOSING ZIP
95813	SACRAMENTO	95815	SACRAMENTO	96310	FPO	00000	NO ENCLOSING ZIP
95840	SACRAMENTO	95814	SACRAMENTO	96311	FPO	00000	NO ENCLOSING ZIP
95851	SACRAMENTO	95815	SACRAMENTO	96313	FPO	00000	NO ENCLOSING ZIP
95852	SACRAMENTO	95815	SACRAMENTO	96319	APO	00000	NO ENCLOSING ZIP
95853	SACRAMENTO	95815	SACRAMENTO	96321	FPO	00000	NO ENCLOSING ZIP
95860	SACRAMENTO	95821	SACRAMENTO	96322	FPO	00000	NO ENCLOSING ZIP
95865	SACRAMENTO	95825	SACRAMENTO	96323	APO	00000	NO ENCLOSING ZIP
95866	SACRAMENTO	95825	SACRAMENTO	96325	APO	00000	NO ENCLOSING ZIP
95867	SACRAMENTO	95814	SACRAMENTO	96326	APO	00000	NO ENCLOSING ZIP
95887	SACRAMENTO	95821	SACRAMENTO	96328	APO	00000	NO ENCLOSING ZIP
95894	SACRAMENTO	95818	SACRAMENTO	96330	APO	00000	NO ENCLOSING ZIP

CALIFORNIA

COLORADO

Point ZIP Code		Enclosing Residential ZIP Code		Point ZIP Code		Enclosing Residential ZIP Code	
	Post Office		Post Office		Post Office		Post Office
ZIP	Name	ZIP	Name	ZIP	Name	ZIP	Name
96336	APO	00000	NO ENCLOSING ZIP	96622	FPO	00000	NO ENCLOSING ZIP
96337	APO	00000	NO ENCLOSING ZIP	96623	FPO	00000	NO ENCLOSING ZIP
96338	APO	00000	NO ENCLOSING ZIP	96624	FPO	00000	NO ENCLOSING ZIP
96343	APO	00000	NO ENCLOSING ZIP	96626	FPO	00000	NO ENCLOSING ZIP
96347	FPO	00000	NO ENCLOSING ZIP	96628	FPO	00000	NO ENCLOSING ZIP
96348	FPO	00000	NO ENCLOSING ZIP	96629	FPO	00000	NO ENCLOSING ZIP
96349	FPO	00000	NO ENCLOSING ZIP	96634	FPO	00000	NO ENCLOSING ZIP
96350	FPO	00000	NO ENCLOSING ZIP	96635	FPO	00000	NO ENCLOSING ZIP
96351	FPO	00000	NO ENCLOSING ZIP	96642	FPO	00000	NO ENCLOSING ZIP
96362	FPO	00000	NO ENCLOSING ZIP	96643	FPO	00000	NO ENCLOSING ZIP
96364	APO	00000	NO ENCLOSING ZIP	96644	FPO	00000	NO ENCLOSING ZIP
96365	APO	00000	NO ENCLOSING ZIP	96647	FPO	00000	NO ENCLOSING ZIP
96367	APO	00000	NO ENCLOSING ZIP	96648	FPO	00000	NO ENCLOSING ZIP
96368	APO	00000	NO ENCLOSING ZIP	96649	FPO	00000	NO ENCLOSING ZIP
96370	FPO	00000	NO ENCLOSING ZIP	96657	FPO	00000	NO ENCLOSING ZIP
96372	FPO	00000	NO ENCLOSING ZIP	96660	FPO	00000	NO ENCLOSING ZIP
96373	FPO	00000	NO ENCLOSING ZIP	96661	FPO	00000	NO ENCLOSING ZIP
96374	FPO	00000	NO ENCLOSING ZIP	96662	FPO	00000	NO ENCLOSING ZIP
96375	FPO	00000	NO ENCLOSING ZIP	96663	FPO	00000	NO ENCLOSING ZIP
96376	APO	00000	NO ENCLOSING ZIP	96664	FPO	00000	NO ENCLOSING ZIP
96377	FPO	00000	NO ENCLOSING ZIP	96665	FPO	00000	NO ENCLOSING ZIP
96378	APO	00000	NO ENCLOSING ZIP	96666	FPO	00000	NO ENCLOSING ZIP
96379	FPO	00000	NO ENCLOSING ZIP	96667	FPO	00000	NO ENCLOSING ZIP
96384	APO	00000	NO ENCLOSING ZIP	96668	FPO	00000	NO ENCLOSING ZIP
96386	APO	00000	NO ENCLOSING ZIP	96669	FPO	00000	NO ENCLOSING ZIP
96387	APO	00000	NO ENCLOSING ZIP	96670	FPO	00000	NO ENCLOSING ZIP
96388	FPO	00000	NO ENCLOSING ZIP	96671	FPO	00000	NO ENCLOSING ZIP
96401	APO	00000	NO ENCLOSING ZIP	96672	FPO	00000	NO ENCLOSING ZIP
96402	APO	00000	NO ENCLOSING ZIP	96673	FPO	00000	NO ENCLOSING ZIP
96426	FPO	00000	NO ENCLOSING ZIP	96674	FPO	00000	NO ENCLOSING ZIP
96427	FPO	00000	NO ENCLOSING ZIP	96675	FPO	00000	NO ENCLOSING ZIP
96490	APO	00000	NO ENCLOSING ZIP	96677	FPO	00000	NO ENCLOSING ZIP
96506	FPO	00000	NO ENCLOSING ZIP	96678	FPO	00000	NO ENCLOSING ZIP
96507	FPO	00000	NO ENCLOSING ZIP	96679	FPO	00000	NO ENCLOSING ZIP
96508	APO	00000	NO ENCLOSING ZIP	96681	FPO	00000	NO ENCLOSING ZIP
96511	FPO	00000	NO ENCLOSING ZIP	96682	FPO	00000	NO ENCLOSING ZIP
96512	APO	00000	NO ENCLOSING ZIP	96683	FPO	00000	NO ENCLOSING ZIP
96515	FPO	00000	NO ENCLOSING ZIP	96684	FPO	00000	NO ENCLOSING ZIP
96517	FPO	00000	NO ENCLOSING ZIP	96686	FPO	00000	NO ENCLOSING ZIP
96518	FPO	00000	NO ENCLOSING ZIP	96687	FPO	00000	NO ENCLOSING ZIP
96520	FPO	00000	NO ENCLOSING ZIP	96698	FPO	00000	NO ENCLOSING ZIP
96521	FPO	00000	NO ENCLOSING ZIP	80001	ARVADA	80004	ARVADA
96522	FPO	00000	NO ENCLOSING ZIP	80006	ARVADA	80005	ARVADA
96529	APO	00000	NO ENCLOSING ZIP	80024	DUPONT	80022	COMMERCE CITY
96530	APO	00000	NO ENCLOSING ZIP	80025	ELDORADO SPRINGS	80305	BOULDER
96531	FPO	00000	NO ENCLOSING ZIP	80028	LOUISVILLE	80027	LOUISVILLE
96534	FPO	00000	NO ENCLOSING ZIP	80034	WHEAT RIDGE	80033	WHEAT RIDGE
96535	APO	00000	NO ENCLOSING ZIP	80035	WESTMINSTER	80030	WESTMINSTER
96536	FPO	00000	NO ENCLOSING ZIP	80036	WESTMINSTER	80030	WESTMINSTER
96537	FPO	00000	NO ENCLOSING ZIP	80037	COMMERCE CITY	80022	COMMERCE CITY
96538	FPO	00000	NO ENCLOSING ZIP	80038	BROOMFIELD	80020	BROOMFIELD
96539	FPO	00000	NO ENCLOSING ZIP	80040	AURORA	80010	AURORA
96540	FPO	00000	NO ENCLOSING ZIP	80041	AURORA	80011	AURORA
96541	APO	00000	NO ENCLOSING ZIP	80042	AURORA	80011	AURORA
96542	APO	00000	NO ENCLOSING ZIP	80044	AURORA	80011	AURORA
96543	APO	00000	NO ENCLOSING ZIP	80045	AURORA	80010	AURORA
96544	FPO	00000	NO ENCLOSING ZIP	80046	AURORA	80015	AURORA
96545	FPO	00000	NO ENCLOSING ZIP	80047	AURORA	80012	AURORA
96546	APO	00000	NO ENCLOSING ZIP	80131	LOUVIERS	80125	LITTLETON
96548	APO	00000	NO ENCLOSING ZIP	80150	ENGLEWOOD	80110	ENGLEWOOD
96549	APO	00000	NO ENCLOSING ZIP	80151	ENGLEWOOD	80113	ENGLEWOOD
96551	APO	00000	NO ENCLOSING ZIP	80155	ENGLEWOOD	80111	ENGLEWOOD
96552	APO	00000	NO ENCLOSING ZIP	80160	LITTLETON	80120	LITTLETON
96553	APO	00000	NO ENCLOSING ZIP	80161	LITTLETON	80121	LITTLETON
96554	APO	00000	NO ENCLOSING ZIP	80162	LITTLETON	80123	LITTLETON
96555	APO	00000	NO ENCLOSING ZIP	80163	LITTLETON	80126	LITTLETON
96557	APO	00000	NO ENCLOSING ZIP	80165	LITTLETON	80120	LITTLETON
96558	APO	00000	NO ENCLOSING ZIP	80166	LITTLETON	80120	LITTLETON
96580	FPO	00000	NO ENCLOSING ZIP	80201	DENVER	80202	DENVER
96594	FPO	00000	NO ENCLOSING ZIP	80217	DENVER	80202	DENVER
96595	FPO	00000	NO ENCLOSING ZIP	80243	DENVER	80205	DENVER
96596	FPO	00000	NO ENCLOSING ZIP	80244	DENVER	80202	DENVER
96597	FPO	00000	NO ENCLOSING ZIP	80248	DENVER	80202	DENVER
96598	FPO	00000	NO ENCLOSING ZIP	80250	DENVER	80210	DENVER
96599	FPO	00000	NO ENCLOSING ZIP	80251	DENVER	80014	AURORA
96601	FPO	00000	NO ENCLOSING ZIP	80252	DENVER	80216	DENVER
96602	FPO	00000	NO ENCLOSING ZIP	80255	DENVER	80202	DENVER
96603	FPO	00000	NO ENCLOSING ZIP	80256	DENVER	80202	DENVER
96604	FPO	00000	NO ENCLOSING ZIP	80257	DENVER	80202	DENVER
96605	FPO	00000	NO ENCLOSING ZIP	80259	DENVER	80202	DENVER
96606	FPO	00000	NO ENCLOSING ZIP	80261	DENVER	80210	DENVER
96607	FPO	00000	NO ENCLOSING ZIP	80263	DENVER	80237	DENVER
96608	FPO	00000	NO ENCLOSING ZIP	80264	DENVER	80203	DENVER
96609	FPO	00000	NO ENCLOSING ZIP	80265	DENVER	80202	DENVER
96610	FPO	00000	NO ENCLOSING ZIP	80266	DENVER	80216	DENVER
96611	FPO	00000	NO ENCLOSING ZIP	80270	DENVER	80202	DENVER
96612	FPO	00000	NO ENCLOSING ZIP	80271	DENVER	80202	DENVER
96613	FPO	00000	NO ENCLOSING ZIP	80273	DENVER	80204	DENVER
96614	FPO	00000	NO ENCLOSING ZIP	80274	DENVER	80202	DENVER
96615	FPO	00000	NO ENCLOSING ZIP	80275	DENVER	80204	DENVER
96617	FPO	00000	NO ENCLOSING ZIP	80279	DENVER	80216	DENVER
96619	FPO	00000	NO ENCLOSING ZIP	80280	DENVER	80230	DENVER
96620	FPO	00000	NO ENCLOSING ZIP	80281	DENVER	80202	DENVER

COLORADO   **CONNECTICUT**

Point ZIP Code		Enclosing Residential ZIP Code		Point ZIP Code		Enclosing Residential ZIP Code	
ZIP	Post Office Name	ZIP	Post Office Name	ZIP	Post Office Name	ZIP	Post Office Name
80285	DENVER	80202	DENVER	80946	COLORADO SPRINGS	80903	COLORADO SPRINGS
80290	DENVER	80205	DENVER	80947	COLORADO SPRINGS	80903	COLORADO SPRINGS
80291	DENVER	80202	DENVER	80949	COLORADO SPRINGS	80919	COLORADO SPRINGS
80292	DENVER	80202	DENVER	80950	COLORADO SPRINGS	80909	COLORADO SPRINGS
80293	DENVER	80202	DENVER	80960	COLORADO SPRINGS	80906	COLORADO SPRINGS
80294	DENVER	80202	DENVER	80962	COLORADO SPRINGS	80920	COLORADO SPRINGS
80295	DENVER	80203	DENVER	80970	COLORADO SPRINGS	80915	COLORADO SPRINGS
80299	DENVER	80202	DENVER	80977	COLORADO SPRINGS	80925	COLORADO SPRINGS
80306	BOULDER	80302	BOULDER	80995	COLORADO SPRINGS	80920	COLORADO SPRINGS
80307	BOULDER	80305	BOULDER	81002	PUEBLO	81003	PUEBLO
80308	BOULDER	80301	BOULDER	81009	PUEBLO	81001	PUEBLO
80310	BOULDER	80302	BOULDER	81010	PUEBLO	81003	PUEBLO
80314	BOULDER	80503	LONGMONT	81011	PUEBLO	81003	PUEBLO
80321	BOULDER	80303	BOULDER	81012	PUEBLO	81003	PUEBLO
80322	BOULDER	80303	BOULDER	81024	BONCARBO	81082	TRINIDAD
80323	BOULDER	80303	BOULDER	81030	CHERAW	81050	LA JUNTA
80328	BOULDER	80303	BOULDER	81033	CROWLEY	81063	ORDWAY
80329	BOULDER	80303	BOULDER	81034	CROWLEY	81063	ORDWAY
80402	GOLDEN	80401	GOLDEN	81038	FORT LYON	81054	LAS ANIMAS
80419	GOLDEN	80401	GOLDEN	81046	HOEHNE	81082	TRINIDAD
80420	ALMA	80440	FAIRPLAY	81077	SWINK	81050	LA JUNTA
80425	BUFFALO CREEK	80470	PINE	81124	CAPULIN	81140	LA JARA
80426	BURNS	81637	GYPSUM	81126	CHAMA	81153	SAN PABLO
80427	CENTRAL CITY	80422	BLACK HAWK	81127	CHIMNEY ROCK	81147	PAGOSA SPRINGS
80432	COMO	80440	FAIRPLAY	81128	CHROMO	81147	PAGOSA SPRINGS
80434	COWDREY	80480	WALDEN	81129	CONEJOS	81120	ANTONITO
80436	DUMONT	80452	IDAHO SPRINGS	81131	CRESTONE	81143	MOFFAT
80437	EVERGREEN	80439	EVERGREEN	81134	GARCIA	81152	SAN LUIS
80438	EMPIRE	80452	IDAHO SPRINGS	81135	HOMELAKE	81144	MONTE VISTA
80442	FRASER	80446	GRANBY	81138	JAROSO	81152	SAN LUIS
80443	FRISCO	80435	DILLON	81141	MANASSA	81151	SANFORD
80444	GEORGETOWN	80452	IDAHO SPRINGS	81148	ROMEO	81151	SANFORD
80448	GRANT	80421	BAILEY	81157	PAGOSA SPRINGS	81147	PAGOSA SPRINGS
80451	HOT SULPHUR SPRINGS	80446	GRANBY	81215	CANON CITY	81212	CANON CITY
80453	IDLEDALE	80401	GOLDEN	81221	COAL CREEK	81226	FLORENCE
80454	INDIAN HILLS	80465	MORRISON	81222	COALDALE	81233	HOWARD
80457	KITTREDGE	80439	EVERGREEN	81225	CRESTED BUTTE	81224	CRESTED BUTTE
80469	PHIPPSBURG	80467	OAK CREEK	81227	MONARCH	81201	SALIDA
80471	PINECLIFFE	80403	GOLDEN	81232	HILLSIDE	81223	COTOPAXI
80473	RAND	80480	WALDEN	81237	OHIO CITY	81239	PARLIN
80474	ROLLINSVILLE	80403	GOLDEN	81242	PONCHA SPRINGS	81201	SALIDA
80475	SHAWNEE	80421	BAILEY	81244	ROCKVALE	81226	FLORENCE
80476	SILVER PLUME	80452	IDAHO SPRINGS	81248	SARGENTS	81149	SAGUACHE
80477	STEAMBOAT SPRINGS	80487	STEAMBOAT SPRINGS	81290	FLORENCE	81226	FLORENCE
80478	TABERNASH	80446	GRANBY	81302	DURANGO	81301	DURANGO
80482	WINTER PARK	80446	GRANBY	81329	MARVEL	81326	HESPERUS
80483	YAMPA	80479	TOPONAS	81330	MESA VERDE NATIONAL	81328	MANCOS
80488	STEAMBOAT SPRINGS	80487	STEAMBOAT SPRINGS	81332	RICO	81320	CAHONE
80497	SILVERTHORNE	80498	SILVERTHORNE	81402	MONTROSE	81401	MONTROSE
80502	LONGMONT	80501	LONGMONT	81414	CORY	81410	AUSTIN
80511	ESTES PARK	80517	ESTES PARK	81420	LAZEAR	81419	HOTCHKISS
80520	FIRESTONE	80621	FORT LUPTON	81429	PARADOX	81411	BEDROCK
80522	FORT COLLINS	80521	FORT COLLINS	81502	GRAND JUNCTION	81501	GRAND JUNCTION
80527	FORT COLLINS	80525	FORT COLLINS	81523	GLADE PARK	81522	GATEWAY
80532	GLEN HAVEN	80515	DRAKE	81602	GLENWOOD SPRINGS	81601	GLENWOOD SPRINGS
80533	HYGIENE	80503	LONGMONT	81612	ASPEN	81611	ASPEN
80539	LOVELAND	80538	LOVELAND	81615	SNOWMASS VILLAGE	81654	SNOWMASS
80541	MASONVILLE	80538	LOVELAND	81620	AVON	81657	VAIL
80544	NIWOT	80501	LONGMONT	81626	CRAIG	81625	CRAIG
80546	SEVERANCE	80550	WINDSOR	81632	EDWARDS	81657	VAIL
80547	TIMNATH	80525	FORT COLLINS	81636	BATTLEMENT MESA	81635	PARACHUTE
80551	WINDSOR	80550	WINDSOR	81645	MINTURN	81657	VAIL
80553	FORT COLLINS	80525	FORT COLLINS	81646	MOLINA	81643	MESA
80614	EASTLAKE	80241	DENVER	81649	RED CLIFF	81657	VAIL
80622	GALETON	80615	EATON	81655	WOLCOTT	81657	VAIL
80623	GILCREST	80651	PLATTEVILLE	81656	WOODY CREEK	81621	BASALT
80632	GREELEY	80631	GREELEY	81658	VAIL	81657	VAIL
80633	GREELEY	80631	GREELEY	06006	WINDSOR	06095	WINDSOR
80638	GREELEY	80631	GREELEY	06011	BRISTOL	06010	BRISTOL
80646	LUCERNE	80631	GREELEY	06020	CANTON CENTER	06019	CANTON
80732	HEREFORD	80729	GROVER	06025	EAST GLASTONBURY	06033	GLASTONBURY
80746	PAOLI	80731	HAXTUN	06028	EAST WINDSOR HILL	06074	SOUTH WINDSOR
80819	GREEN MOUNTAIN FALLS	80809	CASCADE	06030	FARMINGTON	06032	FARMINGTON
80826	LIMON	80828	LIMON	06034	FARMINGTON	06032	FARMINGTON
80841	U S A F ACADEMY	80840	U S A F ACADEMY	06041	MANCHESTER	06040	MANCHESTER
80860	VICTOR	80816	FLORISSANT	06045	MANCHESTER	06040	MANCHESTER
80862	WILD HORSE	80825	KIT CARSON	06050	NEW BRITAIN	06051	NEW BRITAIN
80866	WOODLAND PARK	80863	WOODLAND PARK	06061	PINE MEADOW	06057	NEW HARTFORD
80901	COLORADO SPRINGS	80903	COLORADO SPRINGS	06064	POQUONOCK	06095	WINDSOR
80912	COLORADO SPRINGS	80930	COLORADO SPRINGS	06072	SOMERSVILLE	06071	SOMERS
80931	COLORADO SPRINGS	80911	COLORADO SPRINGS	06075	STAFFORD	06076	STAFFORD SPRINGS
80932	COLORADO SPRINGS	80909	COLORADO SPRINGS	06077	STAFFORDVILLE	06076	STAFFORD SPRINGS
80933	COLORADO SPRINGS	80907	COLORADO SPRINGS	06079	TACONIC	06068	SALISBURY
80934	COLORADO SPRINGS	80904	COLORADO SPRINGS	06080	SUFFIELD	06078	SUFFIELD
80935	COLORADO SPRINGS	80910	COLORADO SPRINGS	06083	ENFIELD	06082	ENFIELD
80936	COLORADO SPRINGS	80918	COLORADO SPRINGS	06087	UNIONVILLE	06085	UNIONVILLE
80937	COLORADO SPRINGS	80903	COLORADO SPRINGS	06091	WEST HARTLAND	06027	EAST HARTLAND
80940	COLORADO SPRINGS	80915	COLORADO SPRINGS	06094	WINCHESTER CENTER	06098	WINSTED
80941	COLORADO SPRINGS	80918	COLORADO SPRINGS	06101	HARTFORD	06120	HARTFORD
80942	COLORADO SPRINGS	80903	COLORADO SPRINGS	06102	HARTFORD	06114	HARTFORD
80943	COLORADO SPRINGS	80903	COLORADO SPRINGS	06104	HARTFORD	06120	HARTFORD
80944	COLORADO SPRINGS	80903	COLORADO SPRINGS	06115	HARTFORD	06105	HARTFORD
80945	COLORADO SPRINGS	80909	COLORADO SPRINGS	06123	HARTFORD	06103	HARTFORD

CONNECTICUT   DISTRICT OF COLUMBIA

Point ZIP Code		Enclosing Residential ZIP Code		Point ZIP Code		Enclosing Residential ZIP Code	
ZIP	Post Office Name	ZIP	Post Office Name	ZIP	Post Office Name	ZIP	Post Office Name
06126	HARTFORD	06105	HARTFORD	06703	WATERBURY	06704	WATERBURY
06127	WEST HARTFORD	06107	WEST HARTFORD	06720	WATERBURY	06702	WATERBURY
06128	EAST HARTFORD	06106	HARTFORD	06721	WATERBURY	06702	WATERBURY
06129	WETHERSFIELD	06109	WETHERSFIELD	06722	WATERBURY	06702	WATERBURY
06131	NEWINGTON	06111	NEWINGTON	06723	WATERBURY	06702	WATERBURY
06132	HARTFORD	06112	HARTFORD	06724	WATERBURY	06702	WATERBURY
06133	WEST HARTFORD	06110	WEST HARTFORD	06725	WATERBURY	06702	WATERBURY
06134	HARTFORD	06114	HARTFORD	06726	WATERBURY	06702	WATERBURY
06137	WEST HARTFORD	06117	WEST HARTFORD	06749	WATERBURY	06762	MIDDLEBURY
06138	EAST HARTFORD	06118	EAST HARTFORD	06753	CORNWALL	06754	CORNWALL BRIDGE
06140	HARTFORD	06120	HARTFORD	06781	PEQUABUCK	06786	TERRYVILLE
06141	HARTFORD	06120	HARTFORD	06813	DANBURY	06810	DANBURY
06142	HARTFORD	06120	HARTFORD	06814	DANBURY	06810	DANBURY
06143	HARTFORD	06120	HARTFORD	06816	DANBURY	06810	DANBURY
06144	HARTFORD	06120	HARTFORD	06817	DANBURY	06810	DANBURY
06145	HARTFORD	06120	HARTFORD	06828	FAIRFIELD	06825	FAIRFIELD
06146	HARTFORD	06120	HARTFORD	06829	GEORGETOWN	06883	WESTON
06147	HARTFORD	06120	HARTFORD	06832	GREENWICH	06831	GREENWICH
06150	HARTFORD	06120	HARTFORD	06836	GREENWICH	06831	GREENWICH
06151	HARTFORD	06120	HARTFORD	06838	GREENS FARMS	06880	WESTPORT
06152	HARTFORD	06002	BLOOMFIELD	06842	NEW CANAAN	06840	NEW CANAAN
06153	HARTFORD	06032	FARMINGTON	06852	NORWALK	06850	NORWALK
06154	HARTFORD	06105	HARTFORD	06856	NORWALK	06854	NORWALK
06155	HARTFORD	06105	HARTFORD	06857	NORWALK	06854	NORWALK
06156	HARTFORD	06105	HARTFORD	06858	NORWALK	06850	NORWALK
06160	HARTFORD	06105	HARTFORD	06859	NORWALK	06851	NORWALK
06161	HARTFORD	06109	WETHERSFIELD	06860	NORWALK	06854	NORWALK
06176	HARTFORD	06103	HARTFORD	06875	REDDING CENTER	06896	REDDING
06180	HARTFORD	06107	WEST HARTFORD	06876	REDDING RIDGE	06896	REDDING
06183	HARTFORD	06103	HARTFORD	06879	RIDGEFIELD	06877	RIDGEFIELD
06199	HARTFORD	06096	WINDSOR LOCKS	06881	WESTPORT	06880	WESTPORT
06230	ABINGTON	06259	POMFRET CENTER	06888	WESTPORT	06880	WESTPORT
06233	BALLOUVILLE	06241	DAYVILLE	06889	WESTPORT	06880	WESTPORT
06244	EAST WOODSTOCK	06281	WOODSTOCK	06904	STAMFORD	06901	STAMFORD
06245	FABYAN	06255	NORTH GROSVENORDALE	06910	STAMFORD	06902	STAMFORD
06246	GROSVENOR DALE	06255	NORTH GROSVENORDALE	06911	STAMFORD	06902	STAMFORD
06251	MANSFIELD DEPOT	06268	STORRS MANSFIELD	06912	STAMFORD	06902	STAMFORD
06258	POMFRET	06259	POMFRET CENTER	06913	STAMFORD	06902	STAMFORD
06263	ROGERS	06241	DAYVILLE	06920	STAMFORD	06902	STAMFORD
06265	SOUTH WILLINGTON	06279	WILLINGTON	06921	STAMFORD	06901	STAMFORD
06267	SOUTH WOODSTOCK	06259	POMFRET CENTER	06922	STAMFORD	06902	STAMFORD
06332	CENTRAL VILLAGE	06374	PLAINFIELD	06925	STAMFORD	06902	STAMFORD
06338	MASHANTUCKET	06320	NEW LONDON	06926	STAMFORD	06902	STAMFORD
06350	HANOVER	06330	BALTIC	06927	STAMFORD	06902	STAMFORD
06372	OLD MYSTIC	06355	MYSTIC	06928	STAMFORD	06902	STAMFORD
06373	ONECO	06377	STERLING	19706	DELAWARE CITY	19720	NEW CASTLE
06376	SOUTH LYME	06371	OLD LYME	19708	KIRKWOOD	19701	BEAR
06383	VERSAILLES	06330	BALTIC	19710	MONTCHANIN	19807	WILMINGTON
06387	WAUREGAN	06374	PLAINFIELD	19712	NEWARK	19711	NEWARK
06388	WEST MYSTIC	06355	MYSTIC	19714	NEWARK	19711	NEWARK
06389	YANTIC	06254	NORTH FRANKLIN	19715	NEWARK	19711	NEWARK
06404	BOTSFORD	06470	NEWTOWN	19718	NEWARK	19713	NEWARK
06408	CHESHIRE	06410	CHESHIRE	19721	NEW CASTLE	19720	NEW CASTLE
06411	CHESHIRE	06410	CHESHIRE	19725	NEWARK	19711	NEWARK
06414	COBALT	06424	EAST HAMPTON	19726	NEWARK	19711	NEWARK
06439	HADLYME	06371	OLD LYME	19730	ODESSA	19709	MIDDLETOWN
06440	HAWLEYVILLE	06470	NEWTOWN	19731	PORT PENN	19709	MIDDLETOWN
06444	MARION	06479	PLANTSVILLE	19732	ROCKLAND	19807	WILMINGTON
06454	MERIDEN	06450	MERIDEN	19733	SAINT GEORGES	19720	NEW CASTLE
06456	MIDDLE HADDAM	06424	EAST HAMPTON	19735	WINTERTHUR	19807	WILMINGTON
06467	MILLDALE	06479	PLANTSVILLE	19850	WILMINGTON	19801	WILMINGTON
06474	NORTH WESTCHESTER	06415	COLCHESTER	19880	WILMINGTON	19801	WILMINGTON
06487	SOUTH BRITAIN	06488	SOUTHBURY	19884	WILMINGTON	19801	WILMINGTON
06491	STEVENSON	06468	MONROE	19885	WILMINGTON	19801	WILMINGTON
06493	WALLINGFORD	06492	WALLINGFORD	19886	WILMINGTON	19801	WILMINGTON
06494	WALLINGFORD	06492	WALLINGFORD	19887	WILMINGTON	19803	WILMINGTON
06495	WALLINGFORD	06492	WALLINGFORD	19889	WILMINGTON	19801	WILMINGTON
06501	NEW HAVEN	06510	NEW HAVEN	19890	WILMINGTON	19801	WILMINGTON
06502	NEW HAVEN	06510	NEW HAVEN	19891	WILMINGTON	19713	NEWARK
06503	NEW HAVEN	06510	NEW HAVEN	19892	WILMINGTON	19720	NEW CASTLE
06504	NEW HAVEN	06510	NEW HAVEN	19893	WILMINGTON	19801	WILMINGTON
06505	NEW HAVEN	06510	NEW HAVEN	19894	WILMINGTON	19801	WILMINGTON
06506	NEW HAVEN	06511	NEW HAVEN	19895	WILMINGTON	19801	WILMINGTON
06507	NEW HAVEN	06510	NEW HAVEN	19896	WILMINGTON	19802	WILMINGTON
06508	NEW HAVEN	06510	NEW HAVEN	19897	WILMINGTON	19803	WILMINGTON
06509	NEW HAVEN	06510	NEW HAVEN	19898	WILMINGTON	19801	WILMINGTON
06520	NEW HAVEN	06510	NEW HAVEN	19899	WILMINGTON	19801	WILMINGTON
06521	NEW HAVEN	06510	NEW HAVEN	19903	DOVER	19901	DOVER
06530	NEW HAVEN	06511	NEW HAVEN	19905	DOVER	19901	DOVER
06531	NEW HAVEN	06511	NEW HAVEN	19906	DOVER	19901	DOVER
06532	NEW HAVEN	06511	NEW HAVEN	19936	CHESWOLD	19901	DOVER
06533	NEW HAVEN	06511	NEW HAVEN	19955	KENTON	19938	CLAYTON
06534	NEW HAVEN	06511	NEW HAVEN	19961	LITTLE CREEK	19901	DOVER
06535	NEW HAVEN	06511	NEW HAVEN	19969	NASSAU	19958	LEWES
06536	NEW HAVEN	06511	NEW HAVEN	19980	WOODSIDE	19943	FELTON
06537	NEW HAVEN	06516	WEST HAVEN	20013	WASHINGTON	20024	WASHINGTON
06538	NEW HAVEN	06516	WEST HAVEN	20022	WASHINGTON	20002	WASHINGTON
06540	NEW HAVEN	06511	NEW HAVEN	20023	WASHINGTON	20003	WASHINGTON
06601	BRIDGEPORT	06604	BRIDGEPORT	20026	WASHINGTON	20019	WASHINGTON
06602	BRIDGEPORT	06604	BRIDGEPORT	20027	WASHINGTON	20007	WASHINGTON
06673	BRIDGEPORT	06615	STRATFORD	20029	WASHINGTON	20019	WASHINGTON
06699	BRIDGEPORT	06615	STRATFORD	20030	WASHINGTON	20020	WASHINGTON
06701	WATERBURY	06702	WATERBURY	20033	WASHINGTON	20002	WASHINGTON

NONRESIDENTIAL ZIP CODES

DISTRICT OF COLUMBIA

Point ZIP Code		Enclosing Residential ZIP Code		Point ZIP Code		Enclosing Residential ZIP Code	
ZIP	Post Office Name	ZIP	Post Office Name	ZIP	Post Office Name	ZIP	Post Office Name
20035	WASHINGTON	20036	WASHINGTON	20372	WASHINGTON	20037	WASHINGTON
20038	WASHINGTON	20005	WASHINGTON	20373	NAVAL ANACOST ANNEX	20020	WASHINGTON
20039	WASHINGTON	20011	WASHINGTON	20374	WASHINGTON NAVY YARD	20003	WASHINGTON
20040	WASHINGTON	20011	WASHINGTON	20375	WASHINGTON	20032	WASHINGTON
20042	WASHINGTON	20018	WASHINGTON	20376	WASHINGTON NAVY YARD	20003	WASHINGTON
20043	WASHINGTON	20005	WASHINGTON	20380	WASHINGTON	20003	WASHINGTON
20044	WASHINGTON	20004	WASHINGTON	20388	WASHINGTON NAVY YARD	20003	WASHINGTON
20045	WASHINGTON	20004	WASHINGTON	20390	WASHINGTON	20003	WASHINGTON
20046	WASHINGTON	20015	WASHINGTON	20391	WASHINGTON NAVY YARD	20003	WASHINGTON
20047	WASHINGTON	20015	WASHINGTON	20392	WASHINGTON	20007	WASHINGTON
20049	WASHINGTON	20004	WASHINGTON	20393	WASHINGTON	20016	WASHINGTON
20050	WASHINGTON	20018	WASHINGTON	20394	WASHINGTON	20016	WASHINGTON
20051	WASHINGTON	20004	WASHINGTON	20398	WASHINGTON NAVY YARD	20003	WASHINGTON
20052	WASHINGTON	20006	WASHINGTON	20401	WASHINGTON	20002	WASHINGTON
20053	WASHINGTON	20024	WASHINGTON	20402	WASHINGTON	20002	WASHINGTON
20055	WASHINGTON	20001	WASHINGTON	20403	WASHINGTON	20024	WASHINGTON
20056	WASHINGTON	20009	WASHINGTON	20404	WASHINGTON	20002	WASHINGTON
20060	WASHINGTON	20001	WASHINGTON	20405	WASHINGTON	20006	WASHINGTON
20061	WASHINGTON	20018	WASHINGTON	20407	WASHINGTON	20002	WASHINGTON
20062	WASHINGTON	20006	WASHINGTON	20408	WASHINGTON	20004	WASHINGTON
20065	WASHINGTON	20024	WASHINGTON	20410	WASHINGTON	20024	WASHINGTON
20066	WASHINGTON	20018	WASHINGTON	20411	WASHINGTON	20024	WASHINGTON
20067	WASHINGTON	20006	WASHINGTON	20412	WASHINGTON	20004	WASHINGTON
20068	WASHINGTON	20006	WASHINGTON	20413	WASHINGTON	20004	WASHINGTON
20071	WASHINGTON	20005	WASHINGTON	20414	WASHINGTON	20024	WASHINGTON
20073	WASHINGTON	20004	WASHINGTON	20415	WASHINGTON	20006	WASHINGTON
20074	WASHINGTON	20018	WASHINGTON	20416	WASHINGTON	20024	WASHINGTON
20075	WASHINGTON	20018	WASHINGTON	20418	WASHINGTON	20004	WASHINGTON
20076	WASHINGTON	20015	WASHINGTON	20419	WASHINGTON	20005	WASHINGTON
20080	WASHINGTON	20005	WASHINGTON	20420	WASHINGTON	20005	WASHINGTON
20081	WASHINGTON	20005	WASHINGTON	20421	WASHINGTON	20005	WASHINGTON
20088	WASHINGTON	20016	WASHINGTON	20422	WASHINGTON	20010	WASHINGTON
20090	WASHINGTON	20018	WASHINGTON	20423	WASHINGTON	20004	WASHINGTON
20091	WASHINGTON	20001	WASHINGTON	20424	WASHINGTON	20004	WASHINGTON
20098	WASHINGTON	20018	WASHINGTON	20425	WASHINGTON	20001	WASHINGTON
20099	WASHINGTON	20002	WASHINGTON	20426	WASHINGTON	20002	WASHINGTON
20201	WASHINGTON	20024	WASHINGTON	20427	WASHINGTON	20006	WASHINGTON
20202	WASHINGTON	20024	WASHINGTON	20428	WASHINGTON	20009	WASHINGTON
20203	WASHINGTON	20036	WASHINGTON	20429	WASHINGTON	20006	WASHINGTON
20204	WASHINGTON	20024	WASHINGTON	20431	WASHINGTON	20006	WASHINGTON
20208	WASHINGTON	20001	WASHINGTON	20433	WASHINGTON	20006	WASHINGTON
20210	WASHINGTON	20004	WASHINGTON	20434	WASHINGTON	20004	WASHINGTON
20211	WASHINGTON	20001	WASHINGTON	20435	WASHINGTON	20007	WASHINGTON
20212	WASHINGTON	20002	WASHINGTON	20436	WASHINGTON	20004	WASHINGTON
20213	WASHINGTON	20004	WASHINGTON	20437	WASHINGTON	20037	WASHINGTON
20215	WASHINGTON	20004	WASHINGTON	20439	WASHINGTON	20006	WASHINGTON
20216	WASHINGTON	20004	WASHINGTON	20440	WASHINGTON	20009	WASHINGTON
20217	WASHINGTON	20001	WASHINGTON	20441	WASHINGTON	20009	WASHINGTON
20218	WASHINGTON	20006	WASHINGTON	20442	WASHINGTON	20001	WASHINGTON
20219	WASHINGTON	20024	WASHINGTON	20444	WASHINGTON	20001	WASHINGTON
20220	WASHINGTON	20005	WASHINGTON	20447	WASHINGTON	20024	WASHINGTON
20221	WASHINGTON	20004	WASHINGTON	20451	WASHINGTON	20006	WASHINGTON
20222	WASHINGTON	20005	WASHINGTON	20456	WASHINGTON	20006	WASHINGTON
20223	WASHINGTON	20036	WASHINGTON	20460	WASHINGTON	20024	WASHINGTON
20224	WASHINGTON	20004	WASHINGTON	20463	WASHINGTON	20004	WASHINGTON
20226	WASHINGTON	20006	WASHINGTON	20469	WASHINGTON	20006	WASHINGTON
20227	WASHINGTON	20004	WASHINGTON	20472	WASHINGTON	20024	WASHINGTON
20228	WASHINGTON	20024	WASHINGTON	20500	WASHINGTON	20005	WASHINGTON
20229	WASHINGTON	20004	WASHINGTON	20502	WASHINGTON	20005	WASHINGTON
20230	WASHINGTON	20005	WASHINGTON	20503	WASHINGTON	20006	WASHINGTON
20232	WASHINGTON	20009	WASHINGTON	20505	WASHINGTON	20006	WASHINGTON
20235	WASHINGTON	20009	WASHINGTON	20506	WASHINGTON	20006	WASHINGTON
20237	WASHINGTON	20024	WASHINGTON	20507	WASHINGTON	20036	WASHINGTON
20238	WASHINGTON	20036	WASHINGTON	20508	WASHINGTON	20006	WASHINGTON
20239	WASHINGTON	20004	WASHINGTON	20509	WASHINGTON	20006	WASHINGTON
20240	WASHINGTON	20006	WASHINGTON	20510	WASHINGTON	20004	WASHINGTON
20241	WASHINGTON	20037	WASHINGTON	20515	WASHINGTON	20004	WASHINGTON
20242	WASHINGTON	20011	WASHINGTON	20520	WASHINGTON	20037	WASHINGTON
20244	WASHINGTON	20018	WASHINGTON	20521	WASHINGTON	20037	WASHINGTON
20245	WASHINGTON	20004	WASHINGTON	20522	WASHINGTON	20037	WASHINGTON
20250	WASHINGTON	20024	WASHINGTON	20523	WASHINGTON	20006	WASHINGTON
20251	WASHINGTON	20024	WASHINGTON	20524	WASHINGTON	20005	WASHINGTON
20254	WASHINGTON	20024	WASHINGTON	20525	WASHINGTON	20005	WASHINGTON
20260	WASHINGTON	20024	WASHINGTON	20526	WASHINGTON	20006	WASHINGTON
20261	WASHINGTON	20024	WASHINGTON	20527	WASHINGTON	20005	WASHINGTON
20262	WASHINGTON	20018	WASHINGTON	20528	WASHINGTON	20018	WASHINGTON
20265	WASHINGTON	20024	WASHINGTON	20530	WASHINGTON	20004	WASHINGTON
20266	WASHINGTON	20024	WASHINGTON	20531	WASHINGTON	20004	WASHINGTON
20268	WASHINGTON	20005	WASHINGTON	20532	WASHINGTON	20001	WASHINGTON
20270	WASHINGTON	20001	WASHINGTON	20533	WASHINGTON	20005	WASHINGTON
20289	WASHINGTON	20024	WASHINGTON	20534	WASHINGTON	20001	WASHINGTON
20299	WASHINGTON	20018	WASHINGTON	20535	WASHINGTON	20004	WASHINGTON
20303	WASHINGTON	20018	WASHINGTON	20536	WASHINGTON	20001	WASHINGTON
20306	WASHINGTON	20012	WASHINGTON	20538	WASHINGTON	20001	WASHINGTON
20307	WASHINGTON	20012	WASHINGTON	20539	WASHINGTON	20005	WASHINGTON
20314	WASHINGTON	20001	WASHINGTON	20540	WASHINGTON	20003	WASHINGTON
20315	WASHINGTON	20018	WASHINGTON	20541	WASHINGTON	20003	WASHINGTON
20317	WASHINGTON	20011	WASHINGTON	20542	WASHINGTON	20011	WASHINGTON
20318	WASHINGTON	20018	WASHINGTON	20543	WASHINGTON	20003	WASHINGTON
20319	WASHINGTON	20024	WASHINGTON	20544	WASHINGTON	20002	WASHINGTON
20340	WASHINGTON	20032	WASHINGTON	20546	WASHINGTON	20024	WASHINGTON
20355	WASHINGTON	20018	WASHINGTON	20547	WASHINGTON	20024	WASHINGTON
20370	WASHINGTON	20003	WASHINGTON	20548	WASHINGTON	20001	WASHINGTON

DISTRICT OF COLUMBIA / FLORIDA

Point ZIP Code ZIP	Post Office Name	Enclosing Residential ZIP Code ZIP	Post Office Name	Point ZIP Code ZIP	Post Office Name	Enclosing Residential ZIP Code ZIP	Post Office Name
20549	WASHINGTON	20001	WASHINGTON	32302	TALLAHASSEE	32301	TALLAHASSEE
20551	WASHINGTON	20004	WASHINGTON	32313	TALLAHASSEE	32304	TALLAHASSEE
20552	WASHINGTON	20006	WASHINGTON	32314	TALLAHASSEE	32301	TALLAHASSEE
20553	WASHINGTON	20024	WASHINGTON	32315	TALLAHASSEE	32303	TALLAHASSEE
20554	WASHINGTON	20009	WASHINGTON	32316	TALLAHASSEE	32304	TALLAHASSEE
20555	WASHINGTON	20006	WASHINGTON	32318	TALLAHASSEE	32305	TALLAHASSEE
20557	WASHINGTON	20003	WASHINGTON	32323	LANARK VILLAGE	32322	CARRABELLE
20559	WASHINGTON	20003	WASHINGTON	32326	CRAWFORDVILLE	32327	CRAWFORDVILLE
20560	WASHINGTON	20004	WASHINGTON	32329	APALACHICOLA	32320	APALACHICOLA
20565	WASHINGTON	20004	WASHINGTON	32330	GREENSBORO	32351	QUINCY
20566	WASHINGTON	20037	WASHINGTON	32337	LLOYD	32317	TALLAHASSEE
20570	WASHINGTON	20006	WASHINGTON	32341	MADISON	32340	MADISON
20571	WASHINGTON	20005	WASHINGTON	32345	MONTICELLO	32344	MONTICELLO
20573	WASHINGTON	20002	WASHINGTON	32353	QUINCY	32351	QUINCY
20575	WASHINGTON	20006	WASHINGTON	32357	SHADY GROVE	32331	GREENVILLE
20576	WASHINGTON	20005	WASHINGTON	32360	TELOGIA	32334	HOSFORD
20577	WASHINGTON	20006	WASHINGTON	32361	WACISSA	32336	LAMONT
20578	WASHINGTON	20001	WASHINGTON	32362	WOODVILLE	32305	TALLAHASSEE
20579	WASHINGTON	20036	WASHINGTON	32395	TALLAHASSEE	32301	TALLAHASSEE
20580	WASHINGTON	20004	WASHINGTON	32399	TALLAHASSEE	32301	TALLAHASSEE
20581	WASHINGTON	20036	WASHINGTON	32402	PANAMA CITY	32401	PANAMA CITY
20585	WASHINGTON	20024	WASHINGTON	32406	PANAMA CITY	32405	PANAMA CITY
20586	WASHINGTON	20037	WASHINGTON	32410	MEXICO BEACH	32401	PANAMA CITY
20590	WASHINGTON	20024	WASHINGTON	32411	PANAMA CITY	32408	PANAMA CITY
20591	WASHINGTON	20024	WASHINGTON	32412	PANAMA CITY	32401	PANAMA CITY
20593	WASHINGTON	20024	WASHINGTON	32417	PANAMA CITY	32407	PANAMA CITY BEACH
20594	WASHINGTON	20024	WASHINGTON	32422	ARGYLE	32433	DEFUNIAK SPRINGS
20597	WASHINGTON	20024	WASHINGTON	32432	CYPRESS	32442	GRAND RIDGE
32004	PONTE VEDRA BEACH	32082	PONTE VEDRA BEACH	32434	MOSSY HEAD	32433	DEFUNIAK SPRINGS
32006	FLEMING ISLAND	32073	ORANGE PARK	32447	MARIANNA	32446	MARIANNA
32007	BOSTWICK	32177	PALATKA	32452	NOMA	32425	BONIFAY
32026	RAIFORD	32083	RAIFORD	32454	POINT WASHINGTON	32459	SANTA ROSA BEACH
32030	DOCTORS INLET	32068	MIDDLEBURG	32457	PORT SAINT JOE	32456	PORT SAINT JOE
32035	FERNANDINA BEACH	32034	FERNANDINA BEACH	32461	ROSEMARY BEACH	32413	PANAMA CITY BEACH
32041	YULEE	32097	YULEE	32463	WAUSAU	32428	CHIPLEY
32042	GRAHAM	32044	HAMPTON	32509	PENSACOLA	32526	PENSACOLA
32050	MIDDLEBURG	32068	MIDDLEBURG	32511	PENSACOLA	32507	PENSACOLA
32056	LAKE CITY	32055	LAKE CITY	32512	PENSACOLA	32507	PENSACOLA
32067	ORANGE PARK	32073	ORANGE PARK	32513	PENSACOLA	32503	PENSACOLA
32072	OLUSTEE	32087	SANDERSON	32516	PENSACOLA	32506	PENSACOLA
32079	PENNEY FARMS	32043	GREEN COVE SPRINGS	32520	PENSACOLA	32501	PENSACOLA
32085	SAINT AUGUSTINE	32084	SAINT AUGUSTINE	32521	PENSACOLA	32507	PENSACOLA
32099	JACKSONVILLE	32220	JACKSONVILLE	32522	PENSACOLA	32502	PENSACOLA
32105	BARBERVILLE	32180	PIERSON	32523	PENSACOLA	32501	PENSACOLA
32111	CANDLER	34472	OCALA	32524	PENSACOLA	32501	PENSACOLA
32115	DAYTONA BEACH	32114	DAYTONA BEACH	32530	BAGDAD	32583	MILTON
32116	DAYTONA BEACH	32118	DAYTONA BEACH	32537	MILLIGAN	32536	CRESTVIEW
32120	DAYTONA BEACH	32114	DAYTONA BEACH	32538	PAXTON	32567	LAUREL HILL
32121	DAYTONA BEACH	32119	DAYTONA BEACH	32540	DESTIN	32541	DESTIN
32122	DAYTONA BEACH	32114	DAYTONA BEACH	32549	FORT WALTON BEACH	32548	FORT WALTON BEACH
32123	PORT ORANGE	32119	DAYTONA BEACH	32559	PENSACOLA	32526	PENSACOLA
32125	DAYTONA BEACH	32117	DAYTONA BEACH	32560	GONZALEZ	32533	CANTONMENT
32126	DAYTONA BEACH	32118	DAYTONA BEACH	32562	GULF BREEZE	32561	GULF BREEZE
32133	EASTLAKE WEIR	32179	OCKLAWAHA	32572	MILTON	32570	MILTON
32135	PALM COAST	32136	FLAGLER BEACH	32588	NICEVILLE	32578	NICEVILLE
32138	GRANDIN	32148	INTERLACHEN	32591	PENSACOLA	32501	PENSACOLA
32142	PALM COAST	32136	FLAGLER BEACH	32602	GAINESVILLE	32601	GAINESVILLE
32147	HOLLISTER	32148	INTERLACHEN	32604	GAINESVILLE	32603	GAINESVILLE
32149	EDGAR	32148	INTERLACHEN	32610	GAINESVILLE	32611	GAINESVILLE
32151	FLAGLER BEACH	32164	PALM COAST	32612	GAINESVILLE	32611	GAINESVILLE
32157	LAKE COMO	32181	POMONA PARK	32614	GAINESVILLE	32608	GAINESVILLE
32158	LADY LAKE	32159	LADY LAKE	32616	ALACHUA	32615	ALACHUA
32160	LAKE GENEVA	32666	MELROSE	32627	GAINESVILLE	32601	GAINESVILLE
32170	NEW SMYRNA BEACH	32169	NEW SMYRNA BEACH	32633	EVINSTON	32640	HAWTHORNE
32173	ORMOND BEACH	32174	ORMOND BEACH	32634	FAIRFIELD	32686	REDDICK
32175	ORMOND BEACH	32174	ORMOND BEACH	32635	GAINESVILLE	32605	GAINESVILLE
32178	PALATKA	32177	PALATKA	32639	GULF HAMMOCK	34449	INGLIS
32182	ORANGE SPRINGS	32134	FORT MC COY	32644	CHIEFLAND	32626	CHIEFLAND
32183	OCKLAWAHA	32179	OCKLAWAHA	32654	ISLAND GROVE	32640	HAWTHORNE
32185	PUTNAM HALL	32148	INTERLACHEN	32655	HIGH SPRINGS	32643	HIGH SPRINGS
32192	SPARR	32617	ANTHONY	32658	LA CROSSE	32615	ALACHUA
32193	WELAKA	32112	CRESCENT CITY	32662	LOCHLOOSA	32640	HAWTHORNE
32198	DAYTONA BEACH	32114	DAYTONA BEACH	32663	LOWELL	32686	REDDICK
32201	JACKSONVILLE	32202	JACKSONVILLE	32664	MC INTOSH	32667	MICANOPY
32203	JACKSONVILLE	32209	JACKSONVILLE	32681	ORANGE LAKE	32667	MICANOPY
32228	JACKSONVILLE	32227	JACKSONVILLE	32683	OTTER CREEK	34449	INGLIS
32229	JACKSONVILLE	32218	JACKSONVILLE	32692	SUWANNEE	32680	OLD TOWN
32231	JACKSONVILLE	32207	JACKSONVILLE	32697	WORTHINGTON SPRINGS	32054	LAKE BUTLER
32232	JACKSONVILLE	32209	JACKSONVILLE	32704	APOPKA	32703	APOPKA
32235	JACKSONVILLE	32206	JACKSONVILLE	32706	CASSADAGA	32744	LAKE HELEN
32236	JACKSONVILLE	32205	JACKSONVILLE	32710	CLARCONA	32818	ORLANDO
32237	JACKSONVILLE	32257	JACKSONVILLE	32715	ALTAMONTE SPRINGS	32714	ALTAMONTE SPRINGS
32238	JACKSONVILLE	32244	JACKSONVILLE	32716	ALTAMONTE SPRINGS	32714	ALTAMONTE SPRINGS
32239	JACKSONVILLE	32277	JACKSONVILLE	32718	CASSELBERRY	32708	WINTER SPRINGS
32240	JACKSONVILLE BEACH	32250	JACKSONVILLE BEACH	32719	WINTER SPRINGS	32708	WINTER SPRINGS
32241	JACKSONVILLE	32223	JACKSONVILLE	32721	DELAND	32720	DELAND
32245	JACKSONVILLE	32216	JACKSONVILLE	32722	GLENWOOD	32720	DELAND
32247	JACKSONVILLE	32207	JACKSONVILLE	32723	DELAND	32724	DELAND
32255	JACKSONVILLE	32207	JACKSONVILLE	32727	EUSTIS	32726	EUSTIS
32260	JACKSONVILLE	32259	JACKSONVILLE	32728	DELTONA	32725	DELTONA
32267	JACKSONVILLE	32233	ATLANTIC BEACH	32733	GOLDENROD	32792	WINTER PARK
32276	JACKSONVILLE	32209	JACKSONVILLE	32739	DELTONA	32738	DELTONA
32290	JACKSONVILLE	32202	JACKSONVILLE	32745	MID FLORIDA	32746	LAKE MARY

FLORIDA   **FLORIDA**

Point ZIP Code		Enclosing Residential ZIP Code		Point ZIP Code		Enclosing Residential ZIP Code	
ZIP	Post Office Name	ZIP	Post Office Name	ZIP	Post Office Name	ZIP	Post Office Name
32747	LAKE MONROE	32771	SANFORD	33097	POMPANO BEACH	33073	POMPANO BEACH
32752	LONGWOOD	32779	LONGWOOD	33101	MIAMI	33128	MIAMI
32753	DEBARY	32713	DEBARY	33110	MIAMI	33150	MIAMI
32756	MOUNT DORA	32757	MOUNT DORA	33111	MIAMI	33131	MIAMI
32762	OVIEDO	32765	OVIEDO	33114	MIAMI	33134	MIAMI
32768	PLYMOUTH	32712	APOPKA	33116	MIAMI	33176	MIAMI
32772	SANFORD	32771	SANFORD	33119	MIAMI BEACH	33139	MIAMI BEACH
32774	ORANGE CITY	32763	ORANGE CITY	33121	MIAMI	33131	MIAMI
32775	SCOTTSMOOR	32754	MIMS	33124	MIAMI	33181	MIAMI
32777	TANGERINE	32757	MOUNT DORA	33148	MIAMI	33131	MIAMI
32781	TITUSVILLE	32780	TITUSVILLE	33151	MIAMI	33127	MIAMI
32782	TITUSVILLE	32796	TITUSVILLE	33153	MIAMI	33138	MIAMI
32783	TITUSVILLE	32780	TITUSVILLE	33159	MIAMI	33139	MIAMI BEACH
32790	WINTER PARK	32789	WINTER PARK	33163	MIAMI	33180	MIAMI
32791	LONGWOOD	32779	LONGWOOD	33164	MIAMI	33162	MIAMI
32793	WINTER PARK	32792	WINTER PARK	33194	MIAMI	33184	MIAMI
32794	MAITLAND	32751	MAITLAND	33195	MIAMI	33125	MIAMI
32795	LAKE MARY	32746	LAKE MARY	33197	MIAMI	33157	MIAMI
32799	MID FLORIDA	32746	LAKE MARY	33231	MIAMI	33131	MIAMI
32802	ORLANDO	32801	ORLANDO	33233	MIAMI	33133	MIAMI
32814	ORLANDO	32803	ORLANDO	33234	MIAMI	33134	MIAMI
32816	ORLANDO	32826	ORLANDO	33238	MIAMI	33150	MIAMI
32834	ORLANDO	32828	ORLANDO	33239	MIAMI BEACH	33139	MIAMI BEACH
32853	ORLANDO	32803	ORLANDO	33242	MIAMI	33142	MIAMI
32854	ORLANDO	32804	ORLANDO	33243	MIAMI	33143	MIAMI
32855	ORLANDO	32805	ORLANDO	33245	MIAMI	33145	MIAMI
32856	ORLANDO	32806	ORLANDO	33255	MIAMI	33155	MIAMI
32857	ORLANDO	32807	ORLANDO	33256	MIAMI	33156	MIAMI
32858	ORLANDO	32808	ORLANDO	33257	MIAMI	33157	MIAMI
32859	ORLANDO	32809	ORLANDO	33261	MIAMI	33161	MIAMI
32860	ORLANDO	32810	ORLANDO	33265	MIAMI	33175	MIAMI
32861	ORLANDO	32811	ORLANDO	33266	MIAMI	33166	MIAMI
32862	ORLANDO	32827	ORLANDO	33269	MIAMI	33169	MIAMI
32867	ORLANDO	32817	ORLANDO	33280	MIAMI	33162	MIAMI
32868	ORLANDO	32818	ORLANDO	33283	MIAMI	33173	MIAMI
32869	ORLANDO	32809	ORLANDO	33296	MIAMI	33156	MIAMI
32872	ORLANDO	32822	ORLANDO	33302	FORT LAUDERDALE	33304	FORT LAUDERDALE
32877	ORLANDO	32837	ORLANDO	33303	FORT LAUDERDALE	33301	FORT LAUDERDALE
32878	ORLANDO	32828	ORLANDO	33307	FORT LAUDERDALE	33334	FORT LAUDERDALE
32885	ORLANDO	32827	ORLANDO	33310	FORT LAUDERDALE	33311	FORT LAUDERDALE
32886	ORLANDO	32801	ORLANDO	33318	FORT LAUDERDALE	33322	FORT LAUDERDALE
32887	ORLANDO	32821	ORLANDO	33320	FORT LAUDERDALE	33321	FORT LAUDERDALE
32890	ORLANDO	32809	ORLANDO	33329	FORT LAUDERDALE	33324	FORT LAUDERDALE
32891	ORLANDO	32803	ORLANDO	33335	FORT LAUDERDALE	33334	FORT LAUDERDALE
32893	ORLANDO	32803	ORLANDO	33336	FORT LAUDERDALE	33301	FORT LAUDERDALE
32896	ORLANDO	32801	ORLANDO	33337	FORT LAUDERDALE	33324	FORT LAUDERDALE
32897	ORLANDO	32801	ORLANDO	33338	FORT LAUDERDALE	33324	FORT LAUDERDALE
32898	ORLANDO	32801	ORLANDO	33339	FORT LAUDERDALE	33306	FORT LAUDERDALE
32902	MELBOURNE	32901	MELBOURNE	33340	FORT LAUDERDALE	33311	FORT LAUDERDALE
32906	PALM BAY	32905	PALM BAY	33345	FORT LAUDERDALE	33351	FORT LAUDERDALE
32910	PALM BAY	32907	PALM BAY	33346	FORT LAUDERDALE	33316	FORT LAUDERDALE
32911	PALM BAY	32905	PALM BAY	33348	FORT LAUDERDALE	33308	FORT LAUDERDALE
32912	MELBOURNE	32904	MELBOURNE	33349	FORT LAUDERDALE	33304	FORT LAUDERDALE
32919	MELBOURNE	32901	MELBOURNE	33355	FORT LAUDERDALE	33325	FORT LAUDERDALE
32923	COCOA	32922	COCOA	33359	FORT LAUDERDALE	33319	FORT LAUDERDALE
32924	COCOA	32922	COCOA	33388	FORT LAUDERDALE	33324	FORT LAUDERDALE
32932	COCOA BEACH	32931	COCOA BEACH	33394	FORT LAUDERDALE	33301	FORT LAUDERDALE
32936	MELBOURNE	32935	MELBOURNE	33402	WEST PALM BEACH	33480	PALM BEACH
32941	MELBOURNE	32901	MELBOURNE	33416	WEST PALM BEACH	33406	WEST PALM BEACH
32954	MERRITT ISLAND	32953	MERRITT ISLAND	33419	WEST PALM BEACH	33404	WEST PALM BEACH
32956	ROCKLEDGE	32955	ROCKLEDGE	33420	WEST PALM BEACH	33410	PALM BEACH GARDENS
32957	ROSELAND	32958	SEBASTIAN	33421	WEST PALM BEACH	33411	WEST PALM BEACH
32959	SHARPES	32927	COCOA	33422	WEST PALM BEACH	33417	WEST PALM BEACH
32961	VERO BEACH	32960	VERO BEACH	33424	BOYNTON BEACH	33426	BOYNTON BEACH
32964	VERO BEACH	32960	VERO BEACH	33425	BOYNTON BEACH	33426	BOYNTON BEACH
32965	VERO BEACH	32962	VERO BEACH	33427	BOCA RATON	33486	BOCA RATON
32969	VERO BEACH	32966	VERO BEACH	33429	BOCA RATON	33432	BOCA RATON
32970	WABASSO	32967	VERO BEACH	33439	BRYANT	33438	CANAL POINT
32971	WINTER BEACH	32967	VERO BEACH	33443	DEERFIELD BEACH	33441	DEERFIELD BEACH
32978	SEBASTIAN	32958	SEBASTIAN	33447	DELRAY BEACH	33444	DELRAY BEACH
33001	LONG KEY	33050	MARATHON	33448	DELRAY BEACH	33446	DELRAY BEACH
33002	HIALEAH	33014	HIALEAH	33454	LAKE WORTH	33467	LAKE WORTH
33008	HALLANDALE	33009	HALLANDALE	33459	LAKE HARBOR	33493	SOUTH BAY
33011	HIALEAH	33010	HIALEAH	33464	BOCA RATON	33460	LAKE WORTH
33017	HIALEAH	33015	HIALEAH	33465	LAKE WORTH	33462	LAKE WORTH
33022	HOLLYWOOD	33020	HOLLYWOOD	33466	LAKE WORTH	33461	LAKE WORTH
33041	KEY WEST	33040	KEY WEST	33468	JUPITER	33458	JUPITER
33044	SUGARLOAF SHORES	33042	SUMMERLAND KEY	33474	BOYNTON BEACH	33436	BOYNTON BEACH
33045	KEY WEST	33040	KEY WEST	33475	HOBE SOUND	33455	HOBE SOUND
33051	KEY COLONY BEACH	33050	MARATHON	33481	BOCA RATON	33431	BOCA RATON
33052	MARATHON SHORES	33050	MARATHON	33482	DELRAY BEACH	33445	DELRAY BEACH
33061	POMPANO BEACH	33060	POMPANO BEACH	33488	BOCA RATON	33433	BOCA RATON
33072	POMPANO BEACH	33062	POMPANO BEACH	33497	BOCA RATON	33428	BOCA RATON
33074	POMPANO BEACH	33064	POMPANO BEACH	33499	BOCA RATON	33487	BOCA RATON
33075	POMPANO BEACH	33067	POMPANO BEACH	33503	BALM	33598	WIMAUMA
33077	POMPANO BEACH	33071	POMPANO BEACH	33508	BRANDON	33511	BRANDON
33081	HOLLYWOOD	33021	HOLLYWOOD	33509	BRANDON	33511	BRANDON
33082	PEMBROKE PINES	33028	HOLLYWOOD	33521	COLEMAN	34785	WILDWOOD
33083	HOLLYWOOD	33023	HOLLYWOOD	33524	CRYSTAL SPRINGS	33540	ZEPHYRHILLS
33084	HOLLYWOOD	33024	HOLLYWOOD	33526	DADE CITY	33525	DADE CITY
33090	HOMESTEAD	33030	HOMESTEAD	33530	DURANT	33567	PLANT CITY
33092	HOMESTEAD	33032	HOMESTEAD	33537	LACOOCHEE	33523	DADE CITY
33093	POMPANO BEACH	33063	POMPANO BEACH	33539	ZEPHYRHILLS	33542	ZEPHYRHILLS

FLORIDA   **FLORIDA**

Point ZIP Code		Enclosing Residential ZIP Code	
ZIP	Post Office Name	ZIP	Post Office Name
33550	MANGO	33584	SEFFNER
33564	PLANT CITY	33566	PLANT CITY
33568	RIVERVIEW	33569	RIVERVIEW
33571	SUN CITY CENTER	33573	SUN CITY CENTER
33574	SAINT LEO	33576	SAN ANTONIO
33575	RUSKIN	33570	RUSKIN
33583	SEFFNER	33584	SEFFNER
33586	SUN CITY	33570	RUSKIN
33587	SYDNEY	33527	DOVER
33593	TRILBY	33523	DADE CITY
33595	VALRICO	33594	VALRICO
33601	TAMPA	33602	TAMPA
33608	TAMPA	33621	TAMPA
33622	TAMPA	33607	TAMPA
33623	TAMPA	33607	TAMPA
33630	TAMPA	33607	TAMPA
33631	TAMPA	33607	TAMPA
33633	TAMPA	33607	TAMPA
33650	TAMPA	33607	TAMPA
33655	TAMPA	33602	TAMPA
33660	TAMPA	33619	TAMPA
33661	TAMPA	33619	TAMPA
33662	TAMPA	33619	TAMPA
33663	TAMPA	33607	TAMPA
33664	TAMPA	33607	TAMPA
33672	TAMPA	33602	TAMPA
33673	TAMPA	33603	TAMPA
33674	TAMPA	33604	TAMPA
33675	TAMPA	33605	TAMPA
33677	TAMPA	33607	TAMPA
33679	TAMPA	33629	TAMPA
33680	TAMPA	33610	TAMPA
33681	TAMPA	33611	TAMPA
33682	TAMPA	33612	TAMPA
33684	TAMPA	33634	TAMPA
33685	TAMPA	33615	TAMPA
33686	TAMPA	33616	TAMPA
33687	TAMPA	33617	TAMPA
33688	TAMPA	33618	TAMPA
33689	TAMPA	33619	TAMPA
33690	TAMPA	33609	TAMPA
33694	TAMPA	33624	TAMPA
33697	TAMPA	33612	TAMPA
33728	SAINT PETERSBURG	33716	SAINT PETERSBURG
33729	SAINT PETERSBURG	33716	SAINT PETERSBURG
33730	SAINT PETERSBURG	33713	SAINT PETERSBURG
33731	SAINT PETERSBURG	33701	SAINT PETERSBURG
33732	SAINT PETERSBURG	33702	SAINT PETERSBURG
33733	SAINT PETERSBURG	33713	SAINT PETERSBURG
33734	SAINT PETERSBURG	33704	SAINT PETERSBURG
33736	SAINT PETERSBURG	33706	SAINT PETERSBURG
33737	SAINT PETERSBURG	33707	SAINT PETERSBURG
33738	SAINT PETERSBURG	33708	SAINT PETERSBURG
33740	SAINT PETERSBURG	33706	SAINT PETERSBURG
33741	SAINT PETERSBURG	33706	SAINT PETERSBURG
33742	SAINT PETERSBURG	33702	SAINT PETERSBURG
33743	SAINT PETERSBURG	33710	SAINT PETERSBURG
33744	BAY PINES	33708	SAINT PETERSBURG
33747	SAINT PETERSBURG	33711	SAINT PETERSBURG
33757	CLEARWATER	33755	CLEARWATER
33758	CLEARWATER	33765	CLEARWATER
33766	CLEARWATER	33763	CLEARWATER
33769	CLEARWATER	33765	CLEARWATER
33775	SEMINOLE	33772	SEMINOLE
33779	LARGO	33771	LARGO
33780	PINELLAS PARK	33781	PINELLAS PARK
33784	SAINT PETERSBURG	33713	SAINT PETERSBURG
33802	LAKELAND	33803	LAKELAND
33804	LAKELAND	33805	LAKELAND
33806	LAKELAND	33803	LAKELAND
33807	LAKELAND	33813	LAKELAND
33820	ALTURAS	33830	BARTOW
33826	AVON PARK	33825	AVON PARK
33831	BARTOW	33830	BARTOW
33835	BRADLEY	33860	MULBERRY
33836	DAVENPORT	33837	DAVENPORT
33840	EATON PARK	33803	LAKELAND
33845	HAINES CITY	33844	HAINES CITY
33846	HIGHLAND CITY	33813	LAKELAND
33847	HOMELAND	33830	BARTOW
33848	INTERCESSION CITY	34758	KISSIMMEE
33851	LAKE HAMILTON	33844	HAINES CITY
33854	FEDHAVEN	33853	LAKE WALES
33855	INDIAN LAKE ESTATES	33853	LAKE WALES
33856	NALCREST	33853	LAKE WALES
33858	LOUGHMAN	33837	DAVENPORT
33862	LAKE PLACID	33852	LAKE PLACID
33863	NICHOLS	33860	MULBERRY
33867	RIVER RANCH	33853	LAKE WALES
33871	SEBRING	33870	SEBRING
33877	WAVERLY	33859	LAKE WALES
33882	WINTER HAVEN	33880	WINTER HAVEN
33883	WINTER HAVEN	33880	WINTER HAVEN
33885	WINTER HAVEN	33881	WINTER HAVEN
33888	WINTER HAVEN	33884	WINTER HAVEN
33902	FORT MYERS	33901	FORT MYERS
33906	FORT MYERS	33907	FORT MYERS
33910	CAPE CORAL	33990	CAPE CORAL
33911	FORT MYERS	33901	FORT MYERS
33915	CAPE CORAL	33990	CAPE CORAL
33918	NORTH FORT MYERS	33903	NORTH FORT MYERS
33930	FELDA	33935	LABELLE
33932	FORT MYERS BEACH	33931	FORT MYERS BEACH
33938	MURDOCK	33948	PORT CHARLOTTE
33944	PALMDALE	33471	MOORE HAVEN
33945	PINELAND	33922	BOKEELIA
33949	PORT CHARLOTTE	33950	PUNTA GORDA
33951	PUNTA GORDA	33950	PUNTA GORDA
33965	FORT MYERS	33912	FORT MYERS
33970	LEHIGH ACRES	33936	LEHIGH ACRES
33975	LABELLE	33935	LABELLE
33994	FORT MYERS	33905	FORT MYERS
34002	APO	00000	NO ENCLOSING ZIP
34020	APO	00000	NO ENCLOSING ZIP
34021	APO	00000	NO ENCLOSING ZIP
34022	APO	00000	NO ENCLOSING ZIP
34023	APO	00000	NO ENCLOSING ZIP
34024	APO	00000	NO ENCLOSING ZIP
34025	APO	00000	NO ENCLOSING ZIP
34030	APO	00000	NO ENCLOSING ZIP
34031	APO	00000	NO ENCLOSING ZIP
34032	APO	00000	NO ENCLOSING ZIP
34033	APO	00000	NO ENCLOSING ZIP
34034	APO	00000	NO ENCLOSING ZIP
34035	APO	00000	NO ENCLOSING ZIP
34036	APO	00000	NO ENCLOSING ZIP
34037	APO	00000	NO ENCLOSING ZIP
34038	APO	00000	NO ENCLOSING ZIP
34039	APO	00000	NO ENCLOSING ZIP
34040	APO	00000	NO ENCLOSING ZIP
34041	APO	00000	NO ENCLOSING ZIP
34042	APO	00000	NO ENCLOSING ZIP
34043	APO	00000	NO ENCLOSING ZIP
34050	FPO	00000	NO ENCLOSING ZIP
34051	FPO	00000	NO ENCLOSING ZIP
34053	FPO	00000	NO ENCLOSING ZIP
34054	FPO	00000	NO ENCLOSING ZIP
34055	FPO	00000	NO ENCLOSING ZIP
34058	FPO	00000	NO ENCLOSING ZIP
34060	FPO	00000	NO ENCLOSING ZIP
34071	FPO	00000	NO ENCLOSING ZIP
34076	APO	00000	NO ENCLOSING ZIP
34077	APO	00000	NO ENCLOSING ZIP
34078	APO	00000	NO ENCLOSING ZIP
34079	FPO	00000	NO ENCLOSING ZIP
34086	FPO	00000	NO ENCLOSING ZIP
34090	FPO	00000	NO ENCLOSING ZIP
34091	FPO	00000	NO ENCLOSING ZIP
34092	FPO	00000	NO ENCLOSING ZIP
34093	FPO	00000	NO ENCLOSING ZIP
34095	FPO	00000	NO ENCLOSING ZIP
34098	FPO	00000	NO ENCLOSING ZIP
34099	FPO	00000	NO ENCLOSING ZIP
34101	NAPLES	34102	NAPLES
34106	NAPLES	34102	NAPLES
34107	VANDERBILT BEACH	34102	NAPLES
34133	BONITA SPRINGS	34135	BONITA SPRINGS
34136	BONITA SPRINGS	34135	BONITA SPRINGS
34137	COPELAND	34114	NAPLES
34138	CHOKOLOSKEE	34141	OCHOPEE
34139	EVERGLADES CITY	34141	OCHOPEE
34140	GOODLAND	34114	NAPLES
34143	IMMOKALEE	34142	IMMOKALEE
34146	MARCO ISLAND	34145	MARCO ISLAND
34204	BRADENTON	34203	BRADENTON
34206	BRADENTON	34205	BRADENTON
34216	ANNA MARIA	34217	BRADENTON BEACH
34218	HOLMES BEACH	34217	BRADENTON BEACH
34220	PALMETTO	34221	PALMETTO
34230	SARASOTA	34236	SARASOTA
34250	TERRA CEIA	34221	PALMETTO
34260	SARASOTA	34243	SARASOTA
34264	ONECO	34203	BRADENTON
34265	ARCADIA	34266	ARCADIA
34267	FORT OGDEN	34266	ARCADIA
34268	NOCATEE	34266	ARCADIA
34270	TALLEVAST	34243	SARASOTA
34272	LAUREL	34275	NOKOMIS
34274	NOKOMIS	34275	NOKOMIS
34276	SARASOTA	34236	SARASOTA
34277	SARASOTA	34231	SARASOTA
34278	SARASOTA	34234	SARASOTA
34280	BRADENTON	34209	BRADENTON
34281	BRADENTON	34207	BRADENTON
34282	BRADENTON	34207	BRADENTON
34284	VENICE	34285	VENICE

FLORIDA   **GEORGIA**

Point ZIP Code	Post Office Name	Enclosing Residential ZIP Code	Post Office Name	Point ZIP Code	Post Office Name	Enclosing Residential ZIP Code	Post Office Name
34289	NORTH PORT	34287	NORTH PORT	30142	HOLLY SPRINGS	30115	CANTON
34295	ENGLEWOOD	34223	ENGLEWOOD	30146	LEBANON	30115	CANTON
34421	BELLEVIEW	34420	BELLEVIEW	30150	MOUNT ZION	30117	CARROLLTON
34423	CRYSTAL RIVER	34429	CRYSTAL RIVER	30151	NELSON	30107	BALL GROUND
34430	DUNNELLON	34432	DUNNELLON	30154	DOUGLASVILLE	30134	DOUGLASVILLE
34445	HOLDER	34442	HERNANDO	30156	KENNESAW	30144	KENNESAW
34447	HOMOSASSA SPRINGS	34448	HOMOSASSA	30160	KENNESAW	30144	KENNESAW
34451	INVERNESS	34453	INVERNESS	30162	ROME	30161	ROME
34460	LECANTO	34461	LECANTO	30163	ROME	30161	ROME
34464	BEVERLY HILLS	34465	BEVERLY HILLS	30164	ROME	30165	ROME
34477	OCALA	34474	OCALA	30169	CANTON	30114	CANTON
34478	OCALA	34474	OCALA	30172	SHANNON	30161	ROME
34483	OCALA	34472	OCALA	30212	EXPERIMENT	30223	GRIFFIN
34487	HOMOSASSA	34448	HOMOSASSA	30219	GLENN	30217	FRANKLIN
34489	SILVER SPRINGS	34488	SILVER SPRINGS	30229	HARALSON	30276	SENOIA
34492	SUMMERFIELD	34491	SUMMERFIELD	30232	INMAN	30214	FAYETTEVILLE
34603	BROOKSVILLE	34601	BROOKSVILLE	30237	JONESBORO	30236	JONESBORO
34605	BROOKSVILLE	34601	BROOKSVILLE	30250	LOVEJOY	30228	HAMPTON
34611	SPRING HILL	34606	SPRING HILL	30261	LAGRANGE	30241	LAGRANGE
34636	ISTACHATTA	34601	BROOKSVILLE	30264	NEWNAN	30263	NEWNAN
34656	NEW PORT RICHEY	34653	NEW PORT RICHEY	30266	ORCHARD HILL	30224	GRIFFIN
34660	OZONA	34683	PALM HARBOR	30270	PEACHTREE CITY	30269	PEACHTREE CITY
34661	NOBLETON	34601	BROOKSVILLE	30271	NEWNAN	30263	NEWNAN
34673	PORT RICHEY	34668	PORT RICHEY	30272	RED OAK	30349	ATLANTA
34674	HUDSON	34667	HUDSON	30275	SARGENT	30263	NEWNAN
34679	ARIPEKA	34667	HUDSON	30284	SUNNY SIDE	30223	GRIFFIN
34680	ELFERS	34652	NEW PORT RICHEY	30287	MORROW	30260	MORROW
34681	CRYSTAL BEACH	34683	PALM HARBOR	30289	TURIN	30276	SENOIA
34682	PALM HARBOR	34683	PALM HARBOR	30298	FOREST PARK	30297	FOREST PARK
34697	DUNEDIN	34698	DUNEDIN	30301	ATLANTA	30354	ATLANTA
34712	CLERMONT	34711	CLERMONT	30302	ATLANTA	30303	ATLANTA
34713	CLERMONT	34711	CLERMONT	30304	ATLANTA	30354	ATLANTA
34729	FERNDALE	34711	CLERMONT	30320	ATLANTA	30337	ATLANTA
34740	KILLARNEY	34787	WINTER GARDEN	30321	ATLANTA	30354	ATLANTA
34742	KISSIMMEE	34741	KISSIMMEE	30325	ATLANTA	30303	ATLANTA
34745	KISSIMMEE	34741	KISSIMMEE	30332	ATLANTA	30313	ATLANTA
34749	LEESBURG	34748	LEESBURG	30333	ATLANTA	30329	ATLANTA
34755	MINNEOLA	34711	CLERMONT	30343	ATLANTA	30303	ATLANTA
34760	OAKLAND	34787	WINTER GARDEN	30347	ATLANTA	30329	ATLANTA
34770	SAINT CLOUD	34769	SAINT CLOUD	30348	ATLANTA	30354	ATLANTA
34777	WINTER GARDEN	34787	WINTER GARDEN	30353	ATLANTA	30303	ATLANTA
34778	WINTER GARDEN	34787	WINTER GARDEN	30355	ATLANTA	30305	ATLANTA
34789	LEESBURG	34788	LEESBURG	30356	ATLANTA	30338	ATLANTA
34948	FORT PIERCE	34950	FORT PIERCE	30357	ATLANTA	30309	ATLANTA
34954	FORT PIERCE	34981	FORT PIERCE	30358	ATLANTA	30328	ATLANTA
34958	JENSEN BEACH	34957	JENSEN BEACH	30359	ATLANTA	30329	ATLANTA
34973	OKEECHOBEE	34972	OKEECHOBEE	30361	ATLANTA	30309	ATLANTA
34979	FORT PIERCE	34950	FORT PIERCE	30362	ATLANTA	30340	ATLANTA
34985	PORT SAINT LUCIE	34952	PORT SAINT LUCIE	30363	ATLANTA	30354	ATLANTA
34991	PALM CITY	34990	PALM CITY	30364	ATLANTA	30344	ATLANTA
34992	PORT SALERNO	34997	STUART	30366	ATLANTA	30341	ATLANTA
34995	STUART	34994	STUART	30368	ATLANTA	30354	ATLANTA
30003	NORCROSS	30013	CONYERS	30369	ATLANTA	30318	ATLANTA
30006	MARIETTA	30067	MARIETTA	30370	ATLANTA	30303	ATLANTA
30007	MARIETTA	30068	MARIETTA	30371	ATLANTA	30303	ATLANTA
30009	ALPHARETTA	30004	ALPHARETTA	30374	ATLANTA	30303	ATLANTA
30010	NORCROSS	30092	NORCROSS	30375	ATLANTA	30308	ATLANTA
30015	COVINGTON	30014	COVINGTON	30376	ATLANTA	30324	ATLANTA
30018	JERSEY	30014	COVINGTON	30377	ATLANTA	30318	ATLANTA
30023	ALPHARETTA	30004	ALPHARETTA	30378	ATLANTA	30331	ATLANTA
30026	NORTH METRO	30044	LAWRENCEVILLE	30379	ATLANTA	30308	ATLANTA
30028	CUMMING	30040	CUMMING	30380	ATLANTA	30354	ATLANTA
30029	NORTH METRO	30096	DULUTH	30384	ATLANTA	30339	ATLANTA
30031	DECATUR	30030	DECATUR	30385	ATLANTA	30344	ATLANTA
30036	DECATUR	30034	DECATUR	30386	ATLANTA	30354	ATLANTA
30037	DECATUR	30034	DECATUR	30387	ATLANTA	30308	ATLANTA
30042	LAWRENCEVILLE	30044	LAWRENCEVILLE	30388	ATLANTA	30354	ATLANTA
30046	LAWRENCEVILLE	30045	LAWRENCEVILLE	30389	ATLANTA	30354	ATLANTA
30048	LILBURN	30047	LILBURN	30390	ATLANTA	30308	ATLANTA
30049	LAWRENCEVILLE	30043	LAWRENCEVILLE	30392	ATLANTA	30303	ATLANTA
30061	MARIETTA	30060	MARIETTA	30394	ATLANTA	30354	ATLANTA
30065	MARIETTA	30062	MARIETTA	30396	ATLANTA	30354	ATLANTA
30070	PORTERDALE	30014	COVINGTON	30398	ATLANTA	30354	ATLANTA
30072	PINE LAKE	30083	STONE MOUNTAIN	30399	ATLANTA	30308	ATLANTA
30074	REDAN	30058	LITHONIA	30412	ALSTON	30473	UVALDA
30077	ROSWELL	30075	ROSWELL	30414	BELLVILLE	30417	CLAXTON
30081	SMYRNA	30080	SMYRNA	30423	DAISY	30417	CLAXTON
30085	TUCKER	30084	TUCKER	30424	DOVER	30467	SYLVANIA
30086	STONE MOUNTAIN	30083	STONE MOUNTAIN	30429	HAGAN	30417	CLAXTON
30090	MARIETTA	30060	MARIETTA	30447	NORRISTOWN	31002	ADRIAN
30091	NORCROSS	30071	NORCROSS	30448	NUNEZ	30401	SWAINSBORO
30095	DULUTH	30096	DULUTH	30449	OLIVER	30446	NEWINGTON
30098	DULUTH	30097	DULUTH	30451	PULASKI	30439	METTER
30099	DULUTH	30096	DULUTH	30459	STATESBORO	30458	STATESBORO
30109	BOWDON JUNCTION	30117	CARROLLTON	30460	STATESBORO	30458	STATESBORO
30111	CLARKDALE	30127	POWDER SPRINGS	30464	STILLMORE	30471	TWIN CITY
30112	CARROLLTON	30117	CARROLLTON	30475	VIDALIA	30474	VIDALIA
30119	CARROLLTON	30117	CARROLLTON	30499	REIDSVILLE	30453	REIDSVILLE
30123	CASSVILLE	30120	CARTERSVILLE	30502	CHESTNUT MOUNTAIN	30542	FLOWERY BRANCH
30129	COOSA	30165	ROME	30503	GAINESVILLE	30501	GAINESVILLE
30133	DOUGLASVILLE	30134	DOUGLASVILLE	30514	BLAIRSVILLE	30512	BLAIRSVILLE
30138	ESOM HILL	30125	CEDARTOWN	30515	BUFORD	30518	BUFORD
30140	FELTON	30113	BUCHANAN	30544	DEMOREST	30535	DEMOREST

Point ZIP Code		Enclosing Residential ZIP Code		Point ZIP Code		Enclosing Residential ZIP Code	
ZIP	Post Office Name	ZIP	Post Office Name	ZIP	Post Office Name	ZIP	Post Office Name
30562	MOUNTAIN CITY	30525	CLAYTON	31416	SAVANNAH	31406	SAVANNAH
30573	TALLULAH FALLS	30552	LAKEMONT	31418	SAVANNAH	31408	SAVANNAH
30580	TURNERVILLE	30523	CLARKESVILLE	31420	SAVANNAH	31419	SAVANNAH
30581	WILEY	30576	TIGER	31421	SAVANNAH	31401	SAVANNAH
30596	ALTO	30510	ALTO	31422	SAVANNAH	31408	SAVANNAH
30598	TOCCOA FALLS	30577	TOCCOA	31502	WAYCROSS	31501	WAYCROSS
30599	COMMERCE	30529	COMMERCE	31515	BAXLEY	31513	BAXLEY
30603	ATHENS	30605	ATHENS	31521	BRUNSWICK	31520	BRUNSWICK
30604	ATHENS	30606	ATHENS	31524	BRUNSWICK	31525	BRUNSWICK
30608	ATHENS	30601	ATHENS	31534	DOUGLAS	31533	DOUGLAS
30612	ATHENS	30605	ATHENS	31556	OFFERMAN	31557	PATTERSON
30623	BOSTWICK	30621	BISHOP	31564	WARESBORO	31503	WAYCROSS
30638	FARMINGTON	30677	WATKINSVILLE	31598	JESUP	31546	JESUP
30639	FRANKLIN SPRINGS	30662	ROYSTON	31599	JESUP	31546	JESUP
30645	HIGH SHOALS	30621	BISHOP	31603	VALDOSTA	31601	VALDOSTA
30647	ILA	30633	DANIELSVILLE	31604	VALDOSTA	31601	VALDOSTA
30664	SHARON	30631	CRAWFORDVILLE	31623	ARGYLE	31634	HOMERVILLE
30665	SILOAM	30678	WHITE PLAINS	31627	CECIL	31620	ADEL
30671	MAXEYS	30667	STEPHENS	31702	ALBANY	31701	ALBANY
30703	CALHOUN	30701	CALHOUN	31703	ALBANY	31701	ALBANY
30719	DALTON	30721	DALTON	31706	ALBANY	31701	ALBANY
30722	DALTON	30720	DALTON	31708	ALBANY	31705	ALBANY
30724	ETON	30705	CHATSWORTH	31710	AMERICUS	31719	AMERICUS
30726	GRAYSVILLE	30736	RINGGOLD	31720	BARWICK	31778	PAVO
30732	OAKMAN	30734	RANGER	31722	BERLIN	31788	MOULTRIE
30756	VARNELL	30710	COHUTTA	31727	BROOKFIELD	31794	TIFTON
30806	BONEVILLE	30808	DEARING	31739	COTTON	31779	PELHAM
30807	CAMAK	30828	WARRENTON	31747	ELLENTON	31771	NORMAN PARK
30811	GOUGH	30816	KEYSVILLE	31753	FUNSTON	31768	MOULTRIE
30812	GRACEWOOD	30906	AUGUSTA	31758	THOMASVILLE	31792	THOMASVILLE
30819	MESENA	30824	THOMSON	31769	MYSTIC	31774	OCILLA
30903	AUGUSTA	30901	AUGUSTA	31776	MOULTRIE	31768	MOULTRIE
30911	AUGUSTA	30901	AUGUSTA	31782	PUTNEY	31705	ALBANY
30914	AUGUSTA	30904	AUGUSTA	31799	THOMASVILLE	31792	THOMASVILLE
30916	AUGUSTA	30906	AUGUSTA	31810	GENEVA	31801	BOX SPRINGS
30917	AUGUSTA	30907	AUGUSTA	31814	LOUVALE	31821	OMAHA
30919	AUGUSTA	30909	AUGUSTA	31902	COLUMBUS	31907	COLUMBUS
30999	AUGUSTA	30909	AUGUSTA	31908	COLUMBUS	31907	COLUMBUS
31004	BOLINGBROKE	31210	MACON	31914	COLUMBUS	31904	COLUMBUS
31010	CORDELE	31015	CORDELE	31917	COLUMBUS	31907	COLUMBUS
31013	CLINCHFIELD	31069	PERRY	31995	FORT BENNING	31905	FORT BENNING
31026	EATONTON	31024	EATONTON	31997	COLUMBUS	31907	COLUMBUS
31034	HARDWICK	31061	MILLEDGEVILLE	31999	COLUMBUS	31906	COLUMBUS
31039	HOWARD	31006	BUTLER	39818	BAINBRIDGE	39819	BAINBRIDGE
31040	DUBLIN	31021	DUBLIN	39829	CALVARY	39828	CAIRO
31051	LILLY	31092	VIENNA	39832	CEDAR SPRINGS	39861	JAKIN
31059	MILLEDGEVILLE	31061	MILLEDGEVILLE	39852	FOWLSTOWN	39819	BAINBRIDGE
31062	MILLEDGEVILLE	31061	MILLEDGEVILLE	39885	SASSER	39824	BLUFFTON
31067	OCONEE	31089	TENNILLE	39901	ATLANTA	30341	ATLANTA
31083	SCOTLAND	31055	MC RAE	96703	ANAHOLA	96746	KAPAA
31084	SEVILLE	31072	PITTS	96709	KAPOLEI	96707	KAPOLEI
31086	SMARR	31029	FORSYTH	96714	HANALEI	96722	PRINCEVILLE
31095	WARNER ROBINS	31098	WARNER ROBINS	96715	HANAMAULU	96766	LIHUE
31099	WARNER ROBINS	31098	WARNER ROBINS	96721	HILO	96720	HILO
31106	ATLANTA	30306	ATLANTA	96733	KAHULUI	96732	KAHULUI
31107	ATLANTA	30306	ATLANTA	96737	OCEAN VIEW	96704	CAPTAIN COOK
31119	ATLANTA	30319	ATLANTA	96739	KEAUHOU	96740	KAILUA KONA
31126	ATLANTA	30096	DULUTH	96745	KAILUA KONA	96740	KAILUA KONA
31131	ATLANTA	30331	ATLANTA	96751	KEALIA	96746	KAPAA
31132	ATLANTA	30331	ATLANTA	96759	KUNIA	96797	WAIPAHU
31139	ATLANTA	30339	ATLANTA	96765	LAWAI	96756	KOLOA
31141	ATLANTA	30341	ATLANTA	96767	LAHAINA	96761	LAHAINA
31145	ATLANTA	30345	ATLANTA	96784	PUUNENE	96732	KAHULUI
31146	ATLANTA	30346	ATLANTA	96788	PUKALANI	96768	MAKAWAO
31150	ATLANTA	30350	ATLANTA	96801	HONOLULU	96813	HONOLULU
31156	ATLANTA	30350	ATLANTA	96802	HONOLULU	96813	HONOLULU
31191	ATLANTA	30318	ATLANTA	96803	HONOLULU	96813	HONOLULU
31192	ATLANTA	30349	ATLANTA	96804	HONOLULU	96813	HONOLULU
31193	ATLANTA	30303	ATLANTA	96805	HONOLULU	96813	HONOLULU
31195	ATLANTA	30318	ATLANTA	96806	HONOLULU	96813	HONOLULU
31196	ATLANTA	30318	ATLANTA	96807	HONOLULU	96813	HONOLULU
31197	ATLANTA	30318	ATLANTA	96808	HONOLULU	96813	HONOLULU
31198	ATLANTA	30318	ATLANTA	96809	HONOLULU	96813	HONOLULU
31199	ATLANTA	30318	ATLANTA	96810	HONOLULU	96813	HONOLULU
31202	MACON	31201	MACON	96811	HONOLULU	96813	HONOLULU
31203	MACON	31204	MACON	96812	HONOLULU	96813	HONOLULU
31205	MACON	31206	MACON	96820	HONOLULU	96819	HONOLULU
31208	MACON	31201	MACON	96823	HONOLULU	96822	HONOLULU
31209	MACON	31204	MACON	96824	HONOLULU	96821	HONOLULU
31212	MACON	31206	MACON	96827	HONOLULU	96817	HONOLULU
31213	MACON	31201	MACON	96828	HONOLULU	96814	HONOLULU
31221	MACON	31201	MACON	96830	HONOLULU	96815	HONOLULU
31295	MACON	31217	MACON	96835	HONOLULU	96815	HONOLULU
31296	MACON	31217	MACON	96836	HONOLULU	96815	HONOLULU
31297	MACON	31210	MACON	96837	HONOLULU	96817	HONOLULU
31307	EDEN	31302	BLOOMINGDALE	96838	HONOLULU	96819	HONOLULU
31310	HINESVILLE	31313	HINESVILLE	96839	HONOLULU	96822	HONOLULU
31318	MELDRIM	31302	BLOOMINGDALE	96840	HONOLULU	96813	HONOLULU
31333	WALTHOURVILLE	31301	ALLENHURST	96841	HONOLULU	96813	HONOLULU
31402	SAVANNAH	31401	SAVANNAH	96842	HONOLULU	96813	HONOLULU
31403	SAVANNAH	31405	SAVANNAH	96843	HONOLULU	96813	HONOLULU
31412	SAVANNAH	31401	SAVANNAH	96846	HONOLULU	96817	HONOLULU
31414	SAVANNAH	31404	SAVANNAH	96847	HONOLULU	96814	HONOLULU

HAWAII   **ILLINOIS**

Point ZIP Code		Enclosing Residential ZIP Code		Point ZIP Code		Enclosing Residential ZIP Code	
ZIP	Post Office Name	ZIP	Post Office Name	ZIP	Post Office Name	ZIP	Post Office Name
96848	HONOLULU	96822	HONOLULU	60055	PALATINE	60067	PALATINE
96849	HONOLULU	96819	HONOLULU	60065	NORTHBROOK	60062	NORTHBROOK
96850	HONOLULU	96813	HONOLULU	60075	RUSSELL	60099	ZION
96854	WHEELER ARMY AIRFIEL	96786	WAHIAWA	60078	PALATINE	60067	PALATINE
96859	TAMC	96819	HONOLULU	60079	WAUKEGAN	60085	WAUKEGAN
96898	WAKE ISLAND	96819	HONOLULU	60086	NORTH CHICAGO	60088	GREAT LAKES
83205	POCATELLO	83201	POCATELLO	60092	LIBERTYVILLE	60048	LIBERTYVILLE
83206	POCATELLO	83201	POCATELLO	60094	PALATINE	60067	PALATINE
83215	ATOMIC CITY	83221	BLACKFOOT	60095	PALATINE	60074	PALATINE
83218	BASALT	83274	SHELLEY	60109	BURLINGTON	60140	HAMPSHIRE
83223	BLOOMINGTON	83261	PARIS	60113	CRESTON	61068	ROCHELLE
83229	COBALT	83469	SHOUP	60116	CAROL STREAM	60188	CAROL STREAM
83233	DINGLE	83254	MONTPELIER	60117	BLOOMINGDALE	60108	BLOOMINGDALE
83239	GEORGETOWN	83254	MONTPELIER	60121	ELGIN	60120	ELGIN
83256	MORELAND	83221	BLACKFOOT	60125	CAROL STREAM	60148	LOMBARD
83277	SPRINGFIELD	83262	PINGREE	60128	CAROL STREAM	60188	CAROL STREAM
83281	SWANLAKE	83234	DOWNEY	60132	CAROL STREAM	60188	CAROL STREAM
83303	TWIN FALLS	83301	TWIN FALLS	60138	GLEN ELLYN	60137	GLEN ELLYN
83311	ALBION	83342	MALTA	60144	KANEVILLE	60119	ELBURN
83312	ALMO	83342	MALTA	60147	LAFOX	60134	GENEVA
83337	HILL CITY	83322	CORRAL	60159	SCHAUMBURG	60194	SCHAUMBURG
83353	SUN VALLEY	83340	KETCHUM	60161	MELROSE PARK	60160	MELROSE PARK
83354	SUN VALLEY	83340	KETCHUM	60168	SCHAUMBURG	60194	SCHAUMBURG
83403	IDAHO FALLS	83401	IDAHO FALLS	60170	PLATO CENTER	60120	ELGIN
83405	IDAHO FALLS	83402	IDAHO FALLS	60179	HOFFMAN ESTATES	60192	SCHAUMBURG
83415	IDAHO FALLS	83402	IDAHO FALLS	60183	WASCO	60175	SAINT CHARLES
83421	CHESTER	83420	ASHTON	60186	WEST CHICAGO	60185	WEST CHICAGO
83433	MACKS INN	83429	ISLAND PARK	60189	WHEATON	60187	WHEATON
83438	PARKER	83445	SAINT ANTHONY	60196	SCHAUMBURG	60173	SCHAUMBURG
83441	REXBURG	83440	REXBURG	60197	CAROL STREAM	60188	CAROL STREAM
83447	SQUIRREL	83420	ASHTON	60199	CAROL STREAM	60188	CAROL STREAM
83454	UCON	83401	IDAHO FALLS	60204	EVANSTON	60201	EVANSTON
83465	LEMHI	83464	LEADORE	60209	EVANSTON	60201	EVANSTON
83468	TENDOY	83464	LEADORE	60303	OAK PARK	60301	OAK PARK
83531	FENN	83530	GRANGEVILLE	60398	FRANKLIN PARK	60131	FRANKLIN PARK
83552	STITES	83539	KOOSKIA	60399	BENSENVILLE	60106	BENSENVILLE
83606	CALDWELL	83605	CALDWELL	60412	CHICAGO HEIGHTS	60411	CHICAGO HEIGHTS
83630	HUSTON	83607	CALDWELL	60434	JOLIET	60436	JOLIET
83635	LAKE FORK	83638	MCCALL	60454	OAK LAWN	60455	BRIDGEVIEW
83652	NAMPA	83651	NAMPA	60474	SOUTH WILMINGTON	60424	GARDNER
83653	NAMPA	83651	NAMPA	60499	BEDFORD PARK	60638	CHICAGO
83656	NOTUS	83607	CALDWELL	60507	AURORA	60505	AURORA
83666	PLACERVILLE	83629	HORSESHOE BEND	60519	EOLA	60504	AURORA
83671	WARREN	83549	RIGGINS	60522	HINSDALE	60523	OAK BROOK
83680	MERIDIAN	83642	MERIDIAN	60536	MILLBROOK	60541	NEWARK
83701	BOISE	83702	BOISE	60537	MILLINGTON	60541	NEWARK
83707	BOISE	83702	BOISE	60557	WEDRON	61350	OTTAWA
83708	BOISE	83702	BOISE	60566	NAPERVILLE	60540	NAPERVILLE
83711	BOISE	83704	BOISE	60567	NAPERVILLE	60540	NAPERVILLE
83715	BOISE	83705	BOISE	60568	AURORA	60505	AURORA
83717	BOISE	83716	BOISE	60570	HINSDALE	60154	WESTCHESTER
83719	BOISE	83702	BOISE	60572	AURORA	60504	AURORA
83720	BOISE	83702	BOISE	60597	FOX VALLEY	60504	AURORA
83721	BOISE	83702	BOISE	60598	AURORA	60505	AURORA
83722	BOISE	83702	BOISE	60599	FOX VALLEY	60504	AURORA
83723	BOISE	83702	BOISE	60663	CHICAGO	60606	CHICAGO
83724	BOISE	83702	BOISE	60664	CHICAGO	60601	CHICAGO
83726	BOISE	83706	BOISE	60665	CHICAGO	60606	CHICAGO
83727	BOISE	83702	BOISE	60667	CHICAGO	60608	CHICAGO
83728	BOISE	83702	BOISE	60668	CHICAGO	60616	CHICAGO
83729	BOISE	83712	BOISE	60670	CHICAGO	60603	CHICAGO
83730	BOISE	83702	BOISE	60671	CHICAGO	60610	CHICAGO
83731	BOISE	83705	BOISE	60673	CHICAGO	60606	CHICAGO
83732	BOISE	83702	BOISE	60674	CHICAGO	60603	CHICAGO
83733	BOISE	83702	BOISE	60675	CHICAGO	60603	CHICAGO
83735	BOISE	83702	BOISE	60677	CHICAGO	60606	CHICAGO
83744	BOISE	83704	BOISE	60678	CHICAGO	60602	CHICAGO
83756	BOISE	83702	BOISE	60679	CHICAGO	60606	CHICAGO
83799	BOISE	83709	BOISE	60680	CHICAGO	60606	CHICAGO
83806	BOVILL	83823	DEARY	60681	CHICAGO	60601	CHICAGO
83816	COEUR D ALENE	83815	COEUR D ALENE	60682	CHICAGO	60607	CHICAGO
83825	DOVER	83864	SANDPOINT	60683	CHICAGO	60609	CHICAGO
83826	EASTPORT	83845	MOYIE SPRINGS	60684	CHICAGO	60606	CHICAGO
83840	KOOTENAI	83864	SANDPOINT	60685	CHICAGO	60604	CHICAGO
83841	LACLEDE	83864	SANDPOINT	60686	CHICAGO	60623	CHICAGO
83844	MOSCOW	83843	MOSCOW	60687	CHICAGO	60603	CHICAGO
83849	OSBURN	83873	WALLACE	60689	CHICAGO	60607	CHICAGO
83852	PONDERAY	83864	SANDPOINT	60690	CHICAGO	60604	CHICAGO
83865	COLBURN	83864	SANDPOINT	60691	CHICAGO	60604	CHICAGO
83866	SANTA	83861	SAINT MARIES	60693	CHICAGO	60604	CHICAGO
83867	SILVERTON	83873	WALLACE	60694	CHICAGO	60603	CHICAGO
83874	MURRAY	83837	KELLOGG	60695	CHICAGO	60607	CHICAGO
83877	POST FALLS	83854	POST FALLS	60696	CHICAGO	60604	CHICAGO
83888	SANDPOINT	83864	SANDPOINT	60697	CHICAGO	60604	CHICAGO
60001	ALDEN	60033	HARVARD	60902	KANKAKEE	60901	KANKAKEE
60006	ARLINGTON HEIGHTS	60005	ARLINGTON HEIGHTS	60910	AROMA PARK	60964	SAINT ANNE
60009	ELK GROVE VILLAGE	60007	ELK GROVE VILLAGE	60920	CAMPUS	60420	DWIGHT
60011	BARRINGTON	60010	BARRINGTON	60926	CLAYTONVILLE	60924	CISSNA PARK
60017	DES PLAINES	60018	DES PLAINES	60932	EAST LYNN	60960	RANKIN
60019	DES PLAINES	60018	DES PLAINES	60933	ELLIOTT	60936	GIBSON CITY
60038	PALATINE	60074	PALATINE	60939	GOODWINE	60953	MILFORD
60039	CRYSTAL LAKE	60014	CRYSTAL LAKE	60944	HOPKINS PARK	60964	SAINT ANNE
60049	LONG GROVE	60047	LAKE ZURICH	60945	IROQUOIS	60966	SHELDON

ILLINOIS   **ILLINOIS**

Point ZIP Code ZIP	Post Office Name	Enclosing Residential ZIP Code ZIP	Post Office Name	Point ZIP Code ZIP	Post Office Name	Enclosing Residential ZIP Code ZIP	Post Office Name
60956	PAPINEAU	60964	SAINT ANNE	61758	MERNA	61761	NORMAL
60967	STOCKLAND	60953	MILFORD	61791	BLOOMINGTON	61701	BLOOMINGTON
60969	UNION HILL	60941	HERSCHER	61799	BLOOMINGTON	61704	BLOOMINGTON
60974	WOODLAND	60970	WATSEKA	61803	URBANA	61801	URBANA
61013	CEDARVILLE	61032	FREEPORT	61815	BONDVILLE	61822	CHAMPAIGN
61027	ELEROY	61048	LENA	61824	CHAMPAIGN	61821	CHAMPAIGN
61037	GALT	61081	STERLING	61825	CHAMPAIGN	61820	CHAMPAIGN
61043	HOLCOMB	61020	DAVIS JUNCTION	61826	CHAMPAIGN	61821	CHAMPAIGN
61057	NACHUSA	61021	DIXON	61848	HENNING	60963	ROSSVILLE
61058	NELSON	61021	DIXON	61857	MUNCIE	61844	FITHIAN
61059	NORA	61087	WARREN	61871	ROYAL	61859	OGDEN
61077	SEWARD	61063	PECATONICA	61936	LA PLACE	61818	CERRO GORDO
61079	SHIRLAND	61072	ROCKTON	61941	MURDOCK	61919	CAMARGO
61091	WOOSUNG	61064	POLO	61949	REDMON	61944	PARIS
61105	ROCKFORD	61101	ROCKFORD	61955	VERMILION	61944	PARIS
61106	ROCKFORD	61104	ROCKFORD	62023	EAGARVILLE	62069	MOUNT OLIVE
61110	ROCKFORD	61104	ROCKFORD	62046	HAMEL	62025	EDWARDSVILLE
61125	ROCKFORD	61108	ROCKFORD	62058	LIVINGSTON	62074	NEW DOUGLAS
61126	ROCKFORD	61111	LOVES PARK	62059	LOVEJOY	62201	EAST SAINT LOUIS
61130	LOVES PARK	61111	LOVES PARK	62071	NATIONAL STOCK YARDS	62201	EAST SAINT LOUIS
61131	LOVES PARK	61111	LOVES PARK	62076	OHLMAN	62075	NOKOMIS
61132	LOVES PARK	61111	LOVES PARK	62077	PANAMA	62019	DONNELLSON
61204	ROCK ISLAND	61201	ROCK ISLAND	62078	PATTERSON	62050	HILLVIEW
61232	ANDALUSIA	61284	TAYLOR RIDGE	62085	SAWYERVILLE	62009	BENLD
61233	ANDOVER	61238	CAMBRIDGE	62089	TAYLOR SPRINGS	62049	HILLSBORO
61236	BARSTOW	61244	EAST MOLINE	62093	WILSONVILLE	62033	GILLESPIE
61237	BUFFALO PRAIRIE	61259	ILLINOIS CITY	62098	WRIGHTS	62092	WHITE HALL
61239	CARBON CLIFF	61282	SILVIS	62202	EAST SAINT LOUIS	62201	EAST SAINT LOUIS
61258	HOOPPOLE	61277	PROPHETSTOWN	62216	AVISTON	62293	TRENTON
61266	MOLINE	61265	MOLINE	62219	BECKEMEYER	62231	CARLYLE
61276	PREEMPTION	61281	SHERRARD	62222	BELLEVILLE	62220	BELLEVILLE
61278	RAPIDS CITY	61275	PORT BYRON	62224	MASCOUTAH	62258	MASCOUTAH
61299	ROCK ISLAND	61201	ROCK ISLAND	62247	HAGARSTOWN	62262	MULBERRY GROVE
61315	BUREAU	61356	PRINCETON	62250	HOFFMAN	62801	CENTRALIA
61316	CEDAR POINT	61354	PERU	62252	HUEY	62231	CARLYLE
61317	CHERRY	61312	ARLINGTON	62256	MAEYSTOWN	62244	FULTS
61322	DEPUE	61356	PRINCETON	62259	MENARD	62233	CHESTER
61323	DOVER	61356	PRINCETON	62266	NEW MEMPHIS	62265	NEW BADEN
61324	ELDENA	61021	DIXON	62273	PIERRON	62275	POCAHONTAS
61328	KASBEER	61349	OHIO	62279	RENAULT	62277	PRAIRIE DU ROCHER
61331	LEE CENTER	61310	AMBOY	62282	SAINT LIBORY	62258	MASCOUTAH
61332	LEONORE	61370	TONICA	62289	SUMMERFIELD	62254	LEBANON
61338	MANLIUS	61361	SHEFFIELD	62292	TILDEN	62286	SPARTA
61340	MARK	61326	GRANVILLE	62306	QUINCY	62301	QUINCY
61359	SEATONVILLE	61356	PRINCETON	62329	COLUSA	62358	NIOTA
61363	STANDARD	61326	GRANVILLE	62336	FERRIS	62321	CARTHAGE
61371	TRIUMPH	61342	MENDOTA	62435	JANESVILLE	62440	LERNA
61372	TROY GROVE	61342	MENDOTA	62444	MODE	62414	BEECHER CITY
61374	VAN ORIN	61330	LA MOILLE	62459	SAINTE MARIE	62480	WILLOW HILL
61402	GALESBURG	61401	GALESBURG	62464	STOY	62454	ROBINSON
61416	BARDOLPH	61455	MACOMB	62519	CORNLAND	62634	ELKHART
61419	BISHOP HILL	61434	GALVA	62524	DECATUR	62526	DECATUR
61424	CAMP GROVE	61421	BRADFORD	62525	DECATUR	62523	DECATUR
61426	CASTLETON	61421	BRADFORD	62532	ELWIN	62521	DECATUR
61430	EAST GALESBURG	61448	KNOXVILLE	62537	HARRISTOWN	62522	DECATUR
61439	HENDERSON	61401	GALESBURG	62540	KINCAID	62568	TAYLORVILLE
61468	OPHEIM	61262	LYNN CENTER	62541	LAKE FORK	62548	MOUNT PULASKI
61539	KINGSTON MINES	61547	MAPLETON	62570	TOVEY	62568	TAYLORVILLE
61541	LA ROSE	61375	VARNA	62610	ALSEY	62694	WINCHESTER
61553	NORRIS	61531	FARMINGTON	62622	BLUFF SPRINGS	62618	BEARDSTOWN
61555	PEKIN	61554	PEKIN	62651	JACKSONVILLE	62650	JACKSONVILLE
61558	PEKIN	61554	PEKIN	62659	LINCOLN S NEW SALEM	62675	PETERSBURG
61562	ROME	61523	CHILLICOTHE	62660	LITERBERRY	62650	JACKSONVILLE
61564	SOUTH PEKIN	61554	PEKIN	62662	LOWDER	62692	WAVERLY
61601	PEORIA	61602	PEORIA	62663	MANCHESTER	62694	WINCHESTER
61612	PEORIA	61614	PEORIA	62689	THAYER	62615	AUBURN
61613	PEORIA	61615	PEORIA	62695	WOODSON	62650	JACKSONVILLE
61628	PEORIA	61602	PEORIA	62705	SPRINGFIELD	62703	SPRINGFIELD
61629	PEORIA	61602	PEORIA	62706	SPRINGFIELD	62704	SPRINGFIELD
61630	PEORIA	61602	PEORIA	62708	SPRINGFIELD	62703	SPRINGFIELD
61632	PEORIA	61614	PEORIA	62713	SPRINGFIELD	62703	SPRINGFIELD
61633	PEORIA	61604	PEORIA	62715	SPRINGFIELD	62701	SPRINGFIELD
61634	PEORIA	61602	PEORIA	62716	SPRINGFIELD	62707	SPRINGFIELD
61636	PEORIA	61602	PEORIA	62719	SPRINGFIELD	62702	SPRINGFIELD
61637	PEORIA	61603	PEORIA	62721	SPRINGFIELD	62701	SPRINGFIELD
61638	PEORIA	61615	PEORIA	62722	SPRINGFIELD	62704	SPRINGFIELD
61639	PEORIA	61603	PEORIA	62723	SPRINGFIELD	62703	SPRINGFIELD
61640	PEORIA	61615	PEORIA	62726	SPRINGFIELD	62702	SPRINGFIELD
61641	PEORIA	61607	PEORIA	62736	SPRINGFIELD	62702	SPRINGFIELD
61643	PEORIA	61614	PEORIA	62739	SPRINGFIELD	62701	SPRINGFIELD
61644	PEORIA	61614	PEORIA	62746	SPRINGFIELD	62702	SPRINGFIELD
61650	PEORIA	61602	PEORIA	62756	SPRINGFIELD	62704	SPRINGFIELD
61651	PEORIA	61602	PEORIA	62757	SPRINGFIELD	62701	SPRINGFIELD
61652	PEORIA	61602	PEORIA	62761	SPRINGFIELD	62702	SPRINGFIELD
61653	PEORIA	61602	PEORIA	62762	SPRINGFIELD	62704	SPRINGFIELD
61654	PEORIA	61602	PEORIA	62763	SPRINGFIELD	62704	SPRINGFIELD
61655	PEORIA	61602	PEORIA	62764	SPRINGFIELD	62703	SPRINGFIELD
61656	PEORIA	61602	PEORIA	62765	SPRINGFIELD	62701	SPRINGFIELD
61702	BLOOMINGTON	61701	BLOOMINGTON	62766	SPRINGFIELD	62703	SPRINGFIELD
61709	BLOOMINGTON	61704	BLOOMINGTON	62767	SPRINGFIELD	62701	SPRINGFIELD
61710	BLOOMINGTON	61701	BLOOMINGTON	62769	SPRINGFIELD	62702	SPRINGFIELD
61750	LANE	61727	CLINTON	62776	SPRINGFIELD	62704	SPRINGFIELD
61751	LAWNDALE	62656	LINCOLN	62777	SPRINGFIELD	62701	SPRINGFIELD

ILLINOIS   **INDIANA**

Point ZIP Code		Enclosing Residential ZIP Code		Point ZIP Code		Enclosing Residential ZIP Code	
ZIP	Post Office Name	ZIP	Post Office Name	ZIP	Post Office Name	ZIP	Post Office Name
62781	SPRINGFIELD	62702	SPRINGFIELD	46513	DONALDSON	46563	PLYMOUTH
62786	SPRINGFIELD	62701	SPRINGFIELD	46515	ELKHART	46516	ELKHART
62791	SPRINGFIELD	62704	SPRINGFIELD	46527	GOSHEN	46526	GOSHEN
62794	SPRINGFIELD	62703	SPRINGFIELD	46537	LAPAZ	46563	PLYMOUTH
62796	SPRINGFIELD	62703	SPRINGFIELD	46546	MISHAWAKA	46544	MISHAWAKA
62805	AKIN	62890	THOMPSONVILLE	46572	TYNER	46563	PLYMOUTH
62811	BELLMONT	62863	MOUNT CARMEL	46581	WARSAW	46580	WARSAW
62825	COELLO	62812	BENTON	46595	WYATT	46506	BREMEN
62834	EMMA	62821	CARMI	46604	SOUTH BEND	46615	SOUTH BEND
62840	FRANKFORT HEIGHTS	62896	WEST FRANKFORT	46620	SOUTH BEND	46619	SOUTH BEND
62841	FREEMAN SPUR	62948	HERRIN	46624	SOUTH BEND	46601	SOUTH BEND
62848	IRVINGTON	62877	RICHVIEW	46626	SOUTH BEND	46601	SOUTH BEND
62852	KEENSBURG	62863	MOUNT CARMEL	46629	SOUTH BEND	46619	SOUTH BEND
62856	LOGAN	62812	BENTON	46634	SOUTH BEND	46601	SOUTH BEND
62857	LOOGOOTEE	62880	SAINT PETER	46660	SOUTH BEND	46615	SOUTH BEND
62861	MAUNIE	62821	CARMI	46680	SOUTH BEND	46614	SOUTH BEND
62874	ORIENT	62896	WEST FRANKFORT	46704	ARCOLA	46818	FORT WAYNE
62876	RADOM	62831	DU BOIS	46713	BIPPUS	46750	HUNTINGTON
62879	SAILOR SPRINGS	62434	INGRAHAM	46769	LINN GROVE	46711	BERNE
62891	VALIER	62822	CHRISTOPHER	46771	MONGO	46746	HOWE
62909	BOLES	62923	CYPRESS	46778	PETROLEUM	46759	KEYSTONE
62915	CAMBRIA	62918	CARTERVILLE	46780	PLEASANT MILLS	46733	DECATUR
62921	COLP	62948	HERRIN	46782	PREBLE	46733	DECATUR
62927	DOWELL	62932	ELKVILLE	46786	SOUTH MILFORD	46795	WOLCOTTVILLE
62949	HURST	62918	CARTERVILLE	46789	STROH	46795	WOLCOTTVILLE
62965	MUDDY	62946	HARRISBURG	46796	WOLFLAKE	46760	KIMMELL
62969	OLIVE BRANCH	62990	THEBES	46799	ZANESVILLE	46783	ROANOKE
62971	ORAVILLE	62966	MURPHYSBORO	46801	FORT WAYNE	46802	FORT WAYNE
62973	PERKS	62992	ULLIN	46850	FORT WAYNE	46802	FORT WAYNE
62993	UNITY	62988	TAMMS	46851	FORT WAYNE	46802	FORT WAYNE
46014	ANDERSON	46011	ANDERSON	46852	FORT WAYNE	46802	FORT WAYNE
46015	ANDERSON	46016	ANDERSON	46853	FORT WAYNE	46802	FORT WAYNE
46018	ANDERSON	46011	ANDERSON	46854	FORT WAYNE	46802	FORT WAYNE
46045	GOLDSMITH	46072	TIPTON	46855	FORT WAYNE	46802	FORT WAYNE
46047	HOBBS	46072	TIPTON	46856	FORT WAYNE	46802	FORT WAYNE
46061	NOBLESVILLE	46060	NOBLESVILLE	46857	FORT WAYNE	46802	FORT WAYNE
46063	ORESTES	46001	ALEXANDRIA	46858	FORT WAYNE	46802	FORT WAYNE
46067	SEDALIA	46041	FRANKFORT	46859	FORT WAYNE	46802	FORT WAYNE
46082	CARMEL	46032	CARMEL	46860	FORT WAYNE	46802	FORT WAYNE
46102	ADVANCE	46147	JAMESTOWN	46861	FORT WAYNE	46802	FORT WAYNE
46103	AMO	46121	COATESVILLE	46862	FORT WAYNE	46802	FORT WAYNE
46111	BROOKLYN	46158	MOORESVILLE	46863	FORT WAYNE	46802	FORT WAYNE
46125	EMINENCE	46151	MARTINSVILLE	46864	FORT WAYNE	46802	FORT WAYNE
46129	FINLY	46130	FOUNTAINTOWN	46865	FORT WAYNE	46802	FORT WAYNE
46144	GWYNNEVILLE	46161	MORRISTOWN	46866	FORT WAYNE	46802	FORT WAYNE
46146	HOMER	46150	MANILLA	46867	FORT WAYNE	46802	FORT WAYNE
46154	MAXWELL	46140	GREENFIELD	46868	FORT WAYNE	46802	FORT WAYNE
46155	MAYS	46173	RUSHVILLE	46869	FORT WAYNE	46802	FORT WAYNE
46170	PUTNAMVILLE	46135	GREENCASTLE	46885	FORT WAYNE	46835	FORT WAYNE
46183	WEST NEWTON	46113	CAMBY	46895	FORT WAYNE	46805	FORT WAYNE
46206	INDIANAPOLIS	46225	INDIANAPOLIS	46896	FORT WAYNE	46806	FORT WAYNE
46207	INDIANAPOLIS	46225	INDIANAPOLIS	46897	FORT WAYNE	46819	FORT WAYNE
46209	INDIANAPOLIS	46225	INDIANAPOLIS	46898	FORT WAYNE	46808	FORT WAYNE
46211	INDIANAPOLIS	46268	INDIANAPOLIS	46899	FORT WAYNE	46809	FORT WAYNE
46230	INDIANAPOLIS	46220	INDIANAPOLIS	46903	KOKOMO	46902	KOKOMO
46242	INDIANAPOLIS	46241	INDIANAPOLIS	46904	KOKOMO	46902	KOKOMO
46244	INDIANAPOLIS	46204	INDIANAPOLIS	46912	ATHENS	46975	ROCHESTER
46247	INDIANAPOLIS	46227	INDIANAPOLIS	46915	BURLINGTON	46920	CUTLER
46249	INDIANAPOLIS	46216	INDIANAPOLIS	46916	BURROWS	46917	CAMDEN
46251	INDIANAPOLIS	46241	INDIANAPOLIS	46921	DEEDSVILLE	46951	MACY
46253	INDIANAPOLIS	46254	INDIANAPOLIS	46922	DELONG	46975	ROCHESTER
46255	INDIANAPOLIS	46204	INDIANAPOLIS	46930	FOWLERTON	46938	JONESBORO
46266	INDIANAPOLIS	46204	INDIANAPOLIS	46931	FULTON	46975	ROCHESTER
46274	INDIANAPOLIS	46268	INDIANAPOLIS	46937	HEMLOCK	46902	KOKOMO
46275	INDIANAPOLIS	46268	INDIANAPOLIS	46942	LAKE CICOTT	46947	LOGANSPORT
46277	INDIANAPOLIS	46204	INDIANAPOLIS	46943	LAKETON	46962	NORTH MANCHESTER
46282	INDIANAPOLIS	46204	INDIANAPOLIS	46945	LEITERS FORD	46975	ROCHESTER
46283	INDIANAPOLIS	46225	INDIANAPOLIS	46946	LIBERTY MILLS	46962	NORTH MANCHESTER
46285	INDIANAPOLIS	46221	INDIANAPOLIS	46957	MATTHEWS	46989	UPLAND
46291	INDIANAPOLIS	46219	INDIANAPOLIS	46958	MEXICO	46970	PERU
46295	INDIANAPOLIS	46225	INDIANAPOLIS	46959	MIAMI	46914	BUNKER HILL
46296	INDIANAPOLIS	46225	INDIANAPOLIS	46961	NEW WAVERLY	46947	LOGANSPORT
46298	INDIANAPOLIS	46268	INDIANAPOLIS	46965	OAKFORD	46902	KOKOMO
46301	BEVERLY SHORES	46304	CHESTERTON	46967	ONWARD	46994	WALTON
46302	BOONE GROVE	46385	VALPARAISO	46968	ORA	46960	MONTEREY
46308	CROWN POINT	46307	CROWN POINT	46971	GRISSOM ARB	46970	PERU
46325	HAMMOND	46320	HAMMOND	46977	ROCKFIELD	46923	DELPHI
46345	KINGSBURY	46350	LA PORTE	46980	SERVIA	46962	NORTH MANCHESTER
46346	KINGSFORD HEIGHTS	46350	LA PORTE	46984	SOMERSET	46940	LA FONTAINE
46352	LA PORTE	46350	LA PORTE	46987	SWEETSER	46952	MARION
46355	LEROY	46307	CROWN POINT	46995	WEST MIDDLETON	46979	RUSSIAVILLE
46361	MICHIGAN CITY	46360	MICHIGAN CITY	46998	YOUNG AMERICA	46932	GALVESTON
46372	ROSELAWN	46310	DEMOTTE	47019	EAST ENTERPRISE	47040	RISING SUN
46376	SCHNEIDER	46356	LOWELL	47021	FRIENDSHIP	47042	VERSAILLES
46377	SHELBY	46356	LOWELL	47033	MORRIS	47006	BATESVILLE
46379	SUMAVA RESORTS	46349	LAKE VILLAGE	47034	NAPOLEON	47037	OSGOOD
46380	TEFFT	46392	WHEATFIELD	47035	NEW TRENTON	47060	WEST HARRISON
46381	THAYER	47963	MOROCCO	47039	PIERCEVILLE	47031	MILAN
46384	VALPARAISO	46383	VALPARAISO	47104	BETHLEHEM	47162	NEW WASHINGTON
46393	WHEELER	46342	HOBART	47107	BRADFORD	47164	PALMYRA
46401	GARY	46407	GARY	47131	JEFFERSONVILLE	47130	JEFFERSONVILLE
46411	MERRILLVILLE	46410	MERRILLVILLE	47139	LITTLE YORK	47170	SCOTTSBURG
46502	ATWOOD	46580	WARSAW	47146	MOUNT SAINT FRANCIS	47119	FLOYDS KNOBS

INDIANA   **IOWA**

| Point ZIP Code | | Enclosing Residential ZIP Code | | Point ZIP Code | | Enclosing Residential ZIP Code | |
| | Post Office | | Post Office | | Post Office | | Post Office |
ZIP	Name	ZIP	Name	ZIP	Name	ZIP	Name
47151	NEW ALBANY	47150	NEW ALBANY	47855	HYMERA	47879	SHELBURN
47199	JEFFERSONVILLE	47130	JEFFERSONVILLE	47856	JUDSON	47872	ROCKVILLE
47202	COLUMBUS	47201	COLUMBUS	47857	KNIGHTSVILLE	47834	BRAZIL
47225	CLARKSBURG	46173	RUSHVILLE	47860	MECCA	47872	ROCKVILLE
47226	CLIFFORD	47203	COLUMBUS	47863	NEW GOSHEN	47885	WEST TERRE HAUTE
47228	CORTLAND	47274	SEYMOUR	47864	NEW LEBANON	47882	SULLIVAN
47245	HAYDEN	47265	NORTH VERNON	47865	PAXTON	47838	CARLISLE
47247	JONESVILLE	47201	COLUMBUS	47869	PRAIRIE CREEK	47802	TERRE HAUTE
47249	KURTZ	47264	NORMAN	47870	PRAIRIETON	47802	TERRE HAUTE
47261	MILLHOUSEN	47240	GREENSBURG	47871	RILEY	47802	TERRE HAUTE
47263	NEW POINT	47240	GREENSBURG	47875	SAINT BERNICE	47842	CLINTON
47280	TAYLORSVILLE	47203	COLUMBUS	47876	SAINT MARY OF THE WO	47885	WEST TERRE HAUTE
47307	MUNCIE	47302	MUNCIE	47878	SEELYVILLE	47803	TERRE HAUTE
47308	MUNCIE	47302	MUNCIE	47880	SHEPARDSVILLE	47842	CLINTON
47322	BENTONVILLE	47331	CONNERSVILLE	47881	STAUNTON	47834	BRAZIL
47324	BOSTON	47374	RICHMOND	47884	UNIVERSAL	47842	CLINTON
47335	DUBLIN	47327	CAMBRIDGE CITY	47902	LAFAYETTE	47905	LAFAYETTE
47337	DUNREITH	47385	SPICELAND	47903	LAFAYETTE	47905	LAFAYETTE
47344	GREENSBORO	46148	KNIGHTSTOWN	47916	ALAMO	47933	CRAWFORDSVILLE
47351	KENNARD	47384	SHIRLEY	47924	BUCK CREEK	47905	LAFAYETTE
47361	MOUNT SUMMIT	47362	NEW CASTLE	47925	BUFFALO	47960	MONTICELLO
47366	NEW LISBON	47387	STRAUGHN	47934	CRAWFORDSVILLE	47933	CRAWFORDSVILLE
47367	OAKVILLE	47302	MUNCIE	47935	CRAWFORDSVILLE	47933	CRAWFORDSVILLE
47370	PERSHING	47327	CAMBRIDGE CITY	47936	CRAWFORDSVILLE	47933	CRAWFORDSVILLE
47375	RICHMOND	47374	RICHMOND	47937	CRAWFORDSVILLE	47933	CRAWFORDSVILLE
47388	SULPHUR SPRINGS	47356	MIDDLETOWN	47938	CRAWFORDSVILLE	47933	CRAWFORDSVILLE
47402	BLOOMINGTON	47401	BLOOMINGTON	47939	CRAWFORDSVILLE	47933	CRAWFORDSVILLE
47407	BLOOMINGTON	47468	UNIONVILLE	47941	DAYTON	47905	LAFAYETTE
47420	AVOCA	47462	SPRINGVILLE	47958	MELLOTT	47987	VEEDERSBURG
47426	CLEAR CREEK	47403	BLOOMINGTON	47962	MONTMORENCI	47906	WEST LAFAYETTE
47430	FORT RITNER	47421	BEDFORD	47964	MOUNT AYR	47963	MOROCCO
47434	HARRODSBURG	47403	BLOOMINGTON	47965	NEW MARKET	47933	CRAWFORDSVILLE
47435	HELMSBURG	47448	NASHVILLE	47966	NEWPORT	47928	CAYUGA
47437	HURON	47470	WILLIAMS	47969	NEWTOWN	47918	ATTICA
47439	KOLEEN	47453	OWENSBURG	47982	STATE LINE	47932	COVINGTON
47445	MIDLAND	47441	LINTON	47983	STOCKWELL	47909	LAFAYETTE
47455	PATRICKSBURG	47833	BOWLING GREEN	47984	TALBOT	47944	FOWLER
47457	SCOTLAND	47424	BLOOMFIELD	47986	TEMPLETON	47944	FOWLER
47458	SMITHVILLE	47401	BLOOMINGTON	47988	WALLACE	47949	HILLSBORO
47463	STANFORD	47403	BLOOMINGTON	47996	WEST LAFAYETTE	47906	WEST LAFAYETTE
47464	STINESVILLE	47429	ELLETTSVILLE	47997	YEOMAN	46923	DELPHI
47467	TUNNELTON	47421	BEDFORD	50012	AMES	50014	AMES
47490	BLOOMINGTON	47401	BLOOMINGTON	50031	BEAVER	50212	OGDEN
47535	FREELANDVILLE	47561	OAKTOWN	50032	BERWICK	50317	DES MOINES
47536	FULDA	47577	SAINT MEINRAD	50037	BOONE	50036	BOONE
47545	IRELAND	47546	JASPER	50078	FERGUSON	50158	MARSHALLTOWN
47547	JASPER	47546	JASPER	50110	GRAY	50025	AUDUBON
47549	JASPER	47546	JASPER	50137	KILLDUFF	50251	SULLY
47573	RAGSDALE	47512	BICKNELL	50142	LE GRAND	50158	MARSHALLTOWN
47584	SPURGEON	47660	OAKLAND CITY	50145	LIBERTY CENTER	50166	MILO
47596	WESTPHALIA	47578	SANDBORN	50160	MARTENSDALE	50229	PROLE
47614	FOLSOMVILLE	47601	BOONVILLE	50163	MELCHER	50062	DALLAS
47617	HATFIELD	47634	RICHLAND	50177	GRINNELL	50112	GRINNELL
47618	INGLEFIELD	47725	EVANSVILLE	50241	SAINT MARYS	50229	PROLE
47629	NEWBURGH	47630	NEWBURGH	50243	SHELDAHL	50226	POLK CITY
47654	MACKEY	47613	ELBERFELD	50255	THORNBURG	50136	KESWICK
47683	SOMERVILLE	47613	ELBERFELD	50259	GIFFORD	50258	UNION
47701	EVANSVILLE	47708	EVANSVILLE	50269	WHITTEN	50258	UNION
47702	EVANSVILLE	47708	EVANSVILLE	50301	DES MOINES	50311	DES MOINES
47703	EVANSVILLE	47708	EVANSVILLE	50302	DES MOINES	50314	DES MOINES
47704	EVANSVILLE	47708	EVANSVILLE	50303	DES MOINES	50311	DES MOINES
47705	EVANSVILLE	47708	EVANSVILLE	50304	DES MOINES	50311	DES MOINES
47706	EVANSVILLE	47708	EVANSVILLE	50305	DES MOINES	50311	DES MOINES
47716	EVANSVILLE	47715	EVANSVILLE	50306	DES MOINES	50311	DES MOINES
47719	EVANSVILLE	47712	EVANSVILLE	50318	DES MOINES	50309	DES MOINES
47721	EVANSVILLE	47712	EVANSVILLE	50319	DES MOINES	50309	DES MOINES
47724	EVANSVILLE	47710	EVANSVILLE	50328	DES MOINES	50309	DES MOINES
47727	EVANSVILLE	47711	EVANSVILLE	50329	DES MOINES	50309	DES MOINES
47728	EVANSVILLE	47714	EVANSVILLE	50330	DES MOINES	50309	DES MOINES
47730	EVANSVILLE	47708	EVANSVILLE	50331	DES MOINES	50309	DES MOINES
47731	EVANSVILLE	47708	EVANSVILLE	50332	DES MOINES	50309	DES MOINES
47732	EVANSVILLE	47708	EVANSVILLE	50333	DES MOINES	50313	DES MOINES
47733	EVANSVILLE	47708	EVANSVILLE	50334	DES MOINES	50322	URBANDALE
47734	EVANSVILLE	47708	EVANSVILLE	50335	DES MOINES	50309	DES MOINES
47735	EVANSVILLE	47708	EVANSVILLE	50336	DES MOINES	50265	WEST DES MOINES
47736	EVANSVILLE	47708	EVANSVILLE	50338	DES MOINES	50310	DES MOINES
47737	EVANSVILLE	47708	EVANSVILLE	50339	DES MOINES	50266	WEST DES MOINES
47739	EVANSVILLE	47710	EVANSVILLE	50340	DES MOINES	50309	DES MOINES
47740	EVANSVILLE	47710	EVANSVILLE	50347	DES MOINES	50265	WEST DES MOINES
47741	EVANSVILLE	47708	EVANSVILLE	50359	DES MOINES	50266	WEST DES MOINES
47744	EVANSVILLE	47712	EVANSVILLE	50360	DES MOINES	50314	DES MOINES
47747	EVANSVILLE	47710	EVANSVILLE	50361	DES MOINES	50266	WEST DES MOINES
47750	EVANSVILLE	47714	EVANSVILLE	50362	DES MOINES	50266	WEST DES MOINES
47801	TERRE HAUTE	47807	TERRE HAUTE	50363	DES MOINES	50266	WEST DES MOINES
47808	TERRE HAUTE	47802	TERRE HAUTE	50364	DES MOINES	50266	WEST DES MOINES
47811	TERRE HAUTE	47804	TERRE HAUTE	50367	DES MOINES	50266	WEST DES MOINES
47812	TERRE HAUTE	47804	TERRE HAUTE	50368	DES MOINES	50266	WEST DES MOINES
47830	BELLMORE	47872	ROCKVILLE	50369	DES MOINES	50266	WEST DES MOINES
47831	BLANFORD	47842	CLINTON	50380	DES MOINES	50309	DES MOINES
47845	COALMONT	47438	JASONVILLE	50381	DES MOINES	50309	DES MOINES
47851	FONTANET	47834	BRAZIL	50391	DES MOINES	50265	WEST DES MOINES
47852	GRAYSVILLE	47882	SULLIVAN	50392	DES MOINES	50309	DES MOINES
47853	HARMONY	47834	BRAZIL	50393	DES MOINES	50309	DES MOINES

IOWA

Point ZIP Code	Post Office Name	Enclosing Residential ZIP Code	Post Office Name
50394	DES MOINES	50322	URBANDALE
50395	DES MOINES	50322	URBANDALE
50396	DES MOINES	50309	DES MOINES
50397	DES MOINES	50309	DES MOINES
50398	WEST DES MOINES	50266	WEST DES MOINES
50402	MASON CITY	50401	MASON CITY
50426	CARPENTER	50472	SAINT ANSGAR
50427	CHAPIN	50475	SHEFFIELD
50431	COULTER	50452	LATIMER
50481	TOETERVILLE	50472	SAINT ANSGAR
50526	CLARION	50525	CLARION
50592	TRUESDALE	50588	STORM LAKE
50593	VARINA	50540	FONDA
50620	COLWELL	50616	CHARLES CITY
50623	DEWAR	50703	WATERLOO
50631	FREDERIKA	50674	SUMNER
50634	GILBERTVILLE	50701	WATERLOO
50657	MORRISON	50669	REINBECK
50661	NORTH WASHINGTON	50659	NEW HAMPTON
50664	ORAN	50629	FAIRBANK
50673	STOUT	50665	PARKERSBURG
50704	WATERLOO	50703	WATERLOO
50799	WATERLOO	50703	WATERLOO
50831	ARISPE	50830	AFTON
50839	CARBON	50841	CORNING
50842	CROMWELL	50801	CRESTON
50936	DES MOINES	50309	DES MOINES
50940	DES MOINES	50309	DES MOINES
50947	DES MOINES	50314	DES MOINES
50950	DES MOINES	50309	DES MOINES
50980	DES MOINES	50309	DES MOINES
50981	DES MOINES	50309	DES MOINES
51008	BRUNSVILLE	51031	LE MARS
51011	CHATSWORTH	51023	HAWARDEN
51015	CLIMBING HILL	51026	HORNICK
51045	OYENS	51031	LE MARS
51102	SIOUX CITY	51101	SIOUX CITY
51242	LESTER	51241	LARCHWOOD
51244	MATLOCK	51201	SHELDON
51340	FOSTORIA	51301	SPENCER
51341	GILLETT GROVE	51343	GREENVILLE
51344	GRUVER	51334	ESTHERVILLE
51459	RALSTON	51443	GLIDDEN
51502	COUNCIL BLUFFS	51503	COUNCIL BLUFFS
51550	MAGNOLIA	51546	LOGAN
51554	MINEOLA	51534	GLENWOOD
51591	RED OAK	51566	RED OAK
51593	HARLAN	51537	HARLAN
51602	SHENANDOAH	51601	SHENANDOAH
51603	SHENANDOAH	51601	SHENANDOAH
52004	DUBUQUE	52001	DUBUQUE
52056	LUXEMBURG	52052	GUTTENBERG
52075	SPRINGBROOK	52031	BELLEVUE
52099	DUBUQUE	52001	DUBUQUE
52149	HIGHLANDVILLE	52101	DECORAH
52163	PROTIVIN	52132	CALMAR
52168	SPILLVILLE	52132	CALMAR
52204	AMANA	52203	AMANA
52235	HILLS	52327	RIVERSIDE
52243	IOWA CITY	52240	IOWA CITY
52244	IOWA CITY	52240	IOWA CITY
52252	LANGWORTHY	52310	MONTICELLO
52312	MORLEY	52205	ANAMOSA
52319	OAKDALE	52240	IOWA CITY
52344	TROY MILLS	52218	COGGON
52350	VIOLA	52336	SPRINGVILLE
52351	WALFORD	52318	NORWAY
52406	CEDAR RAPIDS	52401	CEDAR RAPIDS
52407	CEDAR RAPIDS	52401	CEDAR RAPIDS
52408	CEDAR RAPIDS	52405	CEDAR RAPIDS
52409	CEDAR RAPIDS	52403	CEDAR RAPIDS
52410	CEDAR RAPIDS	52403	CEDAR RAPIDS
52497	CEDAR RAPIDS	52404	CEDAR RAPIDS
52498	CEDAR RAPIDS	52402	CEDAR RAPIDS
52499	CEDAR RAPIDS	52402	CEDAR RAPIDS
52562	HAYESVILLE	52591	SIGOURNEY
52568	MARTINSBURG	52563	HEDRICK
52595	UNIVERSITY PARK	52577	OSKALOOSA
52648	PILOT GROVE	52656	WEST POINT
52652	SWEDESBURG	52641	MOUNT PLEASANT
52728	BUFFALO	52804	DAVENPORT
52733	CLINTON	52732	CLINTON
52736	CLINTON	52732	CLINTON
52737	COLUMBUS CITY	52738	COLUMBUS JUNCTION
52749	FRUITLAND	52761	MUSCATINE
52752	GRANDVIEW	52653	WAPELLO
52757	LOW MOOR	52742	DE WITT
52758	MC CAUSLAND	52748	ELDRIDGE
52767	PLEASANT VALLEY	52722	BETTENDORF
52771	TEEDS GROVE	52732	CLINTON
52805	DAVENPORT	52801	DAVENPORT
52808	DAVENPORT	52802	DAVENPORT
52809	DAVENPORT	52806	DAVENPORT

KENTUCKY

Point ZIP Code	Post Office Name	Enclosing Residential ZIP Code	Post Office Name
66019	CLEARVIEW CITY	66018	DE SOTO
66024	ELWOOD	66090	WATHENA
66031	NEW CENTURY	66030	GARDNER
66036	HILLSDALE	66071	PAOLA
66051	OLATHE	66061	OLATHE
66063	OLATHE	66062	OLATHE
66077	POTTER	66002	ATCHISON
66110	KANSAS CITY	66102	KANSAS CITY
66117	KANSAS CITY	66101	KANSAS CITY
66119	KANSAS CITY	66105	KANSAS CITY
66201	MISSION	66202	MISSION
66222	MISSION	66205	MISSION
66225	OVERLAND PARK	66210	OVERLAND PARK
66250	SHAWNEE MISSION	66215	LENEXA
66251	OVERLAND PARK	66202	MISSION
66276	SHAWNEE MISSION	66202	MISSION
66282	OVERLAND PARK	66202	MISSION
66283	OVERLAND PARK	66223	OVERLAND PARK
66285	LENEXA	66215	LENEXA
66286	SHAWNEE	66226	SHAWNEE
66420	DOVER	66610	TOPEKA
66426	FOSTORIA	66549	WESTMORELAND
66501	MC FARLAND	66401	ALMA
66505	MANHATTAN	66502	MANHATTAN
66601	TOPEKA	66603	TOPEKA
66620	TOPEKA	66619	TOPEKA
66621	TOPEKA	66604	TOPEKA
66622	TOPEKA	66614	TOPEKA
66624	TOPEKA	66619	TOPEKA
66625	TOPEKA	66612	TOPEKA
66626	TOPEKA	66612	TOPEKA
66628	TOPEKA	66612	TOPEKA
66629	TOPEKA	66612	TOPEKA
66636	TOPEKA	66603	TOPEKA
66637	TOPEKA	66608	TOPEKA
66647	TOPEKA	66604	TOPEKA
66652	TOPEKA	66603	TOPEKA
66653	TOPEKA	66603	TOPEKA
66667	TOPEKA	66604	TOPEKA
66675	TOPEKA	66608	TOPEKA
66683	TOPEKA	66603	TOPEKA
66686	TOPEKA	66603	TOPEKA
66692	TOPEKA	66603	TOPEKA
66699	TOPEKA	66612	TOPEKA
66711	GARLAND	66711	ARCADIA
66742	GAS	66749	IOLA
66760	OPOLIS	66762	PITTSBURG
66782	WEST MINERAL	66773	SCAMMON
66863	NEAL	66870	VIRGIL
67012	BEAUMONT	67074	LEON
67041	ELBING	67114	NEWTON
67201	WICHITA	67202	WICHITA
67275	WICHITA	67209	WICHITA
67276	WICHITA	67209	WICHITA
67277	WICHITA	67209	WICHITA
67278	WICHITA	67209	WICHITA
67334	CHAUTAUQUA	67360	PERU
67340	DEARING	67337	COFFEYVILLE
67363	SYCAMORE	67301	INDEPENDENCE
67364	TYRO	67333	CANEY
67402	SALINA	67401	SALINA
67504	HUTCHINSON	67501	HUTCHINSON
67585	YODER	67543	HAVEN
67667	SCHOENCHEN	67601	HAYS
67674	WALKER	67671	VICTORIA
67747	MONUMENT	67764	WINONA
67836	COOLIDGE	67878	SYRACUSE
67843	FORT DODGE	67801	DODGE CITY
67905	LIBERAL	67901	LIBERAL
40018	EASTWOOD	40245	LOUISVILLE
40020	FAIRFIELD	40013	COXS CREEK
40027	HARRODS CREEK	40059	PROSPECT
40032	LA GRANGE	40031	LA GRANGE
40041	MASONIC HOME	40207	LOUISVILLE
40048	NAZARETH	40004	BARDSTOWN
40049	NERINX	40037	LORETTO
40058	PORT ROYAL	40075	TURNERS STATION
40063	SAINT MARY	40033	LEBANON
40066	SHELBYVILLE	40065	SHELBYVILLE
40110	CLERMONT	40165	SHEPHERDSVILLE
40129	HILLVIEW	40229	LOUISVILLE
40153	MC QUADY	40119	FALLS OF ROUGH
40159	RADCLIFF	40160	RADCLIFF
40201	LOUISVILLE	40203	LOUISVILLE
40221	LOUISVILLE	40209	LOUISVILLE
40224	LOUISVILLE	40223	LOUISVILLE
40225	LOUISVILLE	40213	LOUISVILLE
40231	LOUISVILLE	40213	LOUISVILLE
40232	LOUISVILLE	40213	LOUISVILLE
40233	LOUISVILLE	40213	LOUISVILLE
40250	LOUISVILLE	40220	LOUISVILLE
40251	LOUISVILLE	40211	LOUISVILLE
40252	LOUISVILLE	40222	LOUISVILLE

KENTUCKY   **KENTUCKY**

Point ZIP Code		Enclosing Residential ZIP Code		Point ZIP Code		Enclosing Residential ZIP Code	
ZIP	**Post Office Name**	**ZIP**	**Post Office Name**	**ZIP**	**Post Office Name**	**ZIP**	**Post Office Name**
40253	LOUISVILLE	40223	LOUISVILLE	40830	GULSTON	40806	BAXTER
40255	LOUISVILLE	40205	LOUISVILLE	40840	HELTON	40858	MOZELLE
40256	LOUISVILLE	40216	LOUISVILLE	40844	HOSKINSTON	40858	MOZELLE
40257	LOUISVILLE	40207	LOUISVILLE	40849	LEJUNIOR	40828	EVARTS
40259	LOUISVILLE	40219	LOUISVILLE	40854	LOYALL	40831	HARLAN
40261	LOUISVILLE	40218	LOUISVILLE	40856	MIRACLE	40977	PINEVILLE
40266	LOUISVILLE	40258	LOUISVILLE	40874	WARBRANCH	40858	MOZELLE
40268	LOUISVILLE	40258	LOUISVILLE	40932	FALL ROCK	40962	MANCHESTER
40269	LOUISVILLE	40299	LOUISVILLE	40939	FOURMILE	40977	PINEVILLE
40270	LOUISVILLE	40203	LOUISVILLE	40941	GARRARD	40962	MANCHESTER
40280	LOUISVILLE	40206	LOUISVILLE	40944	GOOSE ROCK	40914	BIG CREEK
40281	LOUISVILLE	40258	LOUISVILLE	40951	HIMA	40962	MANCHESTER
40282	LOUISVILLE	40258	LOUISVILLE	40955	INGRAM	40977	PINEVILLE
40283	LOUISVILLE	40258	LOUISVILLE	40981	SAUL	41721	BUCKHORN
40285	LOUISVILLE	40213	LOUISVILLE	41012	COVINGTON	41011	COVINGTON
40289	LOUISVILLE	40213	LOUISVILLE	41019	COVINGTON	41011	COVINGTON
40290	LOUISVILLE	40213	LOUISVILLE	41022	FLORENCE	41042	FLORENCE
40296	LOUISVILLE	40213	LOUISVILLE	41037	ELIZAVILLE	41039	EWING
40297	LOUISVILLE	40202	LOUISVILLE	41053	KENTON	41063	MORNING VIEW
40298	LOUISVILLE	40213	LOUISVILLE	41054	MASON	41097	WILLIAMSTOWN
40310	BURGIN	40330	HARRODSBURG	41061	MILFORD	41004	BROOKSVILLE
40317	ELLIOTTVILLE	40351	MOREHEAD	41062	MINERVA	41056	MAYSVILLE
40319	FARMERS	40351	MOREHEAD	41065	MUSES MILLS	41093	WALLINGFORD
40320	FORD	40391	WINCHESTER	41072	NEWPORT	41071	NEWPORT
40329	HALDEMAN	40351	MOREHEAD	41081	PLUMMERS LANDING	41093	WALLINGFORD
40334	HOPE	40337	JEFFERSONVILLE	41096	WASHINGTON	41056	MAYSVILLE
40339	KEENE	40383	VERSAILLES	41105	ASHLAND	41101	ASHLAND
40340	NICHOLASVILLE	40356	NICHOLASVILLE	41114	ASHLAND	41101	ASHLAND
40348	MILLERSBURG	40361	PARIS	41128	CARTER	41164	OLIVE HILL
40357	NORTH MIDDLETOWN	40361	PARIS	41142	GRAHN	41164	OLIVE HILL
40362	PARIS	40361	PARIS	41156	LLOYD	41144	GREENUP
40363	PERRY PARK	40359	OWENTON	41160	MAZIE	41159	MARTHA
40366	PRESTON	40360	OWINGSVILLE	41173	SOLDIER	41164	OLIVE HILL
40384	VERSAILLES	40383	VERSAILLES	41181	WILLARD	41143	GRAYSON
40386	VERSAILLES	40383	VERSAILLES	41203	BEAUTY	41267	WARFIELD
40392	WINCHESTER	40391	WINCHESTER	41264	ULYSSES	41232	LOWMANSVILLE
40405	BIGHILL	40403	BEREA	41268	WEST VAN LEAR	41260	THELMA
40410	BRYANTSVILLE	40444	LANCASTER	41307	ATHOL	41339	JACKSON
40421	DABOLT	40447	MC KEE	41310	BAYS	41385	VANCLEVE
40423	DANVILLE	40422	DANVILLE	41313	BETHANY	41301	CAMPTON
40434	GRAY HAWK	40447	MC KEE	41333	HEIDELBERG	41311	BEATTYVILLE
40445	LIVINGSTON	40456	MOUNT VERNON	41344	LEROSE	41314	BOONEVILLE
40446	LANCASTER	40444	LANCASTER	41347	LONE	41311	BEATTYVILLE
40448	MC KINNEY	40484	STANFORD	41352	MIZE	41425	EZEL
40452	MITCHELLSBURG	40464	PARKSVILLE	41362	PRIMROSE	41311	BEATTYVILLE
40467	PEOPLES	40402	ANNVILLE	41368	SAINT HELENS	41311	BEATTYVILLE
40473	RENFRO VALLEY	40456	MOUNT VERNON	41408	CANNEL CITY	41332	HAZEL GREEN
40476	RICHMOND	40475	RICHMOND	41410	CISCO	41465	SALYERSVILLE
40488	WANETA	40447	MC KEE	41413	CROCKETT	41472	WEST LIBERTY
40492	WILDIE	40456	MOUNT VERNON	41421	ELKFORK	41472	WEST LIBERTY
40495	WINSTON	40336	IRVINE	41426	FALCON	41465	SALYERSVILLE
40512	LEXINGTON	40511	LEXINGTON	41433	GAPVILLE	41465	SALYERSVILLE
40522	LEXINGTON	40502	LEXINGTON	41451	MALONE	41472	WEST LIBERTY
40523	LEXINGTON	40517	LEXINGTON	41459	OPHIR	41472	WEST LIBERTY
40524	LEXINGTON	40517	LEXINGTON	41477	WRIGLEY	41472	WEST LIBERTY
40526	LEXINGTON	40508	LEXINGTON	41502	PIKEVILLE	41501	PIKEVILLE
40533	LEXINGTON	40504	LEXINGTON	41517	BURDINE	41537	JENKINS
40536	LEXINGTON	40508	LEXINGTON	41520	DORTON	41537	JENKINS
40544	LEXINGTON	40504	LEXINGTON	41526	FORDS BRANCH	41501	PIKEVILLE
40546	LEXINGTON	40508	LEXINGTON	41534	HELLIER	41522	ELKHORN CITY
40555	LEXINGTON	40505	LEXINGTON	41538	JONANCY	41537	JENKINS
40574	LEXINGTON	40511	LEXINGTON	41542	LOOKOUT	41522	ELKHORN CITY
40575	LEXINGTON	40511	LEXINGTON	41547	MAJESTIC	41528	FREEBURN
40576	LEXINGTON	40511	LEXINGTON	41549	MYRA	41537	JENKINS
40577	LEXINGTON	40511	LEXINGTON	41561	ROCKHOUSE	41522	ELKHORN CITY
40578	LEXINGTON	40511	LEXINGTON	41612	BYPRO	41650	MELVIN
40579	LEXINGTON	40511	LEXINGTON	41619	DRIFT	41631	GRETHEL
40580	LEXINGTON	40511	LEXINGTON	41621	DWALE	41653	PRESTONSBURG
40581	LEXINGTON	40511	LEXINGTON	41651	MINNIE	41631	GRETHEL
40582	LEXINGTON	40511	LEXINGTON	41659	STANVILLE	41605	BETSY LAYNE
40583	LEXINGTON	40511	LEXINGTON	41663	TRAM	41642	IVEL
40588	LEXINGTON	40507	LEXINGTON	41667	WEEKSBURY	41606	BEVINSVILLE
40591	LEXINGTON	40513	LEXINGTON	41669	WHEELWRIGHT	41606	BEVINSVILLE
40598	LEXINGTON	40511	LEXINGTON	41702	HAZARD	41701	HAZARD
40602	FRANKFORT	40601	FRANKFORT	41713	AVAWAM	41701	HAZARD
40603	FRANKFORT	40601	FRANKFORT	41739	DWARF	41722	BULAN
40604	FRANKFORT	40601	FRANKFORT	41747	HARDBURLY	41722	BULAN
40618	FRANKFORT	40601	FRANKFORT	41751	JEFF	41701	HAZARD
40619	FRANKFORT	40601	FRANKFORT	41762	SIZEROCK	41714	BEAR BRANCH
40620	FRANKFORT	40601	FRANKFORT	41766	THOUSANDSTICKS	41749	HYDEN
40621	FRANKFORT	40601	FRANKFORT	41778	YERKES	41723	BUSY
40622	FRANKFORT	40601	FRANKFORT	41810	CROMONA	41858	WHITESBURG
40702	CORBIN	40701	CORBIN	41901	MIGRATE	40511	LEXINGTON
40724	BUSH	40744	LONDON	41902	MIGRATE	40511	LEXINGTON
40730	EMLYN	40769	WILLIAMSBURG	41903	MIGRATE	40511	LEXINGTON
40742	LONDON	40741	LONDON	41904	MIGRATE	40511	LEXINGTON
40743	LONDON	40741	LONDON	41905	MIGRATE	40511	LEXINGTON
40745	LONDON	40741	LONDON	41906	MIGRATE	40511	LEXINGTON
40751	MARYDELL	40741	LONDON	42002	PADUCAH	42003	PADUCAH
40755	PITTSBURG	40741	LONDON	42022	BANDANA	42056	LA CENTER
40803	ASHER	40858	MOZELLE	42033	CRAYNE	42064	MARION
40816	CHAPPELL	40858	MOZELLE	42037	DYCUSBURG	42064	MARION
40827	ESSIE	40858	MOZELLE	42060	LOVELACEVILLE	42053	KEVIL

KENTUCKY

LOUISIANA

Point ZIP Code		Enclosing Residential ZIP Code		Point ZIP Code		Enclosing Residential ZIP Code	
ZIP	**Post Office Name**	**ZIP**	**Post Office Name**	**ZIP**	**Post Office Name**	**ZIP**	**Post Office Name**
42061	LOWES	42051	HICKORY	70160	NEW ORLEANS	70113	NEW ORLEANS
42063	LYNNVILLE	42079	SEDALIA	70161	NEW ORLEANS	70113	NEW ORLEANS
42070	MILBURN	42021	ARLINGTON	70162	NEW ORLEANS	70112	NEW ORLEANS
42084	TOLU	42064	MARION	70163	NEW ORLEANS	70112	NEW ORLEANS
42102	BOWLING GREEN	42101	BOWLING GREEN	70164	NEW ORLEANS	70121	NEW ORLEANS
42128	DRAKE	42122	ALVATON	70165	NEW ORLEANS	70130	NEW ORLEANS
42135	FRANKLIN	42134	FRANKLIN	70166	NEW ORLEANS	70112	NEW ORLEANS
42142	GLASGOW	42141	GLASGOW	70167	NEW ORLEANS	70119	NEW ORLEANS
42150	HALFWAY	42164	SCOTTSVILLE	70170	NEW ORLEANS	70130	NEW ORLEANS
42152	HISEVILLE	42141	GLASGOW	70172	NEW ORLEANS	70112	NEW ORLEANS
42201	ABERDEEN	42261	MORGANTOWN	70174	NEW ORLEANS	70114	NEW ORLEANS
42203	ALLEGRE	42280	SHARON GROVE	70175	NEW ORLEANS	70115	NEW ORLEANS
42209	BROOKLYN	42261	MORGANTOWN	70176	NEW ORLEANS	70130	NEW ORLEANS
42216	CLIFTY	42220	ELKTON	70177	NEW ORLEANS	70117	NEW ORLEANS
42219	DUNBAR	42261	MORGANTOWN	70178	NEW ORLEANS	70118	NEW ORLEANS
42221	FAIRVIEW	42266	PEMBROKE	70179	NEW ORLEANS	70119	NEW ORLEANS
42241	HOPKINSVILLE	42240	HOPKINSVILLE	70181	NEW ORLEANS	70121	NEW ORLEANS
42251	HUNTSVILLE	42261	MORGANTOWN	70182	NEW ORLEANS	70122	NEW ORLEANS
42267	PROVO	42273	ROCHESTER	70183	NEW ORLEANS	70123	NEW ORLEANS
42270	RICHARDSVILLE	42101	BOWLING GREEN	70184	NEW ORLEANS	70119	NEW ORLEANS
42283	SOUTH UNION	42206	AUBURN	70185	NEW ORLEANS	70118	NEW ORLEANS
42288	WOODBURY	42261	MORGANTOWN	70186	NEW ORLEANS	70126	NEW ORLEANS
42302	OWENSBORO	42303	OWENSBORO	70187	NEW ORLEANS	70127	NEW ORLEANS
42304	OWENSBORO	42301	OWENSBORO	70189	NEW ORLEANS	70129	NEW ORLEANS
42322	BEECH GROVE	42327	CALHOUN	70190	NEW ORLEANS	70130	NEW ORLEANS
42332	CLEATON	42330	CENTRAL CITY	70195	NEW ORLEANS	70112	NEW ORLEANS
42334	CURDSVILLE	42301	OWENSBORO	70302	THIBODAUX	70301	THIBODAUX
42356	MAPLE MOUNT	42301	OWENSBORO	70310	THIBODAUX	70301	THIBODAUX
42364	PELLVILLE	42348	HAWESVILLE	70340	AMELIA	70380	MORGAN CITY
42370	ROSINE	42349	HORSE BRANCH	70352	DONNER	70395	SCHRIEVER
42374	SOUTH CARROLLTON	42330	CENTRAL CITY	70361	HOUMA	70360	HOUMA
42375	STANLEY	42301	OWENSBORO	70371	KRAEMER	70301	THIBODAUX
42377	WEST LOUISVILLE	42301	OWENSBORO	70373	LAROSE	70345	CUT OFF
42402	BASKETT	42420	HENDERSON	70381	MORGAN CITY	70380	MORGAN CITY
42403	BLACKFORD	42404	CLAY	70391	PAINCOURTVILLE	70390	NAPOLEONVILLE
42419	HENDERSON	42420	HENDERSON	70393	PLATTENVILLE	70341	BELLE ROSE
42440	MORTONS GAP	42431	MADISONVILLE	70404	HAMMOND	70401	HAMMOND
42444	POOLE	42455	SEBREE	70421	AKERS	70454	PONCHATOULA
42457	SMITH MILLS	42406	CORYDON	70429	BOGALUSA	70427	BOGALUSA
42460	SULLIVAN	42459	STURGIS	70434	COVINGTON	70433	COVINGTON
42463	WHEATCROFT	42404	CLAY	70451	NATALBANY	70401	HAMMOND
42502	SOMERSET	42501	SOMERSET	70457	SAINT BENEDICT	70435	COVINGTON
42558	TATEVILLE	42553	SCIENCE HILL	70459	SLIDELL	70458	SLIDELL
42564	WEST SOMERSET	42503	SOMERSET	70463	SUN	70427	BOGALUSA
42631	MARSHES SIDING	42653	WHITLEY CITY	70464	TALISHEEK	70431	BUSH
42702	ELIZABETHTOWN	42701	ELIZABETHTOWN	70465	TANGIPAHOA	70444	KENTWOOD
42719	CAMPBELLSVILLE	42718	CAMPBELLSVILLE	70469	SLIDELL	70460	SLIDELL
42720	CANE VALLEY	42728	COLUMBIA	70470	MANDEVILLE	70471	MANDEVILLE
42755	LEITCHFIELD	42754	LEITCHFIELD	70502	LAFAYETTE	70501	LAFAYETTE
42758	MANNSVILLE	42718	CAMPBELLSVILLE	70505	LAFAYETTE	70503	LAFAYETTE
42759	MARROWBONE	42717	BURKESVILLE	70509	LAFAYETTE	70501	LAFAYETTE
42783	SUMMIT	42732	EASTVIEW	70511	ABBEVILLE	70510	ABBEVILLE
42786	WATERVIEW	42717	BURKESVILLE	70513	AVERY ISLAND	70560	NEW IBERIA
45277	CINCINNATI	41015	LATONIA	70519	CADE	70582	SAINT MARTINVILLE
45298	CINCINNATI	41011	COVINGTON	70521	CECILIA	70517	BREAUX BRIDGE
45944	CINCINNATI	41011	COVINGTON	70522	CENTERVILLE	70538	FRANKLIN
45999	CINCINNATI	41011	COVINGTON	70523	CHARENTON	70544	JEANERETTE
70004	METAIRIE	70001	METAIRIE	70524	CHATAIGNIER	70535	EUNICE
70009	METAIRIE	70002	METAIRIE	70527	CROWLEY	70526	CROWLEY
70010	METAIRIE	70002	METAIRIE	70534	ESTHERWOOD	70559	MORSE
70011	METAIRIE	70002	METAIRIE	70540	GARDEN CITY	70538	FRANKLIN
70033	METAIRIE	70003	METAIRIE	70541	GRAND COTEAU	70570	OPELOUSAS
70038	BOOTHVILLE	70041	BURAS	70550	LAWTELL	70570	OPELOUSAS
70044	CHALMETTE	70043	CHALMETTE	70551	LEONVILLE	70570	OPELOUSAS
70050	EMPIRE	70041	BURAS	70556	MERMENTAU	70559	MORSE
70054	GRETNA	70053	GRETNA	70558	MILTON	70560	NEW IBERIA
70055	METAIRIE	70005	METAIRIE	70562	NEW IBERIA	70560	NEW IBERIA
70059	HARVEY	70058	HARVEY	70569	LYDIA	70560	NEW IBERIA
70060	METAIRIE	70002	METAIRIE	70571	OPELOUSAS	70570	OPELOUSAS
70063	KENNER	70062	KENNER	70575	PERRY	70510	ABBEVILLE
70064	KENNER	70065	KENNER	70576	PINE PRAIRIE	70586	VILLE PLATTE
70069	LA PLACE	70068	LA PLACE	70580	REDDELL	70554	MAMOU
70073	MARRERO	70072	MARRERO	70585	TURKEY CREEK	70586	VILLE PLATTE
70078	NEW SARPY	70047	DESTREHAN	70596	LAFAYETTE	70506	LAFAYETTE
70082	POINTE A LA HACHE	70040	BRAITHWAITE	70598	LAFAYETTE	70508	LAFAYETTE
70096	WESTWEGO	70094	WESTWEGO	70602	LAKE CHARLES	70601	LAKE CHARLES
70139	NEW ORLEANS	70130	NEW ORLEANS	70606	LAKE CHARLES	70605	LAKE CHARLES
70140	NEW ORLEANS	70112	NEW ORLEANS	70612	LAKE CHARLES	70611	LAKE CHARLES
70141	NEW ORLEANS	70126	NEW ORLEANS	70616	LAKE CHARLES	70615	LAKE CHARLES
70142	NEW ORLEANS	70113	NEW ORLEANS	70629	LAKE CHARLES	70601	LAKE CHARLES
70143	NEW ORLEANS	70037	BELLE CHASSE	70638	ELIZABETH	71463	OAKDALE
70145	NEW ORLEANS	70117	NEW ORLEANS	70640	FENTON	70648	KINDER
70146	NEW ORLEANS	70117	NEW ORLEANS	70644	GRANT	70654	MITTIE
70149	NEW ORLEANS	70117	NEW ORLEANS	70646	HAYES	70647	IOWA
70150	NEW ORLEANS	70113	NEW ORLEANS	70651	LEBLANC	70658	REEVES
70151	NEW ORLEANS	70113	NEW ORLEANS	70659	ROSEPINE	71446	LEESVILLE
70152	NEW ORLEANS	70113	NEW ORLEANS	70664	SULPHUR	70663	SULPHUR
70153	NEW ORLEANS	70113	NEW ORLEANS	70704	BAKER	70714	BAKER
70154	NEW ORLEANS	70115	NEW ORLEANS	70707	GONZALES	70737	GONZALES
70156	NEW ORLEANS	70113	NEW ORLEANS	70718	BRITTANY	70737	GONZALES
70157	NEW ORLEANS	70113	NEW ORLEANS	70727	DENHAM SPRINGS	70726	DENHAM SPRINGS
70158	NEW ORLEANS	70113	NEW ORLEANS	70728	DUPLESSIS	70737	GONZALES
70159	NEW ORLEANS	70117	NEW ORLEANS	70738	BURNSIDE	70737	GONZALES

LOUISIANA   **MAINE**

Point ZIP Code		Enclosing Residential ZIP Code		Point ZIP Code		Enclosing Residential ZIP Code	
ZIP	Post Office Name	ZIP	Post Office Name	ZIP	Post Office Name	ZIP	Post Office Name
70743	HESTER	70763	PAULINA	71345	LEBEAU	70589	WASHINGTON
70747	INNIS	70715	BATCHELOR	71348	LIBUSE	71360	PINEVILLE
70765	PLAQUEMINE	70764	PLAQUEMINE	71359	PINEVILLE	71360	PINEVILLE
70782	TUNICA	70775	SAINT FRANCISVILLE	71361	PINEVILLE	71360	PINEVILLE
70784	WAKEFIELD	70775	SAINT FRANCISVILLE	71363	RHINEHART	71340	HARRISONBURG
70786	WATSON	70706	DENHAM SPRINGS	71365	RUBY	71360	PINEVILLE
70787	WEYANOKE	70775	SAINT FRANCISVILLE	71377	WILDSVILLE	71343	JONESVILLE
70804	BATON ROUGE	70802	BATON ROUGE	71405	BALL	71360	PINEVILLE
70821	BATON ROUGE	70802	BATON ROUGE	71410	CALVIN	71483	WINNFIELD
70822	BATON ROUGE	70806	BATON ROUGE	71414	CLARENCE	71457	NATCHITOCHES
70823	BATON ROUGE	70802	BATON ROUGE	71415	CLARKS	71435	GRAYSON
70825	BATON ROUGE	70802	BATON ROUGE	71428	FLORA	71469	ROBELINE
70826	BATON ROUGE	70802	BATON ROUGE	71431	GARDNER	71409	BOYCE
70827	BATON ROUGE	70816	BATON ROUGE	71434	GORUM	71468	PROVENCAL
70831	BATON ROUGE	70802	BATON ROUGE	71440	JOYCE	71483	WINNFIELD
70833	BATON ROUGE	70802	BATON ROUGE	71443	KURTHWOOD	71446	LEESVILLE
70835	BATON ROUGE	70816	BATON ROUGE	71448	LONGLEAF	71430	FOREST HILL
70836	BATON ROUGE	70802	BATON ROUGE	71452	MELROSE	71456	NATCHEZ
70837	BATON ROUGE	70802	BATON ROUGE	71458	NATCHITOCHES	71457	NATCHITOCHES
70874	BATON ROUGE	70811	BATON ROUGE	71460	NEGREET	71429	FLORIEN
70879	BATON ROUGE	70816	BATON ROUGE	71471	SAINT MAURICE	71457	NATCHITOCHES
70883	BATON ROUGE	70806	BATON ROUGE	71474	SIMPSON	71446	LEESVILLE
70884	BATON ROUGE	70810	BATON ROUGE	71475	SLAGLE	71446	LEESVILLE
70892	BATON ROUGE	70805	BATON ROUGE	71477	TIOGA	71360	PINEVILLE
70893	BATON ROUGE	70820	BATON ROUGE	71480	URANIA	71479	TULLOS
70894	BATON ROUGE	70803	BATON ROUGE	71496	LEESVILLE	71446	LEESVILLE
70895	BATON ROUGE	70815	BATON ROUGE	71497	NATCHITOCHES	71457	NATCHITOCHES
70896	BATON ROUGE	70806	BATON ROUGE	03804	PORTSMOUTH	03904	KITTERY
70898	BATON ROUGE	70808	BATON ROUGE	03910	YORK BEACH	03909	YORK
71002	ASHLAND	71016	CASTOR	03911	YORK HARBOR	03909	YORK
71009	BLANCHARD	71107	SHREVEPORT	04004	BAR MILLS	04093	BUXTON
71021	CULLEN	71071	SAREPTA	04007	BIDDEFORD	04005	BIDDEFORD
71025	EAST POINT	71019	COUSHATTA	04014	CAPE PORPOISE	04046	KENNEBUNKPORT
71036	HARMON	71019	COUSHATTA	04028	EAST PARSONFIELD	04047	PARSONSFIELD
71050	LONGSTREET	71049	LOGANSPORT	04033	FREEPORT	04032	FREEPORT
71058	MINDEN	71055	MINDEN	04034	FREEPORT	04032	FREEPORT
71066	POWHATAN	71457	NATCHITOCHES	04053	MEREPOINT	04011	BRUNSWICK
71080	TAYLOR	71028	GIBSLAND	04054	MOODY	04090	WELLS
71102	SHREVEPORT	71103	SHREVEPORT	04056	NEWFIELD	04095	WEST NEWFIELD
71113	BOSSIER CITY	71112	BOSSIER CITY	04057	NORTH BRIDGTON	04040	HARRISON
71120	SHREVEPORT	71101	SHREVEPORT	04063	OCEAN PARK	04064	OLD ORCHARD BEACH
71130	SHREVEPORT	71103	SHREVEPORT	04070	SCARBOROUGH	04074	SCARBOROUGH
71133	SHREVEPORT	71103	SHREVEPORT	04075	SEBAGO LAKE	04084	STANDISH
71134	SHREVEPORT	71104	SHREVEPORT	04077	SOUTH CASCO	04015	CASCO
71135	SHREVEPORT	71105	SHREVEPORT	04078	SOUTH FREEPORT	04032	FREEPORT
71136	SHREVEPORT	71106	SHREVEPORT	04082	SOUTH WINDHAM	04062	WINDHAM
71137	SHREVEPORT	71107	SHREVEPORT	04094	WEST KENNEBUNK	04043	KENNEBUNK
71138	SHREVEPORT	71118	SHREVEPORT	04098	WESTBROOK	04092	WESTBROOK
71148	SHREVEPORT	71108	SHREVEPORT	04104	PORTLAND	04101	PORTLAND
71149	SHREVEPORT	71103	SHREVEPORT	04112	PORTLAND	04101	PORTLAND
71151	SHREVEPORT	71108	SHREVEPORT	04116	SOUTH PORTLAND	04101	PORTLAND
71152	SHREVEPORT	71108	SHREVEPORT	04122	PORTLAND	04102	PORTLAND
71153	SHREVEPORT	71101	SHREVEPORT	04123	PORTLAND	04102	PORTLAND
71154	SHREVEPORT	71101	SHREVEPORT	04124	PORTLAND	04102	PORTLAND
71156	SHREVEPORT	71101	SHREVEPORT	04211	AUBURN	04210	AUBURN
71161	SHREVEPORT	71101	SHREVEPORT	04212	AUBURN	04210	AUBURN
71162	SHREVEPORT	71101	SHREVEPORT	04223	DANVILLE	04210	AUBURN
71163	SHREVEPORT	71101	SHREVEPORT	04227	EAST DIXFIELD	04294	WILTON
71164	SHREVEPORT	71101	SHREVEPORT	04230	EAST POLAND	04274	POLAND
71165	SHREVEPORT	71101	SHREVEPORT	04234	EAST WILTON	04294	WILTON
71166	SHREVEPORT	71101	SHREVEPORT	04241	LEWISTON	04240	LEWISTON
71171	BOSSIER CITY	71111	BOSSIER CITY	04243	LEWISTON	04240	LEWISTON
71172	BOSSIER CITY	71112	BOSSIER CITY	04262	NORTH JAY	04239	JAY
71207	MONROE	71201	MONROE	04271	PARIS	04281	SOUTH PARIS
71208	MONROE	71202	MONROE	04283	TURNER CENTER	04282	TURNER
71210	MONROE	71201	MONROE	04286	WEST BETHEL	04217	BETHEL
71211	MONROE	71201	MONROE	04288	WEST MINOT	04258	MINOT
71212	MONROE	71209	MONROE	04291	WEST POLAND	04274	POLAND
71213	MONROE	71201	MONROE	04332	AUGUSTA	04330	AUGUSTA
71218	ARCHIBALD	71259	MANGHAM	04336	AUGUSTA	04330	AUGUSTA
71221	BASTROP	71220	BASTROP	04338	AUGUSTA	04330	AUGUSTA
71230	CROWVILLE	71295	WINNSBORO	04343	EAST WINTHROP	04364	WINTHROP
71233	DELTA	71282	TALLULAH	04359	SOUTH GARDINER	04345	GARDINER
71240	FAIRBANKS	71201	MONROE	04402	BANGOR	04401	BANGOR
71242	FOREST	71263	OAK GROVE	04415	BROWNVILLE JUNCTION	04414	BROWNVILLE
71247	HODGE	71251	JONESBORO	04420	CASTINE	04421	CASTINE
71249	JIGGER	71295	WINNSBORO	04467	OLAMON	04418	GREENBUSH
71253	KILBOURNE	71263	OAK GROVE	04485	SHIRLEY MILLS	04406	ABBOT
71272	RUSTON	71270	RUSTON	04489	STILLWATER	04468	OLD TOWN
71273	RUSTON	71270	RUSTON	04536	BAYVILLE	04538	BOOTHBAY HARBOR
71279	START	71269	RAYVILLE	04575	WEST BOOTHBAY HARBOR	04538	BOOTHBAY HARBOR
71281	SWARTZ	71201	MONROE	04629	EAST BLUE HILL	04614	BLUE HILL
71284	TALLULAH	71282	TALLULAH	04637	GRAND LAKE STREAM	04668	PRINCETON
71294	WEST MONROE	71291	WEST MONROE	04644	HULLS COVE	04609	BAR HARBOR
71306	ALEXANDRIA	71301	ALEXANDRIA	04662	NORTHEAST HARBOR	04609	BAR HARBOR
71307	ALEXANDRIA	71302	ALEXANDRIA	04664	SULLIVAN	04634	FRANKLIN
71309	ALEXANDRIA	71301	ALEXANDRIA	04672	SALSBURY COVE	04609	BAR HARBOR
71315	ALEXANDRIA	71301	ALEXANDRIA	04674	SEAL COVE	04660	MOUNT DESERT
71320	BORDELONVILLE	71355	MOREAUVILLE	04675	SEAL HARBOR	04609	BAR HARBOR
71324	CHASE	71295	WINNSBORO	04686	WESLEY	04654	MACHIAS
71329	DUPONT	71362	PLAUCHEVILLE	04738	CROUSEVILLE	04786	WASHBURN
71330	ECHO	71351	MARKSVILLE	04739	EAGLE LAKE	04743	FORT KENT
71339	HAMBURG	71369	SIMMESPORT	04744	FORT KENT MILLS	04743	FORT KENT

MAINE   **MARYLAND**

Point ZIP Code ZIP	Post Office Name	Enclosing Residential ZIP Code ZIP	Post Office Name	Point ZIP Code ZIP	Post Office Name	Enclosing Residential ZIP Code ZIP	Post Office Name
04759	MASARDIS	04732	ASHLAND	20918	SILVER SPRING	20901	SILVER SPRING
04770	QUIMBY	04743	FORT KENT	20997	SILVER SPRING	20910	SILVER SPRING
04775	SHERIDAN	04732	ASHLAND	21018	BENSON	21014	BEL AIR
04788	WINTERVILLE	04743	FORT KENT	21020	BORING	21155	UPPERCO
04846	GLEN COVE	04841	ROCKLAND	21022	BROOKLANDVILLE	21093	LUTHERVILLE TIMONIUM
04850	LINCOLNVILLE CENTER	04849	LINCOLNVILLE	21023	BUTLER	21152	SPARKS GLENCOE
04855	PORT CLYDE	04860	TENANTS HARBOR	21027	CHASE	21220	MIDDLE RIVER
04865	WEST ROCKPORT	04856	ROCKPORT	21041	ELLICOTT CITY	21043	ELLICOTT CITY
04903	WATERVILLE	04901	WATERVILLE	21052	FORT HOWARD	21219	SPARROWS POINT
04926	CHINA VILLAGE	04962	NORTH VASSALBORO	21055	GARRISON	21117	OWINGS MILLS
04933	EAST NEWPORT	04969	PLYMOUTH	21062	GLEN BURNIE	21061	GLEN BURNIE
04935	EAST VASSALBORO	04989	VASSALBORO	21065	HUNT VALLEY	21031	HUNT VALLEY
04940	FARMINGTON FALLS	04938	FARMINGTON	21088	LINEBORO CPO	21102	MANCHESTER
04944	HINCKLEY	04937	FAIRFIELD	21092	LONG GREEN	21057	GLEN ARM
04964	OQUOSSOC	04970	RANGELEY	21094	LUTHERVILLE TIMONIUM	21093	LUTHERVILLE TIMONIUM
04972	SANDY POINT	04981	STOCKTON SPRINGS	21098	HANOVER	21076	HANOVER
04975	SHAWMUT	04937	FAIRFIELD	21105	MARYLAND LINE	21053	FREELAND
04992	WEST FARMINGTON	04938	FARMINGTON	21106	MAYO	21037	EDGEWATER
20058	WASHINGTON	20817	BETHESDA	21123	PASADENA	21122	PASADENA
20207	WASHINGTON	20814	BETHESDA	21130	PERRYMAN	21001	ABERDEEN
20233	WASHINGTON	20746	SUITLAND	21139	RIDERWOOD	21286	TOWSON
20389	WASHINGTON	20746	SUITLAND	21150	SIMPSONVILLE	21044	COLUMBIA
20395	WASHINGTON	20746	SUITLAND	21153	STEVENSON	21093	LUTHERVILLE TIMONIUM
20409	WASHINGTON	20746	SUITLAND	21203	BALTIMORE	21202	BALTIMORE
20599	WASHINGTON	20746	SUITLAND	21233	BALTIMORE	21202	BALTIMORE
20604	WALDORF	20602	WALDORF	21235	BALTIMORE	21207	GWYNN OAK
20610	BARSTOW	20678	PRINCE FREDERICK	21241	BALTIMORE	21207	GWYNN OAK
20612	BENEDICT	20637	HUGHESVILLE	21263	BALTIMORE	21202	BALTIMORE
20627	COMPTON	20650	LEONARDTOWN	21264	BALTIMORE	21218	BALTIMORE
20629	DOWELL	20688	SOLOMONS	21265	BALTIMORE	21202	BALTIMORE
20635	HELEN	20659	MECHANICSVILLE	21268	BALTIMORE	21227	HALETHORPE
20643	IRONSIDES	20640	INDIAN HEAD	21270	BALTIMORE	21215	BALTIMORE
20660	MORGANZA	20659	MECHANICSVILLE	21273	BALTIMORE	21202	BALTIMORE
20661	MOUNT VICTORIA	20664	NEWBURG	21274	BALTIMORE	21202	BALTIMORE
20682	ROCK POINT	20618	BUSHWOOD	21275	BALTIMORE	21202	BALTIMORE
20686	SAINT MARYS CITY	20653	LEXINGTON PARK	21278	BALTIMORE	21218	BALTIMORE
20703	LANHAM	20706	LANHAM	21279	BALTIMORE	21202	BALTIMORE
20704	BELTSVILLE	20705	BELTSVILLE	21280	BALTIMORE	21202	BALTIMORE
20709	LAUREL	20708	LAUREL	21281	BALTIMORE	21224	BALTIMORE
20717	BOWIE	20716	BOWIE	21282	BALTIMORE	21208	PIKESVILLE
20718	BOWIE	20715	BOWIE	21283	BALTIMORE	21202	BALTIMORE
20719	BOWIE	20720	BOWIE	21284	BALTIMORE	21204	TOWSON
20725	LAUREL	20707	LAUREL	21285	BALTIMORE	21204	TOWSON
20726	LAUREL	20707	LAUREL	21287	BALTIMORE	21205	BALTIMORE
20731	CAPITOL HEIGHTS	20743	CAPITOL HEIGHTS	21288	BALTIMORE	21202	BALTIMORE
20738	RIVERDALE	20737	RIVERDALE	21289	BALTIMORE	21207	GWYNN OAK
20741	COLLEGE PARK	20740	COLLEGE PARK	21290	BALTIMORE	21201	BALTIMORE
20749	FORT WASHINGTON	20744	FORT WASHINGTON	21297	BALTIMORE	21202	BALTIMORE
20750	OXON HILL	20745	OXON HILL	21298	BALTIMORE	21202	BALTIMORE
20752	SUITLAND	20746	SUITLAND	21404	ANNAPOLIS	21401	ANNAPOLIS
20753	DISTRICT HEIGHTS	20747	DISTRICT HEIGHTS	21405	ANNAPOLIS	21401	ANNAPOLIS
20757	TEMPLE HILLS	20748	TEMPLE HILLS	21411	ANNAPOLIS	21401	ANNAPOLIS
20765	GALESVILLE	20776	HARWOOD	21412	ANNAPOLIS	21402	ANNAPOLIS
20768	GREENBELT	20770	GREENBELT	21501	CUMBERLAND	21502	CUMBERLAND
20773	UPPER MARLBORO	20772	UPPER MARLBORO	21503	CUMBERLAND	21502	CUMBERLAND
20775	UPPER MARLBORO	20774	UPPER MARLBORO	21504	CUMBERLAND	21502	CUMBERLAND
20787	HYATTSVILLE	20912	TAKOMA PARK	21505	CUMBERLAND	21502	CUMBERLAND
20788	HYATTSVILLE	20782	HYATTSVILLE	21524	CORRIGANVILLE	21502	CUMBERLAND
20790	CAPITOL HEIGHTS	20743	CAPITOL HEIGHTS	21528	ECKHART MINES	21532	FROSTBURG
20791	CAPITOL HEIGHTS	20743	CAPITOL HEIGHTS	21529	ELLERSLIE	21502	CUMBERLAND
20792	UPPER MARLBORO	20774	UPPER MARLBORO	21542	MIDLAND	21532	FROSTBURG
20799	CAPITOL HEIGHTS	20743	CAPITOL HEIGHTS	21543	MIDLOTHIAN	21532	FROSTBURG
20810	BETHESDA	20815	CHEVY CHASE	21556	PINTO	21557	RAWLINGS
20811	BETHESDA	20815	CHEVY CHASE	21560	SPRING GAP	21502	CUMBERLAND
20813	BETHESDA	20815	CHEVY CHASE	21606	EASTON	21601	EASTON
20824	BETHESDA	20814	BETHESDA	21609	BETHLEHEM	21655	PRESTON
20825	CHEVY CHASE	20815	CHEVY CHASE	21624	CLAIBORNE	21663	SAINT MICHAELS
20827	BETHESDA	20817	BETHESDA	21627	CROCHERON	21672	TODDVILLE
20830	OLNEY	20832	OLNEY	21641	HILLSBORO	21629	DENTON
20847	ROCKVILLE	20852	ROCKVILLE	21652	NEAVITT	21612	BOZMAN
20848	ROCKVILLE	20851	ROCKVILLE	21653	NEWCOMB	21663	SAINT MICHAELS
20849	ROCKVILLE	20850	ROCKVILLE	21656	PRICE	21623	CHURCH HILL
20857	ROCKVILLE	20852	ROCKVILLE	21664	SECRETARY	21631	EAST NEW MARKET
20859	POTOMAC	20854	POTOMAC	21670	TEMPLEVILLE	21649	MARYDEL
20875	GERMANTOWN	20874	GERMANTOWN	21681	RIDGELY	21660	RIDGELY
20880	WASHINGTON GROVE	20877	GAITHERSBURG	21682	RIDGELY	21660	RIDGELY
20883	GAITHERSBURG	20878	GAITHERSBURG	21683	RIDGELY	21660	RIDGELY
20884	GAITHERSBURG	20877	GAITHERSBURG	21684	RIDGELY	21660	RIDGELY
20885	GAITHERSBURG	20878	GAITHERSBURG	21685	RIDGELY	21660	RIDGELY
20889	BETHESDA	20814	BETHESDA	21687	RIDGELY	21660	RIDGELY
20891	KENSINGTON	20895	KENSINGTON	21690	CHESTERTOWN	21620	CHESTERTOWN
20892	BETHESDA	20814	BETHESDA	21705	FREDERICK	21702	FREDERICK
20894	BETHESDA	20814	BETHESDA	21709	FREDERICK	21701	FREDERICK
20896	GARRETT PARK	20895	KENSINGTON	21714	BRADDOCK HEIGHTS	21702	FREDERICK
20898	GAITHERSBURG	20855	DERWOOD	21715	BROWNSVILLE	21758	KNOXVILLE
20899	GAITHERSBURG	20878	GAITHERSBURG	21717	BUCKEYSTOWN	21704	FREDERICK
20907	SILVER SPRING	20910	SILVER SPRING	21720	CAVETOWN	21783	SMITHSBURG
20908	SILVER SPRING	20906	SILVER SPRING	21721	CHEWSVILLE	21783	SMITHSBURG
20911	SILVER SPRING	20910	SILVER SPRING	21734	FUNKSTOWN	21740	HAGERSTOWN
20913	TAKOMA PARK	20912	TAKOMA PARK	21741	HAGERSTOWN	21740	HAGERSTOWN
20914	SILVER SPRING	20904	SILVER SPRING	21746	HAGERSTOWN	21733	FAIRPLAY
20915	SILVER SPRING	20902	SILVER SPRING	21747	HAGERSTOWN	21742	HAGERSTOWN
20916	SILVER SPRING	20906	SILVER SPRING	21748	HAGERSTOWN	21742	HAGERSTOWN

NONRESIDENTIAL ZIP CODES

MARYLAND   **MASSACHUSETTS**

Point ZIP Code ZIP	Post Office Name	Enclosing Residential ZIP Code ZIP	Post Office Name	Point ZIP Code ZIP	Post Office Name	Enclosing Residential ZIP Code ZIP	Post Office Name
21749	HAGERSTOWN	21742	HAGERSTOWN	01805	BURLINGTON	01803	BURLINGTON
21759	LADIESBURG	21757	KEYMAR	01806	WOBURN	01801	WOBURN
21762	LIBERTYTOWN	21701	FREDERICK	01807	WOBURN	01801	WOBURN
21775	NEW MIDWAY	21757	KEYMAR	01808	WOBURN	01801	WOBURN
21781	SAINT JAMES	21733	FAIRPLAY	01812	ANDOVER	01810	ANDOVER
21792	UNIONVILLE	21791	UNION BRIDGE	01813	WOBURN	01801	WOBURN
21802	SALISBURY	21804	SALISBURY	01815	WOBURN	01801	WOBURN
21803	SALISBURY	21801	SALISBURY	01822	BILLERICA	01824	CHELMSFORD
21810	ALLEN	21822	EDEN	01831	HAVERHILL	01830	HAVERHILL
21836	MANOKIN	21871	WESTOVER	01842	LAWRENCE	01840	LAWRENCE
21843	OCEAN CITY	21842	OCEAN CITY	01853	LOWELL	01854	LOWELL
21852	POWELLVILLE	21850	PITTSVILLE	01865	NUTTING LAKE	01821	BILLERICA
21857	REHOBETH	21871	WESTOVER	01866	PINEHURST	01821	BILLERICA
21861	SHARPTOWN	21837	MARDELA SPRINGS	01885	WEST BOXFORD	01921	BOXFORD
21862	SHOWELL	21811	BERLIN	01888	WOBURN	01801	WOBURN
21867	UPPER FAIRMOUNT	21871	WESTOVER	01889	NORTH READING	01864	NORTH READING
21890	WESTOVER	21871	WESTOVER	01899	ANDOVER	01810	ANDOVER
21902	PERRY POINT	21903	PERRYVILLE	01903	LYNN	01901	LYNN
21916	CHILDS	21921	ELKTON	01910	LYNN	01905	LYNN
21920	ELK MILLS	21921	ELKTON	01931	GLOUCESTER	01930	GLOUCESTER
21922	ELKTON	21921	ELKTON	01936	HAMILTON	01982	SOUTH HAMILTON
21930	GEORGETOWN	21919	EARLEVILLE	01937	HATHORNE	01923	DANVERS
01004	AMHERST	01002	AMHERST	01961	PEABODY	01960	PEABODY
01009	BONDSVILLE	01069	PALMER	01965	PRIDES CROSSING	01915	BEVERLY
01014	CHICOPEE	01013	CHICOPEE	01971	SALEM	01970	SALEM
01021	CHICOPEE	01020	CHICOPEE	02018	ACCORD	02043	HINGHAM
01029	EAST OTIS	01253	OTIS	02020	BRANT ROCK	02050	MARSHFIELD
01037	HARDWICK	01082	WARE	02027	DEDHAM	02026	DEDHAM
01041	HOLYOKE	01040	HOLYOKE	02040	GREENBUSH	02066	SCITUATE
01059	NORTH AMHERST	01002	AMHERST	02041	GREEN HARBOR	02050	MARSHFIELD
01061	NORTHAMPTON	01060	NORTHAMPTON	02044	HINGHAM	02043	HINGHAM
01066	NORTH HATFIELD	01038	HATFIELD	02047	HUMAROCK	02050	MARSHFIELD
01074	SOUTH BARRE	01005	BARRE	02051	MARSHFIELD HILLS	02050	MARSHFIELD
01079	THORNDIKE	01069	PALMER	02055	MINOT	02066	SCITUATE
01083	WARREN	01585	WEST BROOKFIELD	02059	NORTH MARSHFIELD	02050	MARSHFIELD
01086	WESTFIELD	01085	WESTFIELD	02060	NORTH SCITUATE	02066	SCITUATE
01090	WEST SPRINGFIELD	01089	WEST SPRINGFIELD	02065	OCEAN BLUFF	02050	MARSHFIELD
01093	WHATELY	01373	SOUTH DEERFIELD	02070	SHELDONVILLE	02093	WRENTHAM
01094	WHEELWRIGHT	01031	GILBERTVILLE	02101	BOSTON	02109	BOSTON
01097	WORONOCO	01085	WESTFIELD	02102	BOSTON	02109	BOSTON
01101	SPRINGFIELD	01103	SPRINGFIELD	02103	BOSTON	02109	BOSTON
01102	SPRINGFIELD	01103	SPRINGFIELD	02104	BOSTON	02109	BOSTON
01111	SPRINGFIELD	01109	SPRINGFIELD	02105	BOSTON	02109	BOSTON
01114	SPRINGFIELD	01105	SPRINGFIELD	02106	BOSTON	02109	BOSTON
01115	SPRINGFIELD	01103	SPRINGFIELD	02107	BOSTON	02109	BOSTON
01116	LONGMEADOW	01106	LONGMEADOW	02112	BOSTON	02109	BOSTON
01133	SPRINGFIELD	01105	SPRINGFIELD	02117	BOSTON	02116	BOSTON
01138	SPRINGFIELD	01108	SPRINGFIELD	02123	BOSTON	02115	BOSTON
01139	SPRINGFIELD	01109	SPRINGFIELD	02133	BOSTON	02108	BOSTON
01144	SPRINGFIELD	01103	SPRINGFIELD	02137	READVILLE	02136	HYDE PARK
01152	SPRINGFIELD	01151	INDIAN ORCHARD	02156	WEST MEDFORD	02155	MEDFORD
01199	SPRINGFIELD	01105	SPRINGFIELD	02185	BRAINTREE	02184	BRAINTREE
01202	PITTSFIELD	01201	PITTSFIELD	02187	MILTON VILLAGE	02186	MILTON
01203	PITTSFIELD	01201	PITTSFIELD	02196	BOSTON	02111	BOSTON
01227	DALTON	01226	DALTON	02201	BOSTON	02108	BOSTON
01229	GLENDALE	01266	WEST STOCKBRIDGE	02203	BOSTON	02114	BOSTON
01242	LENOX DALE	01238	LEE	02204	BOSTON	02150	CHELSEA
01244	MILL RIVER	01230	GREAT BARRINGTON	02205	BOSTON	02111	BOSTON
01252	NORTH EGREMONT	01230	GREAT BARRINGTON	02206	BOSTON	02150	CHELSEA
01260	SOUTH LEE	01238	LEE	02207	BOSTON	02110	BOSTON
01263	STOCKBRIDGE	01262	STOCKBRIDGE	02208	BOSTON	02109	BOSTON
01264	TYRINGHAM	01238	LEE	02209	BOSTON	02109	BOSTON
01302	GREENFIELD	01301	GREENFIELD	02211	BOSTON	02109	BOSTON
01347	LAKE PLEASANT	01349	TURNERS FALLS	02212	BOSTON	02109	BOSTON
01380	WENDELL DEPOT	01379	WENDELL	02216	BOSTON	02109	BOSTON
01438	EAST TEMPLETON	01468	TEMPLETON	02217	BOSTON	02116	BOSTON
01441	WESTMINSTER	01440	GARDNER	02222	BOSTON	02114	BOSTON
01467	STILL RIVER	01451	HARVARD	02228	EAST BOSTON	02128	BOSTON
01471	GROTON	01450	GROTON	02238	CAMBRIDGE	02139	CAMBRIDGE
01472	WEST GROTON	01464	SHIRLEY	02239	CAMBRIDGE	02139	CAMBRIDGE
01477	WINCHENDON SPRINGS	01475	WINCHENDON	02241	BOSTON	02110	BOSTON
01508	CHARLTON CITY	01507	CHARLTON	02266	BOSTON	02127	BOSTON
01509	CHARLTON DEPOT	01507	CHARLTON	02269	QUINCY	02169	QUINCY
01517	EAST PRINCETON	01541	PRINCETON	02283	BOSTON	02111	BOSTON
01525	LINWOOD	01588	WHITINSVILLE	02284	BOSTON	02111	BOSTON
01526	MANCHAUG	01590	SUTTON	02293	BOSTON	02111	BOSTON
01538	NORTH UXBRIDGE	01569	UXBRIDGE	02295	BOSTON	02116	BOSTON
01546	SHREWSBURY	01545	SHREWSBURY	02297	BOSTON	02111	BOSTON
01561	SOUTH LANCASTER	01523	LANCASTER	02303	BROCKTON	02302	BROCKTON
01580	WESTBOROUGH	01581	WESTBOROUGH	02304	BROCKTON	02301	BROCKTON
01582	WESTBOROUGH	01581	WESTBOROUGH	02305	BROCKTON	02301	BROCKTON
01586	WEST MILLBURY	01527	MILLBURY	02327	BRYANTVILLE	02359	PEMBROKE
01601	WORCESTER	01608	WORCESTER	02331	DUXBURY	02332	DUXBURY
01613	WORCESTER	01604	WORCESTER	02334	EASTON	02375	SOUTH EASTON
01614	WORCESTER	01608	WORCESTER	02337	ELMWOOD	02333	EAST BRIDGEWATER
01615	WORCESTER	01605	WORCESTER	02340	HANOVER	02339	HANOVER
01653	WORCESTER	01605	WORCESTER	02344	MIDDLEBORO	02346	MIDDLEBORO
01654	WORCESTER	01605	WORCESTER	02345	MANOMET	02360	PLYMOUTH
01655	WORCESTER	01605	WORCESTER	02348	MIDDLEBORO	02347	LAKEVILLE
01703	FRAMINGHAM	01701	FRAMINGHAM	02349	MIDDLEBORO	02347	LAKEVILLE
01704	FRAMINGHAM	01701	FRAMINGHAM	02350	MONPONSETT	02341	HANSON
01705	FRAMINGHAM	01701	FRAMINGHAM	02355	NORTH CARVER	02330	CARVER
01784	WOODVILLE	01748	HOPKINTON	02358	NORTH PEMBROKE	02359	PEMBROKE

MASSACHUSETTS   **MICHIGAN**

Point ZIP Code — ZIP	Post Office Name	Enclosing Residential ZIP Code — ZIP	Post Office Name	Point ZIP Code — ZIP	Post Office Name	Enclosing Residential ZIP Code — ZIP	Post Office Name
02361	PLYMOUTH	02360	PLYMOUTH	48279	DETROIT	48226	DETROIT
02362	PLYMOUTH	02360	PLYMOUTH	48288	DETROIT	48212	HAMTRAMCK
02366	SOUTH CARVER	02330	CARVER	48303	BLOOMFIELD HILLS	48304	BLOOMFIELD HILLS
02381	WHITE HORSE BEACH	02360	PLYMOUTH	48308	ROCHESTER	48307	ROCHESTER
02447	BROOKLINE VILLAGE	02445	BROOKLINE	48311	STERLING HEIGHTS	48312	STERLING HEIGHTS
02454	WALTHAM	02451	WALTHAM	48318	UTICA	48316	UTICA
02455	NORTH WALTHAM	02451	WALTHAM	48321	AUBURN HILLS	48326	AUBURN HILLS
02456	NEW TOWN	02472	WATERTOWN	48325	WEST BLOOMFIELD	48322	WEST BLOOMFIELD
02457	BABSON PARK	02481	WELLESLEY HILLS	48330	DRAYTON PLAINS	48329	WATERFORD
02471	WATERTOWN	02472	WATERTOWN	48332	FARMINGTON	48336	FARMINGTON
02475	ARLINGTON HEIGHTS	02474	ARLINGTON	48333	FARMINGTON	48334	FARMINGTON
02477	WATERTOWN	02472	WATERTOWN	48343	PONTIAC	48341	PONTIAC
02479	WAVERLEY	02478	BELMONT	48347	CLARKSTON	48346	CLARKSTON
02495	NONANTUM	02458	NEWTON	48361	LAKE ORION	48362	LAKE ORION
02534	CATAUMET	02559	POCASSET	48366	LAKEVILLE	48367	LEONARD
02541	FALMOUTH	02540	FALMOUTH	48376	NOVI	48375	NOVI
02552	MENEMSHA	02535	CHILMARK	48387	UNION LAKE	48324	WEST BLOOMFIELD
02553	MONUMENT BEACH	02559	POCASSET	48391	WALLED LAKE	48390	WALLED LAKE
02557	OAK BLUFFS	02568	VINEYARD HAVEN	48397	WARREN	48092	WARREN
02558	ONSET	02538	EAST WAREHAM	48410	ARGYLE	48472	SNOVER
02561	SAGAMORE	02532	BUZZARDS BAY	48411	ATLAS	48439	GRAND BLANC
02564	SIASCONSET	02554	NANTUCKET	48434	FORESTVILLE	48456	MINDEN CITY
02565	SILVER BEACH	02556	NORTH FALMOUTH	48437	GENESEE	48458	MOUNT MORRIS
02573	WEST CHOP	02568	VINEYARD HAVEN	48440	HADLEY	48455	METAMORA
02574	WEST FALMOUTH	02540	FALMOUTH	48476	VERNON	48429	DURAND
02584	NANTUCKET	02554	NANTUCKET	48501	FLINT	48503	FLINT
02634	CENTERVILLE	02632	CENTERVILLE	48531	FLINT	48504	FLINT
02637	CUMMAQUID	02675	YARMOUTH PORT	48550	FLINT	48505	FLINT
02641	EAST DENNIS	02660	SOUTH DENNIS	48551	FLINT	48507	FLINT
02643	EAST ORLEANS	02653	ORLEANS	48552	FLINT	48507	FLINT
02647	HYANNIS PORT	02601	HYANNIS	48553	FLINT	48507	FLINT
02651	NORTH EASTHAM	02642	EASTHAM	48554	FLINT	48473	SWARTZ CREEK
02661	SOUTH HARWICH	02645	HARWICH	48555	FLINT	48504	FLINT
02662	SOUTH ORLEANS	02653	ORLEANS	48556	FLINT	48506	FLINT
02663	SOUTH WELLFLEET	02667	WELLFLEET	48557	FLINT	48507	FLINT
02669	WEST CHATHAM	02633	CHATHAM	48605	SAGINAW	48601	SAGINAW
02672	WEST HYANNISPORT	02601	HYANNIS	48606	SAGINAW	48607	SAGINAW
02712	CHARTLEY	02766	NORTON	48608	SAGINAW	48603	SAGINAW
02714	DARTMOUTH	02748	SOUTH DARTMOUTH	48627	HIGGINS LAKE	48653	ROSCOMMON
02722	FALL RIVER	02720	FALL RIVER	48630	HOUGHTON LAKE HEIGHT	48629	HOUGHTON LAKE
02741	NEW BEDFORD	02740	NEW BEDFORD	48633	LAKE GEORGE	48632	LAKE
02742	NEW BEDFORD	02740	NEW BEDFORD	48641	MIDLAND	48640	MIDLAND
02761	NORTH ATTLEBORO	02760	NORTH ATTLEBORO	48663	SAGINAW	48603	SAGINAW
02768	RAYNHAM CENTER	02767	RAYNHAM	48667	MIDLAND	48640	MIDLAND
02783	TAUNTON	02379	WEST BRIDGEWATER	48670	MIDLAND	48640	MIDLAND
02791	WESTPORT POINT	02790	WESTPORT	48674	MIDLAND	48642	MIDLAND
05501	ANDOVER	01810	ANDOVER	48686	MIDLAND	48640	MIDLAND
05544	ANDOVER	01810	ANDOVER	48707	BAY CITY	48708	BAY CITY
48004	ANCHORVILLE	48023	FAIR HAVEN	48724	CARROLLTON	48604	SAGINAW
48007	TROY	48083	TROY	48736	GILFORD	48733	FAIRGROVE
48012	BIRMINGHAM	48009	BIRMINGHAM	48758	RICHVILLE	48768	VASSAR
48037	SOUTHFIELD	48034	SOUTHFIELD	48764	TAWAS CITY	48763	TAWAS CITY
48046	MOUNT CLEMENS	48043	MOUNT CLEMENS	48769	TUSCOLA	48768	VASSAR
48061	PORT HURON	48060	PORT HURON	48787	FRANKENMUTH	48734	FRANKENMUTH
48068	ROYAL OAK	48067	ROYAL OAK	48802	ALMA	48801	ALMA
48086	SOUTHFIELD	48076	SOUTHFIELD	48804	MOUNT PLEASANT	48858	MOUNT PLEASANT
48090	WARREN	48092	WARREN	48805	OKEMOS	48864	OKEMOS
48099	TROY	48083	TROY	48812	CEDAR LAKE	48891	VESTABURG
48102	ALLEN PARK	48101	ALLEN PARK	48816	COHOCTAH	48855	HOWELL
48106	ANN ARBOR	48103	ANN ARBOR	48826	EAST LANSING	48823	EAST LANSING
48107	ANN ARBOR	48104	ANN ARBOR	48830	ELM HALL	48877	RIVERDALE
48110	AZALIA	48159	MAYBEE	48833	EUREKA	48844	HOWELL
48112	BELLEVILLE	48111	BELLEVILLE	48843	HOWELL	48843	HOWELL
48113	ANN ARBOR	48103	ANN ARBOR	48852	MCBRIDES	48829	EDMORE
48115	BRIDGEWATER	48176	SALINE	48853	MAPLE RAPIDS	48879	SAINT JOHNS
48121	DEARBORN	48120	DEARBORN	48859	MOUNT PLEASANT	48858	MOUNT PLEASANT
48123	DEARBORN	48124	DEARBORN	48862	NORTH STAR	48847	ITHACA
48136	GARDEN CITY	48186	WESTLAND	48863	OAK GROVE	48855	HOWELL
48139	HAMBURG	48189	WHITMORE LAKE	48870	PALO	48834	FENWICK
48143	LAKELAND	48169	PINCKNEY	48874	POMPEII	48871	PERRINTON
48151	LIVONIA	48150	LIVONIA	48882	SHAFTSBURG	48872	PERRY
48153	LIVONIA	48150	LIVONIA	48887	SMYRNA	48809	BELDING
48175	SALEM	48167	NORTHVILLE	48894	WESTPHALIA	48835	FOWLER
48177	SAMARIA	48182	TEMPERANCE	48896	WINN	48858	MOUNT PLEASANT
48190	WHITTAKER	48160	MILAN	48901	LANSING	48910	LANSING
48222	DETROIT	48216	DETROIT	48908	LANSING	48917	LANSING
48231	DETROIT	48226	DETROIT	48909	LANSING	48910	LANSING
48232	DETROIT	48226	DETROIT	48913	LANSING	48917	LANSING
48233	DETROIT	48226	DETROIT	48916	LANSING	48911	LANSING
48243	DETROIT	48226	DETROIT	48918	LANSING	48917	LANSING
48244	DETROIT	48226	DETROIT	48919	LANSING	48933	LANSING
48255	DETROIT	48226	DETROIT	48921	LANSING	48933	LANSING
48260	DETROIT	48226	DETROIT	48922	LANSING	48933	LANSING
48264	DETROIT	48226	DETROIT	48924	LANSING	48910	LANSING
48265	DETROIT	48226	DETROIT	48929	LANSING	48933	LANSING
48266	DETROIT	48207	DETROIT	48930	LANSING	48933	LANSING
48267	DETROIT	48226	DETROIT	48937	LANSING	48906	LANSING
48268	DETROIT	48226	DETROIT	48950	LANSING	48917	LANSING
48269	DETROIT	48226	DETROIT	48951	LANSING	48910	LANSING
48272	DETROIT	48226	DETROIT	48956	LANSING	48933	LANSING
48275	DETROIT	48226	DETROIT	48980	LANSING	48917	LANSING
48277	DETROIT	48226	DETROIT	49003	KALAMAZOO	49001	KALAMAZOO
48278	DETROIT	48226	DETROIT				

MICHIGAN

Point ZIP Code ZIP	Post Office Name	Enclosing Residential ZIP Code ZIP	Post Office Name
49005	KALAMAZOO	49001	KALAMAZOO
49016	BATTLE CREEK	49017	BATTLE CREEK
49018	BATTLE CREEK	49017	BATTLE CREEK
49019	KALAMAZOO	49001	KALAMAZOO
49020	BEDFORD	49017	BATTLE CREEK
49023	BENTON HARBOR	49022	BENTON HARBOR
49027	BREEDSVILLE	49056	GRAND JUNCTION
49035	CLOVERDALE	49046	DELTON
49039	HAGAR SHORES	49038	COLOMA
49041	COMSTOCK	49001	KALAMAZOO
49062	KENDALL	49055	GOBLES
49063	LACOTA	49056	GRAND JUNCTION
49069	MARSHALL	49068	MARSHALL
49074	NAZARETH	49006	KALAMAZOO
49075	NOTTAWA	49091	STURGIS
49077	OSHTEMO	49009	KALAMAZOO
49081	PORTAGE	49024	PORTAGE
49084	RIVERSIDE	49038	COLOMA
49115	HARBERT	49128	THREE OAKS
49119	NEW TROY	49125	SAWYER
49121	NILES	49120	NILES
49204	JACKSON	49201	JACKSON
49239	FRONTIER	49242	HILLSDALE
49257	MOSCOW	49250	JONESVILLE
49258	MOSHERVILLE	49250	JONESVILLE
49261	NAPOLEON	49201	JACKSON
49263	NORVELL	49230	BROOKLYN
49281	SOMERSET	49233	CEMENT CITY
49282	SOMERSET CENTER	49233	CEMENT CITY
49289	WESTON	49221	ADRIAN
49311	BRADLEY	49348	WAYLAND
49312	BROHMAN	49309	BITELY
49314	BURNIPS	49323	DORR
49317	CANNONSBURG	49341	ROCKFORD
49320	CHIPPEWA LAKE	49342	RODNEY
49335	MOLINE	49348	WAYLAND
49351	ROCKFORD	49341	ROCKFORD
49355	ADA	49301	ADA
49356	ADA	49301	ADA
49357	ADA	49301	ADA
49406	DOUGLAS	49453	SAUGATUCK
49409	FERRYSBURG	49456	SPRING LAKE
49413	FREMONT	49412	FREMONT
49416	GLENN	49408	FENNVILLE
49422	HOLLAND	49423	HOLLAND
49427	JAMESTOWN	49426	HUDSONVILLE
49429	JENISON	49428	JENISON
49430	LAMONT	49435	MARNE
49434	MACATAWA	49423	HOLLAND
49443	MUSKEGON	49440	MUSKEGON
49458	WALHALLA	49405	CUSTER
49463	WABANINGO	49461	WHITEHALL
49468	GRANDVILLE	49418	GRANDVILLE
49501	GRAND RAPIDS	49503	GRAND RAPIDS
49502	GRAND RAPIDS	49503	GRAND RAPIDS
49510	GRAND RAPIDS	49507	GRAND RAPIDS
49514	GRAND RAPIDS	49504	GRAND RAPIDS
49515	GRAND RAPIDS	49503	GRAND RAPIDS
49516	GRAND RAPIDS	49506	GRAND RAPIDS
49518	GRAND RAPIDS	49508	GRAND RAPIDS
49523	GRAND RAPIDS	49503	GRAND RAPIDS
49530	GRAND RAPIDS	49512	GRAND RAPIDS
49550	GRAND RAPIDS	49544	GRAND RAPIDS
49555	GRAND RAPIDS	49503	GRAND RAPIDS
49560	GRAND RAPIDS	49508	GRAND RAPIDS
49588	GRAND RAPIDS	49512	GRAND RAPIDS
49599	GRAND RAPIDS	49503	GRAND RAPIDS
49610	ACME	49690	WILLIAMSBURG
49611	ALBA	49659	MANCELONA
49626	EASTLAKE	49660	MANISTEE
49627	EASTPORT	49622	CENTRAL LAKE
49628	ELBERTA	49635	FRANKFORT
49634	FILER CITY	49660	MANISTEE
49666	MAYFIELD	49649	KINGSLEY
49673	OLD MISSION	49686	TRAVERSE CITY
49674	OMENA	49682	SUTTONS BAY
49685	TRAVERSE CITY	49684	TRAVERSE CITY
49696	TRAVERSE CITY	49686	TRAVERSE CITY
49711	BAY SHORE	49720	CHARLEVOIX
49717	BURT LAKE	49706	ALANSON
49722	CONWAY	49770	PETOSKEY
49723	CROSS VILLAGE	49740	HARBOR SPRINGS
49734	GAYLORD	49735	GAYLORD
49737	GOOD HART	49740	HARBOR SPRINGS
49739	GRAYLING	49738	GRAYLING
49745	HESSEL	49719	CEDARVILLE
49748	HULBERT	49728	ECKERMAN
49761	MULLETT LAKE	49721	CHEBOYGAN
49764	ODEN	49706	ALANSON
49784	KINCHELOE	49783	SAULT SAINTE MARIE
49785	KINCHELOE	49788	KINCHELOE
49790	STRONGS	49752	KINROSS
49791	TOPINABEE	49749	INDIAN RIVER

MINNESOTA

Point ZIP Code ZIP	Post Office Name	Enclosing Residential ZIP Code ZIP	Post Office Name
49793	TROUT LAKE	49780	RUDYARD
49796	WALLOON LAKE	49712	BOYNE CITY
49797	WATERS	49735	GAYLORD
49805	ALLOUEZ	49913	CALUMET
49808	BIG BAY	49861	MICHIGAMME
49819	ARNOLD	49833	LITTLE LAKE
49845	HARRIS	49896	WILSON
49852	LORETTO	49892	VULCAN
49863	NADEAU	49812	CARNEY
49864	NAHMA	49878	RAPID RIVER
49865	NATIONAL MINE	49849	ISHPEMING
49871	PALMER	49866	NEGAUNEE
49872	PERKINS	49880	ROCK
49877	RALPH	49834	FOSTER CITY
49901	AHMEEK	49913	CALUMET
49902	ALPHA	49920	CRYSTAL FALLS
49903	AMASA	49920	CRYSTAL FALLS
49915	CASPIAN	49935	IRON RIVER
49917	COPPER CITY	49913	CALUMET
49918	COPPER HARBOR	49950	MOHAWK
49922	DOLLAR BAY	49930	HANCOCK
49929	GREENLAND	49953	ONTONAGON
49934	HUBBELL	49945	LAKE LINDEN
49955	PAINESDALE	49905	ATLANTIC MINE
49959	RAMSAY	49911	BESSEMER
49960	ROCKLAND	49953	ONTONAGON
49961	SIDNAW	49967	TROUT CREEK
49963	SOUTH RANGE	49905	ATLANTIC MINE
49964	STAMBAUGH	49935	IRON RIVER
49971	WHITE PINE	49953	ONTONAGON
55010	CASTLE ROCK	55065	RANDOLPH
55029	GRANDY	55008	CAMBRIDGE
55078	STACY	55079	STACY
55083	STILLWATER	55082	STILLWATER
55085	VERMILLION	55033	HASTINGS
55090	WILLERNIE	55115	SAINT PAUL
55133	SAINT PAUL	55101	SAINT PAUL
55144	SAINT PAUL	55119	SAINT PAUL
55146	SAINT PAUL	55107	SAINT PAUL
55155	SAINT PAUL	55101	SAINT PAUL
55161	SAINT PAUL	55113	SAINT PAUL
55164	SAINT PAUL	55101	SAINT PAUL
55165	SAINT PAUL	55101	SAINT PAUL
55166	SAINT PAUL	55101	SAINT PAUL
55168	SAINT PAUL	55101	SAINT PAUL
55169	SAINT PAUL	55101	SAINT PAUL
55170	SAINT PAUL	55101	SAINT PAUL
55172	SAINT PAUL	55101	SAINT PAUL
55175	SAINT PAUL	55101	SAINT PAUL
55177	SAINT PAUL	55113	SAINT PAUL
55182	SAINT PAUL	55113	SAINT PAUL
55187	SAINT PAUL	55125	SAINT PAUL
55188	SAINT PAUL	55125	SAINT PAUL
55190	SAINT PAUL	55112	SAINT PAUL
55191	SAINT PAUL	55112	SAINT PAUL
55199	SAINT PAUL	55101	SAINT PAUL
55323	CRYSTAL BAY	55356	LONG LAKE
55348	MAPLE PLAIN	55359	MAPLE PLAIN
55361	MINNETONKA BEACH	55391	WAYZATA
55365	MONTICELLO	55362	MONTICELLO
55377	SANTIAGO	55319	CLEAR LAKE
55380	SILVER CREEK	55358	MAPLE LAKE
55383	NORWOOD	55368	NORWOOD
55392	NAVARRE	55391	WAYZATA
55393	MAPLE PLAIN	55359	MAPLE PLAIN
55394	YOUNG AMERICA	55397	YOUNG AMERICA
55399	YOUNG AMERICA	55397	YOUNG AMERICA
55440	MINNEAPOLIS	55401	MINNEAPOLIS
55458	MINNEAPOLIS	55401	MINNEAPOLIS
55459	MINNEAPOLIS	55401	MINNEAPOLIS
55460	MINNEAPOLIS	55401	MINNEAPOLIS
55470	MINNEAPOLIS	55401	MINNEAPOLIS
55472	MINNEAPOLIS	55401	MINNEAPOLIS
55474	MINNEAPOLIS	55402	MINNEAPOLIS
55479	MINNEAPOLIS	55401	MINNEAPOLIS
55480	MINNEAPOLIS	55401	MINNEAPOLIS
55483	MINNEAPOLIS	55409	MINNEAPOLIS
55484	MINNEAPOLIS	55401	MINNEAPOLIS
55485	MINNEAPOLIS	55406	MINNEAPOLIS
55486	MINNEAPOLIS	55402	MINNEAPOLIS
55487	MINNEAPOLIS	55415	MINNEAPOLIS
55488	MINNEAPOLIS	55415	MINNEAPOLIS
55550	YOUNG AMERICA	55397	YOUNG AMERICA
55551	YOUNG AMERICA	55397	YOUNG AMERICA
55552	YOUNG AMERICA	55397	YOUNG AMERICA
55553	YOUNG AMERICA	55397	YOUNG AMERICA
55554	NORWOOD	55368	NORWOOD
55556	YOUNG AMERICA	55397	YOUNG AMERICA
55557	YOUNG AMERICA	55397	YOUNG AMERICA
55558	YOUNG AMERICA	55397	YOUNG AMERICA
55559	YOUNG AMERICA	55397	YOUNG AMERICA
55560	YOUNG AMERICA	55397	YOUNG AMERICA
55561	MONTICELLO	55362	MONTICELLO

MINNESOTA   **MISSISSIPPI**

Point ZIP Code ZIP	Point ZIP Code Post Office Name	Enclosing Residential ZIP Code ZIP	Enclosing Residential ZIP Code Post Office Name	Point ZIP Code ZIP	Point ZIP Code Post Office Name	Enclosing Residential ZIP Code ZIP	Enclosing Residential ZIP Code Post Office Name
55562	YOUNG AMERICA	55397	YOUNG AMERICA	56478	NIMROD	56477	SEBEKA
55563	MONTICELLO	55362	MONTICELLO	56502	DETROIT LAKES	56501	DETROIT LAKES
55564	YOUNG AMERICA	55397	YOUNG AMERICA	56538	FERGUS FALLS	56537	FERGUS FALLS
55565	MONTICELLO	55362	MONTICELLO	56541	FLOM	56584	TWIN VALLEY
55566	YOUNG AMERICA	55397	YOUNG AMERICA	56561	MOORHEAD	56560	MOORHEAD
55567	YOUNG AMERICA	55397	YOUNG AMERICA	56591	WHITE EARTH	56569	OGEMA
55568	YOUNG AMERICA	55397	YOUNG AMERICA	56619	BEMIDJI	56601	BEMIDJI
55569	OSSEO	55369	OSSEO	56631	BOWSTRING	56636	DEER RIVER
55570	MAPLE PLAIN	55359	MAPLE PLAIN	56658	MARGIE	56627	BIG FALLS
55571	MAPLE PLAIN	55359	MAPLE PLAIN	56679	SOUTH INTERNATIONAL	56649	INTERNATIONAL FALLS
55572	MAPLE PLAIN	55359	MAPLE PLAIN	56687	WILTON	56601	BEMIDJI
55573	YOUNG AMERICA	55397	YOUNG AMERICA	56731	HUMBOLDT	56755	SAINT VINCENT
55574	MAPLE PLAIN	55359	MAPLE PLAIN	38602	ARKABUTLA	38618	COLDWATER
55575	HOWARD LAKE	55349	HOWARD LAKE	38609	BELEN	38646	MARKS
55576	MAPLE PLAIN	55359	MAPLE PLAIN	38622	CROWDER	38643	LAMBERT
55577	MAPLE PLAIN	55359	MAPLE PLAIN	38623	DARLING	38670	SLEDGE
55578	MAPLE PLAIN	55359	MAPLE PLAIN	38628	FALCON	38670	SLEDGE
55579	MAPLE PLAIN	55359	MAPLE PLAIN	38630	FARRELL	38614	CLARKSDALE
55580	MONTICELLO	55362	MONTICELLO	38631	FRIARS POINT	38614	CLARKSDALE
55581	MONTICELLO	55362	MONTICELLO	38634	HOLLY SPRINGS	38635	HOLLY SPRINGS
55582	MONTICELLO	55362	MONTICELLO	38638	INDEPENDENCE	38668	SENATOBIA
55583	NORWOOD	55368	NORWOOD	38639	JONESTOWN	38617	COAHOMA
55584	MONTICELLO	55362	MONTICELLO	38644	LULA	38617	COAHOMA
55585	MONTICELLO	55362	MONTICELLO	38649	MOUNT PLEASANT	38635	HOLLY SPRINGS
55586	MONTICELLO	55362	MONTICELLO	38669	SHERARD	38614	CLARKSDALE
55587	MONTICELLO	55362	MONTICELLO	38675	TULA	38655	OXFORD
55588	MONTICELLO	55362	MONTICELLO	38679	VICTORIA	38611	BYHALIA
55589	MONTICELLO	55362	MONTICELLO	38686	WALLS	38680	WALLS
55590	MONTICELLO	55362	MONTICELLO	38702	GREENVILLE	38701	GREENVILLE
55591	MONTICELLO	55362	MONTICELLO	38704	GREENVILLE	38701	GREENVILLE
55592	MAPLE PLAIN	55359	MAPLE PLAIN	38722	ARCOLA	38701	GREENVILLE
55593	MAPLE PLAIN	55359	MAPLE PLAIN	38723	AVON	38748	HOLLANDALE
55594	YOUNG AMERICA	55397	YOUNG AMERICA	38738	PARCHMAN	38737	DREW
55595	LORETTO	55357	LORETTO	38739	DUBLIN	38614	CLARKSDALE
55596	LORETTO	55357	LORETTO	38745	GRACE	39113	MAYERSVILLE
55597	LORETTO	55357	LORETTO	38749	HOLLY RIDGE	38751	INDIANOLA
55598	LORETTO	55357	LORETTO	38758	MATTSON	38614	CLARKSDALE
55599	LORETTO	55357	LORETTO	38760	METCALFE	38701	GREENVILLE
55601	BEAVER BAY	55614	SILVER BAY	38764	PACE	38732	CLEVELAND
55609	KNIFE RIVER	55616	TWO HARBORS	38765	PANTHER BURN	38721	ANGUILLA
55701	ADOLPH	55810	DULUTH	38767	RENA LARA	38614	CLARKSDALE
55708	BIWABIK	55741	GILBERT	38768	ROME	38737	DREW
55713	BUHL	55719	CHISHOLM	38772	SCOTT	38725	BENOIT
55716	CALUMET	55709	BOVEY	38776	STONEVILLE	38703	GREENVILLE
55722	COLERAINE	55709	BOVEY	38781	WINSTONVILLE	38762	MOUND BAYOU
55730	GRAND RAPIDS	55744	GRAND RAPIDS	38782	WINTERVILLE	38703	GREENVILLE
55745	GRAND RAPIDS	55744	GRAND RAPIDS	38802	TUPELO	38801	TUPELO
55747	HIBBING	55746	HIBBING	38803	TUPELO	38801	TUPELO
55753	KEEWATIN	55769	NASHWAUK	38820	ALGOMA	38863	PONTOTOC
55758	KINNEY	55719	CHISHOLM	38825	BECKER	38821	AMORY
55764	MARBLE	55709	BOVEY	38835	CORINTH	38834	CORINTH
55772	NETT LAKE	55771	ORR	38839	DERMA	38916	CALHOUN CITY
55777	VIRGINIA	55792	VIRGINIA	38854	MC CONDY	38851	HOUSTON
55782	SOUDAN	55790	TOWER	38869	SHERMAN	38841	ECRU
55786	TACONITE	55709	BOVEY	38874	TOCCOPOLA	38871	THAXTON
55791	TWIG	55779	SAGINAW	38875	TREBLOC	38851	HOUSTON
55796	WINTON	55731	ELY	38877	VAN VLEET	38851	HOUSTON
55814	DULUTH	55811	DULUTH	38879	VERONA	38801	TUPELO
55815	DULUTH	55811	DULUTH	38880	WHEELER	38829	BOONEVILLE
55816	DULUTH	55806	DULUTH	38902	GRENADA	38901	GRENADA
55903	ROCHESTER	55901	ROCHESTER	38926	ELLIOTT	38901	GRENADA
55905	ROCHESTER	55901	ROCHESTER	38928	GLENDORA	38944	MINTER CITY
55931	EITZEN	55921	CALEDONIA	38935	GREENWOOD	38930	GREENWOOD
55942	HOMER	55987	WINONA	38945	MONEY	38930	GREENWOOD
55950	LANSING	55912	AUSTIN	38946	MORGAN CITY	38941	ITTA BENA
55988	STOCKTON	55987	WINONA	38947	NORTH CARROLLTON	38917	CARROLLTON
56002	MANKATO	56001	MANKATO	38955	SLATE SPRING	38916	CALHOUN CITY
56006	MANKATO	56001	MANKATO	38957	SUMNER	38963	TUTWILER
56056	LA SALLE	56081	SAINT JAMES	38958	SWAN LAKE	38921	CHARLESTON
56084	SEARLES	56073	NEW ULM	38959	SWIFTOWN	38941	ITTA BENA
56140	IHLEN	56144	JASPER	38960	TIE PLANT	38901	GRENADA
56177	TROSKY	56164	PIPESTONE	38962	TIPPO	38921	CHARLESTON
56302	SAINT CLOUD	56303	SAINT CLOUD	38966	WEBB	38963	TUTWILER
56317	BUCKMAN	56364	PIERZ	39043	BRANDON	39042	BRANDON
56321	COLLEGEVILLE	56374	SAINT JOSEPH	39054	CARY	39159	ROLLING FORK
56325	ELROSA	56312	BELGRADE	39060	CLINTON	39056	CLINTON
56335	GREENWALD	56352	MELROSE	39061	DELTA CITY	38721	ANGUILLA
56344	LASTRUP	56364	PIERZ	39062	D LO	39114	MENDENHALL
56356	NEW MUNICH	56352	MELROSE	39072	POCAHONTAS	39071	FLORA
56369	ROCKVILLE	56301	SAINT CLOUD	39077	GALLMAN	39059	CRYSTAL SPRINGS
56371	ROSCOE	56368	RICHMOND	39080	HARPERVILLE	39074	FOREST
56372	SAINT CLOUD	56303	SAINT CLOUD	39087	HILLSBORO	39117	MORTON
56376	SAINT MARTIN	56362	PAYNESVILLE	39098	LUDLOW	39117	MORTON
56388	WAITE PARK	56387	WAITE PARK	39107	MC ADAMS	39160	SALLIS
56393	SAINT CLOUD	56303	SAINT CLOUD	39109	MADDEN	39051	CARTHAGE
56395	SAINT CLOUD	56303	SAINT CLOUD	39112	SANATORIUM	39114	MENDENHALL
56396	SAINT CLOUD	56303	SAINT CLOUD	39115	MIDNIGHT	39097	LOUISE
56397	SAINT CLOUD	56301	SAINT CLOUD	39121	NATCHEZ	39120	NATCHEZ
56398	SAINT CLOUD	56301	SAINT CLOUD	39122	NATCHEZ	39120	NATCHEZ
56399	SAINT CLOUD	56387	WAITE PARK	39130	MADISON	39110	MADISON
56430	AH GWAH CHING	56484	WALKER	39148	PINEY WOODS	39044	BRAXTON
56436	BENEDICT	56461	LAPORTE	39151	PUCKETT	39042	BRANDON
56459	LAKE HUBERT	56468	NISSWA	39158	RIDGELAND	39157	RIDGELAND

MISSISSIPPI **MISSOURI**

Point ZIP Code		Enclosing Residential ZIP Code		Point ZIP Code		Enclosing Residential ZIP Code	
ZIP	Post Office Name	ZIP	Post Office Name	ZIP	Post Office Name	ZIP	Post Office Name
39161	SANDHILL	39047	BRANDON	63171	SAINT LOUIS	63119	SAINT LOUIS
39163	SHARON	39046	CANTON	63177	SAINT LOUIS	63103	SAINT LOUIS
39165	SIBLEY	39120	NATCHEZ	63178	SAINT LOUIS	63103	SAINT LOUIS
39167	STAR	39073	FLORENCE	63179	SAINT LOUIS	63103	SAINT LOUIS
39171	THOMASTOWN	39051	CARTHAGE	63180	SAINT LOUIS	63103	SAINT LOUIS
39173	TINSLEY	39194	YAZOO CITY	63182	SAINT LOUIS	63103	SAINT LOUIS
39174	TOUGALOO	39213	JACKSON	63188	SAINT LOUIS	63101	SAINT LOUIS
39181	VICKSBURG	39180	VICKSBURG	63190	SAINT LOUIS	63103	SAINT LOUIS
39182	VICKSBURG	39180	VICKSBURG	63195	SAINT LOUIS	63105	SAINT LOUIS
39190	WASHINGTON	39120	NATCHEZ	63196	SAINT LOUIS	63103	SAINT LOUIS
39193	WHITFIELD	39208	PEARL	63197	SAINT LOUIS	63103	SAINT LOUIS
39205	JACKSON	39201	JACKSON	63198	SAINT LOUIS	63017	CHESTERFIELD
39207	JACKSON	39203	JACKSON	63199	SAINT LOUIS	63102	SAINT LOUIS
39210	JACKSON	39202	JACKSON	63302	SAINT CHARLES	63301	SAINT CHARLES
39215	JACKSON	39201	JACKSON	63338	COTTLEVILLE	63304	SAINT CHARLES
39217	JACKSON	39203	JACKSON	63342	DUTZOW	63357	MARTHASVILLE
39225	JACKSON	39201	JACKSON	63346	FLINTHILL	63385	WENTZVILLE
39235	JACKSON	39201	JACKSON	63365	NEW MELLE	63385	WENTZVILLE
39236	JACKSON	39211	JACKSON	63378	TRELOAR	63357	MARTHASVILLE
39269	JACKSON	39201	JACKSON	63387	WHITESIDE	63377	SILEX
39271	JACKSON	39201	JACKSON	63442	GRANGER	63432	ARBELA
39282	JACKSON	39212	JACKSON	63465	REVERE	63472	WAYLAND
39283	JACKSON	39213	JACKSON	63467	SAVERTON	63401	HANNIBAL
39284	JACKSON	39204	JACKSON	63632	CASCADE	63944	GREENVILLE
39286	JACKSON	39206	JACKSON	63651	KNOB LICK	63640	FARMINGTON
39288	PEARL	39208	PEARL	63661	NEW OFFENBURG	63670	SAINTE GENEVIEVE
39289	JACKSON	39209	JACKSON	63663	PILOT KNOB	63650	IRONTON
39296	JACKSON	39216	JACKSON	63666	REYNOLDS	63638	ELLINGTON
39298	JACKSON	39232	FLOWOOD	63674	TIFF	63630	CADET
39302	MERIDIAN	39301	MERIDIAN	63702	CAPE GIRARDEAU	63701	CAPE GIRARDEAU
39303	MERIDIAN	39301	MERIDIAN	63705	CAPE GIRARDEAU	63701	CAPE GIRARDEAU
39304	MERIDIAN	39307	MERIDIAN	63737	BRAZEAU	63748	FROHNA
39324	CLARA	39367	WAYNESBORO	63738	BROWNWOOD	63730	ADVANCE
39403	HATTIESBURG	39402	HATTIESBURG	63742	COMMERCE	63780	SCOTT CITY
39404	HATTIESBURG	39402	HATTIESBURG	63745	DUTCHTOWN	63701	CAPE GIRARDEAU
39436	EASTABUCHIE	39465	PETAL	63746	FARRAR	63748	FROHNA
39441	LAUREL	39440	LAUREL	63752	GORDONVILLE	63701	CAPE GIRARDEAU
39442	LAUREL	39440	LAUREL	63758	KELSO	63780	SCOTT CITY
39457	MC NEILL	39426	CARRIERE	63767	MORLEY	63736	BENTON
39460	MOSS	39443	LAUREL	63772	PAINTON	63771	ORAN
39463	NICHOLSON	39466	PICAYUNE	63774	PERKINS	63771	ORAN
39477	SANDERSVILLE	39439	HEIDELBERG	63776	MC BRIDE	63775	PERRYVILLE
39502	GULFPORT	39501	GULFPORT	63779	POCAHONTAS	63755	JACKSON
39505	GULFPORT	39501	GULFPORT	63784	VANDUSER	63801	SIKESTON
39506	GULFPORT	39507	GULFPORT	63820	ANNISTON	63845	EAST PRAIRIE
39521	BAY SAINT LOUIS	39520	BAY SAINT LOUIS	63824	BLODGETT	63801	SIKESTON
39533	BILOXI	39540	DIBERVILLE	63826	BRAGGADOCIO	63877	STEELE
39535	BILOXI	39531	BILOXI	63828	CANALOU	63868	MOREHOUSE
39552	ESCATAWPA	39563	MOSS POINT	63839	COOTER	63877	STEELE
39555	HURLEY	39562	MOSS POINT	63840	DEERING	63849	GOBLER
39558	LAKESHORE	39520	BAY SAINT LOUIS	63847	GIBSON	63837	CLARKTON
39566	OCEAN SPRINGS	39564	OCEAN SPRINGS	63850	GRAYRIDGE	63846	ESSEX
39568	PASCAGOULA	39567	PASCAGOULA	63853	HOLLAND	63877	STEELE
39569	PASCAGOULA	39563	MOSS POINT	63860	KEWANEE	63869	NEW MADRID
39595	PASCAGOULA	39567	PASCAGOULA	63874	RISCO	63870	PARMA
39602	BROOKHAVEN	39601	BROOKHAVEN	63875	RIVES	63855	HORNERSVILLE
39603	BROOKHAVEN	39601	BROOKHAVEN	63878	TALLAPOOSA	63873	PORTAGEVILLE
39632	CHATAWA	39652	MAGNOLIA	63880	WHITEOAK	63852	HOLCOMB
39635	FERNWOOD	39648	MCCOMB	63881	WOLF ISLAND	63845	EAST PRAIRIE
39649	MCCOMB	39648	MCCOMB	63882	WYATT	63834	CHARLESTON
39703	COLUMBUS	39705	COLUMBUS	63902	POPLAR BLUFF	63901	POPLAR BLUFF
39704	COLUMBUS	39705	COLUMBUS	63938	FAGUS	63961	QULIN
39736	ARTESIA	39701	COLUMBUS	63962	ROMBAUER	63940	FISK
39737	BELLEFONTAINE	39744	EUPORA	64013	BLUE SPRINGS	64015	BLUE SPRINGS
39753	MAYHEW	39701	COLUMBUS	64028	FARLEY	64079	PLATTE CITY
39754	MONTPELIER	39773	WEST POINT	64051	INDEPENDENCE	64055	INDEPENDENCE
39760	STARKVILLE	39759	STARKVILLE	64065	LEES SUMMIT	64139	KANSAS CITY
39771	WALTHALL	39744	EUPORA	64066	LEVASY	64088	SIBLEY
63001	ALLENTON	63069	PACIFIC	64069	LIBERTY	64068	LIBERTY
63006	CHESTERFIELD	63017	CHESTERFIELD	64072	MISSOURI CITY	64068	LIBERTY
63022	BALLWIN	63011	BALLWIN	64073	MOSBY	64068	LIBERTY
63024	BALLWIN	63011	BALLWIN	64087	LIBERTY	64068	LIBERTY
63032	FLORISSANT	63033	FLORISSANT	64090	STRASBURG	64080	PLEASANT HILL
63047	HEMATITE	63028	FESTUS	64092	WALDRON	64152	KANSAS CITY
63053	KIMMSWICK	63052	IMPERIAL	64121	KANSAS CITY	64127	KANSAS CITY
63057	LIGUORI	63052	IMPERIAL	64141	KANSAS CITY	64108	KANSAS CITY
63065	MAPAVILLE	63050	HILLSBORO	64144	KANSAS CITY	64161	KANSAS CITY
63066	MORSE MILL	63050	HILLSBORO	64148	KANSAS CITY	64108	KANSAS CITY
63073	SAINT ALBANS	63069	PACIFIC	64160	KANSAS CITY	64108	KANSAS CITY
63079	STANTON	63080	SULLIVAN	64168	KANSAS CITY	64150	RIVERSIDE
63099	FENTON	63026	FENTON	64170	KANSAS CITY	64137	KANSAS CITY
63150	SAINT LOUIS	63101	SAINT LOUIS	64171	KANSAS CITY	64111	KANSAS CITY
63151	SAINT LOUIS	63129	SAINT LOUIS	64172	KANSAS CITY	64108	KANSAS CITY
63155	SAINT LOUIS	63103	SAINT LOUIS	64179	KANSAS CITY	64108	KANSAS CITY
63156	SAINT LOUIS	63108	SAINT LOUIS	64180	KANSAS CITY	64106	KANSAS CITY
63157	SAINT LOUIS	63104	SAINT LOUIS	64184	KANSAS CITY	64106	KANSAS CITY
63158	SAINT LOUIS	63118	SAINT LOUIS	64185	KANSAS CITY	64106	KANSAS CITY
63160	SAINT LOUIS	63102	SAINT LOUIS	64187	KANSAS CITY	64106	KANSAS CITY
63163	SAINT LOUIS	63118	SAINT LOUIS	64188	KANSAS CITY	64118	KANSAS CITY
63164	SAINT LOUIS	63102	SAINT LOUIS	64190	KANSAS CITY	64152	KANSAS CITY
63166	SAINT LOUIS	63103	SAINT LOUIS	64191	KANSAS CITY	64124	KANSAS CITY
63167	SAINT LOUIS	63141	SAINT LOUIS	64192	KANSAS CITY	64138	KANSAS CITY
63169	SAINT LOUIS	63101	SAINT LOUIS	64193	KANSAS CITY	64153	KANSAS CITY

MISSOURI

Point ZIP Code ZIP	Post Office Name	Enclosing Residential ZIP Code ZIP	Post Office Name
64194	KANSAS CITY	64106	KANSAS CITY
64195	KANSAS CITY	64152	KANSAS CITY
64196	KANSAS CITY	64105	KANSAS CITY
64197	KANSAS CITY	64131	KANSAS CITY
64198	KANSAS CITY	64106	KANSAS CITY
64199	KANSAS CITY	64106	KANSAS CITY
64420	ALLENDALE	64456	GRANT CITY
64447	FAIRPORT	64469	MAYSVILLE
64502	SAINT JOSEPH	64501	SAINT JOSEPH
64508	SAINT JOSEPH	64505	SAINT JOSEPH
64680	STET	64668	NORBORNE
64743	EAST LYNNE	64701	HARRISONVILLE
64765	METZ	64778	RICHARDS
64766	MILFORD	64759	LAMAR
64781	ROSCOE	64776	OSCEOLA
64802	JOPLIN	64801	JOPLIN
64803	JOPLIN	64801	JOPLIN
64830	ALBA	64855	ORONOGO
64841	DUENWEG	64801	JOPLIN
64849	NECK CITY	64755	JASPER
64853	NEWTONIA	64866	STARK CITY
64857	PURCELL	64755	JASPER
64858	RACINE	64850	NEOSHO
64864	SAGINAW	64804	JOPLIN
64869	WACO	64832	ASBURY
64999	KANSAS CITY	64137	KANSAS CITY
65031	ETTERVILLE	65026	ELDON
65036	GASCONADE	65041	HERMANN
65038	LAURIE	65084	VERSAILLES
65055	MC GIRK	65018	CALIFORNIA
65102	JEFFERSON CITY	65101	JEFFERSON CITY
65103	JEFFERSON CITY	65101	JEFFERSON CITY
65104	JEFFERSON CITY	65101	JEFFERSON CITY
65105	JEFFERSON CITY	65101	JEFFERSON CITY
65106	JEFFERSON CITY	65101	JEFFERSON CITY
65107	JEFFERSON CITY	65101	JEFFERSON CITY
65108	JEFFERSON CITY	65101	JEFFERSON CITY
65110	JEFFERSON CITY	65109	JEFFERSON CITY
65111	JEFFERSON CITY	65101	JEFFERSON CITY
65205	COLUMBIA	65201	COLUMBIA
65212	COLUMBIA	65201	COLUMBIA
65217	COLUMBIA	65201	COLUMBIA
65218	COLUMBIA	65203	COLUMBIA
65278	RENICK	65243	CLARK
65299	COLUMBIA	65201	COLUMBIA
65302	SEDALIA	65301	SEDALIA
65320	ARROW ROCK	65347	NELSON
65327	EMMA	65351	SWEET SPRINGS
65402	ROLLA	65401	ROLLA
65532	LAKE SPRING	65401	ROLLA
65546	MONTIER	65438	BIRCH TREE
65572	SWEDEBORG	65556	RICHLAND
65607	CAPLINGER MILLS	65785	STOCKTON
65615	BRANSON	65616	BRANSON
65636	DIGGINS	65746	SEYMOUR
65645	EUDORA	65770	WALNUT GROVE
65664	HALLTOWN	65612	BOIS D ARC
65673	HOLLISTER	65739	RIDGEDALE
65726	POINT LOOKOUT	65672	HOLLISTER
65741	ROCKBRIDGE	65618	BRIXEY
65765	TURNERS	65809	SPRINGFIELD
65801	SPRINGFIELD	65802	SPRINGFIELD
65805	SPRINGFIELD	65806	SPRINGFIELD
65808	SPRINGFIELD	65804	SPRINGFIELD
65814	SPRINGFIELD	65804	SPRINGFIELD
65817	SPRINGFIELD	65807	SPRINGFIELD
65890	SPRINGFIELD	65804	SPRINGFIELD
65898	SPRINGFIELD	65807	SPRINGFIELD
65899	SPRINGFIELD	65804	SPRINGFIELD
59004	ASHLAND	59003	ASHLAND
59013	BOYD	59041	JOLIET
59018	CLYDE PARK	59086	WILSALL
59020	COOKE CITY	59030	GARDINER
59026	EDGAR	59041	JOLIET
59035	YELLOWTAIL	59050	LODGE GRASS
59036	HARLOWTON	59085	TWO DOT
59054	MELSTONE	59059	MUSSELSHELL
59066	PRYOR	59050	LODGE GRASS
59073	ROUNDUP	59072	ROUNDUP
59081	SILVER GATE	59030	GARDINER
59082	SPRINGDALE	59047	LIVINGSTON
59083	SUMATRA	59039	INGOMAR
59084	TEIGEN	59087	WINNETT
59103	BILLINGS	59101	BILLINGS
59104	BILLINGS	59102	BILLINGS
59107	BILLINGS	59101	BILLINGS
59108	BILLINGS	59102	BILLINGS
59114	BILLINGS	59101	BILLINGS
59115	BILLINGS	59101	BILLINGS
59116	BILLINGS	59102	BILLINGS
59117	BILLINGS	59101	BILLINGS
59217	CRANE	59262	SAVAGE
59231	SAINT MARIE	59230	GLASGOW

NEBRASKA

Point ZIP Code ZIP	Post Office Name	Enclosing Residential ZIP Code ZIP	Post Office Name
59240	GLENTANA	59250	OPHEIM
59273	VANDALIA	59241	HINSDALE
59319	CAPITOL	57724	CAMP CROOK
59323	COLSTRIP	59347	ROSEBUD
59333	HATHAWAY	59347	ROSEBUD
59403	GREAT FALLS	59401	GREAT FALLS
59406	GREAT FALLS	59405	GREAT FALLS
59432	DUPUYER	59486	VALIER
59435	ETHRIDGE	59474	SHELBY
59445	GARNEILL	59418	BUFFALO
59461	LOTHAIR	59522	CHESTER
59477	SIMMS	59421	CASCADE
59485	ULM	59421	CASCADE
59547	ZURICH	59523	CHINOOK
59604	HELENA	59601	HELENA
59620	HELENA	59601	HELENA
59623	HELENA	59601	HELENA
59624	HELENA	59601	HELENA
59626	HELENA	59601	HELENA
59631	BASIN	59634	CLANCY
59636	FORT HARRISON	59602	HELENA
59638	JEFFERSON CITY	59634	CLANCY
59640	MARYSVILLE	59633	CANYON CREEK
59702	BUTTE	59701	BUTTE
59703	BUTTE	59701	BUTTE
59707	BUTTE	59701	BUTTE
59710	ALDER	59749	SHERIDAN
59713	AVON	59731	GARRISON
59716	BIG SKY	59730	GALLATIN GATEWAY
59719	BOZEMAN	59718	BOZEMAN
59728	ELLISTON	59731	GARRISON
59732	GLEN	59725	DILLON
59740	MC ALLISTER	59729	ENNIS
59743	MELROSE	59727	DIVIDE
59746	POLARIS	59725	DILLON
59760	WILLOW CREEK	59752	THREE FORKS
59771	BOZEMAN	59715	BOZEMAN
59772	BOZEMAN	59715	BOZEMAN
59773	BOZEMAN	59718	BOZEMAN
59801	MISSOULA	59801	MISSOULA
59807	MISSOULA	59802	MISSOULA
59830	DE BORGIA	59866	SAINT REGIS
59835	GRANTSDALE	59840	HAMILTON
59841	PINESDALE	59840	HAMILTON
59842	HAUGAN	59866	SAINT REGIS
59851	MILLTOWN	59802	MISSOULA
59855	PABLO	59864	RONAN
59856	PARADISE	59859	PLAINS
59863	RAVALLI	59821	ARLEE
59867	SALTESE	59866	SAINT REGIS
59902	KALISPELL	59901	KALISPELL
59903	KALISPELL	59901	KALISPELL
59904	KALISPELL	59901	KALISPELL
59913	CORAM	59901	KALISPELL
59918	FORTINE	59917	EUREKA
59919	HUNGRY HORSE	59901	KALISPELL
59921	LAKE MC DONALD	59916	ESSEX
59926	MARTIN CITY	59901	KALISPELL
59927	OLNEY	59937	WHITEFISH
59933	STRYKER	59917	EUREKA
59934	TREGO	59917	EUREKA
59936	WEST GLACIER	59901	KALISPELL
68009	BLAIR	68008	BLAIR
68016	CEDAR CREEK	68037	LOUISVILLE
68026	FREMONT	68025	FREMONT
68042	MEMPHIS	68003	ASHLAND
68056	ST COLUMBANS	68005	BELLEVUE
68058	SOUTH BEND	68037	LOUISVILLE
68063	UEHLING	68031	HOOPER
68068	WASHINGTON	68034	KENNARD
68072	WINSLOW	68031	HOOPER
68101	OMAHA	68102	OMAHA
68103	OMAHA	68108	OMAHA
68109	OMAHA	68107	OMAHA
68119	OMAHA	68110	OMAHA
68120	OMAHA	68110	OMAHA
68139	OMAHA	68137	OMAHA
68145	OMAHA	68137	OMAHA
68155	OMAHA	68105	OMAHA
68172	OMAHA	68131	OMAHA
68175	OMAHA	68131	OMAHA
68176	OMAHA	68102	OMAHA
68178	OMAHA	68102	OMAHA
68179	OMAHA	68102	OMAHA
68180	OMAHA	68124	OMAHA
68181	OMAHA	68102	OMAHA
68183	OMAHA	68102	OMAHA
68197	OMAHA	68102	OMAHA
68382	LORTON	68346	DUNBAR
68403	MANLEY	68463	WEEPING WATER
68419	PANAMA	68317	BENNET
68438	SPRAGUE	68404	MARTELL
68501	LINCOLN	68508	LINCOLN

NEBRASKA

NEW JERSEY

Point ZIP Code Post Office		Enclosing Residential ZIP Code Post Office		Point ZIP Code Post Office		Enclosing Residential ZIP Code Post Office	
ZIP	Name	ZIP	Name	ZIP	Name	ZIP	Name
68509	LINCOLN	68508	LINCOLN	89496	FALLON	89406	FALLON
68529	LINCOLN	68507	LINCOLN	89504	RENO	89501	RENO
68542	LINCOLN	68502	LINCOLN	89505	RENO	89501	RENO
68602	COLUMBUS	68601	COLUMBUS	89507	RENO	89503	RENO
68634	DUNCAN	68601	COLUMBUS	89513	RENO	89503	RENO
68664	SNYDER	68633	DODGE	89515	RENO	89502	RENO
68702	NORFOLK	68701	NORFOLK	89520	RENO	89503	RENO
68738	HADAR	68701	NORFOLK	89533	RENO	89523	RENO
68802	GRAND ISLAND	68803	GRAND ISLAND	89555	RENO	89502	RENO
68848	KEARNEY	68847	KEARNEY	89557	RENO	89503	RENO
68902	HASTINGS	68901	HASTINGS	89570	RENO	89502	RENO
69103	NORTH PLATTE	69101	NORTH PLATTE	89595	RENO	89502	RENO
69160	SIDNEY	69162	SIDNEY	89702	CARSON CITY	89701	CARSON CITY
69171	WILLOW ISLAND	69130	COZAD	89711	CARSON CITY	89701	CARSON CITY
69190	OSHKOSH	69154	OSHKOSH	89712	CARSON CITY	89701	CARSON CITY
69219	NENZEL	69216	KILGORE	89713	CARSON CITY	89701	CARSON CITY
69220	SPARKS	69201	VALENTINE	89714	CARSON CITY	89701	CARSON CITY
69353	MCGREW	69341	GERING	89721	CARSON CITY	89701	CARSON CITY
69355	MELBETA	69341	GERING	89802	ELKO	89801	ELKO
69363	SCOTTSBLUFF	69361	SCOTTSBLUFF	89803	ELKO	89801	ELKO
69365	WHITECLAY	69360	RUSHVILLE	89824	HALLECK	89823	DEETH
88901	THE LAKES	89117	LAS VEGAS	89826	JARBIDGE	89825	JACKPOT
88905	THE LAKES	89117	LAS VEGAS	89828	LAMOILLE	89815	SPRING CREEK
89003	BEATTY	89020	AMARGOSA VALLEY	89830	MONTELLO	89835	WELLS
89004	BLUE DIAMOND	89124	LAS VEGAS	89832	OWYHEE	89831	MOUNTAIN CITY
89006	BOULDER CITY	89005	BOULDER CITY	89883	WEST WENDOVER	89835	WELLS
89007	BUNKERVILLE	89040	OVERTON	03040	EAST CANDIA	03034	CANDIA
89009	HENDERSON	89015	HENDERSON	03041	EAST DERRY	03038	DERRY
89010	DYER	89047	SILVERPEAK	03061	NASHUA	03060	NASHUA
89016	HENDERSON	89015	HENDERSON	03073	NORTH SALEM	03079	SALEM
89021	LOGANDALE	89040	OVERTON	03105	MANCHESTER	03104	MANCHESTER
89022	MANHATTAN	89049	TONOPAH	03108	MANCHESTER	03103	MANCHESTER
89023	MERCURY	89020	AMARGOSA VALLEY	03215	WATERVILLE VALLEY	03223	CAMPTON
89024	MESQUITE	89027	MESQUITE	03231	EAST ANDOVER	03216	ANDOVER
89025	MOAPA	89040	OVERTON	03233	ELKINS	03257	NEW LONDON
89026	JEAN	89124	LAS VEGAS	03238	GLENCLIFF	03279	WARREN
89028	LAUGHLIN	89029	LAUGHLIN	03245	HOLDERNESS	03264	PLYMOUTH
89036	NORTH LAS VEGAS	89030	NORTH LAS VEGAS	03247	LACONIA	03246	LACONIA
89039	CAL NEV ARI	89046	SEARCHLIGHT	03252	LOCHMERE	03276	TILTON
89042	PANACA	89043	PIOCHE	03260	NORTH SUTTON	03278	WARNER
89053	HENDERSON	89124	LAS VEGAS	03272	SOUTH NEWBURY	03255	NEWBURY
89070	INDIAN SPRINGS	89018	INDIAN SPRINGS	03273	SOUTH SUTTON	03278	WARNER
89077	HENDERSON	89015	HENDERSON	03274	STINSON LAKE	03266	RUMNEY
89086	NORTH LAS VEGAS	89084	NORTH LAS VEGAS	03289	WINNISQUAM	03220	BELMONT
89111	LAS VEGAS	89119	LAS VEGAS	03293	WOODSTOCK	03262	NORTH WOODSTOCK
89112	LAS VEGAS	89110	LAS VEGAS	03298	TILTON	03253	MEREDITH
89114	LAS VEGAS	89106	LAS VEGAS	03299	TILTON	03253	MEREDITH
89116	LAS VEGAS	89104	LAS VEGAS	03302	CONCORD	03301	CONCORD
89125	LAS VEGAS	89101	LAS VEGAS	03468	WEST PETERBOROUGH	03458	PETERBOROUGH
89126	LAS VEGAS	89102	LAS VEGAS	03469	WEST SWANZEY	03446	SWANZEY
89127	LAS VEGAS	89106	LAS VEGAS	03575	BRETTON WOODS	03598	WHITEFIELD
89132	LAS VEGAS	89119	LAS VEGAS	03587	MEADOWS	03583	JEFFERSON
89133	LAS VEGAS	89128	LAS VEGAS	03595	TWIN MOUNTAIN	03598	WHITEFIELD
89136	LAS VEGAS	89119	LAS VEGAS	03597	WEST STEWARTSTOWN	03576	COLEBROOK
89137	LAS VEGAS	89144	LAS VEGAS	03601	ACWORTH	03605	LEMPSTER
89138	LAS VEGAS	89134	LAS VEGAS	03604	DREWSVILLE	03602	ALSTEAD
89150	LAS VEGAS	89103	LAS VEGAS	03746	CORNISH FLAT	03745	CORNISH
89151	LAS VEGAS	89146	LAS VEGAS	03749	ENFIELD CENTER	03748	ENFIELD
89152	LAS VEGAS	89107	LAS VEGAS	03751	GEORGES MILLS	03782	SUNAPEE
89153	LAS VEGAS	89102	LAS VEGAS	03754	GUILD	03773	NEWPORT
89155	LAS VEGAS	89101	LAS VEGAS	03756	LEBANON	03766	LEBANON
89159	LAS VEGAS	89119	LAS VEGAS	03769	LYME CENTER	03768	LYME
89160	LAS VEGAS	89121	LAS VEGAS	03802	PORTSMOUTH	03801	PORTSMOUTH
89162	LAS VEGAS	89122	LAS VEGAS	03805	ROLLINSFORD	03869	ROLLINSFORD
89163	THE LAKES	89117	LAS VEGAS	03821	DOVER	03820	DOVER
89164	LAS VEGAS	89117	LAS VEGAS	03822	DOVER	03820	DOVER
89170	LAS VEGAS	89154	LAS VEGAS	03832	EATON CENTER	03849	MADISON
89173	LAS VEGAS	89103	LAS VEGAS	03843	HAMPTON	03842	HAMPTON
89177	LAS VEGAS	89106	LAS VEGAS	03847	KEARSARGE	03845	INTERVALE
89180	LAS VEGAS	89103	LAS VEGAS	03850	MELVIN VILLAGE	03816	CENTER TUFTONBORO
89185	LAS VEGAS	89104	LAS VEGAS	03859	NEWTON JUNCTION	03858	NEWTON
89193	LAS VEGAS	89119	LAS VEGAS	03866	ROCHESTER	03867	ROCHESTER
89195	LAS VEGAS	89119	LAS VEGAS	03871	RYE BEACH	03870	RYE
89199	LAS VEGAS	89119	LAS VEGAS	03896	WOLFEBORO FALLS	03894	WOLFEBORO
89314	DUCKWATER	89301	ELY	03897	WONALANCET	03886	TAMWORTH
89315	ELY	89301	ELY	07007	CALDWELL	07006	CALDWELL
89318	MC GILL	89301	ELY	07015	CLIFTON	07011	CLIFTON
89319	RUTH	89301	ELY	07019	EAST ORANGE	07017	EAST ORANGE
89402	CRYSTAL BAY	89451	INCLINE VILLAGE	07051	ORANGE	07050	ORANGE
89407	FALLON	89406	FALLON	07061	PLAINFIELD	07060	PLAINFIELD
89411	GENOA	89413	GLENBROOK	07091	WESTFIELD	07090	WESTFIELD
89421	MC DERMITT	89425	OROVADA	07096	SECAUCUS	07094	SECAUCUS
89422	MINA	89420	LUNING	07097	JERSEY CITY	07307	JERSEY CITY
89428	SILVER CITY	89706	CARSON CITY	07099	KEARNY	07032	KEARNY
89432	SPARKS	89431	SPARKS	07101	NEWARK	07102	NEWARK
89435	SPARKS	89436	SPARKS	07175	NEWARK	07102	NEWARK
89438	VALMY	89414	GOLCONDA	07182	NEWARK	07102	NEWARK
89439	VERDI	89523	RENO	07184	NEWARK	07102	NEWARK
89446	WINNEMUCCA	89445	WINNEMUCCA	07188	NEWARK	07102	NEWARK
89448	ZEPHYR COVE	89413	GLENBROOK	07189	NEWARK	07102	NEWARK
89449	STATELINE	89413	GLENBROOK	07191	NEWARK	07102	NEWARK
89450	INCLINE VILLAGE	89451	INCLINE VILLAGE	07192	NEWARK	07102	NEWARK
89452	INCLINE VILLAGE	89451	INCLINE VILLAGE	07193	NEWARK	07102	NEWARK

NEW JERSEY   **NEW MEXICO**

Point ZIP Code ZIP	Post Office Name	Enclosing Residential ZIP Code ZIP	Post Office Name	Point ZIP Code ZIP	Post Office Name	Enclosing Residential ZIP Code ZIP	Post Office Name
07194	NEWARK	07102	NEWARK	08218	GOSHEN	08210	CAPE MAY COURT HOUSE
07195	NEWARK	07102	NEWARK	08219	GREEN CREEK	08204	CAPE MAY
07197	NEWARK	07102	NEWARK	08220	LEEDS POINT	08205	ABSECON
07198	NEWARK	07102	NEWARK	08224	NEW GRETNA	08087	TUCKERTON
07199	NEWARK	07102	NEWARK	08231	OCEANVILLE	08205	ABSECON
07207	ELIZABETH	07208	ELIZABETH	08240	POMONA	08215	EGG HARBOR CITY
07303	JERSEY CITY	07302	JERSEY CITY	08245	SOUTH DENNIS	08210	CAPE MAY COURT HOUSE
07308	JERSEY CITY	07302	JERSEY CITY	08246	SOUTH SEAVILLE	08230	OCEAN VIEW
07309	JERSEY CITY	07304	JERSEY CITY	08250	TUCKAHOE	08270	WOODBINE
07311	JERSEY CITY	07302	JERSEY CITY	08252	WHITESBORO	08210	CAPE MAY COURT HOUSE
07390	JERSEY CITY	07302	JERSEY CITY	08313	DEERFIELD STREET	08302	BRIDGETON
07399	JERSEY CITY	07306	JERSEY CITY	08315	DIVIDING CREEK	08349	PORT NORRIS
07428	MC AFEE	07462	VERNON	08316	DORCHESTER	08332	MILLVILLE
07451	RIDGEWOOD	07450	RIDGEWOOD	08320	FAIRTON	08302	BRIDGETON
07474	WAYNE	07470	WAYNE	08321	FORTESCUE	08345	NEWPORT
07477	WAYNE	07470	WAYNE	08329	MAURICETOWN	08349	PORT NORRIS
07495	MAHWAH	07430	MAHWAH	08342	MIZPAH	08330	MAYS LANDING
07498	MAHWAH	07430	MAHWAH	08347	NORMA	08318	ELMER
07507	HAWTHORNE	07506	HAWTHORNE	08348	PORT ELIZABETH	08332	MILLVILLE
07509	PATERSON	07501	PATERSON	08352	ROSENHAYN	08302	BRIDGETON
07510	PATERSON	07501	PATERSON	08362	VINELAND	08360	VINELAND
07511	TOTOWA	07512	TOTOWA	08404	ATLANTIC CITY	08401	ATLANTIC CITY
07533	PATERSON	07503	PATERSON	08504	BLAWENBURG	08558	SKILLMAN
07538	HALEDON	07508	HALEDON	08541	PRINCETON	08540	PRINCETON
07543	PATERSON	07513	PATERSON	08543	PRINCETON	08540	PRINCETON
07544	PATERSON	07524	PATERSON	08555	ROOSEVELT	08520	HIGHTSTOWN
07602	HACKENSACK	07601	HACKENSACK	08557	SERGEANTSVILLE	08559	STOCKTON
07653	PARAMUS	07652	PARAMUS	08561	WINDSOR	08520	HIGHTSTOWN
07699	TETERBORO	07601	HACKENSACK	08570	CRANBURY	08512	CRANBURY
07709	ALLENHURST	07711	ALLENHURST	08601	TRENTON	08611	TRENTON
07710	ADELPHIA	07728	FREEHOLD	08602	TRENTON	08691	TRENTON
07715	BELMAR	07719	BELMAR	08603	TRENTON	08691	TRENTON
07752	NAVESINK	07716	ATLANTIC HIGHLANDS	08604	TRENTON	08691	TRENTON
07754	NEPTUNE	07753	NEPTUNE	08605	TRENTON	08691	TRENTON
07763	TENNENT	07728	FREEHOLD	08606	TRENTON	08691	TRENTON
07765	WICKATUNK	07751	MORGANVILLE	08607	TRENTON	08691	TRENTON
07777	HOLMDEL	07733	HOLMDEL	08625	TRENTON	08608	TRENTON
07799	EATONTOWN	07724	EATONTOWN	08645	TRENTON	08608	TRENTON
07802	DOVER	07801	DOVER	08646	TRENTON	08608	TRENTON
07806	PICATINNY ARSENAL	07801	DOVER	08647	TRENTON	08608	TRENTON
07820	ALLAMUCHY	07840	HACKETTSTOWN	08650	TRENTON	08691	TRENTON
07829	BUTTZVILLE	07823	BELVIDERE	08666	TRENTON	08608	TRENTON
07831	CHANGEWATER	08827	HAMPTON	08677	TRENTON	08608	TRENTON
07833	DELAWARE	07832	COLUMBIA	08695	TRENTON	08608	TRENTON
07837	GLASSER	07821	ANDOVER	08720	ALLENWOOD	07719	BELMAR
07839	GREENDELL	07821	ANDOVER	08732	ISLAND HEIGHTS	08753	TOMS RIVER
07842	HIBERNIA	07866	ROCKAWAY	08739	NORMANDY BEACH	08738	MANTOLOKING
07844	HOPE	07825	BLAIRSTOWN	08754	TOMS RIVER	08753	TOMS RIVER
07845	IRONIA	07945	MENDHAM	08756	TOMS RIVER	08721	BAYVILLE
07846	JOHNSONBURG	07825	BLAIRSTOWN	08803	BAPTISTOWN	08825	FRENCHTOWN
07855	MIDDLEVILLE	07860	NEWTON	08808	BROADWAY	07882	WASHINGTON
07870	SCHOOLEYS MOUNTAIN	07853	LONG VALLEY	08818	EDISON	08817	EDISON
07875	STILLWATER	07860	NEWTON	08821	FLAGTOWN	08844	HILLSBOROUGH
07877	SWARTSWOOD	07860	NEWTON	08834	LITTLE YORK	08848	MILFORD
07878	MOUNT TABOR	07834	DENVILLE	08855	PISCATAWAY	08854	PISCATAWAY
07879	TRANQUILITY	07821	ANDOVER	08858	OLDWICK	08889	WHITEHOUSE STATION
07880	VIENNA	07840	HACKETTSTOWN	08862	PERTH AMBOY	08861	PERTH AMBOY
07881	WALLPACK CENTER	07826	BRANCHVILLE	08868	QUAKERTOWN	08867	PITTSTOWN
07890	BRANCHVILLE	07826	BRANCHVILLE	08870	READINGTON	08889	WHITEHOUSE STATION
07902	SUMMIT	07901	SUMMIT	08871	SAYREVILLE	08872	SAYREVILLE
07926	BROOKSIDE	07960	MORRISTOWN	08875	SOMERSET	08873	SOMERSET
07938	LIBERTY CORNER	07920	BASKING RIDGE	08878	SOUTH AMBOY	08879	SOUTH AMBOY
07939	LYONS	07920	BASKING RIDGE	08885	STANTON	08822	FLEMINGTON
07961	MORRISTOWN	07960	MORRISTOWN	08888	WHITEHOUSE	08889	WHITEHOUSE STATION
07962	MORRISTOWN	07960	MORRISTOWN	08890	ZAREPHATH	08873	SOMERSET
07963	MORRISTOWN	07960	MORRISTOWN	08896	RARITAN	08869	RARITAN
07970	MOUNT FREEDOM	07945	MENDHAM	08899	EDISON	08817	EDISON
07977	PEAPACK	07934	GLADSTONE	08903	NEW BRUNSWICK	08901	NEW BRUNSWICK
07978	PLUCKEMIN	07921	BEDMINSTER	08905	NEW BRUNSWICK	08902	NORTH BRUNSWICK
07979	POTTERSVILLE	07830	CALIFON	08906	NEW BRUNSWICK	08817	EDISON
07983	WHIPPANY	07981	WHIPPANY	08922	NEW BRUNSWICK	08902	NORTH BRUNSWICK
07999	WHIPPANY	07981	WHIPPANY	08933	NEW BRUNSWICK	08901	NEW BRUNSWICK
08001	ALLOWAY	08079	SALEM	08988	NEW BRUNSWICK	08817	EDISON
08006	BARNEGAT LIGHT	08008	BEACH HAVEN	08989	NEW BRUNSWICK	08817	EDISON
08011	BIRMINGHAM	08068	PEMBERTON	87011	CLAUNCH	87801	SOCORRO
08018	CEDAR BROOK	08009	BERLIN	87021	MILAN	87014	CUBERO
08023	DEEPWATER	08069	PENNS GROVE	87022	ISLETA	87068	BOSQUE FARMS
08025	EWAN	08062	MULLICA HILL	87032	MC INTOSH	87016	ESTANCIA
08038	HANCOCKS BRIDGE	08079	SALEM	87034	PUEBLO OF ACOMA	87014	CUBERO
08039	HARRISONVILLE	08062	MULLICA HILL	87037	NAGEEZI	87413	BLOOMFIELD
08042	JULIUSTOWN	08068	PEMBERTON	87038	NEW LAGUNA	87007	CASA BLANCA
08064	NEW LISBON	08088	VINCENTOWN	87040	PAGUATE	87014	CUBERO
08072	QUINTON	08079	SALEM	87049	SAN FIDEL	87020	GRANTS
08073	RANCOCAS	08060	MOUNT HOLLY	87051	SAN RAFAEL	87014	CUBERO
08074	RICHWOOD	08062	MULLICA HILL	87061	TORREON	87016	ESTANCIA
08076	RIVERTON	08077	RIVERTON	87064	YOUNGSVILLE	87017	GALLINA
08095	WINSLOW	08037	HAMMONTON	87070	CLINES CORNERS	87035	MORIARTY
08099	BELLMAWR	08031	BELLMAWR	87072	COCHITI PUEBLO	87041	PENA BLANCA
08101	CAMDEN	08102	CAMDEN	87101	ALBUQUERQUE	87102	ALBUQUERQUE
08212	CAPE MAY POINT	08204	CAPE MAY	87103	ALBUQUERQUE	87102	ALBUQUERQUE
08213	COLOGNE	08215	EGG HARBOR CITY	87119	ALBUQUERQUE	87102	ALBUQUERQUE
08214	DENNISVILLE	08270	WOODBINE	87125	ALBUQUERQUE	87102	ALBUQUERQUE
08217	ELWOOD	08037	HAMMONTON	87151	ALBUQUERQUE	87102	ALBUQUERQUE

NEW MEXICO

Point ZIP Code		Enclosing Residential ZIP Code	
ZIP	Post Office Name	ZIP	Post Office Name
87153	ALBUQUERQUE	87112	ALBUQUERQUE
87154	ALBUQUERQUE	87111	ALBUQUERQUE
87158	ALBUQUERQUE	87107	ALBUQUERQUE
87174	RIO RANCHO	87124	RIO RANCHO
87176	ALBUQUERQUE	87110	ALBUQUERQUE
87181	ALBUQUERQUE	87112	ALBUQUERQUE
87184	ALBUQUERQUE	87114	ALBUQUERQUE
87185	ALBUQUERQUE	87117	KIRTLAND AFB
87187	ALBUQUERQUE	87114	ALBUQUERQUE
87190	ALBUQUERQUE	87110	ALBUQUERQUE
87191	ALBUQUERQUE	87111	ALBUQUERQUE
87192	ALBUQUERQUE	87104	ALBUQUERQUE
87193	ALBUQUERQUE	87114	ALBUQUERQUE
87194	ALBUQUERQUE	87104	ALBUQUERQUE
87195	ALBUQUERQUE	87105	ALBUQUERQUE
87196	ALBUQUERQUE	87106	ALBUQUERQUE
87197	ALBUQUERQUE	87107	ALBUQUERQUE
87198	ALBUQUERQUE	87108	ALBUQUERQUE
87199	ALBUQUERQUE	87109	ALBUQUERQUE
87302	GALLUP	87301	GALLUP
87305	GALLUP	87301	GALLUP
87311	CHURCH ROCK	87301	GALLUP
87316	FORT WINGATE	87301	GALLUP
87317	GAMERCO	87301	GALLUP
87319	MENTMORE	87301	GALLUP
87322	REHOBOTH	87301	GALLUP
87326	VANDERWAGEN	87301	GALLUP
87347	JAMESTOWN	87312	CONTINENTAL DIVIDE
87357	PINEHILL	87014	CUBERO
87364	SHEEP SPRINGS	87420	SHIPROCK
87365	SMITH LAKE	87323	THOREAU
87375	YATAHEY	87301	GALLUP
87455	NEWCOMB	87420	SHIPROCK
87461	SANOSTEE	87420	SHIPROCK
87499	FARMINGTON	87401	FARMINGTON
87502	SANTA FE	87501	SANTA FE
87503	SANTA FE	87501	SANTA FE
87504	SANTA FE	87501	SANTA FE
87509	SANTA FE	87505	SANTA FE
87511	ALCALDE	87531	EMBUDO
87512	AMALIA	87524	COSTILLA
87515	CANJILON	87575	TIERRA AMARILLA
87516	CANONES	87017	GALLINA
87517	CARSON	87549	OJO CALIENTE
87518	CEBOLLA	87575	TIERRA AMARILLA
87519	CERRO	87556	QUESTA
87523	CORDOVA	87522	CHIMAYO
87525	TAOS SKI VALLEY	87571	TAOS
87529	EL PRADO	87571	TAOS
87533	ESPANOLA	87532	ESPANOLA
87538	ILFELD	87501	SANTA FE
87543	LLANO	87579	VADITO
87545	LOS ALAMOS	87544	LOS ALAMOS
87548	MEDANALES	87510	ABIQUIU
87551	LOS OJOS	87575	TIERRA AMARILLA
87554	PETACA	87581	VALLECITOS
87558	RED RIVER	87556	QUESTA
87562	ROWE	87565	SAN JOSE
87569	SERAFINA	87560	RIBERA
87574	TESUQUE	87506	SANTA FE
87576	TRAMPAS	87521	CHAMISAL
87577	TRES PIEDRAS	87549	OJO CALIENTE
87578	TRUCHAS	87522	CHIMAYO
87582	VELARDE	87531	EMBUDO
87583	VILLANUEVA	87701	LAS VEGAS
87592	SANTA FE	87507	SANTA FE
87594	SANTA FE	87501	SANTA FE
87710	ANGEL FIRE	87714	CIMARRON
87712	BUENA VISTA	87732	MORA
87723	HOLMAN	87732	MORA
87735	OJO FELIZ	87734	OCATE
87736	RAINSVILLE	87732	MORA
87749	UTE PARK	87714	CIMARRON
87753	WATROUS	87750	VALMORA
87824	LUNA	87830	RESERVE
87832	SAN ANTONIO	87801	SOCORRO
87935	ELEPHANT BUTTE	87901	TRUTH OR CONSEQUENCE
87939	MONTICELLO	87901	TRUTH OR CONSEQUENCE
88003	LAS CRUCES	88001	LAS CRUCES
88004	LAS CRUCES	88001	LAS CRUCES
88006	LAS CRUCES	88001	LAS CRUCES
88009	PLAYAS	88045	LORDSBURG
88024	BERINO	88081	CHAPARRAL
88027	CHAMBERINO	88044	LA MESA
88028	CLIFF	88025	BUCKHORN
88029	COLUMBUS	88030	DEMING
88031	DEMING	88030	DEMING
88032	DONA ANA	88012	LAS CRUCES
88033	FAIRACRES	88007	LAS CRUCES
88034	FAYWOOD	88023	BAYARD
88036	FORT BAYARD	88061	SILVER CITY
88038	GILA	88061	SILVER CITY
88040	HACHITA	88043	HURLEY

NEW YORK

Point ZIP Code		Enclosing Residential ZIP Code	
ZIP	Post Office Name	ZIP	Post Office Name
88046	MESILLA	88005	LAS CRUCES
88051	MULE CREEK	88025	BUCKHORN
88052	ORGAN	88007	LAS CRUCES
88053	PINOS ALTOS	88061	SILVER CITY
88054	RADIUM SPRINGS	87940	RINCON
88055	REDROCK	88025	BUCKHORN
88056	RODEO	88020	ANIMAS
88058	SAN MIGUEL	88044	LA MESA
88062	SILVER CITY	88061	SILVER CITY
88065	TYRONE	88061	SILVER CITY
88102	CLOVIS	88101	CLOVIS
88115	DORA	88130	PORTALES
88122	KENNA	88116	ELIDA
88202	ROSWELL	88201	ROSWELL
88211	ARTESIA	88210	ARTESIA
88221	CARLSBAD	88220	CARLSBAD
88241	HOBBS	88240	HOBBS
88244	HOBBS	88240	HOBBS
88254	LAKEWOOD	88210	ARTESIA
88255	LOCO HILLS	88210	ARTESIA
88262	MC DONALD	88260	LOVINGTON
88263	MALAGA	88256	LOVING
88268	WHITES CITY	88220	CARLSBAD
88311	ALAMOGORDO	88310	ALAMOGORDO
88312	ALTO	88345	RUIDOSO
88325	HIGH ROLLS MOUNTAIN	88317	CLOUDCROFT
88342	OROGRANDE	88317	CLOUDCROFT
88349	SUNSPOT	88317	CLOUDCROFT
88350	TIMBERON	88317	CLOUDCROFT
88355	RUIDOSO	88345	RUIDOSO
88433	QUAY	88401	TUCUMCARI
00501	HOLTSVILLE	11742	HOLTSVILLE
00544	HOLTSVILLE	11742	HOLTSVILLE
09007	APO	00000	NO ENCLOSING ZIP
09009	APO	00000	NO ENCLOSING ZIP
09012	APO	00000	NO ENCLOSING ZIP
09013	APO	00000	NO ENCLOSING ZIP
09014	APO	00000	NO ENCLOSING ZIP
09021	APO	00000	NO ENCLOSING ZIP
09028	APO	00000	NO ENCLOSING ZIP
09031	APO	00000	NO ENCLOSING ZIP
09033	APO	00000	NO ENCLOSING ZIP
09034	APO	00000	NO ENCLOSING ZIP
09036	APO	00000	NO ENCLOSING ZIP
09042	APO	00000	NO ENCLOSING ZIP
09045	APO	00000	NO ENCLOSING ZIP
09046	APO	00000	NO ENCLOSING ZIP
09050	APO	00000	NO ENCLOSING ZIP
09053	APO	00000	NO ENCLOSING ZIP
09054	APO	00000	NO ENCLOSING ZIP
09056	APO	00000	NO ENCLOSING ZIP
09058	APO	00000	NO ENCLOSING ZIP
09059	APO	00000	NO ENCLOSING ZIP
09060	APO	00000	NO ENCLOSING ZIP
09063	APO	00000	NO ENCLOSING ZIP
09067	APO	00000	NO ENCLOSING ZIP
09069	APO	00000	NO ENCLOSING ZIP
09072	APO	00000	NO ENCLOSING ZIP
09074	APO	00000	NO ENCLOSING ZIP
09076	APO	00000	NO ENCLOSING ZIP
09080	APO	00000	NO ENCLOSING ZIP
09081	APO	00000	NO ENCLOSING ZIP
09086	APO	00000	NO ENCLOSING ZIP
09089	APO	00000	NO ENCLOSING ZIP
09090	APO	00000	NO ENCLOSING ZIP
09094	APO	00000	NO ENCLOSING ZIP
09095	APO	00000	NO ENCLOSING ZIP
09096	APO	00000	NO ENCLOSING ZIP
09098	APO	00000	NO ENCLOSING ZIP
09099	APO	00000	NO ENCLOSING ZIP
09100	APO	00000	NO ENCLOSING ZIP
09102	APO	00000	NO ENCLOSING ZIP
09103	APO	00000	NO ENCLOSING ZIP
09104	APO	00000	NO ENCLOSING ZIP
09107	APO	00000	NO ENCLOSING ZIP
09110	APO	00000	NO ENCLOSING ZIP
09111	APO	00000	NO ENCLOSING ZIP
09112	APO	00000	NO ENCLOSING ZIP
09114	APO	00000	NO ENCLOSING ZIP
09123	APO	00000	NO ENCLOSING ZIP
09126	APO	00000	NO ENCLOSING ZIP
09128	APO	00000	NO ENCLOSING ZIP
09131	APO	00000	NO ENCLOSING ZIP
09137	APO	00000	NO ENCLOSING ZIP
09138	APO	00000	NO ENCLOSING ZIP
09139	APO	00000	NO ENCLOSING ZIP
09140	APO	00000	NO ENCLOSING ZIP
09142	APO	00000	NO ENCLOSING ZIP
09143	APO	00000	NO ENCLOSING ZIP
09154	APO	00000	NO ENCLOSING ZIP
09157	APO	00000	NO ENCLOSING ZIP
09165	APO	00000	NO ENCLOSING ZIP
09166	APO	00000	NO ENCLOSING ZIP

NONRESIDENTIAL ZIP CODES

Appendix I

NEW YORK

NEW YORK

Point ZIP Code		Enclosing Residential ZIP Code		Point ZIP Code		Enclosing Residential ZIP Code	
ZIP	Post Office Name	ZIP	Post Office Name	ZIP	Post Office Name	ZIP	Post Office Name
09169	APO	00000	NO ENCLOSING ZIP	09387	APO	00000	NO ENCLOSING ZIP
09172	APO	00000	NO ENCLOSING ZIP	09388	APO	00000	NO ENCLOSING ZIP
09173	APO	00000	NO ENCLOSING ZIP	09389	APO	00000	NO ENCLOSING ZIP
09175	APO	00000	NO ENCLOSING ZIP	09390	APO	00000	NO ENCLOSING ZIP
09177	APO	00000	NO ENCLOSING ZIP	09391	APO	00000	NO ENCLOSING ZIP
09178	APO	00000	NO ENCLOSING ZIP	09392	APO	00000	NO ENCLOSING ZIP
09180	APO	00000	NO ENCLOSING ZIP	09393	APO	00000	NO ENCLOSING ZIP
09182	APO	00000	NO ENCLOSING ZIP	09394	APO	00000	NO ENCLOSING ZIP
09183	APO	00000	NO ENCLOSING ZIP	09397	APO	00000	NO ENCLOSING ZIP
09185	APO	00000	NO ENCLOSING ZIP	09398	APO	00000	NO ENCLOSING ZIP
09186	APO	00000	NO ENCLOSING ZIP	09399	APO	00000	NO ENCLOSING ZIP
09189	APO	00000	NO ENCLOSING ZIP	09409	FPO	00000	NO ENCLOSING ZIP
09211	APO	00000	NO ENCLOSING ZIP	09419	APO	00000	NO ENCLOSING ZIP
09212	APO	00000	NO ENCLOSING ZIP	09421	FPO	00000	NO ENCLOSING ZIP
09213	APO	00000	NO ENCLOSING ZIP	09447	APO	00000	NO ENCLOSING ZIP
09214	APO	00000	NO ENCLOSING ZIP	09449	APO	00000	NO ENCLOSING ZIP
09220	APO	00000	NO ENCLOSING ZIP	09454	APO	00000	NO ENCLOSING ZIP
09225	APO	00000	NO ENCLOSING ZIP	09456	APO	00000	NO ENCLOSING ZIP
09226	APO	00000	NO ENCLOSING ZIP	09459	APO	00000	NO ENCLOSING ZIP
09227	APO	00000	NO ENCLOSING ZIP	09461	APO	00000	NO ENCLOSING ZIP
09229	APO	00000	NO ENCLOSING ZIP	09463	APO	00000	NO ENCLOSING ZIP
09237	APO	00000	NO ENCLOSING ZIP	09464	APO	00000	NO ENCLOSING ZIP
09244	APO	00000	NO ENCLOSING ZIP	09468	APO	00000	NO ENCLOSING ZIP
09245	APO	00000	NO ENCLOSING ZIP	09469	APO	00000	NO ENCLOSING ZIP
09250	APO	00000	NO ENCLOSING ZIP	09470	APO	00000	NO ENCLOSING ZIP
09252	APO	00000	NO ENCLOSING ZIP	09494	APO	00000	NO ENCLOSING ZIP
09261	APO	00000	NO ENCLOSING ZIP	09496	APO	00000	NO ENCLOSING ZIP
09262	APO	00000	NO ENCLOSING ZIP	09498	FPO	00000	NO ENCLOSING ZIP
09263	APO	00000	NO ENCLOSING ZIP	09499	FPO	00000	NO ENCLOSING ZIP
09264	APO	00000	NO ENCLOSING ZIP	09501	FPO	00000	NO ENCLOSING ZIP
09265	APO	00000	NO ENCLOSING ZIP	09502	FPO	00000	NO ENCLOSING ZIP
09266	APO	00000	NO ENCLOSING ZIP	09503	FPO	00000	NO ENCLOSING ZIP
09267	APO	00000	NO ENCLOSING ZIP	09504	FPO	00000	NO ENCLOSING ZIP
09301	APO	00000	NO ENCLOSING ZIP	09505	FPO	00000	NO ENCLOSING ZIP
09302	APO	00000	NO ENCLOSING ZIP	09506	FPO	00000	NO ENCLOSING ZIP
09303	APO	00000	NO ENCLOSING ZIP	09507	FPO	00000	NO ENCLOSING ZIP
09304	APO	00000	NO ENCLOSING ZIP	09508	FPO	00000	NO ENCLOSING ZIP
09305	APO	00000	NO ENCLOSING ZIP	09509	FPO	00000	NO ENCLOSING ZIP
09306	APO	00000	NO ENCLOSING ZIP	09510	FPO	00000	NO ENCLOSING ZIP
09307	APO	00000	NO ENCLOSING ZIP	09517	FPO	00000	NO ENCLOSING ZIP
09308	APO	00000	NO ENCLOSING ZIP	09521	FPO	00000	NO ENCLOSING ZIP
09309	APO	00000	NO ENCLOSING ZIP	09524	FPO	00000	NO ENCLOSING ZIP
09311	APO	00000	NO ENCLOSING ZIP	09532	FPO	00000	NO ENCLOSING ZIP
09314	APO	00000	NO ENCLOSING ZIP	09534	FPO	00000	NO ENCLOSING ZIP
09315	APO	00000	NO ENCLOSING ZIP	09542	FPO	00000	NO ENCLOSING ZIP
09318	APO	00000	NO ENCLOSING ZIP	09543	FPO	00000	NO ENCLOSING ZIP
09320	APO	00000	NO ENCLOSING ZIP	09545	FPO	00000	NO ENCLOSING ZIP
09321	APO	00000	NO ENCLOSING ZIP	09549	FPO	00000	NO ENCLOSING ZIP
09322	APO	00000	NO ENCLOSING ZIP	09550	FPO	00000	NO ENCLOSING ZIP
09323	APO	00000	NO ENCLOSING ZIP	09551	FPO	00000	NO ENCLOSING ZIP
09324	APO	00000	NO ENCLOSING ZIP	09554	FPO	00000	NO ENCLOSING ZIP
09325	APO	00000	NO ENCLOSING ZIP	09556	FPO	00000	NO ENCLOSING ZIP
09326	APO	00000	NO ENCLOSING ZIP	09557	FPO	00000	NO ENCLOSING ZIP
09327	APO	00000	NO ENCLOSING ZIP	09564	FPO	00000	NO ENCLOSING ZIP
09328	APO	00000	NO ENCLOSING ZIP	09565	FPO	00000	NO ENCLOSING ZIP
09329	APO	00000	NO ENCLOSING ZIP	09566	FPO	00000	NO ENCLOSING ZIP
09330	APO	00000	NO ENCLOSING ZIP	09567	FPO	00000	NO ENCLOSING ZIP
09331	APO	00000	NO ENCLOSING ZIP	09568	FPO	00000	NO ENCLOSING ZIP
09332	APO	00000	NO ENCLOSING ZIP	09569	FPO	00000	NO ENCLOSING ZIP
09333	APO	00000	NO ENCLOSING ZIP	09570	FPO	00000	NO ENCLOSING ZIP
09334	APO	00000	NO ENCLOSING ZIP	09573	FPO	00000	NO ENCLOSING ZIP
09335	APO	00000	NO ENCLOSING ZIP	09574	FPO	00000	NO ENCLOSING ZIP
09336	APO	00000	NO ENCLOSING ZIP	09575	FPO	00000	NO ENCLOSING ZIP
09337	APO	00000	NO ENCLOSING ZIP	09576	FPO	00000	NO ENCLOSING ZIP
09338	APO	00000	NO ENCLOSING ZIP	09577	FPO	00000	NO ENCLOSING ZIP
09339	APO	00000	NO ENCLOSING ZIP	09578	FPO	00000	NO ENCLOSING ZIP
09340	APO	00000	NO ENCLOSING ZIP	09579	FPO	00000	NO ENCLOSING ZIP
09342	APO	00000	NO ENCLOSING ZIP	09581	FPO	00000	NO ENCLOSING ZIP
09344	APO	00000	NO ENCLOSING ZIP	09582	FPO	00000	NO ENCLOSING ZIP
09345	APO	00000	NO ENCLOSING ZIP	09586	FPO	00000	NO ENCLOSING ZIP
09346	APO	00000	NO ENCLOSING ZIP	09587	FPO	00000	NO ENCLOSING ZIP
09347	APO	00000	NO ENCLOSING ZIP	09588	FPO	00000	NO ENCLOSING ZIP
09348	APO	00000	NO ENCLOSING ZIP	09589	FPO	00000	NO ENCLOSING ZIP
09351	APO	00000	NO ENCLOSING ZIP	09590	FPO	00000	NO ENCLOSING ZIP
09353	APO	00000	NO ENCLOSING ZIP	09591	FPO	00000	NO ENCLOSING ZIP
09354	APO	00000	NO ENCLOSING ZIP	09593	FPO	00000	NO ENCLOSING ZIP
09355	APO	00000	NO ENCLOSING ZIP	09594	FPO	00000	NO ENCLOSING ZIP
09356	APO	00000	NO ENCLOSING ZIP	09595	FPO	00000	NO ENCLOSING ZIP
09357	APO	00000	NO ENCLOSING ZIP	09596	FPO	00000	NO ENCLOSING ZIP
09358	APO	00000	NO ENCLOSING ZIP	09599	FPO	00000	NO ENCLOSING ZIP
09359	APO	00000	NO ENCLOSING ZIP	09601	APO	00000	NO ENCLOSING ZIP
09360	APO	00000	NO ENCLOSING ZIP	09602	APO	00000	NO ENCLOSING ZIP
09361	APO	00000	NO ENCLOSING ZIP	09603	APO	00000	NO ENCLOSING ZIP
09363	APO	00000	NO ENCLOSING ZIP	09604	APO	00000	NO ENCLOSING ZIP
09365	APO	00000	NO ENCLOSING ZIP	09609	FPO	00000	NO ENCLOSING ZIP
09366	APO	00000	NO ENCLOSING ZIP	09610	APO	00000	NO ENCLOSING ZIP
09368	APO	00000	NO ENCLOSING ZIP	09612	FPO	00000	NO ENCLOSING ZIP
09370	APO	00000	NO ENCLOSING ZIP	09613	APO	00000	NO ENCLOSING ZIP
09372	APO	00000	NO ENCLOSING ZIP	09617	APO	00000	NO ENCLOSING ZIP
09383	APO	00000	NO ENCLOSING ZIP	09618	FPO	00000	NO ENCLOSING ZIP
09384	APO	00000	NO ENCLOSING ZIP	09619	FPO	00000	NO ENCLOSING ZIP
09385	APO	00000	NO ENCLOSING ZIP	09620	FPO	00000	NO ENCLOSING ZIP
09386	APO	00000	NO ENCLOSING ZIP	09621	FPO	00000	NO ENCLOSING ZIP

NONRESIDENTIAL ZIP CODES

NEW YORK

NEW YORK

Point ZIP Code		Enclosing Residential ZIP Code		Point ZIP Code		Enclosing Residential ZIP Code	
ZIP	Post Office Name	ZIP	Post Office Name	ZIP	Post Office Name	ZIP	Post Office Name
09622	FPO	00000	NO ENCLOSING ZIP	09841	APO	00000	NO ENCLOSING ZIP
09623	FPO	00000	NO ENCLOSING ZIP	09842	APO	00000	NO ENCLOSING ZIP
09624	APO	00000	NO ENCLOSING ZIP	09843	APO	00000	NO ENCLOSING ZIP
09625	FPO	00000	NO ENCLOSING ZIP	09844	APO	00000	NO ENCLOSING ZIP
09626	FPO	00000	NO ENCLOSING ZIP	09852	APO	00000	NO ENCLOSING ZIP
09627	FPO	00000	NO ENCLOSING ZIP	09853	APO	00000	NO ENCLOSING ZIP
09628	APO	00000	NO ENCLOSING ZIP	09854	APO	00000	NO ENCLOSING ZIP
09630	APO	00000	NO ENCLOSING ZIP	09855	APO	00000	NO ENCLOSING ZIP
09631	FPO	00000	NO ENCLOSING ZIP	09858	APO	00000	NO ENCLOSING ZIP
09636	FPO	00000	NO ENCLOSING ZIP	09865	FPO	00000	NO ENCLOSING ZIP
09638	FPO	00000	NO ENCLOSING ZIP	09866	APO	00000	NO ENCLOSING ZIP
09642	APO	00000	NO ENCLOSING ZIP	09868	APO	00000	NO ENCLOSING ZIP
09643	APO	00000	NO ENCLOSING ZIP	09871	APO	00000	NO ENCLOSING ZIP
09644	FPO	00000	NO ENCLOSING ZIP	09880	APO	00000	NO ENCLOSING ZIP
09645	FPO	00000	NO ENCLOSING ZIP	09888	APO	00000	NO ENCLOSING ZIP
09647	APO	00000	NO ENCLOSING ZIP	09889	APO	00000	NO ENCLOSING ZIP
09648	FPO	00000	NO ENCLOSING ZIP	09890	APO	00000	NO ENCLOSING ZIP
09649	FPO	00000	NO ENCLOSING ZIP	09892	APO	00000	NO ENCLOSING ZIP
09703	APO	00000	NO ENCLOSING ZIP	09894	APO	00000	NO ENCLOSING ZIP
09704	APO	00000	NO ENCLOSING ZIP	09898	APO	00000	NO ENCLOSING ZIP
09705	APO	00000	NO ENCLOSING ZIP	10008	NEW YORK	10007	NEW YORK
09706	APO	00000	NO ENCLOSING ZIP	10041	NEW YORK	10004	NEW YORK
09707	APO	00000	NO ENCLOSING ZIP	10043	NEW YORK	10005	NEW YORK
09708	APO	00000	NO ENCLOSING ZIP	10045	NEW YORK	10038	NEW YORK
09709	APO	00000	NO ENCLOSING ZIP	10047	NEW YORK	10280	NEW YORK
09710	APO	00000	NO ENCLOSING ZIP	10048	NEW YORK	10280	NEW YORK
09711	APO	00000	NO ENCLOSING ZIP	10055	NEW YORK	10003	NEW YORK
09713	APO	00000	NO ENCLOSING ZIP	10069	NEW YORK	10023	NEW YORK
09714	APO	00000	NO ENCLOSING ZIP	10072	NEW YORK	10001	NEW YORK
09715	APO	00000	NO ENCLOSING ZIP	10080	NEW YORK	10280	NEW YORK
09716	APO	00000	NO ENCLOSING ZIP	10081	NEW YORK	10005	NEW YORK
09717	APO	00000	NO ENCLOSING ZIP	10082	NEW YORK	10023	NEW YORK
09718	APO	00000	NO ENCLOSING ZIP	10087	NEW YORK	10017	NEW YORK
09719	FPO	00000	NO ENCLOSING ZIP	10095	NEW YORK	10001	NEW YORK
09720	APO	00000	NO ENCLOSING ZIP	10098	NEW YORK	10001	NEW YORK
09721	APO	00000	NO ENCLOSING ZIP	10101	NEW YORK	10019	NEW YORK
09722	APO	00000	NO ENCLOSING ZIP	10102	NEW YORK	10019	NEW YORK
09723	APO	00000	NO ENCLOSING ZIP	10103	NEW YORK	10019	NEW YORK
09724	APO	00000	NO ENCLOSING ZIP	10104	NEW YORK	10019	NEW YORK
09725	FPO	00000	NO ENCLOSING ZIP	10105	NEW YORK	10019	NEW YORK
09726	APO	00000	NO ENCLOSING ZIP	10106	NEW YORK	10019	NEW YORK
09727	FPO	00000	NO ENCLOSING ZIP	10107	NEW YORK	10019	NEW YORK
09728	FPO	00000	NO ENCLOSING ZIP	10108	NEW YORK	10036	NEW YORK
09729	FPO	00000	NO ENCLOSING ZIP	10109	NEW YORK	10036	NEW YORK
09732	APO	00000	NO ENCLOSING ZIP	10110	NEW YORK	10017	NEW YORK
09733	FPO	00000	NO ENCLOSING ZIP	10113	NEW YORK	10011	NEW YORK
09734	FPO	00000	NO ENCLOSING ZIP	10114	NEW YORK	10003	NEW YORK
09735	APO	00000	NO ENCLOSING ZIP	10115	NEW YORK	10024	NEW YORK
09777	APO	00000	NO ENCLOSING ZIP	10116	NEW YORK	10027	NEW YORK
09779	APO	00000	NO ENCLOSING ZIP	10117	NEW YORK	10001	NEW YORK
09780	APO	00000	NO ENCLOSING ZIP	10118	NEW YORK	10016	NEW YORK
09782	APO	00000	NO ENCLOSING ZIP	10119	NEW YORK	10001	NEW YORK
09783	APO	00000	NO ENCLOSING ZIP	10120	NEW YORK	10001	NEW YORK
09784	APO	00000	NO ENCLOSING ZIP	10121	NEW YORK	10001	NEW YORK
09788	APO	00000	NO ENCLOSING ZIP	10122	NEW YORK	10001	NEW YORK
09789	APO	00000	NO ENCLOSING ZIP	10123	NEW YORK	10001	NEW YORK
09790	APO	00000	NO ENCLOSING ZIP	10124	NEW YORK	10022	NEW YORK
09791	APO	00000	NO ENCLOSING ZIP	10125	NEW YORK	10001	NEW YORK
09793	APO	00000	NO ENCLOSING ZIP	10126	NEW YORK	10022	NEW YORK
09797	APO	00000	NO ENCLOSING ZIP	10129	NEW YORK	10018	NEW YORK
09801	APO	00000	NO ENCLOSING ZIP	10130	NEW YORK	10001	NEW YORK
09802	APO	00000	NO ENCLOSING ZIP	10131	NEW YORK	10021	NEW YORK
09803	APO	00000	NO ENCLOSING ZIP	10132	NEW YORK	10024	NEW YORK
09804	APO	00000	NO ENCLOSING ZIP	10133	NEW YORK	10023	NEW YORK
09805	APO	00000	NO ENCLOSING ZIP	10138	NEW YORK	10016	NEW YORK
09806	APO	00000	NO ENCLOSING ZIP	10149	NEW YORK	10019	NEW YORK
09807	APO	00000	NO ENCLOSING ZIP	10150	NEW YORK	10022	NEW YORK
09808	APO	00000	NO ENCLOSING ZIP	10151	NEW YORK	10022	NEW YORK
09809	APO	00000	NO ENCLOSING ZIP	10152	NEW YORK	10022	NEW YORK
09810	APO	00000	NO ENCLOSING ZIP	10153	NEW YORK	10022	NEW YORK
09811	APO	00000	NO ENCLOSING ZIP	10154	NEW YORK	10022	NEW YORK
09812	APO	00000	NO ENCLOSING ZIP	10155	NEW YORK	10022	NEW YORK
09813	APO	00000	NO ENCLOSING ZIP	10156	NEW YORK	10016	NEW YORK
09814	APO	00000	NO ENCLOSING ZIP	10157	NEW YORK	10016	NEW YORK
09815	APO	00000	NO ENCLOSING ZIP	10158	NEW YORK	10016	NEW YORK
09819	APO	00000	NO ENCLOSING ZIP	10159	NEW YORK	10010	NEW YORK
09821	APO	00000	NO ENCLOSING ZIP	10160	NEW YORK	10010	NEW YORK
09822	APO	00000	NO ENCLOSING ZIP	10161	NEW YORK	10011	NEW YORK
09823	APO	00000	NO ENCLOSING ZIP	10162	NEW YORK	10021	NEW YORK
09824	APO	00000	NO ENCLOSING ZIP	10163	NEW YORK	10017	NEW YORK
09827	APO	00000	NO ENCLOSING ZIP	10164	NEW YORK	10017	NEW YORK
09828	APO	00000	NO ENCLOSING ZIP	10165	NEW YORK	10017	NEW YORK
09829	APO	00000	NO ENCLOSING ZIP	10166	NEW YORK	10017	NEW YORK
09830	APO	00000	NO ENCLOSING ZIP	10167	NEW YORK	10017	NEW YORK
09831	APO	00000	NO ENCLOSING ZIP	10168	NEW YORK	10017	NEW YORK
09832	APO	00000	NO ENCLOSING ZIP	10169	NEW YORK	10029	NEW YORK
09833	APO	00000	NO ENCLOSING ZIP	10170	NEW YORK	10017	NEW YORK
09834	FPO	00000	NO ENCLOSING ZIP	10171	NEW YORK	10017	NEW YORK
09835	FPO	00000	NO ENCLOSING ZIP	10172	NEW YORK	10010	NEW YORK
09836	FPO	00000	NO ENCLOSING ZIP	10173	NEW YORK	10017	NEW YORK
09837	FPO	00000	NO ENCLOSING ZIP	10174	NEW YORK	10017	NEW YORK
09838	FPO	00000	NO ENCLOSING ZIP	10175	NEW YORK	10017	NEW YORK
09839	APO	00000	NO ENCLOSING ZIP	10176	NEW YORK	10036	NEW YORK

NEW YORK

Point ZIP Code		Enclosing Residential ZIP Code		Point ZIP Code		Enclosing Residential ZIP Code	
ZIP	Post Office Name	ZIP	Post Office Name	ZIP	Post Office Name	ZIP	Post Office Name
10177	NEW YORK	10017	NEW YORK	11424	JAMAICA	11415	KEW GARDENS
10178	NEW YORK	10016	NEW YORK	11425	JAMAICA	11434	JAMAICA
10179	NEW YORK	10017	NEW YORK	11431	JAMAICA	11432	JAMAICA
10185	NEW YORK	10036	NEW YORK	11439	JAMAICA	11432	JAMAICA
10197	NEW YORK	10022	NEW YORK	11484	JAMAICA	11430	JAMAICA
10199	NEW YORK	10001	NEW YORK	11499	JAMAICA	11430	JAMAICA
10213	NEW YORK	10013	NEW YORK	11531	GARDEN CITY	11530	GARDEN CITY
10242	NEW YORK	10007	NEW YORK	11535	GARDEN CITY	11530	GARDEN CITY
10249	NEW YORK	10007	NEW YORK	11536	GARDEN CITY	11530	GARDEN CITY
10256	NEW YORK	10006	NEW YORK	11547	GLENWOOD LANDING	11545	GLEN HEAD
10259	NEW YORK	10017	NEW YORK	11551	HEMPSTEAD	11550	HEMPSTEAD
10260	NEW YORK	10005	NEW YORK	11555	UNIONDALE	11553	UNIONDALE
10261	NEW YORK	10017	NEW YORK	11556	UNIONDALE	11553	UNIONDALE
10265	NEW YORK	10005	NEW YORK	11564	LYNBROOK	11563	LYNBROOK
10268	NEW YORK	10005	NEW YORK	11569	POINT LOOKOUT	11561	LONG BEACH
10269	NEW YORK	10005	NEW YORK	11571	ROCKVILLE CENTRE	11570	ROCKVILLE CENTRE
10270	NEW YORK	10005	NEW YORK	11582	VALLEY STREAM	11580	VALLEY STREAM
10271	NEW YORK	10005	NEW YORK	11583	VALLEY STREAM	11581	VALLEY STREAM
10272	NEW YORK	10038	NEW YORK	11588	UNIONDALE	11530	GARDEN CITY
10273	NEW YORK	10038	NEW YORK	11592	ROCKVILLE CENTRE	11570	ROCKVILLE CENTRE
10274	NEW YORK	10004	NEW YORK	11593	WESTBURY	11554	EAST MEADOW
10275	NEW YORK	10004	NEW YORK	11594	WESTBURY	11590	WESTBURY
10276	NEW YORK	10003	NEW YORK	11595	WESTBURY	11590	WESTBURY
10277	NEW YORK	10007	NEW YORK	11597	WESTBURY	11590	WESTBURY
10278	NEW YORK	10007	NEW YORK	11599	GARDEN CITY	11530	GARDEN CITY
10279	NEW YORK	10007	NEW YORK	11690	FAR ROCKAWAY	11691	FAR ROCKAWAY
10281	NEW YORK	10280	NEW YORK	11695	FAR ROCKAWAY	11693	FAR ROCKAWAY
10282	NEW YORK	10007	NEW YORK	11707	WEST BABYLON	11702	BABYLON
10285	NEW YORK	10280	NEW YORK	11708	AMITYVILLE	11701	AMITYVILLE
10286	NEW YORK	10005	NEW YORK	11736	FARMINGDALE	11735	FARMINGDALE
10292	NEW YORK	10038	NEW YORK	11737	FARMINGDALE	11735	FARMINGDALE
10311	STATEN ISLAND	10314	STATEN ISLAND	11739	GREAT RIVER	11730	EAST ISLIP
10313	STATEN ISLAND	10314	STATEN ISLAND	11745	SMITHTOWN	11787	SMITHTOWN
10499	BRONX	10465	BRONX	11750	HUNTINGTON STATION	11747	MELVILLE
10503	ARDSLEY ON HUDSON	10533	IRVINGTON	11760	ISLANDIA	11788	HAUPPAUGE
10517	CROMPOND	10547	MOHEGAN LAKE	11773	SYOSSET	11791	SYOSSET
10519	CROTON FALLS	10560	NORTH SALEM	11774	FARMINGDALE	11735	FARMINGDALE
10521	CROTON ON HUDSON	10520	CROTON ON HUDSON	11775	MELVILLE	11747	MELVILLE
10540	LINCOLNDALE	10589	SOMERS	11802	HICKSVILLE	11801	HICKSVILLE
10542	MAHOPAC FALLS	10541	MAHOPAC	11805	MID ISLAND	11801	HICKSVILLE
10545	MARYKNOLL	10562	OSSINING	11815	HICKSVILLE	11801	HICKSVILLE
10551	MOUNT VERNON	10550	MOUNT VERNON	11819	HICKSVILLE	11801	HICKSVILLE
10557	MOUNT VERNON	10550	MOUNT VERNON	11854	HICKSVILLE	11801	HICKSVILLE
10558	MOUNT VERNON	10550	MOUNT VERNON	11855	HICKSVILLE	11801	HICKSVILLE
10571	PLEASANTVILLE	10549	MOUNT KISCO	11930	AMAGANSETT	11937	EAST HAMPTON
10572	PLEASANTVILLE	10570	PLEASANTVILLE	11931	AQUEBOGUE	11901	RIVERHEAD
10587	SHENOROCK	10598	YORKTOWN HEIGHTS	11932	BRIDGEHAMPTON	11963	SAG HARBOR
10596	VERPLANCK	10548	MONTROSE	11947	JAMESPORT	11901	RIVERHEAD
10602	WHITE PLAINS	10606	WHITE PLAINS	11956	NEW SUFFOLK	11935	CUTCHOGUE
10610	WHITE PLAINS	10604	WEST HARRISON	11959	QUOGUE	11942	EAST QUOGUE
10650	WHITE PLAINS	10604	WEST HARRISON	11960	REMSENBURG	11977	WESTHAMPTON
10702	YONKERS	10701	YONKERS	11962	SAGAPONACK	11963	SAG HARBOR
10802	NEW ROCHELLE	10801	NEW ROCHELLE	11969	SOUTHAMPTON	11968	SOUTHAMPTON
10910	ARDEN	10975	SOUTHFIELDS	11970	SOUTH JAMESPORT	11901	RIVERHEAD
10912	BELLVALE	10990	WARWICK	11972	SPEONK	11941	EASTPORT
10914	BLOOMING GROVE	10992	WASHINGTONVILLE	11973	UPTON	11961	RIDGE
10915	BULLVILLE	10941	MIDDLETOWN	11975	WAINSCOTT	11937	EAST HAMPTON
10922	FORT MONTGOMERY	10928	HIGHLAND FALLS	12016	AURIESVILLE	12010	AMSTERDAM
10932	HOWELLS	10940	MIDDLETOWN	12040	CHERRY PLAIN	12022	BERLIN
10933	JOHNSON	10973	SLATE HILL	12045	COEYMANS	12143	RAVENA
10943	MIDDLETOWN	10941	MIDDLETOWN	12050	COLUMBIAVILLE	12173	STUYVESANT
10953	MOUNTAINVILLE	12553	NEW WINDSOR	12055	DORMANSVILLE	12193	WESTERLO
10959	NEW MILFORD	10990	WARWICK	12063	EAST SCHODACK	12123	NASSAU
10979	STERLING FOREST	10925	GREENWOOD LAKE	12069	FORT HUNTER	12068	FONDA
10981	SUGAR LOAF	10918	CHESTER	12073	GALLUPVILLE	12157	SCHOHARIE
10982	TALLMAN	10901	SUFFERN	12082	GRAFTON	12052	CROPSEYVILLE
10988	UNIONVILLE	10998	WESTTOWN	12085	GUILDERLAND CENTER	12009	ALTAMONT
10997	WEST POINT	10996	WEST POINT	12089	HOOSICK	12090	HOOSICK FALLS
11002	FLORAL PARK	11001	FLORAL PARK	12107	KNOX	12009	ALTAMONT
11022	GREAT NECK	11021	GREAT NECK	12124	NEW BALTIMORE	12192	WEST COXSACKIE
11041	NEW HYDE PARK	11040	NEW HYDE PARK	12128	NEWTONVILLE	12110	LATHAM
11051	PORT WASHINGTON	11050	PORT WASHINGTON	12132	NORTH CHATHAM	12123	NASSAU
11052	PORT WASHINGTON	11050	PORT WASHINGTON	12133	NORTH HOOSICK	12057	EAGLE BRIDGE
11053	PORT WASHINGTON	11050	PORT WASHINGTON	12141	QUAKER STREET	12053	DELANSON
11054	PORT WASHINGTON	11050	PORT WASHINGTON	12161	SOUTH BETHLEHEM	12054	DELMAR
11055	PORT WASHINGTON	11050	PORT WASHINGTON	12172	STOTTVILLE	12534	HUDSON
11202	BROOKLYN	11201	BROOKLYN	12174	STUYVESANT FALLS	12106	KINDERHOOK
11241	BROOKLYN	11201	BROOKLYN	12177	TRIBES HILL	12068	FONDA
11242	BROOKLYN	11201	BROOKLYN	12181	TROY	12180	TROY
11243	BROOKLYN	11217	BROOKLYN	12195	WEST LEBANON	12125	NEW LEBANON
11245	BROOKLYN	11201	BROOKLYN	12201	ALBANY	12205	ALBANY
11247	BROOKLYN	11216	BROOKLYN	12212	ALBANY	12205	ALBANY
11248	BROOKLYN	11201	BROOKLYN	12220	ALBANY	12206	ALBANY
11249	BROOKLYN	11201	BROOKLYN	12222	ALBANY	12206	ALBANY
11252	BROOKLYN	11209	BROOKLYN	12223	ALBANY	12207	ALBANY
11256	BROOKLYN	11208	BROOKLYN	12224	ALBANY	12207	ALBANY
11351	FLUSHING	11356	COLLEGE POINT	12225	ALBANY	12203	ALBANY
11352	FLUSHING	11355	FLUSHING	12226	ALBANY	12206	ALBANY
11380	ELMHURST	11373	ELMHURST	12227	ALBANY	12207	ALBANY
11381	FLUSHING	11379	MIDDLE VILLAGE	12228	ALBANY	12202	ALBANY
11386	RIDGEWOOD	11385	RIDGEWOOD	12229	ALBANY	12144	RENSSELAER
11390	FLUSHING	11357	WHITESTONE	12230	ALBANY	12207	ALBANY
11405	JAMAICA	11433	JAMAICA	12231	ALBANY	12210	ALBANY

NEW YORK **NEW YORK**

Point ZIP Code		Enclosing Residential ZIP Code		Point ZIP Code		Enclosing Residential ZIP Code	
ZIP	Name	ZIP	Name	ZIP	Name	ZIP	Name
12232	ALBANY	12206	ALBANY	12995	WHIPPLEVILLE	12953	MALONE
12233	ALBANY	12207	ALBANY	12998	WITHERBEE	12956	MINEVILLE
12234	ALBANY	12207	ALBANY	13020	APULIA STATION	13159	TULLY
12235	ALBANY	12207	ALBANY	13022	AUBURN	13021	AUBURN
12236	ALBANY	12207	ALBANY	13024	AUBURN	13021	AUBURN
12237	ALBANY	12207	ALBANY	13043	CLOCKVILLE	13032	CANASTOTA
12238	ALBANY	12207	ALBANY	13051	DELPHI FALLS	13035	CAZENOVIA
12239	ALBANY	12207	ALBANY	13056	EAST HOMER	13045	CORTLAND
12240	ALBANY	12207	ALBANY	13062	ETNA	14850	ITHACA
12241	ALBANY	12207	ALBANY	13064	FAIR HAVEN	13156	STERLING
12242	ALBANY	12207	ALBANY	13065	FAYETTE	13165	WATERLOO
12243	ALBANY	12207	ALBANY	13087	LITTLE YORK	13141	PREBLE
12244	ALBANY	12207	ALBANY	13089	LIVERPOOL	13090	LIVERPOOL
12245	ALBANY	12207	ALBANY	13093	LYCOMING	13126	OSWEGO
12246	ALBANY	12203	ALBANY	13102	MC LEAN	13068	FREEVILLE
12247	ALBANY	12207	ALBANY	13107	MAPLE VIEW	13131	PARISH
12248	ALBANY	12207	ALBANY	13113	MERIDIAN	13033	CATO
12249	ALBANY	12207	ALBANY	13115	MINETTO	13126	OSWEGO
12250	ALBANY	12204	ALBANY	13117	MONTEZUMA	13140	PORT BYRON
12252	ALBANY	12207	ALBANY	13119	MOTTVILLE	13152	SKANEATELES
12255	ALBANY	12207	ALBANY	13121	NEW HAVEN	13114	MEXICO
12256	ALBANY	12207	ALBANY	13123	NORTH BAY	13042	CLEVELAND
12257	ALBANY	12207	ALBANY	13134	PETERBORO	13408	MORRISVILLE
12260	ALBANY	12206	ALBANY	13137	PLAINVILLE	13027	BALDWINSVILLE
12261	ALBANY	12206	ALBANY	13138	POMPEY	13063	FABIUS
12288	ALBANY	12205	ALBANY	13139	POPLAR RIDGE	13147	SCIPIO CENTER
12301	SCHENECTADY	12305	SCHENECTADY	13153	SKANEATELES FALLS	13060	ELBRIDGE
12325	SCHENECTADY	12302	SCHENECTADY	13154	SOUTH BUTLER	13146	SAVANNAH
12345	SCHENECTADY	12306	SCHENECTADY	13157	SYLVAN BEACH	13308	BLOSSVALE
12402	KINGSTON	12401	KINGSTON	13162	VERONA BEACH	13308	BLOSSVALE
12417	CONNELLY	12466	PORT EWEN	13163	WAMPSVILLE	13032	CANASTOTA
12420	CRAGSMOOR	12566	PINE BUSH	13201	SYRACUSE	13202	SYRACUSE
12429	ESOPUS	12528	HIGHLAND	13217	SYRACUSE	13210	SYRACUSE
12432	GLASCO	12477	SAUGERTIES	13218	SYRACUSE	13204	SYRACUSE
12434	GRAND GORGE	12167	STAMFORD	13220	SYRACUSE	13212	SYRACUSE
12436	HAINES FALLS	12485	TANNERSVILLE	13221	SYRACUSE	13212	SYRACUSE
12438	HALCOTTSVILLE	12455	MARGARETVILLE	13225	SYRACUSE	13212	SYRACUSE
12441	HIGHMOUNT	12465	PINE HILL	13235	SYRACUSE	13210	SYRACUSE
12452	LEXINGTON	12492	WEST KILL	13250	SYRACUSE	13212	SYRACUSE
12453	MALDEN ON HUDSON	12477	SAUGERTIES	13251	SYRACUSE	13212	SYRACUSE
12459	NEW KINGSTON	12455	MARGARETVILLE	13252	SYRACUSE	13202	SYRACUSE
12471	RIFTON	12487	ULSTER PARK	13261	SYRACUSE	13202	SYRACUSE
12475	RUBY	12401	KINGSTON	13290	SYRACUSE	13204	SYRACUSE
12483	SPRING GLEN	12428	ELLENVILLE	13305	BEAVER FALLS	13620	CASTORLAND
12489	WAWARSING	12446	KERHONKSON	13312	BRANTINGHAM	13345	GREIG
12490	WEST CAMP	12477	SAUGERTIES	13313	BRIDGEWATER	13318	CASSVILLE
12493	WEST PARK	12528	HIGHLAND	13321	CLARK MILLS	13323	CLINTON
12504	ANNANDALE ON HUDSON	12571	RED HOOK	13341	FRANKLIN SPRINGS	13323	CLINTON
12506	BANGALL	12581	STANFORDVILLE	13352	HINCKLEY	13438	REMSEN
12510	BILLINGS	12540	LAGRANGEVILLE	13362	KNOXBORO	13425	ORISKANY FALLS
12511	CASTLE POINT	12590	WAPPINGERS FALLS	13364	LEONARDSVILLE	13485	WEST EDMESTON
12512	CHELSEA	12590	WAPPINGERS FALLS	13401	MC CONNELLSVILLE	13308	BLOSSVALE
12527	GLENHAM	12524	FISHKILL	13404	MARTINSBURG	13367	LOWVILLE
12530	HOLLOWVILLE	12521	CRARYVILLE	13410	NELLISTON	13428	PALATINE BRIDGE
12537	HUGHSONVILLE	12590	WAPPINGERS FALLS	13426	ORWELL	13144	RICHLAND
12541	LIVINGSTON	12502	ANCRAM	13435	PROSPECT	13438	REMSEN
12544	MELLENVILLE	12075	GHENT	13441	ROME	13440	ROME
12551	NEWBURGH	12550	NEWBURGH	13442	ROME	13440	ROME
12552	NEWBURGH	12550	NEWBURGH	13455	SANGERFIELD	13480	WATERVILLE
12555	MID HUDSON	12550	NEWBURGH	13457	SCHUYLER LAKE	13348	HARTWICK
12565	PHILMONT	12534	HUDSON	13465	SOLSVILLE	13402	MADISON
12568	PLATTEKILL	12589	WALLKILL	13472	THENDARA	13331	EAGLE BAY
12574	RHINECLIFF	12572	RHINEBECK	13479	WASHINGTON MILLS	13413	NEW HARTFORD
12584	VAILS GATE	12553	NEW WINDSOR	13484	WEST EATON	13334	EATON
12588	WALKER VALLEY	12566	PINE BUSH	13503	UTICA	13502	UTICA
12602	POUGHKEEPSIE	12601	POUGHKEEPSIE	13504	UTICA	13501	UTICA
12722	BURLINGHAM	12721	BLOOMINGBURG	13505	UTICA	13502	UTICA
12724	CALLICOON CENTER	12776	ROSCOE	13599	UTICA	13501	UTICA
12749	KAUNEONGA LAKE	12786	WHITE LAKE	13615	BROWNVILLE	13601	WATERTOWN
12767	OBERNBURG	12776	ROSCOE	13623	CHIPPEWA BAY	13646	HAMMOND
12769	PHILLIPSPORT	12790	WURTSBORO	13627	DEER RIVER	13619	CARTHAGE
12778	SMALLWOOD	12701	MONTICELLO	13628	DEFERIET	13619	CARTHAGE
12781	SUMMITVILLE	12790	WURTSBORO	13631	DENMARK	13619	CARTHAGE
12784	THOMPSONVILLE	12701	MONTICELLO	13632	DEPAUVILLE	13622	CHAUMONT
12785	WESTBROOKVILLE	12729	CUDDEBACKVILLE	13641	FISHERS LANDING	13624	CLAYTON
12811	BAKERS MILLS	12843	JOHNSBURG	13643	GREAT BEND	13619	CARTHAGE
12820	CLEVERDALE	12845	LAKE GEORGE	13645	HAILESBORO	13642	GOUVERNEUR
12841	HULETTS LANDING	12887	WHITEHALL	13647	HANNAWA FALLS	13676	POTSDAM
12848	MIDDLE FALLS	12834	GREENWICH	13649	HELENA	13613	BRASHER FALLS
12856	NORTH RIVER	12843	JOHNSBURG	13651	HENDERSON HARBOR	13650	HENDERSON
12862	RIPARIUS	12817	CHESTERTOWN	13657	LIMERICK	13634	DEXTER
12864	SABAEL	12842	INDIAN LAKE	13664	MORRISTOWN	13669	OGDENSBURG
12874	SILVER BAY	12836	HAGUE	13671	OXBOW	13608	ANTWERP
12879	NEWCOMB	12852	NEWCOMB	13674	PIERREPONT MANOR	13605	ADAMS
12884	VICTORY MILLS	12871	SCHUYLERVILLE	13677	PYRITES	13652	HERMON
12915	BRAINARDSVILLE	12920	CHATEAUGAY	13678	RAYMONDVILLE	13667	NORFOLK
12927	CRANBERRY LAKE	13625	COLTON	13683	ROOSEVELTOWN	13655	HOGANSBURG
12929	DANNEMORA	12981	SARANAC	13692	THOUSAND ISLAND PARK	13640	WELLESLEY ISLAND
12933	ELLENBURG	12935	ELLENBURG DEPOT	13737	BIBLE SCHOOL PARK	13760	ENDICOTT
12939	GABRIELS	12983	SARANAC LAKE	13738	BLODGETT MILLS	13045	CORTLAND
12975	PORT KENT	12944	KEESEVILLE	13745	CHENANGO BRIDGE	13901	BINGHAMTON
12976	RAINBOW LAKE	12989	VERMONTVILLE	13747	COLLIERSVILLE	12116	MARYLAND
12977	RAY BROOK	12983	SARANAC LAKE	13749	CORBETTSVILLE	13748	CONKLIN

653

NEW YORK   **NORTH CAROLINA**

Point ZIP Code ZIP	Post Office Name	Enclosing Residential ZIP Code ZIP	Post Office Name	Point ZIP Code ZIP	Post Office Name	Enclosing Residential ZIP Code ZIP	Post Office Name
13758	EAST PHARSALIA	13801	MC DONOUGH	14647	ROCHESTER	14607	ROCHESTER
13761	ENDICOTT	13760	ENDICOTT	14649	ROCHESTER	14604	ROCHESTER
13762	ENDWELL	13760	ENDICOTT	14650	ROCHESTER	14608	ROCHESTER
13763	ENDICOTT	13760	ENDICOTT	14651	ROCHESTER	14608	ROCHESTER
13774	FISHS EDDY	12760	LONG EDDY	14652	ROCHESTER	14608	ROCHESTER
13784	HARFORD	13835	RICHFORD	14653	ROCHESTER	14624	ROCHESTER
13794	KILLAWOG	13797	LISLE	14664	ROCHESTER	14604	ROCHESTER
13814	NORTH NORWICH	13815	NORWICH	14673	ROCHESTER	14614	ROCHESTER
13840	SMITHBORO	13734	BARTON	14683	ROCHESTER	14623	ROCHESTER
13845	TIOGA CENTER	13734	BARTON	14692	ROCHESTER	14623	ROCHESTER
13847	TROUT CREEK	13839	SIDNEY CENTER	14694	ROCHESTER	14623	ROCHESTER
13848	TUNNEL	13833	PORT CRANE	14702	JAMESTOWN	14701	JAMESTOWN
13851	VESTAL	13850	VESTAL	14703	JAMESTOWN	14701	JAMESTOWN
13860	WEST DAVENPORT	13820	ONEONTA	14704	JAMESTOWN	14701	JAMESTOWN
13902	BINGHAMTON	13901	BINGHAMTON	14707	ALLENTOWN	14895	WELLSVILLE
14010	ATHOL SPRINGS	14075	HAMBURG	14720	CELORON	14701	JAMESTOWN
14021	BATAVIA	14020	BATAVIA	14722	CHAUTAUQUA	14757	MAYVILLE
14027	BRANT	14111	NORTH COLLINS	14730	EAST RANDOLPH	14772	RANDOLPH
14029	CENTERVILLE	14065	FREEDOM	14732	ELLINGTON	14747	KENNEDY
14035	COLLINS CENTER	14034	COLLINS	14742	GREENHURST	14701	JAMESTOWN
14038	CRITTENDEN	14004	ALDEN	14745	HUME	14735	FILLMORE
14056	EAST PEMBROKE	14020	BATAVIA	14751	LEON	14726	CONEWANGO VALLEY
14061	FARNHAM	14081	IRVING	14752	LILY DALE	14784	STOCKTON
14095	LOCKPORT	14094	LOCKPORT	14756	MAPLE SPRINGS	14712	BEMUS POINT
14107	MODEL CITY	14092	LEWISTON	14758	NIOBE	14767	PANAMA
14110	NORTH BOSTON	14127	ORCHARD PARK	14766	OTTO	14719	CATTARAUGUS
14112	NORTH EVANS	14057	EDEN	14774	RICHBURG	14715	BOLIVAR
14126	OLCOTT	14028	BURT	14778	SAINT BONAVENTURE	14706	ALLEGANY
14130	PIKE	14066	GAINESVILLE	14783	STEAMBURG	14772	RANDOLPH
14133	SANDUSKY	14065	FREEDOM	14785	STOW	14710	ASHVILLE
14135	SHERIDAN	14136	SILVER CREEK	14786	WEST CLARKSVILLE	14727	CUBA
14140	SPRING BROOK	14059	ELMA	14788	WESTONS MILLS	14760	OLEAN
14144	STELLA NIAGARA	14092	LEWISTON	14827	COOPERS PLAINS	14870	PAINTED POST
14151	TONAWANDA	14150	TONAWANDA	14831	CORNING	14830	CORNING
14166	VAN BUREN POINT	14048	DUNKIRK	14844	HORSEHEADS	14845	HORSEHEADS
14168	VERSAILLES	14129	PERRYSBURG	14851	ITHACA	14850	ITHACA
14169	WALES CENTER	14052	EAST AURORA	14852	ITHACA	14850	ITHACA
14173	YORKSHIRE	14042	DELEVAN	14854	JACKSONVILLE	14886	TRUMANSBURG
14205	BUFFALO	14203	BUFFALO	14856	KANONA	14810	BATH
14231	BUFFALO	14221	BUFFALO	14857	LAKEMONT	14837	DUNDEE
14233	BUFFALO	14203	BUFFALO	14863	MECKLENBURG	14886	TRUMANSBURG
14240	BUFFALO	14206	BUFFALO	14876	READING CENTER	14891	WATKINS GLEN
14241	BUFFALO	14225	BUFFALO	14887	TYRONE	14837	DUNDEE
14261	BUFFALO	14260	BUFFALO	14893	WAYNE	14837	DUNDEE
14263	BUFFALO	14203	BUFFALO	14902	ELMIRA	14901	ELMIRA
14264	BUFFALO	14203	BUFFALO	14925	ELMIRA	14901	ELMIRA
14265	BUFFALO	14221	BUFFALO	27010	BETHANIA	27106	WINSTON SALEM
14267	BUFFALO	14202	BUFFALO	27014	COOLEEMEE	27028	MOCKSVILLE
14269	BUFFALO	14043	DEPEW	27031	WHITE PLAINS	27030	MOUNT AIRY
14270	BUFFALO	14203	BUFFALO	27049	TOAST	27030	MOUNT AIRY
14272	BUFFALO	14043	DEPEW	27094	RURAL HALL	27045	RURAL HALL
14273	BUFFALO	14203	BUFFALO	27098	RURAL HALL	27045	RURAL HALL
14276	BUFFALO	14206	BUFFALO	27099	RURAL HALL	27045	RURAL HALL
14280	BUFFALO	14203	BUFFALO	27102	WINSTON SALEM	27105	WINSTON SALEM
14302	NIAGARA FALLS	14301	NIAGARA FALLS	27108	WINSTON SALEM	27101	WINSTON SALEM
14413	ALTON	14516	NORTH ROSE	27109	WINSTON SALEM	27106	WINSTON SALEM
14429	CLARENDON	14470	HOLLEY	27111	WINSTON SALEM	27101	WINSTON SALEM
14430	CLARKSON	14420	BROCKPORT	27113	WINSTON SALEM	27103	WINSTON SALEM
14443	EAST BLOOMFIELD	14469	BLOOMFIELD	27114	WINSTON SALEM	27103	WINSTON SALEM
14449	EAST WILLIAMSON	14589	WILLIAMSON	27115	WINSTON SALEM	27105	WINSTON SALEM
14452	FANCHER	14470	HOLLEY	27116	WINSTON SALEM	27106	WINSTON SALEM
14453	FISHERS	14564	VICTOR	27117	WINSTON SALEM	27107	WINSTON SALEM
14461	GORHAM	14561	STANLEY	27120	WINSTON SALEM	27105	WINSTON SALEM
14463	HALL	14456	GENEVA	27130	WINSTON SALEM	27103	WINSTON SALEM
14479	KNOWLESVILLE	14411	ALBION	27150	WINSTON SALEM	27101	WINSTON SALEM
14488	LIVONIA CENTER	14487	LIVONIA	27151	WINSTON SALEM	27101	WINSTON SALEM
14508	MORTON	14464	HAMLIN	27155	WINSTON SALEM	27101	WINSTON SALEM
14511	MUMFORD	14482	LE ROY	27156	WINSTON SALEM	27105	WINSTON SALEM
14515	NORTH GREECE	14468	HILTON	27157	WINSTON SALEM	27103	WINSTON SALEM
14518	OAKS CORNERS	14456	GENEVA	27201	ALAMANCE	27215	BURLINGTON
14520	ONTARIO CENTER	14519	ONTARIO	27202	ALTAMAHAW	27244	ELON
14529	PERKINSVILLE	14572	WAYLAND	27204	ASHEBORO	27203	ASHEBORO
14537	PORT GIBSON	14548	SHORTSVILLE	27213	BONLEE	27207	BEAR CREEK
14538	PULTNEYVILLE	14589	WILLIAMSON	27216	BURLINGTON	27215	BURLINGTON
14539	RETSOF	14533	PIFFARD	27228	BYNUM	27312	PITTSBORO
14542	ROSE	14489	LYONS	27230	CEDAR FALLS	27248	FRANKLINVILLE
14547	SENECA CASTLE	14561	STANLEY	27237	CUMNOCK	27330	SANFORD
14549	SILVER LAKE	14550	SILVER SPRINGS	27247	ETHER	27356	STAR
14556	SONYEA	14510	MOUNT MORRIS	27256	GULF	27252	GOLDSTON
14557	SOUTH BYRON	14422	BYRON	27259	HIGHFALLS	27325	ROBBINS
14558	SOUTH LIMA	14487	LIVONIA	27261	HIGH POINT	27260	HIGH POINT
14563	UNION HILL	14519	ONTARIO	27264	HIGH POINT	27263	HIGH POINT
14585	WEST BLOOMFIELD	14469	BLOOMFIELD	27285	KERNERSVILLE	27284	KERNERSVILLE
14588	WILLARD	14521	OVID	27289	EDEN	27288	EDEN
14592	YORK	14533	PIFFARD	27293	LEXINGTON	27292	LEXINGTON
14602	ROCHESTER	14623	ROCHESTER	27294	LEXINGTON	27292	LEXINGTON
14603	ROCHESTER	14605	ROCHESTER	27323	REIDSVILLE	27320	REIDSVILLE
14638	ROCHESTER	14604	ROCHESTER	27331	SANFORD	27330	SANFORD
14639	ROCHESTER	14604	ROCHESTER	27342	SEDALIA	27249	GIBSONVILLE
14643	ROCHESTER	14604	ROCHESTER	27351	SOUTHMONT	27292	LEXINGTON
14644	ROCHESTER	14604	ROCHESTER	27359	SWEPSONVILLE	27253	GRAHAM
14645	ROCHESTER	14604	ROCHESTER	27361	THOMASVILLE	27360	THOMASVILLE
14646	ROCHESTER	14607	ROCHESTER				

NONRESIDENTIAL ZIP CODES

NORTH CAROLINA | NORTH CAROLINA

Point ZIP Code		Enclosing Residential ZIP Code		Point ZIP Code		Enclosing Residential ZIP Code	
ZIP	Post Office Name	ZIP	Post Office Name	ZIP	Post Office Name	ZIP	Post Office Name
27373	WALLBURG	27107	WINSTON SALEM	27895	WILSON	27893	WILSON
27374	WELCOME	27295	LEXINGTON	27906	ELIZABETH CITY	27909	ELIZABETH CITY
27375	WENTWORTH	27320	REIDSVILLE	27907	ELIZABETH CITY	27909	ELIZABETH CITY
27402	GREENSBORO	27401	GREENSBORO	27915	AVON	27959	NAGS HEAD
27404	GREENSBORO	27408	GREENSBORO	27920	BUXTON	27959	NAGS HEAD
27412	GREENSBORO	27403	GREENSBORO	27930	DURANTS NECK	27944	HERTFORD
27415	GREENSBORO	27405	GREENSBORO	27936	FRISCO	27959	NAGS HEAD
27416	GREENSBORO	27406	GREENSBORO	27943	HATTERAS	27959	NAGS HEAD
27417	GREENSBORO	27407	GREENSBORO	27967	POWELLSVILLE	27910	AHOSKIE
27419	GREENSBORO	27409	GREENSBORO	27968	RODANTHE	27959	NAGS HEAD
27420	GREENSBORO	27401	GREENSBORO	27969	RODUCO	27935	EURE
27425	GREENSBORO	27409	GREENSBORO	27972	SALVO	27959	NAGS HEAD
27427	GREENSBORO	27407	GREENSBORO	27982	WAVES	27959	NAGS HEAD
27429	GREENSBORO	27408	GREENSBORO	27985	WINFALL	27944	HERTFORD
27435	GREENSBORO	27401	GREENSBORO	28002	ALBEMARLE	28001	ALBEMARLE
27438	GREENSBORO	27408	GREENSBORO	28007	ANSONVILLE	28170	WADESBORO
27495	GREENSBORO	27407	GREENSBORO	28009	BADIN	28001	ALBEMARLE
27498	GREENSBORO	27401	GREENSBORO	28010	BARIUM SPRINGS	28677	STATESVILLE
27506	BUIES CREEK	27546	LILLINGTON	28017	BOILING SPRINGS	28152	SHELBY
27512	CARY	27511	CARY	28019	CAROLEEN	28043	FOREST CITY
27515	CHAPEL HILL	27514	CHAPEL HILL	28024	CLIFFSIDE	28114	MOORESBORO
27518	CARY	27511	CARY	28026	CONCORD	28025	CONCORD
27532	GOLDSBORO	27530	GOLDSBORO	28035	DAVIDSON	28036	DAVIDSON
27533	GOLDSBORO	27530	GOLDSBORO	28038	EARL	28073	GROVER
27543	KIPLING	27526	FUQUAY VARINA	28039	EAST SPENCER	28144	SALISBURY
27552	MAMERS	27546	LILLINGTON	28041	FAITH	28146	SALISBURY
27555	MICRO	27576	SELMA	28042	FALLSTON	28090	LAWNDALE
27556	MIDDLEBURG	27537	HENDERSON	28053	GASTONIA	28052	GASTONIA
27564	CREEDMOOR	27522	CREEDMOOR	28055	GASTONIA	28054	GASTONIA
27568	PINE LEVEL	27569	PRINCETON	28070	HUNTERSVILLE	28078	HUNTERSVILLE
27570	RIDGEWAY	27589	WARRENTON	28072	GRANITE QUARRY	28146	SALISBURY
27582	STOVALL	27565	OXFORD	28074	HARRIS	28139	RUTHERFORDTON
27584	TOWNSVILLE	27537	HENDERSON	28076	HENRIETTA	28114	MOORESBORO
27586	VAUGHAN	27551	MACON	28077	HIGH SHOALS	28034	DALLAS
27588	WAKE FOREST	27587	WAKE FOREST	28082	KANNAPOLIS	28081	KANNAPOLIS
27593	WILSONS MILLS	27577	SMITHFIELD	28089	LATTIMORE	28150	SHELBY
27594	WISE	27563	NORLINA	28093	LINCOLNTON	28092	LINCOLNTON
27599	CHAPEL HILL	27516	CHAPEL HILL	28101	MC ADENVILLE	28056	GASTONIA
27602	RALEIGH	27601	RALEIGH	28102	MC FARLAN	28119	MORVEN
27611	RALEIGH	27601	RALEIGH	28106	MATTHEWS	28105	MATTHEWS
27619	RALEIGH	27609	RALEIGH	28108	MINERAL SPRINGS	28112	MONROE
27620	RALEIGH	27610	RALEIGH	28109	MISENHEIMER	28137	RICHFIELD
27621	RALEIGH	27606	RALEIGH	28111	MONROE	28112	MONROE
27622	RALEIGH	27612	RALEIGH	28123	MOUNT MOURNE	28117	MOORESVILLE
27623	RALEIGH	27560	MORRISVILLE	28126	NEWELL	28213	CHARLOTTE
27624	RALEIGH	27615	RALEIGH	28130	PAW CREEK	28214	CHARLOTTE
27625	RALEIGH	27604	RALEIGH	28136	POLKVILLE	28150	SHELBY
27626	RALEIGH	27601	RALEIGH	28145	SALISBURY	28144	SALISBURY
27627	RALEIGH	27606	RALEIGH	28151	SHELBY	28150	SHELBY
27628	RALEIGH	27608	RALEIGH	28169	WACO	28021	CHERRYVILLE
27629	RALEIGH	27604	RALEIGH	28201	CHARLOTTE	28202	CHARLOTTE
27634	RALEIGH	27601	RALEIGH	28218	CHARLOTTE	28205	CHARLOTTE
27635	RALEIGH	27604	RALEIGH	28219	CHARLOTTE	28208	CHARLOTTE
27636	RALEIGH	27607	RALEIGH	28220	CHARLOTTE	28209	CHARLOTTE
27640	RALEIGH	27604	RALEIGH	28221	CHARLOTTE	28269	CHARLOTTE
27650	RALEIGH	27607	RALEIGH	28222	CHARLOTTE	28211	CHARLOTTE
27656	RALEIGH	27612	RALEIGH	28223	CHARLOTTE	28213	CHARLOTTE
27658	RALEIGH	27616	RALEIGH	28224	CHARLOTTE	28210	CHARLOTTE
27661	RALEIGH	27616	RALEIGH	28228	CHARLOTTE	28208	CHARLOTTE
27668	RALEIGH	27609	RALEIGH	28229	CHARLOTTE	28212	CHARLOTTE
27675	RALEIGH	27617	RALEIGH	28230	CHARLOTTE	28202	CHARLOTTE
27676	RALEIGH	27601	RALEIGH	28231	CHARLOTTE	28202	CHARLOTTE
27690	RALEIGH	27612	RALEIGH	28232	CHARLOTTE	28202	CHARLOTTE
27697	RALEIGH	27601	RALEIGH	28233	CHARLOTTE	28202	CHARLOTTE
27698	RALEIGH	27601	RALEIGH	28234	CHARLOTTE	28202	CHARLOTTE
27699	RALEIGH	27601	RALEIGH	28235	CHARLOTTE	28202	CHARLOTTE
27702	DURHAM	27701	DURHAM	28236	CHARLOTTE	28202	CHARLOTTE
27708	DURHAM	27705	DURHAM	28237	CHARLOTTE	28202	CHARLOTTE
27710	DURHAM	27705	DURHAM	28240	CHARLOTTE	28208	CHARLOTTE
27711	DURHAM	27713	DURHAM	28241	CHARLOTTE	28273	CHARLOTTE
27715	DURHAM	27705	DURHAM	28242	CHARLOTTE	28202	CHARLOTTE
27717	DURHAM	27707	DURHAM	28243	CHARLOTTE	28208	CHARLOTTE
27722	DURHAM	27712	DURHAM	28244	CHARLOTTE	28202	CHARLOTTE
27802	ROCKY MOUNT	27801	ROCKY MOUNT	28246	CHARLOTTE	28202	CHARLOTTE
27811	BELLARTHUR	27834	GREENVILLE	28247	CHARLOTTE	28226	CHARLOTTE
27813	BLACK CREEK	27893	WILSON	28253	CHARLOTTE	28269	CHARLOTTE
27819	CONETOE	27852	MACCLESFIELD	28254	CHARLOTTE	28208	CHARLOTTE
27825	EVERETTS	27892	WILLIAMSTON	28256	CHARLOTTE	28213	CHARLOTTE
27827	FALKLAND	27834	GREENVILLE	28258	CHARLOTTE	28208	CHARLOTTE
27833	GREENVILLE	27834	GREENVILLE	28260	CHARLOTTE	28208	CHARLOTTE
27835	GREENVILLE	27858	GREENVILLE	28261	CHARLOTTE	28079	INDIAN TRAIL
27836	GREENVILLE	27858	GREENVILLE	28265	CHARLOTTE	28208	CHARLOTTE
27841	HASSELL	27857	OAK CITY	28266	CHARLOTTE	28208	CHARLOTTE
27854	MILWAUKEE	27820	CONWAY	28271	CHARLOTTE	28202	CHARLOTTE
27861	PARMELE	27871	ROBERSONVILLE	28272	CHARLOTTE	28208	CHARLOTTE
27867	POTECASI	27897	WOODLAND	28275	CHARLOTTE	28208	CHARLOTTE
27868	RED OAK	27809	BATTLEBORO	28280	CHARLOTTE	28202	CHARLOTTE
27877	SEVERN	27853	MARGARETTSVILLE	28281	CHARLOTTE	28202	CHARLOTTE
27878	SHARPSBURG	27803	ROCKY MOUNT	28282	CHARLOTTE	28202	CHARLOTTE
27879	SIMPSON	27858	GREENVILLE	28283	CHARLOTTE	28207	CHARLOTTE
27881	SPEED	27843	HOBGOOD	28284	CHARLOTTE	28202	CHARLOTTE
27887	TILLERY	27839	HALIFAX	28285	CHARLOTTE	28202	CHARLOTTE
27894	WILSON	27893	WILSON	28287	CHARLOTTE	28210	CHARLOTTE

NORTH CAROLINA   **OHIO**

Point ZIP	Post Office Name	Enclosing ZIP	Post Office Name	Point ZIP	Post Office Name	Enclosing ZIP	Post Office Name
28289	CHARLOTTE	28208	CHARLOTTE	28784	TUXEDO	28790	ZIRCONIA
28290	CHARLOTTE	28208	CHARLOTTE	28788	WEBSTER	28779	SYLVA
28296	CHARLOTTE	28208	CHARLOTTE	28793	HENDERSONVILLE	28739	HENDERSONVILLE
28297	CHARLOTTE	28216	CHARLOTTE	28802	ASHEVILLE	28801	ASHEVILLE
28299	CHARLOTTE	28205	CHARLOTTE	28810	ASHEVILLE	28806	ASHEVILLE
28302	FAYETTEVILLE	28301	FAYETTEVILLE	28813	ASHEVILLE	28803	ASHEVILLE
28309	FAYETTEVILLE	28314	FAYETTEVILLE	28814	ASHEVILLE	28804	ASHEVILLE
28319	BARNESVILLE	28369	ORRUM	28815	ASHEVILLE	28805	ASHEVILLE
28325	CALYPSO	28365	MOUNT OLIVE	28816	ASHEVILLE	28806	ASHEVILLE
28329	CLINTON	28328	CLINTON	28903	CULBERSON	28906	MURPHY
28330	CORDOVA	28379	ROCKINGHAM	58001	ABERCROMBIE	58075	WAHPETON
28331	CUMBERLAND	28306	FAYETTEVILLE	58002	ABSARAKA	58007	AYR
28332	DUBLIN	28392	TAR HEEL	58065	PILLSBURY	58046	HOPE
28335	DUNN	28334	DUNN	58074	WAHPETON	58075	WAHPETON
28342	FALCON	28344	GODWIN	58105	FARGO	58102	FARGO
28350	LAKEVIEW	28394	VASS	58106	FARGO	58103	FARGO
28353	LAURINBURG	28352	LAURINBURG	58107	FARGO	58102	FARGO
28355	LEMON SPRINGS	27332	SANFORD	58108	FARGO	58102	FARGO
28359	LUMBERTON	28358	LUMBERTON	58109	FARGO	58103	FARGO
28361	MCCAIN	28376	RAEFORD	58121	FARGO	58103	FARGO
28362	MARIETTA	28340	FAIRMONT	58122	FARGO	58102	FARGO
28367	NORMAN	28338	ELLERBE	58124	FARGO	58103	FARGO
28368	OLIVIA	27332	SANFORD	58125	FARGO	58103	FARGO
28370	PINEHURST	28374	PINEHURST	58126	FARGO	58103	FARGO
28375	PROCTORVILLE	28369	ORRUM	58202	GRAND FORKS	58203	GRAND FORKS
28378	REX	28384	SAINT PAULS	58206	GRAND FORKS	58201	GRAND FORKS
28380	ROCKINGHAM	28379	ROCKINGHAM	58207	GRAND FORKS	58204	GRAND FORKS AFB
28388	SOUTHERN PINES	28387	SOUTHERN PINES	58208	GRAND FORKS	58201	GRAND FORKS
28402	WILMINGTON	28401	WILMINGTON	58236	GLASSTON	58276	SAINT THOMAS
28404	WILMINGTON	28411	WILMINGTON	58310	AGATE	58317	BISBEE
28406	WILMINGTON	28403	WILMINGTON	58313	BALTA	58368	RUGBY
28407	WILMINGTON	28405	WILMINGTON	58335	FORT TOTTEN	58370	SAINT MICHAEL
28408	WILMINGTON	28412	WILMINGTON	58355	NEKOMA	58269	OSNABROCK
28424	BRUNSWICK	28472	WHITEVILLE	58359	ORRIN	58368	RUGBY
28446	INGOLD	28328	CLINTON	58379	TOKIO	58370	SAINT MICHAEL
28459	SHALLOTTE	28470	SHALLOTTE	58402	JAMESTOWN	58401	JAMESTOWN
28502	KINSTON	28501	KINSTON	58452	JESSIE	58425	COOPERSTOWN
28503	KINSTON	28501	KINSTON	58502	BISMARCK	58504	BISMARCK
28509	ALLIANCE	28515	BAYBORO	58505	BISMARCK	58501	BISMARCK
28519	BRIDGETON	28560	NEW BERN	58506	BISMARCK	58504	BISMARCK
28522	COMFORT	28585	TRENTON	58507	BISMARCK	58504	BISMARCK
28524	DAVIS	28516	BEAUFORT	58602	DICKINSON	58601	DICKINSON
28533	CHERRY POINT	28532	HAVELOCK	58644	MARSHALL	58652	RICHARDTON
28541	JACKSONVILLE	28546	JACKSONVILLE	58702	MINOT	58701	MINOT
28545	MCCUTCHEON FIELD	28540	JACKSONVILLE	58802	WILLISTON	58801	WILLISTON
28554	MAURY	28538	HOOKERTON	43005	BLADENSBURG	43080	UTICA
28561	NEW BERN	28562	NEW BERN	43007	BROADWAY	43040	MARYSVILLE
28563	NEW BERN	28560	NEW BERN	43010	CATAWBA	43044	MECHANICSBURG
28564	NEW BERN	28560	NEW BERN	43018	ETNA	43062	PATASKALA
28575	SALTER PATH	28512	ATLANTIC BEACH	43027	HOMER	43080	UTICA
28583	STONEWALL	28556	MERRITT	43030	JACKSONTOWN	43076	THORNVILLE
28589	WILLISTON	28579	SMYRNA	43032	KILBOURNE	43015	DELAWARE
28603	HICKORY	28602	HICKORY	43033	KIRKERSVILLE	43062	PATASKALA
28616	CROSSNORE	28657	NEWLAND	43036	MAGNETIC SPRINGS	43040	MARYSVILLE
28619	DREXEL	28655	MORGANTON	43041	MARYSVILLE	43040	MARYSVILLE
28628	GLEN ALPINE	28655	MORGANTON	43047	MINGO	43009	CABLE
28629	GLENDALE SPRINGS	28640	JEFFERSON	43048	MOUNT LIBERTY	43011	CENTERBURG
28633	LENOIR	28645	LENOIR	43058	NEWARK	43055	NEWARK
28641	JONAS RIDGE	28657	NEWLAND	43070	ROSEWOOD	43318	DE GRAFF
28646	LINVILLE	28657	NEWLAND	43073	SUMMIT STATION	43062	PATASKALA
28647	LINVILLE FALLS	28752	MARION	43077	UNIONVILLE CENTER	43064	PLAIN CITY
28652	MINNEAPOLIS	28657	NEWLAND	43083	WESTVILLE	43078	URBANA
28653	MONTEZUMA	28657	NEWLAND	43086	WESTERVILLE	43081	WESTERVILLE
28656	NORTH WILKESBORO	28659	NORTH WILKESBORO	43093	NEWARK	43055	NEWARK
28661	PATTERSON	28645	LENOIR	43098	HEBRON	43025	HEBRON
28662	PINEOLA	28657	NEWLAND	43101	ADELPHI	43135	LAURELVILLE
28664	PLUMTREE	28657	NEWLAND	43109	BRICE	43232	COLUMBUS
28666	ICARD	28612	CONNELLYS SPRINGS	43111	CARBON HILL	45764	NELSONVILLE
28667	RHODHISS	28630	GRANITE FALLS	43117	DERBY	43146	ORIENT
28671	RUTHERFORD COLLEGE	28612	CONNELLYS SPRINGS	43126	HARRISBURG	43146	ORIENT
28680	MORGANTON	28655	MORGANTON	43127	HAYDENVILLE	43138	LOGAN
28687	STATESVILLE	28677	STATESVILLE	43136	LITHOPOLIS	43110	CANAL WINCHESTER
28688	TURNERSBURG	28625	STATESVILLE	43142	MILLEDGEVILLE	43160	WASHINGTON COURT HOU
28699	SCOTTS	28625	STATESVILLE	43144	MURRAY CITY	45732	GLOUSTER
28707	BALSAM	28779	SYLVA	43151	SEDALIA	43140	LONDON
28710	BAT CAVE	28735	GERTON	43156	TARLTON	43135	LAURELVILLE
28720	CHIMNEY ROCK	28746	LAKE LURE	43157	THURSTON	43105	BALTIMORE
28724	DANA	28792	HENDERSONVILLE	43158	UNION FURNACE	45764	NELSONVILLE
28725	DILLSBORO	28779	SYLVA	43163	WEST RUSHVILLE	43130	LANCASTER
28727	EDNEYVILLE	28792	HENDERSONVILLE	43195	GROVEPORT	43125	GROVEPORT
28728	ENKA	28715	CANDLER	43196	GROVEPORT	43125	GROVEPORT
28737	GLENWOOD	28752	MARION	43198	GROVEPORT	43125	GROVEPORT
28738	HAZELWOOD	28786	WAYNESVILLE	43199	GROVEPORT	43125	GROVEPORT
28744	FRANKLIN	28734	FRANKLIN	43216	COLUMBUS	43215	COLUMBUS
28749	LITTLE SWITZERLAND	28752	MARION	43218	COLUMBUS	43215	COLUMBUS
28750	LYNN	28782	TRYON	43226	COLUMBUS	43229	COLUMBUS
28755	MICAVILLE	28714	BURNSVILLE	43234	COLUMBUS	43235	COLUMBUS
28757	MONTREAT	28711	BLACK MOUNTAIN	43236	COLUMBUS	43219	COLUMBUS
28758	MOUNTAIN HOME	28791	HENDERSONVILLE	43251	COLUMBUS	43222	COLUMBUS
28760	NAPLES	28791	HENDERSONVILLE	43260	COLUMBUS	43215	COLUMBUS
28765	PENLAND	28777	SPRUCE PINE	43265	COLUMBUS	43222	COLUMBUS
28770	RIDGECREST	28711	BLACK MOUNTAIN	43268	COLUMBUS	43215	COLUMBUS
28776	SKYLAND	28803	ASHEVILLE	43270	COLUMBUS	43215	COLUMBUS

NONRESIDENTIAL ZIP CODES

OHIO **OHIO**

Point ZIP Code		Enclosing Residential ZIP Code		Point ZIP Code		Enclosing Residential ZIP Code	
ZIP	Post Office Name	ZIP	Post Office Name	ZIP	Post Office Name	ZIP	Post Office Name
43271	COLUMBUS	43215	COLUMBUS	43939	MOUNT PLEASANT	43917	DILLONVALE
43272	COLUMBUS	43215	COLUMBUS	43940	NEFFS	43906	BELLAIRE
43279	COLUMBUS	43215	COLUMBUS	43941	PINEY FORK	43917	DILLONVALE
43287	COLUMBUS	43215	COLUMBUS	43948	SMITHFIELD	43917	DILLONVALE
43291	COLUMBUS	43228	COLUMBUS	43951	LAFFERTY	43977	FLUSHING
43299	COLUMBUS	43219	COLUMBUS	43961	STRATTON	43964	TORONTO
43301	MARION	43302	MARION	43962	SUMMITVILLE	43945	SALINEVILLE
43306	MARION	43302	MARION	43967	WARNOCK	43718	BELMONT
43317	CHESTERVILLE	43019	FREDERICKTOWN	43970	WOLF RUN	43903	AMSTERDAM
43322	GREEN CAMP	43302	MARION	43972	BANNOCK	43950	SAINT CLAIRSVILLE
43325	IBERIA	44833	GALION	43974	HARRISVILLE	43907	CADIZ
43330	KIRBY	43351	UPPER SANDUSKY	43981	NEW ATHENS	43907	CADIZ
43336	MIDDLEBURG	43319	EAST LIBERTY	43984	NEW RUMLEY	43986	JEWETT
43349	SHAUCK	44813	BELLVILLE	43985	HOLLOWAY	43977	FLUSHING
43350	SPARTA	43334	MARENGO	44005	ASHTABULA	44004	ASHTABULA
43408	CLAY CENTER	43430	GENOA	44033	EAST CLARIDON	44024	CHARDON
43414	DUNBRIDGE	43402	BOWLING GREEN	44036	ELYRIA	44035	ELYRIA
43433	GYPSUM	43452	PORT CLINTON	44045	GRAND RIVER	44077	PAINESVILLE
43434	HARBOR VIEW	43616	OREGON	44049	KIPTON	44090	WELLINGTON
43437	JERRY CITY	43413	CYGNET	44061	MENTOR	44060	MENTOR
43439	LACARNE	43452	PORT CLINTON	44068	NORTH KINGSVILLE	44030	CONNEAUT
43441	LEMOYNE	43443	LUCKEY	44073	NOVELTY	44072	NOVELTY
43446	MIDDLE BASS	43452	PORT CLINTON	44080	PARKMAN	44021	BURTON
43458	ROCKY RIDGE	43449	OAK HARBOR	44088	UNIONVILLE	44041	GENEVA
43463	STONY RIDGE	43551	PERRYSBURG	44096	WILLOUGHBY	44094	WILLOUGHBY
43467	WEST MILLGROVE	43466	WAYNE	44097	EASTLAKE	44095	EASTLAKE
43468	WILLISTON	43412	CURTICE	44101	CLEVELAND	44115	CLEVELAND
43505	BLAKESLEE	43518	EDON	44178	CLEVELAND	44114	CLEVELAND
43510	COLTON	43532	LIBERTY CENTER	44181	CLEVELAND	44135	CLEVELAND
43519	EVANSPORT	43512	DEFIANCE	44185	CLEVELAND	44115	CLEVELAND
43520	FARMER	43506	BRYAN	44188	CLEVELAND	44115	CLEVELAND
43523	GRELTON	43534	MC CLURE	44189	CLEVELAND	44115	CLEVELAND
43529	HOYTVILLE	43516	DESHLER	44190	CLEVELAND	44106	CLEVELAND
43530	JEWELL	43512	DEFIANCE	44191	CLEVELAND	44113	CLEVELAND
43531	KUNKLE	43554	PIONEER	44192	CLEVELAND	44115	CLEVELAND
43541	MILTON CENTER	43511	CUSTAR	44193	CLEVELAND	44113	CLEVELAND
43547	NEAPOLIS	43522	GRAND RAPIDS	44194	CLEVELAND	44114	CLEVELAND
43550	OKOLONA	43545	NAPOLEON	44195	CLEVELAND	44106	CLEVELAND
43552	PERRYSBURG	43551	PERRYSBURG	44198	CLEVELAND	44115	CLEVELAND
43553	PETTISVILLE	43567	WAUSEON	44199	CLEVELAND	44114	CLEVELAND
43555	RIDGEVILLE CORNERS	43545	NAPOLEON	44210	BATH	44333	AKRON
43565	TONTOGANY	43402	BOWLING GREEN	44211	BRADY LAKE	44240	KENT
43601	TOLEDO	43602	TOLEDO	44222	CUYAHOGA FALLS	44221	CUYAHOGA FALLS
43603	TOLEDO	43602	TOLEDO	44232	GREEN	44720	CANTON
43635	TOLEDO	43615	TOLEDO	44237	HUDSON	44236	HUDSON
43652	TOLEDO	43604	TOLEDO	44242	KENT	44240	KENT
43654	TOLEDO	43619	NORTHWOOD	44250	LAKEMORE	44312	AKRON
43656	TOLEDO	43623	TOLEDO	44251	WESTFIELD CENTER	44273	SEVILLE
43657	TOLEDO	43610	TOLEDO	44258	MEDINA	44256	MEDINA
43659	TOLEDO	43602	TOLEDO	44265	RANDOLPH	44201	ATWATER
43660	TOLEDO	43604	TOLEDO	44274	SHARON CENTER	44281	WADSWORTH
43661	TOLEDO	43607	TOLEDO	44282	WADSWORTH	44281	WADSWORTH
43666	TOLEDO	43604	TOLEDO	44285	WAYLAND	44266	RAVENNA
43667	TOLEDO	43604	TOLEDO	44309	AKRON	44311	AKRON
43681	TOLEDO	43602	TOLEDO	44315	AKRON	44312	AKRON
43682	TOLEDO	43602	TOLEDO	44316	AKRON	44305	AKRON
43697	TOLEDO	43602	TOLEDO	44317	AKRON	44301	AKRON
43699	TOLEDO	43602	TOLEDO	44322	AKRON	44320	AKRON
43702	ZANESVILLE	43701	ZANESVILLE	44326	AKRON	44308	AKRON
43711	AVA	43732	CUMBERLAND	44328	AKRON	44308	AKRON
43717	BELLE VALLEY	43724	CALDWELL	44334	FAIRLAWN	44312	AKRON
43721	BROWNSVILLE	43076	THORNVILLE	44372	AKRON	44311	AKRON
43722	BUFFALO	43780	SENECAVILLE	44393	AKRON	44310	AKRON
43733	DERWENT	43772	PLEASANT CITY	44396	AKRON	44311	AKRON
43735	EAST FULTONHAM	43777	ROSEVILLE	44398	AKRON	44311	AKRON
43736	FAIRVIEW	43773	QUAKER CITY	44399	AKRON	44308	AKRON
43738	FULTONHAM	43760	MOUNT PERRY	44415	ELKTON	44432	LISBON
43740	GRATIOT	43056	HEATH	44416	ELLSWORTH	44451	NORTH JACKSON
43750	KIPLING	43725	CAMBRIDGE	44422	GREENFORD	44406	CANFIELD
43752	LAINGS	43793	WOODSFIELD	44424	HARTFORD	44404	BURGHILL
43757	MALAGA	43747	JERUSALEM	44439	MESOPOTAMIA	44062	MIDDLEFIELD
43759	MORRISTOWN	43718	BELMONT	44453	ORANGEVILLE	44404	BURGHILL
43761	MOXAHALA	43730	CORNING	44482	WARREN	44481	WARREN
43768	OLD WASHINGTON	43755	LORE CITY	44486	WARREN	44481	WARREN
43786	STAFFORD	43754	LEWISVILLE	44492	WEST POINT	44432	LISBON
43789	SYCAMORE VALLEY	45734	GRAYSVILLE	44493	WINONA	44423	HANOVERTON
43791	WHITE COTTAGE	43701	ZANESVILLE	44501	YOUNGSTOWN	44503	YOUNGSTOWN
43803	BAKERSVILLE	43832	NEWCOMERSTOWN	44513	YOUNGSTOWN	44512	YOUNGSTOWN
43805	BLISSFIELD	43844	WARSAW	44599	YOUNGSTOWN	44503	YOUNGSTOWN
43828	KEENE	43812	COSHOCTON	44607	AUGUSTA	44427	KENSINGTON
43836	PLAINFIELD	43812	COSHOCTON	44610	BERLIN	44654	MILLERSBURG
43842	TRINWAY	43821	DRESDEN	44617	CHARM	43804	BALTIC
43905	BARTON	43912	BRIDGEPORT	44619	DAMASCUS	44460	SALEM
43909	BLAINE	43950	SAINT CLAIRSVILLE	44630	GREENTOWN	44720	CANTON
43914	CAMERON	43716	BEALLSVILLE	44631	HARLEM SPRINGS	44615	CARROLLTON
43916	COLERAIN	43912	BRIDGEPORT	44636	KIDRON	44618	DALTON
43925	EAST SPRINGFIELD	43910	BLOOMINGDALE	44639	LEESVILLE	44621	DENNISON
43926	EMPIRE	43964	TORONTO	44640	LIMAVILLE	44601	ALLIANCE
43927	FAIRPOINT	43950	SAINT CLAIRSVILLE	44648	MASSILLON	44646	MASSILLON
43928	GLENCOE	43950	SAINT CLAIRSVILLE	44650	MAXIMO	44601	ALLIANCE
43931	HANNIBAL	43946	SARDIS	44652	MIDDLEBRANCH	44721	CANTON
43934	LANSING	43935	MARTINS FERRY	44653	MIDVALE	44663	NEW PHILADELPHIA
43937	MAYNARD	43912	BRIDGEPORT	44659	MOUNT EATON	44624	DUNDEE

OHIO **OHIO**

Point ZIP Code		Enclosing Residential ZIP Code		Point ZIP Code		Enclosing Residential ZIP Code	
ZIP	Post Office Name	ZIP	Post Office Name	ZIP	Post Office Name	ZIP	Post Office Name
44660	MOUNT HOPE	44654	MILLERSBURG	45274	CINCINNATI	45225	CINCINNATI
44661	NASHVILLE	44638	LAKEVILLE	45280	CINCINNATI	45214	CINCINNATI
44665	NORTH GEORGETOWN	44609	BELOIT	45296	CINCINNATI	45203	CINCINNATI
44670	ROBERTSVILLE	44669	PARIS	45299	CINCINNATI	45202	CINCINNATI
44671	SANDYVILLE	44656	MINERAL CITY	45301	ALPHA	45434	DAYTON
44678	SOMERDALE	44656	MINERAL CITY	45307	BOWERSVILLE	45335	JAMESTOWN
44679	STILLWATER	44683	UHRICHSVILLE	45310	BURKETTSVILLE	45348	NEW WESTON
44682	TUSCARAWAS	44629	GNADENHUTTEN	45316	CLIFTON	45387	YELLOW SPRINGS
44687	WALNUT CREEK	44681	SUGARCREEK	45319	DONNELSVILLE	45344	NEW CARLISLE
44690	WINESBURG	44624	DUNDEE	45328	GETTYSBURG	45308	BRADFORD
44693	DEERSVILLE	44699	TIPPECANOE	45330	GRATIS	45381	WEST ALEXANDRIA
44697	ZOAR	44612	BOLIVAR	45336	KETTLERSVILLE	45302	ANNA
44701	CANTON	44709	CANTON	45343	MIAMISBURG	45342	MIAMISBURG
44711	CANTON	44709	CANTON	45349	NORTH HAMPTON	45502	SPRINGFIELD
44712	CANTON	44706	CANTON	45350	NORTH STAR	45362	ROSSBURG
44735	CANTON	44720	CANTON	45351	OSGOOD	45388	YORKSHIRE
44750	CANTON	44710	CANTON	45352	PALESTINE	45331	GREENVILLE
44760	CANTON	44718	CANTON	45353	PEMBERTON	45365	SIDNEY
44767	CANTON	44720	CANTON	45354	PHILLIPSBURG	45309	BROOKVILLE
44798	CANTON	44709	CANTON	45358	PITSBURG	45304	ARCANUM
44799	CANTON	44709	CANTON	45360	PORT JEFFERSON	45365	SIDNEY
44809	BASCOM	44883	TIFFIN	45361	POTSDAM	45337	LAURA
44815	BETTSVILLE	44841	KANSAS	45372	TREMONT CITY	45502	SPRINGFIELD
44816	BIRMINGHAM	44889	WAKEMAN	45374	TROY	45373	TROY
44825	CHATFIELD	44818	BLOOMVILLE	45378	VERONA	45338	LEWISBURG
44828	FLAT ROCK	44811	BELLEVUE	45384	WILBERFORCE	45385	XENIA
44838	HAYESVILLE	44805	ASHLAND	45389	CHRISTIANSBURG	45312	CASSTOWN
44845	MELMORE	44882	SYCAMORE	45401	DAYTON	45410	DAYTON
44848	NANKIN	44805	ASHLAND	45412	DAYTON	45402	DAYTON
44850	NEW HAVEN	44865	PLYMOUTH	45413	DAYTON	45414	DAYTON
44856	NORTH ROBINSON	44827	CRESTLINE	45422	DAYTON	45402	DAYTON
44860	OCEOLA	44849	NEVADA	45423	DAYTON	45402	DAYTON
44861	OLD FORT	44883	TIFFIN	45428	DAYTON	45417	DAYTON
44862	ONTARIO	44902	MANSFIELD	45435	DAYTON	45324	FAIRBORN
44871	SANDUSKY	44870	SANDUSKY	45437	DAYTON	45431	DAYTON
44874	SAVANNAH	44805	ASHLAND	45441	DAYTON	45459	DAYTON
44881	SULPHUR SPRINGS	44820	BUCYRUS	45448	DAYTON	45342	MIAMISBURG
44888	WILLARD	44890	WILLARD	45454	DAYTON	45459	DAYTON
44901	MANSFIELD	44902	MANSFIELD	45463	DAYTON	45402	DAYTON
44999	MANSFIELD	44907	MANSFIELD	45469	DAYTON	45409	DAYTON
45004	COLLINSVILLE	45013	HAMILTON	45470	DAYTON	45342	MIAMISBURG
45012	HAMILTON	45011	HAMILTON	45475	DAYTON	45459	DAYTON
45018	FAIRFIELD	45011	HAMILTON	45479	DAYTON	45409	DAYTON
45025	HAMILTON	45011	HAMILTON	45481	DAYTON	45430	DAYTON
45026	HAMILTON	45011	HAMILTON	45482	DAYTON	45430	DAYTON
45032	HARVEYSBURG	45068	WAYNESVILLE	45490	DAYTON	45377	VANDALIA
45033	HOOVEN	45002	CLEVES	45501	SPRINGFIELD	45502	SPRINGFIELD
45041	MIAMITOWN	45002	CLEVES	45617	BOURNEVILLE	45601	CHILLICOTHE
45043	MIDDLETOWN	45042	MIDDLETOWN	45618	CHERRY FORK	45697	WINCHESTER
45051	MOUNT SAINT JOSEPH	45233	CINCINNATI	45621	COALTON	45692	WELLSTON
45055	OVERPECK	45011	HAMILTON	45624	CYNTHIANA	45612	BAINBRIDGE
45061	ROSS	45013	HAMILTON	45630	FRIENDSHIP	45663	WEST PORTSMOUTH
45062	SEVEN MILE	45011	HAMILTON	45633	HALLSVILLE	45644	KINGSTON
45063	SHANDON	45013	HAMILTON	45636	HAVERHILL	45629	FRANKLIN FURNACE
45070	WEST ELKTON	45311	CAMDEN	45642	JASPER	45661	PIKETON
45071	WEST CHESTER	45069	WEST CHESTER	45643	KERR	45614	BIDWELL
45073	MONROE	45050	MONROE	45674	RIO GRANDE	45631	GALLIPOLIS
45099	MONROE	45050	MONROE	45677	SCIOTO FURNACE	45694	WHEELERSBURG
45105	BENTONVILLE	45144	MANCHESTER	45683	STOCKDALE	45613	BEAVER
45110	BUFORD	45171	SARDINIA	45687	WAKEFIELD	45648	LUCASVILLE
45112	CHILO	45120	FELICITY	45698	ZALESKI	45651	MC ARTHUR
45114	CUBA	45107	BLANCHESTER	45699	LUCASVILLE	45648	LUCASVILLE
45115	DECATUR	45168	RUSSELLVILLE	45712	BARLOW	45729	FLEMING
45119	FEESBURG	45130	HAMERSVILLE	45713	BARTLETT	45724	CUTLER
45131	HIGGINSPORT	45121	GEORGETOWN	45716	BUCHTEL	45764	NELSONVILLE
45132	HIGHLAND	45135	LEESBURG	45719	CHAUNCEY	45761	MILLFIELD
45138	LEES CREEK	45169	SABINA	45720	CHESTER	45743	LONG BOTTOM
45145	MARATHON	45176	WILLIAMSBURG	45721	COAL RUN	45744	LOWELL
45147	MIAMIVILLE	45140	LOVELAND	45739	HOCKINGPORT	45723	COOLVILLE
45155	MOWRYSTOWN	45133	HILLSBORO	45740	JACKSONVILLE	45732	GLOUSTER
45156	NEVILLE	45153	MOSCOW	45777	SHARPSBURG	45711	AMESVILLE
45158	NEWTONSVILLE	45122	GOSHEN	45779	SYRACUSE	45771	RACINE
45164	PORT WILLIAM	45177	WILMINGTON	45782	TRIMBLE	45732	GLOUSTER
45166	REESVILLE	45169	SABINA	45783	TUPPERS PLAINS	45723	COOLVILLE
45172	SINKING SPRING	45133	HILLSBORO	45787	WATERTOWN	45786	WATERFORD
45201	CINCINNATI	45203	CINCINNATI	45802	LIMA	45801	LIMA
45210	CINCINNATI	45202	CINCINNATI	45808	BEAVERDAM	45801	LIMA
45222	CINCINNATI	45212	CINCINNATI	45809	GOMER	45807	LIMA
45234	CINCINNATI	45214	CINCINNATI	45815	BELMORE	45856	LEIPSIC
45235	CINCINNATI	45241	CINCINNATI	45816	BENTON RIDGE	45840	FINDLAY
45250	CINCINNATI	45214	CINCINNATI	45819	BUCKLAND	45895	WAPAKONETA
45253	CINCINNATI	45251	CINCINNATI	45820	CAIRO	45807	LIMA
45254	CINCINNATI	45255	CINCINNATI	45826	CHICKASAW	45822	CELINA
45258	CINCINNATI	45248	CINCINNATI	45837	DUPONT	45827	CLOVERDALE
45262	CINCINNATI	45241	CINCINNATI	45838	ELGIN	45894	VENEDOCIA
45263	CINCINNATI	45202	CINCINNATI	45839	FINDLAY	45840	FINDLAY
45264	CINCINNATI	45203	CINCINNATI	45848	GLANDORF	45875	OTTAWA
45267	CINCINNATI	45219	CINCINNATI	45853	KALIDA	45844	FORT JENNINGS
45268	CINCINNATI	45220	CINCINNATI	45854	LAFAYETTE	45801	LIMA
45269	CINCINNATI	45225	CINCINNATI	45855	LATTY	45879	PAULDING
45270	CINCINNATI	45203	CINCINNATI	45859	MC GUFFEY	45812	ALGER
45271	CINCINNATI	45225	CINCINNATI	45861	MELROSE	45873	OAKWOOD
45273	CINCINNATI	45202	CINCINNATI	45864	MILLER CITY	45856	LEIPSIC

OHIO   **OREGON**

Point ZIP Code		Enclosing Residential ZIP Code		Point ZIP Code		Enclosing Residential ZIP Code	
ZIP	Post Office Name	ZIP	Post Office Name	ZIP	Post Office Name	ZIP	Post Office Name
45866	MONTEZUMA	45822	CELINA	74067	SAPULPA	74066	SAPULPA
45870	NEW HAMPSHIRE	45895	WAPAKONETA	74068	SHAMROCK	74030	DRUMRIGHT
45876	OTTOVILLE	45844	FORT JENNINGS	74071	SLICK	74010	BRISTOW
45884	SAINT JOHNS	45895	WAPAKONETA	74076	STILLWATER	74074	STILLWATER
45888	UNIOPOLIS	45895	WAPAKONETA	74082	VERA	74021	COLLINSVILLE
45893	VAUGHNSVILLE	45830	COLUMBUS GROVE	74101	TULSA	74103	TULSA
45897	WILLIAMSTOWN	45843	FOREST	74102	TULSA	74103	TULSA
45899	WREN	45874	OHIO CITY	74121	TULSA	74103	TULSA
45950	CINCINNATI	45214	CINCINNATI	74141	TULSA	74129	TULSA
73001	ALBERT	73038	FORT COBB	74147	TULSA	74145	TULSA
73019	NORMAN	73069	NORMAN	74148	TULSA	74106	TULSA
73022	CONCHO	73036	EL RENO	74149	TULSA	74127	TULSA
73023	CHICKASHA	73018	CHICKASHA	74150	TULSA	74104	TULSA
73031	DIBBLE	73010	BLANCHARD	74152	TULSA	74114	TULSA
73032	DOUGHERTY	73030	DAVIS	74153	TULSA	74135	TULSA
73033	EAKLY	73048	HYDRO	74155	TULSA	74145	TULSA
73050	LANGSTON	73027	COYLE	74156	TULSA	74126	TULSA
73066	NICOMA PARK	73020	CHOCTAW	74157	TULSA	74107	TULSA
73070	NORMAN	73069	NORMAN	74158	TULSA	74115	TULSA
73083	EDMOND	73003	EDMOND	74159	TULSA	74104	TULSA
73085	YUKON	73099	YUKON	74169	TULSA	74134	TULSA
73094	WASHITA	73005	ANADARKO	74170	TULSA	74136	TULSA
73097	WHEATLAND	73169	OKLAHOMA CITY	74172	TULSA	74103	TULSA
73101	OKLAHOMA CITY	73102	OKLAHOMA CITY	74182	TULSA	74103	TULSA
73113	OKLAHOMA CITY	73114	OKLAHOMA CITY	74183	TULSA	74136	TULSA
73123	OKLAHOMA CITY	73132	OKLAHOMA CITY	74184	TULSA	74136	TULSA
73124	OKLAHOMA CITY	73109	OKLAHOMA CITY	74186	TULSA	74103	TULSA
73125	OKLAHOMA CITY	73109	OKLAHOMA CITY	74187	TULSA	74103	TULSA
73126	OKLAHOMA CITY	73109	OKLAHOMA CITY	74189	TULSA	74104	TULSA
73136	OKLAHOMA CITY	73111	OKLAHOMA CITY	74192	TULSA	74103	TULSA
73137	OKLAHOMA CITY	73127	OKLAHOMA CITY	74193	TULSA	74136	TULSA
73140	OKLAHOMA CITY	73110	OKLAHOMA CITY	74194	TULSA	74136	TULSA
73143	OKLAHOMA CITY	73129	OKLAHOMA CITY	74335	CARDIN	74339	COMMERCE
73144	OKLAHOMA CITY	73119	OKLAHOMA CITY	74340	DISNEY	74367	STRANG
73146	OKLAHOMA CITY	73106	OKLAHOMA CITY	74345	GROVE	74344	GROVE
73147	OKLAHOMA CITY	73107	OKLAHOMA CITY	74349	KETCHUM	74301	VINITA
73148	OKLAHOMA CITY	73109	OKLAHOMA CITY	74350	LANGLEY	74367	STRANG
73152	OKLAHOMA CITY	73105	OKLAHOMA CITY	74355	MIAMI	74354	MIAMI
73153	OKLAHOMA CITY	73160	OKLAHOMA CITY	74362	PRYOR	74361	PRYOR
73154	OKLAHOMA CITY	73118	OKLAHOMA CITY	74402	MUSKOGEE	74401	MUSKOGEE
73155	OKLAHOMA CITY	73115	OKLAHOMA CITY	74430	CROWDER	74425	CANADIAN
73156	OKLAHOMA CITY	73120	OKLAHOMA CITY	74431	DEWAR	74437	HENRYETTA
73157	OKLAHOMA CITY	73112	OKLAHOMA CITY	74438	HITCHITA	74428	COUNCIL HILL
73164	OKLAHOMA CITY	73129	OKLAHOMA CITY	74444	MOODYS	74464	TAHLEQUAH
73167	OKLAHOMA CITY	73109	OKLAHOMA CITY	74446	OKAY	74467	WAGONER
73172	OKLAHOMA CITY	73132	OKLAHOMA CITY	74456	PRESTON	74447	OKMULGEE
73178	OKLAHOMA CITY	73112	OKLAHOMA CITY	74458	REDBIRD	74454	PORTER
73184	OKLAHOMA CITY	73114	OKLAHOMA CITY	74459	RENTIESVILLE	74426	CHECOTAH
73185	OKLAHOMA CITY	73102	OKLAHOMA CITY	74460	SCHULTER	74437	HENRYETTA
73189	OKLAHOMA CITY	73159	OKLAHOMA CITY	74465	TAHLEQUAH	74464	TAHLEQUAH
73190	OKLAHOMA CITY	73109	OKLAHOMA CITY	74468	WAINWRIGHT	74450	OKTAHA
73194	OKLAHOMA CITY	73105	OKLAHOMA CITY	74477	WAGONER	74467	WAGONER
73195	OKLAHOMA CITY	73114	OKLAHOMA CITY	74502	MCALESTER	74501	MCALESTER
73196	OKLAHOMA CITY	73102	OKLAHOMA CITY	74521	ALBION	74574	TUSKAHOMA
73198	OKLAHOMA CITY	73112	OKLAHOMA CITY	74522	ALDERSON	74501	MCALESTER
73402	ARDMORE	73401	ARDMORE	74529	BLOCKER	74561	QUINTON
73403	ARDMORE	73401	ARDMORE	74530	BROMIDE	73461	WAPANUCKA
73425	COUNTYLINE	73533	DUNCAN	74535	CLARITA	74572	TUPELO
73435	FOX	73437	GRAHAM	74545	GOWEN	74578	WILBURTON
73436	GENE AUTRY	73458	SPRINGER	74546	HAILEYVILLE	74547	HARTSHORNE
73455	RAVIA	74856	MILL CREEK	74554	KREBS	74501	MCALESTER
73476	PERNELL	73434	FOSTER	74556	LEHIGH	74538	COALGATE
73487	TATUMS	73444	HENNEPIN	74559	PANOLA	74578	WILBURTON
73491	VELMA	73533	DUNCAN	74565	SAVANNA	74501	MCALESTER
73502	LAWTON	73501	LAWTON	74602	PONCA CITY	74601	PONCA CITY
73506	LAWTON	73505	LAWTON	74702	DURANT	74701	DURANT
73520	ADDINGTON	73573	WAURIKA	74720	ACHILLE	74741	HENDRIX
73522	ALTUS	73521	ALTUS	74721	ALBANY	74726	BOKCHITO
73534	DUNCAN	73533	DUNCAN	74722	BATTIEST	74724	BETHEL
73536	DUNCAN	73533	DUNCAN	74737	GOLDEN	74728	BROKEN BOW
73555	MANITOU	73542	FREDERICK	74747	KEMP	74741	HENDRIX
73556	MARTHA	73521	ALTUS	74750	MILLERTON	74764	VALLIANT
73557	MEDICINE PARK	73538	ELGIN	74752	PICKENS	74724	BETHEL
73567	STERLING	73541	FLETCHER	74753	PLATTER	74730	CALERA
73648	ELK CITY	73644	ELK CITY	74761	SWINK	74735	FORT TOWSON
73702	ENID	73701	ENID	74802	SHAWNEE	74801	SHAWNEE
73706	ENID	73703	ENID	74818	SEMINOLE	74868	SEMINOLE
73743	HILLSDALE	73727	CARRIER	74821	ADA	74820	ADA
73746	HOPETON	73731	DACOMA	74830	BOWLEGS	74854	MAUD
73802	WOODWARD	73801	WOODWARD	74836	CONNERVILLE	73460	TISHOMINGO
73901	ADAMS	73945	HOOKER	74837	CROMWELL	74884	WEWOKA
74001	AVANT	74002	BARNSDALL	74844	FRANCIS	74825	ALLEN
74004	BARTLESVILLE	74003	BARTLESVILLE	74866	SAINT LOUIS	74854	MAUD
74005	BARTLESVILLE	74003	BARTLESVILLE	74935	FANSHAWE	74966	WISTER
74013	BROKEN ARROW	74012	BROKEN ARROW	74936	GANS	74948	MULDROW
74018	CLAREMORE	74017	CLAREMORE	74942	LEFLORE	74966	WISTER
74031	FOYIL	74017	CLAREMORE	74943	LEQUIRE	74944	MCCURTAIN
74034	HALLETT	74020	CLEVELAND	74945	MARBLE CITY	74955	SALLISAW
74041	KIEFER	74033	GLENPOOL	74946	MOFFETT	74954	ROLAND
74043	LEONARD	74008	BIXBY	74947	MONROE	74953	POTEAU
74046	MILFAY	74028	DEPEW	74951	PANAMA	74930	BOKOSHE
74050	OAKHURST	74107	TULSA	97020	DONALD	97002	AURORA
74052	OILTON	74030	DRUMRIGHT	97036	MARYLHURST	97034	LAKE OSWEGO

OREGON

Point ZIP Code		Enclosing Residential ZIP Code	
ZIP	Post Office Name	ZIP	Post Office Name
97075	BEAVERTON	97005	BEAVERTON
97076	BEAVERTON	97006	BEAVERTON
97077	BEAVERTON	97005	BEAVERTON
97078	BEAVERTON	97008	BEAVERTON
97102	ARCH CAPE	97138	SEASIDE
97110	CANNON BEACH	97145	TOLOVANA PARK
97118	GARIBALDI	97136	ROCKAWAY BEACH
97130	MANZANITA	97131	NEHALEM
97134	OCEANSIDE	97141	TILLAMOOK
97135	PACIFIC CITY	97112	CLOVERDALE
97143	NETARTS	97141	TILLAMOOK
97147	WHEELER	97136	ROCKAWAY BEACH
97207	PORTLAND	97205	PORTLAND
97208	PORTLAND	97209	PORTLAND
97228	PORTLAND	97209	PORTLAND
97238	PORTLAND	97218	PORTLAND
97240	PORTLAND	97204	PORTLAND
97242	PORTLAND	97202	PORTLAND
97251	PORTLAND	97201	PORTLAND
97253	PORTLAND	97204	PORTLAND
97254	PORTLAND	97210	PORTLAND
97255	PORTLAND	97209	PORTLAND
97258	PORTLAND	97201	PORTLAND
97268	PORTLAND	97267	PORTLAND
97269	PORTLAND	97222	PORTLAND
97271	PORTLAND	97239	PORTLAND
97280	PORTLAND	97219	PORTLAND
97281	PORTLAND	97223	PORTLAND
97282	PORTLAND	97202	PORTLAND
97283	PORTLAND	97203	PORTLAND
97286	PORTLAND	97206	PORTLAND
97290	PORTLAND	97211	PORTLAND
97291	PORTLAND	97210	PORTLAND
97292	PORTLAND	97218	PORTLAND
97293	PORTLAND	97214	PORTLAND
97294	PORTLAND	97213	PORTLAND
97296	PORTLAND	97210	PORTLAND
97298	PORTLAND	97225	PORTLAND
97299	PORTLAND	97213	PORTLAND
97307	KEIZER	97303	SALEM
97308	SALEM	97301	SALEM
97309	SALEM	97301	SALEM
97310	SALEM	97301	SALEM
97311	SALEM	97301	SALEM
97312	SALEM	97302	SALEM
97313	SALEM	97303	SALEM
97314	SALEM	97303	SALEM
97335	CRABTREE	97374	SCIO
97336	CRAWFORDSVILLE	97386	SWEET HOME
97339	CORVALLIS	97333	CORVALLIS
97359	MARION	97392	TURNER
97369	OTTER ROCK	97365	NEWPORT
97372	ROSE LODGE	97367	LINCOLN CITY
97373	SAINT BENEDICT	97362	MOUNT ANGEL
97384	MEHAMA	97383	STAYTON
97388	GLENEDEN BEACH	97341	DEPOE BAY
97407	ALLEGANY	97420	COOS BAY
97409	ALVADORE	97448	JUNCTION CITY
97425	CRESCENT LAKE	97733	CRESCENT
97428	CURTIN	97424	COTTAGE GROVE
97432	DILLARD	97496	WINSTON
97440	EUGENE	97404	EUGENE
97464	OPHIR	97444	GOLD BEACH
97472	SAGINAW	97424	COTTAGE GROVE
97482	THURSTON	97478	SPRINGFIELD
97491	WEDDERBURN	97444	GOLD BEACH
97494	WILBUR	97470	ROSEBURG
97495	WINCHESTER	97470	ROSEBURG
97528	GRANTS PASS	97526	GRANTS PASS
97533	MURPHY	97527	GRANTS PASS
97602	KLAMATH FALLS	97603	KLAMATH FALLS
97604	CRATER LAKE	97731	CHEMULT
97622	BLY	97623	BONANZA
97626	FORT KLAMATH	97624	CHILOQUIN
97634	MIDLAND	97603	KLAMATH FALLS
97641	CHRISTMAS VALLEY	97638	SILVER LAKE
97708	BEND	97701	BEND
97709	BEND	97701	BEND
97722	DIAMOND	97721	PRINCETON
97732	CRANE	97720	BURNS
97736	FRENCHGLEN	97721	PRINCETON
97819	BRIDGEPORT	97837	HEREFORD
97859	MEACHAM	97801	PENDLETON
97861	MIKKALO	97812	ARLINGTON
97880	UKIAH	97868	PILOT ROCK
97902	AROCK	97910	JORDAN VALLEY
97905	DURKEE	97907	HUNTINGTON
15004	ATLASBURG	15021	BURGETTSTOWN
15006	BAIRDFORD	15044	GIBSONIA
15020	BUNOLA	15063	MONONGAHELA
15028	COULTERS	15131	MC KEESPORT
15032	CURTISVILLE	15044	GIBSONIA
15036	ELDERSVILLE	15021	BURGETTSTOWN

PENNSYLVANIA

Point ZIP Code		Enclosing Residential ZIP Code	
ZIP	Post Office Name	ZIP	Post Office Name
15038	ELRAMA	15025	CLAIRTON
15046	CRESCENT	15108	CORAOPOLIS
15047	GREENOCK	15135	MC KEESPORT
15053	JOFFRE	15021	BURGETTSTOWN
15054	LANGELOTH	15078	SLOVAN
15069	NEW KENSINGTON	15613	APOLLO
15072	PRICEDALE	15012	BELLE VERNON
15075	RURAL RIDGE	15024	CHESWICK
15081	SOUTH HEIGHTS	15001	ALIQUIPPA
15082	STURGEON	15057	MC DONALD
15087	WEBSTER	15012	BELLE VERNON
15088	WEST ELIZABETH	15025	CLAIRTON
15091	WILDWOOD	15044	GIBSONIA
15095	WARRENDALE	15090	WEXFORD
15096	WARRENDALE	15086	WARRENDALE
15123	WEST MIFFLIN	15025	CLAIRTON
15127	INGOMAR	15237	PITTSBURGH
15130	MC KEESPORT	15132	MC KEESPORT
15134	MC KEESPORT	15132	MC KEESPORT
15230	PITTSBURGH	15219	PITTSBURGH
15231	PITTSBURGH	15108	CORAOPOLIS
15240	PITTSBURGH	15206	PITTSBURGH
15242	PITTSBURGH	15220	PITTSBURGH
15244	PITTSBURGH	15136	MC KEES ROCKS
15250	PITTSBURGH	15212	PITTSBURGH
15251	PITTSBURGH	15212	PITTSBURGH
15252	PITTSBURGH	15219	PITTSBURGH
15253	PITTSBURGH	15212	PITTSBURGH
15254	PITTSBURGH	15219	PITTSBURGH
15255	PITTSBURGH	15212	PITTSBURGH
15257	PITTSBURGH	15219	PITTSBURGH
15258	PITTSBURGH	15219	PITTSBURGH
15259	PITTSBURGH	15219	PITTSBURGH
15262	PITTSBURGH	15219	PITTSBURGH
15263	PITTSBURGH	15219	PITTSBURGH
15264	PITTSBURGH	15212	PITTSBURGH
15265	PITTSBURGH	15222	PITTSBURGH
15267	PITTSBURGH	15233	PITTSBURGH
15268	PITTSBURGH	15212	PITTSBURGH
15270	PITTSBURGH	15228	PITTSBURGH
15272	PITTSBURGH	15222	PITTSBURGH
15274	PITTSBURGH	15212	PITTSBURGH
15275	PITTSBURGH	15220	PITTSBURGH
15276	PITTSBURGH	15205	PITTSBURGH
15277	PITTSBURGH	15205	PITTSBURGH
15278	PITTSBURGH	15222	PITTSBURGH
15279	PITTSBURGH	15233	PITTSBURGH
15281	PITTSBURGH	15219	PITTSBURGH
15283	PITTSBURGH	15220	PITTSBURGH
15285	PITTSBURGH	15209	PITTSBURGH
15286	PITTSBURGH	15212	PITTSBURGH
15289	PITTSBURGH	15213	PITTSBURGH
15290	PITTSBURGH	15212	PITTSBURGH
15295	PITTSBURGH	15202	PITTSBURGH
15315	BOBTOWN	15327	DILLINER
15316	BRAVE	15362	SPRAGGS
15325	CRUCIBLE	15357	RICES LANDING
15334	GARARDS FORT	15320	CARMICHAELS
15336	GASTONVILLE	15332	FINLEYVILLE
15339	HENDERSONVILLE	15317	CANONSBURG
15347	MEADOW LANDS	15301	WASHINGTON
15348	MILLSBORO	15357	RICES LANDING
15350	MUSE	15317	CANONSBURG
15351	NEMACOLIN	15320	CARMICHAELS
15354	PINE BANK	15362	SPRAGGS
15358	RICHEYVILLE	15427	DAISYTOWN
15361	SOUTHVIEW	15057	MC DONALD
15365	TAYLORSTOWN	15323	CLAYSVILLE
15366	VAN VOORHIS	15022	CHARLEROI
15368	VESTABURG	15333	FREDERICKTOWN
15378	WESTLAND	15340	HICKORY
15379	WEST MIDDLETOWN	15312	AVELLA
15415	BRIER HILL	15442	GRINDSTONE
15416	BROWNFIELD	15401	UNIONTOWN
15420	CARDALE	15463	MERRITTSTOWN
15421	CHALK HILL	15437	FARMINGTON
15422	CHESTNUT RIDGE	15442	GRINDSTONE
15429	DENBO	15417	BROWNSVILLE
15430	DICKERSON RUN	15486	VANDERBILT
15435	FAIRBANK	15468	NEW SALEM
15439	GANS	15451	LAKE LYNN
15443	HIBBS	15458	MC CLELLANDTOWN
15447	ISABELLA	15433	EAST MILLSBORO
15448	JACOBS CREEK	15479	SMITHTON
15449	KEISTERVILLE	15480	SMOCK
15454	LECKRONE	15458	MC CLELLANDTOWN
15455	LEISENRING	15425	CONNELLSVILLE
15460	MARTIN	15478	SMITHFIELD
15465	MOUNT BRADDOCK	15456	LEMONT FURNACE
15466	NEWELL	15438	FAYETTE CITY
15467	NEW GENEVA	15478	SMITHFIELD
15472	OLIVER	15401	UNIONTOWN
15476	RONCO	15461	MASONTOWN

PENNSYLVANIA   **PENNSYLVANIA**

Point ZIP Code		Enclosing Residential ZIP Code		Point ZIP Code		Enclosing Residential ZIP Code	
ZIP	Post Office Name	ZIP	Post Office Name	ZIP	Post Office Name	ZIP	Post Office Name
15484	ULEDI	15401	UNIONTOWN	16054	SAINT PETERSBURG	16036	FOXBURG
15485	URSINA	15424	CONFLUENCE	16058	TURKEY CITY	16036	FOXBURG
15489	WEST LEISENRING	15401	UNIONTOWN	16103	NEW CASTLE	16101	NEW CASTLE
15492	WICKHAVEN	15012	BELLE VERNON	16107	NEW CASTLE	16101	NEW CASTLE
15502	HIDDEN VALLEY	15501	SOMERSET	16108	NEW CASTLE	16101	NEW CASTLE
15510	SOMERSET	15501	SOMERSET	16113	CLARK	16125	GREENVILLE
15520	ACOSTA	15541	FRIEDENS	16132	HILLSVILLE	16116	EDINBURG
15532	BOYNTON	15552	MEYERSDALE	16136	KOPPEL	15010	BEAVER FALLS
15544	GRAY	15531	BOSWELL	16140	NEW BEDFORD	16143	PULASKI
15547	JENNERSTOWN	15531	BOSWELL	16151	SHEAKLEYVILLE	16130	HADLEY
15548	KANTNER	15563	STOYSTOWN	16155	VILLA MARIA	16143	PULASKI
15549	LISTIE	15541	FRIEDENS	16160	WEST PITTSBURG	16157	WAMPUM
15553	NEW BALTIMORE	15530	BERLIN	16161	WHEATLAND	16121	FARRELL
15555	QUECREEK	15501	SOMERSET	16211	BEYER	15747	HOME
15560	SHANKSVILLE	15541	FRIEDENS	16215	KITTANNING	16201	KITTANNING
15561	SIPESVILLE	15501	SOMERSET	16220	CROWN	16260	VOWINCKEL
15564	WELLERSBURG	15545	HYNDMAN	16221	CURLLSVILLE	16232	KNOX
15565	WEST SALISBURY	15558	SALISBURY	16223	DISTANT	16242	NEW BETHLEHEM
15605	GREENSBURG	15601	GREENSBURG	16228	FORD CLIFF	16226	FORD CITY
15606	GREENSBURG	15601	GREENSBURG	16230	HAWTHORN	16224	FAIRMOUNT CITY
15619	BOVARD	15601	GREENSBURG	16236	MC GRANN	16226	FORD CITY
15621	CALUMET	15666	MOUNT PLEASANT	16244	NU MINE	16249	RURAL VALLEY
15623	CLARIDGE	15644	JEANNETTE	16245	OAK RIDGE	16242	NEW BETHLEHEM
15624	CRABTREE	15601	GREENSBURG	16246	PLUMVILLE	15747	HOME
15629	EAST VANDERGRIFT	15690	VANDERGRIFT	16250	SAGAMORE	16249	RURAL VALLEY
15633	FORBES ROAD	15601	GREENSBURG	16253	SEMINOLE	16242	NEW BETHLEHEM
15635	HANNASTOWN	15601	GREENSBURG	16257	SNYDERSBURG	16235	LUCINDA
15638	HOSTETTER	15650	LATROBE	16261	WIDNOON	16259	TEMPLETON
15640	HUTCHINSON	15637	HERMINIE	16263	YATESBORO	16249	RURAL VALLEY
15660	LOWBER	15637	HERMINIE	16312	CHANDLERS VALLEY	16350	SUGAR GROVE
15662	LUXOR	15601	GREENSBURG	16322	ENDEAVOR	16353	TIONESTA
15664	MAMMOTH	15666	MOUNT PLEASANT	16328	HYDETOWN	16354	TITUSVILLE
15671	NEW DERRY	15627	DERRY	16343	RENO	16301	OIL CITY
15673	NORTH APOLLO	15613	APOLLO	16344	ROUSEVILLE	16301	OIL CITY
15674	NORVELT	15666	MOUNT PLEASANT	16352	TIONA	16365	WARREN
15676	PLEASANT UNITY	15650	LATROBE	16361	TYLERSBURG	16233	LEEPER
15680	SALINA	15618	AVONMORE	16366	WARREN	16365	WARREN
15682	SCHENLEY	15656	LEECHBURG	16367	WARREN	16365	WARREN
15685	SOUTHWEST	15666	MOUNT PLEASANT	16368	WARREN	16365	WARREN
15689	UNITED	15666	MOUNT PLEASANT	16369	WARREN	16365	WARREN
15691	WENDEL	15642	IRWIN	16370	WEST HICKORY	16353	TIONESTA
15693	WHITNEY	15650	LATROBE	16375	LAMARTINE	16232	KNOX
15695	WYANO	15089	WEST NEWTON	16388	MEADVILLE	16335	MEADVILLE
15696	YOUNGSTOWN	15650	LATROBE	16413	ELGIN	16407	CORRY
15710	ALVERDA	15714	NORTHERN CAMBRIA	16416	GARLAND	16340	PITTSFIELD
15712	ARCADIA	15724	CHERRY TREE	16422	HARMONSBURG	16316	CONNEAUT LAKE
15715	BIG RUN	15767	PUNXSUTAWNEY	16427	MILL VILLAGE	16441	WATERFORD
15723	CHAMBERSVILLE	15701	INDIANA	16430	NORTH SPRINGFIELD	16411	EAST SPRINGFIELD
15727	CLUNE	15748	HOMER CITY	16432	RICEVILLE	16438	UNION CITY
15731	CORAL	15748	HOMER CITY	16475	ALBION	16401	ALBION
15733	DE LANCEY	15767	PUNXSUTAWNEY	16512	ERIE	16501	ERIE
15734	DIXONVILLE	15759	MARION CENTER	16514	ERIE	16510	ERIE
15736	ELDERTON	15774	SHELOCTA	16515	ERIE	16510	ERIE
15737	ELMORA	15722	CARROLLTOWN	16522	ERIE	16501	ERIE
15738	EMEIGH	15714	NORTHERN CAMBRIA	16530	ERIE	16501	ERIE
15741	GIPSY	15742	GLEN CAMPBELL	16531	ERIE	16511	ERIE
15745	HEILWOOD	15728	CLYMER	16532	ERIE	16501	ERIE
15746	HILLSDALE	15759	MARION CENTER	16533	ERIE	16511	ERIE
15750	JOSEPHINE	15717	BLAIRSVILLE	16534	ERIE	16501	ERIE
15752	KENT	15748	HOMER CITY	16538	ERIE	16501	ERIE
15754	LUCERNEMINES	15748	HOMER CITY	16541	ERIE	16507	ERIE
15756	MC INTYRE	15774	SHELOCTA	16544	ERIE	16510	ERIE
15761	MENTCLE	15714	NORTHERN CAMBRIA	16546	ERIE	16504	ERIE
15779	TORRANCE	15627	DERRY	16550	ERIE	16507	ERIE
15781	WALSTON	15767	PUNXSUTAWNEY	16553	ERIE	16501	ERIE
15783	WEST LEBANON	15681	SALTSBURG	16554	ERIE	16501	ERIE
15822	BRANDY CAMP	15823	BROCKPORT	16563	ERIE	16510	ERIE
15831	DAGUS MINES	15846	KERSEY	16603	ALTOONA	16601	ALTOONA
15841	FORCE	15827	BYRNEDALE	16619	BLANDBURG	16639	FALLENTIMBER
15847	KNOX DALE	15825	BROOKVILLE	16624	CHEST SPRINGS	16668	PATTON
15863	STUMP CREEK	15851	REYNOLDSVILLE	16629	COUPON	16613	ASHVILLE
15866	TROUTVILLE	15848	LUTHERSBURG	16631	CURRYVILLE	16662	MARTINSBURG
15907	JOHNSTOWN	15901	JOHNSTOWN	16633	DEFIANCE	16679	SIX MILE RUN
15921	BEAVERDALE	15955	SIDMAN	16638	ENTRIKEN	16657	JAMES CREEK
15922	BELSANO	15931	EBENSBURG	16644	GLASGOW	16639	FALLENTIMBER
15925	CASSANDRA	15938	LILLY	16654	HUNTINGDON	16652	HUNTINGDON
15929	DILLTOWN	15748	HOMER CITY	16660	MC CONNELLSTOWN	16652	HUNTINGDON
15930	DUNLO	15963	WINDBER	16663	MORANN	16651	HOUTZDALE
15934	ELTON	15963	WINDBER	16665	NEWRY	16635	DUNCANSVILLE
15937	JEROME	15935	HOLLSOPPLE	16670	QUEEN	16655	IMLER
15948	REVLOC	15931	EBENSBURG	16672	RIDDLESBURG	16679	SIX MILE RUN
15959	TIRE HILL	15904	JOHNSTOWN	16675	SAINT BONIFACE	16646	HASTINGS
15962	WILMORE	15946	PORTAGE	16677	SANDY RIDGE	16866	PHILIPSBURG
16003	BUTLER	16001	BUTLER	16681	SMOKERUN	16661	MADERA
16016	BOYERS	16061	WEST SUNBURY	16682	SPROUL	16625	CLAYSBURG
16017	BOYERS	16061	WEST SUNBURY	16684	TIPTON	16617	BELLWOOD
16018	BOYERS	16020	BOYERS	16694	WOOD	16679	SIX MILE RUN
16024	CALLERY	16033	EVANS CITY	16698	HOUTZDALE	16651	HOUTZDALE
16027	CONNOQUENESSING	16033	EVANS CITY	16699	CRESSON	16630	CRESSON
16029	EAST BUTLER	16001	BUTLER	16725	CUSTER CITY	16701	BRADFORD
16035	FORESTVILLE	16038	HARRISVILLE	16728	DE YOUNG	16734	JAMES CITY
16039	HERMAN	16001	BUTLER	16730	EAST SMETHPORT	16749	SMETHPORT
16048	NORTH WASHINGTON	16050	PETROLIA	16733	HAZEL HURST	16749	SMETHPORT

PENNSYLVANIA   **PENNSYLVANIA**

Point ZIP Code		Enclosing Residential ZIP Code		Point ZIP Code		Enclosing Residential ZIP Code	
ZIP	**Post Office Name**	**ZIP**	**Post Office Name**	**ZIP**	**Post Office Name**	**ZIP**	**Post Office Name**
16804	STATE COLLEGE	16801	STATE COLLEGE	17371	YORK NEW SALEM	17404	YORK
16805	STATE COLLEGE	16801	STATE COLLEGE	17405	YORK	17403	YORK
16825	BIGLER	16881	WOODLAND	17415	YORK	17402	YORK
16826	BLANCHARD	16841	HOWARD	17503	BART	17562	PARADISE
16834	DRIFTING	16839	GRASSFLAT	17504	BAUSMAN	17601	LANCASTER
16835	FLEMING	16844	JULIAN	17506	BLUE BALL	17519	EAST EARL
16843	HYDE	16830	CLEARFIELD	17507	BOWMANSVILLE	17517	DENVER
16847	KYLERTOWN	16839	GRASSFLAT	17508	BROWNSTOWN	17522	EPHRATA
16848	LAMAR	17751	MILL HALL	17521	ELM	17543	LITITZ
16849	LANSE	16839	GRASSFLAT	17528	GOODVILLE	17519	EAST EARL
16850	LECONTES MILLS	16836	FRENCHVILLE	17533	HOPELAND	17543	LITITZ
16851	LEMONT	16801	STATE COLLEGE	17534	INTERCOURSE	17529	GORDONVILLE
16853	MILESBURG	16823	BELLEFONTE	17537	LAMPETER	17602	LANCASTER
16855	MINERAL SPRINGS	16881	WOODLAND	17549	MARTINDALE	17522	EPHRATA
16856	MINGOVILLE	16823	BELLEFONTE	17550	MAYTOWN	17547	MARIETTA
16868	PINE GROVE MILLS	16801	STATE COLLEGE	17564	PENRYN	17543	LITITZ
16873	SHAWVILLE	16830	CLEARFIELD	17567	REAMSTOWN	17578	STEVENS
16876	WALLACETON	16878	WEST DECATUR	17568	REFTON	17584	WILLOW STREET
16910	ALBA	17724	CANTON	17570	RHEEMS	17022	ELIZABETHTOWN
16911	ARNOT	16912	BLOSSBURG	17573	RONKS	17572	RONKS
16918	COWANESQUE	16950	WESTFIELD	17575	SILVER SPRING	17512	COLUMBIA
16945	SYLVANIA	16914	COLUMBIA CROSS ROADS	17580	TALMAGE	17540	LEOLA
17001	CAMP HILL	17011	CAMP HILL	17583	WEST WILLOW	17584	WILLOW STREET
17008	BOWMANSDALE	17050	MECHANICSBURG	17585	WITMER	17505	BIRD IN HAND
17010	CAMPBELLTOWN	17078	PALMYRA	17604	LANCASTER	17601	LANCASTER
17012	CAMP HILL	17055	MECHANICSBURG	17605	LANCASTER	17601	LANCASTER
17016	CORNWALL	17042	LEBANON	17606	LANCASTER	17601	LANCASTER
17027	GRANTHAM	17055	MECHANICSBURG	17607	LANCASTER	17601	LANCASTER
17039	KLEINFELTERSVILLE	17073	NEWMANSTOWN	17608	LANCASTER	17601	LANCASTER
17041	LAWN	17078	PALMYRA	17703	WILLIAMSPORT	17701	WILLIAMSPORT
17054	MATTAWANA	17051	MC VEYTOWN	17705	WILLIAMSPORT	17701	WILLIAMSPORT
17056	MEXICO	17059	MIFFLINTOWN	17720	ANTES FORT	17701	WILLIAMSPORT
17064	MOUNT GRETNA	17042	LEBANON	17721	AVIS	17779	WOOLRICH
17069	NEW BUFFALO	17020	DUNCANNON	17726	CASTANEA	17745	LOCK HAVEN
17072	NEW KINGSTOWN	17050	MECHANICSBURG	17727	CEDAR RUN	17723	CAMMAL
17075	NEWTON HAMILTON	17066	MOUNT UNION	17730	DEWART	17777	WATSONTOWN
17077	ONO	17003	ANNVILLE	17731	EAGLES MERE	17758	MUNCY VALLEY
17081	PLAINFIELD	17013	CARLISLE	17735	GROVER	17724	CANTON
17083	QUENTIN	17042	LEBANON	17738	HYNER	17764	RENOVO
17085	REXMONT	17042	LEBANON	17739	JERSEY MILLS	17723	CAMMAL
17088	SCHAEFFERSTOWN	17067	MYERSTOWN	17748	MC ELHATTAN	17745	LOCK HAVEN
17089	CAMP HILL	17011	CAMP HILL	17749	MC EWENSVILLE	17777	WATSONTOWN
17091	LEBANON	17011	CAMP HILL	17750	MACKEYVILLE	17751	MILL HALL
17093	SUMMERDALE	17025	ENOLA	17759	NISBET	17701	WILLIAMSPORT
17105	HARRISBURG	17101	HARRISBURG	17760	NORTH BEND	17764	RENOVO
17106	HARRISBURG	17110	HARRISBURG	17762	PICTURE ROCKS	17737	HUGHESVILLE
17107	HARRISBURG	17110	HARRISBURG	17767	SALONA	17751	MILL HALL
17108	HARRISBURG	17101	HARRISBURG	17769	SLATE RUN	17740	JERSEY SHORE
17120	HARRISBURG	17101	HARRISBURG	17773	TYLERSVILLE	17747	LOGANTON
17121	HARRISBURG	17101	HARRISBURG	17822	DANVILLE	17821	DANVILLE
17122	HARRISBURG	17104	HARRISBURG	17829	HARTLETON	17845	MILLMONT
17123	HARRISBURG	17101	HARRISBURG	17831	HUMMELS WHARF	17870	SELINSGROVE
17124	HARRISBURG	17101	HARRISBURG	17833	KREAMER	17842	MIDDLEBURG
17125	HARRISBURG	17101	HARRISBURG	17839	LIGHT STREET	17815	BLOOMSBURG
17126	HARRISBURG	17101	HARRISBURG	17840	LOCUST GAP	17851	MOUNT CARMEL
17127	HARRISBURG	17101	HARRISBURG	17858	NUMIDIA	17820	CATAWISSA
17128	HARRISBURG	17101	HARRISBURG	17861	PAXTONVILLE	17842	MIDDLEBURG
17129	HARRISBURG	17101	HARRISBURG	17862	PENNS CREEK	17842	MIDDLEBURG
17130	HARRISBURG	17101	HARRISBURG	17865	POTTS GROVE	17847	MILTON
17140	HARRISBURG	17111	HARRISBURG	17876	SHAMOKIN DAM	17870	SELINSGROVE
17177	HARRISBURG	17110	HARRISBURG	17880	SWENGEL	17844	MIFFLINBURG
17210	AMBERSON	17262	SPRING RUN	17882	TROXELVILLE	17813	BEAVERTOWN
17231	LEMASTERS	17236	MERCERSBURG	17883	VICKSBURG	17844	MIFFLINBURG
17235	MARION	17201	CHAMBERSBURG	17884	WASHINGTONVILLE	17821	DANVILLE
17247	QUINCY	17268	WAYNESBORO	17885	WEIKERT	17845	MILLMONT
17249	ROCKHILL FURNACE	17243	ORBISONIA	17886	WEST MILTON	17837	LEWISBURG
17250	ROUZERVILLE	17268	WAYNESBORO	17887	WHITE DEER	17856	NEW COLUMBIA
17251	ROXBURY	17262	SPRING RUN	17920	ARISTES	17888	WILBURTON
17253	SALTILLO	17264	THREE SPRINGS	17930	CUMBOLA	17959	NEW PHILADELPHIA
17254	SCOTLAND	17201	CHAMBERSBURG	17932	FRACKVILLE	17931	FRACKVILLE
17256	SHADY GROVE	17225	GREENCASTLE	17933	FRIEDENSBURG	17972	SCHUYLKILL HAVEN
17261	SOUTH MOUNTAIN	17222	FAYETTEVILLE	17934	GILBERTON	17976	SHENANDOAH
17263	STATE LINE	17268	WAYNESBORO	17936	GORDON	17921	ASHLAND
17270	WILLIAMSON	17225	GREENCASTLE	17942	LANDINGVILLE	17922	AUBURN
17272	ZULLINGER	17268	WAYNESBORO	17943	LAVELLE	17921	ASHLAND
17303	ARENDTSVILLE	17307	BIGLERVILLE	17944	LLEWELLYN	17901	POTTSVILLE
17306	BENDERSVILLE	17304	ASPERS	17945	LOCUSTDALE	17921	ASHLAND
17310	CASHTOWN	17353	ORRTANNA	17946	LOST CREEK	17935	GIRARDVILLE
17311	CODORUS	17362	SPRING GROVE	17949	MAHANOY PLANE	17976	SHENANDOAH
17312	CRALEY	17368	WRIGHTSVILLE	17951	MAR LIN	17901	POTTSVILLE
17317	EAST PROSPECT	17368	WRIGHTSVILLE	17952	MARY D	17925	BROCKTON
17318	EMIGSVILLE	17402	YORK	17953	MIDDLEPORT	17959	NEW PHILADELPHIA
17323	FRANKLINTOWN	17019	DILLSBURG	17966	RAVINE	17963	PINE GROVE
17326	GETTYSBURG	17325	GETTYSBURG	17974	SELTZER	17901	POTTSVILLE
17332	HANOVER	17331	HANOVER	17979	SUMMIT STATION	17922	AUBURN
17333	HANOVER	17331	HANOVER	17982	TUSCARORA	17925	BROCKTON
17334	HANOVER	17331	HANOVER	18001	LEHIGH VALLEY	18101	ALLENTOWN
17337	IDAVILLE	17324	GARDNERS	18002	LEHIGH VALLEY	18017	BETHLEHEM
17342	LOGANVILLE	17403	YORK	18010	ACKERMANVILLE	18013	BANGOR
17343	MC KNIGHTSTOWN	17307	BIGLERVILLE	18012	AQUASHICOLA	18071	PALMERTON
17354	PORTERS SIDELING	17362	SPRING GROVE	18016	BETHLEHEM	18018	BETHLEHEM
17355	RAILROAD	17349	NEW FREEDOM	18025	BETHLEHEM	18018	BETHLEHEM
17358	ROSSVILLE	17019	DILLSBURG	18030	BOWMANSTOWN	18071	PALMERTON

PENNSYLVANIA

PENNSYLVANIA

Point ZIP Code		Enclosing Residential ZIP Code		Point ZIP Code		Enclosing Residential ZIP Code	
ZIP	Post Office Name	ZIP	Post Office Name	ZIP	Post Office Name	ZIP	Post Office Name
18039	DURHAM	18930	KINTNERSVILLE	18911	BLOOMING GLEN	18944	PERKASIE
18043	EASTON	18045	EASTON	18912	BUCKINGHAM	18938	NEW HOPE
18044	EASTON	18042	EASTON	18916	DANBORO	18901	DOYLESTOWN
18046	EAST TEXAS	18062	MACUNGIE	18918	EARLINGTON	18969	TELFORD
18050	FLICKSVILLE	18013	BANGOR	18921	FERNDALE	18972	UPPER BLACK EDDY
18060	LIMEPORT	18036	COOPERSBURG	18922	FOREST GROVE	18925	FURLONG
18063	MARTINS CREEK	18040	EASTON	18924	FRANCONIA	18969	TELFORD
18065	NEFFS	18037	COPLAY	18926	GARDENVILLE	18947	PIPERSVILLE
18068	OLD ZIONSVILLE	18092	ZIONSVILLE	18928	HOLICONG	18901	DOYLESTOWN
18079	SLATEDALE	18080	SLATINGTON	18931	LAHASKA	18938	NEW HOPE
18081	SPRINGTOWN	18055	HELLERTOWN	18935	MILFORD SQUARE	18951	QUAKERTOWN
18083	STOCKERTOWN	18040	EASTON	18943	PENNS PARK	18940	NEWTOWN
18084	SUMNEYTOWN	18054	GREEN LANE	18946	PINEVILLE	18940	NEWTOWN
18085	TATAMY	18040	EASTON	18949	PLUMSTEADVILLE	18947	PIPERSVILLE
18086	TREICHLERS	18088	WALNUTPORT	18950	POINT PLEASANT	18947	PIPERSVILLE
18098	EMMAUS	18049	EMMAUS	18953	REVERE	18942	OTTSVILLE
18099	EMMAUS	18049	EMMAUS	18956	RUSHLAND	18925	FURLONG
18105	ALLENTOWN	18101	ALLENTOWN	18957	SALFORD	19438	HARLEYSVILLE
18175	ALLENTOWN	18104	ALLENTOWN	18958	SALFORDVILLE	19438	HARLEYSVILLE
18195	ALLENTOWN	18106	ALLENTOWN	18962	SILVERDALE	18944	PERKASIE
18212	ASHFIELD	18235	LEHIGHTON	18963	SOLEBURY	18938	NEW HOPE
18221	DRIFTON	18224	FREELAND	18968	SPINNERSTOWN	18951	QUAKERTOWN
18223	EBERVALE	18201	HAZLETON	18970	TRUMBAUERSVILLE	18951	QUAKERTOWN
18225	HARLEIGH	18202	HAZLETON	18971	TYLERSPORT	18969	TELFORD
18230	JUNEDALE	18216	BEAVER MEADOWS	18979	WOXALL	19438	HARLEYSVILLE
18231	KELAYRES	18237	MCADOO	18980	WYCOMBE	18940	NEWTOWN
18234	LATTIMER MINES	18202	HAZLETON	18981	ZIONHILL	18951	QUAKERTOWN
18239	MILNESVILLE	18202	HAZLETON	18991	WARMINSTER	18974	WARMINSTER
18241	NUREMBERG	17985	ZION GROVE	19009	BRYN ATHYN	19006	HUNTINGDON VALLEY
18242	ONEIDA	18248	SHEPPTON	19016	CHESTER	19013	CHESTER
18244	PARRYVILLE	18071	PALMERTON	19017	CHESTER HEIGHTS	19061	MARCUS HOOK
18247	SAINT JOHNS	18222	DRUMS	19019	PHILADELPHIA	19116	PHILADELPHIA
18251	SYBERTSVILLE	18249	SUGARLOAF	19028	EDGEMONT	19073	NEWTOWN SQUARE
18254	TRESCKOW	18216	BEAVER MEADOWS	19037	GLEN RIDDLE LIMA	19063	MEDIA
18256	WESTON	18246	ROCK GLEN	19039	GRADYVILLE	19342	GLEN MILLS
18320	ANALOMINK	18301	EAST STROUDSBURG	19048	FORT WASHINGTON	19053	FEASTERVILLE TREVOSE
18323	BUCK HILL FALLS	18326	CRESCO	19049	FORT WASHINGTON	19053	FEASTERVILLE TREVOSE
18335	MARSHALLS CREEK	18301	EAST STROUDSBURG	19052	LENNI	19063	MEDIA
18341	MINISINK HILLS	18301	EAST STROUDSBURG	19058	LEVITTOWN	19055	LEVITTOWN
18342	MOUNTAINHOME	18326	CRESCO	19059	PHILADELPHIA	19055	LEVITTOWN
18348	POCONO LAKE PRESERVE	18347	POCONO LAKE	19065	MEDIA	19063	MEDIA
18349	POCONO MANOR	18301	EAST STROUDSBURG	19080	WAYNE	19087	WAYNE
18351	PORTLAND	18343	MOUNT BETHEL	19088	WAYNE	19087	WAYNE
18356	SHAWNEE ON DELAWARE	18301	EAST STROUDSBURG	19089	WAYNE	19087	WAYNE
18357	SKYTOP	18325	CANADENSIS	19091	MEDIA	19063	MEDIA
18410	CHINCHILLA	18411	CLARKS SUMMIT	19092	PHILADELPHIA	19104	PHILADELPHIA
18413	CLIFFORD	18421	FOREST CITY	19093	PHILADELPHIA	19104	PHILADELPHIA
18416	ELMHURST	18444	MOSCOW	19098	HOLMES	19043	HOLMES
18420	FLEETVILLE	18419	FACTORYVILLE	19101	PHILADELPHIA	19104	PHILADELPHIA
18440	LA PLUME	18414	DALTON	19105	PHILADELPHIA	19107	PHILADELPHIA
18448	OLYPHANT	18447	OLYPHANT	19108	PHILADELPHIA	19107	PHILADELPHIA
18449	ORSON	18439	LAKEWOOD	19109	PHILADELPHIA	19107	PHILADELPHIA
18454	POYNTELLE	18439	LAKEWOOD	19110	PHILADELPHIA	19107	PHILADELPHIA
18457	ROWLAND	18435	LACKAWAXEN	19155	PHILADELPHIA	19114	PHILADELPHIA
18459	SOUTH CANAAN	18436	LAKE ARIEL	19160	PHILADELPHIA	19120	PHILADELPHIA
18471	WAVERLY	18411	CLARKS SUMMIT	19161	PHILADELPHIA	19104	PHILADELPHIA
18473	WHITE MILLS	18431	HONESDALE	19162	PHILADELPHIA	19104	PHILADELPHIA
18501	SCRANTON	18505	SCRANTON	19170	PHILADELPHIA	19104	PHILADELPHIA
18502	SCRANTON	18503	SCRANTON	19171	PHILADELPHIA	19107	PHILADELPHIA
18514	SCRANTON	18503	SCRANTON	19172	PHILADELPHIA	19106	PHILADELPHIA
18515	SCRANTON	18508	SCRANTON	19173	PHILADELPHIA	19103	PHILADELPHIA
18522	SCRANTON	18509	SCRANTON	19175	PHILADELPHIA	19106	PHILADELPHIA
18577	SCRANTON	18512	SCRANTON	19177	PHILADELPHIA	19106	PHILADELPHIA
18601	BEACH HAVEN	18603	BERWICK	19178	PHILADELPHIA	19104	PHILADELPHIA
18602	BEAR CREEK	18702	WILKES BARRE	19181	PHILADELPHIA	19106	PHILADELPHIA
18611	CAMBRA	17814	BENTON	19182	PHILADELPHIA	19106	PHILADELPHIA
18625	LAKE WINOLA	18414	DALTON	19184	PHILADELPHIA	19104	PHILADELPHIA
18626	LAPORTE	17758	MUNCY VALLEY	19187	PHILADELPHIA	19102	PHILADELPHIA
18627	LEHMAN	18708	SHAVERTOWN	19188	PHILADELPHIA	19123	PHILADELPHIA
18653	RANSOM	18411	CLARKS SUMMIT	19191	PHILADELPHIA	19102	PHILADELPHIA
18654	SHAWANESE	18618	HARVEYS LAKE	19192	PHILADELPHIA	19102	PHILADELPHIA
18690	DALLAS	18612	DALLAS	19193	PHILADELPHIA	19104	PHILADELPHIA
18703	WILKES BARRE	18701	WILKES BARRE	19194	PHILADELPHIA	19104	PHILADELPHIA
18710	WILKES BARRE	18701	WILKES BARRE	19195	PHILADELPHIA	19104	PHILADELPHIA
18711	WILKES BARRE	18706	WILKES BARRE	19196	PHILADELPHIA	19104	PHILADELPHIA
18761	WILKES BARRE	18701	WILKES BARRE	19197	PHILADELPHIA	19104	PHILADELPHIA
18762	WILKES BARRE	18702	WILKES BARRE	19244	PHILADELPHIA	19154	PHILADELPHIA
18763	WILKES BARRE	18701	WILKES BARRE	19255	PHILADELPHIA	19154	PHILADELPHIA
18764	WILKES BARRE	18705	WILKES BARRE	19316	BRANDAMORE	19320	COATESVILLE
18765	WILKES BARRE	18706	WILKES BARRE	19318	CHATHAM	19390	WEST GROVE
18766	WILKES BARRE	18701	WILKES BARRE	19331	CONCORDVILLE	19342	GLEN MILLS
18767	WILKES BARRE	18702	WILKES BARRE	19339	CONCORDVILLE	19373	THORNTON
18769	WILKES BARRE	18702	WILKES BARRE	19345	IMMACULATA	19355	MALVERN
18773	WILKES BARRE	18701	WILKES BARRE	19346	KELTON	19390	WEST GROVE
18774	WILKES BARRE	18701	WILKES BARRE	19347	KEMBLESVILLE	19350	LANDENBERG
18813	BROOKLYN	18826	KINGSLEY	19351	LEWISVILLE	19350	LANDENBERG
18814	BURLINGTON	18848	TOWANDA	19353	LIONVILLE	19341	EXTON
18815	CAMPTOWN	18853	WYALUSING	19354	LYNDELL	19335	DOWNINGTOWN
18816	DIMOCK	18844	SPRINGVILLE	19357	MENDENHALL	19348	KENNETT SQUARE
18820	GIBSON	18823	HARFORD	19358	MODENA	19320	COATESVILLE
18827	LANESBORO	18847	SUSQUEHANNA	19360	NEW LONDON	19352	LINCOLN UNIVERSITY
18843	SOUTH MONTROSE	18801	MONTROSE	19366	POCOPSON	19382	WEST CHESTER
18910	BEDMINSTER	18944	PERKASIE	19367	POMEROY	19365	PARKESBURG

PENNSYLVANIA

Point ZIP Code	Post Office Name	Enclosing Residential ZIP Code	Post Office Name
19369	SADSBURYVILLE	19365	PARKESBURG
19371	SUPLEE	19344	HONEY BROOK
19375	UNIONVILLE	19348	KENNETT SQUARE
19376	WAGONTOWN	19320	COATESVILLE
19381	WEST CHESTER	19380	WEST CHESTER
19395	WESTTOWN	19382	WEST CHESTER
19397	SOUTHEASTERN	19087	WAYNE
19398	SOUTHEASTERN	19087	WAYNE
19399	SOUTHEASTERN	19087	WAYNE
19404	NORRISTOWN	19403	NORRISTOWN
19407	AUDUBON	19403	NORRISTOWN
19408	EAGLEVILLE	19403	NORRISTOWN
19409	FAIRVIEW VILLAGE	19403	NORRISTOWN
19415	EAGLEVILLE	19403	NORRISTOWN
19420	ARCOLA	19426	COLLEGEVILLE
19421	BIRCHRUNVILLE	19425	CHESTER SPRINGS
19423	CEDARS	19426	COLLEGEVILLE
19424	BLUE BELL	19422	BLUE BELL
19429	CONSHOHOCKEN	19428	CONSHOHOCKEN
19430	CREAMERY	19473	SCHWENKSVILLE
19432	DEVAULT	19355	MALVERN
19437	GWYNEDD VALLEY	19002	AMBLER
19441	HARLEYSVILLE	19438	HARLEYSVILLE
19442	KIMBERTON	19460	PHOENIXVILLE
19443	KULPSVILLE	19446	LANSDALE
19450	LEDERACH	19438	HARLEYSVILLE
19451	MAINLAND	19438	HARLEYSVILLE
19455	NORTH WALES	18936	MONTGOMERYVILLE
19456	OAKS	19460	PHOENIXVILLE
19457	PARKER FORD	19475	SPRING CITY
19470	SAINT PETERS	19520	ELVERSON
19472	SASSAMANSVILLE	19525	GILBERTSVILLE
19474	SKIPPACK	19426	COLLEGEVILLE
19478	SPRING MOUNT	19473	SCHWENKSVILLE
19480	UWCHLAND	19425	CHESTER SPRINGS
19481	VALLEY FORGE	19460	PHOENIXVILLE
19482	VALLEY FORGE	19460	PHOENIXVILLE
19483	VALLEY FORGE	19460	PHOENIXVILLE
19484	VALLEY FORGE	19406	KING OF PRUSSIA
19485	VALLEY FORGE	19406	KING OF PRUSSIA
19486	WEST POINT	19446	LANSDALE
19487	KING OF PRUSSIA	19462	PLYMOUTH MEETING
19489	NORRISTOWN	19462	PLYMOUTH MEETING
19490	WORCESTER	19446	LANSDALE
19493	VALLEY FORGE	19355	MALVERN
19494	VALLEY FORGE	19355	MALVERN
19495	VALLEY FORGE	19355	MALVERN
19496	VALLEY FORGE	19355	MALVERN
19511	BOWERS	19539	MERTZTOWN
19516	CENTERPORT	19541	MOHRSVILLE
19519	EARLVILLE	19518	DOUGLASSVILLE
19523	GEIGERTOWN	19508	BIRDSBORO
19535	LIMEKILN	19547	OLEY
19536	LYON STATION	19522	FLEETWOOD
19538	MAXATAWNY	19530	KUTZTOWN
19542	MONOCACY STATION	19508	BIRDSBORO
19544	MOUNT AETNA	17087	RICHLAND
19545	NEW BERLINVILLE	19512	BOYERTOWN
19548	PINE FORGE	19512	BOYERTOWN
19550	REHRERSBURG	19507	BETHEL
19554	SHARTLESVILLE	19506	BERNVILLE
19559	STRAUSSTOWN	19506	BERNVILLE
19564	VIRGINVILLE	19530	KUTZTOWN
19603	READING	19604	READING
19612	READING	19604	READING
19640	READING	19605	READING
02801	ADAMSVILLE	02837	LITTLE COMPTON
02802	ALBION	02865	LINCOLN
02823	FISKEVILLE	02831	HOPE
02824	FORESTDALE	02896	NORTH SMITHFIELD
02826	GLENDALE	02858	OAKLAND
02829	HARMONY	02814	CHEPACHET
02862	PAWTUCKET	02860	PAWTUCKET
02873	ROCKVILLE	02832	HOPE VALLEY
02875	SHANNOCK	02812	CAROLINA
02876	SLATERSVILLE	02896	NORTH SMITHFIELD
02880	WAKEFIELD	02879	WAKEFIELD
02883	PEACE DALE	02879	WAKEFIELD
02887	WARWICK	02886	WARWICK
02901	PROVIDENCE	02903	PROVIDENCE
02902	PROVIDENCE	02903	PROVIDENCE
02940	PROVIDENCE	02904	PROVIDENCE
29002	BALLENTINE	29063	IRMO
29041	DAVIS STATION	29102	MANNING
29062	HORATIO	29128	REMBERT
29071	LEXINGTON	29072	LEXINGTON
29074	LIBERTY HILL	29058	HEATH SPRINGS
29079	LYDIA	29550	HARTSVILLE
29106	MONTICELLO	29015	BLAIR
29116	ORANGEBURG	29115	ORANGEBURG
29122	PEAK	29075	LITTLE MOUNTAIN
29132	RION	29180	WINNSBORO
29143	SARDINIA	29051	GABLE

SOUTH CAROLINA

Point ZIP Code	Post Office Name	Enclosing Residential ZIP Code	Post Office Name
29147	STATE PARK	29150	SUMTER
29151	SUMTER	29150	SUMTER
29171	WEST COLUMBIA	29169	WEST COLUMBIA
29176	WHITE OAK	29180	WINNSBORO
29177	WHITE ROCK	29036	CHAPIN
29202	COLUMBIA	29201	COLUMBIA
29211	COLUMBIA	29201	COLUMBIA
29214	COLUMBIA	29201	COLUMBIA
29215	COLUMBIA	29201	COLUMBIA
29216	COLUMBIA	29201	COLUMBIA
29217	COLUMBIA	29201	COLUMBIA
29218	COLUMBIA	29201	COLUMBIA
29219	COLUMBIA	29223	COLUMBIA
29220	COLUMBIA	29201	COLUMBIA
29221	COLUMBIA	29210	COLUMBIA
29222	COLUMBIA	29201	COLUMBIA
29223	COLUMBIA	29223	COLUMBIA
29224	COLUMBIA	29208	COLUMBIA
29225	COLUMBIA	29210	COLUMBIA
29226	COLUMBIA	29210	COLUMBIA
29227	COLUMBIA	29210	COLUMBIA
29228	COLUMBIA	29201	COLUMBIA
29230	COLUMBIA	29203	COLUMBIA
29240	COLUMBIA	29204	COLUMBIA
29250	COLUMBIA	29205	COLUMBIA
29260	COLUMBIA	29206	COLUMBIA
29290	COLUMBIA	29209	COLUMBIA
29292	COLUMBIA	29201	COLUMBIA
29304	SPARTANBURG	29306	SPARTANBURG
29305	SPARTANBURG	29303	SPARTANBURG
29318	SPARTANBURG	29307	SPARTANBURG
29319	SPARTANBURG	29306	SPARTANBURG
29320	ARCADIA	29301	SPARTANBURG
29324	CLIFTON	29307	SPARTANBURG
29329	CONVERSE	29307	SPARTANBURG
29331	CROSS ANCHOR	29335	ENOREE
29333	DRAYTON	29307	SPARTANBURG
29336	FAIRFOREST	29301	SPARTANBURG
29338	FINGERVILLE	29349	INMAN
29342	GAFFNEY	29341	GAFFNEY
29346	GLENDALE	29307	SPARTANBURG
29348	GRAMLING	29349	INMAN
29364	LOCKHART	29379	UNION
29368	MAYO	29323	CHESNEE
29373	PACOLET MILLS	29372	PACOLET
29375	REIDVILLE	29388	WOODRUFF
29377	STARTEX	29385	WELLFORD
29378	UNA	29301	SPARTANBURG
29386	WHITE STONE	29302	SPARTANBURG
29390	DUNCAN	29334	DUNCAN
29391	DUNCAN	29334	DUNCAN
29395	JONESVILLE	29353	JONESVILLE
29402	CHARLESTON	29401	CHARLESTON
29409	CHARLESTON	29403	CHARLESTON
29410	NORTH CHARLESTON	29406	CHARLESTON
29413	CHARLESTON	29403	CHARLESTON
29415	NORTH CHARLESTON	29405	NORTH CHARLESTON
29416	CHARLESTON	29404	CHARLESTON AFB
29417	CHARLESTON	29407	CHARLESTON
29419	NORTH CHARLESTON	29406	CHARLESTON
29422	CHARLESTON	29412	CHARLESTON
29423	CHARLESTON	29418	NORTH CHARLESTON
29424	CHARLESTON	29401	CHARLESTON
29425	CHARLESTON	29403	CHARLESTON
29430	BETHERA	29453	JAMESTOWN
29433	CANADYS	29474	ROUND O
29439	FOLLY BEACH	29412	CHARLESTON
29442	GEORGETOWN	29440	GEORGETOWN
29447	GROVER	29477	SAINT GEORGE
29452	JACKSONBORO	29446	GREEN POND
29457	JOHNS ISLAND	29455	JOHNS ISLAND
29465	MOUNT PLEASANT	29464	MOUNT PLEASANT
29476	RUSSELLVILLE	29479	SAINT STEPHEN
29484	SUMMERVILLE	29483	SUMMERVILLE
29493	WILLIAMS	29475	RUFFIN
29502	FLORENCE	29501	FLORENCE
29503	FLORENCE	29501	FLORENCE
29504	FLORENCE	29505	FLORENCE
29519	CENTENARY	29571	MARION
29528	CONWAY	29526	CONWAY
29551	HARTSVILLE	29550	HARTSVILLE
29573	MINTURN	29536	DILLON
29578	MYRTLE BEACH	29577	MYRTLE BEACH
29587	MYRTLE BEACH	29582	NORTH MYRTLE BEACH
29589	RAINS	29571	MARION
29594	TATUM	29570	MC COLL
29597	NORTH MYRTLE BEACH	29582	NORTH MYRTLE BEACH
29598	NORTH MYRTLE BEACH	29582	NORTH MYRTLE BEACH
29602	GREENVILLE	29601	GREENVILLE
29603	GREENVILLE	29601	GREENVILLE
29604	GREENVILLE	29605	GREENVILLE
29606	GREENVILLE	29607	GREENVILLE
29608	GREENVILLE	29609	GREENVILLE
29610	GREENVILLE	29611	GREENVILLE

SOUTH CAROLINA   **TENNESSEE**

Point ZIP Code		Enclosing Residential ZIP Code		Point ZIP Code		Enclosing Residential ZIP Code	
ZIP	Post Office Name	ZIP	Post Office Name	ZIP	Post Office Name	ZIP	Post Office Name
29612	GREENVILLE	29651	GREER	24209	BRISTOL	37620	BRISTOL
29614	GREENVILLE	29609	GREENVILLE	37011	ANTIOCH	37013	ANTIOCH
29616	GREENVILLE	29615	GREENVILLE	37024	BRENTWOOD	37027	BRENTWOOD
29622	ANDERSON	29621	ANDERSON	37041	CLARKSVILLE	37040	CLARKSVILLE
29623	ANDERSON	29621	ANDERSON	37044	CLARKSVILLE	37040	CLARKSVILLE
29633	CLEMSON	29631	CLEMSON	37056	DICKSON	37055	DICKSON
29634	CLEMSON	29632	CLEMSON	37063	FOSTERVILLE	37020	BELL BUCKLE
29636	CONESTEE	29605	GREENVILLE	37065	FRANKLIN	37064	FRANKLIN
29641	EASLEY	29640	EASLEY	37068	FRANKLIN	37064	FRANKLIN
29647	GREENWOOD	29653	HODGES	37070	GOODLETTSVILLE	37072	GOODLETTSVILLE
29648	GREENWOOD	29646	GREENWOOD	37071	GLADEVILLE	37122	MOUNT JULIET
29652	GREER	29650	GREER	37077	HENDERSONVILLE	37075	HENDERSONVILLE
29656	LA FRANCE	29670	PENDLETON	37088	LEBANON	37087	LEBANON
29665	NEWRY	29672	SENECA	37089	LA VERGNE	37086	LA VERGNE
29675	RICHLAND	29693	WESTMINSTER	37111	MC MINNVILLE	37110	MC MINNVILLE
29677	SANDY SPRINGS	29670	PENDLETON	37116	MADISON	37115	MADISON
29679	SENECA	29678	SENECA	37119	MITCHELLVILLE	37148	PORTLAND
29683	SLATER	29661	MARIETTA	37121	MOUNT JULIET	37122	MOUNT JULIET
29695	HODGES	29653	HODGES	37131	MURFREESBORO	37129	MURFREESBORO
29698	GREENVILLE	29334	DUNCAN	37133	MURFREESBORO	37130	MURFREESBORO
29703	BOWLING GREEN	29710	CLOVER	37136	NORENE	37184	WATERTOWN
29716	FORT MILL	29715	FORT MILL	37152	RIDGETOP	37073	GREENBRIER
29721	LANCASTER	29720	LANCASTER	37155	SAINT BETHLEHEM	37043	CLARKSVILLE
29722	LANCASTER	29720	LANCASTER	37161	SHELBYVILLE	37160	SHELBYVILLE
29724	LANDO	29729	RICHBURG	37162	SHELBYVILLE	37160	SHELBYVILLE
29731	ROCK HILL	29730	ROCK HILL	37165	SLAYDEN	37051	CUMBERLAND FURNACE
29734	ROCK HILL	29730	ROCK HILL	37202	NASHVILLE	37214	NASHVILLE
29744	VAN WYCK	29720	LANCASTER	37222	NASHVILLE	37211	NASHVILLE
29802	AIKEN	29801	AIKEN	37224	NASHVILLE	37214	NASHVILLE
29804	AIKEN	29803	AIKEN	37227	NASHVILLE	37214	NASHVILLE
29813	HILDA	29812	BARNWELL	37229	NASHVILLE	37214	NASHVILLE
29816	BATH	29851	WARRENVILLE	37230	NASHVILLE	37203	NASHVILLE
29822	CLEARWATER	29842	BEECH ISLAND	37232	NASHVILLE	37212	NASHVILLE
29826	ELKO	29853	WILLISTON	37234	NASHVILLE	37203	NASHVILLE
29834	LANGLEY	29851	WARRENVILLE	37235	NASHVILLE	37240	NASHVILLE
29839	MONTMORENCI	29803	AIKEN	37236	NASHVILLE	37203	NASHVILLE
29844	PARKSVILLE	29845	PLUM BRANCH	37238	NASHVILLE	37201	NASHVILLE
29846	SYCAMORE	29849	ULMER	37239	NASHVILLE	37219	NASHVILLE
29850	VAUCLUSE	29801	AIKEN	37241	NASHVILLE	37214	NASHVILLE
29861	NORTH AUGUSTA	29841	NORTH AUGUSTA	37242	NASHVILLE	37219	NASHVILLE
29901	BEAUFORT	29902	BEAUFORT	37243	NASHVILLE	37203	NASHVILLE
29903	BEAUFORT	29906	BEAUFORT	37244	NASHVILLE	37219	NASHVILLE
29904	BEAUFORT	29906	BEAUFORT	37245	NASHVILLE	37219	NASHVILLE
29905	BEAUFORT	29902	BEAUFORT	37246	NASHVILLE	37203	NASHVILLE
29912	COOSAWATCHIE	29936	RIDGELAND	37247	NASHVILLE	37216	NASHVILLE
29913	CROCKETVILLE	29924	HAMPTON	37248	NASHVILLE	37219	NASHVILLE
29914	DALE	29940	SEABROOK	37249	NASHVILLE	37217	NASHVILLE
29915	DAUFUSKIE ISLAND	29928	HILTON HEAD ISLAND	37250	NASHVILLE	37214	NASHVILLE
29921	FURMAN	29918	ESTILL	37304	BAKEWELL	37373	SALE CREEK
29923	GIFFORD	29932	LURAY	37314	COKERCREEK	37385	TELLICO PLAINS
29925	HILTON HEAD ISLAND	29926	HILTON HEAD ISLAND	37315	COLLEGEDALE	37363	OOLTEWAH
29931	LOBECO	29940	SEABROOK	37316	CONASAUGA	37362	OLDFORT
29933	MILEY	29924	HAMPTON	37320	CLEVELAND	37311	CLEVELAND
29938	HILTON HEAD ISLAND	29928	HILTON HEAD ISLAND	37326	DUCKTOWN	37317	COPPERHILL
29939	SCOTIA	29918	ESTILL	37349	MANCHESTER	37355	MANCHESTER
57041	LYONS	57003	BALTIC	37351	LUPTON CITY	37415	CHATTANOOGA
57061	SINAI	57006	BROOKINGS	37364	CLEVELAND	37311	CLEVELAND
57079	YANKTON	57078	YANKTON	37371	ATHENS	37303	ATHENS
57101	SIOUX FALLS	57104	SIOUX FALLS	37378	SMARTT	37110	MC MINNVILLE
57109	SIOUX FALLS	57105	SIOUX FALLS	37382	SUMMITVILLE	37357	MORRISON
57117	SIOUX FALLS	57104	SIOUX FALLS	37384	SODDY DAISY	37379	SODDY DAISY
57118	SIOUX FALLS	57104	SIOUX FALLS	37389	ARNOLD AFB	37355	MANCHESTER
57186	SIOUX FALLS	57104	SIOUX FALLS	37394	VIOLA	37357	MORRISON
57188	SIOUX FALLS	57104	SIOUX FALLS	37401	CHATTANOOGA	37421	CHATTANOOGA
57189	SIOUX FALLS	57104	SIOUX FALLS	37414	CHATTANOOGA	37411	CHATTANOOGA
57192	SIOUX FALLS	57104	SIOUX FALLS	37422	CHATTANOOGA	37421	CHATTANOOGA
57193	SIOUX FALLS	57104	SIOUX FALLS	37424	CHATTANOOGA	37421	CHATTANOOGA
57194	SIOUX FALLS	57104	SIOUX FALLS	37450	CHATTANOOGA	37402	CHATTANOOGA
57195	SIOUX FALLS	57104	SIOUX FALLS	37501	MEMPHIS	38118	MEMPHIS
57196	SIOUX FALLS	57110	SIOUX FALLS	37602	JOHNSON CITY	37604	JOHNSON CITY
57198	SIOUX FALLS	57030	GARRETSON	37605	JOHNSON CITY	37601	JOHNSON CITY
57214	BADGER	57212	ARLINGTON	37621	BRISTOL	37620	BRISTOL
57253	MILBANK	57252	MILBANK	37625	BRISTOL	37620	BRISTOL
57326	CHAMBERLAIN	57325	CHAMBERLAIN	37644	ELIZABETHTON	37643	ELIZABETHTON
57346	STEPHAN	57345	HIGHMORE	37662	KINGSPORT	37660	KINGSPORT
57365	OACOMA	57569	RELIANCE	37682	MILLIGAN COLLEGE	37601	JOHNSON CITY
57367	PICKSTOWN	57356	LAKE ANDES	37684	MOUNTAIN HOME	37604	JOHNSON CITY
57399	HURON	57350	HURON	37699	PINEY FLATS	37686	PINEY FLATS
57402	ABERDEEN	57401	ABERDEEN	37707	ARTHUR	37724	CUMBERLAND GAP
57439	FERNEY	57434	CONDE	37717	CLINTON	37716	CLINTON
57563	OKREEK	57555	MISSION	37719	COALFIELD	37840	OLIVER SPRINGS
57570	ROSEBUD	57572	SAINT FRANCIS	37730	EAGAN	37715	CLAIRFIELD
57621	BULLHEAD	57642	MC LAUGHLIN	37732	ELGIN	37852	ROBBINS
57636	LANTRY	57633	ISABEL	37733	RUGBY	37852	ROBBINS
57639	LITTLE EAGLE	57642	MC LAUGHLIN	37744	GREENEVILLE	37743	GREENEVILLE
57652	RIDGEVIEW	57625	EAGLE BUTTE	37773	LONE MOUNTAIN	37825	NEW TAZEWELL
57659	WALKER	57642	MC LAUGHLIN	37802	MARYVILLE	37801	MARYVILLE
57661	WHITEHORSE	57625	EAGLE BUTTE	37815	MORRISTOWN	37813	MORRISTOWN
57709	RAPID CITY	57701	RAPID CITY	37816	MORRISTOWN	37813	MORRISTOWN
57764	OGLALA	57770	PINE RIDGE	37822	NEWPORT	37821	NEWPORT
57773	PRINGLE	57730	CUSTER	37824	NEW TAZEWELL	37825	NEW TAZEWELL
57776	REDIG	57720	BUFFALO	37828	NORRIS	37705	ANDERSONVILLE
24203	BRISTOL	37620	BRISTOL	37831	OAK RIDGE	37830	OAK RIDGE

TENNESSEE   **TEXAS**

Point ZIP Code		Enclosing Residential ZIP Code		Point ZIP Code		Enclosing Residential ZIP Code	
ZIP	Post Office Name	ZIP	Post Office Name	ZIP	Post Office Name	ZIP	Post Office Name
37845	PETROS	37840	OLIVER SPRINGS	38393	CHEWALLA	38367	RAMER
37851	PRUDEN	37715	CLAIRFIELD	38402	COLUMBIA	38401	COLUMBIA
37864	SEVIERVILLE	37862	SEVIERVILLE	38455	ELKTON	38449	ARDMORE
37867	SHAWANEE	37752	HARROGATE	38502	COOKEVILLE	38501	COOKEVILLE
37868	PIGEON FORGE	37863	PIGEON FORGE	38503	COOKEVILLE	38501	COOKEVILLE
37901	KNOXVILLE	37902	KNOXVILLE	38550	CAMPAIGN	38581	ROCK ISLAND
37927	KNOXVILLE	37917	KNOXVILLE	38557	CROSSVILLE	38555	CROSSVILLE
37928	KNOXVILLE	37918	KNOXVILLE	73301	AUSTIN	78741	AUSTIN
37929	KNOXVILLE	37902	KNOXVILLE	73344	AUSTIN	78744	AUSTIN
37930	KNOXVILLE	37923	KNOXVILLE	75011	CARROLLTON	75006	CARROLLTON
37933	KNOXVILLE	37922	KNOXVILLE	75014	IRVING	75062	IRVING
37939	KNOXVILLE	37919	KNOXVILLE	75015	IRVING	75061	IRVING
37940	KNOXVILLE	37920	KNOXVILLE	75016	IRVING	75062	IRVING
37950	KNOXVILLE	37909	KNOXVILLE	75017	IRVING	75060	IRVING
37990	KNOXVILLE	37909	KNOXVILLE	75026	PLANO	75075	PLANO
37995	KNOXVILLE	37909	KNOXVILLE	75027	FLOWER MOUND	75067	LEWISVILLE
37996	KNOXVILLE	37916	KNOXVILLE	75029	LEWISVILLE	75057	LEWISVILLE
37997	KNOXVILLE	37915	KNOXVILLE	75030	ROWLETT	75088	ROWLETT
37998	KNOXVILLE	37920	KNOXVILLE	75037	IRVING	75061	IRVING
38007	BOGOTA	38024	DYERSBURG	75044	GARLAND	75044	GARLAND
38010	BRADEN	38068	SOMERVILLE	75045	GARLAND	75040	GARLAND
38014	BRUNSWICK	38002	ARLINGTON	75046	GARLAND	75041	GARLAND
38021	CROCKETT MILLS	38034	FRIENDSHIP	75047	GARLAND	75043	GARLAND
38025	DYERSBURG	38024	DYERSBURG	75049	GARLAND	75051	GRAND PRAIRIE
38027	COLLIERVILLE	38017	COLLIERVILLE	75053	GRAND PRAIRIE	75052	GRAND PRAIRIE
38029	ELLENDALE	38134	MEMPHIS	75054	GRAND PRAIRIE	75080	RICHARDSON
38036	GALLAWAY	38068	SOMERVILLE	75083	RICHARDSON	75081	RICHARDSON
38045	LACONIA	38068	SOMERVILLE	75085	RICHARDSON	75074	PLANO
38046	LA GRANGE	38057	MOSCOW	75086	PLANO	75090	SHERMAN
38047	LENOX	38024	DYERSBURG	75091	SHERMAN	75009	CELINA
38048	MACON	38060	OAKLAND	75097	WESTON	75019	COPPELL
38050	MAURY CITY	38034	FRIENDSHIP	75099	COPPELL	75119	ENNIS
38054	MILLINGTON	38053	MILLINGTON	75101	BARDWELL	75104	CEDAR HILL
38055	MILLINGTON	38053	MILLINGTON	75106	CEDAR HILL	75161	TERRELL
38070	TIGRETT	38059	NEWBERN	75118	ELMO	75119	ENNIS
38071	TIPTON	38004	ATOKA	75120	ENNIS	75173	NEVADA
38074	BOLIVAR	38008	BOLIVAR	75121	COPEVILLE	75115	DESOTO
38077	WYNNBURG	38080	RIDGELY	75123	DESOTO	75189	ROYSE CITY
38083	MILLINGTON	38053	MILLINGTON	75132	FATE	75137	DUNCANVILLE
38088	CORDOVA	38018	CORDOVA	75138	DUNCANVILLE	75110	CORSICANA
38101	MEMPHIS	38126	MEMPHIS	75151	CORSICANA	75158	SCURRY
38124	MEMPHIS	38117	MEMPHIS	75157	ROSSER	75173	NEVADA
38129	MEMPHIS	38103	MEMPHIS	75164	JOSEPHINE	75165	WAXAHACHIE
38130	MEMPHIS	38118	MEMPHIS	75168	WAXAHACHIE	75149	MESQUITE
38136	MEMPHIS	38106	MEMPHIS	75185	MESQUITE	75149	MESQUITE
38137	MEMPHIS	38117	MEMPHIS	75187	MESQUITE	75206	DALLAS
38142	MEMPHIS	38109	MEMPHIS	75221	DALLAS	75208	DALLAS
38145	MEMPHIS	38103	MEMPHIS	75222	DALLAS	75202	DALLAS
38146	MEMPHIS	38103	MEMPHIS	75242	DALLAS	75235	DALLAS
38147	MEMPHIS	38103	MEMPHIS	75245	DALLAS	75202	DALLAS
38148	MEMPHIS	38103	MEMPHIS	75250	DALLAS	75207	DALLAS
38151	MEMPHIS	38112	MEMPHIS	75258	DALLAS	75208	DALLAS
38157	MEMPHIS	38117	MEMPHIS	75260	DALLAS	75208	DALLAS
38159	MEMPHIS	38103	MEMPHIS	75262	DALLAS	75208	DALLAS
38161	MEMPHIS	38134	MEMPHIS	75263	DALLAS	75208	DALLAS
38163	MEMPHIS	38103	MEMPHIS	75264	DALLAS	75208	DALLAS
38165	MEMPHIS	38126	MEMPHIS	75265	DALLAS	75208	DALLAS
38166	MEMPHIS	38120	MEMPHIS	75266	DALLAS	75208	DALLAS
38167	MEMPHIS	38127	MEMPHIS	75267	DALLAS	75208	DALLAS
38168	MEMPHIS	38128	MEMPHIS	75270	DALLAS	75202	DALLAS
38173	MEMPHIS	38103	MEMPHIS	75275	DALLAS	75205	DALLAS
38174	MEMPHIS	38104	MEMPHIS	75277	DALLAS	75215	DALLAS
38175	MEMPHIS	38115	MEMPHIS	75283	DALLAS	75208	DALLAS
38177	MEMPHIS	38117	MEMPHIS	75284	DALLAS	75208	DALLAS
38181	MEMPHIS	38118	MEMPHIS	75285	DALLAS	75208	DALLAS
38182	MEMPHIS	38112	MEMPHIS	75286	DALLAS	75208	DALLAS
38183	GERMANTOWN	38138	GERMANTOWN	75301	DALLAS	75237	DALLAS
38184	MEMPHIS	38134	MEMPHIS	75303	DALLAS	75217	DALLAS
38186	MEMPHIS	38116	MEMPHIS	75310	DALLAS	75202	DALLAS
38187	MEMPHIS	38119	MEMPHIS	75312	DALLAS	75208	DALLAS
38188	MEMPHIS	38119	MEMPHIS	75313	DALLAS	75201	DALLAS
38190	MEMPHIS	38109	MEMPHIS	75315	DALLAS	75215	DALLAS
38193	MEMPHIS	38115	MEMPHIS	75320	DALLAS	75208	DALLAS
38194	MEMPHIS	38131	MEMPHIS	75323	DALLAS	75208	DALLAS
38195	MEMPHIS	38118	MEMPHIS	75326	DALLAS	75208	DALLAS
38197	MEMPHIS	38120	MEMPHIS	75336	DALLAS	75253	DALLAS
38223	COMO	38242	PARIS	75339	DALLAS	75216	DALLAS
38235	MC LEMORESVILLE	38258	TREZEVANT	75342	DALLAS	75212	DALLAS
38254	SAMBURG	38232	HORNBEAK	75353	DALLAS	75217	DALLAS
38271	WOODLAND MILLS	38261	UNION CITY	75354	DALLAS	75220	DALLAS
38281	UNION CITY	38261	UNION CITY	75355	DALLAS	75238	DALLAS
38302	JACKSON	38301	JACKSON	75356	DALLAS	75247	DALLAS
38303	JACKSON	38301	JACKSON	75357	DALLAS	75228	DALLAS
38308	JACKSON	38301	JACKSON	75359	DALLAS	75214	DALLAS
38314	JACKSON	38301	JACKSON	75360	DALLAS	75206	DALLAS
38324	CLARKSBURG	38390	YUMA	75363	DALLAS	75208	DALLAS
38331	EATON	38382	TRENTON	75364	DALLAS	75208	DALLAS
38336	FRUITVALE	38006	BELLS	75367	DALLAS	75230	DALLAS
38338	GIBSON	38343	HUMBOLDT	75368	DALLAS	75063	IRVING
38346	IDLEWILD	38316	BRADFORD	75369	DALLAS	75208	DALLAS
38365	PICKWICK DAM	38326	COUNCE	75370	DALLAS	75287	DALLAS
38378	SPRING CREEK	38305	JACKSON	75371	DALLAS	75246	DALLAS
38389	YORKVILLE	38059	NEWBERN	75372	DALLAS	75206	DALLAS
				75373	DALLAS	75208	DALLAS

Point ZIP Code		Enclosing Residential ZIP Code		Point ZIP Code		Enclosing Residential ZIP Code	
ZIP	Post Office Name	ZIP	Post Office Name	ZIP	Post Office Name	ZIP	Post Office Name
75374	DALLAS	75243	DALLAS	75958	MARTINSVILLE	75961	NACOGDOCHES
75376	DALLAS	75224	DALLAS	75963	NACOGDOCHES	75965	NACOGDOCHES
75378	DALLAS	75229	DALLAS	75978	WODEN	75961	NACOGDOCHES
75379	DALLAS	75244	DALLAS	75990	WOODVILLE	75979	WOODVILLE
75380	DALLAS	75240	DALLAS	76003	ARLINGTON	76017	ARLINGTON
75381	DALLAS	75234	DALLAS	76004	ARLINGTON	76010	ARLINGTON
75382	DALLAS	75231	DALLAS	76005	ARLINGTON	76011	ARLINGTON
75386	DALLAS	75208	DALLAS	76007	ARLINGTON	76010	ARLINGTON
75387	DALLAS	75236	DALLAS	76061	LILLIAN	76009	ALVARADO
75388	DALLAS	75201	DALLAS	76068	MINERAL WELLS	76067	MINERAL WELLS
75389	DALLAS	75042	GARLAND	76094	ARLINGTON	76013	ARLINGTON
75390	DALLAS	75218	DALLAS	76095	BEDFORD	76021	BEDFORD
75391	DALLAS	75254	DALLAS	76096	ARLINGTON	76018	ARLINGTON
75392	DALLAS	75208	DALLAS	76097	BURLESON	76028	BURLESON
75393	DALLAS	75218	DALLAS	76098	AZLE	76020	AZLE
75394	DALLAS	75218	DALLAS	76099	GRAPEVINE	76051	GRAPEVINE
75395	DALLAS	75201	DALLAS	76101	FORT WORTH	76102	FORT WORTH
75396	DALLAS	75211	DALLAS	76113	FORT WORTH	76102	FORT WORTH
75397	DALLAS	75208	DALLAS	76121	FORT WORTH	76116	FORT WORTH
75398	DALLAS	75211	DALLAS	76124	FORT WORTH	76112	FORT WORTH
75403	GREENVILLE	75401	GREENVILLE	76130	FORT WORTH	76109	FORT WORTH
75404	GREENVILLE	75402	GREENVILLE	76136	FORT WORTH	76179	FORT WORTH
75413	BAILEY	75452	LEONARD	76147	FORT WORTH	76107	FORT WORTH
75425	CHICOTA	75486	SUMNER	76161	FORT WORTH	76106	FORT WORTH
75429	COMMERCE	75428	COMMERCE	76162	FORT WORTH	76133	FORT WORTH
75434	CUNNINGHAM	75435	DEPORT	76163	FORT WORTH	76133	FORT WORTH
75441	ENLOE	75432	COOPER	76164	FORT WORTH	76106	FORT WORTH
75443	GOBER	75452	LEONARD	76181	FORT WORTH	76180	NORTH RICHLAND HILLS
75444	GOLDEN	75410	ALBA	76182	NORTH RICHLAND HILLS	76180	NORTH RICHLAND HILLS
75456	MOUNT PLEASANT	75455	MOUNT PLEASANT	76185	FORT WORTH	76109	FORT WORTH
75458	MERIT	75423	CELESTE	76191	FORT WORTH	76102	FORT WORTH
75461	PARIS	75460	PARIS	76192	FORT WORTH	76179	FORT WORTH
75475	RANDOLPH	75418	BONHAM	76193	FORT WORTH	76102	FORT WORTH
75483	SULPHUR SPRINGS	75482	SULPHUR SPRINGS	76195	FORT WORTH	76102	FORT WORTH
75485	WESTMINSTER	75409	ANNA	76196	FORT WORTH	76102	FORT WORTH
75489	TOM BEAN	75090	SHERMAN	76197	FORT WORTH	76102	FORT WORTH
75504	TEXARKANA	75501	TEXARKANA	76198	FORT WORTH	76102	FORT WORTH
75505	TEXARKANA	75501	TEXARKANA	76199	FORT WORTH	76102	FORT WORTH
75507	TEXARKANA	75501	TEXARKANA	76202	DENTON	76201	DENTON
75562	KILDARE	75563	LINDEN	76203	DENTON	76201	DENTON
75564	LODI	75657	JEFFERSON	76204	DENTON	76201	DENTON
75565	MC LEOD	75555	BIVINS	76206	DENTON	76201	DENTON
75573	REDWATER	75567	MAUD	76241	GAINESVILLE	76240	GAINESVILLE
75606	LONGVIEW	75602	LONGVIEW	76244	KELLER	76248	KELLER
75607	LONGVIEW	75602	LONGVIEW	76246	GREENWOOD	76234	DECATUR
75608	LONGVIEW	75605	LONGVIEW	76253	MYRA	76252	MUENSTER
75615	LONGVIEW	75602	LONGVIEW	76267	SLIDELL	76234	DECATUR
75636	CASON	75638	DAINGERFIELD	76268	SOUTHMAYD	75092	SHERMAN
75637	CLAYTON	75633	CARTHAGE	76299	ROANOKE	76262	ROANOKE
75641	EASTON	75603	LONGVIEW	76307	WICHITA FALLS	76301	WICHITA FALLS
75642	ELYSIAN FIELDS	75672	MARSHALL	76352	BLUEGROVE	76365	HENRIETTA
75653	HENDERSON	75654	HENDERSON	76369	KAMAY	76367	IOWA PARK
75658	JOINERVILLE	75652	HENDERSON	76370	MEGARGEL	76366	HOLLIDAY
75659	JONESVILLE	75692	WASKOM	76385	VERNON	76384	VERNON
75660	JUDSON	75605	LONGVIEW	76439	DENNIS	76087	WEATHERFORD
75663	KILGORE	75662	KILGORE	76452	ENERGY	76455	GUSTINE
75666	LAIRD HILL	75662	KILGORE	76461	LINGLEVILLE	76401	STEPHENVILLE
75671	MARSHALL	75670	MARSHALL	76465	MORGAN MILL	76433	BLUFF DALE
75680	MINDEN	75654	HENDERSON	76466	OLDEN	76448	EASTLAND
75682	NEW LONDON	75684	OVERTON	76467	PALUXY	76433	BLUFF DALE
75685	PANOLA	75639	DE BERRY	76468	PROCTOR	76446	DUBLIN
75688	SCOTTSVILLE	75672	MARSHALL	76469	PUTNAM	79504	BAIRD
75694	WOODLAWN	75670	MARSHALL	76481	SOUTH BEND	76450	GRAHAM
75710	TYLER	75702	TYLER	76485	PEASTER	76088	WEATHERFORD
75711	TYLER	75701	TYLER	76503	TEMPLE	76501	TEMPLE
75712	TYLER	75702	TYLER	76505	TEMPLE	76501	TEMPLE
75713	TYLER	75701	TYLER	76508	TEMPLE	76504	TEMPLE
75759	CUNEY	75766	JACKSONVILLE	76533	HEIDENHEIMER	76501	TEMPLE
75764	GALLATIN	75785	RUSK	76540	KILLEEN	76541	KILLEEN
75772	MAYDELLE	75785	RUSK	76547	KILLEEN	76541	KILLEEN
75779	NECHES	75801	PALESTINE	76558	MOUND	76528	GATESVILLE
75780	NEW SUMMERFIELD	75789	TROUP	76564	PENDLETON	76579	TROY
75782	POYNOR	75763	FRANKSTON	76573	SCHWERTNER	76511	BARTLETT
75788	SACUL	75760	CUSHING	76596	GATESVILLE	76689	VALLEY MILLS
75797	BIG SANDY	75755	BIG SANDY	76597	GATESVILLE	76528	GATESVILLE
75802	PALESTINE	75803	PALESTINE	76598	GATESVILLE	76528	GATESVILLE
75832	CAYUGA	75861	TENNESSEE COLONY	76599	GATESVILLE	76528	GATESVILLE
75834	CENTRALIA	75926	APPLE SPRINGS	76623	AVALON	75165	WAXAHACHIE
75848	KIRVIN	76693	WORTHAM	76628	BRANDON	76666	MERTENS
75849	LATEXO	75835	CROCKETT	76644	LAGUNA PARK	76634	CLIFTON
75858	RATCLIFF	75487	KENNARD	76650	IRENE	76666	MERTENS
75865	WOODLAKE	75845	GROVETON	76654	LEROY	76624	AXTELL
75880	TENNESSEE COLONY	75861	TENNESSEE COLONY	76675	OTTO	76682	RIESEL
75882	PALESTINE	75803	PALESTINE	76684	ROSS	76691	WEST
75884	TENNESSEE COLONY	75861	TENNESSEE COLONY	76685	SATIN	76632	CHILTON
75886	TENNESSEE COLONY	75861	TENNESSEE COLONY	76686	TEHUACANA	76667	MEXIA
75902	LUFKIN	75904	LUFKIN	76702	WACO	76712	WOODWAY
75903	LUFKIN	75904	LUFKIN	76703	WACO	76711	WACO
75915	LUFKIN	75904	LUFKIN	76714	WACO	76710	WACO
75934	CAMDEN	75939	CORRIGAN	76715	WACO	76704	WACO
75942	DOUCETTE	75979	WOODVILLE	76716	WACO	76711	WACO
75944	ETOILE	75937	CHIRENO	76795	WACO	76710	WACO
75947	GENEVA	75959	MILAM	76797	WACO	76710	WACO

TEXAS   **TEXAS**

Point ZIP Code		Enclosing Residential ZIP Code		Point ZIP Code		Enclosing Residential ZIP Code	
ZIP	**Post Office Name**	**ZIP**	**Post Office Name**	**ZIP**	**Post Office Name**	**ZIP**	**Post Office Name**
76798	WACO	76706	WACO	77293	HOUSTON	77091	HOUSTON
76799	WACO	76710	WACO	77297	HOUSTON	77002	HOUSTON
76803	BROWNWOOD	76802	EARLY	77298	HOUSTON	77002	HOUSTON
76804	BROWNWOOD	76801	BROWNWOOD	77299	HOUSTON	77007	HOUSTON
76824	BEND	76877	SAN SABA	77305	CONROE	77301	CONROE
76855	LOWAKE	76866	PAINT ROCK	77315	NORTH HOUSTON	77032	HOUSTON
76886	VERIBEST	76905	SAN ANGELO	77325	HUMBLE	77339	HUMBLE
76902	SAN ANGELO	76903	SAN ANGELO	77326	ACE	77351	LIVINGSTON
76906	SAN ANGELO	76904	SAN ANGELO	77332	DALLARDSVILLE	77351	LIVINGSTON
76939	KNICKERBOCKER	76904	SAN ANGELO	77333	DOBBIN	77356	MONTGOMERY
76953	TENNYSON	76933	BRONTE	77334	DODGE	77320	HUNTSVILLE
76958	WATER VALLEY	76934	CARLSBAD	77341	HUNTSVILLE	77340	HUNTSVILLE
77001	HOUSTON	77002	HOUSTON	77342	HUNTSVILLE	77320	HUNTSVILLE
77052	HOUSTON	77002	HOUSTON	77347	HUMBLE	77338	HUMBLE
77097	HOUSTON	77002	HOUSTON	77348	HUNTSVILLE	77340	HUNTSVILLE
77201	HOUSTON	77002	HOUSTON	77350	LEGGETT	77351	LIVINGSTON
77202	HOUSTON	77014	HOUSTON	77353	MAGNOLIA	77355	MAGNOLIA
77203	HOUSTON	77002	HOUSTON	77367	RIVERSIDE	77320	HUNTSVILLE
77204	HOUSTON	77004	HOUSTON	77368	ROMAYOR	77327	CLEVELAND
77205	HOUSTON	77032	HOUSTON	77369	RYE	77327	CLEVELAND
77206	HOUSTON	77018	HOUSTON	77374	THICKET	77585	SARATOGA
77207	HOUSTON	77017	HOUSTON	77376	VOTAW	77585	SARATOGA
77208	HOUSTON	77002	HOUSTON	77383	SPRING	77379	SPRING
77209	HOUSTON	77002	HOUSTON	77387	SPRING	77380	SPRING
77210	HOUSTON	77002	HOUSTON	77391	SPRING	77379	SPRING
77212	HOUSTON	77002	HOUSTON	77393	SPRING	77381	SPRING
77213	HOUSTON	77013	HOUSTON	77399	LIVINGSTON	77351	LIVINGSTON
77215	HOUSTON	77042	HOUSTON	77402	BELLAIRE	77401	BELLAIRE
77216	HOUSTON	77034	HOUSTON	77404	BAY CITY	77414	BAY CITY
77217	HOUSTON	77017	HOUSTON	77406	RICHMOND	77469	RICHMOND
77218	HOUSTON	77094	HOUSTON	77410	CYPRESS	77429	CYPRESS
77219	HOUSTON	77019	HOUSTON	77411	ALIEF	77099	HOUSTON
77220	HOUSTON	77020	HOUSTON	77412	ALTAIR	77442	GARWOOD
77221	HOUSTON	77021	HOUSTON	77413	BARKER	77493	KATY
77222	HOUSTON	77022	HOUSTON	77415	CEDAR LANE	77414	BAY CITY
77223	HOUSTON	77023	HOUSTON	77428	COLLEGEPORT	77465	PALACIOS
77224	HOUSTON	77079	HOUSTON	77431	DANCIGER	77430	DAMON
77225	HOUSTON	77025	HOUSTON	77436	EGYPT	77435	EAST BERNARD
77226	HOUSTON	77026	HOUSTON	77443	GLEN FLORA	77435	EAST BERNARD
77227	HOUSTON	77027	HOUSTON	77446	PRAIRIE VIEW	77484	WALLER
77228	HOUSTON	77078	HOUSTON	77448	HUNGERFORD	77435	EAST BERNARD
77229	HOUSTON	77013	HOUSTON	77451	KENDLETON	77417	BEASLEY
77230	HOUSTON	77054	HOUSTON	77452	KENNEY	77418	BELLVILLE
77231	HOUSTON	77035	HOUSTON	77453	LANE CITY	77488	WHARTON
77233	HOUSTON	77033	HOUSTON	77454	LISSIE	77435	EAST BERNARD
77234	HOUSTON	77075	HOUSTON	77460	NADA	77442	GARWOOD
77235	HOUSTON	77035	HOUSTON	77463	OLD OCEAN	77480	SWEENY
77236	HOUSTON	77036	HOUSTON	77464	ORCHARD	77471	ROSENBERG
77237	HOUSTON	77036	HOUSTON	77466	PATTISON	77423	BROOKSHIRE
77238	HOUSTON	77088	HOUSTON	77467	PIERCE	77437	EL CAMPO
77240	HOUSTON	77040	HOUSTON	77470	ROCK ISLAND	78962	WEIMAR
77241	HOUSTON	77040	HOUSTON	77473	SAN FELIPE	77474	SEALY
77242	HOUSTON	77077	HOUSTON	77475	SHERIDAN	78962	WEIMAR
77243	HOUSTON	77055	HOUSTON	77476	SIMONTON	77485	WALLIS
77244	HOUSTON	77077	HOUSTON	77481	THOMPSONS	77469	RICHMOND
77245	HOUSTON	77089	HOUSTON	77487	SUGAR LAND	77478	SUGAR LAND
77248	HOUSTON	77008	HOUSTON	77491	KATY	77493	KATY
77249	HOUSTON	77009	HOUSTON	77492	KATY	77493	KATY
77251	HOUSTON	77036	HOUSTON	77496	SUGAR LAND	77479	SUGAR LAND
77252	HOUSTON	77002	HOUSTON	77497	STAFFORD	77477	STAFFORD
77253	HOUSTON	77002	HOUSTON	77501	PASADENA	77506	PASADENA
77254	HOUSTON	77054	HOUSTON	77508	PASADENA	77505	PASADENA
77255	HOUSTON	77055	HOUSTON	77512	ALVIN	77511	ALVIN
77256	HOUSTON	77027	HOUSTON	77522	BAYTOWN	77521	BAYTOWN
77257	HOUSTON	77057	HOUSTON	77533	DAISETTA	77564	HULL
77258	HOUSTON	77062	HOUSTON	77542	FREEPORT	77541	FREEPORT
77259	HOUSTON	77062	HOUSTON	77549	FRIENDSWOOD	77546	FRIENDSWOOD
77261	HOUSTON	77017	HOUSTON	77552	GALVESTON	77551	GALVESTON
77262	HOUSTON	77012	HOUSTON	77553	GALVESTON	77550	GALVESTON
77263	HOUSTON	77031	HOUSTON	77555	GALVESTON	77550	GALVESTON
77265	HOUSTON	77005	HOUSTON	77561	HARDIN	77575	LIBERTY
77266	HOUSTON	77006	HOUSTON	77572	LA PORTE	77571	LA PORTE
77267	HOUSTON	77067	HOUSTON	77574	LEAGUE CITY	77573	LEAGUE CITY
77268	HOUSTON	77014	HOUSTON	77580	MONT BELVIEU	77520	BAYTOWN
77269	HOUSTON	77070	HOUSTON	77582	RAYWOOD	77575	LIBERTY
77270	HOUSTON	77002	HOUSTON	77588	PEARLAND	77581	PEARLAND
77271	HOUSTON	77031	HOUSTON	77592	TEXAS CITY	77590	TEXAS CITY
77272	HOUSTON	77072	HOUSTON	77613	CHINA	77713	BEAUMONT
77273	HOUSTON	77090	HOUSTON	77615	EVADALE	77612	BUNA
77274	HOUSTON	77074	HOUSTON	77617	GILCHRIST	77650	PORT BOLIVAR
77275	HOUSTON	77075	HOUSTON	77623	HIGH ISLAND	77650	PORT BOLIVAR
77277	HOUSTON	77027	HOUSTON	77626	MAURICEVILLE	77632	ORANGE
77279	HOUSTON	77079	HOUSTON	77629	NOME	77713	BEAUMONT
77280	HOUSTON	77080	HOUSTON	77631	ORANGE	77630	ORANGE
77281	HOUSTON	77063	HOUSTON	77639	ORANGEFIELD	77630	ORANGE
77282	HOUSTON	77077	HOUSTON	77641	PORT ARTHUR	77640	PORT ARTHUR
77284	HOUSTON	77084	HOUSTON	77643	PORT ARTHUR	77640	PORT ARTHUR
77287	HOUSTON	77017	HOUSTON	77655	SABINE PASS	77640	PORT ARTHUR
77288	HOUSTON	77004	HOUSTON	77661	STOWELL	77665	WINNIE
77289	HOUSTON	77062	HOUSTON	77663	VILLAGE MILLS	77625	KOUNTZE
77290	HOUSTON	77014	HOUSTON	77670	VIDOR	77662	VIDOR
77291	HOUSTON	77091	HOUSTON	77704	BEAUMONT	77701	BEAUMONT
77292	HOUSTON	77018	HOUSTON				

Point ZIP Code		Enclosing Residential ZIP Code		Point ZIP Code		Enclosing Residential ZIP Code	
ZIP	Post Office Name	ZIP	Post Office Name	ZIP	Post Office Name	ZIP	Post Office Name
77720	BEAUMONT	77707	BEAUMONT	78335	ARANSAS PASS	78336	ARANSAS PASS
77725	BEAUMONT	77705	BEAUMONT	78339	BANQUETE	78380	ROBSTOWN
77726	BEAUMONT	77706	BEAUMONT	78341	BENAVIDES	78349	CONCEPCION
77805	BRYAN	77802	BRYAN	78342	BEN BOLT	78332	ALICE
77806	BRYAN	77802	BRYAN	78347	CHAPMAN RANCH	78415	CORPUS CHRISTI
77834	BRENHAM	77833	BRENHAM	78350	DINERO	78022	GEORGE WEST
77838	CHRIESMAN	77836	CALDWELL	78351	DRISCOLL	78380	ROBSTOWN
77841	COLLEGE STATION	77840	COLLEGE STATION	78352	EDROY	78368	MATHIS
77842	COLLEGE STATION	77840	COLLEGE STATION	78358	FULTON	78382	ROCKPORT
77844	COLLEGE STATION	77840	COLLEGE STATION	78359	GREGORY	78374	PORTLAND
77852	DEANVILLE	77836	CALDWELL	78364	KINGSVILLE	78363	KINGSVILLE
77855	FLYNN	77871	NORMANGEE	78371	OILTON	78369	MIRANDO CITY
77857	GAUSE	76556	MILANO	78381	ROCKPORT	78382	ROCKPORT
77862	KURTEN	77808	BRYAN	78403	CORPUS CHRISTI	78401	CORPUS CHRISTI
77863	LYONS	77879	SOMERVILLE	78426	CORPUS CHRISTI	78410	CORPUS CHRISTI
77866	MILLICAN	77845	COLLEGE STATION	78427	CORPUS CHRISTI	78413	CORPUS CHRISTI
77867	MUMFORD	77859	HEARNE	78460	CORPUS CHRISTI	78410	CORPUS CHRISTI
77870	NEW BADEN	77856	FRANKLIN	78463	CORPUS CHRISTI	78404	CORPUS CHRISTI
77875	ROANS PRAIRIE	77830	ANDERSON	78465	CORPUS CHRISTI	78405	CORPUS CHRISTI
77876	SHIRO	77830	ANDERSON	78466	CORPUS CHRISTI	78411	CORPUS CHRISTI
77878	SNOOK	77879	SOMERVILLE	78467	CORPUS CHRISTI	78415	CORPUS CHRISTI
77881	WELLBORN	77845	COLLEGE STATION	78468	CORPUS CHRISTI	78412	CORPUS CHRISTI
77882	WHEELOCK	77856	FRANKLIN	78469	CORPUS CHRISTI	78408	CORPUS CHRISTI
77902	VICTORIA	77901	VICTORIA	78470	CORPUS CHRISTI	78401	CORPUS CHRISTI
77903	VICTORIA	77904	VICTORIA	78471	CORPUS CHRISTI	78401	CORPUS CHRISTI
77950	AUSTWELL	77990	TIVOLI	78472	CORPUS CHRISTI	78411	CORPUS CHRISTI
77960	FANNIN	77963	GOLIAD	78473	CORPUS CHRISTI	78401	CORPUS CHRISTI
77961	FRANCITAS	77971	LOLITA	78474	CORPUS CHRISTI	78401	CORPUS CHRISTI
77967	HOCHHEIM	77995	YOAKUM	78475	CORPUS CHRISTI	78401	CORPUS CHRISTI
77969	LA SALLE	77957	EDNA	78476	CORPUS CHRISTI	78401	CORPUS CHRISTI
77970	LA WARD	77971	LOLITA	78477	CORPUS CHRISTI	78401	CORPUS CHRISTI
77973	MCFADDIN	77905	VICTORIA	78478	CORPUS CHRISTI	78401	CORPUS CHRISTI
77976	NURSERY	77904	VICTORIA	78480	CORPUS CHRISTI	78418	CORPUS CHRISTI
77977	PLACEDO	77951	BLOOMINGTON	78502	MCALLEN	78501	MCALLEN
77978	POINT COMFORT	77971	LOLITA	78505	MCALLEN	78501	MCALLEN
77986	SUBLIME	77964	HALLETTSVILLE	78522	BROWNSVILLE	78520	BROWNSVILLE
77987	SWEET HOME	77995	YOAKUM	78523	BROWNSVILLE	78520	BROWNSVILLE
77988	TELFERNER	77905	VICTORIA	78535	COMBES	78552	HARLINGEN
77989	THOMASTON	77954	CUERO	78540	EDINBURG	78541	EDINBURG
77991	VANDERBILT	77957	EDNA	78543	ELSA	78538	EDCOUCH
77993	WEESATCHE	77963	GOLIAD	78545	FALCON HEIGHTS	78584	ROMA
78001	ARTESIA WELLS	78014	COTULLA	78551	HARLINGEN	78550	HARLINGEN
78012	CHRISTINE	78026	JOURDANTON	78553	HARLINGEN	78550	HARLINGEN
78029	KERRVILLE	78028	KERRVILLE	78558	LA BLANCA	78538	EDCOUCH
78042	LAREDO	78040	LAREDO	78561	LASARA	78580	RAYMONDVILLE
78044	LAREDO	78041	LAREDO	78562	LA VILLA	78538	EDCOUCH
78049	LAREDO	78041	LAREDO	78564	LOPENO	78076	ZAPATA
78050	LEMING	78064	PLEASANTON	78565	LOS EBANOS	78595	SULLIVAN CITY
78054	MACDONA	78002	ATASCOSA	78567	LOS INDIOS	78586	SAN BENITO
78060	OAKVILLE	78071	THREE RIVERS	78568	LOZANO	78583	RIO HONDO
78062	PEGGY	78008	CAMPBELLTON	78573	MISSION	78572	MISSION
78104	BEEVILLE	78102	BEEVILLE	78576	PENITAS	78560	LA JOYA
78107	BERCLAIR	77963	GOLIAD	78579	PROGRESO	78570	MERCEDES
78115	GERONIMO	78155	SEGUIN	78585	SALINENO	78584	ROMA
78125	MINERAL	78102	BEEVILLE	78592	SANTA MARIA	78552	HARLINGEN
78131	NEW BRAUNFELS	78130	NEW BRAUNFELS	78599	WESLACO	78596	WESLACO
78135	NEW BRAUNFELS	78130	NEW BRAUNFELS	78604	BELMONT	78629	GONZALES
78142	NORMANNA	78102	BEEVILLE	78622	FENTRESS	78655	MARTINDALE
78143	PANDORA	78160	STOCKDALE	78627	GEORGETOWN	78626	GEORGETOWN
78144	PANNA MARIA	78116	GILLETT	78630	CEDAR PARK	78613	CEDAR PARK
78145	PAWNEE	78102	BEEVILLE	78646	LEANDER	78641	LEANDER
78146	PETTUS	78102	BEEVILLE	78651	MC NEIL	78728	AUSTIN
78156	SEGUIN	78155	SEGUIN	78658	OTTINE	78629	GONZALES
78162	TULETA	78102	BEEVILLE	78661	PRAIRIE LEA	78655	MARTINDALE
78206	SAN ANTONIO	78210	SAN ANTONIO	78667	SAN MARCOS	78666	SAN MARCOS
78243	SAN ANTONIO	78236	SAN ANTONIO	78670	STAPLES	78638	KINGSBURY
78246	SAN ANTONIO	78216	SAN ANTONIO	78673	WALBURG	76530	GRANGER
78265	SAN ANTONIO	78217	SAN ANTONIO	78674	WEIR	78626	GEORGETOWN
78268	SAN ANTONIO	78238	SAN ANTONIO	78680	ROUND ROCK	78681	ROUND ROCK
78269	SAN ANTONIO	78249	SAN ANTONIO	78682	ROUND ROCK	78728	AUSTIN
78270	SAN ANTONIO	78232	SAN ANTONIO	78683	ROUND ROCK	78664	ROUND ROCK
78275	SAN ANTONIO	78217	SAN ANTONIO	78691	PFLUGERVILLE	78660	PFLUGERVILLE
78278	SAN ANTONIO	78230	SAN ANTONIO	78708	AUSTIN	78758	AUSTIN
78279	SAN ANTONIO	78216	SAN ANTONIO	78709	AUSTIN	78749	AUSTIN
78280	SAN ANTONIO	78233	SAN ANTONIO	78710	AUSTIN	78754	AUSTIN
78283	SAN ANTONIO	78204	SAN ANTONIO	78711	AUSTIN	78701	AUSTIN
78284	SAN ANTONIO	78233	SAN ANTONIO	78713	AUSTIN	78705	AUSTIN
78285	SAN ANTONIO	78217	SAN ANTONIO	78714	AUSTIN	78701	AUSTIN
78286	SAN ANTONIO	78217	SAN ANTONIO	78715	AUSTIN	78745	AUSTIN
78287	SAN ANTONIO	78219	SAN ANTONIO	78716	AUSTIN	78746	AUSTIN
78288	SAN ANTONIO	78230	SAN ANTONIO	78718	AUSTIN	78758	AUSTIN
78289	SAN ANTONIO	78233	SAN ANTONIO	78720	AUSTIN	78759	AUSTIN
78291	SAN ANTONIO	78205	SAN ANTONIO	78755	AUSTIN	78759	AUSTIN
78292	SAN ANTONIO	78205	SAN ANTONIO	78760	AUSTIN	78744	AUSTIN
78293	SAN ANTONIO	78205	SAN ANTONIO	78761	AUSTIN	78752	AUSTIN
78294	SAN ANTONIO	78205	SAN ANTONIO	78762	AUSTIN	78702	AUSTIN
78295	SAN ANTONIO	78205	SAN ANTONIO	78763	AUSTIN	78703	AUSTIN
78296	SAN ANTONIO	78205	SAN ANTONIO	78764	AUSTIN	78704	AUSTIN
78297	SAN ANTONIO	78205	SAN ANTONIO	78765	AUSTIN	78751	AUSTIN
78298	SAN ANTONIO	78205	SAN ANTONIO	78766	AUSTIN	78757	AUSTIN
78299	SAN ANTONIO	78205	SAN ANTONIO	78767	AUSTIN	78701	AUSTIN
78330	AGUA DULCE	78380	ROBSTOWN	78768	AUSTIN	78701	AUSTIN
78333	ALICE	78332	ALICE	78769	AUSTIN	78701	AUSTIN

TEXAS　　　　　　　　　　　　　　　　　　　　　　　　　　**TEXAS**

Point ZIP Code		Enclosing Residential ZIP Code		Point ZIP Code		Enclosing Residential ZIP Code	
ZIP	Post Office Name	ZIP	Post Office Name	ZIP	Post Office Name	ZIP	Post Office Name
78772	AUSTIN	78741	AUSTIN	79493	LUBBOCK	79413	LUBBOCK
78773	AUSTIN	78701	AUSTIN	79499	LUBBOCK	79416	LUBBOCK
78774	AUSTIN	78701	AUSTIN	79505	BENJAMIN	76380	SEYMOUR
78778	AUSTIN	78701	AUSTIN	79516	DUNN	79526	HERMLEIGH
78779	AUSTIN	78731	AUSTIN	79550	SNYDER	79549	SNYDER
78780	AUSTIN	78746	AUSTIN	79604	ABILENE	79601	ABILENE
78781	AUSTIN	78747	AUSTIN	79608	ABILENE	79605	ABILENE
78783	AUSTIN	78723	AUSTIN	79702	MIDLAND	79701	MIDLAND
78785	AUSTIN	78751	AUSTIN	79704	MIDLAND	79701	MIDLAND
78786	AUSTIN	78701	AUSTIN	79708	MIDLAND	79707	MIDLAND
78788	AUSTIN	78754	AUSTIN	79710	MIDLAND	79705	MIDLAND
78789	AUSTIN	78757	AUSTIN	79711	MIDLAND	79706	MIDLAND
78799	AUSTIN	78721	AUSTIN	79712	MIDLAND	79705	MIDLAND
78802	UVALDE	78801	UVALDE	79721	BIG SPRING	79720	BIG SPRING
78836	CATARINA	78827	ASHERTON	79733	FORSAN	79720	BIG SPRING
78841	DEL RIO	78840	DEL RIO	79740	GIRVIN	79735	FORT STOCKTON
78842	DEL RIO	78840	DEL RIO	79759	NOTREES	79741	GOLDSMITH
78847	DEL RIO	78840	DEL RIO	79760	ODESSA	79761	ODESSA
78853	EAGLE PASS	78852	EAGLE PASS	79768	ODESSA	79762	ODESSA
78860	EL INDIO	78852	EAGLE PASS	79769	ODESSA	79761	ODESSA
78871	LANGTRY	78837	COMSTOCK	79770	ORLA	79772	PECOS
78943	GLIDDEN	78934	COLUMBUS	79776	PENWELL	79741	GOLDSMITH
78951	OAKLAND	78962	WEIMAR	79778	RANKIN	79755	MIDKIFF
78952	PLUM	78945	LA GRANGE	79780	SARAGOSA	79718	BALMORHEA
78960	WARDA	78945	LA GRANGE	79785	TOYAH	79772	PECOS
78961	WARRENTON	78954	ROUND TOP	79786	TOYAHVALE	79718	BALMORHEA
79002	ALANREED	79057	MCLEAN	79788	WICKETT	79756	MONAHANS
79003	ALLISON	79011	BRISCOE	79831	ALPINE	79830	ALPINE
79008	BORGER	79007	BORGER	79838	FABENS	79836	CLINT
79010	BOYS RANCH	79092	VEGA	79846	REDFORD	79845	PRESIDIO
79012	BUSHLAND	79124	AMARILLO	79848	SANDERSON	78851	DRYDEN
79013	CACTUS	79029	DUMAS	79853	TORNILLO	79836	CLINT
79021	COTTON CENTER	79311	ABERNATHY	79910	EL PASO	79905	EL PASO
79024	DARROUZETT	79034	FOLLETT	79911	EL PASO	79912	EL PASO
79025	DAWN	79045	HEREFORD	79913	EL PASO	79912	EL PASO
79032	EDMONSON	79072	PLAINVIEW	79914	EL PASO	79924	EL PASO
79033	FARNSWORTH	79070	PERRYTON	79917	EL PASO	79907	EL PASO
79051	KERRICK	79022	DALHART	79920	EL PASO	79930	EL PASO
79053	LAZBUDDIE	79009	BOVINA	79923	EL PASO	79903	EL PASO
79054	LEFORS	79065	PAMPA	79926	EL PASO	79915	EL PASO
79066	PAMPA	79065	PAMPA	79929	EL PASO	79927	EL PASO
79073	PLAINVIEW	79072	PLAINVIEW	79931	EL PASO	79930	EL PASO
79077	SAMNORWOOD	79095	WELLINGTON	79937	EL PASO	79936	EL PASO
79078	SANFORD	79036	FRITCH	79940	EL PASO	79901	EL PASO
79091	UMBARGER	79015	CANYON	79941	EL PASO	79901	EL PASO
79093	WAKA	79070	PERRYTON	79942	EL PASO	79901	EL PASO
79105	AMARILLO	79101	AMARILLO	79943	EL PASO	79901	EL PASO
79114	AMARILLO	79109	AMARILLO	79944	EL PASO	79901	EL PASO
79116	AMARILLO	79106	AMARILLO	79945	EL PASO	79901	EL PASO
79117	AMARILLO	79107	AMARILLO	79946	EL PASO	79901	EL PASO
79120	AMARILLO	79103	AMARILLO	79947	EL PASO	79901	EL PASO
79123	AMARILLO	79103	AMARILLO	79948	EL PASO	79901	EL PASO
79159	AMARILLO	79124	AMARILLO	79949	EL PASO	79901	EL PASO
79165	AMARILLO	79101	AMARILLO	79950	EL PASO	79901	EL PASO
79166	AMARILLO	79101	AMARILLO	79951	EL PASO	79901	EL PASO
79168	AMARILLO	79104	AMARILLO	79952	EL PASO	79901	EL PASO
79170	AMARILLO	79101	AMARILLO	79953	EL PASO	79901	EL PASO
79171	AMARILLO	79101	AMARILLO	79954	EL PASO	79901	EL PASO
79172	AMARILLO	79101	AMARILLO	79955	EL PASO	79901	EL PASO
79174	AMARILLO	79101	AMARILLO	79958	EL PASO	79901	EL PASO
79175	AMARILLO	79103	AMARILLO	79960	EL PASO	79901	EL PASO
79180	AMARILLO	79101	AMARILLO	79961	EL PASO	79925	EL PASO
79181	AMARILLO	79101	AMARILLO	79966	EL PASO	79925	EL PASO
79184	AMARILLO	79101	AMARILLO	79973	EL PASO	79925	EL PASO
79185	AMARILLO	79119	AMARILLO	79974	EL PASO	79925	EL PASO
79186	AMARILLO	79101	AMARILLO	79975	EL PASO	79905	EL PASO
79187	AMARILLO	79103	AMARILLO	79976	EL PASO	79930	EL PASO
79221	AIKEN	79241	LOCKNEY	79977	EL PASO	79925	EL PASO
79223	CEE VEE	79248	PADUCAH	79978	EL PASO	79901	EL PASO
79231	DOUGHERTY	79235	FLOYDADA	79980	EL PASO	79901	EL PASO
79233	ESTELLINE	79245	MEMPHIS	79995	EL PASO	79905	EL PASO
79236	GUTHRIE	79248	PADUCAH	79996	EL PASO	79936	EL PASO
79258	SOUTH PLAINS	79241	LOCKNEY	79997	EL PASO	79905	EL PASO
79314	BLEDSOE	79346	MORTON	79998	EL PASO	79905	EL PASO
79330	JUSTICEBURG	79356	POST	79999	EL PASO	79905	EL PASO
79338	LEVELLAND	79336	LEVELLAND	88510	EL PASO	79906	EL PASO
79350	NEW DEAL	79403	LUBBOCK	88511	EL PASO	79906	EL PASO
79367	SMYER	79336	LEVELLAND	88512	EL PASO	79906	EL PASO
79369	SPADE	79339	LITTLEFIELD	88513	EL PASO	79906	EL PASO
79372	SUNDOWN	79336	LEVELLAND	88514	EL PASO	79906	EL PASO
79378	WELLMAN	79316	BROWNFIELD	88515	EL PASO	79906	EL PASO
79380	WHITHARRAL	79336	LEVELLAND	88516	EL PASO	79925	EL PASO
79383	NEW HOME	79373	TAHOKA	88517	EL PASO	79906	EL PASO
79402	LUBBOCK	79401	LUBBOCK	88518	EL PASO	79906	EL PASO
79406	LUBBOCK	79409	LUBBOCK	88519	EL PASO	79906	EL PASO
79408	LUBBOCK	79401	LUBBOCK	88520	EL PASO	79906	EL PASO
79430	LUBBOCK	79415	LUBBOCK	88521	EL PASO	79906	EL PASO
79452	LUBBOCK	79412	LUBBOCK	88523	EL PASO	79906	EL PASO
79453	LUBBOCK	79423	LUBBOCK	88524	EL PASO	79906	EL PASO
79457	LUBBOCK	79401	LUBBOCK	88525	EL PASO	79906	EL PASO
79464	LUBBOCK	79424	LUBBOCK	88526	EL PASO	79906	EL PASO
79490	LUBBOCK	79407	LUBBOCK	88527	EL PASO	79906	EL PASO
79491	LUBBOCK	79412	LUBBOCK	88528	EL PASO	79906	EL PASO

NONRESIDENTIAL ZIP CODES

TEXAS   **VERMONT**

Point ZIP Code — ZIP	Point ZIP Code — Post Office Name	Enclosing Residential ZIP Code — ZIP	Enclosing Residential ZIP Code — Post Office Name
88529	EL PASO	79906	EL PASO
88530	EL PASO	79906	EL PASO
88531	EL PASO	79906	EL PASO
88532	EL PASO	79906	EL PASO
88533	EL PASO	79906	EL PASO
88534	EL PASO	79906	EL PASO
88535	EL PASO	79906	EL PASO
88536	EL PASO	79906	EL PASO
88538	EL PASO	79906	EL PASO
88539	EL PASO	79906	EL PASO
88540	EL PASO	79925	EL PASO
88541	EL PASO	79925	EL PASO
88542	EL PASO	79925	EL PASO
88543	EL PASO	79925	EL PASO
88544	EL PASO	79925	EL PASO
88545	EL PASO	79925	EL PASO
88546	EL PASO	79925	EL PASO
88547	EL PASO	79925	EL PASO
88548	EL PASO	79925	EL PASO
88549	EL PASO	79925	EL PASO
88550	EL PASO	79925	EL PASO
88553	EL PASO	79925	EL PASO
88554	EL PASO	79925	EL PASO
88555	EL PASO	79925	EL PASO
88556	EL PASO	79925	EL PASO
88557	EL PASO	79925	EL PASO
88558	EL PASO	79925	EL PASO
88559	EL PASO	79925	EL PASO
88560	EL PASO	79925	EL PASO
88561	EL PASO	79925	EL PASO
88562	EL PASO	79925	EL PASO
88563	EL PASO	79925	EL PASO
88565	EL PASO	79925	EL PASO
88566	EL PASO	79925	EL PASO
88567	EL PASO	79925	EL PASO
88568	EL PASO	79925	EL PASO
88569	EL PASO	79925	EL PASO
88570	EL PASO	79925	EL PASO
88571	EL PASO	79925	EL PASO
88572	EL PASO	79925	EL PASO
88573	EL PASO	79925	EL PASO
88574	EL PASO	79925	EL PASO
88575	EL PASO	79925	EL PASO
88576	EL PASO	79925	EL PASO
88577	EL PASO	79925	EL PASO
88578	EL PASO	79925	EL PASO
88579	EL PASO	79925	EL PASO
88580	EL PASO	79925	EL PASO
88581	EL PASO	79925	EL PASO
88582	EL PASO	79925	EL PASO
88583	EL PASO	79925	EL PASO
88584	EL PASO	79925	EL PASO
88585	EL PASO	79925	EL PASO
88586	EL PASO	79925	EL PASO
88587	EL PASO	79925	EL PASO
88588	EL PASO	79925	EL PASO
88589	EL PASO	79925	EL PASO
88590	EL PASO	79925	EL PASO
88595	EL PASO	79905	EL PASO
84008	BONANZA	84078	VERNAL
84011	BOUNTIFUL	84010	BOUNTIFUL
84016	CLEARFIELD	84015	CLEARFIELD
84024	ECHO	84017	COALVILLE
84027	FRUITLAND	84051	MOUNTAIN HOME
84034	IBAPAH	84083	WENDOVER
84055	OAKLEY	84061	PEOA
84059	OREM	84057	OREM
84068	PARK CITY	84060	PARK CITY
84079	VERNAL	84078	VERNAL
84089	CLEARFIELD	84015	CLEARFIELD
84090	SANDY	84093	SANDY
84091	SANDY	84094	SANDY
84110	SALT LAKE CITY	84101	SALT LAKE CITY
84114	SALT LAKE CITY	84103	SALT LAKE CITY
84122	SALT LAKE CITY	84119	SALT LAKE CITY
84125	SALT LAKE CITY	84104	SALT LAKE CITY
84126	SALT LAKE CITY	84104	SALT LAKE CITY
84127	SALT LAKE CITY	84104	SALT LAKE CITY
84130	SALT LAKE CITY	84104	SALT LAKE CITY
84131	SALT LAKE CITY	84104	SALT LAKE CITY
84132	SALT LAKE CITY	84112	SALT LAKE CITY
84133	SALT LAKE CITY	84111	SALT LAKE CITY
84134	SALT LAKE CITY	84116	SALT LAKE CITY
84136	SALT LAKE CITY	84111	SALT LAKE CITY
84138	SALT LAKE CITY	84111	SALT LAKE CITY
84139	SALT LAKE CITY	84111	SALT LAKE CITY
84141	SALT LAKE CITY	84117	SALT LAKE CITY
84143	SALT LAKE CITY	84103	SALT LAKE CITY
84144	SALT LAKE CITY	84111	SALT LAKE CITY
84145	SALT LAKE CITY	84101	SALT LAKE CITY
84147	SALT LAKE CITY	84111	SALT LAKE CITY
84148	SALT LAKE CITY	84108	SALT LAKE CITY
84150	SALT LAKE CITY	84103	SALT LAKE CITY
84151	SALT LAKE CITY	84116	SALT LAKE CITY
84152	SALT LAKE CITY	84105	SALT LAKE CITY
84157	SALT LAKE CITY	84107	SALT LAKE CITY
84158	SALT LAKE CITY	84108	SALT LAKE CITY
84165	SALT LAKE CITY	84115	SALT LAKE CITY
84170	SALT LAKE CITY	84119	SALT LAKE CITY
84171	SALT LAKE CITY	84121	SALT LAKE CITY
84180	SALT LAKE CITY	84101	SALT LAKE CITY
84184	SALT LAKE CITY	84119	SALT LAKE CITY
84189	SALT LAKE CITY	84111	SALT LAKE CITY
84190	SALT LAKE CITY	84115	SALT LAKE CITY
84199	SALT LAKE CITY	84104	SALT LAKE CITY
84201	OGDEN	84404	OGDEN
84244	OGDEN	84404	OGDEN
84301	BEAR RIVER CITY	84314	HONEYVILLE
84304	CACHE JUNCTION	84306	COLLINSTON
84316	HOWELL	84336	SNOWVILLE
84323	LOGAN	84321	LOGAN
84326	MILLVILLE	84332	PROVIDENCE
84327	NEWTON	84335	SMITHFIELD
84334	RIVERSIDE	84312	GARLAND
84402	OGDEN	84404	OGDEN
84407	OGDEN	84404	OGDEN
84409	OGDEN	84404	OGDEN
84412	OGDEN	84404	OGDEN
84415	OGDEN	84403	OGDEN
84512	BLUFF	84511	BLANDING
84513	CASTLE DALE	84528	HUNTINGTON
84515	CISCO	84540	THOMPSON
84516	CLAWSON	84523	FERRON
84518	CLEVELAND	84528	HUNTINGTON
84521	ELMO	84528	HUNTINGTON
84522	EMERY	84523	FERRON
84529	KENILWORTH	84526	HELPER
84530	LA SAL	84535	MONTICELLO
84534	MONTEZUMA CREEK	84510	ANETH
84537	ORANGEVILLE	84528	HUNTINGTON
84539	SUNNYSIDE	84520	EAST CARBON
84603	PROVO	84601	PROVO
84605	PROVO	84601	PROVO
84620	AURORA	84654	SALINA
84623	CHESTER	84647	MOUNT PLEASANT
84626	ELBERTA	84013	CEDAR VALLEY
84632	FOUNTAIN GREEN	84629	FAIRVIEW
84633	GOSHEN	84013	CEDAR VALLEY
84636	HOLDEN	84631	FILLMORE
84637	KANOSH	84631	FILLMORE
84638	LEAMINGTON	84624	DELTA
84639	LEVAN	84648	NEPHI
84640	LYNNDYL	84624	DELTA
84643	MAYFIELD	84642	MANTI
84644	MEADOW	84631	FILLMORE
84646	MORONI	84647	MOUNT PLEASANT
84649	OAK CITY	84624	DELTA
84652	REDMOND	84654	SALINA
84656	SCIPIO	84631	FILLMORE
84657	SIGURD	84701	RICHFIELD
84662	SPRING CITY	84647	MOUNT PLEASANT
84665	STERLING	84642	MANTI
84667	WALES	84647	MOUNT PLEASANT
84711	ANNABELLA	84701	RICHFIELD
84715	BICKNELL	84775	TORREY
84718	CANNONVILLE	84717	BRYCE CANYON
84721	CEDAR CITY	84720	CEDAR CITY
84723	CIRCLEVILLE	84743	KINGSTON
84724	ELSINORE	84754	MONROE
84725	ENTERPRISE	84722	CENTRAL
84730	GLENWOOD	84701	RICHFIELD
84732	GREENWICH	84743	KINGSTON
84733	GUNLOCK	84782	VEYO
84735	HATCH	84759	PANGUITCH
84736	HENRIEVILLE	84717	BRYCE CANYON
84740	JUNCTION	84743	KINGSTON
84742	KANARRAVILLE	84720	CEDAR CITY
84744	KOOSHAREM	84701	RICHFIELD
84746	LEEDS	84737	HURRICANE
84749	LYMAN	84747	LOA
84752	MINERSVILLE	84751	MILFORD
84762	DUCK CREEK VILLAGE	84710	ALTON
84763	ROCKVILLE	84737	HURRICANE
84764	BRYCE	84717	BRYCE CANYON
84767	SPRINGDALE	84737	HURRICANE
84771	SAINT GEORGE	84770	SAINT GEORGE
84774	TOQUERVILLE	84745	LA VERKIN
84776	TROPIC	84717	BRYCE CANYON
84779	VIRGIN	84737	HURRICANE
84784	HILDALE	84741	KANAB
84791	SAINT GEORGE	84790	SAINT GEORGE
05009	WHITE RIVER JUNCTION	05001	WHITE RIVER JUNCTION
05030	ASCUTNEY	05089	WINDSOR
05031	BARNARD	05091	WOODSTOCK
05047	HARTFORD	05001	WHITE RIVER JUNCTION
05049	HARTLAND FOUR CORNER	05089	WINDSOR

VERMONT　　　　　　　　　　　　　　　　　　　　　　　　　　**VIRGINIA**

Point ZIP Code Post Office ZIP	Name	Enclosing Residential ZIP Code Post Office ZIP	Name	Point ZIP Code Post Office ZIP	Name	Enclosing Residential ZIP Code Post Office ZIP	Name
05050	MC INDOE FALLS	05821	BARNET	20199	DULLES	20166	STERLING
05054	NORTH THETFORD	05075	THETFORD CENTER	20206	WASHINGTON	22302	ALEXANDRIA
05059	QUECHEE	05001	WHITE RIVER JUNCTION	20231	WASHINGTON	22202	ARLINGTON
05074	THETFORD	05075	THETFORD CENTER	20301	WASHINGTON	22202	ARLINGTON
05076	TOPSHAM	05040	EAST CORINTH	20310	WASHINGTON	22202	ARLINGTON
05085	WEST NEWBURY	05081	WELLS RIVER	20330	WASHINGTON	22202	ARLINGTON
05088	WILDER	05001	WHITE RIVER JUNCTION	20350	WASHINGTON	22202	ARLINGTON
05144	CHESTER DEPOT	05143	CHESTER	20406	WASHINGTON	22202	ARLINGTON
05159	WESTMINSTER STATION	05158	WESTMINSTER	20453	WASHINGTON	22202	ARLINGTON
05254	MANCHESTER	05255	MANCHESTER CENTER	22009	BURKE	22015	BURKE
05302	BRATTLEBORO	05301	BRATTLEBORO	22035	FAIRFAX	22030	FAIRFAX
05303	BRATTLEBORO	05301	BRATTLEBORO	22037	FAIRFAX	22042	FALLS CHURCH
05304	BRATTLEBORO	05301	BRATTLEBORO	22038	FAIRFAX	22030	FAIRFAX
05344	MARLBORO	05301	BRATTLEBORO	22040	FALLS CHURCH	22046	FALLS CHURCH
05357	WEST DUMMERSTON	05301	BRATTLEBORO	22081	MERRIFIELD	22031	FAIRFAX
05402	BURLINGTON	05401	BURLINGTON	22082	MERRIFIELD	22031	FAIRFAX
05406	BURLINGTON	05401	BURLINGTON	22103	WEST MCLEAN	22182	VIENNA
05407	SOUTH BURLINGTON	05403	SOUTH BURLINGTON	22106	MC LEAN	22101	MC LEAN
05439	COLCHESTER	05446	COLCHESTER	22107	MC LEAN	22101	MC LEAN
05449	COLCHESTER	05446	COLCHESTER	22108	MC LEAN	22101	MC LEAN
05451	ESSEX	05452	ESSEX JUNCTION	22116	MERRIFIELD	22031	FAIRFAX
05453	ESSEX JUNCTION	05452	ESSEX JUNCTION	22118	MERRIFIELD	22031	FAIRFAX
05460	HIGHGATE SPRINGS	05488	SWANTON	22119	MERRIFIELD	22031	FAIRFAX
05466	JONESVILLE	05477	RICHMOND	22121	MOUNT VERNON	22309	ALEXANDRIA
05469	MONKTON	05443	BRISTOL	22122	NEWINGTON	22079	LORTON
05470	MONTGOMERY	05471	MONTGOMERY CENTER	22125	OCCOQUAN	22192	WOODBRIDGE
05479	SAINT ALBANS	05478	SAINT ALBANS	22135	QUANTICO	22556	STAFFORD
05481	SAINT ALBANS BAY	05478	SAINT ALBANS	22156	SPRINGFIELD	22150	SPRINGFIELD
05485	SHELDON SPRINGS	05483	SHELDON	22158	SPRINGFIELD	22151	SPRINGFIELD
05490	UNDERHILL CENTER	05489	UNDERHILL	22159	SPRINGFIELD	22151	SPRINGFIELD
05601	MONTPELIER	05602	MONTPELIER	22160	SPRINGFIELD	22151	SPRINGFIELD
05603	MONTPELIER	05602	MONTPELIER	22161	SPRINGFIELD	22151	SPRINGFIELD
05604	MONTPELIER	05602	MONTPELIER	22183	VIENNA	22180	VIENNA
05609	MONTPELIER	05602	MONTPELIER	22184	VIENNA	22182	VIENNA
05620	MONTPELIER	05602	MONTPELIER	22185	VIENNA	22124	OAKTON
05633	MONTPELIER	05602	MONTPELIER	22194	WOODBRIDGE	22191	WOODBRIDGE
05657	LAKE ELMORE	05680	WOLCOTT	22195	WOODBRIDGE	22193	WOODBRIDGE
05662	MOSCOW	05672	STOWE	22199	LORTON	22079	LORTON
05664	NORTHFIELD FALLS	05663	NORTHFIELD	22210	ARLINGTON	22201	ARLINGTON
05665	NORTH HYDE PARK	05655	HYDE PARK	22214	ARLINGTON	22204	ARLINGTON
05670	SOUTH BARRE	05641	BARRE	22215	ARLINGTON	22202	ARLINGTON
05671	WATERBURY	05676	WATERBURY	22216	ARLINGTON	22201	ARLINGTON
05678	WEBSTERVILLE	05654	GRANITEVILLE	22217	ARLINGTON	22203	ARLINGTON
05702	RUTLAND	05701	RUTLAND	22219	ARLINGTON	22209	ARLINGTON
05731	BENSON	05743	FAIR HAVEN	22222	ARLINGTON	22202	ARLINGTON
05740	EAST MIDDLEBURY	05753	MIDDLEBURY	22226	ARLINGTON	22201	ARLINGTON
05741	EAST POULTNEY	05764	POULTNEY	22227	ARLINGTON	22202	ARLINGTON
05745	FOREST DALE	05733	BRANDON	22229	ARLINGTON	22209	ARLINGTON
05750	HYDEVILLE	05764	POULTNEY	22230	ARLINGTON	22203	ARLINGTON
05768	RUPERT	05776	WEST RUPERT	22234	ARLINGTON	22209	ARLINGTON
05823	BEEBE PLAIN	05855	NEWPORT	22240	ARLINGTON	22202	ARLINGTON
05838	EAST SAINT JOHNSBURY	05819	SAINT JOHNSBURY	22242	ARLINGTON	22202	ARLINGTON
05840	GRANBY	05858	NORTH CONCORD	22243	ARLINGTON	22202	ARLINGTON
05848	LOWER WATERFORD	05819	SAINT JOHNSBURY	22244	ARLINGTON	22202	ARLINGTON
05849	LYNDON	05851	LYNDONVILLE	22245	ARLINGTON	22202	ARLINGTON
05861	PASSUMPSIC	05819	SAINT JOHNSBURY	22246	ARLINGTON	22202	ARLINGTON
05863	SAINT JOHNSBURY CENT	05819	SAINT JOHNSBURY	22313	ALEXANDRIA	22314	ALEXANDRIA
20069	WASHINGTON	22031	FAIRFAX	22320	ALEXANDRIA	22314	ALEXANDRIA
20070	WASHINGTON	22031	FAIRFAX	22331	ALEXANDRIA	22314	ALEXANDRIA
20101	DULLES	20166	STERLING	22332	ALEXANDRIA	22314	ALEXANDRIA
20102	DULLES	20166	STERLING	22333	ALEXANDRIA	22304	ALEXANDRIA
20103	DULLES	20166	STERLING	22334	ALEXANDRIA	22314	ALEXANDRIA
20104	DULLES	20166	STERLING	22336	ALEXANDRIA	22314	ALEXANDRIA
20108	MANASSAS	20110	MANASSAS	22402	FREDERICKSBURG	22401	FREDERICKSBURG
20113	MANASSAS	20111	MANASSAS	22403	FREDERICKSBURG	22405	FREDERICKSBURG
20116	MARSHALL	20115	MARSHALL	22404	FREDERICKSBURG	22401	FREDERICKSBURG
20118	MIDDLEBURG	20117	MIDDLEBURG	22412	FREDERICKSBURG	22406	FREDERICKSBURG
20122	CENTREVILLE	20120	CENTREVILLE	22428	BOWLING GREEN	22427	BOWLING GREEN
20128	ORLEAN	20115	MARSHALL	22430	BROOKE	22554	STAFFORD
20131	PHILOMONT	20132	PURCELLVILLE	22442	COLES POINT	22469	HAGUE
20134	PURCELLVILLE	20132	PURCELLVILLE	22446	CORBIN	22580	WOODFORD
20138	CALVERTON	20119	CATLETT	22451	DOGUE	22485	KING GEORGE
20139	CASANOVA	20187	WARRENTON	22456	EDWARDSVILLE	22473	HEATHSVILLE
20140	RECTORTOWN	20144	DELAPLANE	22463	GARRISONVILLE	22556	STAFFORD
20142	ROUND HILL	20141	ROUND HILL	22471	HARTWOOD	22406	FREDERICKSBURG
20146	ASHBURN	20147	ASHBURN	22472	HAYNESVILLE	22572	WARSAW
20153	CHANTILLY	20151	CHANTILLY	22481	JERSEY	22485	KING GEORGE
20156	GAINESVILLE	20155	GAINESVILLE	22501	LADYSMITH	22546	RUTHER GLEN
20159	HAMILTON	20158	HAMILTON	22507	LIVELY	22503	LANCASTER
20160	LINCOLN	20132	PURCELLVILLE	22513	MERRY POINT	22503	LANCASTER
20163	STERLING	20164	STERLING	22517	MOLLUSK	22503	LANCASTER
20167	STERLING	20164	STERLING	22523	MORATTICO	22503	LANCASTER
20168	HAYMARKET	20169	HAYMARKET	22524	MOUNT HOLLY	22520	MONTROSS
20172	HERNDON	20170	HERNDON	22526	NINDE	22485	KING GEORGE
20177	LEESBURG	20175	LEESBURG	22528	NUTTSVILLE	22503	LANCASTER
20178	LEESBURG	20175	LEESBURG	22529	OLDHAMS	22469	HAGUE
20182	NOKESVILLE	20181	NOKESVILLE	22530	OPHELIA	22473	HEATHSVILLE
20185	UPPERVILLE	20184	UPPERVILLE	22544	ROLLINS FORK	22485	KING GEORGE
20188	WARRENTON	20186	WARRENTON	22545	RUBY	22556	STAFFORD
20189	DULLES	22202	ARLINGTON	22547	SEALSTON	22485	KING GEORGE
20193	RESTON	20190	RESTON	22548	SHARPS	22572	WARSAW
20195	RESTON	20190	RESTON	22552	SPARTA	22514	MILFORD
20196	RESTON	20191	RESTON	22555	STAFFORD	22554	STAFFORD

VIRGINIA   **VIRGINIA**

Point ZIP Code		Enclosing Residential ZIP Code		Point ZIP Code		Enclosing Residential ZIP Code	
ZIP	**Post Office Name**	**ZIP**	**Post Office Name**	**ZIP**	**Post Office Name**	**ZIP**	**Post Office Name**
22558	STRATFORD	22520	MONTROSS	23295	RICHMOND	23230	RICHMOND
22565	THORNBURG	22553	SPOTSYLVANIA	23297	RICHMOND	23237	RICHMOND
22570	VILLAGE	22435	CALLAO	23303	ATLANTIC	23416	OAK HALL
22577	SANDY POINT	22488	KINSALE	23304	BATTERY PARK	23430	SMITHFIELD
22581	ZACATA	22520	MONTROSS	23313	CAPEVILLE	23310	CAPE CHARLES
22604	WINCHESTER	22601	WINCHESTER	23316	CHERITON	23310	CAPE CHARLES
22622	BRUCETOWN	22624	CLEAR BROOK	23326	CHESAPEAKE	23320	CHESAPEAKE
22623	CHESTER GAP	22630	FRONT ROYAL	23327	CHESAPEAKE	23322	CHESAPEAKE
22626	FISHERS HILL	22657	STRASBURG	23328	CHESAPEAKE	23320	CHESAPEAKE
22638	WINCHESTER	22601	WINCHESTER	23341	CRADDOCKVILLE	23306	BELLE HAVEN
22646	MILLWOOD	22620	BOYCE	23345	DAVIS WHARF	23306	BELLE HAVEN
22711	BANCO	22727	MADISON	23347	EASTVILLE	23310	CAPE CHARLES
22721	GRAVES MILL	22727	MADISON	23358	HACKSNECK	23420	PAINTER
22723	HOOD	22727	MADISON	23389	HARBORTON	23420	PAINTER
22739	SOMERVILLE	22728	MIDLAND	23397	ISLE OF WIGHT	23487	WINDSOR
22748	WOLFTOWN	22727	MADISON	23398	JAMESVILLE	23350	EXMORE
22803	HARRISONBURG	22801	HARRISONBURG	23399	JENKINS BRIDGE	23359	HALLWOOD
22833	LACEY SPRING	22802	HARRISONBURG	23401	KELLER	23410	MELFA
22848	PLEASANT VALLEY	22841	MOUNT CRAWFORD	23407	MAPPSVILLE	23308	BLOXOM
22850	SINGERS GLEN	22834	LINVILLE	23408	MARIONVILLE	23413	NASSAWADOX
22905	CHARLOTTESVILLE	22903	CHARLOTTESVILLE	23412	MODEST TOWN	23308	BLOXOM
22906	CHARLOTTESVILLE	22901	CHARLOTTESVILLE	23414	NELSONIA	23308	BLOXOM
22908	CHARLOTTESVILLE	22903	CHARLOTTESVILLE	23419	OYSTER	23310	CAPE CHARLES
22909	CHARLOTTESVILLE	22911	CHARLOTTESVILLE	23422	PUNGOTEAGUE	23410	MELFA
22910	CHARLOTTESVILLE	22903	CHARLOTTESVILLE	23423	QUINBY	23420	PAINTER
22924	BATESVILLE	22903	CHARLOTTESVILLE	23424	RESCUE	23314	CARROLLTON
22945	IVY	22901	CHARLOTTESVILLE	23427	SAXIS	23426	SANFORD
22954	MASSIES MILL	22967	ROSELAND	23429	SEAVIEW	23310	CAPE CHARLES
22957	MONTPELIER STATION	22960	ORANGE	23431	SMITHFIELD	23430	SMITHFIELD
22965	QUINQUE	22968	RUCKERSVILLE	23439	SUFFOLK	23434	SUFFOLK
22987	WHITE HALL	22932	CROZET	23441	TASLEY	23301	ACCOMAC
22989	WOODBERRY FOREST	22732	RADIANT	23443	TOWNSEND	23310	CAPE CHARLES
23001	ACHILLES	23072	HAYES	23450	VIRGINIA BEACH	23454	VIRGINIA BEACH
23003	ARK	23061	GLOUCESTER	23458	VIRGINIA BEACH	23451	VIRGINIA BEACH
23014	BEAUMONT	23063	GOOCHLAND	23465	VIRGINIA BEACH	23464	VIRGINIA BEACH
23017	BELLAMY	23061	GLOUCESTER	23466	VIRGINIA BEACH	23462	VIRGINIA BEACH
23018	BENA	23072	HAYES	23467	VIRGINIA BEACH	23464	VIRGINIA BEACH
23031	CHRISTCHURCH	23149	SALUDA	23471	VIRGINIA BEACH	23455	VIRGINIA BEACH
23058	GLEN ALLEN	23060	GLEN ALLEN	23479	VIRGINIA BEACH	23454	VIRGINIA BEACH
23064	GRIMSTEAD	23066	GWYNN	23480	WACHAPREAGUE	23410	MELFA
23067	HADENSVILLE	23093	LOUISA	23482	WARDTOWN	23350	EXMORE
23068	HALLIEFORD	23035	COBBS CREEK	23483	WATTSVILLE	23415	NEW CHURCH
23076	HUDGINS	23128	NORTH	23486	WILLIS WHARF	23350	EXMORE
23081	JAMESTOWN	23185	WILLIAMSBURG	23488	WITHAMS	23416	OAK HALL
23090	LIGHTFOOT	23188	WILLIAMSBURG	23501	NORFOLK	23510	NORFOLK
23101	MACON	23139	POWHATAN	23506	NORFOLK	23502	NORFOLK
23105	MANNBORO	23002	AMELIA COURT HOUSE	23512	NORFOLK	23505	NORFOLK
23107	MARYUS	23072	HAYES	23514	NORFOLK	23510	NORFOLK
23108	MASCOT	23156	SHACKLEFORDS	23515	NORFOLK	23505	NORFOLK
23115	MILLERS TAVERN	22560	TAPPAHANNOCK	23519	NORFOLK	23518	NORFOLK
23127	NORGE	23188	WILLIAMSBURG	23520	NORFOLK	23521	NORFOLK
23131	ORDINARY	23072	HAYES	23530	NORFOLK	23510	NORFOLK
23147	RUTHVILLE	23030	CHARLES CITY	23541	NORFOLK	23511	NORFOLK
23154	SCHLEY	23061	GLOUCESTER	23551	NORFOLK	23511	NORFOLK
23155	SEVERN	23061	GLOUCESTER	23609	NEWPORT NEWS	23607	NEWPORT NEWS
23162	STUDLEY	23116	MECHANICSVILLE	23612	NEWPORT NEWS	23606	NEWPORT NEWS
23170	TREVILIANS	23093	LOUISA	23628	NEWPORT NEWS	23604	FORT EUSTIS
23178	WARE NECK	23061	GLOUCESTER	23630	HAMPTON	23661	HAMPTON
23183	WHITE MARSH	23061	GLOUCESTER	23631	HAMPTON	23661	HAMPTON
23184	WICOMICO	23072	HAYES	23653	HAMPTON	23661	HAMPTON
23187	WILLIAMSBURG	23185	WILLIAMSBURG	23667	HAMPTON	23668	HAMPTON
23190	WOODS CROSS ROADS	23061	GLOUCESTER	23670	HAMPTON	23661	HAMPTON
23191	ZANONI	23061	GLOUCESTER	23681	HAMPTON	23665	HAMPTON
23218	RICHMOND	23219	RICHMOND	23691	YORKTOWN	23690	YORKTOWN
23232	RICHMOND	23220	RICHMOND	23694	LACKEY	23690	YORKTOWN
23238	RICHMOND	23233	RICHMOND	23705	PORTSMOUTH	23707	PORTSMOUTH
23240	RICHMOND	23219	RICHMOND	23804	PETERSBURG	23803	PETERSBURG
23241	RICHMOND	23219	RICHMOND	23822	AMMON	23850	FORD
23242	RICHMOND	23233	RICHMOND	23870	JARRATT	23847	EMPORIA
23249	RICHMOND	23224	RICHMOND	23873	MEREDITHVILLE	23920	BRODNAX
23255	RICHMOND	23229	RICHMOND	23884	SUSSEX	23890	WAVERLY
23260	RICHMOND	23220	RICHMOND	23891	WAVERLY	23890	WAVERLY
23261	RICHMOND	23220	RICHMOND	23899	CLAREMONT	23881	SPRING GROVE
23269	RICHMOND	23220	RICHMOND	23939	EVERGREEN	24522	APPOMATTOX
23270	RICHMOND	23220	RICHMOND	23941	FORT MITCHELL	23937	DRAKES BRANCH
23272	RICHMOND	23219	RICHMOND	23943	HAMPDEN SYDNEY	23901	FARMVILLE
23273	RICHMOND	23230	RICHMOND	23955	NOTTOWAY	23930	CREWE
23274	RICHMOND	23219	RICHMOND	24001	ROANOKE	24011	ROANOKE
23275	RICHMOND	23220	RICHMOND	24002	ROANOKE	24011	ROANOKE
23276	RICHMOND	23220	RICHMOND	24003	ROANOKE	24011	ROANOKE
23278	RICHMOND	23220	RICHMOND	24004	ROANOKE	24011	ROANOKE
23279	RICHMOND	23230	RICHMOND	24005	ROANOKE	24011	ROANOKE
23280	RICHMOND	23228	RICHMOND	24006	ROANOKE	24011	ROANOKE
23282	RICHMOND	23220	RICHMOND	24007	ROANOKE	24011	ROANOKE
23284	RICHMOND	23220	RICHMOND	24008	ROANOKE	24011	ROANOKE
23285	RICHMOND	23220	RICHMOND	24009	ROANOKE	24011	ROANOKE
23286	RICHMOND	23220	RICHMOND	24010	ROANOKE	24011	ROANOKE
23288	RICHMOND	23229	RICHMOND	24022	ROANOKE	24016	ROANOKE
23289	RICHMOND	23294	RICHMOND	24023	ROANOKE	24016	ROANOKE
23290	RICHMOND	23220	RICHMOND	24024	ROANOKE	24016	ROANOKE
23291	RICHMOND	23219	RICHMOND	24025	ROANOKE	24016	ROANOKE
23292	RICHMOND	23219	RICHMOND	24026	ROANOKE	24016	ROANOKE
23293	RICHMOND	23219	RICHMOND	24027	ROANOKE	24016	ROANOKE

VIRGINIA   **WASHINGTON**

Point ZIP Code	Post Office Name	Enclosing Residential ZIP Code	Post Office Name	Point ZIP Code	Post Office Name	Enclosing Residential ZIP Code	Post Office Name
24028	ROANOKE	24016	ROANOKE	98068	SNOQUALMIE PASS	98922	CLE ELUM
24029	ROANOKE	24016	ROANOKE	98071	AUBURN	98002	AUBURN
24030	ROANOKE	24016	ROANOKE	98073	REDMOND	98052	REDMOND
24031	ROANOKE	24016	ROANOKE	98082	BOTHELL	98012	BOTHELL
24032	ROANOKE	24016	ROANOKE	98083	KIRKLAND	98033	KIRKLAND
24033	ROANOKE	24016	ROANOKE	98089	KENT	98031	KENT
24034	ROANOKE	24016	ROANOKE	98093	FEDERAL WAY	98023	FEDERAL WAY
24035	ROANOKE	24016	ROANOKE	98111	SEATTLE	98101	SEATTLE
24036	ROANOKE	24016	ROANOKE	98113	SEATTLE	98031	KENT
24037	ROANOKE	24016	ROANOKE	98114	SEATTLE	98104	SEATTLE
24038	ROANOKE	24016	ROANOKE	98124	SEATTLE	98108	SEATTLE
24040	ROANOKE	24016	ROANOKE	98127	SEATTLE	98031	KENT
24042	ROANOKE	24016	ROANOKE	98129	SEATTLE	98121	SEATTLE
24044	ROANOKE	24016	ROANOKE	98131	SEATTLE	98188	SEATTLE
24048	ROANOKE	24018	ROANOKE	98132	SEATTLE	98188	SEATTLE
24050	ROANOKE	24019	ROANOKE	98138	SEATTLE	98188	SEATTLE
24058	BELSPRING	24142	RADFORD	98139	SEATTLE	98031	KENT
24061	BLACKSBURG	24060	BLACKSBURG	98141	SEATTLE	98031	KENT
24062	BLACKSBURG	24060	BLACKSBURG	98145	SEATTLE	98105	SEATTLE
24063	BLACKSBURG	24060	BLACKSBURG	98151	SEATTLE	98188	SEATTLE
24068	CHRISTIANSBURG	24073	CHRISTIANSBURG	98154	SEATTLE	98104	SEATTLE
24111	MC COY	24060	BLACKSBURG	98160	SEATTLE	98177	SEATTLE
24113	MARTINSVILLE	24112	MARTINSVILLE	98161	SEATTLE	98101	SEATTLE
24114	MARTINSVILLE	24112	MARTINSVILLE	98164	SEATTLE	98104	SEATTLE
24115	MARTINSVILLE	24112	MARTINSVILLE	98165	SEATTLE	98031	KENT
24126	NEWBERN	24084	DUBLIN	98170	SEATTLE	98101	SEATTLE
24129	NEW RIVER	24142	RADFORD	98171	SEATTLE	98188	SEATTLE
24130	ORISKANY	24085	EAGLE ROCK	98174	SEATTLE	98104	SEATTLE
24132	PARROTT	24142	RADFORD	98175	SEATTLE	98031	KENT
24143	RADFORD	24141	RADFORD	98181	SEATTLE	98101	SEATTLE
24146	REDWOOD	24151	ROCKY MOUNT	98184	SEATTLE	98104	SEATTLE
24155	SALEM	24153	SALEM	98185	SEATTLE	98105	SEATTLE
24156	SALEM	24153	SALEM	98190	SEATTLE	98168	SEATTLE
24177	VESTA	24120	MEADOWS OF DAN	98191	SEATTLE	98101	SEATTLE
24178	VILLAMONT	24064	BLUE RIDGE	98194	SEATTLE	98031	KENT
24212	ABINGDON	24210	ABINGDON	98206	EVERETT	98204	EVERETT
24215	ANDOVER	24216	APPALACHIA	98207	EVERETT	98201	EVERETT
24218	BEN HUR	24263	JONESVILLE	98213	EVERETT	98201	EVERETT
24246	EAST STONE GAP	24219	BIG STONE GAP	98222	BLAKELY ISLAND	98221	ANACORTES
24327	EMORY	24361	MEADOWVIEW	98227	BELLINGHAM	98225	BELLINGHAM
24402	STAUNTON	24401	STAUNTON	98228	BELLINGHAM	98226	BELLINGHAM
24411	AUGUSTA SPRINGS	24430	CRAIGSVILLE	98231	BLAINE	98230	BLAINE
24412	BACOVA	24484	WARM SPRINGS	98235	CLEARLAKE	98284	SEDRO WOOLLEY
24415	BROWNSBURG	24473	ROCKBRIDGE BATHS	98238	CONWAY	98273	MOUNT VERNON
24438	GLEN WILTON	24085	EAGLE ROCK	98243	DEER HARBOR	98245	EASTSOUND
24448	IRON GATE	24422	CLIFTON FORGE	98255	HAMILTON	98284	SEDRO WOOLLEY
24457	LOW MOOR	24426	COVINGTON	98256	INDEX	98294	SULTAN
24463	MINT SPRING	24401	STAUNTON	98259	NORTH LAKEWOOD	98223	ARLINGTON
24469	NEW HOPE	24437	FORT DEFIANCE	98263	LYMAN	98284	SEDRO WOOLLEY
24474	SELMA	24426	COVINGTON	98276	NOOKSACK	98247	EVERSON
24476	STEELES TAVERN	24483	VESUVIUS	98280	ORCAS	98245	EASTSOUND
24505	LYNCHBURG	24501	LYNCHBURG	98286	SHAW ISLAND	98261	LOPEZ ISLAND
24506	LYNCHBURG	24501	LYNCHBURG	98287	SILVANA	98292	STANWOOD
24512	LYNCHBURG	24551	FOREST	98291	SNOHOMISH	98290	SNOHOMISH
24513	LYNCHBURG	24551	FOREST	98293	STARTUP	98294	SULTAN
24514	LYNCHBURG	24502	LYNCHBURG	98297	WALDRON	98245	EASTSOUND
24515	LYNCHBURG	24502	LYNCHBURG	98322	BURLEY	98367	PORT ORCHARD
24533	CLIFFORD	24521	AMHERST	98324	CARLSBORG	98382	SEQUIM
24535	CLUSTER SPRINGS	24520	ALTON	98343	JOYCE	98363	PORT ANGELES
24543	DANVILLE	24541	DANVILLE	98344	KAPOWSIN	98338	GRAHAM
24544	DANVILLE	24541	DANVILLE	98348	LA GRANDE	98328	EATONVILLE
24576	NARUNA	24528	BROOKNEAL	98350	LA PUSH	98331	FORKS
24581	NORWOOD	24599	WINGINA	98352	SUMNER	98390	SUMNER
24585	REPUBLICAN GROVE	24577	NATHALIE	98353	MANCHESTER	98366	PORT ORCHARD
24595	SWEET BRIAR	24521	AMHERST	98357	NEAH BAY	98381	SEKIU
24601	AMONATE	24602	BANDY	98364	PORT GAMBLE	98370	POULSBO
24604	BISHOP	24602	BANDY	98378	RETSIL	98366	PORT ORCHARD
24606	BOISSEVAIN	24605	BLUEFIELD	98384	SOUTH COLBY	98366	PORT ORCHARD
24607	BREAKS	24603	BIG ROCK	98385	SOUTH PRAIRIE	98321	BUCKLEY
24608	BURKES GARDEN	24651	TAZEWELL	98386	SOUTHWORTH	98366	PORT ORCHARD
24612	DORAN	24641	RICHLANDS	98393	TRACYTON	98311	BREMERTON
24618	HARMAN	24614	GRUNDY	98395	WAUNA	98329	GIG HARBOR
24619	HORSEPEN	24602	BANDY	98396	WILKESON	98321	BUCKLEY
24624	KEEN MOUNTAIN	24631	OAKWOOD	98397	LONGMIRE	98321	BUCKLEY
24628	MAXIE	24614	GRUNDY	98398	PARADISE INN	98361	PACKWOOD
24635	POCAHONTAS	24605	BLUEFIELD	98401	TACOMA	98402	TACOMA
24640	RED ASH	24639	RAVEN	98411	TACOMA	98409	TACOMA
24647	SHORTT GAP	24639	RAVEN	98412	TACOMA	98444	TACOMA
24658	WOLFORD	24620	HURLEY	98413	TACOMA	98409	TACOMA
98009	BELLEVUE	98004	BELLEVUE	98415	TACOMA	98405	TACOMA
98013	BURTON	98070	VASHON	98431	TACOMA	98433	TACOMA
98015	BELLEVUE	98004	BELLEVUE	98442	TACOMA	98444	TACOMA
98025	HOBART	98027	ISSAQUAH	98450	TACOMA	98409	TACOMA
98035	KENT	98031	KENT	98455	TACOMA	98409	TACOMA
98041	BOTHELL	98011	BOTHELL	98460	TACOMA	98409	TACOMA
98046	LYNNWOOD	98036	LYNNWOOD	98464	TACOMA	98466	TACOMA
98050	PRESTON	98027	ISSAQUAH	98471	TACOMA	98405	TACOMA
98054	REDONDO	98198	SEATTLE	98477	TACOMA	98405	TACOMA
98057	RENTON	98055	RENTON	98481	TACOMA	98409	TACOMA
98061	ROLLINGBAY	98110	BAINBRIDGE ISLAND	98492	LAKEWOOD	98498	LAKEWOOD
98062	SEAHURST	98166	SEATTLE	98493	TACOMA	98498	LAKEWOOD
98063	FEDERAL WAY	98003	FEDERAL WAY	98497	LAKEWOOD	98498	LAKEWOOD
98064	KENT	98031	KENT	98504	OLYMPIA	98501	OLYMPIA

WASHINGTON   WEST VIRGINIA

Point ZIP Code		Enclosing Residential ZIP Code		Point ZIP Code		Enclosing Residential ZIP Code	
ZIP	Post Office Name	ZIP	Post Office Name	ZIP	Post Office Name	ZIP	Post Office Name
98507	OLYMPIA	98501	OLYMPIA	99345	PATERSON	99350	PROSSER
98508	OLYMPIA	98502	OLYMPIA	99346	PLYMOUTH	99338	KENNEWICK
98509	LACEY	98503	LACEY	99359	STARBUCK	99361	WAITSBURG
98511	TUMWATER	98501	OLYMPIA	99363	WALLULA	99360	TOUCHET
98522	ADNA	98532	CHEHALIS	24716	BUD	24726	HERNDON
98527	BAY CENTER	98586	SOUTH BEND	24719	COVEL	24726	HERNDON
98530	BUCODA	98589	TENINO	24724	FREEMAN	24715	BRAMWELL
98539	DOTY	98532	CHEHALIS	24729	HIAWATHA	24736	MATOAKA
98540	EAST OLYMPIA	98501	OLYMPIA	24732	KELLYSVILLE	24740	PRINCETON
98544	GALVIN	98531	CENTRALIA	24737	MONTCALM	24701	BLUEFIELD
98554	LEBAM	98577	RAYMOND	24738	NEMOURS	24701	BLUEFIELD
98556	LITTLEROCK	98512	OLYMPIA	24739	OAKVALE	24740	PRINCETON
98558	MCKENNA	98580	ROY	24751	WOLFE	24701	BLUEFIELD
98559	MALONE	98541	ELMA	24808	ANAWALT	24801	WELCH
98561	MENLO	98577	RAYMOND	24811	AVONDALE	24844	IAEGER
98565	NAPAVINE	98532	CHEHALIS	24813	BARTLEY	24815	BERWIND
98566	NEILTON	98575	QUINAULT	24816	BIG SANDY	24828	DAVY
98583	SATSOP	98563	MONTESANO	24817	BRADSHAW	24850	JOLO
98599	OLYMPIA	98501	OLYMPIA	24820	CAPELS	24801	WELCH
98609	CARROLLS	98626	KELSO	24821	CARETTA	24873	PAYNESVILLE
98614	CHINOOK	98638	NASELLE	24824	COALWOOD	24873	PAYNESVILLE
98622	HEISSON	98604	BATTLE GROUND	24825	CRUMPLER	24868	NORTHFORK
98623	HUSUM	98672	WHITE SALMON	24826	CUCUMBER	24815	BERWIND
98637	NAHCOTTA	98640	OCEAN PARK	24829	ECKMAN	24801	WELCH
98639	NORTH BONNEVILLE	98648	STEVENSON	24830	ELBERT	24801	WELCH
98641	OYSTERVILLE	98640	OCEAN PARK	24831	ELKHORN	24868	NORTHFORK
98644	SEAVIEW	98631	LONG BEACH	24836	GARY	24801	WELCH
98666	VANCOUVER	98661	VANCOUVER	24842	HEMPHILL	24801	WELCH
98667	VANCOUVER	98660	VANCOUVER	24843	HENSLEY	24828	DAVY
98668	VANCOUVER	98661	VANCOUVER	24845	IKES FORK	24839	HANOVER
98670	WAHKIACUS	98613	CENTERVILLE	24846	ISABAN	24862	MOHAWK
98673	WISHRAM	98613	CENTERVILLE	24847	ITMANN	25882	MULLENS
98687	VANCOUVER	98684	VANCOUVER	24848	JENKINJONES	24801	WELCH
98807	WENATCHEE	98801	WENATCHEE	24851	JUSTICE	24839	HANOVER
98811	ARDENVOIR	98822	ENTIAT	24852	KEYSTONE	24801	WELCH
98817	CHELAN FALLS	98816	CHELAN	24853	KIMBALL	24801	WELCH
98819	CONCONULLY	98849	RIVERSIDE	24854	KOPPERSTON	24870	OCEANA
98821	DRYDEN	98815	CASHMERE	24855	KYLE	24868	NORTHFORK
98824	GEORGE	98848	QUINCY	24856	LECKIE	24801	WELCH
98829	MALOTT	98840	OKANOGAN	24857	LYNCO	24870	OCEANA
98836	MONITOR	98801	WENATCHEE	24861	MAYBEURY	24868	NORTHFORK
98853	STRATFORD	98832	MARLIN	24866	NEWHALL	24884	SQUIRE
98860	WILSON CREEK	98832	MARLIN	24867	NEW RICHMOND	24874	PINEVILLE
98904	YAKIMA	98908	YAKIMA	24871	PAGETON	24801	WELCH
98907	YAKIMA	98902	YAKIMA	24872	PANTHER	24862	MOHAWK
98909	YAKIMA	98902	YAKIMA	24878	PREMIER	24801	WELCH
98920	BROWNSTOWN	98933	HARRAH	24879	RAYSAL	24815	BERWIND
98921	BUENA	98953	ZILLAH	24880	ROCK VIEW	24874	PINEVILLE
98925	EASTON	98922	CLE ELUM	24881	RODERFIELD	24828	DAVY
98929	GOOSE PRAIRIE	98937	NACHES	24887	SWITCHBACK	24747	ROCK
98934	KITTITAS	98926	ELLENSBURG	24888	THORPE	24801	WELCH
98939	PARKER	98951	WAPATO	24892	WAR	24815	BERWIND
98940	RONALD	98922	CLE ELUM	24894	WARRIORMINE	24815	BERWIND
98941	ROSLYN	98922	CLE ELUM	24895	WILCOE	24801	WELCH
98943	SOUTH CLE ELUM	98922	CLE ELUM	24896	WOLF PEN	24874	PINEVILLE
98950	VANTAGE	98926	ELLENSBURG	24897	WORTH	24868	NORTHFORK
99001	AIRWAY HEIGHTS	99224	SPOKANE	24898	WYOMING	24874	PINEVILLE
99014	FOUR LAKES	99004	CHENEY	24899	YUKON	24873	PAYNESVILLE
99015	FREEMAN	99030	ROCKFORD	24902	FAIRLEA	24901	LEWISBURG
99020	MARSHALL	99004	CHENEY	24924	BUCKEYE	24954	MARLINTON
99039	WAVERLY	99012	FAIRFIELD	24961	NEOLA	24986	WHITE SULPHUR SPRING
99102	ALBION	99163	PULLMAN	25002	ALLOY	25136	MONTGOMERY
99104	BELMONT	99158	OAKESDALE	25004	AMEAGLE	25060	DOROTHY
99124	ELMER CITY	99116	COULEE DAM	25011	BANCROFT	25159	POCA
99127	SAINT JOHN	99171	SAINT JOHN	25022	BLAIR	25654	YOLYN
99144	LAMONA	99134	HARRINGTON	25026	BLUE CREEK	25071	ELKVIEW
99146	LAURIER	99141	KETTLE FALLS	25031	BOOMER	25136	MONTGOMERY
99149	MALDEN	99170	ROSALIA	25036	CANNELTON	25136	MONTGOMERY
99151	MARCUS	99141	KETTLE FALLS	25040	CHARLTON HEIGHTS	25136	MONTGOMERY
99152	METALINE	99153	METALINE FALLS	25054	DAWES	25075	ESKDALE
99154	MOHLER	99134	HARRINGTON	25057	DEEP WATER	25136	MONTGOMERY
99155	NESPELEM	99116	COULEE DAM	25061	DRYBRANCH	25015	BELLE
99160	ORIENT	99107	BOYDS	25067	EAST BANK	25015	BELLE
99165	PULLMAN	99163	PULLMAN	25070	ELEANOR	25168	RED HOUSE
99174	STEPTOE	99111	COLFAX	25076	ETHEL	25654	YOLYN
99209	SPOKANE	99205	SPOKANE	25086	GLASGOW	25039	CEDAR GROVE
99210	SPOKANE	99201	SPOKANE	25090	GLEN FERRIS	25136	MONTGOMERY
99211	SPOKANE	99212	SPOKANE	25102	HANDLEY	25083	GALLAGHER
99213	SPOKANE	99212	SPOKANE	25109	HOMETOWN	25168	RED HOUSE
99214	SPOKANE	99206	SPOKANE	25110	HUGHESTON	25015	BELLE
99215	SPOKANE	99216	SPOKANE	25112	INSTITUTE	25143	NITRO
99219	SPOKANE	99224	SPOKANE	25126	LONDON	25039	CEDAR GROVE
99220	SPOKANE	99201	SPOKANE	25134	MIAMI	25075	ESKDALE
99228	SPOKANE	99208	SPOKANE	25147	OHLEY	25075	ESKDALE
99252	SPOKANE	99202	SPOKANE	25149	OTTAWA	25114	JEFFREY
99256	SPOKANE	99201	SPOKANE	25152	PAGE	25136	MONTGOMERY
99258	SPOKANE	99202	SPOKANE	25156	PINCH	25071	ELKVIEW
99260	SPOKANE	99201	SPOKANE	25162	PRATT	25083	GALLAGHER
99299	SPOKANE	99201	SPOKANE	25183	SHARPLES	25654	YOLYN
99302	PASCO	99301	PASCO	25185	MOUNT OLIVE	25136	MONTGOMERY
99329	DIXIE	99361	WAITSBURG	25186	SMITHERS	25136	MONTGOMERY
99333	HOOPER	99143	LACROSSE	25201	TAD	25306	CHARLESTON
99335	KAHLOTUS	99301	PASCO	25203	TURTLE CREEK	25053	DANVILLE

WEST VIRGINIA

Point ZIP Code		Enclosing Residential ZIP Code		Point ZIP Code		Enclosing Residential ZIP Code	
ZIP	**Post Office Name**	**ZIP**	**Post Office Name**	**ZIP**	**Post Office Name**	**ZIP**	**Post Office Name**
25205	UNEEDA	25130	MADISON	25718	HUNTINGTON	25701	HUNTINGTON
25206	VAN	25021	BIM	25719	HUNTINGTON	25701	HUNTINGTON
25208	WHARTON	25021	BIM	25720	HUNTINGTON	25701	HUNTINGTON
25211	WIDEN	26617	DILLE	25721	HUNTINGTON	25701	HUNTINGTON
25247	HARTFORD	25260	MASON	25722	HUNTINGTON	25701	HUNTINGTON
25265	NEW HAVEN	25253	LETART	25723	HUNTINGTON	25701	HUNTINGTON
25305	CHARLESTON	25311	CHARLESTON	25724	HUNTINGTON	25701	HUNTINGTON
25317	CHARLESTON	25311	CHARLESTON	25725	HUNTINGTON	25701	HUNTINGTON
25321	CHARLESTON	25301	CHARLESTON	25726	HUNTINGTON	25704	HUNTINGTON
25322	CHARLESTON	25301	CHARLESTON	25727	HUNTINGTON	25704	HUNTINGTON
25323	CHARLESTON	25301	CHARLESTON	25728	HUNTINGTON	25704	HUNTINGTON
25324	CHARLESTON	25301	CHARLESTON	25729	HUNTINGTON	25701	HUNTINGTON
25325	CHARLESTON	25301	CHARLESTON	25770	HUNTINGTON	25704	HUNTINGTON
25326	CHARLESTON	25301	CHARLESTON	25771	HUNTINGTON	25704	HUNTINGTON
25327	CHARLESTON	25301	CHARLESTON	25772	HUNTINGTON	25704	HUNTINGTON
25328	CHARLESTON	25301	CHARLESTON	25773	HUNTINGTON	25704	HUNTINGTON
25329	CHARLESTON	25301	CHARLESTON	25774	HUNTINGTON	25704	HUNTINGTON
25330	CHARLESTON	25301	CHARLESTON	25775	HUNTINGTON	25704	HUNTINGTON
25331	CHARLESTON	25301	CHARLESTON	25776	HUNTINGTON	25704	HUNTINGTON
25332	CHARLESTON	25301	CHARLESTON	25777	HUNTINGTON	25704	HUNTINGTON
25333	CHARLESTON	25301	CHARLESTON	25778	HUNTINGTON	25704	HUNTINGTON
25334	CHARLESTON	25301	CHARLESTON	25779	HUNTINGTON	25704	HUNTINGTON
25335	CHARLESTON	25301	CHARLESTON	25802	BECKLEY	25801	BECKLEY
25336	CHARLESTON	25301	CHARLESTON	25810	ALLEN JUNCTION	25928	STEPHENSON
25337	CHARLESTON	25301	CHARLESTON	25816	BLUE JAY	25813	BEAVER
25338	CHARLESTON	25301	CHARLESTON	25818	BRADLEY	25801	BECKLEY
25339	CHARLESTON	25301	CHARLESTON	25826	CORINNE	25811	AMIGO
25350	CHARLESTON	25301	CHARLESTON	25833	DOTHAN	25917	SCARBRO
25356	CHARLESTON	25313	CHARLESTON	25836	ECCLES	25801	BECKLEY
25357	CHARLESTON	25312	CHARLESTON	25846	GLEN JEAN	25880	MOUNT HOPE
25358	CHARLESTON	25309	CHARLESTON	25849	GLEN WHITE	25827	CRAB ORCHARD
25360	CHARLESTON	25312	CHARLESTON	25851	HARPER	25801	BECKLEY
25361	CHARLESTON	25311	CHARLESTON	25853	HELEN	25915	RHODELL
25362	CHARLESTON	25071	ELKVIEW	25855	HILLTOP	25901	OAK HILL
25364	CHARLESTON	25304	CHARLESTON	25859	KILSYTH	25880	MOUNT HOPE
25365	CHARLESTON	25315	CHARLESTON	25860	LANARK	25801	BECKLEY
25375	CHARLESTON	25312	CHARLESTON	25866	LOCHGELLY	25901	OAK HILL
25387	CHARLESTON	25304	CHARLESTON	25871	MABSCOTT	25801	BECKLEY
25389	CHARLESTON	25312	CHARLESTON	25873	MAC ARTHUR	25801	BECKLEY
25392	CHARLESTON	25301	CHARLESTON	25875	MC GRAWS	25876	SAULSVILLE
25396	CHARLESTON	25314	CHARLESTON	25878	MIDWAY	25827	CRAB ORCHARD
25402	MARTINSBURG	25401	MARTINSBURG	25879	MINDEN	25901	OAK HILL
25410	BAKERTON	25425	HARPERS FERRY	25904	PAX	25880	MOUNT HOPE
25421	GLENGARY	25427	HEDGESVILLE	25906	PINEY VIEW	25801	BECKLEY
25423	HALLTOWN	25425	HARPERS FERRY	25907	PRINCE	25831	DANESE
25429	KEARNEYSVILLE	25430	KEARNEYSVILLE	25909	PROSPERITY	25880	MOUNT HOPE
25432	MILLVILLE	25425	HARPERS FERRY	25911	RALEIGH	25801	BECKLEY
25440	RIDGEWAY	25413	BUNKER HILL	25914	REDSTAR	25901	OAK HILL
25441	RIPPON	25414	CHARLES TOWN	25916	SABINE	25913	RAVENCLIFF
25507	CEREDO	25530	KENOVA	25919	SKELTON	25801	BECKLEY
25562	SHOALS	25704	HUNTINGTON	25921	SOPHIA	25827	CRAB ORCHARD
25569	TEAYS	25526	HURRICANE	25927	STANAFORD	25801	BECKLEY
25606	ACCOVILLE	25635	MAN	25931	SUMMERLEE	25901	OAK HILL
25611	BRUNO	25635	MAN	25934	TERRY	25864	LAYLAND
25612	CHAUNCEY	25638	OMAR	25942	WINONA	25840	FAYETTEVILLE
25614	CORA	25601	LOGAN	25943	WYCO	25811	AMIGO
25624	HENLAWSON	25601	LOGAN	25961	CRICHTON	25981	QUINWOOD
25625	HOLDEN	25601	LOGAN	25967	HINES	25962	RAINELLE
25628	KISTLER	25635	MAN	25972	LESLIE	25981	QUINWOOD
25630	LORADO	25607	AMHERSTDALE	26030	BEECH BOTTOM	26070	WELLSBURG
25634	MALLORY	25617	DAVIN	26056	NEW MANCHESTER	26034	CHESTER
25636	MONAVILLE	25601	LOGAN	26058	SHORT CREEK	26070	WELLSBURG
25637	MOUNT GAY	25601	LOGAN	26074	WEST LIBERTY	26003	WHEELING
25639	PEACH CREEK	25601	LOGAN	26075	WINDSOR HEIGHTS	26070	WELLSBURG
25644	SARAH ANN	25638	OMAR	26102	PARKERSBURG	26101	PARKERSBURG
25646	STOLLINGS	25601	LOGAN	26103	PARKERSBURG	26101	PARKERSBURG
25647	SWITZER	25047	CLOTHIER	26106	PARKERSBURG	26101	PARKERSBURG
25649	VERDUNVILLE	25508	CHAPMANVILLE	26120	MINERAL WELLS	26150	MINERAL WELLS
25652	WHITMAN	25601	LOGAN	26121	MINERAL WELLS	26150	MINERAL WELLS
25653	WILKINSON	25601	LOGAN	26162	PORTERS FALLS	26167	READER
25665	BORDERLAND	25661	WILLIAMSON	26209	SNOWSHOE	26291	SLATYFORK
25667	CHATTAROY	25661	WILLIAMSON	26229	LORENTZ	26201	BUCKHANNON
25672	EDGARTON	25694	THACKER	26259	DAILEY	26293	VALLEY BEND
25685	NAUGATUCK	25676	LENORE	26275	JUNIOR	26250	BELINGTON
25686	NEWTOWN	25694	THACKER	26285	NORTON	26257	COALTON
25687	NOLAN	25661	WILLIAMSON	26298	BERGOO	26288	WEBSTER SPRINGS
25688	NORTH MATEWAN	25678	MATEWAN	26302	CLARKSBURG	26301	CLARKSBURG
25690	RAGLAND	25670	DELBARTON	26306	CLARKSBURG	26330	BRIDGEPORT
25691	RAWL	25661	WILLIAMSON	26323	ANMOORE	26301	CLARKSBURG
25692	RED JACKET	25678	MATEWAN	26334	BROWNTON	26347	FLEMINGTON
25696	VARNEY	25678	MATEWAN	26349	GALLOWAY	26416	PHILIPPI
25706	HUNTINGTON	25701	HUNTINGTON	26361	GYPSY	26431	SHINNSTON
25707	HUNTINGTON	25701	HUNTINGTON	26366	HAYWOOD	26301	CLARKSBURG
25708	HUNTINGTON	25701	HUNTINGTON	26369	HEPZIBAH	26301	CLARKSBURG
25709	HUNTINGTON	25701	HUNTINGTON	26422	REYNOLDSVILLE	26301	CLARKSBURG
25710	HUNTINGTON	25701	HUNTINGTON	26424	ROSEMONT	26347	FLEMINGTON
25711	HUNTINGTON	25701	HUNTINGTON	26434	SHIRLEY	26320	ALMA
25712	HUNTINGTON	25701	HUNTINGTON	26435	SIMPSON	26347	FLEMINGTON
25713	HUNTINGTON	25701	HUNTINGTON	26436	SMITHBURG	26456	WEST UNION
25714	HUNTINGTON	25701	HUNTINGTON	26438	SPELTER	26330	BRIDGEPORT
25715	HUNTINGTON	25701	HUNTINGTON	26461	WILSONBURG	26301	CLARKSBURG
25716	HUNTINGTON	25701	HUNTINGTON	26463	WYATT	26568	ENTERPRISE
25717	HUNTINGTON	25701	HUNTINGTON	26502	MORGANTOWN	26501	MORGANTOWN

NONRESIDENTIAL ZIP CODES

WEST VIRGINIA | **WISCONSIN**

Point ZIP Code ZIP	Post Office Name	Enclosing Residential ZIP Code ZIP	Post Office Name	Point ZIP Code ZIP	Post Office Name	Enclosing Residential ZIP Code ZIP	Post Office Name
26504	MORGANTOWN	26505	MORGANTOWN	53744	MADISON	53711	MADISON
26507	MORGANTOWN	26505	MORGANTOWN	53774	MADISON	53713	MADISON
26520	ARTHURDALE	26547	REEDSVILLE	53777	MADISON	53704	MADISON
26524	BRETZ	26547	REEDSVILLE	53778	MADISON	53714	MADISON
26527	CASSVILLE	26501	MORGANTOWN	53779	MADISON	53714	MADISON
26531	DELLSLOW	26508	MORGANTOWN	53782	MADISON	53703	MADISON
26534	GRANVILLE	26501	MORGANTOWN	53783	MADISON	53718	MADISON
26543	OSAGE	26501	MORGANTOWN	53784	MADISON	53713	MADISON
26544	PENTRESS	26501	MORGANTOWN	53785	MADISON	53703	MADISON
26555	FAIRMONT	26554	FAIRMONT	53786	MADISON	53703	MADISON
26559	BARRACKVILLE	26554	FAIRMONT	53788	MADISON	53703	MADISON
26563	CAROLINA	26571	FARMINGTON	53789	MADISON	53703	MADISON
26566	COLFAX	26554	FAIRMONT	53790	MADISON	53703	MADISON
26572	FOUR STATES	26591	WORTHINGTON	53791	MADISON	53714	MADISON
26574	GRANT TOWN	26588	RIVESVILLE	53792	MADISON	53726	MADISON
26576	IDAMAY	26571	FARMINGTON	53793	MADISON	53714	MADISON
26578	KINGMONT	26554	FAIRMONT	53794	MADISON	53714	MADISON
26586	MONTANA MINES	26554	FAIRMONT	53802	BEETOWN	53806	CASSVILLE
26671	GILBOA	26651	SUMMERSVILLE	53808	DICKEYVILLE	53807	CUBA CITY
26707	BAYARD	26720	GORMANIA	53812	KIELER	53807	CUBA CITY
26823	CAPON SPRINGS	26808	HIGH VIEW	53817	PATCH GROVE	53821	PRAIRIE DU CHIEN
26886	ONEGO	26884	SENECA ROCKS	53824	SINSINAWA	53811	HAZEL GREEN
53003	ASHIPPUN	53066	OCONOMOWOC	53917	BEAVER DAM	53916	BEAVER DAM
53008	BROOKFIELD	53045	BROOKFIELD	53927	DELLWOOD	54613	ARKDALE
53016	CLYMAN	53039	JUNEAU	53928	DOYLESTOWN	53960	RIO
53026	GREENBUSH	53023	GLENBEULAH	53931	FAIRWATER	53919	BRANDON
53031	HINGHAM	53085	SHEBOYGAN FALLS	53935	FRIESLAND	53923	CAMBRIA
53047	LEBANON	53094	WATERTOWN	53940	LAKE DELTON	53913	BARABOO
53052	MENOMONEE FALLS	53051	MENOMONEE FALLS	53942	LIME RIDGE	53941	LA VALLE
53056	MERTON	53029	HARTLAND	53953	PACKWAUKEE	53949	MONTELLO
53060	NEWBURG	53095	WEST BEND	53957	RANDOLPH	53956	RANDOLPH
53062	NEW HOLSTEIN	53061	NEW HOLSTEIN	53958	REEDSBURG	53959	REEDSBURG
53064	NORTH LAKE	53029	HARTLAND	53962	UNION CENTER	53968	WONEWOC
53082	SHEBOYGAN	53081	SHEBOYGAN	53969	WYOCENA	53954	PARDEEVILLE
53088	STOCKBRIDGE	53014	CHILTON	54010	EAST ELLSWORTH	54011	ELLSWORTH
53099	WOODLAND	53035	IRON RIDGE	54123	FOREST JUNCTION	54110	BRILLION
53101	BASSETT	53128	GENOA CITY	54127	GREEN VALLEY	54154	OCONTO FALLS
53102	BENET LAKE	53104	BRISTOL	54131	FREEDOM	54130	KAUKAUNA
53109	CAMP LAKE	53168	SALEM	54152	NICHOLS	54165	SEYMOUR
53127	GENESEE DEPOT	53189	WAUKESHA	54160	POTTER	53014	CHILTON
53138	HONEY CREEK	53105	BURLINGTON	54182	ZACHOW	54107	BONDUEL
53141	KENOSHA	53140	KENOSHA	54207	COLLINS	54230	REEDSVILLE
53148	LYONS	53105	BURLINGTON	54211	EPHRAIM	54234	SISTER BAY
53152	NEW MUNSTER	53105	BURLINGTON	54214	FRANCIS CREEK	54220	MANITOWOC
53157	PELL LAKE	53128	GENOA CITY	54215	KELLNERSVILLE	54247	WHITELAW
53159	POWERS LAKE	53128	GENOA CITY	54221	MANITOWOC	54220	MANITOWOC
53167	ROCHESTER	53185	WATERFORD	54226	MAPLEWOOD	54235	STURGEON BAY
53171	SOMERS	53144	KENOSHA	54232	SAINT NAZIANZ	53042	KIEL
53176	SPRINGFIELD	53121	ELKHORN	54240	TISCH MILLS	54208	DENMARK
53187	WAUKESHA	53186	WAUKESHA	54305	GREEN BAY	54303	GREEN BAY
53192	WILMOT	53181	TWIN LAKES	54306	GREEN BAY	54303	GREEN BAY
53194	WOODWORTH	53104	BRISTOL	54307	GREEN BAY	54303	GREEN BAY
53195	ZENDA	53147	LAKE GENEVA	54308	GREEN BAY	54302	GREEN BAY
53201	MILWAUKEE	53203	MILWAUKEE	54324	GREEN BAY	54304	GREEN BAY
53234	MILWAUKEE	53219	MILWAUKEE	54344	GREEN BAY	54115	DE PERE
53237	MILWAUKEE	53207	MILWAUKEE	54402	WAUSAU	54403	WAUSAU
53263	MILWAUKEE	53222	MILWAUKEE	54404	MARSHFIELD	54449	MARSHFIELD
53267	MILWAUKEE	53202	MILWAUKEE	54415	BLENKER	54454	MILLADORE
53268	MILWAUKEE	53203	MILWAUKEE	54417	BROKAW	54403	WAUSAU
53270	MILWAUKEE	53202	MILWAUKEE	54429	ELDERON	54499	WITTENBERG
53274	MILWAUKEE	53203	MILWAUKEE	54432	GALLOWAY	54499	WITTENBERG
53277	MILWAUKEE	53202	MILWAUKEE	54434	JUMP RIVER	54433	GILMAN
53278	MILWAUKEE	53202	MILWAUKEE	54439	HANNIBAL	54433	GILMAN
53280	MILWAUKEE	53208	MILWAUKEE	54450	MATTOON	54409	ANTIGO
53281	MILWAUKEE	53208	MILWAUKEE	54458	NELSONVILLE	54407	AMHERST JUNCTION
53284	MILWAUKEE	53212	MILWAUKEE	54464	PHLOX	54409	ANTIGO
53285	MILWAUKEE	53212	MILWAUKEE	54472	MARSHFIELD	54449	MARSHFIELD
53288	MILWAUKEE	53202	MILWAUKEE	54492	STEVENS POINT	54467	PLOVER
53290	MILWAUKEE	53203	MILWAUKEE	54525	GILE	54550	MONTREAL
53293	MILWAUKEE	53203	MILWAUKEE	54532	HEAFFORD JUNCTION	54487	TOMAHAWK
53295	MILWAUKEE	53214	MILWAUKEE	54543	MC NAUGHTON	54501	RHINELANDER
53401	RACINE	53403	RACINE	54561	STAR LAKE	54521	EAGLE RIVER
53407	RACINE	53403	RACINE	54602	LA CROSSE	54601	LA CROSSE
53408	RACINE	53406	RACINE	54620	CATARACT	54656	SPARTA
53490	RACINE	53404	RACINE	54637	HUSTLER	53950	NEW LISBON
53501	AFTON	53548	JANESVILLE	54640	LYNXVILLE	54626	EASTMAN
53512	BELOIT	53511	BELOIT	54643	MILLSTON	54615	BLACK RIVER FALLS
53535	EDMUND	53533	DODGEVILLE	54645	MOUNT STERLING	54631	GAYS MILLS
53537	FOOTVILLE	53545	JANESVILLE	54649	OAKDALE	54660	TOMAH
53540	GOTHAM	53556	LONE ROCK	54654	SENECA	54631	GAYS MILLS
53542	HANOVER	53545	JANESVILLE	54662	TUNNEL CITY	54660	TOMAH
53547	JANESVILLE	53545	JANESVILLE	54702	EAU CLAIRE	54703	EAU CLAIRE
53571	MORRISONVILLE	53532	DE FOREST	54735	DOWNSVILLE	54751	MENOMONIE
53584	SEXTONVILLE	53556	LONE ROCK	54743	GILMANTON	54755	MONDOVI
53591	SUN PRAIRIE	53590	SUN PRAIRIE	54760	PIGEON FALLS	54758	OSSEO
53595	DODGEVILLE	53533	DODGEVILLE	54764	ROCK FALLS	54755	MONDOVI
53596	SUN PRAIRIE	53590	SUN PRAIRIE	54774	CHIPPEWA FALLS	54729	CHIPPEWA FALLS
53599	WOODFORD	53504	ARGYLE	54816	BENOIT	54856	MASON
53701	MADISON	53703	MADISON	54818	BRILL	54868	RICE LAKE
53702	MADISON	53703	MADISON	54834	EDGEWATER	54817	BIRCHWOOD
53707	MADISON	53714	MADISON	54841	HAUGEN	54868	RICE LAKE
53708	MADISON	53714	MADISON	54842	HAWTHORNE	54849	LAKE NEBAGAMON
53725	MADISON	53715	MADISON	54857	MIKANA	54817	BIRCHWOOD

WISCONSIN

WYOMING

Point ZIP Code		Enclosing Residential ZIP Code		Point ZIP Code		Enclosing Residential ZIP Code	
ZIP	Post Office Name	ZIP	Post Office Name	ZIP	Post Office Name	ZIP	Post Office Name
54861	ODANAH	54806	ASHLAND				
54890	WASCOTT	54859	MINONG				
54903	OSHKOSH	54902	OSHKOSH				
54912	APPLETON	54911	APPLETON				
54919	APPLETON	54913	APPLETON				
54926	BIG FALLS	54486	TIGERTON				
54927	BUTTE DES MORTS	54963	OMRO				
54931	DALE	54944	HORTONVILLE				
54933	EMBARRASS	54929	CLINTONVILLE				
54934	EUREKA	54923	BERLIN				
54936	FOND DU LAC	54935	FOND DU LAC				
54946	KING	54981	WAUPACA				
54957	NEENAH	54956	NEENAH				
54969	READFIELD	54940	FREMONT				
54975	ROYALTON	54961	NEW LONDON				
54976	SAXEVILLE	54984	WILD ROSE				
54980	WAUKAU	54963	OMRO				
54985	WINNEBAGO	54902	OSHKOSH				
54990	IOLA	54945	IOLA				
82003	CHEYENNE	82009	CHEYENNE				
82006	CHEYENNE	82009	CHEYENNE				
82008	CHEYENNE	82007	CHEYENNE				
82059	GRANITE CANON	82007	CHEYENNE				
82060	HILLSDALE	82053	BURNS				
82061	HORSE CREEK	82009	CHEYENNE				
82073	LARAMIE	82072	LARAMIE				
82218	HUNTLEY	82240	TORRINGTON				
82324	ELK MOUNTAIN	82327	HANNA				
82335	WALCOTT	82327	HANNA				
82412	BYRON	82431	LOVELL				
82420	COWLEY	82431	LOVELL				
82422	EMBLEM	82426	GREYBULL				
82423	FRANNIE	82421	DEAVER				
82430	KIRBY	82401	WORLAND				
82440	RALSTON	82435	POWELL				
82450	WAPITI	82414	CODY				
82515	HUDSON	82520	LANDER				
82524	SAINT STEPHENS	82501	RIVERTON				
82602	CASPER	82601	CASPER				
82605	CASPER	82609	CASPER				
82615	SHIRLEY BASIN	82609	CASPER				
82630	ARMINTO	82604	CASPER				
82635	EDGERTON	82643	MIDWEST				
82638	HILAND	82642	LYSITE				
82640	LINCH	82639	KAYCEE				
82644	MILLS	82604	CASPER				
82646	NATRONA	82604	CASPER				
82648	POWDER RIVER	82604	CASPER				
82711	ALVA	82720	HULETT				
82717	GILLETTE	82716	GILLETTE				
82833	BIG HORN	82801	SHERIDAN				
82837	LEITER	82835	CLEARMONT				
82840	SADDLESTRING	82834	BUFFALO				
82845	WYARNO	82801	SHERIDAN				
82902	ROCK SPRINGS	82901	ROCK SPRINGS				
82929	LITTLE AMERICA	82938	MC KINNON				
82931	EVANSTON	82930	EVANSTON				
82932	FARSON	82901	ROCK SPRINGS				
82934	GRANGER	82935	GREEN RIVER				
82939	MOUNTAIN VIEW	82933	FORT BRIDGER				
82942	POINT OF ROCKS	82901	ROCK SPRINGS				
82943	RELIANCE	82901	ROCK SPRINGS				
82944	ROBERTSON	82933	FORT BRIDGER				
82945	SUPERIOR	82901	ROCK SPRINGS				
83002	JACKSON	83001	JACKSON				
83025	TETON VILLAGE	83014	WILSON				
83116	DIAMONDVILLE	83101	KEMMERER				
83119	FAIRVIEW	83110	AFTON				
83121	FRONTIER	83101	KEMMERER				
83124	OPAL	83101	KEMMERER				
83128	ALPINE	83118	ETNA				
83414	ALTA	83012	MOOSE				

Appendix II:
NAICS Code Definitions

The Community
Sourcebook
of **ZIP** Code
Demographics

2004
18th EDITION

APPENDIX II
NAICS Codes

111	Crop Production	484	Truck Transportation
112	Animal Production	485	Transit and Ground Passenger Transportation
113	Forestry and Logging	486	Pipeline Transportation
114	Fishing, Hunting and Trapping	487	Scenic and Sightseeing Transportation
115	Support Activities for Agriculture and Forestry	488	Support Activities for Transportation
211	Oil and Gas Extraction	491	Postal Service
212	Mining (except Oil and Gas)	492	Couriers and Messengers
213	Support Activities for Mining	493	Warehousing and Storage
221	Utilities	511	Publishing Industries (except Internet)
236	Construction of Buildings	512	Motion Picture and Sound Recording Industries
237	Heavy and Civil Engineering Construction	515	Broadcasting (except Internet)
238	Specialty Trade Contractors	516	Internet Publishing and Broadcasting
311	Food Manufacturing	517	Telecommunications
312	Beverage and Tobacco Product Manufacturing	518	Internet Service Providers, Web Search Portals, and Data Processing Svcs
313	Textile Mills	519	Other Information Services
314	Textile Product Mills	521	Monetary Authorities - Central Bank
315	Apparel Manufacturing	522	Credit Intermediation and Related Activities
316	Leather and Allied Product Manufacturing	523	Securities/Commodity Contracts/Othr Fin. Inv./Related Activities
321	Wood Product Manufacturing	524	Insurance Carriers and Related Activities
322	Paper Manufacturing	525	Funds, Trusts, and Other Financial Vehicles
323	Printing and Related Support Activities	531	Real Estate
324	Petroleum and Coal Products Manufacturing	532	Rental and Leasing Services
325	Chemical Manufacturing	533	Lessors of Nonfinancial Intangible Assets (except Copyrighted Works)
326	Plastics and Rubber Products Manufacturing	541	Professional, Scientific, and Technical Services
327	Nonmetallic Mineral Product Manufacturing	551	Management of Companies and Enterprises
331	Primary Metal Manufacturing	561	Administrative and Support Services
332	Fabricated Metal Product Manufacturing	562	Waste Management and Remediation Services
333	Machinery Manufacturing	611	Educational Services
334	Computer and Electronic Product Manufacturing	621	Ambulatory Health Care Services
335	Electrical Equipment, Appliance, and Component Manufacturing	622	Hospitals
336	Transportation Equipment Manufacturing	623	Nursing and Residential Care Facilities
337	Furniture and Related Product Manufacturing	624	Social Assistance
339	Miscellaneous Manufacturing	711	Performing Arts, Spectator Sports, and Related Industries
423	Merchant Wholesalers, Durable Goods	712	Museums, Historical Sites, and Similar Institutions
424	Merchant Wholesalers, Nondurable Goods	713	Amusement, Gambling, and Recreation Industries
425	Wholesale Electronic Markets and Agents and Brokers	721	Accommodation
441	Motor Vehicle and Parts Dealers	722	Food Services and Drinking Places
442	Furniture and Home Furnishings Stores	811	Repair and Maintenance
443	Electronics and Appliance Stores	812	Personal and Laundry Services
444	Building Material and Garden Equipment and Supplies Dealers	813	Religious, Grantmaking, Civic, Professional, and Similar Organizations
445	Food and Beverage Stores	814	Private Households
446	Health and Personal Care Stores	921	Executive, Legislative, and Other General Government Support
447	Gasoline Stations	922	Justice, Public Order, and Safety Activities
448	Clothing and Clothing Accessories Stores	923	Administration of Human Resource Programs
451	Sporting Goods, Hobby, Book, and Music Stores	924	Administration of Environmental Quality Programs
452	General Merchandise Stores	925	Administration of Housing Programs, Urban Planning, & Community Dev.
453	Miscellaneous Store Retailers	926	Administration of Economic Programs
454	Nonstore Retailers	927	Space Research and Technology
481	Air Transportation	928	National Security and International Affairs
482	Rail Transportation	999	Unclassified Establishments
483	Water Transportation		

Appendix III:
County FIPS Codes List

The Community
Sourcebook

2004
18th EDITION

of ZIP Code
Demographics

State Name: Alabama
State Abbreviation: AL
State Code: 01

County Name	Code
Autauga	001
Baldwin	003
Barbour	005
Bibb	007
Blount	009
Bullock	011
Butler	013
Calhoun	015
Chambers	017
Cherokee	019
Chilton	021
Choctaw	023
Clarke	025
Clay	027
Cleburne	029
Coffee	031
Colbert	033
Conecuh	035
Coosa	037
Covington	039
Crenshaw	041
Cullman	043
Dale	045
Dallas	047
DeKalb	049
Elmore	051
Escambia	053
Etowah	055
Fayette	057
Franklin	059
Geneva	061
Greene	063
Hale	065
Henry	067
Houston	069
Jackson	071
Jefferson	073
Lamar	075
Lauderdale	077
Lawrence	079
Lee	081
Limestone	083
Lowndes	085
Macon	087
Madison	089
Marengo	091
Marion	093
Marshall	095
Mobile	097
Monroe	099
Montgomery	101
Morgan	103
Perry	105
Pickens	107
Pike	109
Randolph	111
Russell	113
St. Clair	115
Shelby	117
Sumter	119
Talladega	121
Tallapoosa	123
Tuscaloosa	125
Walker	127
Washington	129
Wilcox	131
Winston	133

State Name: Alaska
State Abbreviation: AK
State Code: 02

County Name	Code
Aleutians East	013
Aleutians West	016
Anchorage	020
Bethel	050
Bristol Bay	060
Denali	068
Dillingham	070
Fairbanks North Star	090
Haines	100
Juneau City and	110
Kenai Peninsula	122
Ketchikan Gateway	130
Kodiak Island	150
Lake and Peninsula	164
Matanuska-Susitna	170
Nome	180
North Slope	185
Northwest Arctic	188
Prince of Wales-Outer Ketchika	201
Sitka	220
Skagway-Hoonah-Angoon	232
Southeast Fairbanks	240
Valdez-Cordova	261
Wade Hampton	270
Wrangell-Petersburg	280
Yakutat	282
Yukon-Koyukuk	290

State Name: Arizona
State Abbreviation: AZ
State Code: 04

County Name	Code
Apache	001
Cochise	003
Coconino	005
Gila	007
Graham	009
Greenlee	011
La Paz	012
Maricopa	013
Mohave	015
Navajo	017
Pima	019
Pinal	021
Santa Cruz	023
Yavapai	025
Yuma	027

State Name: Arkansas
State Abbreviation: AR
State Code: 05

County Name	Code
Arkansas	001
Ashley	003
Baxter	005
Benton	007
Boone	009
Bradley	011
Calhoun	013
Carroll	015
Chicot	017
Clark	019
Clay	021
Cleburne	023
Cleveland	025
Columbia	027
Conway	029
Craighead	031
Crawford	033
Crittenden	035
Cross	037
Dallas	039

County Name	Code
Desha	041
Drew	043
Faulkner	045
Franklin	047
Fulton	049
Garland	051
Grant	053
Greene	055
Hempstead	057
Hot Spring	059
Howard	061
Independence	063
Izard	065
Jackson	067
Jefferson	069
Johnson	071
Lafayette	073
Lawrence	075
Lee	077
Lincoln	079
Little River	081
Logan	083
Lonoke	085
Madison	087
Marion	089
Miller	091
Mississippi	093
Monroe	095
Montgomery	097
Nevada	099
Newton	101
Ouachita	103
Perry	105
Phillips	107
Pike	109
Poinsett	111
Polk	113
Pope	115
Prairie	117
Pulaski	119
Randolph	121
St. Francis	123
Saline	125
Scott	127
Searcy	129
Sebastian	131
Sevier	133
Sharp	135
Stone	137
Union	139
Van Buren	141
Washington	143
White	145
Woodruff	147
Yell	149

State Name: California
State Abbreviation: CA
State Code: 06

County Name	Code
Alameda	001
Alpine	003
Amador	005
Butte	007
Calaveras	009
Colusa	011
Contra Costa	013
Del Norte	015
El Dorado	017
Fresno	019
Glenn	021
Humboldt	023
Imperial	025
Inyo	027
Kern	029
Kings	031

County Name	Code
Lake	033
Lassen	035
Los Angeles	037
Madera	039
Marin	041
Mariposa	043
Mendocino	045
Merced	047
Modoc	049
Mono	051
Monterey	053
Napa	055
Nevada	057
Orange	059
Placer	061
Plumas	063
Riverside	065
Sacramento	067
San Benito	069
San Bernardino	071
San Diego	073
San Francisco	075
San Joaquin	077
San Luis Obispo	079
San Mateo	081
Santa Barbara	083
Santa Clara	085
Santa Cruz	087
Shasta	089
Sierra	091
Siskiyou	093
Solano	095
Sonoma	097
Stanislaus	099
Sutter	101
Tehama	103
Trinity	105
Tulare	107
Tuolumne	109
Ventura	111
Yolo	113
Yuba	115

State Name:	Colorado
State Abbreviation:	CO
State Code:	08

County Name	Code
Adams	001
Alamosa	003
Arapahoe	005
Archuleta	007
Baca	009
Bent	011
Boulder	013
Broomfield	014
Chaffee	015
Cheyenne	017
Clear Creek	019
Conejos	021
Costilla	023
Crowley	025
Custer	027
Delta	029
Denver	031
Dolores	033
Douglas	035
Eagle	037
Elbert	039
El Paso	041
Fremont	043
Garfield	045
Gilpin	047
Grand	049
Gunnison	051
Hinsdale	053
Huerfano	055

County Name	Code
Jackson	057
Jefferson	059
Kiowa	061
Kit Carson	063
Lake	065
La Plata	067
Larimer	069
Las Animas	071
Lincoln	073
Logan	075
Mesa	077
Mineral	079
Moffat	081
Montezuma	083
Montrose	085
Morgan	087
Otero	089
Ouray	091
Park	093
Phillips	095
Pitkin	097
Prowers	099
Pueblo	101
Rio Blanco	103
Rio Grande	105
Routt	107
Saguache	109
San Juan	111
San Miguel	113
Sedgwick	115
Summit	117
Teller	119
Washington	121
Weld	123
Yuma	125

State Name:	Connecticut
State Abbreviation:	CT
State Code:	09

County Name	Code
Fairfield	001
Hartford	003
Litchfield	005
Middlesex	007
New Haven	009
New London	011
Tolland	013
Windham	015

State Name:	Delaware
State Abbreviation:	DE
State Code:	10

County Name	Code
Kent	001
New Castle	003
Sussex	005

State Name:	D.C.
State Abbreviation:	DC
State Code:	11

County Name	Code
District of Columbia	001

State Name:	Florida
State Abbreviation:	FL
State Code:	12

County Name	Code
Alachua	001
Baker	003
Bay	005
Bradford	007
Brevard	009
Broward	011
Calhoun	013

County Name	Code
Charlotte	015
Citrus	017
Clay	019
Collier	021
Columbia	023
DeSoto	027
Dixie	029
Duval	031
Escambia	033
Flagler	035
Franklin	037
Gadsden	039
Gilchrist	041
Glades	043
Gulf	045
Hamilton	047
Hardee	049
Hendry	051
Hernando	053
Highlands	055
Hillsborough	057
Holmes	059
Indian River	061
Jackson	063
Jefferson	065
Lafayette	067
Lake	069
Lee	071
Leon	073
Levy	075
Liberty	077
Madison	079
Manatee	081
Marion	083
Martin	085
Miami-Dade	086
Monroe	087
Nassau	089
Okaloosa	091
Okeechobee	093
Orange	095
Osceola	097
Palm Beach	099
Pasco	101
Pinellas	103
Polk	105
Putnam	107
St. Johns	109
St. Lucie	111
Santa Rosa	113
Sarasota	115
Seminole	117
Sumter	119
Suwannee	121
Taylor	123
Union	125
Volusia	127
Wakulla	129
Walton	131
Washington	133

State Name:	Georgia
State Abbreviation:	GA
State Code:	13

County Name	Code
Appling	001
Atkinson	003
Bacon	005
Baker	007
Baldwin	009
Banks	011
Barrow	013
Bartow	015
Ben Hill	017
Berrien	019
Bibb	021

County Name	Code		County Name	Code
Bleckley	023		Liberty	179
Brantley	025		Lincoln	181
Brooks	027		Long	183
Bryan	029		Lowndes	185
Bulloch	031		Lumpkin	187
Burke	033		McDuffie	189
Butts	035		McIntosh	191
Calhoun	037		Macon	193
Camden	039		Madison	195
Candler	043		Marion	197
Carroll	045		Meriwether	199
Catoosa	047		Miller	201
Charlton	049		Mitchell	205
Chatham	051		Monroe	207
Chattahoochee	053		Montgomery	209
Chattooga	055		Morgan	211
Cherokee	057		Murray	213
Clarke	059		Muscogee	215
Clay	061		Newton	217
Clayton	063		Oconee	219
Clinch	065		Oglethorpe	221
Cobb	067		Paulding	223
Coffee	069		Peach	225
Colquitt	071		Pickens	227
Columbia	073		Pierce	229
Cook	075		Pike	231
Coweta	077		Polk	233
Crawford	079		Pulaski	235
Crisp	081		Putnam	237
Dade	083		Quitman	239
Dawson	085		Rabun	241
Decatur	087		Randolph	243
DeKalb	089		Richmond	245
Dodge	091		Rockdale	247
Dooly	093		Schley	249
Dougherty	095		Screven	251
Douglas	097		Seminole	253
Early	099		Spalding	255
Echols	101		Stephens	257
Effingham	103		Stewart	259
Elbert	105		Sumter	261
Emanuel	107		Talbot	263
Evans	109		Taliaferro	265
Fannin	111		Tattnall	267
Fayette	113		Taylor	269
Floyd	115		Telfair	271
Forsyth	117		Terrell	273
Franklin	119		Thomas	275
Fulton	121		Tift	277
Gilmer	123		Toombs	279
Glascock	125		Towns	281
Glynn	127		Treutlen	283
Gordon	129		Troup	285
Grady	131		Turner	287
Greene	133		Twiggs	289
Gwinnett	135		Union	291
Habersham	137		Upson	293
Hall	139		Walker	295
Hancock	141		Walton	297
Haralson	143		Ware	299
Harris	145		Warren	301
Hart	147		Washington	303
Heard	149		Wayne	305
Henry	151		Webster	307
Houston	153		Wheeler	309
Irwin	155		White	311
Jackson	157		Whitfield	313
Jasper	159		Wilcox	315
Jeff Davis	161		Wilkes	317
Jefferson	163		Wilkinson	319
Jenkins	165		Worth	321
Johnson	167			
Jones	169			
Lamar	171			
Lanier	173			
Laurens	175			
Lee	177			

State Name: Hawaii
State Abbreviation: HI
State Code: 15

County Name	Code
Hawaii	001
Honolulu	003
Kalawao	005
Kauai	007
Maui	009

State Name: Idaho
State Abbreviation: ID
State Code: 16

County Name	Code
Ada	001
Adams	003
Bannock	005
Bear Lake	007
Benewah	009
Bingham	011
Blaine	013
Boise	015
Bonner	017
Bonneville	019
Boundary	021
Butte	023
Camas	025
Canyon	027
Caribou	029
Cassia	031
Clark	033
Clearwater	035
Custer	037
Elmore	039
Franklin	041
Fremont	043
Gem	045
Gooding	047
Idaho	049
Jefferson	051
Jerome	053
Kootenai	055
Latah	057
Lemhi	059
Lewis	061
Lincoln	063
Madison	065
Minidoka	067
Nez Perce	069
Oneida	071
Owyhee	073
Payette	075
Power	077
Shoshone	079
Teton	081
Twin Falls	083
Valley	085
Washington	087

State Name: Illinois
State Abbreviation: IL
State Code: 17

County Name	Code
Adams	001
Alexander	003
Bond	005
Boone	007
Brown	009
Bureau	011
Calhoun	013
Carroll	015
Cass	017
Champaign	019
Christian	021
Clark	023
Clay	025
Clinton	027
Coles	029
Cook	031

County Name	Code
Crawford	033
Cumberland	035
DeKalb	037
De Witt	039
Douglas	041
DuPage	043
Edgar	045
Edwards	047
Effingham	049
Fayette	051
Ford	053
Franklin	055
Fulton	057
Gallatin	059
Greene	061
Grundy	063
Hamilton	065
Hancock	067
Hardin	069
Henderson	071
Henry	073
Iroquois	075
Jackson	077
Jasper	079
Jefferson	081
Jersey	083
Jo Daviess	085
Johnson	087
Kane	089
Kankakee	091
Kendall	093
Knox	095
Lake	097
La Salle	099
Lawrence	101
Lee	103
Livingston	105
Logan	107
McDonough	109
McHenry	111
McLean	113
Macon	115
Macoupin	117
Madison	119
Marion	121
Marshall	123
Mason	125
Massac	127
Menard	129
Mercer	131
Monroe	133
Montgomery	135
Morgan	137
Moultrie	139
Ogle	141
Peoria	143
Perry	145
Piatt	147
Pike	149
Pope	151
Pulaski	153
Putnam	155
Randolph	157
Richland	159
Rock Island	161
St. Clair	163
Saline	165
Sangamon	167
Schuyler	169
Scott	171
Shelby	173
Stark	175
Stephenson	177
Tazewell	179
Union	181
Vermilion	183
Wabash	185
Warren	187
Washington	189
Wayne	191
White	193
Whiteside	195
Will	197
Williamson	199
Winnebago	201
Woodford	203

State Name: **Indiana**
State Abbreviation: **IN**
State Code: **18**

County Name	Code
Adams	001
Allen	003
Bartholomew	005
Benton	007
Blackford	009
Boone	011
Brown	013
Carroll	015
Cass	017
Clark	019
Clay	021
Clinton	023
Crawford	025
Daviess	027
Dearborn	029
Decatur	031
DeKalb	033
Delaware	035
Dubois	037
Elkhart	039
Fayette	041
Floyd	043
Fountain	045
Franklin	047
Fulton	049
Gibson	051
Grant	053
Greene	055
Hamilton	057
Hancock	059
Harrison	061
Hendricks	063
Henry	065
Howard	067
Huntington	069
Jackson	071
Jasper	073
Jay	075
Jefferson	077
Jennings	079
Johnson	081
Knox	083
Kosciusko	085
LaGrange	087
Lake	089
LaPorte	091
Lawrence	093
Madison	095
Marion	097
Marshall	099
Martin	101
Miami	103
Monroe	105
Montgomery	107
Morgan	109
Newton	111
Noble	113
Ohio	115
Orange	117
Owen	119
Parke	121
Perry	123
Pike	125
Porter	127
Posey	129
Pulaski	131
Putnam	133
Randolph	135
Ripley	137
Rush	139
St. Joseph	141
Scott	143
Shelby	145
Spencer	147
Starke	149
Steuben	151
Sullivan	153
Switzerland	155
Tippecanoe	157
Tipton	159
Union	161
Vanderburgh	163
Vermillion	165
Vigo	167
Wabash	169
Warren	171
Warrick	173
Washington	175
Wayne	177
Wells	179
White	181
Whitley	183

State Name: **Iowa**
State Abbreviation: **IA**
State Code: **19**

County Name	Code
Adair	001
Adams	003
Allamakee	005
Appanoose	007
Audubon	009
Benton	011
Black Hawk	013
Boone	015
Bremer	017
Buchanan	019
Buena Vista	021
Butler	023
Calhoun	025
Carroll	027
Cass	029
Cedar	031
Cerro Gordo	033
Cherokee	035
Chickasaw	037
Clarke	039
Clay	041
Clayton	043
Clinton	045
Crawford	047
Dallas	049
Davis	051
Decatur	053
Delaware	055
Des Moines	057
Dickinson	059
Dubuque	061
Emmet	063
Fayette	065
Floyd	067
Franklin	069
Fremont	071
Greene	073
Grundy	075
Guthrie	077
Hamilton	079
Hancock	081

County Name	Code	County Name	Code	County Name	Code
Hardin	083	Clay	027	Sherman	181
Harrison	085	Cloud	029	Smith	183
Henry	087	Coffey	031	Stafford	185
Howard	089	Comanche	033	Stanton	187
Humboldt	091	Cowley	035	Stevens	189
Ida	093	Crawford	037	Sumner	191
Iowa	095	Decatur	039	Thomas	193
Jackson	097	Dickinson	041	Trego	195
Jasper	099	Doniphan	043	Wabaunsee	197
Jefferson	101	Douglas	045	Wallace	199
Johnson	103	Edwards	047	Washington	201
Jones	105	Elk	049	Wichita	203
Keokuk	107	Ellis	051	Wilson	205
Kossuth	109	Ellsworth	053	Woodson	207
Lee	111	Finney	055	Wyandotte	209
Linn	113	Ford	057		
Louisa	115	Franklin	059		

State Name: Kentucky
State Abbreviation: KY
State Code: 21

County Name	Code	County Name	Code	County Name	Code
Lucas	117	Geary	061	Adair	001
Lyon	119	Gove	063	Allen	003
Madison	121	Graham	065	Anderson	005
Mahaska	123	Grant	067	Ballard	007
Marion	125	Gray	069	Barren	009
Marshall	127	Greeley	071	Bath	011
Mills	129	Greenwood	073	Bell	013
Mitchell	131	Hamilton	075	Boone	015
Monona	133	Harper	077	Bourbon	017
Monroe	135	Harvey	079	Boyd	019
Montgomery	137	Haskell	081	Boyle	021
Muscatine	139	Hodgeman	083	Bracken	023
O'Brien	141	Jackson	085	Breathitt	025
Osceola	143	Jefferson	087	Breckinridge	027
Page	145	Jewell	089	Bullitt	029
Palo Alto	147	Johnson	091	Butler	031
Plymouth	149	Kearny	093	Caldwell	033
Pocahontas	151	Kingman	095	Calloway	035
Polk	153	Kiowa	097	Campbell	037
Pottawattamie	155	Labette	099	Carlisle	039
Poweshiek	157	Lane	101	Carroll	041
Ringgold	159	Leavenworth	103	Carter	043
Sac	161	Lincoln	105	Casey	045
Scott	163	Linn	107	Christian	047
Shelby	165	Logan	109	Clark	049
Sioux	167	Lyon	111	Clay	051
Story	169	McPherson	113	Clinton	053
Tama	171	Marion	115	Crittenden	055
Taylor	173	Marshall	117	Cumberland	057
Union	175	Meade	119	Daviess	059
Van Buren	177	Miami	121	Edmonson	061
Wapello	179	Mitchell	123	Elliott	063
Warren	181	Montgomery	125	Estill	065
Washington	183	Morris	127	Fayette	067
Wayne	185	Morton	129	Fleming	069
Webster	187	Nemaha	131	Floyd	071
Winnebago	189	Neosho	133	Franklin	073
Winneshiek	191	Ness	135	Fulton	075
Woodbury	193	Norton	137	Gallatin	077
Worth	195	Osage	139	Garrard	079
Wright	197	Osborne	141	Grant	081
		Ottawa	143	Graves	083
		Pawnee	145	Grayson	085

State Name: Kansas
State Abbreviation: KS
State Code: 20

County Name	Code	County Name	Code	County Name	Code
		Phillips	147	Green	087
		Pottawatomie	149	Greenup	089
		Pratt	151	Hancock	091
Allen	001	Rawlins	153	Hardin	093
Anderson	003	Reno	155	Harlan	095
Atchison	005	Republic	157	Harrison	097
Barber	007	Rice	159	Hart	099
Barton	009	Riley	161	Henderson	101
Bourbon	011	Rooks	163	Henry	103
Brown	013	Rush	165	Hickman	105
Butler	015	Russell	167	Hopkins	107
Chase	017	Saline	169	Jackson	109
Chautauqua	019	Scott	171	Jefferson	111
Cherokee	021	Sedgwick	173		
Cheyenne	023	Seward	175		
Clark	025	Shawnee	177		
		Sheridan	179		

County Name	Code
Jessamine	113
Johnson	115
Kenton	117
Knott	119
Knox	121
Larue	123
Laurel	125
Lawrence	127
Lee	129
Leslie	131
Letcher	133
Lewis	135
Lincoln	137
Livingston	139
Logan	141
Lyon	143
McCracken	145
McCreary	147
McLean	149
Madison	151
Magoffin	153
Marion	155
Marshall	157
Martin	159
Mason	161
Meade	163
Menifee	165
Mercer	167
Metcalfe	169
Monroe	171
Montgomery	173
Morgan	175
Muhlenberg	177
Nelson	179
Nicholas	181
Ohio	183
Oldham	185
Owen	187
Owsley	189
Pendleton	191
Perry	193
Pike	195
Powell	197
Pulaski	199
Robertson	201
Rockcastle	203
Rowan	205
Russell	207
Scott	209
Shelby	211
Simpson	213
Spencer	215
Taylor	217
Todd	219
Trigg	221
Trimble	223
Union	225
Warren	227
Washington	229
Wayne	231
Webster	233
Whitley	235
Wolfe	237
Woodford	239

State Name: Louisiana
State Abbreviation: LA
State Code: 22

County Name	Code
Acadia	001
Allen	003
Ascension	005
Assumption	007
Avoyelles	009
Beauregard	011
Bienville	013
Bossier	015
Caddo	017
Calcasieu	019
Caldwell	021
Cameron	023
Catahoula	025
Claiborne	027
Concordia	029
De Soto	031
East Baton Rouge	033
East Carroll	035
East Feliciana	037
Evangeline	039
Franklin	041
Grant	043
Iberia	045
Iberville	047
Jackson	049
Jefferson	051
Jefferson Davis	053
Lafayette	055
Lafourche	057
La Salle	059
Lincoln	061
Livingston	063
Madison	065
Morehouse	067
Natchitoches	069
Orleans	071
Ouachita	073
Plaquemines	075
Pointe Coupee	077
Rapides	079
Red River	081
Richland	083
Sabine	085
St. Bernard	087
St. Charles	089
St. Helena	091
St. James	093
St. John the Baptist	095
St. Landry	097
St. Martin	099
St. Mary	101
St. Tammany	103
Tangipahoa	105
Tensas	107
Terrebonne	109
Union	111
Vermilion	113
Vernon	115
Washington	117
Webster	119
West Baton Rouge	121
West Carroll	123
West Feliciana	125
Winn	127

State Name: Maine
State Abbreviation: ME
State Code: 23

County Name	Code
Androscoggin	001
Aroostook	003
Cumberland	005
Franklin	007
Hancock	009
Kennebec	011
Knox	013
Lincoln	015
Oxford	017
Penobscot	019
Piscataquis	021
Sagadahoc	023
Somerset	025
Waldo	027
Washington	029
York	031

State Name: Maryland
State Abbreviation: MD
State Code: 24

County Name	Code
Allegany	001
Anne Arundel	003
Baltimore	005
Calvert	009
Caroline	011
Carroll	013
Cecil	015
Charles	017
Dorchester	019
Frederick	021
Garrett	023
Harford	025
Howard	027
Kent	029
Montgomery	031
Prince George's	033
Queen Anne's	035
St. Mary's	037
Somerset	039
Talbot	041
Washington	043
Wicomico	045
Worcester	047
Baltimore city	510

State Name: Massachusetts
State Abbreviation: MA
State Code: 25

County Name	Code
Barnstable	001
Berkshire	003
Bristol	005
Dukes	007
Essex	009
Franklin	011
Hampden	013
Hampshire	015
Middlesex	017
Nantucket	019
Norfolk	021
Plymouth	023
Suffolk	025
Worcester	027

State Name: Michigan
State Abbreviation: MI
State Code: 26

County Name	Code
Alcona	001
Alger	003
Allegan	005
Alpena	007
Antrim	009
Arenac	011
Baraga	013
Barry	015
Bay	017
Benzie	019
Berrien	021
Branch	023
Calhoun	025
Cass	027
Charlevoix	029
Cheboygan	031
Chippewa	033
Clare	035
Clinton	037

County Name	Code
Crawford	039
Delta	041
Dickinson	043
Eaton	045
Emmet	047
Genesee	049
Gladwin	051
Gogebic	053
Grand Traverse	055
Gratiot	057
Hillsdale	059
Houghton	061
Huron	063
Ingham	065
Ionia	067
Iosco	069
Iron	071
Isabella	073
Jackson	075
Kalamazoo	077
Kalkaska	079
Kent	081
Keweenaw	083
Lake	085
Lapeer	087
Leelanau	089
Lenawee	091
Livingston	093
Luce	095
Mackinac	097
Macomb	099
Manistee	101
Marquette	103
Mason	105
Mecosta	107
Menominee	109
Midland	111
Missaukee	113
Monroe	115
Montcalm	117
Montmorency	119
Muskegon	121
Newaygo	123
Oakland	125
Oceana	127
Ogemaw	129
Ontonagon	131
Osceola	133
Oscoda	135
Otsego	137
Ottawa	139
Presque Isle	141
Roscommon	143
Saginaw	145
St. Clair	147
St. Joseph	149
Sanilac	151
Schoolcraft	153
Shiawassee	155
Tuscola	157
Van Buren	159
Washtenaw	161
Wayne	163
Wexford	165

State Name: Minnesota
State Abbreviation: MN
State Code: 27

County Name	Code
Aitkin	001
Anoka	003
Becker	005
Beltrami	007
Benton	009
Big Stone	011
Blue Earth	013
Brown	015
Carlton	017
Carver	019
Cass	021
Chippewa	023
Chisago	025
Clay	027
Clearwater	029
Cook	031
Cottonwood	033
Crow Wing	035
Dakota	037
Dodge	039
Douglas	041
Faribault	043
Fillmore	045
Freeborn	047
Goodhue	049
Grant	051
Hennepin	053
Houston	055
Hubbard	057
Isanti	059
Itasca	061
Jackson	063
Kanabec	065
Kandiyohi	067
Kittson	069
Koochiching	071
Lac qui Parle	073
Lake	075
Lake of the Woods	077
Le Sueur	079
Lincoln	081
Lyon	083
McLeod	085
Mahnomen	087
Marshall	089
Martin	091
Meeker	093
Mille Lacs	095
Morrison	097
Mower	099
Murray	101
Nicollet	103
Nobles	105
Norman	107
Olmsted	109
Otter Tail	111
Pennington	113
Pine	115
Pipestone	117
Polk	119
Pope	121
Ramsey	123
Red Lake	125
Redwood	127
Renville	129
Rice	131
Rock	133
Roseau	135
St. Louis	137
Scott	139
Sherburne	141
Sibley	143
Stearns	145
Steele	147
Stevens	149
Swift	151
Todd	153
Traverse	155
Wabasha	157
Wadena	159
Waseca	161
Washington	163
Watonwan	165
Wilkin	167
Winona	169
Wright	171
Yellow Medicine	173

State Name: Mississippi
State Abbreviation: MS
State Code: 28

County Name	Code
Adams	001
Alcorn	003
Amite	005
Attala	007
Benton	009
Bolivar	011
Calhoun	013
Carroll	015
Chickasaw	017
Choctaw	019
Claiborne	021
Clarke	023
Clay	025
Coahoma	027
Copiah	029
Covington	031
DeSoto	033
Forrest	035
Franklin	037
George	039
Greene	041
Grenada	043
Hancock	045
Harrison	047
Hinds	049
Holmes	051
Humphreys	053
Issaquena	055
Itawamba	057
Jackson	059
Jasper	061
Jefferson	063
Jefferson Davis	065
Jones	067
Kemper	069
Lafayette	071
Lamar	073
Lauderdale	075
Lawrence	077
Leake	079
Lee	081
Leflore	083
Lincoln	085
Lowndes	087
Madison	089
Marion	091
Marshall	093
Monroe	095
Montgomery	097
Neshoba	099
Newton	101
Noxubee	103
Oktibbeha	105
Panola	107
Pearl River	109
Perry	111
Pike	113
Pontotoc	115
Prentiss	117
Quitman	119
Rankin	121
Scott	123
Sharkey	125
Simpson	127
Smith	129
Stone	131
Sunflower	133
Tallahatchie	135

County Name	Code
Tate	137
Tippah	139
Tishomingo	141
Tunica	143
Union	145
Walthall	147
Warren	149
Washington	151
Wayne	153
Webster	155
Wilkinson	157
Winston	159
Yalobusha	161
Yazoo	163

State Name: **Missouri**
State Abbreviation: **MO**
State Code: **29**

County Name	Code
Adair	001
Andrew	003
Atchison	005
Audrain	007
Barry	009
Barton	011
Bates	013
Benton	015
Bollinger	017
Boone	019
Buchanan	021
Butler	023
Caldwell	025
Callaway	027
Camden	029
Cape Girardeau	031
Carroll	033
Carter	035
Cass	037
Cedar	039
Chariton	041
Christian	043
Clark	045
Clay	047
Clinton	049
Cole	051
Cooper	053
Crawford	055
Dade	057
Dallas	059
Daviess	061
DeKalb	063
Dent	065
Douglas	067
Dunklin	069
Franklin	071
Gasconade	073
Gentry	075
Greene	077
Grundy	079
Harrison	081
Henry	083
Hickory	085
Holt	087
Howard	089
Howell	091
Iron	093
Jackson	095
Jasper	097
Jefferson	099
Johnson	101
Knox	103
Laclede	105
Lafayette	107
Lawrence	109
Lewis	111
Lincoln	113
Linn	115
Livingston	117
McDonald	119
Macon	121
Madison	123
Maries	125
Marion	127
Mercer	129
Miller	131
Mississippi	133
Moniteau	135
Monroe	137
Montgomery	139
Morgan	141
New Madrid	143
Newton	145
Nodaway	147
Oregon	149
Osage	151
Ozark	153
Pemiscot	155
Perry	157
Pettis	159
Phelps	161
Pike	163
Platte	165
Polk	167
Pulaski	169
Putnam	171
Ralls	173
Randolph	175
Ray	177
Reynolds	179
Ripley	181
St. Charles	183
St. Clair	185
Ste. Genevieve	186
St. Francois	187
St. Louis	189
Saline	195
Schuyler	197
Scotland	199
Scott	201
Shannon	203
Shelby	205
Stoddard	207
Stone	209
Sullivan	211
Taney	213
Texas	215
Vernon	217
Warren	219
Washington	221
Wayne	223
Webster	225
Worth	227
Wright	229
St. Louis city	510

State Name: **Montana**
State Abbreviation: **MT**
State Code: **30**

County Name	Code
Beaverhead	001
Big Horn	003
Blaine	005
Broadwater	007
Carbon	009
Carter	011
Cascade	013
Chouteau	015
Custer	017
Daniels	019
Dawson	021
Deer Lodge	023
Fallon	025
Fergus	027
Flathead	029
Gallatin	031
Garfield	033
Glacier	035
Golden Valley	037
Granite	039
Hill	041
Jefferson	043
Judith Basin	045
Lake	047
Lewis and Clark	049
Liberty	051
Lincoln	053
McCone	055
Madison	057
Meagher	059
Mineral	061
Missoula	063
Musselshell	065
Park	067
Petroleum	069
Phillips	071
Pondera	073
Powder River	075
Powell	077
Prairie	079
Ravalli	081
Richland	083
Roosevelt	085
Rosebud	087
Sanders	089
Sheridan	091
Silver Bow	093
Stillwater	095
Sweet Grass	097
Teton	099
Toole	101
Treasure	103
Valley	105
Wheatland	107
Wibaux	109
Yellowstone	111

State Name: **Nebraska**
State Abbreviation: **NE**
State Code: **31**

County Name	Code
Adams	001
Antelope	003
Arthur	005
Banner	007
Blaine	009
Boone	011
Box Butte	013
Boyd	015
Brown	017
Buffalo	019
Burt	021
Butler	023
Cass	025
Cedar	027
Chase	029
Cherry	031
Cheyenne	033
Clay	035
Colfax	037
Cuming	039
Custer	041
Dakota	043
Dawes	045
Dawson	047
Deuel	049
Dixon	051
Dodge	053
Douglas	055

County Name	Code
Dundy	057
Fillmore	059
Franklin	061
Frontier	063
Furnas	065
Gage	067
Garden	069
Garfield	071
Gosper	073
Grant	075
Greeley	077
Hall	079
Hamilton	081
Harlan	083
Hayes	085
Hitchcock	087
Holt	089
Hooker	091
Howard	093
Jefferson	095
Johnson	097
Kearney	099
Keith	101
Keya Paha	103
Kimball	105
Knox	107
Lancaster	109
Lincoln	111
Logan	113
Loup	115
McPherson	117
Madison	119
Merrick	121
Morrill	123
Nance	125
Nemaha	127
Nuckolls	129
Otoe	131
Pawnee	133
Perkins	135
Phelps	137
Pierce	139
Platte	141
Polk	143
Red Willow	145
Richardson	147
Rock	149
Saline	151
Sarpy	153
Saunders	155
Scotts Bluff	157
Seward	159
Sheridan	161
Sherman	163
Sioux	165
Stanton	167
Thayer	169
Thomas	171
Thurston	173
Valley	175
Washington	177
Wayne	179
Webster	181
Wheeler	183
York	185

State Name: Nevada
State Abbreviation: NV
State Code: 32

County Name	Code
Churchill	001
Clark	003
Douglas	005
Elko	007
Esmeralda	009
Eureka	011
Humboldt	013
Lander	015
Lincoln	017
Lyon	019
Mineral	021
Nye	023
Pershing	027
Storey	029
Washoe	031
White Pine	033
Carson City	510

State Name: New Hampshire
State Abbreviation: NH
State Code: 33

County Name	Code
Belknap	001
Carroll	003
Cheshire	005
Coos	007
Grafton	009
Hillsborough	011
Merrimack	013
Rockingham	015
Strafford	017
Sullivan	019

State Name: New Jersey
State Abbreviation: NJ
State Code: 34

County Name	Code
Atlantic	001
Bergen	003
Burlington	005
Camden	007
Cape May	009
Cumberland	011
Essex	013
Gloucester	015
Hudson	017
Hunterdon	019
Mercer	021
Middlesex	023
Monmouth	025
Morris	027
Ocean	029
Passaic	031
Salem	033
Somerset	035
Sussex	037
Union	039
Warren	041

State Name: New Mexico
State Abbreviation: NM
State Code: 35

County Name	Code
Bernalillo	001
Catron	003
Chaves	005
Cibola	006
Colfax	007
Curry	009
De Baca	011
Dona Ana	013
Eddy	015
Grant	017
Guadalupe	019
Harding	021
Hidalgo	023
Lea	025
Lincoln	027
Los Alamos	028
Luna	029
McKinley	031
Mora	033
Otero	035
Quay	037
Rio Arriba	039
Roosevelt	041
Sandoval	043
San Juan	045
San Miguel	047
Santa Fe	049
Sierra	051
Socorro	053
Taos	055
Torrance	057
Union	059
Valencia	061

State Name: New York
State Abbreviation: NY
State Code: 36

County Name	Code
Albany	001
Allegany	003
Bronx	005
Broome	007
Cattaraugus	009
Cayuga	011
Chautauqua	013
Chemung	015
Chenango	017
Clinton	019
Columbia	021
Cortland	023
Delaware	025
Dutchess	027
Erie	029
Essex	031
Franklin	033
Fulton	035
Genesee	037
Greene	039
Hamilton	041
Herkimer	043
Jefferson	045
Kings	047
Lewis	049
Livingston	051
Madison	053
Monroe	055
Montgomery	057
Nassau	059
New York	061
Niagara	063
Oneida	065
Onondaga	067
Ontario	069
Orange	071
Orleans	073
Oswego	075
Otsego	077
Putnam	079
Queens	081
Rensselaer	083
Richmond	085
Rockland	087
St. Lawrence	089
Saratoga	091
Schenectady	093
Schoharie	095
Schuyler	097
Seneca	099
Steuben	101
Suffolk	103
Sullivan	105
Tioga	107
Tompkins	109

County Name	Code
Ulster	111
Warren	113
Washington	115
Wayne	117
Westchester	119
Wyoming	121
Yates	123

State Name: North Carolina
State Abbreviation: NC
State Code: 37

County Name	Code
Alamance	001
Alexander	003
Alleghany	005
Anson	007
Ashe	009
Avery	011
Beaufort	013
Bertie	015
Bladen	017
Brunswick	019
Buncombe	021
Burke	023
Cabarrus	025
Caldwell	027
Camden	029
Carteret	031
Caswell	033
Catawba	035
Chatham	037
Cherokee	039
Chowan	041
Clay	043
Cleveland	045
Columbus	047
Craven	049
Cumberland	051
Currituck	053
Dare	055
Davidson	057
Davie	059
Duplin	061
Durham	063
Edgecombe	065
Forsyth	067
Franklin	069
Gaston	071
Gates	073
Graham	075
Granville	077
Greene	079
Guilford	081
Halifax	083
Harnett	085
Haywood	087
Henderson	089
Hertford	091
Hoke	093
Hyde	095
Iredell	097
Jackson	099
Johnston	101
Jones	103
Lee	105
Lenoir	107
Lincoln	109
McDowell	111
Macon	113
Madison	115
Martin	117
Mecklenburg	119
Mitchell	121
Montgomery	123
Moore	125
Nash	127

County Name	Code
New Hanover	129
Northampton	131
Onslow	133
Orange	135
Pamlico	137
Pasquotank	139
Pender	141
Perquimans	143
Person	145
Pitt	147
Polk	149
Randolph	151
Richmond	153
Robeson	155
Rockingham	157
Rowan	159
Rutherford	161
Sampson	163
Scotland	165
Stanly	167
Stokes	169
Surry	171
Swain	173
Transylvania	175
Tyrrell	177
Union	179
Vance	181
Wake	183
Warren	185
Washington	187
Watauga	189
Wayne	191
Wilkes	193
Wilson	195
Yadkin	197
Yancey	199

State Name: North Dakota
State Abbreviation: ND
State Code: 38

County Name	Code
Adams	001
Barnes	003
Benson	005
Billings	007
Bottineau	009
Bowman	011
Burke	013
Burleigh	015
Cass	017
Cavalier	019
Dickey	021
Divide	023
Dunn	025
Eddy	027
Emmons	029
Foster	031
Golden Valley	033
Grand Forks	035
Grant	037
Griggs	039
Hettinger	041
Kidder	043
LaMoure	045
Logan	047
McHenry	049
McIntosh	051
McKenzie	053
McLean	055
Mercer	057
Morton	059
Mountrail	061
Nelson	063
Oliver	065
Pembina	067
Pierce	069

County Name	Code
Ramsey	071
Ransom	073
Renville	075
Richland	077
Rolette	079
Sargent	081
Sheridan	083
Sioux	085
Slope	087
Stark	089
Steele	091
Stutsman	093
Towner	095
Traill	097
Walsh	099
Ward	101
Wells	103
Williams	105

State Name: Ohio
State Abbreviation: OH
State Code: 39

County Name	Code
Adams	001
Allen	003
Ashland	005
Ashtabula	007
Athens	009
Auglaize	011
Belmont	013
Brown	015
Butler	017
Carroll	019
Champaign	021
Clark	023
Clermont	025
Clinton	027
Columbiana	029
Coshocton	031
Crawford	033
Cuyahoga	035
Darke	037
Defiance	039
Delaware	041
Erie	043
Fairfield	045
Fayette	047
Franklin	049
Fulton	051
Gallia	053
Geauga	055
Greene	057
Guernsey	059
Hamilton	061
Hancock	063
Hardin	065
Harrison	067
Henry	069
Highland	071
Hocking	073
Holmes	075
Huron	077
Jackson	079
Jefferson	081
Knox	083
Lake	085
Lawrence	087
Licking	089
Logan	091
Lorain	093
Lucas	095
Madison	097
Mahoning	099
Marion	101
Medina	103
Meigs	105

County Name	Code
Mercer	107
Miami	109
Monroe	111
Montgomery	113
Morgan	115
Morrow	117
Muskingum	119
Noble	121
Ottawa	123
Paulding	125
Perry	127
Pickaway	129
Pike	131
Portage	133
Preble	135
Putnam	137
Richland	139
Ross	141
Sandusky	143
Scioto	145
Seneca	147
Shelby	149
Stark	151
Summit	153
Trumbull	155
Tuscarawas	157
Union	159
Van Wert	161
Vinton	163
Warren	165
Washington	167
Wayne	169
Williams	171
Wood	173
Wyandot	175

State Name: Oklahoma
State Abbreviation: OK
State Code: 40

County Name	Code
Adair	001
Alfalfa	003
Atoka	005
Beaver	007
Beckham	009
Blaine	011
Bryan	013
Caddo	015
Canadian	017
Carter	019
Cherokee	021
Choctaw	023
Cimarron	025
Cleveland	027
Coal	029
Comanche	031
Cotton	033
Craig	035
Creek	037
Custer	039
Delaware	041
Dewey	043
Ellis	045
Garfield	047
Garvin	049
Grady	051
Grant	053
Greer	055
Harmon	057
Harper	059
Haskell	061
Hughes	063
Jackson	065
Jefferson	067
Johnston	069
Kay	071
Kingfisher	073
Kiowa	075
Latimer	077
Le Flore	079
Lincoln	081
Logan	083
Love	085
McClain	087
McCurtain	089
McIntosh	091
Major	093
Marshall	095
Mayes	097
Murray	099
Muskogee	101
Noble	103
Nowata	105
Okfuskee	107
Oklahoma	109
Okmulgee	111
Osage	113
Ottawa	115
Pawnee	117
Payne	119
Pittsburg	121
Pontotoc	123
Pottawatomie	125
Pushmataha	127
Roger Mills	129
Rogers	131
Seminole	133
Sequoyah	135
Stephens	137
Texas	139
Tillman	141
Tulsa	143
Wagoner	145
Washington	147
Washita	149
Woods	151
Woodward	153

State Name: Oregon
State Abbreviation: OR
State Code: 41

County Name	Code
Baker	001
Benton	003
Clackamas	005
Clatsop	007
Columbia	009
Coos	011
Crook	013
Curry	015
Deschutes	017
Douglas	019
Gilliam	021
Grant	023
Harney	025
Hood River	027
Jackson	029
Jefferson	031
Josephine	033
Klamath	035
Lake	037
Lane	039
Lincoln	041
Linn	043
Malheur	045
Marion	047
Morrow	049
Multnomah	051
Polk	053
Sherman	055
Tillamook	057
Umatilla	059
Union	061
Wallowa	063
Wasco	065
Washington	067
Wheeler	069
Yamhill	071

State Name: Pennsylvania
State Abbreviation: PA
State Code: 42

County Name	Code
Adams	001
Allegheny	003
Armstrong	005
Beaver	007
Bedford	009
Berks	011
Blair	013
Bradford	015
Bucks	017
Butler	019
Cambria	021
Cameron	023
Carbon	025
Centre	027
Chester	029
Clarion	031
Clearfield	033
Clinton	035
Columbia	037
Crawford	039
Cumberland	041
Dauphin	043
Delaware	045
Elk	047
Erie	049
Fayette	051
Forest	053
Franklin	055
Fulton	057
Greene	059
Huntingdon	061
Indiana	063
Jefferson	065
Juniata	067
Lackawanna	069
Lancaster	071
Lawrence	073
Lebanon	075
Lehigh	077
Luzerne	079
Lycoming	081
McKean	083
Mercer	085
Mifflin	087
Monroe	089
Montgomery	091
Montour	093
Northampton	095
Northumberland	097
Perry	099
Philadelphia	101
Pike	103
Potter	105
Schuylkill	107
Snyder	109
Somerset	111
Sullivan	113
Susquehanna	115
Tioga	117
Union	119
Venango	121
Warren	123
Washington	125
Wayne	127
Westmoreland	129

County Name	Code
Wyoming	131
York	133

State Name: **Rhode Island**
State Abbreviation: **RI**
State Code: **44**

County Name	Code
Bristol	001
Kent	003
Newport	005
Providence	007
Washington	009

State Name: **South Carolina**
State Abbreviation: **SC**
State Code: **45**

County Name	Code
Abbeville	001
Aiken	003
Allendale	005
Anderson	007
Bamberg	009
Barnwell	011
Beaufort	013
Berkeley	015
Calhoun	017
Charleston	019
Cherokee	021
Chester	023
Chesterfield	025
Clarendon	027
Colleton	029
Darlington	031
Dillon	033
Dorchester	035
Edgefield	037
Fairfield	039
Florence	041
Georgetown	043
Greenville	045
Greenwood	047
Hampton	049
Horry	051
Jasper	053
Kershaw	055
Lancaster	057
Laurens	059
Lee	061
Lexington	063
McCormick	065
Marion	067
Marlboro	069
Newberry	071
Oconee	073
Orangeburg	075
Pickens	077
Richland	079
Saluda	081
Spartanburg	083
Sumter	085
Union	087
Williamsburg	089
York	091

State Name: **South Dakota**
State Abbreviation: **SD**
State Code: **46**

County Name	Code
Aurora	003
Beadle	005
Bennett	007
Bon Homme	009
Brookings	011
Brown	013
Brule	015
Buffalo	017
Butte	019
Campbell	021
Charles Mix	023
Clark	025
Clay	027
Codington	029
Corson	031
Custer	033
Davison	035
Day	037
Deuel	039
Dewey	041
Douglas	043
Edmunds	045
Fall River	047
Faulk	049
Grant	051
Gregory	053
Haakon	055
Hamlin	057
Hand	059
Hanson	061
Harding	063
Hughes	065
Hutchinson	067
Hyde	069
Jackson	071
Jerauld	073
Jones	075
Kingsbury	077
Lake	079
Lawrence	081
Lincoln	083
Lyman	085
McCook	087
McPherson	089
Marshall	091
Meade	093
Mellette	095
Miner	097
Minnehaha	099
Moody	101
Pennington	103
Perkins	105
Potter	107
Roberts	109
Sanborn	111
Shannon	113
Spink	115
Stanley	117
Sully	119
Todd	121
Tripp	123
Turner	125
Union	127
Walworth	129
Yankton	135
Ziebach	137

State Name: **Tennessee**
State Abbreviation: **TN**
State Code: **47**

County Name	Code
Anderson	001
Bedford	003
Benton	005
Bledsoe	007
Blount	009
Bradley	011
Campbell	013
Cannon	015
Carroll	017
Carter	019
Cheatham	021
Chester	023
Claiborne	025
Clay	027
Cocke	029
Coffee	031
Crockett	033
Cumberland	035
Davidson	037
Decatur	039
DeKalb	041
Dickson	043
Dyer	045
Fayette	047
Fentress	049
Franklin	051
Gibson	053
Giles	055
Grainger	057
Greene	059
Grundy	061
Hamblen	063
Hamilton	065
Hancock	067
Hardeman	069
Hardin	071
Hawkins	073
Haywood	075
Henderson	077
Henry	079
Hickman	081
Houston	083
Humphreys	085
Jackson	087
Jefferson	089
Johnson	091
Knox	093
Lake	095
Lauderdale	097
Lawrence	099
Lewis	101
Lincoln	103
Loudon	105
McMinn	107
McNairy	109
Macon	111
Madison	113
Marion	115
Marshall	117
Maury	119
Meigs	121
Monroe	123
Montgomery	125
Moore	127
Morgan	129
Obion	131
Overton	133
Perry	135
Pickett	137
Polk	139
Putnam	141
Rhea	143
Roane	145
Robertson	147
Rutherford	149
Scott	151
Sequatchie	153
Sevier	155
Shelby	157
Smith	159
Stewart	161
Sullivan	163
Sumner	165
Tipton	167
Trousdale	169
Unicoi	171
Union	173
Van Buren	175

State Name: **Texas**
State Abbreviation: **TX**
State Code: **48**

County Name	Code
Anderson	001
Andrews	003
Angelina	005
Aransas	007
Archer	009
Armstrong	011
Atascosa	013
Austin	015
Bailey	017
Bandera	019
Bastrop	021
Baylor	023
Bee	025
Bell	027
Bexar	029
Blanco	031
Borden	033
Bosque	035
Bowie	037
Brazoria	039
Brazos	041
Brewster	043
Briscoe	045
Brooks	047
Brown	049
Burleson	051
Burnet	053
Caldwell	055
Calhoun	057
Callahan	059
Cameron	061
Camp	063
Carson	065
Cass	067
Castro	069
Chambers	071
Cherokee	073
Childress	075
Clay	077
Cochran	079
Coke	081
Coleman	083
Collin	085
Collingsworth	087
Colorado	089
Comal	091
Comanche	093
Concho	095
Cooke	097
Coryell	099
Cottle	101
Crane	103
Crockett	105
Crosby	107
Culberson	109
Dallam	111
Dallas	113
Dawson	115
Deaf Smith	117
Delta	119
Denton	121
DeWitt	123
Dickens	125
Dimmit	127
Donley	129
Duval	131
Eastland	133
Ector	135
Edwards	137
Ellis	139
El Paso	141
Erath	143
Falls	145
Fannin	147
Fayette	149
Fisher	151
Floyd	153
Foard	155
Fort Bend	157
Franklin	159
Freestone	161
Frio	163
Gaines	165
Galveston	167
Garza	169
Gillespie	171
Glasscock	173
Goliad	175
Gonzales	177
Gray	179
Grayson	181
Gregg	183
Grimes	185
Guadalupe	187
Hale	189
Hall	191
Hamilton	193
Hansford	195
Hardeman	197
Hardin	199
Harris	201
Harrison	203
Hartley	205
Haskell	207
Hays	209
Hemphill	211
Henderson	213
Hidalgo	215
Hill	217
Hockley	219
Hood	221
Hopkins	223
Houston	225
Howard	227
Hudspeth	229
Hunt	231
Hutchinson	233
Irion	235
Jack	237
Jackson	239
Jasper	241
Jeff Davis	243
Jefferson	245
Jim Hogg	247
Jim Wells	249
Johnson	251
Jones	253
Karnes	255
Kaufman	257
Kendall	259
Kenedy	261
Kent	263
Kerr	265
Kimble	267
King	269
Kinney	271
Kleberg	273
Knox	275
Lamar	277
Lamb	279
Lampasas	281
La Salle	283
Lavaca	285
Lee	287
Leon	289
Liberty	291
Limestone	293
Lipscomb	295
Live Oak	297
Llano	299
Loving	301
Lubbock	303
Lynn	305
McCulloch	307
McLennan	309
McMullen	311
Madison	313
Marion	315
Martin	317
Mason	319
Matagorda	321
Maverick	323
Medina	325
Menard	327
Midland	329
Milam	331
Mills	333
Mitchell	335
Montague	337
Montgomery	339
Moore	341
Morris	343
Motley	345
Nacogdoches	347
Navarro	349
Newton	351
Nolan	353
Nueces	355
Ochiltree	357
Oldham	359
Orange	361
Palo Pinto	363
Panola	365
Parker	367
Parmer	369
Pecos	371
Polk	373
Potter	375
Presidio	377
Rains	379
Randall	381
Reagan	383
Real	385
Red River	387
Reeves	389
Refugio	391
Roberts	393
Robertson	395
Rockwall	397
Runnels	399
Rusk	401
Sabine	403
San Augustine	405
San Jacinto	407
San Patricio	409
San Saba	411
Schleicher	413
Scurry	415
Shackelford	417
Shelby	419
Sherman	421
Smith	423
Somervell	425
Starr	427
Stephens	429
Sterling	431
Stonewall	433
Sutton	435

698

County Name	Code		County Name	Code		County Name	Code
Swisher	437		Addison	001		Mecklenburg	117
Tarrant	439		Bennington	003		Middlesex	119
Taylor	441		Caledonia	005		Montgomery	121
Terrell	443		Chittenden	007		Nelson	125
Terry	445		Essex	009		New Kent	127
Throckmorton	447		Franklin	011		Northampton	131
Titus	449		Grand Isle	013		Northumberland	133
Tom Green	451		Lamoille	015		Nottoway	135
Travis	453		Orange	017		Orange	137
Trinity	455		Orleans	019		Page	139
Tyler	457		Rutland	021		Patrick	141
Upshur	459		Washington	023		Pittsylvania	143
Upton	461		Windham	025		Powhatan	145
Uvalde	463		Windsor	027		Prince Edward	147
Val Verde	465					Prince George	149
Van Zandt	467		**State Name:**	**Virginia**		Prince William	153
Victoria	469		**State Abbreviation:**	**VA**		Pulaski	155
Walker	471		**State Code:**	**51**		Rappahannock	157
Waller	473					Richmond	159
Ward	475		**County Name**	**Code**		Roanoke	161
Washington	477		Accomack	001		Rockbridge	163
Webb	479		Albemarle	003		Rockingham	165
Wharton	481		Alleghany	005		Russell	167
Wheeler	483		Amelia	007		Scott	169
Wichita	485		Amherst	009		Shenandoah	171
Wilbarger	487		Appomattox	011		Smyth	173
Willacy	489		Arlington	013		Southampton	175
Williamson	491		Augusta	015		Spotsylvania	177
Wilson	493		Bath	017		Stafford	179
Winkler	495		Bedford	019		Surry	181
Wise	497		Bland	021		Sussex	183
Wood	499		Botetourt	023		Tazewell	185
Yoakum	501		Brunswick	025		Warren	187
Young	503		Buchanan	027		Washington	191
Zapata	505		Buckingham	029		Westmoreland	193
Zavala	507		Campbell	031		Wise	195
			Caroline	033		Wythe	197
State Name:	**Utah**		Carroll	035		York	199
State Abbreviation:	**UT**		Charles City	036		Alexandria city	510
State Code:	**49**		Charlotte	037		Bedford city	515
			Chesterfield	041		Bristol city	520
County Name	**Code**		Clarke	043		Buena Vista city	530
Beaver	001		Craig	045		Charlottesville city	540
Box Elder	003		Culpeper	047		Chesapeake city	550
Cache	005		Cumberland	049		Colonial Heights city	570
Carbon	007		Dickenson	051		Covington city	580
Daggett	009		Dinwiddie	053		Danville city	590
Davis	011		Essex	057		Emporia city	595
Duchesne	013		Fairfax	059		Fairfax city	600
Emery	015		Fauquier	061		Falls Church city	610
Garfield	017		Floyd	063		Franklin city	620
Grand	019		Fluvanna	065		Fredericksburg city	630
Iron	021		Franklin	067		Galax city	640
Juab	023		Frederick	069		Hampton city	650
Kane	025		Giles	071		Harrisonburg city	660
Millard	027		Gloucester	073		Hopewell city	670
Morgan	029		Goochland	075		Lexington city	678
Piute	031		Grayson	077		Lynchburg city	680
Rich	033		Greene	079		Manassas city	683
Salt Lake	035		Greensville	081		Manassas Park city	685
San Juan	037		Halifax	083		Martinsville city	690
Sanpete	039		Hanover	085		Newport News city	700
Sevier	041		Henrico	087		Norfolk city	710
Summit	043		Henry	089		Norton city	720
Tooele	045		Highland	091		Petersburg city	730
Uintah	047		Isle of Wight	093		Poquoson city	735
Utah	049		James City	095		Portsmouth city	740
Wasatch	051		King and Queen	097		Radford city	750
Washington	053		King George	099		Richmond city	760
Wayne	055		King William	101		Roanoke city	770
Weber	057		Lancaster	103		Salem city	775
			Lee	105		Staunton city	790
State Name:	**Vermont**		Loudoun	107		Suffolk city	800
State Abbreviation:	**VT**		Louisa	109		Virginia Beach city	810
State Code:	**50**		Lunenburg	111		Waynesboro city	820
			Madison	113		Williamsburg city	830
County Name	**Code**		Mathews	115		Winchester city	840

State Name: **Washington**
State Abbreviation: **WA**
State Code: **53**

County Name	Code
Adams	001
Asotin	003
Benton	005
Chelan	007
Clallam	009
Clark	011
Columbia	013
Cowlitz	015
Douglas	017
Ferry	019
Franklin	021
Garfield	023
Grant	025
Grays Harbor	027
Island	029
Jefferson	031
King	033
Kitsap	035
Kittitas	037
Klickitat	039
Lewis	041
Lincoln	043
Mason	045
Okanogan	047
Pacific	049
Pend Oreille	051
Pierce	053
San Juan	055
Skagit	057
Skamania	059
Snohomish	061
Spokane	063
Stevens	065
Thurston	067
Wahkiakum	069
Walla Walla	071
Whatcom	073
Whitman	075
Yakima	077

State Name: **West Virginia**
State Abbreviation: **WV**
State Code: **54**

County Name	Code
Barbour	001
Berkeley	003
Boone	005
Braxton	007
Brooke	009
Cabell	011
Calhoun	013
Clay	015
Doddridge	017
Fayette	019
Gilmer	021
Grant	023
Greenbrier	025
Hampshire	027
Hancock	029
Hardy	031
Harrison	033
Jackson	035
Jefferson	037
Kanawha	039
Lewis	041
Lincoln	043
Logan	045
McDowell	047
Marion	049
Marshall	051
Mason	053
Mercer	055
Mineral	057
Mingo	059
Monongalia	061
Monroe	063
Morgan	065
Nicholas	067
Ohio	069
Pendleton	071
Pleasants	073
Pocahontas	075
Preston	077
Putnam	079
Raleigh	081
Randolph	083
Ritchie	085
Roane	087
Summers	089
Taylor	091
Tucker	093
Tyler	095
Upshur	097
Wayne	099
Webster	101
Wetzel	103
Wirt	105
Wood	107
Wyoming	109

State Name: **Wisconsin**
State Abbreviation: **WI**
State Code: **55**

County Name	Code
Adams	001
Ashland	003
Barron	005
Bayfield	007
Brown	009
Buffalo	011
Burnett	013
Calumet	015
Chippewa	017
Clark	019
Columbia	021
Crawford	023
Dane	025
Dodge	027
Door	029
Douglas	031
Dunn	033
Eau Claire	035
Florence	037
Fond du Lac	039
Forest	041
Grant	043
Green	045
Green Lake	047
Iowa	049
Iron	051
Jackson	053
Jefferson	055
Juneau	057
Kenosha	059
Kewaunee	061
La Crosse	063
Lafayette	065
Langlade	067
Lincoln	069
Manitowoc	071
Marathon	073
Marinette	075
Marquette	077
Menominee	078
Milwaukee	079
Monroe	081
Oconto	083
Oneida	085
Outagamie	087
Ozaukee	089
Pepin	091
Pierce	093
Polk	095
Portage	097
Price	099
Racine	101
Richland	103
Rock	105
Rusk	107
St. Croix	109
Sauk	111
Sawyer	113
Shawano	115
Sheboygan	117
Taylor	119
Trempealeau	121
Vernon	123
Vilas	125
Walworth	127
Washburn	129
Washington	131
Waukesha	133
Waupaca	135
Waushara	137
Winnebago	139
Wood	141

State Name: **Wyoming**
State Abbreviation: **WY**
State Code: **56**

County Name	Code
Albany	001
Big Horn	003
Campbell	005
Carbon	007
Converse	009
Crook	011
Fremont	013
Goshen	015
Hot Springs	017
Johnson	019
Laramie	021
Lincoln	023
Natrona	025
Niobrara	027
Park	029
Platte	031
Sheridan	033
Sublette	035
Sweetwater	037
Teton	039
Uinta	041
Washakie	043
Weston	045

ZIP Code Maps

The Community
Sourcebook
2004
18th EDITION
of ZIP Code
Demographics

Alabama

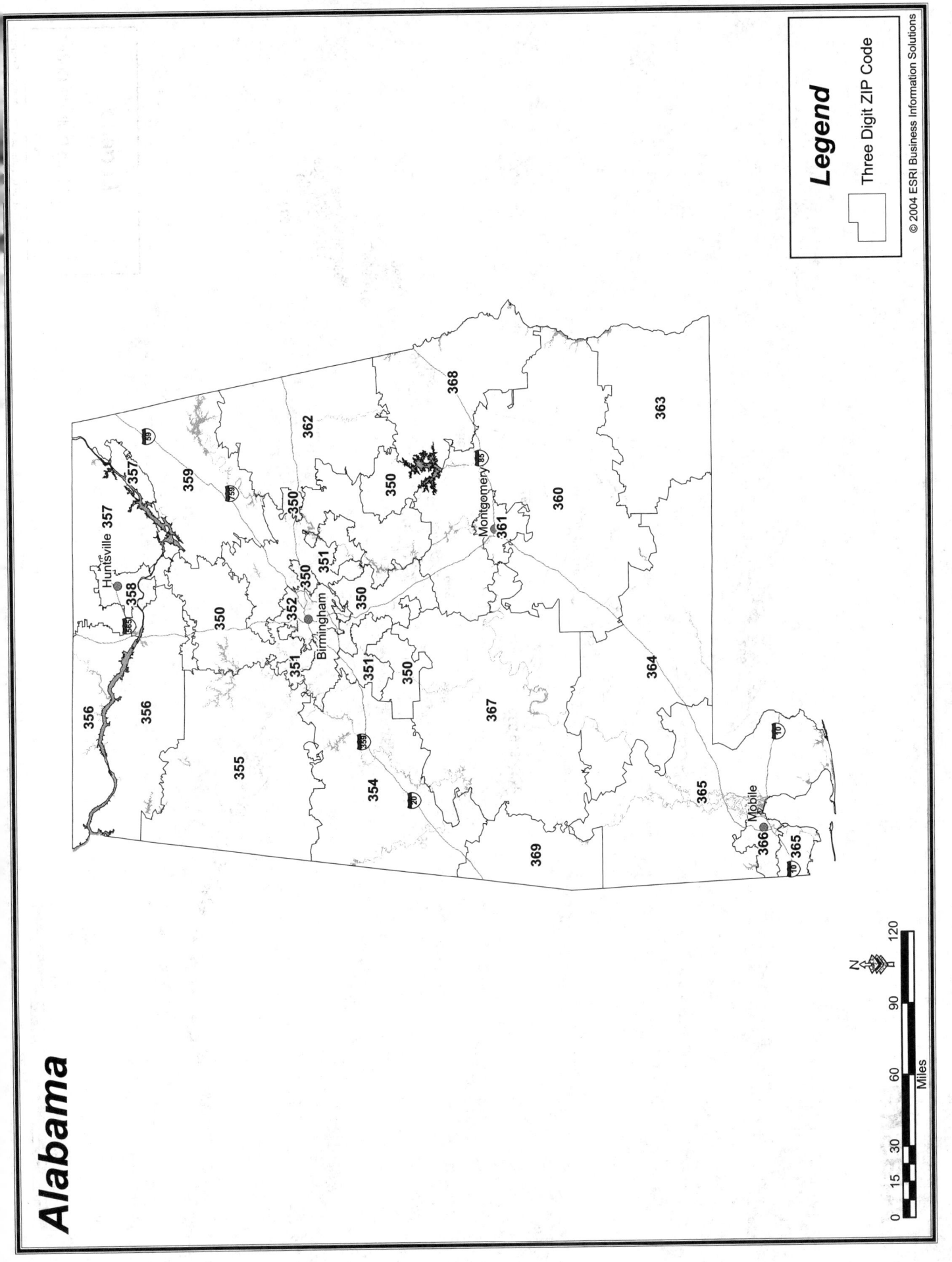

Alaska

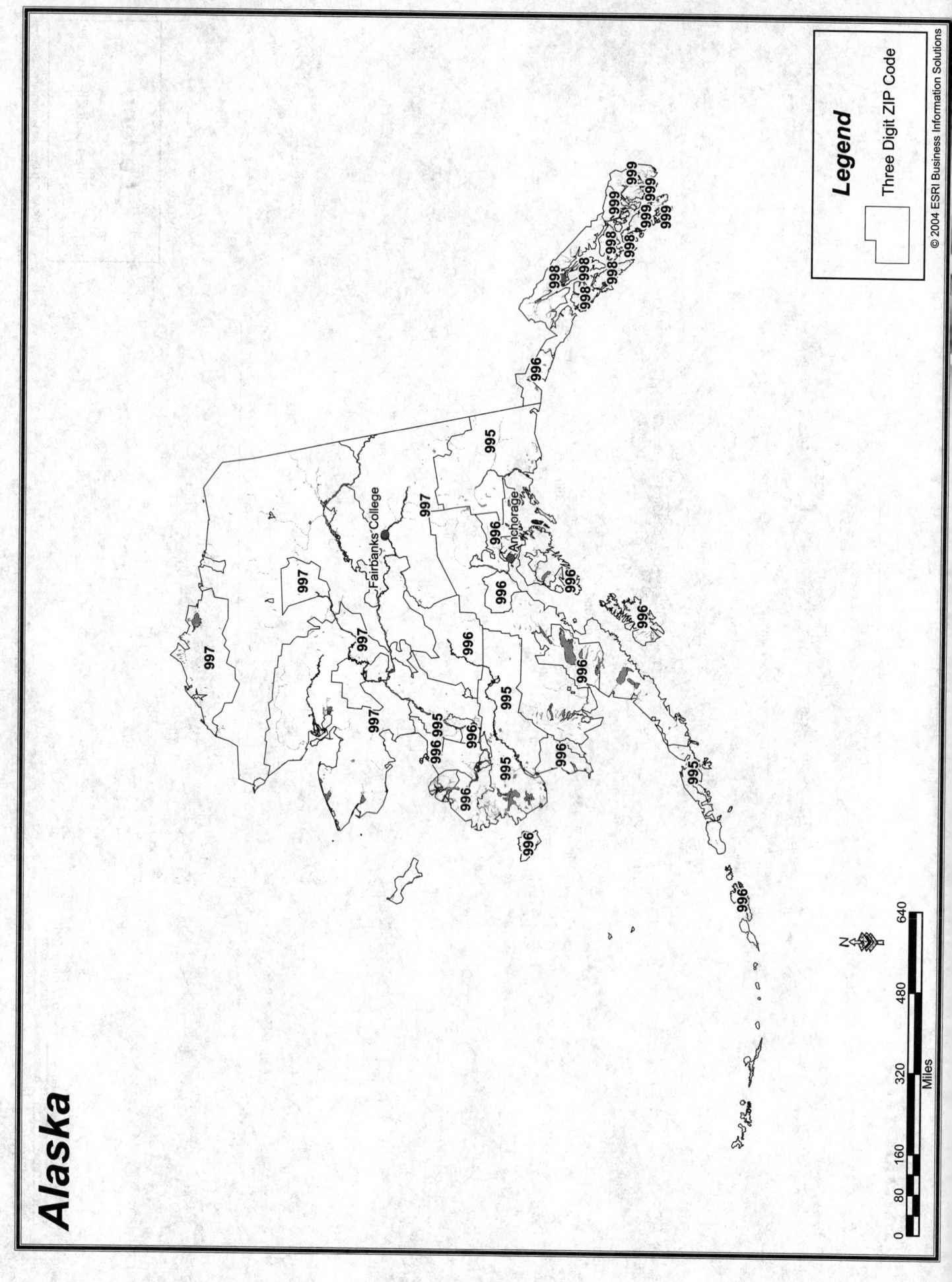

Miles
0   80   160   320   480   640

N

705

Arizona

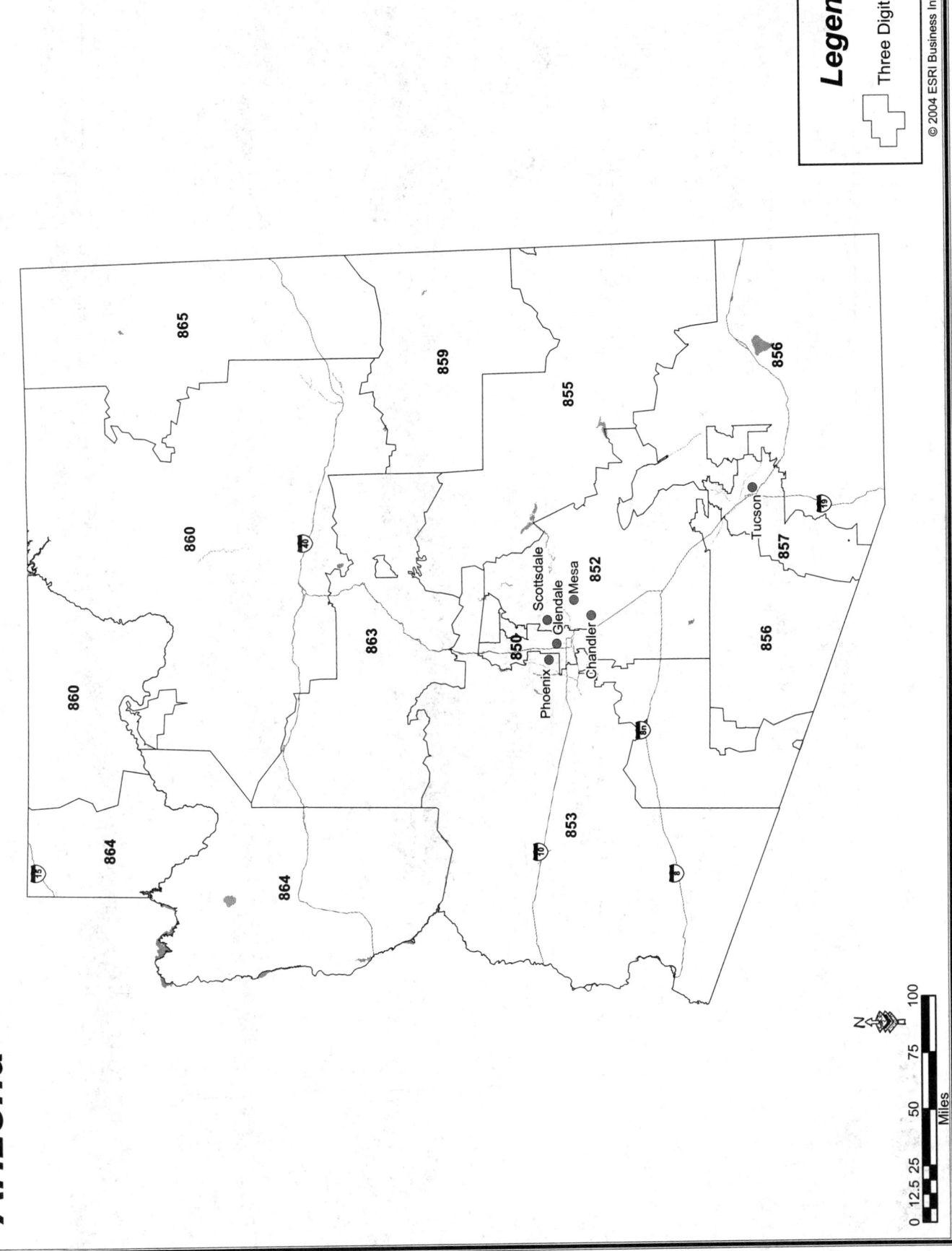

Legend

Three Digit ZIP Code

865

859

855

856

860

863

860

864

864

853

850

857

856

852

Scottsdale

Glendale

Mesa

Chandler

Phoenix

Tucson

N

0 12.5 25   50   75   100

Miles

706

Arkansas

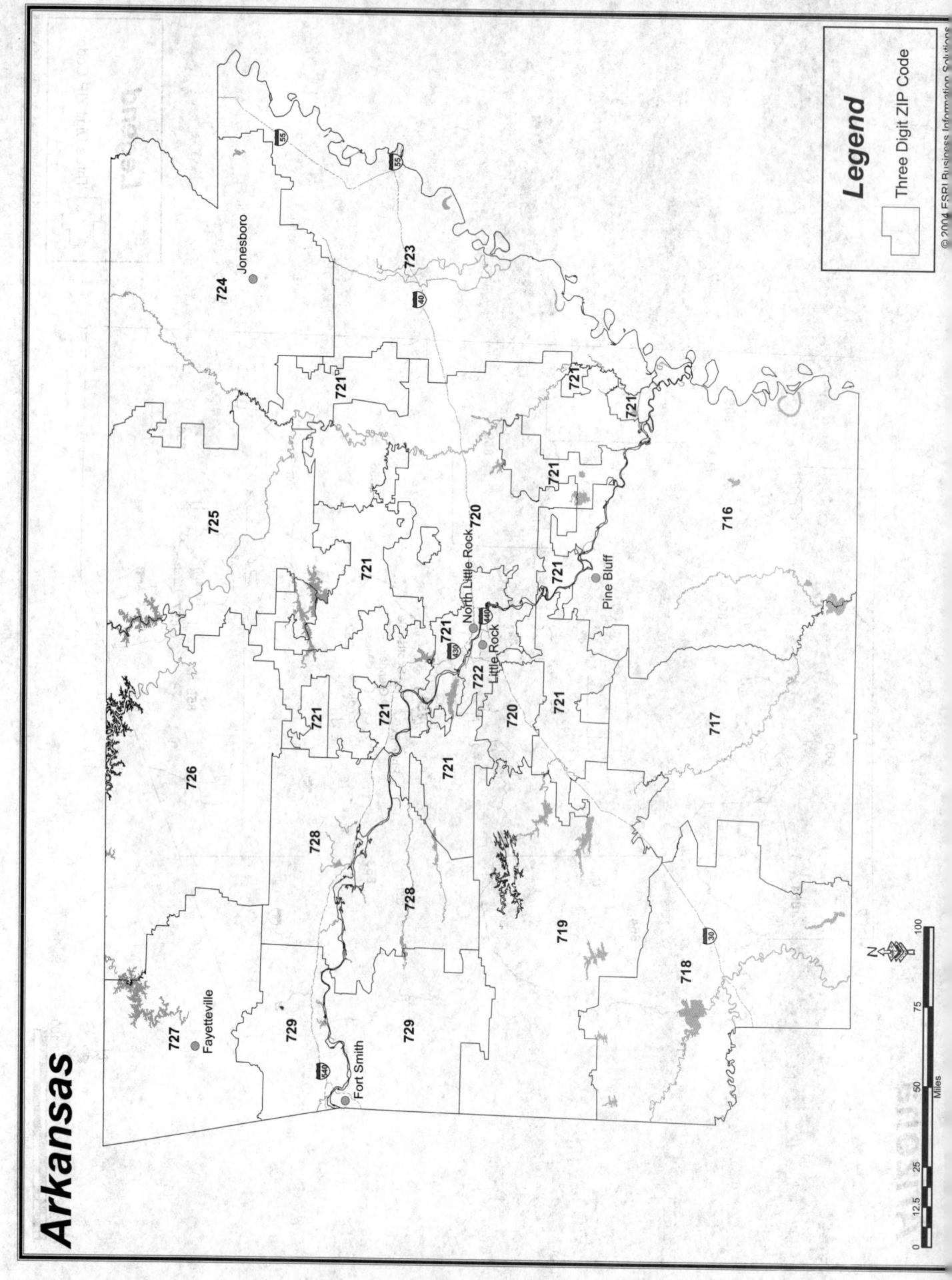

Legend

Three Digit ZIP Code

© 2004 ESRI Business Information Solutions

707

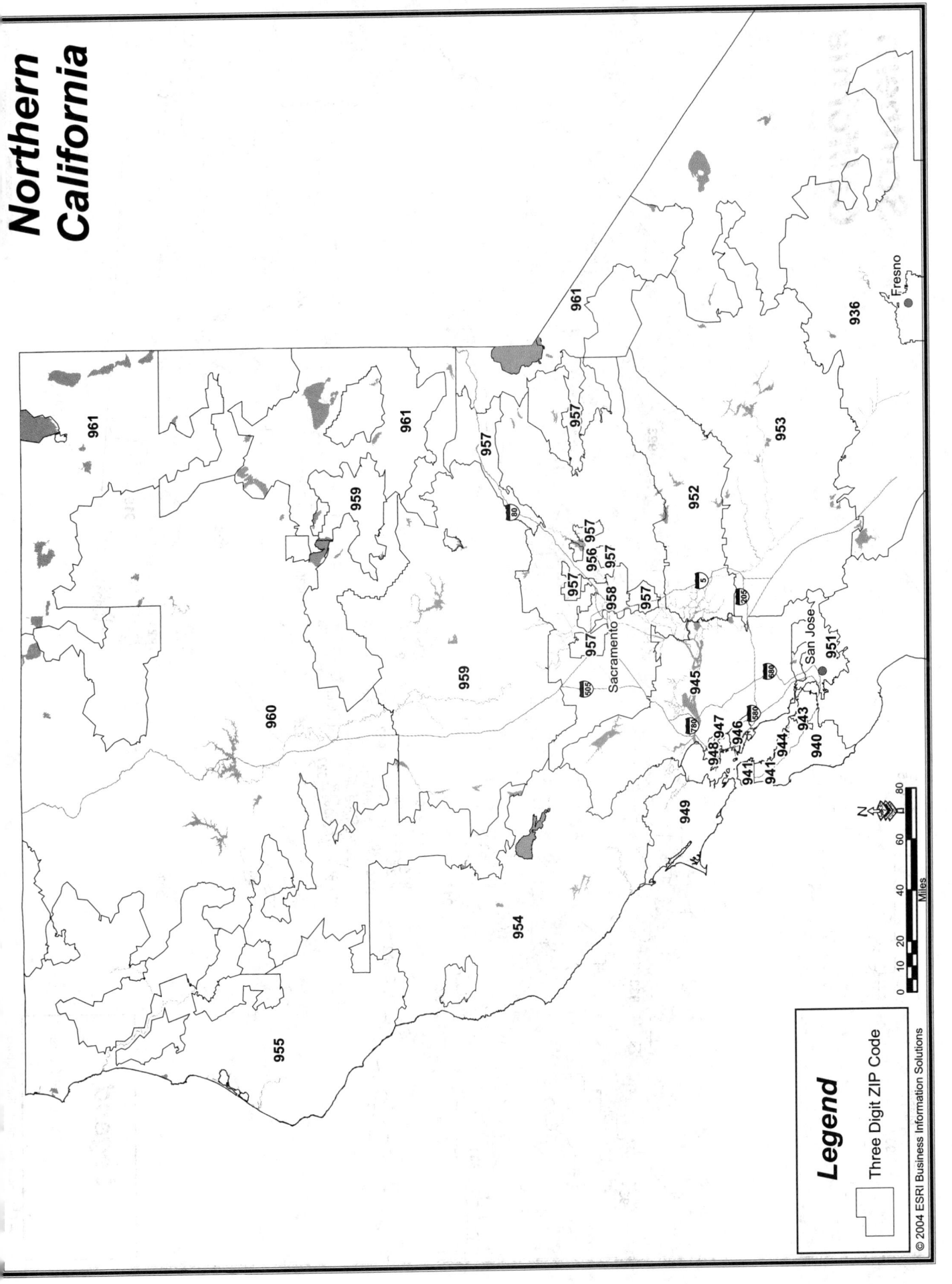

Northern California

Legend

Three Digit ZIP Code

© 2004 ESRI Business Information Solutions

708

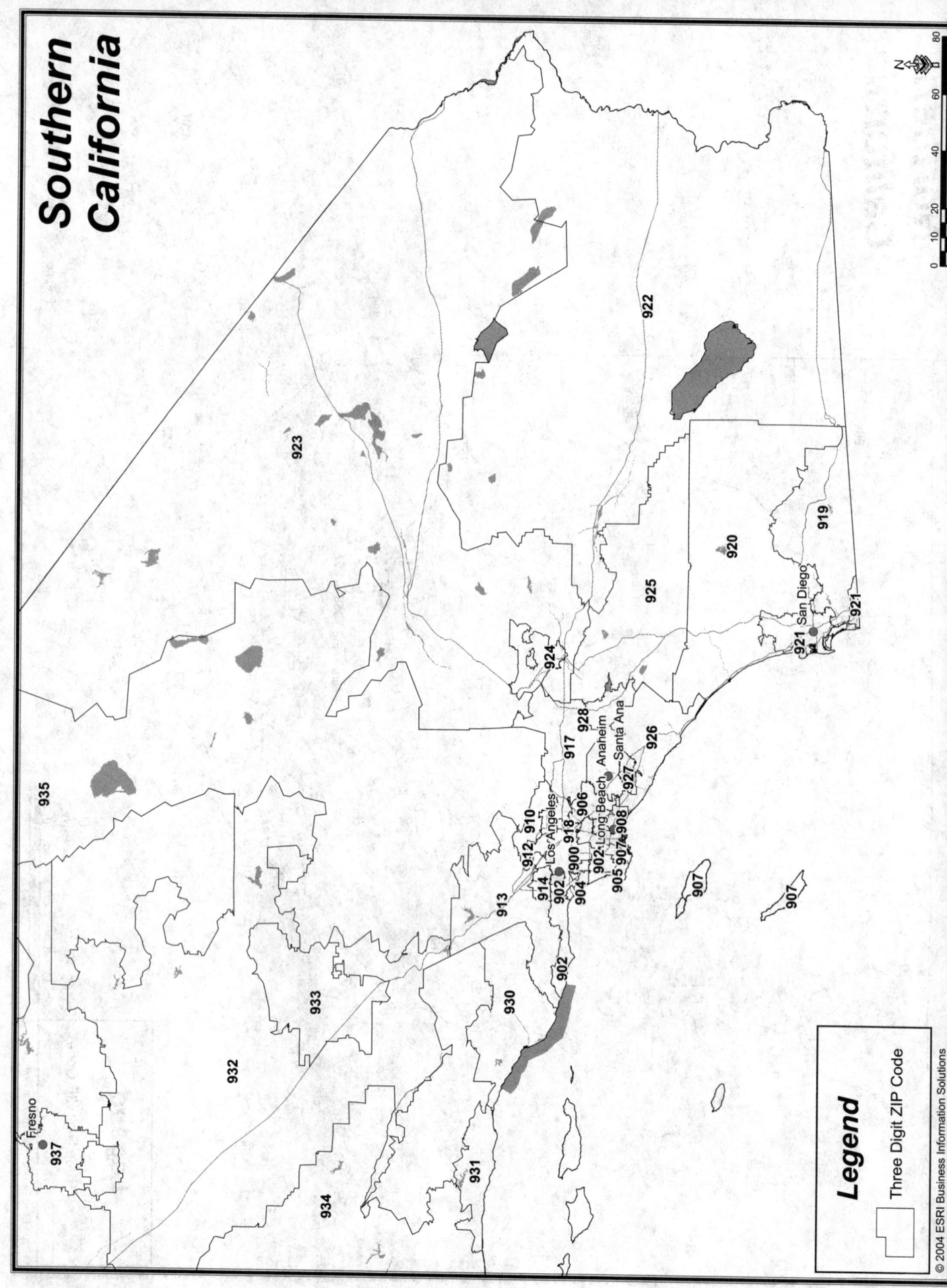

Southern California

Legend

Three Digit ZIP Code

© 2004 ESRI Business Information Solutions

709

Colorado

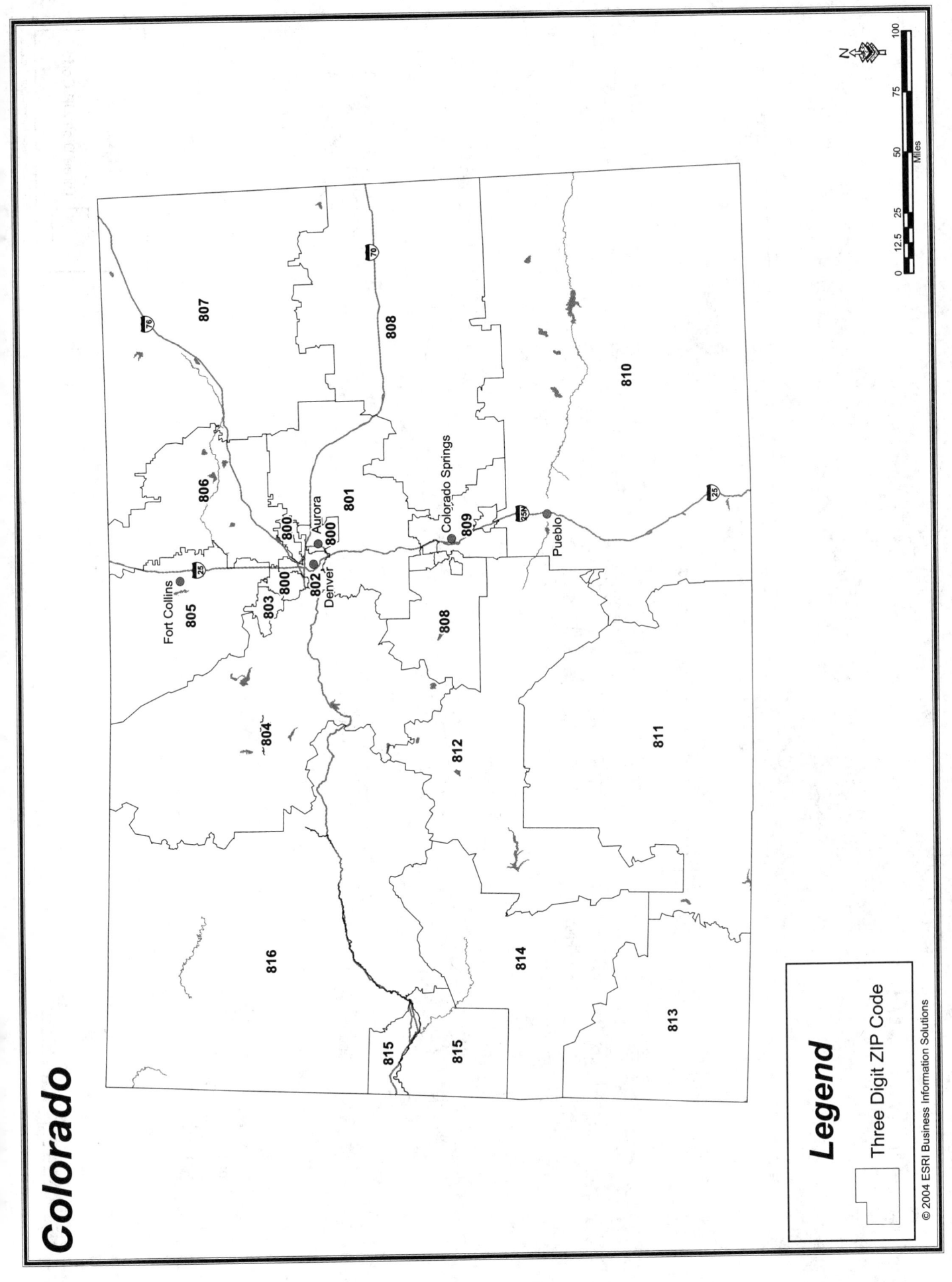

Legend

Three Digit ZIP Code

© 2004 ESRI Business Information Solutions

Connecticut

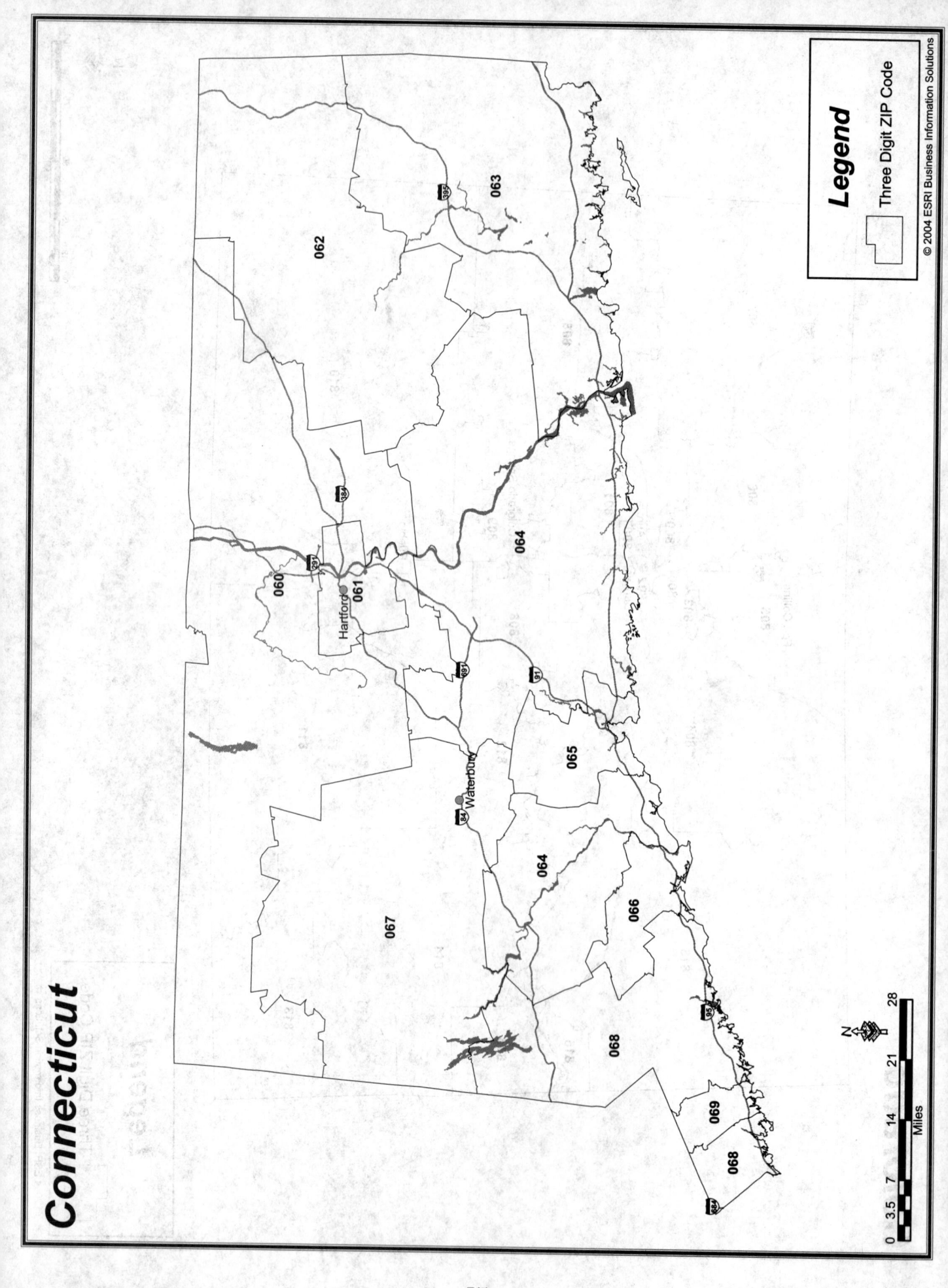

Legend

Three Digit ZIP Code

N

0 3.5 7   14   21   28
Miles

711

Delaware

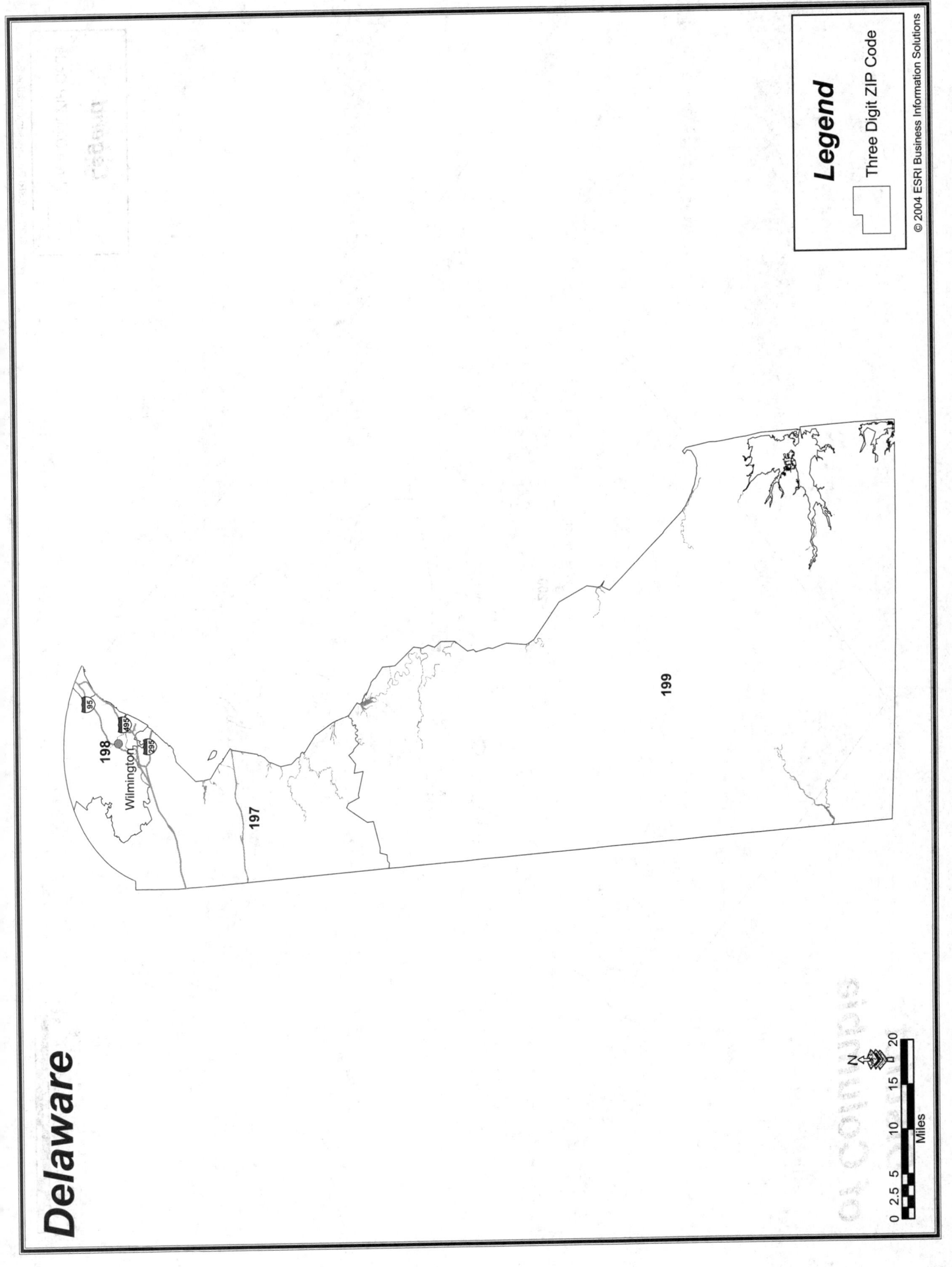

Legend

Three Digit ZIP Code

199

198

197

Wilmington

95

495

295

N

0 2.5 5   10   15   20
Miles

District
of Columbia

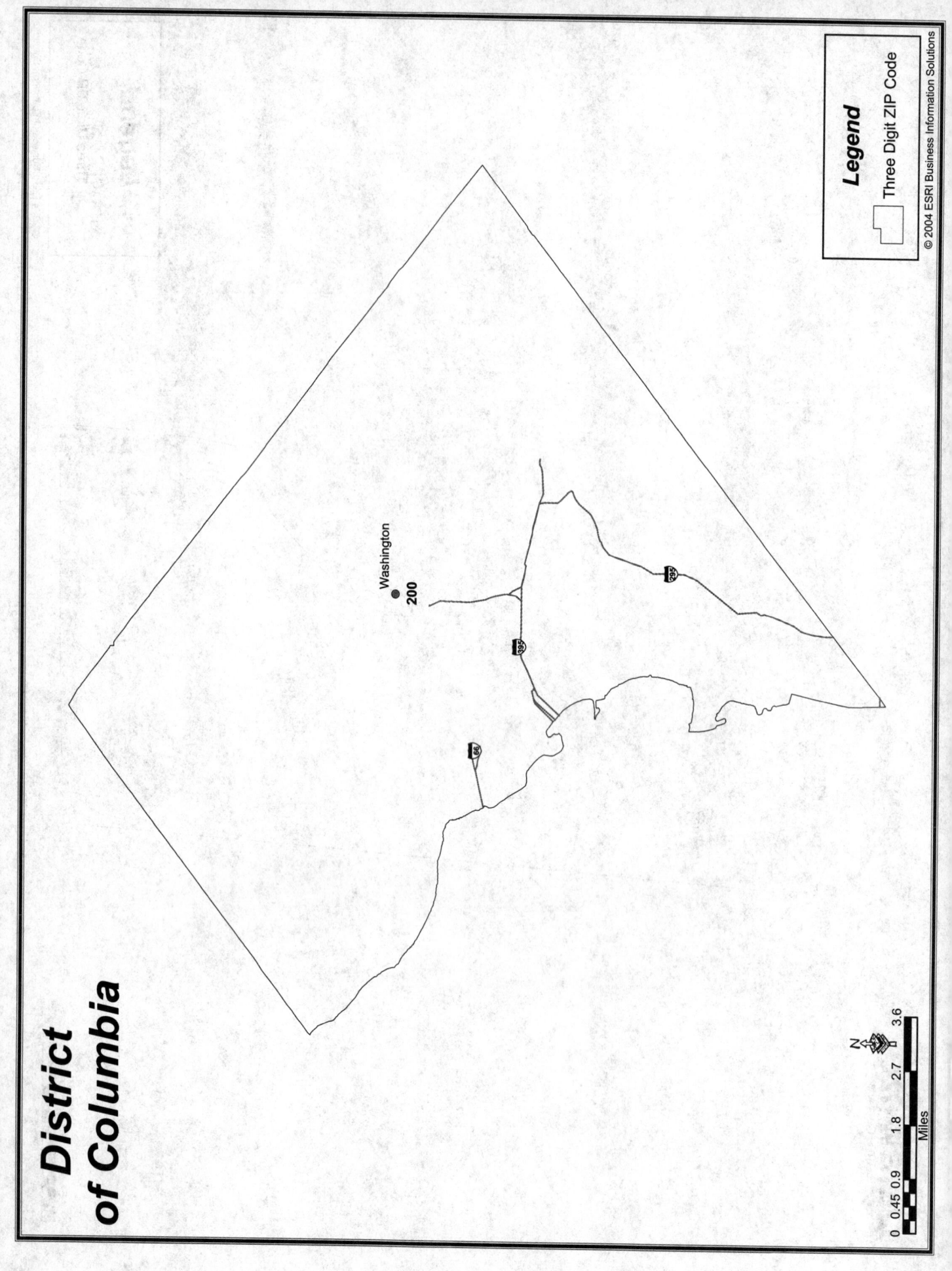

Washington
200

N

0 0.45 0.9   1.8   2.7   3.6
Miles

Florida

322 320 320 323 324 325 321 326 321 344 327 328 346 335 347 338 336 337 341 349 342 339 334 330 333 330 331 330

Jacksonville

Orlando

Tampa
St. Petersburg

Hialeah
Miami

N

0 15 30   60   90   120
Miles

Legend

Three Digit ZIP Code

© 2004 ESRI Business Information Solutions

714

Georgia

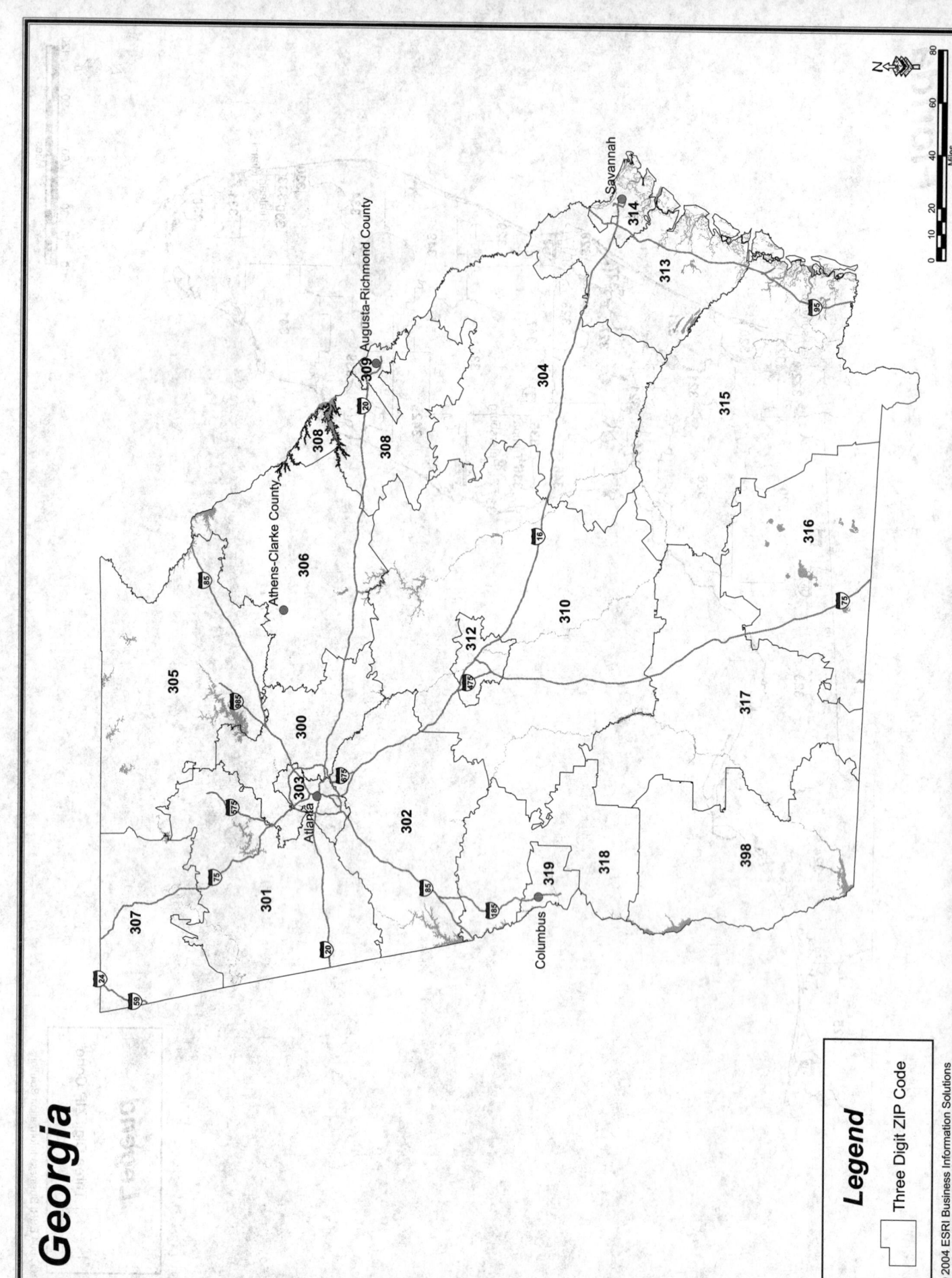

Legend

⬜ Three Digit ZIP Code

© 2004 ESRI Business Information Solutions

715

Hawaii

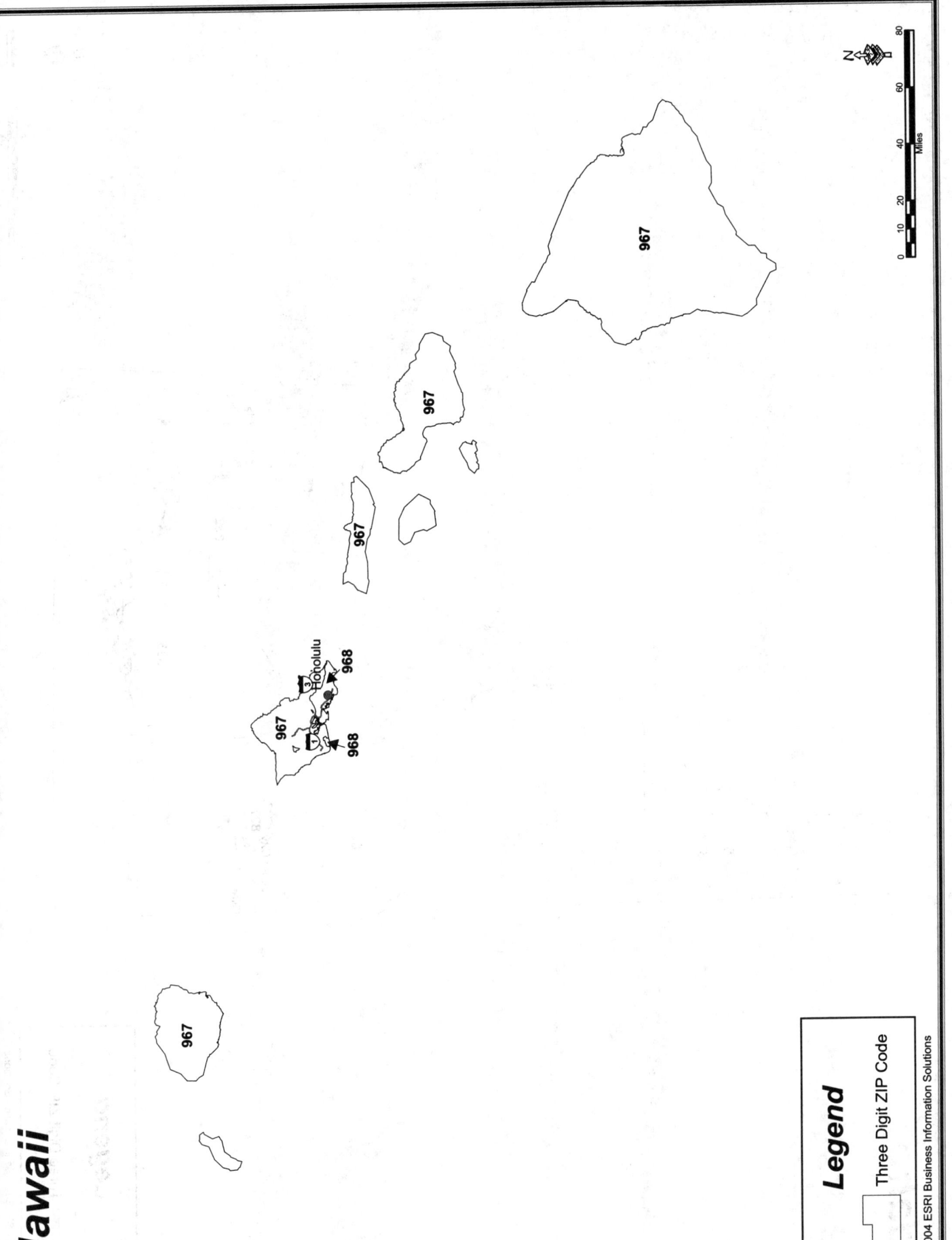

967

967

967

967

Honolulu
3
968
967
968

967

Legend

Three Digit ZIP Code

© 2004 ESRI Business Information Solutions

N

0 10 20 40 60 80
Miles

716

Idaho

838

807

835

834

Idaho Falls

832

Pocatello

833

836

837

Boise City

Nampa

0 15 30 60 90 120
Miles

N

Illinois

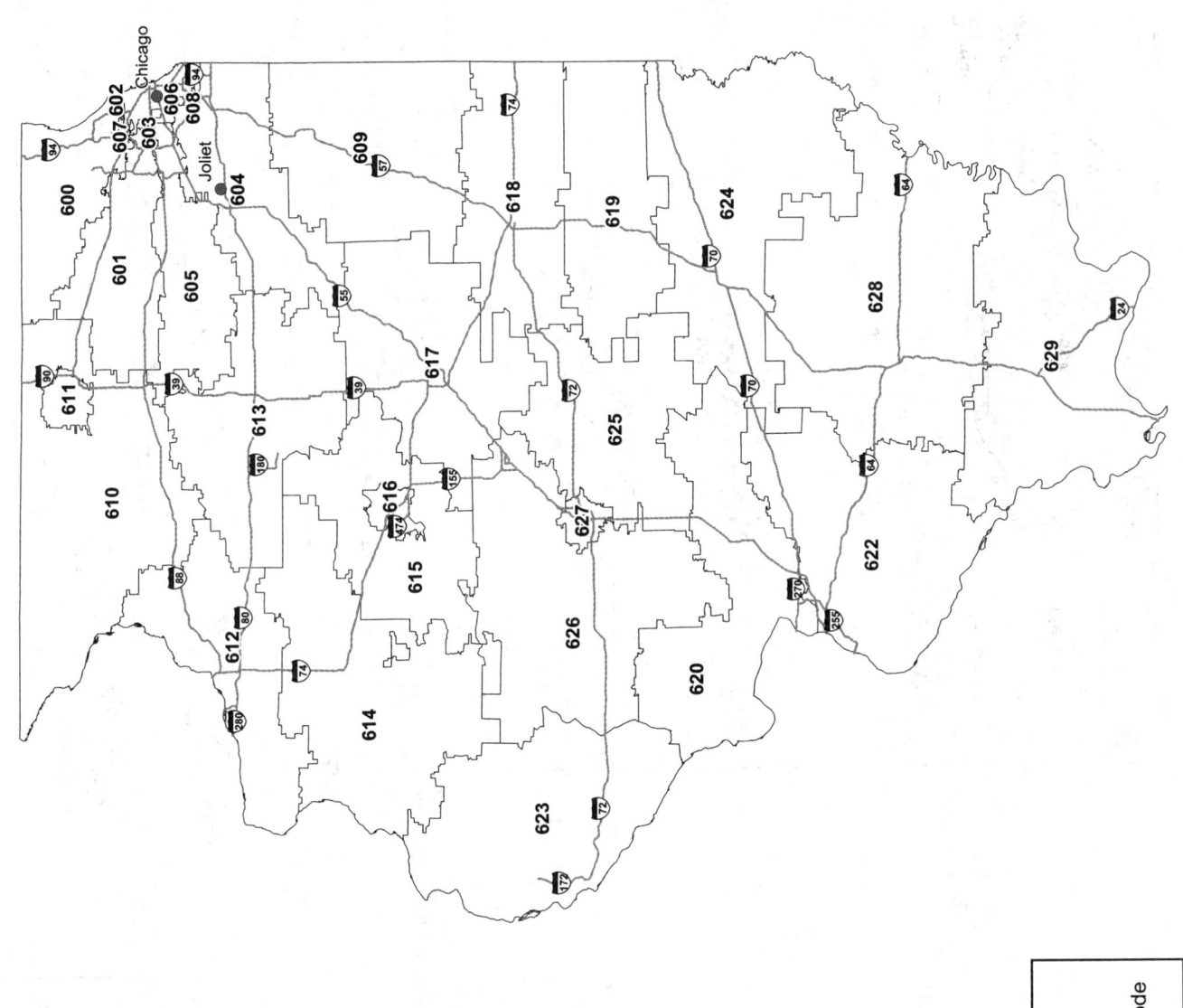

Chicago

Joliet

600
607 602
606
608
603
601
605
604
609
618
619
624
628
629
627
611
610
613
617
625
622
620
626
615
616
623
614
612

Legend

Three Digit ZIP Code

© 2004 ESRI Business Information Solutions

N

0 12.5 25   50   75   100

Miles

718

Indiana

Legend

☐ Three Digit ZIP Code

© 2004 ESRI Business Information Solutions

Miles
0 10 20 40 60 80

South Bend
Gary
Fort Wayne
Indianapolis
Evansville

466
465
463
464
468
467
469
460
462
461
473
472
470
471
474
475
476
477
478
479

Iowa

Three Digit ZIP Code map of Iowa showing cities Dubuque, Davenport, Des Moines, Ames, and Council Bluffs with ZIP code regions including 500, 501, 502, 503, 504, 505, 506, 507, 508, 510, 511, 512, 513, 514, 515, 516, 520, 521, 522, 523, 524, 525, 526, 527, 528.

Legend

☐ Three Digit ZIP Code

© 2004 ESRI Business Information Solutions

Kansas

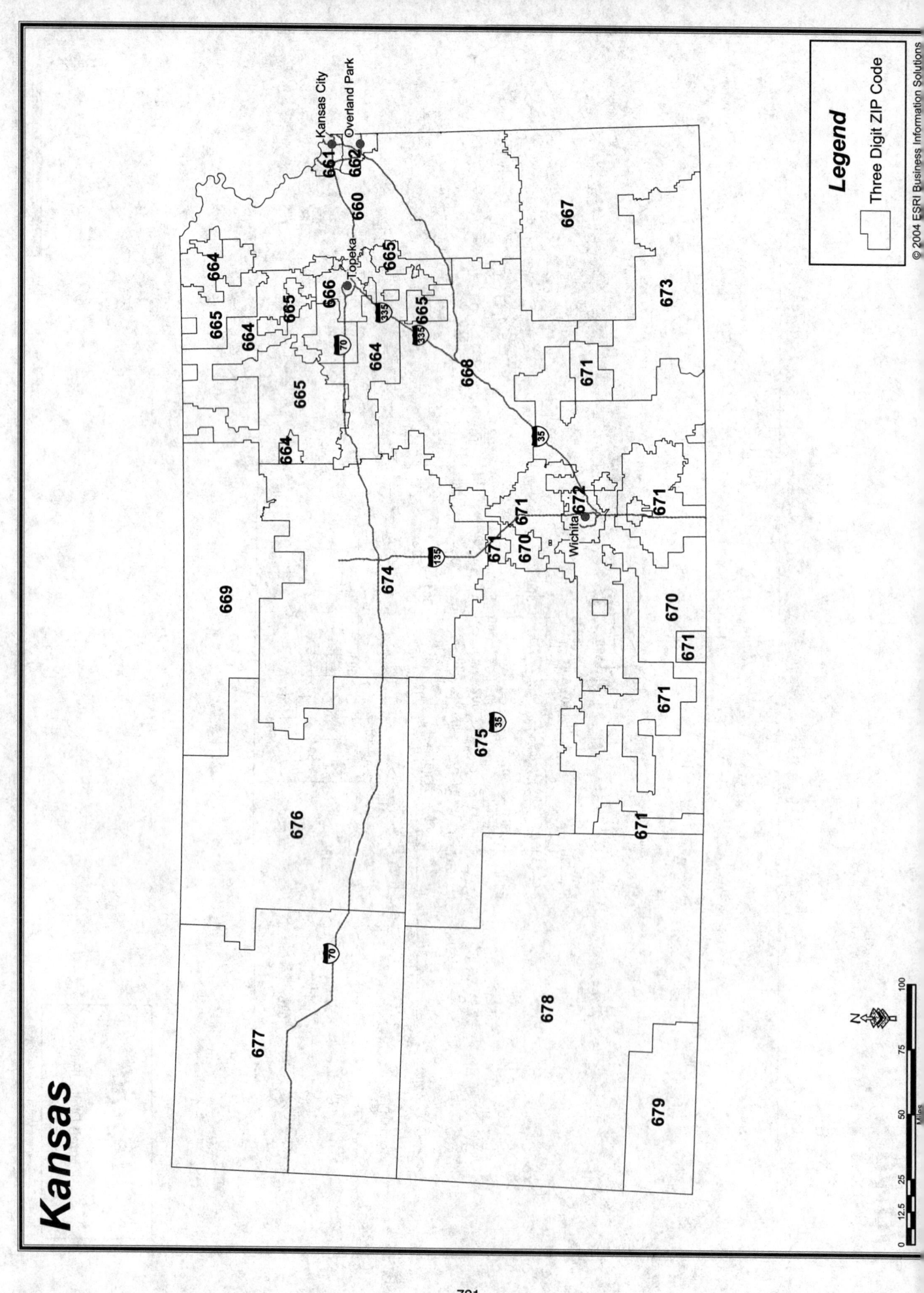

Kentucky

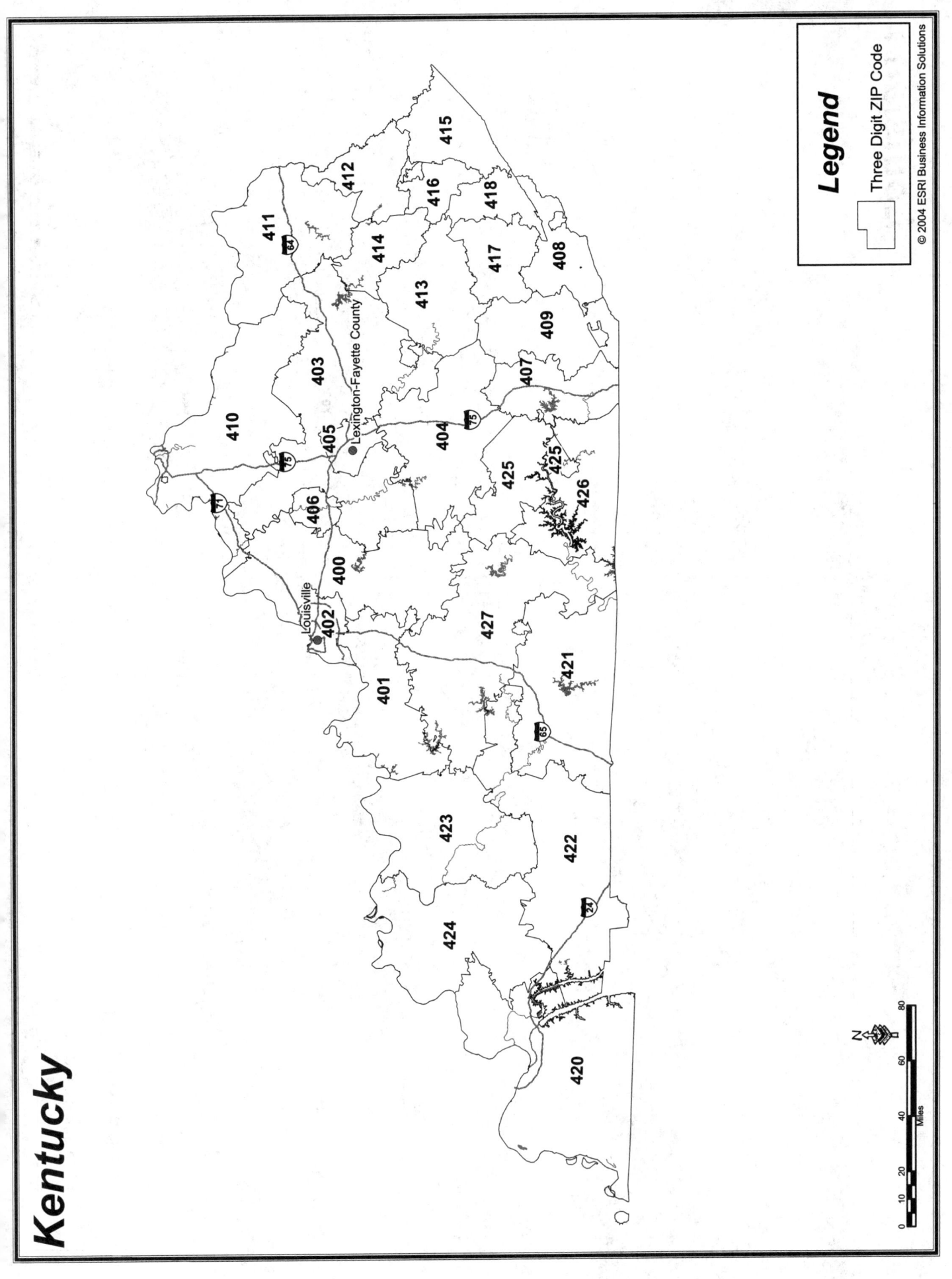

Legend

Three Digit ZIP Code

© 2004 ESRI Business Information Solutions

722

Louisiana

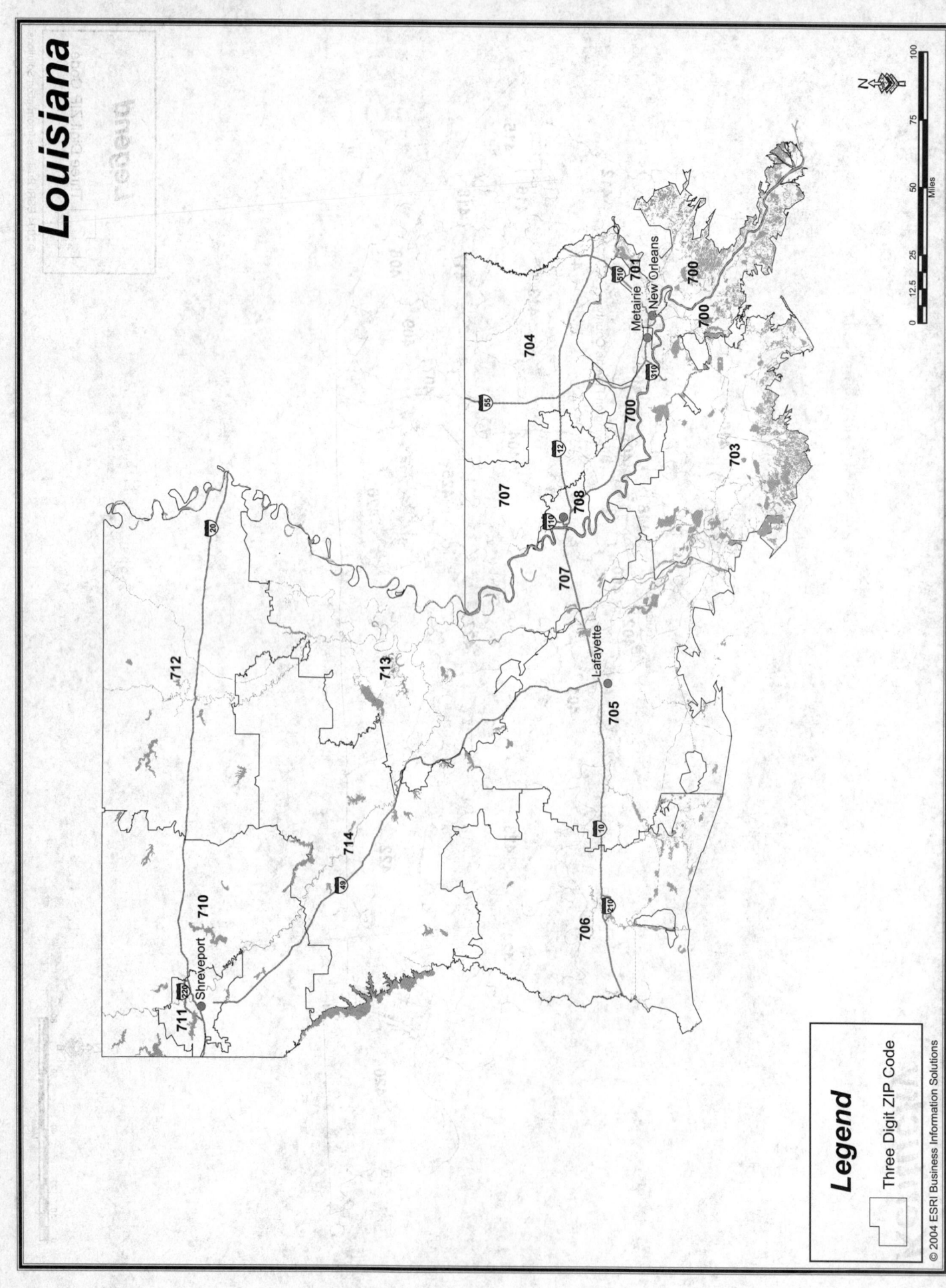

Legend

Three Digit ZIP Code

© 2004 ESRI Business Information Solutions

723

Maine

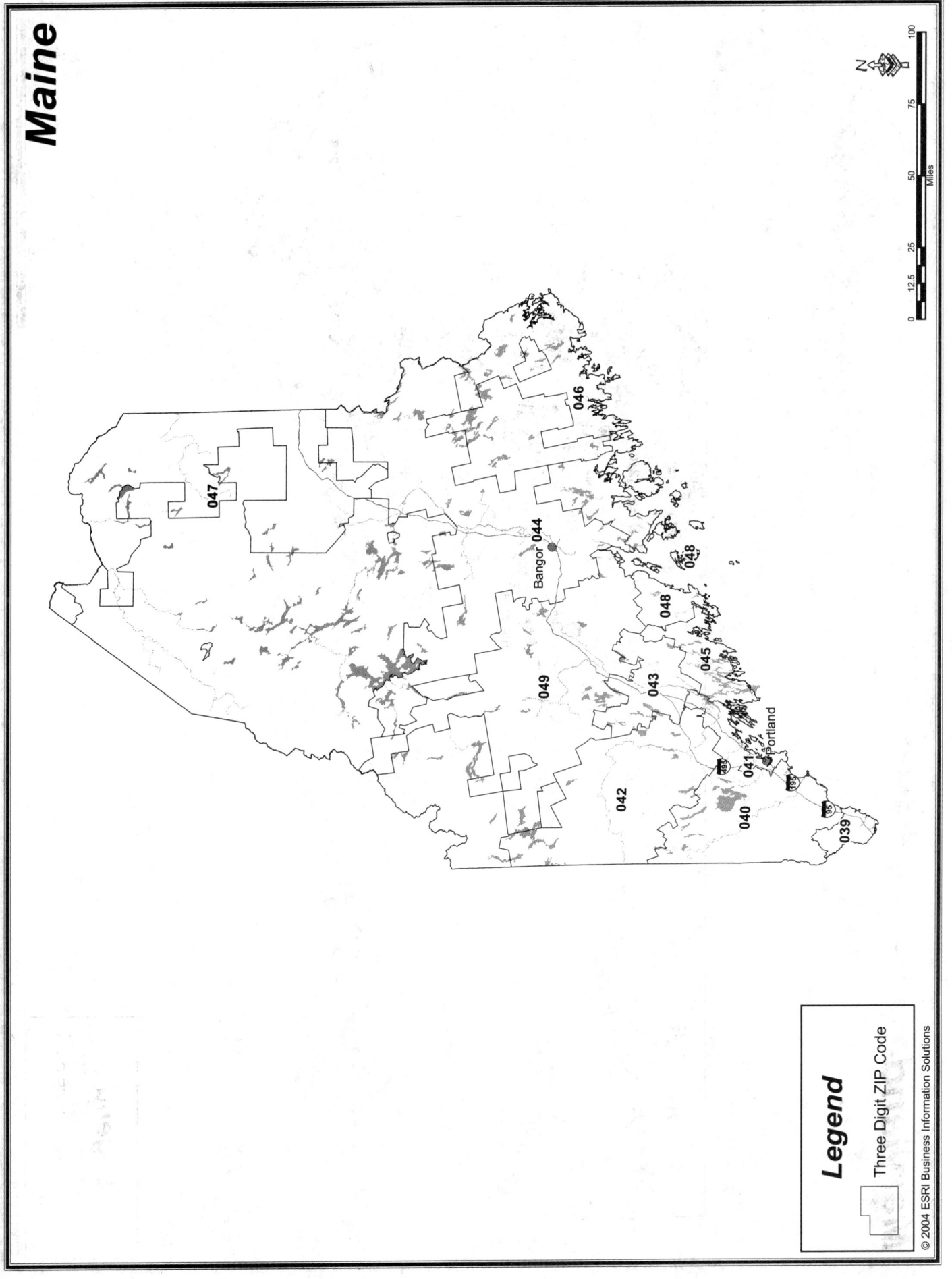

Legend

Three Digit ZIP Code

047

046

044 Bangor

048

048

045

049

043

042

040

041

Portland

039

Maryland

219
210
218
216
214
214A
211
212
95
695
83
211
210
97
211
210
210A
210
695
210
214
210A
210
Baltimore
210
206
95
70
207
209
295
Silver Spring
208
Bethesda
270
217
81
68
215

N

| 0 | 10 | 20 | 40 | 60 | 80 |
Miles

Legend

Three Digit ZIP Code

© 2004 ESRI Business Information Solutions

725

Massachusetts

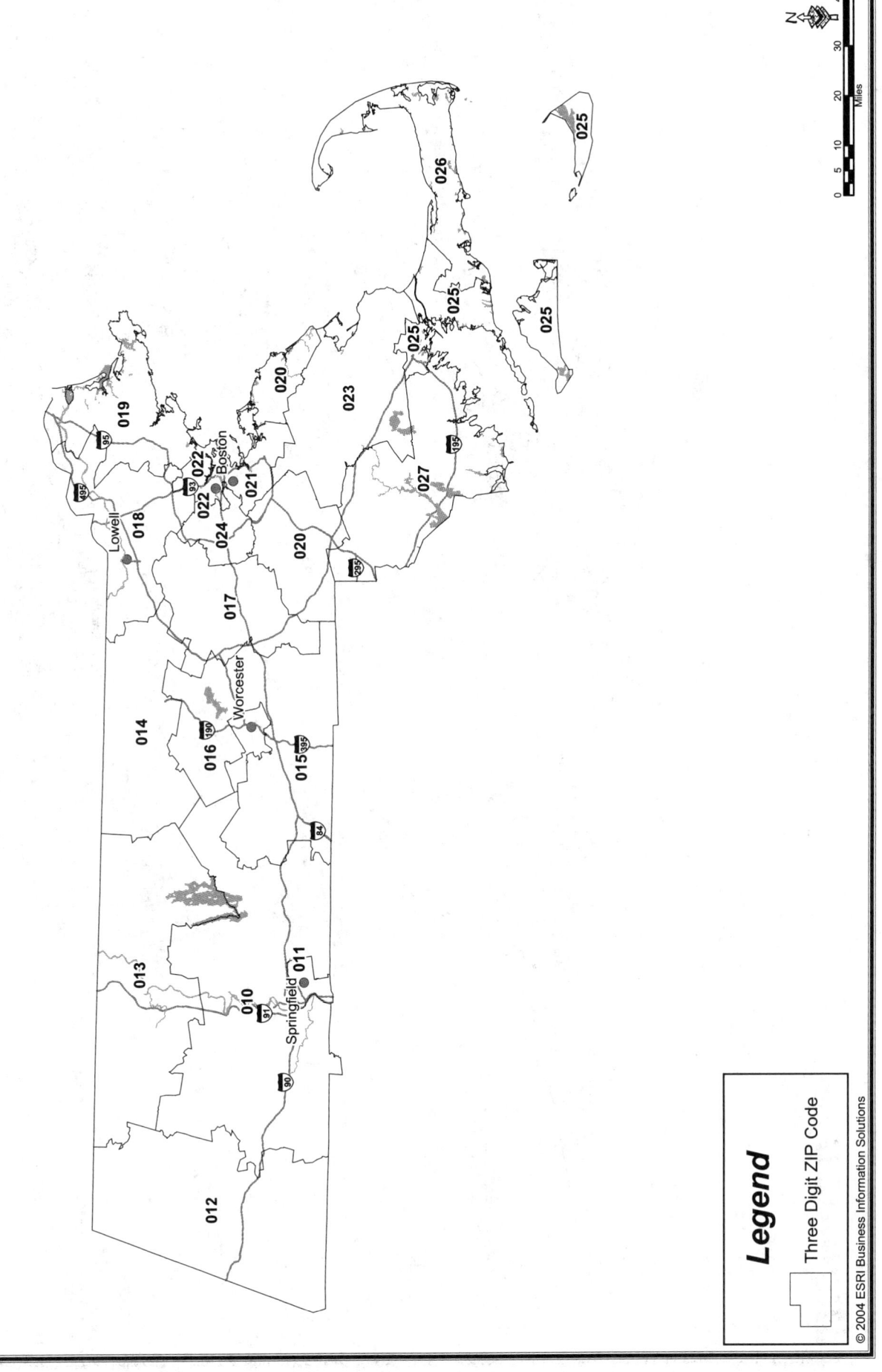

Legend

Three Digit ZIP Code

© 2004 ESRI Business Information Solutions

N

0 5 10 20 30 40
Miles

Michigan

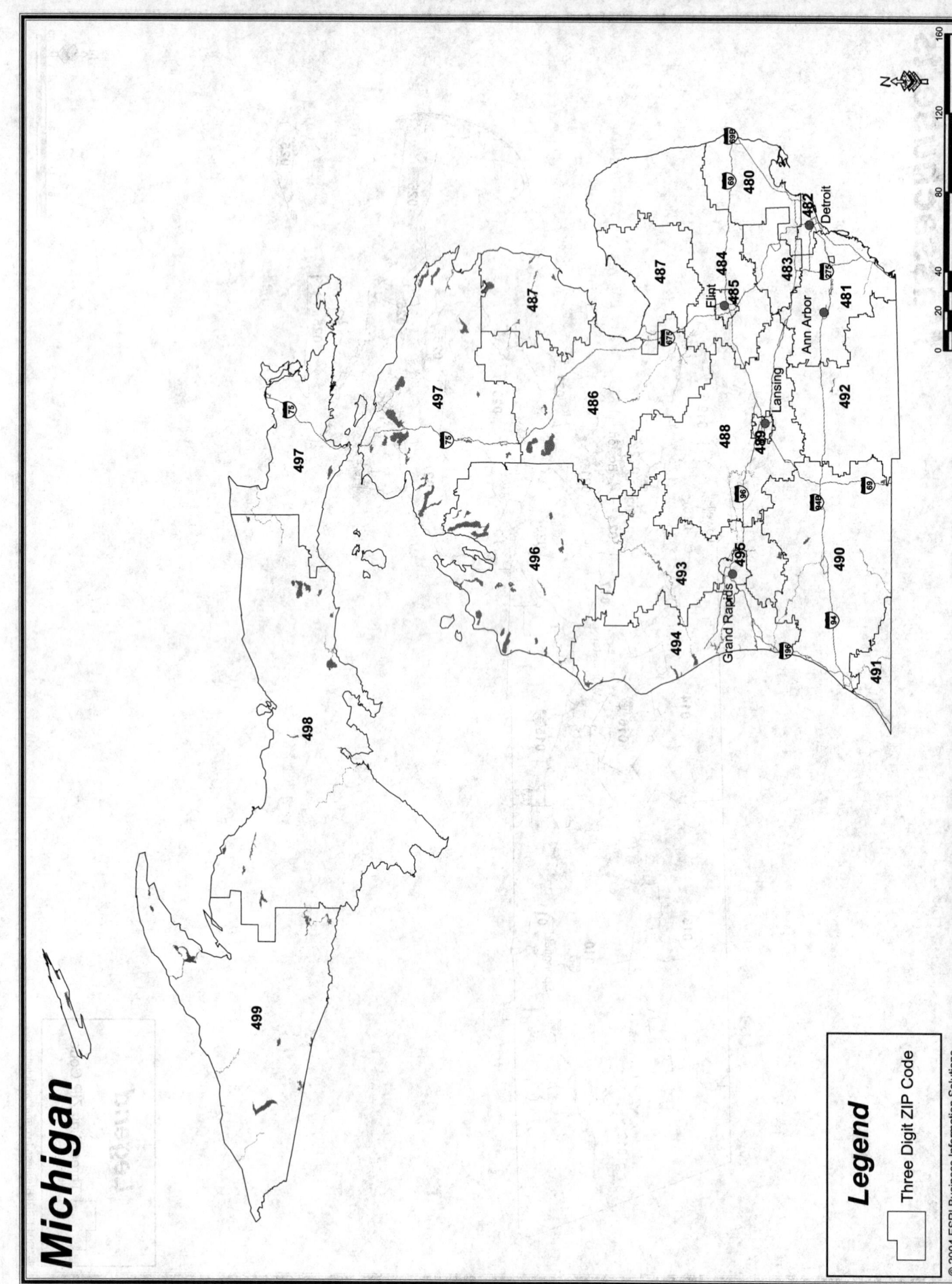

Legend

Three Digit ZIP Code

Minnesota

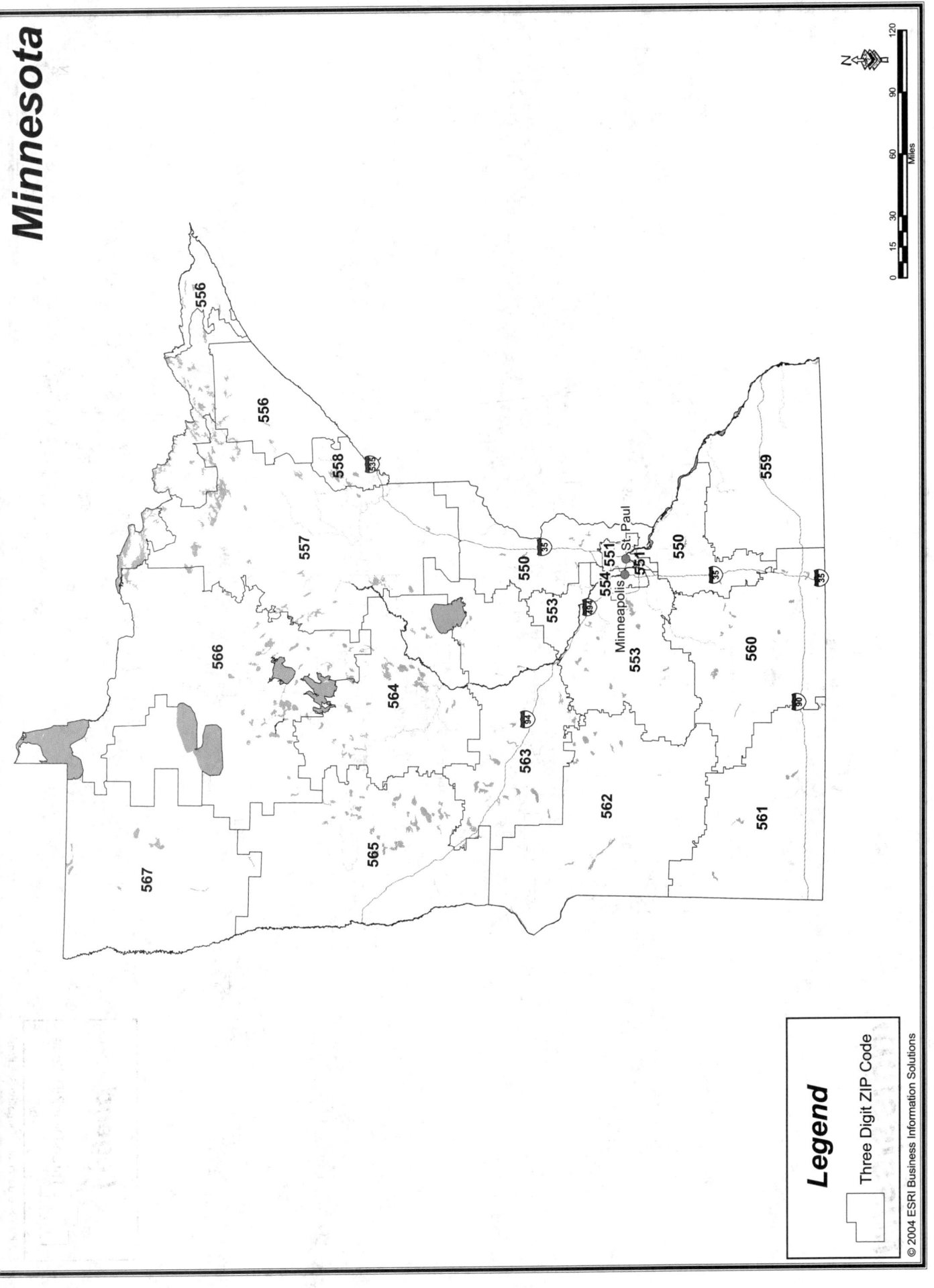

Legend

Three Digit ZIP Code

556
556
558
557
566
567
564
565
563
562
561
560
559
550
553
553
554
551
551
Minneapolis
St. Paul

N

0 15 30 60 90 120
Miles

Mississippi

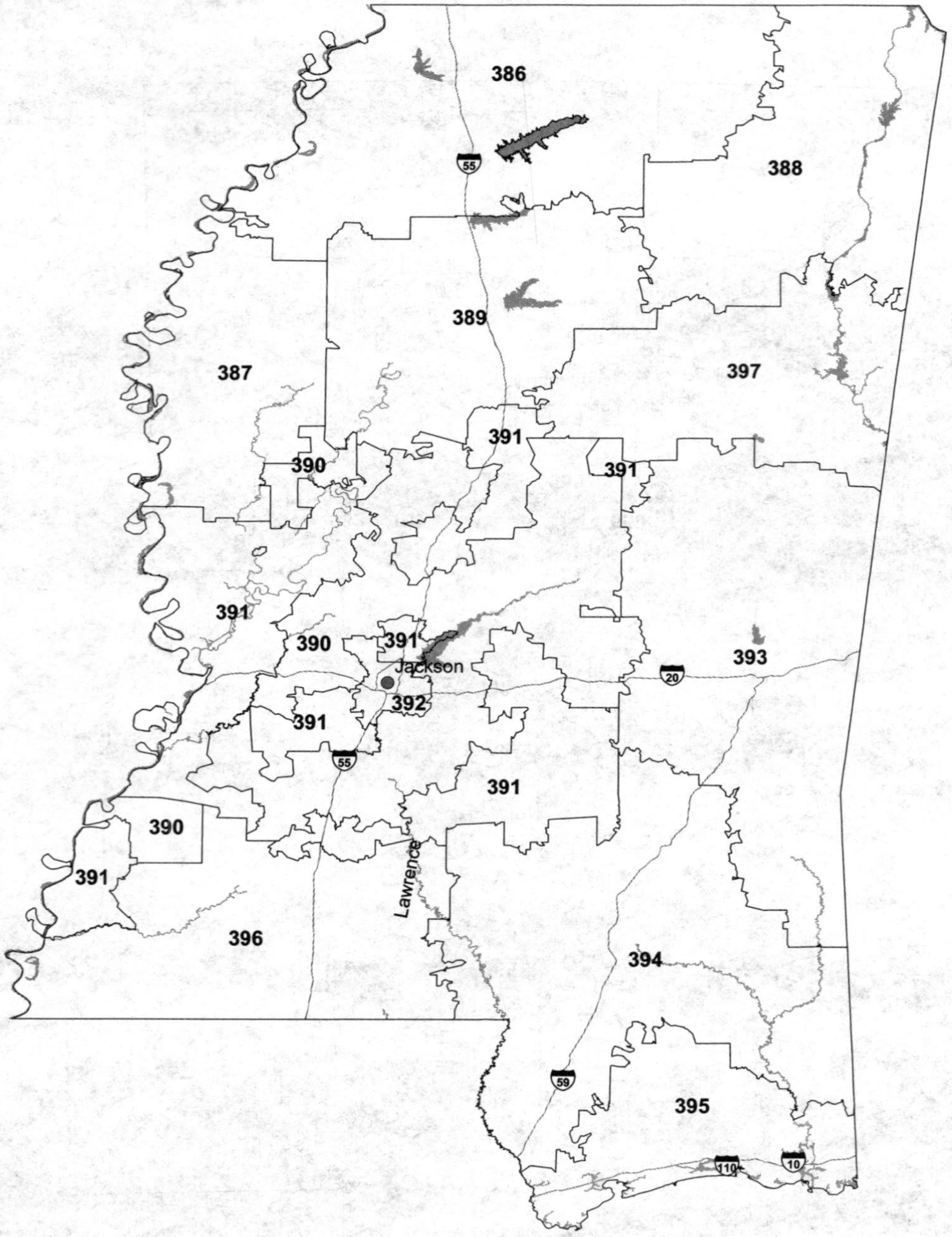

388

397

393

386

389

391

391

391

387

390

390

391

391

Jackson

392

391

391

391

396

390

394

395

20

55

55

55

10

110

Lawrence

Legend

Three Digit ZIP Code

N

0 15 30   60   90   120
Miles

© 2004 ESRI Business Information Solutions

Missouri

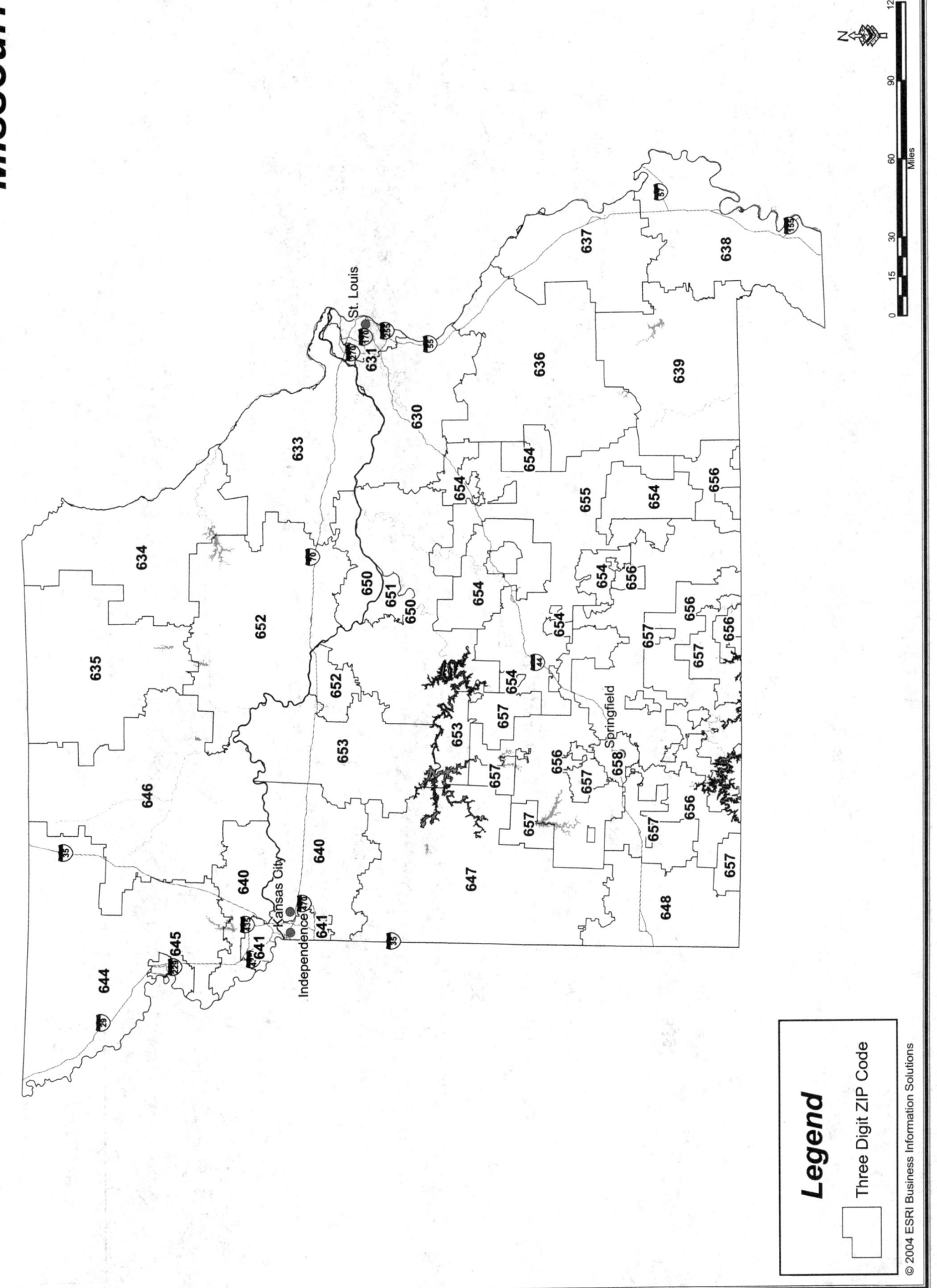

Legend

Three Digit ZIP Code

© 2004 ESRI Business Information Solutions

730

Montana

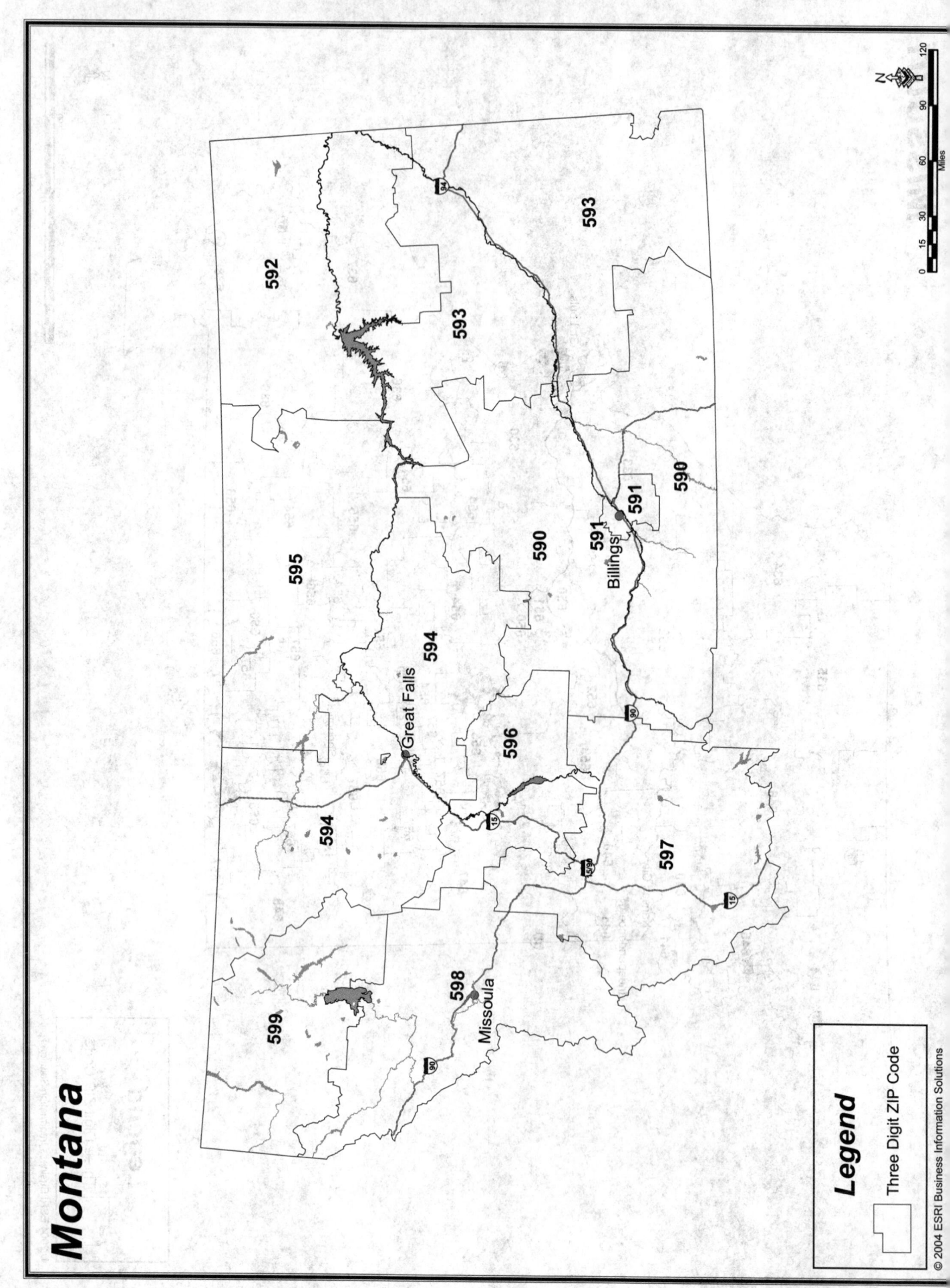

Legend

Three Digit ZIP Code

Nebraska

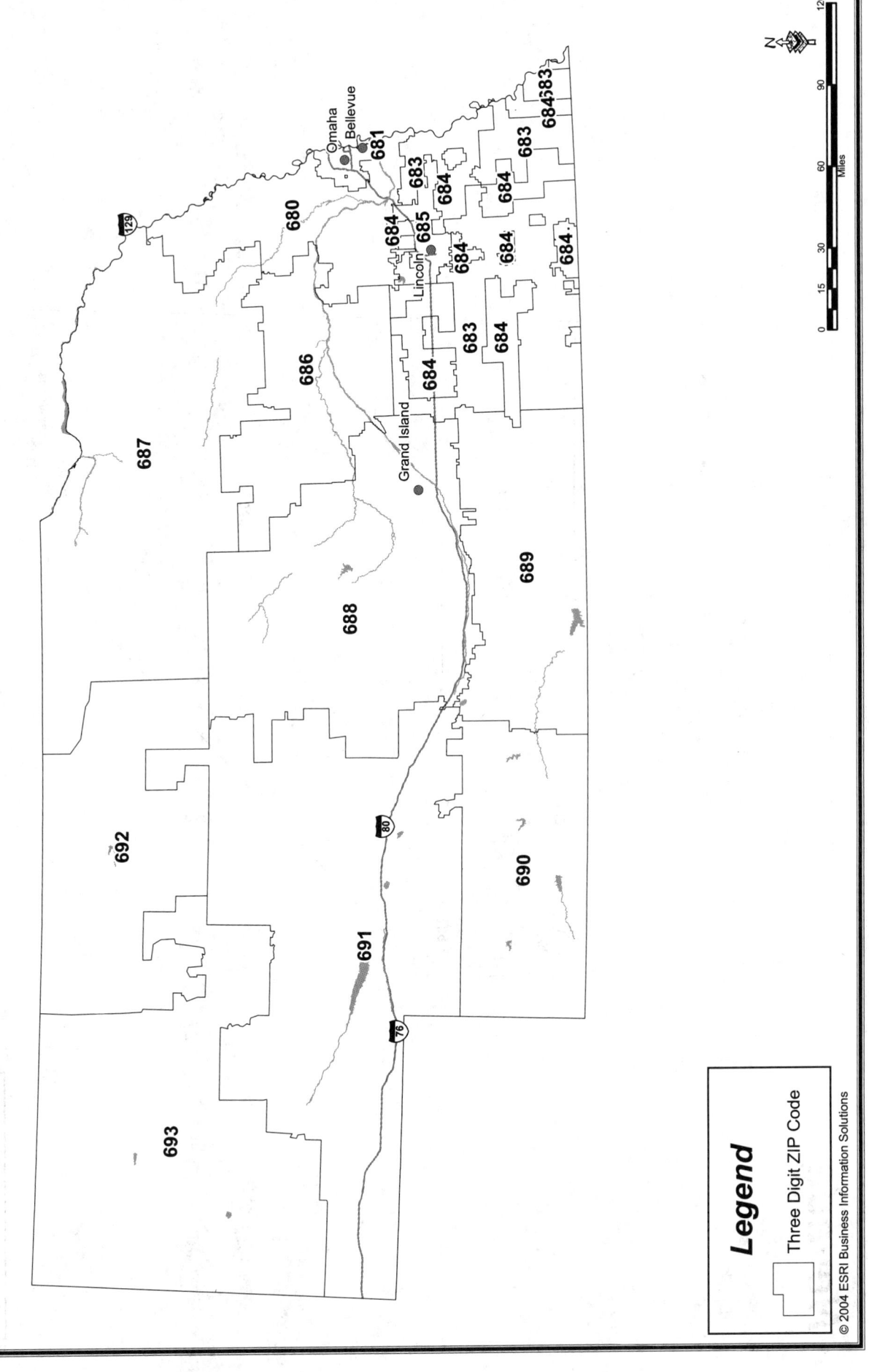

Omaha
Bellevue
681
Omaha
680
683
684
684
683
684 683
684
684
684
684
684
684
685
Lincoln
683
684
684
129
686
687
Grand Island
688
689
692
80
690
691
76
693

N

0 15 30 60 90 120
Miles

732

Nevada

898

890

893

891 Las Vegas

894

895 Reno

897 Carson

Legend

Three Digit ZIP Code

© 2004 ESRI Business Information Solutions

N

0 15 30   60   90   120
Miles

733

New Hampshire

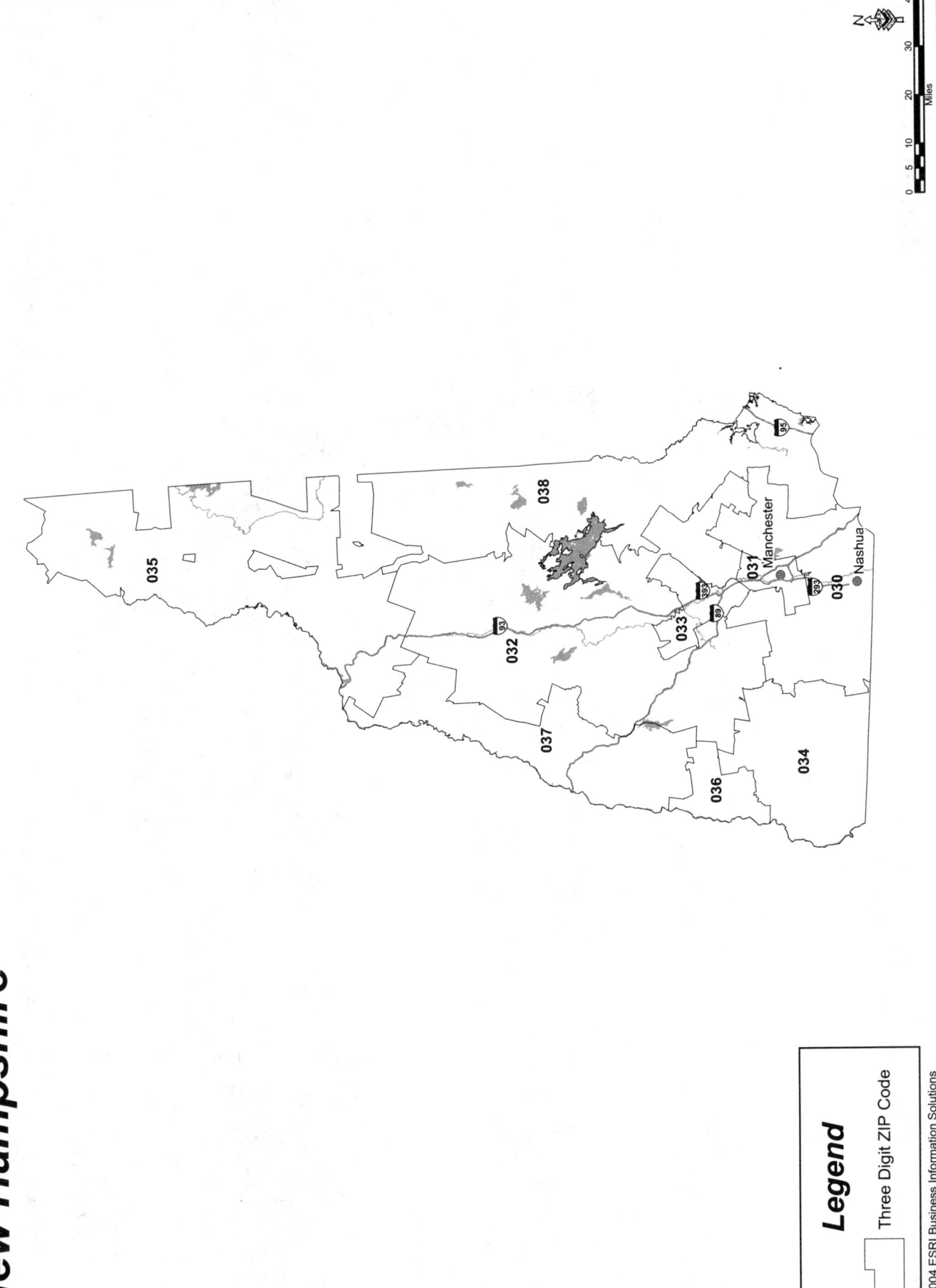

Legend

Three Digit ZIP Code

New Jersey

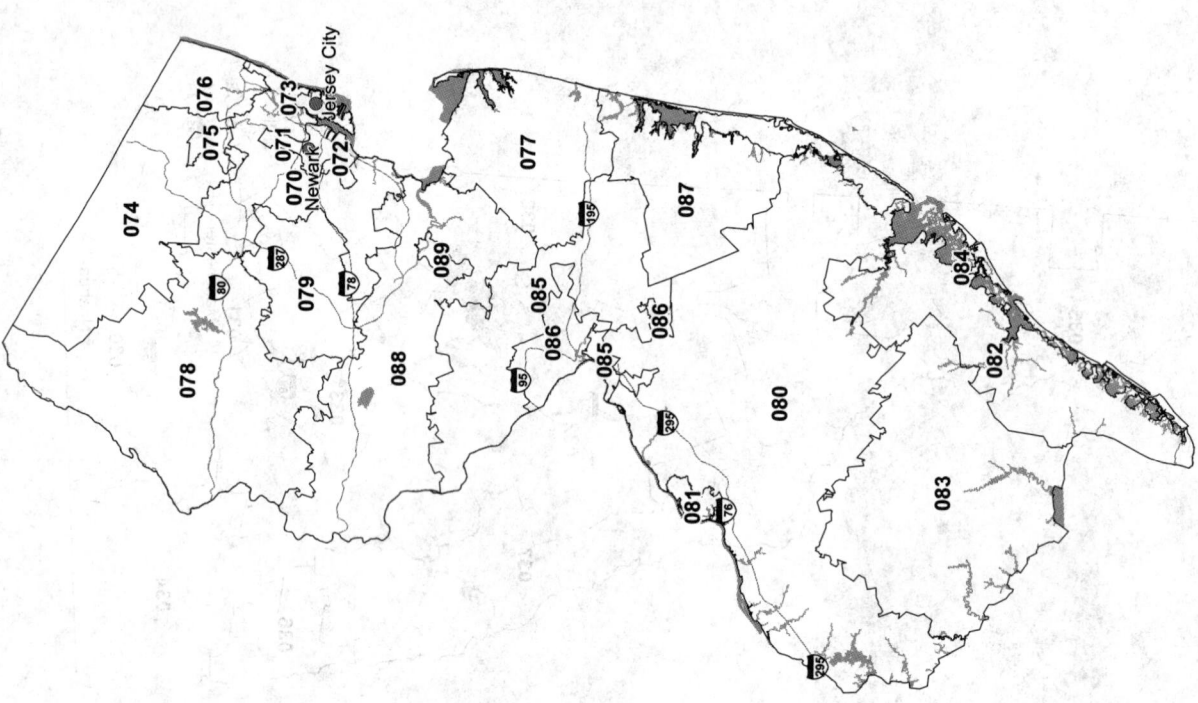

New Mexico

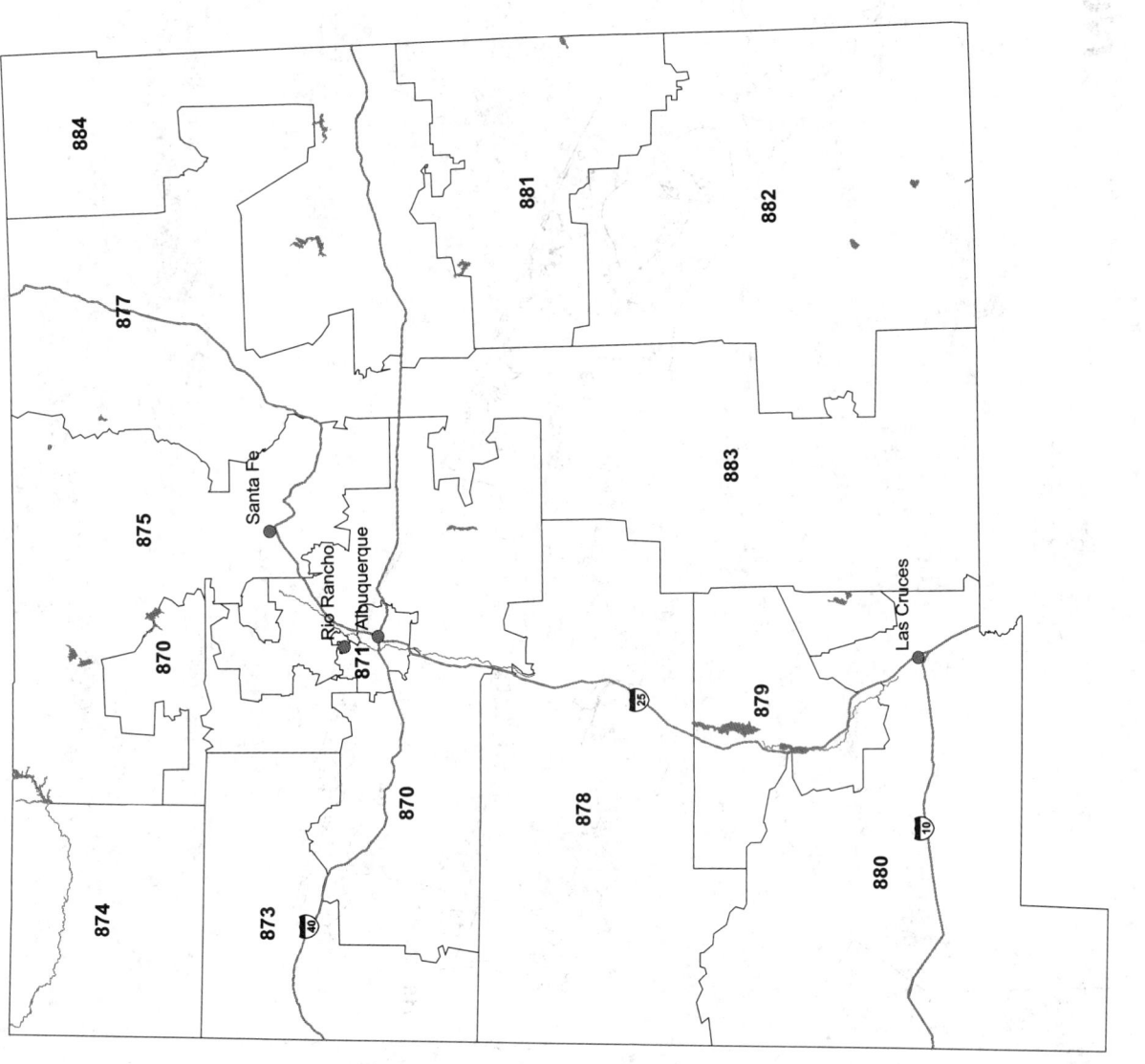

884

877

881

882

875

883

870

Santa Fe

Rio Rancho

Albuquerque

Las Cruces

871

879

870

874

878

873

880

N

0 10 20   40   60   80
Miles

736

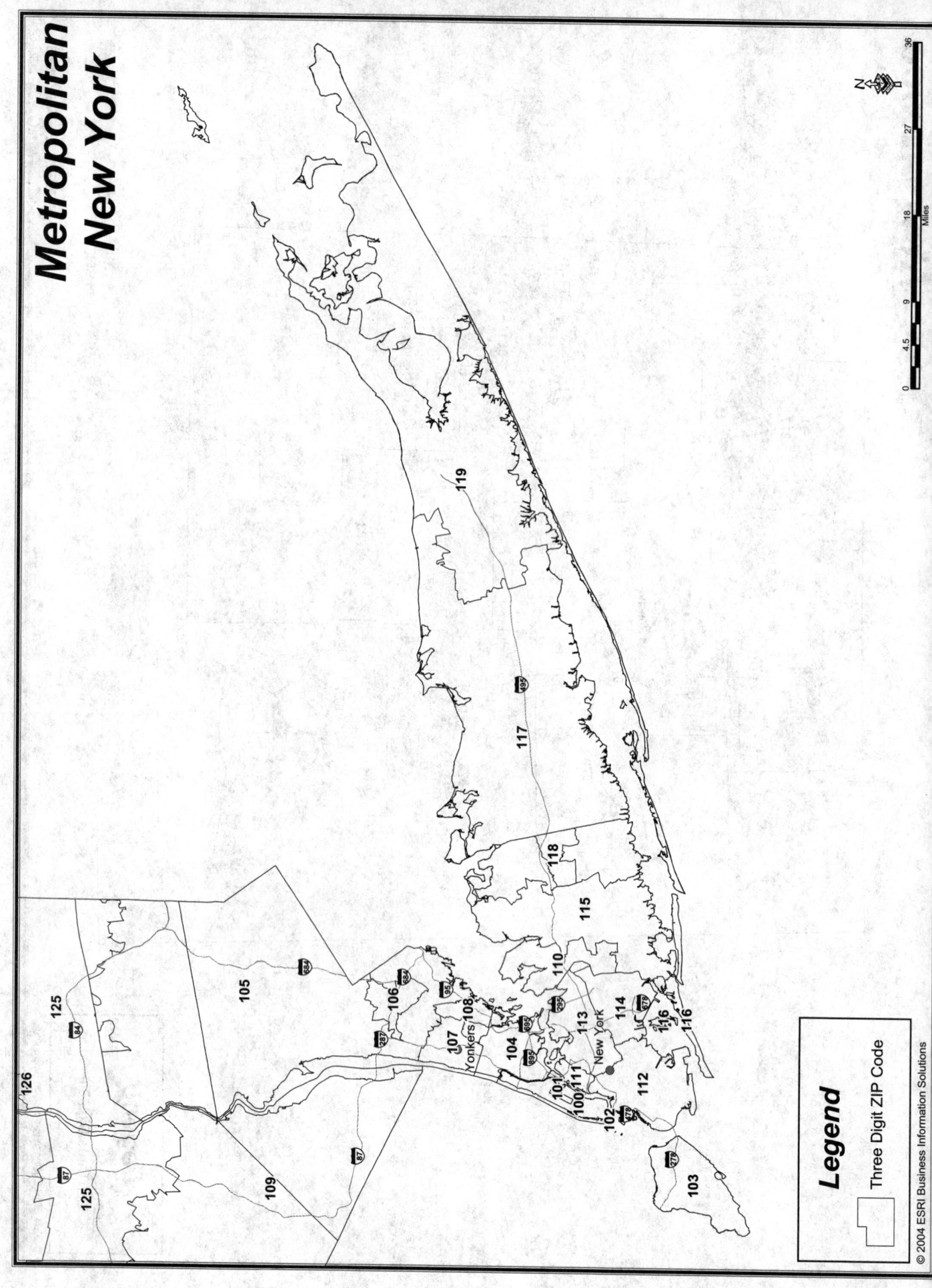

Metropolitan New York

Legend

Three Digit ZIP Code

© 2004 ESRI Business Information Solutions

737

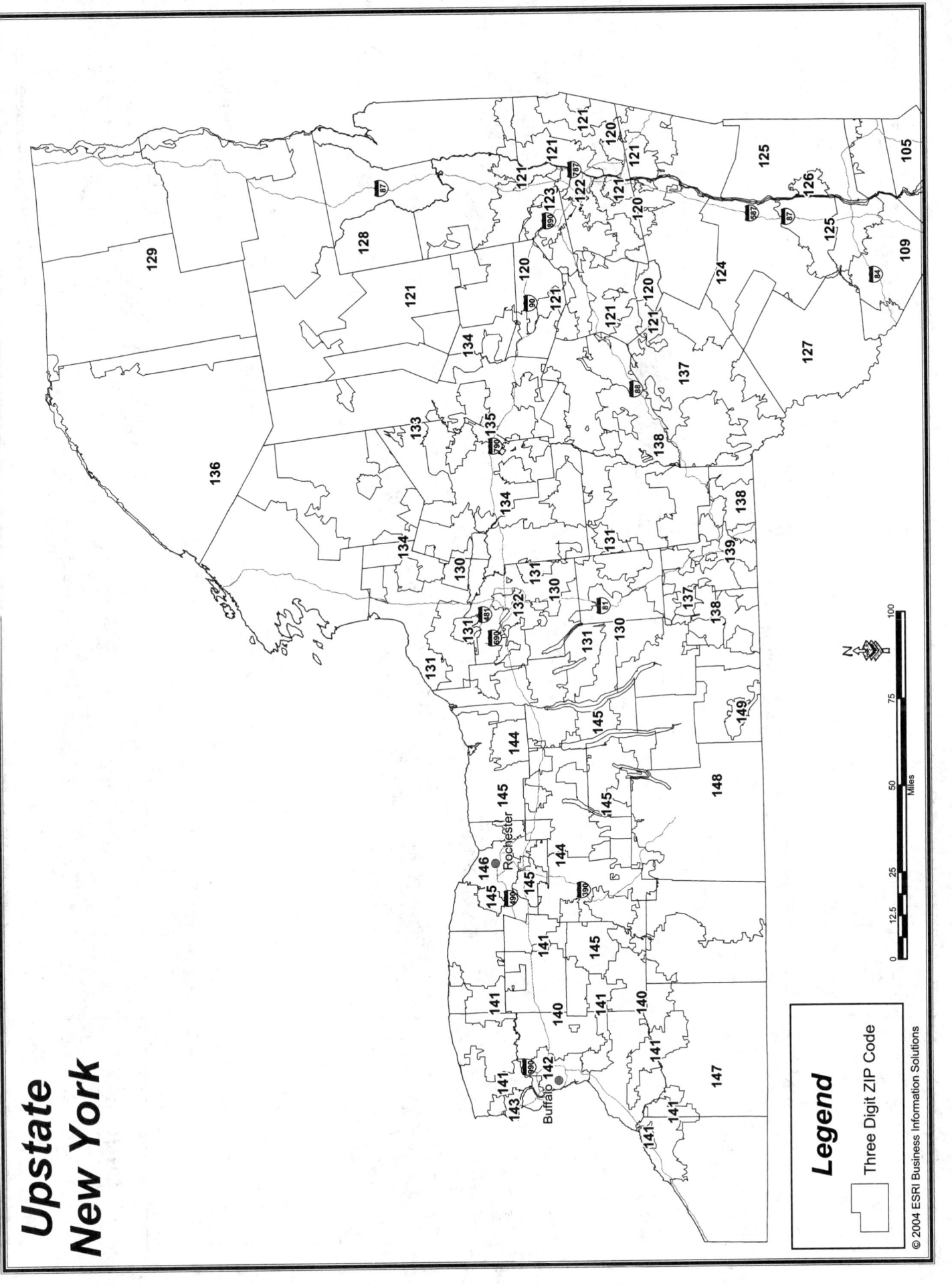

Upstate
New York

Legend

Three Digit ZIP Code

© 2004 ESRI Business Information Solutions

738

North Carolina

279
279
279
278
285
275
276
Raleigh
277
85
272
272
Durham
272
273
272
273
284
95
Fayetteville
283
272
273
274
272
73
272
280
271
272
280
280
270
85
281
286
282
Charlotte
40
280
77
281
288
281
240
26
74
40
287
289

N

0 15 30   60   90   120
Miles

Legend

Three Digit ZIP Code

North Dakota

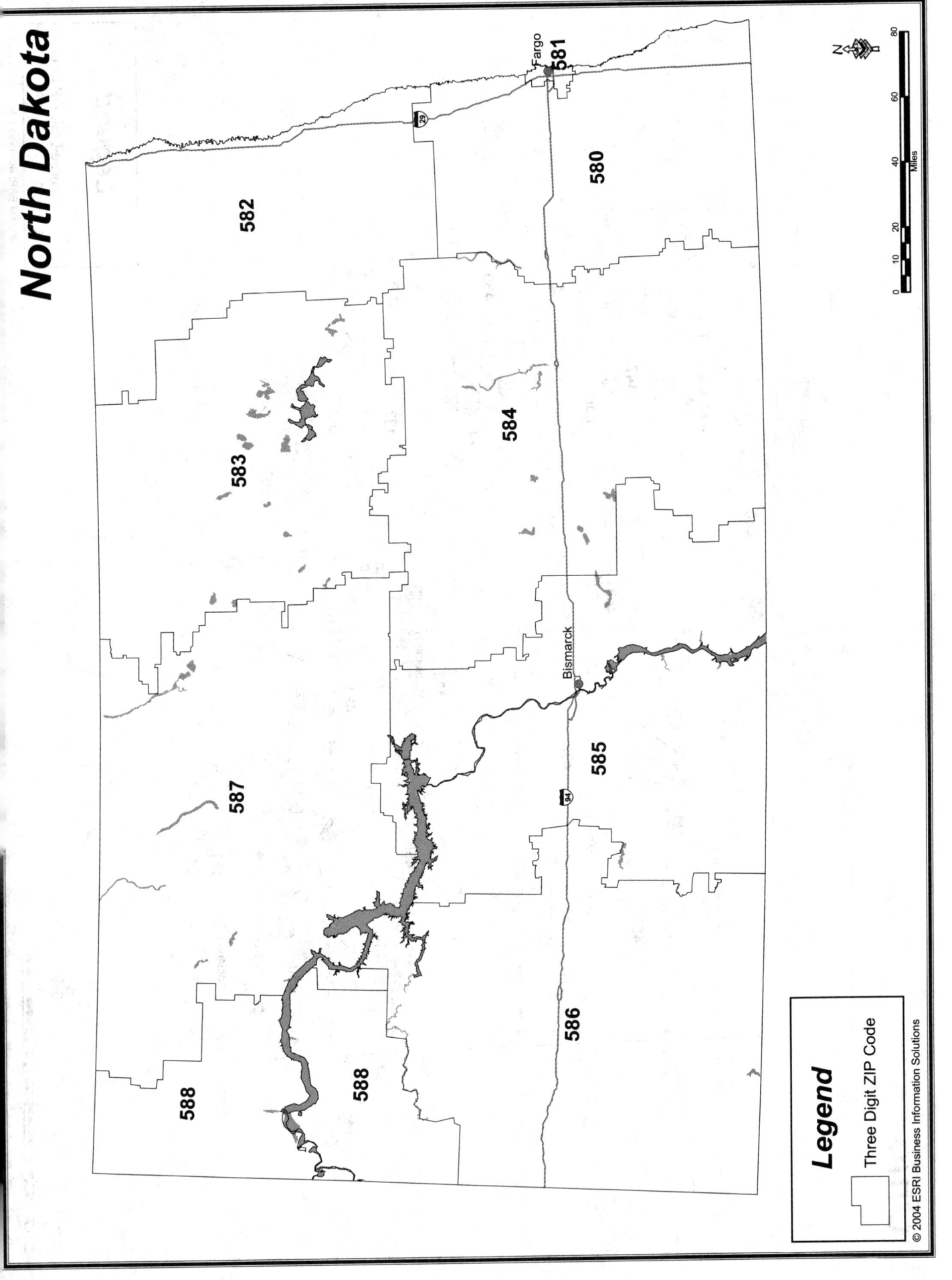

Legend

Three Digit ZIP Code

© 2004 ESRI Business Information Solutions

740

Ohio

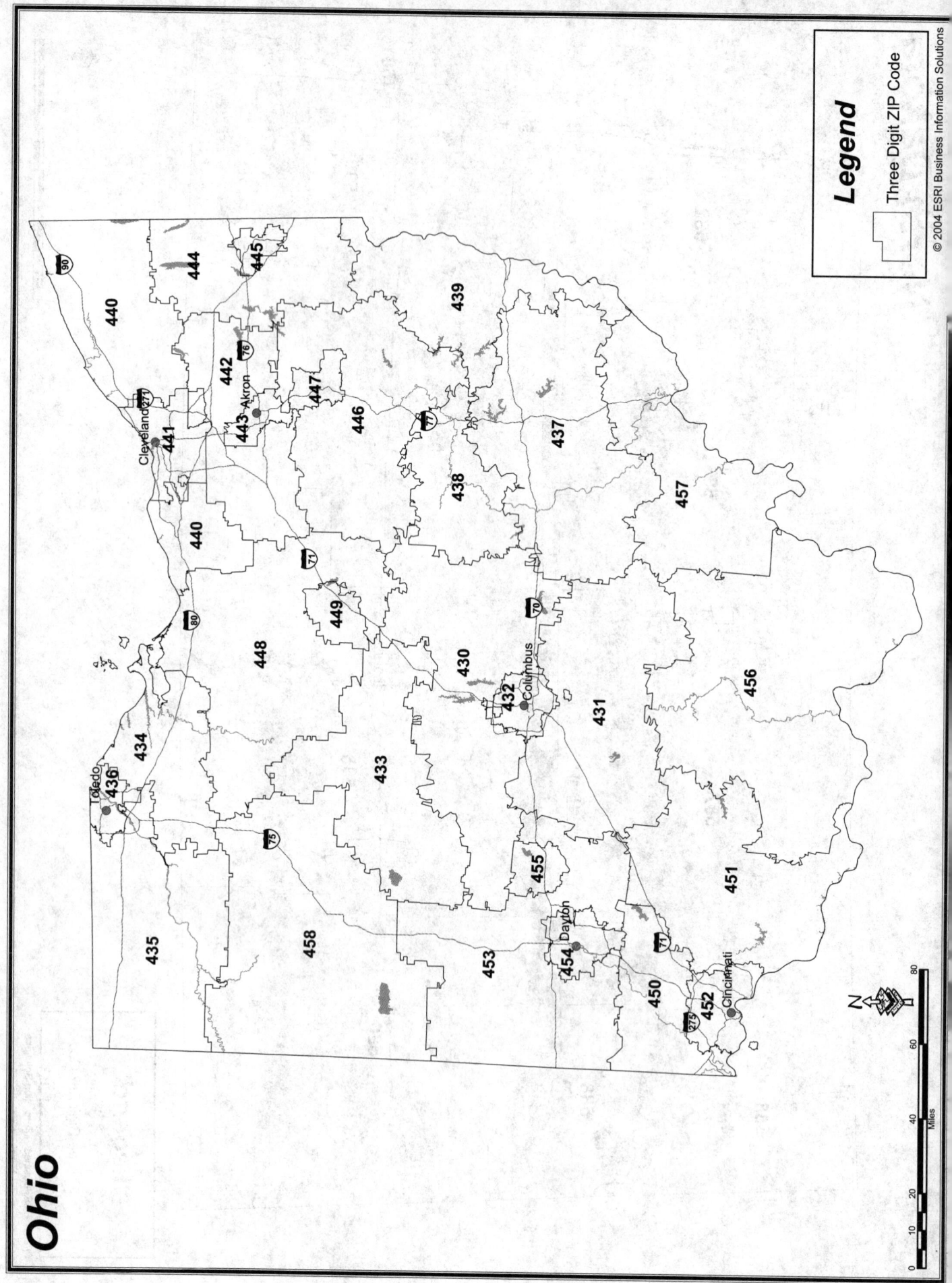

Legend

Three Digit ZIP Code

Oklahoma

Legend

Three Digit ZIP Code

© 2004 ESRI Business Information Solutions

742

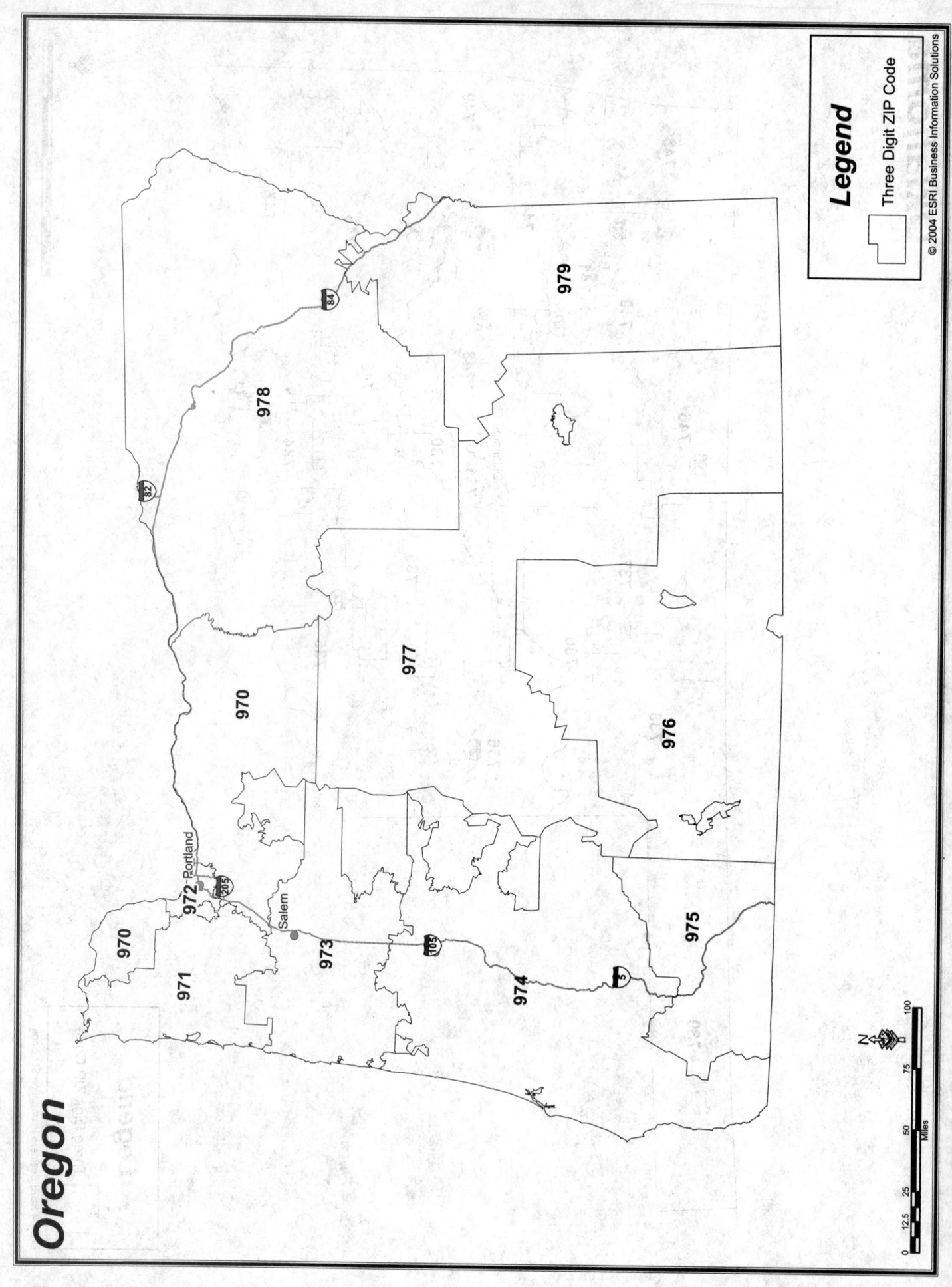

Oregon

Legend

Three Digit ZIP Code

© 2004 ESRI Business Information Solutions

743

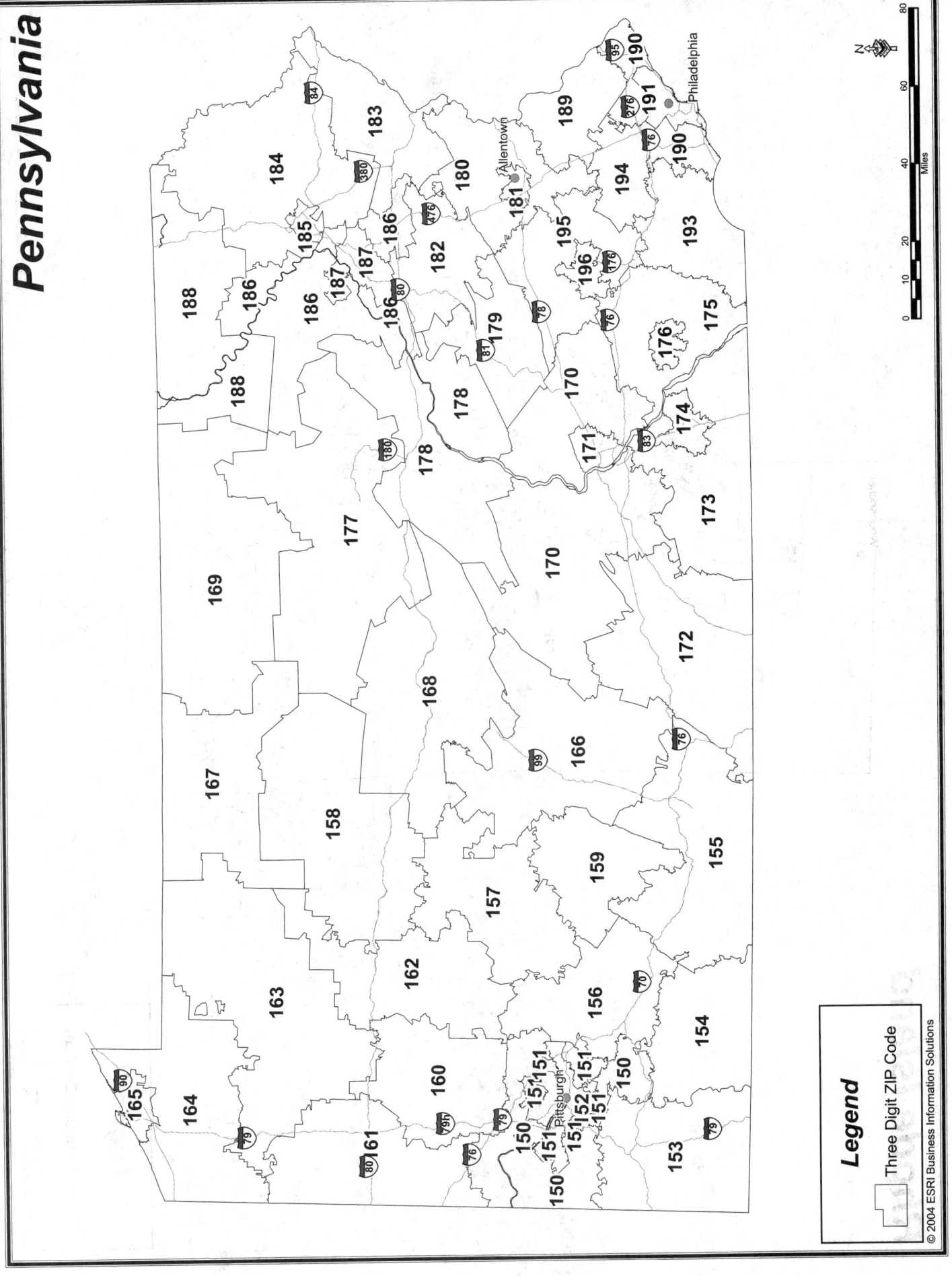

Pennsylvania

Philadelphia

Allentown

Pittsburgh

Legend

Three Digit ZIP Code

© 2004 ESRI Business Information Solutions

Miles
0 10 20 40 60 80

N

Rhode Island

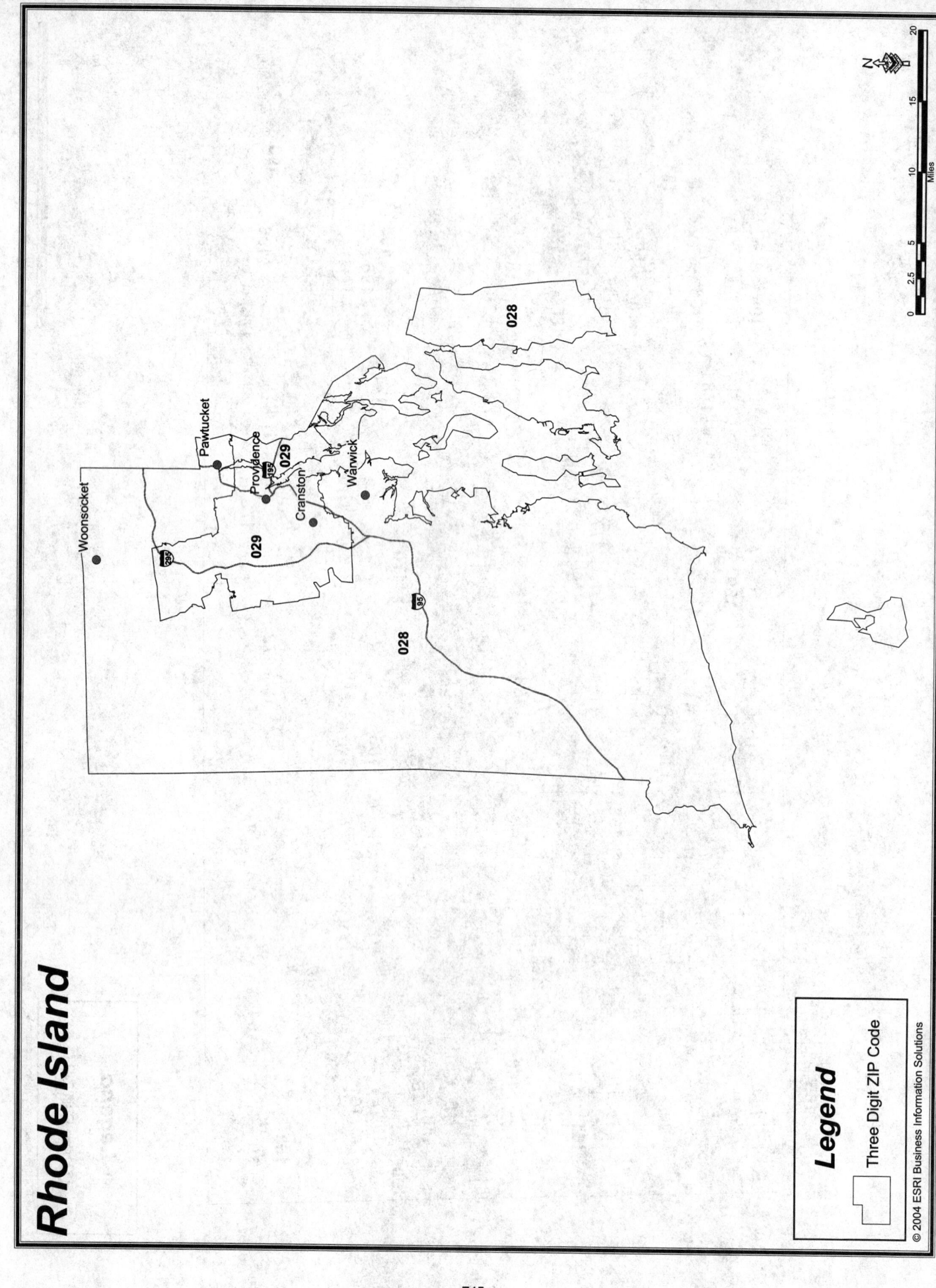

Legend

Three Digit ZIP Code

© 2004 ESRI Business Information Solutions

028

029

029

028

Woonsocket

Pawtucket

Providence

Cranston

Warwick

N

0 2.5 5 10 15 20
Miles

South Carolina

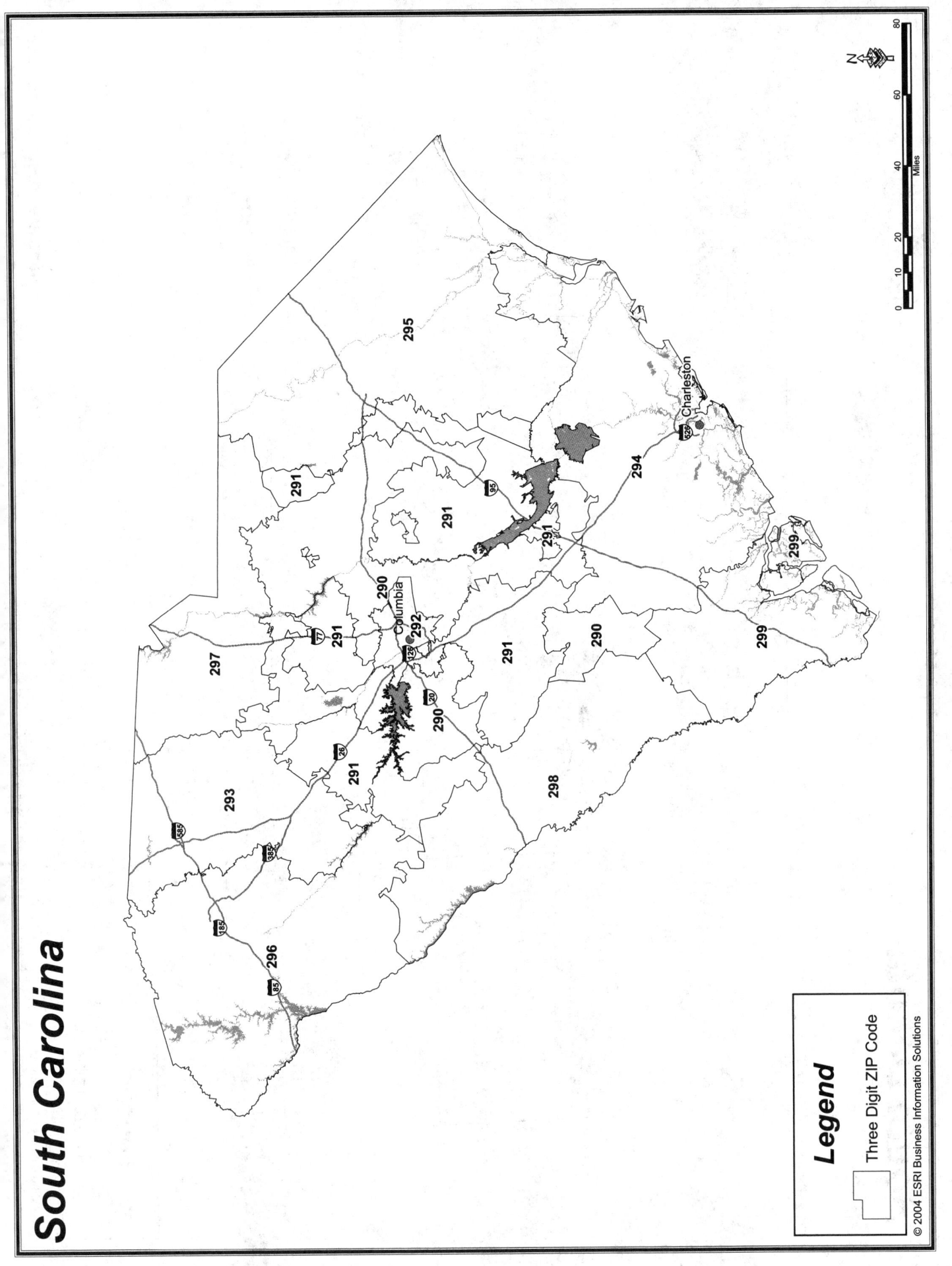

Legend

Three Digit ZIP Code

© 2004 ESRI Business Information Solutions

South Dakota

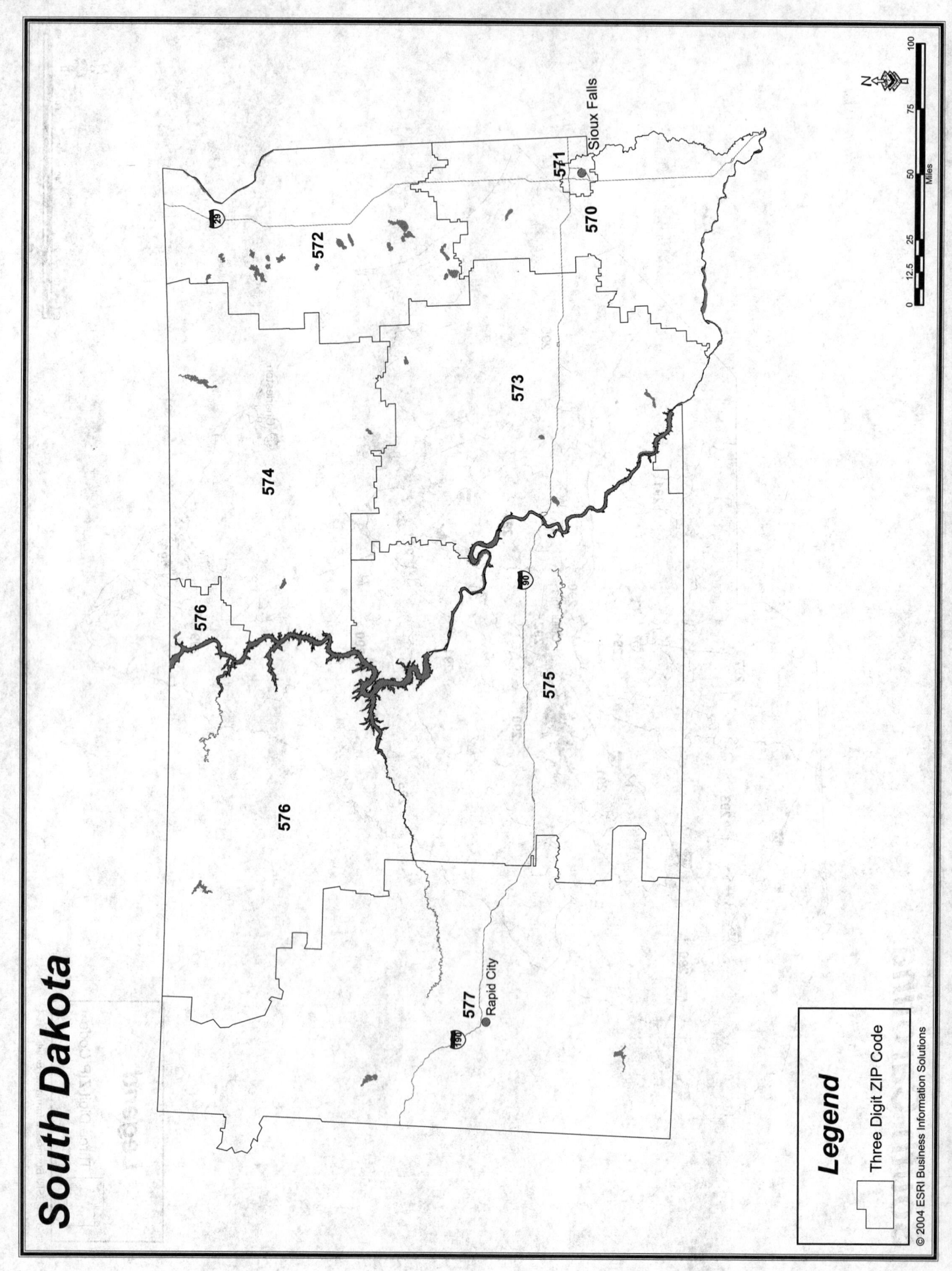

Legend

Three Digit ZIP Code

© 2004 ESRI Business Information Solutions

Tennessee

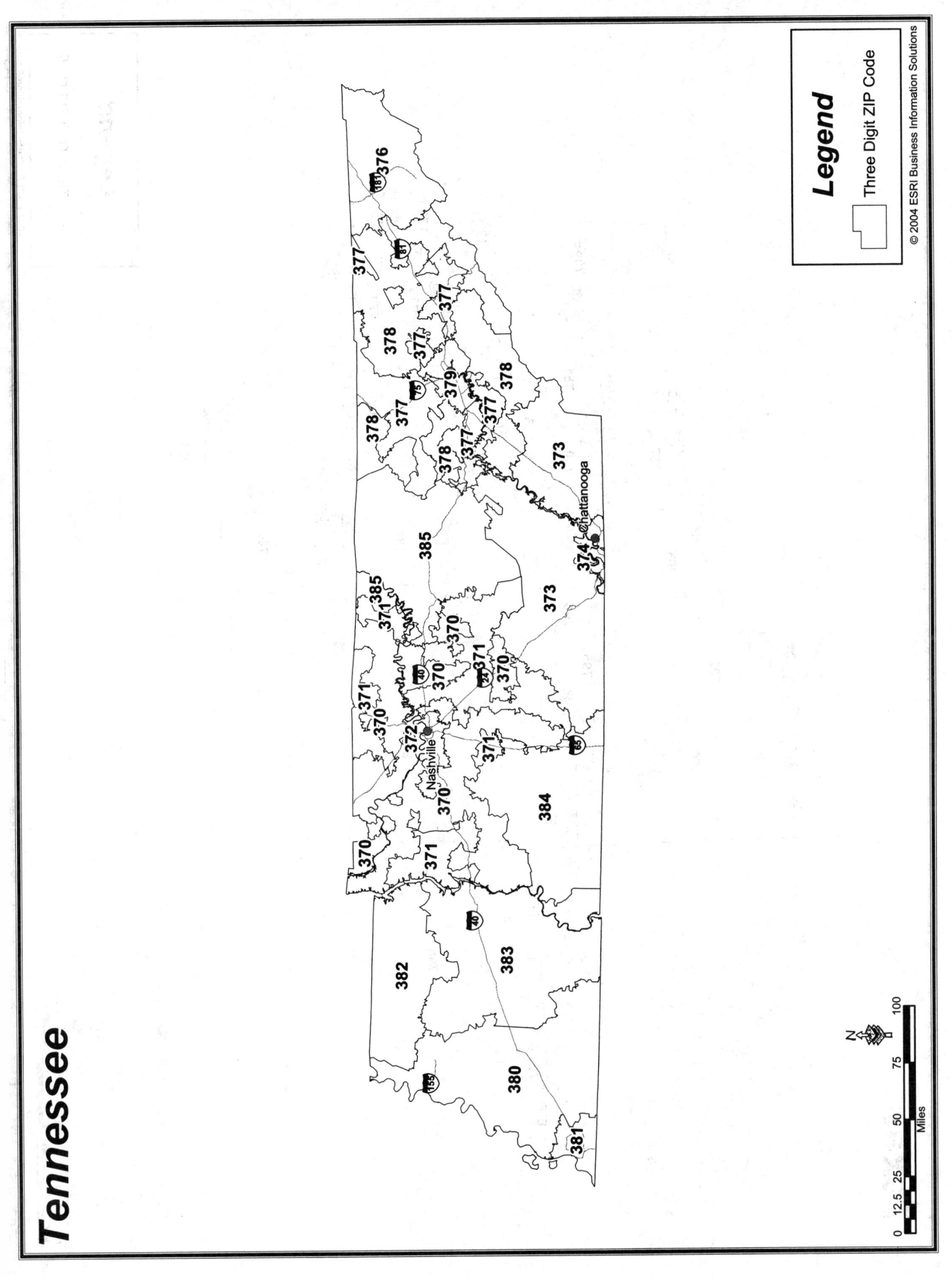

Texas

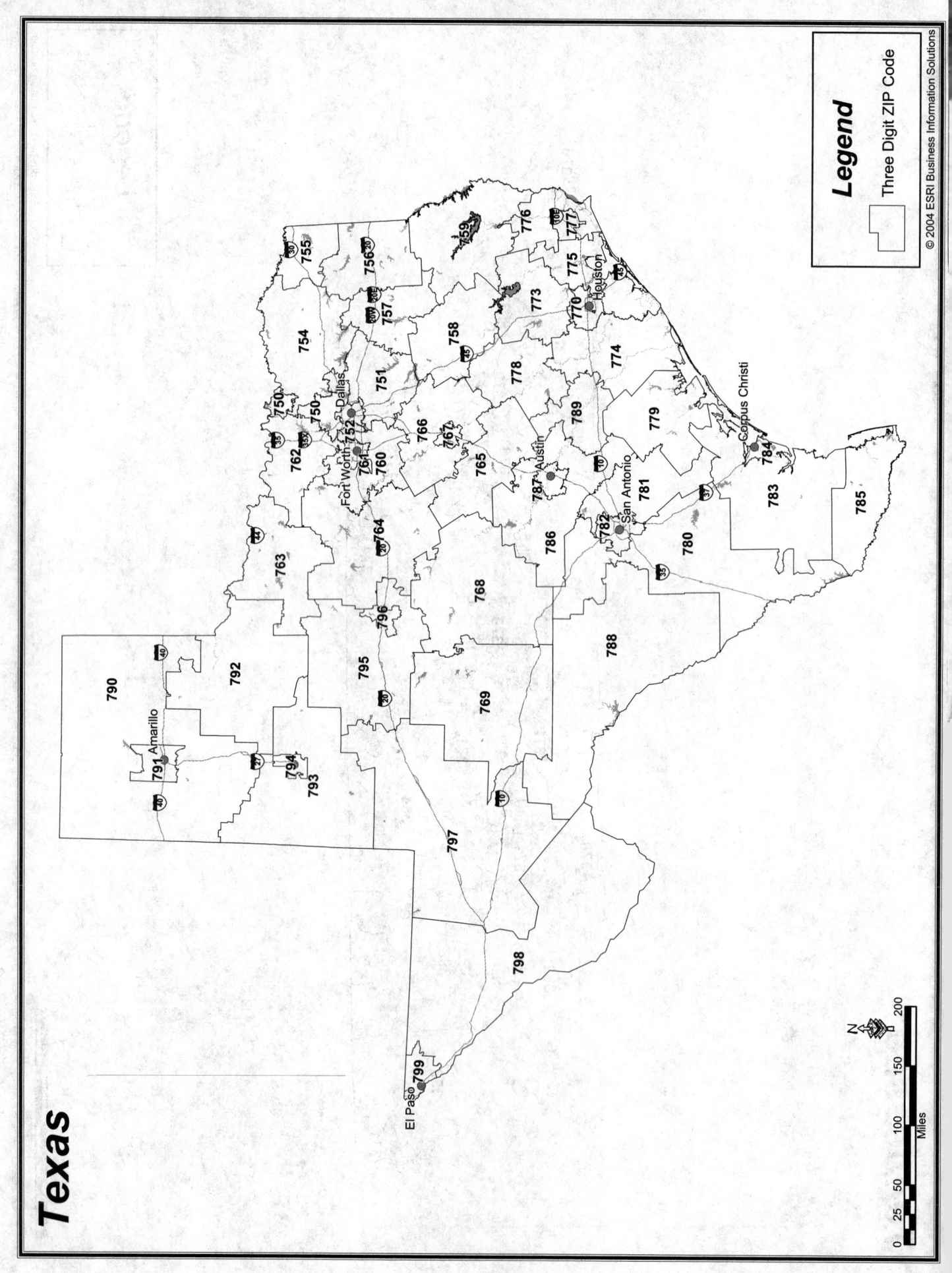

Legend

☐ Three Digit ZIP Code

© 2004 ESRI Business Information Solutions

N

Miles
0 25 50   100   150   200

749

Utah

845

840

845

70

844

15

84

841

Salt Lake City

Sandy

Orem-Provo

West Valley City

846

847

15

843

80

N

0 15 30 60 90 120
Miles

Legend

Three Digit ZIP Code

© 2004 ESRI Business Information Solutions

Vermont

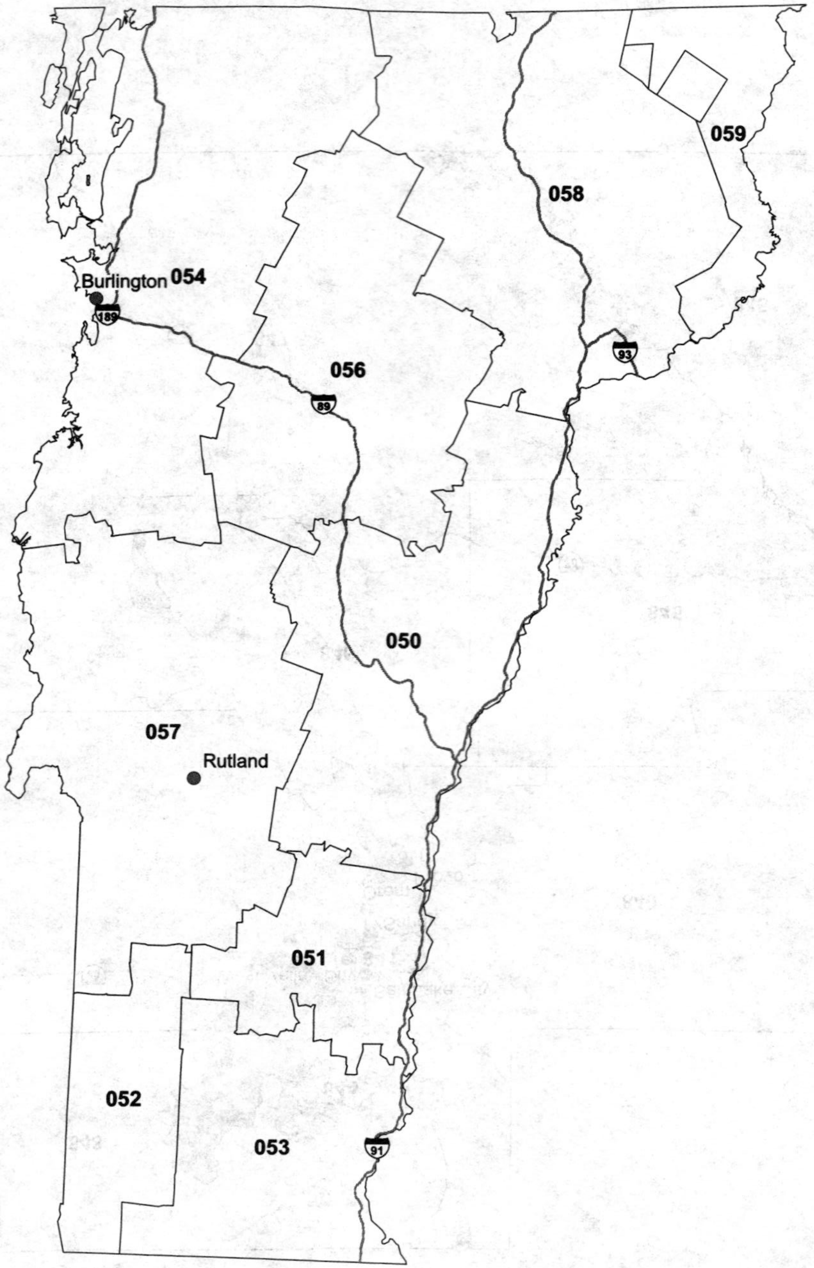

059

058

057

050

056

052

051

053

Burlington 054

Rutland

Legend

Three Digit ZIP Code

© 2004 ESRI Business Information Solutions

Virginia

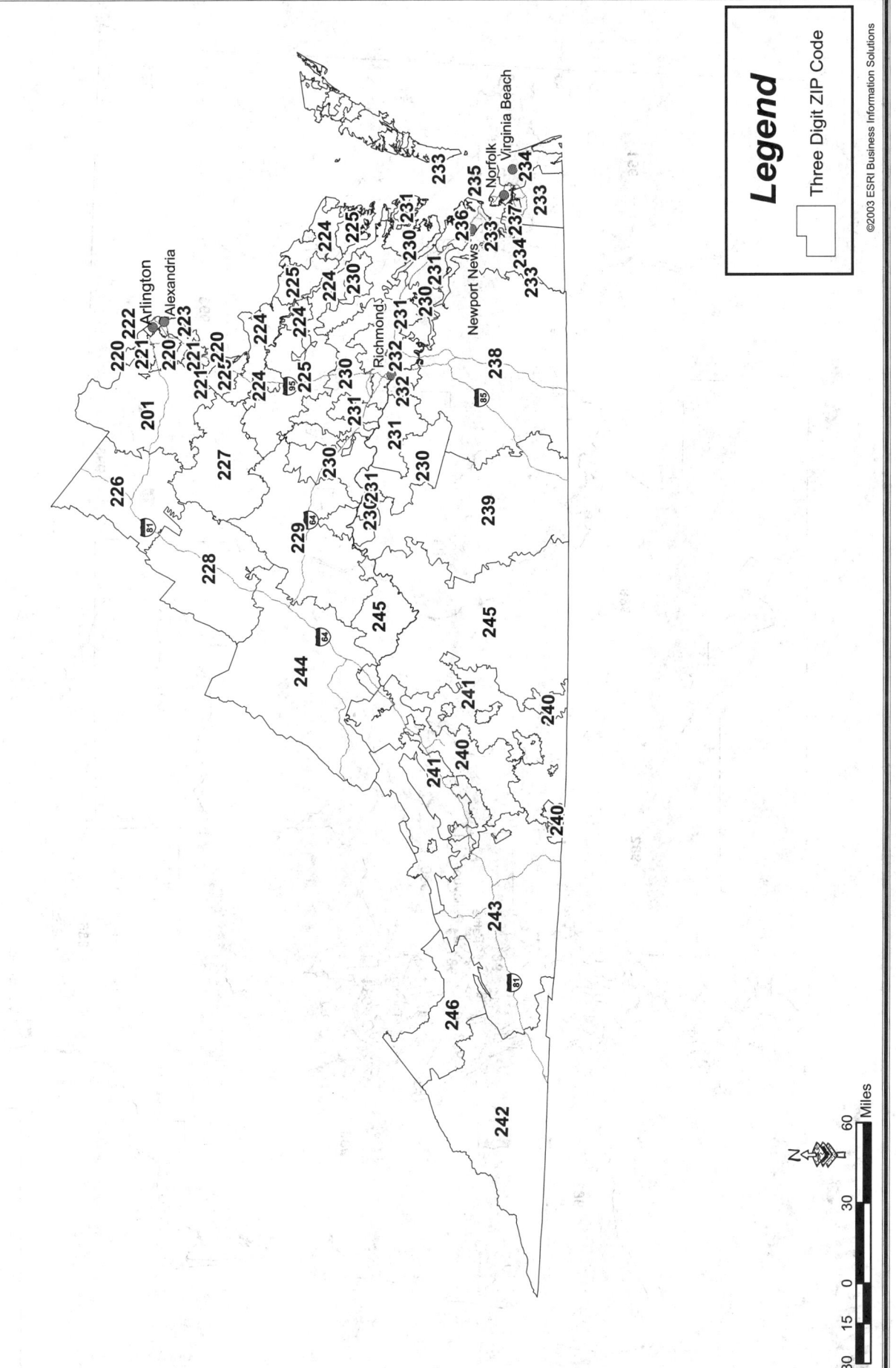

752

Washington

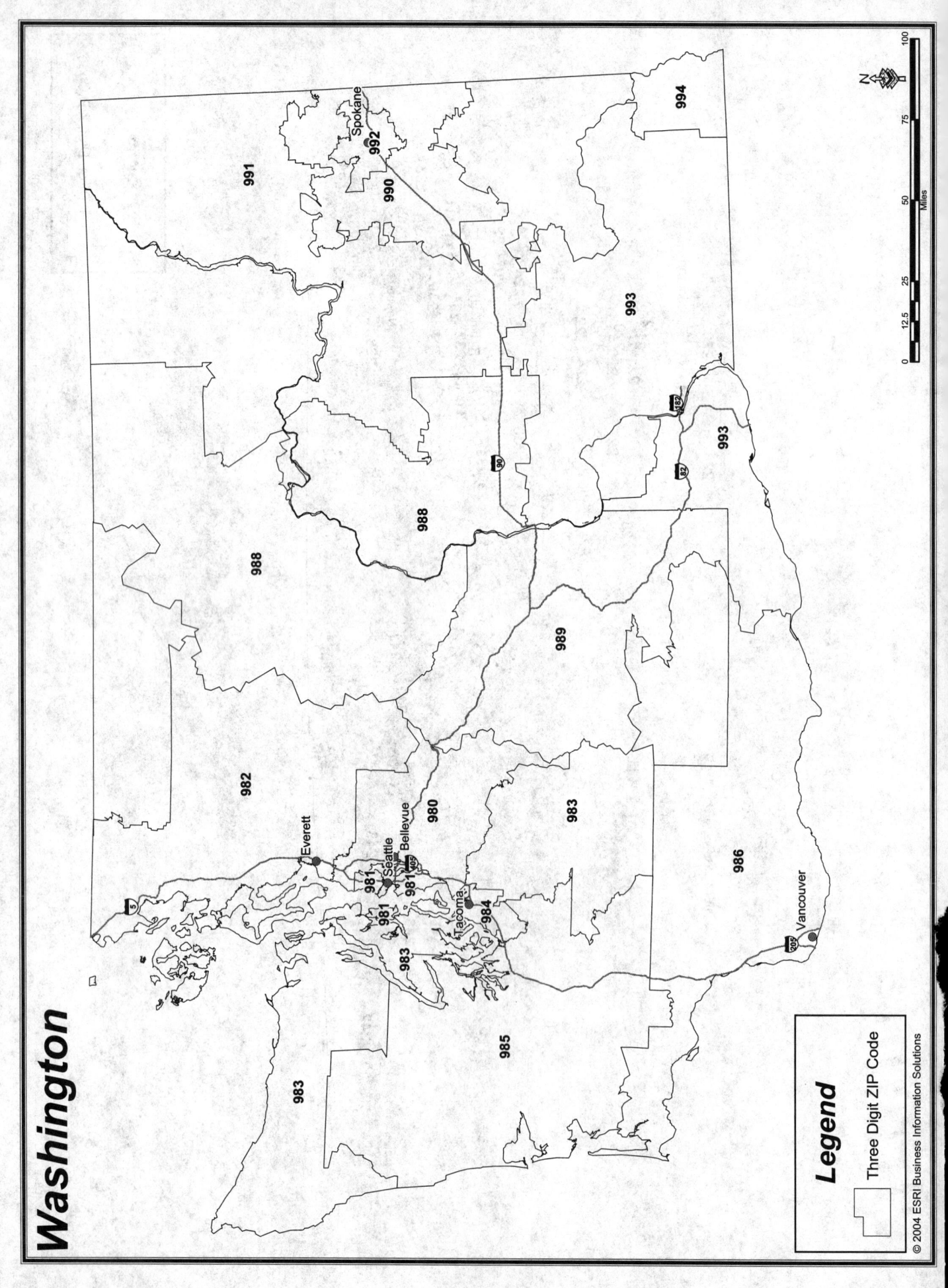

Legend

Three Digit ZIP Code

© 2004 ESRI Business Information Solutions

West Virginia

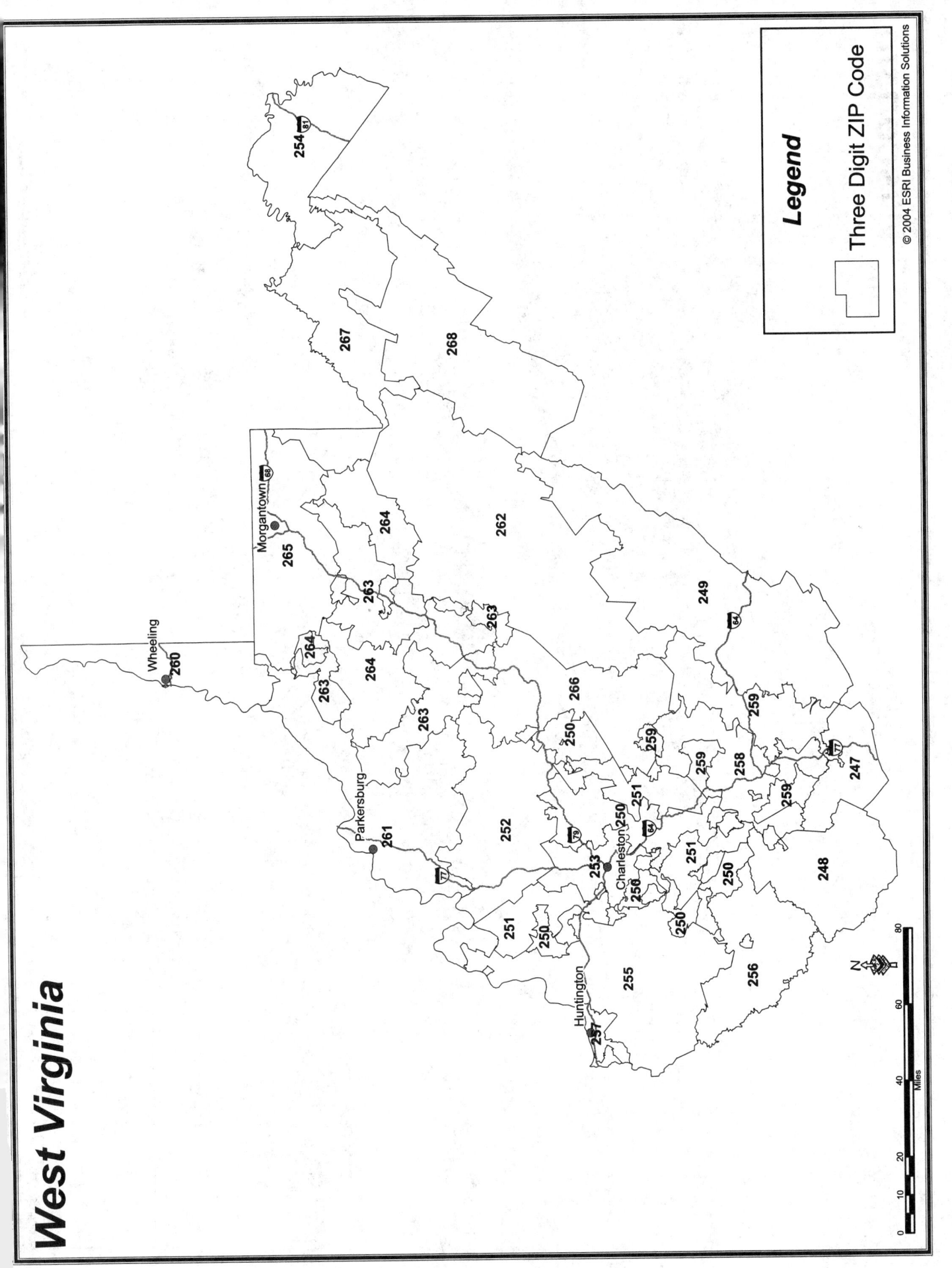

Legend

Three Digit ZIP Code

© 2004 ESRI Business Information Solutions

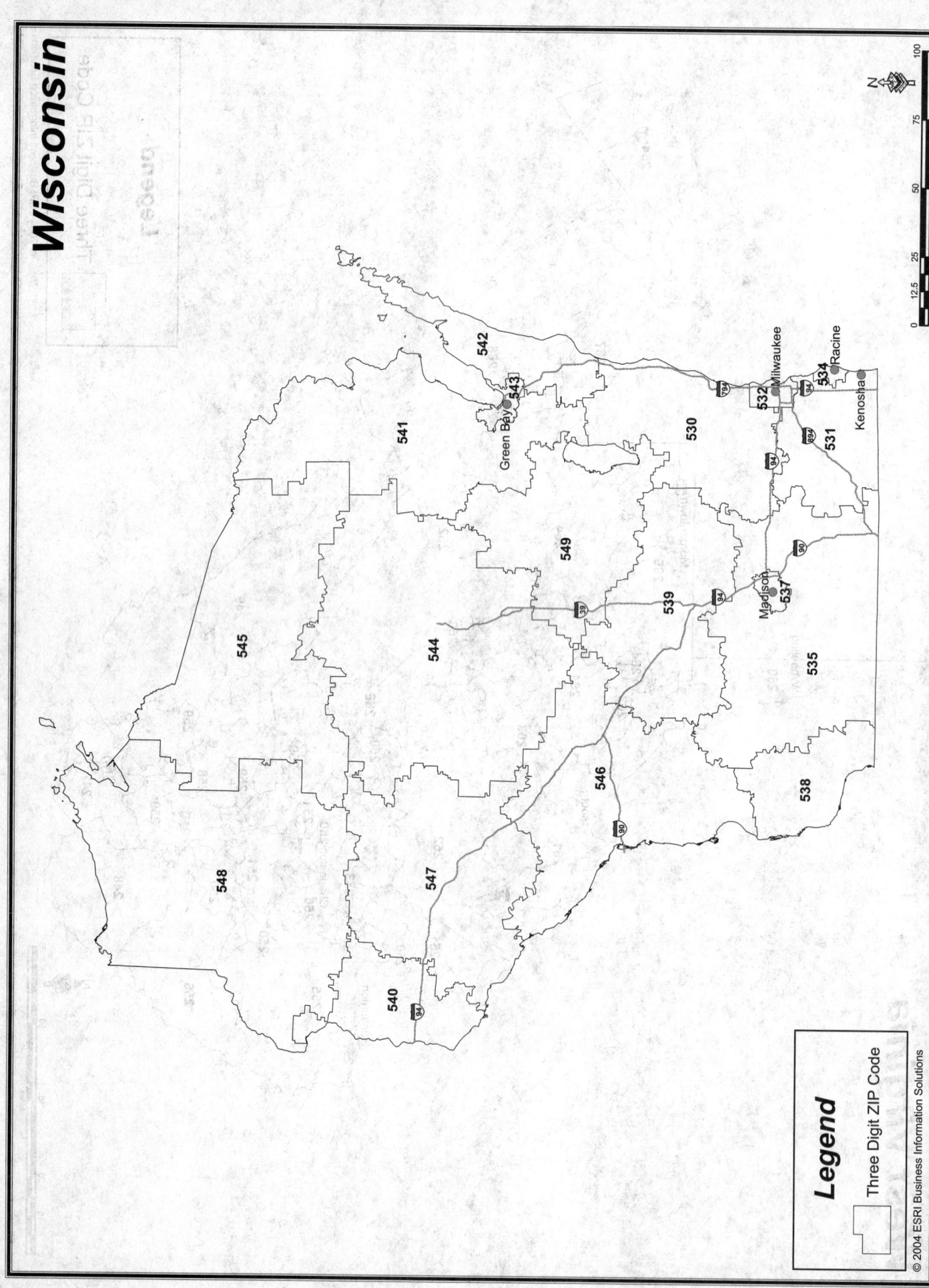

Wisconsin

Three Digit ZIP Code

542

543
Green Bay

541

542

530

Milwaukee
Racine
534
531
Kenosha

549

539

Madison
537

544

545

535

546

548

547

538

540

Legend

Three Digit ZIP Code

N

0 12.5 25   50   75   100
Miles